THE OFFICIAL®

2001 PRICE GUIDE TO

BASEBALL CARDS

BY
DR. JAMES BECKETT

D1479198

TWENTIETH EDITION

HOUSE OF COLLECTIBLES

The Ballantine Publishing Group • New York

Copyright © 1999 by James Beckett III

All rights reserved under International
and Pan-American Copyright Conventions.

House of Collectibles and colophon
are trademarks of Random House, Inc.

Published by:
House of Collectibles
The Ballantine Publishing Group
201 East 50th Street
New York, New York 10022

Distributed by The Ballantine Publishing Group,
a division of Random House, Inc.,
New York, and simultaneously in Canada by
Random House of Canada Limited, Toronto.

Manufactured in the United States of America

Cover photo © T.Derosa / Active Images

ISSN: 1062-7138

ISBN: 0-676-60191-X

Twentieth Edition: April 2000

10 9 8 7 6 5 4 3 2 1

Table of Contents

About the Author ... 10
How to Use This Book ... 10
How to Collect ... 11
    Obtaining Cards ... 11
    Preserving Your Cards ... 12
    Collecting vs. Investing ... 12
Terminology ... 13
Glossary/Legend ... 14
Understanding Card Values ... 18
    Determining Value ... 18
    Regional Variation ... 18
    Set Prices ... 19
    Scarce Series ... 19
Grading Your Cards ... 20
    Centering ... 20
    Corner Wear ... 20
    Creases ... 21
    Alterations ... 21
    Categorization of Defects ... 21
Condition Guide ... 22
    Grades ... 22
Selling Your Cards ... 23
Interesting Notes ... 26
History of Baseball Cards ... 26
    Increasing Popularity ... 27
    Intensified Competition ... 29
    Sharing the Pie ... 30
    Finding Out More ... 33
Additional Reading ... 34
Advertising ... 34
Prices in This Guide ... 34

1948 Bowman ... 35
1949 Bowman ... 35
1950 Bowman ... 36
1951 Bowman ... 37
1952 Bowman ... 38
1953 Bowman B/W ... 40
1953 Bowman Color ... 40
1954 Bowman ... 41
1955 Bowman ... 42
1989 Bowman ... 43
1989 Bowman Tiffany ... 45
1990 Bowman ... 45
1990 Bowman Tiffany ... 48
1991 Bowman ... 48
1992 Bowman ... 51
1993 Bowman ... 53
1994 Bowman Previews ... 56
1994 Bowman ... 56
1995 Bowman ... 59
1995 Bowman Gold Foil ... 61
1996 Bowman ... 61
1996 Bowman Foil ... 63
1996 Bowman Minor League POY ... 63
1997 Bowman ... 63
1997 Bowman International ... 65
1997 Bowman 1998 ROY Favorites ... 65
1997 Bowman Certified Blue Ink Autographs ... 65
1997 Bowman International Best ... 66
1997 Bowman Scout's Honor Roll ... 66
1998 Bowman ... 66
1998 Bowman Golden Anniversary ... 68
1998 Bowman International ... 68
1998 Bowman 1999 ROY Favorites ... 68
1998 Bowman Certified Blue Autographs ... 68
1998 Bowman Minor League MVP's ... 69
1998 Bowman Scout's Choice ... 69
1999 Bowman ... 69
1999 Bowman Gold ... 71
1999 Bowman International ... 71
1999 Bowman Autographs ... 71
1999 Bowman 2000 ROY Favorites ... 72
1999 Bowman Early Risers ... 72
1999 Bowman Late Bloomers ... 72
1999 Bowman Scout's Choice ... 72
1997 Bowman Chrome ... 72
1997 Bowman Chrome International ... 74
1997 Bowman Chrome International Refractors ... 74
1997 Bowman Chrome Refractors ... 74
1997 Bowman Chrome 1998 ROY Favorites ... 74
1997 Bowman Chrome Scout's Honor Roll ... 74
1998 Bowman Chrome ... 74
1998 Bowman Chrome Golden Anniversary ... 76
1998 Bowman Chrome International ... 76
1998 Bowman Chrome International Refractors ... 76
1998 Bowman Chrome Refractors ... 76
1998 Bowman Chrome Reprints ... 76
1999 Bowman Chrome ... 77
1999 Bowman Chrome Gold ... 79
1999 Bowman Chrome Gold Refractors ... 79
1999 Bowman Chrome International ... 79
1999 Bowman Chrome International Refractors ... 79
1999 Bowman Chrome Refractors ... 79
1999 Bowman Chrome 2000 ROY Favorites ... 79
1999 Bowman Chrome Diamond Aces ... 79
1999 Bowman Chrome Impact ... 80
1999 Bowman Chrome Scout's Choice ... 80
1994 Bowman's Best ... 80
1994 Bowman's Best Refractors ... 81
1995 Bowman's Best ... 81
1995 Bowman's Best Refractors ... 82
1996 Bowman's Best Previews ... 82
1996 Bowman's Best ... 82
1996 Bowman's Best Atomic Refractors ... 83
1996 Bowman's Best Refractors ... 83
1996 Bowman's Best Cuts ... 83
1996 Bowman's Best Mirror Image ... 84
1997 Bowman's Best Previews ... 84
1997 Bowman's Best ... 84
1997 Bowman's Best Atomic Refractors ... 85
1997 Bowman's Best Refractors ... 85
1997 Bowman's Best Autographs ... 85
1997 Bowman's Best Best Cuts ... 85
1997 Bowman's Best Mirror Image ... 86
1998 Bowman's Best ... 86
1998 Bowman's Best Atomic Refractors ... 87
1998 Bowman's Best Refractors ... 87
1998 Bowman's Best Autographs ... 87
1998 Bowman's Best Mirror Image Fusion ... 87
1998 Bowman's Best Performers ... 87
1999 Bowman's Best ... 87
1999 Bowman's Best Atomic Refractors ... 88
1999 Bowman's Best Refractors ... 88
1999 Bowman's Best Franchise Best Mach I ... 89
1999 Bowman's Best Franchise Favorites ... 89
1999 Bowman's Best Franchise Favorites Autographs ... 89
1999 Bowman's Best Future Foundations Mach I ... 89
1999 Bowman's Best Mirror Image ... 89
1999 Bowman's Best Rookie Locker Room Autographs ... 89
1999 Bowman's Best Rookie Locker Room Game Used Bats ... 89
1999 Bowman's Best Rookie Locker Room Game Worn Jerseys ... 90
1999 Bowman's Best Rookie of the Year ... 90
1996 Circa ... 90
1996 Circa Rave ... 91
1996 Circa Access ... 91
1996 Circa Boss ... 91
1997 Circa ... 91
1997 Circa Rave ... 93
1997 Circa Boss ... 93
1997 Circa Emerald Autographs ... 93
1997 Circa Fast Track ... 94
1997 Circa Icons ... 94
1997 Circa Limited Access ... 94
1997 Circa Rave Reviews ... 94
1998 Circa Thunder ... 94
1998 Circa Thunder Rave ... 95
1998 Circa Thunder Super Rave ... 96
1998 Circa Thunder Boss ... 96
1998 Circa Thunder Fast Track ... 96
1998 Circa Thunder Limited Access ... 96
1998 Circa Thunder Quick Strike ... 96
1998 Circa Thunder Rave Review ... 96
1998 Circa Thunder Thunder Boomers ... 96
1989 Classic Travel Orange ... 97
1989 Classic Travel Purple ... 97
1994 Collector's Choice ... 97
1994 Collector's Choice Gold Signature ... 100
1994 Collector's Choice Silver Signature ... 100
1994 Collector's Choice Home Run All-Stars ... 100
1995 Collector's Choice ... 100
1995 Collector's Choice Crash the Game ... 103
1996 Collector's Choice ... 103
1996 Collector's Choice Crash the Game ... 107
1996 Collector's Choice Griffey A Cut Above ... 107
1996 Collector's Choice Nomo Scrapbook ... 107
1996 Collector's Choice You Make the Play ... 107
1997 Collector's Choice ... 108
1997 Collector's Choice All-Star Connection ... 110
1997 Collector's Choice Big Shots ... 110
1997 Collector's Choice The Big Show ... 110
1997 Collector's Choice Crash the Game ... 111
1997 Collector's Choice Crash the Game Exchange ... 111
1997 Collector's Choice Griffey Clearly Dominant ... 111
1997 Collector's Choice New Frontier ... 112
1997 Collector's Choice Premier Power ... 112
1997 Collector's Choice Stick'Ums ... 112
1997 Collector's Choice Toast of the Town ... 112
1997 Collector's Choice Update ... 112
1998 Collector's Choice ... 113
1998 Collector's Choice Prime Choice Reserve ... 115
1998 Collector's Choice Crash the Game ... 115
1998 Collector's Choice Evolution Revolution ... 116
1998 Collector's Choice Mini Bobbing Heads ... 116
1998 Collector's Choice StarQuest ... 116
1998 Collector's Choice StarQuest Single ... 117
1998 Collector's Choice Stick 'Ums ... 117
1995 Collector's Choice SE ... 117
1998 Crown Royale ... 118
1998 Crown Royale All-Stars ... 199
1998 Crown Royale Cramer's Choice Premiums ... 119
1998 Crown Royale Diamond Knights ... 119
1998 Crown Royale Firestone on Baseball ... 120
1998 Crown Royale Home Run Fever ... 120
1998 Crown Royale Pillars of the Game ... 120
1999 Crown Royale ... 120
1999 Crown Royale Limited ... 121
1999 Crown Royale Opening Day ... 121
1999 Crown Royale Century 21 ... 121
1999 Crown Royale Cramer's Choice Premiums ... 121
1999 Crown Royale Gold Crown Die Cut Premiums ... 121
1999 Crown Royale Living Legends ... 122
1999 Crown Royale Master Performers ... 122
1999 Crown Royale Pillars of the Game ... 122
1999 Crown Royale Pivotal Players ... 122
1981 Donruss ... 122
1982 Donruss ... 125
1983 Donruss ... 128
1984 Donruss ... 131
1985 Donruss ... 134
1986 Donruss ... 137
1986 Donruss Rookies ... 140
1986 Donruss Highlights ... 140
1987 Donruss ... 141
1987 Donruss Rookies ... 143
1987 Donruss Highlights ... 144
1987 Donruss Opening Day ... 144
1988 Donruss ... 145
1988 Donruss Rookies ... 148
1989 Donruss ... 148
1989 Donruss Rookies ... 151
1989 Donruss Baseball's Best ... 151
1990 Donruss ... 153
1990 Donruss Rookies ... 156
1991 Donruss ... 157
1991 Donruss Elite ... 160
1991 Donruss Rookies ... 160
1992 Donruss ... 161
1992 Donruss Diamond Kings ... 164
1992 Donruss Elite ... 164
1992 Donruss Update ... 164
1992 Donruss Rookies ... 165
1992 Donruss Rookies Phenoms ... 165
1993 Donruss ... 165
1993 Donruss Diamond Kings ... 169
1993 Donruss Elite ... 169
1993 Donruss Long Ball Leaders ... 169
1993 Donruss MVPs ... 169
1993 Donruss Spirit of the Game ... 170
1994 Donruss ... 170
1994 Donruss Anniversary '84 ... 173
1994 Donruss Award Winner Jumbos ... 173
1994 Donruss Diamond Kings ... 173
1994 Donruss Dominators ... 173
1994 Donruss Elite ... 173
1994 Donruss Long Ball Leaders ... 173
1994 Donruss MVPs ... 174
1994 Donruss Spirit of the Game ... 174
1995 Donruss ... 174
1995 Donruss All-Stars ... 176
1995 Donruss Bomb Squad ... 176
1995 Donruss Diamond Kings ... 177
1995 Donruss Dominators ... 177
1995 Donruss Elite ... 177
1995 Donruss Long Ball Leaders ... 177
1995 Donruss Mound Marvels ... 177
1996 Donruss ... 177
1996 Donruss Diamond Kings ... 180
1996 Donruss Elite ... 180
1996 Donruss Freeze Frame ... 180
1996 Donruss Hit List ... 180
1996 Donruss Long Ball Leaders ... 180
1996 Donruss Power Alley ... 180
1996 Donruss Pure Power ... 181
1996 Donruss Round Trippers ... 181
1996 Donruss Showdown ... 181
1997 Donruss ... 181
1997 Donruss Gold Press Proofs ... 183
1997 Donruss Silver Press Proofs ... 183
1997 Donruss Armed and Dangerous ... 183
1997 Donruss Diamond Kings ... 183
1997 Donruss Dominators ... 184
1997 Donruss Elite Inserts ... 184
1997 Donruss Franchise Features ... 184
1997 Donruss Longball Leaders ... 184
1997 Donruss Power Alley ... 184
1997 Donruss Rated Rookies ... 185
1997 Donruss Ripken The Only Way I Know ... 185
1997 Donruss Rocket Launchers ... 185
1997 Donruss Rookie Diamond Kings ... 185
1998 Donruss ... 185
1998 Donruss Gold Press Proofs ... 187

4 / Contents

1998 Donruss Silver Press Proofs	187
1998 Donruss Crusade Green	187
1998 Donruss Diamond Kings	188
1998 Donruss Dominators	188
1998 Donruss Elite Inserts	188
1998 Donruss FANtasy Team	188
1998 Donruss Longball Leaders	189
1998 Donruss MLB 99	189
1998 Donruss Production Line On-Base	189
1998 Donruss Production Line Power Index	189
1998 Donruss Production Line Slugging	189
1998 Donruss Rated Rookies	190
1998 Donruss Rookie Diamond Kings	190
1998 Donruss Signature Series Previews	190
1998 Donruss Collections Donruss	190
1998 Donruss Collections Elite	191
1998 Donruss Collections Leaf	192
1998 Donruss Collections Preferred	193
1998 Donruss Prized Collections Donruss	194
1998 Donruss Prized Collections Elite	194
1998 Donruss Prized Collections Leaf	194
1998 Donruss Prized Collections Preferred	194
1997 Donruss Elite	194
1997 Donruss Elite Leather and Lumber	195
1997 Donruss Elite Passing the Torch	195
1997 Donruss Elite Passing the Torch Autographs	195
1997 Donruss Elite Turn of the Century	195
1998 Donruss Elite	195
1998 Donruss Elite Aspirations	196
1998 Donruss Elite Status	196
1998 Donruss Elite Back to the Future	196
1998 Donruss Elite Back to the Future Autographs	196
1998 Donruss Elite Craftsmen	197
1996 Donruss Elite Prime Numbers	197
1998 Donruss Elite Prime Numbers Die Cuts	197
1997 Donruss Limited	197
1997 Donruss Limited Exposure	199
1997 Donruss Limited Fabric of the Game	199
1997 Donruss Preferred	200
1997 Donruss Preferred Cut to the Chase	200
1997 Donruss Preferred Precious Metals	201
1997 Donruss Preferred Staremasters	201
1997 Donruss Preferred Tin Packs	201
1997 Donruss Preferred X-Potential Power	201
1998 Donruss Preferred	201
1998 Donruss Preferred Seating	202
1998 Donruss Preferred Great X-Pectations	203
1998 Donruss Preferred Precious Metals	203
1998 Donruss Preferred Tin Packs	203
1998 Donruss Preferred Tin Packs Double-Wide	203
1998 Donruss Preferred Tile Waves	204
1997 Donruss Signature	204
1997 Donruss Signature Autographs	204
1997 Donruss Signature Autographs Century	205
1997 Donruss Signature Autographs Millenium	205
1997 Donruss Signature Notable Nicknames	206
1997 Donruss Signature Significant Signatures	206
1998 Donruss Signature	206
1998 Donruss Signature Proofs	207
1998 Donruss Signature Autographs Century	208
1998 Donruss Signature Autographs Millenium	208
1998 Donruss Signature Significant Signatures	209
1998 Donruss Signature Signing Bonus	209
1995 Emotion	209
1995 Emotion Masters	210
1995 Emotion N-Tense	210
1995 Emotion Ripken	210
1995 Emotion Rookies	211
1996 Emotion-XL	211
1996 Emotion-XL D-Fense	212
1996 Emotion-XL Legion of Boom	212
1996 Emotion-XL N-Tense	212
1996 Emotion-XL Rare Breed	212
1997 E-X2000	213
1997 E-X2000 Essential Credentials	213
1997 E-X2000 A Cut Above	213
1997 E-X2000 Emerald Autographs	213
1997 E-X2000 Hall or Nothing	213
1997 E-X2000 Star Date 2000	214
1998 E-X2001	214
1998 E-X2001 Essential Credentials Future	214
1998 E-X2001 Essential Credentials Now	215
1998 E-X2001 Cheap Seat Treats	215
1998 E-X2001 Destination Cooperstown	216
1998 E-X2001 Signature 2001	216
1998 E-X2001 Star Date 2001	216
1999 E-X Century	216
1999 E-X Century Essential Credentials Future	217
1999 E-X Century Essential Credentials Now	217
1999 E-X Century Authen-Kicks	218
1999 E-X Century E-X Quisite	218
1999 E-X Century Favorites for Fenway '99	218
1999 E-X Century Milestones of the Century	219
1993 Finest	219
1993 Finest Refractors	220
1993 Finest Jumbos	220
1994 Finest Pre-Production	220
1994 Finest	220

1995 Finest	222
1995 Finest Flame Throwers	223
1995 Finest Power Kings	224
1996 Finest	224
1996 Finest Refractors	225
1997 Finest	225
1997 Finest Embossed	227
1997 Finest Embossed Refractors	227
1997 Finest Refractors	227
1998 Finest	227
1998 Finest No-Protectors Refractors	229
1998 Finest Oversize	229
1998 Finest Refractors	229
1998 Finest Centurions	229
1998 Finest The Man	229
1998 Finest Mystery Finest 1	229
1998 Finest Mystery Finest 2	230
1998 Finest Power Zone	230
1998 Finest Stadium Stars	230
1999 Finest	231
1999 Finest Gold Refractors	232
1999 Finest Refractors	232
1999 Finest Aaron Award Contenders	232
1999 Finest Aaron Award Contenders Refractors	232
1999 Finest Complements	233
1999 Finest Double Feature	233
1999 Finest Franchise Records	233
1999 Finest Future's Finest	233
1999 Finest Leading Indicators	233
1999 Finest Milestones	233
1999 Finest Peel and Reveal Sparkle	234
1999 Finest Prominent Figures	234
1999 Finest Split Screen	234
1999 Finest Team Finest Blue	234
1993 Flair	235
1993 Flair Wave of the Future	236
1994 Flair	236
1994 Flair Hot Gloves	238
1994 Flair Hot Numbers	238
1994 Flair Infield Power	238
1994 Flair Outfield Power	238
1994 Flair Wave of the Future	239
1995 Flair	239
1995 Flair Hot Gloves	241
1995 Flair Hot Numbers	241
1995 Flair Infield Power	241
1995 Flair Outfield Power	241
1995 Flair Ripken	241
1995 Flair Today's Spotlight	241
1995 Flair Wave of the Future	242
1996 Flair	242
1996 Flair Diamond Cuts	243
1996 Flair Hot Gloves	243
1996 Flair Powerline	244
1996 Flair Wave of the Future	244
1997 Flair Showcase Row 2	244
1997 Flair Showcase Row 1	245
1997 Flair Showcase Row 0	245
1997 Flair Showcase Legacy Collection	245
1997 Flair Showcase Diamond Cuts	245
1997 Flair Showcase Hot Gloves	245
1997 Flair Showcase Wave of the Future	245
1998 Flair Showcase Row 3	246
1998 Flair Showcase Row 2	246
1998 Flair Showcase Row 1	246
1998 Flair Showcase Row 0	247
1998 Flair Showcase Legacy Collection	247
1998 Flair Showcase Perfect 10	247
1998 Flair Showcase Wave of the Future	247
1999 Flair Showcase Row 3	247
1999 Flair Showcase Row 2	248
1999 Flair Showcase Row 1	248
1999 Flair Showcase Legacy Collection	248
1999 Flair Showcase Measure of Greatness	248
1999 Flair Showcase Wave of the Future	248
1963 Fleer	249
1981 Fleer	249
1982 Fleer	252
1983 Fleer	255
1984 Fleer	258
1984 Fleer Update	261
1985 Fleer	261
1985 Fleer Update	264
1986 Fleer	265
1986 Fleer All-Stars	268
1986 Fleer Future Hall of Famers	268
1986 Fleer Update	268
1987 Fleer	269
1987 Fleer Glossy	272
1987 Fleer All-Stars	272
1987 Fleer Headliners	272
1987 Fleer Update	272
1987 Fleer Update Glossy	273
1988 Fleer	273
1988 Fleer Glossy	276
1988 Fleer All-Stars	276
1988 Fleer Headliners	276
1988 Fleer Update	276
1988 Fleer Update Glossy	277

1989 Fleer	277
1989 Fleer Glossy	280
1989 Fleer All-Stars	281
1989 Fleer For The Record	281
1989 Fleer Update	281
1990 Fleer	281
1990 Fleer All-Stars	285
1990 Fleer League Standouts	285
1990 Fleer Soaring Stars	285
1990 Fleer Update	285
1991 Fleer	286
1991 Fleer All-Stars	289
1991 Fleer Pro-Visions	289
1991 Fleer Update	289
1992 Fleer	290
1992 Fleer All-Stars	293
1992 Fleer Clemens	293
1992 Fleer Lumber Company	294
1992 Fleer Rookie Sensations	294
1992 Fleer Smoke 'n Heat	294
1992 Fleer Team Leaders	294
1992 Fleer Update	294
1992 Fleer Update Headliners	295
1993 Fleer	295
1993 Fleer All-Stars	298
1993 Fleer Glavine	298
1993 Fleer Golden Moments	299
1993 Fleer Major League Prospects	299
1993 Fleer Pro-Visions	299
1993 Fleer Pro-Visions	299
1993 Fleer Rookie Sensations	299
1993 Fleer Team Leaders	299
1993 Fleer Final Edition	300
1993 Fleer Final Edition Diamond Tribute	301
1994 Fleer	301
1994 Fleer All-Stars	304
1994 Fleer Award Winners	304
1994 Fleer Golden Moments	304
1994 Fleer League Leaders	305
1994 Fleer Lumber Company	305
1994 Fleer Major League Prospects	305
1994 Fleer Pro-Visions	305
1994 Fleer Rookie Sensations	305
1994 Fleer Salmon	305
1994 Fleer Smoke 'n Heat	306
1994 Fleer Team Leaders	306
1994 Fleer Update	306
1994 Fleer Update Diamond Tribute	307
1995 Fleer	307
1995 Fleer All-Stars	310
1995 Fleer All-Rookies	310
1995 Fleer All-Stars	310
1995 Fleer Award Winners	310
1995 Fleer League Leaders	310
1995 Fleer Lumber Company	310
1995 Fleer Major League Prospects	311
1995 Fleer Pro-Visions	311
1995 Fleer Rookie Sensations	311
1995 Fleer Team Leaders	311
1995 Fleer Update	311
1995 Fleer Update Diamond Tribute	312
1995 Fleer Update Headliners	312
1995 Fleer Update Rookie Update	313
1995 Fleer Update Smooth Leather	313
1995 Fleer Update Soaring Stars	313
1996 Fleer	313
1996 Fleer Tiffany	315
1996 Fleer Checklists	316
1996 Fleer Golden Memories	316
1996 Fleer Lumber Company	316
1996 Fleer Postseason Glory	316
1996 Fleer Prospects	316
1996 Fleer Road Warriors	316
1996 Fleer Rookie Sensations	316
1996 Fleer Smoke 'n Heat	317
1996 Fleer Team Leaders	317
1996 Fleer Tomorrow's Legends	317
1996 Fleer Zone	317
1996 Fleer Update	317
1996 Fleer Update Tiffany	318
1996 Fleer Update Diamond Tribute	318
1996 Fleer Update Headliners	319
1996 Fleer Update New Horizons	319
1996 Fleer Update Smooth Leather	319
1996 Fleer Update Soaring Stars	319
1997 Fleer	319
1997 Fleer Tiffany	322
1997 Fleer Bleacher Blasters	322
1997 Fleer Decade of Excellence	323
1997 Fleer Diamond Tribute	323
1997 Fleer Golden Memories	323
1997 Fleer Goudey Greats	323
1997 Fleer Headliners	323
1997 Fleer Lumber Company	323
1997-98 Fleer Million Dollar Moments	324
1997 Fleer New Horizons	324
1997 Fleer Night and Day	324
1997 Fleer Rookie Sensations	324
1997 Fleer Soaring Stars	324

1997 Fleer Team Leaders 324
1997 Fleer Zone 325
1998 Fleer 325
1998 Fleer Vintage '63 327
1998 Fleer Vintage '63 Classic 328
1998 Fleer Decade of Excellence 328
1998 Fleer Diamond Ink 328
1998 Fleer Diamond Standouts 328
1998 Fleer Diamond Tribute 329
1998 Fleer In The Clutch 329
1998 Fleer Lumber Company 329
1998 Fleer Mickey Mantle Monumental Moments 329
1998 Fleer Power Game 329
1998 Fleer Promising Forecast 329
1998 Fleer Rookie Sensations 330
1998 Fleer Zone 330
1998 Fleer Update 330
1999 Fleer 330
1999 Fleer Starting 9 333
1999 Fleer Vintage '61 333
1999 Fleer Warning Track 333
1999 Fleer Date With Destiny 333
1999 Fleer Diamond Magic 334
1999 Fleer Going Yard 334
1999 Fleer Golden Memories 334
1999 Fleer Stan Musial Monumental Moments 334
1999 Fleer Rookie Flashback 334
1999 Fleer Update 334
1999 Fleer Brilliants 335
1999 Fleer Brilliants 24-Karat Gold 336
1999 Fleer Brilliants Blue 336
1999 Fleer Brilliants Gold 336
1999 Fleer Brilliants Illuminators 336
1999 Fleer Brilliants Shining Stars 336
1999 Fleer Mystique 337
1999 Fleer Mystique Gold 337
1999 Fleer Mystique Destiny 337
1999 Fleer Mystique Established 338
1999 Fleer Mystique Feel the Game 338
1999 Fleer Mystique Fresh Ink 338
1999 Fleer Mystique Prophetic 338
1949 Leaf 338
1990 Leaf 339
1991 Leaf Previews 341
1991 Leaf 341
1991 Leaf Gold Rookies 343
1992 Leaf Previews 344
1992 Leaf 344
1992 Leaf Gold Rookies 346
1993 Leaf 346
1993 Leaf Fasttrack 349
1993 Leaf Gold All-Stars 349
1993 Leaf Gold Rookies 349
1993 Leaf Heading for the Hall 349
1993 Leaf Thomas 349
1994 Leaf 350
1994 Leaf Clean-Up Crew 351
1994 Leaf Gamers 352
1994 Leaf Gold Rookies 352
1994 Leaf Gold Stars 352
1994 Leaf MVP Contenders 352
1994 Leaf Power Brokers 352
1994 Leaf Slideshow 353
1994 Leaf Statistical Standouts 353
1995 Leaf 353
1995 Leaf Checklists 354
1995 Leaf Cornerstones 355
1995 Leaf Gold Rookies 355
1995 Leaf Gold Stars 355
1995 Leaf Great Gloves 355
1995 Leaf Heading for the Hall 355
1995 Leaf Slideshow 355
1995 Leaf Statistical Standouts 356
1995 Leaf Thomas 356
1995 Leaf 300 Club 356
1996 Leaf 356
1996 Leaf All-Star Game MVP Contenders 357
1996 Leaf Gold Stars 357
1996 Leaf Hats Off 357
1996 Leaf Picture Perfect 358
1996 Leaf Statistical Standouts 358
1996 Leaf Thomas Greatest Hits 358
1996 Leaf Total Bases 358
1997 Leaf 358
1997 Leaf Fractal Matrix 360
1997 Leaf Fractal Matrix Die Cuts 361
1997 Leaf Banner Season 363
1997 Leaf Dress for Success 363
1997 Leaf Get-A-Grip 364
1997 Leaf Gold Stars 364
1997 Leaf Knot-Hole Gang 364
1997 Leaf Leagues of the Nation 364
1997 Leaf Statistical Standouts 364
1997 Leaf Thomas Collection 365
1997 Leaf Warning Track 365
1998 Leaf 365
1998 Leaf Fractal Diamond Axis 366
1998 Leaf Fractal Matrix 366
1998 Leaf Fractal Matrix Die Cuts 367
1998 Leaf Crusade Green 368
1998 Leaf Heading for the Hall 368
1998 Leaf State Representatives 368
1998 Leaf Statistical Standouts 368
1998 Leaf Fractal Foundations 369
1998 Leaf Fractal Materials 369
1998 Leaf Fractal Materials Die Cuts 370
1998 Leaf Fractal Materials Z2 Axis 371
1994 Leaf Limited 371
1994 Leaf Limited Gold All-Stars 372
1994 Leaf Limited Rookies 372
1994 Leaf Limited Rookies Phenoms 373
1995 Leaf Limited 373
1995 Leaf Limited Bat Patrol 374
1995 Leaf Limited Lumberjacks 374
1996 Leaf Limited 374
1996 Leaf Limited Lumberjacks 375
1996 Leaf Limited Pennant Craze 375
1996 Leaf Limited Rookies 375
1996 Leaf Preferred 375
1996 Leaf Preferred Staremaster 376
1996 Leaf Preferred Steel 376
1996 Leaf Preferred Steel Power 376
1998 Leaf Rookies and Stars 377
1998 Leaf Rookies and Stars Longevity 378
1998 Leaf Rookies and Stars True Blue 378
1998 Leaf Rookies and Stars Crosstraining 378
1998 Leaf Rookies and Stars Crusade Update Green 378
1998 Leaf Rookies and Stars Extreme Measures 379
1998 Leaf Rookies and Stars Extreme Measures Die Cuts 379
1998 Leaf Rookies and Stars Freshman Orientation 379
1998 Leaf Rookies and Stars Great American Heroes 379
1998 Leaf Rookies and Stars Greatest Hits 379
1998 Leaf Rookies and Stars Home Run Derby 380
1998 Leaf Rookies and Stars Leaf MVP's 380
1998 Leaf Rookies and Stars Major League Hard Drives 380
1998 Leaf Rookies and Stars Standing Ovations 380
1998 Leaf Rookies and Stars Ticket Masters 380
1996 Leaf Signature 381
1996 Leaf Signature Gold Press Proofs 381
1996 Leaf Signature Platinum Press Proofs 381
1996 Leaf Signature Autographs 381
1996 Leaf Signature Extended Autographs 383
1996 Leaf Signature Extended Autographs Century Marks 384
1996 Metal Universe 384
1996 Metal Universe Heavy Metal 385
1996 Metal Universe Mining For Gold 385
1996 Metal Universe Mother Lode 385
1996 Metal Universe Platinum Portraits 385
1996 Metal Universe Titanium 385
1997 Metal Universe 386
1997 Metal Universe Blast Furnace 387
1997 Metal Universe Emerald Autographs 387
1997 Metal Universe Magnetic Field 387
1997 Metal Universe Mining for Gold 387
1997 Metal Universe Mother Lode 387
1997 Metal Universe Platinum Portraits 387
1997 Metal Universe Titanium 388
1998 Metal Universe 388
1998 Metal Universe Precious Metal Gems 389
1998 Metal Universe All-Galactic Team 389
1998 Metal Universe Diamond Heroes 389
1998 Metal Universe Platinum Portraits 389
1998 Metal Universe Titanium 389
1998 Metal Universe Universal Language 389
1999 Metal Universe 390
1999 Metal Universe Precious Metal Gems 391
1999 Metal Universe Boyz With The Wood 391
1999 Metal Universe Diamond Soul 391
1999 Metal Universe Linchpins 391
1999 Metal Universe Neophytes 391
1999 Metal Universe Planet Metal 392
1997 New Pinnacle 392
1997 New Pinnacle Artist's Proofs 393
1997 New Pinnacle Interleague Encounter 394
1997 New Pinnacle Keeping the Pace 394
1997 New Pinnacle Spellbound 394
1994 Pacific 394
1994 Pacific All-Latino 397
1994 Pacific Gold Prisms 397
1994 Pacific Silver Prisms 397
1995 Pacific 398
1995 Pacific Gold Crown Die Cuts 399
1995 Pacific Gold Prisms 400
1995 Pacific Latinos Destacados 400
1996 Pacific 400
1996 Pacific Cramer's Choice 402
1996 Pacific Estrellas Latinas 402
1996 Pacific Gold Crown Die Cuts 402
1996 Pacific Hometowns 403
1996 Pacific Milestones 403
1996 Pacific October Moments 403
1997 Pacific 403
1997 Pacific Card-Supials 405
1997 Pacific Cramer's Choice 405
1997 Pacific Fireworks Die Cuts 405
1997 Pacific Gold Crown Die Cuts 406
1997 Pacific Latinos of the Major Leagues 406
1997 Pacific Triple Crown Die Cuts 406
1998 Pacific 406
1998 Pacific Platinum Blue 408
1998 Pacific Cramer's Choice 408
1998 Pacific Gold Crown Die Cuts 408
1998 Pacific Home Run Hitters 409
1998 Pacific In The Cage 409
1998 Pacific Latinos of the Major Leagues 409
1998 Pacific Team Checklists 409
1999 Pacific 410
1999 Pacific Platinum Blue 412
1999 Pacific Red 412
1999 Pacific Cramer's Choice 412
1999 Pacific Dynagon Diamond 412
1999 Pacific Gold Crown Die Cuts 412
1999 Pacific Hot Cards 412
1999 Pacific Team Checklists 413
1999 Pacific Timelines 413
2000 Pacific 413
2000 Pacific Copper 415
2000 Pacific Platinum Blue 415
2000 Pacific Premiere Date 415
2000 Pacific Cramer's Choice 415
2000 Pacific Diamond Leaders 416
2000 Pacific Gold Crown Die Cuts 416
2000 Pacific Ornaments 416
2000 Pacific Past and Present 416
2000 Pacific Reflections 417
1998 Pacific Aurora 417
1998 Pacific Aurora Cubes 418
1998 Pacific Aurora Hardball Cel-Fusions 418
1998 Pacific Aurora Kings of the Major Leagues 418
1998 Pacific Aurora On Deck Laser Cuts 418
1998 Pacific Aurora Pennant Fever 418
1999 Pacific Aurora 419
1999 Pacific Aurora Opening Day 420
1999 Pacific Aurora Complete Players 420
1999 Pacific Aurora Kings of the Major Leagues 420
1999 Pacific Aurora On Deck Laser-Cuts 420
1999 Pacific Aurora Pennant Fever 420
1999 Pacific Aurora Styrotechs 421
1999 Pacific Crown Collection 421
1999 Pacific Crown Collection Platinum Blue 422
1999 Pacific Crown Collection In The Cage 422
1999 Pacific Crown Collection Latinos of the Major Leagues 422
1999 Pacific Crown Collection Pacific Cup 423
1999 Pacific Crown Collection Tape Measure 423
1999 Pacific Crown Collection Team Checklists 423
1998 Pacific Invincible 423
1998 Pacific Invincible Platinum Blue 424
1998 Pacific Invincible Cramer's Choice Green 424
1998 Pacific Invincible Gems of the Diamond 424
1998 Pacific Invincible Interleague Players 425
1998 Pacific Invincible Moments in Time 425
1998 Pacific Invincible Photoengravings 426
1998 Pacific Invincible Team Checklists 426
1999 Pacific Invincible 426
1999 Pacific Invincible Opening Day 427
1999 Pacific Invincible Platinum Blue 427
1999 Pacific Invincible Diamond Magic 427
1999 Pacific Invincible Flash Point 428
1999 Pacific Invincible Giants of the Game 428
1999 Pacific Invincible Sandlot Heroes 428
1999 Pacific Invincible Seismic Force 428
1999 Pacific Invincible Thunder Alley 428
1998 Pacific Omega 429
1998 Pacific Omega Red 430
1998 Pacific Omega EO Portraits 430
1998 Pacific Omega Face To Face 430
1998 Pacific Omega Online Inserts 430
1998 Pacific Omega Prisms 430
1998 Pacific Omega Rising Stars 431
1999 Pacific Omega 431
1999 Pacific Omega Copper 432
1999 Pacific Omega Gold 432
1999 Pacific Omega Platinum Blue 432
1999 Pacific Omega Premiere Date 432
1999 Pacific Omega 5-Tool Talents 433
1999 Pacific Omega 5-Tool Talents Tiers 433
1999 Pacific Omega Debut Duos 433
1999 Pacific Omega Diamond Masters 433
1999 Pacific Omega EO Portraits 433
1999 Pacific Omega Hit Machine 3000 434
1999 Pacific Omega HR 99 434
1998 Pacific Online 434
1998 Pacific Online Red 437
1998 Pacific Online Web Cards 437
1998 Pacific Paramount 437
1998 Pacific Paramount Copper 439
1998 Pacific Paramount Gold 439
1998 Pacific Paramount Holographic Silver 439
1998 Pacific Paramount Platinum Blue 439
1998 Pacific Paramount Red 439
1998 Pacific Paramount Cooperstown Bound 439
1998 Pacific Paramount Fielder's Choice 439
1998 Pacific Paramount Special Delivery 439
1998 Pacific Paramount Team Checklists 440
1999 Pacific Paramount 440
1999 Pacific Paramount Copper 441
1999 Pacific Paramount Gold 441

1999 Pacific Paramount Holo-Gold 441
1999 Pacific Paramount Holographic Silver 441
1999 Pacific Paramount Opening Day 441
1999 Pacific Paramount Platinum Blue 441
1999 Pacific Paramount Red 441
1999 Pacific Paramount Cooperstown Bound 441
1999 Pacific Paramount Fielder's Choice 441
1999 Pacific Paramount Personal Bests 442
1999 Pacific Paramount Team Checklists 442
1995 Pacific Prisms 442
1996 Pacific Prisms 443
1996 Pacific Prisms Fence Busters 443
1996 Pacific Prisms Flame Throwers 444
1996 Pacific Prisms Red Hot Stars 444
1997 Pacific Prisms 444
1997 Pacific Prisms Gate Attractions 445
1997 Pacific Prisms Gems of the Diamond 445
1997 Pacific Prisms Sizzling Lumber 446
1997 Pacific Prisms Sluggers and Hurlers 446
1999 Pacific Prism 446
1999 Pacific Prism Holographic Blue 447
1999 Pacific Prism Holographic Gold 447
1999 Pacific Prism Holographic Mirror 447
1999 Pacific Prism Holographic Purple 447
1999 Pacific Prism Red 447
1999 Pacific Prism Ahead of the Game 448
1999 Pacific Prism Ballpark Legends 448
1999 Pacific Prism Diamond Glory 448
1999 Pacific Prism Epic Performers 448
1999 Pacific Private Stock 448
1999 Pacific Private Stock Exclusive 449
1999 Pacific Private Stock Platinum 449
1999 Pacific Private Stock Preferred 449
1999 Pacific Private Stock Vintage 449
1999 Pacific Private Stock PS-206 449
1999 Pacific Private Stock PS-206 Red 449
1999 Pacific Private Stock Home Run History 450
1992 Pinnacle 450
1992 Pinnacle Rookie Idols 452
1992 Pinnacle Slugfest 453
1992 Pinnacle Team 2000 453
1992 Pinnacle Team Pinnacle 453
1992 Pinnacle Rookies 453
1993 Pinnacle 454
1993 Pinnacle Expansion Opening Day 456
1993 Pinnacle Rookie Team Pinnacle 456
1993 Pinnacle Slugfest 457
1993 Pinnacle Team 2001 457
1993 Pinnacle Team Pinnacle 457
1993 Pinnacle Tribute 457
1994 Pinnacle 457
1994 Pinnacle Rookie Team Pinnacle 460
1994 Pinnacle Run Creators 460
1994 Pinnacle Team Pinnacle 460
1994 Pinnacle Tribute 460
1995 Pinnacle 460
1995 Pinnacle ETA 462
1995 Pinnacle Gate Attractions 462
1995 Pinnacle New Blood 463
1995 Pinnacle Performers 463
1995 Pinnacle Pin Redemption 463
1995 Pinnacle Red Hot 463
1995 Pinnacle Team Pinnacle 463
1995 Pinnacle Upstarts 464
1996 Pinnacle 464
1996 Pinnacle Christie Brinkley Collection 466
1996 Pinnacle Essence of the Game 466
1996 Pinnacle First Rate 466
1996 Pinnacle Power 466
1996 Pinnacle Project Stardom 466
1996 Pinnacle Skylines 466
1996 Pinnacle Slugfest 467
1996 Pinnacle Team Pinnacle 467
1996 Pinnacle Team Spirit 467
1996 Pinnacle Team Tomorrow 467
1997 Pinnacle 467
1997 Pinnacle Artist's Proofs 468
1997 Pinnacle Cardfrontations 469
1997 Pinnacle Home/Away 469
1997 Pinnacle Passport to the Majors 469
1997 Pinnacle Shades 470
1997 Pinnacle Team Pinnacle 470
1998 Pinnacle 470
1998 Pinnacle Hit It Here 471
1998 Pinnacle Power Pack Jumbos 471
1998 Pinnacle Spellbound 471
1996 Pinnacle Aficionado 472
1996 Pinnacle Aficionado Magic Numbers 473
1996 Pinnacle Aficionado Rivals 473
1996 Pinnacle Aficionado Slick Picks 473
1997 Pinnacle Certified 473
1997 Pinnacle Certified Mirror Blue 474
1997 Pinnacle Certified Mirror Gold 474
1997 Pinnacle Certified Mirror Red 474
1997 Pinnacle Certified Certified Team 474
1997 Pinnacle Certified Lasting Impressions 475
1997 Pinnacle Inside 475
1997 Pinnacle Inside Diamond Edition 475
1997 Pinnacle Inside 40 Something 476
1997 Pinnacle Inside Cans 476
1997 Pinnacle Inside Dueling Dugouts 476
1998 Pinnacle Inside 476
1998 Pinnacle Inside Diamond Edition 477
1998 Pinnacle Inside Behind the Numbers 477
1998 Pinnacle Inside Cans 477
1998 Pinnacle Inside Stand-Up Guys 477
1998 Pinnacle Performers 478
1998 Pinnacle Performers Big Bang 479
1998 Pinnacle Performers Big Bang Seasonal Outburst 479
1998 Pinnacle Performers Launching Pad 479
1998 Pinnacle Performers Power Trip 480
1998 Pinnacle Performers Swing for the Fences 480
1998 Pinnacle Plus 480
1998 Pinnacle Plus Artist's Proofs 481
1998 Pinnacle Plus All-Star Epix 481
1998 Pinnacle Plus Lasting Memories 481
1998 Pinnacle Plus Piece of the Game 482
1998 Pinnacle Plus Team Pinnacle 482
1998 Pinnacle Plus Yardwork 482
1997 Pinnacle Totally Certified Platinum Blue 482
1997 Pinnacle Totally Certified Platinum Gold 482
1997 Pinnacle Totally Certified Platinum Red 482
1997 Pinnacle X-Press 483
1997 Pinnacle X-Press Far and Away 484
1997 Pinnacle X-Press Melting Pot 484
1997 Pinnacle X-Press Metal Works 484
1997 Pinnacle X-Press Swing for the Fences 484
1998 Revolution 485
1998 Revolution Shadow Series 486
1998 Revolution Foul Pole 486
1998 Revolution Major League Icons 486
1998 Revolution Prime Time Performers 486
1998 Revolution Rookies and Hardball Heroes 486
1998 Revolution Rookies and Hardball Heroes Gold 486
1998 Revolution Showstoppers 486
1999 Revolution 487
1999 Revolution Premiere Date 487
1999 Revolution Red 488
1999 Revolution Shadow Series 488
1999 Revolution Diamond Legacy 488
1999 Revolution Foul Pole 488
1999 Revolution MLB Icons 488
1999 Revolution Thorn in the Side 488
1999 Revolution Tripleheader 489
1988 Score 489
1988 Score Glossy 492
1988 Score Rookie/Traded 492
1988 Score Rookie/Traded Glossy 492
1989 Score 492
1989 Score Rookie/Traded 495
1989 Scoremasters 496
1989 Score Young Superstars I 496
1989 Score Young Superstars II 497
1990 Score 497
1990 Score Rookie Dream Team 500
1990 Score Rookie/Traded 500
1990 Score Rising Stars 501
1990 Score Young Superstars I 501
1990 Score Young Superstars II 502
1991 Score 502
1991 Score Cooperstown 506
1991 Score Hot Rookies 506
1991 Score Mantle 506
1991 Score Rookie/Traded 507
1992 Score 507
1992 Score DiMaggio 511
1992 Score Factory Inserts 511
1992 Score Franchise 511
1992 Score Hot Rookies 511
1992 Score Impact Players 511
1992 Score Rookie/Traded 512
1993 Score 512
1993 Score Boys of Summer 515
1993 Score Franchise 515
1993 Score Gold Dream Team 516
1994 Score 516
1994 Score Boys of Summer 518
1994 Score Cycle 519
1994 Score Dream Team 519
1994 Score Gold Stars 519
1994 Score Rookie/Traded 519
1994 Score Rookie/Traded Gold Rush 520
1994 Score Rookie/Traded Changing Places 520
1994 Score Rookie/Traded Super Rookies 521
1995 Score 521
1995 Score Airmail 523
1995 Score Double Gold Champs 523
1995 Score Draft Picks 524
1995 Score Dream Team 524
1995 Score Hall of Gold 524
1995 Score Rookie Dream Team 524
1995 Score Rules 525
1996 Score 525
1996 Score All-Stars 527
1996 Score Big Bats 527
1996 Score Diamond Aces 527
1996 Score Dream Team 528
1996 Score Dugout Collection 528
1996 Score Future Franchise 529
1996 Score Gold Stars 529
1996 Score Numbers Game 529
1996 Score Power Pace 529
1996 Score Reflextions 529
1996 Score Titanic Taters 530
1997 Score 530
1997 Score Blast Masters 532
1997 Score Franchise 532
1997 Score Heart of the Order 533
1997 Score Highlight Zone 533
1997 Score Pitcher Perfect 533
1997 Score Stand and Deliver 533
1997 Score Stellar Season 533
1997 Score Titanic Taters 534
1998 Score 534
1998 Score All Score Team 535
1998 Score Complete Players 535
1998 Score Epix 535
1998 Score First Pitch 535
1998 Score Loaded Lineup 536
1998 Score New Season 536
1998 Score Rookie Traded 536
1998 Score Rookie Traded Showcase Series 537
1998 Score Rookie Traded Showcase Series Artist's Proofs 538
1998 Score Rookie Traded All-Star Epix 538
1998 Score Rookie Traded Complete Players 538
1998 Score Rookie Traded Star Gazing 538
1993 Select 538
1993 Select Aces 540
1993 Select Aces 540
1993 Select Chase Rookies 540
1993 Select Chase Stars 540
1993 Select Stat Leaders 541
1993 Select Triple Crown 541
1993 Select Rookie/Traded 541
1993 Select Rookie/Traded All-Star Rookies 542
1994 Select 542
1994 Select Crown Contenders 544
1994 Select Rookie Surge 544
1994 Select Skills 544
1995 Select 544
1995 Select Big Sticks 545
1995 Select Can't Miss 546
1995 Select Sure Shots 546
1996 Select 546
1996 Select Claim To Fame 547
1996 Select En Fuego 547
1996 Select Team Nucleus 547
1997 Select 548
1997 Select Rookie Autographs 549
1997 Select Rookie Revolution 549
1997 Select Tools of the Trade 549
1995 Select Certified 549
1995 Select Certified Mirror Gold 550
1995 Select Certified Future 550
1995 Select Certified Gold Team 550
1995 Select Certified Potential Unlimited 1975 550
1996 Select Certified 551
1996 Select Certified Mirror Blue 551
1996 Select Certified Mirror Gold 551
1996 Select Certified Mirror Red 551
1996 Select Certified Interleague Preview 552
1996 Select Certified Select Few 552
1998 SkyBox Dugout Axcess 552
1998 SkyBox Dugout Axcess Inside Axcess 553
1998 SkyBox Dugout Axcess Autograph Redemptions 553
1998 SkyBox Dugout Axcess Dishwashers 553
1998 SkyBox Dugout Axcess Double Header 553
1998 SkyBox Dugout Axcess Frequent Flyers 553
1998 SkyBox Dugout Axcess Gronks 553
1998 SkyBox Dugout Axcess SuperHeroes 554
1999 SkyBox Molten Metal 554
1999 SkyBox Molten Metal Xplosion 555
1999 SkyBox Molten Metal Fusion 555
1999 SkyBox Molten Metal Fusion Sterling 555
1999 SkyBox Molten Metal Fusion Titanium 555
1999 SkyBox Molten Metal Oh Atlanta 555
1999 SkyBox Premium 555
1999 SkyBox Premium Star Rubies 557
1999 SkyBox Premium Autographics 557
1999 SkyBox Premium Autographics Blue Ink 557
1999 SkyBox Premium Diamond Debuts 557
1999 SkyBox Premium Intimidation Nation 557
1999 SkyBox Premium Live Bats 558
1999 SkyBox Premium Show Business 558
1999 SkyBox Premium Soul of the Game 558
1999 SkyBox Thunder 558
1999 SkyBox Thunder Rant 559
1999 SkyBox Thunder Rave 559
1999 SkyBox Thunder Super Rave 560
1999 SkyBox Thunder Dial 1 560
1999 SkyBox Thunder Hip-No-Tized 560
1999 SkyBox Thunder In Depth 560
1999 SkyBox Thunder Turbo-Charged 560
1999 SkyBox Thunder Unleashed 560
1999 SkyBox Thunder www.batterz.com 560
1993 SP 561
1993 SP Platinum Power 562

1994 SP Previews 562
1994 SP 562
1994 SP Die Cuts 563
1994 SP Holoviews 563
1994 SP Holoviews Die Cuts 563
1995 SP 563
1995 SP Platinum Power 564
1995 SP Special FX 565
1996 SP 565
1996 SP Baseball Heroes 566
1996 SP Marquee Matchups 566
1996 SP Special FX 566
1997 SP 566
1997 SP Game Film 567
1997 SP Griffey Heroes 567
1997 SP Inside Info 568
1997 SP Marquee Matchups 568
1997 SP Special FX 568
1997 SP SPx Force 568
1997 SP SPx Force Autographs 568
1997 SP Vintage Autographs 569
1998 SP Authentic 569
1998 SP Authentic Chirography 570
1998 SP Authentic Sheer Dominance 570
1998 SP Authentic Trade Cards 570
1999 SP Authentic 570
1999 SP Authentic Chirography 571
1999 SP Authentic Chirography Gold 571
1999 SP Authentic Epic Figures 572
1999 SP Authentic Home Run Chronicles 572
1999 SP Authentic Redemption Cards 572
1999 SP Authentic Reflections 572
1995 SP Championship 573
1995 SP Championship Classic Performances 573
1995 SP Championship Fall Classic 574
1999 SP Signature 574
1999 SP Signature Autographs 575
1999 SP Signature Autographs Gold 575
1999 SP Signature Legendary Cuts 576
1986 Sportflics Rookies 576
1994 Sportflics 576
1994 Sportflics Movers 577
1994 Sportflics Shakers 577
1994 Sportflics Rookie/Traded 577
1994 Sportflics Rookie/Traded Artist's Proofs 578
1994 Sportflics Rookie/Traded Going Going Gone ..578
1994 Sportflics Rookie/Traded Rookie Starflics 578
1995 Sportflix 579
1995 Sportflix Detonators 579
1995 Sportflix Double Take 579
1995 Sportflix Hammer Team 580
1995 Sportflix ProMotion 580
1996 Sportflix 580
1996 Sportflix Double Take 581
1996 Sportflix Hit Parade 581
1996 Sportflix Power Surge 581
1996 Sportflix ProMotion 581
1997 Sports Illustrated 581
1997 Sports Illustrated Extra Edition 582
1997 Sports Illustrated Autographed Mini-Covers ..582
1997 Sports Illustrated Cooperstown Collection 582
1997 Sports Illustrated Great Shots 583
1998 Sports Illustrated 583
1998 Sports Illustrated Extra Edition 584
1998 Sports Illustrated Autographs 584
1998 Sports Illustrated Covers 584
1998 Sports Illustrated Editor's Choice 584
1998 Sports Illustrated Opening Day Mini Posters 584
1999 Sports Illustrated 585
1999 Sports Illustrated Diamond Dominators 586
1999 Sports Illustrated Fabulous 40's 586
1999 Sports Illustrated Fabulous 40's Extra 586
1999 Sports Illustrated Headliners 586
1999 Sports Illustrated One's To Watch 586
1999 Sports Illustrated Greats of the Game 586
1999 Sports Illustrated Greats of the Game Autographs ..587
1999 Sports Illustrated Greats of the Game Cover Collection 587
1999 Sports Illustrated Greats of the Game Record Breakers 588
1998 Sports Illustrated Then and Now 588
1998 Sports Illustrated Then and Now Extra Edition 589
1998 Sports Illustrated Then and Now Art of the Game 589
1998 Sports Illustrated Then and Now Autographs 589
1998 Sports Illustrated Then and Now Covers 589
1998 Sports Illustrated Then and Now Great Shots 589
1998 Sports Illustrated Then and Now Road to Cooperstown 589
1998 Sports Illustrated World Series Fever 589
1998 Sports Illustrated World Series Fever Extra Edition ..590
1998 Sports Illustrated World Series Fever Autumn Excellence 590
1998 Sports Illustrated World Series Fever MVP Collection 590
1998 Sports Illustrated World Series Fever Reggie Jackson's Picks 591
1996 SPx 591
1996 SPx Bound for Glory 591
1997 SPx 591
1997 SPx Grand Finale 592
1997 SPx Bound for Glory 592
1997 SPx Bound for Glory Supreme Signatures 592
1997 SPx Cornerstones of the Game 592
1998 SPx Finite 592
1998 SPx Finite Radiance 594
1998 SPx Finite Spectrum 594
1998 SPx Finite Home Run Hysteria 594
1999 SPx 595
1999 SPx Finite Radiance 595
1999 SPx Finite Spectrum 595
1999 SPx Dominance 595
1999 SPx Power Explosion 595
1999 SPx Premier Stars 596
1999 SPx Star Focus 596
1999 SPx Winning Materials 596
1991 Stadium Club 596
1992 Stadium Club Dome 599
1992 Stadium Club 600
1992 Stadium Club First Draft Picks 603
1993 Stadium Club Murphy 603
1993 Stadium Club Murphy Master Photos 604
1993 Stadium Club 605
1993 Stadium Club Inserts 608
1993 Stadium Club Master Photos 608
1994 Stadium Club 608
1994 Stadium Club Dugout Dirt 611
1994 Stadium Club Finest 611
1994 Stadium Club Super Teams 611
1995 Stadium Club 612
1995 Stadium Club Clear Cut 615
1995 Stadium Club Crunch Time 615
1995 Stadium Club Crystal Ball 615
1995 Stadium Club Power Zone 615
1995 Stadium Club Ring Leaders 615
1995 Stadium Club Super Skills 616
1995 Stadium Club Virtual Extremists 616
1996 Stadium Club 616
1996 Stadium Club Bash and Burn 618
1996 Stadium Club Extreme Players Bronze 618
1996 Stadium Club Extreme Winners Bronze 619
1996 Stadium Club Mantle 619
1996 Stadium Club Megaheroes 619
1996 Stadium Club Metalists 619
1996 Stadium Club Midsummer Matchups 619
1996 Stadium Club Power Packed 620
1996 Stadium Club Power Streak 620
1996 Stadium Club Prime Cuts 620
1996 Stadium Club TSC Awards 620
1997 Stadium Club 620
1997 Stadium Club Co-Signers 622
1997 Stadium Club Firebrand Redemption 622
1997 Stadium Club Instavision 622
1997 Stadium Club Millennium 622
1997 Stadium Club Patent Leather 623
1997 Stadium Club Pure Gold 623
1998 Stadium Club 623
1998 Stadium Club First Day Issue 625
1998 Stadium Club One Of A Kind 625
1998 Stadium Club Bowman Previews 625
1998 Stadium Club Bowman Prospect Previews 625
1998 Stadium Club Co-Signers 625
1998 Stadium Club In The Wings 626
1998 Stadium Club Never Compromise 626
1998 Stadium Club Playing With Passion 626
1998 Stadium Club Royal Court 626
1998 Stadium Club Triumvirate Luminous 626
1999 Stadium Club 627
1999 Stadium Club First Day Issue 628
1999 Stadium Club One of a Kind 628
1999 Stadium Club Printing Plates 628
1999 Stadium Club Autographs 628
1999 Stadium Club Chrome 629
1999 Stadium Club Co-Signers 629
1999 Stadium Club Never Compromise 629
1999 Stadium Club Triumvirate Luminous 630
1999 Stadium Club Video Replay 630
1991 Studio Previews 630
1991 Studio 630
1992 Studio 631
1992 Studio Heritage 633
1993 Studio 633
1993 Studio Heritage 634
1993 Studio Silhouettes 634
1993 Studio Superstars on Canvas 634
1993 Studio Thomas 634
1994 Studio 634
1994 Studio Editor's Choice 635
1994 Studio Heritage 635
1994 Studio Series Stars 635
1995 Studio 636
1996 Studio 636
1996 Studio Hit Parade 637
1996 Studio Masterstrokes 637
1996 Studio Stained Glass Stars 638
1997 Studio 638
1997 Studio Gold Press Proofs 638
1997 Studio Silver Press Proofs 639
1997 Studio Autographs 639
1997 Studio Hard Hats 639
1997 Studio Master Strokes 639
1997 Studio Portraits 8x10 639
1998 Studio 639
1998 Studio Gold Press Proofs 640
1998 Studio Silver Press Proofs 640
1998 Studio Autographs 8 x 10 641
1998 Studio Freeze Frame 641
1998 Studio Hit Parade 641
1998 Studio Masterstrokes 641
1998 Studio Portraits 8 x 10 641
1998 Studio MLB 99 642
1995 Summit 642
1995 Summit Big Bang 643
1995 Summit New Age 643
1995 Summit 21 Club 643
1996 Summit 643
1996 Summit Ballparks 644
1996 Summit Big Bang 644
1996 Summit Hitters Inc. 644
1996 Summit Positions 645
1952 Topps 645
1953 Topps 646
1954 Topps 648
1955 Topps 649
1956 Topps 650
1957 Topps 651
1958 Topps 653
1959 Topps 656
1960 Topps 659
1961 Topps 661
1962 Topps 664
1963 Topps 668
1964 Topps 671
1965 Topps 674
1966 Topps 677
1967 Topps 680
1968 Topps 684
1969 Topps 687
1970 Topps 691
1971 Topps 694
1972 Topps 698
1973 Topps 702
1974 Topps 706
1974 Topps Traded 709
1975 Topps 710
1975 Topps Mini 713
1976 Topps 713
1976 Topps Traded 716
1977 Topps 717
1978 Topps 720
1979 Topps 723
1980 Topps 727
1981 Topps 731
1981 Topps Traded 734
1982 Topps 735
1982 Topps Traded 739
1983 Topps 739
1983 Topps Traded 743
1984 Topps 743
1984 Topps Tiffany 747
1984 Topps Traded 747
1984 Topps Traded Tiffany 748
1985 Topps 748
1985 Topps Tiffany 751
1985 Topps Traded 751
1985 Topps Traded Tiffany 752
1986 Topps 752
1986 Topps Tiffany 755
1986 Topps Traded 755
1986 Topps Traded Tiffany 756
1987 Topps 756
1987 Topps Tiffany 760
1987 Topps Rookies 760
1987 Topps Traded 760
1987 Topps Traded Tiffany 760
1988 Topps 761
1988 Topps Tiffany 764
1988 Topps Rookies 764
1988 Topps Traded 764
1988 Topps Traded Tiffany 765
1989 Topps 765
1989 Topps Tiffany 769
1989 Topps Traded 769
1989 Topps Traded Tiffany 769
1990 Topps 769
1990 Topps Tiffany 773
1990 Topps Rookies 773
1990 Topps Traded 773
1990 Topps Traded Tiffany 774
1990 Topps Big 774
1990 Topps Debut '89 775
1991 Topps 776
1991 Topps Tiffany 780
1991 Topps Traded 780
1991 Topps Traded Tiffany 781
1991 Topps Debut '90 781
1992 Topps 781
1992 Topps Gold 785
1992 Topps Gold Winners 785
1992 Topps Traded 785
1992 Topps Traded Gold 786

1992 Topps Debut '91 786
1993 Topps 787
1993 Topps Gold 790
1993 Topps Inaugural Marlins 791
1993 Topps Inaugural Rockies 791
1993 Topps Black Gold 791
1993 Topps Traded 791
1994 Topps 792
1994 Topps Black Gold 795
1994 Topps Traded 796
1994 Topps Traded Finest Inserts 796
1995 Topps 796
1995 Topps Finest Inserts 799
1995 Topps League Leaders 800
1995 Topps Traded 800
1995 Topps Traded Power Boosters 801
1996 Topps 801
1996 Topps Classic Confrontations 803
1996 Topps Mantle 803
1996 Topps Mantle Case 803
1996 Topps Mantle Finest 803
1996 Topps Mantle Finest Refractors 804
1996 Topps Mantle Redemption 804
1996 Topps Masters of the Game 804
1996 Topps Mystery Finest 804
1996 Topps Power Boosters 804
1996 Topps Profiles 805
1996 Topps Road Warriors 805
1996 Topps Wrecking Crew 805
1997 Topps 805
1997 Topps All-Stars 808
1997 Topps Awesome Impact 808
1997 Topps Hobby Masters 808
1997 Topps Inter-League Finest 808
1997 Topps Mantle 808
1997 Topps Mays 809
1997 Topps Mays Autographs 809
1997 Topps Season's Best 809
1997 Topps Sweet Strokes 809
1997 Topps Team Timber 810
1998 Topps 810
1998 Topps Baby Boomers 812
1998 Topps Clemente 812
1998 Topps Clemente Finest 813
1998 Topps Clemente Tribute 813
1998 Topps Clout Nine 813
1998 Topps Etch-A-Sketch 813
1998 Topps Flashback 813
1998 Topps Focal Points 813
1998 Topps HallBound 813
1998 Topps Milestones 814
1998 Topps Mystery Finest 814
1998 Topps Mystery Finest Bordered 814
1998 Topps Rookie Class 814
1999 Topps 814
1999 Topps MVP Promotion 817
1999 Topps Oversize 817
1999 Topps All-Matrix 817
1999 Topps All-Topps Mystery Finest 818
1999 Topps Autographs 818
1999 Topps Hall of Fame Collection 818
1999 Topps Lords of the Diamond 818
1999 Topps New Breed 818
1999 Topps Picture Perfect 819
1999 Topps Power Brokers 819
1999 Topps Record Numbers 819
1999 Topps Record Numbers Gold 819
1999 Topps Ryan 819
1999 Topps Ryan Autographs 819
1999 Topps Ryan Finest 819
1999 Topps Traded 820
1999 Topps Traded Autographs 820
2000 Topps 821
2000 Topps 20th Century Best Sequential 822
2000 Topps MVP Promotion 822
2000 Topps Oversize 822
2000 Topps 21st Century 822
2000 Topps Aaron 822
2000 Topps Aaron Autograph Exchange 823
2000 Topps Aaron Chrome 823
2000 Topps All-Topps N.L. Team 823
2000 Topps Autographs 823
2000 Topps Hands of Gold 823
2000 Topps Perennial All-Stars 823
2000 Topps Power Players 824
2000 Topps Stadium Relics 824
1996 Topps Chrome 824
1996 Topps Chrome Refractors 825
1996 Topps Chrome Masters of the Game 825
1996 Topps Chrome Wrecking Crew 825
1997 Topps Chrome 825
1997 Topps Chrome Refractors 826
1997 Topps Chrome All-Stars 826
1997 Topps Chrome Diamond Duos 826
1997 Topps Chrome Season's Best 826
1998 Topps Chrome 827
1998 Topps Chrome Refractors 829
1998 Topps Chrome Baby Boomers 829
1998 Topps Chrome Clout Nine 829
1998 Topps Chrome Flashback 829
1998 Topps Chrome HallBound 829
1998 Topps Chrome Milestones 830
1998 Topps Chrome Rookie Class 830
1999 Topps Chrome 830
1999 Topps Chrome Refractors 833
1999 Topps Chrome All-Etch 833
1999 Topps Chrome Early Road to the Hall 833
1999 Topps Chrome Fortune 15 833
1999 Topps Chrome Lords of the Diamond 833
1999 Topps Chrome New Breed 834
1999 Topps Chrome Record Numbers 834
1996 Topps Gallery 834
1996 Topps Gallery Expressionists 835
1996 Topps Gallery Photo Gallery 835
1997 Topps Gallery 835
1997 Topps Gallery Gallery of Heroes 836
1997 Topps Gallery Peter Max Serigraphs 836
1997 Topps Gallery Photo Gallery 836
1998 Topps Gallery 836
1998 Topps Gallery Gallery Proofs 837
1998 Topps Gallery Player's Private Issue 837
1998 Topps Gallery Player's Private Issue Auction 837
1998 Topps Gallery Awards Gallery 837
1998 Topps Gallery Gallery of Heroes 838
1998 Topps Gallery Photo Gallery 838
1999 Topps Gallery 838
1999 Topps Gallery Player's Private Issue 839
1999 Topps Gallery Press Plates 839
1999 Topps Gallery Autographs 839
1999 Topps Gallery Awards Gallery 839
1999 Topps Gallery Exhibitions 839
1999 Topps Gallery Gallery of Heroes 839
1999 Topps Gallery Heritage 839
1998 Topps Gold Label Class 1 840
1998 Topps Gold Label Class 2 840
1998 Topps Gold Label Class 3 840
1998 Topps Gold Label Home Run Race 840
1999 Topps Gold Label Class 1 841
1999 Topps Gold Label Class 2 841
1999 Topps Gold Label Class 3 841
1999 Topps Gold Label Race to Aaron 841
1996 Topps Laser 842
1996 Topps Laser Bright Spots 842
1996 Topps Laser Power Cuts 842
1996 Topps Laser Stadium Stars 843
1999 Topps Opening Day 843
1999 Topps Opening Day Oversize 844
1997 Topps Stars 844
1997 Topps Stars Always Mint 844
1997 Topps Stars '97 All-Stars 844
1997 Topps Stars All-Star Memories 844
1997 Topps Stars Future All-Stars 845
1997 Topps Stars Rookie Reprints 845
1997 Topps Stars Rookie Reprint Autographs 845
1998 Topps Stars 845
1998 Topps Stars Galaxy Bronze 846
1998 Topps Stars Luminaries Bronze 846
1998 Topps Stars Rookie Reprints 846
1998 Topps Stars Rookie Reprints Autographs 846
1998 Topps Stars Supernovas Bronze 847
1999 Topps Stars 847
1999 Topps Stars One Star 848
1999 Topps Stars Two Star 848
1999 Topps Stars Three Star 848
1999 Topps Stars Four Star 849
1999 Topps Stars Bright Futures 849
1999 Topps Stars Galaxy 849
1999 Topps Stars Rookie Reprints 849
1999 Topps Stars Rookie Reprints Autographs 849
1998 Topps Stars 'N Steel 849
1999 Topps Stars 'N Steel 850
1999 Topps Stars 'N Steel Gold 850
1999 Topps Stars 'N Steel Gold Domed Holographic 850
1998 Topps SuperChrome 850
1998 Topps SuperChrome Refractors 850
1999 Topps SuperChrome 850
1999 Topps SuperChrome Refractors 851
1998 Topps Tek 851
1998 Topps Tek Diffractors 851
1999 Topps Tek 851
1999 Topps Tek Gold 852
1999 Topps Tek Fantastek Phenoms 852
1999 Topps Tek Teknicians 852
1995 UC3 852
1995 UC3 Clear Shots 853
1995 UC3 Cyclone Squad 853
1995 UC3 In Motion 853
1997 UD3 853
1997 UD3 Generation Next 854
1997 UD3 Marquee Attraction 854
1997 UD3 Superb Signatures 854
1998 UD3 854
1998 UD3 Die Cuts 856
1999 UD Choice 856
1999 UD Choice Prime Choice Reserve 856
1999 UD Choice Mini Bobbing Head 856
1999 UD Choice StarQuest 857
1999 UD Choice Yard Work 857
1999 UD Ionix 857
1999 UD Ionix Reciprocal 858
1999 UD Ionix Cyber 858
1999 UD Ionix HoloGrFX 858
1999 UD Ionix Hyper 858
1999 UD Ionix Nitro 858
1999 UD Ionix Warp Zone 858
1991 Ultra 859
1991 Ultra Gold 860
1991 Ultra Update 861
1992 Ultra 861
1992 Ultra All-Rookies 864
1992 Ultra All-Stars 864
1992 Ultra Award Winners 864
1992 Ultra Gwynn 864
1993 Ultra 864
1993 Ultra All-Rookies 867
1993 Ultra All-Stars 867
1993 Ultra Award Winners 867
1993 Ultra Eckersley 867
1993 Ultra Home Run Kings 868
1993 Ultra Performers 868
1993 Ultra Strikeout Kings 868
1994 Ultra 868
1994 Ultra All-Rookies 871
1994 Ultra All-Stars 871
1994 Ultra Award Winners 871
1994 Ultra Career Achievement 871
1994 Ultra Firemen 871
1994 Ultra Hitting Machines 871
1994 Ultra Home Run Kings 871
1994 Ultra League Leaders 872
1994 Ultra On-Base Leaders 872
1994 Ultra Phillies Finest 872
1994 Ultra RBI Kings 872
1994 Ultra Rising Stars 872
1994 Ultra Second Year Standouts 873
1994 Ultra Strikeout Kings 873
1995 Ultra 873
1995 Ultra All-Rookies 875
1995 Ultra All-Stars 875
1995 Ultra Award Winners 875
1995 Ultra Gold Medallion Rookies 875
1995 Ultra Golden Prospects 875
1995 Ultra Hitting Machines 876
1995 Ultra Home Run Kings 876
1995 Ultra League Leaders 876
1995 Ultra On-Base Leaders 876
1995 Ultra Power Plus 876
1995 Ultra RBI Kings 876
1995 Ultra Rising Stars 877
1995 Ultra Second Year Standouts 877
1995 Ultra Strikeout Kings 877
1996 Ultra 877
1996 Ultra Gold Medallion 879
1996 Ultra Call to the Hall 880
1996 Ultra Checklists 880
1996 Ultra Diamond Producers 880
1996 Ultra Fresh Foundations 880
1996 Ultra Golden Prospects 880
1996 Ultra Golden Prospects Hobby 880
1996 Ultra Hitting Machines 881
1996 Ultra Home Run Kings 881
1996 Ultra On-Base Leaders 881
1996 Ultra Power Plus 881
1996 Ultra Prime Leather 881
1996 Ultra Rawhide 881
1996 Ultra RBI Kings 881
1996 Ultra Respect 882
1996 Ultra Rising Stars 882
1996 Ultra Season Crowns 882
1996 Ultra Thunderclap 882
1997 Ultra 882
1997 Ultra Gold Medallion 885
1997 Ultra Platinum Medallion 885
1997 Ultra Autographstix Emeralds 885
1997 Ultra Baseball Rules 885
1997 Ultra Checklists 885
1997 Ultra Diamond Producers 885
1997 Ultra Double Trouble 885
1997 Ultra Fame Game 886
1997 Ultra Fielder's Choice 886
1997 Ultra Golden Prospects 886
1997 Ultra Hitting Machines 886
1997 Ultra Home Run Kings 886
1997 Ultra Leather Shop 886
1997 Ultra Power Plus 887
1997 Ultra RBI Kings 887
1997 Ultra Rookie Reflections 887
1997 Ultra Season Crowns 887
1997 Ultra Starring Role 887
1997 Ultra Thunderclap 887
1997 Ultra Top 30 888
1998 Ultra 888
1998 Ultra Gold Medallion 890
1998 Ultra Platinum Medallion 890
1998 Ultra Artistic Talents 890
1998 Ultra Back to the Future 890
1998 Ultra Big Shots 890

1998 Ultra Diamond Immortals 891
1998 Ultra Diamond Producers 891
1998 Ultra Double Trouble 891
1998 Ultra Fall Classics 891
1998 Ultra Kid Gloves 891
1998 Ultra Millennium Men 892
1998 Ultra Notables 892
1998 Ultra Power Plus 892
1998 Ultra Prime Leather 892
1998 Ultra Rocket to Stardom 892
1998 Ultra Ticket Studs 892
1998 Ultra Top 30 893
1998 Ultra Win Now 893
1999 Ultra 893
1999 Ultra Gold Medallion 894
1999 Ultra Masterpiece 894
1999 Ultra Platinum Medallion 894
1999 Ultra The Book On 894
1999 Ultra Damage Inc. 895
1999 Ultra Diamond Producers 895
1999 Ultra RBI Kings 895
1999 Ultra Thunderclap 895
1999 Ultra World Premiere 895
2000 Ultra 895
2000 Ultra Gold Medallion 897
2000 Ultra Masterpiece 897
2000 Ultra Platinum Medallion 897
2000 Ultra Club 3000 897
2000 Ultra Club 3000 Memorabilia 897
2000 Ultra Crunch Time 897
2000 Ultra Diamond Mine 898
2000 Ultra Feel the Game 898
2000 Ultra Fresh Ink 898
2000 Ultra Swing Kings 898
2000 Ultra Talented 898
2000 Ultra World Premiere 898
1989 Upper Deck 899
1990 Upper Deck 902
1990 Upper Deck Jackson Heroes 906
1991 Upper Deck 906
1991 Upper Deck Aaron Heroes 910
1991 Upper Deck Heroes of Baseball 910
1991 Upper Deck Ryan Heroes 910
1991 Upper Deck Silver Sluggers 910
1991 Upper Deck Final Edition 910
1992 Upper Deck 911
1992 Upper Deck Bench/Morgan Heroes 914
1992 Upper Deck Heroes of Baseball 915
1992 Upper Deck Home Run Heroes 915
1992 Upper Deck Scouting Report 915
1992 Upper Deck Williams Best 915
1992 Upper Deck Williams Heroes 915
1993 Upper Deck 915
1993 Upper Deck Gold 919
1993 Upper Deck Clutch Performers 919
1993 Upper Deck Fifth Anniversary 919
1993 Upper Deck Future Heroes 920
1993 Upper Deck Home Run Heroes 920
1993 Upper Deck Iooss Collection 920
1993 Upper Deck Mays Heroes 920
1993 Upper Deck On Deck 920
1993 Upper Deck Season Highlights 921
1993 Upper Deck Then And Now 921
1993 Upper Deck Triple Crown 921
1994 Upper Deck 921
1994 Upper Deck Electric Diamond 923
1994 Upper Deck Diamond Collection 924
1994 Upper Deck Griffey Jumbos 924
1994 Upper Deck Mantle Heroes 924
1994 Upper Deck Mantle's Long Shots 924
1994 Upper Deck Next Generation 924
1994 Upper Deck Next Generation Electric Diamond 924
1995 Upper Deck 925
1995 Upper Deck Autographs 927
1995 Upper Deck Checklists 927
1995 Upper Deck Predictor Award Winners 927
1995 Upper Deck Predictor League Leaders 927
1995 Upper Deck Ruth Heroes 928
1995 Upper Deck Special Edition 928
1995 Upper Deck Steal of a Deal 929
1996 Upper Deck 929
1996 Upper Deck Blue Chip Prospects 931
1996 Upper Deck Diamond Destiny 932
1996 Upper Deck Future Stock Prospects 932
1996 Upper Deck Gameface 932
1996 Upper Deck Hot Commodities 932
1996 Upper Deck V.J. Lovero Showcase 932
1996 Upper Deck Nomo Highlights 933
1996 Upper Deck Power Driven 933
1996 Upper Deck Predictor Hobby 933
1996 Upper Deck Predictor Retail 933
1996 Upper Deck Ripken Collection 934
1996 Upper Deck Run Producers 934
1997 Upper Deck 934
1997 Upper Deck Amazing Greats 937
1997 Upper Deck Blue Chip Prospects 937
1997 Upper Deck Game Jersey 937
1997 Upper Deck Hot Commodities 937
1997 Upper Deck Long Distance Connection 937
1997 Upper Deck Memorable Moments 937
1997 Upper Deck Power Package 938
1997 Upper Deck Predictor 938
1997 Upper Deck Rock Solid Foundation 938
1997 Upper Deck Run Producers 938
1997 Upper Deck Star Attractions 938
1997 Upper Deck Ticket To Stardom 939
1998 Upper Deck 939
1998 Upper Deck 10th Anniversary Preview 942
1998 Upper Deck A Piece of the Action 1 942
1998 Upper Deck A Piece of the Action 2 942
1998 Upper Deck A Piece of the Action 3 943
1998 Upper Deck All-Star Credentials 943
1998 Upper Deck Amazing Greats 943
1998 Upper Deck Blue Chip Prospects 943
1998 Upper Deck Clearly Dominant 943
1998 Upper Deck Destination Stardom 944
1998 Upper Deck Griffey Home Run Chronicles 944
1998 Upper Deck National Pride 944
1998 Upper Deck Prime Nine 945
1998 Upper Deck Retrospectives 945
1998 Upper Deck Rookie Edition Preview 946
1998 Upper Deck Tape Measure Titans 946
1998 Upper Deck Unparalleled 946
1999 Upper Deck 946
1999 Upper Deck Exclusives Level 1 948
1999 Upper Deck Exclusives Level 2 948
1999 Upper Deck 10th Anniversary Team 949
1999 Upper Deck A Piece of History 949
1999 Upper Deck A Piece of History 500 Club 949
1999 Upper Deck A Piece of History 500 Club Autographs 949
1999 Upper Deck Crowning Glory 949
1999 Upper Deck Forte 949
1999 Upper Deck Game Jersey 950
1999 Upper Deck Immaculate Perception 950
1999 Upper Deck Textbook Excellence 950
1999 Upper Deck View to a Thrill 950
1999 Upper Deck Wonder Years 951
2000 Upper Deck 951
2000 Upper Deck Exclusives Gold 952
2000 Upper Deck Exclusives Silver 952
2000 Upper Deck 2K Plus 952
2000 Upper Deck Faces of the Game 952
2000 Upper Deck Game Jersey 953
2000 Upper Deck Game Jersey Patch 953
2000 Upper Deck Game Jersey Patch 1 of 1's 953
2000 Upper Deck Hit Brigade 953
2000 Upper Deck Power MARK 953
2000 Upper Deck Power Rally 953
2000 Upper Deck PowerDeck Inserts 954
2000 Upper Deck Statitude 954
1999 Upper Deck Black Diamond 954
1999 Upper Deck Black Diamond Double 955
1999 Upper Deck Black Diamond Triple 955
1999 Upper Deck Black Diamond Quadruple 955
1999 Upper Deck Black Diamond A Piece of History 955
1999 Upper Deck Black Diamond Dominance 955
1999 Upper Deck Black Diamond Mystery Numbers 955
2000 Upper Deck Black Diamond 956
2000 Upper Deck Black Diamond Final Cut 956
2000 Upper Deck Black Diamond Reciprocal Cut 956
2000 Upper Deck Black Diamond A Piece of History 956
2000 Upper Deck Black Diamond A Piece of History Double 957
2000 Upper Deck Black Diamond A Piece of History Triple 957
2000 Upper Deck Black Diamond Barrage 957
2000 Upper Deck Black Diamond Constant Threat 957
2000 Upper Deck Black Diamond Diamonation 957
2000 Upper Deck Black Diamond Diamond Gallery 957
2000 Upper Deck Black Diamond DiamondMight 957
2000 Upper Deck Black Diamond Diamonds in the Rough 957
1999 Upper Deck Century Legends 958
1999 Upper Deck Century Legends Century Collection 958
1999 Upper Deck Century Legends All-Century Team 958
1999 Upper Deck Century Legends Artifacts 958
1999 Upper Deck Century Legends Epic Milestones 959
1999 Upper Deck Century Legends Epic Signatures 959
1999 Upper Deck Century Legends Epic Signatures Century 959
1999 Upper Deck Century Legends Jerseys of the Century 959
1999 Upper Deck Century Legends Legendary Cuts 959
1999 Upper Deck Century Legends Memorable Shots 960
1999 Upper Deck Century Legends MVPs 960
1999 Upper Deck Challengers for 70 960
1999 Upper Deck Challengers for 70 Challengers Edition 961
1999 Upper Deck Challengers for 70 Challengers Inserts 961
1999 Upper Deck Challengers for 70 Longball Legends 961
1999 Upper Deck Challengers for 70 Mark on History 961
1999 Upper Deck Challengers for 70 Swinging for the Fences 961
1999 Upper Deck Challengers for 70
Swinging for the Fences Autographed 962
1999 Upper Deck Encore 962
1999 Upper Deck Encore FX Gold 963
1999 Upper Deck Encore 2K Countdown 963
1999 Upper Deck Encore Batting Practice Caps 963
1999 Upper Deck Encore Driving Forces 963
1999 Upper Deck Encore McGwired 963
1999 Upper Deck Encore Pure Excitement 963
1999 Upper Deck Encore Rookie Encore 964
1999 Upper Deck Encore UD Authentics 964
1999 Upper Deck Encore Upper Realm 964
1999 Upper Deck HoloGrFX 964
1999 Upper Deck HoloGrFX AuSOME 964
1999 Upper Deck HoloGrFX Future Fame 965
1999 Upper Deck HoloGrFX Launchers 965
1999 Upper Deck HoloGrFX StarView 965
1999 Upper Deck HoloGrFX UD Authentics 965
1999 Upper Deck MVP 965
1999 Upper Deck MVP Gold Script 966
1999 Upper Deck MVP Silver Script 966
1999 Upper Deck MVP Super Script 966
1999 Upper Deck MVP Dynamics 966
1999 Upper Deck MVP Game Used Souvenirs 967
1999 Upper Deck MVP Power Surge 967
1999 Upper Deck MVP ProSign 967
1999 Upper Deck MVP Scout's Choice 967
1999 Upper Deck MVP Super Tools 967
1999 Upper Deck MVP Swing Time 967
1999 Upper Deck Ovation 968
1999 Upper Deck Ovation Standing Ovation 968
1999 Upper Deck Ovation A Piece of History 968
1999 Upper Deck Ovation Curtain Calls 968
1999 Upper Deck Ovation Major Production 969
1999 Upper Deck Ovation ReMarkable Moments 969
1999 Upper Deck PowerDeck 969
1999 Upper Deck PowerDeck Auxiliary 969
1999 Upper Deck PowerDeck A Season To Remember 969
1999 Upper Deck PowerDeck Most Valuable Performances 970
1999 Upper Deck PowerDeck Powerful Moments 970
1999 Upper Deck PowerDeck Time Capsule 970
1998 Upper Deck Retro 970
1998 Upper Deck Retro Big Boppers 971
1998 Upper Deck Retro Groovy Kind of Glove 971
1998 Upper Deck Retro Lunchboxes 971
1998 Upper Deck Retro New Frontier 971
1998 Upper Deck Retro Quantum Leap 971
1998 Upper Deck Retro Sign of the Times 972
1998 Upper Deck Retro Time Capsule 972
1999 Upper Deck Retro 972
1999 Upper Deck Retro Gold 973
1999 Upper Deck Retro Platinum 973
1999 Upper Deck Retro Distant Replay 973
1999 Upper Deck Retro Inkredible 973
1999 Upper Deck Retro Inkredible Level 2 973
1999 Upper Deck Retro Lunchboxes 973
1999 Upper Deck Retro Old School/New School 974
1999 Upper Deck Retro Throwback Attack 974
1998 Upper Deck Special F/X 974
1998 Upper Deck Special F/X Power Zone 975
1998 Upper Deck Special F/X Power Zone OctoberBest 975
1998 Upper Deck Special F/X Power Zone Power Driven 975
1998 Upper Deck Special F/X
Power Zone Superstar Xcitement 975
1999 Upper Deck Ultimate Victory 975
1999 Upper Deck Ultimate Victory Parallel 976
1999 Upper Deck Ultimate Victory Parallel 1 of 1 976
1999 Upper Deck Ultimate Victory Parallel 100 976
1999 Upper Deck Ultimate Victory Bleacher Reachers 976
1999 Upper Deck Ultimate Victory Fame-Used Memorabilia 977
1999 Upper Deck Ultimate Victory Frozen Ropes 977
1999 Upper Deck Ultimate Victory STATure 977
1999 Upper Deck Ultimate Victory Tribute 1999 977
1999 Upper Deck Ultimate Victory Ultimate Competitors 977
1999 Upper Deck Ultimate Victory Ultimate Hit Men 977
1999 Upper Deck Victory 977
1995 Zenith 979
1995 Zenith All-Star Salute 980
1995 Zenith Rookie Roll Call 980
1995 Zenith Z-Team 980
1996 Zenith 981
1996 Zenith Artist's Proofs 981
1996 Zenith Diamond Club 981
1996 Zenith Diamond Club Parallel 982
1996 Zenith Mozaics 982
1996 Zenith Z-Team 982
1997 Zenith 982
1997 Zenith 8 x 10 983
1997 Zenith V-2 983
1997 Zenith Z-Team 983
1998 Zenith 983
1998 Zenith Z-Gold 983
1998 Zenith Z-Silver 984
1998 Zenith 5 x 7 984
1998 Zenith 5 x 7 Gold Impulse 984
1998 Zenith 5 x 7 Impulse 984
1998 Zenith Epix 984
1998 Zenith Raising the Bar 984
1998 Zenith Rookie Thrills 985
1998 Zenith Z-Team 985
1998 Zenith Z-Team 5 x 7 985
Acknowledgments 986

About the Author

Jim Beckett, the leading authority on sport card values in the United States, maintains a wide range of activities in the world of sports. He possesses one of the finest collections of sports cards and autographs in the world, has made numerous appearances on radio and television, and has been frequently cited in many national publications. He was awarded the first "Special Achievement Award" for Contributions to the Hobby by the National Sports Collectors Convention in 1980, the "Jock-Jaspersen Award" for Hobby Dedication in 1983, and the "Buck Barker, Spirit of the Hobby" Award in 1991.

Dr. Beckett is the author of *Beckett Baseball Card Price Guide, The Official Price Guide to Baseball Cards, The Sport Americana Price Guide to Baseball Collectibles, The Sport Americana Baseball Memorabilia and Autograph Price Guide, Beckett Football Card Price Guide, The Official Price Guide to Football Cards, Beckett Hockey Card Price Guide, The Official Price Guide to Hockey Cards, Beckett Basketball Card Price Guide, The Official Price Guide to Basketball Cards,* and *The Sport Americana Baseball Card Alphabetical Checklist.* In addition, he is the founder, publisher, and editor of *Beckett Baseball Card Monthly, Beckett Basketball Monthly, Beckett Football Card Monthly, Beckett Hockey Monthly, Beckett Future Stars, Beckett Racing Monthly,* and *Beckett Tribute* magazines.

Jim Beckett received his Ph.D. in Statistics from Southern Methodist University in 1975. Prior to starting Beckett Publications in 1984, Dr. Beckett served as an Associate Professor of Statistics at Bowling Green State University and as a vice president of a consulting firm in Dallas, Texas.

How to Use This Book

Isn't it great? Every year this book gets bigger and bigger with all the new sets coming out. But even more exciting is that every year there are more collectors, more shows, more stores, and more interest in the cards we love so much. This edition has been enhanced and expanded from the previous edition. The cards you collect — who appears on them, what they look like, where they are from, and (most important to most of you) what their current values are — are enumerated within. Many of the features contained in the other *Beckett Price Guides* have been incorporated into this volume since condition grading, terminology, and many other aspects of collecting are common to the card hobby in general. We hope you find the book both interesting and useful in your collecting pursuits.

The *Beckett Guide* has been successful where other attempts have failed because it is complete, current, and valid. This Price Guide contains not just one, but three prices by condition for all the baseball cards listed. The prices were added to the card lists just prior to printing and reflect not the author's opinions or desires but the going retail prices for each card, based on the marketplace (sports memorabilia conventions and shows, sports card shops, hobby papers, current mail-order catalogs, local club meetings, auction results, and other firsthand reportings of actually realized prices).

What is the best price guide available on the market today? Of course, card sellers prefer the price guide with the highest prices, while card buyers naturally prefer the one with the lowest prices. Accuracy, however, is the true test. Use the price guide trusted by more collectors and dealers than all the others combined. Look for the *Beckett®* name. I won't put my name on anything I won't stake my reputation on. Not the lowest and not the highest — but the most accurate, with integrity.

To facilitate your use of this book, read the complete introductory section on the following pages before going to the pricing pages. Every collectible field has its own terminology; we've tried to capture most of these terms and definitions in our glossary. Please read carefully the section on grading and the condition of your cards, as you cannot determine which price column is appropriate for a given card without first knowing its condition.

Welcome to the world of baseball cards.

How to Collect

Each collection is personal and reflects the individuality of its owner. There are no set rules on how to collect cards. Since card collecting is a hobby or leisure pastime, what you collect, how much you collect, and how much time and money you spend collecting are entirely up to you. The funds you have available for collecting and your own personal taste should determine how you collect. Information and ideas presented here are intended to help you get the most enjoyment from this hobby.

It is impossible to collect every card ever produced. Therefore, beginners as well as intermediate and advanced collectors usually specialize in some way. One of the reasons this hobby is popular is that individual collectors can define and tailor their collecting methods to match their own tastes. To give you some ideas of the various approaches to collecting, we will list some of the more popular areas of specialization.

Many collectors select complete sets from particular years. For example, they may concentrate on assembling complete sets from all the years since their birth or since they became avid sports fans. They may try to collect a card for every player during that specified period of time.

Many others wish to acquire only certain players. Usually such players are the superstars of the sport, but occasionally collectors will specialize in all the cards of players who attended a particular college or came from a certain town. Some collectors are only interested in the first cards or Rookie Cards of certain players. A handy guide for collectors interested in pursuing the hobby this way is the *Sport Americana Baseball Card Alphabetical Checklist*.

Another fun way to collect cards is by team. Most fans have a favorite team, and it is natural for that loyalty to be translated into a desire for cards of the players on that favorite team. For most of the recent years, team sets (all the cards from a given team for that year) are readily available at a reasonable price.

Obtaining Cards

Several avenues are open to card collectors. Cards still can be purchased in the traditional way: by the pack at the local candy, grocery, drug or major discount stores.

But there are also thousands of card shops across the country that specialize in selling cards individually or by the pack, box, or set. Another alternative is the thousands of card shows held each month around the country, which feature anywhere from eight to 800 tables of sports cards and memorabilia for sale.

For many years, it has been possible to purchase complete sets of baseball cards through mail-order advertisers found in traditional sports media publications, such as *The Sporting News, Baseball Digest, Street & Smith* yearbooks, and others. These sets also are advertised in the card collecting periodicals. Many collectors will begin by subscribing to at least one of the hobby

periodicals, all with good up-to-date information. In fact, subscription offers can be found in the advertising section of this book.

Most serious card collectors obtain old (and new) cards from one or more of several main sources: (1) trading or buying from other collectors or dealers; (2) responding to sale or auction ads in the hobby publications; (3) buying at a local hobby store; and/or (4) attending sports collectibles shows or conventions.

We advise that you try all four methods since each has its own distinct advantages: (1) trading is a great way to make new friends; (2) hobby periodicals help you keep up with what's going on in the hobby (including when and where the conventions are happening); (3) stores provide the opportunity to enjoy personalized service and consider a great diversity of material in a relaxed sports-oriented atmosphere; and (4) shows allow you to choose from multiple dealers and thousands of cards under one roof in a competitive situation.

Preserving Your Cards

Cards are fragile. They must be handled properly in order to retain their value. Careless handling can easily result in creased or bent cards. It is, however, not recommended that tweezers or tongs be used to pick up your cards since such utensils might mar or indent card surfaces and thus reduce those cards' conditions and values.

In general, your cards should be handled directly as little as possible. This is sometimes easier to say than to do.

Although there are still many who use custom boxes, storage trays, or even shoe boxes, plastic sheets are the preferred method of many collectors for storing cards.

A collection stored in plastic pages in a three-ring album allows you to view your collection at any time without the need to touch the card itself. Cards can also be kept in single holders (of various types and thickness) designed for the enjoyment of each card individually.

For a large collection, some collectors may use a combination of the above methods. When purchasing plastic sheets for your cards, be sure that you find the pocket size that fits the cards snugly. Don't put your 1951 Bowman in a sheet designed to fit 1981 Topps.

Most hobby and collectibles shops and virtually all collectors' conventions will have these plastic pages available in quantity for the various sizes offered, or you can purchase them directly from the advertisers in this book.

Also, remember that pocket size isn't the only factor to consider when looking for plastic sheets. Other factors such as safety, economy, appearance, availability, or personal preference also may indicate which types of sheets a collector may want to buy.

Damp, sunny and/or hot conditions — no, this is not a weather forecast — are three elements to avoid in extremes if you are interested in preserving your collection. Too much (or too little) humidity can cause the gradual deterioration of a card. Direct, bright sun (or fluorescent light) over time will bleach out the color of a card. Extreme heat accelerates the decomposition of the card. On the other hand, many cards have lasted more than 75 years without much scientific intervention. So be cautious, even if the above factors typically present a problem only when present in the extreme. It never hurts to be prudent.

Collecting vs. Investing

Collecting individual players and collecting complete sets are both popular vehicles for investment and speculation.

Most investors and speculators stock up on complete sets or on quantities of players they think have good investment potential.

There is obviously no guarantee in this book, or anywhere else for that matter, that cards will outperform the stock market or other investment alternatives in the future. After all, baseball cards do not pay quarterly dividends and cards cannot be sold at their "current values" as easily as stocks or bonds.

Nevertheless, investors have noticed a favorable long-term trend in the past performance of baseball and other sports collectibles, and certain cards and sets have outperformed just about any other investment in some years.

Many hobbyists maintain that the best investment is and always will be the building of a collection, which traditionally has held up better than outright speculation.

Some of the obvious questions are: Which cards? When to buy? When to sell? The best investment you can make is in your own education.

The more you know about your collection and the hobby, the more informed the decisions you will be able to make. We're not selling investment tips. We're selling information about the current value of baseball cards. It's up to you to use that information to your best advantage.

Terminology

Each hobby has its own language to describe its area of interest. The nomenclature traditionally used for trading cards is derived from the American Card Catalog, published in 1960 by Nostalgia Press. That catalog, written by Jefferson Burdick (who is called the "Father of Card Collecting" for his pioneering work), uses letter and number designations for each separate set of cards. The letter used in the ACC designation refers to the generic type of card. While both sport and non-sport issues are classified in the ACC, we shall confine ourselves to the sport issues. The following list defines the letters and their meanings as used by the American Card Catalog.

(none) or N - 19th Century U.S. Tobacco
B - Blankets
D - Bakery Inserts Including Bread
E - Early Candy and Gum
F - Food Inserts
H - Advertising
M - Periodicals
PC - Postcards
R - Candy and Gum since 1930

Following the letter prefix and an optional hyphen are one-, two-, or three-digit numbers, R(-)999. These typically represent the company or entity issuing the cards. In several cases, the ACC number is extended by an additional hyphen and another one- or two-digit numerical suffix. For example, the 1957 Topps regular-series baseball card issue carries an ACC designation of R414-11. The "R" indicates a Candy or Gum card produced since 1930. The "414" is the ACC designation for Topps Chewing Gum baseball card issues, and the "11" is the ACC designation for the 1957 regular issue (Topps' eleventh baseball set). Like other traditional methods of identification, this system provides order to the process of cataloging cards; however, most serious collectors learn the ACC designation of the popular sets by repetition and familiarity, rather than by attempting to "figure out" what they might or should be. From 1948 forward, collectors and dealers commonly refer to all sets by their year, maker, type of issue, and any other distinguishing characteristic. For example, such a characteristic could be an unusual issue or one of several

regular issues put out by a specific maker in a single year. Regional issues are usually referred to by year, maker, and sometimes by title or theme of the set.

Glossary/Legend

Our glossary defines terms used in the card collecting hobby and in this book. Many of these terms are also common to other types of sports memorabilia collecting. Some terms may have several meanings depending on use and context.

ACETATE - A transparent plastic.

AS - All-Star card. A card portraying an All-Star Player of the previous year that says "All-Star" on its face.

ATG - All-Time Great card.

ATL - All-Time Leaders card.

AU(TO) - Autographed card.

BC - Bonus Card.

BL - Blue letters.

BOX CARD - Card issued on a box (i.e., 1987 Topps Box Bottoms).

BRICK - A group of 50 or more cards having common characteristics that is intended to be bought, sold or traded as a unit.

CABINETS - Popular and highly valuable photographs on thick card stock produced in the 19th and early 20th century.

CHECKLIST - A list of the cards contained in a particular set. The list is always in numerical order if the cards are numbered. Some unnumbered sets are artificially numbered in alphabetical order, by team and alphabetically within the team, or by uniform number for convenience.

CL - Checklist card. A card that lists in order the cards and players in the set or series. Older checklist cards in Mint condition that have not been marked are very desirable and command premiums.

CO - Coach.

COMM - Commissioner.

COMMON CARD - The typical card of any set; it has no premium value accruing from subject matter, numerical scarcity, popular demand, or anomaly.

CONVENTION - A gathering of dealers and collectors at a single location for the purpose of buying, selling, and trading sports memorabilia items. Conventions are open to the public and sometimes feature autograph guests, door prizes, contests, seminars, etc. They are frequently referred to simply as "shows."

COOP - Cooperstown.

COR - Corrected card.

CY - Cy Young Award.

DEALER - A person who engages in buying, selling, and trading sports collectibles or supplies. A dealer may also be a collector, but as a dealer, his main goal is to earn a profit.

DIE-CUT - A card with part of its stock partially cut, allowing one or more parts to be folded or removed. After removal or appropriate folding, the remaining part of the card can frequently be made to stand

DK - Diamond King.

DL - Division Leaders.

DP - Double Print (a card that was printed in double the quantity compared to the other cards in the same series) or a Draft Pick card.

DUFEX - A method of card manufacturing technology patented by Pinnacle Brands, Inc. It involves a refractive quality to a card with a foil coating.

ERA - Earned Run Average.

ERR - Error card. A card with erroneous information, spelling, or depiction on either side of the card. Most errors are not corrected by the producing card company.

FDP - First or First Round Draft Pick.

FOIL - Foil embossed stamp on card.

FOLD - Foldout.

FS - Father/son card.

FUN - Fun Cards.

GL - Green letters.

GLOSS - A card with luster; a shiny finish as in a card with UV coating.

HIGH NUMBER - The cards in the last series of numbers in a year in which such higher-numbered cards were printed or distributed in significantly lesser amounts than the lower-numbered cards. The high-number designation refers to a scarcity of the high-numbered cards. Not all years have high numbers in terms of this definition.

HL - Highlight card.

HOF - Hall of Fame, or a card that portrays a Hall of Famer (HOFer).

HOLOGRAM - A three-dimensional photographic image.

HOR - Horizontal pose on card as opposed to the standard vertical orientation found on most cards.

IA - In Action card.

IF - Infielder.

INSERT - A card of a different type or any other sports collectible (typically a poster or sticker) contained and sold in the same package along with a card or cards of a major set. An insert card is either unnumbered or not numbered in the same sequence as the major set. Sometimes the inserts are randomly distributed and are not found in every pack.

INTERACTIVE - A concept that involves collector participation.

ISSUE - Synonymous with set, but usually used in conjunction with a manufacturer, e.g., a Topps issue

LHP - Lefthanded pitcher.

LL - League leaders or large letters on card.

MAJOR SET - A set produced by a national manufacturer of cards containing a large number of cards. Usually 100 or more different cards comprise a major set.

MEM - Memorial card. For example, the 1990 Donruss and Topps Bart Giamatti cards.

METALLIC - A glossy design method that enhances card features.

MG - Manager.

MINI - A small card; for example, a 1975 Topps card of identical design but smaller dimensions than the regular Topps issue of 1975.

ML - Major League.

MULTI-PLAYER CARD - A single card depicting two or more players (but not a team card).

MVP - Most Valuable Player.

NAU - No autograph on card.

NH - No-Hitter.

NNOF - No Name on Front.

NOF - Name on Front.

NOTCHING - The grooving of the card, usually caused by fingernails, rubber bands, or bumping card edges against other objects.

OF - Outfield or Outfielder.

OLY - Olympics Card.

P - Pitcher or Pitching pose.

P1 - First Printing.

P2 - Second Printing.

P3 - Third Printing.

PACKS - A means with which cards are issued in terms of pack type (wax, cello, foil, rack, etc.) and channels of distribution (hobby, retail, etc.).

PARALLEL- A card that is similar in design to its counterpart from a basic set, but offers a distinguishing quality.

PF - Profiles.

PLASTIC SHEET - A clear, plastic page that is punched for insertion into a binder (with standard three-ring spacing) containing pockets for displaying cards. Many different styles of sheets exist with pockets of varying sizes to hold the many differing card formats. Also called a display sheet or storage sheet.

PLATINUM - A metallic element used in the process of creating a glossy card.

PR - Printed name on back.

PREMIUM - A card, sometimes on photographic stock, that is purchased or obtained in conjunction with, or redemption for, another card or product. The premium is not packaged in the same unit as the primary item.

PRES - President.

PRISMATIC/PRISM - A glossy or bright design that refracts or disperses light.

PUZZLE CARD - A card whose back contains a part of a picture which, when joined correctly with other puzzle cards, forms the completed picture.

PUZZLE PIECE - A die-cut piece designed to interlock with similar pieces (e.g., early 1980's Donruss).

PVC - Polyvinyl Chloride, a substance used to make many of the popular card display protective sheets. Non-PVC sheets are considered preferable for long-term storage of cards by many.

RARE - A card or series of cards of very limited availability. Unfortunately, "rare" is a subjective term frequently used indiscriminately to hype value. "Rare" cards are harder to obtain than "scarce" cards.

RB - Record Breaker.

REDEMPTION - A program established by multiple card manufacturers that allows collectors to mail in a special card (usually a random insert) in return for special cards, sets or other prizes not available through conventional channels.

REFRACTORS - A card that features a design element which enhances (distorts) its color/appearance through deflecting light.

REV NEG - Reversed or flopped photo side of the card. This is a major type of error card, but only some are corrected.

RHP - Righthanded pitcher.

ROY - Rookie of the Year.

RP - Relief pitcher.

SA - Super Action card.

SASE - Self-Addressed, Stamped Envelope.

SB - Stolen Bases.

SCARCE - A card or series of cards of limited availability. This subjective term is sometimes used indiscriminately to hype value. "Scarce" cards are not as difficult to obtain as "rare" cards.

SCR - Script name on back.

SD - San Diego Padres.

SEMI-HIGH - A card from the next to last series of a sequentially issued set. It has more value than an average card and generally less value than a

high number. A card is not called a semi-high unless the next to last series in which it exists has an additional premium attached to it.

SERIES - The entire set of cards issued by a particular producer in a particular year; e.g., the 1971 Topps series. Also, within a particular set, series can refer to a group of (consecutively numbered) cards printed at the same time; e.g., the first series of the 1957 Topps issue (#1 through #88).

SET - One each of the entire run of cards of the same type produced by a particular manufacturer during a single year. In other words, if you have a complete set of 1976 Topps then you have every card from #1 up to and including #660, i.e., all the different cards that were produced.

SF - Starflics.

SHEEN - Brightness or luster emitted by a card.

SKIP-NUMBERED - A set that has many unissued card numbers between the lowest number in the set and the highest number in the set; e.g., the 1948 Leaf baseball set contains 98 cards skip-numbered from #1 to #168. A major set in which a few numbers were not printed is not considered to be skip-numbered.

SP - Single or Short Print (a card which was printed in lesser quantity compared to the other cards in the same series; see also DP and TP).

SPECIAL CARD - A card that portrays something other than a single player or team; for example, a card that portrays the previous year's statistical leaders or the results from the previous year's World Series.

SS - Shortstop.

STANDARD SIZE - Most modern sports cards measure 2-1/2 by 3-1/2 inches. Exceptions are noted in card descriptions throughout this book.

STAR CARD - A card that portrays a player of some repute, usually determined by his ability, however, sometimes referring to sheer popularity.

STOCK - The cardboard or paper on which the card is printed.

SUPERIMPOSED - To be affixed on top of something, i.e., a player photo over a solid background.

SUPERSTAR CARD - A card that portrays a superstar; e.g., a Hall of Famer or player with strong Hall of Fame potential.

TC - Team Checklist.

TEAM CARD - A card that depicts an entire team.

THREE-DIMENSIONAL (3D) - A visual image that provides an illusion of depth and perspective.

TOPICAL - A subset or group of cards that have a common theme (e.g., MVP award winners).

TP - Triple Print (a card that was printed in triple the quantity compared to the other cards in the same series).

TRANSPARENT - Clear, see through.

TR - Trade reference on card.

UDCA - Upper Deck Classic Alumni.

UER - Uncorrected Error.

UMP - Umpire.

USA - Team USA.

UV - Ultraviolet, a glossy coating used in producing cards.

VAR - Variation card. One of two or more cards from the same series with the same number (or player with identical pose if the series is unnumbered) differing from one another by some aspect, the different feature stemming from the printing or stock of the card. This can be caused when the manufacturer of the cards notices an error in one or more of the cards, makes the changes, and then resumes the print run. In this case there will be two versions or variations of the same card. Sometimes one of the variations is rela-

tively scarce.
    VERT - Vertical pose on card.
    WAS - Washington National League (1974 Topps).
    WC - What's the Call?
    WL - White letter on front.
    WS - World Series card.
    YL - Yellow letters on front
    YT - Yellow team name on front.
    * - To denote multi-sport sets.

Understanding Card Values

Determining Value

Why are some cards more valuable than others? Obviously, the economic laws of supply and demand are applicable to card collecting just as they are to any other field where a commodity is bought, sold or traded in a free, unregulated market.

Supply (the number of cards available on the market) is less than the total number of cards originally produced since attrition diminishes that original quantity. Each year a percentage of cards is typically thrown away, destroyed or otherwise lost to collectors. This percentage is much, much smaller today than it was in the past because more and more people have become increasingly aware of the value of their cards.

For those who collect only Mint condition cards, the supply of older cards can be quite small indeed. Until recently, collectors were not so conscious of the need to preserve the condition of their cards. For this reason, it is difficult to know exactly how many 1953 Topps are currently available, Mint or otherwise. It is generally accepted that there are fewer 1953 Topps available than 1963, 1973 or 1983 Topps cards. If demand were equal for each of these sets, the law of supply and demand would increase the price for the least available sets. Demand, however, is never equal for all sets, so price correlations can be complicated. The demand for a card is influenced by many factors. These include: (1) the age of the card; (2) the number of cards printed; (3) the player(s) portrayed on the card; (4) the attractiveness and popularity of the set; and (5) the physical condition of the card.

In general, (1) the older the card, (2) the fewer the number of the cards printed, (3) the more famous, popular and talented the player, (4) the more attractive and popular the set, and (5) the better the condition of the card, the higher the value of the card will be. There are exceptions to all but one of these factors: the condition of the card. Given two cards similar in all respects except condition, the one in the best condition will always be valued higher.

While those guidelines help to establish the value of a card, the countless exceptions and peculiarities make any simple, direct mathematical formula to determine card values impossible.

Regional Variation

Since the market varies from region to region, card prices of local players may be higher. This is known as a regional premium. How significant the premium is — and if there is any premium at all — depends on the local popularity of the team and the player.

The largest regional premiums usually do not apply to superstars, who often are so well-known nationwide that the prices of their key cards are too high for local dealers to realize a premium.

Lesser stars often command the strongest premiums. Their popularity is concentrated in their home region, creating local demand that greatly exceeds overall demand.

Regional premiums can apply to popular retired players and sometimes can be found in the areas where the players grew up or starred in college.

A regional discount is the converse of a regional premium. Regional discounts occur when a player has been so popular in his region for so long that local collectors and dealers have accumulated quantities of his key cards. The abundant supply may make the cards available in that area at the lowest prices anywhere.

Set Prices

A somewhat paradoxical situation exists in the price of a complete set vs. the combined cost of the individual cards in the set. In nearly every case, the sum of the prices for the individual cards is higher than the cost for the complete set. This is prevalent especially in the cards of the last few years. The reasons for this apparent anomaly stem from the habits of collectors and from the carrying costs to dealers. Today, each card in a set normally is produced in the same quantity as all other cards in its set.

Many collectors pick up only stars, superstars and particular teams. As a result, the dealer is left with a shortage of certain player cards and an abundance of others. He therefore incurs an expense in simply "carrying" these less desirable cards in stock. On the other hand, if he sells a complete set, he gets rid of large numbers of cards at one time. For this reason, he generally is willing to receive less money for a complete set. By doing this, he recovers all of his costs and also makes a profit.

The disparity between the price of the complete set and the sum of the individual cards also has been influenced by the fact that some of the major manufacturers now are pre-collating card sets. Since "pulling" individual cards from the sets involves a specific type of labor (and cost), the singles or star card market is not affected significantly by pre-collation.

Set prices also do not include rare card varieties, unless specifically stated. Of course, the prices for sets do include one example of each type for the given set, but this is the least expensive variety.

Scarce Series

Scarce series occur because cards issued before 1974 were made available to the public each year in several series of finite numbers of cards, rather than all cards of the set being available for purchase at one time. At some point during the year, usually toward the end of the baseball season, interest in current year baseball cards waned. Consequently, the manufacturers produced smaller numbers of these later-series cards.

Nearly all nationwide issues from post-World War II manufacturers (1948 to 1973) exhibit these series variations. In the past, Topps, for example, may have issued series consisting of many different numbers of cards, including 55, 66, 80, 88 and others. Recently, Topps has settled on what is now its standard sheet size of 132 cards, six of which comprise its 792-card set.

While the number of cards within a given series is usually the same as the number of cards on one printed sheet, this is not always the case. For example, Bowman used 36 cards on its standard printed sheets, but in 1948 substituted 12 cards during later print runs of that year's baseball cards. Twelve of the cards from the initial sheet of 36 cards were removed and replaced by 12 different cards giving, in effect, a first series of 36 cards and a second series of 12 new cards. This replacement produced a scarcity of 24 cards — the 12 cards removed from the original sheet and the 12 new cards added to the sheet. A full

sheet of 1948 Bowman cards (second printing) shows that card numbers 37 through 48 have replaced 12 of the cards on the first printing sheet.

The Topps Company also has created scarcities and/or excesses of certain cards in many of its sets. Topps, however, has most frequently gone the other direction by double printing some of the cards. Double printing causes an abundance of cards of the players who are on the same sheet more than one time. During the years from 1978 to 1981, Topps double printed 66 cards out of their large 726-card set. The Topps practice of double printing cards in earlier years is the most logical explanation for the known scarcities of particular cards in some of these Topps sets.

From 1988 through 1990, Donruss short printed and double printed certain cards in its major sets. Ostensibly this was because of its addition of bonus team MVP cards in its regular-issue wax packs. In the last couple of years, card companies have been printing specific subsets (usually young players or rookie cards) in shorter supply than the regular cards.

We are always looking for information or photographs of printing sheets of cards for research. Each year, we try to update the hobby's knowledge of distribution anomalies. Please let us know at the address in this book if you have first-hand knowledge that would be helpful in this pursuit.

Grading Your Cards

Each hobby has its own grading terminology — stamps, coins, comic books, record collecting, etc. Collectors of sports cards are no exception. The one invariable criterion for determining the value of a card is its condition: The better the condition of the card, the more valuable it is. Condition grading, however, is subjective. Individual card dealers and collectors differ in the strictness of their grading, but the stated condition of a card should be determined without regard to whether it is being bought or sold.

No allowance is made for age. A 1952 card is judged by the same standards as a 1992 card. But there are specific sets and cards that are condition sensitive (marked with "!" in the Price Guide) because of their border color, consistently poor centering, etc. Such cards and sets sometimes command premiums above the listed percentages in Mint condition.

Centering

Current centering terminology uses numbers representing the percentage of border on either side of the main design. Obviously, centering is diminished in importance for borderless cards such as Stadium Club.

Slightly Off-Center (60/40): A slightly off-center card is one that, upon close inspection, is found to have one border bigger than the opposite border. This degree once was offensive to only purists, but now some hobbyists try to avoid cards that are anything other than perfectly centered.

Off-Center (70/30): An off-center card has one border that is noticeably more than twice as wide as the opposite border.

Badly Off-Center (80/20 or worse): A badly off-center card has virtually no border on one side of the card.

Miscut: A miscut card actually shows part of the adjacent card in its larger border and consequently a corresponding amount of its card is cut off.

Corner Wear

Corner wear is the most scrutinized grading criteria in the hobby. These are the major categories of corner wear:

Corner with a slight touch of wear: The corner still is sharp, but there is a slight touch of wear showing. On a dark-bordered card, this shows as a dot

of white.

Fuzzy corner: The corner still comes to a point, but the point has just begun to fray. A slightly "dinged" corner is considered the same as a fuzzy corner.

Slightly rounded corner: The fraying of the corner has increased to where there is only a hint of a point. Mild layering may be evident. A "dinged" corner is considered the same as a slightly rounded corner.

Rounded corner: The point is completely gone. Some layering is noticeable.

Badly rounded corner: The corner is completely round and rough. Severe layering is evident.

Creases

A third common defect is the crease. The degree of creasing in a card is difficult to show in a drawing or picture. On giving the specific condition of an expensive card for sale, the seller should note any creases additionally. Creases can be categorized as to severity according to the following scale:

Light Crease: A light crease is a crease that is barely noticeable upon close inspection. In fact, when cards are in plastic sheets or holders, a light crease may not be seen (until the card is taken out of the holder). A light crease on the front is much more serious than a light crease on the card back only.

Medium Crease: A medium crease is noticeable when held and studied at arm's length by the naked eye, but does not overly detract from the appearance of the card. It is an obvious crease, but not one that breaks the picture surface of the card.

Heavy Crease: A heavy crease is one that has torn or broken through the card's picture surface, e.g., puts a tear in the photo surface.

Alterations

Deceptive Trimming: This occurs when someone alters the card in order (1) to shave off edge wear, (2) to improve the sharpness of the corners, or (3) to improve centering — obviously their objective is to falsely increase the perceived value of the card to an unsuspecting buyer. The shrinkage usually is evident only if the trimmed card is compared to an adjacent full-sized card or if the trimmed card is itself measured.

Obvious Trimming: Obvious trimming is noticeable and unfortunate. It is usually performed by non-collectors who give no thought to the present or future value of their cards.

Deceptively Retouched Borders: This occurs when the borders (especially on those cards with dark borders) are touched up on the edges and corners with magic marker or crayons of appropriate color in order to make the card appear Mint.

Categorization of Defects—Miscellaneous Flaws

The following are common minor flaws that, depending on severity, lower a card's condition by one to four grades and often render it no better than Excellent-Mint: bubbles (lumps in surface), gum and wax stains, diamond cutting (slanted borders), notching, off-centered backs, paper wrinkles, scratched-off cartoons or puzzles on back, rubber band marks, scratches, surface impressions and warping.

The following are common serious flaws that, depending on severity,

lower a card's condition at least four grades and often render it no better than Good: chemical or sun fading, erasure marks, mildew, miscutting (severe off-centering), holes, bleached or re-touched borders, tape marks, tears, trimming, water or coffee stains and writing.

Condition Guide

Grades

Mint (Mt) - A card with no flaws or wear. The card has four perfect corners, 60/40 or better centering from top to bottom and from left to right, original gloss, smooth edges and original color borders. A Mint card does not have print spots, color or focus imperfections.

Near Mint-Mint (NrMt-Mt) - A card with one minor flaw. Any one of the following would lower a Mint card to Near Mint-Mint: one corner with a slight touch of wear, barely noticeable print spots, color or focus imperfections. The card must have 60/40 or better centering in both directions, original gloss, smooth edges and original color borders.

Near Mint (NrMt) - A card with one minor flaw. Any one of the following would lower a Mint card to Near Mint: one fuzzy corner or two to four corners with slight touches of wear, 70/30 to 60/40 centering, slightly rough edges, minor print spots, color or focus imperfections. The card must have original gloss and original color borders.

Excellent-Mint (ExMt) - A card with two or three fuzzy, but not rounded, corners and centering no worse than 80/20. The card may have no more than two of the following: slightly rough edges, very slightly discolored borders, minor print spots, color or focus imperfections. The card must have original gloss.

Excellent (Ex) - A card with four fuzzy but definitely not rounded corners and centering no worse than 80/20. The card may have a small amount of original gloss lost, rough edges, slightly discolored borders and minor print spots, color or focus imperfections.

Very Good (Vg) - A card that has been handled but not abused: slightly rounded corners with slight layering, slight notching on edges, a significant amount of gloss lost from the surface but no scuffing and moderate discoloration of borders. The card may have a few light creases.

Good (G), Fair (F), Poor (P) - A well-worn, mishandled or abused card: badly rounded and layered corners, scuffing, most or all original gloss missing, seriously discolored borders, moderate or heavy creases, and one or more serious flaws. The grade of Good, Fair or Poor depends on the severity of wear and flaws. Good, Fair and Poor cards generally are used only as fillers.

The most widely used grades are defined above. Obviously, many cards will not perfectly fit one of the definitions.

Therefore, categories between the major grades known as in-between grades are used, such as Good to Very Good (G-Vg), Very Good to Excellent (VgEx), and Excellent-Mint to Near Mint (ExMt-NrMt). Such grades indicate a card with all qualities of the lower category but with at least a few qualities of the higher category.

The Official Price Guide to Baseball Cards lists each card and set in three grades, with the middle grade valued at about 40-45% of the top grade, and the bottom grade valued at about 10-15% of the top grade.

The value of cards that fall between the listed columns can also be calculated using a percentage of the top grade. For example, a card that falls between the top and middle grades (Ex, ExMt or NrMt in most cases) will generally be valued at anywhere from 50% to 90% of the top grade.

Similarly, a card that falls between the middle and bottom grades (G-Vg, Vg or VgEx in most cases) will generally be valued at anywhere from 20% to 40% of the top grade.

There are also cases where cards are in better condition than the top grade or worse than the bottom grade. Cards that grade worse than the lowest grade are generally valued at 5-10% of the top grade.

When a card exceeds the top grade by one — such as NrMt-Mt when the top grade is NrMt, or Mint when the top grade is NrMt-Mt — a premium of up to 50% is possible, with 10-20% the usual norm.

When a card exceeds the top grade by two — such as Mint when the top grade is NrMt, or NrMt-Mt when the top grade is ExMt — a premium of 25-50% is the usual norm. But certain condition sensitive cards or sets, particularly those from the pre-war era, can bring premiums of up to 100% or even more.

Unopened packs, boxes and factory-collated sets are considered Mint in their unknown (and presumed perfect) state. Once opened, however, each card can be graded (and valued) in its own right by taking into account any defects that may be present in spite of the fact that the card has never been handled.

Selling Your Cards

Just about every collector sells cards or will sell cards eventually. Someday you may be interested in selling your duplicates or maybe even your whole collection. You may sell to other collectors, friends or dealers. You may even sell cards you purchased from a certain dealer back to that same dealer. In any event, it helps to know some of the mechanics of the typical transaction between buyer and seller.

Dealers will buy cards in order to resell them to other collectors who are interested in the cards. Dealers will always pay a higher percentage for items that (in their opinion) can be resold quickly, and a much lower percentage for those items that are perceived as having low demand and hence are slow moving. In either case, dealers must buy at a price that allows for the expense of doing business and a margin for profit.

If you have cards for sale, the best advice we can give is that you get several offers for your cards — either from card shops or at a card show — and take the best offer, all things considered. Note, the "best" offer may not be the one for the highest amount. And remember, if a dealer really wants your cards, he won't let you get away without making his best competitive offer. Another alternative is to place your cards in an auction as one or several lots.

Many people think nothing of going into a department store and paying $15 for an item of clothing for which the store paid $5. But if you were selling your $15 card to a dealer and he offered you $5 for it, you might consider his mark-up unreasonable. To complete the analogy: Most department stores (and card dealers) that consistently pay $10 for $15 items eventually go out of business. An exception is when the dealer has lined up a willing buyer for the item(s) you are attempting to sell, or if the cards are so Hot that it's likely he'll likely have to hold the cards for just a short period of time.

In those cases, an offer of up to 75 percent of book value still will allow the dealer to make a reasonable profit considering the short time he will need to hold the merchandise. In general, however, most cards and collections will bring offers in the range of 25 to 50 percent of retail price. Also consider that most material from the last five to 10 years is plentiful. If that's what you're selling, don't be surprised if your best offer is well below that range.

Centering

Well-centered

Slightly Off-centered

Off-centered

Badly Off-centered

Miscut

Corner Wear

The partial cards here have been photographed at 300%. This was done in order to magnify each card's corner wear to such a degree that differences could be shown on a printed page.

The 1962 Topps Mickey Mantle card definitely has a rounded corner. Some may say that this card is badly rounded, but that is a judgement call.

The 1962 Topps Hank Aaron card has a slightly rounded corner. Note that there is definite corner wear evident by the fraying and that there is no longer a sharp point to which the corner converges.

The 1962 Topps Gil Hodges card has corner wear; it is slightly better than the Aaron card above. Nevertheless, some collectors might classify this Hodges corner as slight-ly rounded.

The 1962 Topps Manager's Dream card showing Mantle and Mays has slight corner wear. This is not a fuzzy corner as very slight wear is noticeable on the card's photo surface.

The 1962 Topps Don Mossi card has very slight corner wear such that it might be called a fuzzy corner. A close look at the original card shows that the corner is not perfect, but almost. However, note that coner wear is somewhat academic on this card. As you can plainly see, the heavy crease going across his name breaks through the photo surface.

Interesting Notes

The first card numerically of an issue is the single card most likely to obtain excessive wear.

Consequently, you typically will find the price on the #1 card (in NrMt or Mint condition) somewhat higher than might otherwise be the case.

Similarly, but to a lesser extent (because normally the less important, reverse side of the card is the one exposed), the last card numerically in an issue also is prone to abnormal wear. This extra wear and tear occurs because the first and last cards are exposed to the elements (human element included) more than any of the other cards. They are generally end cards in any brick formations, rubber bandings, stackings on wet surfaces and like activities.

Sports cards have no intrinsic value. The value of a card, like the value of other collectibles, can be determined only by you and your enjoyment in viewing and possessing these cardboard treasures.

Remember, the buyer ultimately determines the price of each baseball card. You are the determining price factor because you have the ability to say "No" to the price of any card by not exchanging your hard-earned money for a given issue. When the cost of a trading card exceeds the enjoyment you will receive from it, your answer should be "No." We assess and report the prices. You set them!

We are always interested in receiving the price input of collectors and dealers. We happily credit major contributors.

We welcome your opinions, since your contributions assist us in ensuring a better guide each year.

If you would like to join our survey list for the next editions of this book and others authored by Dr. Beckett, please send your name and address to Dr. James Beckett, 15850 Dallas Parkway, Dallas, TX 75248.

History of Baseball Cards

Today's version of the baseball card, with its colorful and oft times high-tech fronts and backs, is a far cry from its earliest predecessors. The issue remains cloudy as to which was the very first baseball card ever produced, but the institution of baseball cards dates from the latter half of the 19th century, more than 100 years ago. Early issues, generally printed on heavy cardboard, were of poor quality, with photographs, drawings, and printing far short of today's standards.

Goodwin & Co., of New York, makers of Gypsy Queen, Old Judge, and other cigarette brands, is considered by many to be the first issuer of baseball and other sports cards. Its issues, predominantly sized 1-1/2 by 2-1/2 inches, generally consisted of photographs of baseball players, boxers, wrestlers, and other subjects mounted on stiff cardboard. More than 2,000 different photos of baseball players alone have been identified. These "Old Judges," a collective name commonly used for the Goodwin & Co. cards, were issued from 1886 to 1890 and are treasured parts of many collections today.

Among the other cigarette companies that issued baseball cards still attracting attention today are Allen & Ginter, D. Buchner & Co. (Gold Coin Chewing Tobacco), and P.H. Mayo & Brother. Cards from the first two companies bear colored line drawings, while the Mayos are sepia photographs on black cardboard. In addition to the small-size cards from this era, several tobacco companies issued cabinet-size baseball cards. These "cabinets" were considerably larger than the small cards, usually about 4-1/4 by 6-1/2 inches, and were printed on heavy stock. Goodwin & Co.'s Old Judge cabinets and the

National Tobacco Works' "Newsboy" baseball photos are two that remain popular today.

By 1895, the American Tobacco Company began to dominate its competition. They discontinued baseball card inserts in their cigarette packages (actually slide boxes in those days). The lack of competition in the cigarette market had made these inserts unnecessary. This marked the end of the first era of baseball cards. At the dawn of the 20th century, few baseball cards were being issued. But once again, it was the cigarette companies — particularly, the American Tobacco Company — followed to a lesser extent by the candy and gum makers that revived the practice of including baseball cards with their products. The bulk of these cards, identified in the American Card Catalog (designated hereafter as ACC) as T or E cards for 20th century "Tobacco" or "Early Candy and Gum" issues, respectively, were released from 1909 to 1915.

This romantic and popular era of baseball card collecting produced many desirable items. The most outstanding is the fabled T-206 Honus Wagner card. Other perennial favorites among collectors are the T-206 Eddie Plank card, and the T-206 Magee error card. The former was once the second most valuable card and only recently relinquished that position to a more distinctive and aesthetically pleasing Napoleon Lajoie card from the 1933-34 Goudey Gum series. The latter misspells the player's name as "Magie," the most famous and most valuable blooper card.

The ingenuity and distinctiveness of this era has yet to be surpassed. Highlights include:

• the T-202 Hassan triple-folders, one of the best looking and the most distinctive cards ever issued;

• the durable T-201 Mecca double-folders, one of the first sets with players' records on the reverse;

• the T-3 Turkey Reds, the hobby's most popular cabinet card;

• the E-145 Cracker Jacks, the only major set containing Federal League player cards;

• the T-204 Ramlys, with their distinctive black-and-white oval photos and ornate gold borders.

These are but a few of the varieties issued during this period.

Increasing Popularity

While the American Tobacco Company dominated the field, several other tobacco companies, as well as clothing manufacturers, newspapers and periodicals, game makers, and companies whose identities remain anonymous, also issued cards during this period. In fact, the Collins-McCarthy Candy Company, makers of Zeenuts Pacific Coast League baseball cards, issued cards yearly from 1911 to 1938. Its record for continuous annual card production has been exceeded only by the Topps Chewing Gum Company. The era of the tobacco card issues closed with the onset of World War I, with the exception of the Red Man chewing tobacco sets produced from 1952 to 1955.

The next flurry of card issues broke out in the roaring and prosperous 1920s, the era of the E card. The caramel companies (National Caramel, American Caramel, York Caramel) were the leading distributors of these E cards. In addition, the strip card, a continous strip with several cards divided by dotted lines or other sectioning features, flourished during this time. While the E cards and the strip cards generally are considered less imaginative than the T cards or the recent candy and gum issues, they still are pursued by many advanced collectors.

Another significant event of the 1920s was the introduction of the arcade card. Taking its designation from its issuer, the Exhibit Supply Company of Chicago, it is usually known as the "Exhibit" card. Once a trademark of the

penny arcades, amusement parks and county fairs across the country, Exhibit machines dispensed nearly postcard-size photos on thick stock for one penny. These picture cards bore likenesses of a favorite cowboy, actor, actress or baseball player. Exhibit Supply and its associated companies produced baseball cards during a longer time span, although discontinuous, than any other manufacturer. Its first cards appeared in 1921, while its last issue was in 1966. In 1979, the Exhibit Supply Company was bought and somewhat revived by a collector/dealer who has since reprinted Exhibit photos of the past.

If the T card period, from 1909 to 1915, can be designated the "Golden Age" of baseball card collecting, then perhaps the "Silver Age" commenced with the introduction of the Big League Gum series of 239 cards in 1933 (a 240th card was added in 1934). These are the forerunners of today's baseball gum cards, and the Goudey Gum Company of Boston is responsible for their success. This era spanned the period from the Depression days of 1933 to America's formal involvement in World War II in 1941.

Goudey's attractive designs, with full-color line drawings on thick card stock, greatly influenced other cards being issued at that time. As a result, the most attractive and popular vintage cards in history were produced in this "Silver Age." The 1933 Goudey Big League Gum series also owes its popularity to the more than 40 Hall of Fame players in the set. These include four cards of Babe Ruth and two of Lou Gehrig. Goudey's reign continued in 1934, when it issued a 96-card set in color, together with the single remaining card from the 1933 series, #106, the Napoleon Lajoie card.

In addition to Goudey, several other bubblegum manufacturers issued baseball cards during this era. DeLong Gum Company issued an extremely attractive set in 1933. National Chicle Company's 192-card "Batter-Up" series of 1934-1936 became the largest die-cut set in card history. In addition, that company offered the popular "Diamond Stars" series during the same period. Other popular sets included the "Tattoo Orbit" set of 60 color cards issued in 1933 and Gum Products' 75-card "Double Play" set, featuring sepia depictions of two players per card.

In 1939, Gum Inc., which later became Bowman Gum, replaced Goudey Gum as the leading baseball card producer. In 1939 and the following year, it issued two important sets of black-and-white cards. In 1939, its "Play Ball America" set consisted of 162 cards. The larger, 240-card "Play Ball" set of 1940 still is considered by many to be the most attractive black-and-white cards ever produced. That firm introduced its only color set in 1941, consisting of 72 cards titled "Play Ball Sports Hall of Fame." Many of these were colored repeats of poses from the black-and-white 1940 series.

In addition to regular gum cards, many manufacturers distributed premium issues during the 1930s. These premiums were printed on paper or photographic stock, rather than card stock. They were much larger than the regular cards and were sold for a penny across the counter with gum (which was packaged separately from the premium). They often were redeemed at the store or through the mail in exchange for the wrappers of previously purchased gum cards, like proof-of-purchase box-top premiums today. The gum premiums are scarcer than the card issues of the 1930s and in most cases no manufacturer's name is present.

World War II brought an end to this popular era of card collecting when paper and rubber shortages curtailed the production of bubblegum baseball cards. They were resurrected again in 1948 by the Bowman Gum Company (the direct descendent of Gum, Inc.). This marked the beginning of the modern era of card collecting.

In 1948, Bowman Gum issued a 48-card set in black and white consist-

ing of one card and one slab of gum in every 1 cent pack. That same year, the Leaf Gum Company also issued a set of cards. Although rather poor in quality, these cards were issued in color. A squabble over the rights to use players' pictures developed between Bowman and Leaf. Eventually Leaf dropped out of the card market, but not before it had left a lasting heritage to the hobby by issuing some of the rarest cards now in existence. Leaf's baseball card series of 1948-49 contained 98 cards, skip numbered to #168 (not all numbers were printed). Of these 98 cards, 49 are relatively plentiful; the other 49, however, are rare and quite valuable.

Bowman continued its production of cards in 1949 with a color series of 240 cards. Because there are many scarce "high numbers," this series remains the most difficult Bowman regular issue to complete. Although the set was printed in color and commands great interest due to its scarcity, it is considered aesthetically inferior to the Goudey and National Chicle issues of the 1930s. In addition to the regular issue of 1949, Bowman also produced a set of 36 Pacific Coast League players. While this was not a regular issue, it still is prized by collectors. In fact, it has become the most valuable Bowman series.

In 1950 (representing Bowman's one-year monopoly of the baseball card market), the company began a string of top quality cards that continued until its demise in 1955. The 1950 series was itself something of an oddity because the low numbers, rather than the traditional high numbers, were the more difficult cards to obtain.

The year 1951 marked the beginning of the most competitive and perhaps the highest quality period of baseball card production. In that year, Topps Chewing Gum Company of Brooklyn entered the market. Topps' 1951 series consisted of two sets of 52 cards each, one set with red backs and the other with blue backs. In addition, Topps also issued 31 insert cards, three of which remain the rarest Topps cards ("Current All-Stars" Konstanty, Roberts and Stanky). The 1951 Topps cards were unattractive and paled in comparison to the 1951 Bowman issues. They were successful, however, and Topps has continued to produce cards ever since.

Intensified Competition

Topps issued a larger and more attractive card set in 1952. This larger size became standard for the next five years. (Bowman followed with larger-size baseball cards in 1953.) This 1952 Topps set has become, like the 1933 Goudey series and the T-206 white border series, the classic set of its era. The 407-card set is a collector's dream of scarcities, rarities, errors and variations. It also contains the first Topps issues of Mickey Mantle and Willie Mays.

As with Bowman and Leaf in the late 1940s, competition over player rights arose. Ensuing court battles occurred between Topps and Bowman. The market split due to stiff competition, and in January 1956, Topps bought out Bowman. (Topps, using the Bowman name, resurrected Bowman as a later label in 1989.) Topps remained essentially unchallenged as the primary producer of baseball cards through 1980. So, the story of major baseball card sets from 1956 through 1980 is by and large the story of Topps' issues. Notable exceptions include the small sets produced by Fleer Gum in 1959, 1960, 1961 and 1963, and the Kellogg's Cereal and Hostess Cakes baseball cards issued to promote their products.

A court decision in 1980 paved the way for two other large gum companies to enter (or reenter, in Fleer's case) the baseball card arena. Fleer, which had last made photo cards in 1963, and the Donruss Company (then a division of General Mills) secured rights to produce baseball cards of current players, thus breaking Topps' monopoly. Each company issued major card sets in 1981 with bubblegum products.

Then a higher court decision in that year overturned the lower court ruling against Topps. It appeared that Topps had regained its sole position as a producer of baseball cards. Undaunted by the revocation ruling, Fleer and Donruss continued to issue cards in 1982 but without bubblegum or any other edible product. Fleer issued its current player baseball cards with "team logo stickers," while Donruss issued its cards with a piece of a baseball jigsaw puzzle.

Sharing the Pie

From 1981 to 1987, the three major companies solidifed their leadership position. The growth and popularity of these newer cards helped in bringing along two new companies by 1989: Score (debut set in 1988) and Upper Deck (debut set in 1989). These five companies were about to embark on a wild ride through the 1990's.

Upper Deck's successful entry into the market turned out to be very important. The company's card stock, photography, packaging and marketing gave baseball cards a new standard for quality, and began the "premium card" trend that continues today. The second premium baseball card set to be issued was the 1990 Leaf set, named for and issued by the parent company of Donruss. To gauge the significance of the premium card trend, one need only note that two of the most valuable post-1986 regular-issue cards in the hobby are the 1989 Upper Deck Ken Griffey Jr. and 1990 Leaf Frank Thomas Rookie Cards.

The impressive debut of Leaf in 1990 was followed by Studio, Ultra, and Stadium Club in 1991. Of those, Stadium Club with its dramatic borderless photo, Un-coated card fronts made the biggest impact. In 1992, Bowman, and Pinnacle joined the premium fray. In 1992, Donruss and Fleer abandoned the traditional 50-cent pack market and instead produced premium sets comparable to (and presumably designed to compete against) Upper Deck's set. Those moves, combined with the almost instantaneous spread of premium cards to the other major team sports cards, serve as strong indicators that premium cards were here to stay. Bowman had been a lower-level product from 1989 to '91.

In 1993, Fleer, Topps and Upper Deck produced the first "super premium" cards with Flair, Finest and SP, respectively. The success of all three products was an indication the baseball card market was headed toward even higher price levels, and that turned out to be the case in 1994 with the introduction of Bowman's Best (a Topps hybrid of prospect-oriented Bowman and the superpremium Finest) and Leaf Limited. Other 1994 debuts included Upper Deck's entry-level Collector's Choice and Pinnacle's hobby-only Select.

Overall, inserts continued to dominate the hobby scene. Specifically, the parallel chase cards first introduced in 1992 with Topps Gold became the latest major hobby trend. Topps Gold was followed by 1993 Finest Refractors (at the time the scarcest insert ever produced and still a landmark set), and the one-per-box Stadium Club First Day Issue.

Of course, the biggest on-field news of 1994 was the owner-provoked players strike that halted the season prematurely. While the baseball card hobby suffered noticeably from the strike, there was no catastrophic market crash as some had feared. However, the strike pulled the plug on a market that was both strong and growing, and contributed to a serious hobby contraction that continues to this day.

By 1995, parallel insert sets were commonplace and had taken on a new complexion: the most popular ones were those that had announced (or at least suspected) print runs of 500 or less, such as Finest Refractors and Select Artist's Proofs.

This trend continued in 1996, with several parallel inserts that were print-

ed in quantities of 250 or less such as Finest Gold Refractors, Fleer Circa Rave, Studio Silver Press Proofs and three of the six Select Certified parallels. It could be argued that the high price tags on these extremely limited parallel cards (many exceeded the $1000 plateau) were driving many single-player collectors to frustration, and even completely out of the hobby. At the same time, average pack prices soared while average number of cards per pack dropped, making the baseball card hobby increasingly more expensive.

On the positive side, two trends from 1996 clearly brought in new collectors: Topps' Mickey Mantle retrospective inserts in both series of Topps and Stadium Club; and Leaf's Signature Series, which included one certified autograph per pack. While the Mantle craze following his passing seemed to be a short-term phenomenon, the inclusion of autographs in packs seemed to have more long-term significance.

In 1997 the print runs in selected sets got even lower. Both Fleer/SkyBox and Pinnacle brands issued cards of which only one exists.

The growth in popularity of autographs also continued. Many products had autographed cards in their packs. A very positive trend was a return to basics. Many collectors bought Rookie Cards as they understood that concept and worked on finishing sets.

There was also an increase in international players collecting. Hideo Nomo was incredibly popular in Japan while Chan Ho Park was in demand in Korea. This bodes well for an international groutih in the hobby.

Nineteen ninety eight was a year of rebirth and growth for the hobby. Led by the home run chase of Mark McGwire and Sammy Sosa as well as the continued brilliance of stalwarts like Ken Griffey Jr. and Roger Clemens. The baseball card hobby got a considerable boost and positive publicity it had not seen in many years.

The Rookie Cards of these players as well as many others showed significant gains as the hobby started accepting Rookie Cards again as the most popular trend in collecting. Also, cards which were professionally graded by companies such as PSA and SGC (and in 1999, BGS) were becoming more heavily traded for both older and newer cards.

In addition, the internet and various services (eBay, Beckett Auction Services (part of the burgeoning Beckett on-line service), as well as many others) contributed to the strong growth in collecting interest over the past year.

There were some down sides in 1998, though. Pinnacle brands went out of buisness, leaving a legacy of innovation and promotions not seen by the other companies. In addition, there was still the problems of collectors being frustrated by the extremely short printed cards of their favorite players, making completion almost impossible. Rookie Cards of the key players of '98 made significant gains in value as the hobby once again turned to Rookie Cards as the collectible of choice. Also, cards professionally graded by companies such as PSA and SGC were becoming more heavily traded in both older and newer material.

In addtion, the internet and various services such as Beckett Auction Services (part of the burgeoning Beckett On-Line service) and eBay, contributed to the strong growth in collecting interest over the last year.

During 1998, Pacific received a full baseball license and added many innovations to the card market. Their 1998 OnLine set for example is the most comprehensive set issued in the last five years and many veteran collectors applauded Pacific's continuing attempts to get as many different players as possible into their sets.

In the last couple of years, card companies have been printing specific subsets (usually young players or Rookie Cards) in shorter supply than the

regular cards. This is not in every set, but in many sets produced since 1998.

In 1999, many of the trends of the last couple of years continued to gain strength. Buying, sellng and trading cards over the Internet became a dominant factor in the secondary market. Beckett Publications began its own Marketplace, offering the collectors a chance to search across inventory from many of the finest dealers nationwide in one comprehensive online database. eBay continued to flourish, while many other parties began to reap the benefits of the burgeoning online auction market.

Also, the boom in Internet trading created a perfect fit for professionally graded cards as buyers and sellers traded cards sight unseen with the confidence established by a third party grader.

From a field of almost a dozen contenders, three companies emerged in 1999 to dominate the field of professional grading - BGS (Beckett Grading Services), PSA (Professional Sports Authenticator) and SGC (Sportscard Guaranty L.L.C.). In 1999 these companies made dramatic expansions in onsite grading and submissions at card shows throughout the nation. In response to the widespread acceptance of graded cards, the line of monthly Beckett Price Guides each added a separate section within the price guide area for professionally graded cards.

As was similar to 1998, four licensed manufacturers (Fleer/SkyBox, Pacific, Topps and Upper Deck) produced slightly more than fifty different products for 1999.

Perhaps the biggest hit of the 1999 card season was created by Topps. Card #220 within the basic issue first series 1999 Topps brand featured Home Run King Mark McGwire in 70 variations, one for each homer he slugged in 1998 and many collectors went after the whole set. Continuing a legacy as strong as the Yankees, the basic Topps issue was the one of the most popular sets released in 1999.

Closely trailing the Topps McGwire promotion was Upper Deck's dynamic A Piece of History bat card promotion. The card that kicked off the frenzy was the Babe Ruth A Piece of History distributed in 1999 Upper Deck series 1 packs. Upper Deck actually purchased a cracked game-used Babe Ruth bat for $24,000 and proceeded to cut it up into approximately 350-400 chips of wood to create the now famous Ruth bat card. The card instantly created polar opposites of opinion amongst hobbyists. Traditional collectors howled at the sacreligious act of destroying such a historic piece of memorabilia while more open-minded collectors jumped at the opportunity to chase such an important card. The Ruth card was followed up by the cross-brand "500 Club" bat card promotion, whereby UD produced bat cards from every major league ballplayer that hit 500 or more home runs in their career (except for Mark McGwire of whom hit his 500th in the midst of the 1999 season and promptly stated that he did not support Upper Deck's promotion).

More memorabilia cards than ever were offered to collectors in 1999 as Fleer/SkyBox kicked up their efforts to match the standards set by Upper Deck in previous years. Batting Gloves, hats and shoes joined the typical bats and jerseys as pieces of game-used equipment to be featured on trading cards. Sets like E-X Century Authen-Kicks and Fleer Mystique Feel the Game typified the new offerings.

Topps only dabbled with memorabilia cards in 1999, but continued to offer some of the hottest autographed inserts highlighted by the Topps Stars Rookie Reprint Autographs and the Topps Nolan Ryan Autographs.

Pacific made a clear decision to steer free of memorabilia and autograph inserts, instead focusing on offering collectors a wide selection of beautifully designed insert and parallel cards. Those themes worked beautifully with

their established presence for making comprehensive sets - providing collectors with the necessary challenge to pursue regional stars and a favorite team in addition to the typical superstars.

An astounding total of 264 different players made their first appearance on a major league licensed trading card in 1999. What may go down as the deepest class of Rookie Cards of all time features a cornucopia of talented youngsters led by Rick Ankiel, Josh Beckett, Pat Burrell, Josh Hamilton, Eric Munson, Corey Patterson and Alfonso Soriano.

As in years past, Topps continued to provide collectors with a fistful of Rookie Cards within their Bowman, Bowman Chrome and Bowman's Best brands. In a trend established in 1998 by Fleer when they released their Fleer Update set (fueled largely by a J.D. Drew Rookie Card), hobbyists enjoyed a bevy of late season sets chock full of RC's. Fleer/SkyBox made an all out effort by stuffing more than 100 Rookie Cards into their 1999 Fleer Update set. Topps produced their first boxed Traded set since 1994. Each 1999 Topps Traded set contained one of 75 different cards autographed by a rookie prospect. Considering how much wider the selection of Rookie Cards became in 1999, it's amazing to see that so few of these RC's were serial numbered. When one looks at the success established with serial numbered Rookie Cards in the basketball and football card markets with brands like SP Authentic and SPx Finite, one can only scratch their head when realizing that Fleer Mystique was the only brand to offer baseball collectors serial numbered RC's. Thus, it's not surprising to see that despite having twenty-five different Rookie Cards issued in 1999, Pat Burrell's Fleer Mystique RC (#'d of 2,999) had been established as his "best" RC by year's end.

Youngsters weren't the only players in the limelight last year as retired stars and Hall of Famers were featured on more cards than any other year in the '90s. Upper Deck's Century Legends brand, featuring the top 50 active and top 50 retired players of the decade as chosen by The Sporting News was a runaway hit.

Perhaps the most popular insert set of the year, outpacing all of the dazzling high dollar memorabilia cards, was Topps Gallery Heritage. Utilizing the design and painting style of artist Gerry Dvorak from the classic 1953 Topps set, these modern masterpieces proved that insert cards can still be a hot commodity in the secondary market - albeit assuming they're well conceived and well made - an unfortunate rarity these days.

The spate of basic issue sets with short-printed subsets continued across many brands in 1999. In reaction to many frustrated dealers and collectors struggling to complete these sets, Fleer/SkyBox created dual versions of each prospect card for the 1999 SkyBox Premium set - an action shot was short-printed and a posed shot was seeded at the same rate as other basic issue cards. The idea was well received by collectors, but enjoyed a surprisingly short-lived period of active trading in the secondary market.

Unfortunately, such positives were clearly overshadowed by the industry's overriding problem: too many products costing too much money, with fewer and fewer buyers willing to ante up. The result? Many dealers going out of business, and a buyer's market in which new products usually were available cheaper to the consumer than original dealer cost from the factory. The hobby still faces this very complex problem with no easy solutions in sight.

Finding Out More

The above has been a thumbnail sketch of card collecting from its inception in the 1880s to the present. It is difficult to tell the whole story in just a few pages — there are several other good sources of information. Serious collectors should subscribe to at least one of the excellent hobby periodicals. We

also suggest that collectors visit their local card shop(s) and also attend a sports collectibles show in their area. Card collecting is still a young and informal hobby. You can learn more about it in either place. After all, smart dealers realize that spending a few minutes teaching beginners about the hobby often pays off in the long run.

Additional Reading

Each year Beckett Publications produces comprehensive annual price guides for each of the four major sports: Beckett Baseball Card Price Guide, Beckett Basketball Card Price Guide, Beckett Football Card Price Guide, Beckett Hockey Card Price Guide, Beckett Racing Price Guide and a line of Beckett Alphabetical Checklists Books have been released as well. The aim of these annual guides is to provide information and accurate pricing on a wide array of sports cards, ranging from main issues by the major card manufacturers to various regional, promotional, and food issues. Also alphabetical checklist books are published to assist the collector in identifying all the cards of any particular player. The seasoned collector will find these tools valuable sources of information that will enable him to pursue his hobby interests.

In addition, abridged editions of the Beckett Price Guides have been published for each of these major sports as part of the House of Collectibles series: The Official Price Guide to Baseball Cards, The Official Price Guide to Football Cards, The Official Price Guide to Basketball Cards. Published in a convenient mass-market paperback format, these price guides provide information and accurate pricing on all the main issues by the major card manufacturers.

Advertising

Within this Price Guide you will find advertisements for sports memorabilia material, mail order, and retail sports collectibles establishments. All advertisements were accepted in good faith based on the reputation of the advertiser; however, neither the author, the publisher, the distributors, nor the other advertisers in this Price Guide accept any responsibility for any particular advertiser not complying with the terms of his or her ad.

Readers also should be aware that prices in advertisements are subject to change over the annual period before a new edition of this volume is issued each spring. When replying to an advertisement late in the baseball year, the reader should take this into account, and contact the dealer by phone or in writing for up-to-date price information. Should you come into contact with any of the advertisers in this guide as a result of their advertisement herein, please mention this source as your contact.

Prices in This Guide

Prices found in this guide reflect current retail rates just prior to the printing of this book. They do not reflect the FOR SALE prices of the author, the publisher, the distributors, the advertisers, or any card dealers associated with this guide. No one is obligated in any way to buy, sell or trade his or her cards based on these prices. The price listings were compiled by the author from actual buy/sell transactions at sports conventions, sports card shops, buy/sell advertisements in the hobby papers, for sale prices from dealer catalogs and price lists, and discussions with leading hobbyists in the U.S. and Canada. All prices are in U.S. dollars.

1948 Bowman

JOHNNY VANDER MEER

	NRMT	VG-E
COMPLETE SET (48)	3400.00	1500.00
COMMON CARD (1-36)	20.00	9.00
MINOR STARS 1-36	25.00	11.00
SEMISTARS 1-36	40.00	18.00
UNLISTED STARS 1-36	50.00	22.00
COMMON CARD (37-48)	30.00	13.50
MINOR STARS 37-48	40.00	18.00
SEMISTARS 37-48	60.00	27.00
UNLISTED STARS 37-48	80.00	36.00

*UNLISTED DODGER/YANKEE: 1.25X VALUE
CARDS PRICED IN NM CONDITION !

❏ 1 Bob Elliott	100.00	15.00
❏ 2 Ewell Blackwell	40.00	18.00
❏ 3 Ralph Kiner	150.00	70.00
❏ 4 Johnny Mize	100.00	45.00
❏ 5 Bob Feller	225.00	100.00
❏ 6 Yogi Berra	450.00	200.00
❏ 7 Pete Reiser SP	120.00	55.00
❏ 8 Phil Rizzuto SP	300.00	135.00
❏ 9 Walker Cooper	20.00	9.00
❏ 10 Buddy Rosar	20.00	9.00
❏ 11 Johnny Lindell	25.00	11.00
❏ 12 Johnny Sain	50.00	22.00
❏ 13 Willard Marshall SP	40.00	18.00
❏ 14 Allie Reynolds	50.00	22.00
❏ 15 Eddie Joost	20.00	9.00
❏ 16 Jack Lohrke SP	40.00	18.00
❏ 17 Enos Slaughter	100.00	45.00
❏ 18 Warren Spahn SP	300.00	135.00
❏ 19 Tommy Henrich	50.00	22.00
❏ 20 Buddy Kerr SP	40.00	18.00
❏ 21 Ferris Fain	40.00	18.00
❏ 22 Floyd Bevens SP	50.00	22.00
❏ 23 Larry Jansen	25.00	11.00
❏ 24 Dutch Leonard SP	40.00	18.00
❏ 25 Barney McCosky	20.00	9.00
❏ 26 Frank Shea SP	50.00	22.00
❏ 27 Sid Gordon	25.00	11.00
❏ 28 Emil Verban SP	40.00	18.00
❏ 29 Joe Page SP	75.00	34.00
❏ 30 Whitey Lockman SP	50.00	22.00
❏ 31 Bill McCahan	20.00	9.00
❏ 32 Bill Rigney	20.00	9.00
❏ 33 Bill Johnson	25.00	11.00
❏ 34 Sheldon Jones SP	40.00	18.00
❏ 35 Snuffy Stirnweiss	40.00	18.00
❏ 36 Stan Musial	800.00	350.00
❏ 37 Clint Hartung	30.00	13.50
❏ 38 Red Schoendienst	150.00	70.00
❏ 39 Augie Galan	30.00	13.50
❏ 40 Marty Marion	80.00	36.00
❏ 41 Rex Barney	60.00	27.00
❏ 42 Ray Poat	30.00	13.50
❏ 43 Bruce Edwards	30.00	13.50
❏ 44 Johnny Wyrostek	30.00	13.50
❏ 45 Hank Sauer	60.00	27.00
❏ 46 Herman Wehmeier	30.00	13.50
❏ 47 Bobby Thomson	100.00	45.00
❏ 48 Dave Kosko	80.00	19.50

1949 Bowman

	NRMT	VG-E
COMPLETE SET (240)	13000.00	5800.00
COMMON CARD (1-144)	15.00	6.75

MINOR STARS 1-144	25.00	11.00
SEMISTARS 1-144	40.00	18.00
UNLISTED STARS 1-144	60.00	27.00
COMMON CARD (145-240)	50.00	22.00
MINOR STARS 145-240	80.00	36.00

*UNLISTED DODGER/YANKEE: 1.25X VALUE
CARDS PRICED IN NM CONDITION

❏ 1 Vern Bickford	100.00	20.00
❏ 2 Whitey Lockman	40.00	18.00
❏ 3 Bob Porterfield	15.00	6.75
❏ 4A Jerry Priddy NNOF	15.00	6.75
❏ 4B Jerry Priddy NOF	50.00	22.00
❏ 5 Hank Sauer	40.00	18.00
❏ 6 Phil Cavarretta	40.00	18.00
❏ 7 Joe Dobson	15.00	6.75
❏ 8 Murry Dickson	15.00	6.75
❏ 9 Ferris Fain	40.00	18.00
❏ 10 Ted Gray	15.00	6.75
❏ 11 Lou Boudreau	60.00	27.00
❏ 12 Cass Michaels	15.00	6.75
❏ 13 Bob Chesnes	15.00	6.75
❏ 14 Curt Simmons	40.00	18.00
❏ 15 Ned Garver	15.00	6.75
❏ 16 Al Kozar	15.00	6.75
❏ 17 Earl Torgeson	15.00	6.75
❏ 18 Bobby Thomson	40.00	18.00
❏ 19 Bobby Brown	40.00	18.00
❏ 20 Gene Hermanski	15.00	6.75
❏ 21 Frank Baumholtz	15.00	6.75
❏ 22 Peanuts Lowrey	15.00	6.75
❏ 23 Bobby Doerr	75.00	34.00
❏ 24 Stan Musial	500.00	220.00
❏ 25 Carl Scheib	15.00	6.75
❏ 26 George Kell	60.00	27.00
❏ 27 Bob Feller	200.00	90.00
❏ 28 Don Kolloway	15.00	6.75
❏ 29 Ralph Kiner	125.00	55.00
❏ 30 Andy Seminick	40.00	18.00
❏ 31 Dick Kokos	15.00	6.75
❏ 32 Eddie Yost	60.00	27.00
❏ 33 Warren Spahn	175.00	80.00
❏ 34 Dave Koslo	15.00	6.75
❏ 35 Vic Raschi	60.00	27.00
❏ 36 Pee Wee Reese	175.00	80.00
❏ 37 Johnny Wyrostek	15.00	6.75
❏ 38 Emil Verban	15.00	6.75
❏ 39 Billy Goodman	25.00	11.00
❏ 40 Red Munger	15.00	6.75
❏ 41 Lou Brissie	15.00	6.75
❏ 42 Hoot Evers	15.00	6.75
❏ 43 Dale Mitchell	40.00	18.00
❏ 44 Dave Philley	15.00	6.75
❏ 45 Wally Westlake	15.00	6.75
❏ 46 Robin Roberts	250.00	110.00
❏ 47 Johnny Sain	40.00	18.00
❏ 48 Willard Marshall	15.00	6.75
❏ 49 Frank Shea	25.00	11.00
❏ 50 Jackie Robinson	1100.00	500.00
❏ 51 Herman Wehmeier	15.00	6.75
❏ 52 Johnny Schmitz	15.00	6.75
❏ 53 Jack Kramer	15.00	6.75
❏ 54 Marty Marion	60.00	27.00
❏ 55 Eddie Joost	15.00	6.75
❏ 56 Pat Mullin	15.00	6.75
❏ 57 Gene Bearden	40.00	18.00
❏ 58 Bob Elliott	40.00	18.00
❏ 59 Jack Lohrke	15.00	6.75
❏ 60 Yogi Berra	275.00	125.00
❏ 61 Rex Barney	40.00	18.00

❏ 62 Grady Hatton	15.00	6.75
❏ 63 Andy Pafko	40.00	18.00
❏ 64 Dom DiMaggio	40.00	18.00
❏ 65 Enos Slaughter	75.00	34.00
❏ 66 Elmer Valo	15.00	6.75
❏ 67 Alvin Dark	40.00	18.00
❏ 68 Sheldon Jones	15.00	6.75
❏ 69 Tommy Henrich	40.00	18.00
❏ 70 Carl Furillo	100.00	45.00
❏ 71 Vern Stephens	15.00	6.75
❏ 72 Tommy Holmes	40.00	18.00
❏ 73 Billy Cox	40.00	18.00
❏ 74 Tom McBride	15.00	6.75
❏ 75 Eddie Mayo	15.00	6.75
❏ 76 Bill Nicholson	25.00	11.00
❏ 77 Ernie Bonham	15.00	6.75
❏ 78A Sam Zoldak NNOF	15.00	6.75
❏ 78B Sam Zoldak NOF	50.00	22.00
❏ 79 Ron Northey	15.00	6.75
❏ 80 Bill McCahan	15.00	6.75
❏ 81 Virgil Stallcup	15.00	6.75
❏ 82 Joe Page	60.00	27.00
❏ 83A Bob Scheffing NNOF	15.00	6.75
❏ 83B Bob Scheffing NOF	50.00	22.00
❏ 84 Roy Campanella	700.00	325.00
❏ 85A Johnny Mize NNOF	80.00	36.00
❏ 85B Johnny Mize NOF	150.00	70.00
❏ 86 Johnny Pesky	60.00	27.00
❏ 87 Randy Gumpert	15.00	6.75
❏ 88A Bill Salkeld NNOF	15.00	6.75
❏ 88B Bill Salkeld NOF	50.00	22.00
❏ 89 Mizell Platt	15.00	6.75
❏ 90 Gil Coan	15.00	6.75
❏ 91 Dick Wakefield	15.00	6.75
❏ 92 Willie Jones	40.00	18.00
❏ 93 Ed Stevens	15.00	6.75
❏ 94 Mickey Vernon	40.00	18.00
❏ 95 Howie Pollet	15.00	6.75
❏ 96 Taft Wright	15.00	6.75
❏ 97 Danny Litwhiler	15.00	6.75
❏ 98A Phil Rizzuto NNOF	150.00	70.00
❏ 98B Phil Rizzuto NOF	200.00	90.00
❏ 99 Frank Gustine	15.00	6.75
❏ 100 Gil Hodges	250.00	110.00
❏ 101 Sid Gordon	15.00	6.75
❏ 102 Stan Spence	15.00	6.75
❏ 103 Joe Tipton	15.00	6.75
❏ 104 Eddie Stanky	40.00	18.00
❏ 105 Bill Kennedy	15.00	6.75
❏ 106 Jake Early	15.00	6.75
❏ 107 Eddie Lake	15.00	6.75
❏ 108 Ken Heintzelman	15.00	6.75
❏ 109A Ed Fitzgerald SCR	15.00	6.75
❏ 109B Ed Fitzgerald PR	50.00	22.00
❏ 110 Early Wynn	125.00	55.00
❏ 111 Red Schoendienst	80.00	36.00
❏ 112 Sam Chapman	40.00	18.00
❏ 113 Ray LaManno	15.00	6.75
❏ 114 Allie Reynolds	40.00	18.00
❏ 115 Dutch Leonard	15.00	6.75
❏ 116 Joe Hatton	15.00	6.75
❏ 117 Walker Cooper	15.00	6.75
❏ 118 Sam Mele	15.00	6.75
❏ 119 Floyd Baker	15.00	6.75
❏ 120 Cliff Fannin	15.00	6.75
❏ 121 Mark Christman	15.00	6.75
❏ 122 George Vico	15.00	6.75
❏ 123 Johnny Blatnick	15.00	6.75
❏ 124A Danny Murtaugh SCR	60.00	27.00
❏ 124B Danny Murtaugh PR	50.00	20.00
❏ 125 Ken Keltner	40.00	18.00
❏ 126A Al Brazle SCR	15.00	6.75
❏ 126B Al Brazle PR	50.00	22.00
❏ 127A Hank Majeski SCR	15.00	6.75
❏ 127B Hank Majeski PR	50.00	22.00
❏ 128 Johnny VanderMeer	40.00	27.00
❏ 129 Bill Johnson	40.00	18.00
❏ 130 Harry Walker	15.00	6.75
❏ 131 Paul Lehner	15.00	6.75
❏ 132A Al Evans SCR	15.00	6.75
❏ 132B Al Evans PR	50.00	22.00
❏ 133 Aaron Robinson	15.00	6.75
❏ 134 Hank Borowy	15.00	6.75
❏ 135 Stan Rojek	15.00	6.75
❏ 136 Hank Edwards	15.00	6.75
❏ 137 Ted Wilks	15.00	6.75

138	Buddy Rosar	15.00	6.75
139	Hank Arft	15.00	6.75
140	Ray Scarborough	15.00	6.75
141	Tony Lupien	15.00	6.75
142	Eddie Waitkus	40.00	18.00
143A	Bob Dillinger SCR	25.00	11.00
143B	Bob Dillinger PR	75.00	34.00
144	Mickey Haefner	15.00	6.75
145	Sylvester Donnelly	50.00	22.00
146	Mike McCormick	50.00	22.00
147	Bert Singleton	50.00	22.00
148	Bob Swift	50.00	22.00
149	Roy Partee	50.00	22.00
150	Allie Clark	50.00	22.00
151	Mickey Harris	50.00	22.00
152	Clarence Maddern	50.00	22.00
153	Phil Masi	50.00	22.00
154	Clint Hartung	80.00	36.00
155	Mickey Guerra	50.00	22.00
156	Al Zarilla	50.00	22.00
157	Walt Masterson	50.00	22.00
158	Harry Brecheen	80.00	36.00
159	Glen Moulder	50.00	22.00
160	Jim Blackburn	50.00	22.00
161	Jocko Thompson	50.00	22.00
162	Preacher Roe	125.00	55.00
163	Clyde McCullough	50.00	22.00
164	Vic Wertz	80.00	36.00
165	Snuffy Stirnweiss	80.00	36.00
166	Mike Tresh	50.00	22.00
167	Babe Martin	50.00	22.00
168	Doyle Lade	50.00	22.00
169	Jeff Heath	80.00	36.00
170	Bill Rigney	80.00	36.00
171	Dick Fowler	50.00	22.00
172	Eddie Pellagrini	50.00	22.00
173	Eddie Stewart	50.00	22.00
174	Terry Moore	75.00	34.00
175	Luke Appling	125.00	55.00
176	Ken Raffensberger	50.00	22.00
177	Stan Lopata	80.00	36.00
178	Tom Brown	80.00	36.00
179	Hugh Casey	100.00	45.00
180	Connie Berry	50.00	22.00
181	Gus Niarhos	50.00	22.00
182	Hal Peck	50.00	22.00
183	Lou Stringer	50.00	22.00
184	Bob Chipman	50.00	22.00
185	Pete Reiser	75.00	34.00
186	Buddy Kerr	50.00	22.00
187	Phil Marchildon	50.00	22.00
188	Karl Drews	50.00	22.00
189	Earl Wooten	50.00	22.00
190	Jim Hearn	50.00	22.00
191	Joe Haynes	50.00	22.00
192	Harry Gumbert	50.00	22.00
193	Ken Trinkle	50.00	22.00
194	Ralph Branca	80.00	36.00
195	Eddie Bockman	50.00	22.00
196	Fred Hutchinson	80.00	36.00
197	Johnny Lindell	80.00	36.00
198	Steve Gromek	50.00	22.00
199	Tex Hughson	50.00	22.00
200	Jess Dobernic	50.00	22.00
201	Sibby Sisti	50.00	22.00
202	Larry Jansen	80.00	36.00
203	Barney McCosky	50.00	22.00
204	Bob Savage	50.00	22.00
205	Dick Sisler	80.00	36.00
206	Bruce Edwards	50.00	22.00
207	Johnny Hopp	50.00	22.00
208	Dizzy Trout	80.00	36.00
209	Charlie Keller	75.00	34.00
210	Joe Gordon	75.00	34.00
211	Boo Ferriss	50.00	22.00
212	Ralph Hamner	50.00	22.00
213	Red Barrett	50.00	22.00
214	Richie Ashburn	550.00	250.00
215	Kirby Higbe	50.00	22.00
216	Schoolboy Rowe	80.00	36.00
217	Marino Pieretti	50.00	22.00
218	Dick Kryhoski	50.00	22.00
219	Virgil Fire Trucks	80.00	36.00
220	Johnny McCarthy	50.00	22.00
221	Bob Muncrief	50.00	22.00
222	Alex Kellner	50.00	22.00
223	Bobby Hofman	50.00	22.00
224	Satchell Paige	1000.00	450.00
225	Jerry Coleman	75.00	34.00
226	Duke Snider	900.00	400.00
227	Fritz Ostermueller	50.00	22.00
228	Jackie Mayo	50.00	22.00
229	Ed Lopat	125.00	55.00
230	Augie Galan	80.00	36.00
231	Earl Johnson	50.00	22.00
232	George McQuinn	80.00	36.00
233	Larry Doby	175.00	80.00
234	Rip Sewell	50.00	22.00
235	Jim Russell	50.00	22.00
236	Fred Sanford	50.00	22.00
237	Monte Kennedy	50.00	22.00
238	Bob Lemon	200.00	90.00
239	Frank McCormick	50.00	22.00
240	Babe Young UER (Photo actually Bobby Young)	100.00	25.00

1950 Bowman

		NRMT	VG-E
COMPLETE SET (252)		8500.00	3800.00
COMMON CARD (1-72)		50.00	22.00
MINOR STARS 1-72		60.00	27.00
SEMISTARS 1-72		80.00	36.00
COMMON CARD (73-252)		15.00	6.75
MINOR STARS 73-252		25.00	11.00
SEMISTARS 73-252		40.00	18.00
UNLISTED STARS 73-252		60.00	27.00

*UNLISTED DODGER/YANKEE: 1.25X VALUE
CARDS PRICED IN NM CONDITION

1	Mel Parnell	150.00	30.00
2	Vern Stephens	60.00	27.00
3	Dom DiMaggio	80.00	36.00
4	Gus Zernial	60.00	27.00
5	Bob Kuzava	50.00	22.00
6	Bob Feller	250.00	110.00
7	Jim Hegan	60.00	27.00
8	George Kell	80.00	36.00
9	Vic Wertz	60.00	27.00
10	Tommy Henrich	80.00	36.00
11	Phil Rizzuto	225.00	100.00
12	Joe Page	80.00	36.00
13	Ferris Fain	60.00	27.00
14	Alex Kellner	50.00	22.00
15	Al Kozar	50.00	22.00
16	Roy Sievers	80.00	36.00
17	Sid Hudson	50.00	22.00
18	Eddie Robinson	50.00	22.00
19	Warren Spahn	225.00	100.00
20	Bob Elliott	60.00	27.00
21	Pee Wee Reese	300.00	135.00
22	Jackie Robinson	800.00	350.00
23	Don Newcombe	150.00	70.00
24	Johnny Schmitz	50.00	22.00
25	Hank Sauer	60.00	27.00
26	Grady Hatton	50.00	22.00
27	Herman Wehmeier	50.00	22.00
28	Bobby Thomson	80.00	36.00
29	Eddie Stanky	60.00	27.00
30	Eddie Waitkus	60.00	27.00
31	Del Ennis	80.00	36.00
32	Robin Roberts	150.00	70.00
33	Ralph Kiner	100.00	45.00
34	Murry Dickson	50.00	22.00
35	Enos Slaughter	100.00	45.00
36	Eddie Kazak	55.00	25.00
37	Luke Appling	80.00	36.00
38	Bill Wight	50.00	22.00
39	Larry Doby	80.00	36.00
40	Bob Lemon	80.00	36.00
41	Hoot Evers	50.00	22.00
42	Art Houtteman	50.00	22.00
43	Bobby Doerr	80.00	36.00
44	Joe Dobson	50.00	22.00
45	Al Zarilla	50.00	22.00
46	Yogi Berra	350.00	160.00
47	Jerry Coleman	80.00	36.00
48	Lou Brissie	50.00	22.00
49	Elmer Valo	50.00	22.00
50	Dick Kokos	50.00	22.00
51	Ned Garver	60.00	27.00
52	Sam Mele	50.00	22.00
53	Clyde Vollmer	50.00	22.00
54	Gil Coan	50.00	22.00
55	Buddy Kerr	50.00	22.00
56	Del Crandall	60.00	27.00
57	Vern Bickford	50.00	22.00
58	Carl Furillo	80.00	36.00
59	Ralph Branca	80.00	36.00
60	Andy Pafko	60.00	27.00
61	Bob Rush	50.00	22.00
62	Ted Kluszewski	125.00	55.00
63	Ewell Blackwell	60.00	27.00
64	Alvin Dark	60.00	27.00
65	Dave Koslo	50.00	22.00
66	Larry Jansen	60.00	27.00
67	Willie Jones	60.00	27.00
68	Curt Simmons	60.00	27.00
69	Wally Westlake	50.00	22.00
70	Bob Chesnes	50.00	22.00
71	Red Schoendienst	80.00	36.00
72	Howie Pollet	50.00	22.00
73	Willard Marshall	15.00	6.75
74	Johnny Antonelli	60.00	27.00
75	Roy Campanella	275.00	125.00
76	Rex Barney	40.00	18.00
77	Duke Snider	275.00	125.00
78	Mickey Owen	25.00	11.00
79	Johnny VanderMeer	40.00	18.00
80	Howard Fox	15.00	6.75
81	Ron Northey	15.00	6.75
82	Whitey Lockman	25.00	11.00
83	Sheldon Jones	15.00	6.75
84	Richie Ashburn	100.00	45.00
85	Ken Heintzelman	15.00	6.75
86	Stan Rojek	15.00	6.75
87	Bill Werle	15.00	6.75
88	Marty Marion	40.00	18.00
89	Red Munger	15.00	6.75
90	Harry Brecheen	40.00	18.00
91	Cass Michaels	15.00	6.75
92	Hank Majeski	15.00	6.75
93	Gene Bearden	40.00	18.00
94	Lou Boudreau	60.00	27.00
95	Aaron Robinson	15.00	6.75
96	Virgil Trucks	25.00	11.00
97	Maurice McDermott	15.00	6.75
98	Ted Williams	850.00	375.00
99	Billy Goodman	25.00	11.00
100	Vic Raschi	60.00	27.00
101	Bobby Brown	60.00	27.00
102	Billy Johnson	25.00	11.00
103	Eddie Joost	15.00	6.75
104	Sam Chapman	15.00	6.75
105	Bob Dillinger	15.00	6.75
106	Cliff Fannin	15.00	6.75
107	Sam Dente	15.00	6.75
108	Ray Scarborough	15.00	6.75
109	Sid Gordon	15.00	6.75
110	Tommy Holmes	25.00	11.00
111	Walker Cooper	15.00	6.75
112	Gil Hodges	100.00	45.00
113	Gene Hermanski	15.00	6.75
114	Wayne Terwilliger	15.00	6.75
115	Roy Smalley	15.00	6.75
116	Virgil Stallcup	15.00	6.75
117	Bill Rigney	15.00	6.75
118	Clint Hartung	15.00	6.75
119	Dick Sisler	25.00	11.00
120	John Thompson	15.00	6.75
121	Andy Seminick	25.00	11.00

		NRMT	VG-E
☐ 122	Johnny Hopp	25.00	11.00
☐ 123	Dino Restelli	15.00	6.75
☐ 124	Clyde McCullough	15.00	6.75
☐ 125	Del Rice	15.00	6.75
☐ 126	Al Brazle	15.00	6.75
☐ 127	Dave Philley	15.00	6.75
☐ 128	Phil Masi	15.00	5.75
☐ 129	Joe Gordon	25.00	11.00
☐ 130	Dale Mitchell	25.00	11.00
☐ 131	Steve Gromek	15.00	6.75
☐ 132	Mickey Vernon	25.00	11.00
☐ 133	Don Kolloway	15.00	6.75
☐ 134	Paul Trout	15.00	6.75
☐ 135	Pat Mullin	15.00	6.75
☐ 136	Warren Rosar	15.00	6.75
☐ 137	Johnny Pesky	25.00	11.00
☐ 138	Allie Reynolds	60.00	27.00
☐ 139	Johnny Mize	75.00	34.00
☐ 140	Pete Suder	15.00	6.75
☐ 141	Joe Coleman	25.00	11.00
☐ 142	Sherman Lollar	40.00	18.00
☐ 143	Eddie Stewart	15.00	6.75
☐ 144	Al Evans	15.00	6.75
☐ 145	Jack Graham	15.00	6.75
☐ 146	Floyd Baker	15.00	6.75
☐ 147	Mike Garcia	40.00	18.00
☐ 148	Early Wynn	75.00	34.00
☐ 149	Bob Swift	15.00	6.75
☐ 150	George Vico	15.00	6.75
☐ 151	Fred Hutchinson	25.00	11.00
☐ 152	Ellis Kinder	15.00	6.75
☐ 153	Walt Masterson	15.00	6.75
☐ 154	Gus Niarhos	15.00	6.75
☐ 155	Frank Shea	25.00	11.00
☐ 156	Fred Sanford	25.00	11.00
☐ 157	Mike Guerra	15.00	6.75
☐ 158	Paul Lehner	15.00	6.75
☐ 159	Joe Tipton	15.00	6.75
☐ 160	Mickey Harris	15.00	6.75
☐ 161	Sherry Robertson	15.00	6.75
☐ 162	Eddie Yost	25.00	11.00
☐ 163	Earl Torgeson	15.00	6.75
☐ 164	Sibby Sisti	15.00	6.75
☐ 165	Bruce Edwards	15.00	6.75
☐ 166	Joe Hatton	15.00	6.75
☐ 167	Preacher Roe	60.00	27.00
☐ 168	Bob Scheffing	15.00	6.75
☐ 169	Hank Edwards	15.00	6.75
☐ 170	Dutch Leonard	15.00	6.75
☐ 171	Harry Gumbert	15.00	6.75
☐ 172	Peanuts Lowrey	15.00	6.75
☐ 173	Lloyd Merriman	15.00	6.75
☐ 174	Hank Thompson	40.00	18.00
☐ 175	Monte Kennedy	15.00	6.75
☐ 176	Sylvester Donnelly	15.00	6.75
☐ 177	Hank Borowy	15.00	6.75
☐ 178	Ed Fitzgerald	15.00	6.75
☐ 179	Chuck Diering	15.00	6.75
☐ 180	Harry Walker	25.00	11.00
☐ 181	Marino Pieretti	15.00	6.75
☐ 182	Sam Zoldak	15.00	6.75
☐ 183	Mickey Haefner	15.00	6.75
☐ 184	Randy Gumpert	15.00	6.75
☐ 185	Howie Judson	15.00	6.75
☐ 186	Ken Keltner	25.00	11.00
☐ 187	Lou Stringer	15.00	6.75
☐ 188	Earl Johnson	15.00	6.75
☐ 189	Owen Friend	15.00	6.75
☐ 190	Ken Wood	15.00	6.75
☐ 191	Dick Starr	15.00	6.75
☐ 192	Bob Chipman	15.00	6.75
☐ 193	Pete Reiser	40.00	18.00
☐ 194	Billy Cox	60.00	27.00
☐ 195	Phil Cavarretta	40.00	18.00
☐ 196	Doyle Lade	15.00	6.75
☐ 197	Johnny Wyrostek	15.00	6.75
☐ 198	Danny Litwhiler	15.00	6.75
☐ 199	Jack Kramer	15.00	6.75
☐ 200	Kirby Higbe	25.00	11.00
☐ 201	Pete Castiglione	15.00	6.75
☐ 202	Cliff Chambers	15.00	6.75
☐ 203	Danny Murtaugh	25.00	11.00
☐ 204	Granny Hamner	40.00	18.00
☐ 205	Mike Goliat	15.00	6.75
☐ 206	Stan Lopata	25.00	11.00
☐ 207	Max Lanier	15.00	6.75
☐ 208	Jim Hearn	15.00	6.75
☐ 209	Johnny Lindell	15.00	6.75
☐ 210	Ted Gray	15.00	6.75
☐ 211	Charlie Keller	25.00	11.00
☐ 212	Jerry Priddy	15.00	6.75
☐ 213	Carl Scheib	15.00	6.75
☐ 214	Dick Fowler	15.00	6.75
☐ 215	Ed Lopat	60.00	27.00
☐ 216	Bob Porterfield	25.00	11.00
☐ 217	Casey Stengel MG	125.00	55.00
☐ 218	Cliff Mapes	25.00	11.00
☐ 219	Hank Bauer	80.00	36.00
☐ 220	Leo Durocher MG	75.00	34.00
☐ 221	Don Mueller	40.00	18.00
☐ 222	Bobby Morgan	15.00	6.75
☐ 223	Jim Russell	15.00	6.75
☐ 224	Jack Banta	15.00	6.75
☐ 225	Eddie Sawyer MG	25.00	11.00
☐ 226	Jim Konstanty	60.00	27.00
☐ 227	Bob Miller	25.00	11.00
☐ 228	Bill Nicholson	25.00	11.00
☐ 229	Frank Frisch MG	60.00	27.00
☐ 230	Bill Serena	15.00	6.75
☐ 231	Preston Ward	15.00	6.75
☐ 232	Al Rosen	60.00	27.00
☐ 233	Allie Clark	15.00	6.75
☐ 234	Bobby Shantz	60.00	27.00
☐ 235	Harold Gilbert	15.00	6.75
☐ 236	Bob Cain	15.00	6.75
☐ 237	Bill Salkeld	15.00	6.75
☐ 238	Nippy Jones	15.00	6.75
☐ 239	Bill Howerton	15.00	6.75
☐ 240	Eddie Lake	15.00	6.75
☐ 241	Neil Berry	15.00	6.75
☐ 242	Dick Kryhoski	15.00	6.75
☐ 243	Johnny Groth	15.00	6.75
☐ 244	Dale Coogan	15.00	6.75
☐ 245	Al Papai	15.00	6.75
☐ 246	Walt Dropo	40.00	18.00
☐ 247	Irv Noren	25.00	11.00
☐ 248	Sam Jethroe	60.00	27.00
☐ 249	Snuffy Stirnweiss	25.00	11.00
☐ 250	Ray Coleman	15.00	6.75
☐ 251	Les Moss	15.00	6.75
☐ 252	Billy DeMars	60.00	16.50

1951 Bowman

PHIL RIZZUTO

	NRMT	VG-E
COMPLETE SET (324)	16000.00	7200.00
COMMON CARD (1-252)	18.00	8.00
MINOR STARS 1-252	25.00	11.00
SEMISTARS 1-252	40.00	18.00
UNLISTED STARS 1-252	60.00	27.00
COMMON CARD (253-324)	50.00	22.00
MINOR STARS 253-324	60.00	27.00
SEMISTARS 253-324	80.00	36.00

*UNLISTED DODGER/YANKEE: 1.25X VALUE
CARDS PRICED IN NM CONDITION

☐ 1	Whitey Ford	800.00	200.00
☐ 2	Yogi Berra	275.00	125.00
☐ 3	Robin Roberts	75.00	34.00
☐ 4	Del Ennis	25.00	11.00
☐ 5	Dale Mitchell	25.00	11.00
☐ 6	Don Newcombe	60.00	27.00
☐ 7	Gil Hodges	90.00	40.00
☐ 8	Paul Lehner	18.00	8.00
☐ 9	Sam Chapman	18.00	8.00
☐ 10	Red Schoendienst	60.00	27.00
☐ 11	Red Munger	18.00	8.00
☐ 12	Hank Majeski	18.00	8.00
☐ 13	Eddie Stanky	25.00	11.00
☐ 14	Alvin Dark	40.00	18.00
☐ 15	Johnny Pesky	25.00	11.00
☐ 16	Maurice McDermott	18.00	8.00
☐ 17	Pete Castiglione	18.00	8.00
☐ 18	Gil Coan	18.00	8.00
☐ 19	Sid Gordon	18.00	8.00
☐ 20	Del Crandall UER	25.00	11.00
	(Misspelled Crandell on card)		
☐ 21	Snuffy Stirnweiss	25.00	11.00
☐ 22	Hank Sauer	25.00	11.00
☐ 23	Hoot Evers	18.00	8.00
☐ 24	Ewell Blackwell	40.00	18.00
☐ 25	Vic Raschi	60.00	27.00
☐ 26	Phil Rizzuto	125.00	55.00
☐ 27	Jim Konstanty	18.00	8.00
☐ 28	Eddie Waitkus	18.00	8.00
☐ 29	Allie Clark	18.00	8.00
☐ 30	Bob Feller	125.00	55.00
☐ 31	Roy Campanella	225.00	100.00
☐ 32	Duke Snider	225.00	100.00
☐ 33	Bob Hooper	18.00	8.00
☐ 34	Marty Marion	40.00	18.00
☐ 35	Al Zarilla	18.00	8.00
☐ 36	Joe Dobson	18.00	8.00
☐ 37	Whitey Lockman	18.00	8.00
☐ 38	Al Evans	18.00	8.00
☐ 39	Ray Scarborough	18.00	8.00
☐ 40	Gus Bell	60.00	27.00
☐ 41	Eddie Yost	25.00	11.00
☐ 42	Vern Bickford	18.00	8.00
☐ 43	Billy DeMars	18.00	8.00
☐ 44	Roy Smalley	18.00	8.00
☐ 45	Art Houtteman	18.00	8.00
☐ 46	George Kell 1941 UER	60.00	27.00
☐ 47	Grady Hatton	18.00	8.00
☐ 48	Ken Raffensberger	18.00	8.00
☐ 49	Jerry Coleman	25.00	11.00
☐ 50	Johnny Mize	60.00	27.00
☐ 51	Andy Seminick	18.00	8.00
☐ 52	Dick Sisler	18.00	8.00
☐ 53	Bob Lemon	60.00	27.00
☐ 54	Ray Boone	30.00	14.00
☐ 55	Gene Hermanski	18.00	8.00
☐ 56	Ralph Branca	60.00	27.00
☐ 57	Alex Kellner	18.00	8.00
☐ 58	Enos Slaughter	60.00	27.00
☐ 59	Randy Gumpert	18.00	8.00
☐ 60	Chico Carrasquel	60.00	27.00
☐ 61	Jim Hearn	25.00	11.00
☐ 62	Lou Boudreau	60.00	27.00
☐ 63	Bob Dillinger	18.00	8.00
☐ 64	Bill Werle	18.00	8.00
☐ 65	Mickey Vernon	40.00	18.00
☐ 66	Bob Elliott	25.00	11.00
☐ 67	Roy Sievers	25.00	11.00
☐ 68	Dick Kokos	18.00	8.00
☐ 69	Johnny Schmitz	18.00	8.00
☐ 70	Ron Northey	18.00	8.00
☐ 71	Jerry Priddy	18.00	8.00
☐ 72	Lloyd Merriman	18.00	8.00
☐ 73	Tommy Byrne	18.00	8.00
☐ 74	Billy Johnson	25.00	11.00
☐ 75	Russ Meyer	25.00	11.00
☐ 76	Stan Lopata	25.00	11.00
☐ 77	Mike Goliat	18.00	8.00
☐ 78	Early Wynn	60.00	27.00
☐ 79	Jim Hegan	25.00	11.00
☐ 80	Pee Wee Reese	125.00	55.00
☐ 81	Carl Furillo	40.00	18.00
☐ 82	Joe Tipton	18.00	8.00
☐ 83	Carl Scheib	18.00	8.00
☐ 84	Barney McCosky	18.00	8.00
☐ 85	Eddie Kazak	18.00	8.00
☐ 86	Harry Brecheen	25.00	11.00
☐ 87	Floyd Baker	18.00	8.00
☐ 88	Eddie Robinson	18.00	8.00
☐ 89	Hank Thompson	25.00	11.00
☐ 90	Dave Koslo	18.00	8.00
☐ 91	Clyde Vollmer	18.00	8.00
☐ 92	Vern Stephens	25.00	11.00

No.	Player	NRMT	VG-E
93	Danny O'Connell	18.00	8.00
94	Clyde McCullough	18.00	8.00
95	Sherry Robertson	18.00	8.00
96	Sandy Consuegra	18.00	8.00
97	Bob Kuzava	18.00	8.00
98	Willard Marshall	18.00	8.00
99	Earl Torgeson	18.00	8.00
100	Sherm Lollar	25.00	11.00
101	Owen Friend	18.00	8.00
102	Dutch Leonard	18.00	8.00
103	Andy Pafko	40.00	18.00
104	Virgil Trucks	25.00	11.00
105	Don Kolloway	18.00	8.00
106	Pat Mullin	18.00	8.00
107	Johnny Wyrostek	18.00	8.00
108	Virgil Stallcup	18.00	8.00
109	Allie Reynolds	60.00	27.00
110	Bobby Brown	40.00	18.00
111	Curt Simmons	18.00	8.00
112	Willie Jones	18.00	8.00
113	Bill Nicholson	25.00	11.00
114	Sam Zoldak	18.00	8.00
115	Steve Gromek	18.00	8.00
116	Bruce Edwards	18.00	8.00
117	Eddie Miksis	18.00	8.00
118	Preacher Roe	60.00	27.00
119	Eddie Joost	18.00	8.00
120	Joe Coleman	25.00	11.00
121	Jerry Staley	18.00	8.00
122	Joe Garagiola	80.00	36.00
123	Howie Judson	18.00	8.00
124	Gus Niarhos	18.00	8.00
125	Bill Rigney	25.00	11.00
126	Bobby Thomson	60.00	27.00
127	Sal Maglie	60.00	27.00
128	Ellis Kinder	18.00	8.00
129	Matt Batts	18.00	8.00
130	Tom Saffell	18.00	8.00
131	Cliff Chambers	18.00	8.00
132	Cass Michaels	18.00	8.00
133	Sam Dente	18.00	8.00
134	Warren Spahn	125.00	55.00
135	Walker Cooper	18.00	8.00
136	Ray Coleman	18.00	8.00
137	Dick Starr	18.00	8.00
138	Phil Cavarretta	25.00	11.00
139	Doyle Lade	18.00	8.00
140	Eddie Lake	18.00	8.00
141	Fred Hutchinson	25.00	11.00
142	Aaron Robinson	18.00	8.00
143	Ted Kluszewski	60.00	27.00
144	Herman Wehmeier	18.00	8.00
145	Fred Sanford	25.00	11.00
146	Johnny Hopp	25.00	11.00
147	Ken Heintzelman	18.00	8.00
148	Granny Hamner	25.00	11.00
149	Bubba Church	18.00	8.00
150	Mike Garcia	25.00	11.00
151	Larry Doby	60.00	27.00
152	Cal Abrams	18.00	8.00
153	Rex Barney	25.00	11.00
154	Pete Suder	18.00	8.00
155	Lou Brissie	18.00	8.00
156	Del Rice	18.00	8.00
157	Al Brazle	18.00	8.00
158	Chuck Diering	18.00	8.00
159	Eddie Stewart	18.00	8.00
160	Phil Masi	18.00	8.00
161	Wes Westrum	18.00	8.00
162	Larry Jansen	25.00	11.00
163	Monte Kennedy	18.00	8.00
164	Bill Wight	18.00	8.00
165	Ted Williams	750.00	350.00
166	Stan Rojek	18.00	8.00
167	Murry Dickson	18.00	8.00
168	Sam Mele	18.00	8.00
169	Sid Hudson	18.00	8.00
170	Sibby Sisti	18.00	8.00
171	Buddy Kerr	18.00	8.00
172	Ned Garver	18.00	8.00
173	Hank Arft	18.00	8.00
174	Mickey Owen	25.00	11.00
175	Wayne Terwilliger	18.00	8.00
176	Vic Wertz	40.00	18.00
177	Charlie Keller	25.00	11.00
178	Ted Gray	18.00	8.00
179	Danny Litwhiler	18.00	8.00
180	Howie Fox	18.00	8.00
181	Casey Stengel MG	75.00	34.00
182	Tom Ferrick	18.00	8.00
183	Hank Bauer	60.00	27.00
184	Eddie Sawyer MG	40.00	18.00
185	Jimmy Bloodworth	18.00	8.00
186	Richie Ashburn	90.00	40.00
187	Al Rosen	40.00	18.00
188	Bobby Avila	25.00	11.00
189	Erv Palica	18.00	8.00
190	Joe Hatten	18.00	8.00
191	Billy Hitchcock	18.00	8.00
192	Hank Wyse	18.00	8.00
193	Ted Wilks	18.00	8.00
194	Peanuts Lowrey	18.00	8.00
195	Paul Richards MG (Caricature)	25.00	11.00
196	Billy Pierce	60.00	27.00
197	Bob Cain	18.00	8.00
198	Monte Irvin	100.00	45.00
199	Sheldon Jones	18.00	8.00
200	Jack Kramer	18.00	8.00
201	Steve O'Neill MG	18.00	8.00
202	Mike Guerra	18.00	8.00
203	Vernon Law	60.00	27.00
204	Vic Lombardi	18.00	8.00
205	Mickey Grasso	18.00	8.00
206	Conrado Marrero	18.00	8.00
207	Billy Southworth MG	18.00	8.00
208	Blix Donnelly	18.00	8.00
209	Ken Wood	18.00	8.00
210	Les Moss	18.00	8.00
211	Hal Jeffcoat	18.00	8.00
212	Bob Rush	18.00	8.00
213	Neil Berry	18.00	8.00
214	Bob Swift	18.00	8.00
215	Ken Peterson	18.00	8.00
216	Connie Ryan	18.00	8.00
217	Joe Page	25.00	11.00
218	Ed Lopat	60.00	27.00
219	Gene Woodling	60.00	27.00
220	Bob Miller	18.00	8.00
221	Dick Whitman	18.00	8.00
222	Thurman Tucker	18.00	8.00
223	Johnny VanderMeer	40.00	18.00
224	Billy Cox	25.00	11.00
225	Dan Bankhead	40.00	18.00
226	Jimmy Dykes MG	25.00	11.00
227	Bobby Shantz UER (Sic, Schantz)	25.00	11.00
228	Cloyd Boyer	25.00	11.00
229	Bill Howerton	18.00	8.00
230	Max Lanier	18.00	8.00
231	Luis Aloma	18.00	8.00
232	Nelson Fox	225.00	100.00
233	Leo Durocher MG	60.00	27.00
234	Clint Hartung	25.00	11.00
235	Jack Lohrke	18.00	8.00
236	Warren Rosar	18.00	8.00
237	Billy Goodman	25.00	11.00
238	Pete Reiser	40.00	18.00
239	Bill MacDonald	18.00	8.00
240	Joe Haynes	18.00	8.00
241	Irv Noren	25.00	11.00
242	Sam Jethroe	25.00	11.00
243	Johnny Antonelli	25.00	11.00
244	Cliff Fannin	18.00	8.00
245	John Berardino	60.00	27.00
246	Bill Serena	18.00	8.00
247	Bob Ramazzotti	18.00	8.00
248	Johnny Klippstein	18.00	8.00
249	Johnny Groth	18.00	8.00
250	Hank Borowy	18.00	8.00
251	Willard Ramsdell	18.00	8.00
252	Dixie Howell	18.00	8.00
253	Mickey Mantle	8500.00	3800.00
254	Jackie Jensen	100.00	45.00
255	Milo Candini	50.00	22.00
256	Ken Sylvestri	50.00	22.00
257	Birdie Tebbetts	60.00	27.00
258	Luke Easter	60.00	27.00
259	Chuck Dressen MG	60.00	27.00
260	Carl Erskine	100.00	45.00
261	Wally Moses	60.00	27.00
262	Gus Zernial	60.00	27.00
263	Howie Pollet	60.00	27.00
264	Don Richmond	50.00	22.00
265	Steve Bilko	60.00	27.00
266	Harry Dorish	50.00	22.00
267	Ken Holcombe	50.00	22.00
268	Don Mueller	60.00	27.00
269	Ray Noble	50.00	22.00
270	Willard Nixon	50.00	22.00
271	Tommy Wright	50.00	22.00
272	Billy Meyer MG	50.00	22.00
273	Danny Murtaugh	60.00	27.00
274	George Metkovich	50.00	22.00
275	Bucky Harris MG	60.00	27.00
276	Frank Quinn	50.00	22.00
277	Roy Hartsfield	50.00	22.00
278	Norman Roy	50.00	22.00
279	Jim Delsing	50.00	22.00
280	Frank Overmire	50.00	22.00
281	Al Widmar	50.00	22.00
282	Frank Frisch MG	80.00	40.00
283	Walt Dubiel	50.00	22.00
284	Gene Bearden	60.00	27.00
285	Johnny Lipon	50.00	22.00
286	Bob Usher	50.00	22.00
287	Jim Blackburn	50.00	22.00
288	Bobby Adams	50.00	22.00
289	Cliff Mapes	50.00	22.00
290	Bill Dickey CO	100.00	45.00
291	Tommy Henrich CO	80.00	36.00
292	Eddie Pellegrini	50.00	22.00
293	Ken Johnson	50.00	22.00
294	Jocko Thompson	50.00	22.00
295	Al Lopez MG	120.00	55.00
296	Bob Kennedy	60.00	27.00
297	Dave Philley	50.00	22.00
298	Joe Astroth	50.00	22.00
299	Clyde King	50.00	22.00
300	Jim Busby	50.00	22.00
301	Tommy Glaviano	50.00	22.00
302	Jim Russell	50.00	22.00
303	Marv Rotblatt	50.00	22.00
304	Al Gettel	50.00	22.00
305	Willie Mays	3000.00	1350.00
306	Jim Piersall	110.00	50.00
307	Walt Masterson	50.00	22.00
308	Ted Beard	50.00	22.00
309	Mel Queen	50.00	22.00
310	Erv Dusak	50.00	22.00
311	Mickey Harris	50.00	22.00
312	Gene Mauch	60.00	27.00
313	Ray Mueller	50.00	22.00
314	Johnny Sain	60.00	27.00
315	Zack Taylor MG	50.00	22.00
316	Duane Pillette	50.00	22.00
317	Smoky Burgess	80.00	36.00
318	Warren Hacker	50.00	22.00
319	Red Rolfe MG	60.00	27.00
320	Hal White	50.00	22.00
321	Earl Johnson	50.00	22.00
322	Luke Sewell MG	60.00	27.00
323	Joe Adcock	80.00	36.00
324	Johnny Pramesa	100.00	30.00

1952 Bowman

	NRMT	VG-E
COMPLETE SET (252)	7500.00	3400.00
COMMON CARD (1-216)	15.00	6.75

MINOR STARS 1-216	25.00	11.00
SEMISTARS 1-216	40.00	18.00
UNLISTED STARS 1-216	60.00	27.00
COMMON CARD (217-252)	27.00	27.00
MINOR STARS 217-252	70.00	32.00
SEMISTARS 217-252	80.00	36.00

*UNLISTED DODGER/YANKEE: 1.25X VALUE
CARDS PRICED IN NM CONDITION

❏ 1	Yogi Berra	550.00	170.00
❏ 2	Bobby Thomson	40.00	18.00
❏ 3	Fred Hutchinson	25.00	11.00
❏ 4	Robin Roberts	60.00	27.00
❏ 5	Minnie Minoso	125.00	55.00
❏ 6	Virgil Stallcup	15.00	6.75
❏ 7	Mike Garcia	25.00	11.00
❏ 8	Pee Wee Reese	135.00	60.00
❏ 9	Vern Stephens	25.00	11.00
❏ 10	Bob Hooper	15.00	6.75
❏ 11	Ralph Kiner	60.00	27.00
❏ 12	Max Surkont	15.00	6.75
❏ 13	Cliff Mapes	15.00	6.75
❏ 14	Cliff Chambers	15.00	6.75
❏ 15	Sam Mele	15.00	6.75
❏ 16	Turk Lown	15.00	6.75
❏ 17	Ed Lopat	40.00	18.00
❏ 18	Don Mueller	25.00	11.00
❏ 19	Bob Cain	15.00	6.75
❏ 20	Willie Jones	15.00	6.75
❏ 21	Nellie Fox	100.00	45.00
❏ 22	Willard Ramsdell	15.00	6.75
❏ 23	Bob Lemon	60.00	27.00
❏ 24	Carl Furillo	40.00	18.00
❏ 25	Mickey McDermott	15.00	6.75
❏ 26	Eddie Joost	15.00	6.75
❏ 27	Joe Garagiola	40.00	18.00
❏ 28	Roy Hartsfield	15.00	6.75
❏ 29	Ned Garver	15.00	6.75
❏ 30	Red Schoendienst	60.00	27.00
❏ 31	Eddie Yost	25.00	11.00
❏ 32	Eddie Miksis	15.00	6.75
❏ 33	Gil McDougald	80.00	36.00
❏ 34	Alvin Dark	25.00	11.00
❏ 35	Granny Hamner	15.00	6.75
❏ 36	Cass Michaels	15.00	6.75
❏ 37	Vic Raschi	25.00	11.00
❏ 38	Whitey Lockman	25.00	11.00
❏ 39	Vic Wertz	25.00	11.00
❏ 40	Bubba Church	15.00	6.75
❏ 41	Chico Carrasquel	25.00	11.00
❏ 42	Johnny Wyrostek	15.00 °	6.75
❏ 43	Bob Feller	125.00	55.00
❏ 44	Roy Campanella	250.00	110.00
❏ 45	Johnny Pesky	25.00	11.00
❏ 46	Carl Scheib	15.00	6.75
❏ 47	Pete Castiglione	15.00	6.75
❏ 48	Vern Bickford	15.00	6.75
❏ 49	Jim Hearn	15.00	6.75
❏ 50	Jerry Staley	15.00	6.75
❏ 51	Gil Coan	15.00	6.75
❏ 52	Phil Rizzuto	150.00	70.00
❏ 53	Richie Ashburn	100.00	45.00
❏ 54	Billy Pierce	25.00	11.00
❏ 55	Ken Raffensberger	15.00	6.75
❏ 56	Clyde King	25.00	11.00
❏ 57	Clyde Vollmer	15.00	6.75
❏ 58	Hank Majeski	15.00	6.75
❏ 59	Murry Dickson	15.00	6.75
❏ 60	Sid Gordon	15.00	6.75
❏ 61	Tommy Byrne	15.00	6.75
❏ 62	Joe Presko	15.00	6.75
❏ 63	Irv Noren	15.00	6.75
❏ 64	Roy Smalley	15.00	6.75
❏ 65	Hank Bauer	25.00	11.00
❏ 66	Sal Maglie	25.00	11.00
❏ 67	Johnny Groth	15.00	6.75
❏ 68	Jim Busby	15.00	6.75
❏ 69	Joe Adcock	25.00	11.00
❏ 70	Carl Erskine	40.00	18.00
❏ 71	Vernon Law	25.00	11.00
❏ 72	Earl Torgeson	15.00	6.75
❏ 73	Jerry Coleman	25.00	11.00
❏ 74	Wes Westrum	25.00	11.00
❏ 75	George Kell	60.00	27.00
❏ 76	Del Ennis	25.00	11.00
❏ 77	Eddie Robinson	15.00	6.75
❏ 78	Lloyd Merriman	15.00	6.75
❏ 79	Lou Brissie	15.00	6.75
❏ 80	Gil Hodges	90.00	40.00
❏ 81	Billy Goodman	25.00	11.00
❏ 82	Gus Zernial	25.00	11.00
❏ 83	Howie Pollet	15.00	6.75
❏ 84	Sam Jethroe	25.00	11.00
❏ 85	Marty Marion CO	25.00	11.00
❏ 86	Cal Abrams	15.00	6.75
❏ 87	Mickey Vernon	25.00	11.00
❏ 88	Bruce Edwards	15.00	6.75
❏ 89	Billy Hitchcock	15.00	6.75
❏ 90	Larry Jansen	25.00	11.00
❏ 91	Don Kolloway	15.00	6.75
❏ 92	Eddie Waitkus	25.00	11.00
❏ 93	Paul Richards MG	25.00	11.00
❏ 94	Luke Sewell MG	25.00	11.00
❏ 95	Luke Easter	25.00	11.00
❏ 96	Ralph Branca	25.00	11.00
❏ 97	Willard Marshall	15.00	6.75
❏ 98	Jimmy Dykes MG	25.00	11.00
❏ 99	Clyde McCullough	15.00	6.75
❏ 100	Sibby Sisti	15.00	6.75
❏ 101	Mickey Mantle	2500.00	1100.00
❏ 102	Peanuts Lowrey	15.00	6.75
❏ 103	Joe Haynes	15.00	6.75
❏ 104	Hal Jeffcoat	15.00	6.75
❏ 105	Bobby Brown	25.00	11.00
❏ 106	Randy Gumpert	15.00	6.75
❏ 107	Del Rice	15.00	6.75
❏ 108	George Metkovich	15.00	6.75
❏ 109	Tom Morgan	15.00	6.75
❏ 110	Max Lanier	15.00	6.75
❏ 111	Hoot Evers	15.00	6.75
❏ 112	Smoky Burgess	25.00	11.00
❏ 113	Al Zarilla	15.00	6.75
❏ 114	Frank Hiller	15.00	6.75
❏ 115	Larry Doby	60.00	27.00
❏ 116	Duke Snider	200.00	90.00
❏ 117	Bill Wight	15.00	6.75
❏ 118	Ray Murray	15.00	6.75
❏ 119	Bill Howerton	15.00	6.75
❏ 120	Chet Nichols	15.00	6.75
❏ 121	Al Corwin	15.00	6.75
❏ 122	Billy Johnson	15.00	6.75
❏ 123	Sid Hudson	15.00	6.75
❏ 124	Birdie Tebbetts	15.00	6.75
❏ 125	Howie Fox	15.00	6.75
❏ 126	Phil Cavarretta	25.00	11.00
❏ 127	Dick Sisler	15.00	6.75
❏ 128	Don Newcombe	40.00	18.00
❏ 129	Gus Niarhos	15.00	6.75
❏ 130	Allie Clark	15.00	6.75
❏ 131	Bob Swift	15.00	6.75
❏ 132	Dave Cole	15.00	6.75
❏ 133	Dick Kryhoski	15.00	6.75
❏ 134	Al Brazle	15.00	6.75
❏ 135	Mickey Harris	15.00	6.75
❏ 136	Gene Hermanski	15.00	6.75
❏ 137	Stan Rojek	15.00	6.75
❏ 138	Ted Wilks	15.00	6.75
❏ 139	Jerry Priddy	15.00	6.75
❏ 140	Ray Scarborough	15.00	6.75
❏ 141	Hank Edwards	15.00	6.75
❏ 142	Early Wynn	60.00	27.00
❏ 143	Sandy Consuegra	15.00	6.75
❏ 144	Joe Hatton	15.00	6.75
❏ 145	Johnny Mize	60.00	27.00
❏ 146	Leo Durocher MG	60.00	27.00
❏ 147	Marlin Stuart	15.00	6.75
❏ 148	Ken Heintzelman	15.00	6.75
❏ 149	Howie Judson	15.00	6.75
❏ 150	Herman Wehmeier	15.00	6.75
❏ 151	Al Rosen	25.00	11.00
❏ 152	Billy Cox	15.00	6.75
❏ 153	Fred Hatfield	15.00	6.75
❏ 154	Ferris Fain	25.00	11.00
❏ 155	Billy Meyer MG	15.00	6.75
❏ 156	Warren Spahn	125.00	55.00
❏ 157	Jim Delsing	15.00	6.75
❏ 158	Bucky Harris MG	25.00	11.00
❏ 159	Dutch Leonard	15.00	6.75
❏ 160	Eddie Stanky	25.00	11.00
❏ 161	Jackie Jensen	40.00	18.00
❏ 162	Monte Irvin	60.00	27.00
❏ 163	Johnny Lipon	15.00	6.75
❏ 164	Connie Ryan	15.00	6.75
❏ 165	Saul Rogovin	15.00	6.75
❏ 166	Bobby Adams	15.00	6.75
❏ 167	Bobby Avila	25.00	11.00
❏ 168	Preacher Roe	25.00	11.00
❏ 169	Walt Dropo	25.00	11.00
❏ 170	Joe Astroth	15.00	6.75
❏ 171	Mel Queen	15.00	6.75
❏ 172	Ebba St.Claire	15.00	6.75
❏ 173	Gene Bearden	15.00	6.75
❏ 174	Mickey Grasso	15.00	6.75
❏ 175	Randy Jackson	15.00	6.75
❏ 176	Harry Brecheen	25.00	11.00
❏ 177	Gene Woodling	25.00	11.00
❏ 178	Dave Williams	25.00	11.00
❏ 179	Pete Suder	15.00	6.75
❏ 180	Ed Fitzgerald	15.00	6.75
❏ 181	Joe Collins	25.00	11.00
❏ 182	Dave Koslo	15.00	6.75
❏ 183	Pat Mullin	15.00	6.75
❏ 184	Curt Simmons	25.00	11.00
❏ 185	Eddie Stewart	15.00	6.75
❏ 186	Frank Smith	15.00	6.75
❏ 187	Jim Hegan	25.00	11.00
❏ 188	Chuck Dressen MG	25.00	11.00
❏ 189	Jimmy Piersall	25.00	11.00
❏ 190	Dick Fowler	15.00	6.75
❏ 191	Bob Friend	40.00	18.00
❏ 192	John Cusick	15.00	6.75
❏ 193	Bobby Young	15.00	6.75
❏ 194	Bob Porterfield	15.00	6.75
❏ 195	Frank Baumholtz	15.00	6.75
❏ 196	Stan Musial	600.00	275.00
❏ 197	Charlie Silvera	15.00	6.75
❏ 198	Chuck Diering	15.00	6.75
❏ 199	Ted Gray	15.00	6.75
❏ 200	Ken Silvestri	15.00	6.75
❏ 201	Ray Coleman	15.00	6.75
❏ 202	Harry Perkowski	15.00	6.75
❏ 203	Steve Gromek	15.00	6.75
❏ 204	Andy Pafko	25.00	11.00
❏ 205	Walt Masterson	15.00	6.75
❏ 206	Elmer Valo	15.00	6.75
❏ 207	George Strickland	15.00	6.75
❏ 208	Walker Cooper	15.00	6.75
❏ 209	Dick Littlefield	15.00	6.75
❏ 210	Archie Wilson	15.00	6.75
❏ 211	Paul Minner	15.00	6.75
❏ 212	Solly Hemus	15.00	6.75
❏ 213	Monte Kennedy	15.00	6.75
❏ 214	Ray Boone	15.00	6.75
❏ 215	Sheldon Jones	15.00	6.75
❏ 216	Matt Batts	15.00	6.75
❏ 217	Casey Stengel MG	150.00	70.00
❏ 218	Willie Mays	1200.00	550.00
❏ 219	Neil Berry	60.00	27.00
❏ 220	Russ Meyer	60.00	27.00
❏ 221	Lou Kretlow	60.00	27.00
❏ 222	Dixie Howell	60.00	27.00
❏ 223	Harry Simpson	60.00	27.00
❏ 224	Johnny Schmitz	60.00	27.00
❏ 225	Del Wilber	60.00	27.00
❏ 226	Alex Kellner	60.00	27.00
❏ 227	Clyde Sukeforth CO	60.00	27.00
❏ 228	Bob Chipman	60.00	27.00
❏ 229	Hank Arft	60.00	27.00
❏ 230	Frank Shea	60.00	27.00
❏ 231	Dee Fondy	60.00	27.00
❏ 232	Enos Slaughter	90.00	40.00
❏ 233	Bob Kuzava	60.00	27.00
❏ 234	Fred Fitzsimmons CO	70.00	32.00
❏ 235	Steve Souchock	60.00	27.00
❏ 236	Tommy Brown	60.00	27.00
❏ 237	Sherm Lollar	70.00	32.00
❏ 238	Roy McMillan	70.00	32.00
❏ 239	Dale Mitchell	70.00	32.00
❏ 240	Billy Loes	70.00	32.00
❏ 241	Mel Parnell	70.00	32.00
❏ 242	Everett Kell	60.00	27.00
❏ 243	Red Munger	60.00	27.00
❏ 244	Lew Burdette	80.00	36.00
❏ 245	George Schmees	60.00	27.00
❏ 246	Jerry Snyder	60.00	27.00
❏ 247	Johnny Pramesa	60.00	27.00
❏ 248	Bill Werle	60.00	27.00

Full name in signature

	NRMT	VG-E
248A Bill Werle	15.00	6.75
Signature on front has no W		
249 Hank Thompson	70.00	32.00
250 Ike Delock	60.00	27.00
251 Jack Lohrke	60.00	27.00
252 Frank Crosetti CO	110.00	28.00

1953 Bowman B/W

	NRMT	VG-E
COMPLETE SET (64)	2400.00	1100.00
COMMON CARD (1-64)	40.00	18.00
MINOR STARS	70.00	32.00

*UNLISTED DODGER/YANKEE: 1.25X VALUE
CARDS PRICED IN NM CONDITION !

	NRMT	VG-E
1 Gus Bell	125.00	25.00
2 Willard Nixon	40.00	18.00
3 Bill Rigney	40.00	18.00
4 Pat Mullin	40.00	18.00
5 Dee Fondy	40.00	18.00
6 Ray Murray	40.00	18.00
7 Andy Seminick	40.00	18.00
8 Pete Suder	40.00	18.00
9 Walt Masterson	40.00	18.00
10 Dick Sisler	70.00	32.00
11 Dick Gernert	40.00	18.00
12 Randy Jackson	40.00	18.00
13 Joe Tipton	40.00	18.00
14 Bill Nicholson	70.00	32.00
15 Johnny Mize	125.00	55.00
16 Stu Miller	70.00	32.00
17 Virgil Trucks	70.00	32.00
18 Billy Hoeft	40.00	18.00
19 Paul LaPalme	40.00	18.00
20 Eddie Robinson	40.00	18.00
21 Clarence Podbielan	40.00	18.00
22 Matt Batts	40.00	18.00
23 Wilmer Mizell	70.00	32.00
24 Del Wilber	40.00	18.00
25 Johnny Sain	70.00	34.00
26 Preacher Roe	75.00	34.00
27 Bob Lemon	125.00	55.00
28 Hoyt Wilhelm	125.00	55.00
29 Sid Hudson	40.00	18.00
30 Walker Cooper	40.00	18.00
31 Gene Woodling	75.00	34.00
32 Rocky Bridges	40.00	18.00
33 Bob Kuzava	40.00	18.00
34 Ebba St Claire	40.00	18.00
35 Johnny Wyrostek	40.00	18.00
36 Jimmy Piersall	75.00	34.00
37 Hal Jeffcoat	40.00	18.00
38 Dave Cole	40.00	18.00
39 Casey Stengel MG	325.00	145.00
40 Larry Jansen	70.00	32.00
41 Bob Ramazzotti	40.00	18.00
42 Howie Judson	40.00	18.00
43 Hal Bevan	40.00	18.00
44 Jim Delsing	40.00	18.00
45 Irv Noren	70.00	32.00
46 Bucky Harris MG	75.00	34.00
47 Jack Lohrke	40.00	18.00
48 Steve Ridzik	40.00	18.00
49 Floyd Baker	40.00	18.00
50 Dutch Leonard	40.00	18.00
51 Lou Burdette	75.00	34.00
52 Ralph Branca	75.00	34.00
53 Morrie Martin	40.00	18.00
54 Bill Miller	40.00	18.00
55 Don Johnson	40.00	18.00
56 Roy Smalley	40.00	18.00
57 Andy Pafko	70.00	32.00
58 Jim Konstanty	70.00	32.00
59 Duane Pillette	40.00	18.00
60 Billy Cox	75.00	34.00
61 Tom Gorman	40.00	18.00
62 Keith Thomas	40.00	18.00
63 Steve Gromek	40.00	18.00
64 Andy Hansen	75.00	24.00

1953 Bowman Color

	NRMT	VG-E
COMPLETE SET (160)	12000.00	5400.00
COMMON CARD (1-112)	40.00	18.00
MINOR STARS 1-112	50.00	22.00
SEMISTARS 1-112	60.00	27.00
*UNLISTED STARS 1-112	80.00	36.00
COMMON CARD (113-128)	80.00	36.00
MINOR STARS 113-128	100.00	45.00
SEMISTARS 113-128	120.00	55.00
COMMON CARD (129-160)	75.00	34.00
MINOR STARS 129-160	90.00	40.00
SEMISTARS 129-160	110.00	50.00

*UNLISTED DODGER/YANKEE: 1.25X VALUE
CARDS PRICED IN NM CONDITION !

	NRMT	VG-E
1 Dave Williams	175.00	35.00
2 Vic Wertz	50.00	22.00
3 Sam Jethroe	50.00	22.00
4 Art Houtteman	40.00	18.00
5 Sid Gordon	40.00	18.00
6 Joe Ginsberg	40.00	18.00
7 Harry Chiti	40.00	18.00
8 Al Rosen	50.00	22.00
9 Phil Rizzuto	225.00	100.00
10 Richie Ashburn	150.00	70.00
11 Bobby Shantz	50.00	22.00
12 Carl Erskine	50.00	22.00
13 Gus Zernial	50.00	22.00
14 Billy Loes	50.00	22.00
15 Jim Busby	40.00	18.00
16 Bob Friend	50.00	22.00
17 Gerry Staley	40.00	18.00
18 Nellie Fox	150.00	70.00
19 Alvin Dark	50.00	22.00
20 Don Lenhardt	40.00	18.00
21 Joe Garagiola	60.00	27.00
22 Bob Porterfield	40.00	18.00
23 Herman Wehmeier	40.00	18.00
24 Jackie Jensen	60.00	27.00
25 Hoot Evers	40.00	18.00
26 Roy McMillan	50.00	22.00
27 Vic Raschi	60.00	27.00
28 Smoky Burgess	50.00	22.00
29 Bobby Avila	50.00	22.00
30 Phil Cavarretta	50.00	22.00
31 Jimmy Dykes MG	50.00	22.00
32 Stan Musial	700.00	325.00
33 Pee Wee Reese	1000.00	450.00
34 Gil Coan	40.00	18.00
35 Maurice McDermott	40.00	18.00
36 Minnie Minoso	75.00	34.00
37 Jim Wilson	40.00	18.00
38 Harry Byrd	40.00	18.00
39 Paul Richards MG	50.00	22.00
40 Larry Doby	80.00	36.00
41 Sammy White	40.00	18.00
42 Tommy Brown	40.00	18.00
43 Mike Garcia	50.00	22.00
44 Yogi Berra	700.00	325.00
Hank Bauer		
Mickey Mantle		
45 Walt Dropo	50.00	22.00
46 Roy Campanella	325.00	145.00
47 Ned Garver	40.00	18.00
48 Hank Sauer	50.00	22.00
49 Eddie Stanky MG	50.00	22.00
50 Lou Kretlow	40.00	18.00
51 Monte Irvin	60.00	27.00
52 Marty Marion MG	50.00	22.00
53 Del Rice	40.00	18.00
54 Chico Carrasquel	40.00	18.00
55 Leo Durocher MG	50.00	36.00
56 Bob Cain	40.00	18.00
57 Lou Boudreau MG	60.00	27.00
58 Willard Marshall	40.00	18.00
59 Mickey Mantle	2500.00	1100.00
60 Granny Hamner	40.00	18.00
61 George Kell	80.00	36.00
62 Ted Kluszewski	80.00	36.00
63 Gil McDougald	60.00	27.00
64 Curt Simmons	50.00	22.00
65 Robin Roberts	110.00	50.00
66 Mel Parnell	50.00	22.00
67 Mel Clark	40.00	18.00
68 Allie Reynolds	50.00	22.00
69 Charlie Grimm MG	50.00	22.00
70 Clint Courtney	40.00	18.00
71 Paul Minner	40.00	18.00
72 Ted Gray	40.00	18.00
73 Billy Pierce	50.00	22.00
74 Don Mueller	50.00	22.00
75 Saul Rogovin	40.00	18.00
76 Jim Hearn	40.00	18.00
77 Mickey Grasso	40.00	18.00
78 Carl Furillo	60.00	27.00
79 Ray Boone	50.00	22.00
80 Ralph Kiner	80.00	36.00
81 Enos Slaughter	60.00	27.00
82 Joe Astroth	40.00	18.00
83 Jack Daniels	40.00	18.00
84 Hank Bauer	60.00	27.00
85 Solly Hemus	40.00	18.00
86 Harry Simpson	40.00	18.00
87 Harry Perkowski	40.00	18.00
88 Joe Dobson	40.00	18.00
89 Sandy Consuegra	40.00	18.00
90 Joe Nuxhall	50.00	22.00
91 Steve Souchock	40.00	18.00
92 Gil Hodges	200.00	90.00
93 Phil Rizzuto and	275.00	125.00
Billy Martin		
94 Bob Addis	40.00	18.00
95 Wally Moses CO	50.00	22.00
96 Sal Maglie	50.00	22.00
97 Eddie Mathews	300.00	135.00
98 Hector Rodriguez	40.00	18.00
99 Warren Spahn	350.00	160.00
100 Bill Wight	40.00	18.00
101 Red Schoendienst	75.00	34.00
102 Jim Hegan	50.00	22.00
103 Del Ennis	50.00	22.00
104 Luke Easter	50.00	22.00
105 Eddie Joost	40.00	18.00
106 Ken Raffensberger	40.00	18.00
107 Alex Kellner	40.00	18.00
108 Bobby Adams	40.00	18.00
109 Ken Wood	40.00	18.00
110 Bob Rush	40.00	18.00
111 Jim Dyck	40.00	18.00
112 Toby Atwell	40.00	18.00
113 Karl Drews	80.00	36.00
114 Bob Feller	350.00	160.00
115 Cloyd Boyer	80.00	36.00
116 Eddie Yost	100.00	45.00
117 Duke Snider	600.00	275.00
118 Billy Martin	350.00	160.00
119 Dale Mitchell	100.00	45.00
120 Marlin Stuart	80.00	36.00
121 Yogi Berra	700.00	325.00

		NRMT	VG-E

❏	122 Bill Serena	80.00	36.00
❏	123 Johnny Lipon	80.00	36.00
❏	124 Charlie Dressen MG	100.00	45.00
❏	125 Fred Hatfield	80.00	36.00
❏	126 Al Corwin	80.00	36.00
❏	127 Dick Kryhoski	80.00	36.00
❏	128 Whitey Lockman	100.00	45.00
❏	129 Russ Meyer	75.00	34.00
❏	130 Cass Michaels	75.00	34.00
❏	131 Connie Ryan	75.00	34.00
❏	132 Fred Hutchinson	90.00	40.00
❏	133 Willie Jones	75.00	34.00
❏	134 Johnny Pesky	90.00	40.00
❏	135 Bobby Morgan	75.00	34.00
❏	136 Jim Brideweser	75.00	34.00
❏	137 Sam Dente	75.00	34.00
❏	138 Bubba Church	75.00	34.00
❏	139 Pete Runnels	90.00	40.00
❏	140 Al Brazle	75.00	34.00
❏	141 Frank Shea	75.00	34.00
❏	142 Larry Miggins	75.00	34.00
❏	143 Al Lopez MG	90.00	40.00
❏	144 Warren Hacker	75.00	34.00
❏	145 George Shuba	90.00	40.00
❏	146 Early Wynn	200.00	90.00
❏	147 Clem Koshorek	75.00	34.00
❏	148 Billy Goodman	90.00	40.00
❏	149 Al Corwin	75.00	34.00
❏	150 Carl Scheib	75.00	34.00
❏	151 Joe Adcock	90.00	40.00
❏	152 Clyde Vollmer	75.00	34.00
❏	153 Whitey Ford	600.00	275.00
❏	154 Turk Lown	75.00	34.00
❏	155 Allie Clark	75.00	34.00
❏	156 Max Surkont	75.00	34.00
❏	157 Sherm Lollar	90.00	40.00
❏	158 Howard Fox	75.00	34.00
❏	159 Mickey Vernon UER	90.00	40.00
	(Photo actually Floyd Baker)		
❏	160 Cal Abrams	200.00	70.00

1954 Bowman

	NRMT	VG-E
COMPLETE SET (224)	4000.00	1800.00
COMMON CARD (1-224)	12.00	5.50
MINOR STARS	20.00	9.00
SEMISTARS	30.00	13.50
UNLISTED STARS	50.00	22.00

*UNLISTED DODGER/YANKEE: 1.25X VALUE
CARDS PRICED IN NM CONDITION !

❏	1 Phil Rizzuto	160.00	47.50
❏	2 Jackie Jensen	20.00	9.00
❏	3 Marion Fricano	12.00	5.50
❏	4 Bob Hooper	12.00	5.50
❏	5 Billy Hunter	12.00	5.50
❏	6 Nellie Fox	75.00	34.00
❏	7 Walt Dropo	20.00	9.00
❏	8 Jim Busby	12.00	5.50
❏	9 Dave Williams	12.00	5.50
❏	10 Carl Erskine	20.00	9.00
❏	11 Sid Gordon	12.00	5.50
❏	12 Roy McMillan	20.00	9.00
❏	13 Paul Minner	12.00	5.50
❏	14 Jerry Staley	12.00	5.50
❏	15 Richie Ashburn	75.00	34.00

❏	16 Jim Wilson	12.00	5.50
❏	17 Tom Gorman	12.00	5.50
❏	18 Hoot Evers	12.00	5.50
❏	19 Bobby Shantz	20.00	9.00
❏	20 Art Houtteman	12.00	5.50
❏	21 Vic Wertz	20.00	9.00
❏	22 Sam Mele	12.00	5.50
❏	23 Harvey Kuenn	30.00	13.50
❏	24 Bob Porterfield	12.00	5.50
❏	25 Wes Westrum	20.00	9.00
❏	26 Billy Cox	20.00	9.00
❏	27 Dick Cole	12.00	5.50
❏	28 Jim Greengrass	12.00	5.50
❏	29 Johnny Klippstein	12.00	5.50
❏	30 Del Rice	12.00	5.50
❏	31 Smoky Burgess	20.00	9.00
❏	32 Del Crandall	20.00	9.00
❏	33A Vic Raschi	20.00	9.00
	(No mention of trade on back)		
❏	33B Vic Raschi	30.00	13.50
	(Traded to St.Louis)		
❏	34 Sammy White	12.00	5.50
❏	35 Eddie Joost	12.00	5.50
❏	36 George Strickland	12.00	5.50
❏	37 Dick Kokos	12.00	5.50
❏	38 Minnie Minoso	30.00	13.50
❏	39 Ned Garver	12.00	5.50
❏	40 Gil Coan	12.00	5.50
❏	41 Alvin Dark	20.00	9.00
❏	42 Billy Loes	20.00	9.00
❏	43 Bob Friend	20.00	9.00
❏	44 Harry Perkowski	12.00	5.50
❏	45 Ralph Kiner	50.00	22.00
❏	46 Rip Repulski	12.00	5.50
❏	47 Granny Hamner	12.00	5.50
❏	48 Jack Dittmer	12.00	5.50
❏	49 Harry Byrd	12.00	5.50
❏	50 George Kell	50.00	22.00
❏	51 Alex Kellner	12.00	5.50
❏	52 Joe Ginsberg	12.00	5.50
❏	53 Don Lenhardt	12.00	5.50
❏	54 Chico Carrasquel	12.00	5.50
❏	55 Jim Delsing	12.00	5.50
❏	56 Maurice McDermott	12.00	5.50
❏	57 Hoyt Wilhelm	50.00	22.00
❏	58 Pee Wee Reese	75.00	34.00
❏	59 Bob Schultz	12.00	5.50
❏	60 Fred Baczewski	12.00	5.50
❏	61 Eddie Miksis	12.00	5.50
❏	62 Enos Slaughter	50.00	22.00
❏	63 Earl Torgeson	12.00	5.50
❏	64 Eddie Mathews	75.00	34.00
❏	65 Mickey Mantle	1400.00	650.00
❏	66A Ted Williams	3500.00	1600.00
❏	66B Jimmy Piersall	75.00	34.00
❏	67 Carl Scheib	12.00	5.50
❏	68 Bobby Avila	20.00	9.00
❏	69 Clint Courtney	12.00	5.50
❏	70 Willard Marshall	12.00	5.50
❏	71 Ted Gray	12.00	5.50
❏	72 Eddie Yost	20.00	9.00
❏	73 Don Mueller	20.00	9.00
❏	74 Jim Gilliam	30.00	13.50
❏	75 Max Surkont	12.00	5.50
❏	76 Joe Nuxhall	20.00	9.00
❏	77 Bob Rush	12.00	5.50
❏	78 Sal Yvars	12.00	5.50
❏	79 Curt Simmons	20.00	5.50
❏	80 Johnny Logan	12.00	5.50
❏	81 Jerry Coleman	20.00	5.50
❏	82 Billy Goodman	20.00	9.00
❏	83 Ray Murray	12.00	5.50
❏	84 Larry Doby	30.00	13.50
❏	85 Jim Dyck	12.00	5.50
❏	86 Harry Dorish	12.00	5.50
❏	87 Don Lund	12.00	5.50
❏	88 Tom Umphlett	12.00	5.50
❏	89 Willie Mays	400.00	180.00
❏	90 Roy Campanella	175.00	80.00
❏	91 Cal Abrams	12.00	5.50
❏	92 Ken Raffensberger	12.00	5.50
❏	93 Bill Serena	12.00	5.50
❏	94 Solly Hemus	12.00	5.50
❏	95 Robin Roberts	50.00	22.00
❏	96 Joe Adcock	20.00	9.00

❏	97 Gil McDougald	20.00	9.00
❏	98 Ellis Kinder	12.00	5.50
❏	99 Pete Suder	12.00	5.50
❏	100 Mike Garcia	20.00	9.00
❏	101 Don Larsen	75.00	34.00
❏	102 Billy Pierce	20.00	9.00
❏	103 Steve Souchock	12.00	5.50
❏	104 Frank Shea	12.00	5.50
❏	105 Sal Maglie	20.00	9.00
❏	106 Clem Labine	20.00	9.00
❏	107 Paul LaPalme	12.00	5.50
❏	108 Bobby Adams	12.00	5.50
❏	109 Roy Smalley	12.00	5.50
❏	110 Red Schoendienst	40.00	18.00
❏	111 Murry Dickson	12.00	5.50
❏	112 Andy Pafko	20.00	9.00
❏	113 Allie Reynolds	30.00	13.50
❏	114 Willard Nixon	12.00	5.50
❏	115 Don Bollweg	12.00	5.50
❏	116 Luke Easter	20.00	9.00
❏	117 Dick Kryhoski	12.00	5.50
❏	118 Bob Boyd	12.00	5.50
❏	119 Fred Hatfield	12.00	5.50
❏	120 Mel Hoderlein	12.00	5.50
❏	121 Ray Katt	12.00	5.50
❏	122 Carl Furillo	30.00	13.50
❏	123 Toby Atwell	12.00	5.50
❏	124 Gus Bell	20.00	9.00
❏	125 Warren Hacker	12.00	5.50
❏	126 Cliff Chambers	12.00	5.50
❏	127 Del Ennis	20.00	9.00
❏	128 Ebba St.Claire	12.00	5.50
❏	129 Hank Bauer	20.00	9.00
❏	130 Milt Bolling	12.00	5.50
❏	131 Joe Astroth	12.00	5.50
❏	132 Bob Feller	75.00	34.00
❏	133 Duane Pillette	12.00	5.50
❏	134 Luis Aloma	12.00	5.50
❏	135 Johnny Pesky	20.00	9.00
❏	136 Clyde Vollmer	12.00	5.50
❏	137 Al Corwin	12.00	5.50
❏	138 Gil Hodges	75.00	34.00
❏	139 Preston Ward	12.00	5.50
❏	140 Saul Rogovin	12.00	5.50
❏	141 Joe Garagiola	30.00	13.50
❏	142 Al Brazle	12.00	5.50
❏	143 Willie Jones	12.00	5.50
❏	144 Ernie Johnson	30.00	13.50
❏	145 Billy Martin	75.00	34.00
❏	146 Dick Gernert	12.00	5.50
❏	147 Joe DeMaestri	12.00	5.50
❏	148 Dale Mitchell	20.00	9.00
❏	149 Bob Young	12.00	5.50
❏	150 Cass Michaels	12.00	5.50
❏	151 Pat Mullin	12.00	5.50
❏	152 Mickey Vernon	20.00	9.00
❏	153 Whitey Ford	200.00	90.00
❏	154 Don Newcombe	30.00	13.50
❏	155 Frank Thomas	20.00	9.00
❏	156 Rocky Bridges	12.00	5.50
❏	157 Turk Lown	12.00	5.50
❏	158 Stu Miller	20.00	9.00
❏	159 Johnny Lindell	12.00	5.50
❏	160 Danny O'Connell	12.00	5.50
❏	161 Yogi Berra	175.00	80.00
❏	162 Ted Lepcio	12.00	5.50
❏	163A Dave Philley	20.00	9.00
	(No mention of trade on back)		
❏	163B Dave Philley	30.00	13.50
	(Traded to Cleveland)		
❏	164 Early Wynn	50.00	22.00
❏	165 Johnny Groth	12.00	5.50
❏	166 Sandy Consuegra	12.00	5.50
❏	167 Billy Hoeft	12.00	5.50
❏	168 Ed Fitzgerald	12.00	5.50
❏	169 Larry Jansen	20.00	9.00
❏	170 Duke Snider	135.00	60.00
❏	171 Carlos Bernier	12.00	5.50
❏	172 Andy Seminick	12.00	5.50
❏	173 Dee Fondy	12.00	5.50
❏	174 Pete Castiglione	12.00	5.50
❏	175 Mel Clark	12.00	5.50
❏	176 Vern Bickford	12.00	5.50
❏	177 Whitey Ford	100.00	45.00

#	Player	NRMT	VG-E
178	Del Wilber	12.00	5.50
179	Morrie Martin	12.00	5.50
180	Joe Tipton	12.00	5.50
181	Les Moss	12.00	5.50
182	Sherm Lollar	20.00	9.00
183	Matt Batts	12.00	5.50
184	Mickey Grasso	12.00	5.50
185	Daryl Spencer	12.00	5.50
186	Russ Meyer	12.00	5.50
187	Vern Law	20.00	9.00
188	Frank Smith	12.00	5.50
189	Randy Jackson	12.00	5.50
190	Joe Presko	12.00	5.50
191	Karl Drews	12.00	5.50
192	Lou Burdette	20.00	9.00
193	Eddie Robinson	12.00	5.50
194	Sid Hudson	12.00	5.50
195	Bob Cain	12.00	5.50
196	Bob Lemon	50.00	22.00
197	Lou Kretlow	12.00	5.50
198	Virgil Trucks	12.00	5.50
199	Steve Gromek	12.00	5.50
200	Conrado Marrero	12.00	5.50
201	Bobby Thomson	30.00	13.50
202	George Shuba	15.00	6.75
203	Vic Janowicz	20.00	9.00
204	Jack Collum	12.00	5.50
205	Hal Jeffcoat	12.00	5.50
206	Steve Bilko	12.00	5.50
207	Stan Lopata	12.00	5.50
208	Johnny Antonelli	20.00	9.00
209	Gene Woodling	20.00	9.00
210	Jimmy Piersall	20.00	9.00
211	Al Robertson	12.00	5.50
212	Owen Friend	12.00	5.50
213	Dick Littlefield	12.00	5.50
214	Ferris Fain	20.00	9.00
215	Johnny Bucha	12.00	5.50
216	Jerry Snyder	12.00	5.50
217	Hank Thompson	20.00	9.00
218	Preacher Roe	20.00	9.00
219	Hal Rice	12.00	5.50
220	Hobie Landrith	12.00	5.50
221	Frank Baumholtz	12.00	5.50
222	Memo Luna	12.00	5.50
223	Steve Ridzik	12.00	5.50
224	Bill Bruton	50.00	12.50

1955 Bowman

	NRMT	VG-E
COMPLETE SET (320)	4600.00	2100.00
COMMON CARD (1-96)	12.00	5.50
COM. CARD (97-224)	10.00	4.50
MINOR STARS 1-224	15.00	6.75
SEMISTARS 1-224	20.00	9.00
UNLISTED STARS 1-224	30.00	13.50
COM. CARD (225-320)	15.00	6.75
COM. UMPIRE (225-320)	30.00	13.50
MINOR STARS 225-320	20.00	9.00
SEMISTARS 225-320	30.00	13.50
UNLISTED STARS 225-320	40.00	18.00

*UNLISTED DODGER/YANKEE: 1.25X VALUE
CARDS PRICED IN NM CONDITION !

#	Player	NRMT	VG-E
1	Hoyt Wilhelm	100.00	22.00
2	Alvin Dark	15.00	6.75
3	Joe Coleman	15.00	6.75
4	Eddie Waitkus	15.00	6.75
5	Jim Robertson	12.00	5.50
6	Pete Suder	12.00	5.50
7	Gene Baker	12.00	5.50
8	Warren Hacker	12.00	5.50
9	Gil McDougald	20.00	9.00
10	Phil Rizzuto	100.00	45.00
11	Bill Bruton	15.00	6.75
12	Andy Pafko	15.00	6.75
13	Clyde Vollmer	12.00	5.50
14	Gus Keriazakos	12.00	5.50
15	Frank Sullivan	12.00	5.50
16	Jimmy Piersall	15.00	6.75
17	Del Ennis	15.00	6.75
18	Stan Lopata	12.00	5.50
19	Bobby Avila	15.00	6.75
20	Al Smith	15.00	6.75
21	Don Hoak	12.00	5.50
22	Roy Campanella	125.00	55.00
23	Al Kaline	150.00	70.00
24	Al Aber	12.00	5.50
25	Minnie Minoso	30.00	13.50
26	Virgil Trucks	15.00	6.75
27	Preston Ward	12.00	5.50
28	Dick Cole	12.00	5.50
29	Red Schoendienst	30.00	13.50
30	Bill Sarni	12.00	5.50
31	Johnny Temple	15.00	6.75
32	Wally Post	15.00	6.75
33	Nellie Fox	45.00	20.00
34	Clint Courtney	12.00	5.50
35	Bill Tuttle	12.00	5.50
36	Wayne Belardi	12.00	5.50
37	Pee Wee Reese	70.00	32.00
38	Early Wynn	30.00	13.50
39	Bob Darnell	15.00	6.75
40	Vic Wertz	15.00	6.75
41	Mel Clark	12.00	5.50
42	Bob Greenwood	12.00	5.50
43	Bob Buhl	15.00	6.75
44	Danny O'Connell	12.00	5.50
45	Tom Umphlett	12.00	5.50
46	Mickey Vernon	15.00	6.75
47	Sammy White	12.00	5.50
48A	Milt Bolling ERR	30.00	13.50
	(Name on back is Frank Bolling)		
48B	Milt Bolling COR	15.00	6.75
49	Jim Greengrass	12.00	5.50
50	Hobie Landrith	12.00	5.50
51	Elvin Tappe	12.00	5.50
52	Hal Rice	12.00	5.50
53	Alex Kellner	12.00	5.50
54	Don Bollweg	12.00	5.50
55	Cal Abrams	12.00	5.50
56	Billy Cox	15.00	6.75
57	Bob Friend	15.00	6.75
58	Frank Thomas	15.00	6.75
59	Whitey Ford	80.00	36.00
60	Enos Slaughter	30.00	13.50
61	Paul LaPalme	12.00	5.50
62	Royce Lint	12.00	5.50
63	Irv Noren	15.00	6.75
64	Curt Simmons	15.00	6.75
65	Don Zimmer	20.00	9.00
66	George Shuba	20.00	9.00
67	Don Larsen	20.00	9.00
68	Elston Howard	75.00	34.00
69	Billy Hunter	12.00	5.50
70	Lou Burdette	15.00	6.75
71	Dave Jolly	12.00	5.50
72	Chet Nichols	12.00	5.50
73	Eddie Yost	15.00	6.75
74	Jerry Snyder	12.00	5.50
75	Brooks Lawrence	12.00	5.50
76	Tom Poholsky	12.00	5.50
77	Jim McDonald	12.00	5.50
78	Gil Coan	12.00	5.50
79	Willie Miranda	12.00	5.50
80	Lou Limmer	12.00	5.50
81	Bobby Morgan	12.00	5.50
82	Lee Walls	12.00	5.50
83	Max Surkont	12.00	5.50
84	George Freese	12.00	5.50
85	Cass Michaels	12.00	5.50
86	Ted Gray	12.00	5.50
87	Randy Jackson	12.00	5.50
88	Steve Bilko	12.00	5.50
89	Lou Boudreau MG	30.00	13.50
90	Art Ditmar	12.00	5.50
91	Dick Marlowe	12.00	5.50
92	George Zuverink	12.00	5.50
93	Andy Seminick	12.00	5.50
94	Hank Thompson	15.00	6.75
95	Sal Maglie	15.00	6.75
96	Ray Narleski	12.00	5.50
97	Johnny Podres	30.00	13.50
98	Jim Gilliam	20.00	9.00
99	Jerry Coleman	15.00	6.75
100	Tom Morgan	10.00	4.50
101A	Don Johnson ERR	15.00	6.75
	(Photo actually Ernie Johnson)		
101B	Don Johnson COR	30.00	13.50
102	Bobby Thomson	15.00	6.75
103	Eddie Mathews	60.00	27.00
104	Bob Porterfield	10.00	4.50
105	Johnny Schmitz	10.00	4.50
106	Del Rice	10.00	4.50
107	Solly Hemus	10.00	4.50
108	Lou Kretlow	10.00	4.50
109	Vern Stephens	15.00	6.75
110	Bob Miller	10.00	4.50
111	Steve Ridzik	10.00	4.50
112	Granny Hamner	10.00	4.50
113	Bob Hall	10.00	4.50
114	Vic Janowicz	15.00	6.75
115	Roger Bowman	10.00	4.50
116	Sandy Consuegra	10.00	4.50
117	Johnny Groth	10.00	4.50
118	Bobby Adams	10.00	4.50
119	Joe Astroth	10.00	4.50
120	Ed Burtschy	10.00	4.50
121	Rufus Crawford	10.00	4.50
122	Al Corwin	10.00	4.50
123	Marv Grissom	10.00	4.50
124	Johnny Antonelli	15.00	6.75
125	Paul Giel	15.00	6.75
126	Billy Goodman	15.00	6.75
127	Hank Majeski	10.00	4.50
128	Mike Garcia	15.00	6.75
129	Hal Naragon	10.00	4.50
130	Richie Ashburn	45.00	20.00
131	Willard Marshall	10.00	4.50
132A	Harvey Kueen ERR	20.00	9.00
	(Sic, Kuenn)		
132B	Harvey Kueen COR	30.00	13.50
133	Charles King	10.00	4.50
134	Bob Feller	70.00	32.00
135	Lloyd Merriman	10.00	4.50
136	Rocky Bridges	10.00	4.50
137	Bob Talbot	10.00	4.50
138	Davey Williams	15.00	6.75
139	Shantz Brothers	15.00	6.75
	Wilmer Shantz		
	Bobby Shantz		
140	Bobby Shantz	15.00	6.75
141	Wes Westrum	15.00	6.75
142	Rudy Regalado	10.00	4.50
143	Don Newcombe	25.00	11.00
144	Art Houtteman	10.00	4.50
145	Bob Nieman	10.00	4.50
146	Don Liddle	10.00	4.50
147	Sam Mele	10.00	4.50
148	Bob Chakales	10.00	4.50
149	Cloyd Boyer	10.00	4.50
150	Billy Klaus	10.00	4.50
151	Jim Bridewesar	10.00	4.50
152	Johnny Klippstein	10.00	4.50
153	Eddie Robinson	10.00	4.50
154	Frank Lary	15.00	6.75
155	Gerry Staley	10.00	4.50
156	Jim Hughes	15.00	6.75
157A	Ernie Johnson ERR	20.00	9.00
	(Photo actually Don Johnson)		
157B	Ernie Johnson COR	12.00	5.50
158	Gil Hodges	50.00	22.00
159	Harry Byrd	10.00	4.50
160	Bill Skowron	20.00	9.00
161	Matt Batts	10.00	4.50
162	Charlie Maxwell	10.00	4.50

#	Player	MINT	NRMT
❏ 163	Sid Gordon	15.00	6.75
❏ 164	Toby Atwell	10.00	4.50
❏ 165	Maurice McDermott	10.00	4.50
❏ 166	Jim Busby	10.00	4.50
❏ 167	Bob Grim	20.00	9.00
❏ 168	Yogi Berra	100.00	45.00
❏ 169	Carl Furillo	20.00	9.00
❏ 170	Carl Erskine	20.00	9.00
❏ 171	Robin Roberts	40.00	18.00
❏ 172	Willie Jones	10.00	4.50
❏ 173	Chico Carrasquel	10.00	4.50
❏ 174	Sherm Lollar	15.00	6.75
❏ 175	Wilmer Shantz	10.00	4.50
❏ 176	Joe DeMaestri	10.00	4.50
❏ 177	Willard Nixon	10.00	4.50
❏ 178	Tom Brewer	10.00	4.50
❏ 179	Hank Aaron	225.00	100.00
❏ 180	Johnny Logan	15.00	6.75
❏ 181	Eddie Miksis	10.00	4.50
❏ 182	Bob Rush	10.00	4.50
❏ 183	Ray Katt	10.00	4.50
❏ 184	Willie Mays	225.00	100.00
❏ 185	Vic Raschi	10.00	4.50
❏ 186	Alex Grammas	10.00	4.50
❏ 187	Fred Hatfield	10.00	4.50
❏ 188	Ned Garver	10.00	4.50
❏ 189	Jack Collum	10.00	4.50
❏ 190	Fred Baczewski	10.00	4.50
❏ 191	Bob Lemon	30.00	13.50
❏ 192	George Strickland	10.00	4.50
❏ 193	Howie Judson	10.00	4.50
❏ 194	Joe Nuxhall	15.00	6.75
❏ 195A	Erv Palica	15.00	6.75
	(Without trade)		
❏ 195B	Erv Palica	30.00	13.50
	(With trade)		
❏ 196	Russ Meyer	15.00	6.75
❏ 197	Ralph Kiner	30.00	13.50
❏ 198	Dave Pope	10.00	4.50
❏ 199	Vern Law	15.00	6.75
❏ 200	Dick Littlefield	10.00	4.50
❏ 201	Allie Reynolds	20.00	9.00
❏ 202	Mickey Mantle UER	900.00	400.00
	Birthdate listed as 10/30/31		
	Should be 10/20/31		
❏ 203	Steve Gromek	10.00	4.50
❏ 204A	Frank Bolling ERR	20.00	9.00
	(Name on back is Milt Bolling)		
❏ 204B	Frank Bolling COR	20.00	9.00
❏ 205	Rip Repulski	10.00	4.50
❏ 206	Ralph Beard	10.00	4.50
❏ 207	Frank Shea	10.00	4.50
❏ 208	Ed Fitzgerald	10.00	4.50
❏ 209	Smoky Burgess	15.00	6.75
❏ 210	Earl Torgeson	10.00	4.50
❏ 211	Sonny Dixon	10.00	4.50
❏ 212	Jack Dittmer	10.00	4.50
❏ 213	George Kell	30.00	13.50
❏ 214	Billy Pierce	15.00	6.75
❏ 215	Bob Kuzava	10.00	4.50
❏ 216	Preacher Roe	15.00	6.75
❏ 217	Del Crandall	15.00	6.75
❏ 218	Joe Adcock	15.00	6.75
❏ 219	Whitey Lockman	10.00	4.50
❏ 220	Jim Hearn	10.00	4.50
❏ 221	Hector Brown	10.00	4.50
❏ 222	Russ Kemmerer	10.00	4.50
❏ 223	Hal Jeffcoat	10.00	4.50
❏ 224	Dee Fondy	10.00	4.50
❏ 225	Paul Richards MG	15.00	6.75
❏ 226	Bill McKinley UMP	30.00	13.50
❏ 227	Frank Baumholtz	15.00	6.75
❏ 228	John Phillips	15.00	6.75
❏ 229	Jim Brosnan	20.00	9.00
❏ 230	Al Brazle	15.00	6.75
❏ 231	Jim Konstanty	20.00	9.00
❏ 232	Birdie Tebbetts MG	20.00	9.00
❏ 233	Bill Serena	15.00	6.75
❏ 234	Dick Bartell CO	20.00	9.00
❏ 235	Joe Paparella UMP	30.00	13.50
❏ 236	Murry Dickson	15.00	6.75
❏ 237	Johnny Wyrostek	15.00	6.75
❏ 238	Eddie Stanky MG	20.00	9.00
❏ 239	Edwin Rommel UMP	40.00	18.00
❏ 240	Billy Loes	20.00	9.00

#	Player	MINT	NRMT
❏ 241	Johnny Pesky CO	20.00	9.00
❏ 242	Ernie Banks	350.00	160.00
❏ 243	Gus Bell	20.00	9.00
❏ 244	Duane Pillette	15.00	6.75
❏ 245	Bill Miller	15.00	6.75
❏ 246	Hank Bauer	30.00	13.50
❏ 247	Dutch Leonard CO	15.00	6.75
❏ 248	Harry Dorish	15.00	6.75
❏ 249	Billy Gardner	20.00	9.00
❏ 250	Larry Napp UMP	30.00	13.50
❏ 251	Stan Jok	15.00	6.75
❏ 252	Roy Smalley	15.00	6.75
❏ 253	Jim Wilson	15.00	6.75
❏ 254	Bennett Flowers	15.00	6.75
❏ 255	Pete Runnels	20.00	9.00
❏ 256	Owen Friend	15.00	6.75
❏ 257	Tom Alston	15.00	6.75
❏ 258	John Stevens UMP	30.00	13.50
❏ 259	Don Mossi	30.00	13.50
❏ 260	Edwin Hurley UMP	30.00	13.50
❏ 261	Walt Moryn	20.00	9.00
❏ 262	Jim Lemon	15.00	6.75
❏ 263	Eddie Joost	15.00	6.75
❏ 264	Bill Henry	15.00	6.75
❏ 265	Albert Barlick UMP	75.00	34.00
❏ 266	Mike Fornieles	15.00	6.75
❏ 267	Jim Honochick UMP	75.00	34.00
❏ 268	Roy Lee Hawes	15.00	6.75
❏ 269	Joe Amalfitano	20.00	9.00
❏ 270	Chico Fernandez	20.00	9.00
❏ 271	Bob Hooper	15.00	6.75
❏ 272	John Flaherty UMP	30.00	13.50
❏ 273	Bubba Church	15.00	6.75
❏ 274	Jim Delsing	15.00	6.75
❏ 275	William Grieve UMP	30.00	13.50
❏ 276	Ike Delock	15.00	6.75
❏ 277	Ed Runge UMP	30.00	13.50
❏ 278	Charlie Neal	40.00	18.00
❏ 279	Hank Soar UMP	30.00	13.50
❏ 280	Clyde McCullough	15.00	6.75
❏ 281	Charles Berry UMP	40.00	18.00
❏ 282	Phil Cavarretta	20.00	9.00
❏ 283	Nestor Chylak UMP	30.00	13.50
❏ 284	Bill Jackowski UMP	30.00	13.50
❏ 285	Walt Dropo	20.00	9.00
❏ 286	Frank Secory UMP	30.00	13.50
❏ 287	Ron Mrozinski	15.00	6.75
❏ 288	Dick Smith	15.00	6.75
❏ 289	Arthur Gore UMP	30.00	13.50
❏ 290	Hershell Freeman	15.00	6.75
❏ 291	Frank Dascoli UMP	30.00	13.50
❏ 292	Marv Blaylock	15.00	6.75
❏ 293	Thomas Gorman UMP	40.00	18.00
❏ 294	Wally Moses CO	15.00	6.75
❏ 295	Lee Ballanfant UMP	30.00	13.50
❏ 296	Bill Virdon	30.00	13.50
❏ 297	Dusty Boggess UMP	30.00	13.50
❏ 298	Charlie Grimm MG	20.00	9.00
❏ 299	Lon Warneke UMP	40.00	18.00
❏ 300	Tommy Byrne	20.00	9.00
❏ 301	William Engeln UMP	30.00	13.50
❏ 302	Frank Malzone	20.00	9.00
❏ 303	Jocko Conlan UMP	75.00	34.00
❏ 304	Harry Chiti	15.00	6.75
❏ 305	Frank Umont UMP	30.00	13.50
❏ 306	Bob Cerv	20.00	9.00
❏ 307	Babe Pinelli UMP	40.00	18.00
❏ 308	Al Lopez MG	50.00	22.00
❏ 309	Hal Dixon UMP	30.00	13.50
❏ 310	Ken Lehman	15.00	6.75
❏ 311	Lawrence Goetz UMP	30.00	13.50
❏ 312	Bill Wight	15.00	6.75
❏ 313	Augie Donatelli UMP	50.00	22.00
❏ 314	Dale Mitchell	20.00	9.00
❏ 315	Cal Hubbard UMP	75.00	34.00
❏ 316	Marion Fricano	15.00	6.75
❏ 317	William Summers UMP	20.00	9.00
❏ 318	Sid Hudson	15.00	6.75
❏ 319	Al Schroll	15.00	6.75
❏ 320	George Susce Jr.	20.00	10.00

1989 Bowman

	MINT	NRMT
COMPLETE SET (484)	35.00	16.00
COMP.FACT.SET (484)	50.00	22.00

	MINT	NRMT
COMMON CARD (1-484)	.05	.02
MINOR STARS	.10	.05
UNLISTED STARS	.20	.09
COMP.REPRINT SET (11)	2.00	.90

REPRINTS: RANDOM INSERTS IN PACKS
1989 TO PRESENT PRICED IN MINT CONDITION

#	Player	MINT	NRMT
❏ 1	Oswald Peraza	.05	.02
❏ 2	Brian Holton	.05	.02
❏ 3	Jose Bautista	.05	.02
❏ 4	Pete Harnisch	.25	.11
❏ 5	Dave Schmidt	.05	.02
❏ 6	Gregg Olson	.20	.09
❏ 7	Jeff Ballard	.05	.02
❏ 8	Bob Melvin	.05	.02
❏ 9	Cal Ripken	.75	.35
❏ 10	Randy Milligan	.05	.02
❏ 11	Juan Bell	.05	.02
❏ 12	Billy Ripken	.05	.02
❏ 13	Jim Traber	.05	.02
❏ 14	Pete Stanicek	.05	.02
❏ 15	Steve Finley	.40	.18
❏ 16	Larry Sheets	.05	.02
❏ 17	Phil Bradley	.05	.02
❏ 18	Brady Anderson	.40	.18
❏ 19	Lee Smith	.10	.05
❏ 20	Tom Fischer	.05	.02
❏ 21	Mike Boddicker	.05	.02
❏ 22	Rob Murphy	.05	.02
❏ 23	Wes Gardner	.05	.02
❏ 24	John Dopson	.05	.02
❏ 25	Bob Stanley	.05	.02
❏ 26	Roger Clemens	.50	.23
❏ 27	Rich Gedman	.05	.02
❏ 28	Marty Barrett	.05	.02
❏ 29	Luis Rivera	.05	.02
❏ 30	Jody Reed	.05	.02
❏ 31	Nick Esasky	.05	.02
❏ 32	Wade Boggs	.20	.09
❏ 33	Jim Rice	.10	.05
❏ 34	Mike Greenwell	.05	.02
❏ 35	Dwight Evans	.10	.05
❏ 36	Ellis Burks	.15	.07
❏ 37	Chuck Finley	.10	.05
❏ 38	Kirk McCaskill	.05	.02
❏ 39	Jim Abbott	.20	.09
❏ 40	Bryan Harvey	.05	.02
❏ 41	Bert Blyleven	.10	.05
❏ 42	Mike Witt	.05	.02
❏ 43	Bob McClure	.05	.02
❏ 44	Bill Schroeder	.05	.02
❏ 45	Lance Parrish	.05	.02
❏ 46	Dick Schofield	.05	.02
❏ 47	Wally Joyner	.10	.05
❏ 48	Jack Howell	.05	.02
❏ 49	Johnny Ray	.05	.02
❏ 50	Chili Davis	.10	.05
❏ 51	Tony Armas	.05	.02
❏ 52	Claudell Washington	.05	.02
❏ 53	Brian Downing	.05	.02
❏ 54	Devon White	.10	.05
❏ 55	Bobby Thigpen	.05	.02
❏ 56	Bill Long	.05	.02
❏ 57	Jerry Reuss	.05	.02
❏ 58	Shawn Hillegas	.05	.02
❏ 59	Melido Perez	.05	.02
❏ 60	Jeff Bittiger	.05	.02

61	Jack McDowell	.10	.05
62	Carlton Fisk	.20	.09
63	Steve Lyons	.05	.02
64	Ozzie Guillen	.05	.02
65	Robin Ventura	.75	.35
66	Fred Manrique	.05	.02
67	Dan Pasqua	.05	.02
68	Ivan Calderon	.05	.02
69	Ron Kittle	.05	.02
70	Daryl Boston	.05	.02
71	Dave Gallagher	.05	.02
72	Harold Baines	.10	.05
73	Charles Nagy	.25	.11
74	John Farrell	.05	.02
75	Kevin Wickander	.05	.02
76	Greg Swindell	.05	.02
77	Mike Walker	.05	.02
78	Doug Jones	.05	.02
79	Rich Yett	.05	.02
80	Tom Candiotti	.05	.02
81	Jesse Orosco	.05	.02
82	Bud Black	.05	.02
83	Andy Allanson	.05	.02
84	Pete O'Brien	.05	.02
85	Jerry Browne	.05	.02
86	Brook Jacoby	.05	.02
87	Mark Lewis	.10	.05
88	Luis Aguayo	.05	.02
89	Cory Snyder	.05	.02
90	Oddibe McDowell	.05	.02
91	Joe Carter	.15	.07
92	Frank Tanana	.05	.02
93	Jack Morris	.10	.05
94	Doyle Alexander	.05	.02
95	Steve Searcy	.05	.02
96	Randy Bockus	.05	.02
97	Jeff M. Robinson	.05	.02
98	Mike Henneman	.05	.02
99	Paul Gibson	.05	.02
100	Frank Williams	.05	.02
101	Matt Nokes	.05	.02
102	Rico Brogna UER (Misspelled Ricco on card back)	.25	.11
103	Lou Whitaker	.10	.05
104	Al Pedrique	.05	.02
105	Alan Trammell	.15	.07
106	Chris Brown	.05	.02
107	Pat Sheridan	.05	.02
108	Chet Lemon	.05	.02
109	Keith Moreland	.05	.02
110	Mel Stottlemyre Jr.	.05	.02
111	Bret Saberhagen	.10	.05
112	Floyd Bannister	.05	.02
113	Jeff Montgomery	.10	.05
114	Steve Farr	.05	.02
115	Tom Gordon UER (Front shows autograph of Don Gordon)	.20	.09
116	Charlie Leibrandt	.05	.02
117	Mark Gubicza	.05	.02
118	Mike Macfarlane	.05	.02
119	Bob Boone	.10	.05
120	Kurt Stillwell	.05	.02
121	George Brett	.40	.18
122	Frank White	.10	.05
123	Kevin Seitzer	.05	.02
124	Willie Wilson	.05	.02
125	Pat Tabler	.05	.02
126	Bo Jackson	.15	.07
127	Hugh Walker	.05	.02
128	Danny Tartabull	.05	.02
129	Teddy Higuera	.05	.02
130	Don August	.05	.02
131	Juan Nieves	.05	.02
132	Mike Birkbeck	.05	.02
133	Dan Plesac	.05	.02
134	Chris Bosio	.05	.02
135	Bill Wegman	.05	.02
136	Chuck Crim	.05	.02
137	B.J. Surhoff	.05	.02
138	Joey Meyer	.05	.02
139	Dale Sveum	.05	.02
140	Paul Molitor	.20	.09
141	Jim Gantner	.05	.02
142	Gary Sheffield	.50	.23
143	Greg Brock	.05	.02
144	Robin Yount	.20	.09
145	Glenn Braggs	.05	.02
146	Rob Deer	.05	.02
147	Fred Toliver	.05	.02
148	Jeff Reardon	.10	.05
149	Allan Anderson	.05	.02
150	Frank Viola	.05	.02
151	Shane Rawley	.05	.02
152	Juan Berenguer	.05	.02
153	Johnny Ard	.05	.02
154	Tim Laudner	.05	.02
155	Brian Harper	.05	.02
156	Al Newman	.05	.02
157	Kent Hrbek	.10	.05
158	Gary Gaetti	.05	.02
159	Wally Backman	.05	.02
160	Gene Larkin	.05	.02
161	Greg Gagne	.05	.02
162	Kirby Puckett	.40	.18
163	Dan Gladden	.05	.02
164	Randy Bush	.05	.02
165	Dave LaPoint	.05	.02
166	Andy Hawkins	.05	.02
167	Dave Righetti	.05	.02
168	Lance McCullers	.05	.02
169	Jimmy Jones	.05	.02
170	Al Leiter	.20	.09
171	John Candelaria	.05	.02
172	Don Slaught	.05	.02
173	Jamie Quirk	.05	.02
174	Rafael Santana	.05	.02
175	Mike Pagliarulo	.05	.02
176	Don Mattingly	.40	.18
177	Ken Phelps	.05	.02
178	Steve Sax	.05	.02
179	Dave Winfield	.20	.09
180	Stan Jefferson	.05	.02
181	Rickey Henderson	.25	.11
182	Bob Brower	.05	.02
183	Roberto Kelly	.10	.05
184	Curt Young	.05	.02
185	Gene Nelson	.05	.02
186	Bob Welch	.05	.02
187	Rick Honeycutt	.05	.02
188	Dave Stewart	.10	.05
189	Mike Moore	.05	.02
190	Dennis Eckersley	.15	.07
191	Eric Plunk	.05	.02
192	Storm Davis	.05	.02
193	Terry Steinbach	.10	.05
194	Ron Hassey	.05	.02
195	Stan Royer	.05	.02
196	Walt Weiss	.05	.02
197	Mark McGwire	1.25	.55
198	Carney Lansford	.10	.05
199	Glenn Hubbard	.05	.02
200	Dave Henderson	.05	.02
201	Jose Canseco	.25	.11
202	Dave Parker	.10	.05
203	Scott Bankhead	.05	.02
204	Tom Niedenfuer	.05	.02
205	Mark Langston	.05	.02
206	Erik Hanson	.10	.05
207	Mike Jackson	.15	.07
208	Dave Valle	.05	.02
209	Scott Bradley	.05	.02
210	Harold Reynolds	.05	.02
211	Tino Martinez	.50	.23
212	Rich Renteria	.05	.02
213	Rey Quinones	.05	.02
214	Jim Presley	.05	.02
215	Alvin Davis	.05	.02
216	Edgar Martinez	.20	.09
217	Darnell Coles	.05	.02
218	Jeffrey Leonard	.05	.02
219	Jay Buhner	.20	.09
220	Ken Griffey Jr.	25.00	11.00
221	Drew Hall	.05	.02
222	Bobby Witt	.05	.02
223	Jamie Moyer	.05	.02
224	Charlie Hough	.10	.05
225	Nolan Ryan	.75	.35
226	Jeff Russell	.05	.02
227	Jim Sundberg	.05	.02
228	Julio Franco	.05	.02
229	Buddy Bell	.10	.05
230	Scott Fletcher	.05	.02
231	Jeff Kunkel	.05	.02
232	Steve Buechele	.05	.02
233	Monty Fariss	.05	.02
234	Rick Leach	.05	.02
235	Ruben Sierra	.05	.02
236	Cecil Espy	.05	.02
237	Rafael Palmeiro	.25	.11
238	Pete Incaviglia	.05	.02
239	Dave Stieb	.05	.02
240	Jeff Musselman	.05	.02
241	Mike Flanagan	.05	.02
242	Todd Stottlemyre	.15	.07
243	Jimmy Key	.10	.05
244	Tony Castillo	.05	.02
245	Alex Sanchez	.05	.02
246	Tom Henke	.05	.02
247	John Cerutti	.05	.02
248	Ernie Whitt	.05	.02
249	Bob Brenly	.05	.02
250	Rance Mulliniks	.05	.02
251	Kelly Gruber	.05	.02
252	Ed Sprague	.25	.11
253	Fred McGriff	.20	.09
254	Tony Fernandez	.05	.02
255	Tom Lawless	.05	.02
256	George Bell	.05	.02
257	Jesse Barfield	.05	.02
258	Roberto Alomar Sandy Alomar	.20	.09
259	Ken Griffey Jr. Ken Griffey Sr.	2.00	.90
260	Cal Ripken Jr. Cal Ripken Sr.	.30	.14
261	Mel Stottlemyre Jr. Mel Stottlemyre Sr.	.05	.02
262	Zane Smith	.05	.02
263	Charlie Puleo	.05	.02
264	Derek Lilliquist	.05	.02
265	Paul Assenmacher	.05	.02
266	John Smoltz	.75	.35
267	Tom Glavine	.20	.09
268	Steve Avery	.20	.09
269	Pete Smith	.05	.02
270	Jody Davis	.05	.02
271	Bruce Benedict	.05	.02
272	Andres Thomas	.05	.02
273	Gerald Perry	.05	.02
274	Ron Gant	.10	.05
275	Darrell Evans	.10	.05
276	Dale Murphy	.05	.02
277	Dion James	.05	.02
278	Lonnie Smith	.05	.02
279	Geronimo Berroa	.05	.02
280	Steve Wilson	.05	.02
281	Rick Sutcliffe	.05	.02
282	Kevin Coffman	.05	.02
283	Mitch Williams	.05	.02
284	Greg Maddux	.60	.25
285	Paul Kilgus	.05	.02
286	Mike Harkey	.05	.02
287	Lloyd McClendon	.05	.02
288	Damon Berryhill	.05	.02
289	Ty Griffin	.05	.02
290	Ryne Sandberg	.25	.11
291	Mark Grace	.20	.09
292	Curt Wilkerson	.05	.02
293	Vance Law	.05	.02
294	Shawon Dunston	.05	.02
295	Jerome Walton	.20	.09
296	Mitch Webster	.05	.02
297	Dwight Smith	.10	.05
298	Andre Dawson	.20	.09
299	Jeff Sellers	.05	.02
300	Jose Rijo	.05	.02
301	John Franco	.10	.05
302	Rick Mahler	.05	.02
303	Ron Robinson	.05	.02
304	Danny Jackson	.05	.02
305	Rob Dibble	.10	.05
306	Tom Browning	.05	.02
307	Bo Diaz	.05	.02
308	Manny Trillo	.05	.02
309	Chris Sabo	.05	.02
310	Ron Oester	.05	.02

❑ 311 Barry Larkin	.20	.09
❑ 312 Todd Benzinger	.05	.02
❑ 313 Paul O'Neill	.10	.05
❑ 314 Kal Daniels	.05	.02
❑ 315 Joel Youngblood	.05	.02
❑ 316 Eric Davis	.10	.05
❑ 317 Dave Smith	.05	.02
❑ 318 Mark Portugal	.05	.02
❑ 319 Brian Meyer	.05	.02
❑ 320 Jim Deshaies	.05	.02
❑ 321 Juan Agosto	.05	.02
❑ 322 Mike Scott	.05	.02
❑ 323 Rick Rhoden	.05	.02
❑ 324 Jim Clancy	.05	.02
❑ 325 Larry Andersen	.05	.02
❑ 326 Alex Trevino	.05	.02
❑ 327 Alan Ashby	.05	.02
❑ 328 Craig Reynolds	.05	.02
❑ 329 Bill Doran	.05	.02
❑ 330 Rafael Ramirez	.05	.02
❑ 331 Glenn Davis	.05	.02
❑ 332 Willie Ansley	.05	.02
❑ 333 Gerald Young	.05	.02
❑ 334 Cameron Drew	.05	.02
❑ 335 Jay Howell	.05	.02
❑ 336 Tim Belcher	.05	.02
❑ 337 Fernando Valenzuela	.05	.02
❑ 338 Ricky Horton	.05	.02
❑ 339 Tim Leary	.05	.02
❑ 340 Bill Bene	.05	.02
❑ 341 Orel Hershiser	.10	.05
❑ 342 Mike Scioscia	.05	.02
❑ 343 Rick Dempsey	.05	.02
❑ 344 Willie Randolph	.10	.05
❑ 345 Alfredo Griffin	.05	.02
❑ 346 Eddie Murray	.20	.09
❑ 347 Mickey Hatcher	.05	.02
❑ 348 Mike Sharperson	.05	.02
❑ 349 John Shelby	.05	.02
❑ 350 Mike Marshall	.05	.02
❑ 351 Kirk Gibson	.10	.05
❑ 352 Mike Davis	.05	.02
❑ 353 Bryn Smith	.05	.02
❑ 354 Pascual Perez	.05	.02
❑ 355 Kevin Gross	.05	.02
❑ 356 Andy McGaffigan	.05	.02
❑ 357 Brian Holman	.05	.02
❑ 358 Dave Wainhouse	.05	.02
❑ 359 Dennis Martinez	.10	.05
❑ 360 Tim Burke	.05	.02
❑ 361 Nelson Santovenia	.05	.02
❑ 362 Tim Wallach	.05	.02
❑ 363 Spike Owen	.05	.02
❑ 364 Rex Hudler	.05	.02
❑ 365 Andres Galarraga	.20	.09
❑ 366 Otis Nixon	.10	.05
❑ 367 Hubie Brooks	.05	.02
❑ 368 Mike Aldrete	.05	.02
❑ 369 Tim Raines	.10	.05
❑ 370 Dave Martinez	.05	.02
❑ 371 Bob Ojeda	.05	.02
❑ 372 Ron Darling	.05	.02
❑ 373 Wally Whitehurst	.05	.02
❑ 374 Randy Myers	.10	.05
❑ 375 David Cone	.20	.09
❑ 376 Dwight Gooden	.10	.05
❑ 377 Sid Fernandez	.05	.02
❑ 378 Dave Proctor	.05	.02
❑ 379 Gary Carter	.15	.07
❑ 380 Keith Miller	.05	.02
❑ 381 Gregg Jefferies	.10	.05
❑ 382 Tim Teufel	.05	.02
❑ 383 Kevin Elster	.05	.02
❑ 384 Dave Magadan	.05	.02
❑ 385 Keith Hernandez	.05	.02
❑ 386 Mookie Wilson	.10	.05
❑ 387 Darryl Strawberry	.10	.05
❑ 388 Kevin McReynolds	.05	.02
❑ 389 Mark Carreon	.05	.02
❑ 390 Jeff Parrett	.05	.02
❑ 391 Mike Maddux	.05	.02
❑ 392 Don Carman	.05	.02
❑ 393 Bruce Ruffin	.05	.02
❑ 394 Ken Howell	.05	.02
❑ 395 Steve Bedrosian	.05	.02
❑ 396 Floyd Youmans	.05	.02

❑ 397 Larry McWilliams	.05	.02
❑ 398 Pat Combs	.05	.02
❑ 399 Steve Lake	.05	.02
❑ 400 Dickie Thon	.05	.02
❑ 401 Ricky Jordan	.05	.02
❑ 402 Mike Schmidt	.30	.14
❑ 403 Tom Herr	.05	.02
❑ 404 Chris James	.05	.02
❑ 405 Juan Samuel	.05	.02
❑ 406 Von Hayes	.05	.02
❑ 407 Ron Jones	.05	.02
❑ 408 Curt Ford	.05	.02
❑ 409 Bob Walk	.05	.02
❑ 410 Jeff D. Robinson	.05	.02
❑ 411 Jim Gott	.05	.02
❑ 412 Scott Medvin	.05	.02
❑ 413 John Smiley	.05	.02
❑ 414 Bob Kipper	.05	.02
❑ 415 Brian Fisher	.05	.02
❑ 416 Doug Drabek	.05	.02
❑ 417 Mike LaValliere	.05	.02
❑ 418 Ken Oberkfell	.05	.02
❑ 419 Sid Bream	.05	.02
❑ 420 Austin Manahan	.05	.02
❑ 421 Jose Lind	.05	.02
❑ 422 Bobby Bonilla	.15	.07
❑ 423 Glenn Wilson	.05	.02
❑ 424 Andy Van Slyke	.10	.05
❑ 425 Gary Redus	.05	.02
❑ 426 Barry Bonds	.40	.18
❑ 427 Don Heinkel	.05	.02
❑ 428 Ken Dayley	.05	.02
❑ 429 Todd Worrell	.05	.02
❑ 430 Brad DuVall	.05	.02
❑ 431 Jose DeLeon	.05	.02
❑ 432 Joe Magrane	.05	.02
❑ 433 John Ericks	.05	.02
❑ 434 Frank DiPino	.05	.02
❑ 435 Tony Pena	.05	.02
❑ 436 Ozzie Smith	.25	.11
❑ 437 Terry Pendleton	.10	.05
❑ 438 Jose Oquendo	.05	.02
❑ 439 Tim Jones	.05	.02
❑ 440 Pedro Guerrero	.05	.02
❑ 441 Milt Thompson	.05	.02
❑ 442 Willie McGee	.05	.05
❑ 443 Vince Coleman	.05	.02
❑ 444 Tom Brunansky	.05	.02
❑ 445 Walt Terrell	.05	.02
❑ 446 Eric Show	.05	.02
❑ 447 Mark Davis	.05	.02
❑ 448 Andy Benes	.20	.09
❑ 449 Ed Whitson	.05	.02
❑ 450 Dennis Rasmussen	.05	.02
❑ 451 Bruce Hurst	.05	.02
❑ 452 Pat Clements	.05	.02
❑ 453 Benito Santiago	.05	.02
❑ 454 Sandy Alomar Jr.	.25	.11
❑ 455 Garry Templeton	.05	.02
❑ 456 Jack Clark	.05	.02
❑ 457 Tim Flannery	.05	.02
❑ 458 Roberto Alomar	.30	.14
❑ 459 Carmelo Martinez	.05	.02
❑ 460 John Kruk	.05	.02
❑ 461 Tony Gwynn	.50	.23
❑ 462 Jerald Clark	.05	.02
❑ 463 Don Robinson	.05	.02
❑ 464 Craig Lefferts	.05	.02
❑ 465 Kelly Downs	.05	.02
❑ 466 Rick Reuschel	.05	.02
❑ 467 Scott Garrelts	.05	.02
❑ 468 Will Tejada	.05	.02
❑ 469 Kirt Manwaring	.05	.02
❑ 470 Terry Kennedy	.05	.02
❑ 471 Jose Uribe	.05	.02
❑ 472 Royce Clayton	.25	.11
❑ 473 Robby Thompson	.05	.02
❑ 474 Kevin Mitchell	.10	.05
❑ 475 Ernie Riles	.05	.02
❑ 476 Will Clark	.20	.09
❑ 477 Donell Nixon	.05	.02
❑ 478 Candy Maldonado	.05	.02
❑ 479 Tracy Jones	.05	.02
❑ 480 Brett Butler	.10	.05
❑ 481 Checklist 1-121	.05	.02
❑ 482 Checklist 122-242	.05	.02

❑ 483 Checklist 243-363	.05	.02
❑ 484 Checklist 364-484	.05	.02

1989 Bowman Tiffany

	MINT	NRMT
COMP.FACT.SET (495)	800.00	350.00
COMMON CARD (1-484)	.25	.11

*STARS: 10X TO 20X BASIC CARDS
*ROOKIES: 12.5X TO 25X BASIC CARDS
STATED PRINT RUN 6000 SETS
DISTRIBUTED ONLY IN FACTORY SET FORM

1990 Bowman

	MINT	NRMT
COMPLETE SET (528)	30.00	13.50
COMP.FACT.SET (528)	40.00	18.00
COMMON CARD (1-528)	.05	.02
MINOR STARS	.10	.05
UNLISTED STARS	.20	.09
COMP.ART SET (11)	2.00	.90

ART CARDS: RANDOM INSERTS IN PACKS.

❑ 1 Tommy Greene	.05	.02
❑ 2 Tom Glavine	.20	.09
❑ 3 Andy Nezelek	.05	.02
❑ 4 Mike Stanton	.05	.02
❑ 5 Rick Luecken	.05	.02
❑ 6 Kent Mercker	.05	.02
❑ 7 Derek Lilliquist	.05	.02
❑ 8 Charlie Leibrandt	.05	.02
❑ 9 Steve Avery	.20	.09
❑ 10 John Smoltz	.20	.09
❑ 11 Mark Lemke	.05	.02
❑ 12 Lonnie Smith	.05	.02
❑ 13 Oddibe McDowell	.05	.02
❑ 14 Tyler Houston	.15	.07
❑ 15 Jeff Blauser	.05	.02
❑ 16 Ernie Whitt	.05	.02
❑ 17 Alexis Infante	.05	.02
❑ 18 Jim Presley	.05	.02
❑ 19 Dale Murphy	.20	.09
❑ 20 Nick Esasky	.05	.02
❑ 21 Rick Sutcliffe	.05	.02
❑ 22 Mike Bielecki	.05	.02
❑ 23 Steve Wilson	.05	.02
❑ 24 Kevin Blankenship	.05	.02
❑ 25 Mitch Williams	.05	.02
❑ 26 Dean Wilkins	.05	.02
❑ 27 Greg Maddux	.50	.23

❑ 28 Mike Harkey	.05	.02
❑ 29 Mark Grace	.20	.09
❑ 30 Ryne Sandberg	.25	.11
❑ 31 Greg Smith	.05	.02
❑ 32 Dwight Smith	.05	.02
❑ 33 Damon Berryhill	.05	.02
❑ 34 Earl Cunningham UER	.05	.02
(Errant " by the word "in")		
❑ 35 Jerome Walton	.05	.02
❑ 36 Lloyd McClendon	.05	.02
❑ 37 Ty Griffin	.05	.02
❑ 38 Shawon Dunston	.05	.02
❑ 39 Andre Dawson	.20	.09
❑ 40 Luis Salazar	.05	.02
❑ 41 Tim Layana	.05	.02
❑ 42 Rob Dibble	.05	.02
❑ 43 Tom Browning	.05	.02
❑ 44 Danny Jackson	.05	.02
❑ 45 Jose Rijo	.05	.02
❑ 46 Scott Scudder	.05	.02
❑ 47 Randy Myers UER	.10	.05
Career ERA .274, should be 2.74		
❑ 48 Brian Lane	.05	.02
❑ 49 Paul O'Neill	.10	.05
❑ 50 Barry Larkin	.20	.09
❑ 51 Reggie Jefferson	.20	.09
❑ 52 Jeff Branson	.05	.02
❑ 53 Chris Sabo	.05	.02
❑ 54 Joe Oliver	.05	.02
❑ 55 Todd Benzinger	.05	.02
❑ 56 Rolando Roomes	.05	.02
❑ 57 Hal Morris	.05	.02
❑ 58 Eric Davis	.10	.05
❑ 59 Scott Bryant	.05	.02
❑ 60 Ken Griffey Sr.	.10	.05
❑ 61 Darryl Kile	.25	.11
❑ 62 Dave Smith	.05	.02
❑ 63 Mark Portugal	.05	.02
❑ 64 Jeff Juden	.05	.02
❑ 65 Bill Gullickson	.05	.02
❑ 66 Danny Darwin	.05	.02
❑ 67 Larry Andersen	.05	.02
❑ 68 Jose Cano	.05	.02
❑ 69 Dan Schatzeder	.05	.02
❑ 70 Jim Deshaies	.05	.02
❑ 71 Mike Scott	.05	.02
❑ 72 Gerald Young	.05	.02
❑ 73 Ken Caminiti	.20	.09
❑ 74 Ken Oberkfell	.05	.02
❑ 75 Dave Rohde	.05	.02
❑ 76 Bill Doran	.05	.02
❑ 77 Andujar Cedeno	.20	.09
❑ 78 Craig Biggio	.20	.09
❑ 79 Karl Rhodes	.05	.02
❑ 80 Glenn Davis	.05	.02
❑ 81 Eric Anthony	.05	.02
❑ 82 John Wetteland	.20	.09
❑ 83 Jay Howell	.05	.02
❑ 84 Orel Hershiser	.10	.05
❑ 85 Tim Belcher	.05	.02
❑ 86 Kiki Jones	.05	.02
❑ 87 Mike Hartley	.05	.02
❑ 88 Ramon Martinez	.15	.07
❑ 89 Mike Scioscia	.05	.02
❑ 90 Willie Randolph	.10	.05
❑ 91 Juan Samuel	.05	.02
❑ 92 Jose Offerman	.50	.23
❑ 93 Dave Hansen	.05	.02
❑ 94 Jeff Hamilton	.05	.02
❑ 95 Alfredo Griffin	.05	.02
❑ 96 Tom Goodwin	.20	.09
❑ 97 Kirk Gibson	.10	.05
❑ 98 Jose Vizcaino	.15	.07
❑ 99 Kal Daniels	.05	.02
❑ 100 Hubie Brooks	.05	.02
❑ 101 Eddie Murray	.20	.09
❑ 102 Dennis Boyd	.05	.02
❑ 103 Tim Burke	.05	.02
❑ 104 Bill Sampen	.05	.02
❑ 105 Brett Gideon	.05	.02
❑ 106 Mark Gardner	.05	.02
❑ 107 Howard Farmer	.05	.02
❑ 108 Mel Rojas	.10	.05
❑ 109 Kevin Gross	.05	.02
❑ 110 Dave Schmidt	.05	.02
❑ 111 Dennis Martinez	.10	.05
❑ 112 Jerry Goff	.05	.02
❑ 113 Andres Galarraga	.20	.09
❑ 114 Tim Wallach	.05	.02
❑ 115 Marquis Grissom	.25	.11
❑ 116 Spike Owen	.05	.02
❑ 117 Larry Walker	2.00	.90
❑ 118 Tim Raines	.05	.02
❑ 119 Delino DeShields	.20	.09
❑ 120 Tom Foley	.05	.02
❑ 121 Dave Martinez	.05	.02
❑ 122 Frank Viola UER	.05	.02
(Career ERA .384 should be 3.84)		
❑ 123 Julio Valera	.05	.02
❑ 124 Alejandro Pena	.05	.02
❑ 125 David Cone	.20	.09
❑ 126 Dwight Gooden	.10	.05
❑ 127 Kevin D. Brown	.05	.02
❑ 128 John Franco	.10	.05
❑ 129 Terry Bross	.05	.02
❑ 130 Blaine Beatty	.05	.02
❑ 131 Sid Fernandez	.05	.02
❑ 132 Mike Marshall	.05	.02
❑ 133 Howard Johnson	.05	.02
❑ 134 Jaime Roseboro	.05	.02
❑ 135 Alan Zinter	.05	.02
❑ 136 Keith Miller	.05	.02
❑ 137 Kevin Elster	.05	.02
❑ 138 Kevin McReynolds	.05	.02
❑ 139 Barry Lyons	.05	.02
❑ 140 Gregg Jefferies	.10	.05
❑ 141 Darryl Strawberry	.05	.02
❑ 142 Todd Hundley	.40	.18
❑ 143 Scott Service	.05	.02
❑ 144 Chuck Malone	.05	.02
❑ 145 Steve Ontiveros	.05	.02
❑ 146 Roger McDowell	.05	.02
❑ 147 Ken Howell	.05	.02
❑ 148 Pat Combs	.05	.02
❑ 149 Jeff Parrett	.05	.02
❑ 150 Chuck McElroy	.05	.02
❑ 151 Jason Grimsley	.05	.02
❑ 152 Len Dykstra	.10	.05
❑ 153 Mickey Morandini	.10	.05
❑ 154 John Kruk	.10	.05
❑ 155 Dickie Thon	.05	.02
❑ 156 Ricky Jordan	.05	.02
❑ 157 Jeff Jackson	.05	.02
❑ 158 Darren Daulton	.10	.05
❑ 159 Tom Herr	.05	.02
❑ 160 Von Hayes	.05	.02
❑ 161 Dave Hollins	.20	.09
❑ 162 Carmelo Martinez	.05	.02
❑ 163 Bob Walk	.05	.02
❑ 164 Doug Drabek	.05	.02
❑ 165 Walt Terrell	.05	.02
❑ 166 Bill Landrum	.05	.02
❑ 167 Scott Ruskin	.05	.02
❑ 168 Bob Patterson	.05	.02
❑ 169 Bobby Bonilla	.10	.05
❑ 170 Jose Lind	.05	.02
❑ 171 Andy Van Slyke	.10	.05
❑ 172 Mike LaValliere	.05	.02
❑ 173 Willie Greene	.05	.02
❑ 174 Jay Bell	.05	.02
❑ 175 Sid Bream	.05	.02
❑ 176 Tom Prince	.05	.02
❑ 177 Wally Backman	.05	.02
❑ 178 Moises Alou	.60	.25
❑ 179 Steve Carter	.05	.02
❑ 180 Gary Redus	.05	.02
❑ 181 Barry Bonds	.25	.11
❑ 182 Don Slaught UER	.05	.02
(Card back shows headings for a pitcher)		
❑ 183 Joe Magrane	.05	.02
❑ 184 Bryn Smith	.05	.02
❑ 185 Todd Worrell	.05	.02
❑ 186 Jose DeLeon	.05	.02
❑ 187 Frank DiPino	.05	.02
❑ 188 John Tudor	.05	.02
❑ 189 Howard Hilton	.05	.02
❑ 190 John Ericks	.05	.02
❑ 191 Ken Dayley	.05	.02
❑ 192 Ray Lankford	.60	.25
❑ 193 Todd Zeile	.10	.05
❑ 194 Willie McGee	.10	.05
❑ 195 Ozzie Smith	.25	.11
❑ 196 Milt Thompson	.05	.02
❑ 197 Terry Pendleton	.10	.05
❑ 198 Vince Coleman	.05	.02
❑ 199 Paul Coleman	.05	.02
❑ 200 Jose Oquendo	.05	.02
❑ 201 Pedro Guerrero	.05	.02
❑ 202 Tom Brunansky	.05	.02
❑ 203 Roger Smithberg	.05	.02
❑ 204 Eddie Whitson	.05	.02
❑ 205 Dennis Rasmussen	.05	.02
❑ 206 Craig Lefferts	.05	.02
❑ 207 Andy Benes	.20	.09
❑ 208 Bruce Hurst	.05	.02
❑ 209 Eric Show	.05	.02
❑ 210 Rafael Valdez	.05	.02
❑ 211 Joey Cora	.10	.05
❑ 212 Thomas Howard	.05	.02
❑ 213 Rob Nelson	.05	.02
❑ 214 Jack Clark	.10	.05
❑ 215 Garry Templeton	.05	.02
❑ 216 Fred Lynn	.05	.02
❑ 217 Tony Gwynn	.50	.23
❑ 218 Benito Santiago	.05	.02
❑ 219 Mike Pagliarulo	.05	.02
❑ 220 Joe Carter	.10	.05
❑ 221 Roberto Alomar	.20	.09
❑ 222 Bip Roberts	.05	.02
❑ 223 Rick Reuschel	.05	.02
❑ 224 Russ Swan	.05	.02
❑ 225 Eric Gunderson	.05	.02
❑ 226 Steve Bedrosian	.05	.02
❑ 227 Mike Remlinger	.05	.02
❑ 228 Scott Garrelts	.05	.02
❑ 229 Ernie Camacho	.05	.02
❑ 230 Andres Santana	.05	.02
❑ 231 Will Clark	.20	.09
❑ 232 Kevin Mitchell	.05	.02
❑ 233 Robby Thompson	.05	.02
❑ 234 Bill Bathe	.05	.02
❑ 235 Tony Perezchica	.05	.02
❑ 236 Gary Carter	.20	.09
❑ 237 Brett Butler	.10	.05
❑ 238 Matt Williams	.20	.09
❑ 239 Earnie Riles	.05	.02
❑ 240 Kevin Bass	.05	.02
❑ 241 Terry Kennedy	.05	.02
❑ 242 Steve Hosey	.05	.02
❑ 243 Ben McDonald	.10	.05
❑ 244 Jeff Ballard	.05	.02
❑ 245 Joe Price	.05	.02
❑ 246 Curt Schilling	.60	.25
❑ 247 Pete Harnisch	.05	.02
❑ 248 Mark Williamson	.05	.02
❑ 249 Gregg Olson	.10	.05
❑ 250 Chris Myers	.05	.02
❑ 251 David Segui ERR	.25	.11
(Missing vital stats "at top of card back under name)		
❑ 251B David Segui COR	.25	.11
❑ 252 Joe Orsulak	.05	.02
❑ 253 Craig Worthington	.05	.02
❑ 254 Mickey Tettleton	.10	.05
❑ 255 Cal Ripken	.75	.35
❑ 256 Bill Ripken	.05	.02
❑ 257 Randy Milligan	.05	.02
❑ 258 Brady Anderson	.20	.09
❑ 259 Chris Hoiles UER	.20	.09
Baltimore is spelled Baltimte		
❑ 260 Mike Devereaux	.05	.02
❑ 261 Phil Bradley	.05	.02
❑ 262 Leo Gomez	.05	.02
❑ 263 Lee Smith	.10	.05
❑ 264 Mike Rochford	.05	.02
❑ 265 Jeff Reardon	.10	.05
❑ 266 Wes Gardner	.05	.02
❑ 267 Mike Boddicker	.05	.02
❑ 268 Roger Clemens	.50	.23
❑ 269 Rob Murphy	.05	.02
❑ 270 Mickey Pina	.05	.02
❑ 271 Tony Pena	.05	.02
❑ 272 Jody Reed	.05	.02

☐ 273	Kevin Romine	.05	.02
☐ 274	Mike Greenwell	.05	.02
☐ 275	Maurice Vaughn	1.50	.70
☐ 276	Danny Heep	.05	.02
☐ 277	Scott Cooper	.05	.02
☐ 278	Greg Blosser	.05	.02
☐ 279	Dwight Evans UER	.10	.05
	* by "1990 Team Breakdown"		
☐ 280	Ellis Burks	.15	.07
☐ 281	Wade Boggs	.20	.09
☐ 282	Marty Barrett	.05	.02
☐ 283	Kirk McCaskill	.05	.02
☐ 284	Mark Langston	.05	.02
☐ 285	Bert Blyleven	.10	.05
☐ 286	Mike Fetters	.05	.02
☐ 287	Kyle Abbott	.05	.02
☐ 288	Jim Abbott	.15	.07
☐ 289	Chuck Finley	.10	.05
☐ 290	Gary DiSarcina	.15	.07
☐ 291	Dick Schofield	.05	.02
☐ 292	Devon White	.05	.02
☐ 293	Bobby Rose	.05	.02
☐ 294	Brian Downing	.05	.02
☐ 295	Lance Parrish	.05	.02
☐ 296	Jack Howell	.05	.02
☐ 297	Claudell Washington	.05	.02
☐ 298	John Orton	.05	.02
☐ 299	Wally Joyner	.05	.02
☐ 300	Lee Stevens	.10	.05
☐ 301	Chili Davis	.10	.05
☐ 302	Johnny Ray	.05	.02
☐ 303	Greg Hibbard	.05	.02
☐ 304	Eric King	.05	.02
☐ 305	Jack McDowell	.05	.02
☐ 306	Bobby Thigpen	.05	.02
☐ 307	Adam Peterson	.05	.02
☐ 308	Scott Radinsky	.05	.02
☐ 309	Wayne Edwards	.05	.02
☐ 310	Melido Perez	.05	.02
☐ 311	Robin Ventura	.20	.09
☐ 312	Sammy Sosa	8.00	3.60
☐ 313	Dan Pasqua	.05	.02
☐ 314	Carlton Fisk	.20	.09
☐ 315	Ozzie Guillen	.05	.02
☐ 316	Ivan Calderon	.05	.02
☐ 317	Daryl Boston	.05	.02
☐ 318	Craig Grebeck	.05	.02
☐ 319	Scott Fletcher	.05	.02
☐ 320	Frank Thomas	4.00	1.80
☐ 321	Steve Lyons	.05	.02
☐ 322	Carlos Martinez	.05	.02
☐ 323	Joe Skalski	.05	.02
☐ 324	Tom Candiotti	.05	.02
☐ 325	Greg Swindell	.05	.02
☐ 326	Steve Olin	.10	.05
☐ 327	Kevin Wickander	.05	.02
☐ 328	Doug Jones	.05	.02
☐ 329	Jeff Shaw	.05	.02
☐ 330	Kevin Bearse	.05	.02
☐ 331	Dion James	.05	.02
☐ 332	Jerry Browne	.05	.02
☐ 333	Joey Belle	1.25	.55
☐ 334	Felix Fermin	.05	.02
☐ 335	Candy Maldonado	.05	.02
☐ 336	Cory Snyder	.05	.02
☐ 337	Sandy Alomar Jr.	.10	.05
☐ 338	Mark Lewis	.05	.02
☐ 339	Carlos Baerga	.20	.09
☐ 340	Chris James	.05	.02
☐ 341	Brook Jacoby	.05	.02
☐ 342	Keith Hernandez	.10	.05
☐ 343	Frank Tanana	.05	.02
☐ 344	Scott Aldred	.05	.02
☐ 345	Mike Henneman	.05	.02
☐ 346	Steve Wapnick	.05	.02
☐ 347	Greg Gohr	.05	.02
☐ 348	Eric Stone	.05	.02
☐ 349	Brian DuBois	.05	.02
☐ 350	Kevin Ritz	.05	.02
☐ 351	Rico Brogna	.20	.09
☐ 352	Mike Heath	.05	.02
☐ 353	Alan Trammell	.15	.07
☐ 354	Chet Lemon	.05	.02
☐ 355	Dave Bergman	.05	.02
☐ 356	Lou Whitaker	.10	.05
☐ 357	Cecil Fielder UER	.10	.05
	* by 1990 Team Breakdown		
☐ 358	Milt Cuyler	.05	.02
☐ 359	Tony Phillips	.05	.02
☐ 360	Travis Fryman	.40	.18
☐ 361	Ed Romero	.05	.02
☐ 362	Lloyd Moseby	.05	.02
☐ 363	Mark Gubicza	.05	.02
☐ 364	Bret Saberhagen	.10	.05
☐ 365	Tom Gordon	.10	.05
☐ 366	Steve Farr	.05	.02
☐ 367	Kevin Appier	.15	.07
☐ 368	Storm Davis	.05	.02
☐ 369	Mark Davis	.05	.02
☐ 370	Jeff Montgomery	.10	.05
☐ 371	Frank White	.10	.05
☐ 372	Brent Mayne	.05	.02
☐ 373	Bob Boone	.10	.05
☐ 374	Jim Eisenreich	.05	.02
☐ 375	Danny Tartabull	.05	.02
☐ 376	Kurt Stillwell	.05	.02
☐ 377	Bill Pecota	.05	.02
☐ 378	Bo Jackson	.10	.05
☐ 379	Bob Hamelin	.20	.09
☐ 380	Kevin Seitzer	.05	.02
☐ 381	Rey Palacios	.05	.02
☐ 382	George Brett	.40	.18
☐ 383	Gerald Perry	.05	.02
☐ 384	Teddy Higuera	.05	.02
☐ 385	Tom Filer	.05	.02
☐ 386	Dan Plesac	.05	.02
☐ 387	Cal Eldred	.10	.05
☐ 388	Jaime Navarro	.05	.02
☐ 389	Chris Bosio	.05	.02
☐ 390	Randy Veres	.05	.02
☐ 391	Gary Sheffield	.20	.09
☐ 392	George Canale	.05	.02
☐ 393	B.J. Surhoff	.10	.05
☐ 394	Tim McIntosh	.05	.02
☐ 395	Greg Brock	.05	.02
☐ 396	Greg Vaughn	.50	.23
☐ 397	Darryl Hamilton	.05	.02
☐ 398	Dave Parker	.10	.05
☐ 399	Paul Molitor	.20	.09
☐ 400	Jim Gantner	.05	.02
☐ 401	Rob Deer	.05	.02
☐ 402	Billy Spiers	.05	.02
☐ 403	Glenn Braggs	.05	.02
☐ 404	Robin Yount	.20	.09
☐ 405	Rick Aguilera	.10	.05
☐ 406	Johnny Ard	.05	.02
☐ 407	Kevin Tapani	.10	.05
☐ 408	Park Pittman	.05	.02
☐ 409	Allan Anderson	.05	.02
☐ 410	Juan Berenguer	.05	.02
☐ 411	Willie Banks	.05	.02
☐ 412	Rich Yett	.05	.02
☐ 413	Dave West	.05	.02
☐ 414	Greg Gagne	.05	.02
☐ 415	Chuck Knoblauch	.75	.35
☐ 416	Randy Bush	.05	.02
☐ 417	Gary Gaetti	.10	.05
☐ 418	Kent Hrbek	.05	.02
☐ 419	Al Newman	.05	.02
☐ 420	Danny Gladden	.05	.02
☐ 421	Paul Sorrento	.15	.07
☐ 422	Derek Parks	.05	.02
☐ 423	Scott Leius	.05	.02
☐ 424	Kirby Puckett	.30	.14
☐ 425	Willie Smith	.05	.02
☐ 426	Dave Righetti	.05	.02
☐ 427	Jeff D. Robinson	.05	.02
☐ 428	Alan Mills	.05	.02
☐ 429	Tim Leary	.05	.02
☐ 430	Pascual Perez	.05	.02
☐ 431	Alvaro Espinoza	.05	.02
☐ 432	Dave Winfield	.20	.09
☐ 433	Jesse Barfield	.05	.02
☐ 434	Randy Velarde	.05	.02
☐ 435	Rick Cerone	.05	.02
☐ 436	Steve Balboni	.05	.02
☐ 437	Mel Hall	.05	.02
☐ 438	Bob Geren	.05	.02
☐ 439	Bernie Williams	2.00	.90
☐ 440	Kevin Maas	.10	.05
☐ 441	Mike Blowers	.10	.05
☐ 442	Steve Sax	.05	.02
☐ 443	Don Mattingly	.40	.18
☐ 444	Roberto Kelly	.05	.02
☐ 445	Mike Moore	.05	.02
☐ 446	Reggie Harris	.05	.02
☐ 447	Scott Sanderson	.05	.02
☐ 448	Dave Otto	.05	.02
☐ 449	Dave Stewart	.10	.05
☐ 450	Rick Honeycutt	.05	.02
☐ 451	Dennis Eckersley	.15	.07
☐ 452	Carney Lansford	.10	.05
☐ 453	Scott Hemond	.05	.02
☐ 454	Mark McGwire	1.00	.45
☐ 455	Felix Jose	.05	.02
☐ 456	Terry Steinbach	.05	.02
☐ 457	Rickey Henderson	.25	.11
☐ 458	Dave Henderson	.05	.02
☐ 459	Mike Gallego	.05	.02
☐ 460	Jose Canseco	.25	.11
☐ 461	Walt Weiss	.05	.02
☐ 462	Ken Phelps	.05	.02
☐ 463	Darren Lewis	.05	.02
☐ 464	Ron Hassey	.05	.02
☐ 465	Roger Salkeld	.05	.02
☐ 466	Scott Bankhead	.05	.02
☐ 467	Keith Comstock	.05	.02
☐ 468	Randy Johnson	.30	.14
☐ 469	Erik Hanson	.05	.02
☐ 470	Mike Schooler	.05	.02
☐ 471	Gary Eave	.05	.02
☐ 472	Jeffrey Leonard	.05	.02
☐ 473	Dave Valle	.05	.02
☐ 474	Omar Vizquel	.20	.09
☐ 475	Pete O'Brien	.05	.02
☐ 476	Henry Cotto	.05	.02
☐ 477	Jay Buhner	.20	.09
☐ 478	Harold Reynolds	.05	.02
☐ 479	Alvin Davis	.05	.02
☐ 480	Darnell Coles	.05	.02
☐ 481	Ken Griffey Jr.	3.00	1.35
☐ 482	Greg Briley	.05	.02
☐ 483	Scott Bradley	.05	.02
☐ 484	Tino Martinez	.20	.09
☐ 485	Jeff Russell	.05	.02
☐ 486	Nolan Ryan	.75	.35
☐ 487	Robb Nen	.25	.11
☐ 488	Kevin Brown	.20	.09
☐ 489	Brian Bohanon	.05	.02
☐ 490	Ruben Sierra	.05	.02
☐ 491	Pete Incaviglia	.05	.02
☐ 492	Juan Gonzalez	4.00	1.80
☐ 493	Steve Buechele	.05	.02
☐ 494	Scott Coolbaugh	.05	.02
☐ 495	Geno Petralli	.05	.02
☐ 496	Rafael Palmeiro	.20	.09
☐ 497	Julio Franco	.05	.02
☐ 498	Gary Pettis	.05	.02
☐ 499	Donald Harris	.05	.02
☐ 500	Monty Fariss	.05	.02
☐ 501	Harold Baines	.10	.05
☐ 502	Cecil Espy	.05	.02
☐ 503	Jack Daugherty	.05	.02
☐ 504	Willie Blair	.05	.02
☐ 505	Dave Stieb	.10	.05
☐ 506	Tom Henke	.05	.02
☐ 507	John Cerutti	.05	.02
☐ 508	Paul Kilgus	.05	.02
☐ 509	Jimmy Key	.10	.05
☐ 510	John Olerud	.75	.35
☐ 511	Ed Sprague	.10	.05
☐ 512	Manuel Lee	.05	.02
☐ 513	Fred McGriff	.20	.09
☐ 514	Glenallen Hill	.05	.02
☐ 515	George Bell	.10	.05
☐ 516	Mookie Wilson	.10	.05
☐ 517	Luis Sojo	.05	.02
☐ 518	Nelson Liriano	.05	.02
☐ 519	Kelly Gruber	.05	.02
☐ 520	Greg Myers	.05	.02
☐ 521	Pat Borders	.05	.02
☐ 522	Junior Felix	.05	.02
☐ 523	Eddie Zosky	.05	.02
☐ 524	Tony Fernandez	.05	.02
☐ 525	Checklist 1-132 UER	.05	.02
	(No copyright mark on the back)		

		MINT	NRMT
❑ 526	Checklist 133-264	.05	.02
❑ 527	Checklist 265-396	.05	.02
❑ 528	Checklist 397-528	.05	.02

1990 Bowman Tiffany

	MINT	NRMT
COMP.FACT.SET (539)	1000.00	450.00
COMMON CARD (1-528)	.25	.11

*STARS: 10X TO 20X BASIC CARDS
*ROOKIES: 10X TO 20X BASIC CARDS
DISTRIBUTED ONLY IN FACTORY SET FORM

1991 Bowman

IVAN RODRIGUEZ

	MINT	NRMT
COMPLETE SET (704)	50.00	22.00
COMP.FACT.SET (704)	60.00	27.00
COMMON CARD (1-704)	.05	.02
MINOR STARS	.10	.05
UNLISTED STARS	.20	.09

❑ 1	Rod Carew I	.20	.09
❑ 2	Rod Carew II	.20	.09
❑ 3	Rod Carew III	.20	.09
❑ 4	Rod Carew IV	.20	.09
❑ 5	Rod Carew V	.20	.09
❑ 6	Willie Fraser	.05	.02
❑ 7	John Olerud	.15	.07
❑ 8	William Suero	.05	.02
❑ 9	Roberto Alomar	.20	.09
❑ 10	Todd Stottlemyre	.10	.05
❑ 11	Joe Carter	.10	.05
❑ 12	Steve Karsay	.50	.23
❑ 13	Mark Whiten	.05	.02
❑ 14	Pat Borders	.05	.02
❑ 15	Mike Timlin	.05	.02
❑ 16	Tom Henke	.05	.02
❑ 17	Eddie Zosky	.05	.02
❑ 18	Kelly Gruber	.05	.02
❑ 19	Jimmy Key	.10	.05
❑ 20	Jerry Schunk	.05	.02
❑ 21	Manuel Lee	.05	.02
❑ 22	Dave Stieb	.05	.02
❑ 23	Pat Hentgen	1.00	.45
❑ 24	Glenallen Hill	.05	.02
❑ 25	Rene Gonzales	.05	.02
❑ 26	Ed Sprague	.05	.02
❑ 27	Ken Dayley	.05	.02
❑ 28	Pat Tabler	.05	.02
❑ 29	Denis Boucher	.05	.02
❑ 30	Devon White	.05	.02
❑ 31	Dante Bichette	.20	.09
❑ 32	Paul Molitor	.20	.09
❑ 33	Greg Vaughn	.20	.09
❑ 34	Dan Plesac	.05	.02
❑ 35	Chris George	.05	.02
❑ 36	Tim McIntosh	.05	.02
❑ 37	Franklin Stubbs	.05	.02
❑ 38	Bo Dodson	.05	.02
❑ 39	Ron Robinson	.05	.02
❑ 40	Ed Nunez	.05	.02
❑ 41	Greg Brock	.05	.02
❑ 42	Jaime Navarro	.05	.02
❑ 43	Chris Bosio	.05	.02
❑ 44	B.J. Surhoff	.05	.02
❑ 45	Chris Johnson	.05	.02
❑ 46	Willie Randolph	.10	.05
❑ 47	Narciso Elvira	.05	.02
❑ 48	Jim Gantner	.05	.02
❑ 49	Kevin Brown	.15	.07
❑ 50	Julio Machado	.05	.02
❑ 51	Chuck Crim	.05	.02
❑ 52	Gary Sheffield	.20	.09
❑ 53	Angel Miranda	.05	.02
❑ 54	Ted Higuera	.05	.02
❑ 55	Robin Yount	.20	.09
❑ 56	Cal Eldred	.05	.02
❑ 57	Sandy Alomar Jr.	.10	.05
❑ 58	Greg Swindell	.05	.02
❑ 59	Brook Jacoby	.05	.02
❑ 60	Efrain Valdez	.05	.02
❑ 61	Ever Magallanes	.05	.02
❑ 62	Tom Candiotti	.05	.02
❑ 63	Eric King	.05	.02
❑ 64	Alex Cole	.05	.02
❑ 65	Charles Nagy	.20	.09
❑ 66	Mitch Webster	.05	.02
❑ 67	Chris James	.05	.02
❑ 68	Jim Thome	4.00	1.80
❑ 69	Carlos Baerga	.10	.05
❑ 70	Mark Lewis	.05	.02
❑ 71	Jerry Browne	.05	.02
❑ 72	Jesse Orosco	.05	.02
❑ 73	Mike Huff	.05	.02
❑ 74	Jose Escobar	.05	.02
❑ 75	Jeff Manto	.05	.02
❑ 76	Turner Ward	.05	.02
❑ 77	Doug Jones	.05	.02
❑ 78	Bruce Egloff	.05	.02
❑ 79	Tim Costo	.05	.02
❑ 80	Beau Allred	.05	.02
❑ 81	Albert Belle	.25	.11
❑ 82	John Farrell	.05	.02
❑ 83	Glenn Davis	.05	.02
❑ 84	Joe Orsulak	.05	.02
❑ 85	Mark Williamson	.05	.02
❑ 86	Ben McDonald	.05	.02
❑ 87	Billy Ripken	.05	.02
❑ 88	Leo Gomez UER	.05	.02
	Baltimore is spelled Baltimore		
❑ 89	Bob Melvin	.05	.02
❑ 90	Jeff M. Robinson	.05	.02
❑ 91	Jose Mesa	.05	.02
❑ 92	Gregg Olson	.05	.02
❑ 93	Mike Devereaux	.05	.02
❑ 94	Luis Mercedes	.10	.05
❑ 95	Arthur Rhodes	.10	.05
❑ 96	Juan Bell	.05	.02
❑ 97	Mike Mussina	4.00	1.80
❑ 98	Jeff Ballard	.05	.02
❑ 99	Chris Hoiles	.05	.02
❑ 100	Brady Anderson	.20	.09
❑ 101	Bob Milacki	.05	.02
❑ 102	David Segui	.10	.05
❑ 103	Dwight Evans	.05	.02
❑ 104	Cal Ripken	.75	.35
❑ 105	Mike Linskey	.05	.02
❑ 106	Jeff Tackett	.05	.02
❑ 107	Jeff Reardon	.10	.05
❑ 108	Dana Kiecker	.05	.02
❑ 109	Ellis Burks	.05	.02
❑ 110	Dave Owen	.05	.02
❑ 111	Danny Darwin	.05	.02
❑ 112	Mo Vaughn	.40	.18
❑ 113	Jeff McNeely	.05	.02
❑ 114	Tom Bolton	.05	.02
❑ 115	Greg Blosser	.05	.02
❑ 116	Mike Greenwell	.05	.02
❑ 117	Phil Plantier	.05	.02
❑ 118	Roger Clemens	.50	.23
❑ 119	John Marzano	.05	.02
❑ 120	Jody Reed	.05	.02
❑ 121	Scott Taylor	.05	.02
❑ 122	Jack Clark	.10	.05
❑ 123	Derek Livernois	.05	.02
❑ 124	Tony Pena	.05	.02
❑ 125	Tom Brunansky	.05	.02
❑ 126	Carlos Quintana	.05	.02
❑ 127	Tim Naehring	.05	.02
❑ 128	Matt Young	.05	.02
❑ 129	Wade Boggs	.20	.09
❑ 130	Kevin Morton	.05	.02
❑ 131	Pete Incaviglia	.05	.02
❑ 132	Rob Deer	.05	.02
❑ 133	Bill Gullickson	.05	.02
❑ 134	Rico Brogna	.15	.07
❑ 135	Lloyd Moseby	.05	.02
❑ 136	Cecil Fielder	.10	.05
❑ 137	Tony Phillips	.05	.02
❑ 138	Mark Leiter	.05	.02
❑ 139	John Cerutti	.05	.02
❑ 140	Mickey Tettleton	.10	.05
❑ 141	Milt Cuyler	.05	.02
❑ 142	Greg Gohr	.05	.02
❑ 143	Tony Bernazard	.05	.02
❑ 144	Dan Gakeler	.05	.02
❑ 145	Travis Fryman	.20	.09
❑ 146	Dan Petry	.05	.02
❑ 147	Scott Aldred	.05	.02
❑ 148	John DeSilva	.05	.02
❑ 149	Rusty Meacham	.05	.02
❑ 150	Lou Whitaker	.10	.05
❑ 151	Dave Haas	.05	.02
❑ 152	Luis de los Santos	.05	.02
❑ 153	Ivan Cruz	.05	.02
❑ 154	Alan Trammell	.15	.07
❑ 155	Pat Kelly	.05	.02
❑ 156	Carl Everett	2.00	.90
❑ 157	Greg Cadaret	.05	.02
❑ 158	Kevin Maas	.05	.02
❑ 159	Jeff Johnson	.05	.02
❑ 160	Willie Smith	.05	.02
❑ 161	Gerald Williams	.05	.02
❑ 162	Mike Humphreys	.05	.02
❑ 163	Alvaro Espinoza	.05	.02
❑ 164	Matt Nokes	.05	.02
❑ 165	Wade Taylor	.05	.02
❑ 166	Roberto Kelly	.05	.02
❑ 167	John Habyan	.05	.02
❑ 168	Steve Farr	.05	.02
❑ 169	Jesse Barfield	.05	.02
❑ 170	Steve Sax	.05	.02
❑ 171	Jim Leyritz	.10	.05
❑ 172	Robert Eenhoorn	.05	.02
❑ 173	Bernie Williams	.50	.23
❑ 174	Scott Lusader	.05	.02
❑ 175	Torey Lovullo	.05	.02
❑ 176	Chuck Cary	.05	.02
❑ 177	Scott Sanderson	.05	.02
❑ 178	Don Mattingly	.40	.18
❑ 179	Mel Hall	.05	.02
❑ 180	Juan Gonzalez	.75	.35
❑ 181	Hensley Meulens	.05	.02
❑ 182	Jose Offerman	.15	.07
❑ 183	Jeff Bagwell	8.00	3.60
❑ 184	Jeff Conine	.50	.23
❑ 185	Henry Rodriguez	2.00	.90
❑ 186	Jimmie Reese CO	.10	.05
❑ 187	Kyle Abbott	.05	.02
❑ 188	Lance Parrish	.05	.02
❑ 189	Rafael Montalvo	.05	.02
❑ 190	Floyd Bannister	.05	.02
❑ 191	Dick Schofield	.05	.02
❑ 192	Scott Lewis	.05	.02
❑ 193	Jeff D. Robinson	.05	.02
❑ 194	Kent Anderson	.05	.02
❑ 195	Wally Joyner	.10	.05
❑ 196	Chuck Finley	.10	.05
❑ 197	Luis Sojo	.05	.02
❑ 198	Jeff Richardson	.05	.02
❑ 199	Dave Parker	.10	.05
❑ 200	Jim Abbott	.10	.05

❑ 201	Junior Felix	.05	.02
❑ 202	Mark Langston	.05	.02
❑ 203	Tim Salmon	3.00	1.35
❑ 204	Cliff Young	.05	.02
❑ 205	Scott Bailes	.05	.02
❑ 206	Bobby Rose	.05	.02
❑ 207	Gary Gaetti	.10	.05
❑ 208	Ruben Amaro	.05	.02
❑ 209	Luis Polonia	.05	.02
❑ 210	Dave Winfield	.20	.09
❑ 211	Bryan Harvey	.05	.02
❑ 212	Mike Moore	.05	.02
❑ 213	Rickey Henderson	.25	.11
❑ 214	Steve Chitren	.05	.02
❑ 215	Bob Welch	.05	.02
❑ 216	Terry Steinbach	.10	.05
❑ 217	Earnest Riles	.05	.02
❑ 218	Todd Van Poppel	.05	.02
❑ 219	Mike Gallego	.05	.02
❑ 220	Curt Young	.05	.02
❑ 221	Todd Burns	.05	.02
❑ 222	Vance Law	.05	.02
❑ 223	Eric Show	.05	.02
❑ 224	Don Peters	.05	.02
❑ 225	Dave Stewart	.10	.05
❑ 226	Dave Henderson	.05	.02
❑ 227	Jose Canseco	.25	.11
❑ 228	Walt Weiss	.05	.02
❑ 229	Dann Howitt	.05	.02
❑ 230	Willie Wilson	.05	.02
❑ 231	Harold Baines	.10	.05
❑ 232	Scott Hemond	.05	.02
❑ 233	Joe Slusarski	.05	.02
❑ 234	Mark McGwire	1.00	.45
❑ 235	Kirk Dressendorfer	.05	.02
❑ 236	Craig Paquette	.05	.02
❑ 237	Dennis Eckersley	.10	.05
❑ 238	Dana Allison	.05	.02
❑ 239	Scott Bradley	.05	.02
❑ 240	Brian Holman	.05	.02
❑ 241	Mike Schooler	.05	.02
❑ 242	Rich DeLucia	.05	.02
❑ 243	Edgar Martinez	.20	.09
❑ 244	Henry Cotto	.05	.02
❑ 245	Omar Vizquel	.20	.09
❑ 246	Ken Griffey Jr.	1.50	.70
	(See also 255)		
❑ 247	Jay Buhner	.20	.09
❑ 248	Bill Krueger	.05	.02
❑ 249	Dave Fleming	.05	.02
❑ 250	Patrick Lennon	.05	.02
❑ 251	Dave Valle	.05	.02
❑ 252	Harold Reynolds	.05	.02
❑ 253	Randy Johnson	.25	.11
❑ 254	Scott Bankhead	.05	.02
❑ 255	Ken Griffey Sr. UER	.05	.02
	(Card number is 246)		
❑ 256	Greg Briley	.05	.02
❑ 257	Tino Martinez	.20	.09
❑ 258	Alvin Davis	.05	.02
❑ 259	Pete O'Brien	.05	.02
❑ 260	Erik Hanson	.05	.02
❑ 261	Bret Boone	1.00	.45
❑ 262	Roger Salkeld	.05	.02
❑ 263	Dave Burba	.05	.02
❑ 264	Kerry Woodson	.05	.02
❑ 265	Julio Franco	.05	.02
❑ 266	Dan Peltier	.05	.02
❑ 267	Jeff Russell	.05	.02
❑ 268	Steve Buechele	.05	.02
❑ 269	Donald Harris	.05	.02
❑ 270	Robb Nen	.20	.09
❑ 271	Rich Gossage	.10	.05
❑ 272	Ivan Rodriguez	6.00	2.70
❑ 273	Jeff Huson	.05	.02
❑ 274	Kevin Brown	.15	.07
❑ 275	Dan Smith	.05	.02
❑ 276	Gary Pettis	.05	.02
❑ 277	Jack Daugherty	.05	.02
❑ 278	Mike Jeffcoat	.05	.02
❑ 279	Brad Arnsberg	.05	.02
❑ 280	Nolan Ryan	.75	.35
❑ 281	Eric McCray	.05	.02
❑ 282	Scott Chiamparino	.05	.02
❑ 283	Ruben Sierra	.05	.02
❑ 284	Geno Petralli	.05	.02
❑ 285	Monty Fariss	.05	.02
❑ 286	Rafael Palmeiro	.20	.09
❑ 287	Bobby Witt	.05	.02
❑ 288	Dean Palmer UER	.10	.05
	Photo is Dan Peltier		
❑ 289	Tony Scruggs	.05	.02
❑ 290	Kenny Rogers	.05	.02
❑ 291	Bret Saberhagen	.10	.05
❑ 292	Brian McRae	.10	.05
❑ 293	Storm Davis	.05	.02
❑ 294	Danny Tartabull	.05	.02
❑ 295	David Howard	.05	.02
❑ 296	Mike Boddicker	.05	.02
❑ 297	Joel Johnston	.05	.02
❑ 298	Tim Spehr	.05	.02
❑ 299	Hector Wagner	.05	.02
❑ 300	George Brett	.40	.18
❑ 301	Mike Macfarlane	.05	.02
❑ 302	Kirk Gibson	.10	.05
❑ 303	Harvey Pulliam	.05	.02
❑ 304	Jim Eisenreich	.05	.02
❑ 305	Kevin Seitzer	.05	.02
❑ 306	Mark Davis	.05	.02
❑ 307	Kurt Stillwell	.05	.02
❑ 308	Jeff Montgomery	.10	.05
❑ 309	Kevin Appier	.10	.05
❑ 310	Bob Hamelin	.05	.02
❑ 311	Tom Gordon	.05	.02
❑ 312	Kerwin Moore	.05	.02
❑ 313	Hugh Walker	.05	.02
❑ 314	Terry Shumpert	.05	.02
❑ 315	Warren Cromartie	.05	.02
❑ 316	Gary Thurman	.05	.02
❑ 317	Steve Bedrosian	.05	.02
❑ 318	Danny Gladden	.05	.02
❑ 319	Jack Morris	.10	.05
❑ 320	Kirby Puckett	.30	.14
❑ 321	Kent Hrbek	.10	.05
❑ 322	Kevin Tapani	.05	.02
❑ 323	Denny Neagle	.75	.35
❑ 324	Rich Garces	.05	.02
❑ 325	Larry Casian	.05	.02
❑ 326	Shane Mack	.05	.02
❑ 327	Allan Anderson	.05	.02
❑ 328	Junior Ortiz	.05	.02
❑ 329	Paul Abbott	.05	.02
❑ 330	Chuck Knoblauch	.20	.09
❑ 331	Chili Davis	.10	.05
❑ 332	Todd Ritchie	.05	.02
❑ 333	Brian Harper	.05	.02
❑ 334	Rick Aguilera	.10	.05
❑ 335	Scott Erickson	.15	.07
❑ 336	Pedro Munoz	.05	.02
❑ 337	Scott Leius	.05	.02
❑ 338	Greg Gagne	.05	.02
❑ 339	Mike Pagliarulo	.05	.02
❑ 340	Terry Leach	.05	.02
❑ 341	Willie Banks	.05	.02
❑ 342	Bobby Thigpen	.05	.02
❑ 343	Roberto Hernandez	.20	.09
❑ 344	Melido Perez	.05	.02
❑ 345	Carlton Fisk	.20	.09
❑ 346	Norberto Martin	.05	.02
❑ 347	Johnny Ruffin	.05	.02
❑ 348	Jeff Carter	.05	.02
❑ 349	Lance Johnson	.05	.02
❑ 350	Sammy Sosa	1.25	.55
❑ 351	Alex Fernandez	.10	.05
❑ 352	Jack McDowell	.05	.02
❑ 353	Bob Wickman	.20	.09
❑ 354	Wilson Alvarez	.20	.09
❑ 355	Charlie Hough	.05	.02
❑ 356	Ozzie Guillen	.05	.02
❑ 357	Cory Snyder	.05	.02
❑ 358	Robin Ventura	.20	.09
❑ 359	Scott Fletcher	.05	.02
❑ 360	Cesar Bernhardt	.05	.02
❑ 361	Dan Pasqua	.05	.02
❑ 362	Tim Raines	.10	.05
❑ 363	Brian Drahman	.05	.02
❑ 364	Wayne Edwards	.05	.02
❑ 365	Scott Radinsky	.05	.02
❑ 366	Frank Thomas	.75	.35
❑ 367	Cecil Fielder SLUG	.10	.05
❑ 368	Julio Franco SLUG	.05	.02
❑ 369	Kelly Gruber SLUG	.05	.02
❑ 370	Alan Trammell SLUG	.10	.05
❑ 371	Rickey Henderson SLUG	.10	.05
❑ 372	Jose Canseco SLUG	.10	.05
❑ 373	Ellis Burks SLUG	.05	.02
❑ 374	Lance Parrish SLUG	.05	.02
❑ 375	Dave Parker SLUG	.05	.02
❑ 376	Eddie Murray SLUG	.10	.05
❑ 377	Ryne Sandberg SLUG	.20	.09
❑ 378	Matt Williams SLUG	.05	.02
❑ 379	Barry Larkin SLUG	.10	.05
❑ 380	Barry Bonds SLUG	.20	.09
❑ 381	Bobby Bonilla SLUG	.05	.02
❑ 382	Darryl Strawberry SLUG	.05	.02
❑ 383	Benny Santiago SLUG	.05	.02
❑ 384	Don Robinson SLUG	.05	.02
❑ 385	Paul Coleman	.05	.02
❑ 386	Milt Thompson	.05	.02
❑ 387	Lee Smith	.10	.05
❑ 388	Ray Lankford	.20	.09
❑ 389	Tom Pagnozzi	.05	.02
❑ 390	Ken Hill	.05	.02
❑ 391	Jamie Moyer	.05	.02
❑ 392	Greg Carmona	.05	.02
❑ 393	John Ericks	.05	.02
❑ 394	Bob Tewksbury	.05	.02
❑ 395	Jose Oquendo	.05	.02
❑ 396	Rheal Cormier	.05	.02
❑ 397	Mike Milchin	.05	.02
❑ 398	Ozzie Smith	.25	.11
❑ 399	Aaron Holbert	.05	.02
❑ 400	Jose DeLeon	.05	.02
❑ 401	Felix Jose	.05	.02
❑ 402	Juan Agosto	.05	.02
❑ 403	Pedro Guerrero	.05	.02
❑ 404	Todd Zeile	.10	.05
❑ 405	Gerald Perry	.05	.02
❑ 406	Donovan Osborne UER	.05	.02
	Card number is 410		
❑ 407	Bryn Smith	.05	.02
❑ 408	Bernard Gilkey	.10	.05
❑ 409	Rex Hudler	.05	.02
❑ 410	Thomson/Branca Shot	.20	.09
	Bobby Thomson		
	Ralph Branca		
	(See also 406)		
❑ 411	Lance Dickson	.05	.02
❑ 412	Danny Jackson	.05	.02
❑ 413	Jerome Walton	.05	.02
❑ 414	Sean Cheetham	.05	.02
❑ 415	Joe Girardi	.10	.05
❑ 416	Ryne Sandberg	.25	.11
❑ 417	Mike Harkey	.05	.02
❑ 418	George Bell	.05	.02
❑ 419	Rick Wilkins	.05	.02
❑ 420	Earl Cunningham	.05	.02
❑ 421	Heathcliff Slocumb	.05	.02
❑ 422	Mike Bielecki	.05	.02
❑ 423	Jessie Hollins	.05	.02
❑ 424	Shawon Dunston	.05	.02
❑ 425	Dave Smith	.05	.02
❑ 426	Greg Maddux	.50	.23
❑ 427	Jose Vizcaino	.05	.02
❑ 428	Luis Salazar	.05	.02
❑ 429	Andre Dawson	.20	.09
❑ 430	Rick Sutcliffe	.05	.02
❑ 431	Paul Assenmacher	.05	.02
❑ 432	Erik Pappas	.05	.02
❑ 433	Mark Grace	.20	.09
❑ 434	Dennis Martinez	.10	.05
❑ 435	Marquis Grissom	.20	.09
❑ 436	Wil Cordero	.05	.02
❑ 437	Tim Wallach	.05	.02
❑ 438	Brian Barnes	.05	.02
❑ 439	Barry Jones	.05	.02
❑ 440	Ivan Calderon	.05	.02
❑ 441	Stan Spencer	.05	.02
❑ 442	Larry Walker	.30	.14
❑ 443	Chris Haney	.05	.02
❑ 444	Hector Rivera	.05	.02
❑ 445	Delino DeShields	.10	.05
❑ 446	Andres Galarraga	.20	.09
❑ 447	Gilberto Reyes	.05	.02
❑ 448	Willie Greene	.10	.05
❑ 449	Greg Colbrunn	.05	.02
❑ 450	Rondell White	1.50	.70
❑ 451	Steve Frey	.05	.02

452	Shane Andrews	.05	.02
453	Mike Fitzgerald	.05	.02
454	Spike Owen	.05	.02
455	Dave Martinez	.05	.02
456	Dennis Boyd	.05	.02
457	Eric Bullock	.05	.02
458	Reid Cornelius	.05	.02
459	Chris Nabholz	.05	.02
460	David Cone	.10	.05
461	Hubie Brooks	.05	.02
462	Sid Fernandez	.05	.02
463	Doug Simons	.05	.02
464	Howard Johnson	.05	.02
465	Chris Donnels	.05	.02
466	Anthony Young	.05	.02
467	Todd Hundley	.20	.09
468	Rick Cerone	.05	.02
469	Kevin Elster	.05	.02
470	Wally Whitehurst	.05	.02
471	Vince Coleman	.05	.02
472	Dwight Gooden	.10	.05
473	Charlie O'Brien	.05	.02
474	Jeromy Burnitz	3.00	1.35
475	John Franco	.10	.05
476	Daryl Boston	.05	.02
477	Frank Viola	.05	.02
478	D.J. Dozier	.05	.02
479	Kevin McReynolds	.05	.02
480	Tom Herr	.05	.02
481	Gregg Jefferies	.05	.02
482	Pete Schourek	.10	.05
483	Ron Darling	.05	.02
484	Dave Magadan	.05	.02
485	Andy Ashby	1.00	.45
486	Dale Murphy	.20	.09
487	Von Hayes	.05	.02
488	Kim Batiste	.05	.02
489	Tony Longmire	.05	.02
490	Wally Backman	.05	.02
491	Jeff Jackson	.05	.02
492	Mickey Morandini	.05	.02
493	Darrel Akerfelds	.05	.02
494	Ricky Jordan	.05	.02
495	Randy Ready	.05	.02
496	Darrin Fletcher	.05	.02
497	Chuck Malone	.05	.02
498	Pat Combs	.05	.02
499	Dickie Thon	.05	.02
500	Roger McDowell	.05	.02
501	Len Dykstra	.10	.05
502	Joe Boever	.05	.02
503	John Kruk	.10	.05
504	Terry Mulholland	.05	.02
505	Wes Chamberlain	.05	.02
506	Mike Lieberthal	2.00	.90
507	Darren Daulton	.10	.05
508	Charlie Hayes	.05	.02
509	John Smiley	.05	.02
510	Gary Varsho	.05	.02
511	Curt Wilkerson	.05	.02
512	Orlando Merced	.05	.02
513	Barry Bonds	.25	.11
514	Mike LaValliere	.05	.02
515	Doug Drabek	.05	.02
516	Gary Redus	.05	.02
517	William Pennyfeather	.05	.02
518	Randy Tomlin	.05	.02
519	Mike Zimmerman	.05	.02
520	Jeff King	.05	.02
521	Kurt Miller	.05	.02
522	Jay Bell	.10	.05
523	Bill Landrum	.05	.02
524	Zane Smith	.05	.02
525	Bobby Bonilla	.10	.05
526	Bob Walk	.05	.02
527	Austin Manahan	.05	.02
528	Joe Ausanio	.05	.02
529	Andy Van Slyke	.10	.05
530	Jose Lind	.05	.02
531	Carlos Garcia	.05	.02
532	Don Slaught	.05	.02
533	Gen.Colin Powell	.75	.35
534	Frank Bolick	.05	.02
535	Gary Scott	.05	.02
536	Nikco Riesgo	.05	.02
537	Reggie Sanders	1.00	.45
538	Tim Howard	.05	.02
539	Ryan Bowen	.05	.02
540	Eric Anthony	.05	.02
541	Jim Deshaies	.05	.02
542	Tom Nevers	.05	.02
543	Ken Caminiti	.20	.09
544	Karl Rhodes	.05	.02
545	Xavier Hernandez	.05	.02
546	Mike Scott	.05	.02
547	Jeff Juden	.05	.02
548	Darryl Kile	.20	.09
549	Willie Ansley	.05	.02
550	Luis Gonzalez	2.00	.90
551	Mike Simms	.05	.02
552	Mark Portugal	.05	.02
553	Jimmy Jones	.05	.02
554	Jim Clancy	.05	.02
555	Pete Harnisch	.05	.02
556	Craig Biggio	.20	.09
557	Eric Yelding	.05	.02
558	Dave Rohde	.05	.02
559	Casey Candaele	.05	.02
560	Curt Schilling	.20	.09
561	Steve Finley	.20	.09
562	Javier Ortiz	.05	.02
563	Andujar Cedeno	.05	.02
564	Rafael Ramirez	.05	.02
565	Kenny Lofton	2.50	1.10
566	Steve Avery	.05	.02
567	Lonnie Smith	.05	.02
568	Kent Mercker	.05	.02
569	Chipper Jones	15.00	6.75
570	Terry Pendleton	.10	.05
571	Otis Nixon	.10	.05
572	Juan Berenguer	.05	.02
573	Charlie Leibrandt	.05	.02
574	David Justice	.20	.09
575	Keith Mitchell	.05	.02
576	Tom Glavine	.20	.09
577	Greg Olson	.05	.02
578	Rafael Belliard	.05	.02
579	Ben Rivera	.05	.02
580	John Smoltz	.20	.09
581	Tyler Houston	.05	.02
582	Mark Wohlers	.10	.05
583	Ron Gant	.05	.02
584	Ramon Caraballo	.05	.02
585	Sid Bream	.05	.02
586	Jeff Treadway	.05	.02
587	Javier Lopez	2.00	.90
588	Deion Sanders	.05	.02
589	Mike Heath	.05	.02
590	Ryan Klesko	1.50	.70
591	Bob Ojeda	.05	.02
592	Alfredo Griffin	.05	.02
593	Raul Mondesi	5.00	2.20
594	Greg Smith	.05	.02
595	Orel Hershiser	.10	.05
596	Juan Samuel	.05	.02
597	Brett Butler	.05	.02
598	Gary Carter	.20	.09
599	Stan Javier	.05	.02
600	Kal Daniels	.05	.02
601	Jamie McAndrew	.05	.02
602	Mike Sharperson	.05	.02
603	Jay Howell	.05	.02
604	Eric Karros	2.00	.90
605	Tim Belcher	.05	.02
606	Dan Opperman	.05	.02
607	Lenny Harris	.05	.02
608	Tom Goodwin	.10	.05
609	Darryl Strawberry	.10	.05
610	Ramon Martinez	.10	.05
611	Kevin Gross	.05	.02
612	Zakary Shinall	.05	.02
613	Mike Scioscia	.05	.02
614	Eddie Murray	.20	.09
615	Ronnie Walden	.05	.02
616	Will Clark	.20	.09
617	Adam Hyzdu	.05	.02
618	Matt Williams	.20	.09
619	Don Robinson	.05	.02
620	Jeff Brantley	.05	.02
621	Greg Litton	.05	.02
622	Steve Decker	.05	.02
623	Robby Thompson	.05	.02
624	Mark Leonard	.05	.02
625	Kevin Bass	.05	.02
626	Scott Garrelts	.05	.02
627	Jose Uribe	.05	.02
628	Eric Gunderson	.05	.02
629	Steve Hosey	.05	.02
630	Trevor Wilson	.05	.02
631	Terry Kennedy	.05	.02
632	Dave Righetti	.05	.02
633	Kelly Downs	.05	.02
634	Johnny Ard	.05	.02
635	Eric Christopherson	.05	.02
636	Kevin Mitchell	.05	.02
637	John Burkett	.05	.02
638	Kevin Rogers	.05	.02
639	Bud Black	.05	.02
640	Willie McGee	.10	.05
641	Royce Clayton	.15	.07
642	Tony Fernandez	.05	.02
643	Ricky Bones	.05	.02
644	Thomas Howard	.05	.02
645	Dave Staton	.05	.02
646	Jim Presley	.05	.02
647	Tony Gwynn	.50	.23
648	Marty Barnett	.05	.02
649	Scott Coolbaugh	.05	.02
650	Craig Lefferts	.05	.02
651	Eddie Whitson	.05	.02
652	Oscar Azocar	.05	.02
653	Wes Gardner	.05	.02
654	Bip Roberts	.05	.02
655	Robbie Beckett	.05	.02
656	Benito Santiago	.05	.02
657	Greg W.Harris	.05	.02
658	Jerald Clark	.05	.02
659	Fred McGriff	.20	.09
660	Larry Andersen	.05	.02
661	Bruce Hurst	.05	.02
662	Steve Martin UER	.05	.02

Card said he pitched at Waterloo
He's an outfielder

663	Rafael Valdez	.05	.02
664	Paul Faries	.05	.02
665	Andy Benes	.10	.05
666	Randy Myers	.10	.05
667	Rob Dibble	.05	.02
668	Glenn Sutko	.05	.02
669	Glenn Braggs	.05	.02
670	Billy Hatcher	.05	.02
671	Joe Oliver	.05	.02
672	Freddy Benavides	.05	.02
673	Barry Larkin	.20	.09
674	Chris Sabo	.05	.02
675	Mariano Duncan	.05	.02
676	Chris Jones	.05	.02
677	Gino Minutelli	.05	.02
678	Reggie Jefferson	.15	.07
679	Jack Armstrong	.05	.02
680	Chris Hammond	.05	.02
681	Jose Rijo	.05	.02
682	Bill Doran	.05	.02
683	Terry Lee	.05	.02
684	Tom Browning	.05	.02
685	Paul O'Neill	.10	.05
686	Eric Davis	.05	.02
687	Dan Wilson	.50	.23
688	Ted Power	.05	.02
689	Tim Layana	.05	.02
690	Norm Charlton	.05	.02
691	Hal Morris	.05	.02
692	Rickey Henderson	.20	.09
693	Sam Militello	.05	.02
694	Matt Mieske	.05	.02
695	Paul Russo	.05	.02
696	Domingo Mota	.05	.02
697	Todd Guggiana	.05	.02
698	Marc Newfield	.05	.02
699	Checklist 1-122	.05	.02
700	Checklist 123-244	.05	.02
701	Checklist 245-366	.05	.02
702	Checklist 367-471	.05	.02
703	Checklist 472-593	.05	.02
704	Checklist 594-704	.05	.02

1992 Bowman

	MINT	NRMT
COMPLETE SET (705)	275.00	125.00
COMMON CARD (1-705)	.25	.11
MINOR STARS	.50	.23
SEMISTARS	1.00	.45
UNLISTED STARS	1.50	.70

☐ 1 Ivan Rodriguez	3.00	1.35
☐ 2 Kirk McCaskill	.25	.11
☐ 3 Scott Livingstone	.25	.11
☐ 4 Salomon Torres	.25	.11
☐ 5 Carlos Hernandez	.25	.11
☐ 6 Dave Hollins	.25	.11
☐ 7 Scott Fletcher	.25	.11
☐ 8 Jorge Fabregas	.25	.11
☐ 9 Andujar Cedeno	.25	.11
☐ 10 Howard Johnson	.25	.11
☐ 11 Trevor Hoffman	3.00	1.35
☐ 12 Roberto Kelly	.25	.11
☐ 13 Gregg Jefferies	.25	.11
☐ 14 Marquis Grissom	.50	.23
☐ 15 Mike Ignasiak	.25	.11
☐ 16 Jack Morris	.50	.23
☐ 17 William Pennyfeather	.25	.11
☐ 18 Todd Stottlemyre	.50	.23
☐ 19 Chito Martinez	.25	.11
☐ 20 Roberto Alomar	1.50	.70
☐ 21 Sam Militello	.25	.11
☐ 22 Hector Fajardo	.25	.11
☐ 23 Paul Quantrill	.25	.11
☐ 24 Chuck Knoblauch	1.50	.70
☐ 25 Reggie Jefferson	.50	.23
☐ 26 Jeremy McGarity	.25	.11
☐ 27 Jerome Walton	.25	.11
☐ 28 Chipper Jones	40.00	18.00
☐ 29 Brian Barber	.25	.11
☐ 30 Ron Darling	.25	.11
☐ 31 Roberto Petagine	.25	.11
☐ 32 Chuck Finley	.25	.23
☐ 33 Edgar Martinez	1.00	.45
☐ 34 Napoleon Robinson	.25	.11
☐ 35 Andy Van Slyke	.50	.23
☐ 36 Bobby Thigpen	.25	.11
☐ 37 Travis Fryman	.50	.23
☐ 38 Eric Christopherson	.25	.11
☐ 39 Terry Mulholland	.25	.11
☐ 40 Darryl Strawberry	.50	.23
☐ 41 Manny Alexander	.25	.11
☐ 42 Tracy Sanders	.25	.11
☐ 43 Pete Incaviglia	.25	.11
☐ 44 Kim Batiste	.25	.11
☐ 45 Frank Rodriguez	.50	.23
☐ 46 Greg Swindell	.25	.11
☐ 47 Delino DeShields	.50	.23
☐ 48 John Ericks	.25	.11
☐ 49 Franklin Stubbs	.25	.11
☐ 50 Tony Gwynn	4.00	1.80
☐ 51 Clifton Garrett	.25	.11
☐ 52 Mike Gardella	.25	.11
☐ 53 Scott Erickson	.50	.23
☐ 54 Gary Caraballo	.25	.11
☐ 55 Jose Oliva	.25	.11
☐ 56 Brook Fordyce	.25	.11
☐ 57 Mark Whiten	.25	.11
☐ 58 Joe Slusarski	.25	.11
☐ 59 J.R. Phillips	.25	.11

☐ 60 Barry Bonds	2.00	.90
☐ 61 Bob Milacki	.25	.11
☐ 62 Keith Mitchell	.25	.11
☐ 63 Angel Miranda	.25	.11
☐ 64 Raul Mondesi	10.00	4.50
☐ 65 Brian Koelling	.25	.11
☐ 66 Brian McRae	.25	.11
☐ 67 John Patterson	.25	.11
☐ 68 John Wetteland	.50	.23
☐ 69 Wilson Alvarez	.50	.23
☐ 70 Wade Boggs	1.50	.70
☐ 71 Darryl Ratliff	.25	.11
☐ 72 Jeff Jackson	.25	.11
☐ 73 Jeremy Hernandez	.25	.11
☐ 74 Darryl Hamilton	.25	.11
☐ 75 Rafael Belliard	.25	.11
☐ 76 Rick Trlicek	.25	.11
☐ 77 Felipe Crespo	.25	.11
☐ 78 Carney Lansford	.50	.23
☐ 79 Ryan Long	.25	.11
☐ 80 Kirby Puckett	2.50	1.10
☐ 81 Earl Cunningham	.25	.11
☐ 82 Pedro Martinez	30.00	13.50
☐ 83 Scott Hatteberg	.25	.11
☐ 84 Juan Gonzalez UER	4.00	1.80
(65 doubles vs. Tigers)		
☐ 85 Robert Nutting	.25	.11
☐ 86 Calvin Reese	1.00	.45
☐ 87 Dave Silvestri	.25	.11
☐ 88 Scott Ruffcorn	.25	.11
☐ 89 Rick Aguilera	.50	.23
☐ 90 Cecil Fielder	.50	.23
☐ 91 Kirk Dressendorfer	.25	.11
☐ 92 Jerry DiPoto	.25	.11
☐ 93 Mike Felder	.25	.11
☐ 94 Craig Paquette	.25	.11
☐ 95 Elvin Paulino	.25	.11
☐ 96 Donovan Osborne	.25	.11
☐ 97 Hubie Brooks	.25	.11
☐ 98 Derek Lowe	1.00	.45
☐ 99 David Zancanaro	.25	.11
☐ 100 Ken Griffey Jr.	10.00	4.50
☐ 101 Todd Hundley	.50	.23
☐ 102 Mike Trombley	.25	.11
☐ 103 Ricky Gutierrez	.25	.11
☐ 104 Braulio Castillo	.25	.11
☐ 105 Craig Lefferts	.25	.11
☐ 106 Rick Sutcliffe	.25	.11
☐ 107 Dean Palmer	.50	.23
☐ 108 Henry Rodriguez	1.50	.70
☐ 109 Mark Clark	.25	.11
☐ 110 Kenny Lofton	4.00	1.80
☐ 111 Mark Carreon	.25	.11
☐ 112 J.T. Bruett	.25	.11
☐ 113 Gerald Williams	.25	.11
☐ 114 Frank Thomas	4.00	1.80
☐ 115 Kevin Reimer	.25	.11
☐ 116 Sammy Sosa	5.00	2.20
☐ 117 Mickey Tettleton	.25	.11
☐ 118 Reggie Sanders	.50	.23
☐ 119 Trevor Wilson	.25	.11
☐ 120 Cliff Brantley	.25	.11
☐ 121 Spike Owen	.25	.11
☐ 122 Jeff Montgomery	.50	.23
☐ 123 Alex Sutherland	.25	.11
☐ 124 Brian Taylor	.25	.11
☐ 125 Brian Williams	.25	.11
☐ 126 Kevin Seitzer	.25	.11
☐ 127 Carlos Delgado	20.00	9.00
☐ 128 Gary Scott	.25	.11
☐ 129 Scott Cooper	.25	.11
☐ 130 Domingo Jean	.25	.11
☐ 131 Pat Mahomes	.25	.11
☐ 132 Mike Boddicker	.25	.11
☐ 133 Roberto Hernandez	1.00	.45
☐ 134 Dave Valle	.25	.11
☐ 135 Kurt Stillwell	.25	.11
☐ 136 Brad Pennington	.25	.11
☐ 137 Jermaine Swinton	.25	.11
☐ 138 Ryan Hawblitzel	.25	.11
☐ 139 Tito Navarro	.25	.11
☐ 140 Sandy Alomar Jr.	.50	.23
☐ 141 Todd Benzinger	.25	.11
☐ 142 Danny Jackson	.25	.11
☐ 143 Melvin Nieves	1.50	.70
☐ 144 Jim Campanis	.25	.11

☐ 145 Luis Gonzalez	1.00	.45
☐ 146 Dave Doorneweerd	.25	.11
☐ 147 Charlie Hayes	.25	.11
☐ 148 Greg Maddux	4.00	1.80
☐ 149 Brian Harper	.25	.11
☐ 150 Brent Miller	.25	.11
☐ 151 Shawn Estes	1.50	.70
☐ 152 Mike Williams	.25	.11
☐ 153 Charlie Hough	.50	.23
☐ 154 Randy Myers	.50	.23
☐ 155 Kevin Young	2.00	.90
☐ 156 Rick Wilkins	.25	.11
☐ 157 Terry Shumpert	.25	.11
☐ 158 Steve Karsay	.25	.11
☐ 159 Gary DiSarcina	.25	.11
☐ 160 Deion Sanders	.50	.23
☐ 161 Tom Browning	.25	.11
☐ 162 Dickie Thon	.25	.11
☐ 163 Luis Mercedes	.25	.11
☐ 164 Riccardo Ingram	.25	.11
☐ 165 Tavo Alvarez	.25	.11
☐ 166 Rickey Henderson	2.00	.90
☐ 167 Jaime Navarro	.25	.11
☐ 168 Billy Ashley	.25	.11
☐ 169 Phil Dauphin	.25	.11
☐ 170 Ivan Cruz	.25	.11
☐ 171 Harold Baines	.50	.23
☐ 172 Bryan Harvey	.25	.11
☐ 173 Alex Cole	.25	.11
☐ 174 Curtis Shaw	.25	.11
☐ 175 Matt Williams	1.00	.45
☐ 176 Felix Jose	.25	.11
☐ 177 Sam Horn	.25	.11
☐ 178 Randy Johnson	1.50	.70
☐ 179 Ivan Calderon	.25	.11
☐ 180 Steve Avery	.25	.11
☐ 181 William Suero	.25	.11
☐ 182 Bill Swift	.25	.11
☐ 183 Howard Battle	.25	.11
☐ 184 Ruben Amaro	.25	.11
☐ 185 Jim Abbott	.50	.23
☐ 186 Mike Fitzgerald	.25	.11
☐ 187 Bruce Hurst	.25	.11
☐ 188 Jeff Juden	.25	.11
☐ 189 Jeromy Burnitz	6.00	2.70
☐ 190 Dave Burba	.25	.11
☐ 191 Kevin Brown	1.00	.45
☐ 192 Patrick Lennon	.25	.11
☐ 193 Jeff McNeely	.25	.11
☐ 194 Wil Cordero	.25	.11
☐ 195 Chili Davis	.50	.23
☐ 196 Milt Cuyler	.25	.11
☐ 197 Von Hayes	.25	.11
☐ 198 Todd Revering	.25	.11
☐ 199 Joel Johnston	.25	.11
☐ 200 Jeff Bagwell	3.00	1.35
☐ 201 Alex Fernandez	.50	.23
☐ 202 Todd Jones	1.00	.45
☐ 203 Charles Nagy	.50	.23
☐ 204 Tim Raines	.50	.23
☐ 205 Kevin Maas	.25	.11
☐ 206 Julio Franco	.25	.11
☐ 207 Randy Velarde	.25	.11
☐ 208 Lance Johnson	.25	.11
☐ 209 Scott Leius	.25	.11
☐ 210 Derek Lee	.25	.11
☐ 211 Joe Sondrini	.25	.11
☐ 212 Royce Clayton	.25	.11
☐ 213 Chris George	.25	.11
☐ 214 Gary Sheffield	1.50	.70
☐ 215 Mark Gubicza	.25	.11
☐ 216 Mike Moore	.25	.11
☐ 217 Rick Huisman	.25	.11
☐ 218 Jeff Russell	.25	.11
☐ 219 D.J. Dozier	.25	.11
☐ 220 Dave Martinez	.25	.11
☐ 221 Alan Newman	.25	.11
☐ 222 Nolan Ryan	6.00	2.70
☐ 223 Teddy Higuera	.25	.11
☐ 224 Damon Buford	.25	.11
☐ 225 Ruben Sierra	.25	.11
☐ 226 Tom Nevers	.25	.11
☐ 227 Tommy Greene	.25	.11
☐ 228 Nigel Wilson	.25	.11
☐ 229 John DeSilva	.25	.11
☐ 230 Bobby Witt	.25	.11

No.	Player	Price	Price
❏ 231	Greg Cadaret	.25	.11
❏ 232	John Vander Wal	.25	.11
❏ 233	Jack Clark	.50	.23
❏ 234	Bill Doran	.25	.11
❏ 235	Bobby Bonilla	.50	.23
❏ 236	Steve Olin	.25	.11
❏ 237	Derek Bell	.50	.23
❏ 238	David Cone	.50	.23
❏ 239	Victor Cole	.25	.11
❏ 240	Rod Bolton	.25	.11
❏ 241	Tom Pagnozzi	.25	.11
❏ 242	Rob Dibble	.25	.11
❏ 243	Michael Carter	.25	.11
❏ 244	Don Peters	.25	.11
❏ 245	Mike LaValliere	.25	.11
❏ 246	Joe Perona	.25	.11
❏ 247	Mitch Williams	.25	.11
❏ 248	Jay Buhner	1.00	.45
❏ 249	Andy Benes	.50	.23
❏ 250	Alex Ochoa	1.50	.70
❏ 251	Greg Blosser	.25	.11
❏ 252	Jack Armstrong	.25	.11
❏ 253	Juan Samuel	.25	.11
❏ 254	Terry Pendleton	.25	.11
❏ 255	Ramon Martinez	.25	.11
❏ 256	Rico Brogna	.50	.23
❏ 257	John Smiley	.25	.11
❏ 258	Carl Everett	1.50	.70
❏ 259	Tim Salmon	5.00	2.20
❏ 260	Will Clark	1.50	.70
❏ 261	Ugueth Urbina	1.00	.45
❏ 262	Jason Wood	.25	.11
❏ 263	Dave Magadan	.25	.11
❏ 264	Dante Bichette	1.00	.45
❏ 265	Jose DeLeon	.25	.11
❏ 266	Mike Neill	.25	.11
❏ 267	Paul O'Neill	.50	.23
❏ 268	Anthony Young	.25	.11
❏ 269	Greg W. Harris	.25	.11
❏ 270	Todd Van Poppel	.25	.11
❏ 271	Pedro Castellano	.25	.11
❏ 272	Tony Phillips	.25	.11
❏ 273	Mike Gallego	.25	.11
❏ 274	Steve Cooke	.25	.11
❏ 275	Robin Ventura	.50	.23
❏ 276	Kevin Mitchell	.50	.23
❏ 277	Doug Linton	.25	.11
❏ 278	Robert Eenhoorn	.25	.11
❏ 279	Gabe White	.25	.11
❏ 280	Dave Stewart	.25	.11
❏ 281	Mo Sanford	.25	.11
❏ 282	Greg Perschke	.25	.11
❏ 283	Kevin Flora	.25	.11
❏ 284	Jeff Williams	.25	.11
❏ 285	Keith Miller	.25	.11
❏ 286	Andy Ashby	.50	.23
❏ 287	Doug Dascenzo	.25	.11
❏ 288	Eric Karros	1.50	.70
❏ 289	Glenn Murray	.25	.11
❏ 290	Troy Percival	2.00	.90
❏ 291	Orlando Merced	.25	.11
❏ 292	Peter Hoy	.25	.11
❏ 293	Tony Fernandez	.25	.11
❏ 294	Juan Guzman	.25	.11
❏ 295	Jesse Barfield	.25	.11
❏ 296	Sid Fernandez	.25	.11
❏ 297	Scott Cepicky	.25	.11
❏ 298	Garret Anderson	3.00	1.35
❏ 299	Cal Eldred	.25	.11
❏ 300	Ryne Sandberg	2.00	.90
❏ 301	Jim Gantner	.25	.11
❏ 302	Mariano Rivera	8.00	3.60
❏ 303	Ron Lockett	.25	.11
❏ 304	Jose Offerman	.50	.23
❏ 305	Dennis Martinez	.50	.23
❏ 306	Luis Ortiz	.25	.11
❏ 307	David Howard	.25	.11
❏ 308	Russ Springer	.25	.11
❏ 309	Chris Howard	.25	.11
❏ 310	Kyle Abbott	.25	.11
❏ 311	Aaron Sele	4.00	1.80
❏ 312	David Justice	1.50	.70
❏ 313	Pete O'Brien	.25	.11
❏ 314	Greg Hansell	.25	.11
❏ 315	Dave Winfield	1.50	.70
❏ 316	Lance Dickson	.25	.11
❏ 317	Eric King	.25	.11
❏ 318	Vaughn Eshelman	.25	.11
❏ 319	Tim Belcher	.25	.11
❏ 320	Andres Galarraga	1.50	.70
❏ 321	Scott Bullett	.25	.11
❏ 322	Doug Strange	.25	.11
❏ 323	Jerald Clark	.25	.11
❏ 324	Dave Righetti	.25	.11
❏ 325	Greg Hibbard	.25	.11
❏ 326	Eric Hillman	.25	.11
❏ 327	Shane Reynolds	2.50	1.10
❏ 328	Chris Hammond	.25	.11
❏ 329	Albert Belle	1.50	.70
❏ 330	Rich Becker	.50	.23
❏ 331	Eddie Williams	.25	.11
❏ 332	Donald Harris	.25	.11
❏ 333	Dave Smith	.25	.11
❏ 334	Steve Fireovid	.25	.11
❏ 335	Steve Buechele	.25	.11
❏ 336	Mike Schooler	.25	.11
❏ 337	Kevin McReynolds	.25	.11
❏ 338	Hensley Meulens	.25	.11
❏ 339	Benji Gil	.25	.11
❏ 340	Don Mattingly	3.00	1.35
❏ 341	Alvin Davis	.25	.11
❏ 342	Alan Mills	.25	.11
❏ 343	Kelly Downs	.25	.11
❏ 344	Leo Gomez	.25	.11
❏ 345	Tarrik Brock	.25	.11
❏ 346	Ryan Turner	.25	.11
❏ 347	John Smoltz	1.00	.45
❏ 348	Bill Sampen	.25	.11
❏ 349	Paul Byrd	2.00	.90
❏ 350	Mike Bordick	.25	.11
❏ 351	Jose Lind	.25	.11
❏ 352	David Wells	.50	.23
❏ 353	Barry Larkin	1.00	.45
❏ 354	Bruce Ruffin	.25	.11
❏ 355	Luis Rivera	.25	.11
❏ 356	Sid Bream	.25	.11
❏ 357	Julian Vasquez	.25	.11
❏ 358	Jason Bere	.25	.11
❏ 359	Ben McDonald	.25	.11
❏ 360	Scott Stahoviak	.25	.11
❏ 361	Kirt Manwaring	.25	.11
❏ 362	Jeff Johnson	.25	.11
❏ 363	Rob Deer	.25	.11
❏ 364	Tony Pena	.25	.11
❏ 365	Melido Perez	.25	.11
❏ 366	Clay Parker	.25	.11
❏ 367	Dale Sveum	.25	.11
❏ 368	Mike Scioscia	.25	.11
❏ 369	Roger Salkeld	.25	.11
❏ 370	Mike Stanley	.25	.11
❏ 371	Jack McDowell	.25	.11
❏ 372	Tim Wallach	.25	.11
❏ 373	Billy Ripken	.25	.11
❏ 374	Mike Christopher	.25	.11
❏ 375	Paul Molitor	1.50	.70
❏ 376	Dave Stieb	.25	.11
❏ 377	Pedro Guerrero	.25	.11
❏ 378	Russ Swan	.25	.11
❏ 379	Bob Ojeda	.25	.11
❏ 380	Donn Pall	.25	.11
❏ 381	Eddie Zosky	.25	.11
❏ 382	Darnell Coles	.25	.11
❏ 383	Tom Smith	.25	.11
❏ 384	Mark McGwire	8.00	3.60
❏ 385	Gary Carter	1.50	.70
❏ 386	Rich Amaral	.25	.11
❏ 387	Alan Embree	.25	.11
❏ 388	Jonathan Hurst	.25	.11
❏ 389	Bobby Jones	1.50	.70
❏ 390	Rico Rossy	.25	.11
❏ 391	Dan Smith	.25	.11
❏ 392	Terry Steinbach	.25	.11
❏ 393	Jon Farrell	.25	.11
❏ 394	Dave Anderson	.25	.11
❏ 395	Benny Santiago	.25	.11
❏ 396	Mark Wohlers	.25	.11
❏ 397	Mo Vaughn	2.00	.90
❏ 398	Randy Kramer	.25	.11
❏ 399	John Jaha	2.00	.90
❏ 400	Cal Ripken	6.00	2.70
❏ 401	Ryan Bowen	.25	.11
❏ 402	Tim McIntosh	.25	.11
❏ 403	Bernard Gilkey	.50	.23
❏ 404	Junior Felix	.25	.11
❏ 405	Cris Colon	.25	.11
❏ 406	Marc Newfield	.25	.11
❏ 407	Bernie Williams	1.50	.70
❏ 408	Jay Howell	.25	.11
❏ 409	Zane Smith	.25	.11
❏ 410	Jeff Shaw	.25	.11
❏ 411	Kerry Woodson	.25	.11
❏ 412	Wes Chamberlain	.25	.11
❏ 413	Dave Mlicki	.25	.11
❏ 414	Benny Distefano	.25	.11
❏ 415	Kevin Rogers	.25	.11
❏ 416	Tim Naehring	.25	.11
❏ 417	Clemente Nunez	.50	.23
❏ 418	Luis Sojo	.25	.11
❏ 419	Kevin Ritz	.25	.11
❏ 420	Omar Olivares	.25	.11
❏ 421	Manuel Lee	.25	.11
❏ 422	Julio Valera	.25	.11
❏ 423	Omar Vizquel	.50	.23
❏ 424	Darren Burton	.25	.11
❏ 425	Mel Hall	.25	.11
❏ 426	Dennis Powell	.25	.11
❏ 427	Lee Stevens	.50	.23
❏ 428	Glenn Davis	.25	.11
❏ 429	Willie Greene	.25	.11
❏ 430	Kevin Wickander	.25	.11
❏ 431	Dennis Eckersley	.50	.23
❏ 432	Joe Orsulak	.25	.11
❏ 433	Eddie Murray	1.50	.70
❏ 434	Matt Stairs	4.00	1.80
❏ 435	Wally Joyner	.50	.23
❏ 436	Rondell White	4.00	1.80
❏ 437	Rob Maurer	.25	.11
❏ 438	Joe Redfield	.25	.11
❏ 439	Mark Lewis	.25	.11
❏ 440	Darren Daulton	.50	.23
❏ 441	Mike Henneman	.25	.11
❏ 442	John Cangelosi	.25	.11
❏ 443	Vince Moore	.25	.11
❏ 444	John Wehner	.25	.11
❏ 445	Kent Hrbek	.50	.23
❏ 446	Mark McLemore	.25	.11
❏ 447	Bill Wegman	.25	.11
❏ 448	Robby Thompson	.25	.11
❏ 449	Mark Anthony	.25	.11
❏ 450	Archi Cianfrocco	.25	.11
❏ 451	Johnny Ruffin	.25	.11
❏ 452	Javier Lopez	6.00	2.70
❏ 453	Greg Gohr	.25	.11
❏ 454	Tim Scott	.25	.11
❏ 455	Stan Belinda	.25	.11
❏ 456	Darrin Jackson	.25	.11
❏ 457	Chris Gardner	.25	.11
❏ 458	Esteban Beltre	.25	.11
❏ 459	Phil Plantier	.25	.11
❏ 460	Jim Thome	12.00	5.50
❏ 461	Mike Piazza	60.00	27.00
❏ 462	Matt Sinatro	.25	.11
❏ 463	Scott Servais	.25	.11
❏ 464	Brian Jordan	6.00	2.70
❏ 465	Doug Drabek	.25	.11
❏ 466	Carl Willis	.25	.11
❏ 467	Bret Barberie	.25	.11
❏ 468	Hal Morris	.25	.11
❏ 469	Steve Sax	.25	.11
❏ 470	Jerry Willard	.25	.11
❏ 471	Dan Wilson	.50	.23
❏ 472	Chris Hoiles	.25	.11
❏ 473	Rheal Cormier	.25	.11
❏ 474	John Morris	.25	.11
❏ 475	Jeff Reardon	.50	.23
❏ 476	Mark Leiter	.25	.11
❏ 477	Tom Gordon	.25	.11
❏ 478	Kent Bottenfield	3.00	1.35
❏ 479	Gene Larkin	.25	.11
❏ 480	Dwight Gooden	.50	.23
❏ 481	B.J. Surhoff	.50	.23
❏ 482	Andy Stankiewicz	.25	.11
❏ 483	Tino Martinez	1.50	.70
❏ 484	Craig Biggio	1.50	.70
❏ 485	Denny Neagle	1.00	.45
❏ 486	Rusty Meacham	.25	.11
❏ 487	Kal Daniels	.25	.11
❏ 488	Dave Henderson	.25	.11

❏ 489 Tim Costo	.25	.11
❏ 490 Doug Davis	.25	.11
❏ 491 Frank Viola	.25	.11
❏ 492 Cory Snyder	.25	.11
❏ 493 Chris Martin	.25	.11
❏ 494 Dion James	.25	.11
❏ 495 Randy Tomlin	.25	.11
❏ 496 Greg Vaughn	1.00	.45
❏ 497 Dennis Cook	.25	.11
❏ 498 Rosario Rodriguez	.25	.11
❏ 499 Dave Staton	.25	.11
❏ 500 George Brett	3.00	1.35
❏ 501 Brian Barnes	.25	.11
❏ 502 Butch Henry	.25	.11
❏ 503 Harold Reynolds	.25	.11
❏ 504 David Nied	.25	.11
❏ 505 Lee Smith	.50	.23
❏ 506 Steve Chitren	.25	.11
❏ 507 Ken Hill	.25	.11
❏ 508 Robbie Beckett	.25	.11
❏ 509 Troy Afenir	.25	.11
❏ 510 Kelly Gruber	.25	.11
❏ 511 Bret Boone	2.50	1.10
❏ 512 Jeff Branson	.25	.11
❏ 513 Mike Jackson	.50	.23
❏ 514 Pete Harnisch	.25	.11
❏ 515 Chad Kreuter	.25	.11
❏ 516 Joe Vitko	.25	.11
❏ 517 Orel Hershiser	.50	.23
❏ 518 John Doherty	.25	.11
❏ 519 Jay Bell	.50	.23
❏ 520 Mark Langston	.25	.11
❏ 521 Dann Howitt	.25	.11
❏ 522 Bobby Reed	.25	.11
❏ 523 Bobby Munoz	.25	.11
❏ 524 Todd Ritchie	.25	.11
❏ 525 Bip Roberts	.25	.11
❏ 526 Pat Listach	.25	.11
❏ 527 Scott Brosius	4.00	1.80
❏ 528 John Roper	.25	.11
❏ 529 Phil Hiatt	.25	.11
❏ 530 Denny Walling	.25	.11
❏ 531 Carlos Baerga	.25	.11
❏ 532 Manny Ramirez	50.00	22.00
❏ 533 Pat Clements UER	.25	.11
(Mistakenly numbered 553)		
❏ 534 Ron Gant	.50	.23
❏ 535 Pat Kelly	.25	.11
❏ 536 Bill Spiers	.25	.11
❏ 537 Darren Reed	.25	.11
❏ 538 Ken Caminiti	1.00	.45
❏ 539 Butch Huskey	2.00	.90
❏ 540 Matt Nokes	.25	.11
❏ 541 John Kruk	.50	.23
❏ 542 John Jaha FOIL	1.50	.70
❏ 543 Justin Thompson	1.50	.70
❏ 544 Steve Hosey	.25	.11
❏ 545 Joe Kmak	.25	.11
❏ 546 John Franco	.50	.23
❏ 547 Devon White	.25	.11
❏ 548 Elston Hansen FOIL	.25	.11
❏ 549 Ryan Klesko	5.00	2.20
❏ 550 Danny Tartabull	.25	.11
❏ 551 Frank Thomas FOIL	4.00	1.80
❏ 552 Kevin Tapani	.25	.11
❏ 553 Willie Banks	.25	.11
(See also 533)		
❏ 554 B.J. Wallace FOIL	.50	.23
❏ 555 Orlando Miller	.25	.11
❏ 556 Mark Smith	.25	.11
❏ 557 Tim Wallach FOIL	.25	.11
❏ 558 Bill Gullickson	.25	.11
❏ 559 Derek Bell FOIL	.50	.23
❏ 560 Joe Randa FOIL	2.00	.90
❏ 561 Frank Seminara	.25	.11
❏ 562 Mark Gardner	.25	.11
❏ 563 Rick Greene FOIL	.25	.11
❏ 564 Gary Gaetti	.25	.11
❏ 565 Ozzie Guillen	.25	.11
❏ 566 Charles Nagy FOIL	.50	.23
❏ 567 Mike Milchin	.25	.11
❏ 568 Ben Shelton	.25	.11
❏ 569 Chris Roberts FOIL	.25	.11
❏ 570 Ellis Burks	.50	.23
❏ 571 Scott Scudder	.25	.11
❏ 572 Jim Abbott FOIL	.25	.11

❏ 573 Joe Carter	.50	.23
❏ 574 Steve Finley	.50	.23
❏ 575 Jim Olander FOIL	.25	.11
❏ 576 Carlos Garcia	.25	.11
❏ 577 Gregg Olson	.25	.11
❏ 578 Greg Swindell FOIL	.25	.11
❏ 579 Matt Williams FOIL	1.00	.45
❏ 580 Mark Grace	1.00	.45
❏ 581 Howard House FOIL	.25	.11
❏ 582 Luis Polonia	.25	.11
❏ 583 Erik Hanson	.25	.11
❏ 584 Salomon Torres FOIL	.25	.11
❏ 585 Carlton Fisk	1.50	.70
❏ 586 Bret Saberhagen	.50	.23
❏ 587 Chad McConnell FOIL	.50	.23
❏ 588 Jimmy Key	.50	.23
❏ 589 Mike Macfarlane	.25	.11
❏ 590 Barry Bonds FOIL	2.00	.90
❏ 591 Jamie McAndrew	.25	.11
❏ 592 Shane Mack	.25	.11
❏ 593 Kerwin Moore	.25	.11
❏ 594 Joe Oliver	.25	.11
❏ 595 Chris Sabo	.25	.11
❏ 596 Alex Gonzalez	1.00	.45
❏ 597 Brett Butler	.50	.23
❏ 598 Mark Hutton	.25	.11
❏ 599 Andy Benes FOIL	.50	.23
❏ 600 Jose Canseco	2.00	.90
❏ 601 Darryl Kile	.25	.11
❏ 602 Matt Stairs FOIL	1.00	.45
❏ 603 Robert Butler FOIL	.25	.11
❏ 604 Willie McGee	.50	.23
❏ 605 Jack McDowell FOIL	.25	.11
❏ 606 Tom Candiotti	.25	.11
❏ 607 Ed Martel	.25	.11
❏ 608 Matt Mieske FOIL	.25	.11
❏ 609 Darrin Fletcher	.25	.11
❏ 610 Rafael Palmeiro	1.50	.70
❏ 611 Bill Swift FOIL	.25	.11
❏ 612 Mike Mussina	2.50	1.10
❏ 613 Vince Coleman	.25	.11
❏ 614 Scott Cepicky FOIL UER	.25	.11
(Bats: LEFT)		
❏ 615 Mike Greenwell	.25	.11
❏ 616 Kevin McGehee	.25	.11
❏ 617 Jeffrey Hammonds FOIL	1.50	.70
❏ 618 Scott Taylor	.25	.11
❏ 619 Dave Otto	.25	.11
❏ 620 Mark McGwire FOIL	8.00	3.60
❏ 621 Kevin Tatar	.25	.11
❏ 622 Steve Farr	.25	.11
❏ 623 Ryan Klesko FOIL	1.50	.70
❏ 624 Dave Fleming	.25	.11
❏ 625 Andre Dawson	1.00	.45
❏ 626 Tino Martinez FOIL	1.50	.70
❏ 627 Chad Curtis	1.00	.45
❏ 628 Mickey Morandini	.25	.11
❏ 629 Gregg Olson FOIL	.25	.11
❏ 630 Lou Whitaker	.50	.23
❏ 631 Arthur Rhodes	.25	.11
❏ 632 Brandon Wilson	.25	.11
❏ 633 Lance Jennings	.25	.11
❏ 634 Allen Watson	.25	.11
❏ 635 Len Dykstra	.50	.23
❏ 636 Joe Girardi	.50	.23
❏ 637 Kiki Hernandez FOIL	.25	.11
❏ 638 Mike Hampton	6.00	2.70
❏ 639 Al Osuna	.25	.11
❏ 640 Kevin Appier	.50	.23
❏ 641 Rick Helling FOIL	3.00	1.35
❏ 642 Jody Reed	.25	.11
❏ 643 Ray Lankford	1.50	.70
❏ 644 John Olerud	.50	.23
❏ 645 Paul Molitor FOIL	1.50	.70
❏ 646 Pat Borders	.25	.11
❏ 647 Mike Morgan	.25	.11
❏ 648 Larry Walker	1.50	.70
❏ 649 Pedro Castellano FOIL	.25	.11
❏ 650 Fred McGriff	1.00	.45
❏ 651 Walt Weiss	.25	.11
❏ 652 Calvin Murray FOIL	.25	.11
❏ 653 Dave Nilsson	.50	.23
❏ 654 Greg Pirkl	.25	.11
❏ 655 Robin Ventura FOIL	.50	.23
❏ 656 Mark Portugal	.25	.11
❏ 657 Roger McDowell	.25	.11

❏ 658 Rick Hirtensteiner	.25	.11
❏ 659 Glenallen Hill	.25	.11
❏ 660 Greg Gagne	.25	.11
❏ 661 Charles Johnson FOIL	3.00	1.35
❏ 662 Brian Hunter	.25	.11
❏ 663 Mark Lemke	.25	.11
❏ 664 Tim Belcher FOIL	.25	.11
❏ 665 Rich DeLucia	.25	.11
❏ 666 Bob Walk	.25	.11
❏ 667 Joe Carter FOIL	.50	.23
❏ 668 Jose Guzman	.25	.11
❏ 669 Otis Nixon	.50	.23
❏ 670 Phil Nevin FOIL	1.50	.70
❏ 671 Eric Davis	.50	.23
❏ 672 Damion Easley	1.50	.70
❏ 673 Will Clark FOIL	1.50	.70
❏ 674 Mark Kiefer	.25	.11
❏ 675 Ozzie Smith	2.00	.90
❏ 676 Manny Ramirez FOIL	8.00	3.60
❏ 677 Gregg Olson	.25	.11
❏ 678 Cliff Floyd	4.00	1.80
❏ 679 Duane Singleton	.25	.11
❏ 680 Jose Rijo	.25	.11
❏ 681 Willie Randolph	.50	.23
❏ 682 Michael Tucker FOIL	2.00	.90
❏ 683 Darren Lewis	.25	.11
❏ 684 Dale Murphy	1.50	.70
❏ 685 Mike Pagliarulo	.25	.11
❏ 686 Paul Miller	.25	.11
❏ 687 Mike Bordick	.25	.11
❏ 688 Mike Devereaux	.25	.11
❏ 689 Pedro Astacio	1.00	.45
❏ 690 Alan Trammell	1.00	.45
❏ 691 Roger Clemens	4.00	1.80
❏ 692 Bud Black	.25	.11
❏ 693 Turk Wendell	.50	.23
❏ 694 Barry Larkin FOIL	1.00	.45
❏ 695 Todd Zeile	.25	.11
❏ 696 Pat Hentgen	1.50	.70
❏ 697 Eddie Taubensee	1.00	.45
❏ 698 Guillermo Velasquez	.25	.11
❏ 699 Tom Glavine	1.00	.45
❏ 700 Robin Yount	1.50	.70
❏ 701 Checklist 1-141	.25	.11
❏ 702 Checklist 142-282	.25	.11
❏ 703 Checklist 283-423	.25	.11
❏ 704 Checklist 424-564	.25	.11
❏ 705 Checklist 565-705	.25	.11

1993 Bowman

	MINT	NRMT
COMPLETE SET (708)	75.00	34.00
COMMON CARD (1-708)	.15	.07
MINOR STARS	.30	.14
UNLISTED STARS	.60	.25

❏ 1 Glenn Davis	.15	.07
❏ 2 Hector Roa	.15	.07
❏ 3 Ken Ryan	.15	.07
❏ 4 Derek Wallace	.15	.07
❏ 5 Jorge Fabregas	.15	.07
❏ 6 Joe Oliver	.15	.07
❏ 7 Brandon Wilson	.15	.07
❏ 8 Mark Thompson	.15	.07
❏ 9 Tracy Sanders	.15	.07
❏ 10 Rich Renteria	.15	.07

#	Name			#	Name			#	Name		
11	Lou Whitaker	.30	.14	97	David Cone	.40	.18	183	John Jaha	.15	.07
12	Brian Hunter	1.00	.45	98	Todd Hollandsworth	.60	.25	184	Mike Lansing	.30	.14
13	Joe Vitiello	.15	.07	99	Matt Mieske	.15	.07	185	Pedro Grifol	.15	.07
14	Eric Karros	.40	.18	100	Larry Walker	.60	.25	186	Vince Coleman	.15	.07
15	Joe Kmak	.15	.07	101	Shane Mack	.15	.07	187	Pat Kelly	.15	.07
16	Tavo Alvarez	.15	.07	102	Aaron Ledesma	.15	.07	188	Clemente Alvarez	.15	.07
17	Steve Dunn	.15	.07	103	Andy Pettitte	4.00	1.80	189	Ron Darling	.15	.07
18	Tony Fernandez	.30	.14	104	Kevin Stocker	.15	.07	190	Orlando Merced	.15	.07
19	Melido Perez	.15	.07	105	Mike Mohler	.15	.07	191	Chris Bosio	.15	.07
20	Mike Lieberthal	.30	.14	106	Tony Menendez	.15	.07	192	Steve Dixon	.15	.07
21	Terry Steinbach	.15	.07	107	Derek Lowe	.40	.18	193	Doug Dascenzo	.15	.07
22	Stan Belinda	.15	.07	108	Basil Shabazz	.15	.07	194	Ray Holbert	.15	.07
23	Jay Buhner	.40	.18	109	Dan Smith	.15	.07	195	Howard Battle	.15	.07
24	Allen Watson	.15	.07	110	Scott Sanders	.15	.07	196	Willie McGee	.30	.14
25	Daryl Henderson	.15	.07	111	Todd Stottlemyre	.15	.07	197	John O'Donoghue	.15	.07
26	Ray McDavid	.15	.07	112	Benji Simonton	.15	.07	198	Steve Avery	.15	.07
27	Shawn Green	2.50	1.10	113	Rick Sutcliffe	.15	.07	199	Greg Blosser	.15	.07
28	Bud Black	.15	.07	114	Lee Heath	.15	.07	200	Ryne Sandberg	.75	.35
29	Sherman Obando	.15	.07	115	Jeff Russell	.15	.07	201	Joe Grahe	.15	.07
30	Mike Hostetler	.15	.07	116	Dave Stevens	.15	.07	202	Dan Wilson	.30	.14
31	Nate Minchey	.15	.07	117	Mark Holzemer	.15	.07	203	Domingo Martinez	.15	.07
32	Randy Myers	.30	.14	118	Tim Belcher	.15	.07	204	Andres Galarraga	.60	.25
33	Brian Grebeck	.15	.07	119	Bobby Thigpen	.15	.07	205	Jamie Taylor	.15	.07
34	John Roper	.15	.07	120	Roger Bailey	.15	.07	206	Darrell Whitmore	.15	.07
35	Larry Thomas	.15	.07	121	Tony Mitchell	.15	.07	207	Ben Blomdahl	.15	.07
36	Alex Cole	.15	.07	122	Junior Felix	.15	.07	208	Doug Drabek	.15	.07
37	Tom Kramer	.15	.07	123	Rich Robertson	.15	.07	209	Keith Miller	.15	.07
38	Matt Whisenant	.15	.07	124	Andy Cook	.15	.07	210	Billy Ashley	.15	.07
39	Chris Gomez	.30	.14	125	Brian Bevil	.15	.07	211	Mike Farrell	.15	.07
40	Luis Gonzalez	.30	.14	126	Darryl Strawberry	.30	.14	212	John Wetteland	.30	.14
41	Kevin Appier	.30	.14	127	Cal Eldred	.30	.14	213	Randy Tomlin	.15	.07
42	Omar Daal	2.00	.90	128	Cliff Floyd	.30	.14	214	Sid Fernandez	.15	.07
43	Duane Singleton	.15	.07	129	Alan Newman	.15	.07	215	Quilvio Veras	1.00	.45
44	Bill Risley	.15	.07	130	Howard Johnson	.15	.07	216	Dave Hollins	.15	.07
45	Pat Meares	.15	.07	131	Jim Abbott	.30	.14	217	Mike Neill	.15	.07
46	Butch Huskey	.40	.18	132	Chad McConnell	.15	.07	218	Andy Van Slyke	.30	.14
47	Bobby Munoz	.15	.07	133	Miguel Jimenez	.15	.07	219	Bret Boone	.30	.14
48	Juan Bell	.15	.07	134	Brett Backlund	.15	.07	220	Tom Pagnozzi	.15	.07
49	Scott Lydy	.15	.07	135	John Cummings	.15	.07	221	Mike Welch	.15	.07
50	Dennis Moeller	.15	.07	136	Brian Barber	.15	.07	222	Frank Seminara	.15	.07
51	Marc Newfield	.15	.07	137	Rafael Palmeiro	.60	.25	223	Ron Villone	.15	.07
52	Tripp Cromer	.15	.07	138	Tim Worrell	.15	.07	224	D.J. Thielen	.15	.07
53	Kurt Miller	.15	.07	139	Jose Pett	.30	.14	225	Cal Ripken	2.50	1.10
54	Jim Pena	.15	.07	140	Barry Bonds	.60	.25	226	Pedro Borbon Jr.	.15	.07
55	Juan Guzman	.15	.07	141	Damon Buford	.15	.07	227	Carlos Quintana	.15	.07
56	Matt Williams	.40	.18	142	Jeff Blauser	.15	.07	228	Tommy Shields	.15	.07
57	Harold Reynolds	.15	.07	143	Frankie Rodriguez	.15	.07	229	Tim Salmon	.60	.25
58	Donnie Elliott	.15	.07	144	Mike Morgan	.15	.07	230	John Smiley	.15	.07
59	Jon Shave	.15	.07	145	Gary DiSarcina	.15	.07	231	Ellis Burks	.30	.14
60	Kevin Roberson	.15	.07	146	Calvin Reese	.30	.14	232	Pedro Castellano	.15	.07
61	Hilly Hathaway	.15	.07	147	Johnny Ruffin	.15	.07	233	Paul Byrd	.15	.07
62	Jose Rijo	.15	.07	148	David Nied	.15	.07	234	Bryan Harvey	.15	.07
63	Kerry Taylor	.15	.07	149	Charles Nagy	.30	.14	235	Scott Livingstone	.15	.07
64	Ryan Hawblitzel	.15	.07	150	Mike Myers	.15	.07	236	James Mouton	.15	.07
65	Glenallen Hill	.15	.07	151	Kenny Carlyle	.15	.07	237	Joe Randa	.15	.07
66	Ramon Martinez	.30	.14	152	Eric Anthony	.15	.07	238	Pedro Astacio	.30	.14
67	Travis Fryman	.30	.14	153	Jose Lind	.15	.07	239	Darryl Hamilton	.15	.07
68	Tom Nevers	.15	.07	154	Pedro Martinez	1.25	.55	240	Joey Eischen	.15	.07
69	Phil Hiatt	.15	.07	155	Mark Kiefer	.15	.07	241	Edgar Herrera	.15	.07
70	Tim Wallach	.15	.07	156	Tim Laker	.15	.07	242	Dwight Gooden	.30	.14
71	B.J. Surhoff	.30	.14	157	Pat Mahomes	.15	.07	243	Sam Militello	.15	.07
72	Rondell White	.40	.18	158	Bobby Bonilla	.30	.14	244	Ron Blazier	.15	.07
73	Denny Hocking	.15	.07	159	Domingo Jean	.15	.07	245	Ruben Sierra	.15	.07
74	Mike Oquist	.15	.07	160	Darren Daulton	.30	.14	246	Al Martin	.15	.07
75	Paul O'Neill	.30	.14	161	Mark McGwire	3.00	1.35	247	Mike Felder	.15	.07
76	Willie Banks	.15	.07	162	Jason Kendall	4.00	1.80	248	Bob Tewksbury	.15	.07
77	Bob Welch	.15	.07	163	Desi Relaford	.30	.14	249	Craig Lefferts	.15	.07
78	Jose Sandoval	.15	.07	164	Ozzie Canseco	.15	.07	250	Luis Lopez	.15	.07
79	Bill Haselman	.15	.07	165	Rick Helling	.40	.18	251	Devon White	.15	.07
80	Rheal Cormier	.15	.07	166	Steve Pegues	.15	.07	252	Will Clark	.60	.25
81	Dean Palmer	.30	.14	167	Paul Molitor	.60	.25	253	Mark Smith	.15	.07
82	Pat Gomez	.15	.07	168	Larry Carter	.15	.07	254	Terry Pendleton	.15	.07
83	Steve Karsay	.30	.14	169	Arthur Rhodes	.15	.07	255	Aaron Sele	.60	.25
84	Carl Hanselman	.15	.07	170	Damon Hollins	.15	.07	256	Jose Viera	.15	.07
85	T.R. Lewis	.15	.07	171	Frank Viola	.15	.07	257	Damion Easley	.30	.14
86	Chipper Jones	2.00	.90	172	Steve Trachsel	.30	.14	258	Rod Lofton	.15	.07
87	Scott Hatteberg	.15	.07	173	J.T. Snow	1.50	.70	259	Chris Snopek	.30	.14
88	Greg Hibbard	.15	.07	174	Keith Gordon	.15	.07	260	Quinton McCracken	.75	.35
89	Lance Painter	.15	.07	175	Carlton Fisk	.60	.25	261	Mike Matthews	.15	.07
90	Chad Mottola	.15	.07	176	Jason Bates	.15	.07	262	Hector Carrasco	.15	.07
91	Jason Bere	.15	.07	177	Mike Crosby	.15	.07	263	Rick Greene	.15	.07
92	Dante Bichette	.30	.14	178	Benny Santiago	.15	.07	264	Chris Holt	.15	.07
93	Sandy Alomar Jr.	.30	.14	179	Mike Moore	.15	.07	265	George Brett	1.25	.55
94	Carl Everett	.40	.18	180	Jeff Juden	.15	.07	266	Rick Gorecki	.15	.07
95	Danny Bautista	.15	.07	181	Darren Burton	.15	.07	267	Francisco Gamez	.15	.07
96	Steve Finley	.30	.14	182	Todd Williams	.15	.07	268	Marquis Grissom	.30	.14

269	Kevin Tapani UER (Misspelled Tapan on card front)	.15	.07
270	Ryan Thompson	.15	.07
271	Gerald Williams	.15	.07
272	Paul Fletcher	.15	.07
273	Lance Blankenship	.15	.07
274	Marty Neff	.15	.07
275	Shawn Estes	.60	.25
276	Rene Arocha	.15	.07
277	Scott Eyre	.15	.07
278	Phil Plantier	.15	.07
279	Paul Spoljaric	.15	.07
280	Chris Gambs	.15	.07
281	Harold Baines	.30	.14
282	Jose Oliva	.15	.07
283	Matt Whiteside	.15	.07
284	Brant Brown	1.00	.45
285	Russ Springer	.15	.07
286	Chris Sabo	.15	.07
287	Ozzie Guillen	.15	.07
288	Marcus Moore	.15	.07
289	Chad Ogea	.30	.14
290	Walt Weiss	.15	.07
291	Brian Edmondson	.15	.07
292	Jimmy Gonzalez	.15	.07
293	Danny Miceli	.15	.07
294	Jose Offerman	.30	.14
295	Greg Vaughn	.30	.14
296	Frank Bolick	.15	.07
297	Mike Maksudian	.15	.07
298	John Franco	.15	.07
299	Danny Tartabull	.30	.14
300	Len Dykstra	.30	.14
301	Bobby Witt	.15	.07
302	Trey Beamon	.50	.23
303	Tino Martinez	.25	
304	Aaron Holbert	.15	.07
305	Juan Gonzalez	1.25	.55
306	Billy Hall	.15	.07
307	Duane Ward	.15	.07
308	Rod Beck	.30	.14
309	Jose Mercedes	.15	.07
310	Otis Nixon	.15	.07
311	Gettys Glaze	.15	.07
312	Candy Maldonado	.15	.07
313	Chad Curtis	.30	.14
314	Tim Costo	.15	.07
315	Mike Robertson	.15	.07
316	Nigel Wilson	.15	.07
317	Greg McMichael	.15	.07
318	Scott Pose	.15	.07
319	Ivan Cruz	.15	.07
320	Greg Swindell	.15	.07
321	Kevin McReynolds	.15	.07
322	Tom Candiotti	.15	.07
323	Rob Wishnevski	.15	.07
324	Ken Hill	.15	.07
325	Kirby Puckett	1.00	.45
326	Tim Bogar	.15	.07
327	Mariano Rivera	.75	.35
328	Mitch Williams	.15	.07
329	Craig Paquette	.15	.07
330	Jay Bell	.30	.14
331	Jose Martinez	.15	.07
332	Rob Deer	.15	.07
333	Brook Fordyce	.15	.07
334	Matt Nokes	.15	.07
335	Derek Lee	.15	.07
336	Paul Ellis	.15	.07
337	Desi Wilson	.15	.07
338	Roberto Alomar	.60	.25
339	Jim Tatum FOIL	.15	.07
340	J.T. Snow FOIL	.60	.25
341	Tim Salmon FOIL	.60	.25
342	Russ Davis FOIL	1.00	.45
343	Javier Lopez FOIL	.25	.25
344	Troy O'Leary FOIL	2.00	.90
345	Marty Cordova FOIL	1.00	.45
346	Bubba Smith FOIL	.15	.07
347	Chipper Jones FOIL	2.00	.90
348	Jessie Hollins FOIL	.15	.07
349	Willie Greene FOIL	.15	.07
350	Mark Thompson FOIL	.15	.07
351	Nigel Wilson FOIL	.15	.07
352	Todd Jones FOIL	.30	.14
353	Raul Mondesi FOIL	.60	.25
354	Cliff Floyd FOIL	.30	.14
355	Bobby Jones FOIL	.30	.14
356	Kevin Stocker FOIL	.15	.07
357	Midre Cummings FOIL	.15	.07
358	Allen Watson FOIL	.15	.07
359	Ray McDavid FOIL	.15	.07
360	Steve Hosey FOIL	.15	.07
361	Brad Pennington FOIL	.15	.07
362	Frankie Rodriguez FOIL	.15	.07
363	Troy Percival FOIL	.40	.18
364	Jason Bere FOIL	.15	.07
365	Manny Ramirez FOIL	2.00	.90
366	Justin Thompson FOIL	.40	.18
367	Joe Vitiello FOIL	.15	.07
368	Tyrone Hill FOIL	.15	.07
369	David McCarty FOIL	.15	.07
370	Brien Taylor FOIL	.15	.07
371	Todd Van Poppel FOIL	.15	.07
372	Marc Newfield FOIL	.15	.07
373	Terrell Lowery FOIL	.15	.07
374	Alex Gonzalez FOIL	.30	.14
375	Ken Griffey Jr.	3.00	1.35
376	Donovan Osborne	.15	.07
377	Ritchie Moody	.15	.07
378	Shane Andrews	.15	.07
379	Carlos Delgado	.60	.25
380	Bill Swift	.15	.07
381	Leo Gomez	.15	.07
382	Ron Gant	.30	.14
383	Scott Fletcher	.15	.07
384	Matt Walbeck	.15	.07
385	Chuck Finley	.30	.14
386	Kevin Mitchell	.30	.14
387	Wilson Alvarez UER (Misspelled Alverez on card front)	.30	.14
388	John Burke	.15	.07
389	Alan Embree	.15	.07
390	Trevor Hoffman	.60	.25
391	Alan Trammell	.40	.18
392	Todd Jones	.30	.14
393	Felix Jose	.15	.07
394	Orel Hershiser	.30	.14
395	Pat Listach	.15	.07
396	Gabe White	.15	.07
397	Dan Serafini	.15	.07
398	Todd Hundley	.40	.18
399	Wade Boggs	.60	.25
400	Tyler Green	.15	.07
401	Mike Bordick	.15	.07
402	Scott Bullett	.15	.07
403	LaGrande Russell	.15	.07
404	Ray Lankford	.40	.18
405	Nolan Ryan	2.50	1.10
406	Robbie Beckett	.15	.07
407	Brent Bowers	.15	.07
408	Adell Davenport	.15	.07
409	Brady Anderson	.30	.14
410	Tom Glavine	.40	.18
411	Doug Hecker	.15	.07
412	Jose Guzman	.15	.07
413	Luis Polonia	.15	.07
414	Brian Williams	.15	.07
415	Bo Jackson	.30	.14
416	Eric Young	.60	.25
417	Kenny Lofton	.60	.25
418	Orestes Destrade	.15	.07
419	Tony Phillips	.15	.07
420	Jeff Bagwell	.75	.35
421	Mark Gardner	.15	.07
422	Brett Butler	.30	.14
423	Graeme Lloyd	.15	.07
424	Delino DeShields	.30	.14
425	Scott Erickson	.15	.07
426	Jeff Kent	.30	.14
427	Jimmy Key	.30	.14
428	Mickey Morandini	.15	.07
429	Marcos Armas	.15	.07
430	Don Slaught	.15	.07
431	Randy Johnson	.60	.25
432	Omar Olivares	.15	.07
433	Charlie Leibrandt	.15	.07
434	Kurt Stillwell	.15	.07
435	Scott Brow	.15	.07
436	Robby Thompson	.15	.07
437	Ben McDonald	.15	.07
438	Deion Sanders	.40	.18
439	Tony Pena	.15	.07
440	Mark Grace	.40	.18
441	Eduardo Perez	.15	.07
442	Tim Pugh	.15	.07
443	Scott Ruffcorn	.15	.07
444	Jay Gainer	.15	.07
445	Albert Belle	.60	.25
446	Brett Barberie	.15	.07
447	Justin Mashore	.15	.07
448	Pete Harnisch	.15	.07
449	Greg Gagne	.15	.07
450	Eric Davis	.30	.14
451	Dave Mlicki	.15	.07
452	Moises Alou	.30	.14
453	Rick Aguilera	.15	.07
454	Eddie Murray	.60	.25
455	Bob Wickman	.15	.07
456	Wes Chamberlain	.15	.07
457	Brent Gates	.15	.07
458	Paul Wagner	.15	.07
459	Mike Hampton	.60	.25
460	Ozzie Smith	.75	.35
461	Tom Henke	.15	.07
462	Ricky Gutierrez	.15	.07
463	Jack Morris	.30	.14
464	Joel Chimelis	.15	.07
465	Gregg Olson	.15	.07
466	Javier Lopez	.60	.25
467	Scott Cooper	.15	.07
468	Willie Wilson	.15	.07
469	Mark Langston	.15	.07
470	Barry Larkin	.60	.25
471	Rod Bolton	.15	.07
472	Freddie Benavides	.15	.07
473	Ken Ramos	.15	.07
474	Chuck Carr	.15	.07
475	Cecil Fielder	.30	.14
476	Eddie Taubensee	.15	.07
477	Chris Eddy	.15	.07
478	Greg Hansell	.15	.07
479	Kevin Reimer	.15	.07
480	Dennis Martinez	.30	.14
481	Chuck Knoblauch	.60	.25
482	Mike Draper	.15	.07
483	Spike Owen	.15	.07
484	Terry Mulholland	.15	.07
485	Dennis Eckersley	.30	.14
486	Blas Minor	.15	.07
487	Dave Fleming	.15	.07
488	Dan Cholowsky	.15	.07
489	Ivan Rodriguez	.75	.35
490	Gary Sheffield	.60	.25
491	Ed Sprague	.15	.07
492	Steve Hosey	.15	.07
493	Jimmy Haynes	.75	.35
494	John Smoltz	.40	.18
495	Andre Dawson	.40	.18
496	Rey Sanchez	.15	.07
497	Ty Van Burkleo	.15	.07
498	Bobby Ayala	.15	.07
499	Tim Raines	.30	.14
500	Charlie Hayes	.15	.07
501	Paul Sorrento	.15	.07
502	Richie Lewis	.15	.07
503	Jason Pfaff	.15	.07
504	Ken Caminiti	.40	.18
505	Mike Macfarlane	.15	.07
506	Jody Reed	.15	.07
507	Bobby Hughes	.15	.07
508	Wil Cordero	.15	.07
509	George Tsamis	.15	.07
510	Bret Saberhagen	.30	.14
511	Derek Jeter	25.00	11.00
512	Gene Schall	.15	.07
513	Curtis Shaw	.15	.07
514	Steve Cooke	.15	.07
515	Edgar Martinez	.40	.18
516	Mike Milchin	.15	.07
517	Billy Ripken	.15	.07
518	Andy Benes	.30	.14
519	Juan de la Rosa	.15	.07
520	John Burkett	.15	.07
521	Alex Ochoa	.15	.07
522	Tony Tarasco	.15	.07

☐ 523	Luis Ortiz	.15	.07
☐ 524	Rick Wilkins	.15	.07
☐ 525	Chris Turner	.15	.07
☐ 526	Rob Dibble	.15	.07
☐ 527	Jack McDowell	.15	.07
☐ 528	Daryl Boston	.15	.07
☐ 529	Bill Wertz	.15	.07
☐ 530	Charlie Hough	.15	.07
☐ 531	Sean Bergman	.15	.07
☐ 532	Doug Jones	.15	.07
☐ 533	Jeff Montgomery	.30	.14
☐ 534	Roger Cedeno	2.50	1.10
☐ 535	Robin Yount	.40	.18
☐ 536	Mo Vaughn	.60	.25
☐ 537	Brian Harper	.15	.07
☐ 538	Juan Castillo	.15	.07
☐ 539	Steve Farr	.15	.07
☐ 540	John Kruk	.30	.14
☐ 541	Troy Neel	.15	.07
☐ 542	Danny Clyburn	.15	.07
☐ 543	Jim Converse	.15	.07
☐ 544	Gregg Williams	.15	.07
☐ 545	Jose Canseco	.75	.35
☐ 546	Julio Bruno	.15	.07
☐ 547	Rob Butler	.15	.07
☐ 548	Royce Clayton	.15	.07
☐ 549	Chris Hoiles	.15	.07
☐ 550	Greg Maddux	1.50	.70
☐ 551	Joe Ciccarella	.30	.14
☐ 552	Ozzie Timmons	.30	.14
☐ 553	Chili Davis	.30	.14
☐ 554	Brian Koelling	.15	.07
☐ 555	Frank Thomas	1.25	.55
☐ 556	Vinny Castilla	2.00	.90
☐ 557	Reggie Jefferson	.30	.14
☐ 558	Rob Natal	.15	.07
☐ 559	Mike Henneman	.15	.07
☐ 560	Craig Biggio	.60	.25
☐ 561	Billy Brewer	.15	.07
☐ 562	Dan Melendez	.15	.07
☐ 563	Kenny Felder	.15	.07
☐ 564	Miguel Batista	.15	.07
☐ 565	Dave Winfield	.40	.18
☐ 566	Al Shirley	.15	.07
☐ 567	Robert Eenhoorn	.15	.07
☐ 568	Mike Williams	.15	.07
☐ 569	Tanyon Sturtze	.15	.07
☐ 570	Tim Wakefield	.30	.14
☐ 571	Greg Pirkl	.15	.07
☐ 572	Sean Lowe	.15	.07
☐ 573	Terry Burrows	.15	.07
☐ 574	Kevin Higgins	.15	.07
☐ 575	Joe Carter	.30	.14
☐ 576	Kevin Rogers	.15	.07
☐ 577	Manny Alexander	.15	.07
☐ 578	David Justice	.60	.25
☐ 579	Brian Conroy	.15	.07
☐ 580	Jessie Hollins	.15	.07
☐ 581	Ron Watson	.15	.07
☐ 582	Bip Roberts	.15	.07
☐ 583	Tom Urbani	.15	.07
☐ 584	Jason Hutchins	.15	.07
☐ 585	Carlos Baerga	.15	.07
☐ 586	Jeff Mutis	.15	.07
☐ 587	Justin Thompson	.40	.18
☐ 588	Orlando Miller	.15	.07
☐ 589	Brian McRae	.15	.07
☐ 590	Ramon Martinez	.30	.14
☐ 591	Dave Nilsson	.30	.14
☐ 592	Jose Vidro	1.00	.45
☐ 593	Rich Becker	.30	.14
☐ 594	Preston Wilson	2.50	1.10
☐ 595	Don Mattingly	1.25	.55
☐ 596	Tony Longmire	.15	.07
☐ 597	Kevin Seitzer	.15	.07
☐ 598	Midre Cummings	.15	.07
☐ 599	Omar Vizquel	.30	.14
☐ 600	Lee Smith	.30	.14
☐ 601	David Hulse	.15	.07
☐ 602	Darrell Sherman	.15	.07
☐ 603	Alex Gonzalez	.30	.14
☐ 604	Geronimo Pena	.15	.07
☐ 605	Mike Devereaux	.15	.07
☐ 606	Sterling Hitchcock	.75	.35
☐ 607	Mike Greenwell	.15	.07
☐ 608	Steve Buechele	.15	.07
☐ 609	Troy Percival	.40	.18
☐ 610	Roberto Kelly	.15	.07
☐ 611	James Baldwin	.75	.35
☐ 612	Jerald Clark	.15	.07
☐ 613	Albie Lopez	.15	.07
☐ 614	Dave Magadan	.15	.07
☐ 615	Mickey Tettleton	.15	.07
☐ 616	Sean Runyan	.15	.07
☐ 617	Bob Hamelin	.15	.07
☐ 618	Raul Mondesi	.60	.25
☐ 619	Tyrone Hill	.15	.07
☐ 620	Darrin Fletcher	.15	.07
☐ 621	Mike Trombley	.15	.07
☐ 622	Jeromy Burnitz	.30	.14
☐ 623	Bernie Williams	.60	.25
☐ 624	Mike Farmer	.15	.07
☐ 625	Rickey Henderson	.75	.35
☐ 626	Carlos Garcia	.15	.07
☐ 627	Jeff Darwin	.15	.07
☐ 628	Todd Zeile	.15	.07
☐ 629	Benji Gil	.15	.07
☐ 630	Tony Gwynn	1.50	.70
☐ 631	Aaron Small	.15	.07
☐ 632	Joe Rosselli	.15	.07
☐ 633	Mike Mussina	.60	.25
☐ 634	Ryan Klesko	.60	.25
☐ 635	Roger Clemens	1.50	.70
☐ 636	Sammy Sosa	2.00	.90
☐ 637	Orlando Palmeiro	.15	.07
☐ 638	Willie Greene	.15	.07
☐ 639	George Bell	.15	.07
☐ 640	Garvin Alston	.15	.07
☐ 641	Pete Janicki	.15	.07
☐ 642	Chris Sheff	.15	.07
☐ 643	Felipe Lira	.15	.14
☐ 644	Roberto Petagine	.15	.07
☐ 645	Wally Joyner	.15	.07
☐ 646	Mike Piazza	3.00	1.35
☐ 647	Jaime Navarro	.15	.07
☐ 648	Jeff Hartsock	.15	.07
☐ 649	David McCarty	.15	.07
☐ 650	Bobby Jones	.30	.14
☐ 651	Mark Hutton	.15	.07
☐ 652	Kyle Abbott	.15	.07
☐ 653	Steve Cox	.50	.23
☐ 654	Jeff King	.15	.07
☐ 655	Norm Charlton	.15	.07
☐ 656	Mike Gulan	.15	.07
☐ 657	Julio Franco	.15	.07
☐ 658	Cameron Cairncross	.15	.07
☐ 659	John Olerud	.40	.18
☐ 660	Salomon Torres	.15	.07
☐ 661	Brad Pennington	.15	.07
☐ 662	Melvin Nieves	.15	.07
☐ 663	Ivan Calderon	.15	.07
☐ 664	Turk Wendell	.15	.07
☐ 665	Chris Pritchett	.15	.07
☐ 666	Reggie Sanders	.30	.14
☐ 667	Robin Ventura	.30	.14
☐ 668	Joe Girardi	.15	.07
☐ 669	Manny Ramirez	2.00	.90
☐ 670	Jeff Conine	.15	.07
☐ 671	Greg Gohr	.15	.07
☐ 672	Andujar Cedeno	.15	.07
☐ 673	Les Norman	.15	.07
☐ 674	Mike James	.15	.07
☐ 675	Marshall Boze	.15	.07
☐ 676	B.J. Wallace	.15	.07
☐ 677	Kent Hrbek	.30	.14
☐ 678	Jack Voigt	.15	.07
☐ 679	Brien Taylor	.30	.14
☐ 680	Curt Schilling	.15	.07
☐ 681	Todd Van Poppel	.30	.14
☐ 682	Kevin Young	.30	.14
☐ 683	Tommy Adams	.15	.07
☐ 684	Bernard Gilkey	.15	.07
☐ 685	Kevin Brown	.40	.18
☐ 686	Fred McGriff	.40	.18
☐ 687	Pat Borders	.15	.07
☐ 688	Kirt Manwaring	.15	.07
☐ 689	Sid Bream	.15	.07
☐ 690	John Valentin	.30	.14
☐ 691	Steve Olsen	.15	.07
☐ 692	Roberto Mejia	.15	.07
☐ 693	Carlos Delgado FOIL	.60	.25
☐ 694	Steve Gibralter FOIL	.30	.14
☐ 695	Gary Mota FOIL	.15	.07
☐ 696	Jose Malave FOIL	.15	.07
☐ 697	Larry Sutton FOIL	.15	.07
☐ 698	Dan Frye FOIL	.15	.07
☐ 699	Tim Clark FOIL	.15	.07
☐ 700	Brian Rupp FOIL	.15	.07
☐ 701	Felipe Alou FOIL	.30	.14
	Moises Alou		
☐ 702	Barry Bonds FOIL	.60	.25
	Bobby Bonds		
☐ 703	Ken Griffey Sr. FOIL	1.00	.45
	Ken Griffey Jr.		
☐ 704	Brian McRae FOIL	.15	.07
	Hal McRae		
☐ 705	Checklist 1	.15	.07
☐ 706	Checklist 2	.15	.07
☐ 707	Checklist 3	.15	.07
☐ 708	Checklist 4	.15	.07

1994 Bowman Previews

	MINT	NRMT
COMPLETE SET (10)	30.00	13.50
COMMON CARD (1-10)	1.00	.45
STATED ODDS 1:24 SER.2 STADIUM CLUB		

☐ 1	Frank Thomas	10.00	4.50
☐ 2	Mike Piazza	12.00	5.50
☐ 3	Albert Belle	4.00	1.80
☐ 4	Javier Lopez	2.50	1.10
☐ 5	Cliff Floyd	2.00	.90
☐ 6	Alex Gonzalez	1.00	.45
☐ 7	Ricky Bottalico	2.00	.90
☐ 8	Tony Clark	5.00	2.20
☐ 9	Mac Suzuki	2.00	.90
☐ 10	James Mouton Foil	1.00	.45

1994 Bowman

	MINT	NRMT
COMPLETE SET (682)	100.00	45.00
COMMON CARD (1-682)	.20	.09
MINOR STARS	.40	.18
UNLISTED STARS	.75	.35

☐ 1	Joe Carter	.40	.18
☐ 2	Marcus Moore	.20	.09
☐ 3	Doug Creek	.20	.09
☐ 4	Pedro Martinez	.20	.09
☐ 5	Ken Griffey Jr.	4.00	1.80
☐ 6	Greg Swindell	.20	.09

❏ 7	J.J. Johnson	.40	.18
❏ 8	Homer Bush	2.50	1.10
❏ 9	Arquimedez Pozo	.40	.18
❏ 10	Bryan Harvey	.20	.09
❏ 11	J.T. Snow	.40	.18
❏ 12	Alan Benes	.75	.35
❏ 13	Chad Kreuter	.20	.09
❏ 14	Eric Karros	.40	.18
❏ 15	Frank Thomas	1.50	.70
❏ 16	Bret Saberhagen	.40	.18
❏ 17	Terrell Lowery	.20	.09
❏ 18	Rod Bolton	.20	.09
❏ 19	Harold Baines	.40	.18
❏ 20	Matt Walbeck	.20	.09
❏ 21	Tom Glavine	.75	.35
❏ 22	Todd Jones	.20	.09
❏ 23	Alberto Castillo	.20	.09
❏ 24	Ruben Sierra	.20	.09
❏ 25	Don Mattingly	1.50	.70
❏ 26	Mike Morgan	.20	.09
❏ 27	Jim Mouswswhite	.20	.09
❏ 28	Matt Brunson	.20	.09
❏ 29	Adam Meinershagen	.20	.09
❏ 30	Joe Girardi	.20	.09
❏ 31	Shane Halter	.20	.09
❏ 32	Jose Paniagua	.40	.18
❏ 33	Paul Perkins	.20	.09
❏ 34	John Hudek	.20	.09
❏ 35	Frank Viola	.20	.09
❏ 36	David Lamb	.20	.09
❏ 37	Marshall Boze	.20	.09
❏ 38	Jorge Posada	3.00	1.35
❏ 39	Brian Anderson	1.50	.70
❏ 40	Mark Whiten	.20	.09
❏ 41	Sean Bergman	.60	.25
❏ 42	Jose Parra	.40	.18
❏ 43	Mike Robertson	.20	.09
❏ 44	Pete Walker	.20	.09
❏ 45	Juan Gonzalez	1.50	.70
❏ 46	Cleveland Ladell	.40	.18
❏ 47	Mark Smith	.20	.09
❏ 48	Kevin Jarvis UER	.20	.09
	(Team listed as Yankees on back)		
❏ 49	Amaury Telemaco	.50	.23
❏ 50	Andy Van Slyke	.40	.18
❏ 51	Rikkert Faneyte	.20	.09
❏ 52	Curtis Shaw	.20	.09
❏ 53	Matt Drews	.50	.23
❏ 54	Wilson Alvarez	.40	.18
❏ 55	Manny Ramirez	1.50	.70
❏ 56	Bobby Munoz	.20	.09
❏ 57	Ed Sprague	.20	.09
❏ 58	Jamey Wright	.50	.23
❏ 59	Jeff Montgomery	.20	.09
❏ 60	Kirk Rueter	.20	.09
❏ 61	Edgar Martinez	.40	.18
❏ 62	Luis Gonzalez	.40	.18
❏ 63	Tim Vanegmond	.20	.09
❏ 64	Bip Roberts	.20	.09
❏ 65	John Jaha	.20	.09
❏ 66	Chuck Carr	.20	.09
❏ 67	Chuck Finley	.40	.18
❏ 68	Aaron Holbert	.20	.09
❏ 69	Cecil Fielder	.40	.18
❏ 70	Tom Engle	.20	.09
❏ 71	Ron Karkovice	.20	.09
❏ 72	Joe Orsulak	.20	.09
❏ 73	Duff Brumley	.20	.09
❏ 74	Craig Clayton	.20	.09
❏ 75	Cal Ripken	3.00	1.35
❏ 76	Brad Fulimer	3.00	1.35
❏ 77	Tony Tarasco	.20	.09
❏ 78	Terry Farrar	.20	.09
❏ 79	Matt Williams	.60	.25
❏ 80	Rickey Henderson	1.00	.45
❏ 81	Terry Mulholland	.20	.09
❏ 82	Sammy Sosa	2.50	1.10
❏ 83	Paul Sorrento	.20	.09
❏ 84	Pete Incaviglia	.20	.09
❏ 85	Darren Hall	.20	.09
❏ 86	Scott Klingenbeck	.20	.09
❏ 87	Dario Perez	.20	.09
❏ 88	Ugueth Urbina	.40	.18
❏ 89	Dave Vanhof	.20	.09
❏ 90	Domingo Jean	.20	.09
❏ 91	Otis Nixon	.20	.09
❏ 92	Andres Berumen	.20	.09
❏ 93	Jose Valentin	.20	.09
❏ 94	Edgar Renteria	2.50	1.10
❏ 95	Chris Turner	.20	.09
❏ 96	Ray Lankford	.40	.18
❏ 97	Danny Bautista	.20	.09
❏ 98	Chan Ho Park	4.00	1.80
❏ 99	Glenn DiSarcina	.20	.18
❏ 100	Butch Huskey	.40	.18
❏ 101	Ivan Rodriguez	1.00	.45
❏ 102	Johnny Ruffin	.20	.09
❏ 103	Alex Ochoa	.20	.09
❏ 104	Torii Hunter	1.00	.45
❏ 105	Ryan Klesko	.40	.18
❏ 106	Jay Bell	.40	.18
❏ 107	Kurt Peltzer	.20	.09
❏ 108	Miguel Jimenez	.20	.09
❏ 109	Russ Davis	.40	.18
❏ 110	Derek Wallace	.20	.09
❏ 111	Keith Lockhart	.20	.09
❏ 112	Mike Lieberthal	.20	.09
❏ 113	Dave Stewart	.40	.18
❏ 114	Tom Schmidt	.20	.09
❏ 115	Brian McRae	.20	.09
❏ 116	Moises Alou	.40	.18
❏ 117	Dave Fleming	.20	.09
❏ 118	Jeff Bagwell	1.00	.45
❏ 119	Luis Ortiz	.20	.09
❏ 120	Tony Gwynn	2.00	.90
❏ 121	Jaime Navarro	.20	.09
❏ 122	Benito Santiago	.20	.09
❏ 123	Darrell Whitmore	.20	.09
❏ 124	John Mabry	.20	.09
❏ 125	Mickey Tettleton	.20	.09
❏ 126	Tom Candiotti	.20	.09
❏ 127	Tim Raines	.40	.18
❏ 128	Bobby Bonilla	.40	.18
❏ 129	John Dettmer	.20	.09
❏ 130	Hector Carrasco	.20	.09
❏ 131	Chris Hoiles	.20	.09
❏ 132	Rick Aguilera	.20	.09
❏ 133	David Justice	.75	.35
❏ 134	Esteban Loaiza	1.00	.45
❏ 135	Barry Bonds	1.00	.45
❏ 136	Bob Welch	.20	.09
❏ 137	Mike Stanley	.20	.09
❏ 138	Roberto Hernandez	.20	.09
❏ 139	Sandy Alomar Jr.	.40	.18
❏ 140	Darren Daulton	.40	.18
❏ 141	Angel Martinez	.20	.09
❏ 142	Howard Johnson	.20	.09
❏ 143	Bob Hamelin UER	.20	.09
	(Name and card number colors don't match)		
❏ 144	J.J. Thobe	.20	.09
❏ 145	Roger Salkeld	.20	.09
❏ 146	Orlando Miller	.20	.09
❏ 147	Dmitri Young	.20	.18
❏ 148	Tim Hyers	.20	.09
❏ 149	Mark Loretta	1.00	.45
❏ 150	Chris Hammond	.20	.09
❏ 151	Joel Moore	.20	.09
❏ 152	Todd Zeile	.20	.09
❏ 153	Wil Cordero	.20	.09
❏ 154	Chris Smith	.20	.09
❏ 155	James Baldwin	.40	.18
❏ 156	Edgardo Alfonzo	10.00	4.50
❏ 157	Kym Ashworth	.20	.18
❏ 158	Paul Bako	.20	.09
❏ 159	Rick Krivda	.20	.09
❏ 160	Pat Mahomes	.20	.09
❏ 161	Damon Hollins	.40	.18
❏ 162	Felix Martinez	.75	.35
❏ 163	Jason Myers	.20	.09
❏ 164	Izzy Molina	.40	.18
❏ 165	Brien Taylor	.20	.09
❏ 166	Kevin Orie	.75	.35
❏ 167	Casey Whitten	.40	.18
❏ 168	Tony Longmire	.20	.09
❏ 169	John Olerud	.40	.18
❏ 170	Mark Thompson	.20	.09
❏ 171	Jorge Fabregas	.20	.09
❏ 172	John Wetteland	.40	.18
❏ 173	Dan Wilson	.20	.09
❏ 174	Doug Drabek	.20	.09
❏ 175	Jeff McNeely	.20	.09
❏ 176	Melvin Nieves	.20	.09
❏ 177	Doug Glanville	4.00	1.80
❏ 178	Javier De La Hoya	.20	.09
❏ 179	Chad Curtis	.20	.09
❏ 180	Brian Barber	.20	.09
❏ 181	Mike Henneman	.20	.09
❏ 182	Jose Offerman	.40	.18
❏ 183	Robert Ellis	.20	.09
❏ 184	John Franco	.40	.18
❏ 185	Benji Gil	.20	.09
❏ 186	Hal Morris	.20	.09
❏ 187	Chris Sabo	.20	.09
❏ 188	Blaise Ilsley	.20	.09
❏ 189	Steve Avery	.20	.09
❏ 190	Rick White	.20	.09
❏ 191	Rod Beck	.20	.09
❏ 192	Mark McGwire UER	4.00	1.80
	(No card number on back)		
❏ 193	Jim Abbott	.40	.18
❏ 194	Randy Myers	.20	.09
❏ 195	Kenny Lofton	.75	.35
❏ 196	Mariano Duncan	.20	.09
❏ 197	Lee Daniels	.20	.09
❏ 198	Armando Reynoso	.20	.09
❏ 199	Joe Randa	.40	.18
❏ 200	Cliff Floyd	.40	.18
❏ 201	Tim Harkrider	.20	.09
❏ 202	Kevin Gallaher	.20	.09
❏ 203	Scott Cooper	.20	.09
❏ 204	Phil Stidham	.20	.09
❏ 205	Jeff D'Amico	.40	.18
❏ 206	Matt Whisenant	.20	.09
❏ 207	De Shawn Warren	.20	.09
❏ 208	Rene Arocha	.20	.09
❏ 209	Tony Clark	5.00	2.20
❏ 210	Jason Jacome	.20	.09
❏ 211	Scott Christman	.20	.09
❏ 212	Bill Pulsipher	.40	.18
❏ 213	Dean Palmer	.40	.18
❏ 214	Chad Mottola	.20	.09
❏ 215	Manny Alexander	.20	.09
❏ 216	Rich Becker	.20	.09
❏ 217	Andre King	.20	.09
❏ 218	Carlos Garcia	.20	.09
❏ 219	Ron Pezzoni	.20	.09
❏ 220	Steve Karsay	.20	.09
❏ 221	Jose Musset	.20	.09
❏ 222	Karl Rhodes	.20	.09
❏ 223	Frank Cimorelli	.20	.09
❏ 224	Kevin Jordan	.20	.09
❏ 225	Duane Ward	.20	.09
❏ 226	John Burke	.20	.09
❏ 227	Mike Macfarlane	.20	.09
❏ 228	Mike Lansing	.40	.18
❏ 229	Chuck Knoblauch	.75	.35
❏ 230	Ken Caminiti	.60	.25
❏ 231	Gar Finnvold	.20	.09
❏ 232	Derrek Lee	2.00	.90
❏ 233	Brady Anderson	.40	.18
❏ 234	Vic Darensbourg	.20	.09
❏ 235	Mark Langston	.40	.18
❏ 236	T.J. Mathews	.40	.18
❏ 237	Lou Whitaker	.40	.18
❏ 238	Roger Cedeno	.40	.18
❏ 239	Alex Fernandez	.20	.09
❏ 240	Ryan Thompson	.20	.09
❏ 241	Kerry Lacy	.20	.09
❏ 242	Reggie Sanders	.40	.18
❏ 243	Brad Pennington	.20	.09
❏ 244	Bryan Eversgerd	.20	.09
❏ 245	Greg Maddux	2.00	.90
❏ 246	Jason Kendall	.75	.35
❏ 247	J.R. Phillips	.20	.09
❏ 248	Bobby Witt	.20	.09
❏ 249	Paul O'Neill	.40	.18
❏ 250	Ryne Sandberg	1.00	.45
❏ 251	Charles Nagy	.20	.09
❏ 252	Kevin Stocker	.20	.09
❏ 253	Shawn Green	1.25	.55
❏ 254	Charlie Hayes	.20	.09
❏ 255	Donnie Elliott	.20	.09
❏ 256	Rob Fitzpatrick	.20	.09
❏ 257	Tim Davis	.20	.09
❏ 258	James Mouton	.20	.09
❏ 259	Mike Greenwell	.20	.09
❏ 260	Ray McDavid	.20	.09

❑ 261	Mike Kelly	.20	.09
❑ 262	Andy Larkin	.20	.09
❑ 263	Marquis Riley UER	.20	.09
	(No card number on back)		
❑ 264	Bob Tewksbury	.20	.09
❑ 265	Brian Edmondson	.20	.09
❑ 266	Eduardo Lantigua	.40	.18
❑ 267	Brandon Wilson	.20	.09
❑ 268	Mike Welch	.20	.09
❑ 269	Tom Henke	.20	.09
❑ 270	Calvin Reese	.60	.25
❑ 271	Greg Zaun	.20	.09
❑ 272	Todd Ritchie	.20	.09
❑ 273	Javier Lopez	.60	.25
❑ 274	Kevin Young	.20	.09
❑ 275	Kirt Manwaring	.20	.09
❑ 276	Bill Taylor	.20	.09
❑ 277	Robert Eenhoorn	.20	.09
❑ 278	Jessie Hollins	.20	.09
❑ 279	Julian Tavarez	.20	.09
❑ 280	Gene Schall	.20	.09
❑ 281	Paul Molitor	.75	.35
❑ 282	Neifi Perez	3.00	1.35
❑ 283	Greg Gagne	.20	.09
❑ 284	Marquis Grissom	.40	.18
❑ 285	Randy Johnson	.75	.35
❑ 286	Pete Harnisch	.20	.09
❑ 287	Joel Bennett	.20	.09
❑ 288	Derek Bell	.40	.18
❑ 289	Darryl Hamilton	.20	.09
❑ 290	Gary Sheffield	.75	.35
❑ 291	Eduardo Perez	.40	.18
❑ 292	Basil Shabazz	.20	.09
❑ 293	Eric Davis	.40	.18
❑ 294	Pedro Astacio	.40	.18
❑ 295	Robin Ventura	.40	.18
❑ 296	Jeff Kent	.40	.18
❑ 297	Rick Helling	.40	.18
❑ 298	Joe Oliver	.20	.09
❑ 299	Lee Smith	.40	.18
❑ 300	Dave Winfield	.75	.35
❑ 301	Deion Sanders	.40	.18
❑ 302	Ravelo Manzanillo	.20	.09
❑ 303	Mark Portugal	.20	.09
❑ 304	Brent Gates	.20	.09
❑ 305	Wade Boggs	.75	.35
❑ 306	Rick Wilkins	.20	.09
❑ 307	Carlos Baerga	.40	.18
❑ 308	Curt Schilling	.40	.18
❑ 309	Shannon Stewart	.75	.35
❑ 310	Darren Holmes	.20	.09
❑ 311	Robert Toth	.20	.09
❑ 312	Gabe White	.20	.09
❑ 313	Mac Suzuki	.40	.18
❑ 314	Alvin Morman	.20	.09
❑ 315	Mo Vaughn	.75	.35
❑ 316	Bryce Florie	.20	.09
❑ 317	Gabby Martinez	.40	.18
❑ 318	Carl Everett	.40	.18
❑ 319	Kerwin Moore	.20	.09
❑ 320	Tom Pagnozzi	.20	.09
❑ 321	Chris Gomez	.20	.09
❑ 322	Todd Williams	.20	.09
❑ 323	Pat Hentgen	.40	.18
❑ 324	Kirk Presley	.20	.09
❑ 325	Kevin Brown	.40	.18
❑ 326	Jason Isringhausen	.75	.35
❑ 327	Rick Forney	.20	.09
❑ 328	Carlos Pulido	.20	.09
❑ 329	Terrell Wade	.20	.09
❑ 330	Al Martin	.20	.09
❑ 331	Dan Carlson	.20	.09
❑ 332	Mark Acre	.20	.09
❑ 333	Sterling Hitchcock	.40	.18
❑ 334	Jon Ratliff	.20	.09
❑ 335	Alex Ramirez	5.00	2.20
❑ 336	Phil Geisler	.20	.09
❑ 337	Eddie Zambrano FOIL	.20	.09
❑ 338	Jim Thome FOIL	.75	.35
❑ 339	James Mouton FOIL	.20	.09
❑ 340	Cliff Floyd FOIL	.40	.18
❑ 341	Carlos Delgado FOIL	.75	.35
❑ 342	Roberto Petagine FOIL	.20	.09
❑ 343	Tim Clark FOIL	.20	.09
❑ 344	Bubba Smith FOIL	.20	.09
❑ 345	Randy Curtis FOIL	.20	.09
❑ 346	Joe Biasucci FOIL	.20	.09
❑ 347	D.J. Boston FOIL	.20	.09
❑ 348	Ruben Rivera FOIL	2.00	.90
❑ 349	Bryan Link FOIL	.20	.09
❑ 350	Mike Bell FOIL	.20	.09
❑ 351	Marty Watson FOIL	.20	.09
❑ 352	Jason Myers FOIL	.20	.09
❑ 353	Chipper Jones FOIL	2.00	.90
❑ 354	Brooks Kieschnick FOIL	.20	.09
❑ 355	Calvin Reese FOIL	.60	.25
❑ 356	John Burke FOIL	.20	.09
❑ 357	Kurt Miller FOIL	.20	.09
❑ 358	Orlando Miller FOIL	.20	.09
❑ 359	Todd Hollandsworth FOIL	.60	.25
❑ 360	Rondell White FOIL	.40	.18
❑ 361	Bill Pulsipher FOIL	.40	.18
❑ 362	Tyler Green FOIL	.20	.09
❑ 363	Midre Cummings FOIL	.20	.09
❑ 364	Brian Barber FOIL	.20	.09
❑ 365	Melvin Nieves FOIL	.20	.09
❑ 366	Salomon Torres FOIL	.20	.09
❑ 367	Alex Ochoa FOIL	.20	.09
❑ 368	Frankie Rodriguez FOIL	.20	.09
❑ 369	Brian Anderson FOIL	1.50	.70
❑ 370	James Baldwin FOIL	.40	.18
❑ 371	Manny Ramirez FOIL	1.50	.70
❑ 372	Justin Thompson FOIL	.75	.35
❑ 373	Johnny Damon FOIL	.75	.35
❑ 374	Jeff D'Amico FOIL	.40	.18
❑ 375	Rich Becker FOIL	.20	.09
❑ 376	Derek Jeter FOIL	3.00	1.35
❑ 377	Steve Karsay FOIL	.20	.09
❑ 378	Mac Suzuki FOIL	.40	.18
❑ 379	Benji Gil FOIL	.20	.09
❑ 380	Alex Gonzalez FOIL	.20	.09
❑ 381	Jason Bere FOIL	.40	.18
❑ 382	Brett Butler FOIL	.40	.18
❑ 383	Jeff Conine FOIL	.20	.09
❑ 384	Darren Daulton FOIL	.40	.18
❑ 385	Jeff Kent FOIL	.40	.18
❑ 386	Don Mattingly FOIL	1.50	.70
❑ 387	Mike Piazza FOIL	2.50	1.10
❑ 388	Ryne Sandberg FOIL	1.00	.45
❑ 389	Rich Amaral	.20	.09
❑ 390	Craig Biggio	.75	.35
❑ 391	Jeff Suppan	1.00	.45
❑ 392	Andy Benes	.40	.18
❑ 393	Cal Eldred	.20	.09
❑ 394	Tim Salmon	.75	.35
❑ 395	Roberto Kelly	.20	.09
❑ 396	Ray Suplee	.20	.09
❑ 397	Tony Phillips	.20	.09
❑ 398	Ramon Martinez	.40	.18
❑ 399	Julio Franco	.20	.09
❑ 400	Dwight Gooden	.40	.18
❑ 401	Kevin Lomon	.20	.09
❑ 402	Jose Rijo	.20	.09
❑ 403	Mike Devereaux	.20	.09
❑ 404	Mike Zolecki	.20	.09
❑ 405	Fred McGriff	.60	.25
❑ 406	Danny Clyburn	.20	.09
❑ 407	Robby Thompson	.20	.09
❑ 408	Terry Steinbach	.20	.09
❑ 409	Luis Polonia	.20	.09
❑ 410	Mark Grace	.60	.25
❑ 411	Albert Belle	.75	.35
❑ 412	John Kruk	.40	.18
❑ 413	Scott Spiezio	.50	.23
❑ 414	Ellis Burks UER	.40	.18
	(Name spelled Elkis on front)		
❑ 415	Joe Vitiello	.20	.09
❑ 416	Tim Costo	.20	.09
❑ 417	Marc Newfield	.20	.09
❑ 418	Oscar Henriquez	.50	.23
❑ 419	Matt Perisho	.75	.35
❑ 420	Julio Bruno	.20	.09
❑ 421	Kenny Felder	.20	.09
❑ 422	Tyler Green	.20	.09
❑ 423	Jim Edmonds	.75	.35
❑ 424	Ozzie Smith	1.00	.45
❑ 425	Rich Greene	.20	.09
❑ 426	Todd Hollandsworth	.60	.25
❑ 427	Eddie Pearson	.40	.18
❑ 428	Quivilio Veras	.40	.18
❑ 429	Kenny Rogers	.20	.09
❑ 430	Willie Greene	.20	.09
❑ 431	Vaughn Eshelman	.20	.09
❑ 432	Pat Meares	.20	.09
❑ 433	Jermaine Dye	6.00	2.70
❑ 434	Steve Cooke	.20	.09
❑ 435	Bill Swift	.20	.09
❑ 436	Fausto Cruz	.20	.09
❑ 437	Mark Hutton	.20	.09
❑ 438	Brooks Kieschnick	.20	.09
❑ 439	Yorkis Perez	.20	.09
❑ 440	Len Dykstra	.40	.18
❑ 441	Pat Borders	.20	.09
❑ 442	Doug Walls	.20	.09
❑ 443	Wally Joyner	.40	.18
❑ 444	Ken Hill	.20	.09
❑ 445	Eric Anthony	.20	.09
❑ 446	Mitch Williams	.20	.09
❑ 447	Cory Bailey	.20	.09
❑ 448	Dave Staton	.20	.09
❑ 449	Greg Vaughn	.40	.18
❑ 450	Dave Magadan	.20	.09
❑ 451	Chili Davis	.40	.18
❑ 452	Gerald Santos	.20	.09
❑ 453	Joe Perona	.20	.09
❑ 454	Delino DeShields	.20	.09
❑ 455	Jack McDowell	.20	.09
❑ 456	Todd Hundley	.40	.18
❑ 457	Ritchie Moody	.20 *	.09
❑ 458	Bret Boone	.40	.18
❑ 459	Ben McDonald	.20	.09
❑ 460	Kirby Puckett	1.25	.55
❑ 461	Gregg Olson	.20	.09
❑ 462	Rich Aude	.20	.09
❑ 463	John Burkett	.20	.09
❑ 464	Troy Neel	.20	.09
❑ 465	Jimmy Key	.40	.18
❑ 466	Ozzie Timmons	.20	.09
❑ 467	Eddie Murray	.75	.35
❑ 468	Mark Tranberg	.20	.09
❑ 469	Alex Gonzalez	.20	.09
❑ 470	David Nied	.20	.09
❑ 471	Barry Larkin	.75	.35
❑ 472	Brian Looney	.20	.09
❑ 473	Shawn Estes	.40	.18
❑ 474	A.J. Sager	.20	.09
❑ 475	Roger Clemens	2.00	.90
❑ 476	Vince Moore	.20	.09
❑ 477	Scott Karl	.40	.18
❑ 478	Kurt Miller	.20	.09
❑ 479	Garret Anderson	.75	.35
❑ 480	Allen Watson	.20	.09
❑ 481	Jose Lima	6.00	2.70
❑ 482	Rick Gorecki	.20	.09
❑ 483	Jimmy Hurst	.20	.09
❑ 484	Preston Wilson	.75	.35
❑ 485	Will Clark	.75	.35
❑ 486	Mike Ferry	.20	.09
❑ 487	Curtis Goodwin	.40	.18
❑ 488	Mike Myers	.20	.09
❑ 489	Chipper Jones	2.00	.90
❑ 490	Jeff King	.20	.09
❑ 491	William VanLandingham	.20	.09
❑ 492	Carlos Reyes	.20	.09
❑ 493	Andy Pettitte	1.00	.45
❑ 494	Brant Brown	.40	.18
❑ 495	Daron Kirkreit	.20	.09
❑ 496	Ricky Bottalico	.50	.23
❑ 497	Devon White	.20	.09
❑ 498	Jason Johnson	.20	.09
❑ 499	Vince Coleman	.20	.09
❑ 500	Larry Walker	.75	.35
❑ 501	Bobby Ayala	.20	.09
❑ 502	Steve Finley	.40	.18
❑ 503	Scott Fletcher	.20	.09
❑ 504	Brad Ausmus	.20	.09
❑ 505	Scott Talanoa	.20	.09
❑ 506	Orestes Destrade	.20	.09
❑ 507	Gary DiSarcina	.20	.09
❑ 508	Willie Smith	.20	.09
❑ 509	Alan Trammell	.60	.25
❑ 510	Mike Piazza	2.50	1.10
❑ 511	Ozzie Guillen	.20	.09
❑ 512	Jeromy Burnitz	.40	.18
❑ 513	Darren Oliver	1.00	.45
❑ 514	Kevin Mitchell	.20	.09
❑ 515	Rafael Palmeiro	.75	.35
❑ 516	David McCarty	.20	.09

517 Jeff Blauser	.20	.09
518 Trey Beamon	.20	.09
519 Royce Clayton	.20	.09
520 Dennis Eckersley	.40	.18
521 Bernie Williams	.75	.35
522 Steve Buechele	.20	.09
523 Dennis Martinez	.40	.18
524 Dave Hollins	.20	.09
525 Joey Hamilton	.75	.35
526 Andres Galarraga	.75	.35
527 Jeff Granger	.20	.09
528 Joey Eischen	.20	.09
529 Desi Relaford	.40	.18
530 Roberto Petagine	.20	.09
531 Andre Dawson	.60	.25
532 Ray Holbert	.20	.09
533 Duane Singleton	.20	.09
534 Kurt Abbott	.20	.09
535 Bo Jackson	.40	.18
536 Gregg Jefferies	.20	.09
537 David Mysel	.20	.09
538 Raul Mondesi	.75	.35
539 Chris Snopek	.20	.09
540 Brook Fordyce	.20	.09
541 Ron Frazier	.20	.09
542 Brian Koelling	.20	.09
543 Jimmy Haynes	.40	.18
544 Marty Cordova	.20	.09
545 Jason Green	.20	.09
546 Orlando Merced	.20	.09
547 Lou Pote	.20	.09
548 Todd Van Poppel	.20	.09
549 Pat Kelly	.20	.09
550 Turk Wendell	.20	.09
551 Herbert Perry	.20	.09
552 Ryan Karp	.20	.09
553 Juan Guzman	.20	.09
554 Bryan Rekar	.60	.25
555 Kevin Appier	.40	.18
556 Chris Schwab	.20	.09
557 Jay Buhner	.40	.18
558 Andujar Cedeno	.20	.09
559 Ryan McGuire	.40	.18
560 Ricky Gutierrez	.20	.09
561 Keith Kimsey	.20	.09
562 Tim Clark	.20	.09
563 Damion Easley	.40	.18
564 Clint Davis	.20	.09
565 Mike Moore	.20	.09
566 Orel Hershiser	.40	.18
567 Jason Bere	.20	.09
568 Kevin McReynolds	.20	.09
569 Leland Macon	.20	.09
570 John Courtright	.20	.09
571 Sid Fernandez	.20	.09
572 Chad Roper	.20	.09
573 Terry Pendleton	.20	.09
574 Danny Miceli	.20	.09
575 Joe Rosselli	.20	.09
576 Mike Bordick	.20	.09
577 Danny Tartabull	.20	.09
578 Jose Guzman	.20	.09
579 Omar Vizquel	.40	.18
580 Tommy Greene	.20	.09
581 Paul Spoljaric	.20	.09
582 Walt Weiss	.20	.09
583 Oscar Jimenez	.20	.09
584 Rod Henderson	.20	.09
585 Derek Lowe	.20	.09
586 Richard Hidalgo	3.00	1.35
587 Shayne Bennett	.40	.18
588 Tim Belk	.20	.09
589 Matt Mieske	.20	.09
590 Nigel Wilson	.20	.09
591 Jeff Knox	.20	.09
592 Bernard Gilkey	.20	.09
593 David Cone	.60	.25
594 Paul LoDuca	.40	.18
595 Scott Ruffcorn	.20	.09
596 Chris Roberts	.40	.18
597 Oscar Munoz	.20	.09
598 Scott Sullivan	.20	.09
599 Matt Jarvis	.20	.09
600 Jose Canseco	1.00	.45
601 Tony Graffanino	.40	.18

602 Don Slaught	.20	.09
603 Brett King	.40	.18
604 Jose Herrera	.40	.18
605 Melido Perez	.20	.09
606 Mike Hubbard	.20	.09
607 Chad Ogea	.20	.09
608 Wayne Gomes	.20	.09
609 Roberto Alomar	.75	.35
610 Angel Echevarria	.20	.09
611 Jose Lind	.20	.09
612 Darrin Fletcher	.20	.09
613 Chris Bosio	.20	.09
614 Darryl Kile	.20	.09
615 Frankie Rodriguez	.20	.09
616 Phil Plantier	.20	.09
617 Pat Listach	.20	.09
618 Charlie Hough	.20	.09
619 Ryan Hancock	.20	.09
620 Darrel Deak	.20	.09
621 Travis Fryman	.40	.18
622 Brett Butler	.40	.18
623 Lance Johnson	.20	.09
624 Pete Smith	.20	.09
625 James Hurst	.20	.09
626 Roberto Kelly	.20	.09
627 Mike Mussina	.75	.35
628 Kevin Tapani	.20	.09
629 John Smoltz	.60	.25
630 Midre Cummings	.20	.09
631 Salomon Torres	.20	.09
632 Willie Adams	.20	.09
633 Derek Jeter	3.00	1.35
634 Steve Trachsel	.20	.09
635 Albie Lopez	.20	.09
636 Jason Moler	.20	.09
637 Carlos Delgado	.75	.35
638 Roberto Mejia	.20	.09
639 Darren Burton	.20	.09
640 B.J. Wallace	.20	.09
641 Brad Clontz	.20	.09
642 Billy Wagner	3.00	1.35
643 Aaron Sele	.40	.18
644 Cameron Cairncross	.20	.09
645 Brian Harper	.20	.09
646 Marc Valdes UER	.20	.09
(No card number on back)		
647 Mark Ratekin	.20	.09
648 Terry Bradshaw	.20	.09
649 Justin Thompson	.75	.35
650 Mike Busch	.40	.18
651 Joe Hall	.20	.09
652 Bobby Jones	.20	.09
653 Kelly Stinnett	.20	.09
654 Rod Steph	.20	.09
655 Jay Powell	.60	.25
656 Keith Garagozzo UER	.20	.09
(No card number on back)		
657 Todd Dunn	.20	.09
658 Charles Peterson	.40	.18
659 Darren Lewis	.20	.09
660 John Wasdin	.40	.18
661 Tate Seefried	.20	.09
662 Hector Trinidad	.40	.18
663 John Carter	.20	.09
664 Larry Mitchell	.20	.09
665 David Catlett	.20	.09
666 Dante Bichette	.40	.18
667 Felix Jose	.20	.09
668 Rondell White	.40	.18
669 Tino Martinez	.75	.35
670 Brian L. Hunter	.40	.18
671 Jose Malave	.20	.09
672 Archi Cianfrocco	.20	.09
673 Mike Matheny	.20	.09
674 Bret Barberie	.20	.09
675 Andrew Lorraine	.20	.09
676 Brian Jordan	.40	.18
677 Tim Belcher	.20	.09
678 Antonio Osuna	.20	.09
679 Checklist	.20	.09
680 Checklist	.20	.09
681 Checklist	.20	.09
682 Checklist	.20	.09

1995 Bowman

	MINT	NRMT
COMPLETE SET (439)	250.00	110.00
COMMON CARD (1-439)	.25	.11
COMMON FOIL (221-274)	.40	.18
MINOR STARS	.50	.23
UNLISTED STARS	1.00	.45

1 Billy Wagner	.75	.35
2 Chris Widger	.25	.11
3 Brent Bowers	.25	.11
4 Bob Abreu	12.00	5.50
5 Lou Collier	.50	.23
6 Juan Acevedo	.25	.11
7 Jason Kelley	.25	.11
8 Brian Sackinsky	.25	.11
9 Scott Christman	.25	.11
10 Damon Hollins	.25	.11
11 Willis Otanez	.25	.11
12 Jason Ryan	.50	.23
13 Jason Giambi	.50	.23
14 Andy Taulbee	.25	.11
15 Mark Thompson	.25	.11
16 Hugo Pivaral	.50	.23
17 Brien Taylor	.25	.11
18 Antonio Osuna	.25	.11
19 Edgardo Alfonzo	1.00	.45
20 Carl Everett	.25	.11
21 Matt Drews	.25	.11
22 Bartolo Colon	8.00	3.60
23 Andruw Jones	40.00	18.00
24 Robert Person	.25	.11
25 Derrek Lee	1.00	.45
26 John Ambrose	.25	.11
27 Eric Knowles	.50	.23
28 Chris Roberts	.25	.11
29 Don Wengert	.25	.11
30 Marcus Jensen	.50	.23
31 Brian Barber	.25	.11
32 Kevin Brown C	.50	.23
33 Benji Gil	.25	.11
34 Mike Hubbard	.25	.11
35 Bart Evans	.25	.11
36 Enrique Wilson	2.00	.90
37 Brian Buchanan	.50	.23
38 Ken Ray	.25	.11
39 Micah Franklin	.25	.11
40 Ricky Otero	.25	.11
41 Jason Kendall	1.00	.45
42 Jimmy Hurst	.25	.11
43 Jerry Wolak	.25	.11
44 Jayson Peterson	.25	.11
45 Allen Battle	.25	.11
46 Scott Stahoviak	.25	.11
47 Steve Schrenk	.25	.11
48 Travis Miller	.25	.11
49 Eddie Rios	.25	.11
50 Mike Hampton	.25	.11
51 Chad Frontera	.25	.11
52 Tom Evans	.50	.23
53 C.J. Nitkowski	.25	.11
54 Clay Caruthers	.25	.11
55 Shannon Stewart	.50	.23
56 Jorge Posada	.50	.23
57 Aaron Holbert	.25	.11
58 Harry Berrios	.25	.11
59 Steve Rodriguez	.25	.11

60	Shane Andrews	.25	.11
61	Will Cunnane	.50	.23
62	Richard Hidalgo	1.00	.45
63	Bill Selby	.25	.11
64	Jay Cranford	.25	.11
65	Jeff Suppan	.50	.23
66	Curtis Goodwin	.25	.11
67	John Thomson	1.00	.45
68	Justin Thompson	.50	.23
69	Troy Percival	.50	.23
70	Matt Wagner	.50	.23
71	Terry Bradshaw	.25	.11
72	Greg Hansell	.25	.11
73	John Burke	.25	.11
74	Jeff D'Amico	.50	.23
75	Ernie Young	.25	.11
76	Jason Bates	.25	.11
77	Chris Stynes	.50	.23
78	Cade Gaspar	.50	.23
79	Melvin Nieves	.25	.11
80	Rick Gorecki	.25	.11
81	Felix Rodriguez	.25	.11
82	Ryan Hancock	.25	.11
83	Chris Carpenter	4.00	1.80
84	Ray McDavid	.25	.11
85	Chris Wimmer	.25	.11
86	Doug Glanville	.25	.11
87	DeShawn Warren	.25	.11
88	Damian Moss	1.00	.45
89	Rafael Orellano	.50	.23
90	Vladimir Guerrero	50.00	22.00
91	Raul Casanova	.25	.11
92	Karim Garcia	2.00	.90
93	Bryce Florie	.25	.11
94	Kevin Orie	.50	.23
95	Ryan Nye	.25	.23
96	Matt Sachse	.50	.23
97	Ivan Arteaga	.25	.11
98	Glenn Murray	.25	.11
99	Stacy Hollins	.25	.11
100	Jim Pittsley	.25	.11
101	Craig Mattson	.25	.11
102	Neifi Perez	.50	.23
103	Keith Williams	.25	.11
104	Roger Cedeno	.25	.11
105	Tony Terry	.25	.11
106	Jose Malave	.25	.11
107	Joe Rosselli	.25	.11
108	Kevin Jordan	.25	.11
109	Sid Roberson	.25	.11
110	Alan Embree	.25	.11
111	Terrell Wade	.25	.11
112	Bob Wolcott	.25	.11
113	Carlos Perez	1.50	.70
114	Mike Bovee	.50	.23
115	Tommy Davis	.25	.11
116	Jeremey Kendall	.25	.11
117	Rich Aude	.25	.11
118	Rick Huisman	.25	.11
119	Tim Belk	.25	.11
120	Edgar Renteria	.50	.23
121	Calvin Maduro	.50	.23
122	Jerry Martin	.25	.11
123	Ramon Fermin	.25	.11
124	Kimera Bartee	.25	.11
125	Mark Farris	.25	.11
126	Frank Rodriguez	.25	.11
127	Bobby Higginson	4.00	1.80
128	Bret Wagner	.25	.11
129	Edwin Diaz	1.00	.45
130	Jimmy Haynes	.25	.11
131	Chris Weinke	3.00	1.35
132	Damian Jackson	1.00	.45
133	Felix Martinez	.50	.23
134	Edwin Hurtado	.25	.11
135	Matt Raleigh	.25	.11
136	Paul Wilson	.25	.11
137	Ron Villone	.25	.11
138	Eric Stuckenschneider	.25	.11
139	Tate Seefried	.25	.11
140	Rey Ordonez	5.00	2.20
141	Eddie Pearson	.25	.11
142	Kevin Gallaher	.25	.11
143	Torii Hunter	.50	.23
144	Daron Kirkreit	.25	.11
145	Craig Wilson	.25	.11
146	Ugueth Urbina	.25	.11
147	Chris Snopek	.25	.11
148	Kym Ashworth	.25	.11
149	Wayne Gomes	.25	.11
150	Mark Loretta	.25	.11
151	Ramon Morel	.50	.23
152	Trot Nixon	.75	.35
153	Desi Relaford	.50	.23
154	Scott Sullivan	.25	.11
155	Marc Barcelo	.25	.11
156	Willie Adams	.25	.11
157	Derrick Gibson	5.00	2.20
158	Brian Meadows	1.00	.45
159	Julian Tavarez	.25	.11
160	Bryan Rekar	.25	.11
161	Steve Gibralter	.50	.23
162	Esteban Loaiza	.25	.11
163	John Wasdin	.25	.11
164	Kirk Presley	.25	.11
165	Mariano Rivera	1.00	.45
166	Andy Larkin	.25	.11
167	Sean Whiteside	.25	.11
168	Matt Apana	.25	.11
169	Shawn Senior	.25	.11
170	Scott Gentile	.25	.11
171	Quilvio Veras	.25	.11
172	Eli Marrero	2.00	.90
173	Mendy Lopez	.25	.11
174	Homer Bush	.25	.11
175	Brian Stephenson	.50	.23
176	Jon Nunnally	.25	.11
177	Jose Herrera	.25	.11
178	Corey Avrard	.50	.23
179	David Bell	.25	.11
180	Jason Isringhausen	.50	.23
181	Jamey Wright	.50	.23
182	Loneil Roberts	.25	.11
183	Marty Cordova	.25	.11
184	Amaury Telemaco	.25	.11
185	John Mabry	.25	.11
186	Andrew Vessel	.25	.11
187	Jim Cole	.25	.11
188	Marquis Riley	.25	.11
189	Todd Dunn	.25	.11
190	John Carter	.25	.11
191	Donnie Sadler	1.50	.70
192	Mike Bell	.50	.23
193	Chris Cumberland	.50	.23
194	Jason Schmidt	.25	.11
195	Matt Brunson	.25	.11
196	James Baldwin	.50	.23
197	Bill Simas	.25	.11
198	Gus Gandarillas	.25	.11
199	Mac Suzuki	.50	.23
200	Rick Holifield	.25	.11
201	Fernando Lunar	.50	.23
202	Kevin Jarvis	.25	.11
203	Everett Stull	.25	.11
204	Steve Wojciechowski	.25	.11
205	Shawn Estes	.25	.23
206	Jermaine Dye	1.00	.45
207	Marc Kroon	.25	.11
208	Peter Munro	.25	.11
209	Pat Watkins	.25	.11
210	Matt Smith	.25	.11
211	Joe Vitiello	.25	.11
212	Gerald Witasick Jr.	.25	.11
213	Freddy Garcia	1.00	.45
214	Glenn Dishman	.50	.23
215	Angel Martinez	.25	.11
216	Angel Martinez	.25	.11
217	Yamil Benitez	.75	.35
218	Fausto Macey	.50	.23
219	Eric Owens	.50	.23
220	Checklist	.25	.11
221	Dwayne Hosey FOIL	.40	.18
222	Brad Woodall FOIL	.40	.18
223	Billy Ashley FOIL	.40	.18
224	Mark Grudzielanek FOIL	1.50	.70
225	Mark Johnson FOIL	.40	.18
226	Tim Unroe FOIL	.40	.18
227	Todd Greene FOIL	1.50	.70
228	Larry Sutton FOIL	.40	.18
229	Derek Jeter FOIL	4.00	1.80
230	Sal Fasano FOIL	.40	.18
231	Ruben Rivera FOIL	.50	.23
232	Chris Truby FOIL	1.50	.70
233	John Donati FOIL	.40	.18
234	Decomba Conner FOIL	.50	.23
235	Sergio Nunez FOIL	.25	.11
236	Ray Brown FOIL	.40	.18
237	Juan Melo FOIL	1.00	.45
238	Hideo Nomo FOIL	8.00	3.60
239	Jamie Bluma FOIL	.40	.18
240	Jay Payton FOIL	.50	.23
241	Paul Konerko FOIL	6.00	2.70
242	Scott Elarton FOIL	4.00	1.80
243	Jeff Abbott FOIL	2.50	1.10
244	Jim Brower FOIL	.40	.18
245	Geoff Blum FOIL	.50	.23
246	Aaron Boone FOIL	1.50	.70
247	J.R. Phillips FOIL	.40	.18
248	Alex Ochoa FOIL	.40	.18
249	Nomar Garciaparra FOIL	20.00	9.00
250	Garret Anderson FOIL	.50	.23
251	Ray Durham FOIL	.50	.23
252	Paul Shuey FOIL	.40	.18
253	Tony Clark FOIL	1.00	.45
254	Johnny Damon FOIL	.75	.35
255	Duane Singleton FOIL	.40	.18
256	LaTroy Hawkins FOIL	.40	.18
257	Andy Pettitte FOIL	1.00	.45
258	Ben Grieve FOIL	10.00	4.50
259	Marc Newfield FOIL	.40	.18
260	Terrell Lowery FOIL	.40	.18
261	Shawn Green FOIL	1.00	.45
262	Chipper Jones FOIL	2.50	1.10
263	Brooks Kieschnick FOIL	.25	.11
264	Calvin Reese FOIL	.40	.18
265	Doug Million FOIL	.40	.18
266	Marc Valdes FOIL	.40	.18
267	Brian L.Hunter FOIL	.50	.23
268	Todd Hollandsworth FOIL	.25	.11
269	Rod Henderson FOIL	.40	.18
270	Bill Pulsipher FOIL	.40	.18
271	Scott Rolen FOIL	50.00	22.00
272	Trey Beamon FOIL	.40	.18
273	Alan Benes FOIL	.25	.11
274	Dustin Hermanson FOIL	.40	.18
275	Ricky Bottalico FOIL	.25	.11
276	Albert Belle	1.00	.45
277	Deion Sanders	.50	.23
278	Matt Williams	1.00	.45
279	Jeff Bagwell	1.25	.55
280	Kirby Puckett	1.50	.70
281	Dave Hollins	.25	.11
282	Don Mattingly	2.00	.90
283	Joey Hamilton	.50	.23
284	Bobby Bonilla	.50	.23
285	Moises Alou	.25	.11
286	Tom Glavine	1.00	.45
287	Brett Butler	.50	.23
288	Chris Hoiles	.25	.11
289	Kenny Rogers	.25	.11
290	Larry Walker	1.00	.45
291	Tim Raines	.50	.23
292	Kevin Appier	.25	.11
293	Roger Clemens	2.50	1.10
294	Chuck Carr	.25	.11
295	Randy Myers	.25	.11
296	Dave Nilsson	.25	.11
297	Joe Carter	.50	.23
298	Chuck Finley	.25	.11
299	Ray Lankford	.50	.23
300	Roberto Kelly	.25	.11
301	Jon Lieber	.25	.11
302	Travis Fryman	.50	.23
303	Mark McGwire	5.00	2.20
304	Tony Gwynn	2.50	1.10
305	Kenny Lofton	.75	.35
306	Mark Whiten	.25	.11
307	Doug Drabek	.25	.11
308	Terry Steinbach	.25	.11
309	Ryan Klesko	.50	.23
310	Mike Piazza	3.00	1.35
311	Ben McDonald	.25	.11
312	Reggie Sanders	.50	.23
313	Alex Fernandez	.25	.11
314	Aaron Sele	.25	.11
315	Gregg Jefferies	.25	.11
316	Rickey Henderson	1.25	.55
317	Brian Anderson	.50	.23

#	Player	MINT	NRMT
318	Jose Valentin	.25	.11
319	Rod Beck	.25	.11
320	Marquis Grissom	.50	.23
321	Ken Griffey Jr.	5.00	2.20
322	Bret Saberhagen	.50	.23
323	Juan Gonzalez	2.00	.90
324	Paul Molitor	1.00	.45
325	Gary Sheffield	.50	.23
326	Darren Daulton	.50	.23
327	Bill Swift	.25	.11
328	Brian McRae	.25	.11
329	Robin Ventura	.50	.23
330	Lee Smith	.50	.23
331	Fred McGriff	.75	.35
332	Delino DeShields	.25	.11
333	Edgar Martinez	.50	.23
334	Mike Mussina	1.00	.45
335	Orlando Merced	.25	.11
336	Carlos Baerga	.25	.11
337	Wil Cordero	.25	.11
338	Tom Pagnozzi	.25	.11
339	Pat Hentgen	.50	.23
340	Chad Curtis	.25	.11
341	Darren Lewis	.25	.11
342	Jeff Kent	.50	.23
343	Bip Roberts	.25	.11
344	Ivan Rodriguez	1.25	.55
345	Jeff Montgomery	.25	.11
346	Hal Morris	.25	.11
347	Danny Tartabull	.25	.11
348	Raul Mondesi	.75	.35
349	Ken Hill	.25	.11
350	Pedro Martinez	1.25	.55
351	Frank Thomas	2.00	.90
352	Manny Ramirez	1.25	.55
353	Tim Salmon	1.00	.45
354	W. VanLandingham	.25	.11
355	Andres Galarraga	1.00	.45
356	Paul O'Neill	.50	.23
357	Brady Anderson	.50	.23
358	Ramon Martinez	.50	.23
359	John Olerud	.50	.23
360	Ruben Sierra	.25	.11
361	Cal Eldred	.25	.11
362	Jay Buhner	.50	.23
363	Jay Bell	.25	.11
364	Wally Joyner	.50	.23
365	Chuck Knoblauch	1.00	.45
366	Len Dykstra	.50	.23
367	John Wetteland	.50	.23
368	Roberto Alomar	1.00	.45
369	Craig Biggio	1.00	.45
370	Ozzie Smith	1.25	.55
371	Terry Pendleton	.25	.11
372	Sammy Sosa	3.00	1.35
373	Carlos Garcia	.25	.11
374	Jose Rijo	.25	.11
375	Chris Gomez	.25	.11
376	Barry Bonds	1.25	.55
377	Steve Avery	.25	.11
378	Rick Wilkins	.25	.11
379	Pete Harnisch	.25	.11
380	Dean Palmer	.50	.23
381	Bob Hamelin	.25	.11
382	Jason Bere	.25	.11
383	Jimmy Key	.25	.11
384	Dante Bichette	.50	.23
385	Rafael Palmeiro	1.00	.45
386	David Justice	1.00	.45
387	Chili Davis	.50	.23
388	Mike Greenwell	.25	.11
389	Todd Zeile	.25	.11
390	Jeff Conine	.25	.11
391	Rick Aguilera	.25	.11
392	Eddie Murray	1.00	.45
393	Mike Stanley	.25	.11
394	Cliff Floyd UER	.50	.23
	(Numbered 294)		
395	Randy Johnson	1.00	.45
396	David Nied	.25	.11
397	Devon White	.50	.23
398	Royce Clayton	.25	.11
399	Andy Benes	.50	.23
400	John Hudek	.25	.11
401	Bobby Jones	.25	.11
402	Eric Karros	.50	.23
403	Will Clark	1.00	.45
404	Mark Langston	.25	.11
405	Kevin Brown	.75	.35
406	Greg Maddux	2.50	1.10
407	David Cone	.75	.35
408	Wade Boggs	1.00	.45
409	Steve Trachsel	.25	.11
410	Greg Vaughn	.50	.23
411	Mo Vaughn	1.00	.45
412	Wilson Alvarez	.25	.11
413	Cal Ripken	4.00	1.80
414	Rico Brogna	.25	.11
415	Barry Larkin	1.00	.45
416	Cecil Fielder	.50	.23
417	Jose Canseco	1.25	.55
418	Jack McDowell	.25	.11
419	Mike Lieberthal	.25	.11
420	Andrew Lorraine	.25	.11
421	Rich Becker	.25	.11
422	Tony Phillips	.25	.11
423	Scott Ruffcorn	.25	.11
424	Jeff Granger	.25	.11
425	Greg Pirkl	.25	.11
426	Dennis Eckersley	.50	.23
427	Jose Lima	.25	.11
428	Russ Davis	.50	.23
429	Armando Benitez	.25	.11
430	Alex Gonzalez	.25	.11
431	Carlos Delgado	1.00	.45
432	Chan Ho Park	1.00	.45
433	Mickey Tettleton	.25	.11
434	Dave Winfield	.50	.23
435	John Burkett	.25	.11
436	Orlando Miller	.25	.11
437	Rondell White	.50	.23
438	Jose Oliva	.25	.11
439	Checklist	.25	.11

1995 Bowman Gold Foil

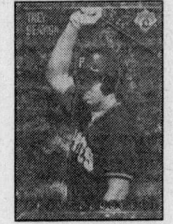

	MINT	NRMT
COMPLETE SET (54)	150.00	70.00
COMMON CARD (221-274)	1.00	.45

*STARS: 1X TO 2.5X BASIC CARDS
*RC's/PROSPECTS: .4X TO 1X BASIC
STATED ODDS 1:6

#	Player	MINT	NRMT
221	Dwayne Hosey	1.00	.45
222	Brad Woodall	1.00	.45
223	Billy Ashley	1.00	.45
224	Mark Grudzielanek	1.00	.45
225	Mark Johnson	1.00	.45
226	Tim Unroe	1.00	.45
227	Todd Greene	1.00	.45
228	Larry Sutton	1.00	.45
229	Derek Jeter	8.00	3.60
230	Sal Fasano	1.00	.45
231	Ruben Rivera	12.00	5.50
232	Chris Truby	1.00	.45
233	John Donati	1.00	.45
234	Decomba Conner	1.00	.45
235	Sergio Nunez	1.00	.45
236	Ray Brown	1.00	.45
237	Juan Melo	1.00	.45
238	Hideo Nomo	6.00	2.70
239	Jaime Bluma	1.00	.45
240	Jay Payton	8.00	3.60
241	Paul Konerko	6.00	2.70
242	Scott Elarton	1.00	.45
243	Jeff Abbott	1.00	.45
244	Jim Brower	1.00	.45
245	Geoff Blum	1.00	.45
246	Aaron Boone	1.00	.45
247	J.R. Phillips	1.00	.45
248	Alex Ochoa	1.00	.45
249	Nomar Garciaparra	20.00	9.00
250	Garret Anderson	1.00	.45
251	Ray Durham	1.00	.45
252	Paul Shuey	1.00	.45
253	Tony Clark	4.00	1.80
254	Johnny Damon	1.00	.45
255	Duane Singleton	1.00	.45
256	LaTroy Hawkins	1.00	.45
257	Andy Pettitte	12.00	5.50
258	Ben Grieve	10.00	4.50
259	Marc Newfield	1.00	.45
260	Terrell Lowery	1.00	.45
261	Shawn Green	1.00	.45
262	Chipper Jones	8.00	3.60
263	Brooks Kieschnick	1.00	.45
264	Calvin Reese	1.00	.45
265	Doug Million	1.00	.45
266	Marc Valdes	1.00	.45
267	Brian L.Hunter	1.00	.45
268	Todd Hollandsworth	1.00	.45
269	Rod Henderson	1.00	.45
270	Bill Pulsipher	1.00	.45
271	Scott Rolen	50.00	22.00
272	Trey Beamon	1.00	.45
273	Alan Benes	1.00	.45
274	Dustin Hermanson	1.00	.45

1996 Bowman

	MINT	NRMT
COMPLETE SET (385)	120.00	55.00
COMMON CARD (1-385)	.20	.09
MINOR STARS	.40	.18
UNLISTED STARS	.75	.35

MANTLE STATED ODDS 1:48

#	Player	MINT	NRMT
1	Cal Ripken	3.00	1.35
2	Ray Durham	.40	.18
3	Ivan Rodriguez	1.00	.45
4	Fred McGriff	.60	.25
5	Hideo Nomo	.75	.35
6	Troy Percival	.40	.18
7	Moises Alou	.40	.18
8	Mike Stanley	.20	.09
9	Jay Buhner	.40	.18
10	Shawn Green	.75	.35
11	Ryan Klesko	.40	.18
12	Andres Galarraga	.75	.35
13	Dean Palmer	.40	.18
14	Jeff Conine	.20	.09
15	Brian L.Hunter	.20	.09
16	J.T. Snow	.40	.18
17	Larry Walker	.75	.35
18	Barry Larkin	.75	.35
19	Alex Gonzalez	.20	.09
20	Edgar Martinez	.40	.18
21	Mo Vaughn	.75	.35
22	Mark McGwire	4.00	1.80
23	Jose Canseco	1.00	.45
24	Jack McDowell	.20	.09
25	Dante Bichette	.40	.18

❑ 26	Wade Boggs	.75	.35
❑ 27	Mike Piazza	2.50	1.10
❑ 28	Ray Lankford	.40	.18
❑ 29	Craig Biggio	.75	.35
❑ 30	Rafael Palmeiro	.75	.35
❑ 31	Ron Gant	.20	.09
❑ 32	Javy Lopez	.40	.18
❑ 33	Brian Jordan	.40	.18
❑ 34	Paul O'Neill	.40	.18
❑ 35	Mark Grace	.60	.25
❑ 36	Matt Williams	.75	.35
❑ 37	Pedro Martinez	1.00	.45
❑ 38	Rickey Henderson	1.00	.45
❑ 39	Bobby Bonilla	.40	.18
❑ 40	Todd Hollandsworth	.20	.09
❑ 41	Jim Thome	.75	.35
❑ 42	Gary Sheffield	.40	.18
❑ 43	Tim Salmon	.60	.25
❑ 44	Gregg Jefferies	.20	.09
❑ 45	Roberto Alomar	.75	.35
❑ 46	Carlos Baerga	.20	.09
❑ 47	Mark Grudzielanek	.20	.09
❑ 48	Randy Johnson	.75	.35
❑ 49	Tino Martinez	.40	.18
❑ 50	Robin Ventura	.40	.18
❑ 51	Ryne Sandberg	1.00	.45
❑ 52	Jay Bell	.40	.18
❑ 53	Jason Schmidt	.20	.09
❑ 54	Frank Thomas	1.50	.70
❑ 55	Kenny Lofton	.60	.25
❑ 56	Ariel Prieto	.20	.09
❑ 57	David Cone	.60	.25
❑ 58	Reggie Sanders	.40	.18
❑ 59	Michael Tucker	.20	.09
❑ 60	Vinny Castilla	.60	.25
❑ 61	Len Dykstra	.40	.18
❑ 62	Todd Hundley	.40	.18
❑ 63	Brian McRae	.20	.09
❑ 64	Dennis Eckersley	.40	.18
❑ 65	Rondell White	.40	.18
❑ 66	Eric Karros	.40	.18
❑ 67	Greg Maddux	2.00	.90
❑ 68	Kevin Appier	.40	.18
❑ 69	Eddie Murray	.75	.35
❑ 70	John Olerud	.40	.18
❑ 71	Tony Gwynn	2.00	.90
❑ 72	David Justice	.75	.35
❑ 73	Ken Caminiti	.40	.18
❑ 74	Terry Steinbach	.20	.09
❑ 75	Alan Benes	.20	.09
❑ 76	Chipper Jones	2.00	.90
❑ 77	Jeff Bagwell	1.00	.45
❑ 78	Barry Bonds	1.00	.45
❑ 79	Ken Griffey Jr.	4.00	1.80
❑ 80	Roger Cedeno	.40	.18
❑ 81	Joe Carter	.40	.18
❑ 82	Henry Rodriguez	.40	.18
❑ 83	Jason Isringhausen	.40	.18
❑ 84	Chuck Knoblauch	.75	.35
❑ 85	Manny Ramirez	1.00	.45
❑ 86	Tom Glavine	.75	.35
❑ 87	Jeffrey Hammonds	.40	.18
❑ 88	Paul Molitor	.75	.35
❑ 89	Roger Clemens	2.00	.90
❑ 90	Greg Vaughn	.40	.18
❑ 91	Marty Cordova	.40	.18
❑ 92	Albert Belle	.75	.35
❑ 93	Mike Mussina	.75	.35
❑ 94	Garret Anderson	.40	.18
❑ 95	Juan Gonzalez	1.50	.70
❑ 96	John Valentin	.40	.18
❑ 97	Jason Giambi	.40	.18
❑ 98	Kirby Puckett	1.25	.55
❑ 99	Jim Edmonds	.60	.25
❑ 100	Cecil Fielder	.40	.18
❑ 101	Mike Aldrete	.20	.09
❑ 102	Marquis Grissom	.40	.18
❑ 103	Derek Bell	.40	.18
❑ 104	Raul Mondesi	.40	.18
❑ 105	Sammy Sosa	2.50	1.10
❑ 106	Travis Fryman	.40	.18
❑ 107	Rico Brogna	.20	.09
❑ 108	Will Clark	.75	.35
❑ 109	Bernie Williams	.75	.35
❑ 110	Brady Anderson	.40	.18
❑ 111	Torii Hunter	.40	.18
❑ 112	Derek Jeter	2.50	1.10
❑ 113	Mike Kusiewicz	.50	.23
❑ 114	Scott Rolen	3.00	1.35
❑ 115	Ramon Castro	.40	.18
❑ 116	Jose Guillen	3.00	1.35
❑ 117	Wade Walker	.20	.09
❑ 118	Shawn Senior	.20	.09
❑ 119	Onan Masaoka	2.00	.90
❑ 120	Marlon Anderson	3.00	1.35
❑ 121	Katsuhiro Maeda	1.00	.45
❑ 122	Garrett Stephenson	.20	.09
❑ 123	Butch Huskey	.20	.09
❑ 124	D'Angelo Jimenez	6.00	2.70
❑ 125	Tony Mounce	.50	.23
❑ 126	Jay Canizaro	.20	.09
❑ 127	Juan Melo	.40	.18
❑ 128	Steve Gibralter	.20	.09
❑ 129	Freddy Garcia	.20	.09
❑ 130	Julio Santana UER	.20	.09
	Card has him born in 1993		
❑ 131	Richard Hidalgo	.40	.18
❑ 132	Jermaine Dye	.40	.18
❑ 133	Willie Adams	.20	.09
❑ 134	Everett Stull	.20	.09
❑ 135	Ramon Morel	.20	.09
❑ 136	Chan Ho Park	.60	.25
❑ 137	Jamey Wright	.20	.09
❑ 138	Luis Garcia	.20	.09
❑ 139	Dan Serafini	.20	.09
❑ 140	Ryan Dempster	1.00	.45
❑ 141	Tate Seefried	.20	.09
❑ 142	Jimmy Hurst	.20	.09
❑ 143	Travis Miller	.20	.09
❑ 144	Curtis Goodwin	.20	.09
❑ 145	Rocky Coppinger	.75	.35
❑ 146	Enrique Wilson	.20	.09
❑ 147	Jaime Bluma	.20	.09
❑ 148	Andrew Vessel	.20	.09
❑ 149	Damian Moss	.20	.09
❑ 150	Shawn Gallagher	2.00	.90
❑ 151	Pat Watkins	.40	.18
❑ 152	Jose Paniagua	.20	.09
❑ 153	Danny Graves	.60	.25
❑ 154	Bryon Gainey	.50	.23
❑ 155	Steve Soderstrom	.20	.09
❑ 156	Cliff Brumbaugh	.20	.09
❑ 157	Eugene Kingsale	1.50	.70
❑ 158	Lou Collier	.20	.09
❑ 159	Todd Walker	1.00	.45
❑ 160	Kris Detmers	1.00	.45
❑ 161	Josh Booty	2.00	.90
❑ 162	Greg Whiteman	.20	.09
❑ 163	Damian Jackson	.20	.09
❑ 164	Tony Clark	.75	.35
❑ 165	Jeff D'Amico	.20	.09
❑ 166	Johnny Damon	.60	.25
❑ 167	Rafael Orellano	.20	.09
❑ 168	Ruben Rivera	.40	.18
❑ 169	Alex Ochoa	.40	.18
❑ 170	Jay Powell	.20	.09
❑ 171	Tom Evans	.20	.09
❑ 172	Ron Villone	.20	.09
❑ 173	Shawn Estes	.40	.18
❑ 174	John Wasdin	.20	.09
❑ 175	Bill Simas	.20	.09
❑ 176	Kevin Brown	.60	.25
❑ 177	Shannon Stewart	.40	.18
❑ 178	Todd Greene	.40	.18
❑ 179	Bob Wolcott	.20	.09
❑ 180	Chris Snopek	.20	.09
❑ 181	Nomar Garciaparra	4.00	1.80
❑ 182	Cameron Smith	.20	.09
❑ 183	Matt Drews	.20	.09
❑ 184	Jimmy Haynes	.20	.09
❑ 185	Chris Carpenter	.40	.18
❑ 186	Desi Relaford	.20	.09
❑ 187	Ben Grieve	1.50	.70
❑ 188	Mike Bell	.20	.09
❑ 189	Luis Castillo	1.50	.70
❑ 190	Ugueth Urbina	.40	.18
❑ 191	Paul Wilson	.20	.09
❑ 192	Andruw Jones	2.50	1.10
❑ 193	Wayne Gomes	.20	.09
❑ 194	Craig Counsell	1.00	.45
❑ 195	Jim Cole	.20	.09
❑ 196	Brooks Kieschnick	.20	.09
❑ 197	Trey Beamon	.20	.09
❑ 198	Marino Santana	.20	.09
❑ 199	Bob Abreu	.60	.25
❑ 200	Calvin Reese	.20	.09
❑ 201	Dante Powell	1.50	.70
❑ 202	George Arias	.20	.09
❑ 203	Jorge Velandia	.20	.09
❑ 204	George Lombard	6.00	2.70
❑ 205	Byron Browne	.20	.09
❑ 206	John Frascatore	.20	.09
❑ 207	Terry Adams	.20	.09
❑ 208	Wilson Delgado	.50	.23
❑ 209	Billy McMillon	.20	.09
❑ 210	Jeff Abbott	.40	.18
❑ 211	Trot Nixon	.40	.18
❑ 212	Amaury Telemaco	.20	.09
❑ 213	Scott Sullivan	.20	.09
❑ 214	Justin Thompson	.40	.18
❑ 215	Decomba Conner	.20	.09
❑ 216	Ryan McGuire	.20	.09
❑ 217	Matt Luke	.20	.09
❑ 218	Doug Million	.20	.09
❑ 219	Jason Dickson	1.50	.70
❑ 220	Ramon Hernandez	4.00	1.80
❑ 221	Mark Bellhorn	1.00	.45
❑ 222	Eric Ludwick	.50	.23
❑ 223	Luke Wilcox	.20	.09
❑ 224	Marty Malloy	.50	.23
❑ 225	Gary Coffee	.40	.18
❑ 226	Wendell Magee	.40	.18
❑ 227	Brett Tomko	1.50	.70
❑ 228	Derek Lowe	.20	.09
❑ 229	Jose Rosado	2.50	1.10
❑ 230	Steve Bourgeois	.20	.09
❑ 231	Neil Weber	.20	.09
❑ 232	Jeff Ware	.20	.09
❑ 233	Calvin Diaz	.40	.18
❑ 234	Greg Norton	.20	.09
❑ 235	Aaron Boone	.20	.09
❑ 236	Jeff Suppan	.20	.09
❑ 237	Bret Wagner	.20	.09
❑ 238	Elieser Marrero	.20	.09
❑ 239	Will Cunnane	.40	.18
❑ 240	Brian Barkley	.50	.23
❑ 241	Jay Payton	.20	.09
❑ 242	Marcus Jensen	.20	.09
❑ 243	Ryan Nye	.20	.09
❑ 244	Chad Mottola	.20	.09
❑ 245	Scott McClain	.20	.09
❑ 246	Jessie Ibarra	.40	.18
❑ 247	Mike Darr	4.00	1.80
❑ 248	Bobby Estalella	1.50	.70
❑ 249	Michael Barrett	1.00	.45
❑ 250	Jamie Lopiccolo	.50	.23
❑ 251	Shane Spencer	6.00	2.70
❑ 252	Ben Petrick	6.00	2.70
❑ 253	Jason Bell	1.00	.45
❑ 254	Arnold Gooch	.50	.23
❑ 255	T.J. Mathews	.20	.09
❑ 256	Jason Ryan	.20	.09
❑ 257	Pat Cline	1.50	.70
❑ 258	Rafael Carmona	.20	.09
❑ 259	Carl Pavano	3.00	1.35
❑ 260	Ben Davis	1.25	.55
❑ 261	Matt Lawton	2.50	1.10
❑ 262	Kevin Sefcik	.20	.09
❑ 263	Chris Fussell	1.00	.45
❑ 264	Mike Cameron	3.00	1.35
❑ 265	Marty Janzen	.20	.09
❑ 266	Livan Hernandez	3.00	1.35
❑ 267	Raul Ibanez	.20	.09
❑ 268	Juan Encarnacion	1.25	.55
❑ 269	David Yocum	.50	.23
❑ 270	Jonathan Johnson	.50	.23
❑ 271	Reggie Taylor	.20	.09
❑ 272	Danny Buxbaum	1.00	.45
❑ 273	Jacob Cruz	.40	.18
❑ 274	Bobby Morris	.20	.09
❑ 275	Andy Fox	.20	.09
❑ 276	Greg Keagle	.20	.09
❑ 277	Charles Peterson	.20	.09
❑ 278	Derrek Lee	.75	.35
❑ 279	Bryant Nelson	.50	.23
❑ 280	Antone Williamson	.20	.09
❑ 281	Scott Elarton	.60	.25
❑ 282	Shad Williams	.20	.09

☐ 283	Rich Hunter	.20	.09
☐ 284	Chris Sheff	.20	.09
☐ 285	Derrick Gibson	.75	.35
☐ 286	Felix Rodriguez	.20	.09
☐ 287	Brian Banks	.20	.09
☐ 288	Jason McDonald	.20	.09
☐ 289	Glendon Rusch	1.00	.45
☐ 290	Gary Rath	.20	.09
☐ 291	Peter Munro	.40	.18
☐ 292	Tom Fordham	.20	.09
☐ 293	Jason Kendall	.75	.35
☐ 294	Russ Johnson	.20	.09
☐ 295	Joe Long	.20	.09
☐ 296	Robert Smith	1.50	.70
☐ 297	Jarrod Washburn	2.00	.90
☐ 298	Dave Coggin	.60	.25
☐ 299	Jeff Yoder	.50	.23
☐ 300	Jed Hansen	.40	.18
☐ 301	Matt Morris	1.50	.70
☐ 302	Josh Bishop	.50	.23
☐ 303	Dustin Hermanson	.20	.09
☐ 304	Mike Gulan	.20	.09
☐ 305	Felipe Crespo	.20	.09
☐ 306	Quinton McCracken	.20	.09
☐ 307	Jim Bonnici	.20	.09
☐ 308	Sal Fasano	.20	.09
☐ 309	Gabe Alvarez	1.25	.55
☐ 310	Heath Murray	.50	.23
☐ 311	Jose Valentin	1.00	.45
☐ 312	Bartolo Colon	.75	.35
☐ 313	Olmedo Saenz	.20	.09
☐ 314	Norm Hutchins	1.50	.70
☐ 315	Chris Holt	.20	.09
☐ 316	David Doster	.20	.09
☐ 317	Robert Person	.20	.09
☐ 318	Donne Wall	.20	.09
☐ 319	Adam Riggs	.20	.09
☐ 320	Homer Bush	.20	.09
☐ 321	Brad Rigby	.20	.09
☐ 322	Lou Merloni	.50	.23
☐ 323	Neifi Perez	.40	.18
☐ 324	Chris Cumberland	.20	.09
☐ 325	Alvie Shepherd	.20	.09
☐ 326	Jarrod Patterson	.20	.09
☐ 327	Ray Ricken	.20	.09
☐ 328	Danny Klassen	1.50	.70
☐ 329	David Miller	.50	.23
☐ 330	Chad Alexander	.75	.35
☐ 331	Matt Beaumont	.20	.09
☐ 332	Damon Hollins	.20	.09
☐ 333	Todd Dunn	.20	.09
☐ 334	Mike Sweeney	4.00	1.80
☐ 335	Richie Sexson	1.25	.55
☐ 336	Billy Wagner	.60	.25
☐ 337	Ron Wright	1.50	.70
☐ 338	Paul Konerko	.75	.35
☐ 339	Tommy Phelps	.50	.23
☐ 340	Karim Garcia	.40	.18
☐ 341	Mike Grace	.20	.09
☐ 342	Russell Branyan	8.00	3.60
☐ 343	Randy Winn	2.50	1.10
☐ 344	A.J. Pierzynski	1.50	.70
☐ 345	Mike Busby	.20	.09
☐ 346	Matt Beech	.50	.23
☐ 347	Jose Cepeda	.50	.23
☐ 348	Brian Stephenson	.20	.09
☐ 349	Rey Ordonez	.75	.35
☐ 350	Rich Aurilia	1.00	.45
☐ 351	Edgard Velazquez	2.50	1.10
☐ 352	Raul Casanova	.20	.09
☐ 353	Carlos Guillen	3.00	1.35
☐ 354	Bruce Aven	2.00	.90
☐ 355	Ryan Jones	.75	.35
☐ 356	Derek Aucoin	.20	.09
☐ 357	Brian Rose	3.00	1.35
☐ 358	Richard Almanzar	.50	.23
☐ 359	Fletcher Bates	.75	.35
☐ 360	Russ Ortiz	4.00	1.80
☐ 361	Wilton Guerrero	1.50	.70
☐ 362	Geoff Jenkins	5.00	2.20
☐ 363	Pete Janicki	.20	.09
☐ 364	Yamil Benitez	.20	.09
☐ 365	Aaron Holbert	.20	.09
☐ 366	Tim Belk	.20	.09
☐ 367	Terrell Wade	.20	.09
☐ 368	Terrence Long	.40	.18

☐ 369	Brad Fullmer	.60	.25
☐ 370	Matt Wagner	.20	.09
☐ 371	Craig Wilson	.20	.09
☐ 372	Mark Loretta	.20	.09
☐ 373	Eric Owens	.20	.09
☐ 374	Vladimir Guerrero	3.00	1.35
☐ 375	Tommy Davis	.20	.09
☐ 376	Donnie Sadler	.40	.18
☐ 377	Edgar Renteria	.40	.18
☐ 378	Todd Helton	4.00	1.80
☐ 379	Ralph Milliard	.20	.09
☐ 380	Darin Blood	1.00	.45
☐ 381	Shayne Bennett	.20	.09
☐ 382	Mark Redman	.20	.09
☐ 383	Felix Martinez	.20	.09
☐ 384	Sean Watkins	.75	.35
☐ 385	Oscar Henriquez	.20	.09
☐ M20	1952 Bowman Mantle	10.00	4.50
☐ NNO	Unnumbered Checklists	.20	.09

1996 Bowman Foil

	MINT	NRMT
COMPLETE SET (385)	300.00	135.00
COMMON CARD (1-385)	.50	.23

*STARS: 1X TO 2.5X BASIC CARDS
*ROOKIES: .6X TO 1.5X BASIC CARDS
ONE FOIL OR INSERT CARD PER HOBBY PACK
TWO FOILS PER RETAIL PACK

1996 Bowman Minor League POY

	MINT	NRMT
COMPLETE SET (15)	30.00	13.50
COMMON CARD (1-15)	1.50	.70
SEMISTARS	2.00	.90

STATED ODDS 1:12

☐ 1	Andruw Jones	8.00	3.60
☐ 2	Derrick Gibson	2.50	1.10
☐ 3	Bob Abreu	2.00	.90
☐ 4	Todd Walker	2.50	1.10
☐ 5	Jamey Wright	1.50	.70
☐ 6	Wes Helms	2.50	1.10
☐ 7	Karim Garcia	1.75	.80
☐ 8	Bartolo Colon	2.50	1.10
☐ 9	Alex Ochoa	1.50	.70
☐ 10	Mike Sweeney	2.50	1.10

☐ 11	Ruben Rivera	1.75	.80
☐ 12	Gabe Alvarez	2.50	1.10
☐ 13	Billy Wagner	2.00	.90
☐ 14	Vladimir Guerrero	10.00	4.50
☐ 15	Edgard Velazquez	3.00	1.35

1997 Bowman

	MINT	NRMT
COMPLETE SET (441)	120.00	55.00
COMPLETE SERIES 1 (221)	60.00	27.00
COMPLETE SERIES 2 (220)	60.00	27.00
COMMON CARD (1-441)	.20	.09
MINOR STARS	.40	.18
UNLISTED STARS	.75	.35

CARDS 155 AND 158 DON'T EXIST
REESE AND ARIAS BOTH NUMBERED 156
CARPENTER 'N MILTON BOTH NUMBER 159
CONDITION SENSITIVE SET

☐ 1	Derek Jeter	2.50	1.10
☐ 2	Edgar Renteria	.40	.18
☐ 3	Chipper Jones	2.00	.90
☐ 4	Hideo Nomo	.75	.35
☐ 5	Tim Salmon	.75	.35
☐ 6	Jason Giambi	.40	.18
☐ 7	Robin Ventura	.40	.18
☐ 8	Tony Clark	.50	.23
☐ 9	Barry Larkin	.75	.35
☐ 10	Paul Molitor	.75	.35
☐ 11	Bernard Gilkey	.20	.09
☐ 12	Jack McDowell	.20	.09
☐ 13	Andy Benes	.40	.18
☐ 14	Ryan Klesko	.40	.18
☐ 15	Mark McGwire	4.00	1.80
☐ 16	Ken Griffey Jr.	4.00	1.80
☐ 17	Robb Nen	.20	.09
☐ 18	Cal Ripken	3.00	1.35
☐ 19	John Valentin	.40	.18
☐ 20	Ricky Bottalico	.40	.18
☐ 21	Mike Lansing	.20	.09
☐ 22	Ryne Sandberg	1.00	.45
☐ 23	Carlos Delgado	.75	.35
☐ 24	Craig Biggio	.75	.35
☐ 25	Eric Karros	.40	.18
☐ 26	Kevin Appier	.40	.18
☐ 27	Mariano Rivera	.40	.18
☐ 28	Vinny Castilla	.50	.23
☐ 29	Juan Gonzalez	1.50	.70
☐ 30	Al Martin	.20	.09
☐ 31	Jeff Cirillo	.40	.18
☐ 32	Eddie Murray	.75	.35
☐ 33	Ray Lankford	.40	.18
☐ 34	Manny Ramirez	1.00	.45
☐ 35	Roberto Alomar	.75	.35
☐ 36	Will Clark	.75	.35
☐ 37	Chuck Knoblauch	.75	.35
☐ 38	Harold Baines	.40	.18
☐ 39	Trevor Hoffman	.40	.18
☐ 40	Edgar Martinez	.40	.18
☐ 41	Geronimo Berroa	.20	.09
☐ 42	Rey Ordonez	.40	.18
☐ 43	Mike Stanley	.20	.09
☐ 44	Mike Mussina	.75	.35
☐ 45	Kevin Brown	.50	.23
☐ 46	Dennis Eckersley	.40	.18
☐ 47	Henry Rodriguez	.40	.18
☐ 48	Tino Martinez	.75	.35

49	Eric Young	.40	.18
50	Bret Boone	.40	.18
51	Raul Mondesi	.40	.18
52	Sammy Sosa	2.50	1.10
53	John Smoltz	.50	.23
54	Billy Wagner	.40	.18
55	Jeff D'Amico	.20	.09
56	Ken Caminiti	.50	.23
57	Jason Kendall	.50	.23
58	Wade Boggs	.75	.35
59	Andres Galarraga	.75	.35
60	Jeff Brantley	.20	.09
61	Mel Rojas	.20	.09
62	Brian L. Hunter	.40	.18
63	Bobby Bonilla	.40	.18
64	Roger Clemens	2.00	.90
65	Jeff Kent	.40	.18
66	Matt Williams	.75	.35
67	Albert Belle	.75	.35
68	Jeff King	.20	.09
69	John Wetteland	.40	.18
70	Deion Sanders	.40	.18
71	Bubba Trammell	.60	.25
72	Felix Heredia	.75	.35
73	Billy Koch	3.00	1.35
74	Sidney Ponson	2.50	1.10
75	Ricky Ledee	3.00	1.35
76	Brett Tomko	.20	.09
77	Braden Looper	.50	.23
78	Damian Jackson	.20	.09
79	Jason Dickson	.20	.09
80	Chad Green	.75	.35
81	R.A. Dickey	.50	.23
82	Jeff Liefer	.40	.18
83	Matt Wagner	.20	.09
84	Richard Hidalgo	.40	.18
85	Adam Riggs	.20	.09
86	Robert Smith	.20	.09
87	Chad Hermansen	3.00	1.35
88	Felix Martinez	.20	.09
89	J.J. Johnson	.20	.09
90	Todd Dunwoody	.40	.18
91	Katsuhiro Maeda	.40	.18
92	Darin Erstad	.75	.35
93	Elieser Marrero	.20	.09
94	Bartolo Colon	.40	.18
95	Chris Fussell	.20	.09
96	Ugueth Urbina	.40	.18
97	Josh Paul	1.00	.45
98	Jaime Bluma	.20	.09
99	Seth Greisinger	1.00	.45
100	Jose Cruz Jr.	2.50	1.10
101	Todd Dunn	.20	.09
102	Joe Young	.50	.23
103	Jonathan Johnson	.20	.09
104	Justin Towle	1.00	.45
105	Brian Rose	.75	.35
106	Jose Guillen	.50	.23
107	Andruw Jones	1.00	.45
108	Mark Kotsay	1.50	.70
109	Wilton Guerrero	.20	.09
110	Jacob Cruz	.20	.09
111	Mike Sweeney	.20	.09
112	Julio Mosquera	.20	.09
113	Matt Morris	.40	.18
114	Wendell Magee	.20	.09
115	John Thomson	.20	.09
116	Javier (Jose) Valentin	.40	.18
117	Tom Fordham	.20	.09
118	Ruben Rivera	.40	.18
119	Mike Drumright	.75	.35
120	Chris Holt	.20	.09
121	Sean Maloney	.20	.09
122	Michael Barrett	.20	.09
123	Tony Saunders	.50	.23
124	Kevin Brown C	.20	.09
125	Richard Almanzar	.20	.09
126	Mark Redman	.20	.09
127	Anthony Sanders	1.00	.45
128	Jeff Abbott	.20	.09
129	Eugene Kingsale	.40	.18
130	Paul Konerko	.75	.35
131	Randall Simon	1.25	.55
132	Andy Larkin	.20	.09
133	Rafael Medina	.40	.18
134	Mendy Lopez	.20	.09
135	Freddy Garcia	.20	.09
136	Karim Garcia	.40	.18
137	Larry Rodriguez	.50	.23
138	Carlos Guillen	.40	.18
139	Aaron Boone	.20	.09
140	Donnie Sadler	.40	.18
141	Brooks Kieschnick	.20	.09
142	Scott Spiezio	.20	.09
143	Everett Stull	.20	.09
144	Enrique Wilson	.40	.18
145	Milton Bradley	4.00	1.80
146	Kevin Orie	.20	.09
147	Derek Wallace	.20	.09
148	Russ Johnson	.20	.09
149	Joe Lagarde	.50	.23
150	Luis Castillo	.40	.18
151	Jay Payton	.20	.09
152	Joe Long	.40	.18
153	Livan Hernandez	.40	.18
154	Vladimir Nunez	1.00	.45
155	Calvin Reese UER	.40	.18
	Card actually numbered 156		
156	George Arias	.20	.09
157	Homer Bush	.40	.18
158	Chris Carpenter UER	.40	.18
	Card numbered 159		
159	Eric Milton	1.25	.55
160	Richie Sexson	.50	.23
161	Carl Pavano	.75	.35
162	Chris Gissell	.50	.23
163	Mac Suzuki	.20	.09
164	Pat Cline	.40	.18
165	Ron Wright	.40	.18
166	Dante Powell	.40	.18
167	Mark Bellhorn	.20	.09
168	George Lombard	.75	.35
169	Pee Wee Lopez	1.00	.45
170	Paul Wilder	.60	.25
171	Brad Fullmer	.40	.18
172	Willie Martinez	1.50	.70
173	Dario Veras	.50	.23
174	Dave Coggin	.20	.09
175	Kris Benson	3.00	1.35
176	Torii Hunter	.20	.09
177	D.T. Cromer	.20	.09
178	Nelson Figueroa	.60	.25
179	Hiram Bocachica	1.00	.45
180	Shane Monahan	.40	.18
181	Jimmy Anderson	.75	.35
182	Juan Melo	.40	.18
183	Pablo Ortega	.75	.35
184	Calvin Pickering	3.00	1.35
185	Reggie Taylor	.20	.09
186	Jeff Farnsworth	.50	.23
187	Terrence Long	.40	.18
188	Geoff Jenkins	.40	.18
189	Steve Rain	.50	.23
190	Nerio Rodriguez	.75	.35
191	Derrick Gibson	.50	.23
192	Darin Blood	.20	.09
193	Ben Davis	.75	.35
194	Adrian Beltre	6.00	2.70
195	Damian Sapp UER	1.50	.70
196	Kerry Wood	8.00	3.60
197	Nate Rolison	1.00	.45
198	Fernando Tatis	5.00	2.20
199	Brad Penny	5.00	2.20
200	Jake Westbrook	1.00	.45
201	Edwin Diaz	.20	.09
202	Joe Fontenot	.75	.35
203	Matt Halloran	.60	.25
204	Blake Stein	1.00	.45
205	Onan Masaoka	.40	.18
206	Ben Petrick	.40	.18
207	Matt Clement	2.50	1.10
208	Todd Greene	.20	.09
209	Ray Ricken	.20	.09
210	Eric Chavez	5.00	2.20
211	Edgard Velazquez	.50	.23
212	Bruce Chen	2.50	1.10
213	Danny Patterson	.20	.09
214	Jeff Yoder	.20	.09
215	Luis Ordaz	.20	.09
216	Chris Widger	.20	.09
217	Jason Brester	.40	.18
218	Carlton Loewer	.40	.18
219	Chris Reitsma	.60	.25
220	Neifi Perez	.40	.18
221	Hideki Irabu	2.00	.90
222	Ellis Burks	.40	.18
223	Pedro Martinez	1.00	.45
224	Kenny Lofton	.50	.23
225	Randy Johnson	.75	.35
226	Terry Steinbach	.20	.09
227	Bernie Williams	.75	.35
228	Dean Palmer	.40	.18
229	Alan Benes	.20	.09
230	Marquis Grissom	.40	.18
231	Gary Sheffield	.40	.18
232	Curt Schilling	.50	.23
233	Reggie Sanders	.40	.18
234	Bobby Higginson	.40	.18
235	Moises Alou	.40	.18
236	Tom Glavine	.75	.35
237	Mark Grace	.50	.23
238	Ramon Martinez	.40	.18
239	Rafael Palmeiro	.75	.35
240	John Olerud	.40	.18
241	Dante Bichette	.40	.18
242	Greg Vaughn	.40	.18
243	Jeff Bagwell	1.00	.45
244	Barry Bonds	1.00	.45
245	Pat Hentgen	.40	.18
246	Jim Thome	.75	.35
247	Jermaine Allensworth	.20	.09
248	Andy Pettitte	.50	.23
249	Jay Bell	.40	.18
250	John Jaha	.20	.09
251	Jim Edmonds	.50	.23
252	Ron Gant	.20	.09
253	David Cone	.50	.23
254	Jose Canseco	1.00	.45
255	Jay Buhner	.40	.18
256	Greg Maddux	2.00	.90
257	Brian McRae	.20	.09
258	Lance Johnson	.20	.09
259	Travis Fryman	.40	.18
260	Paul O'Neill	.40	.18
261	Ivan Rodriguez	1.00	.45
262	Gregg Jefferies	.20	.09
263	Fred McGriff	.50	.23
264	Derek Bell	.40	.18
265	Jeff Conine	.20	.09
266	Mike Piazza	2.50	1.10
267	Mark Grudzielanek	.20	.09
268	Brady Anderson	.40	.18
269	Marty Cordova	.20	.09
270	Ray Durham	.40	.18
271	Joe Carter	.40	.18
272	Brian Jordan	.40	.18
273	David Justice	.75	.35
274	Tony Gwynn	2.00	.90
275	Larry Walker	.75	.35
276	Cecil Fielder	.40	.18
277	Mo Vaughn	.75	.35
278	Alex Fernandez	.20	.09
279	Michael Tucker	.20	.09
280	Jose Vizcaino	.20	.09
281	Sandy Alomar	.40	.18
282	Todd Hollandsworth	.20	.09
283	Rico Brogna	.20	.09
284	Rusty Greer	.40	.18
285	Roberto Hernandez	.20	.09
286	Hal Morris	.20	.09
287	Johnny Damon	.40	.18
288	Todd Hundley	.40	.18
289	Rondell White	.40	.18
290	Frank Thomas	1.50	.70
291	Don Denbow	.20	.09
292	Derrek Lee	.50	.23
293	Todd Walker	.75	.35
294	Scott Rolen	1.25	.55
295	Wes Helms	.20	.09
296	Bob Abreu	.40	.18
297	John Patterson	2.00	.90
298	Alex Gonzalez	2.50	1.10
299	Grant Roberts	1.00	.45
300	Jeff Suppan	.20	.09
301	Luke Wilcox	.20	.09
302	Marlon Anderson	.40	.18
303	Ray Brown	.20	.09
304	Mike Caruso	1.25	.55

❑ 305 Sam Marsonek	.50	.23
❑ 306 Brady Raggio	.20	.09
❑ 307 Kevin McGlinchy	1.00	.45
❑ 308 Roy Halladay	2.50	1.10
❑ 309 Jeremi Gonzalez	.75	.35
❑ 310 Aramis Ramirez	5.00	2.20
❑ 311 Dermal Brown	3.00	1.35
❑ 312 Justin Thompson	.40	.18
❑ 313 Jay Tessmer	.20	.09
❑ 314 Mike Johnson	.50	.23
❑ 315 Danny Clybum	.20	.09
❑ 316 Bruce Aven	.20	.09
❑ 317 Keith Foulke	.20	.09
❑ 318 Jimmy Osting	.50	.23
❑ 319 Valerio De Los Santos	.75	.35
❑ 320 Shannon Stewart	.40	.18
❑ 321 Willie Adams	.20	.09
❑ 322 Larry Barnes	.40	.18
❑ 323 Mark Johnson	.50	.23
❑ 324 Chris Stowers	.50	.23
❑ 325 Brandon Reed	.40	.18
❑ 326 Randy Winn	.20	.09
❑ 327 Steve Chavez	.75	.35
❑ 328 Nomar Garciaparra	2.50	1.10
❑ 329 Jacque Jones	2.50	1.10
❑ 330 Chris Clemons	.20	.09
❑ 331 Todd Helton	1.50	.70
❑ 332 Ryan Brannan	.50	.23
❑ 333 Alex Sanchez	1.00	.45
❑ 334 Arnold Gooch	.75	.35
❑ 335 Russell Branyan	.75	.35
❑ 336 Daryle Ward	2.00	.90
❑ 337 John LeRoy	.50	.23
❑ 338 Steve Cox	.20	.09
❑ 339 Kevin Witt	1.00	.45
❑ 340 Norm Hutchins	.20	.09
❑ 341 Gabby Martinez	.20	.09
❑ 342 Kris Detmers	.20	.09
❑ 343 Mike Villano	.20	.09
❑ 344 Preston Wilson	.40	.18
❑ 345 James Manias	.50	.23
❑ 346 Deivi Cruz	1.00	.45
❑ 347 Donzell McDonald	.60	.25
❑ 348 Rod Myers	.75	.35
❑ 349 Shawn Chacon	1.00	.45
❑ 350 Elvin Hernandez	.50	.23
❑ 351 Orlando Cabrera	.75	.35
❑ 352 Brian Banks	.20	.09
❑ 353 Robbie Bell	.75	.35
❑ 354 Brad Rigby	.40	.18
❑ 355 Scott Elarton	.40	.18
❑ 356 Kevin Sweeney	.50	.23
❑ 357 Steve Soderstrom	.20	.09
❑ 358 Ryan Nye	.40	.18
❑ 359 Marlon Allen	.20	.23
❑ 360 Donny Leon	1.50	.70
❑ 361 Garrett Neubart	.75	.35
❑ 362 Abraham Nunez	1.00	.45
❑ 363 Adam Eaton	1.25	.55
❑ 364 Octavio Dotel	3.00	1.35
❑ 365 Dean Crow	.20	.09
❑ 366 Jason Baker	.50	.23
❑ 367 Sean Casey	8.00	3.60
❑ 368 Joe Lawrence	.75	.35
❑ 369 Adam Johnson	1.00	.45
❑ 370 Scott Schoeneweis	.75	.35
❑ 371 Gerald Witasick Jr.	.20	.09
❑ 372 Ronnie Belliard	1.50	.70
❑ 373 Russ Ortiz	.20	.09
❑ 374 Robert Stratton	2.00	.90
❑ 375 Bobby Estalella	.20	.09
❑ 376 Corey Lee	.60	.25
❑ 377 Carlos Beltran	3.00	1.35
❑ 378 Mike Cameron	.40	.18
❑ 379 Scott Randall	.50	.23
❑ 380 Corey Erickson	.75	.35
❑ 381 Jay Canizaro	.20	.09
❑ 382 Kerry Robinson	.50	.23
❑ 383 Todd Noel	1.00	.45
❑ 384 A.J. Zapp	1.00	.45
❑ 385 Jarrod Washburn	.40	.18
❑ 386 Ben Grieve	1.00	.45
❑ 387 Javier Vazquez	1.00	.45
❑ 388 Tony Graffanino	.20	.09
❑ 389 Travis Lee	4.00	1.80
❑ 390 DaRond Stovall	.20	.09

❑ 391 Dennis Reyes	1.00	.45
❑ 392 Danny Buxbaum	.20	.09
❑ 393 Marc Lewis	1.00	.45
❑ 394 Kelvim Escobar	1.25	.55
❑ 395 Danny Klassen	.20	.09
❑ 396 Ken Cloude	.75	.35
❑ 397 Gabe Alvarez	.40	.18
❑ 398 Jaret Wright	3.00	1.35
❑ 399 Raul Casanova	.20	.09
❑ 400 Clayton Bruner	.75	.35
❑ 401 Jason Marquis	2.00	.90
❑ 402 Marc Kroon	.20	.09
❑ 403 Jamey Wright	.20	.09
❑ 404 Matt Snyder	.50	.23
❑ 405 Josh Garrett	1.00	.45
❑ 406 Juan Encarnacion	.40	.18
❑ 407 Heath Murray	.50	.23
❑ 408 Brett Herbison	.50	.23
❑ 409 Brent Butler	1.00	.45
❑ 410 Danny Peoples	1.00	.45
❑ 411 Miguel Tejada	4.00	1.80
❑ 412 Damian Moss	.20	.09
❑ 413 Jim Pittsley	.20	.09
❑ 414 Dmitri Young	.40	.18
❑ 415 Glendon Rusch	.20	.09
❑ 416 Vladimir Guerrero	1.25	.55
❑ 417 Cole Liniak	.25	.55
❑ 418 Ramon Hernandez UER	.50	.23
Card back says 1st Bowman card in		
1997, he had a 1996 Bowman		
❑ 419 Cliff Politte	.75	.35
❑ 420 Mel Rosario	.50	.23
❑ 421 Jorge Carrion	.50	.23
❑ 422 John Barnes	1.00	.45
❑ 423 Chris Stowe	.50	.23
❑ 424 Vernon Wells	5.00	2.20
❑ 425 Brett Caradonna	1.00	.45
❑ 426 Scott Hodges	.75	.35
❑ 427 Jon Garland	1.25	.55
❑ 428 Nathan Haynes	1.00	.45
❑ 429 Geoff Goetz	.75	.35
❑ 430 Adam Kennedy	2.50	1.10
❑ 431 T.J. Tucker	2.00	.90
❑ 432 Aaron Akin	.60	.25
❑ 433 Jayson Werth	2.50	1.10
❑ 434 Glenn Davis	1.00	.45
❑ 435 Mark Mangum	.60	.25
❑ 436 Troy Cameron	1.50	.70
❑ 437 J.J. Davis	1.50	.70
❑ 438 Lance Berkman	5.00	2.20
❑ 439 Jason Standridge	2.00	.90
❑ 440 Jason Dellaero	1.00	.45
❑ 441 Hideki Irabu	1.00	.45

1997 Bowman International

	MINT	NRMT
COMPLETE SET (441)	240.00	110.00
COMPLETE SERIES 1 (221)	120.00	55.00
COMPLETE SERIES 2 (220)	120.00	55.00
COMMON CARD (1-441)	.50	.23
*STARS: 1X TO 2.5X BASIC CARDS		
*ROOKIES: .6X TO 1.5X BASIC CARDS		
ONE INT'L OR INSERT PER PACK		

1997 Bowman 1998 ROY Favorites

	MINT	NRMT
COMPLETE SET (15)	30.00	13.50
COMMON CARD (1-15)	1.00	.45
MINOR STARS	1.50	.70
SER.2 STATED ODDS 1:12		
❑ ROY1 Jeff Abbott	1.00	.45
❑ ROY2 Karim Garcia	1.50	.70
❑ ROY3 Todd Helton	4.00	1.80
❑ ROY4 Richard Hidalgo	1.50	.70
❑ ROY5 Geoff Jenkins	1.50	.70
❑ ROY6 Russ Johnson	1.00	.45
❑ ROY7 Paul Konerko	2.50	1.10
❑ ROY8 Mark Kotsay	2.00	.90
❑ ROY9 Ricky Ledee	4.00	1.80
❑ ROY10 Travis Lee	5.00	2.20
❑ ROY11 Derrek Lee	2.00	.90
❑ ROY12 Elieser Marrero	1.00	.45
❑ ROY13 Juan Melo	1.50	.70
❑ ROY14 Brian Rose	2.50	1.10
❑ ROY15 Fernando Tatis	6.00	2.70

1997 Bowman Certified Blue Ink Autographs

	MINT	NRMT
COMPLETE SET (90)	1200.00	550.00
COMMON BLUE INK (1-90)	10.00	4.50
BLUE INK SEMISTARS	15.00	6.75
STATED ODDS 1:96, ANCO 1:115		
*BLACK INK: .75X TO 1.5X HI COLUMN		
BLACK STATED ODDS 1:503, ANCO 1:600		
*GOLD INK: 1.5X TO 3X HI COLUMN		
GOLD: STATED ODDS 1:1509, ANCO 1:1795		
D.JETER BLUE SER.1 ODDS 1:1928		
D.JETER GREEN SER.2 ODDS 1:1928		
❑ CA1 Jeff Abbott	10.00	4.50
❑ CA2 Bob Abreu	15.00	6.75
❑ CA3 Willie Adams	10.00	4.50
❑ CA4 Brian Banks	10.00	4.50
❑ CA5 Kris Benson	30.00	13.50
❑ CA6 Darin Blood	10.00	4.50
❑ CA7 Jaime Bluma	10.00	4.50
❑ CA8 Kevin L. Brown	10.00	4.50
❑ CA9 Ray Brown	10.00	4.50
❑ CA10 Homer Bush	15.00	6.75

	MINT	NRMT
❏ CA11 Mike Cameron	15.00	6.75
❏ CA12 Jay Canizaro	10.00	4.50
❏ CA13 Luis Castillo	15.00	6.75
❏ CA14 Dave Coggin	10.00	4.50
❏ CA15 Bartolo Colon	15.00	6.75
❏ CA16 Rocky Coppinger	10.00	4.50
❏ CA17 Jacob Cruz	10.00	4.50
❏ CA18 Jose Cruz Jr.	25.00	11.00
❏ CA19 Jeff D'Amico	10.00	4.50
❏ CA20 Ben Davis	20.00	9.00
❏ CA21 Mike Drumright	15.00	6.75
❏ CA22 Scott Elarton	15.00	6.75
❏ CA23 Darin Erstad	25.00	11.00
❏ CA24 Bobby Estalella	10.00	4.50
❏ CA25 Joe Fontenot	15.00	6.75
❏ CA26 Tom Fordham	10.00	4.50
❏ CA27 Brad Fullmer	15.00	6.75
❏ CA28 Chris Fussell	10.00	4.50
❏ CA29 Karim Garcia	15.00	6.75
❏ CA30 Kris Detmers	10.00	4.50
❏ CA31 Todd Greene	10.00	4.50
❏ CA32 Ben Grieve	30.00	13.50
❏ CA33 Vladimir Guerrero	50.00	22.00
❏ CA34 Jose Guillen	15.00	6.75
❏ CA35 Roy Halladay	25.00	11.00
❏ CA36 Wes Helms	10.00	4.50
❏ CA37 Chad Hermansen	30.00	13.50
❏ CA38 Richard Hidalgo	15.00	6.75
❏ CA39 Todd Hollandsworth	10.00	4.50
❏ CA40 Damian Jackson	10.00	4.50
❏ CA41 Derek Jeter Blue DP	100.00	45.00
❏ CA42 Andruw Jones	40.00	18.00
❏ CA43 Brooks Kieschnick	10.00	4.50
❏ CA44 Eugene Kingsale	15.00	6.75
❏ CA45 Paul Konerko	30.00	13.50
❏ CA46 Marc Kroon	10.00	4.50
❏ CA47 Derrek Lee	15.00	6.75
❏ CA48 Travis Lee	40.00	18.00
❏ CA49 Terrence Long	15.00	6.75
❏ CA50 Curt Lyons	10.00	4.50
❏ CA51 Eli Marrero	10.00	4.50
❏ CA52 Rafael Medina	15.00	6.75
❏ CA53 Juan Melo	10.00	4.50
❏ CA54 Shane Monahan	15.00	6.75
❏ CA55 Julio Mosquera	10.00	4.50
❏ CA56 Heath Murray	10.00	4.50
❏ CA57 Ryan Nye	15.00	6.75
❏ CA58 Kevin Orie	10.00	4.50
❏ CA59 Russ Ortiz	10.00	4.50
❏ CA60 Carl Pavano	20.00	9.00
❏ CA61 Jay Payton	10.00	4.50
❏ CA62 Neifi Perez	15.00	6.75
❏ CA63 Sidney Ponson	15.00	6.75
❏ CA64 Calvin Reese	15.00	6.75
❏ CA65 Ray Ricken	10.00	4.50
❏ CA66 Brad Rigby	10.00	4.50
❏ CA67 Adam Riggs	10.00	4.50
❏ CA68 Ruben Rivera	10.00	4.50
❏ CA69 J.J. Johnson	10.00	4.50
❏ CA70 Scott Rolen	50.00	22.00
❏ CA71 Tony Saunders	15.00	6.75
❏ CA72 Donnie Sadler	15.00	6.75
❏ CA73 Richie Sexson	25.00	11.00
❏ CA74 Scott Spiezio	10.00	4.50
❏ CA75 Everett Stull	10.00	4.50
❏ CA76 Mike Sweeney	15.00	6.75
❏ CA77 Fernando Tatis	50.00	22.00
❏ CA78 Miguel Tejada	40.00	18.00
❏ CA79 Justin Thompson	15.00	6.75
❏ CA80 Justin Towle	15.00	6.75
❏ CA81 Billy Wagner	15.00	6.75
❏ CA82 Todd Walker	30.00	13.50
❏ CA83 Luke Wilcox	10.00	4.50
❏ CA84 Paul Wilder	15.00	6.75
❏ CA85 Enrique Wilson	15.00	6.75
❏ CA86 Kerry Wood	80.00	36.00
❏ CA87 Jamey Wright	10.00	4.50
❏ CA88 Ron Wright	15.00	6.75
❏ CA89 Dmitri Young	15.00	6.75
❏ CA90 Nelson Figueroa	15.00	6.75

1997 Bowman International Best

	MINT	NRMT
COMPLETE SET (20)	80.00	36.00

	MINT	NRMT
COMMON CARD (1-20)	1.50	.70
UNLISTED STARS	3.00	1.35

SER.2 STATED ODDS 1:12
*ATOMIC: 1.5X TO 4X HI COLUMN
ATOMIC SER.2 STATED ODDS 1:96
*REFRACTORS: .75X TO 2X HI COLUMN
REFRACTOR SER.2 STATED ODDS 1:48

	MINT	NRMT
❏ BBI1 Frank Thomas	6.00	2.70
❏ BBI2 Ken Griffey Jr.	15.00	6.75
❏ BBI3 Juan Gonzalez	6.00	2.70
❏ BBI4 Bernie Williams	3.00	1.35
❏ BBI5 Hideo Nomo	3.00	1.35
❏ BBI6 Sammy Sosa	10.00	4.50
❏ BBI7 Larry Walker	3.00	1.35
❏ BBI8 Vinny Castilla	2.00	.90
❏ BBI9 Mariano Rivera	1.50	.70
❏ BBI10 Rafael Palmeiro	3.00	1.35
❏ BBI11 Nomar Garciaparra	10.00	4.50
❏ BBI12 Todd Walker	3.00	1.35
❏ BBI13 Andruw Jones	4.00	1.80
❏ BBI14 Vladimir Guerrero	5.00	2.20
❏ BBI15 Ruben Rivera	1.50	.70
❏ BBI16 Bob Abreu	1.50	.70
❏ BBI17 Karim Garcia	1.50	.70
❏ BBI18 Katsuhiro Maeda	1.50	.70
❏ BBI19 Jose Cruz Jr.	3.00	1.35
❏ BBI20 Damian Moss	1.50	.70

1997 Bowman Scout's Honor Roll

	MINT	NRMT
COMPLETE SET (15)	50.00	22.00
COMMON CARD (1-15)	1.00	.45
UNLISTED STARS	1.50	.70

SER.1 STATED ODDS 1:12

	MINT	NRMT
❏ 1 Dmitri Young	1.25	.55
❏ 2 Bob Abreu	1.25	.55
❏ 3 Vladimir Guerrero	3.00	1.35
❏ 4 Paul Konerko	1.50	.70
❏ 5 Kevin Orie	1.00	.45
❏ 6 Todd Walker	1.50	.70
❏ 7 Ben Grieve	2.50	1.10
❏ 8 Darin Erstad	1.50	.70
❏ 9 Derrek Lee	1.50	.70
❏ 10 Jose Cruz Jr.	3.00	1.35
❏ 11 Scott Rolen	3.00	1.35
❏ 12 Travis Lee	5.00	2.20
❏ 13 Andruw Jones	2.50	1.10
❏ 14 Wilton Guerrero	1.00	.45
❏ 15 Nomar Garciaparra	6.00	2.70

1998 Bowman

	MINT	NRMT
COMPLETE SET (441)	140.00	65.00
COMPLETE SERIES 1 (221)	80.00	36.00
COMPLETE SERIES 2 (220)	60.00	27.00
COMMON CARD (1-441)	.15	.07
MINOR STARS	.25	.11
SEMISTARS	.40	.18
UNLISTED STARS	.60	.25

	MINT	NRMT
❏ 1 Nomar Garciaparra	2.00	.90
❏ 2 Scott Rolen	.75	.35
❏ 3 Andy Pettitte	.25	.11
❏ 4 Ivan Rodriguez	.75	.35
❏ 5 Mark McGwire	4.00	1.80
❏ 6 Jason Dickson	.15	.07
❏ 7 Jose Cruz Jr.	.25	.11
❏ 8 Jeff Kent	.25	.11
❏ 9 Mike Mussina	.60	.25
❏ 10 Jason Kendall	.25	.11
❏ 11 Brett Tomko	.15	.07
❏ 12 Jeff King	.15	.07
❏ 13 Brad Radke	.25	.11
❏ 14 Robin Ventura	.25	.11
❏ 15 Jeff Bagwell	.75	.35
❏ 16 Greg Maddux	1.50	.70
❏ 17 John Jaha	.25	.11
❏ 18 Mike Piazza	2.00	.90
❏ 19 Edgar Martinez	.25	.11
❏ 20 David Justice	.25	.11
❏ 21 Todd Hundley	.25	.11
❏ 22 Tony Gwynn	1.50	.70
❏ 23 Larry Walker	.60	.25
❏ 24 Bernie Williams	.60	.25
❏ 25 Edgar Renteria	.15	.07
❏ 26 Rafael Palmeiro	.60	.25
❏ 27 Tim Salmon	.60	.25
❏ 28 Matt Morris	.15	.07
❏ 29 Shawn Estes	.15	.07
❏ 30 Vladimir Guerrero	.75	.35
❏ 31 Fernando Tatis	.60	.25
❏ 32 Justin Thompson	.15	.07
❏ 33 Ken Griffey Jr.	3.00	1.35
❏ 34 Edgardo Alfonzo	.40	.18
❏ 35 Mo Vaughn	.60	.25
❏ 36 Marty Cordova	.15	.07
❏ 37 Craig Biggio	.60	.25
❏ 38 Roger Clemens	1.50	.70
❏ 39 Mark Grace	.40	.18
❏ 40 Ken Caminiti	.25	.11
❏ 41 Tony Womack	.15	.07
❏ 42 Albert Belle	.60	.25
❏ 43 Tino Martinez	.25	.11
❏ 44 Sandy Alomar Jr.	.25	.11
❏ 45 Jeff Cirillo	.15	.07
❏ 46 Jason Giambi	.25	.11
❏ 47 Darin Erstad	.40	.18
❏ 48 Livan Hernandez	.25	.11
❏ 49 Mark Grudzielanek	.15	.07
❏ 50 Sammy Sosa	2.00	.90
❏ 51 Curt Schilling	.40	.18
❏ 52 Brian Hunter	.15	.07
❏ 53 Neifi Perez	.25	.11

❑ 54	Todd Walker	.25	.11
❑ 55	Jose Guillen	.15	.07
❑ 56	Jim Thome	.60	.25
❑ 57	Tom Glavine	.60	.25
❑ 58	Todd Greene	.15	.07
❑ 59	Rondell White	.25	.11
❑ 60	Roberto Alomar	.60	.25
❑ 61	Tony Clark	.25	.11
❑ 62	Vinny Castilla	.25	.11
❑ 63	Barry Larkin	.60	.25
❑ 64	Hideki Irabu	.25	.11
❑ 65	Johnny Damon	.25	.11
❑ 66	Juan Gonzalez	1.25	.55
❑ 67	John Olerud	.25	.11
❑ 68	Gary Sheffield	.25	.11
❑ 69	Raul Mondesi	.25	.11
❑ 70	Chipper Jones	1.50	.70
❑ 71	David Ortiz	.15	.07
❑ 72	Warren Morris	4.00	1.80
❑ 73	Alex Gonzalez	.25	.11
❑ 74	Nick Bierbrodt	1.00	.45
❑ 75	Roy Halladay	.25	.11
❑ 76	Danny Buxbaum	.15	.07
❑ 77	Adam Kennedy	.25	.11
❑ 78	Jared Sandberg	1.00	.45
❑ 79	Michael Barrett	.40	.18
❑ 80	Gil Meche	1.50	.70
❑ 81	Jayson Werth	.25	.11
❑ 82	Abraham Nunez	.15	.07
❑ 83	Ben Petrick	.25	.11
❑ 84	Brett Caradonna	.15	.07
❑ 85	Mike Lowell	2.00	.90
❑ 86	Clayton Brown	.25	.11
❑ 87	John Curtice	2.00	.90
❑ 88	Bobby Estalella	.15	.07
❑ 89	Juan Melo	.15	.07
❑ 90	Arnold Gooch	.15	.07
❑ 91	Kevin Millwood	6.00	2.70
❑ 92	Richie Sexson	.40	.18
❑ 93	Orlando Cabrera	.15	.07
❑ 94	Pat Cline	.15	.07
❑ 95	Anthony Sanders	.15	.07
❑ 96	Russ Johnson	.15	.07
❑ 97	Ben Grieve	.60	.25
❑ 98	Kevin McGlinchy	.15	.07
❑ 99	Paul Wilder	.15	.07
❑ 100	Russ Ortiz	.25	.11
❑ 101	Ryan Jackson	.75	.35
❑ 102	Heath Murray	.15	.07
❑ 103	Brian Rose	.25	.11
❑ 104	Ryan Radmanovich	.75	.35
❑ 105	Ricky Ledee	.25	.11
❑ 106	Jeff Wallace	1.00	.45
❑ 107	Ryan Minor	2.50	1.10
❑ 108	Dennis Reyes	.15	.07
❑ 109	James Manias	.15	.07
❑ 110	Chris Carpenter	.25	.11
❑ 111	Daryle Ward	.25	.11
❑ 112	Vernon Wells	.40	.18
❑ 113	Chad Green	.15	.07
❑ 114	Mike Stoner	1.25	.55
❑ 115	Brad Fullmer	.15	.07
❑ 116	Adam Eaton	.25	.11
❑ 117	Jeff Liefer	.15	.07
❑ 118	Corey Koskie	2.00	.90
❑ 119	Todd Helton	1.00	.45
❑ 120	Jaime Jones	1.00	.45
❑ 121	Mel Rosario	.15	.07
❑ 122	Geoff Goetz	.15	.07
❑ 123	Adrian Beltre	.60	.25
❑ 124	Jason Dellaero	.15	.07
❑ 125	Gabe Kapler	6.00	2.70
❑ 126	Scott Schoeneweis	.15	.07
❑ 127	Ryan Brannan	.15	.07
❑ 128	Aaron Akin	.15	.07
❑ 129	Ryan Anderson	4.00	1.80
❑ 130	Brad Penny	.25	.11
❑ 131	Bruce Chen	.25	.11
❑ 132	Eli Marrero	.15	.07
❑ 133	Eric Chavez	.60	.25
❑ 134	Troy Glaus	8.00	3.60
❑ 135	Troy Cameron	.25	.11
❑ 136	Brian Sikorski	.75	.35
❑ 137	Mike Kinkade	1.25	.55
❑ 138	Braden Looper	.15	.07
❑ 139	Mark Mangum	.15	.07
❑ 140	Danny Peoples	.15	.07
❑ 141	J.J. Davis	.25	.11
❑ 142	Ben Davis	.40	.18
❑ 143	Jacque Jones	.25	.11
❑ 144	Derrick Gibson	.25	.11
❑ 145	Bronson Arroyo	1.00	.45
❑ 146	Luis De Los Santos UER	1.50	.70
	has hitting stat line instead of pitching		
❑ 147	Jeff Abbott	.15	.07
❑ 148	Mike Cuddyer	3.00	1.35
❑ 149	Jason Romano	.25	.11
❑ 150	Shane Monahan	.15	.07
❑ 151	Ntema Ndungidi	1.50	.70
❑ 152	Alex Sanchez	.15	.07
❑ 153	Jack Cust	4.00	1.80
❑ 154	Brent Butler	.15	.07
❑ 155	Ramon Hernandez	.15	.07
❑ 156	Norm Hutchins	.15	.07
❑ 157	Jason Marquis	.25	.11
❑ 158	Jacob Cruz	.15	.07
❑ 159	Rob Burger	1.00	.45
❑ 160	Dave Coggin	.15	.07
❑ 161	Preston Wilson	.25	.11
❑ 162	Jason Fitzgerald	1.00	.45
❑ 163	Dan Serafini	.15	.07
❑ 164	Peter Munro	.15	.07
❑ 165	Trot Nixon	.25	.11
❑ 166	Homer Bush	.15	.07
❑ 167	Dermal Brown	.25	.11
❑ 168	Chad Hermansen	.60	.25
❑ 169	Julio Moreno	.75	.35
❑ 170	John Roskos	1.50	.70
❑ 171	Grant Roberts	.15	.07
❑ 172	Ken Cloude	.15	.07
❑ 173	Jason Brester	.15	.07
❑ 174	Jason Conti	1.00	.45
❑ 175	Jon Garland	.15	.07
❑ 176	Robbie Bell	.25	.11
❑ 177	Nathan Haynes	.15	.07
❑ 178	Ramon Ortiz	3.00	1.35
❑ 179	Shannon Stewart	.25	.11
❑ 180	Pablo Ortega	.15	.07
❑ 181	Jimmy Rollins	1.50	.70
❑ 182	Sean Casey	1.25	.55
❑ 183	Ted Lilly	1.25	.55
❑ 184	Chris Enochs	1.25	.55
❑ 185	Magglio Ordonez	6.00	2.70
❑ 186	Mike Drumright	.15	.07
❑ 187	Aaron Boone	.15	.07
❑ 188	Matt Clement	.25	.11
❑ 189	Todd Dunwoody	.15	.07
❑ 190	Larry Rodriguez	.15	.07
❑ 191	Todd Noel	.15	.07
❑ 192	Geoff Jenkins	.25	.11
❑ 193	George Lombard	.25	.11
❑ 194	Lance Berkman	.40	.18
❑ 195	Marcus McCain	.25	.11
❑ 196	Ryan McGuire	.15	.07
❑ 197	Jhensy Sandoval	1.25	.55
❑ 198	Corey Lee	.15	.07
❑ 199	Mario Valdez	.15	.07
❑ 200	Robert Fick	2.50	1.10
❑ 201	Donnie Sadler	.15	.07
❑ 202	Marc Kroon	.15	.07
❑ 203	David Miller	.15	.07
❑ 204	Jarrod Washburn	.15	.07
❑ 205	Miguel Tejada	.25	.11
❑ 206	Raul Ibanez	.15	.07
❑ 207	John Patterson	.25	.11
❑ 208	Calvin Pickering	.15	.07
❑ 209	Felix Martinez	.15	.07
❑ 210	Mark Redman	.15	.07
❑ 211	Scott Elarton	.15	.07
❑ 212	Jose Amado	.75	.35
❑ 213	Kerry Wood	1.00	.45
❑ 214	Dante Powell	.15	.07
❑ 215	Aramis Ramirez	.60	.25
❑ 216	A.J. Hinch	.25	.11
❑ 217	Dustin Carr	.75	.35
❑ 218	Mark Kotsay	.25	.11
❑ 219	Jason Standridge	.25	.11
❑ 220	Luis Ordaz	.15	.07
❑ 221	Orlando Hernandez	5.00	2.20
❑ 222	Cal Ripken	2.50	1.10
❑ 223	Paul Molitor	1.00	.45
❑ 224	Derek Jeter	2.00	.90
❑ 225	Barry Bonds	.75	.35
❑ 226	Jim Edmonds	.25	.11
❑ 227	John Smoltz	.40	.18
❑ 228	Eric Karros	.25	.11
❑ 229	Ray Lankford	.25	.11
❑ 230	Rey Ordonez	.25	.11
❑ 231	Kenny Lofton	.40	.18
❑ 232	Alex Rodriguez	2.00	.90
❑ 233	Dante Bichette	.25	.11
❑ 234	Pedro Martinez	.75	.35
❑ 235	Carlos Delgado	.60	.25
❑ 236	Rod Beck	.25	.11
❑ 237	Matt Williams	.60	.25
❑ 238	Charles Johnson	.25	.11
❑ 239	Rico Brogna	.15	.07
❑ 240	Frank Thomas	1.25	.55
❑ 241	Paul O'Neill	.25	.11
❑ 242	Jaret Wright	.25	.11
❑ 243	Brant Brown	.15	.07
❑ 244	Ryan Klesko	.25	.11
❑ 245	Chuck Finley	.25	.11
❑ 246	Derek Bell	.25	.11
❑ 247	Delino DeShields	.15	.07
❑ 248	Chan Ho Park	.25	.11
❑ 249	Wade Boggs	.60	.25
❑ 250	Jay Buhner	.25	.11
❑ 251	Butch Huskey	.15	.07
❑ 252	Steve Finley	.25	.11
❑ 253	Will Clark	.60	.25
❑ 254	John Valentin	.25	.11
❑ 255	Bobby Higginson	.25	.11
❑ 256	Darryl Strawberry	.25	.11
❑ 257	Randy Johnson	.60	.25
❑ 258	Al Martin	.15	.07
❑ 259	Travis Fryman	.25	.11
❑ 260	Fred McGriff	.40	.18
❑ 261	Jose Valentin	.15	.07
❑ 262	Andruw Jones	.60	.25
❑ 263	Kenny Rogers	.15	.07
❑ 264	Moises Alou	.25	.11
❑ 265	Denny Neagle	.15	.07
❑ 266	Ugueth Urbina	.15	.07
❑ 267	Derrek Lee	.15	.07
❑ 268	Ellis Burks	.25	.11
❑ 269	Mariano Rivera	.25	.11
❑ 270	Dean Palmer	.25	.11
❑ 271	Eddie Taubensee	.15	.07
❑ 272	Brady Anderson	.25	.11
❑ 273	Brian Giles	.25	.11
❑ 274	Quinton McCracken	.15	.07
❑ 275	Henry Rodriguez	.25	.11
❑ 276	Andres Galarraga	.40	.18
❑ 277	Jose Canseco	.75	.35
❑ 278	David Segui	.15	.07
❑ 279	Bret Saberhagen	.25	.11
❑ 280	Kevin Brown	.40	.18
❑ 281	Chuck Knoblauch	.25	.11
❑ 282	Jeromy Burnitz	.25	.11
❑ 283	Jay Bell	.25	.11
❑ 284	Manny Ramirez	.75	.35
❑ 285	Rick Helling	.15	.07
❑ 286	Francisco Cordova	.15	.07
❑ 287	Bob Abreu	.25	.11
❑ 288	J.T. Snow	.25	.11
❑ 289	Hideo Nomo	.60	.25
❑ 290	Brian Jordan	.25	.11
❑ 291	Javy Lopez	.25	.11
❑ 292	Travis Lee	.40	.18
❑ 293	Russell Branyan	.25	.11
❑ 294	Paul Konerko	.25	.11
❑ 295	Masato Yoshii	1.25	.55
❑ 296	Kris Benson	.25	.11
❑ 297	Juan Encarnacion	.25	.11
❑ 298	Eric Milton	.25	.11
❑ 299	Mike Caruso	.15	.07
❑ 300	Ricardo Aramboles	2.00	.90
❑ 301	Bobby Smith	.15	.07
❑ 302	Billy Koch	.25	.11
❑ 303	Richard Hidalgo	.25	.11
❑ 304	Justin Baughman	.75	.35
❑ 305	Chris Gissell	.15	.07
❑ 306	Donnie Bridges	.75	.35
❑ 307	Nelson Lara	.75	.35
❑ 308	Randy Wolf	3.00	1.35
❑ 309	Jason LaRue	2.00	.90
❑ 310	Jason Gooding	.75	.35

❑ 311 Edgard Clemente	.15	.07
❑ 312 Andrew Vessel	.15	.07
❑ 313 Chris Reitsma	.15	.07
❑ 314 Jesus Sanchez	1.25	.55
❑ 315 Buddy Carlyle	1.25	.55
❑ 316 Randy Winn	.15	.07
❑ 317 Luis Rivera	1.50	.70
❑ 318 Marcus Thames	1.50	.70
❑ 319 A.J. Pierzynski	.15	.07
❑ 320 Scott Randall	.15	.07
❑ 321 Damian Sapp	.15	.07
❑ 322 Eddie Yarnall	2.50	1.10
❑ 323 Luke Allen	1.50	.70
❑ 324 J.D. Smart	.15	.07
❑ 325 Willie Martinez	.25	.11
❑ 326 Alex Ramirez	.25	.11
❑ 327 Eric DuBose	1.25	.55
❑ 328 Kevin Witt	.15	.07
❑ 329 Dan McKinley	.75	.35
❑ 330 Cliff Politte	.75	.35
❑ 331 Vladimir Nunez	.15	.07
❑ 332 John Halama	2.00	.90
❑ 333 Nerio Rodriguez	.15	.07
❑ 334 Desi Relaford	.15	.07
❑ 335 Robinson Checo	.15	.07
❑ 336 John Nicholson	1.25	.55
❑ 337 Tom LaRosa	.75	.35
❑ 338 Kevin Nicholson	1.25	.55
❑ 339 Javier Vazquez	.15	.07
❑ 340 A.J. Zapp	.15	.07
❑ 341 Tom Evans	.15	.07
❑ 342 Kerry Robinson	.15	.07
❑ 343 Gabe Gonzalez	.15	.07
❑ 344 Ralph Milliard	.15	.07
❑ 345 Enrique Wilson	.15	.07
❑ 346 Elvin Hernandez	.15	.07
❑ 347 Mike Lincoln	1.50	.70
❑ 348 Cesar King	1.25	.55
❑ 349 Cristian Guzman	1.25	.55
❑ 350 Donzell McDonald	.15	.07
❑ 351 Jim Parque	1.25	.55
❑ 352 Mike Saipe	.15	.07
❑ 353 Carlos Febles	4.00	1.80
❑ 354 Dernell Stenson	4.00	1.80
❑ 355 Mark Osborne	1.50	.70
❑ 356 Odalis Perez	2.00	.90
❑ 357 Jason Dewey	1.25	.55
❑ 358 Joe Fontenot	.15	.07
❑ 359 Jason Grilli	1.25	.55
❑ 360 Kevin Haverbusch	1.50	.70
❑ 361 Jay Yennaco	.75	.35
❑ 362 Brian Buchanan	.15	.07
❑ 363 John Barnes	.15	.07
❑ 364 Chris Fussell	.15	.07
❑ 365 Kevin Gibbs	.75	.35
❑ 366 Joe Lawrence	.75	.35
❑ 367 DaRond Stovall	.15	.07
❑ 368 Brian Fuentes	.75	.35
❑ 369 Jimmy Anderson	.15	.07
❑ 370 Lariel Gonzalez	.75	.35
❑ 371 Scott Williamson	2.00	.90
❑ 372 Milton Bradley	.25	.11
❑ 373 Jason Halper	.75	.35
❑ 374 Brent Billingsley	.75	.35
❑ 375 Joe DePastino	.75	.35
❑ 376 Jake Westbrook	.15	.07
❑ 377 Octavio Dotel	.25	.11
❑ 378 Jason Williams	.75	.35
❑ 379 Julio Ramirez	3.00	1.35
❑ 380 Seth Greisinger	.15	.07
❑ 381 Mike Judd	1.25	.55
❑ 382 Ben Ford	.75	.35
❑ 383 Tom Bennett	.75	.35
❑ 384 Adam Butler	.75	.35
❑ 385 Wade Miller	.75	.35
❑ 386 Kyle Peterson	.75	.35
❑ 387 Tommy Peterman	.75	.35
❑ 388 Onan Masaoka	.15	.07
❑ 389 Jason Rakers	.75	.35
❑ 390 Rafael Medina	.15	.07
❑ 391 Luis Lopez	.15	.07
❑ 392 Jeff Yoder	.15	.07
❑ 393 Vance Wilson	.75	.35
❑ 394 Fernando Seguignol	2.50	1.10
❑ 395 Ron Wright	.15	.07
❑ 396 Ruben Mateo	6.00	2.70

❑ 397 Steve Lomasney	1.00	.45
❑ 398 Damian Jackson	.15	.07
❑ 399 Mike Jerzembeck	1.00	.45
❑ 400 Luis Rivas	1.50	.70
❑ 401 Kevin Burford	1.00	.45
❑ 402 Glenn Davis	.15	.07
❑ 403 Robert Luce	.75	.35
❑ 404 Cole Liniak	.15	.07
❑ 405 Matt LeCroy	.75	.35
❑ 406 Jeremy Giambi	2.50	1.10
❑ 407 Shawn Chacon	.15	.07
❑ 408 Dewayne Wise	1.50	.70
❑ 409 Steve Woodard	.15	.07
❑ 410 Francisco Cordero	1.25	.55
❑ 411 Damon Minor	1.00	.45
❑ 412 Lou Collier	.15	.07
❑ 413 Justin Towle	.15	.07
❑ 414 Juan LeBron	.15	.07
❑ 415 Michael Coleman	.25	.11
❑ 416 Felix Rodriguez	.15	.07
❑ 417 Paul Ah Yat	1.00	.45
❑ 418 Kevin Barker	1.25	.55
❑ 419 Brian Meadows	.15	.07
❑ 420 Darnell McDonald	2.50	1.10
❑ 421 Matt Kinney	.75	.35
❑ 422 Mike Vavrek	.75	.35
❑ 423 Courtney Duncan	.75	.35
❑ 424 Kevin Millar	3.00	1.35
❑ 425 Ruben Rivera	.15	.07
❑ 426 Steve Shoemaker	.15	.07
❑ 427 Dan Reichert	1.25	.55
❑ 428 Carlos Lee	4.00	1.80
❑ 429 Rod Barajas	1.50	.70
❑ 430 Pablo Ozuna	3.00	1.35
❑ 431 Todd Belitz	.75	.35
❑ 432 Sidney Ponson	.25	.11
❑ 433 Steve Carver	.15	.07
❑ 434 Esteban Yan	1.50	.70
❑ 435 Cedrick Bowers	1.00	.45
❑ 436 Marlon Anderson	.25	.11
❑ 437 Carl Pavano	.75	.35
❑ 438 Jae Weong Seo	1.00	.45
❑ 439 Jose Taveras	1.00	.45
❑ 440 Matt Anderson	1.50	.70
❑ 441 Darron Ingram	1.50	.70
❑ NNO S.Hasegawa '91 BBM	10.00	4.50
❑ NNO H.Irabu '91 BBM	20.00	9.00
❑ NNO H.Nomo '91 BBM	30.00	13.50

	MINT	NRMT
COMPLETE SERIES 1 (221)	150.00	70.00
COMPLETE SERIES 2 (220)	120.00	55.00
COMMON CARD (1-441)	.50	.23

*STARS: 1.25X TO 3X BASIC CARDS
*RCS/PROSPECTS: .6X TO 1.5X BASIC
ONE PER PACK

1998 Bowman 1999 ROY Favorites

	MINT	NRMT
COMPLETE SET (10)	25.00	11.00
COMMON CARD (ROY1-10)	1.00	.45
SEMISTARS	1.50	.70

SER.2 STATED ODDS 1:12

		MINT	NRMT
❑ ROY1 Adrian Beltre	2.50	1.10
❑ ROY2 Troy Glaus	8.00	3.60
❑ ROY3 Chad Hermansen	2.50	1.10
❑ ROY4 Matt Clement	1.50	.70
❑ ROY5 Eric Chavez	2.00	.90
❑ ROY6 Kris Benson	1.50	.70
❑ ROY7 Richie Sexson	1.50	.70
❑ ROY8 Randy Wolf	2.50	1.10
❑ ROY9 Ryan Minor	2.50	1.10
❑ ROY10 Alex Gonzalez	1.50	.70

1998 Bowman Certified Blue Autographs

Preston Wilson

	MINT	NRMT
COMMON CARD (1-70)	8.00	3.60

1998 Bowman Golden Anniversary

	MINT	NRMT
COMMON CARD (1-441)	15.00	6.75

*STARS: 40X TO 100X BASIC CARDS
*YNG.STARS: 25X TO 60X BASIC CARDS
*PROSPECTS: 20X TO 50X BASIC CARDS
*ROOKIES: 6X TO 15X BASIC CARDS
SER.1 STATED ODDS 1:237
SER.2 STATED ODDS 1:194
STATED PRINT RUN 50 SERIAL #'d SETS

1998 Bowman International

	MINT	NRMT
COMPLETE SET (441)	270.00	120.00

SER.1 STATED ODDS 1:149
SER.2 STATED ODDS 1:122
*GOLD FOIL: 1.5X TO 4X Hi COLUMN
SER.1 GOLD FOIL STATED ODDS 1:2976
SER.2 GOLD FOIL STATED ODDS 1:2445
*SILVER FOIL: .75X TO 2X HI COLUMN
SER.1 SILVER FOIL STATED ODDS 1:992
SER.2 SILVER FOIL STATED ODDS 1:815

1	Adrian Beltre	30.00	13.50
2	Brad Fullmer	8.00	3.60
3	Ricky Ledee	12.00	5.50
4	David Ortiz	8.00	3.60
5	Fernando Tatis	25.00	11.00
6	Kerry Wood	40.00	18.00
7	Mel Rosario	8.00	3.60
8	Cole Liniak	8.00	3.60
9	A.J. Hinch	8.00	3.60
10	Jhensy Sandoval	20.00	9.00
11	Jose Cruz Jr.	15.00	6.75
12	Richard Hidalgo	10.00	4.50
13	Geoff Jenkins	12.00	5.50
14	Carl Pavano	8.00	3.60
15	Richie Sexson	25.00	11.00
16	Tony Womack	8.00	3.60
17	Scott Rolen	50.00	22.00
18	Ryan Minor	20.00	9.00
19	Eli Marrero	8.00	3.60
20	Jason Marquis	12.00	5.50
21	Mike Lowell	20.00	9.00
22	Todd Helton	40.00	18.00
23	Chad Green	8.00	3.60
24	Scott Elarton	10.00	4.50
25	Russell Branyan	20.00	9.00
26	Mike Drumright	8.00	3.60
27	Ben Grieve	30.00	13.50
28	Jacque Jones	12.00	5.50
29	Jared Sandberg	20.00	9.00
30	Grant Roberts	8.00	3.60
31	Mike Stoner	15.00	6.75
32	Brian Rose	8.00	3.60
33	Randy Winn	8.00	3.60
34	Justin Towle	8.00	3.60
35	Anthony Sanders	8.00	3.60
36	Rafael Medina	8.00	3.60
37	Corey Lee	8.00	3.60
38	Mike Kinkade	20.00	9.00
39	Norm Hutchins	8.00	3.60
40	Jason Brester	8.00	3.60
41	Ben Davis	20.00	9.00
42	Nomar Garciaparra	100.00	45.00
43	Jeff Larson	8.00	3.60
44	Eric Milton	8.00	3.60
45	Preston Wilson	12.00	5.50
46	Miguel Tejada	20.00	9.00
47	Luis Ordaz	8.00	3.60
48	Travis Lee	20.00	9.00
49	Kris Benson	12.00	5.50
50	Jason Conti	8.00	3.60
51	Dermal Brown	12.00	5.50
52	Marc Kroon	8.00	3.60
53	Chad Hermansen	20.00	9.00
54	Roy Halladay	15.00	6.75
55	Eric Chavez	25.00	11.00
56	Jason Conti	8.00	3.60
57	Juan Encarnacion	15.00	6.75
58	Paul Wilder	8.00	3.60
59	Aramis Ramirez	30.00	13.50
60	Cliff Politte	8.00	3.60
61	Todd Dunwoody	8.00	3.60
62	Raul Mondesi	20.00	9.00
63	Shane Monahan	8.00	3.60
64	Alex Sanchez	8.00	3.60
65	Jeff Abbott	8.00	3.60
66	John Patterson	15.00	6.75
67	Peter Munro	8.00	3.60
68	Jarrod Washburn	8.00	3.60
69	Derrek Lee	8.00	3.60
70	Ramon Hernandez	8.00	3.60

1998 Bowman Minor League MVP's

	MINT	NRMT
COMPLETE SET (11)	25.00	11.00

COMMON CARD (MVP1-MVP11)	1.00	.45
SER.2 STATED ODDS 1:12		

MVP1	Jeff Bagwell	2.50	1.10
MVP2	Andres Galarraga	1.25	.55
MVP3	Juan Gonzalez	4.00	1.80
MVP4	Tony Gwynn	5.00	2.20
MVP5	Vladimir Guerrero	2.50	1.10
MVP6	Derek Jeter	5.00	2.20
MVP7	Andruw Jones	2.00	.90
MVP8	Tino Martinez	1.00	.45
MVP9	Manny Ramirez	2.50	1.10
MVP10	Gary Sheffield	1.00	.45
MVP11	Jim Thome	1.50	.70

1998 Bowman Scout's Choice

	MINT	NRMT
COMPLETE SET (21)	25.00	11.00
COMMON CARD (SC1-SC21)	1.00	.45
MINOR STARS	1.50	.70
SEMISTARS	2.50	1.10
SER.1 STATED ODDS 1:12		

SC1	Paul Konerko	1.50	.70
SC2	Richard Hidalgo	1.00	.45
SC3	Mark Kotsay	1.50	.70
SC4	Ben Grieve	4.00	1.80
SC5	Chad Hermansen	2.50	1.10
SC6	Matt Clement	1.50	.70
SC7	Brad Fullmer	1.00	.45
SC8	Eli Marrero	1.00	.45
SC9	Kerry Wood	4.00	1.80
SC10	Adrian Beltre	3.00	1.35
SC11	Ricky Ledee	1.50	.70
SC12	Travis Lee	2.50	1.10
SC13	Abraham Nunez	1.00	.45
SC14	Brian Rose	1.00	.45
SC15	Dermal Brown	1.50	.70
SC16	Juan Encarnacion	1.50	.70
SC17	Aramis Ramirez	2.50	1.10
SC18	Todd Helton	4.00	1.80
SC19	Kris Benson	1.50	.70
SC20	Russell Branyan	1.50	.70
SC21	Mike Stoner	2.50	1.10

1999 Bowman

	MINT	NRMT
COMPLETE SET (440)	140.00	65.00

COMPLETE SERIES 1 (220)	60.00	27.00
COMPLETE SERIES 2 (220)	80.00	36.00
COMMON CARD (1-440)	.15	.07
MINOR STARS	.25	.11
SEMISTARS	.40	.18
UNLISTED STARS	.60	.25

1	Ben Grieve	.60	.25
2	Kerry Wood	.60	.25
3	Ruben Rivera	.15	.07
4	Sandy Alomar Jr.	.25	.11
5	Mark McGwire	4.00	1.80
6	Vladimir Guerrero	.75	.35
7	Moises Alou	.25	.11
8	Jim Edmonds	.25	.11
9	Greg Maddux	1.50	.70
10	Gary Sheffield	.25	.11
11	John Valentin	.25	.11
12	Chuck Knoblauch	.25	.11
13	Tony Clark	.25	.11
14	Rusty Greer	.25	.11
15	Al Leiter	.25	.11
16	Travis Lee	.40	.18
17	Jose Cruz Jr.	.25	.11
18	Pedro Martinez	.75	.35
19	Paul O'Neill	.25	.11
20	Todd Walker	.25	.11
21	Vinny Castilla	.25	.11
22	Barry Larkin	.60	.25
23	Curt Schilling	.40	.18
24	Jason Kendall	.25	.11
25	Scott Erickson	.15	.07
26	Andres Galarraga	.40	.18
27	Jeff Shaw	.15	.07
28	John Olerud	.25	.11
29	Orlando Hernandez	.60	.25
30	Larry Walker	.60	.25
31	Andruw Jones	.60	.25
32	Jeff Cirillo	.25	.11
33	Barry Bonds	.75	.35
34	Manny Ramirez	.75	.35
35	Matt Kotsay	.15	.07
36	Ivan Rodriguez	.75	.35
37	Jeff King	.15	.07
38	Brian Hunter	.25	.11
39	Ray Durham	.25	.11
40	Bernie Williams	.60	.25
41	Darin Erstad	.40	.18
42	Chipper Jones	1.50	.70
43	Pat Hentgen	.15	.07
44	Eric Young	.15	.07
45	Jaret Wright	.25	.11
46	Juan Guzman	.15	.07
47	Jorge Posada	.15	.07
48	Bobby Higginson	.25	.11
49	Jose Guillen	.15	.07
50	Trevor Hoffman	.25	.11
51	Ken Griffey Jr.	3.00	1.35
52	David Justice	.25	.11
53	Matt Williams	.60	.25
54	Eric Karros	.25	.11
55	Derek Bell	.25	.11
56	Ray Lankford	.25	.11
57	Mariano Rivera	.25	.11
58	Brett Tomko	.15	.07
59	Mike Mussina	.60	.25
61	Kenny Lofton	.40	.18

62	Chuck Finley	.25	.11
63	Alex Gonzalez	.15	.07
64	Mark Grace	.40	.18
65	Raul Mondesi	.25	.11
66	David Cone	.40	.18
67	Brad Fullmer	.15	.07
68	Andy Benes	.15	.07
69	John Smoltz	.40	.18
70	Shane Reynolds	.15	.11
71	Bruce Chen	.25	.11
72	Adam Kennedy	.25	.11
73	Jack Cust	.25	.11
74	Matt Clement	.25	.11
75	Derrick Gibson	.25	.11
76	Darnell McDonald	.15	.11
77	Adam Everett	1.25	.55
78	Ricardo Aramboles	.25	.11
79	Mark Quinn	2.50	1.10
80	Jason Rakers	.15	.07
81	Seth Etherton	.75	.35
82	Jeff Urban	.75	.35
83	Manny Aybar	.15	.07
84	Mike Nannini	.75	.35
85	Onan Masaoka	.15	.07
86	Rod Barajas	.25	.11
87	Mike Frank	.15	.07
88	Scott Randall	.15	.07
89	Justin Bowles	.50	.23
90	Chris Haas	.15	.07
91	Arturo McDowell	1.00	.45
92	Matt Belisle	1.00	.45
93	Scott Elarton	.15	.07
94	Vernon Wells	.40	.18
95	Pat Cline	.15	.07
96	Ryan Anderson	.25	.11
97	Kevin Barker	.15	.07
98	Ruben Mateo	.60	.25
99	Robert Fick	.25	.11
100	Corey Koskie	.15	.07
101	Ricky Ledee	.25	.11
102	Rick Elder	1.50	.70
103	Jack Cressend	.50	.23
104	Joe Lawrence	.15	.07
105	Mike Lincoln	.15	.07
106	Kit Pellow	1.00	.45
107	Matt Burch	.50	.23
108	Cole Liniak	.15	.07
109	Jason Dewey	.15	.07
110	Cesar King	.15	.07
111	Julio Ramirez	.25	.11
112	Jake Westbrook	.15	.07
113	Eric Valent	2.00	.90
114	Roosevelt Brown	1.25	.55
115	Choo Freeman	1.25	.55
116	Juan Melo	.15	.07
117	Jason Grilli	.15	.07
118	Jared Sandberg	.25	.11
119	Glenn Davis	.15	.07
120	David Riske	.75	.35
121	Jacque Jones	.25	.11
122	Corey Lee	.15	.07
123	Michael Barrett	.40	.18
124	Lariel Gonzalez	.15	.07
125	Mitch Meluskey	.15	.07
126	Freddy Garcia	.15	.07
127	Tony Torcato	1.00	.45
128	Jeff Liefer	.15	.07
129	Ntema Ndungidi	.25	.11
130	Andy Brown	1.00	.45
131	Ryan Mills	.75	.35
132	Andy Abad	.50	.23
133	Carlos Febles	.25	.11
134	Jason Tyner	1.00	.45
135	Mark Osborne	.15	.07
136	Phil Norton	.50	.23
137	Nathan Haynes	.15	.07
138	Roy Halladay	.25	.11
139	Juan Encarnacion	.25	.11
140	Brad Penny	.25	.11
141	Grant Roberts	.15	.07
142	Aramis Ramirez	.40	.18
143	Cristian Guzman	.15	.07
144	Mamon Tucker	1.00	.45
145	Ryan Bradley	.25	.11
146	Brian Simmons	.15	.07
147	Dan Reichert	.15	.07
148	Russ Branyan	.25	.11
149	Victor Valencia	.75	.35
150	Scott Schoeneweis	.15	.07
151	Sean Spencer	.50	.23
152	Odalis Perez	.15	.07
153	Joe Fontenot	.15	.07
154	Milton Bradley	.25	.11
155	Josh McKinley	.75	.35
156	Terrence Long	.75	.35
157	Danny Klassen	.15	.07
158	Paul Hoover	.50	.23
159	Ron Belliard	.25	.11
160	Armando Rios	.15	.07
161	Ramon Hernandez	.15	.07
162	Jason Conti	.15	.07
163	Chad Hermansen	.25	.11
164	Jason Standridge	.25	.11
165	Jason Dellaero	.15	.07
166	John Curtice	.15	.07
167	Clayton Andrews	.75	.35
168	Jeremy Giambi	.25	.11
169	Alex Ramirez	.25	.11
170	Gabe Molina	.50	.23
171	Mario Encarnacion	2.00	.90
172	Mike Zywica	.75	.35
173	Chip Ambres	1.25	.55
174	Trot Nixon	.25	.11
175	Pat Burrell	6.00	2.70
176	Jeff Yoder	.15	.07
177	Chris Jones	.75	.35
178	Kevin Witt	.15	.07
179	Keith Luuloa	.50	.23
180	Billy Koch	.25	.11
181	Damaso Marte	.50	.23
182	Ryan Glynn	.75	.35
183	Calvin Pickering	.15	.11
184	Michael Cuddyer	.25	.11
185	Nick Johnson	5.00	2.20
186	Doug Mientkiewicz	.75	.35
187	Nate Cornejo	1.00	.45
188	Octavio Dotel	.25	.11
189	Wes Helms	.15	.07
190	Nelson Lara	.15	.07
191	Chuck Abbott	.50	.23
192	Tony Armas Jr.	.40	.18
193	Gil Meche	.25	.11
194	Ben Petrick	.25	.11
195	Chris George	1.00	.45
196	Scott Hunter	.75	.35
197	Ryan Brannan	.25	.11
198	Amaury Garcia	.75	.35
199	Chris Gissell	.15	.07
200	Austin Kearns	1.50	.70
201	Alex Gonzalez	.25	.11
202	Wade Miller	.15	.07
203	Scott Williamson	.25	.11
204	Chris Enochs	.15	.07
205	Fernando Seguignol	.25	.11
206	Madison Anderson	.15	.07
207	Todd Sears	.75	.35
208	Nate Bump	.15	.07
209	J.M. Gold	1.00	.45
210	Matt LeCroy	.15	.07
211	Alex Hernandez	.25	.11
212	Luis Rivera	.15	.07
213	Troy Cameron	.15	.07
214	Alex Escobar	3.00	1.35
215	Jason LaRue	.25	.11
216	Kyle Peterson	.15	.07
217	Brent Butler	.25	.11
218	Derrell Stenson	.25	.11
219	Adrian Beltre	.60	.25
220	Daryle Ward	.25	.11
221	Jim Thome	.60	.25
222	Cliff Floyd	.25	.11
223	Rickey Henderson	.75	.35
224	Garret Anderson	.25	.11
225	Ken Caminiti	.25	.11
226	Carlos Beltran	.75	.35
227	Jeromy Burnitz	.25	.11
228	Steve Finley	.25	.11
229	Miguel Tejada	.25	.11
230	Greg Vaughn	.25	.11
231	Jose Offerman	.25	.11
232	Andy Ashby	.15	.07
233	Albert Belle	.60	.25
234	Fernando Tatis	.60	.25
235	Todd Helton	.60	.25
236	Sean Casey	.60	.25
237	Brian Giles	.25	.11
238	Andy Pettitte	.25	.11
239	Fred McGriff	.40	.18
240	Roberto Alomar	.60	.25
241	Edgar Martinez	.25	.11
242	Lee Stevens	.15	.07
243	Shawn Green	.60	.25
244	Ryan Klesko	.25	.11
245	Sammy Sosa	2.00	.90
246	Todd Hundley	.25	.11
247	Shannon Stewart	.25	.11
248	Randy Johnson	.75	.35
249	Rondell White	.25	.11
250	Mike Piazza	2.00	.90
251	Craig Biggio	.60	.25
252	David Wells	.25	.11
253	Brian Jordan	.25	.11
254	Edgar Renteria	.25	.07
255	Bartolo Colon	.25	.11
256	Frank Thomas	1.25	.55
257	Will Clark	.60	.25
258	Dean Palmer	.25	.11
259	Dmitri Young	.25	.11
260	Scott Rolen	.75	.35
261	Jeff Kent	.25	.11
262	Dante Bichette	.25	.11
263	Nomar Garciaparra	2.00	.90
264	Tony Gwynn	1.50	.70
265	Alex Rodriguez	2.00	.90
266	Jose Canseco	.75	.35
267	Jason Giambi	.25	.11
268	Jeff Bagwell	.75	.35
269	Carlos Delgado	.60	.25
270	Tom Glavine	.60	.25
271	Eric Davis	.25	.11
272	Edgardo Alfonzo	.40	.18
273	Tim Salmon	.40	.18
274	Johnny Damon	.25	.11
275	Rafael Palmeiro	.60	.25
276	Denny Neagle	.15	.07
277	Neifi Perez	.25	.11
278	Roger Clemens	1.50	.70
279	Brant Brown	.15	.07
280	Kevin Brown	.40	.18
281	Jay Bell	.25	.11
282	Jay Buhner	.25	.11
283	Matt Lawton	.15	.07
284	Robin Ventura	.25	.11
285	Juan Gonzalez	1.25	.55
286	Mo Vaughn	.60	.25
287	Kevin Millwood	.40	.18
288	Tino Martinez	.25	.11
289	Justin Thompson	.15	.07
290	Derek Jeter	2.00	.90
291	Ben Davis	.25	.11
292	Mike Lowell	.15	.07
293	Calvin Murray	.15	.07
294	Micah Bowie	.75	.35
295	Lance Berkman	.40	.18
296	Jason Marquis	.25	.11
297	Chad Green	.15	.07
298	Dee Brown	.25	.11
299	Jerry Hairston Jr.	.25	.11
300	Gabe Kapler	.60	.25
301	Brent Stentz	.50	.23
302	Scott Mullen	.50	.23
303	Brandon Reed	.15	.07
304	Shea Hillenbrand	1.00	.45
305	J.D. Closser	1.00	.45
306	Gary Matthews Jr.	.15	.07
307	Toby Hall	1.00	.45
308	Jason Phillips	.25	.23
309	Jose Macias	.50	.23
310	Jung Bong	1.00	.45
311	Ramon Soler	.75	.35
312	Kelly Dransfeld	1.00	.45
313	Carlos Hernandez	.50	.23
314	Kevin Haverbusch	.15	.07
315	Aaron Myette	1.25	.55
316	Chad Harville	.50	.23
317	Kyle Farnsworth	1.50	.70
318	Travis Dawkins	1.50	.70
319	Willie Martinez	.15	.07

❑ 320 Carlos Lee	.25	.11
❑ 321 Carlos Pena	1.50	.70
❑ 322 Peter Bergeron	1.50	.70
❑ 323 A.J. Burnett	1.50	.70
❑ 324 Bucky Jacobsen	.75	.35
❑ 325 Mo Bruce	.75	.35
❑ 326 Reggie Taylor	.15	.07
❑ 327 Jackie Rexrode	.25	.11
❑ 328 Alvin Morrow	.25	.11
❑ 329 Carlos Beltran	.75	.35
❑ 330 Eric Chavez	.40	.18
❑ 331 John Patterson	.25	.11
❑ 332 Jayson Werth	.25	.11
❑ 333 Richie Sexson	.40	.18
❑ 334 Randy Wolf	.25	.11
❑ 335 Eli Marrero	.15	.07
❑ 336 Paul LoDuca	.15	.07
❑ 337 J.D Smart	.15	.07
❑ 338 Ryan Minor	.25	.11
❑ 339 Kris Benson	.25	.11
❑ 340 George Lombard	.25	.11
❑ 341 Troy Glaus	.60	.25
❑ 342 Eddie Yarnall	.25	.11
❑ 343 Kip Wells	1.50	.70
❑ 344 C.C. Sabathia	2.50	1.10
❑ 345 Sean Burroughs	6.00	2.70
❑ 346 Felipe Lopez	1.50	.70
❑ 347 Ryan Rupe	1.00	.45
❑ 348 Orber Moreno	1.00	.45
❑ 349 Rafael Roque	1.00	.45
❑ 350 Alfonso Soriano	6.00	2.70
❑ 351 Pablo Ozuna	.25	.11
❑ 352 Corey Patterson	10.00	4.50
❑ 353 Braden Looper	.15	.07
❑ 354 Robbie Bell	.15	.07
❑ 355 Mark Mulder	1.50	.70
❑ 356 Angel Pena	.15	.07
❑ 357 Kevin McGlinchy	.15	.07
❑ 358 Michael Restovich	4.00	1.80
❑ 359 Eric DuBose	.15	.07
❑ 360 Geoff Jenkins	.25	.11
❑ 361 Mark Harriger	.50	.23
❑ 362 Junior Herndon	.50	.23
❑ 363 Tim Raines Jr.	1.00	.45
❑ 364 Rafael Furcal	3.00	1.35
❑ 365 Marcus Giles	2.00	.90
❑ 366 Ted Lilly	.15	.07
❑ 367 Jorge Toca	1.50	.70
❑ 368 David Kelton	1.25	.55
❑ 369 Adam Dunn	1.50	.70
❑ 370 Guillermo Mota	.75	.35
❑ 371 Brett Laxton	.50	.23
❑ 372 Travis Harper	.50	.23
❑ 373 Tom Davey	.50	.23
❑ 374 Darren Blakely	.75	.35
❑ 375 Tim Hudson	3.00	1.35
❑ 376 Jason Romano	.15	.07
❑ 377 Dan Reichert	.15	.07
❑ 378 Julio Lugo	.50	.23
❑ 379 Jose Garcia	.75	.35
❑ 380 Erubiel Durazo	6.00	2.70
❑ 381 Jose Jimenez	.25	.11
❑ 382 Chris Fussell	.15	.07
❑ 383 Steve Lomasney	.75	.35
❑ 384 Juan Pena	.75	.35
❑ 385 Allen Levrault	.75	.35
❑ 386 Juan Rivera	1.25	.55
❑ 387 Steve Colyer	.75	.35
❑ 388 Joe Nathan	.75	.35
❑ 389 Ron Walker	.50	.23
❑ 390 Nick Bierbrodt	.15	.07
❑ 391 Luke Prokopec	.50	.23
❑ 392 Dave Roberts	.75	.35
❑ 393 Mike Darr	.25	.11
❑ 394 Abraham Nunez	2.00	.90
❑ 395 Giuseppe Chiaramonte	1.00	.45
❑ 396 Jermaine Van Buren	.75	.35
❑ 397 Mike Kusiewicz	.15	.07
❑ 398 Matt Wise	.50	.23
❑ 399 Joe McEwing	2.50	1.10
❑ 400 Matt Holliday	1.50	.70
❑ 401 Willi Mo Pena	4.00	1.80
❑ 402 Ruben Quevedo	.75	.35
❑ 403 Rob Ryan	.50	.23
❑ 404 Freddy Garcia	6.00	2.70
❑ 405 Kevin Eberwein	.75	.35

❑ 406 Jesus Colome	1.00	.45
❑ 407 Chris Singleton	.25	.11
❑ 408 Bubba Crosby	.75	.35
❑ 409 Jesus Cordero	.50	.23
❑ 410 Donny Leon	.15	.07
❑ 411 Godfrey Tomlinson	.75	.35
❑ 412 Jeff Winchester	.75	.35
❑ 413 Adam Platt	4.00	1.80
❑ 414 Robert Stratton	.15	.07
❑ 415 T. J Tucker	.15	.07
❑ 416 Ryan Langerhans	.75	.35
❑ 417 Anthony Shumaker	.50	.23
❑ 418 Matt Miller	.50	.23
❑ 419 Doug Clark	1.00	.45
❑ 420 Kory DeHaan	.75	.35
❑ 421 David Eckstein	.50	.23
❑ 422 Brian Cooper	.50	.23
❑ 423 Brady Clark	.50	.23
❑ 424 Chris Magruder	.75	.35
❑ 425 Bobby Seay	1.00	.45
❑ 426 Aubrey Huff	1.00	.45
❑ 427 Mike Jerzembeck	.15	.07
❑ 428 Matt Blank	.75	.35
❑ 429 Benny Agbayani	2.00	.90
❑ 430 Kevin Beirne	.50	.23
❑ 431 Josh Hamilton	8.00	3.60
❑ 432 Josh Girdley	1.00	.45
❑ 433 Kole Strayhorn	1.00	.45
❑ 434 Mike Paradis	.50	.23
❑ 435 Jason Jennings	1.00	.45
❑ 436 David Walling	1.00	.45
❑ 437 Omar Ortiz	.50	.23
❑ 438 Jay Gehrke	.50	.23
❑ 439 Casey Burns	.50	.23
❑ 440 Carl Crawford	1.25	.55

1999 Bowman Gold

	MINT	NRMT
COMMON CARD (1-440)	8.00	3.60
*STARS: 15X TO 40X BASIC CARDS		
*YNG.STARS:12.5X TO 30X BASIC CARDS		
*RC'S: 5X TO 12X BASIC CARDS		
SER.1 STATED ODDS 1:111		
SER.2 STATED ODDS 1:59		
STATED PRINT RUN 99 SERIAL #'d SETS		

1999 Bowman International

	MINT	NRMT
COMPLETE SET (440)	220.00	100.00
COMPLETE SERIES 1 (220)	100.00	45.00
COMPLETE SERIES 2 (220)	120.00	55.00
COMMON CARD (1-440)	.50	.23
*STARS: 1X TO 2.5X BASIC CARDS		
*YNG.STARS: .75X TO 2X BASIC CARDS		
*RC'S: .6X TO 1.5X BASIC CARDS		
ONE PER PACK		

1999 Bowman Autographs

	MINT	NRMT
COMMON CARD (BA1-BA70)	8.00	3.60
MINOR STARS	10.00	4.50
BLUE FOIL SER.1 ODDS 1:162		
BLUE FOIL SER.2 ODDS 1:85		
GOLD FOIL SER.1 ODDS 1:1941		
GOLD FOIL SER.2 ODDS 1:1024		
SILVER FOIL SER.1 ODDS 1:485		
SILVER FOIL SER.2 ODDS 1:256		

❑ BA1 Ruben Mateo B	30.00	13.50
❑ BA2 Troy Glaus G	40.00	18.00
❑ BA3 Ben Davis G	30.00	13.50
❑ BA4 Jayson Werth B	15.00	6.75
❑ BA5 Jerry Hairston Jr. S	10.00	4.50
❑ BA6 Darnell McDonald B	15.00	6.75
❑ BA7 Calvin Pickering S	25.00	11.00
❑ BA8 Ryan Minor S	15.00	6.75
❑ BA9 Alex Escobar B	25.00	11.00
❑ BA10 Grant Roberts B	8.00	3.60
❑ BA11 Carlos Guillen B	8.00	3.60
❑ BA12 Ryan Anderson S	25.00	11.00
❑ BA13 Gil Meche S	20.00	9.00
❑ BA14 Russell Branyan S	20.00	9.00
❑ BA15 Alex Ramirez S	20.00	9.00
❑ BA16 Jason Rakers S	8.00	3.60
❑ BA17 Eddie Yarnall B	15.00	6.75
❑ BA18 Freddy Garcia B	50.00	22.00
❑ BA19 Jason Conti B	8.00	3.60
❑ BA20 Corey Koskie B	8.00	3.60
❑ BA21 Roosevelt Brown B	12.00	5.50
❑ BA22 Willie Martinez B	8.00	3.60
❑ BA23 Mike Jerzembeck B	8.00	3.60
❑ BA24 Lariel Gonzalez B	8.00	3.60
❑ BA25 Fernando Seguignol B	15.00	6.75
❑ BA26 Robert Fick S	12.00	5.50
❑ BA27 J.D. Smart B	8.00	3.60
❑ BA28 Ryan Mills B	10.00	4.50
❑ BA29 Chad Hermansen G	25.00	11.00
❑ BA30 Jason Grilli B	8.00	3.60
❑ BA31 Michael Cuddyer B	15.00	6.75
❑ BA32 Jacque Jones S	15.00	6.75
❑ BA33 Reggie Taylor B	8.00	3.60
❑ BA34 Richie Sexson B	30.00	13.50
❑ BA35 Michael Barrett B	15.00	6.75
❑ BA36 Paul LoDuca B	8.00	3.60
❑ BA37 Adrian Beltre G	30.00	13.50
❑ BA38 Peter Bergeron B	12.00	5.50
❑ BA39 Joe Fontenot B	8.00	3.60
❑ BA40 Randy Wolf B	15.00	6.75
❑ BA41 Nick Johnson B	40.00	18.00
❑ BA42 Ryan Bradley B	10.00	4.50
❑ BA43 Mike Lowell S	8.00	3.60
❑ BA44 Ricky Ledee G	25.00	11.00
❑ BA45 Mike Lincoln S	8.00	3.60

	MINT	NRMT
❑ BA46 Jeremy Giambi B	15.00	6.75
❑ BA47 Dermal Brown S	20.00	9.00
❑ BA48 Derrick Gibson B	10.00	4.50
❑ BA49 Scott Randall B	8.00	3.60
❑ BA50 Ben Petrick S	15.00	6.75
❑ BA51 Jason LaRue B	8.00	3.60
❑ BA52 Cole Liniak B	8.00	3.60
❑ BA53 John Curtice B	8.00	3.60
❑ BA54 Jackie Rexrode B	10.00	4.50
❑ BA55 John Patterson B	15.00	6.75
❑ BA56 Brad Penny S	20.00	9.00
❑ BA57 Jared Sandberg B	10.00	4.50
❑ BA58 Kerry Wood G	40.00	18.00
❑ BA59 Eli Marrero S	8.00	3.60
❑ BA60 Jason Marquis B	12.00	5.50
❑ BA61 George Lombard S	15.00	6.75
❑ BA62 Bruce Chen S	20.00	9.00
❑ BA63 Kevin Witt S	8.00	3.60
❑ BA64 Vernon Wells B	30.00	13.50
❑ BA65 Billy Koch B	15.00	6.75
❑ BA66 Roy Halladay B	25.00	11.00
❑ BA67 Nathan Haynes B	8.00	3.60
❑ BA68 Ben Grieve G	40.00	18.00
❑ BA69 Eric Chavez G	25.00	11.00
❑ BA70 Lance Berkman S	30.00	13.50

1999 Bowman 2000 ROY Favorites

	MINT	NRMT
COMPLETE SET (10)	12.00	5.50
COMMON CARD (ROY1-ROY10)	.50	.23
UNLISTED STARS	.75	.35
SER.2 STATED ODDS 1:12		
❑ ROY1 Ryan Anderson	.50	.23
❑ ROY2 Pat Burrell	3.00	1.35
❑ ROY3 A.J. Burnett	.75	.35
❑ ROY4 Ruben Mateo	.75	.35
❑ ROY5 Alex Escobar	1.50	.70
❑ ROY6 Pablo Ozuna	.50	.23
❑ ROY7 Mark Mulder	.75	.35
❑ ROY8 Corey Patterson	5.00	2.20
❑ ROY9 George Lombard	.50	.23
❑ ROY10 Nick Johnson	2.50	1.10

1999 Bowman Early Risers

	MINT	NRMT
COMPLETE SET (11)	25.00	11.00
COMMON CARD (ER1-ER11)	.50	.23
UNLISTED STARS	1.25	.55
SER.2 STATED ODDS 1:12		
❑ ER1 Mike Piazza	4.00	1.80
❑ ER2 Cal Ripken	5.00	2.20
❑ ER3 Jeff Bagwell	1.50	.70
❑ ER4 Ben Grieve	1.25	.55
❑ ER5 Kerry Wood	1.25	.55
❑ ER6 Mark McGwire	8.00	3.60
❑ ER7 Nomar Garciaparra	4.00	1.80
❑ ER8 Derek Jeter	4.00	1.80
❑ ER9 Scott Rolen	1.50	.70
❑ ER10 Jose Canseco	1.50	.70
❑ ER11 Raul Mondesi	.50	.23

1999 Bowman Late Bloomers

	MINT	NRMT
COMPLETE SET (10)	10.00	4.50
COMMON CARD (LB1-LB10)	.50	.23
SEMISTARS	.75	.35
UNLISTED STARS	1.25	.55
SER.1 STATED ODDS 1:12		
❑ LB1 Mike Piazza	4.00	1.80
❑ LB2 Jim Thome	1.25	.55
❑ LB3 Larry Walker	1.25	.55
❑ LB4 Vinny Castilla	.50	.23
❑ LB5 Andy Pettitte	.50	.23
❑ LB6 Jim Edmonds	.50	.23
❑ LB7 Kenny Lofton	.75	.35
❑ LB8 John Smoltz	.75	.35
❑ LB9 Mark Grace	.75	.35
❑ LB10 Trevor Hoffman	.50	.23

1999 Bowman Scout's Choice

	MINT	NRMT
COMPLETE SET (21)	20.00	9.00
COMMON CARD (SC1-SC21)	.50	.23
MINOR STARS	.75	.35
SEMISTARS	1.25	.55
UNLISTED STARS	2.00	.90
SER.1 STATED ODDS 1:12		
❑ SC1 Ruben Mateo	2.00	.90
❑ SC2 Ryan Anderson	.75	.35
❑ SC3 Pat Burrell	8.00	3.60
❑ SC4 Troy Glaus	2.00	.90
❑ SC5 Eric Chavez	1.25	.55
❑ SC6 Adrian Beltre	2.00	.90
❑ SC7 Bruce Chen	.75	.35
❑ SC8 Carlos Beltran	2.50	1.10
❑ SC9 Alex Gonzalez	.75	.35
❑ SC10 Carlos Lee	.75	.35
❑ SC11 George Lombard	.75	.35
❑ SC12 Matt Clement	.75	.35
❑ SC13 Calvin Pickering	.75	.35
❑ SC14 Marlon Anderson	.50	.23
❑ SC15 Chad Hermansen	.75	.35
❑ SC16 Russell Branyan	.75	.35
❑ SC17 Jeremy Giambi	.75	.35
❑ SC18 Ricky Ledee	.75	.35
❑ SC19 John Patterson	.75	.35
❑ SC20 Roy Halladay	.75	.35
❑ SC21 Michael Barrett	1.25	.55

1997 Bowman Chrome

	MINT	NRMT
COMPLETE SET (300)	300.00	135.00
COMMON RED (1-100)	.40	.18
RED UNLISTED STARS	.75	.35
RED MINOR STARS	1.50	.70
COMMON BLUE (101-300)	1.00	.45
BLUE SEMISTARS	1.50	.70
BLUE UNLISTED STARS	2.00	.90
❑ 1 Derek Jeter	5.00	2.20
❑ 2 Chipper Jones	4.00	1.80
❑ 3 Hideo Nomo	1.50	.70
❑ 4 Tim Salmon	1.50	.70
❑ 5 Robin Ventura	.75	.35
❑ 6 Tony Clark	1.00	.45
❑ 7 Barry Larkin	1.50	.70
❑ 8 Paul Molitor	1.50	.70
❑ 9 Andy Benes	.75	.35
❑ 10 Ryan Klesko	.75	.35
❑ 11 Mark McGwire	8.00	3.60
❑ 12 Ken Griffey Jr.	8.00	3.60
❑ 13 Robb Nen	.40	.18
❑ 14 Cal Ripken	6.00	2.70
❑ 15 John Valentin	.75	.35
❑ 16 Ricky Bottalico	.75	.35
❑ 17 Mike Lansing	.40	.18
❑ 18 Ryne Sandberg	2.00	.90
❑ 19 Carlos Delgado	1.50	.70
❑ 20 Craig Biggio	1.50	.70
❑ 21 Eric Karros	.75	.35
❑ 22 Kevin Appier	.75	.35
❑ 23 Mariano Rivera	.75	.35
❑ 24 Vinny Castilla	1.00	.45
❑ 25 Juan Gonzalez	3.00	1.35
❑ 26 Al Martin	.40	.18
❑ 27 Jeff Cirillo	.75	.35
❑ 28 Ray Lankford	.75	.35
❑ 29 Manny Ramirez	2.00	.90
❑ 30 Roberto Alomar	1.50	.70
❑ 31 Will Clark	1.50	.70
❑ 32 Chuck Knoblauch	1.50	.70
❑ 33 Harold Baines	.75	.35
❑ 34 Edgar Martinez	.75	.35
❑ 35 Mike Mussina	1.50	.70

36	Kevin Brown	1.00	.45
37	Dennis Eckersley	.75	.35
38	Tino Martinez	1.50	.70
39	Raul Mondesi	.75	.35
40	Sammy Sosa	5.00	2.20
41	John Smoltz	1.00	.45
42	Billy Wagner	.75	.35
43	Ken Caminiti	1.00	.45
44	Wade Boggs	1.50	.70
45	Andres Galarraga	1.50	.70
46	Roger Clemens	4.00	1.80
47	Matt Williams	1.50	.70
48	Albert Belle	1.50	.70
49	Jeff King	.40	.18
50	John Wetteland	.75	.35
51	Deion Sanders	.75	.35
52	Ellis Burks	.75	.35
53	Pedro Martinez	2.00	.90
54	Kenny Lofton	1.00	.45
55	Randy Johnson	1.50	.70
56	Bernie Williams	1.50	.70
57	Marquis Grissom	.75	.35
58	Gary Sheffield	.75	.35
59	Curt Schilling	1.00	.45
60	Reggie Sanders	.75	.35
61	Bobby Higginson	.75	.35
62	Moises Alou	.75	.35
63	Tom Glavine	1.50	.70
64	Mark Grace	1.00	.45
65	Rafael Palmeiro	1.50	.70
66	John Olerud	.75	.35
67	Dante Bichette	.75	.35
68	Jeff Bagwell	2.00	.90
69	Barry Bonds	2.00	.90
70	Pat Hentgen	.75	.35
71	Jim Thome	1.50	.70
72	Andy Pettitte	1.00	.45
73	Jay Bell	.75	.35
74	Jim Edmonds	1.00	.45
75	Ron Gant	.40	.18
76	David Cone	1.00	.45
77	Jose Canseco	2.00	.90
78	Jay Buhner	.75	.35
79	Greg Maddux	4.00	1.80
80	Lance Johnson	.40	.18
81	Travis Fryman	.75	.35
82	Paul O'Neill	.75	.35
83	Ivan Rodriguez	2.00	.90
84	Fred McGriff	1.00	.45
85	Mike Piazza	5.00	2.20
86	Brady Anderson	.75	.35
87	Marty Cordova	.40	.18
88	Joe Carter	.75	.35
89	Brian Jordan	.75	.35
90	David Justice	1.50	.70
91	Tony Gwynn	2.50	1.10
92	Larry Walker	1.50	.70
93	Mo Vaughn	1.50	.70
94	Sandy Alomar	.75	.35
95	Rusty Greer	.75	.35
96	Roberto Hernandez	.40	.18
97	Hal Morris	.40	.18
98	Todd Hundley	.75	.35
99	Rondell White	.75	.35
100	Frank Thomas	3.00	1.35
101	Bubba Trammell	2.00	.90
102	Sidney Ponson	8.00	3.60
103	Ricky Ledee	10.00	4.50
104	Brett Tomko	1.25	.55
105	Braden Looper	1.50	.70
106	Jason Dickson	1.00	.45
107	Chad Green	2.50	1.10
108	R.A. Dickey	1.50	.70
109	Jeff Liefer	1.25	.55
110	Richard Hidalgo	1.25	.55
111	Chad Hermansen	10.00	4.50
112	Felix Martinez	1.00	.45
113	J.J. Johnson	1.00	.45
114	Todd Dunwoody	1.25	.55
115	Katsuhiro Maeda	1.25	.55
116	Darin Erstad	2.00	.90
117	Elieser Marrero	1.00	.45
118	Bartolo Colon	1.25	.55
119	Ugueth Urbina	1.25	.55
120	Jaime Bluma	1.00	.45
121	Seth Greisinger	3.00	1.35
122	Jose Cruz Jr.	8.00	3.60
123	Todd Dunn	1.00	.45
124	Justin Towle	3.00	1.35
125	Brian Rose	2.00	.90
126	Jose Guillen	1.50	.70
127	Andruw Jones	2.50	1.10
128	Mark Kotsay	5.00	2.20
129	Wilton Guerrero	1.00	.45
130	Jacob Cruz	1.00	.45
131	Mike Sweeney	1.25	.55
132	Matt Morris	1.25	.55
133	John Thomson	1.00	.45
134	Javier Valentin	1.25	.55
135	Mike Drumright	2.50	1.10
136	Michael Barrett	1.00	.45
137	Tony Saunders	1.50	.70
138	Kevin Brown	1.50	.70
139	Anthony Sanders	3.00	1.35
140	Jeff Abbott	1.00	.45
141	Eugene Kingsale	1.25	.55
142	Paul Konerko	1.50	.70
143	Randall Simon	4.00	1.80
144	Freddy Garcia	1.00	.45
145	Karim Garcia	1.25	.55
146	Carlos Guillen	1.25	.55
147	Aaron Boone	1.25	.55
148	Donnie Sadler	1.25	.55
149	Brooks Kieschnick	1.00	.45
150	Scott Spiezio	1.00	.45
151	Kevin Orie	1.00	.45
152	Russ Johnson	1.00	.45
153	Livan Hernandez	1.25	.55
154	Vladimir Nunez	3.00	1.35
155	Calvin Reese	1.25	.55
156	Chris Carpenter	1.25	.55
157	Eric Milton	4.00	1.80
158	Richie Sexson	2.00	.90
159	Carl Pavano	2.00	.90
160	Pat Cline	1.25	.55
161	Ron Wright	1.25	.55
162	Dante Powell	1.25	.55
163	Mark Bellhorn	1.00	.45
164	George Lombard	2.00	.90
165	Paul Wilder	2.00	.90
166	Brad Fullmer	1.25	.55
167	Kris Benson	10.00	4.50
168	Torii Hunter	1.25	.55
169	D.T. Cromer	1.00	.45
170	Nelson Figueroa	2.00	.90
171	Hiram Bocachica	3.00	1.35
172	Shane Monahan	1.25	.55
173	Juan Melo	1.25	.55
174	Calvin Pickering	10.00	4.50
175	Reggie Taylor	1.25	.55
176	Geoff Jenkins	1.25	.55
177	Steve Rain	1.50	.70
178	Nerio Rodriguez	2.50	1.10
179	Derrick Gibson	1.50	.70
180	Darin Blood	1.00	.45
181	Ben Davis	2.00	.90
182	Adrian Beltre	20.00	9.00
183	Kerry Wood	25.00	11.00
184	Nate Rolison	3.00	1.35
185	Fernando Tatis	15.00	6.75
186	Jake Westbrook	3.00	1.35
187	Edwin Diaz	1.00	.45
188	Joe Fontenot	2.50	1.10
189	Matt Halloran	2.00	.90
190	Matt Clement	8.00	3.60
191	Todd Greene	1.00	.45
192	Eric Chavez	15.00	6.75
193	Edgard Velazquez	1.50	.70
194	Bruce Chen	8.00	3.60
195	Jason Brester	1.25	.55
196	Chris Reitsma	2.00	.90
197	Nerfi Perez	1.25	.55
198	Hideki Irabu	6.00	2.70
199	Don Denbow	1.00	.45
200	Derrek Lee	1.50	.70
201	Todd Walker	2.00	.90
202	Scott Rolen	3.00	1.35
203	Wes Helms	1.00	.45
204	Bob Abreu	1.25	.55
205	John Patterson	6.00	2.70
206	Alex Gonzalez	8.00	3.60
207	Grant Roberts	3.00	1.35
208	Jeff Suppan	1.00	.45
209	Luke Wilson	1.00	.45
210	Marlon Anderson	1.25	.55
211	Mike Caruso	4.00	1.80
212	Roy Halladay	8.00	3.60
213	Jeremi Gonzalez	2.50	1.10
214	Aramis Ramirez	15.00	6.75
215	Dermal Brown	10.00	4.50
216	Justin Thompson	1.25	.55
217	Danny Clyburn	1.00	.45
218	Bruce Aven	1.00	.45
219	Keith Foulke	1.00	.45
220	Shannon Stewart	1.25	.55
221	Larry Barnes	1.25	.55
222	Mark Johnson	1.50	.70
223	Randy Winn	1.00	.45
224	Nomar Garciaparra	5.00	2.20
225	Jacque Jones	8.00	3.60
226	Chris Clemons	1.00	.45
227	Todd Helton	3.00	1.35
228	Ryan Brannan	1.50	.70
229	Alex Sanchez	3.00	1.35
230	Russell Branyan	2.00	.90
231	Daryle Ward	6.00	2.70
232	Kevin Witt	3.00	1.35
233	Gabby Martinez	1.00	.45
234	Preston Wilson	1.25	.55
235	Donzell McDonald	2.00	.90
236	Orlando Cabrera	2.50	1.10
237	Brian Banks	1.00	.45
238	Robbie Bell	2.50	1.10
239	Brad Rigby	1.00	.45
240	Scott Elarton	1.25	.55
241	Donny Leon	5.00	2.20
242	Abraham Nunez	3.00	1.35
243	Adam Eaton	4.00	1.80
244	Octavio Dotel	10.00	4.50
245	Sean Casey	25.00	11.00
246	Joe Lawrence	2.50	1.10
247	Adam Johnson	3.00	1.35
248	Ronnie Belliard	5.00	2.20
249	Bobby Estalella	1.00	.45
250	Corey Lee	2.00	.90
251	Mike Cameron	1.25	.55
252	Kerry Robinson	1.50	.70
253	A.J. Zapp	3.00	1.35
254	Jarrod Washburn	1.25	.55
255	Ben Grieve	2.00	.90
256	Javier Vazquez	3.00	1.35
257	Travis Lee	12.00	5.50
258	Dennis Reyes	3.00	1.35
259	Danny Buxbaum	1.00	.45
260	Kelvim Escobar	4.00	1.80
261	Danny Klassen	1.00	.45
262	Ken Cloude	2.50	1.10
263	Gabe Alvarez	1.25	.55
264	Clayton Bruner	2.50	1.10
265	Jason Marquis	6.00	2.70
266	Jamey Wright	1.00	.45
267	Matt Snyder	1.50	.70
268	Josh Garrett	3.00	1.35
269	Juan Encarnacion	1.25	.55
270	Heath Murray	1.00	.45
271	Brent Butler	1.25	.55
272	Danny Peoples	3.00	1.35
273	Miguel Tejada	12.00	5.50
274	Jim Pittsley	1.00	.45
275	Dmitri Young	1.25	.55
276	Vladimir Guerrero	3.00	1.35
277	Cole Liniak	5.00	2.20
278	Ramon Hernandez	1.50	.70
279	Cliff Politte	2.50	1.10
280	Mel Rosario	1.50	.70
281	Jorge Carrion	1.50	.70
282	John Barnes	3.00	1.35
283	Chris Stowe	1.50	.70
284	Vernon Wells	15.00	6.75
285	Brett Caradonna	3.00	1.35
286	Scott Hodges	2.50	1.10
287	Ron Garland	4.00	1.80
288	Nathan Haynes	3.00	1.35
289	Geoff Goetz	2.50	1.10
290	Adam Kennedy	8.00	3.60
291	T.J. Tucker	6.00	2.70
292	Aaron Akin	2.00	.90
293	Jayson Werth	8.00	3.60

❏ 294 Glenn Davis	3.00	1.35
❏ 295 Mark Mangum	2.00	.90
❏ 296 Troy Cameron	5.00	2.20
❏ 297 J.J. Davis	5.00	2.20
❏ 298 Lance Berkman	15.00	6.75
❏ 299 Jason Standridge	6.00	2.70
❏ 300 Jason Dellaero	3.00	1.35

1997 Bowman Chrome International

JUSTIN
TOWLE

	MINT	NRMT
COMMON RED (1-100)	1.00	.45
COMMON BLUE (101-300)	1.00	.45

*STARS: 1.25X TO 3X BASIC CARDS
*RC'S/PROSPECTS: .4X TO 1X BASIC
STATED ODDS 1:4

1997 Bowman Chrome International Refractors

	MINT	NRMT
COMMON CARD (1-300)	5.00	2.20

*STARS: 5X TO 12X BASIC CARDS
*YOUNG STARS: 4X TO 10X BASIC CARDS
*ROOKIES: 1.5X TO 4X BASIC CARDS
STATED ODDS 1:24

1997 Bowman Chrome Refractors

AL
MARTIN

	MINT	NRMT
COMMON CARD (1-300)	3.00	1.35

*STARS: 3X TO 8X BASIC CARDS
*YOUNG STARS: 2.5X TO 6X BASIC CARDS
*ROOKIES: 1.25X TO 3X BASIC CARDS
STATED ODDS 1:12

1997 Bowman Chrome 1998 ROY Favorites

	MINT	NRMT
COMPLETE SET (15)	50.00	22.00
COMMON CARD (1-15)	1.50	.70
SEMISTARS	2.50	1.10

STATED ODDS 1:24
*REFRACTORS: .75X TO 2X HI COLUMN
REFRACTOR STATED ODDS 1:72

ELVES JOHNSON

❏ ROY1 Jeff Abbott	1.50	.70
❏ ROY2 Karim Garcia	2.00	.90
❏ ROY3 Todd Helton	6.00	2.70
❏ ROY4 Richard Hidalgo	2.00	.90
❏ ROY5 Geoff Jenkins	2.00	.90
❏ ROY6 Russ Johnson	1.50	.70
❏ ROY7 Paul Konerko	4.00	1.80
❏ ROY8 Mark Kotsay	3.00	1.35
❏ ROY9 Ricky Ledee	6.00	2.70
❏ ROY10 Travis Lee	8.00	3.60
❏ ROY11 Derrek Lee	2.50	1.10
❏ ROY12 Elieser Marrero	1.50	.70
❏ ROY13 Juan Melo	2.00	.90
❏ ROY14 Brian Rose	4.00	1.80
❏ ROY15 Fernando Tatis	10.00	4.50

1997 Bowman Chrome Scout's Honor Roll

DERREK
LEE

	MINT	NRMT
COMPLETE SET (15)	50.00	22.00
COMMON CARD (1-15)	1.50	.70

STATED ODDS 1:12
*REFRACTORS: .75X TO 2X HI COLUMN
REFRACTOR STATED ODDS 1:36

❏ SHR1 Dmitri Young	1.50	.70
❏ SHR2 Bob Abreu	1.50	.70
❏ SHR3 Vladimir Guerrero	4.00	1.80
❏ SHR4 Paul Konerko	3.00	1.35
❏ SHR5 Kevin Orie	1.50	.70
❏ SHR6 Todd Walker	3.00	1.35
❏ SHR7 Ben Grieve	3.00	1.35
❏ SHR8 Darin Erstad	3.00	1.35
❏ SHR9 Derrek Lee	2.00	.90
❏ SHR10 Jose Cruz Jr.	4.00	1.80
❏ SHR11 Scott Rolen	4.00	1.80
❏ SHR12 Travis Lee	6.00	2.70
❏ SHR13 Andruw Jones	3.00	1.35
❏ SHR14 Wilton Guerrero	1.50	.70
❏ SHR15 Nomar Garciaparra	8.00	3.60

1998 Bowman Chrome

	MINT	NRMT
COMPLETE SET (441)	250.00	110.00
COMPLETE SERIES 1 (221)	150.00	70.00
COMPLETE SERIES 2 (220)	100.00	45.00
COMMON CARD (1-441)	.40	.18
MINOR STARS	.60	.25

ALEX
HERNANDEZ

SEMISTARS	1.00	.45
UNLISTED STARS	1.50	.70
❏ 1 Nomar Garciaparra	5.00	2.20
❏ 2 Scott Rolen	2.00	.90
❏ 3 Andy Pettitte	.60	.25
❏ 4 Ivan Rodriguez	2.00	.90
❏ 5 Mark McGwire	10.00	4.50
❏ 6 Jason Dickson	.40	.18
❏ 7 Jose Cruz Jr.	.60	.25
❏ 8 Jeff Kent	.60	.25
❏ 9 Mike Mussina	1.50	.70
❏ 10 Jason Kendall	.60	.25
❏ 11 Brett Tomko	.40	.18
❏ 12 Jeff King	.40	.18
❏ 13 Brad Radke	.60	.25
❏ 14 Robin Ventura	.60	.25
❏ 15 Jeff Bagwell	2.00	.90
❏ 16 Greg Maddux	4.00	1.80
❏ 17 John Jaha	.60	.25
❏ 18 Mike Piazza	5.00	2.20
❏ 19 Edgar Martinez	.60	.25
❏ 20 David Justice	.60	.25
❏ 21 Todd Hundley	.60	.25
❏ 22 Tony Gwynn	4.00	1.80
❏ 23 Larry Walker	1.50	.70
❏ 24 Bernie Williams	1.50	.70
❏ 25 Edgar Renteria	.40	.18
❏ 26 Rafael Palmeiro	1.50	.70
❏ 27 Tim Salmon	1.00	.45
❏ 28 Matt Morris	.40	.18
❏ 29 Shawn Estes	.40	.18
❏ 30 Vladimir Guerrero	2.00	.90
❏ 31 Fernando Tatis	1.50	.70
❏ 32 Justin Thompson	.40	.18
❏ 33 Ken Griffey Jr.	8.00	3.60
❏ 34 Edgardo Alfonzo	1.00	.45
❏ 35 Mo Vaughn	1.50	.70
❏ 36 Marty Cordova	.40	.18
❏ 37 Craig Biggio	1.50	.70
❏ 38 Roger Clemens	4.00	1.80
❏ 39 Mark Grace	1.00	.45
❏ 40 Ken Caminiti	.60	.25
❏ 41 Tony Womack	.40	.18
❏ 42 Albert Belle	1.50	.70
❏ 43 Tino Martinez	.60	.25
❏ 44 Sandy Alomar Jr.	.60	.25
❏ 45 Jeff Cirillo	.60	.25
❏ 46 Jason Giambi	.60	.25
❏ 47 Darin Erstad	1.00	.45
❏ 48 Livan Hernandez	.40	.18
❏ 49 Mark Grudzielanek	.40	.18
❏ 50 Sammy Sosa	5.00	2.20
❏ 51 Curt Schilling	1.00	.45
❏ 52 Brian Hunter	.40	.18
❏ 53 Neifi Perez	.60	.25
❏ 54 Todd Walker	.60	.25
❏ 55 Jose Guillen	.40	.18
❏ 56 Jim Thorne	1.50	.70
❏ 57 Tom Glavine	1.50	.70
❏ 58 Todd Greene	.40	.18
❏ 59 Rondell White	.60	.25
❏ 60 Roberto Alomar	1.50	.70
❏ 61 Tony Clark	.60	.25
❏ 62 Vinny Castilla	.60	.25
❏ 63 Barry Larkin	1.50	.70
❏ 64 Hideki Irabu	.60	.25
❏ 65 Johnny Damon	.60	.25

66	Juan Gonzalez	3.00	1.35
67	John Olerud	.60	.25
68	Gary Sheffield	.60	.25
69	Raul Mondesi	.60	.25
70	Chipper Jones	4.00	1.80
71	David Ortiz	.40	.18
72	Warren Morris	10.00	4.50
73	Alex Gonzalez	.60	.25
74	Nick Bierbrodt	2.50	1.10
75	Roy Halladay	.60	.25
76	Danny Buxbaum	.40	.18
77	Adam Kennedy	.60	.25
78	Jared Sandberg	2.50	1.10
79	Michael Barrett	1.00	.45
80	Gil Meche	4.00	1.80
81	Jayson Werth	.60	.25
82	Abraham Nunez	.40	.18
83	Ben Petrick	.60	.25
84	Brett Caradonna	.40	.18
85	Mike Lowell	5.00	2.20
86	Clayton Bruner	.60	.25
87	John Curtice	5.00	2.20
88	Bobby Estalella	.40	.18
89	Juan Melo	.40	.18
90	Arnold Gooch	.40	.18
91	Kevin Millwood	15.00	6.75
92	Richie Sexson	1.00	.45
93	Orlando Cabrera	.40	.18
94	Pat Cline	.40	.18
95	Anthony Sanders	.40	.18
96	Russ Johnson	.40	.18
97	Ben Grieve	1.50	.70
98	Kevin McGlinchy	.40	.18
99	Paul Wilder	.40	.18
100	Russ Ortiz	.60	.25
101	Ryan Jackson	2.00	.90
102	Heath Murray	.40	.18
103	Brian Rose	.40	.18
104	Ryan Radmanovich	.60	.25
105	Ricky Ledee	.60	.25
106	Jeff Wallace	2.50	1.10
107	Ryan Minor	6.00	2.70
108	Dennis Reyes	.40	.18
109	James Manias	.40	.18
110	Chris Carpenter	.60	.25
111	Daryle Ward	.60	.25
112	Vernon Wells	1.00	.45
113	Chad Green	.40	.18
114	Mike Stoner	3.00	1.35
115	Brad Fullmer	.40	.18
116	Adam Eaton	.60	.25
117	Jeff Liefer	.40	.18
118	Corey Koskie	5.00	2.20
119	Todd Helton	2.00	.90
120	Jaime Jones	2.50	1.10
121	Mel Rosario	.40	.18
122	Geoff Goetz	.40	.18
123	Adrian Beltre	1.50	.70
124	Jason Dellaero	.40	.18
125	Gabe Kapler	15.00	6.75
126	Scott Schoeneweis	.40	.18
127	Ryan Brannan	.40	.18
128	Aaron Akin	.40	.18
129	Ryan Anderson	10.00	4.50
130	Brad Penny	.60	.25
131	Bruce Chen	.60	.25
132	Eli Marrero	.40	.18
133	Eric Chavez	1.50	.70
134	Troy Glaus	20.00	9.00
135	Troy Cameron	.60	.25
136	Brian Sikorski	2.00	.90
137	Mike Kinkade	3.00	1.35
138	Braden Looper	.40	.18
139	Mark Mangum	.40	.18
140	Danny Peoples	.40	.18
141	J.J. Davis	.60	.25
142	Ben Davis	1.00	.45
143	Jacque Jones	.60	.25
144	Derrick Gibson	.60	.25
145	Bronson Arroyo	2.50	1.10
146	Luis De Los Santos	4.00	1.80
147	Jeff Abbott	.40	.18
148	Mike Cuddyer	8.00	3.60
149	Jason Romano	.60	.25
150	Shane Monahan	.40	.18
151	Ntema Ndungidi	4.00	1.80
152	Alex Sanchez	.40	.18
153	Jack Cust	10.00	4.50
154	Brent Butler	.40	.18
155	Ramon Hernandez	.40	.18
156	Norm Hutchins	.40	.18
157	Jason Marquis	.60	.25
158	Jacob Cruz	.40	.18
159	Rob Burger	2.50	1.10
160	Dave Coggin	.40	.18
161	Preston Wilson	.60	.25
162	Jason Fitzgerald	2.50	1.10
163	Dan Serafini	.40	.18
164	Peter Munro	.40	.18
165	Trot Nixon	.40	.18
166	Homer Bush	.40	.18
167	Dermal Brown	.60	.25
168	Chad Hermansen	1.50	.70
169	Julio Moreno	2.00	.90
170	John Roskos	4.00	1.80
171	Grant Roberts	.40	.18
172	Ken Cloude	.40	.18
173	Jason Brester	.40	.18
174	Jason Conti	2.00	.90
175	Jon Garland	.40	.18
176	Robbie Bell	.60	.25
177	Nathan Haynes	.40	.18
178	Ramon Ortiz	8.00	3.60
179	Shannon Stewart	.60	.25
180	Pablo Ortega	.40	.18
181	Jimmy Rollins	4.00	1.80
182	Sean Casey	2.50	1.10
183	Ted Lilly	3.00	1.35
184	Chris Enochs	3.00	1.35
185	Magglio Ordonez	15.00	6.75
186	Mike Drumright	.40	.18
187	Aaron Boone	.40	.18
188	Matt Clement	.60	.25
189	Todd Dunwoody	.40	.18
190	Larry Rodriguez	.40	.18
191	Todd Noel	.40	.18
192	Geoff Jenkins	.60	.25
193	George Lombard	.40	.18
194	Lance Berkman	1.00	.45
195	Marcus McCain	.40	.18
196	Ryan McGuire	.40	.18
197	Jhensy Sandoval	3.00	1.35
198	Corey Lee	.40	.18
199	Mario Valdez	2.00	.90
200	Robert Fick	6.00	2.70
201	Donnie Sadler	.40	.18
202	Marc Kroon	.40	.18
203	David Miller	.40	.18
204	Jarrod Washburn	.40	.18
205	Miguel Tejada	.60	.25
206	Raul Ibanez	.60	.25
207	John Patterson	.60	.25
208	Calvin Pickering	.60	.25
209	Felix Martinez	.40	.18
210	Mark Redman	.40	.18
211	Scott Elarton	.40	.18
212	Jose Amado	2.00	.90
213	Kerry Wood	2.00	.90
214	Dante Powell	.40	.18
215	Aramis Ramirez	1.50	.70
216	A.J. Hinch	.40	.18
217	Dustin Carr	2.00	.90
218	Mark Kotsay	.60	.25
219	Jason Standridge	.60	.25
220	Luis Ordaz	.40	.18
221	Orlando Hernandez	12.00	5.50
222	Cal Ripken	6.00	2.70
223	Paul Molitor	1.50	.70
224	Derek Jeter	5.00	2.20
225	Barry Bonds	2.00	.90
226	Jim Edmonds	.60	.25
227	John Smoltz	1.00	.45
228	Eric Karros	.60	.25
229	Ray Lankford	.60	.25
230	Rey Ordonez	.60	.25
231	Kenny Lofton	1.00	.45
232	Alex Rodriguez	5.00	2.20
233	Dante Bichette	.60	.25
234	Pedro Martinez	2.00	.90
235	Carlos Delgado	1.50	.70
236	Rod Beck	.60	.25
237	Matt Williams	1.50	.70
238	Charles Johnson	.60	.25
239	Rico Brogna	.40	.18
240	Frank Thomas	3.00	1.35
241	Paul O'Neill	.60	.25
242	Jaret Wright	.60	.25
243	Brant Brown	.40	.18
244	Ryan Klesko	.60	.25
245	Chuck Finley	.60	.25
246	Derek Bell	.60	.25
247	Delino DeShields	.40	.18
248	Chan Ho Park	.60	.25
249	Wade Boggs	1.50	.70
250	Jay Buhner	.60	.25
251	Butch Huskey	.40	.18
252	Steve Finley	.40	.18
253	Will Clark	1.50	.70
254	John Valentin	.60	.25
255	Bobby Higginson	.60	.25
256	Darryl Strawberry	.60	.25
257	Randy Johnson	1.50	.70
258	Al Martin	.40	.18
259	Travis Fryman	.60	.25
260	Fred McGriff	1.00	.45
261	Jose Valentin	.40	.18
262	Andruw Jones	1.50	.70
263	Kenny Rogers	.40	.18
264	Moises Alou	.60	.25
265	Denny Neagle	.40	.18
266	Ugueth Urbina	.40	.18
267	Derrek Lee	.40	.18
268	Ellis Burks	.60	.25
269	Mariano Rivera	.60	.25
270	Dean Palmer	.40	.18
271	Eddie Taubensee	.40	.18
272	Brady Anderson	.60	.25
273	Brian Giles	.60	.25
274	Quinton McCracken	.40	.18
275	Henry Rodriguez	.60	.25
276	Andres Galarraga	1.00	.45
277	Jose Canseco	2.00	.90
278	David Segui	.40	.18
279	Bret Saberhagen	.60	.25
280	Kevin Brown	1.00	.45
281	Chuck Knoblauch	.60	.25
282	Jeromy Burnitz	.40	.18
283	Jay Bell	.60	.25
284	Manny Ramirez	2.00	.90
285	Rick Helling	.40	.18
286	Francisco Cordova	.40	.18
287	Bob Abreu	.60	.25
288	J.T. Snow	.60	.25
289	Hideo Nomo	1.50	.70
290	Brian Jordan	.60	.25
291	Javy Lopez	.60	.25
292	Travis Lee	1.00	.45
293	Russ Branyan	.60	.25
294	Paul Konerko	.60	.25
295	Masato Yoshii	3.00	1.35
296	Kris Benson	.60	.25
297	Juan Encarnacion	.60	.25
298	Eric Milton	.40	.18
299	Mike Caruso	.40	.18
300	Ricardo Aramboles	5.00	2.20
301	Bobby Smith	.40	.18
302	Billy Koch	.60	.25
303	Richard Hidalgo	.60	.25
304	Justin Baughman	2.00	.90
305	Chris Gissell	.40	.18
306	Donnie Bridges	2.00	.90
307	Nelson Lara	2.00	.90
308	Randy Wolf	8.00	3.60
309	Jason LaRue	5.00	2.20
310	Jason Gooding	2.00	.90
311	Edgard Clemente	.40	.18
312	Andrew Vessel	.40	.18
313	Chris Reitsma	.40	.18
314	Jesus Sanchez	3.00	1.35
315	Buddy Carlyle	3.00	1.35
316	Randy Winn	.40	.18
317	Luis Rivera	4.00	1.80
318	Marcus Thames	4.00	1.80
319	A.J. Pierzynski	.40	.18
320	Scott Randall	.40	.18
321	Damian Sapp	.40	.18
322	Eddie Yarnall	6.00	2.70
323	Luke Allen	4.00	1.80

☐ 324 J.D. Smart	.40	.18
☐ 325 Willie Martinez	.60	.25
☐ 326 Alex Ramirez	.60	.25
☐ 327 Eric DuBose	3.00	1.35
☐ 328 Kevin Witt	.40	.18
☐ 329 Dan McKinley	2.00	.90
☐ 330 Cliff Politte	.40	.18
☐ 331 Vladimir Nunez	.40	.18
☐ 332 John Halama	5.00	2.20
☐ 333 Nerio Rodriguez	.40	.18
☐ 334 Desi Relaford	.40	.18
☐ 335 Robinson Checo	.40	.18
☐ 336 John Nicholson	3.00	1.35
☐ 337 Tom LaRosa	2.00	.90
☐ 338 Kevin Nicholson	3.00	1.35
☐ 339 Javier Vazquez	.40	.18
☐ 340 A.J. Zapp	.40	.18
☐ 341 Tom Evans	.40	.18
☐ 342 Kerry Robinson	.40	.18
☐ 343 Gabe Gonzalez	.40	.18
☐ 344 Ralph Milliard	.40	.18
☐ 345 Enrique Wilson	.40	.18
☐ 346 Elvin Hernandez	.40	.18
☐ 347 Mike Lincoln	4.00	1.80
☐ 348 Cesar King	3.00	1.35
☐ 349 Cristian Guzman	3.00	1.35
☐ 350 Donzell McDonald	.40	.18
☐ 351 Jim Parque	3.00	1.35
☐ 352 Mike Saipe	.40	.18
☐ 353 Carlos Febles	10.00	4.50
☐ 354 Demell Stenson	10.00	4.50
☐ 355 Mark Osborne	.40	1.80
☐ 356 Odalis Perez	5.00	2.20
☐ 357 Jason Dewey	3.00	1.35
☐ 358 Joe Fontenot	.40	.18
☐ 359 Jason Grilli	3.00	1.35
☐ 360 Kevin Haverbusch	4.00	1.80
☐ 361 Jay Yennaco	2.00	.90
☐ 362 Brian Buchanan	.40	.18
☐ 363 John Barnes	.40	.18
☐ 364 Chris Fussell	.40	.18
☐ 365 Kevin Gibbs	2.00	.90
☐ 366 Joe Lawrence	2.00	.90
☐ 367 DaRond Stovall	.40	.18
☐ 368 Brian Fuentes	2.00	.90
☐ 369 Jimmy Anderson	.40	.18
☐ 370 Lariel Gonzalez	2.00	.90
☐ 371 Scott Williamson	5.00	2.20
☐ 372 Milton Bradley	4.00	1.80
☐ 373 Jason Halper	2.00	.90
☐ 374 Brent Billingsley	2.00	.90
☐ 375 Joe DePastino	2.00	.90
☐ 376 Jake Westbrook	.40	.18
☐ 377 Octavio Dotel	.60	.25
☐ 378 Jason Williams	2.00	.90
☐ 379 Julio Ramirez	8.00	3.60
☐ 380 Seth Greisinger	.40	.18
☐ 381 Mike Judd	3.00	1.35
☐ 382 Ben Ford	2.00	.90
☐ 383 Tom Bennett	2.00	.90
☐ 384 Adam Butler	2.00	.90
☐ 385 Wade Miller	2.00	.90
☐ 386 Kyle Peterson	2.00	.90
☐ 387 Tommy Peterman	2.00	.90
☐ 388 Onan Masaoka	.40	.18
☐ 389 Jason Rakers	2.00	.90
☐ 390 Rafael Medina	.40	.18
☐ 391 Luis Lopez	.40	.18
☐ 392 Jeff Yoder	.40	.18
☐ 393 Vance Wilson	2.00	.90
☐ 394 Fernando Seguignol	6.00	2.70
☐ 395 Ron Wright	.40	.18
☐ 396 Ruben Mateo	15.00	6.75
☐ 397 Steve Lomasney	2.50	1.10
☐ 398 Damian Jackson	.40	.18
☐ 399 Mike Jerzembeck	2.50	1.10
☐ 400 Luis Rivas	4.00	1.80
☐ 401 Kevin Burford	3.00	1.35
☐ 402 Glenn Davis	.40	.18
☐ 403 Robert Luce	2.00	.90
☐ 404 Cole Liniak	.40	.18
☐ 405 Matt LeCroy	4.00	1.80
☐ 406 Jeremy Giambi	6.00	2.70
☐ 407 Shawn Chacon	.40	.18
☐ 408 Dewayne Wise	4.00	1.80
☐ 409 Steve Woodard	.40	.18

☐ 410 Francisco Cordero	3.00	1.35
☐ 411 Damon Minor	2.50	1.10
☐ 412 Lou Collier	.40	.18
☐ 413 Justin Towle	.40	.18
☐ 414 Juan LeBron	.40	.18
☐ 415 Michael Coleman	.60	.25
☐ 416 Felix Rodriguez	.40	.18
☐ 417 Paul Ah Yat	2.50	1.10
☐ 418 Kevin Barker	3.00	1.35
☐ 419 Brian Meadows	.40	.18
☐ 420 Darnell McDonald	6.00	2.70
☐ 421 Matt Kinney	2.00	.90
☐ 422 Mike Vavrek	2.00	.90
☐ 423 Courtney Duncan	2.00	.90
☐ 424 Kevin Millar	8.00	3.60
☐ 425 Ruben Rivera	.40	.18
☐ 426 Steve Shoemaker	.40	.18
☐ 427 Dan Reichert	3.00	1.35
☐ 428 Carlos Lee	10.00	4.50
☐ 429 Rod Barajas	4.00	1.80
☐ 430 Pablo Ozuna	8.00	3.60
☐ 431 Todd Belitz	2.00	.90
☐ 432 Sidney Ponson	.60	.25
☐ 433 Steve Carver	.40	.18
☐ 434 Esteban Yan	4.00	1.80
☐ 435 Cedrick Bowers	2.50	1.10
☐ 436 Marlon Anderson	.60	.25
☐ 437 Carl Pavano	.40	.18
☐ 438 Jae Weong Seo	2.50	1.10
☐ 439 Jose Taveras	2.50	1.10
☐ 440 Matt Anderson	4.00	1.80
☐ 441 Darron Ingram	4.00	1.80

1998 Bowman Chrome Golden Anniversary

	MINT	NRMT
COMMON CARD (1-441)	15.00	6.75

*STARS: 15X TO 40X BASIC CARDS
*YOUNG STARS: 12.5X TO 30X BASIC CARDS
*PROSPECTS: 10X TO 25X BASIC CARDS
*ROOKIES: 3X TO 8X BASIC CARDS
SER.1 STATED ODDS 1:164
SER.2 STATED ODDS 1:133
STATED PRINT RUN 50 SERIAL #'d SETS
GOLD.ANN.REF.SER.1 ODDS 1:1279
GOLD.ANN.REF.SER.2 ODDS 1:1022
GOLD.ANN.REF.PRINT RUN 5 SERIAL #'d SETS
GOLD.ANN.REF.NOT PRICED DUE TO SCARCITY

1998 Bowman Chrome International

	MINT	NRMT
COMPLETE SET (441)	700.00	325.00
COMPLETE SERIES 1 (221)	400.00	180.00
COMPLETE SERIES 2 (220)	300.00	135.00
COMMON CARD (1-441)	1.00	.45

*STARS: 1X TO 2.5X BASIC CARDS
*RCS/PROSPECTS: .4X TO 1X BASIC
STATED ODDS 1:4

1998 Bowman Chrome International Refractors

	MINT	NRMT
COMPLETE SET (441)	5000.00	2200.00
COMPLETE SERIES 1 (221)	3000.00	1350.00
COMPLETE SERIES 2 (220)	2000.00	900.00
COMMON CARD (1-441)	6.00	2.70

*STARS: 6X TO 15X BASIC CARDS
*YOUNG STARS: 5X TO 12X BASIC CARDS
*PROSPECTS: 3X TO 8X BASIC CARDS
*ROOKIES: 2X TO 5X BASIC CARDS
STATED ODDS 1:24

1998 Bowman Chrome Refractors

	MINT	NRMT
COMPLETE SET (441)	2500.00	1100.00
COMPLETE SERIES 1 (221)	1500.00	700.00
COMPLETE SERIES 2 (220)	1000.00	450.00
COMMON CARD (1-441)	2.50	1.10

*STARS: 5X TO 6X BASIC CARDS
*YOUNG STARS: 2X TO 5X BASIC CARDS
*PROSPECTS: 1.5X TO 4X BASIC CARDS
*ROOKIES: 1.25X TO 3X BASIC CARDS
STATED ODDS 1:12

1998 Bowman Chrome Reprints

	MINT	NRMT
COMPLETE SET (50)	160.00	70.00
COMPLETE SERIES 1 (25)	80.00	36.00
COMPLETE SERIES 2 (25)	80.00	36.00
COMMON CARD (1-50)	1.00	.45
MINOR STARS	1.50	.70
SEMISTARS	2.00	.90
UNLISTED STARS	3.00	1.35
STATED ODDS 1:12		
*REFRACTORS: 1X TO 2.5X HI COLUMN		
REFRACTOR STATED ODDS 1:36		
ODD NUMBER CARDS DIST.IN SER.1		
EVEN NUMBER CARDS DIST.IN SER.2		
1 Yogi Berra	8.00	3.60
2 Jackie Robinson	12.00	5.50
3 Don Newcombe	1.50	.70
4 Satchell Paige	8.00	3.60
5 Willie Mays	12.00	5.50
6 Gil McDougald	1.50	.70
7 Don Larsen	1.50	.70
8 Elston Howard	1.50	.70
9 Robin Ventura	1.50	.70
10 Brady Anderson	1.50	.70
11 Gary Sheffield	1.50	.70
12 Tino Martinez	1.50	.70
13 Ken Griffey Jr.	15.00	6.75
14 John Smoltz	2.00	.90
15 Sandy Alomar Jr.	1.50	.70
16 Larry Walker	3.00	1.35
17 Todd Hundley	1.50	.70
18 Mo Vaughn	3.00	1.35
19 Sammy Sosa	10.00	4.50
20 Frank Thomas	6.00	2.70
21 Chuck Knoblauch	1.50	.70
22 Bernie Williams	3.00	1.35
23 Juan Gonzalez	6.00	2.70
24 Mike Mussina	3.00	1.35
25 Jeff Bagwell	4.00	1.80
26 Tim Salmon	2.00	.90
27 Ivan Rodriguez	4.00	1.80
28 Kenny Lofton	2.00	.90
29 Chipper Jones	8.00	3.60
30 Javy Lopez	1.50	.70
31 Ryan Klesko	1.50	.70
32 Raul Mondesi	1.50	.70
33 Jim Thome	3.00	1.35
34 Carlos Delgado	3.00	1.35
35 Mike Piazza	10.00	4.50
36 Manny Ramirez	4.00	1.80
37 Andy Pettitte	1.50	.70
38 Derek Jeter	10.00	4.50
39 Brad Fullmer	1.00	.45
40 Richard Hidalgo	1.50	.70
41 Tony Clark	1.50	.70
42 Andruw Jones	3.00	1.35
43 Vladimir Guerrero	4.00	1.80
44 Nomar Garciaparra	10.00	4.50
45 Paul Konerko	1.50	.70
46 Ben Grieve	3.00	1.35
47 Hideo Nomo	3.00	1.35
48 Scott Rolen	4.00	1.80
49 Jose Guillen	1.00	.45
50 Livan Hernandez	1.00	.45

1999 Bowman Chrome

PAT BURRELL

	MINT	NRMT
COMPLETE SET (440)	400.00	180.00
COMPLETE SERIES 1 (220)	150.00	70.00
COMPLETE SERIES 2 (220)	250.00	110.00
COMMON CARD (1-440)	.40	.18
MINOR STARS	.60	.25
SEMISTARS	1.00	.45
UNLISTED STARS	1.50	.70
1 Ben Grieve	1.50	.70
2 Kerry Wood	1.50	.70
3 Ruben Rivera	.40	.18
4 Sandy Alomar Jr	.40	.18
5 Cal Ripken	6.00	2.70
6 Mark McGwire	10.00	4.50
7 Vladimir Guerrero	2.00	.90
8 Moises Alou	.60	.25
9 Jim Edmonds	.60	.25
10 Greg Maddux	4.00	1.80
11 Gary Sheffield	.60	.25
12 John Valentin	.40	.18
13 Chuck Knoblauch	.60	.25
14 Tony Clark	.60	.25
15 Rusty Greer	.60	.25
16 Al Leiter	.60	.25
17 Travis Lee	1.00	.45
18 Jose Cruz Jr.	.60	.25
19 Pedro Martinez	2.00	.90
20 Paul O'Neill	.60	.25
21 Todd Walker	.60	.25
22 Vinny Castilla	.60	.25
23 Barry Larkin	1.50	.70
24 Curt Schilling	1.00	.45
25 Jason Kendall	.40	.18
26 Scott Erickson	.40	.18
27 Andres Galarraga	1.00	.45
28 Jeff Shaw	.40	.18
29 John Olerud	.60	.25
30 Orlando Hernandez	1.50	.70
31 Larry Walker	1.50	.70
32 Andruw Jones	1.50	.70
33 Jeff Cirillo	.40	.18
34 Barry Bonds	2.00	.90
35 Manny Ramirez	2.00	.90
36 Mark Kotsay	.40	.18
37 Ivan Rodriguez	2.00	.90
38 Jeff King	.40	.18
39 Brian Horner	.40*	
40 Ray Durham	.60	.25
41 Bernie Williams	1.50	.70
42 Darin Erstad	1.00	.45
43 Chipper Jones	4.00	1.80
44 Pat Hentgen	.40	.18
45 Eric Young	.40	.18
46 Jaret Wright	.60	.25
47 Juan Guzman	.40	.18
48 Jorge Posada	.40	.18
49 Bobby Higginson	.60	.25
50 Jose Guillen	.40	.18
51 Trevor Hoffman	.60	.25
52 Ken Griffey Jr.	8.00	3.60
53 David Justice	.60	.25
54 Matt Williams	1.50	.70
55 Eric Karros	.60	.25
56 Derek Bell	.60	.25
57 Ray Lankford	.60	.25
58 Mariano Rivera	.60	.25
59 Brett Tomko	.40	.18
60 Mike Mussina	1.50	.70
61 Kenny Lofton	1.00	.45
62 Chuck Finley	.40	.18
63 Alex Gonzalez	.60	.25
64 Mark Grace	1.00	.45
65 Raul Mondesi	.60	.25
66 David Cone	1.00	.45
67 Brad Fullmer	.40	.18
68 Andy Benes	.40	.18
69 John Smoltz	1.00	.45
70 Shane Reynolds	.60	.25
71 Bruce Chen	.60	.25
72 Adam Kennedy	.60	.25
73 Jack Cust	.60	.25
74 Matt Clement	.60	.25
75 Derrick Gibson	.40	.18
76 Darnell McDonald	.60	.25
77 Adam Everett	3.00	1.35
78 Ricardo Aramboles	.40	.18
79 Mark Quinn	6.00	2.70
80 Jason Rakers	.40	.18
81 Seth Etherton	2.00	.90
82 Jeff Urban	2.00	.90
83 Manny Aybar	.40	.18
84 Mike Nannini	2.00	.90
85 Onan Masaoka	.40	.18
86 Rod Barajas	.60	.25
87 Mike Frank	.40	.18
88 Scott Randall	.40	.18
89 Justin Bowles	1.50	.70
90 Chris Haas	.40	.18
91 Arturo McDowell	2.50	1.10
92 Matt Belisle	2.00	.90
93 Scott Elarton	.40	.18
94 Vernon Wells	1.00	.45
95 Pat Cline	.40	.18
96 Ryan Anderson	.60	.25
97 Kevin Barker	.40	.18
98 Ruben Mateo	1.50	.70
99 Robert Fick	.60	.25
100 Corey Koskie	.40	.18
101 Ricky Ledee	.60	.25
102 Rick Elder	4.00	1.80
103 Jack Cressend	1.50	.70
104 Joe Lawrence	.40	.18
105 Mike Lincoln	.40	.18
106 Kit Pellow	3.00	1.35
107 Matt Burch	1.50	.70
108 Cole Liniak	.40	.18
109 Jason Dewey	.40	.18
110 Cesar King	.40	.18
111 Julio Ramirez	.60	.25
112 Jake Westbrook	.40	.18
113 Eric Valent	5.00	2.20
114 Roosevelt Brown	2.50	1.10
115 Choo Freeman	3.00	1.35
116 Juan Melo	.40	.18
117 Jason Grilli	.40	.18
118 Jared Sandberg	.60	.25
119 Glenn Davis	.40	.18
120 David Riske	2.00	.90
121 Jacque Jones	.60	.25
122 Corey Lee	.40	.18
123 Michael Barrett	1.00	.45
124 Lariel Gonzalez	.40	.18
125 Mitch Meluskey	.40	.18
126 Freddy Garcia	.40	.18
127 Tony Torcato	2.50	1.10
128 Jeff Liefer	.40	.18
129 Ntema Ndungidi	.60	.25
130 Andy Brown	2.50	1.10
131 Ryan Mills	2.00	.90
132 Andy Abad	1.50	.70
133 Carlos Febles	.60	.25
134 Jason Tyner	2.50	1.10
135 Mark Osborne	.40	.18
136 Phil Norton	1.50	.70
137 Nathan Haynes	.40	.18
138 Roy Halladay	.60	.25
139 Juan Encarnacion	.60	.25
140 Brad Penny	.60	.25
141 Grant Roberts	.40	.18
142 Aramis Ramirez	1.00	.45
143 Cristian Guzman	.60	.25
144 Mamon Tucker	2.50	1.10
145 Ryan Bradley	.60	.25
146 Brian Simmons	.40	.18
147 Dan Reichert	.40	.18
148 Russ Branyan	.40	.18
149 Victor Valencia	2.00	.90
150 Scott Schoeneweis	.40	.18
151 Sean Spencer	1.50	.70
152 Odalis Perez	.40	.18
153 Joe Fontenot	.60	.25
154 Milton Bradley	.60	.25
155 Josh McKinley	2.00	.90
156 Terrence Long	.60	.25
157 Danny Klassen	.40	.18
158 Paul Hoover	1.50	.70
159 Ron Belliard	.60	.25
160 Armando Rios	.40	.18
161 Ramon Hernandez	.40	.18
162 Jason Conti	.40	.18
163 Chad Hermansen	.60	.25

164	Jason Standridge	.60	.25
165	Jason Dellaero	.40	.18
166	John Curtice	.40	.18
167	Clayton Andrews	2.00	.90
168	Jeremy Giambi	.60	.25
169	Alex Ramirez	.60	.25
170	Gabe Molina	1.50	.70
171	Mario Encarnacion	5.00	2.20
172	Mike Zywica	2.00	.90
173	Chip Ambres	3.00	1.35
174	Trot Nixon	.60	.25
175	Pat Burrell	20.00	9.00
176	Jeff Yoder	.40	.18
177	Chris Jones	2.00	.90
178	Kevin Witt	.40	.18
179	Keith Luuloa	1.50	.70
180	Billy Koch	.60	.25
181	Damaso Marte	1.50	.70
182	Ryan Glynn	2.00	.90
183	Calvin Pickering	.60	.25
184	Michael Cuddyer	.60	.25
185	Nick Johnson	12.00	5.50
186	Doug Mientkiewicz	2.00	.90
187	Nate Cornejo	2.50	1.10
188	Octavio Dotel	.60	.25
189	Wes Helms	.40	.18
190	Nelson Lara	.40	.18
191	Chuck Abbott	1.50	.70
192	Tony Armas Jr.	1.00	.45
193	Gil Meche	.60	.25
194	Ben Petrick	.60	.25
195	Chris George	2.50	1.10
196	Scott Hunter	2.00	.90
197	Ryan Brannan	.40	.18
198	Amaury Garcia	2.00	.90
199	Chris Gissell	.40	.18
200	Austin Kearns	4.00	1.80
201	Alex Gonzalez	.60	.25
202	Wade Miller	.40	.18
203	Scott Williamson	.60	.25
204	Chris Enochs	.40	.18
205	Fernando Seguignol	.60	.25
206	Marlon Anderson	.40	.18
207	Todd Sears	2.00	.90
208	Nate Bump	2.00	.90
209	J.M. Gold	2.50	1.10
210	Matt LeCroy	.40	.18
211	Alex Hernandez	.40	.18
212	Luis Rivera	.40	.18
213	Troy Cameron	.40	.18
214	Alex Escobar	8.00	3.60
215	Jason LaRue	.40	.18
216	Kyle Peterson	.40	.18
217	Brent Butler	.40	.18
218	Dernell Stenson	.60	.25
219	Adrian Beltre	1.50	.70
220	Daryle Ward	.60	.25
221	Jim Thome	1.50	.70
222	Cliff Floyd	.60	.25
223	Rickey Henderson	2.00	.90
224	Garrett Anderson	.60	.25
225	Ken Caminiti	.60	.25
226	Bret Boone	.60	.25
227	Jeromy Burnitz	.60	.25
228	Steve Finley	.60	.25
229	Miguel Tejada	.60	.25
230	Greg Vaughn	.60	.25
231	Jose Offerman	.60	.25
232	Andy Ashby	.40	.18
233	Albert Belle	1.50	.70
234	Fernando Tatis	1.50	.70
235	Todd Helton	1.50	.70
236	Sean Casey	1.50	.70
237	Brian Giles	.60	.25
238	Andy Pettitte	.60	.25
239	Fred McGriff	1.00	.45
240	Roberto Alomar	1.50	.70
241	Edgar Martinez	.60	.25
242	Lee Stevens	.40	.18
243	Shawn Green	1.50	.70
244	Ryan Klesko	.60	.25
245	Sammy Sosa	5.00	2.20
246	Todd Hundley	.60	.25
247	Shannon Stewart	.60	.25
248	Randy Johnson	1.50	.70
249	Rondell White	.60	.25
250	Mike Piazza	5.00	2.20
251	Craig Biggio	1.50	.70
252	David Wells	.60	.25
253	Brian Jordan	.60	.25
254	Edgar Renteria	.40	.18
255	Bartolo Colon	.60	.25
256	Frank Thomas	3.00	1.35
257	Will Clark	1.50	.70
258	Dean Palmer	.60	.25
259	Dmitri Young	.60	.25
260	Scott Rolen	2.00	.90
261	Jeff Kent	.60	.25
262	Dante Bichette	.60	.25
263	Nomar Garciaparra	5.00	2.20
264	Tony Gwynn	4.00	1.80
265	Alex Rodriguez	5.00	2.20
266	Jose Canseco	2.00	.90
267	Jason Giambi	.60	.25
268	Jeff Bagwell	2.00	.90
269	Carlos Delgado	1.50	.70
270	Tom Glavine	1.50	.70
271	Eric Davis	.60	.25
272	Edgardo Alfonzo	1.00	.45
273	Tim Salmon	1.00	.45
274	Johnny Damon	.60	.25
275	Rafael Palmeiro	1.50	.70
276	Denny Neagle	.40	.18
277	Neifi Perez	.40	.18
278	Roger Clemens	4.00	1.80
279	Brant Brown	.40	.18
280	Kevin Brown	1.00	.45
281	Jay Bell	.60	.25
282	Jay Buhner	.60	.25
283	Matt Lawton	.40	.18
284	Robin Ventura	.60	.25
285	Juan Gonzalez	3.00	1.35
286	Mo Vaughn	1.50	.70
287	Kevin Millwood	1.00	.45
288	Tino Martinez	1.00	.45
289	Justin Thompson	.40	.18
290	Derek Jeter	5.00	2.20
291	Ben Davis	1.00	.45
292	Mike Lowell	.40	.18
293	Calvin Murray	.40	.18
294	Micah Bowie	2.00	.90
295	Lance Berkman	1.00	.45
296	Jason Marquis	.40	.18
297	Chad Green	.40	.18
298	Dee Brown	.60	.25
299	Jerry Hairston Jr.	.60	.25
300	Gabe Kapler	1.50	.70
301	Brent Stentz	1.50	.70
302	Scott Mullen	1.50	.70
303	Brandon Reed	.40	.18
304	Shea Hillenbrand	2.50	1.10
305	J.D. Closser	2.50	1.10
306	Gary Matthews Jr.	.40	.18
307	Toby Hall	2.50	1.10
308	Jason Phillips	1.50	.70
309	Jose Macias	1.50	.70
310	Jung Bong	2.50	1.10
311	Ramon Soler	2.00	.90
312	Kelly Dransfeldt	2.50	1.10
313	Carlos Hernandez	1.50	.70
314	Kevin Haverbusch	.40	.18
315	Aaron Myette	3.00	1.35
316	Chad Harville	1.50	.70
317	Kyle Farnsworth	4.00	1.80
318	Travis Dawkins	4.00	1.80
319	Willie Martinez	.40	.18
320	Carlos Lee	.60	.25
321	Carlos Pena	4.00	1.80
322	Peter Bergeron	4.00	1.80
323	A.J. Burnett	4.00	1.80
324	Bucky Jacobsen	2.00	.90
325	Mo Bruce	2.00	.90
326	Reggie Taylor	.40	.18
327	Jackie Rexrode	.40	.25
328	Alvin Morrow	2.00	.90
329	Carlos Beltran	2.00	.90
330	Eric Chavez	1.00	.45
331	John Patterson	.60	.25
332	Jayson Werth	.60	.25
333	Richie Sexson	1.00	.45
334	Randy Wolf	.60	.25
335	Eli Marrero	.40	.18
336	Paul LoDuca	.40	.18
337	J.D Smart	.40	.18
338	Ryan Minor	.60	.25
339	Kris Benson	.60	.25
340	George Lombard	.60	.25
341	Troy Glaus	1.50	.70
342	Eddie Yarnall	.60	.25
343	Kip Wells	4.00	1.80
344	C.C. Sabathia	6.00	2.70
345	Sean Burroughs	15.00	6.75
346	Felipe Lopez	4.00	1.80
347	Ryan Rupe	2.50	1.10
348	Orber Moreno	2.50	1.10
349	Rafael Roque	1.50	.70
350	Alfonso Soriano	15.00	6.75
351	Pablo Ozuna	.60	.25
352	Corey Patterson	25.00	11.00
353	Braden Looper	.40	.18
354	Robbie Bell	.40	.18
355	Mark Mulder	4.00	1.80
356	Angel Pena	.40	.18
357	Kevin McGlinchy	.40	.18
358	Michael Restovich	10.00	4.50
359	Eric DuBose	.40	.18
360	Geoff Jenkins	.60	.25
361	Mark Harriger	1.50	.70
362	Junior Herndon	1.50	.70
363	Tim Raines Jr.	2.50	1.10
364	Rafael Furcal	8.00	3.60
365	Marcus Giles	5.00	2.20
366	Ted Lilly	.40	.18
367	Jorge Toca	4.00	1.80
368	David Kelton	3.00	1.35
369	Adam Dunn	4.00	1.80
370	Guillermo Mota	2.00	.90
371	Brett Laxton	1.50	.70
372	Travis Harper	1.50	.70
373	Tom Davey	1.50	.70
374	Darren Blakely	2.00	.90
375	Tim Hudson	8.00	3.60
376	Jason Romano	.40	.18
377	Dan Reichert	.40	.18
378	Julio Lugo	1.50	.70
379	Jose Garcia	2.00	.90
380	Erubiel Durazo	15.00	6.75
381	Jose Jimenez	.60	.25
382	Chris Fussell	.40	.18
383	Steve Lomasney	.40	.18
384	Juan Pena	2.00	.90
385	Allen Levrault	2.00	.90
386	Juan Rivera	3.00	1.35
387	Steve Colyer	2.00	.90
388	Joe Nathan	2.00	.90
389	Ron Walker	1.50	.70
390	Nick Bierbrodt	.40	.18
391	Luke Prokopec	1.50	.70
392	Dave Roberts	2.00	.90
393	Mike Darr	.60	.25
394	Abraham Nunez	5.00	2.20
395	Giuseppe Chiaramonte	2.50	1.10
396	Jermaine Van Buren	2.00	.90
397	Mike Kusiewicz	.40	.18
398	Matt Wise	1.50	.70
399	Joe McEwing	6.00	2.70
400	Matt Holliday	4.00	1.80
401	Willi Mo Pena	10.00	4.50
402	Ruben Quevedo	2.00	.90
403	Rob Ryan	1.50	.70
404	Freddy Garcia	15.00	6.75
405	Kevin Eberwein	2.00	.90
406	Jesus Colome	2.50	1.10
407	Chris Singleton	.60	.25
408	Bubba Crosby	2.00	.90
409	Jesus Cordero	1.50	.70
410	Donny Leon	.40	.18
411	Goffrey Tomlinson	2.00	.90
412	Jeff Winchester	2.00	.90
413	Adam Platt	10.00	4.50
414	Robert Stratton	.40	.18
415	T. J Tucker	.40	.18
416	Ryan Langerhans	2.00	.90
417	Anthony Shumaker	1.50	.70
418	Matt Miller	1.50	.70
419	Doug Clark	2.50	1.10
420	Kory DeHaan	2.00	.90
421	David Eckstein	1.50	.70

		MINT	NRMT
❑ 422	Brian Cooper	1.50	.70
❑ 423	Brady Clark	1.50	.70
❑ 424	Chris Magruder	2.00	.90
❑ 425	Bobby Seay	2.50	1.10
❑ 426	Aubrey Huff	2.50	1.10
❑ 427	Mike Jerzembeck	.40	.18
❑ 428	Matt Blank	2.00	.90
❑ 429	Benny Agbayani	5.00	2.20
❑ 430	Kevin Beirne	1.50	.70
❑ 431	Josh Hamilton	20.00	9.00
❑ 432	Josh Girdley	2.50	1.10
❑ 433	Kyle Snyder	2.50	1.10
❑ 434	Mike Paradis	1.50	.70
❑ 435	Jason Jennings	2.50	1.10
❑ 436	David Walling	2.50	1.10
❑ 437	Omar Ortiz	1.50	.70
❑ 438	Jay Gehrke	1.50	.70
❑ 439	Casey Burns	1.50	.70
❑ 440	Carl Crawford	3.00	1.35

1999 Bowman Chrome Gold

	MINT	NRMT
COMMON CARD (1-220)	2.00	.90
*SER.1 STARS: 2X TO 5X BASIC CARDS
*SER.1 YNG.STARS: 1.5X TO 4X BASIC
*SER.1 ROOKIES: 1.25X TO 3X BASIC
SER.1 STATED ODDS 1:12

	MINT	NRMT
COMMON CARD (221-440)	2.50	1.10
*SER.2 STARS: 2.5X TO 6X BASIC CARDS
*SER.2 YNG.STARS: 2X TO 5X BASIC
*SER.2 ROOKIES: 1.5X TO 4X BASIC
SER.2 STATED ODDS 1:24

1999 Bowman Chrome Gold Refractors

	MINT	NRMT
COMMON CARD (1-440)	25.00	11.00
*STARS: 25X TO 60X BASIC CARDS
*YNG.STARS: 20X TO 50X BASIC
*ROOKIES: 8X TO 20X BASIC
SER.1 STATED ODDS 1:305
SER.2 STATED ODDS 1:200
STATED PRINT RUN 25 SERIAL #'d SETS

1999 Bowman Chrome International

CARLOS DELGADO

	MINT	NRMT
COMPLETE SET (440)	900.00	400.00
COMPLETE SERIES 1 (220)	300.00	135.00
COMPLETE SERIES 2 (220)	600.00	275.00
COMMON CARD (1-220)	.75	.35
*SER.1 STARS: .75X TO 2X BASIC CARDS
*SER.1 YNG.STARS: .6X TO 1.5X BASIC
*SER.1 ROOKIES: .4X TO 1X BASIC
SER.1 STATED ODDS 1:4

	MINT	NRMT
COMMON CARD (221-440)	1.50	.70
*SER.2 STARS: 1.25X TO 3X BASIC CARDS
*SER.2 YNG.STARS: 1X TO 2.5X BASIC
*SER.2 ROOKIES: .6X TO 1.5X BASIC
SER.2 STATED ODDS 1:12

1999 Bowman Chrome International Refractors

DAN REICHERT

	MINT	NRMT
COMMON CARD (1-440)	6.00	2.70
*STARS: 6X TO 15X BASIC CARDS
*YNG.STARS: 5X TO 12X BASIC
*ROOKIES: 2.5X TO 6X BASIC
SER.1 STATED ODDS 1:76
SER.2 STATED ODDS 1:50
STATED PRINT RUN 100 SERIAL #'d SETS

1999 Bowman Chrome Refractors

DEREK JETER

	MINT	NRMT
COMMON CARD (1-440)	2.50	1.10
*STARS: 2.5X TO 6X BASIC CARDS
*YNG.STARS: 2X TO 5X BASIC
*ROOKIES: 1.5X TO 4X BASIC
SER.1 AND SER.2 STATED ODDS 1:12

1999 Bowman Chrome 2000 ROY Favorites

RYAN ANDERSON

	MINT	NRMT
COMPLETE SET (10)	25.00	11.00
COMMON CARD (ROY1-ROY10)	1.00	.45
UNLISTED STARS	1.50	.70
SER.2 STATED ODDS 1:20
*REFRACTORS: 1X TO 2.5X HI COLUMN
REFRACTOR SER.2 STATED ODDS 1:100

		MINT	NRMT
❑ ROY1	Ryan Anderson	1.00	.45
❑ ROY2	Pat Burrell	6.00	2.70
❑ ROY3	A.J. Burnett	1.50	.70
❑ ROY4	Ruben Mateo	1.50	.70
❑ ROY5	Alex Escobar	3.00	1.35
❑ ROY6	Pablo Ozuna	1.00	.45
❑ ROY7	Mark Mulder	1.50	.70
❑ ROY8	Corey Patterson	10.00	4.50
❑ ROY9	George Lombard	1.00	.45
❑ ROY10	Nick Johnson	5.00	2.20

1999 Bowman Chrome Diamond Aces

DIAMOND ACES

	MINT	NRMT
COMPLETE SET (18)	120.00	55.00
COMMON CARD (DA1-DA18)	2.00	.90
UNLISTED STARS	3.00	1.35
SER.1 STATED ODDS 1:21
*REFRACTORS: 1.25X TO 3X HI COLUMN
REFRACTOR SER.1 ODDS 1:84

		MINT	NRMT
❑ DA1	Troy Glaus	3.00	1.35
❑ DA2	Eric Chavez	2.00	.90
❑ DA3	Fernando Seguignol	1.50	.70
❑ DA4	Ryan Anderson	1.50	.70
❑ DA5	Ruben Mateo	3.00	1.35
❑ DA6	Carlos Beltran	4.00	1.80
❑ DA7	Adrian Beltre	3.00	1.35
❑ DA8	Bruce Chen	1.50	.70
❑ DA9	Pat Burrell	12.00	5.50
❑ DA10	Mike Piazza	10.00	4.50

	MINT	NRMT
DA11 Ken Griffey Jr.	15.00	6.75
DA12 Chipper Jones	8.00	3.60
DA13 Derek Jeter	10.00	4.50
DA14 Mark McGwire	20.00	9.00
DA15 Nomar Garciaparra	10.00	4.50
DA16 Sammy Sosa	10.00	4.50
DA17 Juan Gonzalez	6.00	2.70
DA18 Alex Rodriguez	10.00	4.50

1999 Bowman Chrome Impact

	MINT	NRMT
COMPLETE SET (20)	80.00	36.00
COMMON CARD (I1-I15)	1.00	.45
SEMISTARS	1.25	.55
UNLISTED STARS	2.00	.90

SER.2 STATED ODDS 1:15
*REFRACTORS: 1X TO 2.5X HI COLUMN
REFRACTOR SER.2 STATED ODDS 1:75

I1 Alfonso Soriano	5.00	2.20
I2 Pat Burrell	5.00	2.20
I3 Ruben Mateo	2.00	.90
I4 A.J. Burnett	1.25	.55
I5 Corey Patterson	8.00	3.60
I6 Daryle Ward	1.00	.45
I7 Eric Chavez	1.25	.55
I8 Troy Glaus	2.00	.90
I9 Sean Casey	2.00	.90
I10 Joe McEwing	2.00	.90
I11 Gabe Kapler	2.00	.90
I12 Michael Barrett	1.25	.55
I13 Sammy Sosa	8.00	3.60
I14 Alex Rodriguez	8.00	3.60
I15 Mark McGwire	15.00	6.75
I16 Derek Jeter	8.00	3.60
I17 Nomar Garciaparra	8.00	3.60
I18 Mike Piazza	8.00	3.60
I19 Chipper Jones	6.00	2.70
I20 Ken Griffey Jr.	12.00	5.50

1999 Bowman Chrome Scout's Choice

	MINT	NRMT
COMPLETE SET (21)	30.00	13.50
COMMON CARD (SC1-SC21)	.75	.35
MINOR STARS	1.25	.55
SEMISTARS	2.00	.90

UNLISTED STARS ... 3.00 1.35
SER.1 STATED ODDS 1:12
*REFRACTORS: 1X TO 2.5X HI COLUMN
REFRACTOR SER.1 ODDS 1:48

SC1 Ruben Mateo	3.00	1.35
SC2 Ryan Anderson	1.25	.55
SC3 Pat Burrell	12.00	5.50
SC4 Troy Glaus	3.00	1.35
SC5 Eric Chavez	2.00	.90
SC6 Adrian Beltre	3.00	1.35
SC7 Bruce Chen	1.25	.55
SC8 Carlos Beltran	4.00	1.80
SC9 Alex Gonzalez	1.25	.55
SC10 Carlos Lee	1.25	.55
SC11 George Lombard	1.25	.55
SC12 Matt Clement	1.25	.55
SC13 Calvin Pickering	1.25	.55
SC14 Marlon Anderson	.75	.35
SC15 Chad Hermansen	1.25	.55
SC16 Russell Branyan	1.25	.55
SC17 Jeremy Giambi	1.25	.55
SC18 Ricky Ledee	1.25	.55
SC19 John Patterson	1.25	.55
SC20 Roy Halladay	1.25	.55
SC21 Michael Barrett	2.00	.90

1994 Bowman's Best

	MINT	NRMT
COMPLETE SET (200)	80.00	36.00
COMMON CARD (B1-X110)	.30	.14
MINOR STARS	.60	.25
UNLISTED STARS	1.25	.55

B1 Chipper Jones	3.00	1.35
B2 Derek Jeter	5.00	2.20
B3 Bill Pulsipher	.60	.25
B4 James Baldwin	.60	.25
B5 Brooks Kieschnick	.30	.14
B6 Justin Thompson	1.25	.55
B7 Midre Cummings	.30	.14
B8 Joey Hamilton	1.25	.55
B9 Calvin Reese	.75	.35
B10 Brian Barber	.30	.14
B11 John Burke	.30	.14
B12 DeShawn Warren	.30	.14
B13 Edgardo Alfonzo	12.00	5.50
B14 Eddie Pearson	.60	.25
B15 Jimmy Haynes	.60	.25
B16 Danny Bautista	.30	.14
B17 Roger Cedeno	.60	.25
B18 Jon Lieber	.30	.14
B19 Billy Wagner	4.00	1.80
B20 Tate Seefried	.30	.14
B21 Chad Mottola	.30	.14
B22 Jose Malave	.30	.14
B23 Terrell Wade	.30	.14
B24 Shane Andrews	.30	.14
B25 Chan Ho Park	5.00	2.20
B26 Kirk Presley	.30	.14
B27 Robbie Beckett	.30	.14
B28 Orlando Miller	.30	.14
B29 Jorge Posada	4.00	1.80
B30 Frankie Rodriguez	.30	.14
B31 Brian L. Hunter	.30	.14
B32 Billy Ashley	.30	.14
B33 Rondell White	.60	.25
B34 John Roper	.30	.14
B35 Marc Valdes	.30	.14
B36 Scott Ruffcorn	.30	.14
B37 Rod Henderson	.30	.14
B38 Curtis Goodwin	.60	.25
B39 Russ Davis	.60	.25
B40 Rick Gorecki	.30	.14
B41 Johnny Damon	1.25	.55
B42 Roberto Petagine	.30	.14
B43 Chris Snopek	.30	.14
B44 Mark Acre	.30	.14
B45 Todd Hollandsworth	.75	.35
B46 Shawn Green	2.00	.90
B47 John Carter	.30	.14
B48 Jim Pittsley	.30	.14
B49 John Wasdin	.60	.25
B50 D.J. Boston	.30	.14
B51 Tim Clark	.30	.14
B52 Alex Ochoa	.30	.14
B53 Chad Roper	.30	.14
B54 Mike Kelly	.30	.14
B55 Brad Fullmer	4.00	1.80
B56 Carl Everett	.60	.25
B57 Tim Belk	.30	.14
B58 Jimmy Hurst	.30	.14
B59 Mac Suzuki	.60	.25
B60 Michael Moore	.30	.14
B61 Alan Benes	1.00	.45
B62 Tony Clark	6.00	2.70
B63 Edgar Renteria	3.00	1.35
B64 Trey Beamon	.30	.14
B65 LaTroy Hawkins	.75	.35
B66 Wayne Gomes	.30	.14
B67 Ray McDavid	.30	.14
B68 John Dettmer	.30	.14
B69 Willie Greene	.30	.14
B70 Dave Stevens	.30	.14
B71 Kevin Orie	1.00	.45
B72 Chad Ogea	.30	.14
B73 Ben Van Ryn	.30	.14
B74 Kym Ashworth	.60	.25
B75 Dmitri Young	.60	.25
B76 Herbert Perry	.30	.14
B77 Joey Eischen	.30	.14
B78 Arquimedez Pozo	.30	.14
B79 Ugueth Urbina	.60	.25
B80 Keith Williams	.60	.25
B81 John Frascatore	.30	.14
B82 Garey Ingram	.30	.14
B83 Aaron Small	.30	.14
B84 Olmedo Saenz	.30	.14
B85 Jesus Tavarez	.30	.14
B86 Jose Silva	.30	.14
B87 Jay Witasick	.60	.25
B88 Jay Maldonado	.30	.14
B89 Keith Heberling	.30	.14
B90 Rusty Greer	6.00	2.70
R1 Paul Molitor	1.25	.55
R2 Eddie Murray	1.25	.55
R3 Ozzie Smith	1.50	.70
R4 Rickey Henderson	1.50	.70
R5 Lee Smith	.60	.25
R6 Dave Winfield	1.25	.55
R7 Roberto Alomar	1.25	.55
R8 Matt Williams	.75	.35
R9 Mark Grace	.75	.35
R10 Lance Johnson	.30	.14
R11 Darren Daulton	.60	.25
R12 Tom Glavine	1.25	.55
R13 Gary Sheffield	1.25	.55
R14 Rod Beck	.30	.14
R15 Fred McGriff	.75	.35
R16 Joe Carter	.60	.25
R17 Dante Bichette	.60	.25
R18 Danny Tartabull	.30	.14
R19 Juan Gonzalez	2.50	1.10
R20 Steve Avery	.30	.14
R21 John Wetteland	.60	.25
R22 Ben McDonald	.30	.14
R23 Jack McDowell	.30	.14
R24 Jose Canseco	1.50	.70
R25 Tim Salmon	1.25	.55
R26 Wilson Alvarez	.60	.25
R27 Gregg Jefferies	.30	.14
R28 John Burkett	.30	.14
R29 Greg Vaughn	.60	.25

	MINT	NRMT
R30 Robin Ventura	.60	.25
R31 Paul O'Neill	.60	.25
R32 Cecil Fielder	.60	.25
R33 Kevin Mitchell	.30	.14
R34 Jeff Conine	.30	.14
R35 Carlos Baerga	.60	.25
R36 Greg Maddux	3.00	1.35
R37 Roger Clemens	3.00	1.35
R38 Deion Sanders	.60	.25
R39 Delino DeShields	.30	.14
R40 Ken Griffey Jr.	6.00	2.70
R41 Albert Belle	1.25	.55
R42 Wade Boggs	1.25	.55
R43 Andres Galarraga	1.25	.55
R44 Aaron Sele	.60	.25
R45 Don Mattingly	2.50	1.10
R46 David Cone	.75	.35
R47 Len Dykstra	.60	.25
R48 Brett Butler	.60	.25
R49 Bill Swift	.30	.14
R50 Bobby Bonilla	.60	.25
R51 Rafael Palmeiro	1.25	.55
R52 Moises Alou	.30	.14
R53 Jeff Bagwell	1.50	.70
R54 Mike Mussina	1.25	.55
R55 Frank Thomas	2.50	1.10
R56 Jose Rijo	.30	.14
R57 Ruben Sierra	.30	.14
R58 Randy Myers	.30	.14
R59 Barry Bonds	1.50	.70
R60 Jimmy Key	.60	.25
R61 Travis Fryman	.60	.25
R62 John Olerud	.60	.25
R63 David Justice	1.25	.55
R64 Ray Lankford	.60	.25
R65 Bob Tewksbury	.30	.14
R66 Chuck Carr	.30	.14
R67 Jay Buhner	.60	.25
R68 Kenny Lofton	1.25	.55
R69 Marquis Grissom	.60	.25
R70 Sammy Sosa	4.00	1.80
R71 Cal Ripken	5.00	2.20
R72 Ellis Burks	.60	.25
R73 Jeff Montgomery	.30	.14
R74 Julio Franco	.30	.14
R75 Kirby Puckett	2.00	.90
R76 Larry Walker	1.25	.55
R77 Andy Van Slyke	.60	.25
R78 Tony Gwynn	3.00	1.35
R79 Will Clark	1.25	.55
R80 Mo Vaughn	1.25	.55
R81 Mike Piazza	4.00	1.80
R82 James Mouton	.30	.14
R83 Carlos Delgado	1.25	.55
R84 Ryan Klesko	.60	.25
R85 Javier Lopez	.75	.35
R86 Raul Mondesi	1.25	.55
R87 Cliff Floyd	.60	.25
R88 Manny Ramirez	2.50	1.10
R89 Hector Carrasco	.30	.14
R90 Jeff Granger	.30	.14
X91 Frank Thomas	1.25	.55
Dmitri Young		
X92 Fred McGriff	1.25	.55
Brooks Kieschnick		
X93 Matt Williams	.30	.14
Shane Andrews		
X94 Cal Ripken	2.50	1.10
Kevin Orie		
X95 Barry Larkin	2.50	1.10
Derek Jeter		
X96 Ken Griffey Jr.	3.00	1.35
Johnny Damon		
X97 Barry Bonds	1.25	.55
Rondell White		
X98 Albert Belle	1.25	.55
Jimmy Hurst		
X99 Raul Mondesi	2.50	1.10
Ruben Rivera		
X100 Roger Clemens	1.50	.70
Scott Ruffcorn		
X101 Greg Maddux	1.50	.70
John Wasdin		
X102 Tim Salmon	.75	.35
Chad Mottola		
X103 Carlos Baerga	.60	.25
Arquimedez Pozo		
X104 Mike Piazza	2.00	.90
Bobby Hughes		
X105 Carlos Delgado	1.25	.55
Melvin Nieves		
X106 Javier Lopez	1.00	.45
Jorge Posada		
X107 Manny Ramirez	1.25	.55
Jose Malave		
X108 Travis Fryman	1.50	.70
Chipper Jones		
X109 Steve Avery	.30	.14
Bill Pulsipher		
X110 John Olerud	.60	.25
Shawn Green		

1994 Bowman's Best Refractors

	MINT	NRMT
COMMON CARD	2.50	1.10

*RED STARS: 3X TO 8X BASIC CARDS
*BLUE STARS: 3X TO 8X BASIC CARDS
*BLUE ROOKIES: 2X TO 4X BASIC CARDS
*MIRROR IMAGE: 2.5X TO 6X BASIC CARDS
RANDOM INSERTS IN PACKS

1995 Bowman's Best

	MINT	NRMT
COMPLETE SET (195)	250.00	110.00
COMMON CARD (B1-R90)	.30	.14
COMMON MIR.IM.(X1-X15)	.50	.23
MINOR STARS	.50	.23
SEMISTARS	.75	.35
UNLISTED STARS	1.25	.55
B1 Derek Jeter	4.00	1.80
B2 Vladimir Guerrero	60.00	27.00
B3 Bob Abreu	15.00	6.75
B4 Chan Ho Park	1.25	.55
B5 Paul Wilson	.30	.14
B6 Chad Ogea	.30	.14
B7 Andruw Jones	50.00	22.00
B8 Brian Barber	.30	.14
B9 Andy Larkin	.30	.14
B10 Richie Sexson	20.00	9.00
B11 Everett Stull	.30	.14
B12 Brooks Kieschnick	.30	.14
B13 Matt Murray	.30	.14
B14 John Wasdin	.30	.14
B15 Shannon Stewart	.50	.23
B16 Luis Ortiz	.30	.14
B17 Marc Kroon	.30	.14
B18 Todd Greene	2.00	.90
B19 Juan Acevedo	.30	.14
B20 Tony Clark	1.25	.55
B21 Jermaine Dye	1.25	.55
B22 Derek Lee	1.25	.55
B23 Pat Watkins	.30	.14
B24 Calvin Reese	.30	.14
B25 Ben Grieve	12.00	5.50
B26 Julio Santana	.30	.14
B27 Felix Rodriguez	.30	.14
B28 Paul Konerko	8.00	3.60
B29 Nomar Garciaparra	25.00	11.00
B30 Pat Ahearne	.30	.14
B31 Jason Schmidt	.50	.23
B32 Billy Wagner	.75	.35
B33 Rey Ordonez	6.00	2.70
B34 Curtis Goodwin	.30	.14
B35 Sergio Nunez	.30	.14
B36 Tim Belk	.30	.14
B37 Scott Elarton	5.00	2.20
B38 Jason Isringhausen	.50	.23
B39 Trot Nixon	.75	.35
B40 Sid Roberson	.30	.14
B41 Ron Villone	.30	.14
B42 Ruben Rivera	.50	.23
B43 Rick Huisman	.30	.14
B44 Todd Hollandsworth	.30	.14
B45 Johnny Damon	.75	.35
B46 Garret Anderson	.50	.23
B47 Jeff D'Amico	.50	.23
B48 Dustin Hermanson	.30	.14
B49 Juan Encarnacion	12.00	5.50
B50 Andy Pettitte	1.25	.55
B51 Chris Stynes	.50	.23
B52 Troy Percival	.50	.23
B53 LaTroy Hawkins	.30	.14
B54 Roger Cedeno	.30	.14
B55 Alan Benes	.50	.23
B56 Karim Garcia	2.50	1.10
B57 Andrew Lorraine	.30	.14
B58 Gary Rath	.30	.14
B59 Bret Wagner	.30	.14
B60 Jeff Suppan	.50	.23
B61 Bill Pulsipher	.50	.23
B62 Jay Payton	.50	.23
B63 Alex Ochoa	.30	.14
B64 Ugueth Urbina	.30	.14
B65 Armando Benitez	.30	.14
B66 George Arias	.30	.14
B67 Raul Casanova	.30	.14
B68 Matt Drews	.50	.23
B69 Jimmy Haynes	.30	.14
B70 Jimmy Hurst	.30	.14
B71 C.J. Nitkowski	.30	.14
B72 Tommy Davis	.30	.14
B73 Bartolo Colon	10.00	4.50
B74 Chris Carpenter	5.00	2.20
B75 Trey Beamon	.30	.14
B76 Bryan Rekar	.30	.14
B77 James Baldwin	.50	.23
B78 Marc Valdes	.30	.14
B79 Tom Fordham	.50	.23
B80 Marc Newfield	.30	.14
B81 Angel Martinez	.30	.14
B82 Brian L. Hunter	.30	.23
B83 Jose Herrera	.30	.14
B84 Glenn Dishman	.50	.23
B85 Jacob Cruz	2.50	1.10
B86 Paul Shuey	.30	.14
B87 Scott Rolen	60.00	27.00
B88 Doug Million	.30	.14
B89 Desi Relaford	.50	.23
B90 Michael Tucker	.50	.23
R1 Randy Johnson	1.25	.55
R2 Joe Carter	.50	.23
R3 Chili Davis	.50	.23
R4 Moises Alou	.50	.23
R5 Gary Sheffield	.50	.23
R6 Kevin Appier	.50	.23
R7 Denny Neagle	.50	.23
R8 Ruben Sierra	.30	.14
R9 Darren Daulton	.50	.23

	MINT	NRMT
R10 Cal Ripken	5.00	2.20
R11 Bobby Bonilla	.50	.23
R12 Manny Ramirez	1.50	.70
R13 Gary Sheffield	1.50	.70
R14 Eric Karros	.50	.23
R15 Greg Maddux	3.00	1.35
R16 Jeff Bagwell	1.50	.70
R17 Paul Molitor	1.25	.55
R18 Ray Lankford	.50	.23
R19 Mark Grace	.75	.35
R20 Kenny Lofton	.75	.35
R21 Tony Gwynn	3.00	1.35
R22 Will Clark	1.25	.55
R23 Roger Clemens	3.00	1.35
R24 Dante Bichette	.50	.23
R25 Barry Larkin	1.25	.55
R26 Wade Boggs	1.25	.55
R27 Kirby Puckett	2.00	.90
R28 Cecil Fielder	.50	.23
R29 Jose Canseco	1.50	.70
R30 Juan Gonzalez	2.50	1.10
R31 David Cone	.75	.35
R32 Craig Biggio	1.25	.55
R33 Tim Salmon	1.25	.55
R34 David Justice	1.25	.55
R35 Sammy Sosa	1.50	.70
R36 Mike Piazza	4.00	1.80
R37 Carlos Baerga	.30	.14
R38 Jeff Conine	.30	.14
R39 Rafael Palmeiro	.50	.23
R40 Bret Saberhagen	.50	.23
R41 Len Dykstra	.50	.23
R42 Mo Vaughn	1.25	.55
R43 Wally Joyner	.30	.14
R44 Chuck Knoblauch	1.25	.55
R45 Robin Ventura	.50	.23
R46 Don Mattingly	2.50	1.10
R47 Dave Hollins	.30	.14
R48 Andy Benes	.50	.23
R49 Ken Griffey Jr.	6.00	2.70
R50 Albert Belle	1.25	.55
R51 Matt Williams	1.25	.55
R52 Rondell White	.50	.23
R53 Raul Mondesi	.75	.35
R54 Brian Jordan	.50	.23
R55 Greg Vaughn	.50	.23
R56 Fred McGriff	.75	.35
R57 Roberto Alomar	1.25	.55
R58 Dennis Eckersley	.50	.23
R59 Lee Smith	.50	.23
R60 Eddie Murray	1.25	.55
R61 Kenny Rogers	.30	.14
R62 Ron Gant	.30	.14
R63 Larry Walker	1.25	.55
R64 Chad Curtis	.30	.14
R65 Frank Thomas	2.50	1.10
R66 Paul O'Neill	.50	.23
R67 Kevin Seitzer	.30	.14
R68 Marquis Grissom	.50	.23
R69 Mark McGwire	6.00	2.70
R70 Travis Fryman	.50	.23
R71 Andres Galarraga	1.25	.55
R72 Carlos Perez	2.00	.90
R73 Tyler Green	.30	.14
R74 Marty Cordova	1.25	.55
R75 Shawn Green	1.25	.55
R76 Vaughn Eshelman	.30	.14
R77 John Mabry	.30	.14
R78 Jason Bates	.30	.14
R79 Jon Nunnally	.30	.14
R80 Ray Durham	.50	.23
R81 Edgardo Alfonzo	1.25	.55
R82 Esteban Loaiza	.30	.14
R83 Hideo Nomo	10.00	4.50
R84 Orlando Miller	.30	.14
R85 Alex Gonzalez	.30	.14
R86 Mark Grudzielanek	2.00	.90
R87 Julian Tavarez	.30	.14
R88 Benji Gil	.30	.14
R89 Quilvio Veras	.30	.14
R90 Ricky Bottalico	.30	.14
X1 Ben Davis Ivan Rodriguez	6.00	2.70
X2 Mark Redman Manny Ramirez	1.00	.45
X3 Reggie Taylor Deion Sanders	1.00	.45
X4 Ryan Jaroncyk Shawn Green	1.25	.55
X5 Juan LeBron Juan Gonzalez UER (Card pictures Carlos Beltran instead of Juan LeBron.)	4.00	1.80
X6 Toby McKnight Craig Biggio	1.25	.55
X7 Michael Barrett Travis Fryman	5.00	2.20
X8 Corey Jenkins Mo Vaughn	1.25	.55
X9 Ruben Rivera Frank Thomas	1.50	.70
X10 Curtis Goodwin Kenny Lofton	.50	.23
X11 Brian L. Hunter Tony Gwynn	1.50	.70
X12 Todd Greene Ken Griffey Jr.	3.00	1.35
X13 Karim Garcia Matt Williams	2.00	.90
X14 Billy Wagner Randy Johnson	.50	.23
X15 Pat Watkins Jeff Bagwell	1.50	.70

1995 Bowman's Best Refractors

	MINT	NRMT
COMPLETE SET (195)	2000.00	900.00
COMMON BLUE (B1-B90)	4.00	1.80
COMMON RED (R1-R90)	2.50	1.10
COMMON MIR.IMAGE (X1-X15)	2.50	1.10

*STARS: 3X TO 8X BASIC CARDS
*ROOKIES: 1.25X TO 2.5X BASIC CARDS
*MIRROR IMAGE: 1.25X TO 2.5X BASIC
RED/BLUE REF.STATED ODDS 1:6
MIRROR IMAGE REF.STATED ODDS 1:12

1996 Bowman's Best Previews

	MINT	NRMT
COMPLETE SET (30)	120.00	55.00
COMMON CARD (BBP1-BBP30)	.75	.35
MINOR STARS	1.50	.70
UNLISTED STARS	3.00	1.35

STATED ODDS 1:12 2.50 1.10
*REFRACTORS: .6X TO 1.5X HI COLUMN
REFRACTOR STATED ODDS 1:24
*ATOMIC REF: 1.25X TO 3X HI COLUMN
ATOMIC STATED ODDS 1:48

	MINT	NRMT
BBP1 Chipper Jones	8.00	3.60
BBP2 Alan Benes	.75	.35
BBP3 Brooks Kieschnick	.75	.35
BBP4 Barry Bonds	4.00	1.80
BBP5 Rey Ordonez	3.00	1.35
BBP6 Tim Salmon	2.00	.90
BBP7 Mike Piazza	10.00	4.50
BBP8 Billy Wagner	2.00	.90
BBP9 Andruw Jones	6.00	2.70
BBP10 Tony Gwynn	8.00	3.60
BBP11 Paul Wilson	.75	.35
BBP12 Calvin Reese	.75	.35
BBP13 Frank Thomas	6.00	2.70
BBP14 Greg Maddux	8.00	3.60
BBP15 Derek Jeter	10.00	4.50
BBP16 Jeff Bagwell	4.00	1.80
BBP17 Barry Larkin	3.00	1.35
BBP18 Todd Greene	.75	.35
BBP19 Ruben Rivera	1.50	.70
BBP20 Richard Hidalgo	1.50	.70
BBP21 Larry Walker	3.00	1.35
BBP22 Carlos Baerga	.75	.35
BBP23 Derrick Gibson	3.00	1.35
BBP24 Richie Sexson	3.00	1.35
BBP25 Mo Vaughn	3.00	1.35
BBP26 Hideo Nomo	3.00	1.35
BBP27 Nomar Garciaparra	10.00	4.50
BBP28 Cal Ripken	12.00	5.50
BBP29 Karim Garcia	1.50	.70
BBP30 Ken Griffey Jr.	15.00	6.75

1996 Bowman's Best

	MINT	NRMT
COMPLETE SET (180)	100.00	45.00
COMMON GOLD (1-90)	.25	.11
COMMON SILVER (91-180)	.25	.11
MINOR STARS	.60	.25
UNLISTED STARS	1.25	.55

NUMBER 33 NEVER ISSUED
CLEMENS AND PALMEIRO NUMBERED 32
MANTLE CHROME ODDS 1:24 HOB, 1:20 RET
MANTLE REF.ODDS 1:96 HOB, 1:160 RET
MANTLE ATOMIC ODDS 1:192 HOB,1:320 RET

	MINT	NRMT
1 Hideo Nomo	1.25	.55
2 Edgar Martinez	.60	.25
3 Cal Ripken	5.00	2.20
4 Wade Boggs	1.25	.55
5 Cecil Fielder	.60	.25
6 Albert Belle	1.25	.55
7 Chipper Jones	3.00	1.35
8 Ryne Sandberg	1.50	.70
9 Tim Salmon	.75	.35
10 Barry Bonds	1.50	.70
11 Ken Caminiti	.60	.25
12 Ron Gant	.25	.11
13 Frank Thomas	2.50	1.10
14 Dante Bichette	.60	.25
15 Jason Kendall	1.25	.55
16 Mo Vaughn	1.25	.55
17 Rey Ordonez	1.25	.55

☐ 18	Henry Rodriguez	.60	.25
☐ 19	Ryan Klesko	.60	.25
☐ 20	Jeff Bagwell	1.50	.70
☐ 21	Randy Johnson	1.25	.55
☐ 22	Jim Edmonds	.75	.35
☐ 23	Kenny Lofton	.75	.35
☐ 24	Andy Pettitte	.75	.35
☐ 25	Brady Anderson	.60	.25
☐ 26	Mike Piazza	4.00	1.80
☐ 27	Greg Vaughn	.60	.25
☐ 28	Joe Carter	.60	.25
☐ 29	Jason Giambi	.60	.25
☐ 30	Ivan Rodriguez	1.50	.70
☐ 31	Jeff Conine	.25	.11
☐ 32	Rafael Palmeiro	1.25	.55
☐ 33	Roger Clemens	3.00	1.35
☐ 34	Chuck Knoblauch	1.25	.55
☐ 35	Reggie Sanders	.60	.25
☐ 36	Andres Galarraga	1.25	.55
☐ 37	Paul O'Neill	.60	.25
☐ 38	Tony Gwynn	3.00	1.35
☐ 39	Paul Wilson	.25	.11
☐ 40	Garret Anderson	.60	.25
☐ 41	David Justice	1.25	.55
☐ 42	Eddie Murray	1.25	.55
☐ 43	Mike Grace	.25	.11
☐ 44	Marty Cordova	.25	.11
☐ 45	Kevin Appier	.60	.25
☐ 46	Raul Mondesi	.60	.25
☐ 47	Jim Thome	1.25	.55
☐ 48	Sammy Sosa	4.00	1.80
☐ 49	Craig Biggio	1.25	.55
☐ 50	Marquis Grissom	.25	.11
☐ 51	Alan Benes	.25	.11
☐ 52	Manny Ramirez	1.50	.70
☐ 53	Gary Sheffield	.60	.25
☐ 54	Mike Mussina	1.25	.55
☐ 55	Robin Ventura	.60	.25
☐ 56	Johnny Damon	.75	.35
☐ 57	Jose Canseco	1.50	.70
☐ 58	Juan Gonzalez	2.50	1.10
☐ 59	Tino Martinez	.60	.25
☐ 60	Brian Hunter	.25	.11
☐ 61	Fred McGriff	.75	.35
☐ 62	Jay Buhner	.60	.25
☐ 63	Carlos Delgado	1.25	.55
☐ 64	Moises Alou	.60	.25
☐ 65	Roberto Alomar	1.25	.55
☐ 66	Barry Larkin	1.25	.55
☐ 67	Vinny Castilla	.75	.35
☐ 68	Ray Durham	.60	.25
☐ 69	Travis Fryman	.60	.25
☐ 70	Jason Isringhausen	.25	.11
☐ 71	Ken Griffey Jr.	6.00	2.70
☐ 72	John Smoltz	.75	.35
☐ 73	Matt Williams	1.25	.55
☐ 74	Chan Ho Park	.75	.35
☐ 75	Mark McGwire	6.00	2.70
☐ 76	Jeffrey Hammonds	.60	.25
☐ 77	Will Clark	1.25	.55
☐ 78	Kirby Puckett	2.00	.90
☐ 79	Derek Jeter	4.00	1.80
☐ 80	Derek Bell	.60	.25
☐ 81	Eric Karros	.60	.25
☐ 82	Len Dykstra	.60	.25
☐ 83	Larry Walker	1.25	.55
☐ 84	Mark Grudzielanek	.25	.11
☐ 85	Greg Maddux	3.00	1.35
☐ 86	Carlos Baerga	.25	.11
☐ 87	Paul Molitor	1.25	.55
☐ 88	John Valentin	.60	.25
☐ 89	Mark Grace	.75	.35
☐ 90	Ray Lankford	.60	.25
☐ 91	Andruw Jones	3.00	1.35
☐ 92	Nomar Garciaparra	5.00	2.20
☐ 93	Alex Ochoa	.25	.11
☐ 94	Derrick Gibson	1.25	.55
☐ 95	Jeff D'Amico	.25	.11
☐ 96	Ruben Rivera	.60	.25
☐ 97	Vladimir Guerrero	4.00	1.80
☐ 98	Calvin Reese	.25	.11
☐ 99	Richard Hidalgo	.60	.25
☐ 100	Bartolo Colon	1.25	.55
☐ 101	Karim Garcia	.60	.25
☐ 102	Ben Davis	2.00	.90
☐ 103	Jay Powell	.25	.11
☐ 104	Chris Snopek	.25	.11
☐ 105	Glendon Rusch	1.25	.55
☐ 106	Enrique Wilson	.60	.25
☐ 107	Antonio Alfonseca	.25	.11
☐ 108	Wilton Guerrero	2.00	.90
☐ 109	Jose Guillen	4.00	1.80
☐ 110	Miguel Mejia	.25	.11
☐ 111	Jay Payton	.25	.11
☐ 112	Scott Elarton	.75	.35
☐ 113	Brooks Kieschnick	.25	.11
☐ 114	Dustin Hermanson	.25	.11
☐ 115	Roger Cedeno	.60	.25
☐ 116	Matt Wagner	.25	.11
☐ 117	Lee Daniels	.25	.11
☐ 118	Ben Grieve	2.00	.90
☐ 119	Ugueth Urbina	.60	.25
☐ 120	Danny Graves	.75	.35
☐ 121	Dan Donato	.25	.11
☐ 122	Matt Nueber	.25	.11
☐ 123	Mark Sievert	.25	.11
☐ 124	Chris Stynes	.25	.11
☐ 125	Jeff Abbott	.25	.11
☐ 126	Rocky Coppinger	1.25	.55
☐ 127	Jermaine Dye	.60	.25
☐ 128	Todd Greene	.25	.11
☐ 129	Chris Carpenter	.60	.25
☐ 130	Edgar Renteria	.60	.25
☐ 131	Matt Drews	.25	.11
☐ 132	Edgard Velazquez	3.00	1.35
☐ 133	Casey Whitten	.60	.25
☐ 134	Ryan Jones	1.00	.45
☐ 135	Todd Walker	1.25	.55
☐ 136	Geoff Jenkins	6.00	2.70
☐ 137	Matt Morris	2.00	.90
☐ 138	Richie Sexson	2.00	.90
☐ 139	Todd Dunwoody	2.00	.90
☐ 140	Gabe Alvarez	1.50	.70
☐ 141	J.J. Johnson	.25	.11
☐ 142	Shannon Stewart	.60	.25
☐ 143	Brad Fulmer	.75	.35
☐ 144	Julio Santana	.25	.11
☐ 145	Scott Rolen	4.00	1.80
☐ 146	Amaury Telemaco	.25	.11
☐ 147	Trey Beamon	.25	.11
☐ 148	Billy Wagner	.75	.35
☐ 149	Todd Hollandsworth	.25	.11
☐ 150	Doug Million	.25	.11
☐ 151	Jose Valentin	1.50	.70
☐ 152	Wes Helms	1.50	.70
☐ 153	Jeff Suppan	.25	.11
☐ 154	Luis Castillo	2.00	.90
☐ 155	Bob Abreu	.75	.35
☐ 156	Paul Konerko	1.25	.55
☐ 157	Jamey Wright	.25	.11
☐ 158	Eddie Pearson	.25	.11
☐ 159	Jimmy Haynes	.25	.11
☐ 160	Derek Lee	1.25	.55
☐ 161	Damian Moss	.25	.11
☐ 162	Carlos Guillen	4.00	1.80
☐ 163	Chris Fussell	.25	.11
☐ 164	Mike Sweeney	5.00	2.20
☐ 165	Donnie Sadler	.25	.11
☐ 166	Desi Relaford	.25	.11
☐ 167	Steve Gibralter	.25	.11
☐ 168	Neifi Perez	.60	.25
☐ 169	Antone Williamson	.25	.11
☐ 170	Marty Janzen	.25	.11
☐ 171	Todd Helton	5.00	2.20
☐ 172	Raul Ibanez	.25	.11
☐ 173	Bill Selby	.25	.11
☐ 174	Shane Monahan	2.00	.90
☐ 175	Robin Jennings	.25	.11
☐ 176	Bobby Chouinard	.25	.11
☐ 177	Einar Diaz	.25	.11
☐ 178	Jason Thompson	.25	.11
☐ 179	Rafael Medina	1.00	.45
☐ 180	Kevin Orie	.25	.11
☐ NNO	1952 Mantle Chrome	8.00	3.60
☐ NNO	1952 Mantle Refractor	20.00	9.00
☐ NNO	1952 Mantle Atomic Ref.	40.00	18.00

1996 Bowman's Best Atomic Refractors

	MINT	NRMT
COMMON GOLD (1-90)	5.00	2.20

COMMON SILVER (91-180) 5.00 2.20
*GOLD STARS: 6X TO 15X BASIC CARDS
*SILVER STARS: 6X TO 15X BASIC CARDS
*ROOKIES: 3X TO 8X BASIC CARDS
STATED ODDS 1:48 HOB, 1:80 RET

1996 Bowman's Best Refractors

	MINT	NRMT
COMPLETE SET (180)	1500.00	700.00
COMMON CARD (1-180)	3.00	1.35

*GOLD STARS: 3X TO 8X BASIC CARDS
*SILVER STARS: 3X TO 8X BASIC CARDS
*ROOKIES: 1.5X TO 4X BASIC CARDS
STATED ODDS 1:12 HOB, 1:20 RET

1996 Bowman's Best Cuts

	MINT	NRMT
COMPLETE SET (15)	200.00	90.00
COMMON CARD (1-15)	2.00	.90

STATED ODDS 1:24 HOB, 1:40 RET
*REFRACTORS: 3X TO 8X BASE CARD HI
REF.STATED ODDS 1:48 HOB, 1:80 RET
*ATOMIC: 6X TO 15X BASE CARD HI
ATOMIC STATED ODDS 1:96 HOB, 1:160 RET

☐ 1	Ken Griffey Jr.	30.00	13.50
☐ 2	Jason Isringhausen	2.00	.90
☐ 3	Derek Jeter	20.00	9.00

		MINT	NRMT
❏ 4	Andruw Jones	10.00	4.50
❏ 5	Chipper Jones	15.00	6.75
❏ 6	Ryan Klesko	2.00	.90
❏ 7	Raul Mondesi	2.00	.90
❏ 8	Hideo Nomo	6.00	2.70
❏ 9	Mike Piazza	20.00	9.00
❏ 10	Manny Ramirez	8.00	3.60
❏ 11	Cal Ripken	25.00	11.00
❏ 12	Ruben Rivera	1.50	.70
❏ 13	Tim Salmon	3.00	1.35
❏ 14	Frank Thomas	12.00	5.50
❏ 15	Jim Thome	6.00	2.70

1996 Bowman's Best Mirror Image

	MINT	NRMT
COMPLETE SET (10)	120.00	55.00
COMMON CARD (1-10)	2.50	1.10

STATED ODDS 1:48 HOB, 1:80 RET
*REFRACTORS: .6X TO 1.5X HI COLUMN
REF.STATED ODDS 1:96 HOB, 1:160 RET
*ATOMIC REFRACTORS: 1.25X TO 3X HI
ATOMIC STATED ODDS 1:192 HOB, 1:320 RET

❏ 1	Jeff Bagwell	15.00	6.75
	Todd Helton		
	Frank Thomas		
	Richie Sexson		
❏ 2	Craig Biggio	2.50	1.10
	Luis Castillo		
	Roberto Alomar		
	Desi Relaford		
❏ 3	Chipper Jones	15.00	6.75
	Scott Rolen		
	Wade Boggs		
	George Arias		
❏ 4	Barry Larkin	12.00	5.50
	Neifi Perez		
	Cal Ripken		
	Mark Bellhorn		
❏ 5	Larry Walker	4.00	1.80
	Karim Garcia		
	Albert Belle		
	Ruben Rivera		
❏ 6	Barry Bonds	8.00	3.60
	Andruw Jones		
	Kenny Lofton		
	Donnie Sadler		
❏ 7	Tony Gwynn	30.00	13.50
	Vladimir Guerrero		
	Ken Griffey		
	Ben Grieve		
❏ 8	Mike Piazza	12.00	5.50
	Ben Davis		
	Ivan Rodriguez		
	Jose Valentin		
❏ 9	Greg Maddux	8.00	3.60
	Jamey Wright		
	Mike Mussina		
	Bartolo Colon		
❏ 10	Tom Glavine	2.50	1.10
	Billy Wagner		
	Randy Johnson		
	Jarrod Washburn		

1997 Bowman's Best Previews

	MINT	NRMT
COMPLETE SET (20)	100.00	45.00
COMMON CARD (1-20)	1.50	.70
UNLISTED STARS	2.50	1.10

STATED ODDS 1:12
*REFRACTORS: .75X TO 2X HI COLUMN
REFRACTOR STATED ODDS 1:48
*ATOMIC REFRACTORS: 1.5X TO 4X HI
ATOMIC STATED ODDS 1:96

❏ 1	Frank Thomas	6.00	2.70
❏ 2	Ken Griffey Jr.	15.00	6.75
❏ 3	Barry Bonds	4.00	1.80
❏ 4	Derek Jeter	10.00	4.50
❏ 5	Chipper Jones	8.00	3.60
❏ 6	Mark McGwire	15.00	6.75
❏ 7	Cal Ripken	12.00	5.50
❏ 8	Kenny Lofton	2.00	.90
❏ 9	Gary Sheffield	1.50	.70
❏ 10	Jeff Bagwell	4.00	1.80
❏ 11	Wilton Guerrero	1.50	.70
❏ 12	Scott Rolen	5.00	2.20
❏ 13	Todd Walker	2.50	1.10
❏ 14	Ruben Rivera	1.50	.70
❏ 15	Andruw Jones	4.00	1.80
❏ 16	Nomar Garciaparra	10.00	4.50
❏ 17	Vladimir Guerrero	5.00	2.20
❏ 18	Miguel Tejada	6.00	2.70
❏ 19	Bartolo Colon	1.50	.70
❏ 20	Katsuhiro Maeda	1.50	.70

1997 Bowman's Best

	MINT	NRMT
COMPLETE SET (200)	80.00	36.00
COMMON CARD (1-200)	.25	.11
MINOR STARS	.50	.23
UNLISTED STARS	1.00	.45

❏ 1	Ken Griffey Jr.	5.00	2.20
❏ 2	Cecil Fielder	.50	.23
❏ 3	Albert Belle	1.00	.45
❏ 4	Todd Hundley	.50	.23
❏ 5	Mike Piazza	3.00	1.35
❏ 6	Matt Williams	1.00	.45
❏ 7	Mo Vaughn	1.00	.45
❏ 8	Ryne Sandberg	1.25	.55
❏ 9	Chipper Jones	2.50	1.10
❏ 10	Edgar Martinez	.50	.23
❏ 11	Kenny Lofton	.75	.35
❏ 12	Ron Gant	.25	.11
❏ 13	Moises Alou	.50	.23
❏ 14	Pat Hentgen	.25	.11
❏ 15	Steve Finley	.50	.23
❏ 16	Mark Grace	.75	.35
❏ 17	Jay Buhner	.50	.23
❏ 18	Jeff Conine	.25	.11
❏ 19	Jim Edmonds	.75	.35
❏ 20	Todd Hollandsworth	.25	.11
❏ 21	Andy Pettitte	.75	.35
❏ 22	Jim Thome	1.00	.45
❏ 23	Eric Young	.50	.23
❏ 24	Ray Lankford	.50	.23
❏ 25	Marquis Grissom	.50	.23
❏ 26	Tony Clark	.75	.35
❏ 27	Jermaine Allensworth	.25	.11
❏ 28	Ellis Burks	.50	.23
❏ 29	Tony Gwynn	2.50	1.10
❏ 30	Barry Larkin	1.00	.45
❏ 31	John Olerud	.50	.23
❏ 32	Mariano Rivera	.50	.23
❏ 33	Paul Molitor	1.00	.45
❏ 34	Ken Caminiti	.75	.35
❏ 35	Gary Sheffield	.50	.23
❏ 36	Al Martin	.25	.11
❏ 37	John Valentin	.50	.23
❏ 38	Frank Thomas	2.00	.90
❏ 39	John Jaha	.25	.11
❏ 40	Greg Maddux	2.50	1.10
❏ 41	Alex Fernandez	.25	.11
❏ 42	Dean Palmer	.50	.23
❏ 43	Bernie Williams	1.00	.45
❏ 44	Deion Sanders	.50	.23
❏ 45	Mark McGwire	5.00	2.20
❏ 46	Brian Jordan	.50	.23
❏ 47	Bernard Gilkey	.25	.11
❏ 48	Will Clark	1.00	.45
❏ 49	Kevin Appier	.50	.23
❏ 50	Tom Glavine	1.00	.45
❏ 51	Chuck Knoblauch	1.00	.45
❏ 52	Rondell White	.50	.23
❏ 53	Greg Vaughn	.50	.23
❏ 54	Mike Mussina	1.00	.45
❏ 55	Brian McRae	.25	.11
❏ 56	Chili Davis	.50	.23
❏ 57	Wade Boggs	1.00	.45
❏ 58	Jeff Bagwell	1.25	.55
❏ 59	Roberto Alomar	1.00	.45
❏ 60	Dennis Eckersley	.50	.23
❏ 61	Ryan Klesko	.50	.23
❏ 62	Manny Ramirez	1.25	.55
❏ 63	John Wetteland	.50	.23
❏ 64	Cal Ripken	4.00	1.80
❏ 65	Edgar Renteria	.50	.23
❏ 66	Tino Martinez	1.00	.45
❏ 67	Larry Walker	1.00	.45
❏ 68	Gregg Jefferies	.25	.11
❏ 69	Lance Johnson	.25	.11
❏ 70	Carlos Delgado	1.00	.45
❏ 71	Craig Biggio	1.00	.45
❏ 72	Jose Canseco	1.25	.55
❏ 73	Barry Bonds	1.25	.55
❏ 74	Juan Gonzalez	2.00	.90
❏ 75	Eric Karros	.50	.23
❏ 76	Reggie Sanders	.50	.23
❏ 77	Robin Ventura	.50	.23
❏ 78	Hideo Nomo	1.00	.45
❏ 79	David Justice	1.00	.45
❏ 80	Vinny Castilla	.75	.35
❏ 81	Travis Fryman	.50	.23
❏ 82	Derek Jeter	3.00	1.35
❏ 83	Sammy Sosa	3.00	1.35
❏ 84	Ivan Rodriguez	1.25	.55
❏ 85	Rafael Palmeiro	1.00	.45
❏ 86	Roger Clemens	2.50	1.10
❏ 87	Jason Giambi	.50	.23
❏ 88	Andres Galarraga	1.00	.45
❏ 89	Jermaine Dye	.50	.23
❏ 90	Joe Carter	.50	.23
❏ 91	Brady Anderson	.50	.23
❏ 92	Derek Bell	.50	.23
❏ 93	Randy Johnson	1.00	.45
❏ 94	Fred McGriff	.75	.35

		MINT	NRMT
❑ 95	John Smoltz	.75	.35
❑ 96	Harold Baines	.50	.23
❑ 97	Raul Mondesi	.50	.23
❑ 98	Tim Salmon	1.00	.45
❑ 99	Carlos Baerga	.25	.11
❑ 100	Dante Bichette	.50	.23
❑ 101	Vladimir Guerrero	1.50	.70
❑ 102	Richard Hidalgo	.50	.23
❑ 103	Paul Konerko	1.00	.45
❑ 104	Alex Gonzalez	3.00	1.35
❑ 105	Jason Dickson	.25	.11
❑ 106	Jose Rosado	.25	.11
❑ 107	Todd Walker	.50	.23
❑ 108	Seth Greisinger	1.25	.55
❑ 109	Todd Helton	2.00	.90
❑ 110	Ben Davis	1.00	.45
❑ 111	Bartolo Colon	.50	.23
❑ 112	Elieser Marrero	.25	.11
❑ 113	Jeff D'Amico	.25	.11
❑ 114	Miguel Tejada	5.00	2.20
❑ 115	Darin Erstad	1.00	.45
❑ 116	Kris Benson	4.00	1.80
❑ 117	Adrian Beltre	8.00	3.60
❑ 118	Neifi Perez	.50	.23
❑ 119	Calvin Reese	.50	.23
❑ 120	Carl Pavano	1.00	.45
❑ 121	Juan Melo	.50	.23
❑ 122	Kevin McGlinchy	1.25	.55
❑ 123	Pat Cline	.50	.23
❑ 124	Felix Heredia	1.00	.45
❑ 125	Aaron Boone	.25	.11
❑ 126	Glendon Rusch	.25	.11
❑ 127	Mike Cameron	.50	.23
❑ 128	Justin Thompson	.50	.23
❑ 129	Chad Hermansen	4.00	1.80
❑ 130	Sidney Ponson	3.00	1.35
❑ 131	Willie Martinez	2.00	.90
❑ 132	Paul Wilder	1.00	.45
❑ 133	Geoff Jenkins	.50	.23
❑ 134	Roy Halladay	3.00	1.35
❑ 135	Carlos Guillen	.50	.23
❑ 136	Tony Batista	.75	.35
❑ 137	Todd Greene	.25	.11
❑ 138	Luis Castillo	.50	.23
❑ 139	Jimmy Anderson	1.00	.45
❑ 140	Edgard Velazquez	.75	.35
❑ 141	Chris Snopek	.25	.11
❑ 142	Ruben Rivera	.25	.11
❑ 143	Javier Valentin	.50	.23
❑ 144	Brian Rose	1.00	.45
❑ 145	Fernando Tatis	6.00	2.70
❑ 146	Dean Crow	.25	.11
❑ 147	Karim Garcia	.50	.23
❑ 148	Dante Powell	.50	.23
❑ 149	Hideki Irabu	2.50	1.10
❑ 150	Matt Morris	.50	.23
❑ 151	Wes Helms	.25	.11
❑ 152	Russ Johnson	.25	.11
❑ 153	Jarrod Washburn	.50	.23
❑ 154	Kerry Wood	10.00	4.50
❑ 155	Joe Fontenot	1.00	.45
❑ 156	Eugene Kingsale	1.00	.45
❑ 157	Terrence Long	.50	.23
❑ 158	Calvin Maduro	.25	.11
❑ 159	Jeff Suppan	.25	.11
❑ 160	DaRond Stovall	.25	.11
❑ 161	Mark Redman	.25	.11
❑ 162	Ken Cloude	1.00	.45
❑ 163	Bobby Estalella	.25	.11
❑ 164	Abraham Nunez	1.25	.55
❑ 165	Derrick Gibson	.75	.35
❑ 166	Mike Drumright	1.00	.45
❑ 167	Katsuhiro Maeda	.50	.23
❑ 168	Jeff Liefer	.50	.23
❑ 169	Ben Grieve	1.25	.55
❑ 170	Bob Abreu	.50	.23
❑ 171	Shannon Stewart	.50	.23
❑ 172	Braden Looper	.75	.35
❑ 173	Brant Brown	.50	.23
❑ 174	Marlon Anderson	.50	.23
❑ 175	Brad Fullmer	.50	.23
❑ 176	Carlos Beltran	4.00	1.80
❑ 177	Nomar Garciaparra	3.00	1.35
❑ 178	Derek Lee	.75	.35
❑ 179	Valerio De Los Santos	1.00	.45
❑ 180	Dmitri Young	.50	.23

		MINT	NRMT
❑ 181	Jamey Wright	.25	.11
❑ 182	Hiram Bocachica	1.25	.55
❑ 183	Wilton Guerrero	.25	.11
❑ 184	Chris Carpenter	.50	.23
❑ 185	Scott Spiezio	.25	.11
❑ 186	Andruw Jones	1.25	.55
❑ 187	Travis Lee	5.00	2.20
❑ 188	Jose Cruz Jr.	3.00	1.35
❑ 189	Jose Guillen	.75	.35
❑ 190	Jeff Abbott	.25	.11
❑ 191	Ricky Ledee	4.00	1.80
❑ 192	Mike Sweeney	.50	.23
❑ 193	Donnie Sadler	.50	.23
❑ 194	Scott Rolen	1.50	.70
❑ 195	Kevin Orie	.25	.11
❑ 196	Jason Conti	2.00	.90
❑ 197	Mark Kotsay	2.00	.90
❑ 198	Eric Milton	1.50	.70
❑ 199	Russell Branyan	1.00	.45
❑ 200	Alex Sanchez	1.25	.55

1997 Bowman's Best Atomic Refractors

FRED McGRIFF

	MINT	NRMT
COMMON CARD (1-200)	5.00	2.20

*STARS: 8X TO 20X BASIC CARDS
*YOUNG STARS: 6X TO 15X BASIC CARDS
*ROOKIES: 2.5X TO 6X BASIC CARDS
STATED ODDS 1:24

1997 Bowman's Best Refractors

	MINT	NRMT
COMMON CARD (1-200)	2.50	1.10

*STARS: 4X TO 10X BASIC CARDS
*YOUNG STARS: 3X TO 8X BASIC CARDS
*ROOKIES: 1.25X TO 3X BASIC CARDS
STATED ODDS 1:12

1997 Bowman's Best Autographs

	MINT	NRMT
STATED ODDS 1:170		

*REF.STARS: 1X TO 2.5X HI COLUMN
*REF.CRUZ JR: .6X TO 1.5X HI
REFRACTOR STATED ODDS 1:2036

*ATOMIC STARS: 2.5X TO 5X HI COLUMN
*ATOMIC CRUZ JR: 1.5X TO 3X HI
ATOMIC STATED ODDS 1:6107
SKIP-NUMBERED 10-CARD SET

❑ 29	Tony Gwynn	60.00	27.00
❑ 33	Paul Molitor	25.00	11.00
❑ 82	Derek Jeter	80.00	36.00
❑ 91	Brady Anderson	10.00	4.50
❑ 98	Tim Salmon	15.00	6.75
❑ 107	Todd Walker	8.00	3.60
❑ 183	Wilton Guerrero	5.00	2.20
❑ 185	Scott Spiezio	5.00	2.20
❑ 188	Jose Cruz Jr.	20.00	9.00
❑ 194	Scott Rolen	40.00	18.00

1997 Bowman's Best Best Cuts

	MINT	NRMT
COMPLETE SET (20)	200.00	90.00
COMMON CARD (BC1-BC20)	1.50	.70
SEMISTARS	3.00	1.35
UNLISTED STARS	5.00	2.20

STATED ODDS 1:24
*REFRACTORS: .6X TO 1.5X HI COLUMN
REFRACTOR STATED ODDS 1:48
*ATOMIC REFRACTORS: 1.25X TO 3X HI
ATOMIC STATED ODDS 1:96

❑ BC1	Derek Jeter	15.00	6.75
❑ BC2	Chipper Jones	12.00	5.50
❑ BC3	Frank Thomas	10.00	4.50
❑ BC4	Cal Ripken	20.00	9.00
❑ BC5	Mark McGwire	25.00	11.00
❑ BC6	Ken Griffey Jr.	25.00	11.00
❑ BC7	Jeff Bagwell	6.00	2.70
❑ BC8	Mike Piazza	15.00	6.75
❑ BC9	Ken Caminiti	3.00	1.35
❑ BC10	Albert Belle	5.00	2.20
❑ BC11	Jose Cruz Jr.	5.00	2.20
❑ BC12	Wilton Guerrero	1.50	.70
❑ BC13	Darin Erstad	5.00	2.20
❑ BC14	Andruw Jones	6.00	2.70
❑ BC15	Scott Rolen	8.00	3.60
❑ BC16	Jose Guillen	3.00	1.35
❑ BC17	Bob Abreu	2.00	.90
❑ BC18	Vladimir Guerrero	8.00	3.60
❑ BC19	Todd Walker	5.00	2.20
❑ BC20	Nomar Garciaparra	15.00	6.75

1997 Bowman's Best Mirror Image

	MINT	NRMT
COMPLETE SET (10)	100.00	45.00
COMMON CARD (MI1-MI10)	3.00	1.35

STATED ODDS 1:48
*REFRACTORS: .6X TO 1.5X HI COLUMN
REFRACTOR STATED ODDS 1:96
*ATOMIC REFRACTORS: 1.25X TO 3X HI
ATOMIC STATED ODDS 1:192
*INVERTED: 2X VALUE OF NON-INVERTED
INVERTED: RANDOM INSERTS IN PACKS
INVERTED HAVE LARGER ROOKIE PHOTOS

		MINT	NRMT
☐ MI1	Nomar Garciaparra	15.00	6.75
	Derek Jeter		
	Hiram Bocachica		
	Barry Larkin		
☐ MI2	Travis Lee	8.00	3.60
	Frank Thomas		
	Derrick Lee		
	Jeff Bagwell		
☐ MI3	Kerry Wood	15.00	6.75
	Greg Maddux		
	Kris Benson		
	John Smoltz		
☐ MI4	Kevin Brown	12.00	5.50
	Ivan Rodriguez		
	Eli Marrero		
	Mike Piazza		
☐ MI5	Jose Cruz Jr.	20.00	9.00
	Ken Griffey Jr.		
	Andruw Jones		
	Barry Bonds		
☐ MI6	Jose Guillen	8.00	3.60
	Juan Gonzalez		
	Richard Hidalgo		
	Gary Sheffield		
☐ MI7	Paul Konerko	25.00	11.00
	Mark McGwire		
	Todd Helton		
	Rafael Palmeiro		
☐ MI8	Wilton Guerrero	3.00	1.35
	Craig Biggio		
	Donnie Sadler		
	Chuck Knoblauch		
☐ MI9	Russell Branyan	12.00	5.50
	Matt Williams		
	Adrian Beltre		
	Chipper Jones		
☐ MI10	Bob Abreu	6.00	2.70
	Kenny Lofton		
	Vladimir Guerrero		
	Albert Belle		

1998 Bowman's Best

	MINT	NRMT
COMPLETE SET (200)	80.00	36.00
COMMON CARD (1-200)	.25	.11
MINOR STARS	.40	.18
SEMISTARS	.60	.25
UNLISTED STARS	1.00	.45

☐ 1	Mark McGwire	6.00	2.70
☐ 2	Jeromy Burnitz	.40	.18
☐ 3	Barry Bonds	1.25	.55

☐ 4	Dante Bichette	.40	.18
☐ 5	Chipper Jones	2.50	1.10
☐ 6	Frank Thomas	2.00	.90
☐ 7	Kevin Brown	.60	.25
☐ 8	Juan Gonzalez	2.00	.90
☐ 9	Jay Buhner	.40	.18
☐ 10	Chuck Knoblauch	.40	.18
☐ 11	Cal Ripken	4.00	1.80
☐ 12	Matt Williams	1.00	.45
☐ 13	Jim Edmonds	.40	.18
☐ 14	Manny Ramirez	1.25	.55
☐ 15	Tony Clark	.40	.18
☐ 16	Mo Vaughn	1.00	.45
☐ 17	Bernie Williams	1.00	.45
☐ 18	Scott Rolen	1.25	.55
☐ 19	Gary Sheffield	.40	.18
☐ 20	Albert Belle	1.00	.45
☐ 21	Mike Piazza	3.00	1.35
☐ 22	John Olerud	.40	.18
☐ 23	Tony Gwynn	2.50	1.10
☐ 24	Jay Bell	.40	.18
☐ 25	Jose Cruz Jr.	.40	.18
☐ 26	Justin Thompson	.25	.11
☐ 27	Ken Griffey Jr.	5.00	2.20
☐ 28	Sandy Alomar Jr.	.40	.18
☐ 29	Mark Grudzielanek	.25	.11
☐ 30	Mark Grace	.60	.25
☐ 31	Ron Gant	.40	.18
☐ 32	Javy Lopez	.40	.18
☐ 33	Jeff Bagwell	1.25	.55
☐ 34	Fred McGriff	.60	.25
☐ 35	Rafael Palmeiro	1.00	.45
☐ 36	Vinny Castilla	.40	.18
☐ 37	Andy Benes	.25	.11
☐ 38	Pedro Martinez	1.25	.55
☐ 39	Andy Pettitte	.40	.18
☐ 40	Marty Cordova	.40	.18
☐ 41	Rusty Greer	.40	.18
☐ 42	Kevin Orie	.25	.11
☐ 43	Chan Ho Park	.40	.18
☐ 44	Ryan Klesko	.40	.18
☐ 45	Alex Rodriguez	3.00	1.35
☐ 46	Travis Fryman	.40	.18
☐ 47	Jeff King	.25	.11
☐ 48	Roger Clemens	2.50	1.10
☐ 49	Darin Erstad	.60	.25
☐ 50	Brady Anderson	.40	.18
☐ 51	Jason Kendall	.40	.18
☐ 52	John Valentin	.40	.18
☐ 53	Ellis Burks	.40	.18
☐ 54	Brian Hunter	.25	.11
☐ 55	Paul O'Neill	.40	.18
☐ 56	Ken Caminiti	.40	.18
☐ 57	David Justice	.40	.18
☐ 58	Eric Karros	.40	.18
☐ 59	Pat Hentgen	.25	.11
☐ 60	Greg Maddux	2.50	1.10
☐ 61	Craig Biggio	1.00	.45
☐ 62	Edgar Martinez	.40	.18
☐ 63	Mike Mussina	1.00	.45
☐ 64	Larry Walker	1.00	.45
☐ 65	Tino Martinez	.40	.18
☐ 66	Jim Thome	1.00	.45
☐ 67	Tom Glavine	1.00	.45
☐ 68	Raul Mondesi	.40	.18
☐ 69	Marquis Grissom	.25	.11
☐ 70	Randy Johnson	1.00	.45
☐ 71	Steve Finley	.40	.18

☐ 72	Jose Guillen	.25	.11
☐ 73	Nomar Garciaparra	3.00	1.35
☐ 74	Wade Boggs	1.00	.45
☐ 75	Bobby Higginson	.40	.18
☐ 76	Robin Ventura	.40	.18
☐ 77	Derek Jeter	3.00	1.35
☐ 78	Andruw Jones	1.00	.45
☐ 79	Ray Lankford	.40	.18
☐ 80	Vladimir Guerrero	1.25	.55
☐ 81	Kenny Lofton	.60	.25
☐ 82	Ivan Rodriguez	1.25	.55
☐ 83	Neifi Perez	.40	.18
☐ 84	John Smoltz	.60	.25
☐ 85	Tim Salmon	.60	.25
☐ 86	Carlos Delgado	1.00	.45
☐ 87	Sammy Sosa	3.00	1.35
☐ 88	Jaret Wright	.40	.18
☐ 89	Roberto Alomar	1.00	.45
☐ 90	Paul Molitor	1.00	.45
☐ 91	Dean Palmer	.40	.18
☐ 92	Barry Larkin	1.00	.45
☐ 93	Jason Giambi	.40	.18
☐ 94	Curt Schilling	.60	.25
☐ 95	Eric Young	.25	.11
☐ 96	Denny Neagle	.25	.11
☐ 97	Moises Alou	.40	.18
☐ 98	Livan Hernandez	.25	.11
☐ 99	Todd Hundley	.40	.18
☐ 100	Andres Galarraga	.60	.25
☐ 101	Travis Lee	.60	.25
☐ 102	Lance Berkman	.60	.25
☐ 103	Orlando Cabrera	.25	.11
☐ 104	Mike Lowell	2.50	1.10
☐ 105	Ben Grieve	1.00	.45
☐ 106	Jae Weong Seo	1.25	.55
☐ 107	Richie Sexson	.60	.25
☐ 108	Eli Marrero	.25	.11
☐ 109	Aramis Ramirez	1.00	.45
☐ 110	Paul Konerko	.25	.11
☐ 111	Carl Pavano	.25	.11
☐ 112	Brad Fullmer	.25	.11
☐ 113	Matt Clement	.40	.18
☐ 114	Donzell McDonald	.25	.11
☐ 115	Todd Helton	1.25	.55
☐ 116	Mike Caruso	.25	.11
☐ 117	Donnie Sadler	.25	.11
☐ 118	Bruce Chen	.40	.18
☐ 119	Jarrod Washburn	.25	.11
☐ 120	Adrian Beltre	1.00	.45
☐ 121	Ryan Jackson	1.00	.45
☐ 122	Kevin Millar	4.00	1.80
☐ 123	Corey Koskie	2.50	1.10
☐ 124	Dermal Brown	.40	.18
☐ 125	Kerry Wood	1.25	.55
☐ 126	Juan Melo	.25	.11
☐ 127	Ramon Hernandez	.25	.11
☐ 128	Roy Halladay	.40	.18
☐ 129	Ron Wright	.25	.11
☐ 130	Darnell McDonald	3.00	1.35
☐ 131	Odalis Perez	2.50	1.10
☐ 132	Alex Cora	1.25	.55
☐ 133	Justin Towle	.25	.11
☐ 134	Juan Encarnacion	.40	.18
☐ 135	Brian Rose	.25	.11
☐ 136	Russell Branyan	.40	.18
☐ 137	Cesar King	1.50	.70
☐ 138	Ruben Rivera	.25	.11
☐ 139	Ricky Ledee	.40	.18
☐ 140	Vernon Wells	.60	.25
☐ 141	Luis Rivas	2.00	.90
☐ 142	Brent Butler	.25	.11
☐ 143	Karim Garcia	.25	.11
☐ 144	George Lombard	.40	.18
☐ 145	Masato Yoshii	1.50	.70
☐ 146	Braden Looper	.25	.11
☐ 147	Alex Sanchez	.25	.11
☐ 148	Kris Benson	.40	.18
☐ 149	Mark Kotsay	.40	.18
☐ 150	Richard Hidalgo	.40	.18
☐ 151	Scott Elarton	.25	.11
☐ 152	Ryan Minor	3.00	1.35
☐ 153	Troy Glaus	10.00	4.50
☐ 154	Carlos Lee	5.00	2.20
☐ 155	Michael Coleman	.40	.18
☐ 156	Jason Grilli	1.50	.70
☐ 157	Julio Ramirez	4.00	1.80

	MINT	NRMT
☐ 158 Randy Wolf	4.00	1.80
☐ 159 Ryan Brannan	.25	.11
☐ 160 Edgard Clemente	.25	.11
☐ 161 Miguel Tejada	.40	.18
☐ 162 Chad Hermansen	1.00	.45
☐ 163 Ryan Anderson	5.00	2.20
☐ 164 Ben Petrick	.40	.18
☐ 165 Alex Gonzalez	.40	.18
☐ 166 Ben Davis	.60	.25
☐ 167 John Patterson	.40	.18
☐ 168 Cliff Politte	.25	.11
☐ 169 Randall Simon	.40	.18
☐ 170 Javier Vazquez	.25	.11
☐ 171 Kevin Witt	.25	.11
☐ 172 Geoff Jenkins	.40	.18
☐ 173 David Ortiz	.25	.11
☐ 174 Derrick Gibson	.40	.18
☐ 175 Abraham Nunez	.25	.11
☐ 176 A.J. Hinch	.25	.11
☐ 177 Ruben Mateo	8.00	3.60
☐ 178 Magglio Ordonez	8.00	3.60
☐ 179 Todd Dunwoody	.25	.11
☐ 180 Daryle Ward	.40	.18
☐ 181 Mike Kinkade	1.50	.70
☐ 182 Willie Martinez	.40	.18
☐ 183 Orlando Hernandez	6.00	2.70
☐ 184 Eric Milton	.25	.11
☐ 185 Eric Chavez	1.00	.45
☐ 186 Damian Jackson	.25	.11
☐ 187 Jim Parque	1.50	.70
☐ 188 Dan Reichert	1.50	.70
☐ 189 Mike Drumright	.25	.11
☐ 190 Todd Walker	.40	.18
☐ 191 Shane Monahan	.25	.11
☐ 192 Derrek Lee	.25	.11
☐ 193 Jeremy Giambi	3.00	1.35
☐ 194 Dan McKinley	1.00	.45
☐ 195 Tony Armas Jr.	6.00	2.70
☐ 196 Matt Anderson	2.00	.90
☐ 197 Jim Chamblee	1.00	.45
☐ 198 Francisco Cordero	1.50	.70
☐ 199 Calvin Pickering	.40	.18
☐ 200 Reggie Taylor	.25	.11

1998 Bowman's Best Atomic Refractors

	MINT	NRMT
COMMON CARD (1-200)	15.00	6.75

*STARS: 15X TO 40X BASIC CARDS
*YNG.STARS: 12.5X TO 30X BASIC CARDS
*PROSPECTS: 10X TO 25X BASIC CARDS
*ROOKIES: 4X TO 10X BASIC CARDS
STATED ODDS 1:82
STATED PRINT RUN 100 SERIAL #'d SETS

1998 Bowman's Best Refractors

	MINT	NRMT
COMMON CARD (1-200)	5.00	2.20

*STARS: 6X TO 15X BASIC CARDS
*YOUNG STARS: 5X TO 12X BASIC CARDS
*PROSPECTS: 4X TO 10X BASIC CARDS
*ROOKIES: 2X TO 5X BASIC CARDS
STATED ODDS 1:20
STATED PRINT RUN 400 SERIAL #'d SETS

1998 Bowman's Best Autographs

	MINT	NRMT

STATED ODDS 1:180
*REFRACTORS: 1X TO 2.5X HI COLUMN
REFRACTOR STATED ODDS 1:2158
*ATOMICS: 2X TO 5X HI COLUMN
ATOMIC STATED ODDS 1:6437
SKIP-NUMBERED 10-CARD SET

	MINT	NRMT
☐ 5 Chipper Jones	100.00	45.00
☐ 10 Chuck Knoblauch	20.00	9.00
☐ 15 Tony Clark	15.00	6.75
☐ 20 Albert Belle	30.00	13.50
☐ 25 Jose Cruz Jr.	15.00	6.75
☐ 105 Ben Grieve	30.00	13.50
☐ 110 Paul Konerko	15.00	6.75
☐ 115 Todd Helton	40.00	18.00
☐ 120 Adrian Beltre	25.00	11.00
☐ 125 Kerry Wood	30.00	13.50

1998 Bowman's Best Mirror Image Fusion

	MINT	NRMT
COMPLETE SET (20)	200.00	90.00
COMMON CARD (MI1-MI20)	2.00	.90
UNLISTED STARS	5.00	2.20

STATED ODDS 1:12
*REFRACTORS: 5X TO 12X HI COLUMN
REFRACTOR STATED ODDS 1:809
REF.PRINT RUN 100 SERIAL #'d SETS
*ATOMIC: 12.5X TO 30X HI COLUMN
ATOMIC STATED ODDS 1:3237
ATOMIC PRINT RUN 25 SERIAL #'d SETS

		MINT	NRMT
☐ MI1 Frank Thomas		10.00	4.50
	David Ortiz		
☐ MI2 Chuck Knoblauch		5.00	2.20
	Enrique Wilson		
☐ MI3 Nomar Garciaparra		15.00	6.75
	Miguel Tejada		
☐ MI4 Alex Rodriguez		15.00	6.75
	Mike Caruso		
☐ MI5 Cal Ripken		20.00	9.00
	Ryan Minor		
☐ MI6 Ken Griffey Jr.		25.00	11.00
	Ben Grieve		
☐ MI7 Juan Gonzalez		10.00	4.50

		MINT	NRMT
	Juan Encarnacion		
☐ MI8 Jose Cruz Jr.		10.00	4.50
	Ruben Mateo		
☐ MI9 Randy Johnson		6.00	2.70
	Ryan Anderson		
☐ MI10 Ivan Rodriguez		6.00	2.70
	A.J. Hinch		
☐ MI11 Jeff Bagwell		6.00	2.70
	Paul Konerko		
☐ MI12 Mark McGwire		30.00	13.50
	Travis Lee		
☐ MI13 Craig Biggio		5.00	2.20
	Chad Hermansen		
☐ MI14 Mark Grudzielanek		2.00	.90
	Alex Gonzalez		
☐ MI15 Chipper Jones		12.00	5.50
	Adrian Beltre		
☐ MI16 Larry Walker		5.00	2.20
	Mark Kotsay		
☐ MI17 Tony Gwynn		12.00	5.50
	George Lombard		
☐ MI18 Barry Bonds		6.00	2.70
	Richard Hidalgo		
☐ MI19 Greg Maddux		12.00	5.50
	Kerry Wood		
☐ MI20 Mike Piazza		15.00	6.75
	Ben Petrick		

1998 Bowman's Best Performers

	MINT	NRMT
COMPLETE SET (10)	25.00	11.00
COMMON CARD (BP1-BP10)	1.50	.70
SEMISTARS	2.00	.90

STATED ODDS 1:6
*REFRACTORS: 5X TO 12X HI COLUMN
REFRACTOR STATED ODDS 1:809
REF.PRINT RUN 200 SERIAL #'d SETS
*ATOMIC: 12.5X TO 30X HI COLUMN
ATOMIC STATED ODDS 1:3237
ATOMIC PRINT RUN 50 SERIAL #'d SETS

	MINT	NRMT
☐ BP1 Ben Grieve	2.50	1.10
☐ BP2 Travis Lee	2.00	.90
☐ BP3 Ryan Minor	2.50	1.10
☐ BP4 Todd Helton	3.00	1.35
☐ BP5 Brad Fullmer	1.50	.70
☐ BP6 Paul Konerko	1.50	.70
☐ BP7 Adrian Beltre	2.50	1.10
☐ BP8 Richie Sexson	2.00	.90
☐ BP9 Aramis Ramirez	2.00	.90
☐ BP10 Russell Branyan	1.50	.70

1999 Bowman's Best

	MINT	NRMT
COMPLETE SET (200)	120.00	55.00
COMP.SET w/o SP's (150)	30.00	13.50
COMMON CARD (1-150)	.20	.09
MINOR STARS 1-150	.30	.14
SEMISTARS 1-150	.50	.23
UNLISTED STARS 1-150	.75	.35
COMMON ROOKIE (151-200)	1.00	.45

ONE ROOKIE CARD PER PACK

	MINT	NRMT
☐ 1 Chipper Jones	2.00	.90
☐ 2 Brian Jordan	.30	.14

3	David Justice	.30	.14
4	Jason Kendall	.30	.14
5	Mo Vaughn	.75	.35
6	Jim Edmonds	.30	.14
7	Wade Boggs	.75	.35
8	Jeromy Burnitz	.30	.14
9	Todd Hundley	.30	.14
10	Rondell White	.30	.14
11	Cliff Floyd	.30	.14
12	Sean Casey	.75	.35
13	Bernie Williams	.75	.35
14	Dante Bichette	.30	.14
15	Greg Vaughn	.30	.14
16	Andres Galarraga	.50	.23
17	Ray Durham	.30	.14
18	Jim Thome	.75	.35
19	Gary Sheffield	.75	.35
20	Frank Thomas	1.50	.70
21	Orlando Hernandez	.75	.35
22	Ivan Rodriguez	1.00	.45
23	Jose Cruz Jr.	.30	.14
24	Jason Giambi	.30	.14
25	Craig Biggio	.75	.35
26	Kerry Wood	.75	.35
27	Manny Ramirez	1.00	.45
28	Curt Schilling	.50	.23
29	Mike Mussina	.75	.35
30	Tim Salmon	.50	.23
31	Mike Piazza	2.50	1.10
32	Roberto Alomar	.75	.35
33	Larry Walker	.75	.35
34	Barry Larkin	.75	.35
35	Nomar Garciaparra	2.50	1.10
36	Paul O'Neill	.30	.14
37	Todd Walker	.30	.14
38	Eric Karros	.30	.14
39	Brad Fullmer	.20	.09
40	John Olerud	.30	.14
41	Todd Helton	.75	.35
42	Raul Mondesi	.30	.14
43	Jose Canseco	1.00	.45
44	Matt Williams	.30	.14
45	Ray Lankford	.30	.14
46	Carlos Delgado	.50	.23
47	Darin Erstad	.50	.23
48	Vladimir Guerrero	1.00	.45
49	Robin Ventura	.30	.14
50	Alex Rodriguez	2.50	1.10
51	Vinny Castilla	.30	.14
52	Tony Clark	.30	.14
53	Pedro Martinez	1.00	.45
54	Rafael Palmeiro	.75	.35
55	Scott Rolen	1.00	.45
56	Tino Martinez	.30	.14
57	Tony Gwynn	2.00	.90
58	Barry Bonds	1.00	.45
59	Kenny Lofton	.50	.23
60	Javy Lopez	.30	.14
61	Mark Grace	.50	.23
62	Travis Lee	.50	.23
63	Kevin Brown	.50	.23
64	Al Leiter	.30	.14
65	Albert Belle	.75	.35
66	Sammy Sosa	2.50	1.10
67	Greg Maddux	2.00	.90
68	Mark Kotsay	.20	.09
69	Dmitri Young	.30	.14
70	Mark McGwire	5.00	2.20
71	Juan Gonzalez	1.50	.70
72	Andruw Jones	.75	.35
73	Derek Jeter	2.50	1.10
74	Randy Johnson	.75	.35
75	Cal Ripken	3.00	1.35
76	Shawn Green	.75	.35
77	Moises Alou	.30	.14
78	Tom Glavine	.75	.35
79	Sandy Alomar Jr	.30	.14
80	Ken Griffey Jr.	4.00	1.80
81	Ryan Klesko	.30	.14
82	Jeff Bagwell	1.00	.45
83	Ben Grieve	.75	.35
84	John Smoltz	.50	.23
85	Roger Clemens	2.00	.90
86	Ken Griffey Jr. BP	2.00	.90
87	Roger Clemens BP	1.00	.45
88	Derek Jeter BP	1.25	.55
89	Nomar Garciaparra BP	1.25	.55
90	Mark McGwire BP	2.50	1.10
91	Sammy Sosa BP	1.25	.55
92	Alex Rodriguez BP	1.25	.55
93	Greg Maddux BP	1.00	.45
94	Vladimir Guerrero BP	.50	.23
95	Chipper Jones BP	1.00	.45
96	Kerry Wood BP	.30	.14
97	Ben Grieve BP	.30	.14
98	Tony Gwynn BP	1.00	.45
99	Juan Gonzalez BP	.75	.35
100	Mike Piazza BP	1.25	.55
101	Eric Chavez	.50	.23
102	Billy Koch	.30	.14
103	Dernell Stenson	.30	.14
104	Marlon Anderson	.20	.09
105	Ron Belliard	.30	.14
106	Bruce Chen	.30	.14
107	Carlos Beltran	1.00	.45
108	Chad Hermansen	.30	.14
109	Ryan Anderson	.30	.14
110	Michael Barrett	.50	.23
111	Matt Clement	.30	.14
112	Ben Davis	.50	.23
113	Calvin Pickering	.30	.14
114	Brad Penny	.30	.14
115	Paul Konerko	.30	.14
116	Alex Gonzalez	.30	.14
117	George Lombard	.30	.14
118	John Patterson	.30	.14
119	Rob Bell	.20	.09
120	Ruben Mateo	.75	.35
121	Troy Glaus	.75	.35
122	Ryan Bradley	.30	.14
123	Carlos Lee	.30	.14
124	Gabe Kapler	.75	.35
125	Ramon Hernandez	.20	.09
126	Carlos Febles	.30	.14
127	Mitch Meluskey	.20	.09
128	Michael Cuddyer	.30	.14
129	Pablo Ozuna	.30	.14
130	Jayson Werth	.30	.14
131	Ricky Ledee	.30	.14
132	Jeremy Giambi	.20	.09
133	Danny Klassen	.20	.09
134	Mark DeRosa	.20	.09
135	Randy Wolf	.30	.14
136	Roy Halladay	.30	.14
137	Derrick Gibson	.30	.14
138	Ben Petrick	.30	.14
139	Warren Morris	.30	.14
140	Lance Berkman	.50	.23
141	Russell Branyan	.30	.14
142	Adrian Beltre	.75	.35
143	Juan Encarnacion	.30	.14
144	Fernando Seguignol	.30	.14
145	Corey Koskie	.30	.14
146	Preston Wilson	.30	.14
147	Homer Bush	.30	.14
148	Daryle Ward	.30	.14
149	Joe McEwing	4.00	1.80
150	Peter Bergeron	2.50	1.10
151	Pat Burrell	10.00	4.50
152	Choo Freeman	2.00	.90
153	Matt Belisle	1.25	.55
154	Carlos Pena	2.50	1.10
155	A.J. Burnett	2.50	1.10
156	Doug Mientkiewicz	1.25	.55
157	Sean Burroughs	10.00	4.50
158	Mike Zywica	1.25	.55
159	Corey Patterson	12.00	5.50
160	Austin Kearns	2.50	1.10
161	Chip Ambres	2.00	.90
162	Kelly Dransfeldt	1.50	.70
163	Mike Nannini	1.50	.55
164	Mark Mulder	2.50	1.10
165	Jason Tyner	1.50	.70
166	Bobby Seay	1.50	.70
167	Alex Escobar	5.00	2.20
168	Nick Johnson	8.00	3.60
169	Alfonso Soriano	10.00	4.50
170	Clayton Andrews	1.25	.55
171	C.C. Sabathia	4.00	1.80
172	Matt Holliday	2.50	1.10
173	Brad Lidge	1.50	.70
174	Kit Pellow	2.00	.90
175	J.M. Gold	1.50	.70
176	Roosevelt Brown	1.50	.70
177	Eric Valent	2.50	1.10
178	Adam Everett	2.00	.90
179	Jorge Toca	2.50	1.10
180	Matt Roney	1.50	.70
181	Andy Brown	1.50	.70
182	Phil Norton	1.00	.45
183	Mickey Lopez	1.00	.45
184	Chris George	1.50	.70
185	Arturo McDowell	1.50	.70
186	Jose Fernandez	1.00	.45
187	Seth Etherton	1.25	.55
188	Josh McKinley	1.25	.55
189	Nate Cornejo	1.50	.70
190	Giuseppe Chiaramonte	1.25	.55
191	Mamon Tucker	1.50	.55
192	Ryan Mills	1.50	.70
193	Chad Moeller	1.50	.55
194	Tony Torcato	1.50	.70
195	Jeff Winchester	1.25	.55
196	Rick Elder	2.50	1.10
197	Matt Burch	1.00	.45
198	Jeff Urban	1.25	.55
199	Chris Jones	1.25	.55
200	Masao Kida	2.00	.90

1999 Bowman's Best Atomic Refractors

	MINT	NRMT
COMMON CARD (1-200)	8.00	3.60

*STARS 1-100: 15X TO 40X BASIC 1-100
*PROS. 101-150: 12.5X TO 30X BASIC 101-150
*ROOKIES 151-200: 4X TO 10X BASIC 151-200
STATED ODDS 1:62
STATED PRINT RUN 100 SERIAL #'d SETS

1999 Bowman's Best Refractors

	MINT	NRMT
COMMON CARD (1-200)	3.00	1.35

*STARS 1-100: 6X TO 15X BASIC 1-100
*PROS. 101-150: 5X TO 12X BASIC 101-150
*ROOKIES 151-200: 2X TO 5X BASIC 151-200
STATED ODDS 1:15
STATED PRINT RUN 400 SERIAL #'d SETS

1999 Bowman's Best Franchise Best Mach I

	MINT	NRMT
COMPLETE SET (10)	120.00	55.00
COMMON CARD (FB1-FB10)	8.00	3.60

STATED ODDS 1:41
STATED PRINT RUN 3000 SERIAL #'d SETS
*MACH II: .75X TO 2X HI COLUMN
MACH II STATED ODDS 1:124
MACH II PRINT RUN 1000 SERIAL #'d SETS
*MACH III: 1.25X TO 3X HI COLUMN
MACH III STATED ODDS 1:248
MACH III PRINT RUN 500 SERIAL #'d SETS

		MINT	NRMT
❑ FB1	Mark McGwire	25.00	11.00
❑ FB2	Ken Griffey Jr.	20.00	9.00
❑ FB3	Sammy Sosa	12.00	5.50
❑ FB4	Nomar Garciaparra	12.00	5.50
❑ FB5	Alex Rodriguez	12.00	5.50
❑ FB6	Derek Jeter	15.00	5.50
❑ FB7	Mike Piazza	12.00	5.50
❑ FB8	Frank Thomas	8.00	3.60
❑ FB9	Chipper Jones	10.00	4.50
❑ FB10	Juan Gonzalez	8.00	3.60

1999 Bowman's Best Franchise Favorites

	MINT	NRMT
COMPLETE SET (6)	80.00	36.00
COMMON CARD (1-6)	10.00	4.50

STATED ODD 1:40

		MINT	NRMT
❑ FR1A	Derek Jeter	20.00	9.00
❑ FR1B	Don Mattingly	15.00	6.75
❑ FR1C	Derek Jeter	25.00	11.00
	Don Mattingly		
❑ FR2A	Scott Rolen	10.00	4.50
❑ FR2B	Mike Schmidt	10.00	4.50
❑ FR2C	Scott Rolen	15.00	6.75
	Mike Schmidt		

1999 Bowman's Best Franchise Favorites Autographs

	MINT	NRMT

FR1A/FR2A STATED ODDS 1:1550

FR1B/FR2B STATED ODDS 1:1550
FR1C/FR2C STATED ODDS 1:6174

		MINT	NRMT
❑ FR1A	Derek Jeter	200.00	90.00
❑ FR1B	Don Mattingly	200.00	90.00
❑ FR1C	Derek Jeter	500.00	220.00
	Don Mattingly		
❑ FR2A	Scott Rolen	60.00	27.00
❑ FR2B	Mike Schmidt	120.00	55.00
❑ FR2C	Scott Rolen	400.00	180.00
	Mike Schmidt		

1999 Bowman's Best Future Foundations Mach I

	MINT	NRMT
COMPLETE SET (10)	40.00	18.00
COMMON CARD (FF1-FF10)	1.00	.45
MINOR STARS	1.50	.70
SEMISTARS	2.50	1.10
UNLISTED STARS	4.00	1.80

STATED ODDS 1:41
STATED PRINT RUN 3000 SERIAL #'d SETS
*MACH II: .75X TO 2X HI COLUMN
MACH II STATED ODDS 1:124
MACH II PRINT RUN 1000 SERIAL #'d SETS
*MACH III: 1.25X TO 3X HI COLUMN
MACH III STATED ODDS 1:248
MACH III PRINT RUN 500 SERIAL #'d SETS

		MINT	NRMT
❑ FF1	Ruben Mateo	4.00	1.80
❑ FF2	Troy Glaus	4.00	1.80
❑ FF3	Eric Chavez	2.50	1.10
❑ FF4	Pat Burrell	12.00	5.50
❑ FF5	Adrian Beltre	4.00	1.80
❑ FF6	Ryan Anderson	1.50	.70
❑ FF7	Alfonso Soriano	12.00	5.50
❑ FF8	Brad Penny	1.50	.70
❑ FF9	Derrick Gibson	1.50	.70
❑ FF10	Bruce Chen	1.50	.70

1999 Bowman's Best Mirror Image

	MINT	NRMT
COMPLETE SET (10)	100.00	45.00
COMMON CARD (M1-M10)	3.00	1.35

STATED ODDS 1:24

*REFRACTORS: .75X TO 2X HI COLUMN
REFRACTOR STATED ODDS 1:96
*ATOMIC: 1.25X TO 3X HI COLUMN
ATOMIC STATED ODDS 1:192

		MINT	NRMT
❑ M1	Alex Rodriguez	8.00	3.60
	Alex Gonzalez		
❑ M2	Ken Griffey Jr.	12.00	5.50
	Ruben Mateo		
❑ M3	Derek Jeter	20.00	9.00
	Alfonso Soriano		
❑ M4	Sammy Sosa	20.00	9.00
	Corey Patterson		
❑ M5	Greg Maddux	6.00	2.70
	Bruce Chen		
❑ M6	Chipper Jones	6.00	2.70
	Eric Chavez		
❑ M7	Vladimir Guerrero	3.00	1.35
	Carlos Beltran		
❑ M8	Frank Thomas	10.00	4.50
	Nick Johnson		
❑ M9	Nomar Garciaparra	8.00	3.60
	Pablo Ozuna		
❑ M10	Mark McGwire	20.00	9.00
	Pat Burrell		

1999 Bowman's Best Rookie Locker Room Autographs

	MINT	NRMT
COMPLETE SET (5)	150.00	70.00
COMMON CARD (RA1-RA5)	20.00	9.00

STATED ODDS 1:248

		MINT	NRMT
❑ RA1	Pat Burrell	60.00	27.00
❑ RA2	Michael Barrett	20.00	9.00
❑ RA3	Troy Glaus	30.00	13.50
❑ RA4	Gabe Kapler	25.00	11.00
❑ RA5	Eric Chavez	20.00	9.00

1999 Bowman's Best Rookie Locker Room Game Used Bats

	MINT	NRMT
COMPLETE SET (6)	300.00	135.00
COMMON CARD (RB1-RB6)	30.00	13.50

STATED ODDS 1:517

			MINT	NRMT
❑ RB1	Pat Burrell		100.00	45.00
❑ RB2	Michael Barrett		30.00	13.50
❑ RB3	Troy Glaus		50.00	22.00
❑ RB4	Gabe Kapler		40.00	18.00
❑ RB5	Eric Chavez		30.00	13.50
❑ RB6	Richie Sexson		50.00	22.00

1999 Bowman's Best Rookie Locker Room Game Worn Jerseys

			MINT	NRMT
COMPLETE SET (4)			200.00	90.00
COMMON CARD (1-4)			40.00	18.00
STATED ODDS 1:538				
❑ RJ1	Richie Sexson		60.00	27.00
❑ RJ2	Michael Barrett		40.00	18.00
❑ RJ3	Troy Glaus		60.00	27.00
❑ RJ4	Eric Chavez		40.00	18.00

1999 Bowman's Best Rookie of the Year

	MINT	NRMT
COMPLETE SET (2)	8.00	3.60
COMMON CARD (ROY1-ROY2)	4.00	1.80
STATED ODDS 1:95		
GRIEVE AU STATED ODDS 1:1239		

❑ ROY1	Ben Grieve	4.00	1.80
❑ ROY2	Kerry Wood	4.00	1.80
❑ ROY1A	Ben Grieve AU	40.00	18.00

1996 Circa

	MINT	NRMT
COMPLETE SET (200)	25.00	11.00
COMMON CARD (1-200)	.05	
MINOR STARS	.15	.07
UNLISTED STARS	.40	.18
SUBSET CARDS HALF VALUE OF BASE CARDS		

❑ 1	Roberto Alomar	.40	.18
❑ 2	Brady Anderson	.15	.07
❑ 3	Rocky Coppinger	.40	.18
❑ 4	Eddie Murray	.40	.18
❑ 5	Mike Mussina	.40	.18
❑ 6	Randy Myers	.10	.05
❑ 7	Rafael Palmeiro	.40	.18
❑ 8	Cal Ripken	1.50	.70
❑ 9	Jose Canseco	.50	.23
❑ 10	Roger Clemens	1.00	.45
❑ 11	Mike Greenwell	.10	.05
❑ 12	Tim Naehring	.10	.05
❑ 13	John Valentin	.15	.07
❑ 14	Mo Vaughn	.40	.18
❑ 15	Tim Wakefield	.15	.07
❑ 16	Jim Abbott	.15	.07
❑ 17	Garret Anderson	.40	.18
❑ 18	Jim Edmonds	.40	.18
❑ 19	Darin Erstad	3.00	1.35
❑ 20	Chuck Finley	.15	.07
❑ 21	Troy Percival	.40	.18
❑ 22	Tim Salmon	.40	.18
❑ 23	J.T. Snow	.15	.07
❑ 24	Wilson Alvarez	.10	.05
❑ 25	Harold Baines	.15	.07
❑ 26	Ray Durham	.10	.05
❑ 27	Alex Fernandez	.10	.05
❑ 28	Tony Phillips	.10	.05
❑ 29	Frank Thomas	.75	.35
❑ 30	Robin Ventura	.15	.07
❑ 31	Sandy Alomar Jr.	.15	.07
❑ 32	Albert Belle	.40	.18
❑ 33	Kenny Lofton	.40	.18
❑ 34	Dennis Martinez	.15	.07
❑ 35	Jose Mesa	.10	.05
❑ 36	Charles Nagy	.15	.07
❑ 37	Manny Ramirez	.50	.23
❑ 38	Jim Thome	.40	.18
❑ 39	Travis Fryman	.15	.07
❑ 40	Bob Higginson	.15	.07
❑ 41	Melvin Nieves	.10	.05
❑ 42	Alan Trammell	.40	.18
❑ 43	Kevin Appier	.15	.07
❑ 44	Johnny Damon	.40	.18
❑ 45	Keith Lockhart	.10	.05
❑ 46	Jeff Montgomery	.10	.05
❑ 47	Joe Randa	.10	.05
❑ 48	Bip Roberts	.10	.05
❑ 49	Ricky Bones	.10	.05
❑ 50	Jeff Cirillo	.15	.07
❑ 51	Marc Newfield	.10	.05
❑ 52	Dave Nilsson	.15	.07
❑ 53	Kevin Seitzer	.10	.05
❑ 54	Ron Coomer	.10	.05

❑ 55	Marty Cordova	.10	.05
❑ 56	Roberto Kelly	.10	.05
❑ 57	Chuck Knoblauch	.40	.18
❑ 58	Paul Molitor	.40	.18
❑ 59	Kirby Puckett	.60	.25
❑ 60	Scott Stahoviak	.10	.05
❑ 61	Wade Boggs	.40	.18
❑ 62	David Cone	.40	.18
❑ 63	Cecil Fielder	.15	.07
❑ 64	Dwight Gooden	.15	.07
❑ 65	Derek Jeter	1.25	.55
❑ 66	Tino Martinez	.15	.07
❑ 67	Paul O'Neill	.15	.07
❑ 68	Andy Pettitte	.40	.18
❑ 69	Ruben Rivera	.15	.07
❑ 70	Bernie Williams	.40	.18
❑ 71	Geronimo Berroa	.10	.05
❑ 72	Jason Giambi	.15	.07
❑ 73	Mark McGwire	2.00	.90
❑ 74	Terry Steinbach	.10	.05
❑ 75	Todd Van Poppel	.10	.05
❑ 76	Jay Buhner	.15	.07
❑ 77	Norm Charlton	.10	.05
❑ 78	Ken Griffey Jr.	2.00	.90
❑ 79	Randy Johnson	.40	.18
❑ 80	Edgar Martinez	.15	.07
❑ 81	Alex Rodriguez	1.25	.55
❑ 82	Paul Sorrento	.10	.05
❑ 83	Dan Wilson	.10	.05
❑ 84	Will Clark	.40	.18
❑ 85	Kevin Elster	.10	.05
❑ 86	Juan Gonzalez	.75	.35
❑ 87	Rusty Greer	.15	.07
❑ 88	Ken Hill	.10	.05
❑ 89	Mark McLemore	.10	.05
❑ 90	Dean Palmer	.15	.07
❑ 91	Roger Pavlik	.10	.05
❑ 92	Ivan Rodriguez	.50	.23
❑ 93	Joe Carter	.15	.07
❑ 94	Carlos Delgado	.40	.18
❑ 95	Juan Guzman	.10	.05
❑ 96	John Olerud	.15	.07
❑ 97	Ed Sprague	.10	.05
❑ 98	Jermaine Dye	.15	.07
❑ 99	Tom Glavine	.40	.18
❑ 100	Marquis Grissom	.10	.05
❑ 101	Andruw Jones	1.00	.45
❑ 102	Chipper Jones	1.00	.45
❑ 103	David Justice	.40	.18
❑ 104	Ryan Klesko	.15	.07
❑ 105	Greg Maddux	1.00	.45
❑ 106	Fred McGriff	.40	.18
❑ 107	John Smoltz	.40	.18
❑ 108	Brant Brown	.15	.07
❑ 109	Mark Grace	.40	.18
❑ 110	Brian McRae	.10	.05
❑ 111	Ryne Sandberg	.50	.23
❑ 112	Sammy Sosa	1.25	.55
❑ 113	Steve Trachsel	.10	.05
❑ 114	Bret Boone	.15	.07
❑ 115	Eric Davis	.15	.07
❑ 116	Steve Gibralter	.10	.05
❑ 117	Barry Larkin	.40	.18
❑ 118	Reggie Sanders	.15	.07
❑ 119	John Smiley	.10	.05
❑ 120	Dante Bichette	.15	.07
❑ 121	Ellis Burks	.15	.07
❑ 122	Vinny Castilla	.40	.18
❑ 123	Andres Galarraga	.40	.18
❑ 124	Larry Walker	.40	.18
❑ 125	Eric Young	.10	.05
❑ 126	Kevin Brown	.40	.18
❑ 127	Greg Colbrunn	.15	.07
❑ 128	Jeff Conine	.15	.07
❑ 129	Charles Johnson	.15	.07
❑ 130	Al Leiter	.15	.07
❑ 131	Gary Sheffield	.15	.07
❑ 132	Devon White	.15	.07
❑ 133	Jeff Bagwell	.50	.23
❑ 134	Derek Bell	.15	.07
❑ 135	Craig Biggio	.40	.18
❑ 136	Doug Drabek	.10	.05
❑ 137	Brian L.Hunter	.15	.07
❑ 138	Darryl Kile	.15	.07
❑ 139	Shane Reynolds	.10	.05
❑ 140	Brett Butler	.15	.07

		MINT	NRMT
❑ 141	Eric Karros	.15	.07
❑ 142	Ramon Martinez	.15	.07
❑ 143	Raul Mondesi	.15	.07
❑ 144	Hideo Nomo	.40	.18
❑ 145	Chan Ho Park	.40	.18
❑ 146	Mike Piazza	1.25	.55
❑ 147	Moises Alou	.15	.07
❑ 148	Yamil Benitez	.10	.05
❑ 149	Mark Grudzielanek	.10	.05
❑ 150	Pedro Martinez	.50	.23
❑ 151	Henry Rodriguez	.15	.07
❑ 152	David Segui	.15	.07
❑ 153	Rondell White	.15	.07
❑ 154	Carlos Baerga	.10	.05
❑ 155	John Franco	.15	.07
❑ 156	Bernard Gilkey	.10	.05
❑ 157	Todd Hundley	.15	.07
❑ 158	Jason Isringhausen	.15	.07
❑ 159	Lance Johnson	.10	.05
❑ 160	Alex Ochoa	.10	.05
❑ 161	Rey Ordonez	.40	.18
❑ 162	Paul Wilson	.10	.05
❑ 163	Ron Blazier	.10	.05
❑ 164	Ricky Bottalico	.10	.05
❑ 165	Jim Eisenreich	.10	.05
❑ 166	Pete Incaviglia	.10	.05
❑ 167	Mickey Morandini	.10	.05
❑ 168	Ricky Otero	.10	.05
❑ 169	Curt Schilling	.40	.18
❑ 170	Jay Bell	.15	.07
❑ 171	Charlie Hayes	.10	.05
❑ 172	Jason Kendall	.40	.18
❑ 173	Jeff King	.10	.05
❑ 174	Al Martin	.10	.05
❑ 175	Alan Benes	.10	.05
❑ 176	Royce Clayton	.10	.05
❑ 177	Brian Jordan	.15	.07
❑ 178	Ray Lankford	.15	.07
❑ 179	John Mabry	.10	.05
❑ 180	Willie McGee	.15	.07
❑ 181	Ozzie Smith	.50	.23
❑ 182	Todd Stottlemyre	.10	.05
❑ 183	Andy Ashby	.10	.05
❑ 184	Ken Caminiti	.15	.07
❑ 185	Steve Finley	.15	.07
❑ 186	Tony Gwynn	1.00	.45
❑ 187	Rickey Henderson	.50	.23
❑ 188	Wally Joyner	.15	.07
❑ 189	Fernando Valenzuela	.15	.07
❑ 190	Greg Vaughn	.15	.07
❑ 191	Rod Beck	.10	.05
❑ 192	Barry Bonds	.50	.23
❑ 193	Shawon Dunston	.10	.05
❑ 194	Chris Singleton	2.50	1.10
❑ 195	Robby Thompson	.10	.05
❑ 196	Matt Williams	.40	.18
❑ 197	Barry Bonds CL	.40	.18
❑ 198	Ken Griffey Jr. CL	1.00	.45
❑ 199	Cal Ripken CL	.75	.35
❑ 200	Frank Thomas CL	1.25	.55

1996 Circa Rave

	MINT	NRMT
COMMON CARD (1-200)	6.00	2.70

*STARS: 25X TO 60X BASIC CARDS
*YOUNG STARS: 20X TO 50X BASIC CARDS
*ROOKIES: 6X TO 15X BASIC CARDS

STATED ODDS 1:60
STATED PRINT RUN 150 SERIAL #'d SETS

1996 Circa Access

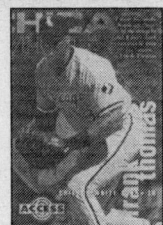

		MINT	NRMT
COMPLETE SET (30)		120.00	55.00
COMMON CARD (1-200)		2.00	.90

STATED ODDS 1:12

		MINT	NRMT
❑ 1	Cal Ripken	15.00	6.75
❑ 2	Mo Vaughn	4.00	1.80
❑ 3	Tim Salmon	3.00	1.35
❑ 4	Frank Thomas	8.00	3.60
❑ 5	Albert Belle	4.00	1.80
❑ 6	Kenny Lofton	3.00	1.35
❑ 7	Manny Ramirez	5.00	2.20
❑ 8	Paul Molitor	4.00	1.80
❑ 9	Kirby Puckett	6.00	2.70
❑ 10	Paul O'Neill	2.00	.90
❑ 11	Mark McGwire	20.00	9.00
❑ 12	Ken Griffey Jr.	20.00	9.00
❑ 13	Randy Johnson	4.00	1.80
❑ 14	Greg Maddux	10.00	4.50
❑ 15	John Smoltz	3.00	1.35
❑ 16	Sammy Sosa	12.00	5.50
❑ 17	Barry Larkin	4.00	1.80
❑ 18	Gary Sheffield	2.00	.90
❑ 19	Jeff Bagwell	5.00	2.20
❑ 20	Hideo Nomo	4.00	1.80
❑ 21	Mike Piazza	12.00	5.50
❑ 22	Moises Alou	2.00	.90
❑ 23	Henry Rodriguez	2.00	.90
❑ 24	Rey Ordonez	4.00	1.80
❑ 25	Jay Bell	2.00	.90
❑ 26	Ozzie Smith	5.00	2.20
❑ 27	Tony Gwynn	10.00	4.50
❑ 28	Rickey Henderson	5.00	2.20
❑ 29	Barry Bonds	5.00	2.20
❑ 30	Matt Williams	4.00	1.80
❑ P30	Matt Williams	1.00	.45
	Promo		

1996 Circa Boss

	MINT	NRMT
COMPLETE SET (50)	100.00	45.00

STATED ODDS 1:6

		MINT	NRMT
❑ 1	Roberto Alomar	3.00	1.35
❑ 2	Cal Ripken	12.00	5.50
❑ 3	Jose Canseco	4.00	1.80
❑ 4	Mo Vaughn	3.00	1.35
❑ 5	Tim Salmon	2.00	.90
❑ 6	Frank Thomas	6.00	2.70
❑ 7	Robin Ventura	1.50	.70
❑ 8	Albert Belle	3.00	1.35
❑ 9	Kenny Lofton	2.00	.90
❑ 10	Manny Ramirez	4.00	1.80
❑ 11	Dave Nilsson	1.00	.45
❑ 12	Chuck Knoblauch	3.00	1.35
❑ 13	Paul Molitor	3.00	1.35
❑ 14	Kirby Puckett	5.00	2.20
❑ 15	Wade Boggs	3.00	1.35
❑ 16	Dwight Gooden	1.50	.70
❑ 17	Paul O'Neill	1.50	.70
❑ 18	Mark McGwire	15.00	6.75
❑ 19	Jay Buhner	1.50	.70
❑ 20	Ken Griffey Jr.	15.00	6.75
❑ 21	Randy Johnson	3.00	1.35
❑ 22	Will Clark	3.00	1.35
❑ 23	Juan Gonzalez	6.00	2.70
❑ 24	Joe Carter	1.50	.70
❑ 25	Tom Glavine	3.00	1.35
❑ 26	Ryan Klesko	1.50	.70
❑ 27	Greg Maddux	8.00	3.60
❑ 28	John Smoltz	2.00	.90
❑ 29	Ryne Sandberg	4.00	1.80
❑ 30	Sammy Sosa	10.00	4.50
❑ 31	Barry Larkin	3.00	1.35
❑ 32	Reggie Sanders	1.50	.70
❑ 33	Dante Bichette	1.50	.70
❑ 34	Andres Galarraga	3.00	1.35
❑ 35	Charles Johnson	1.50	.70
❑ 36	Gary Sheffield	1.50	.70
❑ 37	Jeff Bagwell	4.00	1.80
❑ 38	Hideo Nomo	3.00	1.35
❑ 39	Mike Piazza	10.00	4.50
❑ 40	Moises Alou	1.50	.70
❑ 41	Henry Rodriguez	1.50	.70
❑ 42	Rey Ordonez	3.00	1.35
❑ 43	Ricky Otero	1.00	.45
❑ 44	Jay Bell	1.50	.70
❑ 45	Royce Clayton	1.00	.45
❑ 46	Ozzie Smith	3.00	1.35
❑ 47	Tony Gwynn	8.00	3.60
❑ 48	Rickey Henderson	4.00	1.80
❑ 49	Barry Bonds	3.00	1.35
❑ 50	Matt Williams	3.00	1.35
❑ P2	Cal Ripken	2.00	.90
	Promo		

1997 Circa

	MINT	NRMT
COMPLETE SET (400)	25.00	11.00
COMMON CARD (1-400)	.10	.05
MINOR STARS	.25	.11
UNLISTED STARS	.40	.18
SUBSET CARDS HALF VALUE OF BASE CARDS		

		MINT	NRMT
❑ 1	Kenny Lofton	.30	.14
❑ 2	Ray Durham	.25	.11
❑ 3	Mariano Rivera	.25	.11
❑ 4	Jon Lieber	.10	.05
❑ 5	Tim Salmon	.40	.18
❑ 6	Mark Grudzielanek	.25	.11

7	Neifi Perez	.25	.11
8	Cal Ripken	2.00	.90
9	John Olerud	.25	.11
10	Edgar Renteria	.25	.11
11	Jose Rosado	.10	.05
12	Mickey Morandini	.10	.05
13	Orlando Miller	.10	.05
14	Ben McDonald	.10	.05
15	Hideo Nomo	.40	.18
16	Fred McGriff	.30	.14
17	Sean Berry	.05	.05
18	Roger Pavlik	.10	.05
19	Aaron Sele	.25	.11
20	Joey Hamilton	.25	.11
21	Roger Clemens	1.00	.45
22	Jose Herrera	.10	.05
23	Ryne Sandberg	.50	.23
24	Ken Griffey Jr.	2.00	.90
25	Barry Bonds	.50	.23
26	Dan Naulty	.10	.05
27	Wade Boggs	.40	.18
28	Ray Lankford	.25	.11
29	Rico Brogna	.10	.05
30	Wally Joyner	.25	.11
31	F.P. Santangelo	.10	.05
32	Vinny Castilla	.30	.14
33	Eddie Murray	.40	.18
34	Kevin Elster	.10	.05
35	Mike Macfarlane	.10	.05
36	Jeff Kent	.25	.11
37	Orlando Merced	.10	.05
38	Jason Isringhausen	.10	.05
39	Chad Ogea	.10	.05
40	Greg Gagne	.10	.05
41	Curt Lyons	.10	.05
42	Mo Vaughn	.40	.18
43	Rusty Greer	.10	.05
44	Shane Reynolds	.25	.11
45	Frank Thomas	.75	.35
46	Chris Hoiles	.10	.05
47	Scott Sanders	.10	.05
48	Mark Lemke	.10	.05
49	Fernando Vina	.10	.05
50	Mark McGwire	2.00	.90
51	Bernie Williams	.40	.18
52	Bobby Higginson	.25	.11
53	Kevin Tapani	.10	.05
54	Rich Becker	.10	.05
55	Felix Heredia	.25	.11
56	Delino DeShields	.10	.05
57	Rick Wilkins	.10	.05
58	Edgardo Alfonzo	.30	.14
59	Brett Butler	.25	.11
60	Ed Sprague	.10	.05
61	Joe Randa	.10	.05
62	Ugueth Urbina	.25	.11
63	Todd Greene	.10	.05
64	Devon White	.10	.05
65	Bruce Ruffin	.10	.05
66	Mark Gardner	.10	.05
67	Omar Vizquel	.25	.11
68	Luis Gonzalez	.25	.11
69	Tom Glavine	.40	.18
70	Cal Eldred	.10	.05
71	Wm. VanLandingham	.10	.05
72	Jay Buhner	.25	.11
73	James Baldwin	.25	.11
74	Robin Jennings	.10	.05
75	Terry Steinbach	.10	.05
76	Billy Taylor	.10	.05
77	Armando Benitez	.10	.05
78	Joe Girardi	.10	.05
79	Jay Bell	.25	.11
80	Damon Buford	.10	.05
81	Deion Sanders	.25	.11
82	Bill Haselman	.10	.05
83	John Flaherty	.10	.05
84	Todd Stottlemyre	.10	.05
85	J.T. Snow	.25	.11
86	Felipe Lira	.10	.05
87	Steve Avery	.10	.05
88	Trey Beamon	.10	.05
89	Alex Gonzalez	.10	.05
90	Mark Clark	.10	.05
91	Shane Andrews	.10	.05
92	Randy Myers	.10	.05
93	Gary Gaetti	.25	.11
94	Jeff Blauser	.10	.05
95	Tony Batista	.30	.14
96	Todd Worrell	.10	.05
97	Jim Edmonds	.30	.14
98	Eric Young	.25	.11
99	Roberto Kelly	.10	.05
100	Alex Rodriguez	1.25	.55
101	Julio Franco	.25	.11
102	Jeff Bagwell	.50	.23
103	Bobby Witt	.10	.05
104	Tino Martinez	.40	.18
105	Shannon Stewart	.25	.11
106	Brian Banks	.10	.05
107	Eddie Taubensee	.10	.05
108	Terry Mulholland	.10	.05
109	Lyle Mouton	.10	.05
110	Jeff Conine	.10	.05
111	Johnny Damon	.25	.11
112	Quilvio Veras	.10	.05
113	Wilton Guerrero	.10	.05
114	Dmitri Young	.10	.05
115	Garret Anderson	.25	.11
116	Bill Pulsipher	.10	.05
117	Jacob Brumfield	.10	.05
118	Mike Lansing	.10	.05
119	Jose Canseco	.50	.23
120	Mike Bordick	.10	.05
121	Kevin Stocker	.10	.05
122	Frankie Rodriguez	.10	.05
123	Mike Cameron	.25	.11
124	Tony Womack	.50	.23
125	Bret Boone	.25	.11
126	Moises Alou	.25	.11
127	Tim Naehring	.10	.05
128	Brant Brown	.25	.11
129	Todd Zeile	.10	.05
130	Dave Nilsson	.10	.05
131	Donne Wall	.10	.05
132	Jose Mesa	.10	.05
133	Mark McLemore	.10	.05
134	Mike Stanton	.10	.05
135	Dan Wilson	.10	.05
136	Jose Offerman	.25	.11
137	David Justice	.40	.18
138	Kirt Manwaring	.10	.05
139	Raul Casanova	.10	.05
140	Ron Coomer	.10	.05
141	Dave Hollins	.10	.05
142	Shawn Estes	.25	.11
143	Darren Daulton	.25	.11
144	Turk Wendell	.10	.05
145	Darrin Fletcher	.10	.05
146	Marquis Grissom	.25	.11
147	Andy Benes	.25	.11
148	Nomar Garciaparra	1.25	.55
149	Andy Pettitte	.30	.14
150	Tony Gwynn	1.00	.45
151	Robb Nen	.10	.05
152	Kevin Seitzer	.10	.05
153	Ariel Prieto	.10	.05
154	Scott Karl	.10	.05
155	Carlos Baerga	.10	.05
156	Wilson Alvarez	.25	.11
157	Thomas Howard	.10	.05
158	Kevin Appier	.25	.11
159	Russ Davis	.25	.11
160	Justin Thompson	.25	.11
161	Pete Schourek	.10	.05
162	John Burkett	.10	.05
163	Roberto Alomar	.40	.18
164	Darren Holmes	.10	.05
165	Travis Miller	.10	.05
166	Mark Langston	.25	.11
167	Juan Guzman	.10	.05
168	Pedro Astacio	.10	.05
169	Mark Johnson	.10	.05
170	Mark Leiter	.10	.05
171	Heathcliff Slocumb	.10	.05
172	Dante Bichette	.25	.11
173	Brian Giles	1.25	.55
174	Paul Wilson	.10	.05
175	Eric Davis	.25	.11
176	Charles Johnson	.25	.11
177	Willie Greene	.10	.05
178	Geronimo Berroa	.10	.05
179	Mariano Duncan	.10	.05
180	Robert Person	.10	.05
181	David Segui	.25	.11
182	Ozzie Guillen	.10	.05
183	Osvaldo Fernandez	.10	.05
184	Dean Palmer	.25	.11
185	Bob Wickman	.10	.05
186	Eric Karros	.25	.11
187	Travis Fryman	.25	.11
188	Andy Ashby	.10	.05
189	Scott Stahoviak	.10	.05
190	Norm Charlton	.10	.05
191	Craig Paquette	.10	.05
192	John Smoltz UER	.25	.11
	Name spelled "Smoltz" on back		
193	Orel Hershiser	.25	.11
194	Glenallen Hill	.10	.05
195	George Arias	.10	.05
196	Brian Jordan	.25	.11
197	Greg Vaughn	.25	.11
198	Rafael Palmeiro	.40	.18
199	Darryl Kile	.10	.05
200	Derek Jeter	1.25	.55
201	Jose Vizcaino	.10	.05
202	Rick Aguilera	.10	.05
203	Jason Schmidt	.10	.05
204	Trot Nixon	.25	.11
205	Tom Pagnozzi	.10	.05
206	Mark Wohlers	.10	.05
207	Lance Johnson	.10	.05
208	Carlos Delgado	.40	.18
209	Cliff Floyd	.25	.11
210	Kent Mercker	.10	.05
211	Matt Mieske	.10	.05
212	Ismael Valdes	.25	.11
213	Shawon Dunston	.10	.05
214	Melvin Nieves	.10	.05
215	Tony Phillips	.10	.05
216	Scott Spiezio	.10	.05
217	Michael Tucker	.10	.05
218	Matt Williams	.40	.18
219	Ricky Otero	.10	.05
220	Kevin Ritz	.10	.05
221	Darryl Strawberry	.25	.11
222	Troy Percival	.25	.11
223	Eugene Kingsale	.10	.05
224	Julian Tavarez	.10	.05
225	Jermaine Dye	.25	.11
226	Jason Kendall	.30	.14
227	Sterling Hitchcock	.25	.11
228	Jeff Cirillo	.25	.11
229	Roberto Hernandez	.10	.05
230	Ricky Bottalico	.10	.05
231	Bobby Bonilla	.25	.11
232	Edgar Martinez	.25	.11
233	John Valentin	.25	.11
234	Ellis Burks	.25	.11
235	Benito Santiago	.10	.05
236	Terrell Wade	.10	.05
237	Armando Reynoso	.10	.05
238	Danny Graves	.10	.05
239	Ken Hill	.10	.05
240	Dennis Eckersley	.25	.11
241	Darin Erstad	.40	.18
242	Lee Smith UER	.25	.11
	(Position 2b)		
243	Cecil Fielder	.25	.11
244	Tony Clark	.30	.14
245	Scott Erickson	.25	.11
246	Bob Abreu	.25	.11
247	Ruben Sierra	.10	.05
248	Chili Davis	.10	.05
249	Darryl Hamilton	.10	.05
250	Albert Belle	.40	.18
251	Todd Hollandsworth	.10	.05
252	Terry Adams	.10	.05
253	Rey Ordonez	.25	.11
254	Steve Finley	.25	.11
255	Jose Valentin	.10	.05
256	Royce Clayton	.10	.05
257	Sandy Alomar	.25	.11
258	Mike Lieberthal	.10	.05
259	Ivan Rodriguez	.50	.23
260	Rod Beck	.10	.05
261	Ron Karkovice	.10	.05
262	Mark Gubicza	.10	.05

❑ 263 Chris Holt	.10	.05
❑ 264 Jaime Bluma UER	.10	.05

Name spelled "Jamie" on front and back

❑ 265 Francisco Cordova	.10	.05
❑ 266 Javy Lopez	.25	.11
❑ 267 Reggie Jefferson	.10	.05
❑ 268 Kevin Brown	.30	.14
❑ 269 Scott Brosius	.10	.05
❑ 270 Dwight Gooden	.25	.11
❑ 271 Marty Cordova	.10	.05
❑ 272 Jeff Brantley	.10	.05
❑ 273 Joe Carter	.25	.11
❑ 274 Todd Jones	.10	.05
❑ 275 Sammy Sosa	1.25	.55
❑ 276 Randy Johnson	.40	.18
❑ 277 B.J. Surhoff	.10	.05
❑ 278 Chan Ho Park	.40	.18
❑ 279 Jamey Wright	.10	.05
❑ 280 Manny Ramirez	.50	.23
❑ 281 John Franco	.25	.11
❑ 282 Tim Worrell	.10	.05
❑ 283 Scott Rolen	.60	.25
❑ 284 Reggie Sanders	.25	.11
❑ 285 Mike Fetters	.10	.05
❑ 286 Tim Wakefield	.25	.11
❑ 287 Trevor Hoffman	.25	.11
❑ 288 Donovan Osborne	.10	.05
❑ 289 Phil Nevin	.10	.05
❑ 290 Jermaine Allensworth	.10	.05
❑ 291 Rocky Coppinger	.10	.05
❑ 292 Tim Raines	.25	.11
❑ 293 Henry Rodriguez	.25	.11
❑ 294 Paul Sorrento	.10	.05
❑ 295 Tom Goodwin	.10	.05
❑ 296 Raul Mondesi	.25	.11
❑ 297 Allen Watson	.10	.05
❑ 298 Derek Bell	.25	.11
❑ 299 Gary Sheffield	.25	.11
❑ 300 Paul Molitor	.25	.11
❑ 301 Shawn Green	.40	.18
❑ 302 Darren Oliver	.10	.05
❑ 303 Jack McDowell	.10	.05
❑ 304 Denny Neagle	.25	.11
❑ 305 Doug Drabek	.10	.05
❑ 306 Mel Rojas	.10	.05
❑ 307 Andres Galarraga	.40	.18
❑ 308 Alex Ochoa	.10	.05
❑ 309 Gary DiSarcina	.10	.05
❑ 310 Ron Gant	.25	.11
❑ 311 Gregg Jefferies	.10	.05
❑ 312 Ruben Rivera	.10	.05
❑ 313 Vladimir Guerrero	.60	.25
❑ 314 Willie Adams	.10	.05
❑ 315 Bip Roberts	.10	.05
❑ 316 Mark Grace	.30	.14
❑ 317 Bernard Gilkey	.10	.05
❑ 318 Marc Newfield	.10	.05
❑ 319 Al Leiter	.25	.11
❑ 320 Otis Nixon	.10	.05
❑ 321 Tom Candiotti	.10	.05
❑ 322 Mike Stanley	.10	.05
❑ 323 Jeff Fassero	.10	.05
❑ 324 Billy Wagner	.25	.11
❑ 325 Todd Walker	.40	.18
❑ 326 Chad Curtis	.10	.05
❑ 327 Quinton McCracken	.10	.05
❑ 328 Will Clark	.40	.18
❑ 329 Andruw Jones	.50	.23
❑ 330 Robin Ventura	.25	.11
❑ 331 Curtis Pride	.10	.05
❑ 332 Barry Larkin	.40	.18
❑ 333 Jimmy Key	.25	.11
❑ 334 David Wells	.25	.11
❑ 335 Mike Holtz	.10	.05
❑ 336 Paul Wagner	.10	.05
❑ 337 Greg Maddux	1.00	.45
❑ 338 Curt Schilling	.30	.14
❑ 339 Steve Trachsel	.10	.05
❑ 340 John Wetteland	.25	.11
❑ 341 Rickey Henderson	.50	.23
❑ 342 Ernie Young	.10	.05
❑ 343 Harold Baines	.25	.11
❑ 344 Bobby Jones	.10	.05
❑ 345 Jeff D'Amico	.10	.05
❑ 346 John Mabry	.10	.05

❑ 347 Pedro Martinez	.50	.23
❑ 348 Mark Lewis	.10	.05
❑ 349 Dan Miceli	.10	.05
❑ 350 Chuck Knoblauch	.40	.18
❑ 351 John Smiley	.10	.05
❑ 352 Brady Anderson	.25	.11
❑ 353 Jim Leyritz	.10	.05
❑ 354 Al Martin	.10	.05
❑ 355 Pat Hentgen	.25	.11
❑ 356 Mike Piazza	1.25	.55
❑ 357 Charles Nagy	.25	.11
❑ 358 Luis Castillo	.25	.11
❑ 359 Paul O'Neill	.25	.11
❑ 360 Steve Reed	.10	.05
❑ 361 Tom Gordon	.10	.05
❑ 362 Craig Biggio	.40	.18
❑ 363 Jeff Montgomery	.10	.05
❑ 364 Jamie Moyer	.10	.05
❑ 365 Ryan Klesko	.25	.11
❑ 366 Todd Hundley	.25	.11
❑ 367 Bobby Estalella	.10	.05
❑ 368 Jason Giambi	.25	.11
❑ 369 Brian Hunter	.25	.11
❑ 370 Ramon Martinez	.25	.11
❑ 371 Carlos Garcia	.10	.05
❑ 372 Hal Morris	.10	.05
❑ 373 Juan Gonzalez	.75	.35
❑ 374 Brian McRae	.10	.05
❑ 375 Mike Mussina	.40	.18
❑ 376 John Ericks	.10	.05
❑ 377 Larry Walker	.25	.11
❑ 378 Chris Gomez	.10	.05
❑ 379 John Jaha	.10	.05
❑ 380 Rondell White	.25	.11
❑ 381 Chipper Jones	1.00	.45
❑ 382 David Cone	.30	.14
❑ 383 Alan Benes	.10	.05
❑ 384 Troy O'Leary	.25	.11
❑ 385 Ken Caminiti	.30	.14
❑ 386 Jeff King	.10	.05
❑ 387 Mike Hampton	.25	.11
❑ 388 Jaime Navarro	.10	.05
❑ 389 Brad Radke	.25	.11
❑ 390 Joey Cora	.10	.05
❑ 391 Jim Thome	.40	.18
❑ 392 Alex Fernandez	.25	.11
❑ 393 Chuck Finley	.25	.11
❑ 394 Andruw Jones CL	.30	.14
❑ 395 Ken Griffey Jr. CL	1.00	.45
❑ 396 Frank Thomas CL	.60	.25
❑ 397 Alex Rodriguez CL	.60	.25
❑ 398 Cal Ripken CL	.75	.35
❑ 399 Mike Piazza CL	.60	.25
❑ 400 Greg Maddux CL	.50	.23
❑ P100 Alex Rodriguez Promo	3.00	1.35

1997 Circa Rave

	MINT	NRMT
COMMON CARD (1-400)	6.00	2.70

*STARS: 25X TO 60X BASIC CARDS
*YOUNG STARS: 20X TO 50X BASIC CARDS
*ROOKIES: 12.5X TO 30X BASIC CARDS
STATED ODDS 1:30 HOBBY
STATED PRINT RUN 150 SERIAL #'d SETS

1997 Circa Boss

	MINT	NRMT
COMPLETE SET (20)	40.00	18.00
COMMON CARD (1-20)	.75	.35

STATED ODDS 1:6

COMP.SUPER BOSS SET (20)	150.00	70.00

*SUPER BOSS: 5X TO 12X BASE CARD HI
SUPER BOSS STATED ODDS 1:36

❑ 1 Jeff Bagwell	2.00	.90
❑ 2 Albert Belle	1.25	.55
❑ 3 Barry Bonds	1.50	.70
❑ 4 Ken Caminiti	.75	.35
❑ 5 Juan Gonzalez	2.50	1.10
❑ 6 Ken Griffey Jr.	6.00	2.70
❑ 7 Tony Gwynn	3.00	1.35
❑ 8 Derek Jeter	4.00	1.80
❑ 9 Andruw Jones	1.50	.70
❑ 10 Chipper Jones	3.00	1.35
❑ 11 Greg Maddux	3.00	1.35
❑ 12 Mark McGwire	6.00	2.70
❑ 13 Mike Piazza	4.00	1.80
❑ 14 Manny Ramirez	1.50	.70
❑ 15 Cal Ripken	5.00	2.20
❑ 16 Alex Rodriguez	4.00	1.80
❑ 17 John Smoltz	.75	.35
❑ 18 Frank Thomas	3.00	1.35
❑ 19 Mo Vaughn	1.25	.55
❑ 20 Bernie Williams	1.25	.55

1997 Circa Emerald Autographs

	MINT	NRMT
COMPLETE SET (6)	250.00	110.00
COMMON CARD	8.00	3.60

ONE CARD VIA MAIL PER AU RDMP.CARD
*EXCH CARDS: .1X TO .25X HI COLUMN
EXCH CARDS STATED ODDS 1:1000 PACKS

❑ 100 Alex Rodriguez AU	150.00	70.00
❑ 241 Darin Erstad AU	30.00	13.50
❑ 251 Todd Hollandsworth AU	8.00	3.60
❑ 283 Scott Rolen AU	60.00	27.00
❑ 308 Alex Ochoa AU	8.00	3.60
❑ 325 Todd Walker AU	15.00	6.75

1997 Circa Fast Track

	MINT	NRMT
COMPLETE SET (10)	40.00	18.00
COMMON CARD (1-10)	1.50	.70
STATED ODDS 1:24		

		MINT	NRMT
❏ 1	Vladimir Guerrero	3.00	1.35
❏ 2	Todd Hollandsworth	1.50	.70
❏ 3	Derek Jeter	8.00	3.60
❏ 4	Andruw Jones	4.00	1.80
❏ 5	Chipper Jones	8.00	3.60
❏ 6	Andy Pettitte	2.00	.90
❏ 7	Mariano Rivera	2.00	.90
❏ 8	Alex Rodriguez	10.00	4.50
❏ 9	Scott Rolen	6.00	2.70
❏ 10	Todd Walker	3.00	1.35

1997 Circa Icons

	MINT	NRMT
COMPLETE SET (12)	100.00	45.00
COMMON CARD (1-12)	4.00	1.80
STATED ODDS 1:36		

		MINT	NRMT
❏ 1	Juan Gonzalez	8.00	3.60
❏ 2	Ken Griffey Jr.	20.00	9.00
❏ 3	Tony Gwynn	10.00	4.50
❏ 4	Derek Jeter	10.00	4.50
❏ 5	Chipper Jones	10.00	4.50
❏ 6	Greg Maddux	10.00	4.50
❏ 7	Mark McGwire	20.00	9.00
❏ 8	Mike Piazza	12.00	5.50
❏ 9	Cal Ripken	15.00	6.75
❏ 10	Alex Rodriguez	12.00	5.50
❏ 11	Frank Thomas	8.00	3.60
❏ 12	Matt Williams	4.00	1.80

1997 Circa Limited Access

	MINT	NRMT
COMPLETE SET (15)	180.00	80.00
COMMON CARD (1-15)	6.00	2.70
STATED ODDS 1:18 RETAIL		

		MINT	NRMT
❏ 1	Jeff Bagwell	6.00	2.70
❏ 2	Albert Belle	6.00	2.70
❏ 3	Barry Bonds	6.00	2.70
❏ 4	Juan Gonzalez	10.00	4.50

		MINT	NRMT
❏ 5	Ken Griffey Jr.	25.00	11.00
❏ 6	Tony Gwynn	12.00	5.50
❏ 7	Derek Jeter	12.00	5.50
❏ 8	Chipper Jones	12.00	5.50
❏ 9	Greg Maddux	12.00	5.50
❏ 10	Mark McGwire	25.00	11.00
❏ 11	Mike Piazza	15.00	6.75
❏ 12	Cal Ripken	20.00	9.00
❏ 13	Alex Rodriguez	15.00	6.75
❏ 14	Frank Thomas	10.00	4.50
❏ 15	Mo Vaughn	6.00	2.70

1997 Circa Rave Reviews

	MINT	NRMT
COMPLETE SET (12)	400.00	180.00
COMMON CARD (1-12)	12.00	5.50
STATED ODDS 1:288		

		MINT	NRMT
❏ 1	Albert Belle	12.00	5.50
❏ 2	Barry Bonds	15.00	6.75
❏ 3	Juan Gonzalez	25.00	11.00
❏ 4	Ken Griffey Jr.	60.00	27.00
❏ 5	Tony Gwynn	30.00	13.50
❏ 6	Greg Maddux	30.00	13.50
❏ 7	Mark McGwire	60.00	27.00
❏ 8	Eddie Murray	12.00	5.50
❏ 9	Mike Piazza	40.00	18.00
❏ 10	Cal Ripken	50.00	22.00
❏ 11	Alex Rodriguez	50.00	22.00
❏ 12	Frank Thomas	25.00	11.00

1998 Circa Thunder

	MINT	NRMT
COMPLETE SET (300)	20.00	9.00
COMMON CARD (1-300)	.10	.05
MINOR STARS	.15	.07
SEMISTARS	.25	.11
UNLISTED STARS	.40	.18
CARD 280 DOES NOT EXIST		
RIPKEN AND GRISSOM NUMBERED 8		

		MINT	NRMT
❏ 1	Ben Grieve	.40	.18
❏ 2	Derek Jeter	1.25	.55
❏ 3	Alex Rodriguez	1.25	.55
❏ 4	Paul Molitor	.40	.18
❏ 5	Nomar Garciaparra	1.25	.55
❏ 6	Fred McGriff	.25	.11

		MINT	NRMT
❏ 7	Kenny Lofton	.25	.11
❏ 8	Cal Ripken	1.50	.70
❏ 9	Matt Williams	.40	.18
❏ 10	Chipper Jones	1.00	.45
❏ 11	Barry Larkin	.40	.18
❏ 12	Steve Finley	.15	.07
❏ 13	Billy Wagner	.15	.07
❏ 14	Rico Brogna	.10	.05
❏ 15	Tim Salmon	.25	.11
❏ 16	Hideo Nomo	.40	.18
❏ 17	Tony Clark	.15	.07
❏ 18	Jason Kendall	.15	.07
❏ 19	Juan Gonzalez	.75	.35
❏ 20	Jeromy Burnitz	.15	.07
❏ 21	Roger Clemens	1.00	.45
❏ 22	Mark Grace	.25	.11
❏ 23	Robin Ventura	.15	.07
❏ 24	Manny Ramirez	.50	.23
❏ 25	Mark McGwire	2.50	1.10
❏ 26	Gary Sheffield	.15	.07
❏ 27	Vladimir Guerrero	.50	.23
❏ 28	Butch Huskey	.10	.05
❏ 29	Cecil Fielder	.15	.07
❏ 30	Rod Myers	.10	.05
❏ 31	Greg Maddux	1.00	.45
❏ 32	Bill Mueller	.10	.05
❏ 33	Larry Walker	.40	.18
❏ 34	Henry Rodriguez	.15	.07
❏ 35	Mike Mussina	.40	.18
❏ 36	Ricky Ledee	.15	.07
❏ 37	Bobby Bonilla	.15	.07
❏ 38	Curt Schilling	.25	.11
❏ 39	Luis Gonzalez	.15	.07
❏ 40	Troy Percival	.15	.07
❏ 41	Eric Milton	.10	.05
❏ 42	Mo Vaughn	.40	.18
❏ 43	Raul Mondesi	.15	.07
❏ 44	Kenny Rogers	.10	.05
❏ 45	Frank Thomas	.75	.35
❏ 46	Jose Canseco	.50	.23
❏ 47	Tom Glavine	.40	.18
❏ 48	Scott Rolen	.25	.11
❏ 49	Jay Buhner	.15	.07
❏ 50	Jose Cruz Jr.	.15	.07
❏ 51	Bernie Williams	.40	.18
❏ 52	Doug Glanville	.15	.07
❏ 53	Travis Fryman	.15	.07
❏ 54	Rey Ordonez	.15	.07
❏ 55	Jeff Conine	.10	.05
❏ 56	Trevor Hoffman	.15	.07
❏ 57	Kirk Rueter	.10	.05
	UER back Reuter		
❏ 58	Ron Gant	.15	.07
❏ 59	Carl Everett	.15	.07
❏ 60	Joe Carter	.15	.07
❏ 61	Livan Hernandez	.10	.05
❏ 62	John Jaha	.10	.05
❏ 63	Ivan Rodriguez	.50	.23
❏ 64	Willie Blair	.10	.05
❏ 65	Todd Helton	.50	.23
❏ 66	Kevin Young	.15	.07
❏ 67	Mike Caruso	.10	.05
❏ 68	Steve Trachsel	.10	.05
❏ 69	Marty Cordova	.15	.07
❏ 70	Alex Fernandez	.10	.05
❏ 71	Eric Karros	.15	.07
❏ 72	Reggie Sanders	.10	.05
❏ 73	Russ Davis	.15	.07

❏ 74 Roberto Hernandez	.10	.05	❏ 160 Raul Casanova	.10	.05	❏ 246 Brad Radke	.15	.07
❏ 75 Barry Bonds	.50	.23	❏ 161 Pedro Astacio	.10	.05	❏ 247 Chan Ho Park	.15	.07
❏ 76 Alex Gonzalez	.10	.05	❏ 162 Todd Dunwoody	.10	.05	❏ 248 Lance Johnson	.10	.05
❏ 77 Roberto Alomar	.40	.18	❏ 163 Sammy Sosa	1.25	.55	❏ 249 Rafael Palmeiro	.40	.18
❏ 78 Troy O'Leary	.15	.07	❏ 164 Todd Hundley	.15	.07	❏ 250 Tony Gwynn	1.00	.45
❏ 79 Bernard Gilkey	.10	.05	❏ 165 Wade Boggs	.40	.18	❏ 251 Denny Neagle	.10	.05
❏ 80 Ismael Valdes	.10	.05	❏ 166 Robb Nen	.10	.05	❏ 252 Dean Palmer	.15	.07
❏ 81 Travis Lee	.25	.11	❏ 167 Dan Wilson	.10	.05	❏ 253 Jose Valentin	.10	.05
❏ 82 Brant Brown	.10	.05	❏ 168 Hideki Irabu	.15	.07	❏ 254 Matt Morris	.10	.05
❏ 83 Gary DiSarcina	.10	.05	❏ 169 B.J. Surhoff	.10	.05	❏ 255 Ellis Burks	.15	.07
❏ 84 Joe Randa	.10	.05	❏ 170 Carlos Delgado	.40	.18	❏ 256 Jeff Suppan	.10	.05
❏ 85 Jaret Wright	.15	.07	❏ 171 Fernando Tatis	.40	.18	❏ 257 Jimmy Key	.15	.07
❏ 86 Quilvio Veras	.10	.05	❏ 172 Bob Abreu	.15	.07	❏ 258 Justin Thompson	.10	.05
❏ 87 Rickey Henderson	.50	.23	❏ 173 David Ortiz	.10	.05	❏ 259 Brett Tomko	.10	.05
❏ 88 Randall Simon	.10	.05	❏ 174 Tony Womack	.10	.05	❏ 260 Mark Grudzielanek	.10	.05
❏ 89 Mariano Rivera	.15	.07	❏ 175 Magglio Ordonez	1.25	.55	❏ 261 Mike Hampton	.15	.07
❏ 90 Ugueth Urbina	.10	.05	❏ 176 Aaron Boone	.10	.05	❏ 262 Jeff Fassero	.10	.05
❏ 91 Fernando Vina	.10	.05	❏ 177 Brian Giles	.15	.07	❏ 263 Charles Nagy	.15	.07
❏ 92 Alan Benes	.10	.05	❏ 178 Kevin Appier	.15	.07	❏ 264 Pedro Martinez	.50	.23
❏ 93 Dante Bichette	.15	.07	❏ 179 Chuck Finley	.10	.05	❏ 265 Todd Zeile	.15	.07
❏ 94 Karim Garcia	.10	.05	❏ 180 Brian Rose	.10	.05	❏ 266 Will Clark	.40	.18
❏ 95 A.J. Hinch	.10	.05	❏ 181 Ryan Klesko	.15	.07	❏ 267 Abraham Nunez	.10	.05
❏ 96 Shane Reynolds	.15	.07	❏ 182 Mike Stanley	.10	.05	❏ 268 Dave Martinez	.10	.05
❏ 97 Kevin Stocker	.10	.05	❏ 183 Dave Nilsson	.10	.05	❏ 269 Jason Dickson	.10	.05
❏ 98 John Wetteland	.10	.07	❏ 184 Carlos Perez	.10	.05	❏ 270 Eric Davis	.15	.07
❏ 99 Terry Steinbach	.10	.05	❏ 185 Jeff Blauser	.10	.05	❏ 271 Kevin Orie	.10	.05
❏ 100 Ken Griffey Jr.	2.00	.90	❏ 186 Richard Hidalgo	.15	.07	❏ 272 Derrek Lee	.10	.05
❏ 101 Mike Cameron	.10	.05	❏ 187 Charles Johnson	.15	.07	❏ 273 Andruw Jones	.40	.18
❏ 102 Damion Easley	.15	.07	❏ 188 Vinny Castilla	.15	.07	❏ 274 Juan Encarnacion	.15	.07
❏ 103 Randy Myers	.15	.07	❏ 189 Joey Hamilton	.10	.05	❏ 275 Carlos Baerga	.15	.07
❏ 104 Jason Schmidt	.10	.05	❏ 190 Bubba Trammell	.10	.05	❏ 276 Andy Pettitte	.15	.07
❏ 105 Jeff King	.10	.05	❏ 191 Eli Marrero	.10	.05	❏ 277 Brent Brede	.10	.05
❏ 106 Gregg Jefferies	.15	.07	❏ 192 Scott Erickson	.10	.05	❏ 278 Paul Sorrento	.10	.05
❏ 107 Sean Casey	.60	.25	❏ 193 Pat Hentgen	.10	.05	❏ 279 Mike Lieberthal	.15	.07
❏ 108 Mark Kotsay	.15	.07	❏ 194 Jorge Fabregas	.10	.05	❏ 280 Marquis Grissom	.10	.05
❏ 109 Brad Fullmer	.10	.05	❏ 195 Tino Martinez	.15	.07	UER #'d 8 instead of 280		
❏ 110 Wilson Alvarez	.10	.05	❏ 196 Bobby Higginson	.15	.07	❏ 281 Darin Erstad	.25	.11
❏ 111 Sandy Alomar Jr.	.15	.07	❏ 197 Dave Hollins	.10	.05	❏ 282 Willie Greene	.10	.05
❏ 112 Walt Weiss	.10	.05	❏ 198 Rolando Arrojo	.40	.18	❏ 283 Derek Bell	.15	.07
❏ 113 Doug Jones	.10	.05	❏ 199 Joey Cora	.10	.05	❏ 284 Scott Spiezio	.10	.05
❏ 114 Andy Benes	.10	.05	❏ 200 Mike Piazza	1.25	.55	❏ 285 David Segui	.10	.05
❏ 115 Paul O'Neill	.15	.07	❏ 201 Reggie Jefferson	.10	.05	❏ 286 Albert Belle	.40	.18
❏ 116 Dennis Eckersley	.15	.07	❏ 202 John Smoltz	.25	.11	❏ 287 Ramon Martinez	.10	.05
❏ 117 Todd Greene	.10	.05	❏ 203 Bobby Smith	.10	.05	❏ 288 Jeremi Gonzalez	.10	.05
❏ 118 Bobby Jones	.10	.05	❏ 204 Tom Goodwin	.10	.05	❏ 289 Shawn Estes	.10	.05
❏ 119 Darrin Fletcher	.10	.05	❏ 205 Omar Vizquel	.15	.07	❏ 290 Ron Coomer	.10	.05
❏ 120 Eric Young	.10	.05	❏ 206 John Olerud	.15	.07	❏ 291 John Valentin	.15	.07
❏ 121 Jeffrey Hammonds	.10	.05	❏ 207 Matt Stairs	.15	.07	❏ 292 Kevin Brown	.25	.11
❏ 122 Mickey Morandini	.10	.05	❏ 208 Bobby Estalella	.10	.05	❏ 293 Michael Tucker	.10	.05
❏ 123 Chuck Knoblauch	.15	.07	❏ 209 Miguel Cairo	.10	.05	❏ 294 Brian Jordan	.15	.07
❏ 124 Moises Alou	.15	.07	❏ 210 Shawn Green	.40	.18	❏ 295 Darryl Kile	.10	.05
❏ 125 Miguel Tejada	.15	.07	❏ 211 Jon Nunnally	.10	.05	❏ 296 David Justice	.15	.07
❏ 126 Brian Anderson	.10	.05	❏ 212 Al Leiter	.15	.07	❏ 297 Frank Thomas CL	.60	.25
❏ 127 Edgar Renteria	.15	.07	❏ 213 Matt Lawton	.10	.05	❏ 298 Alex Rodriguez CL	.60	.25
❏ 128 Mike Lansing	.10	.05	❏ 214 Brady Anderson	.15	.07	❏ 299 Ken Griffey Jr. CL	1.00	.45
❏ 129 Quinton McCracken	.10	.05	❏ 215 Jeff Kent	.15	.07	❏ 300 Jose Cruz Jr. CL	.10	.05
❏ 130 Ray Lankford	.15	.07	❏ 216 Ray Durham	.15	.07	❏ P8 Cal Ripken Promo	3.00	1.35
❏ 131 Andy Ashby	.10	.05	❏ 217 Al Martin	.10	.05			
❏ 132 Kelvim Escobar	.10	.05	❏ 218 Jeff D'Amico	.10	.05			
❏ 133 Mike Lowell	.40	.18	❏ 219 Kevin Tapani	.10	.05			
❏ 134 Randy Johnson	.40	.18	❏ 220 Jim Edmonds	.15	.07			
❏ 135 Andres Galarraga	.25	.11	❏ 221 Jose Vizcaino	.10	.05			
❏ 136 Armando Benitez	.10	.05	❏ 222 Jay Bell	.15	.07			
❏ 137 Rusty Greer	.15	.07	❏ 223 Ken Caminiti	.15	.07			
❏ 138 Jose Guillen	.15	.07	❏ 224 Craig Biggio	.40	.18			
❏ 139 Paul Konerko	.15	.07	❏ 225 Bartolo Colon	.15	.07			
❏ 140 Edgardo Alfonzo	.25	.11	❏ 226 Neifi Perez	.10	.05			
❏ 141 Jim Leyritz	.10	.05	❏ 227 Delino DeShields	.10	.05			
❏ 142 Mark Clark	.10	.05	❏ 228 Javier Lopez	.15	.07			
❏ 143 Brian Johnson	.10	.05	❏ 229 David Wells	.15	.07			
❏ 144 Scott Rolen	.50	.23	❏ 230 Brad Rigby	.10	.05			
❏ 145 David Cone	.25	.11	❏ 231 John Franco	.10	.05			
❏ 146 Jeff Shaw	.10	.07	❏ 232 Michael Coleman	.15	.07			
❏ 147 Shannon Stewart	.15	.07	❏ 233 Edgar Martinez	.15	.07			
❏ 148 Brian Hunter	.10	.05	❏ 234 Francisco Cordova	.10	.05			
❏ 149 Garret Anderson	.15	.07	❏ 235 Johnny Damon	.15	.07			
❏ 150 Jeff Bagwell	.50	.23	❏ 236 Devi Cruz	.10	.05			
❏ 151 James Baldwin	.10	.05	❏ 237 J.T. Snow	.15	.07			
❏ 152 Devon White	.10	.05	❏ 238 Enrique Wilson	.10	.05			
❏ 153 Jim Thome	.40	.18	❏ 239 Rondell White	.15	.07			
❏ 154 Wally Joyner	.15	.07	❏ 240 Aaron Sele	.10	.05			
❏ 155 Mark Wohlers	.10	.05	❏ 241 Tony Saunders	.10	.05			
❏ 156 Jeff Cirillo	.15	.07	❏ 242 Ricky Bottalico	.10	.05			
❏ 157 Jason Giambi	.15	.07	❏ 243 Cliff Floyd	.15	.07			
❏ 158 Royce Clayton	.10	.05	❏ 244 Chili Davis	.15	.07			
❏ 159 Dennis Reyes	.10	.05	❏ 245 Brian McRae	.10	.05			

1998 Circa Thunder Rave

Troy Percival
Anaheim Angels

	MINT	NRMT
COMMON CARD (1-296)	6.00	2.70

*STARS: 25X TO 60X BASIC CARDS
*YNG.STARS: 20X TO 50X BASIC CARDS
*RC'S/ PROSPECTS: 15X TO 40X BASIC
RANDOM INSERTS IN PACKS
STATED PRINT RUN 150 SERIAL #'d SETS

1998 Circa Thunder Super Rave

	MINT	NRMT
COMMON CARD (1-296) 25.00		11.00

*STARS: 100X TO 250X BASIC CARDS
*YOUNG STARS: 80X TO 200X BASIC CARDS
*RC'S/PROSPECTS: 50X TO 120X BASIC
RANDOM INSERTS IN PACKS
STATED PRINT RUN 25 SERIAL #'d SETS

		MINT	NRMT
❏ 2	Juan Encarnacion	1.00	.45
❏ 3	Brad Fullmer	.60	.25
❏ 4	Nomar Garciaparra	8.00	3.60
❏ 5	Todd Helton	2.50	1.10
❏ 6	Livan Hernandez	.60	.25
❏ 7	Travis Lee	1.50	.70
❏ 8	Neifi Perez	1.00	.45
❏ 9	Scott Rolen	4.00	1.80
❏ 10	Jaret Wright	1.00	.45

1998 Circa Thunder Boss

	MINT	NRMT
COMPLETE SET (20)	40.00	18.00
COMMON CARD (1-20)	.50	.23
STATED ODDS 1:6		

		MINT	NRMT
❏ 1	Jeff Bagwell	1.50	.70
❏ 2	Barry Bonds	1.50	.70
❏ 3	Roger Clemens	3.00	1.35
❏ 4	Jose Cruz Jr.	.50	.23
❏ 5	Nomar Garciaparra	4.00	1.80
❏ 6	Juan Gonzalez	2.50	1.10
❏ 7	Ken Griffey Jr.	6.00	2.70
❏ 8	Tony Gwynn	3.00	1.35
❏ 9	Derek Jeter	4.00	1.80
❏ 10	Chipper Jones	3.00	1.35
❏ 11	Travis Lee	.75	.35
❏ 12	Greg Maddux	3.00	1.35
❏ 13	Pedro Martinez	1.50	.70
❏ 14	Mark McGwire	8.00	3.60
❏ 15	Mike Piazza	4.00	1.80
❏ 16	Cal Ripken	5.00	2.20
❏ 17	Alex Rodriguez	4.00	1.80
❏ 18	Scott Rolen	2.00	.90
❏ 19	Frank Thomas	2.50	1.10
❏ 20	Larry Walker	1.25	.55

1998 Circa Thunder Fast Track

	MINT	NRMT
COMPLETE SET (10)	20.00	9.00
COMMON CARD (1-10)	.60	.25
STATED ODDS 1:24		

		MINT	NRMT
❏ 1	Jose Cruz Jr.	1.00	.45

1998 Circa Thunder Limited Access

	MINT	NRMT
COMPLETE SET (15)	150.00	70.00
COMMON CARD (1-15)	2.00	.90
STATED ODDS 1:18 RETAIL		

		MINT	NRMT
❏ 1	Jeff Bagwell	6.00	2.70
❏ 2	Roger Clemens	12.00	5.50
❏ 3	Jose Cruz Jr.	2.00	.90
❏ 4	Nomar Garciaparra	15.00	6.75
❏ 5	Juan Gonzalez	10.00	4.50
❏ 6	Ken Griffey Jr.	25.00	11.00
❏ 7	Tony Gwynn	12.00	5.50
❏ 8	Derek Jeter	15.00	6.75
❏ 9	Greg Maddux	12.00	5.50
❏ 10	Pedro Martinez	6.00	2.70
❏ 11	Mark McGwire	30.00	13.50
❏ 12	Mike Piazza	15.00	6.75
❏ 13	Alex Rodriguez	15.00	6.75
❏ 14	Frank Thomas	10.00	4.50
❏ 15	Larry Walker	5.00	2.20

1998 Circa Thunder Quick Strike

	MINT	NRMT
COMPLETE SET (12)	100.00	45.00
COMMON CARD (1-12)	1.50	.70
STATED ODDS 1:36		

		MINT	NRMT
❏ 1	Jeff Bagwell	5.00	2.20
❏ 2	Roger Clemens	10.00	4.50
❏ 3	Jose Cruz Jr.	1.50	.70
❏ 4	Nomar Garciaparra	12.00	5.50
❏ 5	Ken Griffey Jr.	20.00	9.00
❏ 6	Juan Gonzalez	10.00	4.50
❏ 7	Pedro Martinez	5.00	2.20
❏ 8	Mark McGwire	25.00	11.00
❏ 9	Mike Piazza	12.00	5.50

		MINT	NRMT
❏ 10	Alex Rodriguez	12.00	5.50
❏ 11	Frank Thomas	8.00	3.60
❏ 12	Larry Walker	4.00	1.80

1998 Circa Thunder Rave Review

	MINT	NRMT
COMPLETE SET (15)	600.00	275.00
COMMON CARD (1-15)	6.00	2.70
UNLISTED STARS	15.00	6.75
STATED ODDS 1:288		

		MINT	NRMT
❏ 1	Jeff Bagwell	20.00	9.00
❏ 2	Barry Bonds	20.00	9.00
❏ 3	Roger Clemens	40.00	18.00
❏ 4	Jose Cruz Jr.	6.00	2.70
❏ 5	Nomar Garciaparra	50.00	22.00
❏ 6	Juan Gonzalez	30.00	13.50
❏ 7	Ken Griffey Jr.	80.00	36.00
❏ 8	Tony Gwynn	40.00	18.00
❏ 9	Derek Jeter	50.00	22.00
❏ 10	Greg Maddux	40.00	18.00
❏ 11	Mark McGwire	100.00	45.00
❏ 12	Mike Piazza	50.00	22.00
❏ 13	Alex Rodriguez	50.00	22.00
❏ 14	Frank Thomas	30.00	13.50
❏ 15	Larry Walker	15.00	6.75

1998 Circa Thunder Thunder Boomers

	MINT	NRMT
COMPLETE SET (12)	150.00	70.00
COMMON CARD (1-12)	3.00	1.35
SEMISTARS	5.00	2.20
UNLISTED STARS	8.00	3.60
STATED ODDS 1:96		

		MINT	NRMT
❏ 1	Jeff Bagwell	10.00	4.50
❏ 2	Barry Bonds	10.00	4.50
❏ 3	Jay Buhner	3.00	1.35
❏ 4	Andres Galarraga	5.00	2.20
❏ 5	Juan Gonzalez	15.00	6.75
❏ 6	Ken Griffey Jr.	40.00	18.00
❏ 7	Tino Martinez	3.00	1.35
❏ 8	Mark McGwire	50.00	22.00
❏ 9	Mike Piazza	25.00	11.00
❏ 10	Frank Thomas	15.00	6.75
❏ 11	Jim Thome	8.00	3.60
❏ 12	Larry Walker	8.00	3.60

1989 Classic Travel Orange

Roger Clemens

	MINT	NRMT
COMP.FACT.SET (50)	30.00	13.50
COMMON CARD (101-150)	.05	.02
MINOR STARS	.10	.05
UNLISTED STARS	.20	.09

		MINT	NRMT
❏ 101	Gary Sheffield	.50	.23
❏ 102	Wade Boggs	.20	.09
❏ 103	Jose Canseco	.25	.11
❏ 104	Mark McGwire	1.25	.55
❏ 105	Orel Hershiser	.10	.05
❏ 106	Don Mattingly	.40	.18
❏ 107	Dwight Gooden	.10	.05
❏ 108	Darryl Strawberry	.10	.05
❏ 109	Eric Davis	.10	.05
❏ 110	Hensley Meulens UER	.05	.02
	(Listed on card as Bam Bam Muelens)		
❏ 111	Andy Van Slyke	.10	.05
❏ 112	Al Leiter	.10	.05
❏ 113	Matt Nokes	.05	.02
❏ 114	Mike Krukow	.05	.02
❏ 115	Tony Fernandez	.10	.05
❏ 116	Fred McGriff	.20	.09
❏ 117	Barry Bonds	.40	.18
❏ 118	Gerald Perry	.05	.02
❏ 119	Roger Clemens	.50	.23
❏ 120	Kirk Gibson	.10	.05
❏ 121	Greg Maddux	.60	.25
❏ 122	Bo Jackson	.15	.07
❏ 123	Danny Jackson	.05	.02
❏ 124	Dale Murphy	.20	.09
❏ 125	David Cone	.20	.09
❏ 126	Tom Browning	.05	.02
❏ 127	Roberto Alomar	.30	.14
❏ 128	Alan Trammell	.15	.07
❏ 129	Ricky Jordan UER	.05	.02
	(Misspelled Jordon on card back)		
❏ 130	Ramon Martinez	.25	.11
❏ 131	Ken Griffey Jr.	25.00	11.00
❏ 132	Gregg Olson	.20	.09
❏ 133	Carlos Quintana	.05	.02
❏ 134	Dave West	.05	.02
❏ 135	Cameron Drew	.05	.02
❏ 136	Teddy Higuera	.05	.02
❏ 137	Sil Campusano	.05	.02
❏ 138	Mark Gubicza	.05	.02
❏ 139	Mike Boddicker	.05	.02
❏ 140	Paul Gibson	.05	.02
❏ 141	Jose Rijo	.05	.02
❏ 142	John Costello	.05	.02
❏ 143	Cecil Espy	.05	.02
❏ 144	Frank Viola	.05	.02
❏ 145	Erik Hanson	.05	.02
❏ 146	Juan Samuel	.05	.02
❏ 147	Harold Reynolds	.05	.02
❏ 148	Joe Magrane	.05	.02
❏ 149	Mike Greenwell	.05	.02
❏ 150	Darryl Strawberry Will Clark	.10	.05

1989 Classic Travel Purple

Kevin Mitchell

	MINT	NRMT
COMP.FACT.SET (50)	25.00	11.00
COMMON CARD (151-200)	.05	.02
MINOR STARS	.10	.05
UNLISTED STARS	.20	.09

		MINT	NRMT
❏ 151	Jim Abbott	.20	.09
❏ 152	Ellis Burks	.15	.07
❏ 153	Mike Schmidt	.30	.14
❏ 154	Gregg Jefferies	.10	.05
❏ 155	Mark Grace	.20	.09
❏ 156	Jerome Walton	.05	.02
❏ 157	Bo Jackson	.15	.07
❏ 158	Jack Clark	.05	.02
❏ 159	Tom Glavine	.20	.09
❏ 160	Eddie Murray	.20	.09
❏ 161	John Dopson	.05	.02
❏ 162	Ruben Sierra	.05	.02
❏ 163	Rafael Palmeiro	.25	.11
❏ 164	Nolan Ryan	.75	.35
❏ 165	Barry Larkin	.20	.09
❏ 166	Tommy Herr	.05	.02
❏ 167	Roberto Kelly	.10	.05
❏ 168	Glenn Davis	.05	.02
❏ 169	Glenn Braggs	.05	.02
❏ 170	Juan Bell	.05	.02
❏ 171	Todd Burns	.05	.02
❏ 172	Derek Lilliquist	.05	.02
❏ 173	Orel Hershiser	.10	.05
❏ 174	John Smoltz	.75	.35
❏ 175	Ozzie Guillen and Ellis Burks	.05	.02
❏ 176	Kirby Puckett	.40	.18
❏ 177	Robin Ventura	.75	.35
❏ 178	Allan Anderson	.05	.02
❏ 179	Steve Sax	.05	.02
❏ 180	Will Clark	.20	.09
❏ 181	Mike Devereaux	.05	.02
❏ 182	Tom Gordon	.20	.09
❏ 183	Rob Murphy	.05	.02
❏ 184	Pete O'Brien	.05	.02
❏ 185	Cris Carpenter	.05	.02
❏ 186	Tom Brunansky	.05	.02
❏ 187	Bob Boone	.10	.05
❏ 188	Lou Whitaker	.10	.05
❏ 189	Dwight Gooden	.10	.05
❏ 190	Mark McGwire	1.25	.55
❏ 191	John Smiley	.05	.02
❏ 192	Tommy Gregg	.05	.02
❏ 193	Ken Griffey Jr.	20.00	9.00
❏ 194	Bruce Hurst	.05	.02
❏ 195	Greg Swindell	.05	.02
❏ 196	Nelson Liriano	.05	.02
❏ 197	Randy Myers	.10	.05
❏ 198	Kevin Mitchell	.10	.05
❏ 199	Dante Bichette	.40	.18
❏ 200	Deion Sanders	.75	.35

1994 Collector's Choice

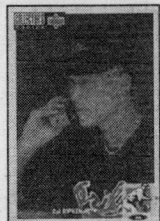

	MINT	NRMT
COMPLETE SET (670)	25.00	11.00
COMP.FACT.SET (675)	30.00	13.50
COMPLETE SERIES 1 (320)	10.00	4.50
COMPLETE SERIES 2 (350)	15.00	6.75
COMMON CARD (1-670)	.10	.05
MINOR STARS	.20	.09
UNLISTED STARS	.40	.18
SUBSET CARDS HALF VALUE OF BASE CARDS		
COMP.TEAM VS. SET (15)	5.00	2.20
ONE TEAM VS.TEAM CARD PER SER.2 PACK		

		MINT	NRMT
❏ 1	Rich Becker	.10	.05
❏ 2	Greg Blosser	.10	.05
❏ 3	Midre Cummings	.10	.05
❏ 4	Carlos Delgado	.40	.18
❏ 5	Steve Dreyer	.10	.05
❏ 6	Carl Everett	.20	.09
❏ 7	Cliff Floyd	.20	.09
❏ 8	Alex Gonzalez	.10	.05
❏ 9	Shawn Green	.60	.25
❏ 10	Butch Huskey	.20	.09
❏ 11	Mark Hutton	.10	.05
❏ 12	Miguel Jimenez	.10	.05
❏ 13	Steve Karsay	.10	.05
❏ 14	Marc Newfield	.10	.05
❏ 15	Luis Ortiz	.10	.05
❏ 16	Manny Ramirez	.75	.35
❏ 17	Johnny Ruffin	.10	.05
❏ 18	Scott Stahoviak	.10	.05
❏ 19	Salomon Torres	.10	.05
❏ 20	Gabe White	.10	.05
❏ 21	Brian Anderson	.30	.14
❏ 22	Wayne Gomes	.10	.05
❏ 23	Jeff Granger	.10	.05
❏ 24	Steve Soderstrom	.10	.05
❏ 25	Trot Nixon	.75	.35
❏ 26	Kirk Presley	.10	.05
❏ 27	Matt Brunson	.10	.05
❏ 28	Brooks Kieschnick	.10	.05
❏ 29	Billy Wagner	.50	.23
❏ 30	Matt Drews	.20	.09
❏ 31	Kurt Abbott	.10	.05
❏ 32	Luis Alicea	.10	.05
❏ 33	Roberto Alomar	.40	.18
❏ 34	Sandy Alomar Jr.	.20	.09
❏ 35	Moises Alou	.20	.09
❏ 36	Wilson Alvarez	.20	.09
❏ 37	Rich Amaral	.10	.05
❏ 38	Eric Anthony	.10	.05
❏ 39	Luis Aquino	.10	.05
❏ 40	Jack Armstrong	.10	.05
❏ 41	Rene Arocha	.10	.05
❏ 42	Rich Aude	.10	.05
❏ 43	Brad Ausmus	.10	.05

#	Player			#	Player			#	Player		
44	Steve Avery	.10	.05	130	Charlie Hayes	.10	.05	213	Jamie Moyer	.10	.05
45	Bob Ayrault	.10	.05	131	Rickey Henderson	.50	.23	214	Bobby Munoz	.10	.05
46	Willie Banks	.10	.05	132	Mike Henneman	.10	.05	215	Troy Neel	.10	.05
47	Bret Barberie	.10	.05	133	Pat Hentgen	.20	.09	216	Dave Nilsson	.10	.05
48	Kim Batiste	.10	.05	134	Roberto Hernandez	.10	.05	217	John O'Donoghue	.10	.05
49	Rod Beck	.10	.05	135	Orel Hershiser	.20	.09	218	Paul O'Neill	.20	.09
50	Jason Bere	.10	.05	136	Phil Hiatt	.10	.05	219	Jose Offerman	.20	.09
51	Sean Berry	.10	.05	137	Glenallen Hill	.10	.05	220	Joe Oliver	.10	.05
52	Dante Bichette	.20	.09	138	Ken Hill	.10	.05	221	Greg Olson	.10	.05
53	Jeff Blauser	.10	.05	139	Eric Hillman	.10	.05	222	Donovan Osborne	.10	.05
54	Mike Blowers	.10	.05	140	Chris Hoiles	.10	.05	223	J. Owens	.10	.05
55	Tim Bogar	.10	.05	141	Dave Hollins	.10	.05	224	Mike Pagliarulo	.10	.05
56	Tom Bolton	.10	.05	142	David Hulse	.10	.05	225	Craig Paquette	.10	.05
57	Ricky Bones	.10	.05	143	Todd Hundley	.20	.09	226	Roger Pavlik	.10	.05
58	Bobby Bonilla	.20	.09	144	Pete Incaviglia	.10	.05	227	Brad Pennington	.10	.05
59	Bret Boone	.20	.09	145	Danny Jackson	.10	.05	228	Eduardo Perez	.10	.05
60	Pat Borders	.10	.05	146	John Jaha	.10	.05	229	Mike Perez	.10	.05
61	Mike Bordick	.10	.05	147	Domingo Jean	.10	.05	230	Tony Phillips	.10	.05
62	Daryl Boston	.10	.05	148	Gregg Jefferies	.10	.05	231	Hipolito Pichardo	.10	.05
63	Ryan Bowen	.10	.05	149	Reggie Jefferson	.10	.05	232	Phil Plantier	.10	.05
64	Jeff Branson	.10	.05	150	Lance Johnson	.10	.05	233	Curtis Pride	.10	.05
65	George Brett	.75	.35	151	Bobby Jones	.10	.05	234	Tim Pugh	.10	.05
66	Steve Buechele	.10	.05	152	Chipper Jones	1.00	.45	235	Scott Radinsky	.10	.05
67	Dave Burba	.10	.05	153	Todd Jones	.10	.05	236	Pat Rapp	.10	.05
68	John Burkett	.10	.05	154	Brian Jordan	.20	.09	237	Kevin Reimer	.10	.05
69	Jeromy Burnitz	.20	.09	155	Wally Joyner	.20	.09	238	Armando Reynoso	.10	.05
70	Brett Butler	.20	.09	156	David Justice	.40	.18	239	Jose Rijo	.10	.05
71	Rob Butler	.10	.05	157	Ron Karkovice	.10	.05	240	Cal Ripken	1.50	.70
72	Ken Caminiti	.30	.14	158	Eric Karros	.20	.09	241	Kevin Roberson	.10	.05
73	Cris Carpenter	.10	.05	159	Jeff Kent	.20	.09	242	Kenny Rogers	.10	.05
74	Vinny Castilla	.20	.09	160	Jimmy Key	.20	.09	243	Kevin Rogers	.10	.05
75	Andujar Cedeno	.10	.05	161	Mark Kiefer	.10	.05	244	Mel Rojas	.10	.05
76	Wes Chamberlain	.10	.05	162	Darryl Kile	.10	.05	245	John Roper	.10	.05
77	Archi Cianfrocco	.10	.05	163	Jeff King	.10	.05	246	Kirk Rueter	.10	.05
78	Dave Clark	.10	.05	164	Wayne Kirby	.10	.05	247	Scott Ruffcorn	.10	.05
79	Jerald Clark	.10	.05	165	Ryan Klesko	.20	.09	248	Ken Ryan	.10	.05
80	Royce Clayton	.10	.05	166	Chuck Knoblauch	.40	.18	249	Nolan Ryan	1.50	.70
81	David Cone	.30	.14	167	Chad Kreuter	.10	.05	250	Bret Saberhagen	.20	.09
82	Jeff Conine	.10	.05	168	John Kruk	.20	.09	251	Tim Salmon	.40	.18
83	Steve Cooke	.10	.05	169	Mark Langston	.10	.05	252	Reggie Sanders	.20	.09
84	Scott Cooper	.10	.05	170	Mike Lansing	.20	.09	253	Curt Schilling	.20	.09
85	Joey Cora	.10	.05	171	Barry Larkin	.40	.18	254	David Segui	.10	.05
86	Tim Costo	.10	.05	172	Manuel Lee	.10	.05	255	Aaron Sele	.20	.09
87	Chad Curtis	.10	.05	173	Phil Leftwich	.10	.05	256	Scott Servais	.10	.05
88	Ron Darling	.10	.05	174	Darren Lewis	.10	.05	257	Gary Sheffield	.40	.18
89	Danny Darwin	.10	.05	175	Derek Lilliquist	.10	.05	258	Ruben Sierra	.10	.05
90	Rob Deer	.10	.05	176	Jose Lind	.10	.05	259	Don Slaught	.10	.05
91	Jim Deshaies	.10	.05	177	Albie Lopez	.10	.05	260	Lee Smith	.20	.09
92	Delino DeShields	.10	.05	178	Javier Lopez	.30	.14	261	Cory Snyder	.10	.05
93	Rob Dibble	.10	.05	179	Torey Lovullo	.10	.05	262	Paul Sorrento	.10	.05
94	Gary DiSarcina	.10	.05	180	Scott Lydy	.10	.05	263	Sammy Sosa	1.25	.55
95	Doug Drabek	.10	.05	181	Mike Macfarlane	.10	.05	264	Bill Spiers	.10	.05
96	Scott Erickson	.20	.09	182	Shane Mack	.10	.05	265	Mike Stanley	.10	.05
97	Rikkert Faneyte	.10	.05	183	Greg Maddux	1.00	.45	266	Dave Staton	.10	.05
98	Jeff Fassero	.10	.05	184	Dave Magadan	.10	.05	267	Terry Steinbach	.10	.05
99	Alex Fernandez	.10	.05	185	Joe Magrane	.10	.05	268	Kevin Stocker	.10	.05
100	Cecil Fielder	.20	.09	186	Kirk Manwaring	.10	.05	269	Todd Stottlemyre	.10	.05
101	Dave Fleming	.10	.05	187	Al Martin	.10	.05	270	Doug Strange	.10	.05
102	Darrin Fletcher	.10	.05	188	Pedro A. Martinez	.10	.05	271	Bill Swift	.10	.05
103	Scott Fletcher	.10	.05	189	Pedro Martinez	.50	.23	272	Kevin Tapani	.10	.05
104	Mike Gallego	.10	.05	190	Ramon Martinez	.20	.09	273	Tony Tarasco	.10	.05
105	Carlos Garcia	.10	.05	191	Tino Martinez	.40	.18	274	Julian Tavarez	.10	.05
106	Jeff Gardner	.10	.05	192	Don Mattingly	.75	.35	275	Mickey Tettleton	.10	.05
107	Brent Gates	.10	.05	193	Derrick May	.10	.05	276	Ryan Thompson	.10	.05
108	Benji Gil	.10	.05	194	David McCarty	.10	.05	277	Chris Turner	.10	.05
109	Bernard Gilkey	.10	.05	195	Ben McDonald	.10	.05	278	John Valentin	.20	.09
110	Chris Gomez	.10	.05	196	Roger McDowell	.10	.05	279	Todd Van Poppel	.10	.05
111	Luis Gonzalez	.20	.09	197	Fred McGriff UER	.30	.14	280	Andy Van Slyke	.20	.09
112	Tom Gordon	.10	.05		(Stats on back have 73			281	Mo Vaughn	.40	.18
113	Jim Gott	.10	.05		stolen bases for 1989; should			282	Robin Ventura	.20	.09
114	Mark Grace	.30	.14		be 7)			283	Frank Viola	.10	.05
115	Tommy Greene	.10	.05	198	Mark McLemore	.10	.05	284	Jose Vizcaino	.10	.05
116	Willie Greene	.10	.05	199	Greg McMichael	.10	.05	285	Omar Vizquel	.10	.05
117	Ken Griffey Jr.	2.00	.90	200	Jeff McNeely	.10	.05	286	Larry Walker	.40	.18
118	Bill Gullickson	.10	.05	201	Brian McRae	.10	.05	287	Duane Ward	.10	.05
119	Ricky Gutierrez	.10	.05	202	Pat Meares	.10	.05	288	Allen Watson	.10	.05
120	Juan Guzman	.10	.05	203	Roberto Mejia	.10	.05	289	Bill Wegman	.10	.05
121	Chris Gwynn	.10	.05	204	Orlando Merced	.10	.05	290	Turk Wendell	.10	.05
122	Tony Gwynn	1.00	.45	205	Jose Mesa	.10	.05	291	Lou Whitaker	.20	.09
123	Jeffrey Hammonds	.20	.09	206	Blas Minor	.10	.05	292	Devon White	.10	.05
124	Erik Hanson	.10	.05	207	Angel Miranda	.10	.05	293	Rondell White	.20	.09
125	Gene Harris	.10	.05	208	Paul Molitor	.40	.18	294	Mark Whiten	.10	.05
126	Greg W. Harris	.10	.05	209	Raul Mondesi	.40	.18	295	Darrel Whitmore	.10	.05
127	Bryan Harvey	.10	.05	210	Jeff Montgomery	.10	.05	296	Bob Wickman	.10	.05
128	Billy Hatcher	.10	.05	211	Mickey Morandini	.10	.05	297	Rick Wilkins	.10	.05
129	Hilly Hathaway	.10	.05	212	Mike Morgan	.10	.05	298	Bernie Williams	.40	.18

299	Matt Williams	.30	.14
300	Woody Williams	.10	.05
301	Nigel Wilson	.10	.05
302	Dave Winfield	.40	.18
303	Anthony Young	.10	.05
304	Eric Young	.10	.05
305	Todd Zeile	.10	.05
306	Jack McDowell TP	.10	.05
	John Burkett		
	Tom Glavine		
307	Randy Johnson TP	.20	.09
308	Randy Myers TP	.10	.05
309	Jack McDowell TP	.10	.05
310	Mike Piazza TP	.60	.25
311	Barry Bonds TP	.40	.18
312	Andres Galarraga TP	.20	.09
313	Juan Gonzalez TP	.40	.18
	Barry Bonds		
314	Albert Belle TP	.20	.09
315	Kenny Lofton TP	.20	.09
316	Barry Bonds CL	.40	.18
317	Ken Griffey Jr. CL	.50	.23
318	Mike Piazza CL	.60	.25
319	Kirby Puckett CL	.40	.18
320	Nolan Ryan CL	.75	.35
321	Roberto Alomar CL	.20	.09
322	Roger Clemens CL	.50	.23
323	Juan Gonzalez CL	.50	.23
324	Ken Griffey Jr. CL	.50	.23
325	David Justice CL	.20	.09
326	John Kruk CL	.10	.05
327	Frank Thomas CL	.40	.18
328	Tim Salmon TC	.20	.09
329	Jeff Bagwell TC	.40	.18
330	Mark McGwire TC	1.00	.45
331	Roberto Alomar TC	.20	.09
332	David Justice TC	.20	.09
333	Pat Listach TC	.10	.05
334	Ozzie Smith TC	.40	.18
335	Ryne Sandberg TC	.30	.14
336	Mike Piazza TC	.60	.25
337	Cliff Floyd TC	.10	.05
338	Barry Bonds TC	.40	.18
339	Albert Belle TC	.20	.09
340	Ken Griffey Jr. TC	1.00	.45
341	Gary Sheffield TC	.20	.09
342	Dwight Gooden TC	.10	.05
343	Cal Ripken TC	.75	.35
344	Tony Gwynn TC	.50	.23
345	Lenny Dykstra TC	.10	.05
346	Andy Van Slyke TC	.10	.05
347	Juan Gonzalez TC	.40	.18
348	Roger Clemens TC	.50	.23
349	Barry Larkin TC	.20	.09
350	Andres Galarraga TC	.20	.09
351	Kevin Appier TC	.10	.05
352	Cecil Fielder TC	.10	.05
353	Kirby Puckett TC	.40	.18
354	Frank Thomas TC	.40	.18
355	Don Mattingly TC	.30	.14
356	Bo Jackson	.20	.09
357	Randy Johnson	.40	.18
358	Darren Daulton	.20	.09
359	Charlie Hough	.10	.05
360	Andres Galarraga	.40	.18
361	Mike Felder	.10	.05
362	Chris Hammond	.10	.05
363	Shawon Dunston	.10	.05
364	Junior Felix	.10	.05
365	Ray Lankford	.20	.09
366	Darryl Strawberry	.20	.09
367	Dave Magadan	.10	.05
368	Gregg Olson	.10	.05
369	Lenny Dykstra	.20	.09
370	Darrin Jackson	.10	.05
371	Dave Stewart	.20	.09
372	Terry Pendleton	.10	.05
373	Arthur Rhodes	.10	.05
374	Benito Santiago	.10	.05
375	Travis Fryman	.20	.09
376	Scott Brosius	.20	.09
377	Stan Belinda	.10	.05
378	Derek Parks	.10	.05
379	Kevin Seitzer	.10	.05
380	Wade Boggs	.40	.18
381	Wally Whitehurst	.10	.05
382	Scott Leius	.10	.05
383	Danny Tartabull	.10	.05
384	Harold Reynolds	.10	.05
385	Tim Raines	.20	.09
386	Darryl Hamilton	.10	.05
387	Felix Fermin	.10	.05
388	Jim Eisenreich	.10	.05
389	Kurt Abbott	.10	.05
390	Kevin Appier	.20	.09
391	Chris Bosio	.10	.05
392	Randy Tomlin	.10	.05
393	Bob Hamelin	.10	.05
394	Kevin Gross	.10	.05
395	Wil Cordero	.20	.09
396	Joe Girardi	.10	.05
397	Orestes Destrade	.10	.05
398	Chris Haney	.10	.05
399	Xavier Hernandez	.10	.05
400	Mike Piazza	1.25	.55
401	Alex Arias	.10	.05
402	Tom Candiotti	.10	.05
403	Kirk Gibson	.20	.09
404	Chuck Carr	.10	.05
405	Brady Anderson	.20	.09
406	Greg Gagne	.10	.05
407	Bruce Ruffin	.10	.05
408	Scott Hemond	.10	.05
409	Keith Miller	.10	.05
410	John Wetteland	.20	.09
411	Eric Anthony	.10	.05
412	Andre Dawson	.30	.14
413	Doug Henry	.10	.05
414	John Franco	.20	.09
415	Julio Franco	.10	.05
416	Dave Hansen	.10	.05
417	Mike Harkey	.10	.05
418	Jack Armstrong	.10	.05
419	Joe Orsulak	.10	.05
420	John Smoltz	.30	.14
421	Scott Livingstone	.10	.05
422	Darren Holmes	.10	.05
423	Ed Sprague	.10	.05
424	Jay Buhner	.20	.09
425	Kirby Puckett	.60	.25
426	Phil Clark	.10	.05
427	Anthony Young	.10	.05
428	Reggie Jefferson	.10	.05
429	Mariano Duncan	.10	.05
430	Tom Glavine	.40	.18
431	Dave Henderson	.10	.05
432	Melido Perez	.10	.05
433	Paul Wagner	.10	.05
434	Tim Worrell	.10	.05
435	Ozzie Guillen	.10	.05
436	Mike Butcher	.10	.05
437	Jim Deshaies	.10	.05
438	Kevin Young	.10	.05
439	Tom Browning	.10	.05
440	Mike Greenwell	.10	.05
441	Mike Stanton	.10	.05
442	John Doherty	.10	.05
443	John Dopson	.10	.05
444	Carlos Baerga	.20	.09
445	Jack McDowell	.10	.05
446	Kent Mercker	.10	.05
447	Ricky Jordan	.10	.05
448	Jerry Browne	.10	.05
449	Fernando Vina	.10	.05
450	Jim Abbott	.20	.09
451	Teddy Higuera	.10	.05
452	Tim Naehring	.10	.05
453	Jim Leyritz	.20	.09
454	Frank Castillo	.10	.05
455	Joe Carter	.20	.09
456	Craig Biggio	.40	.18
457	Geronimo Pena	.10	.05
458	Alejandro Pena	.10	.05
459	Mike Moore	.10	.05
460	Randy Myers	.10	.05
461	Greg Myers	.10	.05
462	Greg Hibbard	.10	.05
463	Jose Guzman	.10	.05
464	Tom Pagnozzi	.10	.05
465	Marquis Grissom	.20	.09
466	Tim Wallach	.10	.05
467	Joe Grahe	.10	.05
468	Bob Tewksbury	.10	.05
469	B.J. Surhoff	.20	.09
470	Kevin Mitchell	.10	.05
471	Bobby Witt	.10	.05
472	Milt Thompson	.10	.05
473	John Smiley	.10	.05
474	Alan Trammell	.30	.14
475	Mike Mussina	.40	.18
476	Rick Aguilera	.10	.05
477	Jose Valentin	.10	.05
478	Harold Baines	.20	.09
479	Bip Roberts	.10	.05
480	Edgar Martinez	.20	.09
481	Rheal Cormier	.10	.05
482	Hal Morris	.10	.05
483	Pat Kelly	.10	.05
484	Roberto Kelly	.10	.05
485	Chris Sabo	.10	.05
486	Kent Hrbek	.20	.09
487	Scott Kamieniecki	.10	.05
488	Walt Weiss	.10	.05
489	Karl Rhodes	.10	.05
490	Derek Bell	.20	.09
491	Chili Davis	.20	.09
492	Brian Harper	.10	.05
493	Felix Jose	.10	.05
494	Trevor Hoffman	.20	.09
495	Dennis Eckersley	.20	.09
496	Pedro Astacio	.10	.05
497	Jay Bell	.20	.09
498	Randy Velarde	.10	.05
499	David Wells	.30	.14
500	Frank Thomas	.75	.35
501	Mark Lemke	.10	.05
502	Mike Devereaux	.10	.05
503	Chuck McElroy	.10	.05
504	Luis Polonia	.10	.05
505	Damion Easley	.20	.09
506	Greg A. Harris	.10	.05
507	Chris James	.10	.05
508	Terry Mulholland	.10	.05
509	Pete Smith	.10	.05
510	Rickey Henderson	.50	.23
511	Sid Fernandez	.10	.05
512	Al Leiter	.20	.09
513	Doug Jones	.10	.05
514	Steve Farr	.10	.05
515	Chuck Finley	.20	.09
516	Bobby Thigpen	.10	.05
517	Jim Edmonds	.40	.18
518	Graeme Lloyd	.10	.05
519	Dwight Gooden	.20	.09
520	Pat Listach	.10	.05
521	Kevin Bass	.10	.05
522	Willie Banks	.10	.05
523	Steve Finley	.20	.09
524	Delino DeShields	.10	.05
525	Mark McGwire	2.00	.90
526	Greg Swindell	.10	.05
527	Chris Nabholz	.10	.05
528	Scott Sanders	.10	.05
529	David Segui	.10	.05
530	Howard Johnson	.10	.05
531	Jaime Navarro	.10	.05
532	Jose Vizcaino	.10	.05
533	Mark Lewis	.10	.05
534	Pete Harnisch	.10	.05
535	Robby Thompson	.10	.05
536	Marcus Moore	.10	.05
537	Kevin Brown	.20	.09
538	Mark Clark	.10	.05
539	Sterling Hitchcock	.10	.05
540	Will Clark	.40	.18
541	Denis Boucher	.10	.05
542	Jack Morris	.20	.09
543	Pedro Munoz	.10	.05
544	Bret Boone	.20	.09
545	Ozzie Smith	.50	.23
546	Dennis Martinez	.20	.09
547	Dan Wilson	.10	.05
548	Rick Sutcliffe	.10	.05
549	Kevin McReynolds	.10	.05
550	Roger Clemens	1.00	.45
551	Todd Benzinger	.10	.05
552	Bill Haselman	.10	.05
553	Bobby Munoz	.10	.05

❏ 554	Ellis Burks	.20	.09
❏ 555	Ryne Sandberg	.50	.23
❏ 556	Lee Smith	.20	.09
❏ 557	Danny Bautista	.10	.05
❏ 558	Rey Sanchez	.10	.05
❏ 559	Norm Charlton	.10	.05
❏ 560	Jose Canseco	.50	.23
❏ 561	Tim Belcher	.10	.05
❏ 562	Denny Neagle	.10	.05
❏ 563	Eric Davis	.20	.09
❏ 564	Jody Reed	.10	.05
❏ 565	Kenny Lofton	.40	.18
❏ 566	Gary Gaetti	.20	.09
❏ 567	Todd Worrell	.10	.05
❏ 568	Mark Portugal	.10	.05
❏ 569	Dick Schofield	.10	.05
❏ 570	Andy Benes	.10	.05
❏ 571	Zane Smith	.10	.05
❏ 572	Bobby Ayala	.10	.05
❏ 573	Chip Hale	.10	.05
❏ 574	Bob Welch	.10	.05
❏ 575	Deion Sanders	.20	.09
❏ 576	David Nied	.10	.05
❏ 577	Pat Mahomes	.10	.05
❏ 578	Charles Nagy	.20	.09
❏ 579	Otis Nixon	.10	.05
❏ 580	Dean Palmer	.20	.09
❏ 581	Roberto Petagine	.10	.05
❏ 582	Dmitrel Smith	.10	.05
❏ 583	Jeff Russell	.10	.05
❏ 584	Mark Dewey	.10	.05
❏ 585	Greg Vaughn	.20	.09
❏ 586	Brian Hunter	.10	.05
❏ 587	Willie McGee	.20	.09
❏ 588	Pedro Martinez	.50	.23
❏ 589	Roger Salkeld	.10	.05
❏ 590	Jeff Bagwell	.50	.23
❏ 591	Spike Owen	.10	.05
❏ 592	Jeff Reardon	.20	.09
❏ 593	Erik Pappas	.10	.05
❏ 594	Brian Williams	.10	.05
❏ 595	Eddie Murray	.40	.18
❏ 596	Henry Rodriguez	.20	.09
❏ 597	Erik Hanson	.10	.05
❏ 598	Stan Javier	.10	.05
❏ 599	Mitch Williams	.10	.05
❏ 600	John Olerud	.20	.09
❏ 601	Vince Coleman	.10	.05
❏ 602	Damon Berryhill	.10	.05
❏ 603	Tom Brunansky	.10	.05
❏ 604	Robb Nen	.10	.05
❏ 605	Rafael Palmeiro	.40	.18
❏ 606	Cal Eldred	.10	.05
❏ 607	Jeff Brantley	.10	.05
❏ 608	Alan Mills	.10	.05
❏ 609	Jeff Nelson	.10	.05
❏ 610	Barry Bonds	.50	.23
❏ 611	Carlos Pulido	.10	.05
❏ 612	Tim Hyers	.10	.05
❏ 613	Steve Howe	.10	.05
❏ 614	Brian Turang	.10	.05
❏ 615	Leo Gomez	.10	.05
❏ 616	Jesse Orosco	.10	.05
❏ 617	Dan Pasqua	.10	.05
❏ 618	Marvin Freeman	.10	.05
❏ 619	Tony Fernandez	.20	.09
❏ 620	Albert Belle	.40	.18
❏ 621	Eddie Taubensee	.10	.05
❏ 622	Mike Jackson	.20	.09
❏ 623	Jose Bautista	.10	.05
❏ 624	Jim Thome	.40	.18
❏ 625	Ivan Rodriguez	.50	.23
❏ 626	Ben Rivera	.10	.05
❏ 627	Dave Valle	.10	.05
❏ 628	Tom Henke	.10	.05
❏ 629	Omar Vizquel	.20	.09
❏ 630	Juan Gonzalez	.75	.35
❏ 631	Roberto Alomar UP	.20	.09
❏ 632	Barry Bonds UP	.40	.18
❏ 633	Juan Gonzalez UP	.40	.18
❏ 634	Ken Griffey Jr. UP	1.00	.45
❏ 635	Michael Jordan UP	2.50	1.10
❏ 636	David Justice UP	.10	.05
❏ 637	Mike Piazza UP	.60	.25
❏ 638	Kirby Puckett UP	.40	.18
❏ 639	Tim Salmon UP	.20	.09

❏ 640	Frank Thomas UP	.40	.18
❏ 641	Alan Benes FF	.20	.09
❏ 642	Johnny Damon FF	.40	.18
❏ 643	Brad Fullmer FF	.60	.25
❏ 644	Derek Jeter FF	1.50	.70
❏ 645	Derek Lee FF	.25	.11
❏ 646	Alex Ochoa	.10	.05
❏ 647	Alex Rodriguez FF	5.00	2.20
❏ 648	Jose Silva FF	.10	.05
❏ 649	Terrell Wade FF	.10	.05
❏ 650	Preston Wilson FF	.40	.18
❏ 651	Shane Andrews	.10	.05
❏ 652	James Baldwin	.20	.09
❏ 653	Ricky Bottalico	.20	.09
❏ 654	Tavo Alvarez	.10	.05
❏ 655	Donnie Elliott	.10	.05
❏ 656	Joey Eischen	.10	.05
❏ 657	Jason Giambi	.30	.14
❏ 658	Todd Hollandsworth	.30	.14
❏ 659	Brian L. Hunter	.20	.09
❏ 660	Charles Johnson	.20	.09
❏ 661	Michael Jordan	5.00	2.20
❏ 662	Jeff Juden	.10	.05
❏ 663	Mike Kelly	.10	.05
❏ 664	James Mouton	.10	.05
❏ 665	Ray Holbert	.10	.05
❏ 666	Pokey Reese	.30	.14
❏ 667	Ruben Santana	.10	.05
❏ 668	Paul Spoljaric	.10	.05
❏ 669	Luis Lopez	.10	.05
❏ 670	Matt Walbeck	.10	.05
❏ P50	Ken Griffey Jr. Promo	1.00	.45

1994 Collector's Choice Gold Signature

	MINT	NRMT
COMMON CARD (1-670)	2.00	.90

*STARS: 15X TO 40X BASIC CARDS
*ROOKIES: 8X TO 20X BASIC CARDS
RANDOM INSERTS IN PACKS
FIVE PER FACTORY SET

1994 Collector's Choice Silver Signature

	MINT	NRMT
COMPLETE SET (670)	200.00	90.00
COMPLETE SERIES 1 (320)	80.00	36.00

COMPLETE SERIES 2 (350)	120.00	55.00
COMMON CARD (1-670)	.25	.11

*STARS: 1.5X TO 4X BASIC CARDS
*ROOKIES: 1.25X TO 3X BASIC CARDS
ONE SILVER SIGNATURE PER PACK

1994 Collector's Choice Home Run All-Stars

	MINT	NRMT
COMPLETE SET (8)	4.00	1.80
COMMON CARD (HA1-HA8)	.25	.11

ONE SET VIA MAIL PER 8TH PRIZE CARD

❏ HA1	Juan Gonzalez	1.25	.55
❏ HA2	Ken Griffey Jr.	3.00	1.35
❏ HA3	Barry Bonds	.75	.35
❏ HA4	Bobby Bonilla	.25	.11
❏ HA5	Cecil Fielder UER	.25	.11
	(Card number is HA4)		
❏ HA6	Albert Belle	.60	.25
❏ HA7	David Justice	.60	.25
❏ HA8	Mike Piazza	2.00	.90

1995 Collector's Choice

	MINT	NRMT
COMPLETE SET (530)	20.00	9.00
COMP.FACT.SET (545)	25.00	11.00
COMMON CARD (1-530)	.10	.05
MINOR STARS	.20	.09
UNLISTED STARS	.40	.18

SUBSET CARDS HALF VALUE OF BASE CARDS

COMP.TRADE SET (55)	10.00	4.50
COMMON TRADE (531-585)	.15	.07

TEN TRADE VIA MAIL PER TRD.EXCH.CARD
ONE 542-552 RUN PER DLR.FACT.SET ORDER

COMP.TRADE EXCH.SET (5)	4.00	1.80
COMMON TRD.EXCH. (TC1-TC5)	1.00	.45

TRD.EXCH.CARDS: RANDOM INS.IN PACKS

COMMON GOLD SIG (1-530)	1.50	.70

*GOLD STARS: 8X TO 20X HI COLUMN
*GOLD YOUNG STARS: 6X TO 15X HI
GOLD STATED ODDS 1:35
12 GOLD CARDS PER SUPER PACK
15 GOLD CARDS PER FACTORY SET

COMP.SILVER SIG.SET (530)	80.00	36.00

COMMON SILVER (1-530) .... 20 .09
*SILV.SIG.STARS: 1.5X TO 4X HI COLUMN
*SILV.SIG.YOUNG STARS: 1.25X TO 3X HI
ONE SILVER PER PACK

#	Player	Hi	Silver
1	Charles Johnson	20	.09
2	Scott Ruffcorn	10	.05
3	Ray Durham	20	.09
4	Armando Benitez	10	.05
5	Alex Rodriguez	1.50	.70
6	Julian Tavarez	10	.05
7	Chad Ogea	10	.05
8	Quilvio Veras	10	.05
9	Phil Nevin	10	.05
10	Michael Tucker	20	.09
11	Mark Thompson	10	.05
12	Rod Henderson	10	.05
13	Andrew Lorraine	10	.05
14	Joe Randa	10	.05
15	Derek Jeter	1.25	.55
16	Tony Clark	40	.18
17	Juan Castillo	10	.05
18	Mark Acre	10	.05
19	Orlando Miller	10	.05
20	Paul Wilson	10	.05
21	John Mabry	10	.05
22	Garey Ingram	10	.05
23	Garret Anderson	20	.09
24	Dave Stevens	10	.05
25	Dustin Hermanson	10	.05
26	Paul Shuey	10	.05
27	J.R. Phillips	10	.05
28	Ruben Rivera FF	20	.09
29	Nomar Garciaparra FF	2.00	.90
30	John Wasdin FF	10	.05
31	Jim Pittsley FF	10	.05
32	Scott Elarton FF	60	.25
33	Raul Casanova FF	10	.05
34	Todd Greene FF	10	.05
35	Bill Pulsipher FF	10	.05
36	Trey Beamon FF	10	.05
37	Curtis Goodwin FF	10	.05
38	Doug Million FF	10	.05
39	Karim Garcia FF	25	.11
40	Ben Grieve FF	1.00	.45
41	Mark Farris FF	10	.05
42	Juan Acevedo FF	10	.05
43	C.J. Nitkowski FF	10	.05
44	Travis Miller FF	10	.05
45	Reid Ryan FF	20	.09
46	Nolan Ryan	1.50	.70
47	Robin Yount	40	.18
48	Ryne Sandberg	50	.23
49	George Brett	75	.35
50	Mike Schmidt	60	.25
51	Cecil Fielder B90	10	.05
52	Nolan Ryan B90	75	.35
53	Rickey Henderson B90	20	.09
54	George Brett B90	40	.18
	Robin Yount		
	Dave Winfield		
55	Sid Bream B90	10	.05
56	Carlos Baerga B90	10	.05
57	Lee Smith B90	10	.05
58	Mark Whiten B90	10	.05
59	Joe Carter B90	20	.09
60	Barry Bonds B90	30	.14
61	Tony Gwynn B90	50	.23
62	Ken Griffey Jr. B90	1.00	.45
63	Greg Maddux B90	50	.23
64	Frank Thomas B90	75	.35
65	Dennis Martinez B90	10	.05
	Kenny Rogers		
66	David Cone	30	.14
67	Greg Maddux	1.00	.45
68	Jimmy Key	20	.09
69	Fred McGriff	30	.14
70	Ken Griffey Jr.	2.00	.90
71	Matt Williams	40	.18
72	Paul O'Neill	20	.09
73	Tony Gwynn	1.00	.45
74	Randy Johnson	40	.18
75	Frank Thomas	75	.35
76	Jeff Bagwell	50	.23
77	Kirby Puckett	60	.25
78	Bob Hamelin	10	.05
79	Raul Mondesi	30	.14
80	Mike Piazza	1.25	.55
81	Kenny Lofton	30	.14
82	Barry Bonds	50	.23
83	Albert Belle	40	.18
84	Juan Gonzalez	75	.35
85	Cal Ripken Jr.	1.50	.70
86	Barry Bonds WC	30	.14
87	Mike Piazza WC	60	.25
88	Ken Griffey Jr. WC	1.00	.45
89	Frank Thomas WC	40	.18
90	Juan Gonzalez WC	40	.18
91	Jorge Fabregas	10	.05
92	J.T. Snow	20	.09
93	Spike Owen	10	.05
94	Eduardo Perez	10	.05
95	Bo Jackson	20	.09
96	Damion Easley	10	.05
97	Gary DiSarcina	10	.05
98	Jim Edmonds	30	.14
99	Chad Curtis	10	.05
100	Tim Salmon	40	.18
101	Chili Davis	20	.09
102	Chuck Finley	10	.05
103	Mark Langston	10	.05
104	Brian Anderson	20	.09
105	Lee Smith	20	.09
106	Phil Leftwich	10	.05
107	Chris Donnels	10	.05
108	John Hudek	10	.05
109	Craig Biggio	40	.18
110	Luis Gonzalez	10	.05
111	Brian L. Hunter	20	.09
112	James Mouton	10	.05
113	Scott Servais	10	.05
114	Tony Eusebio	10	.05
115	Derek Bell	20	.09
116	Doug Drabek	10	.05
117	Shane Reynolds	20	.09
118	Darryl Kile	10	.05
119	Greg Swindell	10	.05
120	Phil Plantier	10	.05
121	Todd Jones	10	.05
122	Steve Ontiveros	10	.05
123	Bobby Witt	10	.05
124	Brent Gates	10	.05
125	Rickey Henderson	50	.23
126	Scott Brosius	10	.05
127	Mike Bordick	10	.05
128	Fausto Cruz	10	.05
129	Stan Javier	10	.05
130	Mark McGwire	2.00	.90
131	Geronimo Berroa	10	.05
132	Terry Steinbach	10	.05
133	Steve Karsay	10	.05
134	Dennis Eckersley	20	.09
135	Ruben Sierra	20	.09
136	Ron Darling	10	.05
137	Todd Van Poppel	10	.05
138	Alex Gonzalez	10	.05
139	John Olerud	20	.09
140	Roberto Alomar	40	.18
141	Darren Hall	10	.05
142	Ed Sprague	10	.05
143	Devon White	20	.09
144	Shawn Green	40	.18
145	Paul Molitor	40	.18
146	Pat Borders	10	.05
147	Carlos Delgado	40	.18
148	Juan Guzman	10	.05
149	Pat Hentgen	20	.09
150	Joe Carter	20	.09
151	Dave Stewart	20	.09
152	Todd Stottlemyre	10	.05
153	Dick Schofield	10	.05
154	Chipper Jones	1.00	.45
155	Ryan Klesko	20	.09
156	David Justice	40	.18
157	Mike Kelly	10	.05
158	Roberto Kelly	20	.09
159	Tony Tarasco	10	.05
160	Javier Lopez	20	.09
161	Steve Avery	10	.05
162	Greg McMichael	10	.05
163	Kent Mercker	10	.05
164	Mark Lemke	10	.05
165	Tom Glavine	40	.18
166	Jose Oliva	10	.05
167	John Smoltz	30	.14
168	Jeff Blauser	10	.05
169	Troy O'Leary	20	.09
170	Greg Vaughn	20	.09
171	Jody Reed	10	.05
172	Kevin Seitzer	10	.05
173	Jeff Cirillo	20	.09
174	B.J. Surhoff	20	.09
175	Cal Eldred	10	.05
176	Jose Valentin	10	.05
177	Turner Ward	10	.05
178	Darryl Hamilton	10	.05
179	Pat Listach	10	.05
180	Matt Mieske	10	.05
181	Brian Harper	10	.05
182	Dave Nilsson	10	.05
183	Mike Fetters	10	.05
184	John Jaha	10	.05
185	Ricky Bones	10	.05
186	Geronimo Pena	10	.05
187	Bob Tewksbury	10	.05
188	Todd Zeile	10	.05
189	Danny Jackson	10	.05
190	Ray Lankford	20	.09
191	Bernard Gilkey	10	.05
192	Brian Jordan	20	.09
193	Tom Pagnozzi	10	.05
194	Rick Sutcliffe	10	.05
195	Mark Whiten	10	.05
196	Tom Henke	10	.05
197	Rene Arocha	10	.05
198	Allen Watson	10	.05
199	Mike Perez	10	.05
200	Ozzie Smith	50	.23
201	Anthony Young	10	.05
202	Rey Sanchez	10	.05
203	Steve Buechele	10	.05
204	Shawon Dunston	10	.05
205	Mark Grace	30	.14
206	Glenallen Hill	10	.05
207	Eddie Zambrano	10	.05
208	Rick Wilkins	10	.05
209	Derrick May	10	.05
210	Sammy Sosa	1.25	.55
211	Kevin Roberson	10	.05
212	Steve Trachsel	10	.05
213	Willie Banks	10	.05
214	Kevin Foster	10	.05
215	Randy Myers	10	.05
216	Mike Morgan	10	.05
217	Rafael Bournigal	10	.05
218	Delino DeShields	10	.05
219	Tim Wallach	10	.05
220	Eric Karros	20	.09
221	Jose Offerman	10	.05
222	Tom Candiotti	10	.05
223	Ismael Valdes	10	.05
224	Henry Rodriguez	20	.09
225	Billy Ashley	10	.05
226	Darren Dreifort	20	.09
227	Ramon Martinez	20	.09
228	Pedro Astacio	10	.05
229	Orel Hershiser	20	.09
230	Brett Butler	20	.09
231	Todd Hollandsworth	10	.05
232	Chan Ho Park	40	.18
233	Mike Lansing	10	.05
234	Sean Berry	10	.05
235	Rondell White	20	.09
236	Ken Hill	10	.05
237	Marquis Grissom	20	.09
238	Larry Walker	40	.18
239	John Wetteland	20	.09
240	Cliff Floyd	20	.09
241	Joey Eischen	10	.05
242	Lou Frazier	10	.05
243	Darrin Fletcher	10	.05
244	Pedro Martinez	50	.23
245	Wil Cordero	20	.09
246	Jeff Fassero	10	.05
247	Butch Henry	10	.05
248	Mel Rojas	10	.05
249	Kirk Rueter	10	.05
250	Moises Alou	20	.09

251	Rod Beck	.10	.05
252	John Patterson	.10	.05
253	Robby Thompson	.10	.05
254	Royce Clayton	.10	.05
255	Wm. VanLandingham	.10	.05
256	Darren Lewis	.10	.05
257	Kirt Manwaring	.10	.05
258	Mark Portugal	.10	.05
259	Bill Swift	.10	.05
260	Rikkert Faneyte	.10	.05
261	Mike Jackson	.20	.09
262	Todd Benzinger	.10	.05
263	Bud Black	.10	.05
264	Salomon Torres	.10	.05
265	Eddie Murray	.40	.18
266	Mark Clark	.10	.05
267	Paul Sorrento	.10	.05
268	Jim Thome	.40	.18
269	Omar Vizquel	.20	.09
270	Carlos Baerga	.10	.05
271	Jeff Russell	.10	.05
272	Herbert Perry	.10	.05
273	Sandy Alomar Jr.	.20	.09
274	Dennis Martinez	.20	.09
275	Manny Ramirez	.50	.23
276	Wayne Kirby	.10	.05
277	Charles Nagy	.20	.09
278	Albie Lopez	.10	.05
279	Jeromy Burnitz	.20	.09
280	Dave Winfield	.40	.18
281	Tim Davis	.10	.05
282	Marc Newfield	.10	.05
283	Tino Martinez	.40	.18
284	Mike Blowers	.10	.05
285	Goose Gossage	.20	.09
286	Luis Sojo	.10	.05
287	Edgar Martinez	.20	.09
288	Rich Amaral	.10	.05
289	Felix Fermin	.10	.05
290	Jay Buhner	.20	.09
291	Dan Wilson	.10	.05
292	Bobby Ayala	.10	.05
293	Dave Fleming	.10	.05
294	Greg Pirkl	.10	.05
295	Reggie Jefferson	.10	.05
296	Greg Hibbard	.10	.05
297	Yorkis Perez	.10	.05
298	Kurt Miller	.10	.05
299	Chuck Carr	.10	.05
300	Gary Sheffield	.20	.09
301	Jerry Browne	.10	.05
302	Dave Magadan	.10	.05
303	Kurt Abbott	.10	.05
304	Pat Rapp	.10	.05
305	Jeff Conine	.10	.05
306	Benito Santiago	.10	.05
307	Dave Weathers	.10	.05
308	Robb Nen	.10	.05
309	Chris Hammond	.10	.05
310	Bryan Harvey	.10	.05
311	Charlie Hough	.10	.05
312	Greg Colbrunn	.10	.05
313	David Segui	.20	.09
314	Rico Brogna	.10	.05
315	Jeff Kent	.20	.09
316	Jose Vizcaino	.10	.05
317	Jim Lindeman	.10	.05
318	Carl Everett	.10	.05
319	Ryan Thompson	.10	.05
320	Bobby Bonilla	.20	.09
321	Joe Orsulak	.10	.05
322	Pete Harnisch	.10	.05
323	Doug Linton	.10	.05
324	Todd Hundley	.20	.09
325	Bret Saberhagen	.20	.09
326	Kelly Stinnett	.10	.05
327	Jason Jacome	.10	.05
328	Bobby Jones	.10	.05
329	John Franco	.20	.09
330	Rafael Palmeiro	.40	.18
331	Chris Hoiles	.10	.05
332	Leo Gomez	.10	.05
333	Chris Sabo	.10	.05
334	Brady Anderson	.20	.09
335	Jeffrey Hammonds	.20	.09
336	Dwight Smith	.10	.05
337	Jack Voigt	.10	.05
338	Harold Baines	.20	.09
339	Ben McDonald	.10	.05
340	Mike Mussina	.40	.18
341	Bret Barberie	.10	.05
342	Jamie Moyer	.10	.05
343	Mike Oquist	.10	.05
344	Sid Fernandez	.10	.05
345	Eddie Williams	.10	.05
346	Joey Hamilton	.20	.09
347	Brian Williams	.10	.05
348	Luis Lopez	.10	.05
349	Steve Finley	.20	.09
350	Andy Benes	.20	.09
351	Andujar Cedeno	.10	.05
352	Bip Roberts	.10	.05
353	Ray McDavid	.10	.05
354	Ken Caminiti	.30	.14
355	Trevor Hoffman	.20	.09
356	Mel Nieves	.10	.05
357	Brad Ausmus	.10	.05
358	Andy Ashby	.10	.05
359	Scott Sanders	.10	.05
360	Gregg Jefferies	.10	.05
361	Mariano Duncan	.10	.05
362	Dave Hollins	.10	.05
363	Kevin Stocker	.10	.05
364	Fernando Valenzuela	.20	.09
365	Lenny Dykstra	.20	.09
366	Jim Eisenreich	.10	.05
367	Ricky Bottalico	.10	.05
368	Doug Jones	.10	.05
369	Ricky Jordan	.10	.05
370	Darren Daulton	.20	.09
371	Mike Lieberthal	.10	.05
372	Bobby Munoz	.10	.05
373	John Kruk	.20	.09
374	Curt Schilling	.30	.14
375	Orlando Merced	.10	.05
376	Carlos Garcia	.10	.05
377	Lance Parrish	.10	.05
378	Steve Cooke	.10	.05
379	Jeff King	.10	.05
380	Jay Bell	.20	.09
381	Al Martin	.10	.05
382	Paul Wagner	.10	.05
383	Rick White	.10	.05
384	Midre Cummings	.10	.05
385	Jon Lieber	.10	.05
386	Dave Clark	.10	.05
387	Don Slaught	.10	.05
388	Denny Neagle	.20	.09
389	Zane Smith	.10	.05
390	Andy Van Slyke	.20	.09
391	Ivan Rodriguez	.50	.23
392	David Hulse	.10	.05
393	John Burkett	.10	.05
394	Kevin Brown	.30	.14
395	Dean Palmer	.20	.09
396	Otis Nixon	.10	.05
397	Rick Helling	.10	.05
398	Kenny Rogers	.10	.05
399	Darren Oliver	.10	.05
400	Will Clark	.40	.18
401	Jeff Frye	.10	.05
402	Kevin Gross	.10	.05
403	John Dettmer	.10	.05
404	Manny Lee	.10	.05
405	Rusty Greer	.40	.18
406	Aaron Sele	.20	.09
407	Carlos Rodriguez	.10	.05
408	Scott Cooper	.10	.05
409	John Valentin	.20	.09
410	Roger Clemens	1.00	.45
411	Mike Greenwell	.10	.05
412	Tim Vanegmond	.10	.05
413	Tom Brunansky	.10	.05
414	Steve Farr	.10	.05
415	Jose Canseco	.50	.23
416	Joe Hesketh	.10	.05
417	Ken Ryan	.10	.05
418	Tim Naehring	.10	.05
419	Frank Viola	.10	.05
420	Andre Dawson	.30	.14
421	Mo Vaughn	.40	.18
422	Jeff Brantley	.10	.05
423	Pete Schourek	.10	.05
424	Hal Morris	.10	.05
425	Deion Sanders	.20	.09
426	Bret R. Hunter	.10	.05
427	Bret Boone	.20	.09
428	Willie Greene	.10	.05
429	Ron Gant	.10	.05
430	Barry Larkin	.40	.18
431	Reggie Sanders	.20	.09
432	Eddie Taubensee	.10	.05
433	Jack Morris	.20	.09
434	Jose Rijo	.10	.05
435	Johnny Ruffin	.10	.05
436	John Smiley	.10	.05
437	John Roper	.10	.05
438	Dave Nied	.10	.05
439	Roberto Mejia	.10	.05
440	Andres Galarraga	.40	.18
441	Mike Kingery	.10	.05
442	Curt Leskanic	.10	.05
443	Walt Weiss	.10	.05
444	Marvin Freeman	.10	.05
445	Charlie Hayes	.10	.05
446	Eric Young	.10	.05
447	Ellis Burks	.20	.09
448	Joe Girardi	.10	.05
449	Lance Painter	.10	.05
450	Dante Bichette	.20	.09
451	Bruce Ruffin	.10	.05
452	Jeff Granger	.10	.05
453	Wally Joyner	.20	.09
454	Jose Lind	.10	.05
455	Jeff Montgomery	.10	.05
456	Gary Gaetti	.20	.09
457	Greg Gagne	.10	.05
458	Vince Coleman	.10	.05
459	Mike Macfarlane	.10	.05
460	Brian McRae	.10	.05
461	Tom Gordon	.10	.05
462	Kevin Appier	.20	.09
463	Billy Brewer	.10	.05
464	Mark Gubicza	.10	.05
465	Travis Fryman	.20	.09
466	Danny Bautista	.10	.05
467	Sean Bergman	.10	.05
468	Mike Henneman	.10	.05
469	Mike Moore	.10	.05
470	Cecil Fielder	.20	.09
471	Alan Trammell	.20	.09
472	Kirk Gibson	.20	.09
473	Tony Phillips	.10	.05
474	Mickey Tettleton	.10	.05
475	Lou Whitaker	.20	.09
476	Chris Gomez	.10	.05
477	John Doherty	.10	.05
478	Greg Gohr	.10	.05
479	Bill Gullickson	.10	.05
480	Rick Aguilera	.10	.05
481	Matt Walbeck	.10	.05
482	Kevin Tapani	.10	.05
483	Scott Erickson	.20	.09
484	Steve Dunn	.10	.05
485	David McCarty	.10	.05
486	Scott Leius	.10	.05
487	Pat Meares	.10	.05
488	Jeff Reboulet	.10	.05
489	Pedro Munoz	.10	.05
490	Chuck Knoblauch	.40	.18
491	Rich Becker	.10	.05
492	Alex Cole	.10	.05
493	Pat Mahomes	.10	.05
494	Ozzie Guillen	.10	.05
495	Tim Raines	.20	.09
496	Kirk McCaskill	.10	.05
497	Olmedo Saenz	.10	.05
498	Scott Sanderson	.10	.05
499	Lance Johnson	.10	.05
500	Michael Jordan	2.50	1.10
501	Warren Newson	.10	.05
502	Ron Karkovice	.10	.05
503	Wilson Alvarez	.20	.09
504	Jason Bere	.20	.09
505	Robin Ventura	.20	.09
506	Alex Fernandez	.10	.05
507	Roberto Hernandez	.10	.05
508	Norberto Martin	.10	.05

		MINT	NRMT
❑ 509	Bob Wickman .10		.05
❑ 510	Don Mattingly .75		.35
❑ 511	Melido Perez .10		.05
❑ 512	Pat Kelly .10		.05
❑ 513	Randy Velarde .10		.05
❑ 514	Tony Fernandez .20		.09
❑ 515	Jack McDowell .10		.05
❑ 516	Luis Polonia .10		.05
❑ 517	Bernie Williams .40		.18
❑ 518	Danny Tartabull .10		.05
❑ 519	Mike Stanley .10		.05
❑ 520	Wade Boggs .40		.18
❑ 521	Jim Leyritz .10		.05
❑ 522	Steve Howe .10		.05
❑ 523	Scott Kamieniecki .10		.05
❑ 524	Russ Davis .20		.09
❑ 525	Jim Abbott .20		.09
❑ 526	Eddie Murray CL .20		.09
❑ 527	Alex Rodriguez CL .75		.35
❑ 528	Jeff Bagwell CL .40		.18
❑ 529	Joe Carter CL .10		.05
❑ 530	Fred McGriff CL .10		.05
❑ 531T	Tony Phillips TRADE .15		.07
❑ 532T	Dave Magadan TRADE .15		.07
❑ 533T	Mike Gallego TRADE .15		.07
❑ 534T	Dave Stewart TRADE .30		.14
❑ 535T	T. Stottlemyre TRADE .15		.07
❑ 536T	David Cone TRADE .50		.23
❑ 537T	M. Grissom TRADE .30		.14
❑ 538T	Derrick May TRADE .15		.07
❑ 539T	Joe Oliver TRADE .15		.07
❑ 540T	Scott Cooper TRADE .15		.07
❑ 541T	Ken Hill TRADE .15		.07
❑ 542T	H. Johnson TRADE DP .15		.07
❑ 543T	B. McRae TRADE DP .15		.07
❑ 544T	J. Navarro TRADE DP .15		.07
❑ 545T	O. Timmons TRADE DP .15		.07
❑ 546T	R. Kelly TRADE DP .15		.07
❑ 547T	Hideo Nomo TRADE DP 2.50		1.10
❑ 548T	S. Andrews TRADE DP .15		.07
❑ 549T	M.Grudzi TRADE DP .75		.35
❑ 550T	C. Perez TRADE DP .15		.07
❑ 551T	H.RodriguezTRADE DP .30		.14
❑ 552T	T. Tarasco TRADE DP .15		.07
❑ 553T	Glenallen Hill TRADE .. .15		.07
❑ 554T	T. Mulholland TRADE .. .15		.07
❑ 555T	Orel Hershiser TRADE .30		.14
❑ 556T	Darren Bragg TRADE .. .15		.07
❑ 557T	John Burkett TRADE .. .15		.07
❑ 558T	Bobby Witt TRADE .15		.07
❑ 559T	Terry Pendleton TRADE.15		.07
❑ 560T	Andre Dawson TRADE .50		.23
❑ 561T	Brett Butler TRADE .30		.14
❑ 562T	Kevin Brown TRADE .. .50		.23
❑ 563T	Doug Jones TRADE .15		.07
❑ 564T	Andy Van Slyke TRADE .15		.07
❑ 565T	Jody Reed TRADE .15		.07
❑ 566T	F. Valenzuela TRADE.. .30		.14
❑ 567T	Charlie Hayes TRADE .. .15		.07
❑ 568T	Benji Gil TRADE .15		.07
❑ 569T	Mark McLemore TRADE.15		.07
❑ 570T	Mickey Tettleton TRADE.15		.07
❑ 571T	Bob Tewksbury TRADE.15		.07
❑ 572T	Rheal Cormier TRADE .15		.07
❑ 573T	V. Eshelman TRADE .. .15		.07
❑ 574T	M. Macfarlane TRADE .15		.07
❑ 575T	Bill Swift TRADE .15		.07
❑ 576T	Mark Whiten TRADE .. .15		.07
❑ 577T	Benito Santiago TRADE .15		.07
❑ 578T	Jason Bates TRADE .15		.07
❑ 579T	Larry Walker TRADE .. .35		.15
❑ 580T	Chad Curtis TRADE .15		.07
❑ 581T	Bob Higginson TRADE 2.00		.90
❑ 582T	Marty Cordova TRADE .15		.07
❑ 583T	Mike Devereaux TRADE.15		.07
❑ 584T	John Kruk TRADE .30		.14
❑ 585T	John Wetteland TRADE .30		.14
❑ P172	Ken Griffey Jr. Promo 3.00		1.35
❑ TC1	Larry Walker EXCH .. 2.00		.90
❑ TC2	David Cone EXCH 2.00		.90
❑ TC3	Marquis Grissom EXCH 1.00		.45
❑ TC4	Terry Pendleton EXCH 1.00		.45
❑ TC5	F.Valenzuela EXCH 1.50		.70

1995 Collector's Choice Crash the Game

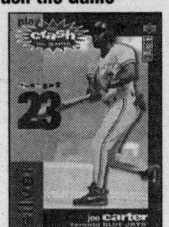

	MINT	NRMT
COMPLETE SET (60)	50.00	22.00
COMMON CARD (CG1-CG30) ..	.10	.05
COMP.GOLD SET (60)	250.00	110.00
*GOLD CARDS: 2X TO 5X BASE CARD HI		
THREE DATES PER PLAYER		
RANDOM INSERTS IN PACKS		
COMP.EXCH.SET (20)	10.00	4.50
*EXCH.CARDS: .25X TO .5X BASE CARD HI		
*GOLD.EXCH.SET (20)	50.00	22.00
*GOLD EXCH: 1.5X TO 4X BASE CARD HI		
ONE EXCH.SET VIA MAIL PER WINNER		

❑ CG1	Jeff Bagwell 7/30	.75	.35
❑ CG1B	Jeff Bagwell 8/13	.75	.35
❑ CG1C	Jeff Bagwell 9/28	.75	.35
❑ CG2	Albert Belle 6/18	.50	.23
❑ CG2B	Albert Belle 8/26	.50	.23
❑ CG2C	Albert Belle 9/14	.50	.23
❑ CG3	Barry Bonds 6/28	.50	.23
❑ CG3B	Barry Bonds 8/8	.50	.23
❑ CG3C	Barry Bonds 9/6	.50	.23
❑ CG4	Jose Canseco 6/30 W	.50	.23
❑ CG4B	Jose Canseco 7/30 W	.50	.23
❑ CG4C	Jose Canseco 9/3	.50	.23
❑ CG5	Joe Carter 7/14	.20	.09
❑ CG5B	Joe Carter 8/9	.20	.09
❑ CG5C	Joe Carter 9/23	.20	.09
❑ CG6	Cecil Fielder 7/4	.20	.09
❑ CG6B	Cecil Fielder 8/2	.20	.09
❑ CG6C	Cecil Fielder 10/1	.20	.09
❑ CG7	Juan Gonzalez 6/29	.75	.35
❑ CG7B	Juan Gonzalez 8/13	.75	.35
❑ CG7C	Juan Gonzalez 9/9	.75	.35
❑ CG8	Ken Griffey Jr. 7/2	2.00	.90
❑ CG8B	Ken Griffey Jr. 8/24 W	2.00	.90
❑ CG8C	Ken Griffey Jr. 9/15	2.00	.90
❑ CG9	Bob Hamelin 7/23	.10	.05
❑ CG9B	Bob Hamelin 8/25	.10	.05
❑ CG9C	Bob Hamelin 9/9	.10	.05
❑ CG10	David Justice 6/24	.50	.23
❑ CG10B	David Justice 7/25	.50	.23
❑ CG10C	David Justice 9/17	.50	.23
❑ CG11	Ryan Klesko 7/13	.20	.09
❑ CG11B	Ryan Klesko 8/20	.20	.09
❑ CG11C	Ryan Klesko 9/10	.20	.09
❑ CG12	Fred McGriff 8/25	.30	.14
❑ CG12B	Fred McGriff 8/26	.30	.14
❑ CG12C	Fred McGriff 9/24	.30	.14
❑ CG13	Mark McGwire 7/23	2.00	.90
❑ CG13B	Mark McGwire 8/3 W	2.00	.90
❑ CG13C	Mark McGwire 9/27	2.00	.90
❑ CG14	Raul Mondesi 7/27 W	.30	.14
❑ CG14B	Raul Mondesi 8/30	.30	.14
❑ CG14C	Raul Mondesi 9/15 W	.30	.14
❑ CG15	Mike Piazza 7/23 W	1.25	.55
❑ CG15B	Mike Piazza 8/27	1.25	.55
❑ CG15C	Mike Piazza 9/19	1.25	.55
❑ CG16	Manny Ramirez 6/21	.75	.35
❑ CG16B	Manny Ramirez 8/13	.75	.35
❑ CG16C	Manny Ramirez 9/26	.75	.35
❑ CG17	Alex Rodriguez 9/10	1.50	.70
❑ CG17B	Alex Rodriguez 9/18	1.50	.70
❑ CG17C	Alex Rodriguez 9/24	1.50	.70
❑ CG18	Gary Sheffield	.20	.09

❑ CG18B	Gary Sheffield 8/13	.20	.09
❑ CG18C	Gary Sheffield 9/4 W	.20	.09
❑ CG19	Frank Thomas 7/26	1.00	.45
❑ CG19B	Frank Thomas 8/17	1.00	.45
❑ CG19C	Frank Thomas 9/23	1.00	.45
❑ CG20	Matt Williams 7/29	.50	.23
❑ CG20B	Matt Williams 8/12	.50	.23
❑ CG20C	Matt Williams 9/19	.50	.23

1996 Collector's Choice

	MINT	NRMT
COMPLETE SET (730)	24.00	11.00
COMP.FACT.SET (790)	30.00	13.50
COMPLETE SERIES 1 (365)	12.00	5.50
COMPLETE SERIES 2 (365) ..	12.00	5.50
COMMON (1-365/396-760)	.10	.05
MINOR STARS	.20	.09
UNLISTED STARS	.40	.18
SUBSET CARDS HALF VALUE OF BASE CARDS		
COMP.TRADE SET (30)	15.00	6.75
COMMON TRADE (366T-395T)..	.15	.07
TRADE SEMISTARS	.50	.23
TRADE UNLISTED STARS	.75	.35
TEN TRADE CARDS PER TRADE EXCH.CARD		
SER.1 TRADE EXCH.STATED ODDS 1:11		
COMP.UPDATE SET (30)	4.00	1.80
COMMON UPDATE (761-790)..	.25	.11
UPDATE SEMISTARS	.50	.23
ONE UPDATE SET PER FACTORY SET		
ONE UPDATE SET VIA SER.2 WRAP.OFFER		
COM.GOLD (1-365/396-760)	2.00	.90
*GOLD STARS: 10X TO 25X HI COLUMN		
*GOLD ROOKIES: 6X TO 15X HI		
GOLD STATED ODDS 1:35		
COMP.SILV.SIG.SET (730) ..	110.00	50.00
COMP.SILV.SIG.SER.1 (365)	60.00	27.00
COMP.SILV.SIG.SER.2 (365)	50.00	22.00
COM.SILVER (1-365/396-760)..	.20	.09
*SILV.SIG.STARS: 1.25X TO 3X HI COLUMN		
*SILV.SIG.ROOKIES: 1X TO 2.5X HI		
ONE SILVER SIGNATURE PER PACK		

❑ 1	Cal Ripken	1.50	.70
❑ 2	Edgar Martinez SL	.40	.18
	Tony Gwynn		
❑ 3	Albert Belle SL	.20	.09
	Dante Bichette		
❑ 4	Albert Belle SL	.20	.09
	Mo Vaughn		
	Dante Bichette		
❑ 5	Kenny Lofton SL	.20	.09
	Quilvio Veras		
❑ 6	Mike Mussina SL	.50	.23
	Greg Maddux		
❑ 7	Randy Johnson SL	.40	.18
	Hideo Nomo		
❑ 8	Randy Johnson SL	.50	.22
	Greg Maddux		
❑ 9	Jose Mesa SL	.10	.05
	Randy Myers		
❑ 10	Johnny Damon	.30	.14
❑ 11	Rick Krivda	.10	.05
❑ 12	Roger Cedeno	.20	.09
❑ 13	Angel Martinez	.10	.05
❑ 14	Ariel Prieto	.10	.05
❑ 15	John Wasdin	.10	.05

☐ 16	Edwin Hurtado	.10	.05
☐ 17	Lyle Mouton	.10	.05
☐ 18	Chris Snopek	.10	.05
☐ 19	Mariano Rivera	.30	.14
☐ 20	Ruben Rivera	.20	.09
☐ 21	Juan Castro	.10	.05
☐ 22	Jimmy Haynes	.10	.05
☐ 23	Bob Wolcott	.10	.05
☐ 24	Brian Barber	.10	.05
☐ 25	Frank Rodriguez	.10	.05
☐ 26	Jesus Tavarez	.10	.05
☐ 27	Glenn Dishman	.10	.05
☐ 28	Jose Herrera	.10	.05
☐ 29	Chan Ho Park	.30	.14
☐ 30	Jason Isringhausen	.20	.09
☐ 31	Doug Johns	.10	.05
☐ 32	Gene Schall	.10	.05
☐ 33	Kevin Jordan	.10	.05
☐ 34	Matt Lawton	.50	.23
☐ 35	Karim Garcia	.20	.09
☐ 36	George Williams	.10	.05
☐ 37	Orlando Palmeiro	.10	.05
☐ 38	Jamie Brewington	.10	.05
☐ 39	Robert Person	.10	.05
☐ 40	Greg Maddux	1.00	.45
☐ 41	Marquis Grissom	.10	.05
☐ 42	Chipper Jones	1.00	.45
☐ 43	David Justice	.40	.18
☐ 44	Mark Lemke	.10	.05
☐ 45	Fred McGriff	.30	.14
☐ 46	Javier Lopez	.20	.09
☐ 47	Mark Wohlers	.10	.05
☐ 48	Jason Schmidt	.10	.05
☐ 49	John Smoltz	.30	.14
☐ 50	Curtis Goodwin	.10	.05
☐ 51	Greg Zaun	.10	.05
☐ 52	Armando Benitez	.10	.05
☐ 53	Manny Alexander	.10	.05
☐ 54	Chris Hoiles	.10	.05
☐ 55	Harold Baines	.20	.09
☐ 56	Ben McDonald	.10	.05
☐ 57	Scott Erickson	.20	.09
☐ 58	Jeff Manto	.10	.05
☐ 59	Luis Alicea	.10	.05
☐ 60	Roger Clemens	1.00	.45
☐ 61	Rheal Cormier	.10	.05
☐ 62	Vaughn Eshelman	.10	.05
☐ 63	Zane Smith	.10	.05
☐ 64	Mike Macfarlane	.10	.05
☐ 65	Erik Hanson	.10	.05
☐ 66	Tim Naehring	.10	.05
☐ 67	Lee Tinsley	.10	.05
☐ 68	Troy O'Leary	.20	.09
☐ 69	Garret Anderson	.20	.09
☐ 70	Chili Davis	.20	.09
☐ 71	Jim Edmonds	.30	.14
☐ 72	Troy Percival	.20	.09
☐ 73	Mark Langston	.10	.05
☐ 74	Spike Owen	.10	.05
☐ 75	Tim Salmon	.30	.14
☐ 76	Brian Anderson	.10	.05
☐ 77	Lee Smith	.20	.09
☐ 78	Jim Abbott	.20	.09
☐ 79	Jim Bullinger	.10	.05
☐ 80	Mark Grace	.30	.14
☐ 81	Todd Zeile	.10	.05
☐ 82	Kevin Foster	.10	.05
☐ 83	Howard Johnson	.10	.05
☐ 84	Brian McRae	.10	.05
☐ 85	Randy Myers	.10	.05
☐ 86	Jaime Navarro	.10	.05
☐ 87	Luis Gonzalez	.20	.09
☐ 88	Ozzie Timmons	.10	.05
☐ 89	Wilson Alvarez	.10	.05
☐ 90	Frank Thomas	.75	.35
☐ 91	James Baldwin	.10	.05
☐ 92	Ray Durham	.20	.09
☐ 93	Alex Fernandez	.10	.05
☐ 94	Ozzie Guillen	.10	.05
☐ 95	Tim Raines	.10	.05
☐ 96	Roberto Hernandez	.10	.05
☐ 97	Lance Johnson	.10	.05
☐ 98	John Kruk	.10	.05
☐ 99	Mark Portugal	.10	.05
☐ 100	Don Mattingly TT	.40	.18
☐ 101	Roger Clemens TT	.40	.18
☐ 102	Raul Mondesi TT	.10	.05
☐ 103	Cecil Fielder TT	.10	.05
☐ 104	Ozzie Smith TT	.40	.18
☐ 105	Frank Thomas TT	.40	.18
☐ 106	Sammy Sosa TT	.60	.25
☐ 107	Fred McGriff TT	.10	.05
☐ 108	Barry Bonds TT	.30	.14
☐ 109	Thomas Howard	.10	.05
☐ 110	Ron Gant	.10	.05
☐ 111	Eddie Taubensee	.10	.05
☐ 112	Hal Morris	.10	.05
☐ 113	Jose Rijo	.10	.05
☐ 114	Pete Schourek	.10	.05
☐ 115	Reggie Sanders	.20	.09
☐ 116	Benito Santiago	.10	.05
☐ 117	Jeff Brantley	.10	.05
☐ 118	Julian Tavarez	.10	.05
☐ 119	Carlos Baerga	.10	.05
☐ 120	Jim Thome	.40	.18
☐ 121	Jose Mesa	.10	.05
☐ 122	Dennis Martinez	.20	.09
☐ 123	Dave Winfield	.40	.18
☐ 124	Eddie Murray	.40	.18
☐ 125	Manny Ramirez	.50	.23
☐ 126	Paul Sorrento	.10	.05
☐ 127	Kenny Lofton	.30	.14
☐ 128	Eric Young	.10	.05
☐ 129	Jason Bates	.10	.05
☐ 130	Bret Saberhagen	.20	.09
☐ 131	Andres Galarraga	.40	.18
☐ 132	Joe Girardi	.10	.05
☐ 133	John VanderWal	.10	.05
☐ 134	David Nied	.10	.05
☐ 135	Dante Bichette	.20	.09
☐ 136	Vinny Castilla	.30	.14
☐ 137	Kevin Ritz	.10	.05
☐ 138	Felipe Lira	.10	.05
☐ 139	Joe Boever	.10	.05
☐ 140	Cecil Fielder	.20	.09
☐ 141	John Flaherty	.10	.05
☐ 142	Kirk Gibson	.20	.09
☐ 143	Brian Maxcy	.10	.05
☐ 144	Lou Whitaker	.20	.09
☐ 145	Alan Trammell	.30	.14
☐ 146	Bobby Higginson	.20	.09
☐ 147	Chad Curtis	.10	.05
☐ 148	Quilvio Veras	.10	.05
☐ 149	Jerry Browne	.10	.05
☐ 150	Andre Dawson	.30	.14
☐ 151	Robb Nen	.10	.05
☐ 152	Greg Colbrunn	.10	.05
☐ 153	Chris Hammond	.10	.05
☐ 154	Kurt Abbott	.10	.05
☐ 155	Charles Johnson	.20	.09
☐ 156	Terry Pendleton	.10	.05
☐ 157	Dave Weathers	.10	.05
☐ 158	Mike Hampton	.20	.09
☐ 159	Craig Biggio	.40	.18
☐ 160	Jeff Bagwell	.50	.23
☐ 161	Brian L.Hunter	.10	.05
☐ 162	Mike Henneman	.10	.05
☐ 163	Dave Magadan	.10	.05
☐ 164	Shane Reynolds	.10	.05
☐ 165	Derek Bell	.20	.09
☐ 166	Orlando Miller	.10	.05
☐ 167	James Mouton	.10	.05
☐ 168	Melvin Bunch	.10	.05
☐ 169	Tom Gordon	.10	.05
☐ 170	Kevin Appier	.20	.09
☐ 171	Tom Goodwin	.10	.05
☐ 172	Greg Gagne	.10	.05
☐ 173	Gary Gaetti	.20	.09
☐ 174	Jeff Montgomery	.10	.05
☐ 175	Jon Nunnally	.10	.05
☐ 176	Michael Tucker	.10	.05
☐ 177	Joe Vitiello	.10	.05
☐ 178	Billy Ashley	.10	.05
☐ 179	Tom Candiotti	.10	.05
☐ 180	Hideo Nomo	.40	.18
☐ 181	Chad Fonville	.10	.05
☐ 182	Todd Hollandsworth	.10	.05
☐ 183	Eric Karros	.20	.09
☐ 184	Roberto Kelly	.10	.05
☐ 185	Mike Piazza	1.25	.55
☐ 186	Ramon Martinez	.10	.05
☐ 187	Tim Wallach	.10	.05
☐ 188	Jeff Cirillo	.20	.09
☐ 189	Sid Roberson	.10	.05
☐ 190	Kevin Seitzer	.10	.05
☐ 191	Mike Fetters	.10	.05
☐ 192	Steve Sparks	.10	.05
☐ 193	Matt Mieske	.10	.05
☐ 194	Joe Oliver	.10	.05
☐ 195	B.J. Surhoff	.20	.09
☐ 196	Alberto Reyes	.10	.05
☐ 197	Fernando Vina	.10	.05
☐ 198	LaTroy Hawkins	.10	.05
☐ 199	Marty Cordova	.10	.05
☐ 200	Kirby Puckett	.60	.25
☐ 201	Brad Radke	.20	.09
☐ 202	Pedro Munoz	.10	.05
☐ 203	Scott Klingenbeck	.10	.05
☐ 204	Pat Meares	.10	.05
☐ 205	Chuck Knoblauch	.40	.18
☐ 206	Scott Stahoviak	.10	.05
☐ 207	Dave Stevens	.10	.05
☐ 208	Shane Andrews	.10	.05
☐ 209	Moises Alou	.20	.09
☐ 210	David Segui	.10	.05
☐ 211	Cliff Floyd	.20	.09
☐ 212	Carlos Perez	.10	.05
☐ 213	Mark Grudzielanek	.10	.05
☐ 214	Butch Henry	.10	.05
☐ 215	Rondell White	.20	.09
☐ 216	Mel Rojas	.10	.05
☐ 217	Ugueth Urbina	.20	.09
☐ 218	Edgardo Alfonzo	.40	.18
☐ 219	Carl Everett	.10	.05
☐ 220	John Franco	.20	.09
☐ 221	Todd Hundley	.20	.09
☐ 222	Bobby Jones	.20	.09
☐ 223	Bill Pulsipher	.20	.09
☐ 224	Rico Brogna	.20	.09
☐ 225	Jeff Kent	.20	.09
☐ 226	Chris Jones	.10	.05
☐ 227	Butch Huskey	.10	.05
☐ 228	Robert Eenhoorn	.10	.05
☐ 229	Sterling Hitchcock	.10	.05
☐ 230	Wade Boggs	.40	.18
☐ 231	Derek Jeter	1.25	.55
☐ 232	Tony Fernandez	.10	.05
☐ 233	Jack McDowell	.10	.05
☐ 234	Andy Pettitte	.30	.14
☐ 235	David Cone	.30	.14
☐ 236	Mike Stanley	.10	.05
☐ 237	Don Mattingly	.75	.35
☐ 238	Geronimo Berroa	.10	.05
☐ 239	Scott Brosius	.20	.09
☐ 240	Rickey Henderson	.50	.23
☐ 241	Terry Steinbach	.10	.05
☐ 242	Mike Gallego	.10	.05
☐ 243	Jason Giambi	.20	.09
☐ 244	Steve Ontiveros	.10	.05
☐ 245	Dennis Eckersley	.20	.09
☐ 246	Dave Stewart	.20	.09
☐ 247	Don Wengert	.10	.05
☐ 248	Paul Quantrill	.10	.05
☐ 249	Ricky Bottalico	.10	.05
☐ 250	Kevin Stocker	.10	.05
☐ 251	Lenny Dykstra	.20	.09
☐ 252	Tony Longmire	.10	.05
☐ 253	Tyler Green	.10	.05
☐ 254	Mike Mimbs	.10	.05
☐ 255	Charlie Hayes	.10	.05
☐ 256	Mickey Morandini	.10	.05
☐ 257	Heathcliff Slocumb	.10	.05
☐ 258	Jeff King	.10	.05
☐ 259	Midre Cummings	.10	.05
☐ 260	Mark Johnson	.10	.05
☐ 261	Freddy Garcia	.10	.05
☐ 262	Jon Lieber	.10	.05
☐ 263	Esteban Loaiza	.10	.05
☐ 264	Dan Miceli	.10	.05
☐ 265	Orlando Merced	.10	.05
☐ 266	Denny Neagle	.20	.09
☐ 267	Steve Parris	.10	.05
☐ 268	Greg Maddux FT	.50	.23
☐ 269	Randy Johnson FT	.20	.09
☐ 270	Hideo Nomo FT	.20	.09
☐ 271	Jose Mesa FT	.10	.05
☐ 272	Mike Piazza FT	.60	.25
☐ 273	Mo Vaughn FT	.20	.09

274	Craig Biggio FT	.20	.09
275	Edgar Martinez FT	.10	.05
276	Barry Larkin FT	.10	.05
277	Sammy Sosa FT	.60	.25
278	Dante Bichette FT	.10	.05
279	Albert Belle FT	.20	.09
280	Ozzie Smith	.50	.23
281	Mark Sweeney	.10	.05
282	Terry Bradshaw	.10	.05
283	Allen Battle	.10	.05
284	Danny Jackson	.10	.05
285	Tom Henke	.10	.05
286	Scott Cooper	.10	.05
287	Tripp Cromer	.10	.05
288	Bernard Gilkey	.10	.05
289	Brian Jordan	.20	.09
290	Tony Gwynn	1.00	.45
291	Brad Ausmus	.10	.05
292	Bryce Florie	.10	.05
293	Andres Berumen	.10	.05
294	Ken Caminiti	.20	.09
295	Bip Roberts	.10	.05
296	Trevor Hoffman	.20	.09
297	Roberto Petagine	.10	.05
298	Jody Reed	.10	.05
299	Fernando Valenzuela	.20	.09
300	Barry Bonds	.50	.23
301	Mark Leiter	.10	.05
302	Mark Carreon	.10	.05
303	Royce Clayton	.10	.05
304	Kirt Manwaring	.10	.05
305	Glenallen Hill	.10	.05
306	Deion Sanders	.20	.09
307	Joe Rosselli	.10	.05
308	Robby Thompson	.10	.05
309	W. VanLandingham	.10	.05
310	Ken Griffey Jr.	2.00	.90
311	Bobby Ayala	.10	.05
312	Joey Cora	.10	.05
313	Mike Blowers	.10	.05
314	Darren Bragg	.40	.18
315	Randy Johnson	.40	.18
316	Alex Rodriguez	1.25	.55
317	Andy Benes	.20	.09
318	Tino Martinez	.20	.09
319	Dan Wilson	.10	.05
320	Will Clark	.40	.18
321	Jeff Frye	.10	.05
322	Benji Gil	.10	.05
323	Rick Helling	.10	.05
324	Mark McLemore	.10	.05
325	Dave Nilsson IF	.10	.05
326	Larry Walker IF	.20	.09
327	Jose Canseco IF	.40	.18
328	Paul Mondesi IF	.40	.18
329	Manny Ramirez IF	.40	.18
330	Robert Eenhoorn IF	.10	.05
331	Chili Davis IF	.10	.05
332	Hideo Nomo IF	.20	.09
333	Benji Gil IF	.10	.05
334	Fernando Valenzuela IF	.10	.05
335	Dennis Martinez IF	.10	.05
336	Roberto Kelly IF	.10	.05
337	Carlos Baerga IF	.10	.05
338	Juan Gonzalez IF	.40	.18
339	Roberto Alomar IF	.20	.09
340	Chan Ho Park IF	.10	.05
341	Andres Galarraga IF	.20	.09
342	Midre Cummings IF	.10	.05
343	Otis Nixon	.10	.05
344	Jeff Russell	.10	.05
345	Ivan Rodriguez	.50	.23
346	Mickey Tettleton	.10	.05
347	Bob Tewksbury	.10	.05
348	Domingo Cedeno	.10	.05
349	Lance Parrish	.10	.05
350	Joe Carter	.20	.09
351	Devon White	.20	.09
352	Carlos Delgado	.40	.18
353	Alex Gonzalez	.10	.05
354	Darren Hall	.10	.05
355	Paul Molitor	.40	.18
356	Al Leiter	.10	.05
357	Randy Knorr	.10	.05
358	Ken Caminiti CL	.10	.05
	Steve Finley		
	Brian Williams		
	Roberto Petagine		
	Andujar Cedeno		
	Phil Plantier		
	Derek Bell		
	Pedro A. Martinez		
	Doug Brocail		
	Craig Shipley		
	Ricky Gutierrez		
359	Hideo Nomo CL	.20	.09
360	Ramon A.Martinez CL	.20	.09
	Ramon J.Martinez		
361	Robin Ventura CL	.10	.05
362	Cal Ripken CL	.75	.35
363	Ken Caminiti CL	.10	.05
364	Albert Belle CL	.30	.14
	Eddie Murray		
365	Randy Johnson CL	.20	.09
366T	Tony Pena TRADE	.15	.07
367T	Jim Thome TRADE	.75	.35
368T	Don Mattingly TRADE	1.50	.70
369T	Jim Leyritz TRADE	.15	.07
370T	Ken Griffey Jr. TRADE	4.00	1.80
371T	Edgar Martinez TRADE	.30	.14
372T	Pete Schourek TRADE	.15	.07
373T	Mark Lewis TRADE	.15	.07
374T	Chipper Jones TRADE	2.00	.90
375T	Fred McGriff TRADE	.50	.23
376T	Javy Lopez TRADE	.30	.14
377T	Fred McGriff TRADE	.50	.23
378T	Charlie O'Brien TRADE	.15	.07
379T	Mike Devereaux TRADE	.15	.07
380T	Mark Wohlers TRADE	.15	.07
381T	Bob Wolcott TRADE	.15	.07
382T	Manny Ramirez TRADE	1.00	.45
383T	Jay Buhner TRADE	.30	.14
384T	Orel Hershiser TRADE	.30	.14
385T	Kenny Lofton TRADE	.30	.14
386T	Greg Maddux TRADE	2.00	.90
387T	Javier Lopez TRADE	.30	.14
388T	Kenny Lofton TRADE	.30	.14
389T	Eddie Murray TRADE	.75	.35
390T	Luis Polonia TRADE	.15	.07
391T	Pedro Borbon TRADE	.15	.07
392T	Jim Thome TRADE	.75	.35
393T	Orel Hershiser TRADE	.30	.14
394T	David Justice TRADE	.30	.14
395T	Tom Glavine TRADE	.75	.35
396	Greg Maddux TC	.50	.23
397	Rico Brogna TC	.10	.05
398	Darren Daulton TC	.10	.05
399	Gary Sheffield TC	.10	.05
400	Moises Alou TC	.10	.05
401	Barry Larkin TC	.10	.05
402	Jeff Bagwell TC	.40	.18
403	Sammy Sosa TC	.60	.25
404	Ozzie Smith TC	.40	.18
405	Jay Bell TC	.10	.05
406	Mike Piazza TC	.60	.25
407	Dante Bichette TC	.10	.05
408	Tony Gwynn TC	.50	.23
409	Barry Bonds TC	.30	.14
410	Kenny Lofton TC	.10	.05
411	Johnny Damon TC	.10	.05
412	Frank Thomas TC	.40	.18
413	Greg Vaughn TC	.10	.05
414	Paul Molitor TC	.20	.09
415	Ken Griffey Jr. TC	1.00	.45
416	Tim Salmon TC	.10	.05
417	Juan Gonzalez TC	.40	.18
418	Mark McGwire TC	1.00	.45
419	Roger Clemens TC	.50	.23
420	Wade Boggs TC	.20	.09
421	Cal Ripken TC	.75	.35
422	Cecil Fielder TC	.10	.05
423	Joe Carter TC	.10	.05
424	Osvaldo Fernandez	.10	.05
425	Billy Wagner	.30	.14
426	George Arias	.10	.05
427	Mendy Lopez	.10	.05
428	Jeff Suppan	.10	.05
429	Rey Ordonez	.40	.18
430	Brooks Kieschnick	.10	.05
431	Raul Ibanez	.10	.05
432	Livan Hernandez	.60	.25
433	Shannon Stewart	.20	.09
434	Steve Cox	.10	.05
435	Trey Beamon	.10	.05
436	Sergio Nunez	.10	.05
437	Jermaine Dye	.20	.09
438	Mike Sweeney	.75	.35
439	Richard Hidalgo	.20	.09
440	Todd Greene	.10	.05
441	Robert Smith	.25	.11
442	Rafael Orellano	.10	.05
443	Wilton Guerrero	.30	.14
444	David Doster	.10	.05
445	Jason Kendall	.40	.18
446	Edgar Renteria	.20	.09
447	Scott Spiezio	.10	.05
448	Jay Canizaro	.10	.05
449	Enrique Wilson	.20	.09
450	Bob Abreu	.30	.14
451	Dwight Smith	.10	.05
452	Jeff Blauser	.10	.05
453	Steve Avery	.10	.05
454	Brad Clontz	.10	.05
455	Tom Glavine	.40	.18
456	Mike Mordecai	.10	.05
457	Rafael Belliard	.10	.05
458	Greg McMichael	.10	.05
459	Pedro Borbon	.10	.05
460	Ryan Klesko	.20	.09
461	Terrell Wade	.10	.05
462	Brady Anderson	.20	.09
463	Roberto Alomar	.40	.18
464	Bobby Bonilla	.20	.09
465	Mike Mussina	.40	.18
466	Cesar Devarez	.10	.05
467	Jeffrey Hammonds	.10	.05
468	Mike Devereaux	.10	.05
469	B.J. Surhoff	.20	.09
470	Rafael Palmeiro	.40	.18
471	John Valentin	.20	.09
472	Mike Greenwell	.10	.05
473	Dwayne Hosey	.10	.05
474	Tim Wakefield	.10	.05
475	Jose Canseco	.50	.23
476	Aaron Sele	.10	.05
477	Stan Belinda	.10	.05
478	Mike Stanley	.10	.05
479	Jamie Moyer	.10	.05
480	Mo Vaughn	.40	.18
481	Randy Velarde	.10	.05
482	Gary DiSarcina	.10	.05
483	Jorge Fabregas	.10	.05
484	Rex Hudler	.10	.05
485	Chuck Finley	.20	.09
486	Tim Wallach	.10	.05
487	Eduardo Perez	.10	.05
488	Scott Sanderson	.10	.05
489	J.T. Snow	.20	.09
490	Sammy Sosa	1.25	.55
491	Terry Adams	.10	.05
492	Matt Franco	.10	.05
493	Scott Servais	.10	.05
494	Frank Castillo	.10	.05
495	Ryne Sandberg	.50	.23
496	Rey Sanchez	.10	.05
497	Steve Trachsel	.10	.05
498	Jose Hernandez	.10	.05
499	Dave Martinez	.10	.05
500	Babe Ruth FC	1.00	.45
501	Ty Cobb FC	.40	.18
502	Walter Johnson FC	.30	.14
503	Christy Mathewson FC	.30	.14
504	Honus Wagner FC	.30	.14
505	Robin Ventura	.20	.09
506	Jason Bere	.10	.05
507	Mike Cameron	.60	.25
508	Ron Karkovice	.10	.05
509	Matt Karchner	.10	.05
510	Harold Baines	.20	.09
511	Kirk McCaskill	.10	.05
512	Larry Thomas	.10	.05
513	Danny Tartabull	.10	.05
514	Steve Gilbralter	.10	.05
515	Bret Boone	.20	.09
516	Jeff Branson	.10	.05
517	Kevin Jarvis	.10	.05
518	Xavier Hernandez	.10	.05
519	Eric Owens	.10	.05

520	Barry Larkin	.40	.18
521	Dave Burba	.10	.05
522	John Smiley	.10	.05
523	Paul Assenmacher	.10	.05
524	Chad Ogea	.10	.05
525	Orel Hershiser	.20	.09
526	Alan Embree	.10	.05
527	Tony Pena	.10	.05
528	Omar Vizquel	.20	.09
529	Mark Clark	.10	.05
530	Albert Belle	.40	.18
531	Charles Nagy	.20	.09
532	Herbert Perry	.10	.05
533	Darren Holmes	.10	.05
534	Ellis Burks	.20	.09
535	Billy Swift	.10	.05
536	Armando Reynoso	.10	.05
537	Curtis Leskanic	.10	.05
538	Quinton McCracken	.10	.05
539	Steve Reed	.10	.05
540	Larry Walker	.40	.18
541	Walt Weiss	.10	.05
542	Bryan Rekar	.10	.05
543	Tony Clark	.40	.18
544	Steve Rodriguez	.10	.05
545	C.J. Nitkowski	.10	.05
546	Todd Steverson	.10	.05
547	Jose Lima	.30	.14
548	Phil Nevin	.20	.09
549	Chris Gomez	.10	.05
550	Travis Fryman	.20	.09
551	Mark Lewis	.10	.05
552	Alex Arias	.10	.05
553	Marc Valdes	.10	.05
554	Kevin Brown	.30	.14
555	Jeff Conine	.10	.05
556	John Burkett	.10	.05
557	Devon White	.20	.09
558	Pat Rapp	.10	.05
559	Jay Powell	.10	.05
560	Gary Sheffield	.20	.09
561	Jim Dougherty	.10	.05
562	Todd Jones	.10	.05
563	Tony Eusebio	.10	.05
564	Darryl Kile	.10	.05
565	Doug Drabek	.10	.05
566	Mike Simms	.10	.05
567	Derrick May	.10	.05
568	Donne Wall	.10	.05
569	Greg Swindell	.10	.05
570	Jim Pittsley	.10	.05
571	Bob Hamelin	.10	.05
572	Mark Gubicza	.10	.05
573	Chris Haney	.10	.05
574	Keith Lockhart	.10	.05
575	Mike Macfarlane	.10	.05
576	Les Norman	.10	.05
577	Joe Randa	.10	.05
578	Chris Stynes	.10	.05
579	Greg Gagne	.10	.05
580	Raul Mondesi	.20	.09
581	Delino DeShields	.10	.05
582	Pedro Astacio	.10	.05
583	Antonio Osuna	.10	.05
584	Brett Butler	.10	.05
585	Todd Worrell	.10	.05
586	Mike Blowers	.10	.05
587	Felix Rodriguez	.10	.05
588	Ismael Valdes	.20	.09
589	Ricky Bones	.10	.05
590	Greg Vaughn	.20	.09
591	Mark Loretta	.10	.05
592	Cal Eldred	.10	.05
593	Chuck Carr	.10	.05
594	Dave Nilsson	.10	.05
595	John Jaha	.10	.05
596	Scott Karl	.10	.05
597	Pat Listach	.10	.05
598	Jose Valentin	.10	.05
599	Mike Trombley	.10	.05
600	Paul Molitor	.40	.18
601	Dave Hollins	.10	.05
602	Ron Coomer	.10	.05
603	Matt Walbeck	.10	.05
604	Roberto Kelly	.10	.05
605	Rick Aguilera	.10	.05
606	Pat Mahomes	.10	.05
607	Jeff Reboulet	.10	.05
608	Rich Becker	.10	.05
609	Tim Scott	.10	.05
610	Pedro Martinez	.50	.23
611	Kirk Rueter	.10	.05
612	Tavo Alvarez	.10	.05
613	Yamil Benitez	.10	.05
614	Darrin Fletcher	.10	.05
615	Mike Lansing	.10	.05
616	Henry Rodriguez	.20	.09
617	Tony Tarasco	.10	.05
618	Alex Ochoa	.10	.05
619	Tim Bogar	.10	.05
620	Bernard Gilkey	.10	.05
621	Dave Mlicki	.10	.05
622	Brent Mayne	.10	.05
623	Ryan Thompson	.10	.05
624	Pete Harnisch	.10	.05
625	Lance Johnson	.10	.05
626	Jose Vizcaino	.10	.05
627	Doug Henry	.10	.05
628	Scott Kamieniecki	.10	.05
629	Jim Leyritz	.10	.05
630	Ruben Sierra	.10	.05
631	Pat Kelly	.10	.05
632	Joe Girardi	.10	.05
633	John Wetteland	.20	.09
634	Melido Perez	.10	.05
635	Paul O'Neill	.20	.09
636	Jorge Posada	.20	.09
637	Bernie Williams	.40	.18
638	Mark Acre	.10	.05
639	Mike Bordick	.10	.05
640	Mark McGwire	2.00	.90
641	Fausto Cruz	.10	.05
642	Ernie Young	.10	.05
643	Todd Van Poppel	.10	.05
644	Craig Paquette	.10	.05
645	Brent Gates	.10	.05
646	Pedro Munoz	.10	.05
647	Andrew Lorraine	.10	.05
648	Sid Fernandez	.10	.05
649	Jim Eisenreich	.10	.05
650	Johnny Damon	.30	.14
651	Dustin Hermanson	.10	.05
652	Joe Randa	.10	.05
653	Michael Tucker	.10	.05
654	Alan Benes	.10	.05
655	Chad Fonville	.10	.05
656	David Bell	.10	.05
657	Jon Nunnally	.10	.05
658	Chan Ho Park	.30	.14
659	LaTroy Hawkins	.10	.05
660	Jamie Brewington	.10	.05
661	Quinton McCracken	.10	.05
662	Tim Unroe	.10	.05
663	Jeff Ware	.10	.05
664	Todd Greene	.10	.05
665	Andrew Lorraine	.10	.05
666	Ernie Young	.10	.05
667	Toby Borland	.10	.05
668	Lenny Webster	.10	.05
669	Benito Santiago	.10	.05
670	Gregg Jefferies	.10	.05
671	Darren Daulton	.20	.09
672	Curt Schilling	.30	.14
673	Mark Whiten	.10	.05
674	Todd Zeile	.10	.05
675	Jay Bell	.20	.09
676	Paul Wagner	.10	.05
677	Dave Clark	.10	.05
678	Nelson Liriano	.10	.05
679	Ramon Morel	.10	.05
680	Charlie Hayes	.10	.05
681	Angelo Encarnacion	.10	.05
682	Al Martin	.10	.05
683	Jacob Brumfield	.10	.05
684	Mike Kingery	.10	.05
685	Carlos Garcia	.10	.05
686	Tom Pagnozzi	.10	.05
687	David Bell	.10	.05
688	Todd Stottlemyre	.10	.05
689	Jose Oliva	.10	.05
690	Ray Lankford	.20	.09
691	Mike Morgan	.10	.05
692	John Frascatore	.10	.05
693	John Mabry	.10	.05
694	Mark Petkovsek	.10	.05
695	Alan Benes	.10	.05
696	Steve Finley	.20	.09
697	Marc Newfield	.10	.05
698	Andy Ashby	.10	.05
699	Marc Kroon	.10	.05
700	Wally Joyner	.10	.05
701	Joey Hamilton	.10	.05
702	Dustin Hermanson	.10	.05
703	Scott Sanders	.10	.05
704	Marty Cordova ROY	.10	.05
705	Hideo Nomo ROY	.20	.09
706	Mo Vaughn MVP	.20	.09
707	Barry Larkin MVP	.20	.09
708	Randy Johnson CY	.20	.09
709	Greg Maddux CY	.50	.23
710	Mark McGwire CB	1.00	.45
711	Ron Gant CB	.10	.05
712	Andujar Cedeno	.10	.05
713	Brian Johnson	.10	.05
714	J.P. Phillips	.10	.05
715	Rod Beck	.10	.05
716	Sergio Valdez	.10	.05
717	Marvin Benard	.10	.05
718	Steve Scarsone	.10	.05
719	Rich Aurilia	.40	.18
720	Matt Williams	.40	.18
721	John Patterson	.10	.05
722	Shawn Estes	.10	.05
723	Russ Davis	.10	.05
724	Rich Amaral	.10	.05
725	Edgar Martinez	.20	.09
726	Norm Charlton	.10	.05
727	Paul Sorrento	.10	.05
728	Luis Sojo	.10	.05
729	Arquimedez Pozo	.10	.05
730	Jay Buhner	.20	.09
731	Chris Bosio	.10	.05
732	Chris Widger	.10	.05
733	Kevin Gross	.10	.05
734	Darren Oliver	.10	.05
735	Dean Palmer	.20	.09
736	Matt Whiteside	.10	.05
737	Luis Ortiz	.10	.05
738	Roger Pavlik	.10	.05
739	Damon Buford	.10	.05
740	Juan Gonzalez	.75	.35
741	Rusty Greer	.20	.09
742	Lou Frazier	.10	.05
743	Pat Hentgen	.20	.09
744	Tomas Perez	.10	.05
745	Juan Guzman	.10	.05
746	Otis Nixon	.10	.05
747	Robert Perez	.10	.05
748	Ed Sprague	.10	.05
749	Tony Castillo	.10	.05
750	John Olerud	.20	.09
751	Shawn Green	.40	.18
752	Jeff Ware	.10	.05
753	Dante Bichette CL	.20	.09
	Vinny Castilla		
	Andres Galarraga		
	Larry Walker		
754	Greg Maddux CL	.50	.23
755	Marty Cordova CL	.10	.05
756	Ozzie Smith CL	.40	.18
757	John Vandernwal CL	.10	.05
758	Andres Galarraga CL	.20	.09
759	Frank Thomas CL	.75	.35
760	Tony Gwynn CL	.50	.23
761	Randy Myers UPD	.25	.11
762	Kent Mercker UPD	.25	.11
763	David Wells UPD	.50	.23
764	Tom Gordon UPD	.25	.11
765	Wil Cordero UPD	.25	.11
766	Dave Magadan UPD	.25	.11
767	Doug Jones UPD	.25	.11
768	Kevin Tapani UPD	.25	.11
769	Curtis Goodwin UPD	.25	.11
770	Julio Franco UPD	.25	.11
771	Jack McDowell UPD	.25	.11
772	Al Leiter UPD	.40	.18
773	Sean Berry UPD	.25	.11
774	Bip Roberts UPD	.25	.11

❏ 775	Jose Offerman UPD	.40	.18
❏ 776	Ben McDonald UPD	.25	.11
❏ 777	Dan Serafini UPD	.25	.11
❏ 778	Ryan McGuire UPD	.25	.11
❏ 779	Tim Raines UPD	.40	.18
❏ 780	Tino Martinez UPD	.40	.18
❏ 781	Kenny Rogers UPD	.25	.11
❏ 782	Bob Tewksbury UPD	.25	.11
❏ 783	Rickey Henderson UPD	1.00	.45
❏ 784	Ron Gant UPD	.25	.11
❏ 785	Gary Gaetti UPD	.40	.18
❏ 786	Andy Benes UPD	.40	.18
❏ 787	Royce Clayton UPD	.25	.11
❏ 788	Darryl Hamilton UPD	.25	.11
❏ 789	Ken Hill UPD	.25	.11
❏ 790	Erik Hanson UPD	.25	.11
❏ P100	Ken Griffey Jr. Promo	3.00	1.35

1996 Collector's Choice Crash the Game

	MINT	NRMT
COMPLETE SET (90)	50.00	22.00
COMMON CARD (CG1-CG30)	.25	.11
SER.2 STATED ODDS 1:5		
*GOLD: 3X TO 8X BASE CARD HI		
GOLD SER.2 STATED ODDS 1:48		
THREE DATES PER PLAYER		
COMP.EXCH.SET (27)	100.00	45.00
*EXCH: 3X TO 8X BASE CARD HI		
*GOLD EXCH: 10X TO 25X BASE CARD HI		
ONE EXCH.CARD VIA MAIL PER WINNER		

❏ CG1	Chipper Jones 7/11 W	1.50	.70
❏ CG1B	Chipper Jones 8/27 W	1.50	.70
❏ CG1C	Chipper Jones 9/19	1.50	.70
❏ CG2	Fred McGriff 7/1	.40	.18
❏ CG2B	Fred McGriff 8/30	.40	.18
❏ CG2C	Fred McGriff 9/10 W	.40	.18
❏ CG3	Rafael Palmeiro 7/4 W	.60	.25
❏ CG3B	Rafael Palmeiro 8/29	.60	.25
❏ CG3C	Rafael Palmeiro 9/26	.60	.25
❏ CG4	Cal Ripken 6/27	2.50	1.10
❏ CG4B	Cal Ripken 7/25 W	2.50	1.10
❏ CG4C	Cal Ripken 9/8	2.50	1.10
❏ CG5	Jose Canseco 6/27	.75	.35
❏ CG5B	Jose Canseco 7/11 W	.75	.35
❏ CG5C	Jose Canseco 8/23	.75	.35
❏ CG6	Mo Vaughn 6/21 W	.60	.25
❏ CG6B	Mo Vaughn 7/18 W	.60	.25
❏ CG6C	Mo Vaughn 9/20	.60	.25
❏ CG7	Jim Edmonds 7/18 W	.40	.18
❏ CG7B	Jim Edmonds 8/16 W	.40	.18
❏ CG7C	Jim Edmonds 9/20	.40	.18
❏ CG8	Tim Salmon 6/20	.40	.18
❏ CG8B	Tim Salmon 7/30	.40	.18
❏ CG8C	Tim Salmon 9/8	.40	.18
❏ CG9	Sammy Sosa 7/4 W	2.00	.90
❏ CG9B	Sammy Sosa 8/1 W	2.00	.90
❏ CG9C	Sammy Sosa 9/2	2.00	.90
❏ CG10	Frank Thomas 6/27	1.25	.55
❏ CG10B	Frank Thomas 7/4	1.25	.55
❏ CG10C	Frank Thomas 9/2 W	1.25	.55
❏ CG11	Albert Belle 6/25	.60	.25
❏ CG11B	Albert Belle 8/4 W	.60	.25
❏ CG11C	Albert Belle 9/6	.60	.25
❏ CG12	Manny Ramirez 7/18 W	.75	.35
❏ CG12B	Manny Ramirez 8/26	.75	.35

❏ CG12C	Manny Ramirez 9/9 W	.75	.35
❏ CG13	Jim Thorne 6/27	.60	.25
❏ CG13B	Jim Thorne 8/14	.60	.25
❏ CG13C	Jim Thorne 9/23	.60	.25
❏ CG14	Dante Bichette 7/11 W	.25	.11
❏ CG14B	Dante Bichette 8/9	.25	.11
❏ CG14C	Dante Bichette 8/9	.25	.11
❏ CG15	Vinny Castilla 7/1	.40	.18
❏ CG15B	Vinny Castilla 8/23 W	.40	.18
❏ CG15C	Vinny Castilla 9/13 W	.40	.18
❏ CG16	Larry Walker 6/24	.60	.25
❏ CG16B	Larry Walker 7/18	.60	.25
❏ CG16C	Larry Walker 9/27	.60	.25
❏ CG17	Cecil Fielder 6/27	.25	.11
❏ CG17B	Cecil Fielder 7/30 W	.25	.11
❏ CG17C	Cecil Fielder 9/17 W	.25	.11
❏ CG18	Gary Sheffield 7/4	.25	.11
❏ CG18B	Gary Sheffield 8/2	.25	.11
❏ CG18C	Gary Sheffield 9/5 W	.25	.11
❏ CG19	Jeff Bagwell 7/4 W	.75	.35
❏ CG19B	Jeff Bagwell 8/16	.75	.35
❏ CG19C	Jeff Bagwell 9/13	.75	.35
❏ CG20	Eric Karros 7/4 W	.25	.11
❏ CG20B	Eric Karros 8/13 W	.25	.11
❏ CG20C	Eric Karros 9/16	.25	.11
❏ CG21	Mike Piazza 6/27 W	2.00	.90
❏ CG21B	Mike Piazza 7/26	2.00	.90
❏ CG21C	Mike Piazza 9/12 W	2.00	.90
❏ CG22	Ken Caminiti 7/11 W	.25	.11
❏ CG22B	Ken Caminiti 8/16 W	.25	.11
❏ CG22C	Ken Caminiti 9/19 W	.25	.11
❏ CG23	Barry Bonds 6/27 W	.75	.35
❏ CG23B	Barry Bonds 7/22	.75	.35
❏ CG23C	Barry Bonds 9/24	.75	.35
❏ CG24	Matt Williams 7/11 W	.60	.25
❏ CG24B	Matt Williams 8/19	.60	.25
❏ CG24C	Matt Williams 9/27	.60	.25
❏ CG25	Jay Buhner 6/20	.25	.11
❏ CG25B	Jay Buhner 7/25	.25	.11
❏ CG25C	Jay Buhner 9/8 W	.25	.11
❏ CG26	Ken Griffey Jr. 7/18 W	3.00	1.35
❏ CG26B	Ken Griffey Jr. 8/16 W	3.00	1.35
❏ CG26C	Ken Griffey Jr. 9/20 W	3.00	1.35
❏ CG27	Ron Gant 6/24 W	.25	.11
❏ CG27B	Ron Gant 7/11 W	.25	.11
❏ CG27C	Ron Gant 9/27 W	.25	.11
❏ CG28	Juan Gonzalez 6/28 W	1.25	.55
❏ CG28B	J. Gonzalez 7/15 W	1.25	.55
❏ CG28C	Juan Gonzalez 8/6	1.25	.55
❏ CG29	Mickey Tettleton 7/4 W	.25	.11
❏ CG29B	Mickey Tettleton 8/6	.25	.11
❏ CG29C	M. Tettleton 9/6 W	.25	.11
❏ CG30	Joe Carter 6/25	.25	.11
❏ CG30B	Joe Carter 8/5	.25	.11
❏ CG30C	Joe Carter 9/25	.25	.11

1996 Collector's Choice Griffey A Cut Above

	MINT	NRMT
COMPLETE SET (10)	8.00	3.60
COMMON CARD (CA1-CA10)	1.00	.45
ONE PER SPECIAL RETAIL PACK		

❏ CA1	Ken Griffey Jr.	1.00	.45
❏ CA2	Ken Griffey Jr.	1.00	.45
❏ CA3	Ken Griffey Jr.	1.00	.45
❏ CA4	Ken Griffey Jr.	1.00	.45

❏ CA5	Ken Griffey Jr.	1.00	.45
❏ CA6	Ken Griffey Jr.	1.00	.45
❏ CA7	Ken Griffey Jr.	1.00	.45
❏ CA8	Ken Griffey Jr.	1.00	.45
❏ CA9	Ken Griffey Jr.	1.00	.45
❏ CA10	Ken Griffey Jr.	1.00	.45

1996 Collector's Choice Nomo Scrapbook

	MINT	NRMT
COMPLETE SET (5)	5.00	2.20
COMMON CARD (1-5)	1.50	.70
SER.2 STATED ODDS 1:12		

❏ 1	Hideo Nomo Hands at Side	1.50	.70
❏ 2	Hideo Nomo Releasing ball	1.50	.70
❏ 3	Hideo Nomo Back turned to batter	1.50	.70
❏ 4	Hideo Nomo Hands over head	1.50	.70
❏ 5	Hideo Nomo Glove at side	1.50	.70

1996 Collector's Choice You Make the Play

	MINT	NRMT
COMPLETE SET (90)	12.00	5.50
COMMON CARD (1-45)	.10	.05
ONE BASIC CARD PER SER.1 PACK		
*GOLD: 6X TO 15X BASE CARD HI		
GOLD SER.1 STATED ODDS 1:35		
TWO MAKE THE PLAY CARDS PER PLAYER		

❏ 1	Kevin Appier	.20	.09
❏ 1A	Kevin Appier	.20	.09
❏ 2	Carlos Baerga	.10	.05
❏ 2A	Carlos Baerga	.10	.05
❏ 3	Jeff Bagwell	.50	.23
❏ 3A	Jeff Bagwell	.50	.23
❏ 4	Jay Bell	.20	.09
❏ 4A	Jay Bell	.20	.09
❏ 5	Albert Belle	.40	.18
❏ 5A	Albert Belle	.40	.18
❏ 6	Craig Biggio	.40	.18
❏ 6A	Craig Biggio	.40	.18
❏ 7	Wade Boggs	.40	.18

❑ 7A Wade Boggs	.40	.18
❑ 8 Barry Bonds	.50	.23
❑ 8A Barry Bonds	.50	.23
❑ 9 Bobby Bonilla	.20	.09
❑ 9A Bobby Bonilla	.20	.09
❑ 10 Jose Canseco	.50	.23
❑ 10A Jose Canseco	.50	.23
❑ 11 Joe Carter	.20	.09
❑ 11A Joe Carter	.20	.09
❑ 12 Darren Daulton	.20	.09
❑ 12A Darren Daulton	.20	.09
❑ 13 Cecil Fielder	.20	.09
❑ 13A Cecil Fielder	.20	.09
❑ 14 Ron Gant	.10	.05
❑ 14A Ron Gant	.10	.05
❑ 15 Juan Gonzalez	.75	.35
❑ 15A Juan Gonzalez	.75	.35
❑ 16 Ken Griffey Jr.	2.00	.90
❑ 16A Ken Griffey Jr.	2.00	.90
❑ 17 Tony Gwynn	1.00	.45
❑ 17A Tony Gwynn	1.00	.45
❑ 18 Randy Johnson	.50	.23
❑ 18A Randy Johnson	.50	.23
❑ 19 Chipper Jones	1.00	.45
❑ 19A Chipper Jones	1.00	.45
❑ 20 Barry Larkin	.40	.18
❑ 20A Barry Larkin	.40	.18
❑ 21 Kenny Lofton	.30	.14
❑ 21A Kenny Lofton	.30	.14
❑ 22 Greg Maddux	1.00	.45
❑ 22A Greg Maddux	1.00	.45
❑ 23 Don Mattingly	.75	.35
❑ 23A Don Mattingly	.75	.35
❑ 24 Fred McGriff	.30	.14
❑ 24A Fred McGriff	.30	.14
❑ 25 Mark McGwire	2.00	.90
❑ 25A Mark McGwire	2.00	.90
❑ 26 Paul Molitor	.40	.18
❑ 26A Paul Molitor	.40	.18
❑ 27 Raul Mondesi	.20	.09
❑ 27A Raul Mondesi	.20	.09
❑ 28 Eddie Murray	.40	.18
❑ 28A Eddie Murray	.40	.18
❑ 29 Hideo Nomo	.40	.18
❑ 29A Hideo Nomo	.40	.18
❑ 30 Jon Nunnally	.10	.05
❑ 30A Jon Nunnally	.10	.05
❑ 31 Mike Piazza	1.25	.55
❑ 31A Mike Piazza	1.25	.55
❑ 32 Kirby Puckett	.75	.35
❑ 32A Kirby Puckett	.75	.35
❑ 33 Cal Ripken	1.50	.70
❑ 33A Cal Ripken	1.50	.70
❑ 34 Alex Rodriguez	1.25	.55
❑ 34A Alex Rodriguez	1.25	.55
❑ 35 Tim Salmon	.30	.14
❑ 35A Tim Salmon	.30	.14
❑ 36 Gary Sheffield	.20	.09
❑ 36A Gary Sheffield	.20	.09
❑ 37 Lee Smith	.20	.09
❑ 37A Lee Smith	.20	.09
❑ 38 Ozzie Smith	.50	.23
❑ 38A Ozzie Smith	.50	.23
❑ 39 Sammy Sosa	1.25	.55
❑ 39A Sammy Sosa	1.25	.55
❑ 40 Frank Thomas	.75	.35
❑ 40A Frank Thomas	.75	.35
❑ 41 Greg Vaughn	.20	.09
❑ 41A Greg Vaughn	.20	.09
❑ 42 Mo Vaughn	.40	.18
❑ 42A Mo Vaughn	.40	.18
❑ 43 Larry Walker	.40	.18
❑ 43A Larry Walker	.40	.18
❑ 44 Rondell White	.20	.09
❑ 44A Rondell White	.20	.09
❑ 45 Matt Williams	.40	.18
❑ 45A Matt Williams	.40	.18

1997 Collector's Choice

	MINT	NRMT
COMPLETE SET (506)	40.00	18.00
COMP.FACT.SET (516)	40.00	18.00
COMPLETE SERIES 1 (246)	20.00	9.00
COMPLETE SERIES 2 (260)	20.00	9.00
COMMON CARD (1-506)	.10	.05

COMMON GRIFFEY CL (244-249)	.25	.11
MINOR STARS	.20	.09
UNLISTED STARS	.40	.18

SUBSET CARDS HALF VALUE OF BASE CARDS
B.WILLIAMS AND D.GOODEN NUMBERED 175
D.GOODEN 176 AVAIL.ONLY IN FACT.SETS
TEN JUMBO PREMIER POWER PER FACT.SET

❑ 1 Andruw Jones	.50	.23
❑ 2 Rocky Coppinger	.10	.05
❑ 3 Jeff D'Amico	.10	.05
❑ 4 Dmitri Young	.20	.09
❑ 5 Darin Erstad	.40	.18
❑ 6 Jermaine Allensworth	.10	.05
❑ 7 Damian Jackson	.10	.05
❑ 8 Bill Mueller	.50	.23
❑ 9 Jacob Cruz	.10	.05
❑ 10 Vladimir Guerrero	.60	.25
❑ 11 Marty Janzen	.10	.05
❑ 12 Kevin L. Brown	.10	.05
❑ 13 Willie Adams	.10	.05
❑ 14 Wendell Magee	.10	.05
❑ 15 Scott Rolen	.60	.25
❑ 16 Matt Beech	.10	.05
❑ 17 Neifi Perez	.20	.09
❑ 18 Jamey Wright	.10	.05
❑ 19 Jose Paniagua	.10	.05
❑ 20 Todd Walker	.40	.18
❑ 21 Justin Thompson	.20	.09
❑ 22 Robin Jennings	.10	.05
❑ 23 Dario Veras	.25	.11
❑ 24 Brian Lesher	.10	.05
❑ 25 Nomar Garciaparra	1.25	.55
❑ 26 Luis Castillo	.20	.09
❑ 27 Brian Giles	1.25	.55
❑ 28 Jermaine Dye	.20	.09
❑ 29 Terrell Wade	.10	.05
❑ 30 Fred McGriff	.30	.14
❑ 31 Marquis Grissom	.20	.09
❑ 32 Ryan Klesko	.20	.09
❑ 33 Javier Lopez	.20	.09
❑ 34 Mark Wohlers	.10	.05
❑ 35 Tom Glavine	.40	.18
❑ 36 Denny Neagle	.20	.09
❑ 37 Scott Erickson	.20	.09
❑ 38 Chris Hoiles	.10	.05
❑ 39 Roberto Alomar	.40	.18
❑ 40 Eddie Murray	.40	.18
❑ 41 Cal Ripken	1.50	.70
❑ 42 Randy Myers	.10	.05
❑ 43 B.J. Surhoff	.20	.09
❑ 44 Rick Krivda	.10	.05
❑ 45 Jose Canseco	.50	.23
❑ 46 Heathcliff Slocumb	.10	.05
❑ 47 Jeff Suppan	.10	.05
❑ 48 Tom Gordon	.10	.05
❑ 49 Aaron Sele	.10	.05
❑ 50 Mo Vaughn	.40	.18
❑ 51 Darren Bragg	.10	.05
❑ 52 Wil Cordero	.10	.05
❑ 53 Scott Bullett	.10	.05
❑ 54 Terry Adams	.10	.05
❑ 55 Jackie Robinson	1.00	.45
❑ 56 Tony Gwynn LL	.50	.23

	Alex Rodriguez	
❑ 57 Andres Galarraga LL	.25	.11
	Mark McGwire	
❑ 58 Andres Galarraga LL	.20	.09
	Albert Belle	
❑ 59 Eric Young LL	.20	.09
	Kenny Lofton	
❑ 60 John Smoltz LL	.10	.05
	Andy Pettitte	
❑ 61 John Smoltz LL	.25	.11
	Roger Clemens	
❑ 62 Kevin Brown LL	.10	.05
	Juan Guzman	
❑ 63 John Wetteland LL	.10	.05
	Todd Worrell	
	Jeff Brantley	
❑ 64 Scott Servais	.10	.05
❑ 65 Sammy Sosa	1.25	.55
❑ 66 Ryne Sandberg	.50	.23
❑ 67 Frank Castillo	.10	.05
❑ 68 Rey Sanchez	.10	.05
❑ 69 Steve Trachsel	.10	.05
❑ 70 Robin Ventura	.20	.09
❑ 71 Wilson Alvarez	.20	.09
❑ 72 Tony Phillips	.10	.05
❑ 73 Lyle Mouton	.10	.05
❑ 74 Mike Cameron	.20	.09
❑ 75 Harold Baines	.20	.09
❑ 76 Albert Belle	.40	.18
❑ 77 Chris Snopek	.10	.05
❑ 78 Reggie Sanders	.20	.09
❑ 79 Jeff Brantley	.10	.05
❑ 80 Barry Larkin	.40	.18
❑ 81 Kevin Jarvis	.10	.05
❑ 82 John Smiley	.10	.05
❑ 83 Pete Schourek	.10	.05
❑ 84 Thomas Howard	.10	.05
❑ 85 Lee Smith	.20	.09
❑ 86 Omar Vizquel	.20	.09
❑ 87 Julio Franco	.20	.09
❑ 88 Orel Hershiser	.20	.09
❑ 89 Charles Nagy	.20	.09
❑ 90 Matt Williams	.40	.18
❑ 91 Dennis Martinez	.20	.09
❑ 92 Jose Mesa	.10	.05
❑ 93 Sandy Alomar Jr.	.20	.09
❑ 94 Jim Thome	.40	.18
❑ 95 Vinny Castilla	.30	.14
❑ 96 Armando Reynoso	.10	.05
❑ 97 Kevin Ritz	.10	.05
❑ 98 Larry Walker	.40	.18
❑ 99 Eric Young	.20	.09
❑ 100 Dante Bichette	.20	.09
❑ 101 Quinton McCracken	.10	.05
❑ 102 John Vander Wal	.10	.05
❑ 103 Phil Nevin	.10	.05
❑ 104 Tony Clark	.30	.14
❑ 105 Alan Trammell	.20	.09
❑ 106 Felipe Lira	.10	.05
❑ 107 Curtis Pride	.10	.05
❑ 108 Bobby Higginson	.20	.09
❑ 109 Mark Lewis	.10	.05
❑ 110 Travis Fryman	.20	.09
❑ 111 Al Leiter	.20	.09
❑ 112 Devon White	.20	.09
❑ 113 Jeff Conine	.20	.09
❑ 114 Charles Johnson	.20	.09
❑ 115 Andre Dawson	.30	.14
❑ 116 Edgar Renteria	.20	.09
❑ 117 Robb Nen	.10	.05
❑ 118 Kevin Brown	.30	.14
❑ 119 Derek Bell	.20	.09
❑ 120 Bob Abreu	.20	.09
❑ 121 Mike Hampton	.20	.09
❑ 122 Todd Jones	.10	.05
❑ 123 Billy Wagner	.20	.09
❑ 124 Shane Reynolds	.20	.09
❑ 125 Jeff Bagwell	.75	.35
❑ 126 Brian L. Hunter	.20	.09
❑ 127 Jeff Montgomery	.10	.05
❑ 128 Rod Myers	.10	.05
❑ 129 Tim Belcher	.10	.05
❑ 130 Kevin Appier	.20	.09
❑ 131 Mike Sweeney	.20	.09
❑ 132 Craig Paquette	.10	.05
❑ 133 Joe Randa	.10	.05

134	Michael Tucker	.10	.05
135	Raul Mondesi	.20	.09
136	Tim Wallach	.10	.05
137	Brett Butler	.20	.09
138	Karim Garcia	.20	.09
139	Todd Hollandsworth	.10	.05
140	Eric Karros	.20	.09
141	Hideo Nomo	.40	.18
142	Ismael Valdes	.20	.09
143	Cal Eldred	.10	.05
144	Scott Karl	.10	.05
145	Matt Mieske	.10	.05
146	Mike Fetters	.10	.05
147	Mark Loretta	.10	.05
148	Fernando Vina	.10	.05
149	Jeff Cirillo	.20	.09
150	Dave Nilsson	.10	.05
151	Kirby Puckett	.60	.25
152	Rich Becker	.10	.05
153	Chuck Knoblauch	.40	.18
154	Marty Cordova	.10	.05
155	Paul Molitor	.40	.18
156	Rick Aguilera	.10	.05
157	Pat Meares	.10	.05
158	Frank Rodriguez	.10	.05
159	David Segui	.20	.09
160	Henry Rodriguez	.20	.09
161	Shane Andrews	.10	.05
162	Pedro Martinez	.50	.23
163	Mark Grudzielanek	.20	.09
164	Mike Lansing	.10	.05
165	Rondell White	.20	.09
166	Ugueth Urbina	.20	.09
167	Rey Ordonez	.20	.09
168	Robert Person	.10	.05
169	Carlos Baerga	.20	.09
170	Bernard Gilkey	.10	.05
171	John Franco	.20	.09
172	Pete Harnisch	.10	.05
173	Butch Huskey	.10	.05
174	Paul Wilson	.10	.05
175	Bernie Williams	.40	.18
175	Dwight Gooden ERR	.20	.09
	Incorrectly numbered 175		
177	Wade Boggs	.40	.18
178	Ruben Rivera	.10	.05
179	Jim Leyritz	.10	.05
180	Derek Jeter	1.25	.55
181	Tino Martinez	.40	.18
182	Tim Raines	.20	.09
183	Scott Brosius	.20	.09
184	Jason Giambi	.20	.09
185	Geronimo Berroa	.10	.05
186	Ariel Prieto	.10	.05
187	Scott Spiezio	.10	.05
188	John Wasdin	.10	.05
189	Ernie Young	.10	.05
190	Mark McGwire	2.00	.90
191	Jim Eisenreich	.10	.05
192	Ricky Bottalico	.20	.09
193	Darren Daulton	.20	.09
194	David Doster	.10	.05
195	Gregg Jefferies	.10	.05
196	Lenny Dykstra	.20	.09
197	Curt Schilling	.30	.14
198	Todd Stottlemyre	.10	.05
199	Willie McGee	.20	.09
200	Ozzie Smith	.50	.23
201	Dennis Eckersley	.20	.09
202	Ray Lankford	.20	.09
203	John Mabry	.10	.05
204	Alan Benes	.10	.05
205	Ron Gant	.20	.09
206	Archi Cianfrocco	.10	.05
207	Fernando Valenzuela	.20	.09
208	Greg Vaughn	.20	.09
209	Steve Finley	.20	.09
210	Tony Gwynn	1.00	.45
211	Rickey Henderson	.50	.23
212	Trevor Hoffman	.20	.09
213	Jason Thompson	.10	.05
214	Osvaldo Fernandez	.10	.05
215	Glenallen Hill	.10	.05
216	William VanLandingham	.10	.05
217	Marvin Benard	.10	.05
218	Juan Gonzalez POST	.40	.18
219	Roberto Alomar POST	.20	.09
220	Brian Jordan POST	.10	.05
221	John Smoltz POST	.20	.09
222	Javy Lopez POST	.10	.05
223	Bernie Williams POST	.20	.09
224	Jim Leyritz POST	.10	.05
	John Wetteland		
225	Barry Bonds	.50	.23
226	Rich Aurilia	.20	.09
227	Jay Canizaro	.10	.05
228	Dan Wilson	.10	.05
229	Bob Wolcott	.10	.05
230	Ken Griffey Jr.	2.00	.90
231	Sterling Hitchcock	.20	.09
232	Edgar Martinez	.20	.09
233	Joey Cora	.10	.05
234	Norm Charlton	.10	.05
235	Alex Rodriguez	1.25	.55
236	Bobby Witt	.10	.05
237	Darren Oliver	.10	.05
238	Kevin Elster	.10	.05
239	Rusty Greer	.20	.09
240	Juan Gonzalez	.75	.35
241	Will Clark	.40	.18
242	Dean Palmer	.20	.09
243	Ivan Rodriguez	.50	.23
244	Ken Griffey Jr. CL	.25	.11
245	Ken Griffey Jr. CL	.25	.11
246	Ken Griffey Jr. CL	.25	.11
247	Ken Griffey Jr. CL	.25	.11
248	Ken Griffey Jr. CL	.25	.11
249	Ken Griffey Jr. CL	.25	.11
250	Eddie Murray	.40	.18
251	Troy Percival	.20	.09
252	Garret Anderson	.20	.09
253	Allen Watson	.10	.05
254	Jason Dickson	.10	.05
255	Jim Edmonds	.30	.14
256	Chuck Finley	.10	.05
257	Randy Velarde	.10	.05
258	Shigetoshi Hasegawa	.20	.09
259	Todd Greene	.10	.05
260	Tim Salmon	.40	.18
261	Mark Langston	.20	.09
262	Dave Hollins	.10	.05
263	Gary DiSarcina	.10	.05
264	Kenny Lofton	.30	.14
265	John Smoltz	.30	.14
266	Greg Maddux	1.00	.45
267	Jeff Blauser	.10	.05
268	Alan Embree	.10	.05
269	Mark Lemke	.10	.05
270	Chipper Jones	1.00	.45
271	Mike Mussina	.40	.18
272	Rafael Palmeiro	.40	.18
273	Jimmy Key	.20	.09
274	Mike Bordick	.10	.05
275	Brady Anderson	.20	.09
276	Eric Davis	.20	.09
277	Jeffrey Hammonds	.20	.09
278	Reggie Jefferson	.10	.05
279	Tim Naehring	.10	.05
280	John Valentin	.20	.09
281	Troy O'Leary	.10	.05
282	Shane Mack	.10	.05
283	Mike Stanley	.10	.05
284	Tim Wakefield	.20	.09
285	Brian McRae	.10	.05
286	Brooks Kieschnick	.10	.05
287	Shawon Dunston	.10	.05
288	Kevin Foster	.10	.05
289	Mel Rojas	.10	.05
290	Mark Grace	.30	.14
291	Brant Brown	.10	.05
292	Amaury Telemaco	.10	.05
293	Dave Martinez	.10	.05
294	Jaime Navarro	.10	.05
295	Ray Durham	.20	.09
296	Ozzie Guillen	.10	.05
297	Roberto Hernandez	.10	.05
298	Ron Karkovice	.10	.05
299	James Baldwin	.20	.09
300	Frank Thomas	.75	.35
301	Eddie Taubensee	.10	.05
302	Bret Boone	.20	.09
303	Willie Greene	.10	.05
304	Dave Burba	.10	.05
305	Deion Sanders	.20	.09
306	Reggie Sanders	.20	.09
307	Hal Morris	.10	.05
308	Pokey Reese	.20	.09
309	Tony Fernandez	.20	.09
310	Manny Ramirez	.50	.23
311	Chad Ogea	.10	.05
312	Jack McDowell	.10	.05
313	Kevin Mitchell	.10	.05
314	Chad Curtis	.10	.05
315	Steve Kline	.10	.05
316	Kevin Seitzer	.10	.05
317	Kirt Manwaring	.10	.05
318	Billy Swift	.10	.05
319	Ellis Burks	.20	.09
320	Andres Galarraga	.40	.18
321	Bruce Ruffin	.10	.05
322	Mark Thompson	.10	.05
323	Walt Weiss	.10	.05
324	Todd Jones	.10	.05
325	Andruw Jones GHL	.30	.14
326	Chipper Jones GHL	.50	.23
327	Mo Vaughn GHL	.20	.09
328	Frank Thomas GHL	.60	.25
329	Albert Belle GHL	.20	.09
330	Mark McGwire GHL	1.00	.45
331	Derek Jeter GHL	.60	.25
332	Alex Rodriguez GHL	.60	.25
333	Jay Buhner GHL	.10	.05
	Ken Griffey Jr.		
334	Ken Griffey Jr. GHL	1.00	.45
335	Brian L. Hunter	.20	.09
336	Brian Johnson	.10	.05
337	Omar Olivares	.10	.05
338	Deivi Cruz	.40	.18
339	Damion Easley	.10	.05
340	Melvin Nieves	.10	.05
341	Moises Alou	.20	.09
342	Jim Eisenreich	.10	.05
343	Mark Hutton	.10	.05
344	Alex Fernandez	.10	.05
345	Gary Sheffield	.20	.09
346	Pat Rapp	.10	.05
347	Brad Ausmus	.10	.05
348	Sean Berry	.10	.05
349	Darryl Kile	.10	.05
350	Craig Biggio	.40	.18
351	Chris Holt	.10	.05
352	Luis Gonzalez	.20	.09
353	Pat Listach	.10	.05
354	Jose Rosado	.10	.05
355	Mike Macfarlane	.10	.05
356	Tom Goodwin	.10	.05
357	Chris Haney	.10	.05
358	Chili Davis	.20	.09
359	Jose Offerman	.10	.05
360	Johnny Damon	.20	.09
361	Bip Roberts	.10	.05
362	Ramon Martinez	.20	.09
363	Pedro Astacio	.10	.05
364	Todd Zeile	.10	.05
365	Mike Piazza	1.25	.55
366	Greg Gagne	.10	.05
367	Chan Ho Park	.40	.18
368	Wilton Guerrero	.10	.05
369	Todd Worrell	.10	.05
370	John Jaha	.10	.05
371	Steve Sparks	.10	.05
372	Mike Matheny	.10	.05
373	Marc Newfield	.10	.05
374	Jeromy Burnitz	.20	.09
375	Jose Valentin	.10	.05
376	Ben McDonald	.10	.05
377	Roberto Kelly	.10	.05
378	Bob Tewksbury	.10	.05
379	Ron Coomer	.10	.05
380	Brad Radke	.20	.09
381	Matt Lawton	.10	.05
382	Dan Naulty	.10	.05
383	Scott Stahoviak	.10	.05
384	Matt Wagner	.10	.05
385	Jim Bullinger	.10	.05
386	Carlos Perez	.10	.05
387	Darrin Fletcher	.10	.05
388	Chris Widger	.10	.05

❑ 389 F.P. Santangelo	.10	.05
❑ 390 Lee Smith	.20	.09
❑ 391 Bobby Jones	.10	.05
❑ 392 John Olerud	.10	.05
❑ 393 Mark Clark	.10	.05
❑ 394 Jason Isringhausen	.10	.05
❑ 395 Todd Hundley	.20	.09
❑ 396 Lance Johnson	.10	.05
❑ 397 Edgardo Alfonzo	.30	.14
❑ 398 Alex Ochoa	.10	.05
❑ 399 Darryl Strawberry	.20	.09
❑ 400 David Cone	.30	.14
❑ 401 Paul O'Neill	.20	.09
❑ 402 Joe Girardi	.10	.05
❑ 403 Charlie Hayes	.10	.05
❑ 404 Andy Pettitte	.30	.14
❑ 405 Mariano Rivera	.20	.09
❑ 406 Mariano Duncan	.10	.05
❑ 407 Kenny Rogers	.10	.05
❑ 408 Cecil Fielder	.20	.09
❑ 409 George Williams	.10	.05
❑ 410 Jose Canseco	.50	.23
❑ 411 Tony Batista	.30	.14
❑ 412 Steve Karsay	.10	.05
❑ 413 Dave Telgheder	.10	.05
❑ 414 Billy Taylor	.10	.05
❑ 415 Mickey Morandini	.10	.05
❑ 416 Calvin Maduro	.10	.05
❑ 417 Mark Leiter	.10	.05
❑ 418 Kevin Stocker	.10	.05
❑ 419 Mike Lieberthal	.10	.05
❑ 420 Rico Brogna	.10	.05
❑ 421 Mark Portugal	.10	.05
❑ 422 Rex Hudler	.10	.05
❑ 423 Mark Johnson	.10	.05
❑ 424 Esteban Loaiza	.10	.05
❑ 425 Lou Collier	.10	.05
❑ 426 Kevin Elster	.10	.05
❑ 427 Francisco Cordova	.10	.05
❑ 428 Marc Wilkins	.10	.05
❑ 429 Joe Randa	.10	.05
❑ 430 Jason Kendall	.30	.14
❑ 431 Jon Lieber	.10	.05
❑ 432 Steve Cooke	.10	.05
❑ 433 Emil Brown	.20	.09
❑ 434 Tony Womack	.30	.14
❑ 435 Al Martin	.10	.05
❑ 436 Jason Schmidt	.10	.05
❑ 437 Andy Benes	.20	.09
❑ 438 Delino DeShields	.10	.05
❑ 439 Royce Clayton	.10	.05
❑ 440 Brian Jordan	.20	.09
❑ 441 Donovan Osborne	.10	.05
❑ 442 Gary Gaetti	.20	.09
❑ 443 Tom Pagnozzi	.10	.05
❑ 444 Joey Hamilton	.20	.09
❑ 445 Wally Joyner	.20	.09
❑ 446 John Flaherty	.10	.05
❑ 447 Chris Gomez	.10	.05
❑ 448 Sterling Hitchcock	.20	.09
❑ 449 Andy Ashby	.10	.05
❑ 450 Ken Caminiti	.30	.14
❑ 451 Tim Worrell	.10	.05
❑ 452 Jose Vizcaino	.10	.05
❑ 453 Rod Beck	.10	.05
❑ 454 Wilson Delgado	.20	.09
❑ 455 Darryl Hamilton	.10	.05
❑ 456 Mark Lewis	.10	.05
❑ 457 Mark Gardner	.10	.05
❑ 458 Rick Wilkins	.10	.05
❑ 459 Scott Sanders	.10	.05
❑ 460 Kevin Orie	.10	.05
❑ 461 Glendon Rusch	.10	.05
❑ 462 Juan Melo	.20	.09
❑ 463 Richie Sexson	.40	.18
❑ 464 Bartolo Colon	.20	.09
❑ 465 Jose Guillen	.30	.14
❑ 466 Heath Murray	.10	.05
❑ 467 Aaron Boone	.10	.05
❑ 468 Bubba Trammell	.40	.18
❑ 469 Jeff Abbott	.10	.05
❑ 470 Derrick Gibson	.30	.14
❑ 471 Matt Morris	.20	.09
❑ 472 Ryan Jones	.10	.05
❑ 473 Pat Cline	.20	.09
❑ 474 Adam Riggs	.10	.05

❑ 475 Jay Payton	.10	.05
❑ 476 Derrek Lee	.30	.14
❑ 477 Eli Marrero	.10	.05
❑ 478 Lee Tinsley	.10	.05
❑ 479 Jamie Moyer	.10	.05
❑ 480 Jay Buhner	.20	.09
❑ 481 Bob Wells	.10	.05
❑ 482 Jeff Fassero	.10	.05
❑ 483 Paul Sorrento	.10	.05
❑ 484 Russ Davis	.20	.09
❑ 485 Randy Johnson	.40	.18
❑ 486 Roger Pavlik	.10	.05
❑ 487 Damon Buford	.10	.05
❑ 488 Julio Santana	.10	.05
❑ 489 Mark McLemore	.10	.05
❑ 490 Mickey Tettleton	.10	.05
❑ 491 Ken Hill	.10	.05
❑ 492 Benji Gil	.10	.05
❑ 493 Ed Sprague	.10	.05
❑ 494 Mike Timlin	.10	.05
❑ 495 Pat Hentgen	.20	.09
❑ 496 Orlando Merced	.10	.05
❑ 497 Carlos Garcia	.10	.05
❑ 498 Carlos Delgado	.40	.18
❑ 499 Juan Guzman	.10	.05
❑ 500 Roger Clemens	1.00	.45
❑ 501 Erik Hanson	.10	.05
❑ 502 Otis Nixon	.10	.05
❑ 503 Shawn Green	.40	.18
❑ 504 Charlie O'Brien	.10	.05
❑ 505 Joe Carter	.20	.09
❑ 506 Alex Gonzalez	.10	.05

1997 Collector's Choice All-Star Connection

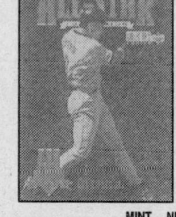

	MINT	NRMT
COMPLETE SET (45)	12.00	5.50
COMMON CARD (1-45)	.10	.05
SER.2 ODDS 1:1 HOBBY, 2:1 RETAIL		

❑ 1 Mark McGwire	2.00	.90
❑ 2 Chuck Knoblauch	.40	.18
❑ 3 Jim Thome	.40	.18
❑ 4 Alex Rodriguez	1.25	.55
❑ 5 Ken Griffey Jr.	2.00	.90
❑ 6 Brady Anderson	.20	.09
❑ 7 Albert Belle	.40	.18
❑ 8 Ivan Rodriguez	.50	.23
❑ 9 Pat Hentgen	.20	.09
❑ 10 Frank Thomas	1.25	.55
❑ 11 Roberto Alomar	.40	.18
❑ 12 Robin Ventura	.20	.09
❑ 13 Cal Ripken	1.50	.70
❑ 14 Juan Gonzalez	.75	.35
❑ 15 Manny Ramirez	.50	.23
❑ 16 Bernie Williams	.40	.18
❑ 17 Terry Steinbach	.10	.05
❑ 18 Andy Pettitte	.30	.14
❑ 19 Jeff Bagwell	.75	.35
❑ 20 Craig Biggio	.40	.18
❑ 21 Ken Caminiti	.30	.14
❑ 22 Barry Larkin	.40	.18
❑ 23 Tony Gwynn	1.00	.45
❑ 24 Barry Bonds	.50	.23
❑ 25 Kenny Lofton	.30	.14
❑ 26 Mike Piazza	1.25	.55
❑ 27 John Smoltz	.30	.14

❑ 28 Andres Galarraga	.40	.18
❑ 29 Ryne Sandberg	.50	.23
❑ 30 Chipper Jones	1.25	.55
❑ 31 Mark Grudzielanek	.20	.09
❑ 32 Sammy Sosa	1.25	.55
❑ 33 Steve Finley	.20	.09
❑ 34 Gary Sheffield	.20	.09
❑ 35 Todd Hundley	.10	.05
❑ 36 Greg Maddux	1.00	.45
❑ 37 Mo Vaughn	.40	.18
❑ 38 Eric Young	.20	.09
❑ 39 Vinny Castilla	.30	.14
❑ 40 Derek Jeter	1.25	.55
❑ 41 Lance Johnson	.10	.05
❑ 42 Ellis Burks	.20	.09
❑ 43 Dante Bichette	.20	.09
❑ 44 Javy Lopez	.20	.09
❑ 45 Hideo Nomo	.40	.18

1997 Collector's Choice Big Shots

	MINT	NRMT
COMPLETE SET (19)	60.00	27.00
COMMON CARD (1-19)	1.25	.55
SER.2 STATED ODDS 1:12		
COMP.GOLD SET (20)	250.00	110.00
*GOLD: 8X TO 20X BASE CARD HI		
SER.2 STATED ODDS 1:144		

❑ 1 Ken Griffey Jr.	10.00	4.50
❑ 2 Nomar Garciaparra	6.00	2.70
❑ 3 Brian Jordan	1.25	.55
❑ 4 Scott Rolen	4.00	1.80
❑ 5 Alex Rodriguez	6.00	2.70
❑ 6 Larry Walker	2.00	.90
❑ 7 Mariano Rivera	1.25	.55
❑ 8 Cal Ripken	8.00	3.60
❑ 9 Deion Sanders	1.25	.55
❑ 10 Frank Thomas	4.00	1.80
❑ 11 Dean Palmer	1.25	.55
❑ 12 Ken Caminiti	1.50	.70
❑ 13 Derek Jeter	5.00	2.20
❑ 14 Barry Bonds	2.00	.90
❑ 15 Chipper Jones	5.00	2.20
❑ 16 Mo Vaughn	2.00	.90
❑ 17 Jay Buhner	1.25	.55
❑ 18 Mike Piazza	6.00	2.70
❑ 19 Tony Gwynn	5.00	2.20

1997 Collector's Choice The Big Show

	MINT	NRMT
COMPLETE SET (45)	10.00	4.50
COMMON CARD (1-45)	.10	.05
SER.1 STATED ODDS 1:5		
COMP.WORLD HQ SET (45)	250.00	110.00
*WHQ STARS: 15X TO 40X BASE CARD HI		
WHQ SER.1 STATED ODDS 1:35		

❑ 1 Greg Maddux	1.00	.45
❑ 2 Chipper Jones	1.00	.45
❑ 3 Andruw Jones	.60	.25
❑ 4 John Smoltz	.30	.14
❑ 5 Cal Ripken	1.50	.70
❑ 6 Roberto Alomar	.40	.18

#	Player	MINT	NRMT
7	Rafael Palmeiro	.40	.18
8	Eddie Murray	.40	.18
9	Jose Canseco	.50	.23
10	Roger Clemens	.75	.35
11	Mo Vaughn	.40	.18
12	Jim Edmonds	.30	.14
13	Tim Salmon	.40	.18
14	Sammy Sosa	1.25	.55
15	Albert Belle	.40	.18
16	Frank Thomas	1.00	.45
17	Barry Larkin	.40	.18
18	Kenny Lofton	.30	.14
19	Manny Ramirez	.50	.23
20	Matt Williams	.40	.18
21	Dante Bichette	.20	.09
22	Gary Sheffield	.20	.09
23	Craig Biggio	.40	.18
24	Jeff Bagwell	.75	.35
25	Todd Hollandsworth	.10	.05
26	Raul Mondesi	.20	.09
27	Hideo Nomo	.40	.18
28	Mike Piazza	1.25	.55
29	Paul Molitor	.50	.23
30	Kirby Puckett	.40	.18
31	Rondell White	.20	.09
32	Rey Ordonez	.20	.09
33	Paul Wilson	.10	.05
34	Derek Jeter	1.25	.55
35	Andy Pettitte	.30	.14
36	Mark McGwire	2.00	.90
37	Jason Kendall	.30	.14
38	Ozzie Smith	.40	.18
39	Tony Gwynn	1.00	.45
40	Barry Bonds	.50	.23
41	Alex Rodriguez	1.25	.55
42	Jay Buhner	.20	.09
43	Ken Griffey Jr.	2.00	.90
44	Randy Johnson	.40	.18
45	Juan Gonzalez	.75	.35

1997 Collector's Choice Crash the Game

	MINT	NRMT
COMPLETE SET (90)	60.00	27.00
COMMON CARD (1-30)	.25	.11

SER.2 STATED ODDS 1:5
*INSTANT WIN: 20X TO 40X BASE CARD HI
INSTANT WIN SER.2 STATED ODDS 1:721

Card	MINT	NRMT
1A R.Klesko July 28-30 L	.50	.23
1B R.Klesko Aug 8-11 L	.50	.23
1C R.Klesko Sept 19-21 L	.50	.23
2A C.Jones Aug 15-17 L	2.50	1.10
2B C.Jones Aug 29-31 L	2.50	1.10
2C C.Jones Sept 12-14 L	2.50	1.10
3A A. Jones Aug 22-24 W	2.00	.90
3B A. Jones Sept 1-3	1.00	.45
3C A.Jones Sept 19-22 L	1.00	.45
4A B. Ander. July 31-Aug 3 W	.25	.11
4B B.Anderson Sept 4-7 L	.25	.11
4C B.Anderson Sept 19-22 L	.25	.11
5A R.Palmeiro July 29-30 L	.50	.23
5B R.Palmeiro Aug 29-31 L	.50	.23
5C R.Palmeiro Sept 26-28 L	.50	.23
6A Cal Ripken Aug 8-10	3.00	1.35
6B C.Ripken Sept 1-3 W	3.00	1.35
6C C.Ripken Sept 19-21 W	3.00	1.35
7A M.Vaughn Aug 14-17 L	1.00	.45
7B M.Vaughn Aug 29-31 W	1.00	.45
7C M.Vaughn Sept 23-25 W	1.00	.45
8A S.Sosa Aug 1-3 W	2.00	.90
8B S.Sosa Aug 29-31 L	2.00	.90
8C S.Sosa Sept 19-21 W	2.00	.90
9A A.Belle Aug 7-10 L	1.00	.45
9B A.Belle Sept 11-14 L	1.00	.45
9C A.Belle Sept 19-21 W	1.00	.45
10A F.Thomas Aug 29-31 L	2.50	1.10
10B F.Thomas Sept 1-3 L	2.50	1.10
10C F.Thomas Sept 23-25 W	2.50	1.10
11A M.Ramirez Aug 14-17 L	.75	.35
11B M.Ramirez Aug 29-31 L	.75	.35
11C M.Ramirez Sept 11-14 W	.75	.35
12A J.Thome July 28-30 L	.75	.35
12B J.Thome Aug 15-18 W	.75	.35
12C J.Thome Sept 19-22 L	.75	.35
13A M.Williams Aug 4-5 L	.50	.23
13B M.Williams Sept 1-3 W	.50	.23
13C M.Williams Sept 23-25 L	.50	.23
14A D.Bichette July 24-27 W	.25	.11
14B D.Bichette Sept 4-7 L	.25	.11
14C D.Bichette Sept 26-28 W	.25	.11
15A V.Castilla Aug 12-13 L	.25	.11
15B V.Castilla Sept 4-7 W	.25	.11
15C V.Castilla Sept 19-21 L	.25	.11
16A A.Galarraga Aug 8-10 W	.75	.35
16B A.Galarraga Aug 30-31 L	.75	.35
16C A.Galarraga Sept 12-14 L	.75	.35
17A G.Sheffield Aug 1-3 W	.50	.23
17B G.Sheffield Sept 1-3 W	.50	.23
17C G.Sheffield Sept 12-14 W	.50	.23
18A J.Bagwell Sept 9-10 L	1.50	.70
18B J.Bagwell Sept 19-22 W	1.50	.70
18C J.Bagwell Sept 23-25 W	1.50	.70
19A E.Karros Aug 1-3 L	.25	.11
19B E.Karros Sept 15-17 L	.25	.11
19C E.Karros Sept 25-28 W	.25	.11
20A M.Piazza Aug 11-12 L	2.50	1.10
20B M.Piazza Sept 5-8 W	2.50	1.10
20C M.Piazza Sept 19-21 W	2.50	1.10
21A V.Guerrero Aug 22-24 L	1.50	.70
21B V.Guerrero Aug 29-31 L	1.50	.70
21C V.Guerrero Sept 19-22 L	1.50	.70
22A C.Fielder Aug 29-31 L	.25	.11
22B C.Fielder Sept 4-7 L	.25	.11
22C C.Fielder Sept 26-28 L	.25	.11
23A J.Canseco Sept 1-3 L	.75	.35
23B J.Canseco Sept 22-24 L	.75	.35
23C J.Canseco Sept 26-28 L	.75	.35
24A McGwire July 31-Aug 3 L	4.00	1.80
24B M.McGwire Aug 30-31 L	4.00	1.80
24C McGwire Sept 19-22 W	4.00	1.80
25A K.Caminiti Aug 8-10 L	.50	.23
25B K.Caminiti Sept 4-7 W	.50	.23
25C K.Caminiti Sept 17-18 W	.50	.23
26A B.Bonds Aug 5-7 L	1.00	.45
26B B.Bonds Sept 4-7 L	1.00	.45
26C B.Bonds Sept 23-24 W	1.00	.45
27A J.Buhner Aug 7-10 L	.25	.11
27B J.Buhner Aug 28-29 L	.25	.11
27C J.Buhner Sept 1-3 L	.25	.11
28A K.Griffey Aug 22-24 W	4.00	1.80
28B K.Griffey Aug 28-29 L	4.00	1.80
28C K.Griffey Sept 19-22 W	4.00	1.80
29A A.Rodriguez Aug 29-31 L	2.50	1.10
29B A.Rodriguez Aug 30-31 L	2.50	1.10
29C A.Rod. Sept 12-15 L	2.50	1.10
30A J.Gonzalez Aug 11-13 W	2.00	.90
30B J.Gonzalez Aug 30-31 L	2.00	.90
30C J.Gonzalez Sept 19-21 W	2.00	.90

1997 Collector's Choice Crash the Game Exchange

	MINT	NRMT
COMPLETE SET (30)	120.00	55.00
COMMON CARD (CG1-CG30)	1.00	.45

*EXCH.WINNERS: 2.5X TO 6X BASE CARD HI
ONE CARD VIA MAIL PER CRASH WINNER
ONE SET VIA MAIL PER INSTANT WIN CARD
SP's AVAIL ONLY W/INSTANT WIN EXCH.

Card	MINT	NRMT
CG1 Ryan Klesko SP	4.00	1.80
CG2 Chipper Jones SP	25.00	11.00
CG3 Andruw Jones	5.00	2.20
CG4 Brady Anderson	1.00	.45
CG5 Rafael Palmeiro SP	10.00	4.50
CG6 Cal Ripken Jr.	10.00	4.50
CG7 Mo Vaughn	3.00	1.35
CG8 Sammy Sosa	6.00	2.70
CG9 Albert Belle	3.00	1.35
CG10 Frank Thomas	10.00	4.50
CG11 Manny Ramirez	2.50	1.10
CG12 Jim Thome	2.50	1.10
CG13 Matt Williams	1.00	.45
CG14 Dante Bichette	1.00	.45
CG15 Vinny Castilla	1.50	.70
CG16 Andres Galarraga	2.00	.90
CG17 Gary Sheffield	1.50	.70
CG18 Jeff Bagwell	5.00	2.20
CG19 Eric Karros	1.00	.45
CG20 Mike Piazza	8.00	3.60
CG21 Vladimir Guerrero SP	15.00	6.75
CG22 Cecil Fielder SP	4.00	1.80
CG23 Jose Canseco SP	12.00	5.50
CG24 Mark McGwire	12.00	5.50
CG25 Ken Caminiti	1.50	.70
CG26 Barry Bonds	3.00	1.35
CG27 Jay Buhner SP	5.00	2.20
CG28 Ken Griffey Jr.	12.00	5.50
CG29 Alex Rodriguez SP	30.00	13.50
CG30 Juan Gonzalez	6.00	2.70

1997 Collector's Choice Griffey Clearly Dominant

	MINT	NRMT
COMPLETE SET (5)	80.00	36.00
COMMON GRIFFEY (CD1-CD5)	20.00	9.00

SER.1 STATED ODDS 1:144

Card	MINT	NRMT
CD1 Ken Griffey Jr. Cap Worn Backwards	20.00	9.00
CD2 Ken Griffey Jr. With Eye Chalk and Flip Sunglasses	20.00	9.00
CD3 Ken Griffey Jr. Portrait	20.00	9.00
CD4 Ken Griffey Jr. Batting	20.00	9.00
CD5 Ken Griffey Jr.	20.00	9.00

1997 Collector's Choice New Frontier

	MINT	NRMT
COMPLETE SET (40)	500.00	220.00
COMMON CARD (NF1-NF40)	5.00	2.20
UNLISTED STARS	10.00	4.50
SER.2 STATED ODDS 1:69		

		MINT	NRMT
❏ NF1	Alex Rodriguez	30.00	13.50
❏ NF2	Tony Gwynn	25.00	11.00
❏ NF3	Jose Canseco	12.00	5.50
❏ NF4	Hideo Nomo	10.00	4.50
❏ NF5	Mark McGwire	50.00	22.00
❏ NF6	Barry Bonds	12.00	5.50
❏ NF7	Juan Gonzalez	20.00	9.00
❏ NF8	Ken Caminiti	5.00	2.20
❏ NF9	Tim Salmon	10.00	4.50
❏ NF10	Mike Piazza	30.00	13.50
❏ NF11	Ken Griffey Jr.	50.00	22.00
❏ NF12	Andres Galarraga	10.00	4.50
❏ NF13	Jay Buhner	5.00	2.20
❏ NF14	Dante Bichette	5.00	2.20
❏ NF15	Frank Thomas	20.00	9.00
❏ NF16	Ryne Sandberg	12.00	5.50
❏ NF17	Roger Clemens	25.00	11.00
❏ NF18	Andruw Jones	12.00	5.50
❏ NF19	Jim Thome	10.00	4.50
❏ NF20	Sammy Sosa	30.00	13.50
❏ NF21	Dave Justice	10.00	4.50
❏ NF22	Deion Sanders	5.00	2.20
❏ NF23	Todd Walker	10.00	4.50
❏ NF24	Kevin Orie	5.00	2.20
❏ NF25	Albert Belle	10.00	4.50
❏ NF26	Jeff Bagwell	12.00	5.50
❏ NF27	Manny Ramirez	12.00	5.50
❏ NF28	Brian Jordan	5.00	2.20
❏ NF29	Derek Jeter	30.00	13.50
❏ NF30	Chipper Jones	25.00	11.00
❏ NF31	Mo Vaughn	10.00	4.50
❏ NF32	Gary Sheffield	5.00	2.20
❏ NF33	Carlos Delgado	10.00	4.50
❏ NF34	Vladimir Guerrero	15.00	6.75
❏ NF35	Cal Ripken	40.00	18.00
❏ NF36	Greg Maddux	25.00	11.00
❏ NF37	Cecil Fielder	5.00	2.20
❏ NF38	Todd Hundley	5.00	2.20
❏ NF39	Mike Mussina	10.00	4.50
❏ NF40	Scott Rolen	15.00	6.75

1997 Collector's Choice Premier Power

	MINT	NRMT
COMPLETE SET (20)	40.00	18.00
COMMON CARD (1-20)	1.00	.45
SER.1 STATED ODDS 1:15		
COMP.GOLD SET (20)	150.00	70.00
*GOLD: 6X TO 15X BASE CARD HI		
GOLD SER.1 STATED ODDS 1:69		

❏ PP1	Mark McGwire	10.00	4.50
❏ PP2	Brady Anderson	1.00	.45
❏ PP3	Ken Griffey Jr.	10.00	4.50
❏ PP4	Albert Belle	2.00	.90
❏ PP5	Juan Gonzalez	4.00	1.80
❏ PP6	Andres Galarraga	2.00	.90

❏ PP7	Jay Buhner	1.00	.45
❏ PP8	Mo Vaughn	2.00	.90
❏ PP9	Barry Bonds	2.00	.90
❏ PP10	Gary Sheffield	1.00	.45
❏ PP11	Todd Hundley	1.00	.45
❏ PP12	Frank Thomas	4.00	1.80
❏ PP13	Sammy Sosa	5.00	2.20
❏ PP14	Ken Caminiti	1.50	.70
❏ PP15	Vinny Castilla	1.50	.70
❏ PP16	Ellis Burks	1.00	.45
❏ PP17	Rafael Palmeiro	2.00	.90
❏ PP18	Alex Rodriguez	6.00	2.70
❏ PP19	Mike Piazza	6.00	2.70
❏ PP20	Eddie Murray	2.00	.90

1997 Collector's Choice Stick'Ums

	MINT	NRMT
COMPLETE SET (30)	15.00	6.75
COMMON CARD (1-30)	.25	.11
SER.1 STATED ODDS 1:3		

❏ 1	Ozzie Smith	.60	.25
❏ 2	Andruw Jones	1.00	.45
❏ 3	Alex Rodriguez	2.00	.90
❏ 4	Paul Molitor	.60	.25
❏ 5	Jeff Bagwell	1.25	.55
❏ 6	Manny Ramirez	.75	.35
❏ 7	Kenny Lofton	.40	.18
❏ 8	Albert Belle	.60	.25
❏ 9	Jay Buhner	.25	.11
❏ 10	Chipper Jones	2.00	.90
❏ 11	Barry Larkin	.60	.25
❏ 12	Dante Bichette	.25	.11
❏ 13	Mike Piazza	2.00	.90
❏ 14	Andres Galarraga	.60	.25
❏ 15	Barry Bonds	.75	.35
❏ 16	Brady Anderson	.25	.11
❏ 17	Gary Sheffield	.25	.11
❏ 18	Jim Thome	.60	.25
❏ 19	Tony Gwynn	1.25	.55
❏ 20	Cal Ripken	2.50	1.10
❏ 21	Sammy Sosa	2.00	.90
❏ 22	Juan Gonzalez	1.25	.55
❏ 23	Greg Maddux	1.50	.70
❏ 24	Ken Griffey Jr.	3.00	1.35
❏ 25	Mark McGwire	3.00	1.35
❏ 26	Kirby Puckett	.60	.25
❏ 27	Mo Vaughn	.60	.25

❏ 28	Vladimir Guerrero	1.25	.55
❏ 29	Ken Caminiti	.40	.18
❏ 30	Frank Thomas	1.50	.70

1997 Collector's Choice Toast of the Town

	MINT	NRMT
COMPLETE SET (30)	200.00	90.00
COMMON CARD (1-30)	2.50	1.10
SER.2 STATED ODDS 1:35		

❏ T1	Andruw Jones	6.00	2.70
❏ T2	Chipper Jones	12.00	5.50
❏ T3	Greg Maddux	12.00	5.50
❏ T4	John Smoltz	4.00	1.80
❏ T5	Kenny Lofton	4.00	1.80
❏ T6	Brady Anderson	2.50	1.10
❏ T7	Cal Ripken	20.00	9.00
❏ T8	Mo Vaughn	5.00	2.20
❏ T9	Sammy Sosa	15.00	6.75
❏ T10	Albert Belle	5.00	2.20
❏ T11	Frank Thomas	10.00	4.50
❏ T12	Barry Larkin	5.00	2.20
❏ T13	Manny Ramirez	6.00	2.70
❏ T14	Jeff Bagwell	6.00	2.70
❏ T15	Mike Piazza	15.00	6.75
❏ T16	Paul Molitor	5.00	2.20
❏ T17	Vladimir Guerrero	8.00	3.60
❏ T18	Todd Hundley	2.50	1.10
❏ T19	Derek Jeter	12.00	5.50
❏ T20	Andy Pettitte	4.00	1.80
❏ T21	Bernie Williams	5.00	2.20
❏ T22	Mark McGwire	25.00	11.00
❏ T23	Scott Rolen	10.00	4.50
❏ T24	Ken Caminiti	4.00	1.80
❏ T25	Tony Gwynn	12.00	5.50
❏ T26	Barry Bonds	5.00	2.20
❏ T27	Ken Griffey Jr.	25.00	11.00
❏ T28	Alex Rodriguez	15.00	6.75
❏ T29	Juan Gonzalez	10.00	4.50
❏ T30	Roger Clemens	12.00	5.50

1997 Collector's Choice Update

	MINT	NRMT
COMPLETE SET (30)	5.00	2.20
COMMON CARD (U1-U30)	.10	.05
MINOR STARS	.20	.09

UNLISTED STARS.................. .40 .18
ONE SET VIA MAIL PER 10 SER.2 WRAPPERS
EXCH.DEADLINE: 12/1/97

	MINT	NRMT
☐ U1 Jim Leyritz	.10	.05
☐ U2 Matt Perisho	.10	.05
☐ U3 Michael Tucker	.10	.05
☐ U4 Mike Johnson	.20	.09
☐ U5 Jaime Navarro	.10	.05
☐ U6 Doug Drabek	.10	.05
☐ U7 Terry Mulholland	.10	.05
☐ U8 Brett Tomko	.20	.09
☐ U9 Marquis Grissom	.20	.09
☐ U10 David Justice	.40	.18
☐ U11 Brian Moehler	.10	.05
☐ U12 Bobby Bonilla	.20	.09
☐ U13 Todd Dunwoody	.20	.09
☐ U14 Tony Saunders	.10	.05
☐ U15 Jay Bell	.20	.09
☐ U16 Jeff King	.10	.05
☐ U17 Terry Steinbach	.10	.05
☐ U18 Steve Bieser	.10	.05
☐ U19 Takashi Kashiwada	.20	.09
☐ U20 Hideki Irabu	1.00	.45
☐ U21 Damon Mashore	.10	.05
☐ U22 Quilvio Veras	.10	.05
☐ U23 Will Cunnane	.10	.05
☐ U24 Jeff Kent	.20	.09
☐ U25 J.T. Snow	.20	.09
☐ U26 Dante Powell	.20	.09
☐ U27 Jose Cruz Jr.	1.25	.55
☐ U28 John Burkett	.10	.05
☐ U29 John Wetteland	.20	.09
☐ U30 Benito Santiago	.10	.05

1998 Collector's Choice

	MINT	NRMT
COMPLETE SET (530)	40.00	18.00
COMPLETE SERIES 1 (265)	20.00	9.00
COMPLETE SERIES 2 (265)	20.00	9.00
COMP.FACT.SET (530)	40.00	18.00
COMMON CARD (1-530)		.05
MINOR STARS	.15	.07
SEMISTARS	.25	.11
UNLISTED STARS	.40	.18

	MINT	NRMT
☐ 1 Nomar Garciaparra CG	.60	.25
☐ 2 Roger Clemens CG	.50	.23
☐ 3 Larry Walker CG	.15	.07
☐ 4 Mike Piazza CG	.60	.25
☐ 5 Mark McGwire CG	1.25	.55
☐ 6 Tony Gwynn CG	.50	.23
☐ 7 Jose Cruz Jr. CG	.10	.05
☐ 8 Frank Thomas CG	.40	.18
☐ 9 Tino Martinez CG	.10	.05
☐ 10 Ken Griffey Jr. CG	1.00	.45
☐ 11 Barry Bonds CG	.25	.11
☐ 12 Scott Rolen CG	.40	.18
☐ 13 Randy Johnson CG	.15	.07
☐ 14 Ryne Sandberg CG	.25	.11
☐ 15 Eddie Murray CG	.15	.07
☐ 16 Kevin Brown CG	.15	.07
☐ 17 Mike Mussina CG	.15	.07
☐ 18 Sandy Alomar Jr. CG	.10	.05
☐ 19 Ken Griffey Jr. CL	.25	.11
Adam Riggs		

	MINT	NRMT
☐ 20 Nomar Garciaparra CL	.15	.07
Charlie O'Brien		
☐ 21 Ben Grieve CL	.15	.07
Frank Thomas		
Tony Gwynn		
☐ 22 Mark McGwire CL	.25	.11
Cal Ripken		
☐ 23 Tino Martinez CL	.10	.05
☐ 24 Jason Dickson	.10	.05
☐ 25 Darin Erstad	.25	.11
☐ 26 Todd Greene	.10	.05
☐ 27 Chuck Finley	.10	.05
☐ 28 Garret Anderson	.15	.07
☐ 29 Dave Hollins	.10	.05
☐ 30 Rickey Henderson	.50	.23
☐ 31 John Smoltz	.25	.11
☐ 32 Michael Tucker	.10	.05
☐ 33 Jeff Blauser	.10	.05
☐ 34 Javier Lopez	.15	.07
☐ 35 Andruw Jones	.40	.18
☐ 36 Denny Neagle	.10	.05
☐ 37 Randall Simon	.15	.07
☐ 38 Mark Wohlers	.10	.05
☐ 39 Harold Baines	.15	.07
☐ 40 Cal Ripken	1.50	.70
☐ 41 Mike Bordick	.10	.05
☐ 42 Jimmy Key	.10	.05
☐ 43 Armando Benitez	.10	.05
☐ 44 Scott Erickson	.10	.05
☐ 45 Eric Davis	.15	.07
☐ 46 Bret Saberhagen	.15	.07
☐ 47 Darren Bragg	.10	.05
☐ 48 Steve Avery	.10	.05
☐ 49 Jeff Frye	.10	.05
☐ 50 Aaron Sele	.15	.07
☐ 51 Scott Hatteberg	.10	.05
☐ 52 Tom Gordon	.15	.07
☐ 53 Kevin Orie	.10	.05
☐ 54 Kevin Foster	.10	.05
☐ 55 Ryne Sandberg	.50	.23
☐ 56 Doug Glanville	.15	.07
☐ 57 Tyler Houston	.10	.05
☐ 58 Steve Trachsel	.10	.05
☐ 59 Mark Grace	.25	.11
☐ 60 Frank Thomas	.75	.35
☐ 61 Scott Eyre	.10	.05
☐ 62 Jeff Abbott	.10	.05
☐ 63 Chris Clemons	.10	.05
☐ 64 Jorge Fabregas	.10	.05
☐ 65 Robin Ventura	.15	.07
☐ 66 Matt Karchner	.10	.05
☐ 67 Jon Nunnally	.10	.05
☐ 68 Aaron Boone	.10	.05
☐ 69 Pokey Reese	.10	.05
☐ 70 Deion Sanders	.15	.07
☐ 71 Jeff Shaw	.10	.05
☐ 72 Eduardo Perez	.10	.05
☐ 73 Brett Tomko	.10	.05
☐ 74 Bartolo Colon	.10	.05
☐ 75 Manny Ramirez	.50	.23
☐ 76 Jose Mesa	.10	.05
☐ 77 Brian Giles	.15	.07
☐ 78 Richie Sexson	.25	.11
☐ 79 Orel Hershiser	.15	.07
☐ 80 Matt Williams	.40	.18
☐ 81 Walt Weiss	.10	.05
☐ 82 Jerry DiPoto	.10	.05
☐ 83 Quinton McCracken	.10	.05
☐ 84 Neifi Perez	.10	.05
☐ 85 Vinny Castilla	.15	.07
☐ 86 Ellis Burks	.15	.07
☐ 87 John Thomson	.10	.05
☐ 88 Willie Blair	.10	.05
☐ 89 Bob Hamelin	.10	.05
☐ 90 Tony Clark	.25	.11
☐ 91 Todd Jones	.10	.05
☐ 92 Deivi Cruz	.10	.05
☐ 93 Frank Catalanotto	.15	.07
☐ 94 Justin Thompson	.10	.05
☐ 95 Gary Sheffield	.25	.11
☐ 96 Kevin Brown	.25	.11
☐ 97 Charles Johnson	.10	.05
☐ 98 Bobby Bonilla	.15	.07
☐ 99 Livan Hernandez	.10	.05
☐ 100 Paul Konerko	.15	.07
☐ 101 Craig Counsell	.10	.05

	MINT	NRMT
☐ 102 Magglio Ordonez	1.25	.55
☐ 103 Garrett Stephenson	.10	.05
☐ 104 Ken Cloude	.10	.05
☐ 105 Miguel Tejada	.15	.07
☐ 106 Juan Encarnacion	.15	.07
☐ 107 Dennis Reyes	.10	.05
☐ 108 Orlando Cabrera	.10	.05
☐ 109 Kelvim Escobar	.15	.07
☐ 110 Ben Grieve	.40	.18
☐ 111 Brian Rose	.10	.05
☐ 112 Fernando Tatis	.40	.18
☐ 113 Tom Evans	.10	.05
☐ 114 Tom Fordham	.10	.05
☐ 115 Mark Kotsay	.15	.07
☐ 116 Mario Valdez	.10	.05
☐ 117 Jeremi Gonzalez	.10	.05
☐ 118 Todd Dunwoody	.10	.05
☐ 119 Javier Valentin	.10	.05
☐ 120 Todd Helton	.50	.23
☐ 121 Jason Varitek	.15	.07
☐ 122 Chris Carpenter	.15	.07
☐ 123 Kevin Millwood	1.25	.55
☐ 124 Brad Fullmer	.10	.05
☐ 125 Jaret Wright	.15	.07
☐ 126 Brad Rigby	.10	.05
☐ 127 Edgar Renteria	.10	.05
☐ 128 Robb Nen	.10	.05
☐ 129 Tony Pena	.10	.05
☐ 130 Craig Biggio	.40	.18
☐ 131 Brad Ausmus	.10	.05
☐ 132 Shane Reynolds	.10	.05
☐ 133 Mike Hampton	.15	.07
☐ 134 Billy Wagner	.15	.07
☐ 135 Richard Hidalgo	.15	.07
☐ 136 Jose Rosado	.10	.05
☐ 137 Yamil Benitez	.10	.05
☐ 138 Felix Martinez	.10	.05
☐ 139 Jeff King	.10	.05
☐ 140 Jose Offerman	.15	.07
☐ 141 Joe Vitiello	.10	.05
☐ 142 Tim Belcher	.10	.05
☐ 143 Brett Butler	.15	.07
☐ 144 Greg Gagne	.10	.05
☐ 145 Mike Piazza	1.25	.55
☐ 146 Ramon Martinez	.10	.05
☐ 147 Raul Mondesi	.15	.07
☐ 148 Adam Riggs	.10	.05
☐ 149 Eddie Murray	.40	.18
☐ 150 Jeff Cirillo	.15	.07
☐ 151 Scott Karl	.10	.05
☐ 152 Mike Fetters	.10	.05
☐ 153 Dave Nilsson	.10	.05
☐ 154 Antone Williamson	.10	.05
☐ 155 Jeff D'Amico	.10	.05
☐ 156 Jose Valentin	.10	.05
☐ 157 Brad Radke	.15	.07
☐ 158 Torii Hunter	.15	.07
☐ 159 Chuck Knoblauch	.15	.07
☐ 160 Paul Molitor	.40	.18
☐ 161 Travis Miller	.10	.05
☐ 162 Rich Robertson	.10	.05
☐ 163 Ron Coomer	.10	.05
☐ 164 Mark Grudzielanek	.10	.05
☐ 165 Lee Smith	.15	.07
☐ 166 Vladimir Guerrero	.50	.23
☐ 167 Dustin Hermanson	.10	.05
☐ 168 Ugueth Urbina	.10	.05
☐ 169 F.P. Santangelo	.10	.05
☐ 170 Rondell White	.15	.07
☐ 171 Bobby Jones	.10	.05
☐ 172 Edgardo Alfonzo	.25	.11
☐ 173 John Franco	.15	.07
☐ 174 Carlos Baerga	.10	.05
☐ 175 Butch Huskey	.10	.05
☐ 176 Rey Ordonez	.15	.07
☐ 177 Matt Franco	.10	.05
☐ 178 Dwight Gooden	.15	.07
☐ 179 Chad Curtis	.10	.05
☐ 180 Tino Martinez	.15	.07
☐ 181 Charlie O'Brien MM	.10	.05
☐ 182 Sandy Alomar Jr. MM	.10	.05
☐ 183 Raul Casanova MM	.10	.05
☐ 184 Javier Lopez MM	.10	.05
☐ 185 Mike Piazza MM	.60	.25
☐ 186 Ivan Rodriguez MM	.25	.11
☐ 187 Charles Johnson MM	.10	.05

❑ 188	Brad Ausmus MM	.10	.05
❑ 189	Brian Johnson MM	.10	.05
❑ 190	Wade Boggs	.40	.18
❑ 191	David Wells	.15	.07
❑ 192	Tim Raines	.15	.07
❑ 193	Ramiro Mendoza	.10	.05
❑ 194	Willie Adams	.10	.05
❑ 195	Matt Stairs	.15	.07
❑ 196	Jason McDonald	.10	.05
❑ 197	Dave Magadan	.10	.05
❑ 198	Mark Bellhorn	.10	.05
❑ 199	Ariel Prieto	.10	.05
❑ 200	Jose Canseco	.50	.23
❑ 201	Bobby Estalella	.10	.05
❑ 202	Tony Barron	.10	.05
❑ 203	Midre Cummings	.10	.05
❑ 204	Ricky Bottalico	.10	.05
❑ 205	Mike Grace	.10	.05
❑ 206	Rico Brogna	.10	.05
❑ 207	Mickey Morandini	.10	.05
❑ 208	Lou Collier	.10	.05
❑ 209	Kevin Polcovich	.10	.05
❑ 210	Kevin Young	.15	.07
❑ 211	Jose Guillen	.15	.07
❑ 212	Esteban Loaiza	.10	.05
❑ 213	Marc Wilkins	.10	.05
❑ 214	Jason Schmidt	.10	.05
❑ 215	Gary Gaetti	.15	.07
❑ 216	Fernando Valenzuela	.15	.07
❑ 217	Willie McGee	.15	.07
❑ 218	Alan Benes	.10	.05
❑ 219	Eli Marrero	.10	.05
❑ 220	Mark McGwire	2.50	1.10
❑ 221	Matt Morris	.15	.07
❑ 222	Trevor Hoffman	.15	.07
❑ 223	Will Cunnane	.10	.05
❑ 224	Joey Hamilton	.10	.05
❑ 225	Ken Caminiti	.15	.07
❑ 226	Derrek Lee	.10	.05
❑ 227	Mark Sweeney	.10	.05
❑ 228	Carlos Hernandez	.10	.05
❑ 229	Brian Johnson	.10	.05
❑ 230	Jeff Kent	.15	.07
❑ 231	Kirk Rueter	.10	.05
❑ 232	Bill Mueller	.10	.05
❑ 233	Dante Powell	.10	.05
❑ 234	J.T. Snow	.15	.07
❑ 235	Shawn Estes	.15	.07
❑ 236	Dennis Martinez	.15	.07
❑ 237	Jamie Moyer	.10	.05
❑ 238	Dan Wilson	.10	.05
❑ 239	Joey Cora	.10	.05
❑ 240	Ken Griffey Jr.	2.00	.90
❑ 241	Paul Sorrento	.10	.05
❑ 242	Jay Buhner	.15	.07
❑ 243	Hanley Frias	.10	.05
❑ 244	John Burkett	.10	.05
❑ 245	Juan Gonzalez	.75	.35
❑ 246	Rick Helling	.10	.05
❑ 247	Darren Oliver	.10	.05
❑ 248	Mickey Tettleton	.10	.05
❑ 249	Ivan Rodriguez	.50	.23
❑ 250	Joe Carter	.15	.07
❑ 251	Pat Hentgen	.10	.05
❑ 252	Marty Janzen	.10	.05
❑ 253	Frank Thomas TOP Tony Gwynn	.40	.18
❑ 254	Mark McGwire TOP Ken Griffey Jr. Larry Walker	1.00	.45
❑ 255	Ken Griffey Jr. TOP Andres Galarraga	.50	.23
❑ 256	Brian L.Hunter TOP Tony Womack	.10	.05
❑ 257	Roger Clemens TOP Denny Neagle	.15	.07
❑ 258	Roger Clemens TOP Curt Schilling	.15	.07
❑ 259	Roger Clemens TOP Pedro Martinez	.25	.11
❑ 260	Randy Myers TOP Jeff Shaw	.10	.05
❑ 261	Nomar Garciaparra TOP Scott Rolen	.40	.18
❑ 262	Charlie O'Brien	.10	.05
❑ 263	Shannon Stewart	.15	.07
❑ 264	Robert Person	.10	.05
❑ 265	Carlos Delgado	.40	.18
❑ 266	Matt Williams CL	.15	.07
❑ 267	Nomar Garciaparra CL Cal Ripken	.25	.11
❑ 268	Mark McGwire CL Mike Piazza	.40	.18
❑ 269	Tony Gwynn CL Ken Griffey Jr.	.40	.18
❑ 270	Fred McGriff CL Jose Cruz Jr.	.10	.05
❑ 271	Andruw Jones GJ	.15	.07
❑ 272	Alex Rodriguez GJ	.60	.25
❑ 273	Juan Gonzalez GJ	.40	.18
❑ 274	Nomar Garciaparra GJ	.60	.25
❑ 275	Ken Griffey Jr. GJ	1.00	.45
❑ 276	Tino Martinez GJ	.10	.05
❑ 277	Roger Clemens GJ	.50	.23
❑ 278	Barry Bonds GJ	.25	.11
❑ 279	Mike Piazza GJ	.60	.25
❑ 280	Tim Salmon	.25	.11
❑ 281	Gary DiSarcina	.10	.05
❑ 282	Cecil Fielder	.15	.07
❑ 283	Ken Hill	.10	.05
❑ 284	Troy Percival	.15	.07
❑ 285	Jim Edmonds	.15	.07
❑ 286	Allen Watson	.10	.05
❑ 287	Brian Anderson	.10	.05
❑ 288	Jay Bell	.15	.07
❑ 289	Jorge Fabregas	.10	.05
❑ 290	Devon White	.10	.05
❑ 291	Yamil Benitez	.10	.05
❑ 292	Jeff Suppan	.10	.05
❑ 293	Tony Batista	.10	.05
❑ 294	Brent Brede	.10	.05
❑ 295	Andy Benes	.15	.07
❑ 296	Felix Rodriguez	.10	.05
❑ 297	Karim Garcia	.10	.05
❑ 298	Omar Daal	.10	.05
❑ 299	Andy Stankiewicz	.10	.05
❑ 300	Matt Williams	.40	.18
❑ 301	Willie Blair	.10	.05
❑ 302	Ryan Klesko	.15	.07
❑ 303	Tom Glavine	.40	.18
❑ 304	Walt Weiss	.15	.07
❑ 305	Greg Maddux	1.00	.45
❑ 306	Chipper Jones	1.00	.45
❑ 307	Keith Lockhart	.10	.05
❑ 308	Andres Galarraga	.25	.11
❑ 309	Chris Hoiles	.10	.05
❑ 310	Roberto Alomar	.40	.18
❑ 311	Joe Carter	.15	.07
❑ 312	Doug Drabek	.10	.05
❑ 313	Jeffrey Hammonds	.10	.05
❑ 314	Rafael Palmeiro	.40	.18
❑ 315	Mike Mussina	.40	.18
❑ 316	Brady Anderson	.15	.07
❑ 317	B.J. Surhoff	.15	.07
❑ 318	Dennis Eckersley	.15	.07
❑ 319	Jim Leyritz	.10	.05
❑ 320	Mo Vaughn	.40	.18
❑ 321	Nomar Garciaparra	1.25	.55
❑ 322	Reggie Jefferson	.10	.05
❑ 323	Tim Naehring	.10	.05
❑ 324	Troy O'Leary	.15	.07
❑ 325	Pedro Martinez	.50	.23
❑ 326	John Valentin	.15	.07
❑ 327	Mark Clark	.10	.05
❑ 328	Rod Beck	.15	.07
❑ 329	Mickey Morandini	.10	.05
❑ 330	Sammy Sosa	1.25	.55
❑ 331	Jeff Blauser	.10	.05
❑ 332	Lance Johnson	.10	.05
❑ 333	Scott Servais	.10	.05
❑ 334	Kevin Tapani	.10	.05
❑ 335	Henry Rodriguez	.15	.07
❑ 336	Jaime Navarro	.10	.05
❑ 337	Benji Gil	.10	.05
❑ 338	James Baldwin	.10	.05
❑ 339	Mike Cameron	.15	.07
❑ 340	Ray Durham	.15	.07
❑ 341	Chris Snopek	.10	.05
❑ 342	Eddie Taubensee	.10	.05
❑ 343	Bret Boone	.15	.07
❑ 344	Willie Greene	.10	.05
❑ 345	Barry Larkin	.40	.18
❑ 346	Chris Stynes	.10	.05
❑ 347	Pete Harnisch	.10	.05
❑ 348	Dave Burba	.10	.05
❑ 349	Sandy Alomar Jr.	.15	.07
❑ 350	Kenny Lofton	.25	.11
❑ 351	Geronimo Berroa	.10	.05
❑ 352	Omar Vizquel	.15	.07
❑ 353	Travis Fryman	.15	.07
❑ 354	Dwight Gooden	.10	.05
❑ 355	Jim Thome	.40	.18
❑ 356	David Justice	.15	.07
❑ 357	Charles Nagy	.15	.07
❑ 358	Chad Ogea	.10	.05
❑ 359	Pedro Astacio	.10	.05
❑ 360	Larry Walker	.40	.18
❑ 361	Mike Lansing	.10	.05
❑ 362	Kirt Manwaring	.10	.05
❑ 363	Dante Bichette	.15	.07
❑ 364	Jamey Wright	.10	.05
❑ 365	Darryl Kile	.10	.05
❑ 366	Luis Gonzalez	.15	.07
❑ 367	Joe Randa	.10	.05
❑ 368	Raul Casanova	.10	.05
❑ 369	Damion Easley	.15	.07
❑ 370	Brian Hunter	.10	.05
❑ 371	Bobby Higginson	.15	.07
❑ 372	Brian Moehler	.10	.05
❑ 373	Scott Sanders	.10	.05
❑ 374	Jim Eisenreich	.10	.05
❑ 375	Derrek Lee	.10	.05
❑ 376	Jay Powell	.10	.05
❑ 377	Cliff Floyd	.15	.07
❑ 378	Alex Fernandez	.10	.05
❑ 379	Felix Heredia	.10	.05
❑ 380	Jeff Bagwell	.50	.23
❑ 381	Bill Spiers	.10	.05
❑ 382	Chris Holt	.10	.05
❑ 383	Carl Everett	.15	.07
❑ 384	Derek Bell	.15	.07
❑ 385	Moises Alou	.15	.07
❑ 386	Ramon Garcia	.10	.05
❑ 387	Mike Sweeney	.15	.07
❑ 388	Glendon Rusch	.10	.05
❑ 389	Kevin Appier	.15	.07
❑ 390	Dean Palmer	.15	.07
❑ 391	Jeff Conine	.15	.07
❑ 392	Johnny Damon	.15	.07
❑ 393	Jose Vizcaino	.10	.05
❑ 394	Todd Hollandsworth	.10	.05
❑ 395	Eric Karros	.15	.07
❑ 396	Todd Zeile	.10	.05
❑ 397	Chan Ho Park	.15	.07
❑ 398	Ismael Valdes	.10	.05
❑ 399	Eric Young	.10	.05
❑ 400	Hideo Nomo	.40	.18
❑ 401	Mark Loretta	.10	.05
❑ 402	Doug Jones	.10	.05
❑ 403	Jeromy Burnitz	.15	.07
❑ 404	John Jaha	.15	.07
❑ 405	Marquis Grissom	.10	.05
❑ 406	Mike Matheny	.10	.05
❑ 407	Todd Walker	.15	.07
❑ 408	Marty Cordova	.10	.05
❑ 409	Matt Lawton	.10	.05
❑ 410	Terry Steinbach	.10	.05
❑ 411	Pat Meares	.10	.05
❑ 412	Rick Aguilera	.10	.05
❑ 413	Otis Nixon	.10	.05
❑ 414	Derrick May	.10	.05
❑ 415	Carl Pavano	.10	.05
❑ 416	A.J. Hinch	.10	.05
❑ 417	Dave Dellucci	.30	.14
❑ 418	Bruce Chen	.15	.07
❑ 419	Darron Ingram	.30	.14
❑ 420	Sean Casey	.60	.25
❑ 421	Mark L. Johnson	.10	.05
❑ 422	Gabe Alvarez	.10	.05
❑ 423	Alex Gonzalez	.10	.05
❑ 424	Daryle Ward	.15	.07
❑ 425	Russell Branyan	.15	.07
❑ 426	Mike Caruso	.10	.05
❑ 427	Mike Kinkade	.25	.11
❑ 428	Ramon Hernandez	.10	.05
❑ 429	Matt Clement	.10	.05
❑ 430	Travis Lee	.25	.11

❏ 431 Shane Monahan	.10	.05
❏ 432 Rich Butler	.25	.11
❏ 433 Chris Widger	.10	.05
❏ 434 Jose Vidro	.10	.05
❏ 435 Carlos Perez	.10	.05
❏ 436 Ryan McGuire	.10	.05
❏ 437 Brian McRae	.10	.05
❏ 438 Al Leiter	.15	.07
❏ 439 Rich Becker	.10	.05
❏ 440 Todd Hundley	.15	.07
❏ 441 Dave Mlicki	.10	.05
❏ 442 Bernard Gilkey	.15	.07
❏ 443 John Olerud	.15	.07
❏ 444 Paul O'Neill	.15	.07
❏ 445 Andy Pettitte	.15	.07
❏ 446 David Cone	.25	.11
❏ 447 Chili Davis	.15	.07
❏ 448 Bernie Williams	.40	.18
❏ 449 Joe Girardi	.10	.05
❏ 450 Derek Jeter	1.25	.55
❏ 451 Mariano Rivera	.15	.07
❏ 452 George Williams	.10	.05
❏ 453 Kenny Rogers	.10	.05
❏ 454 Tom Candiotti	.10	.05
❏ 455 Rickey Henderson	.50	.23
❏ 456 Jason Giambi	.15	.07
❏ 457 Scott Spiezio	.10	.05
❏ 458 Doug Glanville	.15	.07
❏ 459 Desi Relaford	.10	.05
❏ 460 Curt Schilling	.25	.11
❏ 461 Bob Abreu	.15	.07
❏ 462 Gregg Jefferies	.15	.07
❏ 463 Scott Rolen	.50	.23
❏ 464 Mike Lieberthal	.15	.07
❏ 465 Tony Womack	.10	.05
❏ 466 Jermaine Allensworth	.10	.05
❏ 467 Francisco Cordova	.10	.05
❏ 468 Jon Lieber	.10	.05
❏ 469 Al Martin	.10	.05
❏ 470 Jason Kendall	.15	.07
❏ 471 Todd Stottlemyre	.10	.05
❏ 472 Royce Clayton	.10	.05
❏ 473 Brian Jordan	.15	.07
❏ 474 John Mabry	.10	.05
❏ 475 Ray Lankford	.15	.07
❏ 476 Delino DeShields	.10	.05
❏ 477 Ron Gant	.15	.07
❏ 478 Mark Langston	.10	.05
❏ 479 Steve Finley	.15	.07
❏ 480 Tony Gwynn	1.00	.45
❏ 481 Andy Ashby	.10	.05
❏ 482 Wally Joyner	.15	.07
❏ 483 Greg Vaughn	.10	.05
❏ 484 Sterling Hitchcock	.10	.05
❏ 485 Kevin Brown	.25	.11
❏ 486 Orel Hershiser	.15	.07
❏ 487 Charlie Hayes	.10	.05
❏ 488 Darryl Hamilton	.10	.05
❏ 489 Mark Gardner	.10	.05
❏ 490 Barry Bonds	.50	.23
❏ 491 Robb Nen	.10	.05
❏ 492 Kirk Rueter	.10	.05
❏ 493 Randy Johnson	.40	.18
❏ 494 Jeff Fassero	.10	.05
❏ 495 Alex Rodriguez	1.25	.55
❏ 496 David Segui	.10	.05
❏ 497 Rich Amaral	.10	.05
❏ 498 Russ Davis	.15	.07
❏ 499 Bubba Trammell	.10	.05
❏ 500 Wade Boggs	.40	.18
❏ 501 Roberto Hernandez	.10	.05
❏ 502 Dave Martinez	.10	.05
❏ 503 Dennis Springer	.10	.05
❏ 504 Paul Sorrento	.10	.05
❏ 505 Wilson Alvarez	.10	.05
❏ 506 Mike Kelly	.10	.05
❏ 507 Albie Lopez	.10	.05
❏ 508 Tony Saunders	.10	.05
❏ 509 John Flaherty	.10	.05
❏ 510 Fred McGriff	.25	.11
❏ 511 Quinton McCracken	.10	.05
❏ 512 Terrell Wade	.10	.05
❏ 513 Kevin Stocker	.10	.05
❏ 514 Kevin Elster	.10	.05
❏ 515 Will Clark	.40	.18
❏ 516 Bobby Witt	.10	.05
❏ 517 Tom Goodwin	.10	.05
❏ 518 Aaron Sele	.15	.07
❏ 519 Lee Stevens	.10	.05
❏ 520 Rusty Greer	.15	.07
❏ 521 John Wetteland	.15	.07
❏ 522 Darrin Fletcher	.10	.05
❏ 523 Jose Canseco	.50	.23
❏ 524 Randy Myers	.15	.07
❏ 525 Jose Cruz Jr.	.15	.07
❏ 526 Shawn Green	.40	.18
❏ 527 Tony Fernandez	.15	.07
❏ 528 Alex Gonzalez	.10	.05
❏ 529 Ed Sprague	.10	.05
❏ 530 Roger Clemens	1.00	.45

1998 Collector's Choice Prime Choice Reserve

	MINT	NRMT
COMPLETE SET (18)	100.00	45.00
COMMON CARD (415-432)	4.00	1.80

*STARS: 15X TO 40X BASIC CARDS
*ROOKIES: 8X TO 20X BASIC CARDS
RANDOM INSERTS IN SER.2 PACKS
STATED PRINT RUN 500 SERIAL #'d SETS

❏ 415 Carl Pavano	4.00	1.80
❏ 416 A.J. Hinch	4.00	1.80
❏ 417 Dave Dellucci	4.00	1.80
❏ 418 Bruce Chen	4.00	1.80
❏ 419 Darron Ingram	4.00	1.80
❏ 420 Sean Casey	4.00	1.80
❏ 421 Mark L. Johnson	4.00	1.80
❏ 422 Gabe Alvarez	4.00	1.80
❏ 423 Alex Gonzalez	4.00	1.80
❏ 424 Daryle Ward	4.00	1.80
❏ 425 Russell Branyan	4.00	1.80
❏ 426 Mike Caruso	4.00	1.80
❏ 427 Mike Kinkade	4.00	1.80
❏ 428 Ramon Hernandez	4.00	1.80
❏ 429 Matt Clement	4.00	1.80
❏ 430 Travis Lee	4.00	1.80
❏ 431 Shane Monahan	4.00	1.80
❏ 432 Rich Butler	4.00	1.80

1998 Collector's Choice Crash the Game

	MINT	NRMT
COMPLETE SET (90)	80.00	36.00
COMMON CARD (CG1-CG30)	.40	.18

SER.2 STATED ODDS 1:5
THREE VERSIONS AVAIL.FOR EACH CARD
*INSTANT WIN: 15X TO 40X BASE CARD HI
INSTANT WIN SER.2 STATED ODDS 1:721
EXPIRATION DATE: 12/1/98

❏ CG1A K.Griffey June 26-28 W	4.00	1.80
❏ CG1B K.Griffey July 7 L	4.00	1.80
❏ CG1C K.Griffey Sept 21-24 W	4.00	1.80
❏ CG2A T.Lee July 27-30 L	.50	.23
❏ CG2B T.Lee Aug 27-30 L	.50	.23
❏ CG2C T.Lee Sept 17-20 L	.50	.23
❏ CG3A L.Walker July 17-19 L	.75	.35
❏ CG3B L.Walker Aug 27-30 W	.75	.35
❏ CG3C L.Walker Sept 25-27 W	.75	.35
❏ CG4A T.Clark July 9-12 W	.40	.18
❏ CG4B T.Clark June 30-July 2 L	.40	.18
❏ CG4C T.Clark Sept 4-6 L	.40	.18
❏ CG5A C.Ripken June 22-25 W	3.00	1.35
❏ CG5B C.Ripken July 7 L	3.00	1.35
❏ CG5C C.Ripken Sept 4-6 W	3.00	1.35
❏ CG6A T.Salmon June 22-25 L	.50	.23
❏ CG6B T.Salmon Aug 28-30 L	.50	.23
❏ CG6C T.Salmon Sept 14-15 L	.50	.23
❏ CG7A V.Castilla June30-July2 W	.40	.18
❏ CG7B V.Castilla Aug 27-30 W	.40	.18
❏ CG7C V.Castilla Sept 7-10 W	.40	.18
❏ CG8A F.McGriff June 22-25 L	.50	.23
❏ CG8B F.McGriff July 3 L	.50	.23
❏ CG8C F.McGriff Sept 18-20 W	.50	.23
❏ CG9A M.Williams July 17-19 L	.75	.35
❏ CG9B M.Williams Aug 14-16 W	.75	.35
❏ CG9C M.Williams Sept 18-20 L	.75	.35
❏ CG10A M.McGwire July 7 L	5.00	2.20
❏ CG10B M.McGwire July 24-26 W	5.00	2.20
❏ CG10C M.McGwire Aug 18-19 W	5.00	2.20
❏ CG11A A.Belle July 3-5 L	.75	.35
❏ CG11B A.Belle Aug 21-23 W	.75	.35
❏ CG11C A.Belle Sept 11-13 L	.75	.35
❏ CG12A J.Buhner July 9-12 W	.40	.18
❏ CG12B J.Buhner Aug 6-9 L	.40	.18
❏ CG12C J.Buhner Sept 24-27 L	.40	.18
❏ CG13A V.Guerrero June 22-25 L	1.00	.45
❏ CG13B V.Guerrero Aug 10-12 W	1.00	.45
❏ CG13C V.Guerrero Sept 14-16 W	1.00	.45
❏ CG14A A.Jones July 16-19 W	.75	.35
❏ CG14B A.Jones Aug 27-30 W	.75	.35
❏ CG14C A.Jones Sept 17-20 L	.75	.35
❏ CG15A N.Garciaparra July 9-12 L	2.50	1.10
❏ CG15B N.Garciaparra Aug 13-16 W	2.50	1.10
❏ CG15C N.Garciaparra Sept 24-27 W	2.50	1.10
❏ CG16A K.Caminiti June 26-28 W	.40	.18
❏ CG16B K.Caminiti July 13-15 W	.40	.18
❏ CG16C K.Caminiti Sept 10-13 L	.40	.18
❏ CG17A S.Sosa July 9-12 W	2.50	1.10
❏ CG17B S.Sosa July 27-30 W	2.50	1.10
❏ CG17C S.Sosa Sept 18-20 L	2.50	1.10
❏ CG18A B.Grieve June 30-July 2 W	.75	.35
❏ CG18B B.Grieve Aug 14-16 L	.75	.35
❏ CG18C B.Grieve Sept 24-27 L	.75	.35
❏ CG19A M.Vaughn July 7 L	.75	.35
❏ CG19B M.Vaughn Sept 7-9 L	.75	.35
❏ CG19C M.Vaughn Sept 24-27 W	.75	.35

☐ CG20A F.Thomas July 7 L..	1.50	.70
☐ CG20B F.Thomas July 17-19 W	1.50	.70
☐ CG20C F.Thomas Sept 4-6 L	1.50	.70
☐ CG21A M.Ramirez July 9-12 L	1.00	.45
☐ CG21B M.Ramirez Aug 13-16 W	1.00	.45
☐ CG21C M.Ramirez Sept 18-20 W	1.00	.45
☐ CG22A J.Bagwell July 7 L ..	1.00	.45
☐ CG22B J.Bagwell Aug 28-30 W	1.00	.45
☐ CG22C J.Bagwell Sept 4-6 W	1.00	.45
☐ CG23A J.Cruz Jr. July 9-12 L	.40	.18
☐ CG23B J.Cruz Jr. Aug 13-16 L	.40	.18
☐ CG23C J.Cruz Jr. Sept 18-20 L	.40	.18
☐ CG24A A.Rodriguez July 7 W	2.50	1.10
☐ CG24B A.Rodriguez Aug 6-9 W	2.50	1.10
☐ CG24C A.Rodriguez Sept 21-23 W	2.50	1.10
☐ CG25A M.Piazza June 22-25 W	2.50	1.10
☐ CG25B M.Piazza July 7 L ..	2.50	1.10
☐ CG25C M.Piazza Sept 10-13 W	2.50	1.10
☐ CG26A T.Martinez June 26-28 W	.40	.18
☐ CG26B T.Martinez July 9-12 L	.40	.18
☐ CG26C T.Martinez Aug 13-16 L	.40	.18
☐ CG27A C.Jones July 3-5 L..	2.00	.90
☐ CG27B C.Jones Aug 23-30 L	2.00	.90
☐ CG27C C.Jones Sept 17-20 L	2.00	.90
☐ CG28A J.Gonzalez July 7 L	1.50	.70
☐ CG28B J.Gonzalez Aug 6-9 W	1.50	.70
☐ CG28C J.Gonzalez Sept 11-13 W	1.50	.70
☐ CG29A J.Thome June 22-23 L	.75	.35
☐ CG29B J.Thome July 23-26 W	.75	.35
☐ CG29C J.Thome Sept 24-27 L	.75	.35
☐ CG30A B.Bonds July 7 W ..	1.00	.45
☐ CG30B B.Bonds Sept 4-6 L	1.00	.45
☐ CG30C B.Bonds Sept 18-20 W	1.00	.45

1998 Collector's Choice Evolution Revolution

	MINT	NRMT
COMPLETE SET (28)	60.00	27.00
COMMON CARD (ER1-ER28)	.50 .23	.06
SER.1 STATED ODDS 1:13		

☐ ER1 Tim Salmon ..	1.25	.55
☐ ER2 Greg Maddux ..	5.00	2.20
☐ ER3 Cal Ripken ..	8.00	3.60
☐ ER4 Mo Vaughn..	1.50	.70
☐ ER5 Sammy Sosa ..	6.00	2.70
☐ ER6 Frank Thomas	4.00	1.80
☐ ER7 Barry Larkin ..	2.00	.90
☐ ER8 Jim Thome ..	1.50	.70

☐ ER9 Larry Walker ..	2.00	.90
☐ ER10 Travis Fryman ..	.75	.35
☐ ER11 Gary Sheffield ..	.75	.35
☐ ER12 Jeff Bagwell ..	2.50	1.10
☐ ER13 Johnny Damon ..	.75	.35
☐ ER14 Mike Piazza ..	6.00	2.70
☐ ER15 Jeff Cirillo ..	.75	.35
☐ ER16 Paul Molitor ..	2.00	.90
☐ ER17 Vladimir Guerrero ..	2.50	1.10
☐ ER18 Todd Hundley ..	.75	.35
☐ ER19 Tino Martinez ..	.75	.35
☐ ER20 Jose Canseco ..	2.50	1.10
☐ ER21 Scott Rolen ..	2.50	1.10
☐ ER22 Al Martin ..	.50	.23
☐ ER23 Mark McGwire ..	12.00	5.50
☐ ER24 Tony Gwynn ..	5.00	2.20
☐ ER25 Barry Bonds ..	2.50	1.10
☐ ER26 Ken Griffey Jr. ..	10.00	4.50
☐ ER27 Juan Gonzalez ..	4.00	1.80
☐ ER28 Roger Clemens ..	5.00	2.20

1998 Collector's Choice Mini Bobbing Heads

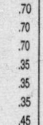

	MINT	NRMT
COMPLETE SET (30)	20.00	9.00
COMMON CARD (1-30)	.25	.11
SER.2 STATED ODDS 1:3		
MADDUX AND RIPKEN BOTH NUMBERED 6		

☐ 1 Tim Salmon ..	.60	.25
☐ 2 Travis Lee ..	1.25	.55
☐ 3 Matt Williams ..	.25	.11
☐ 4 Chipper Jones ..	1.50	.70
☐ 5 Greg Maddux UER6 ..	2.00	.90
☐ 6 Cal Ripken ..	2.50	1.10
☐ 7 Nomar Garciaparra ..	2.00	.90
☐ 8 Mo Vaughn ..	.60	.25
☐ 9 Sammy Sosa ..	1.50	.70
☐ 10 Frank Thomas ..	1.50	.70
☐ 11 Kenny Lofton ..	.60	.25
☐ 12 Jaret Wright ..	.25	.11
☐ 13 Larry Walker ..	.60	.25
☐ 14 Tony Clark ..	.40	.18
☐ 15 Edgar Renteria ..	.25	.11
☐ 16 Jeff Bagwell ..	.75	.35
☐ 17 Mike Piazza ..	2.00	.90
☐ 18 Vladimir Guerrero ..	.60	.25
☐ 19 Derek Jeter ..	1.50	.70
☐ 20 Ben Grieve ..	1.25	.55
☐ 21 Scott Rolen ..	1.50	.70
☐ 22 Mark McGwire ..	4.00	1.80
☐ 23 Tony Gwynn ..	1.50	.70
☐ 24 Barry Bonds ..	.60	.25
☐ 25 Ken Griffey Jr. ..	3.00	1.35
☐ 26 Alex Rodriguez ..	2.00	.90
☐ 27 Fred McGriff ..	.40	.18
☐ 28 Juan Gonzalez ..	1.50	.70
☐ 29 Roger Clemens ..	1.50	.70
☐ 30 Jose Cruz Jr. ..	.60	.25

1998 Collector's Choice StarQuest

	MINT	NRMT
COMP.DELIV.SET (45)	20.00	9.00

COMM.DELIVERY (1-45) ..	.15	.07
DELIVERY MINOR STARS ..	.25	.11
DELIVERY UNLISTED STARS ..	.50	.23
ONE DELIVERY PER SER.1 PACK		
COMP.STUDENT SET (20) ..	60.00	27.00
COMM.STUDENTS (46-65) ..	1.50	.70
STUDENTS SEMISTARS ..	2.00	.90
STUDENTS UNLISTED STARS	3.00	1.35
STUDENTS SER.1 STATED ODDS 1:21		
COMP.POWERS SET (15) ..	100.00	45.00
COMMON POWERS (66-80) ..	3.00	1.35
POWERS SEMISTARS ..	5.00	2.20
POWERS UNLISTED STARS .	8.00	3.60
POWERS SER.1 STATED ODDS 1:71		
COMP.SUPERSTAR SET (10)	300.00	135.00
COM.SUPERSTAR (81-90) ..	5.00	2.20
SUPERSTAR UNLISTED STARS	12.00	5.50
SUPERSTAR SER.1 STATED ODDS 1:145		

☐ SQ1 Nomar Garciaparra SD	1.50	.70
☐ SQ2 Scott Rolen SD ..	.60	.25
☐ SQ3 Jason Dickson SD ..	.15	.07
☐ SQ4 Jaret Wright SD ..	.25	.11
☐ SQ5 Kevin Orie SD ..	.15	.07
☐ SQ6 Jose Guillen SD ..	.15	.07
☐ SQ7 Matt Morris SD ..	.15	.07
☐ SQ8 Mike Cameron SD ..	.25	.11
☐ SQ9 Kevin Polcovich SD ..	.15	.07
☐ SQ10 Jose Cruz Jr. SD ..	.25	.11
☐ SQ11 Miguel Tejada SD ..	.25	.11
☐ SQ12 Fernando Tatis SD ..	.50	.23
☐ SQ13 Todd Helton SD ..	.60	.25
☐ SQ14 Ken Cloude SD ..	.15	.07
☐ SQ15 Ben Grieve SD ..	.50	.23
☐ SQ16 Dante Powell SD ..	.15	.07
☐ SQ17 Bubba Trammell SD ..	.15	.07
☐ SQ18 Juan Encarnacion SD	.25	.11
☐ SQ19 Derek Lee SD ..	.25	.11
☐ SQ20 Paul Konerko SD ..	.25	.11
☐ SQ21 Richard Hidalgo SD ..	.25	.11
☐ SQ22 Denny Neagle SD ..	.15	.07
☐ SQ23 David Justice SD ..	.25	.11
☐ SQ24 Pedro Martinez SD ..	.60	.25
☐ SQ25 Greg Maddux SD ..	1.25	.55
☐ SQ26 Edgar Martinez SD ..	.25	.11
☐ SQ27 Cal Ripken SD ..	2.00	.90
☐ SQ28 Tim Salmon SD ..	.30	.14
☐ SQ29 Shawn Estes SD ..	.15	.07
☐ SQ30 Ken Griffey Jr. SD ..	2.50	1.10
☐ SQ31 Brad Radke SD ..	.25	.11
☐ SQ32 Andy Pettitte SD ..	.25	.11
☐ SQ33 Curt Schilling SD ..	.30	.14
☐ SQ34 Raul Mondesi SD ..	.25	.11
☐ SQ35 Alex Rodriguez SD ..	1.50	.70
☐ SQ36 Jeff Kent SD ..	.25	.11
☐ SQ37 Jeff Bagwell SD ..	.60	.25
☐ SQ38 Juan Gonzalez SD ..	1.00	.45
☐ SQ39 Barry Bonds SD ..	.60	.25
☐ SQ40 Mark McGwire SD ..	3.00	1.35
☐ SQ41 Frank Thomas SD ..	1.00	.45
☐ SQ42 Ray Lankford SD ..	.25	.11
☐ SQ43 Tony Gwynn SD ..	1.25	.55
☐ SQ44 Mike Piazza SD ..	1.50	.70
☐ SQ45 Tino Martinez SD ..	.25	.11
☐ SQ46 Nomar Garciaparra SG	10.00	4.50
☐ SQ47 Paul Molitor SG ..	3.00	1.35
☐ SQ48 Chuck Knoblauch SG	1.50	.70
☐ SQ49 Rusty Greer SG ..	1.50	.70

❏ SQ50 Cal Ripken SG	12.00	5.50
❏ SQ51 Roberto Alomar SG	3.00	1.35
❏ SQ52 Scott Rolen SG	4.00	1.80
❏ SQ53 Derek Jeter SG	10.00	4.50
❏ SQ54 Mark Grace SG	2.00	.90
❏ SQ55 Randy Johnson SG	3.00	1.35
❏ SQ56 Craig Biggio SG	3.00	1.35
❏ SQ57 Kenny Lofton SG	2.00	.90
❏ SQ58 Eddie Murray SG	3.00	1.35
❏ SQ59 Ryne Sandberg SG	4.00	1.80
❏ SQ60 Rickey Henderson SG	4.00	1.80
❏ SQ61 Darin Erstad SG	2.00	.90
❏ SQ62 Jim Edmonds SG	1.50	.70
❏ SQ63 Ken Caminiti SG	1.50	.70
❏ SQ64 Ivan Rodriguez SG	4.00	1.80
❏ SQ65 Tony Gwynn SG	8.00	3.60
❏ SQ66 Tony Clark SP	3.00	1.35
❏ SQ67 Andres Galarraga SP	5.00	2.20
❏ SQ68 Rafael Palmeiro SP	8.00	3.60
❏ SQ69 Manny Ramirez SP	10.00	4.50
❏ SQ70 Albert Belle SP	8.00	3.60
❏ SQ71 Jay Buhner SP	3.00	1.35
❏ SQ72 Mo Vaughn SP	8.00	3.60
❏ SQ73 Barry Bonds SP	10.00	4.50
❏ SQ74 Chipper Jones SP	20.00	9.00
❏ SQ75 Jeff Bagwell SP	10.00	4.50
❏ SQ76 Jim Thome SP	8.00	3.60
❏ SQ77 Sammy Sosa SP	25.00	11.00
❏ SQ78 Todd Hundley SP	3.00	1.35
❏ SQ79 Matt Williams SP	8.00	3.60
❏ SQ80 Vinny Castilla SP	3.00	1.35
❏ SQ81 Jose Cruz Jr. SS	5.00	2.20
❏ SQ82 Frank Thomas SS	25.00	11.00
❏ SQ83 Juan Gonzalez SS	25.00	11.00
❏ SQ84 Mike Piazza SS	40.00	18.00
❏ SQ85 Alex Rodriguez SS	40.00	18.00
❏ SQ86 Larry Walker SS	12.00	5.50
❏ SQ87 Tino Martinez SS	5.00	2.20
❏ SQ88 Greg Maddux SS	30.00	13.50
❏ SQ89 Mark McGwire SS	80.00	36.00
❏ SQ90 Ken Griffey Jr. SS	60.00	27.00

1998 Collector's Choice StarQuest Single

	MINT	NRMT
COMPLETE SET (30)	15.00	6.75
COMMON CARD (1-30)	.15	.07
ONE PER SERIES 2 PACK		
*DOUBLES: 4X TO 10X BASE CARD HI		
DOUBLES SER.2 STATED ODDS 1:21		
*TRIPLES: 12.5X TO 30X BASE CARD HI		
TRIPLES SER.2 STATED ODDS 1:71		
*HOME RUN: 30X TO 80X BASE CARD HI		
HOME RUN: RANDOM INS.IN SER.2 PACKS		
HOME RUN PRINT RUN 100 SERIAL #'d SETS		

❏ 1 Ken Griffey Jr.	2.00	.90
❏ 2 Jose Cruz Jr.	.15	.07
❏ 3 Cal Ripken	1.50	.70
❏ 4 Roger Clemens	1.00	.45
❏ 5 Frank Thomas	.75	.35
❏ 6 Derek Jeter	1.25	.55
❏ 7 Alex Rodriguez	1.25	.55
❏ 8 Andruw Jones	.40	.18
❏ 9 Vladimir Guerrero	.50	.23
❏ 10 Mark McGwire	2.50	1.10
❏ 11 Kenny Lofton	.25	.11

❏ 12 Pedro Martinez	.50	.23
❏ 13 Greg Maddux	1.00	.45
❏ 14 Larry Walker	.40	.18
❏ 15 Barry Bonds	.50	.23
❏ 16 Chipper Jones	1.00	.45
❏ 17 Jeff Bagwell	.50	.23
❏ 18 Juan Gonzalez	.75	.35
❏ 19 Tony Gwynn	1.00	.45
❏ 20 Mike Piazza	1.25	.55
❏ 21 Tino Martinez	.15	.07
❏ 22 Mo Vaughn	.40	.18
❏ 23 Ben Grieve	.40	.18
❏ 24 Scott Rolen	.60	.25
❏ 25 Nomar Garciaparra	1.25	.55
❏ 26 Paul Konerko	.15	.07
❏ 27 Jaret Wright	.15	.07
❏ 28 Gary Sheffield	.15	.07
❏ 29 Todd Helton	.50	.23
❏ 30 Travis Lee	.25	.11

1998 Collector's Choice Stick 'Ums

	MINT	NRMT
COMPLETE SET (30)	20.00	9.00
COMMON (1-30)	.25	.11
SER.1 STATED ODDS 1:3		

❏ 1 Andruw Jones	.60	.25
❏ 2 Chipper Jones	1.50	.70
❏ 3 Cal Ripken	2.50	1.10
❏ 4 Nomar Garciaparra	2.00	.90
❏ 5 Mo Vaughn	.60	.25
❏ 6 Ryne Sandberg	.75	.35
❏ 7 Sammy Sosa	2.00	.90
❏ 8 Frank Thomas	1.25	.55
❏ 9 Albert Belle	.60	.25
❏ 10 Jim Thome	.60	.25
❏ 11 Manny Ramirez	.75	.35
❏ 12 Larry Walker	.60	.25
❏ 13 Gary Sheffield	.25	.11
❏ 14 Jeff Bagwell	.75	.35
❏ 15 Mike Piazza	2.00	.90
❏ 16 Paul Molitor	.60	.25
❏ 17 Pedro Martinez	.75	.35
❏ 18 Todd Hundley	.25	.11
❏ 19 Derek Jeter	2.00	.90
❏ 20 Tino Martinez	.25	.11
❏ 21 Curt Schilling	.40	.18
❏ 22 Mark McGwire	4.00	1.80
❏ 23 Tony Gwynn	1.50	.70
❏ 24 Barry Bonds	.75	.35
❏ 25 Ken Griffey Jr.	3.00	1.35
❏ 26 Alex Rodriguez	2.00	.90
❏ 27 Juan Gonzalez	1.25	.55
❏ 28 Ivan Rodriguez	.75	.35
❏ 29 Roger Clemens	1.50	.70
❏ 30 Jose Cruz Jr.	.25	.11

1995 Collector's Choice SE

	MINT	NRMT
COMPLETE SET (265)	20.00	9.00
COMMON CARD (1-265)	.15	.07
MINOR STARS	.30	.14
UNLISTED STARS	.60	.25

SUBSET CARDS HALF VALUE OF BASE CARDS

COMMON GOLD SIG (1-265)	2.50	1.10
*GOLD STARS: 10X TO 25X HI COLUMN		
*GOLD YNG.STARS: 8X TO 20X HI		
GOLD STATED ODDS 1:35		
12 GOLD PER GOLD SUPER PACK		
COMP.SILV.SIG.SET (265)	60.00	27.00
COMMON SILV.SIG (1-265)	.25	.11
*SILV.SIG.STARS: 1.25X TO 3X HI COLUMN		
*SILV.SIG.YNG.STARS: 1X TO 2.5X HI		
ONE SILVER SIGNATURE PER PACK		
12 SILVER SIGNATURES PER SUPER PACK		

❏ 1 Alex Rodriguez	2.50	1.10
❏ 2 Derek Jeter	2.00	.90
❏ 3 Dustin Hermanson	.15	.07
❏ 4 Bill Pulsipher	.15	.07
❏ 5 Terrell Wade	.15	.07
❏ 6 Darren Dreifort	.30	.14
❏ 7 LaTroy Hawkins	.15	.07
❏ 8 Alex Ochoa	.15	.07
❏ 9 Paul Wilson	.15	.07
❏ 10 Ernie Young	.15	.07
❏ 11 Alan Benes	.15	.07
❏ 12 Garret Anderson	.30	.14
❏ 13 Armando Benitez	.15	.07
❏ 14 Mark Thompson	.15	.07
❏ 15 Herbert Perry	.15	.07
❏ 16 Jose Silva	.15	.07
❏ 17 Orlando Miller	.15	.07
❏ 18 Russ Davis	.30	.14
❏ 19 Jason Isringhausen	.30	.14
❏ 20 Ray McDavid	.15	.07
❏ 21 Duane Singleton	.15	.07
❏ 22 Paul Shuey	.15	.07
❏ 23 Steve Dunn	.15	.07
❏ 24 Mike Lieberthal	.15	.07
❏ 25 Chan Ho Park	.60	.25
❏ 26 Ken Griffey Jr. RP	1.50	.70
❏ 27 Tony Gwynn RP	.75	.35
❏ 28 Chuck Knoblauch RP	.60	.25
❏ 29 Frank Thomas RP	.60	.25
❏ 30 Matt Williams RP	.30	.14
❏ 31 Chili Davis	.30	.14
❏ 32 Chad Curtis	.15	.07
❏ 33 Brian Anderson	.30	.14
❏ 34 Chuck Finley	.30	.14
❏ 35 Tim Salmon	.60	.25
❏ 36 Bo Jackson	.30	.14
❏ 37 Doug Drabek	.15	.07
❏ 38 Craig Biggio	.60	.25
❏ 39 Ken Caminiti	.40	.18
❏ 40 Jeff Bagwell	.75	.35
❏ 41 Darryl Kile	.15	.07
❏ 42 John Hudek	.15	.07
❏ 43 Brian L. Hunter	.30	.14
❏ 44 Dennis Eckersley	.30	.14
❏ 45 Mark McGwire	3.00	1.35
❏ 46 Brent Gates	.15	.07
❏ 47 Steve Karsay	.15	.07
❏ 48 Rickey Henderson	.75	.35
❏ 49 Terry Steinbach	.30	.14
❏ 50 Ruben Sierra	.15	.07
❏ 51 Roberto Alomar	.60	.25
❏ 52 Carlos Delgado	.60	.25
❏ 53 Alex Gonzalez	.15	.07
❏ 54 Joe Carter	.30	.14

No.	Player	MINT	NRMT
☐ 55	Paul Molitor	.60	.25
☐ 56	Juan Guzman	.15	.07
☐ 57	John Olerud	.30	.14
☐ 58	Shawn Green	.60	.25
☐ 59	Tom Glavine	.60	.25
☐ 60	Greg Maddux	1.50	.70
☐ 61	Roberto Kelly	.15	.07
☐ 62	Ryan Klesko	.30	.14
☐ 63	Javier Lopez	.30	.14
☐ 64	Jose Oliva	.15	.07
☐ 65	Fred McGriff	.40	.18
☐ 66	Steve Avery	.15	.07
☐ 67	David Justice	.60	.25
☐ 68	Ricky Bones	.15	.07
☐ 69	Cal Eldred	.15	.07
☐ 70	Greg Vaughn	.30	.14
☐ 71	Dave Nilsson	.15	.07
☐ 72	Jose Valentin	.15	.07
☐ 73	Matt Mieske	.15	.07
☐ 74	Todd Zeile	.15	.07
☐ 75	Ozzie Smith	.75	.35
☐ 76	Bernard Gilkey	.15	.07
☐ 77	Ray Lankford	.30	.14
☐ 78	Bob Tewksbury	.15	.07
☐ 79	Mark Whiten	.15	.07
☐ 80	Gregg Jefferies	.15	.07
☐ 81	Randy Myers	.15	.07
☐ 82	Shawon Dunston	.15	.07
☐ 83	Mark Grace	.40	.18
☐ 84	Derrick May	.15	.07
☐ 85	Sammy Sosa	2.00	.90
☐ 86	Steve Trachsel	.15	.07
☐ 87	Brett Butler	.30	.14
☐ 88	Delino DeShields	.15	.07
☐ 89	Orel Hershiser	.30	.14
☐ 90	Mike Piazza	2.00	.90
☐ 91	Todd Hollandsworth	.15	.07
☐ 92	Eric Karros	.30	.14
☐ 93	Ramon Martinez	.30	.14
☐ 94	Tim Wallach	.15	.07
☐ 95	Raul Mondesi	.40	.18
☐ 96	Larry Walker	.60	.25
☐ 97	Wil Cordero	.15	.07
☐ 98	Marquis Grissom	.30	.14
☐ 99	Ken Hill	.15	.07
☐ 100	Cliff Floyd	.15	.07
☐ 101	Pedro Martinez	.75	.35
☐ 102	John Wetteland	.15	.07
☐ 103	Rondell White	.30	.14
☐ 104	Moises Alou	.30	.14
☐ 105	Barry Bonds	.75	.35
☐ 106	Darren Lewis	.15	.07
☐ 107	Mark Portugal	.15	.07
☐ 108	Matt Williams	.60	.25
☐ 109	William VanLandingham	.15	.07
☐ 110	Bill Swift	.15	.07
☐ 111	Robby Thompson	.15	.07
☐ 112	Rod Beck	.15	.07
☐ 113	Darryl Strawberry	.30	.14
☐ 114	Jim Thome	.60	.25
☐ 115	Dave Winfield	.60	.25
☐ 116	Eddie Murray	.60	.25
☐ 117	Manny Ramirez	.75	.35
☐ 118	Carlos Baerga	.15	.07
☐ 119	Kenny Lofton	.40	.18
☐ 120	Albert Belle	.60	.25
☐ 121	Mark Clark	.15	.07
☐ 122	Dennis Martinez	.30	.14
☐ 123	Randy Johnson	.60	.25
☐ 124	Jay Buhner	.30	.14
☐ 125	Ken Griffey Jr.	3.00	1.35
☐ 126	Goose Gossage	.30	.14
☐ 127	Tino Martinez	.60	.25
☐ 128	Reggie Jefferson	.15	.07
☐ 129	Edgar Martinez	.30	.14
☐ 130	Gary Sheffield	.30	.14
☐ 131	Pat Rapp	.15	.07
☐ 132	Bret Barberie	.15	.07
☐ 133	Chuck Carr	.15	.07
☐ 134	Jeff Conine	.15	.07
☐ 135	Charles Johnson	.30	.14
☐ 136	Benito Santiago	.15	.07
☐ 137	Matt Williams STL	.30	.14
☐ 138	Jeff Bagwell STL	.60	.25
☐ 139	Kenny Lofton STL	.15	.07
☐ 140	Tony Gwynn STL	.75	.35
☐ 141	Jimmy Key STL	.30	.14
☐ 142	Greg Maddux STL	.75	.35
☐ 143	Randy Johnson STL	.30	.14
☐ 144	Lee Smith STL	.15	.07
☐ 145	Bobby Bonilla	.30	.14
☐ 146	Jason Jacome	.15	.07
☐ 147	Jeff Kent	.30	.14
☐ 148	Ryan Thompson	.15	.07
☐ 149	Bobby Jones	.15	.07
☐ 150	Bret Saberhagen	.30	.14
☐ 151	John Franco	.30	.14
☐ 152	Lee Smith	.30	.14
☐ 153	Rafael Palmeiro	.60	.25
☐ 154	Brady Anderson	.30	.14
☐ 155	Cal Ripken Jr.	2.50	1.10
☐ 156	Jeffrey Hammonds	.30	.14
☐ 157	Mike Mussina	.60	.25
☐ 158	Chris Hoiles	.15	.07
☐ 159	Ben McDonald	.15	.07
☐ 160	Tony Gwynn	1.50	.70
☐ 161	Joey Hamilton	.30	.14
☐ 162	Andy Benes	.30	.14
☐ 163	Trevor Hoffman	.30	.14
☐ 164	Phil Plantier	.15	.07
☐ 165	Derek Bell	.30	.14
☐ 166	Bip Roberts	.15	.07
☐ 167	Eddie Williams	.15	.07
☐ 168	Fernando Valenzuela	.30	.14
☐ 169	Mariano Duncan	.15	.07
☐ 170	Lenny Dykstra	.30	.14
☐ 171	Darren Daulton	.30	.14
☐ 172	Danny Jackson	.15	.07
☐ 173	Bobby Munoz	.15	.07
☐ 174	Doug Jones	.15	.07
☐ 175	Jay Bell	.30	.14
☐ 176	Zane Smith	.15	.07
☐ 177	Jon Lieber	.15	.07
☐ 178	Carlos Garcia	.15	.07
☐ 179	Orlando Merced	.15	.07
☐ 180	Andy Van Slyke	.30	.14
☐ 181	Rick Helling	.30	.14
☐ 182	Rusty Greer	.60	.25
☐ 183	Kenny Rogers UER	.15	.07
	Shows 110 wins in 1990		
☐ 184	Will Clark	.60	.25
☐ 185	Jose Canseco	.75	.35
☐ 186	Juan Gonzalez	1.25	.55
☐ 187	Dean Palmer	.30	.14
☐ 188	Ivan Rodriguez	.75	.35
☐ 189	John Valentin	.30	.14
☐ 190	Roger Clemens	1.50	.70
☐ 191	Aaron Sele	.15	.07
☐ 192	Scott Cooper	.15	.07
☐ 193	Mike Greenwell	.15	.07
☐ 194	Mo Vaughn	.60	.25
☐ 195	Andre Dawson	.40	.18
☐ 196	Ron Gant	.15	.07
☐ 197	Jose Rijo	.15	.07
☐ 198	Bret Boone	.15	.07
☐ 199	Deion Sanders	.30	.14
☐ 200	Barry Larkin	.60	.25
☐ 201	Hal Morris	.15	.07
☐ 202	Reggie Sanders	.30	.14
☐ 203	Kevin Mitchell	.15	.07
☐ 204	Marvin Freeman	.15	.07
☐ 205	Andres Galarraga	.60	.25
☐ 206	Walt Weiss	.15	.07
☐ 207	Charlie Hayes	.15	.07
☐ 208	Dave Nied	.15	.07
☐ 209	Dante Bichette	.30	.14
☐ 210	David Cone	.40	.18
☐ 211	Jeff Montgomery	.15	.07
☐ 212	Felix Jose	.15	.07
☐ 213	Mike Macfarlane	.15	.07
☐ 214	Wally Joyner	.30	.14
☐ 215	Bob Hamelin	.15	.07
☐ 216	Brian McRae	.15	.07
☐ 217	Kirk Gibson	.30	.14
☐ 218	Lou Whitaker	.30	.14
☐ 219	Chris Gomez	.15	.07
☐ 220	Cecil Fielder	.30	.14
☐ 221	Mickey Tettleton	.15	.07
☐ 222	Travis Fryman	.30	.14
☐ 223	Tony Phillips	.15	.07
☐ 224	Rick Aguilera	.15	.07
☐ 225	Scott Erickson	.30	.14
☐ 226	Chuck Knoblauch	.60	.25
☐ 227	Kent Hrbek	.15	.07
☐ 228	Shane Mack	.15	.07
☐ 229	Kevin Tapani	.15	.07
☐ 230	Kirby Puckett	1.00	.45
☐ 231	Julio Franco	.15	.07
☐ 232	Jack McDowell	.15	.07
☐ 233	Jason Bere	.15	.07
☐ 234	Alex Fernandez	.15	.07
☐ 235	Frank Thomas	1.25	.55
☐ 236	Ozzie Guillen	.15	.07
☐ 237	Robin Ventura	.30	.14
☐ 238	Michael Jordan	4.00	1.80
☐ 239	Wilson Alvarez	.30	.14
☐ 240	Don Mattingly	1.25	.55
☐ 241	Jim Abbott	.30	.14
☐ 242	Jim Leyritz	.15	.07
☐ 243	Paul O'Neill	.30	.14
☐ 244	Melido Perez	.15	.07
☐ 245	Wade Boggs	.60	.25
☐ 246	Mike Stanley	.15	.07
☐ 247	Danny Tartabull	.15	.07
☐ 248	Jimmy Key	.30	.14
☐ 249	Greg Maddux FT	.75	.35
☐ 250	Randy Johnson FT	.30	.14
☐ 251	Bret Saberhagen FT	.30	.14
☐ 252	John Wetteland FT	.30	.14
☐ 253	Mike Piazza FT	1.00	.45
☐ 254	Jeff Bagwell FT	.60	.25
☐ 255	Craig Biggio FT	.30	.14
☐ 256	Matt Williams FT	.30	.14
☐ 257	Wil Cordero FT	.15	.07
☐ 258	Kenny Lofton FT	.15	.07
☐ 259	Barry Bonds FT	.40	.18
☐ 260	Dante Bichette FT	.15	.07
☐ 261	Ken Griffey Jr. CL	1.50	.70
☐ 262	Goose Gossage CL	.15	.07
☐ 263	Cal Ripken CL	1.25	.55
☐ 264	Kenny Rogers CL	.15	.07
☐ 265	John Valentin CL	.15	.07
☐ P125	Ken Griffey Jr. Promo	3.00	1.35

1998 Crown Royale

	MINT	NRMT
COMPLETE SET (144)	150.00	70.00
COMMON CARD (1-144)	.50	.23
MINOR STARS	.75	.35
SEMISTARS	1.25	.55
UNLISTED STARS	2.00	.90

No.	Player	MINT	NRMT
☐ 1	Garret Anderson	.75	.35
☐ 2	Jim Edmonds	.75	.35
☐ 3	Darin Erstad	1.25	.55
☐ 4	Tim Salmon	1.25	.55
☐ 5	Jarrod Washburn	.50	.23
☐ 6	Dave Dellucci	1.50	.70
☐ 7	Travis Lee	1.25	.55
☐ 8	Devon White	.50	.23
☐ 9	Matt Williams	2.00	.90
☐ 10	Andres Galarraga	1.25	.55
☐ 11	Tom Glavine	2.00	.90
☐ 12	Andruw Jones	2.00	.90
☐ 13	Chipper Jones	5.00	2.20
☐ 14	Ryan Klesko	.75	.35
☐ 15	Javy Lopez	.75	.35
☐ 16	Greg Maddux	5.00	2.20
☐ 17	Walt Weiss	.75	.35

❏ 18 Roberto Alomar	2.00	.90
❏ 19 Harold Baines	.75	.35
❏ 20 Eric Davis	.75	.35
❏ 21 Mike Mussina	2.00	.90
❏ 22 Rafael Palmeiro	2.00	.90
❏ 23 Cal Ripken	8.00	3.60
❏ 24 Nomar Garciaparra	6.00	2.70
❏ 25 Pedro Martinez	2.50	1.10
❏ 26 Troy O'Leary	.75	.35
❏ 27 Mo Vaughn	2.00	.90
❏ 28 Tim Wakefield	.50	.23
❏ 29 Mark Grace	1.25	.55
❏ 30 Mickey Morandini	.50	.23
❏ 31 Sammy Sosa	6.00	2.70
❏ 32 Kerry Wood	2.50	1.10
❏ 33 Albert Belle	2.00	.90
❏ 34 Mike Caruso	.50	.23
❏ 35 Ray Durham	.75	.35
❏ 36 Frank Thomas	4.00	1.80
❏ 37 Robin Ventura	.75	.35
❏ 38 Bret Boone	.75	.35
❏ 39 Sean Casey	3.00	1.35
❏ 40 Barry Larkin	2.00	.90
❏ 41 Reggie Sanders	.50	.23
❏ 42 Sandy Alomar Jr.	.75	.35
❏ 43 David Justice	.75	.35
❏ 44 Kenny Lofton	1.25	.55
❏ 45 Manny Ramirez	2.50	1.10
❏ 46 Jim Thome	2.00	.90
❏ 47 Omar Vizquel	.75	.35
❏ 48 Jaret Wright	.75	.35
❏ 49 Dante Bichette	.75	.35
❏ 50 Ellis Burks	.75	.35
❏ 51 Vinny Castilla	.75	.35
❏ 52 Todd Helton	2.50	1.10
❏ 53 Larry Walker	2.00	.90
❏ 54 Tony Clark	.75	.35
❏ 55 Damion Easley	.75	.35
❏ 56 Bobby Higginson	.75	.35
❏ 57 Cliff Floyd	.75	.35
❏ 58 Livan Hernandez	.50	.23
❏ 59 Derrek Lee	.50	.23
❏ 60 Edgar Renteria	.50	.23
❏ 61 Moises Alou	.75	.35
❏ 62 Jeff Bagwell	2.50	1.10
❏ 63 Derek Bell	.75	.35
❏ 64 Craig Biggio	2.00	.90
❏ 65 Johnny Damon	.75	.35
❏ 66 Jeff King	.50	.23
❏ 67 Hal Morris	.50	.23
❏ 68 Dean Palmer	.75	.35
❏ 69 Bobby Bonilla	.75	.35
❏ 70 Eric Karros	.75	.35
❏ 71 Raul Mondesi	.75	.35
❏ 72 Gary Sheffield	.75	.35
❏ 73 Jeromy Burnitz	.50	.23
❏ 74 Jeff Cirillo	.50	.23
❏ 75 Marquis Grissom	.50	.23
❏ 76 Fernando Vina	.50	.23
❏ 77 Marty Cordova	.50	.23
❏ 78 Pat Meares	.50	.23
❏ 79 Paul Molitor	2.00	.90
❏ 80 Terry Steinbach	.50	.23
❏ 81 Todd Walker	.75	.35
❏ 82 Brad Fullmer	.75	.35
❏ 83 Vladimir Guerrero	2.50	1.10
❏ 84 Carl Pavano	.50	.23
❏ 85 Rondell White	.75	.35
❏ 86 Carlos Baerga	.50	.23
❏ 87 Hideo Nomo	2.00	.90
❏ 88 John Olerud	.75	.35
❏ 89 Rey Ordonez	.75	.35
❏ 90 Mike Piazza	6.00	2.70
❏ 91 Masato Yoshii	1.25	.55
❏ 92 Orlando Hernandez	5.00	2.20
❏ 93 Hideki Irabu	.75	.35
❏ 94 Derek Jeter	6.00	2.70
❏ 95 Chuck Knoblauch	.75	.35
❏ 96 Ricky Ledee	.75	.35
❏ 97 Tino Martinez	.75	.35
❏ 98 Paul O'Neill	.75	.35
❏ 99 Bernie Williams	.90	.90
❏ 100 Jason Giambi	.75	.35
❏ 101 Ben Grieve	2.00	.90
❏ 102 Rickey Henderson	2.50	1.10
❏ 103 Matt Stairs	.75	.35

❏ 104 Bob Abreu	.75	.35
❏ 105 Doug Glanville	.75	.35
❏ 106 Scott Rolen	2.50	1.10
❏ 107 Curt Schilling	1.25	.55
❏ 108 Jose Guillen	.50	.23
❏ 109 Jason Kendall	.75	.35
❏ 110 Jason Schmidt	.50	.23
❏ 111 Kevin Young	.75	.35
❏ 112 Delino DeShields	.50	.23
❏ 113 Brian Jordan	.75	.35
❏ 114 Ray Lankford	.75	.35
❏ 115 Mark McGwire	12.00	5.50
❏ 116 Tony Gwynn	5.00	2.20
❏ 117 Wally Joyner	.75	.35
❏ 118 Ruben Rivera	.50	.23
❏ 119 Greg Vaughn	.75	.35
❏ 120 Rich Aurilia	.50	.23
❏ 121 Barry Bonds	2.50	1.10
❏ 122 Bill Mueller	.50	.23
❏ 123 Robb Nen	.50	.23
❏ 124 Jay Buhner	.75	.35
❏ 125 Ken Griffey Jr.	10.00	4.50
❏ 126 Edgar Martinez	.75	.35
❏ 127 Shane Monahan	.50	.23
❏ 128 Alex Rodriguez	6.00	2.70
❏ 129 David Segui	.50	.23
❏ 130 Rolando Arrojo	2.00	.90
❏ 131 Wade Boggs	2.00	.90
❏ 132 Quinton McCracken	.50	.23
❏ 133 Fred McGriff	1.25	.55
❏ 134 Bobby Smith	.50	.23
❏ 135 Will Clark	2.00	.90
❏ 136 Juan Gonzalez	4.00	1.80
❏ 137 Rusty Greer	.75	.35
❏ 138 Ivan Rodriguez	2.50	1.10
❏ 139 Aaron Sele	.75	.35
❏ 140 John Wetteland	.75	.35
❏ 141 Jose Canseco	2.50	1.10
❏ 142 Roger Clemens	5.00	2.20
❏ 143 Carlos Delgado	2.00	.90
❏ 144 Shawn Green	2.00	.90

1998 Crown Royale All-Stars

	MINT	NRMT
COMPLETE SET (20)	400.00	180.00
COMMON CARD (1-20)	2.50	1.10
MINOR STARS	4.00	1.80
UNLISTED STARS	10.00	4.50
STATED ODDS 1:25		

❏ 1 Roberto Alomar	10.00	4.50
❏ 2 Cal Ripken	40.00	18.00
❏ 3 Kenny Lofton	6.00	2.70
❏ 4 Jim Thome	10.00	4.50
❏ 5 Derek Jeter	30.00	13.50
❏ 6 David Wells	4.00	1.80
❏ 7 Ken Griffey Jr.	50.00	22.00
❏ 8 Alex Rodriguez	30.00	13.50
❏ 9 Juan Gonzalez	20.00	9.00
❏ 10 Ivan Rodriguez	12.00	5.50
❏ 11 Gary Sheffield	4.00	1.80
❏ 12 Chipper Jones	25.00	11.00
❏ 13 Greg Maddux	25.00	11.00
❏ 14 Walt Weiss	2.50	1.10
❏ 15 Larry Walker	10.00	4.50
❏ 16 Craig Biggio	10.00	4.50

❏ 17 Mike Piazza	30.00	13.50
❏ 18 Mark McGwire	60.00	27.00
❏ 19 Tony Gwynn	25.00	11.00
❏ 20 Barry Bonds	12.00	5.50

1998 Crown Royale Cramer's Choice Premiums

	MINT	NRMT
COMPLETE SET (10)	150.00	70.00
COMMON CARD (1-528)	3.00	1.35
ONE PER BOX		

CRAMER AU'S RANDOM INSERTS IN BOXES
CRAMER AU'S PRINT RUN 10 SERIAL #'d SETS
CRAMER AU'S NOT PRICED DUE TO SCARCITY

❏ 1 Cal Ripken	20.00	9.00
❏ 2 Ken Griffey Jr.	25.00	11.00
❏ 3 Alex Rodriguez	15.00	6.75
❏ 4 Juan Gonzalez	10.00	4.50
❏ 5 Travis Lee	3.00	1.35
❏ 6 Chipper Jones	12.00	5.50
❏ 7 Greg Maddux	12.00	5.50
❏ 8 Kerry Wood	5.00	2.20
❏ 9 Mark McGwire	30.00	13.50
❏ 10 Tony Gwynn	12.00	5.50

1998 Crown Royale Diamond Knights

	MINT	NRMT
COMPLETE SET (25)	40.00	18.00
COMMON CARD (1-25)	.40	.18
ONE PER PACK		

❏ 1 Andres Galarraga	.60	.25
❏ 2 Chipper Jones	2.50	1.10
❏ 3 Greg Maddux	2.50	1.10
❏ 4 Cal Ripken	4.00	1.80
❏ 5 Nomar Garciaparra	3.00	1.35
❏ 6 Mo Vaughn	1.00	.45
❏ 7 Kerry Wood	1.00	.45
❏ 8 Frank Thomas	2.00	.90
❏ 9 Vinny Castilla	.40	.18
❏ 10 Jeff Bagwell	1.25	.55
❏ 11 Craig Biggio	1.00	.45

		MINT	NRMT
❑ 12	Paul Molitor	1.00	.45
❑ 13	Mike Piazza	3.00	1.35
❑ 14	Orlando Hernandez	2.50	1.10
❑ 15	Derek Jeter	3.00	1.35
❑ 16	Ricky Ledee	.40	.18
❑ 17	Mark McGwire	6.00	2.70
❑ 18	Tony Gwynn	2.50	1.10
❑ 19	Barry Bonds	1.25	.55
❑ 20	Ken Griffey Jr.	5.00	2.20
❑ 21	Alex Rodriguez	3.00	1.35
❑ 22	Wade Boggs	1.00	.45
❑ 23	Juan Gonzalez	2.00	.90
❑ 24	Ivan Rodriguez	1.25	.55
❑ 25	Jose Canseco	1.25	.55

1998 Crown Royale Firestone on Baseball

	MINT	NRMT
COMPLETE SET (26)	300.00	135.00
COMMON CARD (1-26)	2.50	1.10
SEMISTARS	4.00	1.80
UNLISTED STARS	6.00	2.70

STATED ODDS 2:25
FIRESTONE SIGNED 300 OF CARD 26
FIRESTONE ALSO SIGNED 8 OF EACH 1-25
COMP.SET EXCLUDES FIRESTONE AU'S
FIRESTONE AU'S TOO SCARCE TO PRICE

		MINT	NRMT
❑ 1	Travis Lee	4.00	1.80
❑ 2	Chipper Jones	15.00	6.75
❑ 3	Greg Maddux	15.00	6.75
❑ 4	Cal Ripken	25.00	11.00
❑ 5	Nomar Garciaparra	20.00	9.00
❑ 6	Mo Vaughn	6.00	2.70
❑ 7	Kerry Wood	6.00	2.70
❑ 8	Frank Thomas	12.00	5.50
❑ 9	Manny Ramirez	8.00	3.60
❑ 10	Larry Walker	6.00	2.70
❑ 11	Gary Sheffield	2.50	1.10
❑ 12	Paul Molitor	6.00	2.70
❑ 13	Hideo Nomo	6.00	2.70
❑ 14	Mike Piazza	20.00	9.00
❑ 15	Ben Grieve	6.00	2.70
❑ 16	Mark McGwire	40.00	18.00
❑ 17	Tony Gwynn	15.00	6.75
❑ 18	Barry Bonds	8.00	3.60
❑ 19	Ken Griffey Jr.	30.00	13.50
❑ 20	Randy Johnson	6.00	2.70
❑ 21	Alex Rodriguez	20.00	9.00
❑ 22	Wade Boggs	6.00	2.70
❑ 23	Juan Gonzalez	12.00	5.50
❑ 24	Ivan Rodriguez	8.00	3.60
❑ 25	Roger Clemens	15.00	6.75
❑ 26	Roy Firestone	8.00	3.60
	Tony Gwynn		

1998 Crown Royale Home Run Fever

	MINT	NRMT
COMPLETE SET (10)	350.00	160.00
COMMON CARD (1-10)	8.00	3.60
UNLISTED STARS	15.00	6.75

STATED ODDS 1:73
STATED PRINT RUN 374 SERIAL #'d SETS

		MINT	NRMT
❑ 1	Andres Galarraga	10.00	4.50
❑ 2	Sammy Sosa	50.00	22.00
❑ 3	Albert Belle	15.00	6.75
❑ 4	Jim Thome	15.00	6.75
❑ 5	Mark McGwire	100.00	45.00
❑ 6	Greg Vaughn	8.00	3.60
❑ 7	Ken Griffey Jr.	80.00	36.00
❑ 8	Alex Rodriguez	50.00	22.00
❑ 9	Juan Gonzalez	30.00	13.50
❑ 10	Jose Canseco	20.00	9.00

1998 Crown Royale Pillars of the Game

BERNIE WILLIAMS

	MINT	NRMT
COMPLETE SET (25)	40.00	18.00
COMMON CARD (1-25)	.40	.18

ONE PER PACK

		MINT	NRMT
❑ 1	Jim Edmonds	.40	.18
❑ 2	Travis Lee	.60	.25
❑ 3	Chipper Jones	2.50	1.10
❑ 4	Tom Glavine	2.00	.90
	John Smoltz		
	Greg Maddux		
❑ 5	Cal Ripken	4.00	1.80
❑ 6	Nomar Garciaparra	3.00	1.35
❑ 7	Roberto Alomar	1.00	.45
❑ 8	Sammy Sosa	3.00	1.35
❑ 9	Kerry Wood	1.00	.45
❑ 10	Frank Thomas	2.00	.90
❑ 11	Jim Thome	1.00	.45
❑ 12	Larry Walker	1.00	.45
❑ 13	Moises Alou	.40	.18
❑ 14	Raul Mondesi	.40	.18
❑ 15	Mike Piazza	3.00	1.35
❑ 16	Hideki Irabu	.40	.18
❑ 17	Bernie Williams	1.00	.45
❑ 18	Ben Grieve	1.00	.45
❑ 19	Scott Rolen	1.50	.70
❑ 20	Mark McGwire	6.00	2.70
❑ 21	Tony Gwynn	2.50	1.10
❑ 22	Ken Griffey Jr.	5.00	2.20
❑ 23	Alex Rodriguez	3.00	1.35
❑ 24	Juan Gonzalez	2.00	.90
❑ 25	Roger Clemens	2.50	1.10

1999 Crown Royale

	MINT	NRMT
COMPLETE SET (144)	250.00	110.00

	MINT	NRMT
COMP.SET w/o SP's (126)	120.00	55.00
COMMON CARD (1-144)	.40	.18
MINOR STARS	.60	.25
SEMISTARS	1.00	.45
UNLISTED STARS	1.50	.70
COMMON ROOKIE SP	5.00	2.20

ROOKIE SP ODDS 1:8

		MINT	NRMT
❑ 1	Jim Edmonds	.60	.25
❑ 2	Darin Erstad	1.00	.45
❑ 3	Troy Glaus	1.50	.70
❑ 4	Tim Salmon	1.00	.45
❑ 5	Mo Vaughn	1.50	.70
❑ 6	Jay Bell	.60	.25
❑ 7	Steve Finley	.60	.25
❑ 8	Randy Johnson	1.50	.70
❑ 9	Travis Lee	1.00	.45
❑ 10	Matt Williams	1.50	.70
❑ 11	Andruw Jones	1.50	.70
❑ 12	Chipper Jones	4.00	1.80
❑ 13	Brian Jordan	.60	.25
❑ 14	Ryan Klesko	.60	.25
❑ 15	Javy Lopez	.60	.25
❑ 16	Greg Maddux	4.00	1.80
❑ 17	Randall Simon SP	5.00	2.20
❑ 18	Albert Belle	1.50	.70
❑ 19	Will Clark	1.50	.70
❑ 20	Delino DeShields	.40	.18
❑ 21	Mike Mussina	1.50	.70
❑ 22	Cal Ripken	6.00	2.70
❑ 23	Nomar Garciaparra	5.00	2.20
❑ 24	Pedro Martinez	2.00	.90
❑ 25	Jose Offerman	.60	.25
❑ 26	John Valentin	.60	.25
❑ 27	Mark Grace	1.00	.45
❑ 28	Lance Johnson	.40	.18
❑ 29	Henry Rodriguez	.60	.25
❑ 30	Sammy Sosa	5.00	2.20
❑ 31	Kerry Wood	1.50	.70
❑ 32	Mike Caruso	.40	.18
❑ 33	Ray Durham	.60	.25
❑ 34	Magglio Ordonez	1.50	.70
❑ 35	Brian Simmons SP	5.00	2.20
❑ 36	Frank Thomas	3.00	1.35
❑ 37	Mike Cameron	.40	.18
❑ 38	Barry Larkin	1.50	.70
❑ 39	Greg Vaughn	.60	.25
❑ 40	Dmitri Young	.60	.25
❑ 41	Roberto Alomar	1.50	.70
❑ 42	Sandy Alomar Jr.	.60	.25
❑ 43	David Justice	.60	.25
❑ 44	Kenny Lofton	1.00	.45
❑ 45	Manny Ramirez	2.00	.90
❑ 46	Jim Thome	1.50	.70
❑ 47	Dante Bichette	.60	.25
❑ 48	Vinny Castilla	.60	.25
❑ 49	Todd Helton	1.50	.70
❑ 50	Larry Walker	1.50	.70
❑ 51	Tony Clark	.60	.25
❑ 52	Damion Easley	.60	.25
❑ 53	Bob Higginson	.60	.25
❑ 54	Brian Hunter	.40	.18
❑ 55	Gabe Kapler SP	8.00	3.60
❑ 56	Jeff Weaver SP	10.00	4.50
❑ 57	Cliff Floyd	.60	.25
❑ 58	Alex Gonzalez SP	5.00	2.20
❑ 59	Mark Kotsay	.40	.18
❑ 60	Derrek Lee	.40	.18

		MINT	NRMT
❑ 61	Preston Wilson SP	5.00	2.20
❑ 62	Moises Alou	.60	.25
❑ 63	Jeff Bagwell	2.00	.90
❑ 64	Derek Bell	.60	.25
❑ 65	Craig Biggio	1.50	.70
❑ 66	Ken Caminiti	.60	.25
❑ 67	Carlos Beltran SP	12.00	5.50
❑ 68	Johnny Damon	.60	.25
❑ 69	Carlos Febles SP	5.00	2.20
❑ 70	Jeff King	.40	.18
❑ 71	Kevin Brown	1.00	.45
❑ 72	Todd Hundley	.60	.25
❑ 73	Eric Karros	.60	.25
❑ 74	Raul Mondesi	.60	.25
❑ 75	Gary Sheffield	.60	.25
❑ 76	Jeromy Burnitz	.60	.25
❑ 77	Jeff Cirillo	.60	.25
❑ 78	Marquis Grissom	.40	.18
❑ 79	Fernando Vina	.40	.18
❑ 80	Chad Allen SP	5.00	2.20
❑ 81	Matt Lawton	.40	.18
❑ 82	Doug Mientkiewicz SP	5.00	2.20
❑ 83	Brad Radke	.60	.25
❑ 84	Todd Walker	.60	.25
❑ 85	Michael Barrett SP	5.00	2.20
❑ 86	Brad Fullmer	.40	.18
❑ 87	Vladimir Guerrero	2.00	.90
❑ 88	Wilton Guerrero	.40	.18
❑ 89	Ugueth Urbina	.40	.18
❑ 90	Bobby Bonilla	.60	.25
❑ 91	Rickey Henderson	2.00	.90
❑ 92	Rey Ordonez	.60	.25
❑ 93	Mike Piazza	5.00	2.20
❑ 94	Robin Ventura	.60	.25
❑ 95	Roger Clemens	4.00	1.80
❑ 96	Orlando Hernandez	1.50	.70
❑ 97	Derek Jeter	5.00	2.20
❑ 98	Chuck Knoblauch	.60	.25
❑ 99	Tino Martinez	.60	.25
❑ 100	Bernie Williams	1.50	.70
❑ 101	Eric Chavez SP	5.00	2.20
❑ 102	Jason Giambi	.60	.25
❑ 103	Ben Grieve	1.50	.70
❑ 104	Tim Raines	.60	.25
❑ 105	Marlon Anderson SP	5.00	2.20
❑ 106	Doug Glanville	.60	.25
❑ 107	Scott Rolen	2.00	.90
❑ 108	Curt Schilling	1.00	.45
❑ 109	Brian Giles	.60	.25
❑ 110	Jose Guillen	.40	.18
❑ 111	Jason Kendall	.60	.25
❑ 112	Kevin Young	.60	.25
❑ 113	J.D. Drew SP	15.00	6.75
❑ 114	Jose Jimenez SP	5.00	2.20
❑ 115	Ray Lankford	.60	.25
❑ 116	Mark McGwire	10.00	4.50
❑ 117	Fernando Tatis	1.50	.70
❑ 118	Matt Clement SP	5.00	2.20
❑ 119	Tony Gwynn	4.00	1.80
❑ 120	Trevor Hoffman	.60	.25
❑ 121	Wally Joyner	.60	.25
❑ 122	Reggie Sanders	.40	.18
❑ 123	Barry Bonds	2.00	.90
❑ 124	Ellis Burks	.60	.25
❑ 125	Jeff Kent	.60	.25
❑ 126	J.T. Snow	.60	.25
❑ 127	Freddy Garcia SP	40.00	18.00
❑ 128	Ken Griffey Jr.	8.00	3.60
❑ 129	Edgar Martinez	.60	.25
❑ 130	Alex Rodriguez	5.00	2.20
❑ 131	David Segui	.40	.18
❑ 132	Rolando Arrojo	.40	.18
❑ 133	Wade Boggs	1.50	.70
❑ 134	Jose Canseco	2.00	.90
❑ 135	Quinton McCracken	.40	.18
❑ 136	Fred McGriff	1.00	.45
❑ 137	Juan Gonzalez	3.00	1.35
❑ 138	Rusty Greer	.60	.25
❑ 139	Rafael Palmeiro	1.50	.70
❑ 140	Ivan Rodriguez	2.00	.90
❑ 141	Jose Cruz Jr.	.60	.25
❑ 142	Carlos Delgado	1.50	.70
❑ 143	Shawn Green	1.50	.70
❑ 144	Roy Halladay SP	5.00	2.20

1999 Crown Royale Limited

	MINT	NRMT
COMMON CARD (1-144)	5.00	2.20

*STARS: 5X TO 12X BASIC CARDS
*SP's: .6X TO 1.5X BASIC SP's
RANDOM INSERTS IN PACKS
STATED PRINT RUN 99 SERIAL #'d SETS

1999 Crown Royale Opening Day

	MINT	NRMT
COMMON CARD (1-144)	6.00	2.70

*STARS: 6X TO 15X BASIC CARDS
*SP's: .75X TO 2X BASIC SP's
STATED ODDS 1:25 HOBBY
STATED PRINT RUN 72 SERIAL #'d SETS

1999 Crown Royale Century 21

	MINT	NRMT
COMPLETE SET (10)	150.00	70.00
COMMON CARD (1-10)	6.00	2.70

STATED ODDS 1:25

❑ 1	Cal Ripken	20.00	9.00
❑ 2	Nomar Garciaparra	15.00	6.75
❑ 3	Sammy Sosa	15.00	6.75
❑ 4	Frank Thomas	10.00	4.50

❑ 5	Mike Piazza	15.00	6.75
❑ 6	J.D. Drew	6.00	2.70
❑ 7	Mark McGwire	30.00	13.50
❑ 8	Tony Gwynn	12.00	5.50
❑ 9	Ken Griffey Jr.	25.00	11.00
❑ 10	Alex Rodriguez	15.00	6.75

1999 Crown Royale Cramer's Choice Premiums

	MINT	NRMT
COMPLETE SET (10)	150.00	70.00
COMMON CARD (1-10)	6.00	2.70

ONE PREMIUM PER BOX
*DARK BLUE: 2.5X TO 6X PREMIUMS HI
*GOLD: 8X TO 20X PREMIUMS HI
*GREEN: 3X TO 8X PREMIUMS HI
*LIGHT BLUE: 5X TO 12X PREMIUMS HI
*RED: 4X TO 10X PREMIUMS HI
DARK BLUE PRINT RUN 35 SERIAL #'d SETS
GOLD PRINT RUN 10 SERIAL #'d SETS
GREEN PRINT RUN 30 SERIAL #'d SETS
LIGHT BLUE PRINT RUN 20 SERIAL #'d SETS
PURPLE AU PRINT RUN 1 SERIAL #'d SET
RED PRINT RUN 25 SERIAL #'d SETS
PARALLELS ARE RANDOM INSERTS IN PACKS
PURPLE AU'S NOT PRICED DUE TO SCARCITY
BASIC PREMIUMS LISTED BELOW!

❑ 1	Cal Ripken	20.00	9.00
❑ 2	Nomar Garciaparra	15.00	6.75
❑ 3	Sammy Sosa	15.00	6.75
❑ 4	Frank Thomas	10.00	4.50
❑ 5	Mike Piazza	15.00	6.75
❑ 6	Derek Jeter	15.00	6.75
❑ 7	J.D. Drew	6.00	2.70
❑ 8	Mark McGwire	30.00	13.50
❑ 9	Tony Gwynn	12.00	5.50
❑ 10	Ken Griffey Jr.	25.00	11.00

1999 Crown Royale Gold Crown Die Cut Premiums

	MINT	NRMT
COMPLETE SET (6)	120.00	55.00
COMMON CARD (1-6)	10.00	4.50
STATED ODDS 6:10 BOXES		
STATED PRINT RUN 1036 SERIAL #'d SETS		

❑ 1 Cal Ripken	25.00	11.00
❑ 2 Mike Piazza	20.00	9.00
❑ 3 Ken Griffey Jr.	30.00	13.50
❑ 4 Tony Gwynn	15.00	6.75
❑ 5 Mark McGwire	40.00	18.00
❑ 6 J.D. Drew	10.00	4.50

1999 Crown Royale Living Legends

Sammy Sosa

	MINT	NRMT
COMPLETE SET (10)	300.00	135.00
COMMON CARD (1-10)	20.00	9.00
RANDOM INSERTS IN PACKS		
STATED PRINT RUN 375 SERIAL #'d SETS		

❑ 1 Greg Maddux	25.00	11.00
❑ 2 Cal Ripken	40.00	18.00
❑ 3 Nomar Garciaparra	30.00	13.50
❑ 4 Sammy Sosa	30.00	13.50
❑ 5 Frank Thomas	20.00	9.00
❑ 6 Mike Piazza	30.00	13.50
❑ 7 Mark McGwire	60.00	27.00
❑ 8 Tony Gwynn	25.00	11.00
❑ 9 Ken Griffey Jr.	50.00	22.00
❑ 10 Alex Rodriguez	30.00	13.50

1999 Crown Royale Master Performers

	MINT	NRMT
COMPLETE SET (20)	200.00	90.00
COMMON CARD (1-20)	2.00	.90
STATED ODDS 2:25		

❑ 1 Chipper Jones	10.00	4.50
❑ 2 Greg Maddux	10.00	4.50
❑ 3 Cal Ripken	15.00	6.75
❑ 4 Nomar Garciaparra	12.00	5.50
❑ 5 Sammy Sosa	12.00	5.50
❑ 6 Frank Thomas	8.00	3.60
❑ 7 Raul Mondesi	2.00	.90
❑ 8 Vladimir Guerrero	5.00	2.20
❑ 9 Mike Piazza	12.00	5.50

❑ 10 Roger Clemens	10.00	4.50
❑ 11 Derek Jeter	12.00	5.50
❑ 12 Scott Rolen	5.00	2.20
❑ 13 J.D. Drew	5.00	2.20
❑ 14 Mark McGwire	25.00	11.00
❑ 15 Tony Gwynn	10.00	4.50
❑ 16 Barry Bonds	5.00	2.20
❑ 17 Ken Griffey Jr.	20.00	9.00
❑ 18 Alex Rodriguez	12.00	5.50
❑ 19 Juan Gonzalez	8.00	3.60
❑ 20 Ivan Rodriguez	5.00	2.20

1999 Crown Royale Pillars of the Game

	MINT	NRMT
COMPLETE SET (25)	40.00	18.00
COMMON CARD (1-25)	.50	.23
UNLISTED STARS	1.00	.45
ONE PER PACK		

❑ 1 Mo Vaughn	1.00	.45
❑ 2 Chipper Jones	2.50	1.10
❑ 3 Greg Maddux	2.50	1.10
❑ 4 Albert Belle	1.00	.45
❑ 5 Cal Ripken	4.00	1.80
❑ 6 Nomar Garciaparra	3.00	1.35
❑ 7 Sammy Sosa	3.00	1.35
❑ 8 Frank Thomas	2.00	.90
❑ 9 Manny Ramirez	1.25	.55
❑ 10 Jeff Bagwell	1.25	.55
❑ 11 Raul Mondesi	.50	.23
❑ 12 Vladimir Guerrero	1.25	.55
❑ 13 Mike Piazza	3.00	1.35
❑ 14 Roger Clemens	2.50	1.10
❑ 15 Derek Jeter	3.00	1.35
❑ 16 Bernie Williams	1.00	.45
❑ 17 Ben Grieve	1.00	.45
❑ 18 Scott Rolen	1.25	.55
❑ 19 J.D. Drew	1.50	.70
❑ 20 Mark McGwire	6.00	2.70
❑ 21 Tony Gwynn	3.00	1.35
❑ 22 Ken Griffey Jr.	5.00	2.20
❑ 23 Alex Rodriguez	3.00	1.35
❑ 24 Juan Gonzalez	2.00	.90
❑ 25 Ivan Rodriguez	1.25	.55

1999 Crown Royale Pivotal Players

Pivotal Players

	MINT	NRMT
COMPLETE SET (25)	30.00	13.50
COMMON CARD (1-25)	.50	.23
UNLISTED STARS	1.00	.45
ONE PER PACK		

❑ 1 Mo Vaughn	1.00	.45
❑ 2 Chipper Jones	2.50	1.10
❑ 3 Greg Maddux	2.50	1.10
❑ 4 Albert Belle	1.00	.45
❑ 5 Cal Ripken	4.00	1.80
❑ 6 Nomar Garciaparra	3.00	1.35
❑ 7 Sammy Sosa	3.00	1.35
❑ 8 Frank Thomas	2.00	.90
❑ 9 Manny Ramirez	1.25	.55
❑ 10 Craig Biggio	1.00	.45
❑ 11 Raul Mondesi	.50	.23
❑ 12 Vladimir Guerrero	1.25	.55
❑ 13 Mike Piazza	3.00	1.35
❑ 14 Roger Clemens	2.50	1.10
❑ 15 Derek Jeter	3.00	1.35
❑ 16 Bernie Williams	1.00	.45
❑ 17 Ben Grieve	1.00	.45
❑ 18 Scott Rolen	1.25	.55
❑ 19 J.D. Drew	1.50	.70
❑ 20 Mark McGwire	6.00	2.70
❑ 21 Tony Gwynn	3.00	1.35
❑ 22 Ken Griffey Jr.	5.00	2.20
❑ 23 Alex Rodriguez	3.00	1.35
❑ 24 Juan Gonzalez	2.00	.90
❑ 25 Ivan Rodriguez	1.25	.55

1981 Donruss

FERGUSON JENKINS PITCHER

	NRMT	VG-E
COMPLETE SET (605)	30.00	13.50
COMMON CARD (1-605)	.10	.05
MINOR STARS	.25	.11
SEMISTARS	.50	.23
UNLISTED STARS	1.00	.45

❑ 1 Ozzie Smith	3.00	1.35
❑ 2 Rollie Fingers	1.00	.45
❑ 3 Rick Wise	.10	.05
❑ 4 Gene Richards	.10	.05
❑ 5 Alan Trammell	1.00	.45
❑ 6 Tom Brookens	.10	.05
❑ 7A Duffy Dyer P1	.25	.11
1980 batting average		
has decimal point		
❑ 7B Duffy Dyer P2	.10	.05
1980 batting average		
has no decimal point		
❑ 8 Mark Fidrych	1.00	.45
❑ 9 Dave Rozema	.10	.05
❑ 10 Ricky Peters	.10	.05
❑ 11 Mike Schmidt	1.50	.70
❑ 12 Willie Stargell	1.00	.45
❑ 13 Tim Foli	.10	.05
❑ 14 Manny Sanguillen	.25	.11
❑ 15 Grant Jackson	.10	.05
❑ 16 Eddie Solomon	.10	.05
❑ 17 Omar Moreno	.10	.05
❑ 18 Joe Morgan	1.00	.45
❑ 19 Rafael Landestoy	.10	.05
❑ 20 Bruce Bochy	.10	.05
❑ 21 Joe Sambito	.10	.05
❑ 22 Manny Trillo	.10	.05

Card	Price 1	Price 2
23A Dave Smith P1	.25	.11
(Line box around stats is not complete)		
23B Dave Smith P2	.25	.11
(Box totally encloses stats at top)		
24 Terry Puhl	.10	.05
25 Bump Wills	.10	.05
26A John Ellis P1 ERR	.50	.23
Danny Walton photo on front		
26B John Ellis P2 COR	.25	.11
27 Jim Kern	.10	.05
28 Richie Zisk	.10	.05
29 John Mayberry	.10	.05
30 Bob Davis	.10	.05
31 Jackson Todd	.10	.05
32 Alvis Woods	.10	.05
33 Steve Carlton	1.00	.45
34 Lee Mazzilli	.10	.05
35 John Stearns	.10	.05
36 Roy Lee Jackson	.10	.05
37 Mike Scott	.25	.11
38 Lamar Johnson	.10	.05
39 Kevin Bell	.10	.05
40 Ed Farmer	.10	.05
41 Ross Baumgarten	.10	.05
42 Leo Sutherland	.10	.05
43 Dan Meyer	.10	.05
44 Ron Reed	.10	.05
45 Mario Mendoza	.10	.05
46 Rick Honeycutt	.10	.05
47 Glenn Abbott	.10	.05
48 Leon Roberts	.10	.05
49 Rod Carew	1.00	.45
50 Bert Campaneris	.25	.11
51A Tom Donahue P1 ERR	.25	.11
(Name on front misspelled Donahue)		
51B Tom Donohue	.10	.05
P2 COR		
52 Dave Frost	.10	.05
53 Ed Halicki	.10	.05
54 Dan Ford	.10	.05
55 Garry Maddox	.10	.05
56A Steve Garvey P1	1.00	.45
Surpassed 25 HR		
56B Steve Garvey P2	1.00	.45
Surpassed 21 HR		
57 Bill Russell	.25	.11
58 Don Sutton	1.00	.45
59 Reggie Smith	.25	.11
60 Rick Monday	.10	.05
61 Ray Knight	.25	.11
62 Johnny Bench	1.25	.55
63 Mario Soto	.10	.05
64 Doug Bair	.10	.05
65 George Foster	.25	.11
66 Jeff Burroughs	.10	.05
67 Keith Hernandez	.25	.11
68 Tom Herr	.25	.11
69 Bob Forsch	.10	.05
70 John Fulgham	.10	.05
71A Bobby Bonds P1 ERR	1.00	.45
(986 lifetime HR)		
71B Bobby Bonds P2 COR	.50	.23
(326 lifetime HR)		
72A Rennie Stennett P1	.25	.11
(Breaking broke leg)		
72B Rennie Stennett P2	.10	.05
(Word "broke" deleted)		
73 Joe Strain	.10	.05
74 Ed Whitson	.10	.05
75 Tom Griffin	.10	.05
76 Billy North	.10	.05
77 Gene Garber	.10	.05
78 Mike Hargrove	.25	.11
79 Dave Rosello	.10	.05
80 Ron Hassey	.10	.05
81 Sid Monge	.10	.05
82A Joe Charboneau P1	1.00	.45
'78 highlights		
For some reason		
82B Joe Charboneau P2	1.00	.45
Phrase "For some reason" deleted		
83 Cecil Cooper	.25	.11
84 Sal Bando	.25	.11
85 Moose Haas	.10	.05
86 Mike Caldwell	.10	.05
87A Larry Hisle P1	.25	.11
(77 highlights line ends with "28 RBI")		
87B Larry Hisle P2	.10	.05
(Correct line "28 HR")		
88 Luis Gomez	.10	.05
89 Larry Parrish	.10	.05
90 Gary Carter	1.00	.45
91 Bill Gullickson	.50	.23
92 Fred Norman	.10	.05
93 Tommy Hutton	.10	.05
94 Carl Yastrzemski	1.00	.45
95 Glenn Hoffman	.10	.05
96 Dennis Eckersley	1.00	.45
97A Tom Burgmeier P1	.25	.11
(ERR Throws: Right)		
97B Tom Burgmeier P2	.10	.05
(COR Throws: Left)		
98 Win Remmerswaal	.10	.05
99 Bob Horner	.25	.11
100 George Brett	2.50	1.10
101 Dave Chalk	.10	.05
102 Dennis Leonard	.10	.05
103 Renie Martin	.10	.05
104 Amos Otis	.25	.11
105 Graig Nettles	.25	.11
106 Eric Soderholm	.10	.05
107 Tommy John	.50	.23
108 Tom Underwood	.10	.05
109 Lou Piniella	.25	.11
110 Mickey Klutts	.10	.05
111 Bobby Murcer	.25	.11
112 Eddie Murray	2.00	.90
113 Rick Dempsey	.25	.11
114 Scott McGregor	.10	.05
115 Ken Singleton	.25	.11
116 Gary Roenicke	.10	.05
117 Dave Revering	.10	.05
118 Mike Norris	.10	.05
119 Rickey Henderson	4.00	1.80
120 Mike Heath	.10	.05
121 Dave Cash	.10	.05
122 Randy Jones	.10	.05
123 Eric Rasmussen	.10	.05
124 Jerry Mumphrey	.10	.05
125 Richie Hebner	.10	.05
126 Mark Wagner	.10	.05
127 Jack Morris	1.00	.45
128 Dan Petry	.25	.11
129 Bruce Robbins	.10	.05
130 Champ Summers	.10	.05
131 Pete Rose P1	2.00	.90
Last line ends with see card 251		
131B Pete Rose P2	1.50	.70
Last line corrected see card 371		
132 Willie Stargell	1.00	.45
133 Ed Ott	.10	.05
134 Jim Bibby	.10	.05
135 Bert Blyleven	.50	.23
136 Dave Parker	.25	.11
137 Bill Robinson	.10	.05
138 Enos Cabell	.10	.05
139 Dave Bergman	.10	.05
140 J.R. Richard	.25	.11
141 Ken Forsch	.10	.05
142 Larry Bowa UER	.25	.11
Shortstop on front		
143 Frank LaCorte UER	.10	.05
Photo actually Randy Niemann		
144 Denny Walling	.10	.05
145 Buddy Bell	.25	.11
146 Ferguson Jenkins	1.00	.45
147 Danny Darwin	.25	.11
148 John Grubb	.10	.05
149 Alfredo Griffin	.10	.05
150 Jerry Garvin	.10	.05
151 Paul Mirabella	.10	.05
152 Rick Bosetti	.10	.05
153 Dick Ruthven	.10	.05
154 Frank Tveras	.10	.05
155 Craig Swan	.10	.05
156 Jeff Reardon	1.00	.45
157 Steve Henderson	.10	.05
158 Jim Morrison	.10	.05
159 Glenn Borgmann	.10	.05
160 LaMarr Hoyt	.25	.11
161 Rich Wortham	.10	.05
162 Thad Bosley	.10	.05
163 Julio Cruz	.10	.05
164A Del Unser P1	.25	.11
(No "3B" heading)		
164B Del Unser P2	.10	.05
(Batting record on back corrected "3B")		
165 Jim Anderson	.10	.05
166 Jim Beattie	.10	.05
167 Shane Rawley	.10	.05
168 Joe Simpson	.10	.05
169 Rod Carew	1.00	.45
170 Fred Patek	.10	.05
171 Frank Tanana	.25	.11
172 Alfredo Martinez	.10	.05
173 Chris Knapp	.10	.05
174 Joe Rudi	.25	.11
175 Greg Luzinski	.25	.11
176 Steve Garvey	.50	.23
177 Joe Ferguson	.10	.05
178 Bob Welch	.25	.11
179 Dusty Baker	.50	.23
180 Rudy Law	.10	.05
181 Dave Concepcion	.25	.11
182 Johnny Bench	1.25	.55
183 Mike LaCoss	.10	.05
184 Ken Griffey	.50	.23
185 Dave Collins	.10	.05
186 Brian Asselstine	.10	.05
187 Garry Templeton	.10	.05
188 Mike Phillips	.10	.05
189 Pete Vuckovich	.25	.11
190 John Urrea	.10	.05
191 Tony Scott	.10	.05
192 Darrell Evans	.25	.11
193 Milt May	.10	.05
194 Bob Knepper	.10	.05
195 Randy Moffitt	.10	.05
196 Larry Herndon	.10	.05
197 Rick Camp	.10	.05
198 Andre Thornton	.25	.11
199 Tom Veryzer	.10	.05
200 Gary Alexander	.10	.05
201 Rick Waits	.10	.05
202 Rick Manning	.10	.05
203 Paul Molitor	2.00	.90
204 Jim Gantner	.25	.11
205 Paul Mitchell	.10	.05
206 Reggie Cleveland	.10	.05
207 Sixto Lezcano	.10	.05
208 Bruce Benedict	.10	.05
209 Rodney Scott	.10	.05
210 John Tamargo	.10	.05
211 Bill Lee	.25	.11
212 Andre Dawson UER	1.00	.45
Middle name Fernando should be Nolan		
213 Rowland Office	.10	.05
214 Carl Yastrzemski	1.00	.45
215 Jerry Remy	.10	.05
216 Mike Torrez	.10	.05
217 Skip Lockwood	.10	.05
218 Fred Lynn	.25	.11
219 Chris Chambliss	.10	.05
220 Willie Aikens	.10	.05
221 John Wathan	.10	.05
222 Dan Quisenberry	.25	.11
223 Willie Wilson	.25	.11
224 Clint Hurdle	.10	.05
225 Bob Watson	.10	.05
226 Jim Spencer	.10	.05
227 Ron Guidry	.25	.11
228 Reggie Jackson	1.25	.55
229 Oscar Gamble	.10	.05
230 Jeff Cox	.10	.05
231 Luis Tiant	.25	.11
232 Rich Dauer	.10	.05
233 Dan Graham	.10	.05
234 Mike Flanagan	.25	.11
235 John Lowenstein	.10	.05
236 Benny Ayala	.10	.05

237 Wayne Gross	.10	.05
238 Rick Langford	.10	.05
239 Tony Armas	.25	.11
240A Bob Lacey P1 ERR	.50	.23
Name misspelled Lacy		
240B Bob Lacey P2 COR	.10	.05
241 Gene Tenace	.25	.11
242 Bob Shirley	.10	.05
243 Gary Lucas	.10	.05
244 Jerry Turner	.10	.05
245 John Wockenfuss	.10	.05
246 Stan Papi	.10	.05
247 Milt Wilcox	.10	.05
248 Dan Schatzeder	.10	.05
249 Steve Kemp	.10	.05
250 Jim Lentine	.10	.05
251 Pete Rose	2.00	.90
252 Bill Madlock	.25	.11
253 Dale Berra	.10	.05
254 Kent Tekulve	.25	.11
255 Enrique Romo	.10	.05
256 Mike Easler	.10	.05
257 Chuck Tanner MG	.25	.11
258 Art Howe	.25	.11
259 Alan Ashby	.10	.05
260 Nolan Ryan	5.00	2.20
261A Vern Ruhle P1 ERR	.50	.23
Ken Forsch photo on front		
261B Vern Ruhle P2 COR	.25	.11
262 Bob Boone	.25	.11
263 Cesar Cedeno	.25	.11
264 Jeff Leonard	.25	.11
265 Pat Putnam	.10	.05
266 Jon Matlack	.10	.05
267 Dave Rajsich	.10	.05
268 Billy Sample	.10	.05
269 Damaso Garcia	.10	.05
270 Tom Buskey	.10	.05
271 Joey McLaughlin	.10	.05
272 Barry Bonnell	.10	.05
273 Tug McGraw	.25	.11
274 Mike Jorgensen	.10	.05
275 Pat Zachry	.10	.05
276 Neil Allen	.10	.05
277 Joel Youngblood	.10	.05
278 Greg Pryor	.10	.05
279 Britt Burns	.10	.05
280 Rich Dotson	.10	.05
281 Chet Lemon	.10	.05
282 Rusty Kuntz	.10	.05
283 Ted Cox	.10	.05
284 Sparky Lyle	.25	.11
285 Larry Cox	.10	.05
286 Floyd Bannister	.10	.05
287 Byron McLaughlin	.10	.05
288 Rodney Craig	.10	.05
289 Bobby Grich	.25	.11
290 Dickie Thon	.25	.11
291 Mark Clear	.10	.05
292 Dave Lemanczyk	.10	.05
293 Jason Thompson	.10	.05
294 Rick Miller	.10	.05
295 Lonnie Smith	.25	.11
296 Ron Cey	.25	.11
297 Steve Yeager	.10	.05
298 Bobby Castillo	.10	.05
299 Manny Mota	.25	.11
300 Jay Johnstone	.25	.11
301 Dan Driessen	.10	.05
302 Joe Nolan	.10	.05
303 Paul Householder	.10	.05
304 Harry Spilman	.10	.05
305 Cesar Geronimo	.10	.05
306A Gary Mathews P1 ERR	.50	.23
Name misspelled		
306B Gary Matthews P2 COR	.25	.11
307 Ken Reitz	.10	.05
308 Ted Simmons	.25	.11
309 John Littlefield	.10	.05
310 George Frazier	.10	.05
311 Dane Iorg	.10	.05
312 Mike Ivie	.10	.05
313 Dennis Littlejohn	.10	.05
314 Gary Lavelle	.10	.05
315 Jack Clark	.25	.11
316 Jim Wohlford	.10	.05
317 Rick Matula	.10	.05
318 Toby Harrah	.25	.11
319A Dwane Kuiper P1 ERR	.25	.11
Name misspelled		
319B Duane Kuiper P2 COR	.10	.05
320 Len Barker	.10	.05
321 Victor Cruz	.10	.05
322 Dell Alston	.10	.05
323 Robin Yount	1.00	.45
324 Charlie Moore	.10	.05
325 Lary Sorensen	.10	.05
326A Gorman Thomas P1	.50	.23
2nd line on back:		
"30 HR mark 4th"		
326B Gorman Thomas P2	.25	.11
30 HR mark 3rd		
327 Bob Rodgers MG	.10	.05
328 Phil Niekro	1.00	.45
329 Chris Speier	.10	.05
330A Steve Rodgers P1	.25	.11
ERR Name misspelled		
330B Steve Rogers P2 COR	.10	.05
331 Woodie Fryman	.10	.05
332 Warren Cromartie	.10	.05
333 Jerry White	.10	.05
334 Tony Perez	1.00	.45
335 Carlton Fisk	1.00	.45
336 Dick Drago	.10	.05
337 Steve Renko	.10	.05
338 Jim Rice	.25	.11
339 Jerry Royster	.10	.05
340 Frank White	.25	.11
341 Jamie Quirk	.10	.05
342A Paul Spittorff P1 ERR	.25	.11
Name misspelled		
342B Paul Splittorff	.10	.05
P2 COR		
343 Marty Pattin	.10	.05
344 Pete LaCock	.10	.05
345 Willie Randolph	.25	.11
346 Rick Cerone	.10	.05
347 Rich Gossage	.50	.23
348 Reggie Jackson	1.25	.55
349 Ruppert Jones	.10	.05
350 Dave McKay	.10	.05
351 Yogi Berra CO	.50	.23
352 Doug DeCinces	.25	.11
353 Jim Palmer	1.00	.45
354 Tippy Martinez	.10	.05
355 Al Bumbry	.25	.11
356 Earl Weaver MG	.45	.11
357A Bob Picciolo P1 ERR	.25	.11
Name misspelled		
357B Rob Picciolo P2 COR	.10	.05
358 Matt Keough	.10	.05
359 Dwayne Murphy	.10	.05
360 Brian Kingman	.10	.05
361 Bill Fahey	.10	.05
362 Steve Mura	.10	.05
363 Dennis Kinney	.10	.05
364 Dave Winfield	1.00	.45
365 Lou Whitaker	1.00	.45
366 Lance Parrish	.25	.11
367 Tim Corcoran	.10	.05
368 Pat Underwood	.10	.05
369 Al Cowens	.10	.05
370 Sparky Anderson MG	.25	.11
371 Pete Rose	2.00	.90
372 Phil Garner	.25	.11
373 Steve Nicosia	.10	.05
374 John Candelaria	.25	.11
375 Don Robinson	.10	.05
376 Lee Lacy	.10	.05
377 John Milner	.10	.05
378 Craig Reynolds	.10	.05
379A Luis Pujois P1 ERR	.25	.11
Name misspelled Pujois		
379B Luis Pujols P2 COR	.10	.05
380 Joe Niekro	.25	.11
381 Joaquin Andujar	.25	.11
382 Keith Moreland	.25	.11
383 Jose Cruz	.25	.11
384 Bill Virdon MG	.10	.05
385 Jim Sundberg	.25	.11
386 Doc Medich	.10	.05
387 Al Oliver	.25	.11
388 Jim Norris	.10	.05
389 Bob Bailor	.10	.05
390 Ernie Whitt	.10	.05
391 Otto Velez	.10	.05
392 Roy Howell	.10	.05
393 Bob Walk	.25	.11
394 Doug Flynn	.10	.05
395 Pete Falcone	.10	.05
396 Tom Hausman	.10	.05
397 Elliott Maddox	.10	.05
398 Mike Squires	.10	.05
399 Marvis Foley	.10	.05
400 Steve Trout	.10	.05
401 Wayne Nordhagen	.10	.05
402 Tony LaRussa MG	.25	.11
403 Bruce Bochte	.10	.05
404 Bake McBride	.10	.05
405 Jerry Narron	.10	.05
406 Rob Dressler	.10	.05
407 Dave Heaverlo	.10	.05
408 Tom Paciorek	.25	.11
409 Carney Lansford	.25	.11
410 Brian Downing	.25	.11
411 Don Aase	.10	.05
412 Jim Barr	.10	.05
413 Don Baylor	.50	.23
414 Jim Fregosi MG	.25	.11
415 Dallas Green MG	.10	.05
416 Dave Lopes	.25	.11
417 Jerry Reuss	.25	.11
418 Rick Sutcliffe	.25	.11
419 Derrel Thomas	.10	.05
420 Tom Lasorda MG	1.00	.45
421 Charlie Leibrandt	.50	.23
422 Tom Seaver	1.25	.55
423 Ron Oester	.10	.05
424 Junior Kennedy	.10	.05
425 Tom Seaver	1.25	.55
426 Bobby Cox MG	.25	.11
427 Leon Durham	.25	.11
428 Terry Kennedy	.10	.05
429 Silvio Martinez	.10	.05
430 George Hendrick	.10	.05
431 Red Schoendienst MG	.50	.23
432 Johnnie LeMaster	.10	.05
433 Vida Blue	.25	.11
434 John Montefusco	.10	.05
435 Terry Whitfield	.10	.05
436 Dave Bristol MG	.10	.05
437 Dale Murphy	1.00	.45
438 Jerry Dybzinski	.10	.05
439 Jorge Orta	.10	.05
440 Wayne Garland	.10	.05
441 Miguel Dilone	.10	.05
442 Dave Garcia MG	.10	.05
443 Don Money	.10	.05
444A Buck Martinez P1 ERR	.25	.11
Reverse negative		
444B Buck Martinez	.10	.05
P2 COR		
445 Jerry Augustine	.10	.05
446 Ben Oglivie	.25	.11
447 Jim Slaton	.10	.05
448 Doyle Alexander	.10	.05
449 Tony Bernazard	.10	.05
450 Scott Sanderson	.10	.05
451 David Palmer	.10	.05
452 Stan Bahnsen	.10	.05
453 Dick Williams MG	.10	.05
454 Rick Burleson	.10	.05
455 Gary Allenson	.10	.05
456 Bob Stanley	.10	.05
457A John Tudor P1 ERR	.25	.11
Lifetime W-L 9.7		
457B John Tudor P2 COR	.25	.11
Lifetime W-L 9-7		
458 Dwight Evans	.50	.23
459 Glenn Hubbard	.10	.05
460 U.L. Washington	.10	.05
461 Larry Gura	.10	.05
462 Rich Gale	.10	.05
463 Hal McRae	.25	.11
464 Jim Frey MG	.10	.05
465 Bucky Dent	.25	.11
466 Dennis Werth	.10	.05

☐ 467	Ron Davis	.10	.05
☐ 468	Reggie Jackson UER ..	1.25	.55
	32 HR in 1970		
	should be 23		
☐ 469	Bobby Brown	.10	.05
☐ 470	Mike Davis	.10	.05
☐ 471	Gaylord Perry	1.00	.45
☐ 472	Mark Belanger	.25	.11
☐ 473	Jim Palmer	1.00	.45
☐ 474	Sammy Stewart	.10	.05
☐ 475	Tim Stoddard	.10	.05
☐ 476	Steve Stone	.25	.11
☐ 477	Jeff Newman	.10	.05
☐ 478	Steve McCatty	.10	.05
☐ 479	Billy Martin MG	.50	.23
☐ 480	Mitchell Page	.10	.05
☐ 481	Steve Carlton CY	.50	.23
☐ 482	Bill Buckner	.25	.11
☐ 483A	Ivan DeJesus P1 ERR	.25	.11
	Lifetime hits 702		
☐ 483B	Ivan DeJesus P2 COR	.10	.05
	Lifetime hits 642		
☐ 484	Cliff Johnson	.10	.05
☐ 485	Lenny Randle	.10	.05
☐ 486	Larry Milbourne	.10	.05
☐ 487	Roy Smalley	.10	.05
☐ 488	John Castino	.10	.05
☐ 489	Ron Jackson	.10	.05
☐ 490A	Dave Roberts P1	.25	.11
	Career Highlights		
	Showed pop in		
☐ 490B	Dave Roberts P2	.10	.05
	Declared himself		
☐ 491	George Brett MVP	1.25	.55
☐ 492	Mike Cubbage	.10	.05
☐ 493	Rob Wilfong	.10	.05
☐ 494	Danny Goodwin	.10	.05
☐ 495	Jose Morales	.10	.05
☐ 496	Mickey Rivers	.25	.11
☐ 497	Mike Edwards	.10	.05
☐ 498	Mike Sadek	.10	.05
☐ 499	Lenn Sakata	.10	.05
☐ 500	Gene Michael MG	.10	.05
☐ 501	Dave Roberts	.10	.05
☐ 502	Steve Dillard	.10	.05
☐ 503	Jim Essian	.10	.05
☐ 504	Rance Mulliniks	.10	.05
☐ 505	Darrell Porter	.10	.05
☐ 506	Joe Torre MG	.25	.11
☐ 507	Terry Crowley	.10	.05
☐ 508	Bill Travers	.10	.05
☐ 509	Nelson Norman	.10	.05
☐ 510	Bob McClure	.10	.05
☐ 511	Steve Howe	.25	.11
☐ 512	Dave Rader	.10	.05
☐ 513	Mick Kelleher	.10	.05
☐ 514	Kiko Garcia	.10	.05
☐ 515	Larry Biittner	.10	.05
☐ 516A	Willie Norwood P1	.25	.11
	Career Highlights		
	Spent most of		
☐ 516B	Willie Norwood P2	.10	.05
	Traded to Seattle		
☐ 517	Bo Diaz	.10	.05
☐ 518	Juan Beniquez	.10	.05
☐ 519	Scot Thompson	.10	.05
☐ 520	Jim Tracy	.10	.05
☐ 521	Carlos Lezcano	.10	.05
☐ 522	Joe Amalfitano MG	.10	.05
☐ 523	Preston Hanna	.10	.05
☐ 524A	Ray Burris P1	.25	.11
	Career Highlights		
	Went on a		
☐ 524B	Ray Burris P2	.10	.05
	Drafted by ...		
☐ 525	Broderick Perkins	.10	.05
☐ 526	Mickey Hatcher	.25	.11
☐ 527	John Goryl MG	.10	.05
☐ 528	Dick Davis	.10	.05
☐ 529	Butch Wynegar	.10	.05
☐ 530	Sal Butera	.10	.05
☐ 531	Jerry Koosman	.25	.11
☐ 532A	Geoff Zahn P1	.25	.11
	(Career Highlights		
	Was 2nd in		
☐ 532B	Geoff Zahn P2	.10	.05

☐ 533	Dennis Martinez	.50	.23
☐ 534	Gary Thomasson	.10	.05
☐ 535	Steve Macko	.10	.05
☐ 536	Jim Kaat	.25	.11
☐ 537	Best Hitters	1.50	.70
	George Brett		
	Rod Carew		
☐ 538	Tim Raines	2.00	.90
☐ 539	Keith Smith	.10	.05
☐ 540	Ken Macha	.10	.05
☐ 541	Burt Hooton	.10	.05
☐ 542	Butch Hobson	.10	.05
☐ 543	Bill Stein	.10	.05
☐ 544	Dave Stapleton	.10	.05
☐ 545	Bob Pate	.10	.05
☐ 546	Doug Corbett	.10	.05
☐ 547	Darrell Jackson	.10	.05
☐ 548	Pete Redfern	.10	.05
☐ 549	Roger Erickson	.10	.05
☐ 550	Al Hrabosky	.10	.05
☐ 551	Dick Tidrow	.10	.05
☐ 552	Dave Ford	.10	.05
☐ 553	Dave Kingman	.50	.23
☐ 554A	Mike Vail P1	.25	.11
	Career Highlights		
	After two		
☐ 554B	Mike Vail P2	.10	.05
	Traded to		
☐ 555A	Jerry Martin P1	.25	.11
	Career Highlights		
	Overcame a		
☐ 555B	Jerry Martin P2	.10	.05
☐ 556A	Jesus Figueroa P1	.25	.11
	Career Highlights		
	Had an		
☐ 556B	Jesus Figueroa P2	.10	.05
	Traded to		
☐ 557	Don Stanhouse	.10	.05
☐ 558	Barry Foote	.10	.05
☐ 559	Tim Blackwell	.10	.05
☐ 560	Bruce Sutter	.25	.11
☐ 561	Rick Reuschel	.25	.11
☐ 562	Lynn McGlothen	.10	.05
☐ 563A	Bob Owchinko P1	.25	.11
	Career Highlights		
	Traded to		
☐ 563B	Bob Owchinko P2	.10	.05
	Involved in a		
☐ 564	John Verhoeven	.10	.05
☐ 565	Ken Landreaux	.10	.05
☐ 566A	Glen Adams P1 ERR	.25	.11
	Name misspelled		
☐ 566B	Glenn Adams P2 COR	.10	.05
☐ 567	Hosken Powell	.10	.05
☐ 568	Dick Noles	.10	.05
☐ 569	Danny Ainge	.90	
☐ 570	Bobby Mattick MG	.10	.05
☐ 571	Joe Lefebvre	.10	.05
☐ 572	Bobby Clark	.10	.05
☐ 573	Dennis Lamp	.10	.05
☐ 574	Randy Lerch	.10	.05
☐ 575	Mookie Wilson	.50	.23
☐ 576	Ron LeFlore	.25	.11
☐ 577	Jim Dwyer	.10	.05
☐ 578	Bill Castro	.10	.05
☐ 579	Greg Minton	.10	.05
☐ 580	Mark Littell	.10	.05
☐ 581	Andy Hassler	.10	.05
☐ 582	Dave Stieb	.25	.11
☐ 583	Ken Oberkfell	.10	.05
☐ 584	Larry Bradford	.10	.05
☐ 585	Fred Stanley	.10	.05
☐ 586	Bill Caudill	.10	.05
☐ 587	Doug Capilla	.10	.05
☐ 588	George Riley	.10	.05
☐ 589	Willie Hernandez	.25	.11
☐ 590	Mike Schmidt MVP	1.50	.70
☐ 591	Steve Stone CY	.10	.05
☐ 592	Rick Sofield	.10	.05
☐ 593	Bombo Rivera	.10	.05
☐ 594	Gary Ward	.10	.05
☐ 595A	Dave Edwards P1	.25	.11
	Career Highlights		
	Sidelined the		

☐ 595B	Dave Edwards P2	.10	.05
	Traded to		
☐ 596	Mike Proly	.10	.05
☐ 597	Tommy Boggs	.10	.05
☐ 598	Greg Gross	.10	.05
☐ 599	Elias Sosa	.10	.05
☐ 600	Pat Kelly	.10	.05
☐ 601A	Checklist 1-120 P1	.25	.11
	ERR Unnumbered		
	51 Donahun		
☐ 601B	Checklist 1-120 P2	.50	.23
	COR Unnumbered		
	51 Donohue		
☐ 602	Checklist 121-240	.25	.11
	Unnumbered		
☐ 603A	Checklist 241-360 P1	.25	.11
	ERR Unnumbered		
	306 Mathews		
☐ 603B	Checklist 241-360 P2	.25	.11
	COR Unnumbered		
	306 Matthews		
☐ 604A	Checklist 361-480 P1	.25	.11
	ERR Unnumbered		
	379 Pujois		
☐ 604B	Checklist 361-480 P2	.25	.11
	COR Unnumbered		
	379 Pujols		
☐ 605A	Checklist 481-600 P1	.25	.11
	ERR Unnumbered		
	566 Glen Adams		
☐ 605B	Checklist 481-600 P2	.25	.11
	COR Unnumbered		
	566 Glenn Adams		

1982 Donruss

	NRMT	VG-E
COMPLETE SET (660)	60.00	27.00
COMP.FACT.SET (660)	60.00	27.00
COMMON CARD (1-660)	.10	.05
MINOR STARS	.20	.09
SEMISTARS	.40	.18
UNLISTED STARS	.75	.35

☐ 1	Pete Rose DK	2.00	.90
☐ 2	Gary Carter DK	.20	.09
☐ 3	Steve Garvey DK	.20	.09
☐ 4	Vida Blue DK	.10	.05
☐ 5	Alan Trammell DK	.40	.18
	COR		
☐ 5A	Alan Trammel DK ERR	.75	.35
	(Name misspelled)		
☐ 6	Len Barker DK	.10	.05
☐ 7	Dwight Evans DK	.40	.18
☐ 8	Rod Carew DK	.75	.35
☐ 9	George Hendrick DK	.20	.09
☐ 10	Phil Niekro DK	.40	.18
☐ 11	Richie Zisk DK	.10	.05
☐ 12	Dave Parker DK	.20	.09
☐ 13	Nolan Ryan DK	4.00	1.80
☐ 14	Ivan DeJesus DK	.10	.05
☐ 15	George Brett DK	.75	.35
☐ 16	Tom Seaver DK	1.00	.45
☐ 17	Dave Kingman DK	.20	.09
☐ 18	Dave Winfield DK	.40	.18
☐ 19	Mike Norris DK	.10	.05
☐ 20	Carlton Fisk DK	.40	.18
☐ 21	Ozzie Smith DK	1.25	.55

22	Roy Smalley DK	.20	.09
23	Buddy Bell DK	.20	.09
24	Ken Singleton DK	.10	.05
25	John Mayberry DK	.10	.05
26	Gorman Thomas DK	.20	.09
27	Earl Weaver MG	.40	.18
28	Rollie Fingers	.75	.35
29	Sparky Anderson MG	.20	.09
30	Dennis Eckersley	.75	.35
31	Dave Winfield	.75	.35
32	Burt Hooton	.10	.05
33	Rick Waits	.10	.05
34	George Brett	1.50	.70
35	Steve McCatty	.10	.05
36	Steve Rogers	.10	.05
37	Bill Stein	.10	.05
38	Steve Renko	.10	.05
39	Mike Squires	.10	.05
40	George Hendrick	.10	.05
41	Bob Knepper	.10	.05
42	Steve Carlton	.75	.35
43	Larry Biittner	.10	.05
44	Chris Welsh	.10	.05
45	Steve Nicosia	.10	.05
46	Jack Clark	.20	.09
47	Chris Chambliss	.20	.09
48	Ivan DeJesus	.10	.05
49	Lee Mazzilli	.10	.05
50	Julio Cruz	.10	.05
51	Pete Redfern	.10	.05
52	Dave Stieb	.20	.09
53	Doug Corbett	.10	.05
54	Jorge Bell	.75	.35
55	Joe Simpson	.10	.05
56	Rusty Staub	.20	.09
57	Hector Cruz	.10	.05
58	Claudell Washington	.10	.05
59	Enrique Romo	.10	.05
60	Gary Lavelle	.10	.05
61	Tim Flannery	.10	.05
62	Joe Nolan	.10	.05
63	Larry Bowa	.20	.09
64	Sixto Lezcano	.10	.05
65	Joe Sambito	.10	.05
66	Bruce Kison	.10	.05
67	Wayne Nordhagen	.10	.05
68	Woodie Fryman	.10	.05
69	Billy Sample	.10	.05
70	Amos Otis	.20	.09
71	Matt Keough	.10	.05
72	Toby Harrah	.20	.09
73	Dave Righetti	.75	.35
74	Carl Yastrzemski	.75	.35
75	Bob Welch	.20	.09
76	Alan Trammell COR	.75	.35
76A	Alan Trammel ERR (Name misspelled)	1.00	.45
77	Rick Dempsey	.20	.09
78	Paul Molitor	1.00	.45
79	Dennis Martinez	.40	.18
80	Jim Slaton	.10	.05
81	Champ Summers	.10	.05
82	Carney Lansford	.20	.09
83	Barry Foote	.10	.05
84	Steve Garvey	.40	.18
85	Rick Manning	.10	.05
86	John Wathan	.10	.05
87	Brian Kingman	.10	.05
88	Andre Dawson UER (Middle name Femando should be Nolan)	.75	.35
89	Jim Kern	.10	.05
90	Bobby Grich	.20	.09
91	Bob Forsch	.10	.05
92	Art Howe	.20	.09
93	Marty Bystrom	.10	.05
94	Ozzie Smith	1.50	.70
95	Dave Parker	.20	.09
96	Doyle Alexander	.10	.05
97	Al Hrabosky	.10	.05
98	Frank Taveras	.10	.05
99	Tim Blackwell	.10	.05
100	Floyd Bannister	.10	.05
101	Alfredo Griffin	.10	.05
102	Dave Engle	.10	.05
103	Mario Soto	.10	.05
104	Ross Baumgarten	.10	.05
105	Ken Singleton	.20	.09
106	Ted Simmons	.20	.09
107	Jack Morris	.20	.09
108	Bob Watson	.10	.05
109	Dwight Evans	.40	.18
110	Tom Lasorda MG	.40	.18
111	Bert Blyleven	.40	.18
112	Dan Quisenberry	.20	.09
113	Rickey Henderson	2.00	.90
114	Gary Carter	.75	.35
115	Brian Downing	.10	.05
116	Al Oliver	.20	.09
117	LaMarr Hoyt	.10	.05
118	Cesar Cedeno	.20	.09
119	Keith Moreland	.10	.05
120	Bob Shirley	.10	.05
121	Terry Kennedy	.10	.05
122	Frank Pastore	.10	.05
123	Gene Garber	.10	.05
124	Tony Pena	.20	.09
125	Allen Ripley	.10	.05
126	Randy Martz	.10	.05
127	Richie Zisk	.10	.05
128	Mike Scott	.20	.09
129	Lloyd Moseby	.20	.09
130	Rob Wilfong	.10	.05
131	Tim Stoddard	.10	.05
132	Gorman Thomas	.20	.09
133	Dan Petry	.10	.05
134	Bob Stanley	.10	.05
135	Lou Piniella	.20	.09
136	Pedro Guerrero	.20	.09
137	Len Barker	.10	.05
138	Rich Gale	.10	.05
139	Wayne Gross	.10	.05
140	Tim Wallach	.40	.18
141	Gene Mauch MG	.10	.05
142	Doc Medich	.10	.05
143	Tony Bernazard	.10	.05
144	Bill Virdon MG	.10	.05
145	John Littlefield	.10	.05
146	Dave Bergman	.10	.05
147	Dick Davis	.10	.05
148	Tom Seaver	1.00	.45
149	Matt Sinatro	.10	.05
150	Chuck Tanner MG	.10	.05
151	Leon Durham	.10	.05
152	Gene Tenace	.20	.09
153	Al Bumbry	.10	.05
154	Mark Brouhard	.10	.05
155	Rick Peters	.10	.05
156	Jerry Remy	.10	.05
157	Rick Reuschel	.20	.09
158	Steve Howe	.10	.05
159	Alan Bannister	.10	.05
160	U.L. Washington	.10	.05
161	Rick Langford	.10	.05
162	Bill Gullickson	.20	.09
163	Mark Wagner	.10	.05
164	Geoff Zahn	.10	.05
165	Ron LeFlore	.20	.09
166	Dane Iorg	.10	.05
167	Joe Niekro	.20	.09
168	Pete Rose	1.50	.70
169	Dave Collins	.10	.05
170	Rick Wise	.10	.05
171	Jim Bibby	.10	.05
172	Larry Herndon	.10	.05
173	Bob Horner	.20	.09
174	Steve Dillard	.10	.05
175	Mookie Wilson	.20	.09
176	Dan Meyer	.10	.05
177	Fernando Arroyo	.10	.05
178	Jackson Todd	.10	.05
179	Darrell Jackson	.10	.05
180	Alvis Woods	.10	.05
181	Jim Anderson	.10	.05
182	Dave Kingman	.20	.09
183	Steve Henderson	.10	.05
184	Brian Asselstine	.10	.05
185	Rod Scurry	.10	.05
186	Fred Breining	.10	.05
187	Danny Boone	.10	.05
188	Junior Kennedy	.10	.05
189	Sparky Lyle	.20	.09
190	Whitey Herzog MG	.20	.09
191	Dave Smith	.10	.05
192	Ed Ott	.10	.05
193	Greg Luzinski	.20	.09
194	Bill Lee	.20	.09
195	Don Zimmer MG	.10	.05
196	Hal McRae	.20	.09
197	Mike Norris	.10	.05
198	Duane Kuiper	.10	.05
199	Rick Cerone	.10	.05
200	Jim Rice	.20	.09
201	Steve Yeager	.10	.05
202	Tom Brookens	.10	.05
203	Jose Morales	.10	.05
204	Roy Howell	.10	.05
205	Tippy Martinez	.10	.05
206	Moose Haas	.10	.05
207	Al Cowens	.10	.05
208	Dave Stapleton	.10	.05
209	Bucky Dent	.20	.09
210	Ron Cey	.20	.09
211	Jorge Orta	.10	.05
212	Jamie Quirk	.10	.05
213	Jeff Jones	.10	.05
214	Tim Raines	.75	.35
215	Jon Matlack	.10	.05
216	Rod Carew	.75	.35
217	Jim Kaat	.20	.09
218	Joe Pittman	.10	.05
219	Larry Christenson	.10	.05
220	Juan Bonilla	.10	.05
221	Mike Easler	.10	.05
222	Vida Blue	.20	.09
223	Rick Camp	.10	.05
224	Mike Jorgensen	.10	.05
225	Jody Davis	.10	.05
226	Mike Parrott	.10	.05
227	Jim Clancy	.10	.05
228	Hosken Powell	.10	.05
229	Tom Hume	.10	.05
230	Britt Burns	.10	.05
231	Jim Palmer	.75	.35
232	Bob Rodgers MG	.10	.05
233	Milt Wilcox	.10	.05
234	Dave Revering	.10	.05
235	Mike Torrez	.10	.05
236	Robert Castillo	.10	.05
237	Von Hayes	.20	.09
238	Renie Martin	.10	.05
239	Dwayne Murphy	.10	.05
240	Rodney Scott	.10	.05
241	Fred Patek	.10	.05
242	Mickey Rivers	.10	.05
243	Steve Trout	.10	.05
244	Jose Cruz	.20	.09
245	Manny Trillo	.10	.05
246	Lary Sorensen	.10	.05
247	Dave Edwards	.10	.05
248	Dan Driessen	.10	.05
249	Tommy Boggs	.10	.05
250	Dale Berra	.10	.05
251	Ed Whitson	.10	.05
252	Lee Smith	2.00	.90
253	Tom Paciorek	.10	.05
254	Pat Zachry	.10	.05
255	Luis Leal	.10	.05
256	John Castino	.10	.05
257	Rich Dauer	.10	.05
258	Cecil Cooper	.20	.09
259	Dave Rozema	.10	.05
260	John Tudor	.10	.05
261	Jerry Mumphrey	.10	.05
262	Jay Johnstone	.20	.09
263	Bo Diaz	.10	.05
264	Dennis Leonard	.10	.05
265	Jim Spencer	.10	.05
266	John Milner	.10	.05
267	Don Aase	.10	.05
268	Jim Sundberg	.10	.05
269	Lamar Johnson	.10	.05
270	Frank LaCorte	.10	.05
271	Barry Evans	.10	.05
272	Enos Cabell	.10	.05
273	Del Unser	.10	.05
274	George Foster	.20	.09
275	Brett Butler	1.00	.45

276	Lee Lacy	.10	.05
277	Ken Reitz	.10	.05
278	Keith Hernandez	.20	.09
279	Doug DeCinces	.20	.09
280	Charlie Moore	.10	.05
281	Lance Parrish	.40	.18
282	Ralph Houk MG	.20	.09
283	Rich Gossage	.40	.18
284	Jerry Reuss	.20	.09
285	Mike Stanton	.10	.05
286	Frank White	.20	.09
287	Bob Owchinko	.10	.05
288	Scott Sanderson	.10	.05
289	Bump Wills	.10	.05
290	Dave Frost	.10	.05
291	Chet Lemon	.10	.05
292	Tito Landrum	.10	.05
293	Vern Ruhle	.10	.05
294	Mike Schmidt	1.25	.55
295	Sam Mejias	.10	.05
296	Gary Lucas	.10	.05
297	John Candelaria	.10	.05
298	Jerry Martin	.10	.05
299	Dale Murphy	.75	.35
300	Mike Lum	.10	.05
301	Tom Hausman	.10	.05
302	Glenn Abbott	.10	.05
303	Roger Erickson	.10	.05
304	Otto Velez	.10	.05
305	Danny Goodwin	.10	.05
306	John Mayberry	.10	.05
307	Lenny Randle	.10	.05
308	Bob Bailor	.10	.05
309	Jerry Morales	.10	.05
310	Rufino Linares	.10	.05
311	Kent Tekulve	.20	.09
312	Joe Morgan	.75	.35
313	John Urrea	.10	.05
314	Paul Householder	.10	.05
315	Garry Maddox	.10	.05
316	Mike Ramsey	.10	.05
317	Alan Ashby	.10	.05
318	Bob Clark	.10	.05
319	Tony LaRussa MG	.20	.09
320	Charlie Lea	.10	.05
321	Danny Darwin	.10	.05
322	Cesar Geronimo	.10	.05
323	Tom Underwood	.10	.05
324	Andre Thornton	.10	.05
325	Rudy May	.10	.05
326	Frank Tanana	.20	.09
327	Dave Lopes	.20	.09
328	Richie Hebner	.20	.09
329	Mike Flanagan	.20	.09
330	Mike Caldwell	.10	.05
331	Scott McGregor	.10	.05
332	Jerry Augustine	.10	.05
333	Stan Papi	.10	.05
334	Rick Miller	.10	.05
335	Graig Nettles	.40	.18
336	Dusty Baker	.40	.18
337	Dave Garcia MG	.10	.05
338	Larry Gura	.10	.05
339	Cliff Johnson	.10	.05
340	Warren Cromartie	.10	.05
341	Steve Comer	.10	.05
342	Rick Burleson	.10	.05
343	John Martin	.10	.05
344	Craig Reynolds	.10	.05
345	Mike Proly	.10	.05
346	Ruppert Jones	.10	.05
347	Omar Moreno	.10	.05
348	Greg Minton	.10	.05
349	Rick Mahler	.10	.05
350	Alex Trevino	.10	.05
351	Mike Krukow	.10	.05
352A	Shane Rawley ERR (Photo actually Jim Anderson)	.40	.18
352B	Shane Rawley COR	.10	.05
353	Garth Iorg	.10	.05
354	Pete Mackanin	.10	.05
355	Paul Moskau	.10	.05
356	Richard Dotson	.10	.05
357	Steve Stone	.20	.09
358	Larry Hisle	.10	.05
359	Aurelio Lopez	.10	.05
360	Oscar Gamble	.10	.05
361	Tom Burgmeier	.10	.05
362	Terry Forster	.10	.05
363	Joe Charboneau	.20	.09
364	Ken Brett	.10	.05
365	Tony Armas	.10	.05
366	Chris Speier	.10	.05
367	Fred Lynn	.20	.09
368	Buddy Bell	.20	.09
369	Jim Essian	.10	.05
370	Terry Puhl	.10	.05
371	Greg Gross	.10	.05
372	Bruce Sutter	.20	.09
373	Joe Lefebvre	.10	.05
374	Ray Knight	.20	.09
375	Bruce Benedict	.10	.05
376	Tim Foli	.10	.05
377	Al Holland	.10	.05
378	Ken Kravec	.10	.05
379	Jeff Burroughs	.10	.05
380	Pete Falcone	.10	.05
381	Ernie Whitt	.10	.05
382	Brad Havens	.10	.05
383	Terry Crowley	.10	.05
384	Don Money	.10	.05
385	Dan Schatzeder	.10	.05
386	Gary Allenson	.10	.05
387	Yogi Berra CO	.40	.18
388	Ken Landreaux	.10	.05
389	Mike Hargrove	.20	.09
390	Darryl Motley	.10	.05
391	Dave McKay	.10	.05
392	Stan Bahnsen	.10	.05
393	Ken Forsch	.10	.05
394	Mario Mendoza	.10	.05
395	Jim Morrison	.10	.05
396	Mike Ivie	.10	.05
397	Broderick Perkins	.10	.05
398	Darrell Evans	.20	.09
399	Ron Reed	.10	.05
400	Johnny Bench	1.00	.45
401	Steve Bedrosian	.20	.09
402	Bill Robinson	.10	.05
403	Bill Buckner	.20	.09
404	Ken Oberkfell	.10	.05
405	Cal Ripken	40.00	18.00
406	Jim Gantner	.20	.09
407	Kirk Gibson	.75	.35
408	Tony Perez	.75	.35
409	Tommy John UER (Text says 52-56 as Yankee, should be 52-26)	.40	.18
410	Dave Stewart	1.00	.45
411	Dan Spillner	.10	.05
412	Willie Aikens	.10	.05
413	Mike Heath	.10	.05
414	Ray Burris	.10	.05
415	Leon Roberts	.10	.05
416	Mike Witt	.20	.09
417	Bob Molinaro	.10	.05
418	Steve Braun	.10	.05
419	Nolan Ryan UER (Nisnumbering of Nolan's no-hitters on card back)	5.00	2.20
420	Tug McGraw	.20	.09
421	Dave Concepcion	.20	.09
422A	Juan Eichelberger ERR (Photo actually Gary Lucas)	.40	.18
422B	Juan Eichelberger COR	.10	.05
423	Rick Rhoden	.10	.05
424	Frank Robinson MG	.40	.18
425	Eddie Miller	.10	.05
426	Bill Caudill	.10	.05
427	Doug Flynn	.10	.05
428	Larry Andersen UER (Misspelled Anderson on card front)	.10	.05
429	Al Williams	.10	.05
430	Jerry Garvin	.10	.05
431	Glenn Adams	.10	.05
432	Barry Bonnell	.10	.05
433	Jerry Narron	.10	.05
434	John Stearns	.10	.05
435	Mike Tyson	.10	.05
436	Glenn Hubbard	.10	.05
437	Eddie Solomon	.10	.05
438	Jeff Leonard	.10	.05
439	Randy Bass	.10	.05
440	Mike LaCoss	.10	.05
441	Gary Matthews	.20	.09
442	Mark Littell	.10	.05
443	Don Sutton	.75	.35
444	John Harris	.10	.05
445	Vada Pinson CO	.20	.09
446	Elias Sosa	.10	.05
447	Charlie Hough	.20	.09
448	Willie Wilson	.20	.09
449	Fred Stanley	.10	.05
450	Tom Veryzer	.10	.05
451	Ron Davis	.10	.05
452	Mark Clear	.10	.05
453	Bill Russell	.10	.05
454	Lou Whitaker	.75	.35
455	Dan Graham	.10	.05
456	Reggie Cleveland	.10	.05
457	Sammy Stewart	.10	.05
458	Pete Vuckovich	.10	.05
459	John Wockenfuss	.10	.05
460	Glenn Hoffman	.10	.05
461	Willie Randolph	.20	.09
462	Fernando Valenzuela	.75	.35
463	Ron Hassey	.10	.05
464	Paul Splittorff	.10	.05
465	Rob Picciolo	.10	.05
466	Larry Parrish	.10	.05
467	Johnny Grubb	.10	.05
468	Dan Ford	.10	.05
469	Silvio Martinez	.10	.05
470	Kiko Garcia	.10	.05
471	Bob Boone	.20	.09
472	Luis Salazar	.10	.05
473	Randy Niemann	.10	.05
474	Tom Griffin	.10	.05
475	Phil Niekro	.75	.35
476	Hubie Brooks	.20	.09
477	Dick Tidrow	.10	.05
478	Jim Beattie	.10	.05
479	Damaso Garcia	.10	.05
480	Mickey Hatcher	.10	.05
481	Joe Price	.10	.05
482	Ed Farmer	.10	.05
483	Eddie Murray	1.00	.45
484	Ben Oglivie	.20	.09
485	Kevin Saucier	.10	.05
486	Bobby Murcer	.20	.09
487	Bill Campbell	.10	.05
488	Reggie Smith	.20	.09
489	Wayne Garland	.10	.05
490	Jim Wright	.10	.05
491	Billy Martin MG	.40	.18
492	Jim Fanning MG	.10	.05
493	Don Baylor	.40	.18
494	Rick Honeycutt	.10	.05
495	Carlton Fisk	.75	.35
496	Denny Walling	.10	.05
497	Bake McBride	.10	.05
498	Darrell Porter	.10	.05
499	Gene Richards	.10	.05
500	Ron Oester	.10	.05
501	Ken Dayley	.10	.05
502	Jason Thompson	.10	.05
503	Milt May	.10	.05
504	Doug Bird	.10	.05
505	Bruce Bochte	.10	.05
506	Neil Allen	.10	.05
507	Joey McLaughlin	.10	.05
508	Butch Wynegar	.10	.05
509	Gary Roenicke	.10	.05
510	Robin Yount	.75	.35
511	Dave Tobik	.10	.05
512	Rich Gedman	.20	.09
513	Gene Nelson	.10	.05
514	Rick Monday	.10	.05
515	Miguel Dilone	.10	.05
516	Clint Hurdle	.10	.05
517	Jeff Newman	.10	.05
518	Grant Jackson	.10	.05

#	Player	NRMT	VG-E
519	Andy Hassler	.10	.05
520	Pat Putnam	.10	.05
521	Greg Pryor	.10	.05
522	Tony Scott	.10	.05
523	Steve Mura	.10	.05
524	Johnnie LeMaster	.10	.05
525	Dick Ruthven	.10	.05
526	John McNamara MG	.10	.05
527	Larry McWilliams	.10	.05
528	Johnny Ray	.20	.09
529	Pat Tabler	.20	.09
530	Tom Herr	.20	.09
531A	San Diego Chicken ERR (Without TM)	.75	.35
531B	San Diego Chicken COR (With TM)	.75	.35
532	Sal Butera	.10	.05
533	Mike Griffin	.10	.05
534	Kelvin Moore	.10	.05
535	Reggie Jackson	1.00	.45
536	Ed Romero	.10	.05
537	Derrel Thomas	.10	.05
538	Mike O'Berry	.10	.05
539	Jack O'Connor	.10	.05
540	Bob Ojeda	.40	.18
541	Roy Lee Jackson	.10	.05
542	Lynn Jones	.10	.05
543	Gaylord Perry	.75	.35
544A	Phil Gamer ERR (Reverse negative)	.40	.18
544B	Phil Gamer COR	.20	.09
545	Garry Templeton	.10	.05
546	Rafael Ramirez	.10	.05
547	Jeff Reardon	.40	.18
548	Ron Guidry	.20	.09
549	Tim Laudner	.10	.05
550	John Henry Johnson	.10	.05
551	Chris Bando	.10	.05
552	Bobby Brown	.10	.05
553	Larry Bradford	.10	.05
554	Scott Fletcher	.20	.09
555	Jerry Royster	.10	.05
556	Shooty Babitt UER (Spelled Babbitt on front)	.10	.05
557	Kent Hrbek	1.00	.45
558	Yankee Winners Ron Guidry Tommy John	.20	.09
559	Mark Bomback	.10	.05
560	Julio Valdez	.10	.05
561	Buck Martinez	.10	.05
562	Mike A. Marshall	.20	.09
563	Rennie Stennett	.10	.05
564	Steve Crawford	.10	.05
565	Bob Babcock	.10	.05
566	Johnny Podres CO	.20	.09
567	Paul Serna	.10	.05
568	Harold Baines	.75	.35
569	Dave LaRoche	.10	.05
570	Lee May	.20	.09
571	Gary Ward	.10	.05
572	John Denny	.10	.05
573	Roy Smalley	.10	.05
574	Bob Brenly	.40	.18
575	Bronx Bombers Reggie Jackson Dave Winfield	.75	.35
576	Luis Pujols	.10	.05
577	Butch Hobson	.10	.05
578	Harvey Kuenn MG	.20	.09
579	Cal Ripken Sr. CO	.20	.09
580	Juan Berenguer	.10	.05
581	Benny Ayala	.10	.05
582	Vance Law	.10	.05
583	Rick Leach	.10	.05
584	George Frazier	.10	.05
585	Phillies Finest Pete Rose Mike Schmidt	1.00	.45
586	Joe Rudi	.10	.05
587	Juan Beniquez	.10	.05
588	Luis DeLeon	.10	.05
589	Craig Swan	.10	.05
590	Dave Chalk	.10	.05
591	Billy Gardner MG	.10	.05
592	Sal Bando	.20	.09
593	Bert Campaneris	.20	.09
594	Steve Kemp	.10	.05
595A	Randy Lerch ERR (Braves)	.40	.18
595B	Randy Lerch COR (Brewers)	.10	.05
596	Bryan Clark	.10	.05
597	Dave Ford	.10	.05
598	Mike Scioscia	.20	.09
599	John Lowenstein	.10	.05
600	Rene Lachemann MG	.10	.05
601	Mick Kelleher	.10	.05
602	Ron Jackson	.10	.05
603	Jerry Koosman	.20	.09
604	Dave Goltz	.10	.05
605	Ellis Valentine	.10	.05
606	Lonnie Smith	.20	.09
607	Joaquin Andujar	.20	.09
608	Garry Hancock	.10	.05
609	Jerry Turner	.10	.05
610	Bob Bonner	.10	.05
611	Jim Dwyer	.10	.05
612	Terry Bulling	.10	.05
613	Joel Youngblood	.10	.05
614	Larry Milbourne	.10	.05
615	Gene Roof UER (Name on front is Phil Roof)	.10	.05
616	Keith Drumwright	.10	.05
617	Dave Rosello	.10	.05
618	Rickey Keeton	.10	.05
619	Dennis Lamp	.10	.05
620	Sid Monge	.10	.05
621	Jerry White	.10	.05
622	Luis Aguayo	.10	.05
623	Jamie Easterly	.10	.05
624	Steve Sax	.75	.35
625	Dave Roberts	.10	.05
626	Rick Bosetti	.10	.05
627	Terry Francona	.40	.18
628	Pride of Reds Tom Seaver Johnny Bench	1.00	.45
629	Paul Mirabella	.10	.05
630	Rance Mulliniks	.10	.05
631	Kevin Hickey	.10	.05
632	Reid Nichols	.10	.05
633	Dave Geisel	.10	.05
634	Ken Griffey	.20	.09
635	Bob Lemon MG	.75	.35
636	Orlando Sanchez	.10	.05
637	Bill Almon	.10	.05
638	Danny Ainge	1.00	.45
639	Willie Stargell	.75	.35
640	Bob Sykes	.10	.05
641	Ed Lynch	.10	.05
642	John Ellis	.10	.05
643	Ferguson Jenkins	.75	.35
644	Lenn Sakata	.10	.05
645	Julio Gonzalez	.10	.05
646	Jesse Orosco	.20	.09
647	Jerry Dybzinski	.10	.05
648	Tommy Davis CO	.20	.09
649	Ron Gardenhire	.10	.05
650	Felipe Alou CO	.20	.09
651	Harvey Haddix CO	.20	.09
652	Willie Upshaw	.10	.05
653	Bill Madlock	.20	.09
654A	DK Checklist 1-26 ERR (Unnumbered) (With Trammel)	.75	.35
654B	DK Checklist 1-26 COR (Unnumbered) (With Trammell)	.20	.09
655	Checklist 27-130 (Unnumbered)	.20	.09
656	Checklist 131-234 (Unnumbered)	.20	.09
657	Checklist 235-338 (Unnumbered)	.20	.09
658	Checklist 339-442 (Unnumbered)	.20	.09
659	Checklist 443-544 (Unnumbered)	.20	.09
660	Checklist 545-653 (Unnumbered)	.20	.09

1983 Donruss

MIKE SCHMIDT

	NRMT	VG-E
COMPLETE SET (660)	80.00	36.00
COMP.FACT.SET (660)	80.00	36.00
COMMON CARD (1-660)	.10	.05
MINOR STARS	.20	.09
SEMISTARS	.40	.18
UNLISTED STARS	.75	.35

#	Player	NRMT	VG-E
1	Fernando Valenzuela DK	.40	.18
2	Rollie Fingers DK	.40	.18
3	Reggie Jackson DK	1.00	.45
4	Jim Palmer DK	.40	.18
5	Jack Morris DK	.10	.05
6	George Foster DK	.20	.09
7	Jim Sundberg DK	.10	.05
8	Willie Stargell DK	.40	.18
9	Dave Stieb DK	.20	.09
10	Joe Niekro DK	.20	.09
11	Rickey Henderson DK	1.25	.55
12	Dale Murphy DK	.40	.18
13	Toby Harrah DK	.10	.05
14	Bill Buckner DK	.10	.05
15	Willie Wilson DK	.10	.05
16	Steve Carlton DK	.40	.18
17	Ron Guidry DK	.10	.05
18	Steve Rogers DK	.10	.05
19	Kent Hrbek DK	.20	.09
20	Keith Hernandez DK	.20	.09
21	Floyd Bannister DK	.10	.05
22	Johnny Bench DK	1.00	.45
23	Britt Burns DK	.10	.05
24	Joe Morgan DK	.40	.18
25	Carl Yastrzemski DK	.40	.18
26	Terry Kennedy DK	.10	.05
27	Gary Roenicke	.10	.05
28	Dwight Bernard	.10	.05
29	Pat Underwood	.10	.05
30	Gary Allenson	.10	.05
31	Ron Guidry	.20	.09
32	Burt Hooton	.10	.05
33	Chris Bando	.10	.05
34	Vida Blue	.20	.09
35	Rickey Henderson	1.25	.55
36	Ray Burris	.10	.05
37	John Butcher	.10	.05
38	Don Aase	.10	.05
39	Jerry Koosman	.20	.09
40	Bruce Sutter	.20	.09
41	Jose Cruz	.20	.09
42	Pete Rose	1.25	.55
43	Cesar Cedeno	.20	.09
44	Floyd Chiffer	.10	.05
45	Larry McWilliams	.10	.05
46	Alan Fowlkes	.10	.05
47	Dale Murphy	.75	.35
48	Doug Bird	.10	.05
49	Hubie Brooks	.20	.09
50	Floyd Bannister	.10	.05
51	Jack O'Connor	.10	.05
52	Steve Senteney	.10	.05
53	Gary Gaetti	.75	.35
54	Damaso Garcia	.10	.05
55	Gene Nelson	.10	.05

56	Mookie Wilson	.20	.09
57	Allen Ripley	.10	.05
58	Bob Horner	.10	.05
59	Tony Pena	.10	.05
60	Gary Lavelle	.10	.05
61	Tim Lollar	.10	.05
62	Frank Pastore	.10	.05
63	Garry Maddox	.10	.05
64	Bob Forsch	.10	.05
65	Harry Spilman	.10	.05
66	Geoff Zahn	.10	.05
67	Salome Barojas	.10	.05
68	David Palmer	.10	.05
69	Charlie Hough	.20	.09
70	Dan Quisenberry	.20	.09
71	Tony Armas	.10	.05
72	Rick Sutcliffe	.20	.09
73	Steve Balboni	.10	.05
74	Jerry Remy	.10	.05
75	Mike Scioscia	.10	.05
76	John Wockenfuss	.10	.05
77	Jim Palmer	.75	.35
78	Rollie Fingers	.75	.35
79	Joe Nolan	.10	.05
80	Pete Vuckovich	.10	.05
81	Rick Leach	.10	.05
82	Rick Miller	.10	.05
83	Graig Nettles	.20	.09
84	Ron Cey	.20	.09
85	Miguel Dilone	.10	.05
86	John Wathan	.10	.05
87	Kelvin Moore	.10	.05
88A	Byrn Smith ERR	.20	.09
	(Sic, Bryn)		
88B	Bryn Smith COR	.40	.18
89	Dave Hostetler	.10	.05
90	Rod Carew	.75	.35
91	Lonnie Smith	.10	.05
92	Bob Knepper	.10	.05
93	Marty Bystrom	.10	.05
94	Chris Welsh	.10	.05
95	Jason Thompson	.10	.05
96	Tom O'Malley	.10	.05
97	Phil Niekro	.75	.35
98	Neil Allen	.10	.05
99	Bill Buckner	.20	.09
100	Ed VandeBerg	.10	.05
101	Jim Clancy	.10	.05
102	Robert Castillo	.10	.05
103	Bruce Berenyi	.10	.05
104	Carlton Fisk	.75	.35
105	Mike Flanagan	.20	.09
106	Cecil Cooper	.20	.09
107	Jack Morris	.20	.09
108	Mike Morgan	.10	.05
109	Luis Aponte	.10	.05
110	Pedro Guerrero	.20	.09
111	Len Barker	.10	.05
112	Willie Wilson	.20	.09
113	Dave Beard	.10	.05
114	Mike Gates	.10	.05
115	Reggie Jackson	1.00	.45
116	George Wright	.10	.05
117	Vance Law	.10	.05
118	Nolan Ryan	4.00	1.80
119	Mike Krukow	.10	.05
120	Ozzie Smith	1.25	.55
121	Broderick Perkins	.10	.05
122	Tom Seaver	1.00	.45
123	Chris Chambliss	.20	.09
124	Chuck Tanner MG	.10	.05
125	Johnnie LeMaster	.10	.05
126	Mel Hall	.20	.09
127	Bruce Bochte	.10	.05
128	Charlie Puleo	.10	.05
129	Luis Leal	.10	.05
130	John Pacella	.10	.05
131	Glenn Gulliver	.10	.05
132	Don Money	.10	.05
133	Dave Rozema	.10	.05
134	Bruce Hurst	.10	.05
135	Rudy May	.10	.05
136	Tom Lasorda MG	.40	.18
137	Dan Spillner UER	.10	.05
	(Photo actually		
	Ed Whitson)		
138	Jerry Martin	.10	.05
139	Mike Norris	.10	.05
140	Al Oliver	.20	.09
141	Daryl Sconiers	.10	.05
142	Lamar Johnson	.10	.05
143	Harold Baines	.75	.35
144	Alan Ashby	.10	.05
145	Garry Templeton	.10	.05
146	Al Holland	.10	.05
147	Bo Diaz	.10	.05
148	Dave Concepcion	.20	.09
149	Rick Camp	.10	.05
150	Jim Morrison	.10	.05
151	Randy Martz	.10	.05
152	Keith Hernandez	.20	.09
153	John Lowenstein	.10	.05
154	Mike Caldwell	.10	.05
155	Milt Wilcox	.10	.05
156	Rich Gedman	.10	.05
157	Rich Gossage	.40	.18
158	Jerry Reuss	.10	.05
159	Ron Hassey	.10	.05
160	Larry Gura	.10	.05
161	Dwayne Murphy	.10	.05
162	Woodie Fryman	.10	.05
163	Steve Comer	.10	.05
164	Ken Forsch	.10	.05
165	Dennis Lamp	.10	.05
166	David Green	.10	.05
167	Terry Puhl	.10	.05
168	Mike Schmidt	1.25	.55
	(Wearing 37		
	rather than 20)		
169	Eddie Milner	.10	.05
170	John Curtis	.10	.05
171	Don Robinson	.10	.05
172	Rich Gale	.10	.05
173	Steve Bedrosian	.20	.09
174	Willie Hernandez	.20	.09
175	Ron Gardenhire	.10	.05
176	Jim Beattie	.10	.05
177	Tim Laudner	.10	.05
178	Buck Martinez	.10	.05
179	Kent Hrbek	.20	.09
180	Alfredo Griffin	.10	.05
181	Larry Andersen	.10	.05
182	Pete Falcone	.10	.05
183	Jody Davis	.10	.05
184	Glenn Hubbard	.10	.05
185	Dale Berra	.10	.05
186	Greg Minton	.10	.05
187	Gary Lucas	.10	.05
188	Dave Van Gorder	.10	.05
189	Bob Dernier	.10	.05
190	Willie McGee	1.50	.70
191	Dickie Thon	.10	.05
192	Bob Boone	.20	.09
193	Britt Burns	.10	.05
194	Jeff Reardon	.20	.09
195	Jon Matlack	.10	.05
196	Don Slaught	.40	.18
197	Fred Stanley	.10	.05
198	Rick Manning	.10	.05
199	Dave Righetti	.20	.09
200	Dave Stapleton	.10	.05
201	Steve Yeager	.10	.05
202	Enos Cabell	.10	.05
203	Sammy Stewart	.10	.05
204	Moose Haas	.10	.05
205	Lenn Sakata	.10	.05
206	Charlie Moore	.10	.05
207	Alan Trammell	.75	.35
208	Jim Rice	.20	.09
209	Roy Smalley	.10	.05
210	Bill Russell	.10	.05
211	Andre Thornton	.10	.05
212	Willie Aikens	.10	.05
213	Dave McKay	.10	.05
214	Tim Blackwell	.10	.05
215	Buddy Bell	.20	.09
216	Doug DeCinces	.20	.09
217	Tom Herr	.20	.09
218	Frank LaCorte	.10	.05
219	Steve Carlton	.75	.35
220	Terry Kennedy	.10	.05
221	Mike Easler	.10	.05
222	Jack Clark	.20	.09
223	Gene Garber	.10	.05
224	Scott Holman	.10	.05
225	Mike Proly	.10	.05
226	Terry Bulling	.10	.05
227	Jerry Garvin	.10	.05
228	Ron Davis	.10	.05
229	Tom Hume	.10	.05
230	Marc Hill	.10	.05
231	Dennis Martinez	.20	.09
232	Jim Gantner	.10	.05
233	Larry Pashnick	.10	.05
234	Dave Collins	.10	.05
235	Tom Burgmeier	.10	.05
236	Ken Landreaux	.10	.05
237	John Denny	.10	.05
238	Hal McRae	.20	.09
239	Matt Keough	.10	.05
240	Doug Flynn	.10	.05
241	Fred Lynn	.20	.09
242	Billy Sample	.10	.05
243	Tom Paciorek	.20	.09
244	Joe Sambito	.10	.05
245	Sid Monge	.10	.05
246	Ken Oberkfell	.10	.05
247	Joe Pittman UER	.10	.05
	(Photo actually		
	Juan Eichelberger)		
248	Mario Soto	.10	.05
249	Claudell Washington	.10	.05
250	Rick Rhoden	.10	.05
251	Darrell Evans	.20	.09
252	Steve Henderson	.10	.05
253	Manny Castillo	.10	.05
254	Craig Swan	.10	.05
255	Joey McLaughlin	.10	.05
256	Pete Redfern	.10	.05
257	Ken Singleton	.10	.05
258	Robin Yount	.75	.35
259	Elias Sosa	.10	.05
260	Bob Ojeda	.10	.05
261	Bobby Murcer	.20	.09
262	Candy Maldonado	.20	.09
263	Rick Waits	.10	.05
264	Greg Pryor	.10	.05
265	Bob Owchinko	.10	.05
266	Chris Speier	.10	.05
267	Bruce Kison	.10	.05
268	Mark Wagner	.10	.05
269	Steve Kemp	.10	.05
270	Phil Garner	.20	.09
271	Gene Richards	.10	.05
272	Renie Martin	.10	.05
273	Dave Roberts	.10	.05
274	Dan Driessen	.10	.05
275	Rufino Linares	.10	.05
276	Lee Lacy	.10	.05
277	Ryne Sandberg	12.00	5.50
278	Darrell Porter	.10	.05
279	Cal Ripken	8.00	3.60
280	Jamie Easterly	.10	.05
281	Bill Fahey	.10	.05
282	Glenn Hoffman	.10	.05
283	Willie Randolph	.20	.09
284	Fernando Valenzuela	.40	.18
285	Alan Bannister	.10	.05
286	Paul Splittorff	.10	.05
287	Joe Rudi	.10	.05
288	Bill Gullickson	.10	.05
289	Danny Darwin	.10	.05
290	Andy Hassler	.10	.05
291	Ernesto Escarrega	.10	.05
292	Steve Mura	.10	.05
293	Tony Scott	.10	.05
294	Manny Trillo	.10	.05
295	Greg Harris	.10	.05
296	Luis DeLeon	.10	.05
297	Kent Tekulve	.20	.09
298	Atlee Hammaker	.10	.05
299	Bruce Benedict	.10	.05
300	Fergie Jenkins	.75	.35
301	Dave Kingman	.40	.18
302	Bill Caudill	.10	.05
303	John Castino	.10	.05
304	Ernie Whitt	.10	.05
305	Randy Johnson	.10	.05

□	#	Name		
□	306	Garth Iorg	.10	.05
□	307	Gaylord Perry	.75	.35
□	308	Ed Lynch	.10	.05
□	309	Keith Moreland	.10	.05
□	310	Rafael Ramirez	.10	.05
□	311	Bill Madlock	.20	.09
□	312	Milt May	.10	.05
□	313	John Montefusco	.10	.05
□	314	Wayne Krenchicki	.10	.05
□	315	George Vukovich	.10	.05
□	316	Joaquin Andujar	.10	.05
□	317	Craig Reynolds	.10	.05
□	318	Rick Burleson	.10	.05
□	319	Richard Dotson	.10	.05
□	320	Steve Rogers	.10	.05
□	321	Dave Schmidt	.10	.05
□	322	Bud Black	.20	.09
□	323	Jeff Burroughs	.10	.05
□	324	Von Hayes	.20	.09
□	325	Butch Wynegar	.10	.05
□	326	Carl Yastrzemski	.75	.35
□	327	Ron Roenicke	.10	.05
□	328	Howard Johnson	.75	.35
□	329	Rick Dempsey UER	.20	.09
		(Posing as a left-handed batter)		
□	330A	Jim Slaton	.10	.05
		(Bio printed black on white)		
□	330B	Jim Slaton	.20	.09
		(Bio printed black on yellow)		
□	331	Benny Ayala	.10	.05
□	332	Ted Simmons	.20	.09
□	333	Lou Whitaker	.40	.18
□	334	Chuck Rainey	.10	.05
□	335	Lou Piniella	.20	.09
□	336	Steve Sax	.20	.09
□	337	Toby Harrah	.10	.05
□	338	George Brett	1.50	.70
□	339	Dave Lopes	.20	.09
□	340	Gary Carter	.75	.35
□	341	John Grubb	.10	.05
□	342	Tim Foli	.10	.05
□	343	Jim Kaat	.20	.09
□	344	Mike LaCoss	.10	.05
□	345	Larry Christenson	.10	.05
□	346	Juan Bonilla	.10	.05
□	347	Omar Moreno	.10	.05
□	348	Chili Davis	.75	.35
□	349	Tommy Boggs	.10	.05
□	350	Rusty Staub	.20	.09
□	351	Bump Wills	.10	.05
□	352	Rick Sweet	.10	.05
□	353	Jim Gott	.10	.05
□	354	Terry Felton	.10	.05
□	355	Jim Kern	.10	.05
□	356	Bill Almon UER	.10	.05
		(Expos/Mets in 1983, not Padres/Mets)		
□	357	Tippy Martinez	.10	.05
□	358	Roy Howell	.10	.05
□	359	Dan Petry	.10	.05
□	360	Jerry Mumphrey	.10	.05
□	361	Mark Clear	.10	.05
□	362	Mike Marshall	.10	.05
□	363	Lary Sorensen	.10	.05
□	364	Amos Otis	.20	.09
□	365	Rick Langford	.10	.05
□	366	Brad Mills	.10	.05
□	367	Brian Downing	.10	.05
□	368	Mike Richardt	.10	.05
□	369	Aurelio Rodriguez	.10	.05
□	370	Dave Smith	.10	.05
□	371	Tug McGraw	.20	.09
□	372	Doug Bair	.10	.05
□	373	Ruppert Jones	.10	.05
□	374	Alex Trevino	.10	.05
□	375	Ken Dayley	.10	.05
□	376	Rod Scurry	.10	.05
□	377	Bob Brenly	.10	.05
□	378	Scot Thompson	.10	.05
□	379	Julio Cruz	.10	.05
□	380	John Stearns	.10	.05
□	381	Dale Murray	.10	.05
□	382	Frank Viola	.75	.35
□	383	Al Bumbry	.10	.05
□	384	Ben Oglivie	.10	.05
□	385	Dave Tobik	.10	.05
□	386	Bob Stanley	.10	.05
□	387	Andre Robertson	.10	.05
□	388	Jorge Orta	.10	.05
□	389	Ed Whitson	.10	.05
□	390	Don Hood	.10	.05
□	391	Tom Underwood	.10	.05
□	392	Tim Wallach	.20	.09
□	393	Steve Renko	.10	.05
□	394	Mickey Rivers	.10	.05
□	395	Greg Luzinski	.20	.09
□	396	Art Howe	.10	.05
□	397	Alan Wiggins	.10	.05
□	398	Jim Barr	.10	.05
□	399	Ivan DeJesus	.10	.05
□	400	Tom Lawless	.10	.05
□	401	Bob Walk	.10	.05
□	402	Jimmy Smith	.10	.05
□	403	Lee Smith	.75	.35
□	404	George Hendrick	.10	.05
□	405	Eddie Murray	1.00	.45
□	406	Marshall Edwards	.10	.05
□	407	Lance Parrish	.20	.09
□	408	Carney Lansford	.20	.09
□	409	Dave Winfield	.75	.35
□	410	Bob Welch	.10	.05
□	411	Larry Milbourne	.10	.05
□	412	Dennis Leonard	.10	.05
□	413	Dan Meyer	.10	.05
□	414	Charlie Lea	.10	.05
□	415	Rick Honeycutt	.10	.05
□	416	Mike Witt	.10	.05
□	417	Steve Trout	.10	.05
□	418	Glenn Brummer	.10	.05
□	419	Denny Walling	.10	.05
□	420	Gary Matthews	.20	.09
□	421	Charlie Leibrandt UER	.10	.05
		(Liebrandt on front of card)		
□	422	Juan Eichelberger UER	.10	.05
		(Photo actually Joe Pittman)		
□	423	Cecilio Guante UER	.10	.05
		(Listed as Matt on card)		
□	424	Bill Laskey	.10	.05
□	425	Jerry Royster	.10	.05
□	426	Dickie Noles	.10	.05
□	427	George Foster	.20	.09
□	428	Mike Moore	.20	.09
□	429	Gary Ward	.10	.05
□	430	Barry Bonnell	.10	.05
□	431	Ron Washington	.10	.05
□	432	Rance Mulliniks	.10	.05
□	433	Mike Stanton	.10	.05
□	434	Jesse Orosco	.20	.09
□	435	Larry Bowa	.20	.09
□	436	Biff Pocoroba	.10	.05
□	437	Johnny Ray	.10	.05
□	438	Joe Morgan	.75	.35
□	439	Eric Show	.10	.05
□	440	Larry Biittner	.10	.05
□	441	Greg Gross	.10	.05
□	442	Gene Tenace	.20	.09
□	443	Danny Heep	.10	.05
□	444	Bobby Clark	.10	.05
□	445	Kevin Hickey	.10	.05
□	446	Scott Sanderson	.10	.05
□	447	Frank Tanana	.20	.09
□	448	Cesar Geronimo	.10	.05
□	449	Jimmy Sexton	.10	.05
□	450	Mike Hargrove	.20	.09
□	451	Doyle Alexander	.10	.05
□	452	Dwight Evans	.20	.09
□	453	Terry Forster	.10	.05
□	454	Tom Brookens	.10	.05
□	455	Rich Dauer	.10	.05
□	456	Rob Picciolo	.10	.05
□	457	Terry Crowley	.10	.05
□	458	Ned Yost	.10	.05
□	459	Kirk Gibson	.75	.35
□	460	Reid Nichols	.10	.05
□	461	Oscar Gamble	.10	.05
□	462	Dusty Baker	.20	.09
□	463	Jack Perconte	.10	.05
□	464	Frank White	.20	.09
□	465	Mickey Klutts	.10	.05
□	466	Warren Cromartie	.10	.05
□	467	Larry Parrish	.10	.05
□	468	Bobby Grich	.20	.09
□	469	Dane Iorg	.10	.05
□	470	Joe Niekro	.20	.09
□	471	Ed Farmer	.10	.05
□	472	Tim Flannery	.10	.05
□	473	Dave Parker	.20	.09
□	474	Jeff Leonard	.10	.05
□	475	Al Hrabosky	.10	.05
□	476	Ron Hodges	.10	.05
□	477	Leon Durham	.10	.05
□	478	Jim Essian	.10	.05
□	479	Roy Lee Jackson	.10	.05
□	480	Brad Havens	.10	.05
□	481	Joe Price	.10	.05
□	482	Tony Bernazard	.10	.05
□	483	Scott McGregor	.10	.05
□	484	Paul Molitor	1.00	.45
□	485	Mike Ivie	.10	.05
□	486	Ken Griffey	.20	.09
□	487	Dennis Eckersley	.75	.35
□	488	Steve Garvey	.40	.18
□	489	Mike Fischlin	.10	.05
□	490	U.L. Washington	.10	.05
□	491	Steve McCatty	.10	.05
□	492	Roy Johnson	.10	.05
□	493	Don Baylor	.40	.18
□	494	Bobby Johnson	.10	.05
□	495	Mike Squires	.10	.05
□	496	Bert Roberge	.10	.05
□	497	Dick Ruthven	.10	.05
□	498	Tito Landrum	.10	.05
□	499	Sixto Lezcano	.10	.05
□	500	Johnny Bench	1.00	.45
□	501	Larry Whisenton	.10	.05
□	502	Manny Sarmiento	.10	.05
□	503	Fred Breining	.10	.05
□	504	Bill Campbell	.10	.05
□	505	Todd Cruz	.10	.05
□	506	Bob Bailor	.10	.05
□	507	Dave Stieb	.20	.09
□	508	Al Williams	.10	.05
□	509	Dan Ford	.10	.05
□	510	Gorman Thomas	.10	.05
□	511	Chet Lemon	.10	.05
□	512	Mike Torrez	.10	.05
□	513	Shane Rawley	.10	.05
□	514	Mark Belanger	.10	.05
□	515	Rodney Craig	.10	.05
□	516	Onix Concepcion	.10	.05
□	517	Mike Heath	.10	.05
□	518	Andre Dawson UER	.75	.35
		(Middle name Fernando, should be Nolan)		
□	519	Luis Sanchez	.10	.05
□	520	Terry Bogener	.10	.05
□	521	Rudy Law	.10	.05
□	522	Ray Knight	.20	.09
□	523	Joe Lefebvre	.10	.05
□	524	Jim Wohlford	.10	.05
□	525	Julio Franco	1.00	.45
□	526	Ron Oester	.10	.05
□	527	Rick Mahler	.10	.05
□	528	Steve Nicosia	.10	.05
□	529	Junior Kennedy	.10	.05
□	530A	Whitey Herzog MG	.20	.09
		(Bio printed black on white)		
□	530B	Whitey Herzog MG	.20	.09
		(Bio printed black on yellow)		
□	531A	Don Sutton	.75	.35
		(Blue border on photo)		
□	531B	Don Sutton	.75	.35
		(Green border on photo)		
□	532	Mark Brouhard	.10	.05
□	533A	Sparky Anderson MG	.20	.09
		(Bio printed black on white)		
□	533B	Sparky Anderson MG	.20	.09

(Bio printed black on yellow)

		NRMT	VG-E
❑ 534	Roger LaFrancois	.10	.05
❑ 535	George Frazier	.10	.05
❑ 536	Tom Niedenfuer	.10	.05
❑ 537	Ed Glynn	.10	.05
❑ 538	Lee May	.20	.09
❑ 539	Bob Kearney	.10	.05
❑ 540	Tim Raines	.75	.35
❑ 541	Paul Mirabella	.10	.05
❑ 542	Luis Tiant	.20	.09
❑ 543	Ron LeFlore	.10	.05
❑ 544	Dave LaPoint	.10	.05
❑ 545	Randy Moffitt	.10	.05
❑ 546	Luis Aguayo	.10	.05
❑ 547	Brad Lesley	.20	.09
❑ 548	Luis Salazar	.10	.05
❑ 549	John Candelaria	.10	.05
❑ 550	Dave Bergman	.10	.05
❑ 551	Bob Watson	.20	.09
❑ 552	Pat Tabler	.10	.05
❑ 553	Brent Gaff	.10	.05
❑ 554	Al Cowens	.10	.05
❑ 555	Tom Brunansky	.20	.09
❑ 556	Lloyd Moseby	.10	.05
❑ 557A	Pascual Perez ERR (Twins in glove)	2.00	.90
❑ 557B	Pascual Perez COR (Braves in glove)	.20	.09
❑ 558	Willie Upshaw	.10	.05
❑ 559	Richie Zisk	.10	.05
❑ 560	Pat Zachry	.10	.05
❑ 561	Jay Johnstone	.20	.09
❑ 562	Carlos Diaz	.10	.05
❑ 563	John Tudor	.10	.05
❑ 564	Frank Robinson MG	.40	.18
❑ 565	Dave Edwards	.10	.05
❑ 566	Paul Householder	.10	.05
❑ 567	Ron Reed	.10	.05
❑ 568	Mike Ramsey	.10	.05
❑ 569	Kiko Garcia	.10	.05
❑ 570	Tommy John	.40	.18
❑ 571	Tony LaRussa MG	.20	.09
❑ 572	Joel Youngblood	.10	.05
❑ 573	Wayne Tolleson	.10	.05
❑ 574	Keith Creel	.10	.05
❑ 575	Billy Martin MG	.20	.09
❑ 576	Jerry Dybzinski	.10	.05
❑ 577	Rick Cerone	.10	.05
❑ 578	Tony Perez	.75	.35
❑ 579	Greg Brock	.10	.05
❑ 580	Glenn Wilson	.10	.05
❑ 581	Tim Stoddard	.10	.05
❑ 582	Bob McClure	.10	.05
❑ 583	Jim Dwyer	.10	.05
❑ 584	Ed Romero	.10	.05
❑ 585	Larry Herndon	.10	.05
❑ 586	Wade Boggs	12.00	5.50
❑ 587	Jay Howell	.10	.05
❑ 588	Dave Stewart	.20	.09
❑ 589	Bert Blyleven	.40	.18
❑ 590	Dick Howser MG	.10	.05
❑ 591	Wayne Gross	.10	.05
❑ 592	Terry Francona	.10	.05
❑ 593	Don Werner	.10	.05
❑ 594	Bill Stein	.10	.05
❑ 595	Jesse Barfield	.20	.09
❑ 596	Bob Molinaro	.10	.05
❑ 597	Mike Vail	.10	.05
❑ 598	Tony Gwynn	30.00	13.50
❑ 599	Gary Rajsich	.10	.05
❑ 600	Jerry Ujdur	.10	.05
❑ 601	Cliff Johnson	.10	.05
❑ 602	Jerry White	.10	.05
❑ 603	Bryan Clark	.10	.05
❑ 604	Joe Ferguson	.10	.05
❑ 605	Guy Sularz	.10	.05
❑ 606A	Ozzie Virgil (Green border on photo)	.20	
❑ 606B	Ozzie Virgil (Orange border on photo)	.20	.09
❑ 607	Terry Harper	.10	.05
❑ 608	Harvey Kuenn MG	.10	.05
❑ 609	Jim Sundberg	.20	.09
❑ 610	Willie Stargell	.75	.35
❑ 611	Reggie Smith	.20	.09
❑ 612	Rob Wilfong	.10	.05
❑ 613	The Niekro Brothers Joe Niekro Phil Niekro	.40	.18
❑ 614	Lee Elia MG	.10	.05
❑ 615	Mickey Hatcher	.10	.05
❑ 616	Jerry Hairston	.10	.05
❑ 617	John Martin	.10	.05
❑ 618	Wally Backman	.10	.05
❑ 619	Storm Davis	.10	.05
❑ 620	Alan Knicely	.10	.05
❑ 621	John Stuper	.10	.05
❑ 622	Matt Sinatro	.10	.05
❑ 623	Geno Petralli	.40	.18
❑ 624	Duane Walker	.10	.05
❑ 625	Dick Williams MG	.10	.05
❑ 626	Pat Corrales MG	.10	.05
❑ 627	Vern Ruhle	.10	.05
❑ 628	Joe Torre MG	.20	.09
❑ 629	Anthony Johnson	.10	.05
❑ 630	Steve Howe	.10	.05
❑ 631	Gary Woods	.10	.05
❑ 632	LaMarr Hoyt	.20	.09
❑ 633	Steve Swisher	.10	.05
❑ 634	Terry Leach	.10	.05
❑ 635	Jeff Newman	.10	.05
❑ 636	Brett Butler	.75	.35
❑ 637	Gary Gray	.10	.05
❑ 638	Lee Mazzilli	.10	.05
❑ 639A	Ron Jackson ERR (A's in glove)	5.00	2.20
❑ 639B	Ron Jackson COR (Angels in glove, red border on photo)	.10	.05
❑ 639C	Ron Jackson COR (Angels in glove, green border on photo)	.75	.35
❑ 640	Juan Beniquez	.10	.05
❑ 641	Dave Rucker	.10	.05
❑ 642	Luis Pujols	.10	.05
❑ 643	Rick Monday	.10	.05
❑ 644	Hosken Powell	.10	.05
❑ 645	The Chicken	.75	.35
❑ 646	Dave Engle	.10	.05
❑ 647	Dick Davis	.10	.05
❑ 648	Frank Robinson Vida Blue Joe Morgan	.20	.09
❑ 649	Al Chambers	.10	.05
❑ 650	Jesus Vega	.10	.05
❑ 651	Jeff Jones	.10	.05
❑ 652	Marvis Foley	.10	.05
❑ 653	Ty Cobb Puzzle Card	.75	.35
❑ 654A	Dick Perez/Diamond King Checklist 1-26 (Unnumbered) ERR (Word "checklist" omitted from back)	.75	.35
❑ 654B	Dick Perez/Diamond King Checklist 1-26 (Unnumbered) COR (Word "checklist" is on back)	.75	.35
❑ 655	Checklist 27-130 (Unnumbered)	.10	.05
❑ 656	Checklist 131-234 (Unnumbered)	.10	.05
❑ 657	Checklist 235-338 (Unnumbered)	.10	.05
❑ 658	Checklist 339-442 (Unnumbered)	.10	.05
❑ 659	Checklist 443-544 (Unnumbered)	.10	.05
❑ 660	Checklist 545-653 (Unnumbered)	.10	.05

1984 Donruss

	NRMT	VG-E
COMPLETE SET (660)	120.00	55.00
COMP.FACT.SET (658)	150.00	70.00
COMMON CARD (1-658)	.25	.11

KEITH HERNANDEZ 1B

	NRMT	VG-E
MINOR STARS	.75	.35
SEMISTARS	1.50	.70
UNLISTED STARS	3.00	1.35
DIAMOND KING ERR: 8X VALUE OF CORR		
BEWARE OF COUNTERFEITS		

		NRMT	VG-E
❑ 1	Robin Yount DK COR	4.00	1.80
❑ 1A	Robin Yount DK ERR	3.00	1.35
❑ 2	Dave Concepcion DK COR	1.50	.70
❑ 2A	Dave Concepcion DK ERR (Perez Steel)	.75	.35
❑ 3	Dwayne Murphy DK COR	.75	.35
❑ 3A	Dwayne Murphy DK ERR (Perez Steel)	.25	.11
❑ 4	John Castino DK COR	.75	.35
❑ 4A	John Castino DK ERR (Perez Steel)	.25	.11
❑ 5	Leon Durham DK COR	.75	.35
❑ 5A	Leon Durham DK ERR (Perez Steel)	.25	.11
❑ 6	Rusty Staub DK COR	1.50	.70
❑ 6A	Rusty Staub DK ERR (Perez Steel)	.75	.35
❑ 7	Jack Clark DK COR	.75	.35
❑ 7A	Jack Clark DK ERR (Perez Steel)	.75	.35
❑ 8	Dave Dravecky DK COR	.75	.35
❑ 8A	Dave Dravecky DK ERR (Perez Steel)	.75	.35
❑ 9	Al Oliver DK COR	1.50	.70
❑ 9A	Al Oliver DK ERR (Perez Steel)	.75	.35
❑ 10	Dave Righetti DK COR	.75	.35
❑ 10A	Dave Righetti DK ERR (Perez Steel)	.75	.35
❑ 11	Hal McRae DK COR	1.50	.70
❑ 11A	Hal McRae DK ERR (Perez Steel)	.75	.35
❑ 12	Ray Knight DK COR	.75	.35
❑ 12A	Ray Knight DK ERR (Perez Steel)	.75	.35
❑ 13	Bruce Sutter DK COR	1.50	.70
❑ 13A	Bruce Sutter DK ERR (Perez Steel)	.75	.35
❑ 14	Bob Horner DK COR	.75	.35
❑ 14A	Bob Horner DK ERR (Perez Steel)	.75	.35
❑ 15	Lance Parrish DK COR	1.50	.70
❑ 15A	Lance Parrish DK (Perez Steel)	.75	.35
❑ 16	Matt Young DK COR	.75	.35
❑ 16A	Matt Young DK ERR (Perez Steel)	.25	.11
❑ 17	Fred Lynn DK COR	.75	.35
❑ 17A	Fred Lynn DK ERR (Perez Steel) (A's logo on back)	.25	.11
❑ 18	Ron Kittle DK COR	.75	.35
❑ 18A	Ron Kittle DK ERR (Perez Steel)	.25	.11
❑ 19	Jim Clancy DK COR	.75	.35
❑ 19A	Jim Clancy DK ERR (Perez Steel)	.25	.11

❏ 20	Bill Madlock DK COR	1.50	.70
❏ 20A	Bill Madlock DK ERR (Perez Steel)	.75	.35
❏ 21	Larry Parrish DK COR	.75	.35
❏ 21A	Larry Parrish DK ERR (Perez Steel)	.25	.11
❏ 22	Eddie Murray DK COR	3.00	1.35
❏ 22A	Eddie Murray DK ERR	1.50	.70
❏ 23	Mike Schmidt DK COR	5.00	2.20
❏ 23A	Mike Schmidt DK ERR	3.00	1.35
❏ 24	Pedro Guerrero DK COR	.75	.35
❏ 24A	Pedro Guerrero DK ERR (Perez Steel)	.75	.35
❏ 25	Andre Thornton DK COR	.75	.35
❏ 25A	Andre Thornton DK ERR (Perez Steel)	.75	.35
❏ 26	Wade Boggs DK COR	4.00	1.80
❏ 26A	Wade Boggs DK ERR	2.50	1.10
❏ 27	Joel Skinner RR	.25	.11
❏ 28	Tommy Dunbar RR	.25	.11
❏ 29A	Mike Stenhouse RR ERR No number on back	.25	.11
❏ 29B	Mike Stenhouse RR COR Numbered on back	3.00	1.35
❏ 30A	Ron Darling RR ERR (No number on back)	.75	.35
❏ 30B	Ron Darling RR (Numbered on back)	3.00	1.35
❏ 31	Dion James RR	.25	.11
❏ 32	Tony Fernandez RR	5.00	2.20
❏ 33	Angel Salazar RR	.25	.11
❏ 34	Kevin McReynolds RR	1.50	.70
❏ 35	Dick Schofield RR	.75	.35
❏ 36	Brad Komminsk RR	.25	.11
❏ 37	Tim Teufel RR	.25	.11
❏ 38	Doug Frobel RR	.25	.11
❏ 39	Greg Gagne RR	.75	.35
❏ 40	Mike Fuentes RR	.25	.11
❏ 41	Joe Carter RR	12.00	5.50
❏ 42	Mike Brown RR (Angels OF)	.25	.11
❏ 43	Mike Jeffcoat RR	.25	.11
❏ 44	Sid Fernandez RR	1.50	.70
❏ 45	Brian Dayett RR	.25	.11
❏ 46	Chris Smith RR	.25	.11
❏ 47	Eddie Murray	4.00	1.80
❏ 48	Robin Yount	3.00	1.35
❏ 49	Lance Parrish	1.50	.70
❏ 50	Jim Rice	.75	.35
❏ 51	Dave Winfield	3.00	1.35
❏ 52	Fernando Valenzuela	.75	.35
❏ 53	George Brett	8.00	3.60
❏ 54	Rickey Henderson	5.00	2.20
❏ 55	Gary Carter	3.00	1.35
❏ 56	Buddy Bell	.75	.35
❏ 57	Reggie Jackson	5.00	2.20
❏ 58	Harold Baines	3.00	1.35
❏ 59	Ozzie Smith	5.00	2.20
❏ 60	Nolan Ryan UER (Text on back refers to 1972 as the year he struck out 383; the year was 1973)	20.00	9.00
❏ 61	Pete Rose	8.00	3.60
❏ 62	Ron Oester	.25	.11
❏ 63	Steve Garvey	1.50	.70
❏ 64	Jason Thompson	.25	.11
❏ 65	Jack Clark	.75	.35
❏ 66	Dale Murphy	3.00	1.35
❏ 67	Leon Durham	.25	.11
❏ 68	Darryl Strawberry	8.00	3.60
❏ 69	Richie Zisk	.25	.11
❏ 70	Kent Hrbek	.75	.35
❏ 71	Dave Stieb	.25	.11
❏ 72	Ken Schrom	.25	.11
❏ 73	George Bell	.75	.35
❏ 74	John Moses	.25	.11
❏ 75	Ed Lynch	.25	.11
❏ 76	Chuck Rainey	.25	.11
❏ 77	Biff Pocoroba	.25	.11
❏ 78	Cecilio Guante	.25	.11
❏ 79	Jim Barr	.25	.11
❏ 80	Kurt Bevacqua	.25	.11
❏ 81	Tom Foley	.25	.11
❏ 82	Joe Lefebvre	.25	.11
❏ 83	Andy Van Slyke	3.00	1.35
❏ 84	Bob Lillis MG	.25	.11
❏ 85	Ricky Adams	.25	.11
❏ 86	Jerry Hairston	.25	.11
❏ 87	Bob James	.25	.11
❏ 88	Joe Altobelli MG	.25	.11
❏ 89	Ed Romero	.25	.11
❏ 90	John Grubb	.25	.11
❏ 91	John Henry Johnson	.25	.11
❏ 92	Juan Espino	.25	.11
❏ 93	Candy Maldonado	.25	.11
❏ 94	Andre Thornton	.25	.11
❏ 95	Onix Concepcion	.25	.11
❏ 96	Donnie Hill UER (Listed as P, should be 2B)	.25	.11
❏ 97	Andre Dawson UER (Wrong middle name, should be Nolan)	3.00	1.35
❏ 98	Frank Tanana	.75	.35
❏ 99	Curtis Wilkerson	.25	.11
❏ 100	Larry Gura	.25	.11
❏ 101	Dwayne Murphy	.25	.11
❏ 102	Tom Brennan	.25	.11
❏ 103	Dave Righetti	.75	.35
❏ 104	Steve Sax	.75	.35
❏ 105	Dan Petry	.75	.35
❏ 106	Cal Ripken	25.00	11.00
❏ 107	Paul Molitor UER ('83 stats should say .270 BA, 608 AB, and 164 hits)	4.00	1.80
❏ 108	Fred Lynn	.75	.35
❏ 109	Neil Allen	.25	.11
❏ 110	Joe Niekro	.75	.35
❏ 111	Steve Carlton	4.00	1.80
❏ 112	Terry Kennedy	.25	.11
❏ 113	Bill Madlock	.75	.35
❏ 114	Chili Davis	1.50	.70
❏ 115	Jim Gantner	.25	.11
❏ 116	Tom Seaver	5.00	2.20
❏ 117	Bill Buckner	.75	.35
❏ 118	Bill Caudill	.25	.11
❏ 119	Jim Clancy	.25	.11
❏ 120	John Castino	.25	.11
❏ 121	Dave Concepcion	.75	.35
❏ 122	Greg Luzinski	.75	.35
❏ 123	Mike Boddicker	.25	.11
❏ 124	Pete Ladd	.25	.11
❏ 125	Juan Berenguer	.25	.11
❏ 126	John Montefusco	.25	.11
❏ 127	Ed Jurak	.25	.11
❏ 128	Tom Niedenfuer	.25	.11
❏ 129	Bert Blyleven	.75	.35
❏ 130	Bud Black	.25	.11
❏ 131	Gorman Heimueller	.25	.11
❏ 132	Dan Schatzeder	.25	.11
❏ 133	Ron Jackson	.25	.11
❏ 134	Tom Henke	1.50	.70
❏ 135	Kevin Hickey	.25	.11
❏ 136	Mike Scott	.75	.35
❏ 137	Bo Diaz	.25	.11
❏ 138	Glenn Brummer	.25	.11
❏ 139	Sid Monge	.25	.11
❏ 140	Rich Gale	.25	.11
❏ 141	Brett Butler	1.50	.70
❏ 142	Brian Harper	.75	.35
❏ 143	John Rabb	.25	.11
❏ 144	Gary Woods	.25	.11
❏ 145	Pat Brummer	.25	.11
❏ 146	Jim Acker	.25	.11
❏ 147	Mickey Hatcher	.25	.11
❏ 148	Todd Cruz	.25	.11
❏ 149	Tom Tellmann	.25	.11
❏ 150	John Wockenfuss	.25	.11
❏ 151	Wade Boggs UER 1983 runs 10; should be 100	8.00	3.60
❏ 152	Don Baylor	1.50	.70
❏ 153	Bob Welch	.25	.11
❏ 154	Alan Bannister	.25	.11
❏ 155	Willie Aikens	.25	.11
❏ 156	Jeff Burroughs	.25	.11
❏ 157	Bryan Little	.25	.11
❏ 158	Bob Boone	.75	.35
❏ 159	Dave Hostetler	.25	.11
❏ 160	Jerry Dybzinski	.25	.11
❏ 161	Mike Madden	.25	.11
❏ 162	Luis DeLeon	.25	.11
❏ 163	Willie Hernandez	.75	.35
❏ 164	Frank Pastore	.25	.11
❏ 165	Rick Camp	.25	.11
❏ 166	Lee Mazzilli	.25	.11
❏ 167	Scot Thompson	.25	.11
❏ 168	Bob Forsch	.25	.11
❏ 169	Mike Flanagan	.25	.11
❏ 170	Rick Manning	.25	.11
❏ 171	Chet Lemon	.25	.11
❏ 172	Jerry Remy	.25	.11
❏ 173	Ron Guidry	.75	.35
❏ 174	Pedro Guerrero	.75	.35
❏ 175	Willie Wilson	.25	.11
❏ 176	Carney Lansford	.75	.35
❏ 177	Al Oliver	.75	.35
❏ 178	Jim Sundberg	.25	.11
❏ 179	Bobby Grich	.75	.35
❏ 180	Rich Dotson	.25	.11
❏ 181	Joaquin Andujar	.25	.11
❏ 182	Jose Cruz	.75	.35
❏ 183	Mike Schmidt	6.00	2.70
❏ 184	Gary Redus	.25	.11
❏ 185	Garry Templeton	.25	.11
❏ 186	Tony Pena	.25	.11
❏ 187	Greg Minton	.25	.11
❏ 188	Phil Niekro	3.00	1.35
❏ 189	Ferguson Jenkins	3.00	1.35
❏ 190	Mookie Wilson	.75	.35
❏ 191	Jim Beattie	.25	.11
❏ 192	Gary Ward	.25	.11
❏ 193	Jesse Barfield	.75	.35
❏ 194	Pete Filson	.25	.11
❏ 195	Roy Lee Jackson	.25	.11
❏ 196	Rick Sweet	.25	.11
❏ 197	Jesse Orosco	.25	.11
❏ 198	Steve Lake	.25	.11
❏ 199	Ken Dayley	.25	.11
❏ 200	Manny Sarmiento	.25	.11
❏ 201	Mark Davis	.25	.11
❏ 202	Tim Flannery	.25	.11
❏ 203	Bill Scherrer	.25	.11
❏ 204	Al Holland	.25	.11
❏ 205	Dave Von Ohlen	.25	.11
❏ 206	Mike LaCoss	.25	.11
❏ 207	Juan Beniquez	.25	.11
❏ 208	Juan Agosto	.25	.11
❏ 209	Bobby Ramos	.25	.11
❏ 210	Al Bumbry	.25	.11
❏ 211	Mark Brouhard	.25	.11
❏ 212	Howard Bailey	.25	.11
❏ 213	Bruce Hurst	.25	.11
❏ 214	Bob Shirley	.25	.11
❏ 215	Pat Zachry	.25	.11
❏ 216	Julio Franco	1.50	.70
❏ 217	Mike Armstrong	.25	.11
❏ 218	Dave Beard	.25	.11
❏ 219	Steve Rogers	.25	.11
❏ 220	John Butcher	.25	.11
❏ 221	Mike Smithson	.25	.11
❏ 222	Frank White	.75	.35
❏ 223	Mike Heath	.25	.11
❏ 224	Chris Bando	.25	.11
❏ 225	Roy Smalley	.25	.11
❏ 226	Dusty Baker	.75	.35
❏ 227	Lou Whitaker	3.00	1.35
❏ 228	John Lowenstein	.25	.11
❏ 229	Ben Oglivie	.25	.11
❏ 230	Doug DeCinces	.25	.11
❏ 231	Lonnie Smith	.25	.11
❏ 232	Ray Knight	.75	.35
❏ 233	Gary Matthews	.75	.35
❏ 234	Juan Bonilla	.25	.11
❏ 235	Rod Scurry	.25	.11
❏ 236	Atlee Hammaker	.25	.11
❏ 237	Mike Caldwell	.25	.11
❏ 238	Keith Hernandez	.75	.35
❏ 239	Larry Bowa	.75	.35
❏ 240	Tony Bernazard	.25	.11
❏ 241	Damaso Garcia	.25	.11
❏ 242	Tom Brunansky	.75	.35
❏ 243	Dan Driessen	.25	.11
❏ 244	Ron Kittle	.25	.11
❏ 245	Tim Stoddard	.25	.11

❑ 246	Bob L. Gibson (Brewers Pitcher)	.25	.11
❑ 247	Marty Castillo	.25	.11
❑ 248	Don Mattingly UER ("Trailing" on back)	30.00	13.50
❑ 249	Jeff Newman	.25	.11
❑ 250	Alejandro Pena	.75	.35
❑ 251	Toby Harrah	.75	.35
❑ 252	Cesar Geronimo	.25	.11
❑ 253	Tom Underwood	.25	.11
❑ 254	Doug Flynn	.25	.11
❑ 255	Andy Hassler	.25	.11
❑ 256	Odell Jones	.25	.11
❑ 257	Rudy Law	.25	.11
❑ 258	Harry Spilman	.25	.11
❑ 259	Marty Bystrom	.25	.11
❑ 260	Dave Rucker	.25	.11
❑ 261	Ruppert Jones	.25	.11
❑ 262	Jeff R. Jones (Reds OF)	.25	.11
❑ 263	Gerald Perry	.75	.35
❑ 264	Gene Tenace	.75	.35
❑ 265	Brad Wellman	.25	.11
❑ 266	Dickie Noles	.25	.11
❑ 267	Jamie Allen	.25	.11
❑ 268	Jim Gott	.25	.11
❑ 269	Ron Davis	.25	.11
❑ 270	Benny Ayala	.25	.11
❑ 271	Ned Yost	.25	.11
❑ 272	Dave Rozema	.25	.11
❑ 273	Dave Stapleton	.25	.11
❑ 274	Lou Piniella	.75	.35
❑ 275	Jose Morales	.25	.11
❑ 276	Broderick Perkins	.25	.11
❑ 277	Butch Davis	.25	.11
❑ 278	Tony Phillips	3.00	1.35
❑ 279	Jeff Reardon	.75	.35
❑ 280	Ken Forsch	.25	.11
❑ 281	Pete O'Brien	.75	.35
❑ 282	Tom Paciorek	.75	.35
❑ 283	Frank LaCorte	.25	.11
❑ 284	Tim Lollar	.25	.11
❑ 285	Greg Gross	.25	.11
❑ 286	Alex Trevino	.25	.11
❑ 287	Gene Garber	.25	.11
❑ 288	Dave Parker	.75	.35
❑ 289	Lee Smith	3.00	1.35
❑ 290	Dave LaPoint	.25	.11
❑ 291	John Shelby	.25	.11
❑ 292	Charlie Moore	.25	.11
❑ 293	Alan Trammell	3.00	1.35
❑ 294	Tony Armas	.25	.11
❑ 295	Shane Rawley	.25	.11
❑ 296	Greg Brock	.25	.11
❑ 297	Hal McRae	.75	.35
❑ 298	Mike Davis	.25	.11
❑ 299	Tim Raines	1.50	.70
❑ 300	Bucky Dent	.75	.35
❑ 301	Tommy John	1.50	.70
❑ 302	Carlton Fisk	3.00	1.35
❑ 303	Darrell Porter	.25	.11
❑ 304	Dickie Thon	.25	.11
❑ 305	Garry Maddox	.25	.11
❑ 306	Cesar Cedeno	.75	.35
❑ 307	Gary Lucas	.25	.11
❑ 308	Johnny Ray	.25	.11
❑ 309	Andy McGaffigan	.25	.11
❑ 310	Claudell Washington	.25	.11
❑ 311	Ryne Sandberg	12.00	5.50
❑ 312	George Foster	.75	.35
❑ 313	Spike Owen	.75	.35
❑ 314	Gary Gaetti	1.50	.70
❑ 315	Willie Upshaw	.25	.11
❑ 316	Al Williams	.25	.11
❑ 317	Jorge Orta	.25	.11
❑ 318	Orlando Mercado	.25	.11
❑ 319	Junior Ortiz	.25	.11
❑ 320	Mike Proly	.25	.11
❑ 321	Randy Johnson UER ('72-82 stats are from Twins' Randy Johnson, '83 stats are from Braves' Randy Johnson)	.25	.11
❑ 322	Jim Morrison	.25	.11
❑ 323	Max Venable	.25	.11
❑ 324	Tony Gwynn	25.00	11.00
❑ 325	Duane Walker	.25	.11
❑ 326	Ozzie Virgil	.25	.11
❑ 327	Jeff Lahti	.25	.11
❑ 328	Bill Dawley	.25	.11
❑ 329	Rob Wilfong	.25	.11
❑ 330	Marc Hill	.25	.11
❑ 331	Ray Burris	.25	.11
❑ 332	Allan Ramirez	.25	.11
❑ 333	Chuck Porter	.25	.11
❑ 334	Wayne Krenchicki	.25	.11
❑ 335	Gary Allenson	.25	.11
❑ 336	Bobby Meacham	.25	.11
❑ 337	Joe Beckwith	.25	.11
❑ 338	Rick Sutcliffe	.75	.35
❑ 339	Mark Huismann	.25	.11
❑ 340	Tim Conroy	.25	.11
❑ 341	Scott Sanderson	.25	.11
❑ 342	Larry Biittner	.25	.11
❑ 343	Dave Stewart	.75	.35
❑ 344	Darryl Motley	.25	.11
❑ 345	Chris Codiroli	.25	.11
❑ 346	Rich Behenna	.25	.11
❑ 347	Andre Robertson	.25	.11
❑ 348	Mike Marshall	.25	.11
❑ 349	Larry Herndon	.75	.35
❑ 350	Rich Dauer	.25	.11
❑ 351	Cecil Cooper	.75	.35
❑ 352	Rod Carew	4.00	1.80
❑ 353	Willie McGee	1.50	.70
❑ 354	Phil Garner	.75	.35
❑ 355	Joe Morgan	4.00	1.80
❑ 356	Luis Salazar	.25	.11
❑ 357	John Candelaria	.25	.11
❑ 358	Bill Laskey	.25	.11
❑ 359	Bob McClure	.25	.11
❑ 360	Dave Kingman	1.50	.70
❑ 361	Ron Cey	.75	.35
❑ 362	Matt Young	.25	.11
❑ 363	Lloyd Moseby	.25	.11
❑ 364	Frank Viola	1.50	.70
❑ 365	Eddie Milner	.25	.11
❑ 366	Floyd Bannister	.25	.11
❑ 367	Dan Ford	.25	.11
❑ 368	Moose Haas	.25	.11
❑ 369	Doug Bair	.25	.11
❑ 370	Ray Fontenot	.25	.11
❑ 371	Luis Aponte	.25	.11
❑ 372	Jack Fimple	.25	.11
❑ 373	Neal Heaton	.25	.11
❑ 374	Greg Pryor	.25	.11
❑ 375	Wayne Gross	.25	.11
❑ 376	Charlie Lea	.25	.11
❑ 377	Steve Lubratich	.25	.11
❑ 378	Jon Matlack	.25	.11
❑ 379	Julio Cruz	.25	.11
❑ 380	John Mizerock	.25	.11
❑ 381	Kevin Gross	.25	.11
❑ 382	Mike Ramsey	.25	.11
❑ 383	Doug Gwosdz	.25	.11
❑ 384	Kelly Paris	.25	.11
❑ 385	Pete Falcone	.25	.11
❑ 386	Milt May	.25	.11
❑ 387	Fred Breining	.25	.11
❑ 388	Craig Lefferts	.25	.11
❑ 389	Steve Henderson	.25	.11
❑ 390	Randy Moffitt	.25	.11
❑ 391	Ron Washington	.25	.11
❑ 392	Gary Roenicke	.25	.11
❑ 393	Tom Candiotti	3.00	1.35
❑ 394	Larry Pashnick	.25	.11
❑ 395	Dwight Evans	.75	.35
❑ 396	Rich Gossage	1.50	.70
❑ 397	Derrel Thomas	.25	.11
❑ 398	Juan Eichelberger	.25	.11
❑ 399	Leon Roberts	.25	.11
❑ 400	Dave Lopes	.75	.35
❑ 401	Bill Gullickson	.25	.11
❑ 402	Geoff Zahn	.25	.11
❑ 403	Billy Sample	.25	.11
❑ 404	Mike Squires	.25	.11
❑ 405	Craig Reynolds	.25	.11
❑ 406	Eric Show	.25	.11
❑ 407	Dann Bilardello		
❑ 408	Dann Bilardello	.25	
❑ 409	Bruce Benedict	.25	
❑ 410	Kent Tekulve	.75	.35
❑ 411	Mel Hall	.75	.35
❑ 412	John Stuper	.25	.11
❑ 413	Rick Dempsey	.25	.11
❑ 414	Don Sutton	3.00	1.35
❑ 415	Jack Morris	3.00	1.35
❑ 416	John Tudor	.25	.11
❑ 417	Willie Randolph	.75	.35
❑ 418	Jerry Reuss	.25	.11
❑ 419	Don Slaught	.75	.35
❑ 420	Steve McCatty	.25	.11
❑ 421	Tim Wallach	.75	.35
❑ 422	Larry Parrish	.25	.11
❑ 423	Brian Downing	.25	.11
❑ 424	Britt Burns	.25	.11
❑ 425	David Green	.25	.11
❑ 426	Jerry Mumphrey	.25	.11
❑ 427	Ivan DeJesus	.25	.11
❑ 428	Mario Soto	.25	.11
❑ 429	Gene Richards	.25	.11
❑ 430	Dale Berra	.25	.11
❑ 431	Darrell Evans	.75	.35
❑ 432	Glenn Hubbard	.25	.11
❑ 433	Jody Davis	.25	.11
❑ 434	Danny Heep	.25	.11
❑ 435	Ed Nunez	.25	.11
❑ 436	Bobby Castillo	.25	.11
❑ 437	Ernie Whitt	.25	.11
❑ 438	Scott Ullger	.25	.11
❑ 439	Doyle Alexander	.25	.11
❑ 440	Domingo Ramos	.25	.11
❑ 441	Craig Swan	.25	.11
❑ 442	Warren Brusstar	.25	.11
❑ 443	Len Barker	.25	.11
❑ 444	Mike Easler	.25	.11
❑ 445	Renie Martin	.25	.11
❑ 446	Dennis Rasmussen	.25	.11
❑ 447	Ted Power	.25	.11
❑ 448	Charles Hudson	.25	.11
❑ 449	Danny Cox	.25	.11
❑ 450	Kevin Bass	.25	.11
❑ 451	Daryl Sconiers	.25	.11
❑ 452	Scott Fletcher	.25	.11
❑ 453	Bryn Smith	.25	.11
❑ 454	Jim Dwyer	.25	.11
❑ 455	Rob Picciolo	.25	.11
❑ 456	Enos Cabell	.25	.11
❑ 457	Dennis Boyd	.75	.35
❑ 458	Butch Wynegar	.25	.11
❑ 459	Burt Hooton	.25	.11
❑ 460	Ron Hassey	.25	.11
❑ 461	Danny Jackson	1.50	.70
❑ 462	Bob Kearney	.25	.11
❑ 463	Terry Francona	.25	.11
❑ 464	Wayne Tolleson	.25	.11
❑ 465	Mickey Rivers	.25	.11
❑ 466	John Wathan	.25	.11
❑ 467	Bill Almon	.25	.11
❑ 468	George Vukovich	.25	.11
❑ 469	Steve Kemp	.25	.11
❑ 470	Ken Landreaux	.25	.11
❑ 471	Milt Wilcox	.25	.11
❑ 472	Tippy Martinez	.25	.11
❑ 473	Ted Simmons	.75	.35
❑ 474	Tim Foli	.25	.11
❑ 475	George Hendrick	.25	.11
❑ 476	Terry Puhl	.25	.11
❑ 477	Von Hayes	.25	.11
❑ 478	Bobby Brown	.25	.11
❑ 479	Lee Lacy	.25	.11
❑ 480	Joel Youngblood	.25	.11
❑ 481	Jim Slaton	.25	.11
❑ 482	Mike Fitzgerald	.25	.11
❑ 483	Keith Moreland	.25	.11
❑ 484	Ron Roenicke	.25	.11
❑ 485	Luis Leal	.25	.11
❑ 486	Bryan Oelkers	.25	.11
❑ 487	Bruce Berenyi	.25	.11
❑ 488	LaMarr Hoyt	.25	.11
❑ 489	Joe Nolan	.25	.11
❑ 490	Marshall Edwards	.25	.11
❑ 491	Mike Laga	.75	.35
❑ 492	Rick Cerone	.25	.11
❑ 493	Rick Miller UER (Listed as Mike on card front)	.25	.11
❑ 494	Rick Honeycutt	.25	.11

495 Mike Hargrove	.75	.35
496 Joe Simpson	.25	.11
497 Keith Atherton	.25	.11
498 Chris Welsh	.25	.11
499 Bruce Kison	.25	.11
500 Bobby Johnson	.25	.11
501 Jerry Koosman	.75	.35
502 Frank DiPino	.25	.11
503 Tony Perez	3.00	1.35
504 Ken Oberkfell	.25	.11
505 Mark Thurmond	.25	.11
506 Joe Price	.25	.11
507 Pascual Perez	.25	.11
508 Marvell Wynne	.25	.11
509 Mike Krukow	.25	.11
510 Dick Ruthven	.25	.11
511 Al Cowens	.25	.11
512 Cliff Johnson	.25	.11
513 Randy Bush	.25	.11
514 Sammy Stewart	.25	.11
515 Bill Schroeder	.25	.11
516 Aurelio Lopez	.75	.35
517 Mike G. Brown	.25	.11
518 Graig Nettles	.75	.35
519 Dave Sax	.25	.11
520 Jerry Willard	.25	.11
521 Paul Splittorff	.25	.11
522 Tom Burgmeier	.25	.11
523 Chris Speier	.25	.11
524 Bobby Clark	.25	.11
525 George Wright	.25	.11
526 Dennis Lamp	.25	.11
527 Tony Scott	.25	.11
528 Ed Whitson	.25	.11
529 Ron Reed	.25	.11
530 Charlie Puleo	.25	.11
531 Jerry Royster	.25	.11
532 Don Robinson	.25	.11
533 Steve Trout	.25	.11
534 Bruce Sutter	.75	.35
535 Bob Horner	.75	.35
536 Pat Tabler	.25	.11
537 Chris Chambliss	.75	.35
538 Bob Ojeda	.25	.11
539 Alan Ashby	.25	.11
540 Jay Johnstone	.75	.35
541 Bob Dernier	.25	.11
542 Brook Jacoby	.75	.35
543 U.L. Washington	.25	.11
544 Danny Darwin	.25	.11
545 Kiko Garcia	.25	.11
546 Vance Law UER	.25	.11
(Listed as P on card front)		
547 Tug McGraw	.75	.35
548 Dave Smith	.25	.11
549 Len Matuszek	.25	.11
550 Tom Hume	.25	.11
551 Dave Dravecky	.75	.35
552 Rick Rhoden	.25	.11
553 Duane Kuiper	.25	.11
554 Rusty Staub	.75	.35
555 Bill Campbell	.25	.11
556 Mike Torrez	.25	.11
557 Dave Henderson	.75	.35
558 Len Whitehouse	.25	.11
559 Barry Bonnell	.25	.11
560 Rick Lysander	.25	.11
561 Garth Iorg	.25	.11
562 Bryan Clark	.25	.11
563 Brian Giles	.25	.11
564 Vern Ruhle	.25	.11
565 Steve Bedrosian	.25	.11
566 Larry McWilliams	.25	.11
567 Jeff Leonard UER	.25	.11
(Listed as P on card front)		
568 Alan Wiggins	.25	.11
569 Jeff Russell	.75	.35
570 Salome Barojas	.25	.11
571 Dane Iorg	.25	.11
572 Bob Knepper	.25	.11
573 Gary Lavelle	.25	.11
574 Gorman Thomas	.25	.11
575 Manny Trillo	.25	.11
576 Jim Palmer	4.00	1.80

577 Dale Murray	.25	.11
578 Tom Brookens	.75	.35
579 Rich Gedman	.25	.11
580 Bill Doran	.75	.35
581 Steve Yeager	.25	.11
582 Dan Spillner	.25	.11
583 Dan Quisenberry	.25	.11
584 Rance Mulliniks	.25	.11
585 Storm Davis	.25	.11
586 Dave Schmidt	.25	.11
587 Bill Russell	.25	.11
588 Pat Sheridan	.25	.11
589 Rafael Ramirez UER (A's on front)	.25	.11
590 Bud Anderson	.25	.11
591 George Frazier	.25	.11
592 Lee Tunnell	.25	.11
593 Kirk Gibson	3.00	1.35
594 Scott McGregor	.25	.11
595 Bob Bailor	.25	.11
596 Tom Herr	.75	.35
597 Luis Sanchez	.25	.11
598 Dave Engle	.25	.11
599 Craig McMurtry	.25	.11
600 Carlos Diaz	.25	.11
601 Tom O'Malley	.25	.11
602 Nick Esasky	.25	.11
603 Ron Hodges	.25	.11
604 Ed VandeBerg	.25	.11
605 Alfredo Griffin	.25	.11
606 Glenn Hoffman	.25	.11
607 Hubie Brooks	.25	.11
608 Richard Barnes UER (Photo actually Neal Heaton)	.25	.11
609 Greg Walker	.75	.35
610 Ken Singleton	.25	.11
611 Mark Clear	.25	.11
612 Buck Martinez	.25	.11
613 Ken Griffey	.75	.35
614 Reid Nichols	.25	.11
615 Doug Sisk	.25	.11
616 Bob Brenly	.25	.11
617 Joey McLaughlin	.25	.11
618 Glenn Wilson	.75	.35
619 Bob Stoddard	.25	.11
620 Lenn Sakata UER (Listed as Len on card front)	.25	.11
621 Mike Young	.25	.11
622 John Stefero	.25	.11
623 Carmelo Martinez	.25	.11
624 Dave Bergman	.25	.11
625 Reds UER (Sic, Redbirds) David Green Willie McGee Lonnie Smith Ozzie Smith	3.00	1.35
626 Rudy May	.25	.11
627 Matt Keough	.25	.11
628 Jose DeLeon	.25	.11
629 Jim Essian	.25	.11
630 Darnell Coles	.25	.11
631 Mike Warren	.25	.11
632 Del Crandall MG	.25	.11
633 Dennis Martinez	.75	.35
634 Mike Moore	.75	.35
635 Lary Sorensen	.25	.11
636 Ricky Nelson	.25	.11
637 Omar Moreno	.25	.11
638 Charlie Hough	.75	.35
639 Dennis Eckersley	3.00	1.35
640 Walt Terrell	.25	.11
641 Denny Walling	.25	.11
642 Dave Anderson	.25	.11
643 Jose Oquendo	.75	.35
644 Bob Stanley	.25	.11
645 Dave Geisel	.25	.11
646 Scott Garrelts	.25	.11
647 Gary Pettis	.25	.11
648 Duke Snider Puzzle Card	1.50	.70
649 Johnnie LeMaster	.25	.11
650 Dave Collins	.25	.11
651 The Chicken	1.50	.70

652 DK Checklist 1-26 (Unnumbered)	.75	.35
653 Checklist 27-130 (Unnumbered)	.25	.11
654 Checklist 131-234 (Unnumbered)	.25	.11
655 Checklist 235-338 (Unnumbered)	.25	.11
656 Checklist 339-442 (Unnumbered)	.25	.11
657 Checklist 443-546 (Unnumbered)	.25	.11
658 Checklist 547-651 (Unnumbered)	.25	.11
A Living Legends A Gaylord Perry Rollie Fingers	2.50	1.10
B Living Legends B Carl Yastrzemski Johnny Bench	5.00	2.20

1985 Donruss

	NRMT	VG-E
COMPLETE SET (660)	100.00	45.00
COMP.FACT.SET (660)	125.00	55.00
COMMON CARD (1-660)	.15	.07
MINOR STARS	.40	.18
SEMISTARS	.75	.35
UNLISTED STARS	1.50	.70
CONDITION SENSITIVE SET		

1 Ryne Sandberg DK	2.00	.90
2 Doug DeCinces DK	.15	.07
3 Richard Dotson DK	.15	.07
4 Bert Blyleven DK	.15	.07
5 Lou Whitaker DK	.40	.18
6 Dan Quisenberry DK	.40	.18
7 Don Mattingly DK	2.00	.90
8 Carney Lansford DK	.15	.07
9 Frank Tanana DK	.15	.07
10 Willie Upshaw DK	.15	.07
11 Claudell Washington DK	.15	.07
12 Mike Marshall DK	.15	.07
13 Joaquin Andujar DK	.15	.07
14 Cal Ripken DK	4.00	1.80
15 Jim Rice DK	.40	.18
16 Don Sutton DK	.40	.18
17 Frank Viola DK	.15	.07
18 Alvin Davis DK	.15	.07
19 Mario Soto DK	.15	.07
20 Jose Cruz DK	.15	.07
21 Charlie Lea DK	.15	.07
22 Jesse Orosco DK	.15	.07
23 Juan Samuel DK	.15	.07
24 Tony Pena DK	.15	.07
25 Tony Gwynn DK	3.00	1.35
26 Bob Brenly DK	.15	.07
27 Danny Tartabull RR	1.50	.70
28 Mike Bielecki RR	.15	.07
29 Steve Lyons RR	.40	.18
30 Jeff Reed RR	.15	.07
31 Tony Brewer RR	.15	.07
32 John Morris RR	.15	.07
33 Daryl Boston RR	.15	.07
34 Al Pulido RR	.15	.07
35 Steve Kiefer RR	.15	.07
36 Larry Sheets RR	.15	.07

❏ 37	Scott Bradley RR	.15	.07
❏ 38	Calvin Schiraldi RR	.15	.07
❏ 39	Shawon Dunston RR	1.00	.45
❏ 40	Charlie Mitchell RR	.15	.07
❏ 41	Billy Hatcher RR	.75	.35
❏ 42	Russ Stephans RR	.15	.07
❏ 43	Alejandro Sanchez RR	.15	.07
❏ 44	Steve Jeltz RR	.15	.07
❏ 45	Jim Traber RR	.15	.07
❏ 46	Doug Loman RR	.15	.07
❏ 47	Eddie Murray	1.50	.70
❏ 48	Robin Yount	1.50	.70
❏ 49	Lance Parrish	.40	.18
❏ 50	Jim Rice	.40	.18
❏ 51	Dave Winfield	1.50	.70
❏ 52	Fernando Valenzuela	.40	.18
❏ 53	George Brett	3.00	1.35
❏ 54	Dave Kingman	.40	.18
❏ 55	Gary Carter	1.50	.70
❏ 56	Buddy Bell	.40	.18
❏ 57	Reggie Jackson	2.00	.90
❏ 58	Harold Baines	.40	.18
❏ 59	Ozzie Smith	2.00	.90
❏ 60	Nolan Ryan UER	8.00	3.60
	(Set strikeout record in 1973, not 1972)		
❏ 61	Mike Schmidt	2.50	1.10
❏ 62	Dave Parker	.40	.18
❏ 63	Tony Gwynn	6.00	2.70
❏ 64	Tony Pena	.15	.07
❏ 65	Jack Clark	.40	.18
❏ 66	Dale Murphy	1.50	.70
❏ 67	Ryne Sandberg	3.00	1.35
❏ 68	Keith Hernandez	.40	.18
❏ 69	Alvin Davis	.40	.18
❏ 70	Kent Hrbek	.40	.18
❏ 71	Willie Upshaw	.15	.07
❏ 72	Dave Engle	.15	.07
❏ 73	Alfredo Griffin	.15	.07
❏ 74A	Jack Perconte	.15	.07
	(Career Highlights takes four lines)		
❏ 74B	Jack Perconte	.15	.07
	(Career Highlights takes three lines)		
❏ 75	Jesse Orosco	.15	.07
❏ 76	Jody Davis	.15	.07
❏ 77	Bob Horner	.15	.07
❏ 78	Larry McWilliams	.15	.07
❏ 79	Joel Youngblood	.15	.07
❏ 80	Alan Wiggins	.15	.07
❏ 81	Ron Oester	.15	.07
❏ 82	Ozzie Virgil	.15	.07
❏ 83	Ricky Horton	.15	.07
❏ 84	Bill Doran	.15	.07
❏ 85	Rod Carew	1.50	.70
❏ 86	LaMarr Hoyt	.15	.07
❏ 87	Tim Wallach	.40	.18
❏ 88	Mike Flanagan	.15	.07
❏ 89	Jim Sundberg	.15	.07
❏ 90	Chet Lemon	.15	.07
❏ 91	Bob Stanley	.15	.07
❏ 92	Willie Randolph	.40	.18
❏ 93	Bill Russell	.15	.07
❏ 94	Julio Franco	.75	.35
❏ 95	Dan Quisenberry	.40	.18
❏ 96	Bill Caudill	.15	.07
❏ 97	Bill Gullickson	.15	.07
❏ 98	Danny Darwin	.15	.07
❏ 99	Curtis Wilkerson	.15	.07
❏ 100	Bud Black	.15	.07
❏ 101	Tony Phillips	.15	.07
❏ 102	Tony Bernazard	.15	.07
❏ 103	Jay Howell	.15	.07
❏ 104	Burt Hooton	.15	.07
❏ 105	Milt Wilcox	.15	.07
❏ 106	Rich Dauer	.15	.07
❏ 107	Don Sutton	1.50	.70
❏ 108	Mike Witt	.15	.07
❏ 109	Bruce Sutter	.40	.18
❏ 110	Enos Cabell	.15	.07
❏ 111	John Denny	.15	.07
❏ 112	Dave Dravecky	.40	.18
❏ 113	Marvell Wynne	.15	.07
❏ 114	Johnnie LeMaster	.15	.07
❏ 115	Chuck Porter	.15	.07
❏ 116	John Gibbons	.15	.07
❏ 117	Keith Moreland	.15	.07
❏ 118	Darnell Coles	.15	.07
❏ 119	Dennis Lamp	.15	.07
❏ 120	Ron Davis	.15	.07
❏ 121	Nick Esasky	.15	.07
❏ 122	Vance Law	.15	.07
❏ 123	Gary Roenicke	.15	.07
❏ 124	Bill Schroeder	.15	.07
❏ 125	Dave Rozema	.15	.07
❏ 126	Bobby Meacham	.15	.07
❏ 127	Marty Barrett	.15	.07
❏ 128	R.J. Reynolds	.15	.07
❏ 129	Ernie Camacho UER	.15	.07
	(Photo actually Rich Thompson)		
❏ 130	Jorge Orta	.15	.07
❏ 131	Lary Sorensen	.15	.07
❏ 132	Terry Francona	.15	.07
❏ 133	Fred Lynn	.40	.18
❏ 134	Bob Jones	.15	.07
❏ 135	Jerry Hairston	.15	.07
❏ 136	Kevin Bass	.15	.07
❏ 137	Garry Maddox	.15	.07
❏ 138	Dave LaPoint	.15	.07
❏ 139	Kevin McReynolds	.40	.18
❏ 140	Wayne Krenchicki	.15	.07
❏ 141	Rafael Ramirez	.15	.07
❏ 142	Rod Scurry	.15	.07
❏ 143	Greg Minton	.15	.07
❏ 144	Tim Stoddard	.15	.07
❏ 145	Steve Henderson	.15	.07
❏ 146	George Bell	.40	.18
❏ 147	Dave Meier	.15	.07
❏ 148	Sammy Stewart	.15	.07
❏ 149	Mark Brouhard	.15	.07
❏ 150	Larry Herndon	.15	.07
❏ 151	Oil Can Boyd	.15	.07
❏ 152	Brian Dayett	.15	.07
❏ 153	Tom Niedenfuer	.15	.07
❏ 154	Brook Jacoby	.15	.07
❏ 155	Onix Concepcion	.15	.07
❏ 156	Tim Conroy	.15	.07
❏ 157	Joe Hesketh	.15	.07
❏ 158	Brian Downing	.15	.07
❏ 159	Tommy Dunbar	.15	.07
❏ 160	Marc Hill	.15	.07
❏ 161	Phil Garner	.40	.18
❏ 162	Jerry Davis	.15	.07
❏ 163	Bill Campbell	.15	.07
❏ 164	John Franco	1.50	.70
❏ 165	Len Barker	.15	.07
❏ 166	Benny Distefano	.15	.07
❏ 167	George Frazier	.15	.07
❏ 168	Tito Landrum	.15	.07
❏ 169	Cal Ripken	8.00	3.60
❏ 170	Cecil Cooper	.40	.18
❏ 171	Alan Trammell	.75	.35
❏ 172	Wade Boggs	2.00	.90
❏ 173	Don Baylor	.40	.18
❏ 174	Pedro Guerrero	.40	.18
❏ 175	Frank White	.15	.07
❏ 176	Rickey Henderson	2.00	.90
❏ 177	Charlie Lea	.15	.07
❏ 178	Pete O'Brien	.15	.07
❏ 179	Doug DeCinces	.15	.07
❏ 180	Ron Kittle	.15	.07
❏ 181	George Hendrick	.15	.07
❏ 182	Joe Niekro	.15	.07
❏ 183	Juan Samuel	.15	.07
❏ 184	Mario Soto	.15	.07
❏ 185	Rich Gossage	.40	.18
❏ 186	Johnny Ray	.15	.07
❏ 187	Bob Brenly	.15	.07
❏ 188	Craig McMurtry	.15	.07
❏ 189	Leon Durham	.15	.07
❏ 190	Dwight Gooden	2.00	.90
❏ 191	Barry Bonnell	.15	.07
❏ 192	Tim Teufel	.15	.07
❏ 193	Dave Stieb	.40	.18
❏ 194	Mickey Hatcher	.15	.07
❏ 195	Jesse Barfield	.40	.18
❏ 196	Al Cowens	.15	.07
❏ 197	Hubie Brooks	.15	.07
❏ 198	Steve Trout	.15	.07
❏ 199	Glenn Hubbard	.15	.07
❏ 200	Bill Madlock	.40	.18
❏ 201	Jeff D. Robinson	.15	.07
❏ 202	Eric Show	.15	.07
❏ 203	Dave Concepcion	.40	.18
❏ 204	Ivan DeJesus	.15	.07
❏ 205	Neil Allen	.15	.07
❏ 206	Jerry Mumphrey	.15	.07
❏ 207	Mike C. Brown	.15	.07
❏ 208	Carlton Fisk	1.50	.70
❏ 209	Bryn Smith	.15	.07
❏ 210	Tippy Martinez	.15	.07
❏ 211	Dion James	.15	.07
❏ 212	Willie Hernandez	.15	.07
❏ 213	Mike Easler	.15	.07
❏ 214	Ron Guidry	.40	.18
❏ 215	Rick Honeycutt	.15	.07
❏ 216	Brett Butler	.40	.18
❏ 217	Larry Gura	.15	.07
❏ 218	Ray Burris	.15	.07
❏ 219	Steve Rogers	.15	.07
❏ 220	Frank Tanana UER	.15	.07
	(Bats Left listed twice on card back)		
❏ 221	Ned Yost	.15	.07
❏ 222	Bret Saberhagen UER	1.50	.70
	(18 career IP on back)		
❏ 223	Mike Davis	.15	.07
❏ 224	Bert Blyleven	.40	.18
❏ 225	Steve Kemp	.15	.07
❏ 226	Jerry Reuss	.15	.07
❏ 227	Darrell Evans UER	.40	.18
	(80 homers in 1980)		
❏ 228	Wayne Gross	.15	.07
❏ 229	Jim Gantner	.15	.07
❏ 230	Bob Boone	.40	.18
❏ 231	Lonnie Smith	.15	.07
❏ 232	Frank DiPino	.15	.07
❏ 233	Jerry Koosman	.15	.07
❏ 234	Graig Nettles	.40	.18
❏ 235	John Tudor	.15	.07
❏ 236	John Rabb	.15	.07
❏ 237	Rick Manning	.15	.07
❏ 238	Mike Fitzgerald	.15	.07
❏ 239	Gary Matthews	.15	.07
❏ 240	Jim Presley	.40	.18
❏ 241	Dave Collins	.15	.07
❏ 242	Gary Gaetti	.40	.18
❏ 243	Dann Bilardello	.15	.07
❏ 244	Rudy Law	.15	.07
❏ 245	John Lowenstein	.15	.07
❏ 246	Tom Tellmann	.15	.07
❏ 247	Howard Johnson	.40	.18
❏ 248	Ray Fontenot	.15	.07
❏ 249	Tony Armas	.15	.07
❏ 250	Candy Maldonado	.15	.07
❏ 251	Mike Jeffcoat	.15	.07
❏ 252	Dane Iorg	.15	.07
❏ 253	Bruce Bochte	.15	.07
❏ 254	Pete Rose	3.00	1.35
❏ 255	Don Aase	.15	.07
❏ 256	George Wright	.15	.07
❏ 257	Britt Burns	.15	.07
❏ 258	Mike Scott	.15	.07
❏ 259	Len Matuszek	.15	.07
❏ 260	Dave Rucker	.15	.07
❏ 261	Craig Lefferts	.15	.07
❏ 262	Jay Tibbs	.15	.07
❏ 263	Bruce Benedict	.15	.07
❏ 264	Don Robinson	.15	.07
❏ 265	Gary Lavelle	.15	.07
❏ 266	Scott Sanderson	.15	.07
❏ 267	Matt Young	.15	.07
❏ 268	Ernie Whitt	.15	.07
❏ 269	Houston Jimenez	.15	.07
❏ 270	Ken Dixon	.15	.07
❏ 271	Pete Ladd	.15	.07
❏ 272	Juan Berenguer	.15	.07
❏ 273	Roger Clemens	40.00	18.00
❏ 274	Rick Cerone	.15	.07
❏ 275	Dave Anderson	.15	.07
❏ 276	George Vukovich	.15	.07
❏ 277	Greg Pryor	.15	.07
❏ 278	Mike Warren	.15	.07
❏ 279	Bob James	.15	.07
❏ 280	Bobby Grich	.40	.18
❏ 281	Mike Mason	.15	.07

282	Ron Reed	.15	.07
283	Alan Ashby	.15	.07
284	Mark Thurmond	.15	.07
285	Joe Lefebvre	.15	.07
286	Ted Power	.15	.07
287	Chris Chambliss	.40	.18
288	Lee Tunnell	.15	.07
289	Rich Bordi	.15	.07
290	Glenn Brummer	.15	.07
291	Mike Boddicker	.15	.07
292	Rollie Fingers	1.50	.70
293	Lou Whitaker	.75	.35
294	Dwight Evans	.40	.18
295	Don Mattingly	4.00	1.80
296	Mike Marshall	.15	.07
297	Willie Wilson	.15	.07
298	Mike Heath	.15	.07
299	Tim Raines	.40	.18
300	Larry Parrish	.15	.07
301	Geoff Zahn	.15	.07
302	Rich Dotson	.15	.07
303	David Green	.15	.07
304	Jose Cruz	.40	.18
305	Steve Carlton	1.50	.70
306	Gary Redus	.15	.07
307	Steve Garvey	.75	.35
308	Jose DeLeon	.15	.07
309	Randy Lerch	.15	.07
310	Claudell Washington	.15	.07
311	Lee Smith	.75	.35
312	Darryl Strawberry	1.50	.70
313	Jim Beattie	.15	.07
314	John Butcher	.15	.07
315	Damaso Garcia	.15	.07
316	Mike Smithson	.15	.07
317	Luis Leal	.15	.07
318	Ken Phelps	.15	.07
319	Wally Backman	.15	.07
320	Ron Cey	.40	.18
321	Brad Komminsk	.15	.07
322	Jason Thompson	.15	.07
323	Frank Williams	.15	.07
324	Tim Lollar	.15	.07
325	Eric Davis	3.00	1.35
326	Von Hayes	.15	.07
327	Andy Van Slyke	.75	.35
328	Craig Reynolds	.15	.07
329	Dick Schofield	.15	.07
330	Scott Fletcher	.15	.07
331	Jeff Reardon	.40	.18
332	Rick Dempsey	.15	.07
333	Ben Oglivie	.15	.07
334	Dan Petry	.15	.07
335	Jackie Gutierrez	.15	.07
336	Dave Righetti	.40	.18
337	Alejandro Pena	.15	.07
338	Mel Hall	.15	.07
339	Pat Sheridan	.15	.07
340	Keith Atherton	.15	.07
341	David Palmer	.15	.07
342	Gary Ward	.15	.07
343	Dave Stewart	.40	.18
344	Mark Gubicza	.40	.18
345	Carney Lansford	.40	.18
346	Jerry Willard	.15	.07
347	Ken Griffey	.40	.18
348	Franklin Stubbs	.15	.07
349	Aurelio Lopez	.15	.07
350	Al Bumbry	.15	.07
351	Charlie Moore	.15	.07
352	Luis Sanchez	.15	.07
353	Darrell Porter	.15	.07
354	Bill Dawley	.15	.07
355	Charles Hudson	.15	.07
356	Garry Templeton	.15	.07
357	Cecilio Guante	.15	.07
358	Jeff Leonard	.15	.07
359	Paul Molitor	1.50	.70
360	Ron Gardenhire	.15	.07
361	Larry Bowa	.40	.18
362	Bob Kearney	.15	.07
363	Garth Iorg	.15	.07
364	Tom Brunansky	.40	.18
365	Brad Gulden	.15	.07
366	Greg Walker	.15	.07
367	Mike Young	.15	.07
368	Rick Waits	.15	.07
369	Doug Bair	.15	.07
370	Bob Shirley	.15	.07
371	Bob Ojeda	.15	.07
372	Bob Welch	.15	.07
373	Neal Heaton	.15	.07
374	Danny Jackson UER	.15	.07
	(Photo actually Frank Wills)		
375	Donnie Hill	.15	.07
376	Mike Stenhouse	.15	.07
377	Bruce Kison	.15	.07
378	Wayne Tolleson	.15	.07
379	Floyd Bannister	.15	.07
380	Vern Ruhle	.15	.07
381	Tim Corcoran	.15	.07
382	Kurt Kepshire	.15	.07
383	Bobby Brown	.15	.07
384	Dave Van Gorder	.15	.07
385	Rick Mahler	.15	.07
386	Lee Mazzilli	.15	.07
387	Bill Laskey	.15	.07
388	Thad Bosley	.15	.07
389	Al Chambers	.15	.07
390	Tony Fernandez	.75	.35
391	Ron Washington	.15	.07
392	Bill Swaggerty	.15	.07
393	Bob L. Gibson	.15	.07
394	Marty Castillo	.15	.07
395	Steve Crawford	.15	.07
396	Clay Christiansen	.15	.07
397	Bob Bailor	.15	.07
398	Mike Hargrove	.40	.18
399	Charlie Leibrandt	.15	.07
400	Tom Burgmeier	.15	.07
401	Razor Shines	.15	.07
402	Rob Wilfong	.15	.07
403	Tom Henke	.40	.18
404	Al Jones	.15	.07
405	Mike LaCoss	.15	.07
406	Luis DeLeon	.15	.07
407	Greg Gross	.15	.07
408	Tom Hume	.15	.07
409	Rick Camp	.15	.07
410	Milt May	.15	.07
411	Henry Cotto	.15	.07
412	David Von Ohlen	.15	.07
413	Scott McGregor	.15	.07
414	Ted Simmons	.40	.18
415	Jack Morris	.40	.18
416	Bill Buckner	.40	.18
417	Butch Wynegar	.15	.07
418	Steve Sax	.40	.18
419	Steve Balboni	.15	.07
420	Dwayne Murphy	.15	.07
421	Andre Dawson	1.50	.70
422	Charlie Hough	.40	.18
423	Tommy John	.75	.35
424A	Tom Seaver ERR	2.00	.90
	(Photo actually Floyd Bannister)		
424B	Tom Seaver COR	20.00	9.00
425	Tom Herr	.40	.18
426	Terry Puhl	.15	.07
427	Al Holland	.15	.07
428	Eddie Milner	.15	.07
429	Terry Kennedy	.15	.07
430	John Candelaria	.15	.07
431	Manny Trillo	.15	.07
432	Ken Oberkfell	.15	.07
433	Rick Sutcliffe	.40	.18
434	Ron Darling	.40	.18
435	Spike Owen	.15	.07
436	Frank Viola	.40	.18
437	Lloyd Moseby	.15	.07
438	Kirby Puckett	20.00	9.00
439	Jim Clancy	.15	.07
440	Mike Moore	.15	.07
441	Doug Sisk	.15	.07
442	Dennis Eckersley	1.50	.70
443	Gerald Perry	.15	.07
444	Dale Berra	.15	.07
445	Dusty Baker	.40	.18
446	Ed Whitson	.15	.07
447	Cesar Cedeno	.40	.18
448	Rick Schu	.15	.07
449	Joaquin Andujar	.15	.07
450	Mark Bailey	.15	.07
451	Ron Romanick	.15	.07
452	Julio Cruz	.15	.07
453	Miguel Dilone	.15	.07
454	Storm Davis	.15	.07
455	Jaime Cocanower	.15	.07
456	Barbaro Garbey	.15	.07
457	Rich Gedman	.15	.07
458	Phil Niekro	1.50	.70
459	Mike Scioscia	.15	.07
460	Pat Tabler	.15	.07
461	Darryl Motley	.15	.07
462	Chris Codiroli	.15	.07
463	Doug Flynn	.15	.07
464	Billy Sample	.15	.07
465	Mickey Rivers	.15	.07
466	John Wathan	.15	.07
467	Bill Krueger	.15	.07
468	Andre Thornton	.15	.07
469	Rex Hudler	.15	.07
470	Sid Bream	.40	.18
471	Kirk Gibson	.40	.18
472	John Shelby	.15	.07
473	Moose Haas	.15	.07
474	Doug Corbett	.15	.07
475	Willie McGee	.40	.18
476	Bob Knepper	.15	.07
477	Kevin Gross	.15	.07
478	Carmelo Martinez	.15	.07
479	Kent Tekulve	.15	.07
480	Chili Davis	.40	.18
481	Bobby Clark	.15	.07
482	Mookie Wilson	.40	.18
483	Dave Owen	.15	.07
484	Ed Nunez	.15	.07
485	Rance Mulliniks	.15	.07
486	Ken Schrom	.15	.07
487	Jeff Russell	.15	.07
488	Tom Paciorek	.40	.18
489	Dan Ford	.15	.07
490	Mike Caldwell	.15	.07
491	Scottie Earl	.15	.07
492	Jose Rijo	.75	.35
493	Bruce Hurst	.15	.07
494	Ken Landreaux	.15	.07
495	Mike Fischlin	.15	.07
496	Don Slaught	.15	.07
497	Steve McCatty	.15	.07
498	Gary Lucas	.15	.07
499	Gary Pettis	.15	.07
500	Marvis Foley	.15	.07
501	Mike Squires	.15	.07
502	Jim Pankovits	.15	.07
503	Luis Aguayo	.15	.07
504	Ralph Citarella	.15	.07
505	Bruce Bochy	.15	.07
506	Bob Owchinko	.15	.07
507	Pascual Perez	.15	.07
508	Lee Lacy	.15	.07
509	Atlee Hammaker	.15	.07
510	Bob Demier	.15	.07
511	Ed VandeBerg	.15	.07
512	Cliff Johnson	.15	.07
513	Len Whitehouse	.15	.07
514	Dennis Martinez	.40	.18
515	Ed Romero	.15	.07
516	Rusty Kuntz	.15	.07
517	Rick Miller	.15	.07
518	Dennis Rasmussen	.15	.07
519	Steve Yeager	.15	.07
520	Chris Bando	.15	.07
521	U.L. Washington	.15	.07
522	Curt Young	.15	.07
523	Angel Salazar	.15	.07
524	Curt Kaufman	.15	.07
525	Odell Jones	.15	.07
526	Juan Agosto	.15	.07
527	Denny Walling	.15	.07
528	Andy Hawkins	.15	.07
529	Sixto Lezcano	.15	.07
530	Skeeter Barnes	.15	.07
531	Randy Johnson	.15	.07
532	Jim Morrison	.15	.07
533	Warren Brusstar	.15	.07
534A	Jeff Pendleton ERR	1.50	.70

(Wrong first name)		
❏ 534B Terry Pendleton COR	2.00	.90
❏ 535 Vic Rodriguez	.15	.07
❏ 536 Bob McClure	.15	.07
❏ 537 Dave Bergman	.15	.07
❏ 538 Mark Clear	.15	.07
❏ 539 Mike Pagliarulo	.15	.07
❏ 540 Terry Whitfield	.15	.07
❏ 541 Joe Beckwith	.15	.07
❏ 542 Jeff Burroughs	.15	.07
❏ 543 Dan Schatzeder	.15	.07
❏ 544 Donnie Scott	.15	.07
❏ 545 Jim Slaton	.15	.07
❏ 546 Greg Luzinski	.40	.18
❏ 547 Mark Salas	.15	.07
❏ 548 Dave Smith	.15	.07
❏ 549 John Wockenfuss	.15	.07
❏ 550 Frank Pastore	.15	.07
❏ 551 Tim Flannery	.15	.07
❏ 552 Rick Rhoden	.15	.07
❏ 553 Mark Davis	.15	.07
❏ 554 Jeff Dedmon	.15	.07
❏ 555 Gary Woods	.15	.07
❏ 556 Danny Heep	.15	.07
❏ 557 Mark Langston	.75	.35
❏ 558 Darrell Brown	.15	.07
❏ 559 Jimmy Key	1.50	.70
❏ 560 Rick Lysander	.15	.07
❏ 561 Doyle Alexander	.15	.07
❏ 562 Mike Stanton	.15	.07
❏ 563 Sid Fernandez	.40	.18
❏ 564 Richie Hebner	.15	.07
❏ 565 Alex Trevino	.15	.07
❏ 566 Brian Harper	.15	.07
❏ 567 Dan Gladden	.40	.18
❏ 568 Luis Salazar	.15	.07
❏ 569 Tom Foley	.15	.07
❏ 570 Larry Andersen	.15	.07
❏ 571 Danny Cox	.15	.07
❏ 572 Joe Sambito	.15	.07
❏ 573 Juan Beniquez	.15	.07
❏ 574 Joel Skinner	.15	.07
❏ 575 Randy St.Claire	.15	.07
❏ 576 Floyd Rayford	.15	.07
❏ 577 Roy Howell	.15	.07
❏ 578 John Grubb	.15	.07
❏ 579 Ed Jurak	.15	.07
❏ 580 John Montefusco	.15	.07
❏ 581 Orel Hershiser	2.00	.90
❏ 582 Tom Waddell	.15	.07
❏ 583 Mark Huismann	.15	.07
❏ 584 Joe Morgan	1.50	.70
❏ 585 Jim Wohlford	.15	.07
❏ 586 Dave Schmidt	.15	.07
❏ 587 Jeff Kunkel	.15	.07
❏ 588 Hal McRae	.40	.18
❏ 589 Bill Almon	.15	.07
❏ 590 Carmen Castillo	.15	.07
❏ 591 Omar Moreno	.15	.07
❏ 592 Ken Howell	.15	.07
❏ 593 Tom Brookens	.15	.07
❏ 594 Joe Nolan	.15	.07
❏ 595 Willie Lozado	.15	.07
❏ 596 Tom Nieto	.15	.07
❏ 597 Walt Terrell	.15	.07
❏ 598 Al Jones	.40	.18
❏ 599 Shane Rawley	.15	.07
❏ 600 Denny Gonzalez	.15	.07
❏ 601 Mark Grant	.15	.07
❏ 602 Mike Armstrong	.15	.07
❏ 603 George Foster	.40	.18
❏ 604 Dave Lopes	.40	.18
❏ 605 Salome Barojas	.15	.07
❏ 606 Roy Lee Jackson	.15	.07
❏ 607 Pete Filson	.15	.07
❏ 608 Duane Walker	.15	.07
❏ 609 Glenn Wilson	.15	.07
❏ 610 Rafael Santana	.15	.07
❏ 611 Roy Smith	.15	.07
❏ 612 Ruppert Jones	.15	.07
❏ 613 Joe Cowley	.15	.07
❏ 614 Al Nipper UER	.15	.07
(Photo actually		
Mike Brown)		
❏ 615 Gene Nelson	.15	.07
❏ 616 Joe Carter	1.50	.70

❏ 617 Ray Knight	.15	.07
❏ 618 Chuck Rainey	.15	.07
❏ 619 Dan Driessen	.15	.07
❏ 620 Daryl Sconiers	.15	.07
❏ 621 Bill Stein	.15	.07
❏ 622 Roy Smalley	.15	.07
❏ 623 Ed Lynch	.15	.07
❏ 624 Jeff Stone	.15	.07
❏ 625 Bruce Berenyi	.15	.07
❏ 626 Kelvin Chapman	.15	.07
❏ 627 Joe Price	.15	.07
❏ 628 Steve Bedrosian	.15	.07
❏ 629 Vic Mata	.15	.07
❏ 630 Mike Krukow	.15	.07
❏ 631 Phil Bradley	.40	.18
❏ 632 Jim Gott	.15	.07
❏ 633 Randy Bush	.15	.07
❏ 634 Tom Browning	.40	.18
❏ 635 Lou Gehrig	1.50	.70
Puzzle Card		
❏ 636 Reid Nichols	.15	.07
❏ 637 Dan Pasqua	.40	.18
❏ 638 German Rivera	.15	.07
❏ 639 Don Schulze	.15	.07
❏ 640A Mike Jones	.15	.07
(Career Highlights,		
takes five lines)		
❏ 640B Mike Jones	.15	.07
(Career Highlights,		
takes four lines)		
❏ 641 Pete Rose	3.00	1.35
❏ 642 Wade Rowdon	.15	.07
❏ 643 Jerry Narron	.15	.07
❏ 644 Darrell Miller	.15	.07
❏ 645 Tim Hulett	.15	.07
❏ 646 Andy McGaffigan	.15	.07
❏ 647 Kurt Bevacqua	.15	.07
❏ 648 John Russell	.15	.07
❏ 649 Ron Robinson	.15	.07
❏ 650 Donnie Moore	.15	.07
❏ 651A Two for the Title	2.00	.90
Dave Winfield		
Don Mattingly		
(Yellow letters)		
❏ 651B Two for the Title	4.00	1.80
Dave Winfield		
Don Mattingly		
(White letters)		
❏ 652 Tim Laudner	.15	.07
❏ 653 Steve Farr	.40	.18
❏ 654 DK Checklist 1-26	.15	.07
(Unnumbered)		
❏ 655 Checklist 27-130	.15	.07
(Unnumbered)		
❏ 656 Checklist 131-234	.15	.07
(Unnumbered)		
❏ 657 Checklist 235-338	.15	.07
(Unnumbered)		
❏ 658 Checklist 339-442	.15	.07
(Unnumbered)		
❏ 659 Checklist 443-546	.15	.07
(Unnumbered)		
❏ 660 Checklist 547-653	.15	.07
(Unnumbered)		

1986 Donruss

	MINT	NRMT
COMPLETE SET (660)	50.00	22.00
COMP.FACT.SET (660)	60.00	27.00
COMMON CARD (1-660)	.10	.05
MINOR STARS	.25	.11
SEMISTARS	.50	.23
UNLISTED STARS	1.00	.45
BEWARE CANSECO COUNTERFEITS		

❏ 1 Kirk Gibson DK	.25	.11
❏ 2 Rich Gossage DK	.25	.11
❏ 3 Willie McGee DK	.25	.11
❏ 4 George Bell DK	.10	.05
❏ 5 Tony Armas DK	.10	.05
❏ 6 Chili Davis DK	.50	.23
❏ 7 Cecil Cooper DK	.10	.05
❏ 8 Mike Boddicker DK	.10	.05
❏ 9 Dave Lopes DK	.10	.11
❏ 10 Bill Doran DK	.10	.05
❏ 11 Bret Saberhagen DK	.25	.11
❏ 12 Brett Butler DK	.10	.05
❏ 13 Harold Baines DK	.50	.23
❏ 14 Mike Davis DK	.10	.05
❏ 15 Tony Perez DK	.25	.11
❏ 16 Willie Randolph DK	.10	.05
❏ 17 Bob Boone DK	.10	.05
❏ 18 Orel Hershiser DK	.25	.11
❏ 19 Johnny Ray DK	.10	.05
❏ 20 Gary Ward DK	.10	.05
❏ 21 Rick Mahler DK	.10	.05
❏ 22 Phil Bradley DK	.10	.05
❏ 23 Jerry Koosman DK	.25	.11
❏ 24 Tom Brunansky DK	.10	.05
❏ 25 Andre Dawson DK	.25	.11
❏ 26 Dwight Gooden DK	1.00	.45
❏ 27 Kal Daniels RR	.25	.11
❏ 28 Fred McGriff RR	8.00	3.60
❏ 29 Cory Snyder RR	.10	.05
❏ 30 Jose Guzman RR	.10	.05
❏ 31 Ty Gainey RR	.10	.05
❏ 32 Johnny Abrego RR	.10	.05
❏ 33 Andres Galarraga RR	6.00	2.70
(No accent)		
❏ 33B Andre's Galarraga RR	6.00	2.70
(Accent over e)		
❏ 34 Dave Shipanoff RR	.10	.05
❏ 35 Mark McLemore RR	1.00	.45
❏ 36 Marty Clary RR	.10	.05
❏ 37 Paul O'Neill RR	4.00	1.80
❏ 38 Danny Tartabull RR	.25	.11 *
❏ 39 Jose Canseco RR	30.00	13.50
❏ 40 Juan Nieves RR	.10	.05
❏ 41 Lance McCullers RR	.10	.05
❏ 42 Rick Surhoff RR	.10	.05
❏ 43 Todd Worrell RR	1.00	.45
❏ 44 Bob Kipper RR	.10	.05
❏ 45 John Habyan RR	.10	.05
❏ 46 Mike Woodard RR	.10	.05
❏ 47 Mike Boddicker	.10	.05
❏ 48 Robin Yount	1.00	.45
❏ 49 Lou Whitaker	.25	.11
❏ 50 Oil Can Boyd	.10	.05
❏ 51 Rickey Henderson	1.25	.55
❏ 52 Mike Marshall	.10	.05
❏ 53 George Brett	2.00	.90
❏ 54 Dave Kingman	.25	.11
❏ 55 Hubie Brooks	.10	.05
❏ 56 Oddibe McDowell	.10	.05
❏ 57 Doug DeCinces	.10	.05
❏ 58 Britt Burns	.10	.05
❏ 59 Ozzie Smith	1.25	.55
❏ 60 Jose Cruz	.25	.11
❏ 61 Mike Schmidt	1.50	.70
❏ 62 Pete Rose	2.00	.90
❏ 63 Steve Garvey	.50	.23
❏ 64 Tony Pena	.10	.05
❏ 65 Chili Davis	.50	.23
❏ 66 Dale Murphy	1.00	.45
❏ 67 Ryne Sandberg	1.25	.55
❏ 68 Gary Carter	1.00	.45
❏ 69 Alvin Davis	.10	.05
❏ 70 Kent Hrbek	.25	.11
❏ 71 George Bell	.25	.11
❏ 72 Kirby Puckett	3.00	1.35
❏ 73 Lloyd Moseby	.10	.05
❏ 74 Bob Kearney	.10	.05

75	Dwight Gooden	1.00	.45
76	Gary Matthews	.10	.05
77	Rick Mahler	.10	.05
78	Benny Distefano	.10	.05
79	Jeff Leonard	.10	.05
80	Kevin McReynolds	.25	.11
81	Ron Oester	.10	.05
82	John Russell	.10	.05
83	Tommy Herr	.10	.05
84	Jerry Mumphrey	.10	.05
85	Ron Romanick	.10	.05
86	Daryl Boston	.10	.05
87	Andre Dawson	1.00	.45
88	Eddie Murray	1.00	.45
89	Dion James	.10	.05
90	Chet Lemon	.10	.05
91	Bob Stanley	.10	.05
92	Willie Randolph	.25	.11
93	Mike Scioscia	.10	.05
94	Tom Waddell	.10	.05
95	Danny Jackson	.10	.05
96	Mike Davis	.10	.05
97	Mike Fitzgerald	.10	.05
98	Gary Ward	.10	.05
99	Pete O'Brien	.10	.05
100	Bret Saberhagen	.25	.11
101	Alfredo Griffin	.10	.05
102	Brett Butler	.25	.11
103	Ron Guidry	.25	.11
104	Jerry Reuss	.10	.05
105	Jack Morris	.25	.11
106	Rick Dempsey	.10	.05
107	Ray Burris	.10	.05
108	Brian Downing	.10	.05
109	Willie McGee	.25	.11
110	Bill Doran	.10	.05
111	Kent Tekulve	.10	.05
112	Tony Gwynn	2.50	1.10
113	Marvell Wynne	.10	.05
114	David Green	.10	.05
115	Jim Gantner	.10	.05
116	George Foster	.25	.11
117	Steve Trout	.10	.05
118	Mark Langston	.10	.05
119	Tony Fernandez	.10	.05
120	John Butcher	.10	.05
121	Ron Robinson	.10	.05
122	Dan Spillner	.10	.05
123	Mike Young	.10	.05
124	Paul Molitor	1.00	.45
125	Kirk Gibson	.25	.11
126	Ken Griffey	.25	.11
127	Tony Armas	.10	.05
128	Mariano Duncan	1.00	.45
129	Pat Tabler	.10	.05
130	Frank White	.25	.11
131	Carney Lansford	.25	.11
132	Vance Law	.10	.05
133	Dick Schofield	.10	.05
134	Wayne Tolleson	.10	.05
135	Greg Walker	.10	.05
136	Denny Walling	.10	.05
137	Ozzie Virgil	.10	.05
138	Ricky Horton	.10	.05
139	LaMarr Hoyt	.10	.05
140	Wayne Krenchicki	.10	.05
141	Glenn Hubbard	.10	.05
142	Cecilio Guante	.10	.05
143	Mike Krukow	.10	.05
144	Lee Smith	.50	.23
145	Edwin Nunez	.10	.05
146	Dave Stieb	.10	.05
147	Mike Smithson	.10	.05
148	Ken Dixon	.10	.05
149	Danny Darwin	.10	.05
150	Chris Pittaro	.10	.05
151	Bill Buckner	.25	.11
152	Mike Pagliarulo	.10	.05
153	Bill Russell	.10	.05
154	Brook Jacoby	.10	.05
155	Pat Sheridan	.10	.05
156	Mike Gallego	.25	.11
157	Jim Wohlford	.10	.05
158	Gary Pettis	.10	.05
159	Toby Harrah	.10	.05
160	Richard Dotson	.10	.05
161	Bob Knepper	.10	.05
162	Dave Dravecky	.25	.11
163	Greg Gross	.10	.05
164	Eric Davis	.50	.23
165	Gerald Perry	.10	.05
166	Rick Rhoden	.10	.05
167	Keith Moreland	.10	.05
168	Jack Clark	.25	.11
169	Storm Davis	.10	.05
170	Cecil Cooper	.25	.11
171	Alan Trammell	.50	.23
172	Roger Clemens	5.00	2.20
173	Don Mattingly	2.00	.90
174	Pedro Guerrero	.25	.11
175	Willie Wilson	.10	.05
176	Dwayne Murphy	.10	.05
177	Tim Raines	.25	.11
178	Larry Parrish	.10	.05
179	Mike Witt	.10	.05
180	Harold Baines	.50	.23
181	Vince Coleman UER (BA 2.67 on back)	1.00	.45
182	Jeff Heathcock	.10	.05
183	Steve Carlton	1.00	.45
184	Mario Soto	.10	.05
185	Rich Gossage	.25	.11
186	Johnny Ray	.10	.05
187	Dan Gladden	.10	.05
188	Bob Horner	.10	.05
189	Rick Sutcliffe	.10	.05
190	Keith Hernandez	.25	.11
191	Phil Bradley	.10	.05
192	Tom Brunansky	.10	.05
193	Jesse Barfield	.10	.05
194	Frank Viola	.25	.11
195	Willie Upshaw	.10	.05
196	Jim Beattie	.10	.05
197	Darryl Strawberry	1.00	.45
198	Ron Cey	.25	.11
199	Steve Bedrosian	.10	.05
200	Steve Kemp	.10	.05
201	Manny Trillo	.10	.05
202	Garry Templeton	.10	.05
203	Dave Parker	.25	.11
204	John Denny	.10	.05
205	Terry Pendleton	.50	.23
206	Terry Puhl	.10	.05
207	Bobby Grich	.25	.11
208	Ozzie Guillen	.50	.23
209	Jeff Reardon	.10	.05
210	Cal Ripken	4.00	1.80
211	Bill Schroeder	.10	.05
212	Dan Petry	.10	.05
213	Jim Rice	.25	.11
214	Dave Righetti	.10	.05
215	Fernando Valenzuela	.25	.11
216	Julio Franco	.25	.11
217	Darryl Motley	.10	.05
218	Dave Collins	.10	.05
219	Tim Wallach	.10	.05
220	George Wright	.10	.05
221	Tommy Dunbar	.10	.05
222	Steve Balboni	.10	.05
223	Jay Howell	.10	.05
224	Joe Carter	1.00	.45
225	Ed Whitson	.10	.05
226	Orel Hershiser	.50	.23
227	Willie Hernandez	.10	.05
228	Lee Lacy	.10	.05
229	Rollie Fingers	1.00	.45
230	Bob Boone	.25	.11
231	Joaquin Andujar	.10	.05
232	Craig Reynolds	.10	.05
233	Shane Rawley	.10	.05
234	Eric Show	.10	.05
235	Jose DeLeon	.10	.05
236	Jose Uribe	.10	.05
237	Moose Haas	.10	.05
238	Wally Backman	.10	.05
239	Dennis Eckersley	1.00	.45
240	Mike Moore	.10	.05
241	Damaso Garcia	.10	.05
242	Tim Teufel	.10	.05
243	Dave Concepcion	.25	.11
244	Floyd Bannister	.10	.05
245	Fred Lynn	.25	.11
246	Charlie Moore	.10	.05
247	Walt Terrell	.10	.05
248	Dave Winfield	1.00	.45
249	Dwight Evans	.25	.11
250	Dennis Powell	.10	.05
251	Andre Thornton	.10	.05
252	Onix Concepcion	.10	.05
253	Mike Heath	.10	.05
254A	David Palmer ERR (Position 2B)	.10	.05
254B	David Palmer COR (Position P)	1.00	.45
255	Donnie Moore	.10	.05
256	Curtis Wilkerson	.10	.05
257	Julio Cruz	.10	.05
258	Nolan Ryan	4.00	1.80
259	Jeff Stone	.10	.05
260	John Tudor	.10	.05
261	Mark Thurmond	.10	.05
262	Jay Tibbs	.10	.05
263	Rafael Ramirez	.10	.05
264	Larry McWilliams	.10	.05
265	Mark Davis	.10	.05
266	Bob Dernier	.10	.05
267	Matt Young	.10	.05
268	Jim Clancy	.10	.05
269	Mickey Hatcher	.10	.05
270	Sammy Stewart	.10	.05
271	Bob L. Gibson	.10	.05
272	Nelson Simmons	.10	.05
273	Rich Gedman	.10	.05
274	Butch Wynegar	.10	.05
275	Ken Howell	.10	.05
276	Mel Hall	.10	.05
277	Jim Sundberg	.10	.05
278	Chris Codiroli	.10	.05
279	Herm Winningham	.10	.05
280	Rod Carew	1.00	.45
281	Don Slaught	.10	.05
282	Scott Fletcher	.10	.05
283	Bill Dawley	.10	.05
284	Andy Hawkins	.10	.05
285	Glenn Wilson	.10	.05
286	Nick Esasky	.10	.05
287	Claudell Washington	.10	.05
288	Lee Mazzilli	.10	.05
289	Jody Davis	.10	.05
290	Darrell Porter	.25	.11
291	Scott McGregor	.10	.05
292	Ted Simmons	.25	.11
293	Aurelio Lopez	.10	.05
294	Marty Barrett	.10	.05
295	Dale Berra	.10	.05
296	Greg Brock	.10	.05
297	Charlie Leibrandt	.10	.05
298	Bill Krueger	.10	.05
299	Bryn Smith	.10	.05
300	Burt Hooton	.10	.05
301	Stu Cliburn	.10	.05
302	Luis Salazar	.10	.05
303	Ken Dayley	.10	.05
304	Frank DiPino	.10	.05
305	Von Hayes	.10	.05
306	Gary Redus	.10	.05
307	Craig Lefferts	.10	.05
308	Sammy Khalifa	.10	.05
309	Scott Garrelts	.10	.05
310	Rick Cerone	.10	.05
311	Shawon Dunston	.25	.11
312	Howard Johnson	.25	.11
313	Jim Presley	.10	.05
314	Gary Gaetti	.25	.11
315	Luis Leal	.10	.05
316	Mark Salas	.10	.05
317	Bill Caudill	.10	.05
318	Dave Henderson	.10	.05
319	Rafael Santana	.10	.05
320	Leon Durham	.10	.05
321	Bruce Sutter	.25	.11
322	Jason Thompson	.10	.05
323	Bob Brenly	.10	.05
324	Carmelo Martinez	.10	.05
325	Eddie Milner	.10	.05
326	Juan Samuel	.10	.05
327	Tom Nieto	.10	.05
328	Dave Smith	.10	.05

□ 329 Urbano Lugo	.10	.05
□ 330 Joel Skinner	.10	.05
□ 331 Bill Gullickson	.10	.05
□ 332 Floyd Rayford	.10	.05
□ 333 Ben Oglivie	.10	.05
□ 334 Lance Parrish	.25	.11
□ 335 Jackie Gutierrez	.10	.05
□ 336 Dennis Rasmussen	.10	.05
□ 337 Terry Whitfield	.10	.05
□ 338 Neal Heaton	.10	.05
□ 339 Jorge Orta	.10	.05
□ 340 Donnie Hill	.10	.05
□ 341 Joe Hesketh	.10	.05
□ 342 Charlie Hough	.25	.11
□ 343 Dave Rozema	.10	.05
□ 344 Greg Pryor	.10	.05
□ 345 Mickey Tettleton	1.00	.45
□ 346 George Vukovich	.10	.05
□ 347 Don Baylor	.50	.23
□ 348 Carlos Diaz	.10	.05
□ 349 Barbaro Garbey	.10	.05
□ 350 Larry Sheets	.10	.05
□ 351 Ted Higuera	.25	.11
□ 352 Juan Beniquez	.10	.05
□ 353 Bob Forsch	.10	.05
□ 354 Mark Bailey	.10	.05
□ 355 Larry Andersen	.10	.05
□ 356 Terry Kennedy	.10	.05
□ 357 Don Robinson	.10	.05
□ 358 Jim Gott	.10	.05
□ 359 Earnie Riles	.10	.05
□ 360 John Christensen	.10	.05
□ 361 Ray Fontenot	.10	.05
□ 362 Spike Owen	.10	.05
□ 363 Jim Acker	.10	.05
□ 364 Ron Davis	.10	.05
□ 365 Tom Hume	.10	.05
□ 366 Carlton Fisk	1.00	.45
□ 367 Nate Snell	.10	.05
□ 368 Rick Manning	.10	.05
□ 369 Darrell Evans	.25	.11
□ 370 Ron Hassey	.10	.05
□ 371 Wade Boggs	1.00	.45
□ 372 Rick Honeycutt	.10	.05
□ 373 Chris Bando	.10	.05
□ 374 Bud Black	.10	.05
□ 375 Steve Henderson	.10	.05
□ 376 Charlie Lea	.10	.05
□ 377 Reggie Jackson	1.25	.55
□ 378 Dave Schmidt	.10	.05
□ 379 Bob James	.10	.05
□ 380 Glenn Davis	.25	.11
□ 381 Tim Corcoran	.10	.05
□ 382 Danny Cox	.10	.05
□ 383 Tim Flannery	.10	.05
□ 384 Tom Browning	.10	.05
□ 385 Rick Camp	.10	.05
□ 386 Jim Morrison	.10	.05
□ 387 Dave LaPoint	.10	.05
□ 388 Dave Lopes	.25	.11
□ 389 Al Cowens	.10	.05
□ 390 Doyle Alexander	.10	.05
□ 391 Tim Laudner	.10	.05
□ 392 Don Aase	.10	.05
□ 393 Jaime Cocanower	.10	.05
□ 394 Randy O'Neal	.10	.05
□ 395 Mike Easler	.10	.05
□ 396 Scott Bradley	.10	.05
□ 397 Tom Niedenfuer	.10	.05
□ 398 Jerry Willard	.10	.05
□ 399 Lonnie Smith	.10	.05
□ 400 Bruce Bochte	.10	.05
□ 401 Terry Francona	.10	.05
□ 402 Jim Slaton	.10	.05
□ 403 Bill Stein	.10	.05
□ 404 Tim Hulett	.10	.05
□ 405 Alan Ashby	.10	.05
□ 406 Tim Stoddard	.10	.05
□ 407 Garry Maddox	.10	.05
□ 408 Ted Power	.10	.05
□ 409 Len Barker	.10	.05
□ 410 Denny Gonzalez	.10	.05
□ 411 George Frazier	.10	.05
□ 412 Andy Van Slyke	.25	.11
□ 413 Jim Dwyer	.10	.05
□ 414 Paul Householder	.10	.05
□ 415 Alejandro Sanchez	.10	.05
□ 416 Steve Crawford	.10	.05
□ 417 Dan Pasqua	.10	.05
□ 418 Enos Cabell	.10	.05
□ 419 Mike Jones	.10	.05
□ 420 Steve Kiefer	.10	.05
□ 421 Tim Burke	.10	.05
□ 422 Mike Mason	.10	.05
□ 423 Ruppert Jones	.10	.05
□ 424 Jerry Hairston	.10	.05
□ 425 Tito Landrum	.10	.05
□ 426 Jeff Calhoun	.10	.05
□ 427 Don Carman	.10	.05
□ 428 Tony Perez	1.00	.45
□ 429 Jerry Davis	.10	.05
□ 430 Bob Walk	.10	.05
□ 431 Brad Wellman	.10	.05
□ 432 Terry Forster	.10	.05
□ 433 Billy Hatcher	.10	.05
□ 434 Clint Hurdle	.10	.05
□ 435 Ivan Calderon	.25	.11
□ 436 Pete Filson	.10	.05
□ 437 Tom Henke	.25	.11
□ 438 Dave Engle	.10	.05
□ 439 Tom Filer	.10	.05
□ 440 Gorman Thomas	.10	.05
□ 441 Rick Aguilera	1.00	.45
□ 442 Scott Sanderson	.10	.05
□ 443 Jeff Dedmon	.10	.05
□ 444 Joe Orsulak	.10	.05
□ 445 Atlee Hammaker	.10	.05
□ 446 Jerry Royster	.10	.05
□ 447 Buddy Bell	.25	.11
□ 448 Dave Rucker	.10	.05
□ 449 Ivan DeJesus	.10	.05
□ 450 Jim Pankovits	.10	.05
□ 451 Jerry Narron	.10	.05
□ 452 Bryan Little	.10	.05
□ 453 Gary Lucas	.10	.05
□ 454 Dennis Martinez	.25	.11
□ 455 Ed Romero	.10	.05
□ 456 Bob Melvin	.10	.05
□ 457 Glenn Hoffman	.10	.05
□ 458 Bob Shirley	.10	.05
□ 459 Bob Welch	.10	.05
□ 460 Carmen Castillo	.10	.05
□ 461 Dave Leeper	.10	.05
□ 462 Tim Birtsas	.10	.05
□ 463 Randy St.Claire	.10	.05
□ 464 Chris Welsh	.10	.05
□ 465 Greg Harris	.10	.05
□ 466 Lynn Jones	.10	.05
□ 467 Dusty Baker	.25	.11
□ 468 Roy Smith	.10	.05
□ 469 Andre Robertson	.10	.05
□ 470 Ken Landreaux	.10	.05
□ 471 Dave Bergman	.10	.05
□ 472 Gary Roenicke	.10	.05
□ 473 Pete Vuckovich	.10	.05
□ 474 Kirk McCaskill	.25	.11
□ 475 Jeff Lahti	.10	.05
□ 476 Mike Scott	.10	.05
□ 477 Darren Daulton	2.00	.90
□ 478 Graig Nettles	.25	.11
□ 479 Bill Almon	.10	.05
□ 480 Greg Minton	.10	.05
□ 481 Randy Ready	.10	.05
□ 482 Len Dykstra	2.00	.90
□ 483 Thad Bosley	.10	.05
□ 484 Harold Reynolds	1.00	.45
□ 485 Al Oliver	.25	.11
□ 486 Roy Smalley	.10	.05
□ 487 John Franco	1.00	.45
□ 488 Juan Agosto	.10	.05
□ 489 Al Pardo	.10	.05
□ 490 Bill Wegman	.10	.05
□ 491 Frank Tanana	.10	.05
□ 492 Brian Fisher	.10	.05
□ 493 Mark Clear	.10	.05
□ 494 Len Matuszek	.10	.05
□ 495 Ramon Romero	.10	.05
□ 496 John Wathan	.10	.05
□ 497 Rob Picciolo	.10	.05
□ 498 U.L. Washington	.10	.05
□ 499 John Candelaria	.10	.05
□ 500 Duane Walker	.10	.05
□ 501 Gene Nelson	.10	.05
□ 502 John Mizerock	.10	.05
□ 503 Luis Aguayo	.10	.05
□ 504 Kurt Kepshire	.10	.05
□ 505 Ed Wojna	.10	.05
□ 506 Joe Price	.10	.05
□ 507 Milt Thompson	.25	.11
□ 508 Junior Ortiz	.10	.05
□ 509 Vida Blue	.25	.11
□ 510 Steve Engel	.10	.05
□ 511 Karl Best	.10	.05
□ 512 Cecil Fielder	2.50	1.10
□ 513 Frank Eufemia	.10	.05
□ 514 Tippy Martinez	.10	.05
□ 515 Billy Joe Robidoux	.10	.05
□ 516 Bill Scherrer	.10	.05
□ 517 Bruce Hurst	.10	.05
□ 518 Rich Bordi	.10	.05
□ 519 Steve Yeager	.10	.05
□ 520 Tony Bernazard	.10	.05
□ 521 Hal McRae	.25	.11
□ 522 Jose Rijo	.10	.05
□ 523 Mitch Webster	.10	.05
□ 524 Jack Howell	.10	.05
□ 525 Alan Bannister	.10	.05
□ 526 Ron Kittle	.10	.05
□ 527 Phil Garner	.25	.11
□ 528 Kurt Bevacqua	.10	.05
□ 529 Kevin Gross	.10	.05
□ 530 Bo Diaz	.10	.05
□ 531 Ken Oberkfell	.10	.05
□ 532 Rick Reuschel	.10	.05
□ 533 Ron Meridith	.10	.05
□ 534 Steve Braun	.10	.05
□ 535 Wayne Gross	.10	.05
□ 536 Ray Searage	.10	.05
□ 537 Tom Brookens	.10	.05
□ 538 Al Nipper	.10	.05
□ 539 Billy Sample	.10	.05
□ 540 Steve Sax	.10	.05
□ 541 Dan Quisenberry	.10	.05
□ 542 Tony Phillips	.10	.05
□ 543 Floyd Youmans	.10	.05
□ 544 Steve Buechele	.25	.11
□ 545 Craig Gerber	.10	.05
□ 546 Joe DeSa	.10	.05
□ 547 Brian Harper	.10	.05
□ 548 Kevin Bass	.10	.05
□ 549 Tom Foley	.10	.05
□ 550 Dave Van Gorder	.10	.05
□ 551 Bruce Bochy	.10	.05
□ 552 R.J. Reynolds	.10	.05
□ 553 Chris Brown	.10	.05
□ 554 Bruce Benedict	.10	.05
□ 555 Warren Brusstar	.10	.05
□ 556 Danny Heep	.10	.05
□ 557 Darnell Coles	.10	.05
□ 558 Greg Gagne	.10	.05
□ 559 Ernie Whitt	.10	.05
□ 560 Ron Washington	.10	.05
□ 561 Jimmy Key	1.00	.45
□ 562 Billy Swift	.10	.05
□ 563 Ron Darling	.10	.05
□ 564 Dick Ruthven	.10	.05
□ 565 Zane Smith	.10	.05
□ 566 Sid Bream	.10	.05
□ 567A Joel Youngblood ERR (Position P)	.10	.05
□ 567B Joel Youngblood COR (Position IF)	1.00	.45
□ 568 Mario Ramirez	.10	.05
□ 569 Tom Runnells	.10	.05
□ 570 Rick Schu	.10	.05
□ 571 Bill Campbell	.10	.05
□ 572 Dickie Thon	.10	.05
□ 573 Al Holland	.10	.05
□ 574 Reid Nichols	.10	.05
□ 575 Bert Roberge	.10	.05
□ 576 Mike Flanagan	.10	.05
□ 577 Tim Leary	.10	.05
□ 578 Mike Laga	.10	.05
□ 579 Steve Lyons	.10	.05
□ 580 Phil Niekro	1.00	.45
□ 581 Gilberto Reyes	.10	.05
□ 582 Jamie Easterly	.10	.05
□ 583 Mark Gubicza	.10	.05

☐ 584 Stan Javier	.25	.11
☐ 585 Bill Laskey	.10	.05
☐ 586 Jeff Russell	.10	.05
☐ 587 Dickie Noles	.10	.05
☐ 588 Steve Farr	.10	.05
☐ 589 Steve Ontiveros	.25	.11
☐ 590 Mike Hargrove	.25	.11
☐ 591 Marty Bystrom	.10	.05
☐ 592 Franklin Stubbs	.10	.05
☐ 593 Larry Herndon	.10	.05
☐ 594 Bill Swaggerty	.10	.05
☐ 595 Carlos Ponce	.10	.05
☐ 596 Pat Perry	.10	.05
☐ 597 Ray Knight	.25	.11
☐ 598 Steve Lombardozzi	.10	.05
☐ 599 Brad Havens	.10	.05
☐ 600 Pat Clements	.10	.05
☐ 601 Joe Niekro	.10	.05
☐ 602 Hank Aaron	1.00	.45
Puzzle Card		
☐ 603 Dwayne Henry	.10	.05
☐ 604 Mookie Wilson	.25	.11
☐ 605 Buddy Biancalana	.10	.05
☐ 606 Rance Mulliniks	.10	.05
☐ 607 Alan Wiggins	.10	.05
☐ 608 Joe Cowley	.10	.05
☐ 609 Tom Seaver	1.25	.55
(Green borders		
on name)		
☐ 609B Tom Seaver	2.00	.90
(Yellow borders		
oh name)		
☐ 610 Neil Allen	.10	.05
☐ 611 Don Sutton	1.00	.45
☐ 612 Fred Toliver	.10	.05
☐ 613 Jay Baller	.10	.05
☐ 614 Marc Sullivan	.10	.05
☐ 615 John Grubb	.10	.05
☐ 616 Bruce Kison	.10	.05
☐ 617 Bill Madlock	.10	.05
☐ 618 Chris Chambliss	.25	.11
☐ 619 Dave Stewart	.25	.11
☐ 620 Tim Lollar	.10	.05
☐ 621 Gary Lavelle	.10	.05
☐ 622 Charles Hudson	.10	.05
☐ 623 Joel Davis	.10	.05
☐ 624 Joe Johnson	.10	.05
☐ 625 Sid Fernandez	.25	.11
☐ 626 Dennis Lamp	.10	.05
☐ 627 Terry Harper	.10	.05
☐ 628 Jack Lazorko	.10	.05
☐ 629 Roger McDowell	.25	.11
☐ 630 Mark Funderburk	.10	.05
☐ 631 Ed Lynch	.10	.05
☐ 632 Rudy Law	.10	.05
☐ 633 Roger Mason	.10	.05
☐ 634 Mike Felder	.10	.05
☐ 635 Ken Schrom	.10	.05
☐ 636 Bob Ojeda	.10	.05
☐ 637 Ed VandeBerg	.10	.05
☐ 638 Bobby Meacham	.10	.05
☐ 639 Cliff Johnson	.10	.05
☐ 640 Garth Iorg	.10	.05
☐ 641 Dan Driessen	.10	.05
☐ 642 Mike Brown OF	.10	.05
☐ 643 John Shelby	.10	.05
☐ 644 Pete Rose	1.00	.45
(Ty-Breaking)		
☐ 645 The Knuckle Brothers	.25	.11
Phil Niekro		
Joe Niekro		
☐ 646 Jesse Orosco	.10	.05
☐ 647 Billy Beane	.10	.05
☐ 648 Cesar Cedeno	.25	.11
☐ 649 Bert Blyleven	.25	.11
☐ 650 Max Venable	.10	.05
☐ 651 Fleet Feet	.10	.05
Vince Coleman		
Willie McGee		
☐ 652 Calvin Schiraldi	.10	.05
☐ 653 King of Kings	1.00	.45
(Pete Rose)		
☐ 654 Diamond Kings CL 1-26	.10	.05
(Unnumbered)		
☐ 655A CL 1: 27-130	.10	.05
(Unnumbered)		

(45 Beane ERR)		
☐ 655B CL 1: 27-130	.10	.05
(Unnumbered)		
(45 Habyan COR)		
☐ 656 CL 2: 131-234	.10	.05
(Unnumbered)		
☐ 657 CL 3: 235-338	.10	.05
(Unnumbered)		
☐ 658 CL 4: 339-442	.10	.05
(Unnumbered)		
☐ 659 CL 5: 443-546	.10	.05
(Unnumbered)		
☐ 660 CL 6: 547-653	.10	.05
(Unnumbered)		

1986 Donruss Rookies

KELLY GRUBER

	MINT	NRMT
COMP.FACT.SET (56)	30.00	13.50
COMMON CARD (1-56)	.10	.05
MINOR STARS	.25	.11
SEMISTARS	.50	.23
UNLISTED STARS	1.00	.45
☐ 1 Wally Joyner	1.00	.45
☐ 2 Tracy Jones	.10	.05
☐ 3 Allan Anderson	.10	.05
☐ 4 Ed Correa	.10	.05
☐ 5 Reggie Williams	.10	.05
☐ 6 Charlie Kerfeld	.10	.05
☐ 7 Andres Galarraga	1.50	.70
☐ 8 Bob Tewksbury	.25	.11
☐ 9 Al Newman	.10	.11
☐ 10 Andres Thomas	.10	.05
☐ 11 Barry Bonds	15.00	6.75
☐ 12 Juan Nieves	.10	.05
☐ 13 Mark Eichhorn	.10	.05
☐ 14 Dan Plesac	.10	.05
☐ 15 Cory Snyder	.10	.05
☐ 16 Kelly Gruber	.10	.05
☐ 17 Kevin Mitchell	1.00	.45
☐ 18 Steve Lombardozzi	.10	.05
☐ 19 Mitch Williams	.25	.11
☐ 20 John Cerutti	.10	.05
☐ 21 Todd Worrell	1.00	.45
☐ 22 Jose Canseco	8.00	3.60
☐ 23 Pete Incaviglia	.10	.05
☐ 24 Jose Guzman	.10	.05
☐ 25 Scott Bailes	.10	.05
☐ 26 Greg Mathews	.10	.05
☐ 27 Eric King	.10	.05
☐ 28 Paul Assenmacher	.10	.05
☐ 29 Jeff Sellers	.10	.05
☐ 30 Bobby Bonilla	1.50	.70
☐ 31 Doug Drabek	1.00	.45
☐ 32 Will Clark UER	3.00	1.35
(Listed as throwing		
right, should be left)		
☐ 33 Bip Roberts	1.00	.45
☐ 34 Jim Deshaies	.10	.05
☐ 35 Mike LaValliere	.10	.05
☐ 36 Scott Bankhead	.10	.05
☐ 37 Dale Sveum	.10	.05
☐ 38 Bo Jackson	2.50	1.10
☐ 39 Robby Thompson	.25	.11
☐ 40 Eric Plunk	.10	.05
☐ 41 Bill Bathe	.10	.05
☐ 42 John Kruk	1.00	.45

☐ 43 Andy Allanson	.10	.05
☐ 44 Mark Portugal	.50	.23
☐ 45 Danny Tartabull	.25	.11
☐ 46 Bob Kipper	.10	.05
☐ 47 Gene Walter	.10	.05
☐ 48 Rey Quinones UER	.10	.05
(Misspelled Quinonez)		
☐ 49 Bobby Witt	.50	.23
☐ 50 Bill Mooneyham	.10	.05
☐ 51 John Cangelosi	.10	.05
☐ 52 Ruben Sierra	1.00	.45
☐ 53 Rob Woodward	.10	.05
☐ 54 Ed Hearn	.10	.05
☐ 55 Joel McKeon	.10	.05
☐ 56 Checklist 1-56	.10	.05

1986 Donruss Highlights

	MINT	NRMT
COMP.FACT.SET (56)	6.00	2.70
COMMON CARD (1-56)	.10	.05
MINOR STARS	.15	.07
SEMISTARS	.25	.11
UNLISTED STARS	.40	.18
DISTRIBUTED IN FACTORY SET ONLY		
☐ 1 Will Clark	1.00	.45
☐ 2 Jose Rijo	.10	.05
☐ 3 George Brett	.50	.23
☐ 4 Mike Schmidt	.50	.23
☐ 5 Roger Clemens	.75	.35
☐ 6 Roger Clemens	.75	.35
☐ 7 Kirby Puckett	.50	.23
☐ 8 Dwight Gooden	.40	.18
☐ 9 Johnny Ray	.10	.05
☐ 10 Mickey Mantle	1.00	.45
Reggie Jackson		
☐ 11 Wade Boggs	.40	.18
☐ 12 Don Aase	.10	.05
☐ 13 Wade Boggs	.40	.18
☐ 14 Jeff Reardon	.10	.05
☐ 15 Hubie Brooks	.10	.05
☐ 16 Don Sutton	.40	.18
☐ 17 Roger Clemens	.75	.35
☐ 18 Roger Clemens	.75	.35
☐ 19 Kent Hrbek	.15	.07
☐ 20 Rick Rhoden	.10	.05
☐ 21 Kevin Bass	.10	.05
☐ 22 Bob Horner	.10	.05
☐ 23 Wally Joyner	.40	.18
☐ 24 Darryl Strawberry	.40	.18
☐ 25 Fernando Valenzuela	.15	.07
☐ 26 Roger Clemens	.75	.35
☐ 27 Jack Morris	.25	.11
☐ 28 Scott Fletcher	.10	.05
☐ 29 Todd Worrell	.15	.07
☐ 30 Eric Davis	.25	.11
☐ 31 Bert Blyleven	.15	.07
☐ 32 Bobby Doerr	.15	.07
☐ 33 Ernie Lombardi	.15	.07
☐ 34 Willie McCovey	.40	.18
☐ 35 Steve Carlton	.40	.18
☐ 36 Mike Schmidt	.50	.23
☐ 37 Juan Samuel	.10	.05
☐ 38 Mike Witt	.10	.05
☐ 39 Doug DeCinces	.10	.05
☐ 40 Bill Gullickson	.10	.05
☐ 41 Dale Murphy	.40	.18

❑ 42	Joe Carter	.40	.18
❑ 43	Bo Jackson	.40	.18
❑ 44	Joe Cowley	.10	.05
❑ 45	Jim Deshaies	.10	.05
❑ 46	Mike Scott	.10	.05
❑ 47	Bruce Hurst	.10	.05
❑ 48	Don Mattingly	.50	.23
❑ 49	Mike Krukow	.10	.05
❑ 50	Steve Sax	.10	.05
❑ 51	John Cangelosi	.10	.05
❑ 52	Dave Righetti	.10	.05
❑ 53	Don Mattingly	.50	.23
❑ 54	Todd Worrell	.15	.07
❑ 55	Jose Canseco	4.00	1.80
❑ 56	Checklist Card	.10	.05

1987 Donruss

	MINT	NRMT
COMPLETE SET (660)	70.00	32.00
COMP.FACT.SET (660)	80.00	36.00
COMMON CARD (1-660)	.10	.05
MINOR STARS	.20	.09
UNLISTED STARS	.40	.18

❑ 1	Wally Joyner DK	.40	.18
❑ 2	Roger Clemens DK	.60	.25
❑ 3	Dale Murphy DK	.20	.09
❑ 4	Darryl Strawberry DK	.20	.09
❑ 5	Ozzie Smith DK	.20	.09
❑ 6	Jose Canseco DK	1.00	.45
❑ 7	Charlie Hough DK	.10	.05
❑ 8	Brook Jacoby DK	.10	.05
❑ 9	Fred Lynn DK	.20	.09
❑ 10	Rick Rhoden DK	.10	.05
❑ 11	Chris Brown DK	.10	.05
❑ 12	Von Hayes DK	.10	.05
❑ 13	Jack Morris DK	.20	.09
❑ 14A	Kevin McReynolds DK ERR (Yellow strip missing on back)	.40	.18
❑ 14B	Kevin McReynolds DK COR	.10	.05
❑ 15	George Brett DK	.40	.18
❑ 16	Ted Higuera DK	.10	.05
❑ 17	Hubie Brooks DK	.10	.05
❑ 18	Mike Scott DK	.10	.05
❑ 19	Kirby Puckett DK	.40	.18
❑ 20	Dave Winfield DK	.20	.09
❑ 21	Lloyd Moseby DK	.10	.05
❑ 22A	Eric Davis DK ERR (Yellow strip missing on back)	.40	.18
❑ 22B	Eric Davis DK COR	.20	.09
❑ 23	Jim Presley DK	.10	.05
❑ 24	Keith Moreland DK	.10	.05
❑ 25A	Greg Walker DK ERR (Yellow strip missing on back)	.40	.18
❑ 25B	Greg Walker DK COR	.10	.05
❑ 26	Steve Sax DK	.10	.05
❑ 27	DK Checklist 1-26	.10	.05
❑ 28	B.J. Surhoff RR	1.25	.55
❑ 29	Randy Myers RR	.40	.18
❑ 30	Ken Gerhart RR	.10	.05
❑ 31	Benito Santiago RR	.20	.09
❑ 32	Greg Swindell RR	.20	.09
❑ 33	Mike Birkbeck RR	.10	.05
❑ 34	Terry Steinbach RR	.40	.18
❑ 35	Bo Jackson RR	1.25	.55
❑ 36	Greg Maddux UER (middle name misspelled "Allen")	20.00	9.00
❑ 37	Jim Lindeman RR	.10	.05
❑ 38	Devon White RR	.75	.35
❑ 39	Eric Bell RR	.10	.05
❑ 40	Willie Fraser RR	.10	.05
❑ 41	Jerry Browne RR	.10	.05
❑ 42	Chris James RR	.10	.05
❑ 43	Rafael Palmeiro RR	8.00	3.60
❑ 44	Pat Dodson RR	.10	.05
❑ 45	Duane Ward RR	.20	.09
❑ 46	Mark McGwire RR	30.00	13.50
❑ 47	Bruce Fields RR UER (Photo actually Darnell Coles)	.10	.05
❑ 48	Eddie Murray	.40	.18
❑ 49	Ted Higuera	.10	.05
❑ 50	Kirk Gibson	.20	.09
❑ 51	Oil Can Boyd	.10	.05
❑ 52	Don Mattingly	.75	.35
❑ 53	Pedro Guerrero	.10	.05
❑ 54	George Brett	.75	.35
❑ 55	Jose Rijo	.20	.09
❑ 56	Tim Raines	.20	.09
❑ 57	Ed Correa	.10	.05
❑ 58	Mike Witt	.10	.05
❑ 59	Greg Walker	.10	.05
❑ 60	Ozzie Smith	.50	.23
❑ 61	Glenn Davis	.10	.05
❑ 62	Glenn Wilson	.10	.05
❑ 63	Tom Browning	.10	.05
❑ 64	Tony Gwynn	1.00	.45
❑ 65	R.J. Reynolds	.10	.05
❑ 66	Will Clark	1.50	.70
❑ 67	Ozzie Virgil	.10	.05
❑ 68	Rick Sutcliffe	.10	.05
❑ 69	Gary Carter	.30	.14
❑ 70	Mike Moore	.10	.05
❑ 71	Bert Blyleven	.20	.09
❑ 72	Tony Fernandez	.10	.05
❑ 73	Kent Hrbek	.20	.09
❑ 74	Lloyd Moseby	.10	.05
❑ 75	Alvin Davis	.10	.05
❑ 76	Keith Hernandez	.20	.09
❑ 77	Ryne Sandberg	.50	.23
❑ 78	Dale Murphy	.40	.18
❑ 79	Sid Bream	.10	.05
❑ 80	Chris Brown	.10	.05
❑ 81	Steve Garvey	.30	.14
❑ 82	Mario Soto	.10	.05
❑ 83	Shane Rawley	.10	.05
❑ 84	Willie McGee	.20	.09
❑ 85	Jose Cruz	.10	.05
❑ 86	Brian Downing	.10	.05
❑ 87	Ozzie Guillen	.10	.05
❑ 88	Hubie Brooks	.10	.05
❑ 89	Cal Ripken	1.50	.70
❑ 90	Juan Nieves	.10	.05
❑ 91	Lance Parrish	.20	.09
❑ 92	Jim Rice	.20	.09
❑ 93	Ron Guidry	.20	.09
❑ 94	Fernando Valenzuela	.20	.09
❑ 95	Andy Allanson	.10	.05
❑ 96	Willie Wilson	.10	.05
❑ 97	Jose Canseco	2.00	.90
❑ 98	Jeff Reardon	.20	.09
❑ 99	Bobby Witt	.20	.09
❑ 100	Checklist 26-133	.10	.05
❑ 101	Jose Guzman	.10	.05
❑ 102	Steve Balboni	.10	.05
❑ 103	Tony Phillips	.10	.05
❑ 104	Brook Jacoby	.10	.05
❑ 105	Dave Winfield	.40	.18
❑ 106	Orel Hershiser	.20	.09
❑ 107	Lou Whitaker	.20	.09
❑ 108	Fred Lynn	.10	.05
❑ 109	Bill Wegman	.10	.05
❑ 110	Donnie Moore	.10	.05
❑ 111	Jack Clark	.20	.09
❑ 112	Bob Knepper	.10	.05
❑ 113	Von Hayes	.10	.05
❑ 114	Bip Roberts	.40	.18
❑ 115	Tony Pena	.10	.05
❑ 116	Scott Garrelts	.10	.05
❑ 117	Paul Molitor	.40	.18
❑ 118	Darryl Strawberry	.30	.14
❑ 119	Shawon Dunston	.10	.05
❑ 120	Jim Presley	.10	.05
❑ 121	Jesse Barfield	.10	.05
❑ 122	Gary Gaetti	.20	.09
❑ 123	Kurt Stillwell	.10	.05
❑ 124	Joel Davis	.10	.05
❑ 125	Mike Boddicker	.10	.05
❑ 126	Robin Yount	.40	.18
❑ 127	Alan Trammell	.30	.14
❑ 128	Dave Righetti	.10	.05
❑ 129	Dwight Evans	.20	.09
❑ 130	Mike Scioscia	.10	.05
❑ 131	Julio Franco	.10	.05
❑ 132	Bret Saberhagen	.20	.09
❑ 133	Mike Davis	.10	.05
❑ 134	Joe Hesketh	.10	.05
❑ 135	Wally Joyner	.40	.18
❑ 136	Don Slaught	.10	.05
❑ 137	Daryl Boston	.10	.05
❑ 138	Nolan Ryan	1.50	.70
❑ 139	Mike Schmidt	.60	.25
❑ 140	Tommy Herr	.10	.05
❑ 141	Garry Templeton	.10	.05
❑ 142	Kal Daniels	.10	.05
❑ 143	Billy Sample	.10	.05
❑ 144	Johnny Ray	.10	.05
❑ 145	Rob Thompson	.20	.09
❑ 146	Bob Dernier	.10	.05
❑ 147	Danny Tartabull	.10	.05
❑ 148	Ernie Whitt	.10	.05
❑ 149	Kirby Puckett	.75	.35
❑ 150	Mike Young	.10	.05
❑ 151	Ernest Riles	.10	.05
❑ 152	Frank Tanana	.10	.05
❑ 153	Rich Gedman	.10	.05
❑ 154	Willie Randolph	.20	.09
❑ 155	Bill Madlock	.20	.09
❑ 156	Joe Carter	.40	.18
❑ 157	Danny Jackson	.10	.05
❑ 158	Carney Lansford	.20	.09
❑ 159	Bryn Smith	.10	.05
❑ 160	Gary Pettis	.10	.05
❑ 161	Oddibe McDowell	.10	.05
❑ 162	John Cangelosi	.10	.05
❑ 163	Mike Scott	.20	.09
❑ 164	Eric Show	.10	.05
❑ 165	Juan Samuel	.10	.05
❑ 166	Nick Esasky	.10	.05
❑ 167	Zane Smith	.10	.05
❑ 168	Mike C. Brown OF	.10	.05
❑ 169	Keith Moreland	.10	.05
❑ 170	John Tudor	.10	.05
❑ 171	Ken Dixon	.10	.05
❑ 172	Jim Gantner	.10	.05
❑ 173	Jack Morris	.20	.09
❑ 174	Bruce Hurst	.10	.05
❑ 175	Dennis Rasmussen	.10	.05
❑ 176	Mike Marshall	.10	.05
❑ 177	Dan Quisenberry	.20	.09
❑ 178	Eric Plunk	.10	.05
❑ 179	Tim Wallach	.20	.09
❑ 180	Steve Buechele	.10	.05
❑ 181	Don Sutton	.40	.18
❑ 182	Dave Schmidt	.10	.05
❑ 183	Terry Pendleton	.20	.09
❑ 184	Jim Deshaies	.10	.05
❑ 185	Steve Bedrosian	.10	.05
❑ 186	Pete Rose	.75	.35
❑ 187	Dave Dravecky	.20	.09
❑ 188	Rick Reuschel	.10	.05
❑ 189	Dan Gladden	.10	.05
❑ 190	Rick Mahler	.10	.05
❑ 191	Thad Bosley	.10	.05
❑ 192	Ron Darling	.20	.09
❑ 193	Matt Young	.10	.05
❑ 194	Tom Brunansky	.20	.09
❑ 195	Dave Stieb	.10	.05
❑ 196	Frank Viola	.20	.09
❑ 197	Tom Henke	.10	.05
❑ 198	Karl Best	.10	.05
❑ 199	Dwight Gooden	.30	.14
❑ 200	Checklist 134-239	.10	.05
❑ 201	Steve Trout	.10	.05
❑ 202	Rafael Ramirez	.10	.05

No.	Name	Price 1	Price 2
203	Bob Walk	.10	.05
204	Roger Mason	.10	.05
205	Terry Kennedy	.10	.05
206	Ron Oester	.10	.05
207	John Russell	.10	.05
208	Greg Mathews	.10	.05
209	Charlie Kerfeld	.10	.05
210	Reggie Jackson	.50	.23
211	Floyd Bannister	.10	.05
212	Vance Law	.10	.05
213	Rich Bordi	.10	.05
214	Dan Plesac	.10	.05
215	Dave Collins	.10	.05
216	Bob Stanley	.10	.05
217	Joe Niekro	.10	.05
218	Tom Niedenfuer	.10	.05
219	Brett Butler	.20	.09
220	Charlie Leibrandt	.10	.05
221	Steve Ontiveros	.10	.05
222	Tim Burke	.10	.05
223	Curtis Wilkerson	.10	.05
224	Pete Incaviglia	.20	.09
225	Lonnie Smith	.10	.05
226	Chris Codiroli	.10	.05
227	Scott Bailes	.10	.05
228	Rickey Henderson	.50	.23
229	Ken Howell	.10	.05
230	Darnell Coles	.10	.05
231	Don Aase	.10	.05
232	Tim Leary	.10	.05
233	Bob Boone	.20	.09
234	Ricky Horton	.10	.05
235	Mark Bailey	.10	.05
236	Kevin Gross	.10	.05
237	Lance McCullers	.10	.05
238	Cecilio Guante	.10	.05
239	Bob Melvin	.10	.05
240	Billy Joe Robidoux	.10	.05
241	Roger McDowell	.10	.05
242	Leon Durham	.10	.05
243	Ed Nunez	.10	.05
244	Jimmy Key	.20	.09
245	Mike Smithson	.10	.05
246	Bo Diaz	.10	.05
247	Carlton Fisk	.40	.18
248	Larry Sheets	.10	.05
249	Juan Castillo	.10	.05
250	Eric King	.10	.05
251	Doug Drabek	.40	.18
252	Wade Boggs	.40	.18
253	Mariano Duncan	.10	.05
254	Pat Tabler	.10	.05
255	Frank White	.20	.09
256	Alfredo Griffin	.10	.05
257	Floyd Youmans	.10	.05
258	Rob Wilfong	.10	.05
259	Pete O'Brien	.10	.05
260	Tim Hulett	.10	.05
261	Dickie Thon	.10	.05
262	Darren Daulton	.30	.14
263	Vince Coleman	.10	.05
264	Andy Hawkins	.10	.05
265	Eric Davis	.30	.14
266	Andres Thomas	.10	.05
267	Mike Diaz	.10	.05
268	Chili Davis	.30	.14
269	Jody Davis	.10	.05
270	Phil Bradley	.10	.05
271	George Bell	.10	.05
272	Keith Atherton	.10	.05
273	Storm Davis	.10	.05
274	Rob Deer	.10	.05
275	Walt Terrell	.10	.05
276	Roger Clemens	1.25	.55
277	Mike Easler	.10	.05
278	Steve Sax	.10	.05
279	Andre Thornton	.10	.05
280	Jim Sundberg	.10	.05
281	Bill Bathe	.10	.05
282	Jay Tibbs	.10	.05
283	Dick Schofield	.10	.05
284	Mike Mason	.10	.05
285	Jerry Hairston	.10	.05
286	Bill Doran	.10	.05
287	Tim Flannery	.10	.05
288	Gary Redus	.10	.05
289	John Franco	.20	.09
290	Paul Assenmacher	.30	.14
291	Joe Orsulak	.10	.05
292	Lee Smith	.30	.14
293	Mike Laga	.10	.05
294	Rick Dempsey	.20	.09
295	Mike Felder	.10	.05
296	Tom Brookens	.10	.05
297	Al Nipper	.10	.05
298	Mike Pagliarulo	.10	.05
299	Franklin Stubbs	.10	.05
300	Checklist 240-345	.10	.05
301	Steve Farr	.10	.05
302	Bill Mooneyham	.10	.05
303	Andres Galarraga	.40	.18
304	Scott Fletcher	.10	.05
305	Jack Howell	.10	.05
306	Russ Morman	.10	.05
307	Todd Worrell	.20	.09
308	Dave Smith	.10	.05
309	Jeff Stone	.10	.05
310	Ron Robinson	.10	.05
311	Bruce Bochy	.10	.05
312	Jim Winn	.10	.05
313	Mark Davis	.10	.05
314	Jeff Dedmon	.10	.05
315	Jamie Moyer	.30	.14
316	Wally Backman	.10	.05
317	Ken Phelps	.10	.05
318	Steve Lombardozzi	.10	.05
319	Rance Mulliniks	.10	.05
320	Tim Laudner	.10	.05
321	Mark Eichhorn	.10	.05
322	Lee Guetterman	.10	.05
323	Sid Fernandez	.10	.05
324	Jerry Mumphrey	.10	.05
325	David Palmer	.10	.05
326	Bill Almon	.10	.05
327	Candy Maldonado	.10	.05
328	John Kruk	.40	.18
329	John Denny	.10	.05
330	Milt Thompson	.10	.05
331	Mike LaValliere	.10	.05
332	Alan Ashby	.10	.05
333	Doug Corbett	.10	.05
334	Ron Karkovice	.20	.09
335	Mitch Webster	.10	.05
336	Lee Lacy	.10	.05
337	Glenn Braggs	.10	.05
338	Dwight Lowry	.10	.05
339	Don Baylor	.20	.09
340	Brian Fisher	.10	.05
341	Reggie Williams	.10	.05
342	Tom Candiotti	.10	.05
343	Rudy Law	.10	.05
344	Curt Young	.10	.05
345	Mike Fitzgerald	.10	.05
346	Ruben Sierra	.40	.18
347	Mitch Williams	.20	.09
348	Jorge Orta	.10	.05
349	Mickey Tettleton	.20	.09
350	Ernie Camacho	.10	.05
351	Ron Kittle	.10	.05
352	Ken Landreaux	.10	.05
353	Chet Lemon	.10	.05
354	John Shelby	.10	.05
355	Mark Clear	.10	.05
356	Doug DeCinces	.10	.05
357	Ken Dayley	.10	.05
358	Phil Garner	.10	.05
359	Steve Jeltz	.10	.05
360	Ed Whitson	.10	.05
361	Barry Bonds	8.00	3.60
362	Vida Blue	.20	.09
363	Cecil Cooper	.20	.09
364	Bob Ojeda	.10	.05
365	Dennis Eckersley	.40	.18
366	Mike Morgan	.10	.05
367	Willie Upshaw	.10	.05
368	Allan Anderson	.10	.05
369	Bill Gullickson	.10	.05
370	Bobby Thigpen	.20	.09
371	Juan Beniquez	.10	.05
372	Charlie Moore	.10	.05
373	Dan Petry	.10	.05
374	Rod Scurry	.10	.05
375	Tom Seaver	.40	.18
376	Ed VandeBerg	.10	.05
377	Tony Bernazard	.10	.05
378	Greg Pryor	.10	.05
379	Dwayne Murphy	.10	.05
380	Andy McGaffigan	.10	.05
381	Kirk McCaskill	.10	.05
382	Greg Harris	.10	.05
383	Rich Dotson	.10	.05
384	Craig Reynolds	.10	.05
385	Greg Gross	.10	.05
386	Tito Landrum	.10	.05
387	Craig Lefferts	.10	.05
388	Dave Parker	.20	.09
389	Bob Homer	.10	.05
390	Pat Clements	.10	.05
391	Jeff Leonard	.10	.05
392	Chris Speier	.10	.05
393	John Moses	.10	.05
394	Garth Iorg	.10	.05
395	Greg Gagne	.10	.05
396	Nate Snell	.10	.05
397	Bryan Clutterbuck	.10	.05
398	Darrell Evans	.20	.09
399	Steve Crawford	.10	.05
400	Checklist 346-451	.10	.05
401	Phil Lombardi	.10	.05
402	Rick Honeycutt	.10	.05
403	Ken Schrom	.10	.05
404	Bud Black	.10	.05
405	Donnie Hill	.10	.05
406	Wayne Krenchicki	.10	.05
407	Chuck Finley	.75	.35
408	Toby Harrah	.10	.05
409	Steve Lyons	.10	.05
410	Kevin Bass	.10	.05
411	Marvell Wynne	.10	.05
412	Ron Roenicke	.10	.05
413	Tracy Jones	.10	.05
414	Gene Garber	.10	.05
415	Mike Bielecki	.10	.05
416	Frank DiPino	.10	.05
417	Andy Van Slyke	.20	.09
418	Jim Dwyer	.10	.05
419	Ben Oglivie	.10	.05
420	Dave Bergman	.10	.05
421	Joe Sambito	.10	.05
422	Bob Tewksbury	.20	.09
423	Len Matuszek	.10	.05
424	Mike Kingery	.10	.05
425	Dave Kingman	.20	.09
426	Al Newman	.10	.05
427	Garry Ward	.10	.05
428	Ruppert Jones	.10	.05
429	Harold Baines	.20	.09
430	Pat Perry	.10	.05
431	Terry Puhl	.10	.05
432	Don Carman	.10	.05
433	Eddie Milner	.10	.05
434	LaMarr Hoyt	.10	.05
435	Rick Rhoden	.10	.05
436	Jose Uribe	.10	.05
437	Ken Oberkfell	.10	.05
438	Ron Davis	.10	.05
439	Jesse Orosco	.10	.05
440	Scott Bradley	.10	.05
441	Randy Bush	.10	.05
442	John Cerutti	.10	.05
443	Roy Smalley	.10	.05
444	Kelly Gruber	.10	.05
445	Bob Kearney	.10	.05
446	Ed Hearn	.10	.05
447	Scott Sanderson	.10	.05
448	Bruce Benedict	.10	.05
449	Junior Ortiz	.10	.05
450	Mike Aldrete	.10	.05
451	Kevin McReynolds	.20	.09
452	Rob Murphy	.10	.05
453	Kent Tekulve	.10	.05
454	Curt Ford	.10	.05
455	Dave Lopes	.20	.09
456	Bob Grich	.20	.09
457	Jose DeLeon	.10	.05
458	Andre Dawson	.40	.18
459	Mike Flanagan	.10	.05
460	Joey Meyer	.10	.05

#	Player	MINT	NRMT
461	Chuck Cary	.10	.05
462	Bill Buckner	.20	.09
463	Bob Shirley	.10	.05
464	Jeff Hamilton	.10	.05
465	Phil Niekro	.40	.18
466	Mark Gubicza	.10	.05
467	Jerry Willard	.10	.05
468	Bob Sebra	.10	.05
469	Larry Parrish	.10	.05
470	Charlie Hough	.10	.05
471	Hal McRae	.20	.09
472	Dave Leiper	.10	.05
473	Mel Hall	.10	.05
474	Dan Pasqua	.10	.05
475	Bob Welch	.10	.05
476	Johnny Grubb	.10	.05
477	Jim Traber	.10	.05
478	Chris Bosio	.20	.09
479	Mark McLemore	.20	.09
480	John Morris	.10	.05
481	Billy Hatcher	.10	.05
482	Dan Schatzeder	.10	.05
483	Rich Gossage	.10	.05
484	Jim Morrison	.10	.05
485	Bob Brenly	.10	.05
486	Bill Schroeder	.10	.05
487	Mookie Wilson	.20	.09
488	Dave Martinez	.20	.09
489	Harold Reynolds	.20	.09
490	Jeff Hearron	.10	.05
491	Mickey Hatcher	.10	.05
492	Barry Larkin	2.00	.90
493	Bob James	.10	.05
494	John Habyan	.10	.05
495	Jim Adduci	.10	.05
496	Mike Heath	.10	.05
497	Tim Stoddard	.10	.05
498	Tony Armas	.10	.05
499	Dennis Powell	.10	.05
500	Checklist 452-557	.10	.05
501	Chris Bando	.10	.05
502	David Cone	4.00	1.80
503	Jay Howell	.10	.05
504	Tom Foley	.10	.05
505	Ray Chadwick	.10	.05
506	Mike Loynd	.10	.05
507	Neil Allen	.10	.05
508	Danny Darwin	.10	.05
509	Rick Schu	.10	.05
510	Jose Oquendo	.10	.05
511	Gene Walter	.10	.05
512	Terry McGriff	.10	.09
513	Ken Griffey	.20	.09
514	Benny Distefano	.10	.05
515	Terry Mulholland	.20	.09
516	Ed Lynch	.10	.05
517	Bill Swift	.10	.05
518	Manny Lee	.10	.05
519	Andre David	.10	.05
520	Scott McGregor	.10	.05
521	Rick Manning	.10	.05
522	Willie Hernandez	.10	.05
523	Marty Barrett	.10	.05
524	Wayne Tolleson	.10	.05
525	Jose Gonzalez	.10	.05
526	Cory Snyder	.10	.05
527	Buddy Biancalana	.10	.05
528	Moose Haas	.10	.05
529	Wilfredo Tejada	.10	.05
530	Stu Cliburn	.10	.05
531	Dale Mohorcic	.10	.05
532	Ron Hassey	.10	.05
533	Ty Gainey	.10	.05
534	Jerry Royster	.10	.05
535	Mike Maddux	.10	.05
536	Ted Power	.10	.05
537	Ted Simmons	.20	.09
538	Rafael Belliard	.10	.05
539	Chico Walker	.10	.05
540	Bob Forsch	.10	.05
541	John Stefero	.10	.05
542	Dale Sveum	.10	.05
543	Mark Thurmond	.10	.05
544	Jeff Sellers	.10	.05
545	Joel Skinner	.10	.05
546	Alex Trevino	.10	.05
547	Randy Kutcher	.10	.05
548	Joaquin Andujar	.10	.05
549	Casey Candaele	.10	.05
550	Jeff Russell	.10	.05
551	John Candelaria	.10	.05
552	Joe Cowley	.10	.05
553	Danny Cox	.10	.05
554	Denny Walling	.10	.05
555	Bruce Ruffin	.10	.05
556	Buddy Bell	.20	.09
557	Jimmy Jones	.10	.05
558	Bobby Bonilla	.75	.35
559	Jeff D. Robinson	.10	.05
560	Ed Olwine	.10	.05
561	Glenallen Hill	.40	.18
562	Lee Mazzilli	.10	.05
563	Mike G. Brown P	.10	.05
564	George Frazier	.10	.05
565	Mike Sharperson	.10	.05
566	Mark Portugal	.20	.09
567	Rick Leach	.10	.05
568	Mark Langston	.10	.05
569	Rafael Santana	.10	.05
570	Manny Trillo	.10	.05
571	Cliff Speck	.10	.05
572	Bob Kipper	.10	.05
573	Kelly Downs	.10	.05
574	Randy Asadoor	.10	.05
575	Dave Magadan	.20	.09
576	Marvin Freeman	.10	.05
577	Jeff Lahti	.10	.05
578	Jeff Calhoun	.10	.05
579	Gus Polidor	.10	.05
580	Gene Nelson	.10	.05
581	Tim Teufel	.10	.05
582	Odell Jones	.10	.05
583	Mark Ryal	.10	.05
584	Randy O'Neal	.10	.05
585	Mike Greenwell	.40	.18
586	Ray Knight	.10	.05
587	Ralph Bryant	.10	.05
588	Carmen Castillo	.10	.05
589	Ed Wojna	.10	.05
590	Stan Javier	.10	.05
591	Jeff Musselman	.10	.05
592	Mike Stanley	.40	.18
593	Darrell Porter	.10	.05
594	Drew Hall	.10	.05
595	Rob Nelson	.10	.05
596	Bryan Oelkers	.10	.05
597	Scott Nielsen	.10	.05
598	Brian Holton	.10	.05
599	Kevin Mitchell	.30	.14
600	Checklist 558-660	.10	.05
601	Jackie Gutierrez	.10	.05
602	Barry Jones	.10	.05
603	Jerry Narron	.10	.05
604	Steve Lake	.10	.05
605	Jim Pankovits	.10	.05
606	Ed Romero	.10	.05
607	Dave LaPoint	.10	.05
608	Don Robinson	.10	.05
609	Mike Krukow	.10	.05
610	Dave Valle	.10	.05
611	Len Dykstra	.30	.14
612	Roberto Clemente PUZ	.50	.23
613	Mike Trujillo	.10	.05
614	Damaso Garcia	.10	.05
615	Neal Heaton	.10	.05
616	Juan Berenguer	.10	.05
617	Steve Carlton	.40	.18
618	Gary Lucas	.10	.05
619	Geno Petralli	.10	.05
620	Rick Aguilera	.20	.09
621	Fred McGriff	.50	.23
622	Dave Henderson	.10	.05
623	Dave Clark	.20	.09
624	Angel Salazar	.10	.05
625	Randy Hunt	.10	.05
626	John Gibbons	.10	.05
627	Kevin Brown	3.00	1.35
628	Bill Dawley	.10	.05
629	Aurelio Lopez	.10	.05
630	Charles Hudson	.10	.05
631	Ray Soff	.10	.05
632	Ray Hayward	.10	.05
633	Spike Owen	.10	.05
634	Glenn Hubbard	.10	.05
635	Kevin Elster	.20	.09
636	Mike LaCoss	.10	.05
637	Dwayne Henry	.10	.05
638	Rey Quinones	.10	.05
639	Jim Clancy	.10	.05
640	Larry Andersen	.10	.05
641	Calvin Schiraldi	.10	.05
642	Stan Jefferson	.10	.05
643	Marc Sullivan	.10	.05
644	Mark Grant	.10	.05
645	Cliff Johnson	.10	.05
646	Howard Johnson	.10	.05
647	Dave Sax	.10	.05
648	Dave Stewart	.20	.09
649	Danny Heep	.10	.05
650	Joe Johnson	.10	.05
651	Bob Brower	.10	.05
652	Rob Woodward	.10	.05
653	John Mizerock	.10	.05
654	Tim Pyznarski	.10	.05
655	Luis Aquino	.10	.05
656	Mickey Brantley	.10	.05
657	Doyle Alexander	.10	.05
658	Sammy Stewart	.10	.05
659	Jim Acker	.10	.05
660	Pete Ladd	.10	.05

1987 Donruss Rookies

	MINT	NRMT
COMP.FACT.SET (56)	40.00	18.00
COMMON CARD (1-56)	.10	.05
MINOR STARS	.25	.11
SEMISTARS	.50	.23
UNLISTED STARS	.75	.35

#	Player	MINT	NRMT
1	Mark McGwire	20.00	9.00
2	Eric Bell	.10	.05
3	Mark Williamson	.10	.05
4	Mike Greenwell	.75	.35
5	Ellis Burks	1.50	.70
6	DeWayne Buice	.10	.05
7	Mark McLemore	.25	.11
8	Devon White	.75	.35
9	Willie Fraser	.10	.05
10	Les Lancaster	.10	.05
11	Ken Williams	.10	.05
12	Matt Nokes	.25	.11
13	Jeff M. Robinson	.10	.05
14	Bo Jackson	.75	.35
15	Kevin Seitzer	.75	.35
16	Billy Ripken	.10	.05
17	B.J. Surhoff	.75	.35
18	Chuck Crim	.10	.05
19	Mike Birkbeck	.10	.05
20	Chris Bosio	.25	.11
21	Les Straker	.10	.05
22	Mark Davidson	.10	.05
23	Gene Larkin	.10	.05
24	Ken Gerhart	.10	.05
25	Luis Polonia	.25	.11
26	Terry Steinbach	.75	.35
27	Mickey Brantley	.10	.05
28	Mike Stanley	.75	.35
29	Jerry Browne	.75	.35
30	Todd Benzinger	.10	.05

❏ 31 Fred McGriff	1.00	.45
❏ 32 Mike Henneman	.50	.23
❏ 33 Casey Candaele	.10	.05
❏ 34 Dave Magadan	.25	.11
❏ 35 David Cone	3.00	1.35
❏ 36 Mike Jackson	.75	.35
❏ 37 John Mitchell	.10	.05
❏ 38 Mike Dunne	.10	.05
❏ 39 John Smiley	.10	.05
❏ 40 Joe Magrane	.10	.05
❏ 41 Jim Lindeman	.10	.05
❏ 42 Shane Mack	.25	.11
❏ 43 Stan Jefferson	.10	.05
❏ 44 Benito Santiago	.25	.11
❏ 45 Matt Williams	4.00	1.80
❏ 46 Dave Meads	.10	.05
❏ 47 Rafael Palmeiro	5.00	2.20
❏ 48 Bill Long	.10	.05
❏ 49 Bob Brower	.10	.05
❏ 50 James Steels	.10	.05
❏ 51 Paul Noce	.10	.05
❏ 52 Greg Maddux	15.00	6.75
❏ 53 Jeff Musselman	.10	.05
❏ 54 Brian Holton	.10	.05
❏ 55 Chuck Jackson	.10	.05
❏ 56 Checklist 1-56	.10	.05

❏ 32 Doug Drabek	.40	.18
❏ 33 Dwight Evans	.15	.07
❏ 34 Mark Langston	.10	.05
❏ 35 Wally Joyner	.40	.18
❏ 36 Vince Coleman	.10	.05
❏ 37 Eddie Murray	.40	.18
❏ 38 Cal Ripken	.75	.35
❏ 39 Fred McGriff	.15	.07
Rob Ducey		
Ernie Whitt		
❏ 40 Mark McGwire	2.00	.90
Jose Canseco		
❏ 41 Bob Boone	.15	.07
❏ 42 Darryl Strawberry	.25	.11
❏ 43 Howard Johnson	.10	.05
❏ 44 Wade Boggs	.40	.18
❏ 45 Benito Santiago	.15	.07
❏ 46 Mark McGwire	3.00	1.35
❏ 47 Kevin Seitzer	.40	.18
❏ 48 Don Mattingly	.50	.23
❏ 49 Darryl Strawberry	.25	.11
❏ 50 Pascual Perez	.10	.05
❏ 51 Alan Trammell	.25	.11
❏ 52 Doyle Alexander	.10	.05
❏ 53 Nolan Ryan	.75	.35
❏ 54 Mark McGwire	3.00	1.35
❏ 55 Benito Santiago	.15	.07
❏ 56 Checklist 1-56	.10	.05

❏ 28 Alfredo Griffin	.10	.05
❏ 29 Curt Young	.10	.05
❏ 30 Willie Upshaw	.10	.05
❏ 31 Mike Sharperson	.10	.05
❏ 32 Rance Mullinks	.10	.05
❏ 33 Ernie Whitt	.10	.05
❏ 34 Jesse Barfield	.10	.05
❏ 35 Tony Fernandez	.10	.05
❏ 36 Lloyd Moseby	.10	.05
❏ 37 Jimmy Key	.15	.07
❏ 38 Fred McGriff	.50	.23
❏ 39 George Bell	.10	.05
❏ 40 Dale Murphy	.40	.18
❏ 41 Rick Mahler	.10	.05
❏ 42 Ken Griffey	.15	.07
❏ 43 Andres Thomas	.10	.05
❏ 44 Dion James	.10	.05
❏ 45 Ozzie Virgil	.10	.05
❏ 46 Ken Oberkfell	.10	.05
❏ 47 Gary Roenicke	.10	.05
❏ 48 Glenn Hubbard	.10	.05
❏ 49 Bill Schroeder	.10	.05
❏ 50 Greg Brock	.10	.05
❏ 51 Billy Joe Robidoux	.10	.05
❏ 52 Glenn Braggs	.10	.05
❏ 53 Jim Gantner	.10	.05
❏ 54 Paul Molitor	.40	.18
❏ 55 Dale Sveum	.10	.05
❏ 56 Ted Higuera	.10	.05
❏ 57 Rob Deer	.10	.05
❏ 58 Robin Yount	.40	.18
❏ 59 Jim Lindeman	.10	.05
❏ 60 Vince Coleman	.10	.05
❏ 61 Tommy Herr	.10	.05
❏ 62 Terry Pendleton	.15	.07
❏ 63 John Tudor	.10	.05
❏ 64 Tony Pena	.10	.05
❏ 65 Ozzie Smith	.50	.23
❏ 66 Tito Landrum	.10	.05
❏ 67 Jack Clark	.15	.07
❏ 68 Bob Demier	.10	.05
❏ 69 Rick Sutcliffe	.10	.05
❏ 70 Andre Dawson	.40	.18
❏ 71 Keith Moreland	.10	.05
❏ 72 Jody Davis	.10	.05
❏ 73 Brian Dayett	.10	.05
❏ 74 Leon Durham	.10	.05
❏ 75 Ryne Sandberg	.50	.23
❏ 76 Shawon Dunston	.10	.05
❏ 77 Mike Marshall	.10	.05
❏ 78 Bill Madlock	.15	.07
❏ 79 Orel Hershiser	.15	.07
❏ 80 Mike Ramsey	.10	.05
❏ 81 Ken Landreaux	.10	.05
❏ 82 Mike Scioscia	.10	.05
❏ 83 Franklin Stubbs	.10	.05
❏ 84 Mariano Duncan	.10	.05
❏ 85 Steve Sax	.10	.05
❏ 86 Mitch Webster	.10	.05
❏ 87 Reid Nichols	.10	.05
❏ 88 Tim Wallach	.10	.05
❏ 89 Floyd Youmans	.10	.05
❏ 90 Andres Galarraga	.40	.18
❏ 91 Hubie Brooks	.10	.05
❏ 92 Jeff Reed	.10	.05
❏ 93 Alonzo Powell	.10	.05
❏ 94 Vance Law	.10	.05
❏ 95 Bob Brenly	.10	.05
❏ 96 Will Clark	1.00	.45
❏ 97 Chili Davis	.25	.11
❏ 98 Mike Krukow	.10	.05
❏ 99 Jose Uribe	.10	.05
❏ 100 Chris Brown	.10	.05
❏ 101 Robby Thompson	.15	.07
❏ 102 Candy Maldonado	.10	.05
❏ 103 Jeff Leonard	.10	.05
❏ 104 Tom Candiotti	.10	.05
❏ 105 Chris Bando	.10	.05
❏ 106 Cory Snyder	.10	.05
❏ 107 Pat Tabler	.10	.05
❏ 108 Andre Thornton	.10	.05
❏ 109 Joe Carter	.40	.18
❏ 110 Tony Bernazard	.10	.05
❏ 111 Julio Franco	.15	.07
❏ 112 Brook Jacoby	.10	.05
❏ 113 Brett Butler	.15	.07

1987 Donruss Highlights

	MINT	NRMT
COMP.FACT.SET (56)	12.00	5.50
COMMON CARD (1-56)	.10	.05
MINOR STARS	.15	.07
SEMISTARS	.25	.11
UNLISTED STARS	.40	.18
DISTRIBUTED ONLY IN FACTORY SET FORM		

❏ 1 Juan Nieves	.10	.05
❏ 2 Mike Schmidt	.40	.18
❏ 3 Eric Davis	.25	.11
❏ 4 Sid Fernandez	.10	.05
❏ 5 Brian Downing	.10	.05
❏ 6 Bret Saberhagen	.15	.07
❏ 7 Tim Raines	.15	.07
❏ 8 Eric Davis	.25	.11
❏ 9 Steve Bedrosian	.10	.05
❏ 10 Larry Parrish	.10	.05
❏ 11 Jim Clancy	.10	.05
❏ 12 Tony Gwynn UER	.50	.23
❏ 13 Orel Hershiser	.15	.07
❏ 14 Wade Boggs	.40	.18
❏ 15 Steve Ontiveros	.10	.05
❏ 16 Tim Raines	.15	.07
❏ 17 Don Mattingly	.50	.23
❏ 18 Ray Dandridge	.15	.07
❏ 19 Jim "Catfish" Hunter	.25	.11
❏ 20 Billy Williams	.25	.11
❏ 21 Bo Diaz	.10	.05
❏ 22 Floyd Youmans	.10	.05
❏ 23 Don Mattingly	.50	.23
❏ 24 Frank Viola	.10	.05
❏ 25 Bobby Witt	.10	.05
❏ 26 Kevin Seitzer	.40	.18
❏ 27 Mark McGwire	3.00	1.35
❏ 28 Andre Dawson	.40	.18
❏ 29 Paul Molitor	.40	.18
❏ 30 Kirby Puckett	.40	.18
❏ 31 Andre Dawson	.40	.18

1987 Donruss Opening Day

	MINT	NRMT
COMP.FACT.SET (272)	25.00	11.00
COMMON CARD (1-272)	.10	.05
MINOR STARS	.10	.05
SEMISTARS	.25	.11
UNLISTED STARS	.40	.18
DISTRIBUTED ONLY IN FACTORY SET FORM		
SET PRICE EXCLUDES CARD 163A		

❏ 1 Doug DeCinces	.10	.05
❏ 2 Mike Witt	.10	.05
❏ 3 George Hendrick	.10	.05
❏ 4 Dick Schofield	.10	.05
❏ 5 Devon White	.15	.07
❏ 6 Butch Wynegar	.10	.05
❏ 7 Wally Joyner	.40	.18
❏ 8 Mark McLemore	.15	.07
❏ 9 Brian Downing	.10	.05
❏ 10 Gary Pettis	.10	.05
❏ 11 Bill Doran	.10	.05
❏ 12 Phil Garner	.10	.05
❏ 13 Jose Cruz	.15	.07
❏ 14 Kevin Bass	.10	.05
❏ 15 Mike Scott	.10	.05
❏ 16 Glenn Davis	.10	.05
❏ 17 Alan Ashby	.10	.05
❏ 18 Billy Hatcher	.10	.05
❏ 19 Craig Reynolds	.10	.05
❏ 20 Carney Lansford	.15	.07
❏ 21 Mike Davis	.10	.05
❏ 22 Reggie Jackson	.50	.23
❏ 23 Mickey Tettleton	.15	.07
❏ 24 Jose Canseco	2.00	.90
❏ 25 Rob Nelson	.10	.05
❏ 26 Tony Phillips	.10	.05
❏ 27 Dwayne Murphy	.10	.05

❏ 114 Donell Nixon	.10	.05
❏ 115 Alvin Davis	.10	.05
❏ 116 Mark Langston	.10	.05
❏ 117 Harold Reynolds	.15	.07
❏ 118 Ken Phelps	.10	.05
❏ 119 Mike Kingery	.10	.06
❏ 120 Dave Valle	.10	.05
❏ 121 Rey Quinones	.10	.05
❏ 122 Phil Bradley	.10	.05
❏ 123 Jim Presley	.10	.05
❏ 124 Keith Hernandez	.15	.07
❏ 125 Kevin McReynolds	.10	.05
❏ 126 Rafael Santana	.10	.05
❏ 127 Bob Ojeda	.10	.05
❏ 128 Darryl Strawberry	.25	.11
❏ 129 Mookie Wilson	.15	.07
❏ 130 Gary Carter	.25	.11
❏ 131 Tim Teufel	.10	.05
❏ 132 Howard Johnson	.10	.05
❏ 133 Cal Ripken	1.50	.70
❏ 134 Rick Burleson	.10	.05
❏ 135 Fred Lynn	.15	.07
❏ 136 Eddie Murray	.40	.18
❏ 137 Ray Knight	.10	.05
❏ 138 Alan Wiggins	.10	.05
❏ 139 John Shelby	.10	.05
❏ 140 Mike Boddicker	.10	.05
❏ 141 Ken Gerhart	.10	.05
❏ 142 Terry Kennedy	.10	.05
❏ 143 Steve Garvey	.25	.11
❏ 144 Marvell Wynne	.10	.05
❏ 145 Kevin Mitchell	.25	.11
❏ 146 Tony Gwynn	1.00	.45
❏ 147 Joey Cora	.25	.11
❏ 148 Benito Santiago	.15	.07
❏ 149 Eric Show	.10	.05
❏ 150 Garry Templeton	.10	.05
❏ 151 Carmelo Martinez	.10	.05
❏ 152 Vom Hayes	.10	.05
❏ 153 Lance Parrish	.15	.07
❏ 154 Milt Thompson	.10	.05
❏ 155 Mike Easler	.10	.05
❏ 156 Juan Samuel	.10	.05
❏ 157 Steve Jeltz	.10	.05
❏ 158 Glenn Wilson	.10	.05
❏ 159 Shane Rawley	.10	.05
❏ 160 Mike Schmidt	.60	.25
❏ 161 Andy Van Slyke	.15	.07
❏ 162 Johnny Ray	.10	.05
❏ 163A Barry Bonds ERR ..	100.00	45.00
(Photo actually		
Johnny Ray wearing		
a black shirt)		
❏ 163B Barry Bonds COR ..	5.00	2.20
❏ 164 Junior Ortiz	.10	.05
❏ 165 Rafael Belliard	.10	.05
❏ 166 Bob Patterson	.10	.05
❏ 167 Bobby Bonilla	.40	.18
❏ 168 Sid Bream	.10	.05
❏ 169 Jim Morrison	.10	.05
❏ 170 Jerry Browne	.10	.05
❏ 171 Scott Fletcher	.10	.05
❏ 172 Ruben Sierra	.15	.07
❏ 173 Larry Parrish	.10	.05
❏ 174 Pete O'Brien	.10	.05
❏ 175 Pete Incaviglia	.15	.07
❏ 176 Don Slaught	.10	.05
❏ 177 Oddibe McDowell	.10	.05
❏ 178 Charlie Hough	.10	.05
❏ 179 Steve Buechele	.10	.05
❏ 180 Bob Stanley	.10	.05
❏ 181 Wade Boggs	.40	.18
❏ 182 Jim Rice	.15	.07
❏ 183 Bill Buckner	.15	.07
❏ 184 Dwight Evans	.15	.07
❏ 185 Spike Owen	.10	.05
❏ 186 Don Baylor	.15	.07
❏ 187 Marc Sullivan	.10	.05
❏ 188 Marty Barrett	.10	.05
❏ 189 Dave Henderson	.10	.05
❏ 190 Bo Diaz	.10	.05
❏ 191 Barry Larkin	1.00	.45
❏ 192 Kal Daniels	.10	.05
❏ 193 Terry Francona	.15	.07
❏ 194 Tom Browning	.10	.05
❏ 195 Ron Oester	.10	.05

❏ 196 Buddy Bell	.15	.07
❏ 197 Eric Davis	.25	.11
❏ 198 Dave Parker	.15	.07
❏ 199 Steve Balboni	.10	.05
❏ 200 Danny Tartabull	.10	.05
❏ 201 Ed Hearn	.10	.05
❏ 202 Buddy Biancalana	.10	.05
❏ 203 Danny Jackson	.10	.05
❏ 204 Frank White	.15	.07
❏ 205 Bo Jackson	.40	.18
❏ 206 George Brett	.75	.35
❏ 207 Kevin Seitzer	.40	.18
❏ 208 Willie Wilson	.15	.07
❏ 209 Orlando Mercado	.10	.05
❏ 210 Darrell Evans	.15	.07
❏ 211 Larry Herndon	.10	.05
❏ 212 Jack Morris	.15	.07
❏ 213 Chet Lemon	.10	.05
❏ 214 Mike Heath	.10	.05
❏ 215 Darnell Coles	.10	.05
❏ 216 Alan Trammell	.25	.11
❏ 217 Terry Harper	.10	.05
❏ 218 Lou Whitaker	.15	.07
❏ 219 Gary Gaetti	.10	.05
❏ 220 Tom Nieto	.10	.05
❏ 221 Kirby Puckett	.75	.35
❏ 222 Tom Brunansky	.10	.05
❏ 223 Greg Gagne	.10	.05
❏ 224 Dan Gladden	.10	.05
❏ 225 Mark Davidson	.10	.05
❏ 226 Bert Blyleven	.15	.07
❏ 227 Steve Lombardozzi	.10	.05
❏ 228 Kent Hrbek	.15	.07
❏ 229 Gary Redus	.10	.05
❏ 230 Ivan Calderon	.10	.05
❏ 231 Tim Hulett	.10	.05
❏ 232 Carlton Fisk	.40	.18
❏ 233 Greg Walker	.10	.05
❏ 234 Ron Karkovice	.10	.05
❏ 235 Ozzie Guillen	.10	.05
❏ 236 Harold Baines	.15	.07
❏ 237 Donnie Hill	.10	.05
❏ 238 Rich Dotson	.10	.05
❏ 239 Mike Pagliarulo	.10	.05
❏ 240 Joel Skinner	.10	.05
❏ 241 Don Mattingly	.75	.35
❏ 242 Gary Ward	.10	.05
❏ 243 Dave Winfield	.40	.18
❏ 244 Dan Pasqua	.10	.05
❏ 245 Wayne Tolleson	.10	.05
❏ 246 Willie Randolph	.15	.07
❏ 247 Dennis Rasmussen	.10	.05
❏ 248 Rickey Henderson	.50	.23
❏ 249 Angels Logo	.10	.05
❏ 250 Astros Logo	.10	.05
❏ 251 A's Logo	.10	.05
❏ 252 Blue Jays Logo	.10	.05
❏ 253 Braves Logo	.10	.05
❏ 254 Brewers Logo	.10	.05
❏ 255 Cardinals Logo	.10	.05
❏ 256 Dodgers Logo	.10	.05
❏ 257 Expos Logo	.10	.05
❏ 258 Giants Logo	.10	.05
❏ 259 Indians Logo	.10	.05
❏ 260 Mariners Logo	.10	.05
❏ 261 Orioles Logo	.10	.05
❏ 262 Padres Logo	.10	.05
❏ 263 Phillies Logo	.10	.05
❏ 264 Pirates Logo	.10	.05
❏ 265 Rangers Logo	.10	.05
❏ 266 Red Sox Logo	.10	.05
❏ 267 Reds Logo	.10	.05
❏ 268 Royals Logo	.10	.05
❏ 269 Tigers Logo	.10	.05
❏ 270 Twins Logo	.10	.05
❏ 271 Chicago Logos	.10	.05
❏ 272 New York Logos	.10	.05

1988 Donruss

	MINT	NRMT
COMPLETE SET (660)	10.00	4.50
COMP.FACT.SET (660)	10.00	4.50
COMMON CARD (1-660)	.05	.02
MINOR STARS	.10	.05
UNLISTED STARS	.20	.09

COMP.MVP SET (26) 3.00 1.35
*MVP'S: SAME VALUE AS BASIC CARDS
MVPS: RANDOM INSERTS IN PACKS

❏ 1 Mark McGwire DK	1.00	.45
❏ 2 Tim Raines DK	.07	.02
❏ 3 Benito Santiago DK	.05	.02
❏ 4 Alan Trammell DK	.10	.05
❏ 5 Danny Tartabull DK	.05	.02
❏ 6 Ron Darling DK	.05	.02
❏ 7 Paul Molitor DK	.20	.09
❏ 8 Devon White DK	.05	.02
❏ 9 Andre Dawson DK	.20	.09
❏ 10 Julio Franco DK	.05	.02
❏ 11 Scott Fletcher DK	.05	.02
❏ 12 Tony Fernandez DK	.10	.05
❏ 13 Shane Rawley DK	.05	.02
❏ 14 Kal Daniels DK	.05	.02
❏ 15 Jack Clark DK	.10	.05
❏ 16 Dwight Evans DK	.05	.02
❏ 17 Tommy John DK	.05	.02
❏ 18 Andy Van Slyke DK	.05	.02
❏ 19 Gary Gaetti DK	.05	.02
❏ 20 Mark Langston DK	.05	.02
❏ 21 Will Clark DK	.20	.09
❏ 22 Glenn Hubbard DK	.05	.02
❏ 23 Billy Hatcher DK	.05	.02
❏ 24 Bob Welch DK	.05	.02
❏ 25 Ivan Calderon DK	.05	.02
❏ 26 Cal Ripken DK	.40	.18
❏ 27 DK Checklist 1-26	.05	.02
❏ 28 Mackey Sasser RR	.05	.02
❏ 29 Jeff Treadway RR	.05	.02
❏ 30 Mike Campbell RR	.05	.02
❏ 31 Lance Johnson RR	.20	.09
❏ 32 Nelson Liriano RR	.05	.02
❏ 33 Shawn Abner RR	.05	.02
❏ 34 Roberto Alomar RR	1.25	.55
❏ 35 Shawn Hillegas RR	.05	.02
❏ 36 Joey Meyer RR	.05	.02
❏ 37 Kevin Elster RR	.05	.02
❏ 38 Jose Lind RR	.05	.02
❏ 39 Kirt Manwaring RR	.05	.02
❏ 40 Mark Grace RR	.75	.35
❏ 41 Jody Reed RR	.10	.05
❏ 42 John Farrell RR	.05	.02
❏ 43 Al Leiter RR	.40	.18
❏ 44 Gary Thurman RR	.05	.02
❏ 45 Vicente Palacios RR	.05	.02
❏ 46 Eddie Williams RR	.05	.02
❏ 47 Jack McDowell RR	.20	.09
❏ 48 Ken Dixon	.05	.02
❏ 49 Mike Birkbeck	.05	.02
❏ 50 Eric King	.05	.02
❏ 51 Roger Clemens	.50	.23
❏ 52 Pat Clements	.05	.02
❏ 53 Fernando Valenzuela	.10	.05
❏ 54 Mark Gubicza	.05	.02
❏ 55 Jay Howell	.05	.02
❏ 56 Floyd Youmans	.05	.02
❏ 57 Ed Correa	.05	.02
❏ 58 DeWayne Buice	.05	.02
❏ 59 Jose DeLeon	.05	.02
❏ 60 Danny Cox	.05	.02
❏ 61 Nolan Ryan	.75	.35
❏ 62 Steve Bedrosian	.05	.02
❏ 63 Tom Browning	.05	.02
❏ 64 Mark Davis	.05	.02

65	R.J. Reynolds	.05	.02
66	Kevin Mitchell	.10	.05
67	Ken Oberkfell	.05	.02
68	Rick Sutcliffe	.05	.02
69	Dwight Gooden	.10	.05
70	Scott Bankhead	.05	.02
71	Bert Blyleven	.10	.05
72	Jimmy Key	.05	.02
73	Les Straker	.05	.02
74	Jim Clancy	.05	.02
75	Mike Moore	.05	.02
76	Ron Darling	.05	.02
77	Ed Lynch	.05	.02
78	Dale Murphy	.20	.09
79	Doug Drabek	.05	.02
80	Scott Garrelts	.05	.02
81	Ed Whitson	.05	.02
82	Rob Murphy	.05	.02
83	Shane Rawley	.05	.02
84	Greg Mathews	.05	.02
85	Jim Deshaies	.05	.02
86	Mike Witt	.05	.02
87	Donnie Hill	.05	.02
88	Jeff Reed	.05	.02
89	Mike Boddicker	.05	.02
90	Ted Higuera	.05	.02
91	Walt Terrell	.05	.02
92	Bob Stanley	.05	.02
93	Dave Righetti	.05	.02
94	Orel Hershiser	.10	.05
95	Chris Bando	.05	.02
96	Bret Saberhagen	.10	.05
97	Curt Young	.05	.02
98	Tim Burke	.05	.02
99	Charlie Hough	.10	.05
100A	Checklist 28-137	.05	.02
100B	Checklist 28-133	.05	.02
101	Bobby Witt	.05	.02
102	George Brett	.40	.18
103	Mickey Tettleton	.10	.05
104	Scott Bailes	.05	.02
105	Mike Pagliarulo	.05	.02
106	Mike Scioscia	.05	.02
107	Tom Brookens	.05	.02
108	Ray Knight	.05	.02
109	Dan Plesac	.05	.02
110	Wally Joyner	.15	.07
111	Bob Forsch	.05	.02
112	Mike Scott	.05	.02
113	Kevin Gross	.05	.02
114	Benito Santiago	.05	.02
115	Bob Kipper	.05	.02
116	Mike Krukow	.05	.02
117	Chris Bosio	.05	.02
118	Sid Fernandez	.05	.02
119	Jody Davis	.05	.02
120	Mike Morgan	.05	.02
121	Mark Eichhorn	.05	.02
122	Jeff Reardon	.10	.05
123	John Franco	.05	.02
124	Richard Dotson	.05	.02
125	Eric Bell	.05	.02
126	Juan Nieves	.05	.02
127	Jack Morris	.10	.05
128	Rick Rhoden	.05	.02
129	Rich Gedman	.05	.02
130	Ken Howell	.05	.02
131	Brook Jacoby	.05	.02
132	Danny Jackson	.05	.02
133	Gene Nelson	.05	.02
134	Neal Heaton	.05	.02
135	Willie Fraser	.05	.02
136	Jose Guzman	.05	.02
137	Ozzie Guillen	.05	.02
138	Bob Knepper	.05	.02
139	Mike Jackson	.20	.09
140	Joe Magrane	.05	.02
141	Jimmy Jones	.05	.02
142	Ted Power	.05	.02
143	Ozzie Virgil	.05	.02
144	Felix Fermin	.05	.02
145	Kelly Downs	.05	.02
146	Shawon Dunston	.05	.02
147	Scott Bradley	.05	.02
148	Dave Stieb	.05	.02
149	Frank Viola	.05	.02
150	Terry Kennedy	.05	.02
151	Bill Wegman	.05	.02
152	Matt Nokes	.05	.02
153	Wade Boggs	.20	.09
154	Wayne Tolleson	.05	.02
155	Mariano Duncan	.05	.02
156	Julio Franco	.05	.02
157	Charlie Leibrandt	.05	.02
158	Terry Steinbach	.10	.05
159	Mike Fitzgerald	.05	.02
160	Jack Lazorko	.05	.02
161	Mitch Williams	.05	.02
162	Greg Walker	.05	.02
163	Alan Ashby	.05	.02
164	Tony Gwynn	.50	.23
165	Bruce Ruffin	.05	.02
166	Ron Robinson	.05	.02
167	Zane Smith	.05	.02
168	Junior Ortiz	.05	.02
169	Jamie Moyer	.05	.02
170	Tony Pena	.05	.02
171	Cal Ripken	.75	.35
172	B.J. Surhoff	.10	.05
173	Lou Whitaker	.10	.05
174	Ellis Burks	.25	.11
175	Ron Guidry	.05	.02
176	Steve Sax	.05	.02
177	Danny Tartabull	.10	.05
178	Carney Lansford	.10	.05
179	Casey Candaele	.05	.02
180	Scott Fletcher	.05	.02
181	Mark McLemore	.05	.02
182	Ivan Calderon	.05	.02
183	Jack Clark	.10	.05
184	Glenn Davis	.05	.02
185	Luis Aguayo	.05	.02
186	Bo Diaz	.05	.02
187	Stan Jefferson	.05	.02
188	Sid Bream	.05	.02
189	Bob Brenly	.05	.02
190	Dion James	.05	.02
191	Leon Durham	.05	.02
192	Jesse Orosco	.05	.02
193	Alvin Davis	.05	.02
194	Gary Gaetti	.05	.02
195	Fred McGriff	.20	.09
196	Steve Lombardozzi	.05	.02
197	Rance Mulliniks	.05	.02
198	Rey Quinones	.05	.02
199	Gary Carter	.15	.07
200A	Checklist 138-247	.05	.02
200B	Checklist 134-239	.05	.02
201	Keith Moreland	.05	.02
202	Ken Griffey	.10	.05
203	Tommy Gregg	.05	.02
204	Will Clark	.25	.11
205	John Kruk	.05	.02
206	Buddy Bell	.10	.05
207	Von Hayes	.05	.02
208	Tommy Herr	.05	.02
209	Craig Reynolds	.05	.02
210	Gary Pettis	.05	.02
211	Harold Baines	.10	.05
212	Vance Law	.05	.02
213	Ken Gerhart	.05	.02
214	Jim Gantner	.05	.02
215	Chet Lemon	.05	.02
216	Dwight Evans	.10	.05
217	Don Mattingly	.40	.18
218	Franklin Stubbs	.05	.02
219	Pat Tabler	.05	.02
220	Bo Jackson	.20	.09
221	Tony Phillips	.05	.02
222	Tim Wallach	.05	.02
223	Ruben Sierra	.05	.02
224	Steve Buechele	.05	.02
225	Frank White	.10	.05
226	Alfredo Griffin	.05	.02
227	Greg Swindell	.05	.02
228	Willie Randolph	.10	.05
229	Mike Marshall	.05	.02
230	Alan Trammell	.15	.07
231	Eddie Murray	.20	.09
232	Dale Sveum	.05	.02
233	Dick Schofield	.05	.02
234	Jose Oquendo	.05	.02
235	Bill Doran	.05	.02
236	Milt Thompson	.05	.02
237	Marvell Wynne	.05	.02
238	Bobby Bonilla	.15	.07
239	Chris Speier	.05	.02
240	Glenn Braggs	.05	.02
241	Wally Backman	.05	.02
242	Ryne Sandberg	.25	.11
243	Phil Bradley	.05	.02
244	Kelly Gruber	.05	.02
245	Tom Brunansky	.05	.02
246	Ron Oester	.05	.02
247	Bobby Thigpen	.05	.02
248	Fred Lynn	.05	.02
249	Paul Molitor	.20	.09
250	Darrell Evans	.10	.05
251	Gary Ward	.05	.02
252	Bruce Hurst	.05	.02
253	Bob Welch	.05	.02
254	Joe Carter	.20	.09
255	Willie Wilson	.05	.02
256	Mark McGwire	2.00	.90
257	Mitch Webster	.05	.02
258	Brian Downing	.05	.02
259	Mike Stanley	.10	.05
260	Carlton Fisk	.20	.09
261	Billy Hatcher	.05	.02
262	Glenn Wilson	.05	.02
263	Ozzie Smith	.25	.11
264	Randy Ready	.05	.02
265	Kurt Stillwell	.05	.02
266	David Palmer	.05	.02
267	Mike Diaz	.05	.02
268	Robby Thompson	.05	.02
269	Andre Dawson	.20	.09
270	Lee Guetterman	.05	.02
271	Willie Upshaw	.05	.02
272	Randy Bush	.05	.02
273	Larry Sheets	.05	.02
274	Rob Deer	.05	.02
275	Kirk Gibson	.10	.05
276	Marty Barrett	.05	.02
277	Rickey Henderson	.25	.11
278	Pedro Guerrero	.05	.02
279	Brett Butler	.05	.02
280	Kevin Seitzer	.10	.05
281	Mike Davis	.05	.02
282	Andres Galarraga	.20	.09
283	Devon White	.10	.05
284	Pete O'Brien	.05	.02
285	Jerry Hairston	.05	.02
286	Kevin Bass	.05	.02
287	Carmelo Martinez	.05	.02
288	Juan Samuel	.05	.02
289	Kal Daniels	.05	.02
290	Albert Hall	.05	.02
291	Andy Van Slyke	.10	.05
292	Lee Smith	.10	.05
293	Vince Coleman	.10	.05
294	Tom Niedenfuer	.05	.02
295	Robin Yount	.20	.09
296	Jeff M. Robinson	.05	.02
297	Todd Benzinger	.05	.02
298	Dave Winfield	.20	.09
299	Mickey Hatcher	.05	.02
300A	Checklist 248-357	.05	.02
300B	Checklist 240-345	.05	.02
301	Bud Black	.05	.02
302	Jose Canseco	.40	.18
303	Tom Foley	.05	.02
304	Pete Incaviglia	.05	.02
305	Bob Boone	.10	.05
306	Bill Long	.05	.02
307	Willie McGee	.10	.05
308	Ken Caminiti	.50	.23
309	Darren Daulton	.05	.02
310	Tracy Jones	.05	.02
311	Greg Booker	.05	.02
312	Mike LaValliere	.05	.02
313	Chili Davis	.15	.07
314	Glenn Hubbard	.05	.02
315	Paul Noce	.05	.02
316	Keith Hernandez	.10	.05
317	Mark Langston	.05	.02
318	Keith Atherton	.05	.02
319	Tony Fernandez	.10	.05

320	Kent Hrbek	.10	.05
321	John Cerutti	.05	.02
322	Mike Kingery	.05	.02
323	Dave Magadan	.05	.02
324	Rafael Palmeiro	.40	.18
325	Jeff Dedmon	.05	.02
326	Barry Bonds	.50	.23
327	Jeffrey Leonard	.05	.02
328	Tim Flannery	.05	.02
329	Dave Concepcion	.10	.05
330	Mike Schmidt	.30	.14
331	Bill Dawley	.05	.02
332	Larry Andersen	.05	.02
333	Jack Howell	.05	.02
334	Ken Williams	.05	.02
335	Bryn Smith	.05	.02
336	Bill Ripken	.05	.02
337	Greg Brock	.05	.02
338	Mike Heath	.05	.02
339	Mike Greenwell	.05	.02
340	Claudell Washington	.05	.02
341	Jose Gonzalez	.05	.02
342	Mel Hall	.05	.02
343	Jim Eisenreich	.20	.09
344	Tony Bernazard	.05	.02
345	Tim Raines	.10	.05
346	Bob Brower	.05	.02
347	Larry Parrish	.05	.02
348	Thad Bosley	.05	.02
349	Dennis Eckersley	.10	.05
350	Cory Snyder	.05	.02
351	Rick Cerone	.05	.02
352	John Shelby	.05	.02
353	Larry Herndon	.05	.02
354	John Habyan	.05	.02
355	Chuck Crim	.05	.02
356	Gus Polidor	.05	.02
357	Ken Dayley	.05	.02
358	Danny Darwin	.05	.02
359	Lance Parrish	.05	.02
360	James Steels	.05	.02
361	Al Pedrique	.05	.02
362	Mike Aldrete	.05	.02
363	Juan Castillo	.05	.02
364	Len Dykstra	.10	.05
365	Luis Quinones	.05	.02
366	Jim Presley	.05	.02
367	Lloyd Moseby	.05	.02
368	Kirby Puckett	.30	.14
369	Eric Davis	.10	.05
370	Gary Redus	.05	.02
371	Dave Schmidt	.05	.02
372	Mark Clear	.05	.02
373	Dave Bergman	.05	.02
374	Charles Hudson	.05	.02
375	Calvin Schiraldi	.05	.02
376	Alex Trevino	.05	.02
377	Tom Candiotti	.05	.02
378	Steve Farr	.05	.02
379	Mike Gallego	.05	.02
380	Andy McGaffigan	.05	.02
381	Kirk McCaskill	.05	.02
382	Oddibe McDowell	.05	.02
383	Floyd Bannister	.05	.02
384	Denny Walling	.05	.02
385	Don Carman	.05	.02
386	Todd Worrell	.10	.05
387	Eric Show	.05	.02
388	Dave Parker	.10	.05
389	Rick Mahler	.05	.02
390	Mike Dunne	.05	.02
391	Candy Maldonado	.05	.02
392	Bob Dernier	.05	.02
393	Dave Valle	.05	.02
394	Ernie Whitt	.05	.02
395	Juan Berenguer	.05	.02
396	Mike Young	.05	.02
397	Mike Felder	.05	.02
398	Willie Hernandez	.05	.02
399	Jim Rice	.10	.05
400A	Checklist 358-467	.05	
400B	Checklist 346-451	.05	
401	Tommy John	.10	.05
402	Brian Holton	.05	.02
403	Carmen Castillo	.05	.02
404	Jamie Quirk	.05	.02
405	Dwayne Murphy	.05	.02
406	Jeff Parrett	.05	.02
407	Don Sutton	.20	.09
408	Jerry Browne	.05	.02
409	Jim Winn	.05	.02
410	Dave Smith	.05	.02
411	Shane Mack	.05	.02
412	Greg Gross	.05	.02
413	Nick Esasky	.05	.02
414	Damaso Garcia	.05	.02
415	Brian Fisher	.05	.02
416	Brian Dayett	.05	.02
417	Curt Ford	.05	.02
418	Mark Williamson	.05	.02
419	Bill Schroeder	.05	.02
420	Mike Henneman	.05	.02
421	John Marzano	.05	.02
422	Ron Kittle	.05	.02
423	Matt Young	.05	.02
424	Steve Balboni	.05	.02
425	Luis Polonia	.05	.02
426	Randy St.Claire	.05	.02
427	Greg Harris	.05	.02
428	Johnny Ray	.05	.02
429	Ray Searage	.05	.02
430	Ricky Horton	.05	.02
431	Gerald Young	.05	.02
432	Rick Schu	.05	.02
433	Paul O'Neill	.15	.07
434	Rich Gossage	.10	.05
435	John Cangelosi	.05	.02
436	Mike LaCoss	.05	.02
437	Gerald Perry	.05	.02
438	Dave Martinez	.05	.02
439	Darryl Strawberry	.10	.05
440	John Moses	.05	.02
441	Greg Gagne	.05	.02
442	Jesse Barfield	.05	.02
443	George Frazier	.05	.02
444	Garth Iorg	.05	.02
445	Ed Nunez	.05	.02
446	Rick Aguilera	.10	.05
447	Jerry Mumphrey	.05	.02
448	Rafael Ramirez	.05	.02
449	John Smiley	.10	.05
450	Atlee Hammaker	.05	.02
451	Lance McCullers	.05	.02
452	Guy Hoffman	.05	.02
453	Chris James	.05	.02
454	Terry Pendleton	.10	.05
455	Dave Meads	.05	.02
456	Bill Buckner	.10	.05
457	John Pawlowski	.05	.02
458	Bob Sebra	.05	.02
459	Jim Dwyer	.05	.02
460	Jay Aldrich	.05	.02
461	Frank Tanana	.05	.02
462	Oil Can Boyd	.05	.02
463	Dan Pasqua	.05	.02
464	Tim Crews	.05	.02
465	Andy Allanson	.05	.02
466	Bill Pecota	.05	.02
467	Steve Ontiveros	.05	.02
468	Hubie Brooks	.05	.02
469	Paul Kilgus	.05	.02
470	Dale Mohorcic	.05	.02
471	Dan Quisenberry	.05	.02
472	Dave Stewart	.10	.05
473	Dave Clark	.05	.02
474	Joel Skinner	.05	.02
475	Dave Anderson	.05	.02
476	Dan Petry	.05	.02
477	Carl Nichols	.05	.02
478	Ernest Riles	.05	.02
479	George Hendrick	.05	.02
480	John Morris	.05	.02
481	Manny Hernandez	.05	.02
482	Jeff Stone	.05	.02
483	Chris Brown	.05	.02
484	Mike Bielecki	.05	.02
485	Dave Dravecky	.10	.05
486	Rick Manning	.05	.02
487	Bill Almon	.05	.02
488	Jim Sundberg	.05	.02
489	Ken Phelps	.05	.02
490	Tom Henke	.05	.02
491	Dan Gladden	.05	.02
492	Barry Larkin	.20	.09
493	Fred Manrique	.05	.02
494	Mike Griffin	.05	.02
495	Mark Knudson	.05	.02
496	Bill Madlock	.10	.05
497	Tim Stoddard	.05	.02
498	Sam Horn	.05	.02
499	Tracy Woodson	.05	.02
500A	Checklist 468-577	.05	
500B	Checklist 452-557	.05	
501	Ken Schrom	.05	.02
502	Angel Salazar	.05	.02
503	Eric Plunk	.05	.02
504	Joe Hesketh	.05	.02
505	Greg Minton	.05	.02
506	Geno Petralli	.05	.02
507	Bob James	.05	.02
508	Robbie Wine	.05	.02
509	Jeff Calhoun	.05	.02
510	Steve Lake	.05	.02
511	Mark Grant	.05	.02
512	Frank Williams	.05	.02
513	Jeff Blauser	.20	.09
514	Bob Walk	.05	.02
515	Craig Lefferts	.05	.02
516	Manny Trillo	.05	.02
517	Jerry Reed	.05	.02
518	Rick Leach	.05	.02
519	Mark Davidson	.05	.02
520	Jeff Ballard	.05	.02
521	Dave Stapleton	.05	.02
522	Pat Sheridan	.05	.02
523	Al Nipper	.05	.02
524	Steve Trout	.05	.02
525	Jeff Hamilton	.05	.02
526	Tommy Hinzo	.05	.02
527	Lonnie Smith	.05	.02
528	Greg Cadaret	.05	.02
529	Bob McClure UER (Rob on front)	.05	.02
530	Chuck Finley	.15	.07
531	Jeff Russell	.05	.02
532	Steve Lyons	.05	.02
533	Terry Puhl	.05	.02
534	Eric Nolte	.05	.02
535	Kent Tekulve	.05	.02
536	Pat Pacillo	.05	.02
537	Charlie Puleo	.05	.02
538	Tom Prince	.05	.02
539	Greg Maddux	1.00	.45
540	Jim Lindeman	.05	.02
541	Pete Stanicek	.05	.02
542	Steve Kiefer	.05	.02
543A	Jim Morrison ERR (No decimal before lifetime average)	.20	.09
543B	Jim Morrison COR	.05	.02
544	Spike Owen	.05	.02
545	Jay Buhner	.40	.18
546	Mike Devereaux	.10	.05
547	Jerry Don Gleaton	.05	.02
548	Jose Rijo	.10	.05
549	Dennis Martinez	.10	.05
550	Mike Loynd	.05	.02
551	Darrell Miller	.05	.02
552	Dave LaPoint	.05	.02
553	John Tudor	.05	.02
554	Rocky Childress	.05	.02
555	Wally Ritchie	.05	.02
556	Terry McGriff	.05	.02
557	Dave Leiper	.05	.02
558	Jeff D. Robinson	.05	.02
559	Jose Uribe	.05	.02
560	Ted Simmons	.10	.05
561	Les Lancaster	.05	.02
562	Keith A. Miller	.05	.02
563	Harold Reynolds	.10	.05
564	Gene Larkin	.05	.02
565	Cecil Fielder	.15	.07
566	Roy Smalley	.05	.02
567	Duane Ward	.05	.02
568	Bill Wilkinson	.05	.02
569	Howard Johnson	.05	.02
570	Frank DiPino	.05	.02
571	Pete Smith	.05	.02

	MINT	NRMT
572 Darnell Coles	.05	.02
573 Don Robinson	.05	.02
574 Rob Nelson UER	.05	.02
(Career 0 RBI, but 1 RBI in '87)		
575 Dennis Rasmussen	.05	.02
576 Steve Jeltz UER	.05	.02
(Photo actually Juan Samuel; Samuel noted for one batting glove and black bat)		
577 Tom Pagnozzi	.05	.02
578 Ty Gainey	.05	.02
579 Gary Lucas	.05	.02
580 Ron Hassey	.05	.02
581 Herm Winningham	.05	.02
582 Rene Gonzales	.05	.02
583 Brad Komminsk	.05	.02
584 Doyle Alexander	.05	.02
585 Jeff Sellers	.05	.02
586 Bill Gullickson	.05	.02
587 Tim Belcher	.10	.05
588 Doug Jones	.20	.09
589 Melido Perez	.05	.02
590 Rick Honeycutt	.05	.02
591 Pascual Perez	.05	.02
592 Curt Wilkerson	.05	.02
593 Steve Howe	.05	.02
594 John Davis	.05	.02
595 Storm Davis	.05	.02
596 Sammy Stewart	.05	.02
597 Neil Allen	.05	.02
598 Alejandro Pena	.05	.02
599 Mark Thurmond	.05	.02
600A Checklist 578-660/BC1-BC26		.02
600B Checklist 558-660	.05	.02
601 Jose Mesa	.15	.07
602 Don August	.05	.02
603 Terry Leach SP	.07	.03
604 Tom Newell	.05	.02
605 Randall Byers SP	.07	.03
606 Jim Gott	.05	.02
607 Harry Spilman	.05	.02
608 John Candelaria	.05	.02
609 Mike Brumley	.05	.02
610 Mickey Brantley	.05	.02
611 Jose Nunez SP	.07	.03
612 Tom Nieto	.05	.02
613 Rick Reuschel	.05	.02
614 Lee Mazzilli SP	.07	.03
615 Scott Lusader	.05	.02
616 Bobby Meacham	.05	.02
617 Kevin McReynolds SP	.07	.03
618 Gene Garber	.05	.02
619 Barry Lyons SP	.07	.03
620 Randy Myers	.15	.07
621 Donnie Moore	.05	.02
622 Domingo Ramos	.05	.02
623 Ed Romero	.05	.02
624 Greg Myers	.05	.02
625 Ripken Family	.40	.18
Cal Ripken Sr.		
Cal Ripken Jr.		
Billy Ripken		
626 Pat Perry	.05	.02
627 Andres Thomas SP	.07	.03
628 Matt Williams SP	1.00	.45
629 Dave Hengel	.05	.02
630 Jeff Musselman SP	.07	.03
631 Tim Laudner	.05	.02
632 Bob Ojeda SP	.07	.03
633 Rafael Santana	.05	.02
634 Wes Gardner	.05	.02
635 Roberto Kelly SP	.20	.09
636 Mike Flanagan SP	.07	.03
637 Jay Bell	.50	.23
638 Bob Melvin	.05	.02
639 Damon Berryhill UER	.05	.02
(Bats: Switch)		
640 David Wells SP	.50	.23
641 Stan Musial PUZ	.20	.09
642 Doug Sisk	.05	.02
643 Keith Hughes	.05	.02
644 Tom Glavine	1.00	.45
645 Al Newman	.05	.02
646 Scott Sanderson	.05	.02
647 Scott Terry	.05	.02
648 Tim Teufel SP	.07	.03
649 Garry Templeton SP	.07	.03
650 Manny Lee SP	.07	.03
651 Roger McDowell SP	.07	.03
652 Mookie Wilson SP	.20	.09
653 David Cone SP	.25	.11
654 Ron Gant SP	.25	.11
655 Joe Price SP	.07	.03
656 George Bell SP	.10	.05
657 Gregg Jefferies SP	.20	.09
658 Todd Stottlemyre SP	.20	.09
659 Geronimo Berroa SP	.25	.11
660 Jerry Royster SP	.07	.03

1988 Donruss Rookies

Bryan Harvey

	MINT	NRMT
COMP.FACT.SET (56)	12.00	5.50
COMMON CARD (1-56)	.15	.07
MINOR STARS	.30	.14
UNLISTED STARS	.60	.25
1 Mark Grace	2.50	1.10
2 Mike Campbell	.15	.07
3 Todd Frohwirth	.15	.07
4 Dave Stapleton	.15	.07
5 Shawn Abner	.15	.07
6 Jose Cecena	.15	.07
7 Dave Gallagher	.15	.07
8 Mark Parent	.15	.07
9 Cecil Espy	.15	.07
10 Pete Smith	.15	.07
11 Jay Buhner	1.25	.55
12 Pat Borders	.30	.14
13 Doug Jennings	.15	.07
14 Brady Anderson	1.50	.70
15 Pete Stanicek	.15	.07
16 Roberto Kelly	.40	.18
17 Jeff Treadway	.15	.07
18 Walt Weiss	1.00	.45
19 Paul Gibson	.15	.07
20 Tim Crews	.15	.07
21 Melido Perez	.15	.07
22 Steve Peters	.15	.07
23 Craig Worthington	.15	.07
24 John Trautwein	.15	.07
25 DeWayne Vaughn	.15	.07
26 David Wells	1.50	.70
27 Al Leiter	1.50	.70
28 Tim Belcher	.30	.14
29 Johnny Paredes	.15	.07
30 Chris Sabo	.30	.14
31 Damon Berryhill	.15	.07
32 Randy Milligan	.15	.07
33 Gary Thurman	.15	.07
34 Kevin Elster	.15	.07
35 Roberto Alomar	4.00	1.80
36 Edgar Martinez SP	2.00	.90
(Photo actually Edwin Nunez)		
37 Todd Stottlemyre	.40	.18
38 Joey Meyer	.15	.07
39 Carl Nichols	.15	.07
40 Jack McDowell	.60	.25
41 Jose Bautista	.15	.07
42 Sil Campusano	.15	.07
43 John Dopson	.15	.07
44 Jody Reed	.30	.14
45 Darrin Jackson	.15	.07
46 Mike Capel	.15	.07
47 Ron Gant	.40	.18
48 John Davis	.15	.07
49 Kevin Coffman	.15	.07
50 Cris Carpenter	.15	.07
51 Mackey Sasser	.15	.07
52 Luis Alicea	.15	.07
53 Bryan Harvey	.30	.14
54 Steve Ellsworth	.15	.07
55 Mike Macfarlane	.15	.07
56 Checklist 1-56	.15	.07

1989 Donruss

	MINT	NRMT
COMPLETE SET (660)	35.00	16.00
COMP.FACT.SET (672)	40.00	18.00
COMMON CARD (1-660)	.05	.02
MINOR STARS	.10	.05
UNLISTED STARS	.20	.09
COMP.GRANDSLAMMERS (12)	2.00	.90
*G'SLAMMER: EQUAL VALUE TO BASIC CARD		
ONE G'SLAMMERS SET PER FACT.SET		
COMP.MVP SET (26)	1.50	.70
*MVP'S: SAME VALUE AS BASIC CARDS		
MVP'S: RANDOM INSERTS IN PACKS		
1 Mike Greenwell DK	.05	.02
2 Bobby Bonilla DK DP	.10	.05
3 Pete Incaviglia DK	.05	.02
4 Chris Sabo DK DP	.05	.02
5 Robin Yount DK	.10	.05
6 Tony Gwynn DK DP	.20	.09
7 Carlton Fisk DK UER	.10	.05
(OF on back)		
8 Cory Snyder DK	.05	.02
9 David Cone DK UER	.10	.05
("hurdlers")		
10 Kevin Seitzer DK	.05	.02
11 Rick Reuschel DK	.05	.02
12 Johnny Ray DK	.05	.02
13 Dave Schmidt DK	.05	.02
14 Andres Galarraga DK	.10	.05
15 Kirk Gibson DK	.05	.02
16 Fred McGriff DK	.10	.05
17 Mark Grace DK	.10	.05
18 Jeff M. Robinson DK	.05	.02
19 Vince Coleman DK DP	.05	.02
20 Dave Henderson DK	.05	.02
21 Harold Reynolds DK	.05	.02
22 Gerald Perry DK	.05	.02
23 Frank Viola DK	.05	.02
24 Steve Bedrosian DK	.05	.02
25 Glenn Davis DK	.05	.02
26 Don Mattingly DK UER	.15	.07
(Doesn't mention Don's previous DK in 1985)		
27 DK Checklist 1-26 DP	.05	.02
28 Sandy Alomar Jr. RR	.25	.11
29 Steve Searcy RR	.05	.02
30 Cameron Drew RR	.05	.02
31 Gary Sheffield RR	.50	.23
32 Erik Hanson RR	.10	.05
33 Ken Griffey Jr. RR	25.00	11.00

34	Greg W. Harris RR	.05	.02
35	Gregg Jefferies RR	.10	.05
36	Luis Medina RR	.05	.02
37	Carlos Quintana RR	.05	.02
38	Felix Jose RR	.05	.02
39	Cris Carpenter RR	.05	.02
40	Ron Jones RR	.05	.02
41	Dave West RR	.05	.02
42	Randy Johnson RR UER 2.00		.90
	(Card says born in 1964 he was born in 1963)		
43	Mike Harkey RR	.05	.02
44	Pete Harnisch RR DP	.25	.11
45	Tom Gordon RR DP	.20	.09
46	Gregg Olson RR DP	.20	.09
47	Alex Sanchez RR DP	.05	.02
48	Ruben Sierra	.05	.02
49	Rafael Palmeiro	.25	.11
50	Ron Gant	.10	.05
51	Cal Ripken	.75	.35
52	Wally Joyner	.05	.05
53	Gary Carter	.15	.07
54	Andy Van Slyke	.10	.05
55	Robin Yount	.20	.09
56	Pete Incaviglia	.05	.02
57	Greg Brock	.05	.02
58	Melido Perez	.05	.02
59	Craig Lefferts	.05	.02
60	Gary Pettis	.05	.02
61	Danny Tartabull	.05	.02
62	Guillermo Hernandez	.05	.02
63	Ozzie Smith	.25	.11
64	Gary Gaetti	.10	.05
65	Mark Davis	.05	.02
66	Lee Smith	.10	.05
67	Dennis Eckersley	.15	.07
68	Wade Boggs	.20	.09
69	Mike Scott	.05	.02
70	Fred McGriff	.20	.09
71	Tom Browning	.05	.02
72	Claudell Washington	.05	.02
73	Mel Hall	.05	.02
74	Don Mattingly	.40	.18
75	Steve Bedrosian	.05	.02
76	Juan Samuel	.05	.02
77	Mike Scioscia	.05	.02
78	Dave Righetti	.05	.02
79	Alfredo Griffin	.05	.02
80	Eric Davis UER	.10	.05
	(165 games in 1988, should be 135)		
81	Juan Berenguer	.05	.02
82	Todd Worrell	.05	.02
83	Joe Carter	.15	.07
84	Steve Sax	.10	.05
85	Frank White	.10	.05
86	John Kruk	.05	.02
87	Rance Mulliniks	.05	.02
88	Alan Ashby	.05	.02
89	Charlie Leibrandt	.05	.02
90	Frank Tanana	.05	.02
91	Jose Canseco	.25	.11
92	Barry Bonds	.40	.18
93	Harold Reynolds	.05	.02
94	Mark McLemore	.05	.02
95	Mark McGwire	1.25	.55
96	Eddie Murray	.20	.09
97	Tim Raines	.10	.05
98	Robby Thompson	.05	.02
99	Kevin McReynolds	.05	.02
100	Checklist 28-137	.05	.02
101	Carlton Fisk	.20	.09
102	Dave Martinez	.05	.02
103	Glenn Braggs	.05	.02
104	Dale Murphy	.20	.09
105	Ryne Sandberg	.25	.11
106	Dennis Martinez	.10	.05
107	Pete O'Brien	.05	.02
108	Dick Schofield	.05	.02
109	Henry Cotto	.05	.02
110	Mike Marshall	.05	.02
111	Keith Moreland	.05	.02
112	Tom Brunansky	.05	.02
113	Kelly Gruber UER	.05	.02
	(Wrong birthdate)		
114	Brook Jacoby	.05	.02
115	Keith Brown	.05	.02
116	Matt Nokes	.05	.02
117	Keith Hernandez	.10	.05
118	Bob Forsch	.05	.02
119	Bert Blyleven UER	.10	.05
	(... 3000 strikeouts in 1987, should be 1986)		
120	Willie Wilson	.05	.02
121	Tommy Gregg	.05	.02
122	Jim Rice	.10	.05
123	Bob Knepper	.05	.02
124	Danny Jackson	.05	.02
125	Eric Plunk	.05	.02
126	Brian Fisher	.05	.02
127	Mike Pagliarulo	.05	.02
128	Tony Gwynn	.50	.23
129	Lance McCullers	.05	.02
130	Andres Galarraga	.20	.09
131	Jose Uribe	.05	.02
132	Kirk Gibson UER	.10	.05
	(Wrong birthdate)		
133	David Palmer	.05	.02
134	R.J. Reynolds	.05	.02
135	Greg Walker	.05	.02
136	Kirk McCaskill UER	.05	.02
	(Wrong birthdate)		
137	Shawon Dunston	.05	.02
138	Andy Allanson	.05	.02
139	Rob Murphy	.05	.02
140	Mike Aldrete	.05	.02
141	Terry Kennedy	.05	.02
142	Scott Fletcher	.05	.02
143	Steve Balboni	.05	.02
144	Bret Saberhagen	.10	.05
145	Ozzie Virgil	.05	.02
146	Dale Sveum	.05	.02
147	Darryl Strawberry	.10	.05
148	Harold Baines	.10	.05
149	George Bell	.10	.05
150	Dave Parker	.10	.05
151	Bobby Bonilla	.15	.07
152	Mookie Wilson	.05	.02
153	Ted Power	.05	.02
154	Nolan Ryan	.75	.35
155	Jeff Reardon	.10	.05
156	Tim Wallach	.05	.02
157	Jamie Moyer	.05	.02
158	Rich Gossage	.10	.05
159	Dave Winfield	.20	.09
160	Von Hayes	.05	.02
161	Willie McGee	.10	.05
162	Rich Gedman	.05	.02
163	Tony Pena	.05	.02
164	Mike Morgan	.05	.02
165	Charlie Hough	.05	.02
166	Mike Stanley	.05	.02
167	Andre Dawson	.20	.09
168	Joe Boever	.05	.02
169	Pete Stanicek	.05	.02
170	Bob Boone	.10	.05
171	Ron Darling	.05	.02
172	Bob Walk	.05	.02
173	Rob Deer	.05	.02
174	Steve Buechele	.05	.02
175	Ted Higuera	.05	.02
176	Ozzie Guillen	.05	.02
177	Candy Maldonado	.05	.02
178	Doyle Alexander	.05	.02
179	Mark Gubicza	.05	.02
180	Alan Trammell	.15	.07
181	Vince Coleman	.05	.02
182	Kirby Puckett	.40	.18
183	Chris Brown	.05	.02
184	Marty Barrett	.05	.02
185	Stan Javier	.05	.02
186	Mike Greenwell	.10	.05
187	Billy Hatcher	.05	.02
188	Jimmy Key	.10	.05
189	Nick Esasky	.05	.02
190	Don Slaught	.05	.02
191	Cory Snyder	.05	.02
192	John Candelaria	.05	.02
193	Mike Schmidt	.30	.14
194	Kevin Gross	.05	.02
195	John Tudor	.05	.02
196	Neil Allen	.05	.02
197	Orel Hershiser	.10	.05
198	Kal Daniels	.05	.02
199	Kent Hrbek	.10	.05
200	Checklist 138-247	.05	.02
201	Joe Magrane	.05	.02
202	Scott Bailes	.05	.02
203	Tim Belcher	.05	.02
204	George Brett	.40	.18
205	Benito Santiago	.05	.02
206	Tony Fernandez	.05	.02
207	Gerald Young	.05	.02
208	Bo Jackson	.15	.07
209	Chet Lemon	.05	.02
210	Storm Davis	.05	.02
211	Doug Drabek	.05	.02
212	Mickey Brantley UER	.05	.02
	(Photo actually Nelson Simmons)		
213	Devon White	.10	.05
214	Dave Stewart	.10	.05
215	Dave Schmidt	.05	.02
216	Bryn Smith	.05	.02
217	Brett Butler	.05	.02
218	Bob Ojeda	.05	.02
219	Steve Rosenberg	.05	.02
220	Hubie Brooks	.05	.02
221	B.J. Surhoff	.10	.05
222	Rick Mahler	.05	.02
223	Rick Sutcliffe	.05	.02
224	Neal Heaton	.05	.02
225	Mitch Williams	.05	.02
226	Chuck Finley	.10	.05
227	Mark Langston	.05	.02
228	Jesse Orosco	.05	.02
229	Ed Whitson	.05	.02
230	Terry Pendleton	.10	.05
231	Lloyd Moseby	.05	.02
232	Greg Swindell	.05	.02
233	John Franco	.10	.05
234	Jack Morris	.05	.02
235	Howard Johnson	.05	.02
236	Glenn Davis	.05	.02
237	Frank Viola	.05	.02
238	Kevin Seitzer	.05	.02
239	Gerald Perry	.05	.02
240	Dwight Evans	.10	.05
241	Jim Deshaies	.05	.02
242	Bo Diaz	.05	.02
243	Carney Lansford	.10	.05
244	Mike LaValliere	.05	.02
245	Rickey Henderson	.25	.11
246	Roberto Alomar	.30	.14
247	Jimmy Jones	.05	.02
248	Pascual Perez	.05	.02
249	Will Clark	.20	.09
250	Fernando Valenzuela	.10	.05
251	Shane Rawley	.05	.02
252	Sid Bream	.05	.02
253	Steve Lyons	.05	.02
254	Brian Downing	.05	.02
255	Mark Grace	.20	.09
256	Tom Candiotti	.05	.02
257	Barry Larkin	.20	.09
258	Mike Krukow	.05	.02
259	Billy Ripken	.05	.02
260	Cecilio Guante	.05	.02
261	Scott Bradley	.05	.02
262	Floyd Bannister	.05	.02
263	Pete Smith	.05	.02
264	Jim Gantner UER	.05	.02
	(Wrong birthdate)		
265	Roger McDowell	.05	.02
266	Bobby Thigpen	.05	.02
267	Jim Clancy	.05	.02
268	Terry Steinbach	.10	.05
269	Mike Dunne	.05	.02
270	Dwight Gooden	.10	.05
271	Mike Heath	.05	.02
272	Dave Smith	.05	.02
273	Keith Atherton	.05	.02
274	Tim Burke	.05	.02
275	Damon Berryhill	.05	.02
276	Vance Law	.05	.02
277	Rich Dotson	.05	.02
278	Lance Parrish	.10	.05
279	Denny Walling	.05	.02

❏ 280 Roger Clemens	.50	.23
❏ 281 Greg Mathews	.05	.02
❏ 282 Tom Niedenfuer	.05	.02
❏ 283 Paul Kilgus	.05	.02
❏ 284 Jose Guzman	.05	.02
❏ 285 Calvin Schiraldi	.05	.02
❏ 286 Charlie Puleo UER	.05	.02
(Career ERA 4.24, should be 4.23)		
❏ 287 Joe Orsulak	.05	.02
❏ 288 Jack Howell	.05	.02
❏ 289 Kevin Elster	.05	.02
❏ 290 Jose Lind	.05	.02
❏ 291 Paul Molitor	.20	.09
❏ 292 Cecil Espy	.05	.02
❏ 293 Bill Wegman	.05	.02
❏ 294 Dan Pasqua	.05	.02
❏ 295 Scott Garrelts UER	.05	.02
(Wrong birthdate)		
❏ 296 Walt Terrell	.05	.02
❏ 297 Ed Hearn	.05	.02
❏ 298 Lou Whitaker	.10	.05
❏ 299 Ken Dayley	.05	.02
❏ 300 Checklist 248-357	.05	.02
❏ 301 Tommy Herr	.05	.02
❏ 302 Mike Brumley	.05	.02
❏ 303 Ellis Burks	.15	.07
❏ 304 Curt Young UER	.05	.02
(Wrong birthdate)		
❏ 305 Jody Reed	.05	.02
❏ 306 Bill Doran	.05	.02
❏ 307 David Wells	.05	.02
❏ 308 Ron Robinson	.05	.02
❏ 309 Rafael Santana	.05	.02
❏ 310 Julio Franco	.05	.02
❏ 311 Jack Clark	.05	.02
❏ 312 Chris James	.05	.02
❏ 313 Milt Thompson	.05	.02
❏ 314 John Shelby	.05	.02
❏ 315 Al Leiter	.20	.09
❏ 316 Mike Davis	.05	.02
❏ 317 Chris Sabo	.05	.02
❏ 318 Greg Gagne	.05	.02
❏ 319 Jose Oquendo	.05	.02
❏ 320 John Farrell	.05	.02
❏ 321 Franklin Stubbs	.05	.02
❏ 322 Kurt Stillwell	.05	.02
❏ 323 Shawn Abner	.05	.02
❏ 324 Mike Marshall	.05	.02
❏ 325 Kevin Bass	.05	.02
❏ 326 Pat Tabler	.05	.02
❏ 327 Mike Henneman	.05	.02
❏ 328 Rick Honeycutt	.05	.02
❏ 329 John Smiley	.05	.02
❏ 330 Rey Quinones	.05	.02
❏ 331 Johnny Ray	.05	.02
❏ 332 Bob Welch	.05	.02
❏ 333 Larry Sheets	.05	.02
❏ 334 Jeff Parrett	.05	.02
❏ 335 Rick Reuschel UER	.05	.02
(For Don Robinson, should be Jeff)		
❏ 336 Randy Myers	.10	.05
❏ 337 Ken Williams	.05	.02
❏ 338 Andy McGaffigan	.05	.02
❏ 339 Joey Meyer	.05	.02
❏ 340 Dion James	.05	.02
❏ 341 Les Lancaster	.05	.02
❏ 342 Tom Foley	.05	.02
❏ 343 Geno Petralli	.05	.02
❏ 344 Dan Petry	.05	.02
❏ 345 Alvin Davis	.05	.02
❏ 346 Mickey Hatcher	.05	.02
❏ 347 Marvell Wynne	.05	.02
❏ 348 Danny Cox	.05	.02
❏ 349 Dave Stieb	.05	.02
❏ 350 Jay Bell	.15	.07
❏ 351 Jeff Treadway	.05	.02
❏ 352 Luis Salazar	.05	.02
❏ 353 Len Dykstra	.10	.05
❏ 354 Juan Agosto	.05	.02
❏ 355 Gene Larkin	.05	.02
❏ 356 Steve Farr	.05	.02
❏ 357 Paul Assenmacher	.05	.02
❏ 358 Todd Benzinger	.05	.02
❏ 359 Larry Andersen	.05	.02
❏ 360 Paul O'Neill	.10	.05
❏ 361 Ron Hassey	.05	.02
❏ 362 Jim Gott	.05	.02
❏ 363 Ken Phelps	.05	.02
❏ 364 Tim Flannery	.05	.02
❏ 365 Randy Ready	.05	.02
❏ 366 Nelson Santovenia	.05	.02
❏ 367 Kelly Downs	.05	.02
❏ 368 Danny Heep	.05	.02
❏ 369 Phil Bradley	.05	.02
❏ 370 Jeff D. Robinson	.05	.02
❏ 371 Ivan Calderon	.05	.02
❏ 372 Mike Witt	.05	.02
❏ 373 Greg Maddux	.60	.25
❏ 374 Carmen Castillo	.05	.02
❏ 375 Jose Rijo	.05	.02
❏ 376 Joe Price	.05	.02
❏ 377 Rene Gonzales	.05	.02
❏ 378 Oddibe McDowell	.05	.02
❏ 379 Jim Presley	.05	.02
❏ 380 Brad Wellman	.05	.02
❏ 381 Tom Glavine	.20	.09
❏ 382 Dan Plesac	.05	.02
❏ 383 Wally Backman	.05	.02
❏ 384 Dave Gallagher	.05	.02
❏ 385 Tom Henke	.05	.02
❏ 386 Luis Polonia	.05	.02
❏ 387 Junior Ortiz	.05	.02
❏ 388 David Cone	.20	.09
❏ 389 Dave Bergman	.05	.02
❏ 390 Danny Darwin	.05	.02
❏ 391 Dan Gladden	.05	.02
❏ 392 John Dopson	.05	.02
❏ 393 Frank DiPino	.05	.02
❏ 394 Al Nipper	.05	.02
❏ 395 Willie Randolph	.10	.05
❏ 396 Don Carman	.05	.02
❏ 397 Scott Terry	.05	.02
❏ 398 Rick Cerone	.05	.02
❏ 399 Tom Pagnozzi	.05	.02
❏ 400 Checklist 358-467	.05	.02
❏ 401 Mickey Tettleton	.10	.05
❏ 402 Curtis Wilkerson	.05	.02
❏ 403 Jeff Russell	.05	.02
❏ 404 Pat Perry	.05	.02
❏ 405 Jose Alvarez	.05	.02
❏ 406 Rick Schu	.05	.02
❏ 407 Sherman Corbett	.05	.02
❏ 408 Dave Magadan	.05	.02
❏ 409 Bob Kipper	.05	.02
❏ 410 Don August	.05	.02
❏ 411 Bob Brower	.05	.02
❏ 412 Chris Bosio	.05	.02
❏ 413 Jerry Reuss	.05	.02
❏ 414 Atlee Hammaker	.05	.02
❏ 415 Jim Walewander	.05	.02
❏ 416 Mike Macfarlane	.05	.02
❏ 417 Pat Sheridan	.05	.02
❏ 418 Pedro Guerrero	.05	.02
❏ 419 Allan Anderson	.05	.02
❏ 420 Mark Parent	.05	.02
❏ 421 Bob Stanley	.05	.02
❏ 422 Mike Gallego	.05	.02
❏ 423 Bruce Hurst	.05	.02
❏ 424 Dave Meads	.05	.02
❏ 425 Jesse Barfield	.05	.02
❏ 426 Rob Dibble	.10	.05
❏ 427 Joel Skinner	.05	.02
❏ 428 Ron Kittle	.05	.02
❏ 429 Rick Rhoden	.05	.02
❏ 430 Bob Dernier	.05	.02
❏ 431 Steve Jeltz	.05	.02
❏ 432 Rick Dempsey	.05	.02
❏ 433 Roberto Kelly	.10	.05
❏ 434 Dave Anderson	.05	.02
❏ 435 Herm Winningham	.05	.02
❏ 436 Al Newman	.05	.02
❏ 437 Jose DeLeon	.05	.02
❏ 438 Doug Jones	.05	.02
❏ 439 Brian Holton	.05	.02
❏ 440 Jeff Montgomery	.10	.05
❏ 441 Dickie Thon	.05	.02
❏ 442 Cecil Fielder	.10	.05
❏ 443 John Fishel	.05	.02
❏ 444 Jerry Don Gleaton	.05	.02
❏ 445 Paul Gibson	.05	.02
❏ 446 Walt Weiss	.05	.02
❏ 447 Glenn Wilson	.05	.02
❏ 448 Mike Moore	.05	.02
❏ 449 Chili Davis	.10	.05
❏ 450 Dave Henderson	.05	.02
❏ 451 Jose Bautista	.05	.02
❏ 452 Rex Hudler	.05	.02
❏ 453 Bob Brenly	.05	.02
❏ 454 Mackey Sasser	.05	.02
❏ 455 Daryl Boston	.05	.02
❏ 456 Mike R. Fitzgerald	.05	.02
❏ 457 Jeffrey Leonard	.05	.02
❏ 458 Bruce Sutter	.05	.02
❏ 459 Mitch Webster	.05	.02
❏ 460 Joe Hesketh	.05	.02
❏ 461 Bobby Witt	.05	.02
❏ 462 Stew Cliburn	.05	.02
❏ 463 Scott Bankhead	.05	.02
❏ 464 Ramon Martinez	.25	.11
❏ 465 Dave Leiper	.05	.02
❏ 466 Luis Alicea	.05	.02
❏ 467 John Cerutti	.05	.02
❏ 468 Ron Washington	.05	.02
❏ 469 Jeff Reed	.05	.02
❏ 470 Jeff M. Robinson	.05	.02
❏ 471 Sid Fernandez	.05	.02
❏ 472 Terry Puhl	.05	.02
❏ 473 Charlie Lea	.05	.02
❏ 474 Israel Sanchez	.05	.02
❏ 475 Bruce Benedict	.05	.02
❏ 476 Oil Can Boyd	.05	.02
❏ 477 Craig Reynolds	.05	.02
❏ 478 Frank Williams	.05	.02
❏ 479 Greg Cadaret	.05	.02
❏ 480 Randy Kramer	.05	.02
❏ 481 Dave Eiland	.05	.02
❏ 482 Eric Show	.05	.02
❏ 483 Garry Templeton	.05	.02
❏ 484 Wallace Johnson	.05	.02
❏ 485 Kevin Mitchell	.10	.05
❏ 486 Tim Crews	.05	.02
❏ 487 Mike Maddux	.05	.02
❏ 488 Dave LaPoint	.05	.02
❏ 489 Fred Manrique	.05	.02
❏ 490 Greg Minton	.05	.02
❏ 491 Doug Dascenzo UER	.05	.02
(Photo actually Damon Berryhill)		
❏ 492 Willie Upshaw	.05	.02
❏ 493 Jack Armstrong	.05	.02
❏ 494 Kirt Manwaring	.05	.02
❏ 495 Jeff Ballard	.05	.02
❏ 496 Jeff Kunkel	.05	.02
❏ 497 Mike Campbell	.05	.02
❏ 498 Gary Thurman	.05	.02
❏ 499 Zane Smith	.05	.02
❏ 500 Checklist 468-577 DP	.05	.02
❏ 501 Mike Birkbeck	.05	.02
❏ 502 Terry Leach	.05	.02
❏ 503 Shawn Hillegas	.05	.02
❏ 504 Manny Lee	.05	.02
❏ 505 Doug Jennings	.05	.02
❏ 506 Ken Oberkfell	.05	.02
❏ 507 Tim Teufel	.05	.02
❏ 508 Tom Brookens	.05	.02
❏ 509 Rafael Ramirez	.05	.02
❏ 510 Fred Toliver	.05	.02
❏ 511 Brian Holman	.05	.02
❏ 512 Mike Bielecki	.05	.02
❏ 513 Jeff Pico	.05	.02
❏ 514 Charles Hudson	.05	.02
❏ 515 Bruce Ruffin	.05	.02
❏ 516 Larry McWilliams UER	.05	.02
(New Richland, should be North Richland)		
❏ 517 Jeff Sellers	.05	.02
❏ 518 John Costello	.05	.02
❏ 519 Brady Anderson	.40	.18
❏ 520 Craig McMurtry	.05	.02
❏ 521 Ray Hayward DP	.05	.02
❏ 522 Drew Hall DP	.05	.02
❏ 523 Mark Lemke DP	.15	.07
❏ 524 Oswald Peraza DP	.05	.02
❏ 525 Bryan Harvey DP	.05	.02
❏ 526 Rick Aguilera DP	.10	.05
❏ 527 Tom Prince DP	.05	.02

No.	Player	MINT	NRMT
☐ 528	Mark Clear DP	.05	.02
☐ 529	Jerry Browne DP	.05	.02
☐ 530	Juan Castillo DP	.05	.02
☐ 531	Jack McDowell DP	.10	.05
☐ 532	Chris Speier DP	.05	.02
☐ 533	Darrell Evans DP	.10	.05
☐ 534	Luis Aquino DP	.05	.02
☐ 535	Eric King DP	.05	.02
☐ 536	Ken Hill DP	.20	.09
☐ 537	Randy Bush DP	.05	.02
☐ 538	Shane Mack DP	.05	.02
☐ 539	Tom Bolton DP	.05	.02
☐ 540	Gene Nelson DP	.05	.02
☐ 541	Wes Gardner DP	.05	.02
☐ 542	Ken Caminiti DP	.20	.09
☐ 543	Duane Ward DP	.05	.02
☐ 544	Norm Charlton DP	.10	.05
☐ 545	Hal Morris DP	.20	.09
☐ 546	Rich Yett DP	.05	.02
☐ 547	Hensley Meulens DP	.05	.02
☐ 548	Greg A. Harris DP	.05	.02
☐ 549	Darren Daulton DP	.10	.05
	(Posing as right-handed hitter)		
☐ 550	Jeff Hamilton DP	.05	.02
☐ 551	Luis Aguayo DP	.05	.02
☐ 552	Tim Leary DP	.05	.02
	(Resembles M.Marshall)		
☐ 553	Ron Oester DP	.05	.02
☐ 554	Steve Lombardozzi DP	.05	.02
☐ 555	Tim Jones DP	.05	.02
☐ 556	Bud Black DP	.05	.02
☐ 557	Alejandro Pena DP	.05	.02
☐ 558	Jose DeJesus DP	.05	.02
☐ 559	Dennis Rasmussen DP	.05	.02
☐ 560	Pat Borders DP	.10	.05
☐ 561	Craig Biggio DP	.75	.35
☐ 562	Luis DeLosSantos DP	.05	.02
☐ 563	Fred Lynn DP	.05	.02
☐ 564	Todd Burns DP	.05	.02
☐ 565	Felix Fermin DP	.05	.02
☐ 566	Darnell Coles DP	.05	.02
☐ 567	Willie Fraser DP	.05	.02
☐ 568	Glenn Hubbard DP	.05	.02
☐ 569	Craig Worthington DP	.05	.02
☐ 570	Johnny Paredes DP	.05	.02
☐ 571	Don Robinson DP	.05	.02
☐ 572	Barry Lyons DP	.05	.02
☐ 573	Bill Long DP	.05	.02
☐ 574	Tracy Jones DP	.05	.02
☐ 575	Juan Nieves DP	.05	.02
☐ 576	Andres Thomas DP	.05	.02
☐ 577	Rolando Roomes DP	.05	.02
☐ 578	Luis Rivera UER DP	.05	.02
	(Wrong birthdate)		
☐ 579	Chad Kreuter DP	.05	.02
☐ 580	Tony Armas DP	.05	.02
☐ 581	Jay Buhner DP	.20	.09
☐ 582	Ricky Horton DP	.05	.02
☐ 583	Andy Hawkins DP	.05	.02
☐ 584	Sil Campusano DP	.05	.02
☐ 585	Dave Clark DP	.05	.02
☐ 586	Van Snider DP	.05	.02
☐ 587	Todd Frohwirth DP	.05	.02
☐ 588	Warren Spahn PUZ	.20	.09
☐ 589	William Brennan	.05	.02
☐ 590	German Gonzalez	.05	.02
☐ 591	Ernie Whitt DP	.05	.02
☐ 592	Jeff Blauser	.10	.05
☐ 593	Spike Owen DP	.05	.02
☐ 594	Matt Williams	.20	.09
☐ 595	Lloyd McClendon DP	.05	.02
☐ 596	Steve Ontiveros	.05	.02
☐ 597	Scott Medvin	.05	.02
☐ 598	Hipolito Pena DP	.05	.02
☐ 599	Jerald Clark DP	.05	.02
☐ 600A	Checklist 578-660 DP	.05	.02
	(635 Kurt Schilling)		
☐ 600B	Checklist 578-660 DP	.05	.02
	(635 Curt Schilling; MVP's not listed on checklist card)		
☐ 600C	Checklist 578-660 DP	.05	.02
	(635 Curt Schilling; MVP's listed following 660)		

No.	Player	MINT	NRMT
☐ 601	Carmelo Martinez DP	.05	.02
☐ 602	Mike LaCoss	.05	.02
☐ 603	Mike Devereaux	.05	.02
☐ 604	Alex Madrid DP	.05	.02
☐ 605	Gary Redus DP	.05	.02
☐ 606	Lance Johnson	.10	.05
☐ 607	Terry Clark DP	.05	.02
☐ 608	Manny Trillo DP	.05	.02
☐ 609	Scott Jordan	.10	.05
☐ 610	Jay Howell DP	.05	.02
☐ 611	Francisco Melendez	.05	.02
☐ 612	Mike Boddicker	.05	.02
☐ 613	Kevin Brown DP	.40	.18
☐ 614	Dave Valle	.05	.02
☐ 615	Tim Laudner DP	.05	.02
☐ 616	Andy Nezelek UER	.05	.02
	(Wrong birthdate)		
☐ 617	Chuck Crim	.05	.02
☐ 618	Jack Savage DP	.05	.02
☐ 619	Adam Peterson DP	.05	.02
☐ 620	Todd Stottlemyre	.15	.07
☐ 621	Lance Blankenship	.05	.02
☐ 622	Miguel Garcia DP	.05	.02
☐ 623	Keith A. Miller DP	.05	.02
☐ 624	Ricky Jordan DP	.10	.05
☐ 625	Ernest Riles DP	.05	.02
☐ 626	John Moses DP	.05	.02
☐ 627	Nelson Liriano DP	.05	.02
☐ 628	Mike Smithson DP	.05	.02
☐ 629	Scott Sanderson	.05	.02
☐ 630	Dale Mohorcic	.05	.02
☐ 631	Marvin Freeman DP	.05	.02
☐ 632	Mike Young DP	.05	.02
☐ 633	Dennis Lamp	.05	.02
☐ 634	Dante Bichette DP	.40	.18
☐ 635	Curt Schilling DP	2.00	.90
☐ 636	Scott May DP	.05	.02
☐ 637	Mike Schooler	.05	.02
☐ 638	Rick Leach	.05	.02
☐ 639	Tom Lampkin UER	.05	.02
	(Throws Left, should be Throws Right)		
☐ 640	Brian Meyer	.05	.02
☐ 641	Brian Harper	.05	.02
☐ 642	John Smoltz	.75	.35
☐ 643	Jose Canseco	.10	.05
	(40/40 Club)		
☐ 644	Bill Schroeder	.05	.02
☐ 645	Edgar Martinez	.20	.09
☐ 646	Dennis Cook	.05	.02
☐ 647	Barry Jones	.05	.02
☐ 648	Orel Hershiser	.10	.05
	(59 and Counting)		
☐ 649	Rod Nichols	.05	.02
☐ 650	Jody Davis	.05	.02
☐ 651	Bob Milacki	.05	.02
☐ 652	Mike Jackson	.15	.07
☐ 653	Derek Lilliquist	.05	.02
☐ 654	Paul Mirabella	.05	.02
☐ 655	Mike Diaz	.05	.02
☐ 656	Jeff Musselman	.05	.02
☐ 657	Jerry Reed	.05	.02
☐ 658	Kevin Blankenship	.05	.02
☐ 659	Wayne Tolleson	.05	.02
☐ 660	Eric Hetzel	.05	.02

1989 Donruss Rookies

1989 Donruss Baseball's Best

	MINT	NRMT
COMP.FACT.SET (56)	35.00	16.00
COMMON CARD (1-56)	.05	.02
MINOR STARS	.10	.05
UNLISTED STARS	.20	.09

No.	Player	MINT	NRMT
☐ 1	Gary Sheffield	.50	.23
☐ 2	Gregg Jefferies	.10	.05
☐ 3	Ken Griffey Jr.	25.00	11.00
☐ 4	Tom Gordon	.20	.09
☐ 5	Billy Spiers	.05	.02
☐ 6	Deion Sanders	.75	.35
☐ 7	Donn Pall	.05	.02
☐ 8	Steve Carter	.05	.02
☐ 9	Francisco Oliveras	.05	.02
☐ 10	Steve Wilson	.05	.02
☐ 11	Bob Geren	.05	.02
☐ 12	Tony Castillo	.05	.02
☐ 13	Kenny Rogers	.20	.09
☐ 14	Carlos Martinez	.05	.02
☐ 15	Edgar Martinez	.20	.09
☐ 16	Jim Abbott	.20	.09
☐ 17	Torey Lovullo	.05	.02
☐ 18	Mark Carreon	.05	.02
☐ 19	Geronimo Berroa	.05	.02
☐ 20	Luis Medina	.05	.02
☐ 21	Sandy Alomar Jr.	.25	.11
☐ 22	Bob Milacki	.05	.02
☐ 23	Joe Girardi	.20	.09
☐ 24	German Gonzalez	.05	.02
☐ 25	Craig Worthington	.05	.02
☐ 26	Jerome Walton	.20	.09
☐ 27	Gary Wayne	.05	.02
☐ 28	Tim Jones	.05	.02
☐ 29	Dante Bichette	.40	.18
☐ 30	Alexis Infante	.05	.02
☐ 31	Ken Hill	.20	.09
☐ 32	Dwight Smith	.10	.05
☐ 33	Luis de los Santos	.05	.02
☐ 34	Eric Yelding	.05	.02
☐ 35	Gregg Olson	.20	.09
☐ 36	Phil Stephenson	.05	.02
☐ 37	Ken Patterson	.05	.02
☐ 38	Rick Wrona	.05	.02
☐ 39	Mike Brumley	.05	.02
☐ 40	Cris Carpenter	.05	.02
☐ 41	Jeff Brantley	.15	.07
☐ 42	Ron Jones	.05	.02
☐ 43	Randy Johnson	2.00	.90
☐ 44	Kevin Brown	.40	.18
☐ 45	Ramon Martinez	.20	.09
☐ 46	Greg W.Harris	.05	.02
☐ 47	Steve Finley	.40	.18
☐ 48	Randy Kramer	.05	.02
☐ 49	Erik Hanson	.10	.05
☐ 50	Matt Merullo	.05	.02
☐ 51	Mike Devereaux	.05	.02
☐ 52	Clay Parker	.05	.02
☐ 53	Omar Vizquel	.50	.23
☐ 54	Derek Lilliquist	.05	.02
☐ 55	Junior Felix	.05	.02
☐ 56	Checklist 1-56	.05	.02

	MINT	NRMT
COMP.FACT.SET (336)	100.00	45.00

		Value 1	Value 2
	COMMON PLAYER (1-336)	.15	.07
	MINOR STARS	.25	.11
	UNLISTED STARS	.50	.23
	DISTRIBUTED ONLY IN FACTORY SET FORM		
☐ 1	Don Mattingly	1.00	.45
☐ 2	Tom Glavine	.50	.23
☐ 3	Bert Blyleven	.25	.11
☐ 4	Andre Dawson	.50	.23
☐ 5	Pete O'Brien	.15	.07
☐ 6	Eric Davis	.25	.11
☐ 7	George Brett	1.00	.45
☐ 8	Glenn Davis	.15	.07
☐ 9	Ellis Burks	.30	.14
☐ 10	Kirk Gibson	.25	.11
☐ 11	Carlton Fisk	.50	.23
☐ 12	Andres Galarraga	.50	.23
☐ 13	Alan Trammell	.30	.14
☐ 14	Dwight Gooden	.25	.11
☐ 15	Paul Molitor	.50	.23
☐ 16	Roger McDowell	.15	.07
☐ 17	Doug Drabek	.15	.07
☐ 18	Kent Hrbek	.25	.11
☐ 19	Vince Coleman	.15	.07
☐ 20	Steve Sax	.15	.07
☐ 21	Roberto Alomar	.75	.35
☐ 22	Carney Lansford	.25	.11
☐ 23	Will Clark	.50	.23
☐ 24	Alvin Davis	.15	.07
☐ 25	Bobby Thigpen	.15	.07
☐ 26	Ryne Sandberg	.60	.25
☐ 27	Devon White	.25	.11
☐ 28	Mike Greenwell	.15	.07
☐ 29	Dale Murphy	.50	.23
☐ 30	Jeff Ballard	.15	.07
☐ 31	Kelly Gruber	.15	.07
☐ 32	Julio Franco	.15	.07
☐ 33	Bobby Bonilla	.30	.14
☐ 34	Tim Wallach	.15	.07
☐ 35	Lou Whitaker	.25	.11
☐ 36	Jay Howell	.15	.07
☐ 37	Greg Maddux	1.50	.70
☐ 38	Bill Doran	.15	.07
☐ 39	Danny Tartabull	.15	.07
☐ 40	Darryl Strawberry	.25	.11
☐ 41	Ron Darling	.15	.07
☐ 42	Tony Gwynn	1.25	.55
☐ 43	Mark McGwire	3.00	1.35
☐ 44	Ozzie Smith	.60	.25
☐ 45	Andy Van Slyke	.25	.11
☐ 46	Juan Berenguer	.15	.07
☐ 47	Von Hayes	.15	.07
☐ 48	Tony Fernandez	.15	.07
☐ 49	Eric Plunk	.15	.07
☐ 50	Ernest Riles	.15	.07
☐ 51	Harold Reynolds	.15	.07
☐ 52	Andy Hawkins	.15	.07
☐ 53	Robin Yount	.50	.23
☐ 54	Danny Jackson	.15	.07
☐ 55	Nolan Ryan	2.00	.90
☐ 56	Joe Carter	.30	.14
☐ 57	Jose Canseco	.60	.25
☐ 58	Jody Davis	.15	.07
☐ 59	Lance Parrish	.15	.07
☐ 60	Mitch Williams	.15	.07
☐ 61	Brook Jacoby	.15	.07
☐ 62	Tom Browning	.15	.07
☐ 63	Kurt Stillwell	.15	.07
☐ 64	Rafael Ramirez	.15	.07
☐ 65	Roger Clemens	1.25	.55
☐ 66	Mike Scioscia	.15	.07
☐ 67	Dave Gallagher	.15	.07
☐ 68	Mark Langston	.15	.07
☐ 69	Chet Lemon	.15	.07
☐ 70	Kevin McReynolds	.15	.07
☐ 71	Rob Deer	.15	.07
☐ 72	Tommy Herr	.15	.07
☐ 73	Barry Bonds	1.00	.45
☐ 74	Frank Viola	.15	.07
☐ 75	Pedro Guerrero	.15	.07
☐ 76	Dave Righetti UER (ML total of 7 wins incorrect)	.15	.07
☐ 77	Bruce Hurst	.15	.07
☐ 78	Rickey Henderson	.60	.25
☐ 79	Robby Thompson	.15	.07
☐ 80	Randy Johnson	4.00	1.80
☐ 81	Harold Baines	.25	.11
☐ 82	Calvin Schiraldi	.15	.07
☐ 83	Kirk McCaskill	.15	.07
☐ 84	Lee Smith	.25	.11
☐ 85	John Smoltz	1.50	.70
☐ 86	Mickey Tettleton	.25	.11
☐ 87	Jimmy Key	.25	.11
☐ 88	Rafael Palmeiro	.60	.25
☐ 89	Sid Bream	.15	.07
☐ 90	Dennis Martinez	.25	.11
☐ 91	Frank Tanana	.15	.07
☐ 92	Eddie Murray	.50	.23
☐ 93	Shawon Dunston	.15	.07
☐ 94	Mike Scott	.15	.07
☐ 95	Bret Saberhagen	.25	.11
☐ 96	David Cone	.50	.23
☐ 97	Kevin Elster	.15	.07
☐ 98	Jack Clark	.15	.07
☐ 99	Dave Stewart	.25	.11
☐ 100	Jose Oquendo	.15	.07
☐ 101	Jose Lind	.15	.07
☐ 102	Gary Gaetti	.25	.11
☐ 103	Ricky Jordan	.15	.07
☐ 104	Fred McGriff	.50	.23
☐ 105	Don Slaught	.15	.07
☐ 106	Jose Uribe	.15	.07
☐ 107	Jeffrey Leonard	.15	.07
☐ 108	Lee Guetterman	.15	.07
☐ 109	Chris Bosio	.15	.07
☐ 110	Barry Larkin	.50	.23
☐ 111	Ruben Sierra	.15	.07
☐ 112	Greg Swindell	.15	.07
☐ 113	Gary Sheffield	1.00	.45
☐ 114	Lonnie Smith	.15	.07
☐ 115	Chili Davis	.25	.11
☐ 116	Damon Berryhill	.15	.07
☐ 117	Tom Candiotti	.15	.07
☐ 118	Kal Daniels	.15	.07
☐ 119	Mark Gubicza	.15	.07
☐ 120	Jim Deshaies	.15	.07
☐ 121	Dwight Evans	.25	.11
☐ 122	Mike Morgan	.15	.07
☐ 123	Dan Pasqua	.15	.07
☐ 124	Bryn Smith	.15	.07
☐ 125	Doyle Alexander	.15	.07
☐ 126	Howard Johnson	.15	.07
☐ 127	Chuck Crim	.15	.07
☐ 128	Darren Daulton	.25	.11
☐ 129	Jeff Robinson	.15	.07
☐ 130	Kirby Puckett	1.00	.45
☐ 131	Joe Magrane	.15	.07
☐ 132	Jesse Barfield	.15	.07
☐ 133	Mark Davis UER (Photo actually Dave Leiper)	.15	.07
☐ 134	Dennis Eckersley	.30	.14
☐ 135	Mike Krukow	.15	.07
☐ 136	Jay Buhner	.50	.23
☐ 137	Ozzie Guillen	.15	.07
☐ 138	Rick Sutcliffe	.15	.07
☐ 139	Wally Joyner	.25	.11
☐ 140	Wade Boggs	.50	.23
☐ 141	Jeff Treadway	.15	.07
☐ 142	Cal Ripken	2.00	.90
☐ 143	Dave Stieb	.15	.07
☐ 144	Pete Incaviglia	.15	.07
☐ 145	Bob Walk	.15	.07
☐ 146	Nelson Santovenia	.15	.07
☐ 147	Mike Heath	.15	.07
☐ 148	Willie Randolph	.25	.11
☐ 149	Paul Kilgus	.15	.07
☐ 150	Billy Hatcher	.15	.07
☐ 151	Steve Farr	.15	.07
☐ 152	Gregg Jefferies	.15	.07
☐ 153	Randy Myers	.25	.11
☐ 154	Garry Templeton	.15	.07
☐ 155	Walt Weiss	.15	.07
☐ 156	Terry Pendleton	.25	.11
☐ 157	John Smiley	.15	.07
☐ 158	Greg Gagne	.15	.07
☐ 159	Len Dykstra	.25	.11
☐ 160	Nelson Liriano	.15	.07
☐ 161	Alvaro Espinoza	.15	.07
☐ 162	Rick Reuschel	.15	.07
☐ 163	Omar Vizquel UER (Photo actually Darnell Coles)	.25	.11
☐ 164	Clay Parker	.15	.07
☐ 165	Dan Plesac	.15	.07
☐ 166	John Franco	.25	.11
☐ 167	Scott Fletcher	.15	.07
☐ 168	Cory Snyder	.15	.07
☐ 169	Bo Jackson	.30	.14
☐ 170	Tommy Gregg	.15	.07
☐ 171	Jim Abbott	.25	.11
☐ 172	Jerome Walton	.50	.23
☐ 173	Doug Jones	.15	.07
☐ 174	Todd Benzinger	.15	.07
☐ 175	Frank White	.25	.11
☐ 176	Craig Biggio	2.00	.90
☐ 177	John Dopson	.15	.07
☐ 178	Alfredo Griffin	.15	.07
☐ 179	Melido Perez	.15	.07
☐ 180	Tim Burke	.15	.07
☐ 181	Mark Davis	.15	.07
☐ 182	Gary Carter	.30	.14
☐ 183	Ted Higuera	.15	.07
☐ 184	Ken Howell	.15	.07
☐ 185	Rey Quinones	.15	.07
☐ 186	Wally Backman	.15	.07
☐ 187	Tom Brunansky	.15	.07
☐ 188	Steve Balboni	.15	.07
☐ 189	Marvell Wynne	.15	.07
☐ 190	Dave Henderson	.15	.07
☐ 191	Don Robinson	.15	.07
☐ 192	Ken Griffey Jr.	50.00	22.00
☐ 193	Ivan Calderon	.15	.07
☐ 194	Mike Bielecki	.15	.07
☐ 195	Johnny Ray	.15	.07
☐ 196	Rob Murphy	.15	.07
☐ 197	Andres Thomas	.15	.07
☐ 198	Phil Bradley	.15	.07
☐ 199	Junior Felix	.15	.07
☐ 200	Jeff Russell	.15	.07
☐ 201	Mike LaValliere	.15	.07
☐ 202	Kevin Gross	.15	.07
☐ 203	Keith Moreland	.15	.07
☐ 204	Mike Marshall	.15	.07
☐ 205	Dwight Smith	.25	.11
☐ 206	Jim Clancy	.15	.07
☐ 207	Kevin Seitzer	.15	.07
☐ 208	Keith Hernandez	.25	.11
☐ 209	Bob Ojeda	.15	.07
☐ 210	Ed Whitson	.15	.07
☐ 211	Tony Phillips	.15	.07
☐ 212	Milt Thompson	.15	.07
☐ 213	Randy Kramer	.15	.07
☐ 214	Randy Bush	.15	.07
☐ 215	Randy Ready	.15	.07
☐ 216	Duane Ward	.15	.07
☐ 217	Jimmy Jones	.15	.07
☐ 218	Scott Garrelts	.15	.07
☐ 219	Scott Bankhead	.15	.07
☐ 220	Lance McCullers	.15	.07
☐ 221	B.J. Surhoff	.25	.11
☐ 222	Chris Sabo	.15	.07
☐ 223	Steve Buechele	.15	.07
☐ 224	Joel Skinner	.15	.07
☐ 225	Orel Hershiser	.25	.11
☐ 226	Derek Lilliquist	.15	.07
☐ 227	Claudell Washington	.15	.07
☐ 228	Lloyd McClendon	.15	.07
☐ 229	Felix Fermin	.15	.07
☐ 230	Paul O'Neill	.25	.11
☐ 231	Charlie Leibrandt	.15	.07
☐ 232	Dave Smith	.15	.07
☐ 233	Bob Stanley	.15	.07
☐ 234	Tim Belcher	.15	.07
☐ 235	Eric King	.15	.07
☐ 236	Spike Owen	.15	.07
☐ 237	Mike Henneman	.15	.07
☐ 238	Juan Samuel	.15	.07
☐ 239	Greg Brock	.15	.07
☐ 240	John Kruk	.25	.11
☐ 241	Glenn Wilson	.15	.07
☐ 242	Jeff Reardon	.25	.11
☐ 243	Todd Worrell	.15	.07
☐ 244	Dave LaPoint	.15	.07
☐ 245	Walt Terrell	.15	.07
☐ 246	Mike Moore	.15	.07
☐ 247	Kelly Downs	.15	.07

☐ 248 Dave Valle	.15	.07
☐ 249 Ron Kittle	.15	.07
☐ 250 Steve Wilson	.15	.07
☐ 251 Dick Schofield	.15	.07
☐ 252 Marty Barrett	.15	.07
☐ 253 Dion James	.15	.07
☐ 254 Bob Milacki	.15	.07
☐ 255 Ernie Whitt	.15	.07
☐ 256 Kevin Brown	.60	.25
☐ 257 R.J. Reynolds	.15	.07
☐ 258 Tim Raines	.25	.11
☐ 259 Frank Williams	.15	.07
☐ 260 Jose Gonzalez	.15	.07
☐ 261 Mitch Webster	.15	.07
☐ 262 Ken Caminiti	.50	.23
☐ 263 Bob Boone	.25	.11
☐ 264 Dave Magadan	.15	.07
☐ 265 Rick Aguilera	.25	.11
☐ 266 Chris James	.15	.07
☐ 267 Bob Welch	.15	.07
☐ 268 Ken Dayley	.15	.07
☐ 269 Junior Ortiz	.15	.07
☐ 270 Allan Anderson	.15	.07
☐ 271 Steve Jeltz	.15	.07
☐ 272 George Bell	.15	.07
☐ 273 Roberto Kelly	.25	.11
☐ 274 Brett Butler	.25	.11
☐ 275 Mike Schooler	.15	.07
☐ 276 Ken Phelps	.15	.07
☐ 277 Glenn Braggs	.15	.07
☐ 278 Jose Rijo	.15	.07
☐ 279 Bobby Witt	.15	.07
☐ 280 Jerry Browne	.15	.07
☐ 281 Kevin Mitchell	.25	.11
☐ 282 Craig Worthington	.15	.07
☐ 283 Greg Minton	.15	.07
☐ 284 Nick Esasky	.15	.07
☐ 285 John Farrell	.15	.07
☐ 286 Rick Mahler	.15	.07
☐ 287 Tom Gordon	.50	.23
☐ 288 Gerald Young	.15	.07
☐ 289 Jody Reed	.15	.07
☐ 290 Jeff Hamilton	.15	.07
☐ 291 Gerald Perry	.15	.07
☐ 292 Hubie Brooks	.15	.07
☐ 293 Bo Diaz	.15	.07
☐ 294 Terry Puhl	.15	.07
☐ 295 Jim Gantner	.15	.07
☐ 296 Jeff Parrett	.15	.07
☐ 297 Mike Boddicker	.15	.07
☐ 298 Dan Gladden	.15	.07
☐ 299 Tony Pena	.15	.07
☐ 300 Checklist Card	.15	.07
☐ 301 Tom Henke	.15	.07
☐ 302 Pascual Perez	.15	.07
☐ 303 Steve Bedrosian	.15	.07
☐ 304 Ken Hill	.25	.11
☐ 305 Jerry Reuss	.15	.07
☐ 306 Jim Eisenreich	.15	.07
☐ 307 Jack Howell	.15	.07
☐ 308 Rick Cerone	.15	.07
☐ 309 Tim Leary	.15	.07
☐ 310 Joe Orsulak	.15	.07
☐ 311 Jim Dwyer	.15	.07
☐ 312 Geno Petralli	.15	.07
☐ 313 Rick Honeycutt	.15	.07
☐ 314 Tom Foley	.15	.07
☐ 315 Kenny Rogers	.15	.23
☐ 316 Mike Flanagan	.15	.07
☐ 317 Bryan Harvey	.15	.07
☐ 318 Billy Ripken	.15	.07
☐ 319 Jeff Montgomery	.25	.11
☐ 320 Erik Hanson	.25	.11
☐ 321 Brian Downing	.15	.07
☐ 322 Gregg Olson	.50	.23
☐ 323 Terry Steinbach	.25	.11
☐ 324 Sammy Sosa	50.00	22.00
☐ 325 Gene Harris	.15	.07
☐ 326 Mike Devereaux	.15	.07
☐ 327 Dennis Cook	.15	.07
☐ 328 David Wells	.15	.07
☐ 329 Checklist Card	.15	.07
☐ 330 Kirt Manwaring	.15	.07
☐ 331 Jim Presley	.15	.07
☐ 332 Checklist Card	.15	.07
☐ 333 Chuck Finley	.25	.11

☐ 334 Rob Dibble	.25	.11
☐ 335 Cecil Espy	.15	.07
☐ 336 Dave Parker	.25	.11

1990 Donruss

	MINT	NRMT
COMPLETE SET (716)	12.00	5.50
COMP.FACT.SET (728)	15.00	6.75
COMMON CARD (1-716)	.05	.02
MINOR STARS	.10	.05
UNLISTED STARS	.20	.09
SUBSET CARDS HALF VALUE OF BASE CARDS		
COMP.BONUS MVP SET (26)	1.50	.70
*MVP'S: SAME VALUE AS BASIC CARDS		
MVP'S: RANDOM INSERTS IN PACKS		
COMP.G'SLAMMERS SET (12)	1.50	.70
*G'SLAMMERS: SAME VALUE AS BASIC CARDS		
ONE G.SLAM SET PER FACT.SET		

☐ 1 Bo Jackson DK	.10	.05
☐ 2 Steve Sax DK	.05	.02
☐ 3A Ruben Sierra DK ERR	.05	.02
(No small line on top border on card back)		
☐ 3B Ruben Sierra DK COR	.05	.02
☐ 4 Ken Griffey Jr. DK	1.00	.45
☐ 5 Mickey Tettleton DK	.05	.02
☐ 6 Dave Stewart DK	.05	.02
☐ 7 Jim Deshaies DK DP	.05	.02
☐ 8 John Smoltz DK	.20	.09
☐ 9 Mike Bielecki DK	.05	.02
☐ 10A Brian Downing DK	.20	.09
ERR (Reverse negative on card front)		
☐ 10B Brian Downing DK	.05	.02
COR		
☐ 11 Kevin Mitchell DK	.05	.02
☐ 12 Kelly Gruber DK	.05	.02
☐ 13 Joe Magrane DK	.05	.02
☐ 14 John Franco DK	.05	.02
☐ 15 Ozzie Guillen DK	.05	.02
☐ 16 Lou Whitaker DK	.05	.02
☐ 17 John Smiley DK	.05	.02
☐ 18 Howard Johnson DK	.05	.02
☐ 19 Willie Randolph DK	.10	.05
☐ 20 Chris Bosio DK	.05	.02
☐ 21 Tommy Herr DK DP	.05	.02
☐ 22 Dan Gladden DK	.05	.02
☐ 23 Ellis Burks DK	.10	.05
☐ 24 Pete O'Brien DK	.05	.02
☐ 25 Bryn Smith DK	.05	.02
☐ 26 Ed Whitson DK DP	.05	.02
☐ 27 DK Checklist 1-27 DP	.05	.02
(Comments on Perez-Steele on back)		
☐ 28 Pomin Ventura RR	.20	.09
☐ 29 Todd Zeile RR	.10	.05
☐ 30 Sandy Alomar Jr. RR	.10	.05
☐ 31 Kent Mercker RR	.05	.02
☐ 32 Ben McDonald RR UER	.10	.05
(Middle name Benard, not Benjamin)		
☐ 33A Juan Gonzalez RR ERR	5.00	2.20
(Reverse negative)		
☐ 33B Juan Gonzalez RR COR	2.50	1.10

☐ 34 Eric Anthony RR	.05	.02
☐ 35 Mike Fetters RR	.05	.02
☐ 36 Marquis Grissom RR	.25	.11
☐ 37 Greg Vaughn RR	.40	.18
☐ 38 Brian DuBois RR	.05	.02
☐ 39 Steve Avery RR UER	.05	.02
(Born in MI, not NJ)		
☐ 40 Mark Gardner RR	.05	.02
☐ 41 Andy Benes RR	.20	.09
☐ 42 Delino DeShields RR	.20	.09
☐ 43 Scott Coolbaugh RR	.05	.02
☐ 44 Pat Combs RR DP	.05	.02
☐ 45 Alex Sanchez RR DP	.05	.02
☐ 46 Kelly Mann RR DP	.05	.02
☐ 47 Julio Machado RR DP	.05	.02
☐ 48 Pete Incaviglia	.05	.02
☐ 49 Shawon Dunston	.05	.02
☐ 50 Jeff Treadway	.05	.02
☐ 51 Jeff Ballard	.05	.02
☐ 52 Claudell Washington	.05	.02
☐ 53 Juan Samuel	.05	.02
☐ 54 John Smiley	.05	.02
☐ 55 Rob Deer	.05	.02
☐ 56 Geno Petralli	.05	.02
☐ 57 Chris Bosio	.05	.02
☐ 58 Carlton Fisk	.20	.09
☐ 59 Kirt Manwaring	.05	.02
☐ 60 Chet Lemon	.05	.02
☐ 61 Bo Jackson	.10	.05
☐ 62 Doyle Alexander	.05	.02
☐ 63 Pedro Guerrero	.05	.02
☐ 64 Allan Anderson	.05	.02
☐ 65 Greg W. Harris	.05	.02
☐ 66 Mike Greenwell	.05	.02
☐ 67 Walt Weiss	.05	.02
☐ 68 Wade Boggs	.20	.09
☐ 69 Jim Clancy	.05	.02
☐ 70 Junior Felix	.05	.02
☐ 71 Barry Larkin	.20	.09
☐ 72 Dave LaPoint	.05	.02
☐ 73 Joel Skinner	.05	.02
☐ 74 Jesse Barfield	.05	.02
☐ 75 Tommy Herr	.05	.02
☐ 76 Ricky Jordan	.05	.02
☐ 77 Eddie Murray	.20	.09
☐ 78 Steve Sax	.05	.02
☐ 79 Tim Belcher	.05	.02
☐ 80 Danny Jackson	.05	.02
☐ 81 Kent Hrbek	.10	.05
☐ 82 Milt Thompson	.05	.02
☐ 83 Brook Jacoby	.05	.02
☐ 84 Mike Marshall	.05	.02
☐ 85 Kevin Seitzer	.05	.02
☐ 86 Tony Gwynn	.50	.23
☐ 87 Dave Stieb	.10	.05
☐ 88 Dave Smith	.05	.02
☐ 89 Bret Saberhagen	.10	.05
☐ 90 Alan Trammell	.15	.07
☐ 91 Tony Phillips	.05	.02
☐ 92 Doug Drabek	.05	.02
☐ 93 Jeffrey Leonard	.05	.02
☐ 94 Wally Joyner	.10	.05
☐ 95 Carney Lansford	.10	.05
☐ 96 Cal Ripken	.75	.35
☐ 97 Andres Galarraga	.20	.09
☐ 98 Kevin Mitchell	.05	.02
☐ 99 Howard Johnson	.05	.02
☐ 100A Checklist 28-129	.05	.02
☐ 100B Checklist 28-125	.05	.02
☐ 101 Melido Perez	.05	.02
☐ 102 Spike Owen	.05	.02
☐ 103 Paul Molitor	.20	.09
☐ 104 Geronimo Berroa	.05	.02
☐ 105 Ryne Sandberg	.25	.11
☐ 106 Bryn Smith	.05	.02
☐ 107 Steve Buechele	.05	.02
☐ 108 Jim Abbott	.15	.07
☐ 109 Alvin Davis	.05	.02
☐ 110 Lee Smith	.10	.05
☐ 111 Roberto Alomar	.20	.09
☐ 112 Rick Reuschel	.05	.02
☐ 113A Kelly Gruber ERR	.05	.02
(Born 2/22)		
☐ 113B Kelly Gruber COR	.05	.02
(Born 2/26; corrected in factory sets)		

114	Joe Carter	.10	.05
115	Jose Rijo	.05	.02
116	Greg Minton	.05	.02
117	Bob Ojeda	.05	.02
118	Glenn Davis	.05	.02
119	Jeff Reardon	.10	.05
120	Kurt Stillwell	.05	.02
121	John Smoltz	.20	.09
122	Dwight Evans	.05	.02
123	Eric Yelding	.05	.02
124	John Franco	.10	.05
125	Jose Canseco	.25	.11
126	Barry Bonds	.25	.11
127	Lee Guetterman	.05	.02
128	Jack Clark	.10	.05
129	Dave Valle	.05	.02
130	Hubie Brooks	.05	.02
131	Ernest Riles	.05	.02
132	Mike Morgan	.05	.02
133	Steve Jeltz	.05	.02
134	Jeff D. Robinson	.05	.02
135	Ozzie Guillen	.05	.02
136	Chili Davis	.10	.05
137	Mitch Webster	.05	.02
138	Jerry Browne	.05	.02
139	Bo Diaz	.05	.02
140	Robby Thompson	.05	.02
141	Craig Worthington	.05	.02
142	Julio Franco	.05	.02
143	Brian Holman	.05	.02
144	George Brett	.40	.18
145	Tom Glavine	.20	.09
146	Robin Yount	.20	.09
147	Gary Carter	.20	.09
148	Ron Kittle	.05	.02
149	Tony Fernandez	.05	.02
150	Dave Stewart	.10	.05
151	Gary Gaetti	.10	.05
152	Kevin Elster	.05	.02
153	Gerald Perry	.05	.02
154	Jesse Orosco	.05	.02
155	Wally Backman	.05	.02
156	Dennis Martinez	.10	.05
157	Rick Sutcliffe	.05	.02
158	Greg Maddux	.50	.23
159	Andy Hawkins	.05	.02
160	John Kruk	.10	.05
161	Jose Oquendo	.05	.02
162	John Dopson	.05	.02
163	Joe Magrane	.05	.02
164	Bill Ripken	.05	.02
165	Fred Manrique	.05	.02
166	Nolan Ryan UER (Did not lead NL in K's in '89 as he was in AL in '89)	.75	.35
167	Damon Berryhill	.05	.02
168	Dale Murphy	.20	.09
169	Mickey Tettleton	.10	.05
170A	Kirk McCaskill ERR (Born 4/19)	.05	.02
170B	Kirk McCaskill COR (Born 4/9; corrected in factory sets)	.05	.02
171	Dwight Gooden	.10	.05
172	Jose Lind	.05	.02
173	B.J. Surhoff	.10	.05
174	Ruben Sierra	.20	.09
175	Dan Plesac	.05	.02
176	Dan Pasqua	.05	.02
177	Kelly Downs	.05	.02
178	Matt Nokes	.05	.02
179	Luis Aquino	.05	.02
180	Frank Tanana	.05	.02
181	Tony Pena	.05	.02
182	Dan Gladden	.05	.02
183	Bruce Hurst	.05	.02
184	Roger Clemens	.50	.23
185	Mark McGwire	1.00	.45
186	Rob Murphy	.05	.02
187	Jim Deshaies	.05	.02
188	Fred McGriff	.20	.09
189	Rob Dibble	.05	.02
190	Don Mattingly	.40	.18
191	Felix Fermin	.05	.02
192	Roberto Kelly	.05	.02
193	Dennis Cook	.05	.02
194	Darren Daulton	.10	.05
195	Alfredo Griffin	.05	.02
196	Eric Plunk	.05	.02
197	Orel Hershiser	.10	.05
198	Paul O'Neill	.10	.05
199	Randy Bush	.05	.02
200A	Checklist 130-231	.05	.02
200B	Checklist 126-223	.05	.02
201	Ozzie Smith	.25	.11
202	Pete O'Brien	.05	.02
203	Jay Howell	.05	.02
204	Mark Gubicza	.05	.02
205	Ed Whitson	.05	.02
206	George Bell	.10	.05
207	Mike Scott	.05	.02
208	Charlie Leibrandt	.05	.02
209	Mike Heath	.05	.02
210	Dennis Eckersley	.15	.07
211	Mike LaValliere	.05	.02
212	Darnell Coles	.05	.02
213	Lance Parrish	.05	.02
214	Mike Moore	.05	.02
215	Steve Finley	.20	.09
216	Tim Raines	.10	.05
217A	Scott Garrelts ERR (Born 10/20)	.05	.02
217B	Scott Garrelts COR (Born 10/30; corrected in factory sets)	.05	.02
218	Kevin McReynolds	.05	.02
219	Dave Gallagher	.05	.02
220	Tim Wallach	.05	.02
221	Chuck Crim	.05	.02
222	Lonnie Smith	.05	.02
223	Andre Dawson	.20	.09
224	Nelson Santovenia	.05	.02
225	Rafael Palmeiro	.20	.09
226	Devon White	.05	.02
227	Harold Reynolds	.05	.02
228	Ellis Burks	.15	.07
229	Mark Parent	.05	.02
230	Will Clark	.20	.09
231	Jimmy Key	.10	.05
232	John Farrell	.05	.02
233	Eric Davis	.10	.05
234	Johnny Ray	.05	.02
235	Darryl Strawberry	.10	.05
236	Bill Doran	.05	.02
237	Greg Gagne	.05	.02
238	Jim Eisenreich	.05	.02
239	Tommy Gregg	.05	.02
240	Marty Barrett	.05	.02
241	Rafael Ramirez	.05	.02
242	Chris Sabo	.10	.05
243	Dave Henderson	.05	.02
244	Andy Van Slyke	.10	.05
245	Alvaro Espinoza	.05	.02
246	Garry Templeton	.05	.02
247	Gene Harris	.05	.02
248	Kevin Gross	.05	.02
249	Brett Butler	.10	.05
250	Willie Randolph	.10	.05
251	Roger McDowell	.05	.02
252	Rafael Belliard	.05	.02
253	Steve Rosenberg	.05	.02
254	Jack Howell	.05	.02
255	Marvell Wynne	.05	.02
256	Tom Candiotti	.05	.02
257	Todd Benzinger	.05	.02
258	Don Robinson	.05	.02
259	Phil Bradley	.05	.02
260	Cecil Espy	.05	.02
261	Scott Bankhead	.05	.02
262	Frank White	.10	.05
263	Andres Thomas	.05	.02
264	Glenn Braggs	.05	.02
265	David Cone	.20	.09
266	Bobby Thigpen	.05	.02
267	Nelson Liriano	.05	.02
268	Terry Steinbach	.05	.02
269	Kirby Puckett UER (Back doesn't consider Joe Torre's .363 in '71)	.30	.14
270	Gregg Jefferies	.10	.05
271	Jeff Blauser	.05	.02
272	Cory Snyder	.05	.02
273	Roy Smith	.05	.02
274	Tom Foley	.05	.02
275	Mitch Williams	.05	.02
276	Paul Kilgus	.05	.02
277	Don Slaught	.05	.02
278	Von Hayes	.05	.02
279	Vince Coleman	.05	.02
280	Mike Boddicker	.05	.02
281	Ken Dayley	.05	.02
282	Mike Devereaux	.05	.02
283	Kenny Rogers	.10	.05
284	Jeff Russell	.05	.02
285	Jerome Walton	.05	.02
286	Derek Lilliquist	.05	.02
287	Joe Orsulak	.05	.02
288	Dick Schofield	.05	.02
289	Ron Darling	.05	.02
290	Bobby Bonilla	.10	.05
291	Jim Gantner	.05	.02
292	Bobby Witt	.05	.02
293	Greg Brock	.05	.02
294	Ivan Calderon	.05	.02
295	Steve Bedrosian	.05	.02
296	Mike Henneman	.05	.02
297	Tom Gordon	.10	.05
298	Lou Whitaker	.10	.05
299	Terry Pendleton	.10	.05
300A	Checklist 232-333	.05	.02
300B	Checklist 224-321	.05	.02
301	Juan Berenguer	.05	.02
302	Mark Davis	.05	.02
303	Nick Esasky	.05	.02
304	Rickey Henderson	.25	.11
305	Rick Cerone	.05	.02
306	Craig Biggio	.20	.09
307	Duane Ward	.05	.02
308	Tom Browning	.05	.02
309	Walt Terrell	.05	.02
310	Greg Swindell	.05	.02
311	Dave Righetti	.05	.02
312	Mike Maddux	.05	.02
313	Len Dykstra	.10	.05
314	Jose Gonzalez	.05	.02
315	Steve Balboni	.05	.02
316	Mike Scioscia	.05	.02
317	Ron Oester	.05	.02
318	Gary Wayne	.05	.02
319	Todd Worrell	.05	.02
320	Doug Jones	.05	.02
321	Jeff Hamilton	.05	.02
322	Danny Tartabull	.05	.02
323	Chris James	.05	.02
324	Mike Flanagan	.05	.02
325	Gerald Young	.05	.02
326	Bob Boone	.10	.05
327	Frank Williams	.05	.02
328	Dave Parker	.10	.05
329	Sid Bream	.05	.02
330	Mike Schooler	.05	.02
331	Bert Blyleven	.05	.02
332	Bob Welch	.05	.02
333	Bob Milacki	.05	.02
334	Tim Burke	.05	.02
335	Jose Uribe	.05	.02
336	Randy Myers	.10	.05
337	Eric King	.05	.02
338	Mark Langston	.05	.02
339	Teddy Higuera	.05	.02
340	Oddibe McDowell	.05	.02
341	Lloyd McClendon	.05	.02
342	Pascual Perez	.05	.02
343	Kevin Brown UER (Signed is misspelled as signeed on back)	.20	.09
344	Chuck Finley	.10	.05
345	Erik Hanson	.05	.02
346	Rich Gedman	.05	.02
347	Bip Roberts	.05	.02
348	Matt Williams	.20	.09
349	Tom Henke	.05	.02
350	Brad Komminsk	.05	.02
351	Jeff Reed	.05	.02
352	Brian Downing	.05	.02
353	Frank Viola	.05	.02
354	Terry Puhl	.05	.02

355	Brian Harper	.05	.02
356	Steve Farr	.05	.02
357	Joe Boever	.05	.02
358	Danny Heep	.05	.02
359	Larry Andersen	.05	.02
360	Rolando Roomes	.05	.02
361	Mike Gallego	.05	.02
362	Bob Kipper	.05	.02
363	Clay Parker	.05	.02
364	Mike Pagliarulo	.05	.02
365	Ken Griffey Jr. UER	2.00	.90
	(Signed through 1990, should be 1991)		
366	Rex Hudler	.05	.02
367	Pat Sheridan	.05	.02
368	Kirk Gibson	.10	.05
369	Jeff Parrett	.05	.02
370	Bob Walk	.05	.02
371	Ken Patterson	.05	.02
372	Bryan Harvey	.05	.02
373	Mike Bielecki	.05	.02
374	Tom Magrann	.05	.02
375	Rick Mahler	.05	.02
376	Craig Lefferts	.05	.02
377	Gregg Olson	.10	.05
378	Jamie Moyer	.05	.02
379	Randy Johnson	.30	.14
380	Jeff Montgomery	.10	.05
381	Marty Clary	.05	.02
382	Bill Spiers	.05	.02
383	Dave Magadan	.05	.02
384	Greg Hibbard	.05	.02
385	Ernie Whitt	.05	.02
386	Rick Honeycutt	.05	.02
387	Dave West	.05	.02
388	Keith Hernandez	.10	.05
389	Jose Alvarez	.05	.02
390	Joey Belle	.75	.35
391	Rick Aguilera	.10	.05
392	Mike Fitzgerald	.05	.02
393	Dwight Smith	.05	.02
394	Steve Wilson	.05	.02
395	Bob Geren	.05	.02
396	Randy Ready	.05	.02
397	Ken Hill	.10	.05
398	Jody Reed	.05	.02
399	Tom Brunansky	.05	.02
400A	Checklist 334-435	.05	.02
400B	Checklist 322-419	.05	.02
401	Rene Gonzales	.05	.02
402	Harold Baines	.10	.05
403	Cecilio Guante	.05	.02
404	Joe Girardi	.15	.07
405A	Sergio Valdez ERR	.05	.02
	(Card front shows black line crossing S in Sergio)		
405B	Sergio Valdez COR	.05	.02
406	Mark Williamson	.05	.02
407	Glenn Hoffman	.05	.02
408	Jeff Innis	.05	.02
409	Randy Kramer	.05	.02
410	Charlie O'Brien	.05	.02
411	Charlie Hough	.10	.05
412	Gus Polidor	.05	.02
413	Ron Karkovice	.05	.02
414	Trevor Wilson	.05	.02
415	Kevin Ritz	.05	.02
416	Gary Thurman	.05	.02
417	Jeff M. Robinson	.05	.02
418	Scott Terry	.05	.02
419	Tim Laudner	.05	.02
420	Dennis Rasmussen	.05	.02
421	Luis Rivera	.05	.02
422	Jim Corsi	.05	.02
423	Dennis Lamp	.05	.02
424	Ken Caminiti	.20	.09
425	David Wells	.15	.07
426	Norm Charlton	.05	.02
427	Deion Sanders	.20	.09
428	Dion James	.05	.02
429	Chuck Cary	.05	.02
430	Ken Howell	.05	.02
431	Steve Lake	.05	.02
432	Kal Daniels	.05	.02
433	Lance McCullers	.05	.02
434	Lenny Harris	.05	.02
435	Scott Scudder	.05	.02
436	Gene Larkin	.05	.02
437	Dan Quisenberry	.05	.02
438	Steve Olin	.10	.05
439	Mickey Hatcher	.05	.02
440	Willie Wilson	.05	.02
441	Mark Grant	.05	.02
442	Mookie Wilson	.10	.05
443	Alex Trevino	.05	.02
444	Pat Tabler	.05	.02
445	Dave Bergman	.05	.02
446	Todd Burns	.05	.02
447	R.J. Reynolds	.05	.02
448	Jay Buhner	.20	.09
449	Lee Stevens	.10	.05
450	Ron Hassey	.05	.02
451	Bob Melvin	.05	.02
452	Dave Martinez	.05	.02
453	Greg Litton	.05	.02
454	Mark Carreon	.05	.02
455	Scott Fletcher	.05	.02
456	Otis Nixon	.10	.05
457	Tony Fossas	.05	.02
458	John Russell	.05	.02
459	Paul Assenmacher	.05	.02
460	Zane Smith	.05	.02
461	Jack Daugherty	.05	.02
462	Rich Monteleone	.05	.02
463	Greg Briley	.05	.02
464	Mike Smithson	.05	.02
465	Benito Santiago	.05	.02
466	Jeff Brantley	.05	.02
467	Jose Nunez	.05	.02
468	Scott Bailes	.05	.02
469	Ken Griffey Sr.	.10	.05
470	Bob McClure	.05	.02
471	Mackey Sasser	.05	.02
472	Glenn Wilson	.05	.02
473	Kevin Tapani	.10	.05
474	Bill Buckner	.05	.02
475	Ron Gant	.05	.02
476	Kevin Romine	.05	.02
477	Juan Agosto	.05	.02
478	Herm Winningham	.05	.02
479	Storm Davis	.05	.02
480	Jeff King	.05	.02
481	Kevin Mmahat	.05	.02
482	Carmelo Martinez	.05	.02
483	Omar Vizquel	.20	.09
484	Jim Dwyer	.05	.02
485	Bob Knepper	.05	.02
486	Dave Anderson	.05	.02
487	Ron Jones	.05	.02
488	Jay Bell	.10	.05
489	Sammy Sosa	6.00	2.70
490	Kent Anderson	.05	.02
491	Domingo Ramos	.05	.02
492	Dave Clark	.05	.02
493	Tim Birtsas	.05	.02
494	Ken Oberkfell	.05	.02
495	Larry Sheets	.05	.02
496	Jeff Kunkel	.05	.02
497	Jim Presley	.05	.02
498	Mike Macfarlane	.05	.02
499	Pete Smith	.05	.02
500A	Checklist 436-537 DP	.05	.02
500B	Checklist 420-517	.05	.02
501	Gary Sheffield	.20	.09
502	Terry Bross	.05	.02
503	Jerry Kutzler	.05	.02
504	Lloyd Moseby	.05	.02
505	Curt Young	.05	.02
506	Al Newman	.05	.02
507	Keith Miller	.05	.02
508	Mike Stanton	.05	.02
509	Rich Yett	.05	.02
510	Tim Drummond	.05	.02
511	Joe Hesketh	.05	.02
512	Rick Wrona	.05	.02
513	Luis Salazar	.05	.02
514	Hal Morris	.05	.02
515	Terry Mulholland	.05	.02
516	John Morris	.05	.02
517	Carlos Quintana	.05	.02
518	Frank DiPino	.05	.02
519	Randy Milligan	.05	.02
520	Chad Kreuter	.05	.02
521	Mike Jeffcoat	.05	.02
522	Mike Harkey	.05	.02
523A	Andy Nezelek ERR	.05	.02
	(Wrong birth year)		
523B	Andy Nezelek COR	.20	.09
	(Finally corrected in factory sets)		
524	Dave Schmidt	.05	.02
525	Tony Armas	.05	.02
526	Barry Lyons	.05	.02
527	Rick Reed	.25	.11
528	Jerry Reuss	.05	.02
529	Dean Palmer	.50	.23
530	Jeff Peterek	.05	.02
531	Carlos Martinez	.05	.02
532	Atlee Hammaker	.05	.02
533	Mike Brumley	.05	.02
534	Terry Leach	.05	.02
535	Doug Strange	.05	.02
536	Jose DeLeon	.05	.02
537	Shane Rawley	.05	.02
538	Joey Cora	.10	.05
539	Eric Hetzel	.05	.02
540	Gene Nelson	.05	.02
541	Wes Gardner	.05	.02
542	Mark Portugal	.05	.02
543	Al Leiter	.20	.09
544	Jack Armstrong	.05	.02
545	Greg Cadaret	.05	.02
546	Rod Nichols	.05	.02
547	Luis Polonia	.05	.02
548	Charlie Hayes	.05	.02
549	Dickie Thon	.05	.02
550	Tim Crews	.05	.02
551	Dave Winfield	.20	.09
552	Mike Davis	.05	.02
553	Ron Robinson	.05	.02
554	Carmen Castillo	.05	.02
555	John Costello	.05	.02
556	Bud Black	.05	.02
557	Rick Dempsey	.05	.02
558	Jim Acker	.05	.02
559	Eric Show	.05	.02
560	Pat Borders	.05	.02
561	Danny Darwin	.05	.02
562	Rick Luecken	.05	.02
563	Edwin Nunez	.05	.02
564	Felix Jose	.20	.09
565	John Cangelosi	.05	.02
566	Bill Swift	.05	.02
567	Bill Schroeder	.05	.02
568	Stan Javier	.05	.02
569	Jim Traber	.05	.02
570	Wallace Johnson	.05	.02
571	Donell Nixon	.05	.02
572	Sid Fernandez	.05	.02
573	Lance Johnson	.05	.02
574	Andy McGaffigan	.05	.02
575	Mark Knudson	.05	.02
576	Tommy Greene	.05	.02
577	Mark Grace	.20	.09
578	Larry Walker	1.25	.55
579	Mike Stanley	.05	.02
580	Mike Witt DP	.05	.02
581	Scott Bradley	.05	.02
582	Greg A. Harris	.05	.02
583A	Kevin Hickey ERR	.20	.09
583B	Kevin Hickey COR	.05	.02
584	Lee Mazzilli	.05	.02
585	Jeff Pico	.05	.02
586	Joe Oliver	.05	.02
587	Willie Fraser DP	.05	.02
588	Carl Yastrzemski Puzzle Card DP	.20	.09
589	Kevin Bass DP	.05	.02
590	John Moses DP	.05	.02
591	Tom Pagnozzi DP	.05	.02
592	Tony Castillo DP	.05	.02
593	Jerald Clark DP	.05	.02
594	Dan Schatzeder	.05	.02
595	Luis Quinones DP	.05	.02
596	Pete Harnisch DP	.05	.02
597	Gary Redus	.05	.02
598	Mel Hall	.05	.02

Card	MINT	NRMT
599 Rick Schu	.05	.02
600A Checklist 538-639	.05	.02
600B Checklist 518-617	.05	.02
601 Mike Kingery DP	.05	.02
602 Terry Kennedy DP	.05	.02
603 Mike Sharperson DP	.05	.02
604 Don Carman DP	.05	.02
605 Jim Gott	.05	.02
606 Donn Pall DP	.05	.02
607 Rance Mullinicks	.05	.02
608 Curt Wilkerson DP	.05	.02
609 Mike Felder DP	.05	.02
610 Guillermo Hernandez DP	.05	.02
611 Candy Maldonado DP	.05	.02
612 Mark Thurmond DP	.05	.02
613 Rick Leach DP	.05	.02
614 Jerry Reed DP	.05	.02
615 Franklin Stubbs	.05	.02
616 Billy Hatcher DP	.05	.02
617 Don August DP	.05	.02
618 Tim Teufel	.05	.02
619 Shawn Hillegas DP	.05	.02
620 Manny Lee	.05	.02
621 Gary Ward DP	.05	.02
622 Mark Guthrie DP	.05	.02
623 Jeff Musseiman DP	.05	.02
624 Mark Lemke DP	.05	.02
625 Fernando Valenzuela	.10	.05
626 Paul Sorrento DP	.15	.07
627 Glenallen Hill DP	.05	.02
628 Les Lancaster DP	.05	.02
629 Vance Law DP	.05	.02
630 Randy Velarde DP	.05	.02
631 Todd Frohwirth DP	.05	.02
632 Willie McGee	.10	.05
633 Dennis Boyd DP	.05	.02
634 Cris Carpenter DP	.05	.02
635 Brian Holton	.05	.02
636 Tracy Jones DP	.05	.02
637A Terry Steinbach AS (Recent Major League Performance)	.05	.02
637B Terry Steinbach AS (All-Star Game Performance)	.05	.02
638 Brady Anderson	.20	.09
639A Jack Morris ERR (Card front shows black line crossing J in Jack)	.10	.05
639B Jack Morris COR	.10	.05
640 Jaime Navarro	.05	.02
641 Darrin Jackson	.05	.02
642 Mike Dyer	.05	.02
643 Mike Schmidt	.30	.14
644 Henry Cotto	.05	.02
645 John Cerutti	.05	.02
646 Francisco Cabrera	.05	.02
647 Scott Sanderson	.05	.02
648 Brian Meyer	.05	.02
649 Ray Searage	.05	.02
650A Bo Jackson AS (Recent Major League Performance)	.10	.05
650B Bo Jackson AS (All-Star Game Performance)	.10	.05
651 Steve Lyons	.05	.02
652 Mike LaCoss	.05	.02
653 Ted Power	.05	.02
654A Howard Johnson AS (Recent Major League Performance)	.05	.02
654B Howard Johnson AS (All-Star Game Performance)	.05	.02
655 Mauro Gozzo	.05	.02
656 Mike Blowers	.10	.05
657 Paul Gibson	.05	.02
658 Neal Heaton	.05	.02
659 Nolan Ryan 5000K COR (Still an error as Ryan did not lead AL in K's in '75)	.40	.18
659A Nolan Ryan 5000K (665 King of Kings back) ERR	1.50	.70
660A Harold Baines AS (Black line through star on front; Recent Major League Performance)	.75	.35
660B Harold Baines AS (Black line through star on front; All-Star Game Performance)	1.00	.45
660C Harold Baines AS (Black line behind star on front; Recent Major League Performance)	.20	.09
660D Harold Baines AS (Black line behind star on front; All-Star Game Performance)	.05	.02
661 Gary Pettis	.05	.02
662 Clint Zavaras	.05	.02
663A Rick Reuschel AS (Recent Major League Performance)	.05	.02
663B Rick Reuschel AS (All-Star Game Performance)	.05	.02
664 Alejandro Pena	.05	.02
665 Nolan Ryan KING COR	.40	.18
665A Nolan Ryan KING (659 5000 K back) ERR	1.50	.70
665C Nolan Ryan KING ERR (No number on back; in factory sets)	.75	.35
666 Ricky Horton	.05	.02
667 Curt Schilling	.50	.23
668 Bill Landrum	.05	.02
669 Todd Stottlemyre	.10	.05
670 Tim Leary	.05	.02
671 John Wetteland	.20	.09
672 Calvin Schiraldi	.05	.02
673A Ruben Sierra AS (Recent Major League Performance)	.05	.02
673B Ruben Sierra AS (All-Star Game Performance)	.05	.02
674A Pedro Guerrero AS (Recent Major League Performance)	.05	.02
674B Pedro Guerrero AS (All-Star Game Performance)	.05	.02
675 Ken Phelps	.05	.02
676A Cal Ripken AS (All-Star Game Performance)	.40	.18
676B Cal Ripken AS (Recent Major League Performance)	.75	.35
677 Denny Walling	.05	.02
678 Goose Gossage	.10	.05
679 Gary Mielke	.05	.02
680 Bill Bathe	.05	.02
681 Tom Lawless	.05	.02
682 Xavier Hernandez	.05	.02
683A Kirby Puckett AS (Recent Major League Performance)	.20	.09
683B Kirby Puckett AS (All-Star Game Performance)	.20	.09
684 Mariano Duncan	.05	.02
685 Ramon Martinez	.15	.07
686 Tim Jones	.05	.02
687 Tom Filer	.05	.02
688 Steve Lombardozzi	.05	.02
689 Bernie Williams	1.25	.55
690 Chip Hale	.05	.02
691 Beau Allred	.05	.02
692A Ryne Sandberg AS (Recent Major League Performance)	.20	.09
692B Ryne Sandberg AS (All-Star Game Performance)	.20	.09
693 Jeff Huson	.05	.02
694 Curt Ford	.05	.02
695A Eric Davis AS (Recent Major League Performance)	.05	.02
695B Eric Davis AS (All-Star Game Performance)	.05	.02
696 Scott Lusader	.05	.02
697A Mark McGwire AS (Recent Major League Performance)	.50	.23
697B Mark McGwire AS (All-Star Game Performance)	.20	.09
698 Steve Cummings	.05	.02
699 George Canale	.05	.02
700A Checklist 640-715 and BC1-BC26	.20	.09
700B Checklist 640-716 and BC1-BC26	.10	.05
700C Checklist 618-716	.05	.02
701A Julio Franco AS (Recent Major League Performance)	.05	.02
701B Julio Franco AS (All-Star Game Performance)	.05	.02
702 Dave Johnson (P)	.05	.02
703A Dave Stewart AS (Recent Major League Performance)	.05	.02
703B Dave Stewart AS (All-Star Game Performance)	.05	.02
704 Dave Justice	.50	.23
705 Tony Gwynn AS (All-Star Game Performance)	.20	.09
705A Tony Gwynn AS (Recent Major League Performance)	.20	.09
706 Greg Myers	.05	.02
707A Will Clark AS (Recent Major League Performance)	.05	.02
707B Will Clark AS (All-Star Game Performance)	.20	.09
708A Benito Santiago AS (Recent Major League Performance)	.05	.02
708B Benito Santiago AS (All-Star Game Performance)	.05	.02
709 Larry McWilliams	.05	.02
710A Ozzie Smith AS (Recent Major League Performance)	.20	.09
710B Ozzie Smith AS (All-Star Game Performance)	.10	.05
711 John Olerud	.60	.25
712A Wade Boggs AS (Recent Major League Performance)	.10	.05
712B Wade Boggs AS (All-Star Game Performance)	.10	.05
713 Gary Eave	.05	.02
714 Bob Tewksbury	.05	.02
715A Kevin Mitchell AS (Recent Major League Performance)	.05	.02
715B Kevin Mitchell AS (All-Star Game Performance)	.05	.02
716 Bart Giamatti COMM (In Memoriam)	.20	.09

1990 Donruss Rookies

	MINT	NRMT
COMP.FACT.SET (56)	2.00	.90

	MINT	NRMT
COMMON CARD (1-56)	.05	.02
MINOR STARS	.10	.05
UNLISTED STARS	.20	.09

❏ 1 Sandy Alomar Jr. UER	.10	.05
(No stitches on baseball on Donruss logo on card front)		
❏ 2 John Olerud	.20	.09
❏ 3 Pat Combs	.05	.02
❏ 4 Brian DuBois	.05	.02
❏ 5 Felix Jose	.20	.09
❏ 6 Delino DeShields	.20	.09
❏ 7 Mike Stanton	.05	.02
❏ 8 Mike Munoz	.05	.02
❏ 9 Craig Grebeck	.05	.02
❏ 10 Joe Kraemer	.05	.02
❏ 11 Jeff Huson	.05	.02
❏ 12 Bill Sampen	.05	.02
❏ 13 Brian Bohanon	.05	.02
❏ 14 Dave Justice	.50	.23
❏ 15 Robin Ventura	.20	.09
❏ 16 Greg Vaughn	.40	.18
❏ 17 Wayne Edwards	.05	.02
❏ 18 Shawn Boskie	.05	.02
❏ 19 Carlos Baerga	.20	.09
❏ 20 Mark Gardner	.05	.02
❏ 21 Mike Appier	.15	.07
❏ 22 Mike Harkey	.05	.02
❏ 23 Tim Layana	.05	.02
❏ 24 Glenallen Hill	.05	.02
❏ 25 Jerry Kutzler	.05	.02
❏ 26 Mike Blowers	.10	.05
❏ 27 Scott Ruskin	.05	.02
❏ 28 Dana Kiecker	.05	.02
❏ 29 Willie Blair	.05	.02
❏ 30 Ben McDonald	.20	.09
❏ 31 Todd Zeile	.10	.05
❏ 32 Scott Coolbaugh	.05	.02
❏ 33 Xavier Hernandez	.05	.02
❏ 34 Mike Hartley	.05	.02
❏ 35 Kevin Tapani	.10	.05
❏ 36 Kevin Wickander	.05	.02
❏ 37 Carlos Hernandez	.20	.09
❏ 38 Brian Traxler	.05	.02
❏ 39 Marty Brown	.05	.02
❏ 40 Scott Radinsky	.05	.02
❏ 41 Julio Machado	.05	.02
❏ 42 Steve Avery	.50	.23
❏ 43 Mark Lemke	.05	.02
❏ 44 Alan Mills	.05	.02
❏ 45 Marquis Grissom	.20	.09
❏ 46 Greg Olson	.05	.02
❏ 47 Dave Hollins	.20	.09
❏ 48 Jerald Clark	.05	.02
❏ 49 Eric Anthony	.05	.02
❏ 50 Tim Drummond	.05	.02
❏ 51 John Burkett	.05	.02
❏ 52 Brent Knackert	.05	.02
❏ 53 Jeff Shaw	.05	.02
❏ 54 John Orton	.05	.02
❏ 55 Terry Shumpert	.05	.02
❏ 56 Checklist 1-56	.05	.02

1991 Donruss

	MINT	NRMT
COMPLETE SET (770)	8.00	3.60

COMP.FACT.w/LEAF PREV	10.00	4.50
COMP.FACT.w/STUDIO PREV	10.00	4.50
COMMON CARD (1-770)	.05	.02
MINOR STARS	.10	.05
UNLISTED STARS	.20	.09
SUBSET CARDS HALF VALUE OF BASE CARDS		
COMP.BONUS CARD SET (22)	1.50	.70
*BONUS: SAME VALUE AS BASIC CARDS		
BONUS CARDS: RANDOM INSERTS IN PACKS		
COMP.G'SLAMMERS SET (14)	2.00	.90
*G'SLAMMERS: SAME VALUE AS BASIC CARDS		
ONE G'SLAMMER SET PER FACT.SET		

❏ 1 Dave Stieb DK	.05	.02
❏ 2 Craig Biggio DK	.10	.05
❏ 3 Cecil Fielder DK	.05	.02
❏ 4 Barry Bonds DK	.20	.09
❏ 5 Barry Larkin DK	.10	.05
❏ 6 Dave Parker DK	.05	.02
❏ 7 Len Dykstra DK	.05	.02
❏ 8 Bobby Thigpen DK	.05	.02
❏ 9 Roger Clemens DK	.25	.11
❏ 10 Ron Gant DK UER	.10	.05
(No trademark on team logo on back)		
❏ 11 Delino DeShields DK	.05	.02
❏ 12 Roberto Alomar DK UER	.10	.05
(No trademark on team logo on back)		
❏ 13 Sandy Alomar Jr. DK	.05	.02
❏ 14 Ryne Sandberg DK UER	.20	.09
(Was DK in '85, not '83 as shown)		
❏ 15 Ramon Martinez DK	.05	.02
❏ 16 Edgar Martinez DK	.10	.05
❏ 17 Dave Magadan DK	.05	.02
❏ 18 Matt Williams DK	.10	.05
❏ 19 Rafael Palmeiro DK	.10	.05
UER (No trademark on team logo on back)		
❏ 20 Bob Welch DK	.05	.02
❏ 21 Dave Righetti DK	.05	.02
❏ 22 Brian Harper DK	.05	.02
❏ 23 Gregg Olson DK	.05	.02
❏ 24 Kurt Stillwell DK	.05	.02
❏ 25 Pedro Guerrero DK UER	.05	.02
(No trademark on team logo on back)		
❏ 26 Chuck Finley DK UER	.05	.02
(No trademark on team logo on back)		
❏ 27 DK Checklist 1-27	.05	.02
❏ 28 Tino Martinez RR	.20	.09
❏ 29 Mark Lewis RR	.05	.02
❏ 30 Bernard Gilkey RR	.10	.05
❏ 31 Hensley Meulens RR	.05	.02
❏ 32 Derek Bell RR	.20	.09
❏ 33 Jose Offerman RR	.15	.07
❏ 34 Terry Bross RR	.05	.02
❏ 35 Leo Gomez RR	.05	.02
❏ 36 Derrick May RR	.05	.02
❏ 37 Kevin Morton RR	.05	.02
❏ 38 Moises Alou RR	.20	.09
❏ 39 Julio Valera RR	.05	.02
❏ 40 Milt Cuyler RR	.05	.02

❏ 41 Phil Plantier RR	.05	.02
❏ 42 Scott Chiamparino RR	.05	.02
❏ 43 Ray Lankford RR	.20	.09
❏ 44 Mickey Morandini RR	.05	.02
❏ 45 Dave Hansen RR	.05	.02
❏ 46 Kevin Belcher RR	.05	.02
❏ 47 Darrin Fletcher RR	.05	.02
❏ 48 Steve Sax AS	.05	.02
❏ 49 Ken Griffey Jr. AS	.75	.35
❏ 50A Jose Canseco AS ERR	.10	.05
(Team in stat box should be AL, not A's)		
❏ 50B Jose Canseco AS COR	.75	.35
❏ 51 Sandy Alomar Jr. AS	.05	.02
❏ 52 Cal Ripken AS	.40	.18
❏ 53 Rickey Henderson AS	.10	.05
❏ 54 Bob Welch AS	.05	.02
❏ 55 Wade Boggs AS	.10	.05
❏ 56 Mark McGwire AS	.50	.23
❏ 57A Jack McDowell ERR	.20	.09
(Career stats do not include 1990)		
❏ 57B Jack McDowell COR	.25	.11
(Career stats do not include 1990)		
❏ 58 Jose Lind	.05	.02
❏ 59 Alex Fernandez	.10	.05
❏ 60 Pat Combs	.05	.02
❏ 61 Mike Walker	.05	.02
❏ 62 Juan Samuel	.05	.02
❏ 63 Mike Blowers UER	.05	.02
(Last line has aseball, not baseball)		
❏ 64 Mark Guthrie	.05	.02
❏ 65 Mark Salas	.05	.02
❏ 66 Tim Jones	.05	.02
❏ 67 Tim Leary	.05	.02
❏ 68 Andres Galarraga	.20	.09
❏ 69 Bob Milacki	.05	.02
❏ 70 Tim Belcher	.05	.02
❏ 71 Todd Zeile	.10	.05
❏ 72 Jerome Walton	.05	.02
❏ 73 Kevin Seitzer	.05	.02
❏ 74 Jerald Clark	.05	.02
❏ 75 John Smoltz UER	.20	.09
(Born in Detroit, not Warren)		
❏ 76 Mike Henneman	.05	.02
❏ 77 Ken Griffey Jr.	1.50	.70
❏ 78 Jim Abbott	.10	.05
❏ 79 Gregg Jefferies	.20	.09
❏ 80 Kevin Reimer	.05	.02
❏ 81 Roger Clemens	.50	.23
❏ 82 Mike Fitzgerald	.05	.02
❏ 83 Bruce Hurst UER	.05	.02
(Middle name is Lee, not Vee)		
❏ 84 Eric Davis	.10	.05
❏ 85 Paul Molitor	.20	.09
❏ 86 Will Clark	.20	.09
❏ 87 Mike Bielecki	.05	.02
❏ 88 Bret Saberhagen	.10	.05
❏ 89 Nolan Ryan	.75	.35
❏ 90 Bobby Thigpen	.05	.02
❏ 91 Dickie Thon	.05	.02
❏ 92 Duane Ward	.05	.02
❏ 93 Luis Polonia	.05	.02
❏ 94 Terry Kennedy	.05	.02
❏ 95 Kent Hrbek	.10	.05
❏ 96 Danny Jackson	.05	.02
❏ 97 Sid Fernandez	.05	.02
❏ 98 Jimmy Key	.10	.05
❏ 99 Franklin Stubbs	.05	.02
❏ 100 Checklist 28-103	.05	.02
❏ 101 R.J. Reynolds	.05	.02
❏ 102 Dave Stewart	.10	.05
❏ 103 Dan Pasqua	.05	.02
❏ 104 Dan Plesac	.05	.02
❏ 105 Mark McGwire	1.00	.45
❏ 106 John Farrell	.05	.02
❏ 107 Don Mattingly	.40	.18
❏ 108 Carlton Fisk	.20	.09
❏ 109 Ken Oberkfell	.05	.02
❏ 110 Darrel Akerfelds	.05	.02
❏ 111 Gregg Olson	.05	.02
❏ 112 Mike Scioscia	.05	.02

❑ 113	Bryn Smith	.05	.02
❑ 114	Bob Geren	.05	.02
❑ 115	Tom Candiotti	.05	.02
❑ 116	Kevin Tapani	.05	.02
❑ 117	Jeff Treadway	.05	.02
❑ 118	Alan Trammell	.15	.07
❑ 119	Pete O'Brien	.05	.02
	(Blue shading goes through stats)		
❑ 120	Joel Skinner	.05	.02
❑ 121	Mike LaValliere	.05	.02
❑ 122	Dwight Evans	.10	.05
❑ 123	Jody Reed	.05	.02
❑ 124	Lee Guetterman	.05	.02
❑ 125	Tim Burke	.05	.02
❑ 126	Dave Johnson	.05	.02
❑ 127	Fernando Valenzuela	.10	.05
	(Lower large stripe in yellow instead of blue) UER		
❑ 128	Jose DeLeon	.05	.02
❑ 129	Andre Dawson	.20	.09
❑ 130	Gerald Perry	.05	.02
❑ 131	Greg W. Harris	.05	.02
❑ 132	Tom Glavine	.20	.09
❑ 133	Lance McCullers	.05	.02
❑ 134	Randy Johnson	.25	.11
❑ 135	Lance Parrish UER	.05	.02
	(Born in McKeesport, not Clairton)		
❑ 136	Mackey Sasser	.05	.02
❑ 137	Geno Petralli	.05	.02
❑ 138	Dennis Lamp	.05	.02
❑ 139	Dennis Martinez	.10	.05
❑ 140	Mike Pagliarulo	.05	.02
❑ 141	Hal Morris	.05	.02
❑ 142	Dave Parker	.10	.05
❑ 143	Brett Butler	.10	.05
❑ 144	Paul Assenmacher	.05	.02
❑ 145	Mark Gubicza	.05	.02
❑ 146	Charlie Hough	.10	.05
❑ 147	Sammy Sosa	1.25	.55
❑ 148	Randy Ready	.05	.02
❑ 149	Kelly Gruber	.05	.02
❑ 150	Devon White	.05	.02
❑ 151	Gary Carter	.20	.09
❑ 152	Gene Larkin	.05	.02
❑ 153	Chris Sabo	.05	.02
❑ 154	David Cone	.10	.05
❑ 155	Todd Stottlemyre	.10	.05
❑ 156	Glenn Wilson	.05	.02
❑ 157	Bob Walk	.05	.02
❑ 158	Mike Gallego	.05	.02
❑ 159	Greg Hibbard	.05	.02
❑ 160	Chris Bosio	.05	.02
❑ 161	Mike Moore	.05	.02
❑ 162	Jerry Browne UER	.05	.02
	(Born Christiansted, should be St. Croix)		
❑ 163	Steve Sax UER	.05	.02
	(No asterisk next to his 1989 At Bats)		
❑ 164	Melido Perez	.05	.02
❑ 165	Danny Darwin	.05	.02
❑ 166	Roger McDowell	.05	.02
❑ 167	Bill Ripken	.05	.02
❑ 168	Mike Sharperson	.05	.02
❑ 169	Lee Smith	.10	.05
❑ 170	Matt Nokes	.05	.02
❑ 171	Jesse Orosco	.05	.02
❑ 172	Rick Aguilera	.10	.05
❑ 173	Jim Presley	.05	.02
❑ 174	Lou Whitaker	.10	.05
❑ 175	Harold Reynolds	.05	.02
❑ 176	Brook Jacoby	.05	.02
❑ 177	Wally Backman	.05	.02
❑ 178	Wade Boggs	.20	.09
❑ 179	Chuck Cary	.05	.02
	(Comma after DOB, not on other cards)		
❑ 180	Tom Foley	.05	.02
❑ 181	Pete Harnisch	.05	.02
❑ 182	Mike Morgan	.05	.02
❑ 183	Bob Tewksbury	.05	.02
❑ 184	Joe Girardi	.10	.05
❑ 185	Storm Davis	.05	.02
❑ 186	Ed Whitson	.05	.02
❑ 187	Steve Avery UER	.05	.02
	(Born in New Jersey, should be Michigan)		
❑ 188	Lloyd Moseby	.05	.02
❑ 189	Scott Bankhead	.05	.02
❑ 190	Mark Langston	.05	.02
❑ 191	Kevin McReynolds	.05	.02
❑ 192	Julio Franco	.05	.02
❑ 193	John Dopson	.05	.02
❑ 194	Dennis Boyd	.05	.02
❑ 195	Bip Roberts	.05	.02
❑ 196	Billy Hatcher	.05	.02
❑ 197	Edgar Diaz	.05	.02
❑ 198	Greg Litton	.05	.02
❑ 199	Mark Grace	.20	.09
❑ 200	Checklist 104-179	.05	.02
❑ 201	George Brett	.40	.18
❑ 202	Jeff Russell	.05	.02
❑ 203	Ivan Calderon	.05	.02
❑ 204	Ken Howell	.05	.02
❑ 205	Tom Henke	.05	.02
❑ 206	Bryan Harvey	.05	.02
❑ 207	Steve Bedrosian	.05	.02
❑ 208	Al Newman	.05	.02
❑ 209	Randy Myers	.10	.05
❑ 210	Daryl Boston	.05	.02
❑ 211	Manny Lee	.05	.02
❑ 212	Dave Smith	.05	.02
❑ 213	Don Slaught	.05	.02
❑ 214	Walt Weiss	.05	.02
❑ 215	Donn Pall	.05	.02
❑ 216	Jaime Navarro	.05	.02
❑ 217	Willie Randolph	.10	.05
❑ 218	Rudy Seanez	.05	.02
❑ 219	Jim Leyritz	.10	.05
❑ 220	Ron Karkovice	.05	.02
❑ 221	Ken Caminiti	.20	.09
❑ 222	Von Hayes	.05	.02
❑ 223	Cal Ripken	.75	.35
❑ 224	Lenny Harris	.05	.02
❑ 225	Milt Thompson	.05	.02
❑ 226	Alvaro Espinoza	.05	.02
❑ 227	Chris James	.05	.02
❑ 228	Dan Gladden	.05	.02
❑ 229	Jeff Blauser	.05	.02
❑ 230	Mike Heath	.05	.02
❑ 231	Omar Vizquel	.20	.09
❑ 232	Doug Jones	.05	.02
❑ 233	Jeff King	.05	.02
❑ 234	Luis Rivera	.05	.02
❑ 235	Ellis Burks	.10	.05
❑ 236	Greg Cadaret	.05	.02
❑ 237	Dave Martinez	.05	.02
❑ 238	Mark Williamson	.05	.02
❑ 239	Stan Javier	.05	.02
❑ 240	Ozzie Smith	.25	.11
❑ 241	Shawn Boskie	.05	.02
❑ 242	Tom Gordon	.05	.02
❑ 243	Tony Gwynn	.50	.23
❑ 244	Tommy Gregg	.05	.02
❑ 245	Jeff M. Robinson	.05	.02
❑ 246	Keith Comstock	.05	.02
❑ 247	Jack Howell	.05	.02
❑ 248	Keith Miller	.05	.02
❑ 249	Bobby Witt	.05	.02
❑ 250	Rob Murphy UER	.05	.02
	(Shown as on Reds in '89 stats, should be Red Sox)		
❑ 251	Spike Owen	.05	.02
❑ 252	Garry Templeton	.05	.02
❑ 253	Glenn Braggs	.05	.02
❑ 254	Ron Robinson	.05	.02
❑ 255	Kevin Mitchell	.10	.05
❑ 256	Les Lancaster	.05	.02
❑ 257	Mel Stottlemyre Jr.	.05	.02
❑ 258	Kenny Rogers UER	.05	.02
	(IP listed as 171, should be 172)		
❑ 259	Lance Johnson	.05	.02
❑ 260	John Kruk	.10	.05
❑ 261	Fred McGriff	.20	.09
❑ 262	Dick Schofield	.05	.02
❑ 263	Trevor Wilson	.05	.02
❑ 264	David West	.05	.02
❑ 265	Scott Scudder	.05	.02
❑ 266	Dwight Gooden	.10	.05
❑ 267	Willie Blair	.05	.02
❑ 268	Mark Portugal	.05	.02
❑ 269	Doug Drabek	.05	.02
❑ 270	Dennis Eckersley	.10	.05
❑ 271	Eric King	.05	.02
❑ 272	Robin Yount	.20	.09
❑ 273	Carney Lansford	.10	.05
❑ 274	Carlos Baerga	.10	.05
❑ 275	Dave Righetti	.05	.02
❑ 276	Scott Fletcher	.05	.02
❑ 277	Eric Yelding	.05	.02
❑ 278	Charlie Hayes	.05	.02
❑ 279	Jeff Ballard	.05	.02
❑ 280	Orel Hershiser	.10	.05
❑ 281	Jose Oquendo	.05	.02
❑ 282	Mike Witt	.05	.02
❑ 283	Mitch Webster	.05	.02
❑ 284	Greg Gagne	.05	.02
❑ 285	Greg Olson	.05	.02
❑ 286	Tony Phillips UER	.05	.02
	(Born 4/15 should be 4/25)		
❑ 287	Scott Bradley	.05	.02
❑ 288	Cory Snyder UER	.05	.02
	(In text, led is re-peated and Inglewood is misspelled as Englewood)		
❑ 289	Jay Bell UER	.10	.05
	(Born in Pensacola, not Eglin AFB)		
❑ 290	Kevin Romine	.05	.02
❑ 291	Jeff D. Robinson	.05	.02
❑ 292	Steve Frey UER	.05	.02
	(Bats left, should be right)		
❑ 293	Craig Worthington	.05	.02
❑ 294	Tim Crews	.05	.02
❑ 295	Joe Magrane	.05	.02
❑ 296	Hector Villanueva	.05	.02
❑ 297	Terry Shumpert	.05	.02
❑ 298	Joe Carter	.10	.05
❑ 299	Kent Mercker UER	.05	.02
	(IP listed as 53, should be 52)		
❑ 300	Checklist 180-255	.05	.02
❑ 301	Chet Lemon	.05	.02
❑ 302	Mike Schooler	.05	.02
❑ 303	Dante Bichette	.20	.09
❑ 304	Kevin Elster	.05	.02
❑ 305	Jeff Huson	.05	.02
❑ 306	Greg A. Harris	.05	.02
❑ 307	Marquis Grissom UER	.20	.09
	(Middle name Deon, should be Dean)		
❑ 308	Calvin Schiraldi	.05	.02
❑ 309	Mariano Duncan	.05	.02
❑ 310	Bill Spiers	.05	.02
❑ 311	Scott Garrelts	.05	.02
❑ 312	Mitch Williams	.05	.02
❑ 313	Mike Macfarlane	.05	.02
❑ 314	Kevin Brown	.15	.07
❑ 315	Robin Ventura	.20	.09
❑ 316	Darren Daulton	.10	.05
❑ 317	Pat Borders	.05	.02
❑ 318	Mark Eichhorn	.05	.02
❑ 319	Jeff Brantley	.05	.02
❑ 320	Shane Mack	.05	.02
❑ 321	Rob Dibble	.05	.02
❑ 322	John Franco	.05	.02
❑ 323	Junior Felix	.05	.02
❑ 324	Casey Candaele	.05	.02
❑ 325	Bobby Bonilla	.10	.05
❑ 326	Dave Henderson	.05	.02
❑ 327	Wayne Edwards	.05	.02
❑ 328	Mark Knudson	.05	.02
❑ 329	Terry Steinbach	.05	.02
❑ 330	Colby Ward UER	.05	.02
	(No comma between city and state)		
❑ 331	Oscar Azocar	.05	.02
❑ 332	Scott Radinsky	.05	.02
❑ 333	Eric Anthony	.05	.02
❑ 334	Steve Lake	.05	.02
❑ 335	Bob Melvin	.05	.02

336	Kal Daniels	.05	.02
337	Tom Pagnozzi	.05	.02
338	Alan Mills	.05	.02
339	Steve Olin	.05	.02
340	Juan Berenguer	.05	.02
341	Francisco Cabrera	.05	.02
342	Dave Bergman	.05	.02
343	Henry Cotto	.05	.02
344	Sergio Valdez	.05	.02
345	Bob Patterson	.05	.02
346	John Marzano	.05	.02
347	Dana Kiecker	.05	.02
348	Dion James	.05	.02
349	Hubie Brooks	.05	.02
350	Bill Landrum	.05	.02
351	Bill Sampen	.05	.02
352	Greg Briley	.05	.02
353	Paul Gibson	.05	.02
354	Dave Eiland	.05	.02
355	Steve Finley	.09	.04
356	Bob Boone	.10	.05
357	Steve Buechele	.05	.02
358	Chris Hoiles	.05	.02
359	Larry Walker	.30	.14
360	Frank DiPino	.05	.02
361	Mark Grant	.05	.02
362	Dave Magadan	.05	.02
363	Robby Thompson	.05	.02
364	Lonnie Smith	.05	.02
365	Steve Farr	.05	.02
366	Dave Valle	.05	.02
367	Tim Naehring	.05	.02
368	Jim Acker	.05	.02
369	Jeff Reardon UER (Born in Pittsfield, not Dalton)	.10	.05
370	Tim Teufel	.05	.02
371	Juan Gonzalez	.75	.35
372	Luis Salazar	.05	.02
373	Rick Honeycutt	.05	.02
374	Greg Maddux	.50	.23
375	Jose Uribe UER (Middle name Elta, should be Alta)	.05	.02
376	Donnie Hill	.05	.02
377	Don Carman	.05	.02
378	Craig Grebeck	.05	.02
379	Willie Fraser	.05	.02
380	Glenallen Hill	.05	.02
381	Joe Oliver	.05	.02
382	Randy Bush	.05	.02
383	Alex Cole	.05	.02
384	Norm Charlton	.05	.02
385	Gene Nelson	.05	.02
386	Checklist 256-331	.05	.02
387	Rickey Henderson MVP	.10	.05
388	Lance Parrish MVP	.05	.02
389	Fred McGriff MVP	.05	.02
390	Dave Parker MVP	.05	.02
391	Candy Maldonado MVP	.05	.02
392	Ken Griffey Jr. MVP	.75	.35
393	Gregg Olson MVP	.05	.02
394	Rafael Palmeiro MVP	.10	.05
395	Roger Clemens MVP	.25	.11
396	George Brett MVP	.20	.09
397	Cecil Fielder MVP	.05	.02
398	Brian Harper MVP UER (Major League Performance, should be Career)	.05	.02
399	Bobby Thigpen MVP	.05	.02
400	Roberto Kelly MVP UER (Second Base on front and OF on back)	.05	.02
401	Danny Darwin MVP	.05	.02
402	Dave Justice MVP	.10	.05
403	Lee Smith MVP	.05	.02
404	Ryne Sandberg MVP	.20	.09
405	Eddie Murray MVP	.10	.05
406	Tim Wallach MVP	.05	.02
407	Kevin Mitchell MVP	.05	.02
408	Darryl Strawberry MVP	.05	.02
409	Joe Carter MVP	.05	.02
410	Len Dykstra MVP	.05	.02
411	Doug Drabek MVP	.05	.02
412	Chris Sabo MVP	.05	.02
413	Paul Marak RR	.05	.02
414	Tim McIntosh RR	.05	.02
415	Brian Barnes RR	.05	.02
416	Eric Gunderson RR	.05	.02
417	Mike Gardiner RR	.05	.02
418	Steve Carter RR	.05	.02
419	Gerald Alexander RR	.05	.02
420	Rich Garces RR	.05	.02
421	Chuck Knoblauch RR	.20	.09
422	Scott Aldred RR	.05	.02
423	Wes Chamberlain RR	.05	.02
424	Lance Dickson RR	.05	.02
425	Greg Colbrunn RR	.05	.02
426	Rich DeLucia RR UER (Misspelled Delucia on card)	.05	.02
427	Jeff Conine RR	.20	.09
428	Steve Decker RR	.05	.02
429	Turner Ward RR	.05	.02
430	Mo Vaughn RR	.40	.18
431	Steve Chitren RR	.05	.02
432	Mike Benjamin RR	.05	.02
433	Ryne Sandberg AS	.20	.09
434	Len Dykstra AS	.05	.02
435	Andre Dawson AS	.10	.05
436A	Mike Scioscia AS (White star by name)		
436B	Mike Scioscia AS (Yellow star by name)	.05	.02
437	Ozzie Smith AS	.20	.09
438	Kevin Mitchell AS	.05	.02
439	Jack Armstrong AS	.05	.02
440	Chris Sabo AS	.05	.02
441	Will Clark AS	.10	.05
442	Mel Hall	.05	.02
443	Mark Gardner	.05	.02
444	Mike Devereaux	.05	.02
445	Kirk Gibson	.10	.05
446	Terry Pendleton	.10	.05
447	Mike Harkey	.05	.02
448	Jim Eisenreich	.05	.02
449	Benito Santiago	.05	.02
450	Oddibe McDowell	.05	.02
451	Cecil Fielder	.10	.05
452	Ken Griffey Sr.	.10	.05
453	Bert Blyleven	.10	.05
454	Howard Johnson	.05	.02
455	Monty Fariss UER (Misspelled Farriss on card)	.05	.02
456	Tony Pena	.05	.02
457	Tim Raines	.10	.05
458	Dennis Rasmussen	.05	.02
459	Luis Quinones	.05	.02
460	B.J. Surhoff	.10	.05
461	Ernest Riles	.05	.02
462	Rick Sutcliffe	.05	.02
463	Danny Tartabull	.05	.02
464	Pete Incaviglia	.05	.02
465	Carlos Martinez	.05	.02
466	Ricky Jordan	.05	.02
467	John Cerutti	.05	.02
468	Dave Winfield	.20	.09
469	Francisco Oliveras	.05	.02
470	Roy Smith	.05	.02
471	Barry Larkin	.20	.09
472	Ron Darling	.05	.02
473	David Wells	.10	.05
474	Glenn Davis	.05	.02
475	Neal Heaton	.05	.02
476	Ron Hassey	.05	.02
477	Frank Thomas	.75	.35
478	Greg Vaughn	.20	.09
479	Todd Burns	.05	.02
480	Candy Maldonado	.05	.02
481	Dave LaPoint	.05	.02
482	Alvin Davis	.05	.02
483	Mike Scott	.05	.02
484	Dale Murphy	.20	.09
485	Ben McDonald	.05	.02
486	Jay Howell	.05	.02
487	Vince Coleman	.10	.05
488	Alfredo Griffin	.05	.02
489	Sandy Alomar Jr.	.10	.05
490	Kirby Puckett	.30	.14
491	Andres Thomas	.05	.02
492	Jack Morris	.10	.05
493	Matt Young	.05	.02
494	Greg Myers	.05	.02
495	Barry Bonds	.25	.11
496	Scott Cooper UER (No BA for 1990 and Career)	.05	.02
497	Dan Schatzeder	.05	.02
498	Jesse Barfield	.05	.02
499	Jerry Goff	.05	.02
500	Checklist 332-408	.05	.02
501	Anthony Telford	.05	.02
502	Eddie Murray	.20	.09
503	Omar Olivares	.05	.02
504	Ryne Sandberg	.25	.11
505	Jeff Montgomery	.10	.05
506	Mark Parent	.05	.02
507	Ron Gant	.10	.05
508	Frank Tanana	.05	.02
509	Jay Buhner	.20	.09
510	Max Venable	.05	.02
511	Wally Whitehurst	.05	.02
512	Gary Pettis	.05	.02
513	Tom Brunansky	.05	.02
514	Tim Wallach	.05	.02
515	Craig Lefferts	.05	.02
516	Tim Layana	.05	.02
517	Darryl Hamilton	.05	.02
518	Rick Reuschel	.05	.02
519	Steve Wilson	.05	.02
520	Kurt Stillwell	.05	.02
521	Rafael Palmeiro	.20	.09
522	Ken Patterson	.05	.02
523	Len Dykstra	.10	.05
524	Tony Fernandez	.05	.02
525	Kent Anderson	.05	.02
526	Mark Leonard	.05	.02
527	Allan Anderson	.05	.02
528	Tom Browning	.05	.02
529	Frank Viola	.10	.05
530	John Olerud	.15	.07
531	Juan Agosto	.05	.02
532	Zane Smith	.05	.02
533	Scott Sanderson	.05	.02
534	Barry Jones	.05	.02
535	Mike Felder	.05	.02
536	Jose Canseco	.25	.11
537	Felix Fermin	.05	.02
538	Roberto Kelly	.10	.05
539	Brian Holman	.05	.02
540	Mark Davidson	.05	.02
541	Terry Mulholland	.05	.02
542	Randy Milligan	.05	.02
543	Jose Gonzalez	.05	.02
544	Craig Wilson	.05	.02
545	Mike Hartley	.05	.02
546	Greg Swindell	.05	.02
547	Gary Gaetti	.10	.05
548	Dave Justice	.20	.09
549	Steve Searcy	.05	.02
550	Erik Hanson	.05	.02
551	Dave Stieb	.05	.02
552	Andy Van Slyke	.10	.05
553	Mike Greenwell	.05	.02
554	Kevin Maas	.05	.02
555	Delino DeShields	.10	.05
556	Curt Schilling	.20	.09
557	Ramon Martinez	.10	.05
558	Pedro Guerrero	.05	.02
559	Dwight Smith	.05	.02
560	Mark Davis	.05	.02
561	Shawn Abner	.05	.02
562	Charlie Leibrandt	.05	.02
563	John Shelby	.05	.02
564	Bill Swift	.05	.02
565	Mike Fetters	.05	.02
566	Alejandro Pena	.05	.02
567	Ruben Sierra	.25	.11
568	Carlos Quintana	.05	.02
569	Kevin Gross	.05	.02
570	Derek Lilliquist	.05	.02
571	Jack Armstrong	.05	.02
572	Greg Brock	.05	.02
573	Mike Kingery	.05	.02
574	Greg Smith	.05	.02
575	Brian McRae	.10	.05

576	Jack Daugherty	.05	.02
577	Ozzie Guillen	.05	.02
578	Joe Boever	.05	.02
579	Luis Sojo	.05	.02
580	Chili Davis	.10	.05
581	Don Robinson	.05	.02
582	Brian Harper	.05	.02
583	Paul O'Neill	.10	.05
584	Bob Ojeda	.05	.02
585	Mookie Wilson	.10	.05
586	Rafael Ramirez	.05	.02
587	Gary Redus	.05	.02
588	Jamie Quirk	.05	.02
589	Shawn Hillegas	.05	.02
590	Tom Edens	.05	.02
591	Joe Klink	.05	.02
592	Charles Nagy	.20	.09
593	Eric Plunk	.05	.02
594	Tracy Jones	.05	.02
595	Craig Biggio	.20	.09
596	Jose DeJesus	.05	.02
597	Mickey Tettleton	.10	.05
598	Chris Gwynn	.05	.02
599	Rex Hudler	.05	.02
600	Checklist 409-506	.05	.02
601	Jim Gott	.05	.02
602	Jeff Manto	.05	.02
603	Nelson Liriano	.05	.02
604	Mark Lemke	.05	.02
605	Clay Parker	.05	.02
606	Edgar Martinez	.20	.09
607	Mark Whiten	.05	.02
608	Ted Power	.05	.02
609	Tom Bolton	.05	.02
610	Tom Herr	.05	.02
611	Andy Hawkins UER (Pitched No-Hitter on 7/1, not 7/2)	.05	.02
612	Scott Ruskin	.05	.02
613	Ron Kittle	.05	.02
614	John Wetteland	.20	.09
615	Mike Perez	.05	.02
616	Dave Clark	.05	.02
617	Brent Mayne	.05	.02
618	Jack Clark	.10	.05
619	Marvin Freeman	.05	.02
620	Edwin Nunez	.05	.02
621	Russ Swan	.05	.02
622	Johnny Ray	.05	.02
623	Charlie O'Brien	.05	.02
624	Joe Bitker	.05	.02
625	Mike Marshall	.05	.02
626	Otis Nixon	.10	.05
627	Andy Benes	.10	.05
628	Ron Oester	.05	.02
629	Ted Higuera	.05	.02
630	Kevin Bass	.05	.02
631	Damon Berryhill	.05	.02
632	Bo Jackson	.10	.05
633	Brad Arnsberg	.05	.02
634	Jerry Willard	.05	.02
635	Tommy Greene	.05	.02
636	Bob MacDonald	.05	.02
637	Kirk McCaskill	.05	.02
638	John Burkett	.05	.02
639	Paul Abbott	.05	.02
640	Todd Benzinger	.05	.02
641	Todd Hundley	.20	.09
642	George Bell	.05	.02
643	Javier Ortiz	.05	.02
644	Sid Bream	.05	.02
645	Bob Welch	.05	.02
646	Phil Bradley	.05	.02
647	Bill Krueger	.05	.02
648	Rickey Henderson	.25	.11
649	Kevin Wickander	.05	.02
650	Steve Balboni	.05	.02
651	Gene Harris	.05	.02
652	Jim Deshaies	.05	.02
653	Jason Grimsley	.05	.02
654	Joe Orsulak	.05	.02
655	Jim Poole	.05	.02
656	Felix Jose	.05	.02
657	Denis Cook	.05	.02
658	Tom Brookens	.05	.02
659	Junior Ortiz	.05	.02
660	Jeff Parrett	.05	.02
661	Jerry Don Gleaton	.05	.02
662	Brent Knackert	.05	.02
663	Rance Mulliniks	.05	.02
664	John Smiley	.05	.02
665	Larry Andersen	.05	.02
666	Willie McGee	.10	.05
667	Chris Nabholz	.05	.02
668	Brady Anderson	.20	.09
669	Darren Holmes UER (19 CG's, should be 0)	.05	.02
670	Ken Hill	.05	.02
671	Gary Varsho	.05	.02
672	Bill Pecota	.05	.02
673	Fred Lynn	.05	.02
674	Kevin D. Brown	.05	.02
675	Dan Petry	.05	.02
676	Mike Jackson	.05	.02
677	Wally Joyner	.10	.05
678	Danny Jackson	.05	.02
679	Bill Haselman	.05	.02
680	Mike Boddicker	.05	.02
681	Mel Rojas	.10	.05
682	Roberto Alomar	.20	.09
683	Dave Justice ROY	.10	.05
684	Chuck Crim	.05	.02
685	Matt Williams	.20	.09
686	Shawon Dunston	.05	.02
687	Jeff Schulz	.05	.02
688	John Barfield	.05	.02
689	Gerald Young	.05	.02
690	Luis Gonzalez	.50	.23
691	Frank Wills	.05	.02
692	Chuck Finley	.10	.05
693	Sandy Alomar Jr. ROY	.10	.05
694	Tim Drummond	.05	.02
695	Herm Winningham	.05	.02
696	Darryl Strawberry	.10	.05
697	Al Leiter	.10	.05
698	Karl Rhodes	.05	.02
699	Stan Belinda	.05	.02
700	Checklist 507-604	.05	.02
701	Lance Blankenship	.05	.02
702	Willie Stargell PUZ	.20	.09
703	Jim Gantner	.05	.02
704	Reggie Harris	.05	.02
705	Rob Ducey	.05	.02
706	Tim Hulett	.05	.02
707	Atlee Hammaker	.05	.02
708	Xavier Hernandez	.05	.02
709	Chuck McElroy	.05	.02
710	John Mitchell	.05	.02
711	Carlos Hernandez	.10	.05
712	Geronimo Pena	.05	.02
713	Jim Neidlinger	.05	.02
714	John Orton	.05	.02
715	Terry Leach	.05	.02
716	Mike Stanton	.05	.02
717	Walt Terrell	.05	.02
718	Luis Aquino	.05	.02
719	Bud Black (Blue Jays uniform, but Giants logo)	.05	.02
720	Bob Kipper	.05	.02
721	Jeff Gray	.05	.02
722	Jose Rijo	.05	.02
723	Curt Young	.05	.02
724	Jose Vizcaino	.05	.02
725	Randy Tomlin	.05	.02
726	Junior Noboa	.05	.02
727	Bob Welch CY	.05	.02
728	Gary Ward	.05	.02
729	Rob Deer (Brewers uniform, but Tigers logo)	.05	.02
730	David Segui	.10	.05
731	Mark Carreon	.05	.02
732	Vicente Palacios	.05	.02
733	Sam Horn	.05	.02
734	Howard Farmer	.05	.02
735	Ken Dayley (Cardinals uniform, but Blue Jays logo)	.05	.02
736	Kelly Mann	.05	.02
737	Joe Grahe	.05	.02
738	Kelly Downs	.05	.02
739	Jimmy Kremers	.05	.02
740	Kevin Appier	.10	.05
741	Jeff Reed	.05	.02
742	Jose Rijo WS	.05	.02
743	Dave Rohde	.05	.02
744	Dr.Dirt/Mr.Clean Len Dykstra Dale Murphy UER (No '91 Donruss logo on card front)	.10	.05
745	Paul Sorrento	.10	.05
746	Thomas Howard	.05	.02
747	Matt Stark	.05	.02
748	Harold Baines	.10	.05
749	Doug Dascenzo	.05	.02
750	Doug Drabek CY	.05	.02
751	Gary Sheffield	.20	.09
752	Terry Lee	.05	.02
753	Jim Vatcher	.05	.02
754	Lee Stevens	.10	.05
755	Randy Veres	.05	.02
756	Bill Doran	.05	.02
757	Gary Wayne	.05	.02
758	Pedro Munoz	.05	.02
759	Chris Hammond	.05	.02
760	Checklist 605-702	.05	.02
761	Rickey Henderson MVP	.10	.05
762	Barry Bonds MVP	.20	.09
763	Billy Hatcher WS UER (Line 13, on should be one)	.05	.02
764	Julio Machado	.05	.02
765	Jose Mesa	.05	.02
766	Willie Randolph WS	.05	.02
767	Scott Erickson	.15	.07
768	Travis Fryman	.20	.09
769	Rich Rodriguez	.05	.02
770	Checklist 703-770 and BC1-BC22	.05	.02

1991 Donruss Elite

	MINT	NRMT
COMPLETE SET (10)	500.00	220.00
COMMON CARD (1-8)	12.00	5.50
MINOR STARS	15.00	6.75
SEMISTARS	25.00	11.00
RANDOM INSERTS IN PACKS		
STATED PRINT RUN 10,000 SERIAL #'d SETS		
1 Barry Bonds	50.00	22.00
2 George Brett	80.00	36.00
3 Jose Canseco	50.00	22.00
4 Andre Dawson	40.00	18.00
5 Doug Drabek	12.00	5.50
6 Cecil Fielder	15.00	6.75
7 Rickey Henderson	50.00	22.00
8 Matt Williams	40.00	18.00
L1 Nolan Ryan (Legend)	100.00	45.00
S1 Ryne Sandberg (Signature Series)	200.00	90.00

1991 Donruss Rookies

	MINT	NRMT
COMP.FACT.SET (56)	6.00	2.70
COMMON CARD (1-56)	.10	.05
MINOR STARS	.10	.05

UNLISTED STARS	.20	.09

#	Name	Mint	NrMt
1	Pat Kelly	.05	.02
2	Rich DeLucia	.05	.02
3	Wes Chamberlain	.05	.02
4	Scott Leius	.05	.02
5	Darryl Kile	.20	.09
6	Milt Cuyler	.05	.02
7	Todd Van Poppel	.05	.02
8	Ray Lankford	.20	.09
9	Brian R. Hunter	.05	.02
10	Tony Perezchica	.05	.02
11	Ced Landrum	.05	.02
12	Dave Burba	.05	.02
13	Ramon Garcia	.05	.02
14	Ed Sprague	.05	.02
15	Warren Newson	.05	.02
16	Paul Faries	.05	.02
17	Luis Gonzalez	.50	.23
18	Charles Nagy	.20	.09
19	Chris Hammond	.05	.02
20	Frank Castillo	.05	.02
21	Pedro Munoz	.05	.02
22	Orlando Merced	.05	.02
23	Jose Melendez	.05	.02
24	Kirk Dressendorfer	.05	.02
25	Heathcliff Slocumb	.20	.09
26	Doug Simons	.05	.02
27	Mike Timlin	.05	.02
28	Jeff Fassero	.10	.05
29	Mark Leiter	.05	.02
30	Jeff Bagwell	3.00	1.35
31	Brian McRae	.10	.05
32	Mark Whiten	.05	.02
33	Ivan Rodriguez	3.00	1.35
34	Wade Taylor	.05	.02
35	Darren Lewis	.10	.05
36	Mo Vaughn	.40	.18
37	Mike Remlinger	.05	.02
38	Rick Wilkins	.05	.02
39	Chuck Knoblauch	.20	.09
40	Kevin Morton	.05	.02
41	Carlos Rodriguez	.05	.02
42	Mark Lewis	.05	.02
43	Brent Mayne	.05	.02
44	Chris Haney	.05	.02
45	Denis Boucher	.05	.02
46	Mike Gardiner	.05	.02
47	Jeff Johnson	.05	.02
48	Dean Palmer	.10	.05
49	Chuck McElroy	.05	.02
50	Chris Jones	.05	.02
51	Scott Kamieniecki	.05	.02
52	Al Osuna	.05	.02
53	Rusty Meacham	.05	.02
54	Chito Martinez	.05	.02
55	Reggie Jefferson	.15	.07
56	Checklist 1-56	.05	.02

1992 Donruss

	MINT	NRMT
COMPLETE SET (784)	8.00	3.60
COMP.HOBBY SET (788)	15.00	6.75
COMP.RETAIL SET (788)	8.00	3.60
COMPLETE SERIES 1 (396)	4.00	1.80
COMPLETE SERIES 2 (388)	4.00	1.80
COMMON CARD (1-784)	.05	.02

MINOR STARS	.10	.05
UNLISTED STARS	.20	.09

SUBSET CARDS HALF VALUE OF BASE CARDS

COMP.BONUS CARD SET (8)	2.00	.90

*BONUS: SAME VALUE AS BASIC CARDS
BONUS CARDS: RANDOM INSERTS IN PACKS

#	Name	Mint	NrMt
1	Mark Wohlers RR	.05	.02
2	Wil Cordero RR	.05	.02
3	Kyle Abbott RR	.05	.02
4	Dave Nilsson RR	.10	.05
5	Kenny Lofton RR	.25	.11
6	Luis Mercedes RR	.05	.02
7	Roger Salkeld RR	.05	.02
8	Eddie Zosky RR	.05	.02
9	Todd Van Poppel RR	.05	.02
10	Frank Seminara RR	.05	.02
11	Andy Ashby RR	.10	.05
12	Reggie Jefferson RR	.10	.05
13	Ryan Klesko RR	.20	.09
14	Carlos Garcia RR	.05	.02
15	John Ramos RR	.05	.02
16	Eric Karros RR	.20	.09
17	Patrick Lennon RR	.05	.02
18	Eddie Taubensee RR	.10	.05
19	Roberto Hernandez RR	.15	.07
20	D.J. Dozier RR	.05	.02
21	Dave Henderson AS	.05	.02
22	Cal Ripken AS	.20	.09
23	Wade Boggs AS	.10	.05
24	Ken Griffey Jr. AS	.60	.25
25	Jack Morris AS	.05	.02
26	Danny Tartabull AS	.05	.02
27	Cecil Fielder AS	.05	.02
28	Roberto Alomar AS	.10	.05
29	Sandy Alomar Jr. AS	.05	.02
30	Rickey Henderson AS	.10	.05
31	Ken Hill	.05	.02
32	John Habyan	.05	.02
33	Otis Nixon HL	.05	.02
34	Tim Wallach	.05	.02
35	Cal Ripken	.75	.35
36	Gary Carter	.20	.09
37	Juan Agosto	.05	.02
38	Doug Dascenzo	.05	.02
39	Kirk Gibson	.10	.05
40	Benito Santiago	.05	.02
41	Otis Nixon	.10	.05
42	Andy Allanson	.05	.02
43	Brian Holman	.05	.02
44	Dick Schofield	.05	.02
45	Dave Magadan	.05	.02
46	Rafael Palmeiro	.20	.09
47	Jody Reed	.05	.02
48	Ivan Calderon	.05	.02
49	Greg W. Harris	.05	.02
50	Chris Sabo	.05	.02
51	Paul Molitor	.20	.09
52	Robby Thompson	.05	.02
53	Dave Smith	.05	.02
54	Mark Davis	.05	.02
55	Kevin Brown	.15	.07
56	Donn Pall	.05	.02
57	Len Dykstra	.10	.05
58	Roberto Alomar	.20	.09
59	Jeff D. Robinson	.05	.02
60	Willie McGee	.10	.05
61	Jay Buhner	.15	.07
62	Mike Pagliarulo	.05	.02
63	Paul O'Neill	.10	.05
64	Hubie Brooks	.05	.02
65	Kelly Gruber	.05	.02
66	Ken Caminiti	.15	.07
67	Gary Redus	.05	.02
68	Harold Baines	.10	.05
69	Charlie Hough	.10	.05
70	B.J. Surhoff	.10	.05
71	Walt Weiss	.05	.02
72	Shawn Hillegas	.05	.02
73	Roberto Kelly	.05	.02
74	Jeff Ballard	.05	.02
75	Craig Biggio	.20	.09
76	Pat Combs	.05	.02
77	Jeff M. Robinson	.05	.02
78	Tim Belcher	.05	.02
79	Cris Carpenter	.05	.02
80	Checklist 1-79	.05	.02
81	Steve Avery	.05	.02
82	Chris James	.05	.02
83	Brian Harper	.05	.02
84	Charlie Leibrandt	.05	.02
85	Mickey Tettleton	.05	.02
86	Pete O'Brien	.05	.02
87	Danny Darwin	.05	.02
88	Bob Walk	.05	.02
89	Jeff Reardon	.10	.05
90	Bobby Rose	.05	.02
91	Danny Jackson	.05	.02
92	John Morris	.05	.02
93	Bud Black	.05	.02
94	Tommy Greene HL	.05	.02
95	Rick Aguilera	.10	.05
96	Gary Gaetti	.10	.05
97	David Cone	.05	.02
98	John Olerud	.05	.02
99	Joel Skinner	.05	.02
100	Jay Bell	.10	.05
101	Bob Milacki	.05	.02
102	Norm Charlton	.05	.02
103	Chuck Crim	.05	.02
104	Terry Steinbach	.05	.02
105	Juan Samuel	.05	.02
106	Steve Howe	.05	.02
107	Rafael Belliard	.05	.02
108	Joey Cora	.05	.02
109	Tommy Greene	.05	.02
110	Gregg Olson	.05	.02
111	Frank Tanana	.05	.02
112	Lee Smith	.10	.05
113	Greg A. Harris	.05	.02
114	Dwayne Henry	.05	.02
115	Chili Davis	.05	.02
116	Kent Mercker	.05	.02
117	Brian Barnes	.05	.02
118	Rich DeLucia	.05	.02
119	Andre Dawson	.15	.07
120	Carlos Baerga	.20	.09
121	Mike LaValliere	.05	.02
122	Jeff Gray	.05	.02
123	Bruce Hurst	.05	.02
124	Alvin Davis	.05	.02
125	John Candelaria	.05	.02
126	Matt Nokes	.05	.02
127	George Bell	.10	.05
128	Bret Saberhagen	.10	.05
129	Jeff Russell	.05	.02
130	Jim Abbott	.10	.05
131	Bill Gullickson	.05	.02
132	Todd Zeile	.05	.02
133	Dave Winfield	.20	.09
134	Wally Whitehurst	.05	.02
135	Matt Williams	.15	.07
136	Tom Browning	.05	.02
137	Marquis Grissom	.10	.05
138	Erik Hanson	.05	.02
139	Rob Dibble	.05	.02
140	Don August	.05	.02
141	Tom Henke	.05	.02
142	Dan Pasqua	.05	.02
143	George Brett	.40	.18
144	Jerald Clark	.05	.02
145	Robin Ventura	.10	.05

#	Player			#	Player			#	Player		
146	Dale Murphy	.20	.09	232	Milt Cuyler	.05	.02	318	Al Osuna	.05	.02
147	Dennis Eckersley	.10	.05	233	Felix Jose	.05	.02	319	Darrin Fletcher	.05	.02
148	Eric Yelding	.05	.02	234	Ellis Burks	.10	.05	320	Checklist 238-316	.05	.02
149	Mario Diaz	.05	.02	235	Pete Harnisch	.05	.02	321	David Segui	.10	.05
150	Casey Candaele	.05	.02	236	Kevin Tapani	.05	.02	322	Stan Javier	.05	.02
151	Steve Olin	.05	.02	237	Terry Pendleton	.05	.02	323	Bryn Smith	.05	.02
152	Luis Salazar	.05	.02	238	Mark Gardner	.05	.02	324	Jeff Treadway	.05	.02
153	Kevin Maas	.05	.02	239	Harold Reynolds	.05	.02	325	Mark Whiten	.05	.02
154	Nolan Ryan HL	.40	.18	240	Checklist 158-237	.05	.02	326	Kent Hrbek	.10	.05
155	Barry Jones	.05	.02	241	Mike Harkey	.05	.02	327	Dave Justice	.20	.09
156	Chris Hoiles	.05	.02	242	Felix Fermin	.05	.02	328	Tony Phillips	.05	.02
157	Bob Ojeda	.05	.02	243	Barry Bonds	.25	.11	329	Rob Murphy	.05	.02
158	Pedro Guerrero	.05	.02	244	Roger Clemens	.50	.23	330	Kevin Morton	.05	.02
159	Paul Assenmacher	.05	.02	245	Dennis Rasmussen	.05	.02	331	John Smiley	.05	.02
160	Checklist 80-157	.05	.02	246	Jose DeLeon	.05	.02	332	Luis Rivera	.05	.02
161	Mike Macfarlane	.05	.02	247	Orel Hershiser	.10	.05	333	Wally Joyner	.10	.05
162	Craig Lefferts	.05	.02	248	Mel Hall	.05	.02	334	Heathcliff Slocumb	.05	.02
163	Brian Hunter	.05	.02	249	Rick Wilkins	.05	.02	335	Rick Cerone	.05	.02
164	Alan Trammell	.15	.07	250	Tom Gordon	.05	.02	336	Mike Remlinger	.05	.02
165	Ken Griffey Jr.	1.25	.55	251	Kevin Reimer	.05	.02	337	Mike Moore	.05	.02
166	Lance Parrish	.05	.02	252	Luis Polonia	.05	.02	338	Lloyd McClendon	.05	.02
167	Brian Downing	.05	.02	253	Mike Henneman	.05	.02	339	Al Newman	.05	.02
168	John Barfield	.05	.02	254	Tom Pagnozzi	.05	.02	340	Kirk McCaskill	.05	.02
169	Jack Clark	.10	.05	255	Chuck Finley	.10	.05	341	Howard Johnson	.05	.02
170	Chris Nabholz	.05	.02	256	Mackey Sasser	.05	.02	342	Greg Myers	.05	.02
171	Tim Teufel	.05	.02	257	John Burkett	.05	.02	343	Kal Daniels	.05	.02
172	Chris Hammond	.05	.02	258	Hal Morris	.05	.02	344	Bernie Williams	.20	.09
173	Robin Yount	.20	.09	259	Larry Walker	.20	.09	345	Shane Mack	.05	.02
174	Dave Righetti	.05	.02	260	Bill Swift	.05	.02	346	Gary Thurman	.05	.02
175	Joe Girardi	.10	.05	261	Joe Oliver	.05	.02	347	Dante Bichette	.15	.07
176	Mike Boddicker	.05	.02	262	Julio Machado	.05	.02	348	Mark McGwire	1.00	.45
177	Dean Palmer	.10	.05	263	Todd Stottlemyre	.05	.02	349	Travis Fryman	.10	.05
178	Greg Hibbard	.05	.02	264	Matt Merullo	.05	.02	350	Ray Lankford	.20	.09
179	Randy Ready	.05	.02	265	Brent Mayne	.05	.02	351	Mike Jeffcoat	.05	.02
180	Devon White	.05	.02	266	Thomas Howard	.05	.02	352	Jack McDowell	.05	.02
181	Mark Eichhorn	.05	.02	267	Lance Johnson	.05	.02	353	Mitch Williams	.05	.02
182	Mike Felder	.05	.02	268	Terry Mulholland	.05	.02	354	Mike Devereaux	.05	.02
183	Joe Klink	.05	.02	269	Rick Honeycutt	.05	.02	355	Andres Galarraga	.20	.09
184	Steve Bedrosian	.05	.02	270	Luis Gonzalez	.15	.07	356	Henry Cotto	.05	.02
185	Barry Larkin	.15	.07	271	Jose Guzman	.05	.02	357	Scott Bailes	.05	.02
186	John Franco	.10	.05	272	Jimmy Jones	.05	.02	358	Jeff Bagwell	.40	.18
187	Ed Sprague	.05	.02	273	Mark Lewis	.05	.02	359	Scott Leius	.05	.02
188	Mark Portugal	.05	.02	274	Rene Gonzales	.05	.02	360	Zane Smith	.05	.02
189	Jose Lind	.05	.02	275	Jeff Johnson	.05	.02	361	Bill Pecota	.05	.02
190	Bob Welch	.05	.02	276	Dennis Martinez HL	.05	.02	362	Tony Fernandez	.05	.02
191	Alex Fernandez	.10	.05	277	Delino DeShields	.10	.05	363	Glenn Braggs	.05	.02
192	Gary Sheffield	.20	.09	278	Sam Horn	.05	.02	364	Bill Spiers	.05	.02
193	Rickey Henderson	.25	.11	279	Kevin Gross	.05	.02	365	Vicente Palacios	.05	.02
194	Rod Nichols	.05	.02	280	Jose Oquendo	.05	.02	366	Tim Burke	.05	.02
195	Scott Kamieniecki	.05	.02	281	Mark Grace	.15	.07	367	Randy Tomlin	.05	.02
196	Mike Flanagan	.05	.02	282	Mark Gubicza	.05	.02	368	Kenny Rogers	.05	.02
197	Steve Finley	.10	.05	283	Fred McGriff	.15	.07	369	Brett Butler	.10	.05
198	Darren Daulton	.10	.05	284	Ron Gant	.10	.05	370	Pat Kelly	.05	.02
199	Leo Gomez	.05	.02	285	Lou Whitaker	.10	.05	371	Bip Roberts	.05	.02
200	Mike Morgan	.05	.02	286	Edgar Martinez	.15	.07	372	Gregg Jefferies	.05	.02
201	Bob Tewksbury	.05	.02	287	Ron Tingley	.05	.02	373	Kevin Bass	.05	.02
202	Sid Bream	.05	.02	288	Kevin McReynolds	.05	.02	374	Ron Karkovice	.05	.02
203	Sandy Alomar Jr	.10	.05	289	Ivan Rodriguez	.40	.18	375	Paul Gibson	.05	.02
204	Greg Gagne	.05	.02	290	Mike Gardiner	.05	.02	376	Bernard Gilkey	.10	.05
205	Juan Berenguer	.05	.02	291	Chris Haney	.05	.02	377	Dave Gallagher	.05	.02
206	Cecil Fielder	.10	.05	292	Darrin Jackson	.05	.02	378	Bill Wegman	.05	.02
207	Randy Johnson	.20	.09	293	Bill Doran	.05	.02	379	Pat Borders	.05	.02
208	Tony Pena	.05	.02	294	Ted Higuera	.05	.02	380	Ed Whitson	.05	.02
209	Doug Drabek	.05	.02	295	Jeff Brantley	.05	.02	381	Gilberto Reyes	.05	.02
210	Wade Boggs	.20	.09	296	Les Lancaster	.05	.02	382	Russ Swan	.05	.02
211	Bryan Harvey	.05	.02	297	Jim Eisenreich	.05	.02	383	Andy Van Slyke	.10	.05
212	Jose Vizcaino	.05	.02	298	Ruben Sierra	.15	.07	384	Wes Chamberlain	.05	.02
213	Alonzo Powell	.05	.02	299	Scott Radinsky	.05	.02	385	Steve Chitren	.05	.02
214	Will Clark	.20	.09	300	Jose DeJesus	.05	.02	386	Greg Olson	.05	.02
215	Rickey Henderson HL	.05	.02	301	Mike Nathan	.05	.02	387	Brian McRae	.05	.02
216	Jack Morris	.10	.05	302	Luis Sojo	.05	.02	388	Rich Rodriguez	.05	.02
217	Junior Felix	.05	.02	303	Kelly Downs	.05	.02	389	Steve Decker	.05	.02
218	Vince Coleman	.05	.02	304	Scott Bankhead	.05	.02	390	Chuck Knoblauch	.20	.09
219	Jimmy Key	.10	.05	305	Pedro Munoz	.05	.02	391	Bobby Witt	.05	.02
220	Alex Cole	.05	.02	306	Scott Scudder	.05	.02	392	Eddie Murray	.20	.09
221	Bill Landrum	.05	.02	307	Kevin Elster	.05	.02	393	Juan Gonzalez	.50	.23
222	Randy Milligan	.05	.02	308	Duane Ward	.05	.02	394	Scott Ruskin	.05	.02
223	Jose Rijo	.05	.02	309	Darryl Kile	.10	.05	395	Jay Howell	.05	.02
224	Greg Vaughn	.10	.05	310	Orlando Merced	.10	.05	396	Checklist 317-396	.05	.02
225	Dave Stewart	.10	.05	311	Dave Henderson	.05	.02	397	Royce Clayton RR	.05	.02
226	Lenny Harris	.05	.02	312	Tim Raines	.10	.05	398	John Jaha RR	.25	.11
227	Scott Sanderson	.05	.02	313	Mark Lee	.05	.02	399	Dan Wilson RR	.10	.05
228	Jeff Blauser	.05	.02	314	Mike Gallego	.05	.02	400	Archie Corbin RR	.05	.02
229	Ozzie Guillen	.05	.02	315	Charles Nagy	.10	.05	401	Barry Manuel RR	.05	.02
230	John Kruk	.05	.02	316	Jesse Barfield	.05	.02	402	Kim Batiste RR	.05	.02
231	Bob Melvin	.05	.02	317	Todd Frohwirth	.05	.02	403	Pat Mahomes RR	.05	.02

❑ 404	Dave Fleming RR	.05	.02
❑ 405	Jeff Juden RR	.05	.02
❑ 406	Jim Thome RR	.50	.23
❑ 407	Sam Militello RR	.05	.02
❑ 408	Jeff Nelson RR	.05	.02
❑ 409	Anthony Young RR	.05	.02
❑ 410	Tino Martinez RR	.20	.09
❑ 411	Jeff Mutis RR	.05	.02
❑ 412	Rey Sanchez RR	.05	.02
❑ 413	Chris Gardner RR	.05	.02
❑ 414	John Vander Wal RR	.05	.02
❑ 415	Reggie Sanders RR	.10	.05
❑ 416	Brian Williams RR	.05	.02
❑ 417	Mo Sanford RR	.05	.02
❑ 418	David Weathers RR	.05	.02
❑ 419	Hector Fajardo RR	.05	.02
❑ 420	Steve Foster RR	.05	.02
❑ 421	Lance Dickson RR	.05	.02
❑ 422	Andre Dawson AS	.10	.05
❑ 423	Ozzie Smith AS	.20	.09
❑ 424	Chris Sabo AS	.05	.02
❑ 425	Tony Gwynn AS	.20	.09
❑ 426	Tom Glavine AS	.15	.07
❑ 427	Bobby Bonilla AS	.05	.02
❑ 428	Will Clark AS	.10	.05
❑ 429	Ryne Sandberg AS	.20	.09
❑ 430	Benito Santiago AS	.05	.02
❑ 431	Ivan Calderon AS	.05	.02
❑ 432	Ozzie Smith	.25	.11
❑ 433	Tim Leary	.05	.02
❑ 434	Bret Saberhagen HL	.05	.02
❑ 435	Mel Rojas	.05	.02
❑ 436	Ben McDonald	.05	.02
❑ 437	Tim Crews	.05	.02
❑ 438	Rex Hudler	.05	.02
❑ 439	Chico Walker	.05	.02
❑ 440	Kurt Stillwell	.05	.02
❑ 441	Tony Gwynn	.50	.23
❑ 442	John Smoltz	.15	.07
❑ 443	Lloyd Moseby	.05	.02
❑ 444	Mike Schooler	.05	.02
❑ 445	Joe Grahe	.05	.02
❑ 446	Dwight Gooden	.10	.05
❑ 447	Oil Can Boyd	.05	.02
❑ 448	John Marzano	.05	.02
❑ 449	Bret Barberie	.05	.02
❑ 450	Mike Maddux	.05	.02
❑ 451	Jeff Reed	.05	.02
❑ 452	Dale Sveum	.05	.02
❑ 453	Jose Uribe	.05	.02
❑ 454	Bob Scanlan	.05	.02
❑ 455	Kevin Appier	.10	.05
❑ 456	Jeff Huson	.05	.02
❑ 457	Ken Patterson	.05	.02
❑ 458	Ricky Jordan	.05	.02
❑ 459	Tom Candiotti	.05	.02
❑ 460	Lee Stevens	.05	.02
❑ 461	Riod Beck	.20	.09
❑ 462	Dave Valle	.05	.02
❑ 463	Scott Erickson	.10	.05
❑ 464	Chris Jones	.05	.02
❑ 465	Mark Carreon	.05	.02
❑ 466	Rob Ducey	.05	.02
❑ 467	Jim Corsi	.05	.02
❑ 468	Jeff King	.05	.02
❑ 469	Curt Young	.05	.02
❑ 470	Bo Jackson	.10	.05
❑ 471	Chris Bosio	.05	.02
❑ 472	Jamie Quirk	.05	.02
❑ 473	Jesse Orosco	.05	.02
❑ 474	Alvaro Espinoza	.05	.02
❑ 475	Joe Orsulak	.05	.02
❑ 476	Checklist 397-477	.05	.02
❑ 477	Gerald Young	.05	.02
❑ 478	Wally Backman	.05	.02
❑ 479	Juan Bell	.05	.02
❑ 480	Mike Scioscia	.05	.02
❑ 481	Omar Olivares	.05	.02
❑ 482	Francisco Cabrera	.05	.02
❑ 483	Greg Swindell UER	.05	.02
	(Shown on Indians, but listed on Reds)		
❑ 484	Terry Leach	.05	.02
❑ 485	Tommy Gregg	.05	.02
❑ 486	Scott Aldred	.05	.02
❑ 487	Greg Briley	.05	.02
❑ 488	Phil Plantier	.05	.02
❑ 489	Curtis Wilkerson	.05	.02
❑ 490	Tom Brunansky	.05	.02
❑ 491	Mike Fetters	.05	.02
❑ 492	Frank Castillo	.05	.02
❑ 493	Joe Boever	.05	.02
❑ 494	Kirt Manwaring	.05	.02
❑ 495	Wilson Alvarez HL	.05	.02
❑ 496	Gene Larkin	.05	.02
❑ 497	Gary DiSarcina	.05	.02
❑ 498	Frank Viola	.05	.02
❑ 499	Manuel Lee	.05	.02
❑ 500	Albert Belle	.20	.09
❑ 501	Stan Belinda	.05	.02
❑ 502	Dwight Evans	.05	.02
❑ 503	Eric Davis	.10	.05
❑ 504	Darren Holmes	.05	.02
❑ 505	Mike Bordick	.05	.02
❑ 506	Dave Hansen	.05	.02
❑ 507	Lee Guetterman	.05	.02
❑ 508	Keith Mitchell	.05	.02
❑ 509	Melido Perez	.05	.02
❑ 510	Dickie Thon	.05	.02
❑ 511	Mark Williamson	.05	.02
❑ 512	Mark Salas	.05	.02
❑ 513	Milt Thompson	.05	.02
❑ 514	Mo Vaughn	.25	.11
❑ 515	Jim Deshaies	.05	.02
❑ 516	Rich Garces	.05	.02
❑ 517	Lonnie Smith	.05	.02
❑ 518	Spike Owen	.05	.02
❑ 519	Tracy Jones	.05	.02
❑ 520	Greg Maddux	.50	.23
❑ 521	Carlos Martinez	.05	.02
❑ 522	Neal Heaton	.05	.02
❑ 523	Mike Greenwell	.05	.02
❑ 524	Andy Benes	.10	.05
❑ 525	Jeff Schaefer UER	.05	.02
	(Photo actually Tino Martinez)		
❑ 526	Mike Sharperson	.05	.02
❑ 527	Wade Taylor	.05	.02
❑ 528	Jerome Walton	.05	.02
❑ 529	Storm Davis	.05	.02
❑ 530	Jose Hernandez	.05	.02
❑ 531	Mark Langston	.05	.02
❑ 532	Rob Deer	.05	.02
❑ 533	Geronimo Pena	.05	.02
❑ 534	Juan Guzman	.25	.11
❑ 535	Pete Schourek	.05	.02
❑ 536	Todd Benzinger	.05	.02
❑ 537	Billy Hatcher	.05	.02
❑ 538	Tom Foley	.05	.02
❑ 539	Dave Cochrane	.05	.02
❑ 540	Mariano Duncan	.05	.02
❑ 541	Edwin Nunez	.05	.02
❑ 542	Rance Mulliniks	.05	.02
❑ 543	Carlton Fisk	.20	.09
❑ 544	Luis Aquino	.05	.02
❑ 545	Ricky Bones	.05	.02
❑ 546	Craig Grebeck	.05	.02
❑ 547	Charlie Hayes	.05	.02
❑ 548	Jose Canseco	.25	.11
❑ 549	Andujar Cedeno	.05	.02
❑ 550	Geno Petralli	.05	.02
❑ 551	Javier Ortiz	.05	.02
❑ 552	Rudy Seanez	.05	.02
❑ 553	Rich Gedman	.05	.02
❑ 554	Eric Plunk	.05	.02
❑ 555	Nolan Ryan HL	.25	.11
	(With Rich Gossage)		
❑ 556	Checklist 478-555	.05	.02
❑ 557	Greg Colbrunn	.05	.02
❑ 558	Chito Martinez	.05	.02
❑ 559	Darryl Strawberry	.10	.05
❑ 560	Luis Alicea	.05	.02
❑ 561	Dwight Smith	.05	.02
❑ 562	Jim Vatcher	.05	.02
❑ 563	Deion Sanders	.20	.09
❑ 564	Deion Sanders		
❑ 565	Walt Terrell	.05	.02
❑ 566	Dave Burba	.05	.02
❑ 567	Dave Howard	.05	.02
❑ 568	Todd Hundley	.10	.05
❑ 569	Jack Daugherty	.05	.02
❑ 570	Scott Cooper	.05	.02
❑ 571	Bill Sampen	.05	.02
❑ 572	Jose Melendez	.05	.02
❑ 573	Freddie Benavides	.05	.02
❑ 574	Jim Gantner	.05	.02
❑ 575	Trevor Wilson	.05	.02
❑ 576	Ryne Sandberg	.25	.11
❑ 577	Kevin Seitzer	.05	.02
❑ 578	Gerald Alexander	.05	.02
❑ 579	Mike Huff	.05	.02
❑ 580	Von Hayes	.05	.02
❑ 581	Derek Bell	.10	.05
❑ 582	Mike Stanley	.05	.02
❑ 583	Kevin Mitchell	.10	.05
❑ 584	Mike Jackson	.10	.05
❑ 585	Dan Gladden	.05	.02
❑ 586	Ted Power UER	.05	.02
	(Wrong year given for signing with Reds)		
❑ 587	Jeff Innis	.05	.02
❑ 588	Bob MacDonald	.05	.02
❑ 589	Jose Tolentino	.05	.02
❑ 590	Bob Patterson	.05	.02
❑ 591	Scott Brosius	.25	.11
❑ 592	Frank Thomas	.50	.23
❑ 593	Darryl Hamilton	.05	.02
❑ 594	Kirk Dressendorfer	.05	.02
❑ 595	Jeff Shaw	.05	.02
❑ 596	Don Mattingly	.40	.18
❑ 597	Glenn Davis	.05	.02
❑ 598	Andy Mota	.05	.02
❑ 599	Jason Grimsley	.05	.02
❑ 600	Jim Poole	.05	.02
❑ 601	Jim Gott	.05	.02
❑ 602	Stan Royer	.05	.02
❑ 603	Marvin Freeman	.05	.02
❑ 604	Denis Boucher	.05	.02
❑ 605	Denny Neagle	.15	.07
❑ 606	Mark Lemke	.05	.02
❑ 607	Jerry Don Gleaton	.05	.02
❑ 608	Brent Knackert	.05	.02
❑ 609	Carlos Quintana	.05	.02
❑ 610	Bobby Bonilla	.10	.05
❑ 611	Joe Hesketh	.05	.02
❑ 612	Daryl Boston	.05	.02
❑ 613	Shawon Dunston	.05	.02
❑ 614	Danny Cox	.05	.02
❑ 615	Darren Lewis	.05	.02
❑ 616	Braves No-Hitter UER	.05	.02
	Kent Mercker (Misspelled Merker on card front) Alejandro Pena Mark Wohlers		
❑ 617	Kirby Puckett	.30	.14
❑ 618	Franklin Stubbs	.05	.02
❑ 619	Chris Donnels	.05	.02
❑ 620	David Wells UER	.10	.05
	(Career Highlights in black not red)		
❑ 621	Mike Aldrete	.05	.02
❑ 622	Bob Kipper	.05	.02
❑ 623	Anthony Telford	.05	.02
❑ 624	Randy Myers	.10	.05
❑ 625	Willie Randolph	.10	.05
❑ 626	Joe Slusarski	.05	.02
❑ 627	John Wetteland	.10	.05
❑ 628	Greg Cadaret	.05	.02
❑ 629	Tom Glavine	.15	.07
❑ 630	Wilson Alvarez	.10	.05
❑ 631	Wally Ritchie	.05	.02
❑ 632	Mike Mussina	.30	.14
❑ 633	Mark Leiter	.05	.02
❑ 634	Gerald Perry	.05	.02
❑ 635	Matt Young	.05	.02
❑ 636	Checklist 556-635	.05	.02
❑ 637	Scott Hemond	.05	.02
❑ 638	David West	.05	.02
❑ 639	Jim Clancy	.05	.02
❑ 640	Doug Piatt UER	.05	.02
	(Not born in 1955 as on card; incorrect info on How Acquired)		
❑ 641	Omar Vizquel	.10	.05
❑ 642	Rick Sutcliffe	.05	.02
❑ 643	Gienallen Hill	.05	.02
❑ 644	Gary Varsho	.05	.02

645 Tony Fossas	.05	.02
646 Jack Howell	.05	.02
647 Jim Campanis	.05	.02
648 Chris Gwynn	.05	.02
649 Jim Leyritz	.05	.02
650 Chuck McElroy	.05	.02
651 Sean Berry	.05	.02
652 Donald Harris	.05	.02
653 Don Slaught	.05	.02
654 Rusty Meacham	.05	.02
655 Scott Terry	.05	.02
656 Ramon Martinez	.10	.05
657 Keith Miller	.05	.02
658 Ramon Garcia	.05	.02
659 Milt Hill	.05	.02
660 Steve Frey	.05	.02
661 Bob McClure	.05	.02
662 Ced Landrum	.05	.02
663 Doug Henry	.05	.02
664 Candy Maldonado	.05	.02
665 Carl Willis	.05	.02
666 Jeff Montgomery	.10	.05
667 Craig Shipley	.05	.02
668 Warren Newson	.05	.02
669 Mickey Morandini	.05	.02
670 Brook Jacoby	.05	.02
671 Ryan Bowen	.05	.02
672 Bill Krueger	.05	.02
673 Rob Mallicoat	.05	.02
674 Doug Jones	.05	.02
675 Scott Livingstone	.05	.02
676 Danny Tartabull	.05	.02
677 Joe Carter HL	.05	.02
678 Cecil Espy	.05	.02
679 Randy Velarde	.05	.02
680 Bruce Ruffin	.05	.02
681 Ted Wood	.05	.02
682 Dan Plesac	.05	.02
683 Eric Bullock	.05	.02
684 Junior Ortiz	.05	.02
685 Dave Hollins	.05	.02
686 Dennis Martinez	.10	.05
687 Larry Andersen	.05	.02
688 Doug Simons	.05	.02
689 Tim Spehr	.05	.02
690 Calvin Jones	.05	.02
691 Mark Guthrie	.05	.02
692 Alfredo Griffin	.05	.02
693 Joe Carter	.10	.05
694 Terry Mathews	.05	.02
695 Pascual Perez	.05	.02
696 Gene Nelson	.05	.02
697 Gerald Williams	.05	.02
698 Chris Cron	.05	.02
699 Steve Buechele	.05	.02
700 Paul McClellan	.05	.02
701 Jim Lindeman	.05	.02
702 Francisco Oliveras	.05	.02
703 Rob Maurer	.05	.02
704 Pat Hentgen	.20	.09
705 Jaime Navarro	.05	.02
706 Mike Magnante	.05	.02
707 Nolan Ryan	.75	.35
708 Bobby Thigpen	.05	.02
709 John Cerutti	.05	.02
710 Steve Wilson	.05	.02
711 Hensley Meulens	.05	.02
712 Rheal Cormier	.05	.02
713 Scott Bradley	.05	.02
714 Mitch Webster	.05	.02
715 Roger Mason	.05	.02
716 Checklist 636-716	.05	.02
717 Jeff Fassero	.05	.02
718 Cal Eldred	.05	.02
719 Sid Fernandez	.05	.02
720 Bob Zupcic	.05	.02
721 Jose Offerman	.05	.02
722 Cliff Brantley	.05	.02
723 Ron Darling	.05	.02
724 Dave Stieb	.05	.02
725 Hector Villanueva	.05	.02
726 Mike Hartley	.05	.02
727 Arthur Rhodes	.05	.02
728 Randy Bush	.05	.02
729 Steve Sax	.05	.02
730 Dave Otto	.05	.02

731 John Wehner	.05	.02
732 Dave Martinez	.05	.02
733 Ruben Amaro	.05	.02
734 Billy Ripken	.05	.02
735 Steve Farr	.05	.02
736 Shawn Abner	.05	.02
737 Gil Heredia	.05	.02
738 Ron Jones	.05	.02
739 Tony Castillo	.05	.02
740 Sammy Sosa	.60	.25
741 Julio Franco	.05	.02
742 Tim Naehring	.05	.02
743 Steve Wapnick	.05	.02
744 Craig Wilson	.05	.02
745 Darrin Chapin	.05	.02
746 Chris George	.05	.02
747 Mike Simms	.05	.02
748 Rosario Rodriguez	.05	.02
749 Skeeter Barnes	.05	.02
750 Roger McDowell	.05	.02
751 Dann Howitt	.05	.02
752 Paul Sorrento	.05	.02
753 Braulio Castillo	.05	.02
754 Yorkis Perez	.05	.02
755 Willie Fraser	.05	.02
756 Jeremy Hernandez	.05	.02
757 Curt Schilling	.15	.07
758 Steve Lyons	.05	.02
759 Dave Anderson	.05	.02
760 Willie Banks	.05	.02
761 Mark Leonard	.05	.02
762 Jack Armstrong	.05	.02
(Listed on Indians, but shown on Reds)		
763 Scott Servais	.05	.02
764 Ray Stephens	.05	.02
765 Junior Noboa	.05	.02
766 Jim Olander	.05	.02
767 Joe Magrane	.05	.02
768 Lance Blankenship	.05	.02
769 Mike Humphreys	.05	.02
770 Jarvis Brown	.05	.02
771 Damon Berryhill	.05	.02
772 Alejandro Pena	.05	.02
773 Jose Mesa	.05	.02
774 Gary Cooper	.05	.02
775 Carney Lansford	.10	.05
776 Mike Bielecki	.05	.02
(Shown on Cubs, but listed on Braves)		
777 Charlie O'Brien	.05	.02
778 Carlos Hernandez	.05	.02
779 Howard Farmer	.05	.02
780 Mike Stanton	.05	.02
781 Reggie Harris	.05	.02
782 Xavier Hernandez	.05	.02
783 Bryan Hickerson	.05	.02
784 Checklist 717-784 and BC1-BC8	.05	.02

1992 Donruss Diamond Kings

JOE CARTER

	MINT	NRMT
COMPLETE SET (27)	20.00	9.00
COMPLETE SERIES 1 (14)	16.00	7.25
COMPLETE SERIES 2 (13)	4.00	1.80
COMMON CARD (DK1-DK27)	.50	.23

RANDOM INSERTS IN PACKS

DK1 Paul Molitor	1.50	.70
DK2 Will Clark	1.50	.70
DK3 Joe Carter	.75	.35
DK4 Julio Franco	.50	.23
DK5 Cal Ripken	6.00	2.70
DK6 Dave Justice	1.50	.70
DK7 George Bell	.50	.23
DK8 Frank Thomas	4.00	1.80
DK9 Wade Boggs	1.50	.70
DK10 Scott Sanderson	.50	.23
DK11 Jeff Bagwell	3.00	1.35
DK12 John Kruk	.75	.35
DK13 Felix Jose	.50	.23
DK14 Harold Baines	.75	.35
DK15 Dwight Gooden	.75	.35
DK16 Brian McRae	.50	.23
DK17 Jay Bell	.75	.35
DK18 Brett Butler	.75	.35
DK19 Hal Morris	.50	.23
DK20 Mark Langston	.50	.23
DK21 Scott Erickson	.75	.35
DK22 Randy Johnson	1.50	.70
DK23 Greg Swindell	.50	.23
DK24 Dennis Martinez	.75	.35
DK25 Tony Phillips	.50	.23
DK26 Fred McGriff	1.00	.45
DK27 Checklist 1-26 DP (Dick Perez)	.50	.23

1992 Donruss Elite

	MINT	NRMT
COMPLETE SET (12)	600.00	275.00
COMMON CARD (9-18)	12.00	5.50
SEMISTARS	20.00	9.00
RANDOM INSERTS IN PACKS		
STATED PRINT RUN 10,000 SERIAL #'d SETS		

9 Wade Boggs	25.00	11.00
10 Joe Carter	15.00	6.75
11 Will Clark	25.00	11.00
12 Dwight Gooden	15.00	6.75
13 Ken Griffey Jr.	120.00	55.00
14 Tony Gwynn	50.00	22.00
15 Howard Johnson	12.00	5.50
16 Terry Pendleton	12.00	5.50
17 Kirby Puckett	40.00	18.00
18 Frank Thomas	50.00	22.00
L2 Rickey Henderson	40.00	18.00
(Legend Series)		
S2 Cal Ripken	300.00	135.00
(Signature Series)		

1992 Donruss Update

	MINT	NRMT
COMPLETE SET (22)	50.00	22.00
COMMON CARD (U1-U22)	.50	.23
MINOR STARS	1.00	.45
SEMISTARS	2.00	.90
UNLISTED STARS	3.00	1.35
FOUR PER RETAIL FACTORY SET		

U1 Pat Listach RR	.50	.23
U2 Andy Stankiewicz RR	.50	.23
U3 Brian Jordan RR	3.00	1.35

		MINT	NRMT
❏ U4	Dan Walters RR	1.00	.45
❏ U5	Chad Curtis RR	3.00	1.35
❏ U6	Kenny Lofton RR	8.00	3.60
❏ U7	Mark McGwire HL	15.00	6.75
❏ U8	Eddie Murray HL	3.00	1.35
❏ U9	Jeff Reardon HL	1.00	.45
❏ U10	Frank Viola	.50	.23
❏ U11	Gary Sheffield	3.00	1.35
❏ U12	George Bell	.50	.23
❏ U13	Rick Sutcliffe	.50	.23
❏ U14	Wally Joyner	1.00	.45
❏ U15	Kevin Seitzer	.50	.23
❏ U16	Bill Krueger	.50	.23
❏ U17	Danny Tartabull	.50	.23
❏ U18	Dave Winfield	3.00	1.35
❏ U19	Gary Carter	3.00	1.35
❏ U20	Bobby Bonilla	1.00	.45
❏ U21	Cory Snyder	.50	.23
❏ U22	Bill Swift	.50	.23

1992 Donruss Rookies

	MINT	NRMT
COMPLETE SET (132)	10.00	4.50
COMMON CARD (1-132)	.05	.02
MINOR STARS	.10	.05
UNLISTED STARS	.20	.09

❏ 1	Kyle Abbott	.05	.02
❏ 2	Troy Afenir	.05	.02
❏ 3	Rich Amaral	.05	.02
❏ 4	Ruben Amaro	.05	.02
❏ 5	Billy Ashley	.05	.02
❏ 6	Pedro Astacio	.25	.11
❏ 7	Jim Austin	.05	.02
❏ 8	Robert Ayrault	.05	.02
❏ 9	Kevin Baez	.05	.02
❏ 10	Esteban Beltre	.05	.02
❏ 11	Brian Bohanon	.05	.02
❏ 12	Kent Bottenfield	.75	.35
❏ 13	Jeff Branson	.05	.02
❏ 14	Brad Brink	.05	.02
❏ 15	John Briscoe	.05	.02
❏ 16	Doug Brocail	.05	.02
❏ 17	Rico Brogna	.10	.05
❏ 18	J.T. Bruett	.05	.02
❏ 19	Jacob Brumfield	.05	.02
❏ 20	Jim Bullinger	.05	.02
❏ 21	Kevin Campbell	.05	.02
❏ 22	Pedro Castellano	.05	.02
❏ 23	Mike Christopher	.05	.02

❏ 24	Archi Cianfrocco	.05	.02
❏ 25	Mark Clark	.05	.02
❏ 26	Craig Colbert	.05	.02
❏ 27	Victor Cole	.05	.02
❏ 28	Steve Cooke	.05	.02
❏ 29	Tim Costo	.05	.02
❏ 30	Chad Curtis	.25	.11
❏ 31	Doug Davis	.05	.02
❏ 32	Gary DiSarcina	.05	.02
❏ 33	John Doherty	.05	.02
❏ 34	Mike Draper	.05	.02
❏ 35	Monty Fariss	.05	.02
❏ 36	Bien Figueroa	.05	.02
❏ 37	John Flaherty	.05	.02
❏ 38	Tim Fortugno	.05	.02
❏ 39	Eric Fox	.05	.02
❏ 40	Jeff Frye	.05	.02
❏ 41	Ramon Garcia	.05	.02
❏ 42	Brent Gates	.05	.02
❏ 43	Tom Goodwin	.10	.05
❏ 44	Buddy Groom	.05	.02
❏ 45	Jeff Grotewold	.05	.02
❏ 46	Juan Guerrero	.05	.02
❏ 47	Johnny Guzman	.05	.02
❏ 48	Shawn Hare	.05	.02
❏ 49	Ryan Hawblitzel	.05	.02
❏ 50	Bert Heffernan	.05	.02
❏ 51	Butch Henry	.05	.02
❏ 52	Cesar Hernandez	.05	.02
❏ 53	Vince Horsman	.05	.02
❏ 54	Steve Hosey	.05	.02
❏ 55	Pat Howell	.05	.02
❏ 56	Peter Hoy	.05	.02
❏ 57	Jonathan Hurst	.05	.02
❏ 58	Mark Hutton	.05	.02
❏ 59	Shawn Jeter	.05	.02
❏ 60	Joel Johnston	.05	.02
❏ 61	Jeff Kent	.20	.09
❏ 62	Kurt Knudsen	.05	.02
❏ 63	Kevin Koslofski	.05	.02
❏ 64	Danny Leon	.05	.02
❏ 65	Jesse Levis	.05	.02
❏ 66	Tom Marsh	.05	.02
❏ 67	Ed Martel	.05	.02
❏ 68	Al Martin	.25	.11
❏ 69	Pedro Martinez	3.00	1.35
❏ 70	Derrick May	.05	.02
❏ 71	Matt Maysey	.05	.02
❏ 72	Russ McGinnis	.05	.02
❏ 73	Tim McIntosh	.05	.02
❏ 74	Jim McNamara	.05	.02
❏ 75	Jeff McNeely	.05	.02
❏ 76	Rusty Meacham	.05	.02
❏ 77	Tony Menendez	.05	.02
❏ 78	Henry Mercedes	.05	.02
❏ 79	Paul Miller	.05	.02
❏ 80	Joe Millette	.05	.02
❏ 81	Blas Minor	.05	.02
❏ 82	Dennis Moeller	.05	.02
❏ 83	Raul Mondesi	1.00	.45
❏ 84	Rob Natal	.05	.02
❏ 85	Troy Neel	.05	.02
❏ 86	David Nied	.25	.11
❏ 87	Jerry Nielson	.05	.02
❏ 88	Donovan Osborne	.05	.02
❏ 89	John Patterson	.05	.02
❏ 90	Roger Pavlik	.05	.02
❏ 91	Dan Peltier	.05	.02
❏ 92	Jim Pena	.05	.02
❏ 93	William Pennyfeather	.05	.02
❏ 94	Mike Perez	.05	.02
❏ 95	Hipolito Pichardo	.05	.02
❏ 96	Greg Pirkl	.05	.02
❏ 97	Harvey Pulliam	.05	.02
❏ 98	Manny Ramirez	4.00	1.80
❏ 99	Pat Rapp	.05	.02
❏ 100	Jeff Reboulet	.05	.02
❏ 101	Darren Reed	.05	.02
❏ 102	Shane Reynolds	.50	.23
❏ 103	Bill Risley	.05	.02
❏ 104	Ben Rivera	.05	.02
❏ 105	Henry Rodriguez	.20	.09
❏ 106	Rico Rossy	.05	.02
❏ 107	Johnny Ruffin	.05	.02
❏ 108	Steve Scarsone	.05	.02
❏ 109	Tim Scott	.05	.02

❏ 110	Steve Shifflett	.05	.02
❏ 111	Dave Silvestri	.05	.02
❏ 112	Matt Stairs	.75	.35
❏ 113	William Suero	.05	.02
❏ 114	Jeff Tackett	.05	.02
❏ 115	Eddie Taubensee	.10	.05
❏ 116	Rick Trlicek	.05	.02
❏ 117	Scooter Tucker	.05	.02
❏ 118	Shane Turner	.05	.02
❏ 119	Julio Valera	.05	.02
❏ 120	Paul Wagner	.05	.02
❏ 121	Tim Wakefield	.20	.09
❏ 122	Mike Walker	.05	.02
❏ 123	Bruce Walton	.05	.02
❏ 124	Lenny Webster	.05	.02
❏ 125	Bob Wickman	.05	.02
❏ 126	Mike Williams	.05	.02
❏ 127	Kerry Woodson	.05	.02
❏ 128	Eric Young	.20	.09
❏ 129	Kevin Young	.40	.18
❏ 130	Pete Young	.05	.02
❏ 131	Checklist 1-66	.05	.02
❏ 132	Checklist 67-132	.05	.02

1992 Donruss Rookies Phenoms

	MINT	NRMT
COMP.FOIL SET (12)	30.00	13.50
COMMON FOIL (BC1-BC12)	.50	.23
FOIL MINOR STARS	1.00	.45
FOIL UNLISTED STARS	1.50	.70
FOIL: RANDOM INSERTS IN PACKS		
COMP JUMBO SET (8)	10.00	4.50
COMMON JUMBO (BC13-BC20)	.50	.23
JUMBO MINOR STARS	1.00	.45
JUMBO UNLISTED STARS	1.50	.70
JUMBOS: ONE PER JUMBO PACK		

❏ BC1	Moises Alou	1.50	.70
❏ BC2	Bret Boone	1.50	.70
❏ BC3	Jeff Conine	.50	.23
❏ BC4	Dave Fleming	.50	.23
❏ BC5	Tyler Green	.50	.23
❏ BC6	Eric Karros	1.50	.70
❏ BC7	Pat Listach	.50	.23
❏ BC8	Kenny Lofton	3.00	1.35
❏ BC9	Mike Piazza	25.00	11.00
❏ BC10	Tim Salmon	4.00	1.80
❏ BC11	Andy Stankiewicz	.50	.23
❏ BC12	Dan Walters	.50	.23
❏ BC13	Ramon Caraballo	.50	.23
❏ BC14	Brian Jordan	1.50	.70
❏ BC15	Ryan Klesko	2.00	.90
❏ BC16	Sam Militello	.50	.23
❏ BC17	Frank Seminara	.50	.23
❏ BC18	Salomon Torres	.50	.23
❏ BC19	John Valentin	1.50	.70
❏ BC20	Wil Cordero	.50	.23

1993 Donruss

	MINT	NRMT
COMPLETE SET (792)	30.00	13.50
COMPLETE SERIES 1 (396)	15.00	6.75
COMPLETE SERIES 2 (396)	15.00	6.75
COMMON CARD (1-792)	.10	.05
MINOR STARS	.20	.09

UNLISTED STARS	.40	.18

❏ 1 Craig Lefferts	.10	.05
❏ 2 Kent Mercker	.10	.05
❏ 3 Phil Plantier	.10	.05
❏ 4 Alex Arias	.10	.05
❏ 5 Julio Valera	.10	.05
❏ 6 Dan Wilson	.20	.09
❏ 7 Frank Thomas	.75	.35
❏ 8 Eric Anthony	.10	.05
❏ 9 Derek Lilliquist	.10	.05
❏ 10 Rafael Bournigal	.10	.05
❏ 11 Manny Alexander RR	.10	.05
❏ 12 Bret Barberie	.10	.05
❏ 13 Mickey Tettleton	.10	.05
❏ 14 Anthony Young	.10	.05
❏ 15 Tim Spehr	.10	.05
❏ 16 Bob Ayrault	.10	.05
❏ 17 Bill Wegman	.10	.05
❏ 18 Jay Bell	.20	.09
❏ 19 Rick Aguilera	.10	.05
❏ 20 Todd Zeile	.10	.05
❏ 21 Steve Farr	.10	.05
❏ 22 Andy Benes	.20	.09
❏ 23 Lance Blankenship	.10	.05
❏ 24 Ted Wood	.10	.05
❏ 25 Omar Vizquel	.20	.09
❏ 26 Steve Avery	.10	.05
❏ 27 Brian Bohanon	.10	.05
❏ 28 Roger Pavlik	.10	.05
❏ 29 Devon White	.10	.05
❏ 30 Bobby Ayala	.10	.05
❏ 31 Leo Gomez	.10	.05
❏ 32 Mike Simms	.10	.05
❏ 33 Ellis Burks	.20	.09
❏ 34 Steve Wilson	.10	.05
❏ 35 Jim Abbott	.20	.09
❏ 36 Tim Wallach	.10	.05
❏ 37 Wilson Alvarez	.20	.09
❏ 38 Daryl Boston	.10	.05
❏ 39 Sandy Alomar Jr.	.20	.09
❏ 40 Mitch Williams	.10	.05
❏ 41 Rico Brogna	.20	.09
❏ 42 Gary Varsho	.10	.05
❏ 43 Kevin Appier	.20	.09
❏ 44 Eric Wedge RR	.10	.05
❏ 45 Dante Bichette	.20	.09
❏ 46 Jose Oquendo	.10	.05
❏ 47 Mike Trombley	.10	.05
❏ 48 Dan Walters	.10	.05
❏ 49 Gerald Williams	.10	.05
❏ 50 Bud Black	.10	.05
❏ 51 Bobby Witt	.10	.05
❏ 52 Mark Davis	.10	.05
❏ 53 Shawn Barton	.10	.05
❏ 54 Paul Assenmacher	.10	.05
❏ 55 Kevin Reimer	.10	.05
❏ 56 Billy Ashley RR	.10	.05
❏ 57 Eddie Zosky	.10	.05
❏ 58 Chris Sabo	.10	.05
❏ 59 Billy Ripken	.10	.05
❏ 60 Scooter Tucker	.10	.05
❏ 61 Tim Wakefield RR	.20	.09
❏ 62 Mitch Webster	.10	.05
❏ 63 Jack Clark	.10	.05
❏ 64 Mark Gardner	.10	.05
❏ 65 Lee Stevens	.20	.09
❏ 66 Todd Hundley	.30	.14

❏ 67 Bobby Thigpen	.10	.05
❏ 68 Dave Hollins	.10	.05
❏ 69 Jack Armstrong	.10	.05
❏ 70 Alex Cole	.10	.05
❏ 71 Mark Carreon	.10	.05
❏ 72 Todd Worrell	.10	.05
❏ 73 Steve Shifflett	.10	.05
❏ 74 Jerald Clark	.10	.05
❏ 75 Paul Molitor	.40	.18
❏ 76 Larry Carter	.10	.05
❏ 77 Rich Rowland RR	.10	.05
❏ 78 Damon Berryhill	.10	.05
❏ 79 Willie Banks	.10	.05
❏ 80 Hector Villanueva	.10	.05
❏ 81 Mike Gallego	.10	.05
❏ 82 Tim Belcher	.10	.05
❏ 83 Mike Bordick	.10	.05
❏ 84 Craig Biggio	.40	.18
❏ 85 Lance Parrish	.10	.05
❏ 86 Brett Butler	.20	.09
❏ 87 Mike Timlin	.10	.05
❏ 88 Brian Barnes	.10	.05
❏ 89 Brady Anderson	.20	.09
❏ 90 D.J. Dozier	.10	.05
❏ 91 Frank Viola	.10	.05
❏ 92 Darren Daulton	.20	.09
❏ 93 Chad Curtis	.20	.09
❏ 94 Zane Smith	.10	.05
❏ 95 George Bell	.10	.05
❏ 96 Rex Hudler	.10	.05
❏ 97 Mark Whiten	.10	.05
❏ 98 Tim Teufel	.10	.05
❏ 99 Kevin Ritz	.10	.05
❏ 100 Jeff Brantley	.10	.05
❏ 101 Jeff Conine	.10	.05
❏ 102 Vinny Castilla	.50	.23
❏ 103 Greg Vaughn	.20	.09
❏ 104 Steve Buechele	.10	.05
❏ 105 Darren Reed	.10	.05
❏ 106 Bip Roberts	.10	.05
❏ 107 John Habyan	.10	.05
❏ 108 Scott Servais	.10	.05
❏ 109 Walt Weiss	.10	.05
❏ 110 J.T. Snow RR	.50	.23
❏ 111 Jay Buhner	.30	.14
❏ 112 Darryl Strawberry	.20	.09
❏ 113 Roger Pavlik	.10	.05
❏ 114 Chris Nabholz	.10	.05
❏ 115 Pat Borders	.10	.05
❏ 116 Pat Howell	.10	.05
❏ 117 Gregg Olson	.10	.05
❏ 118 Curt Schilling	.20	.09
❏ 119 Roger Clemens	1.00	.45
❏ 120 Victor Cole	.10	.05
❏ 121 Gary DiSarcina	.10	.05
❏ 122 Checklist 1-80	.20	.09
	Gary Carter and		
	Kirt Manwaring		
❏ 123 Steve Sax	.10	.05
❏ 124 Chuck Carr	.10	.05
❏ 125 Mark Lewis	.10	.05
❏ 126 Tony Gwynn	1.00	.45
❏ 127 Travis Fryman	.20	.09
❏ 128 Dave Burba	.10	.05
❏ 129 Wally Joyner	.20	.09
❏ 130 John Smoltz	.30	.14
❏ 131 Cal Eldred	.20	.09
❏ 132 Checklist 81-159	.20	.09
	Roberto Alomar and		
	Devon White		
❏ 133 Arthur Rhodes	.10	.05
❏ 134 Jeff Blauser	.10	.05
❏ 135 Scott Cooper	.10	.05
❏ 136 Doug Strange	.10	.05
❏ 137 Luis Sojo	.10	.05
❏ 138 Jeff Branson	.10	.05
❏ 139 Alex Fernandez	.20	.09
❏ 140 Ken Caminiti	.30	.14
❏ 141 Charles Nagy	.20	.09
❏ 142 Tom Candiotti	.10	.05
❏ 143 Willie Greene RR	.10	.05
❏ 144 John Vander Wal	.10	.05
❏ 145 Kurt Knudsen	.10	.05
❏ 146 John Franco	.20	.09
❏ 147 Eddie Pierce	.10	.05
❏ 148 Kim Batiste	.10	.05

❏ 149 Darren Holmes	.10	.05
❏ 150 Steve Cooke	.10	.05
❏ 151 Terry Jorgensen	.10	.05
❏ 152 Mark Clark	.10	.05
❏ 153 Randy Velarde	.10	.05
❏ 154 Greg W. Harris	.10	.05
❏ 155 Kevin Campbell	.10	.05
❏ 156 John Burkett	.10	.05
❏ 157 Kevin Mitchell	.20	.09
❏ 158 Deion Sanders	.30	.14
❏ 159 Jose Canseco	.50	.23
❏ 160 Jeff Hartsock	.10	.05
❏ 161 Tom Quinlan	.10	.05
❏ 162 Tim Pugh	.10	.05
❏ 163 Glenn Davis	.10	.05
❏ 164 Shane Reynolds	.20	.09
❏ 165 Jody Reed	.10	.05
❏ 166 Mike Sharperson	.10	.05
❏ 167 Scott Lewis	.10	.05
❏ 168 Dennis Martinez	.20	.09
❏ 169 Scott Radinsky	.10	.05
❏ 170 Dave Gallagher	.10	.05
❏ 171 Jim Thome	.50	.23
❏ 172 Terry Mulholland	.10	.05
❏ 173 Milt Cuyler	.10	.05
❏ 174 Bob Patterson	.10	.05
❏ 175 Jeff Montgomery	.20	.09
❏ 176 Tim Salmon RR	.40	.18
❏ 177 Franklin Stubbs	.10	.05
❏ 178 Donovan Osborne	.10	.05
❏ 179 Jeff Reboulet	.10	.05
❏ 180 Jeremy Hernandez	.10	.05
❏ 181 Charlie Hayes	.10	.05
❏ 182 Matt Williams	.30	.14
❏ 183 Mike Raczka	.10	.05
❏ 184 Francisco Cabrera	.10	.05
❏ 185 Rich DeLucia	.10	.05
❏ 186 Sammy Sosa	1.25	.55
❏ 187 Ivan Rodriguez	.50	.23
❏ 188 Bret Boone RR	.20	.09
❏ 189 Juan Guzman	.20	.09
❏ 190 Tom Browning	.10	.05
❏ 191 Randy Milligan	.10	.05
❏ 192 Steve Finley	.20	.09
❏ 193 John Patterson RR	.10	.05
❏ 194 Kip Gross	.10	.05
❏ 195 Tony Fossas	.10	.05
❏ 196 Ivan Calderon	.10	.05
❏ 197 Junior Felix	.10	.05
❏ 198 Pete Schourek	.10	.05
❏ 199 Craig Grebeck	.10	.05
❏ 200 Juan Bell	.10	.05
❏ 201 Glenallen Hill	.10	.05
❏ 202 Danny Jackson	.10	.05
❏ 203 John Kiely	.10	.05
❏ 204 Bob Tewksbury	.10	.05
❏ 205 Kevin Koslofski	.10	.05
❏ 206 Craig Shipley	.10	.05
❏ 207 John Jaha	.20	.09
❏ 208 Royce Clayton	.10	.05
❏ 209 Mike Piazza RR	2.00	.90
❏ 210 Ron Gant	.20	.09
❏ 211 Scott Erickson	.20	.09
❏ 212 Doug Dascenzo	.10	.05
❏ 213 Andy Stankiewicz	.10	.05
❏ 214 Geronimo Berroa	.10	.05
❏ 215 Dennis Eckersley	.20	.09
❏ 216 Al Osuna	.10	.05
❏ 217 Tino Martinez	.40	.18
❏ 218 Henry Rodriguez	.20	.09
❏ 219 Ed Sprague	.10	.05
❏ 220 Ken Hill	.10	.05
❏ 221 Chito Martinez	.10	.05
❏ 222 Bret Saberhagen	.20	.09
❏ 223 Mike Greenwell	.10	.05
❏ 224 Mickey Morandini	.10	.05
❏ 225 Chuck Finley	.20	.09
❏ 226 Denny Neagle	.20	.09
❏ 227 Kirk McCaskill	.10	.05
❏ 228 Rheal Cormier	.10	.05
❏ 229 Paul Sorrento	.10	.05
❏ 230 Darrin Jackson	.10	.05
❏ 231 Rob Deer	.10	.05
❏ 232 Bill Swift	.10	.05
❏ 233 Kevin McReynolds	.10	.05
❏ 234 Terry Pendleton	.10	.05

❏ 235	Dave Nilsson	.20	.09
❏ 236	Chuck McElroy	.10	.05
❏ 237	Derek Parks	.10	.05
❏ 238	Norm Charlton	.10	.05
❏ 239	Matt Nokes	.10	.05
❏ 240	Juan Guerrero	.10	.05
❏ 241	Jeff Parrett	.10	.05
❏ 242	Ryan Thompson RR	.10	.05
❏ 243	Dave Fleming	.10	.05
❏ 244	Dave Hansen	.10	.05
❏ 245	Monty Fariss	.10	.05
❏ 246	Archi Cianfrocco	.10	.05
❏ 247	Pat Hentgen	.30	.14
❏ 248	Bill Pecota	.10	.05
❏ 249	Ben McDonald	.10	.05
❏ 250	Cliff Brantley	.10	.05
❏ 251	John Valentin	.20	.09
❏ 252	Jeff King	.10	.05
❏ 253	Reggie Williams	.10	.05
❏ 254	Checklist 160-238	.10	.05
	(Damon Berryhill and Alex Arias)		
❏ 255	Ozzie Guillen	.10	.05
❏ 256	Mike Perez	.10	.05
❏ 257	Thomas Howard	.10	.05
❏ 258	Kurt Stillwell	.10	.05
❏ 259	Mike Henneman	.10	.05
❏ 260	Steve Decker	.10	.05
❏ 261	Brent Mayne	.10	.05
❏ 262	Otis Nixon	.10	.05
❏ 263	Mark Kiefer	.10	.05
❏ 264	Checklist 239-317	.30	.14
	(Don Mattingly and Mike Bordick)		
❏ 265	Richie Lewis	.10	.05
❏ 266	Pat Gomez	.10	.05
❏ 267	Scott Taylor	.10	.05
❏ 268	Shawon Dunston	.10	.05
❏ 269	Greg Myers	.10	.05
❏ 270	Tim Costo	.10	.05
❏ 271	Greg Hibbard	.10	.05
❏ 272	Pete Harnisch	.10	.05
❏ 273	Dave Mlicki	.10	.05
❏ 274	Orel Hershiser	.20	.09
❏ 275	Sean Berry RR	.10	.05
❏ 276	Doug Simons	.10	.05
❏ 277	John Doherty	.10	.05
❏ 278	Eddie Murray	.40	.18
❏ 279	Chris Haney	.10	.05
❏ 280	Stan Javier	.10	.05
❏ 281	Jaime Navarro	.10	.05
❏ 282	Orlando Merced	.10	.05
❏ 283	Kent Hrbek	.20	.09
❏ 284	Bernard Gilkey	.10	.05
❏ 285	Russ Springer	.10	.05
❏ 286	Mike Maddux	.10	.05
❏ 287	Eric Fox	.10	.05
❏ 288	Mark Leonard	.10	.05
❏ 289	Tim Leary	.10	.05
❏ 290	Brian Hunter	.10	.05
❏ 291	Donald Harris	.10	.05
❏ 292	Bob Scanlan	.10	.05
❏ 293	Turner Ward	.10	.05
❏ 294	Hal Morris	.10	.05
❏ 295	Jimmy Poole	.10	.05
❏ 296	Doug Jones	.10	.05
❏ 297	Tony Pena	.10	.05
❏ 298	Ramon Martinez	.20	.09
❏ 299	Tim Fortugno	.10	.05
❏ 300	Marquis Grissom	.20	.09
❏ 301	Lance Johnson	.10	.05
❏ 302	Jeff Kent	.20	.09
❏ 303	Reggie Jefferson	.20	.09
❏ 304	Wes Chamberlain	.10	.05
❏ 305	Shawn Hare	.10	.05
❏ 306	Mike LaValliere	.10	.05
❏ 307	Gregg Jefferies	.10	.05
❏ 308	Troy Neel RR	.10	.05
❏ 309	Pat Listach	.10	.05
❏ 310	Geronimo Pena	.10	.05
❏ 311	Pedro Munoz	.10	.05
❏ 312	Guillermo Velasquez	.10	.05
❏ 313	Roberto Kelly	.10	.05
❏ 314	Mike Jackson	.20	.09
❏ 315	Rickey Henderson	.50	.23
❏ 316	Mark Lemke	.10	.05
❏ 317	Erik Hanson	.10	.05
❏ 318	Derrick May	.10	.05
❏ 319	Geno Petralli	.10	.05
❏ 320	Melvin Nieves RR	.10	.05
❏ 321	Doug Linton	.10	.05
❏ 322	Rob Dibble	.10	.05
❏ 323	Chris Hoiles	.10	.05
❏ 324	Jimmy Jones	.10	.05
❏ 325	Dave Staton RR	.10	.05
❏ 326	Pedro Martinez	.75	.35
❏ 327	Paul Quantrill	.10	.05
❏ 328	Greg Colbrunn	.10	.05
❏ 329	Hilly Hathaway	.10	.05
❏ 330	Jeff Innis	.10	.05
❏ 331	Ron Karkovice	.10	.05
❏ 332	Keith Shepherd	.10	.05
❏ 333	Alan Embree	.10	.05
❏ 334	Paul Wagner	.10	.05
❏ 335	Dave Haas	.10	.05
❏ 336	Ozzie Canseco	.10	.05
❏ 337	Bill Sampen	.10	.05
❏ 338	Rich Rodriguez	.10	.05
❏ 339	Dean Palmer	.20	.09
❏ 340	Greg Litton	.10	.05
❏ 341	Jim Tatum RR	.10	.05
❏ 342	Todd Haney	.10	.05
❏ 343	Larry Casian	.10	.05
❏ 344	Ryne Sandberg	.50	.23
❏ 345	Sterling Hitchcock	.40	.18
❏ 346	Chris Hammond	.10	.05
❏ 347	Vince Horsman	.10	.05
❏ 348	Butch Henry	.10	.05
❏ 349	Dann Howitt	.10	.05
❏ 350	Roger McDowell	.10	.05
❏ 351	Jack Morris	.20	.09
❏ 352	Bill Krueger	.10	.05
❏ 353	Cris Colon	.10	.05
❏ 354	Joe Vitko	.10	.05
❏ 355	Willie McGee	.20	.09
❏ 356	Jay Baller	.10	.05
❏ 357	Pat Mahomes	.10	.05
❏ 358	Roger Mason	.10	.05
❏ 359	Jerry Nielsen	.10	.05
❏ 360	Tom Pagnozzi	.10	.05
❏ 361	Kevin Baez	.10	.05
❏ 362	Tim Scott	.10	.05
❏ 363	Domingo Martinez	.10	.05
❏ 364	Kirt Manwaring	.10	.05
❏ 365	Rafael Palmeiro	.40	.18
❏ 366	Ray Lankford	.30	.14
❏ 367	Tim McIntosh	.10	.05
❏ 368	Jessie Hollins	.10	.05
❏ 369	Scott Leius	.10	.05
❏ 370	Bill Doran	.10	.05
❏ 371	Sam Militello	.10	.05
❏ 372	Ryan Bowen	.10	.05
❏ 373	Dave Henderson	.10	.05
❏ 374	Dan Smith RR	.10	.05
❏ 375	Steve Reed RR	.10	.05
❏ 376	Jose Offerman	.20	.09
❏ 377	Kevin Brown	.30	.14
❏ 378	Darrin Fletcher	.10	.05
❏ 379	Duane Ward	.10	.05
❏ 380	Wayne Kirby RR	.10	.05
❏ 381	Steve Scarsone	.10	.05
❏ 382	Mariano Duncan	.10	.05
❏ 383	Ken Ryan	.10	.05
❏ 384	Lloyd McClendon	.10	.05
❏ 385	Brian Holman	.10	.05
❏ 386	Braulio Castillo	.10	.05
❏ 387	Danny Leon	.10	.05
❏ 388	Omar Olivares	.10	.05
❏ 389	Kevin Wickander	.10	.05
❏ 390	Fred McGriff	.30	.14
❏ 391	Phil Clark	.10	.05
❏ 392	Darren Lewis	.10	.05
❏ 393	Phil Hiatt	.10	.05
❏ 394	Mike Morgan	.10	.05
❏ 395	Shane Mack	.10	.05
❏ 396	Checklist 318-396	.20	.09
	(Dennis Eckersley and Art Kusnyer CO)		
❏ 397	David Segui	.10	.05
❏ 398	Rafael Belliard	.10	.05
❏ 399	Tim Naehring	.10	.05
❏ 400	Frank Castillo	.10	.05
❏ 401	Joe Grahe	.10	.05
❏ 402	Reggie Sanders	.20	.09
❏ 403	Roberto Hernandez	.20	.09
❏ 404	Luis Gonzalez	.20	.09
❏ 405	Carlos Baerga	.10	.05
❏ 406	Carlos Hernandez	.10	.05
❏ 407	Pedro Astacio RR	.20	.09
❏ 408	Mel Rojas	.10	.05
❏ 409	Scott Livingstone	.10	.05
❏ 410	Chico Walker	.10	.05
❏ 411	Brian McRae	.10	.05
❏ 412	Ben Rivera	.10	.05
❏ 413	Ricky Bones	.10	.05
❏ 414	Andy Van Slyke	.20	.09
❏ 415	Chuck Knoblauch	.40	.18
❏ 416	Luis Alicea	.10	.05
❏ 417	Bob Wickman	.10	.05
❏ 418	Doug Brocail	.10	.05
❏ 419	Scott Brosius	.20	.09
❏ 420	Rod Beck	.20	.09
❏ 421	Edgar Martinez	.30	.14
❏ 422	Ryan Klesko	.40	.18
❏ 423	Nolan Ryan	1.50	.70
❏ 424	Rey Sanchez	.10	.05
❏ 425	Roberto Alomar	.40	.18
❏ 426	Barry Larkin	.40	.18
❏ 427	Mike Mussina	.40	.18
❏ 428	Jeff Bagwell	.50	.23
❏ 429	Mo Vaughn	.40	.18
❏ 430	Eric Karros	.30	.14
❏ 431	John Orton	.10	.05
❏ 432	Wil Cordero	.10	.05
❏ 433	Jack McDowell	.10	.05
❏ 434	Howard Johnson	.10	.05
❏ 435	Albert Belle	.40	.18
❏ 436	John Kruk	.20	.09
❏ 437	Skeeter Barnes	.10	.05
❏ 438	Don Slaught	.10	.05
❏ 439	Rusty Meacham	.10	.05
❏ 440	Tim Laker RR	.10	.05
❏ 441	Robin Yount	.30	.14
❏ 442	Brian Jordan	.20	.09
❏ 443	Kevin Tapani	.10	.05
❏ 444	Gary Sheffield	.40	.18
❏ 445	Rich Monteleone	.10	.05
❏ 446	Will Clark	.40	.18
❏ 447	Jerry Browne	.10	.05
❏ 448	Jeff Treadway	.10	.05
❏ 449	Mike Schooler	.10	.05
❏ 450	Mike Harkey	.10	.05
❏ 451	Julio Franco	.20	.09
❏ 452	Kevin Young RR	.20	.09
❏ 453	Kelly Gruber	.10	.05
❏ 454	Jose Rijo	.10	.05
❏ 455	Mike Devereaux	.10	.05
❏ 456	Andujar Cedeno	.10	.05
❏ 457	Damion Easley RR	.20	.09
❏ 458	Kevin Gross	.10	.05
❏ 459	Matt Young	.10	.05
❏ 460	Matt Stairs	.30	.14
❏ 461	Luis Polonia	.10	.05
❏ 462	Dwight Gooden	.20	.09
❏ 463	Warren Newson	.10	.05
❏ 464	Jose DeLeon	.10	.05
❏ 465	Jose Mesa	.10	.05
❏ 466	Danny Cox	.10	.05
❏ 467	Dan Gladden	.10	.05
❏ 468	Gerald Perry	.10	.05
❏ 469	Mike Boddicker	.10	.05
❏ 470	Jeff Gardner	.10	.05
❏ 471	Doug Henry	.10	.05
❏ 472	Mike Benjamin	.10	.05
❏ 473	Dan Peltier RR	.10	.05
❏ 474	Mike Stanton	.10	.05
❏ 475	John Smiley	.10	.05
❏ 476	Dwight Smith	.10	.05
❏ 477	Jim Leyritz	.10	.05
❏ 478	Dwayne Henry	.10	.05
❏ 479	Mark McGwire	2.00	.90
❏ 480	Pete Incaviglia	.10	.05
❏ 481	Dave Cochrane	.10	.05
❏ 482	Eric Davis	.20	.09
❏ 483	John Olerud	.30	.14
❏ 484	Kent Bottenfield	.10	.05
❏ 485	Mark McLemore	.10	.05
❏ 486	Dave Magadan	.10	.05

487	John Marzano	.10	.05
488	Ruben Amaro	.10	.05
489	Rob Ducey	.10	.05
490	Stan Belinda	.10	.05
491	Dan Pasqua	.10	.05
492	Joe Magrane	.10	.05
493	Brook Jacoby	.10	.05
494	Gene Harris	.10	.05
495	Mark Leiter	.10	.05
496	Bryan Hickerson	.10	.05
497	Tom Gordon	.10	.05
498	Pete Smith	.10	.05
499	Chris Bosio	.10	.05
500	Shawn Boskie	.10	.05
501	Dave West	.10	.05
502	Milt Hill	.10	.05
503	Pat Kelly	.10	.05
504	Joe Boever	.10	.05
505	Terry Steinbach	.10	.05
506	Butch Huskey RR	.30	.14
507	David Valle	.10	.05
508	Mike Scioscia	.10	.05
509	Kenny Rogers	.10	.05
510	Moises Alou	.20	.09
511	David Wells	.20	.09
512	Mackey Sasser	.10	.05
513	Todd Frohwirth	.10	.05
514	Ricky Jordan	.10	.05
515	Mike Gardiner	.10	.05
516	Gary Redus	.10	.05
517	Gary Gaetti	.20	.09
518	Checklist	.10	.05
519	Carlton Fisk	.18	.05
520	Ozzie Smith	.50	.23
521	Rod Nichols	.10	.05
522	Benito Santiago	.10	.05
523	Bill Gullickson	.10	.05
524	Robby Thompson	.10	.05
525	Mike Macfarlane	.10	.05
526	Sid Bream	.10	.05
527	Darryl Hamilton	.10	.05
528	Checklist	.10	.05
529	Jeff Tackett	.10	.05
530	Greg Olson	.10	.05
531	Bob Zupcic	.10	.05
532	Mark Grace	.30	.14
533	Steve Frey	.10	.05
534	Dave Martinez	.10	.05
535	Robin Ventura	.20	.09
536	Casey Candaele	.10	.05
537	Kenny Lofton	.40	.18
538	Jay Howell	.10	.05
539	Fernando Ramsey RR	.10	.05
540	Larry Walker	.40	.18
541	Cecil Fielder	.20	.09
542	Lee Guetterman	.10	.05
543	Keith Miller	.10	.05
544	Len Dykstra	.20	.09
545	B.J. Surhoff	.20	.05
546	Bob Walk	.10	.05
547	Brian Harper	.10	.05
548	Lee Smith	.20	.09
549	Danny Tartabull	.10	.05
550	Frank Seminara	.10	.05
551	Henry Mercedes	.10	.05
552	Dave Righetti	.10	.05
553	Ken Griffey Jr.	2.00	.90
554	Tom Glavine	.30	.14
555	Juan Gonzalez	.75	.35
556	Jim Bullinger	.10	.05
557	Derek Bell	.20	.09
558	Cesar Hernandez	.10	.05
559	Cal Ripken	1.50	.70
560	Eddie Taubensee	.10	.05
561	John Flaherty	.10	.05
562	Todd Benzinger	.10	.05
563	Hubie Brooks	.10	.05
564	Delino DeShields	.20	.09
565	Tim Raines	.20	.09
566	Sid Fernandez	.10	.05
567	Steve Olin	.10	.05
568	Tommy Greene	.10	.05
569	Buddy Groom	.10	.05
570	Randy Tomlin	.10	.05
571	Hipolito Pichardo	.10	.05
572	Rene Arocha RR	.10	.05
573	Mike Fetters	.10	.05
574	Felix Jose	.10	.05
575	Gene Larkin	.10	.05
576	Bruce Hurst	.10	.05
577	Bernie Williams	.40	.18
578	Trevor Wilson	.10	.05
579	Bob Welch	.10	.05
580	David Justice	.40	.18
581	Randy Johnson	.40	.18
582	Jose Vizcaino	.10	.05
583	Jeff Huson	.10	.05
584	Rob Maurer RR	.10	.05
585	Todd Stottlemyre	.10	.05
586	Joe Oliver	.10	.05
587	Bob Milacki	.10	.05
588	Rob Murphy	.10	.05
589	Greg Pirkl RR	.10	.05
590	Lenny Harris	.10	.05
591	Luis Rivera	.10	.05
592	John Wetteland	.20	.09
593	Mark Langston	.20	.09
594	Bobby Bonilla	.20	.09
595	Esteban Beltre	.10	.05
596	Mike Hartley	.10	.05
597	Felix Fermin	.10	.05
598	Carlos Garcia	.10	.05
599	Frank Tanana	.10	.05
600	Pedro Guerrero	.10	.05
601	Terry Shumpert	.10	.05
602	Wally Whitehurst	.10	.05
603	Kevin Seitzer	.10	.05
604	Chris James	.10	.05
605	Greg Gohr RR	.10	.05
606	Mark Wohlers	.10	.05
607	Kirby Puckett	.60	
608	Greg Maddux	1.00	.45
609	Don Mattingly	.75	.35
610	Greg Cadaret	.10	.05
611	Dave Stewart	.20	.09
612	Mark Portugal	.10	.05
613	Pete O'Brien	.10	.05
614	Bob Ojeda	.10	.05
615	Joe Carter	.20	.09
616	Pete Young	.10	.05
617	Sam Horn	.10	.05
618	Vince Coleman	.10	.05
619	Wade Boggs	.40	.18
620	Todd Pratt	.25	.11
621	Ron Tingley	.10	.05
622	Doug Drabek	.10	.05
623	Scott Hemond	.10	.05
624	Tim Jones	.10	.05
625	Dennis Cook	.10	.05
626	Jose Melendez	.10	.05
627	Mike Munoz	.10	.05
628	Jim Pena	.10	.05
629	Gary Thurman	.10	.05
630	Charlie Leibrandt	.10	.05
631	Scott Fletcher	.10	.05
632	Andre Dawson	.30	.14
633	Greg Gagne	.10	.05
634	Greg Swindell	.10	.05
635	Kevin Maas	.10	.05
636	Xavier Hernandez	.10	.05
637	Ruben Sierra	.30	.14
638	Dmitri Young RR	.40	.18
639	Harold Reynolds	.10	.05
640	Tom Goodwin	.10	.05
641	Todd Burns	.10	.05
642	Jeff Fassero	.10	.05
643	Dave Winfield	.30	.14
644	Willie Randolph	.20	.09
645	Luis Mercedes	.10	.05
646	Dale Murphy	.30	.14
647	Danny Darwin	.10	.05
648	Dennis Moeller	.10	.05
649	Chuck Crim	.10	.05
650	Checklist	.10	.05
651	Shawn Abner	.10	.05
652	Tracy Woodson	.10	.05
653	Scott Scudder	.10	.05
654	Tom Lampkin	.10	.05
655	Alan Trammell	.30	.14
656	Cory Snyder	.10	.05
657	Chris Gwynn	.10	.05
658	Lonnie Smith	.10	.05
659	Jim Austin	.10	.05
660	Checklist	.10	.05
661	Tim Hulett	.10	.05
662	Marvin Freeman	.10	.05
663	Greg A. Harris	.10	.05
664	Heathcliff Slocumb	.10	.05
665	Mike Butcher	.10	.05
666	Steve Foster	.10	.05
667	Donn Pall	.10	.05
668	Darryl Kile	.10	.05
669	Jesse Levis	.10	.05
670	Jim Gott	.10	.05
671	Mark Hutton RR	.10	.05
672	Brian Drahman	.10	.05
673	Chad Kreuter	.10	.05
674	Tony Fernandez	.20	.09
675	Jose Lind	.10	.05
676	Kyle Abbott	.10	.05
677	Dan Plesac	.10	.05
678	Barry Bonds	.50	.23
679	Chili Davis	.20	.09
680	Stan Royer	.10	.05
681	Scott Kamieniecki	.10	.05
682	Carlos Martinez	.10	.05
683	Mike Moore	.10	.05
684	Candy Maldonado	.10	.05
685	Jeff Nelson	.10	.05
686	Lou Whitaker	.20	.09
687	Jose Guzman	.10	.05
688	Manuel Lee	.10	.05
689	Bob MacDonald	.10	.05
690	Scott Bankhead	.10	.05
691	Alan Mills	.10	.05
692	Brian Williams	.10	.05
693	Tom Brunansky	.10	.05
694	Lenny Webster	.10	.05
695	Greg Briley	.10	.05
696	Paul O'Neill	.20	.09
697	Joey Cora	.10	.05
698	Charlie O'Brien	.10	.05
699	Junior Ortiz	.10	.05
700	Ron Darling	.10	.05
701	Tony Phillips	.10	.05
702	William Pennyfeather	.10	.05
703	Mark Gubicza	.10	.05
704	Steve Hosey RR	.10	.05
705	Henry Cotto	.10	.05
706	David Hulse	.10	.05
707	Mike Pagliarulo	.10	.05
708	Dave Stieb	.10	.05
709	Melido Perez	.10	.05
710	Jimmy Key	.20	.09
711	Jeff Russell	.10	.05
712	David Cone	.30	.14
713	Russ Swan	.10	.05
714	Mark Guthrie	.10	.05
715	Checklist	.10	.05
716	Al Martin RR	.10	.05
717	Randy Knorr	.10	.05
718	Mike Stanley	.10	.05
719	Rick Sutcliffe	.10	.05
720	Terry Leach	.10	.05
721	Chipper Jones RR	1.25	.55
722	Jim Eisenreich	.10	.05
723	Tom Henke	.10	.05
724	Jeff Frye	.10	.05
725	Harold Baines	.20	.09
726	Scott Sanderson	.10	.05
727	Tom Foley	.10	.05
728	Bryan Harvey	.10	.05
729	Tom Edens	.10	.05
730	Eric Young	.40	.18
731	Dave Weathers	.10	.05
732	Spike Owen	.10	.05
733	Scott Aldred	.10	.05
734	Cris Carpenter	.10	.05
735	Dion James	.10	.05
736	Joe Girardi	.20	.09
737	Nigel Wilson RR	.10	.05
738	Scott Chiamparino	.10	.05
739	Jeff Reardon	.20	.09
740	Willie Blair	.10	.05
741	Jim Corsi	.10	.05
742	Ken Patterson	.10	.05
743	Andy Ashby	.20	.09
744	Rob Natal	.10	.05

❑ 745 Kevin Bass	.10	.05
❑ 746 Freddie Benavides	.10	.05
❑ 747 Chris Donnels	.10	.05
❑ 748 Kerry Woodson	.10	.05
❑ 749 Calvin Jones	.10	.05
❑ 750 Gary Scott	.10	.05
❑ 751 Joe Orsulak	.10	.05
❑ 752 Armando Reynoso	.10	.05
❑ 753 Monty Fariss	.10	.05
❑ 754 Billy Hatcher	.10	.05
❑ 755 Denis Boucher	.10	.05
❑ 756 Walt Weiss	.10	.05
❑ 757 Mike Fitzgerald	.10	.05
❑ 758 Rudy Seanez	.10	.05
❑ 759 Bret Barberie	.10	.05
❑ 760 Mo Sanford	.10	.05
❑ 761 Pedro Castellano	.10	.05
❑ 762 Chuck Carr	.10	.05
❑ 763 Steve Howe	.10	.05
❑ 764 Andres Galarraga	.40	.18
❑ 765 Jeff Conine	.10	.05
❑ 766 Ted Power	.10	.05
❑ 767 Butch Henry	.10	.05
❑ 768 Steve Decker	.10	.05
❑ 769 Storm Davis	.10	.05
❑ 770 Vinny Castilla	.50	.23
❑ 771 Junior Felix	.10	.05
❑ 772 Walt Terrell	.10	.05
❑ 773 Brad Ausmus	.10	.05
❑ 774 Jamie McAndrew	.10	.05
❑ 775 Milt Thompson	.10	.05
❑ 776 Charlie Hayes	.10	.05
❑ 777 Jack Armstrong	.10	.05
❑ 778 Dennis Rasmussen	.10	.05
❑ 779 Darren Holmes	.10	.05
❑ 780 Alex Arias	.10	.05
❑ 781 Randy Bush	.10	.05
❑ 782 Javier Lopez RR	.40	.18
❑ 783 Dante Bichette	.20	.09
❑ 784 John Johnstone	.10	.05
❑ 785 Rene Gonzales	.10	.05
❑ 786 Alex Cole	.10	.05
❑ 787 Jeromy Burnitz RR	.20	.09
❑ 788 Michael Huff	.10	.05
❑ 789 Anthony Telford	.10	.05
❑ 790 Jerald Clark	.10	.05
❑ 791 Joel Johnston	.10	.05
❑ 792 David Nied RR	.10	.05

1993 Donruss Diamond Kings

	MINT	NRMT
COMPLETE SET (31)	30.00	13.50
COMPLETE SERIES 1 (15)	20.00	9.00
COMPLETE SERIES 2 (16)	10.00	4.50
COMMON CARD (DK1-DK31)	.75	.35
RANDOM INSERTS IN FOIL PACKS		
❑ DK1 Ken Griffey Jr.	12.00	5.50
❑ DK2 Ryne Sandberg	3.00	1.35
❑ DK3 Roger Clemens	6.00	2.70
❑ DK4 Kirby Puckett	4.00	1.80
❑ DK5 Bill Swift	.75	.35
❑ DK6 Larry Walker	2.50	1.10
❑ DK7 Juan Gonzalez	5.00	2.20
❑ DK8 Wally Joyner	1.25	.55
❑ DK9 Andy Van Slyke	.75	.35

❑ DK10 Robin Ventura	1.25	.55
❑ DK11 Bip Roberts	.75	.35
❑ DK12 Roberto Kelly	.75	.35
❑ DK13 Carlos Baerga	.75	.35
❑ DK14 Orel Hershiser	1.25	.55
❑ DK15 Cecil Fielder	1.25	.55
❑ DK16 Robin Yount	2.00	.90
❑ DK17 Darren Daulton	1.25	.55
❑ DK18 Mark McGwire	12.00	5.50
❑ DK19 Tom Glavine	2.00	.90
❑ DK20 Roberto Alomar	2.50	1.10
❑ DK21 Gary Sheffield	2.50	1.10
❑ DK22 Bob Tewksbury	.75	.35
❑ DK23 Brady Anderson	1.25	.55
❑ DK24 Craig Biggio	2.50	1.10
❑ DK25 Eddie Murray	2.50	1.10
❑ DK26 Luis Polonia	.75	.35
❑ DK27 Nigel Wilson	.75	.35
❑ DK28 David Nied	.75	.35
❑ DK29 Pat Listach ROY	.75	.35
❑ DK30 Eric Karros ROY	2.00	.90
❑ DK31 Checklist 1-31	.75	.35

1993 Donruss Elite

	MINT	NRMT
COMPLETE SET (20)	400.00	180.00
COMMON CARD (19-36)	8.00	3.60
SEMISTARS	12.00	5.50
RANDOM INSERTS IN PACKS		
STATED PRINT RUN 10,000 SERIAL #'d SETS		
❑ 19 Fred McGriff	12.00	5.50
❑ 20 Ryne Sandberg	25.00	11.00
❑ 21 Eddie Murray	20.00	9.00
❑ 22 Paul Molitor	20.00	9.00
❑ 23 Barry Larkin	20.00	9.00
❑ 24 Don Mattingly	40.00	18.00
❑ 25 Dennis Eckersley	10.00	4.50
❑ 26 Roberto Alomar	20.00	9.00
❑ 27 Edgar Martinez	12.00	5.50
❑ 28 Gary Sheffield	20.00	9.00
❑ 29 Darren Daulton	10.00	4.50
❑ 30 Larry Walker	20.00	9.00
❑ 31 Barry Bonds	25.00	11.00
❑ 32 Andy Van Slyke	8.00	3.60
❑ 33 Mark McGwire	100.00	45.00
❑ 34 Cecil Fielder	10.00	4.50
❑ 35 Dave Winfield	12.00	5.50
❑ 36 Juan Gonzalez	40.00	18.00
❑ L3 Robin Yount	25.00	11.00
(Legend Series)		
❑ S3 Will Clark AU	80.00	36.00
(Signature Series)		

1993 Donruss Long Ball Leaders

	MINT	NRMT
COMPLETE SET (18)	60.00	27.00
COMPLETE SERIES 1 (9)	30.00	13.50
COMPLETE SERIES 2 (9)	30.00	13.50
COMMON CARD (LL1-LL18)	1.00	.45
RANDOM INSERTS IN 26-CARD JUMBOS		
❑ LL1 Rob Deer	1.00	.45
❑ LL2 Fred McGriff	2.50	1.10
❑ LL3 Albert Belle	4.00	1.80

❑ LL4 Mark McGwire	20.00	9.00
❑ LL5 David Justice	4.00	1.80
❑ LL6 Jose Canseco	5.00	2.20
❑ LL7 Kent Hrbek	2.00	.90
❑ LL8 Roberto Alomar	4.00	1.80
❑ LL9 Ken Griffey Jr.	20.00	9.00
❑ LL10 Frank Thomas	8.00	3.60
❑ LL11 Darryl Strawberry	2.00	.90
❑ LL12 Felix Jose	1.00	.45
❑ LL13 Cecil Fielder	2.00	.90
❑ LL14 Juan Gonzalez	8.00	3.60
❑ LL15 Ryne Sandberg	5.00	2.20
❑ LL16 Gary Sheffield	4.00	1.80
❑ LL17 Jeff Bagwell	5.00	2.20
❑ LL18 Larry Walker	4.00	1.80

1993 Donruss MVPs

	MINT	NRMT
COMPLETE SET (26)	30.00	13.50
COMPLETE SERIES 1 (13)	10.00	4.50
COMPLETE SERIES 2 (13)	20.00	9.00
COMMON CARD (1-26)	.50	.23
ONE PER 23-CARD JUMBO PACK		
❑ 1 Luis Polonia	.50	.23
❑ 2 Frank Thomas	3.00	1.35
❑ 3 George Brett	3.00	1.35
❑ 4 Paul Molitor	1.00	.45
❑ 5 Don Mattingly	3.00	1.35
❑ 6 Roberto Alomar	1.00	.45
❑ 7 Terry Pendleton	.50	.23
❑ 8 Eric Karros	.75	.35
❑ 9 Larry Walker	1.00	.45
❑ 10 Eddie Murray	1.00	.45
❑ 11 Darren Daulton	.60	.25
❑ 12 Ray Lankford	.75	.35
❑ 13 Will Clark	1.00	.45
❑ 14 Cal Ripken	6.00	2.70
❑ 15 Roger Clemens	4.00	1.80
❑ 16 Carlos Baerga	.50	.23
❑ 17 Cecil Fielder	.60	.25
❑ 18 Kirby Puckett	2.50	1.10
❑ 19 Mark McGwire	8.00	3.60
❑ 20 Ken Griffey Jr.	8.00	3.60
❑ 21 Juan Gonzalez	3.00	1.35
❑ 22 Ryne Sandberg	2.00	.90
❑ 23 Bip Roberts	.50	.23
❑ 24 Jeff Bagwell	2.00	.90
❑ 25 Barry Bonds	2.00	.90
❑ 26 Gary Sheffield	1.00	.45

1993 Donruss Spirit of the Game

	MINT	NRMT
COMPLETE SET (20)	20.00	9.00
COMPLETE SERIES 1 (10)	8.00	3.60
COMPLETE SERIES 2 (10)	12.00	5.50
COMMON CARD (SG1-SG20)	.50	.23

RANDOM INSERTS IN FOIL/JUMBO PACKS

		MINT	NRMT
☐ SG1	Mike Bordick Turning Two	.50	.23
☐ SG2	Dave Justice Play at the Plate	1.50	.70
☐ SG3	Roberto Alomar In There	1.50	.70
☐ SG4	Dennis Eckersley Pumped	.75	.35
☐ SG5	Juan Gonzalez and Jose Canseco Dynamic Duo	3.00	1.35
☐ SG6	George Bell Frank Thomas ... Gone	1.50	.70
☐ SG7	Wade Boggs Luis Polonia Safe or Out	1.50	.70
☐ SG8	Will Clark The Thrill	1.50	.70
☐ SG9	Bip Roberts Safe at Home	.50	.23
☐ SG10	Cecil Fielder Rob Deer Mickey Tettleton Thirty 3	.75	.35
☐ SG11	Kenny Lofton Bag Bandit	2.00	.90
☐ SG12	Gary Sheffield Fred McGriff Back to Back	1.50	.70
☐ SG13	Greg Gagne Barry Larkin	.75	.35
☐ SG14	Ryne Sandberg The Ball Stops Here	2.50	1.10
☐ SG15	Carlos Baerga Gary Gaetti Over the Top	.75	.35
☐ SG16	Danny Tartabull At the Wall	.50	.23
☐ SG17	Brady Anderson Head First	.75	.35
☐ SG18	Frank Thomas Big Hurt	6.00	2.70
☐ SG19	Kevin Gross No Hitter	.50	.23
☐ SG20	Robin Yount 3,000 Hits	1.00	.45

1994 Donruss

	MINT	NRMT
COMPLETE SET (660)	40.00	18.00
COMPLETE SERIES 1 (330)	20.00	9.00
COMPLETE SERIES 2 (330)	20.00	9.00
COMMON CARD (1-660)	.15	.07
MINOR STARS	.30	.14
UNLISTED STARS	.60	.25
COMP.SPEC.ED.SET (100)	20.00	9.00
COMP.SPEC.ED.SER.1 (50)	10.00	4.50
COMP.SPEC.ED.SER.2 (50)	10.00	4.50
COMMON SPEC.ED (1-100)	.25	.11

*SPEC.EDITION: 1X TO 2X HI COLUMN
ONE SPECIAL EDITION PER PACK
SE #51-100 CORRESPOND w/ #331-380

☐ 1	Nolan Ryan	3.00	1.35
☐ 2	Mike Piazza	2.00	.90
☐ 3	Moises Alou	.60	.25
☐ 4	Ken Griffey Jr.	3.00	1.35
☐ 5	Gary Sheffield	.60	.25
☐ 6	Roberto Alomar	.60	.25
☐ 7	John Kruk	.30	.14
☐ 8	Gregg Olson	.15	.07
☐ 9	Gregg Jefferies	.15	.07
☐ 10	Tony Gwynn	1.50	.70
☐ 11	Chad Curtis	.15	.07
☐ 12	Craig Biggio	.60	.25
☐ 13	John Burkett	.15	.07
☐ 14	Carlos Baerga	.30	.14
☐ 15	Robin Yount	.60	.25
☐ 16	Dennis Eckersley	.30	.14
☐ 17	Dwight Gooden	.30	.14
☐ 18	Ryne Sandberg	.75	.35
☐ 19	Rickey Henderson	.75	.35
☐ 20	Jack McDowell	.15	.07
☐ 21	Jay Bell	.30	.14
☐ 22	Kevin Brown	.30	.14
☐ 23	Robin Ventura	.30	.14
☐ 24	Paul Molitor	.60	.25
☐ 25	David Justice	.60	.25
☐ 26	Rafael Palmeiro	.60	.25
☐ 27	Cecil Fielder	.30	.14
☐ 28	Chuck Knoblauch	.60	.25
☐ 29	Dave Hollins	.15	.07
☐ 30	Jimmy Key	.30	.14
☐ 31	Mark Langston	.15	.07
☐ 32	Darryl Kile	.15	.07
☐ 33	Ruben Sierra	.30	.14
☐ 34	Ron Gant	.30	.14
☐ 35	Ozzie Smith	.75	.35
☐ 36	Wade Boggs	.60	.25
☐ 37	Marquis Grissom	.30	.14
☐ 38	Will Clark	.60	.25
☐ 39	Kenny Lofton	.60	.25
☐ 40	Cal Ripken	2.50	1.10
☐ 41	Steve Avery	.15	.07
☐ 42	Mo Vaughn	.60	.25
☐ 43	Brian McRae	.15	.07
☐ 44	Mickey Tettleton	.15	.07
☐ 45	Barry Larkin	.60	.25
☐ 46	Charlie Hayes	.15	.07
☐ 47	Kevin Appier	.30	.14
☐ 48	Robby Thompson	.15	.07
☐ 49	Juan Gonzalez	1.25	.55
☐ 50	Paul O'Neill	.30	.14
☐ 51	Marcos Armas	.15	.07
☐ 52	Mike Butcher	.15	.07
☐ 53	Ken Caminiti	.40	.18
☐ 54	Pat Borders	.15	.07
☐ 55	Pedro Munoz	.15	.07
☐ 56	Tim Belcher	.15	.07
☐ 57	Paul Assenmacher	.15	.07
☐ 58	Damon Berryhill	.15	.07
☐ 59	Ricky Bones	.15	.07
☐ 60	Rene Arocha	.15	.07
☐ 61	Shawn Boskie	.15	.07
☐ 62	Pedro Astacio	.15	.07
☐ 63	Frank Bolick	.15	.07
☐ 64	Bud Black	.15	.07
☐ 65	Sandy Alomar Jr.	.30	.14
☐ 66	Rich Amaral	.15	.07
☐ 67	Luis Aquino	.15	.07
☐ 68	Kevin Baez	.15	.07
☐ 69	Mike Devereaux	.15	.07
☐ 70	Andy Ashby	.15	.07
☐ 71	Larry Andersen	.15	.07
☐ 72	Steve Cooke	.15	.07
☐ 73	Mario Diaz	.15	.07
☐ 74	Rob Deer	.15	.07
☐ 75	Bobby Ayala	.15	.07
☐ 76	Freddie Benavides	.15	.07
☐ 77	Stan Belinda	.15	.07
☐ 78	John Doherty	.15	.07
☐ 79	Willie Banks	.15	.07
☐ 80	Spike Owen	.15	.07
☐ 81	Mike Bordick	.15	.07
☐ 82	Chili Davis	.30	.14
☐ 83	Luis Gonzalez	.30	.14
☐ 84	Ed Sprague	.15	.07
☐ 85	Jeff Reboulet	.15	.07
☐ 86	Jason Bere	.15	.07
☐ 87	Mark Hutton	.15	.07
☐ 88	Jeff Blauser	.15	.07
☐ 89	Cal Eldred	.15	.07
☐ 90	Bernard Gilkey	.15	.07
☐ 91	Frank Castillo	.15	.07
☐ 92	Jim Gott	.15	.07
☐ 93	Greg Colbrunn	.15	.07
☐ 94	Jeff Brantley	.15	.07
☐ 95	Jeremy Hernandez	.15	.07
☐ 96	Norm Charlton	.15	.07
☐ 97	Alex Arias	.15	.07
☐ 98	John Franco	.30	.14
☐ 99	Chris Hoiles	.15	.07
☐ 100	Brad Ausmus	.15	.07
☐ 101	Wes Chamberlain	.15	.07
☐ 102	Mark Dewey	.15	.07
☐ 103	Benji Gil	.15	.07
☐ 104	John Dopson	.15	.07
☐ 105	John Smiley	.15	.07
☐ 106	David Nied	.15	.07
☐ 107	George Brett	1.25	.55
☐ 108	Kirk Gibson	.30	.14
☐ 109	Larry Casian	.15	.07
☐ 110	Ryne Sandberg CL	.40	.18
☐ 111	Brent Gates	.15	.07
☐ 112	Damion Easley	.30	.14
☐ 113	Pete Harnisch	.15	.07
☐ 114	Danny Cox	.15	.07
☐ 115	Kevin Tapani	.15	.07
☐ 116	Roberto Hernandez	.15	.07
☐ 117	Domingo Jean	.15	.07
☐ 118	Sid Bream	.15	.07
☐ 119	Doug Henry	.15	.07
☐ 120	Omar Olivares	.15	.07
☐ 121	Mike Harkey	.15	.07
☐ 122	Carlos Hernandez	.15	.07
☐ 123	Jeff Fassero	.15	.07
☐ 124	Dave Burba	.15	.07
☐ 125	Wayne Kirby	.15	.07
☐ 126	John Cummings	.15	.07
☐ 127	Bret Barberie	.15	.07
☐ 128	Todd Hundley	.30	.14
☐ 129	Tim Hulett	.15	.07
☐ 130	Phil Clark	.15	.07
☐ 131	Danny Jackson	.15	.07
☐ 132	Tom Foley	.15	.07
☐ 133	Donald Harris	.15	.07
☐ 134	Scott Fletcher	.15	.07
☐ 135	Johnny Ruffin	.15	.07
☐ 136	Jerald Clark	.15	.07
☐ 137	Billy Brewer	.15	.07
☐ 138	Dan Gladden	.15	.07
☐ 139	Eddie Guardado	.15	.07
☐ 140	Cal Ripken CL	.75	.35
☐ 141	Scott Hemond	.15	.07
☐ 142	Steve Frey	.15	.07
☐ 143	Xavier Hernandez	.15	.07
☐ 144	Mark Eichhorn	.15	.07
☐ 145	Ellis Burks	.30	.14
☐ 146	Jim Leyritz	.30	.14
☐ 147	Mark Lemke	.15	.07
☐ 148	Pat Listach	.15	.07

149	Donovan Osborne	.15	.07
150	Glenallen Hill	.15	.07
151	Orel Hershiser	.30	.14
152	Darrin Fletcher	.15	.07
153	Royce Clayton	.15	.07
154	Derek Lilliquist	.15	.07
155	Mike Felder	.15	.07
156	Jeff Conine	.15	.07
157	Ryan Thompson	.15	.07
158	Ben McDonald	.15	.07
159	Ricky Gutierrez	.15	.07
160	Terry Mulholland	.15	.07
161	Carlos Garcia	.15	.07
162	Tom Henke	.15	.07
163	Mike Greenwell	.15	.07
164	Thomas Howard	.15	.07
165	Joe Girardi	.15	.07
166	Hubie Brooks	.15	.07
167	Greg Gohr	.15	.07
168	Chip Hale	.15	.07
169	Rick Honeycutt	.15	.07
170	Hilly Hathaway	.15	.07
171	Todd Jones	.15	.07
172	Tony Fernandez	.30	.14
173	Bo Jackson	.30	.14
174	Bobby Munoz	.15	.07
175	Greg McMichael	.15	.07
176	Graeme Lloyd	.15	.07
177	Tom Pagnozzi	.15	.07
178	Derrick May	.15	.07
179	Pedro Martinez	.75	.35
180	Ken Hill	.15	.07
181	Bryan Hickerson	.15	.07
182	Jose Mesa	.15	.07
183	Dave Fleming	.15	.07
184	Henry Cotto	.15	.07
185	Jeff Kent	.30	.14
186	Mark McLemore	.15	.07
187	Trevor Hoffman	.30	.14
188	Todd Pratt	.15	.07
189	Blas Minor	.15	.07
190	Charlie Leibrandt	.15	.07
191	Tony Pena	.15	.07
192	Larry Luebbers	.15	.07
193	Greg W. Harris	.15	.07
194	David Cone	.40	.18
195	Bill Gullickson	.15	.07
196	Brian Harper	.15	.07
197	Steve Karsay	.15	.07
198	Greg Myers	.15	.07
199	Mark Portugal	.15	.07
200	Pat Hentgen	.30	.14
201	Mike LaValliere	.15	.07
202	Mike Stanley	.15	.07
203	Kent Mercker	.15	.07
204	Dave Nilsson	.15	.07
205	Erik Pappas	.15	.07
206	Mike Morgan	.15	.07
207	Roger McDowell	.15	.07
208	Mike Lansing	.30	.14
209	Kirt Manwaring	.15	.07
210	Randy Milligan	.15	.07
211	Erik Hanson	.15	.07
212	Orestes Destrade	.15	.07
213	Mike Maddux	.15	.07
214	Alan Mills	.15	.07
215	Tim Mauser	.15	.07
216	Ben Rivera	.15	.07
217	Don Slaught	.15	.07
218	Bob Patterson	.15	.07
219	Carlos Quintana	.15	.07
220	Tim Raines CL	.15	.07
221	Hal Morris	.15	.07
222	Darren Holmes	.15	.07
223	Chris Gwynn	.15	.07
224	Chad Kreuter	.15	.07
225	Mike Hartley	.15	.07
226	Scott Lydy	.15	.07
227	Eduardo Perez	.15	.07
228	Greg Swindell	.15	.07
229	Al Leiter	.30	.14
230	Scott Radinsky	.15	.07
231	Bob Wickman	.15	.07
232	Otis Nixon	.15	.07
233	Kevin Reimer	.15	.07
234	Geronimo Pena	.15	.07
235	Kevin Roberson	.15	.07
236	Jody Reed	.15	.07
237	Kirk Rueter	.15	.07
238	Willie McGee	.30	.14
239	Charles Nagy	.30	.14
240	Tim Leary	.15	.07
241	Carl Everett	.30	.14
242	Charlie O'Brien	.15	.07
243	Mike Pagliarulo	.15	.07
244	Kerry Taylor	.15	.07
245	Kevin Stocker	.15	.07
246	Joel Johnston	.15	.07
247	Geno Petralli	.15	.07
248	Jeff Russell	.15	.07
249	Joe Oliver	.15	.07
250	Roberto Mejia	.15	.07
251	Chris Haney	.15	.07
252	Bill Krueger	.15	.07
253	Shane Mack	.15	.07
254	Terry Steinbach	.15	.07
255	Luis Polonia	.15	.07
256	Eddie Taubensee	.15	.07
257	Dave Stewart	.30	.14
258	Tim Raines	.30	.14
259	Bernie Williams	.60	.25
260	John Smoltz	.40	.18
261	Kevin Seitzer	.15	.07
262	Bob Tewksbury	.15	.07
263	Bob Scanlan	.15	.07
264	Henry Rodriguez	.30	.14
265	Tim Scott	.15	.07
266	Scott Sanderson	.15	.07
267	Eric Plunk	.15	.07
268	Edgar Martinez	.30	.14
269	Charlie Hough	.15	.07
270	Joe Orsulak	.15	.07
271	Harold Reynolds	.15	.07
272	Tim Teufel	.15	.07
273	Bobby Thigpen	.15	.07
274	Randy Tomlin	.15	.07
275	Gary Redus	.15	.07
276	Ken Ryan	.15	.07
277	Tim Pugh	.15	.07
278	J. Owens	.15	.07
279	Phil Hiatt	.15	.07
280	Alan Trammell	.40	.18
281	Dave McCarty	.15	.07
282	Bob Welch	.15	.07
283	J.T. Snow	.30	.14
284	Brian Williams	.15	.07
285	Devon White	.15	.07
286	Steve Sax	.15	.07
287	Tony Tarasco	.15	.07
288	Bill Spiers	.15	.07
289	Allen Watson	.15	.07
290	Rickey Henderson CL	.30	.14
291	Jose Vizcaino	.15	.07
292	Darryl Strawberry	.30	.14
293	John Wetteland	.30	.14
294	Bill Swift	.15	.07
295	Jeff Treadway	.15	.07
296	Tino Martinez	.60	.25
297	Richie Lewis	.15	.07
298	Bret Saberhagen	.30	.14
299	Arthur Rhodes	.15	.07
300	Guillermo Velasquez	.15	.07
301	Milt Thompson	.15	.07
302	Doug Strange	.15	.07
303	Aaron Sele	.30	.14
304	Bip Roberts	.15	.07
305	Bruce Ruffin	.15	.07
306	Jose Lind	.15	.07
307	David Wells	.15	.07
308	Bobby Witt	.15	.07
309	Mark Wohlers	.15	.07
310	B.J. Surhoff	.30	.14
311	Mark Whiten	.15	.07
312	Turk Wendell	.15	.07
313	Raul Mondesi	.60	.25
314	Brian Turang	.15	.07
315	Chris Hammond	.15	.07
316	Tim Bogar	.15	.07
317	Brad Pennington	.15	.07
318	Tim Worrell	.15	.07
319	Mitch Williams	.15	.07
320	Rondell White	.30	.14
321	Frank Viola	.15	.07
322	Manny Ramirez	1.25	.55
323	Gary Wayne	.15	.07
324	Mike Macfarlane	.15	.07
325	Russ Springer	.15	.07
326	Tim Wallach	.15	.07
327	Salomon Torres	.15	.07
328	Omar Vizquel	.30	.14
329	Andy Tomberlin	.15	.07
330	Chris Sabo	.15	.07
331	Mike Mussina	.60	.25
332	Andy Benes	.30	.14
333	Darren Daulton	.30	.14
334	Orlando Merced	.15	.07
335	Mark McGwire	3.00	1.35
336	Dave Winfield	.60	.25
337	Sammy Sosa	2.00	.90
338	Eric Karros	.30	.14
339	Greg Vaughn	.30	.14
340	Don Mattingly	1.25	.55
341	Frank Thomas	1.25	.55
342	Fred McGriff	.40	.18
343	Kirby Puckett	1.00	.45
344	Roberto Kelly	.15	.07
345	Wally Joyner	.30	.14
346	Andres Galarraga	.60	.25
347	Bobby Bonilla	.30	.14
348	Benito Santiago	.15	.07
349	Barry Bonds	.75	.35
350	Delino DeShields	.15	.07
351	Albert Belle	.60	.25
352	Randy Johnson	.60	.25
353	Tim Salmon	.60	.25
354	John Olerud	.30	.14
355	Dean Palmer	.30	.14
356	Roger Clemens	1.50	.70
357	Jim Abbott	.30	.14
358	Mark Grace	.40	.18
359	Ozzie Guillen	.15	.07
360	Lou Whitaker	.30	.14
361	Jose Rijo	.15	.07
362	Jeff Montgomery	.15	.07
363	Chuck Finley	.15	.07
364	Tom Glavine	.60	.25
365	Jeff Bagwell	.75	.35
366	Joe Carter	.30	.14
367	Ray Lankford	.30	.14
368	Ramon Martinez	.30	.14
369	Jay Buhner	.30	.14
370	Matt Williams	.40	.18
371	Larry Walker	.60	.25
372	Jose Canseco	.75	.35
373	Lenny Dykstra	.30	.14
374	Bryan Harvey	.15	.07
375	Andy Van Slyke	.30	.14
376	Ivan Rodriguez	.75	.35
377	Kevin Mitchell	.15	.07
378	Travis Fryman	.30	.14
379	Duane Ward	.15	.07
380	Greg Maddux	1.50	.70
381	Scott Servais	.15	.07
382	Greg Olson	.15	.07
383	Rey Sanchez	.15	.07
384	Tom Kramer	.15	.07
385	David Valle	.15	.07
386	Eddie Murray	.60	.25
387	Kevin Higgins	.15	.07
388	Dan Wilson	.15	.07
389	Todd Frohwirth	.15	.07
390	Gerald Williams	.15	.07
391	Hipolito Pichardo	.15	.07
392	Pat Meares	.15	.07
393	Luis Lopez	.15	.07
394	Ricky Jordan	.15	.07
395	Bob Walk	.15	.07
396	Sid Fernandez	.15	.07
397	Todd Worrell	.15	.07
398	Darryl Hamilton	.15	.07
399	Randy Myers	.15	.07
400	Rod Brewer	.15	.07
401	Lance Blankenship	.15	.07
402	Steve Finley	.30	.14
403	Phil Leftwich	.15	.07
404	Juan Guzman	.30	.14
405	Anthony Young	.15	.07
406	Jeff Gardner	.15	.07

No.	Name			No.	Name			No.	Name		
407	Ryan Bowen	.15	.07	493	Archi Cianfrocco	.15	.07	579	Jerry Spradlin	.15	.07
408	Fernando Valenzuela	.30	.14	494	Al Martin	.15	.07	580	Curt Leskanic	.15	.07
409	David West	.40	.18	495	Mike Gallego	.15	.07	581	Carl Willis	.15	.07
410	Kenny Rogers	.15	.07	496	Mike Henneman	.15	.07	582	Alex Fernandez	.15	.07
411	Bob Zupcic	.15	.07	497	Armando Reynoso	.15	.07	583	Mark Holzemer	.15	.07
412	Eric Young	.15	.07	498	Mickey Morandini	.15	.07	584	Domingo Martinez	.15	.07
413	Bret Boone	.30	.14	499	Rick Renteria	.15	.07	585	Pete Smith	.15	.07
414	Danny Tartabull	.15	.07	500	Rick Sutcliffe	.15	.07	586	Brian Jordan	.30	.14
415	Bob MacDonald	.15	.07	501	Bobby Jones	.15	.07	587	Kevin Gross	.15	.07
416	Ron Karkovice	.15	.07	502	Gary Gaetti	.30	.14	588	J.R. Phillips	.15	.07
417	Scott Cooper	.15	.07	503	Rick Aguilera	.15	.07	589	Chris Nabholz	.15	.07
418	Dante Bichette	.30	.14	504	Todd Stottlemyre	.15	.07	590	Bill Wertz	.15	.07
419	Tripp Cromer	.15	.07	505	Mike Mohler	.15	.07	591	Derek Bell	.30	.14
420	Billy Ashley	.15	.07	506	Mike Stanton	.15	.07	592	Brady Anderson	.30	.14
421	Roger Smithberg	.15	.07	507	Jose Guzman	.15	.07	593	Matt Turner	.15	.07
422	Dennis Martinez	.30	.14	508	Kevin Rogers	.15	.07	594	Pete Incaviglia	.15	.07
423	Mike Blowers	.15	.07	509	Chuck Carr	.15	.07	595	Greg Gagne	.15	.07
424	Darren Lewis	.15	.07	510	Chris Jones	.15	.07	596	John Flaherty	.15	.07
425	Junior Ortiz	.15	.07	511	Brent Mayne	.15	.07	597	Scott Livingstone	.15	.07
426	Butch Huskey	.30	.14	512	Greg Harris	.15	.07	598	Rod Bolton	.15	.07
427	Jimmy Poole	.15	.07	513	Dave Henderson	.15	.07	599	Mike Perez	.15	.07
428	Walt Weiss	.15	.07	514	Eric Hillman	.15	.07	600	Roger Clemens CL	.60	.25
429	Scott Bankhead	.15	.07	515	Dan Peltier	.15	.07	601	Tony Castillo	.15	.07
430	Deion Sanders	.30	.14	516	Craig Shipley	.15	.07	602	Henry Mercedes	.15	.07
431	Scott Bullett	.15	.07	517	John Valentin	.30	.14	603	Mike Fetters	.15	.07
432	Jeff Huson	.15	.07	518	Wilson Alvarez	.30	.14	604	Rod Beck	.15	.07
433	Tyler Green	.15	.07	519	Andujar Cedeno	.15	.07	605	Damon Buford	.15	.07
434	Billy Hatcher	.15	.07	520	Troy Neel	.15	.07	606	Matt Whiteside	.15	.07
435	Bob Hamelin	.15	.07	521	Tom Candiotti	.15	.07	607	Shawn Green	1.00	.45
436	Reggie Sanders	.30	.14	522	Matt Mieske	.15	.07	608	Midre Cummings	.15	.07
437	Scott Erickson	.30	.14	523	Jim Thome	.60	.25	609	Jeff McNeely	.15	.07
438	Steve Reed	.15	.07	524	Lou Frazier	.15	.07	610	Danny Sheaffer	.15	.07
439	Randy Velarde	.15	.07	525	Mike Jackson	.30	.14	611	Paul Wagner	.15	.07
440	Tony Gwynn CL	.60	.25	526	Pedro Martinez	.15	.07	612	Torey Lovullo	.15	.07
441	Terry Leach	.15	.07	527	Roger Pavlik	.15	.07	613	Javier Lopez	.40	.18
442	Danny Bautista	.15	.07	528	Kent Bottenfield	.15	.07	614	Mariano Duncan	.15	.07
443	Kent Hrbek	.30	.14	529	Felix Jose	.15	.07	615	Doug Brocail	.15	.07
444	Rick Wilkins	.15	.07	530	Mark Guthrie	.15	.07	616	Dave Hansen	.15	.07
445	Tony Phillips	.15	.07	531	Steve Farr	.15	.07	617	Ryan Klesko	.30	.14
446	Dion James	.15	.07	532	Craig Paquette	.15	.07	618	Eric Davis	.30	.14
447	Joey Cora	.15	.07	533	Doug Jones	.15	.07	619	Scott Ruffcorn	.15	.07
448	Andre Dawson	.40	.18	534	Luis Alicea	.15	.07	620	Mike Trombley	.15	.07
449	Pedro Castellano	.15	.07	535	Cory Snyder	.15	.07	621	Jaime Navarro	.15	.07
450	Tom Gordon	.15	.07	536	Paul Sorrento	.15	.07	622	Rheal Cormier	.15	.07
451	Rob Dibble	.15	.07	537	Nigel Wilson	.15	.07	623	Jose Offerman	.30	.14
452	Ron Darling	.15	.07	538	Jeff King	.15	.07	624	David Segui	.30	.14
453	Chipper Jones	1.50	.70	539	Willie Greene	.15	.07	625	Robb Nen	.15	.07
454	Joe Grahe	.15	.07	540	Kirk McCaskill	.15	.07	626	Dave Gallagher	.15	.07
455	Domingo Cedeno	.15	.07	541	Al Osuna	.15	.07	627	Julian Tavarez	.15	.07
456	Tom Edens	.15	.07	542	Greg Hibbard	.15	.07	628	Chris Gomez	.15	.07
457	Mitch Webster	.15	.07	543	Brett Butler	.30	.14	629	Jeffrey Hammonds	.30	.14
458	Jose Bautista	.15	.07	544	Jose Valentin	.15	.07	630	Scott Brosius	.30	.14
459	Troy O'Leary	.30	.14	545	Wil Cordero	.15	.07	631	Willie Blair	.15	.07
460	Todd Zeile	.15	.07	546	Chris Bosio	.15	.07	632	Doug Drabek	.15	.07
461	Sean Berry	.15	.07	547	Jamie Moyer	.15	.07	633	Bill Wegman	.15	.07
462	Brad Holman	.15	.07	548	Jim Eisenreich	.15	.07	634	Jeff McKnight	.15	.07
463	Dave Martinez	.15	.07	549	Vinny Castilla	.30	.14	635	Rich Rodriguez	.15	.07
464	Mark Lewis	.15	.07	550	Dave Winfield CL	.30	.14	636	Steve Trachsel	.15	.07
465	Paul Carey	.15	.07	551	John Roper	.15	.07	637	Buddy Groom	.15	.07
466	Jack Armstrong	.15	.07	552	Lance Johnson	.15	.07	638	Sterling Hitchcock	.30	.14
467	David Telgheder	.15	.07	553	Scott Kamieniecki	.15	.07	639	Chuck McElroy	.15	.07
468	Gene Harris	.15	.07	554	Mike Moore	.15	.07	640	Rene Gonzales	.15	.07
469	Danny Darwin	.15	.07	555	Steve Buechele	.15	.07	641	Dan Plesac	.15	.07
470	Kim Batiste	.15	.07	556	Terry Pendleton	.15	.07	642	Jeff Branson	.15	.07
471	Tim Wakefield	.30	.14	557	Todd Van Poppel	.15	.07	643	Darrell Whitmore	.15	.07
472	Craig Lefferts	.15	.07	558	Rob Butler	.15	.07	644	Paul Quantrill	.15	.07
473	Jacob Brumfield	.15	.07	559	Zane Smith	.15	.07	645	Rich Rowland	.15	.07
474	Lance Painter	.15	.07	560	David Hulse	.15	.07	646	Curtis Pride	.15	.07
475	Milt Cuyler	.15	.07	561	Tim Costo	.15	.07	647	Erik Plantenberg	.15	.07
476	Melido Perez	.15	.07	562	John Habyan	.15	.07	648	Abbie Lopez	.15	.07
477	Derek Parks	.15	.07	563	Terry Jorgensen	.15	.07	649	Rich Batchelor	.15	.07
478	Gary DiSarcina	.15	.07	564	Matt Nokes	.15	.07	650	Lee Smith	.30	.14
479	Steve Bedrosian	.15	.07	565	Kevin McReynolds	.15	.07	651	Cliff Floyd	.30	.14
480	Eric Anthony	.15	.07	566	Phil Plantier	.15	.07	652	Pete Schourek	.15	.07
481	Julio Franco	.15	.07	567	Chris Turner	.15	.07	653	Reggie Jefferson	.15	.07
482	Tommy Greene	.15	.07	568	Carlos Delgado	.60	.25	654	Bill Haselman	.15	.07
483	Pat Kelly	.15	.07	569	John Jaha	.15	.07	655	Steve Hosey	.15	.07
484	Nate Minchey	.15	.07	570	Dwight Smith	.15	.07	656	Mark Clark	.15	.07
485	William Pennyfeather	.15	.07	571	John Vander Wal	.15	.07	657	Mark Davis	.15	.07
486	Harold Baines	.30	.14	572	Trevor Wilson	.15	.07	658	Dave Magadan	.15	.07
487	Howard Johnson	.15	.07	573	Felix Fermin	.15	.07	659	Candy Maldonado	.15	.07
488	Angel Miranda	.15	.07	574	Marc Newfield	.15	.07	660	Mark Langston CL	.15	.07
489	Scott Sanders	.15	.07	575	Jeromy Burnitz	.30	.14				
490	Shawon Dunston	.15	.07	576	Leo Gomez	.15	.07				
491	Mel Rojas	.15	.07	577	Curt Schilling	.30	.14				
492	Jeff Nelson	.15	.07	578	Kevin Young	.15	.07				

1994 Donruss Anniversary '84

	MINT	NRMT
COMPLETE SET (10)	50.00	22.00
COMMON CARD (1-10)	2.00	.90
RANDOM INSERTS IN SER.1 HOBBY PACKS		

		MINT	NRMT
❑ 1 Joe Carter		2.00	.90
❑ 2 Robin Yount		4.00	1.80
❑ 3 George Brett		6.00	2.70
❑ 4 Rickey Henderson		5.00	2.20
❑ 5 Nolan Ryan		15.00	6.75
❑ 6 Cal Ripken		15.00	6.75
❑ 7 Wade Boggs UER		4.00	1.80
(1983 runs 10, should be 100)			
❑ 8 Don Mattingly		8.00	3.60
❑ 9 Ryne Sandberg		5.00	2.20
❑ 10 Tony Gwynn		10.00	4.50

1994 Donruss Award Winner Jumbos

	MINT	NRMT
COMPLETE SET (10)	90.00	40.00
COMPLETE SERIES 1 (5)	50.00	22.00
COMPLETE SERIES 2 (5)	40.00	18.00
COMMON CARD (1-10)	1.50	.70
ONE PER JUMBO BOX OR CDN FOIL BOX		
STATED PRINT RUN 10,000 SERIAL #'d SETS		

	MINT	NRMT
❑ 1 Barry Bonds MVP	6.00	2.70
❑ 2 Greg Maddux CY	20.00	9.00
❑ 3 Mike Piazza ROY	20.00	9.00
❑ 4 Barry Bonds HR King	6.00	2.70
❑ 5 Kirby Puckett AS MVP	10.00	4.50
❑ 6 Frank Thomas MVP	15.00	6.75
❑ 7 Jack McDowell CY	1.50	.70
❑ 8 Tim Salmon ROY	6.00	2.70
❑ 9 Juan Gonzalez HR King	15.00	6.75
❑ 10 Paul Molitor WS MVP	6.00	2.70

1994 Donruss Diamond Kings

	MINT	NRMT
COMPLETE SET (30)	50.00	22.00
COMPLETE SERIES 1 (15)	25.00	11.00
COMPLETE SERIES 2 (15)	25.00	11.00

	MINT	NRMT
COMMON CARD (DK1-DK30)	.50	.23
STATED ODDS 1:9		
*JUMBO DK's: 2.5X TO 6X BASE CARD Hi		
ONE JUMBO DK PER RETAIL BOX		

	MINT	NRMT
❑ DK1 Barry Bonds	2.00	.90
❑ DK2 Mo Vaughn	1.50	.70
❑ DK3 Steve Avery	.50	.23
❑ DK4 Tim Salmon	1.50	.70
❑ DK5 Rick Wilkins	.50	.23
❑ DK6 Brian Harper	.50	.23
❑ DK7 Andres Galarraga	1.50	.70
❑ DK8 Albert Belle	1.50	.70
❑ DK9 John Kruk	1.00	.45
❑ DK10 Ivan Rodriguez	2.00	.90
❑ DK11 Tony Gwynn	4.00	1.80
❑ DK12 Brian McRae	.50	.23
❑ DK13 Bobby Bonilla	1.00	.45
❑ DK14 Ken Griffey Jr.	8.00	3.60
❑ DK15 Mike Piazza	5.00	2.20
❑ DK16 Don Mattingly	4.00	1.80
❑ DK17 Barry Larkin	1.50	.70
❑ DK18 Ruben Sierra	.50	.23
❑ DK19 Orlando Merced	.50	.23
❑ DK20 Greg Vaughn	1.00	.45
❑ DK21 Gregg Jefferies	.50	.23
❑ DK22 Cecil Fielder	.50	.23
❑ DK23 Moises Alou	1.00	.45
❑ DK24 John Olerud	1.00	.45
❑ DK25 Gary Sheffield	1.50	.70
❑ DK26 Mike Mussina	1.50	.70
❑ DK27 Jeff Bagwell	2.00	.90
❑ DK28 Frank Thomas	4.00	1.80
❑ DK29 Dave Winfield	1.50	.70
❑ DK30 Checklist	.50	.23

1994 Donruss Dominators

	MINT	NRMT
COMPLETE SET (20)	40.00	18.00
COMPLETE SERIES 1 (10)	20.00	9.00
COMPLETE SERIES 2 (10)	20.00	9.00
COMMON CARD (A1-B10)	.50	.23
RANDOM INSERTS IN PACKS		
*JUMBOS: 3X TO 6X BASE CARD Hi		
ONE JUMBO DOMINATOR PER HOBBY BOX		

	MINT	NRMT
❑ A1 Cecil Fielder	.50	.23
❑ A2 Barry Bonds	2.00	.90

		MINT	NRMT
❑ A3 Fred McGriff		1.25	.55
❑ A4 Matt Williams		1.25	.55
❑ A5 Joe Carter		1.00	.45
❑ A6 Juan Gonzalez		3.00	1.35
❑ A7 Jose Canseco		2.00	.90
❑ A8 Ron Gant		.50	.23
❑ A9 Ken Griffey Jr.		8.00	3.60
❑ A10 Mark McGwire		8.00	3.60
❑ B1 Tony Gwynn		4.00	1.80
❑ B2 Frank Thomas		3.00	1.35
❑ B3 Paul Molitor		1.50	.70
❑ B4 Edgar Martinez		1.00	.45
❑ B5 Kirby Puckett		2.50	1.10
❑ B6 Ken Griffey Jr.		8.00	3.60
❑ B7 Barry Bonds		2.00	.90
❑ B8 Willie McGee		1.00	.45
❑ B9 Lenny Dykstra		.50	.23
❑ B10 John Kruk		1.00	.45

1994 Donruss Elite

	MINT	NRMT
COMPLETE SET (12)	160.00	70.00
COMPLETE SERIES 1 (6)	80.00	36.00
COMPLETE SERIES 2 (6)	80.00	36.00
COMMON CARD (37-48)	8.00	3.60
UNLISTED STARS	10.00	4.50
RANDOM INSERTS IN HOBBY/RETAIL PACKS		
STATED PRINT RUN 10,000 SERIAL #'d SETS		

	MINT	NRMT
❑ 37 Frank Thomas	20.00	9.00
❑ 38 Tony Gwynn	25.00	11.00
❑ 39 Tim Salmon	10.00	4.50
❑ 40 Albert Belle	10.00	4.50
❑ 41 John Kruk	10.00	4.50
❑ 42 Juan Gonzalez	20.00	9.00
❑ 43 John Olerud	10.00	4.50
❑ 44 Barry Bonds	12.00	5.50
❑ 45 Ken Griffey Jr.	50.00	22.00
❑ 46 Mike Piazza	30.00	13.50
❑ 47 Jack McDowell	8.00	3.60
❑ 48 Andres Galarraga	10.00	4.50

1994 Donruss Long Ball Leaders

	MINT	NRMT
COMPLETE SET (10)	40.00	18.00
COMMON CARD (1-10)	1.00	.45
RANDOM INSERTS IN SER.2 HOBBY PACKS		

		MINT	NRMT
☐ 1	Cecil Fielder	1.00	.45
☐ 2	Dean Palmer	1.50	.70
☐ 3	Andres Galarraga	3.00	1.35
☐ 4	Bo Jackson	1.50	.70
☐ 5	Ken Griffey Jr.	15.00	6.75
☐ 6	David Justice	3.00	1.35
☐ 7	Mike Piazza	10.00	4.50
☐ 8	Frank Thomas	6.00	2.70
☐ 9	Barry Bonds	4.00	1.80
☐ 10	Juan Gonzalez	6.00	2.70

1994 Donruss MVPs

	MINT	NRMT
COMPLETE SET (28)	75.00	34.00
COMPLETE SERIES 1 (14)	15.00	6.75
COMPLETE SERIES 2 (14)	60.00	27.00
COMMON CARD (1-28)	.75	.35
ONE PER JUMBO PACK		

		MINT	NRMT
☐ 1	David Justice	2.50	1.10
☐ 2	Mark Grace	1.50	.70
☐ 3	Jose Rijo	.75	.35
☐ 4	Andres Galarraga	2.50	1.10
☐ 5	Bryan Harvey	.75	.35
☐ 6	Jeff Bagwell	4.00	1.80
☐ 7	Mike Piazza	10.00	4.50
☐ 8	Moises Alou	1.00	.45
☐ 9	Bobby Bonilla	1.00	.45
☐ 10	Len Dykstra	1.00	.45
☐ 11	Jeff King	.75	.35
☐ 12	Gregg Jefferies	.75	.35
☐ 13	Tony Gwynn	8.00	3.60
☐ 14	Barry Bonds	4.00	1.80
☐ 15	Cal Ripken Jr.	12.00	5.50
☐ 16	Mo Vaughn	2.50	1.10
☐ 17	Tim Salmon	2.50	1.10
☐ 18	Frank Thomas	6.00	2.70
☐ 19	Albert Belle	2.50	1.10
☐ 20	Cecil Fielder	.75	.35
☐ 21	Wally Joyner	1.00	.45
☐ 22	Greg Vaughn	1.00	.45
☐ 23	Kirby Puckett	5.00	2.20
☐ 24	Don Mattingly	6.00	2.70
☐ 25	Ruben Sierra	.75	.35
☐ 26	Ken Griffey Jr.	15.00	6.75
☐ 27	Juan Gonzalez	6.00	2.70
☐ 28	John Olerud	1.00	.45

1994 Donruss Spirit of the Game

	MINT	NRMT
COMPLETE SET (10)	60.00	27.00
COMPLETE SERIES 1 (5)	30.00	13.50
COMPLETE SERIES 2 (5)	30.00	13.50
COMMON CARD (1-10)		.45
RANDOM INSERTS IN MAG./JUMBO PACKS		
*JUMBOS: 6X TO 12X BASE CARD HI		
ONE JUMBO SPIRIT PER MAG./JUMBO BOX		

		MINT	NRMT
☐ 1	John Olerud	1.50	.70
☐ 2	Barry Bonds	5.00	2.20
☐ 3	Ken Griffey Jr.	20.00	9.00
☐ 4	Mike Piazza	12.00	5.50
☐ 5	Juan Gonzalez	8.00	3.60
☐ 6	Frank Thomas	8.00	3.60
☐ 7	Tim Salmon	4.00	1.80

		MINT	NRMT
☐ 8	David Justice	4.00	1.80
☐ 9	Don Mattingly	8.00	3.60
☐ 10	Lenny Dykstra	1.00	.45

1995 Donruss

	MINT	NRMT
COMPLETE SET (550)	40.00	18.00
COMPLETE SERIES 1 (330)	25.00	11.00
COMPLETE SERIES 2 (220)	15.00	6.75
COMMON CARD (1-550)	.15	.07
MINOR STARS	.30	.14
UNLISTED STARS	.60	.25
COMMON FP (1-550)	2.00	.90
*PP STARS: 6X TO 15X HI COLUMN		
PP SER.1 STAT.ODDS 1:20H/R, 1:18J, 1:24M		
PP SER.2 STAT.ODDS 1:24H/R, 1:18J, 1:24M		
PP STATED PRINT RUN 2000 SETS		

		MINT	NRMT
☐ 1	David Justice	.60	.25
☐ 2	Rene Arocha	.15	.07
☐ 3	Sandy Alomar Jr.	.30	.14
☐ 4	Luis Lopez	.15	.07
☐ 5	Mike Piazza	2.00	.90
☐ 6	Bobby Jones	.15	.07
☐ 7	Damion Easley	.30	.14
☐ 8	Barry Bonds	.75	.35
☐ 9	Mike Mussina	.60	.25
☐ 10	Kevin Seitzer	.15	.07
☐ 11	John Smiley	.15	.07
☐ 12	Wm.VanLandingham	.15	.07
☐ 13	Ron Darling	.15	.07
☐ 14	Walt Weiss	.15	.07
☐ 15	Mike Lansing	.15	.07
☐ 16	Allen Watson	.15	.07
☐ 17	Aaron Sele	.30	.14
☐ 18	Randy Johnson	.60	.25
☐ 19	Dean Palmer	.30	.14
☐ 20	Jeff Bagwell	.75	.35
☐ 21	Curt Schilling	.40	.18
☐ 22	Darrell Whitmore	.15	.07
☐ 23	Steve Trachsel	.15	.07
☐ 24	Dan Wilson	.15	.07
☐ 25	Steve Finley	.30	.14
☐ 26	Bret Boone	.30	.14
☐ 27	Charles Johnson	.30	.14
☐ 28	Mike Stanton	.15	.07
☐ 29	Ismael Valdes	.30	.14
☐ 30	Salomon Torres	.15	.07
☐ 31	Eric Anthony	.15	.07
☐ 32	Spike Owen	.15	.07
☐ 33	Joey Cora	.15	.07
☐ 34	Robert Eenhoorn	.15	.07
☐ 35	Rick White	.15	.07
☐ 36	Omar Vizquel	.30	.14
☐ 37	Carlos Delgado	.60	.25
☐ 38	Eddie Williams	.15	.07
☐ 39	Shawon Dunston	.30	.14
☐ 40	Darrin Fletcher	.15	.07
☐ 41	Leo Gomez	.15	.07
☐ 42	Juan Gonzalez	1.25	.55
☐ 43	Luis Alicea	.15	.07
☐ 44	Ken Ryan	.15	.07
☐ 45	Lou Whitaker	.30	.14
☐ 46	Mike Blowers	.15	.07
☐ 47	Willie Blair	.15	.07
☐ 48	Todd Van Poppel	.15	.07
☐ 49	Roberto Alomar	.60	.25
☐ 50	Ozzie Smith	.75	.35
☐ 51	Sterling Hitchcock	.30	.14
☐ 52	Mo Vaughn	.60	.25
☐ 53	Rick Aguilera	.15	.07
☐ 54	Kent Mercker	.15	.07
☐ 55	Don Mattingly	1.25	.55
☐ 56	Bob Scanlan	.15	.07
☐ 57	Wilson Alvarez	.30	.14
☐ 58	Jose Mesa	.15	.07
☐ 59	Scott Kamienecki	.15	.07
☐ 60	Todd Jones	.15	.07
☐ 61	John Kruk	.30	.14
☐ 62	Mike Stanley	.15	.07
☐ 63	Tino Martinez	.60	.25
☐ 64	Eddie Zambrano	.15	.07
☐ 65	Todd Hundley	.30	.14
☐ 66	Jamie Moyer	.15	.07
☐ 67	Rich Amaral	.15	.07
☐ 68	Alex Gonzalez	.15	.07
☐ 69	Alex Gonzalez	.15	.07
☐ 70	Kurt Abbott	.15	.07
☐ 71	Delino DeShields	.15	.07
☐ 72	Brian Anderson	.30	.14
☐ 73	John Vander Wal	.15	.07
☐ 74	Turner Ward	.15	.07
☐ 75	Tim Raines	.30	.14
☐ 76	Mark Acre	.15	.07
☐ 77	Jose Offerman	.15	.07
☐ 78	Jimmy Key	.30	.14
☐ 79	Mark Whiten	.15	.07
☐ 80	Mark Gubicza	.15	.07
☐ 81	Darren Hall	.15	.07
☐ 82	Travis Fryman	.30	.14
☐ 83	Cal Ripken	2.50	1.10
☐ 84	Geronimo Berroa	.15	.07
☐ 85	Bret Barberie	.15	.07
☐ 86	Andy Ashby	.15	.07
☐ 87	Steve Avery	.15	.07
☐ 88	Rich Becker	.15	.07
☐ 89	John Valentin	.30	.14
☐ 90	Glenallen Hill	.15	.07
☐ 91	Carlos Garcia	.15	.07
☐ 92	Dennis Martinez	.30	.14
☐ 93	Pat Kelly	.15	.07
☐ 94	Orlando Miller	.15	.07
☐ 95	Felix Jose	.15	.07
☐ 96	Mike Kingery	.15	.07
☐ 97	Jeff Kent	.30	.14
☐ 98	Pete Incaviglia	.15	.07
☐ 99	Chad Curtis	.15	.07
☐ 100	Thomas Howard	.15	.07
☐ 101	Hector Carrasco	.15	.07
☐ 102	Tom Pagnozzi	.15	.07
☐ 103	Danny Tartabull	.15	.07
☐ 104	Donnie Elliott	.15	.07
☐ 105	Danny Jackson	.15	.07
☐ 106	Steve Dunn	.15	.07
☐ 107	Roger Salkeld	.15	.07
☐ 108	Jeff King	.15	.07
☐ 109	Cecil Fielder	.30	.14
☐ 110	Paul Molitor Cl	.30	.14
☐ 111	Denny Neagle	.15	.07
☐ 112	Troy Neel	.15	.07
☐ 113	Rod Beck	.15	.07
☐ 114	Alex Rodriguez	2.50	1.10
☐ 115	Joey Eischen	.15	.07
☐ 116	Tom Candiotti	.15	.07
☐ 117	Ray McDavid	.15	.07
☐ 118	Vince Coleman	.15	.07

119	Pete Harnisch	.15	.07
120	David Nied	.15	.07
121	Pat Rapp	.15	.07
122	Sammy Sosa	2.00	.90
123	Steve Reed	.15	.07
124	Jose Oliva	.15	.07
125	Ricky Bottalico	.15	.07
126	Jose DeLeon	.15	.07
127	Pat Hentgen	.15	.14
128	Will Clark	.60	.25
129	Mark Dewey	.15	.07
130	Greg Vaughn	.30	.14
131	Darren Dreifort	.15	.14
132	Ed Sprague	.15	.07
133	Lee Smith	.30	.14
134	Charles Nagy	.30	.14
135	Phil Plantier	.15	.07
136	Jason Jacome	.15	.07
137	Jose Lima	.15	.07
138	J.R. Phillips	.15	.07
139	J.T. Snow	.30	.14
140	Michael Huff	.15	.07
141	Billy Brewer	.15	.07
142	Jeromy Burnitz	.30	.14
143	Ricky Bones	.15	.07
144	Carlos Rodriguez	.15	.07
145	Luis Gonzalez	.15	.07
146	Mark Lemke	.15	.07
147	Al Martin	.15	.07
148	Mike Bordick	.15	.07
149	Robb Nen	.15	.07
150	Wil Cordero	.15	.07
151	Edgar Martinez	.30	.14
152	Gerald Williams	.15	.07
153	Esteban Beltre	.15	.07
154	Mike Moore	.15	.07
155	Mark Langston	.15	.07
156	Mark Clark	.15	.07
157	Bobby Ayala	.15	.07
158	Rick Wilkins	.15	.07
159	Bobby Munoz	.15	.07
160	Brett Butler CL	.30	.14
161	Scott Erickson	.30	.14
162	Paul Molitor	.60	.25
163	Jon Lieber	.15	.07
164	Jason Grimsley	.15	.07
165	Norberto Martin	.15	.07
166	Javier Lopez	.30	.14
167	Brian McRae	.15	.07
168	Gary Sheffield	.30	.14
169	Marcus Moore	.15	.07
170	John Hudek	.15	.07
171	Kelly Stinnett	.15	.07
172	Chris Gomez	.15	.07
173	Rey Sanchez	.15	.07
174	Juan Guzman	.15	.07
175	Chan Ho Park	.60	.25
176	Terry Shumpert	.15	.07
177	Steve Ontiveros	.15	.07
178	Brad Ausmus	.15	.07
179	Tim Davis	.15	.07
180	Billy Ashley	.15	.07
181	Vinny Castilla	.40	.18
182	Bill Spiers	.15	.07
183	Randy Knorr	.15	.07
184	Brian Hunter	.30	.14
185	Pat Meares	.15	.07
186	Steve Buechele	.15	.07
187	Kirt Manwaring	.15	.07
188	Tim Naehring	.15	.07
189	Matt Mieske	.15	.07
190	Josias Manzanillo	.15	.07
191	Greg McMichael	.15	.07
192	Chuck Carr	.15	.07
193	Midre Cummings	.15	.07
194	Darryl Strawberry	.30	.14
195	Greg Gagne	.15	.07
196	Steve Cooke	.15	.07
197	Woody Williams	.15	.07
198	Ron Karkovice	.15	.07
199	Phil Leftwich	.15	.07
200	Jim Thome	.60	.25
201	Brady Anderson	.30	.14
202	Pedro Martinez	.15	.07
203	Steve Karsay	.15	.07
204	Reggie Sanders	.30	.14
205	Bill Risley	.15	.07
206	Jay Bell	.30	.14
207	Kevin Brown	.40	.18
208	Tim Scott	.15	.07
209	Lenny Dykstra	.30	.14
210	Willie Greene	.15	.07
211	Jim Eisenreich	.15	.07
212	Cliff Floyd	.30	.14
213	Otis Nixon	.15	.07
214	Eduardo Perez	.15	.07
215	Manuel Lee	.15	.07
216	Armando Benitez	.15	.07
217	Dave McCarty	.15	.07
218	Scott Livingstone	.15	.07
219	Chad Kreuter	.15	.07
220	Don Mattingly CL	.60	.25
221	Brian Jordan	.30	.14
222	Matt Whiteside	.15	.07
223	Jim Edmonds	.40	.18
224	Tony Gwynn	1.50	.70
225	Jose Lind	.15	.07
226	Marvin Freeman	.15	.07
227	Ken Hill	.15	.07
228	David Hulse	.15	.07
229	Joe Hesketh	.15	.07
230	Roberto Petagine	.15	.07
231	Jeffrey Hammonds	.30	.14
232	John Jaha	.15	.07
233	John Burkett	.15	.07
234	Hal Morris	.15	.07
235	Tony Castillo	.15	.07
236	Ryan Bowen	.15	.07
237	Wayne Kirby	.15	.07
238	Brent Mayne	.15	.07
239	Jim Bullinger	.15	.07
240	Mike Lieberthal	.15	.07
241	Barry Larkin	.60	.25
242	David Segui	.30	.14
243	Jose Bautista	.15	.07
244	Hector Fajardo	.15	.07
245	Orel Hershiser	.30	.14
246	James Mouton	.15	.07
247	Scott Leius	.15	.07
248	Tom Glavine	.60	.25
249	Danny Bautista	.15	.07
250	Jose Mercedes	.15	.07
251	Marquis Grissom	.30	.14
252	Charlie Hayes	.15	.07
253	Ryan Klesko	.30	.14
254	Vicente Palacios	.15	.07
255	Matias Carrillo	.15	.07
256	Guy DiSarcina	.15	.07
257	Kirk Gibson	.30	.14
258	Garey Ingram	.15	.07
259	Alex Fernandez	.15	.07
260	John Mabry	.15	.07
261	Chris Howard	.15	.07
262	Miguel Jimenez	.15	.07
263	Heath Slocumb	.15	.07
264	Albert Belle	.60	.25
265	Dave Clark	.15	.07
266	Joe Orsulak	.15	.07
267	Joey Hamilton	.30	.14
268	Mark Portugal	.15	.07
269	Kevin Tapani	.15	.07
270	Sid Fernandez	.15	.07
271	Steve Dreyer	.15	.07
272	Denny Hocking	.15	.07
273	Troy O'Leary	.30	.14
274	Milt Cuyler	.15	.07
275	Frank Thomas	1.25	.55
276	Jorge Fabregas	.15	.07
277	Mike Gallego	.15	.07
278	Mickey Morandini	.15	.07
279	Roberto Hernandez	.15	.07
280	Henry Rodriguez	.30	.14
281	Garret Anderson	.30	.14
282	Bob Wickman	.15	.07
283	Gar Finnvold	.15	.07
284	Paul O'Neill	.30	.14
285	Royce Clayton	.15	.07
286	Chuck Knoblauch	.60	.25
287	Johnny Ruffin	.15	.07
288	Dave Nilsson	.15	.07
289	David Cone	.30	.18
290	Chuck McElroy	.15	.07
291	Kevin Stocker	.15	.07
292	Jose Rijo	.15	.07
293	Sean Berry	.15	.07
294	Ozzie Guillen	.15	.07
295	Chris Hoiles	.15	.07
296	Kevin Foster	.15	.07
297	Jeff Frye	.15	.07
298	Lance Johnson	.15	.07
299	Mike Kelly	.15	.07
300	Ellis Burks	.30	.14
301	Roberto Kelly	.15	.07
302	Dante Bichette	.30	.14
303	Alvaro Espinoza	.15	.07
304	Alex Cole	.15	.07
305	Rickey Henderson	.75	.35
306	Dave Weathers	.15	.07
307	Shane Reynolds	.30	.14
308	Bobby Bonilla	.30	.14
309	Junior Felix	.15	.07
310	Jeff Fassero	.15	.07
311	Darren Lewis	.15	.07
312	John Doherty	.15	.07
313	Scott Servais	.15	.07
314	Rick Helling	.30	.14
315	Pedro Martinez	.75	.35
316	Wes Chamberlain	.15	.07
317	Bryan Eversgerd	.15	.07
318	Trevor Hoffman	.30	.14
319	John Patterson	.15	.07
320	Matt Walbeck	.15	.07
321	Jeff Montgomery	.15	.07
322	Mel Rojas	.15	.07
323	Eddie Taubensee	.15	.07
324	Ray Lankford	.30	.14
325	Jose Vizcaino	.15	.07
326	Carlos Baerga	.30	.14
327	Jack Voigt	.15	.07
328	Julio Franco	.15	.07
329	Brent Gates	.15	.07
330	Kirby Puckett CL	.60	.25
331	Greg Maddux	1.50	.70
332	Jason Bere	.15	.07
333	Bill Wegman	.15	.07
334	Tuffy Rhodes	.15	.07
335	Kevin Young	.15	.07
336	Andy Benes	.30	.14
337	Pedro Astacio	.15	.07
338	Reggie Jefferson	.15	.07
339	Tim Belcher	.15	.07
340	Ken Griffey Jr.	3.00	1.35
341	Mariano Duncan	.15	.07
342	Andres Galarraga	.60	.25
343	Rondell White	.30	.14
344	Cory Bailey	.15	.07
345	Bryan Harvey	.15	.07
346	John Franco	.30	.14
347	Greg Swindell	.15	.07
348	David West	.40	.18
349	Fred McGriff	.40	.18
350	Jose Canseco	.75	.35
351	Orlando Merced	.15	.07
352	Rheal Cormier	.15	.07
353	Carlos Pulido	.15	.07
354	Terry Steinbach	.15	.07
355	Wade Boggs	.60	.25
356	B.J. Surhoff	.30	.14
357	Rafael Palmeiro	.60	.25
358	Anthony Young	.15	.07
359	Tom Brunansky	.15	.07
360	Todd Stottlemyre	.15	.07
361	Chris Turner	.15	.07
362	Joe Boever	.15	.07
363	Jeff Blauser	.15	.07
364	Derek Bell	.30	.14
365	Matt Williams	.60	.25
366	Jeremy Hernandez	.15	.07
367	Joe Girardi	.15	.07
368	Mike Devereaux	.15	.07
369	Jim Abbott	.30	.14
370	Manny Ramirez	.75	.35
371	Kenny Lofton	.40	.18
372	Mark Smith	.15	.07
373	Dave Fleming	.15	.07
374	Dave Stewart	.30	.14
375	Chuck McElroy	.15	.07
376	Hipolito Pichardo	.15	.07

❑ 377 Bill Taylor	.15	.07
❑ 378 Robin Ventura	.30	.14
❑ 379 Bernard Gilkey	.15	.07
❑ 380 Kirby Puckett	1.00	.45
❑ 381 Steve Howe	.15	.07
❑ 382 Devon White	.30	.14
❑ 383 Roberto Mejia	.15	.07
❑ 384 Darrin Jackson	.15	.07
❑ 385 Mike Morgan	.15	.07
❑ 386 Rusty Meacham	.15	.07
❑ 387 Bill Swift	.15	.07
❑ 388 Lou Frazier	.15	.07
❑ 389 Andy Van Slyke	.30	.14
❑ 390 Brett Butler	.30	.14
❑ 391 Bobby Witt	.15	.07
❑ 392 Jeff Conine	.15	.07
❑ 393 Tim Hyers	.15	.07
❑ 394 Terry Mulholland	.15	.07
❑ 395 Ricky Jordan	.15	.07
❑ 396 Eric Plunk	.15	.07
❑ 397 Melido Perez	.15	.07
❑ 398 Darryl Kile	.15	.07
❑ 399 Mark McLemore	.15	.07
❑ 400 Greg W.Harris	.15	.07
❑ 401 Jim Leyritz	.15	.07
❑ 402 Doug Strange	.15	.07
❑ 403 Tim Salmon	.60	.25
❑ 404 Terry Mulholland	.15	.07
❑ 405 Robby Thompson	.15	.07
❑ 406 Ruben Sierra	.15	.07
❑ 407 Tony Phillips	.15	.07
❑ 408 Moises Alou	.30	.14
❑ 409 Felix Fermin	.15	.07
❑ 410 Pat Listach	.15	.07
❑ 411 Kevin Bass	.15	.07
❑ 412 Ben McDonald	.15	.07
❑ 413 Scott Cooper	.15	.07
❑ 414 Jody Reed	.15	.07
❑ 415 Deion Sanders	.30	.14
❑ 416 Ricky Gutierrez	.15	.07
❑ 417 Gregg Jefferies	.15	.07
❑ 418 Jack McDowell	.15	.07
❑ 419 Al Leiter	.30	.14
❑ 420 Tony Longmire	.15	.07
❑ 421 Paul Wagner	.15	.07
❑ 422 Geronimo Pena	.15	.07
❑ 423 Ivan Rodriguez	.75	.35
❑ 424 Kevin Gross	.15	.07
❑ 425 Kirk McCaskill	.15	.07
❑ 426 Greg Myers	.15	.07
❑ 427 Roger Clemens	1.50	.70
❑ 428 Chris Hammond	.15	.07
❑ 429 Randy Myers	.15	.07
❑ 430 Roger Mason	.15	.07
❑ 431 Bret Saberhagen	.30	.14
❑ 432 Jeff Reboulet	.15	.07
❑ 433 John Olerud	.30	.14
❑ 434 Bill Gullickson	.15	.07
❑ 435 Eddie Murray	.60	.25
❑ 436 Pedro Munoz	.15	.07
❑ 437 Charlie O'Brien	.15	.07
❑ 438 Jeff Nelson	.15	.07
❑ 439 Mike Macfarlane	.15	.07
❑ 440 Don Mattingly CL	.60	.25
❑ 441 Derrick May	.15	.07
❑ 442 John Roper	.15	.07
❑ 443 Darryl Hamilton	.15	.07
❑ 444 Dan Miceli	.15	.07
❑ 445 Tony Eusebio	.15	.07
❑ 446 Jerry Browne	.15	.07
❑ 447 Wally Joyner	.30	.14
❑ 448 Brian Harper	.15	.07
❑ 449 Scott Fletcher	.15	.07
❑ 450 Bip Roberts	.15	.07
❑ 451 Pete Smith	.15	.07
❑ 452 Chili Davis	.30	.14
❑ 453 Dave Hollins	.15	.07
❑ 454 Tony Pena	.15	.07
❑ 455 Butch Henry	.15	.07
❑ 456 Craig Biggio	.60	.25
❑ 457 Zane Smith	.15	.07
❑ 458 Ryan Thompson	.15	.07
❑ 459 Mike Jackson	.30	.14
❑ 460 Mark McGwire	3.00	1.35
❑ 461 John Smoltz	.40	.18
❑ 462 Steve Scarsone	.15	.07

❑ 463 Greg Colbrunn	.15	.07
❑ 464 Shawn Green	.60	.25
❑ 465 David Wells	.40	.18
❑ 466 Jose Hernandez	.15	.07
❑ 467 Chip Hale	.15	.07
❑ 468 Tony Tarasco	.15	.07
❑ 469 Kevin Mitchell	.15	.07
❑ 470 Billy Hatcher	.15	.07
❑ 471 Jay Buhner	.30	.14
❑ 472 Ken Caminiti	.40	.18
❑ 473 Tom Henke	.15	.07
❑ 474 Todd Worrell	.15	.07
❑ 475 Mark Eichhorn	.15	.07
❑ 476 Bruce Ruffin	.15	.07
❑ 477 Chuck Finley	.30	.14
❑ 478 Marc Newfield	.15	.07
❑ 479 Paul Shuey	.15	.07
❑ 480 Bob Tewksbury	.15	.07
❑ 481 Ramon J.Martinez	.30	.14
❑ 482 Melvin Nieves	.15	.07
❑ 483 Todd Zeile	.15	.07
❑ 484 Benito Santiago	.15	.07
❑ 485 Stan Javier	.15	.07
❑ 486 Kirk Rueter	.15	.07
❑ 487 Andre Dawson	.40	.18
❑ 488 Eric Karros	.30	.14
❑ 489 Dave Magadan	.15	.07
❑ 490 Joe Carter CL	.15	.07
❑ 491 Randy Velarde	.15	.07
❑ 492 Larry Walker	.60	.25
❑ 493 Cris Carpenter	.15	.07
❑ 494 Tom Gordon	.15	.07
❑ 495 Dave Burba	.15	.07
❑ 496 Darren Bragg	.15	.07
❑ 497 Darren Daulton	.30	.14
❑ 498 Don Slaught	.15	.07
❑ 499 Pat Borders	.15	.07
❑ 500 Lenny Harris	.15	.07
❑ 501 Joe Ausanio	.15	.07
❑ 502 Alan Trammell	.30	.14
❑ 503 Mike Fetters	.15	.07
❑ 504 Scott Ruffcorn	.15	.07
❑ 505 Rich Rowland	.15	.07
❑ 506 Juan Samuel	.15	.07
❑ 507 Bo Jackson	.30	.14
❑ 508 Jeff Branson	.15	.07
❑ 509 Bernie Williams	.60	.25
❑ 510 Paul Sorrento	.15	.07
❑ 511 Dennis Eckersley	.30	.14
❑ 512 Pat Mahomes	.15	.07
❑ 513 Rusty Greer	.60	.25
❑ 514 Luis Polonia	.15	.07
❑ 515 Willie Banks	.15	.07
❑ 516 John Wetteland	.30	.14
❑ 517 Mike LaValliere	.15	.07
❑ 518 Tommy Greene	.15	.07
❑ 519 Mark Grace	.40	.18
❑ 520 Bob Hamelin	.15	.07
❑ 521 Scott Sanderson	.15	.07
❑ 522 Joe Carter	.30	.14
❑ 523 Jeff Brantley	.15	.07
❑ 524 Andrew Lorraine	.15	.07
❑ 525 Rico Brogna	.15	.07
❑ 526 Shane Mack	.15	.07
❑ 527 Mark Wohlers	.15	.07
❑ 528 Scott Sanders	.15	.07
❑ 529 Chris Bosio	.15	.07
❑ 530 Andujar Cedeno	.15	.07
❑ 531 Kenny Rogers	.15	.07
❑ 532 Doug Drabek	.15	.07
❑ 533 Curt Leskanic	.15	.07
❑ 534 Craig Shipley	.15	.07
❑ 535 Craig Grebeck	.15	.07
❑ 536 Cal Eldred	.15	.07
❑ 537 Mickey Tettleton	.15	.07
❑ 538 Harold Baines	.30	.14
❑ 539 Tim Wallach	.15	.07
❑ 540 Damon Buford	.15	.07
❑ 541 Lenny Webster	.15	.07
❑ 542 Kevin Appier	.30	.14
❑ 543 Raul Mondesi	.40	.18
❑ 544 Eric Young	.15	.07
❑ 545 Russ Davis	.15	.07
❑ 546 Mike Benjamin	.15	.07
❑ 547 Mike Greenwell	.15	.07
❑ 548 Scott Brosius	.30	.14

❑ 549 Brian Dorsett	.15	.07
❑ 550 Chili Davis CL	.15	.07

1995 Donruss All-Stars

	MINT	NRMT
COMPLETE SET (18)	150.00	70.00
COMPLETE SERIES AL (9)	90.00	40.00
COMPLETE SERIES NL (9)	60.00	27.00
COMMON CARD (AL1-NL9)	1.50	.70
STATED ODDS 1:8 JUMBO		

❑ AL1 Jimmy Key	2.50	1.10
❑ AL2 Ivan Rodriguez	8.00	3.60
❑ AL3 Frank Thomas	12.00	5.50
❑ AL4 Roberto Alomar	6.00	2.70
❑ AL5 Wade Boggs	6.00	2.70
❑ AL6 Cal Ripken	25.00	11.00
❑ AL7 Joe Carter	2.50	1.10
❑ AL8 Ken Griffey Jr.	30.00	13.50
❑ AL9 Kirby Puckett	10.00	4.50
❑ NL1 Greg Maddux	15.00	6.75
❑ NL2 Mike Piazza	20.00	9.00
❑ NL3 Gregg Jefferies	1.50	.70
❑ NL4 Mariano Duncan	1.50	.70
❑ NL5 Matt Williams	6.00	2.70
❑ NL6 Ozzie Smith	8.00	3.60
❑ NL7 Barry Bonds	8.00	3.60
❑ NL8 Tony Gwynn	15.00	6.75
❑ NL9 David Justice	6.00	2.70

1995 Donruss Bomb Squad

	MINT	NRMT
COMPLETE SET (6)	15.00	6.75
COMMON CARD (1-6)	1.50	.70
SER.1 STATED ODDS 1:24 RET, 1:16 MAG		

❑ 1 Ken Griffey Matt Williams	8.00	3.60
❑ 2 Frank Thomas Jeff Bagwell	4.00	1.80
❑ 3 Albert Belle Barry Bonds	2.00	.90
❑ 4 Jose Canseco Fred McGriff	2.00	.90
❑ 5 Cecil Fielder Andres Galarraga	1.50	.70
❑ 6 Joe Carter Kevin Mitchell	1.50	.70

1995 Donruss Diamond Kings

	MINT	NRMT
COMPLETE SET (29)	50.00	22.00
COMPLETE SERIES 1 (14)	20.00	9.00
COMPLETE SERIES 2 (15)	30.00	13.50
COMMON CARD (DK1-DK29)	1.00	.45
STATED ODDS 1:10 H/R, 1:9 JUM, 1:10 MAG		

		MINT	NRMT
❑	DK1 Frank Thomas	5.00	2.20
❑	DK2 Jeff Bagwell	4.00	1.80
❑	DK3 Chili Davis	1.50	.70
❑	DK4 Dante Bichette	1.50	.70
❑	DK5 Ruben Sierra	1.00	.45
❑	DK6 Jeff Conine	1.00	.45
❑	DK7 Paul O'Neill	1.50	.70
❑	DK8 Bobby Bonilla	1.50	.70
❑	DK9 Joe Carter	1.50	.70
❑	DK10 Moises Alou	1.50	.70
❑	DK11 Kenny Lofton	2.00	.90
❑	DK12 Matt Williams	2.50	1.10
❑	DK13 Kevin Seitzer	1.00	.45
❑	DK14 Sammy Sosa	8.00	3.60
❑	DK15 Scott Cooper	1.00	.45
❑	DK16 Raul Mondesi	2.00	.90
❑	DK17 Will Clark	2.50	1.10
❑	DK18 Lenny Dykstra	1.50	.70
❑	DK19 Kirby Puckett	2.50	1.10
❑	DK20 Hal Morris	1.00	.45
❑	DK21 Travis Fryman	1.50	.70
❑	DK22 Greg Maddux	6.00	2.70
❑	DK23 Rafael Palmeiro	2.50	1.10
❑	DK24 Tony Gwynn	6.00	2.70
❑	DK25 David Cone	2.00	.90
❑	DK26 Al Martin	1.00	.45
❑	DK27 Ken Griffey Jr.	12.00	5.50
❑	DK28 Gregg Jefferies	1.00	.45
❑	DK29 Checklist	1.00	.45

1995 Donruss Dominators

	MINT	NRMT
COMPLETE SET (9)	25.00	11.00
COMMON CARD (1-9)	1.00	.45
SER.2 STATED ODDS 1:24 HOBBY		

		MINT	NRMT
❑	1 David Cone Mike Mussina	4.00	1.80

	Greg Maddux		
❑ 2	Ivan Rodriguez Mike Piazza Darren Daulton	5.00	2.20
❑ 3	Fred McGriff Frank Thomas Jeff Bagwell	3.00	1.35
❑ 4	Roberto Alomar Carlos Baerga Craig Biggio	1.00	.45
❑ 5	Robin Ventura Travis Fryman Matt Williams	1.00	.45
❑ 6	Cal Ripken Barry Larkin Wil Cordero	6.00	2.70
❑ 7	Albert Belle Barry Bonds Moises Alou	2.00	.90
❑ 8	Ken Griffey Kenny Lofton Marquis Grissom	8.00	3.60
❑ 9	Kirby Puckett Paul O'Neill Tony Gwynn	4.00	1.80

1995 Donruss Elite

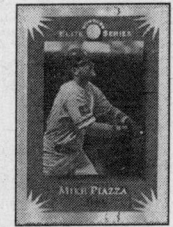

	MINT	NRMT
COMPLETE SET (12)	250.00	110.00
COMPLETE SERIES 1 (6)	150.00	70.00
COMPLETE SERIES 2 (6)	100.00	45.00
COMMON CARD (49-60)	6.00	2.70
SEMISTARS	8.00	3.60
UNLISTED STARS	12.00	5.50
SER.1 STAT.ODDS 1:210H/R, 1:120J, 1:210M		
SER. 2 STAT.ODDS 1:180H/R, 1:120J, 1:180M		
STATED PRINT RUN 10,000 SERIAL #'d SETS		

		MINT	NRMT
❑	49 Jeff Bagwell	15.00	6.75
❑	50 Paul O'Neill	6.00	2.70
❑	51 Greg Maddux	30.00	13.50
❑	52 Mike Piazza	40.00	18.00
❑	53 Matt Williams	12.00	5.50
❑	54 Ken Griffey	60.00	27.00
❑	55 Frank Thomas	25.00	11.00
❑	56 Barry Bonds	15.00	6.75
❑	57 Kirby Puckett	20.00	9.00
❑	58 Fred McGriff	8.00	3.60
❑	59 Jose Canseco	15.00	6.75
❑	60 Albert Belle	12.00	5.50

1995 Donruss Long Ball Leaders

	MINT	NRMT
COMPLETE SET (8)	20.00	9.00
COMMON CARD (1-8)	1.00	.45
SER.1 STATED ODDS 1:24 HOBBY		

		MINT	NRMT
❑	1 Frank Thomas	3.00	1.35
❑	2 Fred McGriff	1.00	.45
❑	3 Ken Griffey	8.00	3.60
❑	4 Matt Williams	1.50	.70
❑	5 Mike Piazza	5.00	2.20
❑	6 Jose Canseco	2.00	.90
❑	7 Barry Bonds	2.00	.90
❑	8 Jeff Bagwell	2.00	.90

1995 Donruss Mound Marvels

	MINT	NRMT
COMPLETE SET (8)	20.00	9.00
COMMON CARD (1-8)	1.00	.45
SER.2 STATED ODDS 1:16 RET/MAG		

		MINT	NRMT
❑	1 Greg Maddux	8.00	3.60
❑	2 David Cone	2.00	.90
❑	3 Mike Mussina	3.00	1.35
❑	4 Bret Saberhagen	1.50	.70
❑	5 Jimmy Key	1.50	.70
❑	6 Doug Drabek	1.00	.45
❑	7 Randy Johnson	3.00	1.35
❑	8 Jason Bere	1.00	.45

1996 Donruss

	MINT	NRMT
COMPLETE SET (550)	40.00	18.00
COMPLETE SERIES 1 (330)	25.00	11.00
COMPLETE SERIES 2 (220)	15.00	6.75
COMMON CARD (1-550)	.15	.07
MINOR STARS	.30	.14
UNLISTED STARS	.60	.25
SUBSET CARDS HALF VALUE OF BASE CARDS		
COMMON PP (1-550)	2.00	.90
*PP STARS: 6X TO 15X HI COLUMN		
*PP ROOKIES: 4X TO 10X HI		
PP SER.1 STATED ODDS 1:12		
PP SER.2 STATED ODDS 1:10		
PP STATED PRINT RUN 2000 SETS		

		MINT	NRMT
❑	1 Frank Thomas	1.25	.55
❑	2 Jason Bates	.15	.07
❑	3 Steve Sparks	.15	.07
❑	4 Scott Servais	.15	.07
❑	5 Angelo Encarnacion	.15	.07
❑	6 Scott Sanders	.15	.07
❑	7 Billy Ashley	.15	.07
❑	8 Alex Rodriguez	2.00	.90
❑	9 Sean Bergman	.15	.07
❑	10 Brad Radke	.30	.14
❑	11 Andy Van Slyke	.15	.07
❑	12 Joe Girard	.15	.07
❑	13 Mark Grudzielanek	.15	.07
❑	14 Rick Aguilera	.15	.07
❑	15 Randy Veres	.15	.07

16	Tim Bogar	.15	.07
17	Dave Veres	.15	.07
18	Kevin Stocker	.15	.07
19	Marquis Grissom	.15	.07
20	Will Clark	.60	.25
21	Jay Bell	.30	.14
22	Allen Battle	.15	.07
23	Frank Rodriguez	.15	.07
24	Terry Steinbach	.15	.07
25	Geronimo Pena	.15	.07
26	Sid Roberson	.15	.07
27	Greg Zaun	.15	.07
28	Ozzie Timmons	.15	.07
29	Vaughn Eshelman	.15	.07
30	Ed Sprague	.15	.07
31	Gary DiSarcina	.15	.07
32	Joe Boever	.15	.07
33	Steve Avery	.15	.07
34	Brad Ausmus	.15	.07
35	Kirt Manwaring	.15	.07
36	Gary Sheffield	.30	.14
37	Jason Bere	.15	.07
38	Jeff Manto	.15	.07
39	David Cone	.40	.18
40	Manny Ramirez	.75	.35
41	Sandy Alomar Jr.	.30	.14
42	Curtis Goodwin	.15	.07
43	Tino Martinez	.30	.14
44	Woody Williams	.15	.07
45	Dean Palmer	.30	.14
46	Hipolito Pichardo	.15	.07
47	Jason Giambi	.30	.14
48	Lance Johnson	.15	.07
49	Bernard Gilkey	.15	.07
50	Kirby Puckett	1.00	.45
51	Tony Fernandez	.15	.07
52	Alex Gonzalez	.15	.07
53	Bret Saberhagen	.30	.14
54	Lyle Mouton	.15	.07
55	Brian McRae	.15	.07
56	Mark Gubicza	.15	.07
57	Sergio Valdez	.15	.07
58	Darrin Fletcher	.15	.07
59	Steve Parris	.15	.07
60	Johnny Damon	.40	.18
61	Rickey Henderson	.75	.35
62	Darrell Whitmore	.15	.07
63	Roberto Petagine	.15	.07
64	Trenidad Hubbard	.15	.07
65	Heathcliff Slocumb	.15	.07
66	Steve Finley	.30	.14
67	Mariano Rivera	.40	.18
68	Brian L.Hunter	.15	.07
69	Jamie Moyer	.15	.07
70	Ellis Burks	.30	.14
71	Pat Kelly	.15	.07
72	Mickey Tettleton	.15	.07
73	Garret Anderson	.30	.14
74	Andy Pettitte	.40	.18
75	Glenallen Hill	.15	.07
76	Brent Gates	.15	.07
77	Lou Whitaker	.30	.14
78	David Segui	.30	.14
79	Dan Wilson	.15	.07
80	Pat Listach	.15	.07
81	Jeff Bagwell	.75	.35
82	Ben McDonald	.15	.07
83	John Valentin	.15	.07
84	John Jaha	.30	.14
85	Pete Schourek	.15	.07
86	Bryce Florie	.15	.07
87	Brian Jordan	.30	.14
88	Ron Karkovice	.15	.07
89	Al Leiter	.30	.14
90	Tony Longmire	.15	.07
91	Nelson Liriano	.15	.07
92	David Bell	.15	.07
93	Kevin Gross	.15	.07
94	Tom Candiotti	.15	.07
95	Dave Martinez	.15	.07
96	Greg Myers	.15	.07
97	Rheal Cormier	.15	.07
98	Chris Hammond	.15	.07
99	Randy Myers	.15	.07
100	Bill Pulsipher	.15	.07
101	Jason Isringhausen	.30	.14
102	Dave Stevens	.15	.07
103	Roberto Alomar	.60	.25
104	Bob Higginson	.30	.14
105	Eddie Murray	.60	.25
106	Matt Walbeck	.15	.07
107	Mark Wohlers	.15	.07
108	Jeff Nelson	.15	.07
109	Tom Goodwin	.15	.07
110	Cal Ripken CL	1.25	.55
111	Rey Sanchez	.15	.07
112	Hector Carrasco	.15	.07
113	B.J. Surhoff	.30	.14
114	Dan Miceli	.15	.07
115	Dean Hartgraves	.15	.07
116	John Burkett	.15	.07
117	Gary Gaetti	.30	.14
118	Ricky Bones	.15	.07
119	Mike Macfarlane	.15	.07
120	Bip Roberts	.15	.07
121	Dave Nilsson	.15	.07
122	Chili Davis	.30	.14
123	Mark Whiten	.15	.07
124	Herbert Perry	.15	.07
125	Butch Henry	.15	.07
126	Derek Bell	.30	.14
127	Al Martin	.15	.07
128	John Franco	.30	.14
129	W. VanLandingham	.15	.07
130	Mike Bordick	.15	.07
131	Mike Mordecai	.15	.07
132	Robby Thompson	.15	.07
133	Greg Colbrunn	.15	.07
134	Domingo Cedeno	.15	.07
135	Chad Curtis	.15	.07
136	Jose Hernandez	.15	.07
137	Scott Klingenbeck	.15	.07
138	Ryan Klesko	.30	.14
139	John Smiley	.15	.07
140	Charlie Hayes	.15	.07
141	Jay Buhner	.30	.14
142	Doug Drabek	.15	.07
143	Roger Pavlik	.15	.07
144	Todd Worrell	.15	.07
145	Cal Ripken	2.50	1.10
146	Steve Reed	.15	.07
147	Chuck Finley	.30	.14
148	Mike Blowers	.15	.07
149	Orel Hershiser	.30	.14
150	Allen Watson	.15	.07
151	Ramon Martinez	.30	.14
152	Melvin Nieves	.15	.07
153	Tripp Cromer	.15	.07
154	Yorkis Perez	.15	.07
155	Stan Javier	.15	.07
156	Mel Rojas	.15	.07
157	Aaron Sele	.30	.14
158	Eric Karros	.30	.14
159	Robb Nen	.15	.07
160	Raul Mondesi	.30	.14
161	John Wetteland	.30	.14
162	Tim Scott	.15	.07
163	Kenny Rogers	.15	.07
164	Melvin Bunch	.15	.07
165	Rod Beck	.15	.07
166	Andy Benes	.15	.07
167	Lenny Dykstra	.30	.14
168	Orlando Merced	.15	.07
169	Tomas Perez	.15	.07
170	Xavier Hernandez	.15	.07
171	Ruben Sierra	.30	.14
172	Alan Trammell	.40	.18
173	Mike Fetters	.15	.07
174	Wilson Alvarez	.15	.07
175	Erik Hanson	.15	.07
176	Travis Fryman	.30	.14
177	Jim Abbott	.30	.14
178	Bret Boone	.30	.14
179	Sterling Hitchcock	.15	.07
180	Pat Mahomes	.15	.07
181	Mark Acre	.15	.07
182	Charles Nagy	.30	.14
183	Rusty Greer	.30	.14
184	Mike Stanley	.15	.07
185	Jim Bullinger	.15	.07
186	Shane Andrews	.15	.07
187	Brian Keyser	.15	.07
188	Tyler Green	.15	.07
189	Mark Grace	.40	.18
190	Bob Hamelin	.15	.07
191	Luis Ortiz	.15	.07
192	Joe Carter	.30	.14
193	Eddie Taubensee	.15	.07
194	Brian Anderson	.15	.07
195	Edgardo Alfonzo	.60	.25
196	Pedro Munoz	.15	.07
197	David Justice	.30	.14
198	Trevor Hoffman	.30	.14
199	Bobby Ayala	.15	.07
200	Tony Eusebio	.15	.07
201	Jeff Russell	.15	.07
202	Mike Hampton	.30	.14
203	Walt Weiss	.15	.07
204	Joey Hamilton	.15	.07
205	Roberto Hernandez	.15	.07
206	Greg Vaughn	.30	.14
207	Felipe Lira	.15	.07
208	Harold Baines	.30	.14
209	Tim Wallach	.15	.07
210	Manny Alexander	.15	.07
211	Tim Laker	.15	.07
212	Chris Haney	.15	.07
213	Brian Maxcy	.15	.07
214	Eric Young	.15	.07
215	Darryl Strawberry	.30	.14
216	Barry Bonds	.75	.35
217	Tim Naehring	.15	.07
218	Scott Brosius	.30	.14
219	Reggie Sanders	.30	.14
220	Eddie Murray CL	.30	.14
221	Luis Alicea	.15	.07
222	Albert Belle	.60	.25
223	Benji Gil	.15	.07
224	Dante Bichette	.30	.14
225	Bobby Bonilla	.30	.14
226	Todd Stottlemyre	.15	.07
227	Jim Edmonds	.30	.14
228	Todd Jones	.15	.07
229	Shawn Green	.60	.25
230	Javier Lopez	.30	.14
231	Ariel Prieto	.15	.07
232	Tony Phillips	.15	.07
233	James Mouton	.15	.07
234	Jose Oquendo	.15	.07
235	Royce Clayton	.15	.07
236	Chuck Carr	.15	.07
237	Doug Jones	.15	.07
238	Mark McLemore	.15	.07
239	Bill Swift	.15	.07
240	Scott Leius	.15	.07
241	Russ Davis	.15	.07
242	Ray Durham	.30	.14
243	Matt Mieske	.15	.07
244	Brent Mayne	.15	.07
245	Thomas Howard	.15	.07
246	Troy O'Leary	.30	.14
247	Jacob Brumfield	.15	.07
248	Mickey Morandini	.15	.07
249	Todd Hundley	.30	.14
250	Chris Bosio	.15	.07
251	Omar Vizquel	.30	.14
252	Mike Lansing	.15	.07
253	John Mabry	.15	.07
254	Mike Perez	.15	.07
255	Delino DeShields	.15	.07
256	Wil Cordero	.15	.07
257	Mike James	.15	.07
258	Todd Van Poppel	.15	.07
259	Joey Cora	.15	.07
260	Andre Dawson	.40	.18
261	Jerry DiPoto	.15	.07
262	Rick Krivda	.15	.07
263	Glenn Dishman	.15	.07
264	Mike Mimbs	.15	.07
265	John Ericks	.15	.07
266	Jose Canseco	.75	.35
267	Jeff Branson	.15	.07
268	Curt Leskanic	.15	.07
269	Jon Nunnally	.15	.07
270	Scott Stahoviak	.15	.07
271	Jeff Montgomery	.15	.07
272	Hal Morris	.15	.07
273	Esteban Loaiza	.15	.07

274	Rico Brogna	.15	.07
275	Dave Winfield	.60	.25
276	J.R. Phillips	.15	.07
277	Todd Zeile	.15	.07
278	Tom Pagnozzi	.15	.07
279	Mark Lemke	.15	.07
280	Dave Magadan	.15	.07
281	Greg McMichael	.15	.07
282	Mike Morgan	.15	.07
283	Moises Alou	.30	.14
284	Dennis Martinez	.30	.14
285	Jeff Kent	.30	.14
286	Mark Johnson	.15	.07
287	Darren Lewis	.15	.07
288	Brad Clontz	.15	.07
289	Chad Fonville	.15	.07
290	Paul Sorrento	.15	.07
291	Lee Smith	.30	.14
292	Tom Glavine	.60	.25
293	Antonio Osuna	.15	.07
294	Kevin Foster	.15	.07
295	Sandy Martinez	.15	.07
296	Mark Leiter	.15	.07
297	Julian Tavarez	.15	.07
298	Mike Kelly	.15	.07
299	Joe Oliver	.15	.07
300	John Flaherty	.15	.07
301	Don Mattingly	1.25	.55
302	Pat Meares	.15	.07
303	John Doherty	.15	.07
304	Joe Vitiello	.15	.07
305	Vinny Castilla	.30	.14
306	Jeff Brantley	.15	.07
307	Mike Greenwell	.15	.07
308	Midre Cummings	.15	.07
309	Curt Schilling	.40	.18
310	Ken Caminiti	.30	.14
311	Scott Erickson	.30	.14
312	Carl Everett	.30	.14
313	Charles Johnson	.30	.14
314	Alex Diaz	.15	.07
315	Jose Mesa	.15	.07
316	Mark Carreon	.15	.07
317	Carlos Perez	.15	.07
318	Ismael Valdes	.30	.14
319	Frank Castillo	.15	.07
320	Tom Henke	.15	.07
321	Spike Owen	.15	.07
322	Joe Orsulak	.15	.07
323	Paul Menhart	.15	.07
324	Pedro Borbon	.15	.07
325	Paul Molitor CL	.30	.14
326	Jeff Cirillo	.30	.14
327	Edwin Hurtado	.15	.07
328	Orlando Miller	.15	.07
329	Steve Ontiveros	.15	.07
330	Kirby Puckett CL	.60	.25
331	Scott Bullett	.15	.07
332	Andres Galarraga	.60	.25
333	Cal Eldred	.15	.07
334	Sammy Sosa	2.00	.90
335	Don Slaught	.15	.07
336	Jody Reed	.15	.07
337	Roger Cedeno	.30	.14
338	Ken Griffey Jr.	3.00	1.35
339	Todd Hollandsworth	.15	.07
340	Mike Trombley	.15	.07
341	Gregg Jefferies	.15	.07
342	Larry Walker	.60	.25
343	Pedro Martinez	.75	.35
344	Dwayne Hosey	.15	.07
345	Terry Pendleton	.15	.07
346	Pete Harnisch	.15	.07
347	Tony Castillo	.15	.07
348	Paul Quantrill	.15	.07
349	Fred McGriff	.40	.18
350	Ivan Rodriguez	.75	.35
351	Butch Huskey	.15	.07
352	Ozzie Smith	.75	.35
353	Marty Cordova	.15	.07
354	John Wasdin	.15	.07
355	Wade Boggs	.60	.25
356	Dave Nilsson	.15	.07
357	Rafael Palmeiro	.60	.25
358	Luis Gonzalez	.30	.14
359	Reggie Jefferson	.15	.07
360	Carlos Delgado	.60	.25
361	Orlando Palmeiro	.15	.07
362	Chris Gomez	.15	.07
363	John Smoltz	.40	.18
364	Marc Newfield	.15	.07
365	Matt Williams	.60	.25
366	Jesus Tavarez	.15	.07
367	Bruce Ruffin	.15	.07
368	Sean Berry	.15	.07
369	Randy Velarde	.15	.07
370	Tony Pena	.15	.07
371	Jim Thome	.60	.25
372	Jeffrey Hammonds	.30	.14
373	Bob Wolcott	.15	.07
374	Juan Guzman	.15	.07
375	Juan Gonzalez	1.25	.55
376	Michael Tucker	.15	.07
377	Doug Johns	.15	.07
378	Mike Cameron	1.00	.45
379	Ray Lankford	.30	.14
380	Jose Parra	.15	.07
381	Jimmy Key	.30	.14
382	John Olerud	.30	.14
383	Kevin Ritz	.15	.07
384	Tim Raines	.30	.14
385	Rich Amaral	.15	.07
386	Keith Lockhart	.15	.07
387	Steve Scarsone	.15	.07
388	Cliff Floyd	.30	.14
389	Rich Aude	.15	.07
390	Hideo Nomo	.60	.25
391	Geronimo Berroa	.15	.07
392	Pat Rapp	.15	.07
393	Dustin Hermanson	.15	.07
394	Greg Maddux	1.50	.70
395	Darren Daulton	.30	.14
396	Kenny Lofton	.40	.18
397	Ruben Rivera	.30	.14
398	Billy Wagner	.40	.18
399	Kevin Brown	.15	.07
400	Mike Kingery	.15	.07
401	Bernie Williams	.60	.25
402	Otis Nixon	.15	.07
403	Damion Easley	.30	.14
404	Paul O'Neill	.30	.14
405	Deion Sanders	.30	.14
406	Dennis Eckersley	.30	.14
407	Tony Clark	.60	.25
408	Rondell White	.30	.14
409	Luis Sojo	.15	.07
410	David Hulse	.15	.07
411	Shane Reynolds	.30	.14
412	Chris Hoiles	.15	.07
413	Lee Tinsley	.15	.07
414	Scott Karl	.15	.07
415	Ron Gant	.15	.07
416	Brian Johnson	.15	.07
417	Jose Oliva	.15	.07
418	Jack McDowell	.15	.07
419	Paul Molitor	.60	.25
420	Ricky Bottalico	.15	.07
421	Paul Wagner	.15	.07
422	Terry Bradshaw	.15	.07
423	Bob Tewksbury	.15	.07
424	Mike Piazza	2.00	.90
425	Luis Andujar	.15	.07
426	Mark Langston	.15	.07
427	Stan Belinda	.15	.07
428	Kurt Abbott	.15	.07
429	Shawon Dunston	.15	.07
430	Bobby Jones	.15	.07
431	Jose Vizcaino	.15	.07
432	Matt Lawton	.75	.35
433	Pat Hentgen	.30	.14
434	Cecil Fielder	.30	.14
435	Carlos Baerga	.15	.07
436	Rich Becker	.15	.07
437	Chipper Jones	1.50	.70
438	Bill Risley	.15	.07
439	Kevin Appier	.30	.14
440	Wade Boggs CL	.30	.14
441	Jaime Navarro	.15	.07
442	Barry Larkin	.60	.25
443	Jose Valentin	.15	.07
444	Bryan Rekar	.15	.07
445	Rick Wilkins	.15	.07
446	Quilvio Veras	.15	.07
447	Greg Gagne	.15	.07
448	Mark Kiefer	.15	.07
449	Bobby Witt	.15	.07
450	Andy Ashby	.15	.07
451	Alex Ochoa	.15	.07
452	Jorge Fabregas	.15	.07
453	Gene Schall	.15	.07
454	Ken Hill	.15	.07
455	Tony Tarasco	.15	.07
456	Donnie Wall	.15	.07
457	Carlos Garcia	.15	.07
458	Ryan Thompson	.15	.07
459	Marvin Benard	.15	.07
460	Jose Herrera	.15	.07
461	Jeff Blauser	.15	.07
462	Chris Hook	.15	.07
463	Jeff Conine	.15	.07
464	Devon White	.30	.14
465	Danny Bautista	.15	.07
466	Steve Trachsel	.15	.07
467	C.J. Nitkowski	.15	.07
468	Mike Devereaux	.15	.07
469	David Wells	.40	.18
470	Jim Eisenreich	.15	.07
471	Edgar Martinez	.30	.14
472	Craig Biggio	.60	.25
473	Jeff Frye	.15	.07
474	Karim Garcia	.30	.14
475	Jimmy Haynes	.15	.07
476	Darren Holmes	.15	.07
477	Tim Salmon	.40	.18
478	Randy Johnson	.60	.25
479	Eric Plunk	.15	.07
480	Scott Cooper	.15	.07
481	Chan Ho Park	.40	.18
482	Ray McDavid	.15	.07
483	Mark Petkovsek	.15	.07
484	Greg Swindell	.15	.07
485	George Williams	.15	.07
486	Yamil Benitez	.15	.07
487	Tim Wakefield	.15	.07
488	Kevin Tapani	.15	.07
489	Derrick May	.15	.07
490	Ken Griffey Jr. CL	1.50	.70
491	Derek Jeter	2.00	.90
492	Jeff Fassero	.15	.07
493	Benito Santiago	.15	.07
494	Tom Gordon	.15	.07
495	Jamie Brewington	.15	.07
496	Vince Coleman	.15	.07
497	Kevin Jordan	.15	.07
498	Jeff King	.15	.07
499	Mike Simms	.15	.07
500	Jose Pijio	.15	.07
501	Denny Neagle	.30	.14
502	Jose Lima	.40	.18
503	Kevin Seitzer	.15	.07
504	Alex Fernandez	.15	.07
505	Mo Vaughn	.60	.25
506	Phil Nevin	.15	.07
507	J.T. Snow	.30	.14
508	Andujar Cedeno	.15	.07
509	Ozzie Guillen	.15	.07
510	Mark Clark	.15	.07
511	Mark McGwire	3.00	1.35
512	Jeff Reboulet	.15	.07
513	Armando Benitez	.15	.07
514	LaTroy Hawkins	.15	.07
515	Brett Butler	.30	.14
516	Tavo Alvarez	.15	.07
517	Chris Snopek	.15	.07
518	Mike Mussina	.60	.25
519	Darryl Kile	.15	.07
520	Wally Joyner	.30	.14
521	Willie McGee	.30	.14
522	Kent Mercker	.15	.07
523	Mike Jackson	.30	.14
524	Troy Percival	.30	.14
525	Tony Gwynn	1.50	.70
526	Ron Coomer	.15	.07
527	Darryl Hamilton	.15	.07
528	Phil Plantier	.15	.07
529	Norm Charlton	.15	.07
530	Craig Paquette	.15	.07
531	Dave Burba	.15	.07

		MINT	NRMT
☐ 532	Mike Henneman	.15	.07
☐ 533	Terrell Wade	.15	.07
☐ 534	Eddie Williams	.15	.07
☐ 535	Robin Ventura	.30	.14
☐ 536	Chuck Knoblauch	.60	.25
☐ 537	Les Norman	.15	.07
☐ 538	Brady Anderson	.30	.14
☐ 539	Roger Clemens	1.50	.70
☐ 540	Mark Portugal	.15	.07
☐ 541	Mike Matheny	.15	.07
☐ 542	Jeff Parrett	.15	.07
☐ 543	Roberto Kelly	.15	.07
☐ 544	Damon Buford	.15	.07
☐ 545	Chad Ogea	.15	.07
☐ 546	Jose Offerman	.30	.14
☐ 547	Brian Barber	.15	.07
☐ 548	Danny Tartabull	.15	.07
☐ 549	Duane Singleton	.15	.07
☐ 550	Tony Gwynn CL	.75	.35

1996 Donruss Diamond Kings

Juan Gonzalez

	MINT	NRMT
COMPLETE SET (31)	200.00	90.00
COMPLETE SERIES 1 (14)	100.00	45.00
COMPLETE SERIES 2 (17)	100.00	45.00
COMMON CARD (1-31)	3.00	1.35
SEMISTARS	5.00	2.20
UNLISTED STARS	8.00	3.60
SER.1 STATED ODDS 1:60		
SER.2 STATED ODDS 1:30		
STATED PRINT RUN 10,000 SERIAL #'d SETS		

		MINT	NRMT
☐ 1	Frank Thomas	15.00	6.75
☐ 2	Mo Vaughn	8.00	3.60
☐ 3	Manny Ramirez	10.00	4.50
☐ 4	Mark McGwire	40.00	18.00
☐ 5	Juan Gonzalez	15.00	6.75
☐ 6	Roberto Alomar	8.00	3.60
☐ 7	Tim Salmon	5.00	2.20
☐ 8	Barry Bonds	10.00	4.50
☐ 9	Tony Gwynn	20.00	9.00
☐ 10	Reggie Sanders	5.00	2.20
☐ 11	Larry Walker	8.00	3.60
☐ 12	Pedro Martinez	10.00	4.50
☐ 13	Jeff King	3.00	1.35
☐ 14	Mark Grace	5.00	2.20
☐ 15	Greg Maddux	20.00	9.00
☐ 16	Don Mattingly	15.00	6.75
☐ 17	Gregg Jefferies	3.00	1.35
☐ 18	Chad Curtis	3.00	1.35
☐ 19	Jason Isringhausen	5.00	2.20
☐ 20	B.J. Surhoff	3.00	1.35
☐ 21	Jeff Conine	5.00	2.20
☐ 22	Kirby Puckett	12.00	5.50
☐ 23	Derek Bell	5.00	2.20
☐ 24	Wally Joyner	5.00	2.20
☐ 25	Brian Jordan	5.00	2.20
☐ 26	Edgar Martinez	5.00	2.20
☐ 27	Hideo Nomo	8.00	3.60
☐ 28	Mike Mussina	8.00	3.60
☐ 29	Eddie Murray	8.00	3.60
☐ 30	Cal Ripken	30.00	13.50
☐ 31	Checklist	3.00	1.35

1996 Donruss Elite

	MINT	NRMT
COMPLETE SET (12)	200.00	90.00
COMPLETE SERIES 1 (6)	100.00	45.00
COMPLETE SERIES 2 (6)	100.00	45.00
COMMON CARD (61-72)	5.00	2.20
UNLISTED STARS	10.00	4.50
SER.1 STATED ODDS 1:140		
SER.2 STATED ODDS 1:75		
STATED PRINT RUN 10,000 SERIAL #'d SETS		

		MINT	NRMT
☐ 61	Cal Ripken	40.00	18.00
☐ 62	Hideo Nomo	10.00	4.50
☐ 63	Reggie Sanders	5.00	2.20
☐ 64	Mo Vaughn	10.00	4.50
☐ 65	Tim Salmon	5.00	2.20
☐ 66	Chipper Jones	25.00	11.00
☐ 67	Manny Ramirez	12.00	5.50
☐ 68	Greg Maddux	20.00	9.00
☐ 69	Frank Thomas	15.00	6.75
☐ 70	Ken Griffey Jr.	40.00	18.00
☐ 71	Dante Bichette	8.00	3.60
☐ 72	Tony Gwynn	20.00	9.00

1996 Donruss Freeze Frame

Nomar: Ken Griffey, Jr.

	MINT	NRMT
COMPLETE SET (8)	150.00	70.00
COMMON CARD (1-8)	10.00	4.50
SER.2 STATED ODDS 1:60		
STATED PRINT RUN 5000 SERIAL #'d SETS		

		MINT	NRMT
☐ 1	Frank Thomas	20.00	9.00
☐ 2	Ken Griffey Jr.	40.00	18.00
☐ 3	Cal Ripken	30.00	13.50
☐ 4	Hideo Nomo	10.00	4.50
☐ 5	Greg Maddux	25.00	11.00
☐ 6	Albert Belle	10.00	4.50
☐ 7	Chipper Jones	20.00	9.00
☐ 8	Mike Piazza	25.00	11.00

1996 Donruss Hit List

	MINT	NRMT
COMPLETE SET (16)	100.00	45.00
COMPLETE SERIES 1 (8)	60.00	27.00
COMPLETE SERIES 2 (8)	40.00	18.00
COMMON CARD (1-16)	2.50	1.10

SER.1 STATED ODDS 1:105		
SER.2 STATED ODDS 1:60		
STATED PRINT RUN 10,000 SERIAL #'d SETS		

		MINT	NRMT
☐ 1	Tony Gwynn	12.00	5.50
☐ 2	Ken Griffey Jr.	25.00	11.00
☐ 3	Will Clark	5.00	2.20
☐ 4	Mike Piazza	15.00	6.75
☐ 5	Carlos Baerga	2.50	1.10
☐ 6	Mo Vaughn	5.00	2.20
☐ 7	Mark Grace	3.00	1.35
☐ 8	Kirby Puckett	8.00	3.60
☐ 9	Frank Thomas	12.00	5.50
☐ 10	Barry Bonds	5.00	2.20
☐ 11	Jeff Bagwell	6.00	2.70
☐ 12	Edgar Martinez	2.50	1.10
☐ 13	Tim Salmon	3.00	1.35
☐ 14	Wade Boggs	5.00	2.20
☐ 15	Don Mattingly	8.00	3.60
☐ 16	Eddie Murray	5.00	2.20

1996 Donruss Long Ball Leaders

	MINT	NRMT
COMPLETE SET (8)	120.00	55.00
COMMON CARD (1-8)	4.00	1.80
SER.1 STATED ODDS 1:96 RETAIL		
STATED PRINT RUN 5000 SERIAL #'d SETS		

		MINT	NRMT
☐ 1	Barry Bonds	10.00	4.50
☐ 2	Ryan Klesko	6.00	2.70
☐ 3	Mark McGwire	50.00	22.00
☐ 4	Raul Mondesi	6.00	2.70
☐ 5	Cecil Fielder	4.00	1.80
☐ 6	Ken Griffey Jr.	50.00	22.00
☐ 7	Larry Walker	10.00	4.50
☐ 8	Frank Thomas	25.00	11.00

1996 Donruss Power Alley

	MINT	NRMT
COMPLETE SET (10)	120.00	55.00
COMMON CARD (1-10)	4.00	1.80
SEMISTARS	6.00	2.70
UNLISTED STARS	10.00	4.50
SER.1 STATED ODDS 1:92 HOBBY		
STATED PRINT RUN 4500 SERIAL #'d SETS		
COMP.DIE CUT SET (10)	400.00	180.00

*DIE CUTS: 1.25X TO 3X HI COLUMN
SER.1 DC STATED ODDS 1:920 HOBBY
DC STATED PRINT RUN 500 SERIAL #'d SETS

❏ 1 Frank Thomas	20.00	9.00
❏ 2 Barry Bonds	12.00	5.50
❏ 3 Reggie Sanders	5.00	2.20
❏ 4 Albert Belle	10.00	4.50
❏ 5 Tim Salmon	6.00	2.70
❏ 6 Dante Bichette	5.00	2.20
❏ 7 Mo Vaughn	10.00	4.50
❏ 8 Jim Edmonds	6.00	2.70
❏ 9 Manny Ramirez	12.00	5.50
❏ 10 Ken Griffey Jr.	50.00	22.00

1996 Donruss Pure Power

	MINT	NRMT
COMPLETE SET (8)	120.00	55.00
COMMON CARD (1-8)	6.00	2.70

RANDOM INSERTS IN SER.2 RETAIL PACKS
STATED PRINT RUN 5000 SETS

❏ 1 Raul Mondesi	6.00	2.70
❏ 2 Barry Bonds	10.00	4.50
❏ 3 Albert Belle	10.00	4.50
❏ 4 Frank Thomas	25.00	11.00
❏ 5 Mike Piazza	30.00	13.50
❏ 6 Dante Bichette	6.00	2.70
❏ 7 Manny Ramirez	10.00	4.50
❏ 8 Mo Vaughn	10.00	4.50

1996 Donruss Round Trippers

	MINT	NRMT
COMPLETE SET (10)	150.00	70.00
COMMON CARD (1-10)	5.0	2.20

SER.2 STATED ODDS 1:55 HOBBY
STATED PRINT RUN 5000 SERIAL #'d SETS

❏ 1 Albert Belle	8.00	3.60
❏ 2 Barry Bonds	8.00	3.60
❏ 3 Jeff Bagwell	10.00	4.50
❏ 4 Tim Salmon	6.00	2.70
❏ 5 Mo Vaughn	8.00	3.60
❏ 6 Ken Griffey Jr.	40.00	18.00
❏ 7 Mike Piazza	25.00	11.00
❏ 8 Cal Ripken	30.00	13.50
❏ 9 Frank Thomas	20.00	9.00
❏ 10 Dante Bichette	5.00	2.20

1996 Donruss Showdown

	MINT	NRMT
COMPLETE SET (8)	100.00	45.00
COMMON CARD (1-8)	3.00	1.35

SER.1 STATED ODDS 1:105
STATED PRINT RUN 10,000 SERIAL #'d SETS

❏ 1 Frank Thomas Hideo Nomo	12.00	5.50
❏ 2 Barry Bonds Randy Johnson	8.00	3.60
❏ 3 Greg Maddux Ken Griffey Jr.	25.00	11.00
❏ 4 Roger Clemens Tony Gwynn	20.00	9.00
❏ 5 Mike Piazza Mike Mussina	20.00	9.00
❏ 6 Cal Ripken Pedro J.Martinez	25.00	11.00
❏ 7 Tim Wakefield Matt Williams	3.00	1.35
❏ 8 Manny Ramirez Carlos Perez	8.00	3.60

1997 Donruss

	MINT	NRMT
COMPLETE SET (450)	45.00	20.00
COMPLETE SERIES 1 (270)	25.00	11.00
COMPLETE UPDATE (180)	20.00	9.00
COMMON CARD (1-450)	.15	.07
MINOR STARS	.30	.14
UNLISTED STARS	.60	.25

SUBSET CARDS HALF VALUE OF BASE CARDS

❏ 1 Juan Gonzalez	1.25	.55
❏ 2 Jim Edmonds	.40	.18
❏ 3 Tony Gwynn	1.50	.70
❏ 4 Andres Galarraga	.60	.25
❏ 5 Joe Carter	.30	.14
❏ 6 Raul Mondesi	.30	.14
❏ 7 Greg Maddux	1.50	.70
❏ 8 Travis Fryman	.30	.14
❏ 9 Brian Jordan	.30	.14
❏ 10 Henry Rodriguez	.30	.14
❏ 11 Manny Ramirez	.75	.35
❏ 12 Mark McGwire	3.00	1.35
❏ 13 Marc Newfield	.15	.07
❏ 14 Craig Biggio	.60	.25
❏ 15 Sammy Sosa	2.00	.90
❏ 16 Brady Anderson	.30	.14
❏ 17 Wade Boggs	.60	.25
❏ 18 Charles Johnson	.30	.14
❏ 19 Matt Williams	.60	.25
❏ 20 Denny Neagle	.30	.14
❏ 21 Ken Griffey Jr.	3.00	1.35
❏ 22 Robin Ventura	.30	.14
❏ 23 Barry Larkin	.60	.25
❏ 24 Todd Zeile	.15	.07
❏ 25 Chuck Knoblauch	.60	.25
❏ 26 Todd Hundley	.30	.14
❏ 27 Roger Clemens	1.50	.70
❏ 28 Michael Tucker	.15	.07
❏ 29 Rondell White	.30	.14
❏ 30 Osvaldo Fernandez	.15	.07
❏ 31 Ivan Rodriguez	.75	.35
❏ 32 Alex Fernandez	.15	.07
❏ 33 Jason Isringhausen	.15	.07
❏ 34 Chipper Jones	1.50	.70
❏ 35 Paul O'Neill	.30	.14
❏ 36 Hideo Nomo	.60	.25
❏ 37 Roberto Alomar	.60	.25
❏ 38 Derek Bell	.30	.14
❏ 39 Paul Molitor	.60	.25
❏ 40 Andy Benes	.30	.14
❏ 41 Steve Trachsel	.15	.07
❏ 42 J.T. Snow	.30	.14
❏ 43 Jason Kendall	.40	.18
❏ 44 Alex Rodriguez	2.00	.90
❏ 45 Joey Hamilton	.30	.14
❏ 46 Carlos Delgado	.60	.25
❏ 47 Jason Giambi	.30	.14
❏ 48 Larry Walker	.60	.25
❏ 49 Derek Jeter	2.00	.90
❏ 50 Kenny Lofton	.40	.18
❏ 51 Devon White	.30	.14
❏ 53 Matt Mieske	.15	.07
❏ 54 Jose Canseco	.75	.35
❏ 55 Tino Martinez	.60	.25
❏ 56 Rafael Palmeiro	.60	.25
❏ 57 Edgardo Alfonzo	.40	.18
❏ 58 Jay Buhner	.30	.14
❏ 59 Shane Reynolds	.30	.14
❏ 60 Steve Finley	.30	.14
❏ 61 Bobby Higginson	.30	.14
❏ 62 Dean Palmer	.30	.14
❏ 63 Terry Pendleton	.15	.07
❏ 64 Marquis Grissom	.30	.14
❏ 65 Mike Stanley	.15	.07
❏ 66 Moises Alou	.30	.14
❏ 67 Ray Lankford	.30	.14
❏ 68 Marty Cordova	.15	.07
❏ 69 John Olerud	.30	.14
❏ 70 David Cone	.40	.18
❏ 71 Benito Santiago	.15	.07
❏ 72 Ryne Sandberg	.75	.35
❏ 73 Rickey Henderson	.75	.35
❏ 74 Roger Cedeno	.30	.14
❏ 75 Wilson Alvarez	.30	.14
❏ 76 Tim Salmon	.60	.25
❏ 77 Orlando Merced	.15	.07
❏ 78 Vinny Castilla	.40	.18
❏ 79 Ismael Valdes	.30	.14
❏ 80 Dante Bichette	.30	.14
❏ 81 Kevin Brown	.40	.18

82	Andy Pettitte	.40	.18
83	Scott Stahoviak	.15	.07
84	Mickey Tettleton	.15	.07
85	Jack McDowell	.15	.07
86	Tom Glavine	.60	.25
87	Gregg Jefferies	.15	.07
88	Chili Davis	.30	.14
89	Randy Johnson	.60	.25
90	John Mabry	.15	.07
91	Billy Wagner	.30	.14
92	Jeff Cirillo	.30	.14
93	Trevor Hoffman	.30	.14
94	Juan Guzman	.15	.07
95	Geronimo Berroa	.15	.07
96	Bernard Gilkey	.15	.07
97	Danny Tartabull	.15	.07
98	Johnny Damon	.30	.14
99	Charlie Hayes	.15	.07
100	Reggie Sanders	.30	.14
101	Robby Thompson	.15	.07
102	Bobby Bonilla	.30	.14
103	Reggie Jefferson	.15	.07
104	John Smoltz	.40	.18
105	Jim Thome	.60	.25
106	Ruben Rivera	.15	.07
107	Darren Oliver	.15	.07
108	Mo Vaughn	.60	.25
109	Roger Pavlik	.15	.07
110	Terry Steinbach	.15	.07
111	Jermaine Dye	.30	.14
112	Mark Grudzielanek	.30	.14
113	Rick Aguilera	.15	.07
114	Jamey Wright	.15	.07
115	Eddie Murray	.60	.25
116	Brian L. Hunter	.30	.14
117	Hal Morris	.15	.07
118	Tom Pagnozzi	.15	.07
119	Mike Mussina	.60	.25
120	Mark Grace	.40	.18
121	Cal Ripken	2.50	1.10
122	Tom Goodwin	.15	.07
123	Paul Sorrento	.15	.07
124	Jay Bell	.30	.14
125	Todd Hollandsworth	.15	.07
126	Edgar Martinez	.30	.14
127	George Arias	.15	.07
128	Greg Vaughn	.30	.14
129	Roberto Hernandez	.15	.07
130	Delino DeShields	.15	.07
131	Bill Pulsipher	.15	.07
132	Joey Cora	.15	.07
133	Mariano Rivera	.30	.14
134	Mike Piazza	2.00	.90
135	Carlos Baerga	.15	.07
136	Jose Mesa	.15	.07
137	Will Clark	.60	.25
138	Frank Thomas	1.25	.55
139	John Wetteland	.15	.07
140	Shawn Estes	.30	.14
141	Garret Anderson	.30	.14
142	Andre Dawson	.40	.18
143	Eddie Taubensee	.15	.07
144	Ryan Klesko	.30	.14
145	Rocky Coppinger	.15	.07
146	Jeff Bagwell	.75	.35
147	Donovan Osborne	.15	.07
148	Greg Myers	.15	.07
149	Brant Brown	.30	.14
150	Kevin Elster	.15	.07
151	Bob Wells	.15	.07
152	Wally Joyner	.30	.14
153	Rico Brogna	.15	.07
154	Dwight Gooden	.30	.14
155	Jermaine Allensworth	.15	.07
156	Ray Durham	.30	.14
157	Cecil Fielder	.30	.14
158	John Burkett	.15	.07
159	Gary Sheffield	.30	.14
160	Albert Belle	.60	.25
161	Tomas Perez	.15	.07
162	David Doster	.15	.07
163	John Valentin	.30	.14
164	Danny Graves	.15	.07
165	Jose Paniagua	.15	.07
166	Brian Giles	2.00	.90
167	Barry Bonds	.75	.35
168	Sterling Hitchcock	.30	.14
169	Bernie Williams	.60	.25
170	Fred McGriff	.40	.18
171	George Williams	.15	.07
172	Amaury Telemaco	.15	.07
173	Ken Caminiti	.40	.18
174	Ron Gant	.30	.14
175	Dave Justice	.60	.25
176	James Baldwin	.30	.14
177	Pat Hentgen	.30	.14
178	Ben McDonald	.15	.07
179	Tim Naehring	.15	.07
180	Jim Eisenreich	.15	.07
181	Ken Hill	.15	.07
182	Paul Wilson	.15	.07
183	Marvin Benard	.15	.07
184	Alan Benes	.15	.07
185	Ellis Burks	.30	.14
186	Scott Servais	.15	.07
187	David Segui	.30	.14
188	Scott Brosius	.15	.07
189	Jose Offerman	.15	.07
190	Eric Davis	.30	.14
191	Brett Butler	.30	.14
192	Curtis Pride	.15	.07
193	Yamil Benitez	.15	.07
194	Chan Ho Park	.60	.25
195	Bret Boone	.30	.14
196	Omar Vizquel	.30	.14
197	Orlando Miller	.15	.07
198	Ramon Martinez	.30	.14
199	Harold Baines	.30	.14
200	Eric Young	.30	.14
201	Fernando Vina	.15	.07
202	Alex Gonzalez	.15	.07
203	Fernando Valenzuela	.30	.14
204	Steve Avery	.15	.07
205	Ernie Young	.30	.14
206	Kevin Appier	.30	.14
207	Randy Myers	.15	.07
208	Jeff Suppan	.15	.07
209	James Mouton	.15	.07
210	Russ Davis	.15	.07
211	Al Martin	.15	.07
212	Troy Percival	.30	.14
213	Al Leiter	.30	.14
214	Dennis Eckersley	.30	.14
215	Mark Johnson	.15	.07
216	Eric Karros	.30	.14
217	Royce Clayton	.15	.07
218	Tony Phillips	.15	.07
219	Tim Wakefield	.30	.14
220	Alan Trammell	.30	.14
221	Eduardo Perez	.15	.07
222	Butch Huskey	.15	.07
223	Tim Belcher	.15	.07
224	Jamie Moyer	.15	.07
225	F.P. Santangelo	.15	.07
226	Rusty Greer	.30	.14
227	Jeff Brantley	.15	.07
228	Mark Langston	.30	.14
229	Ray Montgomery	.15	.07
230	Rich Becker	.15	.07
231	Ozzie Smith	.75	.35
232	Rey Ordonez	.30	.14
233	Ricky Otero	.15	.07
234	Mike Cameron	.30	.14
235	Mike Sweeney	.30	.14
236	Mark Lewis	.15	.07
237	Luis Gonzalez	.30	.14
238	Marcus Jensen	.15	.07
239	Ed Sprague	.15	.07
240	Jose Valentin	.15	.07
241	Jeff Frye	.15	.07
242	Charles Nagy	.30	.14
243	Carlos Garcia	.15	.07
244	Mike Hampton	.30	.14
245	B.J. Surhoff	.30	.14
246	Wilton Guerrero	.15	.07
247	Frank Rodriguez	.15	.07
248	Gary Gaetti	.30	.14
249	Lance Johnson	.30	.14
250	Darren Bragg	.15	.07
251	Darryl Hamilton	.15	.07
252	John Jaha	.15	.07
253	Craig Paquette	.15	.07
254	Jaime Navarro	.15	.07
255	Shawon Dunston	.15	.07
256	Mark Loretta	.15	.07
257	Tim Belk	.15	.07
258	Jeff Darwin	.15	.07
259	Ruben Sierra	.15	.07
260	Chuck Finley	.30	.14
261	Darryl Strawberry	.30	.14
262	Shannon Stewart	.30	.14
263	Pedro Martinez	.75	.35
264	Neifi Perez	.30	.14
265	Jeff Conine	.15	.07
266	Orel Hershiser	.30	.14
267	Eddie Murray CL	.30	.14
268	Paul Molitor CL	.30	.14
269	Barry Bonds CL	.30	.14
270	Mark McGwire CL	1.50	.70
271	Matt Williams	.60	.25
272	Todd Zeile	.15	.07
273	Roger Clemens	1.50	.70
274	Michael Tucker	.15	.07
275	J.T. Snow	.30	.14
276	Kenny Lofton	.40	.18
277	Jose Canseco	.75	.35
278	Marquis Grissom	.30	.14
279	Moises Alou	.30	.14
280	Benito Santiago	.15	.07
281	Willie McGee	.30	.14
282	Chili Davis	.30	.14
283	Ron Coomer	.15	.07
284	Orlando Merced	.15	.07
285	Delino DeShields	.15	.07
286	John Wetteland	.15	.07
287	Darren Daulton	.30	.14
288	Lee Stevens	.15	.07
289	Albert Belle	.60	.25
290	Sterling Hitchcock	.15	.07
291	David Justice	.60	.25
292	Eric Davis	.30	.14
293	Brian Hunter	.30	.14
294	Darryl Hamilton	.15	.07
295	Steve Avery	.15	.07
296	Joe Vitiello	.15	.07
297	Jaime Navarro	.15	.07
298	Eddie Murray	.60	.25
299	Randy Myers	.15	.07
300	Francisco Cordova	.15	.07
301	Javier Lopez	.30	.14
302	Geronimo Berroa	.15	.07
303	Jeffrey Hammonds	.30	.14
304	Deion Sanders	.30	.14
305	Jeff Fassero	.15	.07
306	Curt Schilling	.40	.18
307	Robb Nen	.15	.07
308	Mark McLemore	.15	.07
309	Jimmy Key	.30	.14
310	Quilvio Veras	.15	.07
311	Bip Roberts	.15	.07
312	Esteban Loaiza	.15	.07
313	Andy Ashby	.15	.07
314	Sandy Alomar Jr.	.30	.14
315	Shawn Green	.60	.25
316	Luis Castillo	.30	.14
317	Benji Gil	.15	.07
318	Otis Nixon	.15	.07
319	Aaron Sele	.30	.14
320	Brad Ausmus	.15	.07
321	Troy O'Leary	.15	.07
322	Terrell Wade	.15	.07
323	Jeff King	.15	.07
324	Kevin Seitzer	.15	.07
325	Mark Wohlers	.15	.07
326	Edgar Renteria	.30	.14
327	Dan Wilson	.15	.07
328	Brian McRae	.15	.07
329	Rod Beck	.15	.07
330	Julio Franco	.30	.14
331	Dave Nilsson	.15	.07
332	Glenallen Hill	.15	.07
333	Kevin Elster	.15	.07
334	Joe Girardi	.15	.07
335	David Wells	.30	.14
336	Jeff Blauser	.15	.07
337	Darryl Kile	.30	.14
338	Jeff Kent	.30	.14
339	Jim Leyritz	.15	.07

❏ 340 Todd Stottlemyre	.15		.07
❏ 341 Tony Clark	.40		.18
❏ 342 Chris Hoiles	.15		.07
❏ 343 Mike Lieberthal	.15		.07
❏ 344 Matt Lawton	.30		.14
❏ 345 Alex Ochoa	.15		.07
❏ 346 Chris Snopek	.15		.07
❏ 347 Rudy Pemberton	.15		.07
❏ 348 Eric Owens	.15		.07
❏ 349 Joe Randa	.15		.07
❏ 350 John Olerud	.30		.14
❏ 351 Steve Karsay	.15		.07
❏ 352 Mark Whiten	.15		.07
❏ 353 Bob Abreu	.30		.14
❏ 354 Bartolo Colon	.30		.14
❏ 355 Vladimir Guerrero	1.00		.45
❏ 356 Darin Erstad	.60		.25
❏ 357 Scott Rolen	1.00		.45
❏ 358 Andruw Jones	.75		.35
❏ 359 Scott Spiezio	.15		.07
❏ 360 Karim Garcia	.30		.14
❏ 361 Hideki Irabu	1.00		.45
❏ 362 Nomar Garciaparra	2.00		.90
❏ 363 Dmitri Young	.30		.14
❏ 364 Bubba Trammell	.60		.25
❏ 365 Kevin Orie	.15		.07
❏ 366 Jose Rosado	.15		.07
❏ 367 Jose Guillen	.40		.18
❏ 368 Brooks Kieschnick	.15		.07
❏ 369 Pokey Reese	.30		.14
❏ 370 Glendon Rusch	.15		.07
❏ 371 Jason Dickson	.15		.07
❏ 372 Todd Walker	.60		.25
❏ 373 Justin Thompson	.30		.14
❏ 374 Todd Greene	.15		.07
❏ 375 Jeff Suppan	.15		.07
❏ 376 Trey Beamon	.15		.07
❏ 377 Damon Mashore	.15		.07
❏ 378 Wendell Magee	.15		.07
❏ 379 Shigetoshi Hasegawa	.30		.14
❏ 380 Bill Mueller	.75		.35
❏ 381 Chris Widger	.15		.07
❏ 382 Tony Graffanino	.15		.07
❏ 383 Derrek Lee	.40		.18
❏ 384 Brian Moehler	.15		.07
❏ 385 Quinton McCracken	.15		.07
❏ 386 Matt Morris	.30		.14
❏ 387 Marvin Benard	.15		.07
❏ 388 Deivi Cruz	.60		.25
❏ 389 Javier Valentin	.30		.14
❏ 390 Todd Dunwoody	.30		.14
❏ 391 Derrick Gibson	.40		.18
❏ 392 Raul Casanova	.15		.07
❏ 393 George Arias	.15		.07
❏ 394 Tony Womack	.50		.23
❏ 395 Antone Williamson	.15		.07
❏ 396 Jose Cruz Jr.	1.25		.55
❏ 397 Desi Relaford	.15		.07
❏ 398 Frank Thomas HIT	1.25		.55
❏ 399 Ken Griffey Jr. HIT	1.50		.70
❏ 400 Cal Ripken HIT	1.25		.55
❏ 401 Chipper Jones HIT	.75		.35
❏ 402 Mike Piazza HIT	1.00		.45
❏ 403 Gary Sheffield HIT	.15		.07
❏ 404 Alex Rodriguez HIT	1.00		.45
❏ 405 Wade Boggs HIT	.30		.14
❏ 406 Juan Gonzalez HIT	.75		.35
❏ 407 Tony Gwynn HIT	.75		.35
❏ 408 Edgar Martinez HIT	.15		.07
❏ 409 Jeff Bagwell HIT	.60		.25
❏ 410 Larry Walker HIT	.30		.14
❏ 411 Kenny Lofton HIT	.30		.14
❏ 412 Manny Ramirez HIT	.40		.18
❏ 413 Mark McGwire HIT	1.50		.70
❏ 414 Roberto Alomar HIT	.30		.14
❏ 415 Derek Jeter HIT	1.00		.45
❏ 416 Brady Anderson HIT	.15		.07
❏ 417 Paul Molitor HIT	.30		.14
❏ 418 Dante Bichette HIT	.15		.07
❏ 419 Jim Edmonds HIT	.15		.07
❏ 420 Mo Vaughn HIT	.30		.14
❏ 421 Barry Bonds HIT	.30		.14
❏ 422 Rusty Greer HIT	.15		.07
❏ 423 Greg Maddux KING	.75		.35
❏ 424 Andy Pettitte KING	.15		.07
❏ 425 John Smoltz KING	.30		.14

❏ 426 Randy Johnson KING	.30		.14
❏ 427 Hideo Nomo KING	.75		.35
❏ 428 Roger Clemens KING	.75		.35
❏ 429 Tom Glavine KING	.30		.14
❏ 430 Pat Hentgen KING	.15		.07
❏ 431 Kevin Brown KING	.15		.07
❏ 432 Mike Mussina KING	.30		.14
❏ 433 Alex Fernandez KING	.15		.07
❏ 434 Kevin Appier KING	.15		.07
❏ 435 David Cone KING	.30		.14
❏ 436 Jeff Fassero KING	.15		.07
❏ 437 John Wetteland KING	.15		.07
❏ 438 Barry Bonds IS	.25		.11
	Ivan Rodriguez		
❏ 439 Ken Griffey Jr. IS	1.00		.45
	Andres Galarraga		
❏ 440 Fred McGriff IS	.15		.07
	Rafael Palmeiro		
❏ 441 Barry Larkin IS	.15		.07
	Jim Thome		
❏ 442 Sammy Sosa IS	.25		.11
	Albert Belle		
❏ 443 Bernie Williams IS	.15		.07
	Todd Hundley		
❏ 444 Chuck Knoblauch IS	.15		.07
	Brian Jordan		
❏ 445 Mo Vaughn IS	.60		.25
	Jeff Conine		
❏ 446 Ken Caminiti IS	.15		.07
	Jason Giambi		
❏ 447 Raul Mondesi IS	.15		.07
	Tim Salmon		
❏ 448 Cal Ripken CL	1.25		.55
❏ 449 Greg Maddux CL	.75		.35
❏ 450 Ken Griffey Jr. CL	1.50		.70

1997 Donruss Gold Press Proofs

	MINT	NRMT
COMMON CARD (1-450)	4.00	1.80

*STARS: 10X TO 25X BASIC CARDS
*ROOKIES: 5X TO 12X BASIC CARDS
SER.1 STATED ODDS 1:32
SER.2 STATED ODDS 1:64
STATED PRINT RUN 500 SETS

1997 Donruss Silver Press Proofs

	MINT	NRMT
COMMON CARD (1-450)	1.50	.70

*STARS: 4X TO 10X BASIC CARDS
*ROOKIES: 2X TO 5X BASIC CARDS
SER.1 STATED ODDS 1:16
SER.2 STATED ODDS 1:16
STATED PRINT RUN 2000 SETS

1997 Donruss Armed and Dangerous

	MINT	NRMT
COMPLETE SET (15)	120.00	55.00
COMMON CARD (1-15)	2.50	1.10
UNLISTED STARS	5.00	2.20

SER.1 STATED ODDS 1:58 HOBBY
STATED PRINT RUN 5000 SERIAL #'d SETS

❏ 1 Ken Griffey Jr.	25.00		11.00
❏ 2 Raul Mondesi	2.50		1.10
❏ 3 Chipper Jones	12.00		5.50
❏ 4 Ivan Rodriguez	6.00		2.70
❏ 5 Randy Johnson	5.00		2.20
❏ 6 Alex Rodriguez	15.00		6.75
❏ 7 Larry Walker	5.00		2.20
❏ 8 Cal Ripken	20.00		9.00
❏ 9 Kenny Lofton	4.00		1.80
❏ 10 Barry Bonds	6.00		2.70
❏ 11 Derek Jeter	15.00		6.75
❏ 12 Charles Johnson	2.50		1.10
❏ 13 Greg Maddux	12.00		5.50
❏ 14 Roberto Alomar	5.00		2.20
❏ 15 Barry Larkin	5.00		2.20

1997 Donruss Diamond Kings

	MINT	NRMT
COMPLETE SET (10)	180.00	80.00
COMMON CARD (1-10)	3.00	1.35
SEMISTARS	5.00	2.20
UNLISTED STARS	8.00	3.60

SER.1 STATED ODDS 1:45
STATED PRINT RUN 9500 SERIAL #'d SETS
*CANVAS: 1.25X TO 3X HI COLUMN
CANVAS: RANDOM INS.IN SER.1 PACKS
CANVAS PRINT RUN 500 SERIAL #'d SETS
EACH CARD #1982 WINS ORIGINAL ART

	MINT	NRMT
❑ 1 Ken Griffey Jr.	40.00	18.00
❑ 2 Cal Ripken	30.00	13.50
❑ 3 Mo Vaughn	8.00	3.60
❑ 4 Chuck Knoblauch	8.00	3.60
❑ 5 Jeff Bagwell	10.00	4.50
❑ 6 Henry Rodriguez	3.00	1.35
❑ 7 Mike Piazza	25.00	11.00
❑ 8 Ivan Rodriguez	10.00	4.50
❑ 9 Frank Thomas	15.00	6.75
❑ 10 Chipper Jones	20.00	9.00

1997 Donruss Dominators

	MINT	NRMT
COMPLETE SET (20)	90.00	40.00
COMMON CARD (1-20)	1.50	.70
RANDOM INSERTS IN UPDATE PACKS		

		MINT	NRMT
❑ 1 Frank Thomas		6.00	2.70
❑ 2 Ken Griffey Jr.		15.00	6.75
❑ 3 Greg Maddux		8.00	3.60
❑ 4 Cal Ripken		12.00	5.50
❑ 5 Alex Rodriguez		10.00	4.50
❑ 6 Albert Belle		3.00	1.35
❑ 7 Mark McGwire		15.00	6.75
❑ 8 Juan Gonzalez		6.00	2.70
❑ 9 Chipper Jones		8.00	3.60
❑ 10 Hideo Nomo		3.00	1.35
❑ 11 Roger Clemens		8.00	3.60
❑ 12 John Smoltz		2.00	.90
❑ 13 Mike Piazza		10.00	4.50
❑ 14 Sammy Sosa		10.00	4.50
❑ 15 Matt Williams		3.00	1.35
❑ 16 Kenny Lofton		2.00	.90
❑ 17 Barry Larkin		3.00	1.35
❑ 18 Rafael Palmeiro		3.00	1.35
❑ 19 Ken Caminiti		2.00	.90
❑ 20 Gary Sheffield		1.50	.70

1997 Donruss Elite Inserts

ALEX RODRIGUEZ

	MINT	NRMT
COMPLETE SET (12)	350.00	160.00
COMMON CARD (1-12)	12.00	5.50
SER.1 STATED ODDS 1:144		
STATED PRINT RUN 2500 SERIAL #'d SETS		

	MINT	NRMT
❑ 1 Frank Thomas	25.00	11.00

	MINT	NRMT
❑ 2 Paul Molitor	12.00	5.50
❑ 3 Sammy Sosa	40.00	18.00
❑ 4 Barry Bonds	15.00	6.75
❑ 5 Chipper Jones	30.00	13.50
❑ 6 Alex Rodriguez	40.00	18.00
❑ 7 Ken Griffey Jr.	60.00	27.00
❑ 8 Jeff Bagwell	15.00	6.75
❑ 9 Cal Ripken	50.00	22.00
❑ 10 Mo Vaughn	12.00	5.50
❑ 11 Mike Piazza	40.00	18.00
❑ 12 Juan Gonzalez UER	25.00	11.00
(Name misspelled as Gonzales)		

1997 Donruss Franchise Features

	MINT	NRMT
COMPLETE SET (15)	250.00	110.00
COMMON CARD (1-15)	6.00	2.70
UNLISTED STARS	8.00	3.60
RANDOM INSERTS IN UPDATE PACKS		
STATED PRINT RUN 3000 SERIAL #'d SETS		

		MINT	NRMT
❑ 1	Ken Griffey Jr. / Andruw Jones	40.00	18.00
❑ 2	Frank Thomas / Darin Erstad	15.00	6.75
❑ 3	Alex Rodriguez / Nomar Garciaparra	30.00	13.50
❑ 4	Chuck Knoblauch / Wilton Guerrero	8.00	3.60
❑ 5	Juan Gonzalez / BubbaTrammell	15.00	6.75
❑ 6	Chipper Jones / Todd Walker	20.00	9.00
❑ 7	Barry Bonds / Vladimir Guerrero	12.00	5.50
❑ 8	Mark McGwire / Dmitri Young	40.00	18.00
❑ 9	Mike Piazza / Mike Sweeney	25.00	11.00
❑ 10	Mo Vaughn / Tony Clark	10.00	4.50
❑ 11	Gary Sheffield / Jose Guillen	8.00	3.60
❑ 12	Kenny Lofton / Shannon Stewart	10.00	4.50
❑ 13	Cal Ripken / Scott Rolen	30.00	13.50
❑ 14	Derek Jeter / Pokey Reese	25.00	11.00
❑ 15	Tony Gwynn / Bob Abreu	20.00	9.00

1997 Donruss Longball Leaders

	MINT	NRMT
COMPLETE SET (15)	100.00	45.00
COMMON CARD (1-15)	1.50	.70
SEMISTARS	3.00	1.35
UNLISTED STARS	5.00	2.20
RANDOM INSERTS IN SER.1 RETAIL PACKS		
STATED PRINT RUN 5000 SERIAL #'d SETS		

	MINT	NRMT
❑ 1 Frank Thomas	10.00	4.50
❑ 2 Albert Belle	5.00	2.20

		MINT	NRMT
❑ 3 Mo Vaughn		5.00	2.20
❑ 4 Brady Anderson		2.50	1.10
❑ 5 Greg Vaughn		2.50	1.10
❑ 6 Ken Griffey Jr.		25.00	11.00
❑ 7 Jay Buhner		2.50	1.10
❑ 8 Juan Gonzalez		10.00	4.50
❑ 9 Mike Piazza		15.00	6.75
❑ 10 Jeff Bagwell		6.00	2.70
❑ 11 Sammy Sosa		15.00	6.75
❑ 12 Mark McGwire		25.00	11.00
❑ 13 Cecil Fielder		1.50	.70
❑ 14 Ryan Klesko		2.50	1.10
❑ 15 Jose Canseco		6.00	2.70

1997 Donruss Power Alley

	MINT	NRMT
COMPLETE SET (24)	400.00	180.00
COMMON CARD (1-24)	3.00	1.35
UNLISTED STARS	5.00	2.20
RANDOM INSERTS IN UPDATE PACKS		
GREEN PRINT RUN 3750 SERIAL #'d SETS		
BLUE PRINT RUN 1750 SERIAL #'d SETS		
GOLD PRINT RUN 750 SERIAL #'d SETS		
*GREEN DIE CUT: 2X TO 4X BASIC GREEN		
*BLUE DIE CUT: 1.25X TO 3X BASIC BLUE		
*GOLD DIE CUT: .75X TO 2X BASIC GOLD		
DIE CUTS: RANDOM INS.IN UPDATE PACKS		
DIE CUTS PRINT RUN 250 SERIAL #'d SETS		

		MINT	NRMT
❑ 1 Frank Thomas G		25.00	11.00
❑ 2 Ken Griffey Jr. G		60.00	27.00
❑ 3 Cal Ripken G		50.00	22.00
❑ 4 Jeff Bagwell B		10.00	4.50
❑ 5 Mike Piazza B		25.00	11.00
❑ 6 Andruw Jones GR		6.00	2.70
❑ 7 Alex Rodriguez G		40.00	18.00
❑ 8 Albert Belle GR		5.00	2.20
❑ 9 Mo Vaughn GR		5.00	2.20
❑ 10 Chipper Jones B		20.00	9.00
❑ 11 Juan Gonzalez B		15.00	6.75
❑ 12 Ken Caminiti GR		5.00	2.20
❑ 13 Manny Ramirez GR		6.00	2.70
❑ 14 Mark McGwire GR		25.00	11.00
❑ 15 Kenny Lofton B		5.00	2.20
❑ 16 Barry Bonds GR		6.00	2.70
❑ 17 Gary Sheffield GR		5.00	2.20
❑ 18 Tony Gwynn B		12.00	5.50
❑ 19 Vladimir Guerrero B		12.00	5.50

	MINT	NRMT
❑ 20 Ivan Rodriguez B	10.00	4.50
❑ 21 Paul Molitor B	8.00	3.60
❑ 22 Sammy Sosa GR	15.00	6.75
❑ 23 Matt Williams GR	5.00	2.20
❑ 24 Derek Jeter GR	15.00	6.75

1997 Donruss Rated Rookies

	MINT	NRMT
COMPLETE SET (30)	50.00	22.00
COMMON CARD (1-30)	1.00	.45

RANDOM INSERTS IN SER.1 PACKS

❑ 1 Jason Thompson	1.00	.45
❑ 2 LaTroy Hawkins	1.00	.45
❑ 3 Scott Rolen	8.00	3.60
❑ 4 Trey Beamon	1.00	.45
❑ 5 Kimera Bartee	1.00	.45
❑ 6 Nerio Rodriguez	1.50	.70
❑ 7 Jeff D'Amico	1.00	.45
❑ 8 Quinton McCracken	1.00	.45
❑ 9 John Wasdin	1.00	.45
❑ 10 Robin Jennings	1.00	.45
❑ 11 Steve Gibralter	1.00	.45
❑ 12 Tyler Houston	1.00	.45
❑ 13 Tony Clark	2.50	1.10
❑ 14 Ugueth Urbina	1.50	.70
❑ 15 Karim Garcia	1.50	.70
❑ 16 Raul Casanova	1.00	.45
❑ 17 Brooks Kieschnick	1.00	.45
❑ 18 Luis Castillo	1.50	.70
❑ 19 Edgar Renteria	1.50	.70
❑ 20 Andruw Jones	5.00	2.20
❑ 21 Chad Mottola	1.00	.45
❑ 22 Mac Suzuki	1.00	.45
❑ 23 Justin Thompson	1.50	.70
❑ 24 Darin Erstad	4.00	1.80
❑ 25 Todd Walker	4.00	1.80
❑ 26 Todd Greene	1.00	.45
❑ 27 Vladimir Guerrero	4.00	1.80
❑ 28 Darren Dreifort	1.50	.70
❑ 29 John Burke	1.00	.45
❑ 30 Damon Mashore	1.00	.45

1997 Donruss Ripken The Only Way I Know

	MINT	NRMT
COMPLETE SET (9)	100.00	45.00
COMMON CARD (1-9)	12.00	5.50

RANDOM INSERTS IN UPDATE PACKS
STATED PRINT RUN 5000 SERIAL #'d SETS
CARD #10 DIST.ONLY W/RIPKEN'S BOOK

❑ 1 Cal Ripken	12.00	5.50
❑ 2 Cal Ripken	12.00	5.50
Cal Ripken Sr.		
Memorial Stadium 1978		
❑ 3 Cal Ripken	12.00	5.50
Rochester Red Wings		
❑ 4 Cal Ripken	12.00	5.50
Aberdeen Indians 1970		
❑ 5 Cal Ripken	12.00	5.50
Eddie Murray		
❑ 6 Cal Ripken	12.00	5.50
Cal Ripken Sr.		
Billy Ripken		
Family Reunion at Camden Yards		
❑ 7 Cal Ripken	12.00	5.50
Cal Ripken Sr.		
Billy Ripken		
Family Day Tri-Cities Atoms		
❑ 8 Cal Ripken	12.00	5.50
Victory Lap Game 2131		
❑ 9 Cal Ripken	12.00	5.50
❑ 10 Cal Ripken	6.00	2.70
(distributed exclusively with book)		
❑ 10A Cal Ripken AU/2131	200.00	90.00
(distributed exclusively with book)		

1997 Donruss Rocket Launchers

	MINT	NRMT
COMPLETE SET (15)	100.00	45.00
COMMON CARD (1-15)	1.50	.70
SEMISTARS	3.00	1.35
UNLISTED STARS	5.00	2.20

RANDOM INSERTS IN SER.1 MAG.PACKS
STATED PRINT RUN 5000 SERIAL #'d SETS

❑ 1 Frank Thomas	10.00	4.50
❑ 2 Albert Belle	5.00	2.20
❑ 3 Chipper Jones	12.00	5.50
❑ 4 Mike Piazza	15.00	6.75
❑ 5 Mo Vaughn	5.00	2.20
❑ 6 Juan Gonzalez	10.00	4.50
❑ 7 Fred McGriff	3.00	1.35
❑ 8 Jeff Bagwell	6.00	2.70
❑ 9 Matt Williams	5.00	2.20
❑ 10 Gary Sheffield	2.00	.90
❑ 11 Barry Bonds	6.00	2.70
❑ 12 Manny Ramirez	6.00	2.70
❑ 13 Henry Rodriguez	1.50	.70
❑ 14 Jason Giambi	2.00	.90
❑ 15 Cal Ripken	20.00	9.00

1997 Donruss Rookie Diamond Kings

	MINT	NRMT
COMPLETE SET (10)	100.00	45.00
COMMON CARD (1-10)	4.00	1.80
UNLISTED STARS	6.00	2.70

STATED PRINT RUN 9500 SERIAL #'d SETS
*CANVAS: 1.25X TO 3X HI COLUMN

CANVAS PRINT RUN 500 SERIAL #'d SETS
RANDOM INSERTS IN UPDATE PACKS

❑ 1 Andruw Jones	10.00	4.50
❑ 2 Vladimir Guerrero	12.00	5.50
❑ 3 Scott Rolen	12.00	5.50
❑ 4 Todd Walker	6.00	2.70
❑ 5 Bartolo Colon	4.00	1.80
❑ 6 Jose Guillen	5.00	2.20
❑ 7 Nomar Garciaparra	25.00	11.00
❑ 8 Darin Erstad	6.00	2.70
❑ 9 Dmitri Young	4.00	1.80
❑ 10 Wilton Guerrero	4.00	1.80

1998 Donruss

	MINT	NRMT
COMPLETE SET (420)	50.00	22.00
COMPLETE SERIES 1 (170)	20.00	9.00
COMPLETE UPDATE (250)	30.00	13.50
COMMON CARD (1-420)	.10	.05
MINOR STARS	.20	.09
SEMISTARS	.30	.14
UNLISTED STARS	.50	.23

❑ 1 Paul Molitor	.50	.23
❑ 2 Juan Gonzalez	1.00	.45
❑ 3 Darryl Kile	.10	.05
❑ 4 Randy Johnson	.50	.23
❑ 5 Tom Glavine	.50	.23
❑ 6 Pat Hentgen	.10	.05
❑ 7 David Justice	.20	.09
❑ 8 Kevin Brown	.30	.14
❑ 9 Mike Mussina	.50	.23
❑ 10 Ken Caminiti	.20	.09
❑ 11 Todd Hundley	.20	.09
❑ 12 Frank Thomas	1.00	.45
❑ 13 Ray Lankford	.20	.09
❑ 14 Justin Thompson	.10	.05
❑ 15 Jason Dickson	.10	.05
❑ 16 Kenny Lofton	.30	.14
❑ 17 Ivan Rodriguez	.60	.25
❑ 18 Pedro Martinez	.60	.25
❑ 19 Brady Anderson	.20	.09
❑ 20 Barry Larkin	.50	.23
❑ 21 Chipper Jones	1.25	.55
❑ 22 Tony Gwynn	1.25	.55
❑ 23 Roger Clemens	1.25	.55
❑ 24 Sandy Alomar Jr.	.20	.09
❑ 25 Tino Martinez	.20	.09
❑ 26 Jeff Bagwell	.60	.25

27	Shawn Estes	.10	.05
28	Ken Griffey Jr.	2.50	1.10
29	Javier Lopez	.20	.09
30	Denny Neagle	.10	.05
31	Mike Piazza	1.50	.70
32	Andres Galarraga	.30	.14
33	Larry Walker	.50	.23
34	Alex Rodriguez	1.50	.70
35	Greg Maddux	1.25	.55
36	Albert Belle	.50	.23
37	Barry Bonds	.60	.25
38	Mo Vaughn	.50	.23
39	Kevin Appier	.20	.09
40	Wade Boggs	.50	.23
41	Garret Anderson	.20	.09
42	Jeffrey Hammonds	.10	.05
43	Marquis Grissom	.10	.05
44	Jim Edmonds	.20	.09
45	Brian Jordan	.20	.09
46	Raul Mondesi	.20	.09
47	John Valentin	.20	.09
48	Brad Radke	.20	.09
49	Ismael Valdes	.10	.05
50	Matt Stairs	.20	.09
51	Matt Williams	.50	.23
52	Reggie Jefferson	.10	.05
53	Alan Benes	.10	.05
54	Charles Johnson	.20	.09
55	Chuck Knoblauch	.20	.09
56	Edgar Martinez	.20	.09
57	Nomar Garciaparra	1.50	.70
58	Craig Biggio	.50	.23
59	Bernie Williams	.50	.23
60	David Cone	.30	.14
61	Cal Ripken	2.00	.90
62	Mark McGwire	3.00	1.35
63	Roberto Alomar	.50	.23
64	Fred McGriff	.30	.14
65	Eric Karros	.20	.09
66	Robin Ventura	.20	.09
67	Darin Erstad	.30	.14
68	Michael Tucker	.10	.05
69	Jim Thome	.50	.23
70	Mark Grace	.30	.14
71	Lou Collier	.10	.05
72	Karim Garcia	.10	.05
73	Alex Fernandez	.10	.05
74	J.T. Snow	.20	.09
75	Reggie Sanders	.20	.09
76	John Smoltz	.30	.14
77	Tim Salmon	.30	.14
78	Paul O'Neill	.20	.09
79	Vinny Castilla	.20	.09
80	Rafael Palmeiro	.50	.23
81	Jaret Wright	.50	.23
82	Jay Buhner	.20	.09
83	Brett Butler	.20	.09
84	Todd Greene	.10	.05
85	Scott Rolen	.60	.25
86	Sammy Sosa	1.50	.70
87	Jason Giambi	.20	.09
88	Carlos Delgado	.50	.23
89	Deion Sanders	.50	.23
90	Wilton Guerrero	.10	.05
91	Andy Pettitte	.20	.09
92	Brian Giles	.20	.09
93	Dmitri Young	.20	.09
94	Ron Coomer	.10	.05
95	Mike Cameron	.20	.09
96	Edgardo Alfonzo	.30	.14
97	Jimmy Key	.20	.09
98	Ryan Klesko	.20	.09
99	Andy Benes	.10	.05
100	Derek Jeter	1.50	.70
101	Jeff Fassero	.10	.05
102	Neifi Perez	.20	.09
103	Hideo Nomo	.50	.23
104	Andruw Jones	.50	.23
105	Todd Helton	.60	.25
106	Livan Hernandez	.20	.09
107	Brett Tomko	.10	.05
108	Shannon Stewart	.20	.09
109	Bartolo Colon	.20	.09
110	Matt Morris	.10	.05
111	Miguel Tejada	.20	.09
112	Pokey Reese	.10	.05
113	Fernando Tatis	.50	.23
114	Todd Dunwoody	.10	.05
115	Jose Cruz Jr.	.20	.09
116	Chan Ho Park	.20	.09
117	Kevin Young	.20	.09
118	Rickey Henderson	.60	.25
119	Hideki Irabu	.20	.09
120	Francisco Cordova	.10	.05
121	Al Martin	.10	.05
122	Tony Clark	.20	.09
123	Curt Schilling	.30	.14
124	Rusty Greer	.20	.09
125	Jose Canseco	.60	.25
126	Edgar Renteria	.10	.05
127	Todd Walker	.20	.09
128	Wally Joyner	.20	.09
129	Bill Mueller	.10	.05
130	Jose Guillen	.10	.05
131	Manny Ramirez	.60	.25
132	Bobby Higginson	.20	.09
133	Kevin Orie	.10	.05
134	Will Clark	.50	.23
135	Dave Nilsson	.10	.05
136	Jason Kendall	.20	.09
137	Ivan Cruz	.10	.05
138	Gary Sheffield	.20	.09
139	Bubba Trammell	.10	.05
140	Vladimir Guerrero	.60	.25
141	Dennis Reyes	.10	.05
142	Bobby Bonilla	.20	.09
143	Ruben Rivera	.10	.05
144	Ben Grieve	.50	.23
145	Moises Alou	.20	.09
146	Tony Womack	.10	.05
147	Eric Young	.10	.05
148	Paul Konerko	.20	.09
149	Dante Bichette	.20	.09
150	Joe Carter	.20	.09
151	Rondell White	.20	.09
152	Chris Holt	.10	.05
153	Shawn Green	.50	.23
154	Mark Grudzielanek	.10	.05
	UER back rudzielanek		
155	Jermaine Dye	.20	.09
156	Ken Griffey Jr. FC	1.25	.55
157	Frank Thomas FC	.50	.23
158	Chipper Jones FC	.60	.25
159	Mike Piazza FC	.75	.35
160	Cal Ripken FC	1.00	.45
161	Greg Maddux FC	.60	.25
162	Juan Gonzalez FC	.50	.23
163	Alex Rodriguez FC	.75	.35
164	Mark McGwire FC	1.50	.70
165	Derek Jeter FC	.75	.35
166	Larry Walker CL	.20	.09
167	Tony Gwynn CL	.50	.25
168	Tino Martinez CL	.10	.05
169	Scott Rolen CL	.50	.23
170	Nomar Garciaparra CL	.75	.35
171	Mike Sweeney	.20	.09
172	Dustin Hermanson	.10	.05
173	Darren Dreifort	.10	.05
174	Ron Gant	.20	.09
175	Todd Hollandsworth	.10	.05
176	John Jaha	.10	.05
177	Kerry Wood	.60	.25
178	Chris Stynes	.10	.05
179	Kevin Elster	.10	.05
180	Derek Bell	.20	.09
181	Darryl Strawberry	.20	.09
182	Damion Easley	.20	.09
183	Jeff Cirillo	.20	.09
184	John Thomson	.10	.05
185	Dan Wilson	.10	.05
186	Jay Bell	.20	.09
187	Bernard Gilkey	.10	.05
188	Marc Valdes	.10	.05
189	Ramon Martinez	.10	.05
190	Charles Nagy	.20	.09
191	Derek Lowe	.10	.05
192	Andy Benes	.10	.05
193	Delino DeShields	.10	.05
194	Ryan Jackson	.25	.11
195	Kenny Lofton	.30	.14
196	Chuck Knoblauch	.20	.09
197	Andres Galarraga	.30	.14
198	Jose Canseco	.60	.25
199	John Olerud	.20	.09
200	Lance Johnson	.10	.05
201	Darryl Kile	.10	.05
202	Luis Castillo	.10	.05
203	Joe Carter	.20	.09
204	Dennis Eckersley	.20	.09
205	Steve Finley	.20	.09
206	Esteban Loaiza	.10	.05
207	Ryan Christenson UER	.25	.11
	(Birthdate says 1988)		
208	Deivi Cruz	.10	.05
209	Mariano Rivera	.20	.09
210	Mike Judd	.30	.14
211	Billy Wagner	.20	.09
212	Scott Spiezio	.10	.05
213	Russ Davis	.20	.09
214	Jeff Suppan	.10	.05
215	Doug Glanville	.20	.09
216	Dmitri Young	.20	.09
217	Rey Ordonez	.20	.09
218	Cecil Fielder	.20	.09
219	Masato Yoshii	.30	.14
220	Raul Casanova	.10	.05
221	Rolando Arrojo	.50	.23
222	Ellis Burks	.20	.09
223	Butch Huskey	.10	.05
224	Brian Hunter	.10	.05
225	Marquis Grissom	.10	.05
226	Kevin Brown	.30	.14
227	Joe Randa	.10	.05
228	Henry Rodriguez	.20	.09
229	Omar Vizquel	.20	.09
230	Fred McGriff	.30	.14
231	Matt Williams	.50	.23
232	Moises Alou	.20	.09
233	Travis Fryman	.20	.09
234	Wade Boggs	.50	.23
235	Pedro Martinez	.60	.25
236	Rickey Henderson	.60	.25
237	Bubba Trammell	.10	.05
238	Mike Caruso	.10	.05
239	Wilson Alvarez	.10	.05
240	Geronimo Berroa	.10	.05
241	Eric Milton	.10	.05
242	Scott Erickson	.10	.05
243	Todd Erdos	.10	.05
244	Bobby Hughes	.10	.05
245	Dave Hollins	.10	.05
246	Dean Palmer	.20	.09
247	Carlos Baerga	.10	.05
248	Jose Silva	.10	.05
249	Tom Evans	.10	.05
250	Jose Cabrera	.10	.05
251	Marty Cordova	.10	.05
252	Harley Frias	.10	.05
253	Javier Valentin	.10	.05
254	Mario Valdez	.10	.05
255	Joey Cora	.10	.05
256	Mike Lansing	.10	.05
257	Jeff Kent	.20	.09
258	Dave Dellucci	.40	.18
259	Curtis King	.10	.05
260	David Segui	.10	.05
261	Royce Clayton	.10	.05
262	Jeff Blauser	.10	.05
263	Manny Aybar	.25	.11
264	Mike Cather	.10	.05
265	Todd Zeile	.10	.05
266	Richard Hidalgo	.20	.09
267	Dante Powell	.10	.05
268	Mike DeJean	.10	.05
269	Ken Cloude	.10	.05
270	Danny Klassen	.10	.05
271	Sean Casey	.75	.35
272	A.J. Hinch	.10	.05
273	Rich Butler	.30	.14
274	Ben Ford	.25	.11
275	Billy McMillon	.10	.05
276	Wilson Delgado	.10	.05
277	Orlando Cabrera	.10	.05
278	Geoff Jenkins	.20	.09
279	Enrique Wilson	.10	.05
280	Derrek Lee	.10	.05
281	Marc Pisciotta	.10	.05
282	Abraham Nunez	.10	.05

❏ 283 Aaron Boone	.10	.05
❏ 284 Brad Fullmer	.10	.05
❏ 285 Rob Stanifer	.10	.05
❏ 286 Preston Wilson	.20	.09
❏ 287 Greg Norton	.10	.05
❏ 288 Bobby Smith	.10	.05
❏ 289 Josh Booty	.10	.05
❏ 290 Russell Branyan	.20	.09
❏ 291 Jeremi Gonzalez	.10	.05
❏ 292 Michael Coleman	.20	.09
❏ 293 Cliff Politte	.10	.05
❏ 294 Eric Ludwick	.10	.05
❏ 295 Rafael Medina	.10	.05
❏ 296 Jason Varitek	.20	.09
❏ 297 Ron Wright	.10	.05
❏ 298 Mark Kotsay	.20	.09
❏ 299 David Ortiz	.10	.05
❏ 300 Frank Catalanotto	.20	.09
❏ 301 Robinson Checo	.10	.05
❏ 302 Kevin Millwood	1.50	.70
❏ 303 Jacob Cruz	.10	.05
❏ 304 Javier Vazquez	.10	.05
❏ 305 Magglio Ordonez	1.50	.70
❏ 306 Kevin Witt	.10	.05
❏ 307 Derrick Gibson	.20	.09
❏ 308 Shane Monahan	.10	.05
❏ 309 Brian Rose	.10	.05
❏ 310 Bobby Estalella	.10	.05
❏ 311 Felix Heredia	.10	.05
❏ 312 Desi Relaford	.10	.05
❏ 313 Esteban Yan	.40	.18
❏ 314 Ricky Ledee	.20	.09
❏ 315 Steve Woodard	.10	.05
❏ 316 Pat Watkins	.10	.05
❏ 317 Damian Moss	.10	.05
❏ 318 Bob Abreu	.20	.09
❏ 319 Jeff Abbott	.10	.05
❏ 320 Miguel Cairo	.10	.05
❏ 321 Rigo Beltran	.10	.05
❏ 322 Tony Saunders	.10	.05
❏ 323 Randall Simon	.20	.09
❏ 324 Hiram Bocachica	.10	.05
❏ 325 Richie Sexson	.30	.14
❏ 326 Karim Garcia	.10	.05
❏ 327 Mike Lowell	.50	.23
❏ 328 Pat Cline	.10	.05
❏ 329 Matt Clement	.20	.09
❏ 330 Scott Elarton	.10	.05
❏ 331 Manuel Barrios	.25	.11
❏ 332 Bruce Chen	.20	.09
❏ 333 Juan Encarnacion	.20	.09
❏ 334 Travis Lee	.30	.14
❏ 335 Wes Helms	.10	.05
❏ 336 Chad Fox	.10	.05
❏ 337 Donnie Sadler	.10	.05
❏ 338 Carlos Mendoza	.25	.11
❏ 339 Damian Jackson	.10	.05
❏ 340 Julio Ramirez	.75	.35
❏ 341 John Halama	.50	.23
❏ 342 Edwin Diaz	.10	.05
❏ 343 Felix Martinez	.10	.05
❏ 344 Eli Marrero	.10	.05
❏ 345 Carl Pavano	.20	.09
❏ 346 Vladimir Guerrero HL	.30	.14
❏ 347 Barry Bonds HL	.30	.14
❏ 348 Darin Erstad HL	.20	.09
❏ 349 Albert Belle HL	.20	.09
❏ 350 Kenny Lofton HL	.20	.09
❏ 351 Mo Vaughn HL	.20	.09
❏ 352 Jose Cruz Jr. HL	.10	.05
❏ 353 Tony Clark HL	.10	.05
❏ 354 Roberto Alomar HL	.20	.09
❏ 355 Manny Ramirez HL	.30	.14
❏ 356 Paul Molitor HL	.20	.09
❏ 357 Jim Thome HL	.20	.09
❏ 358 Tino Martinez HL	.10	.05
❏ 359 Tim Salmon HL	.20	.09
❏ 360 David Justice HL	.10	.05
❏ 361 Raul Mondesi HL	.10	.05
❏ 362 Mark Grace HL	.20	.09
❏ 363 Craig Biggio HL	.20	.09
❏ 364 Larry Walker HL	.20	.09
❏ 365 Mark McGwire HL	1.50	.70
❏ 366 Juan Gonzalez HL	.50	.23
❏ 367 Derek Jeter HL	.75	.35
❏ 368 Chipper Jones HL	.60	.25
❏ 369 Frank Thomas HL	.50	.23
❏ 370 Alex Rodriguez HL	.75	.35
❏ 371 Mike Piazza HL	.75	.35
❏ 372 Tony Gwynn HL	.60	.25
❏ 373 Jeff Bagwell HL	.30	.14
❏ 374 Nomar Garciaparra HL	.75	.35
❏ 375 Ken Griffey Jr. HL	1.25	.55
❏ 376 Livan Hernandez UN	.10	.05
❏ 377 Chan Ho Park UN	.10	.05
❏ 378 Mike Mussina UN	.20	.09
❏ 379 Andy Pettitte UN	.10	.05
❏ 380 Greg Maddux UN	.60	.25
❏ 381 Hideo Nomo UN	.20	.09
❏ 382 Roger Clemens UN	.60	.25
❏ 383 Randy Johnson UN	.20	.09
❏ 384 Pedro Martinez UN	.30	.14
❏ 385 Jaret Wright UN	.10	.05
❏ 386 Ken Griffey Jr. SG	1.25	.55
❏ 387 Todd Helton SG	.30	.14
❏ 388 Paul Konerko SG	.10	.05
❏ 389 Cal Ripken SG	1.00	.45
❏ 390 Larry Walker SG	.20	.09
❏ 391 Ken Caminiti SG	.10	.05
❏ 392 Jose Guillen SG	.10	.05
❏ 393 Jim Edmonds SG	.10	.05
❏ 394 Barry Larkin SG	.20	.09
❏ 395 Bernie Williams SG	.20	.09
❏ 396 Tony Clark SG	.10	.05
❏ 397 Jose Cruz Jr. SG	.10	.05
❏ 398 Ivan Rodriguez SG	.30	.14
❏ 399 Darin Erstad SG	.20	.09
❏ 400 Scott Rolen SG	.50	.23
❏ 401 Mark McGwire SG	1.50	.70
❏ 402 Andruw Jones SG	.20	.09
❏ 403 Juan Gonzalez SG	.50	.23
❏ 404 Derek Jeter SG	.75	.35
❏ 405 Chipper Jones SG	.60	.25
❏ 406 Greg Maddux SG	.60	.25
❏ 407 Frank Thomas SG	.50	.23
❏ 408 Alex Rodriguez SG	.75	.35
❏ 409 Mike Piazza SG	.75	.35
❏ 410 Tony Gwynn SG	.60	.25
❏ 411 Jeff Bagwell SG	.30	.14
❏ 412 Nomar Garciaparra SG	.75	.35
❏ 413 Hideo Nomo SG	.20	.09
❏ 414 Barry Bonds CL	.30	.14
❏ 415 Ben Grieve SG	.20	.09
❏ 416 Barry Bonds CL	.30	.14
❏ 417 Mark McGwire CL	1.50	.70
❏ 418 Roger Clemens CL	.60	.25
❏ 419 Livan Hernandez CL	.10	.05
❏ 420 Ken Griffey Jr. CL	1.25	.55

1998 Donruss Gold Press Proofs

	MINT	NRMT
COMMON CARD (1-420)	4.00	1.80

*STARS: 12.5X to 30X BASIC CARDS
*ROOKIES: 6X to 15X BASIC CARDS
RANDOM INSERTS IN PACKS
STATED PRINT RUN 500 SETS

1998 Donruss Silver Press Proofs

	MINT	NRMT
COMMON CARD (1-420)	2.00	.90

*STARS: 6X to 15X BASIC CARDS
*ROOKIES: 3X to 8X BASIC CARDS
RANDOM INSERTS IN PACKS
STATED PRINT RUN 1500 SETS
CONDITION SENSITIVE SET

1998 Donruss Crusade Green

	MINT	NRMT
COMMON CARD (1-100)	8.00	3.60
MINOR STARS	12.00	5.50
SEMISTARS	20.00	9.00
UNLISTED STARS	30.00	13.50

*PURPLE STARS: .6X to 1.5X GREEN HI
*RED STARS: 2X to 4X GREEN HI
GREEN PRINT RUN 250 SERIAL #'d SETS
PURPLE PRINT RUN 100 SERIAL #'d SETS
RED PRINT RUN 25 SERIAL #'d SETS
D SUFFIX ON DONRUSS DISTRIBUTION
L SUFFIX ON LEAF DISTRIBUTION
U SUFFIX ON DON.UPDATE DISTRIBUTION
ALL CTA CARDS ARE UNNUMBERED
ERRORS

❏ 1 Tim Salmon U	20.00	9.00
❏ 2 Garret Anderson U	12.00	5.50
❏ 3 Jim Edmonds CTA L	12.00	5.50
❏ 4 Darin Erstad CTA L	20.00	9.00
❏ 5 Jason Dickson D	8.00	3.60
❏ 6 Todd Greene D	8.00	3.60
❏ 7 Roberto Alomar CTA	30.00	13.50
❏ 8 Cal Ripken D	120.00	55.00
❏ 9 Rafael Palmeiro CTA U	30.00	13.50
❏ 10 Brady Anderson U	12.00	5.50
❏ 11 Mike Mussina L	30.00	13.50
❏ 12 Mo Vaughn CTA	30.00	13.50
❏ 13 Nomar Garciaparra D	100.00	45.00
❏ 14 Frank Thomas CTA U	60.00	27.00
❏ 15 Albert Belle CTA L	30.00	13.50
❏ 16 Mike Cameron D	12.00	5.50
❏ 17 Robin Ventura U	12.00	5.50
❏ 18 Manny Ramirez L	40.00	18.00
❏ 19 Jim Thome CTA L	30.00	13.50
❏ 20 Sandy Alomar Jr. D	12.00	5.50
❏ 21 David Justice D	12.00	5.50
❏ 22 Matt Williams U	30.00	13.50
❏ 23 Tony Clark U	12.00	5.50
❏ 24 Bubba Trammell L	8.00	3.60
❏ 25 Justin Thompson D	8.00	3.60

❏ 26 Bobby Higginson L	12.00	5.50
❏ 27 Kevin Appier D	12.00	5.50
❏ 28 Paul Molitor L	30.00	13.50
❏ 29 Chuck Knoblauch CTA U	12.00	5.50
❏ 30 Todd Walker L	12.00	5.50
❏ 31 Bernie Williams U	30.00	13.50
❏ 32 Derek Jeter CTA U	100.00	45.00
❏ 33 Tino Martinez D	12.00	5.50
❏ 34 Andy Pettitte L	12.00	5.50
❏ 35 Wade Boggs CTA L	30.00	13.50
❏ 36 Hideki Irabu D	12.00	5.50
❏ 37 Jose Canseco D	40.00	18.00
❏ 38 Jason Giambi U	12.00	5.50
❏ 39 Ken Griffey Jr. D	150.00	70.00
❏ 40 Alex Rodriguez CTA L	100.00	45.00
❏ 41 Randy Johnson L	30.00	13.50
❏ 42 Edgar Martinez D	12.00	5.50
❏ 43 Jay Buhner CTA U	12.00	5.50
❏ 44 Juan Gonzalez CTA U	60.00	27.00
❏ 45 Will Clark D	30.00	13.50
❏ 46 Ivan Rodriguez L	40.00	18.00
❏ 47 Rusty Greer D	12.00	5.50
❏ 48 Roger Clemens L	80.00	36.00
❏ 49 Carlos Delgado U	30.00	13.50
❏ 50 Shawn Green D	30.00	13.50
❏ 51 Jose Cruz Jr. D	12.00	5.50
❏ 52 Kenny Lofton D	20.00	9.00
❏ 53 Chipper Jones D	80.00	36.00
❏ 54 Andruw Jones CTA L	30.00	13.50
❏ 55 Greg Maddux U	80.00	36.00
❏ 56 John Smoltz CTA L	20.00	9.00
❏ 57 Tom Glavine U	30.00	13.50
❏ 58 Javier Lopez L	12.00	5.50
❏ 59 Fred McGriff L	20.00	9.00
❏ 60 Mark Grace U	20.00	9.00
❏ 61 Sammy Sosa CTA U	100.00	45.00
❏ 62 Kevin Orie D	8.00	3.60
❏ 63 Barry Larkin CTA U	30.00	13.50
❏ 64 Pokey Reese L	8.00	3.60
❏ 65 Deion Sanders U	12.00	5.50
❏ 66 Andres Galarraga L	20.00	9.00
❏ 67 Larry Walker D	30.00	13.50
❏ 68 Dante Bichette CTA D	12.00	5.50
❏ 69 Neifi Perez U	12.00	5.50
❏ 70 Eric Young L	8.00	3.60
❏ 71 Todd Helton D	30.00	13.50
❏ 72 Gary Sheffield CTA U	12.00	5.50
❏ 73 Moises Alou L	12.00	5.50
❏ 74 Bobby Bonilla D	12.00	5.50
❏ 75 Kevin Brown D	20.00	9.00
❏ 76 Ben Grieve L	30.00	13.50
❏ 77 Jeff Bagwell CTA U	40.00	18.00
❏ 78 Craig Biggio D	30.00	13.50
❏ 79 Mike Piazza L	100.00	45.00
❏ 80 Raul Mondesi U	12.00	5.50
❏ 81 Hideo Nomo CTA U	30.00	13.50
❏ 82 Wilton Guerrero D	8.00	3.60
❏ 83 Rondell White CTA U	12.00	5.50
❏ 84 Vladimir Guerrero CTA U	40.00	18.00
❏ 85 Pedro Martinez D	40.00	18.00
❏ 86 Edgardo Alfonzo D	20.00	9.00
❏ 87 Todd Hundley CTA U	12.00	5.50
❏ 88 Scott Rolen D	40.00	18.00
❏ 89 Francisco Cordova D	8.00	3.60
❏ 90 Jose Guillen D	8.00	3.60
❏ 91 Jason Kendall L	12.00	5.50
❏ 92 Ray Lankford D	12.00	5.50
❏ 93 Mark McGwire CTA D	200.00	90.00
❏ 94 Matt Morris D	8.00	3.60
❏ 95 Alan Benes L	8.00	3.60
❏ 96 Brian Jordan CTA U	12.00	5.50
❏ 97 Tony Gwynn U	80.00	36.00
❏ 98 Ken Caminiti CTA L	12.00	5.50
❏ 99 Barry Bonds CTA U	40.00	18.00
❏ 100 Shawn Estes D	8.00	3.60

1998 Donruss Diamond Kings

	MINT	NRMT
COMPLETE SET (20)	250.00	110.00
COMMON CARD (1-20)	3.00	1.35
SEMISTARS	5.00	2.20
UNLISTED STARS	8.00	3.60
RANDOM INSERTS IN PACKS		

STATED PRINT RUN 9500 SERIAL #'d SETS
*CANVAS: 1.25X TO 3X HI COLUMN
CANVAS: RANDOM INSERTS IN PACKS
CANVAS PRINT RUN 500 SERIAL #'d SETS

❏ 1 Cal Ripken	30.00	13.50
❏ 2 Greg Maddux	20.00	9.00
❏ 3 Ivan Rodriguez	10.00	4.50
❏ 4 Tony Gwynn	20.00	9.00
❏ 5 Paul Molitor	8.00	3.60
❏ 6 Kenny Lofton	5.00	2.20
❏ 7 Andy Pettitte	3.00	1.35
❏ 8 Darin Erstad	5.00	2.20
❏ 9 Randy Johnson	8.00	3.60
❏ 10 Derek Jeter	25.00	11.00
❏ 11 Hideo Nomo	8.00	3.60
❏ 12 David Justice	3.00	1.35
❏ 13 Bernie Williams	8.00	3.60
❏ 14 Roger Clemens	20.00	9.00
❏ 15 Barry Larkin	8.00	3.60
❏ 16 Andruw Jones	8.00	3.60
❏ 17 Mike Piazza	25.00	11.00
❏ 18 Frank Thomas	15.00	6.75
❏ 19 Alex Rodriguez	25.00	11.00
❏ 20 Ken Griffey Jr.	40.00	18.00
❏ S20 Frank Thomas Sample		.90

1998 Donruss Dominators

	MINT	NRMT
COMPLETE SET (30)	150.00	70.00
COMMON CARD (1-30)	1.25	.55
RANDOM INSERTS IN UPDATE PACKS		

❏ 1 Roger Clemens	8.00	3.60
❏ 2 Tony Clark	1.25	.55
❏ 3 Darin Erstad	2.00	.90
❏ 4 Jeff Bagwell	4.00	1.80
❏ 5 Ken Griffey Jr	15.00	6.75
❏ 6 Andruw Jones	3.00	1.35
❏ 7 Juan Gonzalez	6.00	2.70
❏ 8 Ivan Rodriguez	4.00	1.80
❏ 9 Randy Johnson	3.00	1.35
❏ 10 Tino Martinez	1.25	.55
❏ 11 Mark McGwire	20.00	9.00
❏ 12 Chuck Knoblauch	1.25	.55
❏ 13 Jim Thome	3.00	1.35
❏ 14 Alex Rodriguez	10.00	4.50
❏ 15 Hideo Nomo	3.00	1.35

❏ 16 Jose Cruz Jr.	1.25	.55
❏ 17 Chipper Jones	8.00	3.60
❏ 18 Tony Gwynn	8.00	3.60
❏ 19 Barry Bonds	4.00	1.80
❏ 20 Mo Vaughn	3.00	1.35
❏ 21 Cal Ripken	12.00	5.50
❏ 22 Greg Maddux	8.00	3.60
❏ 23 Manny Ramirez	4.00	1.80
❏ 24 Andres Galarraga	2.00	.90
❏ 25 Vladimir Guerrero	4.00	1.80
❏ 26 Albert Belle	3.00	1.35
❏ 27 Nomar Garciaparra	10.00	4.50
❏ 28 Kenny Lofton	2.00	.90
❏ 29 Mike Piazza	10.00	4.50
❏ 30 Frank Thomas	6.00	2.70

1998 Donruss Elite Inserts

	MINT	NRMT
COMPLETE SET (20)	400.00	180.00
COMMON CARD (1-20)	4.00	1.80
UNLISTED STARS	10.00	4.50
RANDOM INSERTS IN UPDATE PACKS		
STATED PRINT RUN 2500 SERIAL #'d SETS		

❏ 1 Jeff Bagwell	12.00	5.50
❏ 2 Andruw Jones	10.00	4.50
❏ 3 Ken Griffey Jr.	50.00	22.00
❏ 4 Derek Jeter	30.00	13.50
❏ 5 Juan Gonzalez	20.00	9.00
❏ 6 Mark McGwire	60.00	27.00
❏ 7 Ivan Rodriguez	12.00	5.50
❏ 8 Paul Molitor	10.00	4.50
❏ 9 Hideo Nomo	10.00	4.50
❏ 10 Mo Vaughn	10.00	4.50
❏ 11 Chipper Jones	25.00	11.00
❏ 12 Nomar Garciaparra	30.00	13.50
❏ 13 Mike Piazza	30.00	13.50
❏ 14 Frank Thomas	20.00	9.00
❏ 15 Greg Maddux	25.00	11.00
❏ 16 Cal Ripken	40.00	18.00
❏ 17 Alex Rodriguez	30.00	13.50
❏ 18 Jose Cruz Jr.	4.00	1.80
❏ 19 Barry Bonds	12.00	5.50
❏ 20 Tony Gwynn	25.00	11.00

1998 Donruss FANtasy Team

	MINT	NRMT
COMPLETE SET (20)	400.00	180.00
COMMON 1ST TEAM (1-10)	4.00	1.80
1ST TEAM PRINT RUN 1750 SERIAL #'d SETS		
COMMON 2ND TEAM (11-20)	1.50	.70
2ND TEAM MINOR STARS	2.50	1.10
2ND TEAM UNLISTED STARS	6.00	2.70
2ND TEAM PRINT RUN 3750 SERIAL #'d SETS		
*1ST TEAM DIE CUTS: 1.25X TO 3X HI COL.		
*2ND TEAM DIE CUTS: 2X TO 5X HI		
DIE CUTS PRINT RUN 250 SERIAL #'d SETS		
RANDOM INSERTS IN UPDATE PACKS		

❑ 1 Frank Thomas	20.00	9.00
❑ 2 Ken Griffey Jr.	50.00	22.00
❑ 3 Cal Ripken	40.00	18.00
❑ 4 Jose Cruz Jr.	4.00	1.80
❑ 5 Travis Lee	6.00	2.70
❑ 6 Greg Maddux	25.00	11.00
❑ 7 Alex Rodriguez	30.00	13.50
❑ 8 Mark McGwire	60.00	27.00
❑ 9 Chipper Jones	25.00	11.00
❑ 10 Andruw Jones	10.00	4.50
❑ 11 Mike Piazza	20.00	9.00
❑ 12 Tony Gwynn	15.00	6.75
❑ 13 Larry Walker	6.00	2.70
❑ 14 Nomar Garciaparra	20.00	9.00
❑ 15 Jaret Wright	2.50	1.10
❑ 16 Livan Hernandez	1.50	.70
❑ 17 Roger Clemens	15.00	6.75
❑ 18 Derek Jeter	20.00	9.00
❑ 19 Scott Rolen	8.00	3.60
❑ 20 Jeff Bagwell	8.00	3.60

1998 Donruss Longball Leaders

	MINT	NRMT
COMPLETE SET (24)	150.00	70.00
COMMON CARD (1-24)	2.00	.90
RANDOM INSERTS IN PACKS		
STATED PRINT RUN 5000 SERIAL #'d SETS		

❑ 1 Ken Griffey Jr.	25.00	11.00
❑ 2 Mark McGwire	30.00	13.50
❑ 3 Tino Martinez	2.00	.90
❑ 4 Barry Bonds	6.00	2.70
❑ 5 Frank Thomas	10.00	4.50
❑ 6 Albert Belle	5.00	2.20
❑ 7 Mike Piazza	15.00	6.75
❑ 8 Chipper Jones	12.00	5.50
❑ 9 Vladimir Guerrero	6.00	2.70
❑ 10 Matt Williams	5.00	2.20
❑ 11 Sammy Sosa	15.00	6.75
❑ 12 Tim Salmon	3.00	1.35
❑ 13 Raul Mondesi	2.00	.90
❑ 14 Jeff Bagwell	6.00	2.70
❑ 15 Mo Vaughn	5.00	2.20
❑ 16 Manny Ramirez	6.00	2.70
❑ 17 Jim Thome	5.00	2.20
❑ 18 Jim Edmonds	2.00	.90
❑ 19 Tony Clark	2.00	.90
❑ 20 Nomar Garciaparra	15.00	6.75
❑ 21 Juan Gonzalez	10.00	4.50
❑ 22 Scott Rolen	8.00	3.60
❑ 23 Larry Walker	5.00	2.20
❑ 24 Andres Galarraga	3.00	1.35

1998 Donruss MLB 99

	MINT	NRMT
COMPLETE SET (20)	10.00	4.50
COMMON CARD (1-20)	.15	.07
UPDATE STATED ODDS 1:2		
DISTRIBUTED IN DON.UPDATE AND STUDIO		

❑ 1 Cal Ripken	2.00	.90
❑ 2 Nomar Garciaparra	1.50	.70
❑ 3 Barry Bonds	.50	.23
❑ 4 Mike Mussina	.40	.18
❑ 5 Pedro Martinez	.50	.23
❑ 6 Derek Jeter	1.50	.70
❑ 7 Andruw Jones	.40	.18
❑ 8 Kenny Lofton	.25	.11
❑ 9 Gary Sheffield	.15	.07
❑ 10 Raul Mondesi	.15	.07
❑ 11 Jeff Bagwell	.50	.23
❑ 12 Tim Salmon	.25	.11
❑ 13 Tom Glavine	.40	.18
❑ 14 Ben Grieve	.40	.18
❑ 15 Matt Williams	.40	.18
❑ 16 Juan Gonzalez	1.00	.45
❑ 17 Mark McGwire	3.00	1.35
❑ 18 Bernie Williams	.40	.18
❑ 19 Andres Galarraga	.25	.11
❑ 20 Jose Cruz Jr.	.15	.07

1998 Donruss Production Line On-Base

	MINT	NRMT
COMPLETE SET (20)	800.00	350.00
COMMON CARD (1-20)	15.00	6.75
SEMISTARS	20.00	9.00
UNLISTED STARS	30.00	13.50
RANDOM INSERTS IN PRE-PRICED PACKS		
PRINT RUN BASED ON PLAYER STATS		

❑ 1 Frank Thomas/456	60.00	27.00
❑ 2 Edgar Martinez/456	15.00	6.75
❑ 3 Roberto Alomar/390	30.00	13.50
❑ 4 Chuck Knoblauch/390	15.00	6.75
❑ 5 Mike Piazza/431	100.00	45.00
❑ 6 Barry Larkin/440	30.00	13.50
❑ 7 Kenny Lofton/409	20.00	9.00
❑ 8 Jeff Bagwell/425	40.00	18.00
❑ 9 Barry Bonds/446	40.00	18.00

❑ 10 Rusty Greer/405	15.00	6.75
❑ 11 Gary Sheffield/424	15.00	6.75
❑ 12 Mark McGwire/393	200.00	90.00
❑ 13 Chipper Jones/371	80.00	36.00
❑ 14 Tony Gwynn/409	80.00	36.00
❑ 15 Craig Biggio/415	30.00	13.50
❑ 16 Mo Vaughn/420	30.00	13.50
❑ 17 Bernie Williams/408	30.00	13.50
❑ 18 Ken Griffey Jr./382	150.00	70.00
❑ 19 Brady Anderson/393	15.00	6.75
❑ 20 Derek Jeter/370	100.00	45.00

1998 Donruss Production Line Power Index

	MINT	NRMT
COMPLETE SET (20)	500.00	220.00
COMMON CARD (1-20)	6.00	2.70
UNLISTED STARS	15.00	6.75
RANDOM INSERTS IN HOBBY PACKS		
PRINT RUN BASED ON PLAYER STATS		

❑ 1 Frank Thomas/1067	30.00	13.50
❑ 2 Mark McGwire/1039	100.00	45.00
❑ 3 Barry Bonds/1031	20.00	9.00
❑ 4 Jeff Bagwell/1017	20.00	9.00
❑ 5 Ken Griffey Jr./1028	80.00	36.00
❑ 6 Alex Rodriguez/846	50.00	22.00
❑ 7 Chipper Jones/850	40.00	18.00
❑ 8 Mike Piazza/1070	50.00	22.00
❑ 9 Mo Vaughn/980	15.00	6.75
❑ 10 Brady Anderson/863	6.00	2.70
❑ 11 Manny Ramirez/953	20.00	9.00
❑ 12 Albert Belle/823	15.00	6.75
❑ 13 Jim Thome/1001	15.00	6.75
❑ 14 Bernie Williams/952	15.00	6.75
❑ 15 Scott Rolen/846	20.00	9.00
❑ 16 Vladimir Guerrero/833	20.00	9.00
❑ 17 Larry Walker/1172	15.00	6.75
❑ 18 David Justice/1013	6.00	2.70
❑ 19 Tino Martinez/948	6.00	2.70
❑ 20 Tony Gwynn/957	40.00	18.00

1998 Donruss Production Line Slugging

	MINT	NRMT
COMPLETE SET (20)	800.00	350.00
COMMON CARD (1-20)	10.00	4.50
SEMISTARS	15.00	6.75
UNLISTED STARS	25.00	11.00

RANDOM INSERTS IN RETAIL PACKS
PRINT RUN BASED ON PLAYER STATS

❏ 1 Mark McGwire/646	150.00	70.00
❏ 2 Ken Griffey Jr./646	120.00	55.00
❏ 3 Andres Galarraga/585	15.00	6.75
❏ 4 Barry Bonds/585	30.00	13.50
❏ 5 Juan Gonzalez/589	50.00	22.00
❏ 6 Mike Piazza/638	80.00	36.00
❏ 7 Jeff Bagwell/592	30.00	13.50
❏ 8 Manny Ramirez/538	30.00	13.50
❏ 9 Jim Thome/579	25.00	11.00
❏ 10 Mo Vaughn/560	25.00	11.00
❏ 11 Larry Walker/720	25.00	11.00
❏ 12 Tino Martinez/577	10.00	4.50
❏ 13 Frank Thomas/611	50.00	22.00
❏ 14 Tim Salmon/517	15.00	6.75
❏ 15 Raul Mondesi/541	10.00	4.50
❏ 16 Alex Rodriguez/496	80.00	36.00
❏ 17 Nomar Garciaparra/534	80.00	36.00
❏ 18 Jose Cruz Jr./499	10.00	4.50
❏ 19 Tony Clark/500	10.00	4.50
❏ 20 Cal Ripken/402	100.00	45.00

1998 Donruss Rated Rookies

	MINT	NRMT
COMPLETE SET (30)	50.00	22.00
COMMON CARD (1-30)	1.00	.45
MINOR STARS	1.50	.70
SEMISTARS	2.50	1.10
UNLISTED STARS	4.00	1.80

*MEDALISTS: 4X TO 10X HI COLUMN
MEDALIST PRINT RUN 250 SETS
RANDOM INSERTS IN PACKS

❏ 1 Mark Kotsay	1.50	.70
❏ 2 Neifi Perez	1.50	.70
❏ 3 Paul Konerko	1.50	.70
❏ 4 Jose Cruz Jr.	1.50	.70
❏ 5 Hideki Irabu	1.50	.70
❏ 6 Mike Cameron	1.50	.70
❏ 7 Jeff Suppan	1.00	.45
❏ 8 Kevin Orie	1.00	.45
❏ 9 Pokey Reese	1.00	.45
❏ 10 Todd Dunwoody	1.00	.45
❏ 11 Miguel Tejada	1.50	.70
❏ 12 Jose Guillen	1.00	.45
❏ 13 Bartolo Colon	1.00	.45
❏ 14 Derrek Lee	1.00	.45
❏ 15 Antone Williamson	1.00	.45
❏ 16 Wilton Guerrero	1.00	.45
❏ 17 Jaret Wright	1.50	.70
❏ 18 Todd Helton	5.00	2.20
❏ 19 Shannon Stewart	1.50	.70
❏ 20 Nomar Garciaparra	12.00	5.50
❏ 21 Brett Tomko	1.00	.45
❏ 22 Fernando Tatis	4.00	1.80
❏ 23 Raul Ibanez	1.00	.45
❏ 24 Dennis Reyes	1.00	.45
❏ 25 Bobby Estalella	1.00	.45
❏ 26 Lou Collier	1.00	.45

❏ 27 Bubba Trammell	1.00	.45
❏ 28 Ben Grieve	4.00	1.80
❏ 29 Ivan Cruz	1.00	.45
❏ 30 Karim Garcia	1.00	.45

1998 Donruss Rookie Diamond Kings

	MINT	NRMT
COMPLETE SET (12)	60.00	27.00
COMMON CARD (1-12)	1.50	.70
MINOR STARS	2.50	1.10
SEMISTARS	4.00	1.80

STATED PRINT RUN 9500 SERIAL #'d SETS
*CANVAS: 1.25X TO 3X HI COLUMN
CANVAS PRINT RUN 500 SERIAL #'d SETS
RANDOM INSERTS IN UPDATE PACKS

❏ 1 Travis Lee	4.00	1.80
❏ 2 Fernando Tatis	6.00	2.70
❏ 3 Livan Hernandez	1.50	.70
❏ 4 Todd Helton	8.00	3.60
❏ 5 Derrek Lee	1.50	.70
❏ 6 Jaret Wright	2.50	1.10
❏ 7 Ben Grieve	6.00	2.70
❏ 8 Paul Konerko	2.50	1.10
❏ 9 Jose Cruz Jr.	2.50	1.10
❏ 10 Mark Kotsay	2.50	1.10
❏ 11 Todd Greene	1.50	.70
❏ 12 Brad Fullmer	1.50	.70

1998 Donruss Signature Series Previews

	MINT	NRMT
COMMON CARD	25.00	11.00

RANDOM INSERTS IN UPDATE PACKS
PRINT RUNS LISTED BELOW
ALOU/CASEY/JENKINS/WILSON
WERE NOT PUBLICLY RELEASED

❏ 1 Sandy Alomar Jr./96	50.00	22.00
❏ 2 Moises Alou/?		
❏ 3 Andy Benes/135	40.00	18.00
❏ 4 Russell Branyan/188	40.00	18.00
❏ 5 Sean Casey/?		
❏ 6 Tony Clark/188	30.00	13.50
❏ 7 Juan Encarnacion/193	40.00	18.00
❏ 8 Brad Fullmer/396	25.00	11.00
❏ 9 Juan Gonzalez/108	250.00	110.00
❏ 10 Ben Grieve/100	80.00	36.00
❏ 11 Todd Helton/101	100.00	45.00
❏ 12 Richard Hidalgo/380	25.00	11.00
❏ 13 A.J. Hinch/400	25.00	11.00
❏ 14 Damian Jackson/15	150.00	70.00
❏ 15 Geoff Jenkins/?		
❏ 16 Chipper Jones/112	300.00	135.00
❏ 17 Chuck Knoblauch/98	80.00	36.00
❏ 18 Travis Lee/101	60.00	27.00
❏ 19 Mike Lowell/450	30.00	13.50
❏ 20 Greg Maddux/92	300.00	135.00
❏ 21 Kevin Millwood/395	100.00	45.00
❏ 22 Magglio Ordonez/420	100.00	45.00
❏ 23 David Ortiz/393	25.00	11.00
❏ 24 Rafael Palmeiro/107	100.00	45.00
❏ 25 Cal Ripken/22	1500.00	700.00
❏ 26 Alex Rodriguez/23	1000.00	450.00
❏ 27 Curt Schilling/100	80.00	36.00
❏ 28 Randall Simon/380	25.00	11.00
❏ 29 Fernando Tatis/400	40.00	18.00
❏ 30 Miguel Tejada/375	30.00	13.50
❏ 31 Robin Ventura/95	60.00	27.00
❏ 32 Dan Wilson/?		
❏ 33 Kerry Wood/373	60.00	27.00

1998 Donruss Collections Donruss

	MINT	NRMT
COMPLETE SET (200)	120.00	55.00
COMMON (1-170/176-205)	.30	.14
MINOR STARS	.50	.23
SEMISTARS	.75	.35
UNLISTED STARS	1.25	.55

TWO PER PACK

❏ 1 Paul Molitor	1.25	.55
❏ 2 Juan Gonzalez	2.50	1.10
❏ 3 Darryl Kile	.30	.14
❏ 4 Randy Johnson	1.25	.55
❏ 5 Tom Glavine	1.25	.55
❏ 6 Pat Hentgen	.30	.14
❏ 7 David Justice	.50	.23
❏ 8 Kevin Brown	.75	.35
❏ 9 Mike Mussina	1.25	.55
❏ 10 Ken Caminiti	.50	.23
❏ 11 Todd Hundley	.50	.23
❏ 12 Frank Thomas	2.50	1.10
❏ 13 Ray Lankford	.50	.23
❏ 14 Justin Thompson	.30	.14
❏ 15 Jason Dickson	.30	.14
❏ 16 Kenny Lofton	.75	.35
❏ 17 Ivan Rodriguez	1.50	.70
❏ 18 Pedro Martinez	1.50	.70
❏ 19 Brady Anderson	.50	.23
❏ 20 Barry Larkin	1.25	.55
❏ 21 Chipper Jones	3.00	1.35
❏ 22 Tony Gwynn	3.00	1.35
❏ 23 Roger Clemens	3.00	1.35
❏ 24 Sandy Alomar Jr.	.50	.23
❏ 25 Tino Martinez	.50	.23
❏ 26 Jeff Bagwell	1.50	.70
❏ 27 Shawn Estes	.30	.14
❏ 28 Ken Griffey Jr.	6.00	2.70
❏ 29 Javier Lopez	.50	.23
❏ 30 Denny Neagle	.30	.14
❏ 31 Mike Piazza	4.00	1.80
❏ 32 Andres Galarraga	.75	.35

#	Player	Mint	Nrmt
33	Larry Walker	1.25	.55
34	Alex Rodriguez	4.00	1.80
35	Greg Maddux	3.00	1.35
36	Albert Belle	1.25	.55
37	Barry Bonds	1.50	.70
38	Mo Vaughn	1.25	.55
39	Kevin Appier	.50	.23
40	Wade Boggs	1.25	.55
41	Garret Anderson	.50	.23
42	Jeffrey Hammonds	.30	.14
43	Marquis Grissom	.30	.14
44	Jim Edmonds	.50	.23
45	Brian Jordan	.50	.23
46	Raul Mondesi	.50	.23
47	John Valentin	.50	.23
48	Brad Radke	.50	.23
49	Ismael Valdes	.30	.14
50	Matt Stairs	.50	.23
51	Matt Williams	1.25	.55
52	Reggie Jefferson	.30	.14
53	Alan Benes	.30	.14
54	Charles Johnson	.50	.23
55	Chuck Knoblauch	.50	.23
56	Edgar Martinez	1.25	.55
57	Nomar Garciaparra	4.00	1.80
58	Craig Biggio	1.25	.55
59	Bernie Williams	1.25	.55
60	David Cone	.75	.35
61	Cal Ripken	5.00	2.20
62	Mark McGwire	8.00	3.60
63	Roberto Alomar	1.25	.55
64	Fred McGriff	.75	.35
65	Eric Karros	.50	.23
66	Robin Ventura	.50	.23
67	Darin Erstad	.75	.35
68	Michael Tucker	.30	.14
69	Jim Thome	1.25	.55
70	Mark Grace	.75	.35
71	Lou Collier	.30	.14
72	Karim Garcia	.30	.14
73	Alex Fernandez	.30	.14
74	J.T. Snow	.50	.23
75	Reggie Sanders	.30	.14
76	John Smoltz	.75	.35
77	Tim Salmon	.75	.35
78	Paul O'Neill	.50	.23
79	Vinny Castilla	.50	.23
80	Rafael Palmeiro	1.25	.55
81	Jaret Wright	.50	.23
82	Jay Buhner	.50	.23
83	Brett Butler	.50	.23
84	Todd Greene	.30	.14
85	Scott Rolen	1.50	.70
86	Sammy Sosa	4.00	1.80
87	Jason Giambi	.50	.23
88	Carlos Delgado	1.25	.55
89	Deion Sanders	.50	.23
90	Wilton Guerrero	.30	.14
91	Andy Pettitte	.50	.23
92	Brian Giles	.50	.23
93	Dmitri Young	.50	.23
94	Ron Coomer	.30	.14
95	Mike Cameron	.50	.23
96	Edgardo Alfonzo	.75	.35
97	Jimmy Key	.50	.23
98	Ryan Klesko	.50	.23
99	Andy Benes	.30	.14
100	Derek Jeter	4.00	1.80
101	Jeff Fassero	.30	.14
102	Neifi Perez	.50	.23
103	Hideo Nomo	1.25	.55
104	Andruw Jones	1.25	.55
105	Todd Helton	1.50	.70
106	Livan Hernandez	.30	.14
107	Brett Tomko	.30	.14
108	Shannon Stewart	.50	.23
109	Bartolo Colon	.50	.23
110	Matt Morris	.50	.23
111	Miguel Tejada	.50	.23
112	Pokey Reese	.30	.14
113	Fernando Tatis	1.25	.55
114	Todd Dunwoody	.30	.14
115	Jose Cruz Jr.	.50	.23
116	Chan Ho Park	.50	.23
117	Kevin Young	.50	.23
118	Rickey Henderson	1.50	.70
119	Hideki Irabu	.50	.23
120	Francisco Cordova	.30	.14
121	Al Martin	.30	.14
122	Tony Clark	.50	.23
123	Curt Schilling	.75	.35
124	Rusty Greer	.50	.23
125	Jose Canseco	1.50	.70
126	Edgar Renteria	.50	.23
127	Todd Walker	.50	.23
128	Wally Joyner	.50	.23
129	Bill Mueller	.30	.14
130	Jose Guillen	.30	.14
131	Manny Ramirez	1.50	.70
132	Bobby Higginson	.50	.23
133	Kevin Orie	.30	.14
134	Will Clark	1.25	.55
135	Dave Nilsson	.30	.14
136	Jason Kendall	.50	.23
137	Ivan Cruz	.30	.14
138	Gary Sheffield	.50	.23
139	Bubba Trammell	.30	.14
140	Vladimir Guerrero	1.50	.70
141	Dennis Reyes	.30	.14
142	Bobby Bonilla	.50	.23
143	Ruben Rivera	.30	.14
144	Ben Grieve	1.25	.55
145	Moises Alou	.50	.23
146	Tony Womack	.30	.14
147	Eric Young	.30	.14
148	Paul Konerko	.50	.23
149	Dante Bichette	.50	.23
150	Joe Carter	.50	.23
151	Rondell White	.50	.23
152	Chris Holt	.30	.14
153	Shawn Green	1.25	.55
154	Mark Grudzielanek	.50	.23
155	Jermaine Dye	.50	.23
156	Ken Griffey Jr. FC	3.00	1.35
157	Frank Thomas FC	1.25	.55
158	Chipper Jones FC	1.50	.70
159	Mike Piazza FC	2.00	.90
160	Cal Ripken FC	2.50	1.10
161	Greg Maddux FC	1.50	.70
162	Juan Gonzalez FC	1.25	.55
163	Alex Rodriguez FC	2.00	.90
164	Mark McGwire FC	4.00	1.80
165	Derek Jeter FC	2.00	.90
166	Larry Walker CL	.50	.23
167	Tony Gwynn CL	1.50	.70
168	Mike Piazza CL	.30	.14
169	Scott Rolen CL	1.25	.55
170	Nomar Garciaparra CL	2.00	.90
176	Mark Kotsay RR	.50	.23
177	Neifi Perez RR	.50	.23
178	Paul Konerko RR	.50	.23
179	Jose Cruz Jr. RR	.50	.23
180	Hideki Irabu RR	.50	.23
181	Mike Cameron RR	.30	.14
182	Jeff Suppan RR	.30	.14
183	Kevin Orie RR	.30	.14
184	Pokey Reese RR	.30	.14
185	Todd Dunwoody RR	.30	.14
186	Miguel Tejada RR	.50	.23
187	Jose Guillen RR	.30	.14
188	Bartolo Colon RR	.50	.23
189	Derek Lee RR	.50	.23
190	Antone Williamson RR	.30	.14
191	Wilton Guerrero RR	.30	.14
192	Jaret Wright RR	.50	.23
193	Todd Helton RR	1.50	.70
194	Shannon Stewart RR	.50	.23
195	Nomar Garciaparra RR	4.00	1.80
196	Brett Tomko RR	.30	.14
197	Fernando Tatis RR	1.25	.55
198	Raul Ibanez RR	.30	.14
199	Dennis Reyes RR	.30	.14
200	Bobby Estalella RR	.30	.14
201	Lou Collier RR	.30	.14
202	Bubba Trammell RR	.30	.14
203	Ben Grieve RR	1.25	.55
204	Ivan Cruz RR	.30	.14
205	Karim Garcia RR	.30	.14

1998 Donruss Collections Elite

	MINT	NRMT
COMPLETE SET (150)	200.00	90.00
COMMON CARD (401-550)	.50	.23
MINOR STARS	.75	.35
SEMISTARS	1.25	.55
UNLISTED STARS	2.00	.90
ONE PER PACK		

#	Player	Mint	Nrmt
401	Ken Griffey Jr.	10.00	4.50
402	Frank Thomas	4.00	1.80
403	Alex Rodriguez	6.00	2.70
404	Mike Piazza	6.00	2.70
405	Greg Maddux	5.00	2.20
406	Cal Ripken	8.00	3.60
407	Chipper Jones	5.00	2.20
408	Derek Jeter	6.00	2.70
409	Tony Gwynn	5.00	2.20
410	Andruw Jones	2.00	.90
411	Juan Gonzalez	4.00	1.80
412	Jeff Bagwell	2.50	1.10
413	Mark McGwire	12.00	5.50
414	Roger Clemens	5.00	2.20
415	Albert Belle	2.00	.90
416	Barry Bonds	2.50	1.10
417	Kenny Lofton	1.25	.55
418	Ivan Rodriguez	2.50	1.10
419	Manny Ramirez	2.50	1.10
420	Jim Thome	2.00	.90
421	Chuck Knoblauch	.75	.35
422	Paul Molitor	2.00	.90
423	Barry Larkin	2.00	.90
424	Andy Pettitte	.75	.35
425	John Smoltz	1.25	.55
426	Randy Johnson	2.00	.90
427	Bernie Williams	2.00	.90
428	Larry Walker	2.00	.90
429	Mo Vaughn	2.00	.90
430	Bobby Higginson	.75	.35
431	Edgardo Alfonzo	1.25	.55
432	Justin Thompson	.50	.23
433	Jeff Suppan	.50	.23
434	Roberto Alomar	2.00	.90
435	Hideo Nomo	2.00	.90
436	Rusty Greer	.75	.35
437	Tim Salmon	1.25	.55
438	Jim Edmonds	.75	.35
439	Gary Sheffield	.75	.35
440	Ken Caminiti	.75	.35
441	Sammy Sosa	6.00	2.70
442	Tony Womack	.50	.23
443	Matt Williams	2.00	.90
444	Andres Galarraga	1.25	.55
445	Garret Anderson	.75	.35
446	Rafael Palmeiro	2.00	.90
447	Mike Mussina	2.00	.90
448	Craig Biggio	2.00	.90
449	Wade Boggs	2.00	.90
450	Tom Glavine	2.00	.90
451	Jason Giambi	.75	.35
452	Will Clark	2.00	.90
453	David Justice	.75	.35
454	Sandy Alomar Jr.	.75	.35
455	Edgar Martinez	.75	.35
456	Brady Anderson	.75	.35
457	Eric Young	.50	.23

#	Player	MINT	NRMT
458	Ray Lankford	.75	.35
459	Kevin Brown	1.25	.55
460	Raul Mondesi	.75	.35
461	Bobby Bonilla	.75	.35
462	Javier Lopez	.75	.35
463	Fred McGriff	1.25	.55
464	Rondell White	.75	.35
465	Todd Hundley	.75	.35
466	Mark Grace	1.25	.55
467	Alan Benes	.50	.23
468	Jeff Abbott	.50	.23
469	Bob Abreu	.75	.35
470	Deion Sanders	.75	.35
471	Tino Martinez	.75	.35
472	Shannon Stewart	.75	.35
473	Homer Bush	.50	.23
474	Carlos Delgado	2.00	.90
475	Raul Ibanez	.50	.23
476	Hideki Irabu	.75	.35
477	Jose Cruz Jr.	.75	.35
478	Tony Clark	.75	.35
479	Wilton Guerrero	.50	.23
480	Vladimir Guerrero	2.50	1.10
481	Scott Rolen	2.50	1.10
482	Nomar Garciaparra	6.00	2.70
483	Darin Erstad	1.25	.55
484	Chan Ho Park	.75	.35
485	Mike Cameron	.75	.35
486	Todd Walker	.75	.35
487	Todd Dunwoody	.50	.23
488	Neifi Perez	.50	.23
489	Brett Tomko	.50	.23
490	Jose Guillen	.50	.23
491	Matt Morris	.50	.23
492	Bartolo Colon	.75	.35
493	Jaret Wright	.75	.35
494	Shawn Estes	.50	.23
495	Livan Hernandez	.50	.23
496	Bobby Estalella	.50	.23
497	Ben Grieve	2.00	.90
498	Paul Konerko	.75	.35
499	David Ortiz	.50	.23
500	Todd Helton	2.50	1.10
501	Juan Encarnacion	.75	.35
502	Bubba Trammell	.50	.23
503	Miguel Tejada	.75	.35
504	Jacob Cruz	.50	.23
505	Todd Greene	.50	.23
506	Kevin Orie	.50	.23
507	Mark Kotsay	.75	.35
508	Fernando Tatis	2.00	.90
509	Jay Payton	.50	.23
510	Pokey Reese	.50	.23
511	Derrek Lee	.50	.23
512	Richard Hidalgo	.75	.35
513	Ricky Ledee	.75	.35
514	Lou Collier	.50	.23
515	Ruben Rivera	.50	.23
516	Shawn Green	2.00	.90
517	Moises Alou	.75	.35
518	Ken Griffey Jr. GEN	5.00	2.20
519	Frank Thomas GEN	2.00	.90
520	Alex Rodriguez GEN	3.00	1.35
521	Mike Piazza GEN	3.00	1.35
522	Greg Maddux GEN	2.50	1.10
523	Cal Ripken GEN	4.00	1.80
524	Chipper Jones GEN	2.50	1.10
525	Derek Jeter GEN	3.00	1.35
526	Tony Gwynn GEN	2.50	1.10
527	Andruw Jones GEN	.75	.35
528	Juan Gonzalez GEN	2.00	.90
529	Jeff Bagwell GEN	1.25	.55
530	Mark McGwire GEN	6.00	2.70
531	Roger Clemens GEN	2.50	1.10
532	Albert Belle GEN	.75	.35
533	Barry Bonds GEN	1.25	.55
534	Kenny Lofton GEN	.75	.35
535	Ivan Rodriguez GEN	1.25	.55
536	Manny Ramirez GEN	1.25	.55
537	Jim Thome GEN	.75	.35
538	Chuck Knoblauch GEN	.50	.23
539	Paul Molitor GEN	.75	.35
540	Barry Larkin GEN	.75	.35
541	Mo Vaughn GEN	.75	.35
542	Hideki Irabu GEN	.50	.23
543	Jose Cruz Jr. GEN	.50	.23
544	Tony Clark GEN	.50	.23
545	Vladimir Guerrero GEN	1.25	.55
546	Scott Rolen GEN	2.00	.90
547	Nomar Garciaparra GEN	3.00	1.35
548	Nomar Garciaparra CL	3.00	1.35
549	Larry Walker CL	.75	.35
550	Tino Martinez CL	.50	.23

1998 Donruss Collections Leaf

	MINT	NRMT
COMPLETE SET (200)	100.00	45.00
COMMON CARD (201-400)	.40	.18
MINOR STARS	.60	.25
SEMISTARS	1.00	.45
UNLISTED STARS	1.50	.70
TWO PER PACK		

#	Player	MINT	NRMT
201	Rusty Greer	.60	.25
202	Tino Martinez	.60	.25
203	Bobby Bonilla	.60	.25
204	Jason Giambi	.60	.25
205	Matt Morris	.40	.18
206	Craig Counsell	.40	.18
207	Reggie Jefferson	.40	.18
208	Brian Rose	.40	.18
209	Ruben Rivera	.40	.18
210	Shawn Estes	.40	.18
211	Tony Gwynn	4.00	1.80
212	Jeff Abbott	.40	.18
213	Jose Cruz Jr.	.60	.25
214	Francisco Cordova	.40	.18
215	Ryan Klesko	.60	.25
216	Tim Salmon	1.00	.45
217	Brett Tomko	.40	.18
218	Matt Williams	1.50	.70
219	Joe Carter	.60	.25
220	Harold Baines	.60	.25
221	Gary Sheffield	.60	.25
222	Charles Johnson	.60	.25
223	Aaron Boone	.40	.18
224	Eddie Murray	1.50	.70
225	Matt Stairs	.40	.18
226	David Cone	1.00	.45
227	Jon Nunnally	.40	.18
228	Chris Stynes	.40	.18
229	Enrique Wilson	.40	.18
230	Randy Johnson	1.50	.70
231	Garret Anderson	.60	.25
232	Manny Ramirez	2.00	.90
233	Jeff Suppan	.40	.18
234	Rickey Henderson	2.00	.90
235	Scott Spiezio	.40	.18
236	Rondell White	.60	.25
237	Todd Greene	.40	.18
238	Delino DeShields	.40	.18
239	Kevin Brown	1.00	.45
240	Chili Davis	.40	.18
241	Jimmy Key	.60	.25
242	Mike Mussina	1.50	.70
243	Joe Randa	.40	.18
244	Chan Ho Park	.60	.25
245	Brad Radke	.40	.18
246	Geronimo Berroa	.40	.18
247	Wade Boggs	1.50	.70
248	Kevin Appier	.40	.18
249	Moises Alou	.60	.25
250	David Justice	.60	.25
251	Ivan Rodriguez	2.00	.90
252	J.T. Snow	.60	.25
253	Brian Giles	.40	.18
254	Will Clark	1.50	.70
255	Justin Thompson	.40	.18
256	Javier Lopez	.60	.25
257	Hideki Irabu	.60	.25
258	Mark Grudzielanek	.40	.18
259	Abraham Nunez	.40	.18
260	Todd Hollandsworth	.40	.18
261	Jay Bell	.60	.25
262	Nomar Garciaparra	5.00	2.20
263	Vinny Castilla	.60	.25
264	Lou Collier	.40	.18
265	Kevin Orie	.40	.18
266	John Valentin	.60	.25
267	Robin Ventura	.60	.25
268	Denny Neagle	.40	.18
269	Tony Womack	.40	.18
270	Dennis Reyes	.40	.18
271	Wally Joyner	.60	.25
272	Kevin Brown	1.00	.45
273	Ray Durham	.60	.25
274	Mike Cameron	.60	.25
275	Dante Bichette	.60	.25
276	Jose Guillen	.40	.18
277	Carlos Delgado	1.50	.70
278	Paul Molitor	1.50	.70
279	Jason Kendall	.60	.25
280	Mark Bellhorn	.40	.18
281	Damian Jackson	.40	.18
282	Bill Mueller	.40	.18
283	Kevin Young	.40	.18
284	Curt Schilling	1.00	.45
285	Jeffrey Hammonds	.40	.18
286	Roberto Alomar Jr.	.60	.25
287	Bartolo Colon	.60	.25
288	Wilton Guerrero	.40	.18
289	Bernie Williams	1.50	.70
290	Deion Sanders	.60	.25
291	Mike Piazza	5.00	2.20
292	Butch Huskey	.40	.18
293	Edgardo Alfonzo	1.00	.45
294	Alan Benes	.40	.18
295	Craig Biggio	1.50	.70
296	Mark Grace	1.00	.45
297	Shawn Green	.70	.35
298	Derek Lee	.40	.18
299	Ken Griffey Jr.	8.00	3.60
300	Tim Raines	.60	.25
301	Pokey Reese	.40	.18
302	Lee Stevens	.40	.18
303	Shannon Stewart	.40	.18
304	John Smoltz	1.00	.45
305	Frank Thomas	3.00	1.35
306	Jeff Fassero	.40	.18
307	Jay Buhner	.60	.25
308	Jose Canseco	2.00	.90
309	Omar Vizquel	.60	.25
310	Travis Fryman	.60	.25
311	Dave Nilsson	.40	.18
312	John Olerud	.60	.25
313	Larry Walker	1.50	.70
314	Jim Edmonds	.60	.25
315	Bobby Higginson	.40	.18
316	Todd Hundley	.60	.25
317	Paul O'Neill	.60	.25
318	Bip Roberts	.40	.18
319	Ismael Valdes	.40	.18
320	Pedro Martinez	2.00	.90
321	Jeff Cirillo	.60	.25
322	Andy Benes	.40	.18
323	Bobby Jones	.40	.18
324	Brian Hunter	.40	.18
325	Darryl Kile	.40	.18
326	Pat Hentgen	.40	.18
327	Marquis Grissom	.40	.18
328	Eric Davis	.60	.25
329	Chipper Jones	4.00	1.80
330	Edgar Martinez	.60	.25
331	Andy Pettitte	.60	.25
332	Cal Ripken	6.00	2.70
333	Scott Rolen	2.00	.90
334	Ron Coomer	.40	.18
335	Luis Castillo	.40	.18
336	Fred McGriff	1.00	.45

#	Card	MINT	NRMT
❑ 337	Neifi Perez	.60	.25
❑ 338	Eric Karros	.60	.25
❑ 339	Alex Fernandez	.40	.18
❑ 340	Jason Dickson	.40	.18
❑ 341	Lance Johnson	.40	.18
❑ 342	Ray Lankford	.60	.25
❑ 343	Sammy Sosa	5.00	2.20
❑ 344	Eric Young	.40	.18
❑ 345	Bubba Trammell	.40	.18
❑ 346	Todd Walker CC	.60	.25
❑ 347	Mo Vaughn CC	.60	.25
❑ 348	Jeff Bagwell CC	1.00	.45
❑ 349	Kenny Lofton CC	.60	.25
❑ 350	Raul Mondesi CC	.40	.18
❑ 351	Mike Piazza CC	2.50	1.10
❑ 352	Chipper Jones CC	2.00	.90
❑ 353	Larry Walker CC	.60	.25
❑ 354	Greg Maddux CC	2.00	.90
❑ 355	Ken Griffey Jr. CC	4.00	1.80
❑ 356	Frank Thomas CC	1.50	.70
❑ 357	Darin Erstad GLS	.60	.25
❑ 358	Roberto Alomar GLS	.60	.25
❑ 359	Albert Belle GLS	.60	.25
❑ 360	Jim Thome GLS	.60	.25
❑ 361	Tony Clark GLS	.40	.18
❑ 362	Chuck Knoblauch GLS	.40	.18
❑ 363	Derek Jeter GLS	2.50	1.10
❑ 364	Alex Rodriguez GLS	2.50	1.10
❑ 365	Tony Gwynn GLS	2.00	.90
❑ 366	Roger Clemens GLS	2.00	.90
❑ 367	Barry Larkin GLS	.60	.25
❑ 368	Andres Galarraga GLS ..	.60	.25
❑ 369	Vladimir Guerrero GLS	1.00	.45
❑ 370	Mark McGwire GLS	5.00	2.20
❑ 371	Barry Bonds GLS	1.00	.45
❑ 372	Juan Gonzalez GLS	1.50	.70
❑ 373	Andruw Jones GLS	.60	.25
❑ 374	Paul Molitor GLS	.60	.25
❑ 375	Hideo Nomo GLS	.60	.25
❑ 376	Cal Ripken GLS	3.00	1.35
❑ 377	Brad Fullmer GLR	.40	.18
❑ 378	Jaret Wright GLR	.40	.18
❑ 379	Bobby Estalella GLR	.40	.18
❑ 380	Ben Grieve GLR	1.50	.70
❑ 381	Paul Konerko GLR	.60	.25
❑ 382	David Ortiz GLR	.40	.18
❑ 383	Todd Helton GLR	2.00	.90
❑ 384	Juan Encarnacion GLR	.60	.25
❑ 385	Miguel Tejada GLR	.60	.25
❑ 386	Jacob Cruz GLR	.40	.18
❑ 387	Mark Kotsay GLR	.60	.25
❑ 388	Fernando Tatis GLR	1.50	.70
❑ 389	Ricky Ledee GLR	.60	.25
❑ 390	Richard Hidalgo GLR	.60	.25
❑ 391	Richie Sexson GLR	1.00	.45
❑ 392	Luis Ordaz GLR	.40	.18
❑ 393	Eli Marrero GLR	.40	.18
❑ 394	Livan Hernandez GLR..	.40	.18
❑ 395	Homer Bush GLR	.40	.18
❑ 396	Raul Ibanez GLR	.40	.18
❑ 397	Nomar Garciaparra CL	2.50	1.10
❑ 398	Scott Rolen CL	1.50	.70
❑ 399	Jose Cruz Jr. CL	.40	.18
❑ 400	Al Martin	.40	.18

1998 Donruss Collections Preferred

	MINT	NRMT
COMPLETE SET (200)	600.00	275.00
COMMON CARD (551-750)	1.50	.70
MINOR STARS	2.50	1.10
SEMISTARS	4.00	1.80
UNLISTED STARS	6.00	2.70
STATED ODDS 1:2		
LESS THAN 1400 SETS PRINTED		

#	Card	MINT	NRMT
❑ 551	Ken Griffey Jr. EX	30.00	13.50
❑ 552	Frank Thomas EX	12.00	5.50
❑ 553	Cal Ripken EX	25.00	11.00
❑ 554	Alex Rodriguez EX	20.00	9.00
❑ 555	Greg Maddux EX	15.00	6.75
❑ 556	Mike Piazza EX	20.00	9.00
❑ 557	Chipper Jones EX	15.00	6.75
❑ 558	Tony Gwynn FB	15.00	6.75
❑ 559	Derek Jeter FB	20.00	9.00
❑ 560	Jeff Bagwell FB	8.00	3.60
❑ 561	Juan Gonzalez EX	12.00	5.50
❑ 562	Nomar Garciaparra EX	20.00	9.00
❑ 563	Andruw Jones FB	6.00	2.70
❑ 564	Hideo Nomo FB	6.00	2.70
❑ 565	Roger Clemens FB	15.00	6.75
❑ 566	Mark McGwire FB	40.00	18.00
❑ 567	Scott Rolen FB	8.00	3.60
❑ 568	Vladimir Guerrero FB	8.00	3.60
❑ 569	Barry Bonds FB	8.00	3.60
❑ 570	Darin Erstad FB	4.00	1.80
❑ 571	Albert Belle FB	6.00	2.70
❑ 572	Kenny Lofton FB	4.00	1.80
❑ 573	Mo Vaughn FB	6.00	2.70
❑ 574	Tony Clark FB	2.50	1.10
❑ 575	Ivan Rodriguez FB	8.00	3.60
❑ 576	Larry Walker CB	6.00	2.70
❑ 577	Eddie Murray CB	6.00	2.70
❑ 578	Andy Pettitte CB	2.50	1.10
❑ 579	Roberto Alomar CB	6.00	2.70
❑ 580	Randy Johnson CB	6.00	2.70
❑ 581	Manny Ramirez CB	8.00	3.60
❑ 582	Paul Molitor CB	6.00	2.70
❑ 583	Mike Mussina CB	6.00	2.70
❑ 584	Jim Thome CB	6.00	2.70
❑ 585	Tino Martinez CB	2.50	1.10
❑ 586	Gary Sheffield CB	2.50	1.10
❑ 587	Chuck Knoblauch CB	2.50	1.10
❑ 588	Bernie Williams CB	6.00	2.70
❑ 589	Tim Salmon CB	4.00	1.80
❑ 590	Sammy Sosa CB	20.00	9.00
❑ 591	Wade Boggs GS	6.00	2.70
❑ 592	Will Clark GS	6.00	2.70
❑ 593	Andres Galarraga GS	4.00	1.80
❑ 594	Raul Mondesi GS	2.50	1.10
❑ 595	Rickey Henderson GS	8.00	3.60
❑ 596	Jose Canseco GS	8.00	3.60
❑ 597	Pedro Martinez GS	8.00	3.60
❑ 598	Jay Buhner GS	2.50	1.10
❑ 599	Ryan Klesko GS	2.50	1.10
❑ 600	Barry Larkin GS	6.00	2.70
❑ 601	Charles Johnson GS	2.50	1.10
❑ 602	Tom Glavine GS	6.00	2.70
❑ 603	Edgar Martinez GS	2.50	1.10
❑ 604	Fred McGriff GS	4.00	1.80
❑ 605	Moises Alou ME	2.50	1.10
❑ 606	Dante Bichette GS	2.50	1.10
❑ 607	Jim Edmonds CB	2.50	1.10
❑ 608	Mark Grace ME	4.00	1.80
❑ 609	Chan Ho Park ME	2.50	1.10
❑ 610	Justin Thompson ME	1.50	.70
❑ 611	John Smoltz ME	4.00	1.80
❑ 612	Craig Biggio GS	6.00	2.70
❑ 613	Ken Caminiti ME	2.50	1.10
❑ 614	Deion Sanders ME	2.50	1.10
❑ 615	Carlos Delgado GS	6.00	2.70
❑ 616	David Justice CB	2.50	1.10
❑ 617	J.T. Snow GS	2.50	1.10
❑ 618	Jason Giambi CB	2.50	1.10
❑ 619	Garret Anderson GS	2.50	1.10
❑ 620	Rondell White ME	2.50	1.10
❑ 621	Matt Williams ME	6.00	2.70
❑ 622	Brady Anderson ME	2.50	1.10
❑ 623	Eric Karros GS	2.50	1.10
❑ 624	Javier Lopez GS	2.50	1.10
❑ 625	Pat Henigen GS	1.50	.70
❑ 626	Todd Hundley GS	2.50	1.10
❑ 627	Ray Lankford GS	2.50	1.10
❑ 628	Denny Neagle GS	1.50	.70
❑ 629	Henry Rodriguez GS	2.50	1.10
❑ 630	Sandy Alomar Jr. ME	2.50	1.10
❑ 631	Rafael Palmeiro ME	6.00	2.70
❑ 632	Robin Ventura GS	2.50	1.10
❑ 633	John Olerud GS	2.50	1.10
❑ 634	Omar Vizquel ME	2.50	1.10
❑ 635	Joe Randa GS	1.50	.70
❑ 636	Lance Johnson GS	1.50	.70
❑ 637	Kevin Brown GS	4.00	1.80
❑ 638	Curt Schilling GS	4.00	1.80
❑ 639	Ismael Valdes GS	1.50	.70
❑ 640	Francisco Cordova GS	1.50	.70
❑ 641	David Cone GS	4.00	1.80
❑ 642	Paul O'Neill GS	2.50	1.10
❑ 643	Jimmy Key GS	2.50	1.10
❑ 644	Brad Radke GS	2.50	1.10
❑ 645	Kevin Appier GS	2.50	1.10
❑ 646	Al Martin GS	1.50	.70
❑ 647	Rusty Greer GS	2.50	1.10
❑ 648	Reggie Jefferson GS	1.50	.70
❑ 649	Ron Coomer GS	1.50	.70
❑ 650	Vinny Castilla GS	2.50	1.10
❑ 651	Bobby Bonilla GS	2.50	1.10
❑ 652	Eric Young GS	1.50	.70
❑ 653	Tony Womack GS	1.50	.70
❑ 654	Jason Kendall GS	2.50	1.10
❑ 655	Jeff Suppan GS	1.50	.70
❑ 656	Shawn Estes ME	1.50	.70
❑ 657	Shawn Green GS	6.00	2.70
❑ 658	Edgardo Alfonzo ME	4.00	1.80
❑ 659	Alan Benes ME	1.50	.70
❑ 660	Bobby Higginson GS	2.50	1.10
❑ 661	Mark Grudzielanek GS	1.50	.70
❑ 662	Wilton Guerrero GS	1.50	.70
❑ 663	Todd Greene ME	1.50	.70
❑ 664	Pokey Reese GS	1.50	.70
❑ 665	Jose Guillen CB	1.50	.70
❑ 666	Neifi Perez ME	2.50	1.10
❑ 667	Luis Castillo GS	1.50	.70
❑ 668	Edgar Renteria GS	2.50	1.10
❑ 669	Karim Garcia GS	1.50	.70
❑ 670	Butch Huskey GS	1.50	.70
❑ 671	Michael Tucker GS	1.50	.70
❑ 672	Jason Dickson GS	1.50	.70
❑ 673	Todd Walker ME	2.50	1.10
❑ 674	Brian Jordan GS	2.50	1.10
❑ 675	Joe Carter ME	2.50	1.10
❑ 676	Matt Morris ME	1.50	.70
❑ 677	Brett Tomko ME	1.50	.70
❑ 678	Mike Cameron ME	2.50	1.10
❑ 679	Russ Davis GS	1.50	.70
❑ 680	Shannon Stewart ME	2.50	1.10
❑ 681	Kevin Orie GS	1.50	.70
❑ 682	Scott Spiezio GS	1.50	.70
❑ 683	Brian Giles GS	2.50	1.10
❑ 684	Raul Casanova GS	1.50	.70
❑ 685	Jose Cruz Jr. GS	6.00	2.70
❑ 686	Hideki Irabu GS	2.50	1.10
❑ 687	Bubba Trammell GS	1.50	.70
❑ 688	Richard Hidalgo CB	2.50	1.10
❑ 689	Paul Konerko GS	2.50	1.10
❑ 690	Todd Helton GS	6.00	3.60
❑ 691	Miguel Tejada GS	2.50	1.10
❑ 692	Fernando Tatis ME	6.00	2.70
❑ 693	Ben Grieve FB	6.00	2.70
❑ 694	Travis Lee FB	4.00	1.80
❑ 695	Mark Kotsay GS	2.50	1.10
❑ 696	Eli Marrero ME	1.50	.70
❑ 697	David Ortiz CB	1.50	.70
❑ 698	Juan Encarnacion ME	2.50	1.10
❑ 699	Jaret Wright ME	2.50	1.10
❑ 700	Livan Hernandez CB	1.50	.70
❑ 701	Ruben Rivera GS	1.50	.70
❑ 702	Brad Fullmer ME	1.50	.70
❑ 703	Dennis Reyes GS	1.50	.70
❑ 704	Enrique Wilson ME	1.50	.70
❑ 705	Todd Dunwoody ME	1.50	.70
❑ 706	Derrick Gibson ME	1.50	.70
❑ 707	Aaron Boone ME	1.50	.70
❑ 708	Ron Wright ME	1.50	.70
❑ 709	Preston Wilson ME	2.50	1.10
❑ 710	Abraham Nunez GS	1.50	.70
❑ 711	Shane Monahan GS	1.50	.70
❑ 712	Carl Pavano GS	1.50	.70
❑ 713	Derrek Lee GS	1.50	.70

	MINT	NRMT
❏ 714 Jeff Abbott GS	1.50	.70
❏ 715 Wes Helms ME	1.50	.70
❏ 716 Brian Rose GS	1.50	.70
❏ 717 Bobby Estaiella GS	1.50	.70
❏ 718 Ken Griffey Jr. PP GS	15.00	6.75
❏ 719 Frank Thomas PP GS	6.00	2.70
❏ 720 Cal Ripken PP GS	12.00	5.50
❏ 721 Alex Rodriguez PP GS	10.00	4.50
❏ 722 Greg Maddux PP GS	8.00	3.60
❏ 723 Mike Piazza PP GS	10.00	4.50
❏ 724 Chipper Jones PP GS	8.00	3.60
❏ 725 Tony Gwynn PP GS	8.00	3.60
❏ 726 Derek Jeter PP GS	10.00	4.50
❏ 727 Jeff Bagwell PP GS	4.00	1.80
❏ 728 Juan Gonzalez PP GS	6.00	2.70
❏ 729 N. Garciaparra PP GS	10.00	4.50
❏ 730 Andruw Jones PP GS	2.50	1.10
❏ 731 Hideo Nomo PP GS	2.50	1.10
❏ 732 Roger Clemens PP GS	8.00	3.60
❏ 733 Mark McGwire PP GS	20.00	9.00
❏ 734 Scott Rolen PP GS	6.00	2.70
❏ 735 Barry Bonds PP GS	4.00	1.80
❏ 736 Darin Erstad PP GS	2.50	1.10
❏ 737 Mo Vaughn PP GS	2.50	1.10
❏ 738 Ivan Rodriguez PP GS	4.00	1.80
❏ 739 Larry Walker PP ME	2.50	1.10
❏ 740 Andy Pettitte PP GS	1.50	.70
❏ 741 Randy Johnson PP ME	2.50	1.10
❏ 742 Paul Molitor PP GS	2.50	1.10
❏ 743 Jim Thome PP GS	2.50	1.10
❏ 744 Tino Martinez PP ME	1.50	.70
❏ 745 Gary Sheffield PP GS	1.50	.70
❏ 746 Albert Belle PP GS	2.50	1.10
❏ 747 Jose Cruz Jr. PP GS	1.50	.70
❏ 748 Todd Helton CL GS	2.50	1.10
❏ 749 Ben Grieve CL GS	2.50	1.10
❏ 750 Paul Konerko CL GS	1.50	.70

1998 Donruss Prized Collections Donruss

	MINT	NRMT
COMMON (1-170/176-205)	2.50	1.10

*STARS: 3X TO 8X BASIC CARDS
*YOUNG STARS: 2.5X TO 6X BASIC CARDS
RANDOM INSERTS IN PACKS
LESS THAN 560 SETS PRINTED

1998 Donruss Prized Collections Elite

	MINT	NRMT
COMMON CARD (401-550)	5.00	2.20

*STARS: 4X TO 10X BASIC CARDS
*YOUNG STARS: 3X TO 8X BASIC CARDS
RANDOM INSERTS IN PACKS
LESS THAN 220 SETS PRINTED

1998 Donruss Prized Collections Leaf

	MINT	NRMT
COMMON CARD (201-400)	3.00	1.35

*STARS: 3X TO 8X BASIC CARDS
*YOUNG STARS: 2.5X TO 6X BASIC CARDS
RANDOM INSERTS IN PACKS
LESS THAN 400 SETS PRINTED

1998 Donruss Prized Collections Preferred

	MINT	NRMT
COMMON CARD (551-750)	20.00	9.00

*STARS: 5X TO 12X BASIC CARDS
*YOUNG STARS: 4X TO 10X BASIC CARDS
RANDOM INSERTS IN PACKS
LESS THAN 55 SETS PRINTED

1997 Donruss Elite

	MINT	NRMT
COMPLETE SET (150)	40.00	18.00
COMMON CARD (1-150)	.20	.09
MINOR STARS	.40	.18
UNLISTED STARS	.75	.35
COMMON GOLD (1-150)	2.00	.90

*GOLD STARS: 6X TO 15X HI COLUMN
GOLD: RANDOM INSERTS IN PACKS

		MINT	NRMT
❏ 1	Juan Gonzalez	1.50	.70
❏ 2	Alex Rodriguez	2.50	1.10
❏ 3	Frank Thomas	1.50	.70
❏ 4	Greg Maddux	2.00	.90
❏ 5	Ken Griffey Jr.	4.00	1.80
❏ 6	Cal Ripken	3.00	1.35
❏ 7	Mike Piazza	2.50	1.10
❏ 8	Chipper Jones	2.00	.90
❏ 9	Albert Belle	.75	.35
❏ 10	Andruw Jones	1.00	.45
❏ 11	Vladimir Guerrero	1.25	.55
❏ 12	Mo Vaughn	.75	.35

		MINT	NRMT
		UER front Gonzales	
❏ 13	Ivan Rodriguez	1.00	.45
❏ 14	Andy Pettitte	.50	.23
❏ 15	Tony Gwynn	2.00	.90
❏ 16	Barry Bonds	1.00	.45
❏ 17	Jeff Bagwell	1.00	.45
❏ 18	Manny Ramirez	1.00	.45
❏ 19	Kenny Lofton	.50	.23
❏ 20	Roberto Alomar	.75	.35
❏ 21	Mark McGwire	4.00	1.80
❏ 22	Ryan Klesko	.40	.18
❏ 23	Tim Salmon	.75	.35
❏ 24	Derek Jeter	2.50	1.10
❏ 25	Eddie Murray	.75	.35
❏ 26	Jermaine Dye	.40	.18
❏ 27	Ruben Rivera	.20	.09
❏ 28	Jim Edmonds	.40	.18
❏ 29	Mike Mussina	.75	.35
❏ 30	Randy Johnson	.75	.35
❏ 31	Sammy Sosa	2.50	1.10
❏ 32	Hideo Nomo	.75	.35
❏ 33	Chuck Knoblauch	.75	.35
❏ 34	Paul Molitor	.75	.35
❏ 35	Rafael Palmeiro	.75	.35
❏ 36	Brady Anderson	.40	.18
❏ 37	Will Clark	.75	.35
❏ 38	Craig Biggio	.75	.35
❏ 39	Jason Giambi	.40	.18
❏ 40	Roger Clemens	2.00	.90
❏ 41	Jay Buhner	.40	.18
❏ 42	Edgar Martinez	.40	.18
❏ 43	Gary Sheffield	.40	.18
❏ 44	Fred McGriff	.50	.23
❏ 45	Bobby Bonilla	.40	.18
❏ 46	Tom Glavine	.75	.35
❏ 47	Wade Boggs	.75	.35
❏ 48	Jeff Conine	.20	.09
❏ 49	John Smoltz	.50	.23
❏ 50	Jim Thome	.75	.35
❏ 51	Billy Wagner	.40	.18
❏ 52	Jose Canseco	1.00	.45
❏ 53	Javy Lopez	.40	.18
❏ 54	Cecil Fielder	.40	.18
❏ 55	Garret Anderson	.40	.18
❏ 56	Alex Ochoa	.20	.09
❏ 57	Scott Rolen	1.25	.55
❏ 58	Darin Erstad	.75	.35
❏ 59	Rey Ordonez	.40	.18
❏ 60	Dante Bichette	.40	.18
❏ 61	Joe Carter	.40	.18
❏ 62	Moises Alou	.40	.18
❏ 63	Jason Isringhausen	.20	.09
❏ 64	Karim Garcia	.40	.18
❏ 65	Brian Jordan	.40	.18
❏ 66	Ruben Sierra	.20	.09
❏ 67	Todd Hollandsworth	.20	.09
❏ 68	Paul Wilson	.20	.09
❏ 69	Ernie Young	.20	.09
❏ 70	Ryne Sandberg	1.00	.45
❏ 71	Raul Mondesi	.40	.18
❏ 72	George Arias	.20	.09
❏ 73	Ray Durham	.40	.18
❏ 74	Dean Palmer	.40	.18
❏ 75	Shawn Green	.75	.35
❏ 76	Eric Young	.40	.18
❏ 77	Jason Kendall	.50	.23
❏ 78	Greg Vaughn	.40	.18
❏ 79	Terrell Wade	.20	.09
❏ 80	Bill Pulsipher	.20	.09
❏ 81	Bobby Higginson	.40	.18
❏ 82	Mark Grudzielanek	.40	.18
❏ 83	Ken Caminiti	.50	.23
❏ 84	Todd Greene	.20	.09
❏ 85	Carlos Delgado	.75	.35
❏ 86	Mark Grace	.50	.23
❏ 87	Rondell White	.40	.18
❏ 88	Barry Larkin	.75	.35
❏ 89	J.T. Snow	.40	.18
❏ 90	Alex Gonzalez	.20	.09
❏ 91	Raul Casanova	.20	.09
❏ 92	Marc Newfield	.20	.09
❏ 93	Jermaine Allensworth	.20	.09
❏ 94	John Mabry	.20	.09
❏ 95	Kirby Puckett	1.25	.55
❏ 96	Travis Fryman	.50	.23
❏ 97	Kevin Brown	.50	.23

		MINT	NRMT
98	Andres Galarraga	.75	.35
99	Marty Cordova	.20	.09
100	Henry Rodriguez	.40	.18
101	Sterling Hitchcock	.40	.18
102	Trey Beamon	.20	.09
103	Brett Butler	.40	.18
104	Rickey Henderson	1.00	.45
105	Tino Martinez	.75	.35
106	Kevin Appier	.40	.18
107	Brian Hunter	.40	.18
108	Eric Karros	.40	.18
109	Andre Dawson	.50	.23
110	Darryl Strawberry	.40	.18
111	James Baldwin	.40	.18
112	Chad Mottola	.20	.09
113	Dave Nilsson	.20	.09
114	Carlos Baerga	.20	.09
115	Chan Ho Park	.75	.35
116	John Jaha	.20	.09
117	Alan Benes	.20	.09
118	Mariano Rivera	.40	.18
119	Ellis Burks	.40	.18
120	Tony Clark	.50	.23
121	Todd Walker	.75	.35
122	Dwight Gooden	.40	.18
123	Ugueth Urbina	.40	.18
124	David Cone	.50	.23
125	Ozzie Smith	1.00	.45
126	Kimera Bartee	.20	.09
127	Rusty Greer	.40	.18
128	Pat Hentgen	.40	.18
129	Charles Johnson	.40	.18
130	Quinton McCracken	.20	.09
131	Troy Percival	.40	.18
132	Shane Reynolds	.20	.09
133	Charles Nagy	.40	.18
134	Tom Goodwin	.20	.09
135	Ron Gant	.40	.18
136	Dan Wilson	.20	.09
137	Matt Williams	.75	.35
138	LaTroy Hawkins	.20	.09
139	Kevin Seitzer	.20	.09
140	Michael Tucker	.20	.09
141	Todd Hundley	.40	.18
142	Alex Fernandez	.20	.09
143	Marquis Grissom	.40	.18
144	Steve Finley	.40	.18
145	Curtis Pride	.20	.09
146	Derek Bell	.40	.18
147	Butch Huskey	.20	.09
148	Dwight Gooden CL	.40	.18
149	Al Leiter CL	.40	.18
150	Hideo Nomo CL	.40	.18

1997 Donruss Elite Leather and Lumber

		MINT	NRMT
	COMPLETE SET (10)	600.00	275.00
	COMMON CARD (1-10)	15.00	6.75
	RANDOM INSERTS IN PACKS		
	STATED PRINT RUN 500 SERIAL #'d SETS		
1	Ken Griffey Jr.	120.00	55.00
2	Alex Rodriguez	80.00	36.00
3	Frank Thomas	50.00	22.00
4	Chipper Jones	60.00	27.00
5	Ivan Rodriguez	30.00	13.50
6	Cal Ripken	100.00	45.00
7	Barry Bonds	30.00	13.50
8	Chuck Knoblauch	15.00	6.75
9	Manny Ramirez	30.00	13.50
10	Mark McGwire	120.00	55.00

1997 Donruss Elite Passing the Torch

		MINT	NRMT
	COMPLETE SET (12)	300.00	135.00
	COMMON CARD (1-12)	5.00	2.20
	RANDOM INSERTS IN PACKS		
	STATED PRINT RUN 1350 SERIAL #'d SETS		
1	Cal Ripken	40.00	18.00
2	Alex Rodriguez	30.00	13.50
3	Cal Ripken	60.00	27.00
	Alex Rodriguez		
4	Kirby Puckett	15.00	6.75
5	Andruw Jones	12.00	5.50
6	Kirby Puckett	15.00	6.75
	Andruw Jones		
7	Cecil Fielder	5.00	2.20
8	Frank Thomas	20.00	9.00
9	Cecil Fielder	20.00	9.00
	Frank Thomas		
10	Ozzie Smith	12.00	5.50
11	Derek Jeter	30.00	13.50
12	Ozzie Smith	30.00	13.50
	Derek Jeter		

1997 Donruss Elite Passing the Torch Autographs

		MINT	NRMT
	COMMON CARD (1-12)	50.00	22.00
	RANDOM INSERTS IN PACKS		
	STATED PRINT RUN 150 SERIAL #'d SETS		
1	Cal Ripken	500.00	220.00
2	Alex Rodriguez	400.00	180.00
3	Cal Ripken	1000.00	450.00
	Alex Rodriguez		
4	Kirby Puckett	250.00	110.00
5	Andruw Jones	100.00	45.00
6	Kirby Puckett	250.00	110.00
	Andruw Jones		
7	Cecil Fielder	50.00	22.00
8	Frank Thomas	250.00	110.00
9	Cecil Fielder	250.00	110.00
	Frank Thomas		
10	Ozzie Smith	200.00	90.00
11	Derek Jeter	300.00	135.00
12	Ozzie Smith	300.00	135.00
	Derek Jeter		

1997 Donruss Elite Turn of the Century

		MINT	NRMT
	COMPLETE SET (20)	120.00	55.00
	COMMON CARD (1-20)	2.00	.90
	MINOR STARS	4.00	1.80
	UNLISTED STARS	8.00	3.60
	STATED PRINT RUN 3000 SERIAL #'d SETS		
	COMP.DIE CUT SET (20)	400.00	180.00
	*DIE CUTS: 1.25X TO 3X HI COLUMN		
	DC STATED PRINT RUN 500 SERIAL #'d SETS		
	RANDOM INSERTS IN PACKS		
1	Alex Rodriguez	25.00	11.00
2	Andruw Jones	10.00	4.50
3	Chipper Jones	20.00	9.00
4	Todd Walker	8.00	3.60
5	Scott Rolen	12.00	5.50
6	Trey Beamon	2.00	.90
7	Derek Jeter	25.00	11.00
8	Darin Erstad	8.00	3.60
9	Tony Clark	6.00	2.70
10	Todd Greene	2.00	.90
11	Jason Giambi	4.00	1.80
12	Justin Thompson	4.00	1.80
13	Ernie Young	2.00	.90
14	Jason Kendall	6.00	2.70
15	Alex Ochoa	2.00	.90
16	Brooks Kieschnick	2.00	.90
17	Bobby Higginson	4.00	1.80
18	Ruben Rivera	2.00	.90
19	Chan Ho Park	8.00	3.60
20	Chad Mottola	2.00	.90
P5	Scott Rolen Promo	5.00	2.20
P7	Derek Jeter Promo	5.00	2.20

1998 Donruss Elite

	MINT	NRMT
COMPLETE SET (150)	30.00	13.50

	MINT	NRMT
COMMON CARD (1-150)	.15	.07
MINOR STARS	.25	.11
SEMISTARS	.40	.18
UNLISTED STARS	.60	.25
THOMAS AU AVAIL VIA MAIL EXCHANGE		

		MINT	NRMT
☐ 1	Ken Griffey Jr.	3.00	1.35
☐ 2	Frank Thomas	1.25	.55
☐ 3	Alex Rodriguez	2.00	.90
☐ 4	Mike Piazza	2.00	.90
☐ 5	Greg Maddux	1.50	.70
☐ 6	Cal Ripken	2.50	1.10
☐ 7	Chipper Jones	1.50	.70
☐ 8	Derek Jeter	2.00	.90
☐ 9	Tony Gwynn	1.50	.70
☐ 10	Andruw Jones	.60	.25
☐ 11	Juan Gonzalez	1.25	.55
☐ 12	Jeff Bagwell	.75	.35
☐ 13	Mark McGwire	4.00	1.80
☐ 14	Roger Clemens	1.50	.70
☐ 15	Albert Belle	.60	.25
☐ 16	Barry Bonds	.75	.35
☐ 17	Kenny Lofton	.40	.18
☐ 18	Ivan Rodriguez	.75	.35
☐ 19	Manny Ramirez	.75	.35
☐ 20	Jim Thome	.60	.25
☐ 21	Chuck Knoblauch	.25	.11
☐ 22	Paul Molitor	.60	.25
☐ 23	Barry Larkin	.60	.25
☐ 24	Andy Pettitte	.25	.11
☐ 25	John Smoltz	.40	.18
☐ 26	Randy Johnson	.60	.25
☐ 27	Bernie Williams	.60	.25
☐ 28	Larry Walker	.60	.25
☐ 29	Mo Vaughn	.60	.25
☐ 30	Bobby Higginson	.25	.11
☐ 31	Edgardo Alfonzo	.40	.18
☐ 32	Justin Thompson	.15	.07
☐ 33	Jeff Suppan	.15	.07
☐ 34	Roberto Alomar	.60	.25
☐ 35	Hideo Nomo	.60	.25
☐ 36	Rusty Greer	.25	.11
☐ 37	Tim Salmon	.40	.18
☐ 38	Jim Edmonds	.25	.11
☐ 39	Gary Sheffield	.25	.11
☐ 40	Ken Caminiti	.25	.11
☐ 41	Sammy Sosa	2.00	.90
☐ 42	Tony Womack	.15	.07
☐ 43	Matt Williams	.60	.25
☐ 44	Andres Galarraga	.40	.18
☐ 45	Garret Anderson	.25	.11
☐ 46	Rafael Palmeiro	.60	.25
☐ 47	Mike Mussina	.60	.25
☐ 48	Craig Biggio	.60	.25
☐ 49	Wade Boggs	.60	.25
☐ 50	Tom Glavine	.60	.25
☐ 51	Jason Giambi	.25	.11
☐ 52	Will Clark	.60	.25
☐ 53	David Justice	.25	.11
☐ 54	Sandy Alomar Jr.	.25	.11
☐ 55	Edgar Martinez	.25	.11
☐ 56	Brady Anderson	.25	.11
☐ 57	Eric Young	.15	.07
☐ 58	Ray Lankford	.25	.11
☐ 59	Kevin Brown	.40	.18
☐ 60	Raul Mondesi	.25	.11
☐ 61	Bobby Bonilla	.25	.11
☐ 62	Javier Lopez	.25	.11
☐ 63	Fred McGriff	.40	.18
☐ 64	Rondell White	.25	.11
☐ 65	Todd Hundley	.25	.11
☐ 66	Mark Grace	.40	.18
☐ 67	Alan Benes	.15	.07
☐ 68	Jeff Abbott	.15	.07
☐ 69	Bob Abreu	.25	.11
☐ 70	Deion Sanders	.25	.11
☐ 71	Tino Martinez	.25	.11
☐ 72	Shannon Stewart	.15	.07
☐ 73	Homer Bush	.15	.07
☐ 74	Carlos Delgado	.60	.25
☐ 75	Raul Ibanez	.15	.07
☐ 76	Hideki Irabu	.25	.11
☐ 77	Jose Cruz Jr.	.25	.11
☐ 78	Tony Clark	.25	.11
☐ 79	Wilton Guerrero	.15	.07
☐ 80	Vladimir Guerrero	.75	.35

		MINT	NRMT
☐ 81	Scott Rolen	.75	.35
☐ 82	Nomar Garciaparra	2.00	.90
☐ 83	Darin Erstad	.40	.18
☐ 84	Chan Ho Park	.25	.11
☐ 85	Mike Cameron	.25	.11
☐ 86	Todd Walker	.25	.11
☐ 87	Todd Dunwoody	.15	.07
☐ 88	Neifi Perez	.25	.11
☐ 89	Brett Tomko	.15	.07
☐ 90	Jose Guillen	.15	.07
☐ 91	Matt Morris	.15	.07
☐ 92	Bartolo Colon	.25	.11
☐ 93	Jaret Wright	.25	.11
☐ 94	Shawn Estes	.15	.07
☐ 95	Livan Hernandez	.15	.07
☐ 96	Bobby Estalella	.15	.07
☐ 97	Ben Grieve	.60	.25
☐ 98	Paul Konerko	.25	.11
☐ 99	David Ortiz	.15	.07
☐ 100	Todd Helton	.75	.35
☐ 101	Juan Encarnacion	.25	.11
☐ 102	Bubba Trammell	.15	.07
☐ 103	Miguel Tejada	.25	.11
☐ 104	Jacob Cruz	.15	.07
☐ 105	Todd Greene	.15	.07
☐ 106	Kevin Orie	.15	.07
☐ 107	Mark Kotsay	.25	.11
☐ 108	Fernando Tatis	.20	.07
☐ 109	Jay Payton	.15	.07
☐ 110	Pokey Reese	.15	.07
☐ 111	Derrek Lee	.15	.07
☐ 112	Richard Hidalgo	.25	.11
☐ 113	Ricky Ledee	.25	.11
	UER front Rickey		
☐ 114	Lou Collier	.15	.07
☐ 115	Ruben Rivera	.15	.07
☐ 116	Shawn Green	.60	.25
☐ 117	Moises Alou	.25	.11
☐ 118	Ken Griffey Jr. GEN	1.50	.70
☐ 119	Frank Thomas GEN	.60	.25
☐ 120	Alex Rodriguez GEN	1.00	.45
☐ 121	Mike Piazza GEN	1.00	.45
☐ 122	Greg Maddux GEN	.75	.35
☐ 123	Cal Ripken GEN	1.25	.55
☐ 124	Chipper Jones GEN	.75	.35
☐ 125	Derek Jeter GEN	1.00	.45
☐ 126	Tony Gwynn GEN	.75	.35
☐ 127	Andruw Jones GEN	.25	.11
☐ 128	Juan Gonzalez GEN	.60	.25
☐ 129	Jeff Bagwell GEN	.40	.18
☐ 130	Mark McGwire GEN	2.00	.90
☐ 131	Roger Clemens GEN	.75	.35
☐ 132	Albert Belle GEN	.25	.11
☐ 133	Barry Bonds GEN	.40	.18
☐ 134	Kenny Lofton GEN	.25	.11
☐ 135	Ivan Rodriguez GEN	.40	.18
☐ 136	Manny Ramirez GEN	.40	.18
☐ 137	Jim Thome GEN	.25	.11
☐ 138	Chuck Knoblauch GEN	.15	.07
☐ 139	Paul Molitor GEN	.25	.11
☐ 140	Barry Larkin GEN	.25	.11
☐ 141	Mo Vaughn GEN	.25	.11
☐ 142	Hideki Irabu GEN	.15	.07
☐ 143	Jose Cruz Jr. GEN	.15	.07
☐ 144	Tony Clark GEN	.15	.07
☐ 145	Vladimir Guerrero GEN	.40	.18
☐ 146	Scott Rolen GEN	.60	.25
☐ 147	Nomar Garciaparra GEN	1.00	.45
☐ 148	Nomar Garciaparra CL	1.00	.45
☐ 149	Larry Walker CL	.25	.11
☐ 150	Tino Martinez GEN	.15	.07
☐ AU2	F.Thomas AUTO/100	250.00	110.00

1998 Donruss Elite Aspirations

	MINT	NRMT
COMMON CARD (1-150)	1.50	.70

*STARS: 4X TO 10X BASIC CARDS
*YNG.STARS: 3X TO 8X BASIC CARDS
RANDOM INSERTS IN PACKS
STATED PRINT RUN 750 SETS

1998 Donruss Elite Status

	MINT	NRMT
COMMON CARD (1-150)	8.00	3.60

*STARS: 20X TO 50X BASIC CARDS
*YNG.STARS: 15X TO 40X BASIC CARDS
RANDOM INSERTS IN PACKS
STATED PRINT RUN 100 SERIAL #'d SETS

1998 Donruss Elite Back to the Future

	MINT	NRMT
COMPLETE SET (8)	200.00	90.00
COMMON CARD (1-8)	10.00	4.50

RANDOM INSERTS IN PACKS
STATED PRINT RUN 1400 SERIAL #'d SETS

		MINT	NRMT
☐ 1	Cal Ripken...... Paul Konerko	30.00	13.50
☐ 2	Jeff Bagwell...... Todd Helton	10.00	4.50
☐ 3	Eddie Mathews...... Chipper Jones	20.00	9.00
☐ 4	Juan Gonzalez...... Ben Grieve	20.00	9.00
☐ 5	Hank Aaron...... Jose Cruz Jr.	20.00	9.00
☐ 6	Frank Thomas...... David Ortiz 1-100	15.00	6.75
☐ 7	Nolan Ryan...... Greg Maddux	40.00	18.00
☐ 8	Alex Rodriguez...... Nomar Garciaparra	30.00	13.50

1998 Donruss Elite Back to the Future Autographs

	MINT	NRMT
COMMON CARD (1A-5/7-8)	40.00	18.00

RANDOM INSERTS IN PACKS
STATED PRINT RUN 100 SERIAL #'d SETS
AU CARD NUMBER 6 DOES NOT EXIST
CARD 1A SIGNED BY KONERKO ONLY
CARD 1B SIGNED BY RIPKEN ONLY

ALL OTHER CARDS SIGNED BY BOTH PLAYERS
COMP.SET INCLUDES CARDS 1A AND 1B

		MINT	NRMT
❑ 1A	Cal Ripken	40.00	18.00
	Paul Konerko Redeemed/100		
	Redeemed card signed only by		
	Konerko		
❑ 1B	C. Ripken AU/200	400.00	180.00
	Redeemed card signed only by		
	Ripken		
❑ 2	Jeff Bagwell	150.00	70.00
	Todd Helton		
❑ 3	Eddie Mathews	300.00	135.00
	Chipper Jones		
❑ 4	Juan Gonzalez	250.00	110.00
	Ben Grieve		
❑ 5	Hank Aaron	300.00	135.00
	Jose Cruz Jr.		
❑ 7	Nolan Ryan	1500.00	700.00
	Greg Maddux		
❑ 8	Alex Rodriguez	600.00	275.00
	Nomar Garciaparra		

1998 Donruss Elite Craftsmen

		MINT	NRMT
COMPLETE SET (30)		200.00	90.00
COMMON CARD (1-30)		2.00	.90
SEMISTARS		3.00	1.35
UNLISTED STARS		5.00	2.20
RANDOM INSERTS IN PACKS			
STATED PRINT RUN 3500 SERIAL #'d SETS			
*MASTERS: 2.5X TO 6X HI COLUMN			
MASTER PRINT RUN 100 SERIAL #'d SETS			

❑ 1	Ken Griffey Jr	25.00	11.00
❑ 2	Frank Thomas	10.00	4.50
❑ 3	Alex Rodriguez	15.00	6.75
❑ 4	Cal Ripken	20.00	9.00
❑ 5	Greg Maddux	12.00	5.50
❑ 6	Mike Piazza	15.00	6.75
❑ 7	Chipper Jones	12.00	5.50
❑ 8	Derek Jeter	15.00	6.75
❑ 9	Tony Gwynn	12.00	5.50
❑ 10	Nomar Garciaparra	15.00	6.75
❑ 11	Scott Rolen	6.00	2.70
❑ 12	Jose Cruz Jr.	2.50	1.10
❑ 13	Tony Clark	2.50	1.10

❑ 14	Vladimir Guerrero	6.00	2.70
❑ 15	Todd Helton	5.00	2.20
❑ 16	Ben Grieve	5.00	2.20
❑ 17	Andruw Jones	5.00	2.20
❑ 18	Jeff Bagwell	6.00	2.70
❑ 19	Mark McGwire	30.00	13.50
❑ 20	Juan Gonzalez	10.00	4.50
❑ 21	Roger Clemens	12.00	5.50
❑ 22	Albert Belle	5.00	2.20
❑ 23	Barry Bonds	6.00	2.70
❑ 24	Kenny Lofton	3.00	1.35
❑ 25	Ivan Rodriguez	6.00	2.70
❑ 26	Paul Molitor	5.00	2.20
❑ 27	Barry Larkin	5.00	2.20
❑ 28	Mo Vaughn	5.00	2.20
❑ 29	Larry Walker	5.00	2.20
❑ 30	Tino Martinez	2.50	1.10

1998 Donruss Elite Prime Numbers

		MINT	NRMT
COMPLETE SET (36)		3000.00	1350.00
COMMON CARD (1-36)		10.00	4.50
RANDOM INSERTS IN PACKS			
PRINT RUNS IN PARENTHESIS BELOW			

❑ 1A	Ken Griffey Jr. 2 (94)	200.00	90.00
❑ 1B	Ken Griffey Jr. 9 (204)	100.00	45.00
❑ 1C	Ken Griffey Jr. 4 (290)	80.00	36.00
❑ 2A	Frank Thomas 4 (56)	100.00	45.00
❑ 2B	Frank Thomas 6 (406)	25.00	11.00
❑ 2C	Frank Thomas 6 (450)	25.00	11.00
❑ 3A	Mark McGwire 3 (87)	250.00	110.00
❑ 3B	Mark McGwire 8 (307)	100.00	45.00
❑ 3C	Mark McGwire 7 (380)	400.00	180.00
❑ 4A	Cal Ripken 5 (17)	600.00	275.00
❑ 4B	Cal Ripken 7 (507)	50.00	22.00
❑ 4C	Cal Ripken 7 (510)	50.00	22.00
❑ 5A	Mike Piazza 5 (76)	120.00	55.00
❑ 5B	Mike Piazza 7 (506)	40.00	18.00
❑ 5C	Mike Piazza 6 (570)	40.00	18.00
❑ 6A	Chipper Jones 4 (89)	100.00	45.00
❑ 6B	Chipper Jones 8 (409)	30.00	13.50
❑ 6C	Chipper Jones 9 (480)	30.00	13.50
❑ 7A	Tony Gwynn 3 (72)	100.00	45.00
❑ 7B	Tony Gwynn 7 (332)	40.00	18.00
❑ 7C	Tony Gwynn 2 (370)	40.00	18.00
❑ 8A	Barry Bonds 3 (74)	50.00	22.00
❑ 8B	Barry Bonds 7 (304)	20.00	9.00
❑ 8C	Barry Bonds 4 (370)	20.00	9.00
❑ 9A	Jeff Bagwell 4 (25)	120.00	55.00
❑ 9B	Jeff Bagwell 2 (405)	15.00	6.75
❑ 9C	Jeff Bagwell 5 (420)	15.00	6.75
❑ 10A	Juan Gonzalez 5 (89)	80.00	36.00
❑ 10B	Juan Gonzalez 8 (509)	25.00	11.00
❑ 10C	Juan Gonzalez 9 (580)	25.00	11.00
❑ 11A	Alex Rodriguez 5 (34)	200.00	90.00
❑ 11B	Alex Rodriguez 3 (504)	40.00	18.00
❑ 11C	Alex Rodriguez 4 (530)	40.00	18.00
❑ 12A	Kenny Lofton 3 (54)	30.00	13.50
❑ 12B	Kenny Lofton 5 (304)	10.00	4.50
❑ 12C	Kenny Lofton 4 (350)	10.00	4.50

1998 Donruss Elite Prime Numbers Die Cuts

		MINT	NRMT
COMMON CARD (1-36)		10.00	4.50
RANDOM INSERTS IN PACKS			
PRINT RUNS IN PARENTHESIS BELOW			

❑ 1A	Ken Griffey Jr. 2 (200)	100.00	45.00
❑ 1B	Ken Griffey Jr. 9 (90)	200.00	90.00
❑ 1C	Ken Griffey Jr. 4 (4)		
❑ 2A	Frank Thomas 4 (400)	25.00	11.00
❑ 2B	Frank Thomas 5 (50)	100.00	45.00
❑ 2C	Frank Thomas 6 (6)		
❑ 3A	Mark McGwire 3 (300)	100.00	45.00
❑ 3B	Mark McGwire 8 (80)	250.00	110.00
❑ 3C	Mark McGwire 7 (7)		
❑ 4A	Cal Ripken 5 (500)	50.00	22.00
❑ 4B	Cal Ripken 1 (10)		
❑ 4C	Cal Ripken 7 (7)		
❑ 5A	Mike Piazza 5 (500)	40.00	18.00
❑ 5B	Mike Piazza 7 (70)	120.00	55.00
❑ 5C	Mike Piazza 6 (6)		
❑ 6A	Chipper Jones 4 (400)	30.00	13.50
❑ 6B	Chipper Jones 8 (80)	100.00	45.00
❑ 6C	Chipper Jones 9 (9)	40.00	18.00
❑ 7A	Tony Gwynn 3 (300)	40.00	18.00
❑ 7B	Tony Gwynn 7 (70)	100.00	45.00
❑ 7C	Tony Gwynn 2 (2)		
❑ 8A	Barry Bonds 3 (300)	20.00	9.00
❑ 8B	Barry Bonds 7 (70)	50.00	22.00
❑ 8C	Barry Bonds 4 (4)		
❑ 9A	Jeff Bagwell 4 (400)	15.00	6.75
❑ 9B	Jeff Bagwell 2 (20)	150.00	70.00
❑ 9C	Jeff Bagwell 5 (5)		
❑ 10A	Juan Gonzalez 5 (500)	25.00	11.00
❑ 10B	Juan Gonzalez 8 (80)	80.00	36.00
❑ 10C	Juan Gonzalez 9 (9)		
❑ 11A	Alex Rodriguez 5 (500)	40.00	18.00
❑ 11B	Alex Rodriguez 3 (30)	250.00	110.00
❑ 11C	Alex Rodriguez 4 (4)		
❑ 12A	Kenny Lofton 3 (300)	10.00	4.50
❑ 12B	Kenny Lofton 5 (50)	30.00	13.50
❑ 12C	Kenny Lofton 4 (4)		

1997 Donruss Limited

	MINT	NRMT
COMP.COUNTER SET (100)..	25.00	11.00
COMMON COUNTERPART	.15	.07

Item	Price 1	Price 2
COUNTERPART MINORS	.25	.11
COUNTERPART UNLISTED	.60	.25
COMP. DOUBLE SET (40)	80.00	36.00
COMMON DOUBLE TEAM	1.00	.45
DOUBLE TEAM MINORS	.20	.90
DOUBLE TEAM UNLISTED	4.00	1.80
COMP.STAR FACT.SET (40)	600.00	275.00
COMMON STAR FACTOR	3.00	1.35
STAR FACTOR MINORS	6.00	2.70
STAR FACTOR UNLISTED	12.00	5.50
COMP.UNLIMITED SET (20)	400.00	180.00
COMMON UNLIMITED	2.00	.90
UNLIMITED MINORS	4.00	1.80
UNLIMITED UNLISTED	8.00	3.60

LESS THAN 1100 OF EACH STAR FACT.MADE

#	Player	Price 1	Price 2
❑ 1	Ken Griffey Jr. C	3.00	1.35
	Rondell White		
❑ 2	Greg Maddux C	1.50	.70
	David Cone		
❑ 3	Gary Sheffield D	4.00	1.80
	Moises Alou		
❑ 4	Frank Thomas S	25.00	11.00
❑ 5	Cal Ripken C	2.50	1.10
	Kevin Orie		
❑ 6	Vladimir Guerrero U	12.00	5.50
	Barry Bonds		
❑ 7	Eddie Murray C	.60	.25
	Reggie Jefferson		
❑ 8	Manny Ramirez D	5.00	2.20
	Marquis Grissom		
❑ 9	Mike Piazza S	40.00	18.00
❑ 10	Barry Larkin C	.75	.35
	Rey Ordonez		
❑ 11	Jeff Bagwell C	.75	.35
	Eric Karros		
❑ 12	Chuck Knoblauch C	.60	.25
	Ray Durham		
❑ 13	Alex Rodriguez C	2.00	.90
	Edgar Renteria		
❑ 14	Matt Williams C	.75	.35
	Vinny Castilla		
❑ 15	Todd Hollandsworth C	.25	.11
	Bob Abreu		
❑ 16	John Smoltz C	.75	.35
	Pedro Martinez		
❑ 17	Jose Canseco C	.75	.35
	Chili Davis		
❑ 18	Jose Cruz Jr. U	50.00	22.00
	Ken Griffey Jr.		
❑ 19	Ken Griffey Jr. S	60.00	27.00
❑ 20	Paul Molitor C	.60	.25
	John Olerud		
❑ 21	Roberto Alomar C	.60	.25
	Luis Castillo		
❑ 22	Derek Jeter C	1.50	.70
	Lou Collier		
❑ 23	Chipper Jones C	1.50	.70
	Robin Ventura		
❑ 24	Gary Sheffield C	.60	.25
	Ron Gant		
❑ 25	Ramon Martinez C	.25	.11
	Bobby Jones		
❑ 26	Mike Piazza D	12.00	5.50
	Raul Mondesi		
❑ 27	Darin Erstad U	12.00	5.50
	Jeff Bagwell		
❑ 28	Ivan Rodriguez S	15.00	6.75
	Kevin Young		
❑ 29	J.T. Snow C	.25	.11
	Julio Franco		
❑ 30	Ryne Sandberg C	.75	.35
	Chris Snopek		
❑ 31	Travis Fryman C	.25	.11
	Chris Snopek		
❑ 32	Wade Boggs C	.60	.25
	Russ Davis		
❑ 33	Brooks Kieschnick C	.25	.11
	Marty Cordova		
❑ 34	Andy Pettitte C	.60	.25
	Denny Neagle		
❑ 35	Paul Molitor D	4.00	1.80
	Matt Lawton		
❑ 36	Scott Rolen U	40.00	18.00
	Cal Ripken		
❑ 37	Cal Ripken S	50.00	22.00
❑ 38	Jim Thome C	.60	.25
	Dave Nilsson		
❑ 39	Tony Womack C	.60	.25
	Carlos Baerga		
❑ 40	Nomar Garciaparra C	2.00	.90
	Mark Grudzielanek		
❑ 41	Todd Greene C	.25	.11
	Chris Widger		
❑ 42	Deion Sanders C	.25	.11
	Bernard Gilkey		
❑ 43	Hideo Nomo C	1.00	.45
	Charles Nagy		
❑ 44	Ivan Rodriguez D	5.00	2.20
	Rusty Greer		
❑ 45	Todd Walker U	20.00	9.00
	Chipper Jones		
❑ 46	Greg Maddux S	30.00	13.50
❑ 47	Mo Vaughn C	.60	.25
	Cecil Fielder		
❑ 48	Craig Biggio C	.75	.35
	Scott Spiezio		
❑ 49	Pokey Reese C	.25	.11
	Jeff Blauser		
❑ 50	Ken Caminiti C	.75	.35
	Joe Randa		
❑ 51	Albert Belle C	.60	.25
	Shawn Green		
❑ 52	Randy Johnson C	.60	.25
	Jason Dickson		
❑ 53	Hideo Nomo D	6.00	2.70
	Chan Ho Park		
❑ 54	Scott Spiezio U	8.00	3.60
	Chuck Knoblauch		
❑ 55	Chipper Jones S	30.00	13.50
❑ 56	Tino Martinez C	.60	.25
	Ryan McGuire		
❑ 57	Eric Young C	.15	.07
	Wilton Guerrero		
❑ 58	Ron Coomer C	.15	.07
	Dave Hollins		
❑ 59	Sammy Sosa C	2.00	.90
	Angel Echevarria		
❑ 60	Dennis Reyes C	.50	.23
	Jimmy Key		
❑ 61	Barry Larkin C	4.00	1.80
	Deion Sanders		
❑ 62	Wilton Guerrero U	8.00	3.60
	Roberto Alomar		
❑ 63	Albert Belle C	12.00	5.50
❑ 64	Mark McGwire C	3.00	1.35
	Andre Galarraga		
❑ 65	Edgar Martinez C	.75	.35
	Todd Walker		
❑ 66	Steve Finley C	.25	.11
	Rich Becker		
❑ 67	Tom Glavine C	.25	.11
	Andy Ashby		
❑ 68	Sammy Sosa D	12.00	5.50
	Ryne Sandberg		
❑ 69	Nomar Garciaparra U	30.00	13.50
	Alex Rodriguez		
❑ 70	Jeff Bagwell S	15.00	6.75
❑ 71	Darin Erstad C	.60	.25
	Mark Grace		
❑ 72	Scott Rolen C	1.00	.45
	Edgardo Alfonzo		
❑ 73	Kenny Lofton C	.60	.25
	Lance Johnson		
❑ 74	Joey Hamilton C	.25	.11
	Brett Tomko		
❑ 75	Eddie Murray D	4.00	1.80
	Tim Salmon		
❑ 76	Dmitri Young U	.25	.11
	Mo Vaughn		
❑ 77	Juan Gonzalez S	25.00	11.00
❑ 78	Frank Thomas C	1.25	.55
	Tony Clark		
❑ 79	Shannon Stewart C	.25	.11
	Bip Roberts		
❑ 80	Shawn Estes C	.25	.11
	Alex Fernandez		
❑ 81	John Smoltz D	2.00	.90
	Javier Lopez		
❑ 82	Todd Greene U	25.00	11.00
	Mike Piazza		
❑ 83	Derek Jeter S	40.00	18.00
❑ 84	Dmitri Young C	.25	.11
	Antone Williamson		
❑ 85	Rickey Henderson C	.75	.35
	Darryl Hamilton		
❑ 86	Billy Wagner C	.25	.11
	Dennis Eckersley		
❑ 87	Larry Walker D	4.00	1.80
	Eric Young		
❑ 88	Mark Kotsay U	20.00	9.00
	Juan Gonzalez		
❑ 89	Barry Bonds S	15.00	6.75
❑ 90	Will Clark C	.75	.35
	Jeff Conine		
❑ 91	Tony Gwynn C	1.50	.70
	Brett Butler		
❑ 92	John Wetteland C	.15	.07
	Rod Beck		
❑ 93	Bernie Williams D	4.00	1.80
	Tony Martinez		
❑ 94	Andruw Jones U	12.00	5.50
	Kenny Lofton		
❑ 95	Mo Vaughn S	12.00	5.50
❑ 96	Joe Carter C	.75	.35
	Derek Lee		
❑ 97	John Mabry C	.15	.07
	F.P. Santangelo		
❑ 98	Esteban Loaiza C	.15	.07
	Wilson Alvarez		
❑ 99	Matt Williams D	4.00	1.80
	David Justice		
❑ 100	Derek Lee U	15.00	6.75
	Frank Thomas		
❑ 101	Mark McGwire S	60.00	27.00
❑ 102	Fred McGriff C	.75	.35
	Paul Sorrento		
❑ 103	Jermaine Allensworth C	.60	.25
	Bernie Williams		
❑ 104	Ismael Valdes C	.25	.11
	Chris Holt		
❑ 105	Fred McGriff D	4.00	1.80
	Ryan Klesko		
❑ 106	Tony Clark U	40.00	18.00
	Mark McGwire		
❑ 107	Tony Gwynn S	30.00	13.50
❑ 108	Jeffrey Hammonds C	.25	.11
	Ellis Burks		
❑ 109	Shane Reynolds C	.25	.11
	Andy Benes		
❑ 110	Roger Clemens D	10.00	4.50
	Carlos Delgado		
❑ 111	Karim Garcia U	8.00	3.60
	Albert Belle		
❑ 112	Paul Molitor S	12.00	5.50
❑ 113	Trey Beamon C	.15	.07
	Eric Owens		
❑ 114	Curt Schilling C	.25	.11
	Darryl Kile		
❑ 115	Tom Glavine D	2.00	.90
	Michael Tucker		
❑ 116	Pokey Reese U	20.00	9.00
	Derek Jeter		
❑ 117	Manny Ramirez S	15.00	6.75
❑ 118	Juan Gonzalez C	1.25	.55
	Brant Brown		
❑ 119	Juan Guzman C	.15	.07
	Francisco Cordova		
❑ 120	Randy Johnson D	4.00	1.80
	Edgar Martinez		
❑ 121	Hideki Irabu U	20.00	9.00
	Greg Maddux		
❑ 122	Alex Rodriguez S	40.00	18.00
❑ 123	Barry Bonds C	.75	.35
	Quinton McCracken		
❑ 124	Roger Clemens S	1.50	.70
	Andy Benes		
❑ 125	Wade Boggs D	4.00	1.80
	Paul O'Neill		
❑ 126	Mike Cameron U	8.00	3.60
	Larry Walker		
❑ 127	Gary Sheffield S	15.00	6.75
❑ 128	Andruw Jones C	.75	.35
	Raul Mondesi		
❑ 129	Brady Anderson C	.25	.11
	Terrell Wade		
❑ 130	Brady Anderson D	4.00	1.80
	Rafael Palmeiro		

#	Player		MINT	NRMT
❑ 131	Neifi Perez U		10.00	4.50
	Barry Larkin			
❑ 132	Ken Caminiti S		12.00	5.50
❑ 133	Larry Walker C		.60	.25
	Rusty Greer			
❑ 134	Mariano Rivera C		.25	.11
	Mark Wohlers			
❑ 135	Hideki Irabu D		4.00	1.80
	Andy Pettitte			
❑ 136	Jose Guillen U		20.00	9.00
	Tony Gwynn			
❑ 137	Hideo Nomo S		.60	.25
❑ 138	Vladimir Guerrero C		1.00	.45
	Jim Edmonds			
❑ 139	Justin Thompson C		.25	.11
	Dwight Gooden			
❑ 140	Andres Galarraga D		4.00	1.80
	Dante Bichette			
❑ 141	Kenny Lofton S		15.00	6.75
	Manny Ramirez			
❑ 142	Tim Salmon C		.75	.35
❑ 143	Kevin Brown C		.25	.11
	Matt Morris			
❑ 144	Craig Biggio D		4.00	1.80
	Bob Abreu			
❑ 145	Roberto Alomar S		12.00	5.50
❑ 146	Jose Guillen C		.60	.25
	Brian Jordan			
❑ 147	Bartolo Colon C		.25	.11
	Kevin Appier			
❑ 148	Ray Lankford D		2.00	.90
	Brian Jordan			
❑ 149	Chuck Knoblauch S		15.00	6.75
❑ 150	Henry Rodriguez C		.25	.11
	Ray Lankford			
❑ 151	Jaret Wright C		1.25	.55
	Ben McDonald			
❑ 152	Bobby Bonilla S		2.00	.90
	Kevin Brown			
❑ 153	Barry Larkin S		12.00	5.50
❑ 154	David Justice C		.25	.11
	Reggie Sanders			
❑ 155	Mike Mussina C		.60	.25
	Ken Hill			
❑ 156	Mark Grace D		4.00	1.80
	Brooks Kieschnick			
❑ 157	Jim Thome S		12.00	5.50
❑ 158	Michael Tucker C		.25	.11
	Curtis Goodwin			
❑ 159	Jeff Suppan C		.25	.11
	Jeff Fassero			
❑ 160	Mike Mussina D		4.00	1.80
	Jeffrey Hammonds			
❑ 161	John Smoltz S		10.00	4.50
❑ 162	Moises Alou C		.25	.11
	Eric Davis			
❑ 163	Sandy Alomar Jr. C		.25	.11
	Dan Wilson			
❑ 164	Rondell White D		2.00	.90
	Henry Rodriguez			
❑ 165	Roger Clemens S		30.00	13.50
	Al Martin			
❑ 166	Brady Anderson C		.25	.11
❑ 167	Jason Kendall C		.25	.11
	Charles Johnson			
❑ 168	Jason Giambi C		5.00	2.20
	Jose Canseco			
❑ 169	Larry Walker S		12.00	5.50
❑ 170	Jay Buhner C		.25	.11
	Geronimo Berroa			
❑ 171	Ivan Rodriguez C		.75	.35
	Mike Sweeney			
❑ 172	Kevin Appier D		2.00	.90
	Jose Rosado			
❑ 173	Bernie Williams S		15.00	6.75
	Brian Giles			
❑ 174	Todd Dunwoody C		2.00	.90
	Javier Lopez			
❑ 175	Javier Lopez C		.25	.11
	Scott Hatteberg			
❑ 176	John Jaha D		2.00	.90
	Jeff Cirillo			
❑ 177	Andy Pettitte S		15.00	6.75
	Dante Bichette			
❑ 178	Dante Bichette C		.25	.11
	Butch Huskey			
❑ 179	Raul Casanova C		.25	.11
	Todd Hundley			
❑ 180	Jim Edmonds D		4.00	1.80
❑ 181	Deion Sanders S		10.00	4.50
❑ 182	Ryan Klesko C		.75	.35
	Paul O'Neill			
❑ 183	Joe Carter D		2.00	.90
	Pat Hentgen			
❑ 184	Brady Anderson S		12.00	5.50
❑ 185	Carlos Delgado C		.25	.11
	Wally Joyner			
❑ 186	Jermaine Dye D		1.00	.45
	Johnny Damon			
❑ 187	Randy Johnson S		12.00	5.50
❑ 188	Todd Hundley D		2.00	.90
	Carlos Baerga			
❑ 189	Tom Glavine S		10.00	4.50
❑ 190	Damon Mashore D		1.00	.45
	Jason McDonald			
❑ 191	Wade Boggs S		12.00	5.50
❑ 192	Al Martin D		2.00	.90
	Jason Kendall			
❑ 193	Matt Williams S		12.00	5.50
❑ 194	Will Clark D		4.00	1.80
	Dean Palmer			
❑ 195	Sammy Sosa S		40.00	18.00
❑ 196	Jose Cruz Jr. D		12.00	5.50
	Jay Buhner			
❑ 197	Eddie Murray S		12.00	5.50
❑ 198	Darin Erstad D		4.00	1.80
	Jason Dickson			
❑ 199	Fred McGriff S		10.00	4.50
❑ 200	Bubba Trammell D		2.50	1.10
	Bobby Higgins			

1997 Donruss Limited Exposure

	MINT	NRMT
*COUNTER.STARS: 5X TO 12X BASIC		
*COUNTER.ROOKIES: 2X TO 5X BASIC		
*DOUBLE TEAM: 3X TO 8X BASIC CARDS		
*STAR FACTOR: 2X TO 5X BASIC CARDS		
*UNLIMITED: 2.5X TO 6X BASIC CARDS		
RANDOM INSERTS IN PACKS		
LESS THAN 40 OF EACH STAR FACTOR MADE		
*NON-GLOSS: .1X TO .25X HI COLUMN		
NON-GLOSS: RANDOM ERRORS IN PACKS		
NO EXCHANGE AVAIL.ON NON-GLOSS CARDS		

1997 Donruss Limited Fabric of the Game

	MINT	NRMT
COMPLETE SET (69)	2000.00	900.00
COMMON MAJOR LG MAT.	4.00	1.80
MAJOR LG.MINORS	6.00	2.70
MAJOR LG.SEMIS	10.00	4.50
MAJOR LG.UNLISTED	15.00	6.75
1000 OF EACH MAJOR LG.MATERIAL		
COMMON STAR MAT.	5.00	2.20
STAR MAT.MINORS	8.00	3.60
STAR MAT.SEMIS	12.00	5.50
STAR MAT.UNLISTED	20.00	9.00
750 OF EACH STAR MATERIAL		
COMMON SUPERSTAR MAT.	12.00	5.50

	MINT	NRMT
SUPERSTAR SEMIS	15.00	6.75
SUPERSTAR UNLISTED	25.00	11.00
500 OF EACH SUPERSTAR MATERIAL		
COMMON HOF MAT	20.00	9.00
250 OF EACH HOF MATERIAL		
COMMON LEGEND	50.00	22.00
100 OF EACH LEGENDARY MATERIAL		
RANDOM INSERTS IN PACKS		
❑ 1 Cal Ripken HF	150.00	70.00
❑ 2 Tony Gwynn SS	60.00	27.00
❑ 3 Ivan Rodriguez S	25.00	11.00
❑ 4 Rickey Henderson L	80.00	36.00
❑ 5 Ken Griffey Jr. SS	120.00	55.00
❑ 6 Chipper Jones ML	40.00	18.00
❑ 7 Sammy Sosa SS	60.00	27.00
❑ 8 Wade Boggs HF	40.00	18.00
❑ 9 Manny Ramirez ML	20.00	9.00
❑ 10 Barry Bonds SS	50.00	22.00
❑ 11 Mike Piazza S	60.00	27.00
❑ 12 Rondell White ML	6.00	2.70
❑ 13 Albert Belle S	20.00	9.00
❑ 14 Tony Clark ML	10.00	4.50
❑ 15 Edgar Martinez SS	15.00	6.75
❑ 16 Deion Sanders S	8.00	3.60
❑ 17 Juan Gonzalez SS	50.00	22.00
❑ 18 Nomar Garciaparra ML	50.00	22.00
❑ 19 Rafael Palmeiro SS	25.00	11.00
❑ 20 Dave Justice S	20.00	9.00
❑ 21 Bob Abreu ML	6.00	2.70
❑ 22 Paul Molitor L	80.00	36.00
❑ 23 Vladimir Guerrero ML	25.00	11.00
❑ 24 Chuck Knoblauch SS	25.00	11.00
❑ 25 Tony Gwynn HF	100.00	45.00
❑ 26 Darin Erstad ML	15.00	6.75
❑ 27 Mark McGwire HF	200.00	90.00
❑ 28 Larry Walker S	20.00	9.00
❑ 29 Gary Sheffield SS	8.00	3.60
❑ 30 Jose Cruz Jr. ML	15.00	6.75
❑ 31 Kenny Lofton SS	25.00	11.00
❑ 32 Andres Galarraga SS	25.00	11.00
❑ 33 Raul Mondesi ML	6.00	2.70
❑ 34 Eddie Murray L	80.00	36.00
❑ 35 Tino Martinez ML	15.00	6.75
❑ 36 Todd Walker ML	15.00	6.75
❑ 37 Frank Thomas SS	50.00	22.00
❑ 38 Ken Caminiti S	12.00	5.50
❑ 39 Pokey Reese ML	6.00	2.70
❑ 40 Barry Bonds HF	50.00	22.00
❑ 41 Barry Larkin SS	25.00	11.00
❑ 42 Bernie Williams S	20.00	9.00
❑ 43 Cal Ripken HF	150.00	70.00
❑ 44 Bobby Bonilla SS	15.00	6.75
❑ 45 Ken Griffey Jr. S	100.00	45.00
❑ 46 Tim Salmon S	20.00	9.00
❑ 47 Ryne Sandberg HF	50.00	22.00
❑ 48 Rusty Greer HF	6.00	2.70
❑ 49 Matt Williams SS	25.00	11.00
❑ 50 Eric Young S	8.00	3.60
❑ 51 Andruw Jones ML	20.00	9.00
❑ 52 Jeff Bagwell S	25.00	11.00
❑ 53 Wilton Guerrero ML	4.00	1.80
❑ 54 Fred McGriff SS	25.00	11.00
❑ 55 Jose Guillen ML	10.00	4.50
❑ 56 Brady Anderson SS	15.00	6.75
❑ 57 Mo Vaughn S	20.00	9.00
❑ 58 Craig Biggio SS	25.00	11.00
❑ 59 Dmitri Young ML	6.00	2.70

	MINT	NRMT
60 Frank Thomas S	40.00	18.00
61 Derek Jeter ML	50.00	22.00
62 Albert Belle SS	25.00	11.00
63 Scott Rolen ML	25.00	11.00
64 Roberto Alomar HF	30.00	13.50
65 Jeff Bagwell S	25.00	11.00
66 Mark Grace SS	15.00	6.75
67 Gary Sheffield S	8.00	3.60
68 Joe Carter HF	20.00	9.00
69 Jim Thome ML	15.00	6.75

1997 Donruss Preferred

	MINT	NRMT
COMP.BRONZE SET (100)	30.00	13.50
COMMON BRONZE	.20	.09
BRONZE MINOR STARS	.40	.18
BRONZE UNLISTED STARS	.75	.35
COMMON SILVER	1.00	.45
SILVER MINOR STARS	1.50	.70
SILVER SEMISTARS	2.50	1.10
SILVER UNLISTED STARS	4.00	1.80
SILVER STATED ODDS 1:3		
COMMON GOLD	2.00	.90
GOLD MINOR STARS	3.00	1.35
GOLD SEMISTARS	5.00	2.20
GOLD UNLISTED STARS	8.00	3.60
GOLD STATED ODDS 1:12		
COMMON PLATINUM	12.00	5.50
PLATINUM STATED ODDS 1:48		

	MINT	NRMT
1 Frank Thomas P	20.00	9.00
2 Ken Griffey Jr. P	50.00	22.00
3 Cecil Fielder B	.40	.18
4 Chuck Knoblauch G	8.00	3.60
5 Garret Anderson B	.40	.18
6 Greg Maddux P	25.00	11.00
7 Matt Williams S	4.00	1.80
8 Marquis Grissom S	1.50	.70
9 Jason Isringhausen B	.20	.09
10 Larry Walker S	4.00	1.80
11 Charles Nagy B	.40	.18
12 Dan Wilson B	.20	.09
13 Albert Belle G	8.00	3.60
14 Javier Lopez B	.40	.18
15 David Cone B	.60	.25
16 Bernard Gilkey B	.20	.09
17 Andres Galarraga S	4.00	1.80
18 Bill Pulsipher B	.20	.09
19 Alex Fernandez B	.20	.09
20 Andy Pettitte S	2.50	1.10
21 Mark Grudzielanek B	.40	.18
22 Juan Gonzalez P	20.00	9.00
23 Reggie Sanders B	.40	.18
24 Kenny Lofton S	5.00	2.20
25 Andy Ashby B	.20	.09
26 John Wetteland B	.40	.18
27 Bobby Bonilla B	.40	.18
28 Hideo Nomo G	8.00	3.60
29 Joe Carter B	.40	.18
30 Jose Canseco B	1.00	.45
31 Ellis Burks B	.40	.18
32 Edgar Martinez S	1.50	.70
33 Chan Ho Park B	.75	.35
34 Dave Justice B	.75	.35
35 Carlos Delgado B	.75	.35
36 Jeff Cirillo B	1.50	.70
37 Charles Johnson B	.40	.18
38 Manny Ramirez G	10.00	4.50
39 Greg Vaughn B	.40	.18
40 Henry Rodriguez B	.40	.18
41 Darryl Strawberry B	.40	.18
42 Jim Thome B	8.00	3.60
43 Ryan Klesko S	1.50	.70
44 Ruben Sierra B	.20	.09
45 Brian Jordan G	3.00	1.35
46 Tony Gwynn S	25.00	11.00
47 Rafael Palmeiro G	8.00	3.60
48 Dante Bichette S	1.50	.70
49 Ivan Rodriguez G	10.00	4.50
50 Mark McGwire G	40.00	18.00
51 Tim Salmon S	4.00	1.80
52 Roger Clemens B	2.00	.90
53 Matt Lawton B	.40	.18
54 Wade Boggs S	4.00	1.80
55 Travis Fryman B	.40	.18
56 Bobby Higginson S	1.50	.70
57 John Jaha S	1.00	.45
58 Rondell White S	1.50	.70
59 Tom Glavine S	4.00	1.80
60 Eddie Murray S	4.00	1.80
61 Vinny Castilla	.60	.25
62 Todd Hundley B	.40	.18
63 Jay Buhner S	1.50	.70
64 Paul O'Neill B	.40	.18
65 Steve Finley S	.40	.18
66 Kevin Appier B	.40	.18
67 Ray Durham B	.40	.18
68 Dave Nilsson B	.20	.09
69 Jeff Bagwell G	10.00	4.50
70 Al Martin S	1.00	.45
71 Paul Molitor G	8.00	3.60
72 Kevin Brown S	2.50	1.10
73 Ron Gant B	.20	.09
74 Dwight Gooden B	.40	.18
75 Quinton McCracken B	.20	.09
76 Rusty Greer S	1.50	.70
77 Juan Guzman B	.20	.09
78 Fred McGriff S	2.50	1.10
79 Tino Martinez B	.75	.35
80 Ray Lankford B	.40	.18
81 Ken Caminiti G	5.00	2.20
82 James Baldwin B	.40	.18
83 Jermaine Dye G	3.00	1.35
84 Mark Grace S	2.50	1.10
85 Pat Hentgen S	1.50	.70
86 Jason Giambi S	1.50	.70
87 Brian Hunter B	.40	.18
88 Andy Benes B	.40	.18
89 Jason Dickson B	.20	.09
90 Shawn Green B	.75	.35
91 Jason Kendall B	.60	.25
92 Alex Rodriguez P	30.00	13.50
93 Chipper Jones P	25.00	11.00
94 Barry Bonds G	10.00	4.50
95 Brady Anderson S	3.00	1.35
96 Ryne Sandberg S	5.00	2.20
97 Lance Johnson B	.20	.09
98 Cal Ripken P	40.00	18.00
99 Craig Biggio S	8.00	3.60
100 Dean Palmer B	.40	.18
101 Gary Sheffield G	3.00	1.35
102 Johnny Damon B	.40	.18
103 Mo Vaughn G	8.00	3.60
104 Randy Johnson S	4.00	1.80
105 Raul Mondesi S	1.50	.70
106 Roberto Alomar G	8.00	3.60
107 Mike Piazza P	30.00	13.50
108 Rey Ordonez B	.40	.18
109 Barry Larkin S	8.00	3.60
110 Tony Clark S	2.50	1.10
111 Bernie Williams S	4.00	1.80
112 John Smoltz G	3.00	1.35
113 Moises Alou B	.40	.18
114 Will Clark B	.75	.35
115 Sammy Sosa G	25.00	11.00
116 Jim Edmonds S	2.50	1.10
117 Jeff Conine B	.20	.09
118 Joey Hamilton B	.40	.18
119 Todd Hollandsworth B	.20	.09
120 Troy Percival B	.40	.18
121 Paul Wilson B	.20	.09
122 Ken Hill B	.20	.09
123 Mariano Rivera S	1.50	.70
124 Eric Karros B	.40	.18
125 Derek Jeter G	25.00	11.00
126 Eric Young S	.40	.18
127 John Mabry B	.20	.09
128 Gregg Jefferies S	.20	.09
129 Ismael Valdes S	1.50	.70
130 Marty Cordova S	.40	.18
131 Omar Vizquel B	.40	.18
132 Mike Mussina S	4.00	1.80
133 Darin Erstad B	.75	.35
134 Edgar Renteria S	1.50	.70
135 Billy Wagner B	.40	.18
136 Alex Ochoa B	.20	.09
137 Luis Castillo B	.40	.18
138 Rocky Coppinger B	.20	.09
139 Mike Sweeney B	.40	.18
140 Michael Tucker B	.20	.09
141 Chris Snopek B	.20	.09
142 Dmitri Young S	1.50	.70
143 Andruw Jones S	12.00	5.50
144 Mike Cameron S	1.50	.70
145 Brant Brown B	.40	.18
146 Todd Walker G	8.00	3.60
147 Nomar Garciaparra G	25.00	11.00
148 Glendon Rusch B	.20	.09
149 Karim Garcia S	1.50	.70
150 Bubba Trammell S	4.00	1.80
151 Todd Greene B	.20	.09
152 Wilton Guerrero G	2.00	.90
153 Scott Spiezio B	.20	.09
154 Brooks Kieschnick B	.20	.09
155 Vladimir Guerrero G	12.00	5.50
156 Brian Giles S	12.00	5.50
157 Pokey Reese B	.40	.18
158 Jason Dickson G	2.00	.90
159 Kevin Orie S	2.00	.90
160 Scott Rolen S	12.00	5.50
161 Bartolo Colon S	1.50	.70
162 Shannon Stewart G	3.00	1.35
163 Wendell Magee B	.20	.09
164 Jose Guillen S	2.50	1.10
165 Bob Abreu S	1.50	.70
166 Deivi Cruz B	.75	.35
167 Alex Rodriguez NT B	2.50	1.10
168 Frank Thomas NT B	1.50	.70
169 Cal Ripken NT B	3.00	1.35
170 Chipper Jones NT B	2.00	.90
171 Mike Piazza NT S	2.50	1.10
172 Tony Gwynn NT S	10.00	4.50
173 Juan Gonzalez NT B	1.50	.70
174 Kenny Lofton NT S	2.50	1.10
175 Ken Griffey Jr. NT B	4.00	1.80
176 Mark McGwire NT S	4.00	1.80
177 Jeff Bagwell NT S	1.00	.45
178 Paul Molitor NT S	4.00	1.80
179 Andruw Jones NT B	1.00	.45
180 Manny Ramirez NT S	5.00	2.20
181 Ken Caminiti NT S	2.50	1.10
182 Barry Bonds NT B	1.00	.45
183 Mo Vaughn NT S	.75	.35
184 Derek Jeter NT B	2.50	1.10
185 Barry Larkin NT S	1.00	.45
186 Ivan Rodriguez NT B	1.00	.45
187 Albert Belle NT S	4.00	1.80
188 John Smoltz NT S	1.50	.70
189 Chuck Knoblauch NT S	1.50	.70
190 Brian Jordan NT S	1.50	.70
191 Gary Sheffield NT S	1.50	.70
192 Jim Thome NT S	4.00	1.80
193 Brady Anderson NT S	1.50	.70
194 Hideo Nomo NT S	.75	.35
195 Sammy Sosa NT S	12.00	5.50
196 Greg Maddux NT B	2.00	.90
197 Vladimir Guerrero CL B	1.25	.55
198 Scott Rolen CL B	1.25	.55
199 Todd Walker CL B	.40	.18
200 Nomar Garciaparra CL B	2.00	.90

1997 Donruss Preferred Cut to the Chase

	MINT	NRMT
*BRONZE STARS: 3X TO 8X BASE CARD HI		
*BRONZE YNG.STARS: 2.5X TO 6X BASE HI		
*SILVER STARS: 1.5X TO 4X BASE CARD HI		

*SILVER YNG.STARS: 1.25X TO 3X BASE HI
*GOLD STARS: 1X TO 2.5X BASE CARD HI
*GOLD YOUNG STARS: .75X TO 2X BASE HI
*PLAT.STARS: 1.25X TO 3X BASE CARD HI
*PLAT.YNG.STARS: 1X TO 2.5X BASE HI
RANDOM INSERTS IN PACKS

1997 Donruss Preferred Precious Metals

	MINT	NRMT
COMPLETE SET (25)	2500.00	1100.00
COMMON CARD (1-25)	25.00	11.00
SEMISTARS	40.00	18.00
UNLISTED STARS	60.00	27.00

RANDOM INSERTS IN PACKS
STATED PRINT RUN 100 SETS
ONE GRAM OF PRECIOUS METAL PER CARD

❑ 1 Frank Thomas P	120.00	55.00
❑ 2 Ken Griffey Jr. P	300.00	135.00
❑ 3 Greg Maddux P	150.00	70.00
❑ 4 Albert Belle G	60.00	27.00
❑ 5 Juan Gonzalez S	120.00	55.00
❑ 6 Kenny Lofton G	40.00	18.00
❑ 7 Tony Gwynn P	150.00	70.00
❑ 8 Ivan Rodriguez G	80.00	36.00
❑ 9 Mark McGwire G	300.00	135.00
❑ 10 Matt Williams S	60.00	27.00
❑ 11 Wade Boggs S	60.00	27.00
❑ 12 Eddie Murray S	60.00	27.00
❑ 13 Jeff Bagwell G	80.00	36.00
❑ 14 Ken Caminiti G	40.00	18.00
❑ 15 Alex Rodriguez P	200.00	90.00
❑ 16 Chipper Jones P	150.00	70.00
❑ 17 Barry Bonds G	80.00	36.00
❑ 18 Cal Ripken P	250.00	110.00
❑ 19 Mo Vaughn G	60.00	27.00
❑ 20 Mike Piazza P	200.00	90.00
❑ 21 Derek Jeter G	200.00	90.00
❑ 22 Bernie Williams S	60.00	27.00
❑ 23 Andruw Jones P	80.00	36.00
❑ 24 Vladimir Guerrero G	100.00	45.00
❑ 25 Jose Guillen S	40.00	18.00

1997 Donruss Preferred Staremasters

	MINT	NRMT
COMPLETE SET (20)	500.00	220.00

	MINT	NRMT
COMMON CARD (1-20)	8.00	3.60
UNLISTED STARS	12.00	5.50

RANDOM INSERTS IN PACKS
STATED PRINT RUN 1500 SERIAL #'d SETS

❑ 1 Alex Rodriguez	40.00	18.00
❑ 2 Frank Thomas	25.00	11.00
❑ 3 Chipper Jones	30.00	13.50
❑ 4 Cal Ripken	50.00	22.00
❑ 5 Mike Piazza	40.00	18.00
❑ 6 Juan Gonzalez	25.00	11.00
❑ 7 Derek Jeter	40.00	18.00
❑ 8 Jeff Bagwell	15.00	6.75
❑ 9 Ken Griffey Jr.	60.00	27.00
❑ 10 Tony Gwynn	30.00	13.50
❑ 11 Barry Bonds	15.00	6.75
❑ 12 Albert Belle	12.00	5.50
❑ 13 Greg Maddux	30.00	13.50
❑ 14 Mark McGwire	60.00	27.00
❑ 15 Ken Caminiti	8.00	3.60
❑ 16 Hideo Nomo	12.00	5.50
❑ 17 Gary Sheffield	8.00	3.60
❑ 18 Andruw Jones	15.00	6.75
❑ 19 Mo Vaughn	12.00	5.50
❑ 20 Ivan Rodriguez	15.00	6.75

1997 Donruss Preferred Tin Packs

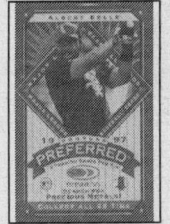

	MINT	NRMT
COMPLETE SET (25)	20.00	9.00
COMMON PACK (1-25)	.25	.11
UNLISTED STARS	.50	.23
COMMON SEALED PACK	5.00	2.20

*SEALED: 1.5X TO 3X HI ON 2.00+ PACKS
COMP.GOLD PACK SET (25) 250.00 110.00
*GOLD PACKS: 4X TO 10X HI COLUMN
*GOLD PACKS: 7.5X TO 15X HI
ONE GOLD PACK PER BOX
GOLD PACKS: 1200 SERIAL #'d SETS
COMP.BLUE BOX SET (25) 150.00 70.00
*BLUE BOXES: 3X TO 8X HI COLUMN
BLUE BOXES: 1200 SERIAL #'d SETS
COMP.GOLD BOX SET (25) 500.00 220.00
*GOLD BOXES: 8X TO 20X HI COLUMN
GOLD BOXES: 299 SERIAL #'d SETS
PRICES BELOW REFER TO OPENED PACKS

❑ 1 Jeff Bagwell	.60	.25
❑ 2 Albert Belle	.50	.23

❑ 3 Barry Bonds	.60	.25
❑ 4 Roger Clemens	1.25	.55
❑ 5 Juan Gonzalez	1.00	.45
❑ 6 Ken Griffey Jr.	2.50	1.10
❑ 7 Tony Gwynn	1.25	.55
❑ 8 Derek Jeter	1.50	.70
❑ 9 Andruw Jones	.60	.25
❑ 10 Chipper Jones	1.25	.55
❑ 11 Kenny Lofton	.40	.18
❑ 12 Greg Maddux	1.25	.55
❑ 13 Mark McGwire	2.50	1.10
❑ 14 Hideo Nomo	.50	.23
❑ 15 Mike Piazza	1.50	.70
❑ 16 Manny Ramirez	.60	.25
❑ 17 Cal Ripken	2.00	.90
❑ 18 Alex Rodriguez	1.50	.70
❑ 19 Ivan Rodriguez	.60	.25
❑ 20 Ryne Sandberg	.60	.25
❑ 21 Gary Sheffield	.25	.11
❑ 22 John Smoltz	.40	.18
❑ 23 Sammy Sosa	1.50	.70
❑ 24 Frank Thomas	1.00	.45
❑ 25 Mo Vaughn	.50	.23

1997 Donruss Preferred X-Ponential Power

	MINT	NRMT
COMPLETE SET (10)	250.00	110.00
COMMON CARD (1A-10B)	5.00	2.20
UNLISTED STARS	8.00	3.60

RANDOM INSERTS IN PACKS
STATED PRINT RUN 3000 SERIAL #'d SETS

❑ 1A Manny Ramirez	10.00	4.50
❑ 1B Jim Thome	8.00	3.60
❑ 2A Paul Molitor	8.00	3.60
❑ 2B Chuck Knoblauch	8.00	3.60
❑ 3A Ivan Rodriguez	10.00	4.50
❑ 3B Juan Gonzalez	15.00	6.75
❑ 4A Albert Belle	8.00	3.60
❑ 4B Frank Thomas	15.00	6.75
❑ 5A Roberto Alomar	8.00	3.60
❑ 5B Cal Ripken	30.00	13.50
❑ 6A Tim Salmon	8.00	3.60
❑ 6B Jim Edmonds	6.00	2.70
❑ 7A Ken Griffey Jr.	40.00	18.00
❑ 7B Alex Rodriguez	25.00	11.00
❑ 8A Chipper Jones	20.00	9.00
❑ 8B Andruw Jones	10.00	4.50
❑ 9A Mike Piazza	25.00	11.00
❑ 9B Raul Mondesi	5.00	2.20
❑ 10A Tony Gwynn	20.00	9.00
❑ 10B Ken Caminiti	5.00	2.20

1998 Donruss Preferred

	MINT	NRMT
COMP.GRAND STAND (100)	25.00	11.00
COMMON GRAND STAND	.15	.07
GRAND STAND MINOR STARS	.25	.11
GRAND STAND SEMISTARS	.40	.18
GRAND STAND UNLISTED STARS	.60	.25
COMP.MEZZANINE (40)	80.00	36.00
COMMON MEZZANINE	1.00	.45
MEZZANINE MINOR STARS	1.50	.70
MEZZANINE SEMISTARS	2.50	1.10

MEZZANINE UNLISTED STARS	4.00	1.80
MEZZANINE STATED ODDS 1:6		
COMP. CLUB LEVEL (30)	120.00	55.00
COMMON CLUB LEVEL	1.50	.70
CLUB LEVEL MINOR STARS	2.50	1.10
CLUB LEVEL SEMISTARS	4.00	1.80
CLUB LEVEL UNLISTED STARS	6.00	2.70
CLUB LEVEL STATED ODDS 1:12		
COMP. FIELD BOX (20)	200.00	90.00
COMMON FIELD BOX	3.00	1.35
FIELD BOX SEMISTARS	5.00	2.20
FIELD BOX UNLISTED STARS	8.00	3.60
FIELD BOX STATED ODDS 1:23		
COMP. EXEC. SUITE (10)	350.00	160.00
COMMON EXEC. SUITE	15.00	6.75
EXECUTIVE SUITE STATED ODDS 1:65		

❑ 1	Ken Griffey Jr. EX	60.00	27.00
❑ 2	Frank Thomas EX	25.00	11.00
❑ 3	Cal Ripken EX	50.00	22.00
❑ 4	Alex Rodriguez EX	40.00	18.00
❑ 5	Greg Maddux EX	30.00	13.50
❑ 6	Mike Piazza EX	40.00	18.00
❑ 7	Chipper Jones EX	30.00	13.50
❑ 8	Tony Gwynn FB	20.00	9.00
❑ 9	Derek Jeter FB	25.00	11.00
❑ 10	Jeff Bagwell EX	15.00	6.75
❑ 11	Juan Gonzalez EX	25.00	11.00
❑ 12	Nomar Garciaparra EX	40.00	18.00
❑ 13	Andruw Jones FB	8.00	3.60
❑ 14	Hideo Nomo FB	8.00	3.60
❑ 15	Roger Clemens FB	20.00	9.00
❑ 16	Mark McGwire FB	50.00	22.00
❑ 17	Scott Rolen FB	10.00	4.50
❑ 18	Vladimir Guerrero FB	10.00	4.50
❑ 19	Barry Bonds FB	10.00	4.50
❑ 20	Darin Erstad FB	5.00	2.20
❑ 21	Albert Belle FB	8.00	3.60
❑ 22	Kenny Lofton FB	5.00	2.20
❑ 23	Mo Vaughn FB	8.00	3.60
❑ 24	Tony Clark FB	3.00	1.35
❑ 25	Ivan Rodriguez FB	10.00	4.50
❑ 26	Larry Walker CB	6.00	2.70
❑ 27	Eddie Murray CB	6.00	2.70
❑ 28	Andy Pettitte CB	2.50	1.10
❑ 29	Roberto Alomar CB	6.00	2.70
❑ 30	Randy Johnson CB	6.00	2.70
❑ 31	Manny Ramirez CB	8.00	3.60
❑ 32	Paul Molitor FB	8.00	3.60
❑ 33	Mike Mussina CB	6.00	2.70
❑ 34	Jim Thome FB	8.00	3.60
❑ 35	Tino Martinez CB	2.50	1.10
❑ 36	Gary Sheffield CB	2.50	1.10
❑ 37	Chuck Knoblauch CB	2.50	1.10
❑ 38	Bernie Williams CB	6.00	2.70
❑ 39	Tim Salmon CB	4.00	1.80
❑ 40	Sammy Sosa CB	20.00	9.00
❑ 41	Wade Boggs ME	4.00	1.80
❑ 42	Will Clark GS	.60	.25
❑ 43	Andres Galarraga CB	4.00	1.80
❑ 44	Raul Mondesi CB	2.50	1.10
❑ 45	Rickey Henderson GS	.75	.35
❑ 46	Jose Canseco CB	.75	.35
❑ 47	Pedro Martinez GS	.75	.35
❑ 48	Jay Buhner GS	.25	.11
❑ 49	Ryan Klesko GS	.25	.11
❑ 50	Barry Larkin CB	6.00	2.70
❑ 51	Charles Johnson GS	.25	.11

❑ 52	Tom Glavine GS	.60	.25
❑ 53	Edgar Martinez CB	2.50	1.10
❑ 54	Fred McGriff GS	.40	.18
❑ 55	Moises Alou ME	1.50	.70
❑ 56	Dante Bichette GS	.25	.11
❑ 57	Jim Edmonds CB	2.50	1.10
❑ 58	Mark Grace ME	2.50	1.10
❑ 59	Chan Ho Park ME	1.50	.70
❑ 60	Justin Thompson ME	1.00	.45
❑ 61	John Smoltz ME	2.50	1.10
❑ 62	Craig Biggio CB	6.00	2.70
❑ 63	Ken Caminiti ME	1.50	.70
❑ 64	Deion Sanders GS	1.50	.70
❑ 65	Carlos Delgado GS	.60	.25
❑ 66	David Justice CB	2.50	1.10
❑ 67	J.T. Snow GS	.25	.11
❑ 68	Jason Giambi CB	2.50	1.10
❑ 69	Garret Anderson ME	1.50	.70
❑ 70	Rondell White ME	1.50	.70
❑ 71	Matt Williams ME	4.00	1.80
❑ 72	Brady Anderson ME	1.50	.70
❑ 73	Eric Karros GS	.25	.11
❑ 74	Javier Lopez GS	.25	.11
❑ 75	Pat Hentgen GS	.15	.07
❑ 76	Todd Hundley GS	.25	.11
❑ 77	Ray Lankford GS	.25	.11
❑ 78	Denny Neagle GS	.15	.07
❑ 79	Henry Rodriguez GS	.25	.11
❑ 80	Sandy Alomar Jr. ME	1.50	.70
❑ 81	Rafael Palmeiro ME	4.00	1.80
❑ 82	Robin Ventura GS	.25	.11
❑ 83	John Olerud GS	.25	.11
❑ 84	Omar Vizquel GS	.25	.11
❑ 85	Joe Randa GS	.15	.07
❑ 86	Lance Johnson GS	.15	.07
❑ 87	Kevin Brown GS	.40	.18
❑ 88	Curt Schilling GS	.40	.18
❑ 89	Ismael Valdes GS	.15	.07
❑ 90	Francisco Cordova GS	.15	.07
❑ 91	David Cone GS	.40	.18
❑ 92	Paul O'Neill GS	.25	.11
❑ 93	Jimmy Key GS	.25	.11
❑ 94	Brad Radke GS	.25	.11
❑ 95	Kevin Appier GS	.25	.11
❑ 96	Al Martin GS	.15	.07
❑ 97	Rusty Greer ME	1.50	.70
❑ 98	Reggie Jefferson GS	.15	.07
❑ 99	Ron Coomer GS	.15	.07
❑ 100	Vinny Castilla GS	.25	.11
❑ 101	Bobby Bonilla ME	1.50	.70
❑ 102	Eric Young GS	.25	.11
❑ 103	Tony Womack GS	.25	.11
❑ 104	Jason Kendall GS	.25	.11
❑ 105	Jeff Suppan GS	.15	.07
❑ 106	Shawn Estes ME	1.00	.45
❑ 107	Shawn Green GS	.40	.18
❑ 108	Edgardo Alfonzo ME	2.50	1.10
❑ 109	Alan Benes ME	1.00	.45
❑ 110	Bobby Higginson GS	.25	.11
❑ 111	Mark Grudzielanek GS	.15	.07
❑ 112	Wilton Guerrero GS	.15	.07
❑ 113	Todd Greene ME	1.00	.45
❑ 114	Pokey Reese GS	.15	.07
❑ 115	Jose Guillen GS	1.50	.70
❑ 116	Neifi Perez ME	1.50	.70
❑ 117	Luis Castillo GS	.15	.07
❑ 118	Edgar Renteria GS	.15	.07
❑ 119	Karim Garcia GS	.15	.07
❑ 120	Butch Huskey GS	.15	.07
❑ 121	Michael Tucker GS	.15	.07
❑ 122	Jason Dickson GS	.15	.07
❑ 123	Todd Walker GS	1.50	.70
❑ 124	Brian Jordan GS	.25	.11
❑ 125	Joe Carter GS	.25	.11
❑ 126	Matt Morris ME	1.00	.45
❑ 127	Brett Tomko ME	1.00	.45
❑ 128	Mike Cameron CB	2.50	1.10
❑ 129	Russ Davis GS	.25	.11
❑ 130	Shannon Stewart ME	1.50	.70
❑ 131	Kevin Orie GS	.15	.07
❑ 132	Scott Spiezio GS	.15	.07
❑ 133	Brian Giles GS	.25	.11
❑ 134	Raul Casanova GS	.15	.07
❑ 135	Jose Cruz Jr. CB	2.50	1.10
❑ 136	Hideki Irabu GS	.15	.11
❑ 137	Bubba Trammell GS	.15	.07

❑ 138	Richard Hidalgo CB	2.50	1.10
❑ 139	Paul Konerko CB	2.50	1.10
❑ 140	Todd Helton FB	8.00	3.60
❑ 141	Miguel Tejada CB	2.50	1.10
❑ 142	Fernando Tatis ME	4.00	1.80
❑ 143	Ben Grieve FB	3.00	1.35
❑ 144	Travis Lee FB	5.00	2.20
❑ 145	Mark Kotsay CB	2.50	1.10
❑ 146	Eli Marrero ME	1.00	.45
❑ 147	David Ortiz CB	1.50	.70
❑ 148	Juan Encarnacion ME	1.50	.70
❑ 149	Jaret Wright ME	1.50	.70
❑ 150	Livan Hernandez CB	1.50	.70
❑ 151	Ruben Rivera GS	.15	.07
❑ 152	Brad Fullmer ME	1.00	.45
❑ 153	Dennis Reyes GS	.15	.07
❑ 154	Enrique Wilson ME	1.00	.45
❑ 155	Todd Dunwoody ME	1.00	.45
❑ 156	Derrick Gibson ME	1.50	.70
❑ 157	Aaron Boone ME	1.00	.45
❑ 158	Matt Morris ME	1.00	.45
❑ 159	Preston Wilson ME	1.50	.70
❑ 160	Abraham Nunez GS	.15	.07
❑ 161	Shane Monahan GS	.15	.07
❑ 162	Carl Pavano GS	.15	.07
❑ 163	Derrek Lee GS	.15	.07
❑ 164	Jeff Abbott GS	.15	.07
❑ 165	Wes Helms ME	1.00	.45
❑ 166	Brian Rose GS	.15	.07
❑ 167	Bobby Estalella GS	.15	.07
❑ 168	Ken Griffey Jr. PP GS	3.00	1.35
❑ 169	Frank Thomas PP GS	1.25	.55
❑ 170	Cal Ripken PP GS	2.50	1.10
❑ 171	Alex Rodriguez PP GS	2.00	.90
❑ 172	Greg Maddux PP GS	1.50	.70
❑ 173	Mike Piazza PP GS	2.00	.90
❑ 174	Chipper Jones PP GS	1.50	.70
❑ 175	Tony Gwynn PP GS	1.50	.70
❑ 176	Derek Jeter PP GS	2.00	.90
❑ 177	Jeff Bagwell PP GS	.75	.35
❑ 178	Juan Gonzalez PP GS	1.25	.55
❑ 179	N. Garciaparra PP GS	2.00	.90
❑ 180	Andruw Jones PP GS	.60	.25
❑ 181	Hideo Nomo PP GS	.60	.25
❑ 182	Roger Clemens PP GS	1.50	.70
❑ 183	Mark McGwire PP GS	4.00	1.80
❑ 184	Scott Rolen PP GS	.75	.35
❑ 185	Barry Bonds PP GS	.75	.35
❑ 186	Darin Erstad PP GS	.40	.18
❑ 187	Mo Vaughn PP GS	.60	.25
❑ 188	Ivan Rodriguez PP GS	.75	.35
❑ 189	Larry Walker PP ME	4.00	1.80
❑ 190	Andy Pettitte PP GS	.25	.11
❑ 191	Randy Johnson PP ME	4.00	1.80
❑ 192	Paul Molitor PP GS	.60	.25
❑ 193	Jim Thome PP GS	.60	.25
❑ 194	Tino Martinez PP ME	1.50	.70
❑ 195	Gary Sheffield PP GS	.25	.11
❑ 196	Albert Belle PP GS	.60	.25
❑ 197	Jose Cruz Jr. PP GS	.25	.11
❑ 198	Todd Helton CL GS	.75	.35
❑ 199	Ben Grieve CL GS	.60	.25
❑ 200	Paul Konerko CL GS	.15	.07

1998 Donruss Preferred Seating

```
                          MINT    NRMT
*GS STARS: 4X TO 10X BASIC CARDS
*GS YOUNG STARS: 3X TO 8X BASIC CARDS
*MEZZ.STARS: .75X TO 2X BASIC CARDS
*CLUB LEV.STARS: .75X TO 2X BASIC CARDS
*FIELD BOX STARS: .75X TO 2X BASIC
CARDS
*EXEC.STARS: .75X TO 2X BASIC CARDS
RANDOM INSERTS IN PACKS
```

		MINT	NRMT
☐ 23	Juan Gonzalez	12.00	5.50
	Andruw Jones		
☐ 24	Barry Bonds	8.00	3.60
	Vladimir Guerrero		
☐ 25	Mark McGwire	40.00	18.00
	Tony Clark		
☐ 26	Bernie Williams	6.00	2.70
	Mike Cameron		

SILVER PACKS: RANDOM INSERTS IN
BOXES
SILVER PACK PRINT RUN 999 SERIAL #'d
SETS
*GREEN BOXES: 3X TO 8X HI COLUMN
GREEN BOX PRINT RUN 999 SERIAL #'d
SETS
*GOLD BOXES: 8X TO 20X HI COLUMN
GOLD BOXES PRINT RUN 199 SERIAL #'d
SETS
PRICES BELOW ARE FOR OPEN GREEN
PACKS

1998 Donruss Preferred Great X-Pectations

	MINT	NRMT
COMPLETE SET (26)	300.00	135.00
COMMON CARD (1-26)	2.50	1.10
SEMISTARS	4.00	1.80
UNLISTED STARS	6.00	2.70

STATED PRINT RUN 2700 SERIAL #'d SETS
*DIE CUT SINGLES: 1.25X TO 3X HI COLUMN
DIE CUT PRINT RUN 300 SERIAL #'d SETS
RANDOM INSERTS IN PACKS

☐ 1	Jeff Bagwell	8.00	3.60
	Travis Lee		
☐ 2	Jose Cruz Jr.	30.00	13.50
	Ken Griffey Jr.		
☐ 3	Larry Walker	10.00	4.50
	Ben Grieve		
☐ 4	Frank Thomas	12.00	5.50
	Todd Helton		
☐ 5	Jim Thome	6.00	2.70
	Paul Konerko		
☐ 6	Alex Rodriguez	20.00	9.00
	Miguel Tejada		
☐ 7	Greg Maddux	15.00	6.75
	Livan Hernandez		
☐ 8	Roger Clemens	15.00	6.75
	Jaret Wright		
☐ 9	Albert Belle	6.00	2.70
	Juan Encarnacion		
☐ 10	Mo Vaughn	6.00	2.70
	David Ortiz		
☐ 11	Manny Ramirez	8.00	3.60
	Mark Kotsay		
☐ 12	Tim Salmon	4.00	1.80
	Brad Fulmer UER		
	misspelled Fulmer		
☐ 13	Cal Ripken	25.00	11.00
	Fernando Tatis		
☐ 14	Hideo Nomo	8.00	3.60
	Hideki Irabu		
☐ 15	Mike Piazza	20.00	9.00
	Todd Greene		
☐ 16	Gary Sheffield	2.50	1.10
	Richard Hidalgo		
☐ 17	Paul Molitor	6.00	2.70
	Darin Erstad		
☐ 18	Ivan Rodriguez	8.00	3.60
	Eli Marrero		
☐ 19	Ken Caminiti	2.50	1.10
	Todd Walker		
☐ 20	Tony Gwynn	15.00	6.75
	Jose Guillen		
☐ 21	Deter Jeter	25.00	11.00
	Nomar Garciaparra		
☐ 22	Chipper Jones	15.00	6.75
	Scott Rolen		

1998 Donruss Preferred Precious Metals

	MINT	NRMT
COMPLETE SET (30)	4000.00	1800.00
COMMON CARD (1-30)	30.00	13.50
SEMISTARS	50.00	22.00
UNLISTED STARS	80.00	36.00

RANDOM INSERTS IN PACKS
STATED PRINT RUN 50 SETS

☐ 1	Ken Griffey Jr.	400.00	180.00
☐ 2	Frank Thomas	150.00	70.00
☐ 3	Cal Ripken	300.00	135.00
☐ 4	Alex Rodriguez	250.00	110.00
☐ 5	Greg Maddux	200.00	90.00
☐ 6	Mike Piazza	250.00	110.00
☐ 7	Chipper Jones	200.00	90.00
☐ 8	Tony Gwynn	200.00	90.00
☐ 9	Derek Jeter	250.00	110.00
☐ 10	Jeff Bagwell	100.00	45.00
☐ 11	Juan Gonzalez	150.00	70.00
☐ 12	Nomar Garciaparra	250.00	110.00
☐ 13	Andruw Jones	80.00	36.00
☐ 14	Hideo Nomo	80.00	36.00
☐ 15	Roger Clemens	200.00	90.00
☐ 16	Mark McGwire	500.00	220.00
☐ 17	Scott Rolen	120.00	55.00
☐ 18	Barry Bonds	100.00	45.00
☐ 19	Darin Erstad	50.00	22.00
☐ 20	Kenny Lofton	50.00	22.00
☐ 21	Mo Vaughn	80.00	36.00
☐ 22	Ivan Rodriguez	100.00	45.00
☐ 23	Randy Johnson	80.00	36.00
☐ 24	Paul Molitor	80.00	36.00
☐ 25	Jose Cruz Jr.	50.00	22.00
☐ 26	Paul Konerko	80.00	36.00
☐ 27	Todd Helton	80.00	36.00
☐ 28	Ben Grieve	80.00	36.00
☐ 29	Travis Lee	50.00	22.00
☐ 30	Mark Kotsay	50.00	22.00

1998 Donruss Preferred Tin Packs

	MINT	NRMT
COMP.GREEN SET (24)	20.00	9.00
COMMON GREEN (1-24)	.25	.11
UNLISTED STARS	.50	.23
COMMON GREEN SEALED	5.00	2.20

*GREEN SEALED: 1.25X TO 3X HI ON 2.00+
*GOLD PACKS: 8X TO 20X HI COLUMN
*GOLD SEALED PACKS: 10X TO 25X HI
GOLD PACKS: RANDOM INSERTS IN BOXES
GOLD PACKS PRINT RUN 199 SERIAL #'d
SETS
*SILVER PACKS: 3X TO 8X HI COLUMN
*SILVER SEALED PACKS: 4X TO 10X HI

☐ 1	Todd Helton	.60	.25
☐ 2	Ben Grieve	.50	.23
☐ 3	Cal Ripken	2.00	.90
☐ 4	Alex Rodriguez	1.50	.70
☐ 5	Greg Maddux	1.25	.55
☐ 6	Mike Piazza	1.50	.70
☐ 7	Chipper Jones	1.25	.55
☐ 8	Travis Lee	.30	.14
☐ 9	Derek Jeter	1.50	.70
☐ 10	Jeff Bagwell	.60	.25
☐ 11	Juan Gonzalez	1.00	.45
☐ 12	Mark McGwire	3.00	1.35
☐ 13	Hideo Nomo	.50	.23
☐ 14	Roger Clemens	1.25	.55
☐ 15	Andruw Jones	.50	.23
☐ 16	Paul Molitor	.50	.23
☐ 17	Vladimir Guerrero	.60	.25
☐ 18	Jose Cruz Jr.	.25	.11
☐ 19	Nomar Garciaparra PH	1.50	.70
☐ 20	Scott Rolen PH	.60	.25
☐ 21	Ken Griffey Jr. PH	2.50	1.10
☐ 22	Larry Walker PH	.50	.23
☐ 23	Frank Thomas PH	1.00	.45
☐ 24	Tony Gwynn PH	1.25	.55

1998 Donruss Preferred Tin Packs Double-Wide

	MINT	NRMT
COMPLETE SET (12)	25.00	11.00
COMMON PACK (1-12)	.75	.35

AVAILABLE ONLY IN RETAIL OUTLETS
PRICES BELOW REFER TO OPENED PACKS

☐ 1	Todd Helton	1.50	.70
	Ben Grieve		
☐ 2	Cal Ripken	3.00	1.35

	MINT	NRMT
Alex Rodriguez		
❑ 3 Greg Maddux	2.00	.90
Mike Piazza		
❑ 4 Chipper Jones	2.00	.90
Travis Lee		
❑ 5 Derek Jeter	2.50	1.10
Jeff Bagwell		
❑ 6 Juan Gonzalez	5.00	2.20
Mark McGwire		
❑ 7 Hideo Nomo	2.00	.90
Roger Clemens		
❑ 8 Andruw Jones	1.00	.45
Paul Molitor		
❑ 9 Vladimir Guerrero	1.00	.45
Jose Cruz Jr.		
❑ 10 Nomar Garciaparra	2.50	1.10
Scott Rolen PH		
❑ 11 Ken Griffey Jr.	4.00	1.80
Larry Walker PH		
❑ 12 Frank Thomas	2.00	.90
Tony Gwynn PH		

1998 Donruss Preferred Title Waves

	MINT	NRMT
COMPLETE SET (30)	500.00	220.00
COMMON CARD (1-30)	4.00	1.80
SEMISTARS	6.00	2.70
UNLISTED STARS	10.00	4.50
RANDOM INSERTS IN PACKS		
PRINT RUN BASED ON TITLE YEAR		
❑ 1 Nomar Garciaparra	30.00	13.50
97 AL ROY		
❑ 2 Scott Rolen	12.00	5.50
97 NL ROY		
❑ 3 Roger Clemens	25.00	11.00
97 AL Cy Young		
❑ 4 Gary Sheffield	4.00	1.80
97 World Series		
❑ 5 Jeff Bagwell	12.00	5.50
97 Wildcard		
❑ 6 Cal Ripken	40.00	18.00
97 AL East Penn.		
❑ 7 Frank Thomas	20.00	9.00
97 AL Batting		
❑ 8 Ken Griffey Jr.	50.00	22.00
97 AL HR		
❑ 9 Larry Walker	10.00	4.50
96 AL ROY		
❑ 10 Derek Jeter	30.00	13.50
96 AL ROY		
❑ 11 Juan Gonzalez	20.00	9.00
96 AL MVP		
❑ 12 Bernie Williams	10.00	4.50
96 ALCS MVP		
❑ 13 Andruw Jones	10.00	4.50
96 NLCS		
❑ 14 Andy Pettitte	4.00	1.80
96 World Series		
❑ 15 Ivan Rodriguez	12.00	5.50
96 AL West Penn.		
❑ 16 Alex Rodriguez	30.00	13.50
96 AL Batting		
❑ 17 Mark McGwire	60.00	27.00
96 AL HR		
❑ 18 Andres Galarraga	6.00	2.70

	MINT	NRMT
96 NL HR		
❑ 19 Hideo Nomo	10.00	4.50
95 ROY		
❑ 20 Mo Vaughn	10.00	4.50
95 AL MVP		
❑ 21 Randy Johnson	10.00	4.50
95 AL Cy Young		
❑ 22 Chipper Jones	25.00	11.00
95 World Series		
❑ 23 Greg Maddux	25.00	11.00
95 World Series		
❑ 24 Manny Ramirez	12.00	5.50
95 ALCS		
❑ 25 Tony Gwynn	25.00	11.00
95 NL Batting		
❑ 26 Albert Belle	10.00	4.50
95 AL HR		
❑ 27 Kenny Lofton	6.00	2.70
95 AL SB		
❑ 28 Mike Piazza	90.00	13.50
93 NL ROY		
❑ 29 Paul Molitor	10.00	4.50
93 World Series		
❑ 30 Barry Bonds	12.00	5.50
93 NL HR		

1997 Donruss Signature

	MINT	NRMT
COMPLETE SET (100)	50.00	22.00
COMMON CARD (1-100)	.25	.11
MINOR STARS	.50	.23
UNLISTED STARS	1.00	.45
COMMON PLAT.PP (1-100)	8.00	3.60
*PLAT.PP STARS: 12.5X TO 30X HI COLUMN		
*PLAT.PP ROOKIES: 5X TO 12X HI		
PLATINUM PP: RANDOM INSERTS IN PACKS		
PLAT.PP STATED PRINT RUN 150 SETS		
❑ 1 Mark McGwire	6.00	2.70
❑ 2 Kenny Lofton	.75	.35
❑ 3 Tony Gwynn	2.50	1.10
❑ 4 Tony Clark	.75	.35
❑ 5 Tim Salmon	1.00	.45
❑ 6 Ken Griffey Jr.	5.00	2.20
❑ 7 Mike Piazza	3.00	1.35
❑ 8 Greg Maddux	2.50	1.10
❑ 9 Roberto Alomar	1.00	.45
❑ 10 Andres Galarraga	1.00	.45
❑ 11 Roger Clemens	2.50	1.10
❑ 12 Bernie Williams	1.00	.45
❑ 13 Rondell White	.50	.23
❑ 14 Kevin Appier	.50	.23
❑ 15 Ray Lankford	.50	.23
❑ 16 Frank Thomas	2.00	.90
❑ 17 Will Clark	1.00	.45
❑ 18 Chipper Jones	2.50	1.10
❑ 19 Jeff Bagwell	1.25	.55
❑ 20 Manny Ramirez	1.25	.55
❑ 21 Ryne Sandberg	1.25	.55
❑ 22 Paul Molitor	1.00	.45
❑ 23 Gary Sheffield	.50	.23
❑ 24 Jim Edmonds	.75	.35
❑ 25 Barry Larkin	1.00	.45
❑ 26 Rafael Palmeiro	1.00	.45
❑ 27 Alan Benes	.25	.11
❑ 28 Dave Justice	1.00	.45
❑ 29 Randy Johnson	1.00	.45

	MINT	NRMT
❑ 30 Barry Bonds	1.25	.55
❑ 31 Mo Vaughn	1.00	.45
❑ 32 Michael Tucker	.25	.11
❑ 33 Larry Walker	1.00	.45
❑ 34 Tino Martinez	1.00	.45
❑ 35 Jose Guillen	.75	.35
❑ 36 Carlos Delgado	1.00	.45
❑ 37 Jason Dickson	.25	.11
❑ 38 Tom Glavine	1.00	.45
❑ 39 Raul Mondesi	.50	.23
❑ 40 Jose Cruz Jr.	2.00	.90
❑ 41 Johnny Damon	.50	.23
❑ 42 Mark Grace	.75	.35
❑ 43 Juan Gonzalez	2.00	.90
❑ 44 Vladimir Guerrero	1.50	.70
❑ 45 Kevin Brown	.75	.35
❑ 46 Justin Thompson	.50	.23
❑ 47 Eric Young	.50	.23
❑ 48 Ron Coomer	.25	.11
❑ 49 Mark Kotsay	1.00	.45
❑ 50 Scott Rolen	1.50	.70
❑ 51 Derek Jeter	3.00	1.35
❑ 52 Jim Thome	1.00	.45
❑ 53 Fred McGriff	.75	.35
❑ 54 Albert Belle	1.00	.45
❑ 55 Garret Anderson	.50	.23
❑ 56 Wilton Guerrero	.25	.11
❑ 57 Jose Canseco	1.25	.55
❑ 58 Cal Ripken	4.00	1.80
❑ 59 Sammy Sosa	3.00	1.35
❑ 60 Dmitri Young	.50	.23
❑ 61 Alex Rodriguez	3.00	1.35
❑ 62 Javier Lopez	.50	.23
❑ 63 Sandy Alomar Jr.	.50	.23
❑ 64 Joe Carter	.50	.23
❑ 65 Dante Bichette	.50	.23
❑ 66 Al Martin	.25	.11
❑ 67 Darin Erstad	1.00	.45
❑ 68 Pokey Reese	.50	.23
❑ 69 Brady Anderson	.50	.23
❑ 70 Andruw Jones	1.25	.55
❑ 71 Ivan Rodriguez	1.25	.55
❑ 72 Nomar Garciaparra	3.00	1.35
❑ 73 Moises Alou	.50	.23
❑ 74 Andy Pettitte	.75	.35
❑ 75 Jay Buhner	.50	.23
❑ 76 Craig Biggio	1.00	.45
❑ 77 Wade Boggs	1.00	.45
❑ 78 Shawn Estes	.50	.23
❑ 79 Neifi Perez	.50	.23
❑ 80 Rusty Greer	.50	.23
❑ 81 Pedro Martinez	1.25	.55
❑ 82 Mike Mussina	1.00	.45
❑ 83 Jason Giambi	1.00	.45
❑ 84 Hideo Nomo	1.00	.45
❑ 85 Todd Hundley	.50	.23
❑ 86 Deion Sanders	.50	.23
❑ 87 Mike Cameron	.50	.23
❑ 88 Bobby Bonilla	.50	.23
❑ 89 Todd Greene	.25	.11
❑ 90 Kevin Orie	.25	.11
❑ 91 Ken Caminiti	.75	.35
❑ 92 Chuck Knoblauch	1.00	.45
❑ 93 Matt Morris	.50	.23
❑ 94 Matt Williams	1.00	.45
❑ 95 Pat Hentgen	.50	.23
❑ 96 John Smoltz	.75	.35
❑ 97 Edgar Martinez	.75	.35
❑ 98 Jason Kendall	.75	.35
❑ 99 Ken Griffey Jr. CL	2.50	1.10
❑ 100 Frank Thomas CL	1.00	.45

1997 Donruss Signature Autographs

	MINT	NRMT
COMPLETE SET (117)	1500.00	700.00
COMMON CARD	4.00	1.80
MINOR STARS	8.00	3.60
ONE AUTOGRAPH PER PACK		
ASTERISK CARDS ARE IN SERIES A AND B		
NNO CARDS LISTED IN ALPH.ORDER		
❑ 1 Jeff Abbott/3900	4.00	1.80
❑ 2 Bob Abreu/3900	10.00	4.50

❏ 3	Edgardo Alfonzo/3900	10.00	4.50
❏ 4	Roberto Alomar/150 *	80.00	36.00
❏ 5	Sandy Alomar Jr./1400	8.00	3.60
❏ 6	Moises Alou/900	10.00	4.50
❏ 7	Garret Anderson/3900	8.00	3.60
❏ 8	Andy Ashby/3900	4.00	1.80
❏ 9	Trey Beamon/3900	4.00	1.80
❏ 10	Alan Benes/3900	4.00	1.80
❏ 11	Geronimo Berroa/3900	4.00	1.80
❏ 12	Wade Boggs/150 *	100.00	45.00
❏ 13	Kevin Brown C/3900	4.00	1.80
❏ 14	Brett Butler/1400	8.00	3.60
❏ 15	Mike Cameron/3900	8.00	3.60
❏ 16	Giovanni Carrara/2900	4.00	1.80
❏ 17	Luis Castillo/3900	8.00	3.60
❏ 18	Tony Clark/3900	10.00	4.50
❏ 19	Will Clark/1400	25.00	11.00
❏ 20	Lou Collier/3900	4.00	1.80
❏ 21	Bartolo Colon/3900	10.00	4.50
❏ 22	Ron Coomer/3900	4.00	1.80
❏ 23	Marty Cordova/3900	4.00	1.80
❏ 24	Jacob Cruz/3900 *	4.00	1.80
❏ 25	Jose Cruz Jr./900 *	20.00	9.00
❏ 26	Russ Davis/3900	8.00	3.60
❏ 27	Jason Dickson/3900	4.00	1.80
❏ 28	Todd Dunwoody/3900	8.00	3.60
❏ 29	Jermaine Dye/3900	8.00	3.60
❏ 30	Jim Edmonds/3900	10.00	4.50
❏ 31	Darin Erstad/3900 *	25.00	11.00
❏ 32	Bobby Estalella/3900	4.00	1.80
❏ 33	Shawn Estes/3900	8.00	3.60
❏ 34	Jeff Fassero/3900	4.00	1.80
❏ 35	Andres Galarraga/900	20.00	9.00
❏ 36	Karim Garcia/3900	4.00	1.80
❏ 37	Derrick Gibson/3900	10.00	4.50
❏ 38	Brian Giles/3900	15.00	6.75
❏ 39	Tom Glavine/150	60.00	27.00
❏ 40	Rick Gorecki/900	4.00	1.80
❏ 41	Shawn Green/1900	25.00	11.00
❏ 42	Todd Greene/3900	8.00	3.60
❏ 43	Rusty Greer/3900	8.00	3.60
❏ 44	Ben Grieve/3900	15.00	6.75
❏ 45	Mark Grudzielanek/3900	8.00	3.60
❏ 46	Vladimir Guerrero/1900 *	30.00	13.50
❏ 47	Wilton Guerrero/2150	4.00	1.80
❏ 48	Jose Guillen/2900	10.00	4.50
❏ 49	Jeffrey Hammonds/2150	8.00	3.60
❏ 50	Todd Helton/1400	25.00	11.00
❏ 51	Todd Hollandsworth/2900	4.00	1.80
❏ 52	Trenidad Hubbard/900	8.00	3.60
❏ 53	Todd Hundley/3900	8.00	3.60
❏ 54	Bobby Jones/3900	4.00	1.80
❏ 55	Brian Jordan/1400	15.00	6.75
❏ 56	David Justice/900	15.00	6.75
❏ 57	Eric Karros/650	20.00	9.00
❏ 58	Jason Kendall/3900	10.00	4.50
❏ 59	Jimmy Key/3900	8.00	3.60
❏ 60	Brooks Kieschnick/3900	4.00	1.80
❏ 61	Ryan Klesko/225	30.00	13.50
❏ 62	Paul Konerko/3900	10.00	4.50
❏ 63	Mark Kotsay/2400	10.00	4.50
❏ 64	Ray Lankford/3900	8.00	3.60
❏ 65	Barry Larkin/150 *	60.00	27.00
❏ 66	Derrek Lee/3900	10.00	4.50
❏ 67	Esteban Loaiza/3900	4.00	1.80
❏ 68	Javier Lopez/1400	12.00	5.50
❏ 69	Edgar Martinez/150 *	40.00	18.00
❏ 70	Pedro Martinez/900	50.00	22.00
❏ 71	Rafael Medina/3900	8.00	3.60
❏ 72	Raul Mondesi EXCH/650	25.00	11.00
❏ 73	Matt Morris/3900	8.00	3.60
❏ 74	Paul O'Neill/900	20.00	9.00
❏ 75	Kevin Orie/3900	4.00	1.80
❏ 76	David Ortiz/3900	12.00	5.50
❏ 77	Rafael Palmeiro/900 *	40.00	18.00
❏ 78	Jay Payton/3900	4.00	1.80
❏ 79	Neifi Perez/3900	8.00	3.60
❏ 80	Manny Ramirez/900	50.00	22.00
❏ 81	Joe Randa/3900	4.00	1.80
❏ 82	Calvin Reese/3900	8.00	3.60
❏ 83	Edgar Renteria EXCH SP	15.00	6.75
❏ 84	Dennis Reyes/3900	10.00	4.50
❏ 85	Henry Rodriguez/3900	8.00	3.60
❏ 86	Scott Rolen/1900 *	30.00	13.50
❏ 87	Kirk Rueter/2900	8.00	3.60
❏ 88	Ryne Sandberg/400	100.00	45.00
❏ 89	Dwight Smith/2900	8.00	3.60
❏ 90	J.T. Snow/3900	12.00	5.50
❏ 91	Scott Spiezio/3900	4.00	1.80
❏ 92	Shannon Stewart/2900	10.00	4.50
❏ 93	Jeff Suppan/1900	4.00	1.80
❏ 94	Mike Sweeney/3900	8.00	3.60
❏ 95	Miguel Tejada/3900	15.00	6.75
❏ 96	Justin Thompson/2400	8.00	3.60
❏ 97	Brett Tomko/3900	8.00	3.60
❏ 98	Bubba Trammell/3900	12.00	5.50
❏ 99	Michael Tucker/3900	4.00	1.80
❏ 100	Javier Valentin/3900	8.00	3.60
❏ 101	Mo Vaughn/150 *	60.00	27.00
❏ 102	Robin Ventura/1400	20.00	9.00
❏ 103	Terrell Wade/3900	4.00	1.80
❏ 104	Billy Wagner/3900	8.00	3.60
❏ 105	Larry Walker/400	40.00	16.00
❏ 106	Todd Walker/2400	12.00	5.50
❏ 107	Rondell White/3900	8.00	3.60
❏ 108	Kevin Wickander/900	4.00	1.80
❏ 109	Chris Widger/3900	4.00	1.80
❏ 110	Matt Williams/150 *	60.00	27.00
❏ 111	Antone Williamson/3900	4.00	1.80
❏ 112	Dan Wilson/3900	4.00	1.80
❏ 113	Tony Womack/3900	12.00	5.50
❏ 114	Jaret Wright/3900	12.00	5.50
❏ 115	Dmitri Young/3900	8.00	3.60
❏ 116	Eric Young/3900	8.00	3.60
❏ 117	Kevin Young/3900	8.00	3.60
❏ NNO	Frank Thomas Sample Fascimile Autograph	5.00	2.20

1997 Donruss Signature Autographs Century

		MINT	NRMT
COMMON CARD		25.00	11.00
MINOR STARS		40.00	18.00
SEMISTARS		60.00	27.00

RANDOM INSERTS IN PACKS
STATED PRINT RUN 100 SERIAL #'d SETS
ASTERISK CARDS ARE IN SERIES A AND B
NNO CARDS LISTED IN ALPH.ORDER

❏ 4	Roberto Alomar *	100.00	45.00
❏ 9	Jeff Bagwell	150.00	70.00
❏ 11	Albert Belle	80.00	36.00
❏ 14	Wade Boggs *	120.00	55.00
❏ 15	Barry Bonds	150.00	70.00
❏ 25	Will Clark	80.00	36.00
❏ 26	Roger Clemens *	250.00	110.00
❏ 32	Jose Cruz Jr. *	80.00	36.00
❏ 38	Darin Erstad *	80.00	36.00
❏ 44	N. Garciaparra SP62 *	300.00	135.00
❏ 46	Brian Giles	60.00	27.00
❏ 48	Juan Gonzalez	200.00	90.00
❏ 50	Shawn Green	80.00	36.00
❏ 53	Ben Grieve	80.00	36.00
❏ 55	Vladimir Guerrero *	120.00	55.00
❏ 58	Tony Gwynn *	200.00	90.00
❏ 60	Todd Helton	80.00	36.00
❏ 64	Derek Jeter *	250.00	110.00
❏ 65	Andruw Jones	100.00	45.00
❏ 67	Chipper Jones *	250.00	110.00
❏ 79	Barry Larkin *	80.00	36.00
❏ 83	Greg Maddux *	250.00	110.00
❏ 85	Pedro Martinez	120.00	55.00
❏ 87	Eddie Murray EXCH*	120.00	55.00
❏ 91	Mike Mussina	100.00	45.00
❏ 95	Rafael Palmeiro	100.00	45.00
❏ 99	Manny Ramirez	120.00	55.00
❏ 104	Cal Ripken	400.00	180.00
❏ 105	Alex Rodriguez	250.00	110.00
❏ 107	Ivan Rodriguez	120.00	55.00
❏ 108	Scott Rolen *	120.00	55.00
❏ 110	Ryne Sandberg	150.00	70.00
❏ 119	Frank Thomas	200.00	90.00
❏ 120	Jim Thome EXCH	80.00	36.00
❏ 126	Mo Vaughn *	80.00	36.00
❏ 130	Larry Walker	100.00	45.00
❏ 135	Bernie Williams	100.00	45.00
❏ 136	Matt Williams *	80.00	36.00

1997 Donruss Signature Autographs Millenium

		MINT	NRMT
COMMON CARD		10.00	4.50
MINOR STARS		15.00	6.75
SEMISTARS		25.00	11.00

RANDOM INSERTS IN PACKS
1000 OF EACH CARD UNLESS NOTED BELOW
ASTERISK CARDS ARE IN SERIES A AND B
NNO CARDS LISTED IN ALPH.ORDER

❏ 1	Jeff Abbott	10.00	4.50
❏ 2	Bob Abreu	15.00	6.75
❏ 3	Edgardo Alfonzo	25.00	11.00
❏ 4	Roberto Alomar *	40.00	18.00
❏ 5	Sandy Alomar Jr.	15.00	6.75
❏ 6	Moises Alou	15.00	6.75
❏ 7	Garret Anderson	15.00	6.75
❏ 8	Andy Ashby	10.00	4.50
❏ 9	Jeff Bagwell/400	100.00	45.00
❏ 10	Trey Beamon	10.00	4.50
❏ 11	Albert Belle/400	60.00	27.00
❏ 12	Alan Benes	10.00	4.50
❏ 13	Geronimo Berroa	10.00	4.50
❏ 14	Wade Boggs *	50.00	22.00
❏ 15	Barry Bonds/400	100.00	45.00
❏ 16	Bobby Bonilla/900 *	15.00	6.75
❏ 17	Kevin Brown/900	25.00	11.00
❏ 18	Kevin Brown C	10.00	4.50
❏ 19	Jay Buhner/900	15.00	6.75
❏ 20	Brett Butler	15.00	6.75
❏ 21	Mike Cameron	10.00	4.50
❏ 22	Giovanni Carrara	10.00	4.50

❏ 23 Luis Castillo	20.00	9.00
❏ 24 Tony Clark	25.00	11.00
❏ 25 Will Clark	30.00	13.50
❏ 26 Roger Clemens/400 *	150.00	70.00
❏ 27 Lou Collier	10.00	4.50
❏ 28 Bartolo Colon	20.00	9.00
❏ 29 Ron Coomer	10.00	4.50
❏ 30 Marty Cordova	10.00	4.50
❏ 31 Jacob Cruz	20.00	9.00
❏ 32 Jose Cruz Jr. *	40.00	18.00
❏ 33 Russ Davis	15.00	6.75
❏ 34 Jason Dickson	10.00	4.50
❏ 35 Todd Dunwoody	30.00	13.50
❏ 36 Jermaine Dye	15.00	6.75
❏ 37 Jim Edmonds	25.00	11.00
❏ 38 Darin Erstad *	40.00	18.00
❏ 39 Bobby Estalella	10.00	4.50
❏ 40 Shawn Estes	15.00	6.75
❏ 41 Jeff Fassero	10.00	4.50
❏ 42 Andres Galarraga	40.00	18.00
❏ 43 Karim Garcia	20.00	9.00
❏ 44 Nomar Garciaparra/650 *	200.00	90.00
❏ 45 Derrick Gibson	30.00	13.50
❏ 46 Brian Giles	25.00	11.00
❏ 47 Tom Glavine	40.00	18.00
❏ 48 Juan Gonzalez/900 *	80.00	36.00
❏ 49 Rick Gorecki	10.00	4.50
❏ 50 Shawn Green	40.00	18.00
❏ 51 Todd Greene	10.00	4.50
❏ 52 Rusty Greer	15.00	6.75
❏ 53 Ben Grieve	30.00	13.50
❏ 54 Mark Grudzielanek	15.00	6.75
❏ 55 Vladimir Guerrero *	50.00	22.00
❏ 56 Wilton Guerrero	10.00	4.50
❏ 57 Jose Guillen	40.00	18.00
❏ 58 Tony Gwynn/900 *	80.00	36.00
❏ 59 Jeffrey Hammonds	15.00	6.75
❏ 60 Todd Helton	30.00	13.50
❏ 61 Todd Hundley	15.00	6.75
❏ 62 Todd Hollandsworth	10.00	4.50
❏ 63 Trenidad Hubbard	10.00	4.50
❏ 64 Derek Jeter/400 *	200.00	90.00
❏ 65 Andruw Jones/900 *	40.00	18.00
❏ 66 Bobby Jones	10.00	4.50
❏ 67 Chipper Jones/900 *	100.00	45.00
❏ 68 Brian Jordan	15.00	6.75
❏ 69 David Justice	40.00	18.00
❏ 70 Eric Karros	15.00	6.75
❏ 71 Jason Kendall	25.00	11.00
❏ 72 Jimmy Key	15.00	6.75
❏ 73 Brooks Kieschnick	10.00	4.50
❏ 74 Ryan Klesko	15.00	6.75
❏ 75 Chuck Knoblauch/900 *	25.00	11.00
❏ 76 Paul Konerko	40.00	18.00
❏ 77 Mark Kotsay	40.00	18.00
❏ 78 Ray Lankford	15.00	6.75
❏ 79 Barry Larkin *	30.00	13.50
❏ 80 Derek Lee	30.00	13.50
❏ 81 Esteban Loaiza	10.00	4.50
❏ 82 Javier Lopez	15.00	6.75
❏ 83 Greg Maddux/400 *	200.00	90.00
❏ 84 Edgar Martinez *	15.00	6.75
❏ 85 Pedro Martinez	50.00	22.00
❏ 86 Tino Martinez/900 *	40.00	18.00
❏ 87 Rafael Medina	15.00	6.75
❏ 88 Raul Mondesi EXCH	15.00	6.75
❏ 89 Matt Morris	20.00	9.00
❏ 90 Eddie Murray/900 *	50.00	22.00
❏ 91 Mike Mussina/900 *	40.00	18.00
❏ 92 Paul O'Neill	15.00	6.75
❏ 93 Kevin Orie	20.00	9.00
❏ 94 David Ortiz	20.00	9.00
❏ 95 Rafael Palmeiro	40.00	18.00
❏ 96 Jay Payton	10.00	4.50
❏ 97 Neifi Perez	15.00	6.75
❏ 98 Andy Pettitte/900 *	25.00	11.00
❏ 99 Manny Ramirez	50.00	22.00
❏ 100 Joe Randa	10.00	4.50
❏ 101 Calvin Reese	15.00	6.75
❏ 102 Edgar Renteria EXCH SP	15.00	6.75
❏ 103 Dennis Reyes	20.00	9.00
❏ 104 Cal Ripken/400	300.00	135.00
❏ 105 Alex Rodriguez/400	200.00	90.00
❏ 106 Henry Rodriguez	15.00	6.75
❏ 107 Ivan Rodriguez/900	50.00	22.00
❏ 108 Scott Rolen *	50.00	22.00
❏ 109 Kirk Rueter	10.00	4.50
❏ 110 Ryne Sandberg	80.00	36.00
❏ 111 Gary Sheffield/400 *	30.00	13.50
❏ 112 Dwight Smith	10.00	4.50
❏ 113 J.T. Snow	15.00	6.75
❏ 114 Scott Spiezio	20.00	9.00
❏ 115 Shannon Stewart	20.00	9.00
❏ 116 Jeff Suppan	20.00	9.00
❏ 117 Mike Sweeney	15.00	6.75
❏ 118 Miguel Tejada	40.00	18.00
❏ 119 Frank Thomas/400	150.00	70.00
❏ 120 Jim Thome EXCH/900	30.00	13.50
❏ 121 Justin Thompson	15.00	6.75
❏ 122 Brett Tomko	20.00	9.00
❏ 123 Bubba Trammell	30.00	13.50
❏ 124 Michael Tucker	10.00	4.50
❏ 125 Javier Valentin	20.00	9.00
❏ 126 Mo Vaughn *	30.00	13.50
❏ 127 Robin Ventura	15.00	6.75
❏ 128 Terrell Wade	10.00	4.50
❏ 129 Billy Wagner	15.00	6.75
❏ 130 Larry Walker	40.00	18.00
❏ 131 Todd Walker	40.00	18.00
❏ 132 Rondell White	15.00	6.75
❏ 133 Kevin Wickander	10.00	4.50
❏ 134 Chris Widger	10.00	4.50
❏ 135 Bernie Williams/400 *	80.00	36.00
❏ 136 Matt Williams *	40.00	18.00
❏ 137 Antone Williamson	10.00	4.50
❏ 138 Dan Wilson	10.00	4.50
❏ 139 Tony Womack	20.00	9.00
❏ 140 Jaret Wright	30.00	13.50
❏ 141 Dmitri Young	15.00	6.75
❏ 142 Eric Young	15.00	6.75
❏ 143 Kevin Young	15.00	6.75

1997 Donruss Signature Notable Nicknames

	MINT	NRMT
RANDOM INSERTS IN PACKS
STATED PRINT RUN 200 SERIAL #'d SETS
NNO CARDS LISTED IN ALPH.ORDER

❏ 1 Ernie Banks	250.00	110.00
Mr. Cub		
❏ 2 Tony Clark	60.00	27.00
The Tiger		
❏ 3 Roger Clemens	300.00	135.00
The Rocket		
❏ 4 Reggie Jackson	250.00	110.00
Mr. October		
❏ 5 Randy Johnson	150.00	70.00
The Big Unit		
❏ 6 Stan Musial	300.00	135.00
The Man		
❏ 7 Ivan Rodriguez	150.00	70.00
Pudge		
❏ 8 Frank Thomas	250.00	110.00
The Big Hurt		
❏ 9 Mo Vaughn	100.00	45.00
The Hit Dog		
❏ 10 Billy Wagner	60.00	27.00
The Kid		

1997 Donruss Signature Significant Signatures

	MINT	NRMT
COMPLETE SET (22)	1000.00	450.00
COMMON CARD	30.00	13.50

RANDOM INSERTS IN PACKS
STATED PRINT RUN 2000 SERIAL #'d SETS
NNO CARDS LISTED IN ALPH.ORDER
COMPLETE SET CONTAINS CARD 11A

❏ 1 Ernie Banks	50.00	22.00
❏ 2 Johnny Bench	60.00	27.00
❏ 3 Yogi Berra	50.00	22.00
❏ 4 George Brett	80.00	36.00
❏ 5 Lou Brock	40.00	18.00
❏ 6 Rod Carew	40.00	18.00
❏ 7 Steve Carlton	40.00	18.00
❏ 8 Larry Doby	30.00	13.50
❏ 9 Carlton Fisk	40.00	18.00
❏ 10 Bob Gibson	40.00	18.00
❏ 11A Reggie Jackson	60.00	27.00
❏ 11B R.Jackson Silver Ink	150.00	70.00
❏ 12 Al Kaline	40.00	18.00
❏ 13 Harmon Killebrew	40.00	18.00
❏ 14 Don Mattingly	80.00	36.00
❏ 15 Stan Musial	80.00	36.00
❏ 16 Jim Palmer	40.00	18.00
❏ 17 Brooks Robinson	40.00	18.00
❏ 18 Frank Robinson	40.00	18.00
❏ 19 Mike Schmidt	80.00	36.00
❏ 20 Tom Seaver	60.00	27.00
❏ 21 Duke Snider	50.00	22.00
❏ 22 Carl Yastrzemski	80.00	36.00

1998 Donruss Signature

	MINT	NRMT
COMPLETE SET (140)	120.00	55.00
COMMON CARD (1-140)	.25	.11
MINOR STARS	.40	.18
SEMISTARS	.60	.25
UNLISTED STARS	1.00	.45

❏ 1 David Justice	.40	.18
❏ 2 Derek Jeter	3.00	1.35
❏ 3 Nomar Garciaparra	3.00	1.35
❏ 4 Ryan Klesko	.40	.18
❏ 5 Jeff Bagwell	1.25	.55
❏ 6 Dante Bichette	.40	.18

	MINT	NRMT
❏ 7 Ivan Rodriguez	1.25	.55
❏ 8 Albert Belle	1.00	.45
❏ 9 Cal Ripken	4.00	1.80
❏ 10 Craig Biggio	1.00	.45
❏ 11 Barry Larkin	1.00	.45
❏ 12 Jose Guillen	.25	.11
❏ 13 Will Clark	1.00	.45
❏ 14 J.T. Snow	.40	.18
❏ 15 Chuck Knoblauch	.40	.18
❏ 16 Todd Walker	.40	.18
❏ 17 Scott Rolen	1.25	.55
❏ 18 Rickey Henderson	1.25	.55
❏ 19 Juan Gonzalez	2.00	.90
❏ 20 Justin Thompson	.25	.11
❏ 21 Roger Clemens	2.50	1.10
❏ 22 Ray Lankford	.40	.18
❏ 23 Jose Cruz Jr.	.40	.18
❏ 24 Ken Griffey Jr.	5.00	2.20
❏ 25 Andruw Jones	1.00	.45
❏ 26 Darin Erstad	.60	.25
❏ 27 Jim Thome	1.00	.45
❏ 28 Wade Boggs	1.00	.45
❏ 29 Ken Caminiti	.40	.18
❏ 30 Todd Hundley	.40	.18
❏ 31 Mike Piazza	3.00	1.35
❏ 32 Sammy Sosa	3.00	1.35
❏ 33 Larry Walker	1.00	.45
❏ 34 Matt Williams	1.00	.45
❏ 35 Frank Thomas	2.00	.90
❏ 36 Gary Sheffield	.40	.18
❏ 37 Alex Rodriguez	3.00	1.35
❏ 38 Hideo Nomo	1.00	.45
❏ 39 Kenny Lofton	.60	.25
❏ 40 John Smoltz	.60	.25
❏ 41 Mo Vaughn	1.00	.45
❏ 42 Edgar Martinez	.40	.18
❏ 43 Paul Molitor	1.00	.45
❏ 44 Rafael Palmeiro	1.00	.45
❏ 45 Barry Bonds	1.25	.55
❏ 46 Vladimir Guerrero	1.25	.55
❏ 47 Carlos Delgado	1.00	.45
❏ 48 Bobby Higginson	.40	.18
❏ 49 Greg Maddux	2.50	1.10
❏ 50 Jim Edmonds	.40	.18
❏ 51 Randy Johnson	1.00	.45
❏ 52 Mark McGwire	6.00	2.70
❏ 53 Rondell White	.40	.18
❏ 54 Raul Mondesi	.40	.18
❏ 55 Manny Ramirez	1.25	.55
❏ 56 Pedro Martinez	1.25	.55
❏ 57 Tim Salmon	.60	.25
❏ 58 Moises Alou	.40	.18
❏ 59 Fred McGriff	.60	.25
❏ 60 Garret Anderson	.40	.18
❏ 61 Sandy Alomar Jr.	.40	.18
❏ 62 Chan Ho Park	.40	.18
❏ 63 Mark Kotsay	.40	.18
❏ 64 Mike Mussina	1.00	.45
❏ 65 Tom Glavine	1.00	.45
❏ 66 Tony Clark	.40	.18
❏ 67 Mark Grace	.60	.25
❏ 68 Tony Gwynn	2.50	1.10
❏ 69 Tino Martinez	.40	.18
❏ 70 Kevin Brown	.60	.25
❏ 71 Todd Greene	.25	.11
❏ 72 Andy Pettitte	.40	.18
❏ 73 Livan Hernandez	.25	.11
❏ 74 Curt Schilling	.60	.25
❏ 75 Andres Galarraga	.60	.25
❏ 76 Rusty Greer	.40	.18
❏ 77 Jay Buhner	.40	.18
❏ 78 Bobby Bonilla	.40	.18
❏ 79 Chipper Jones	2.50	1.10
❏ 80 Eric Young	.25	.11
❏ 81 Jason Giambi	.40	.18
❏ 82 Javy Lopez	.40	.18
❏ 83 Roberto Alomar	1.00	.45
❏ 84 Bernie Williams	1.00	.45
❏ 85 A.J. Hinch	.25	.11
❏ 86 Kerry Wood	1.25	.55
❏ 87 Juan Encarnacion	.40	.18
❏ 88 Brad Fullmer	.25	.11
❏ 89 Ben Grieve	1.00	.45
❏ 90 Magglio Ordonez	8.00	3.60
❏ 91 Todd Helton	1.25	.55
❏ 92 Richard Hidalgo	.40	.18
❏ 93 Paul Konerko	.40	.18
❏ 94 Aramis Ramirez	1.00	.45
❏ 95 Ricky Ledee	.40	.18
❏ 96 Derrek Lee	.25	.11
❏ 97 Travis Lee	.60	.25
❏ 98 Matt Anderson	1.50	.70
❏ 99 Jaret Wright	.40	.18
❏ 100 David Ortiz	.25	.11
❏ 101 Carl Pavano	.25	.11
❏ 102 Orlando Hernandez	6.00	2.70
❏ 103 Fernando Tatis	1.00	.45
❏ 104 Miguel Tejada	.40	.18
❏ 105 Rolando Arrojo	2.00	.90
❏ 106 Kevin Millwood	8.00	3.60
❏ 107 Ken Griffey Jr. CL	2.50	1.10
❏ 108 Frank Thomas CL	1.00	.45
❏ 109 Cal Ripken CL	2.00	.90
❏ 110 Greg Maddux CL	1.25	.55
❏ 111 John Olerud	.40	.18
❏ 112 David Cone	.60	.25
❏ 113 Vinny Castilla	.40	.18
❏ 114 Jason Kendall	.40	.18
❏ 115 Brian Jordan	.40	.18
❏ 116 Hideki Irabu	.40	.18
❏ 117 Bartolo Colon	.40	.18
❏ 118 Greg Vaughn	.40	.18
❏ 119 David Segui	.25	.11
❏ 120 Bruce Chen	.40	.18
❏ 121 Julio Ramirez	5.00	2.20
❏ 122 Troy Glaus	10.00	4.50
❏ 123 Jeremy Giambi	3.00	1.35
❏ 124 Ryan Minor	3.00	1.35
❏ 125 Richie Sexson	.60	.25
❏ 126 Dermal Brown	.40	.18
❏ 127 Adrian Beltre	1.00	.45
❏ 128 Eric Chavez	1.00	.45
❏ 129 J.D. Drew	30.00	13.50
❏ 130 Gabe Kapler	8.00	3.60
❏ 131 Masato Yoshii	1.25	.55
❏ 132 Mike Lowell	2.00	.90
❏ 133 Jim Parque	1.25	.55
❏ 134 Roy Halladay	.40	.18
❏ 135 Carlos Lee	5.00	2.20
❏ 136 Jin Ho Cho	2.50	1.10
❏ 137 Michael Barrett	.60	.25
❏ 138 Fernando Seguignol	3.00	1.35
❏ 139 Odalis Perez	2.00	.90
❏ 140 Mark McGwire CL	3.00	1.35

1998 Donruss Signature Proofs

	MINT	NRMT
COMMON CARD (1-140)	6.00	2.70

*STARS: 10X TO 25X BASIC CARDS
*YOUNG STARS: 8X TO 20X BASIC CARDS
*ROOKIES: 2.5X TO 6X BASIC CARDS
RANDOM INSERTS IN PACKS
STATED PRINT RUN 150 SETS

1998 Donruss Signature Autographs

	MINT	NRMT
COMMON CARD	4.00	1.80
MINOR STARS	8.00	3.60

ONE AUTOGRAPH PER PACK

	MINT	NRMT
❏ 1 Roberto Alomar/150	80.00	36.00
❏ 2 Sandy Alomar Jr./700	10.00	4.50
❏ 3 Moises Alou/900	10.00	4.50
❏ 4 Gabe Alvarez/2900	4.00	1.80
❏ 5 Wilson Alvarez/1600	4.00	1.80
❏ 6 Jay Bell/1500	12.00	5.50
❏ 7 Adrian Beltre/1900	20.00	9.00
❏ 8 Andy Benes/2600	4.00	1.80
❏ 9 Aaron Boone/3400	4.00	1.80
❏ 10 Russell Branyan/1650	12.00	5.50
❏ 11 Orlando Cabrera/3400	4.00	1.80
❏ 12 Mike Cameron/1150	10.00	4.50
❏ 13 Joe Carter/400	30.00	13.50
❏ 14 Sean Casey/2275	30.00	13.50
❏ 15 Bruce Chen/150	30.00	13.50
❏ 16 Tony Clark/2275	8.00	3.60
❏ 17 Will Clark/1400	25.00	11.00
❏ 18 Matt Clement/1400	10.00	4.50
❏ 19 Pat Cline/1400	4.00	1.80
❏ 20 Ken Cloude/3400	4.00	1.80
❏ 21 Michael Coleman/2800	8.00	3.60
❏ 22 David Cone/25	200.00	90.00
❏ 23 Jeff Conine/1400	4.00	1.80
❏ 24 Jacob Cruz/3200	4.00	1.80
❏ 25 Russ Davis/3500	4.00	1.80
❏ 26 Jason Dickson/1400	4.00	1.80
❏ 27 Todd Dunwoody/3500	4.00	1.80
❏ 28 Juan Encarnacion/3400	12.00	5.50
❏ 29 Darin Erstad/700	25.00	11.00
❏ 30 Bobby Estalella/3400	4.00	1.80
❏ 31 Jeff Fassero/3400	4.00	1.80
❏ 32 John Franco/1800	10.00	4.50
❏ 33 Brad Fullmer/3100	4.00	1.80
❏ 34 Jason Giambi/1400	10.00	4.50
❏ 35 Derrick Gibson/1200	10.00	4.50
❏ 36 Todd Greene/1400	4.00	1.80
❏ 37 Ben Grieve/1400	15.00	6.75
❏ 38 Mark Grudzielanek/3200	4.00	1.80
❏ 39 Vladimir Guerrero/2100	30.00	13.50
❏ 40 Wilton Guerrero/1900	4.00	1.80
❏ 41 Jose Guillen/2400	4.00	1.80
❏ 42 Todd Helton/1300	25.00	11.00
❏ 43 Richard Hidalgo/3400	8.00	3.60
❏ 44 A.J. Hinch/2900	4.00	1.80
❏ 45 Butch Huskey/1900	4.00	1.80
❏ 46 Raul Ibanez/3300	4.00	1.80
❏ 47 Damian Jackson/900	10.00	4.50
❏ 48 Geoff Jenkins/3100	10.00	4.50
❏ 49 Eric Karros/650	15.00	6.75
❏ 50 Ryan Klesko/650	20.00	9.00
❏ 51 Mark Kotsay/3600	8.00	3.60
❏ 52 Ricky Ledee/2200	10.00	4.50
❏ 53 Derrek Lee/3400	4.00	1.80
❏ 54 Travis Lee/150	50.00	22.00
❏ 55 Javier Lopez/650	20.00	9.00
❏ 56 Mike Lowell/3500	10.00	4.50
❏ 57 Greg Maddux/12	1000.00	450.00
❏ 58 Eli Marrero/3400	4.00	1.80
❏ 59 Al Martin/1300	4.00	1.80
❏ 60 Rafael Medina/1400	4.00	1.80
❏ 61 Scott Morgan/900	10.00	4.50
❏ 62 Abraham Nunez/3500	4.00	1.80
❏ 63 Paul O'Neill/1500	20.00	9.00
❏ 64 Luis Ordaz/2700	4.00	1.80
❏ 65 Magglio Ordonez/3200	30.00	13.50
❏ 66 Kevin Orie/1350	4.00	1.80
❏ 67 David Ortiz/3400	4.00	1.80
❏ 68 Rafael Palmeiro/1000	40.00	18.00

	MINT	NRMT
69 Carl Pavano/2600	4.00	1.80
70 Neifi Perez/3300	8.00	3.60
71 Dante Powell/3050	4.00	1.80
72 Aramis Ramirez/2800	15.00	6.75
73 Mariano Rivera/900	15.00	6.75
74 Felix Rodriguez/1400	4.00	1.80
75 Henry Rodriguez/3400	8.00	3.60
76 Scott Rolen/1900	30.00	13.50
77 Brian Rose/1400	4.00	1.80
78 Curt Schilling/900	25.00	11.00
79 Richie Sexson/3500	15.00	6.75
80 Randall Simon/3500	8.00	3.60
81 J.T. Snow/400	20.00	9.00
82 Jeff Suppan/1400	4.00	1.80
83 Fernando Tatis/3900	15.00	6.75
84 Miguel Tejada/3800	10.00	4.50
85 Brett Tomko/3400	4.00	1.80
86 Bubba Trammell/3900	4.00	1.80
87 Ismael Valdes/1900	4.00	1.80
88 Robin Ventura/1400	20.00	9.00
89 Billy Wagner/3900	8.00	3.60
90 Todd Walker/1900	8.00	3.60
91 Daryle Ward/400	20.00	9.00
92 Rondell White/3400	8.00	3.60
93 Antone Williamson/3350	4.00	1.80
94 Dan Wilson/2400	4.00	1.80
95 Enrique Wilson/3400	4.00	1.80
96 Preston Wilson/2100	10.00	4.50
97 Tony Womack/3500	4.00	1.80
98 Kerry Wood/3400	20.00	9.00
NNO Travis Lee Sample	2.00	.90

Facsimile Autograph

1998 Donruss Signature Autographs Century

	MINT	NRMT
COMMON CARD	25.00	11.00
MINOR STARS	40.00	18.00
SEMISTARS	60.00	27.00

RANDOM INSERTS IN PACKS
100 OF EACH CARD UNLESS NOTED BELOW
NNO CARDS LISTED IN ALPH.ORDER

	MINT	NRMT
1 Roberto Alomar	100.00	45.00
2 Sandy Alomar Jr.	40.00	18.00
3 Moises Alou	100.00	45.00
4 Gabe Alvarez	25.00	11.00
5 Wilson Alvarez	40.00	18.00
6 Brady Anderson	40.00	18.00
7 Jay Bell	40.00	18.00
8 Albert Belle	80.00	36.00
9 Adrian Beltre	100.00	45.00
10 Andy Benes	25.00	11.00
11 Wade Boggs	120.00	55.00
12 Barry Bonds	150.00	70.00
13 Aaron Boone	25.00	11.00
14 Russell Branyan	40.00	18.00
15 Jay Buhner	40.00	18.00
16 Ellis Burks	40.00	18.00
17 Orlando Cabrera	25.00	11.00
18 Mike Cameron	40.00	18.00
19 Ken Caminiti	100.00	45.00
20 Joe Carter	40.00	18.00
21 Sean Casey	100.00	45.00
22 Bruce Chen	40.00	18.00
23 Tony Clark	40.00	18.00
24 Will Clark	80.00	36.00
25 Roger Clemens	250.00	110.00
26 Matt Clement	40.00	18.00
27 Pat Cline	25.00	11.00
28 Ken Cloude	25.00	11.00
29 Michael Coleman	40.00	18.00
30 David Cone	100.00	45.00
31 Jeff Conine	25.00	11.00
32 Jacob Cruz	25.00	11.00
33 Jose Cruz Jr.	40.00	18.00
34 Russ Davis	40.00	18.00
35 Jason Dickson	25.00	11.00
36 Todd Dunwoody	25.00	11.00
37 Scott Elarton	25.00	11.00
38 Darin Erstad	120.00	55.00
39 Bobby Estalella	25.00	11.00
40 Jeff Fassero	25.00	11.00
41 John Franco	40.00	18.00
42 Brad Fullmer	25.00	11.00
43 Andres Galarraga	60.00	27.00
44 Nomar Garciaparra	300.00	135.00
45 Jason Giambi	40.00	18.00
46 Derrick Gibson	40.00	18.00
47 Tom Glavine	80.00	36.00
48 Juan Gonzalez	200.00	90.00
49 Todd Greene	25.00	11.00
50 Ben Grieve	80.00	36.00
51 Mark Grudzielanek	25.00	11.00
52 Vladimir Guerrero	120.00	55.00
53 Wilton Guerrero	25.00	11.00
54 Jose Guillen	25.00	11.00
55 Tony Gwynn	200.00	90.00
56 Todd Helton	80.00	36.00
57 Richard Hidalgo	40.00	18.00
58 A.J. Hinch	25.00	11.00
59 Butch Huskey	25.00	11.00
60 Raul Ibanez	25.00	11.00
61 Damian Jackson	25.00	11.00
62 Geoff Jenkins	40.00	18.00
63 Derek Jeter	250.00	110.00
64 Randy Johnson	100.00	45.00
65 Chipper Jones	250.00	110.00
66 Eric Karros/50	100.00	45.00
67 Ryan Klesko	40.00	18.00
68 Chuck Knoblauch	100.00	45.00
69 Mark Kotsay	40.00	18.00
70 Ricky Ledee	40.00	18.00
71 Derek Lee	25.00	11.00
72 Travis Lee	60.00	27.00
73 Javier Lopez	40.00	18.00
74 Mike Lowell	100.00	45.00
75 Greg Maddux	250.00	110.00
76 Eli Marrero	25.00	11.00
77 Al Martin	25.00	11.00
78 Rafael Medina	25.00	11.00
79 Paul Molitor	100.00	45.00
80 Scott Morgan	25.00	11.00
81 Mike Mussina	100.00	45.00
82 Abraham Nunez	25.00	11.00
83 Paul O'Neill	40.00	18.00
84 Luis Ordaz	25.00	11.00
85 Magglio Ordonez	100.00	45.00
86 Kevin Orie	25.00	11.00
87 David Ortiz	40.00	18.00
88 Rafael Palmeiro	100.00	45.00
89 Carl Pavano	25.00	11.00
90 Neifi Perez	40.00	18.00
91 Andy Pettitte	100.00	45.00
92 Aramis Ramirez	100.00	45.00
93 Cal Ripken	400.00	180.00
94 Mariano Rivera	40.00	18.00
95 Alex Rodriguez	300.00	135.00
96 Felix Rodriguez	25.00	11.00
97 Henry Rodriguez	40.00	18.00
98 Scott Rolen	120.00	55.00
99 Brian Rose	25.00	11.00
100 Curt Schilling	60.00	27.00
101 Richie Sexson	100.00	45.00
102 Randall Simon	25.00	11.00
103 J.T. Snow	40.00	18.00
104 Darryl Strawberry	40.00	18.00
105 Jeff Suppan	25.00	11.00
106 Fernando Tatis	100.00	45.00
107 Brett Tomko	25.00	11.00
108 Bubba Trammell	25.00	11.00
109 Ismael Valdes	25.00	11.00
110 Robin Ventura	40.00	18.00
111 Billy Wagner	40.00	18.00
112 Todd Walker	40.00	18.00
113 Daryle Ward	40.00	18.00
114 Rondell White	40.00	18.00
115 Matt Williams/80	100.00	45.00
116 Antone Williamson	25.00	11.00
117 Dan Wilson	25.00	11.00
118 Enrique Wilson	25.00	11.00
119 Preston Wilson	40.00	18.00
120 Tony Womack	25.00	11.00
121 Kerry Wood	80.00	36.00

1998 Donruss Signature Autographs Millenium

	MINT	NRMT
COMMON CARD	10.00	4.50
MINOR STARS	15.00	6.75
SEMISTARS	25.00	11.00

RANDOM INSERTS IN PACKS
1000 OF EACH CARD UNLESS NOTED BELOW
NNO CARDS LISTED IN ALPH.ORDER

	MINT	NRMT
1 Roberto Alomar	30.00	13.50
2 Sandy Alomar Jr.	15.00	6.75
3 Moises Alou	40.00	18.00
4 Gabe Alvarez	10.00	4.50
5 Wilson Alvarez	10.00	4.50
6 Brady Anderson/800	25.00	11.00
7 Jay Bell	15.00	6.75
8 Albert Belle/400	60.00	27.00
9 Adrian Beltre	40.00	18.00
10 Andy Benes	10.00	4.50
11 Wade Boggs/900	50.00	22.00
12 Barry Bonds/400	100.00	45.00
13 Aaron Boone	10.00	4.50
14 Russell Branyan	15.00	6.75
15 Jay Buhner/400	30.00	13.50
16 Ellis Burks/900	20.00	9.00
17 Orlando Cabrera	10.00	4.50
18 Mike Cameron	15.00	6.75
19 Ken Caminiti/900	40.00	18.00
20 Joe Carter	15.00	6.75
21 Sean Casey	40.00	18.00
22 Bruce Chen	15.00	6.75
23 Tony Clark	15.00	6.75
24 Will Clark	30.00	13.50
25 Roger Clemens/400	150.00	70.00
26 Matt Clement/900	20.00	9.00
27 Pat Cline	10.00	4.50
28 Ken Cloude	10.00	4.50
29 Michael Coleman	15.00	6.75
30 David Cone	40.00	18.00
31 Jeff Conine	10.00	4.50
32 Jacob Cruz	10.00	4.50
33 Jose Cruz Jr./850	40.00	18.00
34 Russ Davis/950	12.00	5.50
35 Jason Dickson/950	12.00	5.50
36 Todd Dunwoody	10.00	4.50
37 Scott Elarton/900	10.00	4.50
38 Juan Encarnacion	15.00	6.75
39 Darin Erstad	60.00	27.00
40 Bobby Estalella*	10.00	4.50
41 Jeff Fassero	10.00	4.50
42 John Franco/950	20.00	9.00
43 Brad Fullmer	10.00	4.50
44 Andres Galarraga/900	50.00	22.00

		MINT	NRMT
❏ 45	Nomar Garciaparra/400	250.00	110.00
❏ 46	Jason Giambi	15.00	6.75
❏ 47	Derrick Gibson	15.00	6.75
❏ 48	Tom Glavine/700	30.00	13.50
❏ 49	Juan Gonzalez	80.00	36.00
❏ 50	Todd Greene	10.00	4.50
❏ 51	Ben Grieve	30.00	13.50
❏ 52	Mark Grudzielanek	10.00	4.50
❏ 53	Vladimir Guerrero	50.00	22.00
❏ 54	Wilton Guerrero	10.00	4.50
❏ 55	Jose Guillen	10.00	4.50
❏ 56	Tony Gwynn/900	80.00	36.00
❏ 57	Todd Helton	30.00	13.50
❏ 58	Richard Hidalgo	15.00	6.75
❏ 59	A.J. Hinch	10.00	4.50
❏ 60	Butch Huskey	10.00	4.50
❏ 61	Raul Ibanez	10.00	4.50
❏ 62	Damian Jackson	10.00	4.50
❏ 63	Geoff Jenkins	15.00	6.75
❏ 64	Derek Jeter/400	200.00	90.00
❏ 65	Randy Johnson/800	50.00	22.00
❏ 66	Chipper Jones/900	100.00	45.00
❏ 67	Eric Karros	15.00	6.75
❏ 68	Ryan Klesko	15.00	6.75
❏ 69	Chuck Knoblauch/900	40.00	18.00
❏ 70	Mark Kotsay	15.00	6.75
❏ 71	Ricky Ledee	15.00	6.75
❏ 72	Derrek Lee	10.00	4.50
❏ 73	Travis Lee	25.00	11.00
❏ 74	Javier Lopez/800	15.00	6.75
❏ 75	Mike Lowell	40.00	18.00
❏ 76	Greg Maddux/400	200.00	90.00
❏ 77	Eli Marrero	10.00	4.50
❏ 78	Al Martin/950	12.00	5.50
❏ 79	Rafael Medina/850	12.00	5.50
❏ 80	Paul Molitor/900	50.00	22.00
❏ 81	Scott Morgan	10.00	4.50
❏ 82	Mike Mussina/900	40.00	18.00
❏ 83	Abraham Nunez	10.00	4.50
❏ 84	Paul O'Neill/900	30.00	13.50
❏ 85	Luis Ordaz	10.00	4.50
❏ 86	Magglio Ordonez	50.00	22.00
❏ 87	Aaron Orie	10.00	4.50
❏ 88	David Ortiz	10.00	4.50
❏ 89	Rafael Palmeiro/900	40.00	18.00
❏ 90	Carl Pavano	10.00	4.50
❏ 91	Neifi Perez	15.00	6.75
❏ 92	Andy Pettitte/900	40.00	18.00
❏ 93	Dante Powell/950	12.00	5.50
❏ 94	Aramis Ramirez	40.00	18.00
❏ 95	Cal Ripken/375	300.00	135.00
❏ 96	Mariano Rivera	15.00	6.75
❏ 97	Alex Rodriguez/200	200.00	90.00
❏ 98	Felix Rodriguez	10.00	4.50
❏ 99	Henry Rodriguez	15.00	6.75
❏ 100	Scott Rolen	50.00	22.00
❏ 101	Brian Rose	10.00	4.50
❏ 102	Curt Schilling	25.00	11.00
❏ 103	Richie Sexson	30.00	13.50
❏ 104	Randall Simon	15.00	6.75
❏ 105	J.T. Snow	15.00	6.75
❏ 106	Darryl Strawberry/900	40.00	18.00
❏ 107	Jeff Suppan	10.00	4.50
❏ 108	Fernando Tatis	40.00	18.00
❏ 109	Miguel Tejada	15.00	6.75
❏ 110	Brett Tomko	10.00	4.50
❏ 111	Bubba Trammell	10.00	4.50
❏ 112	Ismael Valdes	10.00	4.50
❏ 113	Robin Ventura	15.00	6.75
❏ 114	Billy Wagner/900	12.00	5.50
❏ 115	Todd Walker	15.00	6.75
❏ 116	Daryle Ward	15.00	6.75
❏ 117	Rondell White	10.00	4.50
❏ 118	Matt Williams/820	30.00	13.50
❏ 119	Antone Williamson	10.00	4.50
❏ 120	Dan Wilson	10.00	4.50
❏ 121	Enrique Wilson	10.00	4.50
❏ 122	Preston Wilson/400	25.00	11.00
❏ 123	Tony Womack	10.00	4.50
❏ 124	Kerry Wood	30.00	13.50

1998 Donruss Signature Significant Signatures

MINT NRMT

RANDOM INSERTS IN PACKS

STATED PRINT RUN 2000 SERIAL #'d SETS
CARD NUMBER 8 DOES NOT EXIST
EXCHANGE DEADLINE 12/31/99

		MINT	NRMT
❏ 1	Ernie Banks	40.00	18.00
❏ 2	Yogi Berra	50.00	22.00
❏ 3	George Brett	80.00	36.00
❏ 4	Catfish Hunter	50.00	22.00
❏ 5	Al Kaline	40.00	18.00
❏ 6	Harmon Killebrew	40.00	18.00
❏ 7	Ralph Kiner	25.00	11.00
❏ 9	Eddie Mathews	40.00	18.00
❏ 10	Don Mattingly	80.00	36.00
❏ 11	Willie McCovey	40.00	18.00
❏ 12	Stan Musial	80.00	36.00
❏ 13	Phil Rizzuto SP1000	50.00	22.00
❏ 14	Nolan Ryan EXCH	150.00	70.00
❏ 15	Ozzie Smith EXCH	60.00	27.00
❏ 16	Duke Snider	40.00	18.00
❏ 17	Don Sutton	20.00	9.00
❏ 18	Billy Williams	30.00	13.50
❏ 18A	Billy Williams Redeemed	30.00	13.50
❏ R1	Nolan Ryan	150.00	70.00
❏ R2	Ozzie Smith	60.00	27.00
❏ R3	Sandy Koufax	150.00	70.00

1998 Donruss Signature Signing Bonus

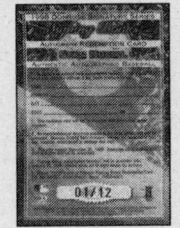

MINT NRMT

RANDOM INSERTS IN PACKS
EXPIRATION DATE 12/31/99

		MINT	NRMT
❏ 1	Roberto Alomar/60	50.00	22.00
❏ 2	Sandy Alomar Jr./60	30.00	13.50
❏ 3	Ernie Banks/12		
❏ 4	Ken Caminiti/60	40.00	18.00
❏ 5	Tony Clark/60	40.00	18.00
❏ 6	Jacob Cruz/12		
❏ 7	Russ Davis/60	25.00	11.00
❏ 8	Juan Encarnacion/60	40.00	18.00
❏ 9	Bobby Estalella/60	25.00	11.00
❏ 10	Jeff Fassero/60	25.00	11.00
❏ 11	Ben Grieve/60		
❏ 12	Mark Grudzielanek/60	25.00	11.00
❏ 13	Jose Guillen/120		
❏ 14	Tony Gwynn/60	150.00	70.00
❏ 15	Al Kaline/12		
❏ 16	Paul Konerko/100	40.00	18.00
❏ 17	Travis Lee/100	80.00	36.00
❏ 18	Mike Lowell/60	30.00	13.50
❏ 19	Eli Marrero/60	25.00	11.00
❏ 20	Eddie Mathews/12		
❏ 21	Paul Molitor/60	80.00	36.00
❏ 22	Stan Musial/12		
❏ 23	Abraham Nunez/12		
❏ 24	Luis Ordaz/12		
❏ 25	Magglio Ordonez/12		
❏ 26	Scott Rolen/60	120.00	55.00
❏ 27	Bubba Trammell/24		
❏ 28	Robin Ventura/60	30.00	13.50
❏ 29	Billy Wagner/60	25.00	11.00
❏ 30	Rondell White/60	30.00	13.50
❏ 31	Antone Williamson/12		
❏ 32	Tony Womack/60	25.00	11.00

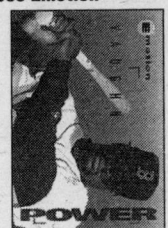

1995 Emotion

	MINT	NRMT
COMPLETE SET (200)	40.00	18.00
COMMON CARD (1-200)	.25	.11
MINOR STARS	.50	.23
UNLISTED STARS	1.00	.45

		MINT	NRMT
❏ 1	Brady Anderson	.50	.23
❏ 2	Kevin Brown	.75	.35
❏ 3	Curtis Goodwin	.25	.11
❏ 4	Jeffrey Hammonds	.50	.23
❏ 5	Ben McDonald	.25	.11
❏ 6	Mike Mussina	1.00	.45
❏ 7	Rafael Palmeiro	1.00	.45
❏ 8	Cal Ripken Jr.	4.00	1.80
❏ 9	Jose Canseco	1.25	.55
❏ 10	Roger Clemens	2.50	1.10
❏ 11	Vaughn Eshelman	.25	.11
❏ 12	Mike Greenwell	.25	.11
❏ 13	Erik Hanson	.25	.11
❏ 14	Tim Naehring	.25	.11
❏ 15	Aaron Sele	.50	.23
❏ 16	John Valentin	.50	.23
❏ 17	Mo Vaughn	1.00	.45
❏ 18	Chili Davis	.50	.23
❏ 19	Gary DiSarcina	.25	.11
❏ 20	Chuck Finley	.50	.23
❏ 21	Tim Salmon	1.00	.45
❏ 22	Lee Smith	.50	.23
❏ 23	J.T. Snow	.50	.23
❏ 24	Jim Abbott	.50	.23
❏ 25	Jason Bere	.25	.11
❏ 26	Ray Durham	.50	.23
❏ 27	Ozzie Guillen	.25	.11
❏ 28	Tim Raines	.50	.23
❏ 29	Frank Thomas	2.00	.90
❏ 30	Robin Ventura	.50	.23
❏ 31	Carlos Baerga	.25	.11
❏ 32	Albert Belle	1.00	.45
❏ 33	Orel Hershiser	.50	.23
❏ 34	Kenny Lofton	.75	.35
❏ 35	Dennis Martinez	.50	.23
❏ 36	Eddie Murray	1.00	.45
❏ 37	Manny Ramirez	1.25	.55
❏ 38	Julian Tavarez	.25	.11
❏ 39	Jim Thome	1.00	.45
❏ 40	Dave Winfield	1.00	.45
❏ 41	Chad Curtis	.25	.11
❏ 42	Cecil Fielder	.50	.23
❏ 43	Travis Fryman	.50	.23
❏ 44	Kirk Gibson	.50	.23
❏ 45	Bobby Higginson	1.50	.70
❏ 46	Alan Trammell	.50	.23
❏ 47	Lou Whitaker	.50	.23
❏ 48	Kevin Appier	.50	.23
❏ 49	Gary Gaetti	.50	.23
❏ 50	Jeff Montgomery	.25	.11
❏ 51	Jon Nunnally	.25	.11
❏ 52	Ricky Bones	.25	.11
❏ 53	Cal Eldred	.25	.11
❏ 54	Joe Oliver	.25	.11
❏ 55	Kevin Seitzer	.25	.11
❏ 56	Marty Cordova	.25	.11
❏ 57	Chuck Knoblauch	1.00	.45
❏ 58	Kirby Puckett	1.50	.70
❏ 59	Wade Boggs	1.00	.45
❏ 60	Derek Jeter	3.00	1.35

#	Player	MINT	NRMT
61	Jimmy Key	.50	.23
62	Don Mattingly	2.00	.90
63	Jack McDowell	.25	.11
64	Paul O'Neill	.50	.23
65	Andy Pettitte	1.00	.45
66	Ruben Rivera	.50	.23
67	Mike Stanley	.25	.11
68	John Wetteland	.50	.23
69	Geronimo Berroa	.25	.11
70	Dennis Eckersley	.50	.23
71	Rickey Henderson	1.25	.55
72	Mark McGwire	5.00	2.20
73	Steve Ontiveros	.25	.11
74	Ruben Sierra	.25	.11
75	Terry Steinbach	.25	.11
76	Jay Buhner	.50	.23
77	Ken Griffey Jr.	5.00	2.20
78	Randy Johnson	1.00	.45
79	Edgar Martinez	.50	.23
80	Tino Martinez	1.00	.45
81	Marc Newfield	.25	.11
82	Alex Rodriguez	4.00	1.80
83	Will Clark	1.00	.45
84	Benji Gil	.25	.11
85	Juan Gonzalez	2.00	.90
86	Rusty Greer	1.00	.45
87	Dean Palmer	.50	.23
88	Ivan Rodriguez	1.25	.55
89	Kenny Rogers	.25	.11
90	Roberto Alomar	1.00	.45
91	Joe Carter	.50	.23
92	David Cone	.75	.35
93	Alex Gonzalez	.25	.11
94	Shawn Green	1.00	.45
95	Pat Hentgen	.50	.23
96	Paul Molitor	1.00	.45
97	John Olerud	.50	.23
98	Devon White	.50	.23
99	Steve Avery	.25	.11
100	Tom Glavine	1.00	.45
101	Marquis Grissom	.50	.23
102	Chipper Jones	2.50	1.10
103	David Justice	1.00	.45
104	Ryan Klesko	.50	.23
105	Javier Lopez	.50	.23
106	Greg Maddux	2.50	1.10
107	Fred McGriff	.75	.35
108	John Smoltz	.75	.35
109	Shawon Dunston	.25	.11
110	Mark Grace	.75	.35
111	Brian McRae	.25	.11
112	Randy Myers	.25	.11
113	Sammy Sosa	3.00	1.35
114	Steve Trachsel	.25	.11
115	Bret Boone	.50	.23
116	Ron Gant	.50	.23
117	Barry Larkin	1.00	.45
118	Deion Sanders	.50	.23
119	Reggie Sanders	.50	.23
120	Pete Schourek	.25	.11
121	John Smiley	.25	.11
122	Jason Bates	.25	.11
123	Dante Bichette	.50	.23
124	Vinny Castilla	.75	.35
125	Andres Galarraga	1.00	.45
126	Larry Walker	1.00	.45
127	Greg Colbrunn	.25	.11
128	Jeff Conine	.25	.11
129	Andre Dawson	.75	.35
130	Chris Hammond	.25	.11
131	Charles Johnson	.50	.23
132	Gary Sheffield	.50	.23
133	Quilvio Veras	.25	.11
134	Jeff Bagwell	1.25	.55
135	Derek Bell	.50	.23
136	Craig Biggio	1.00	.45
137	Jim Dougherty	.25	.11
138	John Hudek	.25	.11
139	Orlando Miller	.25	.11
140	Phil Plantier	.25	.11
141	Eric Karros	.50	.23
142	Ramon Martinez	.50	.23
143	Raul Mondesi	.75	.35
144	Hideo Nomo	2.50	1.10
145	Mike Piazza	3.00	1.35
146	Ismael Valdes	.50	.23
147	Todd Worrell	.25	.11
148	Moises Alou	.50	.23
149	Yamil Benitez	.75	.35
150	Wil Cordero	.25	.11
151	Jeff Fassero	.25	.11
152	Cliff Floyd	.50	.23
153	Pedro Martinez	1.25	.55
154	Carlos Perez	.50	.23
155	Tony Tarasco	.25	.11
156	Rondell White	.50	.23
157	Edgardo Alfonzo	1.00	.45
158	Bobby Bonilla	.50	.23
159	Rico Brogna	.25	.11
160	Bobby Jones	.25	.11
161	Bill Pulsipher	.25	.11
162	Bret Saberhagen	.50	.23
163	Ricky Bottalico	.25	.11
164	Darren Daulton	.50	.23
165	Lenny Dykstra	.50	.23
166	Charlie Hayes	.25	.11
167	Dave Hollins	.25	.11
168	Gregg Jefferies	.25	.11
169	Michael Mimbs	.25	.11
170	Curt Schilling	.75	.35
171	Heathcliff Slocumb	.25	.11
172	Jay Bell	.50	.23
173	Micah Franklin	.25	.11
174	Mark Johnson	.25	.11
175	Jeff King	.25	.11
176	Al Martin	.25	.11
177	Dan Miceli	.25	.11
178	Denny Neagle	.50	.23
179	Bernard Gilkey	.25	.11
180	Ken Hill	.25	.11
181	Brian Jordan	.50	.23
182	Ray Lankford	.50	.23
183	Ozzie Smith	1.25	.55
184	Andy Benes	.50	.23
185	Ken Caminiti	.75	.35
186	Steve Finley	.50	.23
187	Tony Gwynn	2.50	1.10
188	Joey Hamilton	.50	.23
189	Melvin Nieves	.25	.11
190	Scott Sanders	.25	.11
191	Rod Beck	.25	.11
192	Barry Bonds	1.25	.55
193	Royce Clayton	.25	.11
194	Glenallen Hill	.25	.11
195	Darren Lewis	.25	.11
196	Mark Portugal	.25	.11
197	Matt Williams	1.00	.45
198	Checklist 1-82	.25	.11
199	Checklist 83-162	.25	.11
200	Checklist 163-200/Inserts	.25	.11
P8	Cal Ripken Promo	3.00	1.35

1995 Emotion Masters

		MINT	NRMT
	COMPLETE SET (10)	60.00	27.00
	COMMON CARD (1-10)	2.00	.90
	STATED ODDS 1:8		
1	Barry Bonds	3.00	1.35
2	Juan Gonzalez	6.00	2.70
3	Ken Griffey Jr.	15.00	6.75
4	Tony Gwynn	8.00	3.60
5	Kenny Lofton	2.00	.90
6	Greg Maddux	8.00	3.60
7	Raul Mondesi	2.00	.90
8	Cal Ripken	12.00	5.50
9	Frank Thomas	6.00	2.70
10	Matt Williams	3.00	1.35

1995 Emotion N-Tense

		MINT	NRMT
	COMPLETE SET (12)	150.00	70.00
	COMMON CARD (1-12)	3.00	1.35
	STATED ODDS 1:37		
1	Jeff Bagwell	10.00	4.50
2	Albert Belle	8.00	3.60
3	Barry Bonds	8.00	3.60
4	Cecil Fielder	4.00	1.80
5	Ron Gant	3.00	1.35
6	Ken Griffey Jr.	40.00	18.00
7	Mark McGwire	40.00	18.00
8	Mike Piazza	25.00	11.00
9	Manny Ramirez	8.00	3.60
10	Frank Thomas	20.00	9.00
11	Mo Vaughn	8.00	3.60
12	Matt Williams	8.00	3.60

1995 Emotion Ripken

		MINT	NRMT
	COMPLETE SET (10)	50.00	22.00
	COMMON CARD (1-10)	6.00	2.70
	STATED ODDS 1:12		
	COMMON MAIL-IN (11-15)	6.00	2.70
	MAIL-IN CARDS DIST.VIA WRAPPER EXCH.		
1	Cal Ripken High School Pitcher	6.00	2.70
2	Cal Ripken Role Model	6.00	2.70
3	Cal Ripken Rookie of the Year	6.00	2.70
4	Cal Ripken 1st MVP Season	6.00	2.70
5	Cal Ripken 95 Consecutive Errorless Games	6.00	2.70
6	Cal Ripken All-Star MVP	6.00	2.70
7	Cal Ripken Conditioning *	6.00	2.70
8	Cal Ripken Shortstop HR Record	6.00	2.70

		MINT	NRMT
❏ 9	Cal Ripken Literacy Work	6.00	2.70
❏ 10	Cal Ripken 2000th Consecutive Game	6.00	2.70
❏ 11	Cal Ripken 1995 All-Star Selection	6.00	2.70
❏ 12	Cal Ripken 35th Birthday	6.00	2.70
❏ 13	Cal Ripken Game 2,130	6.00	2.70
❏ 14	Cal Ripken Game 2,131	6.00	2.70
❏ 15	Cal Ripken 2,153 and Counting	6.00	2.70

1995 Emotion Rookies

	MINT	NRMT
COMPLETE SET (10)	25.00	11.00
COMMON CARD (1-10)	1.00	.45
STATED ODDS 1:5		

❏ 1	Edgardo Alfonzo	4.00	1.80
❏ 2	Jason Bates	1.00	.45
❏ 3	Marty Cordova	1.00	.45
❏ 4	Ray Durham	2.00	.90
❏ 5	Alex Gonzalez	1.00	.45
❏ 6	Shawn Green	4.00	1.80
❏ 7	Charles Johnson	2.00	.90
❏ 8	Chipper Jones	8.00	3.60
❏ 9	Hideo Nomo	4.00	1.80
❏ 10	Alex Rodriguez	10.00	4.50

1996 Emotion-XL

	MINT	NRMT
COMPLETE SET (300)	80.00	36.00
COMMON CARD (1-300)	.40	.18
MINOR STARS	.75	.35
UNLISTED STARS	1.50	.70
PRODUCED BY FLEER		

❏ 1	Roberto Alomar	1.50	.70
❏ 2	Brady Anderson	.75	.35
❏ 3	Bobby Bonilla	.75	.35
❏ 4	Jeffrey Hammonds	.75	.35
❏ 5	Chris Hoiles	.40	.18
❏ 6	Mike Mussina	1.50	.70
❏ 7	Randy Myers	.40	.18
❏ 8	Rafael Palmeiro	1.50	.70
❏ 9	Cal Ripken	6.00	2.70
❏ 10	B.J. Surhoff	.75	.35
❏ 11	Jose Canseco	2.00	.90
❏ 12	Roger Clemens	4.00	1.80
❏ 13	Wil Cordero	.40	.18
❏ 14	Mike Greenwell	.40	.18
❏ 15	Dwayne Hosey	.40	.18
❏ 16	Tim Naehring	.40	.18
❏ 17	Troy O'Leary	.75	.35
❏ 18	Mike Stanley	.40	.18
❏ 19	John Valentin	.75	.35
❏ 20	Mo Vaughn	1.50	.70
❏ 21	Jim Abbott	.75	.35
❏ 22	Garret Anderson	.75	.35
❏ 23	George Arias	.40	.18
❏ 24	Chili Davis	.75	.35
❏ 25	Jim Edmonds	1.00	.45
❏ 26	Chuck Finley	.75	.35
❏ 27	Todd Greene	.40	.18
❏ 28	Mark Langston	.40	.18
❏ 29	Troy Percival	.75	.35
❏ 30	Tim Salmon	1.00	.45
❏ 31	Lee Smith	.75	.35
❏ 32	J.T. Snow	.75	.35
❏ 33	Harold Baines	.75	.35
❏ 34	Jason Bere	.40	.18
❏ 35	Ray Durham	.75	.35
❏ 36	Alex Fernandez	.40	.18
❏ 37	Ozzie Guillen	.40	.18
❏ 38	Darren Lewis	.40	.18
❏ 39	Lyle Mouton	.40	.18
❏ 40	Tony Phillips	.40	.18
❏ 41	Danny Tartabull	.40	.18
❏ 42	Frank Thomas	3.00	1.35
❏ 43	Robin Ventura	.75	.35
❏ 44	Sandy Alomar Jr.	.75	.35
❏ 45	Carlos Baerga	.75	.35
❏ 46	Albert Belle	1.50	.70
❏ 47	Julio Franco	.40	.18
❏ 48	Orel Hershiser	.75	.35
❏ 49	Kenny Lofton	1.00	.45
❏ 50	Dennis Martinez	.75	.35
❏ 51	Jack McDowell	.40	.18
❏ 52	Jose Mesa	.40	.18
❏ 53	Eddie Murray	1.50	.70
❏ 54	Charles Nagy	.75	.35
❏ 55	Manny Ramirez	2.00	.90
❏ 56	Jim Thome	1.50	.70
❏ 57	Omar Vizquel	.75	.35
❏ 58	Chad Curtis	.40	.18
❏ 59	Cecil Fielder	.75	.35
❏ 60	Travis Fryman	.75	.35
❏ 61	Chris Gomez	.40	.18
❏ 62	Felipe Lira	.40	.18
❏ 63	Alan Trammell	1.00	.45
❏ 64	Kevin Appier	.75	.35
❏ 65	Johnny Damon	1.00	.45
❏ 66	Tom Goodwin	.40	.18
❏ 67	Mark Gubicza	.40	.18
❏ 68	Jeff Montgomery	.40	.18
❏ 69	Jon Nunnally	.40	.18
❏ 70	Bip Roberts	.40	.18
❏ 71	Ricky Bones	.40	.18
❏ 72	Chuck Carr	.40	.18
❏ 73	John Jaha	.40	.18
❏ 74	Ben McDonald	.40	.18
❏ 75	Matt Mieske	.40	.18
❏ 76	Dave Nilsson	.40	.18
❏ 77	Kevin Seitzer	.40	.18
❏ 78	Greg Vaughn	.75	.35
❏ 79	Rick Aguilera	.40	.18
❏ 80	Marty Cordova	.40	.18
❏ 81	Roberto Kelly	.40	.18
❏ 82	Chuck Knoblauch	1.50	.70
❏ 83	Pat Meares	.40	.18
❏ 84	Paul Molitor	1.50	.70
❏ 85	Kirby Puckett	2.50	1.10
❏ 86	Brad Radke	.75	.35
❏ 87	Wade Boggs	1.50	.70
❏ 88	David Cone	1.00	.45
❏ 89	Dwight Gooden	1.00	.45
❏ 90	Derek Jeter	5.00	2.20
❏ 91	Tino Martinez	.75	.35
❏ 92	Paul O'Neill	.75	.35
❏ 93	Andy Pettitte	1.00	.45
❏ 94	Tim Raines	.75	.35
❏ 95	Ruben Rivera	.75	.35
❏ 96	Kenny Rogers	.40	.18
❏ 97	Ruben Sierra	.40	.18
❏ 98	John Wetteland	.75	.35
❏ 99	Bernie Williams	1.50	.70
❏ 100	Allen Battle	.40	.18
❏ 101	Geronimo Berroa	.40	.18
❏ 102	Brent Gates	.40	.18
❏ 103	Doug Johns	.40	.18
❏ 104	Mark McGwire	8.00	3.60
❏ 105	Pedro Munoz	.40	.18
❏ 106	Ariel Prieto	.40	.18
❏ 107	Terry Steinbach	.40	.18
❏ 108	Todd Van Poppel	.40	.18
❏ 109	Chris Bosio	.40	.18
❏ 110	Jay Buhner	.75	.35
❏ 111	Joey Cora	.40	.18
❏ 112	Russ Davis	.40	.18
❏ 113	Ken Griffey Jr.	8.00	3.60
❏ 114	Sterling Hitchcock	.40	.18
❏ 115	Randy Johnson	1.50	.70
❏ 116	Edgar Martinez	.75	.35
❏ 117	Alex Rodriguez	5.00	2.20
❏ 118	Paul Sorrento	.40	.18
❏ 119	Dan Wilson	.40	.18
❏ 120	Will Clark	1.50	.70
❏ 121	Juan Gonzalez	3.00	1.35
❏ 122	Rusty Greer	.75	.35
❏ 123	Kevin Gross	.40	.18
❏ 124	Ken Hill	.40	.18
❏ 125	Dean Palmer	.75	.35
❏ 126	Roger Pavlik	.40	.18
❏ 127	Ivan Rodriguez	2.00	.90
❏ 128	Mickey Tettleton	.40	.18
❏ 129	Joe Carter	.75	.35
❏ 130	Carlos Delgado	1.50	.70
❏ 131	Alex Gonzalez	.40	.18
❏ 132	Shawn Green	1.50	.70
❏ 133	Erik Hanson	.40	.18
❏ 134	Pat Hentgen	.75	.35
❏ 135	Otis Nixon	.40	.18
❏ 136	John Olerud	.75	.35
❏ 137	Ed Sprague	.40	.18
❏ 138	Steve Avery	.40	.18
❏ 139	Jermaine Dye	.75	.35
❏ 140	Tom Glavine	1.50	.70
❏ 141	Marquis Grissom	.40	.18
❏ 142	Chipper Jones	4.00	1.80
❏ 143	David Justice	1.50	.70
❏ 144	Ryan Klesko	.75	.35
❏ 145	Javier Lopez	.75	.35
❏ 146	Greg Maddux	4.00	1.80
❏ 147	Fred McGriff	1.00	.45
❏ 148	Jason Schmidt	.40	.18
❏ 149	John Smoltz	1.00	.45
❏ 150	Mark Wohlers	.40	.18
❏ 151	Jim Bullinger	.40	.18
❏ 152	Frank Castillo	.40	.18
❏ 153	Kevin Foster	.40	.18
❏ 154	Luis Gonzalez	.75	.35
❏ 155	Mark Grace	1.00	.45
❏ 156	Brian McRae	.40	.18
❏ 157	Jaime Navarro	.40	.18
❏ 158	Rey Sanchez	.40	.18
❏ 159	Ryne Sandberg	2.00	.90
❏ 160	Sammy Sosa	5.00	2.20
❏ 161	Bret Boone	.75	.35
❏ 162	Jeff Brantley	.40	.18
❏ 163	Vince Coleman	.40	.18
❏ 164	Steve Gibralter	.40	.18
❏ 165	Barry Larkin	1.50	.70
❏ 166	Hal Morris	.40	.18
❏ 167	Mark Portugal	.40	.18
❏ 168	Reggie Sanders	.75	.35
❏ 169	Pete Schourek	.40	.18
❏ 170	John Smiley	.40	.18
❏ 171	Jason Bates	.40	.18
❏ 172	Dante Bichette	.75	.35
❏ 173	Ellis Burks	.75	.35
❏ 174	Vinny Castilla	1.00	.45
❏ 175	Andres Galarraga	1.50	.70
❏ 176	Kevin Ritz	.40	.18
❏ 177	Bill Swift	.40	.18
❏ 178	Larry Walker	1.50	.70
❏ 179	Walt Weiss	.40	.18
❏ 180	Eric Young	.40	.18
❏ 181	Kurt Abbott	.40	.18

❏ 182 Kevin Brown	1.00	.45	❏ 268 Ray Lankford	.75	.35	
❏ 183 John Burkett	.40	.18	❏ 269 John Mabry	.40	.18	
❏ 184 Greg Colbrunn	.40	.18	❏ 270 Tom Pagnozzi	.40	.18	
❏ 185 Jeff Conine	.40	.18	❏ 271 Ozzie Smith	2.00	.90	
❏ 186 Chris Hammond	.40	.18	❏ 272 Todd Stottlemyre	.40	.18	
❏ 187 Charles Johnson	.75	.35	❏ 273 Andy Ashby	.40	.18	
❏ 188 Terry Pendleton	.40	.18	❏ 274 Brad Ausmus	.40	.18	
❏ 189 Pat Rapp	.40	.18	❏ 275 Ken Caminiti	.75	.35	
❏ 190 Gary Sheffield	.75	.35	❏ 276 Steve Finley	.75	.35	
❏ 191 Quilvio Veras	.40	.18	❏ 277 Tony Gwynn	4.00	1.80	
❏ 192 Devon White	.75	.35	❏ 278 Joey Hamilton	.40	.18	
❏ 193 Jeff Bagwell	2.00	.90	❏ 279 Rickey Henderson	2.00	.90	
❏ 194 Derek Bell	.75	.35	❏ 280 Trevor Hoffman	.75	.35	
❏ 195 Sean Berry	.40	.18	❏ 281 Wally Joyner	.75	.35	
❏ 196 Craig Biggio	1.50	.70	❏ 282 Jody Reed	.40	.18	
❏ 197 Doug Drabek	.40	.18	❏ 283 Bob Tewksbury	.40	.18	
❏ 198 Tony Eusebio	.40	.18	❏ 284 Fernando Valenzuela	.75	.35	
❏ 199 Mike Hampton	.75	.35	❏ 285 Rod Beck	.40	.18	
❏ 200 Brian L.Hunter	.40	.18	❏ 286 Barry Bonds	2.00	.90	
❏ 201 Derrick May	.40	.18	❏ 287 Mark Carreon	.40	.18	
❏ 202 Orlando Miller	.40	.18	❏ 288 Shawon Dunston	.40	.18	
❏ 203 Shane Reynolds	.75	.35	❏ 289 Osvaldo Fernandez	.40	.18	
❏ 204 Mike Blowers	.40	.18	❏ 290 Glenallen Hill	.40	.18	
❏ 205 Tom Candiotti	.40	.18	❏ 291 Stan Javier	.40	.18	
❏ 206 Delino DeShields	.40	.18	❏ 292 Mark Leiter	.40	.18	
❏ 207 Greg Gagne	.40	.18	❏ 293 Kirt Manwaring	.40	.18	
❏ 208 Karim Garcia	.75	.35	❏ 294 Robby Thompson	.40	.18	
❏ 209 Todd Hollandsworth	.40	.18	❏ 295 William VanLandingham	.40	.18	
❏ 210 Eric Karros	.75	.35	❏ 296 Allen Watson	.40	.18	
❏ 211 Ramon Martinez	.75	.35	❏ 297 Matt Williams	1.50	.35	
❏ 212 Raul Mondesi	.75	.35	❏ 298 Checklist	.40	.18	
❏ 213 Hideo Nomo	1.50	.70	❏ 299 Checklist	.40	.18	
❏ 214 Chan Ho Park	1.00	.45	❏ 300 Checklist	.40	.18	
❏ 215 Mike Piazza	5.00	2.20	❏ P55 Manny Ramirez	2.00	.90	
❏ 216 Ismael Valdes	.75	.35			Promo	
❏ 217 Todd Worrell	.40	.18				
❏ 218 Moises Alou	.75	.35				
❏ 219 Yamil Benitez	.40	.18				
❏ 220 Jeff Fassero	.40	.18				
❏ 221 Darrin Fletcher	.40	.18				
❏ 222 Cliff Floyd	.75	.35				
❏ 223 Pedro Martinez	2.00	.90				
❏ 224 Carlos Perez	.40	.18				
❏ 225 Mel Rojas	.40	.18				
❏ 226 David Segui	.75	.35				
❏ 227 Rondell White	.75	.35				
❏ 228 Rico Brogna	.40	.18				
❏ 229 Carl Everett	.75	.35				
❏ 230 John Franco	.75	.35				
❏ 231 Bernard Gilkey	.40	.18				
❏ 232 Todd Hundley	.75	.35				
❏ 233 Jason Isringhausen	.75	.35				
❏ 234 Lance Johnson	.40	.18				
❏ 235 Bobby Jones	.40	.18				
❏ 236 Jeff Kent	.75	.35				
❏ 237 Rey Ordonez	1.50	.70				
❏ 238 Bill Pulsipher	.40	.18				
❏ 239 Jose Vizcaino	.40	.18				
❏ 240 Paul Wilson	.40	.18				
❏ 241 Ricky Bottalico	.40	.18				
❏ 242 Darren Daulton	.75	.35				
❏ 243 Lenny Dykstra	.75	.35				
❏ 244 Jim Eisenreich	.40	.18				
❏ 245 Sid Fernandez	.40	.18				
❏ 246 Gregg Jefferies	.40	.18				
❏ 247 Mickey Morandini	.40	.18				
❏ 248 Benito Santiago	.40	.18				
❏ 249 Curt Schilling	1.00	.45				
❏ 250 Mark Whiten	.40	.18				
❏ 251 Todd Zeile	.40	.18				
❏ 252 Jay Bell	.75	.35				
❏ 253 Carlos Garcia	.40	.18				
❏ 254 Charlie Hayes	.40	.18				
❏ 255 Jason Kendall	1.50	.70				
❏ 256 Jeff King	.40	.18				
❏ 257 Al Martin	.40	.18				
❏ 258 Orlando Merced	.40	.18				
❏ 259 Dan Miceli	.40	.18				
❏ 260 Denny Neagle	.75	.35				
❏ 261 Alan Benes	.40	.18				
❏ 262 Andy Benes	.75	.35				
❏ 263 Royce Clayton	.40	.18				
❏ 264 Dennis Eckersley	.75	.35				
❏ 265 Gary Gaetti	.75	.35				
❏ 266 Ron Gant	.75	.35				
❏ 267 Brian Jordan	.75	.35				

	MINT	NRMT
❏ 5 Mark McGwire	50.00	22.00
❏ 6 Mike Piazza	30.00	13.50
❏ 7 Manny Ramirez	10.00	4.50
❏ 8 Tim Salmon	6.00	2.70
❏ 9 Sammy Sosa	25.00	11.00
❏ 10 Frank Thomas	25.00	11.00
❏ 11 Mo Vaughn	10.00	4.50
❏ 12 Matt Williams	10.00	4.50

1996 Emotion-XL N-Tense

	MINT	NRMT
COMPLETE SET (10)	60.00	27.00
COMMON CARD (1-10)	4.00	1.80
STATED ODDS 1:12		

❏ 1 Albert Belle	4.00	1.80
❏ 2 Barry Bonds	5.00	2.20
❏ 3 Jose Canseco	5.00	2.20
❏ 4 Ken Griffey Jr.	20.00	9.00
❏ 5 Tony Gwynn	10.00	4.50
❏ 6 Randy Johnson	4.00	1.80
❏ 7 Greg Maddux	10.00	4.50
❏ 8 Cal Ripken	15.00	6.75
❏ 9 Frank Thomas	8.00	3.60
❏ 10 Matt Williams	4.00	1.80

1996 Emotion-XL Rare Breed

1996 Emotion-XL D-Fense

	MINT	NRMT
COMPLETE SET (10)	25.00	11.00
COMMON CARD (1-10)	1.00	.45
STATED ODDS 1:4		

❏ 1 Roberto Alomar	1.50	.70
❏ 2 Barry Bonds	1.50	.70
❏ 3 Mark Grace	1.00	.45
❏ 4 Ken Griffey Jr.	10.00	4.50
❏ 5 Kenny Lofton	1.00	.45
❏ 6 Greg Maddux	5.00	2.20
❏ 7 Raul Mondesi	1.00	.45
❏ 8 Cal Ripken	8.00	3.60
❏ 9 Ivan Rodriguez	1.50	.70
❏ 10 Matt Williams	1.50	.70

1996 Emotion-XL Legion of Boom

	MINT	NRMT
COMPLETE SET (12)	200.00	90.00
COMMON CARD (1-12)	6.00	2.70
STATED ODDS 1:36 HOBBY		

❏ 1 Albert Belle	10.00	4.50
❏ 2 Barry Bonds	10.00	4.50
❏ 3 Juan Gonzalez	25.00	11.00
❏ 4 Ken Griffey Jr.	50.00	22.00

	MINT	NRMT
COMPLETE SET (10)	150.00	70.00
COMMON CARD (1-10)	6.00	2.70
MINOR STARS	12.00	5.50
STATED ODDS 1:100		

		MINT	NRMT
❑ 1	Garret Anderson	12.00	5.50
❑ 2	Marty Cordova	6.00	2.70
❑ 3	Brian L. Hunter	6.00	2.70
❑ 4	Jason Isringhausen	12.00	5.50
❑ 5	Charles Johnson	12.00	5.50
❑ 6	Chipper Jones	60.00	27.00
❑ 7	Raul Mondesi	12.00	5.50
❑ 8	Hideo Nomo	25.00	11.00
❑ 9	Manny Ramirez	30.00	13.50
❑ 10	Rondell White	12.00	5.50

1997 E-X2000

	MINT	NRMT
COMPLETE SET (100)	80.00	36.00
COMMON CARD (1-100)	.50	.23
MINOR STARS	1.00	.45
SEMISTARS	1.50	.70
UNLISTED STARS	2.00	.90
COMMON CRED. (1-100)	4.00	1.80
*CRED.STARS: 3X TO 8X HI COLUMN		
*CRED.YNG.STARS: 2.5X TO 6X HI		
CREDENTIALS RANDOM INSERTS IN PACKS		
CRED.PRINT RUN LESS THAN 299 SETS		
A.ROD.BASEBALL EXCH: 5/1/98		

		MINT	NRMT
❑ 1	Jim Edmonds	1.50	.70
❑ 2	Darin Erstad	2.00	.90
❑ 3	Eddie Murray	2.00	.90
❑ 4	Roberto Alomar	2.00	.90
❑ 5	Brady Anderson	1.00	.45
❑ 6	Mike Mussina	2.00	.90
❑ 7	Rafael Palmeiro	2.00	.90
❑ 8	Cal Ripken	8.00	3.60
❑ 9	Steve Avery	.50	.23
❑ 10	Nomar Garciaparra	6.00	2.70
❑ 11	Mo Vaughn	2.00	.90
❑ 12	Albert Belle	2.00	.90
❑ 13	Mike Cameron	1.00	.45
❑ 14	Ray Durham	1.00	.45
❑ 15	Frank Thomas	4.00	1.80
❑ 16	Robin Ventura	1.00	.45
❑ 17	Manny Ramirez	2.50	1.10
❑ 18	Jim Thome	2.00	.90
❑ 19	Matt Williams	2.00	.90
❑ 20	Tony Clark	1.50	.70
❑ 21	Travis Fryman	1.00	.45
❑ 22	Bob Higginson	1.00	.45
❑ 23	Kevin Appier	1.00	.45
❑ 24	Johnny Damon	1.00	.45
❑ 25	Jermaine Dye	1.00	.45
❑ 26	Jeff Cirillo	1.00	.45
❑ 27	Ben McDonald	.50	.23
❑ 28	Chuck Knoblauch	2.00	.90
❑ 29	Paul Molitor	2.00	.90
❑ 30	Todd Walker	2.00	.90
❑ 31	Wade Boggs	2.00	.90
❑ 32	Cecil Fielder	1.00	.45
❑ 33	Derek Jeter	6.00	2.70
❑ 34	Andy Pettitte	1.50	.70
❑ 35	Ruben Rivera	.50	.23
❑ 36	Bernie Williams	2.00	.90

		MINT	NRMT
❑ 37	Jose Canseco	2.50	1.10
❑ 38	Mark McGwire	10.00	4.50
❑ 39	Jay Buhner	1.00	.45
❑ 40	Ken Griffey Jr.	10.00	4.50
❑ 41	Randy Johnson	2.00	.90
❑ 42	Edgar Martinez	1.00	.45
❑ 43	Alex Rodriguez	6.00	2.70
❑ 44	Dan Wilson	.50	.23
❑ 45	Will Clark	2.00	.90
❑ 46	Juan Gonzalez	4.00	1.80
❑ 47	Ivan Rodriguez	2.50	1.10
❑ 48	Joe Carter	1.00	.45
❑ 49	Roger Clemens	5.00	2.20
❑ 50	Juan Guzman	.50	.23
❑ 51	Pat Hentgen	1.00	.45
❑ 52	Tom Glavine	2.00	.90
❑ 53	Andruw Jones	2.50	1.10
❑ 54	Chipper Jones	5.00	2.20
❑ 55	Ryan Klesko	1.00	.45
❑ 56	Kenny Lofton	1.50	.70
❑ 57	Greg Maddux	5.00	2.20
❑ 58	Fred McGriff	1.50	.70
❑ 59	John Smoltz	1.50	.70
❑ 60	Mark Wohlers	.50	.23
❑ 61	Mark Grace	1.50	.70
❑ 62	Ryne Sandberg	2.50	1.10
❑ 63	Sammy Sosa	6.00	2.70
❑ 64	Barry Larkin	2.00	.90
❑ 65	Deion Sanders	1.00	.45
❑ 66	Reggie Sanders	1.00	.45
❑ 67	Dante Bichette	1.00	.45
❑ 68	Ellis Burks	1.00	.45
❑ 69	Andres Galarraga	2.00	.90
❑ 70	Moises Alou	1.00	.45
❑ 71	Kevin Brown	1.50	.70
❑ 72	Cliff Floyd	1.00	.45
❑ 73	Edgar Renteria	1.00	.45
❑ 74	Gary Sheffield	1.00	.45
❑ 75	Bob Abreu	1.00	.45
❑ 76	Jeff Bagwell	2.50	1.10
❑ 77	Craig Biggio	2.00	.90
❑ 78	Todd Hollandsworth	.50	.23
❑ 79	Eric Karros	1.00	.45
❑ 80	Raul Mondesi	1.00	.45
❑ 81	Hideo Nomo	2.00	.90
❑ 82	Mike Piazza	6.00	2.70
❑ 83	Vladimir Guerrero	3.00	1.35
❑ 84	Henry Rodriguez	1.00	.45
❑ 85	Todd Hundley	1.00	.45
❑ 86	Alex Ochoa	.50	.23
❑ 87	Rey Ordonez	1.00	.45
❑ 88	Gregg Jefferies	.50	.23
❑ 89	Scott Rolen	3.00	1.35
❑ 90	Jermaine Allensworth	1.00	.23
❑ 91	Jason Kendall	1.50	.45
❑ 92	Ken Caminiti	1.50	.70
❑ 93	Tony Gwynn	5.00	2.20
❑ 94	Rickey Henderson	2.50	1.10
❑ 95	Barry Bonds	2.50	1.10
❑ 96	J.T. Snow	1.00	.45
❑ 97	Dennis Eckersley	1.00	.45
❑ 98	Ron Gant	.50	.23
❑ 99	Brian Jordan	1.00	.45
❑ 100	Ray Lankford	1.00	.45
❑ 101	Checklist	.50	.23
❑ 102	Checklist	.50	.23
❑ P43	Alex Rodriguez	3.00	1.35
	Three card promo strip		
❑ S43	Alex Rodriguez	20.00	9.00
	Mailed to Dealers who ordered Cases		
	Card is numbered out of 3,000		
❑ NNO	Alex Rodriguez	80.00	36.00
	Ball Exch 100 produced		

1997 E-X2000 Essential Credentials

	MINT	NRMT
COMMON CARD (1-100)	10.00	4.50
*STARS: 8X TO 20X BASIC CARDS		
*YNG.STARS: 6X TO 15X BASIC CARDS		
RANDOM INSERTS IN PACKS		
STATED PRINT RUN LESS THAN 99 SETS		

1997 E-X2000 A Cut Above

	MINT	NRMT
COMPLETE SET (10)	350.00	160.00
COMMON CARD (1-10)	10.00	4.50
UNLISTED STARS	15.00	6.75
STATED ODDS 1:288		

		MINT	NRMT
❑ 1	Frank Thomas	30.00	13.50
❑ 2	Ken Griffey Jr.	80.00	36.00
❑ 3	Alex Rodriguez	50.00	22.00
❑ 4	Albert Belle	15.00	6.75
❑ 5	Juan Gonzalez	30.00	13.50
❑ 6	Mark McGwire	80.00	36.00
❑ 7	Mo Vaughn	15.00	6.75
❑ 8	Manny Ramirez	20.00	9.00
❑ 9	Barry Bonds	20.00	9.00
❑ 10	Fred McGriff	10.00	4.50

1997 E-X2000 Emerald Autographs

	MINT	NRMT
ONE CARD VIA MAIL PER EXCH.CARD		
*EXCH.CARDS: .1X TO .25X HI COLUMN		
EXCH.CARDS STATED ODDS 1:500 PACKS		

		MINT	NRMT
❑ 2	Darin Erstad	40.00	18.00
❑ 30	Todd Walker	20.00	9.00
❑ 43	Alex Rodriguez	200.00	90.00
❑ 78	Todd Hollandsworth	10.00	4.50
❑ 86	Alex Ochoa	10.00	4.50
❑ 89	Scott Rolen	80.00	36.00

1997 E-X2000 Hall or Nothing

	MINT	NRMT
COMPLETE SET (20)	200.00	90.00
COMMON CARD (1-20)	2.00	.90
SEMISTARS	3.00	1.35
UNLISTED STARS	5.00	2.20
STATED ODDS 1:20		

		MINT	NRMT
❑ 1	Frank Thomas	10.00	4.50
❑ 2	Ken Griffey Jr.	25.00	11.00
❑ 3	Eddie Murray	5.00	2.20
❑ 4	Cal Ripken	20.00	9.00

❏ 5 Ryne Sandberg	6.00	2.70
❏ 6 Wade Boggs	5.00	2.20
❏ 7 Roger Clemens	12.00	5.50
❏ 8 Tony Gwynn	12.00	5.50
❏ 9 Alex Rodriguez	15.00	6.75
❏ 10 Mark McGwire	25.00	11.00
❏ 11 Barry Bonds	6.00	2.70
❏ 12 Greg Maddux	12.00	5.50
❏ 13 Juan Gonzalez	10.00	4.50
❏ 14 Albert Belle	5.00	2.20
❏ 15 Mike Piazza	15.00	6.75
❏ 16 Jeff Bagwell	6.00	2.70
❏ 17 Dennis Eckersley	2.00	.90
❏ 18 Mo Vaughn	5.00	2.20
❏ 19 Roberto Alomar	5.00	2.20
❏ 20 Kenny Lofton	3.00	1.35

1997 E-X2000 Star Date 2000

	MINT	NRMT
COMPLETE SET (15)	40.00	18.00
COMMON CARD (1-15)	1.25	.55
STATED ODDS 1:9		

❏ 1 Alex Rodriguez	8.00	3.60
❏ 2 Andruw Jones	3.00	1.35
❏ 3 Andy Pettitte	1.50	.70
❏ 4 Brooks Kieschnick	1.25	.55
❏ 5 Chipper Jones	6.00	2.70
❏ 6 Darin Erstad	2.50	1.10
❏ 7 Derek Jeter	6.00	2.70
❏ 8 Jason Kendall	1.50	.70
❏ 9 Jermaine Dye	1.25	.55
❏ 10 Neifi Perez	1.25	.55
❏ 11 Scott Rolen	5.00	2.20
❏ 12 Todd Hollandsworth	1.25	.55
❏ 13 Todd Walker	2.50	1.10
❏ 14 Tony Clark	1.50	.70
❏ 15 Vladimir Guerrero	4.00	1.80

1998 E-X2001

	MINT	NRMT
COMPLETE SET (100)	120.00	55.00
COMMON CARD (1-100)	.50	.23
MINOR STARS	.75	.35
SEMISTARS	1.25	.55
UNLISTED STARS	2.00	.90
K.WOOD EXCH.DEADLINE 3/31/99		

COMP.SET EXCLUDES WOOD EXCHANGE
COMP.SET EXCLUDES REDEMPTION 101

❏ 1 Alex Rodriguez	6.00	2.70
❏ 2 Barry Bonds	2.50	1.10
❏ 3 Greg Maddux	5.00	2.20
❏ 4 Roger Clemens	5.00	2.20
❏ 5 Juan Gonzalez	4.00	1.80
❏ 6 Chipper Jones	5.00	2.20
❏ 7 Derek Jeter	6.00	2.70
❏ 8 Frank Thomas	4.00	1.80
❏ 9 Cal Ripken	8.00	3.60
❏ 10 Ken Griffey Jr.	10.00	4.50
❏ 11 Mark McGwire	12.00	5.50
❏ 12 Hideo Nomo	2.00	.90
❏ 13 Tony Gwynn	5.00	2.20
❏ 14 Ivan Rodriguez	2.50	1.10
❏ 15 Mike Piazza	6.00	2.70
❏ 16 Roberto Alomar	2.00	.90
❏ 17 Jeff Bagwell	2.50	1.10
❏ 18 Andruw Jones	2.00	.90
❏ 19 Albert Belle	2.00	.90
❏ 20 Mo Vaughn	2.00	.90
❏ 21 Kenny Lofton	1.25	.55
❏ 22 Gary Sheffield	.75	.35
❏ 23 Tony Clark	.75	.35
❏ 24 Mike Mussina	2.00	.90
❏ 25 Barry Larkin	2.00	.90
❏ 26 Moises Alou	.75	.35
❏ 27 Brady Anderson	.75	.35
❏ 28 Andy Pettitte	.75	.35
❏ 29 Sammy Sosa	6.00	2.70
❏ 30 Raul Mondesi	.75	.35
❏ 31 Andres Galarraga	1.25	.55
❏ 32 Chuck Knoblauch	.75	.35
❏ 33 Jim Thome	2.00	.90
❏ 34 Craig Biggio	2.00	.90
❏ 35 Jay Buhner	.75	.35
❏ 36 Rafael Palmeiro	2.00	.90
❏ 37 Curt Schilling	1.25	.55
❏ 38 Tino Martinez	.75	.35
❏ 39 Pedro Martinez	2.50	1.10
❏ 40 Jose Canseco	2.50	1.10
❏ 41 Jeff Cirillo	.75	.35
❏ 42 Dean Palmer	.75	.35
❏ 43 Tim Salmon	1.25	.55
❏ 44 Jason Giambi	.75	.35
❏ 45 Bobby Higginson	.75	.35
❏ 46 Jim Edmonds	.75	.35
❏ 47 David Justice	.75	.35
❏ 48 John Olerud	.75	.35
❏ 49 Ray Lankford	.75	.35
❏ 50 Al Martin	.50	.23
❏ 51 Mike Lieberthal	.50	.23
❏ 52 Henry Rodriguez	.75	.35
❏ 53 Edgar Renteria	.50	.23
❏ 54 Eric Karros	.75	.35
❏ 55 Marquis Grissom	.50	.23
❏ 56 Wilson Alvarez	.50	.23
❏ 57 Darryl Kile	.50	.23
❏ 58 Jeff King	.50	.23
❏ 59 Shawn Estes	.50	.23
❏ 60 Tony Womack	.50	.23
❏ 61 Willie Greene	.50	.23
❏ 62 Ken Caminiti	.75	.35
❏ 63 Vinny Castilla	.75	.35
❏ 64 Mark Grace	1.25	.55
❏ 65 Ryan Klesko	.75	.35

❏ 66 Robin Ventura	.75	.35
❏ 67 Todd Hundley	.75	.35
❏ 68 Travis Fryman	.75	.35
❏ 69 Edgar Martinez	.75	.35
❏ 70 Matt Williams	2.00	.90
❏ 71 Paul Molitor	2.00	.90
❏ 72 Kevin Brown	1.25	.55
❏ 73 Randy Johnson	2.00	.90
❏ 74 Bernie Williams	2.00	.90
❏ 75 Manny Ramirez	2.50	1.10
❏ 76 Fred McGriff	1.25	.55
❏ 77 Tom Glavine	2.00	.90
❏ 78 Carlos Delgado	2.00	.90
❏ 79 Larry Walker	2.00	.90
❏ 80 Hideki Irabu	.75	.35
❏ 81 Ryan McGuire	.50	.23
❏ 82 Justin Thompson	.50	.23
❏ 83 Kevin Orie	.50	.23
❏ 84 Jon Nunnally	.50	.23
❏ 85 Mark Kotsay	.75	.35
❏ 86 Todd Walker	.75	.35
❏ 87 Jason Dickson	.50	.23
❏ 88 Fernando Tatis	2.00	.90
❏ 89 Karim Garcia	.50	.23
❏ 90 Ricky Ledee	.75	.35
❏ 91 Paul Konerko	.75	.35
❏ 92 Jaret Wright	.75	.35
❏ 93 Darin Erstad	1.25	.55
❏ 94 Livan Hernandez	.50	.23
❏ 95 Nomar Garciaparra	6.00	2.70
❏ 96 Jose Cruz Jr.	.75	.35
❏ 97 Scott Rolen	2.50	1.10
❏ 98 Ben Grieve	2.00	.90
❏ 99 Vladimir Guerrero	2.50	1.10
❏ 100 Travis Lee	1.25	.55
❏ 101 Kerry Wood Redemption	8.00	3.60
❏ NNO Kerry Wood EXCH	4.00	1.80
❏ NNO Alex Rodriguez Sample	3.00	1.35

1998 E-X2001 Essential Credentials Future

	MINT	NRMT
COMMON CARD (1-30)	15.00	6.75
SEMISTARS 1-30	25.00	11.00
UNLISTED STARS 1-30	40.00	18.00
COMMON CARD (31-50)	12.00	5.50
MINOR STARS 31-50	20.00	9.00
SEMISTARS 31-50	30.00	13.50
UNLISTED STARS 31-50	50.00	22.00
COMMON CARD (51-65)	15.00	6.75
MINOR STARS 51-65	25.00	11.00
SEMISTARS 51-65	40.00	18.00
UNLISTED STARS 51-65	60.00	27.00
COMMON CARD (66-75)	30.00	13.50
UNLISTED STARS 66-75	50.00	22.00
UNLISTED STARS 76-80	80.00	36.00
COMMON CARD (76-80)	50.00	22.00
SEMISTARS 76-80	60.00	27.00
UNLISTED STARS 76-80	100.00	45.00
COMMON CARD (81-85)	30.00	13.50
MINOR STARS 81-85	50.00	22.00
RANDOM INSERTS IN PACKS		
CARDS 86-100 NOT PRICED DUE TO		
SCARCITY		
PRINT RUNS IN PARENTHESES BELOW		

❏ 1 Alex Rodriguez (100)	120.00	55.00

		MINT	NRMT
❏ 2	Barry Bonds (99)	50.00	22.00
❏ 3	Greg Maddux (98)	100.00	45.00
❏ 4	Roger Clemens (97)	100.00	45.00
❏ 5	Juan Gonzalez (96)	80.00	36.00
❏ 6	Chipper Jones (95)	100.00	45.00
❏ 7	Derek Jeter (94)	120.00	55.00
❏ 8	Frank Thomas (93)	80.00	36.00
❏ 9	Cal Ripken (92)	150.00	70.00
❏ 10	Ken Griffey Jr. (91)	200.00	90.00
❏ 11	Mark McGwire (90)	250.00	110.00
❏ 12	Hideo Nomo (89)	40.00	18.00
❏ 13	Tony Gwynn (88)	100.00	45.00
❏ 14	Ivan Rodriguez (87)	50.00	22.00
❏ 15	Mike Piazza (86)	120.00	55.00
❏ 16	Roberto Alomar (85)	40.00	18.00
❏ 17	Jeff Bagwell (84)	50.00	22.00
❏ 18	Andruw Jones (83)	40.00	18.00
❏ 19	Albert Belle (82)	40.00	18.00
❏ 20	Mo Vaughn (81)	40.00	18.00
❏ 21	Kenny Lofton (80)	25.00	11.00
❏ 22	Gary Sheffield (79)	15.00	6.75
❏ 23	Tony Clark (78)	15.00	6.75
❏ 24	Mike Mussina (77)	40.00	18.00
❏ 25	Barry Larkin (76)	40.00	18.00
❏ 26	Moises Alou (75)	15.00	6.75
❏ 27	Brady Anderson (74)	15.00	6.75
❏ 28	Andy Pettitte (73)	15.00	6.75
❏ 29	Sammy Sosa (72)	120.00	55.00
❏ 30	Raul Mondesi (71)	15.00	6.75
❏ 31	Andres Galarraga (70)	25.00	11.00
❏ 32	Chuck Knoblauch (69)	20.00	9.00
❏ 33	Jim Thome (68)	50.00	22.00
❏ 34	Craig Biggio (67)	50.00	22.00
❏ 35	Jay Buhner (66)	20.00	9.00
❏ 36	Rafael Palmeiro (65)	50.00	22.00
❏ 37	Curt Schilling (64)	30.00	13.50
❏ 38	Tino Martinez (63)	20.00	9.00
❏ 39	Pedro Martinez (62)	60.00	27.00
❏ 40	Jose Canseco (61)	60.00	27.00
❏ 41	Jeff Cirillo (60)	20.00	9.00
❏ 42	Dean Palmer (59)	30.00	13.50
❏ 43	Tim Salmon (58)	30.00	13.50
❏ 44	Jason Giambi (57)	20.00	9.00
❏ 45	Bobby Higginson (56)	20.00	9.00
❏ 46	Jim Edmonds (55)	20.00	9.00
❏ 47	David Justice (54)	20.00	9.00
❏ 48	John Olerud (53)	20.00	9.00
❏ 49	Ray Lankford (52)	20.00	9.00
❏ 50	Al Martin (51)	12.00	5.50
❏ 51	Mike Lieberthal (50)	25.00	11.00
❏ 52	Henry Rodriguez (49)	25.00	11.00
❏ 53	Edgar Renteria (48)	15.00	6.75
❏ 54	Eric Karros (47)	25.00	11.00
❏ 55	Marquis Grissom (46)	15.00	6.75
❏ 56	Wilson Alvarez (45)	15.00	6.75
❏ 57	Darryl Kile (44)	15.00	6.75
❏ 58	Jeff King (43)	15.00	6.75
❏ 59	Shawn Estes (42)	15.00	6.75
❏ 60	Tony Womack (41)	15.00	6.75
❏ 61	Willie Greene (40)	15.00	6.75
❏ 62	Ken Caminiti (39)	25.00	11.00
❏ 63	Vinny Castilla (38)	25.00	11.00
❏ 64	Mark Grace (37)	40.00	18.00
❏ 65	Ryan Klesko (36)	30.00	13.50
❏ 66	Robin Ventura (35)	30.00	13.50
❏ 67	Todd Hundley (34)	30.00	13.50
❏ 68	Travis Fryman (33)	30.00	13.50
❏ 69	Edgar Martinez (32)	30.00	13.50
❏ 70	Matt Williams (31)	80.00	36.00
❏ 71	Paul Molitor (30)	80.00	36.00
❏ 72	Kevin Brown (29)	50.00	22.00
❏ 73	Randy Johnson (28)	80.00	36.00
❏ 74	Bernie Williams (27)	80.00	36.00
❏ 75	Manny Ramirez (26)	100.00	45.00
❏ 76	Fred McGriff (25)	60.00	27.00
❏ 77	Tom Glavine (24)	100.00	45.00
❏ 78	Carlos Delgado (23)	100.00	45.00
❏ 79	Larry Walker (22)	100.00	45.00
❏ 80	Hideki Irabu (21)	50.00	22.00
❏ 81	Ryan McGuire (20)	30.00	13.50
❏ 82	Justin Thompson (19)	30.00	13.50
❏ 83	Kevin Orie (18)	30.00	13.50
❏ 84	Jon Nunnally (17)	30.00	13.50
❏ 85	Mark Kotsay (16)	50.00	22.00
❏ 86	Todd Walker (15)		
❏ 87	Jason Dickson (14)		

❏ 88	Fernando Tatis (13)
❏ 89	Karim Garcia (12)
❏ 90	Ricky Ledee (11)
❏ 91	Paul Konerko (10)
❏ 92	Jaret Wright (9)
❏ 93	Darin Erstad (8)
❏ 94	Livan Hernandez (7)
❏ 95	Nomar Garciaparra (4)
❏ 96	Jose Cruz Jr. (5)
❏ 97	Scott Rolen (4)
❏ 98	Ben Grieve (3)
❏ 99	Vladimir Guerrero (2)
❏ 100	Travis Lee (1)

1998 E-X2001 Essential Credentials Now

	MINT	NRMT
COMMON CARD (16-20)	100.00	45.00
UNLISTED STARS 16-20	120.00	55.00
COMMON CARD (21-25)	40.00	18.00
SEMISTARS 21-25	60.00	27.00
UNLISTED STARS 21-25	100.00	45.00
COMMON CARD (26-35)	30.00	13.50
SEMISTARS 26-35	50.00	22.00
UNLISTED STARS 26-35	60.00	27.00
COMMON CARD (36-50)	15.00	6.75
MINOR STARS 36-50	25.00	11.00
SEMISTARS 36-50	40.00	18.00
COMMON CARD (51-70)	12.00	5.50
MINOR STARS 51-70	20.00	9.00
SEMISTARS 51-70	30.00	13.50
COMMON CARD (71-100)	10.00	4.50
MINOR STARS 71-100	15.00	6.75
SEMISTARS 71-100	25.00	11.00
UNLISTED STARS 71-100	30.00	18.00

RANDOM INSERTS IN PACKS
CARDS 1-15 NOT PRICED DUE TO SCARCITY
PRINT RUNS IN PARENTHESES BELOW

❏ 1	Alex Rodriguez (1)
❏ 2	Barry Bonds (2)
❏ 3	Greg Maddux (3)
❏ 4	Roger Clemens (4)
❏ 5	Juan Gonzalez (5)
❏ 6	Chipper Jones (6)
❏ 7	Derek Jeter (7)
❏ 8	Frank Thomas (8)
❏ 9	Cal Ripken (9)
❏ 10	Ken Griffey Jr. (10)
❏ 11	Mark McGwire (11)
❏ 12	Hideo Nomo (12)
❏ 13	Tony Gwynn (13)
❏ 14	Ivan Rodriguez (14)
❏ 15	Mike Piazza (15)

		MINT	NRMT
❏ 16	Roberto Alomar (16)	100.00	45.00
❏ 17	Jeff Bagwell (17)	150.00	70.00
❏ 18	Andruw Jones (18)	120.00	55.00
❏ 19	Albert Belle (19)	100.00	45.00
❏ 20	Mo Vaughn (20)	100.00	45.00
❏ 21	Kenny Lofton (21)	60.00	27.00
❏ 22	Gary Sheffield (22)	40.00	18.00
❏ 23	Tony Clark (23)	40.00	18.00
❏ 24	Mike Mussina (24)	100.00	45.00
❏ 25	Barry Larkin (25)	100.00	45.00
❏ 26	Moises Alou (26)	50.00	22.00
❏ 27	Brady Anderson (27)	50.00	22.00
❏ 28	Andy Pettitte (28)	50.00	22.00

		MINT	NRMT
❏ 29	Sammy Sosa (29)	250.00	110.00
❏ 30	Raul Mondesi (30)	50.00	22.00
❏ 31	Andres Galarraga (31)	50.00	22.00
❏ 32	Chuck Knoblauch (32)	50.00	22.00
❏ 33	Jim Thome (33)	60.00	27.00
❏ 34	Craig Biggio (34)	60.00	27.00
❏ 35	Jay Buhner (35)	50.00	22.00
❏ 36	Rafael Palmeiro (36)	60.00	27.00
❏ 37	Curt Schilling (37)	40.00	18.00
❏ 38	Tino Martinez (38)	25.00	11.00
❏ 39	Pedro Martinez (39)	80.00	36.00
❏ 40	Jose Canseco (40)	80.00	36.00
❏ 41	Jeff Cirillo (41)	25.00	11.00
❏ 42	Dean Palmer (42)	25.00	11.00
❏ 43	Tim Salmon (43)	40.00	18.00
❏ 44	Jason Giambi (44)	25.00	11.00
❏ 45	Bobby Higginson (45)	25.00	11.00
❏ 46	Jim Edmonds (46)	25.00	11.00
❏ 47	David Justice (47)	25.00	11.00
❏ 48	John Olerud (48)	25.00	11.00
❏ 49	Ray Lankford (49)	25.00	11.00
❏ 50	Al Martin (50)	15.00	6.75
❏ 51	Mike Lieberthal (51)	20.00	9.00
❏ 52	Henry Rodriguez (52)	20.00	9.00
❏ 53	Edgar Renteria (53)	12.00	5.50
❏ 54	Eric Karros (54)	20.00	9.00
❏ 55	Marquis Grissom (55)	12.00	5.50
❏ 56	Wilson Alvarez (56)	12.00	5.50
❏ 57	Darryl Kile (57)	12.00	5.50
❏ 58	Jeff King (58)	12.00	5.50
❏ 59	Shawn Estes (59)	12.00	5.50
❏ 60	Tony Womack (60)	12.00	5.50
❏ 61	Willie Greene (61)	12.00	5.50
❏ 62	Ken Caminiti (62)	20.00	9.00
❏ 63	Vinny Castilla (63)	20.00	9.00
❏ 64	Mark Grace (64)	30.00	13.50
❏ 65	Ryan Klesko (65)	20.00	9.00
❏ 66	Robin Ventura (66)	20.00	9.00
❏ 67	Todd Hundley (67)	20.00	9.00
❏ 68	Travis Fryman (68)	20.00	9.00
❏ 69	Edgar Martinez (69)	20.00	9.00
❏ 70	Matt Williams (70)	50.00	22.00
❏ 71	Paul Molitor (71)	25.00	11.00
❏ 72	Kevin Brown (72)	25.00	11.00
❏ 73	Randy Johnson (73)	40.00	18.00
❏ 74	Bernie Williams (74)	40.00	18.00
❏ 75	Manny Ramirez (75)	50.00	22.00
❏ 76	Fred McGriff (76)	25.00	11.00
❏ 77	Tom Glavine (77)	40.00	18.00
❏ 78	Carlos Delgado (78)	40.00	18.00
❏ 79	Larry Walker (79)	40.00	18.00
❏ 80	Hideki Irabu (80)	15.00	6.75
❏ 81	Ryan McGuire (81)	10.00	4.50
❏ 82	Justin Thompson (82)	10.00	4.50
❏ 83	Kevin Orie (83)	10.00	4.50
❏ 84	Jon Nunnally (84)	10.00	4.50
❏ 85	Mark Kotsay (85)	15.00	6.75
❏ 86	Todd Walker (86)	15.00	6.75
❏ 87	Jason Dickson (87)	10.00	4.50
❏ 88	Fernando Tatis (88)	40.00	18.00
❏ 89	Karim Garcia (89)	10.00	4.50
❏ 90	Ricky Ledee (90)	15.00	6.75
❏ 91	Paul Konerko (91)	15.00	6.75
❏ 92	Jaret Wright (92)	30.00	13.50
❏ 93	Darin Erstad (93)	25.00	11.00
❏ 94	Livan Hernandez (94)	10.00	4.50
❏ 95	Nomar Garciaparra (95)	120.00	55.00
❏ 96	Jose Cruz Jr. (96)	15.00	6.75
❏ 97	Scott Rolen (97)	50.00	22.00
❏ 98	Ben Grieve (98)	40.00	18.00
❏ 99	Vladimir Guerrero (99)	50.00	22.00
❏ 100	Travis Lee (100)	25.00	11.00

1998 E-X2001 Cheap Seat Treats

	MINT	NRMT
COMPLETE SET (20)	200.00	90.00
COMMON CARD (1-20)	2.50	1.10
UNLISTED STARS	6.00	2.70
STATED ODDS 1:24		

		MINT	NRMT
❏ 1	Frank Thomas	12.00	5.50
❏ 2	Ken Griffey Jr.	30.00	13.50
❏ 3	Mark McGwire	40.00	18.00

		MINT	NRMT
❏ 4	Tino Martinez	2.50	1.10
❏ 5	Larry Walker	6.00	2.70
❏ 6	Juan Gonzalez	12.00	5.50
❏ 7	Mike Piazza	20.00	9.00
❏ 8	Jeff Bagwell	8.00	3.60
❏ 9	Tony Clark	2.50	1.10
❏ 10	Albert Belle	6.00	2.70
❏ 11	Andres Galarraga	4.00	1.80
❏ 12	Jim Thome	6.00	2.70
❏ 13	Mo Vaughn	6.00	2.70
❏ 14	Barry Bonds	8.00	3.60
❏ 15	Vladimir Guerrero	8.00	3.60
❏ 16	Scott Rolen	8.00	3.60
❏ 17	Travis Lee	4.00	1.80
❏ 18	David Justice	2.50	1.10
❏ 19	Jose Cruz Jr.	2.50	1.10
❏ 20	Andruw Jones	6.00	2.70

1998 E-X2001 Destination Cooperstown

		MINT	NRMT
COMPLETE SET (15)		1800.00	800.00
COMMON CARD (1-15)		20.00	9.00
UNLISTED STARS		40.00	18.00
STATED ODDS 1:720			
❏ 1	Alex Rodriguez	150.00	70.00
❏ 2	Frank Thomas	100.00	45.00
❏ 3	Cal Ripken	200.00	90.00
❏ 4	Roger Clemens	120.00	55.00
❏ 5	Greg Maddux	120.00	55.00
❏ 6	Chipper Jones	120.00	55.00
❏ 7	Ken Griffey Jr.	250.00	110.00
❏ 8	Mark McGwire	300.00	135.00
❏ 9	Tony Gwynn	120.00	55.00
❏ 10	Mike Piazza	150.00	70.00
❏ 11	Jeff Bagwell	60.00	27.00
❏ 12	Jose Cruz Jr.	20.00	9.00
❏ 13	Derek Jeter	150.00	70.00
❏ 14	Hideo Nomo	40.00	18.00
❏ 15	Ivan Rodriguez	60.00	27.00

1998 E-X2001 Signature 2001

	MINT	NRMT
COMPLETE SET (17)	400.00	180.00

	MINT	NRMT
COMMON CARD (1-17)	10.00	4.50
STATED ODDS 1:60		

		MINT	NRMT
❏ 1	Ricky Ledee	12.00	5.50
❏ 2	Derrick Gibson	15.00	6.75
❏ 3	Mark Kotsay	15.00	6.75
❏ 4	Kevin Millwood	40.00	18.00
❏ 5	Brad Fullmer	10.00	4.50
❏ 6	Todd Walker	15.00	6.75
❏ 7	Ben Grieve	20.00	9.00
❏ 8	Tony Clark	15.00	6.75
❏ 9	Jaret Wright	15.00	6.75
❏ 10	Randall Simon	15.00	6.75
❏ 11	Paul Konerko	15.00	6.75
❏ 12	Todd Helton	25.00	11.00
❏ 13	David Ortiz	10.00	4.50
❏ 14	Alex Gonzalez	12.00	5.50
❏ 15	Bobby Estalella	15.00	6.75
❏ 16	Alex Rodriguez SP	150.00	70.00
❏ 17	Mike Lowell	25.00	11.00

1998 E-X2001 Star Date 2001

		MINT	NRMT
COMPLETE SET (15)		15.00	6.75
COMMON CARD (1-15)		.50	.23
MINOR STARS		.75	.35
SEMISTARS		1.25	.55
UNLISTED STARS		2.00	.90
STATED ODDS 1:12			
❏ 1	Travis Lee	1.25	.55
❏ 2	Jose Cruz Jr.	.75	.35
❏ 3	Paul Konerko	.75	.35
❏ 4	Bobby Estalella	.75	.35
❏ 5	Maggio Ordonez	6.00	2.70
❏ 6	Juan Encarnacion	.75	.35
❏ 7	Richard Hidalgo	.75	.35
❏ 8	Abraham Nunez	.50	.23
❏ 9	Sean Casey	3.00	1.35
❏ 10	Todd Helton	2.50	1.10
❏ 11	Brad Fullmer	.50	.23
❏ 12	Ben Grieve	2.00	.90
❏ 13	Livan Hernandez	.50	.23
❏ 14	Jaret Wright	.75	.35
❏ 15	Todd Dunwoody	.50	.23

1999 E-X Century

	MINT	NRMT
COMPLETE SET (120)	100.00	45.00
COMP.SET w/o SP's (90)	50.00	22.00
COMMON CARD (1-90)	.40	.18
MINOR STARS 1-90	.60	.25
SEMISTARS 1-90	1.00	.45
UNLISTED STARS 1-90	1.50	.70
COMMON SP (91-120)	1.00	.45
SP MINOR STARS 91-120	1.50	.70
SEMISTARS 91-120	2.50	1.10
SP STATED ODDS 1:2		

		MINT	NRMT
❏ 1	Scott Rolen	2.00	.90
❏ 2	Nomar Garciaparra	5.00	2.20
❏ 3	Mike Piazza	5.00	2.20
❏ 4	Tony Gwynn	4.00	1.80
❏ 5	Sammy Sosa	5.00	2.20
❏ 6	Alex Rodriguez	5.00	2.20
❏ 7	Vladimir Guerrero	2.00	.90
❏ 8	Chipper Jones	4.00	1.80
❏ 9	Derek Jeter	5.00	2.20
❏ 10	Kerry Wood	1.50	.70
❏ 11	Juan Gonzalez	3.00	1.35
❏ 12	Frank Thomas	3.00	1.35
❏ 13	Mo Vaughn	1.50	.70
❏ 14	Greg Maddux	4.00	1.80
❏ 15	Jeff Bagwell	2.00	.90
❏ 16	Mark McGwire	10.00	4.50
❏ 17	Ken Griffey Jr.	8.00	3.60
❏ 18	Roger Clemens	4.00	1.80
❏ 19	Cal Ripken	6.00	2.70
❏ 20	Travis Lee	1.00	.45
❏ 21	Todd Helton	1.50	.70
❏ 22	Darin Erstad	1.00	.45
❏ 23	Pedro Martinez	2.00	.90
❏ 24	Barry Bonds	2.00	.90
❏ 25	Andruw Jones	1.50	.70
❏ 26	Larry Walker	1.50	.70
❏ 27	Albert Belle	1.50	.70
❏ 28	Ivan Rodriguez	2.00	.90
❏ 29	Magglio Ordonez	1.50	.70
❏ 30	Andres Galarraga	1.00	.45
❏ 31	Mike Mussina	1.50	.70
❏ 32	Randy Johnson	1.50	.70
❏ 33	Tom Glavine	1.50	.70
❏ 34	Barry Larkin	1.50	.70
❏ 35	Jim Thome	1.50	.70
❏ 36	Gary Sheffield	.60	.25
❏ 37	Bernie Williams	1.50	.70
❏ 38	Carlos Delgado	1.50	.70
❏ 39	Rafael Palmeiro	1.50	.70
❏ 40	Edgar Renteria	.40	.18
❏ 41	Brad Fullmer	.40	.18
❏ 42	David Wells	.60	.25
❏ 43	Dante Bichette	.60	.25
❏ 44	Jaret Wright	.60	.25
❏ 45	Ricky Ledee	.60	.25
❏ 46	Ray Lankford	.60	.25
❏ 47	Mark Grace	1.00	.45
❏ 48	Jeff Cirillo	.60	.25
❏ 49	Rondell White	.60	.25
❏ 50	Jeromy Burnitz	.60	.25
❏ 51	Sean Casey	1.50	.70
❏ 52	Rolando Arrojo	.40	.18
❏ 53	Jason Giambi	.60	.25
❏ 54	John Olerud	.60	.25

55	Will Clark	1.50	.70
56	Raul Mondesi	.60	.25
57	Scott Brosius	.60	.25
58	Bartolo Colon	.60	.25
59	Steve Finley	.60	.25
60	Javy Lopez	.60	.25
61	Tim Salmon	1.00	.45
62	Roberto Alomar	1.50	.70
63	Vinny Castilla	.60	.25
64	Craig Biggio	1.50	.70
65	Jose Guillen	.40	.18
66	Greg Vaughn	.60	.25
67	Jose Canseco	2.00	.90
68	Shawn Green	1.50	.70
69	Curt Schilling	1.00	.45
70	Orlando Hernandez	1.50	.70
71	Jose Cruz Jr.	.60	.25
72	Alex Gonzalez	.60	.25
73	Tino Martinez	.60	.25
74	Todd Hundley	.60	.25
75	Brian Giles	.60	.25
76	Cliff Floyd	.60	.25
77	Paul O'Neill	.60	.25
78	Ken Caminiti	.60	.25
79	Ron Gant	.60	.25
80	Juan Encarnacion	.60	.25
81	Ben Grieve	1.50	.70
82	Brian Jordan	.60	.25
83	Rickey Henderson	2.00	.90
84	Tony Clark	.60	.25
85	Shannon Stewart	.60	.25
86	Robin Ventura	.60	.25
87	Todd Walker	.60	.25
88	Kevin Brown	1.00	.45
89	Moises Alou	.60	.25
90	Manny Ramirez	2.00	.90
91	Gabe Alvarez SP	1.00	.45
92	Jeremy Giambi SP	1.50	.70
93	Adrian Beltre SP	4.00	1.80
94	George Lombard SP	1.50	.70
95	Ryan Minor SP	1.50	.70
96	Kevin Witt SP	1.00	.45
97	Scott Hunter SP	1.50	.70
98	Carlos Beltran SP	1.50	.70
99	Derrick Gibson SP	1.50	.70
100	Trot Nixon SP	1.50	.70
101	Troy Glaus SP	4.00	1.80
102	Armando Rios SP	1.00	.45
103	Preston Wilson SP	1.50	.70
104	Pat Burrell SP	12.00	5.50
105	J.D. Drew SP	6.00	2.70
106	Bruce Chen SP	1.50	.70
107	Matt Clement SP	1.50	.70
108	Carlos Beltran SP	5.00	2.20
109	Carlos Febles SP	1.50	.70
110	Rob Fick SP	1.50	.70
111	Russell Branyan SP	1.50	.70
112	Roosevelt Brown SP	2.50	1.10
113	Corey Koskie SP	1.00	.45
114	Mario Encarnacion SP	4.00	1.80
115	Peter Tucci SP	1.00	.45
116	Eric Chavez SP	2.50	1.10
117	Gabe Kapler SP	3.00	1.35
118	Marlon Anderson SP	1.00	.45
119	A.J. Burnett SP	3.00	1.35
120	Ryan Bradley SP	1.50	.70
P81	Ben Grieve Sample	2.00	.90

1999 E-X Century Essential Credentials Future

	MINT	NRMT
COMMON CARD (1-20)	20.00	9.00
UNLISTED STARS 1-20	30.00	13.50
COMMON CARD (21-50)	15.00	6.75
MINOR STARS 21-50	20.00	9.00
SEMISTARS 21-50	30.00	13.50
UNLISTED STARS 21-50	50.00	22.00
COMMON CARD (51-70)	20.00	9.00
MINOR STARS 51-70	25.00	11.00
SEMISTARS 51-70	40.00	18.00
UNLISTED STARS 51-70	60.00	27.00
COMMON CARD (71-85)	20.00	9.00

MINOR STARS 71-85	30.00	13.50
SEMISTARS 71-85	50.00	22.00
UNLISTED STARS 71-85	80.00	36.00
COMMON CARD (86-95)	25.00	11.00
MINOR STARS 86-95	40.00	18.00
SEMISTARS 86-95	60.00	27.00
COMMON CARD (96-105)	30.00	13.50
MINOR STARS 96-105	50.00	22.00

RANDOM INSERTS IN PACKS
PRINT RUNS IN PARENTHESES BELOW
FUTURE CARDS FEATURE GOLD FOIL FRONTS
106-120 NOT PRICED DUE TO SCARCITY

1	Scott Rolen (120)	50.00	22.00
2	Nomar Garciaparra (119)	120.00	55.00
3	Mike Piazza (118)	120.00	55.00
4	Tony Gwynn (117)	100.00	45.00
5	Sammy Sosa (116)	120.00	55.00
6	Alex Rodriguez (115)	120.00	55.00
7	Vladimir Guerrero (114)	50.00	22.00
8	Chipper Jones (113)	100.00	45.00
9	Derek Jeter (112)	120.00	55.00
10	Kerry Wood (111)	30.00	13.50
11	Juan Gonzalez (110)	80.00	36.00
12	Frank Thomas (109)	80.00	36.00
13	Mo Vaughn (108)	30.00	13.50
14	Greg Maddux (107)	100.00	45.00
15	Jeff Bagwell (106)	50.00	22.00
16	Mark McGwire (105)	250.00	110.00
17	Ken Griffey Jr. (104)	200.00	90.00
18	Roger Clemens (103)	50.00	22.00
19	Cal Ripken (102)	150.00	70.00
20	Travis Lee (101)	25.00	11.00
21	Todd Helton (100)	50.00	22.00
22	Darin Erstad (99)	50.00	22.00
23	Pedro Martinez (98)	60.00	27.00
24	Barry Bonds (97)	60.00	27.00
25	Andruw Jones (96)	50.00	22.00
26	Larry Walker (95)	50.00	22.00
27	Albert Belle (94)	50.00	22.00
28	Ivan Rodriguez (93)	60.00	27.00
29	Magglio Ordonez (92)	50.00	22.00
30	Andres Galarraga (91)	30.00	13.50
31	Mike Mussina (90)	50.00	22.00
32	Randy Johnson (89)	50.00	22.00
33	Tom Glavine (88)	50.00	22.00
34	Barry Larkin (87)	50.00	22.00
35	Jim Thome (86)	50.00	22.00
36	Gary Sheffield (85)	20.00	9.00
37	Bernie Williams (84)	50.00	22.00
38	Carlos Delgado (83)	50.00	22.00
39	Rafael Palmeiro (82)	50.00	22.00
40	Edgar Renteria (81)	15.00	6.75
41	Brad Fullmer (80)	15.00	6.75
42	David Wells (79)	20.00	9.00
43	Dante Bichette (78)	20.00	9.00
44	Jaret Wright (77)	20.00	9.00
45	Ricky Ledee (76)	20.00	9.00
46	Ray Lankford (75)	20.00	9.00
47	Mark Grace (74)	30.00	13.50
48	Jeff Cirillo (73)	20.00	9.00
49	Rondell White (72)	20.00	9.00
50	Jeromy Burnitz (71)	20.00	9.00
51	Sean Casey (70)	60.00	27.00
52	Rolando Arrojo (69)	20.00	9.00
53	Jason Giambi (68)	25.00	11.00
54	John Olerud (67)	25.00	11.00
55	Will Clark (66)	60.00	27.00
56	Raul Mondesi (65)	25.00	11.00
57	Scott Brosius (64)	25.00	11.00
58	Bartolo Colon (63)	25.00	11.00
59	Steve Finley (62)	25.00	11.00
60	Javy Lopez (61)	25.00	11.00
61	Tim Salmon (60)	40.00	18.00
62	Roberto Alomar (59)	50.00	22.00
63	Vinny Castilla (58)	25.00	11.00
64	Craig Biggio (57)	60.00	27.00
65	Jose Guillen (56)	20.00	9.00
66	Greg Vaughn (55)	25.00	11.00
67	Jose Canseco (54)	80.00	36.00
68	Shawn Green (53)	60.00	27.00
69	Curt Schilling (52)	25.00	11.00
70	Orlando Hernandez (51)	60.00	27.00
71	Jose Cruz Jr. (50)	30.00	13.50
72	Alex Gonzalez (49)	30.00	13.50
73	Tino Martinez (48)	30.00	13.50
74	Todd Hundley (47)	30.00	13.50
75	Brian Giles (46)	30.00	13.50
76	Cliff Floyd (45)	30.00	13.50
77	Paul O'Neill (44)	30.00	13.50
78	Ken Caminiti (43)	30.00	13.50
79	Ron Gant (42)	30.00	13.50
80	Juan Encarnacion (41)	30.00	13.50
81	Ben Grieve (40)	80.00	36.00
82	Brian Jordan (39)	30.00	13.50
83	Rickey Henderson (38)	100.00	45.00
84	Tony Clark (37)	30.00	13.50
85	Shannon Stewart (36)	30.00	13.50
86	Robin Ventura (35)	40.00	18.00
87	Todd Walker (34)	40.00	18.00
88	Kevin Brown (33)	60.00	27.00
89	Moises Alou (32)	40.00	18.00
90	Manny Ramirez (31)	120.00	55.00
91	Gabe Alvarez (30)	25.00	11.00
92	Jeremy Giambi (29)	30.00	13.50
93	Adrian Beltre (28)	100.00	45.00
94	George Lombard (27)	40.00	18.00
95	Ryan Minor (26)	40.00	18.00
96	Kevin Witt (25)	30.00	13.50
97	Scott Hunter (24)	50.00	22.50
98	Carlos Guillen (23)	30.00	13.50
99	Derrick Gibson (22)	50.00	22.00
100	Trot Nixon (21)	50.00	22.00
101	Troy Glaus (20)	150.00	70.00
102	Armando Rios (19)	30.00	13.50
103	Preston Wilson (18)	50.00	22.00
104	Pat Burrell (17)	400.00	180.00
105	J.D. Drew (16)	200.00	90.00
106	Bruce Chen (15)		
107	Matt Clement (14)		
108	Carlos Beltran (13)		
109	Carlos Febles (12)		
110	Rob Fick (11)		
111	Russell Branyan (10)		
112	Roosevelt Brown (9)		
113	Corey Koskie (8)		
114	Mario Encarnacion (7)		
115	Peter Tucci (6)		
116	Eric Chavez (5)		
117	Gabe Kapler (4)		
118	Marlon Anderson (3)		
119	A.J. Burnett (2)		
120	Ryan Bradley (1)		

1999 E-X Century Essential Credentials Now

	MINT	NRMT
COMMON CARD (16-20)	100.00	45.00
COMMON CARD (21-25)	80.00	36.00
COMMON CARD (26-35)	60.00	27.00
UNLISTED STARS 26-35	100.00	45.00
COMMON CARD (36-50)	20.00	9.00
MINOR STARS 36-50	30.00	13.50
SEMISTARS 36-50	50.00	22.00
UNLISTED STARS 36-50	80.00	36.00
COMMON CARD (51-70)	20.00	9.00
MINOR STARS 51-70	25.00	11.00
SEMISTARS 51-70	40.00	18.00
UNLISTED STARS 51-70	60.00	27.00

	MINT	NRMT
COMMON CARD (71-100)	15.00	6.75
MINOR STARS 71-100	20.00	9.00
SEMISTARS 71-100	30.00	13.50
UNLISTED STARS 71-100	50.00	22.00
COMMON CARD (101-120)	10.00	4.50
MINOR STARS 101-120	15.00	6.75
SEMISTARS 101-120	25.00	11.00
UNLISTED STARS 101-120	40.00	18.00

*ROOKIES 101-120: 3X TO 8X BASE CARD HI
RANDOM INSERTS IN PACKS
PRINT RUNS IN PARENTHESES BELOW
NOW CARDS FEATURE SILVER FOIL
FRONTS
1-15 NOT PRICED DUE TO SCARCITY

❑ 1 Scott Rolen (1)		
❑ 2 Nomar Garciaparra (2)		
❑ 3 Mike Piazza (3)		
❑ 4 Tony Gwynn (4)		
❑ 5 Sammy Sosa (5)		
❑ 6 Alex Rodriguez (6)		
❑ 7 Vladimir Guerrero (7)		
❑ 8 Chipper Jones (8)		
❑ 9 Derek Jeter (9)		
❑ 10 Kerry Wood (10)		
❑ 11 Juan Gonzalez (11)		
❑ 12 Frank Thomas (12)		
❑ 13 Mo Vaughn (13)		
❑ 14 Greg Maddux (14)		
❑ 15 Jeff Bagwell (15)		
❑ 16 Mark McGwire (16)	1000.00	450.00
❑ 17 Ken Griffey Jr. (17)	800.00	350.00
❑ 18 Roger Clemens (18)	400.00	180.00
❑ 19 Cal Ripken (19)	600.00	275.00
❑ 20 Travis Lee (20)	100.00	45.00
❑ 21 Todd Helton (21)	150.00	70.00
❑ 22 Darin Erstad (22)	100.00	45.00
❑ 23 Pedro Martinez (23)	150.00	70.00
❑ 24 Barry Bonds (24)	150.00	70.00
❑ 25 Andruw Jones (25)	150.00	70.00
❑ 26 Larry Walker (26)	150.00	70.00
❑ 27 Albert Belle (27)	100.00	45.00
❑ 28 Jose Rodriguez (28)	120.00	55.00
❑ 29 Magglio Ordonez (29)	150.00	70.00
❑ 30 Andres Galarraga (30)	100.00	45.00
❑ 31 Mike Mussina (31)	150.00	70.00
❑ 32 Randy Johnson (32)	150.00	70.00
❑ 33 Tom Glavine (33)	150.00	70.00
❑ 34 Barry Larkin (34)	150.00	70.00
❑ 35 Jim Thome (35)	150.00	70.00
❑ 36 Gary Sheffield (36)	100.00	45.00
❑ 37 Bernie Williams (37)	150.00	70.00
❑ 38 Carlos Delgado (38)	100.00	45.00
❑ 39 Rafael Palmeiro (39)	150.00	70.00
❑ 40 Edgar Renteria (40)	100.00	45.00
❑ 41 Brad Fullmer (41)	100.00	45.00
❑ 42 David Wells (42)	100.00	45.00
❑ 43 Dante Bichette (43)	100.00	45.00
❑ 44 Jaret Wright (44)	100.00	45.00
❑ 45 Ricky Ledee (45)	100.00	45.00
❑ 46 Ray Lankford (46)	100.00	45.00
❑ 47 Mark Grace (47)	100.00	45.00
❑ 48 Jeff Cirillo (48)	100.00	45.00
❑ 49 Rondell White (49)	100.00	45.00
❑ 50 Jeromy Burnitz (50)	100.00	45.00
❑ 51 Sean Casey (51)	150.00	70.00
❑ 52 Rolando Arrojo (52)	100.00	45.00
❑ 53 Jason Giambi (53)	100.00	45.00
❑ 54 John Olerud (54)	100.00	45.00
❑ 55 Will Clark (55)	150.00	70.00
❑ 56 Raul Mondesi (56)	100.00	45.00
❑ 57 Scott Brosius (57)	100.00	45.00
❑ 58 Bartolo Colon (58)	100.00	45.00
❑ 59 Steve Finley (59)	100.00	45.00
❑ 60 Javy Lopez (60)	100.00	45.00
❑ 61 Tim Salmon (61)	100.00	45.00
❑ 62 Roberto Alomar (62)	150.00	70.00
❑ 63 Vinny Castilla (63)	100.00	45.00
❑ 64 Craig Biggio (64)	150.00	70.00
❑ 65 Jose Guillen (65)	100.00	45.00
❑ 66 Greg Vaughn (66)	100.00	45.00
❑ 67 Jose Canseco (67)	80.00	36.00
❑ 68 Shawn Green (68)	150.00	70.00
❑ 69 Curt Schilling (69)	100.00	45.00
❑ 70 Orlando Hernandez (70)	150.00	70.00
❑ 71 Jose Cruz Jr. (71)	100.00	45.00
❑ 72 Alex Gonzalez (72)	100.00	45.00
❑ 73 Tino Martinez (73)	100.00	45.00
❑ 74 Todd Hundley (74)	100.00	45.00
❑ 75 Brian Giles (75)	100.00	45.00
❑ 76 Cliff Floyd (76)	100.00	45.00
❑ 77 Paul O'Neill (77)	100.00	45.00
❑ 78 Ken Caminiti (78)	100.00	45.00
❑ 79 Ron Gant (79)	100.00	45.00
❑ 80 Juan Encarnacion (80)	100.00	45.00
❑ 81 Ben Grieve (81)	150.00	70.00
❑ 82 Brian Jordan (82)	100.00	45.00
❑ 83 Rickey Henderson (83)	60.00	27.00
❑ 84 Tony Clark (84)	100.00	45.00
❑ 85 Shannon Stewart (85)	100.00	45.00
❑ 86 Robin Ventura (86)	100.00	45.00
❑ 87 Todd Walker (87)	100.00	45.00
❑ 88 Kevin Brown (88)	100.00	45.00
❑ 89 Moises Alou (89)	100.00	45.00
❑ 90 Manny Ramirez (90)	60.00	27.00
❑ 91 Gabe Alvarez (91)	100.00	45.00
❑ 92 Jeremy Giambi (92)	100.00	45.00
❑ 93 Adrian Beltre (93)	150.00	70.00
❑ 94 George Lombard (94)	100.00	45.00
❑ 95 Ryan Minor (95)	100.00	45.00
❑ 96 Kevin Witt (96)	100.00	45.00
❑ 97 Scott Hunter (97)	100.00	45.00
❑ 98 Carlos Guillen (98)	100.00	45.00
❑ 99 Derrick Gibson (99)	100.00	45.00
❑ 100 Trot Nixon (100)	100.00	45.00
❑ 101 Troy Glaus (101)	150.00	70.00
❑ 102 Armando Rios (102)	100.00	45.00
❑ 103 Preston Wilson (103)	100.00	45.00
❑ 104 Pat Burrell (104)	120.00	55.00
❑ 105 J.D. Drew (105)	50.00	22.00
❑ 106 Bruce Chen (106)	100.00	45.00
❑ 107 Matt Clement (107)	100.00	45.00
❑ 108 Carlos Beltran (108)	150.00	70.00
❑ 109 Carlos Febles (109)	100.00	45.00
❑ 110 Rob Fick (110)	100.00	45.00
❑ 111 Russell Branyan (111)	100.00	45.00
❑ 112 Roosevelt Brown (112)	150.00	70.00
❑ 113 Corey Koskie (113)	100.00	45.00
❑ 114 Mario Encarnacion (114)	150.00	70.00
❑ 115 Peter Tucci (115)	100.00	45.00
❑ 116 Eric Chavez (116)	100.00	45.00
❑ 117 Gabe Kapler (117)	150.00	70.00
❑ 118 Marlon Anderson (118)	100.00	45.00
❑ 119 A.J. Burnett (119)	150.00	70.00
❑ 120 Ryan Bradley (120)	100.00	45.00

1999 E-X Century Authen-Kicks

	MINT	NRMT
COMPLETE SET (9)	600.00	275.00
COMMON CARD (1-9)	40.00	18.00

RANDOM INSERTS IN PACKS
PRINT RUNS LISTED BELOW
COMP.SET EXCLUDES B1 AND R1

❑ 1 J.D. Drew/180	150.00	70.00
❑ 2 Travis Lee/175	40.00	18.00
❑ 3 Kevin Millwood/165	60.00	27.00
❑ 4 Bruce Chen/205	40.00	18.00
❑ 5 Troy Glaus/205	60.00	27.00
❑ 6 Todd Helton/205	80.00	36.00
❑ 7 Ricky Ledee/180	40.00	18.00

❑ 8 Scott Rolen/205	120.00	55.00
❑ 9 Jeremy Giambi/205	40.00	18.00
❑ B1 J.D. Drew Black AU/8		
❑ R1 J.D. Drew Red AU/8		

1999 E-X Century E-X Quisite

	MINT	NRMT
COMPLETE SET (15)	50.00	22.00
COMMON CARD (1-15)	2.00	.90
SEMISTARS	3.00	1.35
UNLISTED STARS	5.00	2.20

STATED ODDS 1:18

❑ 1 Troy Glaus	5.00	2.20
❑ 2 J.D. Drew	8.00	3.60
❑ 3 Pat Burrell	15.00	6.75
❑ 4 Russell Branyan	2.00	.90
❑ 5 Kerry Wood	5.00	2.20
❑ 6 Eric Chavez	3.00	1.35
❑ 7 Ben Grieve	5.00	2.20
❑ 8 Gabe Kapler	5.00	2.20
❑ 9 Adrian Beltre	5.00	2.20
❑ 10 Todd Helton	5.00	2.20
❑ 11 Roosevelt Brown	5.00	2.20
❑ 12 Marlon Anderson	2.00	.90
❑ 13 Jeremy Giambi	2.00	.90
❑ 14 Magglio Ordonez	5.00	2.20
❑ 15 Travis Lee	3.00	1.35

1999 E-X Century Favorites for Fenway '99

	MINT	NRMT
COMPLETE SET (20)	400.00	180.00
COMMON CARD (1-20)	5.00	2.20
UNLISTED STARS	8.00	3.60

STATED ODDS 1:36

❑ 1 Mo Vaughn	8.00	3.60
❑ 2 Nomar Garciaparra	25.00	11.00
❑ 3 Frank Thomas	15.00	6.75
❑ 4 Ken Griffey Jr.	40.00	18.00
❑ 5 Roger Clemens	20.00	9.00
❑ 6 Alex Rodriguez	25.00	11.00
❑ 7 Derek Jeter	25.00	11.00
❑ 8 Juan Gonzalez	15.00	6.75

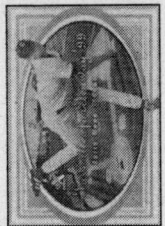

		MINT	NRMT
❑ 9	Cal Ripken	30.00	13.50
❑ 10	Ivan Rodriguez	10.00	4.50
❑ 11	J.D. Drew	10.00	4.50
❑ 12	Barry Bonds	10.00	4.50
❑ 13	Tony Gwynn	20.00	9.00
❑ 14	Vladimir Guerrero	10.00	4.50
❑ 15	Chipper Jones	20.00	9.00
❑ 16	Kerry Wood	5.00	2.20
❑ 17	Mike Piazza	25.00	11.00
❑ 18	Sammy Sosa	25.00	11.00
❑ 19	Scott Rolen	10.00	4.50
❑ 20	Mark McGwire	50.00	22.00

1999 E-X Century Milestones of the Century

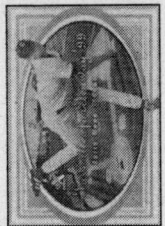

	MINT	NRMT
COMPLETE SET (10)	1500.00	700.00
COMMON CARD (1-10)	15.00	6.75

RANDOM INSERTS IN PACKS
PRINT RUNS LISTED BELOW

❑ 1	Kerry Wood/20	100.00	45.00
❑ 2	Mark McGwire/70	300.00	135.00
❑ 3	Sammy Sosa/66	150.00	70.00
❑ 4	Ken Griffey Jr./350	80.00	36.00
❑ 5	Roger Clemens/98	100.00	45.00
❑ 6	Cal Ripken/17	500.00	220.00
❑ 7	Alex Rodriguez/40	200.00	90.00
❑ 8	Barry Bonds/400	20.00	9.00
❑ 9	N.Y. Yankees/114	120.00	55.00
❑ 10	Travis Lee/98	15.00	6.75

1993 Finest

	MINT	NRMT
COMPLETE SET (199)	200.00	90.00
COMMON CARD (1-199)	1.00	.45
MINOR STARS	1.50	.70
SEMISTARS	3.00	1.35
UNLISTED STARS	5.00	2.20

❑ 1	David Justice	5.00	2.20
❑ 2	Lou Whitaker	1.50	.70
❑ 3	Bryan Harvey	1.00	.45
❑ 4	Carlos Garcia	1.00	.45
❑ 5	Sid Fernandez	1.00	.45
❑ 6	Brett Butler	1.50	.70
❑ 7	Scott Cooper	1.00	.45

❑ 8	B.J. Surhoff	1.50	.70
❑ 9	Steve Finley	1.50	.70
❑ 10	Curt Schilling	1.50	.70
❑ 11	Jeff Bagwell	6.00	2.70
❑ 12	Alex Cole	1.00	.45
❑ 13	John Olerud	3.00	1.35
❑ 14	John Smiley	1.00	.45
❑ 15	Bip Roberts	1.00	.45
❑ 16	Albert Belle	5.00	2.20
❑ 17	Duane Ward	1.00	.45
❑ 18	Alan Trammell	3.00	1.35
❑ 19	Andy Benes	1.50	.70
❑ 20	Reggie Sanders	1.50	.70
❑ 21	Todd Zeile	1.00	.45
❑ 22	Rick Aguilera	1.00	.45
❑ 23	Dave Hollins	1.00	.45
❑ 24	Jose Rijo	1.00	.45
❑ 25	Matt Williams	3.00	1.35
❑ 26	Sandy Alomar Jr.	1.50	.70
❑ 27	Alex Fernandez	1.50	.70
❑ 28	Ozzie Smith	6.00	2.70
❑ 29	Ramon Martinez	1.50	.70
❑ 30	Bernie Williams	5.00	2.20
❑ 31	Gary Sheffield	5.00	2.20
❑ 32	Eric Karros	3.00	1.35
❑ 33	Frank Viola	1.00	.45
❑ 34	Kevin Young	1.50	.70
❑ 35	Ken Hill	1.50	.70
❑ 36	Tony Fernandez	1.50	.70
❑ 37	Tim Wakefield	1.50	.70
❑ 38	John Kruk	1.50	.70
❑ 39	Chris Sabo	1.00	.45
❑ 40	Marquis Grissom	1.50	.70
❑ 41	Glenn Davis	1.00	.45
❑ 42	Jeff Montgomery	1.00	.45
❑ 43	Kenny Lofton	5.00	2.20
❑ 44	John Burkett	1.00	.45
❑ 45	Darryl Hamilton	1.00	.45
❑ 46	Jim Abbott	1.50	.70
❑ 47	Ivan Rodriguez	6.00	2.70
❑ 48	Eric Young	5.00	2.20
❑ 49	Mitch Williams	1.00	.45
❑ 50	Harold Reynolds	1.00	.45
❑ 51	Brian Harper	1.00	.45
❑ 52	Rafael Palmeiro	5.00	2.20
❑ 53	Bret Saberhagen	1.50	.70
❑ 54	Jeff Conine	1.50	.70
❑ 55	Ivan Calderon	1.00	.45
❑ 56	Juan Guzman	1.00	.45
❑ 57	Carlos Baerga	1.00	.45
❑ 58	Charles Nagy	1.50	.70
❑ 59	Wally Joyner	1.00	.45
❑ 60	Charlie Hayes	1.00	.45
❑ 61	Shane Mack	1.00	.45
❑ 62	Pete Harnisch	1.00	.45
❑ 63	George Brett	10.00	4.50
❑ 64	Lance Johnson	1.00	.45
❑ 65	Ben McDonald	1.00	.45
❑ 66	Bobby Bonilla	1.50	.70
❑ 67	Terry Steinbach	1.00	.45
❑ 68	Ron Gant	1.50	.70
❑ 69	Doug Jones	1.00	.45
❑ 70	Paul Molitor	5.00	2.20
❑ 71	Brady Anderson	1.50	.70
❑ 72	Chuck Finley	1.50	.70
❑ 73	Mark Grace	3.00	1.35
❑ 74	Mike Devereaux	1.00	.45
❑ 75	Tony Phillips	1.00	.45
❑ 76	Chuck Knoblauch	5.00	2.20

❑ 77	Tony Gwynn	12.00	5.50
❑ 78	Kevin Appier	1.50	.70
❑ 79	Sammy Sosa	15.00	6.75
❑ 80	Mickey Tettleton	1.00	.45
❑ 81	Felix Jose	1.00	.45
❑ 82	Mark Langston	1.00	.45
❑ 83	Gregg Jefferies	1.00	.45
❑ 84	Andre Dawson AS	3.00	1.35
❑ 85	Greg Maddux AS	12.00	5.50
❑ 86	Rickey Henderson AS	6.00	2.70
❑ 87	Tom Glavine AS	3.00	1.35
❑ 88	Roberto Alomar AS	5.00	2.20
❑ 89	Darryl Strawberry AS	1.50	.70
❑ 90	Wade Boggs AS	5.00	2.20
❑ 91	Bo Jackson AS	1.50	.70
❑ 92	Mark McGwire AS	25.00	11.00
❑ 93	Robin Ventura AS	1.50	.70
❑ 94	Joe Carter AS	1.50	.70
❑ 95	Lee Smith AS	1.50	.70
❑ 96	Cal Ripken AS	20.00	9.00
❑ 97	Larry Walker AS	5.00	2.20
❑ 98	Don Mattingly AS	10.00	4.50
❑ 99	Jose Canseco AS	6.00	2.70
❑ 100	Dennis Eckersley AS	1.00	.45
❑ 101	Terry Pendleton AS	1.00	.45
❑ 102	Frank Thomas AS	10.00	4.50
❑ 103	Barry Bonds AS	6.00	2.70
❑ 104	Roger Clemens AS	12.00	5.50
❑ 105	Ryne Sandberg AS	6.00	2.70
❑ 106	Fred McGriff AS	3.00	1.35
❑ 107	Nolan Ryan AS	20.00	9.00
❑ 108	Will Clark AS	5.00	2.20
❑ 109	Pat Listach AS	1.00	.45
❑ 110	Ken Griffey Jr. AS	25.00	11.00
❑ 111	Cecil Fielder AS	1.50	.70
❑ 112	Kirby Puckett AS	8.00	3.60
❑ 113	Dwight Gooden AS	1.50	.70
❑ 114	Barry Larkin AS	5.00	2.20
❑ 115	David Cone AS	3.00	1.35
❑ 116	Juan Gonzalez AS	10.00	4.50
❑ 117	Kent Hrbek AS	1.50	.70
❑ 118	Tim Wallach	1.00	.45
❑ 119	Craig Biggio	5.00	2.20
❑ 120	Roberto Kelly	1.00	.45
❑ 121	Gregg Olson	1.00	.45
❑ 122	Eddie Murray UER	5.00	2.20
	122 career strikeouts should be 1224		
❑ 123	Wil Cordero	1.00	.45
❑ 124	Jay Buhner	3.00	1.35
❑ 125	Carlton Fisk	5.00	2.20
❑ 126	Eric Davis	1.50	.70
❑ 127	Doug Drabek	1.00	.45
❑ 128	Ozzie Guillen	1.00	.45
❑ 129	John Wetteland	1.50	.70
❑ 130	Andres Galarraga	5.00	2.20
❑ 131	Ken Caminiti	3.00	1.35
❑ 132	Tom Candiotti	1.00	.45
❑ 133	Pat Borders	1.00	.45
❑ 134	Kevin Brown	3.00	1.35
❑ 135	Travis Fryman	1.50	.70
❑ 136	Kevin Mitchell	1.50	.70
❑ 137	Greg Swindell	1.00	.45
❑ 138	Benito Santiago	1.00	.45
❑ 139	Reggie Jefferson	1.00	.45
❑ 140	Chris Bosio	1.00	.45
❑ 141	Deion Sanders	3.00	1.35
❑ 142	Scott Erickson	1.00	.45
❑ 143	Howard Johnson	1.00	.45
❑ 144	Orestes Destrade	1.00	.45
❑ 145	Jose Guzman	1.00	.45
❑ 146	Chad Curtis	1.50	.70
❑ 147	Cal Eldred	1.00	.45
❑ 148	Willie Greene	1.00	.45
❑ 149	Tommy Greene	1.00	.45
❑ 150	Erik Hanson	1.00	.45
❑ 151	Bob Welch	1.00	.45
❑ 152	John Jaha	1.00	.45
❑ 153	Harold Baines	1.50	.70
❑ 154	Randy Johnson	5.00	2.20
❑ 155	Al Martin	1.00	.45
❑ 156	J.T. Snow	6.00	2.70
❑ 157	Mike Mussina	5.00	2.20
❑ 158	Ruben Sierra	1.00	.45
❑ 159	Dean Palmer	1.50	.70
❑ 160	Steve Avery	1.00	.45

		MINT	NRMT
❏ 161	Julio Franco	1.00	.45
❏ 162	Dave Winfield	3.00	1.35
❏ 163	Tim Salmon	5.00	2.20
❏ 164	Tom Henke	1.00	.45
❏ 165	Mo Vaughn	5.00	2.20
❏ 166	John Smoltz	3.00	1.35
❏ 167	Danny Tartabull	1.00	.45
❏ 168	Delino DeShields	1.50	.70
❏ 169	Charlie Hough	1.50	.70
❏ 170	Paul O'Neil	1.50	.70
❏ 171	Darren Daulton	1.50	.70
❏ 172	Jack McDowell	1.00	.45
❏ 173	Junior Felix	1.00	.45
❏ 174	Jimmy Key	1.50	.70
❏ 175	George Bell	1.00	.45
❏ 176	Mike Stanton	1.00	.45
❏ 177	Len Dykstra	1.50	.70
❏ 178	Norm Charlton	1.00	.45
❏ 179	Eric Anthony	1.00	.45
❏ 180	Rob Dibble	1.00	.45
❏ 181	Otis Nixon	1.00	.45
❏ 182	Randy Myers	1.50	.70
❏ 183	Tim Raines	1.50	.70
❏ 184	Orel Hershiser	1.50	.70
❏ 185	Andy Van Slyke	1.50	.70
❏ 186	Mike Lansing	1.50	.70
❏ 187	Ray Lankford	3.00	1.35
❏ 188	Mike Morgan	1.00	.45
❏ 189	Moises Alou	1.50	.70
❏ 190	Edgar Martinez	3.00	1.35
❏ 191	John Franco	1.50	.70
❏ 192	Robin Yount	3.00	1.35
❏ 193	Bob Tewksbury	1.00	.45
❏ 194	Jay Bell	1.50	.70
❏ 195	Luis Gonzalez	1.50	.70
❏ 196	Dave Fleming	1.00	.45
❏ 197	Mike Greenwell	1.00	.45
❏ 198	David Nied	1.00	.45
❏ 199	Mike Piazza	25.00	11.00

1993 Finest Refractors

	MINT	NRMT
COMPLETE SET (199)	12000.00	5400.00
COMMON CARD (1-199)	25.00	11.00
MINOR STARS	40.00	18.00
SEMISTARS	60.00	27.00
UNLISTED STARS	100.00	45.00
STATED ODDS 1:18		
ASTERISK CARDS: PERCEIVED SCARCITY		

1993 Finest Jumbos

	MINT	NRMT
COMPLETE SET (33)	500.00	220.00
*STARS: 1X TO 2.5X BASE CARD HI		
ONE CARD PER SEALED BOX		

1994 Finest Pre-Production

		MINT	NRMT
COMPLETE SET (40)		120.00	55.00
COMMON CARD		2.00	.90
NUMBERS CORRESPOND TO BASIC SET			
TOPPS SER.2 ODDS 1:36H/R,1:15J,1:28 CEL			
THREE PER REGULAR TOPPS FACTORY			
SET			

		MINT	NRMT
❏ 22P	Deion Sanders	4.00	1.80
❏ 23P	Jose Offerman	2.00	.90
❏ 26P	Alex Fernandez	2.00	.90
❏ 31P	Steve Finley	4.00	1.80
❏ 35P	Andres Galarraga	15.00	6.75
❏ 43P	Reggie Sanders	4.00	1.80
❏ 47P	Dave Hollins	2.00	.90
❏ 52P	David Cone	8.00	3.60
❏ 59P	Dante Bichette	4.00	1.80
❏ 61P	Orlando Merced	2.00	.90
❏ 62P	Brian McRae	2.00	.90
❏ 66P	Mike Mussina	15.00	6.75
❏ 76P	Mike Stanley	2.00	.90
❏ 78P	Mark McGwire	60.00	27.00
❏ 79P	Pat Listach	2.00	.90
❏ 82P	Dwight Gooden	4.00	1.80
❏ 84P	Phil Plantier	2.00	.90
❏ 90P	Jeff Russell	2.00	.90
❏ 92P	Gregg Jefferies	2.00	.90
❏ 93P	Jose Guzman	2.00	.90
❏ 100P	John Smoltz	8.00	3.60
❏ 102P	Jim Thome	15.00	6.75
❏ 121P	Moises Alou	4.00	1.80
❏ 125P	Devon White	2.00	.90
❏ 126P	Ivan Rodriguez	15.00	6.75
❏ 130P	Dave Magadan	2.00	.90
❏ 136P	Ozzie Smith	15.00	6.75
❏ 141P	Chris Hoiles	2.00	.90
❏ 149P	Jim Abbott	4.00	1.80
❏ 151P	Bill Swift	2.00	.90
❏ 154P	Edgar Martinez	4.00	1.80
❏ 157P	J.T. Snow	4.00	1.80
❏ 159P	Alan Trammell	8.00	3.60
❏ 163P	Roberto Kelly	2.00	.90
❏ 166P	Scott Erickson	4.00	1.80
❏ 168P	Scott Cooper	2.00	.90
❏ 169P	Rod Beck	2.00	.90
❏ 177P	Dean Palmer	4.00	1.80
❏ 182P	Todd Van Poppel	2.00	.90
❏ 185P	Paul Sorrento	2.00	.90

1994 Finest

	MINT	NRMT
COMPLETE SET (440)	150.00	70.00
COMPLETE SERIES 1 (220)	80.00	36.00
COMPLETE SERIES 2 (220)	80.00	36.00
COMMON CARD (1-440)	.50	.23
MINOR STARS	1.00	.45
SEMISTARS	1.50	.70
UNLISTED STARS	2.50	1.10
COMMON REF. (1-440)	4.00	1.80

		MINT	NRMT
*REF.STARS: 4X TO 8X HI COLUMN			
*REF.ROOKIES: 2X TO 4X HI			
REFRACTOR STATED ODDS 1:9			
COMP.JUMBO SET (80)		350.00	160.00
COMP.JUMBO.SER.1 (40)		200.00	90.00
COMP.JUMBO.SER.2 (40)		150.00	70.00
COMMON 1 (1-20/201-220)		1.00	.45
COMMON 2 (221-240/421-440)		1.00	.45
*JUMBO STARS: 1.5X TO 3X HI COLUMN			
ONE JUMBO PER BOX			

		MINT	NRMT
❏ 1	Mike Piazza FIN	8.00	3.60
❏ 2	Kevin Stocker FIN	.50	.23
❏ 3	Greg McMichael FIN	.50	.23
❏ 4	Jeff Conine FIN	.50	.23
❏ 5	Rene Arocha FIN	.50	.23
❏ 6	Aaron Sele FIN	1.00	.45
❏ 7	Brent Gates FIN	.50	.23
❏ 8	Chuck Carr FIN	.50	.23
❏ 9	Kirk Rueter FIN	.50	.23
❏ 10	Mike Lansing FIN	1.00	.45
❏ 11	Al Martin FIN	.50	.23
❏ 12	Jason Bere FIN	.50	.23
❏ 13	Troy Neel FIN	.50	.23
❏ 14	Armando Reynoso FIN	.50	.23
❏ 15	Jeromy Burnitz FIN	1.00	.45
❏ 16	Rich Amaral FIN	.50	.23
❏ 17	David McCarty FIN	.50	.23
❏ 18	Tim Salmon FIN	2.50	1.10
❏ 19	Steve Cooke FIN	.50	.23
❏ 20	Wil Cordero FIN	.50	.23
❏ 21	Kevin Tapani FIN	.50	.23
❏ 22	Deion Sanders FIN	1.00	.45
❏ 23	Jose Offerman FIN	1.00	.45
❏ 24	Mark Langston FIN	.50	.23
❏ 25	Ken Hill FIN	.50	.23
❏ 26	Alex Fernandez FIN	.50	.23
❏ 27	Jeff Blauser FIN	.50	.23
❏ 28	Royce Clayton FIN	.50	.23
❏ 29	Brad Ausmus FIN	.50	.23
❏ 30	Ryan Bowen FIN	.50	.23
❏ 31	Steve Finley FIN	1.00	.45
❏ 32	Charlie Hayes FIN	.50	.23
❏ 33	Jeff Kent FIN	1.00	.45
❏ 34	Mike Henneman FIN	.50	.23
❏ 35	Andres Galarraga FIN	2.50	1.10
❏ 36	Wayne Kirby FIN	.50	.23
❏ 37	Joe Oliver FIN	.50	.23
❏ 38	Terry Steinbach FIN	.50	.23
❏ 39	Ryan Thompson FIN	.50	.23
❏ 40	Luis Alicea FIN	.50	.23
❏ 41	Randy Velarde FIN	.50	.23
❏ 42	Bob Tewksbury FIN	.50	.23
❏ 43	Reggie Sanders FIN	1.00	.45
❏ 44	Brian Williams FIN	.50	.23
❏ 45	Joe Orsulak FIN	.50	.23
❏ 46	Jose Lind FIN	.50	.23
❏ 47	Dave Hollins FIN	.50	.23
❏ 48	Graeme Lloyd FIN	.50	.23
❏ 49	Jim Gott FIN	.50	.23
❏ 50	Andre Dawson FIN	1.50	.70
❏ 51	Steve Buechele FIN	.50	.23
❏ 52	David Cone FIN	1.50	.70
❏ 53	Ricky Gutierrez FIN	.50	.23
❏ 54	Lance Johnson FIN	.50	.23
❏ 55	Tino Martinez FIN	2.50	1.10
❏ 56	Phil Hiatt FIN	.50	.23
❏ 57	Carlos Garcia FIN	.50	.23

58	Danny Darwin	.50	.23
59	Dante Bichette	1.00	.45
60	Scott Kamieniecki	.50	.23
61	Orlando Merced	.50	.23
62	Brian McRae	.50	.23
63	Pat Kelly	.50	.23
64	Tom Henke	.50	.23
65	Jeff King	.50	.23
66	Mike Mussina	2.50	1.10
67	Tim Pugh	.50	.23
68	Robby Thompson	.50	.23
69	Paul O'Neill	1.00	.45
70	Hal Morris	.50	.23
71	Ron Karkovice	.50	.23
72	Joe Girardi	.50	.23
73	Eduardo Perez	.50	.23
74	Raul Mondesi	2.50	1.10
75	Mike Gallego	.50	.23
76	Mike Stanley	.50	.23
77	Kevin Roberson	.50	.23
78	Mark McGwire	12.00	5.50
79	Pat Listach	.50	.23
80	Eric Davis	1.00	.45
81	Mike Bordick	.50	.23
82	Dwight Gooden	1.00	.45
83	Mike Moore	.50	.23
84	Phil Plantier	.50	.23
85	Darren Lewis	.50	.23
86	Rick Wilkins	.50	.23
87	Darryl Strawberry	1.00	.45
88	Rob Dibble	.50	.23
89	Greg Vaughn	.50	.23
90	Jeff Russell	.50	.23
91	Mark Lewis	.50	.23
92	Gregg Jefferies	.50	.23
93	Jose Guzman	.50	.23
94	Kenny Rogers	.50	.23
95	Mark Lemke	.50	.23
96	Mike Morgan	.50	.23
97	Andujar Cedeno	.50	.23
98	Orel Hershiser	1.00	.45
99	Greg Swindell	.50	.23
100	John Smoltz	1.50	.70
101	Pedro Martinez	.50	.23
102	Jim Thome	2.50	1.10
103	David Segui	1.00	.45
104	Charles Nagy	1.00	.45
105	Shane Mack	.50	.23
106	John Jaha	.50	.23
107	Tom Candiotti	.50	.23
108	David Wells	1.50	.70
109	Bobby Jones	.50	.23
110	Bob Hamelin	.50	.23
111	Bernard Gilkey	.50	.23
112	Chili Davis	1.00	.45
113	Todd Stottlemyre	.50	.23
114	Derek Bell	1.00	.45
115	Mark McLemore	.50	.23
116	Mark Whiten	.50	.23
117	Mike Devereaux	.50	.23
118	Terry Pendleton	.50	.23
119	Pat Meares	.50	.23
120	Pete Harnisch	.50	.23
121	Moises Alou	1.00	.45
122	Jay Buhner	1.00	.45
123	Wes Chamberlain	.50	.23
124	Mike Perez	.50	.23
125	Devon White	.50	.23
126	Ivan Rodriguez	3.00	1.35
127	Don Slaught	.50	.23
128	John Valentin	1.00	.45
129	Jaime Navarro	.50	.23
130	Dave Magadan	.50	.23
131	Brady Anderson	1.00	.45
132	Juan Guzman	.50	.23
133	John Wetteland	1.00	.45
134	Dave Stewart	1.00	.45
135	Scott Servais	.50	.23
136	Ozzie Smith	3.00	1.35
137	Darrin Fletcher	.50	.23
138	Jose Mesa	.50	.23
139	Wilson Alvarez	1.00	.45
140	Pete Incaviglia	.50	.23
141	Chris Hoiles	.50	.23
142	Darryl Hamilton	.50	.23
143	Chuck Finley	1.00	.45
144	Archi Cianfrocco	.50	.23
145	Bill Wegman	.50	.23
146	Joey Cora	.50	.23
147	Darrell Whitmore	.50	.23
148	David Hulse	.50	.23
149	Jim Abbott	1.00	.45
150	Curt Schilling	1.00	.45
151	Bill Swift	.50	.23
152	Tommy Greene	.50	.23
153	Roberto Mejia	.50	.23
154	Edgar Martinez	1.00	.45
155	Roger Pavlik	.50	.23
156	Randy Tomlin	.50	.23
157	J.T. Snow	1.00	.45
158	Bob Welch	.50	.23
159	Alan Trammell	1.50	.70
160	Ed Sprague	.50	.23
161	Ben McDonald	.50	.23
162	Derrick May	.50	.23
163	Roberto Kelly	.50	.23
164	Bryan Harvey	.50	.23
165	Ron Gant	1.00	.45
166	Scott Erickson	1.00	.45
167	Anthony Young	.50	.23
168	Scott Cooper	.50	.23
169	Rod Beck	.50	.23
170	John Franco	1.00	.45
171	Gary DiSarcina	.50	.23
172	Dave Fleming	.50	.23
173	Wade Boggs	2.50	1.10
174	Kevin Appier	1.00	.45
175	Jose Bautista	.50	.23
176	Wally Joyner	1.00	.45
177	Dean Palmer	1.00	.45
178	Tony Phillips	.50	.23
179	John Smiley	.50	.23
180	Charlie Hough	.50	.23
181	Scott Fletcher	.50	.23
182	Todd Van Poppel	.50	.23
183	Mike Blowers	.50	.23
184	Willie McGee	1.00	.45
185	Paul Sorrento	.50	.23
186	Eric Young	.50	.23
187	Bret Barberie	.50	.23
188	Manuel Lee	.50	.23
189	Jeff Branson	.50	.23
190	Jim Deshaies	.50	.23
191	Ken Caminiti	1.50	.70
192	Tim Raines	1.00	.45
193	Joe Grahe	.50	.23
194	Hipolito Pichardo	.50	.23
195	Denny Neagle	.50	.23
196	Jeff Gardner	.50	.23
197	Mike Benjamin	.50	.23
198	Milt Thompson	.50	.23
199	Bruce Ruffin	.50	.23
200	Chris Hammond UER	.50	.23
	(Back of card has Mariners; should be Marlins)		
201	Tony Gwynn FIN	6.00	2.70
202	Robin Ventura FIN	1.00	.45
203	Frank Thomas FIN	5.00	2.20
204	Kirby Puckett FIN	4.00	1.80
205	Roberto Alomar FIN	2.50	1.10
206	Dennis Eckersley FIN	1.00	.45
207	Joe Carter FIN	1.00	.45
208	Albert Belle FIN	2.50	1.10
209	Greg Maddux FIN	6.00	2.70
210	Ryne Sandberg FIN	3.00	1.35
211	Juan Gonzalez FIN	5.00	2.20
212	Jeff Bagwell FIN	3.00	1.35
213	Randy Johnson FIN	2.50	1.10
214	Matt Williams FIN	1.50	.70
215	Dave Winfield FIN	2.50	1.10
216	Larry Walker FIN	2.50	1.10
217	Roger Clemens FIN	6.00	2.70
218	Kenny Lofton FIN	2.50	1.10
219	Cecil Fielder FIN	1.00	.45
220	Darren Daulton FIN	1.00	.45
221	John Olerud FIN	1.00	.45
222	Jose Canseco FIN	3.00	1.35
223	Rickey Henderson FIN	3.00	1.35
224	Fred McGriff FIN	1.50	.70
225	Gary Sheffield FIN	2.50	1.10
226	Jack McDowell FIN	.50	.23
227	Rafael Palmeiro FIN	2.50	1.10
228	Travis Fryman FIN	1.00	.45
229	Marquis Grissom FIN	1.00	.45
230	Barry Bonds FIN	3.00	1.35
231	Carlos Baerga FIN	1.00	.45
232	Ken Griffey Jr. FIN	12.00	5.50
233	David Justice FIN	2.50	1.10
234	Bobby Bonilla FIN	1.00	.45
235	Cal Ripken FIN	10.00	4.50
236	Sammy Sosa FIN	8.00	3.60
237	Len Dykstra FIN	1.00	.45
238	Will Clark FIN	2.50	1.10
239	Paul Molitor FIN	2.50	1.10
240	Barry Larkin FIN	2.50	1.10
241	Bo Jackson	1.00	.45
242	Mitch Williams	.50	.23
243	Ron Darling	.50	.23
244	Darryl Kile	.50	.23
245	Geronimo Berroa	.50	.23
246	Gregg Olson	.50	.23
247	Brian Harper	.50	.23
248	Rheal Cormier	.50	.23
249	Rey Sanchez	.50	.23
250	Jeff Fassero	.50	.23
251	Sandy Alomar Jr.	1.00	.45
252	Chris Bosio	.50	.23
253	Andy Stankiewicz	.50	.23
254	Harold Baines	1.00	.45
255	Andy Ashby	.50	.23
256	Tyler Green	.50	.23
257	Kevin Brown	1.00	.45
258	Mo Vaughn	2.50	1.10
259	Mike Harkey	.50	.23
260	Dave Henderson	.50	.23
261	Kent Hrbek	1.00	.45
262	Darrin Jackson	.50	.23
263	Bob Wickman	.50	.23
264	Spike Owen	.50	.23
265	Todd Jones	.50	.23
266	Pat Borders	.50	.23
267	Tom Glavine	2.50	1.10
268	Dave Nilsson	.50	.23
269	Rich Batchelor	.50	.23
270	Delino DeShields	.50	.23
271	Felix Fermin	.50	.23
272	Orestes Destrade	.50	.23
273	Mickey Morandini	.50	.23
274	Otis Nixon	.50	.23
275	Ellis Burks	1.00	.45
276	Greg Gagne	.50	.23
277	John Doherty	.50	.23
278	Julio Franco	.50	.23
279	Bernie Williams	2.50	1.10
280	Rick Aguilera	.50	.23
281	Mickey Tettleton	.50	.23
282	David Nied	.50	.23
283	Johnny Ruffin	.50	.23
284	Dan Wilson	.50	.23
285	Omar Vizquel	1.00	.45
286	Willie Banks	.50	.23
287	Erik Pappas	.50	.23
288	Cal Eldred	.50	.23
289	Bobby Witt	.50	.23
290	Luis Gonzalez	1.00	.45
291	Greg Pirkl	.50	.23
292	Alex Cole	.50	.23
293	Ricky Bones	.50	.23
294	Denis Boucher	.50	.23
295	John Burkett	.50	.23
296	Steve Trachsel	.50	.23
297	Ricky Jordan	.50	.23
298	Mark Dewey	.50	.23
299	Jimmy Key	1.00	.45
300	Mike Macfarlane	.50	.23
301	Tim Belcher	.50	.23
302	Carlos Reyes	.50	.23
303	Greg A. Harris	.50	.23
304	Brian Anderson	1.50	.70
305	Terry Mulholland	.50	.23
306	Felix Jose	.50	.23
307	Darren Holmes	.50	.23
308	Jose Rijo	.50	.23
309	Paul Wagner	.50	.23
310	Bob Scanlan	.50	.23
311	Mike Jackson	1.00	.45
312	Jose Vizcaino	.50	.23
313	Rob Butler	.50	.23

314 Kevin Seitzer	.50	.23
315 Geronimo Pena	.50	.23
316 Hector Carrasco	.50	.23
317 Eddie Murray	2.50	1.10
318 Roger Salkeld	.50	.23
319 Todd Hundley	1.00	.45
320 Danny Jackson	.50	.23
321 Kevin Young	.50	.23
322 Mike Greenwell	.50	.23
323 Kevin Mitchell	.50	.23
324 Chuck Knoblauch	2.50	1.10
325 Danny Tartabull	.50	.23
326 Vince Coleman	.50	.23
327 Marvin Freeman	.50	.23
328 Andy Benes	1.00	.45
329 Mike Kelly	.50	.23
330 Karl Rhodes	.50	.23
331 Allen Watson	.50	.23
332 Damion Easley	1.00	.45
333 Reggie Jefferson	.50	.23
334 Kevin McReynolds	.50	.23
335 Arthur Rhodes	.50	.23
336 Brian R. Hunter	.50	.23
337 Tom Browning	.50	.23
338 Pedro Munoz	.50	.23
339 Billy Ripken	.50	.23
340 Gene Harris	.50	.23
341 Fernando Vina	.50	.23
342 Sean Berry	.50	.23
343 Pedro Astacio	.50	.23
344 B.J. Surhoff	1.00	.45
345 Doug Drabek	.50	.23
346 Jody Reed	.50	.23
347 Ray Lankford	1.00	.45
348 Steve Farr	.50	.23
349 Eric Anthony	.50	.23
350 Pete Smith	.50	.23
351 Lee Smith	1.00	.45
352 Mariano Duncan	.50	.23
353 Doug Strange	.50	.23
354 Tim Bogar	.50	.23
355 Dave Weathers	.50	.23
356 Eric Karros	1.00	.45
357 Randy Myers	.50	.23
358 Chad Curtis	.50	.23
359 Steve Avery	.50	.23
360 Brian Jordan	1.00	.45
361 Tim Wallach	.50	.23
362 Pedro Martinez	3.00	1.35
363 Bip Roberts	.50	.23
364 Lou Whitaker	1.00	.45
365 Luis Polonia	.50	.23
366 Benito Santiago	.50	.23
367 Brett Butler	1.00	.45
368 Shawon Dunston	.50	.23
369 Kelly Stinnett	.50	.23
370 Chris Turner	.50	.23
371 Ruben Sierra	.50	.23
372 Greg A. Harris	.50	.23
373 Xavier Hernandez	.50	.23
374 Howard Johnson	.50	.23
375 Duane Ward	.50	.23
376 Roberto Hernandez	.50	.23
377 Scott Leius	.50	.23
378 Dave Valle	.50	.23
379 Sid Fernandez	.50	.23
380 Doug Jones	.50	.23
381 Zane Smith	.50	.23
382 Craig Biggio	2.50	1.10
383 Rick White	.50	.23
384 Tom Pagnozzi	.50	.23
385 Chris James	.50	.23
386 Bret Boone	1.00	.45
387 Jeff Montgomery	.50	.23
388 Chad Kreuter	.50	.23
389 Greg Hibbard	.50	.23
390 Mark Grace	1.50	.70
391 Phil Leftwich	.50	.23
392 Don Mattingly	5.00	2.20
393 Ozzie Guillen	.50	.23
394 Gary Gaetti	1.00	.45
395 Erik Hanson	.50	.23
396 Scott Brosius	1.00	.45
397 Tom Gordon	.50	.23
398 Bill Gullickson	.50	.23
399 Matt Mieske	.50	.23

400 Pat Hentgen	1.00	.45
401 Walt Weiss	.50	.23
402 Greg Blosser	.50	.23
403 Stan Javier	.50	.23
404 Doug Henry	.50	.23
405 Ramon Martinez	1.00	.45
406 Frank Viola	.50	.23
407 Mike Hampton	.50	.23
408 Andy Van Slyke	1.00	.45
409 Bobby Ayala	.50	.23
410 Todd Zeile	.50	.23
411 Jay Bell	1.00	.45
412 Dennis Martinez	1.00	.45
413 Mark Portugal	.50	.23
414 Bobby Munoz	.50	.23
415 Kirt Manwaring	.50	.23
416 John Kruk	1.00	.45
417 Trevor Hoffman	1.00	.45
418 Chris Sabo	.50	.23
419 Bret Saberhagen	1.00	.45
420 Chris Nabholz	.50	.23
421 James Mouton FIN	.50	.23
422 Tony Tarasco FIN	.50	.23
423 Carlos Delgado FIN	2.50	1.10
424 Rondell White FIN	1.00	.45
425 Javier Lopez FIN	1.50	.70
426 Chan Ho Park FIN	8.00	3.60
427 Cliff Floyd FIN	1.00	.45
428 Dave Staton FIN	.50	.23
429 J.R. Phillips FIN	.50	.23
430 Manny Ramirez FIN	5.00	2.20
431 Kurt Abbott FIN	.50	.23
432 Melvin Nieves FIN	.50	.23
433 Alex Gonzalez FIN	1.00	.45
434 Rick Helling FIN	1.00	.45
435 Danny Bautista FIN	.50	.23
436 Matt Walbeck FIN	.50	.23
437 Ryan Klesko FIN	1.00	.45
438 Steve Karsay FIN	.50	.23
439 Salomon Torres FIN	.50	.23
440 Scott Ruffcorn FIN	.50	.23

1995 Finest

	MINT	NRMT
COMPLETE SET (330)	100.00	45.00
COMPLETE SERIES 1 (220)	70.00	32.00
COMPLETE SERIES 2 (110)	30.00	13.50
COMMON CARD (1-330)	.40	.18
MINOR STARS	.75	.35
SEMISTARS	1.25	.55
UNLISTED STARS	2.00	.90
COMMON REF. (1-330)	8.00	3.60
*REF.STARS: 6X TO 15X HI COLUMN		
*REF.ROOKIES: 3X TO 8X HI		
REFRACTOR STATED ODDS 1:12		

1 Raul Mondesi	1.25	.55
2 Kurt Abbott	.40	.18
3 Chris Gomez	.40	.18
4 Manny Ramirez	2.50	1.10
5 Rondell White	.75	.35
6 William VanLandingham	.40	.18
7 Jon Lieber	.40	.18
8 Ryan Klesko	.75	.35
9 John Hudek	.40	.18
10 Joey Hamilton	.75	.35
11 Bob Hamelin	.40	.18
12 Brian Anderson	.75	.35
13 Mike Lieberthal	.40	.18

14 Rico Brogna	.40	.18
15 Rusty Greer	2.00	.90
16 Carlos Delgado	2.00	.90
17 Jim Edmonds	1.25	.55
18 Steve Trachsel	.40	.18
19 Matt Walbeck	.40	.18
20 Armando Benitez	.40	.18
21 Steve Karsay	.40	.18
22 Jose Oliva	.40	.18
23 Cliff Floyd	.75	.35
24 Kevin Foster	.40	.18
25 Javier Lopez	.75	.35
26 Jose Valentin	.40	.18
27 James Mouton	.40	.18
28 Hector Carrasco	.40	.18
29 Orlando Miller	.40	.18
30 Garret Anderson	.75	.35
31 Marvin Freeman	.40	.18
32 Brett Butler	.75	.35
33 Roberto Kelly	.40	.18
34 Rod Beck	.40	.18
35 Jose Rijo	.40	.18
36 Edgar Martinez	.75	.35
37 Jim Thome	2.00	.90
38 Rick Wilkins	.40	.18
39 Wally Joyner	.75	.35
40 Wil Cordero	.40	.18
41 Tommy Greene	.40	.18
42 Travis Fryman	.75	.35
43 Don Slaught	.40	.18
44 Brady Anderson	.75	.35
45 Matt Williams	2.00	.90
46 Rene Arocha	.40	.18
47 Rickey Henderson	2.50	1.10
48 Mike Mussina	2.00	.90
49 Greg McMichael	.40	.18
50 Jody Reed	.40	.18
51 Tino Martinez	2.00	.90
52 Dave Clark	.40	.18
53 John Valentin	.75	.35
54 Bret Boone	.75	.35
55 Walt Weiss	.40	.18
56 Kenny Lofton	1.25	.55
57 Scott Leius	.40	.18
58 Eric Karros	.75	.35
59 John Olerud	.75	.35
60 Chris Hoiles	.40	.18
61 Sandy Alomar Jr	.75	.35
62 Tim Wallach	.40	.18
63 Cal Eldred	.40	.18
64 Tom Glavine	2.00	.90
65 Mark Grace	1.25	.55
66 Rey Sanchez	.40	.18
67 Bobby Ayala	.40	.18
68 Dante Bichette	.75	.35
69 Andres Galarraga	2.00	.90
70 Chuck Carr	.40	.18
71 Bobby Witt	.40	.18
72 Steve Avery	.40	.18
73 Bobby Jones	.75	.35
74 Delino DeShields	.40	.18
75 Kevin Tapani	.40	.18
76 Randy Johnson	2.00	.90
77 David Nied	.40	.18
78 Pat Hentgen	.75	.35
79 Tim Salmon	2.00	.90
80 Todd Zeile	.40	.18
81 John Wetteland	.75	.35
82 Albert Belle	2.00	.90
83 Ben McDonald	.40	.18
84 Bobby Munoz	.40	.18
85 Bip Roberts	.40	.18
86 Mo Vaughn	2.00	.90
87 Chuck Finley	.75	.35
88 Chuck Knoblauch	2.00	.90
89 Frank Thomas	4.00	1.80
90 Danny Tartabull	.40	.18
91 Dean Palmer	.75	.35
92 Len Dykstra	.75	.35
93 J.R. Phillips	.40	.18
94 Tom Candiotti	.40	.18
95 Marquis Grissom	.75	.35
96 Barry Larkin	2.00	.90
97 Bryan Harvey	.40	.18
98 David Justice	2.00	.90
99 David Cone	1.25	.55

100	Wade Boggs	2.00	.90
101	Jason Bere	.40	.18
102	Hal Morris	.40	.18
103	Fred McGriff	1.25	.55
104	Bobby Bonilla	.75	.35
105	Jay Buhner	.75	.35
106	Allen Watson	.40	.18
107	Mickey Tettleton	.40	.18
108	Kevin Appier	.75	.35
109	Ivan Rodriguez	2.50	1.10
110	Carlos Garcia	.40	.18
111	Andy Benes	.75	.35
112	Eddie Murray	2.00	.90
113	Mike Piazza	6.00	2.70
114	Greg Vaughn	.75	.35
115	Paul Molitor	2.00	.90
116	Terry Steinbach	.40	.18
117	Jeff Bagwell	2.50	1.10
118	Ken Griffey Jr.	10.00	4.50
119	Gary Sheffield	.75	.35
120	Cal Ripken	8.00	3.60
121	Jeff Kent	.75	.35
122	Jay Bell	.75	.35
123	Will Clark	2.00	.90
124	Cecil Fielder	.75	.35
125	Alex Fernandez	.40	.18
126	Don Mattingly	4.00	1.80
127	Reggie Sanders	.75	.35
128	Moises Alou	.75	.35
129	Craig Biggio	2.00	.90
130	Eddie Williams	.40	.18
131	John Franco	.40	.18
132	John Kruk	.75	.35
133	Jeff King	.40	.18
134	Royce Clayton	.40	.18
135	Doug Drabek	.40	.18
136	Ray Lankford	.75	.35
137	Roberto Alomar	2.00	.90
138	Todd Hundley	.75	.35
139	Alex Cole	.40	.18
140	Shawon Dunston	.40	.18
141	John Roper	.40	.18
142	Mark Langston	.40	.18
143	Tom Pagnozzi	.40	.18
144	Wilson Alvarez	.75	.35
145	Scott Cooper	.40	.18
146	Kevin Mitchell	.40	.18
147	Mark Whiten	.40	.18
148	Jeff Conine	.40	.18
149	Chili Davis	.75	.35
150	Luis Gonzalez	.40	.18
151	Juan Guzman	.40	.18
152	Mike Greenwell	.40	.18
153	Mike Henneman	.40	.18
154	Rick Aguilera	.40	.18
155	Dennis Eckersley	.75	.35
156	Darrin Fletcher	.40	.18
157	Darren Lewis	.40	.18
158	Juan Gonzalez	4.00	1.80
159	Dave Hollins	.40	.18
160	Jimmy Key	.40	.18
161	Roberto Hernandez	.40	.18
162	Randy Myers	.40	.18
163	Joe Carter	.75	.35
164	Darren Daulton	.75	.35
165	Mike Macfarlane	.40	.18
166	Bret Saberhagen	.75	.35
167	Kirby Puckett	3.00	1.35
168	Lance Johnson	.40	.18
169	Mark McGwire	10.00	4.50
170	Jose Canseco	2.50	1.10
171	Mike Stanley	.40	.18
172	Lee Smith	.75	.35
173	Robin Ventura	.75	.35
174	Greg Gagne	.40	.18
175	Brian McRae	.40	.18
176	Mike Bordick	.40	.18
177	Rafael Palmeiro	2.00	.90
178	Kenny Rogers	.40	.18
179	Chad Curtis	.40	.18
180	Devon White	.75	.35
181	Paul O'Neill	.75	.35
182	Ken Caminiti	1.25	.55
183	Dave Nilsson	.40	.18
184	Tim Naehring	.40	.18
185	Roger Clemens	5.00	2.20
186	Otis Nixon	.40	.18
187	Tim Raines	.75	.35
188	Denny Martinez	.75	.35
189	Pedro Martinez	2.50	1.10
190	Jim Abbott	.75	.35
191	Ryan Thompson	.40	.18
192	Barry Bonds	2.50	1.10
193	Joe Girardi	.40	.18
194	Steve Finley	.75	.35
195	John Jaha	.40	.18
196	Tony Gwynn	5.00	2.20
197	Sammy Sosa	6.00	2.70
198	John Burkett	.40	.18
199	Carlos Baerga	.40	.18
200	Ramon Martinez	.75	.35
201	Aaron Sele	.75	.35
202	Eduardo Perez	.40	.18
203	Alan Trammell	.75	.35
204	Orlando Merced	.40	.18
205	Deion Sanders	.75	.35
206	Robb Nen	.40	.18
207	Jack McDowell	.40	.18
208	Ruben Sierra	.40	.18
209	Bernie Williams	2.00	.90
210	Kevin Seitzer	.40	.18
211	Charles Nagy	.75	.35
212	Tony Phillips	.40	.18
213	Greg Maddux	5.00	2.20
214	Jeff Montgomery	.40	.18
215	Larry Walker	2.00	.90
216	Andy Van Slyke	.75	.35
217	Ozzie Smith	2.50	1.10
218	Geronimo Pena	.40	.18
219	Gregg Jefferies	.40	.18
220	Lou Whitaker	.75	.35
221	Chipper Jones	5.00	2.20
222	Benji Gil	.40	.18
223	Tony Phillips	.40	.18
224	Trevor Wilson	.40	.18
225	Tony Tarasco	.40	.18
226	Roberto Petagine	.40	.18
227	Mike Macfarlane	.40	.18
228	Hideo Nomo UER	8.00	3.60
	(in 3rd line against)		
229	Mark McLemore	.40	.18
230	Ron Gant	.40	.18
231	Andujar Cedeno	.40	.18
232	Mike Mimbs	.40	.18
233	Jim Abbott	.75	.35
234	Ricky Bones	.40	.18
235	Marty Cordova	.40	.18
236	Mark Johnson	.40	.18
237	Marquis Grissom	.75	.35
238	Tom Henke	.40	.18
239	Terry Pendleton	.40	.18
240	John Wetteland	.75	.35
241	Lee Smith	.75	.35
242	Jaime Navarro	.40	.18
243	Luis Alicea	.40	.18
244	Scott Cooper	.40	.18
245	Gary Gaetti	.40	.18
246	Edgardo Alfonzo UER	2.00	.90
	(incomplete career BA)		
247	Brad Clontz	.40	.18
248	Dave Milcki	.40	.18
249	Dave Winfield	2.00	.90
250	Mark Grudzielanek	2.00	.90
251	Alex Gonzalez	.40	.18
252	Kevin Brown	1.25	.55
253	Esteban Loaiza	.40	.18
254	Vaughn Eshelman	.40	.18
255	Bill Swift	.40	.18
256	Brian McRae	.40	.18
257	Bobby Higginson	5.00	2.20
258	Jack McDowell	.40	.18
259	Scott Stahoviak	.40	.18
260	Jon Nunnally	.40	.18
261	Charlie Hayes	.40	.18
262	Jacob Brumfield	.40	.18
263	Chad Curtis	.40	.18
264	Heathcliff Slocumb	.40	.18
265	Mark Whiten	.40	.18
266	Mickey Tettleton	.40	.18
267	Jose Mesa	.40	.18
268	Doug Jones	.40	.18
269	Trevor Hoffman	.75	.35
270	Paul Sorrento	.40	.18
271	Shane Andrews	.40	.18
272	Brett Butler	.75	.35
273	Curtis Goodwin	.40	.18
274	Larry Walker	2.00	.90
275	Phil Plantier	.40	.18
276	Ken Hill	.40	.18
277	Vinny Castilla UER	1.25	.55
	Rockies spelled Rockie		
278	Billy Ashley	.40	.18
279	Derek Jeter	6.00	2.70
280	Bob Tewksbury	.40	.18
281	Jose Offerman	.75	.35
282	Glenallen Hill	.40	.18
283	Tony Fernandez	.40	.18
284	Mike Devereaux	.40	.18
285	John Burkett	.40	.18
286	Geronimo Berroa	.40	.18
287	Quilvio Veras	.40	.18
288	Jason Bates	.40	.18
289	Lee Tinsley	.40	.18
290	Derek Bell	.75	.35
291	Jeff Fassero	.40	.18
292	Ray Durham	.75	.35
293	Chad Ogea	.40	.18
294	Bill Pulsipher	.40	.18
295	Phil Nevin	.40	.18
296	Carlos Perez	2.00	.90
297	Roberto Kelly	.40	.18
298	Tim Wakefield	.75	.35
299	Jeff Manto	.40	.18
300	Brian Hunter	.75	.35
301	C.J. Nitkowski	.40	.18
302	Dustin Hermanson	.40	.18
303	John Mabry	.40	.18
304	Orel Hershiser	.75	.35
305	Ron Villone	.40	.18
306	Sean Bergman	.40	.18
307	Tom Goodwin	.40	.18
308	Al Reyes	.40	.18
309	Todd Stottlemyre	.40	.18
310	Rich Becker	.40	.18
311	Joey Cora	.40	.18
312	Ed Sprague	.40	.18
313	John Smoltz UER	1.25	.55
	(3rd line; from spelled as form)		
314	Frank Castillo	.40	.18
315	Chris Hammond	.40	.18
316	Ismael Valdes	.75	.35
317	Pete Harnisch	.40	.18
318	Bernard Gilkey	.40	.18
319	John Kruk	.75	.35
320	Marc Newfield	.40	.18
321	Brian Johnson	.40	.18
322	Mark Portugal	.40	.18
323	David Hulse	.40	.18
324	Luis Ortiz UER	.40	.18
	(Below spelled beloe)		
325	Mike Benjamin	.40	.18
326	Brian Jordan	.75	.35
327	Shawn Green	2.00	.90
328	Joe Oliver	.40	.18
329	Felipe Lira	.40	.18
330	Andre Dawson	1.25	.55

1995 Finest Flame Throwers

	MINT	NRMT
COMPLETE SET (9)	40.00	18.00
COMMON CARD (FT1-FT9)	3.00	1.35
SER.1 STATED ODDS 1:48		
FT1 Jason Bere	3.00	1.35
FT2 Roger Clemens	30.00	13.50
FT3 Juan Guzman	3.00	1.35
FT4 John Hudek	3.00	1.35
FT5 Randy Johnson	8.00	3.60
FT6 Pedro Martinez	8.00	3.60
FT7 Jose Rijo	3.00	1.35
FT8 Bret Saberhagen	4.00	1.80
FT9 John Wetteland	4.00	1.80

1995 Finest Power Kings

	MINT	NRMT
COMPLETE SET (18)	200.00	90.00
COMMON CARD (PK1-PK18)	4.00	1.80
SER.1 STATED ODDS 1:24		
PK1 Bob Hamelin	4.00	1.80
PK2 Raul Mondesi	6.00	2.70
PK3 Ryan Klesko	5.00	2.20
PK4 Carlos Delgado	10.00	4.50
PK5 Manny Ramirez	10.00	4.50
PK6 Mike Piazza	30.00	13.50
PK7 Jeff Bagwell	12.00	5.50
PK8 Mo Vaughn	10.00	4.50
PK9 Frank Thomas	25.00	11.00
PK10 Ken Griffey Jr.	50.00	22.00
PK11 Albert Belle	10.00	4.50
PK12 Sammy Sosa	25.00	11.00
PK13 Dante Bichette	5.00	2.20
PK14 Gary Sheffield	5.00	2.20
PK15 Matt Williams	10.00	4.50
PK16 Fred McGriff	6.00	2.70
PK17 Barry Bonds	10.00	4.50
PK18 Cecil Fielder	5.00	2.20

1996 Finest

	MINT	NRMT
COMP.BRONZE SER.1 (110)	25.00	11.00
COMP.BRONZE SER.2 (110)	30.00	13.50
COMMON BRONZE	.25	.11
BRONZE MINOR STARS	.50	.23
BRONZE UNLISTED STARS	1.00	.45

COMP.GOLD SER.1 (26)	500.00	220.00
COMP.GOLD SER.2 (22)	250.00	110.00
COMMON GOLD	6.00	2.70
GOLD SEMISTARS	8.00	3.60
GOLD UNLISTED STARS	12.00	5.50
GOLD STATED ODDS 1:24		
COMP.SILVER SER.1 (55)	150.00	70.00
COMP.SILVER SER.2 (36)	80.00	36.00
COMMON SILVER	1.50	.70
SILVER MINOR STARS	2.50	1.10
SILVER UNLISTED STARS	5.00	2.20
SILVER STATED ODDS 1:4		
SETS SKIP-NUMBERED BY COLOR		
B5 Roberto Hernandez B	.25	.11
B8 Terry Pendleton B	.25	.11
B12 Ken Caminiti B	.50	.23
B15 Dan Miceli B	.25	.11
B16 Chipper Jones B	2.50	1.10
B17 John Wetteland B	.50	.23
B19 Tim Naehring B	.25	.11
B21 Eddie Murray B	1.00	.45
B23 Kevin Appier B	.50	.23
B24 Ken Griffey Jr. B	5.00	2.20
B26 Brian McRae B	.25	.11
B27 Pedro Martinez B	1.25	.55
B28 Brian Jordan B	.50	.23
B29 Mike Fetters B	.25	.11
B30 Carlos Delgado B	1.00	.45
B31 Shane Reynolds B	.50	.23
B32 Terry Steinbach B	.25	.11
B34 Mark Leiter B	.25	.11
B36 David Segui B	.50	.23
B40 Fred McGriff B	.75	.35
B44 Glenallen Hill B	.25	.11
B45 Brady Anderson B	.50	.23
B47 Jim Thome B	1.00	.45
B48 Frank Thomas B	2.00	.90
B49 Chuck Knoblauch B	1.00	.45
B50 Len Dykstra B	.50	.23
B53 Tom Pagnozzi B	.25	.11
B55 Ricky Bones B	.25	.11
B56 David Justice B	1.00	.45
B57 Steve Avery B	.25	.11
B58 Robby Thompson B	.25	.11
B61 Tony Gwynn B	2.50	1.10
B63 Denny Neagle B	.50	.23
B67 Robin Ventura B	.50	.23
B70 Kevin Seitzer B	.25	.11
B71 Ramon Martinez B	.50	.23
B75 Brian L.Hunter B	.25	.11
B76 Alan Benes B	.25	.11
B80 Ozzie Guillen B	.25	.11
B82 Benji Gil B	.25	.11
B85 Todd Hundley B	.50	.23
B87 Pat Hentgen B	.50	.23
B89 Chuck Finley B	.50	.23
B92 Derek Jeter B	3.00	1.35
B93 Paul O'Neill B	.50	.23
B94 Darrin Fletcher B	.25	.11
B96 Delino DeShields B	.25	.11
B97 Tim Salmon B	.75	.35
B98 John Olerud B	.50	.23
B101 Tim Wakefield B	.25	.11
B103 Dave Stevens B	.25	.11
B104 Orlando Merced B	.25	.11
B106 Jay Bell B	.50	.23
B107 John Burkett B	.25	.11
B108 Chris Hoiles B	.25	.11
B110 Dave Nilsson B	.25	.11
B111 Rod Beck B	.25	.11
B113 Mike Piazza B	3.00	1.35
B114 Mark Langston B	.25	.11
B116 Rico Brogna B	.25	.11
B118 Tom Goodwin B	.25	.11
B119 Bryan Rekar B	.25	.11
B120 David Cone B	.75	.35
B122 Andy Pettitte B	.75	.35
B123 Chili Davis B	.50	.23
B124 John Smoltz B	.75	.35
B125 Heathcliff Slocumb B	.25	.11
B126 Dante Bichette B	.50	.23
B128 Alex Gonzalez B	.25	.11
B129 Jeff Montgomery B	.25	.11
B131 Denny Martinez B	.50	.23
B132 Mel Rojas B	.25	.11

B133 Derek Bell B	.50	.23
B134 Trevor Hoffman B	.50	.23
B136 Darren Daulton B	.50	.23
B137 Pete Schourek B	.25	.11
B138 Phil Nevin B	.25	.11
B139 Andres Galarraga B	1.00	.45
B140 Chad Fonville B	.25	.11
B144 J.T. Snow B	.50	.23
B146 Barry Bonds B	1.25	.55
B147 Orel Hershiser B	.50	.23
B148 Quilvio Veras B	.25	.11
B149 Will Clark B	1.00	.45
B150 Jose Rijo B	.25	.11
B152 Travis Fryman B	.50	.23
B154 Alex Fernandez B	.25	.11
B155 Wade Boggs B	1.00	.45
B156 Troy Percival B	.25	.11
B157 Moises Alou B	.50	.23
B158 Javy Lopez B	.50	.23
B159 Jason Giambi B	.50	.23
B162 Mark McGwire B	5.00	2.20
B163 Eric Karros B	.50	.23
B166 Mickey Tettleton B	.25	.11
B167 Barry Larkin B	1.00	.45
B169 Ruben Sierra B	.25	.11
B170 Bill Swift B	.25	.11
B172 Chad Curtis B	.25	.11
B173 Dean Palmer B	.50	.23
B175 Bobby Bonilla B	.50	.23
B176 Greg Colbrunn B	.25	.11
B177 Jose Mesa B	.25	.11
B178 Mike Greenwell B	.25	.11
B181 Doug Drabek B	.25	.11
B183 Wilson Alvarez B	.25	.11
B184 Marty Cordova B	.25	.11
B185 Hal Morris B	.25	.11
B187 Carlos Garcia B	.25	.11
B190 Marquis Grissom B	.25	.11
B193 Will Clark B	1.00	.45
B194 Paul Molitor B	1.00	.45
B195 Kenny Rogers B	.25	.11
B196 Reggie Sanders B	.50	.23
B199 Raul Mondesi B	.50	.23
B200 Lance Johnson B	.25	.11
B201 Alvin Morman B	.25	.11
B203 Jack McDowell B	.25	.11
B204 Randy Myers B	.25	.11
B205 Harold Baines B	.50	.23
B206 Marty Cordova B	.25	.11
B207 Rich Hunter B	.25	.11
B208 Al Leiter B	.50	.23
B209 Greg Gagne B	.25	.11
B210 Ben McDonald B	.25	.11
B212 Terry Adams B	.25	.11
B213 Paul Sorrento B	.25	.11
B214 Albert Belle B	1.00	.45
B215 Mike Blowers B	.25	.11
B216 Jim Edmonds B	.75	.35
B217 Felipe Crespo B	.25	.11
B219 Shawon Dunston B	.25	.11
B220 Jimmy Haynes B	.25	.11
B221 Jose Canseco B	1.25	.55
B222 Eric Davis B	.50	.23
B224 Tim Raines B	.50	.23
B225 Tony Phillips B	.25	.11
B226 Charlie Hayes B	.25	.11
B227 Eric Owens B	.25	.11
B228 Roberto Alomar B	1.00	.45
B233 Kenny Lofton B	.75	.35
B236 Mark McGwire B	5.00	2.20
B237 Jay Buhner B	.50	.23
B238 Craig Biggio B	1.00	.45
B240 Barry Bonds B	1.25	.55
B244 Ron Gant B	.25	.11
B245 Paul Wilson B	.25	.11
B246 Todd Hollandsworth B	.25	.11
B247 Todd Zeile B	.25	.11
B248 David Justice B	1.00	.45
B250 Moises Alou B	.50	.23
B251 Bob Wolcott B	.25	.11
B252 David Wells B	.75	.35
B253 Juan Gonzalez B	2.00	.90
B254 Andres Galarraga B	1.00	.45
B255 Dave Hollins B	.25	.11
B256 Sammy Sosa B	3.00	1.35
B258 Ivan Rodriguez B	1.00	.45

❑ B259 Bip Roberts B	.25	.11
❑ B260 Tino Martinez B	.50	.23
❑ B262 Mike Stanley B	.25	.11
❑ B264 Butch Huskey B	.25	.11
❑ B265 Jeff Conine B	.25	.11
❑ B267 Mark Grace B	.75	.35
❑ B268 Jason Schmidt B	.25	.11
❑ B269 Otis Nixon B	.25	.11
❑ B271 Kirby Puckett B	1.50	.70
❑ B273 Andy Benes B	.50	.23
❑ B275 Mike Piazza B	3.00	1.35
❑ B276 Rey Ordonez B	1.00	.45
❑ B278 Gary Gaetti B	.25	.11
❑ B280 Robin Ventura B	.50	.23
❑ B281 Cal Ripken B	4.00	1.80
❑ B282 Carlos Baerga B	.25	.11
❑ B283 Roger Cedeno B	.50	.23
❑ B285 Terrell Wade B	.25	.11
❑ B286 Kevin Brown B	.75	.35
❑ B287 Rafael Palmeiro B	1.00	.45
❑ B288 Mo Vaughn B	1.00	.45
❑ B292 Bob Tewksbury B	.25	.11
❑ B297 T.J. Mathews B	.25	.11
❑ B298 Manny Ramirez B	1.25	.55
❑ B299 Jeff Bagwell B	1.25	.55
❑ B301 Wade Boggs B	1.00	.45
❑ B303 Steve Gibralter B	.25	.11
❑ B304 B.J. Surhoff B	.50	.23
❑ B306 Royce Clayton B	.25	.11
❑ B307 Sal Fasano B	.25	.11
❑ B309 Gary Sheffield B	.50	.23
❑ B310 Ken Hill B	.25	.11
❑ B311 Joe Girardi B	.25	.11
❑ B312 Matt Lawton B	1.50	.70
❑ B314 Julio Franco B	.25	.11
❑ B315 Joe Carter B	.50	.23
❑ B316 Brooks Kieschnick B	.25	.11
❑ B318 Heathcliff Slocumb B	.25	.11
❑ B319 Barry Larkin B	1.00	.45
❑ B320 Tony Gwynn B	2.50	1.10
❑ B322 Frank Thomas B	2.00	.90
❑ B323 Edgar Martinez B	.50	.23
❑ B325 Henry Rodriguez B	.50	.23
❑ B326 Marvin Benard B	.25	.11
❑ B329 Ugueth Urbina B	.50	.23
❑ B331 Roger Salkeld B	.25	.11
❑ B332 Edgar Renteria B	.50	.23
❑ B333 Ryan Klesko B	.50	.23
❑ B334 Ray Lankford B	.50	.23
❑ B336 Justin Thompson B	.50	.23
❑ B339 Mark Clark B	.25	.11
❑ B340 Ruben Rivera B	.50	.23
❑ B342 Matt Williams B	1.00	.45
❑ B343 Francisco Cordova B	.25	.11
❑ B344 Cecil Fielder B	.50	.23
❑ B348 Mark Grudzielanek B	.25	.11
❑ B349 Ron Coomer B	.25	.11
❑ B351 Rich Aurilia B	.50	.23
❑ B352 Jose Herrera B	.25	.11
❑ B356 Tony Clark B	1.00	.45
❑ B358 Dan Naulty B	.25	.11
❑ B359 Checklist B	.25	.11
❑ G4 Marty Cordova G	6.00	2.70
❑ G6 Tony Gwynn G	30.00	13.50
❑ G9 Albert Belle G	12.00	5.50
❑ G18 Kirby Puckett G	20.00	9.00
❑ G20 Karim Garcia G	8.00	3.60
❑ G25 Cal Ripken G	50.00	22.00
❑ G33 Hideo Nomo G	12.00	5.50
❑ G39 Ryne Sandberg G	15.00	6.75
❑ G42 Jeff Bagwell G	15.00	6.75
❑ G51 Jason Isringhausen G	8.00	3.60
❑ G64 Mo Vaughn G	12.00	5.50
❑ G66 Dante Bichette G	8.00	3.60
❑ G74 Mark McGwire G	60.00	27.00
❑ G81 Kenny Lofton G	8.00	3.60
❑ G83 Jim Edmonds G	8.00	3.60
❑ G90 Mike Mussina G	12.00	5.50
❑ G100 Jeff Conine G	6.00	2.70
❑ G102 Johnny Damon G	8.00	3.60
❑ G105 Barry Bonds G	15.00	6.75
❑ G117 Jose Canseco G	15.00	6.75
❑ G135 Ken Griffey Jr. G	60.00	27.00
❑ G141 Chipper Jones G	30.00	13.50
❑ G145 Greg Maddux G	30.00	13.50
❑ G164 Jay Buhner G	8.00	3.60

❑ G186 Frank Thomas G	25.00	11.00
❑ G191 Checklist G	6.00	2.70
❑ G192 Chipper Jones G	30.00	13.50
❑ G197 Roberto Alomar G	12.00	5.50
❑ G198 Dennis Eckersley G	8.00	3.60
❑ G202 George Arias G	6.00	2.70
❑ G232 Hideo Nomo G	12.00	5.50
❑ G243 Chris Snopek G	6.00	2.70
❑ G249 Tim Salmon G	8.00	3.60
❑ G266 Matt Williams G	12.00	5.50
❑ G270 Randy Johnson G	12.00	5.50
❑ G279 Paul Molitor G	12.00	5.50
❑ G290 Cecil Fielder G	8.00	3.60
❑ G294 Livan Hernandez G	15.00	6.75
❑ G300 Marty Janzen G	6.00	2.70
❑ G308 Ron Gant G	6.00	2.70
❑ G321 Ryan Klesko G	8.00	3.60
❑ G324 Jermaine Dye G	8.00	3.60
❑ G330 Jason Giambi G	8.00	3.60
❑ G335 Edgar Martinez G	8.00	3.60
❑ G338 Rey Ordonez G	12.00	5.50
❑ G347 Sammy Sosa G	40.00	18.00
❑ G354 Juan Gonzalez G	25.00	11.00
❑ G355 Craig Biggio G	12.00	5.50
❑ S1 Greg Maddux S UER	12.00	5.50
95 stats listed as Mariners		
❑ S2 Bernie Williams S	5.00	2.20
❑ S5 Ivan Rodriguez S	6.00	2.70
❑ S7 Barry Larkin S	5.00	2.20
❑ S10 Ray Lankford S	2.50	1.10
❑ S11 Mike Piazza S	15.00	6.75
❑ S13 Larry Walker S	5.00	2.20
❑ S14 Matt Williams S	5.00	2.20
❑ S22 Tim Salmon S	3.00	1.35
❑ S35 Edgar Martinez S	2.50	1.10
❑ S37 Gregg Jefferies S	1.50	.70
❑ S38 Bill Pulsipher S	1.50	.70
❑ S41 Shawn Green S	5.00	2.20
❑ S43 Jim Abbott S	2.50	1.10
❑ S46 Roger Clemens S	12.00	5.50
❑ S52 Rondell White S	2.50	1.10
❑ S54 Dennis Eckersley S	2.50	1.10
❑ S59 Hideo Nomo S	5.00	2.20
❑ S60 Gary Sheffield S	5.00	2.20
❑ S62 Will Clark S	5.00	2.20
❑ S65 Bret Boone S	2.50	1.10
❑ S68 Rafael Palmeiro S	5.00	2.20
❑ S69 Carlos Baerga S	1.50	.70
❑ S72 Tom Glavine S	5.00	2.20
❑ S73 Garret Anderson S	2.50	1.10
❑ S77 Randy Johnson S	5.00	2.20
❑ S78 Jeff King S	1.50	.70
❑ S79 Kirby Puckett S	8.00	3.60
❑ S84 Cecil Fielder S	2.50	1.10
❑ S86 Reggie Sanders S	2.50	1.10
❑ S88 Ryan Klesko S	5.00	2.20
❑ S91 John Valentin S	2.50	1.10
❑ S95 Manny Ramirez S	6.00	2.70
❑ S99 Vinny Castilla S	3.00	1.35
❑ S109 Carlos Perez S	1.50	.70
❑ S112 Craig Biggio S	5.00	2.20
❑ S115 Juan Gonzalez S	10.00	4.50
❑ S121 Ray Durham S	2.50	1.10
❑ S127 C.J. Nitkowski S	1.50	.70
❑ S130 Raul Mondesi S	2.50	1.10
❑ S142 Lee Smith S	1.50	.70
❑ S143 Joe Carter S	2.50	1.10
❑ S151 Mo Vaughn S	5.00	2.20
❑ S153 Frank Rodriguez S	1.50	.70
❑ S160 Steve Finley S	2.50	1.10
❑ S161 Jeff Bagwell S	6.00	2.70
❑ S165 Cal Ripken S	20.00	9.00
❑ S168 Lyle Mouton S	1.50	.70
❑ S171 Sammy Sosa S	15.00	6.75
❑ S174 John Franco S	2.50	1.10
❑ S179 Greg Vaughn S	2.50	1.10
❑ S180 Mark Wohlers S	1.50	.70
❑ S182 Paul O'Neill S	2.50	1.10
❑ S188 Albert Belle S	5.00	2.20
❑ S189 Mark Grace S	3.00	1.35
❑ S211 Ernie Young S	1.50	.70
❑ S218 Fred McGriff S	3.00	1.35
❑ S223 Kimera Bartee S	1.50	.70
❑ S229 Rickey Henderson S	6.00	2.70
❑ S230 Sterling Hitchcock S	1.50	.70
❑ S231 Bernard Gilkey S	1.50	.70

❑ S234 Ryne Sandberg S	6.00	2.70
❑ S235 Greg Maddux S	12.00	5.50
❑ S239 Todd Stottlemyre S	1.50	.70
❑ S241 Jason Kendall S	5.00	2.20
❑ S242 Paul O'Neill S	2.50	1.10
❑ S256 Devon White S	2.50	1.10
❑ S261 Chuck Knoblauch S	5.00	2.20
❑ S263 Wally Joyner S	2.50	1.10
❑ S272 Andy Fox S	1.50	.70
❑ S274 Sean Berry S	1.50	.70
❑ S277 Benito Santiago S	1.50	.70
❑ S284 Chad Mottola S	1.50	.70
❑ S289 Dante Bichette S	2.50	1.10
❑ S291 Doc Gooden S	2.50	1.10
❑ S293 Kevin Mitchell S	1.50	.70
❑ S295 Russ Davis S	1.50	.70
❑ S296 Chan Ho Park S	3.00	1.35
❑ S302 Larry Walker S	5.00	2.20
❑ S305 Ken Griffey Jr. S	25.00	11.00
❑ S313 Billy Wagner S	3.00	1.35
❑ S317 Mike Grace S	1.50	.70
❑ S327 Kenny Lofton S	3.00	1.35
❑ S328 Derek Bell S	2.50	1.10
❑ S337 Gary Sheffield S	2.50	1.10
❑ S341 Mark Grace S	3.00	1.35
❑ S345 Andres Galarraga S	5.00	2.20
❑ S346 Brady Anderson S	2.50	1.10
❑ S350 Derek Jeter S	12.00	5.50
❑ S353 Jay Buhner S	2.50	1.10
❑ S357 Tino Martinez S	2.50	1.10

1996 Finest Refractors

	MINT	NRMT
COMMON BRONZE	3.00	1.35
*BRONZE STARS: 5X TO 12X HI COLUMN		
BRONZE STATED ODDS 1:12		
COMMON GOLD	20.00	9.00
*GOLD STARS: 1.25X TO 3X HI		
GOLD STATED ODDS 1:288		
COMMON SILVER	5.00	2.20
*SILVER STARS: 1.5X TO 4X HI		
SILVER STATED ODDS 1:48		

1997 Finest

	MINT	NRMT
COMP.BRONZE SER.1 (100)	30.00	13.50
COMP.BRONZE SER.2 (100)	30.00	13.50
COM.BRON.(1-100/176-275)	.25	.11
BRONZE MINOR STARS	.50	.23

BRONZE UNLISTED STARS....	1.00	.45
COMP.SILVER SER.1 (50) ..	120.00	55.00
COMP.SILVER SER.2 (50) ..	150.00	70.00
COM.SILV.(101-150/276-325) .	1.25	.55
SILVER MINOR STARS	2.00	.90
SILVER UNLISTED STARS	4.00	1.80
SILVER STATED ODDS 1:4		
COMP.GOLD SER.1 (25)......	300.00	135.00
COMP.GOLD SER.2 (25)......	250.00	110.00
COM.GOLD (151-175/326-350)	5.00	2.20
GOLD UNLISTED STARS ...	10.00	4.50
GOLD STATED ODDS 1:24		
BICHETTE/MCGWIRE BOTH NUMBERED 155		
BICHETTE UER SHOULD BE NUMBER 5		
❑ 1 Barry Bonds B	1.25	.55
❑ 2 Ryne Sandberg B	1.25	.55
❑ 3 Brian Jordan B	.50	.23
❑ 4 Rocky Coppinger B	.25	.11
❑ 5 Dante Bichette B UER	.50	.23
Card is erroneously numbered 155		
❑ 6 Al Martin B	.25	.11
❑ 7 Charles Nagy B	.50	.23
❑ 8 Otis Nixon B	.25	.11
❑ 9 Mark Johnson B	.25	.11
❑ 10 Jeff Bagwell B	1.25	.55
❑ 11 Ken Hill B	.25	.11
❑ 12 Willie Adams B	.25	.11
❑ 13 Raul Mondesi B	.50	.23
❑ 14 Reggie Sanders B	.50	.23
❑ 15 Derek Jeter B	3.00	1.35
❑ 16 Jermaine Dye B	.50	.23
❑ 17 Edgar Renteria B	.50	.23
❑ 18 Travis Fryman B	.50	.23
❑ 19 Roberto Hernandez B	.25	.11
❑ 20 Sammy Sosa B	3.00	1.35
❑ 21 Garret Anderson B	.50	.23
❑ 22 Rey Ordonez B	.25	.11
❑ 23 Glenallen Hill B	.25	.11
❑ 24 Dave Nilsson B	.25	.11
❑ 25 Kevin Brown B	.75	.35
❑ 26 Brian McRae B	.25	.11
❑ 27 Joey Hamilton B	.50	.23
❑ 28 Jamey Wright B	.25	.11
❑ 29 Frank Thomas B	2.00	.90
❑ 30 Mark McGwire B	5.00	2.20
❑ 31 Ramon Martinez B	.50	.23
❑ 32 Jaime Bluma B	.25	.11
❑ 33 Frank Rodriguez B	.25	.11
❑ 34 Andy Benes B	.50	.23
❑ 35 Jay Buhner B	.50	.23
❑ 36 Justin Thompson B	.25	.11
❑ 37 Darin Erstad B	1.00	.45
❑ 38 Gregg Jefferies B	.25	.11
❑ 39 Jeff D'Amico B	.25	.11
❑ 40 Pedro Martinez B	1.25	.55
❑ 41 Nomar Garciaparra B	3.00	1.35
❑ 42 Jose Valentin B	.25	.11
❑ 43 Pat Hentgen B	.50	.23
❑ 44 Will Clark B	1.00	.45
❑ 45 Bernie Williams B	1.00	.45
❑ 46 Luis Castillo B	.50	.23
❑ 47 B.J. Surhoff B	.50	.23
❑ 48 Greg Gagne B	.25	.11
❑ 49 Pete Schourek B	.25	.11
❑ 50 Mike Piazza B	3.00	1.35
❑ 51 Dwight Gooden B	.50	.23
❑ 52 Javy Lopez B	.50	.23
❑ 53 Chuck Finley B	.25	.23
❑ 54 James Baldwin B	.50	.23
❑ 55 Jack McDowell B	.25	.11
❑ 56 Royce Clayton B	.25	.11
❑ 57 Carlos Delgado B	1.00	.45
❑ 58 Neifi Perez B	.25	.11
❑ 59 Eddie Taubensee B	.25	.11
❑ 60 Rafael Palmeiro B	1.00	.45
❑ 61 Marty Cordova B	.25	.11
❑ 62 Wade Boggs B	1.00	.45
❑ 63 Rickey Henderson B	1.25	.55
❑ 64 Mike Hampton B	.50	.23
❑ 65 Troy Percival B	.50	.23
❑ 66 Barry Larkin B	1.00	.45
❑ 67 Jermaine Allensworth B	.25	.11
❑ 68 Mark Clark B	.25	.11
❑ 69 Mike Lansing B	.25	.11
❑ 70 Mark Grudzielanek B	.50	.23
❑ 71 Todd Stottlemyre B	.25	.11
❑ 72 Juan Guzman B	.25	.11
❑ 73 John Burkett B	.25	.11
❑ 74 Wilson Alvarez B	.50	.23
❑ 75 Ellis Burks B	.50	.23
❑ 76 Bobby Higginson B	.50	.23
❑ 77 Ricky Bottalico B	.50	.23
❑ 78 Omar Vizquel B	.50	.23
❑ 79 Paul Sorrento B	.25	.11
❑ 80 Denny Neagle B	.50	.23
❑ 81 Roger Pavlik B	.25	.11
❑ 82 Mike Lieberthal B	.25	.11
❑ 83 Devon White B	.25	.11
❑ 84 John Olerud B	.50	.23
❑ 85 Kevin Appier B	.25	.23
❑ 86 Joe Girardi B	.25	.11
❑ 87 Paul O'Neill B	.50	.23
❑ 88 Mike Sweeney B	.50	.23
❑ 89 John Smiley B	.25	.11
❑ 90 Ivan Rodriguez B	1.25	.55
❑ 91 Randy Myers B	.25	.11
❑ 92 Bip Roberts B	.25	.11
❑ 93 Jose Mesa B	.25	.11
❑ 94 Paul Wilson B	.25	.11
❑ 95 Mike Mussina B	1.00	.45
❑ 96 Ben McDonald B	.25	.11
❑ 97 John Mabry B	.25	.11
❑ 98 Tom Goodwin B	.25	.11
❑ 99 Edgar Martinez B	.50	.23
❑ 100 Andruw Jones B	1.25	.55
❑ 101 Jose Canseco B	5.00	2.20
❑ 102 Billy Wagner B	2.00	.90
❑ 103 Dante Bichette B	2.00	.90
❑ 104 Curt Schilling B	3.00	1.35
❑ 105 Dean Palmer B	2.00	.90
❑ 106 Larry Walker B	4.00	1.80
❑ 107 Bernie Williams B	4.00	1.80
❑ 108 Chipper Jones B	10.00	4.50
❑ 109 Gary Sheffield B	2.00	.90
❑ 110 Randy Johnson B	4.00	1.80
❑ 111 Roberto Alomar B	4.00	1.80
❑ 112 Todd Walker B	4.00	1.80
❑ 113 Sandy Alomar Jr. B	2.00	.90
❑ 114 John Jaha B	1.25	.55
❑ 115 Ken Caminiti S UER	3.00	1.35
Card is numbered 135		
❑ 116 Ryan Klesko B	2.00	.90
❑ 117 Mariano Rivera S	2.00	.90
❑ 118 Jason Giambi B	2.00	.90
❑ 119 Lance Johnson S	1.25	.55
❑ 120 Robin Ventura B	2.00	.90
❑ 121 Todd Hollandsworth S..	1.25	.55
❑ 122 Johnny Damon S	2.00	.90
❑ 123 W. VanLandingham S ..	.50	.23
❑ 124 Jason Kendall S	3.00	1.35
❑ 125 Vinny Castilla S	3.00	1.35
❑ 126 Harold Baines S	2.00	.90
❑ 127 Joe Carter S	2.00	.90
❑ 128 Craig Biggio S	4.00	1.80
❑ 129 Tony Clark S	3.00	1.35
❑ 130 Ron Gant S	1.25	.55
❑ 131 David Segui S	2.00	.90
❑ 132 Steve Trachsel S	1.25	.55
❑ 133 Scott Rolen S	6.00	2.70
❑ 134 Mike Stanley S	1.25	.55
❑ 135 Cal Ripken S	15.00	6.75
❑ 136 John Smoltz S	2.00	.90
❑ 137 Bobby Jones S	1.25	.55
❑ 138 Manny Ramirez S	5.00	2.20
❑ 139 Ken Griffey Jr. S	20.00	9.00
❑ 140 Chuck Knoblauch S..	4.00	1.80
❑ 141 Mark Grace S	3.00	1.35
❑ 142 Chris Snopek S	1.25	.55
❑ 143 Hideo Nomo S	4.00	1.80
❑ 144 Tim Salmon S	4.00	1.80
❑ 145 David Cone S	3.00	1.35
❑ 146 Eric Young S	2.00	.90
❑ 147 Jeff Brantley S	1.25	.55
❑ 148 Jim Thome S	4.00	1.80
❑ 149 Trevor Hoffman S	2.00	.90
❑ 150 Juan Gonzalez S	8.00	3.60
❑ 151 Mike Piazza G	30.00	13.50
❑ 152 Ivan Rodriguez G	12.00	5.50
❑ 153 Mo Vaughn G	10.00	4.50
❑ 154 Brady Anderson G	8.00	3.60
❑ 155 Mark McGwire G	50.00	22.00
❑ 156 Rafael Palmeiro G	10.00	4.50
❑ 157 Barry Larkin G	10.00	4.50
❑ 158 Greg Maddux G	25.00	11.00
❑ 159 Jeff Bagwell G	12.00	5.50
❑ 160 Frank Thomas G	20.00	9.00
❑ 161 Ken Caminiti G	10.00	4.50
❑ 162 Andruw Jones G	12.00	5.50
❑ 163 Dennis Eckersley G	8.00	3.60
❑ 164 Jeff Conine G	5.00	2.20
❑ 165 Jim Edmonds G	10.00	4.50
❑ 166 Derek Jeter G	30.00	13.50
❑ 167 Vladimir Guerrero G	15.00	6.75
❑ 168 Sammy Sosa G	30.00	13.50
❑ 169 Tony Gwynn G	25.00	11.00
❑ 170 Andres Galarraga G ..	10.00	4.50
❑ 171 Todd Hundley G	8.00	3.60
❑ 172 Jay Buhner G UER	8.00	3.60
Card is numbered 164		
❑ 173 Paul Molitor G	10.00	4.50
❑ 174 Kenny Lofton G	10.00	4.50
❑ 175 Barry Bonds G	12.00	5.50
❑ 176 Gary Sheffield B	.50	.23
❑ 177 Dmitri Young B	.50	.23
❑ 178 Jay Bell B	.50	.23
❑ 179 David Wells B	.50	.23
❑ 180 Walt Weiss B	.25	.11
❑ 181 Paul Molitor B	1.00	.45
❑ 182 Jose Guillen B	.75	.35
❑ 183 Al Leiter B	.50	.23
❑ 184 Mike Fetters B	.25	.11
❑ 185 Mark Langston B	.50	.23
❑ 186 Fred McGriff B	.75	.35
❑ 187 Darrin Fletcher B	.25	.11
❑ 188 Brant Brown B	.50	.23
❑ 189 Geronimo Berroa B	.25	.11
❑ 190 Jim Thome B	1.00	.45
❑ 191 Jose Vizcaino B	.25	.11
❑ 192 Andy Ashby B	.25	.11
❑ 193 Rusty Greer B	.50	.23
❑ 194 Brian Hunter B	.50	.23
❑ 195 Chris Hoiles B	.25	.11
❑ 196 Orlando Merced B	.25	.11
❑ 197 Brett Butler B	.50	.23
❑ 198 Derek Bell B	.50	.23
❑ 199 Bobby Bonilla B	.50	.23
❑ 200 Alex Ochoa B	.25	.11
❑ 201 Wally Joyner B	.50	.23
❑ 202 Mo Vaughn B	1.00	.45
❑ 203 Doug Drabek B	.25	.11
❑ 204 Tino Martinez B	1.00	.45
❑ 205 Roberto Alomar B	1.00	.45
❑ 206 Brian Giles B	5.00	2.20
❑ 207 Todd Worrell B	.25	.11
❑ 208 Alan Benes B	.25	.11
❑ 209 Jim Leyritz B	.25	.11
❑ 210 Darryl Hamilton B	.25	.11
❑ 211 Jimmy Key B	.50	.23
❑ 212 Juan Gonzalez B	2.00	.90
❑ 213 Vinny Castilla B	.75	.35
❑ 214 Chuck Knoblauch B	1.00	.45
❑ 215 Tony Phillips B	.25	.11
❑ 216 Jeff Cirillo B	.50	.23
❑ 217 Carlos Garcia B	.25	.11
❑ 218 Brooks Kieschnick B	.25	.11
❑ 219 Marquis Grissom B	.50	.23
❑ 220 Dan Wilson B	.25	.11
❑ 221 Greg Vaughn B	.50	.23
❑ 222 John Wetteland B	.50	.23
❑ 223 Andres Galarraga B	1.00	.45
❑ 224 Ozzie Guillen B	.25	.11
❑ 225 Kevin Elster B	.25	.11
❑ 226 Bernard Gilkey B	.25	.11
❑ 227 Mike Macfarlane B	.25	.11
❑ 228 Heathcliff Slocumb B	.25	.11
❑ 229 Wendell Magee Jr. B	.25	.11
❑ 230 Carlos Baerga B	.25	.11
❑ 231 Kevin Seitzer B	.25	.11
❑ 232 Henry Rodriguez B	.50	.23
❑ 233 Roger Clemens B	2.50	1.10
❑ 234 Mark Wohlers B	.25	.11
❑ 235 Eddie Murray B	1.00	.45
❑ 236 Todd Zeile B	.25	.11
❑ 237 J.T. Snow B	.50	.23
❑ 238 Ken Griffey Jr. B	5.00	2.20
❑ 239 Sterling Hitchcock B	.25	.11
❑ 240 Albert Belle B	1.00	.45

241	Terry Steinbach B	.25	.11
242	Robb Nen B	.25	.11
243	Mark McLemore B	.25	.11
244	Jeff King B	.25	.11
245	Tony Clark B	.75	.35
246	Tim Salmon B	1.00	.45
247	Benito Santiago B	.25	.11
248	Robin Ventura B	.50	.23
249	Bubba Trammell B	1.00	.45
250	Chili Davis B	.50	.23
251	John Valentin B	.50	.23
252	Cal Ripken B	4.00	1.80
253	Matt Williams B	1.00	.45
254	Jeff Kent B	.50	.23
255	Eric Karros B	.50	.23
256	Ray Lankford B	.50	.23
257	Ed Sprague B	.25	.11
258	Shane Reynolds B	.50	.23
259	Jaime Navarro B	.25	.11
260	Eric Davis B	.50	.23
261	Orel Hershiser B	.50	.23
262	Mark Grace B	.75	.35
263	Rod Beck B	.25	.11
264	Ismael Valdes B	.50	.23
265	Manny Ramirez B	1.25	.55
266	Ken Caminiti B	.75	.35
267	Tim Naehring B	.25	.11
268	Jose Rosado B	.25	.11
269	Greg Colbrunn B	.25	.11
270	Dean Palmer B	.50	.23
271	David Justice B	1.00	.45
272	Scott Spiezio B	.25	.11
273	Chipper Jones B	2.50	1.10
274	Mel Rojas B	.25	.11
275	Bartolo Colon B	.50	.23
276	Darin Erstad S	4.00	1.80
277	Sammy Sosa S	12.00	5.50
278	Rafael Palmeiro S	4.00	1.80
279	Frank Thomas S	8.00	3.60
280	Ruben Rivera S	1.25	.55
281	Hal Morris S	1.25	.55
282	Jay Buhner S	2.00	.90
283	Kenny Lofton S	3.00	1.35
284	Jose Canseco S	5.00	2.20
285	Alex Fernandez S	1.25	.55
286	Todd Helton S	8.00	3.60
287	Andy Pettitte S	3.00	1.35
288	John Franco S	2.00	.90
289	Ivan Rodriguez S	5.00	2.20
290	Ellis Burks S	2.00	.90
291	Julio Franco S	2.00	.90
292	Mike Piazza S	12.00	5.50
293	Brian Jordan S	2.00	.90
294	Greg Maddux S	10.00	4.50
295	Bob Abreu S	2.00	.90
296	Rondell White S	2.00	.90
297	Moises Alou S	2.00	.90
298	Tony Gwynn S	10.00	4.50
299	Deion Sanders S	2.00	.90
300	Jeff Montgomery S	1.25	.55
301	Ray Durham S	2.00	.90
302	John Wasdin S	1.25	.55
303	Ryne Sandberg S	5.00	2.20
304	Delino DeShields S	1.25	.55
305	Mark McGwire S	20.00	9.00
306	Andruw Jones S	5.00	2.20
307	Kevin Orie S	1.25	.55
308	Matt Williams S	4.00	1.80
309	Karim Garcia S	2.00	.90
310	Derek Jeter S	12.00	5.50
311	Mo Vaughn S	4.00	1.80
312	Brady Anderson S	2.00	.90
313	Barry Bonds S	5.00	2.20
314	Steve Finley S	2.00	.90
315	Vladimir Guerrero S	6.00	2.70
316	Matt Morris S	2.00	.90
317	Tom Glavine S	4.00	1.80
318	Jeff Bagwell S	5.00	2.20
319	Albert Belle S	4.00	1.80
320	Hideki Irabu S	6.00	2.70
321	Andres Galarraga S	4.00	1.80
322	Cecil Fielder S	2.00	.90
323	Barry Larkin S	4.00	1.80
324	Todd Hundley S	2.00	.90
325	Fred McGriff S	3.00	1.35
326	Gary Sheffield S	8.00	3.60
327	Craig Biggio G	10.00	4.50
328	Raul Mondesi G	8.00	3.60
329	Edgar Martinez G	8.00	3.60
330	Chipper Jones G	25.00	11.00
331	Bernie Williams G	10.00	4.50
332	Juan Gonzalez G	20.00	9.00
333	Ron Gant G	5.00	2.20
334	Cal Ripken G	40.00	18.00
335	Larry Walker G	10.00	4.50
336	Matt Williams G	10.00	4.50
337	Jose Cruz Jr. G	15.00	6.75
338	Joe Carter G	8.00	3.60
339	Wilton Guerrero G	5.00	2.20
340	Cecil Fielder G	8.00	3.60
341	Todd Walker G	10.00	4.50
342	Ken Griffey Jr. G	50.00	22.00
343	Ryan Klesko G	8.00	3.60
344	Roger Clemens G	25.00	11.00
345	Hideo Nomo G	10.00	4.50
346	Dante Bichette G	8.00	3.60
347	Albert Belle G	10.00	4.50
348	Randy Johnson G	10.00	4.50
349	Manny Ramirez G	12.00	5.50
350	John Smoltz G	8.00	3.60

1997 Finest Embossed

	MINT	NRMT
COM.SILV.(101-150/276-325) ..	2.00	.90

*SILV.STARS: .75X TO 2X BASE CARD HI
*SILV.YNG.STARS: .6X TO 1.5X BASE HI
SILVER STATED ODDS 1:16
ALL SILVER CARDS ARE NON DIE CUT
COM.GOLD (151-175/326-350) 10.00 4.50
*GOLD STARS: .75X TO 2X BASE CARD HI
*GOLD YNG.STARS: .6X TO 1.5X BASE HI
GOLD STATED ODDS 1:96
ALL GOLD CARDS ARE DIE CUT

1997 Finest Embossed Refractors

	MINT	NRMT
COM.SILV.(101-150/276-325)	12.00	5.50

*SILVER STARS: 4X TO 10X BASIC CARDS
*SILVER YNG.STARS: 3X TO 8X BASIC CARDS
SILVER STATED ODDS 1:192
ALL SILVER CARDS ARE NON DIE CUT
COM.SER.1 GOLD (151-175) 25.00 11.00

*SER.1 GOLD STARS: 2.5X TO 6X BASIC CARDS
*SER.1 GOLD YNG.STARS: 2X TO 5X BASIC CARDS
COM.SER.2 GOLD (326-350) 50.00 22.00
*SER.2 GOLD STARS: 5X TO 12X BASIC CARDS
*SER.2 GOLD YNG.STARS: 4X TO 10X BASIC CARDS
GOLD STATED ODDS 1:1152
ALL GOLD CARDS ARE DIE CUT

1997 Finest Refractors

	MINT	NRMT
COM.BRON.(1-100/176-275)	3.00	1.35

*BRONZE STARS: 5X TO 12X BASE CARD HI
*BRONZE RC'S: 1.5X TO 4X BASE HI
BRONZE STATED ODDS 1:12
COM.SILV.(101-150/276-325) .. 4.00 1.80
*SILVER STARS: 1.5X TO 4X BASE CARD HI
*SILVER RC'S: 1.25X TO 3X BASE HI
SILVER STATED ODDS 1:48
COM.GOLD (151-175/326-350) 12.00 5.50
*GOLD STARS: 1.25X TO 3X BASE CARD HI
*GOLD RC'S: 1X TO 2.5X BASE HI
GOLD STATED ODDS 1:288

1998 Finest

	MINT	NRMT
COMPLETE SET (275)	90.00	40.00
COMPLETE SERIES 1 (150)	50.00	22.00
COMPLETE SERIES 2 (125)	40.00	18.00
COMMON CARD (1-275)	.25	.11
MINOR STARS	.40	.18
SEMISTARS	.60	.25
UNLISTED STARS	1.00	.45
COMP.NO-PROT.SET (275)	350.00	160.00
COMP.NO-PROT.SER.1 (150)	150.00	90.00
COMP.NO-PROT.SER.2 (125)	150.00	70.00
COMMON NO-PROT. (1-275)	1.00	.45

*NP.STARS: 1.5X TO 4X HI COLUMN
*NP.YOUNG STARS: 1.25X TO 3X HI
NO-PROTECTOR ODDS 1:2, 1 PER HTA

1	Larry Walker	1.00	.45
2	Andruw Jones	1.00	.45
3	Ramon Martinez	.25	.11
4	Geronimo Berroa	.25	.11
5	David Justice	.40	.18
6	Rusty Greer	.40	.18
7	Chad Ogea	.25	.11

❑ 8	Tom Goodwin	.25	.11
❑ 9	Tino Martinez	.40	.18
❑ 10	Jose Guillen	.25	.11
❑ 11	Jeffrey Hammonds	.25	.11
❑ 12	Brian McRae	.25	.11
❑ 13	Jeremi Gonzalez	.25	.11
❑ 14	Craig Counsell	.25	.11
❑ 15	Mike Piazza	3.00	1.35
❑ 16	Greg Maddux	2.50	1.10
❑ 17	Todd Greene	.25	.11
❑ 18	Rondell White	.40	.18
❑ 19	Kirk Rueter	.25	.11
❑ 20	Tony Clark	.40	.18
❑ 21	Brad Radke	.40	.18
❑ 22	Jaret Wright	.40	.18
❑ 23	Carlos Delgado	1.00	.45
❑ 24	Dustin Hermanson	.25	.11
❑ 25	Gary Sheffield	.40	.18
❑ 26	Jose Canseco	1.25	.55
❑ 27	Kevin Young	.40	.18
❑ 28	David Wells	.40	.18
❑ 29	Mariano Rivera	.40	.18
❑ 30	Reggie Sanders	.25	.11
❑ 31	Mike Cameron	.40	.18
❑ 32	Bobby Witt	.25	.11
❑ 33	Kevin Orie	.25	.11
❑ 34	Royce Clayton	.25	.11
❑ 35	Edgar Martinez	.40	.18
❑ 36	Neifi Perez	.40	.18
❑ 37	Kevin Appier	.40	.18
❑ 38	Darryl Hamilton	.25	.11
❑ 39	Michael Tucker	.25	.11
❑ 40	Roger Clemens	2.50	1.10
❑ 41	Carl Everett	.40	.18
❑ 42	Mike Sweeney	.40	.18
❑ 43	Pat Meares	.25	.11
❑ 44	Brian Giles	.40	.18
❑ 45	Matt Morris	.25	.11
❑ 46	Jason Dickson	.25	.11
❑ 47	Rich Loiselle	.40	.18
❑ 48	Joe Girardi	.25	.11
❑ 49	Steve Trachsel	.25	.11
❑ 50	Ben Grieve	1.00	.45
❑ 51	Brian Johnson	.25	.11
❑ 52	Hideki Irabu	.40	.18
❑ 53	J.T. Snow	.40	.18
❑ 54	Mike Hampton	.40	.18
❑ 55	Dave Nilsson	.25	.11
❑ 56	Alex Fernandez	.25	.11
❑ 57	Brett Tomko	.25	.11
❑ 58	Wally Joyner	.40	.18
❑ 59	Kelvim Escobar	.40	.18
❑ 60	Roberto Alomar	1.00	.45
❑ 61	Todd Jones	.25	.11
❑ 62	Paul O'Neill	.40	.18
❑ 63	Jamie Moyer	.25	.11
❑ 64	Mark Wohlers	.25	.11
❑ 65	Jose Cruz Jr.	.40	.18
❑ 66	Troy Percival	.40	.18
❑ 67	Rick Reed	.25	.11
❑ 68	Will Clark	1.00	.45
❑ 69	Jamey Wright	.25	.11
❑ 70	Mike Mussina	1.00	.45
❑ 71	David Cone	.60	.25
❑ 72	Ryan Klesko	.40	.18
❑ 73	Scott Hatteberg	.25	.11
❑ 74	James Baldwin	.25	.11
❑ 75	Tony Womack	.40	.18
❑ 76	Carlos Perez	.25	.11
❑ 77	Charles Nagy	.40	.18
❑ 78	Jeromy Burnitz	.40	.18
❑ 79	Shane Reynolds	.25	.11
❑ 80	Cliff Floyd	.40	.18
❑ 81	Jason Kendall	.40	.18
❑ 82	Chad Curtis	.25	.11
❑ 83	Matt Karchner	.25	.11
❑ 84	Ricky Bottalico	.25	.11
❑ 85	Sammy Sosa	3.00	1.35
❑ 86	Javy Lopez	.40	.18
❑ 87	Jeff Kent	.40	.18
❑ 88	Shawn Green	1.00	.45
❑ 89	Joey Cora	.25	.11
❑ 90	Tony Gwynn	2.50	1.10
❑ 91	Bob Tewksbury	.25	.11
❑ 92	Derek Jeter	3.00	1.35
❑ 93	Eric Davis	.40	.18
❑ 94	Jeff Fassero	.25	.11
❑ 95	Denny Neagle	.25	.11
❑ 96	Ismael Valdes	.25	.11
❑ 97	Tim Salmon	.60	.25
❑ 98	Mark Grudzielanek	.25	.11
❑ 99	Curt Schilling	.60	.25
❑ 100	Ken Griffey Jr.	5.00	2.20
❑ 101	Edgardo Alfonzo	.60	.25
❑ 102	Vinny Castilla	.40	.18
❑ 103	Jose Rosado	.25	.11
❑ 104	Scott Erickson	.25	.11
❑ 105	Alan Benes	.25	.11
❑ 106	Shannon Stewart	.40	.18
❑ 107	Delino DeShields	.25	.11
❑ 108	Mark Loretta	.25	.11
❑ 109	Todd Hundley	.40	.18
❑ 110	Chuck Knoblauch	.40	.18
❑ 111	Todd Helton	1.25	.55
❑ 112	F.P. Santangelo	.25	.11
❑ 113	Jeff Cirillo	.40	.18
❑ 114	Omar Vizquel	.40	.18
❑ 115	John Valentin	.40	.18
❑ 116	Damion Easley	.25	.11
❑ 117	Matt Lawton	.25	.11
❑ 118	Jim Thome	1.00	.45
❑ 119	Sandy Alomar Jr.	.40	.18
❑ 120	Albert Belle	1.00	.45
❑ 121	Chris Stynes	.25	.11
❑ 122	Butch Huskey	.25	.11
❑ 123	Shawn Estes	.25	.11
❑ 124	Terry Adams	.25	.11
❑ 125	Ivan Rodriguez	1.25	.55
❑ 126	Ron Gant	.40	.18
❑ 127	John Mabry	.25	.11
❑ 128	Jeff Shaw	.25	.11
❑ 129	Jeff Montgomery	.25	.11
❑ 130	Justin Thompson	.25	.11
❑ 131	Livan Hernandez	.25	.11
❑ 132	Ugueth Urbina	.25	.11
❑ 133	Scott Servais	.25	.11
❑ 134	Troy O'Leary	.40	.18
❑ 135	Cal Ripken	4.00	1.80
❑ 136	Quilvio Veras	.25	.11
❑ 137	Pedro Astacio	.25	.11
❑ 138	Willie Greene	.25	.11
❑ 139	Lance Johnson	.25	.11
❑ 140	Nomar Garciaparra	3.00	1.35
❑ 141	Jose Offerman	.40	.18
❑ 142	Scott Rolen	1.25	.55
❑ 143	Derek Bell	.40	.18
❑ 144	Johnny Damon	.40	.18
❑ 145	Mark McGwire	6.00	2.70
❑ 146	Chan Ho Park	.40	.18
❑ 147	Edgar Renteria	.25	.11
❑ 148	Eric Young	.25	.11
❑ 149	Craig Biggio	1.00	.45
❑ 150	Checklist (1-150)	.25	.11
❑ 151	Frank Thomas	2.00	.90
❑ 152	John Wetteland	.40	.18
❑ 153	Mike Lansing	.25	.11
❑ 154	Pedro Martinez	1.25	.55
❑ 155	Rico Brogna	.25	.11
❑ 156	Kevin Brown	.60	.25
❑ 157	Alex Rodriguez	3.00	1.35
❑ 158	Wade Boggs	1.00	.45
❑ 159	Richard Hidalgo	.40	.18
❑ 160	Mark Grace	.60	.25
❑ 161	Jose Mesa	.25	.11
❑ 162	John Olerud	.40	.18
❑ 163	Tim Belcher	.25	.11
❑ 164	Chuck Finley	.40	.18
❑ 165	Brian Hunter	.25	.11
❑ 166	Joe Carter	.40	.18
❑ 167	Stan Javier	.25	.11
❑ 168	Jay Bell	.40	.18
❑ 169	Ray Lankford	.40	.18
❑ 170	John Smoltz	.60	.25
❑ 171	Ed Sprague	.25	.11
❑ 172	Jason Giambi	.40	.18
❑ 173	Todd Walker	.40	.18
❑ 174	Paul Konerko	.40	.18
❑ 175	Rey Ordonez	.40	.18
❑ 176	Dante Bichette	.40	.18
❑ 177	Bernie Williams	1.00	.45
❑ 178	Jon Nunnally	.25	.11
❑ 179	Rafael Palmeiro	1.00	.45
❑ 180	Jay Buhner	.40	.18
❑ 181	Devon White	.25	.11
❑ 182	Jeff D'Amico	.25	.11
❑ 183	Walt Weiss	.40	.18
❑ 184	Scott Spiezio	.40	.18
❑ 185	Moises Alou	.40	.18
❑ 186	Carlos Baerga	.25	.11
❑ 187	Todd Zeile	.40	.18
❑ 188	Gregg Jefferies	.25	.11
❑ 189	Mo Vaughn	1.00	.45
❑ 190	Terry Steinbach	.25	.11
❑ 191	Ray Durham	.40	.18
❑ 192	Robin Ventura	.40	.18
❑ 193	Jeff Reed	.25	.11
❑ 194	Ken Caminiti	.40	.18
❑ 195	Eric Karros	.40	.18
❑ 196	Wilson Alvarez	.25	.11
❑ 197	Gary Gaetti	.40	.18
❑ 198	Andres Galarraga	.60	.25
❑ 199	Alex Gonzalez	.25	.11
❑ 200	Garret Anderson	.40	.18
❑ 201	Andy Benes	.25	.11
❑ 202	Harold Baines	.40	.18
❑ 203	Ron Coomer	.25	.11
❑ 204	Dean Palmer	.40	.18
❑ 205	Reggie Jefferson	.25	.11
❑ 206	John Burkett	.25	.11
❑ 207	Jermaine Allensworth	.25	.11
❑ 208	Bernard Gilkey	.25	.11
❑ 209	Jeff Bagwell	1.25	.55
❑ 210	Kenny Lofton	.60	.25
❑ 211	Bobby Jones	.25	.11
❑ 212	Bartolo Colon	.40	.18
❑ 213	Jim Edmonds	.40	.18
❑ 214	Pat Hentgen	.25	.11
❑ 215	Matt Williams	1.00	.45
❑ 216	Bob Abreu	.40	.18
❑ 217	Jorge Posada	.25	.11
❑ 218	Marty Cordova	.25	.11
❑ 219	Eric Hill	.25	.11
❑ 220	Steve Finley	.40	.18
❑ 221	Jeff King	.25	.11
❑ 222	Quinton McCracken	.25	.11
❑ 223	Matt Stairs	.40	.18
❑ 224	Darin Erstad	.60	.25
❑ 225	Fred McGriff	.60	.25
❑ 226	Marquis Grissom	.25	.11
❑ 227	Doug Glanville	.40	.18
❑ 228	Tom Glavine	1.00	.45
❑ 229	John Franco	.40	.18
❑ 230	Darren Bragg	.25	.11
❑ 231	Barry Larkin	1.00	.45
❑ 232	Trevor Hoffman	.40	.18
❑ 233	Brady Anderson	.40	.18
❑ 234	Al Martin	.25	.11
❑ 235	B.J. Surhoff	.25	.11
❑ 236	Ellis Burks	.40	.18
❑ 237	Randy Johnson	1.00	.45
❑ 238	Mark Clark	.25	.11
❑ 239	Tony Saunders	.25	.11
❑ 240	Hideo Nomo	1.00	.45
❑ 241	Brad Fullmer	.25	.11
❑ 242	Chipper Jones	2.50	1.10
❑ 243	Jose Valentin	.25	.11
❑ 244	Manny Ramirez	1.25	.55
❑ 245	Derrek Lee	.25	.11
❑ 246	Jimmy Key	.40	.18
❑ 247	Tim Naehring	.25	.11
❑ 248	Bobby Higginson	.40	.18
❑ 249	Charles Johnson	.40	.18
❑ 250	Chili Davis	.40	.18
❑ 251	Tom Gordon	.40	.18
❑ 252	Mike Lieberthal	.40	.18
❑ 253	Billy Wagner	.40	.18
❑ 254	Juan Guzman	.25	.11
❑ 255	Todd Stottlemyre	.25	.11
❑ 256	Brian Jordan	.40	.18
❑ 257	Barry Bonds	1.25	.55
❑ 258	Dan Wilson	.25	.11
❑ 259	Paul Molitor	1.00	.45
❑ 260	Juan Gonzalez	2.00	.90
❑ 261	Francisco Cordova	.25	.11
❑ 262	Cecil Fielder	.40	.18
❑ 263	Travis Lee	.60	.25
❑ 264	Kevin Tapani	.25	.11
❑ 265	Raul Mondesi	.40	.18

		MINT	NRMT
❑ 266	Travis Fryman	.40	.18
❑ 267	Armando Benitez	.25	.11
❑ 268	Pokey Reese	.25	.11
❑ 269	Rick Aguilera	.25	.11
❑ 270	Andy Pettitte	.40	.18
❑ 271	Jose Vizcaino	.25	.11
❑ 272	Kerry Wood	1.25	.55
❑ 273	Vladimir Guerrero	1.25	.55
❑ 274	John Smiley	.25	.11
❑ 275	Checklist (151-275)	.25	.11

1998 Finest No-Protectors Refractors

	MINT	NRMT
COMPLETE SET (275)	2200.00	1000.00
COMPLETE SERIES 1 (150)	1200.00	550.00
COMPLETE SERIES 2 (125)	1000.00	450.00
COMMON CARD (1-275)	6.00	2.70

*STARS: 10X TO 25X BASIC CARDS
*YOUNG STARS: 8X TO 20X BASIC CARDS
STATED ODDS 1:24, 1:10 HTA

1998 Finest Oversize

	MINT	NRMT
COMPLETE SERIES 1 (8)	120.00	55.00
COMPLETE SERIES 2 (8)	80.00	36.00
COMMON CARD (A1-B8)	2.50	1.10
UNLISTED STARS	6.00	2.70

STATED ODDS 1:3 HOBBY/HTA BOXES
*REFRACTORS: .75X TO 2X HI COLUMN
REF.ODDS 1:6 HOBBY/HTA BOXES

		MINT	NRMT
❑ A1	Mark McGwire	40.00	18.00
❑ A2	Cal Ripken	25.00	11.00
❑ A3	Nomar Garciaparra	20.00	9.00
❑ A4	Mike Piazza	20.00	9.00
❑ A5	Greg Maddux	15.00	6.75
❑ A6	Jose Cruz Jr.	2.50	1.10
❑ A7	Roger Clemens	15.00	6.75
❑ A8	Ken Griffey Jr.	30.00	13.50
❑ B1	Frank Thomas	12.00	5.50
❑ B2	Bernie Williams	6.00	2.70
❑ B3	Randy Johnson	6.00	2.70
❑ B4	Chipper Jones	15.00	6.75
❑ B5	Manny Ramirez	8.00	3.60
❑ B6	Barry Bonds	8.00	3.60
❑ B7	Juan Gonzalez	12.00	5.50
❑ B8	Jeff Bagwell	8.00	3.60

1998 Finest Refractors

	MINT	NRMT
COMMON CARD (1-275)	3.00	1.35

*STARS: 5X TO 12X BASIC CARDS
*YOUNG STARS: 4X TO 10X BASIC CARDS
STATED ODDS 1:12, 1:5 HTA

1998 Finest Centurions

	MINT	NRMT
COMPLETE SET (20)	200.00	90.00
COMMON CARD (C1-C20)	2.00	.90
MINOR STARS	3.00	1.35
SEMISTARS	5.00	2.20
UNLISTED STARS	8.00	3.60

SER.1 STATED ODDS 1:153 HOBBY, 1:71 HTA
STATED PRINT RUN 500 SERIAL #'d SETS
*REFRACTORS: 2X TO 5X HI COLUMN
SER.1 REF.ODDS 1:1020 HOBBY, 1:471 HTA
REFRACTOR PRINT RUN 75 SERIAL #'d SETS

		MINT	NRMT
❑ C1	Andruw Jones	8.00	3.60
❑ C2	Vladimir Guerrero	10.00	4.50
❑ C3	Nomar Garciaparra	25.00	11.00
❑ C4	Scott Rolen	10.00	4.50
❑ C5	Ken Griffey Jr.	40.00	18.00
❑ C6	Jose Cruz Jr.	3.00	1.35
❑ C7	Barry Bonds	10.00	4.50
❑ C8	Mark McGwire	50.00	22.00
❑ C9	Juan Gonzalez	15.00	6.75
❑ C10	Jeff Bagwell	10.00	4.50
❑ C11	Frank Thomas	15.00	6.75
❑ C12	Paul Konerko	3.00	1.35
❑ C13	Alex Rodriguez	25.00	11.00
❑ C14	Mike Piazza	25.00	11.00
❑ C15	Travis Lee	5.00	2.20
❑ C16	Chipper Jones	20.00	9.00
❑ C17	Larry Walker	8.00	3.60
❑ C18	Mo Vaughn	8.00	3.60
❑ C19	Livan Hernandez	2.00	.90
❑ C20	Jaret Wright	3.00	1.35

1998 Finest The Man

	MINT	NRMT
COMPLETE SET (20)	1000.00	450.00
COMMON CARD (TM1-TM20)	10.00	4.50
SEMISTARS	15.00	6.75
UNLISTED STARS	25.00	11.00

SER.2 STATED ODDS 1:119

*REFRACTORS: 1.25X TO 3X HI COLUMN
REF.SER.2 ODDS 1:793
REFRACTOR PRINT RUN 75 SERIAL #'d SETS

		MINT	NRMT
❑ TM1	Ken Griffey Jr.	120.00	55.00
❑ TM2	Barry Bonds	30.00	13.50
❑ TM3	Frank Thomas	50.00	22.00
❑ TM4	Chipper Jones	60.00	27.00
❑ TM5	Cal Ripken	100.00	45.00
❑ TM6	Nomar Garciaparra	80.00	36.00
❑ TM7	Mark McGwire	150.00	70.00
❑ TM8	Mike Piazza	80.00	36.00
❑ TM9	Derek Jeter	80.00	36.00
❑ TM10	Alex Rodriguez	80.00	36.00
❑ TM11	Jose Cruz Jr.	10.00	4.50
❑ TM12	Larry Walker	25.00	11.00
❑ TM13	Jeff Bagwell	30.00	13.50
❑ TM14	Tony Gwynn	60.00	27.00
❑ TM15	Travis Lee	15.00	6.75
❑ TM16	Juan Gonzalez	50.00	22.00
❑ TM17	Scott Rolen	30.00	13.50
❑ TM18	Randy Johnson	25.00	11.00
❑ TM19	Roger Clemens	60.00	27.00
❑ TM20	Greg Maddux	60.00	27.00

1998 Finest Mystery Finest 1

	MINT	NRMT
COMPLETE SET (50)	1000.00	450.00
COMMON CARD (M1-M50)	4.00	1.80
SEMISTARS	6.00	2.70
UNLISTED STARS	10.00	4.50

SER.1 STAT.ODDS 1:36 HOBBY, 1:15 HTA
*REFRACTORS: 1X TO 2.5X HI COLUMN
REF.SER.1 ODDS 1:144 HOBBY, 1:64 HTA

		MINT	NRMT
❑ M1	Frank Thomas	40.00	18.00
	Ken Griffey Jr.		
❑ M2	Frank Thomas	25.00	11.00
	Mike Piazza		
❑ M3	Frank Thomas	50.00	22.00
	Mark McGwire		
❑ M4	Frank Thomas	20.00	9.00
	Frank Thomas		
❑ M5	Ken Griffey Jr.	40.00	18.00
	Mike Piazza		
❑ M6	Ken Griffey Jr.	60.00	27.00
	Mark McGwire		
❑ M7	Ken Griffey Jr.	50.00	22.00
	Ken Griffey Jr.		

		MINT	NRMT
❏ M8	Mike Piazza / Mark McGwire	50.00	22.00
❏ M9	Mike Piazza / Mike Piazza	30.00	13.50
❏ M10	Mark McGwire / Mark McGwire	60.00	27.00
❏ M11	Nomar Garciaparra / Jose Cruz Jr.	25.00	11.00
❏ M12	Nomar Garciaparra / Derek Jeter	30.00	.13.50
❏ M13	Nomar Garciaparra / Andruw Jones	25.00	11.00
❏ M14	Nomar Garciaparra / Nomar Garciaparra	30.00	13.50
❏ M15	Jose Cruz Jr. / Derek Jeter	20.00	9.00
❏ M16	Jose Cruz Jr. / Andruw Jones	10.00	4.50
❏ M17	Jose Cruz Jr. / Jose Cruz Jr.	4.00	1.80
❏ M18	Derek Jeter / Andruw Jones	20.00	9.00
❏ M19	Derek Jeter / Derek Jeter	30.00	13.50
❏ M20	Andruw Jones / Andruw Jones	10.00	4.50
❏ M21	Cal Ripken / Tony Gwynn	30.00	13.50
❏ M22	Cal Ripken / Barry Bonds	30.00	13.50
❏ M23	Cal Ripken / Greg Maddux	25.00	11.00
❏ M24	Cal Ripken / Cal Ripken	40.00	18.00
❏ M25	Tony Gwynn / Barry Bonds	20.00	9.00
❏ M26	Tony Gwynn / Greg Maddux	20.00	9.00
❏ M27	Tony Gwynn / Tony Gwynn	25.00	11.00
❏ M28	Barry Bonds / Greg Maddux	20.00	9.00
❏ M29	Barry Bonds / Barry Bonds	12.00	5.50
❏ M30	Greg Maddux / Greg Maddux	25.00	11.00
❏ M31	Juan Gonzalez / Larry Walker	15.00	6.75
❏ M32	Juan Gonzalez / Andres Galarraga	15.00	6.75
❏ M33	Juan Gonzalez / Chipper Jones	25.00	11.00
❏ M34	Juan Gonzalez / Juan Gonzalez	20.00	9.00
❏ M35	Larry Walker / Andres Galarraga	10.00	4.50
❏ M36	Larry Walker / Chipper Jones	20.00	9.00
❏ M37	Larry Walker / Larry Walker	10.00	4.50
❏ M38	Andres Galarraga / Chipper Jones	20.00	9.00
❏ M39	Andres Galarraga / Andres Galarraga	10.00	4.50
❏ M40	Chipper Jones / Chipper Jones	25.00	11.00
❏ M41	Gary Sheffield / Sammy Sosa	25.00	11.00
❏ M42	Gary Sheffield / Jeff Bagwell	10.00	4.50
❏ M43	Gary Sheffield / Tino Martinez	4.00	1.80
❏ M44	Gary Sheffield / Gary Sheffield	4.00	1.80
❏ M45	Sammy Sosa / Jeff Bagwell	20.00	9.00
❏ M46	Sammy Sosa / Tino Martinez	25.00	11.00
❏ M47	Sammy Sosa / Sammy Sosa	30.00	13.50
❏ M48	Jeff Bagwell / Tino Martinez	10.00	4.50
❏ M49	Jeff Bagwell / Jeff Bagwell	12.00	5.50
❏ M50	Tino Martinez / Tino Martinez	4.00	1.80

1998 Finest Mystery Finest 2

	MINT	NRMT
COMPLETE SET (40)	800.00	350.00
COMMON CARD (M1-M40)	4.00	1.80
SEMISTARS	6.00	2.70
UNLISTED STARS	10.00	4.50
SER.2 STATED ODDS 1:36		
*REFRACTORS: 1X TO 2.5X HI COLUMN		
REF.SER.2 ODDS 1:144		

		MINT	NRMT
❏ M1	Nomar Garciaparra / Frank Thomas	30.00	13.50
❏ M2	Nomar Garciaparra / Albert Belle	25.00	11.00
❏ M3	Nomar Garciaparra / Scott Rolen	25.00	11.00
❏ M4	Frank Thomas / Albert Belle	20.00	9.00
❏ M5	Frank Thomas / Scott Rolen	20.00	9.00
❏ M6	Albert Belle / Scott Rolen	15.00	6.75
❏ M7	Ken Griffey Jr. / Jose Cruz Jr.	40.00	18.00
❏ M8	Ken Griffey Jr. / Alex Rodriguez	40.00	18.00
❏ M9	Ken Griffey Jr. / Roger Clemens	50.00	22.00
❏ M10	Jose Cruz Jr. / Alex Rodriguez	25.00	11.00
❏ M11	Jose Cruz Jr. / Roger Clemens	20.00	9.00
❏ M12	Alex Rodriguez / Roger Clemens	30.00	13.50
❏ M13	Mike Piazza / Barry Bonds	25.00	11.00
❏ M14	Mike Piazza / Derek Jeter	25.00	11.00
❏ M15	Mike Piazza / Bernie Williams	25.00	11.00
❏ M16	Barry Bonds / Derek Jeter	20.00	9.00
❏ M17	Barry Bonds / Bernie Williams	10.00	4.50
❏ M18	Deter Jeter / Bernie Williams	25.00	11.00
❏ M19	Mark McGwire / Jeff Bagwell	50.00	22.00
❏ M20	Mark McGwire / Mo Vaughn	50.00	22.00
❏ M21	Mark McGwire / Jim Thome	50.00	22.00
❏ M22	Jeff Bagwell / Mo Vaughn	12.00	5.50
❏ M23	Jeff Bagwell / Jim Thome	10.00	4.50
❏ M24	Mo Vaughn / Jim Thome	10.00	4.50
❏ M25	Juan Gonzalez / Travis Lee	15.00	6.75
❏ M26	Juan Gonzalez / Ben Grieve	15.00	6.75
❏ M27	Juan Gonzalez / Fred McGriff	15.00	6.75
❏ M28	Travis Lee / Ben Grieve	10.00	4.50
❏ M29	Travis Lee / Fred McGriff	10.00	4.50
❏ M30	Ben Grieve / Fred McGriff	10.00	4.50
❏ M31	Albert Belle / Albert Belle	10.00	4.50
❏ M32	Scott Rolen / Scott Rolen	12.00	5.50
❏ M33	Alex Rodriguez / Alex Rodriguez	30.00	13.50
❏ M34	Roger Clemens / Roger Clemens	25.00	11.00
❏ M35	Bernie Williams / Bernie Williams	10.00	4.50
❏ M36	Mo Vaughn / Mo Vaughn	10.00	4.50
❏ M37	Jim Thome / Jim Thome	10.00	4.50
❏ M38	Travis Lee / Travis Lee	6.00	2.70
❏ M39	Fred McGriff / Fred McGriff	6.00	2.70
❏ M40	Ben Grieve / Ben Grieve	10.00	4.50

1998 Finest Power Zone

	MINT	NRMT
COMPLETE SET (20)	400.00	180.00
COMMON CARD (P1-P20)	5.00	2.20
SEMISTARS	8.00	3.60
UNLISTED STARS	12.00	5.50
SER.1 STAT.ODDS 1:72 HOBBY, 1:32 HTA		

		MINT	NRMT
❏ P1	Ken Griffey Jr.	60.00	27.00
❏ P2	Jeff Bagwell	15.00	6.75
❏ P3	Jose Cruz Jr.	5.00	2.20
❏ P4	Barry Bonds	15.00	6.75
❏ P5	Mark McGwire	80.00	36.00
❏ P6	Jim Thome	12.00	5.50
❏ P7	Mo Vaughn	12.00	5.50
❏ P8	Gary Sheffield	5.00	2.20
❏ P9	Andres Galarraga	8.00	3.60
❏ P10	Nomar Garciaparra	40.00	18.00
❏ P11	Rafael Palmeiro	12.00	5.50
❏ P12	Sammy Sosa	40.00	18.00
❏ P13	Jay Buhner	5.00	2.20
❏ P14	Tony Clark	5.00	2.20
❏ P15	Mike Piazza	40.00	18.00
❏ P16	Larry Walker	12.00	5.50
❏ P17	Albert Belle	12.00	5.50
❏ P18	Tino Martinez	5.00	2.20
❏ P19	Juan Gonzalez	25.00	11.00
❏ P20	Frank Thomas	25.00	11.00

1998 Finest Stadium Stars

	MINT	NRMT
COMPLETE SET (24)	600.00	275.00
COMMON CARD (SS1-SS24)	6.00	2.70
SEMISTARS	10.00	4.50
UNLISTED STARS	15.00	6.75
SER.2 STATED ODDS 1:72		
*JUMBOS: 2X TO .4X HI COLUMN		
JUMBOS: RANDOM IN SER.2 JUMBO BOXES		

		MINT	NRMT
❏ SS1	Ken Griffey Jr.	80.00	36.00

		MINT	NRMT
SS2	Alex Rodriguez	50.00	22.00
SS3	Mo Vaughn	15.00	6.75
SS4	Nomar Garciaparra	50.00	22.00
SS5	Frank Thomas	30.00	13.50
SS6	Albert Belle	15.00	6.75
SS7	Derek Jeter	50.00	22.00
SS8	Chipper Jones	40.00	18.00
SS9	Cal Ripken	60.00	27.00
SS10	Jim Thome	15.00	6.75
SS11	Mike Piazza	50.00	22.00
SS12	Juan Gonzalez	30.00	13.50
SS13	Jeff Bagwell	20.00	9.00
SS14	Sammy Sosa	50.00	22.00
SS15	Jose Cruz Jr.	6.00	2.70
SS16	Gary Sheffield	6.00	2.70
SS17	Larry Walker	15.00	6.75
SS18	Tony Gwynn	40.00	18.00
SS19	Mark McGwire	100.00	45.00
SS20	Barry Bonds	20.00	9.00
SS21	Tino Martinez	6.00	2.70
SS22	Manny Ramirez	15.00	6.75
SS23	Ken Caminiti	6.00	2.70
SS24	Andres Galarraga	10.00	4.50

1999 Finest

	MINT	NRMT
COMPLETE SET (300)	300.00	135.00
COMPLETE SERIES 1 (150)	150.00	70.00
COMPLETE SERIES 2 (150)	150.00	70.00
COMP.SER.1 w/o SP's (100)	30.00	13.50
COMP.SER.2 w/o SP's (100)	30.00	13.50
COMMON (1-100/151-250)	.20	.09
MINOR STARS 1-100/151-250	.30	.14
SEMISTARS 1-100/151-250	.50	.23
UNLISTED STARS 1-100/151-250	.75	.35
COMMON (101-150/251-300)	.50	.23
SEMISTARS 101-150/251-300	.75	.35
UNLIST.STARS 101-150/251-300	1.25	.55
101-150/251-300 ODDS 1:1 H/R, 2:1 HTA		

#	Player	MINT	NRMT
1	Darin Erstad	.50	.23
2	Javy Lopez	.30	.14
3	Vinny Castilla	.30	.14
4	Jim Thome	.75	.35
5	Tino Martinez	.30	.14
6	Mark Grace	.50	.23
7	Shawn Green	.75	.35
8	Dustin Hermanson	.20	.09
9	Kevin Young	.30	.14
10	Tony Clark	.30	.14
11	Scott Brosius	.30	.14
12	Craig Biggio	.75	.35
13	Brian McRae	.20	.09
14	Chan Ho Park	.30	.14
15	Manny Ramirez	1.00	.45
16	Chipper Jones	2.00	.90
17	Rico Brogna	.20	.09
18	Quinton McCracken	.20	.09
19	J.T. Snow	.30	.14
20	Tony Gwynn	2.00	.90
21	Juan Guzman	.20	.09
22	John Valentin	.30	.14
23	Rick Helling	.20	.09
24	Sandy Alomar Jr.	.30	.14
25	Frank Thomas	1.50	.70
26	Jorge Posada	.20	.09
27	Dmitri Young	.30	.14
28	Rick Reed	.20	.09
29	Kevin Tapani	.20	.09
30	Troy Glaus	.75	.35
31	Kenny Rogers	.20	.09
32	Jeromy Burnitz	.30	.14
33	Mark Grudzielanek	.20	.09
34	Mike Mussina	.75	.35
35	Scott Rolen	1.00	.45
36	Neifi Perez	.30	.14
37	Brad Radke	.30	.14
38	Darryl Strawberry	.30	.14
39	Robb Nen	.20	.09
40	Moises Alou	.30	.14
41	Eric Young	.20	.09
42	Livan Hernandez	.20	.09
43	John Wetteland	.30	.14
44	Matt Lawton	.20	.09
45	Ben Grieve	.75	.35
46	Fernando Tatis	.75	.35
47	Travis Fryman	.30	.14
48	David Segui	.20	.09
49	Bob Abreu	.30	.14
50	Nomar Garciaparra	2.50	1.10
51	Paul O'Neill	.30	.14
52	Jeff King	.20	.09
53	Francisco Cordova	.30	.14
54	John Olerud	.30	.14
55	Vladimir Guerrero	1.00	.45
56	Fernando Vina	.20	.09
57	Shane Reynolds	.30	.14
58	Chuck Finley	.20	.09
59	Rondell White	.30	.14
60	Greg Vaughn	.30	.14
61	Ryan Minor	.30	.14
62	Tom Gordon	.30	.14
63	Damion Easley	.30	.14
64	Ray Durham	.30	.14
65	Orlando Hernandez	.75	.35
66	Bartolo Colon	.30	.14
67	Jaret Wright	.30	.14
68	Royce Clayton	.20	.09
69	Tim Salmon	.50	.23
70	Mark McGwire	5.00	2.20
71	Alex Gonzalez	.30	.14
72	Tom Glavine	.75	.35
73	David Justice	.30	.14
74	Omar Vizquel	.30	.14
75	Juan Gonzalez	1.50	.70
76	Bobby Higginson	.30	.14
77	Todd Walker	.30	.14
78	Dante Bichette	.30	.14
79	Kevin Millwood	.50	.23
80	Roger Clemens	2.00	.90
81	Kerry Wood	.75	.35
82	Cal Ripken	3.00	1.35
83	Jay Bell	.30	.14
84	Barry Bonds	1.00	.45
85	Alex Rodriguez	2.25	1.10
86	Doug Glanville	.30	.14
87	Jason Kendall	.30	.14
88	Sean Casey	.75	.35
89	Aaron Sele	.30	.14
90	Derek Jeter	2.50	1.10
91	Andy Ashby	.20	.09
92	Rusty Greer	.30	.14
93	Rod Beck	.30	.14
94	Matt Williams	.75	.35
95	Mike Piazza	2.50	1.10
96	Wally Joyner	.30	.14
97	Barry Larkin	.75	.35
98	Eric Milton	.20	.09
99	Gary Sheffield	.30	.14
100	Greg Maddux	2.00	.90
101	Ken Griffey Jr. GEM	6.00	2.70
102	Frank Thomas GEM	2.50	1.10
103	Nomar Garciaparra GEM	4.00	1.80
104	Mark McGwire GEM	8.00	3.60
105	Alex Rodriguez GEM	4.00	1.80
106	Tony Gwynn GEM	3.00	1.35
107	Juan Gonzalez GEM	2.50	1.10
108	Jeff Bagwell GEM	1.50	.70
109	Sammy Sosa GEM	4.00	1.80
110	Vladimir Guerrero GEM	1.50	.70
111	Roger Clemens GEM	3.00	1.35
112	Barry Bonds GEM	1.50	.70
113	Darin Erstad GEM	.75	.35
114	Mike Piazza GEM	4.00	1.80
115	Derek Jeter GEM	4.00	1.80
116	Chipper Jones GEM	3.00	1.35
117	Larry Walker GEM	1.25	.55
118	Scott Rolen GEM	1.50	.70
119	Cal Ripken GEM	5.00	2.20
120	Greg Maddux GEM	3.00	1.35
121	Troy Glaus SENS	1.25	.55
122	Ben Grieve SENS	1.25	.55
123	Ryan Minor SENS	.75	.35
124	Kerry Wood SENS	1.25	.55
125	Travis Lee SENS	.75	.35
126	Adrian Beltre SENS	1.25	.55
127	Brad Fullmer SENS	.50	.23
128	Aramis Ramirez SENS	.75	.35
129	Eric Chavez SENS	.75	.35
130	Todd Helton SENS	1.25	.55
131	Pat Burrell	15.00	6.75
132	Ryan Mills	2.50	1.10
133	Austin Kearns	4.00	1.80
134	Josh McKinley	2.00	1.10
135	Adam Everett	4.00	1.80
136	Marlon Anderson	.50	.23
137	Bruce Chen	.75	.35
138	Matt Clement	.75	.35
139	Alex Gonzalez	.75	.35
140	Roy Halladay	.75	.35
141	Calvin Pickering	.75	.35
142	Randy Wolf	.75	.35
143	Ryan Anderson	.75	.35
144	Ruben Mateo	1.25	.55
145	Alex Escobar	8.00	3.60
146	Jeremy Giambi	.75	.35
147	Lance Berkman	.75	.35
148	Michael Barrett	.75	.35
149	Preston Wilson	.75	.35
150	Gabe Kapler	1.25	.55
151	Roger Clemens	2.00	.90
152	Jay Buhner	.30	.14
153	Brad Fullmer	.20	.09
154	Ray Lankford	.20	.09
155	Jim Edmonds	.30	.14
156	Jason Giambi	.30	.14
157	Bret Boone	.30	.14
158	Jeff Cirillo	.30	.14
159	Rickey Henderson	1.00	.45
160	Edgar Martinez	.30	.14
161	Ron Gant	.30	.14
162	Mark Kotsay	.20	.09
163	Trevor Hoffman	.30	.14
164	Jason Schmidt	.20	.09
165	Brett Tomko	.20	.09
166	David Ortiz	.20	.09
167	Dean Palmer	.30	.14
168	Hideki Irabu	.20	.09
169	Mike Cameron	.30	.14
170	Pedro Martinez	1.00	.45
171	Tom Goodwin	.20	.09
172	Brian Hunter	.20	.09
173	Al Leiter	.30	.14
174	Charles Johnson	.30	.14
175	Curt Schilling	.50	.23
176	Robin Ventura	.50	.23
177	Travis Lee	.50	.23
178	Jeff Shaw	.20	.09
179	Ugueth Urbina	.20	.09
180	Roberto Alomar	.75	.35
181	Cliff Floyd	.30	.14

		MINT	NRMT
❏ 182	Adrian Beltre	.75	.35
❏ 183	Tony Womack	.20	.09
❏ 184	Brian Jordan	.30	.14
❏ 185	Randy Johnson	.75	.35
❏ 186	Mickey Morandini	.20	.09
❏ 187	Todd Hundley	.30	.14
❏ 188	Jose Valentin	.20	.09
❏ 189	Eric Davis	.30	.14
❏ 190	Ken Caminiti	.30	.14
❏ 191	David Wells	.30	.14
❏ 192	Ryan Klesko	.30	.14
❏ 193	Garret Anderson	.30	.14
❏ 194	Eric Karros	.30	.14
❏ 195	Ivan Rodriguez	1.00	.45
❏ 196	Aramis Ramirez	.50	.23
❏ 197	Mike Lieberthal	.20	.09
❏ 198	Will Clark	.75	.35
❏ 199	Rey Ordonez	.30	.14
❏ 200	Ken Griffey Jr.	4.00	1.80
❏ 201	Jose Guillen	.20	.09
❏ 202	Scott Erickson	.20	.09
❏ 203	Paul Konerko	.30	.14
❏ 204	Johnny Damon	.30	.14
❏ 205	Larry Walker	.75	.35
❏ 206	Denny Neagle	.20	.09
❏ 207	Jose Offerman	.20	.09
❏ 208	Andy Pettitte	.30	.14
❏ 209	Bobby Jones	.20	.09
❏ 210	Kevin Brown	.50	.23
❏ 211	John Smoltz	.50	.23
❏ 212	Henry Rodriguez	.30	.14
❏ 213	Tim Belcher	.20	.09
❏ 214	Carlos Delgado	.75	.35
❏ 215	Andruw Jones	.75	.35
❏ 216	Andy Benes	.20	.09
❏ 217	Fred McGriff	.50	.23
❏ 218	Edgar Renteria	.20	.09
❏ 219	Miguel Tejada	.30	.14
❏ 220	Bernie Williams	.75	.35
❏ 221	Justin Thompson	.20	.09
❏ 222	Marty Cordova	.20	.09
❏ 223	Delino DeShields	.20	.09
❏ 224	Ellis Burks	.30	.14
❏ 225	Kenny Lofton	.50	.23
❏ 226	Steve Finley	.30	.14
❏ 227	Eric Chavez	.50	.23
❏ 228	Jose Cruz Jr.	.30	.14
❏ 229	Marquis Grissom	.20	.09
❏ 230	Jeff Bagwell	1.00	.45
❏ 231	Jose Canseco	1.00	.45
❏ 232	Edgardo Alfonzo	.50	.23
❏ 233	Richie Sexson	.50	.23
❏ 234	Jeff Kent	.30	.14
❏ 235	Rafael Palmeiro	.75	.35
❏ 236	David Cone	.50	.23
❏ 237	Gregg Jefferies	.20	.09
❏ 238	Mike Lansing	.20	.09
❏ 239	Mariano Rivera	.30	.14
❏ 240	Albert Belle	.75	.35
❏ 241	Chuck Knoblauch	.30	.14
❏ 242	Derek Bell	.30	.14
❏ 243	Pat Hentgen	.20	.09
❏ 244	Andres Galarraga	.50	.23
❏ 245	Mo Vaughn	.75	.35
❏ 246	Wade Boggs	.75	.35
❏ 247	Devon White	.20	.09
❏ 248	Todd Helton	.75	.35
❏ 249	Raul Mondesi	.30	.14
❏ 250	Sammy Sosa	2.50	1.10
❏ 251	Nomar Garciaparra ST	4.00	1.80
❏ 252	Mark McGwire ST	8.00	3.60
❏ 253	Alex Rodriguez ST	4.00	1.80
❏ 254	Juan Gonzalez ST	2.50	1.10
❏ 255	Vladimir Guerrero ST	1.50	.70
❏ 256	Ken Griffey Jr. ST	6.00	2.70
❏ 257	Mike Piazza ST	4.00	1.80
❏ 258	Derek Jeter ST	4.00	1.80
❏ 259	Albert Belle ST	1.25	.55
❏ 260	Greg Vaughn ST	.75	.35
❏ 261	Sammy Sosa ST	4.00	1.80
❏ 262	Greg Maddux ST	3.00	1.35
❏ 263	Frank Thomas ST	2.50	1.10
❏ 264	Mark Grace ST	.75	.35
❏ 265	Ivan Rodriguez ST	1.50	.70
❏ 266	Roger Clemens GM	3.00	1.35
❏ 267	Mo Vaughn GM	1.25	.55
❏ 268	Jim Thome GM	1.25	.55
❏ 269	Darin Erstad GM	.75	.35
❏ 270	Chipper Jones GM	3.00	1.35
❏ 271	Larry Walker GM	1.25	.55
❏ 272	Cal Ripken GM	5.00	2.20
❏ 273	Scott Rolen GM	1.50	.70
❏ 274	Randy Johnson GM	1.25	.55
❏ 275	Tony Gwynn GM	3.00	1.35
❏ 276	Barry Bonds GM	1.50	.70
❏ 277	Sean Burroughs	15.00	6.75
❏ 278	J.M. Gold	2.50	1.10
❏ 279	Carlos Lee	.75	.35
❏ 280	George Lombard	.75	.35
❏ 281	Carlos Beltran	1.50	.70
❏ 282	Fernando Seguignol	.75	.35
❏ 283	Eric Chavez	.75	.35
❏ 284	Carlos Pena	4.00	1.80
❏ 285	Corey Patterson	25.00	11.00
❏ 286	Alfonso Soriano	15.00	6.75
❏ 287	Nick Johnson	12.00	5.50
❏ 288	Jorge Toca	4.00	1.80
❏ 289	A.J. Burnett	4.00	1.80
❏ 290	Andy Brown	2.50	1.10
❏ 291	Doug Mientkiewicz	2.00	.90
❏ 292	Bobby Seay	2.50	1.10
❏ 293	Chip Ambres	3.00	1.35
❏ 294	C.C. Sabathia	6.00	2.70
❏ 295	Choo Freeman	3.00	1.35
❏ 296	Eric Valent	5.00	2.20
❏ 297	Matt Belisle	2.00	.90
❏ 298	Jason Tyner	2.50	1.10
❏ 299	Masao Kida	3.00	1.35
❏ 300	Hank Aaron	8.00	3.60
	Mark McGwire		

1999 Finest Gold Refractors

	MINT	NRMT
COMMON CARD (1-300)	8.00	3.60

*STARS 1-100/151-250: 15X TO 40X BASIC
*YNG.1-100/151-250: 12.5X TO 30X BASIC
*GEMS/STER/GMR: 10X TO 25X BASIC
*SENSATIONS: 8X TO 20X BASIC
*PROSPECTS: 10X TO 25X BASIC
*RC'S: 3X TO 8X BASIC
SER.1 ODDS 1:82 HOB/RET, 1:38 HTA
SER.2 ODDS 1:57 HOB/RET, 1:26 HTA
STATED PRINT RUN 100 SERIAL #'d SETS

1999 Finest Refractors

	MINT	NRMT
COMMON CARD (1-300)	2.50	1.10

*STARS 1-100/151-250: 5X TO 12X BASIC
*YNG.STARS 1-100/151-250: 4X TO 10X BASIC
*GEMS/STERL/GAMER: 3X TO 8X BASIC
*SENSATIONS: 2.5X TO 6X BASIC
*PROSPECTS: 2.5X TO 6X BASIC
*RC'S: 1.5X TO 4X BASIC
STATED ODDS 1:12 HOB/RET, 1:5 HTA

1999 Finest Aaron Award Contenders

	MINT	NRMT
COMPLETE SET (9)	80.00	36.00
COMMON CARD (HA1-HA9)	5.00	2.20

HA1 SER.2 ODDS 1:216, 1:108 HTA
HA2 SER.2 ODDS 1:108, 1:54 HTA
HA3 SER.2 ODDS 1:72, 1:36 HTA
HA4 SER.2 ODDS 1:54, 1:27 HTA
HA5 SER.2 ODDS 1:43, 1:21 HTA
HA6 SER.2 ODDS 1:36, 1:18 HTA
HA7 SER.2 ODDS 1:31, 1:15 HTA
HA8 SER.2 ODDS 1:27, 1:13 HTA
HA9 SER.2 ODDS 1:24, 1:12 HTA

❏ HA1	Juan Gonzalez	20.00	9.00
❏ HA2	Vladimir Guerrero	10.00	4.50
❏ HA3	Nomar Garciaparra	20.00	9.00
❏ HA4	Albert Belle	5.00	2.20
❏ HA5	Frank Thomas	8.00	3.60
❏ HA6	Sammy Sosa	10.00	4.50
❏ HA7	Alex Rodriguez	8.00	3.60
❏ HA8	Ken Griffey Jr.	10.00	4.50
❏ HA9	Mark McGwire	10.00	4.50

1999 Finest Aaron Award Contenders Refractors

	MINT	NRMT
COMPLETE SET (9)	300.00	135.00

*REFRACTORS: 1.5X TO 4X BASIC AARON AW
HA1 SER.2 ODDS 1:1728, 1:864 HTA
HA2 SER.2 ODDS 1:864, 1:432 HTA
HA3 SER.2 ODDS 1:576, 1:288 HTA
HA4 SER.2 ODDS 1:432, 1:216 HTA
HA5 SER.2 ODDS 1:344, 1:172 HTA

HA6 SER.2 ODDS 1:288, 1:144 HTA
HA7 SER.2 ODDS 1:248, 1:124 HTA
HA8 SER.2 ODDS 1:216, 1:108 HTA
HA9 SER.2 ODDS 1:192, 1:96 HTA

1999 Finest Complements

	MINT	NRMT
COMPLETE SET (7)	50.00	22.00
COMMON CARD (C1-C7)	4.00	1.80

SER.2 STATED ODDS 1:56, 1:27 HTA
RIGHT/LEFT REF.VARIATIONS EQUAL VALUE
*DUAL REF: 1.25X TO 3X HI COLUMN
DUAL REF.SER.2 ODDS 1:168, 1:81 HTA

		MINT	NRMT
❏ C1	Mike Piazza Ivan Rodriguez	10.00	4.50
❏ C2	Tony Gwynn Wade Boggs	8.00	3.60
❏ C3	Kerry Wood Roger Clemens	8.00	3.60
❏ C4	Juan Gonzalez Sammy Sosa	10.00	4.50
❏ C5	Derek Jeter Nomar Garciaparra	10.00	4.50
❏ C6	Mark McGwire Frank Thomas	20.00	9.00
❏ C7	Vladimir Guerrero Andruw Jones	4.00	1.80

1999 Finest Double Feature

	MINT	NRMT
COMPLETE SET (7)	40.00	18.00
COMMON CARD (DF1-DF7)	2.50	1.10

SER.2 STATED ODDS 1:56, 1:27 HTA
RIGHT/LEFT REF.VARIATIONS EQUAL VALUE
*DUAL REF: 1.25X TO 3X HI COLUMN
DUAL REF.SER.2 ODDS 1:168, 1:81 HTA

		MINT	NRMT
❏ DF1	Ken Griffey Jr. Alex Rodriguez	15.00	6.75
❏ DF2	Chipper Jones Andruw Jones	8.00	3.60
❏ DF3	Darin Erstad Mo Vaughn	2.50	1.10
❏ DF4	Craig Biggio Jeff Bagwell	4.00	1.80

		MINT	NRMT
❏ DF5	Ben Grieve Eric Chavez	3.00	1.35
❏ DF6	Albert Belle Cal Ripken	12.00	5.50
❏ DF7	Scott Rolen Pat Burrell	10.00	4.50

1999 Finest Franchise Records

	MINT	NRMT
COMPLETE SET (10)	300.00	135.00
COMMON CARD (FR1-FR10)	12.00	5.50

SER.2 STATED ODDS 1:129, 1:64 HTA
*REFRACTORS: .75X TO 2X HI COLUMN
REF.SER.2 ODDS 1:378, 1:189 HTA

		MINT	NRMT
❏ FR1	Frank Thomas	20.00	9.00
❏ FR2	Ken Griffey Jr.	50.00	22.00
❏ FR3	Mark McGwire	60.00	27.00
❏ FR4	Juan Gonzalez	20.00	9.00
❏ FR5	Nomar Garciaparra	30.00	13.50
❏ FR6	Mike Piazza	30.00	13.50
❏ FR7	Cal Ripken	50.00	22.00
❏ FR8	Sammy Sosa	30.00	13.50
❏ FR9	Barry Bonds	12.00	5.50
❏ FR10	Tony Gwynn	25.00	11.00

1999 Finest Future's Finest

	MINT	NRMT
COMPLETE SET (10)	150.00	70.00
COMMON CARD (FF1-FF10)	8.00	3.60

SER.2 STATED ODDS 1:171, 1:79 HTA
STATED PRINT RUN 500 SERIAL #'d SETS

		MINT	NRMT
❏ FF1	Pat Burrell	40.00	18.00
❏ FF2	Troy Glaus	15.00	6.75
❏ FF3	Eric Chavez	10.00	4.50
❏ FF4	Ryan Anderson	8.00	3.60
❏ FF5	Ruben Mateo	12.00	5.50
❏ FF6	Gabe Kapler	8.00	3.60
❏ FF7	Alex Gonzalez	8.00	3.60
❏ FF8	Michael Barrett	10.00	4.50
❏ FF9	Adrian Beltre	10.00	4.50
❏ FF10	Fernando Seguignol	8.00	3.60

1999 Finest Leading Indicators

	MINT	NRMT
COMPLETE SET (10)	60.00	27.00
COMMON CARD (L1-L10)	1.50	.70
UNLISTED STARS	3.00	1.35

SER.1 STATED ODDS 1:24 HOB/RET, 1:11 HTA

		MINT	NRMT
❏ L1	Mark McGwire	20.00	9.00
❏ L2	Sammy Sosa	10.00	4.50
❏ L3	Ken Griffey Jr.	15.00	6.75
❏ L4	Greg Vaughn	1.50	.70
❏ L5	Albert Belle	3.00	1.35
❏ L6	Juan Gonzalez	6.00	2.70
❏ L7	Andres Galarraga	2.00	.90
❏ L8	Alex Rodriguez	10.00	4.50
❏ L9	Barry Bonds	4.00	1.80
❏ L10	Jeff Bagwell	4.00	1.80

1999 Finest Milestones

	MINT	NRMT
COMPLETE SET (40)	800.00	350.00
COMMON HIT (M1-M10)	2.50	1.10
HIT UNLISTED STARS	4.00	1.80

HIT SER.2 ODDS 1:29, 1:13 HTA
HIT PRINT RUN 3000 SERIAL #'d SUBSETS

	MINT	NRMT
COMMON HR (M11-M20)	12.00	5.50

HR SER.2 ODDS 1:171, 1:79 HTA
HR PRINT RUN 500 SERIAL #'d SUBSETS

	MINT	NRMT
COMMON RBI (M21-M30)	3.00	1.35
RBI UNLISTED STARS	6.00	2.70

RBI SER.2 ODDS 1:61, 1:28 HTA
RBI PRINT RUN 1400 SERIAL #'d SUBSETS

	MINT	NRMT
COMMON 2B (M31-M40)	3.00	1.35
2B UNLISTED STARS	10.00	4.50

2B SER.2 ODDS 1:171, 1:79 HTA
2B PRINT RUN 500 SERIAL #'d SUBSETS

		MINT	NRMT
❏ M1	Tony Gwynn HIT	10.00	4.50
❏ M2	Cal Ripken HIT	15.00	6.75
❏ M3	Wade Boggs HIT	4.00	1.80
❏ M4	Ken Griffey Jr. HIT	20.00	9.00
❏ M5	Frank Thomas HIT	8.00	3.60
❏ M6	Barry Bonds HIT	5.00	2.20
❏ M7	Travis Lee HIT	2.50	1.10
❏ M8	Alex Rodriguez HIT	12.00	5.50
❏ M9	Derek Jeter HIT	12.00	5.50

		MINT	NRMT
☐ M10	Vladimir Guerrero HIT	5.00	2.20
☐ M11	Mark McGwire HR	80.00	36.00
☐ M12	Ken Griffey Jr. HR	60.00	27.00
☐ M13	Vladimir Guerrero HR	15.00	6.75
☐ M14	Alex Rodriguez HR	40.00	18.00
☐ M15	Barry Bonds HR	15.00	6.75
☐ M16	Sammy Sosa HR	40.00	18.00
☐ M17	Albert Belle HR	12.00	5.50
☐ M18	Frank Thomas HR	25.00	11.00
☐ M19	Jose Canseco HR	15.00	6.75
☐ M20	Mike Piazza HR	40.00	18.00
☐ M21	Jeff Bagwell RBI	8.00	3.60
☐ M22	Barry Bonds RBI	8.00	3.60
☐ M23	Ken Griffey Jr. RBI	30.00	13.50
☐ M24	Albert Belle RBI	6.00	2.70
☐ M25	Juan Gonzalez RBI	12.00	5.50
☐ M26	Vinny Castilla RBI	3.00	1.35
☐ M27	Mark McGwire RBI	40.00	18.00
☐ M28	Alex Rodriguez RBI	25.00	11.00
☐ M29	Nomar Garciaparra RBI	25.00	11.00
☐ M30	Frank Thomas RBI	12.00	5.50
☐ M31	Barry Bonds 2B	15.00	6.75
☐ M32	Albert Belle 2B	10.00	4.50
☐ M33	Ben Grieve 2B	10.00	4.50
☐ M34	Craig Biggio 2B	10.00	4.50
☐ M35	Vladimir Guerrero 2B	15.00	6.75
☐ M36	Nomar Garciaparra 2B	40.00	18.00
☐ M37	Alex Rodriguez 2B	40.00	18.00
☐ M38	Derek Jeter 2B	40.00	18.00
☐ M39	Ken Griffey Jr. 2B	60.00	27.00
☐ M40	Brad Fullmer 2B	3.00	1.35

1999 Finest Peel and Reveal Sparkle

	MINT	NRMT
COMPLETE SET (20)	150.00	70.00
COMMON CARD (PR1-PR20)	2.50	1.10
UNLISTED STARS	4.00	1.80
SER.1 STATED ODDS 1:30 HOB/RET, 1:15 HTA
*HYPERPLAID: .75X TO 2X SPARKLE
HYPERPLAID SER.1 ODDS 1:60 H/R,1:30 HTA'
*STADIUM STARS: 1.5X TO 4X SPARKLE
STAD.STAR SER.1 ODDS 1:120 H/R, 1:60 HTA

		MINT	NRMT
☐ 1	Kerry Wood	4.00	1.80
☐ 2	Mark McGwire	25.00	11.00
☐ 3	Sammy Sosa	12.00	5.50
☐ 4	Ken Griffey Jr.	20.00	9.00
☐ 5	Nomar Garciaparra	12.00	5.50
☐ 6	Greg Maddux	10.00	4.50
☐ 7	Derek Jeter	12.00	5.50
☐ 8	Andres Galarraga	2.50	1.10
☐ 9	Alex Rodriguez	12.00	5.50
☐ 10	Frank Thomas	8.00	3.60
☐ 11	Roger Clemens	10.00	4.50
☐ 12	Juan Gonzalez	8.00	3.60
☐ 13	Ben Grieve	4.00	1.80
☐ 14	Jeff Bagwell	5.00	2.20
☐ 15	Todd Helton	4.00	1.80
☐ 16	Chipper Jones	10.00	4.50
☐ 17	Barry Bonds	5.00	2.20
☐ 18	Travis Lee	2.50	1.10
☐ 19	Vladimir Guerrero	5.00	2.20
☐ 20	Pat Burrell	15.00	6.75

1999 Finest Prominent Figures

	MINT	NRMT
COMMON HR (PF1-PF10)	25.00	11.00
HR SEMISTARS	30.00	13.50
HR SER.1 ODDS 1:1749 HOB/RET, 1:807 HTA
HR PRINT RUN 70 SERIAL #'d SUBSETS
COMMON SLG (PF11-PP20)	5.00	2.20
SLG SEMISTARS	6.00	2.70
SLG UNLISTED STARS	10.00	4.50
SLUGGING SER.1 ODDS 1:145 H/R, 1:67 HTA
SLG PRINT RUN 847 SERIAL #'d SUBSETS
COMMON BAT (PF21-PF30)	6.00	2.70
BAT UNLISTED STARS	12.00	5.50
BAT SER.1 ODDS 1:289 HOB/RET, 1:133 HTA
BAT PRINT RUN 424 SERIAL #'d SUBSETS
COMMON RBI (PF31-PF40)	10.00	4.50
RBI SER.1 ODDS 1:644 HOB/RET, 1:297 HTA
RBI PRINT RUN 190 SERIAL #'d SUBSETS
COMMON TB (PF41-PF50)	10.00	4.50
TOT.BASES SER.1 ODDS 1:268 H/R, 1:124 HTA
TB PRINT RUN 457 SERIAL #'d SUBSETS

		MINT	NRMT
☐ PF1	Mark McGwire HR	300.00	135.00
☐ PF2	Sammy Sosa HR	150.00	70.00
☐ PF3	Ken Griffey Jr. HR	250.00	110.00
☐ PF4	Mike Piazza HR	150.00	70.00
☐ PF5	Juan Gonzalez HR	100.00	45.00
☐ PF6	Greg Vaughn HR	25.00	11.00
☐ PF7	Alex Rodriguez HR	150.00	70.00
☐ PF8	Manny Ramirez HR	60.00	27.00
☐ PF9	Jeff Bagwell HR	60.00	27.00
☐ PF10	Andres Galarraga HR	30.00	13.50
☐ PF11	Mark McGwire SLG	60.00	27.00
☐ PF12	Sammy Sosa SLG	30.00	13.50
☐ PF13	Juan Gonzalez SLG	20.00	9.00
☐ PF14	Ken Griffey Jr. SLG	50.00	22.00
☐ PF15	Barry Bonds SLG	12.00	5.50
☐ PF16	Greg Vaughn SLG	5.00	2.20
☐ PF17	Larry Walker SLG	10.00	4.50
☐ PF18	Andres Galarraga SLG	6.00	2.70
☐ PF19	Jeff Bagwell SLG	12.00	5.50
☐ PF20	Albert Belle SLG	10.00	4.50
☐ PF21	Tony Gwynn BAT	30.00	13.50
☐ PF22	Mike Piazza BAT	40.00	18.00
☐ PF23	Larry Walker BAT	12.00	5.50
☐ PF24	Alex Rodriguez BAT	40.00	18.00
☐ PF25	John Olerud BAT	6.00	2.70
☐ PF26	Frank Thomas BAT	25.00	11.00
☐ PF27	Bernie Williams BAT	12.00	5.50
☐ PF28	Chipper Jones BAT	30.00	13.50
☐ PF29	Jim Thome BAT	12.00	5.50
☐ PF30	Barry Bonds BAT	15.00	6.75
☐ PF31	Juan Gonzalez RBI	40.00	18.00
☐ PF32	Sammy Sosa RBI	60.00	27.00
☐ PF33	Mark McGwire RBI	120.00	55.00
☐ PF34	Albert Belle RBI	20.00	9.00
☐ PF35	Ken Griffey Jr. RBI	100.00	45.00
☐ PF36	Jeff Bagwell RBI	25.00	11.00
☐ PF37	Chipper Jones RBI	50.00	22.00
☐ PF38	Vinny Castilla RBI	10.00	4.50
☐ PF39	Alex Rodriguez RBI	50.00	22.00
☐ PF40	Andres Galarraga RBI	12.00	5.50
☐ PF41	Sammy Sosa TB	40.00	18.00
☐ PF42	Mark McGwire TB	80.00	36.00
☐ PF43	Albert Belle TB	10.00	4.50
☐ PF44	Ken Griffey Jr. TB	60.00	27.00
☐ PF45	Jeff Bagwell TB	15.00	6.75
☐ PF46	Juan Gonzalez TB	25.00	11.00
☐ PF47	Barry Bonds TB	15.00	6.75
☐ PF48	Vladimir Guerrero TB	15.00	6.75
☐ PF49	Larry Walker TB	12.00	5.50
☐ PF50	Alex Rodriguez TB	40.00	18.00

1999 Finest Split Screen

	MINT	NRMT
COMPLETE SET (14)	100.00	45.00
COMMON CARD (SS1-SS14)	3.00	1.35
SER.1 STATED ODDS 1:28 HOB/RET, 1:14 HTA
RIGHT/LEFT VER.VARIATIONS EQUAL VALUE
*DUAL REF: 1.25X TO 3X HI COLUMN
DUAL REF.SER.1 ODDS 1:82 H/R, 1:42 HTA

		MINT	NRMT
☐ SS1	Mark McGwire Sammy Sosa	20.00	9.00
☐ SS2	Ken Griffey Jr. Alex Rodriguez	15.00	6.75
☐ SS3	Nomar Garciaparra Derek Jeter	10.00	4.50
☐ SS4	Barry Bonds Albert Belle	4.00	1.80
☐ SS5	Cal Ripken Tony Gwynn	12.00	5.50
☐ SS6	Manny Ramirez Juan Gonzalez	6.00	2.70
☐ SS7	Frank Thomas Andres Galarraga	6.00	2.70
☐ SS8	Scott Rolen Chipper Jones	6.00	2.70
☐ SS9	Ivan Rodriguez Mike Piazza	10.00	4.50
☐ SS10	Kerry Wood Roger Clemens	8.00	3.60
☐ SS11	Greg Maddux Tom Glavine	8.00	3.60
☐ SS12	Troy Glaus Eric Chavez	3.00	1.35
☐ SS13	Ben Grieve Todd Helton	3.00	1.35
☐ SS14	Travis Lee Pat Burrell	12.00	5.50

1999 Finest Team Finest Blue

	MINT	NRMT
COMP.BLUE SET (20)	220.00	100.00
COMP.BLUE SER.1 (20)	120.00	55.00
COMP.BLUE SER.2 (10)	100.00	45.00
COMMON CARD (TF1-TF20)	3.00	1.35
UNLISTED STARS	5.00	2.20

BLUE SER.1 ODDS 1:82 HOB/RET, 1:38 HTA
BLUE SER.2 ODDS 1:57 HOB/RET, 1:26 HTA
BLUE PRINT RUN 1500 SERIAL #'d SETS
*BLUE REF: 1.5X TO 4X BASIC BLUE
BLUE REF.SER.1 ODDS 1:816 HOB, 1:377 HTA
BLUE REF.SER.2 ODDS 1:571 HOB, 1:263 HTA
BLUE REF.PRINT RUN 150 SERIAL #'d SETS
*RED: .6X TO 1.5X BASIC BLUE
RED SER.1 ODDS 1:25 HTA
RED SER.2 ODDS 1:18 HTA
RED PRINT RUN 500 SERIAL #'d SETS
*RED REF: 4X TO 10X BASIC BLUE
RED REF.SER.1 ODDS 1:254 HTA
RED REF.SER.2 ODDS 1:184 HTA
RED REF.PRINT RUN 50 SERIAL #'d SETS
*GOLD: 1X TO 2.5X BASIC BLUE
GOLD SER.1 ODDS 1:51 HTA
GOLD SER.2 ODDS 1:37 HTA
GOLD PRINT RUN 250 SERIAL #'d SETS
*GOLD REF: 6X TO 15X BASIC BLUE
GOLD REF.SER.1 ODDS 1:510 HTA
GOLD REF.SER.2 ODDS 1:369 HTA
GOLD REF.PRINT RUN 25 SERIAL #'d SETS

	MINT	NRMT
TF1 Greg Maddux	12.00	5.50
TF2 Mark McGwire	30.00	13.50
TF3 Sammy Sosa	15.00	6.75
TF4 Juan Gonzalez	10.00	4.50
TF5 Alex Rodriguez	15.00	6.75
TF6 Travis Lee	3.00	1.35
TF7 Roger Clemens	12.00	5.50
TF8 Darin Erstad	3.00	1.35
TF9 Todd Helton	5.00	2.20
TF10 Mike Piazza	15.00	6.75
TF11 Kerry Wood	5.00	2.20
TF12 Ken Griffey Jr.	25.00	11.00
TF13 Frank Thomas	10.00	4.50
TF14 Jeff Bagwell	6.00	2.70
TF15 Nomar Garciaparra ..	15.00	6.75
TF16 Derek Jeter	15.00	6.75
TF17 Chipper Jones	12.00	5.50
TF18 Barry Bonds	6.00	2.70
TF19 Tony Gwynn	12.00	5.50
TF20 Ben Grieve	5.00	2.20

1993 Flair

	MINT	NRMT
COMPLETE SET (300)	50.00	22.00
COMMON CARD (1-300)	.40	.18
MINOR STARS	.60	.25
SEMISTARS	1.00	.45
UNLISTED STARS	1.50	.70

1 Steve Avery	.40	.18
2 Jeff Blauser	.40	.18
3 Ron Gant	.60	.25
4 Tom Glavine	1.00	.45
5 David Justice	1.50	.70
6 Mark Lemke	.40	.18
7 Greg Maddux	4.00	1.80
8 Fred McGriff	1.00	.45
9 Terry Pendleton	.40	.18
10 Deion Sanders	1.00	.45
11 John Smoltz	1.00	.45
12 Mike Stanton	.40	.18
13 Steve Buechele	.40	.18
14 Mark Grace	1.00	.45
15 Greg Hibbard	.40	.18
16 Derrick May	.40	.18
17 Chuck McElroy	.40	.18
18 Mike Morgan	.40	.18
19 Randy Myers	.60	.25
20 Ryne Sandberg	2.00	.90
21 Dwight Smith	.40	.18
22 Sammy Sosa	5.00	2.20
23 Jose Vizcaino	.40	.18
24 Tim Belcher	.40	.18
25 Rob Dibble	.40	.18
26 Roberto Kelly	.40	.18
27 Barry Larkin	1.50	.70
28 Kevin Mitchell	.60	.25
29 Hal Morris	.40	.18
30 Joe Oliver	.40	.18
31 Jose Rijo	.40	.18
32 Bip Roberts	.40	.18
33 Chris Sabo	.40	.18
34 Reggie Sanders	.60	.25
35 Dante Bichette	.60	.25
36 Willie Blair	.40	.18
37 Jerald Clark	.40	.18
38 Alex Cole	.40	.18
39 Andres Galarraga	1.50	.70
40 Joe Girardi	.60	.25
41 Charlie Hayes	.40	.18
42 Chris Jones	.40	.18
43 David Nied	.40	.18
44 Eric Young	1.50	.70
45 Alex Arias	.40	.18
46 Jack Armstrong	.40	.18
47 Bret Barberie	.40	.18
48 Chuck Carr	.40	.18
49 Jeff Conine	.60	.25
50 Orestes Destrade	.40	.18
51 Chris Hammond	.40	.18
52 Bryan Harvey	.40	.18
53 Benito Santiago	.40	.18
54 Gary Sheffield	1.50	.70
55 Walt Weiss	.40	.18
56 Eric Anthony	.40	.18
57 Jeff Bagwell	2.00	.90
58 Craig Biggio	1.50	.70
59 Ken Caminiti	1.00	.45
60 Andujar Cedeno	.40	.18
61 Doug Drabek	.40	.18
62 Steve Finley	.60	.25
63 Luis Gonzalez	.60	.25
64 Pete Harnisch	.40	.18
65 Doug Jones	.40	.18
66 Darryl Kile	.40	.18
67 Greg Swindell	.40	.18
68 Brett Butler	.60	.25
69 Jim Gott	.40	.18
70 Orel Hershiser	.60	.25
71 Eric Karros	1.00	.45
72 Pedro Martinez	3.00	1.35
73 Ramon Martinez	.40	.25
74 Roger McDowell	.40	.18
75 Mike Piazza	8.00	3.60
76 Jody Reed	.40	.18
77 Tim Wallach	.40	.18
78 Moises Alou	.60	.25
79 Greg Colbrunn	.40	.18
80 Wil Cordero	.40	.18
81 Delino DeShields	.60	.25
82 Jeff Fassero	.40	.18
83 Marquis Grissom	.60	.25
84 Ken Hill	.40	.18
85 Mike Lansing	.60	.25
86 Dennis Martinez	.60	.25
87 Larry Walker	1.50	.70
88 John Wetteland	.60	.25
89 Bobby Bonilla	.60	.25
90 Vince Coleman	.40	.18
91 Dwight Gooden	.60	.25
92 Todd Hundley	1.00	.45
93 Howard Johnson	.40	.18
94 Eddie Murray	1.50	.70
95 Joe Orsulak	.40	.18
96 Bret Saberhagen	.60	.25
97 Darren Daulton	.60	.25
98 Mariano Duncan	.40	.18
99 Len Dykstra	.60	.25
100 Jim Eisenreich	.40	.18
101 Tommy Greene	.40	.18
102 Dave Hollins	.60	.25
103 Pete Incaviglia	.40	.18
104 Danny Jackson	.40	.18
105 John Kruk	.60	.25
106 Terry Mulholland	.40	.18
107 Curt Schilling	.60	.25
108 Mitch Williams	.40	.18
109 Stan Belinda	.40	.18
110 Jay Bell	.60	.25
111 Steve Cooke	.40	.18
112 Carlos Garcia	.40	.18
113 Jeff King	.40	.18
114 Al Martin	.40	.18
115 Orlando Merced	.40	.18
116 Don Slaught	.40	.18
117 Andy Van Slyke	.60	.25
118 Tim Wakefield	.40	.18
119 Rene Arocha	.40	.18
120 Bernard Gilkey	.40	.18
121 Gregg Jefferies	.60	.25
122 Ray Lankford	1.00	.45
123 Donovan Osborne	.40	.18
124 Tom Pagnozzi	.40	.18
125 Erik Pappas	.40	.18
126 Geronimo Pena	.40	.18
127 Lee Smith	.60	.25
128 Ozzie Smith	2.00	.90
129 Bob Tewksbury	.40	.18
130 Mark Whiten	.40	.18
131 Derek Bell	.60	.25
132 Andy Benes	.40	.18
133 Tony Gwynn	4.00	1.80
134 Gene Harris	.40	.18
135 Trevor Hoffman	1.50	.70
136 Phil Plantier	.40	.18
137 Rod Beck	.60	.25
138 Barry Bonds	2.00	.90
139 John Burkett	.40	.18
140 Will Clark	1.50	.70
141 Royce Clayton	.40	.18
142 Mike Jackson	.40	.18
143 Darren Lewis	.40	.18
144 Kirt Manwaring	.40	.18
145 Willie McGee	.40	.18
146 Bill Swift	.40	.18
147 Robby Thompson	.40	.18
148 Matt Williams	1.00	.45
149 Brady Anderson	.60	.25
150 Mike Devereaux	.40	.18
151 Chris Hoiles	.40	.18
152 Ben McDonald	.40	.18
153 Mark McLemore	.40	.18
154 Mike Mussina	1.50	.70
155 Gregg Olson	.40	.18
156 Harold Reynolds	.40	.18
157 Cal Ripken UER	6.00	2.70

(Back refers to his games streak going into 1992; should be 1993) Also streak is spelled steak

158 Rick Sutcliffe	.40	.18
159 Fernando Valenzuela	.60	.25
160 Roger Clemens	4.00	1.80
161 Scott Cooper	.40	.18
162 Andre Dawson	1.00	.45
163 Scott Fletcher	.40	.18
164 Mike Greenwell	.60	.25
165 Greg A. Harris	.40	.18
166 Billy Hatcher	.40	.18
167 Jeff Russell	.40	.18
168 Mo Vaughn	1.50	.70
169 Frank Viola	.60	.25
170 Chad Curtis	.60	.25
171 Chili Davis	.40	.18
172 Gary DiSarcina	.40	.18
173 Damion Easley	.60	.25
174 Chuck Finley	.60	.25
175 Mark Langston	.40	.18

#	Name	MINT	NRMT
176	Luis Polonia	.40	.18
177	Tim Salmon	1.50	.70
178	Scott Sanderson	.40	.18
179	J.T. Snow	2.00	.90
180	Wilson Alvarez	.40	.18
181	Ellis Burks	.60	.25
182	Joey Cora	.40	.18
183	Alex Fernandez	.40	.25
184	Ozzie Guillen	.40	.18
185	Roberto Hernandez	.60	.25
186	Bo Jackson	.60	.25
187	Lance Johnson	.40	.18
188	Jack McDowell	.40	.18
189	Frank Thomas	3.00	1.35
190	Robin Ventura	.60	.25
191	Carlos Baerga	.40	.18
192	Albert Belle	1.50	.70
193	Wayne Kirby	.40	.18
194	Derek Lilliquist	.40	.18
195	Kenny Lofton	1.50	.70
196	Carlos Martinez	.40	.18
197	Jose Mesa	.40	.18
198	Eric Plunk	.40	.18
199	Paul Sorrento	.40	.18
200	John Doherty	.40	.18
201	Cecil Fielder	.60	.25
202	Travis Fryman	.60	.25
203	Kirk Gibson	.60	.25
204	Mike Henneman	.40	.18
205	Chad Kreuter	.40	.18
206	Scott Livingstone	.40	.18
207	Tony Phillips	.40	.18
208	Mickey Tettleton	.40	.18
209	Alan Trammell	1.00	.45
210	David Wells	.60	.25
211	Lou Whitaker	.60	.25
212	Kevin Appier	.60	.25
213	George Brett	3.00	1.35
214	David Cone	1.00	.45
215	Tom Gordon	.40	.18
216	Phil Hiatt	.40	.18
217	Felix Jose	.40	.18
218	Wally Joyner	.60	.25
219	Jose Lind	.40	.18
220	Mike Macfarlane	.40	.18
221	Brian McRae	.40	.18
222	Jeff Montgomery	.60	.25
223	Cal Eldred	.40	.18
224	Darryl Hamilton	.40	.18
225	John Jaha	.40	.18
226	Pat Listach	.40	.18
227	Graeme Lloyd	.40	.18
228	Kevin Reimer	.40	.18
229	Bill Spiers	.40	.18
230	B.J. Surhoff	.60	.25
231	Greg Vaughn	.60	.25
232	Robin Yount	1.00	.45
233	Rick Aguilera	.40	.18
234	Jim Deshaies	.40	.18
235	Brian Harper	.40	.18
236	Kent Hrbek	.60	.25
237	Chuck Knoblauch	1.50	.70
238	Shane Mack	.40	.18
239	David McCarty	.40	.18
240	Pedro Munoz	.40	.18
241	Mike Pagliarulo	.40	.18
242	Kirby Puckett	2.50	1.10
243	Dave Winfield	1.00	.45
244	Jim Abbott	.60	.25
245	Wade Boggs	1.50	.70
246	Pat Kelly	.40	.18
247	Jimmy Key	.60	.25
248	Jim Leyritz	.40	.18
249	Don Mattingly	3.00	1.35
250	Matt Nokes	.40	.18
251	Paul O'Neill	.60	.25
252	Mike Stanley	.40	.18
253	Danny Tartabull	.40	.18
254	Bob Wickman	.40	.18
255	Bernie Williams	1.50	.70
256	Mike Bordick	.40	.18
257	Dennis Eckersley	.60	.25
258	Brent Gates	.40	.18
259	Rich Gossage	.60	.25
260	Rickey Henderson	2.00	.90
261	Mark McGwire	8.00	3.60
262	Ruben Sierra	.40	.18
263	Terry Steinbach	.40	.18
264	Bob Welch	.40	.18
265	Bobby Witt	.40	.18
266	Rich Amaral	.40	.18
267	Chris Bosio	.40	.18
268	Jay Buhner	1.00	.45
269	Norm Charlton	.40	.18
270	Ken Griffey Jr.	8.00	3.60
271	Erik Hanson	.40	.18
272	Randy Johnson	1.50	.70
273	Edgar Martinez	1.00	.45
274	Tino Martinez	1.50	.70
275	Dave Valle	.40	.18
276	Omar Vizquel	.60	.25
277	Kevin Brown	1.00	.45
278	Jose Canseco	2.00	.90
279	Julio Franco	.40	.18
280	Juan Gonzalez	3.00	1.35
281	Tom Henke	.40	.18
282	David Hulse	.40	.18
283	Rafael Palmeiro	1.50	.70
284	Dean Palmer	.60	.25
285	Ivan Rodriguez	2.00	.90
286	Nolan Ryan	6.00	2.70
287	Roberto Alomar	1.50	.70
288	Pat Borders	.40	.18
289	Joe Carter	.60	.25
290	Juan Guzman	.40	.18
291	Pat Hentgen	1.00	.45
292	Paul Molitor	1.50	.70
293	John Olerud	1.00	.45
294	Ed Sprague	.40	.18
295	Dave Stewart	.60	.25
296	Duane Ward	.40	.18
297	Devon White	.40	.18
298	Checklist 1-100	.40	.18
299	Checklist 101-200	.40	.18
300	Checklist 201-300	.40	.18

1993 Flair Wave of the Future

		MINT	NRMT
COMPLETE SET (20)		40.00	18.00
COMMON CARD (1-20)		1.00	.45
SEMISTARS		2.00	.90
STATED ODDS 1:8			

#	Name	MINT	NRMT
1	Jason Bere	1.00	.45
2	Jeromy Burnitz	1.50	.70
3	Russ Davis	3.00	1.35
4	Jim Edmonds	10.00	4.50
5	Cliff Floyd	1.50	.70
6	Jeffrey Hammonds	1.50	.70
7	Trevor Hoffman	3.00	1.35
8	Domingo Jean	1.00	.45
9	David McCarty	1.00	.45
10	Bobby Munoz	1.00	.45
11	Brad Pennington	1.00	.45
12	Mike Piazza	15.00	6.75
13	Manny Ramirez	12.00	5.50
14	John Roper	1.00	.45
15	Tim Salmon	3.00	1.35
16	Aaron Sele	3.00	1.35
17	Allen Watson	1.00	.45
18	Rondell White	2.00	.90
19	Darrell Whitmore UER	1.00	.45

(Nigel Wilson back)

| 20 | Nigel Wilson UER | 1.00 | .45 |

(Darrell Whitmore back)

1994 Flair

	MINT	NRMT
COMPLETE SET (450)	100.00	45.00
COMPLETE SERIES 1 (250)	25.00	11.00
COMPLETE SERIES 2 (200)	75.00	34.00
COMMON CARD (1-450)	.25	.11
MINOR STARS	.50	.23
UNLISTED STARS	1.00	.45

#	Name	MINT	NRMT
1	Harold Baines	.50	.23
2	Jeffrey Hammonds	.50	.23
3	Chris Hoiles	.25	.11
4	Ben McDonald	.25	.11
5	Mark McLemore	.25	.11
6	Jamie Moyer	.25	.11
7	Jim Poole	.25	.11
8	Cal Ripken Jr.	4.00	1.80
9	Chris Sabo	.25	.11
10	Scott Bankhead	.25	.11
11	Scott Cooper	.25	.11
12	Danny Darwin	.25	.11
13	Andre Dawson	.75	.35
14	Billy Hatcher	.25	.11
15	Aaron Sele	.50	.23
16	John Valentin	.50	.23
17	Dave Valle	.25	.11
18	Mo Vaughn	1.00	.45
19	Brian Anderson	.75	.35
20	Gary DiSarcina	.25	.11
21	Jim Edmonds	1.00	.45
22	Chuck Finley	.50	.23
23	Bo Jackson	.50	.23
24	Mark Leiter	.25	.11
25	Greg Myers	.25	.11
26	Eduardo Perez	.25	.11
27	Tim Salmon	1.00	.45
28	Wilson Alvarez	.50	.23
29	Jason Bere	.25	.11
30	Alex Fernandez	.25	.11
31	Ozzie Guillen	.25	.11
32	Joe Hall	.25	.11
33	Darrin Jackson	.25	.11
34	Kirk McCaskill	.25	.11
35	Tim Raines	.50	.23
36	Frank Thomas	2.00	.90
37	Carlos Baerga	.50	.23
38	Albert Belle	1.00	.45
39	Mark Clark	.25	.11
40	Wayne Kirby	.25	.11
41	Dennis Martinez	.50	.23
42	Charles Nagy	.50	.23
43	Manny Ramirez	2.00	.90
44	Paul Sorrento	.25	.11
45	Jim Thome	1.00	.45
46	Eric Davis	.50	.23
47	John Doherty	.25	.11
48	Junior Felix	.25	.11
49	Cecil Fielder	.50	.23
50	Kirk Gibson	.50	.23
51	Mike Moore	.25	.11
52	Tony Phillips	.25	.11
53	Alan Trammell	.75	.35
54	Kevin Appier	.50	.23

55	Stan Belinda	.25	.11
56	Vince Coleman	.25	.11
57	Greg Gagne	.25	.11
58	Bob Hamelin	.25	.11
59	Dave Henderson	.25	.11
60	Wally Joyner	.50	.23
61	Mike Macfarlane	.25	.11
62	Jeff Montgomery	.25	.11
63	Ricky Bones	.25	.11
64	Jeff Bronkey	.25	.11
65	Alex Diaz	.25	.11
66	Cal Eldred	.25	.11
67	Darryl Hamilton	.25	.11
68	John Jaha	.25	.11
69	Mark Kiefer	.25	.11
70	Kevin Seitzer	.25	.11
71	Turner Ward	.25	.11
72	Rich Becker	.25	.11
73	Scott Erickson	.50	.23
74	Keith Garagozzo	.25	.11
75	Kent Hrbek	.50	.23
76	Scott Leius	.25	.11
77	Kirby Puckett	1.50	.70
78	Matt Walbeck	.25	.11
79	Dave Winfield	1.00	.45
80	Mike Gallego	.25	.11
81	Xavier Hernandez	.25	.11
82	Jimmy Key	.50	.23
83	Jim Leyritz	.50	.23
84	Don Mattingly	2.00	.90
85	Matt Nokes	.25	.11
86	Paul O'Neill	.50	.23
87	Melido Perez	.25	.11
88	Danny Tartabull	.25	.11
89	Mike Bordick	.25	.11
90	Ron Darling	.25	.11
91	Dennis Eckersley	.50	.23
92	Stan Javier	.25	.11
93	Steve Karsay	.25	.11
94	Mark McGwire	5.00	2.20
95	Troy Neel	.25	.11
96	Terry Steinbach	.25	.11
97	Bill Taylor	.25	.11
98	Eric Anthony	.25	.11
99	Chris Bosio	.25	.11
100	Tim Davis	.25	.11
101	Felix Fermin	.25	.11
102	Dave Fleming	.25	.11
103	Ken Griffey Jr.	5.00	2.20
104	Greg Hibbard	.25	.11
105	Reggie Jefferson	.25	.11
106	Tino Martinez	1.00	.45
107	Jack Armstrong	.25	.11
108	Will Clark	1.00	.45
109	Juan Gonzalez	2.00	.90
110	Rick Helling	.50	.23
111	Tom Henke	.25	.11
112	David Hulse	.25	.11
113	Manuel Lee	.25	.11
114	Doug Strange	.25	.11
115	Roberto Alomar	1.00	.45
116	Joe Carter	.50	.23
117	Carlos Delgado	1.00	.45
118	Pat Hentgen	.50	.23
119	Paul Molitor	1.00	.45
120	John Olerud	.50	.23
121	Dave Stewart	.50	.23
122	Todd Stottlemyre	.25	.11
123	Mike Timlin	.25	.11
124	Jeff Blauser	.25	.11
125	Tom Glavine	1.00	.45
126	David Justice	1.00	.45
127	Mike Kelly	.25	.11
128	Ryan Klesko	.50	.23
129	Javier Lopez	.75	.35
130	Greg Maddux	2.50	1.10
131	Fred McGriff	.75	.35
132	Kent Mercker	.25	.11
133	Mark Wohlers	.25	.11
134	Willie Banks	.25	.11
135	Steve Buechele	.25	.11
136	Shawon Dunston	.25	.11
137	Jose Guzman	.25	.11
138	Gienallen Hill	.25	.11
139	Randy Myers	.25	.11
140	Karl Rhodes	.25	.11
141	Ryne Sandberg	1.25	.55
142	Steve Trachsel	.25	.11
143	Bret Boone	.50	.23
144	Tom Browning	.25	.11
145	Hector Carrasco	.25	.11
146	Barry Larkin	1.00	.45
147	Hal Morris	.25	.11
148	Jose Rijo	.25	.11
149	Reggie Sanders	.50	.23
150	John Smiley	.25	.11
151	Dante Bichette	.50	.23
152	Ellis Burks	.25	.11
153	Joe Girardi	.25	.11
154	Mike Harkey	.25	.11
155	Roberto Mejia	.25	.11
156	Marcus Moore	.25	.11
157	Armando Reynoso	.25	.11
158	Bruce Ruffin	.25	.11
159	Eric Young	.25	.11
160	Kurt Abbott	.25	.11
161	Jeff Conine	.25	.11
162	Orestes Destrade	.25	.11
163	Chris Hammond	.25	.11
164	Bryan Harvey	.25	.11
165	Dave Magadan	.25	.11
166	Gary Sheffield	1.00	.45
167	David Weathers	.25	.11
168	Andujar Cedeno	.25	.11
169	Tom Edens	.25	.11
170	Luis Gonzalez	.50	.23
171	Pete Harnisch	.25	.11
172	Todd Jones	.25	.11
173	Darryl Kile	.25	.11
174	James Mouton	.25	.11
175	Scott Servais	.25	.11
176	Mitch Williams	.25	.11
177	Pedro Astacio	.25	.11
178	Orel Hershiser	.50	.23
179	Raul Mondesi	1.00	.45
180	Jose Offerman	.50	.23
181	Chan Ho Park	2.50	1.10
182	Mike Piazza	3.00	1.35
183	Cory Snyder	.25	.11
184	Tim Wallach	.25	.11
185	Todd Worrell	.25	.11
186	Sean Berry	.25	.11
187	Wil Cordero	.25	.11
188	Darrin Fletcher	.25	.11
189	Cliff Floyd	.50	.23
190	Marquis Grissom	.50	.23
191	Rod Henderson	.25	.11
192	Ken Hill	.25	.11
193	Pedro Martinez	1.25	.55
194	Kirk Rueter	.25	.11
195	Jeromy Burnitz	.50	.23
196	John Franco	.25	.11
197	Dwight Gooden	.50	.23
198	Todd Hundley	.25	.11
199	Bobby Jones	.25	.11
200	Jeff Kent	.50	.23
201	Mike Maddux	.25	.11
202	Ryan Thompson	.25	.11
203	Jose Vizcaino	.25	.11
204	Darren Daulton	.50	.23
205	Lenny Dykstra	.50	.23
206	Jim Eisenreich	.25	.11
207	Dave Hollins	.25	.11
208	Danny Jackson	.25	.11
209	Doug Jones	.25	.11
210	Jeff Juden	.25	.11
211	Ben Rivera	.25	.11
212	Kevin Stocker	.25	.11
213	Milt Thompson	.25	.11
214	Jay Bell	.50	.23
215	Steve Cooke	.25	.11
216	Mark Dewey	.25	.11
217	Al Martin	.25	.11
218	Orlando Merced	.25	.11
219	Don Slaught	.25	.11
220	Zane Smith	.25	.11
221	Rick White	.25	.11
222	Kevin Young	.25	.11
223	Rene Arocha	.25	.11
224	Rheal Cormier	.25	.11
225	Brian Jordan	.50	.23
226	Ray Lankford	.50	.23
227	Mike Perez	.25	.11
228	Ozzie Smith	1.25	.55
229	Mark Whiten	.25	.11
230	Todd Zeile	.25	.11
231	Derek Bell	.50	.23
232	Archi Cianfrocco	.25	.11
233	Ricky Gutierrez	.25	.11
234	Trevor Hoffman	.50	.23
235	Phil Plantier	.25	.11
236	Dave Staton	.25	.11
237	Wally Whitehurst	.25	.11
238	Todd Benzinger	.25	.11
239	Barry Bonds	1.25	.55
240	John Burkett	.25	.11
241	Royce Clayton	.25	.11
242	Bryan Hickerson	.25	.11
243	Mike Jackson	.50	.23
244	Darren Lewis	.25	.11
245	Kirt Manwaring	.25	.11
246	Mark Portugal	.25	.11
247	Salomon Torres	.25	.11
248	Checklist	.25	.11
249	Checklist	.25	.11
250	Checklist	.25	.11
251	Brady Anderson	.50	.23
252	Mike Devereaux	.25	.11
253	Sid Fernandez	.25	.11
254	Leo Gomez	.25	.11
255	Mike Mussina	1.00	.45
256	Mike Oquist	.25	.11
257	Rafael Palmeiro	1.00	.45
258	Lee Smith	.50	.23
259	Damon Berryhill	.25	.11
260	Wes Chamberlain	.25	.11
261	Roger Clemens	2.50	1.10
262	Gar Finnvold	.25	.11
263	Mike Greenwell	.25	.11
264	Tim Naehring	.25	.11
265	Otis Nixon	.25	.11
266	Ken Ryan	.25	.11
267	Chad Curtis	.25	.11
268	Chili Davis	.50	.23
269	Damion Easley	.50	.23
270	Jorge Fabregas	.25	.11
271	Mark Langston	.25	.11
272	Phil Leftwich	.25	.11
273	Harold Reynolds	.25	.11
274	J.T. Snow	.50	.23
275	Joey Cora	.25	.11
276	Julio Franco	.25	.11
277	Roberto Hernandez	.25	.11
278	Lance Johnson	.25	.11
279	Ron Karkovice	.25	.11
280	Jack McDowell	.25	.11
281	Robin Ventura	.50	.23
282	Sandy Alomar Jr.	.50	.23
283	Kenny Lofton	1.00	.45
284	Jose Mesa	.25	.11
285	Jack Morris	.50	.23
286	Eddie Murray	1.00	.45
287	Chad Ogea	.25	.11
288	Eric Plunk	.25	.11
289	Paul Shuey	.25	.11
290	Omar Vizquel	.50	.23
291	Danny Bautista	.25	.11
292	Travis Fryman	.50	.23
293	Greg Gohr	.25	.11
294	Chris Gomez	.25	.11
295	Mickey Tettleton	.25	.11
296	Lou Whitaker	.50	.23
297	David Cone	.75	.35
298	Gary Gaetti	.25	.11
299	Tom Gordon	.25	.11
300	Felix Jose	.25	.11
301	Jose Lind	.25	.11
302	Brian McRae	.25	.11
303	Mike Fetters	.25	.11
304	Brian Harper	.25	.11
305	Pat Listach	.25	.11
306	Matt Mieske	.25	.11
307	Dave Nilsson	.25	.11
308	Jody Reed	.25	.11
309	Greg Vaughn	.50	.23
310	Bill Wegman	.25	.11
311	Rick Aguilera	.25	.11
312	Alex Cole	.25	.11

❑ 313 Denny Hocking	.25	.11
❑ 314 Chuck Knoblauch	1.00	.45
❑ 315 Shane Mack	.25	.11
❑ 316 Pat Meares	.25	.11
❑ 317 Kevin Tapani	.25	.11
❑ 318 Jim Abbott	.50	.23
❑ 319 Wade Boggs	1.00	.45
❑ 320 Sterling Hitchcock	.50	.23
❑ 321 Pat Kelly	.25	.11
❑ 322 Terry Mulholland	.25	.11
❑ 323 Luis Polonia	.25	.11
❑ 324 Mike Stanley	.25	.11
❑ 325 Bob Wickman	.25	.11
❑ 326 Bernie Williams	1.00	.45
❑ 327 Mark Acre	.25	.11
❑ 328 Geronimo Berroa	.25	.11
❑ 329 Scott Brosius	.50	.23
❑ 330 Brent Gates	.25	.11
❑ 331 Rickey Henderson	1.25	.55
❑ 332 Carlos Reyes	.25	.11
❑ 333 Ruben Sierra	.25	.11
❑ 334 Bobby Witt	.25	.11
❑ 335 Bobby Ayala	.25	.11
❑ 336 Jay Buhner	.50	.23
❑ 337 Randy Johnson	1.00	.45
❑ 338 Edgar Martinez	.50	.23
❑ 339 Bill Risley	.25	.11
❑ 340 Alex Rodriguez	65.00	29.00
❑ 341 Roger Salkeld	.25	.11
❑ 342 Dan Wilson	.25	.11
❑ 343 Kevin Brown	.50	.23
❑ 344 Jose Canseco	1.25	.55
❑ 345 Dean Palmer	.50	.23
❑ 346 Ivan Rodriguez	1.25	.55
❑ 347 Kenny Rogers	.25	.11
❑ 348 Pat Borders	.25	.11
❑ 349 Juan Guzman	.25	.11
❑ 350 Ed Sprague	.25	.11
❑ 351 Devon White	.25	.11
❑ 352 Steve Avery	.25	.11
❑ 353 Roberto Kelly	.25	.11
❑ 354 Mark Lemke	.25	.11
❑ 355 Greg McMichael	.25	.11
❑ 356 Terry Pendleton	.25	.11
❑ 357 John Smoltz	.75	.35
❑ 358 Mike Stanton	.25	.11
❑ 359 Tony Tarasco	.25	.11
❑ 360 Mark Grace	.75	.35
❑ 361 Derrick May	.25	.11
❑ 362 Rey Sanchez	.25	.11
❑ 363 Sammy Sosa	3.00	1.35
❑ 364 Rick Wilkins	.25	.11
❑ 365 Jeff Brantley	.25	.11
❑ 366 Tony Fernandez	.50	.23
❑ 367 Chuck McElroy	.25	.11
❑ 368 Kevin Mitchell	.25	.11
❑ 369 John Roper	.25	.11
❑ 370 Johnny Ruffin	.25	.11
❑ 371 Deion Sanders	.50	.23
❑ 372 Marvin Freeman	.25	.11
❑ 373 Andres Galarraga	1.00	.45
❑ 374 Charlie Hayes	.25	.11
❑ 375 Nelson Liriano	.25	.11
❑ 376 David Nied	.25	.11
❑ 377 Walt Weiss	.25	.11
❑ 378 Bret Barberie	.25	.11
❑ 379 Jerry Browne	.25	.11
❑ 380 Chuck Carr	.25	.11
❑ 381 Greg Colbrunn	.25	.11
❑ 382 Charlie Hough	.25	.11
❑ 383 Kurt Miller	.25	.11
❑ 384 Benito Santiago	.25	.11
❑ 385 Jeff Bagwell	1.25	.55
❑ 386 Craig Biggio	1.00	.45
❑ 387 Ken Caminiti	.75	.35
❑ 388 Doug Drabek	.25	.11
❑ 389 Steve Finley	.50	.23
❑ 390 John Hudek	.25	.11
❑ 391 Donnie Miller	.25	.11
❑ 392 Shane Reynolds	.50	.23
❑ 393 Brett Butler	.50	.23
❑ 394 Tom Candiotti	.25	.11
❑ 395 Delino DeShields	.25	.11
❑ 396 Kevin Gross	.25	.11
❑ 397 Eric Karros	.50	.23
❑ 398 Ramon Martinez	.50	.23

❑ 399 Henry Rodriguez	.50	.23
❑ 400 Moises Alou	.50	.23
❑ 401 Jeff Fassero	.25	.11
❑ 402 Mike Lansing	.50	.23
❑ 403 Mel Rojas	.25	.11
❑ 404 Larry Walker	1.00	.45
❑ 405 John Wetteland	.50	.23
❑ 406 Gabe White	.25	.11
❑ 407 Bobby Bonilla	.50	.23
❑ 408 Josias Manzanillo	.25	.11
❑ 409 Bret Saberhagen	.50	.23
❑ 410 David Segui	.25	.11
❑ 411 Mariano Duncan	.25	.11
❑ 412 Tommy Greene	.25	.11
❑ 413 Billy Hatcher	.25	.11
❑ 414 Ricky Jordan	.25	.11
❑ 415 John Kruk	.50	.23
❑ 416 Bobby Munoz	.25	.11
❑ 417 Curt Schilling	.50	.23
❑ 418 Fernando Valenzuela	.50	.23
❑ 419 David West	.75	.35
❑ 420 Carlos Garcia	.25	.11
❑ 421 Brian Hunter	.25	.11
❑ 422 Jeff King	.25	.11
❑ 423 Jon Lieber	.25	.11
❑ 424 Ravelo Manzanillo	.25	.11
❑ 425 Denny Neagle	.25	.11
❑ 426 Andy Van Slyke	.50	.23
❑ 427 Bryan Eversgerd	.25	.11
❑ 428 Bernard Gilkey	.25	.11
❑ 429 Gregg Jefferies	.50	.23
❑ 430 Tom Pagnozzi	.25	.11
❑ 431 Bob Tewksbury	.25	.11
❑ 432 Allen Watson	.25	.11
❑ 433 Andy Ashby	.25	.11
❑ 434 Andy Benes	.50	.23
❑ 435 Donnie Elliott	.25	.11
❑ 436 Tony Gwynn	2.50	1.10
❑ 437 Joey Hamilton	1.00	.45
❑ 438 Tim Hyers	.25	.11
❑ 439 Luis Lopez	.25	.11
❑ 440 Bip Roberts	.25	.11
❑ 441 Scott Sanders	.25	.11
❑ 442 Rod Beck	.25	.11
❑ 443 Dave Burba	.25	.11
❑ 444 Darryl Strawberry	.50	.23
❑ 445 Bill Swift	.25	.11
❑ 446 Robby Thompson	.25	.11
❑ 447 Bill VanLandingham	.25	.11
❑ 448 Matt Williams	.75	.35
❑ 449 Checklist	.25	.11
❑ 450 Checklist	.25	.11
❑ P15 Aaron Sele Promo	1.50	.70

1994 Flair Hot Gloves

	MINT	NRMT
COMPLETE SET (10)	120.00	55.00
COMMON CARD (1-10)	6.00	2.70
UNLISTED STARS	10.00	4.50
RANDOM INSERTS IN SER.2 PACKS		

❑ 1 Barry Bonds	12.00	5.50
❑ 2 Will Clark	10.00	4.50
❑ 3 Ken Griffey Jr.	50.00	22.00
❑ 4 Kenny Lofton	10.00	4.50
❑ 5 Greg Maddux	25.00	11.00
❑ 6 Don Mattingly	20.00	9.00

❑ 7 Kirby Puckett	15.00	6.75
❑ 8 Cal Ripken Jr.	40.00	18.00
❑ 9 Tim Salmon	10.00	4.50
❑ 10 Matt Williams	6.00	2.70

1994 Flair Hot Numbers

	MINT	NRMT
COMPLETE SET (10)	80.00	36.00
COMMON CARD (1-10)	1.50	.70
SER.1 STATED ODDS 1:24		

❑ 1 Roberto Alomar	6.00	2.70
❑ 2 Carlos Baerga	1.50	.70
❑ 3 Will Clark	6.00	2.70
❑ 4 Fred McGriff	4.00	1.80
❑ 5 Paul Molitor	6.00	2.70
❑ 6 John Olerud	3.00	1.35
❑ 7 Mike Piazza	20.00	9.00
❑ 8 Cal Ripken Jr.	25.00	11.00
❑ 9 Ryne Sandberg	8.00	3.60
❑ 10 Frank Thomas	12.00	5.50

1994 Flair Infield Power

	MINT	NRMT
COMPLETE SET (10)	18.00	8.00
COMMON CARD (1-528)	.50	.23
RANDOM INSERTS IN SER.2 PACKS		

❑ 1 Jeff Bagwell	2.00	.90
❑ 2 Will Clark	1.50	.70
❑ 3 Darren Daulton	.50	.23
❑ 4 Don Mattingly	2.00	.90
❑ 5 Fred McGriff	1.00	.45
❑ 6 Rafael Palmeiro	1.50	.70
❑ 7 Mike Piazza	5.00	2.20
❑ 8 Cal Ripken Jr.	6.00	2.70
❑ 9 Frank Thomas	3.00	1.35
❑ 10 Matt Williams	1.00	.45

1994 Flair Outfield Power

	MINT	NRMT
COMPLETE SET (10)	25.00	11.00
COMMON CARD (1-528)	.50	.23
RANDOM INSERTS IN SER.1 PACKS		

❑ 1 Albert Belle	2.00	.90

		MINT	NRMT
❏ 2	Barry Bonds	2.50	1.10
❏ 3	Joe Carter	1.00	.45
❏ 4	Lenny Dykstra	.50	.23
❏ 5	Juan Gonzalez	4.00	1.80
❏ 6	Ken Griffey Jr.	10.00	4.50
❏ 7	David Justice	2.00	.90
❏ 8	Kirby Puckett	4.00	1.80
❏ 9	Tim Salmon	2.00	.90
❏ 10	Dave Winfield	2.00	.90

1994 Flair Wave of the Future

	MINT	NRMT
COMPLETE SERIES 1 (10)	15.00	6.75
COMPLETE SERIES 2 (10)	60.00	27.00
COMMON CARD (A1-B10)	1.00	.45
MINOR STARS	2.00	.90
RANDOM INSERTS IN BOTH SERIES PACKS		

❏ A1	Kurt Abbott	1.00	.45
❏ A2	Carlos Delgado	3.00	1.35
❏ A3	Steve Karsay	1.00	.45
❏ A4	Ryan Klesko	2.00	.90
❏ A5	Javier Lopez	2.50	1.10
❏ A6	Raul Mondesi	2.50	1.10
❏ A7	James Mouton	1.00	.45
❏ A8	Chan Ho Park	6.00	2.70
❏ A9	Dave Staton	1.00	.45
❏ A10	Rick White	1.00	.45
❏ B1	Mark Acre	1.00	.45
❏ B2	Chris Gomez	1.00	.45
❏ B3	Joey Hamilton	2.50	1.10
❏ B4	John Hudek	1.00	.45
❏ B5	Jon Lieber	1.00	.45
❏ B6	Matt Mieske	1.00	.45
❏ B7	Orlando Miller	1.00	.45
❏ B8	Alex Rodriguez	50.00	22.00
❏ B9	Tony Tarasco	1.00	.45
❏ B10	William VanLandingham	1.00	.45

1995 Flair

	MINT	NRMT
COMPLETE SET (432)	80.00	36.00
COMPLETE SERIES 1 (216)	50.00	22.00
COMPLETE SERIES 2 (216)	30.00	13.50
COMMON CARD (1-432)	.25	.11
MINOR STARS	.50	.23
UNLISTED STARS	1.00	.45

❏ 1	Brady Anderson	.50	.23
❏ 2	Harold Baines	.50	.23
❏ 3	Leo Gomez	.25	.11
❏ 4	Alan Mills	.25	.11
❏ 5	Jamie Moyer	.25	.11
❏ 6	Mike Mussina	1.00	.45
❏ 7	Mike Oquist	.25	.11
❏ 8	Arthur Rhodes	.25	.11
❏ 9	Cal Ripken Jr.	4.00	1.80
❏ 10	Roger Clemens	2.50	1.10
❏ 11	Scott Cooper	.25	.11
❏ 12	Mike Greenwell	.25	.11
❏ 13	Aaron Sele	.50	.23
❏ 14	John Valentin	.50	.23
❏ 15	Mo Vaughn	1.00	.45
❏ 16	Chad Curtis	.25	.11
❏ 17	Gary DiSarcina	.25	.11
❏ 18	Chuck Finley	.50	.23
❏ 19	Andrew Lorraine	.25	.11
❏ 20	Spike Owen	.25	.11
❏ 21	Tim Salmon	1.00	.45
❏ 22	J.T. Snow	.50	.23
❏ 23	Wilson Alvarez	.50	.23
❏ 24	Jason Bere	.25	.11
❏ 25	Ozzie Guillen	.25	.11
❏ 26	Mike LaValliere	.25	.11
❏ 27	Frank Thomas	2.00	.90
❏ 28	Robin Ventura	.50	.23
❏ 29	Carlos Baerga	.25	.11
❏ 30	Albert Belle	1.00	.45
❏ 31	Jason Grimsley	.25	.11
❏ 32	Dennis Martinez	.50	.23
❏ 33	Eddie Murray	1.00	.45
❏ 34	Charles Nagy	.50	.23
❏ 35	Manny Ramirez	1.25	.55
❏ 36	Paul Sorrento	.25	.11
❏ 37	John Doherty	.25	.11
❏ 38	Cecil Fielder	.50	.23
❏ 39	Travis Fryman	.50	.23
❏ 40	Chris Gomez	.25	.11
❏ 41	Tony Phillips	.25	.11
❏ 42	Lou Whitaker	.50	.23
❏ 43	David Cone	.75	.35
❏ 44	Gary Gaetti	.25	.11
❏ 45	Mark Gubicza	.25	.11
❏ 46	Bob Hamelin	.25	.11
❏ 47	Wally Joyner	.50	.23
❏ 48	Rusty Meacham	.25	.11
❏ 49	Jeff Montgomery	.25	.11
❏ 50	Ricky Bones	.25	.11
❏ 51	Cal Eldred	.25	.11
❏ 52	Pat Listach	.25	.11
❏ 53	Matt Mieske	.25	.11
❏ 54	Dave Nilsson	.25	.11
❏ 55	Greg Vaughn	.50	.23
❏ 56	Bill Wegman	.25	.11
❏ 57	Chuck Knoblauch	1.00	.45
❏ 58	Scott Leius	.25	.11
❏ 59	Pat Mahomes	.25	.11
❏ 60	Pat Meares	.25	.11
❏ 61	Pedro Munoz	.25	.11
❏ 62	Kirby Puckett	1.50	.70
❏ 63	Wade Boggs	1.00	.45
❏ 64	Jimmy Key	.50	.23
❏ 65	Jim Leyritz	.25	.11
❏ 66	Don Mattingly	2.00	.90
❏ 67	Paul O'Neill	.50	.23
❏ 68	Melido Perez	.25	.11

❏ 69	Danny Tartabull	.25	.11
❏ 70	John Briscoe	.25	.11
❏ 71	Scott Brosius	.50	.23
❏ 72	Ron Darling	.25	.11
❏ 73	Brent Gates	.25	.11
❏ 74	Rickey Henderson	1.25	.55
❏ 75	Stan Javier	.25	.11
❏ 76	Mark McGwire	5.00	2.20
❏ 77	Todd Van Poppel	.25	.11
❏ 78	Bobby Ayala	.25	.11
❏ 79	Mike Blowers	.25	.11
❏ 80	Jay Buhner	.50	.23
❏ 81	Ken Griffey Jr.	5.00	2.20
❏ 82	Randy Johnson	1.00	.45
❏ 83	Tino Martinez	1.00	.45
❏ 84	Jeff Nelson	.25	.11
❏ 85	Alex Rodriguez	4.00	1.80
❏ 86	Will Clark	1.00	.45
❏ 87	Jeff Frye	.25	.11
❏ 88	Juan Gonzalez	2.00	.90
❏ 89	Rusty Greer	1.00	.45
❏ 90	Darren Oliver	.25	.11
❏ 91	Dean Palmer	.50	.23
❏ 92	Ivan Rodriguez	1.25	.55
❏ 93	Matt Whiteside	.25	.11
❏ 94	Roberto Alomar	1.00	.45
❏ 95	Joe Carter	.50	.23
❏ 96	Tony Castillo	.25	.11
❏ 97	Juan Guzman	.50	.23
❏ 98	Pat Hentgen	.50	.23
❏ 99	Mike Huff	.25	.11
❏ 100	John Olerud	.50	.23
❏ 101	Woody Williams	.25	.11
❏ 102	Roberto Kelly	.25	.11
❏ 103	Ryan Klesko	.50	.23
❏ 104	Javier Lopez	.50	.23
❏ 105	Greg Maddux	2.50	1.10
❏ 106	Fred McGriff	.75	.35
❏ 107	Jose Oliva	.25	.11
❏ 108	John Smoltz	.75	.35
❏ 109	Tony Tarasco	.25	.11
❏ 110	Mark Wohlers	.25	.11
❏ 111	Jim Bullinger	.25	.11
❏ 112	Shawon Dunston	.25	.11
❏ 113	Derrick May	.25	.11
❏ 114	Randy Myers	.25	.11
❏ 115	Karl Rhodes	.25	.11
❏ 116	Rey Sanchez	.25	.11
❏ 117	Steve Trachsel	.25	.11
❏ 118	Eddie Zambrano	.25	.11
❏ 119	Bret Boone	.50	.23
❏ 120	Brian Dorsett	.25	.11
❏ 121	Hal Morris	.25	.11
❏ 122	Jose Rijo	.25	.11
❏ 123	John Roper	.25	.11
❏ 124	Reggie Sanders	.50	.23
❏ 125	Pete Schourek	.25	.11
❏ 126	John Smiley	.25	.11
❏ 127	Ellis Burks	.50	.23
❏ 128	Vinny Castilla	.75	.35
❏ 129	Marvin Freeman	.25	.11
❏ 130	Andres Galarraga	1.00	.45
❏ 131	Mike Munoz	.25	.11
❏ 132	David Nied	.25	.11
❏ 133	Bruce Ruffin	.25	.11
❏ 134	Walt Weiss	.25	.11
❏ 135	Eric Young	.25	.11
❏ 136	Greg Colbrunn	.25	.11
❏ 137	Jeff Conine	.25	.11
❏ 138	Jeremy Hernandez	.25	.11
❏ 139	Charles Johnson	.50	.23
❏ 140	Robb Nen	.25	.11
❏ 141	Gary Sheffield	.50	.23
❏ 142	Dave Weathers	.25	.11
❏ 143	Jeff Bagwell	1.25	.55
❏ 144	Craig Biggio	1.00	.45
❏ 145	Tony Eusebio	.25	.11
❏ 146	Luis Gonzalez	.25	.11
❏ 147	John Hudek	.25	.11
❏ 148	Darryl Kile	.25	.11
❏ 149	Dave Veres	.25	.11
❏ 150	Billy Ashley	.25	.11
❏ 151	Pedro Astacio	.25	.11
❏ 152	Rafael Bournigal	.25	.11
❏ 153	Delino DeShields	.25	.11
❏ 154	Raul Mondesi	.75	.35

155	Mike Piazza	3.00	1.35
156	Rudy Seanez	.25	.11
157	Ismael Valdes	.50	.23
158	Tim Wallach	.25	.11
159	Todd Worrell	.25	.11
160	Moises Alou	.50	.23
161	Cliff Floyd	.50	.23
162	Gil Heredia	.25	.11
163	Mike Lansing	.25	.11
164	Pedro Martinez	1.25	.55
165	Kirk Rueter	.25	.11
166	Tim Scott	.25	.11
167	Jeff Shaw	.25	.11
168	Rondell White	.50	.23
169	Bobby Bonilla	.50	.23
170	Rico Brogna	.50	.23
171	Todd Hundley	.50	.23
172	Jeff Kent	.50	.23
173	Jim Lindeman	.25	.11
174	Joe Orsulak	.25	.11
175	Bret Saberhagen	.50	.23
176	Toby Borland	.25	.11
177	Darren Daulton	.50	.23
178	Lenny Dykstra	.50	.23
179	Jim Eisenreich	.25	.11
180	Tommy Greene	.25	.11
181	Tony Longmire	.25	.11
182	Bobby Munoz	.25	.11
183	Kevin Stocker	.25	.11
184	Jay Bell	.50	.23
185	Steve Cooke	.25	.11
186	Ravelo Manzanillo	.25	.11
187	Al Martin	.25	.11
188	Denny Neagle	.50	.23
189	Don Slaught	.25	.11
190	Paul Wagner	.25	.11
191	Rene Arocha	.25	.11
192	Bernard Gilkey	.25	.11
193	Jose Oquendo	.25	.11
194	Tom Pagnozzi	.25	.11
195	Ozzie Smith	1.25	.55
196	Allen Watson	.25	.11
197	Mark Whiten	.25	.11
198	Andy Ashby	.25	.11
199	Donnie Elliott	.25	.11
200	Bryce Florie	.25	.11
201	Tony Gwynn	2.50	1.10
202	Trevor Hoffman	.50	.23
203	Brian Johnson	.25	.11
204	Tim Mauser	.25	.11
205	Bip Roberts	.25	.11
206	Rod Beck	.25	.11
207	Barry Bonds	1.25	.55
208	Royce Clayton	.25	.11
209	Darren Lewis	.25	.11
210	Mark Portugal	.25	.11
211	Kevin Rogers	.25	.11
212	Wm. VanLandingham	.25	.11
213	Matt Williams	1.00	.45
214	Checklist	.25	.11
215	Checklist	.25	.11
216	Checklist	.25	.11
217	Bret Barberie	.25	.11
218	Armando Benitez	.25	.11
219	Kevin Brown	.75	.35
220	Sid Fernandez	.25	.11
221	Chris Hoiles	.25	.11
222	Doug Jones	.25	.11
223	Ben McDonald	.25	.11
224	Rafael Palmeiro	1.00	.45
225	Andy Van Slyke	.50	.23
226	Jose Canseco	1.25	.55
227	Vaughn Eshelman	.25	.11
228	Mike Macfarlane	.25	.11
229	Tim Naehring	.25	.11
230	Frank Rodriguez	.25	.11
231	Lee Tinsley	.25	.11
232	Mark Whiten	.25	.11
233	Garret Anderson	.50	.23
234	Chili Davis	.50	.23
235	Jim Edmonds	.75	.35
236	Mark Langston	.25	.11
237	Troy Percival	.25	.11
238	Tony Phillips	.25	.11
239	Lee Smith	.50	.23
240	Jim Abbott	.50	.23
241	James Baldwin	.50	.23
242	Mike Devereaux	.25	.11
243	Ray Durham	.50	.23
244	Alex Fernandez	.25	.11
245	Roberto Hernandez	.25	.11
246	Lance Johnson	.25	.11
247	Ron Karkovice	.25	.11
248	Tim Raines	.50	.23
249	Sandy Alomar Jr.	.50	.23
250	Orel Hershiser	.50	.23
251	Julian Tavarez	.25	.11
252	Jim Thome	1.00	.45
253	Omar Vizquel	.50	.23
254	Dave Winfield	1.00	.45
255	Chad Curtis	.25	.11
256	Kirk Gibson	.50	.23
257	Mike Henneman	.25	.11
258	Bob Higginson	1.50	.70
259	Felipe Lira	.25	.11
260	Rudy Pemberton	.25	.11
261	Alan Trammell	.50	.23
262	Kevin Appier	.50	.23
263	Pat Borders	.25	.11
264	Tom Gordon	.25	.11
265	Jose Lind	.25	.11
266	Jon Nunnally	.25	.11
267	Dilson Torres	.25	.11
268	Michael Tucker	.50	.23
269	Jeff Cirillo	.50	.23
270	Darryl Hamilton	.25	.11
271	David Nilsson	.25	.11
272	Mark Kiefer	.25	.11
273	Graeme Lloyd	.25	.11
274	Joe Oliver	.25	.11
275	Al Reyes	.25	.11
276	Kevin Seitzer	.25	.11
277	Rick Aguilera	.25	.11
278	Marty Cordova	.25	.11
279	Scott Erickson	.50	.23
280	LaTroy Hawkins	.25	.11
281	Brad Radke	1.50	.70
282	Kevin Tapani	.25	.11
283	Tony Fernandez	.50	.23
284	Sterling Hitchcock	.50	.23
285	Pat Kelly	.25	.11
286	Jack McDowell	.25	.11
287	Andy Pettitte	1.00	.45
288	Mike Stanley	.25	.11
289	John Wetteland	.50	.23
290	Bernie Williams	1.00	.45
291	Mark Acre	.25	.11
292	Geronimo Berroa	.25	.11
293	Dennis Eckersley	.50	.23
294	Steve Ontiveros	.25	.11
295	Ruben Sierra	.25	.11
296	Terry Steinbach	.25	.11
297	Dave Stewart	.50	.23
298	Todd Stottlemyre	.25	.11
299	Darren Bragg	.25	.11
300	Joey Cora	.25	.11
301	Edgar Martinez	.50	.23
302	Bill Risley	.25	.11
303	Ron Villone	.25	.11
304	Dan Wilson	.25	.11
305	Benji Gil	.25	.11
306	Wilson Heredia	.25	.11
307	Mark McLemore	.25	.11
308	Otis Nixon	.25	.11
309	Kenny Rogers	.25	.11
310	Jeff Russell	.25	.11
311	Mickey Tettleton	.25	.11
312	Bob Tewksbury	.25	.11
313	David Cone	.75	.35
314	Carlos Delgado	1.00	.45
315	Alex Gonzalez	.25	.11
316	Shawn Green	1.00	.45
317	Paul Molitor	1.00	.45
318	Ed Sprague	.25	.11
319	Devon White	.50	.23
320	Steve Avery	.50	.23
321	Jeff Blauser	.25	.11
322	Brad Clontz	.25	.11
323	Tom Glavine	1.00	.45
324	Marquis Grissom	.50	.23
325	Chipper Jones	2.50	1.10
326	David Justice	1.00	.45
327	Mark Lemke	.25	.11
328	Kent Mercker	.25	.11
329	Jason Schmidt	.50	.23
330	Steve Buechele	.25	.11
331	Kevin Foster	.25	.11
332	Mark Grace	.75	.35
333	Brian McRae	.25	.11
334	Sammy Sosa	3.00	1.35
335	Ozzie Timmons	.25	.11
336	Rick Wilkins	.25	.11
337	Hector Carrasco	.25	.11
338	Ron Gant	.50	.23
339	Barry Larkin	1.00	.45
340	Deion Sanders	.50	.23
341	Benito Santiago	.25	.11
342	Roger Bailey	.25	.11
343	Jason Bates	.25	.11
344	Dante Bichette	.50	.23
345	Joe Girardi	.25	.11
346	Bill Swift	.25	.11
347	Mark Thompson	.25	.11
348	Larry Walker	1.00	.45
349	Kurt Abbott	.25	.11
350	John Burkett	.25	.11
351	Chuck Carr	.25	.11
352	Andre Dawson	.75	.35
353	Chris Hammond	.25	.11
354	Charles Johnson	.50	.23
355	Terry Pendleton	.25	.11
356	Quilvio Veras	.25	.11
357	Derek Bell	.50	.23
358	Jim Dougherty	.25	.11
359	Doug Drabek	.25	.11
360	Todd Jones	.25	.11
361	Orlando Miller	.25	.11
362	James Mouton	.25	.11
363	Phil Plantier	.25	.11
364	Shane Reynolds	.50	.23
365	Todd Hollandsworth	.25	.11
366	Eric Karros	.50	.23
367	Ramon Martinez	.50	.23
368	Hideo Nomo	2.50	1.10
369	Jose Offerman	.50	.23
370	Antonio Osuna	.25	.11
371	Todd Williams	.25	.11
372	Shane Andrews	.25	.11
373	Wil Cordero	.25	.11
374	Jeff Fassero	.25	.11
375	Darrin Fletcher	.25	.11
376	Mark Grudzielanek	.75	.35
377	Carlos Perez	.75	.35
378	Mel Rojas	.25	.11
379	Tony Tarasco	.25	.11
380	Edgardo Alfonzo	1.00	.45
381	Brett Butler	.50	.23
382	Carl Everett	.25	.11
383	John Franco	.50	.23
384	Pete Harnisch	.25	.11
385	Bobby Jones	.25	.11
386	Dave Mlicki	.25	.11
387	Jose Vizcaino	.25	.11
388	Ricky Bottalico	.25	.11
389	Tyler Green	.25	.11
390	Charlie Hayes	.25	.11
391	Dave Hollins	.25	.11
392	Gregg Jefferies	.25	.11
393	Michael Mimbs	.25	.11
394	Mickey Morandini	.25	.11
395	Curt Schilling	.75	.35
396	Heathcliff Slocumb	.25	.11
397	Jason Christiansen	.25	.11
398	Midre Cummings	.25	.11
399	Carlos Garcia	.25	.11
400	Mark Johnson	.25	.11
401	Jeff King	.25	.11
402	Jon Lieber	.25	.11
403	Esteban Loaiza	.25	.11
404	Orlando Merced	.25	.11
405	Gary Wilson	.25	.11
406	Scott Cooper	.25	.11
407	Tom Henke	.25	.11
408	Ken Hill	.25	.11
409	Danny Jackson	.25	.11
410	Brian Jordan	.50	.23
411	Ray Lankford	.50	.23
412	John Mabry	.25	.11

		MINT	NRMT
❏ 413	Todd Zeile	.25	.11
❏ 414	Andy Benes	.50	.23
❏ 415	Andres Berumen	.25	.11
❏ 416	Ken Caminiti	.75	.35
❏ 417	Andujar Cedeno	.25	.11
❏ 418	Steve Finley	.50	.23
❏ 419	Joey Hamilton	.50	.23
❏ 420	Dustin Hermanson	.25	.11
❏ 421	Melvin Nieves	.25	.11
❏ 422	Roberto Petagine	.25	.11
❏ 423	Eddie Williams	.25	.11
❏ 424	Glenallen Hill	.25	.11
❏ 425	Kirt Manwaring	.25	.11
❏ 426	Terry Mulholland	.25	.11
❏ 427	J.R. Phillips	.25	.11
❏ 428	Joe Rosselli	.25	.11
❏ 429	Robby Thompson	.25	.11
❏ 430	Checklist	.25	.11
❏ 431	Checklist	.25	.11
❏ 432	Checklist	.25	.11

1995 Flair Hot Gloves

		MINT	NRMT
COMPLETE SET (12)		120.00	55.00
COMMON CARD (1-12)		4.00	1.80
SEMISTARS		6.00	2.70
UNLISTED STARS		10.00	4.50
SER.2 STATED ODDS 1:25			
❏ 1	Roberto Alomar	10.00	4.50
❏ 2	Barry Bonds	12.00	5.50
❏ 3	Ken Griffey Jr.	50.00	22.00
❏ 4	Marquis Grissom	6.00	2.70
❏ 5	Barry Larkin	10.00	4.50
❏ 6	Darren Lewis	4.00	1.80
❏ 7	Kenny Lofton	6.00	2.70
❏ 8	Don Mattingly	20.00	9.00
❏ 9	Cal Ripken	40.00	18.00
❏ 10	Ivan Rodriguez	12.00	5.50
❏ 11	Devon White	6.00	2.70
❏ 12	Matt Williams	10.00	4.50

1995 Flair Hot Numbers

		MINT	NRMT
COMPLETE SET (10)		60.00	27.00
COMMON CARD (1-10)		2.00	.90
SER.1 STATED ODDS 1:9			
❏ 1	Jeff Bagwell	4.00	1.80
❏ 2	Albert Belle	3.00	1.35
❏ 3	Barry Bonds	3.00	1.35
❏ 4	Ken Griffey Jr.	15.00	6.75
❏ 5	Kenny Lofton	2.00	.90
❏ 6	Greg Maddux	8.00	3.60
❏ 7	Mike Piazza	10.00	4.50
❏ 8	Cal Ripken	8.00	3.60
❏ 9	Frank Thomas	6.00	2.70
❏ 10	Matt Williams	3.00	1.35

1995 Flair Infield Power

		MINT	NRMT
COMPLETE SET (10)		15.00	6.75
COMMON CARD (1-10)		.75	.35
SER.2 STATED ODDS 1:6			
❏ 1	Jeff Bagwell	2.00	.90
❏ 2	Darren Daulton	.75	.35
❏ 3	Cecil Fielder	.75	.35
❏ 4	Andres Galarraga	1.50	.70
❏ 5	Fred McGriff	1.00	.45
❏ 6	Rafael Palmeiro	1.50	.70
❏ 7	Mike Piazza	5.00	2.20
❏ 8	Frank Thomas	3.00	1.35
❏ 9	Mo Vaughn	1.50	.70
❏ 10	Matt Williams	1.50	.70

1995 Flair Outfield Power

		MINT	NRMT
COMPLETE SET (10)		15.00	6.75
COMMON CARD (1-10)		.50	.23
SER.1 STATED ODDS 1:6			
❏ 1	Albert Belle	1.50	.70
❏ 2	Dante Bichette	.75	.35
❏ 3	Barry Bonds	2.00	.90
❏ 4	Jose Canseco	2.00	.90
❏ 5	Joe Carter	.75	.35
❏ 6	Juan Gonzalez	3.00	1.35
❏ 7	Ken Griffey Jr.	8.00	3.60
❏ 8	Kirby Puckett	1.50	.70
❏ 9	Gary Sheffield	.75	.35
❏ 10	Ruben Sierra	.50	.23

1995 Flair Ripken

	MINT	NRMT
COMPLETE SET (10)	80.00	36.00
COMMON CARD (1-10)	10.00	4.50
SER.2 STATED ODDS 1:12		
COMMON MAIL-IN (11-15)	6.00	2.70
MAIL-IN CARDS DIST. VIA WRAPPER EXCH.		

		MINT	NRMT
❏ 1	Cal Ripken Rookie of the Year	10.00	4.50
❏ 2	Cal Ripken 1st MVP Season	10.00	4.50
❏ 3	Cal Ripken World Series Highlight	10.00	4.50
❏ 4	Cal Ripken Family Tradition	10.00	4.50
❏ 5	Cal Ripken 8,243 Consecutive Innings	10.00	4.50
❏ 6	Cal Ripken 95 Consecutive Errorless Games	10.00	4.50
❏ 7	Cal Ripken All-Star MVP	10.00	4.50
❏ 8	Cal Ripken 1,000th RBI	10.00	4.50
❏ 9	Cal Ripken 287th Home Run	10.00	4.50
❏ 10	Cal Ripken 2,000th Consecutive Game	10.00	4.50
❏ 11	Cal Ripken Literacy	6.00	2.70
❏ 12	Cal Ripken Game 2,130	6.00	2.70
❏ 13	Cal Ripken Game 2,131	6.00	2.70
❏ 14	Cal Ripken Defensive Prowess	6.00	2.70
❏ 15	Cal Ripken 2,153 and Counting	6.00	2.70

1995 Flair Today's Spotlight

		MINT	NRMT
COMPLETE SET (12)		100.00	45.00
COMMON CARD (1-12)		4.00	1.80
SER.1 STATED ODDS 1:25			
❏ 1	Jeff Bagwell	12.00	5.50
❏ 2	Jason Bere	4.00	1.80
❏ 3	Cliff Floyd	5.00	2.20
❏ 4	Chuck Knoblauch	10.00	4.50
❏ 5	Kenny Lofton	6.00	2.70
❏ 6	Javier Lopez	5.00	2.20

			MINT	NRMT
❑ 7	Raul Mondesi		6.00	2.70
❑ 8	Mike Mussina		10.00	4.50
❑ 9	Mike Piazza		30.00	13.50
❑ 10	Manny Ramirez		10.00	4.50
❑ 11	Tim Salmon		10.00	4.50
❑ 12	Frank Thomas		25.00	11.00

1995 Flair Wave of the Future

	MINT	NRMT
COMPLETE SET (10)	25.00	11.00
COMMON CARD (1-10)	1.00	.45
SER.2 STATED ODDS 1:9		

		MINT	NRMT
❑ 1	Jason Bates	1.00	.45
❑ 2	Armando Benitez	1.00	.45
❑ 3	Marty Cordova	1.00	.45
❑ 4	Ray Durham	2.00	.90
❑ 5	Vaughn Eshelman	1.00	.45
❑ 6	Carl Everett	1.00	.45
❑ 7	Shawn Green	4.00	1.80
❑ 8	Dustin Hermanson	1.00	.45
❑ 9	Chipper Jones	10.00	4.50
❑ 10	Hideo Nomo	5.00	2.20

1996 Flair

	MINT	NRMT
COMPLETE SET (400)	200.00	90.00
COMMON CARD (1-400)	.50	.23
MINOR STARS	.75	.35
SEMISTARS	1.25	.55
UNLISTED STARS	2.00	.90
GOLD AND SILVER EQUAL VALUE		

❑ 1	Roberto Alomar		2.00	.90
❑ 2	Brady Anderson		.75	.35
❑ 3	Bobby Bonilla		.75	.35
❑ 4	Scott Erickson		.75	.35
❑ 5	Jeffrey Hammonds		.75	.35
❑ 6	Jimmy Haynes		.50	.23
❑ 7	Chris Hoiles		.50	.23
❑ 8	Kent Mercker		.50	.23
❑ 9	Mike Mussina		2.00	.90
❑ 10	Randy Myers		.50	.23
❑ 11	Rafael Palmeiro		2.00	.90
❑ 12	Cal Ripken		8.00	3.60
❑ 13	B.J. Surhoff		.75	.35
❑ 14	David Wells		1.25	.55
❑ 15	Jose Canseco		2.50	1.10
❑ 16	Roger Clemens		5.00	2.20
❑ 17	Wil Cordero		.50	.23
❑ 18	Tom Gordon		.50	.23
❑ 19	Mike Greenwell		.50	.23
❑ 20	Dwayne Hosey		.50	.23
❑ 21	Jose Malave		.50	.23
❑ 22	Tim Naehring		.50	.23
❑ 23	Troy O'Leary		.75	.35
❑ 24	Aaron Sele		.75	.35
❑ 25	Heathcliff Slocumb		.50	.23
❑ 26	Mike Stanley		.50	.23
❑ 27	Jeff Suppan		.50	.23
❑ 28	John Valentin		.75	.35
❑ 29	Mo Vaughn		2.00	.90
❑ 30	Tim Wakefield		.50	.23
❑ 31	Jim Abbott		.75	.35
❑ 32	Garret Anderson		.75	.35
❑ 33	George Arias		.50	.23
❑ 34	Chili Davis		.75	.35
❑ 35	Gary DiSarcina		.50	.23
❑ 36	Jim Edmonds		1.25	.55
❑ 37	Chuck Finley		.75	.35
❑ 38	Todd Greene		.50	.23
❑ 39	Mark Langston		.50	.23
❑ 40	Troy Percival		.75	.35
❑ 41	Tim Salmon		1.25	.55
❑ 42	Lee Smith		.75	.35
❑ 43	J.T. Snow		.75	.35
❑ 44	Randy Velarde		.50	.23
❑ 45	Tim Wallach		.50	.23
❑ 46	Wilson Alvarez		.50	.23
❑ 47	Harold Baines		.75	.35
❑ 48	Jason Bere		.50	.23
❑ 49	Ray Durham		.75	.35
❑ 50	Alex Fernandez		.50	.23
❑ 51	Ozzie Guillen		.50	.23
❑ 52	Roberto Hernandez		.50	.23
❑ 53	Ron Karkovice		.50	.23
❑ 54	Darren Lewis		.50	.23
❑ 55	Lyle Mouton		.50	.23
❑ 56	Tony Phillips		.50	.23
❑ 57	Chris Snopek		.50	.23
❑ 58	Kevin Tapani		.50	.23
❑ 59	Danny Tartabull		.50	.23
❑ 60	Frank Thomas		4.00	1.80
❑ 61	Robin Ventura		.75	.35
❑ 62	Sandy Alomar Jr.		.75	.35
❑ 63	Carlos Baerga		.50	.23
❑ 64	Albert Belle		2.00	.90
❑ 65	Julio Franco		.50	.23
❑ 66	Orel Hershiser		.75	.35
❑ 67	Kenny Lofton		1.25	.55
❑ 68	Dennis Martinez		.75	.35
❑ 69	Jack McDowell		.75	.35
❑ 70	Jose Mesa		.50	.23
❑ 71	Eddie Murray		2.00	.90
❑ 72	Charles Nagy		.75	.35
❑ 73	Tony Pena		.50	.23
❑ 74	Manny Ramirez		2.50	1.10
❑ 75	Julian Tavarez		.50	.23
❑ 76	Jim Thome		2.00	.90
❑ 77	Omar Vizquel		.75	.35
❑ 78	Chad Curtis		.50	.23
❑ 79	Cecil Fielder		.75	.35
❑ 80	Travis Fryman		.75	.35
❑ 81	Chris Gomez		.50	.23
❑ 82	Bob Higginson		.50	.23
❑ 83	Mark Lewis		.50	.23
❑ 84	Felipe Lira		.50	.23
❑ 85	Alan Trammell		1.25	.55
❑ 86	Kevin Appier		.75	.35
❑ 87	Johnny Damon		1.25	.55
❑ 88	Tom Goodwin		.50	.23
❑ 89	Mark Gubicza		.50	.23
❑ 90	Bob Hamelin		.50	.23
❑ 91	Keith Lockhart		.50	.23
❑ 92	Jeff Montgomery		.50	.23
❑ 93	Jon Nunnally		.50	.23
❑ 94	Bip Roberts		.50	.23
❑ 95	Michael Tucker		.50	.23
❑ 96	Joe Vitiello		.50	.23
❑ 97	Ricky Bones		.50	.23
❑ 98	Chuck Carr		.50	.23
❑ 99	Jeff Cirillo		.50	.23
❑ 100	Mike Fetters		.50	.23
❑ 101	John Jaha		.50	.23
❑ 102	Mike Matheny		.50	.23
❑ 103	Ben McDonald		.50	.23
❑ 104	Matt Mieske		.50	.23
❑ 105	Dave Nilsson		.50	.23
❑ 106	Kevin Seitzer		.50	.23
❑ 107	Steve Sparks		.50	.23
❑ 108	Jose Valentin		.50	.23
❑ 109	Greg Vaughn		.75	.35
❑ 110	Rick Aguilera		.50	.23
❑ 111	Rich Becker		.50	.23
❑ 112	Marty Cordova		.50	.23
❑ 113	LaTroy Hawkins		.50	.23
❑ 114	Dave Hollins		.50	.23
❑ 115	Roberto Kelly		.50	.23
❑ 116	Chuck Knoblauch		2.00	.90
❑ 117	Matt Lawton		2.50	1.10
❑ 118	Pat Meares		.50	.23
❑ 119	Paul Molitor		2.00	.90
❑ 120	Kirby Puckett		3.00	1.35
❑ 121	Brad Radke		.75	.35
❑ 122	Frank Rodriguez		.50	.23
❑ 123	Scott Stahoviak		.50	.23
❑ 124	Matt Walbeck		.50	.23
❑ 125	Wade Boggs		2.00	.90
❑ 126	David Cone		1.25	.55
❑ 127	Joe Girardi		.50	.23
❑ 128	Dwight Gooden		.75	.35
❑ 129	Derek Jeter		6.00	2.70
❑ 130	Jimmy Key		.75	.35
❑ 131	Jim Leyritz		.50	.23
❑ 132	Tino Martinez		.75	.35
❑ 133	Paul O'Neill		.75	.35
❑ 134	Andy Pettitte		1.25	.55
❑ 135	Tim Raines		.50	.23
❑ 136	Ruben Rivera		.75	.35
❑ 137	Kenny Rogers		.50	.23
❑ 138	Ruben Sierra		.50	.23
❑ 139	John Wetteland		.75	.35
❑ 140	Bernie Williams		2.00	.90
❑ 141	Tony Batista		4.00	1.80
❑ 142	Allen Battle		.50	.23
❑ 143	Geronimo Berroa		.50	.23
❑ 144	Mike Bordick		.50	.23
❑ 145	Scott Brosius		.75	.35
❑ 146	Steve Cox		.50	.23
❑ 147	Brent Gates		.50	.23
❑ 148	Jason Giambi		.75	.35
❑ 149	Doug Johns		.50	.23
❑ 150	Mark McGwire		10.00	4.50
❑ 151	Pedro Munoz		.50	.23
❑ 152	Ariel Prieto		.50	.23
❑ 153	Terry Steinbach		.50	.23
❑ 154	Todd Van Poppel		.50	.23
❑ 155	Bobby Ayala		.50	.23
❑ 156	Chris Bosio		.50	.23
❑ 157	Jay Buhner		.75	.35
❑ 158	Joey Cora		.50	.23
❑ 159	Russ Davis		.50	.23
❑ 160	Ken Griffey Jr.		10.00	4.50
❑ 161	Sterling Hitchcock		.50	.23
❑ 162	Randy Johnson		2.00	.90
❑ 163	Edgar Martinez		.75	.35
❑ 164	Alex Rodriguez		6.00	2.70
❑ 165	Paul Sorrento		.50	.23
❑ 166	Dan Wilson		.50	.23
❑ 167	Will Clark		2.00	.90
❑ 168	Benji Gil		.50	.23
❑ 169	Juan Gonzalez		4.00	1.80
❑ 170	Rusty Greer		.75	.35
❑ 171	Kevin Gross		.50	.23
❑ 172	Darryl Hamilton		.50	.23
❑ 173	Mike Henneman		.50	.23
❑ 174	Ken Hill		.50	.23
❑ 175	Mark McLemore		.50	.23
❑ 176	Dean Palmer		.75	.35
❑ 177	Roger Pavlik		.50	.23
❑ 178	Ivan Rodriguez		2.50	1.10
❑ 179	Mickey Tettleton		.50	.23
❑ 180	Bobby Witt		.50	.23
❑ 181	Joe Carter		.75	.35
❑ 182	Felipe Crespo		.50	.23
❑ 183	Alex Gonzalez		.50	.23
❑ 184	Shawn Green		2.00	.90
❑ 185	Juan Guzman		.50	.23
❑ 186	Erik Hanson		.50	.23

#	Player	MINT	NRMT
187	Pat Hentgen	.75	.35
188	Sandy Martinez	.50	.23
189	Otis Nixon	.50	.23
190	John Olerud	.75	.35
191	Paul Quantrill	.50	.23
192	Bill Risley	.50	.23
193	Ed Sprague	.50	.23
194	Steve Avery	.50	.23
195	Jeff Blauser	.50	.23
196	Brad Clontz	.50	.23
197	Jermaine Dye	.75	.35
198	Tom Glavine	2.00	.90
199	Marquis Grissom	.50	.23
200	Chipper Jones	5.00	2.20
201	David Justice	2.00	.90
202	Ryan Klesko	.75	.35
203	Mark Lemke	.50	.23
204	Javier Lopez	.75	.35
205	Greg Maddux	5.00	2.20
206	Fred McGriff	1.25	.55
207	Greg McMichael	.50	.23
208	Wonderful Monds	.50	.23
209	Jason Schmidt	.50	.23
210	John Smoltz	1.25	.55
211	Mark Wohlers	.50	.23
212	Jim Bullinger	.50	.23
213	Frank Castillo	.50	.23
214	Kevin Foster	.50	.23
215	Luis Gonzalez	.75	.35
216	Mark Grace	1.25	.55
217	Robin Jennings	.50	.23
218	Doug Jones	.50	.23
219	Dave Magadan	.50	.23
220	Brian McRae	.50	.23
221	Jaime Navarro	.50	.23
222	Rey Sanchez	.50	.23
223	Ryne Sandberg	2.50	1.10
224	Scott Servais	.50	.23
225	Sammy Sosa	6.00	2.70
226	Ozzie Timmons	.50	.23
227	Bret Boone	.75	.35
228	Jeff Branson	.50	.23
229	Jeff Brantley	.50	.23
230	Dave Burba	.50	.23
231	Vince Coleman	.50	.23
232	Steve Gibralter	.50	.23
233	Mike Kelly	.50	.23
234	Barry Larkin	2.00	.90
235	Hal Morris	.50	.23
236	Mark Portugal	.50	.23
237	Jose Rijo	.50	.23
238	Reggie Sanders	.75	.35
239	Pete Schourek	.50	.23
240	John Smiley	.50	.23
241	Eddie Taubensee	.50	.23
242	Jason Bates	.50	.23
243	Dante Bichette	.75	.35
244	Ellis Burks	.75	.35
245	Vinny Castilla	1.25	.55
246	Andres Galarraga	2.00	.90
247	Darren Holmes	.50	.23
248	Curt Leskanic	.50	.23
249	Steve Reed	.50	.23
250	Kevin Ritz	.50	.23
251	Bill Swift	.50	.23
252	Bret Saberhagen	.75	.35
253	Larry Walker	2.00	.90
254	Walt Weiss	.50	.23
255	Eric Young	.50	.23
256	Kurt Abbott	.50	.23
257	Kevin Brown	1.25	.55
258	John Burkett	.50	.23
259	Greg Colbrunn	.50	.23
260	Jeff Conine	.50	.23
261	Andre Dawson	1.25	.55
262	Chris Hammond	.50	.23
263	Charles Johnson	.75	.35
264	Al Leiter	.75	.35
265	Robb Nen	.50	.23
266	Terry Pendleton	.50	.23
267	Pat Rapp	.50	.23
268	Gary Sheffield	.75	.35
269	Quilvio Veras	.50	.23
270	Devon White	.75	.35
271	Bob Abreu	1.25	.55
272	Jeff Bagwell	2.50	1.10
273	Derek Bell	.75	.35
274	Sean Berry	.50	.23
275	Craig Biggio	2.00	.90
276	Doug Drabek	.50	.23
277	Tony Eusebio	.50	.23
278	Richard Hidalgo	.75	.35
279	Brian L.Hunter	.50	.23
280	Todd Jones	.50	.23
281	Derrick May	.50	.23
282	Orlando Miller	.50	.23
283	James Mouton	.50	.23
284	Shane Reynolds	.75	.35
285	Greg Swindell	.50	.23
286	Mike Blowers	.50	.23
287	Brett Butler	.75	.35
288	Tom Candiotti	.50	.23
289	Roger Cedeno	.75	.35
290	Delino DeShields	.50	.23
291	Greg Gagne	.50	.23
292	Karim Garcia	.50	.23
293	Todd Hollandsworth	.75	.35
294	Eric Karros	.75	.35
295	Ramon Martinez	.75	.35
296	Raul Mondesi	.75	.35
297	Hideo Nomo	2.00	.90
298	Mike Piazza	6.00	2.70
299	Ismael Valdes	.75	.35
300	Todd Worrell	.50	.23
301	Moises Alou	.75	.35
302	Shane Andrews	.50	.23
303	Yamil Benitez	.50	.23
304	Jeff Fassero	.50	.23
305	Darrin Fletcher	.50	.23
306	Cliff Floyd	.75	.35
307	Mark Grudzielanek	.50	.23
308	Mike Lansing	.50	.23
309	Pedro Martinez	2.50	1.10
310	Ryan McGuire	.50	.23
311	Carlos Perez	.50	.23
312	Mel Rojas	.50	.23
313	David Segui	.75	.35
314	Rondell White	.75	.35
315	Edgardo Alfonzo	2.00	.90
316	Rico Brogna	.50	.23
317	Carl Everett	.75	.35
318	John Franco	.75	.35
319	Bernard Gilkey	.75	.35
320	Todd Hundley	.75	.35
321	Jason Isringhausen	.75	.35
322	Lance Johnson	.50	.23
323	Bobby Jones	.50	.23
324	Jeff Kent	.75	.35
325	Rey Ordonez	2.00	.90
326	Bill Pulsipher	.50	.23
327	Jose Vizcaino	.50	.23
328	Paul Wilson	.50	.23
329	Ricky Bottalico	.50	.23
330	Darren Daulton	.75	.35
331	David Doster	.50	.23
332	Lenny Dykstra	.75	.35
333	Jim Eisenreich	.50	.23
334	Sid Fernandez	.50	.23
335	Gregg Jefferies	.50	.23
336	Mickey Morandini	.50	.23
337	Benito Santiago	.50	.23
338	Curt Schilling	1.25	.55
339	Kevin Stocker	.50	.23
340	David West	.50	.23
341	Mark Whiten	.50	.23
342	Todd Zeile	.50	.23
343	Jay Bell	.75	.35
344	John Ericks	.50	.23
345	Carlos Garcia	.50	.23
346	Charlie Hayes	.50	.23
347	Jason Kendall	2.00	.90
348	Jeff King	.50	.23
349	Mike Kingery	.50	.23
350	Al Martin	.50	.23
351	Orlando Merced	.50	.23
352	Dan Miceli	.50	.23
353	Denny Neagle	.75	.35
354	Alan Benes	.75	.35
355	Andy Benes	.75	.35
356	Royce Clayton	.50	.23
357	Dennis Eckersley	.75	.35
358	Gary Gaetti	.75	.35
359	Ron Gant	.50	.23
360	Brian Jordan	.75	.35
361	Ray Lankford	.75	.35
362	John Mabry	.50	.23
363	T.J. Mathews	.50	.23
364	Mike Morgan	.50	.23
365	Donovan Osborne	.50	.23
366	Tom Pagnozzi	.50	.23
367	Ozzie Smith	2.50	1.10
368	Todd Stottlemyre	.50	.23
369	Andy Ashby	.50	.23
370	Brad Ausmus	.50	.23
371	Ken Caminiti	.75	.35
372	Andujar Cedeno	.50	.23
373	Steve Finley	.75	.35
374	Tony Gwynn	5.00	2.20
375	Joey Hamilton	.50	.23
376	Rickey Henderson	2.50	1.10
377	Trevor Hoffman	.75	.35
378	Wally Joyner	.75	.35
379	Marc Newfield	.50	.23
380	Jody Reed	.50	.23
381	Bob Tewksbury	.50	.23
382	Fernando Valenzuela	.75	.35
383	Rod Beck	.50	.23
384	Barry Bonds	2.50	1.10
385	Mark Carreon	.50	.23
386	Shawon Dunston	.50	.23
387	Osvaldo Fernandez	.50	.23
388	Glenallen Hill	.50	.23
389	Stan Javier	.50	.23
390	Mark Leiter	.50	.23
391	Kirt Manwaring	.50	.23
392	Robby Thompson	.50	.23
393	William VanLandingham	.50	.23
394	Allen Watson	.50	.23
395	Matt Williams	2.00	.90
396	Checklist 1-92	.50	.23
397	Checklist 93-180	.50	.23
398	Checklist 181-272	.50	.23
399	Checklist 273-365	.50	.23
400	Checklist 366-400/Inserts	.50	.23

1996 Flair Diamond Cuts

	MINT	NRMT
COMPLETE SET (12)	120.00	55.00
COMMON CARD (1-12)	3.00	1.35
STATED ODDS 1:20		
1 Jeff Bagwell	6.00	2.70
2 Albert Belle	3.00	1.35
3 Barry Bonds	6.00	2.70
4 Juan Gonzalez	10.00	4.50
5 Ken Griffey Jr.	25.00	11.00
6 Greg Maddux	12.00	5.50
7 Eddie Murray	3.00	1.35
8 Mike Piazza	15.00	6.75
9 Cal Ripken	20.00	9.00
10 Frank Thomas	10.00	4.50
11 Mo Vaughn	3.00	1.35
12 Matt Williams	3.00	1.35

1996 Flair Hot Gloves

	MINT	NRMT
COMPLETE SET (10)	300.00	135.00

	MINT	NRMT
COMMON CARD (1-10)	12.00	5.50
UNLISTED STARS	20.00	9.00
STATED ODDS 1:90 HOBBY		
❏ 1 Roberto Alomar	20.00	9.00
❏ 2 Barry Bonds	25.00	11.00
❏ 3 Will Clark	20.00	9.00
❏ 4 Ken Griffey Jr.	100.00	45.00
❏ 5 Kenny Lofton	15.00	6.75
❏ 6 Greg Maddux	50.00	22.00
❏ 7 Mike Piazza	60.00	27.00
❏ 8 Cal Ripken	80.00	36.00
❏ 9 Ivan Rodriguez	25.00	11.00
❏ 10 Matt Williams	20.00	9.00

1996 Flair Powerline

	MINT	NRMT
COMPLETE SET (10)	30.00	13.50
COMMON CARD (1-10)	2.00	.90
STATED ODDS 1:6		
❏ 1 Albert Belle	2.00	.90
❏ 2 Barry Bonds	2.00	.90
❏ 3 Juan Gonzalez	4.00	1.80
❏ 4 Ken Griffey Jr.	10.00	4.50
❏ 5 Mark McGwire	10.00	4.50
❏ 6 Mike Piazza	6.00	2.70
❏ 7 Manny Ramirez	2.50	1.10
❏ 8 Sammy Sosa	6.00	2.70
❏ 9 Frank Thomas	4.00	1.80
❏ 10 Matt Williams	2.00	.90

1996 Flair Wave of the Future

WAVE OF THE FUTURE / DAVID DOSTER

	MINT	NRMT
COMPLETE SET (20)	200.00	90.00
COMMON CARD (1-20)	10.00	4.50
STATED ODDS 1:72		
❏ 1 Bob Abreu	25.00	11.00
❏ 2 George Arias	10.00	4.50
❏ 3 Tony Batista	15.00	6.75
❏ 4 Alan Benes	10.00	4.50
❏ 5 Yamil Benitez	10.00	4.50
❏ 6 Steve Cox	10.00	4.50
❏ 7 David Doster	10.00	4.50
❏ 8 Jermaine Dye	25.00	11.00
❏ 9 Osvaldo Fernandez	10.00	4.50
❏ 10 Karim Garcia	15.00	6.75
❏ 11 Steve Gibralter	10.00	4.50
❏ 12 Todd Greene	10.00	4.50
❏ 13 Richard Hidalgo	15.00	6.75
❏ 14 Robin Jennings	10.00	4.50
❏ 15 Jason Kendall	25.00	11.00
❏ 16 Jose Malave	10.00	4.50
❏ 17 Wonderful Monds	10.00	4.50
❏ 18 Rey Ordonez	25.00	11.00
❏ 19 Ruben Rivera	15.00	6.75
❏ 20 Paul Wilson	10.00	4.50

1997 Flair Showcase Row 2

	MINT	NRMT
COMPLETE SET (180)	80.00	36.00
COMMON CARD (1-60)	.25	.11
MINOR STARS 1-60	.40	.18
SEMISTARS 1-60	.60	.25
UNLISTED STARS 1-60	1.00	.45
ROW 2 1-60 ODDS 1.5:1		
COMMON CARD (61-120)	.40	.18
MINOR STARS 61-120	.60	.25
SEMISTARS 61-120	1.00	.45
ROW 2 61-120 ODDS 1:1.5		
COMMON CARD (121-180)	.30	.14
MINOR STARS 121-180°	.50	.23
SEMISTARS 121-180	.75	.35
UNLISTED STARS 121-180°	1.25	.55
ROW 2-121-180 STATED ODDS 1:1		
A.ROD GLOVE EXCH.DEADLINE: 8/1/98		
❏ 1 Andruw Jones	1.25	.55
❏ 2 Derek Jeter	3.00	1.35
❏ 3 Alex Rodriguez	3.00	1.35
❏ 4 Paul Molitor	1.00	.45
❏ 5 Jeff Bagwell	1.25	.55
❏ 6 Scott Rolen	1.50	.70
❏ 7 Kenny Lofton	.60	.25
❏ 8 Cal Ripken	4.00	1.80
❏ 9 Brady Anderson	.40	.18
❏ 10 Chipper Jones	2.50	1.10
❏ 11 Todd Greene	.25	.11
❏ 12 Todd Walker	1.00	.45
❏ 13 Billy Wagner	.40	.18
❏ 14 Craig Biggio	1.00	.45
❏ 15 Kevin Orie	.25	.11
❏ 16 Hideo Nomo	1.00	.45
❏ 17 Kevin Appier	.40	.18
❏ 18 Bubba Trammell STY	1.00	.45
❏ 19 Juan Gonzalez	2.00	.90
❏ 20 Randy Johnson	1.00	.45
❏ 21 Roger Clemens	2.50	1.10
❏ 22 Johnny Damon	.40	.18
❏ 23 Ryne Sandberg	1.25	.55
❏ 24 Ken Griffey Jr.	5.00	2.20
❏ 25 Barry Bonds	1.25	.55
❏ 26 Nomar Garciaparra	3.00	1.35
❏ 27 Vladimir Guerrero	1.50	.70
❏ 28 Ron Gant	.25	.11
❏ 29 Joe Carter	.40	.18
❏ 30 Tim Salmon	1.00	.45
❏ 31 Mike Piazza	3.00	1.35
❏ 32 Barry Larkin	1.00	.45
❏ 33 Manny Ramirez	1.25	.55
❏ 34 Sammy Sosa	3.00	1.35
❏ 35 Frank Thomas	2.00	.90
❏ 36 Melvin Nieves	.25	.11
❏ 37 Tony Gwynn	2.50	1.10
❏ 38 Gary Sheffield	.40	.18
❏ 39 Darin Erstad	1.00	.45
❏ 40 Ken Caminiti	.60	.25
❏ 41 Jermaine Dye	.40	.18
❏ 42 Mo Vaughn	1.00	.45
❏ 43 Raul Mondesi	.40	.18
❏ 44 Greg Maddux	2.50	1.10
❏ 45 Chuck Knoblauch	1.00	.45
❏ 46 Andy Pettitte	.60	.25
❏ 47 Deion Sanders	.40	.18
❏ 48 Albert Belle	1.00	.45
❏ 49 Jamey Wright	.25	.11
❏ 50 Rey Ordonez	.40	.18
❏ 51 Bernie Williams	1.00	.45
❏ 52 Mark McGwire	5.00	2.20
❏ 53 Mike Mussina	1.00	.45
❏ 54 Bob Abreu	.40	.18
❏ 55 Reggie Sanders	.40	.18
❏ 56 Brian Jordan	.40	.18
❏ 57 Ivan Rodriguez	1.25	.55
❏ 58 Roberto Alomar	1.00	.45
❏ 59 Tim Naehring	.25	.11
❏ 60 Edgar Renteria	.40	.18
❏ 61 Dean Palmer	.60	.25
❏ 62 Benito Santiago	.60	.25
❏ 63 David Cone	1.00	.45
❏ 64 Carlos Delgado	1.25	.55
❏ 65 Brian Giles	4.00	1.80
❏ 66 Alex Ochoa	.40	.18
❏ 67 Rondell White	.60	.25
❏ 68 Robin Ventura	.60	.25
❏ 69 Eric Karros	.60	.25
❏ 70 Jose Valentin	.40	.18
❏ 71 Rafael Palmeiro	1.25	.55
❏ 72 Chris Snopek	.40	.18
❏ 73 David Justice	1.25	.55
❏ 74 Tom Glavine	1.25	.55
❏ 75 Rudy Pemberton	.40	.18
❏ 76 Larry Walker	1.50	.70
❏ 77 Jim Thome	1.25	.55
❏ 78 Charles Johnson	.60	.25
❏ 79 Dante Powell	.60	.25
❏ 80 Derrek Lee	1.00	.45
❏ 81 Jason Kendall	1.00	.45
❏ 82 Todd Hollandsworth	.40	.18
❏ 83 Bernard Gilkey	.40	.18
❏ 84 Mel Rojas	.40	.18
❏ 85 Dmitri Young	.60	.25
❏ 86 Bret Boone	.60	.25
❏ 87 Pat Hentgen	.60	.25
❏ 88 Bobby Bonilla	.60	.25
❏ 89 John Wetteland	.60	.25
❏ 90 Todd Hundley	.40	.18
❏ 91 Wilton Guerrero	.40	.18
❏ 92 Geronimo Berroa	.40	.18
❏ 93 Al Martin	.40	.18
❏ 94 Danny Tartabull	.40	.18
❏ 95 Brian McRae	.40	.18
❏ 96 Steve Finley	.60	.25
❏ 97 Todd Stottlemyre	.40	.18
❏ 98 John Smoltz	1.00	.45
❏ 99 Matt Williams	1.25	.55
❏ 100 Eddie Murray	1.50	.70
❏ 101 Henry Rodriguez	.60	.25
❏ 102 Marty Cordova	.40	.18
❏ 103 Juan Guzman	.40	.18
❏ 104 Chili Davis	.60	.25
❏ 105 Eric Young	.60	.25
❏ 106 Jeff Abbott	.40	.18

		MINT	NRMT
❏ 107	Shannon Stewart	.60	.25
❏ 108	Rocky Coppinger	.40	.18
❏ 109	Jose Canseco	1.25	.55
❏ 110	Dante Bichette	.60	.25
❏ 111	Dwight Gooden	.60	.25
❏ 112	Scott Brosius	.40	.18
❏ 113	Steve Avery	.40	.18
❏ 114	Andres Galarraga	1.25	.55
❏ 115	Sandy Alomar Jr.	.60	.25
❏ 116	Ray Lankford	.60	.25
❏ 117	Jorge Posada	.60	.25
❏ 118	Ryan Klesko	.60	.25
❏ 119	Jay Buhner	.60	.25
❏ 120	Jose Guillen	1.00	.45
❏ 121	Paul O'Neill	.50	.23
❏ 122	Jimmy Key	.50	.23
❏ 123	Hal Morris	.30	.14
❏ 124	Travis Fryman	.50	.23
❏ 125	Jim Edmonds	.75	.35
❏ 126	Jeff Cirillo	.50	.23
❏ 127	Fred McGriff	.75	.35
❏ 128	Alan Benes	.30	.14
❏ 129	Derek Bell	.50	.23
❏ 130	Tony Graffanino	.30	.14
❏ 131	Shawn Green	1.25	.55
❏ 132	Denny Neagle	.50	.23
❏ 133	Alex Fernandez	.30	.14
❏ 134	Mickey Morandini	.30	.14
❏ 135	Royce Clayton	.30	.14
❏ 136	Jose Mesa	.30	.14
❏ 137	Edgar Martinez	.50	.23
❏ 138	Curt Schilling	.75	.35
❏ 139	Lance Johnson	.30	.14
❏ 140	Andy Benes	.50	.23
❏ 141	Charles Nagy	.50	.23
❏ 142	Mariano Rivera	.50	.23
❏ 143	Mark Wohlers	.30	.14
❏ 144	Ken Hill	.30	.14
❏ 145	Jay Bell	.50	.23
❏ 146	Bob Higginson	.50	.23
❏ 147	Mark Grudzielanek	.50	.23
❏ 148	Ray Durham	.50	.23
❏ 149	John Olerud	.50	.23
❏ 150	Joey Hamilton	.50	.23
❏ 151	Trevor Hoffman	.50	.23
❏ 152	Dan Wilson	.30	.14
❏ 153	J.T. Snow	.50	.23
❏ 154	Marquis Grissom	.50	.23
❏ 155	Yamil Benitez	.30	.14
❏ 156	Rusty Greer	.50	.23
❏ 157	Darryl Kile	.50	.23
❏ 158	Ismael Valdes	.50	.23
❏ 159	Jeff Conine	.30	.14
❏ 160	Darren Daulton	.50	.23
❏ 161	Chan Ho Park	1.25	.55
❏ 162	Troy Percival	.50	.23
❏ 163	Wade Boggs	1.25	.55
❏ 164	Dave Nilsson	.30	.14
❏ 165	Vinny Castilla	.75	.35
❏ 166	Kevin Brown	.75	.35
❏ 167	Dennis Eckersley	.50	.23
❏ 168	Wendell Magee Jr.	.30	.14
❏ 169	John Jaha	.30	.14
❏ 170	Garret Anderson	.50	.23
❏ 171	Jason Giambi	.50	.23
❏ 172	Mark Grace	.75	.35
❏ 173	Tony Clark	.75	.35
❏ 174	Moises Alou	.50	.23
❏ 175	Brett Butler	.50	.23
❏ 176	Cecil Fielder	.50	.23
❏ 177	Chris Widger	.30	.14
❏ 178	Doug Drabek	.30	.14
❏ 179	Ellis Burks	.50	.23
❏ 180	Shigetoshi Hasegawa	.50	.23
❏ NNO	A. Rod. Glove EXCH/25	300.00	135.00

1997 Flair Showcase Row 1

	MINT	NRMT
COMPLETE SET (180)	200.00	90.00
COMMON CARD (1-60)	.60	.25

*STARS 1-60: 1X TO 2.5X ROW 2
ROW 1 1-60 ODDS 1:2.5

| COMMON CARD (61-120) | .50 | .23 |

*STARS 61-120: .5X TO 1.2X ROW 2
ROW 1 61-120 ODDS 1:2

| COMMON CARD (121-180) | 1.00 | .45 |

*STARS 121-180: 1.25X TO 3X ROW 2
ROW 1 121-180 ODDS 1:3

1997 Flair Showcase Row 0

	MINT	NRMT
COMMON CARD (1-60)	6.00	2.70

*STARS 1-60: 8X TO 20X ROW 2
*YOUNG STARS 1-60: 6X TO 15X ROW 2
ROW 0 1-60 ODDS 1:24

| COMMON CARD (61-120) | 2.50 | 1.10 |

*STARS 61-120: 2.5X TO 6X ROW 2
*YOUNG STARS 61-120: 2X TO 5X ROW 2
ROW 0 61-120 ODDS 1:12

| COMMON CARD (121-180) | 1.00 | .45 |

*STARS 121-180: 1.5X TO 4X ROW 2
*YOUNG STARS 121-180: 1.25X TO 3X ROW 2
ROW 0 121-180 ODDS 1:5

1997 Flair Showcase Legacy Collection

	MINT	NRMT
COMMON CARD (1-180)	15.00	6.75

*STARS 1-60: 25X TO 60X BASIC CARDS
*STARS 61-120: 15X TO 40X BASIC CARDS
*STARS 121-180: 20X TO 50X BASIC CARDS
STATED ODDS 1:30
STATED PRINT RUN 100 SERIAL #'d SETS
THREE CARDS PER PLAYER
MASTERPIECE ONE OF ONE PARALLELS EXIST
MASTERPIECES TOO SCARCE TO PRICE

1997 Flair Showcase Diamond Cuts

	MINT	NRMT
COMPLETE SET (20)	200.00	90.00
COMMON CARD (1-20)	2.50	1.10
STATED ODDS 1:20		
❏ 1 Jeff Bagwell	5.00	2.20
❏ 2 Albert Belle	5.00	2.20
❏ 3 Ken Caminiti	4.00	1.80

		MINT	NRMT
❏ 4	Juan Gonzalez	10.00	4.50
❏ 5	Ken Griffey Jr.	25.00	11.00
❏ 6	Tony Gwynn	12.00	5.50
❏ 7	Todd Hundley	2.50	1.10
❏ 8	Andruw Jones	5.00	2.20
❏ 9	Chipper Jones	12.00	5.50
❏ 10	Greg Maddux	12.00	5.50
❏ 11	Mark McGwire	25.00	11.00
❏ 12	Mike Piazza	15.00	6.75
❏ 13	Derek Jeter	12.00	5.50
❏ 14	Manny Ramirez	6.00	2.70
❏ 15	Cal Ripken	20.00	9.00
❏ 16	Alex Rodriguez	15.00	6.75
❏ 17	Frank Thomas	10.00	4.50
❏ 18	Mo Vaughn	5.00	2.20
❏ 19	Bernie Williams	5.00	2.20
❏ 20	Matt Williams	5.00	2.20

1997 Flair Showcase Hot Gloves

		MINT	NRMT
COMPLETE SET (15)		500.00	220.00
COMMON CARD (1-15)		8.00	3.60
SEMISTARS		10.00	4.50
UNLISTED STARS		15.00	6.75
STATED ODDS 1:90			
❏ 1	Roberto Alomar	15.00	6.75
❏ 2	Barry Bonds	20.00	9.00
❏ 3	Marquis Grissom	30.00	13.50
❏ 4	Ken Griffey Jr.	80.00	36.00
❏ 5	Marquis Grissom	8.00	3.60
❏ 6	Derek Jeter	50.00	22.00
❏ 7	Chipper Jones	40.00	18.00
❏ 8	Barry Larkin	15.00	6.75
❏ 9	Kenny Lofton	10.00	4.50
❏ 10	Greg Maddux	40.00	18.00
❏ 11	Mike Piazza	50.00	22.00
❏ 12	Cal Ripken	60.00	27.00
❏ 13	Alex Rodriguez	50.00	22.00
❏ 14	Ivan Rodriguez	20.00	9.00
❏ 15	Frank Thomas	30.00	13.50

1997 Flair Showcase Wave of the Future

	MINT	NRMT
COMPLETE SET (27)	60.00	27.00
COMMON (1-25/WF1-WF2)	1.00	.45

	MINT	NRMT
MINOR STARS	2.00	.90
SEMISTARS	3.00	1.35
STATED ODDS 1:4		

		MINT	NRMT
❑ 1	Todd Greene	1.00	.45
❑ 2	Andruw Jones	4.00	1.80
❑ 3	Randall Simon	3.00	1.35
❑ 4	Wady Almonte	4.00	1.80
❑ 5	Pat Cline	2.00	.90
❑ 6	Jeff Abbott	1.00	.45
❑ 7	Justin Towle	3.00	1.35
❑ 8	Richie Sexson	4.00	1.80
❑ 9	Bubba Trammell	4.00	1.80
❑ 10	Bob Abreu	2.00	.90
❑ 11	David Arias-Ortiz	3.00	1.35
❑ 12	Todd Walker	4.00	1.80
❑ 13	Orlando Cabrera	2.00	.90
❑ 14	Vladimir Guerrero	5.00	2.20
❑ 15	Ricky Ledee	5.00	2.20
❑ 16	Jorge Posada	2.00	.90
❑ 17	Ruben Rivera	1.00	.45
❑ 18	Scott Spiezio	2.00	.90
❑ 19	Scott Rolen	5.00	2.20
❑ 20	Emil Brown	2.00	.90
❑ 21	Jose Guillen	3.00	1.35
❑ 22	T.J. Staton	2.00	.90
❑ 23	Eli Marrero	2.00	.90
❑ 24	Fernando Tatis	8.00	3.60
❑ 25	Ryan Jones	1.00	.45
❑ WF1	Hideki Irabu	4.00	1.80
❑ WF2	Jose Cruz Jr	4.00	1.80

1998 Flair Showcase Row 3

	MINT	NRMT
COMPLETE SET (120)	80.00	36.00
COMMON CARD (1-30)	.40	.18
SEMISTARS 1-30	.60	.25
UNLISTED STARS 1-30	1.00	.45
ROW 3 1-30 STATED ODDS 1:0.9		
COMMON CARD (31-60)	.40	.18
SEMISTARS 31-60	.60	.25
UNLISTED STARS 31-60	1.00	.45
ROW 3 31-60 STATED ODDS 1:1.1		
COMMON CARD (61-90)	.50	.23
SEMISTARS 61-90	.75	.35
UNLISTED STARS 61-90	1.25	.55
ROW 3 61-90 STATED ODDS 1:1.5		
COMMON CARD (91-120)	.60	.25

		MINT	NRMT
	SEMISTARS 91-120	1.00	.45
	UNLISTED STARS 91-120	1.50	.70
	ROW 3 91-120 STATED ODDS 1:2		
❑ 1	Ken Griffey Jr.	5.00	2.20
❑ 2	Travis Lee	.60	.25
❑ 3	Frank Thomas	2.00	.90
❑ 4	Ben Grieve	1.00	.45
❑ 5	Nomar Garciaparra	3.00	1.35
❑ 6	Jose Cruz Jr.	.40	.18
❑ 7	Alex Rodriguez	3.00	1.35
❑ 8	Cal Ripken	4.00	1.80
❑ 9	Mark McGwire	6.00	2.70
❑ 10	Chipper Jones	2.50	1.10
❑ 11	Paul Konerko	.40	.18
❑ 12	Todd Helton	1.25	.55
❑ 13	Greg Maddux	2.50	1.10
❑ 14	Derek Jeter	3.00	1.35
❑ 15	Jaret Wright	.40	.18
❑ 16	Livan Hernandez	.40	.18
❑ 17	Mike Piazza	3.00	1.35
❑ 18	Juan Encarnacion	.40	.18
❑ 19	Tony Gwynn	2.50	1.10
❑ 20	Scott Rolen	1.25	.55
❑ 21	Roger Clemens	2.50	1.10
❑ 22	Tony Clark	.40	.18
❑ 23	Albert Belle	1.00	.45
❑ 24	Mo Vaughn	1.00	.45
❑ 25	Andruw Jones	1.00	.45
❑ 26	Jason Dickson	.40	.18
❑ 27	Fernando Tatis	1.00	.45
❑ 28	Ivan Rodriguez	1.25	.55
❑ 29	Ricky Ledee	.40	.18
❑ 30	Darin Erstad	.60	.25
❑ 31	Brian Rose	.40	.18
❑ 32	Magglio Ordonez	3.00	1.35
❑ 33	Larry Walker	1.00	.45
❑ 34	Bobby Higginson	.40	.18
❑ 35	Chili Davis	.40	.18
❑ 36	Barry Bonds	1.25	.55
❑ 37	Vladimir Guerrero	1.25	.55
❑ 38	Jeff Bagwell	1.25	.55
❑ 39	Kenny Lofton	.60	.25
❑ 40	Ryan Klesko	.40	.18
❑ 41	Mike Cameron	.40	.18
❑ 42	Charles Johnson	.40	.18
❑ 43	Andy Pettitte	.40	.18
❑ 44	Juan Gonzalez	2.00	.90
❑ 45	Tim Salmon	.60	.25
❑ 46	Hideki Irabu	.40	.18
❑ 47	Paul Molitor	1.00	.45
❑ 48	Edgar Renteria	.40	.18
❑ 49	Manny Ramirez	1.25	.55
❑ 50	Jim Edmonds	.40	.18
❑ 51	Bernie Williams	1.00	.45
❑ 52	Roberto Alomar	1.00	.45
❑ 53	David Justice	.40	.18
❑ 54	Rey Ordonez	.40	.18
❑ 55	Ken Caminiti	.40	.18
❑ 56	Jose Guillen	.40	.18
❑ 57	Randy Johnson	1.00	.45
❑ 58	Brady Anderson	.40	.18
❑ 59	Hideo Nomo	1.00	.45
❑ 60	Tino Martinez	.40	.18
❑ 61	John Smoltz	.75	.23
❑ 62	Joe Carter	.50	.23
❑ 63	Matt Williams	1.25	.55
❑ 64	Robin Ventura	.50	.23
❑ 65	Barry Larkin	1.25	.55
❑ 66	Dante Bichette	.50	.23
❑ 67	Travis Fryman	.50	.23
❑ 68	Gary Sheffield	.50	.23
❑ 69	Eric Karros	.50	.23
❑ 70	Matt Stairs	.50	.23
❑ 71	Al Martin	.50	.23
❑ 72	Jay Buhner	.50	.23
❑ 73	Ray Lankford	.50	.23
❑ 74	Carlos Delgado	1.25	.55
❑ 75	Edgardo Alfonzo	.75	.35
❑ 76	Rondell White	.50	.23
❑ 77	Chuck Knoblauch	.50	.23
❑ 78	Raul Mondesi	.50	.23
❑ 79	Johnny Damon	.50	.23
❑ 80	Matt Morris	.50	.23
❑ 81	Tom Glavine	1.25	.55
❑ 82	Kevin Brown	.75	.35
❑ 83	Garret Anderson	.50	.23
❑ 84	Mike Mussina	1.25	.55
❑ 85	Pedro Martinez	1.25	.55
❑ 86	Craig Biggio	1.25	.55
❑ 87	Darryl Kile	.50	.23
❑ 88	Rafael Palmeiro	1.25	.55
❑ 89	Jim Thome	1.25	.55
❑ 90	Andres Galarraga	.75	.35
❑ 91	Sammy Sosa	5.00	2.20
❑ 92	Willie Greene	.60	.25
❑ 93	Vinny Castilla	.60	.25
❑ 94	Justin Thompson	.60	.25
❑ 95	Jeff King	.60	.25
❑ 96	Jeff Cirillo	.60	.25
❑ 97	Mark Grudzielanek	.60	.25
❑ 98	Brad Radke	.60	.25
❑ 99	John Olerud	.60	.25
❑ 100	Curt Schilling	1.00	.45
❑ 101	Steve Finley	.60	.25
❑ 102	J.T. Snow	.60	.25
❑ 103	Edgar Martinez	.60	.25
❑ 104	Wilson Alvarez	.60	.25
❑ 105	Rusty Greer	.60	.25
❑ 106	Pat Hentgen	.60	.25
❑ 107	David Cone	1.00	.45
❑ 108	Fred McGriff	1.00	.45
❑ 109	Jason Giambi	.60	.25
❑ 110	Tony Womack	.60	.25
❑ 111	Bernard Gilkey	.60	.25
❑ 112	Alan Benes	.60	.25
❑ 113	Mark Grace	1.00	.45
❑ 114	Reggie Sanders	.60	.25
❑ 115	Moises Alou	.60	.25
❑ 116	John Jaha	.60	.25
❑ 117	Henry Rodriguez	.60	.25
❑ 118	Dean Palmer	.60	.25
❑ 119	Mike Lieberthal	.60	.25
❑ 120	Shawn Estes	.60	.25

1998 Flair Showcase Row 2

	MINT	NRMT
COMPLETE SET (120)	150.00	70.00
COMMON CARD (1-30)	1.00	.45
*STARS 1-30: 1X TO 2.5X ROW 3		
ROW 2 1-30 STATED ODDS 1:3		
COMMON CARD (31-60)	.75	.35
*STARS 31-60: .75X TO 2X ROW 3		
ROW 2 31-60 STATED ODDS 1:2.5		
COMMON CARD (61-90)	1.25	.55
*STARS 61-90: 1X TO 2.5X ROW 3		
ROW 2 61-90 STATED ODDS 1:4		
COMMON CARD (91-120)	1.25	.55
*STARS 91-120: .75X TO 2X ROW 3		
ROW 2 91-120 STATED ODDS 1:3.5		

1998 Flair Showcase Row 1

	MINT	NRMT
COMPLETE SET (120)	600.00	275.00
*STARS 1-30: 3X TO 8X ROW 3		
ROW 1 1-30 STATED ODDS 1:16		
COMMON CARD (31-60)	4.00	1.80
*STARS 31-60: 4X TO 10X ROW 3		

ROW 1 31-60 STATED ODDS 1:24
COMMON CARD (61-90) .... 1.50 .70
*STARS 61-90: 1.25X TO 3X ROW 3
ROW 1 61-90 STATED ODDS 1:6
COMMON CARD (91-120) 2.50 1.10
*STARS 91-120: 1.5X TQ 4X ROW 3
ROW 1 91-120 STATED ODDS 1:10

1998 Flair Showcase Row 0

	MINT	NRMT
COMPLETE SET (120)	2500.00	1100.00
COMMON CARD (1-30)	12.00	5.50
*STARS 1-30: 25X TO 30X ROW 3		
ROW 0 1-30 PRINT RUN 250 SERIAL #'d SETS		
COMMON CARD (31-60)	8.00	3.60
*STARS 31-60: 8X TO 20X ROW 3		
ROW 0 31-60 PRINT RUN 500 SERIAL #'d SETS		
COMMON CARD (61-90)	6.00	2.70
*STARS 61-90: 5X TO 12X ROW 3		
ROW 0 61-90 PRINT RUN 1000 SERIAL #'d SETS		
COMMON CARD (91-120)	4.00	1.80
*STARS 91-120: 2.5X TO 6X ROW 3		
ROW 0 91-120 PR.RUN 2000 SERIAL #'d SETS		

1998 Flair Showcase Legacy Collection

	MINT	NRMT
COMMON CARD (1-120)	15.00	6.75
*STARS 1-30: 25X TO 60X ROW 3		
*STARS 31-60: 25X TO 60X ROW 3		
*STARS 61-90: 20X TO 50X ROW 3		
*STARS 91-120: 15X TO 40X ROW 3		

RANDOM INSERTS IN PACKS
STATED PRINT RUN 100 SERIAL #'d SETS
FOUR CARDS PER PLAYER
MASTERPIECE ONE OF ONE PARALLELS
EXIST
NO MASTERPIECE PRICES DUE TO SCARCI-
TY

1998 Flair Showcase Perfect 10

	MINT	NRMT
RANDOM INSERTS IN PACKS		

STATED PRINT RUN 10 SERIAL #'d SETS
NO PRICING AVAILABLE DUE TO SCARCITY

- ❏ 1 Ken Griffey Jr.
- ❏ 2 Cal Ripken
- ❏ 3 Frank Thomas
- ❏ 4 Mike Piazza
- ❏ 5 Greg Maddux
- ❏ 6 Nomar Garciaparra
- ❏ 7 Mark McGwire
- ❏ 8 Scott Rolen
- ❏ 9 Alex Rodriguez
- ❏ 10 Roger Clemens

1998 Flair Showcase Wave of the Future

	MINT	NRMT
COMPLETE SET (12)	30.00	13.50
COMMON CARD (1-12)	1.00	.45
MINOR STARS	2.00	.90
SEMISTARS	3.00	1.35
STATED ODDS 1:20		

		MINT	NRMT
❏ 1 Travis Lee		3.00	1.35
❏ 2 Todd Helton		5.00	2.20
❏ 3 Ben Grieve		4.00	1.80
❏ 4 Juan Encarnacion		2.00	.90
❏ 5 Brad Fullmer		1.00	.45
❏ 6 Ruben Rivera		1.00	.45
❏ 7 Paul Konerko		2.00	.90
❏ 8 Derrek Lee		1.00	.45
❏ 9 Mike Lowell		4.00	1.80
❏ 10 Magglio Ordonez		10.00	4.50
❏ 11 Rich Butler		3.00	1.35
❏ 12 Eli Marrero		1.00	.45

1999 Flair Showcase Row 3

	MINT	NRMT
COMPLETE SET (144)	60.00	27.00
COMMON CARD (1-48)	.25	.11
MINOR STARS 1-48	.40	.18
SEMISTARS 1-48	.60	.25
UNLISTED STARS 1-48	1.00	.45
ROW 3 1-48 STATED ODDS 1:0.9		
COMMON CARD (49-96)	.25	.11
MINOR STARS 49-96	.40	.18
SEMISTARS 49-96	.60	.25
UNLISTED STARS 49-96	1.00	.45
ROW 3 49-96 STATED ODDS 1:1		

	MINT	NRMT
COMMON CARD (97-144)	.30	.14
MINOR STARS 97-144	.50	.23
SEMISTARS 97-144	.75	.35
UNLISTED STARS 97-144	1.25	.55
ROW 3 97-144 STATED ODDS 1:1.2		

		MINT	NRMT
❏ 1 Mark McGwire		6.00	2.70
❏ 2 Sammy Sosa		3.00	1.35
❏ 3 Ken Griffey Jr.		5.00	2.20
❏ 4 Chipper Jones		2.50	1.10
❏ 5 Ben Grieve		1.00	.45
❏ 6 J.D. Drew		1.50	.70
❏ 7 Jeff Bagwell		1.25	.55
❏ 8 Cal Ripken		4.00	1.80
❏ 9 Tony Gwynn		2.50	1.10
❏ 10 Nomar Garciaparra		3.00	1.35
❏ 11 Travis Lee		.60	.25
❏ 12 Troy Glaus		1.00	.45
❏ 13 Mike Piazza		3.00	1.35
❏ 14 Alex Rodriguez		3.00	1.35
❏ 15 Kevin Brown		.60	.25
❏ 16 Darin Erstad		.60	.25
❏ 17 Scott Rolen		1.25	.55
❏ 18 Micah Bowie		.75	.35
❏ 19 Juan Gonzalez		2.00	.90
❏ 20 Kerry Wood		1.00	.45
❏ 21 Roger Clemens		2.50	1.10
❏ 22 Derek Jeter		3.00	1.35
❏ 23 Pat Burrell		6.00	2.70
❏ 24 Tim Salmon		.60	.25
❏ 25 Barry Bonds		1.25	.55
❏ 26 Roosevelt Brown		1.25	.55
❏ 27 Vladimir Guerrero		1.25	.55
❏ 28 Randy Johnson		1.00	.45
❏ 29 Mo Vaughn		1.00	.45
❏ 30 Fernando Seguignol		.40	.18
❏ 31 Greg Maddux		2.50	1.10
❏ 32 Tony Clark		.60	.25
❏ 33 Eric Chavez		.60	.25
❏ 34 Kris Benson		.40	.18
❏ 35 Frank Thomas		2.00	.90
❏ 36 Mario Encarnacion		2.00	.90
❏ 37 Gabe Kapler		1.00	.45
❏ 38 Jeremy Giambi		.40	.18
❏ 39 Peter Tucci		.25	.11
❏ 40 Manny Ramirez		1.25	.55
❏ 41 Albert Belle		1.00	.45
❏ 42 Warren Morris		.40	.18
❏ 43 Michael Barrett		.60	.25
❏ 44 Andruw Jones		1.00	.45
❏ 45 Carlos Delgado		1.00	.45
❏ 46 Jaret Wright		.40	.18
❏ 47 Juan Encarnacion		.40	.18
❏ 48 Scott Hunter		.75	.35
❏ 49 Tino Martinez		1.00	.45
❏ 50 Craig Biggio		1.00	.45
❏ 51 Jim Thome		1.00	.45
❏ 52 Vinny Castilla		.40	.18
❏ 53 Tom Glavine		1.00	.45
❏ 54 Bob Higginson		.40	.18
❏ 55 Moises Alou		.40	.18
❏ 56 Robin Ventura		1.00	.45
❏ 57 Bernie Williams		1.00	.45
❏ 58 Pedro Martinez		1.25	.55
❏ 59 Greg Vaughn		.40	.18
❏ 60 Ray Lankford		.40	.18
❏ 61 Jose Canseco		1.25	.55
❏ 62 Ivan Rodriguez		1.25	.55
❏ 63 Shawn Green		1.00	.45
❏ 64 Rafael Palmeiro		1.00	.45
❏ 65 Ellis Burks		.40	.18
❏ 66 Jason Kendall		.40	.18
❏ 67 David Wells		.40	.18
❏ 68 Rondell White		.40	.18
❏ 69 Gary Sheffield		.40	.18
❏ 70 Ken Caminiti		.40	.18
❏ 71 Cliff Floyd		.40	.18
❏ 72 Larry Walker		1.00	.45
❏ 73 Bartolo Colon		.40	.18
❏ 74 Barry Larkin		1.00	.45
❏ 75 Calvin Pickering		.40	.18
❏ 76 Jim Edmonds		.40	.18
❏ 77 Henry Rodriguez		.40	.18
❏ 78 Roberto Alomar		1.00	.45
❏ 79 Andres Galarraga		.60	.25
❏ 80 Richie Sexson		.60	.25

☐ 81 Todd Helton	1.00	.45
☐ 82 Damion Easley	.40	.18
☐ 83 Livan Hernandez	.25	.11
☐ 84 Carlos Beltran	1.25	.55
☐ 85 Todd Hundley	.40	.18
☐ 86 Todd Walker	.40	.18
☐ 87 Scott Brosius	.40	.18
☐ 88 Bob Abreu	.40	.18
☐ 89 Corey Koskie	.25	.11
☐ 90 Ruben Rivera	.25	.11
☐ 91 Edgar Renteria	.25	.11
☐ 92 Quinton McCracken	.25	.11
☐ 93 Bernard Gilkey	.25	.11
☐ 94 Shannon Stewart	.40	.18
☐ 95 Dustin Hermanson	.25	.11
☐ 96 Mike Caruso	.25	.11
☐ 97 Alex Gonzalez	.50	.23
☐ 98 Raul Mondesi	.50	.23
☐ 99 David Cone	.75	.35
☐ 100 Curt Schilling	.75	.35
☐ 101 Brian Giles	.50	.23
☐ 102 Edgar Martinez	.50	.23
☐ 103 Rolando Arrojo	.30	.14
☐ 104 Derek Bell	.50	.23
☐ 105 Denny Neagle	.30	.14
☐ 106 Marquis Grissom	.30	.14
☐ 107 Bret Boone	.50	.23
☐ 108 Mike Mussina	1.25	.55
☐ 109 John Smoltz	.75	.35
☐ 110 Brett Tomko	.30	.14
☐ 111 David Justice	.50	.23
☐ 112 Andy Pettitte	.50	.23
☐ 113 Eric Karros	.50	.23
☐ 114 Dante Bichette	.50	.23
☐ 115 Jeromy Burnitz	.50	.23
☐ 116 Paul Konerko	.50	.23
☐ 117 Steve Finley	.50	.23
☐ 118 Ricky Ledee	.50	.23
☐ 119 Edgardo Alfonzo	.75	.35
☐ 120 Dean Palmer	.50	.23
☐ 121 Rusty Greer	.50	.23
☐ 122 Luis Gonzalez	.50	.23
☐ 123 Randy Winn	.30	.14
☐ 124 Jeff Kent	.50	.23
☐ 125 Doug Glanville	.50	.23
☐ 126 Justin Thompson	.30	.14
☐ 127 Bret Saberhagen	.50	.23
☐ 128 Wade Boggs	1.25	.55
☐ 129 Al Leiter	.50	.23
☐ 130 Paul O'Neill	.50	.23
☐ 131 Chan Ho Park	.50	.23
☐ 132 Johnny Damon	.50	.23
☐ 133 Darryl Kile	.30	.14
☐ 134 Reggie Sanders	.30	.14
☐ 135 Kevin Millwood	.75	.35
☐ 136 Charles Johnson	.50	.23
☐ 137 Ray Durham	.50	.23
☐ 138 Rico Brogna	.30	.14
☐ 139 Matt Williams	1.25	.55
☐ 140 Sandy Alomar Jr.	.50	.23
☐ 141 Jeff Cirillo	.50	.23
☐ 142 Devon White	.30	.14
☐ 143 Andy Benes	.50	.23
☐ 144 Mike Stanley	.30	.14

1999 Flair Showcase
Row 2

	MINT	NRMT
COMMON CARD (1-144)	8.00	3.60

*STARS 1-48: 12.5X TO 30X ROW 3
*STARS 49-96: 12.5X TO 30X ROW 3
*STARS 97-144: 10X TO 25X ROW 3
RANDOM INSERTS IN PACKS
STATED PRINT RUN 99 SERIAL #'d SETS
THREE CARDS PER PLAYER
MASTERPIECE ONE OF ONE PARALLELS
EXIST
MASTERPIECE NOT PRICED DUE TO
SCARCITY

	MINT	NRMT
COMPLETE SET (144)	150.00	70.00
COMMON CARD (1-48)	.60	.25

*STARS 1-48: 1X TO 2.5X ROW 3
ROW 2 1-48 STATED ODDS 1:3

COMMON CARD (49-96)	.30	.14

*STARS 49-96: .5X TO 1.25X ROW 3
ROW 2 49-96 STATED ODDS 1:1.33

COMMON CARD (97-144)	.40	.18

*STARS 97-144: .5X TO 1.25X ROW 3
ROW 2 97-144 STATED ODDS 1:2

1999 Flair Showcase
Row 1

	MINT	NRMT
COMPLETE SET (144)	1000.00	450.00
COMMON CARD (1-48)	2.50	1.10

*STARS 1-48: 4X TO 10X ROW 3
ROW 1 1-48 PRINT RUN 1500 SERIAL #'d
SETS

COMMON CARD (49-96)	1.50	.70

*STARS 49-96: 2.5X TO 6X ROW 3
ROW 1 49-96 PRINT RUN 3000 SERIAL #'d
SETS

COMMON CARD (97-144)	1.00	.45

*STARS 97-144: 1.25X TO 3X ROW 3
ROW 1 97-144 PRINT RUN 6000 #'d SETS
ROW 1 CARDS RANDOM INSERTS IN PACKS

1999 Flair Showcase
Legacy Collection

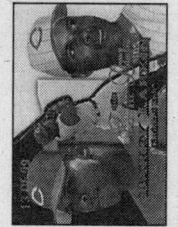

1999 Flair Showcase
Measure of Greatness

	MINT	NRMT
COMPLETE SET (15)	500.00	220.00
COMMON CARD (1-15)	15.00	6.75

RANDOM INSERTS IN PACKS
STATED PRINT RUN 500 SERIAL #'d SETS

☐ 1 Roger Clemens	30.00	13.50
☐ 2 Nomar Garciaparra	40.00	18.00
☐ 3 Juan Gonzalez	25.00	11.00
☐ 4 Ken Griffey Jr.	60.00	27.00
☐ 5 Vladimir Guerrero	15.00	6.75
☐ 6 Tony Gwynn	30.00	13.50
☐ 7 Derek Jeter	40.00	18.00
☐ 8 Chipper Jones	30.00	13.50
☐ 9 Mark McGwire	80.00	36.00
☐ 10 Mike Piazza	40.00	18.00
☐ 11 Manny Ramirez	15.00	6.75
☐ 12 Cal Ripken	50.00	22.00
☐ 13 Alex Rodriguez	40.00	18.00
☐ 14 Sammy Sosa	40.00	18.00
☐ 15 Frank Thomas	25.00	11.00

1999 Flair Showcase
Wave of the Future

	MINT	NRMT
COMPLETE SET (15)	120.00	55.00
COMMON CARD (1-15)	5.00	2.20
SEMISTARS	8.00	3.60

RANDOM INSERTS IN PACKS
STATED PRINT RUN 1000 SERIAL #'d SETS

☐ 1 Kerry Wood	8.00	3.60
☐ 2 Ben Grieve	10.00	4.50
☐ 3 J.D. Drew	15.00	6.75
☐ 4 Juan Encarnacion	5.00	2.20
☐ 5 Travis Lee	8.00	3.60
☐ 6 Todd Helton	10.00	4.50
☐ 7 Troy Glaus	10.00	4.50
☐ 8 Ricky Ledee	5.00	2.20
☐ 9 Eric Chavez	8.00	3.60
☐ 10 Ben Davis	5.00	2.20
☐ 11 George Lombard	5.00	2.20
☐ 12 Jeremy Giambi	5.00	2.20
☐ 13 Roosevelt Brown	5.00	2.20
☐ 14 Pat Burrell	30.00	13.50
☐ 15 Preston Wilson	5.00	2.20

Legacy Collection:

	MINT	NRMT
COMMON CARD (1-144)	8.00	3.60

1963 Fleer

ROBERTO CLEMENTE
Pittsburgh Pirates—Outfield

	NRMT	VG-E
COMPLETE SET (67)	2000.00	900.00
COMMON CARD (1-66)	15.00	6.75
MINOR STARS	20.00	9.00
SEMISTARS	20.00	9.00
UNLISTED STARS	25.00	11.00

CARDS PRICED IN NM CONDITION !

❏ 1	Steve Barber		7.50
❏ 2	Ron Hansen	15.00	6.75
❏ 3	Milt Pappas	20.00	9.00
❏ 4	Brooks Robinson	100.00	45.00
❏ 5	Willie Mays	200.00	90.00
❏ 6	Lou Clinton	15.00	6.75
❏ 7	Bill Monbouquette	15.00	6.75
❏ 8	Carl Yastrzemski	100.00	45.00
❏ 9	Ray Herbert		6.75
❏ 10	Jim Landis	15.00	6.75
❏ 11	Dick Donovan	15.00	6.75
❏ 12	Tito Francona	15.00	6.75
❏ 13	Jerry Kindall	15.00	6.75
❏ 14	Frank Lary	20.00	9.00
❏ 15	Dick Howser	20.00	9.00
❏ 16	Jerry Lumpe	15.00	6.75
❏ 17	Norm Siebern	15.00	6.75
❏ 18	Don Lee	15.00	6.75
❏ 19	Albie Pearson	20.00	9.00
❏ 20	Bob Rodgers	20.00	9.00
❏ 21	Leon Wagner	15.00	6.75
❏ 22	Jim Kaat	20.00	9.00
❏ 23	Vic Power	20.00	9.00
❏ 24	Rich Rollins	15.00	6.75
❏ 25	Bobby Richardson	25.00	11.00
❏ 26	Ralph Terry	20.00	9.00
❏ 27	Tom Cheney	15.00	6.75
❏ 28	Chuck Cottier	15.00	6.75
❏ 29	Jimmy Piersall	20.00	9.00
❏ 30	Dave Stenhouse	15.00	6.75
❏ 31	Glen Hobbie	15.00	6.75
❏ 32	Ron Santo	20.00	9.00
❏ 33	Gene Freese	15.00	6.75
❏ 34	Vada Pinson	20.00	9.00
❏ 35	Bob Purkey	15.00	6.75
❏ 36	Joe Amalfitano	15.00	6.75
❏ 37	Bob Aspromonte	15.00	6.75
❏ 38	Dick Farrell	15.00	6.75
❏ 39	Al Spangler	15.00	6.75
❏ 40	Tommy Davis	20.00	9.00
❏ 41	Don Drysdale	75.00	34.00
❏ 42	Sandy Koufax	200.00	90.00
❏ 43	Maury Wills	100.00	45.00
❏ 44	Frank Bolling	15.00	6.75
❏ 45	Warren Spahn	70.00	32.00
❏ 46	Joe Adcock SP	175.00	80.00
❏ 47	Roger Craig	20.00	9.00
❏ 48	Al Jackson	20.00	9.00
❏ 49	Rod Kanehl	15.00	6.75
❏ 50	Ruben Amaro	15.00	6.75
❏ 51	Johnny Callison	15.00	6.75
❏ 52	Clay Dalrymple	15.00	6.75
❏ 53	Don Demeter	15.00	6.75
❏ 54	Art Mahaffey	15.00	6.75
❏ 55	Smoky Burgess	20.00	9.00
❏ 56	Roberto Clemente	200.00	90.00
❏ 57	Roy Face	20.00	9.00
❏ 58	Vern Law	20.00	9.00
❏ 59	Bill Mazeroski	25.00	11.00
❏ 60	Ken Boyer	20.00	9.00
❏ 61	Bob Gibson	70.00	32.00
❏ 62	Gene Oliver	15.00	6.75
❏ 63	Bill White	20.00	9.00
❏ 64	Orlando Cepeda	25.00	11.00
❏ 65	Jim Davenport	15.00	6.75
❏ 66	Billy O'Dell	25.00	7.50
❏ NNO	Checklist card	500.00	160.00

1981 Fleer

RICKEY HENDERSON
OUTFIELD

	NRMT	VG-E
COMPLETE SET (660)	30.00	13.50
COMMON CARD (1-660)	.10	.05
MINOR STARS	.25	.11
SEMISTARS	.50	.23
UNLISTED STARS	1.00	.45

❏ 1	Pete Rose UER	2.00	.90
	(270 hits in '63,		
	should be 170)		
❏ 2	Larry Bowa	.25	.11
❏ 3	Manny Trillo	.10	.05
❏ 4	Bob Boone	.25	.11
❏ 5	Mike Schmidt	1.50	.70
	(See also 640A)		
❏ 6	Steve Carlton P1	1.00	.45
	Golden Arm		
	(Back "1066 Cardinals-;		
	Number on back 6)		
❏ 6B	Steve Carlton P2	1.50	.70
	Pitcher of Year		
	(Back "1066 Cardinals-)		
❏ 6C	Steve Carlton P3	2.00	.90
	(1966 Cardinals)		
❏ 7	Tug McGraw	.25	.11
	(See 657A)		
❏ 8	Larry Christenson	.10	.05
❏ 9	Bake McBride	.10	.05
❏ 10	Greg Luzinski	.25	.11
❏ 11	Ron Reed	.10	.05
❏ 12	Dickie Noles	.10	.05
❏ 13	Keith Moreland	.25	.11
❏ 14	Bob Walk	.25	.11
❏ 15	Lonnie Smith	.10	.05
❏ 16	Dick Ruthven	.10	.05
❏ 17	Sparky Lyle	.25	.11
❏ 18	Greg Gross	.10	.05
❏ 19	Garry Maddox	.10	.05
❏ 20	Nino Espinosa	.10	.05
❏ 21	George Vukovich	.10	.05
❏ 22	John Vukovich	.10	.05
❏ 23	Ramon Aviles	.10	.05
❏ 24A	Kevin Saucier P1	.10	.05
	(Name on back "Ken-)		
❏ 24B	Kevin Saucier P2	.10	.05
	(Name on back "Ken-)		
❏ 24C	Kevin Saucier P3	1.00	.45
	(Name on back "Kevin-)		
❏ 25	Randy Lerch	.10	.05
❏ 26	Del Unser	.10	.05
❏ 27	Tim McCarver	.50	.23
❏ 28	George Brett	2.50	1.10
	(See also 655A)		
❏ 29	Willie Wilson	.25	.11
	(See also 653A)		
❏ 30	Paul Splittorff	.10	.05
❏ 31	Dan Quisenberry	.25	.11
❏ 32A	Amos Otis P1	.25	.11
	(Batting Pose;		
	"Outfield";		
	32 on back)		
❏ 32B	Amos Otis P2	.25	.11
	Series Starter		
	483 on back		
❏ 33	Steve Busby	.10	.05
❏ 34	U.L. Washington	.10	.05
❏ 35	Dave Chalk	.10	.05
❏ 36	Darrell Porter	.10	.05
❏ 37	Marty Pattin	.10	.05
❏ 38	Larry Gura	.10	.05
❏ 39	Renie Martin	.10	.05
❏ 40	Rich Gale	.10	.05
❏ 41A	Hal McRae P1	.50	.23
	("Royals" on front		
	in black letters)		
❏ 41B	Hal McRae P2	.25	.11
	("Royals" on front		
	in blue letters)		
❏ 42	Dennis Leonard	.10	.05
❏ 43	Willie Aikens	.10	.05
❏ 44	Frank White	.25	.11
❏ 45	Clint Hurdle	.10	.05
❏ 46	John Wathan	.10	.05
❏ 47	Pete LaCock	.10	.05
❏ 48	Rance Mulliniks	.10	.05
❏ 49	Jeff Twitty	.10	.05
❏ 50	Jamie Quirk	.10	.05
❏ 51	Art Howe	.25	.11
❏ 52	Ken Forsch	.10	.05
❏ 53	Vern Ruhle	.10	.05
❏ 54	Joe Niekro	.25	.11
❏ 55	Frank LaCorte	.10	.05
❏ 56	J.R. Richard	.25	.11
❏ 57	Nolan Ryan	5.00	2.20
❏ 58	Enos Cabell	.10	.05
❏ 59	Cesar Cedeno	.25	.11
❏ 60	Jose Cruz	.25	.11
❏ 61	Bill Virdon MG	.10	.05
❏ 62	Terry Puhl	.10	.05
❏ 63	Joaquin Andujar	.25	.11
❏ 64	Alan Ashby	.10	.05
❏ 65	Joe Sambito	.10	.05
❏ 66	Denny Walling	.10	.05
❏ 67	Jeff Leonard	.25	.11
❏ 68	Luis Pujols	.10	.05
❏ 69	Bruce Bochy	.10	.05
❏ 70	Rafael Landestoy	.10	.05
❏ 71	Dave Smith	.25	.11
❏ 72	Danny Heep	.10	.05
❏ 73	Julio Gonzalez	.10	.05
❏ 74	Craig Reynolds	.10	.05
❏ 75	Gary Woods	.10	.05
❏ 76	Dave Bergman	.10	.05
❏ 77	Randy Niemann	.10	.05
❏ 78	Joe Morgan	1.00	.45
❏ 79	Reggie Jackson	1.25	.55
	(See also 650A)		
❏ 80	Bucky Dent	.25	.11
❏ 81	Tommy John	.25	.23
❏ 82	Luis Tiant	.25	.11
❏ 83	Rick Cerone	.10	.05
❏ 84	Dick Howser MG	.10	.05
❏ 85	Lou Piniella	.25	.11
❏ 86	Ron Davis	.10	.05
❏ 87A	Graig Nettles P1	5.00	2.20
	ERR (Name on back		
	misspelled "Craig-)		
❏ 87B	Graig Nettles P2 COR	.25	.11
	("Graig")		
❏ 88	Ron Guidry	.25	.11
❏ 89	Rich Gossage	.50	.23
❏ 90	Rudy May	.10	.05
❏ 91	Gaylord Perry	1.00	.45
❏ 92	Eric Soderholm	.10	.05
❏ 93	Bob Watson	.25	.11
❏ 94	Bobby Murcer	.25	.11
❏ 95	Bobby Brown	.10	.05
❏ 96	Jim Spencer	.10	.05
❏ 97	Tom Underwood	.10	.05
❏ 98	Oscar Gamble	.10	.05
❏ 99	Johnny Oates	.25	.11
❏ 100	Fred Stanley	.10	.05

❏ 101	Ruppert Jones	.10	.05
❏ 102	Dennis Werth	.10	.05
❏ 103	Joe Lefebvre	.10	.05
❏ 104	Brian Doyle	.10	.05
❏ 105	Aurelio Rodriguez	.10	.05
❏ 106	Doug Bird	.10	.05
❏ 107	Mike Griffin	.10	.05
❏ 108	Tim Lollar	.10	.05
❏ 109	Willie Randolph	.25	.11
❏ 110	Steve Garvey	.50	.23
❏ 111	Reggie Smith	.25	.11
❏ 112	Don Sutton	1.00	.45
❏ 113	Burt Hooton	.10	.05
❏ 114A	Dave Lopes P1	.50	.23
	(Small hand on back)		
❏ 114B	Dave Lopes P2	.25	.11
	(No hand)		
❏ 115	Dusty Baker	.50	.23
❏ 116	Tom Lasorda MG	.25	.11
❏ 117	Bill Russell	.25	.11
❏ 118	Jerry Reuss UER	.25	.11
	("Home:" omitted)		
❏ 119	Terry Forster	.10	.05
❏ 120A	Bob Welch P1	.25	.11
	(Name on back is "Bob~)		
❏ 120B	Bob Welch P2	.50	.23
	(Name on back is ""Robert~)		
❏ 121	Don Stanhouse	.10	.05
❏ 122	Rick Monday	.25	.11
❏ 123	Derrel Thomas	.10	.05
❏ 124	Joe Ferguson	.10	.05
❏ 125	Rick Sutcliffe	.25	.11
❏ 126A	Ron Cey P1	.50	.23
	(Small hand on back)		
❏ 126B	Ron Cey P2	.25	.11
	(No hand)		
❏ 127	Dave Goltz	.10	.05
❏ 128	Jay Johnstone	.25	.11
❏ 129	Steve Yeager	.10	.05
❏ 130	Gary Weiss	.10	.05
❏ 131	Mike Scioscia	1.00	.45
❏ 132	Vic Davalillo	.10	.05
❏ 133	Doug Rau	.10	.05
❏ 134	Pepe Frias	.10	.05
❏ 135	Mickey Hatcher	.25	.11
❏ 136	Steve Howe	.25	.11
❏ 137	Robert Castillo	.10	.05
❏ 138	Gary Thomasson	.10	.05
❏ 139	Rudy Law	.10	.05
❏ 140	Fernando Valenzuela	2.00	.90
	UER (Misspelled Femand on card)		
❏ 141	Manny Mota	.25	.11
❏ 142	Gary Carter	1.00	.45
❏ 143	Steve Rogers	.10	.05
❏ 144	Warren Cromartie	.10	.05
❏ 145	Andre Dawson	1.00	.45
❏ 146	Larry Parrish	.10	.05
❏ 147	Rowland Office	.10	.05
❏ 148	Ellis Valentine	.10	.05
❏ 149	Dick Williams MG	.10	.05
❏ 150	Bill Gullickson	.50	.23
❏ 151	Elias Sosa	.10	.05
❏ 152	John Tamargo	.10	.05
❏ 153	Chris Speier	.10	.05
❏ 154	Ron LeFlore	.25	.11
❏ 155	Rodney Scott	.10	.05
❏ 156	Stan Bahnsen	.10	.05
❏ 157	Bill Lee	.25	.11
❏ 158	Fred Norman	.10	.05
❏ 159	Woodie Fryman	.10	.05
❏ 160	David Palmer	.10	.05
❏ 161	Jerry White	.10	.05
❏ 162	Roberto Ramos	.10	.05
❏ 163	John D'Acquisto	.10	.05
❏ 164	Tommy Hutton	.10	.05
❏ 165	Charlie Lea	.10	.05
❏ 166	Scott Sanderson	.10	.05
❏ 167	Ken Macha	.10	.05
❏ 168	Tony Bernazard	.10	.05
❏ 169	Jim Palmer	1.00	.45
❏ 170	Steve Stone	.25	.11
❏ 171	Mike Flanagan	.10	.05
❏ 172	Al Bumbry	.25	.11
❏ 173	Doug DeCinces	.25	.11
❏ 174	Scott McGregor	.10	.05
❏ 175	Mark Belanger	.25	.11
❏ 176	Tim Stoddard	.10	.05
❏ 177A	Rick Dempsey P1	.50	.23
	(Small hand on front)		
❏ 177B	Rick Dempsey P2	.25	.11
	(No hand)		
❏ 178	Earl Weaver MG	1.00	.45
❏ 179	Tippy Martinez	.10	.05
❏ 180	Dennis Martinez	.50	.23
❏ 181	Sammy Stewart	.10	.05
❏ 182	Rich Dauer	.10	.05
❏ 183	Lee May	.25	.11
❏ 184	Eddie Murray	2.00	.90
❏ 185	Benny Ayala	.10	.05
❏ 186	John Lowenstein	.10	.05
❏ 187	Gary Roenicke	.25	.11
❏ 188	Ken Singleton	.25	.11
❏ 189	Dan Graham	.10	.05
❏ 190	Terry Crowley	.10	.05
❏ 191	Kiko Garcia	.10	.05
❏ 192	Dave Ford	.10	.05
❏ 193	Mark Corey	.10	.05
❏ 194	Lenn Sakata	.10	.05
❏ 195	Doug DeCinces	.25	.11
❏ 196	Johnny Bench	1.25	.55
❏ 197	Dave Concepcion	.25	.11
❏ 198	Ray Knight	.25	.11
❏ 199	Ken Griffey	.50	.23
❏ 200	Tom Seaver	1.25	.55
❏ 201	Dave Collins	.10	.05
❏ 202A	George Foster P1 Slugger	.50	.23
	(Number on back 216)		
❏ 202B	George Foster P2 Slugger	.50	.23
	(Number on back 202)		
❏ 203	Junior Kennedy	.10	.05
❏ 204	Frank Pastore	.10	.05
❏ 205	Dan Driessen	.10	.05
❏ 206	Hector Cruz	.10	.05
❏ 207	Paul Moskau	.10	.05
❏ 208	Charlie Leibrandt	.50	.23
❏ 209	Harry Spilman	.10	.05
❏ 210	Joe Price	.10	.05
❏ 211	Tom Hume	.10	.05
❏ 212	Joe Nolan	.10	.05
❏ 213	Doug Bair	.10	.05
❏ 214	Mario Soto	.10	.05
❏ 215A	Bill Bonham P1	.50	.23
	(Small hand on back)		
❏ 215B	Bill Bonham P2	.10	.05
	(No hand)		
❏ 216	George Foster	.25	.11
	(See 202)		
❏ 217	Paul Householder	.10	.05
❏ 218	Ron Oester	.10	.05
❏ 219	Sam Mejias	.10	.05
❏ 220	Sheldon Burnside	.10	.05
❏ 221	Carl Yastrzemski	1.00	.45
❏ 222	Jim Rice	.25	.11
❏ 223	Fred Lynn	.25	.11
❏ 224	Carlton Fisk	1.00	.45
❏ 225	Rick Burleson	.10	.05
❏ 226	Dennis Eckersley	1.00	.45
❏ 227	Butch Hobson	.10	.05
❏ 228	Tom Burgmeier	.10	.05
❏ 229	Garry Hancock	.10	.05
❏ 230	Don Zimmer MG	.25	.11
❏ 231	Steve Renko	.10	.05
❏ 232	Dwight Evans	.50	.23
❏ 233	Mike Torrez	.10	.05
❏ 234	Bob Stanley	.10	.05
❏ 235	Jim Dwyer	.10	.05
❏ 236	Dave Stapleton	.10	.05
❏ 237	Glenn Hoffman	.10	.05
❏ 238	Jerry Remy	.10	.05
❏ 239	Dick Drago	.10	.05
❏ 240	Bill Campbell	.10	.05
❏ 241	Tony Perez	1.00	.45
❏ 242	Phil Niekro	1.00	.45
❏ 243	Dale Murphy	1.00	.45
❏ 244	Bob Horner	.25	.11
❏ 245	Jeff Burroughs	.10	.05
❏ 246	Rick Camp	.10	.05
❏ 247	Bobby Cox MG	.25	.11
❏ 248	Bruce Benedict	.10	.05
❏ 249	Gene Garber	.10	.05
❏ 250	Jerry Royster	.10	.05
❏ 251A	Gary Matthews P1	.50	.23
	(Small hand on front)		
❏ 251B	Gary Matthews P2	.25	.11
	(No hand)		
❏ 252	Chris Chambliss	.25	.11
❏ 253	Luis Gomez	.10	.05
❏ 254	Bill Nahorodny	.10	.05
❏ 255	Doyle Alexander	.10	.05
❏ 256	Brian Asselstine	.10	.05
❏ 257	Biff Pocoroba	.10	.05
❏ 258	Mike Lum	.10	.05
❏ 259	Charlie Spikes	.10	.05
❏ 260	Glenn Hubbard	.25	.11
❏ 261	Tommy Boggs	.10	.05
❏ 262	Al Hrabosky	.25	.11
❏ 263	Rick Matula	.10	.05
❏ 264	Preston Hanna	.10	.05
❏ 265	Larry Bradford	.10	.05
❏ 266	Rafael Ramirez	.10	.05
❏ 267	Larry McWilliams	.10	.05
❏ 268	Rod Carew	1.00	.45
❏ 269	Bobby Grich	.25	.11
❏ 270	Carney Lansford	.25	.11
❏ 271	Don Baylor	.50	.23
❏ 272	Joe Rudi	.25	.11
❏ 273	Dan Ford	.10	.05
❏ 274	Jim Fregosi MG	.10	.05
❏ 275	Dave Frost	.10	.05
❏ 276	Frank Tanana	.25	.11
❏ 277	Dickie Thon	.25	.11
❏ 278	Jason Thompson	.10	.05
❏ 279	Rick Miller	.10	.05
❏ 280	Bert Campaneris	.25	.11
❏ 281	Tom Donohue	.10	.05
❏ 282	Brian Downing	.25	.11
❏ 283	Fred Patek	.10	.05
❏ 284	Bruce Kison	.10	.05
❏ 285	Dave LaRoche	.10	.05
❏ 286	Don Aase	.10	.05
❏ 287	Jim Barr	.10	.05
❏ 288	Alfredo Martinez	.10	.05
❏ 289	Larry Harlow	.10	.05
❏ 290	Andy Hassler	.10	.05
❏ 291	Dave Kingman	.50	.23
❏ 292	Bill Buckner	.25	.11
❏ 293	Rick Reuschel	.25	.11
❏ 294	Bruce Sutter	.50	.23
❏ 295	Jerry Martin	.10	.05
❏ 296	Scot Thompson	.10	.05
❏ 297	Ivan DeJesus	.10	.05
❏ 298	Steve Dillard	.10	.05
❏ 299	Dick Tidrow	.10	.05
❏ 300	Randy Martz	.10	.05
❏ 301	Lenny Randle	.10	.05
❏ 302	Lynn McGlothen	.10	.05
❏ 303	Cliff Johnson	.10	.05
❏ 304	Tim Blackwell	.10	.05
❏ 305	Dennis Lamp	.10	.05
❏ 306	Bill Caudill	.10	.05
❏ 307	Carlos Lezcano	.10	.05
❏ 308	Jim Tracy	.10	.05
❏ 309	Doug Capilla UER	.10	.05
	(Cubs on front but Braves on back)		
❏ 310	Willie Hernandez	.25	.11
❏ 311	Mike Vail	.10	.05
❏ 312	Mike Krukow	.10	.05
❏ 313	Barry Foote	.10	.05
❏ 314	Larry Biittner	.10	.05
❏ 315	Mike Tyson	.10	.05
❏ 316	Lee Mazzilli	.10	.05
❏ 317	John Stearns	.10	.05
❏ 318	Alex Trevino	.10	.05
❏ 319	Craig Swan	.10	.05
❏ 320	Frank Taveras	.10	.05
❏ 321	Steve Henderson	.10	.05
❏ 322	Neil Allen	.10	.05
❏ 323	Mark Bomback	.10	.05
❏ 324	Mike Jorgensen	.10	.05
❏ 325	Joe Torre MG	.25	.11
❏ 326	Elliott Maddox	.10	.05
❏ 327	Pete Falcone	.10	.05

328	Ray Burris	.10	.05
329	Claudell Washington	.10	.05
330	Doug Flynn	.10	.05
331	Joel Youngblood	.10	.05
332	Bill Almon	.10	.05
333	Tom Hausman	.10	.05
334	Pat Zachry	.10	.05
335	Jeff Reardon	1.00	.45
336	Wally Backman	.25	.11
337	Dan Norman	.10	.05
338	Jerry Morales	.10	.05
339	Ed Farmer	.10	.05
340	Bob Molinaro	.10	.05
341	Todd Cruz	.10	.05
342A	Britt Burns P1 (Small hand on front)	.50	.23
342B	Britt Burns P2 (No hand)	.25	.11
343	Kevin Bell	.10	.05
344	Tony LaRussa MG	.25	.11
345	Steve Trout	.10	.05
346	Harold Baines	5.00	2.20
347	Richard Wortham	.10	.05
348	Wayne Nordhagen	.10	.05
349	Mike Squires	.10	.05
350	Lamar Johnson	.10	.05
351	Rickey Henderson (Most Stolen Bases AL)	2.00	.90
352	Francisco Barrios	.10	.05
353	Thad Bosley	.10	.05
354	Chet Lemon	.10	.05
355	Bruce Kimm	.10	.05
356	Richard Dotson	.10	.05
357	Jim Morrison	.10	.05
358	Mike Proly	.10	.05
359	Greg Pryor	.10	.05
360	Dave Parker	.25	.11
361	Omar Moreno	.10	.05
362A	Kent Tekulve P1 Back 1071 Waterbury and 1078 Pirates	.25	.11
362B	Kent Tekulve P2 1971 Waterbury and 1978 Pirates	.25	.11
363	Willie Stargell	1.00	.45
364	Phil Garner	.25	.11
365	Ed Ott	.10	.05
366	Don Robinson	.10	.05
367	Chuck Tanner MG	.25	.11
368	Jim Rooker	.10	.05
369	Dale Berra	.10	.05
370	Jim Bibby	.10	.05
371	Steve Nicosia	.10	.05
372	Mike Easler	.10	.05
373	Bill Robinson	.25	.11
374	Lee Lacy	.10	.05
375	John Candelaria	.25	.11
376	Manny Sanguillen	.25	.11
377	Rick Rhoden	.10	.05
378	Grant Jackson	.10	.05
379	Tim Foli	.10	.05
380	Rod Scurry	.10	.05
381	Bill Madlock	.25	.11
382A	Kurt Bevacqua P1 ERR (P on cap backwards)	.25	.11
382B	Kurt Bevacqua P2 COR	.10	.05
383	Bert Blyleven	.50	.23
384	Eddie Solomon	.10	.05
385	Enrique Romo	.10	.05
386	John Milner	.10	.05
387	Mike Hargrove	.25	.11
388	Jorge Orta	.10	.05
389	Toby Harrah	.25	.11
390	Tom Veryzer	.10	.05
391	Miguel Dilone	.10	.05
392	Dan Spillner	.10	.05
393	Jack Brohamer	.10	.05
394	Wayne Garland	.10	.05
395	Sid Monge	.10	.05
396	Rick Waits	.10	.05
397	Joe Charboneau	1.00	.45
398	Gary Alexander	.10	.05
399	Jerry Dybzinski	.10	.05
400	Mike Stanton	.10	.05
401	Mike Paxton	.10	.05
402	Gary Gray	.10	.05
403	Rick Manning	.10	.05
404	Bo Diaz	.10	.05
405	Ron Hassey	.10	.05
406	Ross Grimsley	.10	.05
407	Victor Cruz	.10	.05
408	Len Barker	.10	.05
409	Bob Bailor	.10	.05
410	Otto Velez	.10	.05
411	Ernie Whitt	.10	.05
412	Jim Clancy	.10	.05
413	Barry Bonnell	.10	.05
414	Dave Stieb	.25	.11
415	Damaso Garcia	.10	.05
416	John Mayberry	.10	.05
417	Roy Howell	.10	.05
418	Danny Ainge	2.00	.90
419A	Jesse Jefferson P1 (Back says Pirates)		
419B	Jesse Jefferson P2 (Back says Pirates)	.10	.05
419C	Jesse Jefferson P3 (Back says Blue Jays)	1.00	.45
420	Joey McLaughlin	.10	.05
421	Lloyd Moseby	.25	.11
422	Alvis Woods	.10	.05
423	Garth Iorg	.10	.05
424	Doug Ault	.10	.05
425	Ken Schrom	.10	.05
426	Mike Willis	.10	.05
427	Steve Braun	.10	.05
428	Bob Davis	.10	.05
429	Jerry Garvin	.10	.05
430	Alfredo Griffin	.10	.05
431	Bob Mattick MG	.10	.05
432	Vida Blue	.25	.11
433	Jack Clark	.25	.11
434	Willie McCovey	1.00	.45
435	Mike Ivie	.10	.05
436A	Darrel Evans P1 ERR (Name on front "Darrel")	.50	.23
436B	Darrell Evans P2 COR (Name on front "Darrell")	.50	.23
437	Terry Whitfield	.10	.05
438	Rennie Stennett	.10	.05
439	John Montefusco	.10	.05
440	Jim Wohlford	.10	.05
441	Bill North	.10	.05
442	Milt May	.10	.05
443	Max Venable	.10	.05
444	Ed Whitson	.10	.05
445	Al Holland	.10	.05
446	Randy Moffitt	.10	.05
447	Bob Knepper	.10	.05
448	Gary Lavelle	.10	.05
449	Greg Minton	.10	.05
450	Johnnie LeMaster	.10	.05
451	Larry Herndon	.10	.05
452	Rich Murray	.10	.05
453	Joe Pettini	.10	.05
454	Allen Ripley	.10	.05
455	Dennis Littlejohn	.10	.05
456	Tom Griffin	.10	.05
457	Alan Hargesheimer	.10	.05
458	Joe Strain	.10	.05
459	Steve Kemp	.10	.05
460	Sparky Anderson MG	.25	.11
461	Alan Trammell	1.00	.45
462	Mark Fidrych	1.00	.45
463	Lou Whitaker	1.00	.45
464	Dave Rozema	.10	.05
465	Milt Wilcox	.10	.05
466	Champ Summers	.10	.05
467	Lance Parrish	.25	.11
468	Dan Petry	.10	.05
469	Pat Underwood	.10	.05
470	Rick Peters	.10	.05
471	Al Cowens	.10	.05
472	John Wockenfuss	.10	.05
473	Tom Brookens	.10	.05
474	Richie Hebner	.10	.05
475	Jack Morris	1.00	.45
476	Jim Lentine	.10	.05
477	Bruce Robbins	.10	.05
478	Mark Wagner	.10	.05
479	Tim Corcoran	.10	.05
480A	Stan Papi P1 (Front as Pitcher)	.25	.11
480B	Stan Papi P2 (Front as Shortstop)	.10	.05
481	Kirk Gibson	2.00	.90
482	Dan Schatzeder	.10	.05
483A	Amos Otis P1 (See card 32)	.25	.11
483B	Amos Otis P2 (See card 32)	.25	.11
484	Dave Winfield	1.00	.45
485	Rollie Fingers	1.00	.45
486	Gene Richards	.10	.05
487	Randy Jones	.10	.05
488	Ozzie Smith	3.00	1.35
489	Gene Tenace	.25	.11
490	Bill Fahey	.10	.05
491	John Curtis	.10	.05
492	Dave Cash	.10	.05
493A	Tim Flannery P1 (Batting right)	.25	.11
493B	Tim Flannery P2 (Batting left)	.10	.05
494	Jerry Mumphrey	.10	.05
495	Bob Shirley	.10	.05
496	Steve Mura	.10	.05
497	Eric Rasmussen	.10	.05
498	Broderick Perkins	.10	.05
499	Barry Evans	.10	.05
500	Chuck Baker	.10	.05
501	Luis Salazar	.10	.05
502	Gary Lucas	.10	.05
503	Mike Armstrong	.10	.05
504	Jerry Turner	.10	.05
505	Dennis Kinney	.10	.05
506	Willie Montanez UER (Misspelled Willy on card front)	.10	.05
507	Gorman Thomas	.25	.11
508	Ben Oglivie	.25	.11
509	Larry Hisle	.10	.05
510	Sal Bando	.25	.11
511	Robin Yount	1.00	.45
512	Mike Caldwell	.10	.05
513	Sixto Lezcano	.10	.05
514A	Bill Travers P1 ERR ("Jerry Augustine" with Augustine back)	.25	.11
514B	Bill Travers P2 COR	.10	.05
515	Paul Molitor	2.00	.90
516	Moose Haas	.10	.05
517	Bill Castro	.10	.05
518	Jim Slaton	.10	.05
519	Lary Sorensen	.10	.05
520	Bob McClure	.10	.05
521	Charlie Moore	.10	.05
522	Jim Gantner	.25	.11
523	Reggie Cleveland	.10	.05
524	Don Money	.10	.05
525	Bill Travers	.10	.05
526	Buck Martinez	.10	.05
527	Dick Davis	.10	.05
528	Ted Simmons	.25	.11
529	Garry Templeton	.25	.11
530	Ken Reitz	.10	.05
531	Tony Scott	.10	.05
532	Ken Oberkfell	.10	.05
533	Bob Sykes	.10	.05
534	Keith Smith	.10	.05
535	John Littlefield	.10	.05
536	Jim Kaat	.25	.11
537	Bob Forsch	.10	.05
538	Mike Phillips	.10	.05
539	Terry Landrum	.10	.05
540	Leon Durham	.25	.11
541	Terry Kennedy	.10	.05
542	George Hendrick	.10	.05
543	Dane Iorg	.10	.05
544	Mark Littell	.10	.05
545	Keith Hernandez	.25	.11
546	Silvio Martinez	.10	.05
547A	Don Hood P1 ERR ("Pete Vuckovich")	.25	.11

with Vuckovich back)

#	Player	NRMT	VG-E
547B	Don Hood P2 COR	.10	.05
548	Bobby Bonds	.25	.11
549	Mike Ramsey	.10	.05
550	Tom Herr	.25	.11
551	Roy Smalley	.10	.05
552	Jerry Koosman	.25	.11
553	Ken Landreaux	.10	.05
554	John Castino	.10	.05
555	Doug Corbett	.10	.05
556	Bombo Rivera	.10	.05
557	Ron Jackson	.10	.05
558	Butch Wynegar	.10	.05
559	Hosken Powell	.10	.05
560	Pete Redfern	.10	.05
561	Roger Erickson	.10	.05
562	Glenn Adams	.10	.05
563	Rick Sofield	.10	.05
564	Geoff Zahn	.10	.05
565	Pete Mackanin	.10	.05
566	Mike Cubbage	.10	.05
567	Darrell Jackson	.10	.05
568	Dave Edwards	.10	.05
569	Rob Wilfong	.10	.05
570	Sal Butera	.10	.05
571	Jose Morales	.10	.05
572	Rick Langford	.10	.05
573	Mike Norris	.10	.05
574	Rickey Henderson	4.00	1.80
575	Tony Armas	.25	.11
576	Dave Revering	.10	.05
577	Jeff Newman	.10	.05
578	Bob Lacey	.10	.05
579	Brian Kingman	.10	.05
580	Mitchell Page	.10	.05
581	Billy Martin MG	.50	.23
582	Rob Picciolo	.10	.05
583	Mike Heath	.10	.05
584	Mickey Klutts	.10	.05
585	Orlando Gonzalez	.10	.05
586	Mike Davis	.10	.05
587	Wayne Gross	.10	.05
588	Matt Keough	.10	.05
589	Steve McCatty	.10	.05
590	Dwayne Murphy	.10	.05
591	Mario Guerrero	.10	.05
592	Dave McKay	.10	.05
593	Jim Essian	.10	.05
594	Dave Heaverlo	.10	.05
595	Maury Wills MG	.25	.11
596	Juan Beniquez	.10	.05
597	Rodney Craig	.10	.05
598	Jim Anderson	.10	.05
599	Floyd Bannister	.10	.05
600	Bruce Bochte	.10	.05
601	Julio Cruz	.10	.05
602	Ted Cox	.10	.05
603	Dan Meyer	.10	.05
604	Larry Cox	.10	.05
605	Bill Stein	.10	.05
606	Steve Garvey (Most Hits NL)	.50	.23
607	Dave Roberts	.10	.05
608	Leon Roberts	.10	.05
609	Reggie Walton	.10	.05
610	Dave Edler	.10	.05
611	Larry Milbourne	.10	.05
612	Kim Allen	.10	.05
613	Mario Mendoza	.10	.05
614	Tom Paciorek	.25	.11
615	Glenn Abbott	.10	.05
616	Joe Simpson	.10	.05
617	Mickey Rivers	.25	.11
618	Jim Kern	.10	.05
619	Jim Sundberg	.25	.11
620	Richie Zisk	.25	.11
621	Jon Matlack	.10	.05
622	Ferguson Jenkins	1.00	.45
623	Pat Corrales MG	.10	.05
624	Ed Figueroa	.10	.05
625	Buddy Bell	.25	.11
626	Al Oliver	.25	.11
627	Doc Medich	.10	.05
628	Bump Wills	.10	.05
629	Rusty Staub	.25	.11
630	Pat Putnam	.10	.05
631	John Grubb	.10	.05
632	Danny Darwin	.10	.05
633	Ken Clay	.10	.05
634	Jim Norris	.10	.05
635	John Butcher	.10	.05
636	Dave Roberts	.10	.05
637	Billy Sample	.10	.05
638	Carl Yastrzemski	1.00	.45
639	Cecil Cooper	.25	.11
640	Mike Schmidt P1 (Portrait; "Third Base"; number on back 5)	1.50	.70
640B	Mike Schmidt P2 ("1980 Home Run King"; 640 on back)	2.00	.90
641A	CL: Phils/Royals P1 41 is Hal McRae	.25	.11
641B	CL: Phils/Royals P2 (41 is Hal McRae, Double Threat)	.25	.11
642	CL: Astros/Yankees	.10	.05
643	CL: Expos/Dodgers	.10	.05
644A	CL: Reds/Orioles P1 (202 is George Foster; Joe Nolan pitcher, should be catcher)	.25	.11
644B	CL: Reds/Orioles P2 (202 is Foster Slugger; Joe Nolan pitcher, should be catcher)	.25	.11
645	Pete Rose / Larry Bowa / Mike Schmidt / Triple Threat P1 (No number on back)	1.25	.55
645B	Pete Rose / Larry Bowa / Mike Schmidt / Triple Threat P2 (Back numbered 645)	2.50	1.10
646	CL: Braves/Red Sox	.10	.05
647	CL: Cubs/Angels	.10	.05
648	CL: Mets/White Sox	.10	.05
649	CL: Indians/Pirates	.10	.05
650	Reggie Jackson / Mr. Baseball P1 (Number on back 79)	1.25	.55
650B	Reggie Jackson / Mr. Baseball P2 (Number on back 650)	1.25	.55
651	CL: Giants/Blue Jays	.10	.05
652A	CL: Tigers/Padres P1 (483 is listed)	.25	.11
652B	CL: Tigers/Padres P2 (483 is deleted)	.25	.11
653A	Willie Wilson P1 Most Hits Most Runs (Number on back 29)	.25	.11
653B	Willie Wilson P2 Most Hits Most Runs (Number on back 28)	.25	.11
654A	CL: Brewers/Cards P1 (514 Jerry Augustine; 547 Pete Vuckovich)	.25	.11
654B	CL:Brewers/Cards P2 (514 Billy Travers; 547 Don Hood)	.25	.11
655	George Brett P1 .390 Average (Number on back 28)	2.50	1.10
655B	George Brett P2 .390 Average (Number on back 655)	4.00	1.80
656	CL: Twins/Oakland A's	.25	.11
657A	Tug McGraw P1 Game Saver (Number on back 7)	.25	.11
657B	Tug McGraw P2 Game Saver (Number on back 657)	.25	.11
658	CL: Rangers/Mariners	.10	.05
659A	Checklist P1 of Special Cards (Last lines on front, Wilson Most Hits)	.10	.05
659B	Checklist P2 of Special Cards (Last lines on front, Otis Series Starter)	.10	.05
660	Steve Carlton P1 Golden Arm (Number on back 660 Back 1066 Cardinals)	1.00	.45
660B	Steve Carlton P2 Golden Arm (1966 Cardinals)	1.50	.70

1982 Fleer

	NRMT	VG-E
COMPLETE SET (660)	60.00	27.00
COMMON CARD (1-660)	.10	.05
MINOR STARS	.20	.09
SEMISTARS	.40	.18
UNLISTED STARS	.75	.35

#	Player	NRMT	VG-E
1	Dusty Baker	.40	.18
2	Robert Castillo	.10	.05
3	Ron Cey	.20	.09
4	Terry Forster	.10	.05
5	Steve Garvey	.40	.18
6	Dave Goltz	.10	.05
7	Pedro Guerrero	.20	.09
8	Burt Hooton	.10	.05
9	Steve Howe	.10	.05
10	Jay Johnstone	.20	.09
11	Ken Landreaux	.10	.05
12	Dave Lopes	.20	.09
13	Mike A. Marshall	.20	.09
14	Bobby Mitchell	.10	.05
15	Rick Monday	.10	.05
16	Tom Niedenfuer	.10	.05
17	Ted Power	.10	.05
18	Jerry Reuss UER ("Home:" omitted)	.20	.09
19	Ron Roenicke	.10	.05
20	Bill Russell	.10	.05
21	Steve Sax	.75	.35
22	Mike Scioscia	.20	.09
23	Reggie Smith	.20	.09
24	Dave Stewart	1.00	.45
25	Rick Sutcliffe	.20	.09
26	Derrel Thomas	.10	.05
27	Fernando Valenzuela	.75	.35
28	Bob Welch	.20	.09
29	Steve Yeager	.10	.05
30	Bobby Brown	.10	.05
31	Rick Cerone	.10	.05
32	Ron Davis	.10	.05
33	Bucky Dent	.20	.09
34	Barry Foote	.10	.05
35	George Frazier	.10	.05
36	Oscar Gamble	.10	.05
37	Rich Gossage	.40	.18
38	Ron Guidry	.20	.09
39	Reggie Jackson	1.00	.45
40	Tommy John	.40	.18
41	Rudy May	.10	.05
42	Larry Milbourne	.10	.05
43	Jerry Mumphrey	.10	.05
44	Bobby Murcer	.20	.09
45	Gene Nelson	.10	.05
46	Graig Nettles	.20	.09

47	Johnny Oates	.20	.09
48	Lou Piniella	.20	.09
49	Willie Randolph	.20	.09
50	Rick Reuschel	.20	.09
51	Dave Revering	.10	.05
52	Dave Righetti	.75	.35
53	Aurelio Rodriguez	.10	.05
54	Bob Watson	.20	.09
55	Dennis Werth	.10	.05
56	Dave Winfield	.75	.35
57	Johnny Bench	1.00	.45
58	Bruce Berenyi	.10	.05
59	Larry Biittner	.10	.05
60	Scott Brown	.10	.05
61	Dave Collins	.10	.05
62	Geoff Combe	.10	.05
63	Dave Concepcion	.20	.09
64	Dan Driessen	.10	.05
65	Joe Edelen	.10	.05
66	George Foster	.20	.09
67	Ken Griffey	.20	.09
68	Paul Householder	.10	.05
69	Tom Hume	.10	.05
70	Junior Kennedy	.10	.05
71	Ray Knight	.20	.09
72	Mike LaCoss	.10	.05
73	Rafael Landestoy	.10	.05
74	Charlie Leibrandt	.10	.05
75	Sam Mejias	.10	.05
76	Paul Moskau	.10	.05
77	Joe Nolan	.10	.05
78	Mike O'Berry	.10	.05
79	Ron Oester	.10	.05
80	Frank Pastore	.10	.05
81	Joe Price	.10	.05
82	Tom Seaver	1.00	.45
83	Mario Soto	.10	.05
84	Mike Vail	.10	.05
85	Tony Armas	.10	.05
86	Shooty Babitt	.10	.05
87	Dave Beard	.10	.05
88	Rick Bosetti	.10	.05
89	Keith Drumwright	.10	.05
90	Wayne Gross	.10	.05
91	Mike Heath	.10	.05
92	Rickey Henderson	2.00	.90
93	Cliff Johnson	.10	.05
94	Jeff Jones	.10	.05
95	Matt Keough	.10	.05
96	Brian Kingman	.10	.05
97	Mickey Klutts	.10	.05
98	Rick Langford	.10	.05
99	Steve McCatty	.10	.05
100	Dave McKay	.10	.05
101	Dwayne Murphy	.10	.05
102	Jeff Newman	.10	.05
103	Mike Norris	.10	.05
104	Bob Owchinko	.10	.05
105	Mitchell Page	.10	.05
106	Rob Picciolo	.10	.05
107	Jim Spencer	.10	.05
108	Fred Stanley	.10	.05
109	Tom Underwood	.10	.05
110	Joaquin Andujar	.20	.09
111	Steve Braun	.10	.05
112	Bob Forsch	.10	.05
113	George Hendrick	.10	.05
114	Keith Hernandez	.20	.09
115	Tom Herr	.10	.05
116	Dane Iorg	.10	.05
117	Jim Kaat	.20	.09
118	Tito Landrum	.10	.05
119	Sixto Lezcano	.10	.05
120	Mark Littell	.10	.05
121	John Martin	.10	.05
122	Silvio Martinez	.10	.05
123	Ken Oberkfell	.10	.05
124	Darrell Porter	.20	.09
125	Mike Ramsey	.10	.05
126	Orlando Sanchez	.10	.05
127	Bob Shirley	.10	.05
128	Lary Sorensen	.10	.05
129	Bruce Sutter	.20	.09
130	Bob Sykes	.10	.05
131	Garry Templeton	.10	.05
132	Gene Tenace	.20	.09
133	Jerry Augustine	.10	.05
134	Sal Bando	.20	.09
135	Mark Brouhard	.10	.05
136	Mike Caldwell	.10	.05
137	Reggie Cleveland	.10	.05
138	Cecil Cooper	.20	.09
139	Jamie Easterly	.10	.05
140	Marshall Edwards	.10	.05
141	Rollie Fingers	.75	.35
142	Jim Gantner	.20	.09
143	Moose Haas	.10	.05
144	Larry Hisle	.10	.05
145	Roy Howell	.10	.05
146	Rickey Keeton	.10	.05
147	Randy Lerch	.10	.05
148	Paul Molitor	1.00	.45
149	Don Money	.10	.05
150	Charlie Moore	.10	.05
151	Ben Oglivie	.20	.09
152	Ted Simmons	.20	.09
153	Jim Slaton	.10	.05
154	Gorman Thomas	.20	.09
155	Robin Yount	.75	.35
156	Pete Vuckovich	.10	.05
	(Should precede Yount in the team order)		
157	Benny Ayala	.10	.05
158	Mark Belanger	.10	.05
159	Al Bumbry	.10	.05
160	Terry Crowley	.10	.05
161	Rich Dauer	.10	.05
162	Doug DeCinces	.20	.09
163	Rick Dempsey	.20	.09
164	Jim Dwyer	.10	.05
165	Mike Flanagan	.20	.09
166	Dave Ford	.10	.05
167	Dan Graham	.10	.05
168	Wayne Krenchicki	.10	.05
169	John Lowenstein	.10	.05
170	Dennis Martinez	.40	.18
171	Tippy Martinez	.10	.05
172	Scott McGregor	.10	.05
173	Jose Morales	.10	.05
174	Eddie Murray	1.00	.45
175	Jim Palmer	.75	.35
176	Cal Ripken	40.00	18.00
	(Fleer Ripken cards from 1982 through 1993 erroneously have 22 games played in 1981; not 23.)		
177	Gary Roenicke	.10	.05
178	Lenn Sakata	.10	.05
179	Ken Singleton	.20	.09
180	Sammy Stewart	.10	.05
181	Tim Stoddard	.10	.05
182	Steve Stone	.20	.09
183	Stan Harman	.10	.05
184	Ray Burris	.10	.05
185	Gary Carter	.75	.35
186	Warren Cromartie	.10	.05
187	Andre Dawson	.75	.35
188	Terry Francona	.40	.18
189	Woodie Fryman	.10	.05
190	Bill Gullickson	.20	.09
191	Grant Jackson	.10	.05
192	Wallace Johnson	.10	.05
193	Charlie Lea	.10	.05
194	Bill Lee	.20	.09
195	Jerry Manuel	.10	.05
196	Brad Mills	.10	.05
197	John Milner	.10	.05
198	Rowland Office	.10	.05
199	David Palmer	.10	.05
200	Larry Parrish	.10	.05
201	Mike Phillips	.10	.05
202	Tim Raines	.75	.35
203	Bobby Ramos	.10	.05
204	Jeff Reardon	.40	.18
205	Steve Rogers	.10	.05
206	Scott Sanderson	.10	.05
207	Rodney Scott UER	.40	.18
	(Photo actually Tim Raines)		
208	Elias Sosa	.10	.05
209	Chris Speier	.10	.05
210	Tim Wallach	.40	.18
211	Jerry White	.10	.05
212	Alan Ashby	.10	.05
213	Cesar Cedeno	.20	.09
214	Jose Cruz	.20	.09
215	Kiko Garcia	.10	.05
216	Phil Garner	.20	.09
217	Danny Heep	.10	.05
218	Art Howe	.20	.09
219	Bob Knepper	.10	.05
220	Frank LaCorte	.10	.05
221	Joe Niekro	.20	.09
222	Joe Pittman	.10	.05
223	Terry Puhl	.10	.05
224	Luis Pujols	.10	.05
225	Craig Reynolds	.10	.05
226	J.R. Richard	.20	.09
227	Dave Roberts	.10	.05
228	Vern Ruhle	.10	.05
229	Nolan Ryan	5.00	2.20
230	Joe Sambito	.10	.05
231	Tony Scott	.10	.05
232	Dave Smith	.10	.05
233	Harry Spilman	.10	.05
234	Don Sutton	.75	.35
235	Dickie Thon	.10	.05
236	Denny Walling	.10	.05
237	Gary Woods	.10	.05
238	Luis Aguayo	.10	.05
239	Ramon Aviles	.10	.05
240	Bob Boone	.20	.09
241	Larry Bowa	.20	.09
242	Warren Brusstar	.10	.05
243	Steve Carlton	.75	.35
244	Larry Christenson	.10	.05
245	Dick Davis	.10	.05
246	Greg Gross	.10	.05
247	Sparky Lyle	.20	.09
248	Garry Maddox	.10	.05
249	Gary Matthews	.20	.09
250	Bake McBride	.10	.05
251	Tug McGraw	.20	.09
252	Keith Moreland	.10	.05
253	Dickie Noles	.10	.05
254	Mike Proly	.10	.05
255	Ron Reed	.10	.05
256	Pete Rose	1.50	.70
257	Dick Ruthven	.10	.05
258	Mike Schmidt	1.25	.55
259	Lonnie Smith	.20	.09
260	Manny Trillo	.10	.05
261	Del Unser	.10	.05
262	George Vukovich	.10	.05
263	Tom Brookens	.10	.05
264	George Cappuzzello	.10	.05
265	Marty Castillo	.10	.05
266	Al Cowens	.10	.05
267	Kirk Gibson	.75	.35
268	Richie Hebner	.20	.09
269	Ron Jackson	.10	.05
270	Lynn Jones	.10	.05
271	Steve Kemp	.10	.05
272	Rick Leach	.10	.05
273	Aurelio Lopez	.10	.05
274	Jack Morris	.10	.05
275	Kevin Saucier	.10	.05
276	Lance Parrish	.40	.18
277	Rick Peters	.10	.05
278	Dan Petry	.10	.05
279	Dave Rozema	.10	.05
280	Stan Papi	.10	.05
281	Dan Schatzeder	.10	.05
282	Champ Summers	.10	.05
283	Alan Trammell	.75	.35
284	Lou Whitaker	.75	.35
285	Milt Wilcox	.10	.05
286	John Wockenfuss	.10	.05
287	Gary Allenson	.10	.05
288	Tom Burgmeier	.10	.05
289	Bill Campbell	.10	.05
290	Mark Clear	.10	.05
291	Steve Crawford	.10	.05
292	Dennis Eckersley	.75	.35
293	Dwight Evans	.40	.18
294	Rich Gedman	.10	.05
295	Gary Hancock	.10	.05
296	Glenn Hoffman	.10	.05
297	Bruce Hurst	.10	.05

298	Carney Lansford	.20	.09
299	Rick Miller	.10	.05
300	Reid Nichols	.10	.05
301	Bob Ojeda	.40	.18
302	Tony Perez	.75	.35
303	Chuck Rainey	.10	.05
304	Jerry Remy	.10	.05
305	Jim Rice	.20	.09
306	Joe Rudi	.10	.05
307	Bob Stanley	.10	.05
308	Dave Stapleton	.10	.05
309	Frank Tanana	.20	.09
310	Mike Torrez	.10	.05
311	John Tudor	.10	.05
312	Carl Yastrzemski	.75	.35
313	Buddy Bell	.20	.09
314	Steve Comer	.10	.05
315	Danny Darwin	.10	.05
316	John Ellis	.10	.05
317	John Grubb	.10	.05
318	Rick Honeycutt	.10	.05
319	Charlie Hough	.20	.09
320	Ferguson Jenkins	.75	.35
321	John Henry Johnson	.10	.05
322	Jim Kern	.10	.05
323	Jon Matlack	.10	.05
324	Doc Medich	.10	.05
325	Mario Mendoza	.10	.05
326	Al Oliver	.20	.09
327	Pat Putnam	.10	.05
328	Mickey Rivers	.10	.05
329	Leon Roberts	.10	.05
330	Billy Sample	.10	.05
331	Bill Stein	.10	.05
332	Jim Sundberg	.10	.05
333	Mark Wagner	.10	.05
334	Bump Wills	.10	.05
335	Bill Almon	.10	.05
336	Harold Baines	.75	.35
337	Ross Baumgarten	.10	.05
338	Tony Bernazard	.10	.05
339	Britt Burns	.10	.05
340	Richard Dotson	.10	.05
341	Jim Essian	.10	.05
342	Ed Farmer	.10	.05
343	Carlton Fisk	.75	.35
344	Kevin Hickey	.10	.05
345	LaMarr Hoyt	.10	.05
346	Lamar Johnson	.10	.05
347	Jerry Koosman	.20	.09
348	Rusty Kuntz	.10	.05
349	Dennis Lamp	.10	.05
350	Ron LeFlore	.20	.09
351	Chet Lemon	.20	.09
352	Greg Luzinski	.20	.09
353	Bob Molinaro	.10	.05
354	Jim Morrison	.10	.05
355	Wayne Nordhagen	.10	.05
356	Greg Pryor	.10	.05
357	Mike Squires	.10	.05
358	Steve Trout	.10	.05
359	Alan Bannister	.10	.05
360	Len Barker	.10	.05
361	Bert Blyleven	.40	.18
362	Joe Charboneau	.20	.09
363	John Denny	.10	.05
364	Bo Diaz	.10	.05
365	Miguel Dilone	.10	.05
366	Jerry Dybzinski	.10	.05
367	Wayne Garland	.10	.05
368	Mike Hargrove	.20	.09
369	Toby Harrah	.20	.09
370	Ron Hassey	.10	.05
371	Von Hayes	.20	.09
372	Pat Kelly	.10	.05
373	Duane Kuiper	.10	.05
374	Rick Manning	.10	.05
375	Sid Monge	.10	.05
376	Jorge Orta	.10	.05
377	Dave Rosello	.10	.05
378	Dan Spillner	.10	.05
379	Mike Stanton	.10	.05
380	Andre Thornton	.10	.05
381	Tom Veryzer	.10	.05
382	Rick Waits	.10	.05
383	Doyle Alexander	.10	.05
384	Vida Blue	.20	.09
385	Fred Breining	.10	.05
386	Enos Cabell	.10	.05
387	Jack Clark	.20	.09
388	Darrell Evans	.20	.09
389	Tom Griffin	.10	.05
390	Larry Herndon	.10	.05
391	Al Holland	.10	.05
392	Gary Lavelle	.10	.05
393	Johnnie LeMaster	.10	.05
394	Jerry Martin	.10	.05
395	Milt May	.10	.05
396	Greg Minton	.10	.05
397	Joe Morgan	.75	.35
398	Joe Pettini	.10	.05
399	Allen Ripley	.10	.05
400	Billy Smith	.10	.05
401	Rennie Stennett	.10	.05
402	Ed Whitson	.10	.05
403	Jim Wohlford	.10	.05
404	Willie Aikens	.10	.05
405	George Brett	1.50	.70
406	Ken Brett	.10	.05
407	Dave Chalk	.10	.05
408	Rich Gale	.10	.05
409	Cesar Geronimo	.10	.05
410	Larry Gura	.10	.05
411	Clint Hurdle	.10	.05
412	Mike Jones	.10	.05
413	Dennis Leonard	.10	.05
414	Renie Martin	.10	.05
415	Lee May	.20	.09
416	Hal McRae	.20	.09
417	Darryl Motley	.10	.05
418	Rance Mulliniks	.10	.05
419	Amos Otis	.20	.09
420	Ken Phelps	.10	.05
421	Jamie Quirk	.10	.05
422	Dan Quisenberry	.20	.09
423	Paul Splittorff	.10	.05
424	U.L. Washington	.10	.05
425	John Wathan	.10	.05
426	Frank White	.20	.09
427	Willie Wilson	.20	.09
428	Brian Asselstine	.10	.05
429	Bruce Benedict	.10	.05
430	Tommy Boggs	.10	.05
431	Larry Bradford	.10	.05
432	Rick Camp	.10	.05
433	Chris Chambliss	.20	.09
434	Gene Garber	.10	.05
435	Preston Hanna	.10	.05
436	Bob Horner	.20	.09
437	Glenn Hubbard	.10	.05
438A	Al Hrabosky ERR (Height 5'1") All on reverse)	8.00	3.60
438B	Al Hrabosky ERR (Height 5'1")	.40	.18
438C	Al Hrabosky (Height 5'10")	.20	.09
439	Rufino Linares	.10	.05
440	Rick Mahler	.10	.05
441	Ed Miller	.10	.05
442	John Montefusco	.10	.05
443	Dale Murphy	.75	.35
444	Phil Niekro	.75	.35
445	Gaylord Perry	.75	.35
446	Biff Pocoroba	.10	.05
447	Rafael Ramirez	.10	.05
448	Jerry Royster	.10	.05
449	Claudell Washington	.10	.05
450	Don Aase	.10	.05
451	Don Baylor	.40	.18
452	Juan Beniquez	.10	.05
453	Rick Burleson	.10	.05
454	Bert Campaneris	.20	.09
455	Rod Carew	.75	.35
456	Bob Clark	.10	.05
457	Brian Downing	.10	.05
458	Dan Ford	.10	.05
459	Ken Forsch	.10	.05
460A	Dave Frost (5 mm space before ERA)	.10	.05
460B	Dave Frost (1 mm space)	.10	.05
461	Bobby Grich	.20	.09
462	Larry Harlow	.10	.05
463	John Harris	.10	.05
464	Andy Hassler	.10	.05
465	Butch Hobson	.10	.05
466	Jesse Jefferson	.10	.05
467	Bruce Kison	.10	.05
468	Fred Lynn	.20	.09
469	Angel Moreno	.10	.05
470	Ed Ott	.10	.05
471	Fred Patek	.10	.05
472	Steve Renko	.10	.05
473	Mike Witt	.20	.09
474	Geoff Zahn	.10	.05
475	Gary Alexander	.10	.05
476	Dale Berra	.10	.05
477	Kurt Bevacqua	.10	.05
478	Jim Bibby	.10	.05
479	John Candelaria	.10	.05
480	Victor Cruz	.10	.05
481	Mike Easler	.10	.05
482	Tim Foli	.10	.05
483	Lee Lacy	.10	.05
484	Vance Law	.10	.05
485	Bill Madlock	.20	.09
486	Willie Montanez	.10	.05
487	Omar Moreno	.10	.05
488	Steve Nicosia	.10	.05
489	Dave Parker	.20	.09
490	Tony Pena	.20	.09
491	Pascual Perez	.20	.09
492	Johnny Ray	.20	.09
493	Rick Rhoden	.10	.05
494	Bill Robinson	.10	.05
495	Don Robinson	.10	.05
496	Enrique Romo	.10	.05
497	Rod Scurry	.10	.05
498	Eddie Solomon	.10	.05
499	Willie Stargell	.75	.35
500	Kent Tekulve	.20	.09
501	Jason Thompson	.10	.05
502	Glenn Abbott	.10	.05
503	Jim Anderson	.10	.05
504	Floyd Bannister	.10	.05
505	Bruce Bochte	.10	.05
506	Jeff Burroughs	.10	.05
507	Bryan Clark	.10	.05
508	Ken Clay	.10	.05
509	Julio Cruz	.10	.05
510	Dick Drago	.10	.05
511	Gary Gray	.10	.05
512	Dan Meyer	.10	.05
513	Jerry Narron	.10	.05
514	Tom Paciorek	.20	.09
515	Casey Parsons	.10	.05
516	Lenny Randle	.10	.05
517	Shane Rawley	.10	.05
518	Joe Simpson	.10	.05
519	Richie Zisk	.10	.05
520	Neil Allen	.10	.05
521	Bob Bailor	.10	.05
522	Hubie Brooks	.20	.09
523	Mike Cubbage	.10	.05
524	Pete Falcone	.10	.05
525	Doug Flynn	.10	.05
526	Tom Hausman	.10	.05
527	Ron Hodges	.10	.05
528	Randy Jones	.10	.05
529	Mike Jorgensen	.10	.05
530	Dave Kingman	.20	.09
531	Ed Lynch	.10	.05
532	Mike G. Marshall	.10	.05
533	Lee Mazzilli	.10	.05
534	Dyar Miller	.10	.05
535	Mike Scott	.20	.09
536	Rusty Staub	.20	.09
537	John Stearns	.10	.05
538	Craig Swan	.10	.05
539	Frank Taveras	.10	.05
540	Alex Trevino	.10	.05
541	Ellis Valentine	.10	.05
542	Mookie Wilson	.20	.09
543	Joel Youngblood	.10	.05
544	Pat Zachry	.10	.05
545	Glenn Adams	.10	.05
546	Fernando Arroyo	.10	.05

❑ 547 John Verhoeven	.10	.05
❑ 548 Sal Butera	.10	.05
❑ 549 John Castino	.10	.05
❑ 550 Don Cooper	.10	.05
❑ 551 Doug Corbett	.10	.05
❑ 552 Dave Engle	.10	.05
❑ 553 Roger Erickson	.10	.05
❑ 554 Danny Goodwin	.10	.05
❑ 555A Darrell Jackson	.40	.18
(Black cap)		
❑ 555B Darrell Jackson	.20	.09
(Red cap with T)		
❑ 555C Darrell Jackson	3.00	1.35
(Red cap, no emblem)		
❑ 556 Pete Mackanin	.10	.05
❑ 557 Jack O'Connor	.10	.05
❑ 558 Hosken Powell	.10	.05
❑ 559 Pete Redfern	.10	.05
❑ 560 Roy Smalley	.10	.05
❑ 561 Chuck Baker UER	.10	.05
(Shortshop on front)		
❑ 562 Gary Ward	.10	.05
❑ 563 Rob Wilfong	.10	.05
❑ 564 Al Williams	.10	.05
❑ 565 Butch Wynegar	.10	.05
❑ 566 Randy Bass	.10	.05
❑ 567 Juan Bonilla	.10	.05
❑ 568 Danny Boone	.10	.05
❑ 569 John Curtis	.10	.05
❑ 570 Juan Eichelberger	.10	.05
❑ 571 Barry Evans	.10	.05
❑ 572 Tim Flannery	.10	.05
❑ 573 Ruppert Jones	.10	.05
❑ 574 Terry Kennedy	.10	.05
❑ 575 Joe Lefebvre	.10	.05
❑ 576A John Littlefield ERR	80.00	36.00
(Left handed;		
reverse negative)		
❑ 576B John Littlefield COR	.20	.09
(Right handed)		
❑ 577 Gary Lucas	.10	.05
❑ 578 Steve Mura	.10	.05
❑ 579 Broderick Perkins	.10	.05
❑ 580 Gene Richards	.10	.05
❑ 581 Luis Salazar	.10	.05
❑ 582 Ozzie Smith	1.50	.70
❑ 583 John Urrea	.10	.05
❑ 584 Chris Welsh	.10	.05
❑ 585 Rick Wise	.10	.05
❑ 586 Doug Bird	.10	.05
❑ 587 Tim Blackwell	.10	.05
❑ 588 Bobby Bonds	.20	.09
❑ 589 Bill Buckner	.20	.09
❑ 590 Bill Caudill	.10	.05
❑ 591 Hector Cruz	.10	.05
❑ 592 Jody Davis	.10	.05
❑ 593 Ivan DeJesus	.10	.05
❑ 594 Steve Dillard	.10	.05
❑ 595 Leon Durham	.10	.05
❑ 596 Rawly Eastwick	.10	.05
❑ 597 Steve Henderson	.10	.05
❑ 598 Mike Krukow	.10	.05
❑ 599 Mike Lum	.10	.05
❑ 600 Randy Martz	.10	.05
❑ 601 Jerry Morales	.10	.05
❑ 602 Ken Reitz	.10	.05
❑ 603 Lee Smith ERR	2.00	.90
(Cubs logo reversed)		
❑ 603B Lee Smith COR	2.50	1.10
❑ 604 Dick Tidrow	.10	.05
❑ 605 Jim Tracy	.10	.05
❑ 606 Mike Tyson	.10	.05
❑ 607 Ty Waller	.10	.05
❑ 608 Danny Ainge	1.00	.45
❑ 609 Jorge Bell	.75	.35
❑ 610 Mark Bomback	.10	.05
❑ 611 Barry Bonnell	.10	.05
❑ 612 Jim Clancy	.10	.05
❑ 613 Damaso Garcia	.10	.05
❑ 614 Jerry Garvin	.10	.05
❑ 615 Alfredo Griffin	.10	.05
❑ 616 Garth Iorg	.10	.05
❑ 617 Luis Leal	.10	.05
❑ 618 Ken Macha	.10	.05
❑ 619 Jim Mayberry	.10	.05
❑ 620 Joey McLaughlin	.10	.05

❑ 621 Lloyd Moseby	.10	.05
❑ 622 Dave Stieb	.20	.09
❑ 623 Jackson Todd	.10	.05
❑ 624 Willie Upshaw	.10	.05
❑ 625 Otto Velez	.10	.05
❑ 626 Ernie Whitt	.10	.05
❑ 627 Alvis Woods	.10	.05
❑ 628 All Star Game	.20	.09
Cleveland, Ohio		
❑ 629 All Star Infielders	.20	.09
Frank White		
Bucky Dent		
❑ 630 Big Red Machine	.20	.09
Dan Driessen		
Dave Concepcion		
George Foster		
❑ 631 Bruce Sutter	.10	.05
Top NL Relief Pitcher		
❑ 632 Steve and Carlton	.40	.18
Steve Carlton		
Carlton Fisk		
❑ 633 Carl Yastrzemski	.75	.35
3000th Game		
❑ 634 Dynamic Duo	1.00	.45
Johnny Bench		
Tom Seaver		
❑ 635 West Meets East	.20	.09
Fernando Valenzuela		
Gary Carter		
❑ 636A Fernando Valenzuela:	.75	.35
NL SO King ("he" NL)		
❑ 636B Fernando Valenzuela:	.75	.35
NL SO King ("the" NL)		
❑ 637 Mike Schmidt	.40	.18
Home Run King		
❑ 638 NL All Stars	.20	.09
Gary Carter		
Dave Parker		
❑ 639 Perfect Game UER	.20	.09
Len Barker		
Bo Diaz		
(Catcher actually		
Ron Hassey)		
❑ 640 Pete and Re-Pete	.75	.35
Pete Rose		
Pete Rose Jr.		
❑ 641 Phillies Finest	.75	.35
Lonnie Smith		
Mike Schmidt		
Steve Carlton		
❑ 642 Red Sox Reunion	.20	.09
Fred Lynn		
Dwight Evans		
❑ 643 Rickey Henderson	1.00	.45
Most Hits and Runs		
❑ 644 Rollie Fingers	.20	.09
Most Saves AL		
❑ 645 Tom Seaver	.40	.18
Most 1981 Wins		
❑ 646 Yankee Powerhouse	.75	.35
Reggie Jackson		
Dave Winfield		
(Comma on back		
after outfielder")		
❑ 646B Yankee Powerhouse..	2.00	.90
Reggie Jackson		
Dave Winfield		
(No comma)		
❑ 647 CL: Yankees/Dodgers	.10	.05
❑ 648 CL: A's/Reds	.10	.05
❑ 649 CL: Cards/Brewers	.10	.05
❑ 650 CL: Expos/Orioles	.10	.05
❑ 651 CL: Astros/Phillies	.10	.05
❑ 652 CL: Tigers/Red Sox	.10	.05
❑ 653 CL: Rangers/White Sox	.10	.05
❑ 654 CL: Giants/Indians	.10	.05
❑ 655 CL: Royals/Braves	.10	.05
❑ 656 CL: Angels/Pirates	.10	.05
❑ 657 CL: Mariners/Mets	.10	.05
❑ 658 CL: Padres/Twins	.10	.05
❑ 659 CL: Blue Jays/Cubs	.10	.05
❑ 660 Specials Checklist	.10	.05

1983 Fleer

	NRMT	VG-E
COMPLETE SET (660)	80.00	36.00

COMMON CARD (1-660)	.10	.05
MINOR STARS	.20	.09
SEMISTARS	.40	.18
UNLISTED STARS	.75	.35
❑ 1 Joaquin Andujar	.10	.05
❑ 2 Doug Bair	.10	.05
❑ 3 Steve Braun	.10	.05
❑ 4 Glenn Brummer	.10	.05
❑ 5 Bob Forsch	.10	.05
❑ 6 David Green	.10	.05
❑ 7 George Hendrick	.10	.05
❑ 8 Keith Hernandez	.20	.09
❑ 9 Tom Herr	.20	.09
❑ 10 Dane Iorg	.10	.05
❑ 11 Jim Kaat	.20	.09
❑ 12 Jeff Lahti	.10	.05
❑ 13 Tito Landrum	.10	.05
❑ 14 Dave LaPoint	.10	.05
❑ 15 Willie McGee	1.50	.70
❑ 16 Steve Mura	.10	.05
❑ 17 Ken Oberkfell	.10	.05
❑ 18 Darrell Porter	.10	.05
❑ 19 Mike Ramsey	.10	.05
❑ 20 Gene Roof	.10	.05
❑ 21 Lonnie Smith	.10	.05
❑ 22 Ozzie Smith	1.25	.55
❑ 23 John Stuper	.10	.05
❑ 24 Bruce Sutter	.20	.09
❑ 25 Gene Tenace	.20	.09
❑ 26 Jerry Augustine	.10	.05
❑ 27 Dwight Bernard	.10	.05
❑ 28 Mark Brouhard	.10	.05
❑ 29 Mike Caldwell	.10	.05
❑ 30 Cecil Cooper	.20	.09
❑ 31 Jamie Easterly	.10	.05
❑ 32 Marshall Edwards	.10	.05
❑ 33 Rollie Fingers	.75	.35
❑ 34 Jim Gantner	.10	.05
❑ 35 Moose Haas	.10	.05
❑ 36 Roy Howell	.10	.05
❑ 37 Pete Ladd	.10	.05
❑ 38 Bob McClure	.10	.05
❑ 39 Doc Medich	.10	.05
❑ 40 Paul Molitor	1.00	.45
❑ 41 Don Money	.10	.05
❑ 42 Charlie Moore	.10	.05
❑ 43 Ben Oglivie	.10	.05
❑ 44 Ed Romero	.10	.05
❑ 45 Ted Simmons	.20	.09
❑ 46 Jim Slaton	.10	.05
❑ 47 Don Sutton	.75	.35
❑ 48 Gorman Thomas	.10	.05
❑ 49 Pete Vuckovich	.10	.05
❑ 50 Ned Yost	.10	.05
❑ 51 Robin Yount	.75	.35
❑ 52 Benny Ayala	.10	.05
❑ 53 Bob Bonner	.10	.05
❑ 54 Al Bumbry	.10	.05
❑ 55 Terry Crowley	.10	.05
❑ 56 Storm Davis	.10	.05
❑ 57 Rich Dauer	.10	.05
❑ 58 Rick Dempsey UER	.20	.09
(Posing batting lefty)		
❑ 59 Jim Dwyer	.10	.05
❑ 60 Mike Flanagan	.10	.05
❑ 61 Dan Ford	.10	.05
❑ 62 Glenn Gulliver	.10	.05
❑ 63 John Lowenstein	.10	.05
❑ 64 Dennis Martinez	.20	.09
❑ 65 Tippy Martinez	.10	.05
❑ 66 Scott McGregor	.10	.05
❑ 67 Eddie Murray	1.00	.45
❑ 68 Joe Nolan	.10	.05
❑ 69 Jim Palmer	.75	.35
❑ 70 Cal Ripken	8.00	3.60
❑ 71 Gary Roenicke	.10	.05
❑ 72 Lenn Sakata	.10	.05
❑ 73 Ken Singleton	.10	.05
❑ 74 Sammy Stewart	.10	.05
❑ 75 Tim Stoddard	.10	.05
❑ 76 Don Aase	.10	.05
❑ 77 Don Baylor	.40	.18
❑ 78 Juan Beniquez	.10	.05
❑ 79 Bob Boone	.20	.09
❑ 80 Rick Burleson	.10	.05

❏ 81	Rod Carew	.75	.35
❏ 82	Bobby Clark	.10	.05
❏ 83	Doug Corbett	.10	.05
❏ 84	John Curtis	.10	.05
❏ 85	Doug DeCinces	.20	.09
❏ 86	Brian Downing	.10	.05
❏ 87	Joe Ferguson	.10	.05
❏ 88	Tim Foli	.10	.05
❏ 89	Ken Forsch	.10	.05
❏ 90	Dave Goltz	.10	.05
❏ 91	Bobby Grich	.20	.09
❏ 92	Andy Hassler	.10	.05
❏ 93	Reggie Jackson	1.00	.45
❏ 94	Ron Jackson	.10	.05
❏ 95	Tommy John	.40	.18
❏ 96	Bruce Kison	.10	.05
❏ 97	Fred Lynn	.20	.09
❏ 98	Ed Ott	.10	.05
❏ 99	Steve Renko	.10	.05
❏ 100	Luis Sanchez	.10	.05
❏ 101	Rob Wilfong	.10	.05
❏ 102	Mike Witt	.10	.05
❏ 103	Geoff Zahn	.10	.05
❏ 104	Willie Aikens	.10	.05
❏ 105	Mike Armstrong	.10	.05
❏ 106	Vida Blue	.20	.09
❏ 107	Bud Black	.20	.09
❏ 108	George Brett	1.50	.70
❏ 109	Bill Castro	.10	.05
❏ 110	Onix Concepcion	.10	.05
❏ 111	Dave Frost	.10	.05
❏ 112	Cesar Geronimo	.10	.05
❏ 113	Larry Gura	.10	.05
❏ 114	Steve Hammond	.10	.05
❏ 115	Don Hood	.10	.05
❏ 116	Dennis Leonard	.10	.05
❏ 117	Jerry Martin	.10	.05
❏ 118	Lee May	.20	.09
❏ 119	Hal McRae	.20	.09
❏ 120	Amos Otis	.20	.09
❏ 121	Greg Pryor	.10	.05
❏ 122	Dan Quisenberry	.20	.09
❏ 123	Don Slaught	.40	.18
❏ 124	Paul Splittorff	.10	.05
❏ 125	U.L. Washington	.10	.05
❏ 126	John Wathan	.10	.05
❏ 127	Frank White	.20	.09
❏ 128	Willie Wilson	.20	.09
❏ 129	Steve Bedrosian UER	.20	.09
	(Height 6'33")		
❏ 130	Bruce Benedict	.10	.05
❏ 131	Tommy Boggs	.10	.05
❏ 132	Brett Butler	.75	.35
❏ 133	Rick Camp	.10	.05
❏ 134	Chris Chambliss	.20	.09
❏ 135	Ken Dayley	.10	.05
❏ 136	Gene Garber	.10	.05
❏ 137	Terry Harper	.10	.05
❏ 138	Bob Horner	.10	.05
❏ 139	Glenn Hubbard	.10	.05
❏ 140	Rufino Linares	.10	.05
❏ 141	Rick Mahler	.10	.05
❏ 142	Dale Murphy	.75	.35
❏ 143	Phil Niekro	.75	.35
❏ 144	Pascual Perez	.10	.05
❏ 145	Biff Pocoroba	.10	.05
❏ 146	Rafael Ramirez	.10	.05
❏ 147	Jerry Royster	.10	.05
❏ 148	Ken Smith	.10	.05
❏ 149	Bob Walk	.10	.05
❏ 150	Claudell Washington	.10	.05
❏ 151	Bob Watson	.20	.09
❏ 152	Larry Whisenton	.10	.05
❏ 153	Porfirio Altamirano	.10	.05
❏ 154	Marty Bystrom	.10	.05
❏ 155	Steve Carlton	.75	.35
❏ 156	Larry Christenson	.10	.05
❏ 157	Ivan DeJesus	.10	.05
❏ 158	John Denny	.10	.05
❏ 159	Bob Dernier	.10	.05
❏ 160	Bo Diaz	.10	.05
❏ 161	Ed Farmer	.10	.05
❏ 162	Greg Gross	.10	.05
❏ 163	Mike Krukow	.10	.05
❏ 164	Garry Maddox	.10	.05
❏ 165	Gary Matthews	.20	.09
❏ 166	Tug McGraw	.20	.09
❏ 167	Bob Molinaro	.10	.05
❏ 168	Sid Monge	.10	.05
❏ 169	Ron Reed	.10	.05
❏ 170	Bill Robinson	.10	.05
❏ 171	Pete Rose	1.25	.55
❏ 172	Dick Ruthven	.10	.05
❏ 173	Mike Schmidt	1.25	.55
❏ 174	Manny Trillo	.10	.05
❏ 175	Ozzie Virgil	.10	.05
❏ 176	George Vukovich	.10	.05
❏ 177	Gary Allenson	.10	.05
❏ 178	Luis Aponte	.10	.05
❏ 179	Wade Boggs	12.00	5.50
❏ 180	Tom Burgmeier	.10	.05
❏ 181	Mark Clear	.10	.05
❏ 182	Dennis Eckersley	.75	.35
❏ 183	Dwight Evans	.20	.09
❏ 184	Rich Gedman	.10	.05
❏ 185	Glenn Hoffman	.10	.05
❏ 186	Bruce Hurst	.10	.05
❏ 187	Carney Lansford	.20	.09
❏ 188	Rick Miller	.10	.05
❏ 189	Reid Nichols	.10	.05
❏ 190	Bob Ojeda	.10	.05
❏ 191	Tony Perez	.75	.35
❏ 192	Chuck Rainey	.10	.05
❏ 193	Jerry Remy	.10	.05
❏ 194	Jim Rice	.20	.09
❏ 195	Bob Stanley	.10	.05
❏ 196	Dave Stapleton	.10	.05
❏ 197	Mike Torrez	.10	.05
❏ 198	John Tudor	.10	.05
❏ 199	Julio Valdez	.10	.05
❏ 200	Carl Yastrzemski	.75	.35
❏ 201	Dusty Baker	.20	.09
❏ 202	Joe Beckwith	.10	.05
❏ 203	Greg Brock	.10	.05
❏ 204	Ron Cey	.20	.09
❏ 205	Terry Forster	.10	.05
❏ 206	Steve Garvey	.40	.18
❏ 207	Pedro Guerrero	.20	.09
❏ 208	Burt Hooton	.10	.05
❏ 209	Steve Howe	.10	.05
❏ 210	Ken Landreaux	.10	.05
❏ 211	Mike Marshall	.10	.05
❏ 212	Candy Maldonado	.20	.09
❏ 213	Rick Monday	.10	.05
❏ 214	Tom Niedenfuer	.10	.05
❏ 215	Jorge Orta	.10	.05
❏ 216	Jerry Reuss UER	.20	.09
	("Home:" omitted)		
❏ 217	Ron Roenicke	.10	.05
❏ 218	Vicente Romo	.10	.05
❏ 219	Bill Russell	.10	.05
❏ 220	Steve Sax	.20	.09
❏ 221	Mike Scioscia	.20	.09
❏ 222	Dave Stewart	.20	.09
❏ 223	Derrel Thomas	.10	.05
❏ 224	Fernando Valenzuela	.40	.18
❏ 225	Bob Welch	.20	.09
❏ 226	Ricky Wright	.10	.05
❏ 227	Steve Yeager	.10	.05
❏ 228	Bill Almon	.10	.05
❏ 229	Harold Baines	.75	.35
❏ 230	Salome Barojas	.10	.05
❏ 231	Tony Bernazard	.10	.05
❏ 232	Britt Burns	.10	.05
❏ 233	Richard Dotson	.10	.05
❏ 234	Ernesto Escarrega	.10	.05
❏ 235	Carlton Fisk	.75	.35
❏ 236	Jerry Hairston	.10	.05
❏ 237	Kevin Hickey	.10	.05
❏ 238	LaMarr Hoyt	.20	.09
❏ 239	Steve Kemp	.10	.05
❏ 240	Jim Kern	.10	.05
❏ 241	Ron Kittle	.40	.18
❏ 242	Jerry Koosman	.20	.09
❏ 243	Dennis Lamp	.10	.05
❏ 244	Rudy Law	.10	.05
❏ 245	Vance Law	.10	.05
❏ 246	Ron LeFlore	.10	.05
❏ 247	Greg Luzinski	.20	.09
❏ 248	Tom Paciorek	.20	.09
❏ 249	Aurelio Rodriguez	.10	.05
❏ 250	Mike Squires	.10	.05
❏ 251	Steve Trout	.10	.05
❏ 252	Jim Barr	.10	.05
❏ 253	Dave Bergman	.10	.05
❏ 254	Fred Breining	.10	.05
❏ 255	Bob Brenly	.10	.05
❏ 256	Jack Clark	.20	.09
❏ 257	Chili Davis	.75	.35
❏ 258	Darrell Evans	.20	.09
❏ 259	Alan Fowlkes	.10	.05
❏ 260	Rich Gale	.10	.05
❏ 261	Atlee Hammaker	.10	.05
❏ 262	Al Holland	.10	.05
❏ 263	Duane Kuiper	.10	.05
❏ 264	Bill Laskey	.10	.05
❏ 265	Gary Lavelle	.10	.05
❏ 266	Johnnie LeMaster	.10	.05
❏ 267	Renie Martin	.10	.05
❏ 268	Milt May	.10	.05
❏ 269	Greg Minton	.10	.05
❏ 270	Joe Morgan	.75	.35
❏ 271	Tom O'Malley	.10	.05
❏ 272	Reggie Smith	.20	.09
❏ 273	Guy Sularz	.10	.05
❏ 274	Champ Summers	.10	.05
❏ 275	Max Venable	.10	.05
❏ 276	Jim Wohlford	.10	.05
❏ 277	Ray Burris	.10	.05
❏ 278	Gary Carter	.75	.35
❏ 279	Warren Cromartie	.10	.05
❏ 280	Andre Dawson	.75	.35
❏ 281	Terry Francona	.10	.05
❏ 282	Doug Flynn	.10	.05
❏ 283	Woodie Fryman	.10	.05
❏ 284	Bill Gullickson	.20	.09
❏ 285	Wallace Johnson	.10	.05
❏ 286	Charlie Lea	.10	.05
❏ 287	Randy Lerch	.10	.05
❏ 288	Brad Mills	.10	.05
❏ 289	Dan Norman	.10	.05
❏ 290	Al Oliver	.20	.09
❏ 291	David Palmer	.10	.05
❏ 292	Tim Raines	.75	.35
❏ 293	Jeff Reardon	.20	.09
❏ 294	Steve Rogers	.10	.05
❏ 295	Scott Sanderson	.10	.05
❏ 296	Dan Schatzeder	.10	.05
❏ 297	Bryn Smith	.10	.05
❏ 298	Chris Speier	.10	.05
❏ 299	Tim Wallach	.20	.09
❏ 300	Jerry White	.10	.05
❏ 301	Joel Youngblood	.10	.05
❏ 302	Ross Baumgarten	.10	.05
❏ 303	Dale Berra	.10	.05
❏ 304	John Candelaria	.20	.09
❏ 305	Dick Davis	.10	.05
❏ 306	Mike Easler	.10	.05
❏ 307	Richie Hebner	.20	.09
❏ 308	Lee Lacy	.10	.05
❏ 309	Bill Madlock	.20	.09
❏ 310	Larry McWilliams	.10	.05
❏ 311	John Milner	.10	.05
❏ 312	Omar Moreno	.10	.05
❏ 313	Jim Morrison	.10	.05
❏ 314	Steve Nicosia	.10	.05
❏ 315	Dave Parker	.20	.09
❏ 316	Tony Pena	.10	.05
❏ 317	Johnny Ray	.10	.05
❏ 318	Rick Rhoden	.10	.05
❏ 319	Don Robinson	.10	.05
❏ 320	Enrique Romo	.10	.05
❏ 321	Manny Sarmiento	.10	.05
❏ 322	Rod Scurry	.10	.05
❏ 323	Jimmy Smith	.10	.05
❏ 324	Willie Stargell	.75	.35
❏ 325	Jason Thompson	.10	.05
❏ 326	Kent Tekulve	.20	.09
❏ 327A	Tom Brookens	.10	.05
	(Short .375" brown box shaded in on card back)		
❏ 327B	Tom Brookens	.10	.05
	(Longer 1.25" brown box shaded in on card back)		
❏ 328	Enos Cabell	.10	.05
❏ 329	Kirk Gibson	.75	.35
❏ 330	Larry Herndon	.10	.05
❏ 331	Mike Ivie	.10	.05

332	Howard Johnson	.75	.35
333	Lynn Jones	.10	.05
334	Rick Leach	.10	.05
335	Chet Lemon	.10	.05
336	Jack Morris	.20	.09
337	Lance Parrish	.20	.09
338	Larry Pashnick	.10	.05
339	Dan Petry	.10	.05
340	Dave Rozema	.10	.05
341	Dave Rucker	.10	.05
342	Elias Sosa	.10	.05
343	Dave Tobik	.10	.05
344	Alan Trammell	.75	.35
345	Jerry Turner	.10	.05
346	Jerry Ujdur	.10	.05
347	Pat Underwood	.10	.05
348	Lou Whitaker	.40	.18
349	Milt Wilcox	.10	.05
350	Glenn Wilson	.20	.09
351	John Wockenfuss	.10	.05
352	Kurt Bevacqua	.10	.05
353	Juan Bonilla	.10	.05
354	Floyd Chiffer	.10	.05
355	Luis DeLeon	.10	.05
356	Dave Dravecky	.75	.35
357	Dave Edwards	.10	.05
358	Juan Eichelberger	.10	.05
359	Tim Flannery	.10	.05
360	Tony Gwynn	30.00	13.50
361	Ruppert Jones	.10	.05
362	Terry Kennedy	.10	.05
363	Joe Lefebvre	.10	.05
364	Sixto Lezcano	.10	.05
365	Tim Lollar	.10	.05
366	Gary Lucas	.10	.05
367	John Montefusco	.10	.05
368	Broderick Perkins	.10	.05
369	Joe Pittman	.10	.05
370	Gene Richards	.10	.05
371	Luis Salazar	.10	.05
372	Eric Show	.10	.05
373	Garry Templeton	.10	.05
374	Chris Welsh	.10	.05
375	Alan Wiggins	.10	.05
376	Rick Cerone	.10	.05
377	Dave Collins	.10	.05
378	Roger Erickson	.10	.05
379	George Frazier	.10	.05
380	Oscar Gamble	.10	.05
381	Rich Gossage	.40	.18
382	Ken Griffey	.20	.09
383	Ron Guidry	.20	.09
384	Dave LaRoche	.10	.05
385	Rudy May	.10	.05
386	John Mayberry	.10	.05
387	Lee Mazzilli	.10	.05
388	Mike Morgan	.10	.05
389	Jerry Mumphrey	.10	.05
390	Bobby Murcer	.20	.09
391	Graig Nettles	.20	.09
392	Lou Piniella	.20	.09
393	Willie Randolph	.20	.09
394	Shane Rawley	.10	.05
395	Dave Righetti	.20	.09
396	Andre Robertson	.10	.05
397	Roy Smalley	.10	.05
398	Dave Winfield	.75	.35
399	Butch Wynegar	.10	.05
400	Chris Bando	.10	.05
401	Alan Bannister	.10	.05
402	Len Barker	.10	.05
403	Tom Brennan	.10	.05
404	Carmelo Castillo	.10	.05
405	Miguel Dilone	.10	.05
406	Jerry Dybzinski	.10	.05
407	Mike Fischlin	.10	.05
408	Ed Glynn UER (Photo actually Bud Anderson)	.10	.05
409	Mike Hargrove	.20	.09
410	Toby Harrah	.10	.05
411	Ron Hassey	.10	.05
412	Von Hayes	.20	.09
413	Rick Manning	.10	.05
414	Bake McBride	.10	.05
415	Larry Milbourne	.10	.05
416	Bill Nahorodny	.10	.05
417	Jack Perconte	.10	.05
418	Lary Sorensen	.10	.05
419	Dan Spillner	.10	.05
420	Rick Sutcliffe	.20	.09
421	Andre Thornton	.10	.05
422	Rick Waits	.10	.05
423	Eddie Whitson	.10	.05
424	Jesse Barfield	.20	.09
425	Barry Bonnell	.10	.05
426	Jim Clancy	.10	.05
427	Damaso Garcia	.10	.05
428	Jerry Garvin	.10	.05
429	Alfredo Griffin	.10	.05
430	Garth Iorg	.10	.05
431	Roy Lee Jackson	.10	.05
432	Luis Leal	.10	.05
433	Buck Martinez	.10	.05
434	Joey McLaughlin	.10	.05
435	Lloyd Moseby	.10	.05
436	Rance Mulliniks	.10	.05
437	Dale Murray	.10	.05
438	Wayne Nordhagen	.10	.05
439	Gene Petralli	.20	.09
440	Hosken Powell	.10	.05
441	Dave Stieb	.20	.09
442	Willie Upshaw	.10	.05
443	Ernie Whitt	.10	.05
444	Alvis Woods	.10	.05
445	Alan Ashby	.10	.05
446	Jose Cruz	.20	.09
447	Kiko Garcia	.10	.05
448	Phil Garner	.20	.09
449	Danny Heep	.10	.05
450	Art Howe	.20	.09
451	Bob Knepper	.10	.05
452	Alan Knicely	.10	.05
453	Ray Knight	.20	.09
454	Frank LaCorte	.10	.05
455	Mike LaCoss	.10	.05
456	Randy Moffitt	.10	.05
457	Joe Niekro	.20	.09
458	Terry Puhl	.10	.05
459	Luis Pujols	.10	.05
460	Craig Reynolds	.10	.05
461	Bert Roberge	.10	.05
462	Vern Ruhle	.10	.05
463	Nolan Ryan	4.00	1.80
464	Joe Sambito	.10	.05
465	Tony Scott	.10	.05
466	Dave Smith	.10	.05
467	Harry Spilman	.10	.05
468	Dickie Thon	.10	.05
469	Denny Walling	.10	.05
470	Larry Andersen	.10	.05
471	Floyd Bannister	.10	.05
472	Jim Beattie	.10	.05
473	Bruce Bochte	.10	.05
474	Manny Castillo	.10	.05
475	Bill Caudill	.10	.05
476	Bryan Clark	.10	.05
477	Al Cowens	.10	.05
478	Julio Cruz	.10	.05
479	Todd Cruz	.10	.05
480	Gary Gray	.10	.05
481	Dave Henderson	.20	.09
482	Mike Moore	.20	.09
483	Gaylord Perry	.75	.35
484	Dave Revering	.10	.05
485	Joe Simpson	.10	.05
486	Mike Stanton	.10	.05
487	Rick Sweet	.10	.05
488	Ed VandeBerg	.10	.05
489	Richie Zisk	.10	.05
490	Doug Bird	.10	.05
491	Larry Bowa	.20	.09
492	Bill Buckner	.20	.09
493	Bill Campbell	.10	.05
494	Jody Davis	.10	.05
495	Leon Durham	.10	.05
496	Steve Henderson	.10	.05
497	Willie Hernandez	.20	.09
498	Ferguson Jenkins	.75	.35
499	Jay Johnstone	.10	.05
500	Junior Kennedy	.10	.05
501	Randy Martz	.10	.05
502	Jerry Morales	.10	.05
503	Keith Moreland	.10	.05
504	Dickie Noles	.10	.05
505	Mike Proly	.10	.05
506	Allen Ripley	.10	.05
507	Ryne Sandberg UER (Should say High School in Spokane, Washington)	12.00	5.50
508	Lee Smith	.75	.35
509	Pat Tabler	.10	.05
510	Dick Tidrow	.10	.05
511	Bump Wills	.10	.05
512	Gary Woods	.10	.05
513	Tony Armas	.10	.05
514	Dave Beard	.10	.05
515	Jeff Burroughs	.10	.05
516	John D'Acquisto	.10	.05
517	Wayne Gross	.10	.05
518	Mike Heath	.10	.05
519	Rickey Henderson UER (Brock record listed as 120 steals)	1.25	.55
520	Cliff Johnson	.10	.05
521	Matt Keough	.10	.05
522	Brian Kingman	.10	.05
523	Rick Langford	.10	.05
524	Dave Lopes	.20	.09
525	Steve McCatty	.10	.05
526	Dave McKay	.10	.05
527	Dan Meyer	.10	.05
528	Dwayne Murphy	.10	.05
529	Jeff Newman	.10	.05
530	Mike Norris	.10	.05
531	Bob Owchinko	.10	.05
532	Joe Rudi	.10	.05
533	Jimmy Sexton	.10	.05
534	Fred Stanley	.10	.05
535	Tom Underwood	.10	.05
536	Neil Allen	.10	.05
537	Wally Backman	.10	.05
538	Bob Bailor	.10	.05
539	Hubie Brooks	.20	.09
540	Carlos Diaz	.10	.05
541	Pete Falcone	.10	.05
542	George Foster	.20	.09
543	Ron Gardenhire	.10	.05
544	Brian Giles	.10	.05
545	Ron Hodges	.10	.05
546	Randy Jones	.10	.05
547	Mike Jorgensen	.10	.05
548	Dave Kingman	.40	.18
549	Ed Lynch	.10	.05
550	Jesse Orosco	.20	.09
551	Rick Ownbey	.10	.05
552	Charlie Puleo	.10	.05
553	Gary Rajsich	.10	.05
554	Mike Scott	.20	.09
555	Rusty Staub	.20	.09
556	John Stearns	.10	.05
557	Craig Swan	.10	.05
558	Ellis Valentine	.10	.05
559	Tom Veryzer	.10	.05
560	Mookie Wilson	.20	.09
561	Pat Zachry	.10	.05
562	Buddy Bell	.20	.09
563	John Butcher	.10	.05
564	Steve Comer	.10	.05
565	Danny Darwin	.10	.05
566	Bucky Dent	.20	.09
567	John Grubb	.10	.05
568	Rick Honeycutt	.10	.05
569	Dave Hostetler	.10	.05
570	Charlie Hough	.20	.09
571	Lamar Johnson	.10	.05
572	Jon Matlack	.10	.05
573	Paul Mirabella	.10	.05
574	Larry Parrish	.10	.05
575	Mike Richardt	.10	.05
576	Mickey Rivers	.10	.05
577	Billy Sample	.10	.05
578	Dave Schmidt	.10	.05
579	Bill Stein	.10	.05
580	Jim Sundberg	.20	.09
581	Frank Tanana	.20	.09
582	Mark Wagner	.10	.05
583	George Wright	.10	.05

❑ 584 Johnny Bench	1.00	.45
❑ 585 Bruce Berenyi	.10	.05
❑ 586 Larry Biittner	.10	.05
❑ 587 Cesar Cedeno	.20	.09
❑ 588 Dave Concepcion	.20	.09
❑ 589 Dan Driessen	.10	.05
❑ 590 Greg Harris	.10	.05
❑ 591 Ben Hayes	.10	.05
❑ 592 Paul Householder	.10	.05
❑ 593 Tom Hume	.10	.05
❑ 594 Wayne Krenchicki	.10	.05
❑ 595 Rafael Landestoy	.10	.05
❑ 596 Charlie Leibrandt	.10	.05
❑ 597 Eddie Milner	.10	.05
❑ 598 Ron Oester	.10	.05
❑ 599 Frank Pastore	.10	.05
❑ 600 Joe Price	.10	.05
❑ 601 Tom Seaver	1.00	.45
❑ 602 Bob Shirley	.10	.05
❑ 603 Mario Soto	.10	.05
❑ 604 Alex Trevino	.10	.05
❑ 605 Mike Vail	.10	.05
❑ 606 Duane Walker	.10	.05
❑ 607 Tom Brunansky	.20	.09
❑ 608 Bobby Castillo	.10	.05
❑ 609 John Castino	.10	.05
❑ 610 Ron Davis	.10	.05
❑ 611 Lenny Faedo	.10	.05
❑ 612 Terry Felton	.10	.05
❑ 613 Gary Gaetti	.75	.35
❑ 614 Mickey Hatcher	.10	.05
❑ 615 Brad Havens	.10	.05
❑ 616 Kent Hrbek	.20	.09
❑ 617 Randy Johnson	.10	.05
❑ 618 Tim Laudner	.10	.05
❑ 619 Jeff Little	.10	.05
❑ 620 Bobby Mitchell	.10	.05
❑ 621 Jack O'Connor	.10	.05
❑ 622 John Pacella	.10	.05
❑ 623 Pete Redfern	.10	.05
❑ 624 Jesus Vega	.10	.05
❑ 625 Frank Viola	.75	.35
❑ 626 Ron Washington	.10	.05
❑ 627 Gary Ward	.10	.05
❑ 628 Al Williams	.10	.05
❑ 629 Red Sox All-Stars	.75	.35
Carl Yastrzemski		
Dennis Eckersley		
Mark Clear		
❑ 630 300 Career Wins	.20	.09
Gaylord Perry		
Terry Bulling 5/6/82		
❑ 631 Pride of Venezuela	.20	.09
Dave Concepcion and		
Manny Trillo		
❑ 632 All-Star Infielders	.75	.35
Robin Yount and		
Buddy Bell		
❑ 633 Mr. Vet and Mr. Rookie	.40	.18
Dave Winfield and		
Kent Hrbek		
❑ 634 Fountain of Youth	.75	.35
Willie Stargell and		
Pete Rose		
❑ 635 Big Chiefs	.20	.09
Toby Harrah and		
Andre Thornton		
❑ 636 Smith Brothers	.75	.35
Ozzie Smith		
Lonnie Smith		
❑ 637 Base Stealers' Threat	.20	.09
Bo Diaz and		
Gary Carter		
❑ 638 All-Star Catchers	.75	.35
Carlton Fisk and		
Gary Carter		
❑ 639 The Silver Shoe	.40	.18
Rickey Henderson		
❑ 640 Home Run Threats	.75	.35
Ben Oglivie and		
Reggie Jackson		
❑ 641 Two Teams Same Day	.10	.05
Joel Youngblood		
August 4, 1982		
❑ 642 Last Perfect Game	.20	.09
Ron Hassey and		

Len Barker		
❑ 643 Black and Blue	.20	.09
Vida Blue		
❑ 644 Black and Blue	.10	.05
Bud Black		
❑ 645 Speed and Power	.40	.18
Reggie Jackson		
❑ 646 Speed and Power	.40	.18
Rickey Henderson		
❑ 647 CL: Cards/Brewers	.10	.05
❑ 648 CL: Orioles/Angels	.10	.05
❑ 649 CL: Royals/Braves	.10	.05
❑ 650 CL: Phillies/Red Sox	.10	.05
❑ 651 CL: Dodgers/White Sox	.10	.05
❑ 652 CL: Giants/Expos	.10	.05
❑ 653 CL: Pirates/Tigers	.10	.05
❑ 654 CL: Padres/Yankees	.10	.05
❑ 655 CL: Indians/Blue Jays	.10	.05
❑ 656 CL: Astros/Mariners	.10	.05
❑ 657 CL: Cubs/A's	.10	.05
❑ 658 CL: Mets/Rangers	.10	.05
❑ 659 CL: Reds/Twins	.10	.05
❑ 660 CL: Specials/Teams	.10	.05

1984 Fleer

	NRMT	VG-E
COMPLETE SET (660)	60.00	27.00
COMMON CARD (1-660)	.15	.07
MINOR STARS	.40	.18
SEMISTARS	.75	.35
UNLISTED STARS	1.50	.70

❑ 1 Mike Boddicker	.15	.07
❑ 2 Al Bumbry	.15	.07
❑ 3 Todd Cruz	.15	.07
❑ 4 Rich Dauer	.15	.07
❑ 5 Storm Davis	.15	.07
❑ 6 Rick Dempsey	.15	.07
❑ 7 Jim Dwyer	.15	.07
❑ 8 Mike Flanagan	.15	.07
❑ 9 Dan Ford	.15	.07
❑ 10 John Lowenstein	.15	.07
❑ 11 Dennis Martinez	.40	.18
❑ 12 Tippy Martinez	.15	.07
❑ 13 Scott McGregor	.15	.07
❑ 14 Eddie Murray	1.50	.70
❑ 15 Joe Nolan	.15	.07
❑ 16 Jim Palmer	1.50	.70
❑ 17 Cal Ripken	10.00	4.50
❑ 18 Gary Roenicke	.15	.07
❑ 19 Lenn Sakata	.15	.07
❑ 20 John Shelby	.15	.07
❑ 21 Ken Singleton	.15	.07
❑ 22 Sammy Stewart	.15	.07
❑ 23 Tim Stoddard	.15	.07
❑ 24 Marty Bystrom	.15	.07
❑ 25 Steve Carlton	1.50	.70
❑ 26 Ivan DeJesus	.15	.07
❑ 27 John Denny	.15	.07
❑ 28 Bob Dernier	.15	.07
❑ 29 Bo Diaz	.15	.07
❑ 30 Kiko Garcia	.15	.07
❑ 31 Greg Gross	.15	.07
❑ 32 Kevin Gross	.15	.07
❑ 33 Von Hayes	.15	.07
❑ 34 Willie Hernandez	.40	.07
❑ 35 Al Holland	.15	.07

❑ 36 Charles Hudson	.15	.07
❑ 37 Joe Lefebvre	.15	.07
❑ 38 Sixto Lezcano	.15	.07
❑ 39 Garry Maddox	.15	.07
❑ 40 Gary Matthews	.40	.18
❑ 41 Len Matuszek	.15	.07
❑ 42 Tug McGraw	.40	.18
❑ 43 Joe Morgan	1.50	.70
❑ 44 Tony Perez	1.50	.70
❑ 45 Ron Reed	.15	.07
❑ 46 Pete Rose	3.00	1.35
❑ 47 Juan Samuel	.75	.35
❑ 48 Mike Schmidt	2.50	1.10
❑ 49 Ozzie Virgil	.15	.07
❑ 50 Juan Agosto	.15	.07
❑ 51 Harold Baines	1.50	.70
❑ 52 Floyd Bannister	.15	.07
❑ 53 Salome Barojas	.15	.07
❑ 54 Britt Burns	.15	.07
❑ 55 Julio Cruz	.15	.07
❑ 56 Richard Dotson	.15	.07
❑ 57 Jerry Dybzinski	.15	.07
❑ 58 Carlton Fisk	1.50	.70
❑ 59 Scott Fletcher	.15	.07
❑ 60 Jerry Hairston	.15	.07
❑ 61 Kevin Hickey	.15	.07
❑ 62 Marc Hill	.15	.07
❑ 63 LaMarr Hoyt	.15	.07
❑ 64 Ron Kittle	.15	.07
❑ 65 Jerry Koosman	.40	.18
❑ 66 Dennis Lamp	.15	.07
❑ 67 Rudy Law	.15	.07
❑ 68 Vance Law	.15	.07
❑ 69 Greg Luzinski	.40	.18
❑ 70 Tom Paciorek	.40	.18
❑ 71 Mike Squires	.15	.07
❑ 72 Dick Tidrow	.15	.07
❑ 73 Greg Walker	.40	.18
❑ 74 Glenn Abbott	.15	.07
❑ 75 Howard Bailey	.15	.07
❑ 76 Doug Bair	.15	.07
❑ 77 Juan Berenguer	.15	.07
❑ 78 Tom Brookens	.40	.18
❑ 79 Enos Cabell	.15	.07
❑ 80 Kirk Gibson	1.50	.70
❑ 81 John Grubb	.15	.07
❑ 82 Larry Herndon	.15	.07
❑ 83 Wayne Krenchicki	.15	.07
❑ 84 Rick Leach	.15	.07
❑ 85 Chet Lemon	.15	.07
❑ 86 Aurelio Lopez	.40	.18
❑ 87 Jack Morris	1.50	.70
❑ 88 Lance Parrish	.75	.35
❑ 89 Dan Petry	.40	.18
❑ 90 Dave Rozema	.15	.07
❑ 91 Alan Trammell	1.50	.70
❑ 92 Lou Whitaker	1.50	.70
❑ 93 Milt Wilcox	.15	.07
❑ 94 Glenn Wilson	.15	.07
❑ 95 John Wockenfuss	.15	.07
❑ 96 Dusty Baker	.40	.18
❑ 97 Joe Beckwith	.15	.07
❑ 98 Greg Brock	.15	.07
❑ 99 Jack Fimple	.15	.07
❑ 100 Pedro Guerrero	.40	.18
❑ 101 Rick Honeycutt	.15	.07
❑ 102 Burt Hooton	.15	.07
❑ 103 Steve Howe	.15	.07
❑ 104 Ken Landreaux	.15	.07
❑ 105 Mike Marshall	.15	.07
❑ 106 Rick Monday	.15	.07
❑ 107 Jose Morales	.15	.07
❑ 108 Tom Niedenfuer	.15	.07
❑ 109 Alejandro Pena	.40	.18
❑ 110 Jerry Reuss UER	.15	.07
("Home:" omitted)		
❑ 111 Bill Russell	.15	.07
❑ 112 Steve Sax	.40	.18
❑ 113 Mike Scioscia	.15	.07
❑ 114 Derrel Thomas	.15	.07
❑ 115 Fernando Valenzuela	.40	.18
❑ 116 Bob Welch	.15	.07
❑ 117 Steve Yeager	.15	.07
❑ 118 Pat Zachry	.15	.07
❑ 119 Don Baylor	.75	.35
❑ 120 Bert Campaneris	.40	.18

121	Rick Cerone	.15	.07
122	Ray Fontenot	.15	.07
123	George Frazier	.15	.07
124	Oscar Gamble	.15	.07
125	Rich Gossage	.75	.35
126	Ken Griffey	.40	.18
127	Ron Guidry	.40	.18
128	Jay Howell	.15	.07
129	Steve Kemp	.15	.07
130	Matt Keough	.15	.07
131	Don Mattingly	20.00	9.00
132	John Montefusco	.15	.07
133	Omar Moreno	.15	.07
134	Dale Murray	.15	.07
135	Graig Nettles	.40	.18
136	Lou Piniella	.40	.18
137	Willie Randolph	.40	.18
138	Shane Rawley	.15	.07
139	Dave Righetti	.40	.18
140	Andre Robertson	.15	.07
141	Bob Shirley	.15	.07
142	Roy Smalley	.15	.07
143	Dave Winfield	1.50	.70
144	Butch Wynegar	.15	.07
145	Jim Acker	.15	.07
146	Doyle Alexander	.15	.07
147	Jesse Barfield	.40	.18
148	Jorge Bell	.40	.18
149	Barry Bonnell	.15	.07
150	Jim Clancy	.15	.07
151	Dave Collins	.15	.07
152	Tony Fernandez	3.00	1.35
153	Damaso Garcia	.15	.07
154	Dave Geisel	.15	.07
155	Jim Gott	.15	.07
156	Alfredo Griffin	.15	.07
157	Garth Iorg	.15	.07
158	Roy Lee Jackson	.15	.07
159	Cliff Johnson	.15	.07
160	Luis Leal	.15	.07
161	Buck Martinez	.15	.07
162	Joey McLaughlin	.15	.07
163	Randy Moffitt	.15	.07
164	Lloyd Moseby	.15	.07
165	Rance Mulliniks	.15	.07
166	Jorge Orta	.15	.07
167	Dave Stieb	.15	.07
168	Willie Upshaw	.15	.07
169	Ernie Whitt	.15	.07
170	Len Barker	.15	.07
171	Steve Bedrosian	.15	.07
172	Bruce Benedict	.15	.07
173	Brett Butler	.75	.35
174	Rick Camp	.15	.07
175	Chris Chambliss	.40	.18
176	Ken Dayley	.15	.07
177	Pete Falcone	.15	.07
178	Terry Forster	.15	.07
179	Gene Garber	.15	.07
180	Terry Harper	.15	.07
181	Bob Horner	.15	.07
182	Glenn Hubbard	.15	.07
183	Randy Johnson	.15	.07
184	Craig McMurtry	.15	.07
185	Donnie Moore	.15	.07
186	Dale Murphy	1.50	.70
187	Phil Niekro	1.50	.70
188	Pascual Perez	.15	.07
189	Biff Pocoroba	.15	.07
190	Rafael Ramirez	.15	.07
191	Jerry Royster	.15	.07
192	Claudell Washington	.15	.07
193	Bob Watson	.40	.18
194	Jerry Augustine	.15	.07
195	Mark Brouhard	.15	.07
196	Mike Caldwell	.15	.07
197	Tom Candiotti	1.50	.70
198	Cecil Cooper	.40	.18
199	Rollie Fingers	1.50	.70
200	Jim Gantner	.15	.07
201	Bob L. Gibson	.15	.07
202	Moose Haas	.15	.07
203	Roy Howell	.15	.07
204	Pete Ladd	.15	.07
205	Rick Manning	.15	.07
206	Bob McClure	.15	.07
207	Paul Molitor UER	1.50	.70
	('83 stats should say .270 BA and 608 AB)		
208	Don Money	.15	.07
209	Charlie Moore	.15	.07
210	Ben Oglivie	.15	.07
211	Chuck Porter	.15	.07
212	Ed Romero	.15	.07
213	Ted Simmons	.40	.18
214	Jim Slaton	.15	.07
215	Don Sutton	1.50	.70
216	Tom Tellmann	.15	.07
217	Pete Vuckovich	.15	.07
218	Ned Yost	.15	.07
219	Robin Yount	1.50	.70
220	Alan Ashby	.15	.07
221	Kevin Bass	.15	.07
222	Jose Cruz	.40	.18
223	Bill Dawley	.15	.07
224	Frank DiPino	.15	.07
225	Bill Doran	.40	.18
226	Phil Garner	.40	.18
227	Art Howe	.40	.18
228	Bob Knepper	.15	.07
229	Ray Knight	.40	.18
230	Frank LaCorte	.15	.07
231	Mike LaCoss	.15	.07
232	Mike Madden	.15	.07
233	Jerry Mumphrey	.15	.07
234	Joe Niekro	.40	.18
235	Terry Puhl	.15	.07
236	Luis Pujols	.15	.07
237	Craig Reynolds	.15	.07
238	Vern Ruhle	.15	.07
239	Nolan Ryan	10.00	4.50
240	Mike Scott	.40	.18
241	Tony Scott	.15	.07
242	Dave Smith	.15	.07
243	Dickie Thon	.15	.07
244	Denny Walling	.15	.07
245	Dale Berra	.15	.07
246	Jim Bibby	.15	.07
247	John Candelaria	.15	.07
248	Jose DeLeon	.15	.07
249	Mike Easler	.15	.07
250	Cecilio Guante	.15	.07
251	Richie Hebner	.15	.07
252	Lee Lacy	.15	.07
253	Bill Madlock	.40	.18
254	Milt May	.15	.07
255	Lee Mazzilli	.15	.07
256	Larry McWilliams	.15	.07
257	Jim Morrison	.15	.07
258	Dave Parker	.40	.18
259	Tony Pena	.15	.07
260	Johnny Ray	.15	.07
261	Rick Rhoden	.15	.07
262	Don Robinson	.15	.07
263	Manny Sarmiento	.15	.07
264	Rod Scurry	.15	.07
265	Kent Tekulve	.40	.18
266	Gene Tenace	.40	.18
267	Jason Thompson	.15	.07
268	Lee Tunnell	.15	.07
269	Marvell Wynne	.15	.07
270	Ray Burris	.15	.07
271	Gary Carter	1.50	.70
272	Warren Cromartie	.15	.07
273	Andre Dawson	1.50	.70
274	Doug Flynn	.15	.07
275	Terry Francona	.15	.07
276	Bill Gullickson	.15	.07
277	Bob James	.15	.07
278	Charlie Lea	.15	.07
279	Bryan Little	.15	.07
280	Al Oliver	.40	.18
281	Tim Raines	.75	.35
282	Bobby Ramos	.15	.07
283	Jeff Reardon	.40	.18
284	Steve Rogers	.15	.07
285	Scott Sanderson	.15	.07
286	Dan Schatzeder	.15	.07
287	Bryn Smith	.15	.07
288	Chris Speier	.15	.07
289	Manny Trillo	.15	.07
290	Mike Vail	.15	.07
291	Tim Wallach	.40	.18
292	Chris Welsh	.15	.07
293	Jim Wohlford	.15	.07
294	Kurt Bevacqua	.15	.07
295	Juan Bonilla	.15	.07
296	Bobby Brown	.15	.07
297	Luis DeLeon	.15	.07
298	Dave Dravecky	.40	.18
299	Tim Flannery	.15	.07
300	Steve Garvey	.75	.35
301	Tony Gwynn	10.00	4.50
302	Andy Hawkins	.15	.07
303	Ruppert Jones	.15	.07
304	Terry Kennedy	.15	.07
305	Tim Lollar	.15	.07
306	Gary Lucas	.15	.07
307	Kevin McReynolds	.75	.35
308	Sid Monge	.15	.07
309	Mario Ramirez	.15	.07
310	Gene Richards	.15	.07
311	Luis Salazar	.15	.07
312	Eric Show	.15	.07
313	Elias Sosa	.15	.07
314	Garry Templeton	.15	.07
315	Mark Thurmond	.15	.07
316	Ed Whitson	.15	.07
317	Alan Wiggins	.15	.07
318	Neil Allen	.15	.07
319	Joaquin Andujar	.15	.07
320	Steve Braun	.15	.07
321	Glenn Brummer	.15	.07
322	Bob Forsch	.15	.07
323	David Green	.15	.07
324	George Hendrick	.15	.07
325	Tom Herr	.40	.18
326	Dane Iorg	.15	.07
327	Jeff Lahti	.15	.07
328	Dave LaPoint	.15	.07
329	Willie McGee	.75	.35
330	Ken Oberkfell	.15	.07
331	Darrell Porter	.15	.07
332	Jamie Quirk	.15	.07
333	Mike Ramsey	.15	.07
334	Floyd Rayford	.15	.07
335	Lonnie Smith	.15	.07
336	Ozzie Smith	2.00	.90
337	John Stuper	.15	.07
338	Bruce Sutter	.40	.18
339	Andy Van Slyke UER	1.50	.70
	(Batting and throwing both wrong on card back)		
340	Dave Von Ohlen	.15	.07
341	Willie Aikens	.15	.07
342	Mike Armstrong	.15	.07
343	Bud Black	.15	.07
344	George Brett	3.00	1.35
345	Onix Concepcion	.15	.07
346	Keith Creel	.15	.07
347	Larry Gura	.15	.07
348	Don Hood	.15	.07
349	Dennis Leonard	.15	.07
350	Hal McRae	.40	.18
351	Amos Otis	.40	.18
352	Gaylord Perry	1.50	.70
353	Greg Pryor	.15	.07
354	Dan Quisenberry	.15	.07
355	Steve Renko	.15	.07
356	Leon Roberts	.15	.07
357	Pat Sheridan	.15	.07
358	Joe Simpson	.15	.07
359	Don Slaught	.40	.18
360	Paul Splittorff	.15	.07
361	U.L. Washington	.15	.07
362	John Wathan	.15	.07
363	Frank White	.40	.18
364	Willie Wilson	.15	.07
365	Jim Barr	.15	.07
366	Dave Bergman	.15	.07
367	Fred Breining	.15	.07
368	Bob Brenly	.15	.07
369	Jack Clark	.40	.18
370	Chili Davis	.75	.35
371	Mark Davis	.15	.07
372	Darrell Evans	.40	.18
373	Atlee Hammaker	.15	.07
374	Mike Krukow	.15	.07

375	Duane Kuiper	.15	.07
376	Bill Laskey	.15	.07
377	Gary Lavelle	.15	.07
378	Johnnie LeMaster	.15	.07
379	Jeff Leonard	.15	.07
380	Randy Lerch	.15	.07
381	Renie Martin	.15	.07
382	Andy McGaffigan	.15	.07
383	Greg Minton	.15	.07
384	Tom O'Malley	.15	.07
385	Max Venable	.15	.07
386	Brad Wellman	.15	.07
387	Joel Youngblood	.15	.07
388	Gary Allenson	.15	.07
389	Luis Aponte	.15	.07
390	Tony Armas	.15	.07
391	Doug Bird	.15	.07
392	Wade Boggs	3.00	1.35
393	Dennis Boyd	.40	.18
394	Mike Brown UER P	.15	.07
	(shown with record of 31-104)		
395	Mark Clear	.15	.07
396	Dennis Eckersley	1.50	.70
397	Dwight Evans	.40	.18
398	Rich Gedman	.15	.07
399	Glenn Hoffman	.15	.07
400	Bruce Hurst	.15	.07
401	John Henry Johnson	.15	.07
402	Ed Jurak	.15	.07
403	Rick Miller	.15	.07
404	Jeff Newman	.15	.07
405	Reid Nichols	.15	.07
406	Bob Ojeda	.15	.07
407	Jerry Remy	.15	.07
408	Jim Rice	.40	.18
409	Bob Stanley	.15	.07
410	Dave Stapleton	.15	.07
411	John Tudor	.15	.07
412	Carl Yastrzemski	1.50	.70
413	Buddy Bell	.40	.18
414	Larry Biittner	.15	.07
415	John Butcher	.15	.07
416	Danny Darwin	.15	.07
417	Bucky Dent	.40	.18
418	Dave Hostetler	.15	.07
419	Charlie Hough	.40	.18
420	Bobby Johnson	.15	.07
421	Odell Jones	.15	.07
422	Jon Matlack	.15	.07
423	Pete O'Brien	.40	.18
424	Larry Parrish	.15	.07
425	Mickey Rivers	.15	.07
426	Billy Sample	.15	.07
427	Dave Schmidt	.15	.07
428	Mike Smithson	.15	.07
429	Bill Stein	.15	.07
430	Dave Stewart	.40	.18
431	Jim Sundberg	.40	.18
432	Frank Tanana	.40	.18
433	Dave Tobik	.15	.07
434	Wayne Tolleson	.15	.07
435	George Wright	.15	.07
436	Bill Almon	.15	.07
437	Keith Atherton	.15	.07
438	Dave Beard	.15	.07
439	Tom Burgmeier	.15	.07
440	Jeff Burroughs	.15	.07
441	Chris Codiroli	.15	.07
442	Tim Conroy	.15	.07
443	Mike Davis	.15	.07
444	Wayne Gross	.15	.07
445	Garry Hancock	.15	.07
446	Mike Heath	.15	.07
447	Rickey Henderson	2.00	.90
448	Donnie Hill	.15	.07
449	Bob Kearney	.15	.07
450	Bill Krueger	.15	.07
451	Rick Langford	.15	.07
452	Carney Lansford	.40	.18
453	Dave Lopes	.40	.18
454	Steve McCatty	.15	.07
455	Dan Meyer	.15	.07
456	Dwayne Murphy	.15	.07
457	Mike Norris	.15	.07
458	Ricky Peters	.15	.07
459	Tony Phillips	1.50	.70
460	Tom Underwood	.15	.07
461	Mike Warren	.15	.07
462	Johnny Bench	2.00	.90
463	Bruce Berenyi	.15	.07
464	Dann Bilardello	.15	.07
465	Cesar Cedeno	.40	.18
466	Dave Concepcion	.40	.18
467	Dan Driessen	.15	.07
468	Nick Esasky	.15	.07
469	Rich Gale	.15	.07
470	Ben Hayes	.15	.07
471	Paul Householder	.15	.07
472	Tom Hume	.15	.07
473	Alan Knicely	.15	.07
474	Eddie Milner	.15	.07
475	Ron Oester	.15	.07
476	Kelly Paris	.15	.07
477	Frank Pastore	.15	.07
478	Ted Power	.15	.07
479	Joe Price	.15	.07
480	Charlie Puleo	.15	.07
481	Gary Redus	.15	.07
482	Bill Scherrer	.15	.07
483	Mario Soto	.15	.07
484	Alex Trevino	.15	.07
485	Duane Walker	.15	.07
486	Larry Bowa	.40	.18
487	Warren Brusstar	.15	.07
488	Bill Buckner	.40	.18
489	Bill Campbell	.15	.07
490	Ron Cey	.40	.18
491	Jody Davis	.15	.07
492	Leon Durham	.15	.07
493	Mel Hall	.40	.18
494	Ferguson Jenkins	1.50	.70
495	Jay Johnstone	.15	.07
496	Craig Lefferts	.15	.07
497	Carmelo Martinez	.15	.07
498	Jerry Morales	.15	.07
499	Keith Moreland	.15	.07
500	Dickie Noles	.15	.07
501	Mike Proly	.15	.07
502	Chuck Rainey	.15	.07
503	Dick Ruthven	.15	.07
504	Ryne Sandberg	5.00	2.20
505	Lee Smith	1.50	.70
506	Steve Trout	.15	.07
507	Gary Woods	.15	.07
508	Juan Beniquez	.15	.07
509	Bob Boone	.40	.18
510	Rick Burleson	.15	.07
511	Rod Carew	1.50	.70
512	Bobby Clark	.15	.07
513	John Curtis	.15	.07
514	Doug DeCinces	.15	.07
515	Brian Downing	.15	.07
516	Tim Foli	.15	.07
517	Ken Forsch	.15	.07
518	Bobby Grich	.40	.18
519	Andy Hassler	.15	.07
520	Reggie Jackson	2.00	.90
521	Ron Jackson	.15	.07
522	Tommy John	.75	.35
523	Bruce Kison	.15	.07
524	Steve Lubratich	.15	.07
525	Fred Lynn	.40	.18
526	Gary Pettis	.15	.07
527	Luis Sanchez	.15	.07
528	Daryl Sconiers	.15	.07
529	Ellis Valentine	.15	.07
530	Rob Wilfong	.15	.07
531	Mike Witt	.15	.07
532	Geoff Zahn	.15	.07
533	Bud Anderson	.15	.07
534	Chris Bando	.15	.07
535	Alan Bannister	.15	.07
536	Bert Blyleven	.40	.18
537	Tom Brennan	.15	.07
538	Jamie Easterly	.15	.07
539	Juan Eichelberger	.15	.07
540	Jim Essian	.15	.07
541	Mike Fischlin	.15	.07
542	Julio Franco	.75	.35
543	Mike Hargrove	.40	.18
544	Toby Harrah	.40	.18
545	Ron Hassey	.15	.07
546	Neal Heaton	.15	.07
547	Bake McBride	.15	.07
548	Broderick Perkins	.15	.07
549	Lary Sorensen	.15	.07
550	Dan Spillner	.15	.07
551	Rick Sutcliffe	.40	.18
552	Pat Tabler	.15	.07
553	Gorman Thomas	.15	.07
554	Andre Thornton	.15	.07
555	George Vukovich	.15	.07
556	Darrell Brown	.15	.07
557	Tom Brunansky	.40	.18
558	Randy Bush	.15	.07
559	Bobby Castillo	.15	.07
560	John Castino	.15	.07
561	Ron Davis	.15	.07
562	Dave Engle	.15	.07
563	Lenny Faedo	.15	.07
564	Pete Filson	.15	.07
565	Gary Gaetti	.75	.35
566	Mickey Hatcher	.15	.07
567	Kent Hrbek	.40	.18
568	Rusty Kuntz	.15	.07
569	Tim Laudner	.15	.07
570	Rick Lysander	.15	.07
571	Bobby Mitchell	.15	.07
572	Ken Schrom	.15	.07
573	Ray Smith	.15	.07
574	Tim Teufel	.15	.07
575	Frank Viola	.75	.35
576	Gary Ward	.15	.07
577	Ron Washington	.15	.07
578	Len Whitehouse	.15	.07
579	Al Williams	.15	.07
580	Bob Bailor	.15	.07
581	Mark Bradley	.15	.07
582	Hubie Brooks	.15	.07
583	Carlos Diaz	.15	.07
584	George Foster	.40	.18
585	Brian Giles	.15	.07
586	Danny Heep	.15	.07
587	Keith Hernandez	.40	.18
588	Ron Hodges	.15	.07
589	Scott Holman	.15	.07
590	Dave Kingman	.75	.35
591	Ed Lynch	.15	.07
592	Jose Oquendo	.40	.18
593	Jesse Orosco	.15	.07
594	Junior Ortiz	.15	.07
595	Tom Seaver	2.00	.90
596	Doug Sisk	.15	.07
597	Rusty Staub	.40	.18
598	John Stearns	.15	.07
599	Darryl Strawberry	5.00	2.20
600	Craig Swan	.15	.07
601	Walt Terrell	.15	.07
602	Mike Torrez	.15	.07
603	Mookie Wilson	.40	.18
604	Jamie Allen	.15	.07
605	Jim Beattie	.15	.07
606	Tony Bernazard	.15	.07
607	Manny Castillo	.15	.07
608	Bill Caudill	.15	.07
609	Bryan Clark	.15	.07
610	Al Cowens	.15	.07
611	Dave Henderson	.40	.18
612	Steve Henderson	.15	.07
613	Orlando Mercado	.15	.07
614	Mike Moore	.15	.07
615	Ricky Nelson UER	.15	.07
	(Jamie Nelson's stats on back)		
616	Spike Owen	.40	.18
617	Pat Putnam	.15	.07
618	Ron Roenicke	.15	.07
619	Mike Stanton	.15	.07
620	Bob Stoddard	.15	.07
621	Rick Sweet	.15	.07
622	Roy Thomas	.15	.07
623	Ed VandeBerg	.15	.07
624	Matt Young	.15	.07
625	Richie Zisk	.15	.07
626	Fred Lynn	.40	.18
	1982 AS Game RB		
627	Manny Trillo	.15	.07

		NRMT	VG-E
	1983 AS Game RB		
☐ 628	Steve Garvey	.40	.18
	NL Iron Man		
☐ 629	Rod Carew	.75	.35
	AL Batting Runner-Up		
☐ 630	Wade Boggs	1.50	.70
	AL Batting Champion		
☐ 631	Tim Raines: Letting	.40	.18
	Go of the Raines		
☐ 632	Al Oliver	.40	.18
	Double Trouble		
☐ 633	Steve Sax	.15	.07
	AS Second Base		
☐ 634	Dickie Thon	.15	.07
	AS Shortstop		
☐ 635	Ace Firemen	.15	.07
	Dan Quisenberry		
	and Tippy Martinez		
☐ 636	Reds Reunited	1.50	.70
	Joe Morgan		
	Pete Rose		
	Tony Perez		
☐ 637	Backstop Stars	.75	.35
	Lance Parrish		
	Bob Boone		
☐ 638	George Brett and	2.00	.90
	Gaylord Perry		
	Pine Tar 7/24/83		
☐ 639	1983 No Hitters	.75	.35
	Dave Righetti		
	Mike Warren		
	Bob Forsch		
☐ 640	Johnny Bench and	2.00	.90
	Carl Yastrzemski		
	Retiring Superstars		
☐ 641	Gaylord Perry	1.50	.70
	Going Out in Style		
☐ 642	Steve Carlton	.75	.35
	300 Club and		
	Strikeout Record		
☐ 643	Joe Altobelli and	.15	.07
	Paul Owens		
	World Series Managers		
☐ 644	Rick Dempsey	.40	.18
	World Series MVP		
☐ 645	Mike Boddicker	.15	.07
	WS Rookie Winner		
☐ 646	Scott McGregor	.15	.07
	WS Clincher		
☐ 647	CL: Orioles/Royals	.15	.07
	Joe Altobelli MG		
☐ 648	CL: Phillies/Giants	.15	.07
	Paul Owens MG		
☐ 649	CL: White Sox/Red Sox	.75	.35
	Tony LaRussa MG		
☐ 650	CL: Tigers/Rangers	.75	.35
	Sparky Anderson MG		
☐ 651	CL: Dodgers/A's	.75	.35
	Tommy Lasorda MG		
☐ 652	CL: Yankees/Reds	.75	.35
	Billy Martin MG		
☐ 653	CL: Blue Jays/Cubs	.40	.18
	Bobby Cox MG		
☐ 654	CL: Braves/Angels	.75	.35
	Joe Torre MG		
☐ 655	CL: Brewers/Indians	.15	.07
	Rene Lachemann MG		
☐ 656	CL: Astros/Twins	.15	.07
	Bob Lillis MG		
☐ 657	CL: Pirates/Mets	.15	.07
	Chuck Tanner MG		
☐ 658	CL: Expos/Mariners	.15	.07
	Bill Virdon MG		
☐ 659	CL: Padres/Specials	.40	.18
	Dick Williams MG		
☐ 660	CL: Cardinals/Teams	.75	.35
	Whitey Herzog MG		

1984 Fleer Update

		NRMT	VG-E
COMP.FACT.SET (132)		400.00	180.00
COMMON CARD (1-132)		1.00	.45
MINOR STARS		2.50	1.10
SEMISTARS		4.00	1.80
BEWARE OF COUNTERFEITS			

John Franco pitcher

☐ 1	Willie Aikens	1.00	.45
☐ 2	Luis Aponte	1.00	.45
☐ 3	Mark Bailey	1.00	.45
☐ 4	Bob Bailor	1.00	.45
☐ 5	Dusty Baker	2.50	1.10
☐ 6	Steve Balboni	1.00	.45
☐ 7	Alan Bannister	1.00	.45
☐ 8	Marty Barrett	2.50	1.10
☐ 9	Dave Beard	1.00	.45
☐ 10	Joe Beckwith	1.00	.45
☐ 11	Dave Bergman	1.00	.45
☐ 12	Tony Bernazard	1.00	.45
☐ 13	Bruce Bochte	1.00	.45
☐ 14	Barry Bonnell	1.00	.45
☐ 15	Phil Bradley	2.50	1.10
☐ 16	Fred Breining	1.00	.45
☐ 17	Mike C. Brown	1.00	.45
☐ 18	Bill Buckner	2.50	1.10
☐ 19	Ray Burris	1.00	.45
☐ 20	John Butcher	1.00	.45
☐ 21	Brett Butler	4.00	1.80
☐ 22	Enos Cabell	1.00	.45
☐ 23	Bill Campbell	1.00	.45
☐ 24	Bill Caudill	1.00	.45
☐ 25	Bobby Clark	1.00	.45
☐ 26	Bryan Clark	1.00	.45
☐ 27	Roger Clemens	200.00	90.00
☐ 28	Jaime Cocanower	1.00	.45
☐ 29	Ron Darling	4.50	1.80
☐ 30	Alvin Davis	2.50	1.10
☐ 31	Bob Dernier	1.00	.45
☐ 32	Carlos Diaz	1.00	.45
☐ 33	Mike Easler	1.00	.45
☐ 34	Dennis Eckersley	5.00	2.20
☐ 35	Jim Essian	1.00	.45
☐ 36	Darrell Evans	2.50	1.10
☐ 37	Mike Fitzgerald	1.00	.45
☐ 38	Tim Foli	1.00	.45
☐ 39	John Franco	8.00	3.60
☐ 40	George Frazier	1.00	.45
☐ 41	Rich Gale	1.00	.45
☐ 42	Barbaro Garbey	1.00	.45
☐ 43	Dwight Gooden	15.00	6.75
☐ 44	Rich Gossage	4.00	1.80
☐ 45	Wayne Gross	1.00	.45
☐ 46	Mark Gubicza	2.50	1.10
☐ 47	Jackie Gutierrez	1.00	.45
☐ 48	Toby Harrah	2.50	1.10
☐ 49	Ron Hassey	1.00	.45
☐ 50	Richie Hebner	1.00	.45
☐ 51	Willie Hernandez	2.50	1.10
☐ 52	Ed Hodge	1.00	.45
☐ 53	Ricky Horton	1.00	.45
☐ 54	Art Howe	2.50	1.10
☐ 55	Dane Iorg	1.00	.45
☐ 56	Brook Jacoby	2.50	1.10
☐ 57	Dion James	1.00	.45
☐ 58	Mike Jeffcoat	1.00	.45
☐ 59	Ruppert Jones	1.00	.45
☐ 60	Bob Kearney	1.00	.45
☐ 61	Jimmy Key	8.00	3.60
☐ 62	Dave Kingman	4.00	1.80
☐ 63	Brad Komminsk	1.00	.45
☐ 64	Jerry Koosman	2.50	1.10
☐ 65	Wayne Krenchicki	1.00	.45
☐ 66	Rusty Kuntz	1.00	.45
☐ 67	Frank LaCorte	1.00	.45
☐ 68	Dennis Lamp	1.00	.45

☐ 69	Tito Landrum	1.00	.45
☐ 70	Mark Langston	5.00	2.20
☐ 71	Rick Leach	1.00	.45
☐ 72	Craig Lefferts	2.50	1.10
☐ 73	Gary Lucas	1.00	.45
☐ 74	Jerry Martin	1.00	.45
☐ 75	Carmelo Martinez	1.00	.45
☐ 76	Mike Mason	1.00	.45
☐ 77	Gary Matthews	2.50	1.10
☐ 78	Andy McGaffigan	1.00	.45
☐ 79	Joey McLaughlin	1.00	.45
☐ 80	Joe Morgan	6.00	2.70
☐ 81	Darryl Motley	1.00	.45
☐ 82	Graig Nettles	2.50	1.10
☐ 83	Phil Niekro	5.00	2.20
☐ 84	Ken Oberkfell	1.00	.45
☐ 85	Al Oliver	2.50	1.10
☐ 86	Jorge Orta	1.00	.45
☐ 87	Amos Otis	2.50	1.10
☐ 88	Bob Owchinko	1.00	.45
☐ 89	Dave Parker	2.50	1.10
☐ 90	Jack Perconte	1.00	.45
☐ 91	Tony Perez	5.00	2.20
☐ 92	Gerald Perry	2.50	1.10
☐ 93	Kirby Puckett	100.00	45.00
☐ 94	Shane Rawley	1.00	.45
☐ 95	Floyd Rayford	1.00	.45
☐ 96	Ron Reed	1.00	.45
☐ 97	R.J. Reynolds	1.00	.45
☐ 98	Gene Richards	1.00	.45
☐ 99	Jose Rijo	5.00	2.20
☐ 100	Jeff D. Robinson	1.00	.45
☐ 101	Ron Romanick	1.00	.45
☐ 102	Pete Rose	12.00	5.50
☐ 103	Bret Saberhagen	12.00	5.50
☐ 104	Scott Sanderson	1.00	.45
☐ 105	Dick Schofield	2.50	1.10
☐ 106	Tom Seaver	10.00	4.50
☐ 107	Jim Slaton	1.00	.45
☐ 108	Mike Smithson	1.00	.45
☐ 109	Lary Sorensen	1.00	.45
☐ 110	Tim Stoddard	1.00	.45
☐ 111	Jeff Stone	1.00	.45
☐ 112	Champ Summers	1.00	.45
☐ 113	Jim Sundberg	2.50	1.10
☐ 114	Rick Sutcliffe	4.00	1.80
☐ 115	Craig Swan	1.00	.45
☐ 116	Derrel Thomas	1.00	.45
☐ 117	Gorman Thomas	2.50	1.10
☐ 118	Alex Trevino	1.00	.45
☐ 119	Manny Trillo	1.00	.45
☐ 120	John Tudor	1.00	.45
☐ 121	Tom Underwood	1.00	.45
☐ 122	Mike Vail	1.00	.45
☐ 123	Tom Waddell	1.00	.45
☐ 124	Gary Ward	1.00	.45
☐ 125	Terry Whitfield	1.00	.45
☐ 126	Curtis Wilkerson	1.00	.45
☐ 127	Frank Williams	1.00	.45
☐ 128	Glenn Wilson	1.00	.45
☐ 129	John Wockenfuss	1.00	.45
☐ 130	Ned Yost	1.00	.45
☐ 131	Mike Young	1.00	.45
☐ 132	Checklist 1-132	1.00	.45

1985 Fleer

KIRBY PUCKETT

	NRMT	VG-E
COMPLETE SET (660)	100.00	45.00
COMMON CARD (1-660)	.15	.07
MINOR STARS	.40	.18
SEMISTARS	.75	.35
UNLISTED STARS	1.50	.70
CONDITION SENSITIVE SET		

#	Player	NRMT	VG-E
1	Doug Bair	.15	.07
2	Juan Berenguer	.15	.07
3	Dave Bergman	.15	.07
4	Tom Brookens	.15	.07
5	Marty Castillo	.15	.07
6	Darrell Evans	.40	.18
7	Barbaro Garbey	.15	.07
8	Kirk Gibson	.40	.18
9	John Grubb	.15	.07
10	Willie Hernandez	.15	.07
11	Larry Herndon	.15	.07
12	Howard Johnson	.40	.18
13	Ruppert Jones	.15	.07
14	Rusty Kuntz	.15	.07
15	Chet Lemon	.15	.07
16	Aurelio Lopez	.15	.07
17	Sid Monge	.15	.07
18	Jack Morris	.40	.18
19	Lance Parrish	.40	.18
20	Dan Petry	.15	.07
21	Dave Rozema	.15	.07
22	Bill Scherrer	.15	.07
23	Alan Trammell	.75	.35
24	Lou Whitaker	.75	.35
25	Milt Wilcox	.15	.07
26	Kurt Bevacqua	.15	.07
27	Greg Booker	.15	.07
28	Bobby Brown	.15	.07
29	Luis DeLeon	.15	.07
30	Dave Dravecky	.40	.18
31	Tim Flannery	.15	.07
32	Steve Garvey	.75	.35
33	Rich Gossage	.40	.18
34	Tony Gwynn	6.00	2.70
35	Greg Harris	.15	.07
36	Andy Hawkins	.15	.07
37	Terry Kennedy	.15	.07
38	Craig Lefferts	.15	.07
39	Tim Lollar	.15	.07
40	Carmelo Martinez	.15	.07
41	Kevin McReynolds	.40	.18
42	Graig Nettles	.40	.18
43	Luis Salazar	.15	.07
44	Eric Show	.15	.07
45	Garry Templeton	.15	.07
46	Mark Thurmond	.15	.07
47	Ed Whitson	.15	.07
48	Alan Wiggins	.15	.07
49	Rich Bordi	.15	.07
50	Larry Bowa	.40	.18
51	Warren Brusstar	.15	.07
52	Ron Cey	.40	.18
53	Henry Cotto	.15	.07
54	Jody Davis	.15	.07
55	Bob Dernier	.15	.07
56	Leon Durham	.15	.07
57	Dennis Eckersley	1.50	.70
58	George Frazier	.15	.07
59	Richie Hebner	.15	.07
60	Dave Lopes	.40	.18
61	Gary Matthews	.15	.07
62	Keith Moreland	.15	.07
63	Rick Reuschel	.15	.07
64	Dick Ruthven	.15	.07
65	Ryne Sandberg	3.00	1.35
66	Scott Sanderson	.15	.07
67	Lee Smith	.75	.35
68	Tim Stoddard	.15	.07
69	Rick Sutcliffe	.15	.07
70	Steve Trout	.15	.07
71	Gary Woods	.15	.07
72	Wally Backman	.15	.07
73	Bruce Berenyi	.15	.07
74	Hubie Brooks UER (Kelvin Chapman's stats on card back)	.15	.07
75	Kelvin Chapman	.15	.07
76	Ron Darling	.40	.18
77	Sid Fernandez	.40	.18
78	Mike Fitzgerald	.15	.07
79	George Foster	.40	.18
80	Brent Gaff	.15	.07
81	Ron Gardenhire	.15	.07
82	Dwight Gooden	2.00	.90
83	Tom Gorman	.15	.07
84	Danny Heep	.15	.07
85	Keith Hernandez	.40	.18
86	Ray Knight	.15	.07
87	Ed Lynch	.15	.07
88	Jose Oquendo	.15	.07
89	Jesse Orosco	.15	.07
90	Rafael Santana	.15	.07
91	Doug Sisk	.15	.07
92	Rusty Staub	.40	.18
93	Darryl Strawberry	1.50	.70
94	Walt Terrell	.15	.07
95	Mookie Wilson	.40	.18
96	Jim Acker	.15	.07
97	Willie Aikens	.15	.07
98	Doyle Alexander	.15	.07
99	Jesse Barfield	.15	.07
100	George Bell	.40	.18
101	Jim Clancy	.15	.07
102	Dave Collins	.15	.07
103	Tony Fernandez	.75	.35
104	Damaso Garcia	.15	.07
105	Jim Gott	.15	.07
106	Alfredo Griffin	.15	.07
107	Garth Iorg	.15	.07
108	Roy Lee Jackson	.15	.07
109	Cliff Johnson	.15	.07
110	Jimmy Key	1.50	.70
111	Dennis Lamp	.15	.07
112	Rick Leach	.15	.07
113	Luis Leal	.15	.07
114	Buck Martinez	.15	.07
115	Lloyd Moseby	.15	.07
116	Rance Mulliniks	.15	.07
117	Dave Stieb	.40	.18
118	Willie Upshaw	.15	.07
119	Ernie Whitt	.15	.07
120	Mike Armstrong	.15	.07
121	Don Baylor	.40	.18
122	Marty Bystrom	.15	.07
123	Rick Cerone	.15	.07
124	Joe Cowley	.15	.07
125	Brian Dayett	.15	.07
126	Tim Foli	.15	.07
127	Ray Fontenot	.15	.07
128	Ken Griffey	.40	.18
129	Ron Guidry	.40	.18
130	Toby Harrah	.15	.07
131	Jay Howell	.15	.07
132	Steve Kemp	.15	.07
133	Don Mattingly	4.00	1.80
134	Bobby Meacham	.15	.07
135	John Montefusco	.15	.07
136	Omar Moreno	.15	.07
137	Dale Murray	.15	.07
138	Phil Niekro	1.50	.70
139	Mike Pagliarulo	.15	.07
140	Willie Randolph	.40	.18
141	Dennis Rasmussen	.15	.07
142	Dave Righetti	.40	.18
143	Jose Rijo	.75	.35
144	Andre Robertson	.15	.07
145	Bob Shirley	.15	.07
146	Dave Winfield	1.50	.70
147	Butch Wynegar	.15	.07
148	Gary Allenson	.15	.07
149	Tony Armas	.15	.07
150	Marty Barrett	.15	.07
151	Wade Boggs	2.00	.90
152	Dennis Boyd	.15	.07
153	Bill Buckner	.40	.18
154	Mark Clear	.15	.07
155	Roger Clemens	40.00	18.00
156	Steve Crawford	.15	.07
157	Mike Easier	.15	.07
158	Dwight Evans	.40	.18
159	Rich Gedman	.15	.07
160	Jackie Gutierrez (Wade Boggs shown on deck)	.40	.18
161	Bruce Hurst	.15	.07
162	John Henry Johnson	.15	.07
163	Rick Miller	.15	.07
164	Reid Nichols	.15	.07
165	Al Nipper	.15	.07
166	Bob Ojeda	.15	.07
167	Jerry Remy	.15	.07
168	Jim Rice	.40	.18
169	Bob Stanley	.15	.07
170	Mike Boddicker	.15	.07
171	Al Bumbry	.15	.07
172	Todd Cruz	.15	.07
173	Rich Dauer	.15	.07
174	Storm Davis	.15	.07
175	Rick Dempsey	.15	.07
176	Jim Dwyer	.15	.07
177	Mike Flanagan	.15	.07
178	Dan Ford	.15	.07
179	Wayne Gross	.15	.07
180	John Lowenstein	.15	.07
181	Dennis Martinez	.40	.18
182	Tippy Martinez	.15	.07
183	Scott McGregor	.15	.07
184	Eddie Murray	1.50	.70
185	Joe Nolan	.15	.07
186	Floyd Rayford	.15	.07
187	Cal Ripken	8.00	3.60
188	Gary Roenicke	.15	.07
189	Lenn Sakata	.15	.07
190	John Shelby	.15	.07
191	Ken Singleton	.15	.07
192	Sammy Stewart	.15	.07
193	Bill Swaggerty	.15	.07
194	Tom Underwood	.15	.07
195	Mike Young	.15	.07
196	Steve Balboni	.15	.07
197	Joe Beckwith	.15	.07
198	Bud Black	.15	.07
199	George Brett	3.00	1.35
200	Onix Concepcion	.15	.07
201	Mark Gubicza	.40	.18
202	Larry Gura	.15	.07
203	Mark Huismann	.15	.07
204	Dane Iorg	.15	.07
205	Danny Jackson	.15	.07
206	Charlie Leibrandt	.15	.07
207	Hal McRae	.40	.18
208	Darryl Motley	.15	.07
209	Jorge Orta	.15	.07
210	Greg Pryor	.15	.07
211	Dan Quisenberry	.40	.18
212	Bret Saberhagen	1.50	.70
213	Pat Sheridan	.15	.07
214	Don Slaught	.15	.07
215	U.L. Washington	.15	.07
216	John Wathan	.15	.07
217	Frank White	.40	.18
218	Willie Wilson	.15	.07
219	Neil Allen	.15	.07
220	Joaquin Andujar	.15	.07
221	Steve Braun	.15	.07
222	Danny Cox	.15	.07
223	Bob Forsch	.15	.07
224	David Green	.15	.07
225	George Hendrick	.15	.07
226	Tom Herr	.15	.07
227	Ricky Horton	.15	.07
228	Art Howe	.15	.07
229	Mike Jorgensen	.15	.07
230	Kurt Kepshire	.15	.07
231	Jeff Lahti	.15	.07
232	Tito Landrum	.15	.07
233	Dave LaPoint	.15	.07
234	Willie McGee	.40	.18
235	Tom Nieto	.15	.07
236	Terry Pendleton	1.50	.70
237	Darrell Porter	.15	.07
238	Dave Rucker	.15	.07
239	Lonnie Smith	.15	.07
240	Ozzie Smith	2.00	.90
241	Bruce Sutter	.40	.18
242	Andy Van Slyke UER (Bats Right, Throws Left)	.75	.35
243	Dave Von Ohlen	.15	.07
244	Larry Andersen	.15	.07

245	Bill Campbell	.15	.07
246	Steve Carlton	1.50	.70
247	Tim Corcoran	.15	.07
248	Ivan DeJesus	.15	.07
249	John Denny	.15	.07
250	Bo Diaz	.15	.07
251	Greg Gross	.15	.07
252	Kevin Gross	.15	.07
253	Von Hayes	.15	.07
254	Al Holland	.15	.07
255	Charles Hudson	.15	.07
256	Jerry Koosman	.40	.18
257	Joe Lefebvre	.15	.07
258	Sixto Lezcano	.15	.07
259	Garry Maddox	.15	.07
260	Len Matuszek	.15	.07
261	Tug McGraw	.40	.18
262	Al Oliver	.40	.18
263	Shane Rawley	.15	.07
264	Juan Samuel	.15	.07
265	Mike Schmidt	2.50	1.10
266	Jeff Stone	.15	.07
267	Ozzie Virgil	.15	.07
268	Glenn Wilson	.15	.07
269	John Wockenfuss	.15	.07
270	Darrell Brown	.15	.07
271	Tom Brunansky	.40	.18
272	Randy Bush	.15	.07
273	John Butcher	.15	.07
274	Bobby Castillo	.15	.07
275	Ron Davis	.15	.07
276	Dave Engle	.15	.07
277	Pete Filson	.15	.07
278	Gary Gaetti	.40	.18
279	Mickey Hatcher	.15	.07
280	Ed Hodge	.15	.07
281	Kent Hrbek	.40	.18
282	Houston Jimenez	.15	.07
283	Tim Laudner	.15	.07
284	Rick Lysander	.15	.07
285	Dave Meier	.15	.07
286	Kirby Puckett	20.00	9.00
287	Pat Putnam	.15	.07
288	Ken Schrom	.15	.07
289	Mike Smithson	.15	.07
290	Tim Teufel	.15	.07
291	Frank Viola	.40	.18
292	Ron Washington	.15	.07
293	Don Aase	.15	.07
294	Juan Beniquez	.15	.07
295	Bob Boone	.40	.18
296	Mike C. Brown	.15	.07
297	Rod Carew	1.50	.70
298	Doug Corbett	.15	.07
299	Doug DeCinces	.15	.07
300	Brian Downing	.15	.07
301	Ken Forsch	.15	.07
302	Bobby Grich	.40	.18
303	Reggie Jackson	2.00	.90
304	Tommy John	.75	.35
305	Curt Kaufman	.15	.07
306	Bruce Kison	.15	.07
307	Fred Lynn	.40	.18
308	Gary Pettis	.15	.07
309	Ron Romanick	.15	.07
310	Luis Sanchez	.15	.07
311	Dick Schofield	.15	.07
312	Daryl Sconiers	.15	.07
313	Jim Slaton	.15	.07
314	Derrel Thomas	.15	.07
315	Rob Wilfong	.15	.07
316	Mike Witt	.15	.07
317	Geoff Zahn	.15	.07
318	Len Barker	.15	.07
319	Steve Bedrosian	.15	.07
320	Bruce Benedict	.15	.07
321	Rick Camp	.15	.07
322	Chris Chambliss	.40	.18
323	Jeff Dedmon	.15	.07
324	Terry Forster	.15	.07
325	Gene Garber	.15	.07
326	Albert Hall	.15	.07
327	Terry Harper	.15	.07
328	Bob Horner	.40	.18
329	Glenn Hubbard	.15	.07
330	Randy Johnson	.15	.07
331	Brad Komminsk	.15	.07
332	Rick Mahler	.15	.07
333	Craig McMurtry	.15	.07
334	Donnie Moore	.15	.07
335	Dale Murphy	1.50	.70
336	Ken Oberkfell	.15	.07
337	Pascual Perez	.15	.07
338	Gerald Perry	.15	.07
339	Rafael Ramirez	.15	.07
340	Jerry Royster	.15	.07
341	Alex Trevino	.15	.07
342	Claudell Washington	.15	.07
343	Alan Ashby	.15	.07
344	Mark Bailey	.15	.07
345	Kevin Bass	.15	.07
346	Enos Cabell	.15	.07
347	Jose Cruz	.40	.18
348	Bill Dawley	.15	.07
349	Frank DiPino	.15	.07
350	Bill Doran	.15	.07
351	Phil Garner	.40	.18
352	Bob Knepper	.15	.07
353	Mike LaCoss	.15	.07
354	Jerry Mumphrey	.15	.07
355	Joe Niekro	.15	.07
356	Terry Puhl	.15	.07
357	Craig Reynolds	.15	.07
358	Vern Ruhle	.15	.07
359	Nolan Ryan	8.00	3.60
360	Joe Sambito	.15	.07
361	Mike Scott	.15	.07
362	Dave Smith	.15	.07
363	Julio Solano	.15	.07
364	Dickie Thon	.15	.07
365	Denny Walling	.15	.07
366	Dave Anderson	.15	.07
367	Bob Bailor	.15	.07
368	Greg Brock	.15	.07
369	Carlos Diaz	.15	.07
370	Pedro Guerrero	.40	.18
371	Orel Hershiser	2.00	.90
372	Rick Honeycutt	.15	.07
373	Burt Hooton	.15	.07
374	Ken Howell	.15	.07
375	Ken Landreaux	.15	.07
376	Candy Maldonado	.15	.07
377	Mike Marshall	.15	.07
378	Tom Niedenfuer	.15	.07
379	Alejandro Pena	.15	.07
380	Jerry Reuss UER	.15	.07
	("Home:" omitted)		
381	R.J. Reynolds	.15	.07
382	German Rivera	.15	.07
383	Bill Russell	.15	.07
384	Steve Sax	.15	.07
385	Mike Scioscia	.15	.07
386	Franklin Stubbs	.15	.07
387	Fernando Valenzuela	.40	.18
388	Bob Welch	.15	.07
389	Terry Whitfield	.15	.07
390	Steve Yeager	.15	.07
391	Pat Zachry	.15	.07
392	Fred Breining	.15	.07
393	Gary Carter	1.50	.70
394	Andre Dawson	1.50	.70
395	Miguel Dilone	.15	.07
396	Dan Driessen	.15	.07
397	Doug Flynn	.15	.07
398	Terry Francona	.15	.07
399	Bill Gullickson	.15	.07
400	Bob James	.15	.07
401	Charlie Lea	.15	.07
402	Bryan Little	.15	.07
403	Gary Lucas	.15	.07
404	David Palmer	.15	.07
405	Tim Raines	.40	.18
406	Mike Ramsey	.15	.07
407	Jeff Reardon	.40	.18
408	Steve Rogers	.15	.07
409	Dan Schatzeder	.15	.07
410	Bryn Smith	.15	.07
411	Mike Stenhouse	.15	.07
412	Tim Wallach	.40	.18
413	Jim Wohlford	.15	.07
414	Bill Almon	.15	.07
415	Keith Atherton	.15	.07
416	Bruce Bochte	.15	.07
417	Tom Burgmeier	.15	.07
418	Ray Burris	.15	.07
419	Bill Caudill	.15	.07
420	Chris Codiroli	.15	.07
421	Tim Conroy	.15	.07
422	Mike Davis	.15	.07
423	Jim Essian	.15	.07
424	Mike Heath	.15	.07
425	Rickey Henderson	2.00	.90
426	Donnie Hill	.15	.07
427	Dave Kingman	.40	.18
428	Bill Krueger	.15	.07
429	Carney Lansford	.40	.18
430	Steve McCatty	.15	.07
431	Joe Morgan	1.50	.70
432	Dwayne Murphy	.15	.07
433	Tony Phillips	.15	.07
434	Lary Sorensen	.15	.07
435	Mike Warren	.15	.07
436	Curt Young	.15	.07
437	Luis Aponte	.15	.07
438	Chris Bando	.15	.07
439	Tony Bernazard	.15	.07
440	Bert Blyleven	.40	.18
441	Brett Butler	.40	.18
442	Ernie Camacho	.15	.07
443	Joe Carter	1.50	.70
444	Carmelo Castillo	.15	.07
445	Jamie Easterly	.15	.07
446	Steve Farr	.40	.18
447	Mike Fischlin	.15	.07
448	Julio Franco	.75	.35
449	Mel Hall	.15	.07
450	Mike Hargrove	.40	.18
451	Neal Heaton	.15	.07
452	Brook Jacoby	.15	.07
453	Mike Jeffcoat	.15	.07
454	Don Schulze	.15	.07
455	Roy Smith	.15	.07
456	Pat Tabler	.15	.07
457	Andre Thornton	.15	.07
458	George Vukovich	.15	.07
459	Tom Waddell	.15	.07
460	Jerry Willard	.15	.07
461	Dale Berra	.15	.07
462	John Candelaria	.15	.07
463	Jose DeLeon	.15	.07
464	Doug Frobel	.15	.07
465	Cecilio Guante	.15	.07
466	Brian Harper	.15	.07
467	Lee Lacy	.15	.07
468	Bill Madlock	.40	.18
469	Lee Mazzilli	.15	.07
470	Larry McWilliams	.15	.07
471	Jim Morrison	.15	.07
472	Tony Pena	.15	.07
473	Johnny Ray	.15	.07
474	Rick Rhoden	.15	.07
475	Don Robinson	.15	.07
476	Rod Scurry	.15	.07
477	Kent Tekulve	.15	.07
478	Jason Thompson	.15	.07
479	John Tudor	.15	.07
480	Lee Tunnell	.15	.07
481	Marvell Wynne	.15	.07
482	Salome Barojas	.15	.07
483	Dave Beard	.15	.07
484	Jim Beattie	.15	.07
485	Barry Bonnell	.15	.07
486	Phil Bradley	.40	.18
487	Al Cowens	.15	.07
488	Alvin Davis	.40	.18
489	Dave Henderson	.15	.07
490	Steve Henderson	.15	.07
491	Bob Kearney	.15	.07
492	Mark Langston	.75	.35
493	Larry Milbourne	.15	.07
494	Paul Mirabella	.15	.07
495	Mike Moore	.15	.07
496	Edwin Nunez	.15	.07
497	Spike Owen	.15	.07
498	Jack Perconte	.15	.07
499	Ken Phelps	.15	.07
500	Jim Presley	.40	.18
501	Mike Stanton	.15	.07

❑ 502 Bob Stoddard .... .15 .07
❑ 503 Gorman Thomas ...... .15 .07
❑ 504 Ed VandeBerg .... .15 .07
❑ 505 Matt Young .... .15 .07
❑ 506 Juan Agosto .... .15 .07
❑ 507 Harold Baines .... .40 .18
❑ 508 Floyd Bannister ...... .15 .07
❑ 509 Britt Burns .... .15 .07
❑ 510 Julio Cruz .... .15 .07
❑ 511 Richard Dotson ...... .15 .07
❑ 512 Jerry Dybzinski ..... .15 .07
❑ 513 Carlton Fisk .... 1.50 .70
❑ 514 Scott Fletcher ...... .15 .07
❑ 515 Jerry Hairston ...... .15 .07
❑ 516 Marc Hill .... .15 .07
❑ 517 LaMarr Hoyt .... .15 .07
❑ 518 Ron Kittle .... .40 .18
❑ 519 Rudy Law .... .15 .07
❑ 520 Vance Law .... .15 .07
❑ 521 Greg Luzinski ...... .40 .18
❑ 522 Gene Nelson .... .15 .07
❑ 523 Tom Paciorek ...... .40 .18
❑ 524 Ron Reed .... .15 .07
❑ 525 Bert Roberge ...... .15 .07
❑ 526 Tom Seaver .... 2.00 .90
❑ 527 Roy Smalley .... .15 .07
❑ 528 Dan Spillner ...... .15 .07
❑ 529 Mike Squires ..... .15 .07
❑ 530 Greg Walker ...... .40 .18
❑ 531 Cesar Cedeno .... .40 .18
❑ 532 Dave Concepcion .. .40 .18
❑ 533 Eric Davis 3.00 1.35
❑ 534 Nick Esasky ...... .15 .07
❑ 535 Tom Foley .... .15 .07
❑ 536 John Franco UER .. 1.50 .70
     (Koufax misspelled
     as Kofax on back)
❑ 537 Brad Gulden ...... .15 .07
❑ 538 Tom Hume .... .15 .07
❑ 539 Wayne Krenchicki . .15 .07
❑ 540 Andy McGaffigan .. .15 .07
❑ 541 Eddie Milner ...... .15 .07
❑ 542 Ron Oester .... .15 .07
❑ 543 Bob Owchinko .... .15 .07
❑ 544 Dave Parker ...... .40 .18
❑ 545 Frank Pastore .... .15 .07
❑ 546 Tony Perez ...... 1.50 .70
❑ 547 Ted Power .... .15 .07
❑ 548 Joe Price .... .15 .07
❑ 549 Gary Redus ...... .15 .07
❑ 550 Pete Rose 3.00 1.35
❑ 551 Jeff Russell ..... .15 .07
❑ 552 Mario Soto ...... .15 .07
❑ 553 Jay Tibbs .... .15 .07
❑ 554 Duane Walker ... .15 .07
❑ 555 Alan Bannister .. .15 .07
❑ 556 Buddy Bell ..... .40 .18
❑ 557 Danny Darwin .. .15 .07
❑ 558 Charlie Hough .. .40 .18
❑ 559 Bobby Jones ... .15 .07
❑ 560 Odell Jones ... .15 .07
❑ 561 Jeff Kunkel ... .15 .07
❑ 562 Mike Mason ... .15 .07
❑ 563 Pete O'Brien .. .15 .07
❑ 564 Larry Parrish . .15 .07
❑ 565 Mickey Rivers . .15 .07
❑ 566 Billy Sample .. .15 .07
❑ 567 Dave Schmidt . .15 .07
❑ 568 Donnie Scott .. .15 .07
❑ 569 Dave Stewart . .40 .18
❑ 570 Frank Tanana . .15 .07
❑ 571 Wayne Tolleson .15 .07
❑ 572 Gary Ward ..... .15 .07
❑ 573 Curtis Wilkerson .15 .07
❑ 574 George Wright . .15 .07
❑ 575 Ned Yost ...... .15 .07
❑ 576 Mark Brouhard .15 .07
❑ 577 Mike Caldwell . .15 .07
❑ 578 Bobby Clark ... .15 .07
❑ 579 Jaime Cocanower .15 .07
❑ 580 Cecil Cooper .. .40 .18
❑ 581 Rollie Fingers .. 1.50 .70
❑ 582 Jim Gantner ... .15 .07
❑ 583 Moose Haas ... .15 .07
❑ 584 Dion James ... .15 .07
❑ 585 Pete Ladd .... .15 .07

❑ 586 Rick Manning .... .15 .07
❑ 587 Bob McClure ..... .15 .07
❑ 588 Paul Molitor ..... 1.50 .70
❑ 589 Charlie Moore .... .15 .07
❑ 590 Ben Oglivie ...... .15 .07
❑ 591 Chuck Porter ..... .15 .07
❑ 592 Randy Ready ..... .15 .07
❑ 593 Ed Romero ...... .15 .07
❑ 594 Bill Schroeder ... .15 .07
❑ 595 Ray Searage .... .15 .07
❑ 596 Ted Simmons .... .40 .18
❑ 597 Jim Sundberg ... .15 .07
❑ 598 Don Sutton ..... 1.50 .70
❑ 599 Tom Tellmann ... .15 .07
❑ 600 Rick Waits ..... .15 .07
❑ 601 Robin Yount .... 1.50 .70
❑ 602 Dusty Baker .... .40 .18
❑ 603 Bob Brenly ..... .15 .07
❑ 604 Jack Clark ..... .40 .18
❑ 605 Chili Davis ..... .40 .18
❑ 606 Mark Davis ..... .15 .07
❑ 607 Dan Gladden ... .40 .18
❑ 608 Atlee Hammaker . .15 .07
❑ 609 Mike Krukow .... .15 .07
❑ 610 Duane Kuiper ... .15 .07
❑ 611 Bob Lacey ...... .15 .07
❑ 612 Bill Laskey ..... .15 .07
❑ 613 Gary Lavelle ... .15 .07
❑ 614 Johnnie LeMaster .15 .07
❑ 615 Jeff Leonard ... .15 .07
❑ 616 Randy Lerch ... .15 .07
❑ 617 Greg Minton ... .15 .07
❑ 618 Steve Nicosia .. .15 .07
❑ 619 Gene Richards .. .15 .07
❑ 620 Jeff D. Robinson .15 .07
❑ 621 Scot Thompson . .15 .07
❑ 622 Manny Trillo ... .15 .07
❑ 623 Brad Wellman .. .15 .07
❑ 624 Frank Williams . .15 .07
❑ 625 Joel Youngblood .15 .07
❑ 626 Cal Ripken IA .. 4.00 1.80
❑ 627 Mike Schmidt IA . .75 .35
❑ 628 Giving The Signs .40 .18
     Sparky Anderson
❑ 629 AL Pitcher's Nightmare 1.50 .70
     Dave Winfield
     Rickey Henderson
❑ 630 NL Pitcher's Nightmare 2.00 .90
     Mike Schmidt
     Ryne Sandberg
❑ 631 NL All-Stars .... 1.50 .70
     Darryl Strawberry
     Gary Carter
     Steve Garvey
     Ozzie Smith
❑ 632 A-S Winning Battery .75 .35
     Gary Carter
     Charlie Lea
❑ 633 NL Pennant Clinchers .75 .35
     Steve Garvey
     Rich Gossage
❑ 634 NL Rookie Phenoms .. 1.50 .70
     Dwight Gooden
     Juan Samuel
❑ 635 Toronto's Big Guns .15 .07
     Willie Upshaw
❑ 636 Toronto's Big Guns .15 .07
     Lloyd Moseby
❑ 637 HOLLAND: Al Holland .15 .07
❑ 638 TUNNELL: Lee Tunnell .15 .07
❑ 639 Reggie Jackson .. 1.50 .70
     500th Homer
❑ 640 4000th Hit ...... 1.50 .70
     Pete Rose
❑ 641 Father and Son .. 4.00 1.80
     Cal Ripken Jr.
     Cal Ripken Sr.
❑ 642 Cubs: Division Champs .40 .18
❑ 643 Two Perfect Games .40 .18
     and One No-Hitter:
     Mike Witt
     David Palmer
     Jack Morris
❑ 644 Willie Lozado and .15 .07
     Vic Mata
❑ 645 Kelly Gruber and . .40 .18

     Randy O'Neal
❑ 646 Jose Roman and .. .15 .07
     Joel Skinner
❑ 647 Steve Kiefer and .. 1.50 .70
     Danny Tartabull
❑ 648 Rob Deer and .... .40 .18
     Alejandro Sanchez
❑ 649 Billy Hatcher and . 1.00 .45
     Shawon Dunston
❑ 650 Ron Robinson and .. .15 .07
     Mike Bielecki
❑ 651 Zane Smith and .. .40 .18
     Paul Zuvella
❑ 652 Joe Hesketh and .. .40 .18
     Glenn Davis
❑ 653 John Russell and .. .15 .07
     Steve Jeltz
❑ 654 CL: Tigers/Padres .15 .07
     and Cubs/Mets
❑ 655 CL: Blue Jays/Yankees .15 .07
     and Red Sox/Orioles
❑ 656 CL: Royals/Cardinals .15 .07
     and Phillies/Twins
❑ 657 CL: Angels/Braves .15 .07
     and Astros/Dodgers
❑ 658 CL: Expos/A's ... .15 .07
     and Indians/Pirates
❑ 659 CL: Mariners/White Sox .15 .07
     and Reds/Rangers
❑ 660 CL: Brewers/Giants .15 .07
     and Special Cards

1985 Fleer Update

	NRMT	VG-E
COMP.FACT.SET (132)	10.00	4.50
COMMON CARD (1-132)	.15	.07
MINOR STARS	.40	.18
SEMISTARS	.75	.35

❑ 1 Don Aase .... .15 .07
❑ 2 Bill Almon ...... .15 .07
❑ 3 Dusty Baker .... .40 .18
❑ 4 Dale Berra ..... .15 .07
❑ 5 Karl Best ...... .15 .07
❑ 6 Tim Birtsas .... .15 .07
❑ 7 Vida Blue ..... .40 .18
❑ 8 Rich Bordi .... .15 .07
❑ 9 Daryl Boston .. .15 .07
❑ 10 Hubie Brooks . .15 .07
❑ 11 Chris Brown .. .15 .07
❑ 12 Tom Browning . .40 .18
❑ 13 Al Bumbry .... .15 .07
❑ 14 Tim Burke .... .15 .07
❑ 15 Ray Burris .... .15 .07
❑ 16 Jeff Burroughs . .15 .07
❑ 17 Ivan Calderon . .15 .07
❑ 18 Jeff Calhoun .. .15 .07
❑ 19 Bill Campbell .. .15 .07
❑ 20 Don Carman .. .15 .07
❑ 21 Gary Carter .. 1.00 .45
❑ 22 Bobby Castillo . .15 .07
❑ 23 Bill Caudill ... .15 .07
❑ 24 Rick Cerone .. .15 .07
❑ 25 Jack Clark ... .40 .18
❑ 26 Pat Clements . .15 .07
❑ 27 Stewart Cliburn .15 .07
❑ 28 Vince Coleman . 1.00 .45

#	Player	MINT	NRMT
29	Dave Collins	.15	.07
30	Fritz Connally	.15	.07
31	Henry Cotto	.15	.07
32	Danny Darwin	.15	.07
33	Darren Daulton	3.00	1.35
34	Jerry Davis	.15	.07
35	Brian Dayett	.15	.07
36	Ken Dixon	.15	.07
37	Tommy Dunbar	.15	.07
38	Mariano Duncan	1.00	.45
39	Bob Fallon	.15	.07
40	Brian Fisher	.15	.07
41	Mike Fitzgerald	.15	.07
42	Ray Fontenot	.15	.07
43	Greg Gagne	.40	.18
44	Oscar Gamble	.15	.07
45	Jim Gott	.15	.07
46	David Green	.15	.07
47	Alfredo Griffin	.15	.07
48	Ozzie Guillen	1.00	.45
49	Toby Harrah	.15	.07
50	Ron Hassey	.15	.07
51	Rickey Henderson	2.00	.90
52	Steve Henderson	.15	.07
53	George Hendrick	.15	.07
54	Teddy Higuera	.40	.18
55	Al Holland	.15	.07
56	Burt Hooton	.15	.07
57	Jay Howell	.15	.07
58	LaMarr Hoyt	.15	.07
59	Tim Hulett	.15	.07
60	Bob James	.15	.07
61	Cliff Johnson	.15	.07
62	Howard Johnson	.40	.18
63	Ruppert Jones	.15	.07
64	Steve Kemp	.15	.07
65	Bruce Kison	.15	.07
66	Mike LaCoss	.15	.07
67	Lee Lacy	.15	.07
68	Dave LaPoint	.15	.07
69	Gary Lavelle	.15	.07
70	Vance Law	.15	.07
71	Manny Lee	.15	.07
72	Sixto Lezcano	.15	.07
73	Tim Lollar	.15	.07
74	Urbano Lugo	.15	.07
75	Fred Lynn	.40	.18
76	Steve Lyons	.15	.07
77	Mickey Mahler	.15	.07
78	Ron Mathis	.15	.07
79	Len Matuszek	.15	.07
80	Oddibe McDowell UER (Part of bio actually Roger's)	.40	.18
81	Roger McDowell UER (Part of bio actually Oddibe's)	.40	.18
82	Donnie Moore	.15	.07
83	Ron Musselman	.15	.07
84	Al Oliver	.40	.18
85	Joe Orsulak	.40	.18
86	Dan Pasqua	.40	.18
87	Chris Pittaro	.15	.07
88	Rick Reuschel	.15	.07
89	Earnie Riles	.15	.07
90	Jerry Royster	.15	.07
91	Dave Rozema	.15	.07
92	Dave Rucker	.15	.07
93	Vern Ruhle	.15	.07
94	Mark Salas	.15	.07
95	Luis Salazar	.15	.07
96	Joe Sambito	.15	.07
97	Billy Sample	.15	.07
98	Alejandro Sanchez	.15	.07
99	Calvin Schiraldi	.15	.07
100	Rick Schu	.15	.07
101	Larry Sheets	.15	.07
102	Ron Shephard	.15	.07
103	Nelson Simmons	.15	.07
104	Don Slaught	.15	.07
105	Roy Smalley	.15	.07
106	Lonnie Smith	.15	.07
107	Nate Snell	.15	.07
108	Lary Sorensen	.15	.07
109	Chris Speier	.15	.07
110	Mike Stenhouse	.15	.07
111	Tim Stoddard	.15	.07
112	John Stuper	.15	.07
113	Jim Sundberg	.15	.07
114	Bruce Sutter	.40	.18
115	Don Sutton	1.00	.45
116	Bruce Tanner	.15	.07
117	Kent Tekulve	.15	.07
118	Walt Terrell	.15	.07
119	Mickey Tettleton	1.00	.45
120	Rich Thompson	.15	.07
121	Louis Thornton	.15	.07
122	Alex Trevino	.15	.07
123	John Tudor	.15	.07
124	Jose Uribe	.15	.07
125	Dave Valle	.15	.07
126	Dave Von Ohlen	.15	.07
127	Curt Wardle	.15	.07
128	U.L. Washington	.15	.07
129	Ed Whitson	.15	.07
130	Herm Winningham	.15	.07
131	Rich Yett	.15	.07
132	Checklist U1-U132	.15	.07

1986 Fleer

MIKE SCHMIDT

	MINT	NRMT
COMPLETE SET (660)	40.00	18.00
COMP.FACT.SET (660)	50.00	22.00
COMMON CARD (1-660)	.10	.05
MINOR STARS	.25	.11
SEMISTARS	.50	.23
UNLISTED STARS	1.00	.45

#	Player	MINT	NRMT
1	Steve Balboni	.10	.05
2	Joe Beckwith	.10	.05
3	Buddy Biancalana	.10	.05
4	Bud Black	.10	.05
5	George Brett	2.00	.90
6	Onix Concepcion	.10	.05
7	Steve Farr	.10	.05
8	Mark Gubicza	.10	.05
9	Dane Iorg	.10	.05
10	Danny Jackson	.10	.05
11	Lynn Jones	.10	.05
12	Mike Jones	.10	.05
13	Charlie Leibrandt	.10	.05
14	Hal McRae	.25	.11
15	Omar Moreno	.10	.06
16	Darryl Motley	.10	.05
17	Jorge Orta	.10	.05
18	Dan Quisenberry	.10	.05
19	Bret Saberhagen	.25	.11
20	Pat Sheridan	.10	.05
21	Lonnie Smith	.10	.05
22	Jim Sundberg	.10	.05
23	John Wathan	.10	.05
24	Frank White	.25	.11
25	Willie Wilson	.10	.05
26	Joaquin Andujar	.10	.05
27	Steve Braun	.10	.05
28	Bill Campbell	.10	.05
29	Cesar Cedeno	.25	.11
30	Jack Clark	.25	.11
31	Vince Coleman	1.00	.45
32	Danny Cox	.10	.05
33	Ken Dayley	.10	.05
34	Ivan DeJesus	.10	.05
35	Bob Forsch	.10	.05
36	Brian Harper	.10	.05
37	Tom Herr	.10	.05
38	Ricky Horton	.10	.05
39	Kurt Kepshire	.10	.05
40	Jeff Lahti	.10	.05
41	Tito Landrum	.10	.05
42	Willie McGee	.25	.11
43	Tom Nieto	.10	.05
44	Terry Pendleton	.50	.23
45	Darrell Porter	.25	.11
46	Ozzie Smith	1.25	.55
47	John Tudor	.10	.05
48	Andy Van Slyke	.25	.11
49	Todd Worrell	1.00	.45
50	Jim Acker	.10	.05
51	Doyle Alexander	.10	.05
52	Jesse Barfield	.10	.05
53	George Bell	.25	.11
54	Jeff Burroughs	.10	.05
55	Bill Caudill	.10	.05
56	Jim Clancy	.10	.05
57	Tony Fernandez	.25	.11
58	Tom Filer	.10	.05
59	Damaso Garcia	.10	.05
60	Tom Henke	.25	.11
61	Garth Iorg	.10	.05
62	Cliff Johnson	.10	.05
63	Jimmy Key	1.00	.45
64	Dennis Lamp	.10	.05
65	Gary Lavelle	.10	.05
66	Buck Martinez	.10	.05
67	Lloyd Moseby	.10	.05
68	Rance Mullniks	.10	.05
69	Al Oliver	.25	.11
70	Dave Stieb	.10	.05
71	Louis Thornton	.10	.05
72	Willie Upshaw	.10	.05
73	Ernie Whitt	.10	.05
74	Rick Aguilera	1.00	.45
75	Wally Backman	.10	.05
76	Gary Carter	1.00	.45
77	Ron Darling	.10	.05
78	Len Dykstra	2.00	.90
79	Sid Fernandez	.25	.11
80	George Foster	.25	.11
81	Dwight Gooden	1.00	.45
82	Tom Gorman	.10	.05
83	Danny Heep	.10	.05
84	Keith Hernandez	.25	.11
85	Howard Johnson	.25	.11
86	Ray Knight	.25	.11
87	Terry Leach	.10	.05
88	Ed Lynch	.10	.05
89	Roger McDowell	.25	.11
90	Jesse Orosco	.10	.05
91	Tom Paciorek	.25	.11
92	Ron Reynolds	.10	.05
93	Rafael Santana	.10	.05
94	Doug Sisk	.10	.05
95	Rusty Staub	.25	.11
96	Darryl Strawberry	1.00	.45
97	Mookie Wilson	.25	.11
98	Neil Allen	.10	.05
99	Don Baylor	.50	.23
100	Dale Berra	.10	.05
101	Rich Bordi	.10	.05
102	Marty Bystrom	.10	.05
103	Joe Cowley	.10	.05
104	Brian Fisher	.10	.05
105	Ken Griffey	.25	.11
106	Ron Guidry	.25	.11
107	Ron Hassey	.10	.05
108	Rickey Henderson UER (SB Record of 120, sic)	1.25	.55
109	Don Mattingly	2.00	.90
110	Bobby Meacham	.10	.05
111	John Montefusco	.10	.05
112	Phil Niekro	1.00	.45
113	Mike Pagliarulo	.10	.05
114	Dan Pasqua	.10	.05
115	Willie Randolph	.25	.11
116	Dave Righetti	.25	.11
117	Andre Robertson	.10	.05
118	Billy Sample	.10	.05
119	Bob Shirley	.10	.05
120	Ed Whitson	.10	.05

121	Dave Winfield	1.00	.45
122	Butch Wynegar	.10	.05
123	Dave Anderson	.10	.05
124	Bob Bailor	.10	.05
125	Greg Brock	.10	.05
126	Enos Cabell	.10	.05
127	Bobby Castillo	.10	.05
128	Carlos Diaz	.10	.05
129	Mariano Duncan	1.00	.45
130	Pedro Guerrero	.25	.11
131	Orel Hershiser	.50	.23
132	Rick Honeycutt	.10	.05
133	Ken Howell	.10	.05
134	Ken Landreaux	.10	.05
135	Bill Madlock	.10	.05
136	Candy Maldonado	.10	.05
137	Mike Marshall	.10	.05
138	Len Matuszek	.10	.05
139	Tom Niedenfuer	.10	.05
140	Alejandro Pena	.10	.05
141	Jerry Reuss	.10	.05
142	Bill Russell	.10	.05
143	Steve Sax	.10	.05
144	Mike Scioscia	.10	.05
145	Fernando Valenzuela	.25	.11
146	Bob Welch	.10	.05
147	Terry Whitfield	.10	.05
148	Juan Beniquez	.10	.05
149	Bob Boone	.25	.11
150	John Candelaria	.10	.05
151	Rod Carew	1.00	.45
152	Stewart Cliburn	.10	.05
153	Doug DeCinces	.10	.05
154	Brian Downing	.10	.05
155	Ken Forsch	.10	.05
156	Craig Gerber	.10	.05
157	Bobby Grich	.25	.11
158	George Hendrick	.10	.05
159	Al Holland	.10	.05
160	Reggie Jackson	1.25	.55
161	Ruppert Jones	.10	.05
162	Urbano Lugo	.10	.05
163	Kirk McCaskill	.25	.11
164	Donnie Moore	.10	.05
165	Gary Pettis	.10	.05
166	Ron Romanick	.10	.05
167	Dick Schofield	.10	.05
168	Daryl Sconiers	.10	.05
169	Jim Slaton	.10	.05
170	Don Sutton	1.00	.45
171	Mike Witt	.10	.05
172	Buddy Bell	.25	.11
173	Tom Browning	.10	.05
174	Dave Concepcion	.25	.11
175	Eric Davis	.50	.23
176	Bo Diaz	.10	.05
177	Nick Esasky	.10	.05
178	John Franco	1.00	.45
179	Tom Hume	.10	.05
180	Wayne Krenchicki	.10	.05
181	Andy McGaffigan	.10	.05
182	Eddie Milner	.10	.05
183	Ron Oester	.10	.05
184	Dave Parker	.25	.11
185	Frank Pastore	.10	.05
186	Tony Perez	1.00	.45
187	Ted Power	.10	.05
188	Joe Price	.10	.05
189	Gary Redus	.10	.05
190	Ron Robinson	.10	.05
191	Pete Rose	2.00	.90
192	Mario Soto	.10	.05
193	John Stuper	.10	.05
194	Jay Tibbs	.10	.05
195	Dave Van Gorder	.10	.05
196	Max Venable	.10	.05
197	Juan Agosto	.10	.05
198	Harold Baines	.50	.23
199	Floyd Bannister	.10	.05
200	Britt Burns	.10	.05
201	Julio Cruz	.10	.05
202	Joel Davis	.10	.05
203	Richard Dotson	.10	.05
204	Carlton Fisk	1.00	.45
205	Scott Fletcher	.10	.05
206	Ozzie Guillen	.50	.23
207	Jerry Hairston	.10	.05
208	Tim Hulett	.10	.05
209	Bob James	.10	.05
210	Ron Kittle	.10	.05
211	Rudy Law	.10	.05
212	Bryan Little	.10	.05
213	Gene Nelson	.10	.05
214	Reid Nichols	.10	.05
215	Luis Salazar	.10	.05
216	Tom Seaver	1.25	.55
217	Dan Spillner	.10	.05
218	Bruce Tanner	.10	.05
219	Greg Walker	.10	.05
220	Dave Wehrmeister	.10	.05
221	Juan Berenguer	.10	.05
222	Dave Bergman	.10	.05
223	Tom Brookens	.10	.05
224	Darrell Evans	.10	.11
225	Barbaro Garbey	.10	.05
226	Kirk Gibson	.25	.11
227	John Grubb	.10	.05
228	Willie Hernandez	.10	.05
229	Larry Herndon	.10	.05
230	Chet Lemon	.10	.05
231	Aurelio Lopez	.10	.05
232	Jack Morris	.25	.11
233	Randy O'Neal	.10	.05
234	Lance Parrish	.25	.11
235	Dan Petry	.10	.05
236	Alejandro Sanchez	.10	.05
237	Bill Scherrer	.10	.05
238	Nelson Simmons	.10	.05
239	Frank Tanana	.10	.05
240	Walt Terrell	.10	.05
241	Alan Trammell	.50	.23
242	Lou Whitaker	.25	.11
243	Milt Wilcox	.10	.05
244	Hubie Brooks	.10	.05
245	Tim Burke	.10	.05
246	Andre Dawson	1.00	.45
247	Mike Fitzgerald	.10	.05
248	Terry Francona	.10	.05
249	Bill Gullickson	.10	.05
250	Joe Hesketh	.10	.05
251	Bill Laskey	.10	.05
252	Vance Law	.10	.05
253	Charlie Lea	.10	.05
254	Gary Lucas	.10	.05
255	David Palmer	.10	.05
256	Tim Raines	.25	.11
257	Jeff Reardon	.10	.05
258	Bert Roberge	.10	.05
259	Dan Schatzeder	.10	.05
260	Bryn Smith	.10	.05
261	Randy St.Claire	.10	.05
262	Scot Thompson	.10	.05
263	Tim Wallach	.10	.05
264	U.L. Washington	.10	.05
265	Mitch Webster	.10	.05
266	Herm Winningham	.10	.05
267	Floyd Youmans	.10	.05
268	Don Aase	.10	.05
269	Mike Boddicker	.10	.05
270	Rich Dauer	.10	.05
271	Storm Davis	.10	.05
272	Rick Dempsey	.10	.05
273	Ken Dixon	.10	.05
274	Jim Dwyer	.10	.05
275	Mike Flanagan	.10	.05
276	Wayne Gross	.10	.05
277	Lee Lacy	.10	.05
278	Fred Lynn	.25	.11
279	Tippy Martinez	.10	.05
280	Dennis Martinez	.25	.11
281	Scott McGregor	.10	.05
282	Eddie Murray	1.00	.45
283	Floyd Rayford	.10	.05
284	Cal Ripken	4.00	1.80
285	Gary Roenicke	.10	.05
286	Larry Sheets	.10	.05
287	John Shelby	.10	.05
288	Nate Snell	.10	.05
289	Sammy Stewart	.10	.05
290	Alan Wiggins	.10	.05
291	Mike Young	.10	.05
292	Alan Ashby	.10	.05
293	Mark Bailey	.10	.05
294	Kevin Bass	.10	.05
295	Jeff Calhoun	.10	.05
296	Jose Cruz	.25	.11
297	Glenn Davis	.25	.11
298	Bill Dawley	.10	.05
299	Frank DiPino	.10	.05
300	Bill Doran	.10	.05
301	Phil Garner	.25	.11
302	Jeff Heathcock	.10	.05
303	Charlie Kerfeld	.10	.05
304	Bob Knepper	.10	.05
305	Ron Mathis	.10	.05
306	Jerry Mumphrey	.10	.05
307	Jim Pankovits	.10	.05
308	Terry Puhl	.10	.05
309	Craig Reynolds	.10	.05
310	Nolan Ryan	4.00	1.80
311	Mike Scott	.10	.05
312	Dave Smith	.10	.05
313	Dickie Thon	.10	.05
314	Denny Walling	.10	.05
315	Kurt Bevacqua	.10	.05
316	Al Bumbry	.10	.05
317	Jerry Davis	.10	.05
318	Luis DeLeon	.10	.05
319	Dave Dravecky	.25	.11
320	Tim Flannery	.10	.05
321	Steve Garvey	.50	.23
322	Rich Gossage	.25	.11
323	Tony Gwynn	2.50	1.10
324	Andy Hawkins	.10	.05
325	LaMarr Hoyt	.10	.05
326	Roy Lee Jackson	.10	.05
327	Terry Kennedy	.10	.05
328	Craig Lefferts	.10	.05
329	Carmelo Martinez	.10	.05
330	Lance McCullers	.10	.05
331	Kevin McReynolds	.10	.05
332	Graig Nettles	.25	.11
333	Jerry Royster	.10	.05
334	Eric Show	.10	.05
335	Tim Stoddard	.10	.05
336	Garry Templeton	.10	.05
337	Mark Thurmond	.10	.05
338	Ed Wojna	.10	.05
339	Tony Armas	.10	.05
340	Marty Barrett	.10	.05
341	Wade Boggs	1.00	.45
342	Dennis Boyd	.10	.05
343	Bill Buckner	.25	.11
344	Mark Clear	.10	.05
345	Roger Clemens	5.00	2.20
346	Steve Crawford	.10	.05
347	Mike Easler	.10	.05
348	Dwight Evans	.25	.11
349	Rich Gedman	.10	.05
350	Jackie Gutierrez	.10	.05
351	Glenn Hoffman	.10	.05
352	Bruce Hurst	.10	.05
353	Bruce Kison	.10	.05
354	Tim Lollar	.10	.05
355	Steve Lyons	.10	.05
356	Al Nipper	.10	.05
357	Bob Ojeda	.10	.05
358	Jim Rice	.25	.11
359	Bob Stanley	.10	.05
360	Mike Trujillo	.10	.05
361	Thad Bosley	.10	.05
362	Warren Brusstar	.10	.05
363	Ron Cey	.25	.11
364	Jody Davis	.10	.05
365	Bob Dernier	.10	.05
366	Shawon Dunston	.25	.11
367	Leon Durham	.10	.05
368	Dennis Eckersley	1.00	.45
369	Ray Fontenot	.10	.05
370	George Frazier	.10	.05
371	Billy Hatcher	.10	.05
372	Dave Lopes	.25	.11
373	Gary Matthews	.10	.05
374	Ron Meridith	.10	.05
375	Keith Moreland	.10	.05
376	Reggie Patterson	.10	.05
377	Dick Ruthven	.10	.05
378	Ryne Sandberg	1.25	.55

379	Scott Sanderson	.10	.05
380	Lee Smith	.50	.23
381	Lary Sorensen	.10	.05
382	Chris Speier	.10	.05
383	Rick Sutcliffe	.10	.05
384	Steve Trout	.10	.05
385	Gary Woods	.10	.05
386	Bert Blyleven	.25	.11
387	Tom Brunansky	.10	.05
388	Randy Bush	.10	.05
389	John Butcher	.10	.05
390	Ron Davis	.10	.05
391	Dave Engle	.10	.05
392	Frank Eufemia	.10	.05
393	Pete Filson	.10	.05
394	Gary Gaetti	.25	.11
395	Greg Gagne	.10	.05
396	Mickey Hatcher	.10	.05
397	Kent Hrbek	.25	.11
398	Tim Laudner	.10	.05
399	Rick Lysander	.10	.05
400	Dave Meier	.10	.05
401	Kirby Puckett UER (Card has him in NL, should be AL)	3.00	1.35
402	Mark Salas	.10	.05
403	Ken Schrom	.10	.05
404	Roy Smalley	.10	.05
405	Mike Smithson	.10	.05
406	Mike Stenhouse	.10	.05
407	Tim Teufel	.10	.05
408	Frank Viola	.25	.11
409	Ron Washington	.10	.05
410	Keith Atherton	.10	.05
411	Dusty Baker	.25	.11
412	Tim Birtsas	.10	.05
413	Bruce Bochte	.10	.05
414	Chris Codiroli	.10	.05
415	Dave Collins	.10	.05
416	Mike Davis	.10	.05
417	Alfredo Griffin	.10	.05
418	Mike Heath	.10	.05
419	Steve Henderson	.10	.05
420	Donnie Hill	.10	.05
421	Jay Howell	.10	.05
422	Tommy John	1.00	.45
423	Dave Kingman	.25	.11
424	Bill Krueger	.10	.05
425	Rick Langford	.10	.05
426	Carney Lansford	.25	.11
427	Steve McCatty	.10	.05
428	Dwayne Murphy	.10	.05
429	Steve Ontiveros	.25	.11
430	Tony Phillips	.10	.05
431	Jose Rijo	.10	.05
432	Mickey Tettleton	1.00	.45
433	Luis Aguayo	.10	.05
434	Larry Andersen	.10	.05
435	Steve Carlton	1.00	.45
436	Don Carman	.10	.05
437	Tim Corcoran	.10	.05
438	Darren Daulton	2.00	.90
439	John Denny	.10	.05
440	Tom Foley	.10	.05
441	Greg Gross	.10	.05
442	Kevin Gross	.10	.05
443	Von Hayes	.10	.05
444	Charles Hudson	.10	.05
445	Garry Maddox	.10	.05
446	Shane Rawley	.10	.05
447	Dave Rucker	.10	.05
448	John Russell	.10	.05
449	Juan Samuel	.10	.05
450	Mike Schmidt	1.50	.70
451	Rick Schu	.10	.05
452	Dave Shipanoff	.10	.05
453	Dave Stewart	.25	.11
454	Jeff Stone	.10	.05
455	Kent Tekulve	.10	.05
456	Ozzie Virgil	.10	.05
457	Glenn Wilson	.10	.05
458	Jim Beattie	.10	.05
459	Karl Best	.10	.05
460	Barry Bonnell	.10	.05
461	Phil Bradley	.10	.05
462	Ivan Calderon	.25	.11
463	Al Cowens	.10	.05
464	Alvin Davis	.10	.05
465	Dave Henderson	.10	.05
466	Bob Kearney	.10	.05
467	Mark Langston	.10	.05
468	Bob Long	.10	.05
469	Mike Moore	.10	.05
470	Edwin Nunez	.10	.05
471	Spike Owen	.10	.05
472	Jack Perconte	.10	.05
473	Jim Presley	.10	.05
474	Donnie Scott	.10	.05
475	Bill Swift	.10	.05
476	Danny Tartabull	.25	.11
477	Gorman Thomas	.10	.05
478	Roy Thomas	.10	.05
479	Ed VandeBerg	.10	.05
480	Frank Wills	.10	.05
481	Matt Young	.10	.05
482	Ray Burris	.10	.05
483	Jaime Cocanower	.10	.05
484	Cecil Copper	.25	.11
485	Danny Darwin	.10	.05
486	Rollie Fingers	1.00	.45
487	Jim Gantner	.10	.05
488	Bob L. Gibson	.10	.05
489	Moose Haas	.10	.05
490	Teddy Higuera	.25	.11
491	Paul Householder	.10	.05
492	Pete Ladd	.10	.05
493	Rick Manning	.10	.05
494	Bob McClure	.10	.05
495	Paul Molitor	1.00	.45
496	Charlie Moore	.10	.05
497	Ben Oglivie	.10	.05
498	Randy Ready	.10	.05
499	Earnie Riles	.10	.05
500	Ed Romero	.10	.05
501	Bill Schroeder	.10	.05
502	Ray Searage	.10	.05
503	Ted Simmons	.25	.11
504	Pete Vuckovich	.10	.05
505	Rick Waits	.10	.05
506	Robin Yount	1.00	.45
507	Len Barker	.10	.05
508	Steve Bedrosian	.10	.05
509	Bruce Benedict	.10	.05
510	Rick Camp	.10	.05
511	Rick Cerone	.10	.05
512	Chris Chambliss	.25	.11
513	Jeff Dedmon	.10	.05
514	Terry Forster	.10	.05
515	Gene Garber	.10	.05
516	Terry Harper	.10	.05
517	Bob Horner	.25	.11
518	Glenn Hubbard	.10	.05
519	Joe Johnson	.10	.05
520	Brad Komminsk	.10	.05
521	Rick Mahler	.10	.05
522	Dale Murphy	1.00	.45
523	Ken Oberkfell	.10	.05
524	Pascual Perez	.10	.05
525	Gerald Perry	.10	.05
526	Rafael Ramirez	.10	.05
527	Steve Shields	.10	.05
528	Zane Smith	.10	.05
529	Bruce Sutter	.25	.11
530	Milt Thompson	.25	.11
531	Claudell Washington	.10	.05
532	Paul Zuvella	.10	.05
533	Vida Blue	.25	.11
534	Bob Brenly	.10	.05
535	Chris Brown	.10	.05
536	Chili Davis	.50	.23
537	Mark Davis	.10	.05
538	Rob Deer	.25	.11
539	Dan Driessen	.10	.05
540	Scott Garrelts	.10	.05
541	Dan Gladden	.10	.05
542	Jim Gott	.10	.05
543	David Green	.10	.05
544	Atlee Hammaker	.10	.05
545	Mike Jeffcoat	.10	.05
546	Mike Krukow	.10	.05
547	Dave LaPoint	.10	.05
548	Jeff Leonard	.10	.05
549	Greg Minton	.10	.05
550	Alex Trevino	.10	.05
551	Manny Trillo	.10	.05
552	Jose Uribe	.10	.05
553	Brad Wellman	.10	.05
554	Frank Williams	.10	.05
555	Joel Youngblood	.10	.05
556	Alan Bannister	.10	.05
557	Glenn Brummer	.10	.05
558	Steve Buechele	.25	.11
559	Jose Guzman	.10	.05
560	Toby Harrah	.10	.05
561	Greg Harris	.10	.05
562	Dwayne Henry	.10	.05
563	Burt Hooton	.10	.05
564	Charlie Hough	.25	.11
565	Mike Mason	.10	.05
566	Oddibe McDowell	.10	.05
567	Dickie Noles	.10	.05
568	Pete O'Brien	.10	.05
569	Larry Parrish	.10	.05
570	Dave Rozema	.10	.05
571	Dave Schmidt	.10	.05
572	Don Slaught	.10	.05
573	Wayne Tolleson	.10	.05
574	Duane Walker	.10	.05
575	Gary Ward	.10	.05
576	Chris Welsh	.10	.05
577	Curtis Wilkerson	.10	.05
578	George Wright	.10	.05
579	Chris Bando	.10	.05
580	Tony Bernazard	.10	.05
581	Brett Butler	.25	.11
582	Ernie Camacho	.10	.05
583	Joe Carter	1.00	.45
584	Carmen Castillo	.10	.05
585	Jamie Easterly	.10	.05
586	Julio Franco	.25	.11
587	Mel Hall	.10	.05
588	Mike Hargrove	.25	.11
589	Neal Heaton	.10	.05
590	Brook Jacoby	.10	.05
591	Otis Nixon	1.00	.45
592	Jerry Reed	.10	.05
593	Vern Ruhle	.10	.05
594	Pat Tabler	.10	.05
595	Rich Thompson	.10	.05
596	Andre Thornton	.10	.05
597	Dave Von Ohlen	.10	.05
598	George Vukovich	.10	.05
599	Tom Waddell	.10	.05
600	Curt Wardle	.10	.05
601	Jerry Willard	.10	.05
602	Bill Almon	.10	.05
603	Mike Bielecki	.10	.05
604	Sid Bream	.10	.05
605	Mike C. Brown	.10	.05
606	Pat Clements	.10	.05
607	Jose DeLeon	.10	.05
608	Denny Gonzalez	.10	.05
609	Cecilio Guante	.10	.05
610	Steve Kemp	.10	.05
611	Sammy Khalifa	.10	.05
612	Lee Mazzilli	.10	.05
613	Larry McWilliams	.10	.05
614	Jim Morrison	.10	.05
615	Joe Orsulak	.10	.05
616	Tony Pena	.10	.05
617	Johnny Ray	.10	.05
618	Rick Reuschel	.10	.05
619	R.J. Reynolds	.10	.05
620	Rick Rhoden	.10	.05
621	Don Robinson	.10	.05
622	Jason Thompson	.10	.05
623	Lee Tunnell	.10	.05
624	Jim Winn	.10	.05
625	Marvell Wynne	.10	.05
626	Dwight Gooden IA	.25	.11
627	Don Mattingly IA	1.00	.45
628	4192 (Pete Rose)	.50	.23
629	3000 Career Hits Rod Carew	1.00	.45
630	300 Career Wins Tom Seaver Phil Niekro	1.00	.45
631	Ouch (Don Baylor)	.25	.11

	MINT	NRMT
❑ 632 Instant Offense	.50	.23
Darryl Strawberry		
Tim Raines		
❑ 633 Shortstops Supreme	2.00	.90
Cal Ripken		
Alan Trammell		
❑ 634 Boggs and "Hero"	1.00	.45
Wade Boggs		
George Brett		
❑ 635 Braves Dynamic Duo	.25	.11
Bob Horner		
Dale Murphy		
❑ 636 Cardinal Ignitors	.25	.11
Willie McGee		
Vince Coleman		
❑ 637 Terror on Basepaths	.25	.11
Vince Coleman		
❑ 638 Charlie Hustle / Dr.K	1.00	.45
Pete Rose		
Dwight Gooden		
❑ 639 1984 and 1985 AL	1.00	.45
Batting Champs		
Wade Boggs		
Don Mattingly		
❑ 640 NL West Sluggers	.25	.11
Dale Murphy		
Steve Garvey		
Dave Parker		
❑ 641 Staff Aces	.25	.11
Fernando Valenzuela		
Dwight Gooden		
❑ 642 Blue Jay Stoppers	.25	.11
Jimmy Key		
Dave Stieb		
❑ 643 AL All-Star Backstops	.25	.11
Carlton Fisk		
Rich Gedman		
❑ 644 Gene Walter and	1.00	.45
Benito Santiago		
❑ 645 Mike Woodard and	.10	.05
Colin Ward		
❑ 646 Kal Daniels and	3.00	1.35
Paul O'Neill		
❑ 647 Andres Galarraga and	5.00	2.20
Fred Toliver		
❑ 648 Bob Kipper and	.10	.05
Curt Ford		
❑ 649 Jose Canseco and	25.00	11.00
Eric Plunk		
❑ 650 Mark McLemore and	1.00	.45
Gus Polidor		
❑ 651 Rob Woodward and	.10	.05
Mickey Brantley		
❑ 652 Billy Joe Robidoux and	.10	.05
Mark Funderburk		
❑ 653 Cecil Fielder and	2.00	.90
Cory Snyder		
❑ 654 CL: Royals/Cardinals	.10	.05
Blue Jays/Mets		
❑ 655 CL: Yankees/Dodgers	.10	.05
Angels/Reds UER		
(168 Darly Sconiers)		
❑ 656 CL: White Sox/Tigers	.10	.05
Expos/Orioles		
(279 Dennis,		
280 Tippy)		
❑ 657 CL: Astros/Padres	.10	.05
Red Sox/Cubs		
❑ 658 CL: Twins/A's	.10	.05
Phillies/Mariners		
❑ 659 CL: Brewers/Braves	.10	.05
Giants/Rangers		
❑ 660 CL: Indians/Pirates	.10	.05
Special Cards		

1986 Fleer All-Stars

	MINT	NRMT
COMPLETE SET (12)	25.00	11.00
COMMON CARD (1-12)	.25	.11
RANDOM INSERTS IN PACKS		
❑ 1 Don Mattingly	5.00	2.20
❑ 2 Tom Herr	.25	.11
❑ 3 George Brett	5.00	2.20
❑ 4 Gary Carter	.75	.35

	MINT	NRMT
❑ 5 Cal Ripken	12.00	5.50
❑ 6 Dave Parker	.35	.16
❑ 7 Rickey Henderson UER	2.00	.90
(Misspelled Ricky on card back)		
❑ 8 Pedro Guerrero	.35	.16
❑ 9 Dan Quisenberry	.25	.11
❑ 10 Dwight Gooden	.75	.35
❑ 11 Gorman Thomas	.25	.11
❑ 12 John Tudor	.25	.11

1986 Fleer Future Hall of Famers

	MINT	NRMT
COMPLETE SET (6)	15.00	6.75
COMMON CARD (1-6)	2.00	.90
ONE PER RACK PACK		
❑ 1 Pete Rose	3.00	1.35
❑ 2 Steve Carlton	2.00	.90
❑ 3 Tom Seaver	2.00	.90
❑ 4 Rod Carew	2.00	.90
❑ 5 Nolan Ryan	10.00	4.50
❑ 6 Reggie Jackson	3.00	1.35

1986 Fleer Update

	MINT	NRMT
COMP.FACT.SET (132)	25.00	11.00
COMMON CARD (1-132)	.10	.05
MINOR STARS	.20	.09
SEMISTARS	.40	.18
UNLISTED STARS	.75	.35
❑ 1 Mike Aldrete	.10	.05
❑ 2 Andy Allanson	.10	.05
❑ 3 Neil Allen	.10	.05
❑ 4 Joaquin Andujar	.10	.05
❑ 5 Paul Assenmacher	.10	.05
❑ 6 Scott Bailes	.10	.05
❑ 7 Jay Baller	.10	.05
❑ 8 Scott Bankhead	.10	.05
❑ 9 Bill Bathe	.10	.05
❑ 10 Don Baylor	.40	.18
❑ 11 Billy Beane	.10	.05
❑ 12 Steve Bedrosian	.10	.05
❑ 13 Juan Beniquez	.10	.05
❑ 14 Barry Bonds	12.00	5.50
❑ 15 Bobby Bonilla UER	1.25	.55
(Wrong birthday)		
❑ 16 Rich Bordi	.10	.05
❑ 17 Bill Campbell	.10	.05
❑ 18 Tom Candiotti	.10	.05
❑ 19 John Cangelosi	.10	.05
❑ 20 Jose Canseco UER	6.00	2.70
(Headings on back for a pitcher)		
❑ 21 Chuck Cary	.10	.05
❑ 22 Juan Castillo	.10	.05
❑ 23 Rick Cerone	.10	.05
❑ 24 John Cerutti	.10	.05
❑ 25 Will Clark	2.50	1.10
❑ 26 Mark Clear	.10	.05
❑ 27 Darnell Coles	.10	.05
❑ 28 Dave Collins	.10	.05
❑ 29 Tim Conroy	.10	.05
❑ 30 Ed Correa	.10	.05
❑ 31 Joe Cowley	.10	.05
❑ 32 Bill Dawley	.10	.05
❑ 33 Rob Deer	.20	.09
❑ 34 John Denny	.10	.05
❑ 35 Jim Deshaies	.10	.05
❑ 36 Doug Drabek	.75	.35
❑ 37 Mike Easler	.10	.05
❑ 38 Mark Eichhorn	.10	.05
❑ 39 Dave Engle	.10	.05
❑ 40 Mike Fischlin	.10	.05
❑ 41 Scott Fletcher	.10	.05
❑ 42 Terry Forster	.10	.05
❑ 43 Terry Francona	.10	.05
❑ 44 Andres Galarraga	1.25	.55
❑ 45 Lee Guetterman	.10	.05
❑ 46 Bill Gullickson	.10	.05
❑ 47 Jackie Gutierrez	.10	.05
❑ 48 Moose Haas	.10	.05
❑ 49 Billy Hatcher	.10	.05
❑ 50 Mike Heath	.10	.05
❑ 51 Guy Hoffman	.10	.05
❑ 52 Tom Hume	.10	.05
❑ 53 Pete Incaviglia	.75	.35
❑ 54 Dane Iorg	.10	.05
❑ 55 Chris James	.10	.05
❑ 56 Stan Javier	.20	.09
❑ 57 Tommy John	.75	.35
❑ 58 Tracy Jones	.10	.05
❑ 59 Wally Joyner	.75	.35
❑ 60 Wayne Krenchicki	.10	.05
❑ 61 John Kruk	.75	.35
❑ 62 Mike LaCoss	.10	.05
❑ 63 Pete Ladd	.10	.05
❑ 64 Dave LaPoint	.10	.05
❑ 65 Mike LaValliere	.10	.05
❑ 66 Rudy Law	.10	.05
❑ 67 Dennis Leonard	.10	.05
❑ 68 Steve Lombardozzi	.10	.05
❑ 69 Aurelio Lopez	.10	.05
❑ 70 Mickey Mahler	.10	.05
❑ 71 Candy Maldonado	.10	.05
❑ 72 Roger Mason	.10	.05
❑ 73 Greg Mathews	.10	.05
❑ 74 Andy McGaffigan	.10	.05
❑ 75 Joel McKeon	.10	.05
❑ 76 Kevin Mitchell	.75	.35
❑ 77 Bill Mooneyham	.10	.05
❑ 78 Omar Moreno	.10	.05
❑ 79 Jerry Mumphrey	.10	.05
❑ 80 Al Newman	.20	.09
❑ 81 Phil Niekro	.75	.35

#	Player	MINT	NRMT
82	Randy Niemann	.10	.05
83	Juan Nieves	.10	.05
84	Bob Ojeda	.10	.05
85	Rick Ownbey	.10	.05
86	Tom Paciorek	.20	.09
87	David Palmer	.10	.05
88	Jeff Parrett	.10	.05
89	Pat Perry	.10	.05
90	Dan Plesac	.10	.05
91	Darrell Porter	.20	.09
92	Luis Quinones	.10	.05
93	Rey Quinones UER	.10	.05
	(Misspelled Quinonez)		
94	Gary Redus	.10	.05
95	Jeff Reed	.10	.05
96	Bip Roberts	.75	.35
97	Billy Joe Robidoux	.10	.05
98	Gary Roenicke	.10	.05
99	Ron Roenicke	.10	.05
100	Angel Salazar	.10	.05
101	Joe Sambito	.10	.05
102	Billy Sample	.10	.05
103	Dave Schmidt	.10	.05
104	Ken Schrom	.10	.05
105	Ruben Sierra	.75	.35
106	Ted Simmons	.20	.09
107	Sammy Stewart	.10	.05
108	Kurt Stillwell	.10	.05
109	Dale Sveum	.10	.05
110	Tim Teufel	.10	.05
111	Bob Tewksbury	.20	.09
112	Andres Thomas	.10	.05
113	Jason Thompson	.10	.05
114	Milt Thompson	.20	.09
115	Robby Thompson	.20	.09
116	Jay Tibbs	.10	.05
117	Fred Toliver	.10	.05
118	Wayne Tolleson	.10	.05
119	Alex Trevino	.10	.05
120	Manny Trillo	.10	.05
121	Ed VandeBerg	.10	.05
122	Ozzie Virgil	.10	.05
123	Tony Walker	.10	.05
124	Gene Walter	.10	.05
125	Duane Ward	.20	.09
126	Jerry Willard	.10	.05
127	Mitch Williams	.20	.09
128	Reggie Williams	.10	.05
129	Bobby Witt	.40	.18
130	Marvell Wynne	.10	.05
131	Steve Yeager	.10	.05
132	Checklist 1-132	.10	.05

1987 Fleer

	MINT	NRMT
COMPLETE SET (660)	50.00	22.00
COMP.FACT.SET (672)	50.00	22.00
COMMON CARD (1-660)	.20	.09
MINOR STARS	.40	.18
UNLISTED STARS	.75	.35
COMP.WORLD SERIES SET (12)	2.00	.90

*WS: EQUAL VALUE TO BASIC CARDS
ONE WORLD SERIES SET PER FACT.SET

#	Player	MINT	NRMT
1	Rick Aguilera	.40	.18
2	Richard Anderson	.20	.09
3	Wally Backman	.20	.09
4	Gary Carter	.60	.25
5	Ron Darling	.20	.09
6	Len Dykstra	.60	.25
7	Kevin Elster	.40	.18
8	Sid Fernandez	.20	.09
9	Dwight Gooden	.60	.25
10	Ed Hearn	.20	.09
11	Danny Heep	.20	.09
12	Keith Hernandez	.40	.18
13	Howard Johnson	.20	.09
14	Ray Knight	.20	.09
15	Lee Mazzilli	.20	.09
16	Roger McDowell	.20	.09
17	Kevin Mitchell	.60	.25
18	Randy Niemann	.20	.09
19	Bob Ojeda	.20	.09
20	Jesse Orosco	.20	.09
21	Rafael Santana	.20	.09
22	Doug Sisk	.20	.09
23	Darryl Strawberry	.60	.25
24	Tim Teufel	.20	.09
25	Mookie Wilson	.40	.18
26	Tony Armas	.20	.09
27	Marty Barrett	.20	.09
28	Don Baylor	.40	.18
29	Wade Boggs	.75	.35
30	Oil Can Boyd	.20	.09
31	Bill Buckner	.40	.18
32	Roger Clemens	2.50	1.10
33	Steve Crawford	.20	.09
34	Dwight Evans	.40	.18
35	Rich Gedman	.20	.09
36	Dave Henderson	.20	.09
37	Bruce Hurst	.20	.09
38	Tim Lollar	.20	.09
39	Al Nipper	.20	.09
40	Spike Owen	.20	.09
41	Jim Rice	.40	.18
42	Ed Romero	.20	.09
43	Joe Sambito	.20	.09
44	Calvin Schiraldi	.20	.09
45	Tom Seaver UER	.75	.35
	Lifetime saves total 0, should be 1		
46	Jeff Sellers	.20	.09
47	Bob Stanley	.20	.09
48	Sammy Stewart	.20	.09
49	Larry Andersen	.20	.09
50	Alan Ashby	.20	.09
51	Kevin Bass	.20	.09
52	Jeff Calhoun	.20	.09
53	Jose Cruz	.40	.18
54	Danny Darwin	.20	.09
55	Glenn Davis	.40	.18
56	Jim Deshaies	.20	.09
57	Bill Doran	.20	.09
58	Phil Garner	.20	.09
59	Billy Hatcher	.20	.09
60	Charlie Kerfeld	.20	.09
61	Bob Knepper	.20	.09
62	Dave Lopes	.40	.18
63	Aurelio Lopez	.20	.09
64	Jim Pankovits	.20	.09
65	Terry Puhl	.20	.09
66	Craig Reynolds	.20	.09
67	Nolan Ryan	3.00	1.35
68	Mike Scott	.20	.09
69	Dave Smith	.20	.09
70	Dickie Thon	.20	.09
71	Tony Walker	.20	.09
72	Denny Walling	.20	.09
73	Bob Boone	.40	.18
74	Rick Burleson	.20	.09
75	John Candelaria	.20	.09
76	Doug Corbett	.20	.09
77	Doug DeCinces	.20	.09
78	Brian Downing	.20	.09
79	Chuck Finley	2.00	.90
80	Terry Forster	.20	.09
81	Bob Grich	.40	.18
82	George Hendrick	.20	.09
83	Jack Howell	.20	.09
84	Reggie Jackson	1.00	.45
85	Ruppert Jones	.20	.09
86	Wally Joyner	1.00	.45
87	Gary Lucas	.20	.09
88	Kirk McCaskill	.20	.09
89	Donnie Moore	.20	.09
90	Gary Pettis	.20	.09
91	Vern Ruhle	.20	.09
92	Dick Schofield	.20	.09
93	Don Sutton	.75	.35
94	Rob Wilfong	.20	.09
95	Mike Witt	.20	.09
96	Doug Drabek	.75	.35
97	Mike Easler	.20	.09
98	Mike Fischlin	.20	.09
99	Brian Fisher	.20	.09
100	Ron Guidry	.40	.18
101	Rickey Henderson	1.00	.45
102	Tommy John	.40	.18
103	Ron Kittle	.20	.09
104	Don Mattingly	1.50	.70
105	Bobby Meacham	.20	.09
106	Joe Niekro	.20	.09
107	Mike Pagliarulo	.20	.09
108	Dan Pasqua	.20	.09
109	Willie Randolph	.40	.18
110	Dennis Rasmussen	.20	.09
111	Dave Righetti	.20	.09
112	Gary Roenicke	.20	.09
113	Rod Scurry	.20	.09
114	Bob Shirley	.20	.09
115	Joel Skinner	.20	.09
116	Tim Stoddard	.20	.09
117	Bob Tewksbury	.40	.18
118	Wayne Tolleson	.20	.09
119	Claudell Washington	.20	.09
120	Dave Winfield	.75	.35
121	Steve Buechele	.20	.09
122	Ed Correa	.20	.09
123	Scott Fletcher	.20	.09
124	Jose Guzman	.20	.09
125	Toby Harrah	.20	.09
126	Greg Harris	.20	.09
127	Charlie Hough	.20	.09
128	Pete Incaviglia	.40	.18
129	Mike Mason	.20	.09
130	Oddibe McDowell	.20	.09
131	Dale Mohorcic	.20	.09
132	Pete O'Brien	.20	.09
133	Tom Paciorek	.40	.18
134	Larry Parrish	.20	.09
135	Geno Petralli	.20	.09
136	Darrell Porter	.20	.09
137	Jeff Russell	.20	.09
138	Ruben Sierra	1.00	.45
139	Don Slaught	.20	.09
140	Gary Ward	.20	.09
141	Curtis Wilkerson	.20	.09
142	Mitch Williams	.40	.18
143	Bobby Witt UER	.40	.18
	(Tulsa misspelled as Tusla; ERA should be 6.43, not .643)		
144	Dave Bergman	.20	.09
145	Tom Brookens	.20	.09
146	Bill Campbell	.20	.09
147	Chuck Cary	.20	.09
148	Darnell Coles	.20	.09
149	Dave Collins	.20	.09
150	Darrell Evans	.40	.18
151	Kirk Gibson	.40	.18
152	John Grubb	.20	.09
153	Willie Hernandez	.20	.09
154	Larry Herndon	.20	.09
155	Eric King	.20	.09
156	Chet Lemon	.20	.09
157	Dwight Lowry	.20	.09
158	Jack Morris	.40	.18
159	Randy O'Neal	.20	.09
160	Lance Parrish	.40	.18
161	Dan Petry	.20	.09
162	Pat Sheridan	.20	.09
163	Jim Slaton	.20	.09
164	Frank Tanana	.20	.09
165	Walt Terrell	.20	.09
166	Mark Thurmond	.20	.09
167	Alan Trammell	.60	.25
168	Lou Whitaker	.40	.18
169	Luis Aguayo	.20	.09
170	Steve Bedrosian	.20	.09
171	Don Carman	.20	.09

172	Darren Daulton	.60	.25
173	Greg Gross	.20	.09
174	Kevin Gross	.20	.09
175	Von Hayes	.20	.09
176	Charles Hudson	.20	.09
177	Tom Hume	.20	.09
178	Steve Jeltz	.20	.09
179	Mike Maddux	.20	.09
180	Shane Rawley	.20	.09
181	Gary Redus	.20	.09
182	Ron Roenicke	.20	.09
183	Bruce Ruffin	.20	.09
184	John Russell	.20	.09
185	Juan Samuel	.20	.09
186	Dan Schatzeder	.20	.09
187	Mike Schmidt	1.25	.55
188	Rick Schu	.20	.09
189	Jeff Stone	.20	.09
190	Kent Tekulve	.20	.09
191	Milt Thompson	.20	.09
192	Glenn Wilson	.20	.09
193	Buddy Bell	.40	.18
194	Tom Browning	.20	.09
195	Sal Butera	.20	.09
196	Dave Concepcion	.40	.18
197	Kal Daniels	.20	.09
198	Eric Davis	.60	.25
199	John Denny	.20	.09
200	Bo Diaz	.20	.09
201	Nick Esasky	.20	.09
202	John Franco	.40	.18
203	Bill Gullickson	.20	.09
204	Barry Larkin	5.00	2.20
205	Eddie Milner	.20	.09
206	Rob Murphy	.20	.09
207	Ron Oester	.20	.09
208	Dave Parker	.40	.18
209	Tony Perez	.75	.35
210	Ted Power	.20	.09
211	Joe Price	.20	.09
212	Ron Robinson	.20	.09
213	Pete Rose	1.50	.70
214	Mario Soto	.20	.09
215	Kurt Stillwell	.20	.09
216	Max Venable	.20	.09
217	Chris Welsh	.20	.09
218	Carl Willis	.20	.09
219	Jesse Barfield	.20	.09
220	George Bell	.40	.18
221	Bill Caudill	.20	.09
222	John Cerutti	.20	.09
223	Jim Clancy	.20	.09
224	Mark Eichhorn	.20	.09
225	Tony Fernandez	.20	.09
226	Damaso Garcia	.20	.09
227	Kelly Gruber ERR (Wrong birth year)	.20	.09
228	Tom Henke	.20	.09
229	Garth Iorg	.20	.09
230	Joe Johnson	.20	.09
231	Cliff Johnson	.20	.09
232	Jimmy Key	.40	.18
233	Dennis Lamp	.20	.09
234	Rick Leach	.20	.09
235	Buck Martinez	.20	.09
236	Lloyd Moseby	.20	.09
237	Rance Mulliniks	.20	.09
238	Dave Stieb	.20	.09
239	Willie Upshaw	.20	.09
240	Ernie Whitt	.20	.09
241	Andy Allanson	.20	.09
242	Scott Bailes	.20	.09
243	Chris Bando	.20	.09
244	Tony Bernazard	.20	.09
245	John Butcher	.20	.09
246	Brett Butler	.40	.18
247	Ernie Camacho	.20	.09
248	Tom Candiotti	.20	.09
249	Joe Carter	.75	.35
250	Carmen Castillo	.20	.09
251	Julio Franco	.40	.18
252	Mel Hall	.20	.09
253	Brook Jacoby	.20	.09
254	Phil Niekro	.75	.35
255	Otis Nixon	.60	.25
256	Dickie Noles	.20	.09
257	Bryan Oelkers	.20	.09
258	Ken Schrom	.20	.09
259	Don Schulze	.20	.09
260	Cory Snyder	.20	.09
261	Pat Tabler	.20	.09
262	Andre Thornton	.20	.09
263	Rich Yatt	.20	.09
264	Mike Aldrete	.20	.09
265	Juan Berenguer	.20	.09
266	Vida Blue	.40	.18
267	Bob Brenly	.20	.09
268	Chris Brown	.20	.09
269	Will Clark	4.00	1.80
270	Chili Davis	.60	.25
271	Mark Davis	.20	.09
272	Kelly Downs	.20	.09
273	Scott Garrelts	.20	.09
274	Dan Gladden	.20	.09
275	Mike Krukow	.20	.09
276	Randy Kutcher	.20	.09
277	Mike LaCoss	.20	.09
278	Jeff Leonard	.20	.09
279	Candy Maldonado	.20	.09
280	Roger Mason	.20	.09
281	Bob Melvin	.20	.09
282	Greg Minton	.20	.09
283	Jeff D. Robinson	.20	.09
284	Harry Spilman	.20	.09
285	Robby Thompson	.40	.18
286	Jose Uribe	.20	.09
287	Frank Williams	.20	.09
288	Joel Youngblood	.20	.09
289	Jack Clark	.40	.18
290	Vince Coleman	.20	.09
291	Tim Conroy	.20	.09
292	Danny Cox	.20	.09
293	Ken Dayley	.20	.09
294	Curt Ford	.20	.09
295	Bob Forsch	.20	.09
296	Tom Herr	.20	.09
297	Ricky Horton	.20	.09
298	Clint Hurdle	.20	.09
299	Jeff Lahti	.20	.09
300	Steve Lake	.20	.09
301	Tito Landrum	.20	.09
302	Mike LaValliere	.20	.09
303	Greg Mathews	.20	.09
304	Willie McGee	.40	.18
305	Jose Oquendo	.20	.09
306	Terry Pendleton	.40	.18
307	Pat Perry	.20	.09
308	Ozzie Smith	1.00	.45
309	Ray Soff	.20	.09
310	John Tudor	.20	.09
311	Andy Van Slyke UER (Bats R, Throws L)	.40	.18
312	Todd Worrell	.40	.18
313	Dann Bilardello	.20	.09
314	Hubie Brooks	.20	.09
315	Tim Burke	.20	.09
316	Andre Dawson	.75	.35
317	Mike Fitzgerald	.20	.09
318	Tom Foley	.20	.09
319	Andres Galarraga	.75	.35
320	Joe Hesketh	.20	.09
321	Wallace Johnson	.20	.09
322	Wayne Krenchicki	.20	.09
323	Vance Law	.20	.09
324	Dennis Martinez	.40	.18
325	Bob McClure	.20	.09
326	Andy McGaffigan	.20	.09
327	Al Newman	.20	.09
328	Tim Raines	.40	.18
329	Jeff Reardon	.40	.18
330	Luis Rivera	.20	.09
331	Bob Sebra	.20	.09
332	Bryn Smith	.20	.09
333	Jay Tibbs	.20	.09
334	Tim Wallach	.20	.09
335	Mitch Webster	.20	.09
336	Jim Wohlford	.20	.09
337	Floyd Youmans	.20	.09
338	Chris Bosio	.40	.18
339	Glenn Braggs	.20	.09
340	Rick Cerone	.20	.09
341	Mark Clear	.20	.09
342	Bryan Clutterbuck	.20	.09
343	Cecil Cooper	.40	.18
344	Rob Deer	.20	.09
345	Jim Gantner	.20	.09
346	Ted Higuera	.20	.09
347	John Henry Johnson	.20	.09
348	Tim Leary	.20	.09
349	Rick Manning	.20	.09
350	Paul Molitor	.75	.35
351	Charlie Moore	.20	.09
352	Juan Nieves	.20	.09
353	Ben Oglivie	.20	.09
354	Dan Plesac	.20	.09
355	Ernest Riles	.20	.09
356	Billy Joe Robidoux	.20	.09
357	Bill Schroeder	.20	.09
358	Dale Sveum	.20	.09
359	Gorman Thomas	.20	.09
360	Bill Wegman	.20	.09
361	Robin Yount	.75	.35
362	Steve Balboni	.20	.09
363	Scott Bankhead	.20	.09
364	Buddy Biancalana	.20	.09
365	Bud Black	.20	.09
366	George Brett	1.50	.70
367	Steve Farr	.20	.09
368	Mark Gubicza	.20	.09
369	Bo Jackson	3.00	1.35
370	Danny Jackson	.20	.09
371	Mike Kingery	.20	.09
372	Rudy Law	.20	.09
373	Charlie Leibrandt	.20	.09
374	Dennis Leonard	.20	.09
375	Hal McRae	.40	.18
376	Jorge Orta	.20	.09
377	Jamie Quirk	.20	.09
378	Dan Quisenberry	.20	.09
379	Bret Saberhagen	.40	.18
380	Angel Salazar	.20	.09
381	Lonnie Smith	.20	.09
382	Jim Sundberg	.20	.09
383	Frank White	.40	.18
384	Willie Wilson	.40	.18
385	Joaquin Andujar	.20	.09
386	Doug Bair	.20	.09
387	Dusty Baker	.40	.18
388	Bruce Bochte	.20	.09
389	Jose Canseco	3.00	1.35
390	Chris Codiroli	.20	.09
391	Mike Davis	.20	.09
392	Alfredo Griffin	.20	.09
393	Moose Haas	.20	.09
394	Donnie Hill	.20	.09
395	Jay Howell	.20	.09
396	Dave Kingman	.40	.18
397	Carney Lansford	.40	.18
398	Dave Leiper	.20	.09
399	Bill Mooneyham	.20	.09
400	Dwayne Murphy	.20	.09
401	Steve Ontiveros	.20	.09
402	Tony Phillips	.20	.09
403	Eric Plunk	.20	.09
404	Jose Rijo	.20	.09
405	Terry Steinbach	1.00	.45
406	Dave Stewart	.40	.18
407	Mickey Tettleton	.40	.18
408	Dave Von Ohlen	.20	.09
409	Jerry Willard	.20	.09
410	Curt Young	.20	.09
411	Bruce Bochy	.20	.09
412	Dave Dravecky	.40	.18
413	Tim Flannery	.20	.09
414	Steve Garvey	.60	.25
415	Rich Gossage	.40	.18
416	Tony Gwynn	2.00	.90
417	Andy Hawkins	.20	.09
418	LaMarr Hoyt	.20	.09
419	Terry Kennedy	.20	.09
420	John Kruk	1.00	.45
421	Dave LaPoint	.20	.09
422	Craig Lefferts	.20	.09
423	Carmelo Martinez	.20	.09
424	Lance McCullers	.20	.09
425	Kevin McReynolds	.20	.09
426	Graig Nettles	.40	.18
427	Bip Roberts	.75	.35

No.	Player	Value	Value
428	Jerry Royster	.20	.09
429	Benito Santiago	.40	.18
430	Eric Show	.20	.09
431	Bob Stoddard	.20	.09
432	Garry Templeton	.20	.09
433	Gene Walter	.20	.09
434	Ed Whitson	.20	.09
435	Marvell Wynne	.20	.09
436	Dave Anderson	.20	.09
437	Greg Brock	.20	.09
438	Enos Cabell	.20	.09
439	Mariano Duncan	.20	.09
440	Pedro Guerrero	.20	.09
441	Orel Hershiser	.40	.18
442	Rick Honeycutt	.20	.09
443	Ken Howell	.20	.09
444	Ken Landreaux	.20	.09
445	Bill Madlock	.40	.18
446	Mike Marshall	.20	.09
447	Len Matuszek	.20	.09
448	Tom Niedenfuer	.20	.09
449	Alejandro Pena	.20	.09
450	Dennis Powell	.20	.09
451	Jerry Reuss	.20	.09
452	Bill Russell	.20	.09
453	Steve Sax	.20	.09
454	Mike Scioscia	.20	.09
455	Franklin Stubbs	.20	.09
456	Alex Trevino	.20	.09
457	Fernando Valenzuela	.40	.18
458	Ed VandeBerg	.20	.09
459	Bob Welch	.20	.09
460	Reggie Williams	.20	.09
461	Don Aase	.20	.09
462	Juan Beniquez	.20	.09
463	Mike Boddicker	.20	.09
464	Juan Bonilla	.20	.09
465	Rich Bordi	.20	.09
466	Storm Davis	.20	.09
467	Rick Dempsey	.40	.18
468	Ken Dixon	.20	.09
469	Jim Dwyer	.20	.09
470	Mike Flanagan	.20	.09
471	Jackie Gutierrez	.20	.09
472	Brad Havens	.20	.09
473	Lee Lacy	.20	.09
474	Fred Lynn	.40	.18
475	Scott McGregor	.20	.09
476	Eddie Murray	.75	.35
477	Tom O'Malley	.20	.09
478	Cal Ripken Jr.	3.00	1.35
479	Larry Sheets	.20	.09
480	John Shelby	.20	.09
481	Nate Snell	.20	.09
482	Jim Traber	.20	.09
483	Mike Young	.20	.09
484	Neil Allen	.20	.09
485	Harold Baines	.40	.18
486	Floyd Bannister	.20	.09
487	Daryl Boston	.20	.09
488	Ivan Calderon	.20	.09
489	John Cangelosi	.20	.09
490	Steve Carlton	.75	.35
491	Joe Cowley	.20	.09
492	Julio Cruz	.20	.09
493	Bill Dawley	.20	.09
494	Jose DeLeon	.20	.09
495	Richard Dotson	.20	.09
496	Carlton Fisk	.75	.35
497	Ozzie Guillen	.20	.09
498	Jerry Hairston	.20	.09
499	Ron Hassey	.20	.09
500	Tim Hulett	.20	.09
501	Bob James	.20	.09
502	Steve Lyons	.20	.09
503	Joel McKeon	.20	.09
504	Gene Nelson	.20	.09
505	Dave Schmidt	.20	.09
506	Ray Searage	.20	.09
507	Bobby Thigpen	.40	.18
508	Greg Walker	.20	.09
509	Jim Acker	.20	.09
510	Doyle Alexander	.20	.09
511	Paul Assenmacher	.60	.25
512	Bruce Benedict	.20	.09
513	Chris Chambliss	.40	.18
514	Jeff Dedmon	.20	.09
515	Gene Garber	.20	.09
516	Ken Griffey	.40	.18
517	Terry Harper	.20	.09
518	Bob Horner	.20	.09
519	Glenn Hubbard	.20	.09
520	Rick Mahler	.20	.09
521	Omar Moreno	.20	.09
522	Dale Murphy	.75	.35
523	Ken Oberkfell	.20	.09
524	Ed Olwine	.20	.09
525	David Palmer	.20	.09
526	Rafael Ramirez	.20	.09
527	Billy Sample	.20	.09
528	Ted Simmons	.40	.18
529	Zane Smith	.20	.09
530	Bruce Sutter	.20	.09
531	Andres Thomas	.20	.09
532	Ozzie Virgil	.20	.09
533	Allan Anderson	.20	.09
534	Keith Atherton	.20	.09
535	Billy Beane	.20	.09
536	Bert Blyleven	.40	.18
537	Tom Brunansky	.20	.09
538	Randy Bush	.20	.09
539	George Frazier	.20	.09
540	Gary Gaetti	.40	.18
541	Greg Gagne	.20	.09
542	Mickey Hatcher	.20	.09
543	Neal Heaton	.20	.09
544	Kent Hrbek	.40	.18
545	Roy Lee Jackson	.20	.09
546	Tim Laudner	.20	.09
547	Steve Lombardozzi	.20	.09
548	Mark Portugal	.40	.18
549	Kirby Puckett	1.50	.70
550	Jeff Reed	.20	.09
551	Mark Salas	.20	.09
552	Roy Smalley	.20	.09
553	Mike Smithson	.20	.09
554	Frank Viola	.40	.18
555	Thad Bosley	.20	.09
556	Ron Cey	.40	.18
557	Jody Davis	.20	.09
558	Ron Davis	.20	.09
559	Bob Dernier	.20	.09
560	Frank DiPino	.20	.09
561	Shawon Dunston UER (Wrong birth year listed on card back)	.20	.09
562	Leon Durham	.20	.09
563	Dennis Eckersley	.75	.35
564	Terry Francona	.40	.18
565	Dave Gumpert	.20	.09
566	Guy Hoffman	.20	.09
567	Ed Lynch	.20	.09
568	Gary Matthews	.20	.09
569	Keith Moreland	.20	.09
570	Jamie Moyer	.60	.25
571	Jerry Mumphrey	.20	.09
572	Ryne Sandberg	1.00	.45
573	Scott Sanderson	.20	.09
574	Lee Smith	.60	.25
575	Chris Speier	.20	.09
576	Rick Sutcliffe	.20	.09
577	Manny Trillo	.20	.09
578	Steve Trout	.20	.09
579	Karl Best	.20	.09
580	Scott Bradley	.20	.09
581	Phil Bradley	.20	.09
582	Mickey Brantley	.20	.09
583	Mike G. Brown P	.20	.09
584	Alvin Davis	.20	.09
585	Lee Guetterman	.20	.09
586	Mark Huismann	.20	.09
587	Bob Kearney	.20	.09
588	Pete Ladd	.20	.09
589	Mark Langston	.20	.09
590	Mike Moore	.20	.09
591	Mike Morgan	.20	.09
592	John Moses	.20	.09
593	Ken Phelps	.20	.09
594	Jim Presley	.20	.09
595	Rey Quinones UER (Quinonez on front)	.20	.09
596	Harold Reynolds	.40	.18
597	Billy Swift	.20	.09
598	Danny Tartabull	.20	.09
599	Steve Yeager	.20	.09
600	Matt Young	.20	.09
601	Bill Almon	.20	.09
602	Rafael Belliard	.20	.09
603	Mike Bielecki	.20	.09
604	Barry Bonds	40.00	18.00
605	Bobby Bonilla	2.00	.90
606	Sid Bream	.20	.09
607	Mike C. Brown	.20	.09
608	Pat Clements	.20	.09
609	Mike Diaz	.20	.09
610	Cecilio Guante	.20	.09
611	Barry Jones	.20	.09
612	Bob Kipper	.20	.09
613	Larry McWilliams	.20	.09
614	Jim Morrison	.20	.09
615	Joe Orsulak	.20	.09
616	Junior Ortiz	.20	.09
617	Tony Pena	.20	.09
618	Johnny Ray	.20	.09
619	Rick Reuschel	.20	.09
620	R.J. Reynolds	.20	.09
621	Rick Rhoden	.20	.09
622	Don Robinson	.20	.09
623	Bob Walk	.20	.09
624	Jim Winn	.20	.09
625	Youthful Power — Pete Incaviglia, Jose Canseco	1.00	.45
626	300 Game Winners — Don Sutton, Phil Niekro	.60	.25
627	AL Firemen — Dave Righetti, Don Aase	.20	.09
628	Rookie All-Stars — Wally Joyner, Jose Canseco	1.00	.45
629	Magic Mets — Gary Carter, Sid Fernandez, Dwight Gooden, Keith Hernandez, Darryl Strawberry	.60	.25
630	NL Best Righties — Mike Scott, Mike Krukow	.20	.09
631	Sensational Southpaws — Fernando Valenzuela, John Franco	.20	.09
632	Count'Em — Bob Horner	.20	.09
633	AL Pitcher's Nightmare — Jose Canseco, Jim Rice, Kirby Puckett	1.00	.45
634	All-Star Battery — Gary Carter, Roger Clemens	1.00	.45
635	4000 Strikeouts — Steve Carlton	.40	.18
636	Big Bats at First — Glenn Davis, Eddie Murray	.75	.35
637	On Base — Wade Boggs, Keith Hernandez	.40	.18
638	Sluggers Left Side — Don Mattingly, Darryl Strawberry	.75	.35
639	Former MVP's — Dave Parker, Ryne Sandberg	.40	.18
640	Dr. K and Super K — Dwight Gooden, Roger Clemens	1.00	.45
641	AL West Stoppers — Mike Witt, Charlie Hough	.20	.09
642	Doubles and Triples — Juan Samuel, Tim Raines	.40	.18
643	Outfielders with Punch — Harold Baines	.40	.18

Jesse Barfield		
❏ 644 Dave Clark and ..... Greg Swindell	.75	.35
❏ 645 Ron Karkovice and ..... Russ Morman	.40	.18
❏ 646 Devon White and ..... Willie Fraser	2.00	.90
❏ 647 Mike Stanley and ..... Jerry Browne	.75	.35
❏ 648 Dave Magadan and ..... Phil Lombardi	.40	.18
❏ 649 Jose Gonzalez and ..... Ralph Bryant	.20	.09
❏ 650 Jimmy Jones and ..... Randy Asadoor	.20	.09
❏ 651 Tracy Jones and ..... Marvin Freeman	.20	.09
❏ 652 John Stefero and ..... Kevin Seitzer	.75	.35
❏ 653 Rob Nelson and ..... Steve Fireovid	.20	.09
❏ 654 CL: Mets/Red Sox ..... Astros/Angels	.20	.09
❏ 655 CL: Yankees/Rangers .... Tigers/Phillies	.20	.09
❏ 656 CL: Reds/Blue Jays .... Indians/Giants ERR (230/231 wrong)	.20	.09
❏ 657 CL: Cardinals/Expos ...... Brewers/Royals	.20	.09
❏ 658 CL: A's/Padres .... Dodgers/Orioles	.20	.09
❏ 659 CL: White Sox/Braves .... Twins/Cubs	.20	.09
❏ 660 CL: Mariners/Pirates ...... Special Cards ER (580/581 wrong)	.20	.09

1987 Fleer Glossy

Mike Schmidt

	MINT	NRMT
COMP.FACT.SET (672)	80.00	36.00
COMMON CARD (1-660)	.20	.09
*STARS: .6X TO 1.2X BASIC CARDS		
*ROOKIES: .6X TO 1.2X BASIC CARDS		
DISTRIBUTED ONLY IN FACTORY SET FORM		

1987 Fleer All-Stars

Steve Sax

	MINT	NRMT
COMPLETE SET (12)	20.00	9.00

COMMON CARD (1-12)	.25	.11
RANDOM INSERTS IN PACKS		

❏ 1 Don Mattingly	5.00	2.20
❏ 2 Gary Carter	1.50	.70
❏ 3 Tony Fernandez	.25	.11
❏ 4 Steve Sax	.25	.11
❏ 5 Kirby Puckett	5.00	2.20
❏ 6 Mike Schmidt	3.00	1.35
❏ 7 Mike Easler	.25	.11
❏ 8 Todd Worrell	.75	.35
❏ 9 George Bell	.25	.11
❏ 10 Fernando Valenzuela ...	.75	.35
❏ 11 Roger Clemens	8.00	3.60
❏ 12 Tim Raines	.75	.35

1987 Fleer Headliners

WADE BOGGS

	MINT	NRMT
COMPLETE SET (6)	6.00	2.70
COMMON CARD (1-6)	.50	.23
ONE PER RACK PACK		

❏ 1 Wade Boggs	1.50	.70
❏ 2 Jose Canseco	5.00	2.20
❏ 3 Dwight Gooden	.75	.35
❏ 4 Rickey Henderson	1.50	.70
❏ 5 Keith Hernandez	.50	.23
❏ 6 Jim Rice	.50	.23

1987 Fleer Update

Matt Williams

	MINT	NRMT
COMP.FACT.SET (132)	30.00	13.50
COMMON CARD (1-132)	.10	.05
MINOR STARS	.15	.07
UNLISTED STARS	.40	.18

❏ 1 Scott Bankhead	.10	.05
❏ 2 Eric Bell	.10	.05
❏ 3 Juan Beniquez	.10	.05
❏ 4 Juan Berenguer	.10	.05
❏ 5 Mike Birkbeck	.10	.05
❏ 6 Randy Bockus	.10	.05
❏ 7 Rod Booker	.10	.05
❏ 8 Thad Bosley	.10	.05
❏ 9 Greg Brock	.10	.05
❏ 10 Bob Brower	.10	.05
❏ 11 Chris Brown	.10	.05
❏ 12 Jerry Browne	.10	.05
❏ 13 Ralph Bryant	.10	.05

❏ 14 DeWayne Buice	.10	.05
❏ 15 Ellis Burks	.75	.35
❏ 16 Casey Candaele	.10	.05
❏ 17 Steve Carlton	.40	.18
❏ 18 Juan Castillo	.10	.05
❏ 19 Chuck Crim	.10	.05
❏ 20 Mark Davidson	.10	.05
❏ 21 Mark Davis	.10	.05
❏ 22 Storm Davis	.10	.05
❏ 23 Bill Dawley	.10	.05
❏ 24 Andre Dawson	.40	.18
❏ 25 Brian Dayett	.10	.05
❏ 26 Rick Dempsey	.15	.07
❏ 27 Ken Dowell	.10	.05
❏ 28 Dave Dravecky	.15	.07
❏ 29 Mike Dunne	.10	.05
❏ 30 Dennis Eckersley	.40	.18
❏ 31 Cecil Fielder	.40	.18
❏ 32 Brian Fisher	.10	.05
❏ 33 Willie Fraser	.10	.05
❏ 34 Ken Gerhart	.10	.05
❏ 35 Jim Gott	.10	.05
❏ 36 Dan Gladden	.10	.05
❏ 37 Mike Greenwell	.40	.18
❏ 38 Cecilio Guante	.10	.05
❏ 39 Albert Hall	.10	.05
❏ 40 Atlee Hammaker	.10	.05
❏ 41 Mickey Hatcher	.10	.05
❏ 42 Mike Heath	.10	.05
❏ 43 Neal Heaton	.10	.05
❏ 44 Mike Henneman	.40	.18
❏ 45 Guy Hoffman	.10	.05
❏ 46 Charles Hudson	.10	.05
❏ 47 Chuck Jackson	.10	.05
❏ 48 Mike Jackson	.40	.18
❏ 49 Reggie Jackson	.60	.25
❏ 50 Chris James	.10	.05
❏ 51 Dion James	.10	.05
❏ 52 Stan Javier	.10	.05
❏ 53 Stan Jefferson	.10	.05
❏ 54 Jimmy Jones	.10	.05
❏ 55 Tracy Jones	.10	.05
❏ 56 Terry Kennedy	.10	.05
❏ 57 Mike Kingery	.10	.05
❏ 58 Ray Knight	.10	.05
❏ 59 Gene Larkin	.10	.05
❏ 60 Mike LaValliere	.10	.05
❏ 61 Jack Lazorko	.10	.05
❏ 62 Terry Leach	.10	.05
❏ 63 Rick Leach	.10	.05
❏ 64 Craig Lefferts	.10	.05
❏ 65 Jim Lindeman	.10	.05
❏ 66 Bill Long	.10	.05
❏ 67 Mike Loynd	.10	.05
❏ 68 Greg Maddux	10.00	4.50
❏ 69 Bill Madlock	.15	.07
❏ 70 Dave Magadan	.15	.07
❏ 71 Joe Magrane	.10	.05
❏ 72 Fred Manrique	.10	.05
❏ 73 Mike Mason	.10	.05
❏ 74 Lloyd McClendon	.10	.05
❏ 75 Fred McGriff	.60	.25
❏ 76 Mark McGwire	20.00	9.00
❏ 77 Mark McLemore	.15	.07
❏ 78 Kevin McReynolds	.10	.05
❏ 79 Dave Meads	.10	.05
❏ 80 Greg Minton	.10	.05
❏ 81 John Mitchell	.10	.05
❏ 82 Kevin Mitchell	.40	.18
❏ 83 John Morris	.10	.05
❏ 84 Jeff Musselman	.10	.05
❏ 85 Randy Myers	.40	.18
❏ 86 Gene Nelson	.10	.05
❏ 87 Joe Niekro	.10	.05
❏ 88 Tom Nieto	.10	.05
❏ 89 Reid Nichols	.10	.05
❏ 90 Matt Nokes	.15	.07
❏ 91 Dickie Noles	.10	.05
❏ 92 Edwin Nunez	.10	.05
❏ 93 Jose Nunez	.10	.05
❏ 94 Paul O'Neill	.40	.18
❏ 95 Jim Paciorek	.10	.05
❏ 96 Lance Parrish	.15	.07
❏ 97 Bill Pecota	.10	.05
❏ 98 Tony Pena	.15	.07
❏ 99 Luis Polonia	.15	.07

			MINT	NRMT
□ 100	Randy Ready	.10		.05
□ 101	Jeff Reardon	.15		.07
□ 102	Gary Redus	.10		.05
□ 103	Rick Rhoden	.10		.05
□ 104	Wally Ritchie	.10		.05
□ 105	Jeff M. Robinson UER	.10		.05
	(Wrong Jeff's stats on back)			
□ 106	Mark Salas	.10		.05
□ 107	Dave Schmidt	.10		.05
□ 108	Kevin Seitzer UER	.15		.07
	(Wrong birth year)			
□ 109	John Shelby	.10		.05
□ 110	John Smiley	.10		.05
□ 111	Lary Sorensen	.10		.05
□ 112	Chris Speier	.10		.05
□ 113	Randy St.Claire	.10		.05
□ 114	Jim Sundberg	.10		.05
□ 115	B.J. Surhoff	.75		.35
□ 116	Greg Swindell	.40		.18
□ 117	Danny Tartabull	.10		.05
□ 118	Dorn Taylor	.10		.05
□ 119	Lee Tunnell	.10		.05
□ 120	Ed VandeBerg	.10		.05
□ 121	Andy Van Slyke	.15		.07
□ 122	Gary Ward	.10		.05
□ 123	Devon White	.40		.18
□ 124	Alan Wiggins	.10		.05
□ 125	Bill Wilkinson	.10		.05
□ 126	Jim Winn	.10		.05
□ 127	Frank Williams	.10		.05
□ 128	Ken Williams	.10		.05
□ 129	Matt Williams	2.50		1.10
□ 130	Herm Winningham	.10		.05
□ 131	Matt Young	.10		.05
□ 132	Checklist 1-132	.10		.05

1987 Fleer Update Glossy

Paul O'Neill

	MINT	NRMT
COMP.FACT.SET (132)	50.00	22.00
COMMON CARD (1-132)	.15	.07

*STARS: .6X TO 1.2X BASIC CARDS
*ROOKIES: .6X TO 1.2X BASIC CARDS
DISTRIBUTED ONLY IN FACTORY SET FORM

1988 Fleer

Danny Tartabull

	MINT	NRMT
COMPLETE SET (660)	15.00	6.75
COMP.RETAIL SET (660)	15.00	6.75
COMP.HOBBY SET (672)	15.00	6.75
COMMON CARD (1-660)	.05	.02
MINOR STARS	.10	.05
UNLISTED STARS	.25	.11
COMP.WORLD SERIES SET (12)	2.00	.90

*WS: EQUAL VALUE TO BASIC CARDS
ONE WORLD SERIES SET PER FACT.SET

□ 1	Keith Atherton	.05		.02
□ 2	Don Baylor	.10		.05
□ 3	Juan Berenguer	.05		.02
□ 4	Bert Blyleven	.10		.05
□ 5	Tom Brunansky	.05		.02
□ 6	Randy Bush	.05		.02
□ 7	Steve Carlton	.25		.11
□ 8	Mark Davidson	.05		.02
□ 9	George Frazier	.05		.02
□ 10	Gary Gaetti	.05		.02
□ 11	Greg Gagne	.05		.02
□ 12	Dan Gladden	.05		.02
□ 13	Kent Hrbek	.10		.05
□ 14	Gene Larkin	.05		.02
□ 15	Tim Laudner	.05		.02
□ 16	Steve Lombardozzi	.05		.02
□ 17	Al Newman	.05		.02
□ 18	Joe Niekro	.05		.02
□ 19	Kirby Puckett	.50		.23
□ 20	Jeff Reardon	.10		.05
□ 21A	Dan Schatzeder ERR	.10		.05
	(Misspelled Schatzeder on card front)			
□ 21B	Dan Schatzeder COR	.05		.02
□ 22	Roy Smalley	.05		.02
□ 23	Mike Smithson	.05		.02
□ 24	Les Straker	.05		.02
□ 25	Frank Viola	.10		.05
□ 26	Jack Clark	.10		.05
□ 27	Vince Coleman	.05		.02
□ 28	Danny Cox	.05		.02
□ 29	Bill Dawley	.05		.02
□ 30	Ken Dayley	.05		.02
□ 31	Doug DeCinces	.05		.02
□ 32	Curt Ford	.05		.02
□ 33	Bob Forsch	.05		.02
□ 34	David Green	.05		.02
□ 35	Tom Herr	.05		.02
□ 36	Ricky Horton	.05		.02
□ 37	Lance Johnson	.25		.11
□ 38	Steve Lake	.05		.02
□ 39	Jim Lindeman	.05		.02
□ 40	Joe Magrane	.05		.02
□ 41	Greg Mathews	.05		.02
□ 42	Willie McGee	.10		.05
□ 43	John Morris	.05		.02
□ 44	Jose Oquendo	.05		.02
□ 45	Tony Pena	.05		.02
□ 46	Terry Pendleton	.10		.05
□ 47	Ozzie Smith	.40		.18
□ 48	John Tudor	.05		.02
□ 49	Lee Tunnell	.05		.02
□ 50	Todd Worrell	.10		.05
□ 51	Doyle Alexander	.05		.02
□ 52	Dave Bergman	.05		.02
□ 53	Tom Brookens	.05		.02
□ 54	Darrell Evans	.10		.05
□ 55	Kirk Gibson	.10		.05
□ 56	Mike Heath	.05		.02
□ 57	Mike Henneman	.10		.05
□ 58	Willie Hernandez	.05		.02
□ 59	Larry Herndon	.05		.02
□ 60	Eric King	.05		.02
□ 61	Chet Lemon	.05		.02
□ 62	Scott Lusader	.05		.02
□ 63	Bill Madlock	.10		.05
□ 64	Jack Morris	.10		.05
□ 65	Jim Morrison	.05		.02
□ 66	Matt Nokes	.05		.02
□ 67	Dan Petry	.05		.02
□ 68A	Jeff M. Robinson ERR	.25		.11
	(Stats for Jeff D. Robinson on card back, Born 12-13-60)			
□ 68B	Jeff M. Robinson COR	.05		.02

	(Born 12-14-61)			
□ 69	Pat Sheridan	.05		.02
□ 70	Nate Snell	.05		.02
□ 71	Frank Tanana	.05		.02
□ 72	Walt Terrell	.05		.02
□ 73	Mark Thurmond	.05		.02
□ 74	Alan Trammell	.30		.14
□ 75	Lou Whitaker	.10		.05
□ 76	Mike Aldrete	.05		.02
□ 77	Bob Brenly	.05		.02
□ 78	Will Clark	.40		.18
□ 79	Chili Davis	.30		.14
□ 80	Kelly Downs	.05		.02
□ 81	Dave Dravecky	.10		.05
□ 82	Scott Garrelts	.05		.02
□ 83	Atlee Hammaker	.05		.02
□ 84	Dave Henderson	.05		.02
□ 85	Mike Krukow	.05		.02
□ 86	Mike LaCoss	.05		.02
□ 87	Craig Lefferts	.05		.02
□ 88	Jeff Leonard	.05		.02
□ 89	Candy Maldonado	.05		.02
□ 90	Eddie Milner	.05		.02
□ 91	Bob Melvin	.05		.02
□ 92	Kevin Mitchell	.10		.05
□ 93	Jon Perlman	.05		.02
□ 94	Rick Reuschel	.05		.02
□ 95	Don Robinson	.05		.02
□ 96	Chris Speier	.05		.02
□ 97	Harry Spilman	.05		.02
□ 98	Robby Thompson	.05		.02
□ 99	Jose Uribe	.05		.02
□ 100	Mark Wasinger	.05		.02
□ 101	Matt Williams	2.00		.90
□ 102	Jesse Barfield	.05		.02
□ 103	George Bell	.10		.05
□ 104	Juan Beniquez	.05		.02
□ 105	John Cerutti	.05		.02
□ 106	Jim Clancy	.05		.02
□ 107	Rob Ducey	.05		.02
□ 108	Mark Eichhorn	.05		.02
□ 109	Tony Fernandez	.10		.05
□ 110	Cecil Fielder	.30		.14
□ 111	Kelly Gruber	.05		.02
□ 112	Tom Henke	.05		.02
□ 113A	Garth Iorg ERR	.25		.11
	(Misspelled Iorg on card front)			
□ 113B	Garth Iorg COR	.05		.02
□ 114	Jimmy Key	.10		.05
□ 115	Rick Leach	.05		.02
□ 116	Manny Lee	.05		.02
□ 117	Nelson Liriano	.05		.02
□ 118	Fred McGriff	.25		.11
□ 119	Lloyd Moseby	.05		.02
□ 120	Rance Mulliniks	.05		.02
□ 121	Jeff Musselman	.05		.02
□ 122	Jose Nunez	.05		.02
□ 123	Dave Stieb	.10		.05
□ 124	Willie Upshaw	.05		.02
□ 125	Duane Ward	.05		.02
□ 126	Ernie Whitt	.05		.02
□ 127	Rick Aguilera	.10		.05
□ 128	Wally Backman	.05		.02
□ 129	Mark Carreon	.10		.05
□ 130	Gary Carter	.30		.14
□ 131	David Cone	.40		.18
□ 132	Ron Darling	.05		.02
□ 133	Len Dykstra	.10		.05
□ 134	Sid Fernandez	.05		.02
□ 135	Dwight Gooden	.10		.05
□ 136	Keith Hernandez	.05		.02
□ 137	Gregg Jefferies	.25		.11
□ 138	Howard Johnson	.05		.02
□ 139	Terry Leach	.05		.02
□ 140	Barry Lyons	.05		.02
□ 141	Dave Magadan	.05		.02
□ 142	Roger McDowell	.05		.02
□ 143	Kevin McReynolds	.05		.02
□ 144	Keith A. Miller	.05		.02
□ 145	John Mitchell	.05		.02
□ 146	Randy Myers	.30		.14
□ 147	Bob Ojeda	.05		.02
□ 148	Jesse Orosco	.05		.02
□ 149	Rafael Santana	.05		.02
□ 150	Doug Sisk	.05		.02

❏ 151	Darryl Strawberry	.10	.05
❏ 152	Tim Teufel	.05	.02
❏ 153	Gene Walter	.05	.02
❏ 154	Mookie Wilson	.10	.05
❏ 155	Jay Aldrich	.05	.02
❏ 156	Chris Bosio	.05	.02
❏ 157	Glenn Braggs	.05	.02
❏ 158	Greg Brock	.05	.02
❏ 159	Juan Castillo	.05	.02
❏ 160	Mark Clear	.05	.02
❏ 161	Cecil Cooper	.10	.05
❏ 162	Chuck Crim	.05	.02
❏ 163	Rob Deer	.05	.02
❏ 164	Mike Felder	.05	.02
❏ 165	Jim Gantner	.05	.02
❏ 166	Ted Higuera	.05	.02
❏ 167	Steve Kiefer	.05	.02
❏ 168	Rick Manning	.05	.02
❏ 169	Paul Molitor	.25	.11
❏ 170	Juan Nieves	.05	.02
❏ 171	Dan Plesac	.05	.02
❏ 172	Earnest Riles	.05	.02
❏ 173	Bill Schroeder	.05	.02
❏ 174	Steve Stanicek	.05	.02
❏ 175	B.J. Surhoff	.10	.05
❏ 176	Dale Sveum	.05	.02
❏ 177	Bill Wegman	.05	.02
❏ 178	Robin Yount	.25	.11
❏ 179	Hubie Brooks	.05	.02
❏ 180	Tim Burke	.05	.02
❏ 181	Casey Candaele	.05	.02
❏ 182	Mike Fitzgerald	.05	.02
❏ 183	Tom Foley	.05	.02
❏ 184	Andres Galarraga	.25	.11
❏ 185	Neal Heaton	.05	.02
❏ 186	Wallace Johnson	.05	.02
❏ 187	Vance Law	.05	.02
❏ 188	Dennis Martinez	.10	.05
❏ 189	Bob McClure	.05	.02
❏ 190	Andy McGaffigan	.05	.02
❏ 191	Reid Nichols	.05	.02
❏ 192	Pascual Perez	.05	.02
❏ 193	Tim Raines	.10	.05
❏ 194	Jeff Reed	.05	.02
❏ 195	Bob Sebra	.05	.02
❏ 196	Bryn Smith	.05	.02
❏ 197	Randy St.Claire	.05	.02
❏ 198	Tim Wallach	.10	.05
❏ 199	Mitch Webster	.05	.02
❏ 200	Herm Winningham	.05	.02
❏ 201	Floyd Youmans	.05	.02
❏ 202	Brad Arnsberg	.05	.02
❏ 203	Rick Cerone	.05	.02
❏ 204	Pat Clements	.05	.02
❏ 205	Henry Cotto	.05	.02
❏ 206	Mike Easler	.05	.02
❏ 207	Ron Guidry	.05	.02
❏ 208	Bill Gullickson	.05	.02
❏ 209	Rickey Henderson	.40	.18
❏ 210	Charles Hudson	.05	.02
❏ 211	Tommy John	.10	.05
❏ 212	Roberto Kelly	.25	.11
❏ 213	Ron Kittle	.05	.02
❏ 214	Don Mattingly	.60	.25
❏ 215	Bobby Meacham	.05	.02
❏ 216	Mike Pagliarulo	.05	.02
❏ 217	Dan Pasqua	.05	.02
❏ 218	Willie Randolph	.10	.05
❏ 219	Rick Rhoden	.05	.02
❏ 220	Dave Righetti	.05	.02
❏ 221	Jerry Royster	.05	.02
❏ 222	Tim Stoddard	.05	.02
❏ 223	Wayne Tolleson	.05	.02
❏ 224	Gary Ward	.05	.02
❏ 225	Claudell Washington	.05	.02
❏ 226	Dave Winfield	.25	.11
❏ 227	Buddy Bell	.10	.05
❏ 228	Tom Browning	.05	.02
❏ 229	Dave Concepcion	.10	.05
❏ 230	Kal Daniels	.05	.02
❏ 231	Eric Davis	.10	.05
❏ 232	Bo Diaz	.05	.02
❏ 233	Nick Esasky	.05	.02
	(Has a dollar sign before '87 SB totals)		
❏ 234	John Franco	.10	.05
❏ 235	Guy Hoffman	.05	.02
❏ 236	Tom Hume	.05	.02
❏ 237	Tracy Jones	.05	.02
❏ 238	Bill Landrum	.05	.02
❏ 239	Barry Larkin	.25	.11
❏ 240	Terry McGriff	.05	.02
❏ 241	Rob Murphy	.05	.02
❏ 242	Ron Oester	.05	.02
❏ 243	Dave Parker	.10	.05
❏ 244	Pat Perry	.05	.02
❏ 245	Ted Power	.05	.02
❏ 246	Dennis Rasmussen	.05	.02
❏ 247	Ron Robinson	.05	.02
❏ 248	Kurt Stillwell	.05	.02
❏ 249	Jeff Treadway	.05	.02
❏ 250	Frank Williams	.05	.02
❏ 251	Steve Balboni	.05	.02
❏ 252	Bud Black	.05	.02
❏ 253	Thad Bosley	.05	.02
❏ 254	George Brett	.60	.25
❏ 255	John Davis	.05	.02
❏ 256	Steve Farr	.05	.02
❏ 257	Gene Garber	.05	.02
❏ 258	Jerry Don Gleaton	.05	.02
❏ 259	Mark Gubicza	.05	.02
❏ 260	Bo Jackson	.25	.11
❏ 261	Danny Jackson	.05	.02
❏ 262	Ross Jones	.05	.02
❏ 263	Charlie Leibrandt	.05	.02
❏ 264	Bill Pecota	.05	.02
❏ 265	Melido Perez	.05	.02
❏ 266	Jamie Quirk	.05	.02
❏ 267	Dan Quisenberry	.05	.02
❏ 268	Bret Saberhagen	.10	.05
❏ 269	Angel Salazar	.05	.02
❏ 270	Kevin Seitzer UER	.10	.05
	(Wrong birth year)		
❏ 271	Danny Tartabull	.05	.02
❏ 272	Gary Thurman	.05	.02
❏ 273	Frank White	.10	.05
❏ 274	Willie Wilson	.05	.02
❏ 275	Tony Bernazard	.05	.02
❏ 276	Jose Canseco	.60	.25
❏ 277	Mike Davis	.05	.02
❏ 278	Storm Davis	.05	.02
❏ 279	Dennis Eckersley	.10	.05
❏ 280	Alfredo Griffin	.05	.02
❏ 281	Rick Honeycutt	.05	.02
❏ 282	Jay Howell	.05	.02
❏ 283	Reggie Jackson	.40	.18
❏ 284	Dennis Lamp	.05	.02
❏ 285	Carney Lansford	.05	.02
❏ 286	Mark McGwire	3.00	1.35
❏ 287	Dwayne Murphy	.05	.02
❏ 288	Gene Nelson	.05	.02
❏ 289	Steve Ontiveros	.05	.02
❏ 290	Tony Phillips	.05	.02
❏ 291	Eric Plunk	.05	.02
❏ 292	Luis Polonia	.05	.02
❏ 293	Rick Rodriguez	.05	.02
❏ 294	Terry Steinbach	.10	.05
❏ 295	Dave Stewart	.10	.05
❏ 296	Curt Young	.05	.02
❏ 297	Luis Aguayo	.05	.02
❏ 298	Steve Bedrosian	.05	.02
❏ 299	Jeff Calhoun	.05	.02
❏ 300	Don Carman	.05	.02
❏ 301	Todd Frohwirth	.05	.02
❏ 302	Greg Gross	.05	.02
❏ 303	Kevin Gross	.05	.02
❏ 304	Von Hayes	.05	.02
❏ 305	Keith Hughes	.05	.02
❏ 306	Mike Jackson	.25	.11
❏ 307	Chris James	.05	.02
❏ 308	Steve Jeltz	.05	.02
❏ 309	Mike Maddux	.05	.02
❏ 310	Lance Parrish	.05	.02
❏ 311	Shane Rawley	.05	.02
❏ 312	Wally Ritchie	.05	.02
❏ 313	Bruce Ruffin	.05	.02
❏ 314	Juan Samuel	.05	.02
❏ 315	Mike Schmidt	.50	.23
❏ 316	Rick Schu	.05	.02
❏ 317	Jeff Stone	.05	.02
❏ 318	Kent Tekulve	.05	.02
❏ 319	Milt Thompson	.05	.02
❏ 320	Glenn Wilson	.05	.02
❏ 321	Rafael Belliard	.05	.02
❏ 322	Barry Bonds	.75	.35
❏ 323	Bobby Bonilla UER	.30	.14
	(Wrong birth year)		
❏ 324	Sid Bream	.05	.02
❏ 325	John Cangelosi	.05	.02
❏ 326	Mike Diaz	.05	.02
❏ 327	Doug Drabek	.05	.02
❏ 328	Mike Dunne	.05	.02
❏ 329	Brian Fisher	.05	.02
❏ 330	Brett Gideon	.05	.02
❏ 331	Terry Harper	.05	.02
❏ 332	Bob Kipper	.05	.02
❏ 333	Mike LaValliere	.05	.02
❏ 334	Jose Lind	.05	.02
❏ 335	Junior Ortiz	.05	.02
❏ 336	Vicente Palacios	.05	.02
❏ 337	Bob Patterson	.05	.02
❏ 338	Al Pedrique	.05	.02
❏ 339	R.J. Reynolds	.05	.02
❏ 340	John Smiley	.10	.05
❏ 341	Andy Van Slyke UER	.10	.05
	(Wrong batting and throwing listed)		
❏ 342	Bob Walk	.05	.02
❏ 343	Marty Barrett	.05	.02
❏ 344	Todd Benzinger	.05	.02
❏ 345	Wade Boggs	.25	.11
❏ 346	Tom Bolton	.05	.02
❏ 347	Oil Can Boyd	.05	.02
❏ 348	Ellis Burks	.50	.23
❏ 349	Roger Clemens	.75	.35
❏ 350	Steve Crawford	.05	.02
❏ 351	Dwight Evans	.10	.05
❏ 352	Wes Gardner	.05	.02
❏ 353	Rich Gedman	.05	.02
❏ 354	Mike Greenwell	.10	.05
❏ 355	Sam Horn	.05	.02
❏ 356	Bruce Hurst	.05	.02
❏ 357	John Marzano	.05	.02
❏ 358	Al Nipper	.05	.02
❏ 359	Spike Owen	.05	.02
❏ 360	Jody Reed	.10	.05
❏ 361	Jim Rice	.10	.05
❏ 362	Ed Romero	.05	.02
❏ 363	Kevin Romine	.05	.02
❏ 364	Joe Sambito	.05	.02
❏ 365	Calvin Schiraldi	.05	.02
❏ 366	Jeff Sellers	.05	.02
❏ 367	Bob Stanley	.05	.02
❏ 368	Scott Bankhead	.05	.02
❏ 369	Phil Bradley	.05	.02
❏ 370	Scott Bradley	.05	.02
❏ 371	Mickey Brantley	.05	.02
❏ 372	Mike Campbell	.05	.02
❏ 373	Alvin Davis	.05	.02
❏ 374	Lee Guetterman	.05	.02
❏ 375	Dave Hengel	.05	.02
❏ 376	Mike Kingery	.05	.02
❏ 377	Mark Langston	.05	.02
❏ 378	Edgar Martinez	1.25	.55
❏ 379	Mike Moore	.05	.02
❏ 380	Mike Morgan	.05	.02
❏ 381	John Moses	.05	.02
❏ 382	Donell Nixon	.05	.02
❏ 383	Edwin Nunez	.05	.02
❏ 384	Ken Phelps	.05	.02
❏ 385	Jim Presley	.05	.02
❏ 386	Rey Quinones	.05	.02
❏ 387	Jerry Reed	.05	.02
❏ 388	Harold Reynolds	.10	.05
❏ 389	Dave Valle	.05	.02
❏ 390	Bill Wilkinson	.05	.02
❏ 391	Harold Baines	.10	.05
❏ 392	Floyd Bannister	.05	.02
❏ 393	Daryl Boston	.05	.02
❏ 394	Ivan Calderon	.05	.02
❏ 395	Jose DeLeon	.05	.02
❏ 396	Richard Dotson	.05	.02
❏ 397	Carlton Fisk	.25	.11
❏ 398	Ozzie Guillen	.05	.02
❏ 399	Ron Hassey	.05	.02
❏ 400	Donnie Hill	.05	.02
❏ 401	Bob James	.05	.02
❏ 402	Dave LaPoint	.05	.02

403	Bill Lindsey	.05	.02
404	Bill Long	.05	.02
405	Steve Lyons	.05	.02
406	Fred Manrique	.05	.02
407	Jack McDowell	.25	.11
408	Gary Redus	.05	.02
409	Ray Searage	.05	.02
410	Bobby Thigpen	.05	.02
411	Greg Walker	.05	.02
412	Ken Williams	.05	.02
413	Jim Winn	.05	.02
414	Jody Davis	.05	.02
415	Andre Dawson	.25	.11
416	Brian Dayett	.05	.02
417	Bob Dernier	.05	.02
418	Frank DiPino	.05	.02
419	Shawon Dunston	.05	.02
420	Leon Durham	.05	.02
421	Les Lancaster	.05	.02
422	Ed Lynch	.05	.02
423	Greg Maddux	1.50	.70
424	Dave Martinez	.05	.02
425A	Keith Moreland ERR (Photo actually Jody Davis)	1.50	.70
425B	Keith Moreland COR (Bat on shoulder)	.10	.05
426	Jamie Moyer	.05	.02
427	Jerry Mumphrey	.05	.02
428	Paul Noce	.05	.02
429	Rafael Palmeiro	.60	.25
430	Wade Rowdon	.05	.02
431	Ryne Sandberg	.40	.18
432	Scott Sanderson	.05	.02
433	Lee Smith	.10	.05
434	Jim Sundberg	.05	.02
435	Rick Sutcliffe	.05	.02
436	Manny Trillo	.05	.02
437	Juan Agosto	.05	.02
438	Larry Andersen	.05	.02
439	Alan Ashby	.05	.02
440	Kevin Bass	.05	.02
441	Ken Caminiti	1.00	.45
442	Rocky Childress	.05	.02
443	Jose Cruz	.05	.02
444	Danny Darwin	.05	.02
445	Glenn Davis	.05	.02
446	Jim Deshaies	.05	.02
447	Bill Doran	.05	.02
448	Ty Gainey	.05	.02
449	Billy Hatcher	.05	.02
450	Jeff Heathcock	.05	.02
451	Bob Knepper	.05	.02
452	Rob Mallicoat	.05	.02
453	Dave Meads	.05	.02
454	Craig Reynolds	.05	.02
455	Nolan Ryan	1.25	.55
456	Mike Scott	.05	.02
457	Dave Smith	.05	.02
458	Denny Walling	.05	.02
459	Robbie Wine	.05	.02
460	Gerald Young	.05	.02
461	Bob Brower	.05	.02
462A	Jerry Browne ERR (Photo actually Bob Brower, white player)	1.50	.70
462B	Jerry Browne COR (Black player)	.10	.05
463	Steve Buechele	.05	.02
464	Edwin Correa	.05	.02
465	Cecil Espy	.05	.02
466	Scott Fletcher	.05	.02
467	Jose Guzman	.05	.02
468	Greg Harris	.05	.02
469	Charlie Hough	.10	.05
470	Pete Incaviglia	.05	.02
471	Paul Kilgus	.05	.02
472	Mike Loynd	.05	.02
473	Oddibe McDowell	.05	.02
474	Dale Mohorcic	.05	.02
475	Pete O'Brien	.05	.02
476	Larry Parrish	.05	.02
477	Geno Petralli	.05	.02
478	Jeff Russell	.05	.02
479	Ruben Sierra	.05	.02
480	Mike Stanley	.10	.05
481	Curtis Wilkerson	.05	.02
482	Mitch Williams	.05	.02
483	Bobby Witt	.05	.02
484	Tony Armas	.05	.02
485	Bob Boone	.10	.05
486	Bill Buckner	.10	.05
487	DeWayne Buice	.05	.02
488	Brian Downing	.05	.02
489	Chuck Finley	.30	.14
490	Willie Fraser UER (Wrong bio stats, for George Hendrick)	.05	.02
491	Jack Howell	.05	.02
492	Ruppert Jones	.05	.02
493	Wally Joyner	.30	.14
494	Jack Lazorko	.05	.02
495	Gary Lucas	.05	.02
496	Kirk McCaskill	.05	.02
497	Mark McLemore	.05	.02
498	Darrell Miller	.05	.02
499	Greg Minton	.05	.02
500	Donnie Moore	.05	.02
501	Gus Polidor	.05	.02
502	Johnny Ray	.05	.02
503	Mark Ryal	.05	.02
504	Dick Schofield	.05	.02
505	Don Sutton	.25	.11
506	Devon White	.10	.05
507	Mike Witt	.05	.02
508	Dave Anderson	.05	.02
509	Tim Belcher	.10	.05
510	Ralph Bryant	.05	.02
511	Tim Crews	.05	.02
512	Mike Devereaux	.10	.05
513	Mariano Duncan	.05	.02
514	Pedro Guerrero	.05	.02
515	Jeff Hamilton	.05	.02
516	Mickey Hatcher	.05	.02
517	Brad Havens	.05	.02
518	Orel Hershiser	.10	.05
519	Shawn Hillegas	.05	.02
520	Ken Howell	.05	.02
521	Tim Leary	.05	.02
522	Mike Marshall	.05	.02
523	Steve Sax	.05	.02
524	Mike Scioscia	.05	.02
525	Mike Sharperson	.05	.02
526	John Shelby	.05	.02
527	Franklin Stubbs	.05	.02
528	Fernando Valenzuela	.10	.05
529	Bob Welch	.05	.02
530	Matt Young	.05	.02
531	Jim Acker	.05	.02
532	Paul Assenmacher	.05	.02
533	Jeff Blauser	.25	.11
534	Joe Boever	.05	.02
535	Martin Clary	.05	.02
536	Kevin Coffman	.05	.02
537	Jeff Dedmon	.05	.02
538	Ron Gant	.40	.18
539	Tom Glavine	2.50	1.10
540	Ken Griffey	.10	.05
541	Albert Hall	.05	.02
542	Glenn Hubbard	.05	.02
543	Dion James	.05	.02
544	Dale Murphy	.25	.11
545	Ken Oberkfell	.05	.02
546	David Palmer	.05	.02
547	Gerald Perry	.05	.02
548	Charlie Puleo	.05	.02
549	Ted Simmons	.10	.05
550	Zane Smith	.05	.02
551	Andres Thomas	.05	.02
552	Ozzie Virgil	.05	.02
553	Don Aase	.05	.02
554	Jeff Ballard	.05	.02
555	Eric Bell	.05	.02
556	Mike Boddicker	.05	.02
557	Ken Dixon	.05	.02
558	Jim Dwyer	.05	.02
559	Ken Gerhart	.05	.02
560	Rene Gonzales	.05	.02
561	Mike Griffin	.05	.02
562	John Habyan UER (Misspelled Hayban on both sides of card)	.05	.02
563	Terry Kennedy	.05	.02
564	Ray Knight	.05	.02
565	Lee Lacy	.05	.02
566	Fred Lynn	.05	.02
567	Eddie Murray	.25	.11
568	Tom Niedenfuer	.05	.02
569	Bill Ripken	.05	.02
570	Cal Ripken	1.25	.55
571	Dave Schmidt	.05	.02
572	Larry Sheets	.05	.02
573	Pete Stanicek	.05	.02
574	Mark Williamson	.05	.02
575	Mike Young	.05	.02
576	Shawn Abner	.05	.02
577	Greg Booker	.05	.02
578	Chris Brown	.05	.02
579	Keith Comstock	.05	.02
580	Joey Cora	.25	.11
581	Mark Davis	.05	.02
582	Tim Flannery (With surfboard)	.25	.11
583	Goose Gossage	.30	.14
584	Mark Grant	.05	.02
585	Tony Gwynn	.75	.35
586	Andy Hawkins	.05	.02
587	Stan Jefferson	.05	.02
588	Jimmy Jones	.05	.02
589	John Kruk	.10	.05
590	Shane Mack	.05	.02
591	Carmelo Martinez	.05	.02
592	Lance McCullers UER (6'11" tall)	.05	.02
593	Eric Nolte	.05	.02
594	Randy Ready	.05	.02
595	Luis Salazar	.05	.02
596	Benito Santiago	.05	.02
597	Eric Show	.05	.02
598	Garry Templeton	.05	.02
599	Ed Whitson	.05	.02
600	Scott Bailes	.05	.02
601	Chris Bando	.05	.02
602	Jay Bell	1.00	.45
603	Brett Butler	.10	.05
604	Tom Candiotti	.05	.02
605	Joe Carter	.25	.11
606	Carmen Castillo	.05	.02
607	Brian Dorsett	.05	.02
608	John Farrell	.05	.02
609	Julio Franco	.05	.02
610	Mel Hall	.05	.02
611	Tommy Hinzo	.05	.02
612	Brook Jacoby	.05	.02
613	Doug Jones	.25	.11
614	Ken Schrom	.05	.02
615	Cory Snyder	.05	.02
616	Greg Swindell	.05	.02
617	Pat Tabler	.05	.02
618	Ed VandeBerg	.05	.02
619	Eddie Williams	.10	.05
620	Rich Yett	.05	.02
621	Slugging Sophomores / Wally Joyner / Cory Snyder	.10	.05
623	Dominican Dynamite / George Bell / Pedro Guerrero	.05	.02
624	Oakland's Power Team / Mark McGwire / Jose Canseco	1.50	.70
625	Classic Relief / Dave Righetti / Dan Plesac	.05	.02
626	All Star Righties / Bret Saberhagen / Mike Witt / Jack Morris	.10	.05
627	Game Closers / John Franco / Steve Bedrosian	.05	.02
628	Masters/Double Play / Ozzie Smith / Ryne Sandberg	.40	.18
629	Rookie Record Setter / Mark McGwire	1.50	.70

		MINT	NRMT
❏ 630	Changing the Guard Mike Greenwell Ellis Burks Todd Benzinger	.25	.11
❏ 631	NL Batting Champs Tony Gwynn Tim Raines	.25	.11
❏ 632	Pitching Magic Mike Scott Orel Hershiser	.10	.05
❏ 633	Big Bats at First Pat Tabler Mark McGwire	1.50	.70
❏ 634	Hitting King/Thief Tony Gwynn Vince Coleman	.25	.11
❏ 635	Slugging Shortstops Tony Fernandez Cal Ripken Alan Trammell	.40	.18
❏ 636	Tried/True Sluggers Mike Schmidt Gary Carter	.30	.14
❏ 637	Crunch Time Darryl Strawberry Eric Davis	.10	.05
❏ 638	AL All-Stars Matt Nokes Kirby Puckett	.30	.14
❏ 639	NL All-Stars Keith Hernandez Dale Murphy	.10	.05
❏ 640	The O's Brothers Billy Ripken Cal Ripken	.60	.25
❏ 641	Mark Grace and Darrin Jackson	1.50	.70
❏ 642	Damon Berryhill and Jeff Montgomery	.25	.11
❏ 643	Felix Fermin and Jesse Reid	.05	.02
❏ 644	Greg Myers and Greg Tabor	.05	.02
❏ 645	Joey Meyer and Jim Eppard	.05	.02
❏ 646	Adam Peterson and Randy Velarde	.10	.05
❏ 647	Pete Smith and Chris Gwynn	.10	.05
❏ 648	Tom Newell and Greg Jelks	.05	.02
❏ 649	Mario Diaz and Clay Parker	.05	.02
❏ 650	Jack Savage and Todd Simmons	.05	.02
❏ 651	John Burkett and Kirt Manwaring	.25	.11
❏ 652	Dave Otto and Walt Weiss	.40	.18
❏ 653	Jeff King and Randell Byers	.40	.18
❏ 654	CL: Twins/Cards Tigers/Giants UER (90 Bob Melvin, 91 Eddie Milner)	.05	.02
❏ 655	CL: Blue Jays/Mets Brewers/Expos UER (Mets listed before Blue Jays on card)	.05	.02
❏ 656	CL: Yankees/Reds Royals/A's	.05	.02
❏ 657	CL: Phillies/Pirates Red Sox/Mariners	.05	.02
❏ 658	CL: White Sox/Cubs Astros/Rangers	.05	.02
❏ 659	CL: Angels/Dodgers Braves/Orioles	.05	.02
❏ 660	CL: Padres/Indians Rookies/Specials	.05	.02

1988 Fleer Glossy

	MINT	NRMT
COMP.FACT.SET (672)	50.00	22.00
COMMON CARD (1-660)	.20	.09
*STARS: 1.5X TO 3X BASIC CARDS		

Dave Stieb

*ROOKIES: 3X TO 6X BASIC CARDS
DISTRIBUTED ONLY IN FACTORY SET FORM

1988 Fleer All-Stars

		MINT	NRMT
COMPLETE SET (12)		6.00	2.70
COMMON CARD (1-12)		.30	.14
RANDOM INSERTS IN PACKS			
❏ 1	Matt Nokes	.30	.14
❏ 2	Tom Henke	.30	.14
❏ 3	Ted Higuera	.30	.14
❏ 4	Roger Clemens	3.00	1.35
❏ 5	George Bell	.30	.14
❏ 6	Andre Dawson	.75	.35
❏ 7	Eric Davis	.40	.18
❏ 8	Wade Boggs	.75	.35
❏ 9	Alan Trammell	.60	.25
❏ 10	Juan Samuel	.30	.14
❏ 11	Jack Clark	.40	.18
❏ 12	Paul Molitor	.75	.35

1988 Fleer Headliners

DARRYL STRAWBERRY

		MINT	NRMT
COMPLETE SET (6)		8.00	3.60
COMMON CARD (1-528)		.50	.23
ONE PER RACK PACK			
❏ 1	Don Mattingly	.75	.35
❏ 2	Mark McGwire	5.00	2.20
❏ 3	Jack Morris	.50	.23
❏ 4	Darryl Strawberry	.50	.23

		MINT	NRMT
❏ 5	Dwight Gooden	.50	.23
❏ 6	Tim Raines	.50	.23

1988 Fleer Update

Ricky Jordan

		MINT	NRMT
COMP.FACT.SET (132)		8.00	3.60
COMMON CARD (1-132)		.10	.05
MINOR STARS		.20	.09
SEMISTARS		.30	.14
UNLISTED STARS		.50	.23
❏ 1	Jose Bautista	.10	.05
❏ 2	Joe Orsulak	.10	.05
❏ 3	Doug Sisk	.10	.05
❏ 4	Craig Worthington	.10	.05
❏ 5	Mike Boddicker	.10	.05
❏ 6	Rick Cerone	.10	.05
❏ 7	Larry Parrish	.10	.05
❏ 8	Lee Smith	.20	.09
❏ 9	Mike Smithson	.10	.05
❏ 10	John Trautwein	.10	.05
❏ 11	Sherman Corbett	.10	.05
❏ 12	Chili Davis	.30	.14
❏ 13	Jim Eppard	.10	.05
❏ 14	Bryan Harvey	.20	.09
❏ 15	John Davis	.10	.05
❏ 16	Dave Gallagher	.10	.05
❏ 17	Ricky Horton	.10	.05
❏ 18	Dan Pasqua	.10	.05
❏ 19	Melido Perez	.10	.05
❏ 20	Jose Segura	.10	.05
❏ 21	Andy Allanson	.10	.05
❏ 22	Jon Perlman	.10	.05
❏ 23	Domingo Ramos	.10	.05
❏ 24	Rick Rodriguez	.10	.05
❏ 25	Willie Upshaw	.10	.05
❏ 26	Paul Gibson	.10	.05
❏ 27	Don Heinkel	.10	.05
❏ 28	Ray Knight	.10	.05
❏ 29	Gary Pettis	.10	.05
❏ 30	Luis Salazar	.10	.05
❏ 31	Mike Macfarlane	.10	.05
❏ 32	Jeff Montgomery	.50	.23
❏ 33	Ted Power	.10	.05
❏ 34	Israel Sanchez	.10	.05
❏ 35	Kurt Stillwell	.10	.05
❏ 36	Pat Tabler	.10	.05
❏ 37	Don August	.10	.05
❏ 38	Darryl Hamilton	.20	.09
❏ 39	Jeff Leonard	.10	.05
❏ 40	Joey Meyer	.10	.05
❏ 41	Allan Anderson	.10	.05
❏ 42	Brian Harper	.10	.05
❏ 43	Tom Herr	.10	.05
❏ 44	Charlie Lea	.10	.05
❏ 45	John Moses (Listed as Hohn on checklist card)	.10	.05
❏ 46	John Candelaria	.10	.05
❏ 47	Jack Clark	.20	.09
❏ 48	Richard Dotson	.10	.05
❏ 49	Al Leiter	1.00	.45
❏ 50	Rafael Santana	.10	.05
❏ 51	Don Slaught	.10	.05
❏ 52	Todd Burns	.10	.05
❏ 53	Dave Henderson	.10	.05
❏ 54	Doug Jennings	.10	.05
❏ 55	Dave Parker	.20	.09

		MINT	NRMT
❑ 56	Walt Weiss	.30	.14
❑ 57	Bob Welch	.10	.05
❑ 58	Henry Cotto	.10	.05
❑ 59	Mario Diaz UER	.10	.05
	(Listed as Marion on card front)		
❑ 60	Mike Jackson	.50	.23
❑ 61	Bill Swift	.10	.05
❑ 62	Jose Cecena	.10	.05
❑ 63	Ray Hayward	.10	.05
❑ 64	Jim Steels UER	.10	.05
	(Listed as Jim Steele on card back)		
❑ 65	Pat Borders	.20	.09
❑ 66	Sil Campusano	.10	.05
❑ 67	Mike Flanagan	.10	.05
❑ 68	Todd Stottlemyre	.50	.23
❑ 69	David Wells	1.50	.70
❑ 70	Jose Alvarez	.10	.05
❑ 71	Paul Runge	.10	.05
❑ 72	Cesar Jimenez	.10	.05
	(Card was intended for German Jimenez, it's his photo)		
❑ 73	Pete Smith	.10	.05
❑ 74	John Smoltz	3.00	1.35
❑ 75	Damon Berryhill	.10	.05
❑ 76	Goose Gossage	.30	.14
❑ 77	Mark Grace	1.50	.70
❑ 78	Darrin Jackson	.10	.05
❑ 79	Vance Law	.10	.05
❑ 80	Jeff Pico	.10	.05
❑ 81	Gary Varsho	.10	.05
❑ 82	Tim Birtsas	.10	.05
❑ 83	Rob Dibble	.20	.09
❑ 84	Danny Jackson	.10	.05
❑ 85	Paul O'Neill	.30	.14
❑ 86	Jose Rijo	.10	.05
❑ 87	Chris Sabo	.20	.09
❑ 88	John Fishel	.10	.05
❑ 89	Craig Biggio	3.00	1.35
❑ 90	Terry Puhl	.10	.05
❑ 91	Rafael Ramirez	.10	.05
❑ 92	Louie Meadows	.10	.05
❑ 93	Kirk Gibson	.50	.23
❑ 94	Alfredo Griffin	.10	.05
❑ 95	Jay Howell	.10	.05
❑ 96	Jesse Orosco	.10	.05
❑ 97	Alejandro Pena	.10	.05
❑ 98	Tracy Woodson	.10	.05
❑ 99	John Dopson	.10	.05
❑ 100	Brian Holman	.10	.05
❑ 101	Rex Hudler	.10	.05
❑ 102	Jeff Parrett	.10	.05
❑ 103	Nelson Santovenia	.10	.05
❑ 104	Kevin Elster	.10	.05
❑ 105	Jeff Innis	.10	.05
❑ 106	Mackey Sasser	.10	.05
❑ 107	Phil Bradley	.10	.05
❑ 108	Danny Clay	.10	.05
❑ 109	Greg A.Harris	.10	.05
❑ 110	Ricky Jordan	.20	.09
❑ 111	David Palmer	.10	.05
❑ 112	Jim Gott	.10	.05
❑ 113	Tommy Gregg UER	.10	.05
	(Photo actually Randy Milligan)		
❑ 114	Barry Jones	.10	.05
❑ 115	Randy Milligan	.10	.05
❑ 116	Luis Alicea	.20	.09
❑ 117	Tom Brunansky	.10	.05
❑ 118	John Costello	.10	.05
❑ 119	Jose DeLeon	.10	.05
❑ 120	Bob Horner	.10	.05
❑ 121	Scott Terry	.10	.05
❑ 122	Roberto Alomar	4.00	1.80
❑ 123	Dave Leiper	.10	.05
❑ 124	Keith Moreland	.10	.05
❑ 125	Mark Parent	.10	.05
❑ 126	Dennis Rasmussen	.10	.05
❑ 127	Randy Bockus	.10	.05
❑ 128	Brett Butler	.20	.09
❑ 129	Donell Nixon	.10	.05
❑ 130	Earnest Riles	.10	.05
❑ 131	Roger Samuels	.10	.05
❑ 132	Checklist U1-U132	.10	.05

1988 Fleer Update Glossy

		MINT	NRMT
COMP.FACT.SET (132)		30.00	13.50
COMMON CARD (1-132)		.25	.11

*STARS: 1X TO 2.5X BASIC CARDS
*ROOKIES: 1.25X TO 3X BASIC CARDS
DISTRIBUTED ONLY IN FACTORY SET FORM

1989 Fleer

	MINT	NRMT
COMPLETE SET (660)	30.00	13.50
COMP.FACT.SET (672)	35.00	16.00
COMMON CARD (1-660)	.05	.02
MINOR STARS	.10	.05
UNLISTED STARS	.20	.09
COMP WORLD SERIES SET (12)	2.00	.90

*WS: EQUAL VALUE TO BASIC CARDS
ONE W.SERIES CARD PER HOBBY SET

❑ 1	Don Baylor	.10	.05
❑ 2	Lance Blankenship	.05	.02
❑ 3	Todd Burns UER	.05	.02
	(Wrong birthdate; before/after All-Star stats missing)		
❑ 4	Greg Cadaret UER	.05	.02
	(All-Star Break stats show 3 losses, should be 2)		
❑ 5	Jose Canseco	.25	.11
❑ 6	Storm Davis	.05	.02
❑ 7	Dennis Eckersley	.15	.07
❑ 8	Mike Gallego	.05	.02
❑ 9	Ron Hassey	.05	.02
❑ 10	Dave Henderson	.05	.02
❑ 11	Rick Honeycutt	.05	.02
❑ 12	Glenn Hubbard	.05	.02
❑ 13	Stan Javier	.05	.02
❑ 14	Doug Jennings	.05	.02
❑ 15	Felix Jose	.05	.02
❑ 16	Carney Lansford	.10	.05
❑ 17	Mark McGwire	1.25	.55
❑ 18	Gene Nelson	.05	.02
❑ 19	Dave Parker	.10	.05
❑ 20	Eric Plunk	.05	.02
❑ 21	Luis Polonia	.05	.02
❑ 22	Terry Steinbach	.05	.02
❑ 23	Dave Stewart	.05	.02
❑ 24	Walt Weiss	.05	.02
❑ 25	Bob Welch	.05	.02
❑ 26	Curt Young	.05	.02
❑ 27	Rick Aguilera	.10	.05
❑ 28	Wally Backman	.05	.02
❑ 29	Mark Carreon UER	.05	.02
	(After All-Star Break batting 7.14)		
❑ 30	Gary Carter	.15	.07
❑ 31	David Cone	.20	.09
❑ 32	Ron Darling	.05	.02
❑ 33	Len Dykstra	.10	.05
❑ 34	Kevin Elster	.05	.02
❑ 35	Sid Fernandez	.05	.02
❑ 36	Dwight Gooden	.10	.05
❑ 37	Keith Hernandez	.10	.05
❑ 38	Gregg Jefferies	.05	.05

❑ 39	Howard Johnson	.05	.02
❑ 40	Terry Leach	.05	.02
❑ 41	Dave Magadan UER	.05	.02
	(Bio says 15 doubles, should be 13)		
❑ 42	Bob McClure	.05	.02
❑ 43	Roger McDowell UER	.05	.02
	(Led Mets with 58, should be 62)		
❑ 44	Kevin McReynolds	.05	.02
❑ 45	Keith A. Miller	.05	.02
❑ 46	Randy Myers	.10	.05
❑ 47	Bob Ojeda	.05	.02
❑ 48	Mackey Sasser	.05	.02
❑ 49	Darryl Strawberry	.10	.05
❑ 50	Tim Teufel	.05	.02
❑ 51	Dave West	.05	.02
❑ 52	Mookie Wilson	.05	.02
❑ 53	Dave Anderson	.05	.02
❑ 54	Tim Belcher	.05	.02
❑ 55	Mike Davis	.05	.02
❑ 56	Mike Devereaux	.05	.02
❑ 57	Kirk Gibson	.10	.05
❑ 58	Alfredo Griffin	.05	.02
❑ 59	Chris Gwynn	.05	.02
❑ 60	Jeff Hamilton	.05	.02
❑ 61A	Danny Heep	.20	.09
	(Home: Lake Hills)		
❑ 61B	Danny Heep	.05	.02
	(Home: San Antonio)		
❑ 62	Orel Hershiser	.10	.05
❑ 63	Brian Holton	.05	.02
❑ 64	Jay Howell	.05	.02
❑ 65	Tim Leary	.05	.02
❑ 66	Mike Marshall	.05	.02
❑ 67	Ramon Martinez	.25	.11
❑ 68	Jesse Orosco	.05	.02
❑ 69	Alejandro Pena	.05	.02
❑ 70	Steve Sax	.05	.02
❑ 71	Mike Scioscia	.05	.02
❑ 72	Mike Sharperson	.05	.02
❑ 73	John Shelby	.05	.02
❑ 74	Franklin Stubbs	.05	.02
❑ 75	John Tudor	.05	.02
❑ 76	Fernando Valenzuela	.10	.05
❑ 77	Tracy Woodson	.05	.02
❑ 78	Marty Barrett	.05	.02
❑ 79	Todd Benzinger	.05	.02
❑ 80	Mike Boddicker UER	.05	.02
	(Rochester in '76, should be '78)		
❑ 81	Wade Boggs	.20	.09
❑ 82	Oil Can Boyd	.05	.02
❑ 83	Ellis Burks	.15	.07
❑ 84	Rick Cerone	.05	.02
❑ 85	Roger Clemens	.50	.23
❑ 86	Steve Curry	.10	.05
❑ 87	Dwight Evans	.05	.02
❑ 88	Wes Gardner	.05	.02
❑ 89	Rich Gedman	.05	.02
❑ 90	Mike Greenwell	.05	.02
❑ 91	Bruce Hurst	.05	.02
❑ 92	Dennis Lamp	.05	.02
❑ 93	Spike Owen	.05	.02
❑ 94	Larry Parrish UER	.05	.02
	(Before All-Star Break batting 1.90)		
❑ 95	Carlos Quintana	.05	.02
❑ 96	Jody Reed	.05	.02
❑ 97	Jim Rice	.10	.05
❑ 98A	Kevin Romine ERR	.20	.09
	(Photo actually Randy Kutcher batting)		
❑ 98B	Kevin Romine COR	.05	.02
	(Arms folded)		
❑ 99	Lee Smith	.10	.05
❑ 100	Mike Smithson	.05	.02
❑ 101	Bob Stanley	.05	.02
❑ 102	Allan Anderson	.05	.02
❑ 103	Keith Atherton	.05	.02
❑ 104	Juan Berenguer	.05	.02
❑ 105	Bert Blyleven	.10	.05
❑ 106	Eric Bullock UER	.05	.02
	(Bats/Throws Right, should be Left)		
❑ 107	Randy Bush	.05	.02

☐ 108 John Christensen	.05	.02
☐ 109 Mark Davidson	.05	.02
☐ 110 Gary Gaetti	.10	.05
☐ 111 Greg Gagne	.05	.02
☐ 112 Dan Gladden	.05	.02
☐ 113 German Gonzalez	.05	.02
☐ 114 Brian Harper	.05	.02
☐ 115 Tom Herr	.05	.02
☐ 116 Kent Hrbek	.10	.05
☐ 117 Gene Larkin	.05	.02
☐ 118 Tim Laudner	.05	.02
☐ 119 Charlie Lea	.05	.02
☐ 120 Steve Lombardozzi	.05	.02
☐ 121A John Moses	.20	.09
(Home: Tempe)		
☐ 121B John Moses	.05	.02
(Home: Phoenix)		
☐ 122 Al Newman	.05	.02
☐ 123 Mark Portugal	.05	.02
☐ 124 Kirby Puckett	.40	.18
☐ 125 Jeff Reardon	.10	.05
☐ 126 Fred Toliver	.05	.02
☐ 127 Frank Viola	.05	.02
☐ 128 Doyle Alexander	.05	.02
☐ 129 Dave Bergman	.05	.02
☐ 130A Tom Brookens ERR	.75	.35
(Mike Heath back)		
☐ 130B Tom Brookens COR	.05	.02
☐ 131 Paul Gibson	.05	.02
☐ 132A Mike Heath ERR	.75	.35
(Tom Brookens back)		
☐ 132B Mike Heath COR	.05	.02
☐ 133 Don Heinkel	.05	.02
☐ 134 Mike Henneman	.05	.02
☐ 135 Guillermo Hernandez	.05	.02
☐ 136 Eric King	.05	.02
☐ 137 Chet Lemon	.05	.02
☐ 138 Fred Lynn UER	.05	.02
(74, 75 stats missing)		
☐ 139 Jack Morris	.10	.05
☐ 140 Matt Nokes	.05	.02
☐ 141 Gary Pettis	.05	.02
☐ 142 Ted Power	.05	.02
☐ 143 Jeff M. Robinson	.05	.02
☐ 144 Luis Salazar	.05	.02
☐ 145 Steve Searcy	.05	.02
☐ 146 Pat Sheridan	.05	.02
☐ 147 Frank Tanana	.05	.02
☐ 148 Alan Trammell	.15	.07
☐ 149 Walt Terrell	.05	.02
☐ 150 Jim Walewander	.05	.02
☐ 151 Lou Whitaker	.10	.05
☐ 152 Tim Birtsas	.05	.02
☐ 153 Tom Browning	.05	.02
☐ 154 Keith Brown	.05	.02
☐ 155 Norm Charlton	.10	.05
☐ 156 Dave Concepcion	.05	.02
☐ 157 Kal Daniels	.05	.02
☐ 158 Eric Davis	.10	.05
☐ 159 Bo Diaz	.05	.02
☐ 160 Rob Dibble	.10	.05
☐ 161 Nick Esasky	.05	.02
☐ 162 John Franco	.10	.05
☐ 163 Danny Jackson	.05	.02
☐ 164 Barry Larkin	.20	.09
☐ 165 Rob Murphy	.05	.02
☐ 166 Paul O'Neill	.10	.05
☐ 167 Jeff Reed	.05	.02
☐ 168 Jose Rijo	.05	.02
☐ 169 Ron Robinson	.05	.02
☐ 170 Chris Sabo	.05	.02
☐ 171 Candy Sierra	.05	.02
☐ 172 Van Snider	.05	.02
☐ 173A Jeff Treadway	5.00	2.20
(Target registration mark above head on front in light blue)		
☐ 173B Jeff Treadway	.05	.02
(No target on front)		
☐ 174 Frank Williams	.05	.02
(After All-Star Break stats are jumbled)		
☐ 175 Herm Winningham	.05	.02
☐ 176 Jim Adduci	.05	.02

☐ 177 Don August	.05	.02
☐ 178 Mike Birkbeck	.05	.02
☐ 179 Chris Bosio	.05	.02
☐ 180 Glenn Braggs	.05	.02
☐ 181 Greg Brock	.05	.02
☐ 182 Mark Clear	.05	.02
☐ 183 Chuck Crim	.05	.02
☐ 184 Rob Deer	.05	.02
☐ 185 Tom Filer	.05	.02
☐ 186 Jim Gantner	.05	.02
☐ 187 Darryl Hamilton	.05	.02
☐ 188 Ted Higuera	.05	.02
☐ 189 Odell Jones	.05	.02
☐ 190 Jeffrey Leonard	.05	.02
☐ 191 Joey Meyer	.05	.02
☐ 192 Paul Mirabella	.05	.02
☐ 193 Paul Molitor	.20	.09
☐ 194 Charlie O'Brien	.05	.02
☐ 195 Dan Plesac	.05	.02
☐ 196 Gary Sheffield	.50	.23
☐ 197 B.J. Surhoff	.10	.05
☐ 198 Dale Sveum	.05	.02
☐ 199 Bill Wegman	.05	.02
☐ 200 Robin Yount	.40	.18
☐ 201 Rafael Belliard	.05	.02
☐ 202 Barry Bonds	.40	.18
☐ 203 Bobby Bonilla	.15	.07
☐ 204 Sid Bream	.05	.02
☐ 205 Benny Distefano	.05	.02
☐ 206 Doug Drabek	.05	.02
☐ 207 Mike Dunne	.05	.02
☐ 208 Felix Fermin	.05	.02
☐ 209 Brian Fisher	.05	.02
☐ 210 Jim Gott	.05	.02
☐ 211 Bob Kipper	.05	.02
☐ 212 Dave LaPoint	.05	.02
☐ 213 Mike LaValliere	.05	.02
☐ 214 Jose Lind	.05	.02
☐ 215 Junior Ortiz	.05	.02
☐ 216 Vicente Palacios	.05	.02
☐ 217 Tom Prince	.05	.02
☐ 218 Gary Redus	.05	.02
☐ 219 R.J. Reynolds	.05	.02
☐ 220 Jeff D. Robinson	.05	.02
☐ 221 John Smiley	.05	.02
☐ 222 Andy Van Slyke	.10	.05
☐ 223 Bob Walk	.05	.02
☐ 224 Glenn Wilson	.05	.02
☐ 225 Jesse Barfield	.05	.02
☐ 226 George Bell	.05	.02
☐ 227 Pat Borders	.10	.05
☐ 228 John Cerutti	.05	.02
☐ 229 Jim Clancy	.05	.02
☐ 230 Mark Eichhorn	.05	.02
☐ 231 Tony Fernandez	.05	.02
☐ 232 Cecil Fielder	.10	.05
☐ 233 Mike Flanagan	.05	.02
☐ 234 Kelly Gruber	.05	.02
☐ 235 Tom Henke	.05	.02
☐ 236 Jimmy Key	.10	.05
☐ 237 Rick Leach	.05	.02
☐ 238 Manny Lee UER	.05	.02
(Bio says regular shortstop, sic, Tony Fernandez)		
☐ 239 Nelson Liriano	.05	.02
☐ 240 Fred McGriff	.20	.09
☐ 241 Lloyd Moseby	.05	.02
☐ 242 Rance Mulliniks	.05	.02
☐ 243 Jeff Musselman	.05	.02
☐ 244 Dave Stieb	.05	.02
☐ 245 Todd Stottlemyre	.15	.07
☐ 246 Duane Ward	.05	.02
☐ 247 David Wells	.20	.09
☐ 248 Ernie Whitt UER	.05	.02
(HR total 21, should be 121)		
☐ 249 Luis Aguayo	.05	.02
☐ 250A Neil Allen	.75	.35
(Home: Sarasota, FL)		
☐ 250B Neil Allen	.05	.02
(Home: Syosset, NY)		
☐ 251 John Candelaria	.05	.02
☐ 252 Jack Clark	.05	.02
☐ 253 Richard Dotson	.05	.02
☐ 254 Rickey Henderson	.25	.11

☐ 255 Tommy John	.10	.05
☐ 256 Roberto Kelly	.05	.05
☐ 257 Al Leiter	.20	.09
☐ 258 Don Mattingly	.40	.18
☐ 259 Dale Mohorcic	.05	.02
☐ 260 Hal Morris	.20	.09
☐ 261 Scott Nielsen	.05	.02
☐ 262 Mike Pagliarulo UER	.05	.02
(Wrong birthdate)		
☐ 263 Hipolito Pena	.05	.02
☐ 264 Ken Phelps	.05	.02
☐ 265 Willie Randolph	.10	.05
☐ 266 Rick Rhoden	.05	.02
☐ 267 Dave Righetti	.05	.02
☐ 268 Rafael Santana	.05	.02
☐ 269 Steve Shields	.05	.02
☐ 270 Joel Skinner	.05	.02
☐ 271 Don Slaught	.05	.02
☐ 272 Claudell Washington	.05	.02
☐ 273 Gary Ward	.05	.02
☐ 274 Dave Winfield	.20	.09
☐ 275 Luis Aquino	.05	.02
☐ 276 Floyd Bannister	.05	.02
☐ 277 George Brett	.40	.18
☐ 278 Bill Buckner	.10	.05
☐ 279 Nick Capra	.05	.02
☐ 280 Jose DeJesus	.05	.02
☐ 281 Steve Farr	.05	.02
☐ 282 Jerry Don Gleaton	.05	.02
☐ 283 Mark Gubicza	.05	.02
☐ 284 Tom Gordon UER	.20	.09
(16.2 innings in '88, should be 15.2)		
☐ 285 Bo Jackson	.15	.07
☐ 286 Charlie Leibrandt	.05	.02
☐ 287 Mike Macfarlane	.05	.02
☐ 288 Jeff Montgomery	.10	.05
☐ 289 Bill Pecota UER	.05	.02
(Photo actually Brad Wellman)		
☐ 290 Jamie Quirk	.05	.02
☐ 291 Bret Saberhagen	.10	.05
☐ 292 Kevin Seitzer	.05	.02
☐ 293 Kurt Stillwell	.05	.02
☐ 294 Pat Tabler	.05	.02
☐ 295 Danny Tartabull	.05	.02
☐ 296 Gary Thurman	.05	.02
☐ 297 Frank White	.10	.05
☐ 298 Willie Wilson	.05	.02
☐ 299 Roberto Alomar	.30	.14
☐ 300 Sandy Alomar Jr. UER	.25	.11
(Wrong birthdate, says 6/16/66, should say 6/18/66)		
☐ 301 Chris Brown	.05	.02
☐ 302 Mike Brumley UER	.05	.02
(133 hits in '88, should be 134)		
☐ 303 Mark Davis	.05	.02
☐ 304 Mark Grant	.05	.02
☐ 305 Tony Gwynn	.50	.23
☐ 306 Greg W. Harris	.05	.02
☐ 307 Andy Hawkins	.05	.02
☐ 308 Jimmy Jones	.05	.02
☐ 309 John Kruk	.10	.05
☐ 310 Dave Leiper	.05	.02
☐ 311 Carmelo Martinez	.05	.02
☐ 312 Lance McCullers	.05	.02
☐ 313 Keith Moreland	.05	.02
☐ 314 Dennis Rasmussen	.05	.02
☐ 315 Randy Ready UER	.05	.02
(1214 games in '88, should be 114)		
☐ 316 Benito Santiago	.05	.02
☐ 317 Eric Show	.05	.02
☐ 318 Todd Simmons	.05	.02
☐ 319 Garry Templeton	.05	.02
☐ 320 Dickie Thon	.05	.02
☐ 321 Ed Whitson	.05	.02
☐ 322 Marvell Wynne	.05	.02
☐ 323 Mike Aldrete	.05	.02
☐ 324 Brett Butler	.10	.05
☐ 325 Will Clark UER	.20	.09
(Three consecutive 100 RBI seasons)		
☐ 326 Kelly Downs UER	.05	.02

('88 stats missing)

❑ 327 Dave Dravecky	.10	.05
❑ 328 Scott Garrelts	.05	.02
❑ 329 Atlee Hammaker	.05	.02
❑ 330 Charlie Hayes	.20	.09
❑ 331 Mike Krukow	.05	.02
❑ 332 Craig Lefferts	.05	.02
❑ 333 Candy Maldonado	.05	.02
❑ 334 Kirt Manwaring UER	.05	.02

(Bats Rights)

❑ 335 Bob Melvin	.05	.02
❑ 336 Kevin Mitchell	.10	.05
❑ 337 Donell Nixon	.05	.02
❑ 338 Tony Perezchica	.05	.02
❑ 339 Joe Price	.05	.02
❑ 340 Rick Reuschel	.05	.02
❑ 341 Earnest Riles	.05	.02
❑ 342 Don Robinson	.05	.02
❑ 343 Chris Speier	.05	.02
❑ 344 Robby Thompson UER	.05	.02

(West Palm Beach)

❑ 345 Jose Uribe	.05	.02
❑ 346 Matt Williams	.20	.09
❑ 347 Trevor Wilson	.05	.02
❑ 348 Juan Agosto	.05	.02
❑ 349 Larry Andersen	.05	.02
❑ 350A Alan Ashby ERR	2.00	.90

(Throws Rig)

❑ 350B Alan Ashby COR	.05	.02
❑ 351 Kevin Bass	.05	.02
❑ 352 Buddy Bell	.05	.02
❑ 353 Craig Biggio	.75	.35
❑ 354 Danny Darwin	.05	.02
❑ 355 Glenn Davis	.05	.02
❑ 356 Jim Deshaies	.05	.02
❑ 357 Bill Doran	.05	.02
❑ 358 John Fishel	.05	.02
❑ 359 Billy Hatcher	.05	.02
❑ 360 Bob Knepper	.05	.02
❑ 361 Louie Meadows UER	.05	.02

(Bio says 10 EBH's
and 6 SB's in '88,
should be 3 and 4)

❑ 362 Dave Meads	.05	.02
❑ 363 Jim Pankovits	.05	.02
❑ 364 Terry Puhl	.05	.02
❑ 365 Rafael Ramirez	.05	.02
❑ 366 Craig Reynolds	.05	.02
❑ 367 Mike Scott	.05	.02

(Card number listed
as 368 on Astros CL)

❑ 368 Nolan Ryan	.75	.35

(Card number listed
as 367 on Astros CL)

❑ 369 Dave Smith	.05	.02
❑ 370 Gerald Young	.05	.02
❑ 371 Hubie Brooks	.05	.02
❑ 372 Tim Burke	.05	.02
❑ 373 John Dopson	.05	.02
❑ 374 Mike R. Fitzgerald	.05	.02
❑ 375 Tom Foley	.05	.02
❑ 376 Andres Galarraga UER	.20	.09

(Home: Caracus)

❑ 377 Neal Heaton	.05	.02
❑ 378 Joe Hesketh	.05	.02
❑ 379 Brian Holman	.05	.02
❑ 380 Rex Hudler	.05	.02
❑ 381 Randy Johnson UER	1.50	.70

(Innings for '85 and
'86 shown as 27 and
120, should be 27.1
and 119.2)

❑ 382 Wallace Johnson	.05	.02
❑ 383 Tracy Jones	.05	.02
❑ 384 Dave Martinez	.05	.02
❑ 385 Dennis Martinez	.10	.05
❑ 386 Andy McGaffigan	.05	.02
❑ 387 Otis Nixon	.10	.05
❑ 388 Johnny Paredes	.05	.02
❑ 389 Jeff Parrett	.05	.02
❑ 390 Pascual Perez	.05	.02
❑ 391 Tim Raines	.10	.05
❑ 392 Luis Rivera	.05	.02
❑ 393 Nelson Santovenia	.05	.02
❑ 394 Bryn Smith	.05	.02
❑ 395 Tim Wallach	.05	.02

❑ 396 Andy Allanson UER	.05	.02

(1214 hits in '88,
should be 114)

❑ 397 Rod Allen	.05	.02
❑ 398 Scott Bailes	.05	.02
❑ 399 Tom Candiotti	.05	.02
❑ 400 Joe Carter	.15	.07
❑ 401 Carmen Castillo UER	.05	.02

(After All-Star Break
batting 2.50)

❑ 402 Dave Clark UER	.05	.02

(Card front shows
position as Rookie;
after All-Star Break
batting 3.14)

❑ 403 John Farrell UER	.05	.02

(Typo in runs
allowed in '88)

❑ 404 Julio Franco	.05	.02
❑ 405 Don Gordon	.05	.02
❑ 406 Mel Hall	.05	.02
❑ 407 Brad Havens	.05	.02
❑ 408 Brook Jacoby	.05	.02
❑ 409 Doug Jones	.05	.02
❑ 410 Jeff Kaiser	.05	.02
❑ 411 Luis Medina	.05	.02
❑ 412 Cory Snyder	.05	.02
❑ 413 Greg Swindell	.05	.02
❑ 414 Ron Tingley UER	.05	.02

(Hit HR in first ML
at-bat, should be
first AL at-bat)

❑ 415 Willie Upshaw	.05	.02
❑ 416 Ron Washington	.05	.02
❑ 417 Rich Yett	.05	.02
❑ 418 Damon Berryhill	.05	.02
❑ 419 Mike Bielecki	.05	.02
❑ 420 Doug Dascenzo	.05	.02
❑ 421 Jody Davis UER	.05	.02

(Braves stats for
'88 missing)

❑ 422 Andre Dawson	.20	.09
❑ 423 Frank DiPino	.05	.02
❑ 424 Shawon Dunston	.05	.02
❑ 425 Rich Gossage	.10	.05
❑ 426 Mark Grace UER	.20	.09

(Minor League stats
for '88 missing)

❑ 427 Mike Harkey	.05	.02
❑ 428 Darrin Jackson	.05	.02
❑ 429 Les Lancaster	.05	.02
❑ 430 Vance Law	.05	.02
❑ 431 Greg Maddux	.60	.25
❑ 432 Jamie Moyer	.05	.02
❑ 433 Al Nipper	.05	.02
❑ 434 Rafael Palmeiro UER	.25	.11

(170 hits in '88,
should be 178)

❑ 435 Pat Perry	.05	.02
❑ 436 Jeff Pico	.05	.02
❑ 437 Ryne Sandberg	.25	.11
❑ 438 Calvin Schiraldi	.05	.02
❑ 439 Rick Sutcliffe	.05	.02
❑ 440A Manny Trillo ERR	2.00	.90

(Throws Rig)

❑ 440B Manny Trillo COR	.05	.02
❑ 441 Gary Varsho UER	.05	.02

(Wrong birthdate;
.303 should be .302;
11/28 should be 9/19)

❑ 442 Mitch Webster	.05	.02
❑ 443 Luis Alicea	.05	.02
❑ 444 Tom Brunansky	.05	.02
❑ 445 Vince Coleman UER	.05	.02

(Third straight with
83, should be fourth
straight with 81)

❑ 446 John Costello UER	.05	.02

(Home California,
should be New York)

❑ 447 Danny Cox	.05	.02
❑ 448 Ken Dayley	.05	.02
❑ 449 Jose DeLeon	.05	.02
❑ 450 Curt Ford	.05	.02
❑ 451 Pedro Guerrero	.05	.02
❑ 452 Bob Horner	.05	.02

❑ 453 Tim Jones	.05	.02
❑ 454 Steve Lake	.05	.02
❑ 455 Joe Magrane UER	.05	.02

(Des Moines, IO)

❑ 456 Greg Mathews	.05	.02
❑ 457 Willie McGee	.10	.05
❑ 458 Larry McWilliams	.05	.02
❑ 459 Jose Oquendo	.05	.02
❑ 460 Tony Pena	.05	.02
❑ 461 Terry Pendleton	.10	.05
❑ 462 Steve Peters UER	.05	.02

(Lives in Harrah,
not Harah)

❑ 463 Ozzie Smith	.25	.11
❑ 464 Scott Terry	.05	.02
❑ 465 Denny Walling	.05	.02
❑ 466 Todd Worrell	.05	.02
❑ 467 Tony Armas UER	.05	.02

(Before All-Star
batting 2.39)

❑ 468 Dante Bichette	.40	.18
❑ 469 Bob Boone	.10	.05
❑ 470 Terry Clark	.05	.02
❑ 471 Stew Cliburn	.05	.02
❑ 472 Mike Cook UER	.05	.02

(TM near Angels logo
missing from front)

❑ 473 Sherman Corbett	.05	.02
❑ 474 Chili Davis	.10	.05
❑ 475 Brian Downing	.05	.02
❑ 476 Jim Eppard	.05	.02
❑ 477 Chuck Finley	.05	.02
❑ 478 Willie Fraser	.05	.02
❑ 479 Bryan Harvey UER	.05	.02

(ML record shows 0-0,
should be 7-5)

❑ 480 Jack Howell	.05	.02
❑ 481 Wally Joyner UER	.10	.05

(Yorba Linda, GA)

❑ 482 Jack Lazorko	.05	.02
❑ 483 Kirk McCaskill	.05	.02
❑ 484 Mark McLemore	.05	.02
❑ 485 Greg Minton	.05	.02
❑ 486 Dan Petry	.05	.02
❑ 487 Johnny Ray	.05	.02
❑ 488 Dick Schofield	.05	.02
❑ 489 Devon White	.10	.05
❑ 490 Mike Witt	.05	.02
❑ 491 Harold Baines	.05	.02
❑ 492 Daryl Boston	.05	.02
❑ 493 Ivan Calderon UER	.05	.02

('60 stats shifted)

❑ 494 Mike Diaz	.05	.02
❑ 495 Carlton Fisk	.20	.09
❑ 496 Dave Gallagher	.05	.02
❑ 497 Ozzie Guillen	.05	.02
❑ 498 Shawn Hillegas	.05	.02
❑ 499 Lance Johnson	.10	.05
❑ 500 Barry Jones	.05	.02
❑ 501 Bill Long	.05	.02
❑ 502 Steve Lyons	.05	.02
❑ 503 Fred Manrique	.05	.02
❑ 504 Jack McDowell	.10	.05
❑ 505 Donn Pall	.05	.02
❑ 506 Kelly Paris	.05	.02
❑ 507 Dan Pasqua	.05	.02
❑ 508 Ken Patterson	.05	.02
❑ 509 Melido Perez	.05	.02
❑ 510 Jerry Reuss	.05	.02
❑ 511 Mark Salas	.05	.02
❑ 512 Bobby Thigpen UER	.05	.02

('86 ERA 4.69,
should be 4.88)

❑ 513 Mike Woodard	.05	.02
❑ 514 Bob Brower	.05	.02
❑ 515 Steve Buechele	.05	.02
❑ 516 Jose Cecena	.05	.02
❑ 517 Cecil Espy	.05	.02
❑ 518 Scott Fletcher	.05	.02
❑ 519 Cecilio Guante	.05	.02

('87 Yankee stats
are off-centered)

❑ 520 Jose Guzman	.05	.02
❑ 521 Ray Hayward	.05	.02
❑ 522 Charlie Hough	.10	.05
❑ 523 Pete Incaviglia	.05	.02

□ 524 Mike Jeffcoat .... .05 .02
□ 525 Paul Kilgus .... .05 .02
□ 526 Chad Kreuter .... .05 .02
□ 527 Jeff Kunkel .... .05 .02
□ 528 Oddibe McDowell .... .05 .02
□ 529 Pete O'Brien .... .05 .02
□ 530 Geno Petralli .... .05 .02
□ 531 Jeff Russell .... .05 .02
□ 532 Ruben Sierra .... .05 .02
□ 533 Mike Stanley .... .05 .02
□ 534A Ed VandeBerg ERR .. 2.00 .90
    (Throws Left)
□ 534B Ed VandeBerg COR .. .05 .02
□ 535 Curtis Wilkerson ERR ... .05 .02
    (Pitcher headings
    at bottom)
□ 536 Mitch Williams .... .05 .02
□ 537 Bobby Witt UER .... .05 .02
    ('85 ERA .643,
    should be 6.43)
□ 538 Steve Balboni .... .05 .02
□ 539 Scott Bankhead .... .05 .02
□ 540 Scott Bradley .... .05 .02
□ 541 Mickey Brantley .... .05 .02
□ 542 Jay Buhner .... .20 .09
□ 543 Mike Campbell .... .05 .02
□ 544 Darnell Coles .... .05 .02
□ 545 Henry Cotto .... .05 .02
□ 546 Alvin Davis .... .05 .02
□ 547 Mario Diaz .... .05 .02
□ 548 Ken Griffey Jr. 25.00 11.00
□ 549 Erik Hanson .... .10 .05
□ 550 Mike Jackson UER ...... .15 .07
    (Lifetime ERA 3.345,
    should be 3.45)
□ 551 Mark Langston .... .05 .02
□ 552 Edgar Martinez .... .20 .09
□ 553 Bill McGuire .... .05 .02
□ 554 Mike Moore .... .05 .02
□ 555 Jim Presley .... .05 .02
□ 556 Rey Quinones .... .05 .02
□ 557 Jerry Reed .... .05 .02
□ 558 Harold Reynolds .... .05 .02
□ 559 Mike Schooler .... .05 .02
□ 560 Bill Swift .... .05 .02
□ 561 Dave Valle .... .05 .02
□ 562 Steve Bedrosian .... .05 .02
□ 563 Phil Bradley .... .05 .02
□ 564 Don Carman .... .05 .02
□ 565 Bob Dernier .... .05 .02
□ 566 Marvin Freeman .... .05 .02
□ 567 Todd Frohwirth .... .05 .02
□ 568 Greg Gross .... .05 .02
□ 569 Kevin Gross .... .05 .02
□ 570 Greg A. Harris .... .05 .02
□ 571 Von Hayes .... .05 .02
□ 572 Chris James .... .05 .02
□ 573 Steve Jeltz .... .05 .02
□ 574 Ron Jones UER .... .05 .02
    (Led IL in '88 with
    85, should be 75)
□ 575 Ricky Jordan .... .10 .05
□ 576 Mike Maddux .... .05 .02
□ 577 David Palmer .... .05 .02
□ 578 Lance Parrish .... .05 .02
□ 579 Shane Rawley .... .05 .02
□ 580 Bruce Ruffin .... .05 .02
□ 581 Juan Samuel .... .05 .02
□ 582 Mike Schmidt .... .30 .14
□ 583 Kent Tekulve .... .05 .02
□ 584 Milt Thompson UER ..... .05 .02
    (19 hits in '88,
    should be 109)
□ 585 Jose Alvarez .... .05 .02
□ 586 Paul Assenmacher ...... .05 .02
□ 587 Bruce Benedict .... .05 .02
□ 588 Jeff Blauser .... .10 .05
□ 589 Terry Blocker .... .05 .02
□ 590 Ron Gant .... .10 .05
□ 591 Tom Glavine .... .20 .09
□ 592 Tommy Gregg .... .05 .02
□ 593 Albert Hall .... .05 .02
□ 594 Dion James .... .05 .02
□ 595 Rick Mahler .... .05 .02
□ 596 Dale Murphy .... .20 .09
□ 597 Gerald Perry .... .05 .02

□ 598 Charlie Puleo .... .05 .02
□ 599 Ted Simmons .... .10 .05
□ 600 Pete Smith .... .05 .02
□ 601 Zane Smith .... .05 .02
□ 602 John Smoltz .... .75 .35
□ 603 Bruce Sutter .... .05 .02
□ 604 Andres Thomas .... .05 .02
□ 605 Ozzie Virgil .... .05 .02
□ 606 Brady Anderson .... .40 .18
□ 607 Jeff Ballard .... .05 .02
□ 608 Jose Bautista .... .05 .02
□ 609 Ken Gerhart .... .05 .02
□ 610 Terry Kennedy .... .05 .02
□ 611 Eddie Murray .... .20 .09
□ 612 Carl Nichols UER .... .05 .02
    (Before All-Star Break
    batting 1.86)
□ 613 Tom Niedenfuer .... .05 .02
□ 614 Joe Orsulak .... .05 .02
□ 615 Oswald Peraza UER ..... .05 .02
    (Shown as Oswaldo)
□ 616A Bill Ripken ERR 6.00 2.70
    (Rick Face written
    on knob of bat)
□ 616B Bill Ripken 25.00 11.00
    (Bat knob
    whited out)
□ 616C Bill Ripken 5.00 2.20
    (Words on bat knob
    scribbled out)
□ 616D Bill Ripken DP .... .10 .05
    (Black box covering
    bat knob)
□ 617 Cal Ripken .... .75 .35
□ 618 Dave Schmidt .... .05 .02
□ 619 Rick Schu .... .05 .02
□ 620 Larry Sheets .... .05 .02
□ 621 Doug Sisk .... .05 .02
□ 622 Pete Stanicek .... .05 .02
□ 623 Mickey Tettleton .... .10 .05
□ 624 Jay Tibbs .... .05 .02
□ 625 Jim Traber .... .05 .02
□ 626 Mark Williamson .... .05 .02
□ 627 Craig Worthington ...... .05 .02
□ 628 Speed/Power .... .10 .05
    Jose Canseco
□ 629 Pitcher Perfect .... .05 .02
    Tom Browning
□ 630 Like Father/Like Sons .. .20 .09
    Roberto Alomar
    Sandy Alomar Jr.
    (Names on card listed
    in wrong order) UER
□ 631 NL All Stars UER .... .20 .09
    Will Clark
    Rafael Palmeiro
    (Gallaraga, sic;
    Clark 3 consecutive
    100 RBI seasons;
    third with 102 RBI's)
□ 632 Homeruns - Coast ...... .10 .05
    to Coast UER
    Darryl Strawberry
    Will Clark (Homeruns
    should be two words)
□ 633 Hot Corners - Hot ...... .10 .05
    Hitters UER
    Wade Boggs
    Carney Lansford
    (Boggs hit .366 in
    '86, should be '88)
□ 634 Triple A's .... .50 .23
    Jose Canseco
    Terry Steinbach
    Mark McGwire
□ 635 Dual Heat .... .10 .05
    Mark Davis
    Dwight Gooden
□ 636 NL Pitching Power UER .. .10 .05
    Danny Jackson
    David Cone
    (Hersheiser, sic)
□ 637 Cannon Arms UER .... .10 .05
    Chris Sabo
    Bobby Bonilla
    (Bobby Bonds, sic)

□ 638 Double Trouble UER ..... .10 .05
    Andres Galarraga
    (Misspelled Gallaraga
    on card back)
    Gerald Perry
□ 639 Power Center .... .20 .09
    Kirby Puckett
    Eric Davis
□ 640 Steve Wilson and .... .05 .02
    Cameron Drew
□ 641 Kevin Brown and .... .40 .18
    Kevin Reimer
□ 642 Brad Pounders and ..... .05 .02
    Jerald Clark
□ 643 Mike Capel and .... .05 .02
    Drew Hall
□ 644 Joe Girardi and .... .20 .09
    Rolando Roomes
□ 645 Lenny Harris and .... .10 .05
    Marty Brown
□ 646 Luis DeLosSantos .... .05 .02
    and Jim Campbell
□ 647 Randy Kramer and ...... .05 .02
    Miguel Garcia
□ 648 Torey Lovullo and ...... .05 .02
    Robert Palacios
□ 649 Jim Corsi and .... .05 .02
    Bob Milacki
□ 650 Grady Hall and .... .05 .02
    Mike Rochford
□ 651 Terry Taylor and .... .05 .02
    Vance Lovelace
□ 652 Ken Hill and .... .20 .09
    Dennis Cook
□ 653 Scott Service and .... .05 .02
    Shane Turner
□ 654 CL: Oakland/Mets ...... .05 .02
    Dodgers/Red Sox
    (10 Hendersor;
    68 Jess Orosco)
□ 655A CL: Twins/Tigers ERR .05 .02
    Reds/Brewers
    (179 Boslo and
    Twins/Tigers positions
    listed)
□ 655B CL: Twins/Tigers COR .05 .02
    Reds/Brewers
    (179 Boslo but
    Twins/Tigers positions
    not listed)
□ 656 CL: Pirates/Blue Jays .. .05 .02
    Yankees/Royals
    (225 Jess Barfield)
□ 657 CL: Padres/Giants ...... .05 .02
    Astros/Expos
    (367/368 wrong)
□ 658 CL: Indians/Cubs........ .05 .02
    Cardinals/Angels
    (449 Deleon)
□ 659 CL: White Sox/Rangers.. .05 .02
    Mariners/Phillies
□ 660 CL: Braves/Orioles ..... .05 .02
    Specials/Checklists
    (632 hyphenated diff-
    erently and 650 Hall;
    595 Rich Mahler;
    619 Rich Schu)

1989 Fleer Glossy

	MINT	NRMT
COMP.FACT.SET (672)	300.00	135.00
COMMON CARD (1-660)	.15	.07

*STARS: 4X TO 8X BASIC CARDS
*ROOKIES: 6X TO 12X BASIC CARDS
DISTRIBUTED ONLY IN FACTORY SET FORM

1989 Fleer All-Stars

WILL CLARK
FIRST BASE-GIANTS

	MINT	NRMT
COMPLETE SET (12)	5.00	2.20
COMMON CARD (1-12)	.25	.11

RANDOM INSERTS IN PACKS

☐ 1 Bobby Bonilla	.40	.18
☐ 2 Jose Canseco	2.00	.90
☐ 3 Will Clark	.50	.23
☐ 4 Dennis Eckersley	.40	.18
☐ 5 Julio Franco	.25	.11
☐ 6 Mike Greenwell	.25	.11
☐ 7 Orel Hershiser	.40	.18
☐ 8 Paul Molitor	.50	.23
☐ 9 Mike Scioscia	.25	.11
☐ 10 Darryl Strawberry	.35	.16
☐ 11 Alan Trammell	.40	.18
☐ 12 Frank Viola	.25	.11

1989 Fleer For The Record

Roger Clemens RED SOX PITCHER

	MINT	NRMT
COMPLETE SET (6)	8.00	3.60
COMMON CARD (1-6)	.30	.14

ONE PER RACK PACK

☐ 1 Wade Boggs	.75	.35
☐ 2 Roger Clemens	3.00	1.35
☐ 3 Andres Galarraga	.75	.35
☐ 4 Kirk Gibson	.30	.14
☐ 5 Greg Maddux	5.00	2.20
☐ 6 Don Mattingly UER	2.50	1.10
(Won batting title '83, should say '84)		

1989 Fleer Update

	MINT	NRMT
COMP.FACT.SET (132)	6.00	2.70
COMMON CARD (1-132)	.05	.02
MINOR STARS	.10	.05

MARK LANGSTON
PITCHER

UNLISTED STARS	.20	.09
☐ 1 Phil Bradley	.05	.02
☐ 2 Mike Devereaux	.05	.02
☐ 3 Steve Finley	.40	.18
☐ 4 Kevin Hickey	.05	.02
☐ 5 Brian Holton	.05	.02
☐ 6 Bob Milacki	.05	.02
☐ 7 Randy Milligan	.05	.02
☐ 8 John Dopson	.05	.02
☐ 9 Nick Esasky	.05	.02
☐ 10 Rob Murphy	.05	.02
☐ 11 Jim Abbott	.20	.09
☐ 12 Bert Blyleven	.10	.05
☐ 13 Jeff Manto	.05	.02
☐ 14 Bob McClure	.05	.02
☐ 15 Lance Parrish	.05	.02
☐ 16 Lee Stevens	.25	.11
☐ 17 Claudell Washington	.05	.02
☐ 18 Mark Davis	.05	.02
☐ 19 Eric King	.05	.02
☐ 20 Ron Kittle	.05	.02
☐ 21 Matt Merullo	.05	.02
☐ 22 Steve Rosenberg	.05	.02
☐ 23 Robin Ventura	.75	.35
☐ 24 Keith Atherton	.05	.02
☐ 25 Joey Belle	3.00	1.35
☐ 26 Jerry Browne	.05	.02
☐ 27 Felix Fermin	.05	.02
☐ 28 Brad Komminsk	.05	.02
☐ 29 Pete O'Brien	.05	.02
☐ 30 Mike Brumley	.05	.02
☐ 31 Tracy Jones	.05	.02
☐ 32 Mike Schwabe	.05	.02
☐ 33 Gary Ward	.05	.02
☐ 34 Frank Williams	.05	.02
☐ 35 Kevin Appier	.25	.11
☐ 36 Bob Boone	.10	.05
☐ 37 Luis DeLosSantos	.05	.02
☐ 38 Jim Eisenreich	.05	.02
☐ 39 Jaime Navarro	.05	.02
☐ 40 Bill Spiers	.05	.02
☐ 41 Greg Vaughn	1.50	.70
☐ 42 Randy Veres	.05	.02
☐ 43 Wally Backman	.05	.02
☐ 44 Shane Rawley	.05	.02
☐ 45 Steve Balboni	.05	.02
☐ 46 Jesse Barfield	.05	.02
☐ 47 Alvaro Espinoza	.05	.02
☐ 48 Bob Geren	.05	.02
☐ 49 Mel Hall	.05	.02
☐ 50 Andy Hawkins	.05	.02
☐ 51 Hensley Meulens	.05	.02
☐ 52 Steve Sax	.05	.02
☐ 53 Deion Sanders	.75	.35
☐ 54 Rickey Henderson	.25	.11
☐ 55 Mike Moore	.05	.02
☐ 56 Tony Phillips	.05	.02
☐ 57 Greg Briley	.05	.02
☐ 58 Gene Harris	.05	.02
☐ 59 Randy Johnson	1.50	.70
☐ 60 Jeffrey Leonard	.05	.02
☐ 61 Dennis Powell	.05	.02
☐ 62 Omar Vizquel	.50	.23
☐ 63 Kevin Brown	.40	.18
☐ 64 Julio Franco	.05	.02
☐ 65 Jamie Moyer	.05	.02
☐ 66 Rafael Palmeiro	.25	.11

☐ 67 Nolan Ryan	1.50	.70
☐ 68 Francisco Cabrera	.10	.05
☐ 69 Junior Felix	.05	.02
☐ 70 Al Leiter	.20	.09
☐ 71 Alex Sanchez	.05	.02
☐ 72 Geronimo Berroa	.05	.02
☐ 73 Derek Lilliquist	.05	.02
☐ 74 Lonnie Smith	.05	.02
☐ 75 Jeff Treadway	.05	.02
☐ 76 Paul Kilgus	.05	.02
☐ 77 Lloyd McClendon	.05	.02
☐ 78 Scott Sanderson	.05	.02
☐ 79 Dwight Smith	.10	.05
☐ 80 Jerome Walton	.20	.09
☐ 81 Mitch Williams	.05	.02
☐ 82 Steve Wilson	.05	.02
☐ 83 Todd Benzinger	.05	.02
☐ 84 Ken Griffey Sr.	.10	.05
☐ 85 Rick Mahler	.05	.02
☐ 86 Rolando Roomes	.05	.02
☐ 87 Scott Scudder	.05	.02
☐ 88 Jim Clancy	.05	.02
☐ 89 Rick Rhoden	.05	.02
☐ 90 Dan Schatzeder	.05	.02
☐ 91 Mike Morgan	.05	.02
☐ 92 Eddie Murray	.20	.09
☐ 93 Willie Randolph	.10	.05
☐ 94 Ray Searage	.05	.02
☐ 95 Mike Aldrete	.05	.02
☐ 96 Kevin Gross	.05	.02
☐ 97 Mark Langston	.05	.02
☐ 98 Spike Owen	.05	.02
☐ 99 Zane Smith	.05	.02
☐ 100 Don Aase	.05	.02
☐ 101 Barry Lyons	.05	.02
☐ 102 Juan Samuel	.05	.02
☐ 103 Wally Whitehurst	.05	.02
☐ 104 Dennis Cook	.05	.02
☐ 105 Len Dykstra	.10	.05
☐ 106 Charlie Hayes	.20	.09
☐ 107 Tommy Herr	.05	.02
☐ 108 Ken Howell	.05	.02
☐ 109 John Kruk	.10	.05
☐ 110 Roger McDowell	.05	.02
☐ 111 Terry Mulholland	.05	.02
☐ 112 Jeff Parrett	.05	.02
☐ 113 Neal Heaton	.05	.02
☐ 114 Jeff King	.05	.02
☐ 115 Randy Kramer	.05	.02
☐ 116 Bill Landrum	.05	.02
☐ 117 Cris Carpenter	.05	.02
☐ 118 Frank DiPino	.05	.02
☐ 119 Ken Hill	.20	.09
☐ 120 Dan Quisenberry	.05	.02
☐ 121 Milt Thompson	.05	.02
☐ 122 Todd Zeile	.25	.11
☐ 123 Jack Clark	.05	.02
☐ 124 Bruce Hurst	.05	.02
☐ 125 Mark Parent	.05	.02
☐ 126 Bip Roberts	.10	.05
☐ 127 Jeff Brantley UER	.15	.07
(Photo actually Joe Kmak)		
☐ 128 Terry Kennedy	.05	.02
☐ 129 Mike LaCoss	.05	.02
☐ 130 Greg Litton	.05	.02
☐ 131 Mike Schmidt	.60	.25
☐ 132 Checklist 1-132	.05	.02

1990 Fleer

	MINT	NRMT
COMPLETE SET (660)	12.00	5.50
COMP.HOBBY SET (672)	15.00	6.75
COMMON CARD (1-660)	.05	.02
MINOR STARS	.10	.05
UNLISTED STARS	.20	.09
COMP.WORLD SERIES SET (12)	2.00	.90

*WS: EQUAL VALUE TO BASIC CARDS
ONE WORLD SERIES SET PER FACT.SET

☐ 1 Lance Blankenship	.05	.02
☐ 2 Todd Burns	.05	.02
☐ 3 Jose Canseco	.25	.11
☐ 4 Jim Corsi	.05	.02
☐ 5 Storm Davis	.05	.02

- ☐ 6 Dennis Eckersley .... .15 .07
- ☐ 7 Mike Gallego .... .05 .02
- ☐ 8 Ron Hassey .... .05 .02
- ☐ 9 Dave Henderson .... .05 .02
- ☐ 10 Rickey Henderson .... .25 .11
- ☐ 11 Rick Honeycutt .... .05 .02
- ☐ 12 Stan Javier .... .05 .02
- ☐ 13 Felix Jose .... .05 .02
- ☐ 14 Carney Lansford .... .10 .05
- ☐ 15 Mark McGwire UER .... 1.00 .45
   (1989 runs listed as
   4, should be 74)
- ☐ 16 Mike Moore .... .05 .02
- ☐ 17 Gene Nelson .... .05 .02
- ☐ 18 Dave Parker .... .10 .05
- ☐ 19 Tony Phillips .... .05 .02
- ☐ 20 Terry Steinbach .... .05 .02
- ☐ 21 Dave Stewart .... .10 .05
- ☐ 22 Walt Weiss .... .05 .02
- ☐ 23 Bob Welch .... .05 .02
- ☐ 24 Curt Young .... .05 .02
- ☐ 25 Paul Assenmacher .... .05 .02
- ☐ 26 Damon Berryhill .... .05 .02
- ☐ 27 Mike Bielecki .... .05 .02
- ☐ 28 Kevin Blankenship .... .05 .02
- ☐ 29 Andre Dawson .... .20 .09
- ☐ 30 Shawon Dunston .... .05 .02
- ☐ 31 Joe Girardi .... .15 .07
- ☐ 32 Mark Grace .... .20 .09
- ☐ 33 Mike Harkey .... .05 .02
- ☐ 34 Paul Kilgus .... .05 .02
- ☐ 35 Les Lancaster .... .05 .02
- ☐ 36 Vance Law .... .05 .02
- ☐ 37 Greg Maddux .... .50 .23
- ☐ 38 Lloyd McClendon .... .05 .02
- ☐ 39 Jeff Pico .... .05 .02
- ☐ 40 Ryne Sandberg .... .25 .11
- ☐ 41 Scott Sanderson .... .05 .02
- ☐ 42 Dwight Smith .... .05 .02
- ☐ 43 Rick Sutcliffe .... .05 .02
- ☐ 44 Jerome Walton .... .05 .02
- ☐ 45 Mitch Webster .... .05 .02
- ☐ 46 Curt Wilkerson .... .05 .02
- ☐ 47 Dean Wilkins .... .05 .02
- ☐ 48 Mitch Williams .... .05 .02
- ☐ 49 Steve Wilson .... .05 .02
- ☐ 50 Steve Bedrosian .... .05 .02
- ☐ 51 Mike Benjamin .... .05 .02
- ☐ 52 Jeff Brantley .... .05 .02
- ☐ 53 Brett Butler .... .10 .05
- ☐ 54 Will Clark UER .... .10 .05
   (Did You Know says
   first in runs, should
   say tied for first)
- ☐ 55 Kelly Downs .... .05 .02
- ☐ 56 Scott Garrelts .... .05 .02
- ☐ 57 Atlee Hammaker .... .05 .02
- ☐ 58 Terry Kennedy .... .05 .02
- ☐ 59 Mike LaCoss .... .05 .02
- ☐ 60 Craig Lefferts .... .05 .02
- ☐ 61 Greg Litton .... .05 .02
- ☐ 62 Candy Maldonado .... .05 .02
- ☐ 63 Kirt Manwaring UER .... .05 .02
   (No '88 Phoenix stats
   as noted in box)
- ☐ 64 Randy McCament .... .05 .02
- ☐ 65 Kevin Mitchell .... .05 .02
- ☐ 66 Donell Nixon .... .05 .02

- ☐ 67 Ken Oberkfell .... .05 .02
- ☐ 68 Rick Reuschel .... .05 .02
- ☐ 69 Ernest Riles .... .05 .02
- ☐ 70 Don Robinson .... .05 .02
- ☐ 71 Pat Sheridan .... .05 .02
- ☐ 72 Chris Speier .... .05 .02
- ☐ 73 Robby Thompson .... .05 .02
- ☐ 74 Jose Uribe .... .05 .02
- ☐ 75 Matt Williams .... .20 .09
- ☐ 76 George Bell .... .05 .02
- ☐ 77 Pat Borders .... .05 .02
- ☐ 78 John Cerutti .... .05 .02
- ☐ 79 Junior Felix .... .05 .02
- ☐ 80 Tony Fernandez .... .05 .02
- ☐ 81 Mike Flanagan .... .05 .02
- ☐ 82 Mauro Gozzo .... .05 .02
- ☐ 83 Kelly Gruber .... .05 .02
- ☐ 84 Tom Henke .... .05 .02
- ☐ 85 Jimmy Key .... .10 .05
- ☐ 86 Manny Lee .... .05 .02
- ☐ 87 Nelson Liriano UER .... .05 .02
   (Should say "led the
   IL" instead of "led
   the TL")
- ☐ 88 Lee Mazzilli .... .05 .02
- ☐ 89 Fred McGriff .... .20 .09
- ☐ 90 Lloyd Moseby .... .05 .02
- ☐ 91 Rance Mulliniks .... .05 .02
- ☐ 92 Alex Sanchez .... .05 .02
- ☐ 93 Dave Stieb .... .10 .05
- ☐ 94 Todd Stottlemyre .... .10 .05
- ☐ 95 Duane Ward UER .... .05 .02
   (Double line of '87
   Syracuse stats)
- ☐ 96 David Wells .... .15 .07
- ☐ 97 Ernie Whitt .... .05 .02
- ☐ 98 Frank Wills .... .05 .02
- ☐ 99 Mookie Wilson .... .10 .05
- ☐ 100 Kevin Appier .... .15 .07
- ☐ 101 Luis Aquino .... .05 .02
- ☐ 102 Bob Boone .... .10 .05
- ☐ 103 George Brett .... .40 .18
- ☐ 104 Jose DeJesus .... .05 .02
- ☐ 105 Luis De Los Santos .... .05 .02
- ☐ 106 Jim Eisenreich .... .05 .02
- ☐ 107 Steve Farr .... .05 .02
- ☐ 108 Tom Gordon .... .10 .05
- ☐ 109 Mark Gubicza .... .05 .02
- ☐ 110 Bo Jackson .... .10 .05
- ☐ 111 Terry Leach .... .05 .02
- ☐ 112 Charlie Leibrandt .... .05 .02
- ☐ 113 Rick Luecken .... .05 .02
- ☐ 114 Mike Macfarlane .... .05 .02
- ☐ 115 Jeff Montgomery .... .10 .05
- ☐ 116 Bret Saberhagen .... .10 .05
- ☐ 117 Kevin Seitzer .... .05 .02
- ☐ 118 Kurt Stillwell .... .05 .02
- ☐ 119 Pat Tabler .... .05 .02
- ☐ 120 Danny Tartabull .... .05 .02
- ☐ 121 Gary Thurman .... .05 .02
- ☐ 122 Frank White .... .10 .05
- ☐ 123 Willie Wilson .... .05 .02
- ☐ 124 Matt Winters .... .05 .02
- ☐ 125 Jim Abbott .... .15 .07
- ☐ 126 Tony Armas .... .05 .02
- ☐ 127 Dante Bichette .... .20 .09
- ☐ 128 Bert Blyleven .... .10 .05
- ☐ 129 Chili Davis .... .05 .02
- ☐ 130 Brian Downing .... .05 .02
- ☐ 131 Mike Fetters .... .05 .02
- ☐ 132 Chuck Finley .... .10 .05
- ☐ 133 Willie Fraser .... .05 .02
- ☐ 134 Bryan Harvey .... .05 .02
- ☐ 135 Jack Howell .... .05 .02
- ☐ 136 Wally Joyner .... .10 .05
- ☐ 137 Jeff Manto .... .05 .02
- ☐ 138 Kirk McCaskill .... .05 .02
- ☐ 139 Bob McClure .... .05 .02
- ☐ 140 Greg Minton .... .05 .02
- ☐ 141 Lance Parrish .... .05 .02
- ☐ 142 Dan Petry .... .05 .02
- ☐ 143 Johnny Ray .... .05 .02
- ☐ 144 Dick Schofield .... .05 .02
- ☐ 145 Lee Stevens .... .10 .05
- ☐ 146 Claudell Washington ...... .05 .02
- ☐ 147 Devon White .... .05 .02

- ☐ 148 Mike Witt .... .05 .02
- ☐ 149 Roberto Alomar .... .20 .09
- ☐ 150 Sandy Alomar Jr .... .10 .05
- ☐ 151 Andy Benes .... .20 .09
- ☐ 152 Jack Clark .... .10 .05
- ☐ 153 Pat Clements .... .05 .02
- ☐ 154 Joey Cora .... .05 .02
- ☐ 155 Mark Davis .... .05 .02
- ☐ 156 Mark Grant .... .05 .02
- ☐ 157 Tony Gwynn .... .50 .23
- ☐ 158 Greg W. Harris .... .05 .02
- ☐ 159 Bruce Hurst .... .05 .02
- ☐ 160 Darrin Jackson .... .05 .02
- ☐ 161 Chris James .... .05 .02
- ☐ 162 Carmelo Martinez .... .05 .02
- ☐ 163 Mike Pagliarulo .... .05 .02
- ☐ 164 Mark Parent .... .05 .02
- ☐ 165 Dennis Rasmussen .... .05 .02
- ☐ 166 Bip Roberts .... .05 .02
- ☐ 167 Benito Santiago .... .05 .02
- ☐ 168 Calvin Schiraldi .... .05 .02
- ☐ 169 Eric Show .... .05 .02
- ☐ 170 Garry Templeton .... .05 .02
- ☐ 171 Ed Whitson .... .05 .02
- ☐ 172 Brady Anderson .... .20 .09
- ☐ 173 Jeff Ballard .... .05 .02
- ☐ 174 Phil Bradley .... .05 .02
- ☐ 175 Mike Devereaux .... .05 .02
- ☐ 176 Steve Finley .... .20 .09
- ☐ 177 Pete Harnisch .... .05 .02
- ☐ 178 Kevin Hickey .... .05 .02
- ☐ 179 Brian Holton .... .05 .02
- ☐ 180 Ben McDonald .... .10 .05
- ☐ 181 Bob Melvin .... .05 .02
- ☐ 182 Bob Milacki .... .05 .02
- ☐ 183 Randy Milligan UER .... .05 .02
   (Double line of
   '87 stats)
- ☐ 184 Gregg Olson .... .10 .05
- ☐ 185 Joe Orsulak .... .05 .02
- ☐ 186 Bill Ripken .... .05 .02
- ☐ 187 Cal Ripken .... .75 .35
- ☐ 188 Dave Schmidt .... .05 .02
- ☐ 189 Larry Sheets .... .05 .02
- ☐ 190 Mickey Tettleton .... .10 .05
- ☐ 191 Mark Thurmond .... .05 .02
- ☐ 192 Jay Tibbs .... .05 .02
- ☐ 193 Jim Traber .... .05 .02
- ☐ 194 Mark Williamson .... .05 .02
- ☐ 195 Craig Worthington .... .05 .02
- ☐ 196 Don Aase .... .05 .02
- ☐ 197 Blaine Beatty .... .05 .02
- ☐ 198 Mark Carreon .... .05 .02
- ☐ 199 Gary Carter .... .20 .09
- ☐ 200 David Cone .... .20 .09
- ☐ 201 Ron Darling .... .05 .02
- ☐ 202 Kevin Elster .... .05 .02
- ☐ 203 Sid Fernandez .... .05 .02
- ☐ 204 Dwight Gooden .... .10 .05
- ☐ 205 Keith Hernandez .... .10 .05
- ☐ 206 Jeff Innis .... .05 .02
- ☐ 207 Gregg Jefferies .... .10 .05
- ☐ 208 Howard Johnson .... .05 .02
- ☐ 209 Barry Lyons UER .... .05 .02
   (Double line of
   '87 stats)
- ☐ 210 Dave Magadan .... .05 .02
- ☐ 211 Kevin McReynolds .... .05 .02
- ☐ 212 Jeff Musselman .... .05 .02
- ☐ 213 Randy Myers .... .10 .05
- ☐ 214 Bob Ojeda .... .05 .02
- ☐ 215 Juan Samuel .... .05 .02
- ☐ 216 Mackey Sasser .... .05 .02
- ☐ 217 Darryl Strawberry .... .10 .05
- ☐ 218 Tim Teufel .... .05 .02
- ☐ 219 Frank Viola .... .05 .02
- ☐ 220 Juan Agosto .... .05 .02
- ☐ 221 Larry Andersen .... .05 .02
- ☐ 222 Eric Anthony .... .20 .09
- ☐ 223 Kevin Bass .... .05 .02
- ☐ 224 Craig Biggio .... .20 .09
- ☐ 225 Ken Caminiti .... .20 .09
- ☐ 226 Jim Clancy .... .05 .02
- ☐ 227 Danny Darwin .... .05 .02
- ☐ 228 Glenn Davis .... .05 .02
- ☐ 229 Jim Deshaies .... .05 .02

☐ 230	Bill Doran	.05	.02
☐ 231	Bob Forsch	.05	.02
☐ 232	Brian Meyer	.05	.02
☐ 233	Terry Puhl	.05	.02
☐ 234	Rafael Ramirez	.05	.02
☐ 235	Rick Rhoden	.05	.02
☐ 236	Dan Schatzeder	.05	.02
☐ 237	Mike Scott	.05	.02
☐ 238	Dave Smith	.05	.02
☐ 239	Alex Trevino	.05	.02
☐ 240	Glenn Wilson	.05	.02
☐ 241	Gerald Young	.05	.02
☐ 242	Tom Brunansky	.05	.02
☐ 243	Cris Carpenter	.05	.02
☐ 244	Alex Cole	.05	.02
☐ 245	Vince Coleman	.05	.02
☐ 246	John Costello	.05	.02
☐ 247	Ken Dayley	.05	.02
☐ 248	Jose DeLeon	.05	.02
☐ 249	Frank DiPino	.05	.02
☐ 250	Pedro Guerrero	.05	.02
☐ 251	Ken Hill	.10	.05
☐ 252	Joe Magrane	.05	.02
☐ 253	Willie McGee UER	.10	.05
	(No decimal point before 353)		
☐ 254	John Morris	.05	.02
☐ 255	Jose Oquendo	.05	.02
☐ 256	Tony Pena	.05	.02
☐ 257	Terry Pendleton	.10	.05
☐ 258	Ted Power	.05	.02
☐ 259	Dan Quisenberry	.05	.02
☐ 260	Ozzie Smith	.25	.11
☐ 261	Scott Terry	.05	.02
☐ 262	Milt Thompson	.05	.02
☐ 263	Denny Walling	.05	.02
☐ 264	Todd Worrell	.05	.02
☐ 265	Todd Zeile	.10	.05
☐ 266	Marty Barrett	.05	.02
☐ 267	Mike Boddicker	.05	.02
☐ 268	Wade Boggs	.20	.09
☐ 269	Ellis Burks	.15	.07
☐ 270	Rick Cerone	.05	.02
☐ 271	Roger Clemens	.50	.23
☐ 272	John Dopson	.05	.02
☐ 273	Nick Esasky	.05	.02
☐ 274	Dwight Evans	.10	.05
☐ 275	Wes Gardner	.05	.02
☐ 276	Rich Gedman	.05	.02
☐ 277	Mike Greenwell	.05	.02
☐ 278	Danny Heep	.05	.02
☐ 279	Eric Hetzel	.05	.02
☐ 280	Dennis Lamp	.05	.02
☐ 281	Rob Murphy UER	.05	.02
	('89 stats say Reds, should say Red Sox)		
☐ 282	Joe Price	.05	.02
☐ 283	Carlos Quintana	.05	.02
☐ 284	Jody Reed	.05	.02
☐ 285	Luis Rivera	.05	.02
☐ 286	Kevin Romine	.05	.02
☐ 287	Lee Smith	.10	.05
☐ 288	Mike Smithson	.05	.02
☐ 289	Bob Stanley	.05	.02
☐ 290	Harold Baines	.05	.02
☐ 291	Kevin Brown	.20	.09
☐ 292	Steve Buechele	.05	.02
☐ 293	Scott Coolbaugh	.05	.02
☐ 294	Jack Daugherty	.05	.02
☐ 295	Cecil Espy	.05	.02
☐ 296	Julio Franco	.05	.02
☐ 297	Juan Gonzalez	2.50	1.10
☐ 298	Cecilio Guante	.05	.02
☐ 299	Drew Hall	.05	.02
☐ 300	Charlie Hough	.10	.05
☐ 301	Pete Incaviglia	.05	.02
☐ 302	Mike Jeffcoat	.05	.02
☐ 303	Chad Kreuter	.05	.02
☐ 304	Jeff Kunkel	.05	.02
☐ 305	Rick Leach	.05	.02
☐ 306	Fred Manrique	.05	.02
☐ 307	Jamie Moyer	.05	.02
☐ 308	Rafael Palmeiro	.20	.09
☐ 309	Geno Petralli	.05	.02
☐ 310	Kevin Reimer	.05	.02
☐ 311	Kenny Rogers	.10	.05
☐ 312	Jeff Russell	.05	.02
☐ 313	Nolan Ryan	.75	.35
☐ 314	Ruben Sierra	.05	.02
☐ 315	Bobby Witt	.05	.02
☐ 316	Chris Bosio	.05	.02
☐ 317	Glenn Braggs UER	.05	.02
	(Stats say 111 K's, but bio says 117 K's)		
☐ 318	Greg Brock	.05	.02
☐ 319	Chuck Crim	.05	.02
☐ 320	Rob Deer	.05	.02
☐ 321	Mike Felder	.05	.02
☐ 322	Tom Filer	.05	.02
☐ 323	Tony Fossas	.05	.02
☐ 324	Jim Gantner	.05	.02
☐ 325	Darryl Hamilton	.05	.02
☐ 326	Teddy Higuera	.05	.02
☐ 327	Mark Knudson	.05	.02
☐ 328	Bill Krueger UER	.05	.02
	('86 stats missing)		
☐ 329	Tim McIntosh	.05	.02
☐ 330	Paul Molitor	.20	.09
☐ 331	Jaime Navarro	.05	.02
☐ 332	Charlie O'Brien	.05	.02
☐ 333	Jeff Peterek	.05	.02
☐ 334	Dan Plesac	.05	.02
☐ 335	Jerry Reuss	.05	.02
☐ 336	Gary Sheffield UER	.20	.09
	(Bio says played for 3 teams in '87, but stats say in '88)		
☐ 337	Bill Spiers	.05	.02
☐ 338	B.J. Surhoff	.05	.02
☐ 339	Greg Vaughn	.40	.18
☐ 340	Robin Yount	.20	.09
☐ 341	Hubie Brooks	.05	.02
☐ 342	Tim Burke	.05	.02
☐ 343	Mike Fitzgerald	.05	.02
☐ 344	Tom Foley	.05	.02
☐ 345	Andres Galarraga	.20	.09
☐ 346	Damaso Garcia	.05	.02
☐ 347	Marquis Grissom	.25	.11
☐ 348	Kevin Gross	.05	.02
☐ 349	Joe Hesketh	.05	.02
☐ 350	Jeff Huson	.05	.02
☐ 351	Wallace Johnson	.05	.02
☐ 352	Mark Langston	.05	.02
☐ 353A	Dave Martinez	2.00	.90
	(Yellow on front)		
☐ 353B	Dave Martinez	.05	.02
	(Red on front)		
☐ 354	Dennis Martinez UER	.10	.05
	('87 ERA is 616, should be 6.16)		
☐ 355	Andy McGaffigan	.05	.02
☐ 356	Otis Nixon	.10	.05
☐ 357	Spike Owen	.05	.02
☐ 358	Pascual Perez	.05	.02
☐ 359	Tim Raines	.10	.05
☐ 360	Nelson Santovenia	.05	.02
☐ 361	Bryn Smith	.05	.02
☐ 362	Zane Smith	.05	.02
☐ 363	Larry Walker	1.25	.55
☐ 364	Tim Wallach	.10	.05
☐ 365	Rick Aguilera	.10	.05
☐ 366	Allan Anderson	.05	.02
☐ 367	Wally Backman	.05	.02
☐ 368	Doug Baker	.05	.02
☐ 369	Juan Berenguer	.05	.02
☐ 370	Randy Bush	.05	.02
☐ 371	Carmen Castillo	.05	.02
☐ 372	Mike Dyer	.05	.02
☐ 373	Gary Gaetti	.10	.05
☐ 374	Greg Gagne	.05	.02
☐ 375	Dan Gladden	.05	.02
☐ 376	German Gonzalez UER	.05	.02
	(Bio says 31 saves in '88, but stats says 30)		
☐ 377	Brian Harper	.05	.02
☐ 378	Kent Hrbek	.10	.05
☐ 379	Gene Larkin	.05	.02
☐ 380	Tim Laudner UER	.05	.02
	(No decimal point before '85 BA of 238)		
☐ 381	John Moses	.05	.02
☐ 382	Al Newman	.05	.02
☐ 383	Kirby Puckett	.30	.14
☐ 384	Shane Rawley	.05	.02
☐ 385	Jeff Reardon	.10	.05
☐ 386	Roy Smith	.05	.02
☐ 387	Gary Wayne	.05	.02
☐ 388	Dave West	.05	.02
☐ 389	Tim Belcher	.05	.02
☐ 390	Tim Crews UER	.05	.02
	(Stats say 163 IP for '83, but bio says 136)		
☐ 391	Mike Davis	.05	.02
☐ 392	Rick Dempsey	.05	.02
☐ 393	Kirk Gibson	.10	.05
☐ 394	Jose Gonzalez	.05	.02
☐ 395	Alfredo Griffin	.05	.02
☐ 396	Jeff Hamilton	.05	.02
☐ 397	Lenny Harris	.05	.02
☐ 398	Mickey Hatcher	.05	.02
☐ 399	Orel Hershiser	.10	.05
☐ 400	Jay Howell	.05	.02
☐ 401	Mike Marshall	.05	.02
☐ 402	Ramon Martinez	.15	.07
☐ 403	Mike Morgan	.05	.02
☐ 404	Eddie Murray	.20	.09
☐ 405	Alejandro Pena	.05	.02
☐ 406	Willie Randolph	.10	.05
☐ 407	Mike Scioscia	.05	.02
☐ 408	Ray Searage	.05	.02
☐ 409	Fernando Valenzuela	.10	.05
☐ 410	Jose Vizcaino	.15	.07
☐ 411	John Wetteland	.20	.09
☐ 412	Jack Armstrong	.05	.02
☐ 413	Todd Benzinger UER	.05	.02
	(Bio says .323 at Pawtucket, but stats say .321)		
☐ 414	Tim Birtsas	.05	.02
☐ 415	Tom Browning	.05	.02
☐ 416	Norm Charlton	.05	.02
☐ 417	Eric Davis	.10	.05
☐ 418	Rob Dibble	.05	.02
☐ 419	John Franco	.10	.05
☐ 420	Ken Griffey Sr.	.05	.02
☐ 421	Chris Hammond	.05	.02
	(No 1989 used for "Did Not Play" stat, actually did play for Nashville in 1989)		
☐ 422	Danny Jackson	.05	.02
☐ 423	Barry Larkin	.20	.09
☐ 424	Tim Leary	.05	.02
☐ 425	Rick Mahler	.05	.02
☐ 426	Joe Oliver	.05	.02
☐ 427	Paul O'Neill	.10	.05
☐ 428	Luis Quinones UER	.05	.02
	('86-'88 stats are omitted from card but included in totals)		
☐ 429	Jeff Reed	.05	.02
☐ 430	Jose Rijo	.05	.02
☐ 431	Ron Robinson	.05	.02
☐ 432	Rolando Roomes	.05	.02
☐ 433	Chris Sabo	.05	.02
☐ 434	Scott Scudder	.05	.02
☐ 435	Herm Winningham	.05	.02
☐ 436	Steve Balboni	.05	.02
☐ 437	Jesse Barfield	.05	.02
☐ 438	Mike Blowers	.10	.05
☐ 439	Tom Brookens	.05	.02
☐ 440	Greg Cadaret	.05	.02
☐ 441	Alvaro Espinoza UER	.05	.02
	(Career games say 218, should be 219)		
☐ 442	Bob Geren	.05	.02
☐ 443	Lee Guetterman	.05	.02
☐ 444	Mel Hall	.05	.02
☐ 445	Andy Hawkins	.05	.02
☐ 446	Roberto Kelly	.05	.02
☐ 447	Don Mattingly	.40	.18
☐ 448	Lance McCullers	.05	.02
☐ 449	Hensley Meulens	.05	.02
☐ 450	Dale Mohorcic	.05	.02
☐ 451	Clay Parker	.05	.02
☐ 452	Eric Plunk	.05	.02
☐ 453	Dave Righetti	.05	.02
☐ 454	Deion Sanders	.20	.09

☐ 455 Steve Sax	.05	.02
☐ 456 Don Slaught	.05	.02
☐ 457 Walt Terrell	.05	.02
☐ 458 Dave Winfield	.20	.09
☐ 459 Jay Bell	.10	.05
☐ 460 Rafael Belliard	.05	.02
☐ 461 Barry Bonds	.25	.11
☐ 462 Bobby Bonilla	.10	.05
☐ 463 Sid Bream	.05	.02
☐ 464 Benny Distefano	.05	.02
☐ 465 Doug Drabek	.05	.02
☐ 466 Jim Gott	.05	.02
☐ 467 Billy Hatcher UER	.05	.02
(.1 hits for Cubs		
in 1984)		
☐ 468 Neal Heaton	.05	.02
☐ 469 Jeff King	.05	.02
☐ 470 Bob Kipper	.05	.02
☐ 471 Randy Kramer	.05	.02
☐ 472 Bill Landrum	.05	.02
☐ 473 Mike LaValliere	.05	.02
☐ 474 Jose Lind	.05	.02
☐ 475 Junior Ortiz	.05	.02
☐ 476 Gary Redus	.05	.02
☐ 477 Rick Reed	.25	.11
☐ 478 R.J. Reynolds	.05	.02
☐ 479 Jeff D. Robinson	.05	.02
☐ 480 John Smiley	.05	.02
☐ 481 Andy Van Slyke	.10	.05
☐ 482 Bob Walk	.05	.02
☐ 483 Andy Allanson	.05	.02
☐ 484 Scott Bailes	.05	.02
☐ 485 Joey Belle UER	.75	.35
(Has Jay Bell		
"Did You Know")		
☐ 486 Bud Black	.05	.02
☐ 487 Jerry Browne	.05	.02
☐ 488 Tom Candiotti	.05	.02
☐ 489 Joe Carter	.10	.05
☐ 490 Dave Clark	.05	.02
(No '84 stats)		
☐ 491 John Farrell	.05	.02
☐ 492 Felix Fermin	.05	.02
☐ 493 Brook Jacoby	.05	.02
☐ 494 Dion James	.05	.02
☐ 495 Doug Jones	.05	.02
☐ 496 Brad Komminsk	.05	.02
☐ 497 Rod Nichols	.05	.02
☐ 498 Pete O'Brien	.05	.02
☐ 499 Steve Olin	.10	.05
☐ 500 Jesse Orosco	.05	.02
☐ 501 Joel Skinner	.05	.02
☐ 502 Cory Snyder	.05	.02
☐ 503 Greg Swindell	.05	.02
☐ 504 Rich Yett	.05	.02
☐ 505 Scott Bankhead	.05	.02
☐ 506 Scott Bradley	.05	.02
☐ 507 Greg Briley UER	.05	.02
(28 SB's in bio,		
but 27 in stats)		
☐ 508 Jay Buhner	.20	.09
☐ 509 Darnell Coles	.05	.02
☐ 510 Keith Comstock	.05	.02
☐ 511 Henry Cotto	.05	.02
☐ 512 Alvin Davis	.05	.02
☐ 513 Ken Griffey Jr.	2.00	.90
☐ 514 Erik Hanson	.05	.02
☐ 515 Gene Harris	.05	.02
☐ 516 Brian Holman	.05	.02
☐ 517 Mike Jackson	.10	.05
☐ 518 Randy Johnson	.30	.14
☐ 519 Jeffrey Leonard	.05	.02
☐ 520 Edgar Martinez	.20	.09
☐ 521 Dennis Powell	.05	.02
☐ 522 Jim Presley	.05	.02
☐ 523 Jerry Reed	.05	.02
☐ 524 Harold Reynolds	.05	.02
☐ 525 Mike Schooler	.05	.02
☐ 526 Bill Swift	.05	.02
☐ 527 Dave Valle	.05	.02
☐ 528 Omar Vizquel	.20	.09
☐ 529 Ivan Calderon	.05	.02
☐ 530 Carlton Fisk UER	.20	.09
(Bellow Falls, should		
be Bellows Falls)		
☐ 531 Scott Fletcher	.05	.02

☐ 532 Dave Gallagher	.05	.02
☐ 533 Ozzie Guillen	.05	.02
☐ 534 Greg Hibbard	.05	.02
☐ 535 Shawn Hillegas	.05	.02
☐ 536 Lance Johnson	.05	.02
☐ 537 Eric King	.05	.02
☐ 538 Ron Kittle	.05	.02
☐ 539 Steve Lyons	.05	.02
☐ 540 Carlos Martinez	.05	.02
☐ 541 Tom McCarthy	.05	.02
☐ 542 Matt Merullo	.05	.02
(Had 5 ML runs scored		
entering '90, not 6)		
☐ 543 Donn Pall UER	.05	.02
(Stats say pro career		
began in '85,		
bio says '88)		
☐ 544 Dan Pasqua	.05	.02
☐ 545 Ken Patterson	.05	.02
☐ 546 Melido Perez	.05	.02
☐ 547 Steve Rosenberg	.05	.02
☐ 548 Sammy Sosa	6.00	2.70
☐ 549 Bobby Thigpen	.05	.02
☐ 550 Robin Ventura	.20	.09
☐ 551 Greg Walker	.05	.02
☐ 552 Don Carman	.05	.02
☐ 553 Pat Combs	.05	.02
(6 walks for Phillies		
in '89 in stats,		
brief bio says 4)		
☐ 554 Dennis Cook	.05	.02
☐ 555 Darren Daulton	.10	.05
☐ 556 Len Dykstra	.10	.05
☐ 557 Curt Ford	.05	.02
☐ 558 Charlie Hayes	.05	.02
☐ 559 Von Hayes	.05	.02
☐ 560 Tommy Herr	.05	.02
☐ 561 Ken Howell	.05	.02
☐ 562 Steve Jeltz	.05	.02
☐ 563 Ron Jones	.05	.02
☐ 564 Ricky Jordan UER	.05	.02
(Duplicate line of		
statistics on back)		
☐ 565 John Kruk	.10	.05
☐ 566 Steve Lake	.05	.02
☐ 567 Roger McDowell	.05	.02
☐ 568 Terry Mulholland UER	.05	.02
(Did You Know refers		
to Dave Magadan)		
☐ 569 Dwayne Murphy	.05	.02
☐ 570 Jeff Parrett	.05	.02
☐ 571 Randy Ready	.05	.02
☐ 572 Bruce Ruffin	.05	.02
☐ 573 Dickie Thon	.05	.02
☐ 574 Jose Alvarez UER	.05	.02
(78 and 79 stats		
are reversed)		
☐ 575 Geronimo Berroa	.05	.02
☐ 576 Jeff Blauser	.05	.02
☐ 577 Joe Boever	.05	.02
☐ 578 Marty Clary UER	.05	.02
(No comma between		
city and state)		
☐ 579 Jody Davis	.05	.02
☐ 580 Mark Eichhorn	.05	.02
☐ 581 Darrell Evans	.10	.05
☐ 582 Ron Gant	.10	.05
☐ 583 Tom Glavine	.20	.09
☐ 584 Tommy Greene	.05	.02
☐ 585 Tommy Gregg	.05	.02
☐ 586 Dave Justice UER	.50	.23
(Actually had 16 2B		
in Sumter in '86)		
☐ 587 Mark Lemke	.05	.02
☐ 588 Derek Lilliquist	.05	.02
☐ 589 Oddibe McDowell	.05	.02
☐ 590 Kent Mercker ERA	.05	.02
(Bio says 2.75 ERA,		
stats say 2.68 ERA)		
☐ 591 Dale Murphy	.20	.09
☐ 592 Gerald Perry	.05	.02
☐ 593 Lonnie Smith	.05	.02
☐ 594 Pete Smith	.05	.02
☐ 595 John Smoltz	.20	.09
☐ 596 Mike Stanton UER	.05	.02
(No comma between		

city and state)		
☐ 597 Andres Thomas	.05	.02
☐ 598 Jeff Treadway	.05	.02
☐ 599 Doyle Alexander	.05	.02
☐ 600 Dave Bergman	.05	.02
☐ 601 Brian DuBois	.05	.02
☐ 602 Paul Gibson	.05	.02
☐ 603 Mike Heath	.05	.02
☐ 604 Mike Henneman	.05	.02
☐ 605 Guillermo Hernandez	.05	.02
☐ 606 Shawn Holman	.05	.02
☐ 607 Tracy Jones	.05	.02
☐ 608 Chet Lemon	.05	.02
☐ 609 Fred Lynn	.05	.02
☐ 610 Jack Morris	.10	.05
☐ 611 Matt Nokes	.05	.02
☐ 612 Gary Pettis	.05	.02
☐ 613 Kevin Ritz	.05	.02
☐ 614 Jeff M. Robinson	.05	.02
(88 stats are		
not in line)		
☐ 615 Steve Searcy	.05	.02
☐ 616 Frank Tanana	.05	.02
☐ 617 Alan Trammell	.15	.07
☐ 618 Gary Ward	.05	.02
☐ 619 Lou Whitaker	.10	.05
☐ 620 Frank Williams	.05	.02
☐ 621A George Brett '80	1.50	.70
ERR (Had 10 .390		
hitting seasons)		
☐ 621B George Brett '80	.20	.09
COR		
☐ 622 Fern.Valenzuela '81	.05	.02
☐ 623 Dale Murphy '82	.10	.05
☐ 624A Cal Ripken '83 ERR	5.00	2.20
(Misspelled Ripkin		
on card back)		
☐ 624B Cal Ripken '83 COR	.40	.18
☐ 625 Ryne Sandberg '84	.20	.09
☐ 626 Don Mattingly '85	.20	.09
☐ 627 Roger Clemens '86	.25	.11
☐ 628 George Bell '87	.05	.02
☐ 629 Jose Canseco '88 UER	.10	.05
(Reggie won MVP in		
'83, should say '73)		
☐ 630A Will Clark '89 ERR	1.00	.45
(32 total bases		
on card back)		
☐ 630B Will Clark '89 COR	.20	.09
(321 total bases;		
technically still		
an error, listing		
only 24 runs)		
☐ 631 Game Savers	.05	.02
Mark Davis		
Mitch Williams		
☐ 632 Boston Igniters	.20	.09
Wade Boggs		
Mike Greenwell		
☐ 633 Starter and Stopper	.05	.02
Mark Gubicza		
Jeff Russell		
☐ 634 League's Best	.25	.11
Shortstops		
Tony Fernandez		
Cal Ripken		
☐ 635 Human Dynamos	.20	.09
Kirby Puckett		
Bo Jackson		
☐ 636 300 Strikeout Club	.25	.11
Nolan Ryan		
Mike Scott		
☐ 637 The Dynamic Duo	.10	.05
Will Clark		
Kevin Mitchell		
☐ 638 AL All-Stars	.50	.23
Don Mattingly		
Mark McGwire		
☐ 639 NL East Rivals	.20	.09
Howard Johnson		
Ryne Sandberg		
☐ 640 Rudy Seanez	.05	.02
Colin Charland		
☐ 641 George Canale	.10	.05
Kevin Maas UER		
(Canale listed as INF		

on front, 1B on back)			
❏ 642 Kelly Mann	.05	.02	
and Dave Hansen			
❏ 643 Greg Smith	.05	.02	
and Stu Tate			
❏ 644 Tom Drees	.05	.02	
and Dann Howitt			
❏ 645 Mike Roesler	.20	.09	
and Derrick May			
❏ 646 Scott Hemond	.05	.02	
and Mark Gardner			
❏ 647 John Orton	.05	.02	
and Scott Leius			
❏ 648 Rich Monteleone	.05	.02	
and Dana Williams			
❏ 649 Mike Huff	.05	.02	
and Steve Frey			
❏ 650 Chuck McElroy	.40	.18	
and Moises Alou			
❏ 651 Bobby Rose	.05	.02	
and Mike Hartley			
❏ 652 Matt Kinzer	.05	.02	
and Wayne Edwards			
❏ 653 Delino DeShields	.20	.09	
and Jason Grimsley			
❏ 654 CL: A's/Cubs	.05	.02	
Giants/Blue Jays			
❏ 655 CL: Royals/Angels	.05	.02	
Padres/Orioles			
❏ 656 CL: Mets/Astros	.05	.02	
Cards/Red Sox			
❏ 657 CL: Rangers/Brewers	.05	.02	
Expos/Twins			
❏ 658 CL: Dodgers/Reds	.05	.02	
Yankees/Pirates			
❏ 659 CL: Indians/Mariners	.05	.02	
White Sox/Phillies			
❏ 660A CL: Braves/Tigers	.05	.02	
Specials/Checklists			
(Checklist-660 in small-			
er print on card front)			
❏ 660B CL: Braves/Tigers	.05	.02	
Specials/Checklists			
(Checklist-660 in nor-			
mal print on card front)			

1990 Fleer All-Stars

	MINT	NRMT
COMPLETE SET (12)	3.00	1.35
COMMON CARD (1-12)	.15	.07
RANDOM INSERTS IN PACKS		
❏ 1 Harold Baines	.25	.11
❏ 2 Will Clark	.75	.35
❏ 3 Mark Davis	.15	.07
❏ 4 Howard Johnson UER	.15	.07
(In middle of 5th		
line, the is		
misspelled th)		
❏ 5 Joe Magrane	.15	.07
❏ 6 Kevin Mitchell	.15	.07
❏ 7 Kirby Puckett	.75	.35
❏ 8 Cal Ripken	2.00	.90
❏ 9 Ryne Sandberg	.60	.25
❏ 10 Mike Scott UER	.15	.07
Astros spelled Astroos		
❏ 11 Ruben Sierra	.15	.07
❏ 12 Mickey Tettleton	.25	.11

1990 Fleer League Standouts

	MINT	NRMT
COMPLETE SET (6)	6.00	2.70
COMMON CARD (1-6)	.50	.23
ONE PER RACK PACK		
❏ 1 Barry Larkin	1.50	.70
❏ 2 Don Mattingly	3.00	1.35
❏ 3 Darryl Strawberry	.50	.23
❏ 4 Jose Canseco	2.00	.90
❏ 5 Wade Boggs	1.50	.70
❏ 6 Mark Grace UER	1.50	.70
(Chris Sabo misspelled		
as Cris)		

1990 Fleer Soaring Stars

	MINT	NRMT
COMPLETE SET (12)	25.00	11.00
COMMON CARD (1-12)	.50	.23
MINOR STARS	1.00	.45
SEMISTARS	1.50	.70
RANDOM INSERTS IN JUMBO PACKS		
❏ 1 Todd Zeile	1.00	.45
❏ 2 Mike Stanton	.50	.23
❏ 3 Larry Walker	6.00	2.70
❏ 4 Robin Ventura	2.00	.90
❏ 5 Scott Coolbaugh	.50	.23
❏ 6 Ken Griffey Jr.	15.00	6.75
❏ 7 Tom Gordon	1.00	.45
❏ 8 Jerome Walton	.50	.23
❏ 9 Junior Felix	.50	.23
❏ 10 Jim Abbott	1.50	.70
❏ 11 Ricky Jordan	.50	.23
❏ 12 Dwight Smith	.50	.23

1990 Fleer Update

	MINT	NRMT
COMP.FACT.SET (132)	5.00	2.20
COMMON CARD (1-132)	.05	.02
MINOR STARS	.10	.05
UNLISTED STARS	.20	.09
❏ 1 Steve Avery	.05	.02
❏ 2 Francisco Cabrera	.05	.02

❏ 3 Nick Esasky	.05	.02	
❏ 4 Jim Kremers	.05	.02	
❏ 5 Greg Olson	.05	.02	
❏ 6 Jim Presley	.05	.02	
❏ 7 Shawn Boskie	.05	.02	
❏ 8 Joe Kraemer	.05	.02	
❏ 9 Luis Salazar	.05	.02	
❏ 10 Hector Villanueva	.05	.02	
❏ 11 Glenn Braggs	.05	.02	
❏ 12 Mariano Duncan	.05	.02	
❏ 13 Billy Hatcher	.05	.02	
❏ 14 Tim Layana	.05	.02	
❏ 15 Hal Morris	.20	.09	
❏ 16 Javier Ortiz	.05	.02	
❏ 17 Dave Rohde	.05	.02	
❏ 18 Eric Yelding	.05	.02	
❏ 19 Hubie Brooks	.05	.02	
❏ 20 Kal Daniels	.05	.02	
❏ 21 Dave Hansen	.05	.02	
❏ 22 Mike Hartley	.05	.02	
❏ 23 Stan Javier	.05	.02	
❏ 24 Jose Offerman	.40	.18	
❏ 25 Juan Samuel	.05	.02	
❏ 26 Dennis Boyd	.05	.02	
❏ 27 Delino DeShields	.20	.09	
❏ 28 Steve Frey	.05	.02	
❏ 29 Mark Gardner	.05	.02	
❏ 30 Chris Nabholz	.05	.02	
❏ 31 Bill Sampen	.05	.02	
❏ 32 Dave Schmidt	.05	.02	
❏ 33 Daryl Boston	.05	.02	
❏ 34 Chuck Carr	.20	.09	
❏ 35 John Franco	.10	.05	
❏ 36 Todd Hundley	.25	.11	
❏ 37 Julio Machado	.05	.02	
❏ 38 Alejandro Pena	.05	.02	
❏ 39 Darren Reed	.05	.02	
❏ 40 Kelvin Torve	.05	.02	
❏ 41 Darrel Akerfelds	.05	.02	
❏ 42 Jose DeJesus	.05	.02	
❏ 43 Dave Hollins UER	.20	.09	
(Misspelled Dane			
on card back)			
❏ 44 Carmelo Martinez	.05	.02	
❏ 45 Brad Moore	.05	.02	
❏ 46 Dale Murphy	.20	.09	
❏ 47 Wally Backman	.05	.02	
❏ 48 Stan Belinda	.05	.02	
❏ 49 Bob Patterson	.05	.02	
❏ 50 Ted Power	.05	.02	
❏ 51 Don Slaught	.05	.02	
❏ 52 Geronimo Pena	.05	.02	
❏ 53 Lee Smith	.10	.05	
❏ 54 John Tudor	.05	.02	
❏ 55 Joe Carter	.10	.05	
❏ 56 Thomas Howard	.05	.02	
❏ 57 Craig Lefferts	.05	.02	
❏ 58 Rafael Valdez	.05	.02	
❏ 59 Dave Anderson	.05	.02	
❏ 60 Kevin Bass	.05	.02	
❏ 61 John Burkett	.05	.02	
❏ 62 Gary Carter	.20	.09	
❏ 63 Rick Parker	.05	.02	
❏ 64 Trevor Wilson	.05	.02	
❏ 65 Chris Holles	.05	.02	
❏ 66 Tim Hulett	.05	.02	
❏ 67 Dave Johnson	.05	.02	
❏ 68 Curt Schilling	.50	.23	

❏ 69 David Segui	.25	.11
❏ 70 Tom Brunansky	.05	.02
❏ 71 Greg A. Harris	.05	.02
❏ 72 Dana Kiecker	.05	.02
❏ 73 Tim Naehring	.10	.05
❏ 74 Tony Pena	.05	.02
❏ 75 Jeff Reardon	.10	.05
❏ 76 Jerry Reed	.05	.02
❏ 77 Mark Eichhorn	.05	.02
❏ 78 Mark Langston	.05	.02
❏ 79 John Orton	.05	.02
❏ 80 Luis Polonia	.05	.02
❏ 81 Dave Winfield	.20	.09
❏ 82 Cliff Young	.05	.02
❏ 83 Wayne Edwards	.05	.02
❏ 84 Alex Fernandez	.25	.11
❏ 85 Craig Grebeck	.05	.02
❏ 86 Scott Radinsky	.05	.02
❏ 87 Frank Thomas	2.50	1.10
❏ 88 Beau Allred	.05	.02
❏ 89 Sandy Alomar Jr.	.10	.05
❏ 90 Carlos Baerga	.20	.09
❏ 91 Kevin Bearse	.05	.02
❏ 92 Chris James	.05	.02
❏ 93 Candy Maldonado	.05	.02
❏ 94 Jeff Manto	.05	.02
❏ 95 Cecil Fielder	.10	.05
❏ 96 Travis Fryman	.25	.11
❏ 97 Lloyd Moseby	.05	.02
❏ 98 Edwin Nunez	.05	.02
❏ 99 Tony Phillips	.05	.02
❏ 100 Larry Sheets	.05	.02
❏ 101 Mark Davis	.05	.02
❏ 102 Storm Davis	.05	.02
❏ 103 Gerald Perry	.05	.02
❏ 104 Terry Shumpert	.05	.02
❏ 105 Edgar Diaz	.05	.02
❏ 106 Dave Parker	.10	.05
❏ 107 Tim Drummond	.05	.02
❏ 108 Junior Ortiz	.05	.02
❏ 109 Park Pittman	.05	.02
❏ 110 Kevin Tapani	.10	.05
❏ 111 Oscar Azocar	.05	.02
❏ 112 Jim Leyritz	.25	.11
❏ 113 Kevin Maas	.10	.05
❏ 114 Alan Mills	.05	.02
❏ 115 Matt Nokes	.05	.02
❏ 116 Pascual Perez	.05	.02
❏ 117 Ozzie Canseco	.05	.02
❏ 118 Scott Sanderson	.05	.02
❏ 119 Tino Martinez	.25	.11
❏ 120 Jeff Schaefer	.05	.02
❏ 121 Matt Young	.05	.02
❏ 122 Brian Bohanon	.05	.02
❏ 123 Jeff Huson	.05	.02
❏ 124 Ramon Manon	.05	.02
❏ 125 Gary Mielke UER	.05	.02
(Shown as Blue Jay on front)		
❏ 126 Willie Blair	.05	.02
❏ 127 Glenallen Hill	.05	.02
❏ 128 John Olerud UER	.60	.25
(Listed as throwing right, should be left)		
❏ 129 Luis Sojo	.05	.02
❏ 130 Mark Whiten	.05	.02
❏ 131 Nolan Ryan	.75	.35
❏ 132 Checklist U1-U132	.05	.02

1991 Fleer

	MINT	NRMT
COMPLETE SET (720)	8.00	3.60
COMP.RETAIL SET (732)	10.00	4.50
COMP.HOBBY SET (732)	10.00	4.50
COMMON CARD (1-720)	.05	.02
MINOR STARS	.10	.05
UNLISTED STARS	.20	.09
COMP.WORLD SERIES SET (8)	2.00	.90
*WS: EQUAL VALUE TO BASIC CARDS		
ONE WORLD SERIES SET PER FACT.SET		

❏ 1 Troy Afenir	.05	.02
❏ 2 Harold Baines	.10	.05
❏ 3 Lance Blankenship	.05	.02
❏ 4 Todd Burns	.05	.02

KEVIN BROWN — RANGERS P

❏ 5 Jose Canseco	.25	.11
❏ 6 Dennis Eckersley	.10	.05
❏ 7 Mike Gallego	.05	.02
❏ 8 Ron Hassey	.05	.02
❏ 9 Dave Henderson	.05	.02
❏ 10 Rickey Henderson	.25	.11
❏ 11 Rick Honeycutt	.05	.02
❏ 12 Doug Jennings	.05	.02
❏ 13 Joe Klink	.05	.02
❏ 14 Carney Lansford	.10	.05
❏ 15 Darren Lewis	.10	.05
❏ 16 Willie McGee UER	.05	.02
(Height 6'11")		
❏ 17 Mark McGwire UER	1.00	.45
(183 extra base hits in 1987)		
❏ 18 Mike Moore	.05	.02
❏ 19 Gene Nelson	.05	.02
❏ 20 Dave Otto	.05	.02
❏ 21 Jamie Quirk	.05	.02
❏ 22 Willie Randolph	.05	.02
❏ 23 Scott Sanderson	.05	.02
❏ 24 Terry Steinbach	.10	.05
❏ 25 Dave Stewart	.10	.05
❏ 26 Walt Weiss	.05	.02
❏ 27 Bob Welch	.05	.02
❏ 28 Curt Young	.05	.02
❏ 29 Wally Backman	.05	.02
❏ 30 Stan Belinda UER	.05	.02
(Born in Huntington, should be State College)		
❏ 31 Jay Bell	.10	.05
❏ 32 Rafael Belliard	.05	.02
❏ 33 Barry Bonds	.25	.11
❏ 34 Bobby Bonilla	.10	.05
❏ 35 Sid Bream	.05	.02
❏ 36 Doug Drabek	.05	.02
❏ 37 Carlos Garcia	.05	.02
❏ 38 Neal Heaton	.05	.02
❏ 39 Jeff King	.05	.02
❏ 40 Bob Kipper	.05	.02
❏ 41 Bill Landrum	.05	.02
❏ 42 Mike LaValliere	.05	.02
❏ 43 Jose Lind	.05	.02
❏ 44 Carmelo Martinez	.05	.02
❏ 45 Bob Patterson	.05	.02
❏ 46 Ted Power	.05	.02
❏ 47 Gary Redus	.05	.02
❏ 48 R.J. Reynolds	.05	.02
❏ 49 Don Slaught	.05	.02
❏ 50 John Smiley	.05	.02
❏ 51 Zane Smith	.05	.02
❏ 52 Randy Tomlin	.10	.05
❏ 53 Andy Van Slyke	.10	.05
❏ 54 Bob Walk	.05	.02
❏ 55 Jack Armstrong	.05	.02
❏ 56 Todd Benzinger	.05	.02
❏ 57 Glenn Braggs	.05	.02
❏ 58 Keith Brown	.05	.02
❏ 59 Tom Browning	.05	.02
❏ 60 Norm Charlton	.05	.02
❏ 61 Eric Davis	.10	.05
❏ 62 Rob Dibble	.05	.02
❏ 63 Bill Doran	.05	.02
❏ 64 Mariano Duncan	.05	.02
❏ 65 Chris Hammond	.05	.02
❏ 66 Billy Hatcher	.05	.02
❏ 67 Danny Jackson	.05	.02

❏ 68 Barry Larkin	.20	.09
❏ 69 Tim Layana	.05	.02
(Black line over made in first text line)		
❏ 70 Terry Lee	.05	.02
❏ 71 Rick Mahler	.05	.02
❏ 72 Hal Morris	.05	.02
❏ 73 Randy Myers	.10	.05
❏ 74 Ron Oester	.05	.02
❏ 75 Joe Oliver	.05	.02
❏ 76 Paul O'Neill	.10	.05
❏ 77 Luis Quinones	.05	.02
❏ 78 Jeff Reed	.05	.02
❏ 79 Jose Rijo	.05	.02
❏ 80 Chris Sabo	.05	.02
❏ 81 Scott Scudder	.05	.02
❏ 82 Herm Winningham	.05	.02
❏ 83 Larry Andersen	.05	.02
❏ 84 Marty Barrett	.05	.02
❏ 85 Mike Boddicker	.05	.02
❏ 86 Wade Boggs	.20	.09
❏ 87 Tom Bolton	.05	.02
❏ 88 Tom Brunansky	.05	.02
❏ 89 Ellis Burks	.05	.02
❏ 90 Roger Clemens	.50	.23
❏ 91 Scott Cooper	.05	.02
❏ 92 John Dopson	.05	.02
❏ 93 Dwight Evans	.10	.05
❏ 94 Wes Gardner	.05	.02
❏ 95 Jeff Gray	.05	.02
❏ 96 Mike Greenwell	.05	.02
❏ 97 Greg A. Harris	.05	.02
❏ 98 Daryl Irvine	.05	.02
❏ 99 Dana Kiecker	.05	.02
❏ 100 Randy Kutcher	.05	.02
❏ 101 Dennis Lamp	.05	.02
❏ 102 Mike Marshall	.05	.02
❏ 103 John Marzano	.05	.02
❏ 104 Rob Murphy	.05	.02
❏ 105 Tim Naehring	.05	.02
❏ 106 Tony Pena	.05	.02
❏ 107 Phil Plantier	.05	.02
❏ 108 Carlos Quintana	.05	.02
❏ 109 Jeff Reardon	.10	.05
❏ 110 Jerry Reed	.05	.02
❏ 111 Jody Reed	.05	.02
❏ 112 Luis Rivera UER	.05	.02
(Born 1/3/84)		
❏ 113 Kevin Romine	.05	.02
❏ 114 Phil Bradley	.05	.02
❏ 115 Ivan Calderon	.05	.02
❏ 116 Wayne Edwards	.05	.02
❏ 117 Alex Fernandez	.10	.05
❏ 118 Carlton Fisk	.20	.09
❏ 119 Scott Fletcher	.05	.02
❏ 120 Craig Grebeck	.05	.02
❏ 121 Ozzie Guillen	.05	.02
❏ 122 Greg Hibbard	.05	.02
❏ 123 Lance Johnson UER	.05	.02
(Born Cincinnati; should be Lincoln Heights)		
❏ 124 Barry Jones	.05	.02
❏ 125 Ron Karkovice	.05	.02
❏ 126 Eric King	.05	.02
❏ 127 Steve Lyons	.05	.02
❏ 128 Carlos Martinez	.05	.02
❏ 129 Jack McDowell UER	.05	.02
(Stanford misspelled as Standford on back)		
❏ 130 Donn Pall	.05	.02
(No dots over any i's in text)		
❏ 131 Dan Pasqua	.05	.02
❏ 132 Ken Patterson	.05	.02
❏ 133 Melido Perez	.05	.02
❏ 134 Adam Peterson	.05	.02
❏ 135 Scott Radinsky	.05	.02
❏ 136 Sammy Sosa	1.25	.55
❏ 137 Bobby Thigpen	.05	.02
❏ 138 Frank Thomas	.75	.35
❏ 139 Robin Ventura	.05	.02
❏ 140 Daryl Boston	.05	.02
❏ 141 Chuck Carr	.05	.02
❏ 142 Mark Carreon	.05	.02
❏ 143 David Cone	.10	.05
❏ 144 Ron Darling	.05	.02

☐ 145	Kevin Elster	.05	.02
☐ 146	Sid Fernandez	.05	.02
☐ 147	John Franco	.10	.05
☐ 148	Dwight Gooden	.10	.05
☐ 149	Tom Herr	.05	.02
☐ 150	Todd Hundley	.20	.09
☐ 151	Gregg Jefferies	.05	.02
☐ 152	Howard Johnson	.05	.02
☐ 153	Dave Magadan	.05	.02
☐ 154	Kevin McReynolds	.05	.02
☐ 155	Keith Miller UER	.05	.02

(Text says Rochester in '87, stats say Tidewater, mixed up with other Keith Miller)

☐ 156	Bob Ojeda	.05	.02
☐ 157	Tom O'Malley	.05	.02
☐ 158	Alejandro Pena	.05	.02
☐ 159	Darren Reed	.05	.02
☐ 160	Mackey Sasser	.05	.02
☐ 161	Darryl Strawberry	.10	.05
☐ 162	Tim Teufel	.05	.02
☐ 163	Kelvin Torve	.05	.02
☐ 164	Julio Valera	.05	.02
☐ 165	Frank Viola	.05	.02
☐ 166	Wally Whitehurst	.05	.02
☐ 167	Jim Acker	.05	.02
☐ 168	Derek Bell	.20	.09
☐ 169	George Bell	.05	.02
☐ 170	Willie Blair	.05	.02
☐ 171	Pat Borders	.05	.02
☐ 172	John Cerutti	.05	.02
☐ 173	Junior Felix	.05	.02
☐ 174	Tony Fernandez	.05	.02
☐ 175	Kelly Gruber UER	.05	.02

(Born in Houston, should be Bellaire)

☐ 176	Tom Henke	.05	.02
☐ 177	Glenallen Hill	.05	.02
☐ 178	Jimmy Key	.10	.05
☐ 179	Manny Lee	.05	.02
☐ 180	Fred McGriff	.20	.09
☐ 181	Rance Mulliniks	.05	.02
☐ 182	Greg Myers	.05	.02
☐ 183	Jim Olerud UER	.15	.07

(Listed as throwing right, should be left)

☐ 184	Luis Sojo	.05	.02
☐ 185	Dave Stieb	.05	.02
☐ 186	Todd Stottlemyre	.10	.05
☐ 187	Duane Ward	.05	.02
☐ 188	David Wells	.10	.05
☐ 189	Mark Whiten	.05	.02
☐ 190	Ken Williams	.05	.02
☐ 191	Frank Wills	.05	.02
☐ 192	Mookie Wilson	.05	.02
☐ 193	Don Aase	.05	.02
☐ 194	Tim Belcher UER	.05	.02

(Born Sparta, Ohio, should say Mt. Gilead)

☐ 195	Hubie Brooks	.05	.02
☐ 196	Dennis Cook	.05	.02
☐ 197	Tim Crews	.05	.02
☐ 198	Kal Daniels	.05	.02
☐ 199	Kirk Gibson	.10	.05
☐ 200	Jim Gott	.05	.02
☐ 201	Alfredo Griffin	.05	.02
☐ 202	Chris Gwynn	.05	.02
☐ 203	Dave Hansen	.05	.02
☐ 204	Lenny Harris	.05	.02
☐ 205	Mike Hartley	.05	.02
☐ 206	Mickey Hatcher	.05	.02
☐ 207	Carlos Hernandez	.05	.02
☐ 208	Orel Hershiser	.10	.05
☐ 209	Jay Howell UER	.05	.02

(No 1982 Yankee stats)

☐ 210	Mike Huff	.05	.02
☐ 211	Stan Javier	.05	.02
☐ 212	Ramon Martinez	.10	.05
☐ 213	Mike Morgan	.05	.02
☐ 214	Eddie Murray	.20	.09
☐ 215	Jim Neidlinger	.05	.02
☐ 216	Jose Offerman	.15	.07
☐ 217	Jim Poole	.05	.02
☐ 218	Juan Samuel	.05	.02
☐ 219	Mike Scioscia	.05	.02
☐ 220	Ray Searage	.05	.02
☐ 221	Mike Sharperson	.05	.02
☐ 222	Fernando Valenzuela	.10	.05
☐ 223	Jose Vizcaino	.05	.02
☐ 224	Mike Aldrete	.05	.02
☐ 225	Scott Anderson	.05	.02
☐ 226	Dennis Boyd	.05	.02
☐ 227	Tim Burke	.05	.02
☐ 228	Delino DeShields	.10	.05
☐ 229	Mike Fitzgerald	.05	.02
☐ 230	Tom Foley	.05	.02
☐ 231	Steve Frey	.05	.02
☐ 232	Andres Galarraga	.05	.02
☐ 233	Mark Gardner	.05	.02
☐ 234	Marquis Grissom	.20	.09
☐ 235	Kevin Gross	.05	.02

(No date given for first Expos win)

☐ 236	Drew Hall	.05	.02
☐ 237	Dave Martinez	.05	.02
☐ 238	Dennis Martinez	.05	.02
☐ 239	Dale Mohorcic	.05	.02
☐ 240	Chris Nabholz	.05	.02
☐ 241	Otis Nixon	.10	.05
☐ 242	Junior Noboa	.05	.02
☐ 243	Spike Owen	.05	.02
☐ 244	Tim Raines	.10	.05
☐ 245	Mel Rojas UER	.10	.05

(Stats show 3.60 ERA, bio says 3.19 ERA)

☐ 246	Scott Ruskin	.05	.02
☐ 247	Bill Sampen	.05	.02
☐ 248	Nelson Santovenia	.05	.02
☐ 249	Dave Schmidt	.05	.02
☐ 250	Larry Walker	.30	.14
☐ 251	Tim Wallach	.05	.02
☐ 252	Dave Anderson	.05	.02
☐ 253	Kevin Bass	.05	.02
☐ 254	Steve Bedrosian	.05	.02
☐ 255	Jeff Brantley	.05	.02
☐ 256	John Burkett	.05	.02
☐ 257	Brett Butler	.10	.05
☐ 258	Gary Carter	.20	.09
☐ 259	Will Clark	.30	.14
☐ 260	Steve Decker	.05	.02
☐ 261	Kelly Downs	.05	.02
☐ 262	Scott Garrelts	.05	.02
☐ 263	Terry Kennedy	.05	.02
☐ 264	Mike LaCoss	.05	.02
☐ 265	Mark Leonard	.05	.02
☐ 266	Greg Litton	.05	.02
☐ 267	Kevin Mitchell	.10	.05
☐ 268	Randy O'Neal	.05	.02
☐ 269	Rick Parker	.05	.02
☐ 270	Rick Reuschel	.05	.02
☐ 271	Ernest Riles	.05	.02
☐ 272	Don Robinson	.05	.02
☐ 273	Robby Thompson	.05	.02
☐ 274	Mark Thurmond	.05	.02
☐ 275	Jose Uribe	.05	.02
☐ 276	Matt Williams	.20	.09
☐ 277	Trevor Wilson	.05	.02
☐ 278	Gerald Alexander	.05	.02
☐ 279	Brad Arnsberg	.05	.02
☐ 280	Kevin Belcher	.05	.02
☐ 281	Joe Bitker	.05	.02
☐ 282	Kevin Brown	.15	.07
☐ 283	Steve Buechele	.05	.02
☐ 284	Jack Daugherty	.05	.02
☐ 285	Julio Franco	.05	.02
☐ 286	Juan Gonzalez	.75	.35
☐ 287	Bill Haselman	.05	.02
☐ 288	Charlie Hough	.10	.05
☐ 289	Jeff Huson	.05	.02
☐ 290	Pete Incaviglia	.05	.02
☐ 291	Mike Jeffcoat	.05	.02
☐ 292	Jeff Kunkel	.05	.02
☐ 293	Gary Mielke	.05	.02
☐ 294	Jamie Moyer	.05	.02
☐ 295	Rafael Palmeiro	.20	.09
☐ 296	Geno Petralli	.05	.02
☐ 297	Gary Pettis	.05	.02
☐ 298	Kevin Reimer	.05	.02
☐ 299	Kenny Rogers	.05	.02
☐ 300	Jeff Russell	.05	.02
☐ 301	John Russell	.05	.02
☐ 302	Nolan Ryan	.75	.35
☐ 303	Ruben Sierra	.05	.02
☐ 304	Bobby Witt	.05	.02
☐ 305	Jim Abbott UER	.10	.05

(Text on back states he won Sullivan Award (outstanding amateur athlete) in 1989; should be '88)

☐ 306	Kent Anderson	.05	.02
☐ 307	Dante Bichette	.20	.09
☐ 308	Bert Blyleven	.10	.05
☐ 309	Chili Davis	.10	.05
☐ 310	Brian Downing	.05	.02
☐ 311	Mark Eichhorn	.05	.02
☐ 312	Mike Fetters	.05	.02
☐ 313	Chuck Finley	.10	.05
☐ 314	Willie Fraser	.05	.02
☐ 315	Bryan Harvey	.05	.02
☐ 316	Donnie Hill	.05	.02
☐ 317	Wally Joyner	.10	.05
☐ 318	Mark Langston	.05	.02
☐ 319	Kirk McCaskill	.05	.02
☐ 320	John Orton	.05	.02
☐ 321	Lance Parrish	.05	.02
☐ 322	Luis Polonia UER	.05	.02

(1984 Madison, should be Madison)

☐ 323	Johnny Ray	.05	.02
☐ 324	Bobby Rose	.05	.02
☐ 325	Dick Schofield	.05	.02
☐ 326	Rick Schu	.05	.02
☐ 327	Lee Stevens	.10	.05
☐ 328	Devon White	.05	.02
☐ 329	Dave Winfield	.20	.09
☐ 330	Cliff Young	.05	.02
☐ 331	Dave Bergman	.05	.02
☐ 332	Phil Clark	.05	.02
☐ 333	Darnell Coles	.05	.02
☐ 334	Milt Cuyler	.05	.02
☐ 335	Cecil Fielder	.10	.05
☐ 336	Travis Fryman	.20	.09
☐ 337	Paul Gibson	.05	.02
☐ 338	Jerry Don Gleaton	.05	.02
☐ 339	Mike Heath	.05	.02
☐ 340	Mike Henneman	.05	.02
☐ 341	Chet Lemon	.05	.02
☐ 342	Lance McCullers	.05	.02
☐ 343	Jack Morris	.10	.05
☐ 344	Lloyd Moseby	.05	.02
☐ 345	Edwin Nunez	.05	.02
☐ 346	Clay Parker	.05	.02
☐ 347	Dan Petry	.05	.02
☐ 348	Tony Phillips	.05	.02
☐ 349	Jeff M. Robinson	.05	.02
☐ 350	Mark Salas	.05	.02
☐ 351	Mike Schwabe	.05	.02
☐ 352	Larry Sheets	.05	.02
☐ 353	John Shelby	.05	.02
☐ 354	Frank Tanana	.05	.02
☐ 355	Alan Trammell	.15	.07
☐ 356	Gary Ward	.05	.02
☐ 357	Lou Whitaker	.10	.05
☐ 358	Beau Allred	.05	.02
☐ 359	Sandy Alomar Jr.	.10	.05
☐ 360	Carlos Baerga	.10	.05
☐ 361	Kevin Bearse	.05	.02
☐ 362	Tom Brookens	.05	.02
☐ 363	Jerry Browne UER	.05	.02

(No dot over i in first text line)

☐ 364	Tom Candiotti	.05	.02
☐ 365	Alex Cole	.05	.02
☐ 366	John Farrell UER	.05	.02

(Born in Neptune, should be Monmouth)

☐ 367	Felix Fermin	.05	.02
☐ 368	Keith Hernandez	.10	.05
☐ 369	Brook Jacoby	.05	.02
☐ 370	Chris James	.05	.02
☐ 371	Dion James	.05	.02
☐ 372	Doug Jones	.05	.02
☐ 373	Candy Maldonado	.05	.02
☐ 374	Steve Olin	.05	.02
☐ 375	Jesse Orosco	.05	.02
☐ 376	Rudy Seanez	.05	.02
☐ 377	Joel Skinner	.05	.02
☐ 378	Cory Snyder	.05	.02

☐ 379	Greg Swindell	.05	.02
☐ 380	Sergio Valdez	.05	.02
☐ 381	Mike Walker	.05	.02
☐ 382	Colby Ward	.05	.02
☐ 383	Turner Ward	.05	.02
☐ 384	Mitch Webster	.05	.02
☐ 385	Kevin Wickander	.05	.02
☐ 386	Darrel Akerfelds	.05	.02
☐ 387	Joe Boever	.05	.02
☐ 388	Rod Booker	.05	.02
☐ 389	Sil Campusano	.05	.02
☐ 390	Don Carman	.05	.02
☐ 391	Wes Chamberlain	.05	.02
☐ 392	Pat Combs	.05	.02
☐ 393	Darren Daulton	.10	.05
☐ 394	Jose DeJesus	.05	.02
☐ 395A	Len Dykstra	.05	.02
	Name spelled Lenny on back		
☐ 395B	Len Dykstra	.10	.05
	Name spelled Len on back		
☐ 396	Jason Grimsley	.05	.02
☐ 397	Charlie Hayes	.05	.02
☐ 398	Von Hayes	.05	.02
☐ 399	David Hollins UER	.05	.02
	(All-bats, should say at-bats)		
☐ 400	Ken Howell	.05	.02
☐ 401	Ricky Jordan	.05	.02
☐ 402	John Kruk	.10	.05
☐ 403	Steve Lake	.05	.02
☐ 404	Chuck Malone	.05	.02
☐ 405	Roger McDowell UER	.05	.02
	(Says Phillies is saves, should say in)		
☐ 406	Chuck McElroy	.05	.02
☐ 407	Mickey Morandini	.05	.02
☐ 408	Terry Mulholland	.05	.02
☐ 409	Dale Murphy	.20	.09
☐ 410A	Randy Ready ERR	.05	.02
	(No Brewers stats listed for 1983)		
☐ 410B	Randy Ready COR	.05	.02
☐ 411	Bruce Ruffin	.05	.02
☐ 412	Dickie Thon	.05	.02
☐ 413	Paul Assenmacher	.05	.02
☐ 414	Damon Berryhill	.05	.02
☐ 415	Mike Bielecki	.05	.02
☐ 416	Shawn Boskie	.05	.02
☐ 417	Dave Clark	.05	.02
☐ 418	Doug Dascenzo	.05	.02
☐ 419A	Andre Dawson ERR	.20	.09
	(No stats for 1976)		
☐ 419B	Andre Dawson COR	.20	.09
☐ 420	Shawon Dunston	.05	.02
☐ 421	Joe Girardi	.10	.05
☐ 422	Mark Grace	.20	.09
☐ 423	Mike Harkey	.05	.02
☐ 424	Les Lancaster	.05	.02
☐ 425	Bill Long	.05	.02
☐ 426	Greg Maddux	.50	.23
☐ 427	Derrick May	.05	.02
☐ 428	Jeff Pico	.05	.02
☐ 429	Domingo Ramos	.05	.02
☐ 430	Luis Salazar	.05	.02
☐ 431	Ryne Sandberg	.25	.11
☐ 432	Dwight Smith	.05	.02
☐ 433	Greg Smith	.05	.02
☐ 434	Rick Sutcliffe	.05	.02
☐ 435	Gary Varsho	.05	.02
☐ 436	Hector Villanueva	.05	.02
☐ 437	Jerome Walton	.05	.02
☐ 438	Curtis Wilkerson	.05	.02
☐ 439	Mitch Williams	.05	.02
☐ 440	Steve Wilson	.05	.02
☐ 441	Marvell Wynne	.05	.02
☐ 442	Scott Bankhead	.05	.02
☐ 443	Scott Bradley	.05	.02
☐ 444	Greg Briley	.05	.02
☐ 445	Mike Brumley UER	.05	.02
	(Text 40 SB's in 1988, stats say 41)		
☐ 446	Jay Buhner	.20	.09
☐ 447	Dave Burba	.05	.02
☐ 448	Henry Cotto	.05	.02
☐ 449	Alvin Davis	.05	.02
☐ 450	Ken Griffey Jr.	1.50	.70

	(Bat around .300)		
☐ 450A	Ken Griffey Jr.	1.50	.70
	(Bat .300)		
☐ 451	Erik Hanson	.05	.02
☐ 452	Gene Harris UER	.05	.02
	(63 career runs, should be 73)		
☐ 453	Brian Holman	.05	.02
☐ 454	Mike Jackson	.10	.05
☐ 455	Randy Johnson	.25	.11
☐ 456	Jeffrey Leonard	.05	.02
☐ 457	Edgar Martinez	.20	.09
☐ 458	Tino Martinez	.20	.09
☐ 459	Pete O'Brien UER	.05	.02
	(1987 BA .266, should be .286)		
☐ 460	Harold Reynolds	.05	.02
☐ 461	Mike Schooler	.05	.02
☐ 462	Bill Swift	.05	.02
☐ 463	David Valle	.05	.02
☐ 464	Omar Vizquel	.20	.09
☐ 465	Matt Young	.05	.02
☐ 466	Brady Anderson	.20	.09
☐ 467	Jeff Ballard UER	.05	.02
	(Missing top of right parenthesis after Saberhagen in last text line)		
☐ 468	Juan Bell	.05	.02
☐ 469A	Mike Devereaux	.10	.05
	(First line of text ends with six)		
☐ 469B	Mike Devereaux	.10	.05
	(First line of text ends with runs)		
☐ 470	Steve Finley	.20	.09
☐ 471	Dave Gallagher	.05	.02
☐ 472	Leo Gomez	.20	.09
☐ 473	Rene Gonzales	.05	.02
☐ 474	Pete Harnisch	.05	.02
☐ 475	Kevin Hickey	.05	.02
☐ 476	Chris Hoiles	.05	.02
☐ 477	Sam Horn	.05	.02
☐ 478	Tim Hulett	.05	.02
	(Photo shows National Leaguer sliding into second base)		
☐ 479	Dave Johnson	.05	.02
☐ 480	Ron Kittle UER	.05	.02
	(Edmonton misspelled as Edmundton)		
☐ 481	Ben McDonald	.05	.02
☐ 482	Bob Melvin	.05	.02
☐ 483	Bob Milacki	.05	.02
☐ 484	Randy Milligan	.05	.02
☐ 485	John Mitchell	.05	.02
☐ 486	Gregg Olson	.05	.02
☐ 487	Joe Orsulak	.05	.02
☐ 488	Joe Price	.05	.02
☐ 489	Bill Ripken	.05	.02
☐ 490	Cal Ripken	.75	.35
☐ 491	Curt Schilling	.20	.09
☐ 492	David Segui	.10	.05
☐ 493	Anthony Telford	.05	.02
☐ 494	Mickey Tettleton	.10	.05
☐ 495	Mark Williamson	.05	.02
☐ 496	Craig Worthington	.05	.02
☐ 497	Juan Agosto	.05	.02
☐ 498	Eric Anthony	.05	.02
☐ 499	Craig Biggio	.20	.09
☐ 500	Ken Caminiti UER	.20	.09
	(Born 4/4, should be 4/21)		
☐ 501	Casey Candaele	.05	.02
☐ 502	Andujar Cedeno	.05	.02
☐ 503	Danny Darwin	.05	.02
☐ 504	Mark Davidson	.05	.02
☐ 505	Glenn Davis	.05	.02
☐ 506	Jim Deshaies	.05	.02
☐ 507	Luis Gonzalez	.50	.23
☐ 508	Bill Gullickson	.05	.02
☐ 509	Xavier Hernandez	.05	.02
☐ 510	Brian Meyer	.05	.02
☐ 511	Ken Oberkfell	.05	.02
☐ 512	Mark Portugal	.05	.02
☐ 513	Rafael Ramirez	.05	.02

☐ 514	Karl Rhodes	.05	.02
☐ 515	Mike Scott	.05	.02
☐ 516	Mike Simms	.05	.02
☐ 517	Dave Smith	.05	.02
☐ 518	Franklin Stubbs	.05	.02
☐ 519	Glenn Wilson	.05	.02
☐ 520	Eric Yelding UER	.05	.02
	(Text has 63 steals, stats have 64, which is correct)		
☐ 521	Gerald Young	.05	.02
☐ 522	Shawn Abner	.05	.02
☐ 523	Roberto Alomar	.20	.09
☐ 524	Andy Benes	.10	.05
☐ 525	Joe Carter	.10	.05
☐ 526	Jack Clark	.10	.05
☐ 527	Joey Cora	.05	.02
☐ 528	Paul Faries	.05	.02
☐ 529	Tony Gwynn	.50	.23
☐ 530	Atlee Hammaker	.05	.02
☐ 531	Greg W. Harris	.05	.02
☐ 532	Thomas Howard	.05	.02
☐ 533	Bruce Hurst	.05	.02
☐ 534	Craig Lefferts	.05	.02
☐ 535	Derek Lilliquist	.05	.02
☐ 536	Fred Lynn	.05	.02
☐ 537	Mike Pagliarulo	.05	.02
☐ 538	Mark Parent	.05	.02
☐ 539	Dennis Rasmussen	.05	.02
☐ 540	Bip Roberts	.05	.02
☐ 541	Richard Rodriguez	.05	.02
☐ 542	Benito Santiago	.05	.02
☐ 543	Calvin Schiraldi	.05	.02
☐ 544	Eric Show	.05	.02
☐ 545	Phil Stephenson	.05	.02
☐ 546	Garry Templeton UER	.05	.02
	(Born 3/24/57, should be 3/24/56)		
☐ 547	Ed Whitson	.05	.02
☐ 548	Eddie Williams	.05	.02
☐ 549	Kevin Appier	.10	.05
☐ 550	Luis Aquino	.05	.02
☐ 551	Bob Boone	.10	.05
☐ 552	George Brett	.40	.18
☐ 553	Jeff Conine	.20	.09
☐ 554	Steve Crawford	.05	.02
☐ 555	Mark Davis	.05	.02
☐ 556	Storm Davis	.05	.02
☐ 557	Jim Eisenreich	.05	.02
☐ 558	Steve Farr	.05	.02
☐ 559	Tom Gordon	.05	.02
☐ 560	Mark Gubicza	.05	.02
☐ 561	Bo Jackson	.10	.05
☐ 562	Mike Macfarlane	.05	.02
☐ 563	Brian McRae	.10	.05
☐ 564	Jeff Montgomery	.05	.02
☐ 565	Bill Pecota	.05	.02
☐ 566	Gerald Perry	.05	.02
☐ 567	Bret Saberhagen	.10	.05
☐ 568	Jeff Schulz	.05	.02
☐ 569	Kevin Seitzer	.05	.02
☐ 570	Terry Shumpert	.05	.02
☐ 571	Kurt Stillwell	.05	.02
☐ 572	Danny Tartabull	.05	.02
☐ 573	Gary Thurman	.05	.02
☐ 574	Frank White	.10	.05
☐ 575	Willie Wilson	.05	.02
☐ 576	Chris Bosio	.05	.02
☐ 577	Greg Brock	.05	.02
☐ 578	George Canale	.05	.02
☐ 579	Chuck Crim	.05	.02
☐ 580	Rob Deer	.05	.02
☐ 581	Edgar Diaz	.05	.02
☐ 582	Tom Edens	.05	.02
☐ 583	Mike Felder	.05	.02
☐ 584	Jim Gantner	.05	.02
☐ 585	Darryl Hamilton	.05	.02
☐ 586	Ted Higuera	.05	.02
☐ 587	Mark Knudson	.05	.02
☐ 588	Bill Krueger	.05	.02
☐ 589	Tim McIntosh	.05	.02
☐ 590	Paul Mirabella	.05	.02
☐ 591	Paul Molitor	.20	.09
☐ 592	Jaime Navarro	.05	.02
☐ 593	Dave Parker	.10	.05
☐ 594	Dan Plesac	.05	.02

❑ 595 Ron Robinson	.05	.02
❑ 596 Gary Sheffield	.20	.09
❑ 597 Bill Spiers	.05	.02
❑ 598 B.J. Surhoff	.10	.05
❑ 599 Greg Vaughn	.20	.09
❑ 600 Randy Veres	.05	.02
❑ 601 Robin Yount	.20	.09
❑ 602 Rick Aguilera	.10	.05
❑ 603 Allan Anderson	.05	.02
❑ 604 Juan Berenguer	.05	.02
❑ 605 Randy Bush	.05	.02
❑ 606 Carmen Castillo	.05	.02
❑ 607 Tim Drummond	.05	.02
❑ 608 Scott Erickson	.15	.07
❑ 609 Gary Gaetti	.10	.05
❑ 610 Greg Gagne	.05	.02
❑ 611 Dan Gladden	.05	.02
❑ 612 Mark Guthrie	.05	.02
❑ 613 Brian Harper	.05	.02
❑ 614 Kent Hrbek	.10	.05
❑ 615 Gene Larkin	.05	.02
❑ 616 Terry Leach	.05	.02
❑ 617 Nelson Liriano	.05	.02
❑ 618 Shane Mack	.05	.02
❑ 619 John Moses	.05	.02
❑ 620 Pedro Munoz	.05	.02
❑ 621 Al Newman	.05	.02
❑ 622 Junior Ortiz	.05	.02
❑ 623 Kirby Puckett	.30	.14
❑ 624 Roy Smith	.05	.02
❑ 625 Kevin Tapani	.05	.02
❑ 626 Gary Wayne	.05	.02
❑ 627 David West	.05	.02
❑ 628 Cris Carpenter	.05	.02
❑ 629 Vince Coleman	.05	.02
❑ 630 Ken Dayley	.05	.02
❑ 631A Jose DeLeon ERR	.05	.02
(missing '79 Bradenton stats)		
❑ 631B Jose DeLeon COR	.05	.02
(with '79 Bradenton stats)		
❑ 632 Frank DiPino	.05	.02
❑ 633 Bernard Gilkey	.10	.05
❑ 634A Pedro Guerrero ERR	.15	.07
(career SB shown as "$91")		
❑ 634B Pedro Guerrero COR	.10	.05
❑ 635 Ken Hill	.05	.02
❑ 636 Felix Jose	.05	.02
❑ 637 Ray Lankford	.20	.09
❑ 638 Joe Magrane	.05	.02
❑ 639 Tom Niedenfuer	.05	.02
❑ 640 Jose Oquendo	.05	.02
❑ 641 Tom Pagnozzi	.05	.02
❑ 642 Terry Pendleton	.10	.05
❑ 643 Mike Perez	.05	.02
❑ 644 Bryn Smith	.05	.02
❑ 645 Lee Smith	.10	.05
❑ 646 Ozzie Smith	.25	.11
❑ 647 Scott Terry	.05	.02
❑ 648 Bob Tewksbury	.05	.02
❑ 649 Milt Thompson	.05	.02
❑ 650 John Tudor	.05	.02
❑ 651 Denny Walling	.05	.02
❑ 652 Craig Wilson	.05	.02
❑ 653 Todd Worrell	.05	.02
❑ 654 Todd Zeile	.10	.05
❑ 655 Oscar Azocar	.05	.02
❑ 656 Steve Balboni UER	.05	.02
(Born 1/5/57,		
should be 1/16)		
❑ 657 Jesse Barfield	.05	.02
❑ 658 Greg Cadaret	.05	.02
❑ 659 Chuck Cary	.05	.02
❑ 660 Rick Cerone	.05	.02
❑ 661 Dave Eiland	.05	.02
❑ 662 Alvaro Espinoza	.05	.02
❑ 663 Bob Geren	.05	.02
❑ 664 Lee Guetterman	.05	.02
❑ 665 Mel Hall	.05	.02
❑ 666 Andy Hawkins	.05	.02
❑ 667 Jimmy Jones	.05	.02
❑ 668 Roberto Kelly	.05	.02
❑ 669 Dave LaPoint UER	.05	.02
(No '81 Brewers stats,		
totals also are wrong)		
❑ 670 Tim Leary	.05	.02
❑ 671 Jim Leyritz	.10	.05

❑ 672 Kevin Maas	.05	.02
❑ 673 Don Mattingly	.40	.18
❑ 674 Matt Nokes	.05	.02
❑ 675 Pascual Perez	.05	.02
❑ 676 Eric Plunk	.05	.02
❑ 677 Dave Righetti	.05	.02
❑ 678 Jeff D. Robinson	.05	.02
❑ 679 Steve Sax	.05	.02
❑ 680 Mike Witt	.05	.02
❑ 681 Steve Avery UER	.05	.02
(Born in New Jersey,		
should say Michigan)		
❑ 682 Mike Bell	.05	.02
❑ 683 Jeff Blauser	.05	.02
❑ 684 Francisco Cabrera UER	.05	.02
(Born 10/16,		
should say 10/10)		
❑ 685 Tony Castillo	.05	.02
❑ 686 Marty Clary UER	.05	.02
(Shown pitching righty,		
but bio has left)		
❑ 687 Nick Esasky	.05	.02
❑ 688 Ron Gant	.10	.05
❑ 689 Tom Glavine	.20	.09
❑ 690 Mark Grant	.05	.02
❑ 691 Tommy Gregg	.05	.02
❑ 692 Dwayne Henry	.05	.02
❑ 693 Dave Justice	.20	.09
❑ 694 Jimmy Kremers	.05	.02
❑ 695 Charlie Leibrandt	.05	.02
❑ 696 Mark Lemke	.05	.02
❑ 697 Oddibe McDowell	.05	.02
❑ 698 Greg Olson	.05	.02
❑ 699 Jeff Parrett	.05	.02
❑ 700 Jim Presley	.05	.02
❑ 701 Victor Rosario	.05	.02
❑ 702 Lonnie Smith	.05	.02
❑ 703 Pete Smith	.05	.02
❑ 704 John Smoltz	.20	.09
❑ 705 Mike Stanton	.05	.02
❑ 706 Andres Thomas	.05	.02
❑ 707 Jeff Treadway	.05	.02
❑ 708 Jim Vatcher	.05	.02
❑ 709 Ryne Sandberg	.20	.09
Cecil Fielder		
Home Run Kings		
❑ 710 Barry Bonds	.50	.23
Ken Griffey Jr.		
2nd Generation Stars		
❑ 711 Bobby Bonilla	.20	.09
Barry Larkin		
NLCS Team Leaders		
❑ 712 Bobby Thigpen	.05	.02
John Franco		
Top Game Savers		
❑ 713 Chicago's 100 Club	.10	.05
Andre Dawson		
Ryne Sandberg UER		
(Ryno misspelled Rhino)		
❑ 714 CL:A's/Pirates	.05	.02
Reds/Red Sox		
❑ 715 CL:White Sox/Mets	.05	.02
Blue Jays/Dodgers		
❑ 716 CL:Expos/Giants	.05	.02
Rangers/Angels		
❑ 717 CL:Tigers/Indians	.05	.02
Phillies/Cubs		
❑ 718 CL:Braves/Orioles	.05	.02
Astros/Padres		
❑ 719 CL:Royals/Brewers	.05	.02
Twins/Cardinals		
❑ 720 CL:Yankees/Braves	.05	.02
Superstars/Specials		

1991 Fleer All-Stars

	MINT	NRMT
COMPLETE SET (10)	15.00	6.75
COMMON CARD (1-10)	.50	.23
RANDOM INSERTS IN CELLO PACKS		
❑ 1 Ryne Sandberg	2.00	.90
❑ 2 Barry Larkin	2.00	.90
❑ 3 Matt Williams	2.00	.90
❑ 4 Cecil Fielder	1.00	.45
❑ 5 Barry Bonds	2.00	.90

❑ 6 Rickey Henderson	2.00	.90
❑ 7 Ken Griffey Jr.	12.00	5.50
❑ 8 Jose Canseco	2.00	.90
❑ 9 Benito Santiago	.50	.23
❑ 10 Roger Clemens	4.00	1.80

1991 Fleer Pro-Visions

	MINT	NRMT
COMP.WAX SET (12)	4.00	1.80
COMP.FACT.SET (4)	2.00	.90
COMMON CARD	.20	.09
1-12: RANDOM INSERTS IN PACKS		
F1-F4: ONE SET PER FACT.SET		
❑ 1 Kirby Puckett UER	1.00	.45
(.326 average,		
should be .328)		
❑ 2 Will Clark UER	.50	.23
(On tenth line, pennant		
misspelled pennent)		
❑ 3 Ruben Sierra UER	.20	.09
(No apostrophe		
in hasn't)		
❑ 4 Mark McGwire UER	3.00	1.35
(Fisk won ROY in		
72, not '82)		
❑ 5 Bo Jackson	.30	.14
(Bio says 6', others		
have him at 6'1-)		
❑ 6 Jose Canseco	.75	.35
(Bio 6'3-, 230,		
text has 6'4-, 240)		
❑ 7 Dwight Gooden UER	.30	.14
(2.80 ERA in Lynchburg,		
should be 2.50)		
❑ 8 Mike Greenwell UER	.20	.09
(.328 BA and 87 RBI,		
should be .325 and 95)		
❑ 9 Roger Clemens	1.50	.70
❑ 10 Eric Davis	.30	.14
❑ 11 Don Mattingly	1.25	.55
❑ 12 Darryl Strawberry	.30	.14
❑ F1 Barry Bonds	.75	.35
❑ F2 Rickey Henderson	.75	.35
❑ F3 Ryne Sandberg	.75	.35
❑ F4 Dave Stewart	.25	.11

1991 Fleer Update

	MINT	NRMT
COMP.FACT.SET (132)	5.00	2.20

	MINT	NRMT

COMMON CARD (1-132) ..... .05 .02
MINOR STARS ..... .10 .05
UNLISTED STARS ..... .20 .09

□ 1 Glenn Davis ..... .05 .02
□ 2 Dwight Evans ..... .10 .02
□ 3 Jose Mesa ..... .05 .02
□ 4 Jack Clark ..... .10 .02
□ 5 Danny Darwin ..... .05 .02
□ 6 Steve Lyons ..... .05 .02
□ 7 Mo Vaughn ..... .40 .18
□ 8 Floyd Bannister ..... .05 .02
□ 9 Gary Gaetti ..... .10 .05
□ 10 Dave Parker ..... .05 .02
□ 11 Joey Cora ..... .05 .02
□ 12 Charlie Hough ..... .10 .05
□ 13 Matt Merullo ..... .05 .02
□ 14 Warren Newson ..... .05 .02
□ 15 Tim Raines ..... .10 .05
□ 16 Albert Belle ..... .25 .11
□ 17 Glenallen Hill ..... .05 .02
□ 18 Shawn Hillegas ..... .05 .02
□ 19 Mark Lewis ..... .05 .02
□ 20 Charles Nagy ..... .20 .09
□ 21 Mark Whiten ..... .05 .02
□ 22 John Cerutti ..... .05 .02
□ 23 Rob Deer ..... .05 .02
□ 24 Mickey Tettleton ..... .10 .05
□ 25 Warren Cromartie ..... .05 .02
□ 26 Kirk Gibson ..... .10 .05
□ 27 David Howard ..... .05 .02
□ 28 Brent Mayne ..... .05 .02
□ 29 Dante Bichette ..... .20 .09
□ 30 Mark Lee ..... .05 .02
□ 31 Julio Machado ..... .05 .02
□ 32 Edwin Nunez ..... .05 .02
□ 33 Willie Randolph ..... .10 .05
□ 34 Franklin Stubbs ..... .05 .02
□ 35 Bill Wegman ..... .05 .02
□ 36 Chili Davis ..... .10 .05
□ 37 Chuck Knoblauch ..... .20 .09
□ 38 Scott Leius ..... .05 .02
□ 39 Jack Morris ..... .05 .02
□ 40 Mike Pagliarulo ..... .05 .02
□ 41 Lenny Webster ..... .05 .02
□ 42 John Habyan ..... .05 .02
□ 43 Steve Howe ..... .05 .02
□ 44 Jeff Johnson ..... .05 .02
□ 45 Scott Kamieniecki ..... .05 .02
□ 46 Pat Kelly ..... .05 .02
□ 47 Hensley Meulens ..... .05 .02
□ 48 Wade Taylor ..... .05 .02
□ 49 Bernie Williams ..... .50 .23
□ 50 Kirk Dressendorfer ..... .05 .02
□ 51 Ernest Riles ..... .05 .02
□ 52 Rich DeLucia ..... .05 .02
□ 53 Tracy Jones ..... .05 .02
□ 54 Bill Krueger ..... .05 .02
□ 55 Alonzo Powell ..... .05 .02
□ 56 Jeff Schaefer ..... .05 .02
□ 57 Russ Swan ..... .05 .02
□ 58 John Barfield ..... .05 .02
□ 59 Rich Gossage ..... .10 .05
□ 60 Jose Guzman ..... .05 .02
□ 61 Dean Palmer ..... .10 .05
□ 62 Ivan Rodriguez 2.50 1.10
□ 63 Roberto Alomar ..... .20 .09
□ 64 Tom Candiotti ..... .05 .02

□ 65 Joe Carter ..... .10 .05
□ 66 Ed Sprague ..... .05 .02
□ 67 Pat Tabler ..... .05 .02
□ 68 Mike Timlin ..... .05 .02
□ 69 Devon White ..... .05 .02
□ 70 Rafael Belliard ..... .05 .02
□ 71 Juan Berenguer ..... .05 .02
□ 72 Sid Bream ..... .05 .02
□ 73 Marvin Freeman ..... .05 .02
□ 74 Kent Mercker ..... .05 .02
□ 75 Otis Nixon ..... .10 .05
□ 76 Terry Pendleton ..... .10 .05
□ 77 George Bell ..... .05 .02
□ 78 Danny Jackson ..... .05 .02
□ 79 Chuck McElroy ..... .05 .02
□ 80 Gary Scott ..... .05 .02
□ 81 Heathcliff Slocumb ..... .20 .09
□ 82 Dave Smith ..... .05 .02
□ 83 Rick Wilkins ..... .05 .02
□ 84 Freddie Benavides ..... .05 .02
□ 85 Ted Power ..... .05 .02
□ 86 Mo Sanford ..... .05 .02
□ 87 Jeff Bagwell 2.50 1.10
□ 88 Steve Finley ..... .20 .09
□ 89 Pete Harnisch ..... .05 .02
□ 90 Darryl Kile ..... .20 .09
□ 91 Brett Butler ..... .10 .05
□ 92 John Candelaria ..... .05 .02
□ 93 Gary Carter ..... .20 .09
□ 94 Kevin Gross ..... .05 .02
□ 95 Bob Ojeda ..... .05 .02
□ 96 Darryl Strawberry ..... .10 .05
□ 97 Ivan Calderon ..... .05 .02
□ 98 Ron Hassey ..... .05 .02
□ 99 Gilberto Reyes ..... .05 .02
□ 100 Hubie Brooks ..... .05 .02
□ 101 Rick Cerone ..... .05 .02
□ 102 Vince Coleman ..... .05 .02
□ 103 Jeff Innis ..... .05 .02
□ 104 Pete Schourek ..... .10 .05
□ 105 Andy Ashby ..... .20 .09
□ 106 Wally Backman ..... .05 .02
□ 107 Darrin Fletcher ..... .05 .02
□ 108 Tommy Greene ..... .05 .02
□ 109 John Morris ..... .05 .02
□ 110 Mitch Williams ..... .05 .02
□ 111 Lloyd McClendon ..... .05 .02
□ 112 Orlando Merced ..... .05 .02
□ 113 Vicente Palacios ..... .05 .02
□ 114 Gary Varsho ..... .05 .02
□ 115 John Wehner ..... .05 .02
□ 116 Rex Hudler ..... .05 .02
□ 117 Tim Jones ..... .05 .02
□ 118 Geronimo Pena ..... .05 .02
□ 119 Gerald Perry ..... .05 .02
□ 120 Larry Andersen ..... .05 .02
□ 121 Jerald Clark ..... .05 .02
□ 122 Scott Coolbaugh ..... .05 .02
□ 123 Tony Fernandez ..... .05 .02
□ 124 Darrin Jackson ..... .05 .02
□ 125 Fred McGriff ..... .05 .02
□ 126 Jose Mota ..... .05 .02
□ 127 Tim Teufel ..... .05 .02
□ 128 Bud Black ..... .05 .02
□ 129 Mike Felder ..... .05 .02
□ 130 Willie McGee ..... .10 .05
□ 131 Dave Righetti ..... .05 .02
□ 132 Checklist U1-U132 ..... .05 .02

1992 Fleer

	MINT	NRMT
COMPLETE SET (720)	10.00	4.50
COMP.HOBBY SET (732)	20.00	9.00
COMP.RETAIL SET (732)	20.00	9.00
COMMON CARD (1-720)	.05	.02
MINOR STARS	.10	.05
UNLISTED STARS	.20	.09

SUBSET CARDS HALF VALUE OF BASE CARDS

□ 1 Brady Anderson ..... .15 .07
□ 2 Jose Bautista ..... .05 .02
□ 3 Juan Bell ..... .05 .02
□ 4 Glenn Davis ..... .05 .02
□ 5 Mike Devereaux ..... .05 .02

□ 6 Dwight Evans ..... .10 .05
□ 7 Mike Flanagan ..... .05 .02
□ 8 Leo Gomez ..... .05 .02
□ 9 Chris Hoiles ..... .05 .02
□ 10 Sam Horn ..... .05 .02
□ 11 Tim Hulett ..... .05 .02
□ 12 Dave Johnson ..... .05 .02
□ 13 Chito Martinez ..... .05 .02
□ 14 Ben McDonald ..... .05 .02
□ 15 Bob Melvin ..... .05 .02
□ 16 Luis Mercedes ..... .05 .02
□ 17 Jose Mesa ..... .05 .02
□ 18 Bob Milacki ..... .05 .02
□ 19 Randy Milligan ..... .05 .02
□ 20 Mike Mussina UER ..... .30 .14
    (Card back refers
    to him as Jeff)
□ 21 Gregg Olson ..... .05 .02
□ 22 Joe Orsulak ..... .05 .02
□ 23 Jim Poole ..... .05 .02
□ 24 Arthur Rhodes ..... .05 .02
□ 25 Billy Ripken ..... .05 .02
□ 26 Cal Ripken ..... .75 .35
□ 27 David Segui ..... .10 .05
□ 28 Roy Smith ..... .05 .02
□ 29 Anthony Telford ..... .05 .02
□ 30 Mark Williamson ..... .05 .02
□ 31 Craig Worthington ..... .05 .02
□ 32 Wade Boggs ..... .20 .09
□ 33 Tom Bolton ..... .05 .02
□ 34 Tom Brunansky ..... .05 .02
□ 35 Ellis Burks ..... .10 .05
□ 36 Jack Clark ..... .10 .05
□ 37 Roger Clemens ..... .50 .23
□ 38 Danny Darwin ..... .05 .02
□ 39 Mike Greenwell ..... .05 .02
□ 40 Joe Hesketh ..... .05 .02
□ 41 Daryl Irvine ..... .05 .02
□ 42 Dennis Lamp ..... .05 .02
□ 43 Tony Pena ..... .05 .02
□ 44 Phil Plantier ..... .05 .02
□ 45 Carlos Quintana ..... .05 .02
□ 46 Jeff Reardon ..... .10 .05
□ 47 Jody Reed ..... .05 .02
□ 48 Luis Rivera ..... .05 .02
□ 49 Mo Vaughn ..... .25 .11
□ 50 Jim Abbott ..... .10 .05
□ 51 Kyle Abbott ..... .05 .02
□ 52 Ruben Amaro ..... .05 .02
□ 53 Scott Bailes ..... .05 .02
□ 54 Chris Beasley ..... .05 .02
□ 55 Mark Eichhorn ..... .05 .02
□ 56 Mike Fetters ..... .05 .02
□ 57 Chuck Finley ..... .10 .05
□ 58 Gary Gaetti ..... .05 .02
□ 59 Dave Gallagher ..... .05 .02
□ 60 Donnie Hill ..... .05 .02
□ 61 Bryan Harvey UER ..... .05 .02
    (Lee Smith led the
    Majors with 47 saves)
□ 62 Wally Joyner ..... .10 .05
□ 63 Mark Langston ..... .05 .02
□ 64 Kirk McCaskill ..... .05 .02
□ 65 John Orton ..... .05 .02
□ 66 Lance Parrish ..... .05 .02
□ 67 Luis Polonia ..... .05 .02
□ 68 Bobby Rose ..... .05 .02
□ 69 Dick Schofield ..... .05 .02

70	Luis Sojo	.05	.02
71	Lee Stevens	.10	.05
72	Dave Winfield	.20	.09
73	Cliff Young	.05	.02
74	Wilson Alvarez	.10	.05
75	Esteban Beltre	.05	.02
76	Joey Cora	.05	.02
77	Brian Drahman	.05	.02
78	Alex Fernandez	.10	.05
79	Carlton Fisk	.20	.09
80	Scott Fletcher	.05	.02
81	Craig Grebeck	.05	.02
82	Ozzie Guillen	.05	.02
83	Greg Hibbard	.05	.02
84	Charlie Hough	.10	.05
85	Mike Huff	.05	.02
86	Bo Jackson	.10	.05
87	Lance Johnson	.05	.02
88	Ron Karkovice	.05	.02
89	Jack McDowell	.05	.02
90	Matt Merullo	.05	.02
91	Warren Newson	.05	.02
92	Donn Pall UER	.05	.02
	(Called Dunn on card back)		
93	Dan Pasqua	.05	.02
94	Ken Patterson	.05	.02
95	Melido Perez	.05	.02
96	Scott Radinsky	.05	.02
97	Tim Raines	.10	.05
98	Sammy Sosa	.60	.25
99	Bobby Thigpen	.05	.02
100	Frank Thomas	.50	.23
101	Robin Ventura	.10	.05
102	Mike Aldrete	.05	.02
103	Sandy Alomar Jr.	.10	.05
104	Carlos Baerga	.20	.09
105	Albert Belle	.20	.09
106	Willie Blair	.05	.02
107	Jerry Browne	.05	.02
108	Alex Cole	.05	.02
109	Felix Fermin	.05	.02
110	Glenallen Hill	.05	.02
111	Shawn Hillegas	.05	.02
112	Chris James	.05	.02
113	Reggie Jefferson	.10	.05
114	Doug Jones	.05	.02
115	Eric King	.05	.02
116	Mark Lewis	.05	.02
117	Carlos Martinez	.05	.02
118	Charles Nagy UER	.10	.05
	(Throws right, but card says left)		
119	Rod Nichols	.05	.02
120	Steve Olin	.05	.02
121	Jesse Orosco	.05	.02
122	Rudy Seanez	.05	.02
123	Joel Skinner	.05	.02
124	Greg Swindell	.05	.02
125	Jim Thome	.50	.23
126	Mark Whiten	.05	.02
127	Scott Aldred	.05	.02
128	Andy Allanson	.05	.02
129	John Cerutti	.05	.02
130	Milt Cuyler	.05	.02
131	Mike Dalton	.05	.02
132	Rob Deer	.05	.02
133	Cecil Fielder	.10	.05
134	Travis Fryman	.10	.05
135	Dan Gakeler	.05	.02
136	Paul Gibson	.05	.02
137	Bill Gullickson	.05	.02
138	Mike Henneman	.05	.02
139	Pete Incaviglia	.05	.02
140	Mark Leiter	.05	.02
141	Scott Livingstone	.05	.02
142	Lloyd Moseby	.05	.02
143	Tony Phillips	.05	.02
144	Mark Salas	.05	.02
145	Frank Tanana	.05	.02
146	Walt Terrell	.05	.02
147	Mickey Tettleton	.05	.02
148	Alan Trammell	.15	.07
149	Lou Whitaker	.10	.05
150	Kevin Appier	.05	.02
151	Luis Aquino	.05	.02
152	Todd Benzinger	.05	.02
153	Mike Boddicker	.05	.02
154	George Brett	.40	.18
155	Storm Davis	.05	.02
156	Jim Eisenreich	.05	.02
157	Kirk Gibson	.10	.05
158	Tom Gordon	.05	.02
159	Mark Gubicza	.05	.02
160	David Howard	.05	.02
161	Mike Macfarlane	.05	.02
162	Brent Mayne	.05	.02
163	Brian McRae	.05	.02
164	Jeff Montgomery	.10	.05
165	Bill Pecota	.05	.02
166	Harvey Pulliam	.05	.02
167	Bret Saberhagen	.10	.05
168	Kevin Seitzer	.05	.02
169	Terry Shumpert	.05	.02
170	Kurt Stillwell	.05	.02
171	Danny Tartabull	.15	.07
172	Gary Thurman	.05	.02
173	Dante Bichette	.15	.07
174	Kevin D. Brown	.05	.02
175	Chuck Crim	.05	.02
176	Jim Gantner	.05	.02
177	Darryl Hamilton	.05	.02
178	Ted Higuera	.05	.02
179	Darren Holmes	.05	.02
180	Mark Lee	.05	.02
181	Julio Machado	.05	.02
182	Paul Molitor	.20	.09
183	Jaime Navarro	.05	.02
184	Edwin Nunez	.05	.02
185	Dan Plesac	.05	.02
186	Willie Randolph	.10	.05
187	Ron Robinson	.05	.02
188	Gary Sheffield	.20	.09
189	Bill Spiers	.05	.02
190	B.J. Surhoff	.10	.05
191	Dale Sveum	.05	.02
192	Greg Vaughn	.15	.07
193	Bill Wegman	.05	.02
194	Robin Yount	.20	.09
195	Rick Aguilera	.10	.05
196	Allan Anderson	.05	.02
197	Steve Bedrosian	.05	.02
198	Randy Bush	.05	.02
199	Larry Casian	.05	.02
200	Chili Davis	.05	.02
201	Scott Erickson	.10	.05
202	Greg Gagne	.05	.02
203	Dan Gladden	.05	.02
204	Brian Harper	.05	.02
205	Kent Hrbek	.10	.05
206	Chuck Knoblauch UER	.20	.09
	(Career hit total of 59 is wrong)		
207	Gene Larkin	.05	.02
208	Terry Leach	.05	.02
209	Scott Leius	.05	.02
210	Shane Mack	.05	.02
211	Jack Morris	.10	.05
212	Pedro Munoz	.05	.02
213	Denny Neagle	.15	.07
214	Al Newman	.05	.02
215	Junior Ortiz	.05	.02
216	Mike Pagliarulo	.05	.02
217	Kirby Puckett	.30	.14
218	Paul Sorrento	.05	.02
219	Kevin Tapani	.05	.02
220	Lenny Webster	.05	.02
221	Jesse Barfield	.05	.02
222	Greg Cadaret	.05	.02
223	Dave Eiland	.05	.02
224	Alvaro Espinoza	.05	.02
225	Steve Farr	.05	.02
226	Bob Geren	.05	.02
227	Lee Guetterman	.05	.02
228	John Habyan	.05	.02
229	Mel Hall	.05	.02
230	Steve Howe	.05	.02
231	Mike Humphreys	.05	.02
232	Scott Kamieniecki	.05	.02
233	Pat Kelly	.05	.02
234	Roberto Kelly	.05	.02
235	Tim Leary	.05	.02
236	Kevin Maas	.05	.02
237	Don Mattingly	.40	.18
238	Hensley Meulens	.05	.02
239	Matt Nokes	.05	.02
240	Pascual Perez	.05	.02
241	Eric Plunk	.05	.02
242	John Ramos	.05	.02
243	Scott Sanderson	.05	.02
244	Steve Sax	.05	.02
245	Wade Taylor	.05	.02
246	Randy Velarde	.05	.02
247	Bernie Williams	.20	.09
248	Troy Afenir	.05	.02
249	Harold Baines	.10	.05
250	Lance Blankenship	.05	.02
251	Mike Bordick	.05	.02
252	Jose Canseco	.25	.11
253	Steve Chitren	.05	.02
254	Ron Darling	.05	.02
255	Dennis Eckersley	.10	.05
256	Mike Gallego	.05	.02
257	Dave Henderson	.05	.02
258	Rickey Henderson UER	.25	.11
	(Wearing 24 on front and 22 on back)		
259	Rick Honeycutt	.05	.02
260	Brook Jacoby	.05	.02
261	Carney Lansford	.10	.05
262	Mark McGwire	1.00	.45
263	Mike Moore	.05	.02
264	Gene Nelson	.05	.02
265	Jamie Quirk	.05	.02
266	Joe Slusarski	.05	.02
267	Terry Steinbach	.05	.02
268	Dave Stewart	.10	.05
269	Todd Van Poppel	.05	.02
270	Walt Weiss	.05	.02
271	Bob Welch	.05	.02
272	Curt Young	.05	.02
273	Scott Bradley	.05	.02
274	Greg Briley	.05	.02
275	Jay Buhner	.15	.07
276	Henry Cotto	.05	.02
277	Alvin Davis	.05	.02
278	Rich DeLucia	.05	.02
279	Ken Griffey Jr.	1.25	.55
280	Erik Hanson	.05	.02
281	Brian Holman	.05	.02
282	Mike Jackson	.10	.05
283	Randy Johnson	.20	.09
284	Tracy Jones	.05	.02
285	Bill Krueger	.05	.02
286	Edgar Martinez	.15	.07
287	Tino Martinez	.20	.09
288	Rob Murphy	.05	.02
289	Pete O'Brien	.05	.02
290	Alonzo Powell	.05	.02
291	Harold Reynolds	.05	.02
292	Mike Schooler	.05	.02
293	Russ Swan	.05	.02
294	Bill Swift	.05	.02
295	Dave Valle	.05	.02
296	Omar Vizquel	.10	.05
297	Gerald Alexander	.05	.02
298	Brad Arnsberg	.05	.02
299	Kevin Brown	.15	.07
300	Jack Daugherty	.05	.02
301	Mario Diaz	.05	.02
302	Brian Downing	.05	.02
303	Julio Franco	.05	.02
304	Juan Gonzalez	.50	.23
305	Rich Gossage	.10	.05
306	Jose Guzman	.05	.02
307	Jose Hernandez	.05	.02
308	Jeff Huson	.05	.02
309	Mike Jeffcoat	.05	.02
310	Terry Mathews	.05	.02
311	Rafael Palmeiro	.20	.09
312	Dean Palmer	.10	.05
313	Geno Petralli	.05	.02
314	Gary Pettis	.05	.02
315	Kevin Reimer	.05	.02
316	Ivan Rodriguez	.40	.18
317	Kenny Rogers	.05	.02
318	Wayne Rosenthal	.05	.02
319	Jeff Russell	.05	.02

320	Nolan Ryan	.75	.35
321	Ruben Sierra	.05	.02
322	Jim Acker	.05	.02
323	Roberto Alomar	.20	.09
324	Derek Bell	.10	.05
325	Pat Borders	.05	.02
326	Tom Candiotti	.05	.02
327	Joe Carter	.10	.05
328	Rob Ducey	.05	.02
329	Kelly Gruber	.05	.02
330	Juan Guzman	.05	.02
331	Tom Henke	.05	.02
332	Jimmy Key	.10	.05
333	Manny Lee	.05	.02
334	Al Leiter	.10	.05
335	Bob MacDonald	.05	.02
336	Candy Maldonado	.05	.02
337	Rance Mulliniks	.05	.02
338	Greg Myers	.05	.02
339	John Olerud UER (1991 BA has .256, but text says .258)	.10	.05
340	Ed Sprague	.05	.02
341	Dave Stieb	.05	.02
342	Todd Stottlemyre	.10	.05
343	Mike Timlin	.05	.02
344	Duane Ward	.05	.02
345	David Wells	.05	.02
346	Devon White	.05	.02
347	Mookie Wilson	.10	.05
348	Eddie Zosky	.05	.02
349	Steve Avery	.05	.02
350	Mike Bell	.05	.02
351	Rafael Belliard	.05	.02
352	Juan Berenguer	.05	.02
353	Jeff Blauser	.05	.02
354	Sid Bream	.05	.02
355	Francisco Cabrera	.05	.02
356	Marvin Freeman	.05	.02
357	Ron Gant	.10	.05
358	Tom Glavine	.15	.07
359	Brian Hunter	.05	.02
360	Dave Justice	.20	.09
361	Charlie Leibrandt	.05	.02
362	Mark Lemke	.05	.02
363	Kent Mercker	.05	.02
364	Keith Mitchell	.05	.02
365	Greg Olson	.05	.02
366	Terry Pendleton	.05	.02
367	Armando Reynoso	.05	.02
368	Deion Sanders	.20	.09
369	Lonnie Smith	.05	.02
370	Pete Smith	.05	.02
371	John Smoltz	.15	.07
372	Mike Stanton	.05	.02
373	Jeff Treadway	.05	.02
374	Mark Wohlers	.05	.02
375	Paul Assenmacher	.05	.02
376	George Bell	.05	.02
377	Shawn Boskie	.05	.02
378	Frank Castillo	.05	.02
379	Andre Dawson	.15	.07
380	Shawon Dunston	.05	.02
381	Mark Grace	.15	.07
382	Mike Harkey	.05	.02
383	Danny Jackson	.05	.02
384	Les Lancaster	.05	.02
385	Ced Landrum	.05	.02
386	Greg Maddux	.50	.23
387	Derrick May	.05	.02
388	Chuck McElroy	.05	.02
389	Ryne Sandberg	.25	.11
390	Heathcliff Slocumb	.05	.02
391	Dave Smith	.05	.02
392	Dwight Smith	.05	.02
393	Rick Sutcliffe	.05	.02
394	Hector Villanueva	.05	.02
395	Chico Walker	.05	.02
396	Jerome Walton	.05	.02
397	Rick Wilkins	.05	.02
398	Jack Armstrong	.05	.02
399	Freddie Benavides	.05	.02
400	Glenn Braggs	.05	.02
401	Tom Browning	.05	.02
402	Norm Charlton	.05	.02
403	Eric Davis	.10	.05
404	Rob Dibble	.05	.02
405	Bill Doran	.05	.02
406	Mariano Duncan	.05	.02
407	Kip Gross	.05	.02
408	Chris Hammond	.05	.02
409	Billy Hatcher	.05	.02
410	Chris Jones	.05	.02
411	Barry Larkin	.15	.07
412	Hal Morris	.05	.02
413	Randy Myers	.10	.05
414	Joe Oliver	.05	.02
415	Paul O'Neill	.10	.05
416	Ted Power	.05	.02
417	Luis Quinones	.05	.02
418	Jeff Reed	.05	.02
419	Jose Rijo	.05	.02
420	Chris Sabo	.05	.02
421	Reggie Sanders	.10	.05
422	Scott Scudder	.05	.02
423	Glenn Sutko	.05	.02
424	Eric Anthony	.05	.02
425	Jeff Bagwell	.40	.18
426	Craig Biggio	.20	.09
427	Ken Caminiti	.15	.07
428	Casey Candaele	.05	.02
429	Mike Capel	.05	.02
430	Andujar Cedeno	.05	.02
431	Jim Corsi	.05	.02
432	Mark Davidson	.05	.02
433	Steve Finley	.05	.02
434	Luis Gonzalez	.15	.07
435	Pete Harnisch	.05	.02
436	Dwayne Henry	.05	.02
437	Xavier Hernandez	.05	.02
438	Jimmy Jones	.05	.02
439	Darryl Kile	.10	.05
440	Rob Mallicoat	.05	.02
441	Andy Mota	.05	.02
442	Al Osuna	.05	.02
443	Mark Portugal	.05	.02
444	Scott Servais	.05	.02
445	Mike Simms	.05	.02
446	Gerald Young	.05	.02
447	Tim Belcher	.05	.02
448	Brett Butler	.10	.05
449	John Candelaria	.05	.02
450	Gary Carter	.20	.09
451	Dennis Cook	.05	.02
452	Tim Crews	.05	.02
453	Kal Daniels	.05	.02
454	Jim Gott	.05	.02
455	Alfredo Griffin	.05	.02
456	Kevin Gross	.05	.02
457	Chris Gwynn	.05	.02
458	Lenny Harris	.05	.02
459	Orel Hershiser	.10	.05
460	Jay Howell	.05	.02
461	Stan Javier	.05	.02
462	Eric Karros	.20	.09
463	Ramon Martinez UER (Card says bats right, should be left)	.10	.05
464	Roger McDowell UER (Wins add up to 50, totals have 51)	.05	.02
465	Mike Morgan	.05	.02
466	Eddie Murray	.20	.09
467	Jose Offerman	.05	.02
468	Bob Ojeda	.05	.02
469	Juan Samuel	.05	.02
470	Mike Scioscia	.05	.02
471	Darryl Strawberry	.10	.05
472	Bret Barberie	.05	.02
473	Brian Barnes	.05	.02
474	Eric Bullock	.05	.02
475	Ivan Calderon	.05	.02
476	Delino DeShields	.10	.05
477	Jeff Fassero	.05	.02
478	Mike Fitzgerald	.05	.02
479	Steve Frey	.05	.02
480	Andres Galarraga	.05	.02
481	Mark Gardner	.05	.02
482	Marquis Grissom	.10	.05
483	Chris Haney	.05	.02
484	Barry Jones	.05	.02
485	Dave Martinez	.05	.02
486	Dennis Martinez	.10	.05
487	Chris Nabholz	.05	.02
488	Spike Owen	.05	.02
489	Gilberto Reyes	.05	.02
490	Mel Rojas	.05	.02
491	Scott Ruskin	.05	.02
492	Bill Sampen	.05	.02
493	Larry Walker	.20	.09
494	Tim Wallach	.05	.02
495	Daryl Boston	.05	.02
496	Hubie Brooks	.05	.02
497	Tim Burke	.05	.02
498	Mark Carreon	.05	.02
499	Tony Castillo	.05	.02
500	Vince Coleman	.05	.02
501	David Cone	.10	.05
502	Kevin Elster	.05	.02
503	Sid Fernandez	.05	.02
504	John Franco	.05	.02
505	Dwight Gooden	.10	.05
506	Todd Hundley	.05	.02
507	Jeff Innis	.05	.02
508	Gregg Jefferies	.05	.02
509	Howard Johnson	.05	.02
510	Dave Magadan	.05	.02
511	Terry McDaniel	.05	.02
512	Kevin McReynolds	.05	.02
513	Keith Miller	.05	.02
514	Charlie O'Brien	.05	.02
515	Mackey Sasser	.05	.02
516	Pete Schourek	.05	.02
517	Julio Valera	.05	.02
518	Frank Viola	.05	.02
519	Wally Whitehurst	.05	.02
520	Anthony Young	.05	.02
521	Andy Ashby	.10	.05
522	Kim Batiste	.05	.02
523	Joe Boever	.05	.02
524	Wes Chamberlain	.05	.02
525	Pat Combs	.05	.02
526	Danny Cox	.05	.02
527	Darren Daulton	.10	.05
528	Jose DeJesus	.05	.02
529	Len Dykstra	.10	.05
530	Darrin Fletcher	.05	.02
531	Tommy Greene	.05	.02
532	Jason Grimsley	.05	.02
533	Charlie Hayes	.05	.02
534	Von Hayes	.05	.02
535	Dave Hollins	.10	.05
536	Ricky Jordan	.05	.02
537	John Kruk	.10	.05
538	Jim Lindeman	.05	.02
539	Mickey Morandini	.05	.02
540	Terry Mulholland	.05	.02
541	Dale Murphy	.20	.09
542	Randy Ready	.05	.02
543	Wally Ritchie UER (Letters in data are cut off on card)	.05	.02
544	Bruce Ruffin	.05	.02
545	Steve Searcy	.05	.02
546	Dickie Thon	.05	.02
547	Mitch Williams	.05	.02
548	Stan Belinda	.05	.02
549	Jay Bell	.10	.05
550	Barry Bonds	.25	.11
551	Bobby Bonilla	.10	.05
552	Steve Buechele	.05	.02
553	Doug Drabek	.10	.05
554	Neal Heaton	.05	.02
555	Jeff King	.05	.02
556	Bob Kipper	.05	.02
557	Bill Landrum	.05	.02
558	Mike LaValliere	.05	.02
559	Jose Lind	.05	.02
560	Lloyd McClendon	.05	.02
561	Orlando Merced	.05	.02
562	Bob Patterson	.05	.02
563	Joe Redfield	.05	.02
564	Gary Redus	.05	.02
565	Rosario Rodriguez	.05	.02
566	Don Slaught	.05	.02
567	John Smiley	.10	.05
568	Zane Smith	.05	.02
569	Randy Tomlin	.05	.02

❏ 570 Andy Van Slyke	.10	.05	
❏ 571 Gary Varsho	.05	.02	
❏ 572 Bob Walk	.05	.02	
❏ 573 John Wehner UER	.05	.02	
(Actually played for			
Carolina in 1991,			
not Cards)			
❏ 574 Juan Agosto	.05	.02	
❏ 575 Cris Carpenter	.05	.02	
❏ 576 Jose DeLeon	.05	.02	
❏ 577 Rich Gedman	.05	.02	
❏ 578 Bernard Gilkey	.10	.05	
❏ 579 Pedro Guerrero	.05	.02	
❏ 580 Ken Hill	.05	.02	
❏ 581 Rex Hudler	.05	.02	
❏ 582 Felix Jose	.05	.02	
❏ 583 Ray Lankford	.20	.09	
❏ 584 Omar Olivares	.05	.02	
❏ 585 Jose Oquendo	.05	.02	
❏ 586 Tom Pagnozzi	.05	.02	
❏ 587 Geronimo Pena	.05	.02	
❏ 588 Mike Perez	.05	.02	
❏ 589 Gerald Perry	.05	.02	
❏ 590 Bryn Smith	.05	.02	
❏ 591 Lee Smith	.10	.05	
❏ 592 Ozzie Smith	.25	.11	
❏ 593 Scott Terry	.05	.02	
❏ 594 Bob Tewksbury	.05	.02	
❏ 595 Milt Thompson	.05	.02	
❏ 596 Todd Zeile	.05	.02	
❏ 597 Larry Andersen	.05	.02	
❏ 598 Oscar Azocar	.05	.02	
❏ 599 Andy Benes	.10	.05	
❏ 600 Ricky Bones	.05	.02	
❏ 601 Jerald Clark	.05	.02	
❏ 602 Pat Clements	.05	.02	
❏ 603 Paul Faries	.05	.02	
❏ 604 Tony Fernandez	.05	.02	
❏ 605 Tony Gwynn	.50	.23	
❏ 606 Greg W. Harris	.05	.02	
❏ 607 Thomas Howard	.05	.02	
❏ 608 Bruce Hurst	.05	.02	
❏ 609 Darrin Jackson	.05	.02	
❏ 610 Tom Lampkin	.05	.02	
❏ 611 Craig Lefferts	.05	.02	
❏ 612 Jim Lewis	.05	.02	
❏ 613 Mike Maddux	.05	.02	
❏ 614 Fred McGriff	.15	.07	
❏ 615 Jose Melendez	.05	.02	
❏ 616 Jose Mota	.05	.02	
❏ 617 Dennis Rasmussen	.05	.02	
❏ 618 Bip Roberts	.05	.02	
❏ 619 Rich Rodriguez	.05	.02	
❏ 620 Benito Santiago	.05	.02	
❏ 621 Craig Shipley	.05	.02	
❏ 622 Tim Teufel	.05	.02	
❏ 623 Kevin Ward	.05	.02	
❏ 624 Ed Whitson	.05	.02	
❏ 625 Dave Anderson	.05	.02	
❏ 626 Kevin Bass	.05	.02	
❏ 627 Rod Beck	.20	.09	
❏ 628 Bud Black	.05	.02	
❏ 629 Jeff Brantley	.05	.02	
❏ 630 John Burkett	.05	.02	
❏ 631 Will Clark	.20	.09	
❏ 632 Royce Clayton	.05	.02	
❏ 633 Steve Decker	.05	.02	
❏ 634 Kelly Downs	.05	.02	
❏ 635 Mike Felder	.05	.02	
❏ 636 Scott Garrelts	.05	.02	
❏ 637 Eric Gunderson	.05	.02	
❏ 638 Bryan Hickerson	.05	.02	
❏ 639 Darren Lewis	.05	.02	
❏ 640 Greg Litton	.05	.02	
❏ 641 Kirt Manwaring	.05	.02	
❏ 642 Paul McClellan	.05	.02	
❏ 643 Willie McGee	.10	.05	
❏ 644 Kevin Mitchell	.10	.05	
❏ 645 Francisco Oliveras	.05	.02	
❏ 646 Mike Remlinger	.05	.02	
❏ 647 Dave Righetti	.05	.02	
❏ 648 Robby Thompson	.05	.02	
❏ 649 Jose Uribe	.05	.02	
❏ 650 Matt Williams	.15	.07	
❏ 651 Trevor Wilson	.05	.02	
❏ 652 Tom Goodwin MLP UER	.10	.05	

(Timed in 3.5,			
should be be timed)			
❏ 653 Terry Bross MLP	.05	.02	
❏ 654 Mike Christopher MLP	.05	.02	
❏ 655 Kenny Lofton MLP	.25	.11	
❏ 656 Chris Cron MLP	.05	.02	
❏ 657 Willie Banks MLP	.05	.02	
❏ 658 Pat Rice MLP	.05	.02	
❏ 659A Rob Maurer MLP ERR	.75	.35	
(Name misspelled as			
Mauer on card front)			
❏ 659B Rob Maurer MLP COR	.10	.05	
❏ 660 Don Harris MLP	.05	.02	
❏ 661 Henry Rodriguez MLP	.20	.09	
❏ 662 Cliff Brantley MLP	.05	.02	
❏ 663 Mike Linskey MLP UER	.05	.02	
(220 pounds in data,			
200 in text)			
❏ 664 Gary DiSarcina MLP	.05	.02	
❏ 665 Gil Heredia MLP	.05	.02	
❏ 666 Vinny Castilla MLP	2.50	1.10	
❏ 667 Paul Abbott MLP	.05	.02	
❏ 668 Monty Fariss MLP UER	.05	.02	
(Called Paul on back)			
❏ 669 Jarvis Brown MLP	.05	.02	
❏ 670 Wayne Kirby MLP	.05	.02	
❏ 671 Scott Brosius MLP	.25	.11	
❏ 672 Bob Hamelin MLP	.05	.02	
❏ 673 Joel Johnston MLP	.05	.02	
❏ 674 Tim Spehr MLP	.05	.02	
❏ 675A Jeff Gardner MLP ERR	.75	.35	
(P on front,			
should be SS)			
❏ 675B Jeff Gardner MLP COR	.25	.11	
❏ 676 Rico Rossy MLP	.05	.02	
❏ 677 Roberto Hernandez MLP	.15	.07	
❏ 678 Ted Wood MLP	.05	.02	
❏ 679 Cal Eldred MLP	.05	.02	
❏ 680 Sean Berry MLP	.05	.02	
❏ 681 Rickey Henderson RS	.10	.05	
❏ 682 Nolan Ryan RS	.20	.09	
❏ 683 Dennis Martinez RS	.05	.02	
❏ 684 Wilson Alvarez RS	.05	.02	
❏ 685 Joe Carter RS	.05	.02	
❏ 686 Dave Winfield RS	.10	.05	
❏ 687 David Cone RS	.05	.02	
❏ 688 Jose Canseco LL UER	.10	.05	
(Text on back has 42 stolen			
bases in '88; should be 40)			
❏ 689 Howard Johnson LL	.05	.02	
❏ 690 Julio Franco LL	.05	.02	
❏ 691 Terry Pendleton LL	.05	.02	
❏ 692 Cecil Fielder LL	.05	.02	
❏ 693 Scott Erickson LL	.05	.02	
❏ 694 Tom Glavine LL	.05	.02	
❏ 695 Dennis Martinez LL	.05	.02	
❏ 696 Bryan Harvey LL	.05	.02	
❏ 697 Lee Smith LL	.05	.02	
❏ 698 Super Siblings	.10	.05	
Roberto Alomar			
Sandy Alomar Jr.			
❏ 699 The Indispensables	.10	.05	
Bobby Bonilla			
Will Clark			
❏ 700 Teamwork	.05	.02	
Mark Wohlers			
Kent Mercker			
Alejandro Pena			
❏ 701 Tiger Tandems	.25	.11	
Stacy Jones			
Bo Jackson			
Gregg Olson			
Frank Thomas			
❏ 702 The Ignitors	.20	.09	
Paul Molitor			
Brett Butler			
❏ 703 Indispensables II	.40	.18	
Cal Ripken			
Joe Carter			
❏ 704 Power Packs	.20	.09	
Barry Larkin			
Kirby Puckett			
❏ 705 Today and Tomorrow	.20	.09	
Mo Vaughn			
Cecil Fielder			
❏ 706 Teenage Sensations	.10	.05	

Ramon Martinez			
Ozzie Guillen			
❏ 707 Designated Hitters	.15	.07	
Harold Baines			
Wade Boggs			
❏ 708 Robin Yount PV	.10	.05	
❏ 709 Ken Griffey Jr. PV UER	.60	.25	
(Missing quotations on			
back; BA has .322, but			
was actually .327)			
❏ 710 Nolan Ryan PV	.40	.18	
❏ 711 Cal Ripken PV	.40	.18	
❏ 712 Frank Thomas PV	.25	.11	
❏ 713 Dave Justice PV	.10	.05	
❏ 714 Checklist 1-101	.05	.02	
❏ 715 Checklist 102-194	.05	.02	
❏ 716 Checklist 195-296	.05	.02	
❏ 717 Checklist 297-397	.05	.02	
❏ 718 Checklist 398-494	.05	.02	
❏ 719 Checklist 495-596	.05	.02	
❏ 720A Checklist 597-720 ERR	.05	.02	
(659 Rob Maurer)			
❏ 720B Checklist 597-720 COR	.05	.02	
(659 Rob Maurer)			

1992 Fleer All-Stars

	MINT	NRMT
COMPLETE SET (24)	35.00	16.00
COMMON CARD (1-24)	.50	.23
RANDOM INSERTS IN WAX PACKS		
❏ 1 Felix Jose	.50	.23
❏ 2 Tony Gwynn	4.00	1.80
❏ 3 Barry Bonds	2.00	.90
❏ 4 Bobby Bonilla	1.00	.45
❏ 5 Mike LaValliere	.50	.23
❏ 6 Tom Glavine	1.50	.70
❏ 7 Ramon Martinez	1.00	.45
❏ 8 Lee Smith	1.00	.45
❏ 9 Mickey Tettleton	.50	.23
❏ 10 Scott Erickson	1.00	.45
❏ 11 Frank Thomas	4.00	1.80
❏ 12 Danny Tartabull	.50	.23
❏ 13 Will Clark	2.00	.90
❏ 14 Ryne Sandberg	2.00	.90
❏ 15 Terry Pendleton	.50	.23
❏ 16 Barry Larkin	1.50	.70
❏ 17 Rafael Palmeiro	2.00	.90
❏ 18 Julio Franco	.50	.23
❏ 19 Robin Ventura	1.00	.45
❏ 20 Cal Ripken UER	6.00	2.70
(Candice; total bases		
misspelled as based)		
❏ 21 Joe Carter	1.00	.45
❏ 22 Kirby Puckett	2.50	1.10
❏ 23 Ken Griffey Jr.	10.00	4.50
❏ 24 Jose Canseco	2.00	.90

1992 Fleer Clemens

	MINT	NRMT
COMPLETE SET (12)	10.00	4.50
COMMON CLEMENS (1-12)	1.00	.45
RANDOM INSERTS IN PACKS		
AUTOGRAPH CARD IS NOT CERTIFIED		
COMMON MAIL-IN (13-15)	1.00	.45
MAIL-IN CARDS DIST.VIA WRAPPER EXCH.		

AU CARD RANDOM INSERT IN PACKS

❑ 1	Roger Clemens	1.00	.45
	Quiet Storm		
❑ 2	Roger Clemens	1.00	.45
	Courted By Mets and Twins		
❑ 3	Roger Clemens	1.00	.45
	The Show		
❑ 4	Roger Clemens	1.00	.45
	Rocket Launched		
❑ 5	Roger Clemens	1.00	.45
	Time Of Trial		
❑ 6	Roger Clemens	1.00	.45
	Break Through		
❑ 7	Roger Clemens	1.00	.45
	Play It Again Roger		
❑ 8	Roger Clemens	1.00	.45
	Business As Usual		
❑ 9	Roger Clemens	1.00	.45
	Heeee's Back		
❑ 10	Roger Clemens	1.00	.45
	Blood, Sweat and Tears		
❑ 11	Roger Clemens	1.00	.45
	Prime Of Life		
❑ 12	Roger Clemens	1.00	.45
	Man For Every Season		
❑ 13	Roger Clemens EXCH	1.00	.45
	Cooperstown Bound		
❑ 14	Roger Clemens EXCH	1.00	.45
	The Heat of the Moment		
❑ 15	Roger Clemens EXCH	1.00	.45
	Final Words Q and A with "The Rocket"		
❑ AU	Roger Clemens AU	60.00	27.00
	Uncertified Signature		
❑ NNO	Roger Clemens Promo	6.00	2.70
	with Paul Mulian		

1992 Fleer Lumber Company

	MINT	NRMT
COMPLETE SET (9)	10.00	4.50
COMMON CARD (L1-L9)	.50	.23

ONE SET PER HOBBY FACTORY SET

❑ L1	Cecil Fielder	.75	.35
❑ L2	Mickey Tettleton	.50	.23
❑ L3	Darryl Strawberry	.75	.35
❑ L4	Ryne Sandberg	2.00	.90

❑ L5	Jose Canseco	2.00	.90
❑ L6	Matt Williams UER	1.00	.45
	In 17th line, cycle is spelled cycle		
❑ L7	Cal Ripken	6.00	2.70
❑ L8	Barry Bonds	2.00	.90
❑ L9	Ron Gant	.75	.35

1992 Fleer Rookie Sensations

	MINT	NRMT
COMPLETE SET (20)	50.00	22.00
COMMON CARD (1-20)	1.00	.45
MINOR STARS	2.00	.90
SEMISTARS	3.00	1.35

RANDOM INSERTS IN CELLO PACKS

❑ 1	Frank Thomas	15.00	6.75
❑ 2	Todd Van Poppel	1.00	.45
❑ 3	Orlando Merced	1.00	.45
❑ 4	Jeff Bagwell	8.00	3.60
❑ 5	Jeff Fassero	1.00	.45
❑ 6	Darren Lewis	1.00	.45
❑ 7	Milt Cuyler	1.00	.45
❑ 8	Mike Timlin	1.00	.45
❑ 9	Brian McRae	1.00	.45
❑ 10	Chuck Knoblauch	4.00	1.80
❑ 11	Rich DeLucia	1.00	.45
❑ 12	Ivan Rodriguez	8.00	3.60
❑ 13	Juan Guzman	1.00	.45
❑ 14	Steve Chitren	1.00	.45
❑ 15	Mark Wohlers	1.00	.45
❑ 16	Wes Chamberlain	1.00	.45
❑ 17	Ray Lankford	4.00	1.80
❑ 18	Chito Martinez	1.00	.45
❑ 19	Phil Plantier	1.00	.45
❑ 20	Scott Leius UER	1.00	.45
	(Misspelled Lieus on card front)		

1992 Fleer Smoke 'n Heat

	MINT	NRMT
COMPLETE SET (12)	10.00	4.50
COMMON CARD (S1-S12)	.50	.23

ONE SET PER RETAIL FACTORY SET

❑ S1	Lee Smith	.75	.35
❑ S2	Jack McDowell	.50	.23

❑ S3	David Cone	.75	.35
❑ S4	Roger Clemens	4.00	1.80
❑ S5	Nolan Ryan	6.00	2.70
❑ S6	Scott Erickson	.75	.35
❑ S7	Tom Glavine	1.00	.45
❑ S8	Dwight Gooden	.75	.35
❑ S9	Andy Benes	.75	.35
❑ S10	Steve Avery	.50	.23
❑ S11	Randy Johnson	1.50	.70
❑ S12	Jim Abbott	.75	.35

1992 Fleer Team Leaders

	MINT	NRMT
COMPLETE SET (20)	40.00	18.00
COMMON CARD (1-20)	1.00	.45

ONE TL OR CLEMENS PER RACK PACK

❑ 1	Don Mattingly	6.00	2.70
❑ 2	Howard Johnson	1.00	.45
❑ 3	Chris Sabo UER	1.00	.45
	(Where he it, should be Where he hit)		
❑ 4	Carlton Fisk	4.00	1.80
❑ 5	Kirby Puckett	5.00	2.20
❑ 6	Cecil Fielder	2.00	.90
❑ 7	Tony Gwynn	8.00	3.60
❑ 8	Will Clark	4.00	1.80
❑ 9	Bobby Bonilla	2.00	.90
❑ 10	Len Dykstra	2.00	.90
❑ 11	Tom Glavine	2.50	1.10
❑ 12	Rafael Palmeiro	4.00	1.80
❑ 13	Wade Boggs	4.00	1.80
❑ 14	Joe Carter	2.00	.90
❑ 15	Ken Griffey Jr.	20.00	9.00
❑ 16	Darryl Strawberry	2.00	.90
❑ 17	Cal Ripken	12.00	5.50
❑ 18	Danny Tartabull	1.00	.45
❑ 19	Jose Canseco	4.00	1.80
❑ 20	Andre Dawson	2.50	1.10

1992 Fleer Update

	MINT	NRMT
COMP.FACT.SET (136)	150.00	70.00
COMPLETE SET (132)	140.00	65.00
COMMON CARD (U1-U132)	.25	.11
MINOR STARS	.75	.35
SEMISTARS	1.50	.70

		MINT	NRMT
❏ 1	Todd Frohwirth	.25	.11
❏ 2	Alan Mills	.25	.11
❏ 3	Rick Sutcliffe	.25	.11
❏ 4	John Valentin	2.50	1.10
❏ 5	Frank Viola	.25	.11
❏ 6	Bob Zupcic	.25	.11
❏ 7	Mike Butcher	.25	.11
❏ 8	Chad Curtis	1.50	.70
❏ 9	Damion Easley	1.50	.70
❏ 10	Tim Salmon	12.00	5.50
❏ 11	Julio Valera	.25	.11
❏ 12	George Bell	.25	.11
❏ 13	Roberto Hernandez	1.50	.70
❏ 14	Shawn Jeter	.25	.11
❏ 15	Thomas Howard	.25	.11
❏ 16	Jesse Levis	.25	.11
❏ 17	Kenny Lofton	10.00	4.50
❏ 18	Paul Sorrento	.25	.11
❏ 19	Rico Brogna	.75	.35
❏ 20	John Doherty	.25	.11
❏ 21	Dan Gladden	.25	.11
❏ 22	Buddy Groom	.25	.11
❏ 23	Shawn Hare	.25	.11
❏ 24	John Kiely	.25	.11
❏ 25	Kurt Knudsen	.25	.11
❏ 26	Gregg Jefferies	.25	.11
❏ 27	Wally Joyner	.75	.35
❏ 28	Kevin Koslofski	.25	.11
❏ 29	Kevin McReynolds	.25	.11
❏ 30	Rusty Meacham	.25	.11
❏ 31	Keith Miller	.25	.11
❏ 32	Hipolito Pichardo	.25	.11
❏ 33	James Austin	.25	.11
❏ 34	Scott Fletcher	.25	.11
❏ 35	John Jaha	2.50	1.10
❏ 36	Pat Listach	.25	.11
❏ 37	Dave Nilsson	2.50	1.10
❏ 38	Kevin Seitzer	.25	.11
❏ 39	Tom Edens	.25	.11
❏ 40	Pat Mahomes	.25	.11
❏ 41	John Smiley	.25	.11
❏ 42	Charlie Hayes	.25	.11
❏ 43	Sam Militello	.25	.11
❏ 44	Andy Stankiewicz	.25	.11
❏ 45	Danny Tartabull	.25	.11
❏ 46	Bob Wickman	.25	.11
❏ 47	Jerry Browne	.25	.11
❏ 48	Kevin Campbell	.25	.11
❏ 49	Vince Horsman	.25	.11
❏ 50	Troy Neel	.25	.11
❏ 51	Ruben Sierra	.25	.11
❏ 52	Bruce Walton	.25	.11
❏ 53	Willie Wilson	.25	.11
❏ 54	Bret Boone	4.00	1.80
❏ 55	Dave Fleming	.25	.11
❏ 56	Kevin Mitchell	.75	.35
❏ 57	Jeff Nelson	.25	.11
❏ 58	Shane Turner	.25	.11
❏ 59	Jose Canseco	3.00	1.35
❏ 60	Jeff Frye	.25	.11
❏ 61	Danny Leon	.25	.11
❏ 62	Roger Pavlik	.25	.11
❏ 63	David Cone	.75	.35
❏ 64	Pat Hentgen	2.00	.90
❏ 65	Randy Knorr	.25	.11
❏ 66	Jack Morris	.75	.35
❏ 67	Dave Winfield	2.00	.90
❏ 68	David Nied	.25	.11
❏ 69	Otis Nixon	.75	.35
❏ 70	Alejandro Pena	.25	.11
❏ 71	Jeff Reardon	.75	.35
❏ 72	Alex Arias	.25	.11
❏ 73	Jim Bullinger	.25	.11
❏ 74	Mike Morgan	.25	.11
❏ 75	Rey Sanchez	.25	.11
❏ 76	Bob Scanlan	.25	.11
❏ 77	Sammy Sosa	10.00	4.50
❏ 78	Scott Bankhead	.25	.11
❏ 79	Tim Belcher	.25	.11
❏ 80	Steve Foster	.25	.11
❏ 81	Willie Greene	.25	.11
❏ 82	Bip Roberts	.25	.11
❏ 83	Scott Ruskin	.25	.11
❏ 84	Greg Swindell	.25	.11
❏ 85	Juan Guerrero	.25	.11
❏ 86	Butch Henry	.25	.11
❏ 87	Doug Jones	.25	.11
❏ 88	Brian Williams	.25	.11
❏ 89	Tom Candiotti	.25	.11
❏ 90	Eric Davis	.75	.35
❏ 91	Carlos Hernandez	.25	.11
❏ 92	Mike Piazza	100.00	45.00
❏ 93	Mike Sharperson	.25	.11
❏ 94	Eric Young	1.50	.70
❏ 95	Moises Alou	5.00	2.20
❏ 96	Greg Colbrunn	.25	.11
❏ 97	Wil Cordero	.25	.11
❏ 98	Ken Hill	.25	.11
❏ 99	John Vander Wal	.25	.11
❏ 100	John Wetteland	.75	.35
❏ 101	Bobby Bonilla	.75	.35
❏ 102	Eric Hillman	.25	.11
❏ 103	Pat Howell	.25	.11
❏ 104	Jeff Kent	5.00	2.20
❏ 105	Dick Schofield	.25	.11
❏ 106	Ryan Thompson	.25	.11
❏ 107	Chico Walker	.25	.11
❏ 108	Juan Bell	.25	.11
❏ 109	Mariano Duncan	.25	.11
❏ 110	Jeff Grotewold	.25	.11
❏ 111	Ben Rivera	.25	.11
❏ 112	Curt Schilling	5.00	2.20
❏ 113	Victor Cole	.25	.11
❏ 114	Al Martin	1.50	.70
❏ 115	Roger Mason	.25	.11
❏ 116	Blas Minor	.25	.11
❏ 117	Tim Wakefield	1.50	.70
❏ 118	Mark Clark	.25	.11
❏ 119	Rheal Cormier	.25	.11
❏ 120	Donovan Osborne	.25	.11
❏ 121	Todd Worrell	.25	.11
❏ 122	Jeremy Hernandez	.25	.11
❏ 123	Randy Myers	.75	.35
❏ 124	Frank Seminara	.25	.11
❏ 125	Gary Sheffield	2.00	.90
❏ 126	Dan Walters	.25	.11
❏ 127	Steve Hosey	.25	.11
❏ 128	Mike Jackson	.75	.35
❏ 129	Jim Pena	.25	.11
❏ 130	Cory Snyder	.25	.11
❏ 131	Bill Swift	.25	.11
❏ 132	Checklist U1-U132	.25	.11

1992 Fleer Update Headliners

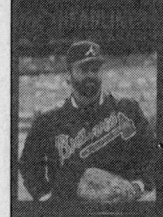

	MINT	NRMT
COMPLETE SET (4)	10.00	4.50
COMMON CARD (1-528)	.25	.11
ONE SET PER FACTORY SET		

		MINT	NRMT
❏ 1	Ken Griffey Jr.	10.00	4.50
❏ 2	Robin Yount	1.50	.70
❏ 3	Jeff Reardon	.25	.11
❏ 4	Cecil Fielder	.50	.23

1993 Fleer

	MINT	NRMT
COMPLETE SET (720)	40.00	18.00
COMPLETE SERIES 1 (360)	20.00	9.00
COMPLETE SERIES 2 (360)	20.00	9.00
COMMON CARD (1-720)	.10	.05

		MINT	NRMT
MINOR STARS		.20	.09
UNLISTED STARS		.40	.18
❏ 1	Steve Avery	.10	.05
❏ 2	Sid Bream	.10	.05
❏ 3	Ron Gant	.20	.09
❏ 4	Tom Glavine	.30	.14
❏ 5	Brian Hunter	.10	.05
❏ 6	Ryan Klesko	.40	.18
❏ 7	Charlie Leibrandt	.10	.05
❏ 8	Kent Mercker	.10	.05
❏ 9	David Nied	.10	.05
❏ 10	Otis Nixon	.10	.05
❏ 11	Greg Olson	.10	.05
❏ 12	Terry Pendleton	.10	.05
❏ 13	Deion Sanders	.30	.14
❏ 14	John Smoltz	.30	.14
❏ 15	Mike Stanton	.10	.05
❏ 16	Mark Wohlers	.10	.05
❏ 17	Paul Assenmacher	.10	.05
❏ 18	Steve Buechele	.10	.05
❏ 19	Shawon Dunston	.10	.05
❏ 20	Mark Grace	.30	.14
❏ 21	Derrick May	.10	.05
❏ 22	Chuck McElroy	.10	.05
❏ 23	Mike Morgan	.10	.05
❏ 24	Rey Sanchez	.10	.05
❏ 25	Ryne Sandberg	.50	.23
❏ 26	Bob Scanlan	.10	.05
❏ 27	Sammy Sosa	1.25	.55
❏ 28	Rick Wilkins	.10	.05
❏ 29	Bobby Ayala	.10	.05
❏ 30	Tim Belcher	.10	.05
❏ 31	Jeff Branson	.10	.05
❏ 32	Norm Charlton	.10	.05
❏ 33	Steve Foster	.10	.05
❏ 34	Willie Greene	.10	.05
❏ 35	Chris Hammond	.10	.05
❏ 36	Milt Hill	.10	.05
❏ 37	Hal Morris	.10	.05
❏ 38	Joe Oliver	.10	.05
❏ 39	Paul O'Neill	.20	.09
❏ 40	Tim Pugh	.10	.05
❏ 41	Jose Rijo	.10	.05
❏ 42	Bip Roberts	.10	.05
❏ 43	Chris Sabo	.10	.05
❏ 44	Reggie Sanders	.20	.09
❏ 45	Eric Anthony	.10	.05
❏ 46	Jeff Bagwell	.50	.23
❏ 47	Craig Biggio	.40	.18
❏ 48	Joe Boever	.10	.05
❏ 49	Casey Candaele	.10	.05
❏ 50	Steve Finley	.20	.09
❏ 51	Luis Gonzalez	.20	.09
❏ 52	Pete Harnisch	.10	.05
❏ 53	Xavier Hernandez	.10	.05
❏ 54	Doug Jones	.10	.05
❏ 55	Eddie Taubensee	.10	.05
❏ 56	Brian Williams	.10	.05
❏ 57	Pedro Astacio	.20	.09
❏ 58	Todd Benzinger	.10	.05
❏ 59	Brett Butler	.20	.09
❏ 60	Tom Candiotti	.10	.05
❏ 61	Lenny Harris	.10	.05
❏ 62	Carlos Hernandez	.10	.05
❏ 63	Orel Hershiser	.20	.09
❏ 64	Eric Karros	.30	.14
❏ 65	Ramon Martinez	.20	.09

66	Jose Offerman	.20	.09
67	Mike Scioscia	.10	.05
68	Mike Sharperson	.10	.05
69	Eric Young	.40	.18
70	Moises Alou	.20	.09
71	Ivan Calderon	.10	.05
72	Archi Cianfrocco	.10	.05
73	Wil Cordero	.10	.05
74	Delino DeShields	.20	.09
75	Mark Gardner	.10	.05
76	Ken Hill	.10	.05
77	Tim Laker	.10	.05
78	Chris Nabholz	.10	.05
79	Mel Rojas	.10	.05
80	John Vander Wal UER	.10	.05
	(Misspelled Vander Wall in letters on back)		
81	Larry Walker	.40	.18
82	Tim Wallach	.10	.05
83	John Wetteland	.20	.09
84	Bobby Bonilla	.20	.09
85	Daryl Boston	.10	.05
86	Sid Fernandez	.10	.05
87	Eric Hillman	.10	.05
88	Todd Hundley	.30	.14
89	Howard Johnson	.10	.05
90	Jeff Kent	.20	.09
91	Eddie Murray	.40	.18
92	Bill Pecota	.10	.05
93	Bret Saberhagen	.20	.09
94	Dick Schofield	.10	.05
95	Pete Schourek	.10	.05
96	Anthony Young	.10	.05
97	Ruben Amaro	.10	.05
98	Juan Bell	.10	.05
99	Wes Chamberlain	.10	.05
100	Darren Daulton	.20	.09
101	Mariano Duncan	.10	.05
102	Mike Hartley	.10	.05
103	Ricky Jordan	.10	.05
104	John Kruk	.20	.09
105	Mickey Morandini	.10	.05
106	Terry Mulholland	.10	.05
107	Ben Rivera	.10	.05
108	Curt Schilling	.20	.09
109	Keith Shepherd	.10	.05
110	Stan Belinda	.10	.05
111	Jay Bell	.20	.09
112	Barry Bonds	.50	.23
113	Jeff King	.10	.05
114	Mike LaValliere	.10	.05
115	Jose Lind	.10	.05
116	Roger Mason	.10	.05
117	Orlando Merced	.10	.05
118	Bob Patterson	.10	.05
119	Don Slaught	.10	.05
120	Zane Smith	.10	.05
121	Randy Tomlin	.10	.05
122	Andy Van Slyke	.20	.09
123	Tim Wakefield	.20	.09
124	Rheal Cormier	.10	.05
125	Bernard Gilkey	.10	.05
126	Felix Jose	.10	.05
127	Ray Lankford	.30	.14
128	Bob McClure	.10	.05
129	Donovan Osborne	.10	.05
130	Tom Pagnozzi	.10	.05
131	Geronimo Pena	.10	.05
132	Mike Perez	.10	.05
133	Lee Smith	.20	.09
134	Bob Tewksbury	.10	.05
135	Todd Worrell	.10	.05
136	Todd Zeile	.10	.05
137	Jerald Clark	.10	.05
138	Tony Gwynn	1.00	.45
139	Greg W. Harris	.10	.05
140	Jeremy Hernandez	.10	.05
141	Darrin Jackson	.10	.05
142	Mike Maddux	.10	.05
143	Fred McGriff	.30	.14
144	Jose Melendez	.10	.05
145	Rich Rodriguez	.10	.05
146	Frank Seminara	.10	.05
147	Gary Sheffield	.40	.18
148	Kurt Stillwell	.10	.05
149	Dan Walters	.10	.05
150	Rod Beck	.20	.09
151	Bud Black	.10	.05
152	Jeff Brantley	.10	.05
153	John Burkett	.10	.05
154	Will Clark	.40	.18
155	Royce Clayton	.10	.05
156	Mike Jackson	.20	.05
157	Darren Lewis	.10	.05
158	Kirt Manwaring	.10	.05
159	Willie McGee	.20	.09
160	Cory Snyder	.10	.05
161	Bill Swift	.10	.05
162	Trevor Wilson	.10	.05
163	Brady Anderson	.20	.09
164	Glenn Davis	.10	.05
165	Mike Devereaux	.10	.05
166	Todd Frohwirth	.10	.05
167	Leo Gomez	.10	.05
168	Chris Hoiles	.20	.09
169	Ben McDonald	.10	.05
170	Randy Milligan	.10	.05
171	Alan Mills	.10	.05
172	Mike Mussina	.40	.18
173	Gregg Olson	.10	.05
174	Arthur Rhodes	.20	.09
175	David Segui	.10	.05
176	Ellis Burks	.10	.09
177	Roger Clemens	1.00	.45
178	Scott Cooper	.10	.05
179	Danny Darwin	.10	.05
180	Tony Fossas	.10	.05
181	Paul Quantrill	.10	.05
182	Jody Reed	.10	.05
183	John Valentin	.20	.09
184	Mo Vaughn	.40	.18
185	Frank Viola	.10	.05
186	Bob Zupcic	.10	.05
187	Jim Abbott	.20	.09
188	Gary DiSarcina	.10	.05
189	Damion Easley	.10	.05
190	Junior Felix	.10	.05
191	Chuck Finley	.20	.09
192	Joe Grahe	.10	.05
193	Bryan Harvey	.10	.05
194	Mark Langston	.10	.05
195	John Orton	.10	.05
196	Luis Polonia	.10	.05
197	Tim Salmon	.40	.18
198	Luis Sojo	.10	.05
199	Wilson Alvarez	.20	.09
200	George Bell	.20	.09
201	Alex Fernandez	.20	.09
202	Craig Grebeck	.10	.05
203	Ozzie Guillen	.10	.05
204	Lance Johnson	.10	.05
205	Ron Karkovice	.10	.05
206	Kirk McCaskill	.10	.05
207	Jack McDowell	.20	.09
208	Scott Radinsky	.10	.05
209	Tim Raines	.20	.09
210	Frank Thomas	.75	.35
211	Robin Ventura	.20	.09
212	Sandy Alomar Jr.	.20	.09
213	Carlos Baerga	.20	.09
214	Dennis Cook	.10	.05
215	Thomas Howard	.10	.05
216	Mark Lewis	.10	.05
217	Derek Lilliquist	.10	.05
218	Kenny Lofton	.40	.18
219	Charles Nagy	.20	.09
220	Steve Olin	.10	.05
221	Paul Sorrento	.10	.05
222	Jim Thome	.50	.23
223	Mark Whiten	.10	.05
224	Milt Cuyler	.10	.05
225	Rob Deer	.10	.05
226	John Doherty	.10	.05
227	Cecil Fielder	.20	.09
228	Travis Fryman	.20	.09
229	Mike Henneman	.10	.05
230	John Kelly UER	.10	.05
	(Card has batting stats of Pat Kelly)		
231	Kurt Knudsen	.10	.05
232	Scott Livingstone	.10	.05
233	Tony Phillips	.10	.05
234	Mickey Tettleton	.10	.05
235	Kevin Appier	.20	.09
236	George Brett	.75	.35
237	Tom Gordon	.10	.05
238	Gregg Jefferies	.10	.05
239	Wally Joyner	.20	.09
240	Kevin Koslofski	.10	.05
241	Mike Macfarlane	.10	.05
242	Brian McRae	.10	.05
243	Rusty Meacham	.10	.05
244	Keith Miller	.10	.05
245	Jeff Montgomery	.20	.09
246	Hipolito Pichardo	.10	.05
247	Ricky Bones	.10	.05
248	Cal Eldred	.20	.09
249	Mike Fetters	.10	.05
250	Darryl Hamilton	.10	.05
251	Doug Henry	.10	.05
252	John Jaha	.20	.09
253	Pat Listach	.10	.05
254	Paul Molitor	.40	.18
255	Jaime Navarro	.10	.05
256	Kevin Seitzer	.10	.05
257	B.J. Surhoff	.20	.09
258	Greg Vaughn	.20	.09
259	Bill Wegman	.10	.05
260	Robin Yount	.30	.14
261	Rick Aguilera	.10	.05
262	Chili Davis	.20	.09
263	Scott Erickson	.10	.05
264	Greg Gagne	.10	.05
265	Mark Guthrie	.10	.05
266	Brian Harper	.10	.05
267	Kent Hrbek	.20	.09
268	Terry Jorgensen	.10	.05
269	Gene Larkin	.10	.05
270	Scott Leius	.10	.05
271	Pat Mahomes	.10	.05
272	Pedro Munoz	.10	.05
273	Kirby Puckett	.60	.25
274	Kevin Tapani	.10	.05
275	Carl Willis	.10	.05
276	Steve Farr	.10	.05
277	John Habyan	.10	.05
278	Mel Hall	.10	.05
279	Charlie Hayes	.10	.05
280	Pat Kelly	.10	.05
281	Don Mattingly	.75	.35
282	Sam Militello	.10	.05
283	Matt Nokes	.10	.05
284	Melido Perez	.10	.05
285	Andy Stankiewicz	.10	.05
286	Danny Tartabull	.20	.09
287	Randy Velarde	.10	.05
288	Bob Wickman	.10	.05
289	Bernie Williams	.40	.18
290	Lance Blankenship	.10	.05
291	Mike Bordick	.10	.05
292	Jerry Browne	.10	.05
293	Dennis Eckersley	.20	.09
294	Rickey Henderson	.50	.23
295	Vince Horsman	.10	.05
296	Mark McGwire	2.00	.90
297	Jeff Parrett	.10	.05
298	Ruben Sierra	.20	.09
299	Terry Steinbach	.10	.05
300	Walt Weiss	.10	.05
301	Bob Welch	.10	.05
302	Willie Wilson	.10	.05
303	Bobby Witt	.10	.05
304	Bret Boone	.20	.09
305	Jay Buhner	.30	.14
306	Dave Fleming	.10	.05
307	Ken Griffey Jr.	2.00	.90
308	Erik Hanson	.10	.05
309	Edgar Martinez	.30	.14
310	Tino Martinez	.40	.18
311	Jeff Nelson	.10	.05
312	Dennis Powell	.10	.05
313	Mike Schooler	.10	.05
314	Russ Swan	.10	.05
315	Dave Valle	.10	.05
316	Omar Vizquel	.20	.09
317	Kevin Brown	.30	.14
318	Todd Burns	.10	.05
319	Jose Canseco	.50	.23

320	Julio Franco	.10	.05
321	Jeff Frye	.10	.05
322	Juan Gonzalez	.75	.35
323	Jose Guzman	.10	.05
324	Jeff Huson	.10	.05
325	Dean Palmer	.20	.09
326	Kevin Reimer	.10	.05
327	Ivan Rodriguez	.50	.23
328	Kenny Rogers	.10	.05
329	Dan Smith	.10	.05
330	Roberto Alomar	.40	.18
331	Derek Bell	.20	.09
332	Pat Borders	.10	.05
333	Joe Carter	.20	.09
334	Kelly Gruber	.10	.05
335	Tom Henke	.10	.05
336	Jimmy Key	.20	.09
337	Manuel Lee	.10	.05
338	Candy Maldonado	.10	.05
339	John Olerud	.30	.14
340	Todd Stottlemyre	.10	.05
341	Duane Ward	.10	.05
342	Devon White	.10	.05
343	Dave Winfield	.30	.14
344	Edgar Martinez LL	.20	.09
345	Cecil Fielder LL	.10	.05
346	Kenny Lofton LL	.20	.09
347	Jack Morris LL	.10	.05
348	Roger Clemens LL	.50	.23
349	Fred McGriff RT	.20	.09
350	Barry Bonds RT	.30	.14
351	Gary Sheffield RT	.10	.05
352	Darren Daulton RT	.10	.05
353	Dave Hollins RT	.10	.05
354	Brothers in Blue	.50	.23
	Pedro Martinez		
	Ramon Martinez		
355	Power Packs	.50	.23
	Ivan Rodriguez		
	Kirby Puckett		
356	Triple Threats	1.00	.45
	Ryne Sandberg		
	Gary Sheffield		
357	Infield Trifecta	.40	.18
	Roberto Alomar		
	Chuck Knoblauch		
	Carlos Baerga		
358	Checklist 1-120	.10	.05
359	Checklist 121-240	.10	.05
360	Checklist 241-360	.10	.05
361	Rafael Belliard	.10	.05
362	Damon Berryhill	.10	.05
363	Mike Bielecki	.10	.05
364	Jeff Blauser	.10	.05
365	Francisco Cabrera	.10	.05
366	Marvin Freeman	.10	.05
367	David Justice	.40	.18
368	Mark Lemke	.10	.05
369	Alejandro Pena	.10	.05
370	Jeff Reardon	.20	.09
371	Lonnie Smith	.10	.05
372	Pete Smith	.10	.05
373	Shawn Boskie	.10	.05
374	Jim Bullinger	.10	.05
375	Frank Castillo	.10	.05
376	Doug Dascenzo	.10	.05
377	Andre Dawson	.30	.14
378	Mike Harkey	.10	.05
379	Greg Hibbard	.10	.05
380	Greg Maddux	1.00	.45
381	Ken Patterson	.10	.05
382	Jeff D. Robinson	.10	.05
383	Luis Salazar	.10	.05
384	Dwight Smith	.10	.05
385	Jose Vizcaino	.10	.05
386	Scott Bankhead	.10	.05
387	Tom Browning	.10	.05
388	Darnell Coles	.10	.05
389	Rob Dibble	.10	.05
390	Bill Doran	.10	.05
391	Dwayne Henry	.10	.05
392	Cesar Hernandez	.10	.05
393	Roberto Kelly	.20	.09
394	Barry Larkin	.40	.18
395	Dave Martinez	.10	.05
396	Kevin Mitchell	.20	.09
397	Jeff Reed	.10	.05
398	Scott Ruskin	.10	.05
399	Greg Swindell	.10	.05
400	Dan Wilson	.20	.09
401	Andy Ashby	.20	.09
402	Freddie Benavides	.10	.05
403	Dante Bichette	.20	.09
404	Willie Blair	.10	.05
405	Denis Boucher	.10	.05
406	Vinny Castilla	.50	.23
407	Braulio Castillo	.10	.05
408	Alex Cole	.10	.05
409	Andres Galarraga	.40	.18
410	Joe Girardi	.20	.09
411	Butch Henry	.10	.05
412	Darren Holmes	.10	.05
413	Calvin Jones	.10	.05
414	Steve Reed	.10	.05
415	Kevin Ritz	.10	.05
416	Jim Tatum	.10	.05
417	Jack Armstrong	.10	.05
418	Bret Barberie	.10	.05
419	Ryan Bowen	.10	.05
420	Cris Carpenter	.10	.05
421	Chuck Carr	.10	.05
422	Scott Chiamparino	.10	.05
423	Jeff Conine	.10	.05
424	Jim Corsi	.10	.05
425	Steve Decker	.10	.05
426	Chris Donnels	.10	.05
427	Monty Fariss	.10	.05
428	Bob Natal	.10	.05
429	Pat Rapp	.10	.05
430	Dave Weathers	.10	.05
431	Nigel Wilson	.10	.05
432	Ken Caminiti	.30	.14
433	Andujar Cedeno	.10	.05
434	Tom Edens	.10	.05
435	Juan Guerrero	.10	.05
436	Pete Incaviglia	.10	.05
437	Jimmy Jones	.10	.05
438	Darryl Kile	.10	.05
439	Rob Murphy	.10	.05
440	Al Osuna	.10	.05
441	Mark Portugal	.10	.05
442	Scott Servais	.10	.05
443	John Candelaria	.10	.05
444	Tim Crews	.10	.05
445	Eric Davis	.20	.09
446	Tom Goodwin	.10	.05
447	Jim Gott	.10	.05
448	Kevin Gross	.10	.05
449	Dave Hansen	.10	.05
450	Jay Howell	.10	.05
451	Roger McDowell	.10	.05
452	Bob Ojeda	.10	.05
453	Henry Rodriguez	.20	.09
454	Darryl Strawberry	.20	.09
455	Mitch Webster	.10	.05
456	Steve Wilson	.10	.05
457	Brian Barnes	.10	.05
458	Sean Berry	.10	.05
459	Jeff Fassero	.10	.05
460	Darrin Fletcher	.10	.05
461	Marquis Grissom	.20	.09
462	Dennis Martinez	.20	.09
463	Spike Owen	.10	.05
464	Matt Stairs	.30	.14
465	Sergio Valdez	.10	.05
466	Kevin Bass	.10	.05
467	Vince Coleman	.10	.05
468	Mark Dewey	.10	.05
469	Kevin Elster	.10	.05
470	Tony Fernandez	.20	.09
471	John Franco	.10	.05
472	Dave Gallagher	.10	.05
473	Paul Gibson	.10	.05
474	Dwight Gooden	.20	.09
475	Lee Guetterman	.10	.05
476	Jeff Innis	.10	.05
477	Dave Magadan	.10	.05
478	Charlie O'Brien	.10	.05
479	Willie Randolph	.20	.09
480	Mackey Sasser	.10	.05
481	Ryan Thompson	.10	.05
482	Chico Walker	.10	.05
483	Kyle Abbott	.10	.05
484	Bob Ayrault	.10	.05
485	Kim Batiste	.10	.05
486	Cliff Brantley	.10	.05
487	Jose DeLeon	.10	.05
488	Len Dykstra	.20	.09
489	Tommy Greene	.10	.05
490	Jeff Grotewold	.10	.05
491	Dave Hollins	.10	.05
492	Danny Jackson	.10	.05
493	Stan Javier	.10	.05
494	Tom Marsh	.10	.05
495	Greg Mathews	.10	.05
496	Dale Murphy	.30	.14
497	Todd Pratt	.25	.11
498	Mitch Williams	.10	.05
499	Danny Cox	.10	.05
500	Doug Drabek	.10	.05
501	Carlos Garcia	.10	.05
502	Lloyd McClendon	.10	.05
503	Denny Neagle	.20	.09
504	Gary Redus	.10	.05
505	Bob Walk	.10	.05
506	John Wehner	.10	.05
507	Luis Alicea	.10	.05
508	Mark Clark	.10	.05
509	Pedro Guerrero	.10	.05
510	Rex Hudler	.10	.05
511	Brian Jordan	.20	.09
512	Omar Olivares	.10	.05
513	Jose Oquendo	.10	.05
514	Gerald Perry	.10	.05
515	Bryn Smith	.10	.05
516	Craig Wilson	.10	.05
517	Tracy Woodson	.10	.05
518	Larry Andersen	.10	.05
519	Andy Benes	.20	.09
520	Jim Deshaies	.10	.05
521	Bruce Hurst	.10	.05
522	Randy Myers	.20	.09
523	Benito Santiago	.10	.05
524	Tim Scott	.10	.05
525	Tim Teufel	.10	.05
526	Mike Benjamin	.10	.05
527	Dave Burba	.10	.05
528	Craig Colbert	.10	.05
529	Mike Felder	.10	.05
530	Bryan Hickerson	.10	.05
531	Chris James	.10	.05
532	Mark Leonard	.10	.05
533	Greg Litton	.10	.05
534	Francisco Oliveras	.10	.05
535	John Patterson	.10	.05
536	Jim Pena	.10	.05
537	Dave Righetti	.10	.05
538	Robby Thompson	.10	.05
539	Jose Uribe	.10	.05
540	Matt Williams	.30	.14
541	Storm Davis	.10	.05
542	Sam Horn	.10	.05
543	Tim Hulett	.10	.05
544	Craig Lefferts	.10	.05
545	Chito Martinez	.10	.05
546	Mark McLemore	.10	.05
547	Luis Mercedes	.10	.05
548	Bob Milacki	.10	.05
549	Joe Orsulak	.10	.05
550	Billy Ripken	.10	.05
551	Cal Ripken Jr.	1.50	.70
552	Rick Sutcliffe	.10	.05
553	Jeff Tackett	.10	.05
554	Wade Boggs	.40	.18
555	Tom Brunansky	.10	.05
556	Jack Clark	.10	.05
557	John Dopson	.10	.05
558	Mike Gardiner	.10	.05
559	Mike Greenwell	.10	.05
560	Greg A. Harris	.10	.05
561	Billy Hatcher	.10	.05
562	Joe Hesketh	.10	.05
563	Tony Pena	.10	.05
564	Phil Plantier	.10	.05
565	Luis Rivera	.10	.05
566	Herm Winningham	.10	.05
567	Matt Young	.10	.05
568	Bert Blyleven	.20	.09

❑ 569	Mike Butcher	.10	.05
❑ 570	Chuck Crim	.10	.05
❑ 571	Chad Curtis	.20	.09
❑ 572	Tim Fortugno	.10	.05
❑ 573	Steve Frey	.10	.05
❑ 574	Gary Gaetti	.20	.09
❑ 575	Scott Lewis	.10	.05
❑ 576	Lee Stevens	.20	.09
❑ 577	Ron Tingley	.10	.05
❑ 578	Julio Valera	.10	.05
❑ 579	Shawn Abner	.10	.05
❑ 580	Joey Cora	.10	.05
❑ 581	Chris Cron	.10	.05
❑ 582	Carlton Fisk	.40	.18
❑ 583	Roberto Hernandez	.20	.09
❑ 584	Charlie Hough	.20	.09
❑ 585	Terry Leach	.10	.05
❑ 586	Donn Pall	.10	.05
❑ 587	Dan Pasqua	.10	.05
❑ 588	Steve Sax	.10	.05
❑ 589	Bobby Thigpen	.10	.05
❑ 590	Albert Belle	.40	.18
❑ 591	Felix Fermin	.10	.05
❑ 592	Glenallen Hill	.10	.05
❑ 593	Brook Jacoby	.10	.05
❑ 594	Reggie Jefferson	.20	.09
❑ 595	Carlos Martinez	.10	.05
❑ 596	Jose Mesa	.10	.05
❑ 597	Rod Nichols	.10	.05
❑ 598	Junior Ortiz	.10	.05
❑ 599	Eric Plunk	.10	.05
❑ 600	Ted Power	.10	.05
❑ 601	Scott Scudder	.10	.05
❑ 602	Kevin Wickander	.10	.05
❑ 603	Skeeter Barnes	.10	.05
❑ 604	Mark Carreon	.10	.05
❑ 605	Dan Gladden	.10	.05
❑ 606	Bill Gullickson	.10	.05
❑ 607	Chad Kreuter	.10	.05
❑ 608	Mark Leiter	.10	.05
❑ 609	Mike Munoz	.10	.05
❑ 610	Rich Rowland	.10	.05
❑ 611	Frank Tanana	.10	.05
❑ 612	Walt Terrell	.10	.05
❑ 613	Alan Trammell	.30	.14
❑ 614	Lou Whitaker	.20	.09
❑ 615	Luis Aquino	.10	.05
❑ 616	Mike Boddicker	.10	.05
❑ 617	Jim Eisenreich	.10	.05
❑ 618	Mark Gubicza	.10	.05
❑ 619	David Howard	.10	.05
❑ 620	Mike Magnante	.10	.05
❑ 621	Brent Mayne	.10	.05
❑ 622	Kevin McReynolds	.10	.05
❑ 623	Ed Pierce	.10	.05
❑ 624	Bill Sampen	.10	.05
❑ 625	Steve Shifflett	.10	.05
❑ 626	Gary Thurman	.10	.05
❑ 627	Curt Wilkerson	.10	.05
❑ 628	Chris Bosio	.10	.05
❑ 629	Scott Fletcher	.10	.05
❑ 630	Jim Gantner	.10	.05
❑ 631	Dave Nilsson	.20	.09
❑ 632	Jesse Orosco	.10	.05
❑ 633	Dan Plesac	.10	.05
❑ 634	Ron Robinson	.10	.05
❑ 635	Bill Spiers	.10	.05
❑ 636	Franklin Stubbs	.10	.05
❑ 637	Willie Banks	.10	.05
❑ 638	Randy Bush	.10	.05
❑ 639	Chuck Knoblauch	.40	.18
❑ 640	Shane Mack	.10	.05
❑ 641	Mike Pagliarulo	.10	.05
❑ 642	Jeff Reboulet	.10	.05
❑ 643	John Smiley	.10	.05
❑ 644	Mike Trombley	.10	.05
❑ 645	Gary Wayne	.10	.05
❑ 646	Lenny Webster	.10	.05
❑ 647	Tim Burke	.10	.05
❑ 648	Mike Gallego	.10	.05
❑ 649	Dion James	.10	.05
❑ 650	Jeff Johnson	.10	.05
❑ 651	Scott Kamieniecki	.10	.05
❑ 652	Kevin Maas	.10	.05
❑ 653	Rich Monteleone	.10	.05
❑ 654	Jerry Nielsen	.10	.05

❑ 655	Scott Sanderson	.10	.05
❑ 656	Mike Stanley	.10	.05
❑ 657	Gerald Williams	.10	.05
❑ 658	Curt Young	.10	.05
❑ 659	Harold Baines	.20	.09
❑ 660	Kevin Campbell	.10	.05
❑ 661	Ron Darling	.10	.05
❑ 662	Kelly Downs	.10	.05
❑ 663	Eric Fox	.10	.05
❑ 664	Dave Henderson	.10	.05
❑ 665	Rick Honeycutt	.10	.05
❑ 666	Mike Moore	.10	.05
❑ 667	Jamie Quirk	.10	.05
❑ 668	Jeff Russell	.10	.05
❑ 669	Dave Stewart	.20	.09
❑ 670	Walt Weiss	.10	.05
❑ 671	Dave Cochrane	.10	.05
❑ 672	Henry Cotto	.10	.05
❑ 673	Rich DeLucia	.10	.05
❑ 674	Brian Fisher	.10	.05
❑ 675	Mark Grant	.10	.05
❑ 676	Randy Johnson	.40	.18
❑ 677	Tim Leary	.10	.05
❑ 678	Pete O'Brien	.10	.05
❑ 679	Lance Parrish	.10	.05
❑ 680	Harold Reynolds	.10	.05
❑ 681	Shane Turner	.10	.05
❑ 682	Jack Daugherty	.10	.05
❑ 683	David Hulse	.10	.05
❑ 684	Terry Mathews	.10	.05
❑ 685	Al Newman	.10	.05
❑ 686	Edwin Nunez	.10	.05
❑ 687	Rafael Palmeiro	.40	.18
❑ 688	Roger Pavlik	.10	.05
❑ 689	Geno Petralli	.10	.05
❑ 690	Nolan Ryan	1.50	.70
❑ 691	David Cone	.30	.14
❑ 692	Alfredo Griffin	.10	.05
❑ 693	Juan Guzman	.10	.05
❑ 694	Pat Hentgen	.30	.14
❑ 695	Randy Knorr	.10	.05
❑ 696	Bob MacDonald	.10	.05
❑ 697	Jack Morris	.20	.09
❑ 698	Ed Sprague	.10	.05
❑ 699	Dave Stieb	.10	.05
❑ 700	Pat Tabler	.10	.05
❑ 701	Mike Timlin	.10	.05
❑ 702	David Wells	.20	.09
❑ 703	Eddie Zosky	.10	.05
❑ 704	Gary Sheffield LL	.20	.09
❑ 705	Darren Daulton LL	.10	.05
❑ 706	Marquis Grissom LL	.10	.05
❑ 707	Greg Maddux LL	.50	.23
❑ 708	Bill Swift LL	.10	.05
❑ 709	Juan Gonzalez RT	.40	.18
❑ 710	Mark McGwire RT	1.00	.45
❑ 711	Cecil Fielder RT	.20	.09
❑ 712	Albert Belle RT	.20	.09
❑ 713	Joe Carter RT	.10	.05
❑ 714	Cecil Fielder SS	.40	.18
	Frank Thomas		
	Power Brokers		
❑ 715	Larry Walker SS	.40	.18
	Darren Daulton		
	Unsung Heroes		
❑ 716	Edgar Martinez SS	.20	.09
	Robin Ventura		
	Hot Corner Hammers		
❑ 717	Roger Clemens SS	.40	.18
	Dennis Eckersley		
	Start to Finish		
❑ 718	Checklist 361-480	.10	.05
❑ 719	Checklist 481-600	.10	.05
❑ 720	Checklist 601-720	.10	.05

1993 Fleer All-Stars

	MINT	NRMT
COMPLETE SET (24)	40.00	18.00
COMPLETE SERIES 1 (12)	25.00	11.00
COMPLETE SERIES 2 (12)	15.00	6.75
COMMON CARD (AL1-NL12)	.50	.23
AL: RANDOM INSERTS IN SER.1 PACKS		
NL: RANDOM INSERTS IN SER.2 PACKS		

❑ AL1	Frank Thomas	5.00	2.20

❑ AL2	Roberto Alomar	2.50	1.10
❑ AL3	Edgar Martinez	1.50	.70
❑ AL4	Pat Listach	.50	.23
❑ AL5	Cecil Fielder	1.00	.45
❑ AL6	Juan Gonzalez	5.00	2.20
❑ AL7	Ken Griffey Jr.	12.00	5.50
❑ AL8	Joe Carter	1.00	.45
❑ AL9	Kirby Puckett	4.00	1.80
❑ AL10	Brian Harper	.50	.23
❑ AL11	Dave Fleming	.50	.23
❑ AL12	Jack McDowell	.50	.23
❑ NL1	Fred McGriff	1.50	.70
❑ NL2	Delino DeShields	.50	.23
❑ NL3	Gary Sheffield	2.50	1.10
❑ NL4	Barry Larkin	2.50	1.10
❑ NL5	Felix Jose	.50	.23
❑ NL6	Larry Walker	2.50	1.10
❑ NL7	Barry Bonds	3.00	1.35
❑ NL8	Andy Van Slyke	.50	.23
❑ NL9	Darren Daulton	1.00	.45
❑ NL10	Greg Maddux	6.00	2.70
❑ NL11	Tom Glavine	1.50	.70
❑ NL12	Lee Smith	1.00	.45

1993 Fleer Glavine

	MINT	NRMT
COMPLETE SET (12)	4.00	1.80
COMMON GLAVINE (1-12)	.50	.23
RANDOM INSERTS IN ALL PACKS		
COMMON MAIL-IN (13-15)	2.00	.90
MAIL-IN CARDS DIST.VIA WRAPPER EXCH.		

❑ 1	Tom Glavine	.50	.23
	The Glavine family ...		
	(Throwing to first)		
❑ 2	Tom Glavine	.50	.23
	High School baseball ...		
	(Pitching, with arm		
	behind head, shot from		
	left side)		
❑ 3	Tom Glavine	.50	.23
	Despite being drafted ...		
	(Pitching, close-up		
	shot from left side)		
❑ 4	Tom Glavine	.50	.23
	Unflappable is ...		
	(Pitching, shot from		
	almost directly in front)		
❑ 5	Tom Glavine	.50	.23
	In 1989 Tom ...		

(Pitching, shot from
right angle)

❏ 6	Tom Glavine .... .50		.23
	Tom Glavine had ...		
	(Pitching, with ball		
	below waist)		
❏ 7	Tom Glavine .... .50		.23
	Tom Glavine's dream ...		
	(Pitching, close-up shot		
	with ball behind head)		
❏ 8	Tom Glavine .... .50		.23
	After Winning ...		
	(Pitching, shot from		
	directly in front)		
❏ 9	Tom Glavine .... .50		.23
	Little Leaguers ...		
	(Pitching, just after re-		
	lease with left leg in air)		
❏ 10	Tom Glavine .... .50		.23
	Will success spoil ...		
	(Pitching, ball below		
	waist and right leg		
	slightly raised)		
❏ 11	Tom Glavine .... .50		.23
	What makes Tom ...		
	(Batting)		
❏ 12	Tom Glavine .... .50		.23
	It was a day ...		
	(Pitching, close-up shot		
	wearing dark blue top)		
❏ 13	Tom Glavine 2.00		.90
	Send-Off 1		
❏ 14	Tom Glavine 2.00		.90
	Send-Off 2		
❏ 15	Tom Glavine 2.00		.90
	Send-Off 3		
❏ AU	Tom Glavine AU 80.00		36.00
	(Certified signature)		

1993 Fleer Golden Moments

	MINT	NRMT
COMPLETE SET (6)	12.00	5.50
COMPLETE SERIES 1 (3)	4.00	1.80
COMPLETE SERIES 2 (3)	8.00	3.60
COMMON CARD (A1-B3)	.50	.23

RANDOM INSERTS IN WAX PACKS

❏ A1	George Brett	4.00	1.80
❏ A2	Mickey Morandini	.50	.23
❏ A3	Dave Winfield	1.50	.70
❏ B1	Dennis Eckersley	1.00	.45
❏ B2	Bip Roberts	.50	.23
❏ B3	Frank Thomas	8.00	3.60
	and Juan Gonzalez		

1993 Fleer Major League Prospects

	MINT	NRMT
COMPLETE SET (36)	30.00	13.50
COMPLETE SERIES 1 (18)	20.00	9.00
COMPLETE SERIES 2 (18)	10.00	4.50
COMMON SERIES 1 (A1-A18) ..	.50	.23
COMMON SERIES 2 (B1-B18) ..	.50	.23
SEMISTARS	1.00	.45

RANDOM INSERTS IN WAX PACKS

❏ A1	Melvin Nieves	.50	.23
❏ A2	Sterling Hitchcock ...	.50	.23
❏ A3	Tim Costo	.50	.23
❏ A4	Manny Alexander	.50	.23
❏ A5	Alan Embree	.50	.23
❏ A6	Kevin Young	.75	.35
❏ A7	J.T. Snow	1.50	.70
❏ A8	Russ Springer	.50	.23
❏ A9	Billy Ashley	.50	.23
❏ A10	Kevin Rogers	.50	.23
❏ A11	Steve Hosey	.50	.23
❏ A12	Eric Wedge	.50	.23
❏ A13	Mike Piazza	15.00	6.75
❏ A14	Jesse Levis	.50	.23
❏ A15	Rico Brogna	.75	.35
❏ A16	Alex Arias	.50	.23
❏ A17	Rod Brewer	.50	.23
❏ A18	Troy Neel	.50	.23
❏ B1	Scooter Tucker	.50	.23
❏ B2	Kerry Woodson	.50	.23
❏ B3	Greg Colbrunn	.50	.23
❏ B4	Pedro Martinez	8.00	3.60
❏ B5	Dave Silvestri	.50	.23
❏ B6	Kent Bottenfield	.50	.23
❏ B7	Rafael Bournigal	.50	.23
❏ B8	J.T. Bruett	.50	.23
❏ B9	Dave Mlicki	.50	.23
❏ B10	Paul Wagner	.50	.23
❏ B11	Mike Williams	.50	.23
❏ B12	Henry Mercedes	.50	.23
❏ B13	Scott Taylor	.50	.23
❏ B14	Steve Moeller	.50	.23
❏ B15	Javier Lopez	2.00	.90
❏ B16	Steve Cooke	.50	.23
❏ B17	Pete Young	.50	.23
❏ B18	Ken Ryan	.50	.23

1993 Fleer Pro-Visions

	MINT	NRMT
COMPLETE SET (6)	5.00	2.20
COMPLETE SERIES 1 (3)	3.00	1.35
COMPLETE SERIES 2 (3)	2.00	.90
COMMON CARD (A1-B3)	.75	.35

RANDOM INSERTS IN WAX PACKS

❏ A1	Roberto Alomar	2.00	.90
❏ A2	Dennis Eckersley	1.00	.45
❏ A3	Gary Sheffield	2.00	.90
❏ B1	Andy Van Slyke	.75	.35
❏ B2	Tom Glavine	1.50	.70
❏ B3	Cecil Fielder	1.00	.45

1993 Fleer Rookie Sensations

	MINT	NRMT
COMPLETE SET (20)	25.00	11.00
COMPLETE SERIES 1 (10)	15.00	6.75
COMPLETE SERIES 2 (10)	10.00	4.50
COMMON CARD (RSA1-RSB10)	1.00	.45

RANDOM INSERTS IN CELLO PACKS

❏ RSA1	Kenny Lofton	2.50	1.10
❏ RSA2	Cal Eldred	1.00	.45
❏ RSA3	Pat Listach	1.00	.45
❏ RSA4	Roberto Hernandez	1.50	.70
❏ RSA5	Dave Fleming	1.00	.45
❏ RSA6	Eric Karros	3.00	1.35
❏ RSA7	Reggie Sanders	1.50	.70
❏ RSA8	Derrick May	1.00	.45
❏ RSA9	Mike Perez	1.00	.45
❏ RSA10	Donovan Osborne ..	1.00	.45
❏ RSB1	Moises Alou	5.00	2.20
❏ RSB2	Pedro Astacio	1.50	.70
❏ RSB3	Jim Austin	1.00	.45
❏ RSB4	Chad Curtis	1.50	.70
❏ RSB5	Gary DiSarcina	1.00	.45
❏ RSB6	Scott Livingstone ..	1.00	.45
❏ RSB7	Sam Militello	1.00	.45
❏ RSB8	Arthur Rhodes	1.00	.45
❏ RSB9	Tim Wakefield	1.50	.70
❏ RSB10	Bob Zupcic	1.00	.45

1993 Fleer Team Leaders

	MINT	NRMT
COMPLETE SET (20)	70.00	32.00
COMPLETE SERIES 1 (10)	50.00	22.00
COMPLETE SERIES 2 (10)	20.00	9.00

COMMON CARD (AL1-NL10) ... 1.00 .45
ONE TL OR GLAVINE PER RACK PACK
AL: RANDOM INSERTS IN SER.1 PACKS
NL: RANDOM INSERTS IN SER.2 PACKS

		MINT	NRMT
❑ AL1	Kirby Puckett	6.00	2.70
❑ AL2	Mark McGwire	20.00	9.00
❑ AL3	Pat Listach	1.00	.45
❑ AL4	Roger Clemens	10.00	4.50
❑ AL5	Frank Thomas	8.00	3.60
❑ AL6	Carlos Baerga	1.00	.45
❑ AL7	Brady Anderson	2.00	.90
❑ AL8	Juan Gonzalez	8.00	3.60
❑ AL9	Roberto Alomar	4.00	1.80
❑ AL10	Ken Griffey Jr.	20.00	9.00
❑ NL1	Will Clark	4.00	1.80
❑ NL2	Terry Pendleton	1.00	.45
❑ NL3	Ray Lankford	3.00	1.35
❑ NL4	Eric Karros	3.00	1.35
❑ NL5	Gary Sheffield	4.00	1.80
❑ NL6	Ryne Sandberg	5.00	2.20
❑ NL7	Marquis Grissom	2.00	.90
❑ NL8	John Kruk	2.00	.90
❑ NL9	Jeff Bagwell	5.00	2.20
❑ NL10	Andy Van Slyke	1.00	.45

1993 Fleer Final Edition

	MINT	NRMT
COMP.FACT.SET (310)	10.00	4.50
COMPLETE SET (300)	6.00	2.70
COMMON CARD (F1-F300)	.10	.05
MINOR STARS	.20	.09
SEMISTARS	.30	.14
UNLISTED STARS	.40	.18

❑ 1	Steve Bedrosian	.10	.05
❑ 2	Jay Howell	.10	.05
❑ 3	Greg Maddux	1.00	.45
❑ 4	Greg McMichael	.10	.05
❑ 5	Tony Tarasco	.10	.05
❑ 6	Jose Bautista	.10	.05
❑ 7	Jose Guzman	.10	.05
❑ 8	Greg Hibbard	.10	.05
❑ 9	Candy Maldonado	.10	.05
❑ 10	Randy Myers	.20	.09
❑ 11	Matt Walbeck	.10	.05
❑ 12	Turk Wendell	.10	.05
❑ 13	Willie Wilson	.10	.05
❑ 14	Greg Cadaret	.10	.05
❑ 15	Roberto Kelly	.10	.05
❑ 16	Randy Milligan	.10	.05
❑ 17	Kevin Mitchell	.20	.09
❑ 18	Jeff Reardon	.20	.09
❑ 19	John Roper	.10	.05
❑ 20	John Smiley	.10	.05
❑ 21	Andy Ashby	.20	.09
❑ 22	Dante Bichette	.20	.09
❑ 23	Willie Blair	.10	.05
❑ 24	Pedro Castellano	.10	.05
❑ 25	Vinny Castilla	.50	.23
❑ 26	Jerald Clark	.10	.05
❑ 27	Alex Cole	.10	.05
❑ 28	Scott Fredrickson	.10	.05
❑ 29	Jay Gainer	.10	.05
❑ 30	Andres Galarraga	.40	.18
❑ 31	Joe Girardi	.20	.09
❑ 32	Ryan Hawblitzel	.10	.05

❑ 33	Charlie Hayes	.10	.05
❑ 34	Darren Holmes	.10	.05
❑ 35	Chris Jones	.10	.05
❑ 36	David Nied	.10	.05
❑ 37	J.Owens	.10	.05
❑ 38	Lance Painter	.10	.05
❑ 39	Jeff Parrett	.10	.05
❑ 40	Steve Reed	.10	.05
❑ 41	Armando Reynoso	.10	.05
❑ 42	Bruce Ruffin	.10	.05
❑ 43	Danny Sheaffer	.10	.05
❑ 44	Keith Shepherd	.10	.05
❑ 45	Jim Tatum	.10	.05
❑ 46	Gary Wayne	.10	.05
❑ 47	Eric Young	.40	.18
❑ 48	Luis Aquino	.10	.05
❑ 49	Alex Arias	.10	.05
❑ 50	Jack Armstrong	.10	.05
❑ 51	Bret Barberie	.10	.05
❑ 52	Geronimo Berroa	.10	.05
❑ 53	Ryan Bowen	.10	.05
❑ 54	Greg Briley	.10	.05
❑ 55	Cris Carpenter	.10	.05
❑ 56	Chuck Carr	.10	.05
❑ 57	Jeff Conine	.10	.05
❑ 58	Jim Corsi	.10	.05
❑ 59	Orestes Destrade	.10	.05
❑ 60	Junior Felix	.10	.05
❑ 61	Chris Hammond	.10	.05
❑ 62	Bryan Harvey	.10	.05
❑ 63	Charlie Hough	.20	.09
❑ 64	Joe Klink	.10	.05
❑ 65	Richie Lewis UER	.10	.05
	(Refers to place of birth and		
	residence as Illinois instead of		
Indiana)			
❑ 66	Mitch Lyden	.10	.05
❑ 67	Bob Natal	.10	.05
❑ 68	Scott Pose	.10	.05
❑ 69	Rich Renteria	.10	.05
❑ 70	Benito Santiago	.10	.05
❑ 71	Gary Sheffield	.40	.18
❑ 72	Matt Turner	.10	.05
❑ 73	Walt Weiss	.10	.05
❑ 74	Darrell Whitmore	.10	.05
❑ 75	Nigel Wilson	.10	.05
❑ 76	Kevin Bass	.10	.05
❑ 77	Doug Drabek	.10	.05
❑ 78	Tom Edens	.10	.05
❑ 79	Chris James	.10	.05
❑ 80	Greg Swindell	.10	.05
❑ 81	Omar Daal	.60	.25
❑ 82	Raul Mondesi	.40	.18
❑ 83	Jody Reed	.10	.05
❑ 84	Cory Snyder	.10	.05
❑ 85	Rick Trlicek	.10	.05
❑ 86	Tim Wallach	.10	.05
❑ 87	Todd Worrell	.10	.05
❑ 88	Tavo Alvarez	.10	.05
❑ 89	Frank Bolick	.10	.05
❑ 90	Kent Bottenfield	.10	.05
❑ 91	Greg Colbrunn	.10	.05
❑ 92	Cliff Floyd	.20	.09
❑ 93	Lou Frazier	.10	.05
❑ 94	Mike Gardiner	.10	.05
❑ 95	Mike Lansing	.20	.09
❑ 96	Bill Risley	.10	.05
❑ 97	Jeff Shaw	.10	.05
❑ 98	Kevin Baez	.10	.05
❑ 99	Tim Bogar	.10	.05
❑ 100	Jeromy Burnitz	.20	.09
❑ 101	Mike Draper	.10	.05
❑ 102	Darrin Jackson	.10	.05
❑ 103	Mike Maddux	.10	.05
❑ 104	Joe Orsulak	.10	.05
❑ 105	Doug Saunders	.10	.05
❑ 106	Frank Tanana	.10	.05
❑ 107	Dave Telgheder	.10	.05
❑ 108	Larry Andersen	.10	.05
❑ 109	Jim Eisenreich	.10	.05
❑ 110	Pete Incaviglia	.10	.05
❑ 111	Danny Jackson	.10	.05
❑ 112	David West	.10	.05
❑ 113	Al Martin	.10	.05
❑ 114	Blas Minor	.10	.05
❑ 115	Dennis Moeller	.10	.05

❑ 116	William Pennyfeather	.10	.05
❑ 117	Rich Robertson	.10	.05
❑ 118	Ben Shelton	.10	.05
❑ 119	Lonnie Smith	.10	.05
❑ 120	Freddie Toliver	.10	.05
❑ 121	Paul Wagner	.10	.05
❑ 122	Kevin Young	.20	.09
❑ 123	Rene Arocha	.10	.05
❑ 124	Gregg Jefferies	.10	.05
❑ 125	Paul Kilgus	.10	.05
❑ 126	Les Lancaster	.10	.05
❑ 127	Joe Magrane	.10	.05
❑ 128	Rob Murphy	.10	.05
❑ 129	Erik Pappas	.10	.05
❑ 130	Stan Royer	.10	.05
❑ 131	Ozzie Smith	.50	.23
❑ 132	Tom Urbani	.10	.05
❑ 133	Mark Whiten	.10	.05
❑ 134	Derek Bell	.20	.09
❑ 135	Doug Brocail	.10	.05
❑ 136	Phil Clark	.10	.05
❑ 137	Mark Ettles	.10	.05
❑ 138	Jeff Gardner	.10	.05
❑ 139	Pat Gomez	.10	.05
❑ 140	Ricky Gutierrez	.10	.05
❑ 141	Gene Harris	.10	.05
❑ 142	Kevin Higgins	.10	.05
❑ 143	Trevor Hoffman	.40	.18
❑ 144	Phil Plantier	.10	.05
❑ 145	Kerry Taylor	.10	.05
❑ 146	Guillermo Velasquez	.10	.05
❑ 147	Wally Whitehurst	.10	.05
❑ 148	Tim Worrell	.10	.05
❑ 149	Todd Benzinger	.10	.05
❑ 150	Barry Bonds	.50	.23
❑ 151	Greg Brummett	.10	.05
❑ 152	Mark Carreon	.10	.05
❑ 153	Dave Martinez	.10	.05
❑ 154	Jeff Reed	.10	.05
❑ 155	Kevin Rogers	.10	.05
❑ 156	Harold Baines	.20	.09
❑ 157	Damon Buford	.10	.05
❑ 158	Paul Carey	.10	.05
❑ 159	Jeffrey Hammonds	.20	.09
❑ 160	Jamie Moyer	.10	.05
❑ 161	Sherman Obando	.10	.05
❑ 162	John O'Donoghue	.10	.05
❑ 163	Brad Pennington	.10	.05
❑ 164	Jim Poole	.10	.05
❑ 165	Harold Reynolds	.10	.05
❑ 166	Fernando Valenzuela	.20	.09
❑ 167	Jack Voigt	.10	.05
❑ 168	Mark Williamson	.10	.05
❑ 169	Scott Bankhead	.10	.05
❑ 170	Greg Blosser	.10	.05
❑ 171	Jim Byrd	.10	.05
❑ 172	Ivan Calderon	.10	.05
❑ 173	Andre Dawson	.30	.14
❑ 174	Scott Fletcher	.10	.05
❑ 175	Jose Melendez	.10	.05
❑ 176	Carlos Quintana	.10	.05
❑ 177	Jeff Russell	.10	.05
❑ 178	Aaron Sele	.40	.18
❑ 179	Rod Correia	.10	.05
❑ 180	Chili Davis	.20	.09
❑ 181	Jim Edmonds	1.00	.45
❑ 182	Rene Gonzales	.10	.05
❑ 183	Hilly Hathaway	.10	.05
❑ 184	Torey Lovullo	.10	.05
❑ 185	Greg Myers	.10	.05
❑ 186	Gene Nelson	.10	.05
❑ 187	Troy Percival	.30	.14
❑ 188	Scott Sanderson	.10	.05
❑ 189	Darryl Scott	.10	.05
❑ 190	J.T. Snow	.50	.23
❑ 191	Russ Springer	.10	.05
❑ 192	Jason Bere	.10	.05
❑ 193	Rodney Bolton	.10	.05
❑ 194	Ellis Burks	.20	.09
❑ 195	Bo Jackson	.20	.09
❑ 196	Mike LaValliere	.10	.05
❑ 197	Scott Ruffcorn	.10	.05
❑ 198	Jeff Schwartz	.10	.05
❑ 199	Jerry DiPoto	.10	.05
❑ 200	Alvaro Espinoza	.10	.05
❑ 201	Wayne Kirby	.10	.05

❏ 202 Tom Kramer	.10	.05
❏ 203 Jesse Levis	.10	.05
❏ 204 Manny Ramirez	1.00	.45
❏ 205 Jeff Treadway	.10	.05
❏ 206 Bill Wertz	.10	.05
❏ 207 Cliff Young	.10	.05
❏ 208 Matt Young	.10	.05
❏ 209 Kirk Gibson	.20	.09
❏ 210 Greg Gohr	.10	.05
❏ 211 Bill Krueger	.10	.05
❏ 212 Bob MacDonald	.10	.05
❏ 213 Mike Moore	.10	.05
❏ 214 David Wells	.20	.09
❏ 215 Billy Brewer	.10	.05
❏ 216 David Cone	.30	.14
❏ 217 Greg Gagne	.10	.05
❏ 218 Mark Gardner	.10	.05
❏ 219 Chris Haney	.10	.05
❏ 220 Phil Hiatt	.10	.05
❏ 221 Jose Lind	.10	.05
❏ 222 Juan Bell	.10	.05
❏ 223 Tom Brunansky	.10	.05
❏ 224 Mike Ignasiak	.10	.05
❏ 225 Joe Kmak	.10	.05
❏ 226 Tom Lampkin	.10	.05
❏ 227 Graeme Lloyd	.10	.05
❏ 228 Carlos Maldonado	.10	.05
❏ 229 Matt Mieske	.10	.05
❏ 230 Angel Miranda	.10	.05
❏ 231 Troy O'Leary	.75	.35
❏ 232 Kevin Reimer	.10	.05
❏ 233 Larry Casian	.10	.05
❏ 234 Jim Deshaies	.10	.05
❏ 235 Eddie Guardado	.10	.05
❏ 236 Chip Hale	.10	.05
❏ 237 Mike Maksudian	.10	.05
❏ 238 David McCarty	.10	.05
❏ 239 Pat Meares	.10	.05
❏ 240 George Tsamis	.10	.05
❏ 241 Dave Winfield	.30	.14
❏ 242 Jim Abbott	.20	.09
❏ 243 Wade Boggs	.40	.18
❏ 244 Andy Cook	.10	.05
❏ 245 Russ Davis	.40	.18
❏ 246 Mike Humphreys	.10	.05
❏ 247 Jimmy Key	.20	.09
❏ 248 Jim Leyritz	.10	.05
❏ 249 Bobby Munoz	.10	.05
❏ 250 Paul O'Neill	.20	.09
❏ 251 Spike Owen	.10	.05
❏ 252 Dave Silvestri	.10	.05
❏ 253 Marcos Armas	.10	.05
❏ 254 Brent Gates	.10	.05
❏ 255 Rich Gossage	.20	.09
❏ 256 Scott Lydy	.10	.05
❏ 257 Henry Mercedes	.10	.05
❏ 258 Mike Mohler	.10	.05
❏ 259 Troy Neel	.10	.05
❏ 260 Edwin Nunez	.10	.05
❏ 261 Craig Paquette	.10	.05
❏ 262 Kevin Seitzer	.10	.05
❏ 263 Rich Amaral	.10	.05
❏ 264 Mike Blowers	.10	.05
❏ 265 Chris Bosio	.10	.05
❏ 266 Norm Charlton	.10	.05
❏ 267 Jim Converse	.10	.05
❏ 268 John Cummings	.10	.05
❏ 269 Mike Felder	.10	.05
❏ 270 Mike Hampton	.40	.18
❏ 271 Bill Haselman	.10	.05
❏ 272 Dwayne Henry	.10	.05
❏ 273 Greg Litton	.10	.05
❏ 274 Mackey Sasser	.10	.05
❏ 275 Lee Tinsley	.10	.05
❏ 276 David Wainhouse	.10	.05
❏ 277 Jeff Bronkey	.10	.05
❏ 278 Benji Gil	.10	.05
❏ 279 Tom Henke	.10	.05
❏ 280 Charlie Leibrandt	.10	.05
❏ 281 Robb Nen	.30	.14
❏ 282 Bill Ripken	.10	.05
❏ 283 Jon Shave	.10	.05
❏ 284 Doug Strange	.10	.05
❏ 285 Matt Whiteside	.10	.05
❏ 286 Scott Brow	.10	.05
❏ 287 Willie Canate	.10	.05

❏ 288 Tony Castillo	.10	.05
❏ 289 Domingo Cedeno	.10	.05
❏ 290 Darnell Coles	.10	.05
❏ 291 Danny Cox	.10	.05
❏ 292 Mark Eichhorn	.10	.05
❏ 293 Tony Fernandez	.20	.09
❏ 294 Al Leiter	.20	.09
❏ 295 Paul Molitor	.40	.18
❏ 296 Dave Stewart	.20	.09
❏ 297 Woody Williams	.30	.14
❏ 298 Checklist F1-F100	.10	.05
❏ 299 Checklist F101-F200	.10	.05
❏ 300 Checklist F201-F300	.10	.05

1993 Fleer Final Edition Diamond Tribute

	MINT	NRMT
COMPLETE SET (10)	4.00	1.80
COMMON CARD (1-10)	.20	.09
ONE SET PER FINAL EDITION FACTORY SET		

❏ 1 Wade Boggs	.50	.23
❏ 2 George Brett	1.25	.55
❏ 3 Andre Dawson	.30	.14
❏ 4 Carlton Fisk	.50	.23
❏ 5 Paul Molitor	.50	.23
❏ 6 Nolan Ryan	2.00	.90
❏ 7 Lee Smith	.20	.09
❏ 8 Ozzie Smith	.75	.35
❏ 9 Dave Winfield	.30	.14
❏ 10 Robin Yount	.30	.14

1994 Fleer

	MINT	NRMT
COMPLETE SET (720)	50.00	22.00
COMMON CARD (1-720)	.15	.07
MINOR STARS	.30	.14
UNLISTED STARS	.60	.25
COMP.ALL-ROOKIE SET (9)	8.00	3.60
ONE SET PER EXCHANGE CARD VIA MAIL		

❏ 1 Brady Anderson	.30	.14
❏ 2 Harold Baines	.30	.14
❏ 3 Mike Devereaux	.15	.07
❏ 4 Todd Frohwirth	.15	.07
❏ 5 Jeffrey Hammonds	.30	.14
❏ 6 Chris Hoiles	.15	.07
❏ 7 Tim Hulett	.15	.07

❏ 8 Ben McDonald	.15	.07
❏ 9 Mark McLemore	.15	.07
❏ 10 Alan Mills	.15	.07
❏ 11 Jamie Moyer	.15	.07
❏ 12 Mike Mussina	.60	.25
❏ 13 Gregg Olson	.15	.07
❏ 14 Mike Pagliarulo	.15	.07
❏ 15 Brad Pennington	.15	.07
❏ 16 Jim Poole	.15	.07
❏ 17 Harold Reynolds	.15	.07
❏ 18 Arthur Rhodes	.15	.07
❏ 19 Cal Ripken Jr.	2.50	1.10
❏ 20 David Segui	.30	.14
❏ 21 Rick Sutcliffe	.15	.07
❏ 22 Fernando Valenzuela	.30	.14
❏ 23 Jack Voigt	.15	.07
❏ 24 Mark Williamson	.15	.07
❏ 25 Scott Bankhead	.15	.07
❏ 26 Roger Clemens	1.50	.70
❏ 27 Scott Cooper	.15	.07
❏ 28 Danny Darwin	.15	.07
❏ 29 Andre Dawson	.40	.18
❏ 30 Rob Deer	.15	.07
❏ 31 John Dopson	.15	.07
❏ 32 Scott Fletcher	.15	.07
❏ 33 Mike Greenwell	.15	.07
❏ 34 Greg A. Harris	.15	.07
❏ 35 Billy Hatcher	.15	.07
❏ 36 Bob Melvin	.15	.07
❏ 37 Tony Pena	.15	.07
❏ 38 Paul Quantrill	.15	.07
❏ 39 Carlos Quintana	.15	.07
❏ 40 Ernest Riles	.15	.07
❏ 41 Jeff Russell	.15	.07
❏ 42 Ken Ryan	.15	.07
❏ 43 Aaron Sele	.30	.14
❏ 44 John Valentin	.30	.14
❏ 45 Mo Vaughn	.60	.25
❏ 46 Frank Viola	.15	.07
❏ 47 Bob Zupcic	.15	.07
❏ 48 Mike Butcher	.15	.07
❏ 49 Rod Correia	.15	.07
❏ 50 Chad Curtis	.15	.07
❏ 51 Chili Davis	.30	.14
❏ 52 Gary DiSarcina	.15	.07
❏ 53 Damion Easley	.30	.14
❏ 54 Jim Edmonds	.60	.25
❏ 55 Chuck Finley	.30	.14
❏ 56 Steve Frey	.15	.07
❏ 57 Rene Gonzales	.15	.07
❏ 58 Joe Grahe	.15	.07
❏ 59 Hilly Hathaway	.15	.07
❏ 60 Stan Javier	.15	.07
❏ 61 Mark Langston	.15	.07
❏ 62 Phil Leftwich	.15	.07
❏ 63 Torey Lovullo	.15	.07
❏ 64 Joe Magrane	.15	.07
❏ 65 Greg Myers	.15	.07
❏ 66 Ken Patterson	.15	.07
❏ 67 Eduardo Perez	.15	.07
❏ 68 Luis Polonia	.15	.07
❏ 69 Tim Salmon	.60	.25
❏ 70 J.T. Snow	.30	.14
❏ 71 Ron Tingley	.15	.07
❏ 72 Julio Valera	.15	.07
❏ 73 Wilson Alvarez	.30	.14
❏ 74 Tim Belcher	.15	.07
❏ 75 George Bell	.15	.07
❏ 76 Jason Bere	.15	.07
❏ 77 Rod Bolton	.15	.07
❏ 78 Ellis Burks	.30	.14
❏ 79 Joey Cora	.15	.07
❏ 80 Alex Fernandez	.30	.14
❏ 81 Craig Grebeck	.15	.07
❏ 82 Ozzie Guillen	.15	.07
❏ 83 Roberto Hernandez	.15	.07
❏ 84 Bo Jackson	.30	.14
❏ 85 Lance Johnson	.15	.07
❏ 86 Ron Karkovice	.15	.07
❏ 87 Mike LaValliere	.15	.07
❏ 88 Kirk McCaskill	.15	.07
❏ 89 Jack McDowell	.15	.07
❏ 90 Warren Newson	.15	.07
❏ 91 Dan Pasqua	.15	.07
❏ 92 Scott Radinsky	.15	.07
❏ 93 Tim Raines	.30	.14

❑ 94 Steve Sax	.15	.07
❑ 95 Jeff Schwarz	.15	.07
❑ 96 Frank Thomas	1.25	.55
❑ 97 Robin Ventura	.30	.14
❑ 98 Sandy Alomar Jr.	.30	.14
❑ 99 Carlos Baerga	.30	.14
❑ 100 Albert Belle	.60	.25
❑ 101 Mark Clark	.15	.07
❑ 102 Jerry DiPoto	.15	.07
❑ 103 Alvaro Espinoza	.15	.07
❑ 104 Felix Fermin	.15	.07
❑ 105 Jeremy Hernandez	.15	.07
❑ 106 Reggie Jefferson	.15	.07
❑ 107 Wayne Kirby	.15	.07
❑ 108 Tom Kramer	.15	.07
❑ 109 Mark Lewis	.15	.07
❑ 110 Derek Lilliquist	.15	.07
❑ 111 Kenny Lofton	.60	.25
❑ 112 Candy Maldonado	.15	.07
❑ 113 Jose Mesa	.15	.07
❑ 114 Jeff Mutis	.15	.07
❑ 115 Charles Nagy	.30	.14
❑ 116 Bob Ojeda	.15	.07
❑ 117 Junior Ortiz	.15	.07
❑ 118 Eric Plunk	.15	.07
❑ 119 Manny Ramirez	1.25	.55
❑ 120 Paul Sorrento	.15	.07
❑ 121 Jim Thome	.60	.25
❑ 122 Jeff Treadway	.15	.07
❑ 123 Bill Wertz	.15	.07
❑ 124 Skeeter Barnes	.15	.07
❑ 125 Milt Cuyler	.15	.07
❑ 126 Eric Davis	.30	.14
❑ 127 John Doherty	.15	.07
❑ 128 Cecil Fielder	.30	.14
❑ 129 Travis Fryman	.30	.14
❑ 130 Kirk Gibson	.30	.14
❑ 131 Dan Gladden	.15	.07
❑ 132 Greg Gohr	.15	.07
❑ 133 Chris Gomez	.15	.07
❑ 134 Bill Gullickson	.15	.07
❑ 135 Mike Henneman	.15	.07
❑ 136 Kurt Knudsen	.15	.07
❑ 137 Chad Kreuter	.15	.07
❑ 138 Bill Krueger	.15	.07
❑ 139 Scott Livingstone	.15	.07
❑ 140 Bob MacDonald	.15	.07
❑ 141 Mike Moore	.15	.07
❑ 142 Tony Phillips	.15	.07
❑ 143 Mickey Tettleton	.15	.07
❑ 144 Alan Trammell	.40	.18
❑ 145 David Wells	.40	.18
❑ 146 Lou Whitaker	.30	.14
❑ 147 Kevin Appier	.30	.14
❑ 148 Stan Belinda	.15	.07
❑ 149 George Brett	1.25	.55
❑ 150 Billy Brewer	.15	.07
❑ 151 Hubie Brooks	.15	.07
❑ 152 David Cone	.40	.18
❑ 153 Gary Gaetti	.30	.14
❑ 154 Greg Gagne	.15	.07
❑ 155 Tom Gordon	.15	.07
❑ 156 Mark Gubicza	.15	.07
❑ 157 Chris Gwynn	.15	.07
❑ 158 John Habyan	.15	.07
❑ 159 Chris Haney	.15	.07
❑ 160 Phil Hiatt	.15	.07
❑ 161 Felix Jose	.15	.07
❑ 162 Wally Joyner	.30	.14
❑ 163 Jose Lind	.15	.07
❑ 164 Mike Macfarlane	.15	.07
❑ 165 Mike Magnante	.15	.07
❑ 166 Brent Mayne	.15	.07
❑ 167 Brian McRae	.15	.07
❑ 168 Kevin McReynolds	.15	.07
❑ 169 Keith Miller	.15	.07
❑ 170 Jeff Montgomery	.15	.07
❑ 171 Hipolito Pichardo	.15	.07
❑ 172 Rico Rossy	.15	.07
❑ 173 Juan Bell	.15	.07
❑ 174 Ricky Bones	.15	.07
❑ 175 Cal Eldred	.15	.07
❑ 176 Mike Fetters	.15	.07
❑ 177 Darryl Hamilton	.15	.07
❑ 178 Doug Henry	.15	.07
❑ 179 Mike Ignasiak	.15	.07
❑ 180 John Jaha	.15	.07
❑ 181 Pat Listach	.15	.07
❑ 182 Graeme Lloyd	.15	.07
❑ 183 Matt Mieske	.15	.07
❑ 184 Angel Miranda	.15	.07
❑ 185 Jaime Navarro	.15	.07
❑ 186 Dave Nilsson	.15	.07
❑ 187 Troy O'Leary	.30	.14
❑ 188 Jesse Orosco	.15	.07
❑ 189 Kevin Reimer	.15	.07
❑ 190 Kevin Seitzer	.15	.07
❑ 191 Bill Spiers	.15	.07
❑ 192 B.J. Surhoff	.30	.14
❑ 193 Dickie Thon	.15	.07
❑ 194 Jose Valentin	.15	.07
❑ 195 Greg Vaughn	.30	.14
❑ 196 Bill Wegman	.15	.07
❑ 197 Robin Yount	.60	.25
❑ 198 Rick Aguilera	.15	.07
❑ 199 Willie Banks	.15	.07
❑ 200 Bernardo Brito	.15	.07
❑ 201 Larry Casian	.15	.07
❑ 202 Scott Erickson	.30	.14
❑ 203 Eddie Guardado	.15	.07
❑ 204 Mark Guthrie	.15	.07
❑ 205 Chip Hale	.15	.07
❑ 206 Brian Harper	.15	.07
❑ 207 Mike Hartley	.15	.07
❑ 208 Kent Hrbek	.30	.14
❑ 209 Terry Jorgensen	.15	.07
❑ 210 Chuck Knoblauch	.60	.25
❑ 211 Gene Larkin	.15	.07
❑ 212 Shane Mack	.15	.07
❑ 213 David McCarty	.15	.07
❑ 214 Pat Meares	.15	.07
❑ 215 Pedro Munoz	.15	.07
❑ 216 Derek Parks	.15	.07
❑ 217 Kirby Puckett	1.00	.45
❑ 218 Jeff Reboulet	.15	.07
❑ 219 Kevin Tapani	.15	.07
❑ 220 Mike Trombley	.15	.07
❑ 221 George Tsamis	.15	.07
❑ 222 Carl Willis	.15	.07
❑ 223 Dave Winfield	.60	.25
❑ 224 Jim Abbott	.30	.14
❑ 225 Paul Assenmacher	.15	.07
❑ 226 Wade Boggs	.60	.25
❑ 227 Russ Davis	.30	.14
❑ 228 Steve Farr	.15	.07
❑ 229 Mike Gallego	.15	.07
❑ 230 Paul Gibson	.15	.07
❑ 231 Steve Howe	.15	.07
❑ 232 Dion James	.15	.07
❑ 233 Domingo Jean	.15	.07
❑ 234 Scott Kamieniecki	.15	.07
❑ 235 Pat Kelly	.15	.07
❑ 236 Jimmy Key	.30	.14
❑ 237 Jim Leyritz	.30	.14
❑ 238 Kevin Maas	.15	.07
❑ 239 Don Mattingly	1.25	.55
❑ 240 Rich Monteleone	.15	.07
❑ 241 Bobby Munoz	.15	.07
❑ 242 Matt Nokes	.15	.07
❑ 243 Paul O'Neill	.30	.14
❑ 244 Spike Owen	.15	.07
❑ 245 Melido Perez	.15	.07
❑ 246 Lee Smith	.30	.14
❑ 247 Mike Stanley	.15	.07
❑ 248 Danny Tartabull	.15	.07
❑ 249 Randy Velarde	.15	.07
❑ 250 Bob Wickman	.15	.07
❑ 251 Bernie Williams	.60	.25
❑ 252 Mike Aldrete	.15	.07
❑ 253 Marcos Armas	.15	.07
❑ 254 Lance Blankenship	.15	.07
❑ 255 Mike Bordick	.15	.07
❑ 256 Scott Brosius	.30	.14
❑ 257 Jerry Browne	.15	.07
❑ 258 Ron Darling	.15	.07
❑ 259 Kelly Downs	.15	.07
❑ 260 Dennis Eckersley	.30	.14
❑ 261 Brent Gates	.15	.07
❑ 262 Rich Gossage	.30	.14
❑ 263 Scott Hemond	.15	.07
❑ 264 Dave Henderson	.15	.07
❑ 265 Rick Honeycutt	.15	.07
❑ 266 Vince Horsman	.15	.07
❑ 267 Scott Lydy	.15	.07
❑ 268 Mark McGwire	3.00	1.35
❑ 269 Mike Mohler	.15	.07
❑ 270 Troy Neel	.15	.07
❑ 271 Edwin Nunez	.15	.07
❑ 272 Craig Paquette	.15	.07
❑ 273 Ruben Sierra	.15	.07
❑ 274 Terry Steinbach	.15	.07
❑ 275 Todd Van Poppel	.15	.07
❑ 276 Bob Welch	.15	.07
❑ 277 Bobby Witt	.15	.07
❑ 278 Rich Amaral	.15	.07
❑ 279 Mike Blowers	.15	.07
❑ 280 Bret Boone UER	.30	.14
(Name spelled Brett on front)		
❑ 281 Chris Bosio	.15	.07
❑ 282 Jay Buhner	.30	.14
❑ 283 Norm Charlton	.15	.07
❑ 284 Mike Felder	.15	.07
❑ 285 Dave Fleming	.15	.07
❑ 286 Ken Griffey Jr.	3.00	1.35
❑ 287 Erik Hanson	.15	.07
❑ 288 Bill Haselman	.15	.07
❑ 289 Brad Holman	.15	.07
❑ 290 Randy Johnson	.60	.25
❑ 291 Tim Leary	.15	.07
❑ 292 Greg Litton	.15	.07
❑ 293 Dave Magadan	.15	.07
❑ 294 Edgar Martinez	.30	.14
❑ 295 Tino Martinez	.60	.25
❑ 296 Jeff Nelson	.15	.07
❑ 297 Erik Plantenberg	.15	.07
❑ 298 Mackey Sasser	.15	.07
❑ 299 Brian Turang	.15	.07
❑ 300 Dave Valle	.15	.07
❑ 301 Omar Vizquel	.30	.14
❑ 302 Brian Bohanon	.15	.07
❑ 303 Kevin Brown	.30	.14
❑ 304 Jose Canseco UER	.75	.35
(Back mentions 1991 as his		
40/40 MVP season; should be '88)		
❑ 305 Mario Diaz	.15	.07
❑ 306 Julio Franco	.15	.07
❑ 307 Juan Gonzalez	1.25	.55
❑ 308 Tom Henke	.15	.07
❑ 309 David Hulse	.15	.07
❑ 310 Manuel Lee	.15	.07
❑ 311 Craig Lefferts	.15	.07
❑ 312 Charlie Leibrandt	.15	.07
❑ 313 Rafael Palmeiro	.60	.25
❑ 314 Dean Palmer	.30	.14
❑ 315 Roger Pavlik	.15	.07
❑ 316 Dan Peltier	.15	.07
❑ 317 Gene Petralli	.15	.07
❑ 318 Gary Redus	.15	.07
❑ 319 Ivan Rodriguez	.75	.35
❑ 320 Kenny Rogers	.15	.07
❑ 321 Nolan Ryan	2.50	1.10
❑ 322 Doug Strange	.15	.07
❑ 323 Matt Whiteside	.15	.07
❑ 324 Roberto Alomar	.60	.25
❑ 325 Pat Borders	.15	.07
❑ 326 Joe Carter	.30	.14
❑ 327 Tony Castillo	.15	.07
❑ 328 Darnell Coles	.15	.07
❑ 329 Danny Cox	.15	.07
❑ 330 Mark Eichhorn	.15	.07
❑ 331 Tony Fernandez	.30	.14
❑ 332 Alfredo Griffin	.15	.07
❑ 333 Juan Guzman	.30	.14
❑ 334 Rickey Henderson	.75	.35
❑ 335 Pat Hentgen	.30	.14
❑ 336 Randy Knorr	.15	.07
❑ 337 Al Leiter	.30	.14
❑ 338 Paul Molitor	.60	.25
❑ 339 Jack Morris	.30	.14
❑ 340 John Olerud	.30	.14
❑ 341 Dick Schofield	.15	.07
❑ 342 Ed Sprague	.15	.07
❑ 343 Dave Stewart	.30	.14
❑ 344 Todd Stottlemyre	.15	.07
❑ 345 Mike Timlin	.15	.07
❑ 346 Duane Ward	.15	.07
❑ 347 Turner Ward	.15	.07
❑ 348 Devon White	.15	.07

#	Name	V1	V2
349	Woody Williams	.15	.07
350	Steve Avery	.15	.07
351	Steve Bedrosian	.15	.07
352	Rafael Belliard	.15	.07
353	Damon Berryhill	.15	.07
354	Jeff Blauser	.15	.07
355	Sid Bream	.15	.07
356	Francisco Cabrera	.15	.07
357	Marvin Freeman	.15	.07
358	Ron Gant	.30	.14
359	Tom Glavine	.60	.25
360	Jay Howell	.15	.07
361	David Justice	.60	.25
362	Ryan Klesko	.30	.14
363	Mark Lemke	.15	.07
364	Javier Lopez	.40	.18
365	Greg Maddux	1.50	.70
366	Fred McGriff	.40	.18
367	Greg McMichael	.15	.07
368	Kent Mercker	.15	.07
369	Otis Nixon	.15	.07
370	Greg Olson	.15	.07
371	Bill Pecota	.15	.07
372	Terry Pendleton	.15	.07
373	Deion Sanders	.30	.14
374	Pete Smith	.15	.07
375	John Smoltz	.40	.18
376	Mike Stanton	.15	.07
377	Tony Tarasco	.15	.07
378	Mark Wohlers	.15	.07
379	Jose Bautista	.15	.07
380	Shawn Boskie	.15	.07
381	Steve Buechele	.15	.07
382	Frank Castillo	.15	.07
383	Mark Grace	.40	.18
384	Jose Guzman	.15	.07
385	Mike Harkey	.15	.07
386	Greg Hibbard	.15	.07
387	Glenallen Hill	.15	.07
388	Steve Lake	.15	.07
389	Derrick May	.15	.07
390	Chuck McElroy	.15	.07
391	Mike Morgan	.15	.07
392	Randy Myers	.15	.07
393	Dan Plesac	.15	.07
394	Kevin Roberson	.15	.07
395	Rey Sanchez	.15	.07
396	Ryne Sandberg	.75	.35
397	Bob Scanlan	.15	.07
398	Dwight Smith	.15	.07
399	Sammy Sosa	2.50	1.10
400	Jose Vizcaino	.15	.07
401	Rick Wilkins	.15	.07
402	Willie Wilson	.15	.07
403	Eric Yelding	.15	.07
404	Bobby Ayala	.15	.07
405	Jeff Branson	.15	.07
406	Tom Browning	.15	.07
407	Jacob Brumfield	.15	.07
408	Tim Costo	.15	.07
409	Rob Dibble	.15	.07
410	Willie Greene	.15	.07
411	Thomas Howard	.15	.07
412	Roberto Kelly	.15	.07
413	Bill Landrum	.15	.07
414	Barry Larkin	.60	.25
415	Larry Luebbers	.15	.07
416	Kevin Mitchell	.15	.07
417	Hal Morris	.15	.07
418	Joe Oliver	.15	.07
419	Tim Pugh	.15	.07
420	Jeff Reardon	.30	.14
421	Jose Rijo	.15	.07
422	Bip Roberts	.15	.07
423	John Roper	.15	.07
424	Johnny Ruffin	.15	.07
425	Chris Sabo	.15	.07
426	Juan Samuel	.15	.07
427	Reggie Sanders	.30	.14
428	Scott Service	.15	.07
429	John Smiley	.15	.07
430	Jerry Spradlin	.15	.07
431	Kevin Wickander	.15	.07
432	Freddie Benavides	.15	.07
433	Dante Bichette	.30	.14
434	Willie Blair	.15	.07
435	Daryl Boston	.15	.07
436	Kent Bottenfield	.15	.07
437	Vinny Castilla	.30	.14
438	Jerald Clark	.15	.07
439	Alex Cole	.15	.07
440	Andres Galarraga	.60	.25
441	Joe Girardi	.15	.07
442	Greg W. Harris	.15	.07
443	Charlie Hayes	.15	.07
444	Darren Holmes	.15	.07
445	Chris Jones	.15	.07
446	Roberto Mejia	.15	.07
447	David Nied	.15	.07
448	J. Owens	.15	.07
449	Jeff Parrett	.15	.07
450	Steve Reed	.15	.07
451	Armando Reynoso	.15	.07
452	Bruce Ruffin	.15	.07
453	Mo Sanford	.15	.07
454	Danny Sheaffer	.15	.07
455	Jim Tatum	.15	.07
456	Gary Wayne	.15	.07
457	Eric Young	.15	.07
458	Luis Aquino	.15	.07
459	Alex Arias	.15	.07
460	Jack Armstrong	.15	.07
461	Bret Barberie	.15	.07
462	Ryan Bowen	.15	.07
463	Chuck Carr	.15	.07
464	Jeff Conine	.15	.07
465	Henry Cotto	.15	.07
466	Orestes Destrade	.15	.07
467	Chris Hammond	.15	.07
468	Bryan Harvey	.15	.07
469	Charlie Hough	.15	.07
470	Joe Klink	.15	.07
471	Richie Lewis	.15	.07
472	Bob Natal	.15	.07
473	Pat Rapp	.15	.07
474	Rich Renteria	.15	.07
475	Rich Rodriguez	.15	.07
476	Benito Santiago	.15	.07
477	Gary Sheffield	.60	.25
478	Matt Turner	.15	.07
479	David Weathers	.15	.07
480	Walt Weiss	.15	.07
481	Darrell Whitmore	.15	.07
482	Eric Anthony	.15	.07
483	Jeff Bagwell	.75	.35
484	Kevin Bass	.15	.07
485	Craig Biggio	.60	.25
486	Ken Caminiti	.40	.18
487	Andujar Cedeno	.15	.07
488	Chris Donnels	.15	.07
489	Doug Drabek	.15	.07
490	Steve Finley	.30	.14
491	Luis Gonzalez	.30	.14
492	Pete Harnisch	.15	.07
493	Xavier Hernandez	.15	.07
494	Doug Jones	.15	.07
495	Todd Jones	.15	.07
496	Darryl Kile	.15	.07
497	Al Osuna	.15	.07
498	Mark Portugal	.15	.07
499	Scott Servais	.15	.07
500	Greg Swindell	.15	.07
501	Eddie Taubensee	.15	.07
502	Jose Uribe	.15	.07
503	Brian Williams	.15	.07
504	Billy Ashley	.15	.07
505	Pedro Astacio	.15	.07
506	Brett Butler	.30	.14
507	Tom Candiotti	.15	.07
508	Omar Daal	.15	.07
509	Jim Gott	.15	.07
510	Kevin Gross	.15	.07
511	Dave Hansen	.15	.07
512	Carlos Hernandez	.15	.07
513	Orel Hershiser	.30	.14
514	Eric Karros	.30	.14
515	Pedro Martinez	.75	.35
516	Ramon Martinez	.30	.14
517	Roger McDowell	.15	.07
518	Raul Mondesi	.60	.25
519	Jose Offerman	.30	.14
520	Mike Piazza	2.00	.90
521	Jody Reed	.15	.07
522	Henry Rodriguez	.30	.14
523	Mike Sharperson	.15	.07
524	Cory Snyder	.15	.07
525	Darryl Strawberry	.30	.14
526	Rick Trlicek	.15	.07
527	Tim Wallach	.15	.07
528	Mitch Webster	.15	.07
529	Steve Wilson	.15	.07
530	Todd Worrell	.15	.07
531	Moises Alou	.30	.14
532	Brian Barnes	.15	.07
533	Sean Berry	.15	.07
534	Greg Colbrunn	.15	.07
535	Delino DeShields	.15	.07
536	Jeff Fassero	.15	.07
537	Darrin Fletcher	.15	.07
538	Cliff Floyd	.30	.14
539	Lou Frazier	.15	.07
540	Marquis Grissom	.30	.14
541	Butch Henry	.15	.07
542	Ken Hill	.15	.07
543	Mike Lansing	.30	.14
544	Brian Looney	.15	.07
545	Dennis Martinez	.15	.07
546	Chris Nabholz	.15	.07
547	Randy Ready	.15	.07
548	Mel Rojas	.15	.07
549	Kirk Rueter	.15	.07
550	Tim Scott	.15	.07
551	Jeff Shaw	.15	.07
552	Tim Spehr	.15	.07
553	John VanderWal	.15	.07
554	Larry Walker	.60	.25
555	John Wetteland	.30	.14
556	Rondell White	.30	.14
557	Tim Bogar	.15	.07
558	Bobby Bonilla	.30	.14
559	Jeromy Burnitz	.30	.14
560	Sid Fernandez	.15	.07
561	John Franco	.15	.07
562	Dave Gallagher	.15	.07
563	Dwight Gooden	.30	.14
564	Eric Hillman	.15	.07
565	Todd Hundley	.30	.14
566	Jeff Innis	.15	.07
567	Darrin Jackson	.15	.07
568	Howard Johnson	.15	.07
569	Bobby Jones	.15	.07
570	Jeff Kent	.30	.14
571	Mike Maddux	.15	.07
572	Jeff McKnight	.15	.07
573	Eddie Murray	.60	.25
574	Charlie O'Brien	.15	.07
575	Joe Orsulak	.15	.07
576	Bret Saberhagen	.30	.14
577	Pete Schourek	.15	.07
578	Dave Telgheder	.15	.07
579	Ryan Thompson	.15	.07
580	Anthony Young	.15	.07
581	Ruben Amaro	.15	.07
582	Larry Andersen	.15	.07
583	Kim Batiste	.15	.07
584	Wes Chamberlain	.15	.07
585	Darren Daulton	.30	.14
586	Mariano Duncan	.15	.07
587	Lenny Dykstra	.30	.14
588	Jim Eisenreich	.15	.07
589	Tommy Greene	.15	.07
590	Dave Hollins	.15	.07
591	Pete Incaviglia	.15	.07
592	Danny Jackson	.15	.07
593	Ricky Jordan	.15	.07
594	John Kruk	.30	.14
595	Roger Mason	.15	.07
596	Mickey Morandini	.15	.07
597	Terry Mulholland	.15	.07
598	Todd Pratt	.15	.07
599	Ben Rivera	.15	.07
600	Curt Schilling	.30	.14
601	Kevin Stocker	.15	.07
602	Milt Thompson	.15	.07
603	David West	.40	.18
604	Mitch Williams	.15	.07
605	Jay Bell	.30	.14
606	Dave Clark	.15	.07

❏ 607 Steve Cooke	.15	.07
❏ 608 Tom Foley	.15	.07
❏ 609 Carlos Garcia	.15	.07
❏ 610 Joel Johnston	.15	.07
❏ 611 Jeff King	.15	.07
❏ 612 Al Martin	.15	.07
❏ 613 Lloyd McClendon	.15	.07
❏ 614 Orlando Merced	.15	.07
❏ 615 Blas Minor	.15	.07
❏ 616 Denny Neagle	.15	.07
❏ 617 Mark Petkovsek	.15	.07
❏ 618 Tom Prince	.15	.07
❏ 619 Don Slaught	.15	.07
❏ 620 Zane Smith	.15	.07
❏ 621 Randy Tomlin	.15	.07
❏ 622 Andy Van Slyke	.30	.14
❏ 623 Paul Wagner	.15	.07
❏ 624 Tim Wakefield	.30	.14
❏ 625 Bob Walk	.15	.07
❏ 626 Kevin Young	.15	.07
❏ 627 Luis Alicea	.15	.07
❏ 628 Rene Arocha	.15	.07
❏ 629 Rod Brewer	.15	.07
❏ 630 Rheal Cormier	.15	.07
❏ 631 Bernard Gilkey	.15	.07
❏ 632 Lee Guetterman	.15	.07
❏ 633 Gregg Jefferies	.15	.07
❏ 634 Brian Jordan	.30	.14
❏ 635 Les Lancaster	.15	.07
❏ 636 Ray Lankford	.30	.14
❏ 637 Rob Murphy	.15	.07
❏ 638 Omar Olivares	.15	.07
❏ 639 Jose Oquendo	.15	.07
❏ 640 Donovan Osborne	.15	.07
❏ 641 Tom Pagnozzi	.15	.07
❏ 642 Erik Pappas	.15	.07
❏ 643 Geronimo Pena	.15	.07
❏ 644 Mike Perez	.15	.07
❏ 645 Gerald Perry	.15	.07
❏ 646 Ozzie Smith	.75	.35
❏ 647 Bob Tewksbury	.15	.07
❏ 648 Allen Watson	.15	.07
❏ 649 Mark Whiten	.15	.07
❏ 650 Tracy Woodson	.15	.07
❏ 651 Todd Zeile	.15	.07
❏ 652 Andy Ashby	.15	.07
❏ 653 Brad Ausmus	.15	.07
❏ 654 Billy Bean	.15	.07
❏ 655 Derek Bell	.30	.14
❏ 656 Andy Benes	.30	.14
❏ 657 Doug Brocail	.15	.07
❏ 658 Jarvis Brown	.15	.07
❏ 659 Archi Cianfrocco	.15	.07
❏ 660 Phil Clark	.15	.07
❏ 661 Mark Davis	.15	.07
❏ 662 Jeff Gardner	.15	.07
❏ 663 Pat Gomez	.15	.07
❏ 664 Ricky Gutierrez	.15	.07
❏ 665 Tony Gwynn	1.50	.70
❏ 666 Gene Harris	.15	.07
❏ 667 Kevin Higgins	.15	.07
❏ 668 Trevor Hoffman	.30	.14
❏ 669 Pedro Martinez	.15	.07
❏ 670 Tim Mauser	.15	.07
❏ 671 Melvin Nieves	.15	.07
❏ 672 Phil Plantier	.15	.07
❏ 673 Frank Seminara	.15	.07
❏ 674 Craig Shipley	.15	.07
❏ 675 Kerry Taylor	.15	.07
❏ 676 Tim Teufel	.15	.07
❏ 677 Guillermo Velasquez	.15	.07
❏ 678 Wally Whitehurst	.15	.07
❏ 679 Tim Worrell	.15	.07
❏ 680 Rod Beck	.15	.07
❏ 681 Mike Benjamin	.15	.07
❏ 682 Todd Benzinger	.15	.07
❏ 683 Bud Black	.15	.07
❏ 684 Barry Bonds	.75	.35
❏ 685 Jeff Brantley	.15	.07
❏ 686 Dave Burba	.15	.07
❏ 687 John Burkett	.15	.07
❏ 688 Mark Carreon	.15	.07
❏ 689 Will Clark	.60	.25
❏ 690 Royce Clayton	.15	.07
❏ 691 Bryan Hickerson	.15	.07
❏ 692 Mike Jackson	.30	.14

❏ 693 Darren Lewis	.15	.07
❏ 694 Kirt Manwaring	.15	.07
❏ 695 Dave Martinez	.15	.07
❏ 696 Willie McGee	.30	.14
❏ 697 John Patterson	.15	.07
❏ 698 Jeff Reed	.15	.07
❏ 699 Kevin Rogers	.15	.07
❏ 700 Scott Sanderson	.15	.07
❏ 701 Steve Scarsone	.15	.07
❏ 702 Billy Swift	.15	.07
❏ 703 Robby Thompson	.15	.07
❏ 704 Matt Williams	.40	.18
❏ 705 Trevor Wilson	.15	.07
❏ 706 Brave New World	.60	.25
Fred McGriff		
Ron Gant		
David Justice		
❏ 707 1-2 Punch	.30	.14
John Olerud		
Paul Molitor		
❏ 708 American Heat	.30	.14
Mike Mussina		
Jack McDowell		
❏ 709 Together Again	.40	.18
Lou Whitaker		
Alan Trammell		
❏ 710 Lone Star Lumber	.40	.18
Rafael Palmeiro		
Juan Gonzalez		
❏ 711 Batmen	.40	.18
Brett Butler		
Tony Gwynn		
❏ 712 Twin Peaks	.60	.25
Kirby Puckett		
Chuck Knoblauch		
❏ 713 Back to Back	.75	.35
Mike Piazza		
Eric Karros		
❏ 714 Checklist 1	.15	.07
❏ 715 Checklist 2	.15	.07
❏ 716 Checklist 3	.15	.07
❏ 717 Checklist 4	.15	.07
❏ 718 Checklist 5	.15	.07
❏ 719 Checklist 6	.15	.07
❏ 720 Checklist 7	.15	.07
❏ P69 Tim Salmon Promo	1.00	.45

1994 Fleer All-Stars

	MINT	NRMT
COMPLETE SET (50)	25.00	11.00
COMMON CARD (1-50)	.25	.11
RANDOM INSERTS IN ALL PACKS		

❏ 1 Roberto Alomar	.75	.35
❏ 2 Carlos Baerga	.25	.11
❏ 3 Albert Belle	.75	.35
❏ 4 Wade Boggs	.75	.35
❏ 5 Joe Carter	.40	.18
❏ 6 Scott Cooper	.25	.11
❏ 7 Cecil Fielder	.25	.11
❏ 8 Travis Fryman	.40	.18
❏ 9 Juan Gonzalez	1.50	.70
❏ 10 Ken Griffey Jr.	4.00	1.80
❏ 11 Pat Hentgen	.40	.18
❏ 12 Randy Johnson	.75	.35
❏ 13 Jimmy Key	.40	.18
❏ 14 Mark Langston	.25	.11

❏ 15 Jack McDowell	.25	.11
❏ 16 Paul Molitor	.75	.35
❏ 17 Jeff Montgomery	.25	.11
❏ 18 Mike Mussina	.75	.35
❏ 19 John Olerud	.40	.18
❏ 20 Kirby Puckett	1.50	.70
❏ 21 Cal Ripken	3.00	1.35
❏ 22 Ivan Rodriguez	1.00	.45
❏ 23 Frank Thomas	2.00	.90
❏ 24 Greg Vaughn	.40	.18
❏ 25 Duane Ward	.25	.11
❏ 26 Steve Avery	.25	.11
❏ 27 Rod Beck	.25	.11
❏ 28 Jay Bell	.40	.18
❏ 29 Andy Benes	.40	.18
❏ 30 Jeff Blauser	.25	.11
❏ 31 Barry Bonds	.75	.35
❏ 32 Bobby Bonilla	.40	.18
❏ 33 John Burkett	.25	.11
❏ 34 Darren Daulton	.40	.18
❏ 35 Andres Galarraga	.75	.35
❏ 36 Tom Glavine	.75	.35
❏ 37 Mark Grace	.50	.23
❏ 38 Marquis Grissom	.25	.11
❏ 39 Tony Gwynn	2.50	1.10
❏ 40 Bryan Harvey	.25	.11
❏ 41 Dave Hollins	.25	.11
❏ 42 David Justice	.75	.35
❏ 43 Darryl Kile	.25	.11
❏ 44 John Kruk	.40	.18
❏ 45 Barry Larkin	.75	.35
❏ 46 Terry Mulholland	.25	.11
❏ 47 Mike Piazza	3.00	1.35
❏ 48 Ryne Sandberg	1.00	.45
❏ 49 Gary Sheffield	.75	.35
❏ 50 John Smoltz	.50	.23

1994 Fleer Award Winners

	MINT	NRMT
COMPLETE SET (6)	12.00	5.50
COMMON CARD (1-6)	.25	.11
RANDOM INSERTS IN ALL PACKS		

❏ 1 Frank Thomas	2.00	.90
❏ 2 Barry Bonds	1.25	.55
❏ 3 Jack McDowell	.25	.11
❏ 4 Greg Maddux	2.50	1.10
❏ 5 Tim Salmon	1.00	.45
❏ 6 Mike Piazza	3.00	1.35

1994 Fleer Golden Moments

	MINT	NRMT
COMPLETE SET (10)	40.00	18.00
COMMON CARD (1-10)	.75	.35
ONE PER BLUE RETAIL JUMBO PACK		
*JUMBOS: 1.5X TO 4X BASE CARD HI		
ONE JUMBO SET PER HOBBY CASE		

❏ 1 Mark Whiten	.75	.35
❏ 2 Carlos Baerga	.75	.35
❏ 3 Dave Winfield	2.50	1.10
❏ 4 Ken Griffey Jr.	12.00	5.50
❏ 5 Bo Jackson	1.00	.45

CARLOS BAERGA
AND FRIEND

		MINT	NRMT
❏ 6	George Brett	5.00	2.20
❏ 7	Nolan Ryan	10.00	4.50
❏ 8	Fred McGriff	1.50	.70
❏ 9	Frank Thomas	5.00	2.20
❏ 10	Chris Bosio	.75	.35
	Jim Abbott		
	Darryl Kile		

1994 Fleer League Leaders

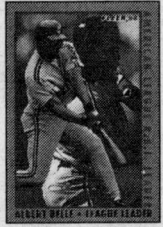

ALBERT BELLE • LEAGUE LEADER

		MINT	NRMT
	COMPLETE SET (12)	5.00	2.20
	COMMON CARD (1-528)	.25	.11
	RANDOM INSERTS IN ALL PACKS		
❏ 1	John Olerud	.40	.18
❏ 2	Albert Belle	.75	.35
❏ 3	Rafael Palmeiro	.75	.35
❏ 4	Kenny Lofton	.75	.35
❏ 5	Jack McDowell	.25	.11
❏ 6	Kevin Appier	.40	.18
❏ 7	Andres Galarraga	.75	.35
❏ 8	Barry Bonds	1.00	.45
❏ 9	Lenny Dykstra	.40	.18
❏ 10	Chuck Carr	.25	.11
❏ 11	Tom Glavine UER	.75	.35
	No number on back of card		
❏ 12	Greg Maddux	2.50	1.10

1994 Fleer Lumber Company

		MINT	NRMT
	COMPLETE SET (10)	12.00	5.50
	COMMON CARD (1-528)	.40	.18
	RANDOM INSERTS IN JUMBO PACKS		
❏ 1	Albert Belle	1.00	.45
❏ 2	Barry Bonds	1.25	.55
❏ 3	Ron Gant	.40	.18
❏ 4	Juan Gonzalez	2.00	.90
❏ 5	Ken Griffey Jr.	5.00	2.20
❏ 6	David Justice	1.00	.45
❏ 7	Fred McGriff	.75	.35
❏ 8	Rafael Palmeiro	1.00	.45
❏ 9	Frank Thomas	2.00	.90
❏ 10	Matt Williams	.75	.35

1994 Fleer Major League Prospects

MAJOR LEAGUE PROSPECTS

		MINT	NRMT
	COMPLETE SET (35)	15.00	6.75
	COMMON CARD (1-35)	.25	.11
	MINOR STARS	.50	.23
	SEMISTARS	1.00	.45
	RANDOM INSERTS IN ALL PACKS		
❏ 1	Kurt Abbott	.25	.11
❏ 2	Brian Anderson	1.00	.45
❏ 3	Rich Aude	.25	.11
❏ 4	Cory Bailey	.25	.11
❏ 5	Danny Bautista	.25	.11
❏ 6	Marty Cordova	.50	.23
❏ 7	Tripp Cromer	.25	.11
❏ 8	Midre Cummings	.25	.11
❏ 9	Carlos Delgado	2.50	1.10
❏ 10	Steve Dreyer	.25	.11
❏ 11	Steve Dunn	.25	.11
❏ 12	Jeff Granger	.25	.11
❏ 13	Tyrone Hill	.25	.11
❏ 14	Denny Hocking	.25	.11
❏ 15	John Hope	.25	.11
❏ 16	Butch Huskey	.50	.23
❏ 17	Miguel Jimenez	.25	.11
❏ 18	Chipper Jones	5.00	2.20
❏ 19	Steve Karsay	.25	.11
❏ 20	Mike Kelly	.25	.11
❏ 21	Mike Lieberthal	.25	.11
❏ 22	Albie Lopez	.25	.11
❏ 23	Jeff McNeely	.25	.11
❏ 24	Danny Miceli	.25	.11
❏ 25	Nate Minchey	.25	.11
❏ 26	Marc Newfield	.25	.11
❏ 27	Darren Oliver	1.50	.70
❏ 28	Luis Ortiz	.25	.11
❏ 29	Curtis Pride	.25	.11
❏ 30	Roger Salkeld	.25	.11
❏ 31	Scott Sanders	.25	.11
❏ 32	Dave Staton	.25	.11
❏ 33	Salomon Torres	.25	.11
❏ 34	Steve Trachsel	.25	.11
❏ 35	Chris Turner	.25	.11

1994 Fleer Pro-Visions

		MINT	NRMT
	COMPLETE SET (9)	4.00	1.80
	COMMON CARD (1-9)	.40	.18
	RANDOM INSERTS IN ALL PACKS		

		MINT	NRMT
❏ 1	Darren Daulton	.40	.18
❏ 2	John Olerud	.40	.18
❏ 3	Matt Williams	.60	.25
❏ 4	Carlos Baerga	.40	.18
❏ 5	Ozzie Smith	1.00	.45
❏ 6	Juan Gonzalez	1.50	.70
❏ 7	Jack McDowell	.25	.11
❏ 8	Mike Piazza	2.50	1.10
❏ 9	Tony Gwynn	2.00	.90

1994 Fleer Rookie Sensations

		MINT	NRMT
	COMPLETE SET (20)	18.00	8.00
	COMMON CARD (1-20)	.75	.35
	STATED ODDS 1:4 JUMBO		
❏ 1	Rene Arocha	.75	.35
❏ 2	Jason Bere	.75	.35
❏ 3	Jeromy Burnitz	1.50	.70
❏ 4	Chuck Carr	.75	.35
❏ 5	Jeff Conine	.75	.35
❏ 6	Steve Cooke	.75	.35
❏ 7	Cliff Floyd	1.50	.70
❏ 8	Jeffrey Hammonds	1.50	.70
❏ 9	Wayne Kirby	.75	.35
❏ 10	Mike Lansing	1.50	.70
❏ 11	Al Martin	.75	.35
❏ 12	Greg McMichael	.75	.35
❏ 13	Troy Neel	.75	.35
❏ 14	Mike Piazza	12.00	5.50
❏ 15	Armando Reynoso	.75	.35
❏ 16	Kirk Rueter	.75	.35
❏ 17	Tim Salmon	2.50	1.10
❏ 18	Aaron Sele	1.50	.70
❏ 19	J.T. Snow	1.50	.70
❏ 20	Kevin Stocker	.75	.35

1994 Fleer Salmon

		MINT	NRMT
	COMPLETE SET (12)	20.00	9.00
	COMMON CARD (1-12)	2.00	.90
	RANDOM INSERTS IN ALL PACKS		
	COMMON MAIL-IN (13-15)	2.00	.90
	MAIL-IN CARDS DIST.VIA WRAPPER EXCH.		
❏ 1	Tim Salmon	2.00	.90
	Watching flight of		

	ball after hit	
❑ 2 Tim Salmon	2.00	.90
	Trotting in to catch ball	
❑ 3 Tim Salmon	2.00	.90
	Follow through	
	weight on front leg	
❑ 4 Tim Salmon	2.00	.90
	Middle of swing	
	horizontal pose	
❑ 5 Tim Salmon	2.00	.90
	Sliding into base	
❑ 6 Tim Salmon	2.00	.90
	Pose swing	
	end of bat in camera angle	
❑ 7 Tim Salmon	2.00	.90
	Running with shades on	
❑ 8 Tim Salmon	2.00	.90
	Bat cocked	
	awaiting pitch	
❑ 9 Tim Salmon	2.00	.90
	Adjusting batting gloves	
	bat under arm	
❑ 10 Tim Salmon	2.00	.90
	Running to base	
❑ 11 Tim Salmon	2.00	.90
	Awaiting pitch	
	shot from left side	
	with catcher in view	
❑ 12 Tim Salmon	2.00	.90
	Ready to play	
❑ 13 Tim Salmon	2.00	.90
	Awaiting a pitch	
❑ 14 Tim Salmon	2.00	.90
	Fielding	
❑ 15 Tim Salmon	2.00	.90
	Running the bases	
❑ AU Tim Salmon AU	60.00	27.00
	(Certified autograph)	

1994 Fleer Smoke 'n Heat

	MINT	NRMT
COMPLETE SET (12)	60.00	27.00
COMMON CARD (1-12)	1.50	.70
STATED ODDS 1:36		
❑ 1 Roger Clemens	15.00	6.75
❑ 2 David Cone	4.00	1.80
❑ 3 Juan Guzman	1.50	.70

❑ 4 Pete Harnisch	1.50	.70
❑ 5 Randy Johnson	6.00	2.70
❑ 6 Mark Langston	1.50	.70
❑ 7 Greg Maddux	15.00	6.75
❑ 8 Mike Mussina	6.00	2.70
❑ 9 Jose Rijo	1.50	.70
❑ 10 Nolan Ryan	25.00	11.00
❑ 11 Curt Schilling	2.50	1.10
❑ 12 John Smoltz	4.00	1.80

1994 Fleer Team Leaders

	MINT	NRMT
COMPLETE SET (28)	25.00	11.00
COMMON CARD (1-28)	.25	.11
RANDOM INSERTS IN ALL PACKS		
❑ 1 Cal Ripken	4.00	1.80
❑ 2 Mo Vaughn	1.00	.45
❑ 3 Tim Salmon	1.00	.45
❑ 4 Frank Thomas	2.00	.90
❑ 5 Carlos Baerga	.25	.11
❑ 6 Cecil Fielder	.25	.11
❑ 7 Brian McRae	.25	.11
❑ 8 Greg Vaughn	.50	.23
❑ 9 Kirby Puckett	1.50	.70
❑ 10 Don Mattingly	2.00	.90
❑ 11 Mark McGwire	5.00	2.20
❑ 12 Ken Griffey Jr.	5.00	2.20
❑ 13 Juan Gonzalez	2.00	.90
❑ 14 Paul Molitor	1.00	.45
❑ 15 David Justice	1.00	.45
❑ 16 Ryne Sandberg	1.25	.55
❑ 17 Barry Larkin	1.00	.45
❑ 18 Andres Galarraga	1.00	.45
❑ 19 Gary Sheffield	1.00	.45
❑ 20 Jeff Bagwell	1.25	.55
❑ 21 Mike Piazza	3.00	1.35
❑ 22 Marquis Grissom	.25	.11
❑ 23 Bobby Bonilla	.50	.23
❑ 24 Lenny Dykstra	.50	.23
❑ 25 Jay Bell	.50	.23
❑ 26 Gregg Jefferies	.25	.11
❑ 27 Tony Gwynn	2.50	1.10
❑ 28 Will Clark	1.00	.45

1994 Fleer Update

	MINT	NRMT
COMP.FACT.SET (210)	60.00	27.00
COMMON CARD (U1-U200)	.15	.07
MINOR STARS	.25	.11
SEMISTARS	.50	.23
UNLISTED STARS	1.00	.45
❑ 1 Mark Eichhorn	.15	.07
❑ 2 Sid Fernandez	.15	.07
❑ 3 Leo Gomez	.15	.07
❑ 4 Mike Oquist	.15	.07
❑ 5 Rafael Palmeiro	1.00	.45
❑ 6 Chris Sabo	.15	.07
❑ 7 Dwight Smith	.15	.07
❑ 8 Lee Smith	.25	.11
❑ 9 Damon Berryhill	.15	.07
❑ 10 Wes Chamberlain	.15	.07
❑ 11 Gar Finnvold	.15	.07
❑ 12 Chris Howard	.15	.07
❑ 13 Tim Naehring	.15	.07
❑ 14 Otis Nixon	.15	.07
❑ 15 Brian Anderson	.50	.23
❑ 16 Jorge Fabregas	.15	.07
❑ 17 Rex Hudler	.15	.07
❑ 18 Bo Jackson	.25	.11
❑ 19 Mark Leiter	.15	.07
❑ 20 Spike Owen	.15	.07
❑ 21 Harold Reynolds	.15	.07
❑ 22 Chris Turner	.15	.07
❑ 23 Dennis Cook	.15	.07
❑ 24 Jose DeLeon	.15	.07
❑ 25 Julio Franco	.15	.07
❑ 26 Joe Hall	.15	.07
❑ 27 Darrin Jackson	.15	.07
❑ 28 Dane Johnson	.15	.07
❑ 29 Norberto Martin	.15	.07
❑ 30 Scott Sanderson	.15	.07
❑ 31 Jason Grimsley	.15	.07
❑ 32 Dennis Martinez	.25	.11
❑ 33 Jack Morris	.25	.11
❑ 34 Eddie Murray	1.00	.45
❑ 35 Chad Ogea	.15	.07
❑ 36 Tony Pena	.15	.07
❑ 37 Paul Shuey	.15	.07
❑ 38 Omar Vizquel	.25	.11
❑ 39 Danny Bautista	.15	.07
❑ 40 Tim Belcher	.15	.07
❑ 41 Joe Boever	.15	.07
❑ 42 Storm Davis	.15	.07
❑ 43 Junior Felix	.15	.07
❑ 44 Mike Gardiner	.15	.07
❑ 45 Buddy Groom	.15	.07
❑ 46 Juan Samuel	.15	.07
❑ 47 Vince Coleman	.15	.07
❑ 48 Bob Hamelin	.15	.07
❑ 49 Dave Henderson	.15	.07
❑ 50 Rusty Meacham	.15	.07
❑ 51 Terry Shumpert	.15	.07
❑ 52 Jeff Bronkey	.15	.07
❑ 53 Alex Diaz	.15	.07
❑ 54 Brian Harper	.15	.07
❑ 55 Jose Mercedes	.15	.07
❑ 56 Jody Reed	.15	.07
❑ 57 Bob Scanlan	.15	.07
❑ 58 Turner Ward	.15	.07
❑ 59 Rich Becker	.15	.07
❑ 60 Alex Cole	.15	.07
❑ 61 Denny Hocking	.15	.07
❑ 62 Scott Leius	.15	.07
❑ 63 Pat Mahomes	.15	.07
❑ 64 Carlos Pulido	.15	.07
❑ 65 Dave Stevens	.15	.07
❑ 66 Matt Walbeck	.15	.07
❑ 67 Xavier Hernandez	.15	.07
❑ 68 Sterling Hitchcock	.25	.11
❑ 69 Terry Mulholland	.15	.07
❑ 70 Luis Polonia	.15	.07
❑ 71 Gerald Williams	.15	.07
❑ 72 Mark Acre	.15	.07
❑ 73 Geronimo Berroa	.15	.07
❑ 74 Rickey Henderson	1.25	.55
❑ 75 Stan Javier	.15	.07
❑ 76 Steve Karsay	.15	.07
❑ 77 Carlos Reyes	.15	.07
❑ 78 Bill Taylor	.15	.07
❑ 79 Eric Anthony	.15	.07

#	Player	MINT	NRMT
❏ 80	Bobby Ayala	.15	.07
❏ 81	Tim Davis	.15	.07
❏ 82	Felix Fermin	.15	.07
❏ 83	Reggie Jefferson	.15	.07
❏ 84	Keith Mitchell	.15	.07
❏ 85	Bill Risley	.15	.07
❏ 86	Alex Rodriguez	50.00	22.00
❏ 87	Roger Salkeld	.15	.07
❏ 88	Dan Wilson	.15	.07
❏ 89	Cris Carpenter	.15	.07
❏ 90	Will Clark	1.00	.45
❏ 91	Jeff Frye	.15	.07
❏ 92	Rick Helling	.25	.11
❏ 93	Chris James	.15	.07
❏ 94	Oddibe McDowell	.15	.07
❏ 95	Billy Ripken	.15	.07
❏ 96	Carlos Delgado	1.00	.45
❏ 97	Alex Gonzalez	.15	.07
❏ 98	Shawn Green	1.50	.70
❏ 99	Darren Hall	.15	.07
❏ 100	Mike Huff	.15	.07
❏ 101	Mike Kelly	.15	.07
❏ 102	Roberto Kelly	.15	.07
❏ 103	Charlie O'Brien	.15	.07
❏ 104	Jose Oliva	.15	.07
❏ 105	Gregg Olson	.15	.07
❏ 106	Willie Banks	.15	.07
❏ 107	Jim Bullinger	.15	.07
❏ 108	Chuck Crim	.15	.07
❏ 109	Shawon Dunston	.15	.07
❏ 110	Karl Rhodes	.15	.07
❏ 111	Steve Trachsel	.15	.07
❏ 112	Anthony Young	.15	.07
❏ 113	Eddie Zambrano	.15	.07
❏ 114	Bret Boone	.25	.11
❏ 115	Jeff Brantley	.15	.07
❏ 116	Hector Carrasco	.15	.07
❏ 117	Tony Fernandez	.25	.11
❏ 118	Tim Fortugno	.15	.07
❏ 119	Erik Hanson	.15	.07
❏ 120	Chuck McElroy	.15	.07
❏ 121	Deion Sanders	.25	.11
❏ 122	Ellis Burks	.15	.07
❏ 123	Marvin Freeman	.15	.07
❏ 124	Mike Harkey	.15	.07
❏ 125	Howard Johnson	.15	.07
❏ 126	Mike Kingery	.15	.07
❏ 127	Nelson Liriano	.15	.07
❏ 128	Marcus Moore	.15	.07
❏ 129	Mike Munoz	.15	.07
❏ 130	Kevin Ritz	.15	.07
❏ 131	Walt Weiss	.15	.07
❏ 132	Kurt Abbott	.15	.07
❏ 133	Jerry Browne	.15	.07
❏ 134	Greg Colbrunn	.15	.07
❏ 135	Jeremy Hernandez	.15	.07
❏ 136	Dave Magadan	.15	.07
❏ 137	Kurt Miller	.15	.07
❏ 138	Robb Nen	.15	.07
❏ 139	Jesus Tavarez	.15	.07
❏ 140	Sid Bream	.15	.07
❏ 141	Tom Edens	.15	.07
❏ 142	Tony Eusebio	.15	.07
❏ 143	John Hudek	.15	.07
❏ 144	Brian L. Hunter	.25	.11
❏ 145	Orlando Miller	.15	.07
❏ 146	James Mouton	.15	.07
❏ 147	Shane Reynolds	.25	.11
❏ 148	Rafael Bournigal	.15	.07
❏ 149	Delino DeShields	.15	.07
❏ 150	Garey Ingram	.15	.07
❏ 151	Chan Ho Park	1.50	.70
❏ 152	Wil Cordero	.15	.07
❏ 153	Pedro Martinez	1.25	.55
❏ 154	Randy Milligan	.15	.07
❏ 155	Lenny Webster	.15	.07
❏ 156	Rico Brogna	.15	.07
❏ 157	Josias Manzanillo	.15	.07
❏ 158	Kevin McReynolds	.15	.07
❏ 159	Mike Remlinger	.15	.07
❏ 160	David Segui	.25	.11
❏ 161	Pete Smith	.15	.07
❏ 162	Kelly Stinnett	.15	.07
❏ 163	Jose Vizcaino	.15	.07
❏ 164	Billy Hatcher	.15	.07
❏ 165	Doug Jones	.15	.07
❏ 166	Mike Lieberthal	.15	.07
❏ 167	Tony Longmire	.15	.07
❏ 168	Bobby Munoz	.15	.07
❏ 169	Paul Quantrill	.15	.07
❏ 170	Heathcliff Slocumb	.15	.07
❏ 171	Fernando Valenzuela	.25	.11
❏ 172	Mark Dewey	.15	.07
❏ 173	Brian R. Hunter	.15	.07
❏ 174	Jon Lieber	.15	.07
❏ 175	Ravelo Manzanillo	.15	.07
❏ 176	Dan Miceli	.15	.07
❏ 177	Rick White	.15	.07
❏ 178	Bryan Eversgerd	.15	.07
❏ 179	John Habyan	.15	.07
❏ 180	Terry McGriff	.15	.07
❏ 181	Vicente Palacios	.15	.07
❏ 182	Rich Rodriguez	.15	.07
❏ 183	Rick Sutcliffe	.15	.07
❏ 184	Donnie Elliott	.15	.07
❏ 185	Joey Hamilton	1.00	.45
❏ 186	Tim Hyers	.15	.07
❏ 187	Luis Lopez	.15	.07
❏ 188	Ray McDavid	.15	.07
❏ 189	Bip Roberts	.15	.07
❏ 190	Scott Sanders	.15	.07
❏ 191	Eddie Williams	.15	.07
❏ 192	Steve Frey	.15	.07
❏ 193	Pat Gomez	.15	.07
❏ 194	Rich Monteleone	.15	.07
❏ 195	Mark Portugal	.15	.07
❏ 196	Darryl Strawberry	.25	.11
❏ 197	Salomon Torres	.15	.07
❏ 198	W.VanLandingham	.15	.07
❏ 199	Checklist	.15	.07
❏ 200	Checklist	.15	.07

1994 Fleer Update Diamond Tribute

	MINT	NRMT
COMPLETE SET (10)	2.00	.90
COMMON CARD (1-10)	.15	.07
ONE SET PER UPDATE FACTORY SET		

#	Player	MINT	NRMT
❏ 1	Barry Bonds	.40	.18
❏ 2	Joe Carter	.15	.07
❏ 3	Will Clark	.30	.14
❏ 4	Roger Clemens	.60	.25
❏ 5	Tony Gwynn	.75	.35
❏ 6	Don Mattingly	.50	.23
❏ 7	Fred McGriff	.25	.11
❏ 8	Eddie Murray	.30	.14
❏ 9	Kirby Puckett	.50	.23
❏ 10	Cal Ripken	1.25	.55

1995 Fleer

	MINT	NRMT
COMPLETE SET (600)	50.00	22.00
COMMON CARD (1-600)	.15	.07
MINOR STARS	.30	.14
UNLISTED STARS	.60	.25

#	Player	MINT	NRMT
❏ 1	Brady Anderson	.30	.14
❏ 2	Harold Baines	.30	.14
❏ 3	Damon Buford	.15	.07
❏ 4	Mike Devereaux	.15	.07
❏ 5	Mark Eichhorn	.15	.07

#	Player	MINT	NRMT
❏ 6	Sid Fernandez	.15	.07
❏ 7	Leo Gomez	.15	.07
❏ 8	Jeffrey Hammonds	.30	.14
❏ 9	Chris Hoiles	.15	.07
❏ 10	Rick Krivda	.15	.07
❏ 11	Ben McDonald	.15	.07
❏ 12	Mark McLemore	.15	.07
❏ 13	Alan Mills	.15	.07
❏ 14	Jamie Moyer	.15	.07
❏ 15	Mike Mussina	.60	.25
❏ 16	Mike Oquist	.15	.07
❏ 17	Rafael Palmeiro	.60	.25
❏ 18	Arthur Rhodes	.15	.07
❏ 19	Cal Ripken Jr.	2.50	1.10
❏ 20	Chris Sabo	.15	.07
❏ 21	Lee Smith	.30	.14
❏ 22	Jack Voigt	.15	.07
❏ 23	Damon Berryhill	.15	.07
❏ 24	Tom Brunansky	.15	.07
❏ 25	Wes Chamberlain	.15	.07
❏ 26	Roger Clemens	1.50	.70
❏ 27	Scott Cooper	.15	.07
❏ 28	Andre Dawson	.40	.18
❏ 29	Gar Finnvold	.15	.07
❏ 30	Tony Fossas	.15	.07
❏ 31	Mike Greenwell	.15	.07
❏ 32	Joe Hesketh	.15	.07
❏ 33	Chris Howard	.15	.07
❏ 34	Chris Nabholz	.15	.07
❏ 35	Tim Naehring	.15	.07
❏ 36	Otis Nixon	.15	.07
❏ 37	Carlos Rodriguez	.15	.07
❏ 38	Rich Rowland	.15	.07
❏ 39	Ken Ryan	.15	.07
❏ 40	Aaron Sele	.30	.14
❏ 41	John Valentin	.30	.14
❏ 42	Mo Vaughn	.60	.25
❏ 43	Frank Viola	.15	.07
❏ 44	Danny Bautista	.15	.07
❏ 45	Joe Boever	.15	.07
❏ 46	Milt Cuyler	.15	.07
❏ 47	Storm Davis	.15	.07
❏ 48	John Doherty	.15	.07
❏ 49	Junior Felix	.15	.07
❏ 50	Cecil Fielder	.30	.14
❏ 51	Travis Fryman	.30	.14
❏ 52	Mike Gardiner	.15	.07
❏ 53	Kirk Gibson	.30	.14
❏ 54	Chris Gomez	.15	.07
❏ 55	Buddy Groom	.15	.07
❏ 56	Mike Henneman	.15	.07
❏ 57	Chad Kreuter	.15	.07
❏ 58	Mike Moore	.15	.07
❏ 59	Tony Phillips	.15	.07
❏ 60	Juan Samuel	.15	.07
❏ 61	Mickey Tettleton	.30	.14
❏ 62	Alan Trammell	.30	.14
❏ 63	David Wells	.40	.18
❏ 64	Lou Whitaker	.30	.14
❏ 65	Jim Abbott	.15	.07
❏ 66	Joe Ausanio	.15	.07
❏ 67	Wade Boggs	.60	.25
❏ 68	Mike Gallego	.15	.07
❏ 69	Xavier Hernandez	.15	.07
❏ 70	Sterling Hitchcock	.30	.14
❏ 71	Steve Howe	.15	.07
❏ 72	Scott Kamieniecki	.15	.07
❏ 73	Pat Kelly	.15	.07

74	Jimmy Key	.30	.14
75	Jim Leyritz	.15	.07
76	Don Mattingly UER	1.25	.55
	Photo is a reversed negative		
77	Terry Mulholland	.15	.07
78	Paul O'Neill	.30	.14
79	Melido Perez	.15	.07
80	Luis Polonia	.15	.07
81	Mike Stanley	.15	.07
82	Danny Tartabull	.15	.07
83	Randy Velarde	.15	.07
84	Bob Wickman	.15	.07
85	Bernie Williams	.60	.25
86	Gerald Williams	.15	.07
87	Roberto Alomar	.60	.25
88	Pat Borders	.15	.07
89	Joe Carter	.30	.14
90	Tony Castillo	.15	.07
91	Brad Cornett	.15	.07
92	Carlos Delgado	.60	.25
93	Alex Gonzalez	.15	.07
94	Shawn Green	.60	.25
95	Juan Guzman	.15	.07
96	Darren Hall	.15	.07
97	Pat Hentgen	.30	.14
98	Mike Huff	.15	.07
99	Randy Knorr	.15	.07
100	Al Leiter	.30	.14
101	Paul Molitor	.60	.25
102	John Olerud	.30	.14
103	Dick Schofield	.15	.07
104	Ed Sprague	.15	.07
105	Dave Stewart	.30	.14
106	Todd Stottlemyre	.15	.07
107	Devon White	.30	.14
108	Woody Williams	.15	.07
109	Wilson Alvarez	.30	.14
110	Paul Assenmacher	.15	.07
111	Jason Bere	.15	.07
112	Dennis Cook	.15	.07
113	Joey Cora	.15	.07
114	Jose DeLeon	.15	.07
115	Alex Fernandez	.15	.07
116	Julio Franco	.15	.07
117	Craig Grebeck	.15	.07
118	Ozzie Guillen	.15	.07
119	Roberto Hernandez	.15	.07
120	Darrin Jackson	.15	.07
121	Lance Johnson	.15	.07
122	Ron Karkovice	.15	.07
123	Mike LaValliere	.15	.07
124	Norberto Martin	.15	.07
125	Kirk McCaskill	.15	.07
126	Jack McDowell	.15	.07
127	Tim Raines	.30	.14
128	Frank Thomas	1.25	.55
129	Robin Ventura	.30	.14
130	Sandy Alomar Jr.	.30	.14
131	Carlos Baerga	.15	.07
132	Albert Belle	.60	.25
133	Mark Clark	.15	.07
134	Alvaro Espinoza	.15	.07
135	Jason Grimsley	.15	.07
136	Wayne Kirby	.15	.07
137	Kenny Lofton	.40	.18
138	Albie Lopez	.15	.07
139	Dennis Martinez	.30	.14
140	Jose Mesa	.15	.07
141	Eddie Murray	.60	.25
142	Charles Nagy	.30	.14
143	Tony Pena	.15	.07
144	Eric Plunk	.15	.07
145	Manny Ramirez	.75	.35
146	Jeff Russell	.15	.07
147	Paul Shuey	.15	.07
148	Paul Sorrento	.15	.07
149	Jim Thome	.60	.25
150	Omar Vizquel	.30	.14
151	Dave Winfield	.60	.25
152	Kevin Appier	.30	.14
153	Billy Brewer	.15	.07
154	Vince Coleman	.15	.07
155	David Cone	.40	.18
156	Gary Gaetti	.30	.14
157	Greg Gagne	.15	.07
158	Tom Gordon	.15	.07
159	Mark Gubicza	.15	.07
160	Bob Hamelin	.15	.07
161	Dave Henderson	.15	.07
162	Felix Jose	.15	.07
163	Wally Joyner	.30	.14
164	Jose Lind	.15	.07
165	Mike Macfarlane	.15	.07
166	Mike Magnante	.15	.07
167	Brent Mayne	.15	.07
168	Brian McRae	.15	.07
169	Rusty Meacham	.15	.07
170	Jeff Montgomery	.15	.07
171	Hipolito Pichardo	.15	.07
172	Terry Shumpert	.15	.07
173	Michael Tucker	.30	.14
174	Ricky Bones	.15	.07
175	Jeff Cirillo	.30	.14
176	Alex Diaz	.15	.07
177	Cal Eldred	.30	.14
178	Mike Fetters	.15	.07
179	Darryl Hamilton	.15	.07
180	Brian Harper	.15	.07
181	John Jaha	.15	.07
182	Pat Listach	.15	.07
183	Graeme Lloyd	.15	.07
184	Jose Mercedes	.15	.07
185	Matt Mieske	.15	.07
186	Dave Nilsson	.15	.07
187	Jody Reed	.15	.07
188	Bob Scanlan	.15	.07
189	Kevin Seitzer	.15	.07
190	Bill Spiers	.15	.07
191	B.J. Surhoff	.30	.14
192	Jose Valentin	.15	.07
193	Greg Vaughn	.30	.14
194	Turner Ward	.15	.07
195	Bill Wegman	.15	.07
196	Rick Aguilera	.15	.07
197	Rich Becker	.15	.07
198	Alex Cole	.15	.07
199	Marty Cordova	.15	.07
200	Steve Dunn	.15	.07
201	Scott Erickson	.30	.14
202	Mark Guthrie	.15	.07
203	Chip Hale	.15	.07
204	LaTroy Hawkins	.15	.07
205	Denny Hocking	.15	.07
206	Chuck Knoblauch	.60	.25
207	Scott Leius	.15	.07
208	Shane Mack	.15	.07
209	Pat Mahomes	.15	.07
210	Pat Meares	.15	.07
211	Pedro Munoz	.15	.07
212	Kirby Puckett	1.00	.45
213	Jeff Reboulet	.15	.07
214	Dave Stevens	.15	.07
215	Kevin Tapani	.15	.07
216	Matt Walbeck	.15	.07
217	Carl Willis	.15	.07
218	Brian Anderson	.30	.14
219	Chad Curtis	.15	.07
220	Chili Davis	.30	.14
221	Gary DiSarcina	.15	.07
222	Damion Easley	.30	.14
223	Jim Edmonds	.40	.18
224	Chuck Finley	.15	.07
225	Joe Grahe	.15	.07
226	Rex Hudler	.15	.07
227	Bo Jackson	.30	.14
228	Mark Langston	.15	.07
229	Phil Leftwich	.15	.07
230	Mark Leiter	.15	.07
231	Spike Owen	.15	.07
232	Bob Patterson	.15	.07
233	Troy Percival	.30	.14
234	Eduardo Perez	.15	.07
235	Tim Salmon	.60	.25
236	J.T. Snow	.30	.14
237	Chris Turner	.15	.07
238	Mark Acre	.15	.07
239	Geronimo Berroa	.15	.07
240	Mike Bordick	.15	.07
241	John Briscoe	.15	.07
242	Scott Brosius	.30	.14
243	Ron Darling	.15	.07
244	Dennis Eckersley	.30	.14
245	Brent Gates	.15	.07
246	Rickey Henderson	.75	.35
247	Stan Javier	.15	.07
248	Steve Karsay	.15	.07
249	Mark McGwire	3.00	1.35
250	Troy Neel	.15	.07
251	Steve Ontiveros	.15	.07
252	Carlos Reyes	.15	.07
253	Ruben Sierra	.15	.07
254	Terry Steinbach	.15	.07
255	Bill Taylor	.15	.07
256	Todd Van Poppel	.15	.07
257	Bobby Witt	.15	.07
258	Rich Amaral	.15	.07
259	Eric Anthony	.15	.07
260	Bobby Ayala	.15	.07
261	Mike Blowers	.15	.07
262	Chris Bosio	.15	.07
263	Jay Buhner	.30	.14
264	John Cummings	.15	.07
265	Tim Davis	.15	.07
266	Felix Fermin	.15	.07
267	Dave Fleming	.15	.07
268	Goose Gossage	.30	.14
269	Ken Griffey Jr.	3.00	1.35
270	Reggie Jefferson	.15	.07
271	Randy Johnson	.60	.25
272	Edgar Martinez	.30	.14
273	Tino Martinez	.60	.25
274	Greg Pirkl	.15	.07
275	Bill Risley	.15	.07
276	Roger Salkeld	.15	.07
277	Luis Sojo	.15	.07
278	Mac Suzuki	.30	.14
279	Dan Wilson	.15	.07
280	Kevin Brown	.40	.18
281	Jose Canseco	.75	.35
282	Cris Carpenter	.15	.07
283	Will Clark	.60	.25
284	Jeff Frye	.15	.07
285	Juan Gonzalez	1.25	.55
286	Rick Helling	.30	.14
287	Tom Henke	.15	.07
288	David Hulse	.15	.07
289	Chris James	.15	.07
290	Manuel Lee	.15	.07
291	Oddibe McDowell	.15	.07
292	Dean Palmer	.30	.14
293	Roger Pavlik	.15	.07
294	Bill Ripken	.15	.07
295	Ivan Rodriguez	.75	.35
296	Kenny Rogers	.15	.07
297	Doug Strange	.15	.07
298	Matt Whiteside	.15	.07
299	Steve Avery	.15	.07
300	Steve Bedrosian	.15	.07
301	Rafael Belliard	.15	.07
302	Jeff Blauser	.15	.07
303	Dave Gallagher	.15	.07
304	Tom Glavine	.60	.25
305	David Justice	.60	.25
306	Mike Kelly	.15	.07
307	Roberto Kelly	.15	.07
308	Ryan Klesko	.30	.14
309	Mark Lemke	.15	.07
310	Javier Lopez	.30	.14
311	Greg Maddux	1.50	.70
312	Fred McGriff	.40	.18
313	Greg McMichael	.15	.07
314	Kent Mercker	.15	.07
315	Charlie O'Brien	.15	.07
316	Jose Oliva	.15	.07
317	Terry Pendleton	.15	.07
318	John Smoltz	.40	.18
319	Mike Stanton	.15	.07
320	Tony Tarasco	.15	.07
321	Terrell Wade	.15	.07
322	Mark Wohlers	.15	.07
323	Kurt Abbott	.15	.07
324	Luis Aquino	.15	.07
325	Bret Barberie	.15	.07
326	Ryan Bowen	.15	.07
327	Jerry Browne	.15	.07
328	Chuck Carr	.15	.07
329	Matias Carrillo	.15	.07
330	Greg Colbrunn	.15	.07

331	Jeff Conine	.15	.07
332	Mark Gardner	.15	.07
333	Chris Hammond	.15	.07
334	Bryan Harvey	.15	.07
335	Richie Lewis	.15	.07
336	Dave Magadan	.15	.07
337	Terry Mathews	.15	.07
338	Robb Nen	.15	.07
339	Yorkis Perez	.15	.07
340	Pat Rapp	.15	.07
341	Benito Santiago	.15	.07
342	Gary Sheffield	.30	.14
343	Dave Weathers	.15	.07
344	Moises Alou	.30	.14
345	Sean Berry	.15	.07
346	Wil Cordero	.15	.07
347	Joey Eischen	.15	.07
348	Jeff Fassero	.15	.07
349	Darrin Fletcher	.15	.07
350	Cliff Floyd	.30	.14
351	Marquis Grissom	.30	.14
352	Butch Henry	.15	.07
353	Gil Heredia	.15	.07
354	Ken Hill	.15	.07
355	Mike Lansing	.15	.07
356	Pedro Martinez	.75	.35
357	Mel Rojas	.15	.07
358	Kirk Rueter	.15	.07
359	Tim Scott	.15	.07
360	Jeff Shaw	.15	.07
361	Larry Walker	.60	.25
362	Lenny Webster	.15	.07
363	John Wetteland	.30	.14
364	Rondell White	.30	.14
365	Bobby Bonilla	.30	.14
366	Rico Brogna	.15	.07
367	Jeromy Burnitz	.30	.14
368	John Franco	.30	.14
369	Dwight Gooden	.30	.14
370	Todd Hundley	.30	.14
371	Jason Jacome	.15	.07
372	Bobby Jones	.15	.07
373	Jeff Kent	.30	.14
374	Jim Lindeman	.15	.07
375	Josias Manzanillo	.15	.07
376	Roger Mason	.15	.07
377	Kevin McReynolds	.15	.07
378	Joe Orsulak	.15	.07
379	Bill Pulsipher	.15	.07
380	Bret Saberhagen	.30	.14
381	David Segui	.30	.14
382	Pete Smith	.15	.07
383	Kelly Stinnett	.15	.07
384	Ryan Thompson	.15	.07
385	Jose Vizcaino	.15	.07
386	Toby Borland	.15	.07
387	Ricky Bottalico	.15	.07
388	Darren Daulton	.30	.14
389	Mariano Duncan	.15	.07
390	Lenny Dykstra	.30	.14
391	Jim Eisenreich	.15	.07
392	Tommy Greene	.15	.07
393	Dave Hollins	.15	.07
394	Pete Incaviglia	.15	.07
395	Danny Jackson	.15	.07
396	Doug Jones	.15	.07
397	Ricky Jordan	.15	.07
398	John Kruk	.30	.14
399	Mike Lieberthal	.15	.07
400	Tony Longmire	.15	.07
401	Mickey Morandini	.15	.07
402	Bobby Munoz	.15	.07
403	Curt Schilling	.40	.18
404	Heathcliff Slocumb	.15	.07
405	Kevin Stocker	.15	.07
406	Fernando Valenzuela	.30	.14
407	David West	.40	.18
408	Willie Banks	.15	.07
409	Dante Bautista	.15	.07
410	Steve Buechele	.15	.07
411	Jim Bullinger	.15	.07
412	Chuck Crim	.15	.07
413	Shawon Dunston	.15	.07
414	Kevin Foster	.15	.07
415	Mark Grace	.40	.18
416	Jose Hernandez	.15	.07
417	Glenallen Hill	.15	.07
418	Brooks Kieschnick	.15	.07
419	Derrick May	.15	.07
420	Randy Myers	.15	.07
421	Dan Plesac	.15	.07
422	Karl Rhodes	.15	.07
423	Rey Sanchez	.15	.07
424	Sammy Sosa	2.00	.90
425	Steve Trachsel	.15	.07
426	Rick Wilkins	.15	.07
427	Anthony Young	.15	.07
428	Eddie Zambrano	.15	.07
429	Bret Boone	.30	.14
430	Jeff Branson	.15	.07
431	Jeff Brantley	.15	.07
432	Hector Carrasco	.15	.07
433	Brian Dorsett	.15	.07
434	Tony Fernandez	.30	.14
435	Tim Fortugno	.15	.07
436	Erik Hanson	.15	.07
437	Thomas Howard	.15	.07
438	Kevin Jarvis	.15	.07
439	Barry Larkin	.60	.25
440	Chuck McElroy	.15	.07
441	Kevin Mitchell	.15	.07
442	Hal Morris	.15	.07
443	Jose Rijo	.15	.07
444	John Roper	.15	.07
445	Johnny Ruffin	.15	.07
446	Deion Sanders	.30	.14
447	Reggie Sanders	.30	.14
448	Pete Schourek	.15	.07
449	John Smiley	.15	.07
450	Eddie Taubensee	.15	.07
451	Jeff Bagwell	.75	.35
452	Kevin Bass	.15	.07
453	Craig Biggio	.60	.25
454	Ken Caminiti	.40	.18
455	Andujar Cedeno	.15	.07
456	Doug Drabek	.15	.07
457	Tony Eusebio	.15	.07
458	Mike Felder	.15	.07
459	Steve Finley	.30	.14
460	Luis Gonzalez	.15	.07
461	Mike Hampton	.15	.07
462	Pete Harnisch	.15	.07
463	John Hudek	.15	.07
464	Todd Jones	.15	.07
465	Darryl Kile	.15	.07
466	James Mouton	.15	.07
467	Shane Reynolds	.30	.14
468	Scott Servais	.15	.07
469	Greg Swindell	.15	.07
470	Dave Veres	.15	.07
471	Brian Williams	.15	.07
472	Jay Bell	.30	.14
473	Jacob Brumfield	.15	.07
474	Dave Clark	.15	.07
475	Steve Cooke	.15	.07
476	Midre Cummings	.15	.07
477	Mark Dewey	.15	.07
478	Tom Foley	.15	.07
479	Carlos Garcia	.15	.07
480	Jeff King	.15	.07
481	Jon Lieber	.15	.07
482	Ravelo Manzanillo	.15	.07
483	Al Martin	.15	.07
484	Orlando Merced	.15	.07
485	Danny Miceli	.15	.07
486	Denny Neagle	.30	.14
487	Lance Parrish	.15	.07
488	Don Slaught	.15	.07
489	Zane Smith	.15	.07
490	Andy Van Slyke	.30	.14
491	Paul Wagner	.15	.07
492	Rick White	.15	.07
493	Luis Alicea	.15	.07
494	Rene Arocha	.15	.07
495	Rheal Cormier	.15	.07
496	Bryan Eversgerd	.15	.07
497	Bernard Gilkey	.15	.07
498	John Habyan	.15	.07
499	Gregg Jefferies	.15	.07
500	Brian Jordan	.30	.14
501	Ray Lankford	.30	.14
502	John Mabry	.15	.07
503	Terry McGriff	.15	.07
504	Tom Pagnozzi	.15	.07
505	Vicente Palacios	.15	.07
506	Geronimo Pena	.15	.07
507	Gerald Perry	.15	.07
508	Rich Rodriguez	.15	.07
509	Ozzie Smith	.75	.35
510	Bob Tewksbury	.15	.07
511	Allen Watson	.15	.07
512	Mark Whiten	.15	.07
513	Todd Zeile	.15	.07
514	Dante Bichette	.30	.14
515	Willie Blair	.15	.07
516	Ellis Burks	.30	.14
517	Marvin Freeman	.15	.07
518	Andres Galarraga	.60	.25
519	Joe Girardi	.15	.07
520	Greg W. Harris	.15	.07
521	Charlie Hayes	.15	.07
522	Mike Kingery	.15	.07
523	Nelson Liriano	.15	.07
524	Mike Munoz	.15	.07
525	David Nied	.15	.07
526	Steve Reed	.15	.07
527	Kevin Ritz	.15	.07
528	Bruce Ruffin	.15	.07
529	John Vander Wal	.15	.07
530	Walt Weiss	.15	.07
531	Eric Young	.15	.07
532	Billy Ashley	.15	.07
533	Pedro Astacio	.15	.07
534	Rafael Bournigal	.15	.07
535	Brett Butler	.30	.14
536	Tom Candiotti	.15	.07
537	Omar Daal	.15	.07
538	Delino DeShields	.15	.07
539	Darren Dreifort	.30	.14
540	Kevin Gross	.15	.07
541	Orel Hershiser	.30	.14
542	Garey Ingram	.15	.07
543	Eric Karros	.30	.14
544	Ramon Martinez	.30	.14
545	Raul Mondesi	.40	.18
546	Chan Ho Park	.60	.25
547	Mike Piazza	2.00	.90
548	Henry Rodriguez	.30	.14
549	Rudy Seanez	.15	.07
550	Ismael Valdes	.30	.14
551	Tim Wallach	.15	.07
552	Todd Worrell	.15	.07
553	Andy Ashby	.15	.07
554	Brad Ausmus	.15	.07
555	Derek Bell	.30	.14
556	Andy Benes	.30	.14
557	Phil Clark	.15	.07
558	Donnie Elliott	.15	.07
559	Ricky Gutierrez	.15	.07
560	Tony Gwynn	1.50	.70
561	Joey Hamilton	.30	.14
562	Trevor Hoffman	.30	.14
563	Luis Lopez	.15	.07
564	Pedro A. Martinez	.15	.07
565	Tim Mauser	.15	.07
566	Phil Plantier	.15	.07
567	Bip Roberts	.15	.07
568	Scott Sanders	.15	.07
569	Craig Shipley	.15	.07
570	Jeff Tabaka	.15	.07
571	Eddie Williams	.15	.07
572	Rod Beck	.15	.07
573	Mike Benjamin	.15	.07
574	Barry Bonds	.75	.35
575	Dave Burba	.15	.07
576	John Burkett	.15	.07
577	Mark Carreon	.15	.07
578	Royce Clayton	.15	.07
579	Steve Frey	.15	.07
580	Bryan Hickerson	.15	.07
581	Mike Jackson	.30	.14
582	Darren Lewis	.15	.07
583	Kirt Manwaring	.15	.07
584	Rich Monteleone	.15	.07
585	John Patterson	.15	.07
586	J.R. Phillips	.15	.07
587	Mark Portugal	.15	.07
588	Joe Rosselli	.15	.07

		MINT	NRMT
❏ 589	Darryl Strawberry	.30	.14
❏ 590	Bill Swift	.15	.07
❏ 591	Robby Thompson	.15	.07
❏ 592	William VanLandingham	.15	.07
❏ 593	Matt Williams	.60	.25
❏ 594	Checklist	.15	.07
❏ 595	Checklist	.15	.07
❏ 596	Checklist	.15	.07
❏ 597	Checklist	.15	.07
❏ 598	Checklist	.15	.07
❏ 599	Checklist	.15	.07
❏ 600	Checklist	.15	.07

1995 Fleer All-Fleer

	MINT	NRMT
COMPLETE SET (9)	10.00	4.50
COMMON CARD (1-9)	.60	.25

SETS WERE AVAILABLE VIA WRAPPER OFFER

❏ 1	Mike Piazza	2.00	.90
❏ 2	Frank Thomas	1.25	.55
❏ 3	Roberto Alomar	.60	.25
❏ 4	Cal Ripken	2.50	1.10
❏ 5	Matt Williams	.60	.25
❏ 6	Barry Bonds	.75	.35
❏ 7	Ken Griffey Jr.	3.00	1.35
❏ 8	Tony Gwynn	1.50	.70
❏ 9	Greg Maddux	1.50	.70

1995 Fleer All-Rookies

	MINT	NRMT
COMPLETE SET (9)	3.00	1.35
COMMON CARD (M1-M9)	.25	.11
MINOR STARS	.50	.23

ONE SET PER EXCHANGE CARD VIA MAIL

❏ M1	Edgardo Alfonzo	1.50	.70
❏ M2	Jason Bates	.25	.11
❏ M3	Brian Boehringer	.25	.11
❏ M4	Darren Bragg	.25	.11
❏ M5	Brad Clontz	.25	.11
❏ M6	Jim Dougherty	.25	.11
❏ M7	Todd Hollandsworth	.25	.11
❏ M8	Rudy Pemberton	.25	.11
❏ M9	Frank Rodriguez	.25	.11
❏ NNO	Expired All-Rookie Exch.	1.00	.45

1995 Fleer All-Stars

	MINT	NRMT
COMPLETE SET (25)	12.00	5.50
COMMON CARD (1-25)	.25	.11
SEMISTARS	.50	.23

RANDOM INSERTS IN PACKS

❏ 1	Ivan Rodriguez	2.00	.90
	Mike Piazza		
❏ 2	Frank Thomas	1.25	.55
	Gregg Jefferies		
❏ 3	Robert Alomar	.60	.25
	Mariano Duncan		
❏ 4	Wade Boggs	.60	.25
	Matt Williams		
❏ 5	Cal Ripken Jr.	2.50	1.10
	Ozzie Smith		
❏ 6	Joe Carter	.75	.35
	Barry Bonds		
❏ 7	Ken Griffey Jr.	4.00	1.80
	Tony Gwynn		
❏ 8	Kirby Puckett	1.00	.45
	David Justice		
❏ 9	Jimmy Key	1.50	.70
	Greg Maddux		
❏ 10	Chuck Knoblauch	.60	.25
	Wil Cordero		
❏ 11	Scott Cooper	.40	.18
	Ken Caminiti		
❏ 12	Will Clark	.50	.23
	Carlos Garcia		
❏ 13	Paul Molitor	.75	.35
	Jeff Bagwell		
❏ 14	Travis Fryman	.50	.23
	Craig Biggio		
❏ 15	Mickey Tettleton	.50	.23
	Fred McGriff		
❏ 16	Kenny Lofton	.75	.35
	Moises Alou		
❏ 17	Albert Belle	.60	.25
	Marquis Grissom		
❏ 18	Paul O'Neill	.40	.18
	Dante Bichette		
❏ 19	David Cone	.50	.23
	Ken Hill		
❏ 20	Mike Mussina	.60	.25
	Doug Drabek		
❏ 21	Randy Johnson	.60	.25
	John Hudek		
❏ 22	Pat Hentgen	.25	.11
	Danny Jackson		
❏ 23	Wilson Alvarez	.25	.11
	Rod Beck		
❏ 24	Lee Smith	.25	.11
	Randy Myers		
❏ 25	Jason Bere	.25	.11
	Doug Jones		

1995 Fleer Award Winners

	MINT	NRMT
COMPLETE SET (6)	8.00	3.60
COMMON CARD (1-6)	.50	.23

STATED ODDS 1:24

❏ 1	Frank Thomas	2.00	.90

❏ 2	Jeff Bagwell	1.25	.55
❏ 3	David Cone	1.00	.45
❏ 4	Greg Maddux	2.50	1.10
❏ 5	Bob Hamelin	.50	.23
❏ 6	Raul Mondesi	1.00	.45

1995 Fleer League Leaders

	MINT	NRMT
COMPLETE SET (10)	8.00	3.60
COMMON CARD (1-10)	.50	.23

STATED ODDS 1:12

❏ 1	Paul O'Neill	.50	.23
❏ 2	Ken Griffey Jr.	5.00	2.20
❏ 3	Kirby Puckett	1.00	.45
❏ 4	Jimmy Key	.50	.23
❏ 5	Randy Johnson	1.00	.45
❏ 6	Tony Gwynn	2.50	1.10
❏ 7	Matt Williams	1.00	.45
❏ 8	Jeff Bagwell	1.25	.55
❏ 9	Greg Maddux	1.50	.70
	Ken Hill		
❏ 10	Andy Benes	.50	.23

1995 Fleer Lumber Company

	MINT	NRMT
COMPLETE SET (10)	40.00	18.00
COMMON CARD (1-10)	1.00	.45

STATED ODDS 1:24 RETAIL

	MINT	NRMT
☐ 1 Jeff Bagwell	4.00	1.80
☐ 2 Albert Belle	2.50	1.10
☐ 3 Barry Bonds	4.00	1.80
☐ 4 Jose Canseco	4.00	1.80
☐ 5 Joe Carter	1.50	.70
☐ 6 Ken Griffey Jr.	15.00	6.75
☐ 7 Fred McGriff	2.00	.90
☐ 8 Kevin Mitchell	1.00	.45
☐ 9 Frank Thomas	6.00	2.70
☐ 10 Matt Williams	2.50	1.10

1995 Fleer Major League Prospects

CHARLES JOHNSON ▪ MARLINS

	MINT	NRMT
COMPLETE SET (10)	10.00	4.50
COMMON CARD (1-10)	.50	.23
SEMISTARS	1.00	.45

STATED ODDS 1:6

☐ 1 Garret Anderson	.75	.35
☐ 2 James Baldwin	.75	.35
☐ 3 Alan Benes	.50	.23
☐ 4 Armando Benitez	.50	.23
☐ 5 Ray Durham	.75	.35
☐ 6 Brian L. Hunter	.75	.35
☐ 7 Derek Jeter	5.00	2.20
☐ 8 Charles Johnson	.75	.35
☐ 9 Orlando Miller	.50	.23
☐ 10 Alex Rodriguez	5.00	2.20

1995 Fleer Pro-Visions

	MINT	NRMT
COMPLETE SET (6)	3.00	1.35
COMMON CARD (1-6)	.50	.23

STATED ODDS 1:9

☐ 1 Mike Mussina	.60	.25
☐ 2 Raul Mondesi	.50	.23
☐ 3 Jeff Bagwell	1.00	.45
☐ 4 Greg Maddux	1.50	.70
☐ 5 Tim Salmon	.60	.25
☐ 6 Manny Ramirez	.75	.35

1995 Fleer Rookie Sensations

	MINT	NRMT
COMPLETE SET (20)	40.00	18.00
COMMON CARD (1-20)	2.00	.90
MINOR STARS	4.00	1.80

RANDOM INSERTS IN JUMBO PACKS

☐ 1 Kurt Abbott	2.00	.90
☐ 2 Rico Brogna	2.00	.90
☐ 3 Hector Carrasco	2.00	.90
☐ 4 Kevin Foster	2.00	.90
☐ 5 Chris Gomez	2.00	.90
☐ 6 Darren Hall	2.00	.90
☐ 7 Bob Hamelin	2.00	.90
☐ 8 Joey Hamilton	4.00	1.80
☐ 9 John Hudek	2.00	.90
☐ 10 Ryan Klesko	4.00	1.80
☐ 11 Javier Lopez	4.00	1.80
☐ 12 Matt Mieske	2.00	.90
☐ 13 Raul Mondesi	4.00	1.80
☐ 14 Manny Ramirez	10.00	4.50
☐ 15 Shane Reynolds	4.00	1.80
☐ 16 Bill Risley	2.00	.90
☐ 17 Johnny Ruffin	2.00	.90
☐ 18 Steve Trachsel	2.00	.90
☐ 19 William VanLandingham	2.00	.90
☐ 20 Rondell White	4.00	1.80

1995 Fleer Team Leaders

MATT WILLIAMS

	MINT	NRMT
COMPLETE SET (28)	200.00	90.00
COMMON CARD (1-28)	2.50	1.10
SEMISTARS	5.00	2.20
UNLISTED STARS	8.00	3.60

STATED ODDS 1:24 HOBBY

☐ 1 Cal Ripken Jr.	30.00	13.50
Mike Mussina		
☐ 2 Mo Vaughn	20.00	9.00
Roger Clemens		
☐ 3 Tim Salmon	2.50	1.10
Chuck Finley		
☐ 4 Frank Thomas	15.00	6.75
Jack McDowell		
☐ 5 Albert Belle	8.00	3.60
Dennis Martinez		

☐ 6 Cecil Fielder	4.00	1.80
Mike Moore		
☐ 7 Bob Hamelin	2.50	1.10
David Cone		
☐ 8 Greg Vaughn	2.50	1.10
Ricky Bones		
☐ 9 Kirby Puckett	12.00	5.50
Rick Aguilera		
☐ 10 Don Mattingly	15.00	6.75
Jimmy Key		
☐ 11 Ruben Sierra	2.50	1.10
Dennis Eckersley		
☐ 12 Ken Griffey Jr.	40.00	18.00
Randy Johnson		
☐ 13 Jose Canseco	10.00	4.50
Kenny Rogers		
☐ 14 Joe Carter	4.00	1.80
Pat Hentgen		
☐ 15 David Justice	20.00	9.00
Greg Maddux		
☐ 16 Sammy Sosa	25.00	11.00
Steve Trachsel		
☐ 17 Kevin Mitchell	2.50	1.10
Jose Rijo		
☐ 18 Dante Bichette	2.50	1.10
Bruce Ruffin		
☐ 19 Jeff Conine	2.50	1.10
Robb Nen		
☐ 20 Jeff Bagwell	10.00	4.50
Doug Drabek		
☐ 21 Mike Piazza	20.00	9.00
Ramon Martinez		
☐ 22 Moises Alou	4.00	1.80
Ken Hill		
☐ 23 Bobby Bonilla	2.50	1.10
Bret Saberhagen		
☐ 24 Darren Daulton	4.00	1.80
Danny Jackson		
☐ 25 Jay Bell	4.00	1.80
Zane Smith		
☐ 26 Gregg Jefferies	2.50	1.10
Bob Tewksbury		
☐ 27 Tony Gwynn	20.00	9.00
Andy Benes		
☐ 28 Matt Williams	2.50	1.10
Rod Beck		

1995 Fleer Update

	MINT	NRMT
COMPLETE SET (200)	15.00	6.75
COMMON CARD (1-200)	.10	.05
MINOR STARS	.20	.09
UNLISTED STARS	.40	.18

☐ 1 Manny Alexander	.10	.05
☐ 2 Bret Barberie	.10	.05
☐ 3 Armando Benitez	.10	.05
☐ 4 Kevin Brown	.30	.14
☐ 5 Doug Jones	.10	.05
☐ 6 Sherman Obando	.10	.05
☐ 7 Andy Van Slyke	.20	.09
☐ 8 Stan Belinda	.10	.05
☐ 9 Jose Canseco	.50	.23
☐ 10 Vaughn Eshelman	.10	.05
☐ 11 Mike Macfarlane	.10	.05
☐ 12 Troy O'Leary	.20	.09
☐ 13 Steve Rodriguez	.10	.05

❑ 14 Lee Tinsley	.10	.05
❑ 15 Tim Vanegmond	.10	.05
❑ 16 Mark Whiten	.10	.05
❑ 17 Sean Bergman	.10	.05
❑ 18 Chad Curtis	.10	.05
❑ 19 John Flaherty	.10	.05
❑ 20 Bob Higginson	.60	.25
❑ 21 Felipe Lira	.10	.05
❑ 22 Shannon Penn	.10	.05
❑ 23 Todd Stevenson	.10	.05
❑ 24 Sean Whiteside	.10	.05
❑ 25 Tony Fernandez	.20	.09
❑ 26 Jack McDowell	.10	.05
❑ 27 Andy Pettitte	.40	.18
❑ 28 John Wetteland	.20	.09
❑ 29 David Cone	.30	.14
❑ 30 Mike Timlin	.10	.05
❑ 31 Duane Ward	.10	.05
❑ 32 Jim Abbott	.20	.09
❑ 33 James Baldwin	.20	.09
❑ 34 Mike Devereaux	.10	.05
❑ 35 Ray Durham	.20	.09
❑ 36 Tim Fortugno	.10	.05
❑ 37 Scott Ruffcorn	.10	.05
❑ 38 Chris Sabo	.10	.05
❑ 39 Paul Assenmacher	.10	.05
❑ 40 Bud Black	.10	.05
❑ 41 Orel Hershiser	.20	.09
❑ 42 Julian Tavarez	.10	.05
❑ 43 Dave Winfield	.40	.18
❑ 44 Pat Borders	.10	.05
❑ 45 Melvin Bunch	.10	.05
❑ 46 Tom Goodwin	.10	.05
❑ 47 Jon Nunnally	.10	.05
❑ 48 Joe Randa	.10	.05
❑ 49 Dilson Torres	.10	.05
❑ 50 Joe Vitiello	.10	.05
❑ 51 David Hulse	.10	.05
❑ 52 Scott Karl	.10	.05
❑ 53 Mark Kiefer	.10	.05
❑ 54 Derrick May	.10	.05
❑ 55 Joe Oliver	.10	.05
❑ 56 Al Reyes	.10	.05
❑ 57 Steve Sparks	.10	.05
❑ 58 Jerald Clark	.10	.05
❑ 59 Eddie Guardado	.10	.05
❑ 60 Kevin Maas	.10	.05
❑ 61 David McCarty	.10	.05
❑ 62 Brad Radke	.60	
❑ 63 Scott Stahoviak	.20	.09
❑ 64 Garret Anderson	.20	.09
❑ 65 Shawn Boskie	.10	.05
❑ 66 Mike James	.10	.05
❑ 67 Tony Phillips	.10	.05
❑ 68 Lee Smith	.20	.09
❑ 69 Mitch Williams	.10	.05
❑ 70 Jim Corsi	.10	.05
❑ 71 Mark Harkey	.10	.05
❑ 72 Dave Stewart	.20	.09
❑ 73 Todd Stottlemyre	.10	.05
❑ 74 Joey Cora	.10	.05
❑ 75 Chad Kreuter	.10	.05
❑ 76 Jeff Nelson	.10	.05
❑ 77 Alex Rodriguez	1.50	.70
❑ 78 Ron Villone	.10	.05
❑ 79 Bob Wells	.10	.05
❑ 80 Jose Alberro	.10	.05
❑ 81 Terry Burrows	.10	.05
❑ 82 Kevin Gross	.10	.05
❑ 83 Wilson Heredia	.10	.05
❑ 84 Mark McLemore	.10	.05
❑ 85 Otis Nixon	.10	.05
❑ 86 Jeff Russell	.10	.05
❑ 87 Mickey Tettleton	.10	.05
❑ 88 Bob Tewksbury	.10	.05
❑ 89 Pedro Borbon	.10	.05
❑ 90 Marquis Grissom	.20	.09
❑ 91 Chipper Jones	1.00	.45
❑ 92 Mike Mordecai	.10	.05
❑ 93 Jason Schmidt	.20	.09
❑ 94 John Burkett	.10	.05
❑ 95 Andre Dawson	.30	.14
❑ 96 Matt Dunbar	.10	.05
❑ 97 Charles Johnson	.20	.09
❑ 98 Terry Pendleton	.10	.05
❑ 99 Rich Scheid	.10	.05
❑ 100 Quilvio Veras	.10	.05
❑ 101 Bobby Witt	.10	.05
❑ 102 Eddie Zosky	.10	.05
❑ 103 Shane Andrews	.10	.05
❑ 104 Reid Cornelius	.10	.05
❑ 105 Chad Fonville	.10	.05
❑ 106 Mark Grudzielanek	.30	.14
❑ 107 Roberto Kelly	.10	.05
❑ 108 Carlos Perez	.30	.14
❑ 109 Tony Tarasco	.10	.05
❑ 110 Brett Butler	.20	.09
❑ 111 Carl Everett	.10	.05
❑ 112 Pete Harnisch	.10	.05
❑ 113 Doug Henry	.10	.05
❑ 114 Kevin Lomon	.10	.05
❑ 115 Blas Minor	.10	.05
❑ 116 Dave Mlicki	.10	.05
❑ 117 Ricky Otero	.10	.05
❑ 118 Norm Charlton	.10	.05
❑ 119 Tyler Green	.10	.05
❑ 120 Gene Harris	.10	.05
❑ 121 Charlie Hayes	.10	.05
❑ 122 Gregg Jefferies	.10	.05
❑ 123 Michael Mimbs	.10	.05
❑ 124 Paul Quantrill	.10	.05
❑ 125 Frank Castillo	.10	.05
❑ 126 Brian McRae	.10	.05
❑ 127 Jaime Navarro	.10	.05
❑ 128 Mike Perez	.10	.05
❑ 129 Tanyon Sturtze	.10	.05
❑ 130 Ozzie Timmons	.10	.05
❑ 131 John Courtright	.10	.05
❑ 132 Ron Gant	.10	.05
❑ 133 Xavier Hernandez	.10	.05
❑ 134 Brian Hunter	.10	.05
❑ 135 Benito Santiago	.10	.05
❑ 136 Pete Smith	.10	.05
❑ 137 Scott Sullivan	.10	.05
❑ 138 Derek Bell	.20	.09
❑ 139 Doug Brocail	.10	.05
❑ 140 Ricky Gutierrez	.10	.05
❑ 141 Pedro Martinez	.10	.05
❑ 142 Orlando Miller	.10	.05
❑ 143 Phil Plantier	.10	.05
❑ 144 Craig Shipley	.10	.05
❑ 145 Rich Aude	.10	.05
❑ 146 Jason Christiansen	.10	.05
❑ 147 Freddy Garcia	.10	.05
❑ 148 Jim Gott	.10	.05
❑ 149 Mark Johnson	.10	.05
❑ 150 Esteban Loaiza	.10	.05
❑ 151 Dan Plesac	.10	.05
❑ 152 Gary Wilson	.10	.05
❑ 153 Allen Battle	.10	.05
❑ 154 Terry Bradshaw	.10	.05
❑ 155 Scott Cooper	.10	.05
❑ 156 Tripp Cromer	.10	.05
❑ 157 John Frascatore	.10	.05
❑ 158 John Habyan	.10	.05
❑ 159 Tom Henke	.10	.05
❑ 160 Ken Hill	.10	.05
❑ 161 Danny Jackson	.10	.05
❑ 162 Donovan Osborne	.10	.05
❑ 163 Tom Urbani	.10	.05
❑ 164 Roger Bailey	.10	.05
❑ 165 Jorge Brito	.10	.05
❑ 166 Vinny Castilla	.30	.14
❑ 167 Darren Holmes	.10	.05
❑ 168 Roberto Mejia	.10	.05
❑ 169 Bill Swift	.10	.05
❑ 170 Mark Thompson	.10	.05
❑ 171 Larry Walker	.40	.18
❑ 172 Greg Hansell	.10	.05
❑ 173 Dave Hansen	.10	.05
❑ 174 Carlos Hernandez	.10	.05
❑ 175 Hideo Nomo	1.00	.45
❑ 176 Jose Offerman	.20	.09
❑ 177 Antonio Osuna	.10	.05
❑ 178 Reggie Williams	.10	.05
❑ 179 Todd Williams	.10	.05
❑ 180 Andres Berumen	.10	.05
❑ 181 Ken Caminiti	.30	.14
❑ 182 Andujar Cedeno	.10	.05
❑ 183 Steve Finley	.20	.09
❑ 184 Bryce Florie	.10	.05
❑ 185 Dustin Hermanson	.10	.05
❑ 186 Ray Holbert	.10	.05
❑ 187 Melvin Nieves	.10	.05
❑ 188 Roberto Petagine	.10	.05
❑ 189 Jody Reed	.10	.05
❑ 190 Fernando Valenzuela	.20	.09
❑ 191 Brian Williams	.10	.05
❑ 192 Mark Dewey	.10	.05
❑ 193 Glenallen Hill	.10	.05
❑ 194 Chris Hook	.10	.05
❑ 195 Terry Mulholland	.10	.05
❑ 196 Steve Scarsone	.10	.05
❑ 197 Trevor Wilson	.10	.05
❑ 198 Checklist	.10	.05
❑ 199 Checklist	.10	.05
❑ 200 Checklist	.10	.05

1995 Fleer Update Diamond Tribute

	MINT	NRMT
COMPLETE SET (10)	8.00	3.60
COMMON CARD (1-10)	.30	.14
STATED ODDS 1:5 HOB/RET		

❑ 1 Jeff Bagwell	.75	.35
❑ 2 Albert Belle	.60	.25
❑ 3 Barry Bonds	.75	.35
❑ 4 David Cone	.50	.23
❑ 5 Dennis Eckersley	.30	.14
❑ 6 Ken Griffey Jr.	3.00	1.35
❑ 7 Rickey Henderson	.75	.35
❑ 8 Greg Maddux	1.50	.70
❑ 9 Frank Thomas	1.25	.55
❑ 10 Matt Williams	.60	.25

1995 Fleer Update Headliners

	MINT	NRMT
COMPLETE SET (20)	12.00	5.50
COMMON CARD (1-20)	.25	.11
STATED ODDS 1:3		

❑ 1 Jeff Bagwell	.75	.35
❑ 2 Albert Belle	.60	.25
❑ 3 Barry Bonds	.75	.35
❑ 4 Jose Canseco	.75	.35
❑ 5 Joe Carter	.25	.11
❑ 6 Will Clark	.50	.25
❑ 7 Roger Clemens	1.25	.55
❑ 8 Lenny Dykstra	.25	.11

❑ 9 Cecil Fielder	.25	.11
❑ 10 Juan Gonzalez	1.25	.55
❑ 11 Ken Griffey Jr.	3.00	1.35
❑ 12 Kenny Lofton	.50	.23
❑ 13 Greg Maddux	1.50	.70
❑ 14 Fred McGriff	.50	.23
❑ 15 Mike Piazza	2.00	.90
❑ 16 Kirby Puckett	.75	.35
❑ 17 Tim Salmon	.60	.25
❑ 18 Frank Thomas	1.25	.55
❑ 19 Mo Vaughn	.60	.25
❑ 20 Matt Williams	.60	.25

1995 Fleer Update Rookie Update

	MINT	NRMT
COMPLETE SET (10)	15.00	6.75
COMMON CARD (1-10)	.25	.11
MINOR STARS	.50	.23
UNLISTED STARS	1.00	.45
STATED ODDS 1:4		

❑ 1 Shane Andrews	.25	.11
❑ 2 Ray Durham	.50	.23
❑ 3 Shawn Green	1.00	.45
❑ 4 Charles Johnson	.50	.23
❑ 5 Chipper Jones	4.00	1.80
❑ 6 Esteban Loaiza	.25	.11
❑ 7 Hideo Nomo	2.00	.90
❑ 8 Jon Nunnally	.25	.11
❑ 9 Alex Rodriguez	5.00	2.20
❑ 10 Julian Tavarez	.25	.11

1995 Fleer Update Smooth Leather

	MINT	NRMT
COMPLETE SET (10)	25.00	11.00
COMMON CARD (1-10)	.75	.35
STATED ODDS 1:5 JUMBO		

❑ 1 Roberto Alomar	2.00	.90
❑ 2 Barry Bonds	2.50	1.10
❑ 3 Ken Griffey Jr.	10.00	4.50
❑ 4 Marquis Grissom	.75	.35
❑ 5 Darren Lewis	.75	.35
❑ 6 Kenny Lofton	1.25	.55
❑ 7 Don Mattingly	4.00	1.80
❑ 8 Cal Ripken	8.00	3.60

❑ 9 Ivan Rodriguez	2.50	1.10
❑ 10 Matt Williams	2.00	.90

1995 Fleer Update Soaring Stars

	MINT	NRMT
COMPLETE SET (10)	30.00	13.50
COMMON CARD (1-10)	2.00	.90
STATED ODDS 1:36		

❑ 1 Moises Alou UER	3.00	1.35
(says .399 BA in 1994)		
❑ 2 Jason Bere	2.00	.90
❑ 3 Jeff Conine	2.00	.90
❑ 4 Cliff Floyd	3.00	1.35
❑ 5 Pat Hentgen	3.00	1.35
❑ 6 Kenny Lofton	4.00	1.80
❑ 7 Raul Mondesi	4.00	1.80
❑ 8 Mike Piazza	25.00	11.00
❑ 9 Tim Salmon	8.00	3.60

1996 Fleer

	MINT	NRMT
COMPLETE SET (600)	80.00	36.00
COMMON CARD (1-600)	.15	.07
MINOR STARS	.30	.14
UNLISTED STARS	.60	.25

❑ 1 Manny Alexander	.15	.07
❑ 2 Brady Anderson	.30	.14
❑ 3 Harold Baines	.30	.14
❑ 4 Armando Benitez	.15	.07
❑ 5 Bobby Bonilla	.30	.14
❑ 6 Kevin Brown	.40	.18
❑ 7 Scott Erickson	.30	.14
❑ 8 Curtis Goodwin	.15	.07
❑ 9 Jeffrey Hammonds	.30	.14
❑ 10 Jimmy Haynes	.15	.07
❑ 11 Chris Hoiles	.15	.07
❑ 12 Doug Jones	.15	.07
❑ 13 Rick Krivda	.15	.07
❑ 14 Jeff Manto	.15	.07
❑ 15 Ben McDonald	.15	.07
❑ 16 Jamie Moyer	.15	.07
❑ 17 Mike Mussina	.60	.25
❑ 18 Jesse Orosco	.15	.07
❑ 19 Rafael Palmeiro	.60	.25
❑ 20 Cal Ripken	2.50	1.10

❑ 21 Rick Aguilera	.15	.07
❑ 22 Luis Alicea	.15	.07
❑ 23 Stan Belinda	.15	.07
❑ 24 Jose Canseco	.75	.35
❑ 25 Roger Clemens	1.50	.70
❑ 26 Vaughn Eshelman	.15	.07
❑ 27 Mike Greenwell	.15	.07
❑ 28 Erik Hanson	.15	.07
❑ 29 Dwayne Hosey	.15	.07
❑ 30 Mike Macfarlane UER	.15	.07
❑ 31 Tim Naehring	.15	.07
❑ 32 Troy O'Leary	.30	.14
❑ 33 Aaron Sele	.30	.14
❑ 34 Zane Smith	.15	.07
❑ 35 Jeff Suppan	.15	.07
❑ 36 Lee Tinsley	.15	.07
❑ 37 John Valentin	.30	.14
❑ 38 Mo Vaughn	.60	.25
❑ 39 Tim Wakefield	.15	.07
❑ 40 Jim Abbott	.30	.14
❑ 41 Brian Anderson	.15	.07
❑ 42 Garret Anderson	.30	.14
❑ 43 Chili Davis	.30	.14
❑ 44 Gary DiSarcina	.15	.07
❑ 45 Damion Easley	.30	.14
❑ 46 Jim Edmonds	.40	.18
❑ 47 Chuck Finley	.30	.14
❑ 48 Todd Greene	.15	.07
❑ 49 Mike Harkey	.15	.07
❑ 50 Mike James	.15	.07
❑ 51 Mark Langston	.15	.07
❑ 52 Greg Myers	.15	.07
❑ 53 Orlando Palmeiro	.15	.07
❑ 54 Bob Patterson	.15	.07
❑ 55 Troy Percival	.30	.14
❑ 56 Tony Phillips	.15	.07
❑ 57 Tim Salmon	.40	.18
❑ 58 Lee Smith	.30	.14
❑ 59 J.T. Snow	.30	.14
❑ 60 Randy Velarde	.15	.07
❑ 61 Wilson Alvarez	.15	.07
❑ 62 Luis Andujar	.15	.07
❑ 63 Jason Bere	.15	.07
❑ 64 Ray Durham	.30	.14
❑ 65 Alex Fernandez	.15	.07
❑ 66 Ozzie Guillen	.15	.07
❑ 67 Roberto Hernandez	.15	.07
❑ 68 Lance Johnson	.15	.07
❑ 69 Matt Karchner	.15	.07
❑ 70 Ron Karkovice	.15	.07
❑ 71 Norberto Martin	.15	.07
❑ 72 Dave Martinez	.15	.07
❑ 73 Kirk McCaskill	.15	.07
❑ 74 Lyle Mouton	.15	.07
❑ 75 Tim Raines	.30	.14
❑ 76 Mike Sirotka	.50	.23
❑ 77 Frank Thomas	1.25	.55
❑ 78 Larry Thomas	.15	.07
❑ 79 Robin Ventura	.30	.14
❑ 80 Sandy Alomar Jr.	.30	.14
❑ 81 Paul Assenmacher	.15	.07
❑ 82 Carlos Baerga	.30	.14
❑ 83 Albert Belle	.60	.25
❑ 84 Mark Clark	.15	.07
❑ 85 Alan Embree	.15	.07
❑ 86 Alvaro Espinoza	.15	.07
❑ 87 Orel Hershiser	.30	.14
❑ 88 Ken Hill	.15	.07
❑ 89 Kenny Lofton	.40	.18
❑ 90 Dennis Martinez	.30	.14
❑ 91 Jose Mesa	.15	.07
❑ 92 Eddie Murray	.60	.25
❑ 93 Charles Nagy	.30	.14
❑ 94 Chad Ogea	.15	.07
❑ 95 Tony Pena	.15	.07
❑ 96 Herb Perry	.15	.07
❑ 97 Eric Plunk	.15	.07
❑ 98 Jim Poole	.15	.07
❑ 99 Manny Ramirez	.75	.35
❑ 100 Paul Sorrento	.15	.07
❑ 101 Julian Tavarez	.15	.07
❑ 102 Jim Thome	.60	.25
❑ 103 Omar Vizquel	.30	.14
❑ 104 Dave Winfield	.60	.25
❑ 105 Danny Bautista	.15	.07
❑ 106 Joe Boever	.15	.07

107	Chad Curtis	.15	.07
108	John Doherty	.15	.07
109	Cecil Fielder	.30	.14
110	John Flaherty	.15	.07
111	Travis Fryman	.30	.14
112	Chris Gomez	.15	.07
113	Bob Higginson	.30	.14
114	Mark Lewis	.15	.07
115	Jose Lima	.40	.18
116	Felipe Lira	.15	.07
117	Brian Maxcy	.15	.07
118	C.J. Nitkowski	.15	.07
119	Phil Plantier	.15	.07
120	Clint Sodowsky	.15	.07
121	Alan Trammell	.40	.18
122	Lou Whitaker	.30	.14
123	Kevin Appier	.30	.14
124	Johnny Damon	.40	.18
125	Gary Gaetti	.30	.14
126	Tom Goodwin	.15	.07
127	Tom Gordon	.15	.07
128	Mark Gubicza	.15	.07
129	Bob Hamelin	.15	.07
130	David Howard	.15	.07
131	Jason Jacome	.15	.07
132	Wally Joyner	.30	.14
133	Keith Lockhart	.15	.07
134	Brent Mayne	.15	.07
135	Jeff Montgomery	.15	.07
136	Jon Nunnally	.15	.07
137	Juan Samuel	.15	.07
138	Mike Sweeney	1.25	.55
139	Michael Tucker	.15	.07
140	Joe Vitiello	.15	.07
141	Ricky Bones	.15	.07
142	Chuck Carr	.15	.07
143	Jeff Cirillo	.30	.14
144	Mike Fetters	.15	.07
145	Darryl Hamilton	.15	.07
146	David Hulse	.15	.07
147	John Jaha	.15	.07
148	Scott Karl	.15	.07
149	Mark Kiefer	.15	.07
150	Pat Listach	.15	.07
151	Mark Loretta	.15	.07
152	Mike Matheny	.15	.07
153	Matt Mieske	.15	.07
154	Dave Nilsson	.15	.07
155	Joe Oliver	.15	.07
156	Al Reyes	.15	.07
157	Kevin Seitzer	.15	.07
158	Steve Sparks	.15	.07
159	B.J. Surhoff	.30	.14
160	Jose Valentin	.15	.07
161	Greg Vaughn	.30	.14
162	Fernando Vina	.15	.07
163	Rich Becker	.15	.07
164	Ron Coomer	.15	.07
165	Marty Cordova	.15	.07
166	Chuck Knoblauch	.60	.25
167	Matt Lawton	.35	.15
168	Pat Meares	.15	.07
169	Paul Molitor	.60	.25
170	Pedro Munoz	.15	.07
171	Jose Parra	.15	.07
172	Kirby Puckett	1.00	.45
173	Brad Radke	.30	.14
174	Jeff Reboulet	.15	.07
175	Rich Robertson	.15	.07
176	Frank Rodriguez	.15	.07
177	Scott Stahoviak	.15	.07
178	Dave Stevens	.15	.07
179	Matt Walbeck	.15	.07
180	Wade Boggs	.60	.25
181	David Cone	.40	.18
182	Tony Fernandez	.15	.07
183	Joe Girardi	.15	.07
184	Derek Jeter	2.00	.90
185	Scott Kamieniecki	.15	.07
186	Pat Kelly	.15	.07
187	Jim Leyritz	.15	.07
188	Tino Martinez	.30	.14
189	Don Mattingly	1.25	.55
190	Jack McDowell	.15	.07
191	Jeff Nelson	.15	.07
192	Paul O'Neill	.30	.14
193	Melido Perez	.15	.07
194	Andy Pettitte	.40	.18
195	Mariano Rivera	.40	.18
196	Ruben Sierra	.15	.07
197	Mike Stanley	.15	.07
198	Darryl Strawberry	.30	.14
199	John Wetteland	.30	.14
200	Bob Wickman	.15	.07
201	Bernie Williams	.60	.25
202	Mark Acre	.15	.07
203	Geronimo Berroa	.15	.07
204	Mike Bordick	.15	.07
205	Scott Brosius	.30	.14
206	Dennis Eckersley	.30	.14
207	Brent Gates	.15	.07
208	Jason Giambi	.30	.14
209	Rickey Henderson	.75	.35
210	Jose Herrera	.15	.07
211	Stan Javier	.15	.07
212	Doug Johns	.15	.07
213	Mark McGwire	3.00	1.35
214	Steve Ontiveros	.15	.07
215	Craig Paquette	.15	.07
216	Ariel Prieto	.15	.07
217	Carlos Reyes	.15	.07
218	Terry Steinbach	.15	.07
219	Todd Stottlemyre	.15	.07
220	Danny Tartabull	.15	.07
221	Todd Van Poppel	.15	.07
222	John Wasdin	.15	.07
223	George Williams	.15	.07
224	Steve Wojciechowski	.15	.07
225	Rich Amaral	.15	.07
226	Bobby Ayala	.15	.07
227	Tim Belcher	.15	.07
228	Andy Benes	.30	.14
229	Chris Bosio	.15	.07
230	Darren Bragg	.15	.07
231	Jay Buhner	.30	.14
232	Norm Charlton	.15	.07
233	Vince Coleman	.15	.07
234	Joey Cora	.15	.07
235	Russ Davis	.15	.07
236	Alex Diaz	.15	.07
237	Felix Fermin	.15	.07
238	Ken Griffey Jr.	3.00	1.35
239	Sterling Hitchcock	.15	.07
240	Randy Johnson	.60	.25
241	Edgar Martinez	.30	.14
242	Bill Risley	.15	.07
243	Alex Rodriguez	2.00	.90
244	Luis Sojo	.15	.07
245	Dan Wilson	.15	.07
246	Bob Wolcott	.15	.07
247	Will Clark	.60	.25
248	Jeff Frye	.15	.07
249	Benji Gil	.15	.07
250	Juan Gonzalez	1.25	.55
251	Rusty Greer	.30	.14
252	Kevin Gross	.15	.07
253	Roger McDowell	.15	.07
254	Mark McLemore	.15	.07
255	Otis Nixon	.15	.07
256	Luis Ortiz	.15	.07
257	Mike Pagliarulo	.15	.07
258	Dean Palmer	.30	.14
259	Roger Pavlik	.15	.07
260	Ivan Rodriguez	.75	.35
261	Kenny Rogers	.15	.07
262	Jeff Russell	.15	.07
263	Mickey Tettleton	.15	.07
264	Bob Tewksbury	.15	.07
265	Dave Valle	.15	.07
266	Matt Whiteside	.15	.07
267	Roberto Alomar	.60	.25
268	Joe Carter	.30	.14
269	Tony Castillo	.15	.07
270	Domingo Cedeno	.15	.07
271	Tim Crabtree UER	.15	.07
272	Carlos Delgado	.60	.25
273	Alex Gonzalez	.15	.07
274	Shawn Green	.60	.25
275	Juan Guzman	.15	.07
276	Pat Hentgen	.30	.14
277	Al Leiter	.30	.14
278	Sandy Martinez	.15	.07
279	Paul Menhart	.15	.07
280	John Olerud	.30	.14
281	Paul Quantrill	.15	.07
282	Ken Robinson	.15	.07
283	Ed Sprague	.15	.07
284	Mike Timlin	.15	.07
285	Steve Avery	.15	.07
286	Rafael Belliard	.15	.07
287	Jeff Blauser	.15	.07
288	Pedro Borbon	.15	.07
289	Brad Clontz	.15	.07
290	Mike Devereaux	.15	.07
291	Tom Glavine	.60	.25
292	Marquis Grissom	.15	.07
293	Chipper Jones	1.50	.70
294	David Justice	.60	.25
295	Mike Kelly	.15	.07
296	Ryan Klesko	.30	.14
297	Mark Lemke	.15	.07
298	Javier Lopez	.30	.14
299	Greg Maddux	1.50	.70
300	Fred McGriff	.40	.18
301	Greg McMichael	.15	.07
302	Kent Mercker	.15	.07
303	Mike Mordecai	.15	.07
304	Charlie O'Brien	.15	.07
305	Eduardo Perez	.15	.07
306	Luis Polonia	.15	.07
307	Jason Schmidt	.15	.07
308	John Smoltz	.40	.18
309	Terrell Wade	.15	.07
310	Mark Wohlers	.15	.07
311	Scott Bullett	.15	.07
312	Jim Bullinger	.15	.07
313	Larry Casian	.15	.07
314	Frank Castillo	.15	.07
315	Shawon Dunston	.15	.07
316	Kevin Foster	.15	.07
317	Matt Franco	.15	.07
318	Luis Gonzalez	.30	.14
319	Mark Grace	.40	.18
320	Jose Hernandez	.15	.07
321	Mike Hubbard	.15	.07
322	Brian McRae	.15	.07
323	Randy Myers	.15	.07
324	Jaime Navarro	.15	.07
325	Mark Parent	.15	.07
326	Mike Perez	.15	.07
327	Rey Sanchez	.15	.07
328	Ryne Sandberg	.75	.35
329	Scott Servais	.15	.07
330	Sammy Sosa	2.00	.90
331	Ozzie Timmons	.15	.07
332	Steve Trachsel	.15	.07
333	Todd Zeile	.15	.07
334	Bret Boone	.30	.14
335	Jeff Branson	.15	.07
336	Jeff Brantley	.15	.07
337	Dave Burba	.15	.07
338	Hector Carrasco	.15	.07
339	Mariano Duncan	.15	.07
340	Ron Gant	.30	.14
341	Lenny Harris	.15	.07
342	Xavier Hernandez	.15	.07
343	Thomas Howard	.15	.07
344	Mike Jackson	.30	.14
345	Barry Larkin	.60	.25
346	Darren Lewis	.15	.07
347	Hal Morris	.15	.07
348	Eric Owens	.15	.07
349	Mark Portugal	.15	.07
350	Jose Rijo	.15	.07
351	Reggie Sanders	.30	.14
352	Benito Santiago	.15	.07
353	Pete Schourek	.15	.07
354	John Smiley	.15	.07
355	Eddie Taubensee	.15	.07
356	Jerome Walton	.15	.07
357	David Wells	.40	.18
358	Roger Bailey	.15	.07
359	Jason Bates	.15	.07
360	Dante Bichette	.30	.14
361	Ellis Burks	.30	.14
362	Vinny Castilla	.40	.18
363	Andres Galarraga	.60	.25
364	Darren Holmes	.15	.07

❑ 365	Mike Kingery	.15	.07
❑ 366	Curt Leskanic	.15	.07
❑ 367	Quinton McCracken	.15	.07
❑ 368	Mike Munoz	.15	.07
❑ 369	David Nied	.15	.07
❑ 370	Steve Reed	.15	.07
❑ 371	Bryan Rekar	.15	.07
❑ 372	Kevin Ritz	.15	.07
❑ 373	Bruce Ruffin	.15	.07
❑ 374	Bret Saberhagen	.30	.14
❑ 375	Bill Swift	.15	.07
❑ 376	John Vander Wal	.15	.07
❑ 377	Larry Walker	.60	.25
❑ 378	Walt Weiss	.15	.07
❑ 379	Eric Young	.15	.07
❑ 380	Kurt Abbott	.15	.07
❑ 381	Alex Arias	.15	.07
❑ 382	Jerry Browne	.15	.07
❑ 383	John Burkett	.15	.07
❑ 384	Greg Colbrunn	.15	.07
❑ 385	Jeff Conine	.15	.07
❑ 386	Andre Dawson	.40	.18
❑ 387	Chris Hammond	.15	.07
❑ 388	Charles Johnson	.30	.14
❑ 389	Terry Mathews	.15	.07
❑ 390	Robb Nen	.15	.07
❑ 391	Joe Orsulak	.15	.07
❑ 392	Terry Pendleton	.15	.07
❑ 393	Pat Rapp	.15	.07
❑ 394	Gary Sheffield	.30	.14
❑ 395	Jesus Tavarez	.15	.07
❑ 396	Marc Valdes	.15	.07
❑ 397	Quilvio Veras	.15	.07
❑ 398	Randy Veres	.15	.07
❑ 399	Devon White	.30	.14
❑ 400	Jeff Bagwell	.75	.35
❑ 401	Derek Bell	.30	.14
❑ 402	Craig Biggio	.60	.25
❑ 403	John Cangelosi	.15	.07
❑ 404	Jim Dougherty	.15	.07
❑ 405	Doug Drabek	.15	.07
❑ 406	Tony Eusebio	.15	.07
❑ 407	Ricky Gutierrez	.15	.07
❑ 408	Mike Hampton	.30	.14
❑ 409	Dean Hartgraves	.15	.07
❑ 410	John Hudek	.15	.07
❑ 411	Brian L. Hunter	.15	.07
❑ 412	Todd Jones	.15	.07
❑ 413	Darryl Kile	.15	.07
❑ 414	Dave Magadan	.15	.07
❑ 415	Derrick May	.15	.07
❑ 416	Orlando Miller	.15	.07
❑ 417	James Mouton	.15	.07
❑ 418	Shane Reynolds	.30	.14
❑ 419	Greg Swindell	.15	.07
❑ 420	Jeff Tabaka	.15	.07
❑ 421	Dave Veres	.15	.07
❑ 422	Billy Wagner	.40	.18
❑ 423	Donne Wall	.15	.07
❑ 424	Rick Wilkins	.15	.07
❑ 425	Billy Ashley	.15	.07
❑ 426	Mike Blowers	.15	.07
❑ 427	Brett Butler	.30	.14
❑ 428	Tom Candiotti	.15	.07
❑ 429	Juan Castro	.15	.07
❑ 430	John Cummings	.15	.07
❑ 431	Delino DeShields	.15	.07
❑ 432	Joey Eischen	.15	.07
❑ 433	Chad Fonville	.15	.07
❑ 434	Greg Gagne	.15	.07
❑ 435	Dave Hansen	.15	.07
❑ 436	Carlos Hernandez	.15	.07
❑ 437	Todd Hollandsworth	.15	.07
❑ 438	Eric Karros	.30	.14
❑ 439	Roberto Kelly	.15	.07
❑ 440	Ramon Martinez	.30	.14
❑ 441	Raul Mondesi	.30	.14
❑ 442	Hideo Nomo	.60	.25
❑ 443	Antonio Osuna	.15	.07
❑ 444	Chan Ho Park	.40	.18
❑ 445	Mike Piazza	2.00	.90
❑ 446	Felix Rodriguez	.15	.07
❑ 447	Kevin Tapani	.15	.07
❑ 448	Ismael Valdes	.30	.14
❑ 449	Todd Worrell	.15	.07
❑ 450	Moises Alou	.30	.14
❑ 451	Shane Andrews	.15	.07
❑ 452	Yamil Benitez	.15	.07
❑ 453	Sean Berry	.15	.07
❑ 454	Wil Cordero	.15	.07
❑ 455	Jeff Fassero	.15	.07
❑ 456	Darrin Fletcher	.15	.07
❑ 457	Cliff Floyd	.30	.14
❑ 458	Mark Grudzielanek	.15	.07
❑ 459	Gil Heredia	.15	.07
❑ 460	Tim Laker	.15	.07
❑ 461	Mike Lansing	.15	.07
❑ 462	Pedro J.Martinez	.75	.35
❑ 463	Carlos Perez	.15	.07
❑ 464	Curtis Pride	.15	.07
❑ 465	Mel Rojas	.15	.07
❑ *466	Kirk Rueter	.15	.07
❑ 467	F.P. Santangelo	.15	.07
❑ 468	Tim Scott	.15	.07
❑ 469	David Segui	.30	.14
❑ 470	Tony Tarasco	.15	.07
❑ 471	Rondell White	.30	.14
❑ 472	Edgardo Alfonzo	.60	.25
❑ 473	Tim Bogar	.15	.07
❑ 474	Rico Brogna	.15	.07
❑ 475	Damon Buford	.15	.07
❑ 476	Paul Byrd	.15	.07
❑ 477	Carl Everett	.30	.14
❑ 478	John Franco	.30	.14
❑ 479	Todd Hundley	.30	.14
❑ 480	Butch Huskey	.15	.07
❑ 481	Jason Isringhausen	.30	.14
❑ 482	Bobby Jones	.15	.07
❑ 483	Chris Jones	.15	.07
❑ 484	Jeff Kent	.30	.14
❑ 485	Dave Mlicki	.15	.07
❑ 486	Robert Person	.15	.07
❑ 487	Bill Pulsipher	.15	.07
❑ 488	Kelly Stinnett	.15	.07
❑ 489	Ryan Thompson	.15	.07
❑ 490	Jose Vizcaino	.15	.07
❑ 491	Howard Battle	.15	.07
❑ 492	Toby Borland	.15	.07
❑ 493	Ricky Bottalico	.15	.07
❑ 494	Darren Daulton	.30	.14
❑ 495	Lenny Dykstra	.30	.14
❑ 496	Jim Eisenreich	.15	.07
❑ 497	Sid Fernandez	.15	.07
❑ 498	Tyler Green	.15	.07
❑ 499	Charlie Hayes	.15	.07
❑ 500	Gregg Jefferies	.15	.07
❑ 501	Kevin Jordan	.15	.07
❑ 502	Tony Longmire	.15	.07
❑ 503	Tom Marsh	.15	.07
❑ 504	Michael Mimbs	.15	.07
❑ 505	Mickey Morandini	.15	.07
❑ 506	Gene Schall	.15	.07
❑ 507	Curt Schilling	.40	.18
❑ 508	Heathcliff Slocumb	.15	.07
❑ 509	Kevin Stocker	.15	.07
❑ 510	Andy Van Slyke	.15	.07
❑ 511	Lenny Webster	.15	.07
❑ 512	Mark Whiten	.15	.07
❑ 513	Mike Williams	.15	.07
❑ 514	Jay Bell	.30	.14
❑ 515	Jacob Brumfield	.15	.07
❑ 516	Jason Christiansen	.15	.07
❑ 517	Dave Clark	.15	.07
❑ 518	Midre Cummings	.15	.07
❑ 519	Angelo Encarnacion	.15	.07
❑ 520	John Ericks	.15	.07
❑ 521	Carlos Garcia	.15	.07
❑ 522	Mark Johnson	.15	.07
❑ 523	Jeff King	.15	.07
❑ 524	Nelson Liriano	.15	.07
❑ 525	Esteban Loaiza	.15	.07
❑ 526	Al Martin	.15	.07
❑ 527	Orlando Merced	.15	.07
❑ 528	Dan Miceli	.15	.07
❑ 529	Ramon Morel	.15	.07
❑ 530	Denny Neagle	.30	.14
❑ 531	Steve Parris	.15	.07
❑ 532	Dan Plesac	.15	.07
❑ 533	Don Slaught	.15	.07
❑ 534	Paul Wagner	.15	.07
❑ 535	John Wehner	.15	.07
❑ 536	Kevin Young	.15	.07
❑ 537	Allen Battle	.15	.07
❑ 538	David Bell	.15	.07
❑ 539	Alan Benes	.15	.07
❑ 540	Scott Cooper	.15	.07
❑ 541	Tripp Cromer	.15	.07
❑ 542	Tony Fossas	.15	.07
❑ 543	Bernard Gilkey	.15	.07
❑ 544	Tom Henke	.15	.07
❑ 545	Brian Jordan	.30	.14
❑ 546	Ray Lankford	.30	.14
❑ 547	John Mabry	.15	.07
❑ 548	T.J. Mathews	.15	.07
❑ 549	Mike Morgan	.15	.07
❑ 550	Jose Oliva	.15	.07
❑ 551	Jose Oquendo	.15	.07
❑ 552	Donovan Osborne	.15	.07
❑ 553	Tom Pagnozzi	.15	.07
❑ 554	Mark Petkovsek	.15	.07
❑ 555	Danny Sheaffer	.15	.07
❑ 556	Ozzie Smith	.75	.35
❑ 557	Mark Sweeney	.15	.07
❑ 558	Allen Watson	.15	.07
❑ 559	Andy Ashby	.15	.07
❑ 560	Brad Ausmus	.15	.07
❑ 561	Willie Blair	.15	.07
❑ 562	Ken Caminiti	.30	.14
❑ 563	Andujar Cedeno	.15	.07
❑ 564	Glenn Dishman	.15	.07
❑ 565	Steve Finley	.30	.14
❑ 566	Bryce Florie	.15	.07
❑ 567	Tony Gwynn	1.50	.70
❑ 568	Joey Hamilton	.15	.07
❑ 569	Dustin Hermanson UER	.15	.07
❑ 570	Trevor Hoffman	.30	.14
❑ 571	Brian Johnson	.15	.07
❑ 572	Marc Kroon	.15	.07
❑ 573	Scott Livingstone	.15	.07
❑ 574	Marc Newfield	.15	.07
❑ 575	Melvin Nieves	.15	.07
❑ 576	Jody Reed	.15	.07
❑ 577	Bip Roberts	.15	.07
❑ 578	Scott Sanders	.15	.07
❑ 579	Fernando Valenzuela	.30	.14
❑ 580	Eddie Williams	.15	.07
❑ 581	Rod Beck	.15	.07
❑ 582	Marvin Benard	.15	.07
❑ 583	Barry Bonds	.75	.35
❑ 584	Jamie Brewington	.15	.07
❑ 585	Mark Carreon	.15	.07
❑ 586	Royce Clayton	.15	.07
❑ 587	Shawn Estes	.30	.14
❑ 588	Glenallen Hill	.15	.07
❑ 589	Mark Leiter	.15	.07
❑ 590	Kirt Manwaring	.15	.07
❑ 591	David McCarty	.15	.07
❑ 592	Terry Mulholland	.15	.07
❑ 593	John Patterson	.15	.07
❑ 594	J.R. Phillips	.15	.07
❑ 595	Deion Sanders	.30	.14
❑ 596	Steve Scarsone	.15	.07
❑ 597	Robby Thompson	.15	.07
❑ 598	Sergio Valdez	.15	.07
❑ 599	William Van Landingham	.15	.07
❑ 600	Matt Williams	.60	.25
❑ P20	Cal Ripken	3.00	1.35
	Promo		

1996 Fleer Tiffany

	MINT	NRMT
COMPLETE SET (600)	200.00	90.00
COMMON CARD (1-600)	.25	.11
*STARS: 1.5X TO 4X BASIC CARDS		
*ROOKIES: 1.25X TO 3X BASIC CARDS		
ONE PER PACK		

1996 Fleer Checklists

	MINT	NRMT
COMPLETE SET (10)	4.00	1.80
COMMON CARD (1-10)	.40	.18
STATED ODDS 1:6		
❑ 1 Barry Bonds	.40	.18
❑ 2 Ken Griffey Jr.	1.50	.70
❑ 3 Chipper Jones	.75	.35
❑ 4 Greg Maddux	.75	.35
❑ 5 Mike Piazza	1.00	.45
❑ 6 Manny Ramirez	.50	.23
❑ 7 Cal Ripken	1.25	.55
❑ 8 Frank Thomas	.60	.25
❑ 9 Mo Vaughn	.40	.18
❑ 10 Matt Williams	.40	.18

1996 Fleer Golden Memories

	MINT	NRMT
COMPLETE SET (10)	8.00	3.60
COMMON CARD (1-10)	.30	.14
STATED ODDS 1:10		
❑ 1 Albert Belle	.75	.35
❑ 2 Barry Bonds	1.50	.70
Sammy Sosa		
❑ 3 Greg Maddux	2.00	.90
❑ 4 Edgar Martinez	.30	.14
❑ 5 Ramon Martinez	.30	.14
❑ 6 Mark McGwire	4.00	1.80
❑ 7 Eddie Murray	.75	.35
❑ 8 Cal Ripken	3.00	1.35
❑ 9 Frank Thomas	2.00	.90
❑ 10 Alan Trammell	.50	.23
Lou Whitaker		

1996 Fleer Lumber Company

	MINT	NRMT
COMPLETE SET (12)	25.00	11.00

COMMON CARD (1-12)	1.00	.45
STATED ODDS 1:9 RETAIL		
❑ 1 Albert Belle	2.00	.90
❑ 2 Dante Bichette	1.00	.45
❑ 3 Barry Bonds	2.50	1.10
❑ 4 Ken Griffey Jr.	10.00	4.50
❑ 5 Mark McGwire	10.00	4.50
❑ 6 Mike Piazza	6.00	2.70
❑ 7 Manny Ramirez	2.50	1.10
❑ 8 Tim Salmon	1.50	.70
❑ 9 Sammy Sosa	6.00	2.70
❑ 10 Frank Thomas	4.00	1.80
❑ 11 Mo Vaughn	2.00	.90
❑ 12 Matt Williams	2.00	.90

1996 Fleer Postseason Glory

	MINT	NRMT
COMPLETE SET (5)	2.00	.90
COMMON CARD (1-5)	.10	.05
STATED ODDS 1:5		
❑ 1 Tom Glavine	.30	.14
❑ 2 Ken Griffey Jr.	1.50	.70
❑ 3 Orel Hershiser	.10	.05
❑ 4 Randy Johnson	.30	.14
❑ 5 Jim Thome	.30	.14

1996 Fleer Prospects

	MINT	NRMT
COMPLETE SET (10)	5.00	2.20
COMMON CARD (1-10)	.25	.11
MINOR STARS	.50	.23
SEMISTARS	1.00	.45
STATED ODDS 1:6		
❑ 1 Yamil Benitez	.25	.11
❑ 2 Roger Cedeno	.50	.23
❑ 3 Tony Clark	1.50	.70
❑ 4 Micah Franklin	.25	.11
❑ 5 Karim Garcia	.50	.23
❑ 6 Todd Greene	.25	.11
❑ 7 Alex Ochoa	.25	.11
❑ 8 Ruben Rivera	.50	.23
❑ 9 Chris Snopek	.25	.11
❑ 10 Shannon Stewart	.50	.23

1996 Fleer Road Warriors

	MINT	NRMT
COMPLETE SET (10)	12.00	5.50
COMMON CARD (1-10)	.40	.18
STATED ODDS 1:13		
❑ 1 Derek Bell	.40	.18
❑ 2 Tony Gwynn	2.50	1.10
❑ 3 Greg Maddux	2.50	1.10
❑ 4 Mark McGwire	5.00	2.20
❑ 5 Mike Piazza	3.00	1.35
❑ 6 Manny Ramirez	1.00	.45
❑ 7 Tim Salmon	.60	.25
❑ 8 Frank Thomas	2.00	.90
❑ 9 Mo Vaughn	.75	.35
❑ 10 Matt Williams	.75	.35

1996 Fleer Rookie Sensations

	MINT	NRMT
COMPLETE SET (15)	15.00	6.75
COMMON CARD (1-15)	1.00	.45
STATED ODDS 1:11		
❑ 1 Garret Anderson	1.50	.70
❑ 2 Marty Cordova	1.00	.45
❑ 3 Johnny Damon	2.00	.90
❑ 4 Ray Durham	1.50	.70
❑ 5 Carl Everett	1.50	.70
❑ 6 Shawn Green	3.00	1.35
❑ 7 Brian L.Hunter	1.00	.45
❑ 8 Jason Isringhausen	1.50	.70
❑ 9 Charles Johnson	1.50	.70
❑ 10 Chipper Jones	8.00	3.60
❑ 11 John Mabry	1.00	.45
❑ 12 Hideo Nomo	3.00	1.35
❑ 13 Troy Percival	1.50	.70
❑ 14 Andy Pettitte	2.00	.90
❑ 15 Quilvio Veras	1.00	.45

1996 Fleer Smoke 'n Heat

	MINT	NRMT
COMPLETE SET (10)	6.00	2.70
COMMON CARD (1-10)	.25	.11
STATED ODDS 1:9		

		MINT	NRMT
❏ 1	Kevin Appier	.40	.18
❏ 2	Roger Clemens	2.50	1.10
❏ 3	David Cone	.75	.35
❏ 4	Chuck Finley	.40	.18
❏ 5	Randy Johnson	1.00	.45
❏ 6	Greg Maddux	2.50	1.10
❏ 7	Pedro Martinez	1.25	.55
❏ 8	Hideo Nomo	1.00	.45
❏ 9	John Smoltz	.75	.35
❏ 10	Todd Stottlemyre	.25	.11

1996 Fleer Team Leaders

	MINT	NRMT
COMPLETE SET (28)	60.00	27.00
COMMON CARD (1-28)	.75	.35
STATED ODDS 1:9 HOBBY		

		MINT	NRMT
❏ 1	Cal Ripken	12.00	5.50
❏ 2	Mo Vaughn	3.00	1.35
❏ 3	Jim Edmonds	2.00	.90
❏ 4	Frank Thomas	6.00	2.70
❏ 5	Kenny Lofton	2.00	.90
❏ 6	Travis Fryman	1.50	.70
❏ 7	Gary Gaetti	1.50	.70
❏ 8	B.J. Surhoff	1.50	.70
❏ 9	Kirby Puckett	5.00	2.20
❏ 10	Don Mattingly	6.00	2.70
❏ 11	Mark McGwire	15.00	6.75
❏ 12	Ken Griffey Jr.	15.00	6.75
❏ 13	Juan Gonzalez	6.00	2.70
❏ 14	Joe Carter	1.50	.70
❏ 15	Greg Maddux	8.00	3.60
❏ 16	Sammy Sosa	10.00	4.50
❏ 17	Barry Larkin	3.00	1.35
❏ 18	Dante Bichette	1.50	.70
❏ 19	Jeff Conine	.75	.35
❏ 20	Jeff Bagwell	4.00	1.80
❏ 21	Mike Piazza	10.00	4.50
❏ 22	Rondell White	1.50	.70
❏ 23	Rico Brogna	.75	.35
❏ 24	Darren Daulton	1.50	.70
❏ 25	Jeff King	.75	.35
❏ 26	Ray Lankford	1.50	.70
❏ 27	Tony Gwynn	8.00	3.60
❏ 28	Barry Bonds	4.00	1.80

1996 Fleer Tomorrow's Legends

	MINT	NRMT
COMPLETE SET (10)	10.00	4.50
COMMON CARD (1-10)	1.09	.45
STATED ODDS 1:13		

		MINT	NRMT
❏ 1	Garret Anderson	1.25	.55
❏ 2	Jim Edmonds	1.50	.70
❏ 3	Brian L.Hunter	1.00	.45
❏ 4	Jason Isringhausen	1.25	.55
❏ 5	Charles Johnson	1.25	.55
❏ 6	Chipper Jones	5.00	2.20
❏ 7	Ryan Klesko	1.25	.55
❏ 8	Hideo Nomo	2.00	.90
❏ 9	Manny Ramirez	2.50	1.10
❏ 10	Rondell White	1.25	.55

1996 Fleer Zone

	MINT	NRMT
COMPLETE SET (12)	100.00	45.00
COMMON CARD (1-12)	5.00	2.20
STATED ODDS 1:90		

		MINT	NRMT
❏ 1	Albert Belle	8.00	3.60
❏ 2	Barry Bonds	10.00	4.50
❏ 3	Ken Griffey Jr.	40.00	18.00
❏ 4	Tony Gwynn	20.00	9.00
❏ 5	Randy Johnson	8.00	3.60
❏ 6	Kenny Lofton	5.00	2.20
❏ 7	Greg Maddux	20.00	9.00
❏ 8	Edgar Martinez	5.00	2.20
❏ 9	Mike Piazza	25.00	11.00
❏ 10	Frank Thomas	15.00	6.75
❏ 11	Mo Vaughn	8.00	3.60
❏ 12	Matt Williams	8.00	3.60

1996 Fleer Update

	MINT	NRMT
COMPLETE SET (250)	30.00	13.50
COMMON CARD (U1-U250)	.15	.07

		MINT	NRMT
MINOR STARS		.30	.14
UNLISTED STARS		.60	.25
❏ U1	Roberto Alomar	.60	.25
❏ U2	Mike Devereaux	.15	.07
❏ U3	Scott McClain	.15	.07
❏ U4	Roger McDowell	.15	.07
❏ U5	Kent Mercker	.15	.07
❏ U6	Jimmy Myers	.15	.07
❏ U7	Randy Myers	.15	.07
❏ U8	B.J. Surhoff	.30	.14
❏ U9	Tony Tarasco	.15	.07
❏ U10	David Wells	.40	.18
❏ U11	Wil Cordero	.15	.07
❏ U12	Tom Gordon	.15	.07
❏ U13	Reggie Jefferson	.15	.07
❏ U14	Jose Malave	.15	.07
❏ U15	Kevin Mitchell	.15	.07
❏ U16	Jamie Moyer	.15	.07
❏ U17	Heathcliff Slocumb	.15	.07
❏ U18	Mike Stanley	.15	.07
❏ U19	George Arias	.15	.07
❏ U20	Jorge Fabregas	.15	.07
❏ U21	Don Slaught	.15	.07
❏ U22	Randy Velarde	.15	.07
❏ U23	Harold Baines	.30	.14
❏ U24	Mike Cameron	1.50	.70
❏ U25	Darren Lewis	.15	.07
❏ U26	Tony Phillips	.15	.07
❏ U27	Bill Simas	.15	.07
❏ U28	Chris Snopek	.15	.07
❏ U29	Kevin Tapani	.15	.07
❏ U30	Danny Tartabull	.15	.07
❏ U31	Julio Franco	.15	.07
❏ U32	Jack McDowell	.15	.07
❏ U33	Kimera Bartee	.15	.07
❏ U34	Mark Lewis	.15	.07
❏ U35	Melvin Nieves	.15	.07
❏ U36	Mark Parent	.15	.07
❏ U37	Eddie Williams	.15	.07
❏ U38	Tim Belcher	.15	.07
❏ U39	Sal Fasano	.15	.07
❏ U40	Chris Haney	.15	.07
❏ U41	Mike Macfarlane	.15	.07
❏ U42	Jose Offerman	.30	.14
❏ U43	Joe Randa	.15	.07
❏ U44	Bip Roberts	.15	.07
❏ U45	Chuck Carr	.15	.07
❏ U46	Bobby Hughes	.15	.07
❏ U47	Graeme Lloyd	.15	.07
❏ U48	Ben McDonald	.15	.07
❏ U49	Kevin Wickander	.15	.07
❏ U50	Rick Aguilera	.15	.07
❏ U51	Mike Durant	.15	.07
❏ U52	Chip Hale	.15	.07
❏ U53	LaTroy Hawkins	.15	.07
❏ U54	Dave Hollins	.15	.07
❏ U55	Roberto Kelly	.15	.07
❏ U56	Paul Molitor	.60	.25
❏ U57	Dan Naulty	.15	.07
❏ U58	Mariano Duncan	.15	.07
❏ U59	Andy Fox	.15	.07
❏ U60	Joe Girardi	.15	.07
❏ U61	Dwight Gooden	.30	.14
❏ U62	Jimmy Key	.30	.14
❏ U63	Matt Luke	.15	.07
❏ U64	Tino Martinez	.30	.14
❏ U65	Jeff Nelson	.15	.07

☐ U66 Tim Raines	.30	.14
☐ U67 Ruben Rivera	.30	.14
☐ U68 Kenny Rogers	.15	.07
☐ U69 Gerald Williams	.15	.07
☐ U70 Tony Batista	2.00	.90
☐ U71 Allen Battle	.15	.07
☐ U72 Jim Corsi	.15	.07
☐ U73 Steve Cox	.15	.07
☐ U74 Pedro Munoz	.15	.07
☐ U75 Phil Plantier	.15	.07
☐ U76 Scott Spiezio	.15	.07
☐ U77 Ernie Young	.15	.07
☐ U78 Russ Davis	.15	.07
☐ U79 Sterling Hitchcock	.15	.07
☐ U80 Edwin Hurtado	.15	.07
☐ U81 Raul Ibanez	.15	.07
☐ U82 Mike Jackson	.30	.14
☐ U83 Ricky Jordan	.15	.07
☐ U84 Paul Sorrento	.15	.07
☐ U85 Doug Strange	.15	.07
☐ U86 Mark Brandenburg	.15	.07
☐ U87 Damon Buford	.15	.07
☐ U88 Kevin Elster	.15	.07
☐ U89 Darryl Hamilton	.15	.07
☐ U90 Ken Hill	.15	.07
☐ U91 Ed Vosberg	.15	.07
☐ U92 Craig Worthington	.15	.07
☐ U93 Tilson Brito	.15	.07
☐ U94 Giovanni Carrara	.15	.07
☐ U95 Felipe Crespo	.15	.07
☐ U96 Erik Hanson	.15	.07
☐ U97 Marty Janzen	.15	.07
☐ U98 Otis Nixon	.15	.07
☐ U99 Charlie O'Brien	.15	.07
☐ U100 Robert Perez	.15	.07
☐ U101 Paul Quantrill	.15	.07
☐ U102 Bill Risley	.15	.07
☐ U103 Juan Samuel	.15	.07
☐ U104 Jermaine Dye	.30	.14
☐ U105 Wonderful Monds	.15	.07
☐ U106 Dwight Smith	.15	.07
☐ U107 Jerome Walton	.15	.07
☐ U108 Terry Adams	.15	.07
☐ U109 Leo Gomez	.15	.07
☐ U110 Robin Jennings	.15	.07
☐ U111 Doug Jones	.15	.07
☐ U112 Brooks Kieschnick	.15	.07
☐ U113 Dave Magadan	.15	.07
☐ U114 Jason Maxwell	.15	.07
☐ U115 Rodney Myers	.15	.07
☐ U116 Eric Anthony	.15	.07
☐ U117 Vince Coleman	.15	.07
☐ U118 Eric Davis	.30	.14
☐ U119 Steve Gibralter	.15	.07
☐ U120 Curtis Goodwin	.15	.07
☐ U121 Willie Greene	.30	.14
☐ U122 Mike Kelly	.15	.07
☐ U123 Marcus Moore	.15	.07
☐ U124 Chad Mottola	.15	.07
☐ U125 Chris Sabo	.15	.07
☐ U126 Roger Salkeld	.15	.07
☐ U127 Pedro Castellano	.15	.07
☐ U128 Trenidad Hubbard	.15	.07
☐ U129 Jayhawk Owens	.15	.07
☐ U130 Jeff Reed	.15	.07
☐ U131 Kevin Brown	.40	.18
☐ U132 Al Leiter	.30	.14
☐ U133 Matt Mantei	1.00	.45
☐ U134 Dave Weathers	.15	.07
☐ U135 Devon White	.30	.14
☐ U136 Bob Abreu	.40	.18
☐ U137 Sean Berry	.15	.07
☐ U138 Doug Brocail	.15	.07
☐ U139 Richard Hidalgo	.30	.14
☐ U140 Alvin Morman	.15	.07
☐ U141 Mike Blowers	.15	.07
☐ U142 Roger Cedeno	.30	.14
☐ U143 Greg Gagne	.15	.07
☐ U144 Karim Garcia	.30	.14
☐ U145 Wilton Guerrero	.75	.35
☐ U146 Israel Alcantara	.15	.07
☐ U147 Omar Daal	.30	.14
☐ U148 Ryan McGuire	.15	.07
☐ U149 Sherman Obando	.15	.07
☐ U150 Jose Paniagua	.15	.07
☐ U151 Henry Rodriguez	.30	.14
☐ U152 Andy Stankiewicz	.15	.07
☐ U153 Dave Veres	.15	.07
☐ U154 Juan Acevedo	.15	.07
☐ U155 Mark Clark	.15	.07
☐ U156 Bernard Gilkey	.15	.07
☐ U157 Pete Harnisch	.15	.07
☐ U158 Lance Johnson	.15	.07
☐ U159 Brent Mayne	.15	.07
☐ U160 Rey Ordonez	.60	.25
☐ U161 Kevin Roberson	.15	.07
☐ U162 Paul Wilson	.15	.07
☐ U163 David Doster	.15	.07
☐ U164 Mike Grace	.15	.07
☐ U165 Rich Hunter	.15	.07
☐ U166 Pete Incaviglia	.15	.07
☐ U167 Mike Lieberthal	.15	.07
☐ U168 Terry Mulholland	.15	.07
☐ U169 Ken Ryan	.15	.07
☐ U170 Benito Santiago	.15	.07
☐ U171 Kevin Sefcik	.15	.07
☐ U172 Lee Tinsley	.15	.07
☐ U173 Todd Zeile	.15	.07
☐ U174 Francisco Cordova	.15	.07
☐ U175 Danny Darwin	.15	.07
☐ U176 Charlie Hayes	.15	.07
☐ U177 Jason Kendall	.60	.25
☐ U178 Mike Kingery	.15	.07
☐ U179 Jon Lieber	.15	.07
☐ U180 Zane Smith	.15	.07
☐ U181 Luis Alicea	.15	.07
☐ U182 Cory Bailey	.15	.07
☐ U183 Andy Benes	.30	.14
☐ U184 Pat Borders	.15	.07
☐ U185 Mike Busby	.15	.07
☐ U186 Royce Clayton	.15	.07
☐ U187 Dennis Eckersley	.30	.14
☐ U188 Gary Gaetti	.30	.14
☐ U189 Ron Gant	.15	.07
☐ U190 Aaron Holbert	.15	.07
☐ U191 Willie McGee	.30	.14
☐ U192 Miguel Mejia	.15	.07
☐ U193 Jeff Parrett	.15	.07
☐ U194 Todd Stottlemyre	.15	.07
☐ U195 Sean Bergman	.15	.07
☐ U196 Archi Cianfrocco	.15	.07
☐ U197 Rickey Henderson	.75	.35
☐ U198 Wally Joyner	.30	.14
☐ U199 Craig Shipley	.15	.07
☐ U200 Bob Tewksbury	.15	.07
☐ U201 Tim Worrell	.15	.07
☐ U202 Rich Aurilia	.50	.23
☐ U203 Doug Creek	.15	.07
☐ U204 Shawon Dunston	.15	.07
☐ U205 Osvaldo Fernandez	.15	.07
☐ U206 Mark Gardner	.15	.07
☐ U207 Stan Javier	.15	.07
☐ U208 Marcus Jensen	.15	.07
☐ U209 Chris Singleton	8.00	3.60
☐ U210 Allen Watson	.15	.07
☐ U211 Jeff Bagwell ENC	.75	.35
☐ U212 Derek Bell ENC	.15	.07
☐ U213 Albert Belle ENC	.30	.14
☐ U214 Wade Boggs ENC	.30	.14
☐ U215 Barry Bonds ENC	.75	.35
☐ U216 Jose Canseco ENC	.75	.35
☐ U217 Marty Cordova ENC	.15	.07
☐ U218 Jim Edmonds ENC	.15	.07
☐ U219 Cecil Fielder ENC	.15	.07
☐ U220 Andres Galarraga ENC	.30	.14
☐ U221 Juan Gonzalez ENC	1.25	.55
☐ U222 Mark Grace ENC	.15	.07
☐ U223 Ken Griffey Jr. ENC	3.00	1.35
☐ U224 Tony Gwynn ENC	1.50	.70
☐ U225 J. Isringhausen ENC	.15	.07
☐ U226 Derek Jeter ENC	2.00	.90
☐ U227 Randy Johnson ENC	1.50	.70
☐ U228 Chipper Jones ENC	1.50	.70
☐ U229 Ryan Klesko ENC	.15	.07
☐ U230 Barry Larkin ENC	.15	.07
☐ U231 Kenny Lofton ENC	.15	.07
☐ U232 Greg Maddux ENC	1.50	.70
☐ U233 Raul Mondesi ENC	.15	.07
☐ U234 Hideo Nomo ENC	.30	.14
☐ U235 Mike Piazza ENC	2.00	.90
☐ U236 Manny Ramirez ENC	.75	.35
☐ U237 Cal Ripken ENC	1.50	.70
☐ U238 Tim Salmon ENC	.15	.07
☐ U239 Ryne Sandberg ENC	.75	.35
☐ U240 Reggie Sanders ENC	.15	.07
☐ U241 Gary Sheffield ENC	.15	.07
☐ U242 Sammy Sosa ENC	2.00	.90
☐ U243 Frank Thomas ENC	1.25	.55
☐ U244 Mo Vaughn ENC	.30	.14
☐ U245 Matt Williams ENC	.30	.14
☐ U246 Barry Bonds CL	.40	.18
☐ U247 Ken Griffey Jr. CL	1.50	.70
☐ U248 Rey Ordonez CL	.30	.14
☐ U249 Ryne Sandberg CL	.60	.25
☐ U250 Frank Thomas CL	.60	.25

1996 Fleer Update Tiffany

	MINT	NRMT
COMPLETE SET (250)	120.00	55.00
COMMON CARD (U1-U250)	.25	.11

*STARS: 1.5X TO 4X BASIC CARDS
*ROOKIES: 1X TO 2.5X BASIC CARDS
ONE TIFFANY PER PACK

1996 Fleer Update Diamond Tribute

	MINT	NRMT
COMPLETE SET (10)	150.00	70.00
COMMON CARD (1-10)	5.00	2.20
UNLISTED STARS	8.00	3.60

STATED ODDS 1:100

☐ 1 Wade Boggs	8.00	3.60
☐ 2 Barry Bonds	10.00	4.50
☐ 3 Ken Griffey Jr.	40.00	18.00
☐ 4 Tony Gwynn	15.00	6.75
☐ 5 Rickey Henderson	10.00	4.50
☐ 6 Greg Maddux	20.00	9.00
☐ 7 Eddie Murray	5.00	2.20
☐ 8 Cal Ripken	30.00	13.50
☐ 9 Ozzie Smith	10.00	4.50
☐ 10 Frank Thomas	15.00	6.75

1996 Fleer Update Headliners

	MINT	NRMT
COMPLETE SET (20)	40.00	18.00
COMMON CARD (1-20)	.75	.35
STATED ODDS 1:5 RETAIL		

		MINT	NRMT
❏ 1	Roberto Alomar	1.50	.70
❏ 2	Jeff Bagwell	2.00	.90
❏ 3	Albert Belle	1.50	.70
❏ 4	Barry Bonds	2.00	.90
❏ 5	Cecil Fielder	.75	.35
❏ 6	Juan Gonzalez	3.00	1.35
❏ 7	Ken Griffey Jr.	8.00	3.60
❏ 8	Tony Gwynn	4.00	1.80
❏ 9	Randy Johnson	1.50	.70
❏ 10	Chipper Jones	4.00	1.80
❏ 11	Ryan Klesko	.75	.35
❏ 12	Kenny Lofton	1.00	.45
❏ 13	Greg Maddux	4.00	1.80
❏ 14	Hideo Nomo	1.50	.70
❏ 15	Mike Piazza	5.00	2.20
❏ 16	Manny Ramirez	2.00	.90
❏ 17	Cal Ripken	6.00	2.70
❏ 18	Tim Salmon	1.00	.45
❏ 19	Frank Thomas	3.00	1.35
❏ 20	Matt Williams	1.50	.70

1996 Fleer Update New Horizons

	MINT	NRMT
COMPLETE SET (20)	15.00	6.75
COMMON CARD (1-20)	.25	.11
MINOR STARS	.50	.23
SEMISTARS	1.00	.45
STATED ODDS 1:5 HOBBY		

		MINT	NRMT
❏ 1	Bob Abreu	1.00	.45
❏ 2	George Arias	.25	.11
❏ 3	Tony Batista	2.00	.90
❏ 4	Steve Cox	.25	.11
❏ 5	Jermaine Dye	.50	.23
❏ 6	Andy Fox	.25	.11
❏ 7	Mike Grace	.25	.11
❏ 8	Todd Greene	.25	.11

		MINT	NRMT
❏ 9	Wilton Guerrero	2.00	.90
❏ 10	Richard Hidalgo	.50	.23
❏ 11	Raul Ibanez	.25	.11
❏ 12	Robin Jennings	.25	.11
❏ 13	Marcus Jensen	.25	.11
❏ 14	Jason Kendall	2.00	.90
❏ 15	Jason Maxwell	.25	.11
❏ 16	Ryan McGuire	.25	.11
❏ 17	Miguel Mejia	.25	.11
❏ 18	Wonderful Monds	.25	.11
❏ 19	Rey Ordonez	1.25	.55
❏ 20	Paul Wilson	.25	.11

1996 Fleer Update Smooth Leather

	MINT	NRMT
COMPLETE SET (10)	10.00	4.50
COMMON CARD (1-10)	.25	.11
STATED ODDS 1:5		

		MINT	NRMT
❏ 1	Roberto Alomar	.75	.35
❏ 2	Barry Bonds	1.00	.45
❏ 3	Will Clark	.75	.35
❏ 4	Ken Griffey Jr	4.00	1.80
❏ 5	Kenny Lofton	.50	.23
❏ 6	Greg Maddux	2.00	.90
❏ 7	Raul Mondesi	.25	.11
❏ 8	Rey Ordonez	.75	.35
❏ 9	Cal Ripken	3.00	1.35
❏ 10	Matt Williams	.75	.35

1996 Fleer Update Soaring Stars

	MINT	NRMT
COMPLETE SET (10)	25.00	11.00
COMMON CARD (1-10)	1.50	.70
STATED ODDS 1:11		

		MINT	NRMT
❏ 1	Jeff Bagwell	2.00	.90
❏ 2	Barry Bonds	2.00	.90
❏ 3	Juan Gonzalez	3.00	1.35
❏ 4	Ken Griffey Jr.	8.00	3.60
❏ 5	Chipper Jones	4.00	1.80
❏ 6	Greg Maddux	4.00	1.80
❏ 7	Mike Piazza	5.00	2.20

		MINT	NRMT
❏ 8	Manny Ramirez	2.00	.90
❏ 9	Frank Thomas	3.00	1.35
❏ 10	Matt Williams	1.50	.70

1997 Fleer

	MINT	NRMT
COMPLETE SET (761)	90.00	40.00
COMPLETE SERIES 1 (500)	50.00	22.00
COMPLETE SERIES 2 (261)	40.00	18.00
COMMON CARD (1-750)	.15	.07
COMMON CARD (751-761)	.25	.11
MINOR STARS	.30	.14
UNLISTED STARS	.60	.25
SUBSET CARDS HALF VALUE OF BASE CARDS		

		MINT	NRMT
❏ 1	Roberto Alomar	.60	.25
❏ 2	Brady Anderson	.30	.14
❏ 3	Bobby Bonilla	.30	.14
❏ 4	Rocky Coppinger	.15	.07
❏ 5	Cesar Devarez	.15	.07
❏ 6	Scott Erickson	.30	.14
❏ 7	Jeffrey Hammonds	.15	.07
❏ 8	Chris Hoiles	.15	.07
❏ 9	Eddie Murray	.60	.25
❏ 10	Mike Mussina	.60	.25
❏ 11	Randy Myers	.15	.07
❏ 12	Rafael Palmeiro	.60	.25
❏ 13	Cal Ripken	2.50	1.10
❏ 14	B.J. Surhoff	.30	.14
❏ 15	David Wells	.30	.14
❏ 16	Todd Zeile	.15	.07
❏ 17	Darren Bragg	.15	.07
❏ 18	Jose Canseco	.75	.35
❏ 19	Roger Clemens	1.50	.70
❏ 20	Wil Cordero	.15	.07
❏ 21	Jeff Frye	.15	.07
❏ 22	Nomar Garciaparra	2.00	.90
❏ 23	Tom Gordon	.15	.07
❏ 24	Mike Greenwell	.15	.07
❏ 25	Reggie Jefferson	.15	.07
❏ 26	Jose Malave	.15	.07
❏ 27	Tim Naehring	.15	.07
❏ 28	Troy O'Leary	.30	.14
❏ 29	Heathcliff Slocumb	.15	.07
❏ 30	Mike Stanley	.15	.07
❏ 31	John Valentin	.30	.14
❏ 32	Mo Vaughn	.60	.25
❏ 33	Tim Wakefield	.30	.14
❏ 34	Garret Anderson	.30	.14
❏ 35	George Arias	.15	.07
❏ 36	Shawn Boskie	.15	.07
❏ 37	Chili Davis	.30	.14
❏ 38	Jason Dickson	.15	.07
❏ 39	Gary DiSarcina	.15	.07
❏ 40	Jim Edmonds	.40	.18
❏ 41	Darin Erstad	.60	.25
❏ 42	Jorge Fabregas	.15	.07
❏ 43	Chuck Finley	.30	.14
❏ 44	Todd Greene	.15	.07
❏ 45	Mike Holtz	.15	.07
❏ 46	Rex Hudler	.15	.07
❏ 47	Mike James	.15	.07
❏ 48	Mark Langston	.30	.14
❏ 49	Troy Percival	.30	.14
❏ 50	Tim Salmon	.60	.25
❏ 51	Jeff Schmidt	.15	.07

❏ 52 J.T. Snow	.30	.14	
❏ 53 Randy Velarde	.15	.07	
❏ 54 Wilson Alvarez	.30	.14	
❏ 55 Harold Baines	.30	.14	
❏ 56 James Baldwin	.30	.14	
❏ 57 Jason Bere	.15	.07	
❏ 58 Mike Cameron	.30	.14	
❏ 59 Ray Durham	.30	.14	
❏ 60 Alex Fernandez	.15	.07	
❏ 61 Ozzie Guillen	.15	.07	
❏ 62 Roberto Hernandez	.15	.07	
❏ 63 Ron Karkovice	.15	.07	
❏ 64 Darren Lewis	.15	.07	
❏ 65 Dave Martinez	.15	.07	
❏ 66 Lyle Mouton	.15	.07	
❏ 67 Greg Norton	.15	.07	
❏ 68 Tony Phillips	.15	.07	
❏ 69 Chris Snopek	.15	.07	
❏ 70 Kevin Tapani	.15	.07	
❏ 71 Danny Tartabull	.15	.07	
❏ 72 Frank Thomas	1.25	.55	
❏ 73 Robin Ventura	.30	.14	
❏ 74 Sandy Alomar Jr.	.30	.14	
❏ 75 Albert Belle	.60	.25	
❏ 76 Mark Carreon	.15	.07	
❏ 77 Julio Franco	.30	.14	
❏ 78 Brian Giles	2.00	.90	
❏ 79 Orel Hershiser	.30	.14	
❏ 80 Kenny Lofton	.40	.18	
❏ 81 Dennis Martinez	.30	.14	
❏ 82 Jack McDowell	.15	.07	
❏ 83 Jose Mesa	.15	.07	
❏ 84 Charles Nagy	.30	.14	
❏ 85 Chad Ogea	.15	.07	
❏ 86 Eric Plunk	.15	.07	
❏ 87 Manny Ramirez	.75	.35	
❏ 88 Kevin Seitzer	.15	.07	
❏ 89 Julian Tavarez	.15	.07	
❏ 90 Jim Thome	.60	.25	
❏ 91 Jose Vizcaino	.15	.07	
❏ 92 Omar Vizquel	.30	.14	
❏ 93 Brad Ausmus	.15	.07	
❏ 94 Kimera Bartee	.15	.07	
❏ 95 Raul Casanova	.15	.07	
❏ 96 Tony Clark	.40	.18	
❏ 97 John Cummings	.15	.07	
❏ 98 Travis Fryman	.30	.14	
❏ 99 Bob Higginson	.30	.14	
❏ 100 Mark Lewis	.15	.07	
❏ 101 Felipe Lira	.15	.07	
❏ 102 Phil Nevin	.15	.07	
❏ 103 Melvin Nieves	.15	.07	
❏ 104 Curtis Pride	.15	.07	
❏ 105 A.J. Sager	.15	.07	
❏ 106 Ruben Sierra	.15	.07	
❏ 107 Justin Thompson	.30	.14	
❏ 108 Alan Trammell	.30	.14	
❏ 109 Kevin Appier	.30	.14	
❏ 110 Tim Belcher	.15	.07	
❏ 111 Jaime Bluma	.15	.07	
❏ 112 Johnny Damon	.30	.14	
❏ 113 Tom Goodwin	.15	.07	
❏ 114 Chris Haney	.15	.07	
❏ 115 Keith Lockhart	.15	.07	
❏ 116 Mike Macfarlane	.15	.07	
❏ 117 Jeff Montgomery	.15	.07	
❏ 118 Jose Offerman	.30	.14	
❏ 119 Craig Paquette	.15	.07	
❏ 120 Joe Randa	.15	.07	
❏ 121 Bip Roberts	.15	.07	
❏ 122 Jose Rosado	.15	.07	
❏ 123 Mike Sweeney	.30	.14	
❏ 124 Michael Tucker	.15	.07	
❏ 125 Jeromy Burnitz	.30	.14	
❏ 126 Jeff Cirillo	.30	.14	
❏ 127 Jeff D'Amico	.15	.07	
❏ 128 Mike Fetters	.15	.07	
❏ 129 John Jaha	.15	.07	
❏ 130 Scott Karl	.15	.07	
❏ 131 Jesse Levis	.15	.07	
❏ 132 Mark Loretta	.15	.07	
❏ 133 Mike Matheny	.15	.07	
❏ 134 Ben McDonald	.15	.07	
❏ 135 Matt Mieske	.15	.07	
❏ 136 Marc Newfield	.15	.07	
❏ 137 Dave Nilsson	.15	.07	
❏ 138 Jose Valentin	.15	.07	
❏ 139 Fernando Vina	.15	.07	
❏ 140 Bob Wickman	.15	.07	
❏ 141 Gerald Williams	.15	.07	
❏ 142 Rick Aguilera	.15	.07	
❏ 143 Rich Becker	.15	.07	
❏ 144 Ron Coomer	.15	.07	
❏ 145 Marty Cordova	.15	.07	
❏ 146 Roberto Kelly	.15	.07	
❏ 147 Chuck Knoblauch	.60	.25	
❏ 148 Matt Lawton	.30	.14	
❏ 149 Pat Meares	.15	.07	
❏ 150 Travis Miller	.15	.07	
❏ 151 Paul Molitor	.60	.25	
❏ 152 Greg Myers	.15	.07	
❏ 153 Dan Naulty	.15	.07	
❏ 154 Kirby Puckett	1.00	.45	
❏ 155 Brad Radke	.30	.14	
❏ 156 Frank Rodriguez	.15	.07	
❏ 157 Scott Stahoviak	.15	.07	
❏ 158 Dave Stevens	.15	.07	
❏ 159 Matt Walbeck	.15	.07	
❏ 160 Todd Walker	.60	.25	
❏ 161 Wade Boggs	.60	.25	
❏ 162 David Cone	.40	.18	
❏ 163 Mariano Duncan	.15	.07	
❏ 164 Cecil Fielder	.30	.14	
❏ 165 Joe Girardi	.15	.07	
❏ 166 Dwight Gooden	.30	.14	
❏ 167 Charlie Hayes	.15	.07	
❏ 168 Derek Jeter	2.00	.90	
❏ 169 Jimmy Key	.30	.14	
❏ 170 Jim Leyritz	.15	.07	
❏ 171 Tino Martinez	.60	.25	
❏ 172 Ramiro Mendoza	.50	.23	
❏ 173 Jeff Nelson	.15	.07	
❏ 174 Paul O'Neill	.30	.14	
❏ 175 Andy Pettitte	.40	.18	
❏ 176 Mariano Rivera	.30	.14	
❏ 177 Ruben Rivera	.15	.07	
❏ 178 Kenny Rogers	.15	.07	
❏ 179 Darryl Strawberry	.30	.14	
❏ 180 John Wetteland	.30	.14	
❏ 181 Bernie Williams	.60	.25	
❏ 182 Willie Adams	.15	.07	
❏ 183 Tony Batista	.40	.18	
❏ 184 Geronimo Berroa	.15	.07	
❏ 185 Mike Bordick	.15	.07	
❏ 186 Scott Brosius	.30	.14	
❏ 187 Bobby Chouinard	.15	.07	
❏ 188 Jim Corsi	.15	.07	
❏ 189 Brent Gates	.15	.07	
❏ 190 Jason Giambi	.30	.14	
❏ 191 Jose Herrera	.15	.07	
❏ 192 Damon Mashore	.15	.07	
❏ 193 Mark McGwire	3.00	1.35	
❏ 194 Mike Mohler	.15	.07	
❏ 195 Scott Spiezio	.15	.07	
❏ 196 Terry Steinbach	.15	.07	
❏ 197 Bill Taylor	.15	.07	
❏ 198 John Wasdin	.15	.07	
❏ 199 Steve Wojciechowski	.15	.07	
❏ 200 Ernie Young	.15	.07	
❏ 201 Rich Amaral	.15	.07	
❏ 202 Jay Buhner	.30	.14	
❏ 203 Norm Charlton	.15	.07	
❏ 204 Joey Cora	.15	.07	
❏ 205 Russ Davis	.30	.14	
❏ 206 Ken Griffey Jr.	3.00	1.35	
❏ 207 Sterling Hitchcock	.30	.14	
❏ 208 Brian Hunter	.30	.14	
❏ 209 Raul Ibanez	.15	.07	
❏ 210 Randy Johnson	.60	.25	
❏ 211 Edgar Martinez	.30	.14	
❏ 212 Jamie Moyer	.15	.07	
❏ 213 Alex Rodriguez	2.00	.90	
❏ 214 Paul Sorrento	.15	.07	
❏ 215 Matt Wagner	.15	.07	
❏ 216 Bob Wells	.15	.07	
❏ 217 Dan Wilson	.15	.07	
❏ 218 Damon Buford	.15	.07	
❏ 219 Will Clark	.60	.25	
❏ 220 Kevin Elster	.15	.07	
❏ 221 Juan Gonzalez	1.25	.55	
❏ 222 Rusty Greer	.30	.14	
❏ 223 Kevin Gross	.15	.07	
❏ 224 Darryl Hamilton	.15	.07	
❏ 225 Mike Henneman	.15	.07	
❏ 226 Ken Hill	.15	.07	
❏ 227 Mark McLemore	.15	.07	
❏ 228 Darren Oliver	.15	.07	
❏ 229 Dean Palmer	.30	.14	
❏ 230 Roger Pavlik	.15	.07	
❏ 231 Ivan Rodriguez	.75	.35	
❏ 232 Mickey Tettleton	.15	.07	
❏ 233 Bobby Witt	.15	.07	
❏ 234 Jacob Brumfield	.15	.07	
❏ 235 Joe Carter	.30	.14	
❏ 236 Tim Crabtree	.15	.07	
❏ 237 Carlos Delgado	.60	.25	
❏ 238 Huck Flener	.15	.07	
❏ 239 Alex Gonzalez	.15	.07	
❏ 240 Shawn Green	.60	.25	
❏ 241 Juan Guzman	.15	.07	
❏ 242 Pat Hentgen	.30	.14	
❏ 243 Marty Janzen	.15	.07	
❏ 244 Sandy Martinez	.15	.07	
❏ 245 Otis Nixon	.15	.07	
❏ 246 Charlie O'Brien	.15	.07	
❏ 247 John Olerud	.30	.14	
❏ 248 Robert Perez	.15	.07	
❏ 249 Ed Sprague	.15	.07	
❏ 250 Mike Timlin	.15	.07	
❏ 251 Steve Avery	.15	.07	
❏ 252 Jeff Blauser	.15	.07	
❏ 253 Brad Clontz	.15	.07	
❏ 254 Jermaine Dye	.30	.14	
❏ 255 Tom Glavine	.60	.25	
❏ 256 Marquis Grissom	.30	.14	
❏ 257 Andruw Jones	.75	.35	
❏ 258 Chipper Jones	1.50	.70	
❏ 259 David Justice	.60	.25	
❏ 260 Ryan Klesko	.30	.14	
❏ 261 Mark Lemke	.15	.07	
❏ 262 Javier Lopez	.30	.14	
❏ 263 Greg Maddux	1.50	.70	
❏ 264 Fred McGriff	.40	.18	
❏ 265 Greg McMichael	.15	.07	
❏ 266 Denny Neagle	.30	.14	
❏ 267 Terry Pendleton	.15	.07	
❏ 268 Eddie Perez	.15	.07	
❏ 269 John Smoltz	.40	.18	
❏ 270 Terrell Wade	.15	.07	
❏ 271 Mark Wohlers	.15	.07	
❏ 272 Terry Adams	.15	.07	
❏ 273 Brant Brown	.30	.14	
❏ 274 Leo Gomez	.15	.07	
❏ 275 Luis Gonzalez	.30	.14	
❏ 276 Mark Grace	.40	.18	
❏ 277 Tyler Houston	.15	.07	
❏ 278 Robin Jennings	.15	.07	
❏ 279 Brooks Kieschnick	.15	.07	
❏ 280 Brian McRae	.15	.07	
❏ 281 Jaime Navarro	.15	.07	
❏ 282 Ryne Sandberg	.75	.35	
❏ 283 Scott Servais	.15	.07	
❏ 284 Sammy Sosa	2.00	.90	
❏ 285 Dave Swartzbaugh	.15	.07	
❏ 286 Amaury Telemaco	.15	.07	
❏ 287 Steve Trachsel	.15	.07	
❏ 288 Pedro Valdes	.15	.07	
❏ 289 Turk Wendell	.15	.07	
❏ 290 Bret Boone	.30	.14	
❏ 291 Jeff Branson	.15	.07	
❏ 292 Jeff Brantley	.15	.07	
❏ 293 Eric Davis	.30	.14	
❏ 294 Willie Greene	.15	.07	
❏ 295 Thomas Howard	.15	.07	
❏ 296 Barry Larkin	.60	.25	
❏ 297 Kevin Mitchell	.15	.07	
❏ 298 Hal Morris	.15	.07	
❏ 299 Chad Mottola	.15	.07	
❏ 300 Joe Oliver	.15	.07	
❏ 301 Mark Portugal	.15	.07	
❏ 302 Roger Salkeld	.15	.07	
❏ 303 Reggie Sanders	.30	.14	
❏ 304 Pete Schourek	.15	.07	
❏ 305 John Smiley	.15	.07	
❏ 306 Eddie Taubensee	.15	.07	
❏ 307 Dante Bichette	.30	.14	
❏ 308 Ellis Burks	.30	.14	
❏ 309 Vinny Castilla	.40	.18	

#	Player	Value	
310	Andres Galarraga	.60	.25
311	Curt Leskanic	.15	.07
312	Quinton McCracken	.15	.07
313	Neifi Perez	.30	.14
314	Jeff Reed	.15	.07
315	Steve Reed	.15	.07
316	Armando Reynoso	.15	.07
317	Kevin Ritz	.15	.07
318	Bruce Ruffin	.15	.07
319	Larry Walker	.60	.25
320	Walt Weiss	.15	.07
321	Jamey Wright	.15	.07
322	Eric Young	.30	.14
323	Kurt Abbott	.15	.07
324	Alex Arias	.15	.07
325	Kevin Brown	.40	.18
326	Luis Castillo	.30	.14
327	Greg Colbrunn	.15	.07
328	Jeff Conine	.15	.07
329	Andre Dawson	.40	.18
330	Charles Johnson	.30	.14
331	Al Leiter	.30	.14
332	Ralph Milliard	.15	.07
333	Robb Nen	.15	.07
334	Pat Rapp	.15	.07
335	Edgar Renteria	.30	.14
336	Gary Sheffield	.30	.14
337	Devon White	.30	.14
338	Bob Abreu	.30	.14
339	Jeff Bagwell	.75	.35
340	Derek Bell	.30	.14
341	Sean Berry	.15	.07
342	Craig Biggio	.60	.25
343	Doug Drabek	.15	.07
344	Tony Eusebio	.15	.07
345	Ricky Gutierrez	.15	.07
346	Mike Hampton	.30	.14
347	Brian Hunter	.30	.14
348	Todd Jones	.15	.07
349	Darryl Kile	.15	.07
350	Derrick May	.15	.07
351	Orlando Miller	.15	.07
352	James Mouton	.15	.07
353	Shane Reynolds	.30	.14
354	Billy Wagner	.30	.14
355	Donne Wall	.15	.07
356	Mike Blowers	.15	.07
357	Brett Butler	.30	.14
358	Roger Cedeno	.30	.14
359	Chad Curtis	.15	.07
360	Delino DeShields	.15	.07
361	Greg Gagne	.15	.07
362	Karim Garcia	.30	.14
363	Wilton Guerrero	.15	.07
364	Todd Hollandsworth	.15	.07
365	Eric Karros	.30	.14
366	Ramon Martinez	.30	.14
367	Raul Mondesi	.60	.25
368	Hideo Nomo	.60	.25
369	Antonio Osuna	.15	.07
370	Chan Ho Park	.60	.25
371	Mike Piazza	2.00	.90
372	Ismael Valdes	.30	.14
373	Todd Worrell	.15	.07
374	Moises Alou	.30	.14
375	Shane Andrews	.15	.07
376	Yamil Benitez	.15	.07
377	Jeff Fassero	.15	.07
378	Darrin Fletcher	.15	.07
379	Cliff Floyd	.30	.14
380	Mark Grudzielanek	.30	.14
381	Mike Lansing	.15	.07
382	Barry Manuel	.15	.07
383	Pedro Martinez	.75	.35
384	Henry Rodriguez	.30	.14
385	Mel Rojas	.15	.07
386	F.P. Santangelo	.15	.07
387	David Segui	.30	.14
388	Ugueth Urbina	.30	.14
389	Rondell White	.30	.14
390	Edgardo Alfonzo	.40	.18
391	Carlos Baerga	.15	.07
392	Mark Clark	.15	.07
393	Alvaro Espinoza	.15	.07
394	John Franco	.30	.14
395	Bernard Gilkey	.15	.07
396	Pete Harnisch	.15	.07
397	Todd Hundley	.30	.14
398	Butch Huskey	.15	.07
399	Jason Isringhausen	.15	.07
400	Lance Johnson	.15	.07
401	Bobby Jones	.15	.07
402	Alex Ochoa	.15	.07
403	Rey Ordonez	.30	.14
404	Robert Person	.15	.07
405	Paul Wilson	.15	.07
406	Matt Beech	.15	.07
407	Ron Blazier	.15	.07
408	Ricky Bottalico	.30	.14
409	Lenny Dykstra	.30	.14
410	Jim Eisenreich	.15	.07
411	Bobby Estalella	.15	.07
412	Mike Grace	.15	.07
413	Gregg Jefferies	.15	.07
414	Mike Lieberthal	.15	.07
415	Wendell Magee	.15	.07
416	Mickey Morandini	.15	.07
417	Ricky Otero	.15	.07
418	Scott Rolen	1.00	.45
419	Ken Ryan	.15	.07
420	Benito Santiago	.15	.07
421	Curt Schilling	.40	.18
422	Kevin Sefcik	.15	.07
423	Jermaine Allensworth	.15	.07
424	Trey Beamon	.15	.07
425	Jay Bell	.30	.14
426	Francisco Cordova	.15	.07
427	Carlos Garcia	.15	.07
428	Mark Johnson	.15	.07
429	Jason Kendall	.40	.18
430	Jeff King	.15	.07
431	Jon Lieber	.15	.07
432	Al Martin	.15	.07
433	Orlando Merced	.15	.07
434	Ramon Morel	.15	.07
435	Matt Ruebel	.15	.07
436	Jason Schmidt	.15	.07
437	Marc Wilkins	.15	.07
438	Alan Benes	.15	.07
439	Andy Benes	.30	.14
440	Royce Clayton	.15	.07
441	Dennis Eckersley	.30	.14
442	Gary Gaetti	.15	.07
443	Ron Gant	.30	.14
444	Aaron Holbert	.15	.07
445	Brian Jordan	.30	.14
446	Ray Lankford	.30	.14
447	John Mabry	.15	.07
448	T.J. Mathews	.15	.07
449	Willie McGee	.30	.14
450	Donovan Osborne	.15	.07
451	Tom Pagnozzi	.15	.07
452	Ozzie Smith	.75	.35
453	Todd Stottlemyre	.15	.07
454	Mark Sweeney	.15	.07
455	Dmitri Young	.30	.14
456	Andy Ashby	.15	.07
457	Ken Caminiti	.40	.18
458	Archi Cianfrocco	.15	.07
459	Steve Finley	.30	.14
460	John Flaherty	.15	.07
461	Chris Gomez	.15	.07
462	Tony Gwynn	1.50	.70
463	Joey Hamilton	.30	.14
464	Rickey Henderson	.75	.35
465	Trevor Hoffman	.30	.14
466	Brian Johnson	.15	.07
467	Wally Joyner	.30	.14
468	Jody Reed	.15	.07
469	Scott Sanders	.15	.07
470	Bob Tewksbury	.15	.07
471	Fernando Valenzuela	.30	.14
472	Greg Vaughn	.30	.14
473	Tim Worrell	.15	.07
474	Rich Aurilia	.30	.14
475	Rod Beck	.15	.07
476	Marvin Benard	.15	.07
477	Barry Bonds	.75	.35
478	Jay Canizaro	.15	.07
479	Shawn Dunston	.30	.14
480	Shawn Estes	.30	.14
481	Mark Gardner	.15	.07
482	Glenallen Hill	.15	.07
483	Stan Javier	.15	.07
484	Marcus Jensen	.15	.07
485	Bill Mueller	.75	.35
486	Wm. VanLandingham	.15	.07
487	Allen Watson	.15	.07
488	Rick Wilkins	.15	.07
489	Matt Williams	.60	.25
490	Desi Wilson	.15	.07
491	Albert Belle CL	.30	.14
492	Ken Griffey Jr. CL	1.50	.70
493	Andruw Jones CL	.40	.18
494	Chipper Jones CL	.75	.35
495	Mark McGwire CL	1.50	.70
496	Paul Molitor CL	.30	.14
497	Mike Piazza CL	1.00	.45
498	Cal Ripken CL	1.25	.55
499	Alex Rodriguez CL	1.00	.45
500	Frank Thomas CL	.60	.25
501	Kenny Lofton	.40	.18
502	Carlos Perez	.15	.07
503	Tim Raines	.30	.14
504	Danny Patterson	.15	.07
505	Derrick May	.15	.07
506	Dave Hollins	.15	.07
507	Felipe Crespo	.15	.07
508	Brian Banks	.15	.07
509	Jeff Kent	.30	.14
510	Bubba Trammell	.60	.25
511	Robert Person	.15	.07
512	David Arias-Ortiz	.75	.35
513	Ryan Jones	.15	.07
514	David Justice	.60	.25
515	Will Cunnane	.15	.07
516	Russ Johnson	.15	.07
517	John Burkett	.15	.07
518	Robinson Checo	.15	.07
519	Ricardo Rincon	.15	.07
520	Woody Williams	.15	.07
521	Rick Helling	.30	.14
522	Jorge Posada	.30	.14
523	Kevin Orie	.15	.07
524	Fernando Tatis	2.50	1.10
525	Jermaine Dye	.30	.14
526	Brian Hunter	.30	.14
527	Greg McMichael	.15	.07
528	Matt Wagner	.15	.07
529	Richie Sexson	.60	.25
530	Scott Ruffcorn	.15	.07
531	Luis Gonzalez	.30	.14
532	Mike Johnson	.40	.18
533	Mark Petkovsek	.15	.07
534	Doug Drabek	.15	.07
535	Jose Canseco	.75	.35
536	Bobby Bonilla	.30	.14
537	J.T. Snow	.30	.14
538	Shawon Dunston	.15	.07
539	John Ericks	.15	.07
540	Terry Steinbach	.15	.07
541	Jay Bell	.30	.14
542	Joe Borowski	.15	.07
543	David Wells	.30	.14
544	Justin Towle	.40	.18
545	Mike Blowers	.15	.07
546	Shannon Stewart	.30	.14
547	Rudy Pemberton	.15	.07
548	Bill Swift	.15	.07
549	Osvaldo Fernandez	.15	.07
550	Eddie Murray	.60	.25
551	Don Wengert	.15	.07
552	Brad Ausmus	.15	.07
553	Carlos Garcia	.15	.07
554	Jose Guillen	.40	.18
555	Rheal Cormier	.15	.07
556	Doug Brocail	.15	.07
557	Rex Hudler	.15	.07
558	Armando Benitez	.15	.07
559	Eli Marrero	.15	.07
560	Ricky Ledee	1.50	.70
561	Bartolo Colon	.30	.14
562	Quilvio Veras	.15	.07
563	Alex Fernandez	.15	.07
564	Darren Dreifort	.30	.14
565	Benji Gil	.15	.07
566	Kent Mercker	.15	.07
567	Glendon Rusch	.15	.07

❏ 568 Ramon Tatis	.15	.07
❏ 569 Roger Clemens	1.50	.70
❏ 570 Mark Lewis	.15	.07
❏ 571 Emil Brown	.40	.18
❏ 572 Jaime Navarro	.15	.07
❏ 573 Sherman Obando	.15	.07
❏ 574 John Wasdin	.15	.07
❏ 575 Calvin Maduro	.15	.07
❏ 576 Todd Jones	.15	.07
❏ 577 Orlando Merced	.15	.07
❏ 578 Cal Eldred	.15	.07
❏ 579 Mark Gubicza	.15	.07
❏ 580 Michael Tucker	.15	.07
❏ 581 Tony Saunders	.15	.07
❏ 582 Garvin Alston	.15	.07
❏ 583 Joe Roa	.15	.07
❏ 584 Brady Raggio	.15	.07
❏ 585 Jimmy Key	.30	.14
❏ 586 Marc Sagmoen	.15	.07
❏ 587 Jim Bullinger	.15	.07
❏ 588 Yorkis Perez	.15	.07
❏ 589 Jose Cruz Jr.	1.25	.55
❏ 590 Mike Stanton	.15	.07
❏ 591 Deivi Cruz	.60	.25
❏ 592 Steve Karsay	.15	.07
❏ 593 Mike Trombley	.15	.07
❏ 594 Doug Glanville	.40	.18
❏ 595 Scott Sanders	.15	.07
❏ 596 Thomas Howard	.15	.07
❏ 597 T.J. Staton	.40	.18
❏ 598 Garrett Stephenson	.15	.07
❏ 599 Rico Brogna	.15	.07
❏ 600 Albert Belle	.60	.25
❏ 601 Jose Vizcaino	.15	.07
❏ 602 Chili Davis	.30	.14
❏ 603 Shane Mack	.15	.07
❏ 604 Jim Eisenreich	.15	.07
❏ 605 Todd Zeile	.15	.07
❏ 606 Brian Boehringer	.15	.07
❏ 607 Paul Shuey	.15	.07
❏ 608 Kevin Tapani	.15	.07
❏ 609 John Wetteland	.30	.14
❏ 610 Jim Leyritz	.15	.07
❏ 611 Ray Montgomery	.15	.07
❏ 612 Doug Bochtler	.15	.07
❏ 613 Wady Almonte	.30	.14
❏ 614 Danny Tartabull	.15	.07
❏ 615 Orlando Miller	.15	.07
❏ 616 Bobby Ayala	.15	.07
❏ 617 Tony Graffanino	.15	.07
❏ 618 Marc Valdes	.15	.07
❏ 619 Ron Villone	.15	.07
❏ 620 Derek Lee	.40	.18
❏ 621 Greg Colbrunn	.15	.07
❏ 622 Felix Heredia	.30	.14
❏ 623 Carl Everett	.30	.14
❏ 624 Mark Thompson	.15	.07
❏ 625 Jeff Granger	.15	.07
❏ 626 Damian Jackson	.15	.07
❏ 627 Mark Leiter	.15	.07
❏ 628 Chris Holt	.15	.07
❏ 629 Dario Veras	.40	.18
❏ 630 Dave Burba	.15	.07
❏ 631 Darryl Hamilton	.15	.07
❏ 632 Mark Acre	.15	.07
❏ 633 Fernando Hernandez	.15	.07
❏ 634 Terry Mulholland	.15	.07
❏ 635 Dustin Hermanson	.15	.07
❏ 636 Delino DeShields	.15	.07
❏ 637 Steve Avery	.15	.07
❏ 638 Tony Womack	.50	.23
❏ 639 Mark Whiten	.15	.07
❏ 640 Marquis Grissom	.30	.14
❏ 641 Xavier Hernandez	.15	.07
❏ 642 Eric Davis	.30	.14
❏ 643 Bob Tewksbury	.15	.07
❏ 644 Dante Powell	.30	.14
❏ 645 Carlos Castillo	.40	.18
❏ 646 Chris Widger	.15	.07
❏ 647 Moises Alou	.30	.14
❏ 648 Pat Listach	.15	.07
❏ 649 Edgar Ramos	.40	.18
❏ 650 Deion Sanders	.30	.14
❏ 651 John Olerud	.30	.14
❏ 652 Todd Dunwoody	.30	.14
❏ 653 Randall Simon	.60	.25

❏ 654 Dan Carlson	.15	.07
❏ 655 Matt Williams	.60	.25
❏ 656 Jeff King	.15	.07
❏ 657 Luis Alicea	.15	.07
❏ 658 Brian Moehler	.15	.07
❏ 659 Ariel Prieto	.15	.07
❏ 660 Kevin Elster	.15	.07
❏ 661 Mark Hutton	.15	.07
❏ 662 Aaron Sele	.30	.14
❏ 663 Graeme Lloyd	.15	.07
❏ 664 John Burke	.15	.07
❏ 665 Mel Rojas	.15	.07
❏ 666 Sid Fernandez	.15	.07
❏ 667 Pedro Astacio	.15	.07
❏ 668 Jeff Abbott	.15	.07
❏ 669 Darren Daulton	.30	.14
❏ 670 Mike Bordick	.15	.07
❏ 671 Sterling Hitchcock	.15	.07
❏ 672 Damian Easley	.30	.14
❏ 673 Armando Reynoso	.15	.07
❏ 674 Pat Cline	.30	.14
❏ 675 Orlando Cabrera	.30	.14
❏ 676 Alan Embree	.15	.07
❏ 677 Brian Bevil	.15	.07
❏ 678 David Weathers	.15	.07
❏ 679 Cliff Floyd	.30	.14
❏ 680 Joe Randa	.15	.07
❏ 681 Bill Haselman	.15	.07
❏ 682 Jeff Fassero	.15	.07
❏ 683 Matt Morris	.30	.14
❏ 684 Mark Portugal	.15	.07
❏ 685 Lee Smith	.30	.14
❏ 686 Pokey Reese	.30	.14
❏ 687 Benito Santiago	.15	.07
❏ 688 Brian Johnson	.15	.07
❏ 689 Brent Brede	.15	.07
❏ 690 Shigetoshi Hasegawa	.30	.14
❏ 691 Julio Santana	.15	.07
❏ 692 Steve Kline	.15	.07
❏ 693 Julian Tavarez	.15	.07
❏ 694 John Hudek	.15	.07
❏ 695 Manny Alexander	.15	.07
❏ 696 Roberto Alomar ENC	.30	.14
❏ 697 Jeff Bagwell ENC	.30	.14
❏ 698 Barry Bonds ENC	.30	.14
❏ 699 Ken Caminiti ENC	.15	.07
❏ 700 Juan Gonzalez ENC	.60	.25
❏ 701 Ken Griffey Jr. ENC	1.50	.70
❏ 702 Tony Gwynn ENC	.75	.35
❏ 703 Derek Jeter ENC	1.00	.45
❏ 704 Andruw Jones ENC	.40	.18
❏ 705 Chipper Jones ENC	.75	.35
❏ 706 Barry Larkin ENC	.30	.14
❏ 707 Greg Maddux ENC	.75	.35
❏ 708 Mark McGwire ENC	1.50	.70
❏ 709 Paul Molitor ENC	.30	.14
❏ 710 Hideo Nomo ENC	.30	.14
❏ 711 Andy Pettitte ENC	.15	.07
❏ 712 Mike Piazza ENC	1.00	.45
❏ 713 Manny Ramirez ENC	.40	.18
❏ 714 Cal Ripken ENC	1.25	.55
❏ 715 Alex Rodriguez ENC	1.00	.45
❏ 716 Ryne Sandberg ENC	.60	.25
❏ 717 John Smoltz ENC	.30	.14
❏ 718 Frank Thomas ENC	.60	.25
❏ 719 Mo Vaughn ENC	.30	.14
❏ 720 Bernie Williams ENC	.30	.14
❏ 721 Tim Salmon CL	.30	.14
❏ 722 Greg Maddux CL	.75	.35
❏ 723 Cal Ripken CL	1.25	.55
❏ 724 Mo Vaughn CL	.30	.14
❏ 725 Ryne Sandberg CL	.60	.25
❏ 726 Frank Thomas CL	.60	.25
❏ 727 Barry Larkin CL	.15	.07
❏ 728 Manny Ramirez CL	.40	.18
❏ 729 Andres Galarraga CL	.30	.14
❏ 730 Tony Clark CL	.15	.07
❏ 731 Gary Sheffield CL	.15	.07
❏ 732 Jeff Bagwell CL	.30	.14
❏ 733 Kevin Appier CL	.15	.07
❏ 734 Mike Piazza CL	1.00	.45
❏ 735 Jeff Cirillo CL	.15	.07
❏ 736 Paul Molitor CL	.30	.14
❏ 737 Henry Rodriguez CL	.15	.07
❏ 738 Todd Hundley CL	.15	.07
❏ 739 Derek Jeter CL	1.00	.45

❏ 740 Mark McGwire CL	1.50	.70
❏ 741 Curt Schilling CL	.30	.14
❏ 742 Jason Kendall CL	.15	.07
❏ 743 Tony Gwynn CL	.75	.35
❏ 744 Barry Bonds CL	.30	.14
❏ 745 Ken Griffey Jr. CL	1.50	.70
❏ 746 Brian Jordan CL	.15	.07
❏ 747 Juan Gonzalez CL	.60	.25
❏ 748 Joe Carter CL	.15	.07
❏ 749 Arizona Diamondbacks ..	.30	.14
	CL	
❏ 750 Tampa Bay Devil Rays ..	.30	.14
	CL	
❏ 751 Hideki Irabu	2.00	.90
❏ 752 Jeremi Gonzalez	.60	.25
❏ 753 Mario Valdez	.75	.35
❏ 754 Aaron Boone	.25	.11
❏ 755 Brett Tomko	.25	.11
❏ 756 Jaret Wright	1.50	.70
❏ 757 Ryan McGuire	.25	.11
❏ 758 Jason McDonald	.25	.11
❏ 759 Adrian Brown	.25	.11
❏ 760 Keith Foulke	.25	.11
❏ 761 Bonus Checklist	.25	.11
❏ P489 Matt Williams Promo..	1.00	.45
❏ NNO Andruw Jones	80.00	36.00
	Circa AU/200	

1997 Fleer Tiffany

	MINT	NRMT
COMMON CARD (1-761)	4.00	1.80

*STARS: 12.5X TO 30X BASIC CARDS
*ROOKIES: 5X TO 12X BASIC CARDS
*751-761: 3X TO 8X BASIC CARDS
STATED ODDS 1:20

1997 Fleer Bleacher Blasters

	MINT	NRMT
COMPLETE SET (10)	100.00	45.00
COMMON CARD (1-10)	5.00	2.20

SER.2 STATED ODDS 1:36 RETAIL

❏ 1 Albert Belle		5.00	2.20
❏ 2 Barry Bonds		6.00	2.70
❏ 3 Juan Gonzalez		10.00	4.50
❏ 4 Ken Griffey Jr.		25.00	11.00
❏ 5 Mark McGwire		25.00	11.00

	MINT	NRMT
❑ 6 Mike Piazza	15.00	6.75
❑ 7 Alex Rodriguez	15.00	6.75
❑ 8 Frank Thomas	10.00	4.50
❑ 9 Mo Vaughn	5.00	2.20
❑ 10 Matt Williams	5.00	2.20

1997 Fleer Decade of Excellence

	MINT	NRMT
COMPLETE SET (12)	60.00	27.00
COMMON CARD (1-12)	4.00	1.80

SER.2 STATED ODDS 1:36 HOBBY
*RARE TRAD: 12.5X TO 30X BASE CARD HI
RARE TRAD.STATED ODDS 1:360 HOBBY

	MINT	NRMT
❑ 1 Wade Boggs	4.00	1.80
❑ 2 Barry Bonds	5.00	2.20
❑ 3 Roger Clemens	10.00	4.50
❑ 4 Tony Gwynn	10.00	4.50
❑ 5 Rickey Henderson	5.00	2.20
❑ 6 Greg Maddux	10.00	4.50
❑ 7 Mark McGwire	20.00	9.00
❑ 8 Paul Molitor	4.00	1.80
❑ 9 Eddie Murray	4.00	1.80
❑ 10 Cal Ripken	15.00	6.75
❑ 11 Ryne Sandberg	5.00	2.20
❑ 12 Matt Williams	4.00	1.80

1997 Fleer Diamond Tribute

	MINT	NRMT
COMPLETE SET (12)	500.00	220.00
COMMON CARD (1-12)	15.00	6.75

SER.2 STATED ODDS 1:288

	MINT	NRMT
❑ 1 Albert Belle	15.00	6.75
❑ 2 Barry Bonds	20.00	9.00
❑ 3 Juan Gonzalez	30.00	13.50
❑ 4 Ken Griffey Jr.	80.00	36.00
❑ 5 Tony Gwynn	40.00	18.00
❑ 6 Greg Maddux	40.00	18.00
❑ 7 Mark McGwire	80.00	36.00
❑ 8 Eddie Murray	15.00	6.75
❑ 9 Mike Piazza	50.00	22.00
❑ 10 Cal Ripken	60.00	27.00
❑ 11 Alex Rodriguez	50.00	22.00
❑ 12 Frank Thomas	30.00	13.50

1997 Fleer Golden Memories

	MINT	NRMT
COMPLETE SET (10)	10.00	4.50
COMMON CARD (1-10)	.50	.23

SER.1 STATED ODDS 1:16 HOBBY

	MINT	NRMT
❑ 1 Barry Bonds	1.25	.55
❑ 2 Dwight Gooden	.50	.23
❑ 3 Todd Hundley	.50	.23
❑ 4 Mark McGwire	5.00	2.20
❑ 5 Paul Molitor	1.00	.45
❑ 6 Eddie Murray	1.00	.45
❑ 7 Hideo Nomo	1.00	.45
❑ 8 Mike Piazza	4.00	1.80
❑ 9 Cal Ripken	4.00	1.80
❑ 10 Ozzie Smith	1.50	.70

1997 Fleer Goudey Greats

	MINT	NRMT
COMPLETE SET (15)	30.00	13.50
COMMON CARD (1-15)	1.00	.45

SER.2 STATED ODDS 1:8
*FOIL CARDS: 15X TO 40X BASE CARD HI
FOIL SER.2 STATED ODDS 1:800

	MINT	NRMT
❑ 1 Barry Bonds	1.25	.55
❑ 2 Ken Griffey Jr.	5.00	2.20
❑ 3 Tony Gwynn	2.50	1.10
❑ 4 Derek Jeter	3.00	1.35
❑ 5 Chipper Jones	2.50	1.10
❑ 6 Kenny Lofton	1.00	.45
❑ 7 Greg Maddux	2.50	1.10
❑ 8 Mark McGwire	5.00	2.20
❑ 9 Eddie Murray	1.00	.45
❑ 10 Mike Piazza	3.00	1.35
❑ 11 Cal Ripken	4.00	1.80
❑ 12 Alex Rodriguez	3.00	1.35
❑ 13 Ryne Sandberg	1.25	.55
❑ 14 Frank Thomas	2.50	1.10
❑ 15 Mo Vaughn	1.00	.45

1997 Fleer Headliners

	MINT	NRMT
COMPLETE SET (20)	12.00	5.50
COMMON CARD (1-20)	.30	.14

SER.2 STATED ODDS 1:2

	MINT	NRMT
❑ 1 Jeff Bagwell	.50	.23
❑ 2 Albert Belle	.40	.18
❑ 3 Barry Bonds	.50	.23
❑ 4 Ken Caminiti	.30	.14
❑ 5 Juan Gonzalez	.75	.35
❑ 6 Ken Griffey Jr.	2.00	.90
❑ 7 Tony Gwynn	1.00	.45
❑ 8 Derek Jeter	1.25	.55
❑ 9 Andruw Jones	.75	.35
❑ 10 Chipper Jones	1.00	.45
❑ 11 Greg Maddux	1.00	.45
❑ 12 Mark McGwire	2.00	.90
❑ 13 Paul Molitor	.40	.18
❑ 14 Eddie Murray	.40	.18
❑ 15 Mike Piazza	1.25	.55
❑ 16 Cal Ripken	1.50	.70
❑ 17 Alex Rodriguez	1.25	.55
❑ 18 Ryne Sandberg	.50	.23
❑ 19 John Smoltz	.30	.14
❑ 20 Frank Thomas	1.00	.45

1997 Fleer Lumber Company

	MINT	NRMT
COMPLETE SET (18)	180.00	80.00
COMMON CARD (1-528)	3.00	1.35

SER.1 STATED ODDS 1:48 RETAIL

	MINT	NRMT
❑ 1 Brady Anderson	3.00	1.35
❑ 2 Jeff Bagwell	6.00	2.70
❑ 3 Albert Belle	6.00	2.70
❑ 4 Barry Bonds	6.00	2.70
❑ 5 Jay Buhner	3.00	1.35
❑ 6 Ellis Burks	3.00	1.35
❑ 7 Andres Galarraga	6.00	2.70
❑ 8 Juan Gonzalez	12.00	5.50
❑ 9 Ken Griffey Jr.	30.00	13.50
❑ 10 Todd Hundley	3.00	1.35
❑ 11 Ryan Klesko	3.00	1.35
❑ 12 Mark McGwire	30.00	13.50
❑ 13 Mike Piazza	20.00	9.00
❑ 14 Alex Rodriguez	20.00	9.00
❑ 15 Gary Sheffield	3.00	1.35
❑ 16 Sammy Sosa	20.00	9.00
❑ 17 Frank Thomas	12.00	5.50
❑ 18 Mo Vaughn	6.00	2.70

1997-98 Fleer Million Dollar Moments

	MINT	NRMT
COMPLETE SET (45)	8.00	3.60
COMMON CARD (1-45)	.10	.05

#'s 1-45: ONE PER '97 FLEER 2/FLAIR PACK
#'s 1-45: ONE PER '98 FLEER 1/ULT.1 PACK
#'s 46-50: RAND.IN '97 FLEER 2/FLAIR PACKS
#'s 46-50: RAND.IN '98 FLEER 1/ULT.1 PACKS
1-45 SET REDEEMABLE FOR 1-50 EXCH.SET
EXCHANGE DEADLINE: 7/31/98

❏ 1	Checklist	.10	.05
❏ 2	Derek Jeter	.60	.25
❏ 3	Babe Ruth	1.50	.70
❏ 4	Barry Bonds	.30	.14
❏ 5	Brooks Robinson	.20	.09
❏ 6	Todd Hundley	.10	.05
❏ 7	Johnny Vander Meer	.10	.05
❏ 8	Cal Ripken	.75	.35
❏ 9	Bill Mazeroski	.10	.05
❏ 10	Chipper Jones	.50	.23
❏ 11	Frank Robinson	.20	.09
❏ 12	Roger Clemens	.50	.23
❏ 13	Bob Feller	.20	.09
❏ 14	Mike Piazza	.60	.25
❏ 15	Joe Nuxhall	.10	.05
❏ 16	Hideo Nomo	.20	.09
❏ 17	Jackie Robinson	1.00	.45
❏ 18	Orel Hershiser	.10	.05
❏ 19	Bobby Thomson	.10	.05
❏ 20	Joe Carter	.10	.05
❏ 21	Al Kaline	.20	.09
❏ 22	Bernie Williams	.20	.09
❏ 23	Don Larsen	.10	.05
❏ 24	Rickey Henderson	.25	.11
❏ 25	Maury Wills	.10	.05
❏ 26	Andruw Jones	.20	.09
❏ 27	Bobby Richardson	.10	.05
❏ 28	Alex Rodriguez	.60	.25
❏ 29	Jim Bunning	.10	.05
❏ 30	Ken Caminiti	.15	.07
❏ 31	Bob Gibson	.20	.09
❏ 32	Frank Thomas	.40	.18
❏ 33	Mickey Lolich	.15	.07
❏ 34	John Smoltz	.15	.07
❏ 35	Ron Swoboda	.10	.05
❏ 36	Albert Belle	.20	.09
❏ 37	Chris Chambliss	.10	.05
❏ 38	Juan Gonzalez	.40	.18
❏ 39	Ron Blomberg	.10	.05
❏ 40	John Wetteland	.10	.05
❏ 41	Carlton Fisk	.20	.09
❏ 42	Mo Vaughn	.20	.09
❏ 43	Bucky Dent	.10	.05
❏ 44	Greg Maddux	.50	.23
❏ 45	Willie Stargell	.20	.09
❏ 46	Tony Gwynn SP		
❏ 47	Joel Youngblood SP		
❏ 48	Andy Pettitte SP		
❏ 49	Mookie Wilson SP		
❏ 50	Jeff Bagwell SP		

1997 Fleer New Horizons

	MINT	NRMT
COMPLETE SET (15)	5.00	2.20

	MINT	NRMT
COMMON CARD (1-15)	.25	.11

SER.2 STATED ODDS 1:4

❏ 1	Bob Abreu	.25	.11
❏ 2	Jose Cruz Jr.	1.00	.45
❏ 3	Darin Erstad	.75	.35
❏ 4	Nomar Garciaparra	2.50	1.10
❏ 5	Vladimir Guerrero	2.00	.90
❏ 6	Wilton Guerrero	.25	.11
❏ 7	Jose Guillen	.50	.23
❏ 8	Hideki Irabu	1.00	.45
❏ 9	Andruw Jones	1.25	.55
❏ 10	Kevin Orie	.25	.11
❏ 11	Scott Rolen	1.50	.70
❏ 12	Scott Spiezio	.25	.11
❏ 13	Bubba Trammell	.75	.35
❏ 14	Todd Walker	.75	.35
❏ 15	Dmitri Young	.25	.11

1997 Fleer Night and Day

	MINT	NRMT
COMPLETE SET (10)	250.00	110.00
COMMON CARD (1-10)	6.00	2.70
UNLISTED STARS	12.00	5.50

SER.1 STATED ODDS 1:240

❏ 1	Barry Bonds	15.00	6.75
❏ 2	Ellis Burks	6.00	2.70
❏ 3	Juan Gonzalez	25.00	11.00
❏ 4	Ken Griffey Jr.	60.00	27.00
❏ 5	Mark McGwire	60.00	27.00
❏ 6	Mike Piazza	40.00	18.00
❏ 7	Manny Ramirez	15.00	6.75
❏ 8	Alex Rodriguez	40.00	18.00
❏ 9	John Smoltz	10.00	4.50
❏ 10	Frank Thomas	25.00	11.00

1997 Fleer Rookie Sensations

	MINT	NRMT
COMPLETE SET (20)	25.00	11.00
COMMON CARD (1-20)	.40	.18

SER.1 STATED ODDS 1:6

❏ 1	Jermaine Allensworth	.40	.18
❏ 2	James Baldwin	.60	.25
❏ 3	Alan Benes	.40	.18

❏ 4	Jermaine Dye	.60	.25
❏ 5	Darin Erstad	1.50	.70
❏ 6	Todd Hollandsworth	.40	.18
❏ 7	Derek Jeter	6.00	2.70
❏ 8	Jason Kendall	1.00	.45
❏ 9	Alex Ochoa	.40	.18
❏ 10	Rey Ordonez	.60	.25
❏ 11	Edgar Renteria	.60	.25
❏ 12	Bob Abreu	.60	.25
❏ 13	Nomar Garciaparra	5.00	2.20
❏ 14	Wilton Guerrero	.40	.18
❏ 15	Andruw Jones	3.00	1.35
❏ 16	Wendell Magee	.40	.18
❏ 17	Neifi Perez	.40	.18
❏ 18	Scott Rolen	3.00	1.35
❏ 19	Scott Spiezio	.40	.18
❏ 20	Todd Walker	1.50	.70

1997 Fleer Soaring Stars

	MINT	NRMT
COMPLETE SET (12)	40.00	18.00
COMMON CARD (1-12)	1.50	.70

SER.2 STATED ODDS 1:12
*GLOWING: 8X TO 20X BASE CARD HI
GLOWING: RANDOM INS.IN SER.2 PACKS

❏ 1	Albert Belle	1.50	.70
❏ 2	Barry Bonds	1.50	.70
❏ 3	Juan Gonzalez	3.00	1.35
❏ 4	Ken Griffey Jr.	6.00	2.70
❏ 5	Derek Jeter	4.00	1.80
❏ 6	Andruw Jones	2.00	.90
❏ 7	Chipper Jones	3.00	1.35
❏ 8	Greg Maddux	3.00	1.35
❏ 9	Mark McGwire	6.00	2.70
❏ 10	Mike Piazza	4.00	1.80
❏ 11	Alex Rodriguez	4.00	1.80
❏ 12	Frank Thomas	3.00	1.35

1997 Fleer Team Leaders

	MINT	NRMT
COMPLETE SET (28)	100.00	45.00
COMMON CARD (1-28)	1.00	.45

SER.1 STATED ODDS 1:20

❏ 1	Cal Ripken	15.00	6.75

		MINT	NRMT
❏ 2	Mo Vaughn	4.00	1.80
❏ 3	Jim Edmonds	2.50	1.10
❏ 4	Frank Thomas	8.00	3.60
❏ 5	Albert Belle	4.00	1.80
❏ 6	Bob Higginson	2.00	.90
❏ 7	Kevin Appier	2.00	.90
❏ 8	John Jaha	1.00	.45
❏ 9	Paul Molitor	4.00	1.80
❏ 10	Andy Pettitte	2.50	1.10
❏ 11	Mark McGwire	20.00	9.00
❏ 12	Ken Griffey Jr.	20.00	9.00
❏ 13	Juan Gonzalez	8.00	3.60
❏ 14	Pat Hentgen	2.00	.90
❏ 15	Chipper Jones	10.00	4.50
❏ 16	Mark Grace	2.50	1.10
❏ 17	Barry Larkin	4.00	1.80
❏ 18	Ellis Burks	2.00	.90
❏ 19	Gary Sheffield	2.00	.90
❏ 20	Jeff Bagwell	5.00	2.20
❏ 21	Mike Piazza	12.00	5.50
❏ 22	Henry Rodriguez	1.00	.45
❏ 23	Todd Hundley	1.00	.45
❏ 24	Curt Schilling	2.50	1.10
❏ 25	Jeff King	1.00	.45
❏ 26	Brian Jordan	2.00	.90
❏ 27	Tony Gwynn	10.00	4.50
❏ 28	Barry Bonds	5.00	2.20

1997 Fleer Zone

		MINT	NRMT
COMPLETE SET (20)		250.00	110.00
COMMON CARD (1-20)		2.00	.90
MINOR STARS		4.00	1.80
UNLISTED STARS		8.00	3.60
SER.1 STATED ODDS 1:80 HOBBY			
❏ 1	Jeff Bagwell	10.00	4.50
❏ 2	Albert Belle	8.00	3.60
❏ 3	Barry Bonds	10.00	4.50
❏ 4	Ken Caminiti	5.00	2.20
❏ 5	Andres Galarraga	8.00	3.60
❏ 6	Juan Gonzalez	15.00	6.75
❏ 7	Ken Griffey Jr.	40.00	18.00
❏ 8	Tony Gwynn	20.00	9.00
❏ 9	Chipper Jones	20.00	9.00
❏ 10	Greg Maddux	20.00	9.00
❏ 11	Mark McGwire	40.00	18.00
❏ 12	Dean Palmer	2.00	.90
❏ 13	Andy Pettitte	5.00	2.20
❏ 14	Mike Piazza	25.00	11.00

❏ 15	Alex Rodriguez	25.00	11.00
❏ 16	Gary Sheffield	5.00	2.20
❏ 17	John Smoltz	4.00	1.80
❏ 18	Frank Thomas	15.00	6.75
❏ 19	Jim Thome	8.00	3.60
❏ 20	Matt Williams	4.00	1.80

1998 Fleer

	MINT	NRMT
COMPLETE SET (600)	170.00	75.00
COMPLETE SERIES 1 (350)	100.00	45.00
COMPLETE SERIES 2 (250)	70.00	32.00
COMMON CARD (1-600)	.15	.07
MINOR STARS	.25	.11
SEMISTARS	.40	.18
UNLISTED STARS	.60	.25
COMMON GM (311-320)	.40	.18
GM SEMISTARS	.60	.25
GM UNLISTED STARS	1.00	.45
GOLDEN MOMENT SER.1 STATED ODDS 1:6		
COMMON TT (321-340)	.50	.23
TT SEMISTARS	.75	.35
TT UNLISTED STARS	1.25	.55
TALE OF TAPE SER.1 STATED ODDS 1:4		
COMMON UM (576-600)	.60	.25
UM SEMISTARS	1.00	.45
UM UNLISTED STARS	1.50	.70
UNF.MOMENTS SER.2 STATED ODDS 1:4		

❏ 1	Ken Griffey Jr.	3.00	1.35
❏ 2	Derek Jeter	2.00	.90
❏ 3	Gerald Williams	.15	.07
❏ 4	Carlos Delgado	.60	.25
❏ 5	Nomar Garciaparra	2.00	.90
❏ 6	Gary Sheffield	.25	.11
❏ 7	Jeff King	.15	.07
❏ 8	Cal Ripken	2.50	1.10
❏ 9	Matt Williams	.60	.25
❏ 10	Chipper Jones	1.50	.70
❏ 11	Chuck Knoblauch	.25	.11
❏ 12	Mark Grudzielanek	.15	.07
❏ 13	Edgardo Alfonzo	.40	.18
❏ 14	Andres Galarraga	.40	.18
❏ 15	Tim Salmon	.40	.18
❏ 16	Reggie Sanders	.15	.07
❏ 17	Tony Clark	.25	.11
❏ 18	Jason Kendall	.15	.11
❏ 19	Juan Gonzalez	1.25	.55
❏ 20	Ben Grieve	.60	.25
❏ 21	Roger Clemens	1.50	.70
❏ 22	Raul Mondesi	.25	.11
❏ 23	Robin Ventura	.25	.11
❏ 24	Derrek Lee	.15	.07
❏ 25	Mark McGwire	4.00	1.80
❏ 26	Luis Gonzalez	.25	.11
❏ 27	Kevin Brown	.40	.18
❏ 28	Kirk Rueter	.15	.07
❏ 29	Bobby Estalella	.15	.07
❏ 30	Shawn Green	.60	.25
❏ 31	Greg Maddux	1.50	.70
❏ 32	Jorge Velandia	.15	.07
❏ 33	Larry Walker	.60	.25
❏ 34	Joey Cora	.15	.07
❏ 35	Frank Thomas	1.25	.55
❏ 36	Curtis King	.15	.07
❏ 37	Aaron Boone	.25	.07
❏ 38	Curt Schilling	.40	.18

❏ 39	Bruce Aven	.15	.07
❏ 40	Ben McDonald	.15	.07
❏ 41	Andy Ashby	.15	.07
❏ 42	Jason McDonald	.15	.07
❏ 43	Eric Davis	.25	.11
❏ 44	Mark Grace	.40	.18
❏ 45	Pedro Martinez	.75	.35
❏ 46	Lou Collier	.15	.07
❏ 47	Chan Ho Park	.25	.11
❏ 48	Shane Halter	.15	.07
❏ 49	Brian Hunter	.15	.07
❏ 50	Jeff Bagwell	.75	.35
❏ 51	Bernie Williams	.60	.25
❏ 52	J.T. Snow	.25	.11
❏ 53	Todd Greene	.15	.07
❏ 54	Shannon Stewart	.25	.11
❏ 55	Darren Bragg	.15	.07
❏ 56	Fernando Tatis	.60	.25
❏ 57	Darryl Kile	.15	.07
❏ 58	Chris Stynes	.15	.07
❏ 59	Javier Valentin	.15	.07
❏ 60	Brian McRae	.15	.07
❏ 61	Tom Evans	.15	.07
❏ 62	Randall Simon	.25	.11
❏ 63	Darrin Fletcher	.15	.07
❏ 64	Jaret Wright	.25	.11
❏ 65	Luis Ordaz	.15	.07
❏ 66	Jose Canseco	.75	.35
❏ 67	Edgar Renteria	.15	.07
❏ 68	Jay Buhner	.25	.11
❏ 69	Paul Konerko	.25	.11
❏ 70	Adrian Brown	.15	.07
❏ 71	Chris Carpenter	.25	.11
❏ 72	Mike Lieberthal	.15	.07
❏ 73	Dean Palmer	.15	.07
❏ 74	Jorge Fabregas	.15	.07
❏ 75	Stan Javier	.15	.07
❏ 76	Damion Easley	.25	.11
❏ 77	David Cone	.40	.18
❏ 78	Aaron Sele	.15	.07
❏ 79	Antonio Alfonseca	.15	.07
❏ 80	Bobby Jones	.15	.07
❏ 81	David Justice	.25	.11
❏ 82	Jeffrey Hammonds	.15	.07
❏ 83	Doug Glanville	.25	.11
❏ 84	Jason Dickson	.15	.07
❏ 85	Brad Radke	.25	.11
❏ 86	David Segui	.15	.07
❏ 87	Greg Vaughn	.25	.11
❏ 88	Mike Cather	.15	.07
❏ 89	Alex Fernandez	.15	.07
❏ 90	Billy Taylor	.15	.07
❏ 91	Jason Schmidt	.15	.07
❏ 92	Mike DeJean	.15	.07
❏ 93	Domingo Cedeno	.15	.07
❏ 94	Jeff Cirillo	.15	.07
❏ 95	Manny Aybar	.25	.11
❏ 96	Jaime Navarro	.15	.07
❏ 97	Dennis Reyes	.15	.07
❏ 98	Barry Larkin	.60	.25
❏ 99	Troy O'Leary	.25	.11
❏ 100	Alex Rodriguez	2.00	.90
❏ 101	Pat Hentgen	.15	.07
❏ 102	Bubba Trammell	.15	.07
❏ 103	Glendon Rusch	.15	.07
❏ 104	Kenny Lofton	.40	.18
❏ 105	Craig Biggio	.60	.25
❏ 106	Kelvim Escobar	.25	.11
❏ 107	Mark Kotsay	.25	.11
❏ 108	Rondell White	.25	.11
❏ 109	Darren Oliver	.15	.07
❏ 110	Jim Thome	.60	.25
❏ 111	Rich Becker	.15	.07
❏ 112	Chad Curtis	.15	.07
❏ 113	Dave Hollins	.15	.07
❏ 114	Bill Mueller	.15	.07
❏ 115	Antone Williamson	.15	.07
❏ 116	Tony Womack	.15	.07
❏ 117	Randy Myers	.25	.11
❏ 118	Rico Brogna	.15	.07
❏ 119	Pat Watkins	.15	.07
❏ 120	Eli Marrero	.15	.07
❏ 121	Jay Bell	.25	.11
❏ 122	Kevin Tapani	.15	.07
❏ 123	Todd Erdos	.25	.11
❏ 124	Neifi Perez	.25	.11

125	Todd Hundley	.25	.11
126	Jeff Abbott	.15	.07
127	Todd Zeile	.25	.11
128	Travis Fryman	.25	.11
129	Sandy Alomar Jr.	.25	.11
130	Fred McGriff	.40	.18
131	Richard Hidalgo	.25	.11
132	Scott Spiezio	.15	.07
133	John Valentin	.25	.11
134	Quilvio Veras	.15	.07
135	Mike Lansing	.15	.07
136	Paul Molitor	.60	.25
137	Randy Johnson	.60	.25
138	Harold Baines	.25	.11
139	Doug Jones	.15	.07
140	Abraham Nunez	.15	.07
141	Alan Benes	.15	.07
142	Matt Perisho	.15	.07
143	Chris Clemons	.15	.07
144	Andy Pettitte	.25	.11
145	Jason Giambi	.25	.11
146	Moises Alou	.25	.11
147	Chad Fox	.15	.07
148	Felix Martinez	.15	.07
149	Carlos Mendoza	.25	.11
150	Scott Rolen	.75	.35
151	Jose Cabrera	.15	.07
152	Justin Thompson	.15	.07
153	Ellis Burks	.25	.11
154	Pokey Reese	.15	.07
155	Bartolo Colon	.25	.11
156	Ray Durham	.25	.11
157	Ugueth Urbina	.15	.07
158	Tom Goodwin	.15	.07
159	Dave Dellucci	.50	.23
160	Rod Beck	.25	.11
161	Ramon Martinez	.25	.11
162	Joe Carter	.25	.11
163	Kevin Orie	.15	.07
164	Trevor Hoffman	.25	.11
165	Emil Brown	.15	.07
166	Robb Nen	.15	.07
167	Paul O'Neill	.25	.11
168	Ryan Long	.15	.07
169	Ray Lankford	.25	.11
170	Ivan Rodriguez	.75	.35
171	Rick Aguilera	.15	.07
172	Delvi Cruz	.15	.07
173	Ricky Bottalico	.15	.07
174	Garret Anderson	.25	.11
175	Jose Vizcaino	.15	.07
176	Omar Vizquel	.25	.11
177	Jeff Blauser	.15	.07
178	Orlando Cabrera	.15	.07
179	Russ Johnson	.15	.07
180	Matt Stairs	.25	.11
181	Will Cunnane	.15	.07
182	Adam Riggs	.15	.07
183	Matt Morris	.15	.07
184	Mario Valdez	.15	.07
185	Larry Sutton	.15	.07
186	Marc Pisciotta	.15	.07
187	Dan Wilson	.25	.11
188	John Franco	.25	.11
189	Darren Daulton	.25	.11
190	Todd Helton	.75	.35
191	Brady Anderson	.25	.11
192	Ricardo Rincon	.15	.07
193	Kevin Stocker	.15	.07
194	Jose Valentin	.15	.07
195	Ed Sprague	.15	.07
196	Ryan McGuire	.15	.07
197	Scott Eyre	.15	.07
198	Steve Finley	.25	.11
199	T.J. Mathews	.15	.07
200	Mike Piazza	2.00	.90
201	Mark Wohlers	.25	.11
202	Brian Giles	.25	.11
203	Eduardo Perez	.15	.07
204	Shigetoshi Hasegawa	.25	.11
205	Mariano Rivera	.25	.11
206	Jose Rosado	.15	.07
207	Michael Coleman	.25	.11
208	James Baldwin	.15	.07
209	Russ Davis	.15	.07
210	Billy Wagner	.25	.11
211	Sammy Sosa	2.00	.90
212	Frank Catalanotto	.25	.11
213	Delino DeShields	.25	.07
214	John Olerud	.25	.11
215	Heath Murray	.15	.07
216	Jose Vidro	.15	.07
217	Jim Edmonds	.25	.11
218	Shawon Dunston	.15	.07
219	Homer Bush	.15	.07
220	Midre Cummings	.15	.07
221	Tony Saunders	.15	.07
222	Jeromy Burnitz	.25	.11
223	Enrique Wilson	.15	.07
224	Chili Davis	.25	.11
225	Jerry DiPoto	.15	.07
226	Dante Powell	.15	.07
227	Javier Lopez	.25	.11
228	Kevin Polcovich	.15	.07
229	Deion Sanders	.25	.11
230	Jimmy Key	.25	.11
231	Rusty Greer	.25	.11
232	Reggie Jefferson	.15	.07
233	Ron Coomer	.15	.07
234	Bobby Higginson	.25	.11
235	Magglio Ordonez	2.00	.90
236	Miguel Tejada	.25	.11
237	Rick Gorecki	.15	.07
238	Carlos Johnson	.25	.11
239	Lance Johnson	.15	.07
240	Derek Bell	.25	.11
241	Will Clark	.60	.25
242	Brady Raggio	.15	.07
243	Orel Hershiser	.25	.11
244	Vladimir Guerrero	.75	.35
245	John LeRoy	.15	.07
246	Shawn Estes	.15	.07
247	Brett Tomko	.15	.07
248	Dave Nilsson	.15	.07
249	Edgar Martinez	.25	.11
250	Tony Gwynn	1.50	.70
251	Mark Bellhorn	.15	.07
252	Jed Hansen	.15	.07
253	Butch Huskey	.15	.07
254	Eric Young	.15	.07
255	Vinny Castilla	.25	.11
256	Hideki Irabu	.25	.11
257	Mike Cameron	.25	.11
258	Juan Encarnacion	.25	.11
259	Brian Rose	.15	.07
260	Brad Ausmus	.15	.07
261	Dan Serafini	.15	.07
262	Willie Greene	.15	.07
263	Troy Percival	.25	.11
264	Jeff Wallace	.25	.11
265	Richie Sexson	.40	.18
266	Rafael Palmeiro	.60	.25
267	Brad Fullmer	.25	.11
268	Jeremi Gonzalez	.15	.07
269	Rob Stanifer	.15	.07
270	Mickey Morandini	.15	.07
271	Andruw Jones	.60	.25
272	Royce Clayton	.15	.07
273	Takashi Kashiwada	.40	.18
274	Steve Woodard	.15	.07
275	Jose Cruz Jr.	.25	.11
276	Keith Foulke	.25	.11
277	Brad Rigby	.15	.07
278	Tino Martinez	.25	.11
279	Todd Jones	.15	.07
280	John Wetteland	.25	.11
281	Alex Gonzalez	.15	.07
282	Ken Cloude	.15	.07
283	Jose Guillen	.25	.11
284	Danny Clyburn	.15	.07
285	David Ortiz	.15	.07
286	John Thomson	.15	.07
287	Kevin Appier	.25	.11
288	Ismael Valdes	.15	.07
289	Gary DiSarcina	.15	.07
290	Todd Dunwoody	.15	.07
291	Wally Joyner	.25	.11
292	Charles Nagy	.25	.11
293	Jeff Shaw	.15	.07
294	Kevin Millwood	2.00	.90
295	Rigo Beltran	.15	.07
296	Jeff Frye	.15	.07
297	Oscar Henriquez	.15	.07
298	Mike Thurman	.15	.07
299	Garrett Stephenson	.15	.07
300	Barry Bonds	.75	.35
301	Roger Clemens SH	.75	.35
302	David Cone SH	.25	.11
303	Hideki Irabu SH	.15	.07
304	Randy Johnson SH	.25	.11
305	Greg Maddux SH	.75	.35
306	Pedro Martinez SH	.40	.18
307	Mike Mussina SH	.25	.11
308	Andy Pettitte SH	.15	.07
309	Curt Schilling SH	.25	.11
310	John Smoltz SH	.25	.11
311	Roger Clemens GM	2.50	1.10
312	Jose Cruz JR. GM	.40	.18
313	Nomar Garciaparra GM	3.00	1.35
314	Ken Griffey Jr. GM	5.00	2.20
315	Tony Gwynn GM	2.50	1.10
316	Hideki Irabu GM	.40	.18
317	Randy Johnson GM	1.00	.45
318	Mark McGwire GM	6.00	2.70
319	Curt Schilling GM	.60	.25
320	Larry Walker GM	1.00	.45
321	Jeff Bagwell TT	1.50	.70
322	Albert Belle TT	1.25	.55
323	Barry Bonds TT	1.50	.70
324	Jay Buhner TT	.50	.23
325	Tony Clark TT	.50	.23
326	Jose Cruz Jr. TT	.50	.23
327	Andres Galarraga TT	.75	.35
328	Juan Gonzalez TT	2.50	1.10
329	Ken Griffey Jr. TT	6.00	2.70
330	Andruw Jones TT	1.25	.55
331	Tino Martinez TT	.50	.23
332	Mark McGwire TT	8.00	3.60
333	Rafael Palmeiro TT	1.25	.55
334	Mike Piazza TT	4.00	1.80
335	Manny Ramirez TT	1.50	.70
336	Alex Rodriguez TT	4.00	1.80
337	Frank Thomas TT	2.50	1.10
338	Jim Thome TT	1.25	.55
339	Mo Vaughn TT	1.25	.55
340	Larry Walker TT	1.25	.55
341	Jose Cruz Jr. CL	.15	.07
342	Ken Griffey Jr. CL	1.50	.70
343	Derek Jeter CL	1.00	.45
344	Andruw Jones CL	.25	.11
345	Chipper Jones CL	.75	.35
346	Greg Maddux CL	.75	.35
347	Mike Piazza CL	1.00	.45
348	Cal Ripken CL	1.25	.55
349	Alex Rodriguez CL	1.00	.45
350	Frank Thomas CL	.60	.25
351	Mo Vaughn	.60	.25
352	Andres Galarraga	.40	.18
353	Roberto Alomar	.40	.18
354	Darin Erstad	.40	.18
355	Albert Belle	.60	.25
356	Matt Williams	.60	.25
357	Darryl Kile	.15	.07
358	Kenny Lofton	.40	.18
359	Orel Hershiser	.25	.11
360	Bob Abreu	.25	.11
361	Chris Widger	.15	.07
362	Glenallen Hill	.15	.07
363	Chili Davis	.25	.11
364	Kevin Brown	.40	.18
365	Marquis Grissom	.15	.07
366	Livan Hernandez	.15	.07
367	Moises Alou	.25	.11
368	Matt Lawton	.15	.07
369	Rey Ordonez	.25	.11
370	Kenny Rogers	.15	.07
371	Lee Stevens	.15	.07
372	Wade Boggs	.60	.25
373	Luis Gonzalez	.25	.11
374	Jeff Conine	.15	.07
375	Esteban Loaiza	.15	.07
376	Jose Canseco	.75	.35
377	Henry Rodriguez	.25	.11
378	Dave Burba	.15	.07
379	Todd Hollandsworth	.15	.07
380	Ron Gant	.25	.11
381	Pedro Martinez	.75	.35
382	Ryan Klesko	.25	.11

383	Derek Lee	.15	.07
384	Doug Glanville	.25	.11
385	David Wells	.25	.11
386	Ken Caminiti	.25	.11
387	Damon Hollins	.15	.07
388	Manny Ramirez	.75	.35
389	Mike Mussina	.60	.25
390	Jay Bell	.25	.11
391	Mike Piazza	2.00	.90
392	Mike Lansing	.15	.07
393	Mike Hampton	.25	.11
394	Geoff Jenkins	.25	.11
395	Jimmy Haynes	.15	.07
396	Scott Servais	.15	.07
397	Kent Mercker	.15	.07
398	Jeff Kent	.25	.11
399	Kevin Elster	.15	.07
400	Masato Yoshii	.40	.18
401	Jose Vizcaino	.15	.07
402	Javier Martinez	.40	.18
403	David Segui	.15	.07
404	Tony Saunders	.15	.07
405	Karim Garcia	.15	.07
406	Armando Benitez	.15	.07
407	Joe Randa	.15	.07
408	Vic Darensbourg	.15	.07
409	Sean Casey	1.00	.45
410	Eric Milton	.15	.07
411	Trey Moore	.15	.07
412	Mike Stanley	.15	.07
413	Tom Gordon	.25	.11
414	Hal Morris	.15	.07
415	Braden Looper	.15	.07
416	Mike Kelly	.15	.07
417	John Smoltz	.40	.18
418	Roger Cedeno	.15	.07
419	Al Leiter	.25	.11
420	Chuck Knoblauch	.25	.11
421	Felix Rodriguez	.15	.07
422	Bip Roberts	.15	.07
423	Ken Hill	.15	.07
424	Jermaine Allensworth	.15	.07
425	Esteban Yan	.50	.23
426	Scott Karl	.15	.07
427	Sean Berry	.15	.07
428	Rafael Medina	.15	.07
429	Javier Vazquez	.15	.07
430	Rickey Henderson	.75	.35
431	Adam Butler	.25	.11
432	Todd Stottlemyre	.15	.07
433	Yamil Benitez	.15	.07
434	Sterling Hitchcock	.15	.07
435	Paul Sorrento	.15	.07
436	Bobby Ayala	.15	.07
437	Tim Raines	.25	.11
438	Chris Hoiles	.15	.07
439	Rod Beck	.15	.07
440	Donnie Sadler	.25	.11
441	Charles Johnson	.25	.11
442	Russ Ortiz	.25	.11
443	Pedro Astacio	.15	.07
444	Wilson Alvarez	.15	.07
445	Mike Blowers	.15	.07
446	Todd Zeile	.15	.11
447	Mel Rojas	.15	.07
448	F.P. Santangelo	.15	.07
449	Dmitri Young	.25	.11
450	Brian Anderson	.15	.07
451	Cecil Fielder	.25	.11
452	Roberto Hernandez	.15	.07
453	Todd Walker	.25	.11
454	Tyler Green	.15	.07
455	Jorge Posada	.25	.11
456	Geronimo Berroa	.15	.07
457	Jose Silva	.15	.07
458	Bobby Bonilla	.25	.11
459	Walt Weiss	.15	.11
460	Darren Dreifort	.15	.07
461	B.J. Surhoff	.15	.07
462	Quinton McCracken	.15	.07
463	Derek Lowe	.15	.07
464	Jorge Fabregas	.15	.07
465	Joey Hamilton	.25	.07
466	Brian Jordan	.25	.11
467	Allen Watson	.15	.07
468	John Jaha	.25	.11

469	Heathcliff Slocumb	.15	.07
470	Gregg Jefferies	.15	.07
471	Scott Brosius	.25	.11
472	Chad Ogea	.15	.07
473	A.J. Hinch	.15	.07
474	Bobby Smith	.15	.07
475	Brian Moehler	.15	.07
476	DaRond Stovall	.15	.07
477	Kevin Young	.25	.11
478	Jeff Suppan	.15	.07
479	Marty Cordova	.15	.07
480	John Halama	.60	.25
481	Bubba Trammell	.25	.11
482	Mike Caruso	.15	.07
483	Eric Karros	.25	.11
484	Jamey Wright	.15	.07
485	Mike Sweeney	.15	.07
486	Aaron Sele	.25	.11
487	Cliff Floyd	.25	.11
488	Jeff Brantley	.15	.07
489	Jim Leyritz	.15	.07
490	Denny Neagle	.15	.07
491	Travis Fryman	.25	.11
492	Carlos Baerga	.15	.07
493	Eddie Taubensee	.15	.07
494	Darryl Strawberry	.25	.11
495	Brian Johnson	.15	.07
496	Randy Myers	.25	.11
497	Jeff Blauser	.15	.07
498	Jason Wood	.15	.07
499	Rolando Arrojo	.60	.25
500	Johnny Damon	.25	.11
501	Jose Mercedes	.15	.07
502	Tony Batista	.15	.07
503	Mike Piazza Mets	2.00	.90
504	Hideo Nomo	.60	.25
505	Chris Gomez	.15	.07
506	Jesus Sanchez	.40	.18
507	Al Martin	.15	.07
508	Brian Edmondson	.15	.07
509	Joe Girardi	.15	.07
510	Shayne Bennett	.15	.07
511	Joe Carter	.25	.11
512	Dave Mlicki	.15	.07
513	Rich Butler	.40	.18
514	Dennis Eckersley	.25	.11
515	Travis Lee	.40	.18
516	John Mabry	.15	.07
517	Jose Mesa	.15	.07
518	Phil Nevin	.15	.07
519	Raul Casanova	.15	.07
520	Mike Fetters	.15	.07
521	Gary Sheffield	.25	.11
522	Terry Steinbach	.15	.07
523	Steve Trachsel	.15	.07
524	Josh Booty	.15	.07
525	Darryl Hamilton	.15	.07
526	Mark McLemore	.15	.07
527	Kevin Stocker	.15	.07
528	Bret Boone	.25	.11
529	Shane Andrews	.15	.07
530	Robb Nen	.15	.07
531	Carl Everett	.25	.11
532	LaTroy Hawkins	.15	.07
533	Fernando Tatis	.15	.07
534	Michael Tucker	.15	.07
535	Mark Langston	.15	.07
536	Mickey Mantle	5.00	2.20
537	Bernard Gilkey	.15	.07
538	Francisco Cordova	.15	.07
539	Mike Bordick	.15	.07
540	Fred McGriff	.40	.18
541	Cliff Politte	.15	.07
542	Jason Varitek	.25	.11
543	Shawon Dunston	.15	.07
544	Brian Meadows	.15	.07
545	Pat Meares	.15	.07
546	Carlos Perez	.15	.07
547	Desi Relaford	.15	.07
548	Antonio Osuna	.15	.07
549	Devon White	.15	.07
550	Sean Runyan	.15	.07
551	Mickey Morandini	.15	.07
552	Dave Martinez	.15	.07
553	Jeff Jackson	.25	.11
554	Ryan Jackson	.25	.11

555	Stan Javier	.15	.07
556	Jaime Navarro	.15	.07
557	Jose Offerman	.25	.11
558	Mike Lowell	.60	.25
559	Darrin Fletcher	.15	.07
560	Mark Lewis	.15	.07
561	Dante Bichette	.25	.11
562	Chuck Finley	.25	.11
563	Kerry Wood	.75	.35
564	Andy Benes	.15	.07
565	Freddy Garcia	.15	.07
566	Tom Glavine	.60	.25
567	Jon Nunnally	.15	.07
568	Miguel Cairo	.15	.07
569	Shane Reynolds	.25	.11
570	Roberto Kelly	.15	.07
571	Jose Cruz Jr. CL	.15	.07
572	Ken Griffey Jr. CL	1.50	.70
573	Mark McGwire UM	2.00	.90
574	Cal Ripken UM	1.25	.55
575	Frank Thomas CL	.60	.25
576	Jeff Bagwell UM	2.00	.90
577	Barry Bonds UM	2.00	.90
578	Tony Clark UM	.60	.25
579	Roger Clemens UM	4.00	1.80
580	Jose Cruz Jr. UM	.60	.25
581	Nomar Garciaparra UM	5.00	2.20
582	Juan Gonzalez UM	3.00	1.35
583	Ben Grieve UM	1.50	.70
584	Ken Griffey Jr. UM	8.00	3.60
585	Tony Gwynn UM	4.00	1.80
586	Derek Jeter UM	5.00	2.20
587	Randy Johnson UM	1.50	.70
588	Chipper Jones UM	4.00	1.80
589	Greg Maddux UM	4.00	1.80
590	Mark McGwire UM	10.00	4.50
591	Paul Molitor UM	1.50	.70
592	Andy Pettitte UM	.60	.25
593	Cal Ripken UM	6.00	2.70
594	Alex Rodriguez UM	5.00	2.20
595	Scott Rolen UM	2.00	.90
596	Curt Schilling UM	1.00	.45
597	Frank Thomas UM	3.00	1.35
598	Jim Thome UM	1.50	.70
599	Larry Walker UM	1.50	.70
600	Bernie Williams UM	1.50	.70
P100	Alex Rodriguez Promo	3.00	1.35

1998 Fleer Vintage '63

CHIPPER JONES
Atlanta Braves - 3B

	MINT	NRMT
COMPLETE SET (128)	50.00	22.00
COMPLETE SERIES 1 (64)	25.00	11.00
COMPLETE SERIES 2 (64)	25.00	11.00
COMMON CARD (1-126/CL'S)	.20	.09
MINOR STARS	.30	.14
SEMISTARS	.50	.23
UNLISTED STARS	.75	.35
STATED ODDS 1:1 HOBBY		

1	Jason Dickson	.20	.09
2	Tim Salmon	.50	.23
3	Andruw Jones	.75	.35
4	Chipper Jones	2.00	.90
5	Kenny Lofton	.50	.23
6	Greg Maddux	2.00	.90
7	Rafael Palmeiro	.75	.35
8	Cal Ripken	3.00	1.35

❑ 9 Nomar Garciaparra	2.50	1.10
❑ 10 Mark Grace	.50	.23
❑ 11 Sammy Sosa	2.50	1.10
❑ 12 Frank Thomas	1.50	.70
❑ 13 Deion Sanders	.30	.14
❑ 14 Sandy Alomar Jr.	.30	.14
❑ 15 David Justice	.30	.14
❑ 16 Jim Thome	.75	.35
❑ 17 Matt Williams	.75	.35
❑ 18 Jaret Wright	.30	.14
❑ 19 Vinny Castilla	.30	.14
❑ 20 Andres Galarraga	.50	.23
❑ 21 Todd Helton	1.00	.45
❑ 22 Larry Walker	.75	.35
❑ 23 Tony Clark	.30	.14
❑ 24 Moises Alou	.30	.14
❑ 25 Kevin Brown	.50	.23
❑ 26 Charles Johnson	.30	.14
❑ 27 Edgar Renteria	.20	.09
❑ 28 Gary Sheffield	.30	.14
❑ 29 Jeff Bagwell	1.00	.45
❑ 30 Craig Biggio	.75	.35
❑ 31 Raul Mondesi	.30	.14
❑ 32 Mike Piazza	2.50	1.10
❑ 33 Chuck Knoblauch	.30	.14
❑ 34 Paul Molitor	.75	.35
❑ 35 Vladimir Guerrero	1.00	.45
❑ 36 Pedro Martinez	1.00	.45
❑ 37 Todd Hundley	.30	.14
❑ 38 Derek Jeter	2.50	1.10
❑ 39 Tino Martinez	.30	.14
❑ 40 Paul O'Neill	.30	.14
❑ 41 Andy Pettitte	.30	.14
❑ 42 Mariano Rivera	.30	.14
❑ 43 Bernie Williams	.75	.35
❑ 44 Ben Grieve	.75	.35
❑ 45 Scott Rolen	1.00	.45
❑ 46 Curt Schilling	.50	.23
❑ 47 Jason Kendall	.30	.14
❑ 48 Tony Womack	.20	.09
❑ 49 Ray Lankford	.30	.14
❑ 50 Mark McGwire	5.00	2.20
❑ 51 Matt Morris	.20	.09
❑ 52 Tony Gwynn	2.00	.90
❑ 53 Barry Bonds	1.00	.45
❑ 54 Jay Buhner	.30	.14
❑ 55 Ken Griffey Jr.	4.00	1.80
❑ 56 Randy Johnson	.75	.35
❑ 57 Edgar Martinez	.30	.14
❑ 58 Alex Rodriguez	2.50	1.10
❑ 59 Juan Gonzalez	1.50	.70
❑ 60 Rusty Greer	.30	.14
❑ 61 Ivan Rodriguez	1.00	.45
❑ 62 Roger Clemens	2.00	.90
❑ 63 Jose Cruz Jr.	.30	.14
❑ 64 Darin Erstad	.50	.23
❑ 65 Jay Bell	.30	.14
❑ 66 Andy Benes	.20	.09
❑ 67 Mickey Mantle	5.00	2.20
❑ 68 Karim Garcia	.20	.09
❑ 69 Travis Lee	.50	.23
❑ 70 Matt Williams	.75	.35
❑ 71 Andres Galarraga	.50	.23
❑ 72 Tom Glavine	.75	.35
❑ 73 Ryan Klesko	.30	.14
❑ 74 Denny Neagle	.20	.09
❑ 75 John Smoltz	.50	.23
❑ 76 Roberto Alomar	.75	.35
❑ 77 Joe Carter	.30	.14
❑ 78 Mike Mussina	.75	.35
❑ 79 B.J. Surhoff	.30	.14
❑ 80 Dennis Eckersley	.30	.14
❑ 81 Pedro Martinez	1.00	.45
❑ 82 Mo Vaughn	.75	.35
❑ 83 Henry Rodriguez	.30	.14
❑ 84 Kerry Wood	1.00	.45
❑ 85 Albert Belle	.75	.35
❑ 86 Sean Casey	1.25	.55
❑ 87 Travis Fryman	.50	.14
❑ 88 Kenny Lofton	.50	.23
❑ 89 Darryl Kile	.20	.09
❑ 90 Mike Lansing	.20	.09
❑ 91 Bobby Bonilla	.30	.14
❑ 92 Cliff Floyd	.30	.14
❑ 93 Livan Hernandez	.30	.14
❑ 94 Derrek Lee	.20	.09

❑ 95 Moises Alou	.30	.14
❑ 96 Shane Reynolds	.30	.14
❑ 97 Mike Piazza	2.50	1.10
❑ 98 Johnny Damon	.30	.14
❑ 99 Eric Karros	.30	.14
❑ 100 Hideo Nomo	.75	.35
❑ 101 Marquis Grissom	.20	.09
❑ 102 Matt Lawton	.20	.09
❑ 103 Todd Walker	.30	.14
❑ 104 Gary Sheffield	.30	.14
❑ 105 Bernard Gilkey	.20	.09
❑ 106 Rey Ordonez	.30	.14
❑ 107 Chili Davis	.30	.14
❑ 108 Chuck Knoblauch	.30	.14
❑ 109 Charles Johnson	.30	.14
❑ 110 Rickey Henderson	1.00	.45
❑ 111 Bob Abreu	.30	.14
❑ 112 Doug Glanville	.30	.14
❑ 113 Gregg Jefferies	.20	.09
❑ 114 Al Martin	.20	.09
❑ 115 Kevin Young	.30	.14
❑ 116 Ron Gant	.30	.14
❑ 117 Kevin Brown	.50	.23
❑ 118 Ken Caminiti	.30	.14
❑ 119 Joey Hamilton	.20	.09
❑ 120 Jeff Kent	.30	.14
❑ 121 Wade Boggs	.75	.35
❑ 122 Quinton McCracken	.20	.09
❑ 123 Fred McGriff	.50	.23
❑ 124 Paul Sorrento	.20	.09
❑ 125 Jose Canseco	1.00	.45
❑ 126 Randy Myers	.30	.14
❑ NNO Checklist 1	.20	.09
❑ NNO Checklist 2	.20	.09

1998 Fleer Vintage '63 Classic

CAL RIPKEN JR.
Baltimore Orioles – 38

	MINT	NRMT
COMMON CARD (1-126/CL'S)	15.00	6.75
*STARS: 30X TO 80X BASIC '63 VIN		
*YOUNG STARS: 25X TO 60X BASIC '63 VIN		
RANDOM INSERTS IN HOBBY PACKS		
STATED PRINT RUN 63 SERIAL #'d SETS		

1998 Fleer Decade of Excellence

Randy Johnson

	MINT	NRMT
COMPLETE SET (12)	120.00	55.00

COMMON CARD (1-12)	4.00	1.80
SEMISTARS	5.00	2.20
UNLISTED STARS	8.00	3.60
STATED ODDS 1:72 HOBBY		
*RARE TRADITIONS: 2X TO 5X HI COLUMN		
RARE TRAD. STATED ODDS 1:720 HOBBY		

❑ 1 Roberto Alomar	8.00	3.60
❑ 2 Barry Bonds	10.00	4.50
❑ 3 Roger Clemens	20.00	9.00
❑ 4 David Cone	5.00	2.20
❑ 5 Andres Galarraga	5.00	2.20
❑ 6 Mark Grace	5.00	2.20
❑ 7 Tony Gwynn	20.00	9.00
❑ 8 Randy Johnson	8.00	3.60
❑ 9 Greg Maddux	20.00	9.00
❑ 10 Mark McGwire	50.00	22.00
❑ 11 Paul O'Neill	4.00	1.80
❑ 12 Cal Ripken	30.00	13.50

1998 Fleer Diamond Ink

	MINT	NRMT
ONE PER FLEER 1 AND ULTRA 1 PACK		
EXCHANGE 500 PTS. FOR SIGNED BALL		
EXCHANGE DEADLINE: 12/31/98		

1998 Fleer Diamond Standouts

Jeff Bagwell

	MINT	NRMT
COMPLETE SET (20)	50.00	22.00
COMMON CARD (1-20)	.75	.35
STATED ODDS 1:12		

❑ 1 Jeff Bagwell	2.00	.90
❑ 2 Barry Bonds	2.00	.90
❑ 3 Roger Clemens	4.00	1.80
❑ 4 Jose Cruz Jr.	.75	.35
❑ 5 Andres Galarraga	1.00	.45
❑ 6 Nomar Garciaparra	5.00	2.20
❑ 7 Juan Gonzalez	3.00	1.35
❑ 8 Ken Griffey Jr.	8.00	3.60
❑ 9 Derek Jeter	5.00	2.20
❑ 10 Randy Johnson	1.50	.70
❑ 11 Chipper Jones	4.00	1.80
❑ 12 Kenny Lofton	1.00	.45
❑ 13 Greg Maddux	4.00	1.80
❑ 14 Pedro Martinez	2.00	.90
❑ 15 Mark McGwire	10.00	4.50

		MINT	NRMT
❑ 16	Mike Piazza	5.00	2.20
❑ 17	Alex Rodriguez	5.00	2.20
❑ 18	Curt Schilling	1.00	.45
❑ 19	Frank Thomas	3.00	1.35
❑ 20	Larry Walker	1.50	.70

1998 Fleer Diamond Tribute

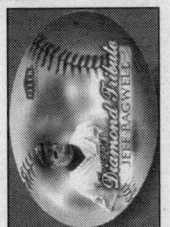

	MINT	NRMT
COMPLETE SET (10)	500.00	220.00
COMMON CARD (DT1-DT10)	20.00	9.00
SER.2 STATED ODDS 1:300		

		MINT	NRMT
❑ DT1	Jeff Bagwell	20.00	9.00
❑ DT2	Roger Clemens	40.00	18.00
❑ DT3	Nomar Garciaparra	50.00	22.00
❑ DT4	Juan Gonzalez	30.00	13.50
❑ DT5	Ken Griffey Jr.	80.00	36.00
❑ DT6	Mark McGwire	100.00	45.00
❑ DT7	Mike Piazza	50.00	22.00
❑ DT8	Cal Ripken	60.00	27.00
❑ DT9	Alex Rodriguez	50.00	22.00
❑ DT10	Frank Thomas	30.00	13.50

1998 Fleer In The Clutch

	MINT	NRMT
COMPLETE SET (15)	100.00	45.00
COMMON CARD (IC1-IC15)	1.25	.55
SER.2 STATED ODDS 1:20		

		MINT	NRMT
❑ IC1	Jeff Bagwell	4.00	1.80
❑ IC2	Barry Bonds	4.00	1.80
❑ IC3	Roger Clemens	8.00	3.60
❑ IC4	Jose Cruz Jr.	1.25	.55
❑ IC5	Nomar Garciaparra	10.00	4.50
❑ IC6	Juan Gonzalez	6.00	2.70
❑ IC7	Ken Griffey Jr.	15.00	6.75
❑ IC8	Tony Gwynn	8.00	3.60
❑ IC9	Derek Jeter	10.00	4.50
❑ IC10	Chipper Jones	8.00	3.60
❑ IC11	Greg Maddux	8.00	3.60
❑ IC12	Mark McGwire	20.00	9.00
❑ IC13	Mike Piazza	10.00	4.50
❑ IC14	Frank Thomas	6.00	2.70
❑ IC15	Larry Walker	3.00	1.35

1998 Fleer Lumber Company

	MINT	NRMT
COMPLETE SET (15)	150.00	70.00
COMMON CARD (1-15)	2.00	.90
STATED ODDS 1:36 RETAIL		

		MINT	NRMT
❑ 1	Jeff Bagwell	6.00	2.70
❑ 2	Barry Bonds	6.00	2.70
❑ 3	Jose Cruz Jr.	2.00	.90
❑ 4	Nomar Garciaparra	15.00	6.75
❑ 5	Juan Gonzalez	10.00	4.50
❑ 6	Ken Griffey Jr.	25.00	11.00
❑ 7	Tony Gwynn	12.00	5.50
❑ 8	Chipper Jones	12.00	5.50
❑ 9	Tino Martinez	2.00	.90
❑ 10	Mark McGwire	30.00	13.50
❑ 11	Mike Piazza	15.00	6.75
❑ 12	Cal Ripken	20.00	9.00
❑ 13	Alex Rodriguez	15.00	6.75
❑ 14	Frank Thomas	10.00	4.50
❑ 15	Larry Walker	5.00	2.20

1998 Fleer Mickey Mantle Monumental Moments

	MINT	NRMT
COMPLETE SET (10)	225.00	100.00
COMMON CARD (1-10)	25.00	11.00
SER.2 STATED ODDS 1:68		
COMMON GOLD (1-10)	250.00	110.00
GOLD: RANDOM INSERTS IN SER.2 PACKS		
GOLD PRINT RUN 51 SERIAL #'d SETS		

		MINT	NRMT
❑ 1	Mickey Mantle	25.00	11.00
	Armed and Dangerous		
❑ 2	Mickey Mantle	25.00	11.00
	Getting Ready in Spring Training		
❑ 3	Mickey Mantle	25.00	11.00
	Phil Rizzuto		
	Mantle and Rizzuto Celebrate		
❑ 4	Mickey Mantle	25.00	11.00
	Posed for Action		
❑ 5	Mickey Mantle	25.00	11.00
	Signed, Sealed and Ready to Deliver		
❑ 6	Mickey Mantle	25.00	11.00
	Triple Crown 1956 Season		
❑ 7	Mickey Mantle	25.00	11.00
	Number 7 on Yankee Pinstripes		
	Never to be Worn Again		
❑ 8	Mickey Mantle	25.00	11.00
	Mantle's Powerful Swing Produces		
	Another Homer		
❑ 9	Mickey Mantle	25.00	11.00
	Old-Timer's Day Introduction		
❑ 10	Mickey Mantle	25.00	11.00
	Portrait of Determination		

1998 Fleer Power Game

	MINT	NRMT
COMPLETE SET (20)	120.00	55.00
COMMON CARD (1-20)	2.00	.90
STATED ODDS 1:36		

		MINT	NRMT
❑ 1	Jeff Bagwell	5.00	2.20
❑ 2	Albert Belle	5.00	2.20
❑ 3	Barry Bonds	5.00	2.20
❑ 4	Tony Clark	2.00	.90
❑ 5	Roger Clemens	12.00	5.50
❑ 6	Jose Cruz Jr.	2.00	.90
❑ 7	Andres Galarraga	3.00	1.35
❑ 8	Nomar Garciaparra	15.00	6.75
❑ 9	Juan Gonzalez	10.00	4.50
❑ 10	Ken Griffey Jr.	25.00	11.00
❑ 11	Randy Johnson	5.00	2.20
❑ 12	Greg Maddux	12.00	5.50
❑ 13	Pedro Martinez	5.00	2.20
❑ 14	Tino Martinez	2.00	.90
❑ 15	Mark McGwire	30.00	13.50
❑ 16	Mike Piazza	15.00	6.75
❑ 17	Curt Schilling	3.00	1.35
❑ 18	Frank Thomas	10.00	4.50
❑ 19	Jim Thome	5.00	2.20
❑ 20	Larry Walker	5.00	2.20

1998 Fleer Promising Forecast

	MINT	NRMT
COMPLETE SET (20)	15.00	6.75
COMMON CARD (PF1-PF20)	.50	.23
SEMISTARS	.75	.35
UNLISTED STARS	1.25	.55
SER.2 STATED ODDS 1:12		

		MINT	NRMT
❑ PF1	Rolando Arrojo	1.25	.55

☐ PF2 Sean Casey	2.00	.90
☐ PF3 Brad Fullmer	.50	.23
☐ PF4 Karim Garcia	.50	.23
☐ PF5 Ben Grieve	1.25	.55
☐ PF6 Todd Helton	1.50	.70
☐ PF7 Richard Hidalgo	.50	.23
☐ PF8 A.J. Hinch	.50	.23
☐ PF9 Paul Konerko	.50	.23
☐ PF10 Mark Kotsay	.50	.23
☐ PF11 Derrek Lee	.50	.23
☐ PF12 Travis Lee	.75	.35
☐ PF13 Eric Milton	.50	.23
☐ PF14 Magglio Ordonez	4.00	1.80
☐ PF15 David Ortiz	.50	.23
☐ PF16 Brian Rose	.50	.23
☐ PF17 Miguel Tejada	.50	.23
☐ PF18 Jason Varitek	.50	.23
☐ PF19 Enrique Wilson	.50	.23
☐ PF20 Kerry Wood	1.50	.70

1998 Fleer Rookie Sensations

	MINT	NRMT
COMPLETE SET (20)	40.00	18.00
COMMON CARD (1-20)	.75	.35
STATED ODDS 1:18		
☐ 1 Mike Cameron	1.25	.55
☐ 2 Jose Cruz Jr.	1.25	.55
☐ 3 Jason Dickson	.75	.35
☐ 4 Kelvim Escobar	1.25	.55
☐ 5 Nomar Garciaparra	10.00	4.50
☐ 6 Ben Grieve	3.00	1.35
☐ 7 Vladimir Guerrero	4.00	1.80
☐ 8 Wilton Guerrero	.75	.35
☐ 9 Jose Guillen	.75	.35
☐ 10 Todd Helton	3.00	1.35
☐ 11 Livan Hernandez	.75	.35
☐ 12 Hideki Irabu	1.25	.55
☐ 13 Andruw Jones	3.00	1.35
☐ 14 Matt Morris	.75	.35
☐ 15 Magglio Ordonez	3.00	1.35
☐ 16 Neifi Perez	1.25	.55
☐ 17 Scott Rolen	5.00	2.20
☐ 18 Fernando Tatis	3.00	1.35
☐ 19 Brett Tomko	.75	.35
☐ 20 Jaret Wright	1.25	.55

1998 Fleer Zone

	MINT	NRMT
COMPLETE SET (15)	600.00	275.00
COMMON CARD (1-15)	6.00	2.70
UNLISTED STARS	15.00	6.75
STATED ODDS 1:288		
☐ 1 Jeff Bagwell	20.00	9.00
☐ 2 Barry Bonds	20.00	9.00
☐ 3 Roger Clemens	40.00	18.00
☐ 4 Jose Cruz Jr.	6.00	2.70
☐ 5 Nomar Garciaparra	30.00	13.50
☐ 6 Juan Gonzalez	30.00	13.50
☐ 7 Ken Griffey Jr.	80.00	36.00
☐ 8 Tony Gwynn	40.00	18.00
☐ 9 Chipper Jones	40.00	18.00
☐ 10 Greg Maddux	40.00	18.00
☐ 11 Mark McGwire	100.00	45.00
☐ 12 Mike Piazza	50.00	22.00
☐ 13 Alex Rodriguez	50.00	22.00
☐ 14 Frank Thomas	30.00	13.50
☐ 15 Larry Walker	15.00	6.75

1998 Fleer Update

	MINT	NRMT
COMP.FACT.SET (100)	50.00	22.00
COMMON CARD (1-100)	.10	.05
MINOR STARS	.15	.07
SEMISTARS	.25	.11
UNLISTED STARS	.40	.18
DISTRIBUTED ONLY IN FACTORY SET FORM		
☐ U1 Mark McGwire HL	2.50	1.10
☐ U2 Sammy Sosa HL	1.25	.55
☐ U3 Roger Clemens HL	1.00	.45
☐ U4 Barry Bonds HL	.60	.25
☐ U5 Kerry Wood HL	.50	.23
☐ U6 Paul Molitor HL	.15	.07
☐ U7 Ken Griffey Jr. HL	2.00	.90
☐ U8 Cal Ripken HL	1.50	.70
☐ U9 David Wells HL	.15	.07
☐ U10 Alex Rodriguez HL	1.25	.55
☐ U11 Angel Pena	1.50	.70
☐ U12 Bruce Chen	.15	.07
☐ U13 Craig Wilson	.10	.05
☐ U14 Orlando Hernandez	3.00	1.35
☐ U15 Aramis Ramirez	.40	.18
☐ U16 Aaron Boone	.10	.05
☐ U17 Bob Henley	.10	.05
☐ U18 Juan Guzman	.10	.05
☐ U19 Darryl Hamilton	.10	.05
☐ U20 Jay Payton	.10	.05
☐ U21 Jeremy Powell	.10	.05
☐ U22 Ben Davis	.25	.11
☐ U23 Preston Wilson	.15	.07
☐ U24 Jim Parque	.75	.35
☐ U25 Odalis Perez	1.25	.55
☐ U26 Ronnie Belliard	.15	.07
☐ U27 Royce Clayton	.10	.05
☐ U28 George Lombard	.15	.07
☐ U29 Tony Phillips	.10	.05
☐ U30 Fernando Seguignol	1.50	.70
☐ U31 Armando Rios	.75	.35
☐ U32 Jerry Hairston Jr.	1.50	.70
☐ U33 Justin Baughman	.50	.23
☐ U34 Seth Greisinger	.10	.05
☐ U35 Alex Gonzalez	.15	.07
☐ U36 Michael Barrett	.25	.11
☐ U37 Carlos Beltran	.75	.35
☐ U38 Ellis Burks	.15	.07
☐ U39 Jose Jimenez	1.50	.70
☐ U40 Carlos Guillen	.10	.05
☐ U41 Marlon Anderson	.15	.07
☐ U42 Scott Elarton	.10	.05
☐ U43 Glenallen Hill	.10	.05
☐ U44 Shane Monahan	.10	.05
☐ U45 Dennis Martinez	.15	.07
☐ U46 Carlos Febles	2.50	1.10
☐ U47 Carlos Perez	.10	.05
☐ U48 Wilton Guerrero	.10	.05
☐ U49 Randy Johnson	.40	.18
☐ U50 Brian Simmons	.50	.23
☐ U51 Carlton Loewer	.10	.05
☐ U52 Mark DeRosa	.50	.23
☐ U53 Tim Young	.50	.23
☐ U54 Gary Gaetti	.15	.07
☐ U55 Eric Chavez	.40	.18
☐ U56 Carl Pavano	.10	.05
☐ U57 Mike Stanley	.10	.05
☐ U58 Todd Stottlemyre	.10	.05
☐ U59 Gabe Kapler	4.00	1.80
☐ U60 Mike Jerzembeck	.60	.25
☐ U61 Mitch Meluskey	.75	.35
☐ U62 Bill Pulsipher	.10	.05
☐ U63 Derrick Gibson	.15	.07
☐ U64 John Rocker	3.00	1.35
☐ U65 Calvin Pickering	.15	.07
☐ U66 Blake Stein	.10	.05
☐ U67 Fernando Tatis	.40	.18
☐ U68 Gabe Alvarez	.10	.05
☐ U69 Jeffrey Hammonds	.10	.05
☐ U70 Adrian Beltre	.40	.18
☐ U71 Ryan Bradley	1.50	.70
☐ U72 Edgard Clemente	.10	.05
☐ U73 Rick Croushore	.10	.05
☐ U74 Matt Clement	.15	.07
☐ U75 Dermal Brown	.15	.07
☐ U76 Paul Bako	.10	.05
☐ U77 Placido Polanco	.50	.23
☐ U78 Jay Tessmer	.10	.05
☐ U79 Jarrod Washburn	.10	.05
☐ U80 Kevin Witt	.10	.05
☐ U81 Mike Metcalfe	.10	.05
☐ U82 Daryle Ward	.15	.07
☐ U83 Benj Sampson	.75	.35
☐ U84 Mike Kinkade	.75	.35
☐ U85 Randy Winn	.10	.05
☐ U86 Jeff Shaw	.10	.05
☐ U87 Troy Glaus	5.00	2.20
☐ U88 Hideo Nomo	.40	.18
☐ U89 Mark Grudzielanek	.10	.05
☐ U90 Mike Frank	1.00	.45
☐ U91 Bobby Howry	.75	.35
☐ U92 Ryan Minor	1.50	.70
☐ U93 Corey Koskie	1.25	.55
☐ U94 Matt Anderson	1.25	.55
☐ U95 Joe Carter	.15	.07
☐ U96 Paul Konerko	.15	.07
☐ U97 Sidney Ponson	.15	.07
☐ U98 Jeremy Giambi	1.50	.70
☐ U99 Jeff Kubenka	.50	.23
☐ U100 J.D. Drew	25.00	11.00

1999 Fleer

	MINT	NRMT
COMPLETE SET (600)	75.00	34.00
COMMON CARD (1-600)	.15	.07
MINOR STARS	.25	.11
SEMISTARS	.40	.18
UNLISTED STARS	.50	.25

#	Player	MINT	NRMT
1	Mark McGwire	4.00	1.80
2	Sammy Sosa	2.00	.90
3	Ken Griffey Jr.	3.00	1.35
4	Kerry Wood	.50	.25
5	Derek Jeter	2.00	.90
6	Stan Musial	2.00	.90
7	J.D. Drew	1.00	.45
8	Cal Ripken	2.50	1.10
9	Alex Rodriguez	2.00	.90
10	Travis Lee	.40	.18
11	Andres Galarraga	.40	.18
12	Nomar Garciaparra	2.00	.90
13	Albert Belle	.60	.25
14	Barry Larkin	.25	.11
15	Dante Bichette	.25	.11
16	Tony Clark	.25	.11
17	Moises Alou	.25	.11
18	Rafael Palmeiro	.50	.25
19	Raul Mondesi	.25	.11
20	Vladimir Guerrero	.75	.35
21	John Olerud	.25	.11
22	Bernie Williams	.60	.25
23	Ben Grieve	.60	.25
24	Scott Rolen	.75	.35
25	Jeromy Burnitz	.25	.11
26	Ken Caminiti	.25	.11
27	Barry Bonds	.75	.35
28	Todd Helton	.60	.25
29	Juan Gonzalez	1.25	.55
30	Roger Clemens	1.50	.70
31	Andruw Jones	.60	.25
32	Mo Vaughn	.60	.25
33	Larry Walker	.60	.25
34	Frank Thomas	1.25	.55
35	Manny Ramirez	.75	.35
36	Randy Johnson	.60	.25
37	Vinny Castilla	.25	.11
38	Juan Encarnacion	.25	.11
39	Jeff Bagwell	.75	.35
40	Gary Sheffield	.25	.11
41	Mike Piazza	2.00	.90
42	Richie Sexson	.40	.18
43	Tony Gwynn	1.50	.70
44	Chipper Jones	1.50	.70
45	Jim Thome	.60	.25
46	Craig Biggio	.60	.25
47	Carlos Delgado	.60	.25
48	Greg Vaughn	.25	.11
49	Greg Maddux	1.50	.70
50	Troy Glaus	.60	.25
51	Roberto Alomar	.60	.25
52	Dennis Eckersley	.25	.11
53	Mike Caruso	.15	.07
54	Bruce Chen	.25	.11
55	Aaron Boone	.15	.07
56	Bartolo Colon	.25	.11
57	Derrick Gibson	.25	.11
58	Brian Anderson	.15	.07
59	Gabe Alvarez	.15	.07
60	Todd Dunwoody	.15	.07
61	Rod Beck	.25	.11
62	Derek Bell	.25	.11
63	Francisco Cordova	.15	.07
64	Johnny Damon	.25	.11
65	Adrian Beltre	.60	.25
66	Garret Anderson	.25	.11
67	Armando Benitez	.15	.07
68	Edgardo Alfonzo	.40	.18
69	Ryan Bradley	.15	.07
70	Eric Chavez	.40	.18
71	Bobby Abreu	.25	.11
72	Andy Ashby	.15	.07
73	Ellis Burks	.25	.11
74	Jeff Cirillo	.25	.11
75	Jay Buhner	.25	.11
76	Ron Gant	.25	.11
77	Rolando Arrojo	.15	.07
78	Will Clark	.60	.25
79	Chris Carpenter	.15	.07
80	Jim Edmonds	.25	.11
81	Tony Batista	.15	.07
82	Shane Andrews	.15	.07
83	Mark DeRosa	.15	.07
84	Brady Anderson	.25	.11
85	Tom Gordon	.25	.11
86	Brant Brown	.15	.07
87	Ray Durham	.25	.11
88	Ron Coomer	.25	.11
89	Bret Boone	.25	.11
90	Travis Fryman	.25	.11
91	Darryl Kile	.15	.07
92	Paul Bako	.15	.07
93	Cliff Floyd	.25	.11
94	Scott Elarton	.15	.07
95	Jeremy Giambi	.25	.11
96	Darren Dreifort	.15	.07
97	Marquis Grissom	.15	.07
98	Marty Cordova	.15	.07
99	Fernando Seguignol	.25	.11
100	Orlando Hernandez	.60	.25
101	Jose Cruz Jr.	.25	.11
102	Jason Giambi	.25	.11
103	Damion Easley	.15	.07
104	Freddy Garcia	.15	.07
105	Marlon Anderson	.15	.07
106	Kevin Brown	.40	.18
107	Joe Carter	.25	.11
108	Russ Davis	.15	.07
109	Brian Jordan	.25	.11
110	Wade Boggs	.60	.25
111	Tom Goodwin	.15	.07
112	Scott Brosius	.25	.11
113	Darin Erstad	.40	.18
114	Jay Bell	.25	.11
115	Tom Glavine	.60	.25
116	Pedro Martinez	.75	.35
117	Mark Grace	.40	.18
118	Russ Ortiz	.15	.07
119	Magglio Ordonez	.60	.25
120	Sean Casey	.60	.25
121	Rafael Roque	.25	.11
122	Brian Giles	.25	.11
123	Mike Lansing	.15	.07
124	David Cone	.40	.18
125	Alex Gonzalez	.25	.11
126	Carl Everett	.25	.11
127	Jeff King	.15	.07
128	Charles Johnson	.25	.11
129	Geoff Jenkins	.25	.11
130	Corey Koskie	.15	.07
131	Brad Fullmer	.15	.07
132	Al Leiter	.25	.11
133	Rickey Henderson	.75	.35
134	Rico Brogna	.15	.07
135	Jose Guillen	.15	.07
136	Matt Clement	.25	.11
137	Carlos Guillen	.15	.07
138	Orel Hershiser	.25	.11
139	Ray Lankford	.25	.11
140	Miguel Cairo	.15	.07
141	Chuck Finley	.25	.11
142	Rusty Greer	.25	.11
143	Kelvim Escobar	.25	.11
144	Ryan Klesko	.25	.11
145	Andy Benes	.15	.07
146	Eric Davis	.25	.11
147	David Wells	.25	.11
148	Trot Nixon	.25	.11
149	Jose Hernandez	.15	.07
150	Mark Johnson	.15	.07
151	Mike Frank	.15	.07
152	Joey Hamilton	.15	.07
153	David Justice	.25	.11
154	Mike Mussina	.60	.25
155	Neifi Perez	.15	.07
156	Luis Gonzalez	.25	.11
157	Livan Hernandez	.25	.11
158	Dermal Brown	.25	.11
159	Jose Lima	.25	.11
160	Eric Karros	.25	.11
161	Ronnie Belliard	.25	.11
162	Matt Lawton	.15	.07
163	Dustin Hermanson	.15	.07
164	Brian McRae	.15	.07
165	Mike Kinkade	.15	.07
166	A.J. Hinch	.15	.07
167	Doug Glanville	.25	.11
168	Hideo Nomo	.60	.25
169	Jason Kendall	.25	.11
170	Steve Finley	.25	.11
171	Jeff Kent	.25	.11
172	Ben Davis	.40	.18
173	Edgar Martinez	.25	.11
174	Eli Marrero	.15	.07
175	Quinton McCracken	.15	.07
176	Rick Helling	.15	.07
177	Tom Evans	.15	.07
178	Carl Pavano	.15	.07
179	Todd Greene	.15	.07
180	Omar Daal	.15	.07
181	George Lombard	.25	.11
182	Ryan Minor	.25	.11
183	Troy O'Leary	.25	.11
184	Robb Nen	.15	.07
185	Manny Morandini	.15	.07
186	Robin Ventura	.25	.11
187	Pete Harnisch	.15	.07
188	Kenny Lofton	.40	.18
189	Eric Milton	.15	.07
190	Bobby Higginson	.25	.11
191	Jamie Moyer	.15	.07
192	Mark Kotsay	.15	.07
193	Shane Reynolds	.25	.11
194	Carlos Febles	.25	.11
195	Jeff Kubenka	.15	.07
196	Chuck Knoblauch	.25	.11
197	Kenny Rogers	.15	.07
198	Bill Mueller	.15	.07
199	Shane Monahan	.15	.07
200	Matt Morris	.15	.07
201	Fred McGriff	.40	.18
202	Ivan Rodriguez	.75	.35
203	Kevin Witt	.15	.07
204	Troy Percival	.25	.11
205	David Dellucci	.15	.07
206	Kevin Millwood	.40	.18
207	Jerry Hairston Jr.	.25	.11
208	Mike Stanley	.15	.07
209	Henry Rodriguez	.25	.11
210	Trevor Hoffman	.25	.11
211	Craig Wilson	.15	.07
212	Reggie Sanders	.25	.11
213	Carlton Loewer	.15	.07
214	Omar Vizquel	.25	.11
215	Gabe Kapler	.60	.25
216	Derrek Lee	.25	.11
217	Billy Wagner	.25	.11
218	Dean Palmer	.25	.11
219	Chan Ho Park	.25	.11
220	Fernando Vina	.15	.07
221	Roy Halladay	.25	.11
222	Paul Molitor	.60	.25
223	Ugueth Urbina	.15	.07
224	Rey Ordonez	.25	.11
225	Ricky Ledee	.25	.11
226	Scott Spiezio	.15	.07
227	Wendell Magee	.15	.07
228	Aramis Ramirez	.40	.18
229	Brian Simmons	.15	.07
230	Fernando Tatis	.60	.25
231	Bobby Smith	.15	.07
232	Aaron Sele	.25	.11
233	Shawn Green	.60	.25
234	Mariano Rivera	.25	.11
235	Tim Salmon	.40	.18
236	Andy Fox	.15	.07
237	Denny Neagle	.15	.07
238	John Valentin	.15	.07
239	Kevin Tapani	.15	.07
240	Paul Konerko	.25	.11
241	Robert Fick	.25	.11
242	Edgar Renteria	.15	.07
243	Brett Tomko	.15	.07
244	Daryle Ward	.25	.11
245	Carlos Beltran	.60	.25
246	Angel Pena	.15	.07
247	Steve Woodard	.15	.07
248	David Ortiz	.15	.07
249	Justin Thompson	.15	.07
250	Rondell White	.25	.11
251	Jaret Wright	.25	.11

252	Ed Sprague	.15	.07
253	Jay Payton	.15	.07
254	Mike Lowell	.15	.07
255	Orlando Cabrera	.15	.07
256	Jason Schmidt	.15	.07
257	David Segui	.15	.07
258	Paul Sorrento	.15	.07
259	John Wetteland	.25	.11
260	Devon White	.15	.07
261	Odalis Perez	.15	.07
262	Calvin Pickering	.25	.11
263	Tyler Green	.15	.07
264	Preston Wilson	.25	.11
265	Brad Radke	.25	.11
266	Walt Weiss	.15	.07
267	Tim Young	.15	.07
268	Tino Martinez	.25	.11
269	Matt Stairs	.25	.11
270	Curt Schilling	.40	.18
271	Tony Womack	.15	.07
272	Ismael Valdes	.15	.07
273	Wally Joyner	.25	.11
274	Armando Rios	.15	.07
275	Andy Pettitte	.25	.11
276	Bubba Trammell	.15	.07
277	Todd Zeile	.15	.07
278	Shannon Stewart	.25	.11
279	Matt Williams	.60	.25
280	John Rocker	.40	.18
281	B.J. Surhoff	.25	.11
282	Eric Young	.15	.07
283	Dmitri Young	.25	.11
284	John Smoltz	.40	.18
285	Todd Walker	.25	.11
286	Paul O'Neill	.25	.11
287	Blake Stein	.15	.07
288	Kevin Young	.25	.11
289	Quilvio Veras	.15	.07
290	Kirk Rueter	.15	.07
291	Randy Winn	.15	.07
292	Miguel Tejada	.25	.11
293	J.T. Snow	.25	.11
294	Michael Tucker	.15	.07
295	Jay Tessmer	.15	.07
296	Scott Erickson	.15	.07
297	Tim Wakefield	.15	.07
298	Jeff Abbott	.15	.07
299	Eddie Taubensee	.15	.07
300	Darryl Hamilton	.15	.07
301	Kevin Orie	.15	.07
302	Jose Offerman	.25	.11
303	Scott Karl	.15	.07
304	Chris Widger	.15	.07
305	Todd Hundley	.25	.11
306	Desi Relaford	.15	.07
307	Sterling Hitchcock	.15	.07
308	Delino DeShields	.15	.07
309	Alex Gonzalez	.25	.11
310	Justin Baughman	.15	.07
311	Jamey Wright	.15	.07
312	Wes Helms	.15	.07
313	Dante Powell	.15	.07
314	Jim Abbott	.25	.11
315	Manny Alexander	.15	.07
316	Harold Baines	.25	.11
317	Danny Graves	.15	.07
318	Sandy Alomar Jr.	.25	.11
319	Pedro Astacio	.15	.07
320	Jermaine Allensworth	.15	.07
321	Matt Anderson	.15	.07
322	Chad Curtis	.15	.07
323	Antonio Osuna	.15	.07
324	Brad Ausmus	.15	.07
325	Steve Trachsel	.15	.07
326	Mike Blowers	.15	.07
327	Brian Bohanon	.15	.07
328	Chris Gomez	.15	.07
329	Valerio De Los Santos	.15	.07
330	Rich Aurilia	.15	.07
331	Michael Barrett	.40	.18
332	Rick Aguilera	.15	.07
333	Adrian Brown	.15	.07
334	Bill Spiers	.15	.07
335	Matt Beech	.15	.07
336	David Bell	.15	.07
337	Juan Acevedo	.15	.07
338	Jose Canseco	.75	.35
339	Wilson Alvarez	.15	.07
340	Luis Alicea	.15	.07
341	Jason Dickson	.15	.07
342	Mike Bordick	.15	.07
343	Ben Ford	.15	.07
344	Javy Lopez	.25	.11
345	Jason Christiansen	.15	.07
346	Darren Bragg	.15	.07
347	Doug Brocail	.15	.07
348	Jeff Blauser	.15	.07
349	James Baldwin	.15	.07
350	Jeffrey Hammonds	.15	.07
351	Ricky Bottalico	.15	.07
352	Russ Branyan	.25	.11
353	Mark Brownson	.25	.11
354	Dave Berg	.15	.07
355	Sean Bergman	.15	.07
356	Jeff Conine	.15	.07
357	Shayne Bennett	.15	.07
358	Bobby Bonilla	.25	.11
359	Bob Wickman	.15	.07
360	Carlos Baerga	.15	.07
361	Chris Fussell	.15	.07
362	Chili Davis	.25	.11
363	Jerry Spradlin	.15	.07
364	Carlos Hernandez	.15	.07
365	Roberto Hernandez	.15	.07
366	Marvin Benard	.15	.07
367	Ken Cloude	.15	.07
368	Tony Fernandez	.25	.11
369	John Burkett	.15	.07
370	Gary DiSarcina	.15	.07
371	Alan Benes	.15	.07
372	Karim Garcia	.15	.07
373	Carlos Perez	.15	.07
374	Damon Buford	.15	.07
375	Mark Clark	.15	.07
376	Edgard Clemente	.15	.07
377	Chad Bradford	.25	.11
378	Frank Catalanotto	.15	.07
379	Vic Darensbourg	.15	.07
380	Sean Berry	.15	.07
381	Dave Burba	.15	.07
382	Sal Fasano	.15	.07
383	Steve Parris	.15	.07
384	Roger Cedeno	.25	.11
385	Chad Fox	.15	.07
386	Wilton Guerrero	.15	.07
387	Dennis Cook	.15	.07
388	Joe Girardi	.15	.07
389	LaTroy Hawkins	.15	.07
390	Ryan Christenson	.15	.07
391	Paul Byrd	.15	.07
392	Lou Collier	.15	.07
393	Jeff Fassero	.15	.07
394	Jim Leyritz	.15	.07
395	Shawn Estes	.15	.07
396	Mike Kelly	.15	.07
397	Rich Croushore	.15	.07
398	Royce Clayton	.15	.07
399	Rudy Seanez	.15	.07
400	Darrin Fletcher	.15	.07
401	Shigetoshi Hasegawa	.15	.07
402	Bernard Gilkey	.15	.07
403	Juan Guzman	.15	.07
404	Jeff Frye	.15	.07
405	Donovan Osborne	.15	.07
406	Alex Fernandez	.15	.07
407	Gary Gaetti	.25	.11
408	Dan Miceli	.15	.07
409	Mike Cameron	.15	.07
410	Mike Remlinger	.15	.07
411	Joey Cora	.15	.07
412	Mark Gardner	.15	.07
413	Aaron Ledesma	.15	.07
414	Jerry Dipoto	.15	.07
415	Ricky Gutierrez	.15	.07
416	John Franco	.25	.11
417	Mendy Lopez	.15	.07
418	Hideki Irabu	.25	.11
419	Mark Grudzielanek	.15	.07
420	Bobby Hughes	.15	.07
421	Pat Meares	.15	.07
422	Jimmy Haynes	.15	.07
423	Bob Henley	.15	.07
424	Bobby Estalella	.15	.07
425	Jon Lieber	.15	.07
426	Giomar Guevara	.25	.11
427	Jose Jimenez	.25	.11
428	Deivi Cruz	.15	.07
429	Jonathan Johnson	.15	.07
430	Ken Hill	.15	.07
431	Craig Grebeck	.15	.07
432	Jose Rosado	.15	.07
433	Danny Klassen	.15	.07
434	Bobby Howry	.15	.07
435	Gerald Williams	.15	.07
436	Omar Olivares	.15	.07
437	Chris Holles	.15	.07
438	Seth Greisinger	.15	.07
439	Scott Hatteberg	.15	.07
440	Jeremi Gonzalez	.15	.07
441	Wil Cordero	.15	.07
442	Jeff Montgomery	.15	.07
443	Chris Stynes	.15	.07
444	Tony Saunders	.15	.07
445	Einar Diaz	.15	.07
446	Lariel Gonzalez	.15	.07
447	Ryan Jackson	.15	.07
448	Mike Hampton	.25	.11
449	Todd Hollandsworth	.15	.07
450	Gabe White	.15	.07
451	John Jaha	.25	.11
452	Bret Saberhagen	.25	.11
453	Otis Nixon	.15	.07
454	Steve Kline	.15	.07
455	Butch Huskey	.15	.07
456	Mike Jerzembeck	.15	.07
457	Wayne Gomes	.15	.07
458	Mike Macfarlane	.15	.07
459	Jesus Sanchez	.15	.07
460	Al Martin	.15	.07
461	Dwight Gooden	.25	.11
462	Ruben Rivera	.15	.07
463	Pat Hentgen	.15	.07
464	Jose Valentin	.15	.07
465	Vladimir Nunez	.15	.07
466	Charlie Hayes	.15	.07
467	Jay Powell	.15	.07
468	Raul Ibanez	.15	.07
469	Kent Mercker	.15	.07
470	John Mabry	.15	.07
471	Woody Williams	.15	.07
472	Roberto Kelly	.15	.07
473	Jim Mecir	.15	.07
474	Dave Hollins	.15	.07
475	Rafael Medina	.15	.07
476	Darren Lewis	.15	.07
477	Felix Heredia	.15	.07
478	Brian Hunter	.15	.07
479	Matt Mantei	.25	.11
480	Richard Hidalgo	.15	.07
481	Bobby Jones	.15	.07
482	Hal Morris	.15	.07
483	Ramiro Mendoza	.15	.07
484	Matt Luke	.15	.07
485	Esteban Loaiza	.15	.07
486	Mark Loretta	.15	.07
487	A.J. Pierzynski	.15	.07
488	Charles Nagy	.25	.11
489	Kevin Sefcik	.15	.07
490	Jason McDonald	.15	.07
491	Jeremy Powell	.15	.07
492	Scott Servais	.15	.07
493	Abraham Nunez	.15	.07
494	Stan Spencer	.15	.07
495	Stan Javier	.15	.07
496	Jose Paniagua	.15	.07
497	Gregg Jefferies	.15	.07
498	Gregg Olson	.15	.07
499	Derek Lowe	.15	.07
500	Willie Otanez	.15	.07
501	Brian Moehler	.15	.07
502	Glenallen Hill	.15	.07
503	Bobby M. Jones	.15	.07
504	Greg Norton	.15	.07
505	Mike Jackson	.15	.07
506	Kirt Manwaring	.15	.07
507	Eric Weaver	.25	.11
508	Mitch Meluskey	.15	.07
509	Todd Jones	.15	.07

❏ 510 Mike Matheny	.15	.07
❏ 511 Benj Sampson	.15	.07
❏ 512 Tony Phillips	.15	.07
❏ 513 Mike Thurman	.15	.07
❏ 514 Jorge Posada	.15	.07
❏ 515 Bill Taylor	.15	.07
❏ 516 Mike Sweeney	.25	.11
❏ 517 Jose Silva	.15	.07
❏ 518 Mark Lewis	.15	.07
❏ 519 Chris Peters	.15	.07
❏ 520 Brian Johnson	.15	.07
❏ 521 Mike Timlin	.15	.07
❏ 522 Mark McLemore	.15	.07
❏ 523 Dan Plesac	.15	.07
❏ 524 Kelly Stinnett	.15	.07
❏ 525 Sidney Ponson	.15	.07
❏ 526 Jim Parque	.15	.07
❏ 527 Tyler Houston	.15	.07
❏ 528 John Thomson	.15	.07
❏ 529 Reggie Jefferson	.15	.07
❏ 530 Robert Person	.15	.07
❏ 531 Marc Newfield	.15	.07
❏ 532 Javier Vazquez	.15	.07
❏ 533 Terry Steinbach	.15	.07
❏ 534 Turk Wendell	.15	.07
❏ 535 Tim Raines	.25	.11
❏ 536 Brian Meadows	.15	.07
❏ 537 Mike Lieberthal	.25	.11
❏ 538 Ricardo Rincon	.15	.07
❏ 539 Dan Wilson	.15	.07
❏ 540 John Johnstone	.15	.07
❏ 541 Todd Stottlemyre	.15	.07
❏ 542 Kevin Stocker	.15	.07
❏ 543 Ramon Martinez	.15	.07
❏ 544 Mike Simms	.15	.07
❏ 545 Paul Quantrill	.15	.07
❏ 546 Matt Walbeck	.15	.07
❏ 547 Turner Ward	.15	.07
❏ 548 Bill Pulsipher	.15	.07
❏ 549 Donnie Sadler	.15	.07
❏ 550 Lance Johnson	.15	.07
❏ 551 Bill Simas	.15	.07
❏ 552 Jeff Reed	.15	.07
❏ 553 Jeff Shaw	.15	.07
❏ 554 Joe Randa	.15	.07
❏ 555 Paul Shuey	.15	.07
❏ 556 Mike Redmond	.25	.07
❏ 557 Sean Runyan	.15	.07
❏ 558 Enrique Wilson	.15	.07
❏ 559 Scott Radinsky	.15	.07
❏ 560 Larry Sutton	.15	.07
❏ 561 Masato Yoshii	.25	.11
❏ 562 David Nilsson	.15	.07
❏ 563 Mike Trombley	.15	.07
❏ 564 Darryl Strawberry	.25	.11
❏ 565 Dave Mlicki	.15	.07
❏ 566 Placido Polanco	.15	.07
❏ 567 Yorkis Perez	.15	.07
❏ 568 Esteban Yan	.15	.07
❏ 569 Lee Stevens	.15	.07
❏ 570 Steve Sinclair	.15	.07
❏ 571 Jarrod Washburn	.15	.07
❏ 572 Lenny Webster	.15	.07
❏ 573 Mike Sirotka	.15	.07
❏ 574 Jason Varitek	.25	.11
❏ 575 Terry Mulholland	.15	.07
❏ 576 Adrian Beltre FF	.25	.11
❏ 577 Eric Chavez FF	.25	.11
❏ 578 J.D. Drew FF	.60	.25
❏ 579 Juan Encarnacion FF	.15	
❏ 580 Nomar Garciaparra FF	1.00	.45
❏ 581 Troy Glaus FF	.25	.11
❏ 582 Ben Grieve FF	.25	.11
❏ 583 Vladimir Guerrero FF	.40	.18
❏ 584 Todd Helton FF	.25	.11
❏ 585 Derek Jeter FF	1.00	.45
❏ 586 Travis Lee FF	.25	.11
❏ 587 Alex Rodriguez FF	1.00	.45
❏ 588 Scott Rolen FF	.60	.25
❏ 589 Richie Sexson FF	.15	.07
❏ 590 Kerry Wood FF	.25	.11
❏ 591 Ken Griffey Jr. CL	1.50	.70
❏ 592 Chipper Jones CL	.75	.35
❏ 593 Alex Rodriguez CL	1.00	.45
❏ 594 Sammy Sosa CL	1.00	.45
❏ 595 Mark McGwire CL	2.00	.90

❏ 596 Cal Ripken CL	1.25	.55
❏ 597 Nomar Garciaparra CL	1.00	.45
❏ 598 Derek Jeter CL	1.00	.45
❏ 599 Kerry Wood CL	.25	.11
❏ 600 J.D. Drew CL	.60	.25
❏ P7 J.D. Drew Promo	2.00	.90

1999 Fleer Starting 9

	MINT	NRMT

RANDOM INSERTS IN HOBBY PACKS
STATED PRINT RUN 9 SERIAL #'d SETS
NO PRICING DUE TO SCARCITY

1999 Fleer Vintage '61

	MINT	NRMT
COMPLETE SET (50)	25.00	11.00
COMMON CARD (1-50)	.25	.11

ONE PER HOBBY PACK

❏ 1 Mark McGwire	4.00	1.80
❏ 2 Sammy Sosa	2.00	.90
❏ 3 Ken Griffey Jr.	3.00	1.35
❏ 4 Kerry Wood	.60	.25
❏ 5 Derek Jeter	2.00	.90
❏ 6 Stan Musial	1.50	.70
❏ 7 J.D. Drew	1.25	.55
❏ 8 Cal Ripken	2.50	1.10
❏ 9 Alex Rodriguez	2.00	.90
❏ 10 Travis Lee	.40	.18
❏ 11 Andres Galarraga	.40	.18
❏ 12 Nomar Garciaparra	2.00	.90
❏ 13 Albert Belle	.60	.25
❏ 14 Barry Larkin	.60	.25
❏ 15 Dante Bichette	.25	.11
❏ 16 Tony Clark	.25	.11
❏ 17 Moises Alou	.25	.11
❏ 18 Rafael Palmeiro	.60	.25
❏ 19 Raul Mondesi	.25	.11
❏ 20 Vladimir Guerrero	.75	.35
❏ 21 John Olerud	.25	.11
❏ 22 Bernie Williams	.60	.25
❏ 23 Ben Grieve	.60	.25
❏ 24 Scott Rolen	1.00	.45
❏ 25 Jeromy Burnitz	.25	.11
❏ 26 Ken Caminiti	.25	.11
❏ 27 Barry Bonds	.75	.35
❏ 28 Todd Helton	.60	.25
❏ 29 Juan Gonzalez	1.25	.55
❏ 30 Roger Clemens	1.50	.70

❏ 31 Andruw Jones	.60	.25
❏ 32 Mo Vaughn	.60	.25
❏ 33 Larry Walker	.60	.25
❏ 34 Frank Thomas	1.25	.55
❏ 35 Manny Ramirez	.75	.35
❏ 36 Randy Johnson	.60	.25
❏ 37 Vinny Castilla	.25	.11
❏ 38 Juan Encarnacion	.25	.11
❏ 39 Jeff Bagwell	.75	.35
❏ 40 Gary Sheffield	.25	.11
❏ 41 Mike Piazza	2.00	.90
❏ 42 Richie Sexson	.40	.18
❏ 43 Tony Gwynn	1.50	.70
❏ 44 Chipper Jones	1.50	.70
❏ 45 Jim Thome	.60	.25
❏ 46 Craig Biggio	.60	.25
❏ 47 Carlos Delgado	.60	.25
❏ 48 Greg Vaughn	.25	.11
❏ 49 Greg Maddux	2.00	.90
❏ 50 Troy Glaus	.60	.25

1999 Fleer Warning Track

	MINT	NRMT
COMPLETE SET (600)	450.00	200.00
COMMON CARD (1-600)	.25	.11

*STARS: 2.5X TO 6X BASIC CARDS
*YOUNG STARS: 2X TO 5X BASIC CARDS
ONE PER RETAIL PACK

1999 Fleer Date With Destiny

	MINT	NRMT
COMPLETE SET (10)	1200.00	550.00
COMMON CARD (1-10)	50.00	22.00

RANDOM INSERTS IN PACKS
STATED PRINT RUN 100 SERIAL #'d SETS

❏ 1 Barry Bonds	50.00	22.00
❏ 2 Roger Clemens	100.00	45.00
❏ 3 Ken Griffey Jr.	200.00	90.00
❏ 4 Tony Gwynn	100.00	45.00
❏ 5 Greg Maddux	100.00	45.00
❏ 6 Mark McGwire	250.00	110.00
❏ 7 Mike Piazza	120.00	55.00
❏ 8 Cal Ripken	150.00	70.00
❏ 9 Alex Rodriguez	120.00	55.00
❏ 10 Frank Thomas	80.00	36.00

1999 Fleer Diamond Magic

	MINT	NRMT
COMPLETE SET (15)	250.00	110.00
COMMON CARD (1-15)	8.00	3.60
STATED ODDS 1:96		

		MINT	NRMT
❏ 1	Barry Bonds	10.00	4.50
❏ 2	Roger Clemens	20.00	9.00
❏ 3	Nomar Garciaparra	25.00	11.00
❏ 4	Ken Griffey Jr.	40.00	18.00
❏ 5	Tony Gwynn	20.00	9.00
❏ 6	Orlando Hernandez	8.00	3.60
❏ 7	Derek Jeter	25.00	11.00
❏ 8	Randy Johnson	8.00	3.60
❏ 9	Chipper Jones	20.00	9.00
❏ 10	Greg Maddux	20.00	9.00
❏ 11	Mark McGwire	50.00	22.00
❏ 12	Alex Rodriguez	25.00	11.00
❏ 13	Sammy Sosa	25.00	11.00
❏ 14	Bernie Williams	8.00	3.60
❏ 15	Kerry Wood	8.00	3.60

1999 Fleer Going Yard

	MINT	NRMT
COMPLETE SET (15)	50.00	22.00
COMMON CARD (1-15)	.75	.35
SEMISTARS	1.25	.55
UNLISTED STARS	2.00	.90
STATED ODDS 1:18		

		MINT	NRMT
❏ 1	Moises Alou	.75	.35
❏ 2	Albert Belle	2.00	.90
❏ 3	Jose Canseco	2.50	1.10
❏ 4	Vinny Castilla	.75	.35
❏ 5	Andres Galarraga	1.25	.55
❏ 6	Juan Gonzalez	4.00	1.80
❏ 7	Ken Griffey Jr.	10.00	4.50
❏ 8	Chipper Jones	5.00	2.20
❏ 9	Mark McGwire	12.00	5.50
❏ 10	Rafael Palmeiro	2.00	.90
❏ 11	Mike Piazza	6.00	2.70
❏ 12	Alex Rodriguez	6.00	2.70
❏ 13	Sammy Sosa	6.00	2.70
❏ 14	Greg Vaughn	.75	.35
❏ 15	Mo Vaughn	2.00	.90

1999 Fleer Golden Memories

	MINT	NRMT
COMPLETE SET (15)	175.00	80.00
COMMON CARD (1-15)	2.00	.90
UNLISTED STARS	5.00	2.20
STATED ODDS 1:54		

		MINT	NRMT
❏ 1	Albert Belle	5.00	2.20
❏ 2	Barry Bonds	6.00	2.70
❏ 3	Roger Clemens	12.00	5.50
❏ 4	Nomar Garciaparra	15.00	6.75
❏ 5	Juan Gonzalez	10.00	4.50
❏ 6	Ken Griffey Jr.	25.00	11.00
❏ 7	Randy Johnson	5.00	2.20
❏ 8	Greg Maddux	12.00	5.50
❏ 9	Mark McGwire	30.00	13.50
❏ 10	Mike Piazza	15.00	6.75
❏ 11	Cal Ripken	20.00	9.00
❏ 12	Alex Rodriguez	15.00	6.75
❏ 13	Sammy Sosa	15.00	6.75
❏ 14	David Wells	2.00	.90
❏ 15	Kerry Wood	5.00	2.20

1999 Fleer Stan Musial Monumental Moments

	MINT	NRMT
COMPLETE SET (10)	50.00	22.00
COMMON CARD (1-10)	5.00	2.20
STATED ODDS 1:36		
MUSIAL SIGNED 50 OF EACH CARD		

		MINT	NRMT
❏ 1	Stan Musial	5.00	2.20
	Life in Donora		
❏ 2	Stan Musial	5.00	2.20
	Mrs. Stan Musial Values		
❏ 3	Stan Musial	5.00	2.20
	In the Beginning		
❏ 4	Stan Musial	5.00	2.20
	In the Navy		
❏ 5	Stan Musial	5.00	2.20
	Red Schoendienst 1948 Season		
❏ 6	Stan Musial	5.00	2.20
	John. F. Kennedy Success Stories		
❏ 7	Stan Musial	5.00	2.20
	Mr. Cardinal		
❏ 8	Stan Musial	5.00	2.20
	Most Valuable Player		
❏ 9	Stan Musial	5.00	2.20
	Statue's Caption		
❏ 10	Stan Musial	5.00	2.20
	Hall of Fame		

1999 Fleer Rookie Flashback

	MINT	NRMT
COMPLETE SET (15)	10.00	4.50
COMMON CARD (1-15)	.50	.23
SEMISTARS	1.00	.45
UNLISTED STARS	1.50	.70
STATED ODDS 1:6		

		MINT	NRMT
❏ 1	Matt Anderson	.50	.23
❏ 2	Rolando Arrojo	.50	.23
❏ 3	Adrian Beltre	1.50	.70
❏ 4	Mike Caruso	.50	.23
❏ 5	Eric Chavez	1.00	.45
❏ 6	J.D. Drew	2.50	1.10
❏ 7	Juan Encarnacion	.50	.23
❏ 8	Brad Fullmer	.50	.23
❏ 9	Troy Glaus	1.50	.70
❏ 10	Ben Grieve	1.50	.70
❏ 11	Todd Helton	1.50	.70
❏ 12	Orlando Hernandez	1.50	.70
❏ 13	Travis Lee	1.00	.45
❏ 14	Richie Sexson	1.00	.45
❏ 15	Kerry Wood	1.50	.70

1999 Fleer Update

	MINT	NRMT
COMP.FACT.SET (150)	40.00	18.00
COMMON CARD (1-150)	.10	.05
MINOR STARS	.15	.07
SEMISTARS	.25	.11
UNLISTED STARS	.40	.18
DISTRIBUTED ONLY IN FACTORY SET FORM		

		MINT	NRMT
❏ U1	Rick Ankiel	15.00	6.75
❏ U2	Peter Bergeron	1.00	.45
❏ U3	Pat Burrell	4.00	1.80
❏ U4	Eric Munson	5.00	2.20
❏ U5	Alfonso Soriano	4.00	1.80
❏ U6	Tim Hudson	2.00	.90

❏ U7 Erubiel Durazo	4.00	1.80
❏ U8 Chad Hermansen	.15	.07
❏ U9 Jeff Zimmerman	1.00	.45
❏ U10 Jesus Pena	.40	.18
❏ U11 Ramon Hernandez	.10	.05
❏ U12 Trent Durrington	.40	.18
❏ U13 Tony Armas Jr.	.25	.11
❏ U14 Mike Fyhrie	.10	.05
❏ U15 Danny Kolb	.50	.23
❏ U16 Mike Porzio	.10	.05
❏ U17 Will Brunson	.10	.05
❏ U18 Mike Duvall	.40	.18
❏ U19 Doug Mientkiewicz	.50	.23
❏ U20 Gabe Molina	.25	.11
❏ U21 Luis Vizcaino	.50	.23
❏ U22 Robinson Cancel	.40	.18
❏ U23 Brett Laxton	.25	.11
❏ U24 Joe McEwing	1.50	.70
❏ U25 Justin Speier	.10	.05
❏ U26 Kip Wells	1.00	.45
❏ U27 Armando Almanza	.10	.05
❏ U28 Joe Davenport	.40	.18
❏ U29 Yamid Haad	.25	.11
❏ U30 John Halama	.10	.05
❏ U31 Adam Kennedy	.15	.07
❏ U32 Micah Bowie	.50	.23
❏ U33 Travis Dawkins	1.00	.45
❏ U34 Ryan Rupe	.60	.25
❏ U35 B.J. Ryan	.50	.23
❏ U36 Chance Sanford	.10	.05
❏ U37 Anthony Shumaker	.25	.11
❏ U38 Ryan Glynn	.50	.23
❏ U39 Roosevelt Brown	.75	.35
❏ U40 Ben Molina	.40	.18
❏ U41 Scott Williamson	.15	.07
❏ U42 Eric Gagne	1.25	.55
❏ U43 John McDonald	.40	.18
❏ U44 Scott Sauerbeck	.25	.11
❏ U45 Mike Venafro	.10	.05
❏ U46 Edwards Guzman	.50	.23
❏ U47 Richard Barker	.10	.05
❏ U48 Braden Looper	.10	.05
❏ U49 Chad Meyers	.25	.11
❏ U50 Scott Strickland	.40	.18
❏ U51 Billy Koch	.15	.07
❏ U52 David Newhan	.10	.05
❏ U53 David Riske	.50	.23
❏ U54 Jose Santiago	.10	.05
❏ U55 Miguel Del Toro	.10	.05
❏ U56 Orber Moreno	.50	.23
❏ U57 Dave Roberts	.50	.23
❏ U58 Tim Byrdak	.10	.05
❏ U59 David Lee	.10	.05
❏ U60 Guillermo Mota	.50	.23
❏ U61 Wilton Veras	2.50	1.10
❏ U62 Joe Mays	1.25	.55
❏ U63 Jose Fernandez	.40	.18
❏ U64 Ray King	.10	.05
❏ U65 Chris Petersen	.10	.05
❏ U66 Vernon Wells	.25	.11
❏ U67 Ruben Mateo	.40	.18
❏ U68 Ben Petrick	.15	.07
❏ U69 Chris Tremie	.25	.11
❏ U70 Lance Berkman	.25	.11
❏ U71 Dan Smith	.50	.23
❏ U72 Carlos Hernandez	.25	.11
❏ U73 Chad Harville	.40	.18
❏ U74 Damaso Marte	.25	.11
❏ U75 Aaron Myette	.75	.35
❏ U76 Willis Roberts	.25	.11
❏ U77 Erik Sabel	.25	.11
❏ U78 Hector Almonte	.25	.11
❏ U79 Kris Benson	.15	.07
❏ U80 Pat Daneker	.50	.23
❏ U81 Freddy Garcia	4.00	1.80
❏ U82 Byung-Hyun Kim	1.50	.70
❏ U83 Wily Mo Pena	2.50	1.10
❏ U84 Dan Wheeler	.50	.23
❏ U85 Tim Harikkala	.10	.05
❏ U86 Derrin Ebert	.50	.23
❏ U87 Horacio Estrada	.25	.11
❏ U88 Liu Rodriguez	.40	.18
❏ U89 Jordan Zimmerman	.25	.11
❏ U90 A.J. Burnett	1.00	.45
❏ U91 Doug Davis	.50	.23
❏ U92 Robert Ramsey	.10	.05

❏ U93 Clay Bellinger	.10	.05
❏ U94 Charlie Greene	.10	.05
❏ U95 Bo Porter	.10	.05
❏ U96 Jorge Toca	1.00	.45
❏ U97 Casey Blake	.50	.23
❏ U98 Amaury Garcia	.40	.18
❏ U99 Jose Molina	.40	.18
❏ U100 Melvin Mora	1.50	.70
❏ U101 Joe Nathan	.50	.23
❏ U102 Juan Pena	.50	.23
❏ U103 Dave Borkowski	.50	.23
❏ U104 Eddie Gaillard	.10	.05
❏ U105 Glen Barker	.10	.05
❏ U106 Brett Hinchliffe	.50	.23
❏ U107 Carlos Lee	.15	.07
❏ U108 Rob Ryan	.25	.11
❏ U109 Jeff Weaver	1.00	.45
❏ U110 Ed Yarnall	.15	.07
❏ U111 Nelson Cruz	.10	.05
❏ U112 Cleatus Davidson	.50	.23
❏ U113 Tim Kubinski	.10	.05
❏ U114 Sean Spencer	.25	.11
❏ U115 Joe Winkelsas	.10	.05
❏ U116 Mike Colangelo	.50	.23
❏ U117 Tom Davey	.25	.11
❏ U118 Warren Morris	.15	.07
❏ U119 Dan Murray	.25	.11
❏ U120 Jose Nieves	.50	.23
❏ U121 Mark Quinn	1.50	.70
❏ U122 Josh Beckett	5.00	2.20
❏ U123 Chad Allen	.50	.23
❏ U124 Mike Figga	.10	.05
❏ U125 Beiker Graterol	.25	.11
❏ U126 Aaron Scheffer	.25	.11
❏ U127 Wiki Gonzalez	.75	.35
❏ U128 Ramon E.Martinez	.10	.05
❏ U129 Matt Riley	3.00	1.35
❏ U130 Chris Woodward	.40	.18
❏ U131 Albert Belle	.40	.18
❏ U132 Roger Cedeno	.15	.07
❏ U133 Roger Clemens	1.00	.45
❏ U134 Brian Giles	.15	.07
❏ U135 Rickey Henderson	.50	.23
❏ U136 Randy Johnson	.40	.18
❏ U137 Brian Jordan	.15	.07
❏ U138 Paul Konerko	.15	.07
❏ U139 Hideo Nomo	.40	.18
❏ U140 Kenny Rogers	.10	.05
❏ U141 Wade Boggs HL	.15	.07
❏ U142 Jose Canseco HL	.25	.11
❏ U143 Roger Clemens HL	1.00	.45
❏ U144 David Cone HL	.15	.07
❏ U145 Tony Gwynn HL	1.00	.45
❏ U146 Mark McGwire HL	2.50	1.10
❏ U147 Cal Ripken HL	1.50	.70
❏ U148 Alex Rodriguez HL	1.25	.55
❏ U149 Fernando Tatis HL	.15	.07
❏ U150 Robin Ventura HL	.15	.07

1999 Fleer Brilliants

	MINT	NRMT
COMPLETE SET (175)	150.00	70.00
COMP.SET w/o SP's (125)	60.00	27.00
COMMON CARD (1-125)	.30	.14
MINOR STARS 1-125	.50	.23
SEMISTARS 1-125	.75	.35
UNLISTED STARS 1-125	1.25	.55

COMMON CARD (126-175)	1.00	.45
MINOR STARS 126-175	1.50	.70
SEMISTARS 126-175	2.50	1.10
CARDS 126-175 STATED ODDS 1:2		

❏ 1 Mark McGwire	8.00	3.60
❏ 2 Derek Jeter	4.00	1.80
❏ 3 Nomar Garciaparra	4.00	1.80
❏ 4 Travis Lee	.75	.35
❏ 5 Jeff Bagwell	1.50	.70
❏ 6 Andres Galarraga	.75	.35
❏ 7 Pedro Martinez	1.50	.70
❏ 8 Cal Ripken	5.00	2.20
❏ 9 Vladimir Guerrero	1.50	.70
❏ 10 Chipper Jones	3.00	1.35
❏ 11 Rusty Greer	.50	.23
❏ 12 Omar Vizquel	.50	.23
❏ 13 Quinton McCracken	.30	.14
❏ 14 Jaret Wright	.50	.23
❏ 15 Mike Mussina	1.25	.55
❏ 16 Jason Giambi	.50	.23
❏ 17 Tony Clark	.50	.23
❏ 18 Troy O'Leary	.50	.23
❏ 19 Troy Percival	.50	.23
❏ 20 Kerry Wood	1.25	.55
❏ 21 Vinny Castilla	.50	.23
❏ 22 Chris Carpenter	.30	.14
❏ 23 Richie Sexson	.75	.35
❏ 24 Ken Griffey Jr.	6.00	2.70
❏ 25 Barry Bonds	1.50	.70
❏ 26 Carlos Delgado	1.25	.55
❏ 27 Frank Thomas	2.50	1.10
❏ 28 Manny Ramirez	1.50	.70
❏ 29 Shawn Green	1.25	.55
❏ 30 Mike Piazza	4.00	1.80
❏ 31 Tino Martinez	.50	.23
❏ 32 Dante Bichette	.50	.23
❏ 33 Scott Rolen	1.50	.70
❏ 34 Gabe Alvarez	.30	.14
❏ 35 Raul Mondesi	.50	.23
❏ 36 Damion Easley	.50	.23
❏ 37 Jeff Kent	.50	.23
❏ 38 Al Leiter	.50	.23
❏ 39 Alex Rodriguez	4.00	1.80
❏ 40 Jeff King	.30	.14
❏ 41 Mark Grace	.75	.35
❏ 42 Larry Walker	1.25	.55
❏ 43 Moises Alou	.50	.23
❏ 44 Juan Gonzalez	2.50	1.10
❏ 45 Rolando Arrojo	.30	.14
❏ 46 Tom Glavine	1.25	.55
❏ 47 Johnny Damon	.50	.23
❏ 48 Livan Hernandez	.30	.14
❏ 49 Craig Biggio	1.25	.55
❏ 50 Dmitri Young	.50	.23
❏ 51 Chan Ho Park	.50	.23
❏ 52 Todd Walker	.50	.23
❏ 53 Derrek Lee	.30	.14
❏ 54 Todd Helton	1.25	.55
❏ 55 Ray Lankford	.50	.23
❏ 56 Jim Thome	1.25	.55
❏ 57 Matt Lawton	.30	.14
❏ 58 Matt Anderson	.50	.23
❏ 59 Eric Karros	.50	.23
❏ 60 Orlando Hernandez	1.25	.55
❏ 61 Ben Grieve	1.25	.55
❏ 62 Bobby Abreu	.50	.23
❏ 63 Kevin Young	.50	.23
❏ 64 John Olerud	.50	.23
❏ 65 Sammy Sosa	4.00	1.80
❏ 66 Andy Ashby	.30	.14
❏ 67 Juan Encarnacion	.50	.23
❏ 68 Shane Reynolds	.50	.23
❏ 69 Bernie Williams	1.25	.55
❏ 70 Mike Cameron	.30	.14
❏ 71 Troy Glaus	1.25	.55
❏ 72 Gary Sheffield	.50	.23
❏ 73 Jeromy Burnitz	.50	.23
❏ 74 Mike Caruso	.30	.14
❏ 75 Chuck Knoblauch	.50	.23
❏ 76 Kenny Rogers	.30	.14
❏ 77 David Cone	.75	.35
❏ 78 Tony Gwynn	3.00	1.35
❏ 79 Jay Buhner	.50	.23
❏ 80 Paul O'Neill	.50	.23

☐ 82 Charles Nagy	.50	.23
☐ 83 Javy Lopez	.50	.23
☐ 84 Scott Erickson	.30	.14
☐ 85 Trevor Hoffman	.50	.23
☐ 86 Andruw Jones	1.25	.55
☐ 87 Ray Durham	.50	.23
☐ 88 Jorge Posada	.30	.14
☐ 89 Edgar Martinez	.50	.23
☐ 90 Tim Salmon	.75	.35
☐ 91 Bobby Higginson	.50	.23
☐ 92 Adrian Beltre	1.25	.55
☐ 93 Jason Kendall	.50	.23
☐ 94 Henry Rodriguez	.50	.23
☐ 95 Greg Maddux	3.00	1.35
☐ 96 David Justice	.50	.23
☐ 97 Ivan Rodriguez	1.50	.70
☐ 98 Curt Schilling	.75	.35
☐ 99 Matt Williams	1.25	.55
☐ 100 Darin Erstad	.75	.35
☐ 101 Rafael Palmeiro	1.25	.55
☐ 102 David Wells	.50	.23
☐ 103 Barry Larkin	1.25	.55
☐ 104 Robin Ventura	.50	.23
☐ 105 Edgar Renteria	.30	.14
☐ 106 Andy Pettitte	.50	.23
☐ 107 Albert Belle	1.25	.55
☐ 108 Steve Finley	.50	.23
☐ 109 Fernando Vina	.30	.14
☐ 110 Rondell White	.50	.23
☐ 111 Kevin Brown	.75	.35
☐ 112 Jose Canseco	1.50	.70
☐ 113 Roger Clemens	3.00	1.35
☐ 114 Todd Hundley	.50	.23
☐ 115 Will Clark	1.25	.55
☐ 116 Jim Edmonds	.50	.23
☐ 117 Randy Johnson	1.25	.55
☐ 118 Denny Neagle	.30	.14
☐ 119 Brian Jordan	.50	.23
☐ 120 Dean Palmer	.50	.23
☐ 121 Roberto Alomar	1.25	.55
☐ 122 Ken Caminiti	.50	.23
☐ 123 Brian Giles	.50	.23
☐ 124 Todd Stottlemyre	.30	.14
☐ 125 Mo Vaughn	1.25	.55
☐ 126 J.D. Drew	6.00	2.70
☐ 127 Ryan Minor	1.50	.70
☐ 128 Gabe Kapler	3.00	1.35
☐ 129 Jeremy Giambi	1.50	.70
☐ 130 Eric Chavez	2.50	1.10
☐ 131 Ben Davis	2.50	1.10
☐ 132 Rob Fick	1.50	.70
☐ 133 George Lombard	1.50	.70
☐ 134 Calvin Pickering	1.50	.70
☐ 135 Preston Wilson	1.50	.70
☐ 136 Corey Koskie	1.00	.45
☐ 137 Russell Branyan	1.50	.70
☐ 138 Bruce Chen	1.50	.70
☐ 139 Matt Clement	1.50	.70
☐ 140 Pat Burrell	12.00	5.50
☐ 141 Freddy Garcia	12.00	5.50
☐ 142 Brian Simmons	1.00	.45
☐ 143 Carlos Febles	1.50	.70
☐ 144 Carlos Guillen	1.00	.45
☐ 145 Fernando Seguignol	1.50	.70
☐ 146 Carlos Beltran	5.00	2.20
☐ 147 Edgard Clemente	1.00	.45
☐ 148 Mitch Meluskey	1.00	.45
☐ 149 Ryan Bradley	1.50	.70
☐ 150 Marlon Anderson	1.00	.45
☐ 151 A.J. Burnett	3.00	1.35
☐ 152 Scott Hunter	1.50	.70
☐ 153 Mark Johnson	1.00	.45
☐ 154 Angel Pena	1.00	.45
☐ 155 Roy Halladay	1.50	.70
☐ 156 Chad Allen	1.50	.70
☐ 157 Trot Nixon	1.50	.70
☐ 158 Ricky Ledee	1.50	.70
☐ 159 Gary Bennett	1.00	.45
☐ 160 Micah Bowie	1.50	.70
☐ 161 Doug Mientkiewicz	1.50	.70
☐ 162 Danny Klassen	1.00	.45
☐ 163 Willis Otanez	1.00	.45
☐ 164 Jin Ho Cho	1.50	.70
☐ 165 Mike Lowell	1.50	.70
☐ 166 Armando Rios	1.00	.45
☐ 167 Warren Morris	1.50	.70

☐ 168 Michael Barrett	2.50	1.10
☐ 169 Alex Gonzalez	1.50	.70
☐ 170 Masao Kida	2.50	1.10
☐ 171 Peter Tucci	1.00	.45
☐ 172 Luis Saturria	1.50	.70
☐ 173 Kris Benson	1.50	.70
☐ 174 Mario Encarnacion	4.00	1.80
☐ 175 Roosevelt Brown	2.50	1.10
☐ NNO J.D. Drew Sample	3.00	1.35

1999 Fleer Brilliants 24-Karat Gold

	MINT	NRMT
COMMON CARD (1-175)	30.00	13.50

*STARS 1-125: 40X TO 100X BASIC CARDS
*ROOKIES: 126-175: 8X TO 20X BASIC CARDS
RANDOM INSERTS IN PACKS
STATED PRINT RUN 24 SERIAL #'d SETS

1999 Fleer Brilliants Blue

	MINT	NRMT
COMPLETE SET (175)	500.00	220.00
COMMON CARD (1-175)	1.00	.45

*STARS 1-125: 1.25X TO 3X BASIC CARDS
*ROOKIES: 126-175: .5X TO 1.25X BASIC
STARS 1-125 STATED ODDS 1:3
ROOKIES 126-175 STATED ODDS 1:6

1999 Fleer Brilliants Gold

	MINT	NRMT
COMMON CARD (1-175)	8.00	3.60

*STARS 1-125: 10X TO 25X BASIC
*ROOKIES 126-175: 2.5X TO 6X BASIC
RANDOM INSERTS IN PACKS
STATED PRINT RUN 99 SERIAL #'d SETS

1999 Fleer Brilliants Illuminators

	MINT	NRMT
COMPLETE SET (15)	30.00	13.50
COMMON CARD (1-15)	1.50	.70
SEMISTARS	2.50	1.10
UNLISTED STARS	4.00	1.80
STATED ODDS 1:10		

☐ 1 Kerry Wood	4.00	1.80
☐ 2 Ben Grieve	4.00	1.80
☐ 3 J.D. Drew	6.00	2.70
☐ 4 Juan Encarnacion	1.50	.70
☐ 5 Travis Lee	2.50	1.10
☐ 6 Todd Helton	4.00	1.80
☐ 7 Troy Glaus	4.00	1.80
☐ 8 Ricky Ledee	1.50	.70
☐ 9 Eric Chavez	2.50	1.10
☐ 10 Ben Davis	2.50	1.10
☐ 11 George Lombard	1.50	.70
☐ 12 Jeremy Giambi	1.50	.70
☐ 13 Richie Sexson	2.50	1.10
☐ 14 Corey Koskie	1.50	.70
☐ 15 Russell Branyan	1.50	.70

1999 Fleer Brilliants Shining Stars

	MINT	NRMT
COMPLETE SET (15)	150.00	70.00
COMMON CARD (1-15)	5.00	2.20
STATED ODDS 1:20		

*PULSAR: 2X TO 5X HI COLUMN
PULSAR STATED ODDS 1:400

☐ 1 Ken Griffey Jr.	20.00	9.00
☐ 2 Mark McGwire	25.00	11.00
☐ 3 Sammy Sosa	12.00	5.50
☐ 4 Derek Jeter	12.00	5.50
☐ 5 Nomar Garciaparra	12.00	5.50
☐ 6 Alex Rodriguez	12.00	5.50

☐ 7 Mike Piazza	12.00	5.50
☐ 8 Juan Gonzalez	8.00	3.60
☐ 9 Chipper Jones	10.00	4.50
☐ 10 Cal Ripken	15.00	6.75
☐ 11 Frank Thomas	8.00	3.60
☐ 12 Greg Maddux	10.00	4.50
☐ 13 Roger Clemens	10.00	4.50
☐ 14 Vladimir Guerrero	5.00	2.20
☐ 15 Manny Ramirez	5.00	2.20

1999 Fleer Mystique

	MINT	NRMT
COMPLETE SET (160)	400.00	180.00
COMP. SHORT SET (100)	50.00	22.00
COMMON CARD (1-100)	.20	.09
MINOR STARS 1-100	.30	.14
SEMISTARS 1-100	.50	.23
UNLISTED STARS 1-100	.75	.35
COMMON (1-100)	.75	.35
SP UNLISTED STARS	1.25	.55

SP CARDS DISTRIBUTED ONLY AS PEEL OFFS

COMMON (101-150)	3.00	1.35
MINOR STARS 101-150	4.00	1.80
SEMISTARS 101-150	6.00	2.70

101-150 PRINT RUN 2999 SERIAL #'d SUBSETS

COMMON CARD (151-160)	12.00	5.50

151-160 PRINT RUN 2500 SERIAL #'d SUBSETS
MASTERPIECE ONE OF ONE PARALLELS EXIST
MASTERPIECE NOT PRICED DUE TO SCARCITY

☐ 1 Ken Griffey Jr. SP	6.00	2.70
☐ 2 Livan Hernandez	.20	.09
☐ 3 Jeff Kent	.30	.14
☐ 4 Brian Jordan	.30	.14
☐ 5 Kevin Young	.30	.14
☐ 6 Vinny Castilla	.30	.14
☐ 7 Orlando Hernandez SP	1.25	.55
☐ 8 Bobby Abreu	.30	.14
☐ 9 Vladimir Guerrero SP	1.50	.70
☐ 10 Chuck Knoblauch	.30	.14
☐ 11 Nomar Garciaparra SP	4.00	1.80
☐ 12 Jeff Bagwell	1.00	.45
☐ 13 Todd Walker	.30	.14
☐ 14 Johnny Damon	.30	.14
☐ 15 Mike Caruso	.20	.09
☐ 16 Cliff Floyd	.30	.14
☐ 17 Andy Pettitte	.30	.14
☐ 18 Cal Ripken SP	5.00	2.20
☐ 19 Brian Giles	.30	.14
☐ 20 Robin Ventura	.30	.14
☐ 21 Alex Gotzalez	.30	.14
☐ 22 Randy Johnson	.75	.35
☐ 23 Raul Mondesi	.30	.14
☐ 24 Ken Caminiti	.30	.14
☐ 25 Tom Glavine	.75	.35
☐ 26 Derek Jeter SP	4.00	1.80
☐ 27 Carlos Delgado	.75	.35
☐ 28 Adrian Beltre	.75	.35
☐ 29 Tino Martinez	.30	.14
☐ 30 Todd Helton	.75	.35
☐ 31 Juan Gonzalez SP	2.50	1.10
☐ 32 Henry Rodriguez	.30	.14
☐ 33 Jim Thome	.75	.35
☐ 34 Paul O'Neill	.30	.14
☐ 35 Scott Rolen SP	1.50	.70
☐ 36 Rafael Palmeiro	.75	.35
☐ 37 Will Clark	.75	.35
☐ 38 Todd Hundley	.30	.14
☐ 39 Andruw Jones SP	1.25	.55
☐ 40 Rolando Arrojo	.20	.09
☐ 41 Barry Larkin	.75	.35
☐ 42 Tim Salmon	.50	.23
☐ 43 Rondell White	.30	.14
☐ 44 Curt Schilling	.50	.23
☐ 45 Chipper Jones SP	3.00	1.35
☐ 46 Jeromy Burnitz	.30	.14
☐ 47 Mo Vaughn	.75	.35
☐ 48 Tony Clark	.30	.14
☐ 49 Fernando Tatis	.75	.35
☐ 50 Dmitri Young	.30	.14
☐ 51 Wade Boggs	.75	.35
☐ 52 Rickey Henderson	1.00	.45
☐ 53 Manny Ramirez SP	1.50	.70
☐ 54 Edgar Martinez	.30	.14
☐ 55 Jason Giambi	.30	.14
☐ 56 Jason Kendall	.30	.14
☐ 57 Eric Karros	.30	.14
☐ 58 Jose Canseco SP	1.50	.70
☐ 59 Shawn Green	.75	.35
☐ 60 Ellis Burks	.30	.14
☐ 61 Derek Bell	.30	.14
☐ 62 Shannon Stewart	.30	.14
☐ 63 Roger Clemens SP	3.00	1.35
☐ 64 Sean Casey SP	1.25	.55
☐ 65 Jose Offerman	.30	.14
☐ 66 Sammy Sosa SP	4.00	1.80
☐ 67 Frank Thomas SP	2.50	1.10
☐ 68 Tony Gwynn SP	3.00	1.35
☐ 69 Roberto Alomar	.75	.35
☐ 70 Mark McGwire SP	8.00	3.60
☐ 71 Troy Glaus	.75	.35
☐ 72 Ray Durham	.30	.14
☐ 73 Jeff Cirillo	.30	.14
☐ 74 Alex Rodriguez SP	4.00	1.80
☐ 75 Jose Cruz Jr.	.30	.14
☐ 76 Juan Encarnacion	.30	.14
☐ 77 Mark Grace	.50	.23
☐ 78 Barry Bonds SP	1.50	.70
☐ 79 Ivan Rodriguez SP	1.50	.70
☐ 80 Greg Vaughn	.30	.14
☐ 81 Greg Maddux SP	3.00	1.35
☐ 82 Albert Belle	.75	.35
☐ 83 John Olerud	.30	.14
☐ 84 Kenny Lofton	.50	.23
☐ 85 Bernie Williams	.75	.35
☐ 86 Matt Williams	.75	.35
☐ 87 Ray Lankford	.30	.14
☐ 88 Darin Erstad	.50	.23
☐ 89 Ben Grieve	.75	.35
☐ 90 Craig Biggio	.75	.35
☐ 91 Dean Palmer	.30	.14
☐ 92 Reggie Sanders	.20	.09
☐ 93 Dante Bichette	.30	.14
☐ 94 Pedro Martinez SP	1.50	.70
☐ 95 Larry Walker	.75	.35
☐ 96 David Wells	.30	.14
☐ 97 Travis Lee SP	.75	.35
☐ 98 Mike Piazza SP	4.00	1.80
☐ 99 Mike Mussina	.75	.35
☐ 100 Kevin Brown	.50	.23
☐ 101 Ruben Mateo PROS	8.00	3.60
☐ 102 Roberto Ramirez PROS	3.00	1.35
☐ 103 Glen Barker PROS	3.00	1.35
☐ 104 Clay Bellinger PROS	3.00	1.35
☐ 105 Carlos Guillen PROS	3.00	1.35
☐ 106 Scott Schoeneweis PROS	3.00	1.35
☐ 107 C.Gubanich PROS	3.00	1.35
☐ 108 Scott Williamson PROS	4.00	1.80
☐ 109 Edwards Guzman PROS	4.00	1.80
☐ 110 A.J. Burnett PROS	8.00	3.60
☐ 111 Jeremy Giambi PROS	4.00	1.80
☐ 112 Trot Nixon PROS	4.00	1.80
☐ 113 CC Sabathia PROS	15.00	6.75
☐ 114 Roy Halladay PROS	4.00	1.80
☐ 115 Jose Macias PROS	3.00	1.35
☐ 116 Corey Koskie PROS	3.00	1.35
☐ 117 Ryan Rupe PROS	5.00	2.20
☐ 118 Scott Hunter PROS	4.00	1.80
☐ 119 Rob Fick PROS	4.00	1.80
☐ 120 McKay Christensen PROS.	3.00	1.35
☐ 121 Carlos Febles PROS	4.00	1.80
☐ 122 Gabe Kapler PROS	8.00	3.60
☐ 123 Jeff Liefer PROS	3.00	1.35
☐ 124 Warren Morris PROS	4.00	1.80
☐ 125 Chris Pritchett PROS	3.00	1.35
☐ 126 Torii Hunter PROS	4.00	1.80
☐ 127 Armando Rios PROS	3.00	1.35
☐ 128 Ricky Ledee PROS	4.00	1.80
☐ 129 Kelly Dransfeldt PROS	5.00	2.20
☐ 130 Jeff Zimmerman PROS	8.00	3.60
☐ 131 Eric Chavez PROS	6.00	2.70
☐ 132 Freddy Garcia PROS	30.00	13.50
☐ 133 Jose Jimenez PROS	4.00	1.80
☐ 134 Pat Burrell PROS	50.00	22.00
☐ 135 Joe McEwing PROS	12.00	5.50
☐ 136 Kris Benson PROS	10.00	4.50
☐ 137 Joe Mays PROS	10.00	4.50
☐ 138 Rafael Roque PROS	3.00	1.35
☐ 139 Cristian Guzman PROS	3.00	1.35
☐ 140 Michael Barrett PROS	6.00	2.70
☐ 141 Doug Mientkiewicz PROS	4.00	1.80
☐ 142 Jeff Weaver PROS	8.00	3.60
☐ 143 Mike Lowell PROS	3.00	1.35
☐ 144 Jason Phillips PROS	3.00	1.35
☐ 145 Marlon Anderson PROS	3.00	1.35
☐ 146 Brett Hinchliffe PROS	4.00	1.80
☐ 147 Matt Clement PROS	4.00	1.80
☐ 148 Terrence Long PROS	3.00	1.35
☐ 149 Carlos Beltran PROS	12.00	5.50
☐ 150 Preston Wilson PROS	4.00	1.80
☐ 151 Ken Griffey Jr. STAR.	25.00	11.00
☐ 152 Mark McGwire STAR	30.00	13.50
☐ 153 Sammy Sosa STAR	15.00	6.75
☐ 154 Mike Piazza STAR	15.00	6.75
☐ 155 Alex Rodriguez STAR	15.00	6.75
☐ 156 Nomar Garciaparra STAR	15.00	6.75
☐ 157 Cal Ripken STAR	20.00	9.00
☐ 158 Greg Maddux STAR	12.00	5.50
☐ 159 Derek Jeter STAR	15.00	6.75
☐ 160 Juan Gonzalez STAR	10.00	4.50
☐ P113 J.D. Drew Promo	3.00	1.35

1999 Fleer Mystique Gold

	MINT	NRMT
COMPLETE SET (100)	800.00	350.00
COMMON CARD (1-100)	2.50	1.10

*GOLD: 5X TO 12X BASIC CARDS
*GOLD: 3X TO 8X BASIC SPs
STATED ODDS 1:

1999 Fleer Mystique Destiny

	MINT	NRMT
COMPLETE SET (10)	150.00	70.00
COMMON CARD (1-10)	6.00	2.70
UNLISTED STARS	10.00	4.50

RANDOM INSERTS IN PACKS
STATED PRINT RUN 999 SERIAL #'d SETS

☐ 1 Tony Gwynn	25.00	11.00

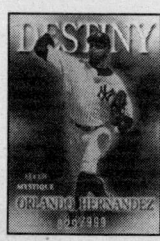

	MINT	NRMT
❑ 2 Juan Gonzalez	20.00	9.00
❑ 3 Scott Rolen	12.00	5.50
❑ 4 Nomar Garciaparra	30.00	13.50
❑ 5 Orlando Hernandez	10.00	4.50
❑ 6 Andruw Jones	10.00	4.50
❑ 7 Vladimir Guerrero	12.00	5.50
❑ 8 Darin Erstad	6.00	2.70
❑ 9 Manny Ramirez	12.00	5.50
❑ 10 Roger Clemens	25.00	11.00

1999 Fleer Mystique Established

	MINT	NRMT
COMPLETE SET (10)	1000.00	450.00
COMMON CARD (1-10)	60.00	27.00

RANDOM INSERTS IN PACKS
STATED PRINT RUN 100 SERIAL #'d SETS

❑ 1 Ken Griffey Jr.	150.00	70.00
❑ 2 Derek Jeter	100.00	45.00
❑ 3 Chipper Jones	80.00	36.00
❑ 4 Greg Maddux	80.00	36.00
❑ 5 Mark McGwire	200.00	90.00
❑ 6 Mike Piazza	100.00	45.00
❑ 7 Cal Ripken	120.00	55.00
❑ 8 Alex Rodriguez	100.00	45.00
❑ 9 Sammy Sosa	100.00	45.00
❑ 10 Frank Thomas	60.00	27.00

1999 Fleer Mystique Feel the Game

	MINT	NRMT
RANDOM INSERTS IN PACKS PRINT RUNS LISTED BELOW		
❑ 1 A.Beltre Shoe/430	50.00	22.00
❑ 2 J.D.Drew Jersey/450	120.00	55.00
❑ 3 J.Gonzalez Btg.Glove/415	80.00	36.00
❑ 4 T.Gwynn Jersey/435	120.00	55.00
❑ 5 K.Millwood Jersey/435	80.00	36.00
❑ 6 A.Rodriguez Btg.Glove/345	250.00	110.00
❑ 7 F.Thomas Jersey/450	150.00	70.00

1999 Fleer Mystique Fresh Ink

	MINT	NRMT
COMMON CARD	10.00	4.50

STATED ODDS 1:48
PRINT RUNS LISTED BELOW
UNNNUMBERED CARDS LISTED IN ALPH.ORDER

❑ 1 Roberto Alomar/500	50.00	22.00
❑ 2 Michael Barrett/1000	15.00	6.75
❑ 3 Kris Benson/500	15.00	6.75
❑ 4 Micah Bowie/1000	10.00	4.50
❑ 5 A.J. Burnett/1000	15.00	6.75
❑ 6 Pat Burrell/500	60.00	27.00
❑ 7 Ken Caminiti/250	25.00	11.00
❑ 8 Jose Canseco/250	150.00	70.00
❑ 9 Sean Casey/1000	30.00	13.50
❑ 10 Edgard Clemente/1000	10.00	4.50
❑ 11 Bartolo Colon/500	20.00	9.00
❑ 12 J.D. Drew/400	50.00	22.00
❑ 13 Juan Encarnacion/1000	10.00	4.50
❑ 14 Troy Glaus/400	30.00	13.50
❑ 15 Juan Gonzalez/250	80.00	36.00
❑ 16 Shawn Green/250	50.00	22.00
❑ 17 Tony Gwynn/250	100.00	45.00
❑ 18 Chipper Jones/500	100.00	45.00
❑ 19 Gabe Kapler/750	25.00	11.00
❑ 20 Barry Larkin/250	30.00	13.50
❑ 21 Doug Mientkiewicz/500	10.00	4.50
❑ 22 Alex Rodriguez/200	250.00	110.00
❑ 23 Scott Rolen/140	120.00	55.00
❑ 24 Fernando Tatis/750	20.00	9.00
❑ 25 Robin Ventura/500	30.00	13.50
❑ 26 Todd Walker/1000	10.00	4.50

1999 Fleer Mystique Prophetic

	MINT	NRMT
COMPLETE SET (10)	50.00	22.00
COMMON CARD (1-10)	4.00	1.80
UNLISTED STARS	6.00	2.70

RANDOM INSERTS IN PACKS
STATED PRINT RUN 1999 SERIAL #'d SETS

❑ 1 Eric Chavez	4.00	1.80
❑ 2 J.D. Drew	10.00	4.50
❑ 3 A.J. Burnett	5.00	2.20
❑ 4 Ben Grieve	6.00	2.70
❑ 5 Gabe Kapler	6.00	2.70

❑ 6 Todd Helton	6.00	2.70
❑ 7 Troy Glaus	6.00	2.70
❑ 8 Travis Lee	4.00	1.80
❑ 9 Pat Burrell	20.00	9.00
❑ 10 Kerry Wood	6.00	2.70

1949 Leaf

	NRMT	VG-E
COMPLETE SET (98)	25000.00	11200.00
COMMON CARD (1-168)	25.00	11.00
MINOR STARS	40.00	18.00
SEMISTARS	60.00	27.00
UNLISTED STARS	100.00	45.00
COMMON SP's	300.00	135.00
MINOR STAR SP's	400.00	180.00

*UNLISTED DODGER/YANKEE: 1.25X VALUE
SET IS SKIP NUMBERED
CARDS PRICED IN NM CONDITION !

❑ 1 Joe DiMaggio	2200.00	900.00
❑ 3 Babe Ruth	2500.00	1100.00
❑ 4 Stan Musial	850.00	375.00
❑ 5 Virgil Trucks SP	400.00	180.00
❑ 8 Satchel Paige SP	2500.00	1100.00
❑ 10 Dizzy Trout	40.00	18.00
❑ 11 Phil Rizzuto	300.00	135.00
❑ 13 Cass Michaels SP	300.00	135.00
❑ 14 Billy Johnson	40.00	18.00
❑ 17 Frank Overmire	25.00	11.00
❑ 19 Johnny Wyrostek SP	300.00	135.00
❑ 20 Hank Sauer SP	400.00	180.00
❑ 22 Al Evans	25.00	11.00
❑ 26 Sam Chapman	40.00	18.00
❑ 27 Mickey Harris	25.00	11.00
❑ 28 Jim Hegan	40.00	18.00
❑ 29 Elmer Valo	40.00	18.00
❑ 30 Billy Goodman SP	300.00	135.00
❑ 31 Lou Brissie	25.00	11.00
❑ 32 Warren Spahn	275.00	125.00
❑ 33 Peanuts Lowrey SP	300.00	135.00
❑ 36 Al Zarilla SP	300.00	135.00
❑ 38 Ted Kluszewski	150.00	70.00
❑ 39 Ewell Blackwell	60.00	27.00
❑ 42 Kent Peterson	25.00	11.00
❑ 43 Ed Stevens SP	300.00	135.00
❑ 45 Ken Keltner SP	300.00	135.00
❑ 46 Johnny Mize	100.00	45.00
❑ 47 George Vico	25.00	11.00
❑ 48 Johnny Schmitz SP	300.00	135.00
❑ 49 Del Ennis	60.00	27.00

#	Card	MINT	NRMT
50	Dick Wakefield	25.00	11.00
51	Al Dark SP	500.00	220.00
53	Johnny VanderMeer	100.00	45.00
54	Bobby Adams SP	300.00	135.00
55	Tommy Henrich SP	500.00	220.00
56	Larry Jansen UER (Misspelled Jensen)	40.00	18.00
57	Bob McCall	25.00	11.00
59	Luke Appling	100.00	45.00
61	Jake Early	25.00	11.00
62	Eddie Joost SP	300.00	135.00
63	Barney McCosky SP	300.00	135.00
65	Robert Elliott UER (Misspelled Elliot on card front)	100.00	45.00
66	Orval Grove SP	300.00	135.00
68	Eddie Miller SP	300.00	135.00
70	Honus Wagner CO	300.00	135.00
72	Hank Edwards	25.00	11.00
73	Pat Seerey	25.00	11.00
75	Dom DiMaggio SP	550.00	250.00
76	Ted Williams	1000.00	450.00
77	Roy Smalley	25.00	11.00
78	Hoot Evers SP	300.00	135.00
79	Jackie Robinson	1100.00	500.00
81	Whitey Kurowski SP	300.00	135.00
82	Johnny Lindell	40.00	18.00
83	Bobby Doerr	100.00	45.00
84	Sid Hudson	25.00	11.00
85	Dave Philley SP	300.00	135.00
86	Ralph Weigel	25.00	11.00
88	Frank Gustine SP	300.00	135.00
91	Ralph Kiner	200.00	90.00
93	Bob Feller SP	1300.00	575.00
95	George Stirnweiss	40.00	18.00
97	Marty Marion	60.00	27.00
98	Hal Newhouser SP	550.00	250.00
102A	Gene Hermansk ERR	250.00	110.00
102B	Gene Hermanski COR	40.00	18.00
104	Eddie Stewart SP	300.00	135.00
106	Lou Boudreau	100.00	45.00
108	Matt Batts SP	300.00	135.00
111	Jerry Priddy	25.00	11.00
113	Dutch Leonard SP	300.00	135.00
117	Joe Gordon	40.00	18.00
120	George Kell SP	550.00	250.00
121	Johnny Pesky SP	400.00	180.00
123	Cliff Fannin SP	300.00	135.00
125	Andy Pafko	25.00	11.00
127	Enos Slaughter SP	650.00	300.00
128	Buddy Rosar	25.00	11.00
129	Kirby Higbe SP	400.00	180.00
131	Sid Gordon SP	400.00	180.00
133	Tommy Holmes SP	500.00	220.00
136A	Cliff Aberson (Full sleeve)	25.00	11.00
136B	Cliff Aberson (Short sleeve)	250.00	110.00
137	Harry Walker SP	400.00	180.00
138	Larry Doby SP	650.00	300.00
139	Johnny Hopp	25.00	11.00
142	Danny Murtaugh SP	400.00	180.00
143	Dick Sisler SP	300.00	135.00
144	Bob Dillinger SP	400.00	180.00
146	Pete Reiser SP	500.00	220.00
149	Hank Majeski SP	300.00	135.00
153	Floyd Baker SP	300.00	135.00
158	Harry Brecheen SP	400.00	180.00
159	Mizell Platt	25.00	11.00
160	Bob Scheffing SP	300.00	135.00
161	Vern Stephens SP	400.00	180.00
163	Fred Hutchinson SP	400.00	180.00
165	Dale Mitchell SP	400.00	180.00
168	Phil Cavarretta SP UER (Name spelled Cavaretta)	500.00	200.00

1990 Leaf

	MINT	NRMT
COMPLETE SET (528)	250.00	110.00
COMPLETE SERIES 1 (264)	150.00	70.00
COMPLETE SERIES 2 (264)	100.00	45.00
COMMON CARD (1-528)	.25	.11
MINOR STARS	.50	.23
SEMISTARS	1.00	.45
UNLISTED STARS	1.50	.70

BEWARE THOMAS COUNTERFEIT

#	Card	MINT	NRMT
1	Introductory Card	.25	.11
2	Mike Henneman	.25	.11
3	Steve Bedrosian	.25	.11
4	Mike Scott	.25	.11
5	Allan Anderson	.25	.11
6	Rick Sutcliffe	.25	.11
7	Gregg Olson	.50	.23
8	Kevin Elster	.25	.11
9	Pete O'Brien	.25	.11
10	Carlton Fisk	1.50	.70
11	Joe Magrane	.25	.11
12	Roger Clemens	4.00	1.80
13	Tom Glavine	4.00	1.80
14	Tom Gordon	.50	.23
15	Todd Benzinger	.25	.11
16	Hubie Brooks	.25	.11
17	Roberto Kelly	.25	.11
18	Barry Larkin	1.50	.70
19	Mike Boddicker	.25	.11
20	Roger McDowell	.25	.11
21	Nolan Ryan	6.00	2.70
22	John Farrell	.25	.11
23	Bruce Hurst	.25	.11
24	Wally Joyner	.50	.23
25	Greg Maddux	10.00	4.50
26	Chris Bosio	.25	.11
27	John Cerutti	.25	.11
28	Tim Burke	.25	.11
29	Dennis Eckersley	1.00	.45
30	Glenn Davis	.25	.11
31	Jim Abbott	1.00	.45
32	Mike LaValliere	.25	.11
33	Andres Thomas	.25	.11
34	Lou Whitaker	.50	.23
35	Alvin Davis	.25	.11
36	Melido Perez	.25	.11
37	Craig Biggio	1.50	.70
38	Rick Aguilera	.50	.23
39	Pete Harnisch	.25	.11
40	David Cone	1.50	.70
41	Scott Garrelts	.25	.11
42	Jay Howell	.25	.11
43	Eric King	.25	.11
44	Pedro Guerrero	.25	.11
45	Mike Bielecki	.25	.11
46	Bob Boone	.50	.23
47	Kevin Brown	2.00	.90
48	Jerry Browne	.25	.11
49	Mike Scioscia	.25	.11
50	Chuck Cary	.25	.11
51	Wade Boggs	1.50	.70
52	Von Hayes	.25	.11
53	Tony Fernandez	.25	.11
54	Dennis Martinez	.50	.23
55	Tom Candiotti	.25	.11
56	Andy Benes	1.50	.70
57	Rob Dibble	.25	.11
58	Chuck Crim	.25	.11
59	John Smoltz	3.00	1.35
60	Mike Heath	.25	.11
61	Kevin Gross	.25	.11
62	Mark McGwire	8.00	3.60
63	Bert Blyleven	.50	.23
64	Bob Walk	.25	.11
65	Mickey Tettleton	.50	.23
66	Sid Fernandez	.25	.11
67	Terry Kennedy	.25	.11
68	Fernando Valenzuela	.50	.23
69	Don Mattingly	3.00	1.35
70	Paul O'Neill	.50	.23
71	Robin Yount	1.50	.70
72	Bret Saberhagen	.50	.23
73	Geno Petralli	.25	.11
74	Brook Jacoby	.25	.11
75	Roberto Alomar	1.50	.70
76	Devon White	.25	.11
77	Jose Lind	.25	.11
78	Pat Combs	.25	.11
79	Dave Stieb	.50	.23
80	Tim Wallach	.25	.11
81	Dave Stewart	.50	.23
82	Eric Anthony	.25	.11
83	Randy Bush	.25	.11
84	Rickey Henderson CL	.50	.23
85	Jaime Navarro	.25	.11
86	Tommy Gregg	.25	.11
87	Frank Tanana	.25	.11
88	Omar Vizquel	2.00	.90
89	Ivan Calderon	.25	.11
90	Vince Coleman	.25	.11
91	Barry Bonds	2.00	.90
92	Randy Milligan	.25	.11
93	Frank Viola	.25	.11
94	Matt Williams	1.50	.70
95	Alfredo Griffin	.25	.11
96	Steve Sax	.25	.11
97	Gary Gaetti	.50	.23
98	Ryne Sandberg	2.00	.90
99	Danny Tartabull	.25	.11
100	Rafael Palmeiro	2.00	.90
101	Jesse Orosco	.25	.11
102	Garry Templeton	.25	.11
103	Frank DiPino	.25	.11
104	Tony Pena	.25	.11
105	Dickie Thon	.25	.11
106	Kelly Gruber	.25	.11
107	Marquis Grissom	2.00	.90
108	Jose Canseco	2.00	.90
109	Mike Blowers	.50	.23
110	Tom Browning	.25	.11
111	Greg Vaughn	6.00	2.70
112	Oddibe McDowell	.25	.11
113	Gary Ward	.25	.11
114	Jay Buhner	1.50	.70
115	Eric Show	.25	.11
116	Bryan Harvey	.25	.11
117	Andy Van Slyke	.50	.23
118	Jeff Ballard	.25	.11
119	Barry Lyons	.25	.11
120	Kevin Mitchell	.25	.11
121	Mike Gallego	.25	.11
122	Dave Smith	.25	.11
123	Kirby Puckett	2.50	1.10
124	Jerome Walton	.50	.23
125	Bo Jackson	.50	.23
126	Harold Baines	.50	.23
127	Scott Bankhead	.25	.11
128	Ozzie Guillen	.25	.11
129	Jose Oquendo UER (League misspelled as Legue)	.25	.11
130	John Dopson	.25	.11
131	Charlie Hayes	.25	.11
132	Fred McGriff	1.50	.70
133	Chet Lemon	.25	.11
134	Gary Carter	1.50	.70
135	Rafael Ramirez	.25	.11
136	Shane Mack	.25	.11
137	Mark Grace UER (Card back has OB:L, should be B:L)	1.50	.70
138	Phil Bradley	.25	.11
139	Dwight Gooden	.50	.23
140	Harold Reynolds	.25	.11
141	Scott Fletcher	.25	.11
142	Ozzie Smith	2.00	.90
143	Mike Greenwell	.25	.11
144	Pete Smith	.25	.11
145	Mark Gubicza	.25	.11
146	Chris Sabo	.25	.11

147	Ramon Martinez	1.00	.45
148	Tim Leary	.25	.11
149	Randy Myers	.50	.23
150	Jody Reed	.25	.11
151	Bruce Ruffin	.25	.11
152	Jeff Russell	.25	.11
153	Doug Jones	.25	.11
154	Tony Gwynn	4.00	1.80
155	Mark Langston	.25	.11
156	Mitch Williams	.25	.11
157	Gary Sheffield	2.50	1.10
158	Tom Henke	.25	.11
159	Oil Can Boyd	.25	.11
160	Rickey Henderson	2.00	.90
161	Bill Doran	.25	.11
162	Chuck Finley	.50	.23
163	Jeff King	.25	.11
164	Nick Esasky	.25	.11
165	Cecil Fielder	.50	.23
166	Dave Valle	.25	.11
167	Robin Ventura	2.50	1.10
168	Jim Deshaies	.25	.11
169	Juan Berenguer	.25	.11
170	Craig Worthington	.25	.11
171	Gregg Jefferies	.50	.23
172	Will Clark	1.50	.70
173	Kirk Gibson	.50	.23
174	Carlton Fisk CL	1.00	.45
175	Bobby Thigpen	.25	.11
176	John Tudor	.25	.11
177	Andre Dawson	1.50	.70
178	George Brett	3.00	1.35
179	Steve Buechele	.25	.11
180	Joey Belle	15.00	6.75
181	Eddie Murray	1.50	.70
182	Bob Geren	.25	.11
183	Rob Murphy	.25	.11
184	Tom Herr	.25	.11
185	George Bell	.50	.23
186	Spike Owen	.25	.11
187	Cory Snyder	.25	.11
188	Fred Lynn	.25	.11
189	Eric Davis	.50	.23
190	Dave Parker	.50	.23
191	Jeff Blauser	.25	.11
192	Matt Nokes	.25	.11
193	Delino DeShields	1.50	.70
194	Scott Sanderson	.25	.11
195	Lance Parrish	.25	.11
196	Bobby Bonilla	.50	.23
197	Cal Ripken UER (Reisterstown, should be Reisterstown)	6.00	2.70
198	Kevin McReynolds	.25	.11
199	Robby Thompson	.25	.11
200	Tim Belcher	.25	.11
201	Jesse Barfield	.25	.11
202	Mariano Duncan	.25	.11
203	Bill Spiers	.25	.11
204	Frank White	.50	.23
205	Julio Franco	.25	.11
206	Greg Swindell	.25	.11
207	Benito Santiago	.25	.11
208	Johnny Ray	.25	.11
209	Gary Redus	.25	.11
210	Jeff Parrett	.25	.11
211	Jimmy Key	.25	.11
212	Tim Raines	.50	.23
213	Carney Lansford	.25	.11
214	Gerald Young	.25	.11
215	Gene Larkin	.25	.11
216	Dan Plesac	.25	.11
217	Lonnie Smith	.25	.11
218	Alan Trammell	1.00	.45
219	Jeffrey Leonard	.25	.11
220	Sammy Sosa	80.00	36.00
221	Todd Zeile	.50	.23
222	Bill Landrum	.25	.11
223	Mike Devereaux	.25	.11
224	Mike Marshall	.25	.11
225	Jose Uribe	.25	.11
226	Juan Samuel	.25	.11
227	Mel Hall	.25	.11
228	Kent Hrbek	.50	.23
229	Shawon Dunston	.25	.11
230	Kevin Seitzer	.25	.11
231	Pete Incaviglia	.25	.11
232	Sandy Alomar Jr.	.50	.23
233	Bip Roberts	.25	.11
234	Scott Terry	.25	.11
235	Dwight Evans	.50	.23
236	Ricky Jordan	.25	.11
237	Jon Olerud	6.00	2.70
238	Zane Smith	.25	.11
239	Walt Weiss	.25	.11
240	Alvaro Espinoza	.25	.11
241	Billy Hatcher	.25	.11
242	Paul Molitor	1.50	.70
243	Dale Murphy	1.50	.70
244	Dave Bergman	.25	.11
245	Ken Griffey Jr.	30.00	13.50
246	Ed Whitson	.25	.11
247	Kirk McCaskill	.25	.11
248	Jay Bell	.50	.23
249	Ben McDonald	.50	.23
250	Darryl Strawberry	.50	.23
251	Brett Butler	.50	.23
252	Terry Steinbach	.25	.11
253	Ken Caminiti	2.50	1.10
254	Dan Gladden	.25	.11
255	Dwight Smith	.25	.11
256	Kurt Stillwell	.25	.11
257	Ruben Sierra	.25	.11
258	Mike Schooler	.25	.11
259	Lance Johnson	.25	.11
260	Terry Pendleton	.50	.23
261	Ellis Burks	1.00	.45
262	Len Dykstra	.25	.11
263	Mookie Wilson	.25	.11
264	Nolan Ryan CL UER (No TM after Ranger logo)	1.50	.70
265	Nolan Ryan (No Hit King)	3.00	1.35
266	Brian DuBois	.25	.11
267	Don Robinson	.25	.11
268	Glenn Wilson	.25	.11
269	Kevin Tapani	.50	.23
270	Marvell Wynne	.25	.11
271	Bill Ripken	.25	.11
272	Howard Johnson	.25	.11
273	Brian Holman	.25	.11
274	Dan Pasqua	.25	.11
275	Ken Dayley	.25	.11
276	Jeff Reardon	.50	.23
277	Jim Presley	.25	.11
278	Jim Eisenreich	.25	.11
279	Danny Jackson	.25	.11
280	Orel Hershiser	.50	.23
281	Andy Hawkins	.25	.11
282	Jose Rijo	.25	.11
283	Luis Rivera	.25	.11
284	John Kruk	.50	.23
285	Jeff Huson	.25	.11
286	Joel Skinner	.25	.11
287	Jack Clark	.50	.23
288	Chili Davis	.25	.11
289	Joe Girardi	1.00	.45
290	B.J. Surhoff	.50	.23
291	Luis Sojo	.25	.11
292	Tom Foley	.25	.11
293	Mike Moore	.25	.11
294	Ken Oberkfell	.25	.11
295	Luis Polonia	.25	.11
296	Doug Drabek	.25	.11
297	Dave Justice	5.00	2.20
298	Paul Gibson	.25	.11
299	Edgar Martinez	1.50	.70
300	Frank Thomas UER (No B in front of birthdate)	40.00	18.00
301	Eric Yelding	.25	.11
302	Greg Gagne	.25	.11
303	Brad Komminsk	.25	.11
304	Ron Darling	.25	.11
305	Kevin Bass	.25	.11
306	Jeff Hamilton	.25	.11
307	Ron Karkovice	.25	.11
308	Milt Thompson UER (Ray Lankford pictured on card back)	1.50	.70
309	Mike Harkey	.25	.11
310	Mel Stottlemyre Jr.	.25	.11
311	Kenny Rogers	.50	.23
312	Mitch Webster	.25	.11
313	Kal Daniels	.25	.11
314	Matt Nokes	.25	.11
315	Dennis Lamp	.25	.11
316	Ken Howell	.25	.11
317	Glenallen Hill	.25	.11
318	Dave Martinez	.25	.11
319	Chris James	.25	.11
320	Mike Pagliarulo	.25	.11
321	Hal Morris	.25	.11
322	Rob Deer	.25	.11
323	Greg Olson	.25	.11
324	Tony Phillips	.25	.11
325	Larry Walker	20.00	9.00
326	Ron Hassey	.25	.11
327	Jack Howell	.25	.11
328	John Smiley	.25	.11
329	Steve Finley	1.50	.70
330	Dave Magadan	.25	.11
331	Greg Litton	.25	.11
332	Mickey Hatcher	.25	.11
333	Lee Guetterman	.25	.11
334	Norm Charlton	.25	.11
335	Edgar Diaz	.25	.11
336	Willie Wilson	.25	.11
337	Bobby Witt	.25	.11
338	Candy Maldonado	.25	.11
339	Craig Lefferts	.25	.11
340	Dante Bichette	2.00	.90
341	Wally Backman	.25	.11
342	Dennis Cook	.25	.11
343	Pat Borders	.25	.11
344	Wallace Johnson	.25	.11
345	Willie Randolph	.50	.23
346	Danny Darwin	.25	.11
347	Al Newman	.25	.11
348	Mark Knudson	.25	.11
349	Joe Boever	.25	.11
350	Larry Sheets	.25	.11
351	Mike Jackson	.50	.23
352	Wayne Edwards	.25	.11
353	Bernard Gilkey	2.00	.90
354	Don Slaught	.25	.11
355	Joe Orsulak	.25	.11
356	John Franco	.50	.23
357	Jeff Brantley	.25	.11
358	Mike Morgan	.25	.11
359	Deion Sanders	2.00	.90
360	Terry Leach	.25	.11
361	Les Lancaster	.25	.11
362	Storm Davis	.25	.11
363	Scott Coolbaugh	.25	.11
364	Ozzie Smith CL	1.00	.45
365	Cecilio Guante	.25	.11
366	Joey Cora	.50	.23
367	Willie McGee	.50	.23
368	Jerry Reed	.25	.11
369	Darren Daulton	.25	.11
370	Manny Lee	.25	.11
371	Mark Gardner	.25	.11
372	Rick Honeycutt	.25	.11
373	Steve Balboni	.25	.11
374	Jack Armstrong	.25	.11
375	Charlie O'Brien	.25	.11
376	Ron Gant	.50	.23
377	Lloyd Moseby	.25	.11
378	Gene Harris	.25	.11
379	Joe Carter	.50	.23
380	Scott Bailes	.25	.11
381	R.J. Reynolds	.25	.11
382	Bob Melvin	.25	.11
383	Tim Teufel	.25	.11
384	John Burkett	.25	.11
385	Felix Jose	.25	.11
386	Larry Andersen	.25	.11
387	David West	.25	.11
388	Luis Salazar	.25	.11
389	Mike Macfarlane	.25	.11
390	Charlie Hough	.50	.23
391	Greg Briley	.25	.11
392	Donn Pall	.25	.11
393	Bryn Smith	.25	.11
394	Carlos Quintana	.25	.11
395	Steve Lake	.25	.11
396	Mark Whiten	.25	.11

❑ 397 Edwin Nunez	.25	.11
❑ 398 Rick Parker	.25	.11
❑ 399 Mark Portugal	.25	.11
❑ 400 Roy Smith	.25	.11
❑ 401 Hector Villanueva	.25	.11
❑ 402 Bob Milacki	.25	.11
❑ 403 Alejandro Pena	.25	.11
❑ 404 Scott Bradley	.25	.11
❑ 405 Ron Kittle	.25	.11
❑ 406 Bob Tewksbury	.25	.11
❑ 407 Wes Gardner	.25	.11
❑ 408 Ernie Whitt	.25	.11
❑ 409 Terry Shumpert	.25	.11
❑ 410 Tim Layana	.25	.11
❑ 411 Chris Gwynn	.25	.11
❑ 412 Jeff D. Robinson	.25	.11
❑ 413 Scott Scudder	.25	.11
❑ 414 Kevin Romine	.25	.11
❑ 415 Jose DeJesus	.25	.11
❑ 416 Mike Jeffcoat	.25	.11
❑ 417 Rudy Seanez	.25	.11
❑ 418 Mike Dunne	.25	.11
❑ 419 Dick Schofield	.25	.11
❑ 420 Steve Wilson	.25	.11
❑ 421 Bill Krueger	.25	.11
❑ 422 Junior Felix	.25	.11
❑ 423 Drew Hall	.25	.11
❑ 424 Curt Young	.25	.11
❑ 425 Franklin Stubbs	.25	.11
❑ 426 Dave Winfield	1.50	.70
❑ 427 Rick Reed	2.00	.90
❑ 428 Charlie Leibrandt	.25	.11
❑ 429 Jeff M. Robinson	.25	.11
❑ 430 Erik Hanson	.25	.11
❑ 431 Barry Jones	.25	.11
❑ 432 Alex Trevino	.25	.11
❑ 433 John Moses	.25	.11
❑ 434 Dave Johnson	.25	.11
❑ 435 Mackey Sasser	.25	.11
❑ 436 Rick Leach	.25	.11
❑ 437 Lenny Harris	.25	.11
❑ 438 Carlos Martinez	.25	.11
❑ 439 Rex Hudler	.25	.11
❑ 440 Domingo Ramos	.25	.11
❑ 441 Gerald Perry	.25	.11
❑ 442 Jeff Russell	.25	.11
❑ 443 Carlos Baerga	1.50	.70
❑ 444 Will Clark CL	.50	.23
❑ 445 Stan Javier	.25	.11
❑ 446 Kevin Maas	.50	.23
❑ 447 Tom Brunansky	.25	.11
❑ 448 Carmelo Martinez	.25	.11
❑ 449 Willie Blair	.50	.23
❑ 450 Andres Galarraga	1.50	.70
❑ 451 Bud Black	.25	.11
❑ 452 Greg W. Harris	.25	.11
❑ 453 Joe Oliver	.25	.11
❑ 454 Greg Brock	.25	.11
❑ 455 Jeff Treadway	.25	.11
❑ 456 Lance McCullers	.25	.11
❑ 457 Dave Schmidt	.25	.11
❑ 458 Todd Burns	.25	.11
❑ 459 Max Venable	.25	.11
❑ 460 Neal Heaton	.25	.11
❑ 461 Mark Williamson	.25	.11
❑ 462 Keith Miller	.25	.11
❑ 463 Mike LaCoss	.25	.11
❑ 464 Jose Offerman	4.00	1.80
❑ 465 Jim Leyritz	2.00	.90
❑ 466 Glenn Braggs	.25	.11
❑ 467 Ron Robinson	.25	.11
❑ 468 Mark Davis	.25	.11
❑ 469 Gary Pettis	.25	.11
❑ 470 Keith Hernandez	.50	.23
❑ 471 Dennis Rasmussen	.25	.11
❑ 472 Mark Eichhorn	.25	.11
❑ 473 Ted Power	.25	.11
❑ 474 Terry Mulholland	.25	.11
❑ 475 Todd Stottlemyre	.50	.23
❑ 476 Jerry Goff	.25	.11
❑ 477 Gene Nelson	.25	.11
❑ 478 Rich Gedman	.25	.11
❑ 479 Brian Harper	.25	.11
❑ 480 Mike Felder	.25	.11
❑ 481 Steve Avery	1.50	.70
❑ 482 Jack Morris	.50	.23

❑ 483 Randy Johnson	5.00	2.20
❑ 484 Scott Radinsky	.25	.11
❑ 485 Jose DeLeon	.25	.11
❑ 486 Stan Belinda	.25	.11
❑ 487 Brian Holton	.25	.11
❑ 488 Mark Carreon	.25	.11
❑ 489 Trevor Wilson	.25	.11
❑ 490 Mike Sharperson	.25	.11
❑ 491 Alan Mills	.25	.11
❑ 492 John Candelaria	.25	.11
❑ 493 Paul Assenmacher	.25	.11
❑ 494 Steve Crawford	.25	.11
❑ 495 Brad Arnsberg	.25	.11
❑ 496 Sergio Valdez	.25	.11
❑ 497 Mark Parent	.25	.11
❑ 498 Tom Pagnozzi	.25	.11
❑ 499 Greg A. Harris	.25	.11
❑ 500 Randy Ready	.25	.11
❑ 501 Duane Ward	.25	.11
❑ 502 Nelson Santovenia	.25	.11
❑ 503 Joe Klink	.25	.11
❑ 504 Eric Plunk	.25	.11
❑ 505 Jeff Reed	.25	.11
❑ 506 Ted Higuera	.25	.11
❑ 507 Joe Hesketh	.25	.11
❑ 508 Dan Petry	.25	.11
❑ 509 Matt Young	.25	.11
❑ 510 Jerald Clark	.25	.11
❑ 511 John Orton	.25	.11
❑ 512 Scott Ruskin	.25	.11
❑ 513 Chris Hoiles	1.50	.70
❑ 514 Daryl Boston	.25	.11
❑ 515 Francisco Oliveras	.25	.11
❑ 516 Ozzie Canseco	.25	.11
❑ 517 Xavier Hernandez	.25	.11
❑ 518 Fred Manrique	.25	.11
❑ 519 Shawn Boskie	.25	.11
❑ 520 Jeff Montgomery	.50	.23
❑ 521 Jack Daugherty	.25	.11
❑ 522 Keith Comstock	.25	.11
❑ 523 Greg Hibbard	.25	.11
❑ 524 Lee Smith	.50	.23
❑ 525 Dana Kiecker	.25	.11
❑ 526 Darrel Akerfelds	.25	.11
❑ 527 Greg Myers	.25	.11
❑ 528 Ryne Sandberg CL	1.50	.70

1991 Leaf Previews

DAVE JUSTICE 8F

	MINT	NRMT
COMPLETE SET (26)	30.00	13.50
COMMON CARD (1-26)	1.00	.45
FOUR PER DONRUSS HOBBY FACT.SET		

❑ 1 Dave Justice	3.00	1.35
❑ 2 Ryne Sandberg	4.00	1.80
❑ 3 Barry Larkin	3.00	1.35
❑ 4 Craig Biggio	3.00	1.35
❑ 5 Ramon Martinez	1.50	.70
❑ 6 Tim Wallach	1.00	.45
❑ 7 Dwight Gooden	1.50	.70
❑ 8 Len Dykstra	1.50	.70
❑ 9 Barry Bonds	4.00	1.80
❑ 10 Ray Lankford	3.00	1.35
❑ 11 Tony Gwynn	8.00	3.60
❑ 12 Will Clark	3.00	1.35
❑ 13 Leo Gomez	1.00	.45

❑ 14 Wade Boggs	3.00	1.35
❑ 15 Chuck Finley UER	1.00	.45
(Position on card		
back is First Base)		
❑ 16 Carlton Fisk	3.00	1.35
❑ 17 Sandy Alomar Jr.	1.50	.70
❑ 18 Cecil Fielder	1.50	.70
❑ 19 Bo Jackson	1.50	.70
❑ 20 Paul Molitor	3.00	1.35
❑ 21 Kirby Puckett	5.00	2.20
❑ 22 Don Mattingly	6.00	2.70
❑ 23 Rickey Henderson	4.00	1.80
❑ 24 Tino Martinez	3.00	1.35
❑ 25 Nolan Ryan	12.00	5.50
❑ 26 Dave Stieb	1.00	.45

1991 Leaf

JOSE CANSECO 8F

	MINT	NRMT
COMPLETE SET (528)	15.00	6.75
COMPLETE SERIES 1 (264)	5.00	2.20
COMPLETE SERIES 2 (264)	10.00	4.50
COMMON CARD (1-528)	.10	.05
MINOR STARS	.20	.09
UNLISTED STARS	.40	.18

❑ 1 The Leaf Card	.10	.05
❑ 2 Kurt Stillwell	.10	.05
❑ 3 Bobby Witt	.10	.05
❑ 4 Tony Phillips	.10	.05
❑ 5 Scott Garrelts	.10	.05
❑ 6 Greg Swindell	.10	.05
❑ 7 Billy Ripken	.10	.05
❑ 8 Dave Martinez	.10	.05
❑ 9 Kelly Gruber	.10	.05
❑ 10 Juan Samuel	.10	.05
❑ 11 Brian Holman	.10	.05
❑ 12 Craig Biggio	.40	.18
❑ 13 Lonnie Smith	.10	.05
❑ 14 Ron Robinson	.10	.05
❑ 15 Mike LaValliere	.10	.05
❑ 16 Mark Davis	.10	.05
❑ 17 Jack Daugherty	.10	.05
❑ 18 Mike Henneman	.10	.05
❑ 19 Mike Greenwell	.10	.05
❑ 20 Dave Magadan	.10	.05
❑ 21 Mark Williamson	.10	.05
❑ 22 Marquis Grissom	.40	.18
❑ 23 Pat Borders	.10	.05
❑ 24 Mike Scioscia	.10	.05
❑ 25 Shawon Dunston	.10	.05
❑ 26 Randy Bush	.10	.05
❑ 27 John Smoltz	.40	.18
❑ 28 Chuck Crim	.10	.05
❑ 29 Don Slaught	.10	.05
❑ 30 Mike Macfarlane	.10	.05
❑ 31 Wally Joyner	.30	.14
❑ 32 Pat Combs	.10	.05
❑ 33 Tony Pena	.10	.05
❑ 34 Howard Johnson	.10	.05
❑ 35 Lee Gomez	.10	.05
❑ 36 Spike Owen	.10	.05
❑ 37 Eric Davis	.30	.14
❑ 38 Roberto Kelly	.10	.05
❑ 39 Jerome Walton	.10	.05
❑ 40 Shane Mack	.10	.05
❑ 41 Kent Mercker	.10	.05

42	B.J. Surhoff	.30	.14
43	Jerry Browne	.10	.05
44	Lee Smith	.20	.09
45	Chuck Finley	.30	.14
46	Terry Mulholland	.10	.05
47	Tom Bolton	.10	.05
48	Tom Herr	.10	.05
49	Jim Deshaies	.10	.05
50	Walt Weiss	.10	.05
51	Hal Morris	.10	.05
52	Lee Guetterman	.10	.05
53	Paul Assenmacher	.10	.05
54	Brian Harper	.10	.05
55	Paul Gibson	.10	.05
56	John Burkett	.10	.05
57	Doug Jones	.10	.05
58	Jose Oquendo	.10	.05
59	Dick Schofield	.10	.05
60	Dickie Thon	.10	.05
61	Ramon Martinez	.30	.14
62	Jay Buhner	.40	.18
63	Mark Portugal	.10	.05
64	Bob Welch	.10	.05
65	Chris Sabo	.10	.05
66	Chuck Cary	.10	.05
67	Mark Langston	.10	.05
68	Joe Boever	.10	.05
69	Jody Reed	.10	.05
70	Alejandro Pena	.10	.05
71	Jeff King	.10	.05
72	Tom Pagnozzi	.10	.05
73	Joe Oliver	.10	.05
74	Mike Witt	.10	.05
75	Hector Villanueva	.10	.05
76	Dan Gladden	.10	.05
77	Dave Justice	.40	.18
78	Mike Gallego	.10	.05
79	Tom Candiotti	.10	.05
80	Ozzie Smith	.50	.23
81	Luis Polonia	.10	.05
82	Randy Ready	.10	.05
83	Greg A. Harris	.10	.05
84	David Justice CL	.20	.09
85	Kevin Mitchell	.10	.05
86	Mark McLemore	.10	.05
87	Terry Steinbach	.30	.14
88	Tom Browning	.10	.05
89	Matt Nokes	.10	.05
90	Mike Harkey	.10	.05
91	Omar Vizquel	.40	.18
92	Dave Bergman	.10	.05
93	Matt Williams	.40	.18
94	Steve Olin	.10	.05
95	Craig Wilson	.10	.05
96	Dave Stieb	.10	.05
97	Ruben Sierra	.10	.05
98	Jay Howell	.10	.05
99	Scott Bradley	.10	.05
100	Eric Yelding	.10	.05
101	Rickey Henderson	.50	.23
102	Jeff Reed	.10	.05
103	Jimmy Key	.30	.14
104	Terry Shumpert	.10	.05
105	Kenny Rogers	.10	.05
106	Cecil Fielder	.30	.14
107	Robby Thompson	.10	.05
108	Alex Cole	.10	.05
109	Randy Milligan	.10	.05
110	Andres Galarraga	.40	.18
111	Bill Spiers	.10	.05
112	Kal Daniels	.10	.05
113	Henry Cotto	.10	.05
114	Casey Candaele	.10	.05
115	Jeff Blauser	.10	.05
116	Robin Yount	.40	.18
117	Ben McDonald	.10	.05
118	Bret Saberhagen	.20	.09
119	Juan Gonzalez	1.50	.70
120	Lou Whitaker	.30	.14
121	Ellis Burks	.20	.09
122	Charlie O'Brien	.10	.05
123	John Smiley	.10	.05
124	Tim Burke	.10	.05
125	John Olerud	.30	.14
126	Eddie Murray	.40	.18
127	Greg Maddux	1.00	.45
128	Kevin Tapani	.10	.05
129	Ron Gant	.30	.14
130	Jay Bell	.30	.14
131	Chris Hoiles	.10	.05
132	Tom Gordon	.10	.05
133	Kevin Seitzer	.10	.05
134	Jeff Huson	.10	.05
135	Jerry Don Gleaton	.10	.05
136	Jeff Brantley UER (Photo actually Rick Leach on back)	.10	.05
137	Felix Fermin	.10	.05
138	Mike Devereaux	.10	.05
139	Delino DeShields	.20	.09
140	David Wells	.20	.09
141	Tim Crews	.10	.05
142	Erik Hanson	.10	.05
143	Mark Davidson	.10	.05
144	Tommy Gregg	.10	.05
145	Jim Gantner	.10	.05
146	Jose Lind	.10	.05
147	Danny Tartabull	.20	.09
148	Geno Petralli	.10	.05
149	Travis Fryman	.40	.18
150	Tim Naehring	.10	.05
151	Kevin McReynolds	.10	.05
152	Joe Orsulak	.10	.05
153	Steve Frey	.10	.05
154	Duane Ward	.10	.05
155	Stan Javier	.10	.05
156	Damon Berryhill	.10	.05
157	Gene Larkin	.10	.05
158	Greg Olson	.10	.05
159	Mark Knudson	.10	.05
160	Carmelo Martinez	.10	.05
161	Storm Davis	.10	.05
162	Jim Abbott	.20	.09
163	Len Dykstra	.30	.14
164	Tom Brunansky	.10	.05
165	Dwight Gooden	.30	.14
166	Jose Mesa	.10	.05
167	Oil Can Boyd	.10	.05
168	Barry Larkin	.40	.18
169	Scott Sanderson	.10	.05
170	Mark Grace	.40	.18
171	Mark Guthrie	.10	.05
172	Tom Glavine	.40	.18
173	Gary Sheffield	.40	.18
174	Roger Clemens CL	.40	.18
175	Chris James	.10	.05
176	Milt Thompson	.10	.05
177	Donnie Hill	.10	.05
178	Wes Chamberlain	.10	.05
179	John Marzano	.10	.05
180	Frank Viola	.10	.05
181	Eric Anthony	.10	.05
182	Jose Canseco	.50	.23
183	Scott Scudder	.10	.05
184	Dave Elland	.10	.05
185	Luis Salazar	.10	.05
186	Pedro Munoz	.10	.05
187	Steve Searcy	.10	.05
188	Don Robinson	.10	.05
189	Sandy Alomar Jr.	.20	.09
190	Jose DeLeon	.10	.05
191	Jim Orton	.10	.05
192	Darren Daulton	.30	.14
193	Mike Morgan	.10	.05
194	Greg Briley	.10	.05
195	Karl Rhodes	.10	.05
196	Harold Baines	.20	.09
197	Bill Doran	.10	.05
198	Alvaro Espinoza	.10	.05
199	Kirk McCaskill	.10	.05
200	Jose DeJesus	.10	.05
201	Jack Clark	.20	.09
202	Daryl Boston	.10	.05
203	Randy Tomlin	.10	.05
204	Pedro Guerrero	.10	.05
205	Billy Hatcher	.10	.05
206	Tim Leary	.10	.05
207	Ryne Sandberg	.50	.23
208	Kirby Puckett	.60	.25
209	Charlie Leibrandt	.10	.05
210	Rick Honeycutt	.10	.05
211	Joel Skinner	.10	.05
212	Rex Hudler	.10	.05
213	Bryan Harvey	.10	.05
214	Charlie Hayes	.10	.05
215	Matt Young	.10	.05
216	Terry Kennedy	.10	.05
217	Carl Nichols	.10	.05
218	Mike Moore	.10	.05
219	Paul O'Neill	.30	.14
220	Steve Sax	.10	.05
221	Shawn Boskie	.10	.05
222	Rich DeLucia	.10	.05
223	Lloyd Moseby	.10	.05
224	Mike Kingery	.10	.05
225	Carlos Baerga	.30	.14
226	Bryn Smith	.10	.05
227	Todd Stottlemyre	.20	.09
228	Julio Franco	.10	.05
229	Jim Gott	.10	.05
230	Mike Schooler	.10	.05
231	Steve Finley	.40	.18
232	Dave Henderson	.10	.05
233	Luis Quinones	.10	.05
234	Mark Whiten	.10	.05
235	Brian McRae	.20	.09
236	Rich Gossage	.10	.05
237	Rob Deer	.10	.05
238	Will Clark	.40	.18
239	Albert Belle	.50	.23
240	Bob Melvin	.10	.05
241	Larry Walker	.60	.25
242	Dante Bichette	.40	.18
243	Orel Hershiser	.30	.14
244	Pete O'Brien	.10	.05
245	Pete Harnisch	.10	.05
246	Jeff Treadway	.10	.05
247	Julio Machado	.10	.05
248	Dave Johnson	.10	.05
249	Kirk Gibson	.30	.14
250	Kevin Brown	.30	.14
251	Milt Cuyler	.10	.05
252	Jeff Reardon	.20	.09
253	David Cone	.30	.14
254	Gary Redus	.10	.05
255	Junior Noboa	.10	.05
256	Greg Myers	.10	.05
257	Dennis Cook	.10	.05
258	Joe Girardi	.30	.14
259	Allan Anderson	.10	.05
260	Paul Marak	.10	.05
261	Barry Bonds	.50	.23
262	Juan Bell	.10	.05
263	Russ Morman	.10	.05
264	George Brett CL	.40	.18
265	Jerald Clark	.10	.05
266	Dwight Evans	.30	.14
267	Roberto Alomar	.40	.18
268	Danny Jackson	.10	.05
269	Brian Downing	.10	.05
270	John Candelaria	.10	.05
271	Robin Ventura	.40	.18
272	Gerald Perry	.10	.05
273	Wade Boggs	.40	.18
274	Dennis Martinez	.30	.14
275	Andy Benes	.20	.09
276	Tony Fossas	.10	.05
277	Franklin Stubbs	.10	.05
278	John Kruk	.30	.14
279	Kevin Gross	.10	.05
280	Von Hayes	.10	.05
281	Frank Thomas	1.50	.70
282	Rob Dibble	.10	.05
283	Mel Hall	.10	.05
284	Rick Mahler	.10	.05
285	Dennis Eckersley	.20	.09
286	Bernard Gilkey	.30	.14
287	Dan Plesac	.10	.05
288	Jason Grimsley	.10	.05
289	Mark Lewis	.10	.05
290	Tony Gwynn	1.00	.45
291	Jeff Russell	.10	.05
292	Curt Schilling	.40	.18
293	Pascual Perez	.10	.05
294	Jack Morris	.30	.14
295	Hubie Brooks	.10	.05
296	Alex Fernandez	.20	.09
297	Harold Reynolds	.10	.05

296	Craig Worthington	.10	.05
299	Willie Wilson	.10	.05
300	Mike Maddux	.10	.05
301	Dave Righetti	.10	.05
302	Paul Molitor	.40	.18
303	Gary Gaetti	.20	.09
304	Terry Pendleton	.30	.14
305	Kevin Elster	.10	.05
306	Scott Fletcher	.10	.05
307	Jeff Robinson	.10	.05
308	Jesse Barfield	.10	.05
309	Mike LaCoss	.10	.05
310	Andy Van Slyke	.30	.14
311	Glenallen Hill	.10	.05
312	Bud Black	.10	.05
313	Kent Hrbek	.30	.14
314	Tim Teufel	.10	.05
315	Tony Fernandez	.10	.05
316	Beau Allred	.10	.05
317	Curtis Wilkerson	.10	.05
318	Bill Sampen	.10	.05
319	Randy Johnson	.50	.23
320	Mike Heath	.10	.05
321	Sammy Sosa	2.50	1.10
322	Mickey Tettleton	.30	.14
323	Jose Vizcaino	.10	.05
324	John Candelaria	.10	.05
325	Dave Howard	.10	.05
326	Jose Rijo	.10	.05
327	Todd Zeile	.30	.14
328	Gene Nelson	.10	.05
329	Dwayne Henry	.10	.05
330	Mike Boddicker	.10	.05
331	Ozzie Guillen	.10	.05
332	Sam Horn	.10	.05
333	Wally Whitehurst	.10	.05
334	Dave Parker	.30	.14
335	George Brett	.75	.35
336	Bobby Thigpen	.10	.05
337	Ed Whitson	.10	.05
338	Ivan Calderon	.10	.05
339	Mike Pagliarulo	.10	.05
340	Jack McDowell	.10	.05
341	Dana Kiecker	.10	.05
342	Fred McGriff	.40	.18
343	Mark Lee	.10	.05
344	Alfredo Griffin	.10	.05
345	Scott Bankhead	.10	.05
346	Darrin Jackson	.10	.05
347	Rafael Palmeiro	.40	.18
348	Steve Farr	.10	.05
349	Hensley Meulens	.10	.05
350	Danny Cox	.10	.05
351	Alan Trammell	.20	.09
352	Edwin Nunez	.10	.05
353	Joe Carter	.20	.09
354	Eric Show	.10	.05
355	Vance Law	.10	.05
356	Jeff Gray	.10	.05
357	Bobby Bonilla	.20	.09
358	Ernest Riles	.10	.05
359	Ron Hassey	.10	.05
360	Willie McGee	.20	.09
361	Mackey Sasser	.10	.05
362	Glenn Braggs	.10	.05
363	Mario Diaz	.10	.05
364	Barry Bonds CL	.40	.18
365	Kevin Bass	.10	.05
366	Pete Incaviglia	.10	.05
367	Luis Sojo UER	.10	.05
	(1989 stats interspersed with 1990's)		
368	Lance Parrish	.10	.05
369	Mark Leonard	.10	.05
370	Heathcliff Slocumb	.40	.18
371	Jimmy Jones	.10	.05
372	Ken Griffey Jr.	3.00	1.35
373	Chris Hammond	.10	.05
374	Chili Davis	.30	.14
375	Joey Cora	.10	.05
376	Ken Hill	.10	.05
377	Darryl Strawberry	.30	.14
378	Ron Darling	.10	.05
379	Sid Bream	.10	.05
380	Bill Swift	.10	.05
381	Shawn Abner	.10	.05
382	Eric King	.10	.05
383	Mickey Morandini	.10	.05
384	Carlton Fisk	.40	.18
385	Steve Lake	.10	.05
386	Mike Jeffcoat	.10	.05
387	Darren Holmes	.10	.05
388	Tim Wallach	.10	.05
389	George Bell	.10	.05
390	Craig Lefferts	.10	.05
391	Ernie Whitt	.10	.05
392	Felix Jose	.10	.05
393	Kevin Maas	.10	.05
394	Devon White	.10	.05
395	Otis Nixon	.30	.14
396	Chuck Knoblauch	.40	.18
397	Scott Coolbaugh	.10	.05
398	Glenn Davis	.10	.05
399	Manny Lee	.10	.05
400	Andre Dawson	.40	.18
401	Scott Chiamparino	.10	.05
402	Bill Gullickson	.10	.05
403	Lance Johnson	.10	.05
404	Juan Agosto	.10	.05
405	Danny Darwin	.10	.05
406	Barry Jones	.10	.05
407	Larry Andersen	.10	.05
408	Luis Rivera	.10	.05
409	Jaime Navarro	.10	.05
410	Roger McDowell	.10	.05
411	Brett Butler	.30	.14
412	Dale Murphy	.40	.18
413	Tim Raines UER	.20	.09
	(Listed as hitting .500 in 1980, should be .050)		
414	Norm Charlton	.10	.05
415	Greg Cadaret	.10	.05
416	Chris Nabholz	.10	.05
417	Dave Stewart	.30	.14
418	Rich Gedman	.10	.05
419	Willie Randolph	.30	.14
420	Mitch Williams	.10	.05
421	Brook Jacoby	.10	.05
422	Greg W. Harris	.10	.05
423	Nolan Ryan	1.50	.70
424	Dave Rohde	.10	.05
425	Don Mattingly	.75	.35
426	Greg Gagne	.10	.05
427	Vince Coleman	.10	.05
428	Dan Pasqua	.10	.05
429	Alvin Davis	.10	.05
430	Cal Ripken	1.50	.70
431	Jamie Quirk	.10	.05
432	Benito Santiago	.10	.05
433	Jose Uribe	.10	.05
434	Candy Maldonado	.10	.05
435	Junior Felix	.10	.05
436	Deion Sanders	.20	.09
437	John Franco	.20	.09
438	Greg Hibbard	.10	.05
439	Floyd Bannister	.10	.05
440	Steve Howe	.10	.05
441	Steve Decker	.10	.05
442	Vicente Palacios	.10	.05
443	Pat Tabler	.10	.05
444	Darryl Strawberry CL	.30	.14
445	Mike Felder	.10	.05
446	Al Newman	.10	.05
447	Chris Donnels	.10	.05
448	Rich Rodriguez	.10	.05
449	Turner Ward	.10	.05
450	Bob Walk	.10	.05
451	Gilberto Reyes	.10	.05
452	Mike Jackson	.20	.09
453	Rafael Belliard	.10	.05
454	Wayne Edwards	.10	.05
455	Andy Allanson	.10	.05
456	Dave Smith	.10	.05
457	Gary Carter	.40	.18
458	Warren Cromartie	.10	.05
459	Jack Armstrong	.10	.05
460	Bob Tewksbury	.10	.05
461	Joe Klink	.10	.05
462	Xavier Hernandez	.10	.05
463	Scott Radinsky	.10	.05
464	Jeff Robinson	.10	.05
465	Gregg Jefferies	.10	.05
466	Denny Neagle	.40	.18
467	Carmelo Martinez	.10	.05
468	Donn Pall	.10	.05
469	Bruce Hurst	.10	.05
470	Eric Bullock	.10	.05
471	Rick Aguilera	.30	.14
472	Charlie Hough	.20	.09
473	Carlos Quintana	.10	.05
474	Marty Barrett	.10	.05
475	Kevin D. Brown	.10	.05
476	Bobby Ojeda	.10	.05
477	Edgar Martinez	.40	.18
478	Bip Roberts	.10	.05
479	Mike Flanagan	.10	.05
480	John Habyan	.10	.05
481	Larry Casian	.10	.05
482	Wally Backman	.10	.05
483	Doug Dascenzo	.10	.05
484	Rick Dempsey	.10	.05
485	Ed Sprague	.10	.05
486	Steve Chitren	.10	.05
487	Mark McGwire	2.00	.90
488	Roger Clemens	1.00	.45
489	Orlando Merced	.10	.05
490	Rene Gonzales	.10	.05
491	Mike Stanton	.10	.05
492	Al Osuna	.10	.05
493	Rick Cerone	.10	.05
494	Mariano Duncan	.10	.05
495	Zane Smith	.10	.05
496	John Morris	.10	.05
497	Frank Tanana	.10	.05
498	Junior Ortiz	.10	.05
499	Dave Winfield	.40	.18
500	Gary Varsho	.10	.05
501	Chico Walker	.10	.05
502	Ken Caminiti	.40	.18
503	Ken Griffey Sr.	.20	.09
504	Randy Myers	.20	.09
505	Steve Bedrosian	.10	.05
506	Cory Snyder	.10	.05
507	Cris Carpenter	.10	.05
508	Tim Belcher	.10	.05
509	Jeff Hamilton	.10	.05
510	Steve Avery	.10	.05
511	Dave Valle	.10	.05
512	Tom Lampkin	.10	.05
513	Shawn Hillegas	.10	.05
514	Reggie Jefferson	.30	.14
515	Ron Karkovice	.10	.05
516	Doug Drabek	.10	.05
517	Tom Henke	.10	.05
518	Chris Bosio	.10	.05
519	Gregg Olson	.10	.05
520	Bob Scanlan	.10	.05
521	Alonzo Powell	.10	.05
522	Jeff Ballard	.10	.05
523	Ray Lankford	.40	.18
524	Tommy Greene	.10	.05
525	Mike Timlin	.10	.05
526	Juan Berenguer	.10	.05
527	Scott Erickson	.30	.14
528	Sandy Alomar Jr. CL	.10	.05

1991 Leaf Gold Rookies

	MINT	NRMT
COMPLETE SET (26)	20.00	9.00
COMMON CARD (BC1-BC26)	.50	.23
SEMISTARS	1.00	.45
RANDOM INSERTS IN BOTH SERIES		
BC1 Scott Leius	.50	.23
BC2 Luis Gonzalez	1.50	.70
BC3 Wil Cordero	.50	.23
BC4 Gary Scott	.50	.23
BC5 Willie Banks	.50	.23
BC6 Arthur Rhodes	.75	.35
BC7 Mo Vaughn	3.00	1.35
BC8 Henry Rodriguez	1.50	.70

KIRK DRESSENDORFER P

☐ BC9	Todd Van Poppel	.50	.23
☐ BC10	Reggie Sanders	1.25	.55
☐ BC11	Rico Brogna	1.00	.45
☐ BC12	Mike Mussina	3.00	1.35
☐ BC13	Kirk Dressendorfer	.50	.23
☐ BC14	Jeff Bagwell	5.00	2.20
☐ BC15	Pete Schourek	.75	.35
☐ BC16	Wade Taylor	.50	.23
☐ BC17	Pat Kelly	.50	.23
☐ BC18	Tim Costo	.50	.23
☐ BC19	Roger Salkeld	.50	.23
☐ BC20	Andujar Cedeno	.50	.23
☐ BC21	Ryan Klesko UER	1.50	.70
	(1990 Sumter BA .289;		
	should be .368)		
☐ BC22	Mike Huff	.50	.23
☐ BC23	Anthony Young	.50	.23
☐ BC24	Eddie Zosky	.50	.23
☐ BC25	Nolan Ryan DP UER	1.50	.70
	No Hitter 7		
	(Word other repeated		
	in 7th line)		
☐ BC26	Rickey Henderson DP	.75	.35
	Record Steal		

1992 Leaf Previews

MARK WHITEN RF

		MINT	NRMT
COMPLETE SET (26)		50.00	22.00
COMMON CARD (1-26)		.50	.23
FOUR PER DONRUSS HOBBY FACTORY SET			

☐ 1	Steve Avery	.50	.23
☐ 2	Ryne Sandberg	2.50	1.10
☐ 3	Chris Sabo	.50	.23
☐ 4	Jeff Bagwell	4.00	1.80
☐ 5	Darryl Strawberry	1.00	.45
☐ 6	Bret Barberie	.50	.23
☐ 7	Howard Johnson	.50	.23
☐ 8	John Kruk	1.00	.45
☐ 9	Andy Van Slyke	1.00	.45
☐ 10	Felix Jose	.50	.23
☐ 11	Fred McGriff	1.50	.70
☐ 12	Will Clark	2.00	.90
☐ 13	Cal Ripken	8.00	3.60
☐ 14	Phil Plantier	.50	.23
☐ 15	Lee Stevens	1.00	.45
☐ 16	Frank Thomas	5.00	2.20
☐ 17	Mark Whiten	.50	.23
☐ 18	Cecil Fielder	1.00	.45
☐ 19	George Brett	4.00	1.80

☐ 20	Robin Yount	2.00	.90
☐ 21	Scott Erickson	1.00	.45
☐ 22	Don Mattingly	4.00	1.80
☐ 23	Jose Canseco	2.50	1.10
☐ 24	Ken Griffey Jr.	12.00	5.50
☐ 25	Nolan Ryan	8.00	3.60
☐ 26	Joe Carter	1.00	.45

1992 Leaf

STEVE SAX 2B

	MINT	NRMT
COMPLETE SET (528)	15.00	6.75
COMPLETE SERIES 1 (264)	5.00	2.20
COMPLETE SERIES 2 (264)	10.00	4.50
COMMON CARD (1-528)	.05	.02
MINOR STARS	.15	.07
UNLISTED STARS	.30	.14
COMP.B.GOLD SET (528)	80.00	36.00
COMP.B.GOLD SER.1 (264)	30.00	13.50
COMP.B.GOLD SER.2 (264)	50.00	22.00
COMMON BLACK GOLD (1-528)	.15	.07
*B.GOLD STARS: 2X TO 5X HI COLUMN		
*BLACK GOLD RCs: 1.25X TO 3X HI		
ONE BLACK GOLD IN EVERY PACK		

☐ 1	Jim Abbott	.15	.07
☐ 2	Cal Eldred	.05	.02
☐ 3	Bud Black	.05	.02
☐ 4	Dave Howard	.05	.02
☐ 5	Luis Sojo	.05	.02
☐ 6	Gary Scott	.05	.02
☐ 7	Joe Oliver	.05	.02
☐ 8	Chris Gardner	.05	.02
☐ 9	Sandy Alomar Jr.	.15	.07
☐ 10	Greg W. Harris	.05	.02
☐ 11	Doug Drabek	.05	.02
☐ 12	Darryl Hamilton	.05	.02
☐ 13	Mike Mussina	.50	.23
☐ 14	Kevin Tapani	.05	.02
☐ 15	Ron Gant	.15	.07
☐ 16	Mark McGwire	1.50	.70
☐ 17	Robin Ventura	.15	.07
☐ 18	Pedro Guerrero	.05	.02
☐ 19	Roger Clemens	.75	.35
☐ 20	Steve Farr	.05	.02
☐ 21	Frank Tanana	.05	.02
☐ 22	Joe Hesketh	.05	.02
☐ 23	Erik Hanson	.05	.02
☐ 24	Greg Cadaret	.05	.02
☐ 25	Rex Hudler	.05	.02
☐ 26	Mark Grace	.20	.09
☐ 27	Kelly Gruber	.05	.02
☐ 28	Bill Gullickson	.05	.02
☐ 29	Darryl Strawberry	.15	.07
☐ 30	Dave Smith	.05	.02
☐ 31	Kevin Appier	.15	.07
☐ 32	Steve Chitren	.05	.02
☐ 33	Kevin Gross	.05	.02
☐ 34	Rick Aguilera	.05	.02
☐ 35	Juan Guzman	.05	.02
☐ 36	Joe Orsulak	.05	.02
☐ 37	Tim Raines	.05	.02
☐ 38	Harold Reynolds	.05	.02
☐ 39	Charlie Hough	.05	.02
☐ 40	Tony Phillips	.05	.02
☐ 41	Nolan Ryan	1.25	.55
☐ 42	Vince Coleman	.05	.02
☐ 43	Andy Van Slyke	.15	.07

☐ 44	Tim Burke	.05	.02
☐ 45	Luis Polonia	.05	.02
☐ 46	Tom Browning	.05	.02
☐ 47	Willie McGee	.15	.07
☐ 48	Gary DiSarcina	.05	.02
☐ 49	Mark Lewis	.05	.02
☐ 50	Phil Plantier	.05	.02
☐ 51	Doug Dascenzo	.05	.02
☐ 52	Cal Ripken	1.25	.55
☐ 53	Pedro Munoz	.05	.02
☐ 54	Carlos Hernandez	.05	.02
☐ 55	Jerald Clark	.05	.02
☐ 56	Jeff Brantley	.05	.02
☐ 57	Don Mattingly	.60	.25
☐ 58	Roger McDowell	.05	.02
☐ 59	Steve Avery	.05	.02
☐ 60	John Olerud	.15	.07
☐ 61	Bill Gullickson	.05	.02
☐ 62	Juan Gonzalez	.75	.35
☐ 63	Felix Jose	.05	.02
☐ 64	Robin Yount	.30	.14
☐ 65	Greg Briley	.05	.02
☐ 66	Steve Finley	.15	.07
☐ 67	Frank Thomas CL	.30	.14
☐ 68	Tom Gordon	.05	.02
☐ 69	Rob Dibble	.05	.02
☐ 70	Glenallen Hill	.05	.02
☐ 71	Calvin Jones	.05	.02
☐ 72	Joe Girardi	.15	.07
☐ 73	Barry Larkin	.20	.09
☐ 74	Andy Benes	.15	.07
☐ 75	Milt Cuyler	.05	.02
☐ 76	Kevin Bass	.05	.02
☐ 77	Pete Harnisch	.05	.02
☐ 78	Wilson Alvarez	.15	.07
☐ 79	Mike Devereaux	.05	.02
☐ 80	Doug Henry	.05	.02
☐ 81	Orel Hershiser	.15	.07
☐ 82	Shane Mack	.05	.02
☐ 83	Mike Macfarlane	.05	.02
☐ 84	Thomas Howard	.05	.02
☐ 85	Alex Fernandez	.15	.07
☐ 86	Reggie Jefferson	.15	.07
☐ 87	Leo Gomez	.15	.07
☐ 88	Mel Hall	.05	.02
☐ 89	Mike Greenwell	.05	.02
☐ 90	Jeff Russell	.05	.02
☐ 91	Steve Buechele	.05	.02
☐ 92	David Cone	.15	.07
☐ 93	Kevin Reimer	.05	.02
☐ 94	Mark Lemke	.05	.02
☐ 95	Bob Tewksbury	.05	.02
☐ 96	Zane Smith	.05	.02
☐ 97	Mark Eichhorn	.05	.02
☐ 98	Kirby Puckett	.50	.23
☐ 99	Paul O'Neill	.15	.07
☐ 100	Dennis Eckersley	.15	.07
☐ 101	Duane Ward	.05	.02
☐ 102	Matt Nokes	.05	.02
☐ 103	Mo Vaughn	.40	.18
☐ 104	Pat Kelly	.05	.02
☐ 105	Ron Karkovice	.05	.02
☐ 106	Bill Spiers	.05	.02
☐ 107	Gary Gaetti	.15	.07
☐ 108	Mackey Sasser	.05	.02
☐ 109	Robby Thompson	.05	.02
☐ 110	Marvin Freeman	.05	.02
☐ 111	Jimmy Key	.15	.07
☐ 112	Dwight Gooden	.15	.07
☐ 113	Charlie Leibrandt	.05	.02
☐ 114	Devon White	.05	.02
☐ 115	Charles Nagy	.15	.07
☐ 116	Rickey Henderson	.40	.18
☐ 117	Paul Assenmacher	.05	.02
☐ 118	Junior Felix	.05	.02
☐ 119	Julio Franco	.05	.02
☐ 120	Norm Charlton	.05	.02
☐ 121	Scott Servais	.05	.02
☐ 122	Gerald Perry	.05	.02
☐ 123	Brian McRae	.05	.02
☐ 124	Don Slaught	.05	.02
☐ 125	Juan Samuel	.05	.02
☐ 126	Harold Baines	.15	.07
☐ 127	Scott Livingstone	.05	.02
☐ 128	Jay Buhner	.20	.09
☐ 129	Darrin Jackson	.05	.02

#	Player	Price	Price
❏ 130	Luis Mercedes	.05	.02
❏ 131	Brian Harper	.05	.02
❏ 132	Howard Johnson	.05	.02
❏ 133	Nolan Ryan CL	.30	.14
❏ 134	Dante Bichette	.20	.09
❏ 135	Dave Righetti	.05	.02
❏ 136	Jeff Montgomery	.15	.07
❏ 137	Joe Grahe	.05	.02
❏ 138	Delino DeShields	.15	.07
❏ 139	Jose Rijo	.05	.02
❏ 140	Ken Caminiti	.20	.09
❏ 141	Steve Olin	.05	.02
❏ 142	Kurt Stillwell	.05	.02
❏ 143	Jay Bell	.15	.07
❏ 144	Jaime Navarro	.05	.02
❏ 145	Ben McDonald	.05	.02
❏ 146	Greg Gagne	.05	.02
❏ 147	Jeff Blauser	.05	.02
❏ 148	Carney Lansford	.15	.07
❏ 149	Ozzie Guillen	.05	.02
❏ 150	Milt Thompson	.05	.02
❏ 151	Jeff Reardon	.15	.07
❏ 152	Scott Sanderson	.05	.02
❏ 153	Cecil Fielder	.15	.07
❏ 154	Greg A. Harris	.05	.02
❏ 155	Rich DeLucia	.05	.02
❏ 156	Roberto Kelly	.05	.02
❏ 157	Bryn Smith	.05	.02
❏ 158	Chuck McElroy	.05	.02
❏ 159	Tom Henke	.05	.02
❏ 160	Luis Gonzalez	.20	.09
❏ 161	Steve Wilson	.05	.02
❏ 162	Shawn Boskie	.05	.02
❏ 163	Mark Davis	.05	.02
❏ 164	Mike Moore	.05	.02
❏ 165	Mike Scioscia	.05	.02
❏ 166	Scott Erickson	.15	.07
❏ 167	Todd Stottlemyre	.15	.07
❏ 168	Alvin Davis	.05	.02
❏ 169	Greg Hibbard	.05	.02
❏ 170	David Valle	.05	.02
❏ 171	Dave Winfield	.30	.14
❏ 172	Alan Trammell	.20	.09
❏ 173	Kenny Rogers	.05	.02
❏ 174	John Franco	.15	.07
❏ 175	Jose Lind	.05	.02
❏ 176	Pete Schourek	.05	.02
❏ 177	Von Hayes	.05	.02
❏ 178	Chris Hammond	.05	.02
❏ 179	John Burkett	.05	.02
❏ 180	Dickie Thon	.05	.02
❏ 181	Joel Skinner	.05	.02
❏ 182	Scott Cooper	.05	.02
❏ 183	Andre Dawson	.20	.09
❏ 184	Billy Ripken	.05	.02
❏ 185	Kevin Mitchell	.15	.07
❏ 186	Brett Butler	.15	.07
❏ 187	Tony Fernandez	.05	.02
❏ 188	Cory Snyder	.05	.02
❏ 189	John Habyan	.05	.02
❏ 190	Dennis Martinez	.15	.07
❏ 191	John Smoltz	.20	.09
❏ 192	Greg Myers	.05	.02
❏ 193	Rob Deer	.05	.02
❏ 194	Ivan Rodriguez	.60	.25
❏ 195	Ray Lankford	.30	.14
❏ 196	Bill Wegman	.05	.02
❏ 197	Edgar Martinez	.20	.09
❏ 198	Darryl Kile	.15	.07
❏ 199	Cal Ripken CL	.30	.14
❏ 200	Brent Mayne	.05	.02
❏ 201	Larry Walker	.30	.14
❏ 202	Carlos Baerga	.05	.02
❏ 203	Russ Swan	.05	.02
❏ 204	Mike Morgan	.05	.02
❏ 205	Hal Morris	.05	.02
❏ 206	Tony Gwynn	.75	.35
❏ 207	Mark Leiter	.05	.02
❏ 208	Kirt Manwaring	.05	.02
❏ 209	Al Osuna	.05	.02
❏ 210	Bobby Thigpen	.05	.02
❏ 211	Chris Hoiles	.05	.02
❏ 212	B.J. Surhoff	.15	.07
❏ 213	Lenny Harris	.05	.02
❏ 214	Scott Leius	.05	.02
❏ 215	Gregg Jefferies	.05	.02
❏ 216	Bruce Hurst	.05	.02
❏ 217	Steve Sax	.05	.02
❏ 218	Dave Otto	.05	.02
❏ 219	Sam Horn	.05	.02
❏ 220	Charlie Hayes	.05	.02
❏ 221	Frank Viola	.05	.02
❏ 222	Jose Guzman	.05	.02
❏ 223	Gary Redus	.05	.02
❏ 224	Dave Gallagher	.05	.02
❏ 225	Dean Palmer	.15	.07
❏ 226	Greg Olson	.05	.02
❏ 227	Jose DeLeon	.05	.02
❏ 228	Mike LaValliere	.05	.02
❏ 229	Mark Langston	.05	.02
❏ 230	Chuck Knoblauch	.30	.14
❏ 231	Bill Doran	.05	.02
❏ 232	Dave Henderson	.05	.02
❏ 233	Roberto Alomar	.30	.14
❏ 234	Scott Fletcher	.05	.02
❏ 235	Tim Naehring	.05	.02
❏ 236	Mike Gallego	.05	.02
❏ 237	Lance Johnson	.05	.02
❏ 238	Paul Molitor	.30	.14
❏ 239	Dan Gladden	.05	.02
❏ 240	Willie Randolph	.15	.07
❏ 241	Will Clark	.30	.14
❏ 242	Sid Bream	.05	.02
❏ 243	Derek Bell	.15	.07
❏ 244	Bill Pecota	.05	.02
❏ 245	Terry Pendleton	.05	.02
❏ 246	Randy Ready	.05	.02
❏ 247	Jack Armstrong	.05	.02
❏ 248	Todd Van Poppel	.05	.02
❏ 249	Shawon Dunston	.05	.02
❏ 250	Bobby Rose	.05	.02
❏ 251	Jeff Huson	.05	.02
❏ 252	Bip Roberts	.05	.02
❏ 253	Doug Jones	.05	.02
❏ 254	Lee Smith	.15	.07
❏ 255	George Brett	.60	.25
❏ 256	Randy Tomlin	.05	.02
❏ 257	Todd Benzinger	.05	.02
❏ 258	Dave Stewart	.15	.07
❏ 259	Mark Carreon	.05	.02
❏ 260	Pete O'Brien	.05	.02
❏ 261	Tim Teufel	.05	.02
❏ 262	Bob Milacki	.05	.02
❏ 263	Mark Guthrie	.05	.02
❏ 264	Darrin Fletcher	.05	.02
❏ 265	Omar Vizquel	.15	.07
❏ 266	Chris Bosio	.05	.02
❏ 267	Jose Canseco	.40	.18
❏ 268	Mike Boddicker	.05	.02
❏ 269	Lance Parrish	.05	.02
❏ 270	Jose Vizcaino	.05	.02
❏ 271	Chris Sabo	.05	.02
❏ 272	Royce Clayton	.05	.02
❏ 273	Marquis Grissom	.15	.07
❏ 274	Fred McGriff	.20	.09
❏ 275	Barry Bonds	.40	.18
❏ 276	Greg Vaughn	.20	.09
❏ 277	Gregg Olson	.05	.02
❏ 278	Dave Hollins	.05	.02
❏ 279	Tom Glavine	.20	.09
❏ 280	Bryan Hickerson UER	.05	.02
	Name spelled Brian on front		
❏ 281	Scott Radinsky	.05	.02
❏ 282	Omar Olivares	.05	.02
❏ 283	Ivan Calderon	.05	.02
❏ 284	Kevin Maas	.05	.02
❏ 285	Mickey Tettleton	.05	.02
❏ 286	Wade Boggs	.30	.14
❏ 287	Stan Belinda	.05	.02
❏ 288	Bret Barberie	.05	.02
❏ 289	Jose Oquendo	.05	.02
❏ 290	Frank Castillo	.05	.02
❏ 291	Dave Stieb	.05	.02
❏ 292	Tommy Greene	.05	.02
❏ 293	Eric Karros	.30	.14
❏ 294	Greg Maddux	.75	.35
❏ 295	Jim Eisenreich	.05	.02
❏ 296	Rafael Palmeiro	.30	.14
❏ 297	Ramon Martinez	.15	.07
❏ 298	Tim Wallach	.05	.02
❏ 299	Jim Thome	.75	.35
❏ 300	Chito Martinez	.05	.02
❏ 301	Mitch Williams	.05	.02
❏ 302	Randy Johnson	.30	.14
❏ 303	Carlton Fisk	.30	.14
❏ 304	Travis Fryman	.15	.07
❏ 305	Bobby Witt	.05	.02
❏ 306	Dave Magadan	.05	.02
❏ 307	Alex Cole	.05	.02
❏ 308	Bobby Bonilla	.15	.07
❏ 309	Bryan Harvey	.05	.02
❏ 310	Rafael Belliard	.05	.02
❏ 311	Mariano Duncan	.05	.02
❏ 312	Chuck Crim	.05	.02
❏ 313	John Kruk	.15	.07
❏ 314	Ellis Burks	.15	.07
❏ 315	Craig Biggio	.30	.14
❏ 316	Glenn Davis	.05	.02
❏ 317	Ryne Sandberg	.40	.18
❏ 318	Mike Sharperson	.05	.02
❏ 319	Rich Rodriguez	.05	.02
❏ 320	Lee Guetterman	.05	.02
❏ 321	Benito Santiago	.05	.02
❏ 322	Jose Offerman	.15	.07
❏ 323	Tony Pena	.05	.02
❏ 324	Pat Borders	.05	.02
❏ 325	Mike Henneman	.05	.02
❏ 326	Kevin Brown	.20	.09
❏ 327	Chris Nabholz	.05	.02
❏ 328	Franklin Stubbs	.05	.02
❏ 329	Tino Martinez	.30	.14
❏ 330	Mickey Morandini	.05	.02
❏ 331	Ryne Sandberg CL	.30	.14
❏ 332	Mark Gubicza	.05	.02
❏ 333	Bill Landrum	.05	.02
❏ 334	Mark Whiten	.05	.02
❏ 335	Darren Daulton	.15	.07
❏ 336	Rick Wilkins	.05	.02
❏ 337	Brian Jordan	1.00	.45
❏ 338	Kevin Ward	.05	.02
❏ 339	Ruben Amaro	.05	.02
❏ 340	Trevor Wilson	.05	.02
❏ 341	Andujar Cedeno	.05	.02
❏ 342	Michael Huff	.05	.02
❏ 343	Brady Anderson	.20	.09
❏ 344	Craig Grebeck	.05	.02
❏ 345	Bob Ojeda	.05	.02
❏ 346	Mike Pagliarulo	.05	.02
❏ 347	Terry Shumpert	.05	.02
❏ 348	Dann Bilardello	.05	.02
❏ 349	Frank Thomas	.75	.35
❏ 350	Albert Belle	.30	.14
❏ 351	Jose Mesa	.05	.02
❏ 352	Rich Monteleone	.05	.02
❏ 353	Bob Walk	.05	.02
❏ 354	Monty Fariss	.05	.02
❏ 355	Luis Rivera	.05	.02
❏ 356	Anthony Young	.05	.02
❏ 357	Geno Petralli	.05	.02
❏ 358	Otis Nixon	.15	.07
❏ 359	Tom Pagnozzi	.05	.02
❏ 360	Reggie Sanders	.15	.07
❏ 361	Lee Stevens	.05	.02
❏ 362	Kent Hrbek	.15	.07
❏ 363	Orlando Merced	.05	.02
❏ 364	Mike Bordick	.05	.02
❏ 365	Dion James UER	.05	.02
	(Blue Jays logo on card back)		
❏ 366	Jack Clark	.15	.07
❏ 367	Matt Stairs	.05	.02
❏ 368	Randy Velarde	.05	.02
❏ 369	Dan Pasqua	.05	.02
❏ 370	Pat Listach	.05	.02
❏ 371	Mike Fitzgerald	.05	.02
❏ 372	Tom Foley	.05	.02
❏ 373	Matt Williams	.20	.09
❏ 374	Brian Hunter	.05	.02
❏ 375	Joe Carter	.15	.07
❏ 376	Bret Saberhagen	.15	.07
❏ 377	Mike Stanton	.05	.02
❏ 378	Hubie Brooks	.05	.02
❏ 379	Eric Bell	.05	.02
❏ 380	Walt Weiss	.05	.02
❏ 381	Danny Jackson	.05	.02
❏ 382	Manuel Lee	.05	.02
❏ 383	Ruben Sierra	.05	.02
❏ 384	Greg Swindell	.05	.02

❑ 385 Ryan Bowen	.05	.02
❑ 386 Kevin Ritz	.05	.02
❑ 387 Curtis Wilkerson	.05	.02
❑ 388 Gary Varsho	.05	.02
❑ 389 Dave Hansen	.05	.02
❑ 390 Bob Welch	.05	.02
❑ 391 Lou Whitaker	.15	.07
❑ 392 Ken Griffey Jr.	2.00	.90
❑ 393 Mike Maddux	.05	.02
❑ 394 Arthur Rhodes	.05	.02
❑ 395 Chili Davis	.15	.07
❑ 396 Eddie Murray	.30	.14
❑ 397 Robin Yount CL	.20	.09
❑ 398 Dave Cochrane	.05	.02
❑ 399 Kevin Seitzer	.05	.02
❑ 400 Ozzie Smith	.40	.18
❑ 401 Paul Sorrento	.05	.02
❑ 402 Les Lancaster	.05	.02
❑ 403 Junior Noboa	.05	.02
❑ 404 David Justice	.30	.14
❑ 405 Andy Ashby	.15	.07
❑ 406 Danny Tartabull	.05	.02
❑ 407 Bill Swift	.05	.02
❑ 408 Craig Lefferts	.05	.02
❑ 409 Tom Candiotti	.05	.02
❑ 410 Lance Blankenship	.05	.02
❑ 411 Jeff Tackett	.05	.02
❑ 412 Sammy Sosa	1.00	.45
❑ 413 Jody Reed	.05	.02
❑ 414 Bruce Ruffin	.05	.02
❑ 415 Gene Larkin	.05	.02
❑ 416 John Vander Wal	.05	.02
❑ 417 Tim Belcher	.05	.02
❑ 418 Steve Frey	.05	.02
❑ 419 Dick Schofield	.05	.02
❑ 420 Jeff King	.05	.02
❑ 421 Kim Batiste	.05	.02
❑ 422 Jack McDowell	.05	.02
❑ 423 Damon Berryhill	.05	.02
❑ 424 Gary Wayne	.05	.02
❑ 425 Jack Morris	.15	.07
❑ 426 Moises Alou	.05	.02
❑ 427 Mark McLemore	.05	.02
❑ 428 Juan Guerrero	.05	.02
❑ 429 Scott Scudder	.05	.02
❑ 430 Eric Davis	.15	.07
❑ 431 Joe Slusarski	.05	.02
❑ 432 Todd Zeile	.05	.02
❑ 433 Dwayne Henry	.05	.02
❑ 434 Cliff Brantley	.05	.02
❑ 435 Butch Henry	.05	.02
❑ 436 Todd Worrell	.05	.02
❑ 437 Bob Scanlan	.05	.02
❑ 438 Wally Joyner	.15	.07
❑ 439 John Flaherty	.05	.02
❑ 440 Brian Downing	.05	.02
❑ 441 Darren Lewis	.05	.02
❑ 442 Gary Carter	.30	.14
❑ 443 Wally Ritchie	.05	.02
❑ 444 Chris Jones	.05	.02
❑ 445 Jeff Kent	.30	.14
❑ 446 Gary Sheffield	.30	.14
❑ 447 Ron Darling	.05	.02
❑ 448 Delon Sanders	.30	.14
❑ 449 Andres Galarraga	.30	.14
❑ 450 Chuck Finley	.15	.07
❑ 451 Derek Lilliquist	.05	.02
❑ 452 Carl Willis	.05	.02
❑ 453 Wes Chamberlain	.05	.02
❑ 454 Roger Mason	.05	.02
❑ 455 Spike Owen	.05	.02
❑ 456 Thomas Howard	.05	.02
❑ 457 Dave Martinez	.05	.02
❑ 458 Pete Incaviglia	.05	.02
❑ 459 Keith A. Miller	.05	.02
❑ 460 Mike Fetters	.05	.02
❑ 461 Paul Gibson	.05	.02
❑ 462 George Bell	.05	.02
❑ 463 Bobby Bonilla CL	.15	.07
❑ 464 Terry Mulholland	.05	.02
❑ 465 Storm Davis	.05	.02
❑ 466 Gary Pettis	.05	.02
❑ 467 Randy Bush	.05	.02
❑ 468 Ken Hill	.05	.02
❑ 469 Rheal Cormier	.05	.02
❑ 470 Andy Stankiewicz	.05	.02

❑ 471 Dave Burba	.05	.02
❑ 472 Henry Cotto	.05	.02
❑ 473 Dale Sveum	.05	.02
❑ 474 Rich Gossage	.15	.07
❑ 475 William Suero	.05	.02
❑ 476 Doug Strange	.05	.02
❑ 477 Bill Krueger	.05	.02
❑ 478 John Wetteland	.15	.07
❑ 479 Melido Perez	.05	.02
❑ 480 Lonnie Smith	.05	.02
❑ 481 Mike Jackson	.15	.07
❑ 482 Mike Gardiner	.05	.02
❑ 483 David Wells	.15	.07
❑ 484 Barry Jones	.05	.02
❑ 485 Scott Bankhead	.05	.02
❑ 486 Terry Leach	.05	.02
❑ 487 Vince Horsman	.05	.02
❑ 488 Dave Eiland	.05	.02
❑ 489 Alejandro Pena	.05	.02
❑ 490 Julio Valera	.05	.02
❑ 491 Joe Boever	.05	.02
❑ 492 Paul Miller	.05	.02
❑ 493 Archi Cianfrocco	.05	.02
❑ 494 Dave Fleming	.05	.02
❑ 495 Kyle Abbott	.05	.02
❑ 496 Chad Kreuter	.05	.02
❑ 497 Chris James	.05	.02
❑ 498 Donnie Hill	.05	.02
❑ 499 Jacob Brumfield	.05	.02
❑ 500 Ricky Bones	.05	.02
❑ 501 Terry Steinbach	.05	.02
❑ 502 Bernard Gilkey	.15	.07
❑ 503 Dennis Cook	.05	.02
❑ 504 Len Dykstra	.15	.07
❑ 505 Mike Bielecki	.05	.02
❑ 506 Bob Kipper	.05	.02
❑ 507 Jose Melendez	.05	.02
❑ 508 Rick Sutcliffe	.05	.02
❑ 509 Ken Patterson	.05	.02
❑ 510 Andy Allanson	.05	.02
❑ 511 Al Newman	.05	.02
❑ 512 Mark Gardner	.05	.02
❑ 513 Jeff Schaefer	.05	.02
❑ 514 Jim McNamara	.05	.02
❑ 515 Peter Hoy	.05	.02
❑ 516 Curt Schilling	.20	.09
❑ 517 Kirk McCaskill	.05	.02
❑ 518 Chris Gwynn	.05	.02
❑ 519 Sid Fernandez	.05	.02
❑ 520 Jeff Parrett	.05	.02
❑ 521 Scott Ruskin	.05	.02
❑ 522 Kevin McReynolds	.05	.02
❑ 523 Rick Cerone	.05	.02
❑ 524 Jesse Orosco	.05	.02
❑ 525 Troy Afenir	.05	.02
❑ 526 John Smiley	.05	.02
❑ 527 Dale Murphy	.30	.14
❑ 528 Leaf Set Card	.05	.02

1992 Leaf Gold Rookies

	MINT	NRMT
COMPLETE SET (24)	18.00	8.00
COMPLETE SERIES 1 (12)	12.00	5.50
COMPLETE SERIES 2 (12)	6.00	2.70
COMMON CARD (BC1-BC24)	.50	.23
MINOR STARS	1.00	.45
RANDOM INSERTS IN BOTH SERIES		

❑ BC1 Chad Curtis	1.50	.70
❑ BC2 Brent Gates	.50	.23
❑ BC3 Pedro Martinez	10.00	4.50
❑ BC4 Kenny Lofton	2.50	1.10
❑ BC5 Turk Wendell	1.00	.45
❑ BC6 Mark Hutton	.50	.23
❑ BC7 Todd Hundley	1.00	.45
❑ BC8 Matt Stairs	2.50	1.10
❑ BC9 Eddie Taubensee	1.00	.45
❑ BC10 David Nied	.50	.23
❑ BC11 Salomon Torres	.50	.23
❑ BC12 Bret Boone	1.50	.70
❑ BC13 Johnny Ruffin	.50	.23
❑ BC14 Ed Martel	.50	.23
❑ BC15 Rick Trlicek	.50	.23
❑ BC16 Raul Mondesi	4.00	1.80
❑ BC17 Pat Mahomes	.50	.23
❑ BC18 Dan Wilson	1.00	.45
❑ BC19 Donovan Osborne	.50	.23
❑ BC20 Dave Silvestri	.50	.23
❑ BC21 Gary DiSarcina	.50	.23
❑ BC22 Denny Neagle	1.25	.55
❑ BC23 Steve Hosey	.50	.23
❑ BC24 John Doherty	.50	.23

1993 Leaf

	MINT	NRMT
COMPLETE SET (550)	35.00	16.00
COMPLETE SERIES 1 (220)	15.00	6.75
COMPLETE SERIES 2 (220)	15.00	6.75
COMPLETE UPDATE (110)	5.00	2.20
COMMON CARD (1-550)	.15	.07
MINOR STARS	.30	.14
UNLISTED STARS	.60	.25

❑ 1 Ben McDonald	.15	.07
❑ 2 Sid Fernandez	.15	.07
❑ 3 Juan Guzman	.15	.07
❑ 4 Curt Schilling	.30	.14
❑ 5 Ivan Rodriguez	.75	.35
❑ 6 Don Slaught	.15	.07
❑ 7 Terry Steinbach	.15	.07
❑ 8 Todd Zeile	.15	.07
❑ 9 Andy Stankiewicz	.15	.07
❑ 10 Tim Teufel	.15	.07
❑ 11 Marvin Freeman	.15	.07
❑ 12 Jim Austin	.15	.07
❑ 13 Bob Scanlan	.15	.07
❑ 14 Rusty Meacham	.15	.07
❑ 15 Casey Candaele	.15	.07
❑ 16 Travis Fryman	.30	.14
❑ 17 Jose Offerman	.30	.14
❑ 18 Albert Belle	.60	.25
❑ 19 John Vander Wal	.15	.07
❑ 20 Dan Pasqua	.15	.07
❑ 21 Frank Viola	.15	.07
❑ 22 Terry Mulholland	.15	.07
❑ 23 Gregg Olson	.15	.07
❑ 24 Randy Tomlin	.15	.07
❑ 25 Todd Stottlemyre	.15	.07
❑ 26 Jose Oquendo	.15	.07
❑ 27 Julio Franco	.15	.07
❑ 28 Tony Gwynn	1.50	.70
❑ 29 Ruben Sierra	.15	.07
❑ 30 Bobby Thompson	.15	.07
❑ 31 Jim Bullinger	.15	.07
❑ 32 Rick Aguilera	.15	.07

33	Scott Servais	.15	.07
34	Cal Eldred	.15	.07
35	Mike Piazza	3.00	1.35
36	Brent Mayne	.15	.07
37	Wil Cordero	.15	.07
38	Milt Cuyler	.15	.07
39	Howard Johnson	.15	.07
40	Kenny Lofton	.60	.25
41	Alex Fernandez	.30	.14
42	Denny Neagle	.30	.14
43	Tony Pena	.15	.07
44	Bob Tewksbury	.15	.07
45	Glenn Davis	.15	.07
46	Fred McGriff	.40	.18
47	John Olerud	.40	.18
48	Steve Hosey	.15	.07
49	Rafael Palmeiro	.60	.25
50	David Justice	.60	.25
51	Pete Harnisch	.15	.07
52	Sam Militello	.15	.07
53	Orel Hershiser	.30	.14
54	Pat Mahomes	.15	.07
55	Greg Colbrunn	.15	.07
56	Greg Vaughn	.30	.14
57	Vince Coleman	.15	.07
58	Brian McRae	.15	.07
59	Len Dykstra	.30	.14
60	Dan Gladden	.15	.07
61	Ted Power	.15	.07
62	Donovan Osborne	.15	.07
63	Ron Karkovice	.15	.07
64	Frank Seminara	.15	.07
65	Bob Zupcic	.15	.07
66	Kirt Manwaring	.15	.07
67	Mike Devereaux	.15	.07
68	Mark Lemke	.15	.07
69	Devon White	.15	.07
70	Sammy Sosa	2.00	.90
71	Pedro Astacio	.30	.14
72	Dennis Eckersley	.30	.14
73	Chris Nabholz	.15	.07
74	Melido Perez	.15	.07
75	Todd Hundley	.40	.18
76	Kent Hrbek	.30	.14
77	Mickey Morandini	.15	.07
78	Tim McIntosh	.15	.07
79	Andy Van Slyke	.30	.14
80	Kevin McReynolds	.15	.07
81	Mike Henneman	.15	.07
82	Greg W. Harris	.15	.07
83	Sandy Alomar Jr	.30	.14
84	Mike Jackson	.30	.14
85	Ozzie Guillen	.15	.07
86	Jeff Blauser	.15	.07
87	John Valentin	.30	.14
88	Rey Sanchez	.15	.07
89	Rick Sutcliffe	.15	.07
90	Luis Gonzalez	.30	.14
91	Jeff Fassero	.15	.07
92	Kenny Rogers	.15	.07
93	Bret Saberhagen	.30	.14
94	Bob Welch	.15	.07
95	Darren Daulton	.30	.14
96	Mike Gallego	.15	.07
97	Orlando Merced	.15	.07
98	Chuck Knoblauch	.60	.25
99	Bernard Gilkey	.15	.07
100	Billy Ashley	.15	.07
101	Kevin Appier	.30	.14
102	Jeff Brantley	.15	.07
103	Bill Gullickson	.15	.07
104	John Smoltz	.40	.18
105	Paul Sorrento	.15	.07
106	Steve Buechele	.15	.07
107	Steve Sax	.15	.07
108	Andujar Cedeno	.15	.07
109	Billy Hatcher	.15	.07
110	Checklist	.15	.07
111	Alan Mills	.15	.07
112	John Franco	.30	.14
113	Jack Morris	.30	.14
114	Mitch Williams	.15	.07
115	Nolan Ryan	2.50	1.10
116	Jay Bell	.30	.14
117	Mike Bordick	.15	.07
118	Geronimo Pena	.15	.07
119	Danny Tartabull	.15	.07
120	Checklist	.15	.07
121	Steve Avery	.15	.07
122	Ricky Bones	.15	.07
123	Mike Morgan	.15	.07
124	Jeff Montgomery	.30	.14
125	Jeff Bagwell	.75	.35
126	Tony Phillips	.15	.07
127	Lenny Harris	.15	.07
128	Glenallen Hill	.15	.07
129	Marquis Grissom	.30	.14
130	Gerald Williams UER	.15	.07
	(Bernie William's picture and stats)		
131	Greg A. Harris	.15	.07
132	Tommy Greene	.15	.07
133	Chris Hoiles	.15	.07
134	Bob Walk	.15	.07
135	Duane Ward	.15	.07
136	Tom Pagnozzi	.15	.07
137	Jeff Huson	.15	.07
138	Kurt Stillwell	.15	.07
139	Dave Henderson	.15	.07
140	Darrin Jackson	.15	.07
141	Frank Castillo	.15	.07
142	Scott Erickson	.15	.07
143	Darryl Kile	.15	.07
144	Bill Wegman	.15	.07
145	Steve Wilson	.15	.07
146	George Brett	1.25	.55
147	Moises Alou	.30	.14
148	Lou Whitaker	.30	.14
149	Chico Walker	.15	.07
150	Jerry Browne	.15	.07
151	Kirk McCaskill	.15	.07
152	Zane Smith	.15	.07
153	Matt Young	.15	.07
154	Lee Smith	.30	.14
155	Leo Gomez	.15	.07
156	Dan Walters	.15	.07
157	Pat Borders	.15	.07
158	Matt Williams	.40	.18
159	Dean Palmer	.30	.14
160	John Patterson	.15	.07
161	Doug Jones	.15	.07
162	John Habyan	.15	.07
163	Pedro Martinez	1.25	.55
164	Carl Willis	.15	.07
165	Darrin Fletcher	.15	.07
166	B.J. Surhoff	.30	.14
167	Eddie Murray	.60	.25
168	Keith Miller	.15	.07
169	Ricky Jordan	.15	.07
170	Juan Gonzalez	1.25	.55
171	Charles Nagy	.30	.14
172	Mark Clark	.15	.07
173	Bobby Thigpen	.15	.07
174	Tim Scott	.15	.07
175	Scott Cooper	.30	.14
176	Royce Clayton	.15	.07
177	Brady Anderson	.30	.14
178	Sid Bream	.15	.07
179	Derek Bell	.30	.14
180	Otis Nixon	.15	.07
181	Kevin Gross	.15	.07
182	Ron Darling	.15	.07
183	John Wetteland	.30	.14
184	Mike Stanley	.15	.07
185	Jeff Kent	.30	.14
186	Brian Harper	.15	.07
187	Mariano Duncan	.15	.07
188	Robin Yount	1.00	.45
189	Al Martin	.15	.07
190	Eddie Zosky	.15	.07
191	Mike Munoz	.15	.07
192	Andy Benes	.30	.14
193	Dennis Cook	.15	.07
194	Bill Swift	.15	.07
195	Frank Thomas	1.25	.55
195A	Frank Thomas	1.25	.55
	Franklin visible on batting glove		
196	Damon Berryhill	.15	.07
197	Mike Greenwell	.15	.07
198	Mark Grace	.40	.18
199	Darryl Hamilton	.15	.07
200	Derrick May	.15	.07
201	Ken Hill	.15	.07
202	Kevin Brown	.40	.18
203	Dwight Gooden	.30	.14
204	Bobby Witt	.15	.07
205	Juan Bell	.15	.07
206	Kevin Maas	.15	.07
207	Jeff King	.15	.07
208	Scott Leius	.15	.07
209	Rheal Cormier	.15	.07
210	Darryl Strawberry	.30	.14
211	Tom Gordon	.15	.07
212	Bud Black	.15	.07
213	Mickey Tettleton	.15	.07
214	Pete Smith	.15	.07
215	Felix Fermin	.15	.07
216	Rick Wilkins	.15	.07
217	George Bell	.15	.07
218	Eric Anthony	.15	.07
219	Pedro Munoz	.15	.07
220	Checklist	.15	.07
221	Lance Blankenship	.15	.07
222	Deion Sanders	.40	.18
223	Craig Biggio	.60	.25
224	Ryne Sandberg	.75	.35
225	Ron Gant	.30	.14
226	Tom Brunansky	.15	.07
227	Chad Curtis	.30	.14
228	Joe Carter	.30	.14
229	Brian Jordan	.30	.14
230	Brett Butler	.30	.14
231	Frank Bolick	.15	.07
232	Rod Beck	.30	.14
233	Carlos Baerga	.40	.18
234	Eric Karros	.40	.18
235	Jack Armstrong	.15	.07
236	Bobby Bonilla	.30	.14
237	Don Mattingly	1.25	.55
238	Jeff Gardner	.15	.07
239	Dave Hollins	.30	.14
240	Steve Cooke	.15	.07
241	Jose Canseco	.75	.35
242	Ivan Calderon	.15	.07
243	Tim Belcher	.15	.07
244	Freddie Benavides	.15	.07
245	Roberto Alomar	.60	.25
246	Rob Deer	.15	.07
247	Will Clark	.60	.25
248	Mike Felder	.15	.07
249	Harold Baines	.30	.14
250	David Cone	.40	.18
251	Mark Guthrie	.15	.07
252	Ellis Burks	.30	.14
253	Jim Abbott	.30	.14
254	Chili Davis	.30	.14
255	Chris Bosio	.15	.07
256	Bret Barberie	.15	.07
257	Hal Morris	.15	.07
258	Dante Bichette	.30	.14
259	Storm Davis	.15	.07
260	Gary DiSarcina	.15	.07
261	Ken Caminiti	.40	.18
262	Paul Molitor	.60	.25
263	Joe Oliver	.15	.07
264	Pat Listach	.15	.07
265	Gregg Jefferies	.15	.07
266	Jose Guzman	.15	.07
267	Eric Davis	.30	.14
268	Delino DeShields	.30	.14
269	Barry Bonds	.75	.35
270	Mike Bielecki	.15	.07
271	Jay Buhner	.40	.18
272	Scott Pose	.15	.07
273	Tony Fernandez	.30	.14
274	Chito Martinez	.15	.07
275	Phil Plantier	.15	.07
276	Pete Incaviglia	.15	.07
277	Carlos Garcia	.15	.07
278	Tom Henke	.15	.07
279	Roger Clemens	1.50	.70
280	Rob Dibble	.15	.07
281	Daryl Boston	.15	.07
282	Greg Gagne	.15	.07
283	Cecil Fielder	.30	.14
284	Carlton Fisk	.60	.25
285	Wade Boggs	.60	.25
286	Damion Easley	.30	.14

❏ 287	Norm Charlton	.15	.07
❏ 288	Jeff Conine	.15	.07
❏ 289	Roberto Kelly	.15	.07
❏ 290	Jerald Clark	.15	.07
❏ 291	Rickey Henderson	.75	.35
❏ 292	Chuck Finley	.30	.14
❏ 293	Doug Drabek	.15	.07
❏ 294	Dave Stewart	.30	.14
❏ 295	Tom Glavine	.40	.18
❏ 296	Jaime Navarro	.15	.07
❏ 297	Ray Lankford	.40	.18
❏ 298	Greg Hibbard	.15	.07
❏ 299	Jody Reed	.15	.07
❏ 300	Dennis Martinez	.30	.14
❏ 301	Dave Martinez	.15	.07
❏ 302	Reggie Jefferson	.30	.14
❏ 303	John Cummings	.15	.07
❏ 304	Orestes Destrade	.15	.07
❏ 305	Mike Maddux	.15	.07
❏ 306	David Segui	.15	.07
❏ 307	Gary Sheffield	.60	.25
❏ 308	Danny Jackson	.15	.07
❏ 309	Craig Lefferts	.15	.07
❏ 310	Andre Dawson	.40	.18
❏ 311	Barry Larkin	.60	.25
❏ 312	Alex Cole	.15	.07
❏ 313	Mark Gardner	.15	.07
❏ 314	Kirk Gibson	.30	.14
❏ 315	Shane Mack	.15	.07
❏ 316	Bo Jackson	.30	.14
❏ 317	Jimmy Key	.30	.14
❏ 318	Greg Myers	.15	.07
❏ 319	Ken Griffey Jr.	3.00	1.35
❏ 320	Monty Fariss	.15	.07
❏ 321	Kevin Mitchell	.30	.14
❏ 322	Andres Galarraga	.60	.25
❏ 323	Mark McGwire	3.00	1.35
❏ 324	Mark Langston	.15	.07
❏ 325	Steve Finley	.30	.14
❏ 326	Greg Maddux	1.50	.70
❏ 327	Dave Nilsson	.30	.14
❏ 328	Ozzie Smith	.75	.35
❏ 329	Candy Maldonado	.15	.07
❏ 330	Checklist	.15	.07
❏ 331	Tim Pugh	.15	.07
❏ 332	Joe Girardi	.30	.14
❏ 333	Junior Felix	.15	.07
❏ 334	Greg Swindell	.15	.07
❏ 335	Ramon Martinez	.30	.14
❏ 336	Sean Berry	.15	.07
❏ 337	Joe Orsulak	.15	.07
❏ 338	Wes Chamberlain	.15	.07
❏ 339	Stan Belinda	.15	.07
❏ 340	Checklist UER	.15	.07
	(306 Luis Mercedes)		
❏ 341	Bruce Hurst	.15	.07
❏ 342	John Burkett	.15	.07
❏ 343	Mike Mussina	.60	.25
❏ 344	Scott Fletcher	.15	.07
❏ 345	Rene Gonzales	.15	.07
❏ 346	Roberto Hernandez	.30	.14
❏ 347	Carlos Martinez	.15	.07
❏ 348	Bill Krueger	.15	.07
❏ 349	Felix Jose	.15	.07
❏ 350	John Jaha	.15	.07
❏ 351	Willie Banks	.15	.07
❏ 352	Matt Nokes	.15	.07
❏ 353	Kevin Seitzer	.15	.07
❏ 354	Erik Hanson	.15	.07
❏ 355	David Hulse	.15	.07
❏ 356	Domingo Martinez	.15	.07
❏ 357	Greg Olson	.15	.07
❏ 358	Randy Myers	.30	.14
❏ 359	Tom Browning	.15	.07
❏ 360	Charlie Hayes	.15	.07
❏ 361	Bryan Harvey	.15	.07
❏ 362	Eddie Taubensee	.15	.07
❏ 363	Tim Wallach	.15	.07
❏ 364	Mel Rojas	.15	.07
❏ 365	Frank Tanana	.15	.07
❏ 366	John Kruk	.30	.14
❏ 367	Tim Laker	.07	.07
❏ 368	Rich Rodriguez	.15	.07
❏ 369	Darren Lewis	.15	.07
❏ 370	Harold Reynolds	.15	.07
❏ 371	Jose Melendez	.15	.07
❏ 372	Joe Grahe	.15	.07
❏ 373	Lance Johnson	.15	.07
❏ 374	Jose Mesa	.15	.07
❏ 375	Scott Livingstone	.15	.07
❏ 376	Wally Joyner	.30	.14
❏ 377	Kevin Reimer	.15	.07
❏ 378	Kirby Puckett	1.00	.45
❏ 379	Paul O'Neill	.30	.14
❏ 380	Randy Johnson	.60	.25
❏ 381	Manuel Lee	.15	.07
❏ 382	Dick Schofield	.15	.07
❏ 383	Darren Holmes	.15	.07
❏ 384	Charlie Hough	.30	.14
❏ 385	John Orton	.15	.07
❏ 386	Edgar Martinez	.40	.18
❏ 387	Terry Pendleton	.15	.07
❏ 388	Dan Plesac	.15	.07
❏ 389	Jeff Reardon	.30	.14
❏ 390	David Nied	.15	.07
❏ 391	Dave Magadan	.15	.07
❏ 392	Larry Walker	.60	.25
❏ 393	Ben Rivera	.15	.07
❏ 394	Lonnie Smith	.15	.07
❏ 395	Craig Shipley	.15	.07
❏ 396	Willie McGee	.30	.14
❏ 397	Arthur Rhodes	.15	.07
❏ 398	Mike Stanton	.15	.07
❏ 399	Luis Polonia	.15	.07
❏ 400	Jack McDowell	.15	.07
❏ 401	Mike Moore	.15	.07
❏ 402	Jose Lind	.15	.07
❏ 403	Bill Spiers	.15	.07
❏ 404	Kevin Tapani	.15	.07
❏ 405	Spike Owen	.15	.07
❏ 406	Tino Martinez	.60	.25
❏ 407	Charlie Leibrandt	.15	.07
❏ 408	Ed Sprague	.15	.07
❏ 409	Bryn Smith	.15	.07
❏ 410	Benito Santiago	.15	.07
❏ 411	Jose Rijo	.15	.07
❏ 412	Pete O'Brien	.15	.07
❏ 413	Willie Wilson	.15	.07
❏ 414	Bip Roberts	.15	.07
❏ 415	Eric Young	.60	.25
❏ 416	Walt Weiss	.15	.07
❏ 417	Milt Thompson	.15	.07
❏ 418	Chris Sabo	.15	.07
❏ 419	Scott Sanderson	.15	.07
❏ 420	Tim Raines	.30	.14
❏ 421	Alan Trammell	.40	.18
❏ 422	Mike Macfarlane	.15	.07
❏ 423	Dave Winfield	.40	.18
❏ 424	Bob Wickman	.15	.07
❏ 425	David Valle	.15	.07
❏ 426	Gary Redus	.15	.07
❏ 427	Turner Ward	.15	.07
❏ 428	Reggie Sanders	.30	.14
❏ 429	Todd Worrell	.15	.07
❏ 430	Julio Valera	.15	.07
❏ 431	Cal Ripken Jr.	2.50	1.10
❏ 432	Mo Vaughn	.60	.25
❏ 433	John Smiley	.15	.07
❏ 434	Omar Vizquel	.30	.14
❏ 435	Billy Ripken	.15	.07
❏ 436	Cory Snyder	.15	.07
❏ 437	Carlos Quintana	.15	.07
❏ 438	Omar Olivares	.15	.07
❏ 439	Robin Ventura	.30	.14
❏ 440	Checklist	.15	.07
❏ 441	Kevin Higgins	.15	.07
❏ 442	Carlos Hernandez	.15	.07
❏ 443	Dan Peltier	.15	.07
❏ 444	Derek Lilliquist	.15	.07
❏ 445	Tim Salmon	.60	.25
❏ 446	Sherman Obando	.15	.07
❏ 447	Pat Kelly	.15	.07
❏ 448	Todd Van Poppel	.15	.07
❏ 449	Mark Whiten	.15	.07
❏ 450	Checklist	.15	.07
❏ 451	Pat Meares	.15	.07
❏ 452	Tony Tarasco	.15	.07
❏ 453	Chris Gwynn	.15	.07
❏ 454	Armando Reynoso	.15	.07
❏ 455	Danny Darwin	.15	.07
❏ 456	Willie Greene	.15	.07
❏ 457	Mike Blowers	.15	.07
❏ 458	Kevin Roberson	.15	.07
❏ 459	Graeme Lloyd	.15	.07
❏ 460	David West	.15	.07
❏ 461	Joey Cora	.15	.07
❏ 462	Alex Arias	.15	.07
❏ 463	Chad Kreuter	.15	.07
❏ 464	Mike Lansing	.30	.14
❏ 465	Mike Timlin	.15	.07
❏ 466	Paul Wagner	.15	.07
❏ 467	Mark Portugal	.15	.07
❏ 468	Jim Leyritz	.15	.07
❏ 469	Ryan Klesko	.60	.25
❏ 470	Mario Diaz	.15	.07
❏ 471	Guillermo Velasquez	.15	.07
❏ 472	Fernando Valenzuela	.30	.14
❏ 473	Raul Mondesi	.60	.25
❏ 474	Mike Pagliarulo	.15	.07
❏ 475	Chris Hammond	.15	.07
❏ 476	Torey Lovullo	.15	.07
❏ 477	Trevor Wilson	.15	.07
❏ 478	Marcos Armas	.15	.07
❏ 479	Dave Gallagher	.15	.07
❏ 480	Jeff Treadway	.15	.07
❏ 481	Jeff Branson	.15	.07
❏ 482	Dickie Thon	.15	.07
❏ 483	Eduardo Perez	.15	.07
❏ 484	David Wells	.30	.14
❏ 485	Brian Williams	.15	.07
❏ 486	Domingo Cedeno	.15	.07
❏ 487	Tom Candiotti	.15	.07
❏ 488	Steve Frey	.15	.07
❏ 489	Greg McMichael	.15	.07
❏ 490	Marc Newfield	.15	.07
❏ 491	Larry Andersen	.15	.07
❏ 492	Damon Buford	.15	.07
❏ 493	Ricky Gutierrez	.15	.07
❏ 494	Jeff Russell	.15	.07
❏ 495	Vinny Castilla	.75	.35
❏ 496	Wilson Alvarez	.30	.14
❏ 497	Scott Bullett	.15	.07
❏ 498	Larry Casian	.15	.07
❏ 499	Jose Vizcaino	.15	.07
❏ 500	J.T. Snow	.75	.35
❏ 501	Bryan Hickerson	.15	.07
❏ 502	Jeremy Hernandez	.15	.07
❏ 503	Jeromy Burnitz	.30	.14
❏ 504	Steve Farr	.15	.07
❏ 505	J. Owens	.15	.07
❏ 506	Craig Paquette	.15	.07
❏ 507	Jim Eisenreich	.15	.07
❏ 508	Matt Whiteside	.15	.07
❏ 509	Luis Aquino	.15	.07
❏ 510	Mike LaValliere	.15	.07
❏ 511	Jim Gott	.15	.07
❏ 512	Mark McLemore	.15	.07
❏ 513	Randy Milligan	.15	.07
❏ 514	Gary Gaetti	.30	.14
❏ 515	Lou Frazier	.15	.07
❏ 516	Rich Amaral	.15	.07
❏ 517	Gene Harris	.15	.07
❏ 518	Aaron Sele	.60	.25
❏ 519	Mark Wohlers	.15	.07
❏ 520	Scott Kamieniecki	.15	.07
❏ 521	Kent Mercker	.15	.07
❏ 522	Jim Deshaies	.15	.07
❏ 523	Kevin Stocker	.15	.07
❏ 524	Jason Bere	.15	.07
❏ 525	Tim Bogar	.15	.07
❏ 526	Brad Pennington	.15	.07
❏ 527	Curt Leskanic	.15	.07
❏ 528	Wayne Kirby	.15	.07
❏ 529	Tim Costo	.15	.07
❏ 530	Doug Henry	.15	.07
❏ 531	Trevor Hoffman	.60	.25
❏ 532	Kelly Gruber	.15	.07
❏ 533	Mike Harkey	.15	.07
❏ 534	John Doherty	.15	.07
❏ 535	Erik Pappas	.15	.07
❏ 536	Brent Gates	.15	.07
❏ 537	Roger McDowell	.15	.07
❏ 538	Chris Haney	.15	.07
❏ 539	Blas Minor	.15	.07
❏ 540	Pat Hentgen	.40	.18
❏ 541	Chuck Carr	.15	.07
❏ 542	Doug Strange	.15	.07
❏ 543	Xavier Hernandez	.15	.07

		MINT	NRMT
544	Paul Quantrill	.15	.07
545	Anthony Young	.15	.07
546	Bret Boone	.30	.14
547	Dwight Smith	.15	.07
548	Bobby Munoz	.15	.07
549	Russ Springer	.15	.07
550	Roger Pavlik	.15	.07
DW	Dave Winfield 3000 Hits	1.00	.45
FT	Frank Thomas AU/3500 (Certified autograph)	100.00	45.00

1993 Leaf Fasttrack

	MINT	NRMT
COMPLETE SET (20)	100.00	45.00
COMPLETE SERIES 1 (10)	60.00	27.00
COMPLETE SERIES 2 (10)	40.00	18.00
COMMON CARD (1-20)	2.00	.90
RANDOM INSERTS IN RETAIL PACKS		

		MINT	NRMT
1	Frank Thomas	20.00	9.00
2	Tim Wakefield	3.00	1.35
3	Kenny Lofton	8.00	3.60
4	Mike Mussina	8.00	3.60
5	Juan Gonzalez	20.00	9.00
6	Chuck Knoblauch	8.00	3.60
7	Eric Karros	5.00	2.20
8	Ray Lankford	5.00	2.20
9	Juan Guzman	2.00	.90
10	Pat Listach	2.00	.90
11	Carlos Baerga	2.00	.90
12	Felix Jose	2.00	.90
13	Steve Avery	2.00	.90
14	Robin Ventura	3.00	1.35
15	Ivan Rodriguez	8.00	3.60
16	Cal Eldred	2.00	.90
17	Jeff Bagwell	8.00	3.60
18	David Justice	8.00	3.60
19	Travis Fryman	3.00	1.35
20	Marquis Grissom	3.00	1.35

1993 Leaf Gold All-Stars

	MINT	NRMT
COMPLETE REG.SET (20)	40.00	18.00
COMPLETE UPDATE SET (10)	12.00	5.50
COMMON CARD (R1-U10)	.50	.23
SEMISTARS	1.00	.45
R1-R20 ONE PER JUMBO PACK		
U1-U10 INSERTS IN UPDATE PACKS		

		MINT	NRMT
R1	Ivan Rodriguez / Darren Daulton	.75	.35
R2	Don Mattingly / Fred McGriff	2.00	.90
R3	Cecil Fielder / Jeff Bagwell	1.25	.55
R4	Carlos Baerga / Ryne Sandberg	1.50	.70
R5	Chuck Knoblauch / Delino DeShields	1.00	.45
R6	Robin Ventura / Andy Van Slyke	.50	.23
R7	Ken Griffey Jr. / Andy Van Slyke	5.00	2.20
R8	Joe Carter / Dave Justice	.75	.35
R9	Jose Canseco / Tony Gwynn	2.50	1.10
R10	Dennis Eckersley / Rob Dibble	.50	.23
R11	Mark McGwire / Will Clark	5.00	2.20
R12	Frank Thomas / Mark Grace	2.00	.90
R13	Roberto Alomar / Craig Biggio	1.50	.70
R14	Cal Ripken / Barry Larkin	4.00	1.80
R15	Edgar Martinez / Gary Sheffield	1.00	.45
R16	Juan Gonzalez / Barry Bonds	2.00	.90
R17	Kirby Puckett / Marquis Grissom	1.50	.70
R18	Jim Abbott / Tom Glavine	.75	.35
R19	Nolan Ryan / Greg Maddux	8.00	3.60
R20	Roger Clemens / Doug Drabek	2.50	1.10
U1	Mark Langston / Terry Mulholland	.50	.23
U2	Ivan Rodriguez / Darren Daulton	.75	.35
U3	John Olerud / John Kruk	.50	.23
U4	Roberto Alomar / Ryne Sandberg	1.50	.70
U5	Wade Boggs / Gary Sheffield	1.50	.70
U6	Cal Ripken / Barry Larkin	4.00	1.80
U7	Kirby Puckett / Barry Bonds	2.00	.90
U8	Ken Griffey Jr. / Marquis Grissom	5.00	2.20
U9	Joe Carter / David Justice	1.00	.45
U10	Paul Molitor / Mark Grace	1.00	.45

1993 Leaf Gold Rookies

	MINT	NRMT
COMPLETE REG.SET (20)	40.00	18.00
COMPLETE UPDATE SET (5)	20.00	9.00
COMMON CARD (R1-U5)	1.00	.45
SEMISTARS	1.50	.70

R1-R20 INSERTS IN HOBBY FOIL PACKS
U1-U5 INSERTS IN UPDATE PACKS
*JUMBOS:2X BASIC GOLD ROOKIES

		MINT	NRMT
R1	Kevin Young	1.25	.55
R2	Wil Cordero	1.00	.45
R3	Mark Kiefer	1.00	.45
R4	Gerald Williams	1.00	.45
R5	Brandon Wilson	1.00	.45
R6	Greg Gohr	1.00	.45
R7	Ryan Thompson	1.00	.45
R8	Tim Wakefield	1.25	.55
R9	Troy Neel	1.00	.45
R10	Tim Salmon	4.00	1.80
R11	Kevin Rogers	1.00	.45
R12	Rod Bolton	1.00	.45
R13	Ken Ryan	1.00	.45
R14	Phil Hiatt	1.00	.45
R15	Rene Arocha	1.00	.45
R16	Nigel Wilson	1.00	.45
R17	J.T. Snow	3.00	1.35
R18	Benji Gil	1.00	.45
R19	Chipper Jones	15.00	6.75
R20	Darrell Sherman	1.00	.45
U1	Allen Watson	1.00	.45
U2	Jeffrey Hammonds	1.25	.55
U3	David McCarty	1.00	.45
U4	Mike Piazza	15.00	6.75
U5	Roberto Mejia	1.00	.45

1993 Leaf Heading for the Hall

	MINT	NRMT
COMPLETE SET (10)	30.00	13.50
COMPLETE SERIES 1 (5)	20.00	9.00
COMPLETE SERIES 2 (5)	10.00	4.50
COMMON CARD (1-10)	2.00	.90
RANDOM INSERTS IN PACKS		

		MINT	NRMT
1	Nolan Ryan	10.00	4.50
2	Tony Gwynn	6.00	2.70
3	Robin Yount	2.00	.90
4	Eddie Murray	2.00	.90
5	Cal Ripken	10.00	4.50
6	Roger Clemens	6.00	2.70
7	George Brett	5.00	2.20
8	Ryne Sandberg	3.00	1.35
9	Kirby Puckett	4.00	1.80
10	Ozzie Smith	3.00	1.35

1993 Leaf Thomas

	MINT	NRMT
COMPLETE SET (10)	40.00	18.00
COMMON THOMAS (1-10)	5.00	2.20
RANDOM INSERTS IN BOTH SERIES PACKS		
COMPLETE JUMBO SET (10)	60.00	27.00
COMMON JUMBO (1-10)	6.00	2.70
ONE JUMBO CARD PER UPDATE BOX		

		MINT	NRMT
1	Frank Thomas (Aggressive)	5.00	2.20
2	Frank Thomas (Serious)	5.00	2.20
3	Frank Thomas (Intense)	5.00	2.20
4	Frank Thomas	5.00	2.20

Confident
		MINT	NRMT
❑ 5	Frank Thomas	5.00	2.20

Assertive
| ❑ 6 | Frank Thomas | 5.00 | 2.20 |

Power
| ❑ 7 | Frank Thomas | 5.00 | 2.20 |

Control
| ❑ 8 | Frank Thomas | 5.00 | 2.20 |

Strength
| ❑ 9 | Frank Thomas | 5.00 | 2.20 |

Concentration
| ❑ 10 | Frank Thomas | 5.00 | 2.20 |

Preparation

1994 Leaf

	MINT	NRMT
COMPLETE SET (440)	24.00	11.00
COMPLETE SERIES 1 (220)	12.00	5.50
COMPLETE SERIES 2 (220)	12.00	5.50
COMMON CARD (1-440)	.15	.07
MINOR STARS	.30	.14
UNLISTED STARS	.60	.25
THOMAS ANN. STATED ODDS 1:36		

❑ 1	Cal Ripken Jr.	2.50	1.10
❑ 2	Tony Tarasco	.15	.07
❑ 3	Joe Girardi	.15	.07
❑ 4	Bernie Williams	.60	.25
❑ 5	Chad Kreuter	.15	.07
❑ 6	Troy Neel	.15	.07
❑ 7	Tom Pagnozzi	.15	.07
❑ 8	Kirk Rueter	.15	.07
❑ 9	Chris Bosio	.15	.07
❑ 10	Dwight Gooden	.30	.14
❑ 11	Mariano Duncan	.15	.07
❑ 12	Jay Bell	.30	.14
❑ 13	Lance Johnson	.15	.07
❑ 14	Richie Lewis	.15	.07
❑ 15	Dave Martinez	.15	.07
❑ 16	Orel Hershiser	.30	.14
❑ 17	Rob Butler	.15	.07
❑ 18	Glenallen Hill	.15	.07
❑ 19	Chad Curtis	.15	.07
❑ 20	Mike Stanton	.15	.07
❑ 21	Tim Wallach	.15	.07
❑ 22	Milt Thompson	.15	.07
❑ 23	Kevin Young	.15	.07
❑ 24	John Smiley	.15	.07
❑ 25	Jeff Montgomery	.15	.07
❑ 26	Robin Ventura	.30	.14
❑ 27	Scott Lydy	.15	.07
❑ 28	Todd Stottlemyre	.15	.07
❑ 29	Mark Whiten	.15	.07
❑ 30	Robby Thompson	.15	.07
❑ 31	Bobby Bonilla	.30	.14
❑ 32	Andy Ashby	.15	.07
❑ 33	Greg Myers	.15	.07
❑ 34	Billy Hatcher	.15	.07
❑ 35	Brad Holman	.15	.07
❑ 36	Mark McLemore	.15	.07
❑ 37	Scott Sanders	.15	.07
❑ 38	Jim Abbott	.30	.14
❑ 39	David Wells	.40	.18
❑ 40	Roberto Kelly	.15	.07
❑ 41	Jeff Conine	.15	.07
❑ 42	Sean Berry	.15	.07
❑ 43	Mark Grace	.40	.18
❑ 44	Eric Young	.15	.07
❑ 45	Rick Aguilera	.15	.07
❑ 46	Chipper Jones	1.50	.70
❑ 47	Mel Rojas	.15	.07
❑ 48	Ryan Thompson	.15	.07
❑ 49	Al Martin	.15	.07
❑ 50	Cecil Fielder	.30	.14
❑ 51	Pat Kelly	.15	.07
❑ 52	Kevin Tapani	.15	.07
❑ 53	Tim Costo	.15	.07
❑ 54	Dave Hollins	.15	.07
❑ 55	Kirt Manwaring	.15	.07
❑ 56	Gregg Jefferies	.15	.07
❑ 57	Ron Darling	.15	.07
❑ 58	Bill Haselman	.15	.07
❑ 59	Phil Plantier	.15	.07
❑ 60	Frank Viola	.15	.07
❑ 61	Todd Zeile	.15	.07
❑ 62	Bret Barberie	.15	.07
❑ 63	Roberto Mejia	.15	.07
❑ 64	Chuck Knoblauch	.60	.25
❑ 65	Jose Lind	.15	.07
❑ 66	Brady Anderson	.30	.14
❑ 67	Ruben Sierra	.15	.07
❑ 68	Jose Vizcaino	.15	.07
❑ 69	Joe Grahe	.15	.07
❑ 70	Kevin Appier	.30	.14
❑ 71	Wilson Alvarez	.30	.14
❑ 72	Tom Candiotti	.15	.07
❑ 73	John Burkett	.15	.07
❑ 74	Anthony Young	.15	.07
❑ 75	Scott Cooper	.15	.07
❑ 76	Nigel Wilson	.15	.07
❑ 77	John Valentin	.30	.14
❑ 78	David McCarty	.15	.07
❑ 79	Archi Cianfrocco	.15	.07
❑ 80	Lou Whitaker	.30	.14
❑ 81	Dante Bichette	.30	.14
❑ 82	Mark Dewey	.15	.07
❑ 83	Danny Jackson	.15	.07
❑ 84	Harold Baines	.30	.14
❑ 85	Todd Benzinger	.15	.07
❑ 86	Damion Easley	.30	.14
❑ 87	Danny Cox	.15	.07
❑ 88	Jose Bautista	.15	.07
❑ 89	Mike Lansing	.30	.14
❑ 90	Phil Hiatt	.15	.07
❑ 91	Tim Pugh	.15	.07
❑ 92	Tino Martinez	.60	.25
❑ 93	Raul Mondesi	.60	.25
❑ 94	Greg Maddux	1.50	.70
❑ 95	Al Leiter	.30	.14
❑ 96	Benito Santiago	.15	.07
❑ 97	Lenny Dykstra	.30	.14
❑ 98	Sammy Sosa	2.50	1.10
❑ 99	Tim Bogar	.15	.07
❑ 100	Checklist	.15	.07
❑ 101	Deion Sanders	.30	.14
❑ 102	Bobby Witt	.15	.07
❑ 103	Wil Cordero	.15	.07
❑ 104	Rich Amaral	.15	.07
❑ 105	Mike Mussina	.60	.25
❑ 106	Reggie Sanders	.30	.14
❑ 107	Ozzie Guillen	.15	.07
❑ 108	Paul O'Neill	.30	.14
❑ 109	Tim Salmon	.60	.25
❑ 110	Rheal Cormier	.15	.07
❑ 111	Billy Ashley	.15	.07
❑ 112	Jeff Kent	.30	.14
❑ 113	Derek Bell	.30	.14
❑ 114	Danny Darwin	.15	.07
❑ 115	Chip Hale	.15	.07
❑ 116	Tim Raines	.30	.14
❑ 117	Ed Sprague	.15	.07
❑ 118	Darrin Fletcher	.15	.07
❑ 119	Darren Holmes	.15	.07
❑ 120	Alan Trammell	.40	.18
❑ 121	Don Mattingly	1.25	.55
❑ 122	Greg Gagne	.15	.07
❑ 123	Jose Offerman	.30	.14
❑ 124	Joe Orsulak	.15	.07
❑ 125	Jack McDowell	.15	.07
❑ 126	Barry Larkin	.60	.25
❑ 127	Ben McDonald	.15	.07
❑ 128	Mike Bordick	.15	.07
❑ 129	Devon White	.15	.07
❑ 130	Mike Perez	.15	.07
❑ 131	Jay Buhner	.30	.14
❑ 132	Phil Leftwich	.15	.07
❑ 133	Tommy Greene	.15	.07
❑ 134	Charlie Hayes	.15	.07
❑ 135	Don Slaught	.15	.07
❑ 136	Mike Gallego	.15	.07
❑ 137	Dave Winfield	.60	.25
❑ 138	Steve Avery	.15	.07
❑ 139	Derrick May	.15	.07
❑ 140	Bryan Harvey	.15	.07
❑ 141	Wally Joyner	.30	.14
❑ 142	Andre Dawson	.40	.18
❑ 143	Andy Benes	.30	.14
❑ 144	John Franco	.30	.14
❑ 145	Jeff King	.15	.07
❑ 146	Joe Oliver	.15	.07
❑ 147	Bill Gullickson	.15	.07
❑ 148	Armando Reynoso	.15	.07
❑ 149	Dave Fleming	.15	.07
❑ 150	Checklist	.15	.07
❑ 151	Todd Van Poppel	.15	.07
❑ 152	Bernard Gilkey	.15	.07
❑ 153	Kevin Gross	.15	.07
❑ 154	Mike Devereaux	.15	.07
❑ 155	Tim Wakefield	.30	.14
❑ 156	Andres Galarraga	.60	.25
❑ 157	Pat Meares	.15	.07
❑ 158	Jim Leyritz	.30	.14
❑ 159	Mike Macfarlane	.15	.07
❑ 160	Tony Phillips	.15	.07
❑ 161	Brent Gates	.15	.07
❑ 162	Mark Langston	.15	.07
❑ 163	Allen Watson	.15	.07
❑ 164	Randy Johnson	.60	.25
❑ 165	Doug Brocail	.15	.07
❑ 166	Rob Dibble	.15	.07
❑ 167	Roberto Hernandez	.15	.07
❑ 168	Felix Jose	.15	.07
❑ 169	Steve Cooke	.15	.07
❑ 170	Darren Daulton	.30	.14
❑ 171	Eric Karros	.30	.14
❑ 172	Geronimo Pena	.15	.07
❑ 173	Gary DiSarcina	.15	.07
❑ 174	Marquis Grissom	.30	.14
❑ 175	Joey Cora	.15	.07
❑ 176	Jim Eisenreich	.15	.07
❑ 177	Brad Pennington	.15	.07
❑ 178	Terry Steinbach	.15	.07
❑ 179	Pat Borders	.15	.07
❑ 180	Steve Buechele	.15	.07
❑ 181	Jeff Fassero	.15	.07
❑ 182	Mike Greenwell	.15	.07
❑ 183	Mike Henneman	.15	.07
❑ 184	Ron Karkovice	.15	.07
❑ 185	Pat Hentgen	.30	.14
❑ 186	Jose Guzman	.15	.07
❑ 187	Brett Butler	.30	.14
❑ 188	Charlie Hough	.15	.07
❑ 189	Terry Pendleton	.15	.07
❑ 190	Melido Perez	.15	.07
❑ 191	Orestes Destrade	.15	.07
❑ 192	Mike Morgan	.15	.07
❑ 193	Joe Carter	.30	.14
❑ 194	Jeff Blauser	.15	.07
❑ 195	Chris Hoiles	.15	.07
❑ 196	Ricky Gutierrez	.15	.07
❑ 197	Mike Moore	.15	.07
❑ 198	Carl Willis	.15	.07

❏ 199	Aaron Sele	.30	.14
❏ 200	Checklist	.15	.07
❏ 201	Tim Naehring	.15	.07
❏ 202	Scott Livingstone	.15	.07
❏ 203	Luis Alicea	.15	.07
❏ 204	Torey Lovullo	.15	.07
❏ 205	Jim Gott	.15	.07
❏ 206	Bob Wickman	.15	.07
❏ 207	Greg McMichael	.15	.07
❏ 208	Scott Brosius	.30	.14
❏ 209	Chris Gwynn	.15	.07
❏ 210	Steve Sax	.15	.07
❏ 211	Dick Schofield	.15	.07
❏ 212	Robb Nen	.15	.07
❏ 213	Ben Rivera	.15	.07
❏ 214	Vinny Castilla	.30	.14
❏ 215	Jamie Moyer	.15	.07
❏ 216	Wally Whitehurst	.15	.07
❏ 217	Frank Castillo	.15	.07
❏ 218	Mike Blowers	.15	.07
❏ 219	Tim Scott	.15	.07
❏ 220	Paul Wagner	.15	.07
❏ 221	Jeff Bagwell	.75	.35
❏ 222	Ricky Bones	.15	.07
❏ 223	Sandy Alomar Jr.	.30	.14
❏ 224	Rod Beck	.15	.07
❏ 225	Roberto Alomar	.25	.11
❏ 226	Jack Armstrong	.15	.07
❏ 227	Scott Erickson	.30	.14
❏ 228	Rene Arocha	.15	.07
❏ 229	Eric Anthony	.15	.07
❏ 230	Jeromy Burnitz	.30	.14
❏ 231	Kevin Brown	.30	.14
❏ 232	Tim Belcher	.15	.07
❏ 233	Bret Boone	.30	.14
❏ 234	Dennis Eckersley	.30	.14
❏ 235	Tom Glavine	.60	.25
❏ 236	Craig Biggio	.60	.25
❏ 237	Pedro Astacio	.15	.07
❏ 238	Ryan Bowen	.15	.07
❏ 239	Brad Ausmus	.15	.07
❏ 240	Vince Coleman	.15	.07
❏ 241	Jason Bere	.15	.07
❏ 242	Ellis Burks	.30	.14
❏ 243	Wes Chamberlain	.15	.07
❏ 244	Ken Caminiti	.40	.18
❏ 245	Willie Banks	.15	.07
❏ 246	Sid Fernandez	.15	.07
❏ 247	Carlos Baerga	.30	.14
❏ 248	Carlos Garcia	.15	.07
❏ 249	Jose Canseco	.75	.35
❏ 250	Alex Diaz	.15	.07
❏ 251	Albert Belle	.60	.25
❏ 252	Moises Alou	.30	.14
❏ 253	Bobby Ayala	.15	.07
❏ 254	Tony Gwynn	1.50	.70
❏ 255	Roger Clemens	1.50	.70
❏ 256	Eric Davis	.30	.14
❏ 257	Wade Boggs	.60	.25
❏ 258	Chili Davis	.15	.07
❏ 259	Rickey Henderson	.75	.35
❏ 260	Andujar Cedeno	.15	.07
❏ 261	Cris Carpenter	.15	.07
❏ 262	Juan Guzman	.15	.07
❏ 263	David Justice	.60	.25
❏ 264	Barry Bonds	.75	.35
❏ 265	Pete Incaviglia	.15	.07
❏ 266	Tony Fernandez	.30	.14
❏ 267	Cal Eldred	.15	.07
❏ 268	Alex Fernandez	.15	.07
❏ 269	Kent Hrbek	.30	.14
❏ 270	Steve Farr	.15	.07
❏ 271	Doug Drabek	.15	.07
❏ 272	Brian Jordan	.30	.14
❏ 273	Xavier Hernandez	.15	.07
❏ 274	David Cone	.40	.18
❏ 275	Brian Hunter	.15	.07
❏ 276	Mike Harkey	.15	.07
❏ 277	Delino DeShields	.15	.07
❏ 278	David Hulse	.15	.07
❏ 279	Mickey Tettleton	.15	.07
❏ 280	Kevin McReynolds	.15	.07
❏ 281	Darryl Hamilton	.15	.07
❏ 282	Ken Hill	.15	.07
❏ 283	Wayne Kirby	.15	.07
❏ 284	Chris Hammond	.15	.07
❏ 285	Mo Vaughn	.60	.25
❏ 286	Ryan Klesko	.30	.14
❏ 287	Rick Wilkins	.15	.07
❏ 288	Bill Swift	.15	.07
❏ 289	Rafael Palmeiro	.60	.25
❏ 290	Brian Harper	.15	.07
❏ 291	Chris Turner	.15	.07
❏ 292	Luis Gonzalez	.30	.14
❏ 293	Kenny Rogers	.15	.07
❏ 294	Kirby Puckett	1.00	.45
❏ 295	Mike Stanley	.15	.07
❏ 296	Carlos Reyes	.15	.07
❏ 297	Charles Nagy	.30	.14
❏ 298	Reggie Jefferson	.15	.07
❏ 299	Bip Roberts	.15	.07
❏ 300	Darrin Jackson	.15	.07
❏ 301	Mike Jackson	.15	.07
❏ 302	Dave Nilsson	.30	.14
❏ 303	Ramon Martinez	.30	.14
❏ 304	Bobby Jones	.15	.07
❏ 305	Johnny Ruffin	.15	.07
❏ 306	Brian McRae	.15	.07
❏ 307	Bo Jackson	.30	.14
❏ 308	Dave Stewart	.30	.14
❏ 309	John Smoltz	.40	.18
❏ 310	Dennis Martinez	.15	.07
❏ 311	Dean Palmer	.30	.14
❏ 312	David Nied	.15	.07
❏ 313	Eddie Murray	.60	.25
❏ 314	Darryl Kile	.15	.07
❏ 315	Rick Sutcliffe	.15	.07
❏ 316	Shawon Dunston	.15	.07
❏ 317	John Jaha	.15	.07
❏ 318	Salomon Torres	.15	.07
❏ 319	Gary Sheffield	.60	.25
❏ 320	Curt Schilling	.30	.14
❏ 321	Greg Vaughn	.30	.14
❏ 322	Jay Howell	.15	.07
❏ 323	Todd Hundley	.30	.14
❏ 324	Chris Sabo	.15	.07
❏ 325	Stan Javier	.15	.07
❏ 326	Willie Greene	.15	.07
❏ 327	Hipolito Pichardo	.15	.07
❏ 328	Doug Strange	.15	.07
❏ 329	Dan Wilson	.15	.07
❏ 330	Checklist	.15	.07
❏ 331	Omar Vizquel	.30	.14
❏ 332	Scott Servais	.15	.07
❏ 333	Bob Tewksbury	.15	.07
❏ 334	Matt Williams	.40	.18
❏ 335	Tom Foley	.15	.07
❏ 336	Jeff Russell	.15	.07
❏ 337	Scott Leius	.15	.07
❏ 338	Ivan Rodriguez	.75	.35
❏ 339	Kevin Seitzer	.15	.07
❏ 340	Jose Rijo	.15	.07
❏ 341	Eduardo Perez	.15	.07
❏ 342	Kirk Gibson	.30	.14
❏ 343	Randy Milligan	.15	.07
❏ 344	Edgar Martinez	.30	.14
❏ 345	Fred McGriff	.40	.18
❏ 346	Kurt Abbott	.15	.07
❏ 347	John Kruk	.30	.14
❏ 348	Mike Felder	.15	.07
❏ 349	Dave Staton	.15	.07
❏ 350	Kenny Lofton	.60	.25
❏ 351	Graeme Lloyd	.15	.07
❏ 352	David Segui	.30	.14
❏ 353	Danny Tartabull	.15	.07
❏ 354	Bob Welch	.15	.07
❏ 355	Duane Ward	.15	.07
❏ 356	Karl Rhodes	.15	.07
❏ 357	Lee Smith	.30	.14
❏ 358	Chris James	.15	.07
❏ 359	Walt Weiss	.15	.07
❏ 360	Pedro Munoz	.15	.07
❏ 361	Paul Sorrento	.15	.07
❏ 362	Todd Worrell	.15	.07
❏ 363	Bob Hamelin	.30	.14
❏ 364	Julio Franco	.15	.07
❏ 365	Roberto Petagine	.15	.07
❏ 366	Willie McGee	.30	.14
❏ 367	Pedro Martinez	.75	.35
❏ 368	Ken Griffey Jr.	3.00	1.35
❏ 369	B.J. Surhoff	.15	.07
❏ 370	Kevin Mitchell	.15	.07
❏ 371	John Doherty	.15	.07
❏ 372	Manuel Lee	.15	.07
❏ 373	Terry Mulholland	.15	.07
❏ 374	Zane Smith	.15	.07
❏ 375	Otis Nixon	.15	.07
❏ 376	Jody Reed	.15	.07
❏ 377	Doug Jones	.15	.07
❏ 378	John Olerud	.30	.14
❏ 379	Greg Swindell	.15	.07
❏ 380	Checklist	.15	.07
❏ 381	Royce Clayton	.15	.07
❏ 382	Jim Thome	.60	.25
❏ 383	Steve Finley	.30	.14
❏ 384	Ray Lankford	.30	.14
❏ 385	Henry Rodriguez	.30	.14
❏ 386	Dave Magadan	.15	.07
❏ 387	Gary Redus	.15	.07
❏ 388	Orlando Merced	.15	.07
❏ 389	Tom Gordon	.15	.07
❏ 390	Luis Polonia	.15	.07
❏ 391	Mark McGwire	3.00	1.35
❏ 392	Mark Lemke	.15	.07
❏ 393	Doug Henry	.15	.07
❏ 394	Chuck Finley	.30	.14
❏ 395	Paul Molitor	.60	.25
❏ 396	Randy Myers	.15	.07
❏ 397	Larry Walker	.60	.25
❏ 398	Pete Harnisch	.15	.07
❏ 399	Darren Lewis	.15	.07
❏ 400	Frank Thomas	1.25	.55
❏ 401	Jack Morris	.30	.14
❏ 402	Greg Hibbard	.15	.07
❏ 403	Jeffrey Hammonds	.30	.14
❏ 404	Will Clark	.60	.25
❏ 405	Travis Fryman	.30	.14
❏ 406	Scott Sanderson	.15	.07
❏ 407	Gene Harris	.15	.07
❏ 408	Chuck Carr	.15	.07
❏ 409	Ozzie Smith	.75	.35
❏ 410	Kent Mercker	.15	.07
❏ 411	Andy Van Slyke	.30	.14
❏ 412	Jimmy Key	.30	.14
❏ 413	Pat Mahomes	.15	.07
❏ 414	John Wetteland	.30	.14
❏ 415	Todd Jones	.15	.07
❏ 416	Greg Harris	.15	.07
❏ 417	Kevin Stocker	.15	.07
❏ 418	Juan Gonzalez	1.25	.55
❏ 419	Pete Smith	.15	.07
❏ 420	Pat Listach	.15	.07
❏ 421	Trevor Hoffman	.30	.14
❏ 422	Scott Fletcher	.15	.07
❏ 423	Mark Lewis	.15	.07
❏ 424	Mickey Morandini	.15	.07
❏ 425	Ryne Sandberg	.75	.35
❏ 426	Erik Hanson	.15	.07
❏ 427	Gary Gaetti	.30	.14
❏ 428	Harold Reynolds	.15	.07
❏ 429	Mark Portugal	.15	.07
❏ 430	David Valle	.15	.07
❏ 431	Mitch Williams	.15	.07
❏ 432	Howard Johnson	.15	.07
❏ 433	Hal Morris	.15	.07
❏ 434	Tom Henke	.15	.07
❏ 435	Shane Mack	.15	.07
❏ 436	Mike Piazza	2.00	.90
❏ 437	Bret Saberhagen	.30	.14
❏ 438	Jose Mesa	.15	.07
❏ 439	Jaime Navarro	.15	.07
❏ 440	Checklist	.15	.07
❏ A300	Frank Thomas	1.50	.70
	Leaf 5th Anniversary		

1994 Leaf Clean-Up Crew

	MINT	NRMT
COMPLETE SET (12)	35.00	16.00
COMPLETE SERIES 1 (6)	10.00	4.50
COMPLETE SERIES 2 (6)	25.00	11.00
COMMON CARD (1-12)	2.50	1.10
STATED ODDS 1:12 MAG-JUMBOS		

❏ 1	Larry Walker	6.00	2.70
❏ 2	Andres Galarraga	6.00	2.70

	MINT	NRMT
3 Dave Hollins	2.50	1.10
4 Bobby Bonilla	3.00	1.35
5 Cecil Fielder	2.50	1.10
6 Danny Tartabull	2.50	1.10
7 Juan Gonzalez	12.00	5.50
8 Joe Carter	3.00	1.35
9 Fred McGriff	4.00	1.80
10 Matt Williams	4.00	1.80
11 Albert Belle	6.00	2.70
12 Harold Baines	3.00	1.35

1994 Leaf Gamers

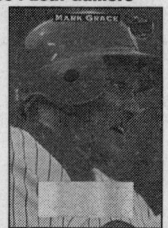

	MINT	NRMT
COMPLETE SET (12)	80.00	36.00
COMPLETE SERIES 1 (6)	40.00	18.00
COMPLETE SERIES 2 (6)	40.00	18.00
COMMON CARD (1-12)	1.50	.70
STATED ODDS 1:8 JUMBO		
1 Ken Griffey Jr.	25.00	11.00
2 Lenny Dykstra	1.50	.70
3 Juan Gonzalez	10.00	4.50
4 Don Mattingly	10.00	4.50
5 David Justice	3.00	1.35
6 Mark Grace	3.00	1.35
7 Frank Thomas	10.00	4.50
8 Barry Bonds	6.00	2.70
9 Kirby Puckett	8.00	3.60
10 Will Clark	5.00	2.20
11 John Kruk	2.50	1.10
12 Mike Piazza	15.00	6.75

1994 Leaf Gold Rookies

	MINT	NRMT
COMPLETE SET (20)	16.00	7.25
COMPLETE SERIES 1 (10)	12.00	5.50
COMPLETE SERIES 2 (10)	4.00	1.80
COMMON CARD (1-20)	.50	.23
MINOR STARS	1.00	.45
STAT.ODDS 1:18 SER.1, 1:12 SER.2		
1 Javier Lopez	1.50	.70
2 Rondell White	1.00	.45
3 Butch Huskey	1.00	.45
4 Midre Cummings	.50	.23
5 Scott Ruffcorn	.50	.23
6 Manny Ramirez	6.00	2.70
7 Danny Bautista	.50	.23
8 Russ Davis	1.00	.45
9 Steve Karsay	.50	.23
10 Carlos Delgado	2.50	1.10
11 Bob Hamelin	1.00	.45
12 Marcus Moore	.50	.23
13 Miguel Jimenez	.50	.23
14 Matt Walbeck	.50	.23
15 James Mouton	.50	.23
16 Rich Becker	.50	.23
17 Brian Anderson	1.50	.70
18 Cliff Floyd	1.00	.45
19 Steve Trachsel	.50	.23
20 Hector Carrasco	.50	.23

1994 Leaf Gold Stars

	MINT	NRMT
COMPLETE SET (15)	200.00	90.00
COMPLETE SERIES 1 (8)	120.00	55.00
COMPLETE SERIES 2 (7)	80.00	36.00
COMMON CARD (1-15)	5.00	2.20
UNLISTED STARS	10.00	4.50
SER.1 STAT.ODDS 1:90H/R, 1:28BJ, 1:240M		
STATED PRINT RUN 10,000 SERIAL #'d SETS		
1 Roberto Alomar	10.00	4.50
2 Barry Bonds	12.00	5.50
3 David Justice	10.00	4.50
4 Ken Griffey Jr.	50.00	22.00
5 Lenny Dykstra	6.00	2.70
6 Don Mattingly	20.00	9.00
7 Andres Galarraga	10.00	4.50
8 Greg Maddux	25.00	11.00
9 Carlos Baerga	5.00	2.20
10 Paul Molitor	10.00	4.50
11 Frank Thomas	20.00	9.00
12 John Olerud	6.00	2.70
13 Juan Gonzalez	20.00	9.00
14 Fred McGriff	8.00	3.60
15 Jack McDowell	5.00	2.20

1994 Leaf MVP Contenders

	MINT	NRMT
COMPLETE SET (30)	150.00	70.00
COMMON CARD (1-30)	1.50	.70
SER.2 STAT.ODDS 1:36H/R, 1:90J, 1:90MAG		
STATED PRINT RUN 10,000 SERIAL #'d SETS		
COMP.GOLD SET (30)	150.00	70.00

*GOLD: SAME PRICE AS BASIC MVPS
ONE GOLD SET PER A13 OR N1 VIA MAIL
ONE THOMAS J400 PER A13 OR N1 VIA MAIL

THOMAS JUMBO PRINT RUN 20,000 #'d CARDS

	MINT	NRMT
A1 Albert Belle	6.00	2.70
A2 Jose Canseco	8.00	3.60
A3 Joe Carter	2.50	1.10
A4 Will Clark	6.00	2.70
A5 Cecil Fielder	1.50	.70
A6 Juan Gonzalez	12.00	5.50
A7 Ken Griffey Jr	30.00	13.50
A8 Paul Molitor	6.00	2.70
A9 Rafael Palmeiro	6.00	2.70
A10 Kirby Puckett	10.00	4.50
A11 Cal Ripken Jr	25.00	11.00
A12 Frank Thomas W	12.00	5.50
A13 Mo Vaughn	6.00	2.70
A14 Carlos Baerga	1.50	.70
A15 AL Bonus Card	1.50	.70
N1 Gary Sheffield	2.50	1.10
N2 Jeff Bagwell W	8.00	3.60
N3 Dante Bichette	2.50	1.10
N4 Barry Bonds	8.00	3.60
N5 Darren Daulton	1.50	.70
N6 Andres Galarraga	6.00	2.70
N7 Gregg Jefferies	1.50	.70
N8 David Justice	6.00	2.70
N9 Ray Lankford	2.50	1.10
N10 Fred McGriff	4.00	1.80
N11 Barry Larkin	6.00	2.70
N12 Mike Piazza	20.00	9.00
N13 Deion Sanders	2.50	1.10
N14 Matt Williams	6.00	2.70
N15 NL Bonus Card	1.50	.70
J400 Frank Thomas Jumbo	6.00	2.70

1994 Leaf Power Brokers

	MINT	NRMT
COMPLETE SET (10)	20.00	9.00
COMMON CARD (1-10)	.75	.35
SER.2 STATED ODDS 1:12 HOB/RET		
1 Frank Thomas	3.00	1.35
2 David Justice	1.50	.70
3 Barry Bonds	2.00	.90
4 Juan Gonzalez	3.00	1.35
5 Ken Griffey Jr.	8.00	3.60
6 Mike Piazza	5.00	2.20
7 Cecil Fielder	.75	.35

		MINT	NRMT
❏ 8	Fred McGriff	1.00	.45
❏ 9	Joe Carter	.75	.35
❏ 10	Albert Belle	1.50	.70

1994 Leaf Slideshow

	MINT	NRMT
COMPLETE SET (10)	60.00	27.00
COMPLETE SERIES 1 (5)	30.00	13.50
COMPLETE SERIES 2 (5)	30.00	13.50
COMMON CARD (1-10)	2.00	.90
STATED ODDS 1:54H/R, 1:36J, 1:36M		

❏ 1	Frank Thomas	8.00	3.60
❏ 2	Mike Piazza	12.00	5.50
❏ 3	Darren Daulton	2.00	.90
❏ 4	Ryne Sandberg	5.00	2.20
❏ 5	Roberto Alomar	4.00	1.80
❏ 6	Barry Bonds	5.00	2.20
❏ 7	Juan Gonzalez	8.00	3.60
❏ 8	Tim Salmon	4.00	1.80
❏ 9	Ken Griffey Jr.	20.00	9.00
❏ 10	David Justice	4.00	1.80

1994 Leaf Statistical Standouts

	MINT	NRMT
COMPLETE SET (10)	20.00	9.00
*.6X TO 1.5X BASE CARD HI		
SER.1 STATED ODDS 1:12 HOB/RET		

❏ 1	Frank Thomas	2.00	.90
❏ 2	Barry Bonds	1.25	.55
❏ 3	Juan Gonzalez	2.00	.90
❏ 4	Mike Piazza	3.00	1.35
❏ 5	Greg Maddux	2.50	1.10
❏ 6	Ken Griffey Jr.	5.00	2.20
❏ 7	Joe Carter	.50	.23
❏ 8	Dave Winfield	1.00	.45
❏ 9	Tony Gwynn	2.50	1.10
❏ 10	Cal Ripken	4.00	1.80

1995 Leaf

	MINT	NRMT
COMPLETE SET (400)	40.00	18.00
COMPLETE SERIES 1 (200)	15.00	6.75
COMPLETE SERIES 2 (200)	25.00	11.00
COMMON CARD (1-400)	.15	.07

MINOR STARS		.30	.14
UNLISTED STARS		.60	.25
❏ 1	Frank Thomas	1.25	.55
❏ 2	Carlos Garcia	.15	.07
❏ 3	Todd Hundley	.30	.14
❏ 4	Damion Easley	.30	.14
❏ 5	Roberto Mejia	.15	.07
❏ 6	John Mabry	.15	.07
❏ 7	Aaron Sele	.30	.14
❏ 8	Kenny Lofton	.40	.18
❏ 9	John Doherty	.15	.07
❏ 10	Joe Carter	.30	.14
❏ 11	Mike Lansing	.15	.07
❏ 12	John Valentin	.15	.07
❏ 13	Ismael Valdes	.30	.14
❏ 14	Dave McCarty	.15	.07
❏ 15	Melvin Nieves	.15	.07
❏ 16	Bobby Jones	.15	.07
❏ 17	Trevor Hoffman	.30	.14
❏ 18	John Smoltz	.40	.18
❏ 19	Leo Gomez	.15	.07
❏ 20	Roger Pavlik	.15	.07
❏ 21	Dean Palmer	.30	.14
❏ 22	Rickey Henderson	.75	.35
❏ 23	Eddie Taubensee	.15	.07
❏ 24	Damon Buford	.15	.07
❏ 25	Mark Wohlers	.15	.07
❏ 26	Jim Edmonds	.40	.18
❏ 27	Wilson Alvarez	.30	.14
❏ 28	Matt Williams	.60	.25
❏ 29	Jeff Montgomery	.15	.07
❏ 30	Shawon Dunston	.15	.07
❏ 31	Tom Pagnozzi	.15	.07
❏ 32	Jose Lind	.15	.07
❏ 33	Royce Clayton	.15	.07
❏ 34	Cal Eldred	.15	.07
❏ 35	Chris Gomez	.15	.07
❏ 36	Henry Rodriguez	.30	.14
❏ 37	Dave Fleming	.15	.07
❏ 38	Jon Lieber	.15	.07
❏ 39	Scott Servais	.15	.07
❏ 40	Wade Boggs	.60	.25
❏ 41	John Olerud	.30	.14
❏ 42	Eddie Williams	.15	.07
❏ 43	Paul Sorrento	.15	.07
❏ 44	Ron Karkovice	.15	.07
❏ 45	Kevin Foster	.15	.07
❏ 46	Miguel Jimenez	.15	.07
❏ 47	Reggie Sanders	.30	.14
❏ 48	Rondell White	.30	.14
❏ 49	Scott Leius	.15	.07
❏ 50	Jose Valentin	.15	.07
❏ 51	Wm. VanLandingham	.15	.07
❏ 52	Denny Hocking	.15	.07
❏ 53	Jeff Fassero	.15	.07
❏ 54	Chris Hoiles	.15	.07
❏ 55	Walt Weiss	.15	.07
❏ 56	Geronimo Berroa	.15	.07
❏ 57	Rich Rowland	.15	.07
❏ 58	Dave Weathers	.15	.07
❏ 59	Sterling Hitchcock	.30	.14
❏ 60	Raul Mondesi	.40	.18
❏ 61	Rusty Greer	.60	.25
❏ 62	David Justice	.60	.25
❏ 63	Cecil Fielder	.30	.14
❏ 64	Brian Jordan	.30	.14
❏ 65	Mike Lieberthal	.15	.07
❏ 66	Rick Aguilera	.15	.07
❏ 67	Chuck Finley	.30	.14
❏ 68	Andy Ashby	.15	.07
❏ 69	Alex Fernandez	.15	.07
❏ 70	Ed Sprague	.15	.07
❏ 71	Steve Buechele	.15	.07
❏ 72	Willie Greene	.15	.07
❏ 73	Dave Nilsson	.15	.07
❏ 74	Bret Saberhagen	.30	.14
❏ 75	Jimmy Key	.30	.14
❏ 76	Darren Lewis	.15	.07
❏ 77	Steve Cooke	.15	.07
❏ 78	Kirk Gibson	.30	.14
❏ 79	Ray Lankford	.30	.14
❏ 80	Paul O'Neill	.30	.14
❏ 81	Mike Bordick	.15	.07
❏ 82	Wes Chamberlain	.15	.07
❏ 83	Rico Brogna	.15	.07
❏ 84	Kevin Appier	.30	.14
❏ 85	Juan Guzman	.15	.07
❏ 86	Kevin Seitzer	.15	.07
❏ 87	Mickey Morandini	.15	.07
❏ 88	Pedro Martinez	.75	.35
❏ 89	Matt Mieske	.15	.07
❏ 90	Tino Martinez	.60	.25
❏ 91	Paul Shuey	.15	.07
❏ 92	Bip Roberts	.15	.07
❏ 93	Chili Davis	.30	.14
❏ 94	Deion Sanders	.30	.14
❏ 95	Darrell Whitmore	.15	.07
❏ 96	Joe Orsulak	.15	.07
❏ 97	Bret Boone	.30	.14
❏ 98	Kent Mercker	.15	.07
❏ 99	Scott Livingstone	.15	.07
❏ 100	Brady Anderson	.30	.14
❏ 101	James Mouton	.15	.07
❏ 102	Jose Rijo	.15	.07
❏ 103	Kenny Munoz	.15	.07
❏ 104	Ramon Martinez	.30	.14
❏ 105	Bernie Williams	.60	.25
❏ 106	Troy Neel	.15	.07
❏ 107	Ivan Rodriguez	.75	.35
❏ 108	Salomon Torres	.15	.07
❏ 109	Johnny Ruffin	.15	.07
❏ 110	Darryl Kile	.15	.07
❏ 111	Bobby Ayala	.15	.07
❏ 112	Ron Darling	.15	.07
❏ 113	Jose Lima	.15	.07
❏ 114	Joey Hamilton	.30	.14
❏ 115	Greg Maddux	1.50	.70
❏ 116	Greg Colbrunn	.15	.07
❏ 117	Ozzie Guillen	.15	.07
❏ 118	Brian Anderson	.30	.14
❏ 119	Jeff Bagwell	.75	.35
❏ 120	Pat Listach	.15	.07
❏ 121	Sandy Alomar Jr.	.30	.14
❏ 122	Jose Vizcaino	.15	.07
❏ 123	Rick Helling	.30	.14
❏ 124	Allen Watson	.15	.07
❏ 125	Pedro Munoz	.15	.07
❏ 126	Craig Biggio	.60	.25
❏ 127	Kevin Stocker	.15	.07
❏ 128	Wil Cordero	.15	.07
❏ 129	Rafael Palmeiro	.60	.25
❏ 130	Gar Finnvold	.15	.07
❏ 131	Darren Hall	.15	.07
❏ 132	Heath Slocumb	.15	.07
❏ 133	Darrin Fletcher	.15	.07
❏ 134	Cal Ripken	2.50	1.10
❏ 135	Dante Bichette	.30	.14
❏ 136	Don Slaught	.15	.07
❏ 137	Pedro Astacio	.15	.07
❏ 138	Ryan Thompson	.15	.07
❏ 139	Greg Gohr	.15	.07
❏ 140	Javier Lopez	.30	.14
❏ 141	Lenny Dykstra	.15	.07
❏ 142	Pat Rapp	.15	.07
❏ 143	Mark Kiefer	.15	.07
❏ 144	Greg Gagne	.15	.07
❏ 145	Eduardo Perez	.15	.07
❏ 146	Felix Fermin	.15	.07
❏ 147	Jeff Frye	.15	.07
❏ 148	Terry Steinbach	.15	.07
❏ 149	Jim Eisenreich	.15	.07
❏ 150	Brad Ausmus	.15	.07
❏ 151	Randy Myers	.15	.07

#	Player	Mint	Nrmt
152	Rick White	.15	.07
153	Mark Portugal	.15	.07
154	Delino DeShields	.15	.07
155	Scott Cooper	.15	.07
156	Pat Hentgen	.30	.14
157	Mark Gubicza	.15	.07
158	Carlos Baerga	.15	.07
159	Joe Girardi	.15	.07
160	Rey Sanchez	.15	.07
161	Todd Jones	.15	.07
162	Luis Polonia	.15	.07
163	Steve Trachsel	.15	.07
164	Roberto Hernandez	.15	.07
165	John Patterson	.15	.07
166	Rene Arocha	.15	.07
167	Will Clark	.60	.25
168	Jim Leyritz	.15	.07
169	Todd Van Poppel	.15	.07
170	Robb Nen	.15	.07
171	Midre Cummings	.15	.07
172	Jay Buhner	.30	.14
173	Kevin Tapani	.15	.07
174	Mark Lemke	.15	.07
175	Marcus Moore	.15	.07
176	Wayne Kirby	.15	.07
177	Rich Amaral	.15	.07
178	Lou Whitaker	.30	.14
179	Jay Bell	.15	.07
180	Rick Wilkins	.15	.07
181	Paul Molitor	.60	.25
182	Gary Sheffield	.30	.14
183	Kirby Puckett	1.00	.45
184	Cliff Floyd	.30	.14
185	Darren Oliver	.15	.07
186	Tim Naehring	.15	.07
187	John Hudek	.15	.07
188	Eric Young	.15	.07
189	Roger Salkeld	.15	.07
190	Kirt Manwaring	.15	.07
191	Kurt Abbott	.15	.07
192	David Nied	.15	.07
193	Todd Zeile	.15	.07
194	Wally Joyner	.30	.14
195	Dennis Martinez	.30	.14
196	Billy Ashley	.15	.07
197	Ben McDonald	.15	.07
198	Bob Hamelin	.15	.07
199	Chris Turner	.15	.07
200	Lance Johnson	.15	.07
201	Willie Banks	.15	.07
202	Juan Gonzalez	1.25	.55
203	Scott Sanders	.15	.07
204	Scott Brosius	.30	.14
205	Curt Schilling	.40	.18
206	Alex Gonzalez	.15	.07
207	Travis Fryman	.30	.14
208	Tim Raines	.30	.14
209	Steve Avery	.15	.07
210	Hal Morris	.15	.07
211	Ken Griffey Jr.	3.00	1.35
212	Ozzie Smith	.75	.35
213	Chuck Carr	.15	.07
214	Ryan Klesko	.30	.14
215	Robin Ventura	.30	.14
216	Luis Gonzalez	.15	.07
217	Ken Ryan	.15	.07
218	Mike Piazza	2.00	.90
219	Matt Walbeck	.15	.07
220	Jeff Kent	.30	.14
221	Orlando Miller	.15	.07
222	Kenny Rogers	.15	.07
223	J.T. Snow	.15	.07
224	Alan Trammell	.30	.14
225	John Franco	.15	.07
226	Gerald Williams	.15	.07
227	Andy Benes	.30	.14
228	Dan Wilson	.15	.07
229	Dave Hollins	.15	.07
230	Vinny Castilla	.40	.18
231	Devon White	.30	.14
232	Fred McGriff	.40	.18
233	Quilvio Veras	.15	.07
234	Tom Candiotti	.15	.07
235	Jason Bere	.15	.07
236	Mark Langston	.15	.07
237	Mel Rojas	.15	.07
238	Chuck Knoblauch	.60	.25
239	Bernard Gilkey	.15	.07
240	Mark McGwire	3.00	1.35
241	Kirk Rueter	.15	.07
242	Pat Kelly	.15	.07
243	Ruben Sierra	.15	.07
244	Randy Johnson	.60	.25
245	Shane Reynolds	.30	.14
246	Danny Tartabull	.15	.07
247	Darryl Hamilton	.15	.07
248	Danny Bautista	.15	.07
249	Tom Gordon	.15	.07
250	Tom Glavine	.60	.25
251	Orlando Merced	.15	.07
252	Eric Karros	.30	.14
253	Benji Gil	.15	.07
254	Sean Bergman	.15	.07
255	Roger Clemens	1.50	.70
256	Roberto Alomar	.60	.25
257	Benito Santiago	.15	.07
258	Bobby Thompson	.15	.07
259	Marvin Freeman	.15	.07
260	Jose Offerman	.30	.14
261	Greg Vaughn	.15	.07
262	David Segui	.15	.07
263	Geronimo Pena	.15	.07
264	Tim Salmon	.60	.25
265	Eddie Murray	.60	.25
266	Mariano Duncan	.15	.07
267	Hideo Nomo	1.50	.70
268	Derek Bell	.30	.14
269	Mo Vaughn	.60	.25
270	Jeff King	.15	.07
271	Edgar Martinez	.30	.14
272	Sammy Sosa	2.00	.90
273	Scott Ruffcorn	.15	.07
274	Darren Daulton	.30	.14
275	John Jaha	.15	.07
276	Andres Galarraga	.60	.25
277	Mark Grace	.40	.18
278	Mike Moore	.15	.07
279	Barry Bonds	.75	.35
280	Manny Ramirez	.75	.35
281	Ellis Burks	.30	.14
282	Greg Swindell	.15	.07
283	Barry Larkin	.60	.25
284	Albert Belle	.75	.35
285	Shawn Green	.60	.25
286	John Roper	.15	.07
287	Scott Erickson	.30	.14
288	Moises Alou	.30	.14
289	Mike Blowers	.15	.07
290	Brent Gates	.15	.07
291	Sean Berry	.15	.07
292	Mike Stanley	.15	.07
293	Jeff Conine	.15	.07
294	Tim Wallach	.15	.07
295	Bobby Bonilla	.30	.14
296	Bruce Ruffin	.15	.07
297	Chad Curtis	.15	.07
298	Mike Greenwell	.15	.07
299	Tony Gwynn	1.50	.70
300	Russ Davis	.30	.14
301	Danny Jackson	.15	.07
302	Pete Harnisch	.15	.07
303	Don Mattingly	1.25	.55
304	Rheal Cormier	.15	.07
305	Larry Walker	.60	.25
306	Hector Carrasco	.15	.07
307	Jason Jacome	.15	.07
308	Phil Plantier	.15	.07
309	Harold Baines	.30	.14
310	Mitch Williams	.15	.07
311	Charles Nagy	.30	.14
312	Ken Caminiti	.40	.18
313	Alex Rodriguez	2.50	1.10
314	Chris Sabo	.15	.07
315	Gary Gaetti	.15	.07
316	Andre Dawson	.40	.18
317	Mark Gubicza	.15	.07
318	Vince Coleman	.15	.07
319	Brad Clontz	.15	.07
320	Steve Finley	.30	.14
321	Doug Drabek	.15	.07
322	Mark McLemore	.15	.07
323	Stan Javier	.15	.07
324	Ron Gant	.15	.07
325	Charlie Hayes	.15	.07
326	Carlos Delgado	.60	.25
327	Ricky Bottalico	.15	.07
328	Rod Beck	.15	.07
329	Mark Acre	.15	.07
330	Chris Bosio	.15	.07
331	Tony Phillips	.15	.07
332	Garret Anderson	.30	.14
333	Pat Meares	.15	.07
334	Todd Worrell	.15	.07
335	Marquis Grissom	.30	.14
336	Brent Mayne	.15	.07
337	Lee Tinsley	.15	.07
338	Terry Pendleton	.15	.07
339	David Cone	.40	.18
340	Tony Fernandez	.30	.14
341	Jim Bullinger	.15	.07
342	Armando Benitez	.15	.07
343	John Smiley	.15	.07
344	Dan Miceli	.15	.07
345	Charles Johnson	.30	.14
346	Lee Smith	.30	.14
347	Brian McRae	.15	.07
348	Jim Thome	.60	.25
349	Jose Oliva	.15	.07
350	Terry Mulholland	.15	.07
351	Tom Henke	.15	.07
352	Dennis Eckersley	.30	.14
353	Sid Fernandez	.15	.07
354	Paul Wagner	.15	.07
355	John Dettmer	.15	.07
356	John Wetteland	.30	.14
357	John Burkett	.15	.07
358	Marty Cordova	.15	.07
359	Norm Charlton	.15	.07
360	Mike Devereaux	.15	.07
361	Alex Cole	.15	.07
362	Brett Butler	.30	.14
363	Mickey Tettleton	.15	.07
364	Al Martin	.15	.07
365	Tony Tarasco	.15	.07
366	Pat Mahomes	.15	.07
367	Gary DiSarcina	.15	.07
368	Bill Swift	.15	.07
369	Chipper Jones	1.50	.70
370	Orel Hershiser	.30	.14
371	Kevin Gross	.15	.07
372	Dave Winfield	.60	.25
373	Andujar Cedeno	.15	.07
374	Jim Abbott	.30	.14
375	Glenallen Hill	.15	.07
376	Otis Nixon	.15	.07
377	Roberto Kelly	.15	.07
378	Chris Hammond	.15	.07
379	Mike Macfarlane	.15	.07
380	J.R. Phillips	.15	.07
381	Luis Alicea	.15	.07
382	Bret Barberie	.15	.07
383	Tom Goodwin	.15	.07
384	Mark Whiten	.15	.07
385	Jeffrey Hammonds	.30	.14
386	Omar Vizquel	.30	.14
387	Mike Mussina	.60	.25
388	Ricky Bones	.15	.07
389	Steve Ontiveros	.15	.07
390	Jeff Blauser	.15	.07
391	Jose Canseco	.75	.35
392	Bob Tewksbury	.15	.07
393	Jacob Brumfield	.15	.07
394	Doug Jones	.15	.07
395	Ken Hill	.15	.07
396	Pat Borders	.15	.07
397	Carl Everett	.15	.07
398	Gregg Jefferies	.15	.07
399	Jack McDowell	.15	.07
400	Denny Neagle	.30	.14

1995 Leaf Checklists

	MINT	NRMT
COMPLETE SET (8)	8.00	3.60
COMPLETE SERIES 1 (4)	4.00	1.80
COMPLETE SERIES 2 (4)	4.00	1.80
COMMON CARD (1-8)	.15	.07
RANDOM INSERTS IN BOTH SERIES PACKS		

		MINT	NRMT
❏ 1	Bob Hamelin UER .... (Name spelled Hamlin)	.15	.07
❏ 2	David Cone	.40	.18
❏ 3	Frank Thomas	1.25	.55
❏ 4	Paul O'Neill	.25	.11
❏ 5	Raul Mondesi	.40	.18
❏ 6	Greg Maddux	1.50	.70
❏ 7	Tony Gwynn	1.50	.70
❏ 8	Jeff Bagwell	.75	.35

1995 Leaf Cornerstones

		MINT	NRMT
	COMPLETE SET (6)	10.00	4.50
	COMMON CARD (1-6)	1.00	.45
	SER.1 STATED ODDS 1:18 HOB/RET		
❏ 1	Frank Thomas .... Robin Ventura	2.50	1.10
❏ 2	Cecil Fielder .... Travis Fryman	1.00	.45
❏ 3	Don Mattingly .... Wade Boggs	2.50	1.10
❏ 4	Jeff Bagwell .... Ken Caminiti	1.50	.70
❏ 5	Will Clark .... Dean Palmer	1.50	.70
❏ 6	J.R. Phillips .... Matt Williams	1.00	.45

1995 Leaf Gold Rookies

	MINT	NRMT
COMPLETE SET (16)	6.00	2.70

		MINT	NRMT
	COMMON CARD (1-25)	.25	.11
	SER.1 STATED ODDS 1:2 HOB/RET		
❏ 1	Alex Rodriguez	4.00	1.80
❏ 2	Garret Anderson	.50	.23
❏ 3	Shawn Green	1.50	.70
❏ 4	Armando Benitez	.25	.11
❏ 5	Darren Dreifort	.50	.23
❏ 6	Orlando Miller	.25	.11
❏ 7	Jose Oliva	.25	.11
❏ 8	Ricky Bottalico	.25	.11
❏ 9	Charles Johnson	.50	.23
❏ 10	Brian L.Hunter	.50	.23
❏ 11	Ray McDavid	.25	.11
❏ 12	Chan Ho Park	1.50	.70
❏ 13	Mike Kelly	.25	.11
❏ 14	Cory Bailey	.25	.11
❏ 15	Alex Gonzalez	.25	.11
❏ 16	Andrew Lorraine	.25	.11

1995 Leaf Gold Stars

		MINT	NRMT
	COMPLETE SET (14)	160.00	70.00
	COMPLETE SERIES 1 (8)	80.00	36.00
	COMPLETE SERIES 2 (6)	80.00	38.00
	COMMON CARD (1-14)	6.00	2.70
	STATED ODDS 1:110 HOB/RET		
	STATED PRINT RUN 10,000 SERIAL #'d SETS		
❏ 1	Jeff Bagwell	8.00	3.60
❏ 2	Albert Belle	8.00	3.60
❏ 3	Tony Gwynn	20.00	9.00
❏ 4	Ken Griffey Jr.	40.00	18.00
❏ 5	Barry Bonds	8.00	3.60
❏ 6	Don Mattingly	12.00	5.50
❏ 7	Raul Mondesi	6.00	2.70
❏ 8	Joe Carter	6.00	2.70
❏ 9	Greg Maddux	25.00	11.00
❏ 10	Frank Thomas	20.00	9.00
❏ 11	Mike Piazza	25.00	11.00
❏ 12	Jose Canseco	8.00	3.60
❏ 13	Kirby Puckett	8.00	3.60
❏ 14	Matt Williams	8.00	3.60

1995 Leaf Great Gloves

		MINT	NRMT
	COMPLETE SET (16)	10.00	4.50
	COMMON CARD (1-16)	.25	.11
	SER.2 STATED ODDS 1:2		

		MINT	NRMT
❏ 1	Jeff Bagwell	.75	.35
❏ 2	Roberto Alomar	.60	.25
❏ 3	Barry Bonds	.75	.35
❏ 4	Wade Boggs	.60	.25
❏ 5	Andres Galarraga	.60	.25
❏ 6	Ken Griffey Jr.	3.00	1.35
❏ 7	Marquis Grissom	.25	.11
❏ 8	Kenny Lofton	.40	.18
❏ 9	Barry Larkin	.60	.25
❏ 10	Don Mattingly	1.25	.55
❏ 11	Greg Maddux	1.50	.70
❏ 12	Kirby Puckett	.75	.35
❏ 13	Ozzie Smith	.75	.35
❏ 14	Cal Ripken Jr.	2.50	1.10
❏ 15	Matt Williams	.60	.25
❏ 16	Ivan Rodriguez	.75	.35

1995 Leaf Heading for the Hall

		MINT	NRMT
	COMPLETE SET (8)	180.00	80.00
	COMMON CARD (1-8)	10.00	4.50
	SER.2 STATED ODDS 1:75 HOBBY		
	STATED PRINT RUN 5000 SERIAL #'d SETS		
❏ 1	Frank Thomas	20.00	9.00
❏ 2	Ken Griffey Jr.	50.00	22.00
❏ 3	Jeff Bagwell	12.00	5.50
❏ 4	Barry Bonds	12.00	5.50
❏ 5	Kirby Puckett	15.00	6.75
❏ 6	Cal Ripken	40.00	18.00
❏ 7	Tony Gwynn	25.00	11.00
❏ 8	Paul Molitor	10.00	4.50

1995 Leaf Slideshow

		MINT	NRMT
	COMPLETE SET (16)	80.00	36.00
	COMPLETE SERIES 1 (8)	40.00	18.00
	COMPLETE SERIES 2 (8)	40.00	18.00
	COMMON CARD (1-8)	2.00	.90
	SERIES 1 AND 2 CARDS SAME VALUE		
	STATED ODDS 1:30 HOB, 1:36 RET		
❏ 1A	Raul Mondesi	2.00	.90
❏ 1B	Raul Mondesi	2.00	.90
❏ 2A	Frank Thomas	6.00	2.70
❏ 2B	Frank Thomas	6.00	2.70
❏ 3A	Fred McGriff	2.00	.90

		MINT	NRMT
❑ 3B	Fred McGriff	2.00	.90
❑ 4A	Cal Ripken	12.00	5.50
❑ 4B	Cal Ripken	12.00	5.50
❑ 5A	Jeff Bagwell	4.00	1.80
❑ 5B	Jeff Bagwell	4.00	1.80
❑ 6A	Will Clark	2.50	1.10
❑ 6B	Will Clark	2.50	1.10
❑ 7A	Matt Williams	2.50	1.10
❑ 7B	Matt Williams	2.50	1.10
❑ 8A	Ken Griffey Jr.	15.00	6.75
❑ 8B	Ken Griffey Jr.	15.00	6.75

1995 Leaf Statistical Standouts

	MINT	NRMT
COMPLETE SET (9)	350.00	160.00
COMMON CARD (1-9)	12.00	5.50
UNLISTED STARS	20.00	9.00
SER.1 STATED ODDS 1:70 HOBBY		

		MINT	NRMT
❑ 1	Joe Carter	12.00	5.50
❑ 2	Ken Griffey Jr.	100.00	45.00
❑ 3	Don Mattingly	40.00	18.00
❑ 4	Fred McGriff	12.00	5.50
❑ 5	Paul Molitor	20.00	9.00
❑ 6	Kirby Puckett	30.00	13.50
❑ 7	Cal Ripken	80.00	36.00
❑ 8	Frank Thomas	50.00	22.00
❑ 9	Matt Williams	20.00	9.00

1995 Leaf Thomas

	MINT	NRMT
COMPLETE SET (6)	25.00	11.00
COMMON CARD (1-6)	5.00	2.20
SER.2 STATED ODDS 1:18		

		MINT	NRMT
❑ 1	Frank Thomas The Rookie	5.00	2.20
❑ 2	Frank Thomas Sophomore Stardom	5.00	2.20
❑ 3	Frank Thomas Superstar	5.00	2.20
❑ 4	Frank Thomas AL MVP	5.00	2.20
❑ 5	Frank Thomas Back-To-Back	5.00	2.20
❑ 6	Frank Thomas The Big Hurt	5.00	2.20

1995 Leaf 300 Club

	MINT	NRMT
COMPLETE SET (18)	120.00	55.00
COMPLETE SERIES 1 (9)	50.00	22.00
COMPLETE SERIES 2 (9)	70.00	32.00
COMMON CARD (1-18)	1.50	.70
STATED ODDS 1:12 RETAIL/MINI		

		MINT	NRMT
❑ 1	Frank Thomas	10.00	4.50
❑ 2	Paul Molitor	5.00	2.20
❑ 3	Mike Piazza	15.00	6.75
❑ 4	Moises Alou	3.00	1.35
❑ 5	Mike Greenwell	1.50	.70
❑ 6	Will Clark	5.00	2.20
❑ 7	Hal Morris	1.50	.70
❑ 8	Edgar Martinez	3.00	1.35
❑ 9	Carlos Baerga	1.50	.70
❑ 10	Ken Griffey Jr.	25.00	11.00
❑ 11	Wade Boggs	5.00	2.20
❑ 12	Jeff Bagwell	6.00	2.70
❑ 13	Tony Gwynn	12.00	5.50
❑ 14	John Kruk	3.00	1.35
❑ 15	Don Mattingly	10.00	4.50
❑ 16	Mark Grace	4.00	1.80
❑ 17	Kirby Puckett	6.00	2.70
❑ 18	Kenny Lofton	4.00	1.80

1996 Leaf

	MINT	NRMT
COMPLETE SET (220)	20.00	9.00
COMMON CARD (1-220)	.15	.07
MINOR STARS	.30	.14
UNLISTED STARS	.60	.25
COMMON BRZ.PP (1-220)	1.50	.70
*BRONZE PP STARS: 5X TO 12X HI COLUMN		
*BRONZE PP YOUNG STARS: 3X TO 8X HI		
BRONZE PP STATED PRINT RUN 2000 SETS		
COMMON GOLD PP (1-220)	5.00	2.20
*GOLD PP STARS: 15X TO 40X HI COLUMN		
*GOLD PP YOUNG STARS: 12.5X TO 30X HI		
GOLD PP STATED PRINT RUN 500 SETS		
COMMON SILV.PP (1-220)	3.00	1.35
*SILV.PP STARS: 10X TO 25X HI COLUMN		
*SILV.PP YOUNG STARS: 8X TO 20X HI		
SILVER PP STATED PRINT RUN 1000 SETS		
1:10 PACKS CONTAINS EITHER B, G OR S PP		

		MINT	NRMT
❑ 1	John Smoltz	.40	.18
❑ 2	Dennis Eckersley	.30	.14

❑ 3	Delino DeShields	.15	.07
❑ 4	Cliff Floyd	.30	.14
❑ 5	Chuck Finley	.30	.14
❑ 6	Cecil Fielder	.30	.14
❑ 7	Tim Naehring	.15	.07
❑ 8	Carlos Perez	.15	.07
❑ 9	Brad Ausmus	.15	.07
❑ 10	Matt Lawton	.75	.35
❑ 11	Alan Trammell	.40	.18
❑ 12	Steve Finley	.30	.14
❑ 13	Paul O'Neill	.30	.14
❑ 14	Gary Sheffield	.30	.14
❑ 15	Mark McGwire	3.00	1.35
❑ 16	Bernie Williams	.60	.25
❑ 17	Jeff Montgomery	.15	.07
❑ 18	Chan Ho Park	.40	.18
❑ 19	Greg Vaughn	.30	.14
❑ 20	Jeff Kent	.30	.14
❑ 21	Cal Ripken	2.50	1.10
❑ 22	Charles Johnson	.30	.14
❑ 23	Eric Karros	.30	.14
❑ 24	Alex Rodriguez	2.00	.90
❑ 25	Chris Snopek	.15	.07
❑ 26	Jason Isringhausen	.30	.14
❑ 27	Chili Davis	.15	.07
❑ 28	Chipper Jones	1.50	.70
❑ 29	Bret Saberhagen	.30	.14
❑ 30	Tony Clark	.60	.25
❑ 31	Marty Cordova	.15	.07
❑ 32	Dwayne Hosey	.15	.07
❑ 33	Fred McGriff	.40	.18
❑ 34	Deion Sanders	.30	.14
❑ 35	Orlando Merced	.15	.07
❑ 36	Brady Anderson	.30	.14
❑ 37	Ray Lankford	.30	.14
❑ 38	Manny Ramirez	.75	.35
❑ 39	Alex Fernandez	.15	.07
❑ 40	Greg Colbrunn	.15	.07
❑ 41	Ken Griffey, Jr.	3.00	1.35
❑ 42	Mickey Morandini	.15	.07
❑ 43	Chuck Knoblauch	.60	.25
❑ 44	Quinton McCracken	.15	.07
❑ 45	Tim Salmon	.40	.18
❑ 46	Jose Mesa	.15	.07
❑ 47	Marquis Grissom	.15	.07
❑ 48	Checklist	.15	.07
❑ 49	Raul Mondesi	.30	.14
❑ 50	Mark Grudzielanek	.15	.07
❑ 51	Ray Durham	.30	.14
❑ 52	Matt Williams	.60	.25
❑ 53	Bob Hamelin	.15	.07
❑ 54	Lenny Dykstra	.15	.07
❑ 55	Jeff King	.15	.07
❑ 56	LaTroy Hawkins	.15	.07
❑ 57	Terry Pendleton	.15	.07
❑ 58	Kevin Stocker	.15	.07
❑ 59	Ozzie Timmons	.15	.07
❑ 60	David Justice	.60	.25
❑ 61	Ricky Bottalico	.15	.07
❑ 62	Andy Ashby	.15	.07
❑ 63	Larry Walker	.60	.25
❑ 64	Jose Canseco	.75	.35
❑ 65	Bret Boone	.15	.07
❑ 66	Shawn Green	.60	.25
❑ 67	Chad Curtis	.15	.07
❑ 68	Travis Fryman	.30	.14
❑ 69	Roger Clemens	1.50	.70
❑ 70	David Bell	.15	.07
❑ 71	Rusty Greer	.30	.14
❑ 72	Bob Higginson	.30	.14
❑ 73	Joey Hamilton	.15	.07
❑ 74	Kevin Seitzer	.15	.07
❑ 75	Julian Tavarez	.15	.07
❑ 76	Troy Percival	.30	.14
❑ 77	Kirby Puckett	1.00	.45
❑ 78	Barry Bonds	.75	.35
❑ 79	Michael Tucker	.15	.07
❑ 80	Paul Molitor	.60	.25
❑ 81	Carlos Garcia	.15	.07
❑ 82	Johnny Damon	.40	.18
❑ 83	Mike Hampton	.30	.14
❑ 84	Ariel Prieto	.15	.07
❑ 85	Tony Tarasco	.15	.07
❑ 86	Pete Schourek	.15	.07
❑ 87	Tom Glavine	.60	.25
❑ 88	Rondell White	.30	.14

#	Player	MINT	NRMT
89	Jim Edmonds	.40	.18
90	Robby Thompson	.15	.07
91	Wade Boggs	.60	.25
92	Pedro Martinez	.75	.35
93	Gregg Jefferies	.15	.07
94	Albert Belle	.60	.25
95	Benji Gil	.15	.07
96	Denny Neagle	.30	.14
97	Mark Langston	.15	.07
98	Sandy Alomar Jr.	.30	.14
99	Tony Gwynn	1.50	.70
100	Todd Hundley	.30	.14
101	Dante Bichette	.30	.14
102	Eddie Murray	.60	.25
103	Lyle Mouton	.15	.07
104	Jon Jaha	.15	.07
105	Checklist	.15	.07
106	Jon Nunnally	.15	.07
107	Juan Gonzalez	1.25	.55
108	Kevin Appier	.30	.14
109	Brian McRae	.15	.07
110	Lee Smith	.30	.14
111	Tim Wakefield	.15	.07
112	Sammy Sosa	2.00	.90
113	Jay Buhner	.30	.14
114	Garret Anderson	.30	.14
115	Edgar Martinez	.30	.14
116	Edgardo Alfonzo	.60	.25
117	Billy Ashley	.15	.07
118	Joe Carter	.30	.14
119	Javy Lopez	.30	.14
120	Bobby Bonilla	.30	.14
121	Ken Caminiti	.30	.14
122	Barry Larkin	.60	.25
123	Shannon Stewart	.30	.14
124	Orel Hershiser	.30	.14
125	Jeff Conine	.15	.07
126	Mark Grace	.40	.18
127	Kenny Lofton	.40	.18
128	Luis Gonzalez	.30	.14
129	Rico Brogna	.15	.07
130	Mo Vaughn	.60	.25
131	Brad Radke	.30	.14
132	Jose Herrera	.15	.07
133	Rick Aguilera	.15	.07
134	Gary DiSarcina	.15	.07
135	Andres Galarraga	.60	.25
136	Carl Everett	.30	.14
137	Steve Avery	.15	.07
138	Vinny Castilla	.40	.18
139	Dennis Martinez	.30	.14
140	John Wetteland	.30	.14
141	Alex Gonzalez	.15	.07
142	Brian Jordan	.30	.14
143	Todd Hollandsworth	.15	.07
144	Terrell Wade	.15	.07
145	Wilson Alvarez	.15	.07
146	Reggie Sanders	.30	.14
147	Will Clark	.60	.25
148	Hideo Nomo	.60	.25
149	J.T.Snow	.30	.14
150	Frank Thomas	1.25	.55
151	Ivan Rodriguez	.75	.35
152	Jay Bell	.30	.14
153	Checklist	.15	.07
154	David Cone	.40	.18
155	Roberto Alomar	.60	.25
156	Carlos Delgado	.60	.25
157	Carlos Baerga		.25
158	Geronimo Berroa	.15	.07
159	Joe Vitiello	.15	.07
160	Terry Steinbach	.15	.07
161	Doug Drabek	.15	.07
162	David Segui	.30	.14
163	Ozzie Smith	.75	.35
164	Kurt Abbott	.15	.07
165	Randy Johnson	.60	.25
166	John Valentin	.30	.14
167	Mickey Tettleton	.15	.07
168	Ruben Sierra	.15	.07
169	Jim Thome	.60	.25
170	Mike Greenwell	.15	.07
171	Quilvio Veras	.15	.07
172	Robin Ventura	.30	.14
173	Bill Pulsipher	.15	.07
174	Rafael Palmeiro	.60	.25
175	Hal Morris	.15	.07
176	Ryan Klesko	.30	.14
177	Eric Young	.15	.07
178	Shane Andrews	.15	.07
179	Brian L.Hunter	.15	.07
180	Brett Butler	.30	.14
181	John Olerud	.30	.14
182	Moises Alou	.30	.14
183	Glenallen Hill	.15	.07
184	Ismael Valdes	.30	.14
185	Andy Pettitte	.40	.18
186	Yamil Benitez	.15	.07
187	Jason Bere	.15	.07
188	Dean Palmer	.30	.14
189	Jimmy Haynes	.15	.07
190	Trevor Hoffman	.30	.14
191	Mike Mussina	.60	.25
192	Greg Maddux	1.50	.70
193	Ozzie Guillen	.15	.07
194	Pat Listach	.15	.07
195	Derek Bell	.30	.14
196	Darren Daulton	.30	.14
197	John Mabry	.15	.07
198	Ramon Martinez	.30	.14
199	Jeff Bagwell	.75	.35
200	Mike Piazza	2.00	.90
201	Al Martin	.15	.07
202	Aaron Sele	.30	.14
203	Ed Sprague	.15	.07
204	Rod Beck	.15	.07
205	Checklist	.15	.07
206	Mike Lansing	.15	.07
207	Craig Biggio	.60	.25
208	Jeffrey Hammonds	.30	.14
209	Dave Nilsson	.15	.07
210	Checklist	.15	.07
211	Derek Jeter	2.00	.90
212	Alan Benes	.15	.07
213	Jason Schmidt	.15	.07
214	Alex Ochoa	.15	.07
215	Ruben Rivera	.30	.14
216	Roger Cedeno	.15	.07
217	Jeff Suppan	.15	.07
218	Billy Wagner	.40	.18
219	Mark Loretta	.15	.07
220	Karim Garcia	.30	.14

1996 Leaf All-Star Game MVP Contenders

		MINT	NRMT
	COMPLETE SET (20)	40.00	18.00
	COMMON CARD (1-20)	.25	.11
	RANDOM INSERTS IN PACKS		
	COMP.GOLD SET (20)	40.00	18.00
	*GOLD CARDS: .75X TO 2X BASE CARD HI		
	ONE GOLD SET PER PIAZZA VIA MAIL		
1	Frank Thomas	2.50	1.10
2	Mike Piazza W	6.00	2.70
3	Sammy Sosa	4.00	1.80
4	Cal Ripken	5.00	2.20
5	Jeff Bagwell	1.50	.70
6	Reggie Sanders	.50	.23
7	Mo Vaughn	1.25	.55
8	Tony Gwynn	3.00	1.35
9	Dante Bichette	.50	.23
10	Tim Salmon	.75	.35
11	Chipper Jones	3.00	1.35
12	Kenny Lofton	.75	.35
13	Manny Ramirez	1.50	.70
14	Barry Bonds	1.50	.70
15	Raul Mondesi	.50	.23
16	Kirby Puckett	2.50	1.10
17	Albert Belle	1.25	.55
18	Ken Griffey Jr.	6.00	2.70
19	Greg Maddux	3.00	1.35
20	Bonus Card	.25	.11

1996 Leaf Gold Stars

		MINT	NRMT
	COMPLETE SET (15)	450.00	200.00
	COMMON CARD (1-15)	10.00	4.50
	UNLISTED STARS	15.00	6.75
	STATED ODDS 1:190		
	STATED PRINT RUN 2500 SERIAL #'d SETS		
1	Frank Thomas	30.00	13.50
2	Dante Bichette	10.00	4.50
3	Sammy Sosa	50.00	22.00
4	Ken Griffey Jr.	80.00	36.00
5	Mike Piazza	50.00	22.00
6	Tim Salmon	12.00	5.50
7	Hideo Nomo	15.00	6.75
8	Cal Ripken	60.00	27.00
9	Chipper Jones	40.00	18.00
10	Albert Belle	15.00	6.75
11	Tony Gwynn	40.00	18.00
12	Mo Vaughn	15.00	6.75
13	Barry Larkin	15.00	6.75
14	Manny Ramirez	20.00	9.00
15	Greg Maddux	40.00	18.00

1996 Leaf Hats Off

		MINT	NRMT
	COMPLETE SET (8)	200.00	90.00
	COMMON CARD (1-8)	8.00	3.60
	STATED ODDS 1:72 RETAIL		
	STATED PRINT RUN 5000 SERIAL #'d SETS		
1	Cal Ripken	30.00	13.50
2	Barry Larkin	8.00	3.60
3	Frank Thomas	20.00	9.00
4	Mo Vaughn	8.00	3.60
5	Ken Griffey Jr.	40.00	18.00
6	Hideo Nomo	8.00	3.60
7	Albert Belle	8.00	3.60
8	Greg Maddux	25.00	11.00

1996 Leaf Picture Perfect

	MINT	NRMT
COMPLETE SET (12)	250.00	110.00
COMMON CARD (1-12)	8.00	3.60

CARDS 1-6 STATED ODDS 1:140 HOBBY
CARDS 7-12 RANDOM INS.IN RET.PACKS
STATED PRINT RUN 5000 SERIAL #'d SETS

		MINT	NRMT
❏ 1	Frank Thomas	20.00	9.00
❏ 2	Cal Ripken	30.00	13.50
❏ 3	Greg Maddux	25.00	11.00
❏ 4	Manny Ramirez	8.00	3.60
❏ 5	Chipper Jones	20.00	9.00
❏ 6	Tony Gwynn	8.00	3.60
❏ 7	Ken Griffey Jr.	40.00	18.00
❏ 8	Albert Belle	8.00	3.60
❏ 9	Jeff Bagwell	8.00	3.60
❏ 10	Mike Piazza	25.00	11.00
❏ 11	Mo Vaughn	8.00	3.60
❏ 12	Barry Bonds	8.00	3.60
❏ P10	Mike Piazza Promo	3.00	1.35

1996 Leaf Statistical Standouts

	MINT	NRMT
COMPLETE SET (8)	250.00	110.00
COMMON CARD (1-8)	12.00	5.50

STATED ODDS 1:210 HOBBY
STATED PRINT RUN 2500 SERIAL #'d SETS

		MINT	NRMT
❏ 1	Cal Ripken	50.00	22.00
❏ 2	Tony Gwynn	30.00	13.50
❏ 3	Frank Thomas	25.00	11.00
❏ 4	Ken Griffey Jr.	60.00	27.00
❏ 5	Hideo Nomo	20.00	9.00
❏ 6	Greg Maddux	30.00	13.50
❏ 7	Albert Belle	8.00	3.60
❏ 8	Chipper Jones	30.00	13.50

1996 Leaf Thomas Greatest Hits

	MINT	NRMT
COMPLETE SET (8)	150.00	70.00
COMMON CARD (1-7)	25.00	11.00
COMMON EXCHANGE (8)	30.00	13.50

CARDS 1-4 STATED ODDS 1:210 HOBBY
CARDS 5-7 STATED ODDS 1:210 RETAIL
CARD 8 WAS AVAIL.VIA MAIL-IN OFFER
STATED PRINT RUN 5000 SETS

		MINT	NRMT
❏ 1	Frank Thomas 1990	25.00	11.00
❏ 2	Frank Thomas 1991	25.00	11.00
❏ 3	Frank Thomas 1992	25.00	11.00
❏ 4	Frank Thomas 1993	25.00	11.00
❏ 5	Frank Thomas 1994	25.00	11.00
❏ 6	Frank Thomas 1995	25.00	11.00
❏ 7	Frank Thomas Career	25.00	11.00
❏ 8	Frank Thomas MVP	30.00	13.50

1996 Leaf Total Bases

PAUL MOLITOR

	MINT	NRMT
COMPLETE SET (12)	120.00	55.00
COMMON CARD (1-12)	3.00	1.35

STATED ODDS 1:72 HOBBY
STATED PRINT RUN 5000 SERIAL #'d SETS

		MINT	NRMT
❏ 1	Frank Thomas	15.00	6.75
❏ 2	Albert Belle	6.00	2.70
❏ 3	Rafael Palmeiro	6.00	2.70
❏ 4	Barry Bonds	6.00	2.70
❏ 5	Kirby Puckett	10.00	4.50
❏ 6	Joe Carter	4.00	1.80
❏ 7	Paul Molitor	6.00	2.70
❏ 8	Fred McGriff	5.00	2.20
❏ 9	Ken Griffey Jr.	30.00	13.50
❏ 10	Carlos Baerga	3.00	1.35
❏ 11	Juan Gonzalez	15.00	6.75
❏ 12	Cal Ripken	25.00	11.00

1997 Leaf

	MINT	NRMT
COMPLETE SET (400)	40.00	18.00
COMPLETE SERIES 1 (200)	20.00	9.00
COMPLETE SERIES 2 (200)	20.00	9.00
COMMON CARD (1-400)	.15	.07
MINOR STARS	.30	.14
UNLISTED STARS	.60	.25

SUBSET CARDS HALF VALUE OF BASE CARDS

		MINT	NRMT
❏ 1	Wade Boggs	.60	.25
❏ 2	Brian McRae	.15	.07
❏ 3	Jeff D'Amico	.15	.07
❏ 4	George Arias	.15	.07

		MINT	NRMT
❏ 5	Billy Wagner	.30	.14
❏ 6	Ray Lankford	.30	.14
❏ 7	Will Clark	.60	.25
❏ 8	Edgar Renteria	.30	.14
❏ 9	Alex Ochoa	.15	.07
❏ 10	Roberto Hernandez	.15	.07
❏ 11	Joe Carter	.30	.14
❏ 12	Gregg Jefferies	.15	.07
❏ 13	Mark Grace	.40	.18
❏ 14	Roberto Alomar	.60	.25
❏ 15	Joe Randa	.15	.07
❏ 16	Alex Rodriguez	2.00	.90
❏ 17	Tony Gwynn	1.50	.70
❏ 18	Steve Gibralter	.15	.07
❏ 19	Scott Stahoviak	.15	.07
❏ 20	Matt Williams	.60	.25
❏ 21	Quinton McCracken	.15	.07
❏ 22	Ugueth Urbina	.30	.14
❏ 23	Jermaine Allensworth	.15	.07
❏ 24	Paul Molitor	.60	.25
❏ 25	Carlos Delgado	.60	.25
❏ 26	Bob Abreu	.30	.14
❏ 27	John Jaha	.15	.07
❏ 28	Rusty Greer	.30	.14
❏ 29	Kimera Bartee	.15	.07
❏ 30	Ruben Rivera	.15	.07
❏ 31	Jason Kendall	.40	.18
❏ 32	Lance Johnson	.15	.07
❏ 33	Robin Ventura	.30	.14
❏ 34	Kevin Appier	.30	.14
❏ 35	John Mabry	.15	.07
❏ 36	Ricky Otero	.15	.07
❏ 37	Mike Lansing	.15	.07
❏ 38	Mark McGwire	3.00	1.35
❏ 39	Tim Naehring	.15	.07
❏ 40	Tom Glavine	.60	.25
❏ 41	Rey Ordonez	.30	.14
❏ 42	Tony Clark	.40	.18
❏ 43	Rafael Palmeiro	.60	.25
❏ 44	Pedro Martinez	.75	.35
❏ 45	Keith Lockhart	.15	.07
❏ 46	Dan Wilson	.15	.07
❏ 47	John Wetteland	.30	.14
❏ 48	Chan Ho Park	.60	.25
❏ 49	Gary Sheffield	.30	.14
❏ 50	Shawn Estes	.30	.14
❏ 51	Royce Clayton	.15	.07
❏ 52	Jaime Navarro	.15	.07
❏ 53	Raul Casanova	.15	.07
❏ 54	Jeff Bagwell	.75	.35
❏ 55	Barry Larkin	.60	.25
❏ 56	Charles Nagy	.30	.14
❏ 57	Ken Caminiti	.40	.18
❏ 58	Todd Hollandsworth	.15	.07
❏ 59	Pat Hentgen	.30	.14
❏ 60	Jose Valentin	.15	.07
❏ 61	Rafael Palmeiro	.15	.07
❏ 62	Mickey Tettleton	.15	.07
❏ 63	Marty Cordova	.15	.07
❏ 64	Cecil Fielder	.30	.14
❏ 65	Barry Bonds	.75	.35
❏ 66	Scott Servais	.15	.07
❏ 67	Ernie Young	.15	.07
❏ 68	Wilson Alvarez	.30	.14
❏ 69	Mike Grace	.15	.07
❏ 70	Shane Reynolds	.30	.14
❏ 71	Henry Rodriguez	.30	.14
❏ 72	Eric Karros	.30	.14

73	Mark Langston	.30	.14
74	Scott Karl	.15	.07
75	Trevor Hoffman	.30	.14
76	Orel Hershiser	.30	.14
77	John Smoltz	.40	.18
78	Raul Mondesi	.30	.14
79	Jeff Brantley	.15	.07
80	Donne Wall	.15	.07
81	Joey Cora	.15	.07
82	Mel Rojas	.15	.07
83	Chad Mottola	.15	.07
84	Omar Vizquel	.30	.14
85	Greg Maddux	1.50	.70
86	Jamey Wright	.15	.07
87	Chuck Finley	.30	.14
88	Brady Anderson	.30	.14
89	Alex Gonzalez	.15	.07
90	Andy Benes	.30	.14
91	Reggie Jefferson	.15	.07
92	Paul O'Neill	.30	.14
93	Javier Lopez	.30	.14
94	Mark Grudzielanek	.30	.14
95	Marc Newfield	.15	.07
96	Kevin Ritz	.15	.07
97	Fred McGriff	.40	.18
98	Dwight Gooden	.30	.14
99	Hideo Nomo	.60	.25
100	Steve Finley	.30	.14
101	Juan Gonzalez	1.25	.55
102	Jay Buhner	.30	.14
103	Paul Wilson	.15	.07
104	Alan Benes	.15	.07
105	Manny Ramirez	.75	.35
106	Kevin Elster	.15	.07
107	Frank Thomas	1.25	.55
108	Orlando Miller	.15	.07
109	Ramon Martinez	.30	.14
110	Kenny Lofton	.40	.18
111	Bernie Williams	.60	.25
112	Robby Thompson	.15	.07
113	Bernard Gilkey	.15	.07
114	Ray Durham	.30	.14
115	Jeff Cirillo	.30	.14
116	Brian Jordan	.30	.14
117	Rich Becker	.15	.07
118	Al Leiter	.30	.14
119	Mark Johnson	.15	.07
120	Ellis Burks	.30	.14
121	Sammy Sosa	2.00	.90
122	Willie Greene	.15	.07
123	Michael Tucker	.15	.07
124	Eddie Murray	.60	.25
125	Joey Hamilton	.30	.14
126	Antonio Osuna	.15	.07
127	Bobby Higginson	.30	.14
128	Tomas Perez	.15	.07
129	Tim Salmon	.60	.25
130	Mark Wohlers	.15	.07
131	Charles Johnson	.30	.14
132	Randy Johnson	.60	.25
133	Brooks Kieschnick	.15	.07
134	Al Martin	.15	.07
135	Dante Bichette	.30	.14
136	Andy Pettitte	.40	.18
137	Jason Giambi	.30	.14
138	James Baldwin	.30	.14
139	Ben McDonald	.15	.07
140	Shawn Green	.60	.25
141	Geronimo Berroa	.15	.07
142	Jose Offerman	.30	.14
143	Curtis Pride	.15	.07
144	Terrell Wade	.15	.07
145	Ismael Valdes	.30	.14
146	Mike Mussina	.60	.25
147	Mariano Rivera	.30	.14
148	Ken Hill	.15	.07
149	Darin Erstad	.60	.25
150	Jay Bell	.30	.14
151	Mo Vaughn	.60	.25
152	Ozzie Smith	.75	.35
153	Jose Mesa	.15	.07
154	Osvaldo Fernandez	.15	.07
155	Vinny Castilla	.40	.18
156	Jason Isringhausen	.15	.07
157	B.J. Surhoff	.30	.14
158	Robert Perez	.15	.07
159	Ron Coomer	.15	.07
160	Darren Oliver	.15	.07
161	Mike Mohler	.15	.07
162	Russ Davis	.30	.14
163	Bret Boone	.30	.14
164	Ricky Bottalico	.30	.14
165	Derek Jeter	2.00	.90
166	Orlando Merced	.15	.07
167	John Valentin	.30	.14
168	Andruw Jones	.75	.35
169	Angel Echevarria	.15	.07
170	Todd Walker	.60	.25
171	Desi Relaford	.15	.07
172	Trey Beamon	.15	.07
173	Brian Giles	2.00	.90
174	Scott Rolen	1.00	.45
175	Shannon Stewart	.30	.14
176	Dmitri Young	.30	.14
177	Justin Thompson	.30	.14
178	Trot Nixon	.30	.14
179	Josh Booty	.15	.07
180	Robin Jennings	.15	.07
181	Marvin Benard	.15	.07
182	Luis Castillo	.30	.14
183	Wendell Magee	.15	.07
184	Vladimir Guerrero	1.00	.45
185	Nomar Garciaparra	2.00	.90
186	Ryan Hancock	.15	.07
187	Mike Cameron	.30	.14
188	Cal Ripken LG	1.25	.55
189	Chipper Jones LG	.75	.35
190	Albert Belle LG	.30	.14
191	Mike Piazza LG	1.00	.45
192	Chuck Knoblauch LG	.30	.14
193	Ken Griffey Jr. LG	1.50	.70
194	Ivan Rodriguez LG	.40	.18
195	Jose Canseco LG	.60	.25
196	Ryne Sandberg LG	.60	.25
197	Jim Thome LG	.30	.14
198	Andy Pettitte CL	.15	.07
199	Andruw Jones CL	.40	.18
200	Derek Jeter CL	1.00	.45
201	Chipper Jones	1.50	.70
202	Albert Belle	.60	.25
203	Mike Piazza	2.00	.90
204	Ken Griffey Jr.	3.00	1.35
205	Ryne Sandberg	.75	.35
206	Jose Canseco	.75	.35
207	Chili Davis	.30	.14
208	Roger Clemens	1.50	.70
209	Deion Sanders	.50	.14
210	Darryl Hamilton	.15	.07
211	Jermaine Dye	.30	.14
212	Matt Williams	.60	.25
213	Kevin Elster	.15	.07
214	John Wetteland	.30	.14
215	Garret Anderson	.30	.14
216	Kevin Brown	.40	.18
217	Matt Lawton	.30	.14
218	Cal Ripken	2.50	1.10
219	Moises Alou	.30	.14
220	Chuck Knoblauch	.60	.25
221	Ivan Rodriguez	.75	.35
222	Travis Fryman	.30	.14
223	Jim Thome	.60	.25
224	Eddie Murray	.60	.25
225	Eric Young	.30	.14
226	Ron Gant	.15	.07
227	Tony Phillips	.15	.07
228	Reggie Sanders	.30	.14
229	Johnny Damon	.30	.14
230	Bill Pulsipher	.15	.07
231	Jim Edmonds	.40	.18
232	Melvin Nieves	.15	.07
233	Ryan Klesko	.30	.14
234	David Cone	.40	.18
235	Derek Bell	.30	.14
236	Julio Franco	.30	.14
237	Juan Guzman	.15	.07
238	Larry Walker	.60	.25
239	Delino DeShields	.15	.07
240	Troy Percival	.30	.14
241	Andres Galarraga	.60	.25
242	Rondell White	.30	.14
243	John Burkett	.15	.07
244	J.T. Snow	.30	.14
245	Alex Fernandez	.15	.07
246	Edgar Martinez	.30	.14
247	Craig Biggio	.60	.25
248	Todd Hundley	.30	.14
249	Jimmy Key	.30	.14
250	Cliff Floyd	.30	.14
251	Jeff Conine	.15	.07
252	Curt Schilling	.40	.18
253	Jeff King	.15	.07
254	Tino Martinez	.60	.25
255	Carlos Baerga	.15	.07
256	Jeff Fassero	.15	.07
257	Dean Palmer	.30	.14
258	Robb Nen	.15	.07
259	Sandy Alomar Jr.	.30	.14
260	Carlos Perez	.15	.07
261	Rickey Henderson	.75	.35
262	Bobby Bonilla	.30	.14
263	Darren Daulton	.30	.14
264	Jim Leyritz	.15	.07
265	Dennis Martinez	.15	.07
266	Butch Huskey	.15	.07
267	Joe Vitiello	.15	.07
268	Steve Trachsel	.15	.07
269	Gienallin Hill	.15	.07
270	Terry Steinbach	.15	.07
271	Mark McLemore	.15	.07
272	Devon White	.30	.14
273	Jeff Kent	.30	.14
274	Tim Raines	.30	.14
275	Carlos Garcia	.15	.07
276	Hal Morris	.15	.07
277	Gary Gaetti	.30	.14
278	John Olerud	.30	.14
279	Wally Joyner	.30	.14
280	Brian Hunter	.30	.14
281	Steve Karsay	.15	.07
282	Denny Neagle	.15	.07
283	Jose Herrera	.15	.07
284	Todd Stottlemyre	.15	.07
285	Bip Roberts	.15	.07
286	Kevin Seitzer	.15	.07
287	Benji Gil	.15	.07
288	Dennis Eckersley	.30	.14
289	Brad Ausmus	.15	.07
290	Otis Nixon	.15	.07
291	Darryl Strawberry	.30	.14
292	Marquis Grissom	.30	.14
293	Darryl Kile	.15	.07
294	Quilvio Veras	.15	.07
295	Tom Goodwin	.15	.07
296	Benito Santiago	.15	.07
297	Mike Bordick	.15	.07
298	Roberto Kelly	.15	.07
299	David Justice	.60	.25
300	Carl Everett	.15	.07
301	Mark Whiten	.15	.07
302	Aaron Sele	.30	.14
303	Darren Dreifort	.15	.07
304	Bobby Jones	.15	.07
305	Fernando Vina	.15	.07
306	Ed Sprague	.15	.07
307	Andy Ashby	.15	.07
308	Tony Fernandez	.30	.14
309	Roger Pavlik	.15	.07
310	Mark Clark	.15	.07
311	Mariano Duncan	.15	.07
312	Tyler Houston	.15	.07
313	Eric Davis	.30	.14
314	Greg Vaughn	.30	.14
315	David Segui	.30	.14
316	Dave Nilsson	.15	.07
317	F.P. Santangelo	.15	.07
318	Wilton Guerrero	.15	.07
319	Jose Guillen	.40	.18
320	Kevin Orie	.15	.07
321	Derek Lee	.40	.18
322	Bubba Trammell	.60	.25
323	Pokey Reese	.30	.14
324	Hideki Irabu	1.00	.45
325	Scott Spiezio	.15	.07
326	Bartolo Colon	.30	.14
327	Damon Mashore	.15	.07
328	Chris Carpenter	.30	.14
330	Jose Cruz Jr.	1.25	.55
331	Todd Greene	.15	.07

❏ 332 Brian Moehler	.15		.07
❏ 333 Mike Sweeney	.30		.14
❏ 334 Neifi Perez	.30		.14
❏ 335 Matt Morris	.30		.14
❏ 336 Marvin Benard	.15		.07
❏ 337 Karim Garcia	.30		.14
❏ 338 Jason Dickson	.15		.07
❏ 339 Brant Brown	.15		.07
❏ 340 Jeff Suppan	.15		.07
❏ 341 Delvi Cruz	.60		.25
❏ 342 Antone Williamson	.15		.07
❏ 343 Curtis Goodwin	.15		.07
❏ 344 Brooks Kieschnick	.15		.07
❏ 345 Tony Womack	.50		.23
❏ 346 Rudy Pemberton	.15		.07
❏ 347 Todd Dunwoody	.30		.14
❏ 348 Frank Thomas LG	.60		.25
❏ 349 Andruw Jones LG	.40		.18
❏ 350 Alex Rodriguez LG	1.00		.45
❏ 351 Greg Maddux LG	.75		.35
❏ 352 Jeff Bagwell LG	.60		.25
❏ 353 Juan Gonzalez LG	.60		.25
❏ 354 Barry Bonds LG	.30		.14
❏ 355 Mark McGwire LG	1.50		.70
❏ 356 Tony Gwynn LG	.75		.35
❏ 357 Gary Sheffield LG	.15		.07
❏ 358 Derek Jeter LG	1.00		.45
❏ 359 Manny Ramirez LG	.40		.18
❏ 360 Hideo Nomo LG	.30		.14
❏ 361 Sammy Sosa LG	1.00		.45
❏ 362 Paul Molitor LG	.30		.14
❏ 363 Kenny Lofton LG	.30		.14
❏ 364 Eddie Murray LG	.30		.14
❏ 365 Barry Larkin LG	.30		.14
❏ 366 Roger Clemens LG	.75		.35
❏ 367 John Smoltz LG	.30		.14
❏ 368 Alex Rodriguez GM	1.00		.45
❏ 369 Frank Thomas GM	.60		.25
❏ 370 Cal Ripken GM	1.25		.55
❏ 371 Ken Griffey Jr. GM	1.50		.70
❏ 372 Greg Maddux GM	.75		.35
❏ 373 Mike Piazza GM	1.00		.45
❏ 374 Chipper Jones GM	.30		.14
❏ 375 Albert Belle GM	.60		.25
❏ 376 Chuck Knoblauch GM	.30		.14
❏ 377 Brady Anderson GM	.15		.07
❏ 378 David Justice GM	.30		.14
❏ 379 Randy Johnson GM	.30		.14
❏ 380 Wade Boggs GM	.30		.14
❏ 381 Kevin Brown GM	.15		.07
❏ 382 Tom Glavine GM	.30		.14
❏ 383 Raul Mondesi GM	.15		.07
❏ 384 Ivan Rodriguez GM	.40		.18
❏ 385 Larry Walker GM	.30		.14
❏ 386 Bernie Williams GM	.30		.14
❏ 387 Rusty Greer GM	.30		.14
❏ 388 Rafael Palmeiro GM	.30		.14
❏ 389 Matt Williams GM	.30		.14
❏ 390 Eric Young GM	.15		.07
❏ 391 Fred McGriff GM	.30		.14
❏ 392 Ken Caminiti GM	.45		.07
❏ 393 Roberto Alomar GM	.30		.14
❏ 394 Brian Jordan GM	.15		.07
❏ 395 Mark Grace GM	.15		.07
❏ 396 Jim Edmonds GM	.15		.07
❏ 397 Deion Sanders GM	.30		.14
❏ 398 Vladimir Guerrero CL	.75		.35
❏ 399 Darin Erstad CL	.60		.25
❏ 400 N. Garciaparra CL	1.00		.45
❏ NNO J.Robinson Reprint	30.00		13.50

1997 Leaf Fractal Matrix

	MINT	NRMT
COMMON BRONZE	1.00	.45
BRONZE MINOR STARS	1.50	.70
BRONZE SEMISTARS	2.50	1.10
BRONZE UNLISTED STARS	4.00	1.80
COMMON SILVER	2.50	1.10
SILVER MINOR STARS	4.00	1.80
SILVER SEMISTARS	6.00	2.70
SILVER UNLISTED STARS	10.00	4.50
COMMON GOLD	4.00	1.80
GOLD MINOR STARS	6.00	2.70

GOLD SEMISTARS	10.00	4.50
GOLD UNLISTED STARS	15.00	6.75
RANDOM INSERTS IN PACKS		

❏ 1 Wade Boggs GY	40.00		18.00
❏ 2 Brian McRae SY	1.00		.45
❏ 3 Jeff D'Amico SY	1.00		.45
❏ 4 George Arias SY	2.50		1.10
❏ 5 Billy Wagner SY	4.00		1.80
❏ 6 Ray Lankford BZ	1.50		.70
❏ 7 Will Clark SY	10.00		4.50
❏ 8 Edgar Renteria SY	4.00		1.80
❏ 9 Alex Ochoa SY	2.50		1.10
❏ 10 Roberto Hernandez BX	1.00		.45
❏ 11 Joe Carter SY	4.00		1.80
❏ 12 Gregg Jefferies BY	1.00		.45
❏ 13 Mark Grace SY	6.00		2.70
❏ 14 Roberto Alomar SY	15.00		6.75
❏ 15 Joe Randa BX	1.00		.45
❏ 16 Alex Rodriguez GZ	50.00		22.00
❏ 17 Tony Gwynn GZ	40.00		18.00
❏ 18 Steve Gibralter BY	1.00		.45
❏ 19 Scott Stahoviak BX	1.00		.45
❏ 20 Matt Williams SZ	4.00		1.80
❏ 21 Quinton McCracken BY	1.50		.70
❏ 22 Ugueth Urbina BX	1.50		.70
❏ 23 Jermaine Allensworth SX	2.50		1.10
❏ 24 Paul Molitor GX	40.00		18.00
❏ 25 Carlos Delgado SY	4.00		1.80
❏ 26 Bob Abreu SY	4.00		1.80
❏ 27 John Jaha SY	2.50		1.10
❏ 28 Rusty Greer SY	4.00		1.80
❏ 29 Kimera Bartee SY	1.00		.45
❏ 30 Ruben Rivera SY	4.00		1.80
❏ 31 Jason Kendall SY	6.00		2.70
❏ 32 Lance Johnson BX	1.00		.45
❏ 33 Robin Ventura BY	1.50		.70
❏ 34 Kevin Appier SX	4.00		1.80
❏ 35 John Mabry SY	2.50		1.10
❏ 36 Ricky Otero BX	1.00		.45
❏ 37 Mike Lansing BX	1.00		.45
❏ 38 Mark McGwire GZ	80.00		36.00
❏ 39 Tim Naehring BX	1.00		.45
❏ 40 Tom Glavine GZ	10.00		4.50
❏ 41 Rey Ordonez SY	4.00		1.80
❏ 42 Tony Clark SY	6.00		2.70
❏ 43 Rafael Palmeiro SZ	5.00		2.20
❏ 44 Pedro Martinez BX	5.00		2.20
❏ 45 Keith Lockhart BX	1.00		.45
❏ 46 Dan Wilson BY	1.00		.45
❏ 47 John Wetteland BY	1.50		.70
❏ 48 Chan Ho Park BX	4.00		1.80
❏ 49 Gary Sheffield GZ	10.00		4.50
❏ 50 Shawn Estes SY	1.50		.70
❏ 51 Royce Clayton BX	1.00		.45
❏ 52 Jaime Navarro BX	1.00		.45
❏ 53 Raul Casanova BX	1.00		.45
❏ 54 Jeff Bagwell GZ	20.00		9.00
❏ 55 Barry Larkin GX	25.00		11.00
❏ 56 Charles Nagy BY	1.50		.70
❏ 57 Ken Caminiti GY	10.00		4.50
❏ 58 Todd Hollandsworth SZ	2.50		1.10
❏ 59 Pat Hentgen SX	4.00		1.80
❏ 60 Jose Valentin BX	1.00		.45
❏ 61 Frank Rodriguez BX	1.00		.45
❏ 62 Mickey Tettleton BX	1.00		.45
❏ 63 Marty Cordova GX	4.00		1.80
❏ 64 Cecil Fielder SX	4.00		1.80

❏ 65 Barry Bonds GZ	20.00		9.00
❏ 66 Scott Servais BX	1.00		.45
❏ 67 Ernie Young SY	1.00		.45
❏ 68 Wilson Alvarez BX	1.50		.70
❏ 69 Mike Grace BX	1.00		.45
❏ 70 Shane Reynolds SX	4.00		1.80
❏ 71 Henry Rodriguez SY	4.00		1.80
❏ 72 Eric Karros BX	1.50		.70
❏ 73 Mark Langston BX	1.50		.70
❏ 74 Scott Karl BX	1.00		.45
❏ 75 Trevor Hoffman BX	1.50		.70
❏ 76 Orel Hershiser SX	4.00		1.80
❏ 77 John Smoltz GY	6.00		2.70
❏ 78 Raul Mondesi GZ	10.00		4.50
❏ 79 Jeff Brantley BX	1.00		.45
❏ 80 Donne Wall BX	1.00		.45
❏ 81 Joey Cora BX	1.50		.70
❏ 82 Mel Rojas BX	1.00		.45
❏ 83 Chad Mottola BX	1.00		.45
❏ 84 Omar Vizquel BX	1.50		.70
❏ 85 Greg Maddux GZ	40.00		18.00
❏ 86 Jamey Wright SY	2.50		1.10
❏ 87 Chuck Finley SX	1.50		.70
❏ 88 Brady Anderson GY	6.00		2.70
❏ 89 Alex Gonzalez SY	2.50		1.10
❏ 90 Andy Benes BX	1.50		.70
❏ 91 Reggie Jefferson BX	1.00		.45
❏ 92 Paul O'Neill BY	1.50		.70
❏ 93 Javier Lopez SX	4.00		1.80
❏ 94 Mark Grudzielanek SX	4.00		1.80
❏ 95 Marc Newfield BX	1.00		.45
❏ 96 Kevin Ritz BX	1.00		.45
❏ 97 Fred McGriff GY	10.00		4.50
❏ 98 Dwight Gooden SX	4.00		1.80
❏ 99 Hideo Nomo SY	20.00		9.00
❏ 100 Steve Finley SY	1.50		.70
❏ 101 Juan Gonzalez GZ	30.00		13.50
❏ 102 Jay Buhner SX	4.00		1.80
❏ 103 Paul Wilson SY	2.50		1.10
❏ 104 Alan Benes SY	1.50		.70
❏ 105 Manny Ramirez GZ	20.00		9.00
❏ 106 Kevin Elster BX	1.00		.45
❏ 107 Frank Thomas GZ	30.00		13.50
❏ 108 Orlando Miller BX	1.00		.45
❏ 109 Ramon Martinez BX	1.50		.70
❏ 110 Kenny Lofton GZ	15.00		6.75
❏ 111 Bernie Williams GY	15.00		6.75
❏ 112 Robby Thompson BX	1.00		.45
❏ 113 Bernard Gilkey BZ	1.00		.45
❏ 114 Ray Durham BX	1.50		.70
❏ 115 Jeff Cirillo SZ	4.00		1.80
❏ 116 Brian Jordan GZ	6.00		2.70
❏ 117 Rich Becker SY	2.50		1.10
❏ 118 Al Leiter BX	1.50		.70
❏ 119 Mark Johnson BX	1.00		.45
❏ 120 Ellis Burks BY	1.50		.70
❏ 121 Sammy Sosa GZ	50.00		22.00
❏ 122 Willie Greene BX	1.50		.70
❏ 123 Michael Tucker BX	1.50		.70
❏ 124 Eddie Murray GY	20.00		9.00
❏ 125 Joey Hamilton SY	4.00		1.80
❏ 126 Antonio Osuna BX	1.00		.45
❏ 127 Bobby Higginson SY	6.00		2.70
❏ 128 Tomas Perez BX	1.00		.45
❏ 129 Tim Salmon GX	15.00		6.75
❏ 130 Mark Wohlers BX	1.00		.45
❏ 131 Charles Johnson SX	4.00		1.80
❏ 132 Randy Johnson GY	10.00		4.50
❏ 133 Brooks Kieschnick SZ	2.50		1.10
❏ 134 Al Martin SY	4.00		1.80
❏ 135 Dante Bichette BX	1.50		.70
❏ 136 Andy Pettitte GZ	10.00		4.50
❏ 137 Jason Giambi GY	6.00		2.70
❏ 138 James Baldwin SX	4.00		1.80
❏ 139 Ben McDonald SX	4.00		1.80
❏ 140 Shawn Green SX	4.00		1.80
❏ 141 Geronimo Berroa BY	1.00		.45
❏ 142 Jose Offerman BX	1.00		.45
❏ 143 Curtis Pride BX	1.00		.45
❏ 144 Terrell Wade BX	1.00		.45
❏ 145 Ismael Valdes SX	4.00		1.80
❏ 146 Mike Mussina SY	10.00		4.50
❏ 147 Mariano Rivera SX	4.00		1.80
❏ 148 Ken Hill BY	1.00		.45
❏ 149 Darin Erstad GZ	15.00		6.75
❏ 150 Jay Bell BX	1.50		.70

#	Player	Mint	NRMT
151	Mo Vaughn GZ	15.00	6.75
152	Ozzie Smith GY	25.00	11.00
153	Jose Mesa BX	1.00	.45
154	Osvaldo Fernandez BX	1.00	.45
155	Vinny Castilla BY	2.50	1.10
156	Jason Isringhausen SY	2.50	1.10
157	B.J. Surhoff BX	1.50	.70
158	Robert Perez BX	1.00	.45
159	Ron Coomer BX	1.00	.45
160	Darren Oliver BX	1.00	.45
161	Mike Mohler BX	1.00	.45
162	Russ Davis BX	1.50	.70
163	Bret Boone BX	1.50	.70
164	Ricky Bottalico BX	1.50	.70
165	Derek Jeter GZ	50.00	22.00
166	Orlando Merced BX	1.00	.45
167	John Valentin BX	1.50	.70
168	Andruw Jones GZ	20.00	9.00
169	Angel Echevarria BX	1.00	.45
170	Todd Walker GZ	15.00	6.75
171	Desi Relaford BY	1.00	.45
172	Trey Beamon SX	2.50	1.10
173	Brian Giles SY	4.00	1.80
174	Scott Rolen GZ	25.00	11.00
175	Shannon Stewart SZ	4.00	1.80
176	Dmitri Young GZ	6.00	2.70
177	Justin Thompson BY	1.50	.70
178	Trot Nixon SY	4.00	1.80
179	Josh Booty SY	2.50	1.10
180	Robin Jennings BX	1.00	.45
181	Marvin Benard BX	1.00	.45
182	Luis Castillo BY	1.50	.70
183	Wendell Magee BX	1.00	.45
184	Vladimir Guerrero GX	50.00	22.00
185	Nomar Garciaparra GX	120.00	55.00
186	Ryan Hancock BX	1.00	.45
187	Mike Cameron SX	4.00	1.80
188	Cal Ripken LG BZ	15.00	6.75
189	Chipper Jones LG SZ	25.00	11.00
190	Albert Belle LG SZ	10.00	4.50
191	Mike Piazza LG BZ	12.00	5.50
192	Chuck Knoblauch LG SY	10.00	4.50
193	Ken Griffey Jr. LG BZ	20.00	9.00
194	Ivan Rodriguez LG GZ	20.00	9.00
195	Jose Canseco LG SX	12.00	5.50
196	Ryne Sandberg LG SX	12.00	5.50
197	Jim Thome LG GY	15.00	6.75
198	Andy Pettitte CL BY	2.50	1.10
199	Andruw Jones CL BY	5.00	2.20
200	Derek Jeter CL SY	30.00	13.50
201	Chipper Jones GZ	120.00	55.00
202	Albert Belle GY	15.00	6.75
203	Mike Piazza GY	60.00	27.00
204	Ken Griffey Jr. GX	250.00	110.00
205	Ryne Sandberg GZ	20.00	9.00
206	Jose Canseco SZ	12.00	5.50
207	Chili Davis BX	1.50	.70
208	Roger Clemens GZ	40.00	18.00
209	Deion Sanders GZ	6.00	2.70
210	Darryl Hamilton BX	1.00	.45
211	Jermaine Dye SX	2.50	1.10
212	Matt Williams GY	6.00	2.70
213	Kevin Elster BX	1.00	.45
214	John Wetteland SX	4.00	1.80
215	Garret Anderson SX	6.00	2.70
216	Kevin Brown GY	10.00	4.50
217	Matt Lawton SY	4.00	1.80
218	Cal Ripken GX	200.00	90.00
219	Moises Alou GY	10.00	4.50
220	Chuck Knoblauch GZ	15.00	6.75
221	Ivan Rodriguez GY	25.00	11.00
222	Travis Fryman BY	1.50	.70
223	Jim Thome GZ	15.00	6.75
224	Eddie Murray SZ	10.00	4.50
225	Eric Young GZ	6.00	2.70
226	Ron Gant SX	2.50	1.10
227	Tony Phillips BX	1.00	.45
228	Reggie Sanders BY	1.50	.70
229	Johnny Damon SZ	4.00	1.80
230	Bill Pulsipher BX	1.00	.45
231	Jim Edmonds GZ	10.00	4.50
232	Melvin Nieves BX	1.00	.45
233	Ryan Klesko GZ	6.00	2.70
234	David Cone SX	4.00	1.80
235	Derek Bell BY	1.50	.70
236	Julio Franco SX	4.00	1.80
237	Juan Guzman BX	1.00	.45
238	Larry Walker GZ	15.00	6.75
239	Delino DeShields BX	1.00	.45
240	Troy Percival BY	1.50	.70
241	Andres Galarraga GZ	15.00	6.75
242	Rondell White BZ	6.00	2.70
243	John Burkett BX	1.00	.45
244	J.T. Snow BY	1.00	.45
245	Alex Fernandez SY	2.50	*1.10
246	Edgar Martinez GZ	6.00	2.70
247	Craig Biggio GZ	15.00	6.75
248	Todd Hundley GY	6.00	2.70
249	Jimmy Key SX	4.00	1.80
250	Cliff Floyd BY	1.50	.70
251	Jeff Conine BY	1.50	.70
252	Curt Schilling BX	1.50	.70
253	Jeff King BX	1.00	.45
254	Tino Martinez GZ	15.00	6.75
255	Carlos Baerga SY	4.00	1.80
256	Jeff Fassero BY	1.00	.45
257	Dean Palmer SY	4.00	1.80
258	Robb Nen BX	1.00	.45
259	Sandy Alomar Jr. SY	4.00	1.80
260	Carlos Perez BX	1.00	.45
261	Rickey Henderson SY	12.00	5.50
262	Bobby Bonilla SY	4.00	1.80
263	Darren Daulton BX	1.50	.70
264	Dennis Martinez BX	1.50	.70
265	Butch Huskey BX	1.00	.45
266	Joe Vitiello SY	2.50	1.10
267	Steve Trachsel BX	1.00	.45
268	Glenallen Hill BX	1.00	.45
269	Terry Steinbach BX	1.50	.70
270	Mark McLemore BX	1.00	.45
271	Devon White BX	1.50	.70
272	Jeff Kent BX	1.50	.70
273	Tim Raines BX	1.50	.70
274	Carlos Garcia BX	1.00	.45
275	Hal Morris BX	1.00	.45
276	Gary Gaetti BX	1.00	.45
277	John Olerud SX	4.00	1.80
278	Wally Joyner BX	1.50	.70
279	Brian Hunter SX	4.00	1.80
280	Steve Karsay BX	1.00	.45
281	Denny Neagle SX	4.00	1.80
282	Jose Herrera BX	1.00	.45
283	Todd Stottlemyre BX	1.00	.45
284	Bip Roberts SX	2.50	1.10
285	Kevin Seitzer BX	1.00	.45
286	Benji Gil BX	1.00	.45
287	Dennis Eckersley SX	4.00	1.80
288	Brad Ausmus BX	1.00	.45
289	Otis Nixon BX	1.00	.45
290	Darryl Strawberry BX	1.50	.70
291	Marquis Grissom SY	4.00	1.80
292	Darryl Kile BX	1.50	.70
293	Quilvio Veras BX	1.00	.45
294	Tom Goodwin BX	1.00	.45
295	Benito Santiago BX	1.00	.45
296	Mike Bordick BX	1.00	.45
297	Roberto Kelly BX	1.00	.45
298	David Justice GX	15.00	6.75
299	Carl Everett BX	1.00	.45
300	Mark Whiten BX	1.00	.45
301	Aaron Sele BX	1.00	.70
302	Darren Dreifort BX	1.50	.70
303	Bobby Jones BX	1.00	.45
304	Fernando Vina BX	1.00	.45
305	Ed Sprague BX	1.00	.45
306	Andy Ashby SX	2.50	1.10
307	Tony Fernandez BX	1.00	.45
308	Roger Pavlik BX	1.00	.45
309	Mark Clark BX	1.00	.45
310	Mariano Duncan BX	1.00	.45
311	Tyler Houston BX	1.00	.45
312	Eric Davis SY	4.00	1.80
313	Greg Vaughn BY	1.50	.70
314	David Segui SY	4.00	1.80
315	Dave Nilsson SX	2.50	1.10
316	F.P. Santangelo SX	2.50	1.10
317	Wilton Guerrero GZ	4.00	1.80
318	Jose Guillen GZ	15.00	6.75
319	Kevin Orie SY	2.50	1.10
320	Derrek Lee GZ	10.00	4.50
322	Bubba Trammell SY	10.00	4.50
323	Pokey Reese GZ	4.00	1.80
324	Hideki Irabu GX	25.00	11.00
325	Scott Spiezio GZ	2.50	1.10
326	Bartolo Colon GZ	6.00	2.70
327	Damon Mashore SY	2.50	1.10
328	Ryan McGuire GY	1.50	.70
329	Chris Carpenter BX	1.50	.70
330	Jose Cruz Jr. GX	25.00	11.00
331	Todd Greene SZ	4.00	1.80
332	Brian Moehler BX	1.00	.45
333	Mike Sweeney BY	1.00	.45
334	Neifi Perez GZ	4.00	1.80
335	Matt Morris SY	4.00	1.80
336	Marvin Benard BY	1.00	.45
337	Karim Garcia SZ	4.00	1.80
338	Jason Dickson SY	4.00	1.80
339	Brant Brown SY	4.00	1.80
340	Jeff Suppan SZ	2.50	1.10
341	Deivi Cruz BX	1.00	.45
342	Antone Williamson GZ	4.00	1.80
343	Curtis Goodwin BX	1.00	.45
344	Brooks Kieschnick SY	2.50	1.10
345	Tony Womack SX	4.00	1.80
346	Rudy Pemberton BX	1.00	.45
347	Todd Dunwoody BX	1.50	.70
348	Frank Thomas LG SY	20.00	9.00
349	Andruw Jones LG SY	12.00	5.50
350	Alex Rodriguez LG BY	12.00	5.50
351	Greg Maddux LG SY	25.00	11.00
352	Jeff Bagwell LG BY	5.00	2.20
353	Juan Gonzalez LG SY	20.00	9.00
354	Barry Bonds LG BY	5.00	2.20
355	Mark McGwire LG BY	20.00	9.00
356	Tony Gwynn LG BY	10.00	4.50
357	Gary Sheffield LG SX	4.00	1.80
358	Derek Jeter LG SX	30.00	13.50
359	Manny Ramirez LG SY	12.00	5.50
360	Hideo Nomo LG GZ	30.00	13.50
361	Sammy Sosa LG SX	12.00	5.50
362	Paul Molitor LG SY	5.00	2.20
363	Kenny Lofton LG BY	4.00	1.80
364	Eddie Murray LG BX	4.00	1.80
365	Barry Larkin LG SZ	6.00	2.70
366	Roger Clemens LG SY	25.00	11.00
367	John Smoltz LG BZ	1.50	.70
368	Alex Rodriguez GM SX	30.00	13.50
369	Frank Thomas GM BX	8.00	3.60
370	Cal Ripken GM SY	40.00	18.00
371	Ken Griffey Jr. GM SY	50.00	22.00
372	Greg Maddux GM BX	10.00	4.50
373	Mike Piazza GM SX	30.00	13.50
374	Chipper Jones GM BY	10.00	4.50
375	Albert Belle GM BY	4.00	1.80
376	Chuck Knoblauch GM BX	4.00	1.80
377	Brady Anderson GM BZ	1.50	.70
378	David Justice GM SX	10.00	4.50
379	Randy Johnson GM BZ	4.00	1.80
380	Wade Boggs GM BX	4.00	1.80
381	Kevin Brown GM BX	1.00	.45
382	Tom Glavine GM GY	15.00	6.75
383	Raul Mondesi GM SX	6.00	2.70
384	Ivan Rodriguez GM SX	12.00	5.50
385	Larry Walker GM BY	4.00	1.80
386	Bernie Williams GM BZ	4.00	1.80
387	Rusty Greer GM BY	6.00	2.70
388	Rafael Palmeiro GM GY	6.00	2.70
389	Matt Williams GM BX	1.50	.70
390	Eric Young GM BX	1.50	.70
391	Fred McGriff GM BX	2.50	1.10
392	Ken Caminiti GM BX	2.50	1.10
393	Roberto Alomar GM BZ	4.00	1.80
394	Brian Jordan GM BX	1.50	.70
395	Mark Grace GM GZ	2.50	1.10
396	Jim Edmonds GM BY	2.50	1.10
397	Deion Sanders GM SY	4.00	1.80
398	Vladimir Guerrero CL SZ	15.00	6.75
399	Darin Erstad CL SY	10.00	4.50
400	N. Garciaparra CL SZ	30.00	13.50

1997 Leaf Fractal Matrix Die Cuts

	MINT	NRMT
COMMON X-AXIS	4.00	1.80
X-AXIS MINOR STARS	6.00	2.70

X-AXIS SEMISTARS	10.00	4.50
X-AXIS UNLISTED STARS	15.00	6.75
COMMON X-AXIS	6.00	2.70
Y-AXIS MINOR STARS	10.00	4.50
Y-AXIS SEMISTARS	15.00	6.75
Y-AXIS UNLISTED STARS	25.00	11.00
COMMON Z-AXIS	10.00	4.50
Z-AXIS MINOR STARS	15.00	6.75
Z-AXIS SEMISTARS	25.00	11.00
Z-AXIS UNLISTED STARS	40.00	18.00

RANDOM INSERTS IN PACKS

❏ 1	Wade Boggs GY	40.00	18.00
❏ 2	Brian McRae BY	4.00	1.80
❏ 3	Jeff D'Amico BY	4.00	1.80
❏ 4	George Arias SY	6.00	2.70
❏ 5	Billy Wagner SY	10.00	4.50
❏ 6	Ray Lankford BZ	6.00	2.70
❏ 7	Will Clark SY	25.00	11.00
❏ 8	Edgar Renteria SY	10.00	4.50
❏ 9	Alex Ochoa SY	6.00	2.70
❏ 10	Roberto Hernandez BX	4.00	1.80
❏ 11	Joe Carter SY	10.00	4.50
❏ 12	Gregg Jefferies BY	4.00	1.80
❏ 13	Mark Grace SY	15.00	6.75
❏ 14	Roberto Alomar GY	40.00	18.00
❏ 15	Joe Randa BX	4.00	1.80
❏ 16	Alex Rodriguez GY	120.00	55.00
❏ 17	Tony Gwynn GZ	100.00	45.00
❏ 18	Steve Gibralter BY	4.00	1.80
❏ 19	Scott Stahoviak BX	4.00	1.80
❏ 20	Matt Williams SZ	10.00	4.50
❏ 21	Quinton McCracken BY	6.00	2.70
❏ 22	Ugueth Urbina BX	6.00	2.70
❏ 23	Jermaine Allensworth SX	6.00	2.70
❏ 24	Paul Molitor GX	40.00	18.00
❏ 25	Carlos Delgado SY	10.00	4.50
❏ 26	Bob Abreu SY	10.00	4.50
❏ 27	John Jaha SY	6.00	2.70
❏ 28	Rusty Greer SY	10.00	4.50
❏ 29	Kimera Bartee BX	4.00	1.80
❏ 30	Ruben Rivera SY	10.00	4.50
❏ 31	Jason Kendall SY	15.00	6.75
❏ 32	Lance Johnson BX	4.00	1.80
❏ 33	Robin Ventura BX	6.00	2.70
❏ 34	Kevin Appier SX	10.00	4.50
❏ 35	John Mabry SY	6.00	2.70
❏ 36	Ricky Otero BX	4.00	1.80
❏ 37	Mike Lansing BX	4.00	1.80
❏ 38	Mark McGwire GZ	200.00	90.00
❏ 39	Tim Naehring BX	4.00	1.80
❏ 40	Tom Glavine SZ	25.00	11.00
❏ 41	Rey Ordonez SY	10.00	4.50
❏ 42	Tony Clark SY	15.00	6.75
❏ 43	Rafael Palmeiro SY	15.00	6.75
❏ 44	Pedro Martinez BX	20.00	9.00
❏ 45	Keith Lockhart BY	4.00	1.80
❏ 46	Dan Wilson BY	4.00	1.80
❏ 47	John Wetteland BY	6.00	2.70
❏ 48	Chan Ho Park BX	15.00	6.75
❏ 49	Gary Sheffield GZ	25.00	11.00
❏ 50	Shawn Estes BX	6.00	2.70
❏ 51	Royce Clayton BX	4.00	1.80
❏ 52	Jaime Navarro BX	4.00	1.80
❏ 53	Raul Casanova BX	4.00	1.80
❏ 54	Jeff Bagwell GZ	50.00	22.00
❏ 55	Barry Larkin GX	25.00	11.00
❏ 56	Charles Nagy BY	6.00	2.70
❏ 57	Ken Caminiti GY	25.00	11.00

❏ 58	Todd Hollandsworth SZ	6.00	2.70
❏ 59	Pat Hentgen SX	10.00	4.50
❏ 60	Jose Valentin BX	4.00	1.80
❏ 61	Frank Rodriguez BX	4.00	1.80
❏ 62	Mickey Tettleton BX	4.00	1.80
❏ 63	Marty Cordova GX	10.00	4.50
❏ 64	Cecil Fielder SY	10.00	4.50
❏ 65	Barry Bonds GZ	50.00	22.00
❏ 66	Scott Servais BX	4.00	1.80
❏ 67	Ernie Young BX	4.00	1.80
❏ 68	Wilson Alvarez BX	6.00	2.70
❏ 69	Mike Grace BX	4.00	1.80
❏ 70	Shane Reynolds SX	10.00	4.50
❏ 71	Henry Rodriguez SY	10.00	4.50
❏ 72	Eric Karros BX	6.00	2.70
❏ 73	Mark Langston BX	6.00	2.70
❏ 74	Scott Karl BX	4.00	1.80
❏ 75	Trevor Hoffman BX	6.00	2.70
❏ 76	Orel Hershiser SX	10.00	4.50
❏ 77	John Smoltz GY	15.00	6.75
❏ 78	Raul Mondesi GZ	25.00	11.00
❏ 79	Jeff Brantley BX	4.00	1.80
❏ 80	Donne Wall BX	4.00	1.80
❏ 81	Joey Cora BX	6.00	2.70
❏ 82	Mel Rojas BX	4.00	1.80
❏ 83	Chad Mottola BX	4.00	1.80
❏ 84	Omar Vizquel BX	6.00	2.70
❏ 85	Greg Maddux GY	100.00	45.00
❏ 86	Jamey Wright SY		
❏ 87	Chuck Finley BX	6.00	2.70
❏ 88	Brady Anderson GY	15.00	6.75
❏ 89	Alex Gonzalez SX	6.00	2.70
❏ 90	Andy Benes BX	6.00	2.70
❏ 91	Reggie Jefferson BX	4.00	1.80
❏ 92	Paul O'Neill BY	6.00	2.70
❏ 93	Javier Lopez SX	10.00	4.50
❏ 94	Mark Grudzielanek SX	10.00	4.50
❏ 95	Marc Newfield BX	4.00	1.80
❏ 96	Kevin Ritz BX	4.00	1.80
❏ 97	Fred McGriff GY	25.00	11.00
❏ 98	Dwight Gooden SX	10.00	4.50
❏ 99	Hideo Nomo SY	50.00	22.00
❏ 100	Steve Finley BX	6.00	2.70
❏ 101	Juan Gonzalez GZ	80.00	36.00
❏ 102	Jay Buhner SZ	10.00	4.50
❏ 103	Paul Wilson SY	6.00	2.70
❏ 104	Alan Benes BY	6.00	2.70
❏ 105	Manny Ramirez GZ	50.00	22.00
❏ 106	Kevin Elster BX	4.00	1.80
❏ 107	Frank Thomas GZ	80.00	36.00
❏ 108	Orlando Miller BX	4.00	1.80
❏ 109	Ramon Martinez BX	6.00	2.70
❏ 110	Kenny Lofton GZ	40.00	18.00
❏ 111	Bernie Williams GY	40.00	18.00
❏ 112	Robby Thompson BX	4.00	1.80
❏ 113	Bernard Gilkey BZ	6.00	2.70
❏ 114	Ray Durham BX	6.00	2.70
❏ 115	Jeff Cirillo SZ	10.00	4.50
❏ 116	Brian Jordan GY	15.00	6.75
❏ 117	Rich Becker SY	6.00	2.70
❏ 118	Al Leiter BX	6.00	2.70
❏ 119	Mark Johnson BX	4.00	1.80
❏ 120	Ellis Burks BY	6.00	2.70
❏ 121	Sammy Sosa GZ	120.00	55.00
❏ 122	Willie Greene BX	6.00	2.70
❏ 123	Michael Tucker BX	6.00	2.70
❏ 124	Eddie Murray GY	40.00	18.00
❏ 125	Joey Hamilton SY	10.00	4.50
❏ 126	Antonio Osuna BX	4.00	1.80
❏ 127	Bobby Higginson SY	15.00	6.75
❏ 128	Tomas Perez BX	4.00	1.80
❏ 129	Tim Salmon GZ	40.00	18.00
❏ 130	Mark Wohlers BX	4.00	1.80
❏ 131	Charles Johnson SX	10.00	4.50
❏ 132	Randy Johnson GY	25.00	11.00
❏ 133	Brooks Kieschnick SX	6.00	2.70
❏ 134	Al Martin SY	10.00	4.50
❏ 135	Dante Bichette BX	6.00	2.70
❏ 136	Andy Pettitte GZ	25.00	11.00
❏ 137	Jason Giambi SY	15.00	6.75
❏ 138	James Baldwin SX	10.00	4.50
❏ 139	Ben McDonald BX	6.00	2.70
❏ 140	Shawn Green SX	10.00	4.50
❏ 141	Geronimo Berroa BY	4.00	1.80
❏ 142	Jose Offerman BX	4.00	1.80
❏ 143	Curtis Pride BX		1.80

❏ 144	Terrell Wade BX	4.00	1.80
❏ 145	Ismael Valdes SX	10.00	4.50
❏ 146	Mike Mussina SY	25.00	11.00
❏ 147	Mariano Rivera SX	10.00	4.50
❏ 148	Ken Hill BY	4.00	1.80
❏ 149	Darin Erstad GZ	50.00	22.00
❏ 150	Jay Bell BX	6.00	2.70
❏ 151	Mo Vaughn GZ	50.00	22.00
❏ 152	Ozzie Smith GY	30.00	13.50
❏ 153	Jose Mesa BX	4.00	1.80
❏ 154	Osvaldo Fernandez BX	4.00	1.80
❏ 155	Vinny Castilla BY	10.00	4.50
❏ 156	Jason Isringhausen SY	6.00	2.70
❏ 157	B.J. Surhoff BX	4.00	1.80
❏ 158	Robert Perez BX	4.00	1.80
❏ 159	Ron Coomer BX	4.00	1.80
❏ 160	Darren Oliver BX	4.00	1.80
❏ 161	Mike Mohler BX	4.00	1.80
❏ 162	Russ Davis BX	6.00	2.70
❏ 163	Bret Boone BX	6.00	2.70
❏ 164	Ricky Bottalico BX	6.00	2.70
❏ 165	Derek Jeter GZ	120.00	55.00
❏ 166	Orlando Merced BX	4.00	1.80
❏ 167	John Valentin BX	6.00	2.70
❏ 168	Andruw Jones GZ	50.00	22.00
❏ 169	Angel Echevarria BX	4.00	1.80
❏ 170	Todd Walker GZ	40.00	18.00
❏ 171	Desi Relaford BY	4.00	1.80
❏ 172	Trey Beamon SX	6.00	2.70
❏ 173	Brian Giles SY	10.00	4.50
❏ 174	Scott Rolen GZ	60.00	27.00
❏ 175	Shannon Stewart SZ	10.00	4.50
❏ 176	Dmitri Young GZ	15.00	6.75
❏ 177	Justin Thompson BX	6.00	2.70
❏ 178	Trot Nixon SY	10.00	4.50
❏ 179	Josh Booty SY	6.00	2.70
❏ 180	Robin Jennings BX	4.00	1.80
❏ 181	Marvin Benard BX	4.00	1.80
❏ 182	Luis Castillo BY	6.00	2.70
❏ 183	Wendell Magee BX	4.00	1.80
❏ 184	Vladimir Guerrero GX	25.00	11.00
❏ 185	Nomar Garciaparra GX	50.00	22.00
❏ 186	Ryan Hancock BX	4.00	1.80
❏ 187	Mike Cameron SX	10.00	4.50
❏ 188	Cal Ripken LGD BZ	150.00	70.00
❏ 189	Chipper Jones LGD SZ	100.00	45.00
❏ 190	Albert Belle LGD SZ	25.00	11.00
❏ 191	Mike Piazza LGD BZ	120.00	55.00
❏ 192	Chuck Knoblauch LGD SY	25.00	11.00
❏ 193	Ken Griffey Jr. LGD BZ	200.00	90.00
❏ 194	Ivan Rodriguez LGD GZ	50.00	22.00
❏ 195	Jose Canseco LGD SX	20.00	9.00
❏ 196	Ryne Sandberg LGD SX	20.00	9.00
❏ 197	Jim Thome LGD GY	40.00	18.00
❏ 198	Andy Pettitte CL BY	10.00	4.50
❏ 199	Andruw Jones CL BY	30.00	13.50
❏ 200	Derek Jeter CL SY	80.00	36.00
❏ 201	Chipper Jones GX	40.00	18.00
❏ 202	Albert Belle GY	40.00	18.00
❏ 203	Mike Piazza GY	80.00	36.00
❏ 204	Ken Griffey Jr. GX	80.00	36.00
❏ 205	Ryne Sandberg GZ	50.00	22.00
❏ 206	Jose Canseco SY	30.00	13.50
❏ 207	Chili Davis BX	6.00	2.70
❏ 208	Roger Clemens GX	100.00	45.00
❏ 209	Deion Sanders GZ	15.00	6.75
❏ 210	Darryl Hamilton BX	4.00	1.80
❏ 211	Jermaine Dye SX	6.00	2.70
❏ 212	Matt Williams GY	15.00	6.75
❏ 213	Kevin Elster BX	4.00	1.80
❏ 214	John Wetteland SX	10.00	4.50
❏ 215	Garret Anderson GZ	15.00	6.75
❏ 216	Kevin Brown GY	25.00	11.00
❏ 217	Matt Lawton SY	10.00	4.50
❏ 218	Cal Ripken GD	60.00	27.00
❏ 219	Moises Alou GY	25.00	11.00
❏ 220	Chuck Knoblauch GZ	40.00	18.00
❏ 221	Ivan Rodriguez GY	30.00	13.50
❏ 222	Travis Fryman BY	6.00	2.70
❏ 223	Jim Thome GZ	40.00	18.00
❏ 224	Eddie Murray SZ	25.00	11.00
❏ 225	Eric Young GZ	15.00	6.75
❏ 226	Ron Gant SX	6.00	2.70
❏ 227	Tony Phillips BX	4.00	1.80
❏ 228	Reggie Sanders BY	6.00	2.70

❑ 229	Johnny Damon SZ	10.00	4.50
❑ 230	Bill Pulsipher BX	4.00	1.80
❑ 231	Jim Edmonds GZ	25.00	11.00
❑ 232	Melvin Nieves BX	4.00	1.80
❑ 233	Ryan Klesko GZ	15.00	6.75
❑ 234	David Cone SX	15.00	6.75
❑ 235	Derek Bell BY	6.00	2.70
❑ 236	Julio Franco BX	10.00	4.50
❑ 237	Juan Guzman BX	4.00	1.80
❑ 238	Larry Walker GZ	40.00	18.00
❑ 239	Delino DeShields BX ..	4.00	1.80
❑ 240	Troy Percival BY	6.00	2.70
❑ 241	Andres Galarraga GZ	40.00	18.00
❑ 242	Rondell White GZ	15.00	6.75
❑ 243	John Burkett BX	4.00	1.80
❑ 244	J.T. Snow BY	6.00	2.70
❑ 245	Alex Fernandez SY	6.00	2.70
❑ 246	Edgar Martinez GZ	15.00	6.75
❑ 247	Craig Biggio GZ	40.00	18.00
❑ 248	Todd Hundley GY	15.00	6.75
❑ 249	Jimmy Key SX	10.00	4.50
❑ 250	Cliff Floyd BY	6.00	2.70
❑ 251	Jeff Conine BY	6.00	2.70
❑ 252	Curt Schilling BX	6.00	2.70
❑ 253	Jeff King BX	4.00	1.80
❑ 254	Tino Martinez GZ	40.00	18.00
❑ 255	Carlos Baerga SY	10.00	4.50
❑ 256	Jeff Fassero BY	4.00	1.80
❑ 257	Dean Palmer SY	10.00	4.50
❑ 258	Robb Nen BX	4.00	1.80
❑ 259	Sandy Alomar Jr. SY ..	10.00	4.50
❑ 260	Carlos Perez BX	6.00	2.70
❑ 261	Rickey Henderson SY	30.00	13.50
❑ 262	Bobby Bonilla SY	10.00	4.50
❑ 263	Darren Daulton BX	6.00	2.70
❑ 264	Jim Leyritz BX	4.00	1.80
❑ 265	Dennis Martinez BX ..	6.00	2.70
❑ 266	Butch Huskey BX	4.00	1.80
❑ 267	Joe Vitiello SY	6.00	2.70
❑ 268	Steve Trachsel BX	4.00	1.80
❑ 269	Glenallen Hill BX	4.00	1.80
❑ 270	Terry Steinbach BX	6.00	2.70
❑ 271	Mark McLemore BX	4.00	1.80
❑ 272	Devon White BX	4.00	1.80
❑ 273	Jeff Kent BX	6.00	2.70
❑ 274	Tim Raines SY	6.00	2.70
❑ 275	Carlos Garcia BX	4.00	1.80
❑ 276	Hal Morris BX	4.00	1.80
❑ 277	Gary Gaetti BX	4.00	1.80
❑ 278	John Olerud SY	10.00	4.50
❑ 279	Wally Joyner BX	6.00	2.70
❑ 280	Brian Hunter SX	10.00	4.50
❑ 281	Steve Karsay BX	4.00	1.80
❑ 282	Denny Neagle SX	10.00	4.50
❑ 283	Jose Herrera BX	4.00	1.80
❑ 284	Todd Stottlemyre BX ..	4.00	1.80
❑ 285	Bip Roberts BX	6.00	2.70
❑ 286	Kevin Seitzer BX	4.00	1.80
❑ 287	Benji Gil BX	4.00	1.80
❑ 288	Dennis Eckersley SX..	10.00	4.50
❑ 289	Brad Ausmus BX	4.00	1.80
❑ 290	Otis Nixon BX	4.00	1.80
❑ 291	Darryl Strawberry BX	6.00	2.70
❑ 292	Marquis Grissom SY ..	10.00	4.50
❑ 293	Darryl Kile BX	6.00	2.70
❑ 294	Quilvio Veras BX	4.00	1.80
❑ 295	Tom Goodwin BX	4.00	1.80
❑ 296	Benito Santiago BX	4.00	1.80
❑ 297	Mike Bordick BX	4.00	1.80
❑ 298	Roberto Kelly BX	4.00	1.80
❑ 299	David Justice GZ	40.00	18.00
❑ 300	Carl Everett BX	4.00	1.80
❑ 301	Mark Whiten BX	4.00	1.80
❑ 302	Aaron Sele BX	6.00	2.70
❑ 303	Darren Bragg BX	6.00	2.70
❑ 304	Bobby Jones BX	6.00	2.70
❑ 305	Fernando Vina BX	4.00	1.80
❑ 306	Ed Sprague BX	4.00	1.80
❑ 307	Andy Ashby SX	6.00	2.70
❑ 308	Tony Fernandez BX	6.00	2.70
❑ 309	Roger Pavlik BX	4.00	1.80
❑ 310	Mark Clark BX	4.00	1.80
❑ 311	Mariano Duncan BX ..	4.00	1.80
❑ 312	Tyler Houston BX	4.00	1.80
❑ 313	Eric Davis SY	10.00	4.50
❑ 314	Greg Vaughn BY	6.00	2.70
❑ 315	David Segui SY	10.00	4.50
❑ 316	Dave Nilsson SX	6.00	2.70
❑ 317	F.P. Santangelo SX....	6.00	2.70
❑ 318	Wilton Guerrero SY	10.00	4.50
❑ 319	Jose Guillen GZ	40.00	18.00
❑ 320	Kevin Orie SY	6.00	2.70
❑ 321	Derrek Lee GZ	25.00	11.00
❑ 322	Bubba Trammell SY ..	25.00	11.00
❑ 323	Pokey Reese GZ	10.00	4.50
❑ 324	Hideki Irabu GX	20.00	9.00
❑ 325	Scott Spiezio SZ	6.00	2.70
❑ 326	Bartolo Colon GZ	15.00	6.75
❑ 327	Damon Mashore SY ..	6.00	2.70
❑ 328	Ryan McGuire SY	6.00	2.70
❑ 329	Chris Carpenter BX	6.00	2.70
❑ 330	Jose Cruz Jr. GX	25.00	11.00
❑ 331	Todd Greene SZ	10.00	4.50
❑ 332	Brian Moehler BX	4.00	1.80
❑ 333	Mike Sweeney BX	4.00	1.80
❑ 334	Neifi Perez GZ	10.00	4.50
❑ 335	Matt Morris SY	10.00	4.50
❑ 336	Marvin Benard BY	4.00	1.80
❑ 337	Karim Garcia SZ	10.00	4.50
❑ 338	Jason Dickson SY	10.00	4.50
❑ 339	Brant Brown SY	10.00	4.50
❑ 340	Jeff Suppan SZ	6.00	2.70
❑ 341	Deivi Cruz SX	15.00	6.75
❑ 342	Antone Williamson GZ	10.00	4.50
❑ 343	Curtis Goodwin BX	4.00	1.80
❑ 344	Brooks Kieschnick SY	6.00	2.70
❑ 345	Tony Womack BX	15.00	6.75
❑ 346	Rudy Pemberton BX ..	4.00	1.80
❑ 347	Todd Dunwoody BX	6.00	2.70
❑ 348	Frank Thomas LG SY	50.00	22.00
❑ 349	Andruw Jones LG SX	20.00	9.00
❑ 350	Alex Rodriguez LG SY	80.00	36.00
❑ 351	Greg Maddux LG SY..	60.00	27.00
❑ 352	Jeff Bagwell LG SY	30.00	13.50
❑ 353	Juan Gonzalez LG SY	50.00	22.00
❑ 354	Barry Bonds LG SY	30.00	13.50
❑ 355	Mark McGwire LG BY	120.00	55.00
❑ 356	Tony Gwynn LG BY	60.00	27.00
❑ 357	Gary Sheffield LG BX	10.00	4.50
❑ 358	Derek Jeter LG SX	50.00	22.00
❑ 359	Manny Ramirez LG SY	30.00	13.50
❑ 360	Hideo Nomo LG GZ	80.00	36.00
❑ 361	Sammy Sosa LG BX ..	50.00	22.00
❑ 362	Paul Molitor LG SY	25.00	11.00
❑ 363	Kenny Lofton LG BY ..	15.00	6.75
❑ 364	Eddie Murray LG BX ..	15.00	6.75
❑ 365	Barry Larkin LG GZ	15.00	6.75
❑ 366	Roger Clemens LG SY	60.00	27.00
❑ 367	John Smoltz LG BZ	6.00	2.70
❑ 368	Alex Rodriguez GM SX	50.00	22.00
❑ 369	Frank Thomas GM SX	30.00	13.50
❑ 370	Cal Ripken GM GY	100.00	45.00
❑ 371	Ken Griffey Jr. GM SY	120.00	55.00
❑ 372	Greg Maddux GM GX	40.00	18.00
❑ 373	Mike Piazza GM SX ..	50.00	22.00
❑ 374	Chipper Jones GM BY	60.00	27.00
❑ 375	Albert Belle GM BX	15.00	6.75
❑ 376	Chuck Knoblauch GM BX	15.00	6.75
❑ 377	Brady Anderson GM BZ	6.00	2.70
❑ 378	David Justice GM SX	15.00	6.75
❑ 379	Randy Johnson GM BZ	15.00	6.75
❑ 380	Wade Boggs GM BX ..	15.00	6.75
❑ 381	Kevin Brown GM BX ..	4.00	1.80
❑ 382	Tom Glavine GM GY ..	40.00	18.00
❑ 383	Raul Mondesi GM SX	15.00	6.75
❑ 384	Ivan Rodriguez GM SX	20.00	9.00
❑ 385	Larry Walker GM SX ..	15.00	6.75
❑ 386	Bernie Williams GM BZ	15.00	6.75
❑ 387	Rusty Greer GM GY ..	15.00	6.75
❑ 388	Rafael Palmeiro GM GY	15.00	6.75
❑ 389	Matt Williams GM BX	6.00	2.70
❑ 390	Eric Young GM BZ	6.00	2.70
❑ 391	Fred McGriff GM BX ..	10.00	4.50
❑ 392	Ken Caminiti GM BX ..	10.00	4.50
❑ 393	Roberto Alomar GM BZ	15.00	6.75
❑ 394	Brian Jordan GM BX ..	6.00	2.70
❑ 395	Mark Grace GM GZ	10.00	4.50
❑ 396	Jim Edmonds GM SY	10.00	4.50
❑ 397	Deion Sanders GM SY	10.00	4.50
❑ 398	Vladimir Guerrero CL SZ	60.00	27.00
❑ 399	Darin Erstad CL SY	25.00	11.00
❑ 400	N. Garciaparra CL SZ	120.00	55.00

1997 Leaf Banner Season

	MINT	NRMT
COMPLETE SET (15)	250.00	110.00
COMMON CARD (1-15)	2.50	1.10
MINOR STARS	5.00	2.20
UNLISTED STARS	10.00	4.50
RANDOM INS.IN SER.1 MAGAZINE PACKS		
STATED PRINT RUN 2500 SERIAL #'d SETS		

❑ 1	Jeff Bagwell	12.00	5.50
❑ 2	Ken Griffey Jr.	50.00	22.00
❑ 3	Juan Gonzalez	20.00	9.00
❑ 4	Frank Thomas	20.00	9.00
❑ 5	Alex Rodriguez	30.00	13.50
❑ 6	Kenny Lofton	6.00	2.70
❑ 7	Chuck Knoblauch	10.00	4.50
❑ 8	Mo Vaughn	10.00	4.50
❑ 9	Chipper Jones	25.00	11.00
❑ 10	Ken Caminiti	6.00	2.70
❑ 11	Craig Biggio..............	10.00	4.50
❑ 12	John Smoltz	5.00	2.20
❑ 13	Pat Hentgen	5.00	2.20
❑ 14	Derek Jeter	30.00	13.50
❑ 15	Todd Hollandsworth ..	2.50	1.10

1997 Leaf Dress for Success

	MINT	NRMT
COMPLETE SET (18)	200.00	90.00
COMMON CARD (1-18)	2.50	1.10
UNLISTED STARS	5.00	2.20
RANDOM INS.IN SER.1 RETAIL PACKS		
STATED PRINT RUN 3500 SERIAL #'d SETS		

❑ 1	Greg Maddux	12.00	5.50
❑ 2	Cal Ripken	20.00	9.00
❑ 3	Albert Belle	5.00	2.20
❑ 4	Frank Thomas	10.00	4.50
❑ 5	Dante Bichette	2.50	1.10
❑ 6	Gary Sheffield	2.50	1.10
❑ 7	Jeff Bagwell	6.00	2.70
❑ 8	Mike Piazza	10.00	4.50
❑ 9	Mark McGwire	25.00	11.00
❑ 10	Ken Caminiti	3.00	1.35
❑ 11	Alex Rodriguez	15.00	6.75
❑ 12	Ken Griffey Jr.	25.00	11.00
❑ 13	Juan Gonzalez	10.00	4.50

☐ 14 Brian Jordan	2.50	1.10
☐ 15 Mo Vaughn	5.00	2.20
☐ 16 Ivan Rodriguez	6.00	2.70
☐ 17 Andruw Jones	6.00	2.70
☐ 18 Chipper Jones	12.00	5.50

1997 Leaf Get-A-Grip

	MINT	NRMT
COMPLETE SET (16)	250.00	110.00
COMMON CARD (1-16)	6.00	2.70

RANDOM INS.IN SER.1 HOBBY PACKS
STATED PRINT RUN 3500 SERIAL #'d SETS

☐ 1 Ken Griffey Jr. Greg Maddux	40.00	18.00
☐ 2 John Smoltz Frank Thomas	12.00	5.50
☐ 3 Mike Piazza Andy Pettitte	20.00	9.00
☐ 4 Randy Johnson Chipper Jones	15.00	6.75
☐ 5 Tom Glavine Alex Rodriguez	20.00	9.00
☐ 6 Pat Hentgen Jeff Bagwell	8.00	3.60
☐ 7 Kevin Brown Juan Gonzalez	12.00	5.50
☐ 8 Barry Bonds Mike Mussina	8.00	3.60
☐ 9 Hideo Nomo Albert Belle	8.00	3.60
☐ 10 Troy Percival Andruw Jones	8.00	3.60
☐ 11 Roger Clemens Brian Jordan	15.00	6.75
☐ 12 Paul Wilson Ivan Rodriguez	8.00	3.60
☐ 13 Andy Benes Mo Vaughn	8.00	3.60
☐ 14 Al Leiter Derek Jeter	20.00	9.00
☐ 15 Bill Pulsipher Cal Ripken	25.00	11.00
☐ 16 Mariano Rivera Ken Caminiti	6.00	2.70

1997 Leaf Gold Stars

	MINT	NRMT
COMPLETE SET (36)	500.00	220.00

COMMON CARD (1-36)	2.50	1.10
MINOR STARS	4.00	1.80
SEMISTARS	6.00	2.70
UNLISTED STARS	10.00	4.50

RANDOM INSERTS IN SER.2 PACKS
STATED PRINT RUN 2500 SERIAL #'d SETS

☐ 1 Frank Thomas	20.00	9.00
☐ 2 Alex Rodriguez	30.00	13.50
☐ 3 Ken Griffey Jr.	50.00	22.00
☐ 4 Andruw Jones	12.00	5.50
☐ 5 Chipper Jones	25.00	11.00
☐ 6 Jeff Bagwell	12.00	5.50
☐ 7 Derek Jeter	30.00	13.50
☐ 8 Deion Sanders	4.00	1.80
☐ 9 Ivan Rodriguez	12.00	5.50
☐ 10 Juan Gonzalez	20.00	9.00
☐ 11 Greg Maddux	25.00	11.00
☐ 12 Andy Pettitte	6.00	2.70
☐ 13 Roger Clemens	25.00	11.00
☐ 14 Hideo Nomo	10.00	4.50
☐ 15 Tony Gwynn	25.00	11.00
☐ 16 Barry Bonds	12.00	5.50
☐ 17 Kenny Lofton	6.00	2.70
☐ 18 Paul Molitor	10.00	4.50
☐ 19 Jim Thome	10.00	4.50
☐ 20 Albert Belle	10.00	4.50
☐ 21 Cal Ripken	40.00	18.00
☐ 22 Mark McGwire	50.00	22.00
☐ 23 Barry Larkin	10.00	4.50
☐ 24 Mike Piazza	30.00	13.50
☐ 25 Darin Erstad	10.00	4.50
☐ 26 Chuck Knoblauch	10.00	4.50
☐ 27 Vladimir Guerrero	15.00	6.75
☐ 28 Tony Clark	6.00	2.70
☐ 29 Scott Rolen	15.00	6.75
☐ 30 Nomar Garciaparra	30.00	13.50
☐ 31 Eric Young	2.50	1.10
☐ 32 Ryne Sandberg	12.00	5.50
☐ 33 Roberto Alomar	10.00	4.50
☐ 34 Eddie Murray	10.00	4.50
☐ 35 Rafael Palmeiro	10.00	4.50
☐ 36 Jose Guillen	6.00	2.70

1997 Leaf Knot-Hole Gang

	MINT	NRMT
COMPLETE SET (12)	120.00	55.00
COMMON CARD (1-12)	2.50	1.10
UNLISTED STARS	5.00	2.20

RANDOM INSERTS IN SER.1 PACKS
STATED PRINT RUN 5000 SERIAL #'d SETS

☐ 1 Chuck Knoblauch	5.00	2.20
☐ 2 Ken Griffey Jr.	25.00	11.00
☐ 3 Frank Thomas	10.00	4.50
☐ 4 Tony Gwynn	12.00	5.50
☐ 5 Mike Piazza	15.00	6.75
☐ 6 Jeff Bagwell	6.00	2.70
☐ 7 Rusty Greer	2.50	1.10
☐ 8 Cal Ripken	20.00	9.00
☐ 9 Chipper Jones	12.00	5.50
☐ 10 Ryan Klesko	2.50	1.10
☐ 11 Barry Larkin	5.00	2.20
☐ 12 Paul Molitor	5.00	2.20
☐ P10 Ryan Klesko Promo	2.00	.90

1997 Leaf Leagues of the Nation

	MINT	NRMT
COMPLETE SET (15)	300.00	135.00
COMMON CARD (1-15)	10.00	4.50

RANDOM INSERTS IN SER.2 PACKS
STATED PRINT RUN 2500 SERIAL #'d SETS

☐ 1 Juan Gonzalez Barry Bonds	20.00	9.00
☐ 2 Cal Ripken Chipper Jones	40.00	18.00
☐ 3 Mark McGwire Ken Caminiti	50.00	22.00
☐ 4 Derek Jeter Kenny Lofton	30.00	13.50
☐ 5 Ivan Rodriguez Mike Piazza	30.00	13.50
☐ 6 Ken Griffey Jr. Larry Walker	50.00	22.00
☐ 7 Frank Thomas Sammy Sosa	40.00	18.00
☐ 8 Paul Molitor Barry Larkin	10.00	4.50
☐ 9 Albert Belle Deion Sanders	10.00	4.50
☐ 10 Matt Williams Jeff Bagwell	12.00	5.50
☐ 11 Mo Vaughn Gary Sheffield	10.00	4.50
☐ 12 Alex Rodriguez Tony Gwynn	40.00	18.00
☐ 13 Tino Martinez Scott Rolen	15.00	6.75
☐ 14 Darin Erstad Wilton Guerrero	10.00	4.50
☐ 15 Tony Clark Vladimir Guerrero	15.00	6.75

1997 Leaf Statistical Standouts

	MINT	NRMT
COMPLETE SET (15)	750.00	350.00
COMMON CARD (1-15)	10.00	4.50
SEMISTARS	12.00	5.50
UNLISTED STARS	20.00	9.00

RANDOM INSERTS IN SER.1 PACKS
STATED PRINT RUN 1000 SERIAL #'d SETS

		MINT	NRMT
❏ 1	Albert Belle	20.00	9.00
❏ 2	Juan Gonzalez	40.00	18.00
❏ 3	Ken Griffey Jr.	100.00	45.00
❏ 4	Alex Rodriguez	60.00	27.00
❏ 5	Frank Thomas	40.00	18.00
❏ 6	Chipper Jones	50.00	22.00
❏ 7	Greg Maddux	50.00	22.00
❏ 8	Mike Piazza	60.00	27.00
❏ 9	Cal Ripken	80.00	36.00
❏ 10	Mark McGwire	100.00	45.00
❏ 11	Barry Bonds	25.00	11.00
❏ 12	Derek Jeter	60.00	27.00
❏ 13	Ken Caminiti	12.00	5.50
❏ 14	John Smoltz	12.00	5.50
❏ 15	Paul Molitor	20.00	9.00

1997 Leaf Thomas Collection

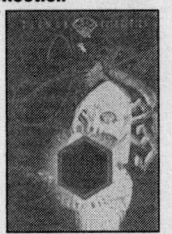

	MINT	NRMT
COMPLETE SET (6)	2500.00	1100.00
COMMON CARD (1-6)	400.00	180.00
RANDOM INSERTS IN SER.2 PACKS		
STATED PRINT RUN 100 SETS		

		MINT	NRMT
❏ 1	Frank Thomas	400.00	180.00
	Game Hat/Blue Text		
❏ 2	Frank Thomas	500.00	220.00
	Home Jersey/Orange Text		
❏ 3	Frank Thomas	400.00	180.00
	Batting Glove/Yellow Text		
❏ 4	Frank Thomas	400.00	180.00
	Bat/Green Text		
❏ 5	Frank Thomas	400.00	180.00
	Sweatband/Purple Text		
❏ 6	Frank Thomas	500.00	220.00
	Away Jersey/Red Text		

1997 Leaf Warning Track

	MINT	NRMT
COMPLETE SET (18)	100.00	45.00
COMMON CARD (1-18)	3.00	1.35
UNLISTED STARS	6.00	2.70
RANDOM INSERTS IN SER.2 PACKS		
STATED PRINT RUN 3500 SERIAL #'d SETS		

		MINT	NRMT
❏ 1	Ken Griffey Jr.	30.00	13.50
❏ 2	Albert Belle	6.00	2.70

❏ 3	Barry Bonds	8.00	3.60
❏ 4	Andruw Jones	8.00	3.60
❏ 5	Kenny Lofton	4.00	1.80
❏ 6	Tony Gwynn	15.00	6.75
❏ 7	Manny Ramirez	8.00	3.60
❏ 8	Rusty Greer	3.00	1.35
❏ 9	Bernie Williams	6.00	2.70
❏ 10	Gary Sheffield	3.00	1.35
❏ 11	Juan Gonzalez	12.00	5.50
❏ 12	Raul Mondesi	3.00	1.35
❏ 13	Brady Anderson	3.00	1.35
❏ 14	Rondell White	3.00	1.35
❏ 15	Sammy Sosa	20.00	9.00
❏ 16	Deion Sanders	3.00	1.35
❏ 17	Dave Justice	6.00	2.70
❏ 18	Jim Edmonds	4.00	1.80

1998 Leaf

	MINT	NRMT
COMPLETE SET (200)	175.00	80.00
COMP.SET w/o SPs (147)	15.00	6.75
COMMON CARD (1-201)	.15	.07
MINOR CARD	.25	.11
UNLISTED STARS	.40	.18
SEMISTARS	.60	.25
COMMON SP (148-197)	1.00	.45
SP MINOR STARS	1.50	.70
SP SEMISTARS	2.00	.90
SP UNLISTED STARS	3.00	1.35
CARDS 148-197 ARE SHORTPRINTED		
CARD NUMBER 42 DOES NOT EXIST		

❏ 1	Rusty Greer	.25	.11
❏ 2	Tino Martinez	.25	.11
❏ 3	Bobby Bonilla	.25	.11
❏ 4	Jason Giambi	.25	.11
❏ 5	Matt Morris	.15	.07
❏ 6	Craig Counsell	.15	.07
❏ 7	Reggie Jefferson	.15	.07
❏ 8	Brian Rose	.15	.07
❏ 9	Ruben Rivera	.15	.07
❏ 10	Shawn Estes	.15	.07
❏ 11	Tony Gwynn	1.50	.70
❏ 12	Jeff Abbott	.15	.07
❏ 13	Jose Cruz Jr.	.25	.11
❏ 14	Francisco Cordova	.15	.07
❏ 15	Ryan Klesko	.25	.11
❏ 16	Tim Salmon	.40	.18
❏ 17	Brett Tomko	.15	.07
❏ 18	Matt Williams	.60	.25
❏ 19	Joe Carter	.25	.11
❏ 20	Harold Baines	.25	.11
❏ 21	Gary Sheffield	.25	.11
❏ 22	Charles Johnson	.15	.07
❏ 23	Aaron Boone	.25	.11
❏ 24	Eddie Murray	.60	.25
❏ 25	Matt Stairs	.15	.11
❏ 26	David Cone	.40	.18
❏ 27	Jon Nunnally	.15	.07
❏ 28	Chris Stynes	.15	.07
❏ 29	Enrique Wilson	.15	.07
❏ 30	Randy Johnson	.60	.25
❏ 31	Garret Anderson	.25	.11
❏ 32	Manny Ramirez	.75	.35
❏ 33	Jeff Suppan	.15	.07
❏ 34	Rickey Henderson	.75	.35
❏ 35	Scott Spiezio	.15	.07

❏ 36	Rondell White	.25	.11
❏ 37	Todd Greene	.15	.07
❏ 38	Delino DeShields	.15	.07
❏ 39	Kevin Brown	.40	.18
❏ 40	Chili Davis	.25	.11
❏ 41	Jimmy Key	.25	.11
❏ 43	Mike Mussina	.60	.25
❏ 44	Joe Randa	.15	.07
❏ 45	Chan Ho Park	.25	.11
❏ 46	Brad Radke	.25	.11
❏ 47	Geronimo Berroa	.15	.07
❏ 48	Wade Boggs	.60	.25
❏ 49	Kevin Appier	.25	.11
❏ 50	Moises Alou	.25	.11
❏ 51	David Justice	.25	.11
❏ 52	Ivan Rodriguez	.75	.35
❏ 53	J.T. Snow	.25	.11
❏ 54	Brian Giles	.25	.11
❏ 55	Will Clark	.60	.25
❏ 56	Justin Thompson	.15	.07
❏ 57	Javier Lopez	.25	.11
❏ 58	Hideki Irabu	.25	.11
❏ 59	Mark Grudzielanek	.15	.07
❏ 60	Abraham Nunez	.15	.07
❏ 61	Todd Hollandsworth	.15	.07
❏ 62	Jay Bell	.25	.11
❏ 63	Nomar Garciaparra	2.00	.90
❏ 64	Vinny Castilla	.25	.11
❏ 65	Lou Collier	.15	.07
❏ 66	Kevin Orie	.15	.07
❏ 67	John Valentin	.25	.11
❏ 68	Robin Ventura	.25	.11
❏ 69	Denny Neagle	.15	.07
❏ 70	Tony Womack	.25	.11
❏ 71	Dennis Reyes	.15	.07
❏ 72	Wally Joyner	.25	.11
❏ 73	Kevin Brown	.40	.18
❏ 74	Ray Durham	.25	.11
❏ 75	Mike Cameron	.15	.07
❏ 76	Dante Bichette	.25	.11
❏ 77	Jose Guillen	.15	.07
❏ 78	Carlos Delgado	.60	.25
❏ 79	Paul Molitor	.60	.25
❏ 80	Jason Kendall	.25	.11
❏ 81	Mark Bellhorn	.15	.07
❏ 82	Damian Jackson	.15	.07
❏ 83	Bill Mueller	.15	.07
❏ 84	Kevin Young	.15	.07
❏ 85	Curt Schilling	.40	.18
❏ 86	Jeffrey Hammonds	.15	.07
❏ 87	Sandy Alomar Jr.	.25	.11
❏ 88	Bartolo Colon	.25	.11
❏ 89	Wilton Guerrero	.15	.07
❏ 90	Bernie Williams	.60	.25
❏ 91	Deion Sanders	.25	.11
❏ 92	Mike Piazza	2.00	.90
❏ 93	Butch Huskey	.15	.07
❏ 94	Edgardo Alfonzo	.40	.18
❏ 95	Alan Benes	.15	.07
❏ 96	Craig Biggio	.60	.25
❏ 97	Mark Grace	.40	.18
❏ 98	Shawn Green	.60	.25
❏ 99	Derek Lee	.15	.07
❏ 100	Ken Griffey Jr.	3.00	1.35
❏ 101	Tim Raines	.25	.11
❏ 102	Pokey Reese	.15	.07
❏ 103	Lee Stevens	.15	.07
❏ 104	Shannon Stewart	.25	.11
❏ 105	John Smoltz	.40	.18
❏ 106	Frank Thomas	1.25	.55
❏ 107	Jeff Fassero	.15	.07
❏ 108	Jay Buhner	.25	.11
❏ 109	Jose Canseco	.75	.35
❏ 110	Omar Vizquel	.25	.11
❏ 111	Travis Fryman	.25	.11
❏ 112	Dave Nilsson	.15	.07
❏ 113	John Olerud	.25	.11
❏ 114	Larry Walker	.60	.25
❏ 115	Jim Edmonds	.25	.11
❏ 116	Bobby Higginson	.25	.11
❏ 117	Todd Hundley	.25	.11
❏ 118	Paul O'Neill	.25	.11
❏ 119	Bip Roberts	.15	.07
❏ 120	Ismael Valdes	.15	.07
❏ 121	Pedro Martinez	.75	.35
❏ 122	Jeff Cirillo	.25	.11

☐ 123 Andy Benes	.15	.07
☐ 124 Bobby Jones	.15	.07
☐ 125 Brian Hunter	.15	.07
☐ 126 Darryl Kile	.15	.07
☐ 127 Pat Hentgen	.15	.07
☐ 128 Marquis Grissom	.15	.07
☐ 129 Eric Davis	.25	.11
☐ 130 Chipper Jones	1.50	.70
☐ 131 Edgar Martinez	.25	.11
☐ 132 Andy Pettitte	.25	.11
☐ 133 Cal Ripken	2.50	1.10
☐ 134 Scott Rolen	.75	.35
☐ 135 Ron Coomer	.15	.07
☐ 136 Luis Castillo	.15	.07
☐ 137 Fred McGriff	.40	.18
☐ 138 Neifi Perez	.25	.11
☐ 139 Eric Karros	.25	.11
☐ 140 Alex Fernandez	.15	.07
☐ 141 Jason Dickson	.15	.07
☐ 142 Lance Johnson	.15	.07
☐ 143 Ray Lankford	.25	.11
☐ 144 Sammy Sosa	2.00	.90
☐ 145 Eric Young	.15	.07
☐ 146 Bubba Trammell	.15	.07
☐ 147 Todd Walker	.25	.11
☐ 148 Mo Vaughn	3.00	1.35
☐ 149 Jeff Bagwell CC	4.00	1.80
☐ 150 Kenny Lofton CC	2.00	.90
☐ 151 Raul Mondesi CC	1.50	.70
☐ 152 Mike Piazza CC	10.00	4.50
☐ 153 Chipper Jones CC	8.00	3.60
☐ 154 Larry Walker CC	3.00	1.35
☐ 155 Greg Maddux CC	8.00	3.60
☐ 156 Ken Griffey Jr. CC	15.00	6.75
☐ 157 Frank Thomas CC	6.00	2.70
☐ 158 Darin Erstad GLS	2.00	.90
☐ 159 Roberto Alomar GLS	3.00	1.35
☐ 160 Albert Belle GLS	3.00	1.35
☐ 161 Jim Thome GLS	3.00	1.35
☐ 162 Tony Clark GLS	1.50	.70
☐ 163 Chuck Knoblauch GLS	1.50	.70
☐ 164 Derek Jeter GLS	10.00	4.50
☐ 165 Alex Rodriguez GLS	10.00	4.50
☐ 166 Tony Gwynn GLS	8.00	3.60
☐ 167 Roger Clemens GLS	8.00	3.60
☐ 168 Barry Larkin GLS	3.00	1.35
☐ 169 Andres Galarraga GLS	2.00	.90
☐ 170 Vladimir Guerrero GLS	4.00	1.80
☐ 171 Mark McGwire GLS	20.00	9.00
☐ 172 Barry Bonds GLS	4.00	1.80
☐ 173 Juan Gonzalez GLS	6.00	2.70
☐ 174 Andruw Jones GLS	3.00	1.35
☐ 175 Paul Molitor GLS	3.00	1.35
☐ 176 Hideo Nomo GLS	3.00	1.35
☐ 177 Cal Ripken GLS	12.00	5.50
☐ 178 Brad Fullmer GLR	1.00	.45
☐ 179 Jaret Wright GLR	1.50	.70
☐ 180 Bobby Estalella GLR	1.00	.45
☐ 181 Ben Grieve GLR	3.00	1.35
☐ 182 Paul Konerko GLR	1.50	.70
☐ 183 David Ortiz GLR	1.00	.45
☐ 184 Todd Helton GLR	4.00	1.80
☐ 185 Juan Encarnacion GLR	1.50	.70
☐ 186 Miguel Tejada GLR	1.50	.70
☐ 187 Jacob Cruz GLR	1.00	.45
☐ 188 Mark Kotsay GLR	1.50	.70
☐ 189 Fernando Tatis GLR	3.00	1.35
☐ 190 Ricky Ledee GLR	1.50	.70
☐ 191 Richard Hidalgo GLR	1.00	.70
☐ 192 Richie Sexson GLR	2.00	.90
☐ 193 Luis Ordaz GLR	1.00	.45
☐ 194 Eli Marrero GLR	1.00	.45
☐ 195 Livan Hernandez GLR	1.00	.45
☐ 196 Homer Bush GLR	1.00	.45
☐ 197 Raul Ibanez GLR	1.00	.45
☐ 198 Nomar Garciaparra CL	1.00	.45
☐ 199 Scott Rolen CL	.60	.25
☐ 200 Jose Cruz Jr. CL	.15	.07
☐ 201 Al Martin	.15	.07

1998 Leaf Fractal Diamond Axis

	MINT	NRMT
COMMON (1-41/43-201)	12.00	5.50

*STARS 1-147/198-201: 30X TO 80X HI
*YNG.STARS 1-147/198-201: 25X TO 60X HI
*SP STARS 148-177: 6X TO 15X BASIC SPS
*SP YG.STARS 148-177: 5X TO 12X BASE SPS
RANDOM INSERTS IN PACKS
STATED PRINT RUN 50 SERIAL #'d SETS
CARD NUMBER 42 DOES NOT EXIST

1998 Leaf Fractal Matrix

	MINT	NRMT
COMMON BRONZE	1.00	.45
BRONZE MINOR STARS	1.50	.70
BRONZE SEMISTARS	2.50	1.10
BRONZE UNLISTED STARS	4.00	1.80
BRONZE X STATED PRINT RUN 1600 SETS		
BRONZE Y STATED PRINT RUN 1700 SETS		
BRONZE Z STATED PRINT RUN 1900 SETS		
COMMON SILVER	2.00	.90
SILVER MINOR STARS	3.00	1.35
SILVER SEMISTARS	5.00	2.20
SILVER UNLISTED STARS	8.00	3.60
SILVER X STATED PRINT RUN 600 SETS		
SILVER Y STATED PRINT RUN 800 SETS		
SILVER Z STATED PRINT RUN 900 SETS		
COMMON GOLD	5.00	2.20
GOLD SEMISTARS	8.00	3.60
GOLD UNLISTED STARS	12.00	5.50
GOLD X STATED PRINT RUN 100 SETS		
GOLD Y STATED PRINT RUN 300 SETS		
GOLD Z STATED PRINT RUN 400 SETS		
RANDOM INSERTS IN PACKS		
CARD NUMBER 42 DOES NOT EXIST		

☐ 1 Rusty Greer GZ	5.00	2.20
☐ 2 Tino Martinez GZ	5.00	2.20
☐ 3 Bobby Bonilla GZ	3.00	1.35
☐ 4 Jason Giambi GZ	3.00	1.35
☐ 5 Matt Morris GZ	2.00	.90
☐ 6 Craig Counsell BX	1.00	.45
☐ 7 Reggie Jefferson BX	1.00	.45
☐ 8 Brian Rose SY	2.00	.90
☐ 9 Ruben Rivera BX	1.00	.45
☐ 10 Shawn Estes SY	2.00	.90
☐ 11 Tony Gwynn GZ	30.00	13.50
☐ 12 Jeff Abbott BY	1.00	.45
☐ 13 Jose Cruz Jr. GZ	5.00	2.20
☐ 14 Francisco Cordova BX	1.00	.45
☐ 15 Ryan Klesko BX	1.50	.70
☐ 16 Tim Salmon GY	8.00	3.60
☐ 17 Brett Tomko BX	1.00	.45
☐ 18 Matt Williams SY	8.00	3.60
☐ 19 Joe Carter BX	1.50	.70
☐ 20 Harold Baines BX	1.50	.70
☐ 21 Gary Sheffield SZ	3.00	1.35
☐ 22 Charles Johnson SX	3.00	1.35
☐ 23 Aaron Boone SY	1.00	.45
☐ 24 Eddie Murray GY	12.00	5.50
☐ 25 Matt Stairs BY	1.50	.70
☐ 26 David Cone BX	2.50	1.10
☐ 27 Jon Nunnally BY	1.00	.45
☐ 28 Chris Stynes BX	1.00	.45
☐ 29 Enrique Wilson BY	1.00	.45
☐ 30 Randy Johnson SZ	8.00	3.60
☐ 31 Garret Anderson SY	3.00	1.35
☐ 32 Manny Ramirez GZ	15.00	6.75
☐ 33 Jeff Suppan SX	2.00	.90
☐ 34 Rickey Henderson BX	5.00	2.20
☐ 35 Scott Spiezio BX	1.00	.45
☐ 36 Rondell White SY	3.00	1.35
☐ 37 Todd Greene SZ	2.00	.90
☐ 38 Delino DeShields SX	1.00	.45
☐ 39 Kevin Brown P SX	5.00	2.20
☐ 40 Chili Davis SY	1.50	.70
☐ 41 Jimmy Key BX	1.50	.70
☐ 43 Mike Mussina GY	12.00	5.50
☐ 44 Joe Randa BX	1.00	.45
☐ 45 Chan Ho Park SZ	3.00	1.35
☐ 46 Brad Radke BX	1.50	.70
☐ 47 Geronimo Berroa BX	1.00	.45
☐ 48 Wade Boggs SY	8.00	3.60
☐ 49 Kevin Appier BX	1.00	.45
☐ 50 Moises Alou SY	3.00	1.35
☐ 51 David Justice BX	5.00	2.20
☐ 52 Ivan Rodriguez GZ	15.00	6.75
☐ 53 J.T. Snow BX	1.50	.70
☐ 54 Brian Giles BX	1.50	.70
☐ 55 Will Clark BY	4.00	1.80
☐ 56 Justin Thompson SY	2.00	.90
☐ 57 Javier Lopez SX	1.50	.70
☐ 58 Hideki Irabu BZ	1.50	.70
☐ 59 Mark Grudzielanek BX	1.00	.45
☐ 60 Abraham Nunez SX	2.00	.90
☐ 61 Todd Hollandsworth BX	1.00	.45
☐ 62 Jay Bell BX	1.50	.70
☐ 63 Nomar Garciaparra GZ	40.00	18.00
☐ 64 Vinny Castilla BY	1.50	.70
☐ 65 Lou Collier BY	1.00	.45
☐ 66 Kevin Orie SY	2.00	.90
☐ 67 John Valentin BX	1.00	.45
☐ 68 Robin Ventura SY	1.50	.70
☐ 69 Denny Neagle BX	1.00	.45
☐ 70 Tony Womack SY	2.00	.90
☐ 71 Dennis Reyes SY	2.00	.90
☐ 72 Wally Joyner BX	1.50	.70
☐ 73 Kevin Brown C BY	1.00	.45
☐ 74 Ray Durham SY	1.50	.70
☐ 75 Mike Cameron SZ	3.00	1.35
☐ 76 Dante Bichette SY	1.50	.70
☐ 77 Jose Guillen GY	5.00	2.20
☐ 78 Carlos Delgado BY	4.00	1.80
☐ 79 Paul Molitor GZ	12.00	5.50
☐ 80 Jason Kendall BX	1.50	.70
☐ 81 Mark Bellhorn BX	1.00	.45
☐ 82 Damian Jackson BX	1.00	.45
☐ 83 Bill Mueller BX	1.00	.45
☐ 84 Kevin Young BX	1.50	.70
☐ 85 Curt Schilling BX	2.50	1.10
☐ 86 Jeffrey Hammonds BX	1.00	.45
☐ 87 Sandy Alomar Jr. SY	3.00	1.35
☐ 88 Bartolo Colon BY	1.50	.70
☐ 89 Wilton Guerrero BY	1.00	.45
☐ 90 Bernie Williams GY	12.00	5.50
☐ 91 Deion Sanders SY	3.00	1.35
☐ 92 Mike Piazza GX	100.00	45.00
☐ 93 Butch Huskey BX	1.00	.45
☐ 94 Edgardo Alfonzo SX	5.00	2.20
☐ 95 Alan Benes SY	2.00	.90
☐ 96 Craig Biggio SY	8.00	3.60
☐ 97 Mark Grace SY	5.00	2.20
☐ 98 Shawn Green SY	8.00	3.60
☐ 99 Derek Lee SY	2.00	.90
☐ 100 Ken Griffey Jr. GZ	60.00	27.00
☐ 101 Tim Raines BX	1.50	.70

❏ 102	Pokey Reese SX ..	2.00	.90
❏ 103	Lee Stevens BX ..	1.00	.45
❏ 104	Shannon Stewart SY ..	3.00	1.35
❏ 105	John Smoltz SY ..	5.00	2.20
❏ 106	Frank Thomas GX ..	60.00	27.00
❏ 107	Jeff Fassero BX ..	1.00	.45
❏ 108	Jay Buhner BY ..	1.50	.70
❏ 109	Jose Canseco BX ..	5.00	2.20
❏ 110	Omar Vizquel BX ..	1.50	.70
❏ 111	Travis Fryman BX ..	1.50	.70
❏ 112	Dave Nilsson BX ..	1.00	.45
❏ 113	John Olerud BX ..	1.50	.70
❏ 114	Larry Walker GZ ..	12.00	5.50
❏ 115	Jim Edmonds SX ..	3.00	1.35
❏ 116	Bobby Higginson SX ..	3.00	1.35
❏ 117	Todd Hundley BX ..	3.00	1.35
❏ 118	Paul O'Neill BX ..	1.50	.70
❏ 119	Bip Roberts BX ..	1.00	.45
❏ 120	Ismael Valdes BX ..	1.00	.45
❏ 121	Pedro Martinez SY ..	10.00	4.50
❏ 122	Jeff Cirillo BX ..	1.50	.70
❏ 123	Andy Benes BX ..	1.00	.45
❏ 124	Bobby Jones BX ..	1.00	.45
❏ 125	Brian Hunter BX ..	1.00	.45
❏ 126	Darryl Kile BX ..	1.00	.45
❏ 127	Pat Hentgen BX ..	1.00	.45
❏ 128	Marquis Grissom BX ..	1.00	.45
❏ 129	Eric Davis BY ..	1.50	.70
❏ 130	Chipper Jones GZ ..	30.00	13.50
❏ 131	Edgar Martinez SZ ..	3.00	1.35
❏ 132	Andy Pettitte GZ ..	5.00	2.20
❏ 133	Cal Ripken GX ..	120.00	55.00
❏ 134	Scott Rolen GZ ..	15.00	6.75
❏ 135	Ron Coomer BX ..	1.00	.45
❏ 136	Luis Castillo BY ..	1.00	.45
❏ 137	Fred McGriff BY ..	2.50	1.10
❏ 138	Neifi Perez SY ..	3.00	1.35
❏ 139	Eric Karros BX ..	1.50	.70
❏ 140	Alex Fernandez BX ..	1.00	.45
❏ 141	Jason Dickson BX ..	1.00	.45
❏ 142	Lance Johnson BX ..	1.00	.45
❏ 143	Ray Lankford BY ..	1.50	.70
❏ 144	Sammy Sosa GY ..	50.00	22.00
❏ 145	Eric Young BY ..	1.00	.45
❏ 146	Bubba Trammell SY ..	2.00	.90
❏ 147	Todd Walker SY ..	3.00	1.35
❏ 148	Mo Vaughn CC SX ..	8.00	3.60
❏ 149	Jeff Bagwell CC SX ..	10.00	4.50
❏ 150	Kenny Lofton CC SX ..	5.00	2.20
❏ 151	Raul Mondesi CC SX ..	3.00	1.35
❏ 152	Mike Piazza CC SX ..	25.00	11.00
❏ 153	Chipper Jones CC SX ..	20.00	9.00
❏ 154	Larry Walker CC SX ..	8.00	3.60
❏ 155	Greg Maddux CC SX ..	20.00	9.00
❏ 156	Ken Griffey Jr. CC SX	40.00	18.00
❏ 157	Frank Thomas CC SX	15.00	6.75
❏ 158	Darin Erstad GLS BZ ..	2.50	1.10
❏ 159	Roberto Alomar GLS SY	4.00	1.80
❏ 160	Albert Belle GLS GY ..	12.00	5.50
❏ 161	Jim Thome GLS GY ..	12.00	5.50
❏ 162	Tony Clark GLS GY ..	5.00	2.20
❏ 163	C. Knoblauch GLS BY ..	1.50	.70
❏ 164	Derek Jeter GLS GZ ..	40.00	18.00
❏ 165	Alex Rodriguez GLS GZ	40.00	18.00
❏ 166	Tony Gwynn GLS SY	10.00	4.50
❏ 167	Roger Clemens GLS GZ	30.00	13.50
❏ 168	Barry Larkin GLS BY ..	4.00	1.80
❏ 169	A. Galarraga GLS BY ..	2.50	1.10
❏ 170	V. Guerrero GLS GZ ..	15.00	6.75
❏ 171	Mark McGwire GLS BZ	25.00	11.00
❏ 172	Barry Bonds GLS GZ ..	5.00	2.20
❏ 173	Juan Gonzalez GLS GZ	25.00	11.00
❏ 174	Andruw Jones GLS SY ..	12.00	5.50
❏ 175	Paul Molitor GLS BX ..	4.00	1.80
❏ 176	Hideo Nomo GLS BZ ..	4.00	1.80
❏ 177	Cal Ripken GLS GX ..	15.00	6.75
❏ 178	Brad Fullmer GLR SZ ..	2.00	.90
❏ 179	Jaret Wright GLR GZ ..	5.00	2.20
❏ 180	Bobby Estalella GLR BY	1.00	.45
❏ 181	Ben Grieve GLR GZ ..	25.00	11.00
❏ 182	Paul Konerko GLR GZ ..	5.00	2.20
❏ 183	David Ortiz GLR BZ ..	5.00	2.20
❏ 184	Todd Helton GLR GX ..	30.00	13.50
❏ 185	J. Encarnacion GLR GZ	5.00	2.20
❏ 186	Miguel Tejada GLR GZ	5.00	2.20
❏ 187	Jacob Cruz GLR BY ..	1.00	.45

❏ 188	Mark Kotsay GLR GZ ..	5.00	2.20
❏ 189	Fernando Tatis GLR SZ	8.00	3.60
❏ 190	Ricky Ledee GLR SY ..	3.00	1.35
❏ 191	Richard Hidalgo GLR SY	3.00	1.35
❏ 192	Richie Sexson GLR SY	5.00	2.20
❏ 193	Luis Ordaz GLR BX ..	1.00	.45
❏ 194	Eli Marrero GLR SZ ..	2.00	.90
❏ 195	Livan Hernandez GLR SZ	2.00	.90
❏ 196	Homer Bush GLR BX ..	1.00	.45
❏ 197	Raul Ibanez GLR BX ..	1.00	.45
❏ 198	N. Garciaparra CL BX	12.00	5.50
❏ 199	Scott Rolen CL BX ..	5.00	2.20
❏ 200	Jose Cruz Jr. CL BX ..	1.00	.45
❏ 201	Al Martin BX ..	1.00	.45

1998 Leaf Fractal Matrix Die Cuts

	MINT	NRMT
COMMON X-AXIS	3.00	1.35
X-AXIS MINOR STARS ..	5.00	2.20
X-AXIS SEMISTARS	8.00	3.60
X-AXIS UNLISTED STARS	12.00	5.50
X-AXIS STATED PRINT RUN 400 SETS		
COMMON Y-AXIS	5.00	2.20
Y-AXIS- MINOR STARS ..	8.00	3.60
Y-AXIS SEMISTARS	12.00	5.50
Y-AXIS UNLISTED STARS	20.00	9.00
Y-AXIS STATED PRINT RUN 200 SETS		
COMMON Z-AXIS	8.00	3.60
Z-AXIS MINOR STARS	12.00	5.50
Z-AXIS SEMISTARS	20.00	9.00
Z-AXIS UNLISTED STARS ..	30.00	13.50
Z-AXIS STATED PRINT RUN 100 SETS		
RANDOM INSERTS IN PACKS		
CARD NUMBER 42 DOES NOT EXIST		

❏ 1	Rusty Greer GZ ..	12.00	5.50
❏ 2	Tino Martinez GZ ..	5.00	2.20
❏ 3	Bobby Bonilla SY ..	8.00	3.60
❏ 4	Jason Giambi BY ..	8.00	3.60
❏ 5	Matt Morris SY ..	5.00	2.20
❏ 6	Craig Counsell BX ..	3.00	1.35
❏ 7	Reggie Jefferson BX ..	5.00	2.20
❏ 8	Brian Rose SY ..	5.00	2.20
❏ 9	Ruben Rivera BX ..	5.00	2.20
❏ 10	Shawn Estes SY ..	5.00	2.20
❏ 11	Tony Gwynn GZ ..	80.00	36.00
❏ 12	Jeff Abbott BY ..	5.00	2.20
❏ 13	Jose Cruz Jr. GZ ..	12.00	5.50
❏ 14	Francisco Cordova BX ..	3.00	1.35
❏ 15	Ryan Klesko BX ..	5.00	2.20
❏ 16	Tim Salmon GY ..	12.00	5.50
❏ 17	Brett Tomko BX ..	3.00	1.35
❏ 18	Matt Williams SY ..	20.00	9.00
❏ 19	Joe Carter BX ..	5.00	2.20
❏ 20	Harold Baines BX ..	5.00	2.20
❏ 21	Gary Sheffield SZ ..	12.00	5.50
❏ 22	Charles Johnson SX ..	5.00	2.20
❏ 23	Aaron Boone BX ..	3.00	1.35
❏ 24	Eddie Murray GY ..	20.00	9.00
❏ 25	Matt Stairs BX ..	5.00	2.20
❏ 26	David Cone BX ..	8.00	3.60
❏ 27	Jon Nunnally BX ..	3.00	1.35
❏ 28	Chris Stynes BX ..	3.00	1.35
❏ 29	Enrique Wilson BY ..	5.00	2.20
❏ 30	Randy Johnson SZ ..	30.00	13.50
❏ 31	Garret Anderson BX ..	8.00	3.60

❏ 32	Manny Ramirez GZ ..	40.00	18.00
❏ 33	Jeff Suppan SX ..	3.00	1.35
❏ 34	Rickey Henderson BX ..	40.00	18.00
❏ 35	Scott Spiezio BX ..	3.00	1.35
❏ 36	Rondell White SY ..	8.00	3.60
❏ 37	Todd Greene SZ ..	8.00	3.60
❏ 38	Delino DeShields BX ..	3.00	1.35
❏ 39	Kevin Brown P SX ..	8.00	3.60
❏ 40	Chili Davis BX ..	5.00	2.20
❏ 41	Jimmy Key BX ..	5.00	2.20
❏ 43	Mike Mussina GY ..	20.00	9.00
❏ 44	Joe Randa BX ..	3.00	1.35
❏ 45	Chan Ho Park GZ ..	12.00	5.50
❏ 46	Brad Radke BX ..	5.00	2.20
❏ 47	Geronimo Berroa BX ..	3.00	1.35
❏ 48	Wade Boggs SY ..	20.00	9.00
❏ 49	Kevin Appier BX ..	5.00	2.20
❏ 50	Moises Alou GY ..	8.00	3.60
❏ 51	David Justice GY ..	8.00	3.60
❏ 52	Ivan Rodriguez GZ ..	40.00	18.00
❏ 53	J.T. Snow BX ..	5.00	2.20
❏ 54	Brian Giles SX ..	5.00	2.20
❏ 55	Will Clark BY ..	20.00	9.00
❏ 56	Justin Thompson SY ..	5.00	2.20
❏ 57	Javier Lopez SX ..	5.00	2.20
❏ 58	Hideki Irabu BZ ..	12.00	5.50
❏ 59	Mark Grudzielanek BX ..	3.00	1.35
❏ 60	Abraham Nunez SX ..	3.00	1.35
❏ 61	Todd Hollandsworth BX	3.00	1.35
❏ 62	Jay Bell BX ..	5.00	2.20
❏ 63	Nomar Garciaparra GZ	100.00	45.00
❏ 64	Vinny Castilla BY ..	8.00	3.60
❏ 65	Lou Collier BY ..	5.00	2.20
❏ 66	Kevin Orie SX ..	3.00	1.35
❏ 67	John Valentin BX ..	5.00	2.20
❏ 68	Robin Ventura BX ..	8.00	3.60
❏ 69	Denny Neagle SY ..	3.00	1.35
❏ 70	Tony Womack SY ..	5.00	2.20
❏ 71	Dennis Reyes SY ..	5.00	2.20
❏ 72	Wally Joyner BX ..	5.00	2.20
❏ 73	Kevin Brown C BY ..	5.00	2.20
❏ 74	Ray Durham BX ..	5.00	2.20
❏ 75	Mike Cameron SZ ..	12.00	5.50
❏ 76	Dante Bichette BX ..	5.00	2.20
❏ 77	Jose Guillen GY ..	5.00	2.20
❏ 78	Carlos Delgado BY ..	20.00	9.00
❏ 79	Paul Molitor GZ ..	30.00	13.50
❏ 80	Jason Kendall BX ..	5.00	2.20
❏ 81	Mark Bellhorn BX ..	3.00	1.35
❏ 82	Damian Jackson BX ..	3.00	1.35
❏ 83	Bill Mueller BX ..	3.00	1.35
❏ 84	Kevin Young BX ..	5.00	2.20
❏ 85	Curt Schilling BX ..	8.00	3.60
❏ 86	Jeffrey Hammonds BX ..	3.00	1.35
❏ 87	Sandy Alomar Jr. SY ..	8.00	3.60
❏ 88	Bartolo Colon BY ..	8.00	3.60
❏ 89	Wilton Guerrero BY ..	5.00	2.20
❏ 90	Bernie Williams GY ..	20.00	9.00
❏ 91	Deion Sanders BY ..	8.00	3.60
❏ 92	Mike Piazza GX ..	40.00	18.00
❏ 93	Butch Huskey BX ..	3.00	1.35
❏ 94	Edgardo Alfonzo SX ..	8.00	3.60
❏ 95	Alan Benes SY ..	5.00	2.20
❏ 96	Craig Biggio SY ..	20.00	9.00
❏ 97	Mark Grace SY ..	12.00	5.50
❏ 98	Shawn Green SY ..	20.00	9.00
❏ 99	Derrek Lee SY ..	5.00	2.20
❏ 100	Ken Griffey Jr. GZ ..	150.00	70.00
❏ 101	Tim Raines BX ..	5.00	2.20
❏ 102	Pokey Reese SX ..	3.00	1.35
❏ 103	Lee Stevens BX ..	3.00	1.35
❏ 104	Shannon Stewart SY ..	8.00	3.60
❏ 105	John Smoltz SY ..	12.00	5.50
❏ 106	Frank Thomas GX ..	25.00	11.00
❏ 107	Jeff Fassero BX ..	3.00	1.35
❏ 108	Jay Buhner BY ..	8.00	3.60
❏ 109	Jose Canseco BX ..	15.00	6.75
❏ 110	Omar Vizquel BX ..	5.00	2.20
❏ 111	Travis Fryman BX ..	5.00	2.20
❏ 112	Dave Nilsson BX ..	5.00	2.20
❏ 113	John Olerud BX ..	5.00	2.20
❏ 114	Larry Walker SZ ..	30.00	13.50
❏ 115	Jim Edmonds SX ..	8.00	3.60
❏ 116	Bobby Higginson SX ..	5.00	2.20
❏ 117	Todd Hundley SX ..	5.00	2.20
❏ 118	Paul O'Neill BX ..	5.00	2.20

		MINT	NRMT
❑ 119	Bip Roberts BX	3.00	1.35
❑ 120	Ismael Valdes BX	3.00	1.35
❑ 121	Pedro Martinez SY	25.00	11.00
❑ 122	Jeff Cirillo BX	5.00	2.20
❑ 123	Andy Benes BX	3.00	1.35
❑ 124	Bobby Jones BX	3.00	1.35
❑ 125	Brian Hunter BX	3.00	1.35
❑ 126	Darryl Kile BX	3.00	1.35
❑ 127	Pat Hentgen BX	3.00	1.35
❑ 128	Marquis Grissom BX	3.00	1.35
❑ 129	Eric Davis BX	5.00	2.20
❑ 130	Chipper Jones GZ	80.00	36.00
❑ 131	Edgar Martinez GZ	12.00	5.50
❑ 132	Andy Pettitte GZ	12.00	5.50
❑ 133	Cal Ripken GZ	50.00	22.00
❑ 134	Scott Rolen GZ	40.00	18.00
❑ 135	Ron Coomer BX	3.00	1.35
❑ 136	Luis Castillo BY	5.00	2.20
❑ 137	Fred McGriff BY	12.00	5.50
❑ 138	Neifi Perez SY	8.00	3.60
❑ 139	Eric Karros BX	5.00	2.20
❑ 140	Alex Fernandez BX	3.00	1.35
❑ 141	Jason Dickson BX	3.00	1.35
❑ 142	Lance Johnson BX	3.00	1.35
❑ 143	Ray Lankford BY	8.00	3.60
❑ 144	Sammy Sosa GY	60.00	27.00
❑ 145	Eric Young BY	5.00	2.20
❑ 146	Bubba Trammell SY	5.00	2.20
❑ 147	Todd Walker SY	8.00	3.60
❑ 148	Mo Vaughn CC SX	12.00	5.50
❑ 149	Jeff Bagwell CC SX	15.00	6.75
❑ 150	Kenny Lofton CC SX	5.00	2.20
❑ 151	Raul Mondesi CC SX	5.00	2.20
❑ 152	Mike Piazza CC SX	40.00	18.00
❑ 153	Chipper Jones CC SX	30.00	13.50
❑ 154	Larry Walker CC SX	5.00	2.20
❑ 155	Greg Maddux CC SX	30.00	13.50
❑ 156	Ken Griffey Jr. CC SX	60.00	27.00
❑ 157	Frank Thomas CC SX	25.00	11.00
❑ 158	Darin Erstad GLS BZ	20.00	9.00
❑ 159	Roberto Alomar GLS BY	20.00	9.00
❑ 160	Albert Belle GLS GY	20.00	9.00
❑ 161	Jim Thome GLS GY	20.00	9.00
❑ 162	Tony Clark GLS GY	8.00	3.60
❑ 163	C. Knoblauch GLS BY	8.00	3.60
❑ 164	Derek Jeter GLS GZ	100.00	45.00
❑ 165	Alex Rodriguez GLS GZ	100.00	45.00
❑ 166	Tony Gwynn GLS BX	30.00	13.50
❑ 167	Roger Clemens GLS GZ	80.00	36.00
❑ 168	Barry Larkin GLS GY	20.00	9.00
❑ 169	A. Galarraga GLS BY	8.00	3.60
❑ 170	Vladimir Guerrero GLS GZ	40.00	18.00
❑ 171	Mark McGwire GLS BZ	200.00	90.00
❑ 172	Barry Bonds BZ	40.00	18.00
❑ 173	Juan Gonzalez GZ	60.00	27.00
❑ 174	Andruw Jones GLS GZ	30.00	13.50
❑ 175	Paul Molitor GLS BX	12.00	5.50
❑ 176	Hideo Nomo GLS BZ	30.00	13.50
❑ 177	Cal Ripken GLS BX	50.00	22.00
❑ 178	Brad Fullmer GLR GZ	8.00	3.60
❑ 179	Jaret Wright GLR GZ	8.00	3.60
❑ 180	Bobby Estalella GLR BY	5.00	2.20
❑ 181	Ben Grieve GLR GX	12.00	5.50
❑ 182	Paul Konerko GLR GZ	12.00	5.50
❑ 183	David Ortiz GLR GZ	8.00	3.60
❑ 184	Todd Helton GLR GX	12.00	5.50
❑ 185	J. Encarnacion GLR GZ	12.00	5.50
❑ 186	Miguel Tejada GLR GZ	12.00	5.50
❑ 187	Jacob Cruz GLR BY	5.00	2.20
❑ 188	Mark Kotsay GLR GZ	12.00	5.50
❑ 189	Fernando Tatis GLR SZ	30.00	13.50
❑ 190	Ricky Ledee GLR SY	8.00	3.60
❑ 191	Richard Hidalgo GLR SY	8.00	3.60
❑ 192	Richie Sexson GLR SY	12.00	5.50
❑ 193	Luis Ordaz GLR BX	3.00	1.35
❑ 194	Eli Marrero GLR SZ	8.00	3.60
❑ 195	Livan Hernandez GLR SZ	8.00	3.60
❑ 196	Homer Bush GLR BX	3.00	1.35
❑ 197	Raul Ibanez GLR BX	3.00	1.35
❑ 198	N. Garciaparra GLR BX	20.00	9.00
❑ 199	Scott Rolen CL BX	12.00	5.50
❑ 200	Jose Cruz Jr. CL BX	3.00	1.35
❑ 201	Al Martin BX	3.00	1.35

1998 Leaf Crusade Green

MINT NRMT
PLEASE SEE 1998 DONRUSS CRUSADE

1998 Leaf Heading for the Hall

		MINT	NRMT
COMPLETE SET (20)		200.00	90.00
COMMON CARD (1-20)		4.00	1.80
UNLISTED STARS		6.00	2.70

RANDOM INSERTS IN PACKS
STATED PRINT RUN 3500 SERIAL #'d SETS

❑ 1	Roberto Alomar	6.00	2.70
❑ 2	Jeff Bagwell	8.00	3.60
❑ 3	Albert Belle	6.00	2.70
❑ 4	Wade Boggs	6.00	2.70
❑ 5	Barry Bonds	8.00	3.60
❑ 6	Roger Clemens	15.00	6.75
❑ 7	Juan Gonzalez	12.00	5.50
❑ 8	Ken Griffey Jr.	30.00	13.50
❑ 9	Tony Gwynn	15.00	6.75
❑ 10	Barry Larkin	6.00	2.70
❑ 11	Kenny Lofton	4.00	1.80
❑ 12	Greg Maddux	15.00	6.75
❑ 13	Mark McGwire	40.00	18.00
❑ 14	Paul Molitor	6.00	2.70
❑ 15	Eddie Murray	6.00	2.70
❑ 16	Mike Piazza	20.00	9.00
❑ 17	Cal Ripken	25.00	11.00
❑ 18	Ivan Rodriguez	8.00	3.60
❑ 19	Ryne Sandberg	8.00	3.60
❑ 20	Frank Thomas	12.00	5.50

1998 Leaf State Representatives

		MINT	NRMT
COMPLETE SET (30)		250.00	110.00
COMMON CARD (1-30)		2.00	.90
SEMISTARS		3.00	1.35
UNLISTED STARS		5.00	2.20

RANDOM INSERTS IN PACKS
STATED PRINT RUN 5000 SERIAL #'d SETS

❑ 1	Ken Griffey Jr.	25.00	11.00

❑ 2	Frank Thomas	10.00	4.50
❑ 3	Alex Rodriguez	15.00	6.75
❑ 4	Cal Ripken	20.00	9.00
❑ 5	Chipper Jones	12.00	5.50
❑ 6	Andruw Jones	5.00	2.20
❑ 7	Scott Rolen	6.00	2.70
❑ 8	Nomar Garciaparra	15.00	6.75
❑ 9	Tim Salmon	3.00	1.35
❑ 10	Manny Ramirez	6.00	2.70
❑ 11	Jose Cruz Jr.	2.00	.90
❑ 12	Vladimir Guerrero	6.00	2.70
❑ 13	Tino Martinez	2.00	.90
❑ 14	Larry Walker	5.00	2.20
❑ 15	Mo Vaughn	5.00	2.20
❑ 16	Jim Thome	5.00	2.20
❑ 17	Tony Clark	2.00	.90
❑ 18	Derek Jeter	15.00	6.75
❑ 19	Juan Gonzalez	10.00	4.50
❑ 20	Jeff Bagwell	6.00	2.70
❑ 21	Ivan Rodriguez	6.00	2.70
❑ 22	Mark McGwire	30.00	13.50
❑ 23	David Justice	2.00	.90
❑ 24	Chuck Knoblauch	2.00	.90
❑ 25	Andy Pettitte	2.00	.90
❑ 26	Raul Mondesi	2.00	.90
❑ 27	Randy Johnson	5.00	2.20
❑ 28	Greg Maddux	12.00	5.50
❑ 29	Bernie Williams	5.00	2.20
❑ 30	Rusty Greer	2.00	.90

1998 Leaf Statistical Standouts

		MINT	NRMT
COMPLETE SET (24)		300.00	135.00
COMMON CARD (1-24)		3.00	1.35
SEMISTARS		5.00	2.20
UNLISTED STARS		8.00	3.60

STATED PRINT RUN 2250 SERIAL #'d SETS
*DIE CUTS: 1.25X TO 3X HI COLUMN
DIE CUT PRINT RUN 250 SERIAL #'d SETS
RANDOM INSERTS IN PACKS

❑ 1	Frank Thomas	15.00	6.75
❑ 2	Ken Griffey Jr.	40.00	18.00
❑ 3	Alex Rodriguez	25.00	11.00
❑ 4	Mike Piazza	25.00	11.00
❑ 5	Greg Maddux	20.00	9.00
❑ 6	Cal Ripken	30.00	13.50
❑ 7	Chipper Jones	20.00	9.00
❑ 8	Juan Gonzalez	15.00	6.75
❑ 9	Jeff Bagwell	10.00	4.50
❑ 10	Mark McGwire	50.00	22.00
❑ 11	Tony Gwynn	20.00	9.00
❑ 12	Mo Vaughn	8.00	3.60
❑ 13	Nomar Garciaparra	25.00	11.00
❑ 14	Jose Cruz Jr.	4.00	1.80
❑ 15	Vladimir Guerrero	10.00	4.50
❑ 16	Scott Rolen	10.00	4.50
❑ 17	Andy Pettitte	4.00	1.80
❑ 18	Randy Johnson	8.00	3.60
❑ 19	Larry Walker	8.00	3.60
❑ 20	Kenny Lofton	5.00	2.20
❑ 21	Tony Clark	4.00	1.80
❑ 22	David Justice	4.00	1.80
❑ 23	Derek Jeter	25.00	11.00
❑ 24	Barry Bonds	10.00	4.50

1998 Leaf Fractal Foundations

	MINT	NRMT
COMPLETE SET (200)	300.00	135.00
COMMON (1-41/43-201)	1.00	.45
MINOR STARS	1.50	.70
SEMISTARS	2.50	1.10
UNLISTED STARS	4.00	1.80

STATED PRINT RUN 3,999 SERIAL #'d SETS
CARD NUMBER 42 DOES NOT EXIST

		MINT	NRMT
❑ 1	Rusty Greer	1.50	.70
❑ 2	Tino Martinez	1.50	.70
❑ 3	Bobby Bonilla	1.50	.70
❑ 4	Jason Giambi	1.50	.70
❑ 5	Matt Morris	1.00	.45
❑ 6	Craig Counsell	1.00	.45
❑ 7	Reggie Jefferson	1.00	.45
❑ 8	Brian Rose	1.00	.45
❑ 9	Ruben Rivera	1.00	.45
❑ 10	Shawn Estes	1.00	.45
❑ 11	Tony Gwynn	10.00	4.50
❑ 12	Jeff Abbott	1.00	.45
❑ 13	Jose Cruz Jr.	1.50	.70
❑ 14	Francisco Cordova	1.00	.45
❑ 15	Ryan Klesko	1.50	.70
❑ 16	Tim Salmon	2.50	1.10
❑ 17	Brett Tomko	1.00	.45
❑ 18	Matt Williams	4.00	1.80
❑ 19	Joe Carter	1.50	.70
❑ 20	Harold Baines	1.50	.70
❑ 21	Gary Sheffield	1.50	.70
❑ 22	Charles Johnson	1.50	.70
❑ 23	Aaron Boone	1.00	.45
❑ 24	Eddie Murray	4.00	1.80
❑ 25	Matt Stairs	1.50	.70
❑ 26	David Cone	2.50	1.10
❑ 27	Jon Nunnally	1.00	.45
❑ 28	Chris Stynes	1.00	.45
❑ 29	Enrique Wilson	1.00	.45
❑ 30	Randy Johnson	4.00	1.80
❑ 31	Garret Anderson	1.50	.70
❑ 32	Manny Ramirez	5.00	2.20
❑ 33	Jeff Suppan	1.00	.45
❑ 34	Rickey Henderson	5.00	2.20
❑ 35	Scott Spiezio	1.00	.45
❑ 36	Rondell White	1.50	.70
❑ 37	Todd Greene	1.00	.45
❑ 38	Delino DeShields	1.00	.45
❑ 39	Kevin Brown	2.50	1.10
❑ 40	Chili Davis	1.50	.70
❑ 41	Jimmy Key	1.50	.70
❑ 43	Mike Mussina	4.00	1.80
❑ 44	Joe Randa	1.00	.45
❑ 45	Chan Ho Park	1.50	.70
❑ 46	Brad Radke	1.50	.70
❑ 47	Geronimo Berroa	1.00	.45
❑ 48	Wade Boggs	4.00	1.80
❑ 49	Kevin Appier	1.50	.70
❑ 50	Moises Alou	1.50	.70
❑ 51	David Justice	1.50	.70
❑ 52	Ivan Rodriguez	5.00	2.20
❑ 53	J.T. Snow	1.50	.70
❑ 54	Brian Giles	1.50	.70
❑ 55	Will Clark	4.00	1.80
❑ 56	Justin Thompson	1.00	.45
❑ 57	Javier Lopez	1.50	.70
❑ 58	Hideki Irabu	1.50	.70
❑ 59	Mark Grudzielanek	1.00	.45
❑ 60	Abraham Nunez	1.00	.45
❑ 61	Todd Hollandsworth	1.00	.45
❑ 62	Jay Bell	1.50	.70
❑ 63	Nomar Garciaparra	12.00	5.50
❑ 64	Vinny Castilla	1.50	.70
❑ 65	Lou Collier	1.00	.45
❑ 66	Kevin Orie	1.00	.45
❑ 67	John Valentin	1.50	.70
❑ 68	Robin Ventura	1.50	.70
❑ 69	Denny Neagle	1.00	.45
❑ 70	Tony Womack	1.00	.45
❑ 71	Dennis Reyes	1.00	.45
❑ 72	Wally Joyner	1.50	.70
❑ 73	Kevin Brown	2.50	1.10
❑ 74	Ray Durham	1.50	.70
❑ 75	Mike Cameron	1.50	.70
❑ 76	Dante Bichette	1.50	.70
❑ 77	Jose Guillen	1.00	.45
❑ 78	Carlos Delgado	4.00	1.80
❑ 79	Paul Molitor	4.00	1.80
❑ 80	Jason Kendall	1.50	.70
❑ 81	Mark Bellhorn	1.00	.45
❑ 82	Damian Jackson	1.00	.45
❑ 83	Bill Mueller	1.00	.45
❑ 84	Kevin Young	1.50	.70
❑ 85	Curt Schilling	2.50	1.10
❑ 86	Jeffrey Hammonds	1.00	.45
❑ 87	Sandy Alomar Jr.	1.50	.70
❑ 88	Bartolo Colon	1.50	.70
❑ 89	Wilton Guerrero	1.00	.45
❑ 90	Bernie Williams	4.00	1.80
❑ 91	Deion Sanders	1.50	.70
❑ 92	Mike Piazza	12.00	5.50
❑ 93	Butch Huskey	1.00	.45
❑ 94	Edgardo Alfonzo	2.50	1.10
❑ 95	Alan Benes	1.00	.45
❑ 96	Craig Biggio	4.00	1.80
❑ 97	Mark Grace	2.50	1.10
❑ 98	Shawn Green	4.00	1.80
❑ 99	Derrek Lee	1.00	.45
❑ 100	Ken Griffey Jr.	20.00	9.00
❑ 101	Tim Raines	1.50	.70
❑ 102	Pokey Reese	1.00	.45
❑ 103	Lee Stevens	1.00	.45
❑ 104	Shannon Stewart	1.50	.70
❑ 105	John Smoltz	2.50	1.10
❑ 106	Frank Thomas	8.00	3.60
❑ 107	Jeff Fassero	1.00	.45
❑ 108	Jay Buhner	1.50	.70
❑ 109	Jose Canseco	5.00	2.20
❑ 110	Omar Vizquel	1.50	.70
❑ 111	Travis Fryman	1.50	.70
❑ 112	Dave Nilsson	1.00	.45
❑ 113	John Olerud	1.50	.70
❑ 114	Larry Walker	4.00	1.80
❑ 115	Jim Edmonds	1.50	.70
❑ 116	Bobby Higginson	1.50	.70
❑ 117	Todd Hundley	1.50	.70
❑ 118	Paul O'Neill	1.50	.70
❑ 119	Bip Roberts	1.00	.45
❑ 120	Ismael Valdes	1.00	.45
❑ 121	Pedro Martinez	5.00	2.20
❑ 122	Jeff Cirillo	1.50	.70
❑ 123	Andy Benes	1.00	.45
❑ 124	Bobby Jones	1.00	.45
❑ 125	Brian Hunter	1.00	.45
❑ 126	Darryl Kile	1.00	.45
❑ 127	Pat Hentgen	1.00	.45
❑ 128	Marquis Grissom	1.00	.45
❑ 129	Eric Davis	1.50	.70
❑ 130	Chipper Jones	10.00	4.50
❑ 131	Edgar Martinez	1.50	.70
❑ 132	Andy Pettitte	1.50	.70
❑ 133	Cal Ripken	15.00	6.75
❑ 134	Scott Rolen	5.00	2.20
❑ 135	Ron Coomer	1.00	.45
❑ 136	Luis Castillo	1.00	.45
❑ 137	Fred McGriff	2.50	1.10
❑ 138	Neifi Perez	1.00	.45
❑ 139	Eric Karros	1.50	.70
❑ 140	Alex Fernandez	1.00	.45
❑ 141	Jason Dickson	1.00	.45
❑ 142	Lance Johnson	1.00	.45
❑ 143	Ray Lankford	1.50	.70
❑ 144	Sammy Sosa	12.00	5.50
❑ 145	Eric Young	1.00	.45
❑ 146	Bubba Trammell	1.00	.45
❑ 147	Todd Walker	1.50	.70
❑ 148	Mo Vaughn CC	4.00	1.80
❑ 149	Jeff Bagwell CC	5.00	2.20
❑ 150	Kenny Lofton CC	2.50	1.10
❑ 151	Raul Mondesi CC	1.50	.70
❑ 152	Mike Piazza CC	12.00	5.50
❑ 153	Chipper Jones CC	10.00	4.50
❑ 154	Larry Walker CC	4.00	1.80
❑ 155	Greg Maddux CC	10.00	4.50
❑ 156	Ken Griffey Jr. CC	20.00	9.00
❑ 157	Frank Thomas CC	8.00	3.60
❑ 158	Darin Erstad GLS	2.50	1.10
❑ 159	Roberto Alomar GLS	4.00	1.80
❑ 160	Albert Belle GLS	4.00	1.80
❑ 161	Jim Thome GLS	4.00	1.80
❑ 162	Tony Clark GLS	1.50	.70
❑ 163	Chuck Knoblauch GLS	1.50	.70
❑ 164	Derek Jeter GLS	12.00	5.50
❑ 165	Alex Rodriguez GLS	12.00	5.50
❑ 166	Tony Gwynn GLS	10.00	4.50
❑ 167	Roger Clemens GLS	10.00	4.50
❑ 168	Barry Larkin GLS	4.00	1.80
❑ 169	A. Galarraga GLS	5.00	2.20
❑ 170	Vladimir Guerrero GLS	5.00	2.20
❑ 171	Mark McGwire GLS	25.00	11.00
❑ 172	Barry Bonds GLS	5.00	2.20
❑ 173	Juan Gonzalez GLS	8.00	3.60
❑ 174	Andruw Jones GLS	4.00	1.80
❑ 175	Paul Molitor GLS	4.00	1.80
❑ 176	Hideo Nomo GLS	4.00	1.80
❑ 177	Cal Ripken GLS	15.00	6.75
❑ 178	Brad Fullmer GLR	1.00	.45
❑ 179	Jaret Wright GLR	1.50	.70
❑ 180	Bobby Estalella GLR	1.00	.45
❑ 181	Ben Grieve GLR	4.00	1.80
❑ 182	Paul Konerko GLR	1.50	.70
❑ 183	David Ortiz GLR	1.00	.45
❑ 184	Todd Helton GLR	4.00	1.80
❑ 185	Juan Encarnacion GLR	1.50	.70
❑ 186	Miguel Tejada GLR	1.50	.70
❑ 187	Jacob Cruz GLR	1.00	.45
❑ 188	Mark Kotsay GLR	1.50	.70
❑ 189	Fernando Tatis GLR	4.00	1.80
❑ 190	Ricky Ledee GLR	1.00	.70
❑ 191	Richard Hidalgo GLR	1.50	.70
❑ 192	Richie Sexson GLR	2.50	1.10
❑ 193	Luis Ordaz GLR	1.00	.45
❑ 194	Eli Marrero GLR	1.00	.45
❑ 195	Livan Hernandez GLR	1.00	.45
❑ 196	Homer Bush GLR	1.00	.45
❑ 197	Raul Ibanez GLR	1.00	.45
❑ 198	N. Garciaparra CL	6.00	2.70
❑ 199	Scott Rolen CL	4.00	1.80
❑ 200	Jose Cruz Jr. CL	1.00	.45
❑ 201	Al Martin CL	1.00	.45

1998 Leaf Fractal Materials

	MINT	NRMT
COMMON PLASTIC	1.50	.70
PLASTIC MINOR STARS	2.00	.90
PLASTIC SEMISTARS	3.00	1.35
PLASTIC UNLISTED STARS	5.00	2.20

PLASTIC X PRINT RUN 3050 SERIAL #'d

CARDS
PLASTIC Y PRINT RUN 3150 SERIAL #'d CARDS
PLASTIC Z PRINT RUN 3200 SERIAL #'d CARDS
COMMON LEATHER .... 2.50 ... 1.10
LEATHER MINOR STARS ... 4.00 ... 1.80
LEATHER SEMISTARS ...... 6.00 ... 2.70
LEATHER UNLISTED STARS 10.00 ... 4.50
LEATHER X PRINT RUN 800 SERIAL #'d CARDS
LEATHER Y PRINT RUN 900 SERIAL #'d CARDS
LEATHER Z PRINT RUN 950 SERIAL #'d CARDS
COMMON NYLON .... 4.00 ... 1.80
NYLON MINOR STARS .... 6.00 ... 2.70
NYLON SEMISTARS .... 10.00 ... 4.50
NYLON UNLISTED STARS ... 15.00 ... 6.75
NYLON Y PRINT RUN 300 SERIAL #'d CARDS
NYLON Y PRINT RUN 400 SERIAL #'d CARDS
NYLON Z PRINT RUN 450 SERIAL #'d CARDS
COMMON WOOD .... 10.00 ... 4.50
WOOD SEMISTARS .... 15.00 ... 6.75
WOOD UNLISTED STARS ... 25.00 ... 11.00
WOOD X PRINT RUN 50 SERIAL #'d CARDS
WOOD Y PRINT RUN 150 SERIAL #'d CARDS
WOOD Z PRINT RUN 200 SERIAL #'d CARDS
CARD NUMBER 42 DOES NOT EXIST

#	Card	Mint	Nrmt
1	Rusty Greer NZ	6.00	2.70
2	Tino Martinez WY	12.00	5.50
3	Bobby Bonilla NZ	6.00	2.70
4	Jason Giambi NZ	6.00	2.70
5	Matt Morris LY	2.50	1.10
6	Craig Counsell PX	1.50	.70
7	Reggie Jefferson PX	1.50	.70
8	Brian Rose PX	1.50	.70
9	Ruben Rivera LY	2.50	1.10
10	Shawn Estes LY	2.50	1.10
11	Tony Gwynn WX	150.00	70.00
12	Jeff Abbott PY	1.50	.70
13	Jose Cruz Jr. WZ	10.00	4.50
14	Francisco Cordova PY	1.50	.70
15	Ryan Klesko LX	4.00	1.80
16	Tim Salmon WY	20.00	9.00
17	Brett Tomko LY	2.50	1.10
18	Matt Williams NY	15.00	6.75
19	Joe Carter PX	2.00	.90
20	Harold Baines PX	2.00	.90
21	Gary Sheffield NZ	6.00	2.70
22	Charles Johnson LY	4.00	1.80
23	Aaron Boone PY	1.50	.70
24	Eddie Murray NX	15.00	6.75
25	Matt Stairs PX	2.00	.90
26	David Cone PX	3.00	1.35
27	Jon Nunnally PX	1.50	.70
28	Chris Stynes PX	1.50	.70
29	Enrique Wilson PY	1.50	.70
30	Randy Johnson WY	30.00	13.50
31	Garret Anderson NY	6.00	2.70
32	Manny Ramirez WY	40.00	18.00
33	Jeff Suppan LY	2.50	1.10
34	Rickey Henderson NX	20.00	9.00
35	Scott Spiezio PY	1.50	.70
36	Rondell White LY	4.00	1.80
37	Todd Greene NZ	4.00	1.80
38	Delino DeShields PY	1.50	.70
39	Kevin Brown LX	6.00	2.70
40	Chili Davis PX	2.00	.90
41	Jimmy Key PX	2.00	.90
43	Mike Mussina NX	15.00	6.75
43	Joe Randa PX	1.50	.70
44	Chan Ho Park NY	6.00	2.70
46	Brad Radke PX	2.00	.90
47	Geronimo Berroa PX	1.50	.70
48	Wade Boggs NY	15.00	6.75
49	Kevin Appier PX	2.00	.90
50	Moises Alou NX	6.00	2.70
51	David Justice NZ	6.00	2.70
52	Ivan Rodriguez WX	80.00	36.00
53	J.T. Snow LX	4.00	1.80
54	Brian Giles PY	2.00	.90
55	Will Clark LX	10.00	4.50
56	Justin Thompson NY	4.00	1.80
57	Javier Lopez PY	2.00	.90
58	Hideki Irabu LX	4.00	1.80
59	Mark Grudzielanek PX	1.50	.70
60	Abraham Nunez PZ	1.50	.70
61	Todd Hollandsworth PX	1.50	.70
62	Jay Bell PX	2.00	.90
63	Nomar Garciaparra WZ	80.00	36.00
64	Vinny Castilla PY	2.00	.90
65	Lou Collier PY	1.50	.70
66	Kevin Orie LX	2.50	1.10
67	John Valentin PY	2.00	.90
68	Robin Ventura PX	2.00	.90
69	Denny Neagle PY	1.50	.70
70	Tony Womack LX	2.50	1.10
71	Dennis Reyes LY	2.50	1.10
72	Wally Joyner PX	2.00	.90
73	Kevin Brown PX	3.00	1.35
74	Ray Durham PX	2.00	.90
75	Mike Cameron NY	6.00	2.70
76	Dante Bichette LX	4.00	1.80
77	Jose Guillen NZ	4.00	1.80
78	Carlos Delgado LY	10.00	4.50
79	Paul Molitor WX	60.00	27.00
80	Jason Kendall PX	2.00	.90
81	Mark Bellhorn LX	2.50	1.10
82	Damian Jackson PY	1.50	.70
83	Bill Mueller PX	1.50	.70
84	Kevin Young PX	2.00	.90
85	Curt Schilling PX	3.00	1.35
86	Jeffrey Hammonds PX	1.50	.70
87	Sandy Alomar Jr. LY	4.00	1.80
88	Bartolo Colon PY	2.00	.90
89	Wilton Guerrero LY	2.50	1.10
90	Bernie Williams NZ	15.00	6.75
91	Deion Sanders NY	6.00	2.70
92	Mike Piazza WX	80.00	36.00
93	Butch Huskey LX	2.50	1.10
94	Edgardo Alfonzo LY	6.00	2.70
95	Alan Benes LZ	2.50	1.10
96	Craig Biggio NX	15.00	6.75
97	Mark Grace LY	10.00	4.50
98	Shawn Green LY	10.00	4.50
99	Derrek Lee LY	2.50	1.10
100	Ken Griffey Jr. WZ	120.00	55.00
101	Tim Raines PX	2.00	.90
102	Pokey Reese PY	1.50	.70
103	Lee Stevens PX	1.50	.70
104	Shannon Stewart NX	6.00	2.70
105	John Smoltz LY	6.00	2.70
106	Frank Thomas WZ	50.00	22.00
107	Jeff Fassero PX	1.50	.70
108	Jay Buhner LY	4.00	1.80
109	Jose Canseco LX	12.00	5.50
110	Omar Vizquel PX	2.00	.90
111	Travis Fryman PX	2.00	.90
112	Dave Nilsson PX	1.50	.70
113	John Olerud PX	2.00	.90
114	Larry Walker NX	50.00	22.00
115	Jim Edmonds NX	6.00	2.70
116	Bobby Higginson LY	4.00	1.80
117	Todd Hundley LZ	4.00	1.80
118	Paul O'Neill PX	2.00	.90
119	Bip Roberts PX	1.50	.70
120	Ismael Valdes PX	1.50	.70
121	Pedro Martinez LX	20.00	9.00
122	Jeff Cirillo PX	2.00	.90
123	Andy Benes PX	1.50	.70
124	Bobby Jones PX	1.50	.70
125	Brian Hunter PX	1.50	.70
126	Darryl Kile PX	1.50	.70
127	Pat Hentgen PX	1.50	.70
128	Marquis Grissom PX	1.50	.70
129	Eric Davis PX	2.00	.90
130	Chipper Jones WZ	60.00	27.00
131	Edgar Martinez NZ	6.00	2.70
132	Andy Pettitte WY	12.00	5.50
133	Cal Ripken WZ	100.00	45.00
134	Scott Rolen WX	80.00	36.00
135	Ron Coomer PX	1.50	.70
136	Luis Castillo LX	2.50	1.10
137	Fred McGriff LX	6.00	2.70
138	Neifi Perez LY	4.00	1.80
139	Eric Karros PX	2.00	.90
140	Alex Fernandez PX	1.50	.70
141	Jason Dickson PX	1.50	.70
142	Lance Johnson PX	1.50	.70
143	Ray Lankford PY	2.00	.90
144	Sammy Sosa NY	50.00	22.00
145	Eric Young PY	1.50	.70
146	Bubba Trammell LZ	2.50	1.10
147	Todd Walker LZ	4.00	1.80
148	Mo Vaughn CC PX	5.00	2.20
149	Jeff Bagwell CC PX	6.00	2.70
150	Kenny Lofton CC PX	3.00	1.35
151	Raul Mondesi CC PX	2.00	.90
152	Mike Piazza CC PX	15.00	6.75
153	Chipper Jones CC PX	12.00	5.50
154	Larry Walker CC PX	5.00	2.20
155	Greg Maddux CC PX	12.00	5.50
156	Ken Griffey Jr. CC PX	25.00	11.00
157	Frank Thomas CC PX	10.00	4.50
158	Darin Erstad GLS LY	4.00	1.80
159	Roberto Alomar GLS PX	5.00	2.20
160	Albert Belle GLS LX	10.00	4.50
161	Jim Thome GLS LX	10.00	4.50
162	Tony Clark GLS LZ	4.00	1.80
163	Chuck Knoblauch GLS LZ	4.00	1.80
164	Derek Jeter GLS PX	15.00	6.75
165	Alex Rodriguez GLS PY	15.00	6.75
166	Tony Gwynn GLS PX	12.00	5.50
167	Roger Clemens GLS PX	25.00	11.00
168	Barry Larkin GLS PY	3.00	1.35
169	Andres Galarraga GLS PY	3.00	1.35
170	Vladimir Guerrero GLS LY	12.00	5.50
171	Mark McGwire GLS LZ	60.00	27.00
172	Barry Bonds GLS LY	12.00	5.50
173	Juan Gonzalez GLS PY	10.00	4.50
174	Andruw Jones GLS PX	5.00	2.20
175	Paul Molitor GLS PY	5.00	2.20
176	Hideo Nomo GLS LZ	10.00	4.50
177	Cal Ripken GLS PX...	20.00	9.00
178	Brad Fullmer GLR PZ	1.50	.70
179	Jaret Wright GLR NZ	6.00	2.70
180	Bobby Estalella GLR PY	1.50	.70
181	Ben Grieve GLR WZ	25.00	11.00
182	Paul Konerko GLR WZ	10.00	4.50
183	David Ortiz GLR NZ	4.00	1.80
184	Todd Helton GLR WZ	25.00	11.00
185	J. Encarnacion GLR NZ	6.00	2.70
186	Miguel Tejada GLR NZ	6.00	2.70
187	Jacob Cruz GLR PX	1.50	.70
188	Mark Kotsay GLR NZ	6.00	2.70
189	Fernando Tatis GLR LY	10.00	4.50
190	Ricky Ledee GLR PX	2.00	.90
191	Richard Hidalgo GLR PZ	2.00	.90
192	Richie Sexson GLR PZ	3.00	1.35
193	Luis Ordaz GLR PX	1.50	.70
194	Eli Marrero GLR LZ	2.50	1.10
195	Livan Hernandez GLR LZ	2.50	1.10
196	Homer Bush GLR PX	1.50	.70
197	Raul Ibanez GLR PX	1.50	.70
198	N. Garciaparra CL PX	15.00	6.75
199	Scott Rolen CL PZ	6.00	2.70
200	Jose Cruz Jr. CL PX	2.00	.90
201	Al Martin LY	2.50	1.10

1998 Leaf Fractal Materials Die Cuts

	MINT	NRMT
COMMON X-AXIS	6.00	2.70
X-AXIS MINOR STARS	10.00	4.50
X-AXIS SEMISTARS	15.00	6.75

	MINT	NRMT
X-AXIS UNLISTED STARS	25.00	11.00
X-AXIS PRINT RUN 200 SERIAL #'d SETS		
COMMON Y-AXIS	12.00	5.50
Y-AXIS MINOR STARS	20.00	9.00
Y-AXIS SEMISTARS	30.00	13.50
Y-AXIS UNLISTED STARS	50.00	22.00
Y-AXIS PRINT RUN 100 SERIAL #'d SETS		
COMMON Z-AXIS	25.00	11.00
Z-AXIS SEMISTARS	40.00	18.00
Z-AXIS UNLISTED STARS	60.00	27.00
Z-AXIS PRINT RUN 50 SERIAL #'d SETS		
CARD NUMBER 42 DOES NOT EXIST		

		MINT	NRMT
❏ 1	Rusty Greer NZ	25.00	11.00
❏ 2	Tino Martinez WY	20.00	9.00
❏ 3	Bobby Bonilla NY	20.00	9.00
❏ 4	Jason Giambi NZ	25.00	11.00
❏ 5	Mark Morris LY	12.00	5.50
❏ 6	Craig Counsell PX	6.00	2.70
❏ 7	Reggie Jefferson PX	6.00	2.70
❏ 8	Brian Rose LY	6.00	2.70
❏ 9	Ruben Rivera LY	12.00	5.50
❏ 10	Shawn Estes LY	12.00	5.50
❏ 11	Tony Gwynn WX	60.00	27.00
❏ 12	Jeff Abbott PY	20.00	9.00
❏ 13	Jose Cruz Jr. WZ	25.00	11.00
❏ 14	Francisco Cordova PY	12.00	5.50
❏ 15	Ryan Klesko LX	10.00	4.50
❏ 16	Tim Salmon WY	30.00	13.50
❏ 17	Brett Tomko LY	10.00	4.50
❏ 18	Matt Williams LY	50.00	22.00
❏ 19	Joe Carter PX	10.00	4.50
❏ 20	Harold Baines PX	10.00	4.50
❏ 21	Gary Sheffield NZ	25.00	11.00
❏ 22	Charles Johnson LY	20.00	9.00
❏ 23	Aaron Boone PY	12.00	5.50
❏ 24	Eddie Murray NY	50.00	22.00
❏ 25	Matt Stairs PX	10.00	4.50
❏ 26	David Cone PX	15.00	6.75
❏ 27	Jon Nunnally PX	6.00	2.70
❏ 28	Chris Stynes PX	6.00	2.70
❏ 29	Enrique Wilson PY	12.00	5.50
❏ 30	Randy Johnson WY	50.00	22.00
❏ 31	Garret Anderson NY	20.00	9.00
❏ 32	Manny Ramirez WY	60.00	27.00
❏ 33	Jeff Suppan LY	6.00	2.70
❏ 34	Rickey Henderson NX	30.00	13.50
❏ 35	Scott Spiezio PY	12.00	5.50
❏ 36	Rondell White LY	20.00	9.00
❏ 37	Todd Greene NZ	25.00	11.00
❏ 38	Delino DeShields PY	12.00	5.50
❏ 39	Kevin Brown P LX	15.00	6.75
❏ 40	Chili Davis PX	10.00	4.50
❏ 41	Jimmy Key PX	10.00	4.50
❏ 43	Mike Mussina PX	60.00	27.00
❏ 44	Joe Randa PX	6.00	2.70
❏ 45	Chan Ho Park NY	20.00	9.00
❏ 46	Brad Radke PX	10.00	4.50
❏ 47	Geronimo Berroa PX	6.00	2.70
❏ 48	Wade Boggs NY	50.00	22.00
❏ 49	Kevin Appier PX	10.00	4.50
❏ 50	Moises Alou NX	10.00	4.50
❏ 51	David Justice NZ	25.00	11.00
❏ 52	Ivan Rodriguez WX	30.00	13.50
❏ 53	J.T. Snow LX	10.00	4.50
❏ 54	Brian Giles PY	20.00	9.00
❏ 55	Will Clark LX	25.00	11.00
❏ 56	Justin Thompson NY	20.00	9.00
❏ 57	Javier Lopez PY	20.00	9.00
❏ 58	Hideki Irabu LX	10.00	4.50
❏ 59	Mark Grudzielanek PX	10.00	4.50
❏ 60	Abraham Nunez NZ	25.00	11.00
❏ 61	Todd Hollandsworth PX	6.00	2.70
❏ 62	Jay Bell PX	10.00	4.50
❏ 63	Nomar Garciaparra WZ	200.00	90.00
❏ 64	Vinny Castilla PY	20.00	9.00
❏ 65	Lou Collier PY	12.00	5.50
❏ 66	Kevin Orie LX	6.00	2.70
❏ 67	John Valentin PX	10.00	4.50
❏ 68	Robin Ventura PX	10.00	4.50
❏ 69	Denny Neagle PX	10.00	4.50
❏ 70	Tony Womack LY	10.00	4.50
❏ 71	Dennis Reyes LY	12.00	5.50
❏ 72	Wally Joyner PX	10.00	4.50
❏ 73	Kevin Brown C PX	6.00	2.70
❏ 74	Ray Durham PX	10.00	4.50
❏ 75	Mike Cameron NY	20.00	9.00
❏ 76	Dante Bichette LX	10.00	4.50
❏ 77	Jose Guillen NZ	25.00	11.00
❏ 78	Carlos Delgado LY	50.00	22.00
❏ 79	Paul Molitor WX	25.00	11.00
❏ 80	Jason Kendall PX	10.00	4.50
❏ 81	Mark Bellhorn LX	6.00	2.70
❏ 82	Damian Jackson PY	12.00	5.50
❏ 83	Bill Mueller PX	6.00	2.70
❏ 84	Kevin Young PX	10.00	4.50
❏ 85	Curt Schilling PX	10.00	4.50
❏ 86	Jeffrey Hammonds PX	6.00	2.70
❏ 87	Sandy Alomar Jr. LY	20.00	9.00
❏ 88	Bartolo Colon PY	20.00	9.00
❏ 89	Wilton Guerrero LY	12.00	5.50
❏ 90	Bernie Williams NZ	60.00	27.00
❏ 91	Deion Sanders NY	20.00	9.00
❏ 92	Mike Piazza WZ	200.00	90.00
❏ 93	Butch Huskey LX	6.00	2.70
❏ 94	Edgardo Alfonzo LY	30.00	13.50
❏ 95	Alan Benes LZ	25.00	11.00
❏ 96	Craig Biggio NX	30.00	13.50
❏ 97	Mark Grace LY	30.00	13.50
❏ 98	Shawn Green LY	50.00	22.00
❏ 99	Derrek Lee LY	12.00	5.50
❏ 100	Ken Griffey Jr. WZ	300.00	135.00
❏ 101	Tim Hamm PX	10.00	4.50
❏ 102	Pokey Reese PY	20.00	9.00
❏ 103	Lee Stevens PX	6.00	2.70
❏ 104	Shannon Stewart NX	10.00	4.50
❏ 105	John Smoltz LY	30.00	13.50
❏ 106	Frank Thomas WZ	120.00	55.00
❏ 107	Jeff Fassero PX	6.00	2.70
❏ 108	Jay Buhner LY	20.00	9.00
❏ 109	Jose Canseco LX	30.00	13.50
❏ 110	Omar Vizquel PX	10.00	4.50
❏ 111	Travis Fryman PX	10.00	4.50
❏ 112	Dave Nilsson PX	6.00	2.70
❏ 113	John Olerud PX	10.00	4.50
❏ 114	Larry Walker WX	25.00	11.00
❏ 115	Jim Edmonds NZ	25.00	11.00
❏ 116	Bobby Higginson LY	20.00	9.00
❏ 117	Todd Hundley LZ	25.00	11.00
❏ 118	Paul O'Neill PX	10.00	4.50
❏ 119	Bip Roberts PX	6.00	2.70
❏ 120	Ismael Valdes PX	6.00	2.70
❏ 121	Pedro Martinez NX	30.00	13.50
❏ 122	Jeff Cirillo PX	10.00	4.50
❏ 123	Andy Benes PX	10.00	4.50
❏ 124	Bobby Jones PX	6.00	2.70
❏ 125	Brian Hunter PX	6.00	2.70
❏ 126	Darryl Kile PX	6.00	2.70
❏ 127	Pat Hentgen PX	6.00	2.70
❏ 128	Marquis Grissom PX	10.00	4.50
❏ 129	Eric Davis PX	10.00	4.50
❏ 130	Chipper Jones WZ	150.00	70.00
❏ 131	Edgar Martinez NY	20.00	11.00
❏ 132	Andy Pettitte WY	20.00	9.00
❏ 133	Cal Ripken WZ	250.00	110.00
❏ 134	Scott Rolen WX	30.00	13.50
❏ 135	Ron Coomer PX	6.00	2.70
❏ 136	Luis Castillo LX	6.00	2.70
❏ 137	Fred McGriff LX	15.00	6.75
❏ 138	Neifi Perez LY	20.00	9.00
❏ 139	Eric Karros PX	10.00	4.50
❏ 140	Alex Fernandez PX	6.00	2.70
❏ 141	Jason Dickson PX	6.00	2.70
❏ 142	Lance Johnson PX	6.00	2.70
❏ 143	Ray Lankford PY	20.00	9.00
❏ 144	Sammy Sosa NY	120.00	55.00
❏ 145	Eric Young PY	12.00	5.50
❏ 146	Bubba Trammell LZ	20.00	9.00
❏ 147	Todd Walker LZ	25.00	11.00
❏ 148	Mo Vaughn CC PX	25.00	11.00
❏ 149	Jeff Bagwell CC PX	30.00	13.50
❏ 150	Kenny Lofton CC PX	10.00	4.50
❏ 151	Raul Mondesi CC PX	10.00	4.50
❏ 152	Mike Piazza CC PX	80.00	36.00
❏ 153	Chipper Jones CC PX	60.00	27.00
❏ 154	Larry Walker CC PX	25.00	11.00
❏ 155	Greg Maddux CC PX	60.00	27.00
❏ 156	Ken Griffey Jr. CC PX	120.00	55.00
❏ 157	Frank Thomas CC PX	50.00	22.00
❏ 158	Darin Erstad GLS LY	20.00	9.00
❏ 159	Roberto Alomar GLS PX	25.00	11.00
❏ 160	Albert Belle GLS LX	25.00	11.00
❏ 161	Jim Thome GLS LX	25.00	11.00
❏ 162	Tony Clark GLS LZ	25.00	11.00
❏ 163	Chuck Knoblauch GLS LZ	25.00	11.00
❏ 164	Derek Jeter GLS PX	80.00	36.00
❏ 165	Alex Rodriguez GLS PY	120.00	55.00
❏ 166	Tony Gwynn GLS PX	60.00	27.00
❏ 167	Roger Clemens GLS LY	100.00	45.00
❏ 168	Barry Larkin GLS PX	50.00	22.00
❏ 169	Andres Galarraga GLS PY	20.00	9.00
❏ 170	V. Guerrero GLS LY	50.00	22.00
❏ 171	Mark McGwire GLS LZ	300.00	135.00
❏ 172	Barry Bonds GLS LY	50.00	22.00
❏ 173	Juan Gonzalez GLS PY	80.00	36.00
❏ 174	Andruw Jones GLS PX	25.00	11.00
❏ 175	Paul Molitor GLS PX	25.00	11.00
❏ 176	Hideo Nomo GLS LZ	60.00	27.00
❏ 177	Cal Ripken GLS PX	100.00	45.00
❏ 178	Brad Fullmer GLR PZ	25.00	11.00
❏ 179	Jaret Wright GLR WZ	25.00	11.00
❏ 180	Bobby Estalella GLR PY	12.00	5.50
❏ 181	Ben Grieve GLR WZ	60.00	27.00
❏ 182	Paul Konerko GLR WZ	25.00	11.00
❏ 183	David Ortiz GLR NZ	25.00	11.00
❏ 184	Todd Helton GLR WZ	60.00	27.00
❏ 185	Juan Encarnacion GLR NZ	25.00	11.00
❏ 186	Miguel Tejada GLR NZ	25.00	11.00
❏ 187	Jacob Cruz GLR PX	6.00	2.70
❏ 188	Mark Kotsay GLR NZ	25.00	11.00
❏ 189	Fernando Tatis GLR LY	30.00	13.50
❏ 190	Ricky Ledee GLR PX	10.00	4.50
❏ 191	Richard Hidalgo GLR PZ	25.00	11.00
❏ 192	Richie Sexson GLR PZ	40.00	18.00
❏ 193	Luis Ordaz GLR PX	6.00	2.70
❏ 194	Eli Marrero GLR LZ	25.00	11.00
❏ 195	Livan Hernandez GLR LZ	25.00	11.00
❏ 196	Homer Bush GLR PX	6.00	2.70
❏ 197	Raul Ibanez GLR PX	6.00	2.70
❏ 198	N. Garciaparra CL PX	50.00	22.00
❏ 199	Scott Rolen CL PZ	50.00	22.00
❏ 200	Jose Cruz Jr. CL PX	10.00	4.50
❏ 201	Al Martin LY	12.00	5.50

1998 Leaf Fractal Materials Z2 Axis

	MINT	NRMT
COMMON (1-41/43-201)	25.00	11.00
*STARS: 10X TO 25X BASIC FOUNDATION		
STATED PRINT RUN 20 SERIAL #'d SETS		
CARD NUMBER 42 DOES NOT EXIST		

1994 Leaf Limited

	MINT	NRMT
COMPLETE SET (160) *	80.00	36.00
COMMON CARD (1-160)	.50	.23
MINOR STARS	.75	.35
SEMISTARS	1.25	.55
UNLISTED STARS	2.00	.90

		MINT	NRMT
❏ 1	Jeffrey Hammonds	.75	.35
❏ 2	Ben McDonald	.50	.23
❏ 3	Mike Mussina	2.00	.90
❏ 4	Rafael Palmeiro	2.00	.90
❏ 5	Cal Ripken Jr.	8.00	3.60
❏ 6	Lee Smith	.75	.35

❑ 7	Roger Clemens	5.00	2.20
❑ 8	Scott Cooper	.50	.23
❑ 9	Andre Dawson	1.25	.55
❑ 10	Mike Greenwell	.50	.23
❑ 11	Aaron Sele	.75	.35
❑ 12	Mo Vaughn	2.00	.90
❑ 13	Brian Anderson	1.25	.55
❑ 14	Chad Curtis	.50	.23
❑ 15	Chili Davis	.75	.35
❑ 16	Gary DiSarcina	.50	.23
❑ 17	Mark Langston	.50	.23
❑ 18	Tim Salmon	2.00	.90
❑ 19	Wilson Alvarez	.75	.35
❑ 20	Jason Bere	.50	.23
❑ 21	Julio Franco	.50	.23
❑ 22	Jack McDowell	.75	.35
❑ 23	Tim Raines	.75	.35
❑ 24	Frank Thomas	4.00	1.80
❑ 25	Robin Ventura	.75	.35
❑ 26	Carlos Baerga	.75	.35
❑ 27	Albert Belle	2.00	.90
❑ 28	Kenny Lofton	2.00	.90
❑ 29	Eddie Murray	2.00	.90
❑ 30	Manny Ramirez	4.00	1.80
❑ 31	Cecil Fielder	.75	.35
❑ 32	Travis Fryman	.75	.35
❑ 33	Mickey Tettleton	.50	.23
❑ 34	Alan Trammell	1.25	.55
❑ 35	Lou Whitaker	.75	.35
❑ 36	David Cone	1.25	.55
❑ 37	Gary Gaetti	.75	.35
❑ 38	Greg Gagne	.50	.23
❑ 39	Bob Hamelin	.50	.23
❑ 40	Wally Joyner	.75	.35
❑ 41	Brian McRae	.50	.23
❑ 42	Ricky Bones	.50	.23
❑ 43	Brian Harper	.50	.23
❑ 44	John Jaha	.50	.23
❑ 45	Pat Listach	.50	.23
❑ 46	Dave Nilsson	.50	.23
❑ 47	Greg Vaughn	.75	.35
❑ 48	Kent Hrbek	.75	.35
❑ 49	Chuck Knoblauch	2.00	.90
❑ 50	Shane Mack	.50	.23
❑ 51	Kirby Puckett	3.00	1.35
❑ 52	Dave Winfield	2.00	.90
❑ 53	Jim Abbott	.75	.35
❑ 54	Wade Boggs	2.00	.90
❑ 55	Jimmy Key	.75	.35
❑ 56	Don Mattingly	4.00	1.80
❑ 57	Paul O'Neill	.75	.35
❑ 58	Danny Tartabull	.50	.23
❑ 59	Dennis Eckersley	1.25	.55
❑ 60	Rickey Henderson	2.50	1.10
❑ 61	Mark McGwire	10.00	4.50
❑ 62	Troy Neel	.50	.23
❑ 63	Ruben Sierra	.50	.23
❑ 64	Eric Anthony	.50	.23
❑ 65	Jay Buhner	.75	.35
❑ 66	Ken Griffey Jr.	10.00	4.50
❑ 67	Randy Johnson	2.00	.90
❑ 68	Edgar Martinez	.75	.35
❑ 69	Tino Martinez	2.00	.90
❑ 70	Jose Canseco	2.50	1.10
❑ 71	Will Clark	2.00	.90
❑ 72	Juan Gonzalez	4.00	1.80
❑ 73	Dean Palmer	.75	.35
❑ 74	Ivan Rodriguez	2.50	1.10

❑ 75	Roberto Alomar	2.00	.90
❑ 76	Joe Carter	.75	.35
❑ 77	Carlos Delgado	2.00	.90
❑ 78	Paul Molitor	2.00	.90
❑ 79	John Olerud	.75	.35
❑ 80	Devon White	.50	.23
❑ 81	Steve Avery	.50	.23
❑ 82	Tom Glavine	2.00	.90
❑ 83	David Justice	2.00	.90
❑ 84	Roberto Kelly	.50	.23
❑ 85	Ryan Klesko	.75	.35
❑ 86	Javier Lopez	1.25	.55
❑ 87	Greg Maddux	5.00	2.20
❑ 88	Fred McGriff	1.25	.55
❑ 89	Shawon Dunston	.50	.23
❑ 90	Mark Grace	1.25	.55
❑ 91	Derrick May	.50	.23
❑ 92	Sammy Sosa	8.00	3.60
❑ 93	Rick Wilkins	.50	.23
❑ 94	Bret Boone	.75	.35
❑ 95	Barry Larkin	2.00	.90
❑ 96	Kevin Mitchell	.50	.23
❑ 97	Hal Morris	.50	.23
❑ 98	Deion Sanders	.75	.35
❑ 99	Reggie Sanders	.75	.35
❑ 100	Dante Bichette	.75	.35
❑ 101	Ellis Burks	.50	.23
❑ 102	Andres Galarraga	2.00	.90
❑ 103	Joe Girardi	.50	.23
❑ 104	Charlie Hayes	.50	.23
❑ 105	Chuck Carr	.50	.23
❑ 106	Jeff Conine	.50	.23
❑ 107	Bryan Harvey	.50	.23
❑ 108	Benito Santiago	.50	.23
❑ 109	Gary Sheffield	2.00	.90
❑ 110	Jeff Bagwell	2.50	1.10
❑ 111	Craig Biggio	2.00	.90
❑ 112	Ken Caminiti	1.25	.55
❑ 113	Andujar Cedeno	.50	.23
❑ 114	Doug Drabek	.50	.23
❑ 115	Luis Gonzalez	.75	.35
❑ 116	Brett Butler	.75	.35
❑ 117	Delino DeShields	.50	.23
❑ 118	Eric Karros	.75	.35
❑ 119	Raul Mondesi	2.00	.90
❑ 120	Mike Piazza	6.00	2.70
❑ 121	Henry Rodriguez	.75	.35
❑ 122	Tim Wallach	.50	.23
❑ 123	Moises Alou	.50	.23
❑ 124	Cliff Floyd	.75	.35
❑ 125	Marquis Grissom	.75	.35
❑ 126	Ken Hill	.50	.23
❑ 127	Larry Walker	2.00	.90
❑ 128	John Wetteland	.75	.35
❑ 129	Bobby Bonilla	.75	.35
❑ 130	John Franco	.50	.23
❑ 131	Jeff Kent	.50	.23
❑ 132	Bret Saberhagen	.75	.35
❑ 133	Ryan Thompson	.50	.23
❑ 134	Darren Daulton	.75	.35
❑ 135	Mariano Duncan	.50	.23
❑ 136	Lenny Dykstra	.75	.35
❑ 137	Danny Jackson	.50	.23
❑ 138	John Kruk	.75	.35
❑ 139	Jay Bell	.50	.23
❑ 140	Jeff King	.50	.23
❑ 141	Al Martin	.50	.23
❑ 142	Orlando Merced	.50	.23
❑ 143	Andy Van Slyke	.75	.35
❑ 144	Bernard Gilkey	.50	.23
❑ 145	Gregg Jefferies	.50	.23
❑ 146	Ray Lankford	.75	.35
❑ 147	Ozzie Smith	2.50	1.10
❑ 148	Mark Whiten	.50	.23
❑ 149	Todd Zeile	.50	.23
❑ 150	Derek Bell	.75	.35
❑ 151	Andy Benes	.75	.35
❑ 152	Tony Gwynn	5.00	2.20
❑ 153	Phil Plantier	.50	.23
❑ 154	Bip Roberts	.50	.23
❑ 155	Rod Beck	.50	.23
❑ 156	Barry Bonds	2.50	1.10
❑ 157	John Burkett	.50	.23
❑ 158	Royce Clayton	.50	.23
❑ 159	Bill Swift	.50	.23
❑ 160	Matt Williams	1.25	.55

1994 Leaf Limited Gold All-Stars

	MINT	NRMT
COMPLETE SET (18)	120.00	55.00
COMMON CARD (1-18)	1.25	.55
STATED ODDS 1:7		
STATED PRINT RUN 10,000 SERIAL #'d SETS		

❑ 1	Frank Thomas	12.00	5.50
❑ 2	Gregg Jefferies	1.25	.55
❑ 3	Roberto Alomar	5.00	2.20
❑ 4	Mariano Duncan	1.25	.55
❑ 5	Wade Boggs	5.00	2.20
❑ 6	Matt Williams	3.00	1.35
❑ 7	Cal Ripken Jr.	20.00	9.00
❑ 8	Ozzie Smith	5.00	2.20
❑ 9	Kirby Puckett	8.00	3.60
❑ 10	Barry Bonds	5.00	2.20
❑ 11	Ken Griffey Jr.	25.00	11.00
❑ 12	Tony Gwynn	12.00	5.50
❑ 13	Joe Carter	2.00	.90
❑ 14	David Justice	3.00	1.35
❑ 15	Ivan Rodriguez	5.00	2.20
❑ 16	Mike Piazza	15.00	6.75
❑ 17	Jimmy Key	2.00	.90
❑ 18	Greg Maddux	15.00	6.75

1994 Leaf Limited Rookies

	MINT	NRMT
COMPLETE SET (80)	25.00	11.00
COMMON CARD (1-80)	.40	.18
MINOR STARS	.75	.35
UNLISTED STARS	1.50	.70

❑ 1	Charles Johnson	.75	.35
❑ 2	Rico Brogna	.40	.18
❑ 3	Melvin Nieves	.40	.18
❑ 4	Rich Becker	.40	.18
❑ 5	Russ Davis	.75	.35
❑ 6	Matt Mieske	.40	.18
❑ 7	Paul Shuey	.40	.18
❑ 8	Hector Carrasco	.40	.18
❑ 9	J.R. Phillips	.40	.18
❑ 10	Scott Ruffcorn	.40	.18
❑ 11	Kurt Abbott	.40	.18
❑ 12	Danny Bautista	.40	.18
❑ 13	Rick White	.40	.18
❑ 14	Steve Dunn	.40	.18
❑ 15	Joe Ausanio	.40	.18
❑ 16	Salomon Torres	.40	.18

❏ 17 Ricky Bottalico	.75	.35
❏ 18 Johnny Ruffin	.40	.18
❏ 19 Kevin Foster	.40	.18
❏ 20 W.VanLandingham	.40	.18
❏ 21 Troy O'Leary	.75	.35
❏ 22 Mark Acre	.40	.18
❏ 23 Norberto Martin	.40	.18
❏ 24 Jason Jacome	.40	.18
❏ 25 Steve Trachsel	.40	.18
❏ 26 Denny Hocking	.40	.18
❏ 27 Mike Lieberthal	.40	.18
❏ 28 Gerald Williams	.40	.18
❏ 29 John Mabry	.40	.18
❏ 30 Greg Blosser	.40	.18
❏ 31 Carl Everett	.75	.35
❏ 32 Steve Karsay	.40	.18
❏ 33 Jose Valentin	.40	.18
❏ 34 Jon Lieber	.40	.18
❏ 35 Chris Gomez	.40	.18
❏ 36 Jesus Tavarez	.40	.18
❏ 37 Tony Longmire	.40	.18
❏ 38 Luis Lopez	.40	.18
❏ 39 Matt Walbeck	.40	.18
❏ 40 Rikkert Faneyte	.40	.18
❏ 41 Shane Reynolds	.75	.35
❏ 42 Joey Hamilton	1.50	.70
❏ 43 Ismael Valdes	1.00	.45
❏ 44 Danny Miceli	.40	.18
❏ 45 Darren Bragg	.40	.18
❏ 46 Alex Gonzalez	.40	.18
❏ 47 Rick Helling	.75	.35
❏ 48 Jose Oliva	.40	.18
❏ 49 Jim Edmonds	1.50	.70
❏ 50 Miguel Jimenez	.40	.18
❏ 51 Tony Eusebio	.40	.18
❏ 52 Shawn Green	2.50	1.10
❏ 53 Billy Ashley	.40	.18
❏ 54 Rondell White	.75	.35
❏ 55 Cory Bailey	.40	.18
❏ 56 Tim Davis	.40	.18
❏ 57 John Hudek	.40	.18
❏ 58 Darren Hall	.40	.18
❏ 59 Darren Dreifort	.75	.35
❏ 60 Mike Kelly	.40	.18
❏ 61 Marcus Moore	.40	.18
❏ 62 Garret Anderson	1.50	.70
❏ 63 Brian L. Hunter	.75	.35
❏ 64 Mark Smith	.40	.18
❏ 65 Garey Ingram	.40	.18
❏ 66 Rusty Greer	6.00	2.70
❏ 67 Marc Newfield	.40	.18
❏ 68 Gar Finnvold	.40	.18
❏ 69 Paul Spoljaric	.40	.18
❏ 70 Ray McDavid	.40	.18
❏ 71 Orlando Miller	.40	.18
❏ 72 Jorge Fabregas	.40	.18
❏ 73 Ray Holbert	.40	.18
❏ 74 Armando Benitez	1.00	.45
❏ 75 Ernie Young	.40	.18
❏ 76 James Mouton	.40	.18
❏ 77 Robert Perez	.40	.18
❏ 78 Chan Ho Park	4.00	1.80
❏ 79 Roger Salkeld	.40	.18
❏ 80 Tony Tarasco	.40	.18

1994 Leaf Limited Rookies Phenoms

	MINT	NRMT
COMPLETE SET (10)	120.00	55.00
COMMON CARD (1-10)	4.00	1.80
MINOR STARS	8.00	3.60
STATED ODDS 1:12		
STATED PRINT RUN 5000 SERIAL #'d SETS		

❏ 1 Raul Mondesi	10.00	4.50
❏ 2 Bob Hamelin	4.00	1.80
❏ 3 Midre Cummings	4.00	1.80
❏ 4 Carlos Delgado	12.00	5.50
❏ 5 Cliff Floyd	8.00	3.60
❏ 6 Jeffrey Hammonds	4.00	1.80
❏ 7 Ryan Klesko	8.00	3.60
❏ 8 Javier Lopez	8.00	3.60
❏ 9 Manny Ramirez	30.00	13.50
❏ 10 Alex Rodriguez	80.00	36.00

1995 Leaf Limited

	MINT	NRMT
COMPLETE SET (192)	50.00	22.00
COMPLETE SERIES 1 (96)	25.00	11.00
COMPLETE SERIES 2 (96)	25.00	11.00
COMMON CARD (1-192)	.25	.11
MINOR STARS	.50	.23
SEMISTARS	.75	.35
UNLISTED STARS	1.25	.55
COMP.GOLD SET (24)	30.00	13.50
*GOLD: 4X TO 1X HI COLUMN		
ONE GOLD PER SERIES 1 PACK		

❏ 1 Frank Thomas	2.50	1.10
❏ 2 Geronimo Berroa	.25	.11
❏ 3 Tony Phillips	.25	.11
❏ 4 Roberto Alomar	1.25	.55
❏ 5 Steve Avery	.25	.11
❏ 6 Darryl Hamilton	.25	.11
❏ 7 Scott Cooper	.25	.11
❏ 8 Mark Grace	.75	.35
❏ 9 Billy Ashley	.25	.11
❏ 10 Wil Cordero	.25	.11
❏ 11 Barry Bonds	1.50	.70
❏ 12 Kenny Lofton	.75	.35
❏ 13 Jay Buhner	.50	.23
❏ 14 Alex Rodriguez	5.00	2.20
❏ 15 Bobby Bonilla	.50	.23
❏ 16 Brady Anderson	.50	.23
❏ 17 Ken Caminiti	.75	.35
❏ 18 Charlie Hayes	.25	.11
❏ 19 Jay Bell	.50	.23
❏ 20 Will Clark	1.25	.55
❏ 21 Jose Canseco	1.50	.70
❏ 22 Bret Boone	.50	.23
❏ 23 Dante Bichette	.50	.23
❏ 24 Kevin Appier	.50	.23
❏ 25 Chad Curtis	.25	.11
❏ 26 Marty Cordova	.25	.11
❏ 27 Jason Bere	.25	.11
❏ 28 Jimmy Key	.50	.23
❏ 29 Rickey Henderson	1.50	.70
❏ 30 Tim Salmon	1.25	.55
❏ 31 Joe Carter	.50	.23
❏ 32 Tom Glavine	1.25	.55
❏ 33 Pat Listach	.25	.11
❏ 34 Brian Jordan	.50	.23
❏ 35 Brian McRae	.25	.11
❏ 36 Eric Karros	.50	.23
❏ 37 Pedro Martinez	1.50	.70
❏ 38 Royce Clayton	.25	.11
❏ 39 Eddie Murray	1.25	.55
❏ 40 Randy Johnson	1.25	.55
❏ 41 Jeff Conine	.25	.11
❏ 42 Brett Butler	.50	.23
❏ 43 Jeffrey Hammonds	.50	.23
❏ 44 Andujar Cedeno	.25	.11
❏ 45 Dave Hollins	.25	.11
❏ 46 Jeff King	.25	.11
❏ 47 Benji Gil	.25	.11
❏ 48 Roger Clemens	3.00	1.35
❏ 49 Barry Larkin	1.25	.55
❏ 50 Joe Girardi	.25	.11
❏ 51 Bob Hamelin	.25	.11
❏ 52 Travis Fryman	.50	.23
❏ 53 Chuck Knoblauch	1.25	.55
❏ 54 Ray Durham	.50	.23
❏ 55 Don Mattingly	2.50	1.10
❏ 56 Ruben Sierra	.25	.11
❏ 57 J.T. Snow	.50	.23
❏ 58 Derek Bell	.50	.23
❏ 59 David Cone	.75	.35
❏ 60 Marquis Grissom	.50	.23
❏ 61 Kevin Seitzer	.25	.11
❏ 62 Ozzie Smith	1.50	.70
❏ 63 Rick Wilkins	.25	.11
❏ 64 Hideo Nomo	3.00	1.35
❏ 65 Tony Tarasco	.25	.11
❏ 66 Manny Ramirez	1.50	.70
❏ 67 Charles Johnson	.50	.23
❏ 68 Craig Biggio	1.25	.55
❏ 69 Bobby Jones	.25	.11
❏ 70 Mike Mussina	1.25	.55
❏ 71 Alex Gonzalez	.25	.11
❏ 72 Gregg Jefferies	.25	.11
❏ 73 Rusty Greer	.25	.11
❏ 74 Mike Greenwell	.25	.11
❏ 75 Hal Morris	.25	.11
❏ 76 Paul O'Neill	.50	.23
❏ 77 Luis Gonzalez	.25	.11
❏ 78 Chipper Jones	3.00	1.35
❏ 79 Mike Piazza	4.00	1.80
❏ 80 Rondell White	.50	.23
❏ 81 Glenallen Hill	.25	.11
❏ 82 Shawn Green	1.25	.55
❏ 83 Bernie Williams	1.25	.55
❏ 84 Jim Thome	1.25	.55
❏ 85 Terry Pendleton	.25	.11
❏ 86 Rafael Palmeiro	1.25	.55
❏ 87 Tony Gwynn	3.00	1.35
❏ 88 Mickey Tettleton	.25	.11
❏ 89 John Valentin	.50	.23
❏ 90 Deion Sanders	.50	.23
❏ 91 Larry Walker	1.25	.55
❏ 92 Michael Tucker	.50	.23
❏ 93 Alan Trammell	.50	.23
❏ 94 Tim Raines	.50	.23
❏ 95 David Justice	1.25	.55
❏ 96 Tino Martinez	1.25	.55
❏ 97 Cal Ripken Jr.	5.00	2.20
❏ 98 Deion Sanders	.50	.23
❏ 99 Darren Daulton	.50	.23
❏ 100 Paul Molitor	1.25	.55
❏ 101 Randy Myers	.25	.11
❏ 102 Wally Joyner	.50	.23
❏ 103 Carlos Perez	.25	.11
❏ 104 Brian Hunter	.50	.23
❏ 105 Wade Boggs	1.25	.55
❏ 106 Bob Higginson	2.00	.90
❏ 107 Jeff Kent	.50	.23
❏ 108 Jose Offerman	.25	.11
❏ 109 Dennis Eckersley	.50	.23
❏ 110 Dave Nilsson	.25	.11
❏ 111 Chuck Finley	.25	.11
❏ 112 Devon White	.25	.11
❏ 113 Bip Roberts	.25	.11
❏ 114 Ramon Martinez	.50	.23
❏ 115 Greg Maddux	3.00	1.35
❏ 116 Curtis Goodwin	.25	.11
❏ 117 John Jaha	.25	.11
❏ 118 Ken Griffey Jr.	6.00	2.70
❏ 119 Geronimo Pena	.25	.11
❏ 120 Shawon Dunston	.25	.11
❏ 121 Ariel Prieto	.25	.11
❏ 122 Kirby Puckett	2.00	.90

		MINT	NRMT
❑ 123 Carlos Baerga	.25		.11
❑ 124 Todd Hundley	.50		.23
❑ 125 Tim Naehring	.25		.11
❑ 126 Gary Sheffield	.50		.23
❑ 127 Dean Palmer	.50		.23
❑ 128 Rondell White	.50		.23
❑ 129 Greg Gagne	.25		.11
❑ 130 Jose Rijo	.25		.11
❑ 131 Ivan Rodriguez	1.50		.70
❑ 132 Jeff Bagwell	1.50		.70
❑ 133 Greg Vaughn	.50		.23
❑ 134 Chili Davis	.50		.23
❑ 135 Al Martin	.25		.11
❑ 136 Kenny Rogers	.25		.11
❑ 137 Aaron Sele	.50		.23
❑ 138 Raul Mondesi	.75		.35
❑ 139 Cecil Fielder	.50		.23
❑ 140 Tim Wallach	.25		.11
❑ 141 Andres Galarraga	1.25		.55
❑ 142 Lou Whitaker	.50		.23
❑ 143 Jack McDowell	.25		.11
❑ 144 Matt Williams	1.25		.55
❑ 145 Ryan Klesko	.50		.23
❑ 146 Carlos Garcia	.25		.11
❑ 147 Albert Belle	1.25		.55
❑ 148 Ryan Thompson	.25		.11
❑ 149 Roberto Kelly	.25		.11
❑ 150 Edgar Martinez	.50		.23
❑ 151 Robby Thompson	.25		.11
❑ 152 Mo Vaughn	1.25		.55
❑ 153 Todd Zeile	.25		.11
❑ 154 Harold Baines	.50		.23
❑ 155 Phil Plantier	.25		.11
❑ 156 Mike Stanley	.25		.11
❑ 157 Ed Sprague	.25		.11
❑ 158 Moises Alou	.50		.23
❑ 159 Quivio Veras	.25		.11
❑ 160 Reggie Sanders	.50		.23
❑ 161 Delino DeShields	.25		.11
❑ 162 Rico Brogna	.25		.11
❑ 163 Greg Colbrunn	.25		.11
❑ 164 Steve Finley	.50		.23
❑ 165 Orlando Merced	.25		.11
❑ 166 Mark McGwire	6.00		2.70
❑ 167 Garret Anderson	.50		.23
❑ 168 Paul Sorrento	.25		.11
❑ 169 Mark Langston	.25		.11
❑ 170 Danny Tartabull	.25		.11
❑ 171 Vinny Castilla	.75		.35
❑ 172 Javier Lopez	.50		.23
❑ 173 Bret Saberhagen	.50		.23
❑ 174 Eddie Williams	.25		.11
❑ 175 Scott Leius	.25		.11
❑ 176 Juan Gonzalez	2.50		1.10
❑ 177 Gary Gaetti	.50		.23
❑ 178 Jim Edmonds	.75		.35
❑ 179 John Olerud	.50		.23
❑ 180 Lenny Dykstra	.50		.23
❑ 181 Ray Lankford	.50		.23
❑ 182 Ron Gant	.25		.11
❑ 183 Doug Drabek	.25		.11
❑ 184 Fred McGriff	.75		.35
❑ 185 Andy Benes	.50		.23
❑ 186 Kurt Abbott	.25		.11
❑ 187 Bernard Gilkey	.25		.11
❑ 188 Sammy Sosa	4.00		1.80
❑ 189 Lee Smith	.50		.23
❑ 190 Dennis Martinez	.50		.23
❑ 191 Ozzie Guillen	.25		.11
❑ 192 Robin Ventura	.50		.23

1995 Leaf Limited Bat Patrol

	MINT	NRMT
COMPLETE SET (24)	25.00	11.00
COMMON CARD (1-24)	.50	.23
ONE PER SERIES 2 PACK		
❑ 1 Frank Thomas	3.00	1.35
❑ 2 Tony Gwynn	4.00	1.80
❑ 3 Wade Boggs	1.50	.70
❑ 4 Larry Walker	1.50	.70
❑ 5 Ken Griffey, Jr.	8.00	3.60
❑ 6 Jeff Bagwell	2.00	.90

		MINT	NRMT
❑ 7 Manny Ramirez	2.00		.90
❑ 8 Mark Grace	1.25		.55
❑ 9 Kenny Lofton	1.25		.55
❑ 10 Mike Piazza	5.00		2.20
❑ 11 Will Clark	1.50		.70
❑ 12 Mo Vaughn	1.50		.70
❑ 13 Carlos Baerga	.50		.23
❑ 14 Rafael Palmeiro	1.50		.70
❑ 15 Barry Bonds	2.00		.90
❑ 16 Kirby Puckett	2.00		.90
❑ 17 Roberto Alomar	1.50		.70
❑ 18 Barry Larkin	1.50		.70
❑ 19 Eddie Murray	1.50		.70
❑ 20 Tim Salmon	1.50		.70
❑ 21 Don Mattingly	3.00		1.35
❑ 22 Fred McGriff	1.25		.55
❑ 23 Albert Belle	1.50		.70
❑ 24 Dante Bichette	.75		.35

1995 Leaf Limited Lumberjacks

	MINT	NRMT
COMPLETE SET (16)	250.00	110.00
COMPLETE SERIES 1 (8)	150.00	70.00
COMPLETE SERIES 2 (8)	100.00	45.00
COMMON CARD (1-16)	5.00	2.20
UNLISTED STARS	10.00	4.50
STATED ODDS 1:23		
STATED PRINT RUN 5000 SERIAL #'d SETS		
❑ 1 Albert Belle	10.00	4.50
❑ 2 Barry Bonds	12.00	5.50
❑ 3 Juan Gonzalez	20.00	9.00
❑ 4 Ken Griffey Jr.	50.00	22.00
❑ 5 Fred McGriff	8.00	3.60
❑ 6 Mike Piazza	30.00	13.50
❑ 7 Kirby Puckett	15.00	6.75
❑ 8 Mo Vaughn	10.00	4.50
❑ 9 Frank Thomas	20.00	9.00
❑ 10 Jeff Bagwell	12.00	5.50
❑ 11 Matt Williams	10.00	4.50
❑ 12 Jose Canseco	12.00	5.50
❑ 13 Raul Mondesi	8.00	3.60
❑ 14 Manny Ramirez	12.00	5.50
❑ 15 Cecil Fielder	5.00	2.20
❑ 16 Cal Ripken Jr.	40.00	18.00

1996 Leaf Limited

	MINT	NRMT
COMPLETE SET (90)	50.00	22.00
COMMON CARD (1-90)	.30	.14
MINOR STARS	.50	.23
SEMISTARS	.75	.35
UNLISTED STARS	1.25	.55
COMMON GOLD (1-90)	2.50	1.10
*GOLD: 3X TO 8X HI COLUMN		
GOLD STATED ODDS 1:11		
❑ 1 Ivan Rodriguez	1.50	.70
❑ 2 Roger Clemens	3.00	1.35
❑ 3 Gary Sheffield	.50	.23
❑ 4 Tino Martinez	.50	.23
❑ 5 Sammy Sosa	4.00	1.80
❑ 6 Reggie Sanders	.50	.23
❑ 7 Ray Lankford	.50	.23
❑ 8 Manny Ramirez	1.50	.70
❑ 9 Jeff Bagwell	1.50	.70
❑ 10 Greg Maddux	3.00	1.35
❑ 11 Ken Griffey Jr.	6.00	2.70
❑ 12 Rondell White	.50	.23
❑ 13 Mike Piazza	4.00	1.80
❑ 14 Marc Newfield	.30	.14
❑ 15 Cal Ripken	5.00	2.20
❑ 16 Carlos Delgado	1.25	.55
❑ 17 Tim Salmon	.75	.35
❑ 18 Andres Galarraga	1.25	.55
❑ 19 Chuck Knoblauch	1.25	.55
❑ 20 Matt Williams	1.25	.55
❑ 21 Mark McGwire	6.00	2.70
❑ 22 Ben McDonald	.30	.14
❑ 23 Frank Thomas	2.50	1.10
❑ 24 Johnny Damon	.75	.35
❑ 25 Gregg Jefferies	.30	.14
❑ 26 Travis Fryman	.50	.23
❑ 27 Chipper Jones	3.00	1.35
❑ 28 David Cone	.75	.35
❑ 29 Kenny Lofton	.75	.35
❑ 30 Mike Mussina	1.25	.55
❑ 31 Alex Rodriguez	4.00	1.80
❑ 32 Carlos Baerga	.30	.14
❑ 33 Brian Hunter	.30	.14
❑ 34 Juan Gonzalez	2.50	1.10
❑ 35 Bernie Williams	1.25	.55
❑ 36 Wally Joyner	.50	.23
❑ 37 Fred McGriff	.75	.35
❑ 38 Randy Johnson	1.25	.55
❑ 39 Marty Cordova	.30	.14
❑ 40 Garret Anderson	.50	.23
❑ 41 Albert Belle	1.25	.55
❑ 42 Edgar Martinez	.50	.23
❑ 43 Barry Larkin	1.25	.55
❑ 44 Paul O'Neill	.50	.23
❑ 45 Cecil Fielder	.50	.23
❑ 46 Rusty Greer	.50	.23
❑ 47 Mo Vaughn	1.25	.55
❑ 48 Dante Bichette	.50	.23
❑ 49 Ryan Klesko	.50	.23
❑ 50 Roberto Alomar	1.25	.55
❑ 51 Raul Mondesi	.50	.23
❑ 52 Robin Ventura	.50	.23
❑ 53 Tony Gwynn	3.00	1.35
❑ 54 Mark Grace	.75	.35
❑ 55 Jim Thome	1.25	.55
❑ 56 Jason Giambi	.50	.23

❏ 57 Tom Glavine	1.25	.55
❏ 58 Jim Edmonds	.75	.35
❏ 59 Pedro Martinez	1.50	.70
❏ 60 Charles Johnson	.50	.23
❏ 61 Wade Boggs	1.25	.55
❏ 62 Orlando Merced	.30	.14
❏ 63 Craig Biggio	1.25	.55
❏ 64 Brady Anderson	.50	.23
❏ 65 Hideo Nomo	1.25	.55
❏ 66 Ozzie Smith	1.50	.70
❏ 67 Eddie Murray	1.25	.55
❏ 68 Will Clark	1.25	.55
❏ 69 Jay Buhner	.50	.23
❏ 70 Kirby Puckett	2.00	.90
❏ 71 Barry Bonds	1.50	.70
❏ 72 Ray Durham	.50	.23
❏ 73 Sterling Hitchcock	.30	.14
❏ 74 John Smoltz	.75	.35
❏ 75 Andre Dawson	.75	.35
❏ 76 Joe Carter	.50	.23
❏ 77 Ryne Sandberg	1.50	.70
❏ 78 Rickey Henderson	1.50	.70
❏ 79 Brian Jordan	.50	.23
❏ 80 Greg Vaughn	.50	.23
❏ 81 Andy Pettitte	.75	.35
❏ 82 Dean Palmer	.50	.23
❏ 83 Paul Molitor	1.25	.55
❏ 84 Rafael Palmeiro	1.25	.55
❏ 85 Henry Rodriguez	.50	.23
❏ 86 Larry Walker	1.25	.55
❏ 87 Ismael Valdes	.50	.23
❏ 88 Derek Bell	.50	.23
❏ 89 J.T. Snow	.50	.23
❏ 90 Jack McDowell	.30	.14

1996 Leaf Limited Lumberjacks

	MINT	NRMT
COMPLETE SET (10)	150.00	70.00
COMMON CARD (1-10)	8.00	3.60
RANDOM INSERTS IN PACKS		
STATED PRINT RUN 4500 SERIAL #'d SETS		
*BLACK: 1.5X TO 4X HI COLUMN		
BLACK PRINT RUN 500 SERIAL #'d SETS		

❏ 1 Ken Griffey Jr.	30.00	13.50
❏ 2 Sammy Sosa	20.00	9.00
❏ 3 Cal Ripken	25.00	11.00
❏ 4 Frank Thomas	12.00	5.50
❏ 5 Alex Rodriguez	20.00	9.00
❏ 6 Mo Vaughn	10.00	4.50
❏ 7 Chipper Jones	15.00	6.75
❏ 8 Mike Piazza	20.00	9.00
❏ 9 Jeff Bagwell	8.00	3.60
❏ 10 Mark McGwire	30.00	13.50
❏ P8 Mike Piazza Promo	5.00	2.20

1996 Leaf Limited Pennant Craze

	MINT	NRMT
COMPLETE SET (10)	300.00	135.00
COMMON CARD (1-10)	12.00	5.50
STATED PRINT RUN 2500 SERIAL #'d SETS		

❏ 1 Juan Gonzalez	30.00	13.50

❏ 2 Cal Ripken	50.00	22.00
❏ 3 Frank Thomas	30.00	13.50
❏ 4 Ken Griffey Jr.	60.00	27.00
❏ 5 Albert Belle	12.00	5.50
❏ 6 Greg Maddux	40.00	18.00
❏ 7 Paul Molitor	12.00	5.50
❏ 8 Alex Rodriguez	40.00	18.00
❏ 9 Barry Bonds	12.00	5.50
❏ 10 Chipper Jones	30.00	13.50

1996 Leaf Limited Rookies

	MINT	NRMT
COMPLETE SET (10)	50.00	22.00
COMMON CARD (1-10)	2.50	1.10
UNLISTED STARS	5.00	2.20
STATED ODDS 1:7		
*GOLD: 1X TO 2.5X HI COLUMN		
GOLD: RANDOM INSERTS IN PACKS		

❏ 1 Alex Ochoa	2.50	1.10
❏ 2 Darin Erstad	12.00	5.50
❏ 3 Ruben Rivera	3.00	1.35
❏ 4 Derek Jeter	15.00	6.75
❏ 5 Jermaine Dye	3.00	1.35
❏ 6 Jason Kendall	5.00	2.20
❏ 7 Mike Grace	2.50	1.10
❏ 8 Andruw Jones	8.00	3.60
❏ 9 Rey Ordonez	5.00	2.20
❏ 10 George Arias	2.50	1.10

1996 Leaf Preferred

	MINT	NRMT
COMPLETE SET (150)	25.00	11.00
COMMON CARD (1-150)	.15	.07
MINOR STARS	.30	.14
UNLISTED STARS	.60	.25
SUBSET CARDS HALF VALUE OF BASE CARDS		
COMMON PP (1-150)	5.00	2.20
*PP STARS: 15X TO 40X HI COLUMN		
*PP ROOKIES: 10X TO 25X HI		
PRESS PROOFS: RANDOM INS.IN PACKS		
PP STATED PRINT RUN 500 SETS		

❏ 1 Ken Griffey Jr.	3.00	1.35
❏ 2 Rico Brogna	.15	.07
❏ 3 Gregg Jefferies	.15	.07
❏ 4 Reggie Sanders	.30	.14
❏ 5 Manny Ramirez	.75	.35
❏ 6 Shawn Green	.60	.25
❏ 7 Tino Martinez	.30	.14
❏ 8 Jeff Bagwell	.75	.35
❏ 9 Marc Newfield	.15	.07
❏ 10 Ray Lankford	.30	.14
❏ 11 Jay Bell	.30	.14
❏ 12 Greg Maddux	1.50	.70
❏ 13 Frank Thomas	1.25	.55
❏ 14 Travis Fryman	.30	.14
❏ 15 Mark McGwire	3.00	1.35
❏ 16 Chuck Knoblauch	.60	.25
❏ 17 Sammy Sosa	2.00	.90
❏ 18 Matt Williams	.60	.25
❏ 19 Roger Clemens	1.50	.70
❏ 20 Rondell White	.30	.14
❏ 21 Ivan Rodriguez	.75	.35
❏ 22 Cal Ripken	2.50	1.10
❏ 23 Ben McDonald	.15	.07
❏ 24 Kenny Lofton	.40	.18
❏ 25 Mike Piazza	2.00	.90
❏ 26 David Cone	.40	.18
❏ 27 Gary Sheffield	.30	.14
❏ 28 Tim Salmon	.40	.18
❏ 29 Andres Galarraga	.60	.25
❏ 30 Johnny Damon	.40	.18
❏ 31 Ozzie Smith	.75	.35
❏ 32 Carlos Baerga	.15	.07
❏ 33 Raul Mondesi	.30	.14
❏ 34 Moises Alou	.30	.14
❏ 35 Alex Rodriguez	2.00	.90
❏ 36 Mike Mussina	.60	.25
❏ 37 Jason Isringhausen	.30	.14
❏ 38 Barry Larkin	.60	.25
❏ 39 Bernie Williams	.60	.25
❏ 40 Chipper Jones	1.50	.70
❏ 41 Joey Hamilton	.15	.07
❏ 42 Charles Johnson	.30	.14
❏ 43 Juan Gonzalez	1.25	.55
❏ 44 Greg Vaughn	.30	.14
❏ 45 Robin Ventura	.30	.14
❏ 46 Albert Belle	.60	.25
❏ 47 Rafael Palmeiro	.60	.25
❏ 48 Brian L.Hunter	.15	.07
❏ 49 Mo Vaughn	.60	.25
❏ 50 Paul O'Neill	.30	.14
❏ 51 Mark Grace	.40	.18
❏ 52 Randy Johnson	.60	.25
❏ 53 Pedro Martinez	.75	.35
❏ 54 Marty Cordova	.15	.07
❏ 55 Garret Anderson	.30	.14
❏ 56 Joe Carter	.30	.14
❏ 57 Jim Thome	.60	.25
❏ 58 Edgardo Alfonzo	.30	.14
❏ 59 Dante Bichette	.30	.14
❏ 60 Darryl Hamilton	.15	.07
❏ 61 Roberto Alomar	.60	.25
❏ 62 Fred McGriff	.40	.18
❏ 63 Kirby Puckett	1.00	.45
❏ 64 Hideo Nomo	.60	.25
❏ 65 Alex Fernandez	.15	.07
❏ 66 Ryan Klesko	.30	.14
❏ 67 Wade Boggs	.60	.25
❏ 68 Eddie Murray	.60	.25
❏ 69 Eric Karros	.30	.14
❏ 70 Jim Edmonds	.40	.18
❏ 71 Edgar Martinez	.30	.14
❏ 72 Andy Pettitte	.40	.18
❏ 73 Mark Grudzielanek	.15	.07

❏ 74 Tom Glavine	.60	.25
❏ 75 Ken Caminiti	.30	.14
❏ 76 Will Clark	.60	.25
❏ 77 Craig Biggio	.60	.25
❏ 78 Brady Anderson	.30	.14
❏ 79 Tony Gwynn	1.50	.70
❏ 80 Larry Walker	.60	.25
❏ 81 Brian Jordan	.30	.14
❏ 82 Lenny Dykstra	.30	.14
❏ 83 Butch Huskey	.15	.07
❏ 84 Jack McDowell	.15	.07
❏ 85 Cecil Fielder	.30	.14
❏ 86 Jose Canseco	.75	.35
❏ 87 Jason Giambi	.30	.14
❏ 88 Rickey Henderson	.75	.35
❏ 89 Kevin Seitzer	.15	.07
❏ 90 Carlos Delgado	.60	.25
❏ 91 Ryne Sandberg	.75	.35
❏ 92 Dwight Gooden	.30	.14
❏ 93 Michael Tucker	.15	.07
❏ 94 Barry Bonds	.75	.35
❏ 95 Eric Young	.15	.07
❏ 96 Dean Palmer	.30	.14
❏ 97 Henry Rodriguez	.30	.14
❏ 98 John Mabry	.15	.07
❏ 99 J.T. Snow	.30	.14
❏ 100 Andre Dawson	.40	.18
❏ 101 Ismael Valdes	.30	.14
❏ 102 Charles Nagy	.30	.14
❏ 103 Jay Buhner	.30	.14
❏ 104 Derek Bell	.30	.14
❏ 105 Paul Molitor	.60	.25
❏ 106 Hal Morris	.15	.07
❏ 107 Ray Durham	.15	.07
❏ 108 Bernard Gilkey	.15	.07
❏ 109 John Valentin	.30	.14
❏ 110 Melvin Nieves	.15	.07
❏ 111 John Smoltz	.40	.18
❏ 112 Terrell Wade	.15	.07
❏ 113 Chad Mottola	.15	.07
❏ 114 Tony Clark	.60	.25
❏ 115 John Wasdin	.15	.07
❏ 116 Derek Jeter	2.00	.90
❏ 117 Rey Ordonez	.60	.25
❏ 118 Jason Thompson	.15	.07
❏ 119 Robin Jennings	.15	.07
❏ 120 Rocky Coppinger	.60	.25
❏ 121 Billy Wagner	.40	.18
❏ 122 Steve Gibralter	.15	.07
❏ 123 Jermaine Dye	.30	.14
❏ 124 Jason Kendall	.60	.25
❏ 125 Mike Grace	.15	.07
❏ 126 Jason Schmidt	.15	.07
❏ 127 Paul Wilson	.15	.07
❏ 128 Alan Benes	.15	.07
❏ 129 Justin Thompson	.30	.14
❏ 130 Brooks Kieschnick	.15	.07
❏ 131 George Arias	.15	.07
❏ 132 Osvaldo Fernandez	.15	.07
❏ 133 Todd Hollandsworth	.15	.07
❏ 134 Eric Owens	.15	.07
❏ 135 Chan Ho Park	.40	.18
❏ 136 Mark Loretta	.15	.07
❏ 137 Ruben Rivera	.30	.14
❏ 138 Jeff Suppan	.30	.14
❏ 139 Ugueth Urbina	.30	.14
❏ 140 LaTroy Hawkins	.15	.07
❏ 141 Chris Snopek	.15	.07
❏ 142 Edgar Renteria	.30	.14
❏ 143 Raul Casanova	.15	.07
❏ 144 Jose Herrera	.15	.07
❏ 145 Matt Lawton	.75	.35
❏ 146 Wade Milliard	.15	.07
❏ 147 Frank Thomas CL	.60	.25
❏ 148 Jeff Bagwell CL	.60	.25
❏ 149 Ken Griffey Jr. CL	1.50	.70
❏ 150 Mike Piazza CL	1.00	.45

1996 Leaf Preferred Staremaster

	MINT	NRMT
COMPLETE SET (12)	400.00	180.00
COMMON CARD (1-25)	15.00	6.75
RANDOM INSERTS IN PACKS		

STATED PRINT RUN 2500 SERIAL #'d SETS

❏ 1 Chipper Jones	30.00	13.50
❏ 2 Alex Rodriguez	40.00	18.00
❏ 3 Derek Jeter	30.00	13.50
❏ 4 Tony Gwynn	15.00	6.75
❏ 5 Frank Thomas	30.00	13.50
❏ 6 Ken Griffey Jr.	60.00	27.00
❏ 7 Cal Ripken	50.00	22.00
❏ 8 Greg Maddux	40.00	18.00
❏ 9 Albert Belle	15.00	6.75
❏ 10 Barry Bonds	15.00	6.75
❏ 11 Jeff Bagwell	15.00	6.75
❏ 12 Mike Piazza	40.00	18.00

1996 Leaf Preferred Steel

	MINT	NRMT
COMPLETE SET (77)	120.00	55.00
COMMON CARD (1-77)	.50	.23
MINOR STARS	.75	.35
SEMISTARS	1.25	.55
UNLISTED STARS	2.00	.90
ONE SILVER STEEL PER PACK		
*GOLD STARS: 4X TO 10X HI COLUMN		
GOLD: RANDOM INSERTS IN PACKS		

❏ 1 Frank Thomas	4.00	1.80
❏ 2 Paul Molitor	2.00	.90
❏ 3 Kenny Lofton	1.25	.55
❏ 4 Travis Fryman	.75	.35
❏ 5 Jeff Conine	.50	.23
❏ 6 Barry Bonds	2.50	1.10
❏ 7 Gregg Jefferies	.50	.23
❏ 8 Alex Rodriguez	6.00	2.70
❏ 9 Wade Boggs	2.00	.90
❏ 10 David Justice	2.00	.90
❏ 11 Hideo Nomo	2.00	.90
❏ 12 Roberto Alomar	2.00	.90
❏ 13 Todd Hollandsworth	.50	.23
❏ 14 Mark McGwire	10.00	4.50
❏ 15 Rafael Palmeiro	2.00	.90
❏ 16 Will Clark	2.00	.90
❏ 17 Cal Ripken	8.00	3.60
❏ 18 Derek Bell	.75	.35
❏ 19 Gary Sheffield	.75	.35
❏ 20 Juan Gonzalez	4.00	1.80
❏ 21 Garret Anderson	.75	.35
❏ 22 Mo Vaughn	2.00	.90
❏ 23 Robin Ventura	.75	.35
❏ 24 Carlos Baerga	.50	.23
❏ 25 Tim Salmon	1.25	.55
❏ 26 Matt Williams	2.00	.90
❏ 27 Fred McGriff	1.25	.55
❏ 28 Rondell White	.75	.35
❏ 29 Ray Lankford	.75	.35
❏ 30 Lenny Dykstra	.75	.35
❏ 31 J.T. Snow	.75	.35
❏ 32 Sammy Sosa	6.00	2.70
❏ 33 Chipper Jones	5.00	2.20
❏ 34 Bobby Bonilla	.75	.35
❏ 35 Paul Wilson	.50	.23
❏ 36 Darren Daulton	.75	.35
❏ 37 Larry Walker	2.00	.90
❏ 38 Raul Mondesi	.75	.35
❏ 39 Jeff Bagwell	2.50	1.10
❏ 40 Derek Jeter	6.00	2.70
❏ 41 Kirby Puckett	3.00	1.35
❏ 42 Jason Isringhausen	.75	.35
❏ 43 Vinny Castilla	1.25	.55
❏ 44 Jim Edmonds	1.25	.55
❏ 45 Ron Gant	.50	.23
❏ 46 Carlos Delgado	2.00	.90
❏ 47 Jose Canseco	2.50	1.10
❏ 48 Tony Gwynn	5.00	2.20
❏ 49 Mike Mussina	2.00	.90
❏ 50 Charles Johnson	.75	.35
❏ 51 Mike Piazza	6.00	2.70
❏ 52 Ken Griffey Jr.	10.00	4.50
❏ 53 Greg Maddux	5.00	2.20
❏ 54 Mark Grace	1.25	.55
❏ 55 Ryan Klesko	.75	.35
❏ 56 Dennis Eckersley	.75	.35
❏ 57 Rickey Henderson	2.50	1.10
❏ 58 Michael Tucker	.50	.23
❏ 59 Joe Carter	.75	.35
❏ 60 Randy Johnson	2.00	.90
❏ 61 Brian Jordan	.75	.35
❏ 62 Shawn Green	2.00	.90
❏ 63 Roger Clemens	5.00	2.20
❏ 64 Andres Galarraga	2.00	.90
❏ 65 Johnny Damon	1.25	.55
❏ 66 Ryne Sandberg	2.50	1.10
❏ 67 Alan Benes	.50	.23
❏ 68 Albert Belle	2.00	.90
❏ 69 Barry Larkin	2.00	.90
❏ 70 Marty Cordova	.50	.23
❏ 71 Dante Bichette	.75	.35
❏ 72 Craig Biggio	2.00	.90
❏ 73 Reggie Sanders	.75	.35
❏ 74 Moises Alou	.75	.35
❏ 75 Chuck Knoblauch	2.00	.90
❏ 76 Cecil Fielder	.75	.35
❏ 77 Manny Ramirez	2.50	1.10

1996 Leaf Preferred Steel Power

	MINT	NRMT
COMPLETE SET (8)	150.00	70.00
COMMON CARD (1-8)	10.00	4.50
RANDOM INSERTS IN PACKS		
STATED PRINT RUN 5000 SERIAL #'d SETS		

❏ 1 Albert Belle	10.00	4.50
❏ 2 Mo Vaughn	10.00	4.50
❏ 3 Ken Griffey Jr.	40.00	18.00

		MINT	NRMT
❏ 4	Cal Ripken	30.00	13.50
❏ 5	Mike Piazza	25.00	11.00
❏ 6	Barry Bonds	10.00	4.50
❏ 7	Jeff Bagwell	10.00	4.50
❏ 8	Frank Thomas	20.00	9.00

1998 Leaf Rookies and Stars

	MINT	NRMT
COMPLETE SET (339)	800.00	350.00
COMP.SET w/o SP's (200)	30.00	13.50
COMMON (1-130/231-300)	.15	.07
MINOR STARS	.25	.11
SEMISTARS	.40	.18
UNLISTED STARS	.60	.25
COMMON LO SP (131-230)	.50	.23
LO SP MINOR STARS	.75	.35
LO SP SEMISTARS	1.25	.55
LO SP UNLISTED STARS	2.00	.90
COMMON HI SP (301-339)	2.00	.90
HI SP MINOR STARS	3.00	1.35
SP STATED ODDS 1:2		

❏ 1	Andy Pettitte	.25	.11
❏ 2	Roberto Alomar	.60	.25
❏ 3	Randy Johnson	.60	.25
❏ 4	Manny Ramirez	.75	.35
❏ 5	Paul Molitor	.60	.25
❏ 6	Mike Mussina	.60	.25
❏ 7	Jim Thome	.25	.11
❏ 8	Tino Martinez	.25	.11
❏ 9	Gary Sheffield	.25	.11
❏ 10	Chuck Knoblauch	.25	.11
❏ 11	Bernie Williams	.60	.25
❏ 12	Tim Salmon	.40	.18
❏ 13	Sammy Sosa	2.00	.90
❏ 14	Wade Boggs	.25	.11
❏ 15	Andres Galarraga	.40	.18
❏ 16	Pedro Martinez	.75	.35
❏ 17	David Justice	.25	.11
❏ 18	Chan Ho Park	.25	.11
❏ 19	Jay Buhner	.25	.11
❏ 20	Ryan Klesko	.25	.11
❏ 21	Barry Larkin	.60	.25
❏ 22	Will Clark	.60	.25
❏ 23	Raul Mondesi	.25	.11
❏ 24	Rickey Henderson	.75	.35
❏ 25	Jim Edmonds	.25	.11
❏ 26	Ken Griffey Jr.	3.00	1.35
❏ 27	Frank Thomas	1.25	.55
❏ 28	Cal Ripken	2.50	1.10
❏ 29	Alex Rodriguez	2.00	.90
❏ 30	Mike Piazza	2.00	.90
❏ 31	Greg Maddux	1.50	.70
❏ 32	Chipper Jones	1.50	.70
❏ 33	Tony Gwynn	1.50	.70
❏ 34	Derek Jeter	2.00	.90
❏ 35	Jeff Bagwell	.75	.35
❏ 36	Juan Gonzalez	1.25	.55
❏ 37	Nomar Garciaparra	2.00	.90
❏ 38	Andruw Jones	.60	.25
❏ 39	Hideo Nomo	.25	.11
❏ 40	Roger Clemens	1.50	.70
❏ 41	Mark McGwire	4.00	1.80
❏ 42	Scott Rolen	.75	.35
❏ 43	Vladimir Guerrero	.75	.35
❏ 44	Barry Bonds	.75	.35
❏ 45	Darin Erstad	.40	.18
❏ 46	Albert Belle	.60	.25
❏ 47	Kenny Lofton	.40	.18
❏ 48	Mo Vaughn	.60	.25
❏ 49	Ivan Rodriguez	.75	.35
❏ 50	Jose Cruz Jr.	.25	.11
❏ 51	Tony Clark	.25	.11
❏ 52	Larry Walker	.60	.25
❏ 53	Mark Grace	.40	.18
❏ 54	Edgar Martinez	.25	.11
❏ 55	Fred McGriff	.40	.18
❏ 56	Rafael Palmeiro	.60	.25
❏ 57	Matt Williams	.25	.11
❏ 58	Craig Biggio	.60	.25
❏ 59	Ken Caminiti	.25	.11
❏ 60	Jose Canseco	.75	.35
❏ 61	Brady Anderson	.25	.11
❏ 62	Moises Alou	.25	.11
❏ 63	Justin Thompson	.15	.07
❏ 64	John Smoltz	.40	.18
❏ 65	Carlos Delgado	.60	.25
❏ 66	J.T. Snow	.25	.11
❏ 67	Jason Giambi	.25	.11
❏ 68	Garret Anderson	.25	.11
❏ 69	Rondell White	.25	.11
❏ 70	Eric Karros	.25	.11
❏ 71	Javier Lopez	.25	.11
❏ 72	Pat Hentgen	.15	.07
❏ 73	Dante Bichette	.25	.11
❏ 74	Charles Johnson	.25	.11
❏ 75	Tom Glavine	.60	.25
❏ 76	Rusty Greer	.25	.11
❏ 77	Travis Fryman	.25	.11
❏ 78	Todd Hundley	.25	.11
❏ 79	Ray Lankford	.25	.11
❏ 80	Denny Neagle	.15	.07
❏ 81	Henry Rodriguez	.25	.11
❏ 82	Sandy Alomar Jr.	.25	.11
❏ 83	Robin Ventura	.25	.11
❏ 84	John Olerud	.25	.11
❏ 85	Omar Vizquel	.25	.11
❏ 86	Darren Dreifort	.15	.07
❏ 87	Kevin Brown	.40	.18
❏ 88	Curt Schilling	.40	.18
❏ 89	Francisco Cordova	.15	.07
❏ 90	Brad Radke	.25	.11
❏ 91	David Cone	.40	.18
❏ 92	Paul O'Neill	.25	.11
❏ 93	Vinny Castilla	.25	.11
❏ 94	Marquis Grissom	.15	.07
❏ 95	Brian L. Hunter	.15	.07
❏ 96	Kevin Appier	.25	.11
❏ 97	Bobby Bonilla	.25	.11
❏ 98	Eric Young	.25	.11
❏ 99	Jason Kendall	.25	.11
❏ 100	Shawn Green	.60	.25
❏ 101	Edgardo Alfonzo	.40	.18
❏ 102	Alan Benes	.25	.11
❏ 103	Bobby Higginson	.25	.11
❏ 104	Todd Greene	.15	.07
❏ 105	Jose Guillen	.15	.07
❏ 106	Neifi Perez	.25	.11
❏ 107	Edgar Renteria	.15	.07
❏ 108	Chris Stynes	.15	.07
❏ 109	Todd Walker	.25	.11
❏ 110	Brian Jordan	.25	.11
❏ 111	Joe Carter	.25	.11
❏ 112	Ellis Burks	.25	.11
❏ 113	Brett Tomko	.15	.07
❏ 114	Mike Cameron	.25	.11
❏ 115	Shannon Stewart	.25	.11
❏ 116	Kevin Orie	.15	.07
❏ 117	Brian Giles	.25	.11
❏ 118	Hideki Irabu	.25	.11
❏ 119	Delino DeShields	.15	.07
❏ 120	David Segui	.15	.07
❏ 121	Dustin Hermanson	.15	.07
❏ 122	Kevin Young	.25	.11
❏ 123	Jay Bell	.25	.11
❏ 124	Doug Glanville	.25	.11
❏ 125	John Roskos	.50	.23
❏ 126	Damon Hollins	.25	.11
❏ 127	Matt Stairs	.25	.11
❏ 128	Cliff Floyd	.25	.11
❏ 129	Derek Bell	.25	.11
❏ 130	Darryl Strawberry	.25	.11
❏ 131	Ken Griffey Jr. PT SP	10.00	4.50
❏ 132	Tim Salmon PT SP	1.25	.55
❏ 133	Manny Ramirez PT SP	2.50	1.10
❏ 134	Paul Konerko PT SP	.75	.35
❏ 135	Frank Thomas PT SP	4.00	1.80
❏ 136	Todd Helton PT SP	2.50	1.10
❏ 137	Larry Walker PT SP	2.00	.90
❏ 138	Mo Vaughn PT SP	2.00	.90
❏ 139	Travis Lee PT SP	1.25	.55
❏ 140	Ivan Rodriguez PT SP	2.50	1.10
❏ 141	Ben Grieve PT SP	2.00	.90
❏ 142	Brad Fullmer PT SP	.50	.23
❏ 143	Alex Rodriguez PT SP	6.00	2.70
❏ 144	Mike Piazza PT SP	6.00	2.70
❏ 145	Greg Maddux PT SP	5.00	2.20
❏ 146	Chipper Jones PT SP	5.00	2.20
❏ 147	Kenny Lofton PT SP	1.25	.55
❏ 148	Albert Belle PT SP	2.00	.90
❏ 149	Barry Bonds PT SP	2.50	1.10
❏ 150	Vladimir Guerrero PT SP	2.50	1.10
❏ 151	Tony Gwynn PT SP	5.00	2.20
❏ 152	Derek Jeter PT SP	6.00	2.70
❏ 153	Jeff Bagwell PT SP	2.50	1.10
❏ 154	Juan Gonzalez PT SP	4.00	1.80
❏ 155	Nomar Garciaparra PT SP	6.00	2.70
❏ 156	Andruw Jones PT SP	2.00	.90
❏ 157	Hideo Nomo PT SP	.50	.23
❏ 158	Roger Clemens PT SP	5.00	2.20
❏ 159	Mark McGwire PT SP	12.00	5.50
❏ 160	Scott Rolen PT SP	2.50	1.10
❏ 161	Travis Lee TLU SP	1.25	.55
❏ 162	Ben Grieve TLU SP	2.00	.90
❏ 163	Jose Guillen TLU SP	.50	.23
❏ 164	Mike Piazza TLU SP	6.00	2.70
❏ 165	Kevin Appier TLU SP	.75	.35
❏ 166	Marquis Grissom TLU SP	.50	.23
❏ 167	Rusty Greer TLU SP	.75	.35
❏ 168	Ken Caminiti TLU SP	.75	.35
❏ 169	Craig Biggio TLU SP	2.00	.90
❏ 170	Ken Griffey Jr. TLU SP	10.00	4.50
❏ 171	Larry Walker TLU SP	2.00	.90
❏ 172	Barry Larkin TLU SP	2.00	.90
❏ 173	Andres Galarraga TLU SP	1.25	.55
❏ 174	Wade Boggs TLU SP	2.00	.90
❏ 175	Sammy Sosa TLU SP	6.00	2.70
❏ 176	Todd Dunwoody TLU SP	.50	.23
❏ 177	Jim Thome TLU SP	2.00	.90
❏ 178	Paul Molitor TLU SP	2.00	.90
❏ 179	Tony Clark TLU SP	.75	.35
❏ 180	Jose Cruz Jr. TLU SP	.75	.35
❏ 181	Darin Erstad TLU SP	1.25	.55
❏ 182	Barry Bonds TLU SP	2.50	1.10
❏ 183	Vladimir Guerrero TLU SP	2.50	1.10
❏ 184	Scott Rolen TLU SP	2.50	1.10
❏ 185	Mark McGwire TLU SP	12.00	5.50
❏ 186	Nomar Garciaparra TLU SP	6.00	2.70
❏ 187	Gary Sheffield TLU SP	.75	.35
❏ 188	Cal Ripken TLU SP	8.00	3.60
❏ 189	Frank Thomas TLU SP	4.00	1.80
❏ 190	Andy Pettitte TLU SP	.75	.35
❏ 191	Paul Konerko SP	.75	.35
❏ 192	Todd Helton SP	2.50	1.10
❏ 193	Mark Kotsay SP	.75	.35
❏ 194	Brad Fullmer SP	.50	.23
❏ 195	Kevin Millwood SP	40.00	18.00
❏ 196	David Ortiz SP	.50	.23
❏ 197	Kerry Wood SP	2.00	.90
❏ 198	Miguel Tejada SP	.75	.35
❏ 199	Fernando Tatis SP	2.00	.90
❏ 200	Jaret Wright SP	.75	.35
❏ 201	Ben Grieve SP	2.00	.90
❏ 202	Travis Lee SP	1.25	.55
❏ 203	Wes Helms SP	.50	.23
❏ 204	Geoff Jenkins SP	.75	.35
❏ 205	Russell Branyan SP	.75	.35
❏ 206	Esteban Yan SP	4.00	1.80
❏ 207	Ben Ford SP	2.50	1.10
❏ 208	Rich Butler SP	4.00	1.80
❏ 209	Ryan Jackson SP	.50	.23
❏ 210	A.J. Hinch SP	.50	.23
❏ 211	Maggio Ordonez SP	40.00	18.00
❏ 212	Dave Dellucci SP	5.00	2.20
❏ 213	Billy McMillon SP	.50	.23
❏ 214	Mike Lowell SP	8.00	3.60

❏ 215 Todd Erdos SP	2.50	1.10
❏ 216 Carlos Mendoza SP	2.50	1.10
❏ 217 Frank Catalanotto SP	2.50	1.10
❏ 218 Julio Ramirez SP	20.00	9.00
❏ 219 John Halama SP	12.00	5.50
❏ 220 Wilson Delgado SP	.50	.23
❏ 221 Mike Judd SP	5.00	2.20
❏ 222 Rolando Arrojo SP	8.00	3.60
❏ 223 Jason LaRue SP	8.00	3.60
❏ 224 Manny Aybar SP	2.50	1.10
❏ 225 Jorge Velandia SP	.50	.23
❏ 226 Mike Kinkade SP	4.00	1.80
❏ 227 Carlos Lee SP	25.00	11.00
❏ 228 Bobby Hughes SP	.50	.23
❏ 229 Ryan Christenson SP	2.50	1.10
❏ 230 Masato Yoshii SP	4.00	1.80
❏ 231 Richard Hidalgo	.15	.11
❏ 232 Rafael Medina	.15	.07
❏ 233 Damian Jackson	.15	.07
❏ 234 Derek Lowe	.15	.07
❏ 235 Mario Valdez	.15	.07
❏ 236 Eli Marrero	.25	.11
❏ 237 Juan Encarnacion	.25	.11
❏ 238 Livan Hernandez	.25	.11
❏ 239 Bruce Chen	.25	.11
❏ 240 Eric Milton	.15	.07
❏ 241 Jason Varitek	.25	.11
❏ 242 Scott Elarton	.15	.07
❏ 243 Manuel Barrios	.15	.07
❏ 244 Mike Caruso	.15	.07
❏ 245 Tom Evans	.15	.07
❏ 246 Pat Cline	.15	.07
❏ 247 Matt Clement	.40	.18
❏ 248 Karim Garcia	.15	.07
❏ 249 Richie Sexson	.40	.18
❏ 250 Sidney Ponson	.25	.11
❏ 251 Randall Simon	.25	.11
❏ 252 Tony Saunders	.15	.07
❏ 253 Javier Valentin	.15	.07
❏ 254 Danny Clyburn	.15	.07
❏ 255 Michael Coleman	.25	.11
❏ 256 Hanley Frias	.15	.07
❏ 257 Miguel Cairo	.15	.07
❏ 258 Rob Stanifer	.15	.07
❏ 259 Lou Collier	.15	.07
❏ 260 Abraham Nunez	.15	.07
❏ 261 Ricky Ledee	.25	.11
❏ 262 Carl Pavano	.15	.07
❏ 263 Derek Lee	.15	.07
❏ 264 Jeff Abbott	.15	.07
❏ 265 Bob Abreu	.25	.11
❏ 266 Bartolo Colon	.25	.11
❏ 267 Mike Drumright	.15	.07
❏ 268 Daryle Ward	.15	.11
❏ 269 Gabe Alvarez	.15	.07
❏ 270 Josh Booty	.15	.07
❏ 271 Damian Moss	.15	.07
❏ 272 Brian Rose	.15	.07
❏ 273 Jarrod Washburn	.15	.07
❏ 274 Bobby Estalella	.15	.07
❏ 275 Enrique Wilson	.15	.07
❏ 276 Derrick Gibson	.15	.11
❏ 277 Ken Cloude	.15	.07
❏ 278 Kevin Witt	.15	.07
❏ 279 Donnie Sadler	.15	.07
❏ 280 Sean Casey	1.00	.45
❏ 281 Jacob Cruz	.15	.07
❏ 282 Ron Wright	.15	.07
❏ 283 Jeremi Gonzalez	.15	.07
❏ 284 Desi Relaford	.15	.07
❏ 285 Bobby Smith	.15	.07
❏ 286 Javier Vazquez	.15	.07
❏ 287 Steve Woodard	.15	.07
❏ 288 Greg Norton	.15	.07
❏ 289 Cliff Politte	.15	.07
❏ 290 Felix Heredia	.15	.07
❏ 291 Braden Looper	.15	.07
❏ 292 Felix Martinez	.15	.07
❏ 293 Brian Meadows	.15	.07
❏ 294 Edwin Diaz	.15	.07
❏ 295 Pat Watkins	.15	.07
❏ 296 Marc Pisciotta	.15	.07
❏ 297 Rick Gorecki	.15	.07
❏ 298 DaRond Stovall	.15	.07
❏ 299 Andy Larkin	.15	.07
❏ 300 Felix Rodriguez	.15	.07

❏ 301 Blake Stein SP	2.00	.90
❏ 302 John Rocker SP	20.00	9.00
❏ 303 Justin Baughman SP	4.00	1.80
❏ 304 Jesus Sanchez SP	4.00	1.80
❏ 305 Randy Winn SP	2.00	.90
❏ 306 Lou Merloni SP	2.00	.90
❏ 307 Jim Parque SP	5.00	2.20
❏ 308 Dennis Reyes SP	2.00	.90
❏ 309 Orlando Hernandez SP	25.00	11.00
❏ 310 Jason Johnson SP	2.00	.90
❏ 311 Torii Hunter SP	2.00	.90
❏ 312 Mike Piazza Marlins SP	20.00	9.00
❏ 313 Mike Frank SP	5.00	2.20
❏ 314 Troy Glaus SP	80.00	36.00
❏ 315 Jin Ho Cho SP	10.00	4.50
❏ 316 Ruben Mateo SP	50.00	22.00
❏ 317 Ryan Minor SP	60.00	27.00
❏ 318 Aramis Ramirez SP	5.00	2.20
❏ 319 Adrian Beltre SP	6.00	2.70
❏ 320 Matt Anderson SP	5.00	2.20
❏ 321 Gabe Kapler SP	50.00	22.00
❏ 322 Jeremy Giambi SP	15.00	6.75
❏ 323 Carlos Beltran SP	10.00	4.50
❏ 324 Dermal Brown SP	3.00	1.35
❏ 325 Ben Davis SP	6.00	2.70
❏ 326 Eric Chavez SP	5.00	2.20
❏ 327 Bob Howry SP	5.00	2.20
❏ 328 Roy Halladay SP	3.00	1.35
❏ 329 George Lombard SP	5.00	2.20
❏ 330 Michael Barrett SP	5.00	2.20
❏ 331 Fernando Seguignol SP	15.00	6.75
❏ 332 J.D. Drew SP	100.00	45.00
❏ 333 Odalis Perez SP	10.00	4.50
❏ 334 Alex Cora SP	4.00	1.80
❏ 335 Placido Polanco SP	4.00	1.80
❏ 336 Armando Rios SP	5.00	2.20
❏ 337 Sammy Sosa HR SP	20.00	9.00
❏ 338 Mark McGwire HR SP	30.00	13.50
❏ 339 Sammy Sosa	25.00	11.00
Mark McGwire CL SP		

1998 Leaf Rookies and Stars Longevity

	MINT	NRMT
COMMON CARD (1-339)	15.00	6.75

*STARS 1-130/231-300: 40X TO 100X BASIC
*YOUNG 1-130/231-300: 30X TO 80X BASIC
*ROOKIES 1-130/231-300: 20X TO 50X BASIC
*LO SP STARS 131-190: 5X TO 12X BASIC
*LO SP YNG.131-190: 4X TO 10X BASIC
*LO SP YNG.191-230: 6X TO 15X BASIC
*LO SP RC's 191-230: 1.25X TO 3X BASIC
*HI SP STARS 301-339: 4X TO 10X BASIC
*HI SP PROSP 301-339: 2.5X TO 6X BASIC
*HI SP RC'S 301-339: 1.25X TO 3X BASIC
RANDOM INSERTS IN PACKS
STATED PRINT RUN 50 SERIAL #'d SETS
LONGEVITY HOLOGRAPHIC 1 OF 1 SET
EXISTS

1998 Leaf Rookies and Stars True Blue

	MINT	NRMT
COMMON CARD (1-339)	3.00	1.35

*STARS 1-130/231-300: 8X TO 20X BASIC
*YOUNG 1-130/231-300: 6X TO 15X BASIC
*ROOKIES 1-130/231-300: 3X TO 8X BASIC
*LO SP STARS 131-190: .75X TO 2X BASIC
*LO SP YNG.131-190: .5X TO 1.25X BASIC
*LO SP YNG.191-230: .1X TO 2.5X BASIC
*LO SP RC's 191-230: .3X TO .8X BASIC
*HI SP STARS 301-339: .75X TO 2X BASIC
*HI SP PROSP 301-339: .4X TO 1X BASIC
*HI SP RC's 301-339: .3X TO .8X BASIC
RANDOM INSERTS IN PACKS
STATED PRINT RUN 500 SETS

1998 Leaf Rookies and Stars Crosstraining

	MINT	NRMT
COMPLETE SET (10)	200.00	90.00
COMMON CARD (1-10)	6.00	2.70
RANDOM INSERTS IN PACKS
STATED PRINT RUN 1000 SERIAL #'d SETS

❏ 1 Kenny Lofton	6.00	2.70
❏ 2 Ken Griffey Jr.	50.00	22.00
❏ 3 Alex Rodriguez	30.00	13.50
❏ 4 Greg Maddux	25.00	11.00
❏ 5 Barry Bonds	12.00	5.50
❏ 6 Ivan Rodriguez	12.00	5.50
❏ 7 Chipper Jones	25.00	11.00
❏ 8 Jeff Bagwell	12.00	5.50
❏ 9 Nomar Garciaparra	30.00	13.50
❏ 10 Derek Jeter	30.00	13.50

1998 Leaf Rookies and Stars Crusade Update Green

	MINT	NRMT
COMPLETE SET (30)	300.00	135.00
COMMON CARD (101-130)	6.00	2.70
MINOR STARS	10.00	4.50
SEMISTARS	15.00	6.75
*PURPLE STARS: .6X TO 1.5X GREEN HI
*RED STARS: 1.5X TO 4X GREEN HI
GREEN PRINT RUN 250 SERIAL #'d SETS
PURPLE PRINT RUN 100 SERIAL #'d SETS
RED PRINT RUN 25 SERIAL #'d SETS
RANDOM INSERTS IN PACKS

		MINT	NRMT
❏ 101	Richard Hidalgo	10.00	4.50
❏ 102	Paul Konerko	10.00	4.50
❏ 103	Miguel Tejada	10.00	4.50
❏ 104	Fernando Tatis	25.00	11.00
❏ 105	Travis Lee	15.00	6.75
❏ 106	Wes Helms	6.00	2.70
❏ 107	Rich Butler	15.00	6.75
❏ 108	Mark Kotsay	10.00	4.50
❏ 109	Eli Marrero	6.00	2.70
❏ 110	David Ortiz	6.00	2.70
❏ 111	Juan Encarnacion	10.00	4.50
❏ 112	Jaret Wright	10.00	4.50
❏ 113	Livan Hernandez	6.00	2.70
❏ 114	Ron Wright	6.00	2.70
❏ 115	Ryan Christenson	10.00	4.50
❏ 116	Eric Milton	6.00	2.70
❏ 117	Brad Fullmer	6.00	2.70
❏ 118	Karim Garcia	6.00	2.70
❏ 119	Abraham Nunez	6.00	2.70
❏ 120	Ricky Ledee	10.00	4.50
❏ 121	Carl Pavano	6.00	2.70
❏ 122	Derrek Lee	6.00	2.70
❏ 123	A.J. Hinch	6.00	2.70
❏ 124	Brian Rose	6.00	2.70
❏ 125	Bobby Estalella	6.00	2.70
❏ 126	Kevin Millwood	40.00	18.00
❏ 127	Kerry Wood	25.00	11.00
❏ 128	Sean Casey	30.00	13.50
❏ 129	Russell Branyan	10.00	4.50
❏ 130	Magglio Ordonez	40.00	18.00

1998 Leaf Rookies and Stars Extreme Measures

		MINT	NRMT
COMPLETE SET (10)		250.00	110.00
COMMON CARD (1-10)		12.00	5.50
RANDOM INSERTS IN PACKS			
PRINT RUNS LISTED BELOW			
❏ 1	Ken Griffey Jr./944	50.00	22.00
❏ 2	Frank Thomas/653	25.00	11.00
❏ 3	Tony Gwynn	30.00	13.50
❏ 4	Mark McGwire/942	60.00	27.00
❏ 5	Larry Walker/280	20.00	9.00
❏ 6	Mike Piazza/960	30.00	13.50
❏ 7	Roger Clemens/706	30.00	13.50
❏ 8	Greg Maddux/980	25.00	11.00
❏ 9	Jeff Bagwell/873	12.00	5.50
❏ 10	Nomar Garciaparra/989	30.00	13.50

1998 Leaf Rookies and Stars Extreme Measures Die Cuts

		MINT	NRMT
RANDOM INSERTS IN PACKS			
PRINT RUNS LISTED BELOW			
❏ 1	Ken Griffey Jr./56	300.00	135.00
❏ 2	Frank Thomas/347	40.00	18.00
❏ 3	Tony Gwynn/372	50.00	22.00
❏ 4	Mark McGwire/58	400.00	180.00
❏ 5	Larry Walker/720	12.00	5.50
❏ 6	Mike Piazza/40	200.00	90.00
❏ 7	Roger Clemens/292	50.00	22.00
❏ 8	Greg Maddux/20		
❏ 9	Jeff Bagwell/127	50.00	22.00
❏ 10	Nomar Garciaparra/11		

1998 Leaf Rookies and Stars Freshman Orientation

		MINT	NRMT
COMPLETE SET (20)		30.00	13.50
COMMON CARD (1-20)		1.00	.45
SEMISTARS		1.50	.70
UNLISTED STARS		2.50	1.10
RANDOM INSERTS IN PACKS			
STATED PRINT RUN 5000 SERIAL #'d SETS			
❏ 1	Todd Helton	3.00	1.35
❏ 2	Ben Grieve	2.50	1.10
❏ 3	Travis Lee	1.50	.70
❏ 4	Paul Konerko	1.50	.70
❏ 5	Jaret Wright	1.50	.70
❏ 6	Livan Hernandez	1.00	.45
❏ 7	Brad Fullmer	1.00	.45
❏ 8	Carl Pavano	1.00	.45
❏ 9	Richard Hidalgo	1.50	.70
❏ 10	Miguel Tejada	1.50	.70
❏ 11	Mark Kotsay	1.50	.70
❏ 12	David Ortiz	1.00	.45
❏ 13	Juan Encarnacion	1.50	.70
❏ 14	Fernando Tatis	2.50	1.10
❏ 15	Kevin Millwood	6.00	2.70
❏ 16	Kerry Wood	2.50	1.10
❏ 17	Magglio Ordonez	6.00	2.70
❏ 18	Derrek Lee	1.00	.45
❏ 19	Jose Cruz Jr.	1.50	.70
❏ 20	A.J. Hinch	1.00	.45

1998 Leaf Rookies and Stars Great American Heroes

		MINT	NRMT
COMPLETE SET (20)		150.00	70.00
COMMON CARD (1-20)		3.00	1.35
RANDOM INSERTS IN PACKS			
STATED PRINT RUN 2500 SERIAL #'d SETS			
THREE DIFT.PIAZZA VERSIONS EXIST			
PIAZZA PRINT RUNS: 2500 OF EACH			
ALL THREE PIAZZA'S VALUED EQUALLY			
❏ 1	Frank Thomas	10.00	4.50
❏ 2	Cal Ripken	20.00	9.00
❏ 3	Ken Griffey Jr.	25.00	11.00
❏ 4	Alex Rodriguez	15.00	6.75
❏ 5	Greg Maddux	12.00	5.50
❏ 6	Mike Piazza Dodgers	15.00	6.75
❏ 6B	Mike Piazza Marlins	15.00	6.75
❏ 6C	Mike Piazza Mets	15.00	6.75
❏ 7	Chipper Jones	12.00	5.50
❏ 8	Tony Gwynn	12.00	5.50
❏ 9	Jeff Bagwell	6.00	2.70
❏ 10	Juan Gonzalez	10.00	4.50
❏ 11	Hideo Nomo	5.00	2.20
❏ 12	Roger Clemens	12.00	5.50
❏ 13	Mark McGwire	30.00	13.50
❏ 14	Barry Bonds	6.00	2.70
❏ 15	Kenny Lofton	3.00	1.35
❏ 16	Larry Walker	5.00	2.20
❏ 17	Paul Molitor	5.00	2.20
❏ 18	Wade Boggs	5.00	2.20
❏ 19	Barry Larkin	5.00	2.20
❏ 20	Andres Galarraga	3.00	1.35

1998 Leaf Rookies and Stars Greatest Hits

		MINT	NRMT
COMPLETE SET (20)		150.00	70.00
COMMON CARD (1-20)		2.00	.90
RANDOM INSERTS IN PACKS			
STATED PRINT RUN 2500 SERIAL #'d SETS			

		MINT	NRMT
❑ 1	Ken Griffey Jr.	25.00	11.00
❑ 2	Frank Thomas	10.00	4.50
❑ 3	Cal Ripken	20.00	9.00
❑ 4	Alex Rodriguez	15.00	6.75
❑ 5	Ben Grieve	5.00	2.20
❑ 6	Mike Piazza	15.00	6.75
❑ 7	Chipper Jones	12.00	5.50
❑ 8	Tony Gwynn	12.00	5.50
❑ 9	Derek Jeter	15.00	6.75
❑ 10	Jeff Bagwell	6.00	2.70
❑ 11	Tino Martinez	2.00	.90
❑ 12	Juan Gonzalez	10.00	4.50
❑ 13	Nomar Garciaparra	15.00	6.75
❑ 14	Mark McGwire	30.00	13.50
❑ 15	Scott Rolen	8.00	3.60
❑ 16	David Justice	2.00	.90
❑ 17	Darin Erstad	3.00	1.35
❑ 18	Mo Vaughn	5.00	2.20
❑ 19	Ivan Rodriguez	6.00	2.70
❑ 20	Travis Lee	3.00	1.35

1998 Leaf Rookies and Stars Home Run Derby

	MINT	NRMT
COMPLETE SET (20)	120.00	55.00
COMMON CARD (1-20)	2.00	.90

RANDOM INSERTS IN PACKS
STATED PRINT RUN 2500 SERIAL #'d SETS

		MINT	NRMT
❑ 1	Tino Martinez	2.00	.90
❑ 2	Jim Thome	5.00	2.20
❑ 3	Larry Walker	5.00	2.20
❑ 4	Tony Clark	2.00	.90
❑ 5	Jose Cruz Jr.	2.00	.90
❑ 6	Barry Bonds	6.00	2.70
❑ 7	Scott Rolen	8.00	3.60
❑ 8	Paul Konerko	2.00	.90
❑ 9	Travis Lee	3.00	1.35
❑ 10	Todd Helton	5.00	2.20
❑ 11	Mark McGwire	30.00	13.50
❑ 12	Andruw Jones	5.00	2.20
❑ 13	Nomar Garciaparra	15.00	6.75
❑ 14	Juan Gonzalez	10.00	4.50
❑ 15	Jeff Bagwell	6.00	2.70
❑ 16	Chipper Jones	12.00	5.50
❑ 17	Mike Piazza	15.00	6.75
❑ 18	Frank Thomas	10.00	4.50
❑ 19	Ken Griffey Jr.	25.00	11.00
❑ 20	Albert Belle	5.00	2.20

1998 Leaf Rookies and Stars Leaf MVP's

	MINT	NRMT
COMPLETE SET (20)	100.00	45.00
COMMON CARD (1-20)	1.25	.55

RANDOM INSERTS IN PACKS
STATED PRINT RUN 5000 SERIAL #'d SETS
*PENNANT ED: 8X TO 20X BASE CARD HI
PENNANT ED.1ST 500 SERIAL #'d SETS
RANDOM INSERTS IN PACKS

		MINT	NRMT
❑ 1	Frank Thomas	6.00	2.70
❑ 2	Chuck Knoblauch	1.25	.55
❑ 3	Cal Ripken	12.00	5.50
❑ 4	Alex Rodriguez	10.00	4.50

		MINT	NRMT
❑ 5	Ivan Rodriguez	4.00	1.80
❑ 6	Albert Belle	3.00	1.35
❑ 7	Ken Griffey Jr.	15.00	6.75
❑ 8	Juan Gonzalez	6.00	2.70
❑ 9	Roger Clemens	8.00	3.60
❑ 10	Mo Vaughn	3.00	1.35
❑ 11	Jeff Bagwell	4.00	1.80
❑ 12	Craig Biggio	3.00	1.35
❑ 13	Chipper Jones	8.00	3.60
❑ 14	Barry Larkin	3.00	1.35
❑ 15	Mike Piazza	10.00	4.50
❑ 16	Barry Bonds	4.00	1.80
❑ 17	Andruw Jones	3.00	1.35
❑ 18	Tony Gwynn	8.00	3.60
❑ 19	Greg Maddux	8.00	3.60
❑ 20	Mark McGwire	20.00	9.00

1998 Leaf Rookies and Stars Major League Hard Drives

	MINT	NRMT
COMPLETE SET (20)	150.00	70.00
COMMON CARD (1-20)	1.25	.55

RANDOM INSERTS IN PACKS
STATED PRINT RUN 2500 SERIAL #'d SETS
THREE DIFT.PIAZZA VERSIONS EXIST
PIAZZA PRINT RUNS: 2500 OF EACH
ALL THREE PIAZZA'S VALUED EQUALLY

		MINT	NRMT
❑ 1	Jeff Bagwell	6.00	2.70
❑ 2	Juan Gonzalez	10.00	4.50
❑ 3	Nomar Garciaparra	15.00	6.75
❑ 4	Ken Griffey Jr.	25.00	11.00
❑ 5	Frank Thomas	10.00	4.50
❑ 6	Cal Ripken	20.00	9.00
❑ 7	Alex Rodriguez	15.00	6.75
❑ 8A	Mike Piazza Dodgers	15.00	6.75
❑ 8B	Mike Piazza Marlins	15.00	6.75
❑ 8C	Mike Piazza Mets	15.00	6.75
❑ 9	Chipper Jones	12.00	5.50
❑ 10	Tony Gwynn	12.00	5.50
❑ 11	Derek Jeter	15.00	6.75
❑ 12	Mo Vaughn	5.00	2.20
❑ 13	Ben Grieve	5.00	2.20
❑ 14	Manny Ramirez	6.00	2.70
❑ 15	Vladimir Guerrero	6.00	2.70
❑ 16	Scott Rolen	8.00	3.60
❑ 17	Darin Erstad	3.00	1.35
❑ 18	Kenny Lofton	3.00	1.35
❑ 19	Brad Fullmer	1.25	.55
❑ 20	David Justice	2.00	.90

1998 Leaf Rookies and Stars Standing Ovations

	MINT	NRMT
COMPLETE SET (10)	60.00	27.00
COMMON CARD (1-10)	3.00	1.35

RANDOM INSERTS IN PACKS
STATED PRINT RUN 5000 SERIAL #'d SETS

		MINT	NRMT
❑ 1	Barry Bonds	4.00	1.80
❑ 2	Mark McGwire	20.00	9.00
❑ 3	Ken Griffey Jr.	15.00	6.75
❑ 4	Frank Thomas	6.00	2.70
❑ 5	Tony Gwynn	8.00	3.60
❑ 6	Cal Ripken	12.00	5.50
❑ 7	Greg Maddux	8.00	3.60
❑ 8	Roger Clemens	8.00	3.60
❑ 9	Paul Molitor	3.00	1.35
❑ 10	Ivan Rodriguez	4.00	1.80

1998 Leaf Rookies and Stars Ticket Masters

	MINT	NRMT
COMPLETE SET (20)	200.00	90.00
COMMON CARD (1-20)	2.50	1.10
SEMISTARS	4.00	1.80
UNLISTED STARS	6.00	2.70

STATED PRINT RUN 2500 SERIAL #'d SETS
*DIE CUTS: 1.25X TO 3X HI COLUMN
DIE CUTS 1ST 250 SERIAL #'d SETS
RANDOM INSERTS IN PACKS

		MINT	NRMT
❑ 1	Ken Griffey Jr. / Alex Rodriguez	30.00	13.50
❑ 2	Frank Thomas / Albert Belle	12.00	5.50
❑ 3	Cal Ripken / Roberto Alomar	25.00	11.00
❑ 4	Greg Maddux / Chipper Jones	15.00	6.75
❑ 5	Tony Gwynn / Ken Caminiti	15.00	6.75
❑ 6	Derek Jeter / Andy Pettitte	20.00	9.00
❑ 7	Jeff Bagwell / Craig Biggio	8.00	3.60

		MINT	NRMT
❏ 8	Juan Gonzalez	12.00	5.50
	Ivan Rodriguez		
❏ 9	Nomar Garciaparra	20.00	9.00
	Mo Vaughn		
❏ 10	Vladimir Guerrero	8.00	3.60
	Brad Fullmer		
❏ 11	Andruw Jones	6.00	2.70
	Andres Galarraga		
❏ 12	Tino Martinez	2.50	1.10
	Chuck Knoblauch		
❏ 13	Raul Mondesi	2.50	1.10
	Paul Konerko		
❏ 14	Roger Clemens	15.00	6.75
	Jose Cruz Jr.		
❏ 15	Mark McGwire	40.00	18.00
	Brian Jordan		
❏ 16	Kenny Lofton	8.00	3.60
	Manny Ramirez		
❏ 17	Larry Walker	6.00	2.70
	Todd Helton		
❏ 18	Darin Erstad	4.00	1.80
	Tim Salmon		
❏ 19	Travis Lee	6.00	2.70
	Matt Williams		
❏ 20	Ben Grieve	10.00	4.50
	Jason Giambi		

1996 Leaf Signature

	MINT	NRMT
COMPLETE SET (150)	100.00	45.00
COMPLETE SERIES 1 (100)	60.00	27.00
COMMON CARD (1-100)	.25	.11
SERIES 1 MINOR STARS	.50	.23
SERIES 1 UNLISTED STARS	1.00	.45
COMPLETE SERIES 2 (50)	40.00	18.00
COMMON CARD (101-150)	.25	.11
SERIES 2 MINOR STARS	1.00	.45
SERIES 2 UNLISTED STARS	2.00	.90

❏ 1	Mike Piazza	3.00	1.35
❏ 2	Juan Gonzalez	2.00	.90
❏ 3	Greg Maddux	2.50	1.10
❏ 4	Marc Newfield	.25	.11
❏ 5	Wade Boggs	1.00	.45
❏ 6	Ray Lankford	.50	.23
❏ 7	Frank Thomas	2.00	.90
❏ 8	Rico Brogna	.25	.11
❏ 9	Tim Salmon	.75	.35
❏ 10	Ken Griffey Jr.	5.00	2.20
❏ 11	Manny Ramirez	1.25	.55
❏ 12	Cecil Fielder	.50	.23
❏ 13	Gregg Jefferies	.25	.11
❏ 14	Rondell White	.50	.23
❏ 15	Cal Ripken	4.00	1.80
❏ 16	Alex Rodriguez	3.00	1.35
❏ 17	Bernie Williams	1.00	.45
❏ 18	Andres Galarraga	1.00	.45
❏ 19	Mike Mussina	1.00	.45
❏ 20	Chuck Knoblauch	1.00	.45
❏ 21	Joe Carter	.50	.23
❏ 22	Jeff Bagwell	1.25	.55
❏ 23	Mark McGwire	5.00	2.20
❏ 24	Sammy Sosa	3.00	1.35
❏ 25	Reggie Sanders	.50	.23
❏ 26	Chipper Jones	2.50	1.10
❏ 27	Jeff Cirillo	.50	.23
❏ 28	Roger Clemens	2.50	1.10
❏ 29	Craig Biggio	1.00	.45
❏ 30	Gary Sheffield	.50	.23
❏ 31	Paul O'Neill	.50	.23
❏ 32	Johnny Damon	.75	.35
❏ 33	Jason Isringhausen	.50	.23
❏ 34	Jay Bell	.50	.23
❏ 35	Henry Rodriguez	.50	.23
❏ 36	Matt Williams	1.00	.45
❏ 37	Randy Johnson	1.00	.45
❏ 38	Fred McGriff	.75	.35
❏ 39	Jason Giambi	.50	.23
❏ 40	Ivan Rodriguez	1.25	.55
❏ 41	Raul Mondesi	.50	.23
❏ 42	Barry Larkin	1.00	.45
❏ 43	Ryan Klesko	.50	.23
❏ 44	Joey Hamilton	.25	.11
❏ 45	Todd Hundley	.50	.23
❏ 46	Jim Edmonds	.75	.35
❏ 47	Dante Bichette	.50	.23
❏ 48	Roberto Alomar	1.00	.45
❏ 49	Mark Grace	.75	.35
❏ 50	Brady Anderson	.50	.23
❏ 51	Hideo Nomo	1.00	.45
❏ 52	Ozzie Smith	1.25	.55
❏ 53	Robin Ventura	.50	.23
❏ 54	Andy Pettitte	.75	.35
❏ 55	Kenny Lofton	.75	.35
❏ 56	John Mabry	.25	.11
❏ 57	Paul Molitor	1.00	.45
❏ 58	Rey Ordonez	.50	.23
❏ 59	Albert Belle	1.00	.45
❏ 60	Charles Johnson	.50	.23
❏ 61	Edgar Martinez	.50	.23
❏ 62	Derek Bell	.50	.23
❏ 63	Carlos Delgado	1.00	.45
❏ 64	Raul Casanova	.25	.11
❏ 65	Ismael Valdes	.50	.23
❏ 66	J.T. Snow	.50	.23
❏ 67	Derek Jeter	3.00	1.35
❏ 68	Jason Kendall	1.00	.45
❏ 69	John Smoltz	.75	.35
❏ 70	Chad Mottola	.25	.11
❏ 71	Jim Thome	1.00	.45
❏ 72	Will Clark	1.00	.45
❏ 73	Mo Vaughn	1.00	.45
❏ 74	John Wasdin	.25	.11
❏ 75	Rafael Palmeiro	1.00	.45
❏ 76	Mark Grudzielanek	.25	.11
❏ 77	Larry Walker	1.00	.45
❏ 78	Alan Benes	.25	.11
❏ 79	Michael Tucker	.25	.11
❏ 80	Billy Wagner	.75	.35
❏ 81	Paul Wilson	.25	.11
❏ 82	Greg Vaughn	.50	.23
❏ 83	Dean Palmer	.50	.23
❏ 84	Ryne Sandberg	1.25	.55
❏ 85	Eric Young	.25	.11
❏ 86	Jay Buhner	.50	.23
❏ 87	Tony Clark	1.00	.45
❏ 88	Jermaine Dye	.50	.23
❏ 89	Barry Bonds	1.25	.55
❏ 90	Ugueth Urbina	.50	.23
❏ 91	Charles Nagy	.50	.23
❏ 92	Ruben Rivera	.50	.23
❏ 93	Todd Hollandsworth	.25	.11
❏ 94	Darin Erstad	8.00	3.60
❏ 95	Brooks Kieschnick	.25	.11
❏ 96	Edgar Renteria	.50	.23
❏ 97	Lenny Dykstra	.50	.23
❏ 98	Tony Gwynn	2.50	1.10
❏ 99	Kirby Puckett	1.50	.70
❏ 100	Checklist	.25	.11
❏ 101	Andruw Jones	3.00	1.35
❏ 102	Alex Ochoa	.50	.23
❏ 103	David Cone	1.50	.70
❏ 104	Rusty Greer	.50	.23
❏ 105	Jose Canseco	1.25	.55
❏ 106	Ken Caminiti	.50	.23
❏ 107	Mariano Rivera	1.50	.70
❏ 108	Ron Gant	.50	.23
❏ 109	Darryl Strawberry	1.00	.45
❏ 110	Vladimir Guerrero	4.00	1.80
❏ 111	George Arias	.50	.23
❏ 112	Jeff Conine	.50	.23
❏ 113	Bobby Higginson	1.00	.45
❏ 114	Eric Karros	1.00	.45
❏ 115	Brian Hunter	.50	.23
❏ 116	Eddie Murray	2.00	.90
❏ 117	Todd Walker	1.50	.70
❏ 118	Chan Ho Park	1.50	.70
❏ 119	John Jaha	.50	.23
❏ 120	Dave Justice	2.00	.90
❏ 121	Makoto Suzuki	1.00	.45
❏ 122	Scott Rolen	4.00	1.80
❏ 123	Tino Martinez	1.00	.45
❏ 124	Kimera Bartee	.50	.23
❏ 125	Garret Anderson	1.00	.45
❏ 126	Brian Jordan	1.00	.45
❏ 127	Andre Dawson	1.50	.70
❏ 128	Javier Lopez	1.00	.45
❏ 129	Bill Pulsipher	.50	.23
❏ 130	Dwight Gooden	1.00	.45
❏ 131	Al Martin	.50	.23
❏ 132	Terrell Wade	.50	.23
❏ 133	Steve Gibralter	.50	.23
❏ 134	Tom Glavine	2.00	.90
❏ 135	Kevin Appier	1.00	.45
❏ 136	Tim Raines	1.00	.45
❏ 137	Curtis Pride	.50	.23
❏ 138	Todd Greene	.50	.23
❏ 139	Bobby Bonilla	1.00	.45
❏ 140	Trey Beamon	.50	.23
❏ 141	Marty Cordova	1.00	.45
❏ 142	Rickey Henderson	1.25	.55
❏ 143	Ellis Burks	1.00	.45
❏ 144	Dennis Eckersley	1.00	.45
❏ 145	Kevin Brown	.75	.35
❏ 146	Carlos Baerga	.50	.23
❏ 147	Brett Butler	1.00	.45
❏ 148	Marquis Grissom	.50	.23
❏ 149	Karim Garcia	1.00	.45
❏ 150	Frank Thomas CL	2.00	.90

1996 Leaf Signature Gold Press Proofs

	MINT	NRMT
COMMON CARD (1-150)	3.00	1.35

*SER.1 STARS: 5X TO 12X BASIC CARDS
*SER.1 ROOKIES: 1.25X TO 3X BASIC
*SER.2 STARS: 2.5X TO 6X BASIC CARDS
STATED ODDS 1:12

1996 Leaf Signature Platinum Press Proofs

	MINT	NRMT
COMMON CARD (1-150)	8.00	3.60

*SER.1 STARS: 12.5X TO 30X BASIC
*SER.1 ROOKIES: 3X TO 8X BASIC
*SER.2 STARS: 6X TO 15X BASIC
RANDOM INSERTS IN EXTENDED PACKS

1996 Leaf Signature Autographs

	MINT	NRMT
COMP. BRONZE SET (251)	2000.00	900.00
COMMON BRONZE (1-251)	2.50	1.10
BRONZE MINOR STARS	8.00	3.60

*SILVER: .6X TO 1.2X HI COLUMN
*GOLD: .6X TO 1.2X HI COLUMN

ONE OR MORE AUTOGRAPHS PER PACK
NON-SP: 3500 BRONZE/1000 SILV/500 GOLD
SP: 700 BRONZE/200 SILV/100 GOLD

❑ 1 Kurt Abbott	2.50	1.10
❑ 2 Juan Acevedo	2.50	1.10
❑ 3 Terry Adams	2.50	1.10
❑ 4 Manny Alexander	2.50	1.10
❑ 5 Roberto Alomar SP	50.00	22.00
❑ 6 Moises Alou	8.00	3.60
❑ 7 Wilson Alvarez	2.50	1.10
❑ 8 Garret Anderson	8.00	3.60
❑ 9 Shane Andrews	2.50	1.10
❑ 10 Andy Ashby	2.50	1.10
❑ 11 Pedro Astacio	2.50	1.10
❑ 12 Brad Ausmus	2.50	1.10
❑ 13 Bobby Ayala	2.50	1.10
❑ 14 Carlos Baerga	2.50	1.10
❑ 15 Harold Baines	10.00	4.50
❑ 16 Jason Bates	2.50	1.10
❑ 17 Allen Battle	2.50	1.10
❑ 18 Rich Becker	2.50	1.10
❑ 19 David Bell	2.50	1.10
❑ 20 Rafael Belliard	2.50	1.10
❑ 21 Andy Benes	8.00	3.60
❑ 22 Armando Benitez	2.50	1.10
❑ 23 Jason Bere	2.50	1.10
❑ 24 Geronimo Berroa	2.50	1.10
❑ 25 Willie Blair	2.50	1.10
❑ 26 Mike Blowers	2.50	1.10
❑ 27 Wade Boggs SP	150.00	70.00
❑ 28 Ricky Bones	2.50	1.10
❑ 29 Mike Bordick	2.50	1.10
❑ 30 Toby Borland	2.50	1.10
❑ 31 Ricky Bottalico	2.50	1.10
❑ 32 Darren Bragg	2.50	1.10
❑ 33 Jeff Branson	2.50	1.10
❑ 34 Tilson Brito	2.50	1.10
❑ 35 Rico Brogna	2.50	1.10
❑ 36 Scott Brosius	8.00	3.60
❑ 37 Damon Buford	2.50	1.10
❑ 38 Mike Busby	2.50	1.10
❑ 39 Tom Candiotti	2.50	1.10
❑ 40 Frank Castillo	2.50	1.10
❑ 41 Andujar Cedeno	2.50	1.10
❑ 42 Domingo Cedeno	2.50	1.10
❑ 43 Roger Cedeno	8.00	3.60
❑ 44 Norm Charlton	2.50	1.10
❑ 45 Jeff Cirillo	8.00	3.60
❑ 46 Will Clark	20.00	9.00
❑ 47 Jeff Conine	2.50	1.10
❑ 48 Steve Cooke	2.50	1.10
❑ 49 Joey Cora	2.50	1.10
❑ 50 Marty Cordova	2.50	1.10
❑ 51 Rheal Cormier	2.50	1.10
❑ 52 Felipe Crespo	2.50	1.10
❑ 53 Chad Curtis	2.50	1.10
❑ 54 Johnny Damon	12.00	5.50
❑ 55 Russ Davis	2.50	1.10
❑ 56 Andre Dawson	15.00	6.75
❑ 57 Carlos Delgado	20.00	9.00
❑ 58 Doug Drabek	2.50	1.10
❑ 59 Darren Dreifort	8.00	3.60
❑ 60 Shawon Dunston	2.50	1.10
❑ 61 Ray Durham	8.00	3.60
❑ 62 Jim Edmonds	10.00	4.50
❑ 63 Joey Eischen	2.50	1.10
❑ 64 Jim Eisenreich	2.50	1.10

❑ 65 Sal Fasano	2.50	1.10
❑ 66 Jeff Fassero	2.50	1.10
❑ 67 Alex Fernandez	2.50	1.10
❑ 68 Darrin Fletcher	2.50	1.10
❑ 69 Chad Fonville	2.50	1.10
❑ 70 Kevin Foster	2.50	1.10
❑ 71 John Franco	8.00	3.60
❑ 72 Julio Franco	2.50	1.10
❑ 73 Marvin Freeman	2.50	1.10
❑ 74 Travis Fryman	8.00	3.60
❑ 75 Gary Gaetti	8.00	3.60
❑ 76 Carlos Garcia	2.50	1.10
❑ 77 Jason Giambi	10.00	4.50
❑ 78 Benji Gil	2.50	1.10
❑ 79 Greg Gohr	2.50	1.10
❑ 80 Chris Gomez	2.50	1.10
❑ 81 Leo Gomez	2.50	1.10
❑ 82 Tom Goodwin	2.50	1.10
❑ 83 Mike Grace	2.50	1.10
❑ 84 Mike Greenwell	2.50	1.10
❑ 85 Rusty Greer	10.00	4.50
❑ 86 Mark Grudzielanek	2.50	1.10
❑ 87 Mark Gubicza	2.50	1.10
❑ 88 Juan Guzman	2.50	1.10
❑ 89 Darryl Hamilton	2.50	1.10
❑ 90 Joey Hamilton	2.50	1.10
❑ 91 Chris Hammond	2.50	1.10
❑ 92 Mike Hampton	10.00	4.50
❑ 93 Chris Haney	2.50	1.10
❑ 94 Todd Haney	2.50	1.10
❑ 95 Erik Hanson	2.50	1.10
❑ 96 Pete Harnisch	2.50	1.10
❑ 97 LaTroy Hawkins	2.50	1.10
❑ 98 Charlie Hayes	2.50	1.10
❑ 99 Jimmy Haynes	2.50	1.10
❑ 100 Roberto Hernandez	2.50	1.10
❑ 101 Bobby Higginson	8.00	3.60
❑ 102 Glenallen Hill	2.50	1.10
❑ 103 Ken Hill	2.50	1.10
❑ 104 Sterling Hitchcock	2.50	1.10
❑ 105 Trevor Hoffman	8.00	3.60
❑ 106 Dave Hollins	2.50	1.10
❑ 107 Dwayne Hosey	2.50	1.10
❑ 108 Thomas Howard	2.50	1.10
❑ 109 Steve Howe	2.50	1.10
❑ 110 John Hudek	2.50	1.10
❑ 111 Rex Hudler	2.50	1.10
❑ 112 Brian L.Hunter	2.50	1.10
❑ 113 Butch Huskey	2.50	1.10
❑ 114 Mark Hutton	2.50	1.10
❑ 115 Jason Jacome	2.50	1.10
❑ 116 John Jaha	2.50	1.10
❑ 117 Reggie Jefferson	2.50	1.10
❑ 118 Derek Jeter SP	150.00	70.00
❑ 119 Bobby Jones	2.50	1.10
❑ 120 Todd Jones	2.50	1.10
❑ 121 Brian Jordan	10.00	4.50
❑ 122 Kevin Jordan	2.50	1.10
❑ 123 Jeff Juden	2.50	1.10
❑ 124 Ron Karkovice	2.50	1.10
❑ 125 Roberto Kelly	2.50	1.10
❑ 126 Mark Kiefer	2.50	1.10
❑ 127 Brooks Kieschnick	2.50	1.10
❑ 128 Jeff King	2.50	1.10
❑ 129 Mike Lansing	2.50	1.10
❑ 130 Matt Lawton	20.00	9.00
❑ 131 Al Leiter	8.00	3.60
❑ 132 Mark Leiter	2.50	1.10
❑ 133 Curtis Leskanic	2.50	1.10
❑ 134 Darren Lewis	2.50	1.10
❑ 135 Mark Lewis	2.50	1.10
❑ 136 Felipe Lira	2.50	1.10
❑ 137 Pat Listach	2.50	1.10
❑ 138 Keith Lockhart	2.50	1.10
❑ 139 Kenny Lofton SP	25.00	11.00
❑ 140 John Mabry	2.50	1.10
❑ 141 Mike Macfarlane	2.50	1.10
❑ 142 Kirt Manwaring	2.50	1.10
❑ 143 Al Martin	2.50	1.10
❑ 144 Norberto Martin	2.50	1.10
❑ 145 Dennis Martinez	8.00	3.60
❑ 146 Pedro Martinez	40.00	18.00
❑ 147 Sandy Martinez	2.50	1.10
❑ 148 Mike Matheny	2.50	1.10
❑ 149 T.J. Mathews	2.50	1.10
❑ 150 David McCarty	2.50	1.10

❑ 151 Ben McDonald	2.50	1.10
❑ 152 Pat Meares	2.50	1.10
❑ 153 Orlando Merced	2.50	1.10
❑ 154 Jose Mesa	2.50	1.10
❑ 155 Matt Mieske	2.50	1.10
❑ 156 Orlando Miller	2.50	1.10
❑ 157 Mike Mimbs	2.50	1.10
❑ 158 Paul Molitor SP	50.00	22.00
❑ 159 Raul Mondesi SP	25.00	11.00
❑ 160 Jeff Montgomery	2.50	1.10
❑ 161 Mickey Morandini	2.50	1.10
❑ 162 Lyle Mouton	2.50	1.10
❑ 163 James Mouton	2.50	1.10
❑ 164 Jamie Moyer	2.50	1.10
❑ 165 Rodney Myers	2.50	1.10
❑ 166 Denny Neagle	8.00	3.60
❑ 167 Robb Nen	2.50	1.10
❑ 168 Marc Newfield	2.50	1.10
❑ 169 Dave Nilsson	2.50	1.10
❑ 170 Jon Nunnally	2.50	1.10
❑ 171 Chad Ogea	2.50	1.10
❑ 172 Troy O'Leary	8.00	3.60
❑ 173 Rey Ordonez	12.00	5.50
❑ 174 Jayhawk Owens	2.50	1.10
❑ 175 Tom Pagnozzi	2.50	1.10
❑ 176 Dean Palmer	8.00	3.60
❑ 177 Roger Pavlik	2.50	1.10
❑ 178 Troy Percival	8.00	3.60
❑ 179 Carlos Perez	2.50	1.10
❑ 180 Robert Perez	2.50	1.10
❑ 181 Andy Pettitte	10.00	4.50
❑ 182 Phil Plantier	2.50	1.10
❑ 183 Mike Potts	2.50	1.10
❑ 184 Curtis Pride	2.50	1.10
❑ 185 Ariel Prieto	2.50	1.10
❑ 186 Bill Pulsipher	2.50	1.10
❑ 187 Brad Radke	8.00	3.60
❑ 188 Manny Ramirez SP	50.00	22.00
❑ 189 Joe Randa	2.50	1.10
❑ 190 Pat Rapp	2.50	1.10
❑ 191 Bryan Rekar	2.50	1.10
❑ 192 Shane Reynolds	8.00	3.60
❑ 193 Arthur Rhodes	2.50	1.10
❑ 194 Mariano Rivera	15.00	6.75
❑ 195 Alex Rodriguez SP	150.00	70.00
❑ 196 Frank Rodriguez	2.50	1.10
❑ 197 Mel Rojas	2.50	1.10
❑ 198 Ken Ryan	2.50	1.10
❑ 199 Bret Saberhagen	8.00	3.60
❑ 200 Tim Salmon	15.00	6.75
❑ 201 Rey Sanchez	2.50	1.10
❑ 202 Scott Sanders	2.50	1.10
❑ 203 Steve Scarsone	2.50	1.10
❑ 204 Curt Schilling	15.00	6.75
❑ 205 Jason Schmidt	2.50	1.10
❑ 206 David Segui	8.00	3.60
❑ 207 Kevin Seitzer	2.50	1.10
❑ 208 Scott Servais	2.50	1.10
❑ 209 Don Slaught	2.50	1.10
❑ 210 Zane Smith	2.50	1.10
❑ 211 Paul Sorrento	2.50	1.10
❑ 212 Scott Stahoviak	2.50	1.10
❑ 213 Mike Stanley	2.50	1.10
❑ 214 Terry Steinbach	2.50	1.10
❑ 215 Kevin Stocker	2.50	1.10
❑ 216 Jeff Suppan	2.50	1.10
❑ 217 Bill Swift	2.50	1.10
❑ 218 Greg Swindell	2.50	1.10
❑ 219 Kevin Tapani	2.50	1.10
❑ 220 Danny Tartabull	2.50	1.10
❑ 221 Julian Tavarez	2.50	1.10
❑ 222 Frank Thomas SP	100.00	45.00
❑ 223 Ozzie Timmons	2.50	1.10
❑ 224 Michael Tucker	2.50	1.10
❑ 225 Ismael Valdes	8.00	3.60
❑ 226 Jose Valentin	2.50	1.10
❑ 227 Todd Van Poppel	2.50	1.10
❑ 228 Mo Vaughn SP	40.00	18.00
❑ 229 Quilvio Veras	2.50	1.10
❑ 230 Fernando Vina	2.50	1.10
❑ 231 Joe Vitiello	2.50	1.10
❑ 232 Jose Vizcaino	2.50	1.10
❑ 233 Omar Vizquel	15.00	6.75
❑ 234 Terrell Wade	2.50	1.10
❑ 235 Paul Wagner	2.50	1.10
❑ 236 Matt Walbeck	2.50	1.10

		MINT	NRMT
❑ 237	Jerome Walton	2.50	1.10
❑ 238	Turner Ward	2.50	1.10
❑ 239	Allen Watson	2.50	1.10
❑ 240	David Weathers	2.50	1.10
❑ 241	Walt Weiss	2.50	1.10
❑ 242	Turk Wendell	2.50	1.10
❑ 243	Rondell White	8.00	3.60
❑ 244	Brian Williams	2.50	1.10
❑ 245	George Williams	2.50	1.10
❑ 246	Paul Wilson	2.50	1.10
❑ 247	Bobby Witt	2.50	1.10
❑ 248	Bob Wolcott	2.50	1.10
❑ 249	Eric Young	2.50	1.10
❑ 250	Ernie Young	2.50	1.10
❑ 251	Greg Zaun	2.50	1.10
❑ NNO	F.Thomas Jumbo AU	60.00	27.00

1996 Leaf Signature Extended Autographs

	MINT	NRMT
COMPLETE SET (217)	2500.00	1100.00
COMMON CARD (1-217)	2.50	1.10
MINOR STARS	5.00	2.20
TWO OR MORE AUTOGRAPHS PER PACK		
NON-SP PRINT RUN 5000 OF EACH CARD		
EXCH.DEADLINE: 12/31/98		

❑ 1	Scott Aldred	2.50	1.10
❑ 2	Mike Aldrete	2.50	1.10
❑ 3	Rich Amaral	2.50	1.10
❑ 4	Alex Arias	2.50	1.10
❑ 5	Paul Assenmacher	2.50	1.10
❑ 6	Roger Bailey	2.50	1.10
❑ 7	Erik Bennett	2.50	1.10
❑ 8	Sean Bergman	2.50	1.10
❑ 9	Doug Bochtler	2.50	1.10
❑ 10	Tim Bogar	2.50	1.10
❑ 11	Pat Borders	2.50	1.10
❑ 12	Pedro Borbon	2.50	1.10
❑ 13	Shawn Boskie	2.50	1.10
❑ 14	Rafael Bournigal	2.50	1.10
❑ 15	Mark Brandenburg	2.50	1.10
❑ 16	John Briscoe	2.50	1.10
❑ 17	Jorge Brito	2.50	1.10
❑ 18	Doug Brocail	2.50	1.10
❑ 19	Jay Buhner SP1000	20.00	9.00
❑ 20	Scott Bullett	2.50	1.10
❑ 21	Dave Burba	2.50	1.10
❑ 22	Ken Caminiti SP1000	20.00	9.00
❑ 23	John Cangelosi	2.50	1.10
❑ 24	Cris Carpenter	2.50	1.10
❑ 25	Chuck Carr	2.50	1.10
❑ 26	Larry Casian	2.50	1.10
❑ 27	Tony Castillo	2.50	1.10
❑ 28	Jason Christiansen	2.50	1.10
❑ 29	Archi Cianfrocco	2.50	1.10
❑ 30	Mark Clark	2.50	1.10
❑ 31	Terry Clark	2.50	1.10
❑ 32	Roger Clemens SP1000	120.00	55.00
❑ 33	Jim Converse	2.50	1.10
❑ 34	Dennis Cook	2.50	1.10
❑ 35	Francisco Cordova	2.50	1.10
❑ 36	Jim Corsi	2.50	1.10
❑ 37	Tim Crabtree	2.50	1.10
❑ 38	Doug Creek SP1950	8.00	3.60
❑ 39	Jim Cummings	2.50	1.10
❑ 40	Omar Daal	5.00	2.20

❑ 41	Rich DeLucia	2.50	1.10
❑ 42	Mark Dewey	2.50	1.10
❑ 43	Alex Diaz	2.50	1.10
❑ 44	Jermaine Dye SP2500	12.00	5.50
❑ 45	Ken Edenfield	2.50	1.10
❑ 46	Mark Eichhorn	2.50	1.10
❑ 47	John Ericks	2.50	1.10
❑ 48	Darin Erstad	30.00	13.50
❑ 49	Alvaro Espinoza	2.50	1.10
❑ 50	Jorge Fabregas	2.50	1.10
❑ 51	Mike Fetters	2.50	1.10
❑ 52	John Flaherty	2.50	1.10
❑ 53	Bryce Florie	2.50	1.10
❑ 54	Tony Fossas	2.50	1.10
❑ 55	Lou Frazier	2.50	1.10
❑ 56	Mike Gallego	2.50	1.10
❑ 57	Karim Garcia SP2500	5.00	2.20
❑ 58	Jason Giambi	5.00	2.20
❑ 59	Ed Giovanola	2.50	1.10
❑ 60	Tom Glavine SP1250	40.00	18.00
❑ 61	Juan Gonzalez SP1000	100.00	45.00
❑ 62	Craig Grebeck	2.50	1.10
❑ 63	Buddy Groom	2.50	1.10
❑ 64	Kevin Gross	2.50	1.10
❑ 65	Eddie Guardado	2.50	1.10
❑ 66	Mark Guthrie	2.50	1.10
❑ 67	Tony Gwynn SP1000	100.00	45.00
❑ 68	Chip Hale	2.50	1.10
❑ 69	Darren Hall	2.50	1.10
❑ 70	Lee Hancock	2.50	1.10
❑ 71	Dave Hansen	2.50	1.10
❑ 72	Bryan Harvey	2.50	1.10
❑ 73	Bill Haselman	2.50	1.10
❑ 74	Mike Henneman	2.50	1.10
❑ 75	Doug Henry	2.50	1.10
❑ 76	Gil Heredia	2.50	1.10
❑ 77	Carlos Hernandez	2.50	1.10
❑ 78	Jose Hernandez	2.50	1.10
❑ 79	Darren Holmes	2.50	1.10
❑ 80	Mark Holzemer	2.50	1.10
❑ 81	Rick Honeycutt	2.50	1.10
❑ 82	Chris Hook	2.50	1.10
❑ 83	Chris Howard	2.50	1.10
❑ 84	Jack Howell	2.50	1.10
❑ 85	David Hulse	2.50	1.10
❑ 86	Edwin Hurtado	2.50	1.10
❑ 87	Jeff Huson	2.50	1.10
❑ 88	Mike James	2.50	1.10
❑ 89	Derek Jeter SP1000	120.00	55.00
❑ 90	Brian Johnson	2.50	1.10
❑ 91	Randy Johnson SP1000	50.00	22.00
❑ 92	Mark Johnson	2.50	1.10
❑ 93	Andruw Jones SP2000	40.00	18.00
❑ 94	Chris Jones	2.50	1.10
❑ 95	Ricky Jordan	2.50	1.10
❑ 96	Matt Karchner	2.50	1.10
❑ 97	Scott Karl	2.50	1.10
❑ 98	Jason Kendall SP2500	25.00	11.00
❑ 99	Brian Keyser	2.50	1.10
❑ 100	Mike Kingery	2.50	1.10
❑ 101	Wayne Kirby	2.50	1.10
❑ 102	Ryan Klesko SP1000	20.00	9.00
❑ 103	Chuck Knoblauch SP1000	25.00	11.00
❑ 104	Chad Kreuter	2.50	1.10
❑ 105	Tom Lampkin	2.50	1.10
❑ 106	Scott Leius	2.50	1.10
❑ 107	Jon Lieber	2.50	1.10
❑ 108	Nelson Liriano	2.50	1.10
❑ 109	Scott Livingstone	2.50	1.10
❑ 110	Graeme Lloyd	2.50	1.10
❑ 111	Kenny Lofton SP1000	25.00	11.00
❑ 112	Luis Lopez	2.50	1.10
❑ 113	Torey Lovullo	2.50	1.10
❑ 114	Greg Maddux SP500	250.00	110.00
❑ 115	Mike Maddux	2.50	1.10
❑ 116	Dave Magadan	2.50	1.10
❑ 117	Mike Magnante	2.50	1.10
❑ 118	Joe Magrane	2.50	1.10
❑ 119	Pat Mahomes	2.50	1.10
❑ 120	Matt Mantei	5.00	2.20
❑ 121	John Marzano	2.50	1.10
❑ 122	Terry Mathews	2.50	1.10
❑ 123	Chuck McElroy	2.50	1.10
❑ 124	Fred McGriff SP1000	30.00	13.50
❑ 125	Mark McLemore	2.50	1.10

❑ 126	Greg McMichael	2.50	1.10
❑ 127	Blas Minor	2.50	1.10
❑ 128	Dave Mlicki	2.50	1.10
❑ 129	Mike Mohler	2.50	1.10
❑ 130	Paul Molitor SP1000	50.00	22.00
❑ 131	Steve Montgomery	2.50	1.10
❑ 132	Mike Mordecai	2.50	1.10
❑ 133	Mike Morgan	2.50	1.10
❑ 134	Mike Munoz	2.50	1.10
❑ 135	Greg Myers	2.50	1.10
❑ 136	Jimmy Myers	2.50	1.10
❑ 137	Mike Myers	2.50	1.10
❑ 138	Bob Natal	2.50	1.10
❑ 139	Dan Naulty	2.50	1.10
❑ 140	Jeff Nelson	2.50	1.10
❑ 141	Warren Newson	2.50	1.10
❑ 142	Chris Nichting	2.50	1.10
❑ 143	Melvin Nieves	2.50	1.10
❑ 144	Charlie O'Brien	2.50	1.10
❑ 145	Alex Ochoa	2.50	1.10
❑ 146	Omar Olivares	2.50	1.10
❑ 147	Joe Oliver	2.50	1.10
❑ 148	Lance Painter	2.50	1.10
❑ 149	Rafael Palmeiro SP2000	30.00	13.50
❑ 150	Mark Parent	2.50	1.10
❑ 151	Steve Parris SP1800	8.00	3.60
❑ 152	Bob Patterson	2.50	1.10
❑ 153	Tony Pena	2.50	1.10
❑ 154	Eddie Perez	2.50	1.10
❑ 155	Yorkis Perez	2.50	1.10
❑ 156	Robert Person	2.50	1.10
❑ 157	Mark Petkovsek	2.50	1.10
❑ 158	Andy Pettitte SP1000	25.00	11.00
❑ 159	J.R. Phillips	2.50	1.10
❑ 160	Hipolito Pichardo	2.50	1.10
❑ 161	Eric Plunk	2.50	1.10
❑ 162	Jimmy Poole	2.50	1.10
❑ 163	Kirby Puckett SP1000	100.00	45.00
❑ 164	Paul Quantrill	2.50	1.10
❑ 165	Tom Quinlan	2.50	1.10
❑ 166	Jeff Reboulet	2.50	1.10
❑ 167	Jeff Reed	2.50	1.10
❑ 168	Steve Reed	2.50	1.10
❑ 169	Carlos Reyes	2.50	1.10
❑ 170	Bill Risley	2.50	1.10
❑ 171	Kevin Ritz	2.50	1.10
❑ 172	Kevin Roberson	2.50	1.10
❑ 173	Rich Robertson	2.50	1.10
❑ 174	Alex Rodriguez SP500	250.00	110.00
❑ 175	Ivan Rodriguez SP1250	60.00	27.00
❑ 176	Bruce Ruffin	2.50	1.10
❑ 177	Juan Samuel	2.50	1.10
❑ 178	Tim Scott	2.50	1.10
❑ 179	Kevin Sefcik	2.50	1.10
❑ 180	Jeff Shaw	2.50	1.10
❑ 181	Danny Sheaffer	2.50	1.10
❑ 182	Craig Shipley	2.50	1.10
❑ 183	Dave Silvestri	2.50	1.10
❑ 184	Aaron Small	2.50	1.10
❑ 185	John Smoltz SP1000	30.00	13.50
❑ 186	Luis Sojo	2.50	1.10
❑ 187	Sammy Sosa SP1000	300.00	135.00
❑ 188	Steve Sparks	2.50	1.10
❑ 189	Tim Spehr	2.50	1.10
❑ 190	Russ Springer	2.50	1.10
❑ 191	Matt Stairs	5.00	2.20
❑ 192	Andy Stankiewicz	2.50	1.10
❑ 193	Mike Stanton	2.50	1.10
❑ 194	Kelly Stinnett	2.50	1.10
❑ 195	Doug Strange	2.50	1.10
❑ 196	Mark Sweeney	2.50	1.10
❑ 197	Jeff Tabaka	2.50	1.10
❑ 198	Jesus Tavarez	2.50	1.10
❑ 199	Frank Thomas SP1000	100.00	45.00
❑ 200	Larry Thomas	2.50	1.10
❑ 201	Mark Thompson	2.50	1.10
❑ 202	Mike Timlin	2.50	1.10
❑ 203	Steve Trachsel	2.50	1.10
❑ 204	Tom Urbani	2.50	1.10
❑ 205	Julio Valera	2.50	1.10
❑ 206	Dave Valle	2.50	1.10
❑ 207	William VanLandingham	2.50	1.10
❑ 208	Mo Vaughn SP1000	40.00	18.00
❑ 209	Dave Veres	2.50	1.10
❑ 210	Ed Vosberg	2.50	1.10
❑ 211	Don Wengert	2.50	1.10

☐ 212 Matt Whiteside 2.50   1.10
☐ 213 Bob Wickman 2.50   1.10
☐ 214 Matt Williams SP1250 30.00   13.50
☐ 215 Mike Williams 2.50   1.10
☐ 216 Woody Williams 2.50   1.10
☐ 217 Craig Worthington 2.50   1.10
☐ NNO F.Thomas Jumbo AU 60.00   27.00

1996 Leaf Signature Extended Autographs Century Marks

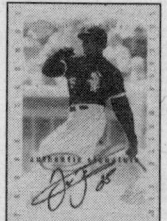

	MINT	NRMT
COMPLETE SET (31)	3500.00	1600.00
COMMON CARD (1-31)	15.00	6.75

RANDOM INSERTS IN PACKS
STATED PRINT RUN 100 SETS

☐ 1 Jay Buhner 50.00   22.00
☐ 2 Ken Caminiti 50.00   22.00
☐ 3 Roger Clemens 300.00   135.00
☐ 4 Jermaine Dye 40.00   18.00
☐ 5 Darin Erstad 120.00   55.00
☐ 6 Karim Garcia 15.00   6.75
☐ 7 Jason Giambi 50.00   22.00
☐ 8 Tom Glavine 100.00   45.00
☐ 9 Juan Gonzalez 250.00   110.00
☐ 10 Tony Gwynn 250.00   110.00
☐ 11 Derek Jeter 300.00   135.00
☐ 12 Randy Johnson 120.00   55.00
☐ 13 Andruw Jones 150.00   70.00
☐ 14 Jason Kendall 80.00   36.00
☐ 15 Ryan Klesko 40.00   18.00
☐ 16 Chuck Knoblauch 60.00   27.00
☐ 17 Kenny Lofton 60.00   27.00
☐ 18 Greg Maddux 400.00   180.00
☐ 19 Fred McGriff 80.00   36.00
☐ 20 Paul Molitor 120.00   55.00
☐ 21 Alex Ochoa 15.00   6.75
☐ 22 Rafael Palmeiro 100.00   45.00
☐ 23 Andy Pettitte 60.00   27.00
☐ 24 Kirby Puckett 200.00   90.00
☐ 25 Alex Rodriguez 400.00   180.00
☐ 26 Ivan Rodriguez 150.00   70.00
☐ 27 John Smoltz 80.00   36.00
☐ 28 Sammy Sosa 500.00   220.00
☐ 29 Frank Thomas 250.00   110.00
☐ 30 Mo Vaughn 100.00   45.00
☐ 31 Matt Williams 80.00   36.00

1996 Metal Universe

	MINT	NRMT
COMPLETE SET (250)	40.00	18.00
COMMON CARD (1-250)	.15	.07
MINOR STARS	.30	.14
UNLISTED STARS	.60	.25
COMP.PLAT.SET (250)	150.00	70.00
COMMON PLATINUM (1-250)	.25	.11

*PLAT.STARS: 2X TO 4X HI COLUMN
*PLAT.YOUNG STARS: 1.5X TO 3X HI
ONE PLATINUM PER PACK

☐ 1 Roberto Alomar .... .60   .25
☐ 2 Brady Anderson .... .30   .14
☐ 3 Bobby Bonilla .... .30   .14
☐ 4 Chris Hoiles .... .15   .07

☐ 5 Ben McDonald .... .15   .07
☐ 6 Mike Mussina .... .60   .25
☐ 7 Randy Myers .... .15   .07
☐ 8 Rafael Palmeiro .... .60   .25
☐ 9 Cal Ripken 2.50   1.10
☐ 10 B.J. Surhoff .... .30   .14
☐ 11 Luis Alicea .... .15   .07
☐ 12 Jose Canseco .... .75   .35
☐ 13 Roger Clemens .... 1.50   .70
☐ 14 Wil Cordero .... .15   .07
☐ 15 Tom Gordon .... .15   .07
☐ 16 Mike Greenwell .... .15   .07
☐ 17 Tim Naehring .... .15   .07
☐ 18 Troy O'Leary .... .30   .14
☐ 19 Mike Stanley .... .15   .07
☐ 20 John Valentin .... .30   .14
☐ 21 Mo Vaughn .... .60   .25
☐ 22 Tim Wakefield .... .15   .07
☐ 23 Garret Anderson ...... .30   .14
☐ 24 Chili Davis .... .30   .14
☐ 25 Gary DiSarcina .... .15   .07
☐ 26 Jim Edmonds .... .40   .18
☐ 27 Chuck Finley .... .30   .14
☐ 28 Todd Greene .... .15   .07
☐ 29 Mark Langston .... .15   .07
☐ 30 Troy Percival .... .30   .14
☐ 31 Tony Phillips .... .15   .07
☐ 32 Tim Salmon .... .40   .18
☐ 33 Lee Smith .... .30   .14
☐ 34 J.T. Snow .... .30   .14
☐ 35 Ray Durham .... .30   .14
☐ 36 Alex Fernandez .... .15   .07
☐ 37 Ozzie Guillen .... .15   .07
☐ 38 Roberto Hernandez .... .15   .07
☐ 39 Lyle Mouton .... .15   .07
☐ 40 Frank Thomas .... 1.25   .55
☐ 41 Robin Ventura .... .30   .14
☐ 42 Sandy Alomar Jr ...... .30   .14
☐ 43 Carlos Baerga .... .15   .07
☐ 44 Albert Belle .... .60   .25
☐ 45 Orel Hershiser .... .30   .14
☐ 46 Kenny Lofton .... .40   .18
☐ 47 Dennis Martinez ...... .30   .14
☐ 48 Jack McDowell .... .15   .07
☐ 49 Jose Mesa .... .15   .07
☐ 50 Eddie Murray .... .60   .25
☐ 51 Charles Nagy .... .30   .14
☐ 52 Manny Ramirez .... .75   .35
☐ 53 Julian Tavarez .... .15   .07
☐ 54 Jim Thome .... .60   .25
☐ 55 Omar Vizquel .... .30   .14
☐ 56 Chad Curtis .... .15   .07
☐ 57 Cecil Fielder .... .30   .14
☐ 58 John Flaherty .... .15   .07
☐ 59 Travis Fryman .... .30   .14
☐ 60 Chris Gomez .... .15   .07
☐ 61 Felipe Lira .... .15   .07
☐ 62 Kevin Appier .... .30   .14
☐ 63 Johnny Damon .... .40   .18
☐ 64 Tom Gordon .... .15   .07
☐ 65 Mark Gubicza .... .15   .07
☐ 66 Jeff Montgomery ...... .15   .07
☐ 67 Jon Nunnally .... .15   .07
☐ 68 Ricky Bones .... .15   .07
☐ 69 Jeff Cirillo .... .30   .14
☐ 70 John Jaha .... .15   .07
☐ 71 Dave Nilsson .... .15   .07
☐ 72 Joe Oliver .... .15   .07

☐ 73 Kevin Seitzer .... .15   .07
☐ 74 Greg Vaughn .... .30   .14
☐ 75 Marty Cordova .... .15   .07
☐ 76 Chuck Knoblauch ...... .60   .25
☐ 77 Pat Meares .... .15   .07
☐ 78 Paul Molitor .... .60   .25
☐ 79 Pedro Munoz .... .15   .07
☐ 80 Kirby Puckett .... 1.00   .45
☐ 81 Brad Radke .... .30   .14
☐ 82 Scott Stahoviak ...... .15   .07
☐ 83 Matt Walbeck .... .15   .07
☐ 84 Wade Boggs .... .60   .25
☐ 85 David Cone .... .30   .18
☐ 86 Joe Girardi .... .15   .07
☐ 87 Derek Jeter .... 2.00   .90
☐ 88 Jim Leyritz .... .15   .07
☐ 89 Tino Martinez .... .30   .14
☐ 90 Don Mattingly .... 1.25   .55
☐ 91 Paul O'Neil .... .30   .14
☐ 92 Andy Pettitte .... .40   .18
☐ 93 Tim Raines .... .30   .14
☐ 94 Kenny Rogers .... .15   .07
☐ 95 Ruben Sierra .... .15   .07
☐ 96 John Wetteland .... .30   .14
☐ 97 Bernie Williams ...... .60   .25
☐ 98 Geronimo Berroa ...... .15   .07
☐ 99 Dennis Eckersley ..... .30   .14
☐ 100 Brent Gates .... .15   .07
☐ 101 Mark McGwire 3.00   1.35
☐ 102 Steve Ontiveros ..... .15   .07
☐ 103 Terry Steinbach ..... .15   .07
☐ 104 Jay Buhner .... .30   .14
☐ 105 Vince Coleman .... .15   .07
☐ 106 Joey Cora .... .15   .07
☐ 107 Ken Griffey, Jr. 3.00   1.35
☐ 108 Randy Johnson .... .60   .25
☐ 109 Edgar Martinez ...... .30   .14
☐ 110 Alex Rodriguez ...... 2.00   .90
☐ 111 Paul Sorrento .... .15   .07
☐ 112 Will Clark .... .60   .25
☐ 113 Juan Gonzalez .... 1.25   .55
☐ 114 Rusty Greer .... .30   .14
☐ 115 Dean Palmer .... .30   .14
☐ 116 Ivan Rodriguez ...... .75   .35
☐ 117 Mickey Tettleton .... .15   .07
☐ 118 Joe Carter .... .30   .14
☐ 119 Alex Gonzalez .... .15   .07
☐ 120 Shawn Green .... .60   .25
☐ 121 Erik Hanson .... .15   .07
☐ 122 Pat Hentgen .... .30   .14
☐ 123 Sandy Martinez ...... .15   .07
☐ 124 Otis Nixon .... .15   .07
☐ 125 John Olerud .... .30   .14
☐ 126 Steve Avery .... .15   .07
☐ 127 Tom Glavine .... .60   .25
☐ 128 Marquis Grissom ..... .15   .07
☐ 129 Chipper Jones .... 1.50   .70
☐ 130 David Justice .... .60   .25
☐ 131 Ryan Klesko .... .30   .14
☐ 132 Mark Lemke .... .15   .07
☐ 133 Javier Lopez .... .30   .14
☐ 134 Greg Maddux .... 1.50   .70
☐ 135 Fred McGriff .... .40   .18
☐ 136 John Smoltz .... .40   .18
☐ 137 Mark Wohlers .... .15   .07
☐ 138 Frank Castillo ...... .15   .07
☐ 139 Shawon Dunston ...... .15   .07
☐ 140 Luis Gonzalez .... .15   .07
☐ 141 Mark Grace .... .40   .18
☐ 142 Brian McRae .... .15   .07
☐ 143 Jaime Navarro .... .15   .07
☐ 144 Rey Sanchez .... .15   .07
☐ 145 Ryne Sandberg .... .75   .35
☐ 146 Sammy Sosa .... 2.00   .90
☐ 147 Bret Boone .... .30   .14
☐ 148 Curtis Goodwin ...... .15   .07
☐ 149 Barry Larkin .... .60   .25
☐ 150 Hal Morris .... .15   .07
☐ 151 Reggie Sanders ...... .30   .14
☐ 152 Pete Schourek .... .15   .07
☐ 153 John Smiley .... .15   .07
☐ 154 Dante Bichette ...... .40   .18
☐ 155 Vinny Castilla ...... .40   .18
☐ 156 Andres Galarraga .... .60   .25
☐ 157 Bret Saberhagen ..... .30   .14
☐ 158 Bill Swift .... .15   .07

		MINT	NRMT
☐ 159 Larry Walker	.60	.25	
☐ 160 Walt Weiss	.15	.07	
☐ 161 Kurt Abbott	.15	.07	
☐ 162 John Burkett	.15	.07	
☐ 163 Greg Colbrunn	.15	.07	
☐ 164 Jeff Conine	.15	.07	
☐ 165 Chris Hammond	.15	.07	
☐ 166 Charles Johnson	.30	.14	
☐ 167 Al Leiter	.30	.14	
☐ 168 Pat Rapp	.15	.07	
☐ 169 Gary Sheffield	.30	.14	
☐ 170 Quilvio Veras	.15	.07	
☐ 171 Devon White	.15	.07	
☐ 172 Jeff Bagwell	.75	.35	
☐ 173 Derek Bell	.30	.14	
☐ 174 Sean Berry	.15	.07	
☐ 175 Craig Biggio	.60	.25	
☐ 176 Doug Drabek	.15	.07	
☐ 177 Tony Eusebio	.15	.07	
☐ 178 Brian L. Hunter	.15	.07	
☐ 179 Orlando Miller	.15	.07	
☐ 180 Shane Reynolds	.30	.14	
☐ 181 Mike Blowers	.15	.07	
☐ 182 Roger Cedeno	.30	.14	
☐ 183 Eric Karros	.30	.14	
☐ 184 Ramon Martinez	.30	.14	
☐ 185 Raul Mondesi	.30	.14	
☐ 186 Hideo Nomo	.60	.25	
☐ 187 Mike Piazza	2.00	.90	
☐ 188 Moises Alou	.30	.14	
☐ 189 Yamil Benitez	.15	.07	
☐ 190 Darrin Fletcher	.15	.07	
☐ 191 Cliff Floyd	.30	.14	
☐ 192 Pedro Martinez	.75	.35	
☐ 193 Carlos Perez	.15	.07	
☐ 194 David Segui	.30	.14	
☐ 195 Tony Tarasco	.15	.07	
☐ 196 Rondell White	.30	.14	
☐ 197 Edgardo Alfonzo	.60	.25	
☐ 198 Rico Brogna	.15	.07	
☐ 199 Carl Everett	.30	.14	
☐ 200 Todd Hundley	.30	.14	
☐ 201 Jason Isringhausen	.30	.14	
☐ 202 Lance Johnson	.15	.07	
☐ 203 Bobby Jones	.15	.07	
☐ 204 Jeff Kent	.30	.14	
☐ 205 Bill Pulsipher	.15	.07	
☐ 206 Jose Vizcaino	.15	.07	
☐ 207 Ricky Bottalico	.15	.07	
☐ 208 Darren Daulton	.30	.14	
☐ 209 Lenny Dykstra	.30	.14	
☐ 210 Jim Eisenreich	.15	.07	
☐ 211 Gregg Jefferies	.15	.07	
☐ 212 Mickey Morandini	.15	.07	
☐ 213 Heathcliff Slocumb	.15	.07	
☐ 214 Jay Bell	.30	.14	
☐ 215 Carlos Garcia	.15	.07	
☐ 216 Jeff King	.15	.07	
☐ 217 Al Martin	.15	.07	
☐ 218 Orlando Merced	.15	.07	
☐ 219 Dan Miceli	.15	.07	
☐ 220 Denny Neagle	.30	.14	
☐ 221 Andy Benes	.30	.14	
☐ 222 Royce Clayton	.15	.07	
☐ 223 Gary Gaetti	.30	.14	
☐ 224 Ron Gant	.15	.07	
☐ 225 Bernard Gilkey	.15	.07	
☐ 226 Brian Jordan	.30	.14	
☐ 227 Ray Lankford	.30	.14	
☐ 228 John Mabry	.15	.07	
☐ 229 Ozzie Smith	.75	.35	
☐ 230 Todd Stottlemyre	.15	.07	
☐ 231 Andy Ashby	.15	.07	
☐ 232 Brad Ausmus	.15	.07	
☐ 233 Ken Caminiti	.30	.14	
☐ 234 Steve Finley	.30	.14	
☐ 235 Tony Gwynn	1.50	.70	
☐ 236 Joey Hamilton	.15	.07	
☐ 237 Rickey Henderson	.75	.35	
☐ 238 Trevor Hoffman	.30	.14	
☐ 239 Wally Joyner	.30	.14	
☐ 240 Rod Beck	.15	.07	
☐ 241 Barry Bonds	.75	.35	
☐ 242 Glenallen Hill	.15	.07	
☐ 243 Stan Javier	.15	.07	
☐ 244 Mark Leiter	.15	.07	
☐ 245 Deion Sanders	.30	.14	
☐ 246 William Van Landingham	.15	.07	
☐ 247 Matt Williams	.60	.25	
☐ 248 Checklist	.15	.07	
☐ 249 Checklist	.15	.07	
☐ 250 Checklist	.15	.07	

1996 Metal Universe Heavy Metal

	MINT	NRMT
COMPLETE SET (10)	25.00	11.00
COMMON CARD (1-10)	1.50	.70
STATED ODDS 1:8		

		MINT	NRMT
☐ 1 Albert Belle	1.50	.70	
☐ 2 Barry Bonds	1.50	.70	
☐ 3 Juan Gonzalez	4.00	1.80	
☐ 4 Ken Griffey Jr.	10.00	4.50	
☐ 5 Mark McGwire	10.00	4.50	
☐ 6 Mike Piazza	6.00	2.70	
☐ 7 Sammy Sosa	6.00	2.70	
☐ 8 Frank Thomas	4.00	.70	
☐ 9 Mo Vaughn	1.50	.70	
☐ 10 Matt Williams	1.50	.70	

1996 Metal Universe Mining For Gold

	MINT	NRMT
COMPLETE SET (12)	60.00	27.00
COMMON CARD (1-12)	1.50	.70
STATED ODDS 1:12 RETAIL		

		MINT	NRMT
☐ 1 Yamil Benitez	1.50	.70	
☐ 2 Marty Cordova	1.50	.70	
☐ 3 Shawn Green	6.00	2.70	
☐ 4 Todd Greene	1.50	.70	
☐ 5 Brian Hunter	1.50	.70	
☐ 6 Derek Jeter	15.00	6.75	
☐ 7 Charles Johnson	2.50	1.10	
☐ 8 Chipper Jones	15.00	6.75	
☐ 9 Hideo Nomo	6.00	2.70	
☐ 10 Alex Ochoa	1.50	.70	
☐ 11 Andy Pettitte	4.00	1.80	
☐ 12 Quilvio Veras	1.50	.70	

1996 Metal Universe Mother Lode

	MINT	NRMT
COMPLETE SET (12)	60.00	27.00
COMMON CARD (1-12)	2.00	.90
STATED ODDS 1:12 HOBBY		

		MINT	NRMT
☐ 1 Barry Bonds	4.00	1.80	
☐ 2 Jim Edmonds	2.00	.90	
☐ 3 Ken Griffey Jr.	15.00	6.75	
☐ 4 Kenny Lofton	2.00	.90	
☐ 5 Raul Mondesi	2.00	.90	
☐ 6 Rafael Palmeiro	3.00	1.35	
☐ 7 Manny Ramirez	4.00	1.80	
☐ 8 Cal Ripken	12.00	5.50	
☐ 9 Tim Salmon	2.00	.90	
☐ 10 Ryne Sandberg	4.00	1.80	
☐ 11 Frank Thomas	8.00	3.60	
☐ 12 Matt Williams	3.00	1.35	

1996 Metal Universe Platinum Portraits

	MINT	NRMT
COMPLETE SET (10)	12.00	5.50
COMMON CARD (1-10)	.50	.23
STATED ODDS 1:4		

		MINT	NRMT
☐ 1 Garret Anderson	.75	.35	
☐ 2 Marty Cordova	.50	.23	
☐ 3 Jim Edmonds	1.00	.45	
☐ 4 Jason Isringhausen	.75	.35	
☐ 5 Chipper Jones	5.00	2.20	
☐ 6 Ryan Klesko	.75	.35	
☐ 7 Hideo Nomo	1.50	.70	
☐ 8 Carlos Perez	.50	.23	
☐ 9 Manny Ramirez	2.00	.90	
☐ 10 Rondell White	.75	.35	

1996 Metal Universe Titanium

	MINT	NRMT
COMPLETE SET (10)	120.00	55.00
COMMON CARD (1-10)	5.00	2.20
STATED ODDS 1:24		

		MINT	NRMT
☐ 1 Albert Belle	5.00	2.20	

		MINT	NRMT
❏ 2	Barry Bonds	6.00	2.70
❏ 3	Ken Griffey Jr.	25.00	11.00
❏ 4	Tony Gwynn	12.00	5.50
❏ 5	Greg Maddux	12.00	5.50
❏ 6	Mike Piazza	15.00	6.75
❏ 7	Cal Ripken	20.00	9.00
❏ 8	Frank Thomas	10.00	4.50
❏ 9	Mo Vaughn	5.00	2.20
❏ 10	Matt Williams	5.00	2.20

1997 Metal Universe

	MINT	NRMT
COMPLETE SET (250)	40.00	18.00
COMMON CARD (1-250)	.15	.07
MINOR STARS	.30	.14
UNLISTED STARS	.60	.25

		MINT	NRMT
❏ 1	Roberto Alomar	.60	.25
❏ 2	Brady Anderson	.30	.14
❏ 3	Rocky Coppinger	.15	.07
❏ 4	Chris Hoiles	.15	.07
❏ 5	Eddie Murray	.60	.25
❏ 6	Mike Mussina	.60	.25
❏ 7	Rafael Palmeiro	.60	.25
❏ 8	Cal Ripken	2.50	1.10
❏ 9	B.J. Surhoff	.30	.14
❏ 10	Brant Brown	.30	.14
❏ 11	Mark Grace	.40	.18
❏ 12	Brian McRae	.15	.07
❏ 13	Jaime Navarro	.15	.07
❏ 14	Ryne Sandberg	.75	.35
❏ 15	Sammy Sosa	2.00	.90
❏ 16	Amaury Telemaco	.15	.07
❏ 17	Steve Trachsel	.15	.07
❏ 18	Darren Bragg	.15	.07
❏ 19	Jose Canseco	.75	.35
❏ 20	Roger Clemens	1.50	.70
❏ 21	Nomar Garciaparra	2.00	.90
❏ 22	Tom Gordon	.15	.07
❏ 23	Tim Naehring	.15	.07
❏ 24	Mike Stanley	.15	.07
❏ 25	John Valentin	.30	.14
❏ 26	Mo Vaughn	.60	.25
❏ 27	Jermaine Dye	.30	.14
❏ 28	Tom Glavine	.60	.25
❏ 29	Marquis Grissom	.30	.14
❏ 30	Andruw Jones	.75	.35
❏ 31	Chipper Jones	1.50	.70
❏ 32	Ryan Klesko	.30	.14
❏ 33	Greg Maddux	1.50	.70
❏ 34	Fred McGriff	.40	.18
❏ 35	John Smoltz	.40	.18
❏ 36	Garret Anderson	.30	.14
❏ 37	George Arias	.15	.07
❏ 38	Gary DiSarcina	.15	.07
❏ 39	Jim Edmonds	.40	.18
❏ 40	Darin Erstad	.60	.25
❏ 41	Chuck Finley	.30	.14
❏ 42	Troy Percival	.30	.14
❏ 43	Tim Salmon	.60	.25
❏ 44	Bret Boone	.30	.14
❏ 45	Jeff Brantley	.15	.07
❏ 46	Eric Davis	.30	.14
❏ 47	Barry Larkin	.60	.25
❏ 48	Hal Morris	.15	.07
❏ 49	Mark Portugal	.15	.07
❏ 50	Reggie Sanders	.30	.14
❏ 51	John Smiley	.15	.07
❏ 52	Wilson Alvarez	.30	.14
❏ 53	Harold Baines	.30	.14
❏ 54	James Baldwin	.30	.14
❏ 55	Albert Belle	.60	.25
❏ 56	Mike Cameron	.30	.14
❏ 57	Ray Durham	.30	.14
❏ 58	Alex Fernandez	.15	.07
❏ 59	Roberto Hernandez	.15	.07
❏ 60	Tony Phillips	.15	.07
❏ 61	Frank Thomas	1.25	.55
❏ 62	Robin Ventura	.30	.14
❏ 63	Jeff Cirillo	.30	.14
❏ 64	Jeff D'Amico	.15	.07
❏ 65	John Jaha	.15	.07
❏ 66	Scott Karl	.15	.07
❏ 67	Ben McDonald	.15	.07
❏ 68	Marc Newfield	.15	.07
❏ 69	Dave Nilsson	.15	.07
❏ 70	Jose Valentin	.15	.07
❏ 71	Dante Bichette	.30	.14
❏ 72	Ellis Burks	.30	.14
❏ 73	Vinny Castilla	.40	.18
❏ 74	Andres Galarraga	.60	.25
❏ 75	Kevin Ritz	.15	.07
❏ 76	Larry Walker	.60	.25
❏ 77	Walt Weiss	.15	.07
❏ 78	Jamey Wright	.15	.07
❏ 79	Eric Young	.30	.14
❏ 80	Julio Franco	.15	.07
❏ 81	Orel Hershiser	.30	.14
❏ 82	Kenny Lofton	.40	.18
❏ 83	Jack McDowell	.15	.07
❏ 84	Jose Mesa	.15	.07
❏ 85	Charles Nagy	.30	.14
❏ 86	Manny Ramirez	.75	.35
❏ 87	Jim Thome	.60	.25
❏ 88	Omar Vizquel	.30	.14
❏ 89	Matt Williams	.60	.25
❏ 90	Kevin Appier	.30	.14
❏ 91	Johnny Damon	.30	.14
❏ 92	Chili Davis	.30	.14
❏ 93	Tom Goodwin	.15	.07
❏ 94	Keith Lockhart	.15	.07
❏ 95	Jeff Montgomery	.15	.07
❏ 96	Craig Paquette	.15	.07
❏ 97	Jose Rosado	.15	.07
❏ 98	Michael Tucker	.15	.07
❏ 99	Wilton Guerrero	.15	.07
❏ 100	Todd Hollandsworth	.15	.07
❏ 101	Eric Karros	.30	.14
❏ 102	Ramon Martinez	.30	.14
❏ 103	Raul Mondesi	.30	.14
❏ 104	Hideo Nomo	.60	.25
❏ 105	Mike Piazza	2.00	.90
❏ 106	Ismael Valdes	.30	.14
❏ 107	Todd Worrell	.15	.07
❏ 108	Tony Clark	.40	.18
❏ 109	Travis Fryman	.30	.14
❏ 110	Bob Higginson	.30	.14
❏ 111	Mark Lewis	.15	.07
❏ 112	Melvin Nieves	.15	.07
❏ 113	Justin Thompson	.30	.14
❏ 114	Wade Boggs	.60	.25
❏ 115	David Cone	.40	.18
❏ 116	Cecil Fielder	.30	.14
❏ 117	Dwight Gooden	.30	.14
❏ 118	Derek Jeter	2.00	.90
❏ 119	Tino Martinez	.60	.25
❏ 120	Paul O'Neill	.30	.14
❏ 121	Andy Pettitte	.40	.18
❏ 122	Mariano Rivera	.30	.14
❏ 123	Darryl Strawberry	.30	.14
❏ 124	John Wetteland	.30	.14
❏ 125	Bernie Williams	.60	.25
❏ 126	Tony Batista	.40	.18
❏ 127	Geronimo Berroa	.15	.07
❏ 128	Scott Brosius	.30	.14
❏ 129	Jason Giambi	.30	.14
❏ 130	Jose Herrera	.15	.07
❏ 131	Mark McGwire	3.00	1.35
❏ 132	John Wasdin	.15	.07
❏ 133	Bob Abreu	.30	.14
❏ 134	Jeff Bagwell	.75	.35
❏ 135	Derek Bell	.30	.14
❏ 136	Craig Biggio	.60	.25
❏ 137	Brian Hunter	.30	.14
❏ 138	Darryl Kile	.15	.07
❏ 139	Orlando Miller	.15	.07
❏ 140	Shane Reynolds	.30	.14
❏ 141	Billy Wagner	.30	.14
❏ 142	Donne Wall	.15	.07
❏ 143	Jay Buhner	.30	.14
❏ 144	Jeff Fassero	.15	.07
❏ 145	Ken Griffey Jr.	3.00	1.35
❏ 146	Sterling Hitchcock	.30	.14
❏ 147	Randy Johnson	.60	.25
❏ 148	Edgar Martinez	.30	.14
❏ 149	Alex Rodriguez	2.00	.90
❏ 150	Paul Sorrento	.15	.07
❏ 151	Dan Wilson	.15	.07
❏ 152	Moises Alou	.30	.14
❏ 153	Darrin Fletcher	.15	.07
❏ 154	Cliff Floyd	.30	.14
❏ 155	Mark Grudzielanek	.30	.14
❏ 156	Vladimir Guerrero	1.00	.45
❏ 157	Mike Lansing	.15	.07
❏ 158	Pedro Martinez	.75	.35
❏ 159	Henry Rodriguez	.30	.14
❏ 160	Rondell White	.30	.14
❏ 161	Will Clark	.60	.25
❏ 162	Juan Gonzalez	1.25	.55
❏ 163	Rusty Greer	.15	.07
❏ 164	Ken Hill	.15	.07
❏ 165	Mark McLemore	.15	.07
❏ 166	Dean Palmer	.30	.14
❏ 167	Roger Pavlik	.15	.07
❏ 168	Ivan Rodriguez	.75	.35
❏ 169	Mickey Tettleton	.15	.07
❏ 170	Bobby Bonilla	.30	.14
❏ 171	Kevin Brown	.40	.18
❏ 172	Greg Colbrunn	.15	.07
❏ 173	Jeff Conine	.15	.07
❏ 174	Jim Eisenreich	.15	.07
❏ 175	Charles Johnson	.30	.14
❏ 176	Al Leiter	.15	.07
❏ 177	Robb Nen	.15	.07
❏ 178	Edgar Renteria	.30	.14
❏ 179	Gary Sheffield	.30	.14
❏ 180	Devon White	.15	.07
❏ 181	Joe Carter	.30	.14
❏ 182	Carlos Delgado	.60	.25
❏ 183	Alex Gonzalez	.15	.07
❏ 184	Shawn Green	.60	.25
❏ 185	Juan Guzman	.30	.14
❏ 186	Pat Hentgen	.30	.14
❏ 187	Orlando Merced	.15	.07
❏ 188	John Olerud	.30	.14
❏ 189	Robert Perez	.15	.07
❏ 190	Ed Sprague	.15	.07
❏ 191	Mark Clark	.15	.07
❏ 192	John Franco	.30	.14
❏ 193	Bernard Gilkey	.15	.07
❏ 194	Todd Hundley	.30	.14
❏ 195	Lance Johnson	.15	.07
❏ 196	Bobby Jones	.15	.07
❏ 197	Alex Ochoa	.15	.07
❏ 198	Rey Ordonez	.30	.14
❏ 199	Paul Wilson	.15	.07
❏ 200	Ricky Bottalico	.30	.14
❏ 201	Gregg Jefferies	.15	.07
❏ 202	Wendell Magee	.15	.07
❏ 203	Mickey Morandini	.15	.07
❏ 204	Ricky Otero	.15	.07
❏ 205	Scott Rolen	1.00	.45

			MINT	NRMT
☐ 206	Benito Santiago	.15		.07
☐ 207	Curt Schilling	.40		.18
☐ 208	Rich Becker	.15		.07
☐ 209	Marty Cordova	.15		.07
☐ 210	Chuck Knoblauch	.60		.25
☐ 211	Pat Meares	.15		.07
☐ 212	Paul Molitor	.60		.25
☐ 213	Frank Rodriguez	.15		.07
☐ 214	Terry Steinbach	.15		.07
☐ 215	Todd Walker	.60		.25
☐ 216	Andy Ashby	.15		.07
☐ 217	Ken Caminiti	.40		.18
☐ 218	Steve Finley	.30		.14
☐ 219	Tony Gwynn	1.50		.70
☐ 220	Joey Hamilton	.30		.14
☐ 221	Rickey Henderson	.75		.35
☐ 222	Trevor Hoffman	.30		.14
☐ 223	Wally Joyner	.30		.14
☐ 224	Scott Sanders	.15		.07
☐ 225	Fernando Valenzuela	.30		.14
☐ 226	Greg Vaughn	.30		.14
☐ 227	Alan Benes	.15		.07
☐ 228	Andy Benes	.30		.14
☐ 229	Dennis Eckersley	.30		.14
☐ 230	Ron Gant	.30		.14
☐ 231	Brian Jordan	.30		.14
☐ 232	Ray Lankford	.30		.14
☐ 233	John Mabry	.15		.07
☐ 234	Tom Pagnozzi	.15		.07
☐ 235	Todd Stottlemyre	.15		.07
☐ 236	Jermaine Allensworth	.15		.07
☐ 237	Francisco Cordova	.15		.07
☐ 238	Jason Kendall	.40		.18
☐ 239	Jeff King	.15		.07
☐ 240	Al Martin	.15		.07
☐ 241	Rod Beck	.15		.07
☐ 242	Barry Bonds	.75		.35
☐ 243	Shawn Estes	.30		.14
☐ 244	Mark Gardner	.15		.07
☐ 245	Glenallen Hill	.15		.07
☐ 246	Bill Mueller	.75		.35
☐ 247	J.T. Snow	.30		.14
☐ 248	Checklist 1-107	.15		.07
☐ 249	Checklist 108-207	.15		.07
☐ 250	Checklist 208-250/inserts	.15		.07
☐ P149	Alex Rodriguez Promo	2.00		.90

1997 Metal Universe Blast Furnace

		MINT	NRMT
COMPLETE SET (12)		120.00	55.00
COMMON CARD (1-12)		4.00	1.80
STATED ODDS 1:48 HOBBY			

		MINT	NRMT
☐ 1	Jeff Bagwell	10.00	4.50
☐ 2	Albert Belle	6.00	2.70
☐ 3	Barry Bonds	10.00	4.50
☐ 4	Andres Galarraga	6.00	2.70
☐ 5	Juan Gonzalez	15.00	6.75
☐ 6	Ken Griffey Jr.	40.00	18.00
☐ 7	Todd Hundley	4.00	1.80
☐ 8	Mark McGwire	40.00	18.00
☐ 9	Mike Piazza	25.00	11.00
☐ 10	Alex Rodriguez	25.00	11.00
☐ 11	Frank Thomas	15.00	6.75
☐ 12	Mo Vaughn	6.00	2.70

1997 Metal Universe Emerald Autographs

	MINT	NRMT
COMPLETE SET (6)	250.00	110.00
COMMON CARD	8.00	3.60
ONE CARD VIA MAIL PER EXCH.CARD		
*EXCH.CARDS: .1X TO .25X HI COLUMN		
EXCHANGE CARDS: 1:20 BOXES		8.00
3.60		

		MINT	NRMT
☐ AU1	Darin Erstad	30.00	13.50
☐ AU2	Todd Hollandsworth	8.00	3.60
☐ AU3	Alex Ochoa	8.00	3.60
☐ AU4	Alex Rodriguez	150.00	70.00
☐ AU5	Scott Rolen	60.00	27.00
☐ AU6	Todd Walker	15.00	6.75

1997 Metal Universe Magnetic Field

		MINT	NRMT
COMPLETE SET (10)		25.00	11.00
COMMON CARD (1-10)		1.00	.45
STATED ODDS 1:12			

		MINT	NRMT
☐ 1	Roberto Alomar	2.50	1.10
☐ 2	Jeff Bagwell	3.00	1.35
☐ 3	Barry Bonds	3.00	1.35
☐ 4	Ken Griffey Jr.	12.00	5.50
☐ 5	Derek Jeter	6.00	2.70
☐ 6	Kenny Lofton	1.50	.70
☐ 7	Edgar Renteria	1.00	.45
☐ 8	Cal Ripken	10.00	4.50
☐ 9	Alex Rodriguez	8.00	3.60
☐ 10	Matt Williams	2.50	1.10

1997 Metal Universe Mining for Gold

	MINT	NRMT
COMPLETE SET (10)	20.00	9.00
COMMON CARD (1-25)	1.00	.45
STATED ODDS 1:8		

		MINT	NRMT
☐ 1	Bob Abreu	1.00	.45
☐ 2	Kevin Brown C	1.00	.45
☐ 3	Nomar Garciaparra	6.00	2.70
☐ 4	Vladimir Guerrero	1.50	.70

			MINT	NRMT
☐ 5	Wilton Guerrero	1.00		.45
☐ 6	Andruw Jones	2.50		1.10
☐ 7	Curt Lyons	1.00		.45
☐ 8	Neifi Perez	1.00		.45
☐ 9	Scott Rolen	4.00		1.80
☐ 10	Todd Walker	1.50		.70

1997 Metal Universe Mother Lode

	MINT	NRMT
COMPLETE SET (12)	400.00	180.00
COMMON CARD (1-12)	12.00	5.50
UNLISTED STARS	15.00	6.75
STATED ODDS 1:288		

		MINT	NRMT
☐ 1	Roberto Alomar	15.00	6.75
☐ 2	Jeff Bagwell	20.00	9.00
☐ 3	Barry Bonds	20.00	9.00
☐ 4	Ken Griffey Jr.	80.00	36.00
☐ 5	Andruw Jones	20.00	9.00
☐ 6	Chipper Jones	40.00	18.00
☐ 7	Kenny Lofton	12.00	5.50
☐ 8	Mike Piazza	50.00	22.00
☐ 9	Cal Ripken	60.00	27.00
☐ 10	Alex Rodriguez	50.00	22.00
☐ 11	Frank Thomas	30.00	13.50
☐ 12	Matt Williams	15.00	6.75

1997 Metal Universe Platinum Portraits

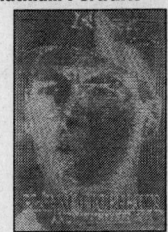

	MINT	NRMT
COMPLETE SET (10)	50.00	22.00
COMMON CARD (1-10)	3.00	1.35
STATED ODDS 1:36		
☐ 1 James Baldwin	3.00	1.35
☐ 2 Jermaine Dye	3.00	1.35
☐ 3 Todd Hollandsworth	1.50	.70
☐ 4 Derek Jeter	15.00	6.75
☐ 5 Chipper Jones	15.00	6.75
☐ 6 Jason Kendall	4.00	1.80
☐ 7 Rey Ordonez	3.00	1.35
☐ 8 Andy Pettitte	4.00	1.80
☐ 9 Edgar Renteria	3.00	1.35
☐ 10 Alex Rodriguez	20.00	9.00

1997 Metal Universe Titanium

	MINT	NRMT
COMPLETE SET (10)	100.00	45.00
COMMON CARD (1-25)	4.00	1.80
STATED ODDS 1:24 RETAIL		
☐ 1 Jeff Bagwell	5.00	2.20
☐ 2 Albert Belle	4.00	1.80
☐ 3 Ken Griffey Jr.	20.00	9.00
☐ 4 Chipper Jones	10.00	4.50
☐ 5 Greg Maddux	10.00	4.50
☐ 6 Mark McGwire	20.00	9.00
☐ 7 Mike Piazza	12.00	5.50
☐ 8 Cal Ripken	15.00	6.75
☐ 9 Alex Rodriguez	12.00	5.50
☐ 10 Frank Thomas	8.00	3.60

1998 Metal Universe

ROBIN VENTURA

	MINT	NRMT
COMPLETE SET (220)	40.00	18.00
COMMON CARD (1-220)	.15	.07
MINOR STARS	.25	.11
SEMISTARS	.40	.18
UNLISTED STARS	.60	.25
☐ 1 Jose Cruz Jr.	.25	.11
☐ 2 Jeff Abbott	.15	.07
☐ 3 Rafael Palmeiro	.60	.25
☐ 4 Ivan Rodriguez	.75	.35
☐ 5 Jaret Wright	.25	.11
☐ 6 Derek Bell	.25	.11

☐ 7 Chuck Finley	.25	.11
☐ 8 Travis Fryman	.25	.11
☐ 9 Randy Johnson	.60	.25
☐ 10 Derek Lee	.15	.07
☐ 11 Bernie Williams	.60	.25
☐ 12 Carlos Baerga	.25	.11
☐ 13 Ricky Bottalico	.15	.07
☐ 14 Ellis Burks	.25	.11
☐ 15 Russ Davis	.15	.07
☐ 16 Nomar Garciaparra	2.00	.90
☐ 17 Joey Hamilton	.15	.07
☐ 18 Jason Kendall	.25	.11
☐ 19 Darryl Kile	.15	.07
☐ 20 Edgardo Alfonzo	.40	.18
☐ 21 Moises Alou	.25	.11
☐ 22 Bobby Bonilla	.25	.11
☐ 23 Jim Edmonds	.25	.11
☐ 24 Jose Guillen	.15	.07
☐ 25 Chuck Knoblauch	.25	.11
☐ 26 Javy Lopez	.25	.11
☐ 27 Billy Wagner	.25	.11
☐ 28 Kevin Appier	.25	.11
☐ 29 Joe Carter	.25	.11
☐ 30 Todd Dunwoody	.15	.07
☐ 31 Gary Gaetti	.15	.07
☐ 32 Juan Gonzalez	1.25	.55
☐ 33 Jeffrey Hammonds	.15	.07
☐ 34 Roberto Hernandez	.15	.07
☐ 35 Dave Nilsson	.15	.07
☐ 36 Manny Ramirez	.75	.35
☐ 37 Robin Ventura	.25	.11
☐ 38 Rondell White	.25	.11
☐ 39 Vinny Castilla	.25	.11
☐ 40 Will Clark	.60	.25
☐ 41 Scott Hatteberg	.15	.07
☐ 42 Russ Johnson	.15	.07
☐ 43 Ricky Ledee	.25	.11
☐ 44 Kenny Lofton	.40	.18
☐ 45 Paul Molitor	.60	.25
☐ 46 Justin Thompson	.15	.07
☐ 47 Craig Biggio	.25	.11
☐ 48 Damion Easley	.25	.11
☐ 49 Brad Radke	.25	.11
☐ 50 Ben Grieve	.60	.25
☐ 51 Mark Bellhorn	.15	.07
☐ 52 Henry Blanco	.15	.07
☐ 53 Mariano Rivera	.25	.11
☐ 54 Reggie Sanders	.15	.07
☐ 55 Paul Sorrento	.15	.07
☐ 56 Terry Steinbach	.25	.11
☐ 57 Mo Vaughn	.60	.25
☐ 58 Brady Anderson	.25	.11
☐ 59 Tom Glavine	.60	.25
☐ 60 Sammy Sosa	2.00	.90
☐ 61 Larry Walker	.60	.25
☐ 62 Rod Beck	.15	.07
☐ 63 Jose Canseco	.75	.35
☐ 64 Steve Finley	.25	.11
☐ 65 Pedro Martinez	.75	.35
☐ 66 John Olerud	.25	.11
☐ 67 Scott Rolen	.75	.35
☐ 68 Ismael Valdes	.15	.07
☐ 69 Andrew Vessel	.15	.07
☐ 70 Mark Grudzielanek	.15	.07
☐ 71 Eric Karros	.25	.11
☐ 72 Jeff Shaw	.15	.07
☐ 73 Lou Collier	.15	.07
☐ 74 Edgar Martinez	.25	.11
☐ 75 Vladimir Guerrero	.75	.35
☐ 76 Paul Konerko	.25	.11
☐ 77 Kevin Orie	.15	.07
☐ 78 Kevin Polcovich	.15	.07
☐ 79 Brett Tomko	.15	.07
☐ 80 Jeff Bagwell	.75	.35
☐ 81 Barry Bonds	.75	.35
☐ 82 David Justice	.25	.11
☐ 83 Hideo Nomo	.25	.11
☐ 84 Ryne Sandberg	.75	.35
☐ 85 Shannon Stewart	.15	.07
☐ 86 Derek Wallace	.15	.07
☐ 87 Tony Womack	.25	.11
☐ 88 Jason Giambi	.25	.11
☐ 89 Mark Grace	.40	.18
☐ 90 Pat Hentgen	.25	.11
☐ 91 Raul Mondesi	.25	.11
☐ 92 Matt Morris	.15	.07

☐ 93 Matt Perisho	.15	.07
☐ 94 Tim Salmon	.40	.18
☐ 95 Jeremi Gonzalez	.15	.07
☐ 96 Shawn Green	.60	.25
☐ 97 Todd Greene	.15	.07
☐ 98 Ruben Rivera	.15	.07
☐ 99 Deion Sanders	.25	.11
☐ 100 Alex Rodriguez	2.00	.90
☐ 101 Will Cunnane	.15	.07
☐ 102 Ray Lankford	.25	.11
☐ 103 Ryan McGuire	.15	.07
☐ 104 Charles Nagy	.25	.11
☐ 105 Rey Ordonez	.25	.11
☐ 106 Mike Piazza	2.00	.90
☐ 107 Tony Saunders	.15	.07
☐ 108 Curt Schilling	.40	.18
☐ 109 Fernando Tatis	.60	.25
☐ 110 Mark McGwire	4.00	1.80
☐ 111 Dave Dellucci	.50	.23
☐ 112 Garret Anderson	.25	.11
☐ 113 Shane Bowers	.15	.07
☐ 114 David Cone	.40	.18
☐ 115 Jeff King	.15	.07
☐ 116 Matt Williams	.60	.25
☐ 117 Aaron Boone	.25	.11
☐ 118 Dennis Eckersley	.25	.11
☐ 119 Livan Hernandez	.15	.07
☐ 120 Richard Hidalgo	.25	.11
☐ 121 Bobby Higginson	.25	.11
☐ 122 Tino Martinez	.25	.11
☐ 123 Tim Naehring	.15	.07
☐ 124 Jose Vidro	.15	.07
☐ 125 John Wetteland	.25	.11
☐ 126 Jay Bell	.25	.11
☐ 127 Albert Belle	.60	.25
☐ 128 Marty Cordova	.25	.11
☐ 129 Chili Davis	.25	.11
☐ 130 Jason Dickson	.15	.07
☐ 131 Rusty Greer	.25	.11
☐ 132 Hideki Irabu	.25	.11
☐ 133 Greg Maddux	1.50	.70
☐ 134 Billy Taylor	.15	.07
☐ 135 Jim Thome	.60	.25
☐ 136 Gerald Williams	.15	.07
☐ 137 Jeff Cirillo	.25	.11
☐ 138 Delino DeShields	.15	.07
☐ 139 Andres Galarraga	.40	.18
☐ 140 Willie Greene	.15	.07
☐ 141 John Jaha	.25	.11
☐ 142 Charles Johnson	.25	.11
☐ 143 Ryan Klesko	.25	.11
☐ 144 Paul O'Neill	.25	.11
☐ 145 Roberto Alomar	.60	.25
☐ 146 Wilson Alvarez	.15	.07
☐ 147 Bobby Jones	.15	.07
☐ 148 Raul Casanova	.15	.07
☐ 149 Andruw Jones	.60	.25
☐ 150 Mike Lansing	.15	.07
☐ 151 Mickey Morandini	.15	.07
☐ 152 Neifi Perez	.25	.11
☐ 153 Pokey Reese	.15	.07
☐ 154 Edgar Renteria	.15	.07
☐ 155 Eric Young	.15	.07
☐ 156 Darin Erstad	.40	.18
☐ 157 Kelvim Escobar	.25	.11
☐ 158 Carl Everett	.25	.11
☐ 159 Tom Gordon	.25	.11
☐ 160 Ken Griffey Jr.	3.00	1.35
☐ 161 Al Martin	.35	.16
☐ 162 Bubba Trammell	.15	.07
☐ 163 Carlos Delgado	.40	.18
☐ 164 Kevin Brown	.40	.18
☐ 165 Ken Caminiti	.25	.11
☐ 166 Roger Clemens	1.50	.70
☐ 167 Ron Gant	.25	.11
☐ 168 Jeff Kent	.25	.11
☐ 169 Mike Mussina	.60	.25
☐ 170 Dean Palmer	.25	.11
☐ 171 Henry Rodriguez	.25	.11
☐ 172 Matt Stairs	.25	.11
☐ 173 Jay Buhner	.25	.11
☐ 174 Frank Thomas	1.25	.55
☐ 175 Mike Cameron	.25	.11
☐ 176 Johnny Damon	.25	.11
☐ 177 Tony Gwynn	1.50	.70
☐ 178 John Smoltz	.40	.18

		MINT	NRMT
❑ 180	B.J. Surhoff .... .25		.11
❑ 181	Antone Williamson .15		.07
❑ 182	Alan Benes .... .15		.07
❑ 183	Jeromy Burnitz ...... .25		.11
❑ 184	Tony Clark .... .25		.11
❑ 185	Shawn Estes .... .15		.07
❑ 186	Todd Helton .... .75		.35
❑ 187	Todd Hundley ...... .25		.11
❑ 188	Chipper Jones 1.50		.70
❑ 189	Mark Kotsay .... .25		.11
❑ 190	Barry Larkin .... .60		.25
❑ 191	Mike Lieberthal .... .25		.11
❑ 192	Andy Pettitte ...... .25		.11
❑ 193	Gary Sheffield ..... .25		.11
❑ 194	Jeff Suppan .... .15		.07
❑ 195	Mark Wohlers ...... .15		.07
❑ 196	Dante Bichette ..... .25		.11
❑ 197	Trevor Hoffman .... .25		.11
❑ 198	J.T. Snow .... .25		.11
❑ 199	Derek Jeter 2.00		.90
❑ 200	Cal Ripken 2.50		1.10
❑ 201	Steve Woodard .... .15		.07
❑ 202	Ray Durham .... .25		.11
❑ 203	Barry Bonds HG .... .40		.18
❑ 204	Tony Clark HG ..... .15		.07
❑ 205	Roger Clemens HG .. .75		.35
❑ 206	Ken Griffey Jr. HG .. 1.50		.70
❑ 207	Deion Sanders HG .. .25		.11
❑ 208	Derek Jeter HG 1.00		.45
❑ 209	Randy Johnson HG .. .25		.11
❑ 210	Brady Anderson HG . .15		.07
❑ 211	Hideo Nomo HG .... .25		.11
❑ 212	Mike Piazza HG 1.00		.45
❑ 213	Cal Ripken HG 1.25		.55
❑ 214	Alex Rodriguez HG . 1.00		.45
❑ 215	Frank Thomas HG ... .60		.25
❑ 216	Mo Vaughn HG ..... .25		.11
❑ 217	Larry Walker HG ... .25		.11
❑ 218	Ken Griffey Jr. CL .. 1.50		.70
❑ 219	Alex Rodriguez CL . 1.00		.45
❑ 220	Frank Thomas CL ... .60		.25
❑ NNO	Alex Rodriguez Promo 3.00		1.35

1998 Metal Universe Precious Metal Gems

	MINT	NRMT
COMMON CARD (1-217) 12.00		5.50

*STARS: 30X TO 80X BASIC CARDS
*YNG.STARS: 25X TO 60X BASIC CARDS
*ROOKIES: 20X TO 50X BASIC CARDS
RANDOM INSERTS IN PACKS
STATED PRINT RUN 50 SERIAL #'d SETS

1998 Metal Universe All-Galactic Team

	MINT	NRMT
COMPLETE SET (18)	600.00	275.00
COMMON CARD (1-18)	6.00	2.70
SEMISTARS	10.00	4.50
UNLISTED STARS	15.00	6.75
STATED ODDS 1:192		
❑ 1 Ken Griffey Jr.	80.00	36.00
❑ 2 Frank Thomas	30.00	13.50
❑ 3 Chipper Jones	40.00	18.00

	MINT	NRMT
❑ 4 Albert Belle	15.00	6.75
❑ 5 Juan Gonzalez	30.00	13.50
❑ 6 Jeff Bagwell	20.00	9.00
❑ 7 Andruw Jones	15.00	6.75
❑ 8 Cal Ripken	60.00	27.00
❑ 9 Derek Jeter	50.00	22.00
❑ 10 Nomar Garciaparra	50.00	22.00
❑ 11 Darin Erstad	10.00	4.50
❑ 12 Greg Maddux	40.00	18.00
❑ 13 Alex Rodriguez	50.00	22.00
❑ 14 Mike Piazza	50.00	22.00
❑ 15 Vladimir Guerrero	20.00	9.00
❑ 16 Jose Cruz Jr.	6.00	2.70
❑ 17 Mark McGwire	100.00	45.00
❑ 18 Scott Rolen	20.00	9.00

1998 Metal Universe Diamond Heroes

	MINT	NRMT
COMPLETE SET (6)	20.00	9.00
COMMON CARD (1-6)	.75	.35
STATED ODDS 1:18		
❑ 1 Ken Griffey Jr.	8.00	3.60
❑ 2 Frank Thomas	3.00	1.35
❑ 3 Andruw Jones	1.50	.70
❑ 4 Alex Rodriguez	5.00	2.20
❑ 5 Jose Cruz Jr.	.75	.35
❑ 6 Cal Ripken	6.00	2.70

1998 Metal Universe Platinum Portraits

		MINT	NRMT
COMPLETE SET (12)		550.00	250.00
COMMON CARD (1-12)		8.00	3.60
SEMISTARS		12.00	5.50
UNLISTED STARS		20.00	9.00
STATED ODDS 1:360			
❑ 1	Ken Griffey Jr.	100.00	45.00
❑ 2	Frank Thomas	40.00	18.00
❑ 3	Chipper Jones	50.00	22.00
❑ 4	Jose Cruz Jr.	8.00	3.60
❑ 5	Andruw Jones	20.00	9.00
❑ 6	Cal Ripken	80.00	36.00
❑ 7	Derek Jeter	60.00	27.00
❑ 8	Darin Erstad	12.00	5.50
❑ 9	Greg Maddux	50.00	22.00
❑ 10	Alex Rodriguez	60.00	27.00
❑ 11	Mike Piazza	60.00	27.00
❑ 12	Vladimir Guerrero	25.00	11.00

1998 Metal Universe Titanium

		MINT	NRMT
COMPLETE SET (15)		250.00	110.00
COMMON CARD (1-15)		3.00	1.35
STATED ODDS 1:96			
❑ 1	Ken Griffey Jr.	40.00	18.00
❑ 2	Frank Thomas	15.00	6.75
❑ 3	Chipper Jones	20.00	9.00
❑ 4	Jose Cruz Jr.	3.00	1.35
❑ 5	Juan Gonzalez	15.00	6.75
❑ 6	Scott Rolen	10.00	4.50
❑ 7	Andruw Jones	8.00	3.60
❑ 8	Cal Ripken	30.00	13.50
❑ 9	Derek Jeter	25.00	11.00
❑ 10	Nomar Garciaparra	25.00	11.00
❑ 11	Darin Erstad	5.00	2.20
❑ 12	Greg Maddux	20.00	9.00
❑ 13	Alex Rodriguez	25.00	11.00
❑ 14	Mike Piazza	25.00	11.00
❑ 15	Vladimir Guerrero	10.00	4.50

1998 Metal Universe Universal Language

	MINT	NRMT
COMPLETE SET (20)	50.00	22.00

COMMON CARD (1-20) .75 .35
STATED ODDS 1:6

□ 1	Ken Griffey Jr.	8.00	3.60
□ 2	Frank Thomas	3.00	1.35
□ 3	Chipper Jones	4.00	1.80
□ 4	Albert Belle	1.50	.70
□ 5	Juan Gonzalez	3.00	1.35
□ 6	Jeff Bagwell	2.00	.90
□ 7	Andruw Jones	1.50	.70
□ 8	Cal Ripken	6.00	2.70
□ 9	Derek Jeter	5.00	2.20
□ 10	Nomar Garciaparra	5.00	2.20
□ 11	Darin Erstad	1.00	.45
□ 12	Greg Maddux	4.00	1.80
□ 13	Alex Rodriguez	5.00	2.20
□ 14	Mike Piazza	5.00	2.20
□ 15	Vladimir Guerrero	2.00	.90
□ 16	Jose Cruz Jr.	.75	.35
□ 17	Hideo Nomo	1.50	.70
□ 18	Kenny Lofton	1.00	.45
□ 19	Tony Gwynn	4.00	1.80
□ 20	Scott Rolen	2.50	1.10

1999 Metal Universe

	MINT	NRMT
COMPLETE SET (300)	50.00	22.00
COMMON CARD (1-300)	.15	.07
MINOR STARS	.25	.11
SEMISTARS	.40	.18
UNLISTED STARS	.60	.25

□ 1	Mark McGwire	4.00	1.80
□ 2	Jim Edmonds	.25	.11
□ 3	Travis Fryman	.25	.11
□ 4	Tom Gordon	.25	.11
□ 5	Jeff Bagwell	.75	.35
□ 6	Rico Brogna	.15	.07
□ 7	Tom Evans	.15	.07
□ 8	John Franco	.25	.11
□ 9	Juan Gonzalez	1.25	.55
□ 10	Paul Molitor	.60	.25
□ 11	Roberto Alomar	.60	.25
□ 12	Mike Hampton	.25	.11
□ 13	Orel Hershiser	.25	.11
□ 14	Todd Stottlemyre	.15	.07
□ 15	Robin Ventura	.25	.11
□ 16	Todd Walker	.25	.11
□ 17	Bernie Williams	.60	.25
□ 18	Shawn Estes	.15	.07
□ 19	Richie Sexson	.40	.18
□ 20	Kevin Millwood	.40	.18
□ 21	David Ortiz	.15	.07
□ 22	Mariano Rivera	.25	.11
□ 23	Ivan Rodriguez	.75	.35
□ 24	Mike Sirotka	.15	.07
□ 25	David Justice	.25	.11
□ 26	Carl Pavano	.15	.07
□ 27	Albert Belle	.60	.25
□ 28	Will Clark	.60	.25
□ 29	Jose Cruz Jr.	.25	.11
□ 30	Trevor Hoffman	.25	.11
□ 31	Dean Palmer	.15	.07
□ 32	Edgar Renteria	.25	.11
□ 33	David Segui	.15	.07
□ 34	B.J. Surhoff	.25	.11
□ 35	Miguel Tejada	.25	.11
□ 36	Bob Wickman	.15	.07
□ 37	Charles Johnson	.25	.11
□ 38	Andruw Jones	.60	.25
□ 39	Mike Lieberthal	.25	.11
□ 40	Eli Marrero	.15	.07
□ 41	Neifi Perez	.25	.11
□ 42	Jim Thome	.60	.25
□ 43	Barry Bonds	.75	.35
□ 44	Carlos Delgado	.60	.25
□ 45	Chuck Finley	.15	.07
□ 46	Brian Meadows	.15	.07
□ 47	Tony Gwynn	1.50	.70
□ 48	Jose Offerman	.25	.11
□ 49	Cal Ripken	2.50	1.10
□ 50	Alex Rodriguez	2.00	.90
□ 51	Esteban Yan	.15	.07
□ 52	Matt Stairs	.25	.11
□ 53	Fernando Vina	.15	.07
□ 54	Rondell White	.25	.11
□ 55	Kerry Wood	.60	.25
□ 56	Dmitri Young	.25	.11
□ 57	Ken Caminiti	.25	.11
□ 58	Alex Gonzalez	.15	.07
□ 59	Matt Mantei	.25	.11
□ 60	Tino Martinez	.25	.11
□ 61	Hal Morris	.15	.07
□ 62	Rafael Palmeiro	.60	.25
□ 63	Troy Percival	.25	.11
□ 64	Bobby Smith	.15	.07
□ 65	Ed Sprague	.15	.07
□ 66	Brett Tomko	.15	.07
□ 67	Steve Trachsel	.15	.07
□ 68	Ugueth Urbina	.15	.07
□ 69	Jose Valentin	.15	.07
□ 70	Kevin Brown	.40	.18
□ 71	Shawn Green	.25	.11
□ 72	Dustin Hermanson	.15	.07
□ 73	Livan Hernandez	.15	.07
□ 74	Geoff Jenkins	.25	.11
□ 75	Jeff King	.15	.07
□ 76	Chuck Knoblauch	.25	.11
□ 77	Edgar Martinez	.25	.11
□ 78	Fred McGriff	.40	.18
□ 79	Mike Mussina	.60	.25
□ 80	Dave Nilsson	.15	.07
□ 81	Kenny Rogers	.15	.07
□ 82	Tim Salmon	.40	.18
□ 83	Reggie Sanders	.15	.07
□ 84	Wilson Alvarez	.15	.07
□ 85	Rod Beck	.25	.11
□ 86	Jose Guillen	.25	.11
□ 87	Bob Higginson	.25	.11
□ 88	Gregg Olson	.15	.07
□ 89	Jeff Shaw	.15	.07
□ 90	Masato Yoshii	.15	.07
□ 91	Todd Helton	.60	.25
□ 92	David Dellucci	.15	.07
□ 93	Johnny Damon	.25	.11
□ 94	Cliff Floyd	.25	.11
□ 95	Ken Griffey Jr.	3.00	1.35
□ 96	Juan Guzman	.15	.07
□ 97	Derek Jeter	2.00	.90
□ 98	Barry Larkin	.60	.25
□ 99	Quinton McCracken	.15	.07
□ 100	Sammy Sosa	2.00	.90
□ 101	Kevin Young	.15	.07
□ 102	Jay Bell	.25	.11
□ 103	Jay Buhner	.25	.11
□ 104	Jeff Conine	.15	.07
□ 105	Ryan Jackson	.15	.07
□ 106	Sidney Ponson	.15	.07
□ 107	Jeromy Burnitz	.25	.11
□ 108	Roberto Hernandez	.15	.07
□ 109	A.J. Hinch	.25	.11
□ 110	Hideki Irabu	.25	.11
□ 111	Paul Konerko	.25	.11
□ 112	Henry Rodriguez	.25	.11
□ 113	Shannon Stewart	.25	.11
□ 114	Tony Womack	.25	.11
□ 115	Wilton Guerrero	.15	.07
□ 116	Andy Benes	.25	.11
□ 117	Jeff Cirillo	.25	.11
□ 118	Chili Davis	.25	.11
□ 119	Eric Davis	.25	.11
□ 120	Vladimir Guerrero	.75	.35
□ 121	Dennis Reyes	.15	.07
□ 122	Rickey Henderson	.75	.35
□ 123	Mickey Morandini	.15	.07
□ 124	Jason Schmidt	.25	.11
□ 125	J.T. Snow	.25	.11
□ 126	Justin Thompson	.15	.07
□ 127	Billy Wagner	.25	.11
□ 128	Armando Benitez	.15	.07
□ 129	Sean Casey	.60	.25
□ 130	Brad Fullmer	.25	.11
□ 131	Ben Grieve	.60	.25
□ 132	Robb Nen	.15	.07
□ 133	Shane Reynolds	.25	.11
□ 134	Todd Zeile	.25	.11
□ 135	Brady Anderson	.25	.11
□ 136	Aaron Boone	.15	.07
□ 137	Orlando Cabrera	.15	.07
□ 138	Jason Giambi	.25	.11
□ 139	Randy Johnson	.60	.25
□ 140	Jeff Kent	.25	.11
□ 141	John Wetteland	.25	.11
□ 142	Rolando Arrojo	.15	.07
□ 143	Scott Brosius	.25	.11
□ 144	Mark Grace	.40	.18
□ 145	Jason Kendall	.25	.11
□ 146	Travis Lee	.25	.11
□ 147	Gary Sheffield	.25	.11
□ 148	David Cone	.40	.18
□ 149	Jose Hernandez	.15	.07
□ 150	Todd Jones	.15	.07
□ 151	Al Martin	.15	.07
□ 152	Ismael Valdes	.15	.07
□ 153	Wade Boggs	.60	.25
□ 154	Garret Anderson	.25	.11
□ 155	Bobby Bonilla	.25	.11
□ 156	Darryl Kile	.15	.07
□ 157	Ryan Klesko	.25	.11
□ 158	Tim Wakefield	.25	.11
□ 159	Kenny Lofton	.40	.18
□ 160	Jose Canseco	.75	.35
□ 161	Doug Glanville	.25	.11
□ 162	Todd Hundley	.25	.11
□ 163	Brian Jordan	.25	.11
□ 164	Steve Finley	.25	.11
□ 165	Tom Glavine	.60	.25
□ 166	Al Leiter	.25	.11
□ 167	Raul Mondesi	.25	.11
□ 168	Desi Relaford	.15	.07
□ 169	Bret Saberhagen	.15	.07
□ 170	Omar Vizquel	.25	.11
□ 171	Larry Walker	.60	.25
□ 172	Bobby Abreu	.25	.11
□ 173	Moises Alou	.25	.11
□ 174	Mike Caruso	.15	.07
□ 175	Royce Clayton	.15	.07
□ 176	Bartolo Colon	.25	.11
□ 177	Marty Cordova	.15	.07
□ 178	Darin Erstad	.25	.11
□ 179	Nomar Garciaparra	2.00	.90
□ 180	Andy Ashby	.15	.07
□ 181	Dan Wilson	.15	.07
□ 182	Larry Sutton	.15	.07
□ 183	Tony Clark	.25	.11
□ 184	Andres Galarraga	.40	.18
□ 185	Ray Durham	.25	.11
□ 186	Hideo Nomo	.60	.25
□ 187	Steve Woodard	.15	.07
□ 188	Scott Rolen	.75	.35
□ 189	Mike Stanley	.15	.07
□ 190	Jaret Wright	.25	.11
□ 191	Vinny Castilla	.25	.11
□ 192	Jason Christiansen	.15	.07
□ 193	Paul Bako	.15	.07
□ 194	Carlos Perez	.15	.07
□ 195	Mike Piazza	2.00	.90
□ 196	Fernando Tatis	.60	.25
□ 197	Mo Vaughn	.60	.25
□ 198	Devon White	.15	.07
□ 199	Ricky Gutierrez	.15	.07
□ 200	Charlie Hayes	.15	.07
□ 201	Brad Radke	.25	.11
□ 202	Rick Helling	.15	.07
□ 203	John Smoltz	.40	.18
□ 204	Frank Thomas	1.25	.55
□ 205	David Wells	.25	.11
□ 206	Roger Clemens	1.50	.70
□ 207	Mark Grudzielanek	.15	.07

❏ 208 Chipper Jones	1.50	.70
❏ 209 Ray Lankford	.25	.11
❏ 210 Pedro Martinez	.75	.35
❏ 211 Manny Ramirez	.75	.35
❏ 212 Greg Vaughn	.25	.11
❏ 213 Craig Biggio	.60	.25
❏ 214 Rusty Greer	.25	.11
❏ 215 Greg Maddux	1.50	.70
❏ 216 Rick Aguilera	.15	.07
❏ 217 Andy Pettitte	.25	.11
❏ 218 Dante Bichette	.25	.11
❏ 219 Damion Easley	.25	.11
❏ 220 Matt Morris	.15	.07
❏ 221 John Olerud	.25	.11
❏ 222 Chan Ho Park	.25	.11
❏ 223 Curt Schilling	.40	.18
❏ 224 John Valentin	.25	.11
❏ 225 Matt Williams	.60	.25
❏ 226 Ellis Burks	.25	.11
❏ 227 Tom Goodwin	.15	.07
❏ 228 Javy Lopez	.25	.11
❏ 229 Eric Milton	.15	.07
❏ 230 Paul O'Neill	.25	.11
❏ 231 Magglio Ordonez	.60	.25
❏ 232 Derrek Lee	.15	.07
❏ 233 Ken Griffey Jr. FLY	1.50	.70
❏ 234 Randy Johnson FLY	.25	.11
❏ 235 Alex Rodriguez FLY	1.00	.45
❏ 236 Darin Erstad FLY	.25	.11
❏ 237 Juan Gonzalez FLY	.60	.25
❏ 238 Derek Jeter FLY	1.00	.45
❏ 239 Tony Gwynn FLY	.75	.35
❏ 240 Kerry Wood FLY	.25	.11
❏ 241 Cal Ripken FLY	1.25	.55
❏ 242 Sammy Sosa FLY	1.00	.45
❏ 243 Greg Maddux FLY	.75	.35
❏ 244 Mark McGwire FLY	2.00	.90
❏ 245 Chipper Jones FLY	.75	.35
❏ 246 Barry Bonds FLY	.40	.18
❏ 247 Ben Grieve FLY	.25	.11
❏ 248 Ben Davis BB	.40	.18
❏ 249 Robert Fick BB	.25	.11
❏ 250 Carlos Guillen BB	.15	.07
❏ 251 Mike Frank BB	.15	.07
❏ 252 Ryan Minor BB	.25	.11
❏ 253 Troy Glaus BB	.60	.25
❏ 254 Matt Anderson BB	.15	.07
❏ 255 Josh Booty BB	.15	.07
❏ 256 Gabe Alvarez BB	.15	.07
❏ 257 Gabe Kapler BB	.60	.25
❏ 258 Enrique Wilson BB	.15	.07
❏ 259 Alex Gonzalez BB	.25	.11
❏ 260 Preston Wilson BB	.25	.11
❏ 261 Eric Chavez BB	.40	.18
❏ 262 Adrian Beltre BB	.60	.25
❏ 263 Corey Koskie BB	.15	.07
❏ 264 Robert Machado BB	.15	.07
❏ 265 Orlando Hernandez BB	.60	.25
❏ 266 Matt Clement BB	.25	.11
❏ 267 Luis Ordaz BB	.15	.07
❏ 268 Jeremy Giambi BB	.25	.11
❏ 269 J.D. Drew BB	1.00	.45
❏ 270 Cliff Politte BB	.15	.07
❏ 271 Carlton Loewer BB	.15	.07
❏ 272 Aramis Ramirez BB	.40	.18
❏ 273 Ken Griffey Jr. MLPD	1.50	.70
❏ 274 Randy Johnson MLPD	.25	.11
❏ 275 Alex Rodriguez MLPD	1.00	.45
❏ 276 Darin Erstad MLPD	.25	.11
❏ 277 Scott Rolen MLPD	.60	.25
❏ 278 Juan Gonzalez MLPD	.60	.25
❏ 279 Jeff Bagwell MLPD	.40	.18
❏ 280 Mike Piazza MLPD	1.00	.45
❏ 281 Derek Jeter MLPD	1.00	.45
❏ 282 Travis Lee MLPD	.25	.11
❏ 283 Tony Gwynn MLPD	.75	.35
❏ 284 Kerry Wood MLPD	.25	.11
❏ 285 Albert Belle MLPD	.25	.11
❏ 286 Sammy Sosa MLPD	1.00	.45
❏ 287 Mo Vaughn MLPD	.25	.11
❏ 288 Nomar Garciaparra MLPD	1.00	.45
❏ 289 Frank Thomas MLPD	.75	.35
❏ 290 Cal Ripken MLPD	1.25	.55
❏ 291 Greg Maddux MLPD	.75	.35
❏ 292 Chipper Jones MLPD	.75	.35
❏ 293 Ben Grieve MLPD	.60	.25
❏ 294 Andruw Jones MLPD	.25	.11
❏ 295 Mark McGwire MLPD	2.00	.90
❏ 296 Roger Clemens MLPD	.75	.35
❏ 297 Barry Bonds MLPD	.40	.18
❏ 298 Ken Griffey Jr. CL	1.50	.70
❏ 299 Kerry Wood CL	.25	.11
❏ 300 Alex Rodriguez CL	1.00	.45

1999 Metal Universe Precious Metal Gems

	MINT	NRMT
COMMON CARD (1-300)	12.00	5.50

*STARS: 30X TO 80X BASIC CARDS
*YNG.STARS: 25X TO 60X BASIC CARDS
RANDOM INSERTS IN PACKS
STATED PRINT RUN 50 SERIAL #'D SETS
GEM MASTER 1 OF 1 PARALLELS EXIST

1999 Metal Universe Boyz With The Wood

	MINT	NRMT
COMPLETE SET (15)	80.00	36.00
COMMON CARD (1-15)	1.50	.70
UNLISTED STARS	2.50	1.10
STATED ODDS 1:18		
❏ 1 Ken Griffey Jr.	12.00	5.50
❏ 2 Frank Thomas	5.00	2.20
❏ 3 Jeff Bagwell	3.00	1.35
❏ 4 Juan Gonzalez	5.00	2.20
❏ 5 Mark McGwire	15.00	6.75
❏ 6 Scott Rolen	3.00	1.35
❏ 7 Travis Lee	1.50	.70
❏ 8 Tony Gwynn	6.00	2.70
❏ 9 Mike Piazza	8.00	3.60
❏ 10 Chipper Jones	6.00	2.70
❏ 11 Nomar Garciaparra	8.00	3.60
❏ 12 Derek Jeter	8.00	3.60
❏ 13 Cal Ripken	10.00	4.50
❏ 14 Andruw Jones	2.50	1.10
❏ 15 Alex Rodriguez	8.00	3.60

1999 Metal Universe Diamond Soul

	MINT	NRMT
COMPLETE SET (15)	300.00	135.00

COMMON CARD (1-15)	5.00	2.20
UNLISTED STARS	8.00	3.60
STATED ODDS 1:72		
❏ 1 Cal Ripken	30.00	13.50
❏ 2 Alex Rodriguez	25.00	11.00
❏ 3 Chipper Jones	20.00	9.00
❏ 4 Derek Jeter	25.00	11.00
❏ 5 Frank Thomas	15.00	6.75
❏ 6 Greg Maddux	20.00	9.00
❏ 7 Juan Gonzalez	15.00	6.75
❏ 8 Ken Griffey Jr.	40.00	18.00
❏ 9 Kerry Wood	8.00	3.60
❏ 10 Mark McGwire	50.00	22.00
❏ 11 Mike Piazza	25.00	11.00
❏ 12 Nomar Garciaparra	25.00	11.00
❏ 13 Scott Rolen	10.00	4.50
❏ 14 Tony Gwynn	20.00	9.00
❏ 15 Travis Lee	5.00	2.20

1999 Metal Universe Linchpins

	MINT	NRMT
COMPLETE SET (10)	500.00	220.00
COMMON CARD (1-10)	12.00	5.50
STATED ODDS 1:360		
❏ 1 Mike Piazza	50.00	22.00
❏ 2 Mark McGwire	100.00	45.00
❏ 3 Kerry Wood	12.00	5.50
❏ 4 Ken Griffey Jr.	80.00	36.00
❏ 5 Greg Maddux	40.00	18.00
❏ 6 Frank Thomas	30.00	13.50
❏ 7 Derek Jeter	50.00	22.00
❏ 8 Chipper Jones	40.00	18.00
❏ 9 Cal Ripken	60.00	27.00
❏ 10 Alex Rodriguez	50.00	22.00

1999 Metal Universe Neophytes

	MINT	NRMT
COMPLETE SET (15)	10.00	4.50
COMMON CARD (1-15)	.40	.18
MINOR STARS	.60	.25
SEMISTARS	1.00	.45
UNLISTED STARS	1.50	.70
STATED ODDS 1:6		

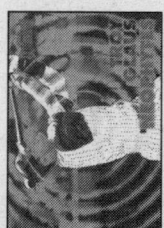

		MINT	NRMT
❑ 1	Troy Glaus	1.50	.70
❑ 2	Travis Lee	1.00	.45
❑ 3	Scott Elarton	.40	.18
❑ 4	Ricky Ledee	.60	.25
❑ 5	Richard Hidalgo	.60	.25
❑ 6	J.D. Drew	2.50	1.10
❑ 7	Paul Konerko	.60	.25
❑ 8	Orlando Hernandez	1.50	.70
❑ 9	Mike Caruso	.40	.18
❑ 10	Mike Frank	.40	.18
❑ 11	Miguel Tejada	.60	.25
❑ 12	Matt Anderson	.40	.18
❑ 13	Kerry Wood	1.50	.70
❑ 14	Gabe Alvarez	.40	.18
❑ 15	Adrian Beltre	1.50	.70

1999 Metal Universe Planet Metal

	MINT	NRMT
COMPLETE SET (15)	150.00	70.00
COMMON CARD (1-15)	2.00	.90
UNLISTED STARS	5.00	2.20
STATED ODDS 1:36		

		MINT	NRMT
❑ 1	Alex Rodriguez	15.00	6.75
❑ 2	Andruw Jones	5.00	2.20
❑ 3	Cal Ripken	20.00	9.00
❑ 4	Chipper Jones	12.00	5.50
❑ 5	Darin Erstad	3.00	1.35
❑ 6	Derek Jeter	15.00	6.75
❑ 7	Frank Thomas	10.00	4.50
❑ 8	Travis Lee	3.00	1.35
❑ 9	Scott Rolen	6.00	2.70
❑ 10	Nomar Garciaparra	15.00	6.75
❑ 11	Mike Piazza	15.00	6.75
❑ 12	Mark McGwire	30.00	13.50
❑ 13	Ken Griffey Jr.	25.00	11.00
❑ 14	Juan Gonzalez	10.00	4.50
❑ 15	Jeff Bagwell	6.00	2.70

1997 New Pinnacle

	MINT	NRMT
COMPLETE SET (200)	25.00	11.00
COMMON CARD (1-200)	.15	.07
MINOR STARS	.30	.14
UNLISTED STARS	.60	.25
SUBSET CARDS HALF VALUE OF BASE CARDS		

COMMON MUSEUM (1-200)	1.50	.70
*MUSEUM STARS: 5X TO 12X HI COLUMN		
*MUSEUM ROOKIES: 3X TO 8X HI		
MUSEUM STATED ODDS 1:9		

❑ 1	Ken Griffey Jr.	3.00	1.35
❑ 2	Sammy Sosa	2.00	.90
❑ 3	Greg Maddux	1.50	.70
❑ 4	Matt Williams	.60	.25
❑ 5	Jason Isringhausen	.15	.07
❑ 6	Gregg Jefferies	.15	.07
❑ 7	Chili Davis	.30	.14
❑ 8	Paul O'Neill	.30	.14
❑ 9	Larry Walker	.60	.25
❑ 10	Ellis Burks	.30	.14
❑ 11	Cliff Floyd	.30	.14
❑ 12	Albert Belle	.60	.25
❑ 13	Javier Lopez	.30	.14
❑ 14	David Cone	.40	.18
❑ 15	Jose Canseco	.75	.35
❑ 16	Todd Zeile	.15	.07
❑ 17	Bernard Gilkey	.15	.07
❑ 18	Andres Galarraga	.60	.25
❑ 19	Chris Snopek	.15	.07
❑ 20	Tim Salmon	.60	.25
❑ 21	Roger Clemens	1.50	.70
❑ 22	Reggie Sanders	.30	.14
❑ 23	John Jaha	.15	.07
❑ 24	Andy Pettitte	.40	.18
❑ 25	Kenny Lofton	.40	.18
❑ 26	Robb Nen	.15	.07
❑ 27	John Wetteland	.30	.14
❑ 28	Bobby Bonilla	.30	.14
❑ 29	Hideo Nomo	.60	.25
❑ 30	Cecil Fielder	.30	.14
❑ 31	Garret Anderson	.30	.14
❑ 32	Pat Hentgen	.30	.14
❑ 33	Dave Justice	.60	.25
❑ 34	Billy Wagner	.30	.14
❑ 35	Al Leiter	.30	.14
❑ 36	Mark Wohlers	.15	.07
❑ 37	Rondell White	.30	.14
❑ 38	Charles Johnson	.30	.14
❑ 39	Mark Grace	.40	.18
❑ 40	Pedro Martinez	.75	.35
❑ 41	Tom Goodwin	.15	.07
❑ 42	Manny Ramirez	.75	.35
❑ 43	Greg Vaughn	.30	.14
❑ 44	Brian Jordan	.30	.14
❑ 45	Mike Piazza	2.00	.90
❑ 46	Roberto Hernandez	.15	.07
❑ 47	Wade Boggs	.60	.25
❑ 48	Scott Sanders	.15	.07
❑ 49	Alex Gonzalez	.15	.07
❑ 50	Kevin Brown	.40	.18
❑ 51	Bob Higginson	.30	.14
❑ 52	Ken Caminiti	.40	.18
❑ 53	Derek Jeter	2.00	.90
❑ 54	Carlos Baerga	.15	.07
❑ 55	Jay Buhner	.30	.14
❑ 56	Tim Naehring	.15	.07
❑ 57	Jeff Bagwell	.75	.35
❑ 58	Steve Finley	.30	.14
❑ 59	Kevin Appier	.30	.14
❑ 60	Jay Bell	.30	.14
❑ 61	Ivan Rodriguez	.75	.35
❑ 62	Terrell Wade	.15	.07
❑ 63	Rusty Greer	.30	.14
❑ 64	Juan Guzman	.15	.07
❑ 65	Fred McGriff	.40	.18
❑ 66	Tino Martinez	.60	.25
❑ 67	Ray Lankford	.30	.14
❑ 68	Juan Gonzalez	1.25	.55
❑ 69	Ron Gant	.15	.07
❑ 70	Jack McDowell	.15	.07
❑ 71	Tony Gwynn	1.50	.70
❑ 72	Joe Carter	.30	.14
❑ 73	Wilson Alvarez	.30	.14
❑ 74	Jason Giambi	.30	.14
❑ 75	Brian Hunter	.30	.14
❑ 76	Michael Tucker	.15	.07
❑ 77	Andy Benes	.30	.14
❑ 78	Brady Anderson	.30	.14
❑ 79	Ramon Martinez	.30	.14
❑ 80	Troy Percival	.30	.14
❑ 81	Alex Rodriguez	2.00	.90
❑ 82	Jim Thome	.60	.25
❑ 83	Denny Neagle	.30	.14
❑ 84	Rafael Palmeiro	.60	.25
❑ 85	Jose Valentin	.15	.07
❑ 86	Marc Newfield	.15	.07
❑ 87	Mariano Rivera	.30	.14
❑ 88	Alan Benes	.15	.07
❑ 89	Jimmy Key	.30	.14
❑ 90	Joe Randa	.15	.07
❑ 91	Cal Ripken	2.50	1.10
❑ 92	Craig Biggio	.60	.25
❑ 93	Dean Palmer	.30	.14
❑ 94	Gary Sheffield	.30	.14
❑ 95	Ismael Valdes	.30	.14
❑ 96	John Valentin	.30	.14
❑ 97	Johnny Damon	.30	.14
❑ 98	Mo Vaughn	.60	.25
❑ 99	Paul Sorrento	.15	.07
❑ 100	Randy Johnson	.60	.25
❑ 101	Raul Mondesi	.30	.14
❑ 102	Roberto Alomar	.60	.25
❑ 103	Royce Clayton	.15	.07
❑ 104	Mark Grudzielanek	.30	.14
❑ 105	Wally Joyner	.30	.14
❑ 106	Wil Cordero	.15	.07
❑ 107	Will Clark	.60	.25
❑ 108	Chuck Knoblauch	.60	.25
❑ 109	Derek Bell	.30	.14
❑ 110	Henry Rodriguez	.30	.14
❑ 111	Edgar Renteria	.30	.14
❑ 112	Travis Fryman	.30	.14
❑ 113	Eric Young	.30	.14
❑ 114	Sandy Alomar Jr.	.30	.14
❑ 115	Darin Erstad	.60	.25
❑ 116	Barry Larkin	.60	.25
❑ 117	Barry Bonds	.75	.35
❑ 118	Frank Thomas	1.25	.55
❑ 119	Carlos Delgado	.60	.25
❑ 120	Jason Kendall	.40	.18
❑ 121	Todd Hollandsworth	.15	.07
❑ 122	Jim Edmonds	.40	.18
❑ 123	Chipper Jones	1.50	.70
❑ 124	Jeff Fassero	.15	.07
❑ 125	Deion Sanders	.30	.14
❑ 126	Matt Lawton	.30	.14
❑ 127	Ryan Klesko	.30	.14
❑ 128	Mike Mussina	.60	.25
❑ 129	Paul Molitor	.60	.25
❑ 130	Dante Bichette	.30	.14
❑ 131	Bill Pulsipher	.15	.07
❑ 132	Todd Hundley	.30	.14
❑ 133	J.T. Snow	.30	.14
❑ 134	Chuck Finley	.30	.14
❑ 135	Shawn Green	.60	.25
❑ 136	Charles Nagy	.30	.14
❑ 137	Willie Greene	.15	.07
❑ 138	Marty Cordova	.15	.07
❑ 139	Eddie Murray	.60	.25
❑ 140	Ryne Sandberg	.75	.35
❑ 141	Alex Fernandez	.15	.07
❑ 142	Mark McGwire	3.00	1.35
❑ 143	Eric Davis	.30	.14
❑ 144	Jermaine Dye	.30	.14
❑ 145	Ruben Sierra	.30	.14
❑ 146	Damon Buford	.15	.07
❑ 147	John Smoltz	.40	.18
❑ 148	Alex Ochoa	.15	.07
❑ 149	Moises Alou	.30	.14

#	Player	MINT	NRMT
150	Rico Brogna	.15	.07
151	Terry Steinbach	.15	.07
152	Jeff King	.15	.07
153	Carlos Garcia	.15	.07
154	Tom Glavine	.60	.25
155	Edgar Martinez	.30	.14
156	Kevin Elster	.15	.07
157	Darryl Hamilton	.15	.07
158	Jason Dickson	.15	.07
159	Kevin Orie	.15	.07
160	Bubba Trammell	.60	.25
161	Jose Guillen	.40	.18
162	Brant Brown	.30	.14
163	Wendell Magee	.15	.07
164	Scott Spiezio	.15	.07
165	Todd Walker	.60	.25
166	Rod Myers	.15	.07
167	Damon Mashore	.15	.07
168	Wilton Guerrero	.15	.07
169	Vladimir Guerrero	1.00	.45
170	Nomar Garciaparra	2.00	.90
171	Shannon Stewart	.30	.14
172	Scott Rolen	1.00	.45
173	Bob Abreu	.30	.14
174	Danny Patterson	.15	.07
175	Andruw Jones	.75	.35
176	Brian Giles	2.00	.90
177	Dmitri Young	.30	.14
178	Cal Ripken EMW	1.25	.55
179	Chuck Knoblauch EMW	.30	.14
180	Alex Rodriguez EMW	1.00	.45
181	Andres Galarraga EMW	.30	.14
182	Pedro Martinez EMW	.40	.18
183	Brady Anderson EMW	.15	.07
184	Barry Bonds EMW	.30	.14
185	Ivan Rodriguez EMW	.40	.18
186	Gary Sheffield EMW	.15	.07
187	Denny Neagle EMW	.15	.07
188	Mark McGwire AURA	1.50	.70
189	Ellis Burks AURA	.15	.07
190	Alex Rodriguez AURA	1.00	.45
191	Mike Piazza AURA	1.00	.45
192	Barry Bonds AURA	.30	.14
193	Albert Belle AURA	.30	.14
194	Chipper Jones AURA	.75	.35
195	Juan Gonzalez AURA	.60	.25
196	Brady Anderson AURA	.15	.07
197	Frank Thomas AURA	.60	.25
198	Vladimir Guerrero CL	.30	.14
199	Todd Walker CL	.30	.14
200	Scott Rolen CL	.60	.25

1997 New Pinnacle Artist's Proofs

	MINT	NRMT
*RED CARDS: 8X TO 20X HI COLUMN
*BLUE CARDS: 20X TO 50X HI COLUMN
*GREEN CARDS: 25X TO 60X HI COLUMN
STATED ODDS 1:39

#	Player	MINT	NRMT
1	Ken Griffey Jr. G	200.00	90.00
2	Sammy Sosa B	80.00	36.00
3	Greg Maddux G	120.00	55.00
4	Matt Williams B	15.00	6.75
5	Jason Isringhausen R	4.00	1.80
6	Gregg Jefferies R	4.00	1.80
7	Chili Davis R	6.00	2.70
8	Paul O'Neill R	6.00	2.70
9	Larry Walker R	12.00	5.50
10	Ellis Burks B	15.00	6.75
11	Cliff Floyd R	6.00	2.70
12	Albert Belle G	50.00	22.00
13	Javier Lopez R	10.00	4.50
14	David Cone R	10.00	4.50
15	Jose Canseco B	30.00	13.50
16	Todd Zeile R	4.00	1.80
17	Bernard Gilkey B	8.00	3.60
18	Andres Galarraga R	30.00	13.50
19	Chris Snopek R	4.00	1.80
20	Tim Salmon B	30.00	13.50
21	Roger Clemens B	80.00	36.00
22	Reggie Sanders R	6.00	2.70
23	John Jaha R	4.00	1.80
24	Andy Pettitte R	25.00	11.00
25	Kenny Lofton G	50.00	22.00
26	Robb Nen R	4.00	1.80
27	John Wetteland B	15.00	6.75
28	Bobby Bonilla R	6.00	2.70
29	Hideo Nomo G	50.00	22.00
30	Cecil Fielder R	6.00	2.70
31	Garret Anderson R	6.00	2.70
32	Pat Hentgen R	6.00	2.70
33	Dave Justice R	12.00	5.50
34	Billy Wagner R	4.00	1.80
35	Al Leiter R	6.00	2.70
36	Mark Wohlers R	4.00	1.80
37	Rondell White R	6.00	2.70
38	Charles Johnson R	6.00	2.70
39	Mark Grace R	10.00	4.50
40	Pedro Martinez R	12.00	5.50
41	Tom Goodwin R	4.00	1.80
42	Manny Ramirez R	30.00	13.50
43	Greg Vaughn R	6.00	2.70
44	Brian Jordan B	15.00	6.75
45	Mike Piazza G	120.00	55.00
46	Roberto Hernandez R	4.00	1.80
47	Wade Boggs B	30.00	13.50
48	Scott Sanders R	4.00	1.80
49	Alex Gonzalez R	4.00	1.80
50	Kevin Brown R	10.00	4.50
51	Bob Higginson R	25.00	11.00
52	Ken Caminiti B	25.00	11.00
53	Derek Jeter G	100.00	45.00
54	Carlos Baerga R	6.00	2.70
55	Jay Buhner B	15.00	6.75
56	Tim Naehring R	4.00	1.80
57	Jeff Bagwell G	50.00	22.00
58	Steve Finley R	6.00	2.70
59	Kevin Appier R	6.00	2.70
60	Jay Bell R	6.00	2.70
61	Ivan Rodriguez B	30.00	13.50
62	Terrell Wade R	4.00	1.80
63	Rusty Greer R	6.00	2.70
64	Juan Guzman R	4.00	1.80
65	Fred McGriff R	10.00	4.50
66	Tino Martinez R	12.00	5.50
67	Ray Lankford R	6.00	2.70
68	Juan Gonzalez G	100.00	45.00
69	Ron Gant R	4.00	1.80
70	Jack McDowell R	4.00	1.80
71	Tony Gwynn B	80.00	36.00
72	Joe Carter B	15.00	6.75
73	Wilson Alvarez R	6.00	2.70
74	Jason Giambi R	6.00	2.70
75	Brian Hunter R	6.00	2.70
76	Michael Tucker R	6.00	2.70
77	Andy Benes R	6.00	2.70
78	Brady Anderson B	15.00	6.75
79	Ramon Martinez R	6.00	2.70
80	Troy Percival B	15.00	6.75
81	Alex Rodriguez G	120.00	55.00
82	Jim Thome B	30.00	13.50
83	Denny Neagle R	6.00	2.70
84	Rafael Palmeiro B	25.00	11.00
85	Jose Valentin R	4.00	1.80
86	Marc Newfield R	4.00	1.80
87	Mariano Rivera B	15.00	6.75
88	Alan Benes R	6.00	2.70
89	Jimmy Key R	6.00	2.70
90	Joe Randa R	4.00	1.80
91	Cal Ripken G	150.00	70.00
92	Craig Biggio R	12.00	5.50
93	Dean Palmer R	6.00	2.70
94	Gary Sheffield B	25.00	11.00
95	Ismael Valdes R	6.00	2.70
96	John Valentin R	6.00	2.70
97	Johnny Damon R	6.00	2.70
98	Mo Vaughn G	50.00	22.00
99	Paul Sorrento R	4.00	1.80
100	Randy Johnson B	30.00	13.50
101	Raul Mondesi B	25.00	11.00
102	Roberto Alomar B	30.00	13.50
103	Royce Clayton R	4.00	1.80
104	Mark Grudzielanek R	6.00	2.70
105	Wally Joyner R	6.00	2.70
106	Wil Cordero R	4.00	1.80
107	Will Clark B	30.00	13.50
108	Chuck Knoblauch B	30.00	13.50
109	Derek Bell R	6.00	2.70
110	Henry Rodriguez R	6.00	2.70
111	Edgar Renteria R	6.00	2.70
112	Travis Fryman R	6.00	2.70
113	Eric Young R	6.00	2.70
114	Sandy Alomar Jr. R	6.00	2.70
115	Darin Erstad B	30.00	13.50
116	Barry Larkin B	25.00	11.00
117	Barry Bonds B	30.00	13.50
118	Frank Thomas G	100.00	45.00
119	Carlos Delgado R	6.00	2.70
120	Jason Kendall R	10.00	4.50
121	Todd Hollandsworth R	4.00	1.80
122	Jim Edmonds R	10.00	4.50
123	Chipper Jones G	100.00	45.00
124	Jeff Fassero R	4.00	1.80
125	Deion Sanders R	15.00	6.75
126	Matt Lawton R	6.00	2.70
127	Ryan Klesko R	6.00	2.70
128	Mike Mussina R	12.00	5.50
129	Paul Molitor B	30.00	13.50
130	Dante Bichette R	6.00	2.70
131	Bill Pulsipher R	4.00	1.80
132	Todd Hundley B	15.00	6.75
133	J.T. Snow R	6.00	2.70
134	Chuck Finley R	6.00	2.70
135	Shawn Green R	6.00	2.70
136	Charles Nagy R	6.00	2.70
137	Willie Greene R	6.00	2.70
138	Marty Cordova R	4.00	1.80
139	Eddie Murray R	12.00	5.50
140	Ryne Sandberg R	12.00	5.50
141	Alex Fernandez R	4.00	1.80
142	Mark McGwire G	200.00	90.00
143	Eric Davis R	6.00	2.70
144	Jermaine Dye R	4.00	1.80
145	Ruben Sierra R	4.00	1.80
146	Damon Buford R	4.00	1.80
147	John Smoltz B	15.00	6.75
148	Alex Ochoa R	4.00	1.80
149	Moises Alou R	10.00	4.50
150	Rico Brogna R	4.00	1.80
151	Terry Steinbach R	6.00	2.70
152	Jeff King R	4.00	1.80
153	Carlos Garcia R	4.00	1.80
154	Tom Glavine R	12.00	5.50
155	Edgar Martinez B	15.00	6.75
156	Kevin Elster R	4.00	1.80
157	Darryl Hamilton R	4.00	1.80
158	Jason Dickson R	6.00	2.70
159	Kevin Orie R	4.00	1.80
160	Bubba Trammell R	12.00	5.50
161	Jose Guillen B	30.00	13.50
162	Brant Brown R	6.00	2.70
163	Wendell Magee R	4.00	1.80
164	Scott Spiezio R	4.00	1.80
165	Todd Walker B	30.00	13.50
166	Rod Myers R	4.00	1.80
167	Damon Mashore R	4.00	1.80
168	Wilton Guerrero R	8.00	3.60
169	Vladimir Guerrero G	60.00	27.00
170	Nomar Garciaparra G	100.00	45.00
171	Shannon Stewart R	6.00	2.70
172	Scott Rolen R	25.00	11.00
173	Bob Abreu R	6.00	2.70
174	Danny Patterson R	4.00	1.80
175	Andruw Jones G	50.00	22.00
176	Brian Giles R	6.00	2.70
177	Dmitri Young R	6.00	2.70
178	Cal Ripken EMW G	80.00	36.00
179	Chuck Knoblauch EMW B	15.00	6.75

❑ 180 Alex Rodriguez EMW G	60.00	27.00
❑ 181 A. Galarraga EMW R ..	6.00	2.70
❑ 182 Pedro Martinez EMW R	6.00	2.70
❑ 183 Brady Anderson EMW R	6.00	2.70
❑ 184 Barry Bonds EMW B ..	15.00	6.75
❑ 185 Ivan Rodriguez EMW B	25.00	11.00
❑ 186 Gary Sheffield EMW B	8.00	3.60
❑ 187 Denny Neagle EMW B	15.00	6.75
❑ 188 Mark McGwire AURA R	100.00	45.00
❑ 189 Ellis Burks AURA R	6.00	2.70
❑ 190 Alex Rodriguez AURA G	60.00	27.00
❑ 191 Mike Piazza AURA G	60.00	27.00
❑ 192 Barry Bonds AURA B	15.00	6.75
❑ 193 Albert Belle AURA G ..	30.00	13.50
❑ 194 Chipper Jones AURA G	50.00	22.00
❑ 195 Juan Gonzalez AURA G	50.00	22.00
❑ 196 Brady Anderson AURA B	15.00	6.75
❑ 197 Frank Thomas AURA G	50.00	22.00
❑ 198 Vladimir Guerrero CL R	12.00	5.50
❑ 199 Todd Walker CL R......	6.00	2.70
❑ 200 Scott Rolen CL R	12.00	5.50

1997 New Pinnacle Interleague Encounter

	MINT	NRMT
COMPLETE SET (10)	500.00	220.00
COMMON CARD (1-10)	20.00	9.00
STATED ODDS 1:240		
❑ 1 Albert Belle	30.00	13.50
Brian Jordan		
❑ 2 Andruw Jones	25.00	11.00
Brady Anderson		
❑ 3 Ken Griffey Jr.	100.00	45.00
Tony Gwynn		
❑ 4 Cal Ripken	80.00	36.00
Chipper Jones		
❑ 5 Mike Piazza	60.00	27.00
Ivan Rodriguez		
❑ 6 Derek Jeter	60.00	27.00
Vladimir Guerrero		
❑ 7 Greg Maddux	50.00	22.00
Mo Vaughn		
❑ 8 Alex Rodriguez	60.00	27.00
Hideo Nomo		
❑ 9 Juan Gonzalez	40.00	18.00
Barry Bonds		
❑ 10 Frank Thomas	40.00	18.00
Jeff Bagwell		

1997 New Pinnacle Keeping the Pace

	MINT	NRMT
COMPLETE SET (18)	600.00	275.00
COMMON CARD (1-18)	4.00	1.80
MINOR STARS	8.00	3.60
UNLISTED STARS	15.00	6.75
STATED ODDS 1:89		
❑ 1 Juan Gonzalez	30.00	13.50
❑ 2 Greg Maddux	40.00	18.00
❑ 3 Ivan Rodriguez	20.00	9.00
❑ 4 Ken Griffey Jr.	80.00	36.00
❑ 5 Alex Rodriguez	50.00	22.00
❑ 6 Barry Bonds	20.00	9.00

❑ 7 Frank Thomas	30.00	13.50
❑ 8 Chuck Knoblauch	15.00	6.75
❑ 9 Derek Jeter	50.00	22.00
❑ 10 Roger Clemens	40.00	18.00
❑ 11 Kenny Lofton	10.00	4.50
❑ 12 Tony Gwynn	40.00	18.00
❑ 13 Troy Percival	8.00	3.60
❑ 14 Cal Ripken	60.00	27.00
❑ 15 Andy Pettitte	10.00	4.50
❑ 16 Hideo Nomo	15.00	6.75
❑ 17 Randy Johnson	15.00	6.75
❑ 18 Mike Piazza	50.00	22.00

1997 New Pinnacle Spellbound

	MINT	NRMT
COMMON A.BELLE	4.00	1.80
COMMON A.JONES	5.00	2.20
COMMON A.RODRIGUEZ	15.00	6.75
COMMON C.JONES	12.00	5.50
COMMON C.RIPKEN	20.00	9.00
COMMON F.THOMAS	10.00	4.50
COMMON I.RODRIGUEZ	6.00	2.70
COMMON K.GRIFFEY JR.	25.00	11.00
COMMON M.PIAZZA	15.00	6.75
STATED ODDS 1:19		
HOBBY: JUNIOR, ANDRUW, RIPKEN, CHIPPER		
RETAIL: FRANK,PIAZZA,ALEX,PUDGE,BELLE		
❑ AB1 Albert Belle B	15.00	6.75
❑ AB2 Albert Belle B	15.00	6.75
❑ AB3 Albert Belle L	15.00	6.75
❑ AB4 Albert Belle B	15.00	6.75
❑ AB5 Albert Belle E	15.00	6.75
❑ AJ1 Andruw Jones A	5.00	2.20
❑ AJ2 Andruw Jones N	5.00	2.20
❑ AJ3 Andruw Jones D	5.00	2.20
❑ AJ4 Andruw Jones R	5.00	2.20
❑ AJ5 Andruw Jones U	5.00	2.20
❑ AJ6 Andruw Jones W	5.00	2.20
❑ AR1 Alex Rodriguez A	15.00	6.75
❑ AR2 Alex Rodriguez L	15.00	6.75
❑ AR3 Alex Rodriguez R	15.00	6.75
❑ AR4 Alex Rodriguez X	15.00	6.75
❑ CJ1 Chipper Jones C	12.00	5.50
❑ CJ2 Chipper Jones H	12.00	5.50
❑ CJ3 Chipper Jones I	12.00	5.50
❑ CJ4 Chipper Jones P	12.00	5.50

❑ CJ5 Chipper Jones P	12.00	5.50
❑ CJ6 Chipper Jones E	12.00	5.50
❑ CJ7 Chipper Jones P	12.00	5.50
❑ CR1 Cal Ripken R	20.00	9.00
❑ CR2 Cal Ripken I	20.00	9.00
❑ CR3 Cal Ripken B	20.00	9.00
❑ CR4 Cal Ripken K	20.00	9.00
❑ CR5 Cal Ripken E	20.00	9.00
❑ CR6 Cal Ripken N	20.00	9.00
❑ FT1 Frank Thomas R	10.00	4.50
❑ FT2 Frank Thomas A	10.00	4.50
❑ FT3 Frank Thomas R	10.00	4.50
❑ FT4 Frank Thomas N	10.00	4.50
❑ FT5 Frank Thomas K	10.00	4.50
❑ IR1 Ivan Rodriguez R	6.00	2.70
❑ IR2 Ivan Rodriguez U	6.00	2.70
❑ IR3 Ivan Rodriguez I	6.00	2.70
❑ IR4 Ivan Rodriguez G	6.00	2.70
❑ IR5 Ivan Rodriguez E	6.00	2.70
❑ KG1 Ken Griffey Jr. J	25.00	11.00
❑ KG2 Ken Griffey Jr. U	25.00	11.00
❑ KG3 Ken Griffey Jr. N	25.00	11.00
❑ KG4 Ken Griffey Jr. I	25.00	11.00
❑ KG5 Ken Griffey Jr. O	25.00	11.00
❑ KG6 Ken Griffey Jr. R	25.00	11.00
❑ MP1 Mike Piazza P	15.00	6.75
❑ MP2 Mike Piazza I	15.00	6.75
❑ MP3 Mike Piazza A	15.00	6.75
❑ MP4 Mike Piazza Z	15.00	6.75
❑ MP5 Mike Piazza Z	15.00	6.75
❑ MP6 Mike Piazza A	15.00	6.75

1994 Pacific

	MINT	NRMT
COMPLETE SET (660)	35.00	16.00
COMMON CARD (1-660)	.10	.05
MINOR STARS	.20	.09
UNLISTED STARS	.40	.18
SUBSET CARDS HALF VALUE OF BASE CARDS		
COMP.CHECKLIST SET (6)	2.00	.90
CL: RANDOM INSERTS IN PACKS		
❑ 1 Steve Avery	.10	.05
❑ 2 Steve Bedrosian	.10	.05
❑ 3 Damon Berryhill	.10	.05
❑ 4 Jeff Blauser	.10	.05
❑ 5 Sid Bream	.10	.05
❑ 6 Francisco Cabrera	.10	.05
❑ 7 Ramon Caraballo	.10	.05
❑ 8 Ron Gant	.20	.09
❑ 9 Tom Glavine	.40	.18
❑ 10 Chipper Jones	1.00	.45
❑ 11 Dave Justice	.40	.18
❑ 12 Ryan Klesko	.20	.09
❑ 13 Mark Lemke	.10	.05
❑ 14 Javier Lopez	.30	.14
❑ 15 Greg Maddux	1.00	.45
❑ 16 Fred McGriff	.30	.14
❑ 17 Greg McMichael	.10	.05
❑ 18 Kent Mercker	.10	.05
❑ 19 Otis Nixon	.10	.05
❑ 20 Terry Pendleton	.10	.05
❑ 21 Deion Sanders	.20	.09
❑ 22 John Smoltz	.30	.14
❑ 23 Tony Tarasco	.10	.05
❑ 24 Manny Alexander	.10	.05

❑ 25 Brady Anderson	.20	.09	❑ 109 Ryne Sandberg	.50	.23	❑ 195 Andres Galarraga	.40	.18
❑ 26 Harold Baines	.20	.09	❑ 110 Tommy Shields	.10	.05	❑ 196 Joe Girardi	.10	.05
❑ 27 Damon Buford	.10	.05	❑ 111 Dwight Smith	.10	.05	❑ 197 Charlie Hayes	.10	.05
❑ 28 Paul Carey	.10	.05	❑ 112 Sammy Sosa	1.25	.55	❑ 198 Darren Holmes	.10	.05
❑ 29 Mike Devereaux	.10	.05	❑ 113 Jose Vizcaino	.10	.05	❑ 199 Chris Jones	.10	.05
❑ 30 Todd Frohwirth	.10	.05	❑ 114 Turk Wendell	.10	.05	❑ 200 Curt Leskanic	.10	.05
❑ 31 Leo Gomez	.10	.05	❑ 115 Rick Wilkins	.10	.05	❑ 201 Roberto Mejia	.10	.05
❑ 32 Jeffrey Hammonds	.20	.09	❑ 116 Willie Wilson	.10	.05	❑ 202 David Nied	.10	.05
❑ 33 Chris Hoiles	.10	.05	❑ 117 Eduardo Zambrano	.10	.05	❑ 203 J. Owens	.10	.05
❑ 34 Tim Hulett	.10	.05	❑ 118 Wilson Alvarez	.20	.09	❑ 204 Steve Reed	.10	.05
❑ 35 Ben McDonald	.10	.05	❑ 119 Tim Belcher	.10	.05	❑ 205 Armando Reynoso	.10	.05
❑ 36 Mark McLemore	.10	.05	❑ 120 Jason Bere	.10	.05	❑ 206 Bruce Ruffin	.10	.05
❑ 37 Alan Mills	.10	.05	❑ 121 Rodney Bolton	.10	.05	❑ 207 Keith Shepherd	.10	.05
❑ 38 Mike Mussina	.40	.18	❑ 122 Ellis Burks	.20	.09	❑ 208 Jim Tatum	.10	.05
❑ 39 Sherman Obando	.10	.05	❑ 123 Joey Cora	.10	.05	❑ 209 Eric Young	.10	.05
❑ 40 Gregg Olson	.10	.05	❑ 124 Alex Fernandez	.10	.05	❑ 210 Skeeter Barnes	.10	.05
❑ 41 Mike Pagliarulo	.10	.05	❑ 125 Ozzie Guillen	.10	.05	❑ 211 Danny Bautista	.10	.05
❑ 42 Jim Poole	.10	.05	❑ 126 Craig Grebeck	.10	.05	❑ 212 Tom Bolton	.10	.05
❑ 43 Harold Reynolds	.10	.05	❑ 127 Roberto Hernandez	.10	.05	❑ 213 Eric Davis	.20	.09
❑ 44 Cal Ripken	1.50	.70	❑ 128 Bo Jackson	.20	.09	❑ 214 Storm Davis	.10	.05
❑ 45 David Segui	.20	.09	❑ 129 Lance Johnson	.10	.05	❑ 215 Cecil Fielder	.20	.09
❑ 46 Fernando Valenzuela	.20	.09	❑ 130 Ron Karkovice	.10	.05	❑ 216 Travis Fryman	.20	.09
❑ 47 Jack Voigt	.10	.05	❑ 131 Mike LaValliere	.10	.05	❑ 217 Kirk Gibson	.20	.09
❑ 48 Scott Bankhead	.10	.05	❑ 132 Norberto Martin	.10	.05	❑ 218 Dan Gladden	.10	.05
❑ 49 Roger Clemens	1.00	.45	❑ 133 Kirk McCaskill	.10	.05	❑ 219 John Doherty	.10	.05
❑ 50 Scott Cooper	.10	.05	❑ 134 Jack McDowell	.20	.09	❑ 220 Chris Gomez	.10	.05
❑ 51 Danny Darwin	.10	.05	❑ 135 Scott Radinsky	.10	.05	❑ 221 David Haas	.10	.05
❑ 52 Andre Dawson	.30	.14	❑ 136 Tim Raines	.20	.09	❑ 222 Bill Krueger	.10	.05
❑ 53 John Dopson	.10	.05	❑ 137 Steve Sax	.10	.05	❑ 223 Chad Kreuter	.10	.05
❑ 54 Scott Fletcher	.10	.05	❑ 138 Frank Thomas	.75	.35	❑ 224 Mark Leiter	.10	.05
❑ 55 Tony Fossas	.10	.05	❑ 139 Dan Pasqua	.10	.05	❑ 225 Bob MacDonald	.10	.05
❑ 56 Mike Greenwell	.10	.05	❑ 140 Robin Ventura	.20	.09	❑ 226 Mike Moore	.10	.05
❑ 57 Billy Hatcher	.10	.05	❑ 141 Jeff Branson	.10	.05	❑ 227 Tony Phillips	.10	.05
❑ 58 Jeff McNeely	.10	.05	❑ 142 Tom Browning	.10	.05	❑ 228 Rich Rowland	.10	.05
❑ 59 Jose Melendez	.10	.05	❑ 143 Jacob Brumfield	.10	.05	❑ 229 Mickey Tettleton	.10	.05
❑ 60 Tim Naehring	.10	.05	❑ 144 Tim Costo	.10	.05	❑ 230 Alan Trammell	.30	.14
❑ 61 Tony Pena	.10	.05	❑ 145 Rob Dibble	.10	.05	❑ 231 David Wells	.30	.14
❑ 62 Paul Quantrill	.10	.05	❑ 146 Brian Dorsett	.10	.05	❑ 232 Lou Whitaker	.20	.09
❑ 63 Carlos Quintana	.10	.05	❑ 147 Steve Foster	.10	.05	❑ 233 Luis Aquino	.10	.05
❑ 64 Luis Rivera	.10	.05	❑ 148 Cesar Hernandez	.10	.05	❑ 234 Alex Arias	.10	.05
❑ 65 Jeff Russell	.10	.05	❑ 149 Roberto Kelly	.10	.05	❑ 235 Jack Armstrong	.10	.05
❑ 66 Aaron Sele	.20	.09	❑ 150 Barry Larkin	.40	.18	❑ 236 Ryan Bowen	.10	.05
❑ 67 John Valentin	.20	.09	❑ 151 Larry Luebbers	.10	.05	❑ 237 Chuck Carr	.10	.05
❑ 68 Mo Vaughn	.40	.18	❑ 152 Kevin Mitchell	.10	.05	❑ 238 Matias Carrillo	.10	.05
❑ 69 Frank Viola	.10	.05	❑ 153 Joe Oliver	.10	.05	❑ 239 Jeff Conine	.10	.05
❑ 70 Bob Zupcic	.10	.05	❑ 154 Tim Pugh	.10	.05	❑ 240 Henry Cotto	.10	.05
❑ 71 Mike Butcher	.10	.05	❑ 155 Jeff Reardon	.20	.09	❑ 241 Orestes Destrade	.10	.05
❑ 72 Rod Correia	.10	.05	❑ 156 Jose Rijo	.10	.05	❑ 242 Chris Hammond	.10	.05
❑ 73 Chad Curtis	.10	.05	❑ 157 Bip Roberts	.10	.05	❑ 243 Bryan Harvey	.10	.05
❑ 74 Chili Davis	.20	.09	❑ 158 Chris Sabo	.10	.05	❑ 244 Charlie Hough	.10	.05
❑ 75 Gary DiSarcina	.10	.05	❑ 159 Juan Samuel	.10	.05	❑ 245 Richie Lewis	.10	.05
❑ 76 Damion Easley	.20	.09	❑ 160 Reggie Sanders	.20	.09	❑ 246 Mitch Lyden	.10	.05
❑ 77 John Farrell	.10	.05	❑ 161 John Smiley	.10	.05	❑ 247 Dave Magadan	.10	.05
❑ 78 Chuck Finley	.20	.09	❑ 162 Jerry Spradlin	.10	.05	❑ 248 Bob Natal	.10	.05
❑ 79 Joe Grahe	.10	.05	❑ 163 Gary Varsho	.10	.05	❑ 249 Benito Santiago	.10	.05
❑ 80 Stan Javier	.10	.05	❑ 164 Sandy Alomar Jr.	.20	.09	❑ 250 Gary Sheffield	.40	.18
❑ 81 Mark Langston	.10	.05	❑ 165 Albert Belle	.40	.18	❑ 251 Matt Turner	.10	.05
❑ 82 Phil Leftwich	.10	.05	❑ 166 Carlos Baerga	.20	.09	❑ 252 David Weathers	.10	.05
❑ 83 Torey Lovullo	.10	.05	❑ 167 Mark Clark	.10	.05	❑ 253 Walt Weiss	.10	.05
❑ 84 Joe Magrane	.10	.05	❑ 168 Alvaro Espinoza	.10	.05	❑ 254 Darrell Whitmore	.10	.05
❑ 85 Greg Myers	.10	.05	❑ 169 Felix Fermin	.10	.05	❑ 255 Nigel Wilson	.10	.05
❑ 86 Eduardo Perez	.10	.05	❑ 170 Reggie Jefferson	.10	.05	❑ 256 Eric Anthony	.10	.05
❑ 87 Luis Polonia	.10	.05	❑ 171 Wayne Kirby	.10	.05	❑ 257 Jeff Bagwell	.50	.23
❑ 88 Tim Salmon	.40	.18	❑ 172 Tom Kramer	.10	.05	❑ 258 Kevin Bass	.10	.05
❑ 89 J.T. Snow	.20	.09	❑ 173 Kenny Lofton	.40	.18	❑ 259 Craig Biggio	.40	.18
❑ 90 Kurt Stillwell	.10	.05	❑ 174 Jesse Levis	.10	.05	❑ 260 Ken Caminiti	.30	.14
❑ 91 Ron Tingley	.10	.05	❑ 175 Candy Maldonado	.10	.05	❑ 261 Andujar Cedeno	.10	.05
❑ 92 Chris Turner	.10	.05	❑ 176 Carlos Martinez	.10	.05	❑ 262 Chris Donnels	.10	.05
❑ 93 Julio Valera	.10	.05	❑ 177 Jose Mesa	.10	.05	❑ 263 Doug Drabek	.10	.05
❑ 94 Jose Bautista	.10	.05	❑ 178 Jeff Mutis	.10	.05	❑ 264 Tom Edens	.10	.05
❑ 95 Shawn Boskie	.10	.05	❑ 179 Charles Nagy	.20	.09	❑ 265 Steve Finley	.20	.09
❑ 96 Steve Buechele	.10	.05	❑ 180 Bob Ojeda	.10	.05	❑ 266 Luis Gonzalez	.20	.09
❑ 97 Frank Castillo	.10	.05	❑ 181 Junior Ortiz	.10	.05	❑ 267 Pete Harnisch	.10	.05
❑ 98 Mark Grace UER	.30	.14	❑ 182 Eric Plunk	.10	.05	❑ 268 Xavier Hernandez	.10	.05
(stats have 98 home runs in 1993; should be 14)			❑ 183 Manny Ramirez	.75	.35	❑ 269 Todd Jones	.10	.05
❑ 99 Jose Guzman	.10	.05	❑ 184 Paul Sorrento	.10	.05	❑ 270 Darryl Kile	.10	.05
❑ 100 Mike Harkey	.10	.05	❑ 185 Jeff Treadway	.10	.05	❑ 271 Al Osuna	.10	.05
❑ 101 Greg Hibbard	.10	.05	❑ 186 Bill Wertz	.10	.05	❑ 272 Rick Parker	.10	.05
❑ 102 Doug Jennings	.10	.05	❑ 187 Freddie Benavides	.10	.05	❑ 273 Mark Portugal	.10	.05
❑ 103 Derrick May	.10	.05	❑ 188 Dante Bichette	.20	.09	❑ 274 Scott Servais	.10	.05
❑ 104 Mike Morgan	.10	.05	❑ 189 Willie Blair	.10	.05	❑ 275 Greg Swindell	.10	.05
❑ 105 Randy Myers	.10	.05	❑ 190 Daryl Boston	.10	.05	❑ 276 Eddie Taubensee	.10	.05
❑ 106 Karl Rhodes	.10	.05	❑ 191 Pedro Castellano	.10	.05	❑ 277 Jose Uribe	.10	.05
❑ 107 Kevin Roberson	.10	.05	❑ 192 Vinny Castilla	.20	.09	❑ 278 Brian Williams	.10	.05
❑ 108 Rey Sanchez	.10	.05	❑ 193 Jerald Clark	.10	.05	❑ 279 Kevin Appier	.20	.09
			❑ 194 Alex Cole	.10	.05	❑ 280 Billy Brewer	.10	.05

281	David Cone	.30	.14
282	Greg Gagne	.10	.05
283	Tom Gordon	.10	.05
284	Chris Gwynn	.10	.05
285	John Habyan	.10	.05
286	Chris Haney	.10	.05
287	Phil Hiatt	.10	.05
288	David Howard	.10	.05
289	Felix Jose	.10	.05
290	Wally Joyner	.20	.09
291	Kevin Koslofski	.10	.05
292	Jose Lind	.10	.05
293	Brent Mayne	.10	.05
294	Mike Macfarlane	.10	.05
295	Brian McRae	.10	.05
296	Kevin McReynolds	.10	.05
297	Keith Miller	.10	.05
298	Jeff Montgomery	.10	.05
299	Hipolito Pichardo	.10	.05
300	Rico Rossy	.10	.05
301	Curtis Wilkerson	.10	.05
302	Pedro Astacio	.10	.05
303	Rafael Boumigal	.10	.05
304	Brett Butler	.20	.09
305	Tom Candiotti	.10	.05
306	Omar Daal	.10	.05
307	Jim Gott	.10	.05
308	Kevin Gross	.10	.05
309	Dave Hansen	.10	.05
310	Carlos Hernandez	.10	.05
311	Orel Hershiser	.20	.09
312	Eric Karros	.20	.09
313	Pedro Martinez	.50	.23
314	Ramon Martinez	.20	.09
315	Roger McDowell	.10	.05
316	Raul Mondesi	.40	.18
317	Jose Offerman	.20	.09
318	Mike Piazza	1.25	.55
319	Jody Reed	.10	.05
320	Henry Rodriguez	.20	.09
321	Cory Snyder	.10	.05
322	Darryl Strawberry	.20	.09
323	Tim Wallach	.10	.05
324	Steve Wilson	.10	.05
325	Juan Bell	.10	.05
326	Ricky Bones	.10	.05
327	Alex Diaz	.10	.05
328	Cal Eldred	.10	.05
329	Darryl Hamilton	.10	.05
330	Doug Henry	.10	.05
331	John Jaha	.10	.05
332	Pat Listach	.10	.05
333	Graeme Lloyd	.10	.05
334	Carlos Maldonado	.10	.05
335	Angel Miranda	.10	.05
336	Jaime Navarro	.10	.05
337	Dave Nilsson	.10	.05
338	Rafael Novoa	.10	.05
339	Troy O'Leary	.20	.09
340	Jesse Orosco	.10	.05
341	Kevin Seitzer	.10	.05
342	Bill Spiers	.10	.05
343	William Suero	.10	.05
344	B.J. Surhoff	.20	.09
345	Dickie Thon	.10	.05
346	Jose Valentin	.10	.05
347	Greg Vaughn	.20	.09
348	Robin Yount	.40	.18
349	Willie Banks	.10	.05
350	Bernardo Brito	.10	.05
351	Scott Erickson	.20	.09
352	Mark Guthrie	.10	.05
353	Chip Hale	.10	.05
354	Brian Harper	.10	.05
355	Kent Hrbek	.20	.09
356	Terry Jorgensen	.10	.05
357	Chuck Knoblauch	.40	.18
358	Gene Larkin	.10	.05
359	Scott Leius	.10	.05
360	Shane Mack	.10	.05
361	David McCarty	.10	.05
362	Pat Meares	.10	.05
363	Pedro Munoz	.10	.05
364	Derek Parks	.10	.05
365	Kirby Puckett	.60	.25
366	Jeff Reboulet	.10	.05
367	Kevin Tapani	.10	.05
368	Mike Trombley	.10	.05
369	George Tsamis	.10	.05
370	Carl Willis	.10	.05
371	Dave Winfield	.40	.18
372	Moises Alou	.20	.09
373	Brian Barnes	.10	.05
374	Sean Berry	.10	.05
375	Frank Bolick	.10	.05
376	Wil Cordero	.10	.05
377	Delino DeShields	.10	.05
378	Jeff Fassero	.10	.05
379	Darrin Fletcher	.10	.05
380	Cliff Floyd	.20	.09
381	Lou Frazier	.10	.05
382	Marquis Grissom	.20	.09
383	Gil Heredia	.10	.05
384	Mike Lansing	.20	.09
385	Oreste Marrero	.10	.05
386	Dennis Martinez	.20	.09
387	Curtis Pride	.10	.05
388	Mel Rojas	.10	.05
389	Kirk Rueter	.10	.05
390	Joe Siddall	.10	.05
391	John Vander Wal	.10	.05
392	Larry Walker	.40	.18
393	John Wetteland	.20	.09
394	Rondell White	.20	.09
395	Tim Bogar	.10	.05
396	Bobby Bonilla	.20	.09
397	Jeromy Burnitz	.20	.09
398	Mike Draper	.10	.05
399	Sid Fernandez	.10	.05
400	John Franco	.20	.09
401	Dave Gallagher	.10	.05
402	Dwight Gooden	.20	.09
403	Eric Hillman	.10	.05
404	Todd Hundley	.20	.09
405	Butch Huskey	.20	.09
406	Jeff Innis	.10	.05
407	Howard Johnson	.20	.09
408	Jeff Kent	.20	.09
409	Ced Landrum	.10	.05
410	Mike Maddux	.10	.05
411	Josias Manzanillo	.10	.05
412	Jeff McKnight	.10	.05
413	Eddie Murray	.40	.18
414	Tito Navarro	.10	.05
415	Joe Orsulak	.10	.05
416	Bret Saberhagen	.20	.09
417	Dave Telgheder	.10	.05
418	Ryan Thompson	.10	.05
419	Chico Walker	.10	.05
420	Jim Abbott	.20	.09
421	Wade Boggs	.40	.18
422	Mike Gallego	.10	.05
423	Mark Hutton	.10	.05
424	Dion James	.10	.05
425	Domingo Jean	.10	.05
426	Pat Kelly	.10	.05
427	Jimmy Key	.20	.09
428	Jim Leyritz	.20	.09
429	Kevin Maas	.10	.05
430	Don Mattingly	.75	.35
431	Bobby Munoz	.10	.05
432	Matt Nokes	.10	.05
433	Paul O'Neill	.20	.09
434	Spike Owen	.10	.05
435	Melido Perez	.10	.05
436	Lee Smith	.20	.09
437	Andy Stankiewicz	.10	.05
438	Mike Stanley	.10	.05
439	Danny Tartabull	.10	.05
440	Randy Velarde	.10	.05
441	Bernie Williams	.40	.18
442	Gerald Williams	.10	.05
443	Mike Witt	.10	.05
444	Marcos Armas	.10	.05
445	Lance Blankenship	.10	.05
446	Mike Bordick	.10	.05
447	Ron Darling UER	.10	.05
	Reversed negative on front		
448	Dennis Eckersley	.20	.09
449	Brent Gates	.10	.05
450	Rich Gossage	.20	.09
451	Scott Hemond	.10	.05
452	Dave Henderson	.10	.05
453	Shawn Hillegas	.10	.05
454	Rick Honeycutt	.10	.05
455	Scott Lydy	.10	.05
456	Mark McGwire	2.00	.90
457	Henry Mercedes	.10	.05
458	Mike Mohler	.10	.05
459	Troy Neel	.10	.05
460	Edwin Nunez	.10	.05
461	Craig Paquette	.10	.05
462	Ruben Sierra	.10	.05
463	Terry Steinbach	.10	.05
464	Todd Van Poppel	.10	.05
465	Bob Welch	.10	.05
466	Bobby Witt	.10	.05
467	Ruben Amaro	.10	.05
468	Larry Andersen	.10	.05
469	Kim Batiste	.10	.05
470	Wes Chamberlain	.10	.05
471	Darren Daulton	.20	.09
472	Mariano Duncan	.10	.05
473	Len Dykstra	.20	.09
474	Jim Eisenreich	.10	.05
475	Tommy Greene	.10	.05
476	Dave Hollins	.10	.05
477	Pete Incaviglia	.10	.05
478	Danny Jackson	.10	.05
479	John Kruk	.20	.09
480	Tony Longmire	.10	.05
481	Jeff Manto	.10	.05
482	Mickey Morandini	.10	.05
483	Terry Mulholland	.10	.05
484	Todd Pratt	.10	.05
485	Ben Rivera	.10	.05
486	Curt Schilling	.20	.09
487	Kevin Stocker	.10	.05
488	Milt Thompson	.10	.05
489	David West	.30	.14
490	Mitch Williams	.10	.05
491	Jeff Ballard	.10	.05
492	Jay Bell	.20	.09
493	Scott Bullett	.10	.05
494	Dave Clark	.10	.05
495	Steve Cooke	.10	.05
496	Midre Cummings	.10	.05
497	Mark Dewey	.10	.05
498	Carlos Garcia	.10	.05
499	Jeff King	.10	.05
500	Al Martin	.10	.05
501	Lloyd McClendon	.10	.05
502	Orlando Merced	.10	.05
503	Blas Minor	.10	.05
504	Denny Neagle	.10	.05
505	Tom Prince	.10	.05
506	Don Slaught	.10	.05
507	Zane Smith	.10	.05
508	Randy Tomlin	.10	.05
509	Andy Van Slyke	.20	.09
510	Paul Wagner	.10	.05
511	Tim Wakefield	.20	.09
512	Bob Walk	.10	.05
513	John Wehner	.10	.05
514	Kevin Young	.10	.05
515	Billy Bean	.10	.05
516	Andy Benes	.20	.09
517	Derek Bell	.20	.09
518	Doug Brocail	.10	.05
519	Jarvis Brown	.10	.05
520	Phil Clark	.10	.05
521	Mark Davis	.10	.05
522	Jeff Gardner	.10	.05
523	Pat Gomez	.10	.05
524	Ricky Gutierrez	.10	.05
525	Tony Gwynn	1.00	.45
526	Gene Harris	.10	.05
527	Kevin Higgins	.10	.05
528	Trevor Hoffman	.20	.09
529	Luis Lopez	.10	.05
530	Pedro A.Martinez	.10	.05
531	Melvin Nieves	.10	.05
532	Phil Plantier	.10	.05
533	Frank Seminara	.10	.05
534	Craig Shipley	.10	.05
535	Tim Teufel	.10	.05
536	Guillermo Velasquez	.10	.05
537	Wally Whitehurst	.10	.05

☐ 538 Rod Beck	.10	.05
☐ 539 Todd Benzinger	.10	.05
☐ 540 Barry Bonds	.50	.23
☐ 541 Jeff Brantley	.10	.05
☐ 542 Dave Burba	.10	.05
☐ 543 John Burkett	.10	.05
☐ 544 Will Clark	.40	.18
☐ 545 Royce Clayton	.10	.05
☐ 546 Bryan Hickerson	.10	.05
☐ 547 Mike Jackson	.20	.09
☐ 548 Darren Lewis	.10	.05
☐ 549 Kirt Manwaring	.10	.05
☐ 550 Dave Martinez	.10	.05
☐ 551 Willie McGee	.20	.09
☐ 552 Jeff Reed	.10	.05
☐ 553 Dave Righetti	.10	.05
☐ 554 Kevin Rogers	.10	.05
☐ 555 Steve Scarsone	.10	.05
☐ 556 Bill Swift	.10	.05
☐ 557 Robby Thompson	.10	.05
☐ 558 Salomon Torres	.10	.05
☐ 559 Matt Williams	.30	.14
☐ 560 Trevor Wilson	.10	.05
☐ 561 Rich Amaral	.10	.05
☐ 562 Mike Blowers	.10	.05
☐ 563 Chris Bosio	.10	.05
☐ 564 Jay Buhner	.20	.09
☐ 565 Norm Charlton	.10	.05
☐ 566 Jim Converse	.10	.05
☐ 567 Rich DeLucia	.10	.05
☐ 568 Mike Felder	.10	.05
☐ 569 Dave Fleming	.10	.05
☐ 570 Ken Griffey Jr.	2.00	.90
☐ 571 Bill Haselman	.10	.05
☐ 572 Dwayne Henry	.10	.05
☐ 573 Brad Holman	.10	.05
☐ 574 Randy Johnson	.40	.18
☐ 575 Greg Litton	.10	.05
☐ 576 Edgar Martinez	.20	.09
☐ 577 Tino Martinez	.10	.05
☐ 578 Jeff Nelson	.10	.05
☐ 579 Marc Newfield	.10	.05
☐ 580 Roger Salkeld	.10	.05
☐ 581 Mackey Sasser	.10	.05
☐ 582 Brian Turang	.10	.05
☐ 583 Omar Vizquel	.20	.09
☐ 584 Dave Valle	.10	.05
☐ 585 Luis Alicea	.10	.05
☐ 586 Rene Arocha	.10	.05
☐ 587 Rheal Cormier	.10	.05
☐ 588 Tripp Cromer	.10	.05
☐ 589 Bernard Gilkey	.10	.05
☐ 590 Lee Guetterman	.10	.05
☐ 591 Gregg Jefferies	.10	.05
☐ 592 Tim Jones	.10	.05
☐ 593 Paul Kilgus	.10	.05
☐ 594 Les Lancaster	.10	.05
☐ 595 Omar Olivares	.10	.05
☐ 596 Jose Oquendo	.10	.05
☐ 597 Donovan Osborne	.10	.05
☐ 598 Tom Pagnozzi	.10	.05
☐ 599 Erik Pappas	.10	.05
☐ 600 Geronimo Pena	.10	.05
☐ 601 Mike Perez	.10	.05
☐ 602 Gerald Perry	.10	.05
☐ 603 Stan Royer	.10	.05
☐ 604 Ozzie Smith	.50	.23
☐ 605 Bob Tewksbury	.10	.05
☐ 606 Allen Watson	.10	.05
☐ 607 Mark Whiten	.10	.05
☐ 608 Todd Zeile	.10	.05
☐ 609 Jeff Bronkey	.10	.05
☐ 610 Kevin Brown	.20	.09
☐ 611 Jose Canseco	.50	.23
☐ 612 Doug Dascenzo	.10	.05
☐ 613 Butch Davis	.10	.05
☐ 614 Mario Diaz	.10	.05
☐ 615 Julio Franco	.10	.05
☐ 616 Benji Gil	.10	.05
☐ 617 Juan Gonzalez	.75	.35
☐ 618 Tom Henke	.10	.05
☐ 619 Jeff Huson	.10	.05
☐ 620 David Hulse	.10	.05
☐ 621 Craig Lefferts	.10	.05
☐ 622 Rafael Palmeiro	.40	.18
☐ 623 Dean Palmer	.20	.09

☐ 624 Bob Patterson	.10	.05
☐ 625 Roger Pavlik	.10	.05
☐ 626 Gary Redus	.10	.05
☐ 627 Ivan Rodriguez	.50	.23
☐ 628 Kenny Rogers	.10	.05
☐ 629 Jon Shave	.10	.05
☐ 630 Doug Strange	.10	.05
☐ 631 Matt Whiteside	.10	.05
☐ 632 Roberto Alomar	.40	.18
☐ 633 Pat Borders	.10	.05
☐ 634 Scott Brow	.10	.05
☐ 635 Rob Butler	.10	.05
☐ 636 Joe Carter	.20	.09
☐ 637 Tony Castillo	.10	.05
☐ 638 Mark Eichhorn	.10	.05
☐ 639 Tony Fernandez	.20	.09
☐ 640 Huck Flener	.10	.05
☐ 641 Alfredo Griffin	.10	.05
☐ 642 Juan Guzman	.10	.05
☐ 643 Rickey Henderson	.50	.23
☐ 644 Pat Hentgen	.20	.09
☐ 645 Randy Knorr	.10	.05
☐ 646 Al Leiter	.20	.09
☐ 647 Domingo Martinez	.10	.05
☐ 648 Paul Molitor	.40	.18
☐ 649 Jack Morris	.20	.09
☐ 650 John Olerud	.20	.09
☐ 651 Ed Sprague	.10	.05
☐ 652 Dave Stewart	.20	.09
☐ 653 Devon White	.10	.05
☐ 654 Woody Williams	.10	.05
☐ 655 Barry Bonds MVP	.40	.18
☐ 656 Greg Maddux CY	.50	.23
☐ 657 Jack McDowell CY	.10	.05
☐ 658 Mike Piazza ROY	.60	.25
☐ 659 Tim Salmon ROY	.40	.18
☐ 660 Frank Thomas MVP	.40	.18

1994 Pacific All-Latino

	MINT	NRMT
COMPLETE SET (20)	25.00	11.00
COMMON CARD (1-20)	1.00	.45
RANDOM INSERTS IN PURPLE PACKS		

☐ 1 Benito Santiago	1.00	.45
☐ 2 Dave Magadan	1.00	.45
☐ 3 Andres Galarraga	4.00	1.80
☐ 4 Luis Gonzalez	2.00	.90
☐ 5 Jose Offerman	2.00	.90
☐ 6 Bobby Bonilla	2.00	.90
☐ 7 Dennis Martinez	2.00	.90
☐ 8 Mariano Duncan	1.00	.45
☐ 9 Orlando Merced	1.00	.45
☐ 10 Jose Rijo	1.00	.45
☐ 11 Danny Tartabull	1.00	.45
☐ 12 Ruben Sierra	1.00	.45
☐ 13 Ivan Rodriguez	6.00	2.70
☐ 14 Juan Gonzalez	10.00	4.50
☐ 15 Jose Canseco	6.00	2.70
☐ 16 Rafael Palmeiro	4.00	1.80
☐ 17 Roberto Alomar	4.00	1.80
☐ 18 Eduardo Perez	1.00	.45
☐ 19 Alex Fernandez	1.00	.45
☐ 20 Omar Vizquel	2.00	.90

1994 Pacific Gold Prisms

	MINT	NRMT
COMPLETE SET (20)	90.00	40.00
COMMON CARD (1-20)	1.00	.45
RANDOM INSERTS IN PURPLE PACKS		

☐ 1 Juan Gonzalez	10.00	4.50
☐ 2 Ken Griffey Jr.	25.00	11.00
☐ 3 Frank Thomas	10.00	4.50
☐ 4 Albert Belle	4.00	1.80
☐ 5 Rafael Palmeiro	4.00	1.80
☐ 6 Joe Carter	2.00	.90
☐ 7 Dean Palmer	2.00	.90
☐ 8 Mickey Tettleton	1.00	.45
☐ 9 Tim Salmon	4.00	1.80
☐ 10 Danny Tartabull	1.00	.45
☐ 11 Barry Bonds	6.00	2.70
☐ 12 Dave Justice	4.00	1.80
☐ 13 Matt Williams	3.00	1.35
☐ 14 Fred McGriff	3.00	1.35
☐ 15 Ron Gant	1.00	.45
☐ 16 Mike Piazza	15.00	6.75
☐ 17 Bobby Bonilla	2.00	.90
☐ 18 Phil Plantier	1.00	.45
☐ 19 Sammy Sosa	15.00	6.75
☐ 20 Rick Wilkins	1.00	.45

1994 Pacific Silver Prisms

	MINT	NRMT
COMPLETE SET (36)	125.00	55.00
COMMON CARD (1-36)	1.00	.45
TRIANGULAR INSERTS IN PURPLE PACKS		
COMP. CIRCULAR SET (36)	60.00	27.00
*CIRCULAR STARS: 2X TO 5X BASE CARD HI		
ONE CIRCULAR PER BLACK RETAIL PACK		

☐ 1 Robin Yount	3.00	1.35
☐ 2 Juan Gonzalez	8.00	3.60
☐ 3 Rafael Palmeiro	3.00	1.35
☐ 4 Paul Molitor	3.00	1.35
☐ 5 Roberto Alomar	3.00	1.35
☐ 6 John Olerud	2.00	.90
☐ 7 Randy Johnson	3.00	1.35
☐ 8 Ken Griffey Jr.	20.00	9.00
☐ 9 Wade Boggs	3.00	1.35
☐ 10 Don Mattingly	8.00	3.60

#	Player	MINT	NRMT
11	Kirby Puckett	6.00	2.70
12	Tim Salmon	3.00	1.35
13	Frank Thomas	8.00	3.60
14	Fernando Valenzuela	2.00	.90
15	Cal Ripken	15.00	6.75
16	Carlos Baerga	1.00	.45
17	Kenny Lofton	3.00	1.35
18	Cecil Fielder	1.00	.45
19	John Burkett	1.00	.45
20	Andres Galarraga	3.00	1.35
21	Charlie Hayes	1.00	.45
22	Orestes Destrade	1.00	.45
23	Jeff Conine	1.00	.45
24	Jeff Bagwell	5.00	2.20
25	Mark Grace	2.50	1.10
26	Ryne Sandberg	5.00	2.20
27	Gregg Jefferies	1.00	.45
28	Barry Bonds	5.00	2.20
29	Mike Piazza	12.00	5.50
30	Greg Maddux	10.00	4.50
31	Darren Daulton	2.00	.90
32	John Kruk	2.00	.90
33	Lenny Dykstra	2.00	.90
34	Orlando Merced	1.00	.45
35	Tony Gwynn	10.00	4.50
36	Robby Thompson	1.00	.45

1995 Pacific

	MINT	NRMT
COMPLETE SET (450)	30.00	13.50
COMMON CARD (1-450)	.10	.05
MINOR STARS	.20	.09
UNLISTED STARS	.40	.18

#	Player	MINT	NRMT
1	Steve Avery	.10	.05
2	Rafael Belliard	.10	.05
3	Jeff Blauser	.10	.05
4	Tom Glavine	.40	.18
5	David Justice	.40	.18
6	Mike Kelly	.10	.05
7	Roberto Kelly	.10	.05
8	Ryan Klesko	.20	.09
9	Mark Lemke	.10	.05
10	Javier Lopez	.20	.09
11	Greg Maddux	1.00	.45
12	Fred McGriff	.30	.14
13	Greg McMichael	.10	.05
14	Jose Oliva	.10	.05
15	John Smoltz	.30	.14
16	Tony Tarasco	.10	.05
17	Brady Anderson	.20	.09
18	Harold Baines	.20	.09
19	Armando Benitez	.10	.05
20	Mike Devereaux	.10	.05
21	Leo Gomez	.10	.05
22	Jeffrey Hammonds	.20	.09
23	Chris Hoiles	.10	.05
24	Ben McDonald	.10	.05
25	Mark McLemore	.10	.05
26	Jamie Moyer	.10	.05
27	Mike Mussina	.40	.18
28	Rafael Palmeiro	.40	.18
29	Jim Poole	.10	.05
30	Cal Ripken Jr.	1.50	.70
31	Lee Smith	.20	.09
32	Mark Smith	.10	.05
33	Jose Canseco	.50	.23
34	Roger Clemens	1.00	.45
35	Scott Cooper	.10	.05
36	Andre Dawson	.30	.14
37	Tony Fossas	.10	.05
38	Mike Greenwell	.10	.05
39	Chris Howard	.10	.05
40	Jose Melendez	.10	.05
41	Nate Minchey	.10	.05
42	Tim Naehring	.10	.05
43	Otis Nixon	.10	.05
44	Carlos Rodriguez	.10	.05
45	Aaron Sele	.20	.09
46	Lee Tinsley	.10	.05
47	Sergio Valdez	.10	.05
48	John Valentin	.20	.09
49	Mo Vaughn	.40	.18
50	Brian Anderson	.10	.05
51	Garret Anderson	.20	.09
52	Rod Correia	.10	.05
53	Chad Curtis	.10	.05
54	Mark Dalesandro	.10	.05
55	Chili Davis	.20	.09
56	Gary DiSarcina	.10	.05
57	Damion Easley	.10	.05
58	Jim Edmonds	.30	.14
59	Jorge Fabregas	.10	.05
60	Chuck Finley	.20	.09
61	Bo Jackson	.20	.09
62	Mark Langston	.10	.05
63	Eduardo Perez	.10	.05
64	Tim Salmon	.40	.18
65	J.T. Snow	.20	.09
66	Willie Banks	.10	.05
67	Jose Bautista	.10	.05
68	Shawon Dunston	.10	.05
69	Kevin Foster	.10	.05
70	Mark Grace	.30	.14
71	Jose Guzman	.10	.05
72	Jose Hernandez	.10	.05
73	Blaise Ilsley	.10	.05
74	Derrick May	.10	.05
75	Randy Myers	.10	.05
76	Karl Rhodes	.10	.05
77	Kevin Roberson	.10	.05
78	Rey Sanchez	.10	.05
79	Sammy Sosa	1.25	.55
80	Steve Trachsel	.10	.05
81	Eddie Zambrano	.10	.05
82	Wilson Alvarez	.20	.09
83	Jason Bere	.10	.05
84	Joey Cora	.10	.05
85	Jose DeLeon	.10	.05
86	Alex Fernandez	.10	.05
87	Julio Franco	.10	.05
88	Ozzie Guillen	.10	.05
89	Joe Hall	.10	.05
90	Roberto Hernandez	.10	.05
91	Darrin Jackson	.10	.05
92	Lance Johnson	.10	.05
93	Norberto Martin	.10	.05
94	Jack McDowell	.10	.05
95	Tim Raines	.20	.09
96	Olmedo Saenz	.10	.05
97	Frank Thomas	.75	.35
98	Robin Ventura	.20	.09
99	Bret Boone	.20	.09
100	Jeff Brantley	.10	.05
101	Jacob Brumfield	.10	.05
102	Hector Carrasco	.10	.05
103	Brian Dorsett	.10	.05
104	Tony Fernandez	.20	.09
105	Willie Greene	.10	.05
106	Erik Hanson	.10	.05
107	Kevin Jarvis	.10	.05
108	Barry Larkin	.40	.18
109	Kevin Mitchell	.10	.05
110	Hal Morris	.10	.05
111	Jose Rijo	.10	.05
112	Johnny Ruffin	.10	.05
113	Deion Sanders	.20	.09
114	Reggie Sanders	.20	.09
115	Sandy Alomar Jr.	.20	.09
116	Ruben Amaro	.10	.05
117	Carlos Baerga	.10	.05
118	Albert Belle	.40	.18
119	Alvaro Espinoza	.10	.05
120	Rene Gonzales	.10	.05
121	Wayne Kirby	.10	.05
122	Kenny Lofton	.30	.14
123	Candy Maldonado	.10	.05
124	Dennis Martinez	.20	.09
125	Eddie Murray	.40	.18
126	Charles Nagy	.20	.09
127	Tony Pena	.10	.05
128	Manny Ramirez	.50	.23
129	Paul Sorrento	.10	.05
130	Jim Thome	.40	.18
131	Omar Vizquel	.20	.09
132	Dante Bichette	.20	.09
133	Ellis Burks	.20	.09
134	Vinny Castilla	.30	.14
135	Marvin Freeman	.10	.05
136	Andres Galarraga	.40	.18
137	Joe Girardi	.10	.05
138	Charlie Hayes	.10	.05
139	Mike Kingery	.10	.05
140	Nelson Liriano	.10	.05
141	Roberto Mejia	.10	.05
142	David Nied	.10	.05
143	Steve Reed	.10	.05
144	Armando Reynoso	.10	.05
145	Bruce Ruffin	.10	.05
146	John VanderWal	.10	.05
147	Walt Weiss	.10	.05
148	Skeeter Barnes	.10	.05
149	Tim Belcher	.10	.05
150	Junior Felix	.10	.05
151	Cecil Fielder	.20	.09
152	Travis Fryman	.20	.09
153	Kirk Gibson	.10	.05
154	Chris Gomez	.10	.05
155	Buddy Groom	.10	.05
156	Chad Kreuter	.10	.05
157	Mike Moore	.10	.05
158	Tony Phillips	.10	.05
159	Juan Samuel	.10	.05
160	Mickey Tettleton	.10	.05
161	Alan Trammell	.20	.09
162	David Wells	.30	.14
163	Lou Whitaker	.20	.09
164	Kurt Abbott	.10	.05
165	Luis Aquino	.10	.05
166	Alex Arias	.10	.05
167	Bret Barberie	.10	.05
168	Jerry Browne	.10	.05
169	Chuck Carr	.10	.05
170	Matias Carrillo	.10	.05
171	Greg Colbrunn	.10	.05
172	Jeff Conine	.20	.09
173	Carl Everett	.10	.05
174	Robb Nen	.10	.05
175	Yorkis Perez	.10	.05
176	Pat Rapp	.10	.05
177	Benito Santiago	.10	.05
178	Gary Sheffield	.20	.09
179	Darrell Whitmore	.10	.05
180	Jeff Bagwell	.50	.23
181	Kevin Bass	.10	.05
182	Craig Biggio	.40	.18
183	Andujar Cedeno	.10	.05
184	Doug Drabek	.10	.05
185	Tony Eusebio	.10	.05
186	Steve Finley	.20	.09
187	Luis Gonzalez	.10	.05
188	Pete Harnisch	.10	.05
189	John Hudek	.10	.05
190	Orlando Miller	.10	.05
191	James Mouton	.10	.05
192	Roberto Petagine	.10	.05
193	Shane Reynolds	.20	.09
194	Greg Swindell	.10	.05
195	Dave Veres	.10	.05
196	Kevin Appier	.20	.09
197	Stan Belinda	.10	.05
198	Vince Coleman	.10	.05
199	David Cone	.30	.14
200	Gary Gaetti	.10	.05
201	Greg Gagne	.10	.05
202	Mark Gubicza	.10	.05
203	Bob Hamelin	.10	.05
204	Dave Henderson	.10	.05
205	Felix Jose	.10	.05

206	Wally Joyner	.20	.09
207	Jose Lind	.10	.05
208	Mike Macfarlane	.10	.05
209	Brian McRae	.10	.05
210	Jeff Montgomery	.10	.05
211	Hipolito Pichardo	.10	.05
212	Pedro Astacio	.10	.05
213	Brett Butler	.20	.09
214	Omar Daal	.10	.05
215	Delino DeShields	.20	.09
216	Darren Dreifort	.20	.09
217	Carlos Hernandez	.10	.05
218	Orel Hershiser	.20	.09
219	Garey Ingram	.10	.05
220	Eric Karros	.20	.09
221	Ramon Martinez	.20	.09
222	Raul Mondesi	.30	.14
223	Jose Offerman	.20	.09
224	Mike Piazza	1.25	.55
225	Henry Rodriguez	.20	.09
226	Ismael Valdes	.20	.09
227	Tim Wallach	.10	.05
228	Jeff Cirillo	.20	.09
229	Alex Diaz	.10	.05
230	Cal Eldred	.10	.05
231	Mike Fetters	.10	.05
232	Brian Harper	.10	.05
233	Ted Higuera	.10	.05
234	John Jaha	.10	.05
235	Graeme Lloyd	.10	.05
236	Jose Mercedes	.10	.05
237	Jaime Navarro	.10	.05
238	Dave Nilsson	.10	.05
239	Jesse Orosco	.10	.05
240	Jody Reed	.10	.05
241	Jose Valentin	.10	.05
242	Greg Vaughn	.20	.09
243	Turner Ward	.10	.05
244	Rick Aguilera	.10	.05
245	Rich Becker	.10	.05
246	Jim Deshaies	.10	.05
247	Steve Dunn	.10	.05
248	Scott Erickson	.20	.09
249	Kent Hrbek	.20	.09
250	Chuck Knoblauch	.40	.18
251	Scott Leius	.10	.05
252	David McCarty	.10	.05
253	Pat Meares	.10	.05
254	Pedro Munoz	.10	.05
255	Kirby Puckett	.60	.25
256	Carlos Pulido	.10	.05
257	Kevin Tapani	.10	.05
258	Matt Walbeck	.10	.05
259	Dave Winfield	.40	.18
260	Moises Alou	.20	.09
261	Juan Bell	.10	.05
262	Freddie Benavides	.10	.05
263	Sean Berry	.10	.05
264	Wil Cordero	.10	.05
265	Jeff Fassero	.10	.05
266	Darrin Fletcher	.10	.05
267	Cliff Floyd	.20	.09
268	Marquis Grissom	.20	.09
269	Gil Heredia	.10	.05
270	Ken Hill	.10	.05
271	Pedro Martinez	.50	.23
272	Mel Rojas	.10	.05
273	Larry Walker	.40	.18
274	John Wetteland	.20	.09
275	Rondell White	.20	.09
276	Tim Bogar	.10	.05
277	Bobby Bonilla	.20	.09
278	Rico Brogna	.20	.09
279	Jeromy Burnitz	.20	.09
280	John Franco	.20	.09
281	Eric Hillman	.10	.05
282	Todd Hundley	.10	.05
283	Jeff Kent	.20	.09
284	Mike Maddux	.10	.05
285	Joe Orsulak	.10	.05
286	Luis Rivera	.10	.05
287	Bret Saberhagen	.20	.09
288	David Segui	.10	.05
289	Ryan Thompson	.20	.09
290	Fernando Vina	.10	.05
291	Jose Vizcaino	.10	.05
292	Jim Abbott	.20	.09
293	Wade Boggs	.40	.18
294	Russ Davis	.20	.09
295	Mike Gallego	.10	.05
296	Xavier Hernandez	.10	.05
297	Steve Howe	.10	.05
298	Jimmy Key	.20	.09
299	Don Mattingly	.75	.35
300	Terry Mulholland	.10	.05
301	Paul O'Neill	.20	.09
302	Luis Polonia	.10	.05
303	Mike Stanley	.10	.05
304	Danny Tartabull	.10	.05
305	Randy Velarde	.10	.05
306	Bob Wickman	.10	.05
307	Bernie Williams	.40	.18
308	Mark Acre	.10	.05
309	Geronimo Berroa	.10	.05
310	Mike Bordick	.10	.05
311	Dennis Eckersley	.20	.09
312	Rickey Henderson	.50	.23
313	Stan Javier	.10	.05
314	Miguel Jimenez	.10	.05
315	Francisco Matos	.10	.05
316	Mark McGwire	2.00	.90
317	Troy Neel	.10	.05
318	Steve Ontiveros	.10	.05
319	Carlos Reyes	.10	.05
320	Ruben Sierra	.10	.05
321	Terry Steinbach	.10	.05
322	Bob Welch	.10	.05
323	Bobby Witt	.10	.05
324	Larry Andersen	.10	.05
325	Kim Batiste	.10	.05
326	Darren Daulton	.20	.09
327	Mariano Duncan	.10	.05
328	Lenny Dykstra	.20	.09
329	Jim Eisenreich	.10	.05
330	Danny Jackson	.10	.05
331	John Kruk	.20	.09
332	Tony Longmire	.10	.05
333	Tom Marsh	.10	.05
334	Mickey Morandini	.10	.05
335	Bobby Munoz	.10	.05
336	Todd Pratt	.10	.05
337	Tom Quinlan	.10	.05
338	Kevin Stocker	.10	.05
339	Fernando Valenzuela	.20	.09
340	Jay Bell	.20	.09
341	Dave Clark	.10	.05
342	Steve Cooke	.10	.05
343	Carlos Garcia	.10	.05
344	Jeff King	.10	.05
345	Jon Lieber	.10	.05
346	Ravelo Manzanillo	.10	.05
347	Al Martin	.10	.05
348	Orlando Merced	.10	.05
349	Denny Neagle	.20	.09
350	Alejandro Pena	.10	.05
351	Don Slaught	.10	.05
352	Zane Smith	.10	.05
353	Andy Van Slyke	.20	.09
354	Rick White	.10	.05
355	Kevin Young	.10	.05
356	Andy Ashby	.10	.05
357	Derek Bell	.20	.09
358	Andy Benes	.20	.09
359	Phil Clark	.10	.05
360	Donnie Elliott	.10	.05
361	Ricky Gutierrez	.10	.05
362	Tony Gwynn	1.00	.45
363	Trevor Hoffman	.20	.09
364	Tim Hyers	.10	.05
365	Luis Lopez	.10	.05
366	Jose Martinez	.10	.05
367	Pedro A. Martinez	.10	.05
368	Phil Plantier	.20	.09
369	Bip Roberts	.10	.05
370	A.J. Sager	.10	.05
371	Jeff Tabaka	.10	.05
372	Todd Benzinger	.10	.05
373	Barry Bonds	.50	.23
374	John Burkett	.10	.05
375	Mark Carreon	.10	.05
376	Royce Clayton	.10	.05
377	Pat Gomez	.10	.05
378	Erik Johnson	.10	.05
379	Darren Lewis	.10	.05
380	Kirt Manwaring	.10	.05
381	Dave Martinez	.10	.05
382	John Patterson	.10	.05
383	Mark Portugal	.10	.05
384	Darryl Strawberry	.20	.09
385	Salomon Torres	.10	.05
386	Wm. VanLandingham	.10	.05
387	Matt Williams	.40	.18
388	Rich Amaral	.10	.05
389	Bobby Ayala	.10	.05
390	Mike Blowers	.10	.05
391	Chris Bosio	.10	.05
392	Jay Buhner	.20	.09
393	Jim Converse	.10	.05
394	Tim Davis	.10	.05
395	Felix Fermin	.10	.05
396	Dave Fleming	.10	.05
397	Goose Gossage	.20	.09
398	Ken Griffey Jr.	2.00	.90
399	Randy Johnson	.40	.18
400	Edgar Martinez	.20	.09
401	Tino Martinez	.40	.18
402	Alex Rodriguez	1.50	.70
403	Dan Wilson	.10	.05
404	Luis Alicea	.10	.05
405	Rene Arocha	.10	.05
406	Bernard Gilkey	.10	.05
407	Gregg Jefferies	.20	.09
408	Ray Lankford	.20	.09
409	Terry McGriff	.10	.05
410	Omar Olivares	.10	.05
411	Jose Oquendo	.10	.05
412	Vicente Palacios	.10	.05
413	Geronimo Pena	.10	.05
414	Mike Perez	.10	.05
415	Gerald Perry	.10	.05
416	Ozzie Smith	.50	.23
417	Bob Tewksbury	.10	.05
418	Mark Whiten	.10	.05
419	Todd Zeile	.10	.05
420	Esteban Beltre	.10	.05
421	Kevin Brown	.30	.14
422	Cris Carpenter	.10	.05
423	Will Clark	.40	.18
424	Hector Fajardo	.10	.05
425	Jeff Frye	.10	.05
426	Juan Gonzalez	.75	.35
427	Rusty Greer	.40	.18
428	Rick Honeycutt	.10	.05
429	David Hulse	.10	.05
430	Manny Lee	.10	.05
431	Junior Ortiz	.10	.05
432	Dean Palmer	.20	.09
433	Ivan Rodriguez	.50	.23
434	Dan Smith	.10	.05
435	Roberto Alomar	.40	.18
436	Pat Borders	.10	.05
437	Scott Brow	.10	.05
438	Rob Butler	.10	.05
439	Joe Carter	.20	.09
440	Tony Castillo	.10	.05
441	Domingo Cedeno	.10	.05
442	Brad Cornett	.10	.05
443	Carlos Delgado	.40	.18
444	Alex Gonzalez	.10	.05
445	Juan Guzman	.10	.05
446	Darren Hall	.10	.05
447	Paul Molitor	.40	.18
448	John Olerud	.20	.09
449	Robert Perez	.20	.09
450	Devon White	.10	.05

1995 Pacific Gold Crown Die Cuts

	MINT	NRMT
COMPLETE SET (20)	150.00	70.00
COMMON CARD (1-20)	2.50	1.10
STATED ODDS 1:18		
1 Greg Maddux	15.00	6.75
2 Fred McGriff	2.50	1.10
3 Rafael Palmeiro	4.00	1.80

		MINT	NRMT
❏ 25	Paul Molitor	4.00	1.80
❏ 26	Kirby Puckett	8.00	3.60
❏ 27	David Justice	4.00	1.80
❏ 28	Jeff Conine	1.25	.55
❏ 29	Bret Boone	2.00	.90
❏ 30	Larry Walker	4.00	1.80
❏ 31	Cecil Fielder	2.00	.90
❏ 32	Manny Ramirez	5.00	2.20
❏ 33	Javier Lopez	2.00	.90
❏ 34	Jimmy Key	2.00	.90
❏ 35	Andres Galarraga	4.00	1.80
❏ 36	Tony Gwynn	12.00	5.50

1995 Pacific Latinos Destacados

		MINT	NRMT
❏ 4	Cal Ripken Jr.	25.00	11.00
❏ 5	Jose Canseco	8.00	3.60
❏ 6	Frank Thomas	12.00	5.50
❏ 7	Albert Belle	4.00	1.80
❏ 8	Manny Ramirez	8.00	3.60
❏ 9	Andres Galarraga	4.00	1.80
❏ 10	Jeff Bagwell	8.00	3.60
❏ 11	Chan Ho Park	4.00	1.80
❏ 12	Raul Mondesi	2.50	1.10
❏ 13	Mike Piazza	20.00	9.00
❏ 14	Kirby Puckett	10.00	4.50
❏ 15	Barry Bonds	4.00	1.80
❏ 16	Ken Griffey Jr.	30.00	13.50
❏ 17	Alex Rodriguez	25.00	11.00
❏ 18	Juan Gonzalez	12.00	5.50
❏ 19	Roberto Alomar	4.00	1.80
❏ 20	Carlos Delgado	4.00	1.80

1995 Pacific Gold Prisms

		MINT	NRMT
COMPLETE SET (36)		120.00	55.00
COMMON CARD (1-36)		1.25	.55
STATED ODDS 1:12			
❏ 1	Jose Canseco	5.00	2.20
❏ 2	Gregg Jefferies	1.25	.55
❏ 3	Fred McGriff	3.00	1.35
❏ 4	Joe Carter	2.00	.90
❏ 5	Tim Salmon	4.00	1.80
❏ 6	Wade Boggs	4.00	1.80
❏ 7	Dave Winfield	4.00	1.80
❏ 8	Bob Hamelin	1.25	.55
❏ 9	Cal Ripken Jr.	20.00	9.00
❏ 10	Don Mattingly	10.00	4.50
❏ 11	Juan Gonzalez	10.00	4.50
❏ 12	Carlos Delgado	4.00	1.80
❏ 13	Barry Bonds	5.00	2.20
❏ 14	Albert Belle	4.00	1.80
❏ 15	Raul Mondesi	3.00	1.35
❏ 16	Jeff Bagwell	5.00	2.20
❏ 17	Mike Piazza	15.00	6.75
❏ 18	Rafael Palmeiro	4.00	1.80
❏ 19	Frank Thomas	10.00	4.50
❏ 20	Matt Williams	4.00	1.80
❏ 21	Ken Griffey Jr.	25.00	11.00
❏ 22	Will Clark	4.00	1.80
❏ 23	Bobby Bonilla	2.00	.90
❏ 24	Kenny Lofton	3.00	1.35

		MINT	NRMT
COMPLETE SET (36)		50.00	22.00
COMMON CARD (1-36)		1.00	.45
STATED ODDS 1:9			
❏ 1	Roberto Alomar	3.00	1.35
❏ 2	Moises Alou	1.50	.70
❏ 3	Wilson Alvarez	1.50	.70
❏ 4	Carlos Baerga	1.00	.45
❏ 5	Geronimo Berroa	1.00	.45
❏ 6	Jose Canseco	4.00	1.80
❏ 7	Hector Carrasco	1.00	.45
❏ 8	Wil Cordero	1.00	.45
❏ 9	Carlos Delgado	3.00	1.35
❏ 10	Damion Easley	1.50	.70
❏ 11	Tony Eusebio	1.00	.45
❏ 12	Hector Fajardo	1.00	.45
❏ 13	Andres Galarraga	3.00	1.35
❏ 14	Carlos Garcia	1.00	.45
❏ 15	Chris Gomez	1.00	.45
❏ 16	Alex Gonzalez	1.00	.45
❏ 17	Juan Gonzalez	8.00	3.60
❏ 18	Luis Gonzalez	1.00	.45
❏ 19	Felix Jose	1.00	.45
❏ 20	Javier Lopez	1.50	.70
❏ 21	Luis Lopez	1.00	.45
❏ 22	Dennis Martinez	1.50	.70
❏ 23	Orlando Miller	1.00	.45
❏ 24	Raul Mondesi	2.50	1.10
❏ 25	Jose Oliva	1.00	.45
❏ 26	Rafael Palmeiro	3.00	1.35
❏ 27	Yorkis Perez	1.00	.45
❏ 28	Manny Ramirez	4.00	1.80
❏ 29	Jose Rijo	1.00	.45
❏ 30	Alex Rodriguez	15.00	6.75
❏ 31	Ivan Rodriguez	3.00	1.35
❏ 32	Carlos Rodriguez	1.00	.45
❏ 33	Sammy Sosa	12.00	5.50
❏ 34	Tony Tarasco	1.00	.45
❏ 35	Ismael Valdes	1.50	.70
❏ 36	Bernie Williams	3.00	1.35

1996 Pacific

	MINT	NRMT
COMPLETE SET (450)	35.00	16.00
COMMON CARD (1-450)	.10	.05
MINOR STARS	.20	.09
UNLISTED STARS	.40	.18
SUBSET CARDS HALF VALUE OF BASE CARDS		

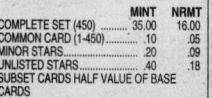

		MINT	NRMT
❏ 1	Steve Avery	.10	.05
❏ 2	Ryan Klesko	.20	.09
❏ 3	Pedro Borbon	.10	.05
❏ 4	Chipper Jones	1.00	.45
❏ 5	Kent Mercker	.10	.05
❏ 6	Greg Maddux	1.00	.45
❏ 7	Greg McMichael	.10	.05
❏ 8	Mark Wohlers	.10	.05
❏ 9	Fred McGriff	.30	.14
❏ 10	John Smoltz	.30	.14
❏ 11	Rafael Bellard	.10	.05
❏ 12	Mark Lemke	.10	.05
❏ 13	Tom Glavine	.40	.18
❏ 14	Javier Lopez	.20	.09
❏ 15	Jeff Blauser	.10	.05
❏ 16	David Justice	.40	.18
❏ 17	Marquis Grissom	.10	.05
❏ 18	Greg Maddux CY	.50	.23
❏ 19	Randy Myers	.10	.05
❏ 20	Scott Servais	.10	.05
❏ 21	Sammy Sosa	1.25	.55
❏ 22	Kevin Foster	.10	.05
❏ 23	Jose Hernandez	.10	.05
❏ 24	Jim Bullinger	.10	.05
❏ 25	Mike Perez	.10	.05
❏ 26	Shawon Dunston	.10	.05
❏ 27	Rey Sanchez	.10	.05
❏ 28	Frank Castillo	.10	.05
❏ 29	Jaime Navarro	.10	.05
❏ 30	Brian McRae	.10	.05
❏ 31	Mark Grace	.30	.14
❏ 32	Roberto Rivera	.10	.05
❏ 33	Luis Gonzalez	.20	.09
❏ 34	Hector Carrasco	.10	.05
❏ 35	Bret Boone	.20	.09
❏ 36	Thomas Howard	.10	.05
❏ 37	Hal Morris	.10	.05
❏ 38	John Smiley	.10	.05
❏ 39	Jeff Brantley	.10	.05
❏ 40	Barry Larkin	.40	.18
❏ 41	Mariano Duncan	.10	.05
❏ 42	Xavier Hernandez	.10	.05
❏ 43	Pete Schourek	.10	.05
❏ 44	Reggie Sanders	.20	.09
❏ 45	Dave Burba	.10	.05
❏ 46	Jeff Branson	.10	.05
❏ 47	Mark Portugal	.10	.05
❏ 48	Ron Gant	.20	.09
❏ 49	Benito Santiago	.10	.05
❏ 50	Barry Larkin MVP	.30	.14
❏ 51	Steve Reed	.10	.05
❏ 52	Kevin Ritz	.10	.05
❏ 53	Dante Bichette	.20	.09
❏ 54	Darren Holmes	.10	.05
❏ 55	Ellis Burks	.20	.09
❏ 56	Walt Weiss	.10	.05
❏ 57	Armando Reynoso	.10	.05
❏ 58	Vinny Castilla	.30	.14
❏ 59	Jason Bates	.10	.05
❏ 60	Mike Kingery	.10	.05
❏ 61	Bryan Rekar	.10	.05
❏ 62	Curtis Leskanic	.10	.05
❏ 63	Bret Saberhagen	.20	.09
❏ 64	Andres Galarraga	.40	.18
❏ 65	Larry Walker	.40	.18
❏ 66	Joe Girardi	.10	.05
❏ 67	Quilvio Veras	.10	.05
❏ 68	Robb Nen	.10	.05

69	Mario Diaz	.10	.05
70	Chuck Carr	.10	.05
71	Alex Arias	.10	.05
72	Pat Rapp	.10	.05
73	Rich Garces	.10	.05
74	Kurt Abbott	.10	.05
75	Andre Dawson	.30	.14
76	Greg Colbrunn	.10	.05
77	John Burkett	.10	.05
78	Terry Pendleton	.10	.05
79	Jesus Tavarez	.10	.05
80	Charles Johnson	.20	.09
81	Yorkis Perez	.10	.05
82	Jeff Conine	.10	.05
83	Gary Sheffield	.20	.09
84	Brian L. Hunter	.10	.05
85	Derrick May	.10	.05
86	Greg Swindell	.10	.05
87	Derek Bell	.20	.09
88	Dave Veres	.10	.05
89	Jeff Bagwell	.50	.23
90	Todd Jones	.10	.05
91	Orlando Miller	.10	.05
92	Pedro A. Martinez	.10	.05
93	Tony Eusebio	.10	.05
94	Craig Biggio	.40	.18
95	Shane Reynolds	.20	.09
96	James Mouton	.10	.05
97	Doug Drabek	.10	.05
98	Dave Magadan	.10	.05
99	Ricky Gutierrez	.10	.05
100	Hideo Nomo	.40	.18
101	Delino DeShields	.10	.05
102	Tom Candiotti	.10	.05
103	Mike Piazza	1.25	.55
104	Ramon Martinez	.10	.05
105	Pedro Astacio	.10	.05
106	Chad Fonville	.10	.05
107	Raul Mondesi	.20	.09
108	Ismael Valdes	.20	.09
109	Jose Offerman	.20	.09
110	Todd Worrell	.10	.05
111	Eric Karros	.20	.09
112	Brett Butler	.20	.09
113	Juan Castro	.10	.05
114	Roberto Kelly	.10	.05
115	Omar Daal	.10	.05
116	Antonio Osuna	.10	.05
117	Hideo Nomo ROY	.20	.09
118	Mike Lansing	.10	.05
119	Mel Rojas	.10	.05
120	Sean Berry	.10	.05
121	David Segui	.20	.09
122	Tavo Alvarez	.10	.05
123	Pedro J.Martinez	.50	.23
124	F.P. Santangelo	.10	.05
125	Rondell White	.20	.09
126	Cliff Floyd	.20	.09
127	Henry Rodriguez	.20	.09
128	Tony Tarasco	.10	.05
129	Yamil Benitez	.10	.05
130	Carlos Perez	.10	.05
131	Wil Cordero	.10	.05
132	Jeff Fassero	.10	.05
133	Moises Alou	.20	.09
134	John Franco	.20	.09
135	Rico Brogna	.10	.05
136	Dave Mlicki	.10	.05
137	Bill Pulsipher	.10	.05
138	Jose Vizcaino	.10	.05
139	Carl Everett	.20	.09
140	Edgardo Alfonzo	.40	.18
141	Bobby Jones	.10	.05
142	Alberto Castillo	.10	.05
143	Joe Orsulak	.10	.05
144	Jeff Kent	.20	.09
145	Ryan Thompson	.10	.05
146	Jason Isringhausen	.20	.09
147	Todd Hundley	.10	.05
148	Alex Ochoa	.10	.05
149	Charlie Hayes	.10	.05
150	Michael Mimbs	.10	.05
151	Darren Daulton	.20	.09
152	Toby Borland	.10	.05
153	Andy Van Slyke	.10	.05
154	Mickey Morandini	.10	.05
155	Sid Fernandez	.10	.05
156	Tom Marsh	.10	.05
157	Kevin Stocker	.10	.05
158	Paul Quantrill	.10	.05
159	Gregg Jefferies	.10	.05
160	Ricky Bottalico	.10	.05
161	Lenny Dykstra	.20	.09
162	Mark Whiten	.10	.05
163	Tyler Green	.10	.05
164	Jim Eisenreich	.10	.05
165	Heathcliff Slocumb	.10	.05
166	Esteban Loaiza	.10	.05
167	Rich Aude	.10	.05
168	Jason Christiansen	.10	.05
169	Ramon Morel	.10	.05
170	Orlando Merced	.10	.05
171	Paul Wagner	.10	.05
172	Jeff King	.10	.05
173	Jay Bell	.20	.09
174	Jacob Brumfield	.10	.05
175	Nelson Liriano	.10	.05
176	Dan Miceli	.10	.05
177	Carlos Garcia	.10	.05
178	Denny Neagle	.20	.09
179	Angelo Encarnacion	.10	.05
180	Al Martin	.10	.05
181	Midre Cummings	.10	.05
182	Eddie Williams	.10	.05
183	Roberto Petagine	.10	.05
184	Tony Gwynn	1.00	.45
185	Andy Ashby	.10	.05
186	Melvin Nieves	.10	.05
187	Phil Clark	.10	.05
188	Brad Ausmus	.10	.05
189	Bip Roberts	.10	.05
190	Fernando Valenzuela	.20	.09
191	Marc Newfield	.10	.05
192	Steve Finley	.20	.09
193	Trevor Hoffman	.20	.09
194	Andujar Cedeno	.10	.05
195	Jody Reed	.10	.05
196	Ken Caminiti	.20	.09
197	Joey Hamilton	.10	.05
198	Tony Gwynn BAC	.50	.23
199	Shawn Barton	.10	.05
200	Deion Sanders	.20	.09
201	Rikkert Faneyte	.10	.05
202	Barry Bonds	.50	.23
203	Matt Williams	.40	.18
204	Jose Bautista	.10	.05
205	Mark Leiter	.10	.05
206	Mark Carreon	.10	.05
207	Robby Thompson	.10	.05
208	Terry Mulholland	.10	.05
209	Rod Beck	.10	.05
210	Royce Clayton	.10	.05
211	J.R. Phillips	.10	.05
212	Kirt Manwaring	.10	.05
213	Glenallen Hill	.10	.05
214	William VanLandingham	.10	.05
215	Scott Cooper	.10	.05
216	Bernard Gilkey	.10	.05
217	Allen Watson	.10	.05
218	Donovan Osborne	.10	.05
219	Ray Lankford	.20	.09
220	Tony Fossas	.10	.05
221	Tom Pagnozzi	.10	.05
222	John Mabry	.10	.05
223	Tripp Cromer	.10	.05
224	Mark Petkovsek	.10	.05
225	Mike Morgan	.10	.05
226	Ozzie Smith	.50	.23
227	Tom Henke	.10	.05
228	Jose Oquendo	.10	.05
229	Brian Jordan	.20	.09
230	Cal Ripken	1.50	.70
231	Scott Erickson	.20	.09
232	Harold Baines	.20	.09
233	Jeff Manto	.10	.05
234	Jesse Orosco	.10	.05
235	Jeffrey Hammonds	.20	.09
236	Brady Anderson	.20	.09
237	Manny Alexander	.10	.05
238	Chris Hoiles	.10	.05
239	Rafael Palmeiro	.40	.18
240	Ben McDonald	.10	.05
241	Curtis Goodwin	.10	.05
242	Bobby Bonilla	.20	.09
243	Mike Mussina	.40	.18
244	Kevin Brown	.30	.14
245	Armando Benitez	.10	.05
246	Jose Canseco	.50	.23
247	Erik Hanson	.10	.05
248	Mo Vaughn	.40	.18
249	Tim Naehring	.10	.05
250	Vaughn Eshelman	.10	.05
251	Mike Greenwell	.10	.05
252	Troy O'Leary	.20	.09
253	Tim Wakefield	.10	.05
254	Dwayne Hosey	.10	.05
255	John Valentin	.20	.09
256	Rick Aguilera	.10	.05
257	Mike Macfarlane	.10	.05
258	Roger Clemens	1.00	.45
259	Luis Alicea	.10	.05
260	Mo Vaughn MVP	.20	.09
261	Mark Langston	.10	.05
262	Jim Edmonds	.30	.14
263	Rod Correia	.10	.05
264	Tim Salmon	.30	.14
265	J.T. Snow	.20	.09
266	Orlando Palmeiro	.10	.05
267	Jorge Fabregas	.10	.05
268	Jim Abbott	.20	.09
269	Eduardo Perez	.10	.05
270	Lee Smith	.20	.09
271	Gary DiSarcina	.10	.05
272	Damon Easley	.20	.09
273	Tony Phillips	.10	.05
274	Garret Anderson	.20	.09
275	Chuck Finley	.10	.05
276	Chili Davis	.20	.09
277	Lance Johnson	.10	.05
278	Alex Fernandez	.10	.05
279	Robin Ventura	.20	.09
280	Chris Snopek	.10	.05
281	Brian Keyser	.10	.05
282	Lyle Mouton	.10	.05
283	Luis Andujar	.10	.05
284	Tim Raines	.20	.09
285	Larry Thomas	.10	.05
286	Ozzie Guillen	.10	.05
287	Frank Thomas	.75	.35
288	Roberto Hernandez	.10	.05
289	Dave Martinez	.10	.05
290	Ray Durham	.20	.09
291	Ron Karkovice	.10	.05
292	Wilson Alvarez	.10	.05
293	Omar Vizquel	.20	.09
294	Eddie Murray	.40	.18
295	Sandy Alomar Jr.	.20	.09
296	Orel Hershiser	.20	.09
297	Jose Mesa	.10	.05
298	Julian Tavarez	.10	.05
299	Dennis Martinez	.20	.09
300	Carlos Baerga	.20	.09
301	Manny Ramirez	.50	.23
302	Jim Thome	.40	.18
303	Kenny Lofton	.30	.14
304	Tony Pena	.10	.05
305	Alvaro Espinoza	.10	.05
306	Paul Sorrento	.10	.05
307	Albert Belle	.40	.18
308	Danny Bautista	.10	.05
309	Chris Gomez	.10	.05
310	Jose Lima	.30	.14
311	Phil Nevin	.10	.05
312	Alan Trammell	.30	.14
313	Chad Curtis	.10	.05
314	John Flaherty	.10	.05
315	Travis Fryman	.20	.09
316	Todd Steverson	.10	.05
317	Brian Bohanon	.10	.05
318	Lou Whitaker	.20	.09
319	Bobby Higginson	.20	.09
320	Steve Rodriguez	.10	.05
321	Cecil Fielder	.20	.09
322	Felipe Lira	.10	.05
323	Juan Samuel	.10	.05
324	Bob Hamelin	.10	.05
325	Tom Goodwin	.10	.05
326	Johnny Damon	.30	.14

❑ 327 Hipolito Pichardo	.10	.05
❑ 328 Dilson Torres	.10	.05
❑ 329 Kevin Appier	.20	.09
❑ 330 Mark Gubicza	.10	.05
❑ 331 Jon Nunnally	.10	.05
❑ 332 Gary Gaetti	.20	.09
❑ 333 Brent Mayne	.10	.05
❑ 334 Brent Cookson	.10	.05
❑ 335 Tom Gordon	.10	.05
❑ 336 Wally Joyner	.20	.09
❑ 337 Greg Gagne	.10	.05
❑ 338 Fernando Vina	.10	.05
❑ 339 Joe Oliver	.10	.05
❑ 340 John Jaha	.10	.05
❑ 341 Jeff Cirillo	.20	.09
❑ 342 Pat Listach	.10	.05
❑ 343 Dave Nilsson	.10	.05
❑ 344 Steve Sparks	.10	.05
❑ 345 Ricky Bones	.10	.05
❑ 346 David Hulse	.10	.05
❑ 347 Scott Karl	.10	.05
❑ 348 Darryl Hamilton	.10	.05
❑ 349 B.J. Surhoff	.20	.09
❑ 350 Angel Miranda	.10	.05
❑ 351 Sid Roberson	.10	.05
❑ 352 Matt Mieske	.10	.05
❑ 353 Jose Valentin	.10	.05
❑ 354 Matt Lawton	.50	.23
❑ 355 Eddie Guardado	.10	.05
❑ 356 Brad Radke	.20	.09
❑ 357 Pedro Munoz	.10	.05
❑ 358 Scott Stahoviak	.10	.05
❑ 359 Erik Schullstrom	.10	.05
❑ 360 Pat Meares	.10	.05
❑ 361 Marty Cordova	.10	.05
❑ 362 Scott Leius	.10	.05
❑ 363 Matt Walbeck	.10	.05
❑ 364 Rich Becker	.10	.05
❑ 365 Kirby Puckett	.60	.25
❑ 366 Oscar Munoz	.10	.05
❑ 367 Chuck Knoblauch	.40	.18
❑ 368 Marty Cordova ROY	.10	.05
❑ 369 Bernie Williams	.40	.18
❑ 370 Mike Stanley	.10	.05
❑ 371 Andy Pettitte	.30	.14
❑ 372 Jack McDowell	.10	.05
❑ 373 Sterling Hitchcock	.10	.05
❑ 374 David Cone	.30	.14
❑ 375 Randy Velarde	.10	.05
❑ 376 Don Mattingly	.75	.35
❑ 377 Melido Perez	.10	.05
❑ 378 Wade Boggs	.40	.18
❑ 379 Ruben Sierra	.10	.05
❑ 380 Tony Fernandez	.10	.05
❑ 381 John Wetteland	.20	.09
❑ 382 Mariano Rivera	.30	.14
❑ 383 Derek Jeter	1.25	.55
❑ 384 Paul O'Neill	.20	.09
❑ 385 Mark McGwire	2.00	.90
❑ 386 Scott Brosius	.10	.05
❑ 387 Don Wengert	.10	.05
❑ 388 Terry Steinbach	.10	.05
❑ 389 Brent Gates	.10	.05
❑ 390 Craig Paquette	.10	.05
❑ 391 Mike Bordick	.10	.05
❑ 392 Ariel Prieto	.10	.05
❑ 393 Dennis Eckersley	.20	.09
❑ 394 Carlos Reyes	.10	.05
❑ 395 Todd Stottlemyre	.10	.05
❑ 396 Rickey Henderson	.50	.23
❑ 397 Geronimo Berroa	.10	.05
❑ 398 Steve Ontiveros	.10	.05
❑ 399 Mike Gallego	.10	.05
❑ 400 Stan Javier	.10	.05
❑ 401 Randy Johnson	.40	.18
❑ 402 Norm Charlton	.10	.05
❑ 403 Mike Blowers	.10	.05
❑ 404 Tino Martinez	.20	.09
❑ 405 Dan Wilson	.10	.05
❑ 406 Andy Benes	.20	.09
❑ 407 Alex Diaz	.10	.05
❑ 408 Edgar Martinez	.20	.09
❑ 409 Chris Bosio	.10	.05
❑ 410 Ken Griffey, Jr.	2.00	.90
❑ 411 Luis Sojo	.10	.05
❑ 412 Bob Wolcott	.10	.05

❑ 413 Vince Coleman	.10	.05
❑ 414 Rich Amaral	.10	.05
❑ 415 Jay Buhner	.20	.09
❑ 416 Alex Rodriguez	1.25	.55
❑ 417 Joey Cora	.10	.05
❑ 418 Randy Johnson CY	.20	.09
❑ 419 Edgar Martinez BAC	.10	.05
❑ 420 Ivan Rodriguez	.50	.23
❑ 421 Mark McLemore	.10	.05
❑ 422 Mickey Tettleton	.10	.05
❑ 423 Juan Gonzalez	.75	.35
❑ 424 Will Clark	.40	.18
❑ 425 Kevin Gross	.10	.05
❑ 426 Dean Palmer	.20	.09
❑ 427 Kenny Rogers	.10	.05
❑ 428 Bob Tewksbury	.10	.05
❑ 429 Benji Gil	.10	.05
❑ 430 Jeff Russell	.10	.05
❑ 431 Rusty Greer	.20	.09
❑ 432 Roger Pavlik	.10	.05
❑ 433 Esteban Beltre	.10	.05
❑ 434 Otis Nixon	.10	.05
❑ 435 Paul Molitor	.40	.18
❑ 436 Carlos Delgado	.40	.18
❑ 437 Ed Sprague	.10	.05
❑ 438 Juan Guzman	.10	.05
❑ 439 Domingo Cedeno	.10	.05
❑ 440 Pat Hentgen	.20	.09
❑ 441 Tomas Perez	.10	.05
❑ 442 John Olerud	.20	.09
❑ 443 Shawn Green	.40	.18
❑ 444 Al Leiter	.20	.09
❑ 445 Joe Carter	.20	.09
❑ 446 Robert Perez	.10	.05
❑ 447 Devon White	.20	.09
❑ 448 Tony Castillo	.10	.05
❑ 449 Alex Gonzalez	.10	.05
❑ 450 Roberto Alomar	.40	.18

1996 Pacific Cramer's Choice

	MINT	NRMT
COMPLETE SET (10)	1000.00	450.00
COMMON CARD (CC1-CC10)	20.00	9.00
UNLISTED STARS	40.00	18.00
STATED ODDS 1:721		

❑ CC1 Roberto Alomar	40.00	18.00
❑ CC2 Wade Boggs	40.00	18.00
❑ CC3 Cal Ripken	150.00	70.00
❑ CC4 Greg Maddux	100.00	45.00
❑ CC5 Frank Thomas	80.00	36.00
❑ CC6 Tony Gwynn	100.00	45.00
❑ CC7 Mike Piazza	120.00	55.00
❑ CC8 Ken Griffey Jr.	200.00	90.00
❑ CC9 Manny Ramirez	50.00	22.00
❑ CC10 Edgar Martinez	20.00	9.00

1996 Pacific Estrellas Latinas

	MINT	NRMT
COMPLETE SET (36)	40.00	18.00
COMMON CARD (EL1-EL36)	.50	.23
STATED ODDS 1:9		

❑ EL1 Roberto Alomar	2.00	.90
❑ EL2 Moises Alou	1.00	.45
❑ EL3 Carlos Baerga	.50	.23
❑ EL4 Geronimo Berroa	.50	.23
❑ EL5 Ricky Bones	.50	.23
❑ EL6 Bobby Bonilla	1.00	.45
❑ EL7 Jose Canseco	2.50	1.10
❑ EL8 Vinny Castilla	1.50	.70
❑ EL9 Pedro Martinez	2.50	1.10
❑ EL10 John Valentin	1.00	.45
❑ EL11 Andres Galarraga	2.00	.90
❑ EL12 Juan Gonzalez	5.00	2.20
❑ EL13 Ozzie Guillen	.50	.23
❑ EL14 Esteban Loaiza	.50	.23
❑ EL15 Javier Lopez	1.00	.45
❑ EL16 Dennis Martinez	1.00	.45
❑ EL17 Edgar Martinez	1.00	.45
❑ EL18 Tino Martinez	1.00	.45
❑ EL19 Orlando Merced	.50	.23
❑ EL20 Jose Mesa	1.00	.45
❑ EL21 Raul Mondesi	1.00	.45
❑ EL22 Jaime Navarro	.50	.23
❑ EL23 Rafael Palmeiro	2.00	.90
❑ EL24 Carlos Perez	.50	.23
❑ EL25 Manny Ramirez	2.50	1.10
❑ EL26 Alex Rodriguez	8.00	3.60
❑ EL27 Ivan Rodriguez	2.50	1.10
❑ EL28 David Segui	1.00	.45
❑ EL29 Ruben Sierra	.50	.23
❑ EL30 Sammy Sosa	8.00	3.60
❑ EL31 Julian Tavarez	.50	.23
❑ EL32 Ismael Valdes	1.00	.45
❑ EL33 Fernando Valenzuela	1.00	.45
❑ EL34 Quilvio Veras	.50	.23
❑ EL35 Omar Vizquel	1.00	.45
❑ EL36 Bernie Williams	2.00	.90

1996 Pacific Gold Crown Die Cuts

	MINT	NRMT
COMPLETE SET (36)	250.00	110.00
COMMON CARD (DC1-DC36)	2.50	1.10
STATED ODDS 1:37		

❑ DC1 Roberto Alomar	6.00	2.70
❑ DC2 Will Clark	6.00	2.70
❑ DC3 Johnny Damon	4.00	1.80
❑ DC4 Don Mattingly	12.00	5.50
❑ DC5 Edgar Martinez	3.00	1.35

❑ DC6 Manny Ramirez	8.00	3.60
❑ DC7 Mike Piazza	20.00	9.00
❑ DC8 Quilvio Veras	2.50	1.10
❑ DC9 Rickey Henderson	8.00	3.60
❑ DC10 Jeff Bagwell	8.00	3.60
❑ DC11 Andres Galarraga	6.00	2.70
❑ DC12 Tim Salmon	4.00	1.80
❑ DC13 Ken Griffey Jr.	30.00	13.50
❑ DC14 Sammy Sosa	20.00	9.00
❑ DC15 Cal Ripken	25.00	11.00
❑ DC16 Raul Mondesi	3.00	1.35
❑ DC17 Jose Canseco	8.00	3.60
❑ DC18 Frank Thomas	12.00	5.50
❑ DC19 Hideo Nomo	6.00	2.70
❑ DC20 Wade Boggs	6.00	2.70
❑ DC21 Reggie Sanders	3.00	1.35
❑ DC22 Carlos Baerga	2.50	1.10
❑ DC23 Mo Vaughn	6.00	2.70
❑ DC24 Ivan Rodriguez	8.00	3.60
❑ DC25 Kirby Puckett	8.00	3.60
❑ DC26 Albert Belle	6.00	2.70
❑ DC27 Vinny Castilla	4.00	1.80
❑ DC28 Greg Maddux	15.00	6.75
❑ DC29 Dante Bichette	3.00	1.35
❑ DC30 Deion Sanders	3.00	1.35
❑ DC31 Chipper Jones	15.00	6.75
❑ DC32 Cecil Fielder	2.50	1.10
❑ DC33 Randy Johnson	6.00	2.70
❑ DC34 Mark McGwire	30.00	13.50
❑ DC35 Tony Gwynn	15.00	6.75
❑ DC36 Barry Bonds	8.00	3.60

1996 Pacific Hometowns

	MINT	NRMT
COMPLETE SET (20)	80.00	36.00
COMMON CARD (HP1-HP20)	1.25	.55
STATED ODDS 1:18		

❑ HP1 Mike Piazza	10.00	4.50
❑ HP2 Greg Maddux	8.00	3.60
❑ HP3 Tony Gwynn	8.00	3.60
❑ HP4 Carlos Baerga	1.25	.55
❑ HP5 Don Mattingly	6.00	2.70
❑ HP6 Cal Ripken	12.00	5.50
❑ HP7 Chipper Jones	8.00	3.60
❑ HP8 Andres Galarraga	3.00	1.35
❑ HP9 Manny Ramirez	4.00	1.80
❑ HP10 Roberto Alomar	3.00	1.35
❑ HP11 Ken Griffey Jr.	15.00	6.75
❑ HP12 Jose Canseco	4.00	1.80
❑ HP13 Frank Thomas	6.00	2.70
❑ HP14 Vinny Castilla	2.00	.90
❑ HP15 Roberto Kelly	1.25	.55
❑ HP16 Dennis Martinez	1.50	.70
❑ HP17 Kirby Puckett	5.00	2.20
❑ HP18 Raul Mondesi	1.50	.70
❑ HP19 Hideo Nomo	3.00	1.35
❑ HP20 Edgar Martinez	1.50	.70

1996 Pacific Milestones

	MINT	NRMT
COMPLETE SET (10)	50.00	22.00
COMMON CARD (M1-M10)	2.00	.90
STATED ODDS 1:37		

❑ M1 Albert Belle	3.00	1.35
❑ M2 Don Mattingly	6.00	2.70
❑ M3 Tony Gwynn	8.00	3.60
❑ M4 Jose Canseco	4.00	1.80
❑ M5 Marty Cordova	2.00	.90
❑ M6 Wade Boggs	3.00	1.35
❑ M7 Greg Maddux	8.00	3.60
❑ M8 Eddie Murray	3.00	1.35
❑ M9 Ken Griffey Jr.	15.00	6.75
❑ M10 Cal Ripken	12.00	5.50

1996 Pacific October Moments

	MINT	NRMT
COMPLETE SET (20)	100.00	45.00
COMMON CARD (OM1-OM20)	1.50	.70
STATED ODDS 1:37		

❑ OM1 Carlos Baerga	1.50	.70
❑ OM2 Albert Belle	5.00	2.20
❑ OM3 Dante Bichette	2.00	.90
❑ OM4 Jose Canseco	6.00	2.70
❑ OM5 Tom Glavine	5.00	2.20
❑ OM6 Ken Griffey Jr.	25.00	11.00
❑ OM7 Randy Johnson	5.00	2.20
❑ OM8 Chipper Jones	12.00	5.50
❑ OM9 David Justice	5.00	2.20
❑ OM10 Ryan Klesko	2.00	.90
❑ OM11 Kenny Lofton	3.00	1.35
❑ OM12 Javier Lopez	2.00	.90
❑ OM13 Greg Maddux	12.00	5.50
❑ OM14 Edgar Martinez	2.00	.90
❑ OM15 Don Mattingly	10.00	4.50
❑ OM16 Hideo Nomo	5.00	2.20
❑ OM17 Mike Piazza	15.00	6.75
❑ OM18 Manny Ramirez	6.00	2.70
❑ OM19 Reggie Sanders	2.00	.90
❑ OM20 Jim Thome	5.00	2.20

1997 Pacific

	MINT	NRMT
COMPLETE SET (450)	40.00	18.00
COMMON CARD (1-450)	.15	.07
MINOR STARS	.30	.14
UNLISTED STARS	.60	.25
COMMON LT.BLUE (1-450)	.25	.11
*LT.BLUE STARS: 2.5X TO 6X HI COLUMN		
*LT.BLUE ROOKIES: 1.5X TO 4X HI		

ONE LT.BLUE PER WAL-MART PACK		
COMMON SILVER (1-450)	8.00	3.60
*SILVER STARS: 25X TO 60X HI COLUMN		
*SILVER ROOKIES: 12.5X TO 30X HI		
SILVER STATED ODDS 1:73		
SILVER STATED PRINT RUN 67 SETS		

❑ 1 Garret Anderson	.30	.14
❑ 2 George Arias	.15	.07
❑ 3 Chili Davis	.30	.14
❑ 4 Gary DiSarcina	.15	.07
❑ 5 Jim Edmonds	.40	.18
❑ 6 Darin Erstad	.60	.25
❑ 7 Jorge Fabregas	.15	.07
❑ 8 Chuck Finley	.30	.14
❑ 9 Rex Hudler	.15	.07
❑ 10 Mark Langston	.30	.14
❑ 11 Orlando Palmeiro	.15	.07
❑ 12 Troy Percival	.30	.14
❑ 13 Tim Salmon	.60	.25
❑ 14 J.T. Snow	.30	.14
❑ 15 Randy Velarde	.15	.07
❑ 16 Manny Alexander	.15	.07
❑ 17 Roberto Alomar	.60	.25
❑ 18 Brady Anderson	.30	.14
❑ 19 Armando Benitez	.15	.07
❑ 20 Bobby Bonilla	.30	.14
❑ 21 Rocky Coppinger	.15	.07
❑ 22 Scott Erickson	.30	.14
❑ 23 Jeffrey Hammonds	.30	.14
❑ 24 Chris Hoiles	.30	.14
❑ 25 Eddie Murray	.60	.25
❑ 26 Mike Mussina	.60	.25
❑ 27 Randy Myers	.15	.07
❑ 28 Rafael Palmeiro	.60	.25
❑ 29 Cal Ripken	2.50	1.10
❑ 30 B.J. Surhoff	.30	.14
❑ 31 Tony Tarasco	.15	.07
❑ 32 Esteban Beltre	.15	.07
❑ 33 Darren Bragg	.15	.07
❑ 34 Jose Canseco	.75	.35
❑ 35 Roger Clemens	1.50	.70
❑ 36 Wil Cordero	.15	.07
❑ 37 Alex Delgado	.15	.07
❑ 38 Jeff Frye	.15	.07
❑ 39 Nomar Garciaparra	2.00	.90
❑ 40 Tom Gordon	.15	.07
❑ 41 Mike Greenwell	.15	.07
❑ 42 Reggie Jefferson	.15	.07
❑ 43 Tim Naehring	.15	.07
❑ 44 Troy O'Leary	.30	.14
❑ 45 Heathcliff Slocumb	.15	.07
❑ 46 Lee Tinsley	.15	.07
❑ 47 John Valentin	.30	.14
❑ 48 Mo Vaughn	.60	.25
❑ 49 Wilson Alvarez	.30	.14
❑ 50 Harold Baines	.30	.14
❑ 51 Ray Durham	.30	.14
❑ 52 Alex Fernandez	.15	.07
❑ 53 Ozzie Guillen	.15	.07
❑ 54 Roberto Hernandez	.15	.07
❑ 55 Ron Karkovice	.15	.07
❑ 56 Darren Lewis	.15	.07
❑ 57 Norberto Martin	.15	.07
❑ 58 Dave Martinez	.15	.07
❑ 59 Lyle Mouton	.15	.07
❑ 60 Jose Munoz	.15	.07
❑ 61 Tony Phillips	.15	.07

❏ 62	Kevin Tapani	.15	.07
❏ 63	Danny Tartabull	.15	.07
❏ 64	Frank Thomas	1.25	.55
❏ 65	Robin Ventura	.30	.14
❏ 66	Sandy Alomar Jr.	.30	.14
❏ 67	Albert Belle	.60	.25
❏ 68	Julio Franco	.30	.14
❏ 69	Brian Giles	2.00	.90
❏ 70	Danny Graves	.15	.07
❏ 71	Orel Hershiser	.30	.14
❏ 72	Jeff Kent	.30	.14
❏ 73	Kenny Lofton	.40	.18
❏ 74	Dennis Martinez	.30	.14
❏ 75	Jack McDowell	.15	.07
❏ 76	Jose Mesa	.15	.07
❏ 77	Charles Nagy	.30	.14
❏ 78	Manny Ramirez	.75	.35
❏ 79	Julian Tavarez	.15	.07
❏ 80	Jim Thome	.60	.25
❏ 81	Jose Vizcaino	.15	.07
❏ 82	Omar Vizquel	.30	.14
❏ 83	Brad Ausmus	.15	.07
❏ 84	Kimera Bartee	.15	.07
❏ 85	Raul Casanova	.15	.07
❏ 86	Tony Clark	.40	.18
❏ 87	Travis Fryman	.30	.14
❏ 88	Bobby Higginson	.30	.14
❏ 89	Mark Lewis	.15	.07
❏ 90	Jose Lima	.30	.14
❏ 91	Felipe Lira	.15	.07
❏ 92	Phil Nevin	.15	.07
❏ 93	Melvin Nieves	.15	.07
❏ 94	Curtis Pride	.15	.07
❏ 95	Ruben Sierra	.15	.07
❏ 96	Alan Trammell	.30	.14
❏ 97	Kevin Appier	.30	.14
❏ 98	Tim Belcher	.15	.07
❏ 99	Johnny Damon	.30	.14
❏ 100	Tom Goodwin	.15	.07
❏ 101	Bob Hamelin	.15	.07
❏ 102	David Howard	.15	.07
❏ 103	Jason Jacome	.15	.07
❏ 104	Keith Lockhart	.15	.07
❏ 105	Mike Macfarlane	.15	.07
❏ 106	Jeff Montgomery	.15	.07
❏ 107	Jose Offerman	.30	.14
❏ 108	Hipolito Pichardo	.15	.07
❏ 109	Joe Randa	.15	.07
❏ 110	Bip Roberts	.15	.07
❏ 111	Chris Stynes	.15	.07
❏ 112	Mike Sweeney	.30	.14
❏ 113	Joe Vitiello	.15	.07
❏ 114	Jeromy Burnitz	.30	.14
❏ 115	Chuck Carr	.15	.07
❏ 116	Jeff Cirillo	.30	.14
❏ 117	Mike Fetters	.15	.07
❏ 118	David Hulse	.15	.07
❏ 119	John Jaha	.15	.07
❏ 120	Scott Karl	.15	.07
❏ 121	Jesse Levis	.15	.07
❏ 122	Mark Loretta	.15	.07
❏ 123	Mike Matheny	.15	.07
❏ 124	Ben McDonald	.15	.07
❏ 125	Matt Mieske	.15	.07
❏ 126	Angel Miranda	.15	.07
❏ 127	Dave Nilsson	.15	.07
❏ 128	Jose Valentin	.15	.07
❏ 129	Fernando Vina	.15	.07
❏ 130	Ron Villone	.15	.07
❏ 131	Gerald Williams	.15	.07
❏ 132	Rick Aguilera	.15	.07
❏ 133	Rich Becker	.15	.07
❏ 134	Ron Coomer	.15	.07
❏ 135	Marty Cordova	.15	.07
❏ 136	Eddie Guardado	.15	.07
❏ 137	Denny Hocking	.15	.07
❏ 138	Roberto Kelly	.15	.07
❏ 139	Chuck Knoblauch	.60	.25
❏ 140	Matt Lawton	.30	.14
❏ 141	Pat Meares	.15	.07
❏ 142	Paul Molitor	.60	.25
❏ 143	Greg Myers	.15	.07
❏ 144	Jeff Reboulet	.15	.07
❏ 145	Scott Stahoviak	.15	.07
❏ 146	Todd Walker	.60	.25
❏ 147	Wade Boggs	.60	.25
❏ 148	David Cone	.40	.18
❏ 149	Mariano Duncan	.15	.07
❏ 150	Cecil Fielder	.30	.14
❏ 151	Dwight Gooden	.30	.14
❏ 152	Derek Jeter	2.00	.90
❏ 153	Jim Leyritz	.15	.07
❏ 154	Tino Martinez	.60	.25
❏ 155	Paul O'Neill	.30	.14
❏ 156	Andy Pettitte	.40	.18
❏ 157	Tim Raines	.30	.14
❏ 158	Mariano Rivera	.30	.14
❏ 159	Ruben Rivera	.15	.07
❏ 160	Kenny Rogers	.15	.07
❏ 161	Darryl Strawberry	.30	.14
❏ 162	John Wetteland	.30	.14
❏ 163	Bernie Williams	.60	.25
❏ 164	Tony Batista	.40	.18
❏ 165	Geronimo Berroa	.15	.07
❏ 166	Mike Bordick	.15	.07
❏ 167	Scott Brosius	.30	.14
❏ 168	Brent Gates	.15	.07
❏ 169	Jason Giambi	.30	.14
❏ 170	Jose Herrera	.15	.07
❏ 171	Brian Lesher	.15	.07
❏ 172	Damon Mashore	.15	.07
❏ 173	Mark McGwire	3.00	1.35
❏ 174	Ariel Prieto	.15	.07
❏ 175	Carlos Reyes	.15	.07
❏ 176	Matt Stairs	.30	.14
❏ 177	Terry Steinbach	.15	.07
❏ 178	John Wasdin	.15	.07
❏ 179	Ernie Young	.15	.07
❏ 180	Rich Amaral	.15	.07
❏ 181	Bobby Ayala	.15	.07
❏ 182	Jay Buhner	.30	.14
❏ 183	Rafael Carmona	.15	.07
❏ 184	Norm Charlton	.15	.07
❏ 185	Joey Cora	.15	.07
❏ 186	Ken Griffey Jr.	3.00	1.35
❏ 187	Sterling Hitchcock	.30	.14
❏ 188	Dave Hollins	.15	.07
❏ 189	Randy Johnson	.60	.25
❏ 190	Edgar Martinez	.30	.14
❏ 191	Jamie Moyer	.15	.07
❏ 192	Alex Rodriguez	2.00	.90
❏ 193	Paul Sorrento	.15	.07
❏ 194	Salomon Torres	.15	.07
❏ 195	Bob Wells	.15	.07
❏ 196	Dan Wilson	.15	.07
❏ 197	Will Clark	.60	.25
❏ 198	Kevin Elster	.15	.07
❏ 199	Rene Gonzales	.15	.07
❏ 200	Juan Gonzalez	1.25	.55
❏ 201	Rusty Greer	.30	.14
❏ 202	Darryl Hamilton	.15	.07
❏ 203	Mike Henneman	.15	.07
❏ 204	Ken Hill	.15	.07
❏ 205	Mark McLemore	.15	.07
❏ 206	Darren Oliver	.15	.07
❏ 207	Dean Palmer	.30	.14
❏ 208	Roger Pavlik	.15	.07
❏ 209	Ivan Rodriguez	.75	.35
❏ 210	Kurt Stillwell	.15	.07
❏ 211	Mickey Tettleton	.15	.07
❏ 212	Bobby Witt	.15	.07
❏ 213	Tilson Brito	.15	.07
❏ 214	Jacob Brumfield	.15	.07
❏ 215	Miguel Cairo	.30	.14
❏ 216	Joe Carter	.30	.14
❏ 217	Felipe Crespo	.15	.07
❏ 218	Carlos Delgado	.60	.25
❏ 219	Alex Gonzalez	.15	.07
❏ 220	Shawn Green	.60	.25
❏ 221	Juan Guzman	.15	.07
❏ 222	Pat Hentgen	.30	.14
❏ 223	Charlie O'Brien	.15	.07
❏ 224	John Olerud	.30	.14
❏ 225	Robert Perez	.15	.07
❏ 226	Tomas Perez	.15	.07
❏ 227	Juan Samuel	.15	.07
❏ 228	Ed Sprague	.15	.07
❏ 229	Mike Timlin	.15	.07
❏ 230	Rafael Bellard	.15	.07
❏ 231	Jermaine Dye	.30	.14
❏ 232	Tom Glavine	.60	.25
❏ 233	Marquis Grissom	.30	.14
❏ 234	Andruw Jones	.75	.35
❏ 235	Chipper Jones	1.50	.70
❏ 236	David Justice	.60	.25
❏ 237	Ryan Klesko	.30	.14
❏ 238	Mark Lemke	.15	.07
❏ 239	Javier Lopez	.30	.14
❏ 240	Greg Maddux	1.50	.70
❏ 241	Fred McGriff	.40	.18
❏ 242	Denny Neagle	.30	.14
❏ 243	Eddie Perez	.15	.07
❏ 244	John Smoltz	.40	.18
❏ 245	Mark Wohlers	.15	.07
❏ 246	Brant Brown	.30	.14
❏ 247	Scott Bullett	.15	.07
❏ 248	Leo Gomez	.15	.07
❏ 249	Luis Gonzalez	.30	.14
❏ 250	Mark Grace	.40	.18
❏ 251	Jose Hernandez	.15	.07
❏ 252	Brooks Kieschnick	.15	.07
❏ 253	Brian McRae	.15	.07
❏ 254	Jaime Navarro	.15	.07
❏ 255	Mike Perez	.15	.07
❏ 256	Rey Sanchez	.15	.07
❏ 257	Ryne Sandberg	.75	.35
❏ 258	Scott Servais	.15	.07
❏ 259	Sammy Sosa	2.00	.90
❏ 260	Pedro Valdes	.15	.07
❏ 261	Turk Wendell	.15	.07
❏ 262	Bret Boone	.30	.14
❏ 263	Jeff Branson	.15	.07
❏ 264	Jeff Brantley	.15	.07
❏ 265	Dave Burba	.15	.07
❏ 266	Hector Carrasco	.15	.07
❏ 267	Eric Davis	.30	.14
❏ 268	Willie Greene	.15	.07
❏ 269	Lenny Harris	.15	.07
❏ 270	Thomas Howard	.15	.07
❏ 271	Barry Larkin	.60	.25
❏ 272	Hal Morris	.15	.07
❏ 273	Joe Oliver	.15	.07
❏ 274	Eric Owens	.15	.07
❏ 275	Jose Rijo	.15	.07
❏ 276	Reggie Sanders	.30	.14
❏ 277	Eddie Taubensee	.15	.07
❏ 278	Jason Bates	.15	.07
❏ 279	Dante Bichette	.30	.14
❏ 280	Ellis Burks	.30	.14
❏ 281	Vinny Castilla	.40	.18
❏ 282	Andres Galarraga	.60	.25
❏ 283	Quinton McCracken	.15	.07
❏ 284	Jayhawk Owens	.15	.07
❏ 285	Jeff Reed	.15	.07
❏ 286	Bryan Rekar	.15	.07
❏ 287	Armando Reynoso	.15	.07
❏ 288	Kevin Ritz	.15	.07
❏ 289	Bruce Ruffin	.15	.07
❏ 290	John Vander Wal	.15	.07
❏ 291	Larry Walker	.60	.25
❏ 292	Walt Weiss	.15	.07
❏ 293	Eric Young	.30	.14
❏ 294	Kurt Abbott	.15	.07
❏ 295	Alex Arias	.15	.07
❏ 296	Miguel Batista	.15	.07
❏ 297	Kevin Brown	.40	.18
❏ 298	Luis Castillo	.30	.14
❏ 299	Greg Colbrunn	.15	.07
❏ 300	Jeff Conine	.30	.14
❏ 301	Charles Johnson	.30	.14
❏ 302	Al Leiter	.30	.14
❏ 303	Robb Nen	.15	.07
❏ 304	Jose Orsulak	.15	.07
❏ 305	Yorkis Perez	.15	.07
❏ 306	Edgar Renteria	.30	.14
❏ 307	Gary Sheffield	.30	.14
❏ 308	Jesus Tavarez	.15	.07
❏ 309	Quilvio Veras	.15	.07
❏ 310	Devon White	.30	.14
❏ 311	Jeff Bagwell	.75	.35
❏ 312	Derek Bell	.30	.14
❏ 313	Sean Berry	.15	.07
❏ 314	Craig Biggio	.60	.25
❏ 315	Doug Drabek	.15	.07
❏ 316	Tony Eusebio	.15	.07
❏ 317	Ricky Gutierrez	.15	.07
❏ 318	Xavier Hernandez	.15	.07
❏ 319	Brian L. Hunter	.30	.14

❑ 320 Darryl Kile	.15	.07
❑ 321 Derrick May	.15	.07
❑ 322 Orlando Miller	.15	.07
❑ 323 James Mouton	.15	.07
❑ 324 Bill Spiers	.15	.07
❑ 325 Pedro Astacio	.15	.07
❑ 326 Brett Butler	.30	.14
❑ 327 Juan Castro	.15	.07
❑ 328 Roger Cedeno	.30	.14
❑ 329 Delino DeShields	.15	.07
❑ 330 Karim Garcia	.30	.14
❑ 331 Todd Hollandsworth	.15	.07
❑ 332 Eric Karros	.30	.14
❑ 333 Oreste Marrero	.15	.07
❑ 334 Ramon Martinez	.30	.14
❑ 335 Raul Mondesi	.30	.14
❑ 336 Hideo Nomo	.60	.25
❑ 337 Antonio Osuna	.15	.07
❑ 338 Chan Ho Park	.60	.25
❑ 339 Mike Piazza	2.00	.90
❑ 340 Ismael Valdes	.30	.14
❑ 341 Moises Alou	.30	.14
❑ 342 Omar Daal	.15	.07
❑ 343 Jeff Fassero	.15	.07
❑ 344 Cliff Floyd	.30	.14
❑ 345 Mark Grudzielanek	.30	.14
❑ 346 Mike Lansing	.15	.07
❑ 347 Pedro Martinez	.75	.35
❑ 348 Sherman Obando	.15	.07
❑ 349 Jose Paniagua	.15	.07
❑ 350 Henry Rodriguez	.30	.14
❑ 351 Mel Rojas	.15	.07
❑ 352 F.P. Santangelo	.15	.07
❑ 353 David Segui	.30	.14
❑ 354 Dave Silvestri	.15	.07
❑ 355 Ugueth Urbina	.30	.14
❑ 356 Rondell White	.30	.14
❑ 357 Edgardo Alfonzo	.40	.18
❑ 358 Carlos Baerga	.15	.07
❑ 359 Tim Bogar	.15	.07
❑ 360 Rico Brogna	.15	.07
❑ 361 Alvaro Espinoza	.15	.07
❑ 362 Carl Everett	.30	.14
❑ 363 John Franco	.30	.14
❑ 364 Bernard Gilkey	.15	.07
❑ 365 Todd Hundley	.30	.14
❑ 366 Butch Huskey	.15	.07
❑ 367 Jason Isringhausen	.15	.07
❑ 368 Bobby Jones	.15	.07
❑ 369 Lance Johnson	.15	.07
❑ 370 Brent Mayne	.15	.07
❑ 371 Alex Ochoa	.15	.07
❑ 372 Rey Ordonez	.30	.14
❑ 373 Ron Blazier	.15	.07
❑ 374 Ricky Bottalico	.30	.14
❑ 375 David Doster	.15	.07
❑ 376 Lenny Dykstra	.30	.14
❑ 377 Jim Eisenreich	.15	.07
❑ 378 Bobby Estalella	.15	.07
❑ 379 Gregg Jefferies	.15	.07
❑ 380 Kevin Jordan	.15	.07
❑ 381 Ricardo Jordan	.15	.07
❑ 382 Mickey Morandini	.15	.07
❑ 383 Ricky Otero	.15	.07
❑ 384 Benito Santiago	.15	.07
❑ 385 Gene Schall	.15	.07
❑ 386 Curt Schilling	.40	.18
❑ 387 Kevin Sefcik	.15	.07
❑ 388 Kevin Stocker	.15	.07
❑ 389 Jermaine Allensworth	.15	.07
❑ 390 Jay Bell	.30	.14
❑ 391 Jason Christiansen	.15	.07
❑ 392 Francisco Cordova	.15	.07
❑ 393 Mark Johnson	.15	.07
❑ 394 Jason Kendall	.40	.18
❑ 395 Jeff King	.15	.07
❑ 396 Jon Lieber	.15	.07
❑ 397 Nelson Liriano	.15	.07
❑ 398 Esteban Loaiza	.15	.07
❑ 399 Al Martin	.15	.07
❑ 400 Orlando Merced	.15	.07
❑ 401 Ramon Morel	.15	.07
❑ 402 Luis Alicea	.15	.07
❑ 403 Alan Benes	.15	.07
❑ 404 Andy Benes	.30	.14
❑ 405 Terry Bradshaw	.15	.07

❑ 406 Royce Clayton	.15	.07
❑ 407 Dennis Eckersley	.30	.14
❑ 408 Gary Gaetti	.30	.14
❑ 409 Mike Gallego	.15	.07
❑ 410 Ron Gant	.15	.07
❑ 411 Brian Jordan	.30	.14
❑ 412 Ray Lankford	.30	.14
❑ 413 John Mabry	.15	.07
❑ 414 Willie McGee	.30	.14
❑ 415 Tom Pagnozzi	.15	.07
❑ 416 Ozzie Smith	.75	.35
❑ 417 Todd Stottlemyre	.15	.07
❑ 418 Mark Sweeney	.15	.07
❑ 419 Andy Ashby	.15	.07
❑ 420 Ken Caminiti	.40	.18
❑ 421 Archi Cianfrocco	.15	.07
❑ 422 Steve Finley	.30	.14
❑ 423 Chris Gomez	.15	.07
❑ 424 Tony Gwynn	1.50	.70
❑ 425 Joey Hamilton	.30	.14
❑ 426 Rickey Henderson	.75	.35
❑ 427 Trevor Hoffman	.30	.14
❑ 428 Brian Johnson	.15	.07
❑ 429 Wally Joyner	.30	.14
❑ 430 Scott Livingstone	.15	.07
❑ 431 Jody Reed	.15	.07
❑ 432 Craig Shipley	.15	.07
❑ 433 Fernando Valenzuela	.30	.14
❑ 434 Greg Vaughn	.30	.14
❑ 435 Rich Aurilia	.30	.14
❑ 436 Kim Batiste	.15	.07
❑ 437 Jose Bautista	.15	.07
❑ 438 Rod Beck	.15	.07
❑ 439 Marvin Benard	.15	.07
❑ 440 Barry Bonds	.75	.35
❑ 441 Shawon Dunston	.15	.07
❑ 442 Shawn Estes	.30	.14
❑ 443 Osvaldo Fernandez	.15	.07
❑ 444 Stan Javier	.15	.07
❑ 445 David McCarty	.15	.07
❑ 446 Bill Mueller	.75	.35
❑ 447 Steve Scarsone	.15	.07
❑ 448 Robby Thompson	.15	.07
❑ 449 Rick Wilkins	.15	.07
❑ 450 Matt Williams	.60	.25

1997 Pacific Card-Supials

	MINT	NRMT
COMP.LARGE SET (36)	250.00	110.00
*LARGE SINGLES: 3X TO 8X BASE CARD HI		
COMP.MINI SET (36)	150.00	70.00
*MINI SINGLES: 2X TO 5X BASE CARD HI		
STATED ODDS 1:37		
❑ 1 Roberto Alomar	5.00	2.20
❑ 2 Brady Anderson	2.50	1.10
❑ 3 Eddie Murray	5.00	2.20
❑ 4 Cal Ripken	20.00	9.00
❑ 5 Jose Canseco	5.00	2.20
❑ 6 Mo Vaughn	5.00	2.20
❑ 7 Frank Thomas	10.00	4.50
❑ 8 Albert Belle	5.00	2.20
❑ 9 Omar Vizquel	2.50	1.10
❑ 10 Chuck Knoblauch	5.00	2.20
❑ 11 Paul Molitor	5.00	2.20
❑ 12 Wade Boggs	5.00	2.20

❑ 13 Derek Jeter	12.00	5.50
❑ 14 Andy Pettitte	3.00	1.35
❑ 15 Mark McGwire	25.00	11.00
❑ 16 Jay Buhner	2.50	1.10
❑ 17 Ken Griffey Jr.	25.00	11.00
❑ 18 Alex Rodriguez	15.00	6.75
❑ 19 Juan Gonzalez	10.00	4.50
❑ 20 Ivan Rodriguez	6.00	2.70
❑ 21 Andruw Jones	5.00	2.20
❑ 22 Chipper Jones	12.00	5.50
❑ 23 Ryan Klesko	2.50	1.10
❑ 24 Greg Maddux	12.00	5.50
❑ 25 Ryne Sandberg	5.00	2.20
❑ 26 Andres Galarraga	5.00	2.20
❑ 27 Gary Sheffield	2.50	1.10
❑ 28 Jeff Bagwell	6.00	2.70
❑ 29 Todd Hollandsworth	1.25	.55
❑ 30 Hideo Nomo	5.00	2.20
❑ 31 Mike Piazza	15.00	6.75
❑ 32 Todd Hundley	2.50	1.10
❑ 33 Dennis Eckersley	2.50	1.10
❑ 34 Ken Caminiti	3.00	1.35
❑ 35 Tony Gwynn	12.00	5.50
❑ 36 Barry Bonds	6.00	2.70

1997 Pacific Cramer's Choice

	MINT	NRMT
COMPLETE SET (10)	600.00	275.00
COMMON CARD (1-10)	15.00	6.75
STATED ODDS 1:721		
❑ 1 Roberto Alomar	30.00	13.50
❑ 2 Frank Thomas	60.00	27.00
❑ 3 Albert Belle	25.00	11.00
❑ 4 Andy Pettitte	20.00	9.00
❑ 5 Ken Griffey Jr.	150.00	70.00
❑ 6 Alex Rodriguez	100.00	45.00
❑ 7 Chipper Jones	80.00	36.00
❑ 8 John Smoltz	20.00	9.00
❑ 9 Mike Piazza	100.00	45.00
❑ 10 Tony Gwynn	80.00	36.00

1997 Pacific Fireworks Die Cuts

	MINT	NRMT
COMPLETE SET (20)	300.00	135.00
COMMON CARD (1-20)	1.50	.70

STATED ODDS 1:73

		MINT	NRMT
❏ 1	Roberto Alomar	6.00	2.70
❏ 2	Brady Anderson	2.00	.90
❏ 3	Eddie Murray	6.00	2.70
❏ 4	Cal Ripken	25.00	11.00
❏ 5	Frank Thomas	12.00	5.50
❏ 6	Albert Belle	6.00	2.70
❏ 7	Derek Jeter	15.00	6.75
❏ 8	Andy Pettitte	4.00	1.80
❏ 9	Bernie Williams	6.00	2.70
❏ 10	Mark McGwire	30.00	13.50
❏ 11	Ken Griffey Jr.	30.00	13.50
❏ 12	Alex Rodriguez	20.00	9.00
❏ 13	Juan Gonzalez	12.00	5.50
❏ 14	Andruw Jones	6.00	2.70
❏ 15	Chipper Jones	15.00	6.75
❏ 16	Hideo Nomo	6.00	2.70
❏ 17	Mike Piazza	20.00	9.00
❏ 18	Henry Rodriguez	1.50	.70
❏ 19	Tony Gwynn	15.00	6.75
❏ 20	Barry Bonds	8.00	3.60

1997 Pacific Gold Crown Die Cuts

	MINT	NRMT
COMPLETE SET (36)	300.00	135.00
COMMON CARD (1-36)	1.50	.70

STATED ODDS 1:37

		MINT	NRMT
❏ 1	Roberto Alomar	6.00	2.70
❏ 2	Brady Anderson	3.00	1.35
❏ 3	Mike Mussina	6.00	2.70
❏ 4	Eddie Murray	6.00	2.70
❏ 5	Cal Ripken	25.00	11.00
❏ 6	Jose Canseco	6.00	2.70
❏ 7	Frank Thomas	12.00	5.50
❏ 8	Albert Belle	6.00	2.70
❏ 9	Omar Vizquel	3.00	1.35
❏ 10	Wade Boggs	6.00	2.70
❏ 11	Derek Jeter	15.00	6.75
❏ 12	Andy Pettitte	4.00	1.80
❏ 13	Mariano Rivera	3.00	1.35
❏ 14	Bernie Williams	6.00	2.70
❏ 15	Mark McGwire	30.00	13.50
❏ 16	Ken Griffey Jr.	30.00	13.50
❏ 17	Edgar Martinez	3.00	1.35
❏ 18	Alex Rodriguez	20.00	9.00
❏ 19	Juan Gonzalez	12.00	5.50
❏ 20	Ivan Rodriguez	8.00	3.60
❏ 21	Andruw Jones	6.00	2.70
❏ 22	Chipper Jones	15.00	6.75
❏ 23	Ryan Klesko	3.00	1.35
❏ 24	John Smoltz	4.00	1.80
❏ 25	Ryne Sandberg	6.00	2.70
❏ 26	Andres Galarraga	6.00	2.70
❏ 27	Edgar Renteria	3.00	1.35
❏ 28	Jeff Bagwell	8.00	3.60
❏ 29	Todd Hollandsworth	1.50	.70
❏ 30	Hideo Nomo	6.00	2.70
❏ 31	Mike Piazza	20.00	9.00
❏ 32	Todd Hundley	1.50	.70
❏ 33	Brian Jordan	3.00	1.35
❏ 34	Ken Caminiti	4.00	1.80
❏ 35	Tony Gwynn	15.00	6.75
❏ 36	Barry Bonds	8.00	3.60

1997 Pacific Latinos of the Major Leagues

	MINT	NRMT
COMPLETE SET (36)	60.00	27.00
COMMON CARD (1-36)	.75	.35

STATED ODDS 1:18

		MINT	NRMT
❏ 1	George Arias	.75	.35
❏ 2	Roberto Alomar	3.00	1.35
❏ 3	Rafael Palmeiro	3.00	1.35
❏ 4	Bobby Bonilla	1.50	.70
❏ 5	Jose Canseco	3.00	1.35
❏ 6	Wilson Alvarez	1.50	.70
❏ 7	Dave Martinez	.75	.35
❏ 8	Julio Franco	1.50	.70
❏ 9	Manny Ramirez	4.00	1.80
❏ 10	Omar Vizquel	1.50	.70
❏ 11	Marty Cordova	.75	.35
❏ 12	Roberto Kelly	.75	.35
❏ 13	Tino Martinez	3.00	1.35
❏ 14	Mariano Rivera	1.50	.70
❏ 15	Ruben Rivera	.75	.35
❏ 16	Bernie Williams	3.00	1.35
❏ 17	Geronimo Berroa	.75	.35
❏ 18	Joey Cora	.75	.35
❏ 19	Edgar Martinez	1.50	.70
❏ 20	Alex Rodriguez	10.00	4.50
❏ 21	Juan Gonzalez	6.00	2.70
❏ 22	Ivan Rodriguez	4.00	1.80
❏ 23	Andruw Jones	4.00	1.80
❏ 24	Javier Lopez	1.50	.70
❏ 25	Sammy Sosa	10.00	4.50
❏ 26	Vinny Castilla	2.00	.90
❏ 27	Andres Galarraga	3.00	1.35
❏ 28	Ramon Martinez	1.50	.70
❏ 29	Raul Mondesi	1.50	.70
❏ 30	Ismael Valdes	1.50	.70
❏ 31	Pedro Martinez	4.00	1.80
❏ 32	Henry Rodriguez	.75	.35
❏ 33	Carlos Baerga	.75	.35
❏ 34	Rey Ordonez	1.50	.70
❏ 35	Fernando Valenzuela	1.50	.70
❏ 36	Osvaldo Fernandez	.75	.35

1997 Pacific Triple Crown Die Cuts

	MINT	NRMT
COMPLETE SET (20)	500.00	220.00

		MINT	NRMT
COMMON CARD (1-20)		6.00	2.70
SEMISTARS		8.00	3.60
UNLISTED STARS		12.00	5.50

STATED ODDS 1:145

		MINT	NRMT
❏ 1	Brady Anderson	6.00	2.70
❏ 2	Rafael Palmeiro	12.00	5.50
❏ 3	Mo Vaughn	12.00	5.50
❏ 4	Frank Thomas	25.00	11.00
❏ 5	Albert Belle	12.00	5.50
❏ 6	Jim Thome	12.00	5.50
❏ 7	Cecil Fielder	6.00	2.70
❏ 8	Mark McGwire	60.00	27.00
❏ 9	Ken Griffey Jr.	60.00	27.00
❏ 10	Alex Rodriguez	40.00	18.00
❏ 11	Juan Gonzalez	25.00	11.00
❏ 12	Andruw Jones	15.00	6.75
❏ 13	Chipper Jones	30.00	13.50
❏ 14	Dante Bichette	6.00	2.70
❏ 15	Ellis Burks	6.00	2.70
❏ 16	Andres Galarraga	12.00	5.50
❏ 17	Jeff Bagwell	15.00	6.75
❏ 18	Mike Piazza	40.00	18.00
❏ 19	Ken Caminiti	8.00	3.60
❏ 20	Barry Bonds	15.00	6.75

1998 Pacific

	MINT	NRMT
COMPLETE SET (450)	60.00	27.00
COMMON CARD (1-450)	.15	.07
MINOR STARS	.25	.11
SEMISTARS	.40	.18
UNLISTED STARS	.60	.25
COMMON RED (1-450)	.30	.14
*RED STARS: 2.5X TO 6X HI COLUMN		
*RED YOUNG STARS: 2X TO 5X HI		
ONE RED PER WAL-MART PACK		
COMMON SILVER (1-450)	.25	.11
*SILVER STARS: 2X TO 5X HI COLUMN		
*SILVER YOUNG STARS: 1.5X TO 4X HI		
ONE SILVER PER HOBBY PACK		

		MINT	NRMT
❏ 1	Luis Alicea	.15	.07
❏ 2	Garret Anderson	.25	.11
❏ 3	Jason Dickson	.15	.07
❏ 4	Gary DiSarcina	.15	.07
❏ 5	Jim Edmonds	.25	.11
❏ 6	Darin Erstad	.40	.18
❏ 7	Chuck Finley	.25	.11
❏ 8	Shigetoshi Hasegawa	.25	.11
❏ 9	Rickey Henderson	.75	.35
❏ 10	Dave Hollins	.15	.07
❏ 11	Mark Langston	.15	.07
❏ 12	Orlando Palmeiro	.15	.07
❏ 13	Troy Percival	.25	.11
❏ 14	Tony Phillips	.15	.07
❏ 15	Tim Salmon	.40	.18
❏ 16	Allen Watson	.15	.07
❏ 17	Roberto Alomar	.60	.25
❏ 18	Brady Anderson	.25	.11
❏ 19	Harold Baines	.25	.11
❏ 20	Armando Benitez	.15	.07
❏ 21	Geronimo Berroa	.15	.07
❏ 22	Mike Bordick	.15	.07
❏ 23	Eric Davis	.25	.11
❏ 24	Scott Erickson	.15	.07
❏ 25	Chris Hoiles	.15	.07

26	Jimmy Key	.25	.11
27	Aaron Ledesma	.15	.07
28	Mike Mussina	.60	.25
29	Randy Myers	.25	.11
30	Jesse Orosco	.15	.07
31	Rafael Palmeiro	.60	.25
32	Jeff Reboulet	.15	.07
33	Cal Ripken	2.50	1.10
34	B.J. Surhoff	.25	.11
35	Steve Avery	.15	.07
36	Darren Bragg	.15	.07
37	Wil Cordero	.15	.07
38	Jeff Frye	.15	.07
39	Nomar Garciaparra	2.00	.90
40	Tom Gordon	.25	.11
41	Bill Haselman	.15	.07
42	Scott Hatteberg	.15	.07
43	Butch Henry	.15	.07
44	Reggie Jefferson	.15	.07
45	Tim Naehring	.15	.07
46	Troy O'Leary	.25	.11
47	Jeff Suppan	.15	.07
48	John Valentin	.25	.11
49	Mo Vaughn	.60	.25
50	Tim Wakefield	.15	.07
51	James Baldwin	.15	.07
52	Albert Belle	.60	.25
53	Tony Castillo	.15	.07
54	Doug Drabek	.15	.07
55	Ray Durham	.25	.11
56	Jorge Fabregas	.15	.07
57	Ozzie Guillen	.15	.07
58	Matt Karchner	.15	.07
59	Norberto Martin	.15	.07
60	Dave Martinez	.15	.07
61	Lyle Mouton	.15	.07
62	Jaime Navarro	.15	.07
63	Frank Thomas	1.25	.55
64	Mario Valdez	.15	.07
65	Robin Ventura	.25	.11
66	Sandy Alomar Jr.	.25	.11
67	Paul Assenmacher	.15	.07
68	Tony Fernandez	.25	.11
69	Brian Giles	.25	.11
70	Marquis Grissom	.25	.11
71	Orel Hershiser	.25	.11
72	Mike Jackson	.15	.07
73	David Justice	.25	.11
74	Albie Lopez	.15	.07
75	Jose Mesa	.15	.07
76	Charles Nagy	.15	.07
77	Chad Ogea	.15	.07
78	Manny Ramirez	.75	.35
79	Jim Thome	.60	.25
80	Omar Vizquel	.25	.11
81	Matt Williams	.60	.25
82	Jaret Wright	.25	.11
83	Willie Blair	.15	.07
84	Raul Casanova	.15	.07
85	Tony Clark	.25	.11
86	Deivi Cruz	.15	.07
87	Damion Easley	.15	.07
88	Travis Fryman	.25	.11
89	Bobby Higginson	.25	.11
90	Brian L. Hunter	.15	.07
91	Todd Jones	.15	.07
92	Dan Miceli	.15	.07
93	Brian Moehler	.15	.07
94	Mel Nieves	.15	.07
95	Jody Reed	.15	.07
96	Justin Thompson	.25	.11
97	Bubba Trammell	.15	.07
98	Kevin Appier	.25	.11
99	Jay Bell	.25	.11
100	Yamil Benitez	.15	.07
101	Johnny Damon	.25	.11
102	Chili Davis	.25	.11
103	Jermaine Dye	.25	.11
104	Jed Hansen	.15	.07
105	Jeff King	.15	.07
106	Mike Macfarlane	.15	.07
107	Felix Martinez	.15	.07
108	Jeff Montgomery	.15	.07
109	Jose Offerman	.25	.11
110	Dean Palmer	.15	.07
111	Hipolito Pichardo	.15	.07
112	Jose Rosado	.15	.07
113	Jeromy Burnitz	.25	.11
114	Jeff Cirillo	.25	.11
115	Cal Eldred	.15	.07
116	John Jaha	.15	.07
117	Doug Jones	.15	.07
118	Scott Karl	.15	.07
119	Jesse Levis	.15	.07
120	Mark Loretta	.15	.07
121	Ben McDonald	.15	.07
122	Jose Mercedes	.15	.07
123	Matt Mieske	.15	.07
124	Dave Nilsson	.15	.07
125	Jose Valentin	.15	.07
126	Fernando Vina	.15	.07
127	Gerald Williams	.15	.07
128	Rick Aguilera	.15	.07
129	Rich Becker	.15	.07
130	Ron Coomer	.15	.07
131	Marty Cordova	.15	.07
132	Eddie Guardado	.15	.07
133	LaTroy Hawkins	.15	.07
134	Denny Hocking	.15	.07
135	Chuck Knoblauch	.25	.11
136	Matt Lawton	.15	.07
137	Pat Meares	.15	.07
138	Paul Molitor	.60	.25
139	David Ortiz	.15	.07
140	Brad Radke	.25	.11
141	Terry Steinbach	.25	.11
142	Bob Tewksbury	.15	.07
143	Javier Valentin	.15	.07
144	Wade Boggs	.60	.25
145	David Cone	.40	.18
146	Chad Curtis	.15	.07
147	Cecil Fielder	.25	.11
148	Joe Girardi	.15	.07
149	Dwight Gooden	.25	.11
150	Hideki Irabu	.25	.11
151	Derek Jeter	2.00	.90
152	Tino Martinez	.25	.11
153	Ramiro Mendoza	.15	.07
154	Paul O'Neill	.25	.11
155	Andy Pettitte	.25	.11
156	Jorge Posada	.15	.07
157	Mariano Rivera	.25	.11
158	Rey Sanchez	.15	.07
159	Luis Sojo	.15	.07
160	David Wells	.25	.11
161	Bernie Williams	.60	.25
162	Rafael Bournigal	.15	.07
163	Scott Brosius	.25	.11
164	Jose Canseco	.75	.35
165	Jason Giambi	.25	.11
166	Ben Grieve	.60	.25
167	Dave Magadan	.15	.07
168	Brent Mayne	.15	.07
169	Jason McDonald	.15	.07
170	Izzy Molina	.15	.07
171	Ariel Prieto	.15	.07
172	Carlos Reyes	.15	.07
173	Scott Spiezio	.15	.07
174	Matt Stairs	.25	.11
175	Bill Taylor	.15	.07
176	Dave Telgheder	.15	.07
177	Steve Wojciechowski	.15	.07
178	Rich Amaral	.15	.07
179	Bobby Ayala	.15	.07
180	Jay Buhner	.25	.11
181	Rafael Carmona	.15	.07
182	Ken Cloude	.15	.07
183	Joey Cora	.15	.07
184	Russ Davis	.25	.11
185	Jeff Fassero	.15	.07
186	Ken Griffey Jr.	3.00	1.35
187	Raul Ibanez	.15	.07
188	Randy Johnson	.60	.25
189	Roberto Kelly	.15	.07
190	Edgar Martinez	.25	.11
191	Jamie Moyer	.15	.07
192	Omar Olivares	.15	.07
193	Alex Rodriguez	2.00	.90
194	Heathcliff Slocumb	.15	.07
195	Paul Sorrento	.15	.07
196	Dan Wilson	.15	.07
197	Scott Bailes	.15	.07
198	John Burkett	.15	.07
199	Domingo Cedeno	.15	.07
200	Will Clark	.60	.25
201	Hanley Frias	.15	.07
202	Juan Gonzalez	1.25	.55
203	Tom Goodwin	.15	.07
204	Rusty Greer	.25	.11
205	Wilson Heredia	.15	.07
206	Darren Oliver	.15	.07
207	Bill Ripken	.15	.07
208	Ivan Rodriguez	.60	.25
209	Lee Stevens	.15	.07
210	Fernando Tatis	.60	.25
211	John Wetteland	.25	.11
212	Bobby Witt	.15	.07
213	Jacob Brumfield	.15	.07
214	Joe Carter	.25	.11
215	Roger Clemens	1.50	.70
216	Felipe Crespo	.15	.07
217	Jose Cruz Jr.	.25	.11
218	Carlos Delgado	.60	.25
219	Mariano Duncan	.15	.07
220	Carlos Garcia	.15	.07
221	Alex Gonzalez	.15	.07
222	Juan Guzman	.15	.07
223	Pat Hentgen	.15	.07
224	Orlando Merced	.15	.07
225	Tomas Perez	.15	.07
226	Paul Quantrill	.15	.07
227	Benito Santiago	.15	.07
228	Woody Williams	.15	.07
229	Rafael Belliard	.15	.07
230	Jeff Blauser	.25	.11
231	Pedro Borbon	.15	.07
232	Tom Glavine	.60	.25
233	Tony Graffanino	.15	.07
234	Andruw Jones	.60	.25
235	Chipper Jones	1.50	.70
236	Ryan Klesko	.25	.11
237	Mark Lemke	.15	.07
238	Kenny Lofton	.40	.18
239	Javier Lopez	.25	.11
240	Fred McGriff	.40	.18
241	Greg Maddux	1.50	.70
242	Denny Neagle	.15	.07
243	John Smoltz	.40	.18
244	Michael Tucker	.15	.07
245	Mark Wohlers	.15	.07
246	Manny Alexander	.15	.07
247	Miguel Batista	.15	.07
248	Mark Clark	.15	.07
249	Doug Glanville	.25	.11
250	Jeremi Gonzalez	.15	.07
251	Mark Grace	.40	.18
252	Jose Hernandez	.15	.07
253	Lance Johnson	.15	.07
254	Brooks Kieschnick	.15	.07
255	Kevin Orie	.15	.07
256	Ryne Sandberg	.75	.35
257	Scott Servais	.15	.07
258	Sammy Sosa	2.00	.90
259	Kevin Tapani	.15	.07
260	Ramon Tatis	.15	.07
261	Bret Boone	.25	.11
262	Dave Burba	.15	.07
263	Brook Fordyce	.15	.07
264	Willie Greene	.15	.07
265	Barry Larkin	.60	.25
266	Pedro A. Martinez	.15	.07
267	Hal Morris	.15	.07
268	Joe Oliver	.15	.07
269	Eduardo Perez	.15	.07
270	Pokey Reese	.15	.07
271	Felix Rodriguez	.15	.07
272	Deion Sanders	.25	.11
273	Reggie Sanders	.15	.07
274	Jeff Shaw	.15	.07
275	Scott Sullivan	.15	.07
276	Brett Tomko	.15	.07
277	Roger Bailey	.15	.07
278	Dante Bichette	.25	.11
279	Ellis Burks	.25	.11
280	Vinny Castilla	.25	.11
281	Frank Castillo	.15	.07
282	Mike DeJean	.15	.07
283	Andres Galarraga	.40	.18

❏ 284 Darren Holmes	.15	.07
❏ 285 Kirt Manwaring	.15	.07
❏ 286 Quinton McCracken	.15	.07
❏ 287 Neifi Perez	.25	.11
❏ 288 Steve Reed	.15	.07
❏ 289 John Thomson	.15	.07
❏ 290 Larry Walker	.60	.25
❏ 291 Walt Weiss	.25	.11
❏ 292 Kurt Abbott	.15	.07
❏ 293 Antonio Alfonseca	.15	.07
❏ 294 Moises Alou	.25	.11
❏ 295 Alex Arias	.15	.07
❏ 296 Bobby Bonilla	.25	.11
❏ 297 Kevin Brown	.40	.18
❏ 298 Craig Counsell	.15	.07
❏ 299 Darren Daulton	.25	.11
❏ 300 Jim Eisenreich	.15	.07
❏ 301 Alex Fernandez	.15	.07
❏ 302 Felix Heredia	.15	.07
❏ 303 Livan Hernandez	.15	.07
❏ 304 Charles Johnson	.25	.11
❏ 305 Al Leiter	.25	.11
❏ 306 Robb Nen	.15	.07
❏ 307 Edgar Renteria	.15	.07
❏ 308 Gary Sheffield	.25	.11
❏ 309 Devon White	.15	.07
❏ 310 Bob Abreu	.25	.11
❏ 311 Brad Ausmus	.15	.07
❏ 312 Jeff Bagwell	.75	.35
❏ 313 Derek Bell	.25	.11
❏ 314 Sean Berry	.15	.07
❏ 315 Craig Biggio	.60	.25
❏ 316 Ramon Garcia	.15	.07
❏ 317 Luis Gonzalez	.25	.11
❏ 318 Ricky Gutierrez	.15	.07
❏ 319 Mike Hampton	.25	.11
❏ 320 Richard Hidalgo	.25	.11
❏ 321 Thomas Howard	.15	.07
❏ 322 Darryl Kile	.15	.07
❏ 323 Jose Lima	.15	.07
❏ 324 Shane Reynolds	.25	.11
❏ 325 Bill Spiers	.15	.07
❏ 326 Tom Candiotti	.15	.07
❏ 327 Roger Cedeno	.25	.11
❏ 328 Greg Gagne	.15	.07
❏ 329 Karim Garcia	.15	.07
❏ 330 Wilton Guerrero	.15	.07
❏ 331 Todd Hollandsworth	.15	.07
❏ 332 Eric Karros	.25	.11
❏ 333 Ramon Martinez	.15	.07
❏ 334 Raul Mondesi	.25	.11
❏ 335 Otis Nixon	.15	.07
❏ 336 Hideo Nomo	.60	.25
❏ 337 Antonio Osuna	.15	.07
❏ 338 Chan Ho Park	.25	.11
❏ 339 Mike Piazza	2.00	.90
❏ 340 Dennis Reyes	.15	.07
❏ 341 Ismael Valdes	.15	.07
❏ 342 Todd Worrell	.15	.07
❏ 343 Todd Zeile	.25	.11
❏ 344 Darrin Fletcher	.15	.07
❏ 345 Mark Grudzielanek	.15	.07
❏ 346 Vladimir Guerrero	.75	.35
❏ 347 Dustin Hermanson	.15	.07
❏ 348 Mike Lansing	.15	.07
❏ 349 Pedro Martinez	.75	.35
❏ 350 Ryan McGuire	.15	.07
❏ 351 Jose Paniagua	.15	.07
❏ 352 Carlos Perez	.15	.07
❏ 353 Henry Rodriguez	.25	.11
❏ 354 F.P. Santangelo	.15	.07
❏ 355 David Segui	.15	.07
❏ 356 Ugueth Urbina	.15	.07
❏ 357 Marc Valdes	.15	.07
❏ 358 Jose Vidro	.15	.07
❏ 359 Rondell White	.25	.11
❏ 360 Juan Acevedo	.15	.07
❏ 361 Edgardo Alfonzo	.40	.18
❏ 362 Carlos Baerga	.25	.11
❏ 363 Carl Everett	.25	.11
❏ 364 John Franco	.25	.11
❏ 365 Bernard Gilkey	.15	.07
❏ 366 Todd Hundley	.25	.11
❏ 367 Butch Huskey	.15	.07
❏ 368 Bobby Jones	.15	.07
❏ 369 Takashi Kashiwada	.40	.18

❏ 370 Greg McMichael	.15	.07
❏ 371 Brian McRae	.15	.07
❏ 372 Alex Ochoa	.15	.07
❏ 373 John Olerud	.25	.11
❏ 374 Rey Ordonez	.25	.11
❏ 375 Turk Wendell	.15	.07
❏ 376 Ricky Bottalico	.15	.07
❏ 377 Rico Brogna	.15	.07
❏ 378 Len Dykstra	.25	.11
❏ 379 Bobby Estalella	.15	.07
❏ 380 Wayne Gomes	.15	.07
❏ 381 Tyler Green	.15	.07
❏ 382 Gregg Jefferies	.15	.07
❏ 383 Mark Leiter	.15	.07
❏ 384 Mike Lieberthal	.25	.11
❏ 385 Mickey Morandini	.15	.07
❏ 386 Scott Rolen	.75	.35
❏ 387 Curt Schilling	.40	.18
❏ 388 Kevin Stocker	.15	.07
❏ 389 Danny Tartabull	.15	.07
❏ 390 Jermaine Allensworth	.15	.07
❏ 391 Adrian Brown	.15	.07
❏ 392 Jason Christiansen	.15	.07
❏ 393 Steve Cooke	.15	.07
❏ 394 Francisco Cordova	.15	.07
❏ 395 Jose Guillen	.15	.07
❏ 396 Jason Kendall	.25	.11
❏ 397 Jon Lieber	.15	.07
❏ 398 Esteban Loaiza	.15	.07
❏ 399 Al Martin	.15	.07
❏ 400 Kevin Polcovich	.15	.07
❏ 401 Joe Randa	.15	.07
❏ 402 Ricardo Rincon	.15	.07
❏ 403 Tony Womack	.15	.07
❏ 404 Kevin Young	.25	.11
❏ 405 Andy Benes	.25	.11
❏ 406 Royce Clayton	.15	.07
❏ 407 Delino DeShields	.15	.07
❏ 408 Mike Difelice	.15	.07
❏ 409 Dennis Eckersley	.25	.11
❏ 410 John Frascatore	.15	.07
❏ 411 Gary Gaetti	.25	.11
❏ 412 Ron Gant	.25	.11
❏ 413 Brian Jordan	.25	.11
❏ 414 Ray Lankford	.25	.11
❏ 415 Willie McGee	.25	.11
❏ 416 Mark McGwire	4.00	1.80
❏ 417 Matt Morris	.15	.07
❏ 418 Luis Ordaz	.15	.07
❏ 419 Todd Stottlemyre	.15	.07
❏ 420 Andy Ashby	.15	.07
❏ 421 Jim Bruske	.15	.07
❏ 422 Ken Caminiti	.25	.11
❏ 423 Will Cunnane	.15	.07
❏ 424 Steve Finley	.25	.11
❏ 425 John Flaherty	.15	.07
❏ 426 Chris Gomez	.15	.07
❏ 427 Tony Gwynn	1.50	.70
❏ 428 Joey Hamilton	.15	.07
❏ 429 Carlos Hernandez	.15	.07
❏ 430 Sterling Hitchcock	.15	.07
❏ 431 Trevor Hoffman	.25	.11
❏ 432 Wally Joyner	.25	.11
❏ 433 Greg Vaughn	.25	.11
❏ 434 Quilvio Veras	.15	.07
❏ 435 Wilson Alvarez	.15	.07
❏ 436 Rod Beck	.25	.11
❏ 437 Barry Bonds	.75	.35
❏ 438 Jacob Cruz	.15	.07
❏ 439 Shawn Estes	.15	.07
❏ 440 Darryl Hamilton	.15	.07
❏ 441 Roberto Hernandez	.15	.07
❏ 442 Glenallen Hill	.15	.07
❏ 443 Stan Javier	.15	.07
❏ 444 Brian Johnson	.15	.07
❏ 445 Jeff Kent	.25	.11
❏ 446 Bill Mueller	.15	.07
❏ 447 Kirk Rueter	.15	.07
❏ 448 J.T. Snow	.25	.11
❏ 449 Julian Tavarez	.15	.07
❏ 450 Jose Vizcaino	.15	.07

1998 Pacific Platinum Blue

	MINT	NRMT
COMMON CARD (1-450)	10.00	4.50

*STARS: 25X TO 60X BASIC CARDS
*YNG.STARS: 20X TO 50X BASIC CARDS
STATED ODDS 1:73
STATED PRINT RUN 67 SETS

1998 Pacific Cramer's Choice

	MINT	NRMT
COMPLETE SET (10)	1000.00	450.00
COMMON CARD (1-10)	40.00	18.00

STATED ODDS 1:721

		MINT	NRMT
❏ 1 Greg Maddux	100.00	45.00
❏ 2 Roberto Alomar	30.00	13.50
❏ 3 Cal Ripken	150.00	70.00
❏ 4 Nomar Garciaparra	120.00	55.00
❏ 5 Larry Walker	30.00	13.50
❏ 6 Mike Piazza	120.00	55.00
❏ 7 Mark McGwire	250.00	110.00
❏ 8 Tony Gwynn	100.00	45.00
❏ 9 Ken Griffey Jr.	200.00	90.00
❏ 10 Roger Clemens	100.00	45.00

1998 Pacific Gold Crown Die Cuts

	MINT	NRMT
COMPLETE SET (36)	450.00	200.00
COMMON CARD (1-36)	2.00	.90
MINOR STARS	3.00	1.35
SEMISTARS	5.00	2.20
UNLISTED STARS	8.00	3.60
STATED ODDS 1:37		
❏ 1 Chipper Jones	20.00	9.00
❏ 2 Greg Maddux	20.00	9.00
❏ 3 Denny Neagle	2.00	.90
❏ 4 Roberto Alomar	8.00	3.60
❏ 5 Rafael Palmeiro	8.00	3.60
❏ 6 Cal Ripken	30.00	13.50
❏ 7 Nomar Garciaparra	25.00	11.00
❏ 8 Mo Vaughn	8.00	3.60
❏ 9 Frank Thomas	15.00	6.75
❏ 10 Sandy Alomar Jr	3.00	1.35
❏ 11 David Justice	3.00	1.35
❏ 12 Manny Ramirez	10.00	4.50
❏ 13 Andres Galarraga	5.00	2.20
❏ 14 Larry Walker	8.00	3.60
❏ 15 Moises Alou	3.00	1.35
❏ 16 Hideo Nomo	2.00	.90
❏ 17 Gary Sheffield	3.00	1.35
❏ 18 Jeff Bagwell	10.00	4.50
❏ 19 Raul Mondesi	3.00	1.35
❏ 20 Hideo Nomo	8.00	3.60
❏ 21 Mike Piazza	25.00	11.00
❏ 22 Derek Jeter	25.00	11.00
❏ 23 Tino Martinez	3.00	1.35
❏ 24 Bernie Williams	8.00	3.60
❏ 25 Ben Grieve	8.00	3.60
❏ 26 Mark McGwire	50.00	22.00
❏ 27 Tony Gwynn	20.00	9.00
❏ 28 Barry Bonds	10.00	4.50
❏ 29 Ken Griffey Jr	40.00	18.00
❏ 30 Randy Johnson	8.00	3.60
❏ 31 Edgar Martinez	3.00	1.35
❏ 32 Alex Rodriguez	25.00	11.00
❏ 33 Juan Gonzalez	15.00	6.75
❏ 34 Ivan Rodriguez	10.00	4.50
❏ 35 Roger Clemens	20.00	9.00
❏ 36 Jose Cruz Jr	3.00	1.35

1998 Pacific Home Run Hitters

	MINT	NRMT
COMPLETE SET (20)	300.00	135.00
COMMON CARD (1-20)	4.00	1.80
SEMISTARS	6.00	2.70
UNLISTED STARS	10.00	4.50
STATED ODDS 1:73		
❏ 1 Rafael Palmeiro	10.00	4.50
❏ 2 Mo Vaughn	10.00	4.50
❏ 3 Sammy Sosa	30.00	13.50
❏ 4 Albert Belle	10.00	4.50
❏ 5 Frank Thomas	20.00	9.00
❏ 6 David Justice	4.00	1.80
❏ 7 Jim Thome	10.00	4.50
❏ 8 Matt Williams	10.00	4.50
❏ 9 Vinny Castilla	4.00	1.80
❏ 10 Andres Galarraga	6.00	2.70
❏ 11 Larry Walker	10.00	4.50
❏ 12 Jeff Bagwell	12.00	5.50
❏ 13 Mike Piazza	30.00	13.50
❏ 14 Tino Martinez	4.00	1.80
❏ 15 Mark McGwire	60.00	27.00
❏ 16 Barry Bonds	12.00	5.50
❏ 17 Jay Buhner	4.00	1.80
❏ 18 Ken Griffey Jr.	50.00	22.00
❏ 19 Alex Rodriguez	30.00	13.50
❏ 20 Juan Gonzalez	20.00	9.00

1998 Pacific In The Cage

	MINT	NRMT
COMPLETE SET (20)	600.00	275.00
COMMON CARD (1-20)	6.00	2.70
SEMISTARS	10.00	4.50
UNLISTED STARS	15.00	6.75
STATED ODDS 1:145		
❏ 1 Chipper Jones	40.00	18.00
❏ 2 Roberto Alomar	15.00	6.75
❏ 3 Cal Ripken	60.00	27.00
❏ 4 Nomar Garciaparra	50.00	22.00
❏ 5 Frank Thomas	30.00	13.50
❏ 6 Sandy Alomar Jr.	6.00	2.70
❏ 7 David Justice	6.00	2.70
❏ 8 Larry Walker	15.00	6.75
❏ 9 Bobby Bonilla	6.00	2.70
❏ 10 Mike Piazza	50.00	22.00
❏ 11 Tino Martinez	6.00	2.70
❏ 12 Bernie Williams	15.00	6.75
❏ 13 Mark McGwire	100.00	45.00
❏ 14 Tony Gwynn	40.00	18.00
❏ 15 Barry Bonds	20.00	9.00
❏ 16 Ken Griffey Jr.	80.00	36.00
❏ 17 Edgar Martinez	6.00	2.70
❏ 18 Alex Rodriguez	50.00	22.00
❏ 19 Juan Gonzalez	30.00	13.50
❏ 20 Ivan Rodriguez	20.00	9.00

1998 Pacific Latinos of the Major Leagues

	MINT	NRMT
COMPLETE SET (36)	80.00	36.00
COMMON CARD (1-36)	1.00	.45
STATED ODDS 2:37		
❏ 1 Andruw Jones	4.00	1.80
❏ 2 Javier Lopez	1.50	.70
❏ 3 Roberto Alomar	4.00	1.80
❏ 4 Geronimo Berroa	1.00	.45
❏ 5 Rafael Palmeiro	4.00	1.80
❏ 6 Nomar Garciaparra	12.00	5.50
❏ 7 Sammy Sosa	12.00	5.50
❏ 8 Ozzie Guillen	1.00	.45
❏ 9 Sandy Alomar Jr.	1.50	.70
❏ 10 Manny Ramirez	5.00	2.20
❏ 11 Omar Vizquel	1.50	.70
❏ 12 Vinny Castilla	1.50	.70
❏ 13 Andres Galarraga	2.50	1.10
❏ 14 Moises Alou	1.50	.70
❏ 15 Bobby Bonilla	1.00	.70
❏ 16 Livan Hernandez	1.00	.45
❏ 17 Edgar Renteria	1.00	.45
❏ 18 Wilton Guerrero	1.00	.45
❏ 19 Raul Mondesi	1.50	.70
❏ 20 Ismael Valdes	1.00	.45
❏ 21 Fernando Vina	1.00	.45
❏ 22 Pedro Martinez	5.00	2.20
❏ 23 Edgardo Alfonzo	2.50	1.10
❏ 24 Carlos Baerga	1.00	.45
❏ 25 Rey Ordonez	1.50	.70
❏ 26 Tino Martinez	1.50	.70
❏ 27 Mariano Rivera	1.50	.70
❏ 28 Bernie Williams	4.00	1.80
❏ 29 Jose Canseco	5.00	2.20
❏ 30 Joey Cora	1.00	.45
❏ 31 Roberto Kelly	1.00	.45
❏ 32 Edgar Martinez	1.50	.70
❏ 33 Alex Rodriguez	12.00	5.50
❏ 34 Juan Gonzalez	8.00	3.60
❏ 35 Ivan Rodriguez	5.00	2.20
❏ 36 Jose Cruz Jr.	1.50	.70

1998 Pacific Team Checklists

	MINT	NRMT
COMPLETE SET (30)	300.00	135.00
COMMON CARD (1-30)	1.50	.70
MINOR STARS	2.50	1.10
SEMISTARS	4.00	1.80
UNLISTED STARS	6.00	2.70
STATED ODDS 1:37		
❏ 1 Tim Salmon	4.00	1.80
Jim Edmonds		
❏ 2 Cal Ripken	25.00	11.00
Roberto Alomar		
❏ 3 Nomar Garciaparra	20.00	9.00
Mo Vaughn		
❏ 4 Frank Thomas	12.00	5.50
Albert Belle		
❏ 5 Sandy Alomar Jr.	8.00	3.60
Manny Ramirez		
❏ 6 Justin Thompson	2.50	1.10
Tony Clark		
❏ 7 Johnny Damon	2.50	1.10
Jermaine Dye		
❏ 8 Dave Nilsson	2.50	1.10
Jeff Cirillo		
❏ 9 Paul Molitor	6.00	2.70
Chuck Knoblauch		
❏ 10 Tino Martinez	15.00	6.75
Derek Jeter		
❏ 11 Ben Grieve	10.00	4.50
Jose Canseco		
❏ 12 Ken Griffey Jr.	40.00	18.00

Alex Rodriguez
☐ 13 Juan Gonzalez 12.00 5.50
Ivan Rodriguez
☐ 14 Jose Cruz Jr. 15.00 6.75
Roger Clemens
☐ 15 Greg Maddux 20.00 9.00
Chipper Jones
☐ 16 Sammy Sosa 20.00 9.00
Mark Grace
☐ 17 Barry Larkin 6.00 2.70
Deion Sanders
☐ 18 Larry Walker 6.00 2.70
Andres Galarraga
☐ 19 Moises Alou 2.50 1.10
Bobby Bonilla
☐ 20 Jeff Bagwell 8.00 3.60
Craig Biggio
☐ 21 Mike Piazza 20.00 9.00
Hideo Nomo
☐ 22 Pedro Martinez 8.00 3.60
Henry Rodriguez
☐ 23 Rey Ordonez 2.50 1.10
Carlos Baerga
☐ 24 Curt Schilling 8.00 3.60
Scott Rolen
☐ 25 Al Martin ...... 1.50 .70
Tony Womack
☐ 26 Mark McGwire 40.00 18.00
Dennis Eckersley
☐ 27 Tony Gwynn 15.00 6.75
Wally Joyner
☐ 28 Barry Bonds 8.00 3.60
J.T.Snow
☐ 29 Matt Williams 6.00 2.70
Jay Bell
☐ 30 Fred McGriff 4.00 1.80
Roberto Hernandez

1999 Pacific

	MINT	NRMT
COMPLETE SET (500)	80.00	36.00
COMMON CARD (1-450)	.15	.07
MINOR STARS	.25	.11
SEMISTARS	.40	.18
UNLISTED STARS	.60	.25

EACH ASTERISK CARD HAS TWO VERSIONS
BOTH VERSIONS EQUALLY VALUED
ASTERISK CARDS AS FOLLOWS: 12/22/27/28
32/36/37/40/45/49/54/57/60/65/66/70/87/106
134/136/141/142/143/144/146/154/184/186
196/204/250/270/286/293/294/296/305/308
311/322/352/368/378/387/396/423/429/436
438/440

☐ 1 Garret Anderson ...... .25 .11
☐ 2 Jason Dickson ...... .15 .07
☐ 3 Gary DiSarcina ...... .15 .07
☐ 4 Jim Edmonds ...... .25 .11
☐ 5 Darin Erstad ...... .40 .18
☐ 6 Chuck Finley ...... .25 .11
☐ 7 Shigetoshi Hasegawa ...... .15 .07
☐ 8 Ken Hill ...... .15 .07
☐ 9 Dave Hollins ...... .15 .07
☐ 10 Phil Nevin ...... .15 .07
☐ 11 Troy Percival ...... .25 .11
☐ 12 Tim Salmon * ...... .40 .18
☐ 12A Tim Salmon Headshot .. .40 .18
☐ 13 Brian Anderson ...... .15 .07

☐ 14 Tony Batista ...... .15 .07
☐ 15 Jay Bell ...... .25 .11
☐ 16 Andy Benes ...... .15 .07
☐ 17 Yamil Benitez ...... .15 .07
☐ 18 Omar Daal ...... .15 .07
☐ 19 David Dellucci ...... .15 .07
☐ 20 Karim Garcia ...... .15 .07
☐ 21 Bernard Gilkey ...... .15 .07
☐ 22 Travis Lee * ...... .40 .18
☐ 22A Travis Lee Headshot ...... .40 .18
☐ 23 Aaron Small ...... .15 .07
☐ 24 Kelly Stinnett ...... .15 .07
☐ 25 Devon White ...... .15 .07
☐ 26 Matt Williams ...... .60 .25
☐ 27 Bruce Chen * ...... .25 .11
☐ 27A Bruce Chen Headshot ...... .25 .11
☐ 28 Andres Galarraga * ...... .40 .18
☐ 28A A. Galarraga Headshot * .. .40 .18
☐ 29 Tom Glavine ...... .60 .25
☐ 30 Ozzie Guillen ...... .15 .07
☐ 31 Andruw Jones ...... .60 .25
☐ 32 Chipper Jones * ...... 1.50 .70
☐ 32A Chipper Jones Headshot 1.50 .70
☐ 33 Ryan Klesko ...... .25 .11
☐ 34 George Lombard ...... .25 .11
☐ 35 Javy Lopez ...... .25 .11
☐ 36 Greg Maddux * ...... 1.50 .70
☐ 36A Greg Maddux Headshot 1.50 .70
☐ 37 Marty Malloy ...... .15 .07
☐ 37A Marty Malloy Headshot .. .15 .07
☐ 38 Dennis Martinez ...... .25 .11
☐ 39 Kevin Millwood ...... .40 .18
☐ 40 Alex Rodriguez * ...... 2.00 .90
☐ 40A Alex Rodriguez Headshot 2.00 .90
☐ 41 Denny Neagle ...... .15 .07
☐ 42 John Smoltz ...... .40 .18
☐ 43 Michael Tucker ...... .15 .07
☐ 44 Walt Weiss ...... .15 .07
☐ 45 Roberto Alomar * ...... .60 .25
☐ 45A R. Alomar Headshot ...... .60 .25
☐ 46 Brady Anderson ...... .25 .11
☐ 47 Harold Baines ...... .25 .11
☐ 48 Mike Bordick ...... .15 .07
☐ 49 Danny Clyburn * ...... .15 .07
☐ 49A Danny Clyburn Headshot .. .15 .07
☐ 50 Eric Davis ...... .25 .11
☐ 51 Scott Erickson ...... .15 .07
☐ 52 Chris Hoiles ...... .15 .07
☐ 53 Jimmy Key ...... .25 .11
☐ 54 Ryan Minor * ...... .25 .11
☐ 54A Ryan Minor Headshot * .. .25 .11
☐ 55 Mike Mussina ...... .60 .25
☐ 56 Jesse Orosco ...... .15 .07
☐ 57 Rafael Palmeiro * ...... .60 .25
☐ 57A R. Palmeiro Headshot ...... .60 .25
☐ 58 Sidney Ponson ...... .15 .07
☐ 59 Arthur Rhodes ...... .15 .07
☐ 60 Cal Ripken * 2.50 1.10
☐ 60A Cal Ripken Headshot 2.50 1.10
☐ 61 B.J. Surhoff ...... .25 .11
☐ 62 Steve Avery ...... .15 .07
☐ 63 Darren Bragg ...... .15 .07
☐ 64 Dennis Eckersley ...... .25 .11
☐ 65 Nomar Garciaparra * .. 2.00 .90
☐ 65A N.Garciaparra Headshot 2.00 .90
☐ 66 Sammy Sosa * ...... 2.00 .90
☐ 66A Sammy Sosa Headshot 2.00 .90
☐ 67 Tom Gordon ...... .25 .11
☐ 68 Reggie Jefferson ...... .15 .07
☐ 69 Darren Lewis ...... .15 .07
☐ 70 Mark McGwire * 4.00 1.80
☐ 70A Mark McGwire Headshot 4.00 1.80
☐ 71 Pedro Martinez ...... .75 .35
☐ 72 Troy O'Leary ...... .15 .07
☐ 73 Bret Saberhagen ...... .25 .11
☐ 74 Mike Stanley ...... .15 .07
☐ 75 John Valentin ...... .25 .11
☐ 76 Jason Varitek ...... .25 .11
☐ 77 Mo Vaughn ...... .60 .25
☐ 78 Tim Wakefield ...... .15 .07
☐ 79 Manny Alexander ...... .15 .07
☐ 80 Rod Beck ...... .15 .07
☐ 81 Brant Brown ...... .15 .07
☐ 82 Mark Clark ...... .15 .07
☐ 83 Gary Gaetti ...... .25 .11
☐ 84 Mark Grace ...... .40 .18

☐ 85 Jose Hernandez ...... .15 .07
☐ 86 Lance Johnson ...... .15 .07
☐ 87 Jason Maxwell * ...... .15 .07
☐ 87A Jason Maxwell Headshot .15 .07
☐ 88 Mickey Morandini ...... .15 .07
☐ 89 Terry Mulholland ...... .15 .07
☐ 90 Henry Rodriguez ...... .25 .11
☐ 91 Scott Servais ...... .15 .07
☐ 92 Kevin Tapani ...... .15 .07
☐ 93 Pedro Valdes ...... .15 .07
☐ 94 Kerry Wood ...... .60 .25
☐ 95 Jeff Abbott ...... .15 .07
☐ 96 James Baldwin ...... .15 .07
☐ 97 Albert Belle ...... .60 .25
☐ 98 Mike Cameron ...... .15 .07
☐ 99 Mike Caruso ...... .15 .07
☐ 100 Wil Cordero ...... .15 .07
☐ 101 Ray Durham ...... .25 .11
☐ 102 Jaime Navarro ...... .15 .07
☐ 103 Greg Norton ...... .15 .07
☐ 104 Magglio Ordonez ...... .60 .25
☐ 105 Mike Sirotka ...... .15 .07
☐ 106 Frank Thomas * ...... 1.25 .55
☐ 106A F. Thomas Headshot 1.25 .55
☐ 107 Robin Ventura ...... .25 .11
☐ 108 Craig Wilson ...... .15 .07
☐ 109 Aaron Boone ...... .15 .07
☐ 110 Bret Boone ...... .25 .11
☐ 111 Sean Casey ...... .60 .25
☐ 112 Pete Harnisch ...... .15 .07
☐ 113 John Hudek ...... .15 .07
☐ 114 Barry Larkin ...... .60 .25
☐ 115 Eduardo Perez ...... .15 .07
☐ 116 Mike Remlinger ...... .15 .07
☐ 117 Reggie Sanders ...... .15 .07
☐ 118 Chris Stynes ...... .15 .07
☐ 119 Eddie Taubensee ...... .15 .07
☐ 120 Brett Tomko ...... .15 .07
☐ 121 Pat Watkins ...... .15 .07
☐ 122 Dmitri Young ...... .25 .11
☐ 123 Sandy Alomar Jr. ...... .25 .11
☐ 124 Dave Burba ...... .15 .07
☐ 125 Bartolo Colon ...... .25 .11
☐ 126 Joey Cora ...... .15 .07
☐ 127 Brian Giles ...... .25 .11
☐ 128 Dwight Gooden ...... .25 .11
☐ 129 Mike Jackson ...... .15 .07
☐ 130 David Justice ...... .25 .11
☐ 131 Kenny Lofton ...... .40 .18
☐ 132 Charles Nagy ...... .25 .11
☐ 133 Chad Ogea ...... .15 .07
☐ 134 Manny Ramirez * ...... .75 .35
☐ 134A M. Ramirez Headshot .75 .35
☐ 135 Richie Sexson ...... .40 .18
☐ 136 Jim Thome * ...... .60 .25
☐ 136A Jim Thome Headshot .. .60 .25
☐ 137 Omar Vizquel ...... .25 .11
☐ 138 Jaret Wright ...... .25 .11
☐ 139 Pedro Astacio ...... .15 .07
☐ 140 Jason Bates ...... .15 .07
☐ 141 Dante Bichette * ...... .25 .11
☐ 141A D. Bichette Headshot .. .25 .11
☐ 142 Vinny Castilla * ...... .25 .11
☐ 142A Vinny Castilla Headshot .25 .11
☐ 143 Edgard Clemente * ...... .15 .07
☐ 143A E. Clemente Headshot .15 .07
☐ 144 Derrick Gibson * ...... .25 .11
☐ 144A D. Gibson Headshot ...... .25 .11
☐ 145 Curtis Goodwin ...... .15 .07
☐ 146 Todd Helton * ...... .60 .25
☐ 146A Todd Helton Headshot .60 .25
☐ 147 Bobby Jones ...... .15 .07
☐ 148 Darryl Kile ...... .15 .07
☐ 149 Mike Lansing ...... .15 .07
☐ 150 Chuck McElroy ...... .15 .07
☐ 151 Neifi Perez ...... .25 .11
☐ 152 Jeff Reed ...... .15 .07
☐ 153 John Thomson ...... .15 .07
☐ 154 Larry Walker * ...... .60 .25
☐ 154A Larry Walker Headshot .60 .25
☐ 155 Jamey Wright ...... .15 .07
☐ 156 Kimera Bartee ...... .15 .07
☐ 157 Geronimo Berroa ...... .15 .07
☐ 158 Raul Casanova ...... .15 .07
☐ 159 Frank Catalanotto ...... .15 .07
☐ 160 Tony Clark ...... .25 .11

161	Deivi Cruz	.15	.07
162	Damion Easley	.25	.11
163	Juan Encarnacion	.25	.11
164	Luis Gonzalez	.25	.11
165	Seth Greisinger	.15	.07
166	Bob Higginson	.25	.11
167	Brian L.Hunter	.15	.07
168	Todd Jones	.15	.07
169	Justin Thompson	.15	.07
170	Antonio Alfonseca	.15	.07
171	Dave Berg	.15	.07
172	John Cangelosi	.15	.07
173	Craig Counsell	.15	.07
174	Todd Dunwoody	.15	.07
175	Cliff Floyd	.25	.11
176	Alex Gonzalez	.25	.11
177	Livan Hernandez	.15	.07
178	Ryan Jackson	.15	.07
179	Mark Kotsay	.15	.07
180	Derek Lee	.15	.07
181	Matt Mantei	.25	.11
182	Brian Meadows	.15	.07
183	Edgar Renteria	.15	.07
184	Moises Alou *	.15	.11
184A	Moises Alou Headshot	.25	.11
185	Brad Ausmus	.15	.07
186	Jeff Bagwell	.75	.35
186A	Jeff Bagwell Headshot	.75	.35
187	Derek Bell	.15	.07
188	Sean Berry	.15	.07
189	Craig Biggio	.60	.25
190	Carl Everett	.25	.11
191	Ricky Gutierrez	.15	.07
192	Mike Hampton	.25	.11
193	Doug Henry	.15	.07
194	Richard Hidalgo	.15	.07
195	Randy Johnson	.60	.25
196	Russ Johnson *	.15	.07
196A	Russ Johnson Headshot	.15	.07
197	Shane Reynolds	.25	.11
198	Bill Spiers	.15	.07
199	Kevin Appier	.25	.11
200	Tim Belcher	.15	.07
201	Jeff Conine	.25	.11
202	Johnny Damon	.25	.11
203	Jermaine Dye	.25	.11
204	Jeremy Giambi *	.15	.07
204A	Je. Giambi Headshot	.15	.07
205	Jeff King	.15	.07
206	Shane Mack	.15	.07
207	Jeff Montgomery	.15	.07
208	Hal Morris	.15	.07
209	Jose Offerman	.25	.11
210	Dean Palmer	.25	.11
211	Jose Rosado	.15	.07
212	Glendon Rusch	.15	.07
213	Larry Sutton	.15	.07
214	Mike Sweeney	.15	.07
215	Bobby Bonilla	.25	.11
216	Alex Cora	.15	.07
217	Darren Dreifort	.15	.07
218	Mark Grudzielanek	.15	.07
219	Todd Hollandsworth	.15	.07
220	Trenidad Hubbard	.15	.07
221	Charles Johnson	.25	.11
222	Eric Karros	.25	.11
223	Matt Luke	.15	.07
224	Ramon Martinez	.15	.07
225	Raul Mondesi	.25	.11
226	Chan Ho Park	.25	.11
227	Jeff Shaw	.15	.07
228	Gary Sheffield	.25	.11
229	Eric Young	.15	.07
230	Jeromy Burnitz	.25	.11
231	Jeff Cirillo	.25	.11
232	Marquis Grissom	.15	.07
233	Bobby Hughes	.15	.07
234	John Jaha	.25	.11
235	Geoff Jenkins	.15	.07
236	Scott Karl	.15	.07
237	Mark Loretta	.15	.07
238	Mike Matheny	.15	.07
239	Mike Myers	.15	.07
240	Dave Nilsson	.25	.11
241	Bob Wickman	.15	.07
242	Jose Valentin	.15	.07
243	Fernando Vina	.15	.07
244	Rick Aguilera	.15	.07
245	Ron Coomer	.15	.07
246	Marty Cordova	.15	.07
247	Denny Hocking	.15	.07
248	Matt Lawton	.15	.07
249	Pat Meares	.15	.07
250	Paul Molitor *	.60	.25
250A	Paul Molitor Headshot	.60	.25
251	Otis Nixon	.15	.07
252	Alex Ochoa	.15	.07
253	David Ortiz	.15	.07
254	A.J. Pierzynski	.15	.07
255	Brad Radke	.25	.11
256	Terry Steinbach	.15	.07
257	Bob Tewksbury	.15	.07
258	Todd Walker	.25	.11
259	Shane Andrews	.15	.07
260	Shayne Bennett	.15	.07
261	Orlando Cabrera	.15	.07
262	Brad Fullmer	.15	.07
263	Vladimir Guerrero	.75	.35
264	Wilton Guerrero	.15	.07
265	Dustin Hermanson	.15	.07
266	Terry Jones	.15	.07
267	Steve Kline	.15	.07
268	Carl Pavano	.15	.07
269	F.P. Santangelo	.15	.07
270	Fernando Seguignol *	.25	.11
270A	F. Seguignol Headshot	.25	.11
271	Ugueth Urbina	.15	.07
272	Jose Vidro	.15	.07
273	Chris Widger	.15	.07
274	Edgardo Alfonzo	.40	.18
275	Carlos Baerga	.25	.11
276	John Franco	.15	.07
277	Todd Hundley	.25	.11
278	Butch Huskey	.15	.07
279	Bobby Jones	.15	.07
280	Al Leiter	.25	.11
281	Greg McMichael	.15	.07
282	Brian McRae	.15	.07
283	Hideo Nomo	.25	.11
284	John Olerud	.25	.11
285	Rey Ordonez	.25	.11
286	Mike Piazza	2.00	.90
286A	Mike Piazza Headshot	2.00	.90
287	Turk Wendell	.15	.07
288	Masato Yoshii	.25	.11
289	David Cone	.40	.18
290	Chad Curtis	.15	.07
291	Joe Girardi	.15	.07
292	Orlando Hernandez	.60	.25
293	Hideki Irabu	.25	.11
293A	Hideki Irabu Headshot	.25	.11
294	Derek Jeter *	2.00	.90
294A	Derek Jeter Headshot	2.00	.90
295	Chuck Knoblauch	.25	.11
296	Mike Lowell *	.15	.07
296A	Mike Lowell Headshot	.15	.07
297	Tino Martinez	.25	.11
298	Ramiro Mendoza	.15	.07
299	Paul O'Neill	.25	.11
300	Andy Pettitte	.25	.11
301	Jorge Posada	.15	.07
302	Tim Raines	.25	.11
303	Mariano Rivera	.25	.11
304	David Wells	.25	.11
305	Bernie Williams *	.60	.25
305A	B. Williams Headshot	.60	.25
306	Mike Blowers	.15	.07
307	Tom Candiotti	.15	.07
308	Eric Chavez *	.40	.18
308A	Eric Chavez Headshot	.40	.18
309	Ryan Christenson	.15	.07
310	Jason Giambi	.25	.11
311	Ben Grieve *	.60	.25
311A	Ben Grieve Headshot	.60	.25
312	Rickey Henderson	.75	.35
313	A.J. Hinch	.15	.07
314	Jason McDonald	.15	.07
315	Bip Roberts	.15	.07
316	Kenny Rogers	.15	.07
317	Scott Spiezio	.15	.07
318	Matt Stairs	.25	.11
319	Miguel Tejada	.25	.11
320	Bob Abreu	.25	.11
321	Alex Arias	.15	.07
322	Gary Bennett	.15	.07
322A	Gary Bennett Headshot	.15	.07
323	Ricky Bottalico	.15	.07
324	Rico Brogna	.15	.07
325	Bobby Estalella	.15	.07
326	Doug Glanville	.25	.11
327	Kevin Jordan	.15	.07
328	Mark Leiter	.15	.07
329	Wendell Magee	.15	.07
330	Mark Portugal	.15	.07
331	Desi Relaford	.15	.07
332	Scott Rolen	.75	.35
333	Curt Schilling	.40	.18
334	Kevin Sefcik	.15	.07
335	Adrian Brown	.15	.07
336	Emil Brown	.15	.07
337	Lou Collier	.15	.07
338	Francisco Cordova	.15	.07
339	Freddy Garcia	.15	.07
340	Jose Guillen	.15	.07
341	Jason Kendall	.25	.11
342	Al Martin	.15	.07
343	Abraham Nunez	.15	.07
344	Aramis Ramirez	.40	.18
345	Ricardo Rincon	.15	.07
346	Jason Schmidt	.15	.07
347	Turner Ward	.15	.07
348	Tony Womack	.15	.07
349	Kevin Young	.25	.11
350	Juan Acevedo	.15	.07
351	Delino DeShields	.15	.07
352	J.D. Drew *	1.00	.45
352A	J.D. Drew Headshot	1.00	.45
353	Ron Gant	.25	.11
354	Brian Jordan	.25	.11
355	Ray Lankford	.25	.11
356	Eli Marrero	.15	.07
357	Kent Mercker	.15	.07
358	Matt Morris	.25	.11
359	Luis Ordaz	.15	.07
360	Donovan Osborne	.15	.07
361	Placido Polanco	.15	.07
362	Fernando Tatis	.60	.25
363	Andy Ashby	.15	.07
364	Kevin Brown	.40	.18
365	Ken Caminiti	.25	.11
366	Steve Finley	.25	.11
367	Chris Gomez	.15	.07
368	Tony Gwynn *	1.50	.70
368A	Tony Gwynn Headshot	1.50	.70
369	Joey Hamilton	.15	.07
370	Carlos Hernandez	.15	.07
371	Trevor Hoffman	.25	.11
372	Wally Joyner	.15	.07
373	Jim Leyritz	.15	.07
374	Ruben Rivera	.15	.07
375	Greg Vaughn	.25	.11
376	Quilvio Veras	.15	.07
377	Rich Aurilia	.15	.07
378	Barry Bonds *	.75	.35
378A	Barry Bonds Headshot	.75	.35
379	Ellis Burks	.25	.11
380	Joe Carter	.25	.11
381	Stan Javier	.15	.07
382	Brian Johnson	.15	.07
383	Jeff Kent	.25	.11
384	Jose Mesa	.15	.07
385	Bill Mueller	.15	.07
386	Robb Nen	.15	.07
387	Armando Rios *	.15	.07
387A	Armando Rios Headshot	.15	.07
388	Kirk Rueter	.15	.07
389	Rey Sanchez	.15	.07
390	J.T. Snow	.25	.11
391	David Bell	.15	.07
392	Jay Buhner	.25	.11
393	Ken Cloude	.15	.07
394	Russ Davis	.15	.07
395	Jeff Fassero	.15	.07
396	Ken Griffey Jr. *	3.00	1.35
396A	K. Griffey Jr. Headshot	3.00	1.35
397	Giomar Guevara	.15	.07
398	Carlos Guillen	.15	.07
399	Edgar Martinez	.25	.11

❑ 400	Shane Monahan	.15	.07
❑ 401	Jamie Moyer	.15	.07
❑ 402	David Segui	.15	.07
❑ 403	Makoto Suzuki	.15	.07
❑ 404	Mike Timlin	.15	.07
❑ 405	Dan Wilson	.15	.07
❑ 406	Wilson Alvarez	.15	.07
❑ 407	Rolando Arrojo	.15	.07
❑ 408	Wade Boggs	.60	.25
❑ 409	Miguel Cairo	.15	.07
❑ 410	Roberto Hernandez	.15	.07
❑ 411	Mike Kelly	.15	.07
❑ 412	Aaron Ledesma	.15	.07
❑ 413	Albie Lopez	.15	.07
❑ 414	Dave Martinez	.15	.07
❑ 415	Quinton McCracken	.15	.07
❑ 416	Fred McGriff	.40	.18
❑ 417	Bryan Rekar	.15	.07
❑ 418	Paul Sorrento	.15	.07
❑ 419	Randy Winn	.15	.07
❑ 420	John Burkett	.15	.07
❑ 421	Will Clark	.60	.25
❑ 422	Royce Clayton	.15	.07
❑ 423	Juan Gonzalez *	1.25	.55
❑ 423A	J. Gonzalez Headshot	1.25	.55
❑ 424	Tom Goodwin	.15	.07
❑ 425	Rusty Greer	.25	.11
❑ 426	Rick Helling	.15	.07
❑ 427	Roberto Kelly	.15	.07
❑ 428	Mark McLemore	.15	.07
❑ 429	Ivan Rodriguez *	.75	.35
❑ 429A	Ivan Rodriguez Headshot	.75	.35
❑ 430	Aaron Sele	.25	.11
❑ 431	Lee Stevens	.15	.07
❑ 432	Todd Stottlemyre	.15	.07
❑ 433	John Wetteland	.25	.11
❑ 434	Todd Zeile	.25	.11
❑ 435	Jose Canseco *	.75	.35
❑ 435A	Jose Canseco Headshot	.75	.35
❑ 436	Roger Clemens *	1.50	.70
❑ 436A	R. Clemens Headshot	1.50	.70
❑ 437	Felipe Crespo	.15	.07
❑ 438	Jose Cruz Jr.	.25	.11
❑ 439	Carlos Delgado	.60	.25
❑ 440	Tom Evans *	.15	.07
❑ 440A	Tom Evans Headshot	.15	.07
❑ 441	Tony Fernandez	.25	.11
❑ 442	Darrin Fletcher	.15	.07
❑ 443	Alex Gonzalez	.25	.11
❑ 444	Shawn Green	.60	.25
❑ 445	Roy Halladay	.25	.11
❑ 446	Pat Hentgen	.25	.11
❑ 447	Juan Samuel	.15	.07
❑ 448	Benito Santiago	.25	.11
❑ 449	Shannon Stewart	.25	.11
❑ 450	Woody Williams	.15	.07
❑ NNO	Tony Gwynn Sample	2.00	.90

1999 Pacific Platinum Blue

	MINT	NRMT
COMMON CARD (1-450)	5.00	2.20

*STARS: 12.5X TO 30X BASIC CARDS
*YNG.STARS: 10X TO 25X BASIC CARDS
STATED ODDS 1:73

1999 Pacific Red

	MINT	NRMT
COMPLETE SET (500)	300.00	135.00
COMMON CARD (1-450)	.30	.14

*STARS: 2.5X TO 6X BASIC CARDS
*YOUNG STARS: 2X TO 5X BASIC CARDS
ONE PER RETAIL PACK

1999 Pacific Cramer's Choice

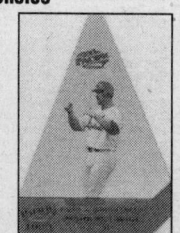

	MINT	NRMT
COMPLETE SET (10)	600.00	275.00
COMMON CARD (1-10)	15.00	6.75

RANDOM INSERTS IN PACKS
STATED PRINT RUN 299 SERIAL #'d SETS

❑ 1	Cal Ripken	80.00	36.00
❑ 2	Nomar Garciaparra	60.00	27.00
❑ 3	Frank Thomas	40.00	18.00
❑ 4	Ken Griffey Jr.	100.00	45.00
❑ 5	Alex Rodriguez	60.00	27.00
❑ 6	Greg Maddux	50.00	22.00
❑ 7	Sammy Sosa	60.00	27.00
❑ 8	Kerry Wood	15.00	6.75
❑ 9	Mark McGwire	120.00	55.00
❑ 10	Tony Gwynn	50.00	22.00

1999 Pacific Dynagon Diamond

	MINT	NRMT
COMPLETE SET (20)	120.00	55.00
COMMON CARD (1-20)	1.50	.70
UNLISTED STARS	2.50	1.10

STATED ODDS 4:37
*TITANIUM: 4X TO 10X BASIC DYN.DIAM.
TITANIUM: RANDOM INS.IN HOBBY PACKS
TITANIUM PRINT RUN 99 SERIAL #'d SETS

❑ 1	Cal Ripken	10.00	4.50
❑ 2	Nomar Garciaparra	8.00	3.60
❑ 3	Frank Thomas	5.00	2.20
❑ 4	Derek Jeter	8.00	3.60
❑ 5	Ben Grieve	2.50	1.10
❑ 6	Ken Griffey Jr.	12.00	5.50
❑ 7	Alex Rodriguez	8.00	3.60
❑ 8	Juan Gonzalez	5.00	2.20
❑ 9	Travis Lee	1.50	.70
❑ 10	Chipper Jones	6.00	2.70
❑ 11	Greg Maddux	6.00	2.70

❑ 12	Sammy Sosa	8.00	3.60
❑ 13	Kerry Wood	2.50	1.10
❑ 14	Jeff Bagwell	3.00	1.35
❑ 15	Hideo Nomo	2.50	1.10
❑ 16	Mike Piazza	8.00	3.60
❑ 17	J.D. Drew	3.00	1.35
❑ 18	Mark McGwire	15.00	6.75
❑ 19	Tony Gwynn	6.00	2.70
❑ 20	Barry Bonds	3.00	1.35

1999 Pacific Gold Crown Die Cuts

	MINT	NRMT
COMPLETE SET (36)	500.00	220.00
COMMON CARD (1-36)	3.00	1.35
SEMISTARS	5.00	2.20
UNLISTED STARS	8.00	3.60

STATED ODDS 1:37

❑ 1	Darin Erstad	5.00	2.20
❑ 2	Cal Ripken	30.00	13.50
❑ 3	Nomar Garciaparra	25.00	11.00
❑ 4	Pedro Martinez	10.00	4.50
❑ 5	Mo Vaughn	8.00	3.60
❑ 6	Frank Thomas	15.00	6.75
❑ 7	Kenny Lofton	5.00	2.20
❑ 8	Manny Ramirez	10.00	4.50
❑ 9	Paul Molitor	8.00	3.60
❑ 10	Derek Jeter	25.00	11.00
❑ 11	Bernie Williams	8.00	3.60
❑ 12	Ben Grieve	8.00	3.60
❑ 13	Ken Griffey Jr.	40.00	18.00
❑ 14	Alex Rodriguez	25.00	11.00
❑ 15	Wade Boggs	8.00	3.60
❑ 16	Juan Gonzalez	15.00	6.75
❑ 17	Ivan Rodriguez	10.00	4.50
❑ 18	Jose Canseco	10.00	4.50
❑ 19	Roger Clemens	20.00	9.00
❑ 20	Travis Lee	5.00	2.20
❑ 21	Chipper Jones	20.00	9.00
❑ 22	Greg Maddux	20.00	9.00
❑ 23	Sammy Sosa	25.00	11.00
❑ 24	Kerry Wood	8.00	3.60
❑ 25	Todd Helton	8.00	3.60
❑ 26	Larry Walker	8.00	3.60
❑ 27	Jeff Bagwell	10.00	4.50
❑ 28	Craig Biggio	8.00	3.60
❑ 29	Raul Mondesi	4.00	1.80
❑ 30	Vladimir Guerrero	10.00	4.50
❑ 31	Mike Piazza	25.00	11.00
❑ 32	Scott Rolen	10.00	4.50
❑ 33	J.D. Drew	10.00	4.50
❑ 34	Mark McGwire	50.00	22.00
❑ 35	Tony Gwynn	20.00	9.00
❑ 36	Barry Bonds	10.00	4.50

1999 Pacific Hot Cards

	MINT	NRMT
COMPLETE SET (10)	200.00	90.00
COMMON CARD (1-10)	8.00	3.60

ONE PER HOT CARD REGISTRY EXCHANGE
STATED PRINT RUN 500 SERIAL #'d SETS

❑ 1	Alex Rodriguez	20.00	9.00
❑ 2	Tony Gwynn	15.00	6.75
❑ 3	Ken Griffey Jr.	40.00	18.00

		MINT	NRMT
❑ 4	Sammy Sosa	20.00	9.00
❑ 5	Ivan Rodriguez	10.00	4.50
❑ 6	Derek Jeter	20.00	9.00
❑ 7	Cal Ripken	30.00	13.50
❑ 8	Mark McGwire	40.00	18.00
❑ 9	J.D. Drew	10.00	4.50
❑ 10	Bernie Williams	8.00	3.60

1999 Pacific Team Checklists

	MINT	NRMT
COMPLETE SET (30)	150.00	70.00
COMMON CARD (1-30)	1.00	.45
MINOR STARS	1.50	.70
SEMISTARS	2.50	1.10
UNLISTED STARS	4.00	1.80
STATED ODDS 2:37		

		MINT	NRMT
❑ 1	Darin Erstad	2.50	1.10
❑ 2	Cal Ripken	15.00	6.75
❑ 3	Nomar Garciaparra	12.00	5.50
❑ 4	Frank Thomas	8.00	3.60
❑ 5	Manny Ramirez	5.00	2.20
❑ 6	Damion Easley	1.50	.70
❑ 7	Jeff King	1.00	.45
❑ 8	Paul Molitor	4.00	1.80
❑ 9	Derek Jeter	12.00	5.50
❑ 10	Ben Grieve	4.00	1.80
❑ 11	Ken Griffey Jr.	20.00	9.00
❑ 12	Wade Boggs	4.00	1.80
❑ 13	Juan Gonzalez	8.00	3.60
❑ 14	Roger Clemens	10.00	4.50
❑ 15	Travis Lee	2.50	1.10
❑ 16	Chipper Jones	10.00	4.50
❑ 17	Sammy Sosa	12.00	5.50
❑ 18	Barry Larkin	4.00	1.80
❑ 19	Todd Helton	4.00	1.80
❑ 20	Mark Kotsay	1.00	.45
❑ 21	Jeff Bagwell	5.00	2.20
❑ 22	Paul Mondesi	1.50	.70
❑ 23	Jeff Cirillo	1.50	.70
❑ 24	Vladimir Guerrero	5.00	2.20
❑ 25	Mike Piazza	12.00	5.50
❑ 26	Scott Rolen	5.00	2.20
❑ 27	Jason Kendall	1.50	.70
❑ 28	Mark McGwire	25.00	11.00
❑ 29	Tony Gwynn	10.00	4.50
❑ 30	Barry Bonds	5.00	2.20

1999 Pacific Timelines

	MINT	NRMT
COMPLETE SET (20)	1200.00	550.00
COMMON CARD (1-20)	20.00	9.00
UNLISTED STARS	30.00	13.50
STATED ODDS 1:181 HOBBY		
STATED PRINT RUN 199 SERIAL #'d SETS		

		MINT	NRMT
❑ 1	Cal Ripken	120.00	55.00
❑ 2	Frank Thomas	60.00	27.00
❑ 3	Jim Thome	30.00	13.50
❑ 4	Paul Molitor	30.00	13.50
❑ 5	Bernie Williams	30.00	13.50
❑ 6	Derek Jeter	100.00	45.00
❑ 7	Ken Griffey Jr.	150.00	70.00
❑ 8	Alex Rodriguez	100.00	45.00
❑ 9	Wade Boggs	30.00	13.50
❑ 10	Jose Canseco	40.00	18.00
❑ 11	Roger Clemens	80.00	36.00
❑ 12	Andres Galarraga	20.00	9.00
❑ 13	Chipper Jones	80.00	36.00
❑ 14	Greg Maddux	80.00	36.00
❑ 15	Sammy Sosa	100.00	45.00
❑ 16	Larry Walker	30.00	13.50
❑ 17	Randy Johnson	30.00	13.50
❑ 18	Mike Piazza	100.00	45.00
❑ 19	Mark McGwire	200.00	90.00
❑ 20	Tony Gwynn	80.00	36.00

2000 Pacific

DEREK JETER
SS / TEAM: NEW YORK YANKEES

	MINT	NRMT
COMPLETE SET (500)	80.00	36.00
COMMON CARD (1-450)	.15	.07
MINOR STARS	.25	.11
SEMISTARS	.40	.18
DUAL VERSIONS EXIST FOR FOLLOWING:		
BOTH VERSIONS VALUED EQUALLY		
6/16/31/37/38/42/49/60/64/68/91/107/111		
114/123/132/134/143/154/190/201/214/224		
230/263/282/284/289/294/304/331/332/341		
352/356/357/363/373/377/381/392/393/402		
406/408/415/420/429/440/444		

		MINT	NRMT
❑ 1	Garret Anderson	.25	.11
❑ 2	Tim Belcher	.15	.07
❑ 3	Gary DiSarcina	.15	.07
❑ 4	Trent Durrington	.15	.07
❑ 5	Jim Edmonds	.25	.11
❑ 6	Darin Erstad ACTION	.25	.11
❑ 6A	Darin Erstad POR	.25	.11
❑ 7	Chuck Finley	.25	.11
❑ 8	Troy Glaus	.50	.23
❑ 9	Todd Greene	.15	.07
❑ 10	Bret Hemphill	.15	.07
❑ 11	Ken Hill	.15	.07
❑ 12	Ramon Ortiz	.25	.11
❑ 13	Troy Percival	.25	.11
❑ 14	Mark Petkovsek	.15	.07
❑ 15	Tim Salmon	.40	.18
❑ 16	Mo Vaughn ACTION	.50	.23
❑ 16A	Mo Vaughn POR	.50	.23
❑ 17	Jay Bell	.15	.07
❑ 18	Omar Daal	.25	.11
❑ 19	Erubiel Durazo	1.50	.70
❑ 20	Steve Finley	.25	.11
❑ 21	Bernard Gilkey	.15	.07
❑ 22	Luis Gonzalez	.25	.11
❑ 23	Randy Johnson	.60	.25
❑ 24	Byung-Hyun Kim	.40	.18
❑ 25	Travis Lee	.25	.11
❑ 26	Matt Mantei	.25	.11
❑ 27	Armando Reynoso	.15	.07
❑ 28	Rob Ryan	.15	.07
❑ 29	Kelly Stinnett	.15	.07
❑ 30	Todd Stottlemyre	.25	.11
❑ 31	Matt Williams ACTION	.50	.23
❑ 31A	Matt Williams POR	.50	.23
❑ 32	Tony Womack	.15	.07
❑ 33	Bret Boone	.25	.11
❑ 34	Andres Galarraga	.50	.23
❑ 35	Tom Glavine	.50	.23
❑ 36	Ozzie Guillen	.15	.07
❑ 37	Andruw Jones ACTION	.60	.25
❑ 37A	Andruw Jones POR	.60	.25
❑ 38	Chipper Jones ACTION	1.50	.70
❑ 38A	Chipper Jones POR	1.50	.70
❑ 39	Brian Jordan	.25	.11
❑ 40	Ryan Klesko	.25	.11
❑ 41	Javy Lopez	.25	.11
❑ 42	Greg Maddux ACTION	1.50	.70
❑ 42A	Greg Maddux POR	1.50	.70
❑ 43	Kevin Millwood	.40	.18
❑ 44	John Rocker	.15	.07
❑ 45	Randall Simon	.25	.11
❑ 46	John Smoltz	.40	.18
❑ 47	Gerald Williams	.15	.07
❑ 48	Brady Anderson	.25	.11
❑ 49	Albert Belle ACTION	.50	.23
❑ 49A	Albert Belle POR	.50	.23
❑ 50	Mike Bordick	.15	.07
❑ 51	Will Clark	.50	.23
❑ 52	Jeff Conine	.25	.11
❑ 53	Delino DeShields	.15	.07
❑ 54	Jerry Hairston Jr.	.25	.11
❑ 55	Charles Johnson	.25	.11
❑ 56	Eugene Kingsale	.15	.07
❑ 57	Ryan Minor	.25	.11
❑ 58	Mike Mussina	.60	.25
❑ 59	Sidney Ponson	.25	.11
❑ 60	Cal Ripken ACTION	2.50	1.10
❑ 60A	Cal Ripken POR	2.50	1.10
❑ 61	B.J. Surhoff	.25	.11
❑ 62	Mike Timlin	.15	.07
❑ 63	Rod Beck	.25	.11
❑ 64	Nomar Garciaparra ACTION	2.00	.90
❑ 64A	Nomar Garciaparra POR	2.00	.90
❑ 65	Tom Gordon	.15	.07
❑ 66	Butch Huskey	.15	.07
❑ 67	Derek Lowe	.15	.07
❑ 68	Pedro Martinez ACTION	.75	.35
❑ 68A	Pedro Martinez POR	.75	.35
❑ 69	Trot Nixon	.25	.11
❑ 70	Jose Offerman	.25	.11
❑ 71	Troy O'Leary	.25	.11
❑ 72	Pat Rapp	.15	.07
❑ 73	Donnie Sadler	.15	.07
❑ 74	Mike Stanley	.15	.07
❑ 75	John Valentin	.15	.07
❑ 76	Jason Varitek	.25	.11
❑ 77	Wilton Veras	1.00	.45
❑ 78	Tim Wakefield	.25	.11
❑ 79	Rick Aguilera	.25	.11
❑ 80	Manny Alexander	.15	.07
❑ 81	Roosevelt Brown	.25	.11
❑ 82	Mark Grace	.40	.18
❑ 83	Glenallen Hill	.15	.07

#	Player	Price	Price2
❏ 84	Lance Johnson	.15	.07
❏ 85	Jon Lieber	.15	.07
❏ 86	Cole Liniak	.15	.07
❏ 87	Chad Meyers	.25	.11
❏ 88	Mickey Morandini	.15	.07
❏ 89	Jose Nieves	.15	.07
❏ 90	Henry Rodriguez	.15	.07
❏ 91	Sammy Sosa ACTION	2.00	.90
❏ 91A	Sammy Sosa POR	2.00	.90
❏ 92	Kevin Tapani	.15	.07
❏ 93	Kerry Wood	.50	.23
❏ 94	Mike Caruso	.15	.07
❏ 95	Ray Durham	.25	.11
❏ 96	Brook Fordyce	.15	.07
❏ 97	Bobby Howry	.15	.07
❏ 98	Paul Konerko	.25	.11
❏ 99	Carlos Lee	.15	.07
❏ 100	Aaron Myette	.15	.07
❏ 101	Greg Norton	.15	.07
❏ 102	Magglio Ordonez	.40	.18
❏ 103	Jim Parque	.15	.07
❏ 104	Liu Rodriguez	.15	.07
❏ 105	Chris Singleton	.25	.11
❏ 106	Mike Sirotka	.15	.07
❏ 107	Frank Thomas ACTION	1.25	.55
❏ 107A	Frank Thomas POR	1.25	.55
❏ 108	Kip Wells	.15	.07
❏ 109	Aaron Boone	.15	.07
❏ 110	Mike Cameron	.15	.07
❏ 111	Sean Casey ACTION	.50	.23
❏ 111A	Sean Casey POR	.50	.23
❏ 112	Jeffrey Hammonds	.25	.11
❏ 113	Pete Harnisch	.15	.07
❏ 114	Barry Larkin ACTION	.50	.23
❏ 114A	Barry Larkin POR	.50	.23
❏ 115	Jason LaRue	.15	.07
❏ 116	Denny Neagle	.15	.07
❏ 117	Pokey Reese	.15	.07
❏ 118	Scott Sullivan	.15	.07
❏ 119	Eddie Taubensee	.15	.07
❏ 120	Greg Vaughn	.25	.11
❏ 121	Scott Williamson	.15	.07
❏ 122	Dmitri Young	.15	.07
❏ 123	Roberto Alomar ACTION	.60	.25
❏ 123A	Roberto Alomar POR	.60	.25
❏ 124	Sandy Alomar Jr.	.25	.11
❏ 125	Harold Baines	.25	.11
❏ 126	Russell Branyan	.25	.11
❏ 127	Dave Burba	.15	.07
❏ 128	Bartolo Colon	.25	.11
❏ 129	Travis Fryman	.25	.11
❏ 130	Mike Jackson	.25	.11
❏ 131	David Justice	.25	.11
❏ 132	Kenny Lofton ACTION	.25	.11
❏ 132A	Kenny Lofton POR	.25	.11
❏ 133	Charles Nagy	.25	.11
❏ 134	Manny Ramirez ACTION	.75	.35
❏ 134A	Manny Ramirez POR	.75	.35
❏ 135	Dave Roberts	.15	.07
❏ 136	Richie Sexson	.25	.11
❏ 137	Jim Thome	.50	.23
❏ 138	Omar Vizquel	.25	.11
❏ 139	Jaret Wright	.15	.07
❏ 140	Pedro Astacio	.15	.07
❏ 141	Dante Bichette	.25	.11
❏ 142	Brian Bohanon	.15	.07
❏ 143	Vinny Castilla ACTION	.25	.11
❏ 143A	Vinny Castilla POR	.25	.11
❏ 144	Edgard Clemente	.15	.07
❏ 145	Derrick Gibson	.15	.07
❏ 146	Todd Helton	.50	.23
❏ 147	Darryl Kile	.15	.07
❏ 148	Mike Lansing	.15	.07
❏ 149	Kirt Manwaring	.15	.07
❏ 150	Neifi Perez	.25	.11
❏ 151	Ben Petrick	.15	.07
❏ 152	Juan Sosa	.25	.11
❏ 153	Dave Veres	.15	.07
❏ 154	Larry Walker ACTION	.60	.25
❏ 154A	Larry Walker POR	.60	.25
❏ 155	Brad Ausmus	.15	.07
❏ 156	Dave Borkowski	.15	.07
❏ 157	Tony Clark	.25	.11
❏ 158	Francisco Cordero	.15	.07
❏ 159	Deivi Cruz	.15	.07
❏ 160	Damion Easley	.25	.11
❏ 161	Juan Encarnacion	.25	.11
❏ 162	Robert Fick	.15	.07
❏ 163	Bobby Higginson	.15	.07
❏ 164	Gabe Kapler	.40	.18
❏ 165	Brian Moehler	.15	.07
❏ 166	Dean Palmer	.25	.11
❏ 167	Luis Polonia	.15	.07
❏ 168	Justin Thompson	.15	.07
❏ 169	Jeff Weaver	.25	.11
❏ 170	Antonio Alfonseca	.15	.07
❏ 171	Bruce Aven	.15	.07
❏ 172	A.J. Burnett	.15	.07
❏ 173	Luis Castillo	.15	.07
❏ 174	Ramon Castro	.15	.07
❏ 175	Ryan Dempster	.15	.07
❏ 176	Alex Fernandez	.15	.07
❏ 177	Cliff Floyd	.25	.11
❏ 178	Amaury Garcia	.15	.07
❏ 179	Alex Gonzalez	.15	.07
❏ 180	Mark Kotsay	.15	.07
❏ 181	Mike Lowell	.25	.11
❏ 182	Brian Meadows	.15	.07
❏ 183	Kevin Orie	.15	.07
❏ 184	Julio Ramirez	.15	.07
❏ 185	Preston Wilson	.25	.11
❏ 186	Moises Alou	.25	.11
❏ 187	Jeff Bagwell	.75	.35
❏ 188	Glen Barker	.15	.07
❏ 189	Derek Bell	.25	.11
❏ 190	Craig Biggio ACTION	.50	.23
❏ 190A	Craig Biggio POR	.50	.23
❏ 191	Ken Caminiti	.25	.11
❏ 192	Scott Elarton	.25	.11
❏ 193	Carl Everett	.25	.11
❏ 194	Mike Hampton	.25	.11
❏ 195	Carlos Hernandez	.15	.07
❏ 196	Richard Hidalgo	.25	.11
❏ 197	Jose Lima	.25	.11
❏ 198	Shane Reynolds	.15	.07
❏ 199	Bill Spiers	.15	.07
❏ 200	Billy Wagner	.25	.11
❏ 201	Carlos Beltran ACTION	.60	.25
❏ 201A	Carlos Beltran POR	.60	.25
❏ 202	Dermal Brown	.25	.11
❏ 203	Johnny Damon	.25	.11
❏ 204	Jermaine Dye	.25	.11
❏ 205	Carlos Febles	.25	.11
❏ 206	Jeremy Giambi	.25	.11
❏ 207	Mark Quinn	.25	.11
❏ 208	Joe Randa	.15	.07
❏ 209	Dan Reichert	.15	.07
❏ 210	Jose Rosado	.15	.07
❏ 211	Rey Sanchez	.15	.07
❏ 212	Jeff Suppan	.15	.07
❏ 213	Mike Sweeney	.15	.07
❏ 214	Kevin Brown ACTION	.40	.18
❏ 214A	Kevin Brown POR	.40	.18
❏ 215	Darren Dreifort	.15	.07
❏ 216	Eric Gagne	.25	.11
❏ 217	Mark Grudzielanek	.15	.07
❏ 218	Todd Hollandsworth	.15	.07
❏ 219	Todd Hundley	.15	.07
❏ 220	Eric Karros	.25	.11
❏ 221	Raul Mondesi	.25	.11
❏ 222	Chan Ho Park	.25	.11
❏ 223	Jeff Shaw	.15	.07
❏ 224	Gary Sheffield ACTION	.25	.11
❏ 224A	Gary Sheffield POR	.25	.11
❏ 225	Ismael Valdes	.25	.11
❏ 226	Devon White	.25	.11
❏ 227	Eric Young	.15	.07
❏ 228	Kevin Barker	.15	.07
❏ 229	Ron Belliard	.15	.07
❏ 230	Jeromy Burnitz ACTION	.25	.11
❏ 230A	Jeromy Burnitz POR	.25	.11
❏ 231	Jeff Cirillo	.15	.07
❏ 232	Marquis Grissom	.25	.11
❏ 233	Geoff Jenkins	.25	.11
❏ 234	Mark Loretta	.15	.07
❏ 235	David Nilsson	.15	.07
❏ 236	Hideo Nomo	.50	.23
❏ 237	Alex Ochoa	.15	.07
❏ 238	Kyle Peterson	.25	.11
❏ 239	Fernando Vina	.15	.07
❏ 240	Bob Wickman	.15	.07
❏ 241	Steve Woodard	.15	.07
❏ 242	Chad Allen	.15	.07
❏ 243	Ron Coomer	.15	.07
❏ 244	Marty Cordova	.15	.07
❏ 245	Cristian Guzman	.15	.07
❏ 246	Denny Hocking	.15	.07
❏ 247	Jacque Jones	.25	.11
❏ 248	Corey Koskie	.15	.07
❏ 249	Matt Lawton	.15	.07
❏ 250	Joe Mays	.15	.07
❏ 251	Eric Milton	.15	.07
❏ 252	Brad Radke	.15	.07
❏ 253	Mark Redman	.15	.07
❏ 254	Terry Steinbach	.15	.07
❏ 255	Todd Walker	.25	.11
❏ 256	Tony Armas Jr.	.15	.07
❏ 257	Michael Barrett	.25	.11
❏ 258	Peter Bergeron	.25	.11
❏ 259	Geoff Blum	.15	.07
❏ 260	Orlando Cabrera	.15	.07
❏ 261	Trace Coquillette	.25	.11
❏ 262	Brad Fullmer	.15	.07
❏ 263	Vladimir Guerrero ACTION	.75	.35
❏ 263A	Vladimir Guerrero POR	.75	.35
❏ 264	Wilton Guerrero	.15	.07
❏ 265	Dustin Hermanson	.15	.07
❏ 266	Manny Martinez	.25	.11
❏ 267	Ryan McGuire	.15	.07
❏ 268	Ugueth Urbina	.15	.07
❏ 269	Jose Vidro	.15	.07
❏ 270	Rondell White	.25	.11
❏ 271	Chris Widger	.15	.07
❏ 272	Edgardo Alfonzo	.40	.18
❏ 273	Armando Benitez	.25	.11
❏ 274	Roger Cedeno	.25	.11
❏ 275	Dennis Cook	.15	.07
❏ 276	Octavio Dotel	.25	.11
❏ 277	John Franco	.25	.11
❏ 278	Darryl Hamilton	.15	.07
❏ 279	Rickey Henderson	.75	.35
❏ 280	Orel Hershiser	.25	.11
❏ 281	Al Leiter	.15	.07
❏ 282	John Olerud ACTION	.25	.11
❏ 282A	John Olerud POR	.25	.11
❏ 283	Rey Ordonez	.25	.11
❏ 284	Mike Piazza ACTION	2.00	.90
❏ 284A	Mike Piazza POR	2.00	.90
❏ 285	Kenny Rogers	.15	.07
❏ 286	Jorge Toca	.25	.11
❏ 287	Robin Ventura	.25	.11
❏ 288	Scott Brosius	.15	.07
❏ 289	Roger Clemens ACTION	1.50	.70
❏ 289A	Roger Clemens POR	1.50	.70
❏ 290	David Cone	.40	.18
❏ 291	Chili Davis	.25	.11
❏ 292	Orlando Hernandez	.50	.23
❏ 293	Hideki Irabu	.25	.11
❏ 294	Derek Jeter ACTION	2.00	.90
❏ 294A	Derek Jeter POR	2.00	.90
❏ 295	Chuck Knoblauch	.25	.11
❏ 296	Ricky Ledee	.25	.11
❏ 297	Jim Leyritz	.15	.07
❏ 298	Tino Martinez	.25	.11
❏ 299	Paul O'Neill	.25	.11
❏ 300	Andy Pettitte	.25	.11
❏ 301	Jorge Posada	.15	.07
❏ 302	Mariano Rivera	.25	.11
❏ 303	Alfonso Soriano	1.50	.70
❏ 304	Bernie Williams ACTION	.60	.25
❏ 304A	Bernie Williams POR	.60	.25
❏ 305	Ed Yarnall	.25	.11
❏ 306	Kevin Appier	.15	.07
❏ 307	Rich Becker	.15	.07
❏ 308	Eric Chavez	.25	.11
❏ 309	Jason Giambi	.25	.11
❏ 310	Ben Grieve	.50	.23
❏ 311	Ramon Hernandez	.15	.07
❏ 312	Tim Hudson	.75	.35
❏ 313	John Jaha	.15	.07
❏ 314	Doug Jones	.15	.07
❏ 315	Omar Olivares	.15	.07
❏ 316	Mike Oquist	.15	.07
❏ 317	Matt Stairs	.15	.07
❏ 318	Miguel Tejada	.25	.11
❏ 319	Randy Velarde	.15	.07
❏ 320	Bob Abreu	.25	.11

❑ 321 Marlon Anderson	.15	.07
❑ 322 Alex Arias	.15	.07
❑ 323 Rico Brogna	.25	.11
❑ 324 Paul Byrd	.15	.07
❑ 325 Ron Gant	.25	.11
❑ 326 Doug Glanville	.25	.11
❑ 327 Wayne Gomes	.15	.07
❑ 328 Mike Lieberthal	.25	.11
❑ 329 Robert Person	.15	.07
❑ 330 Desi Relaford	.15	.07
❑ 331 Scott Rolen ACTION	.75	.35
❑ 331A Scott Rolen POR	.75	.35
❑ 332 Curt Schilling ACTION	.40	.18
❑ 332A Curt Schilling POR	.40	.18
❑ 333 Kris Benson	.25	.11
❑ 334 Adrian Brown	.15	.07
❑ 335 Brant Brown	.15	.07
❑ 336 Brian Giles	.25	.11
❑ 337 Chad Hermansen	.25	.11
❑ 338 Jason Kendall	.25	.11
❑ 339 Al Martin	.15	.07
❑ 340 Pat Meares	.15	.07
❑ 341 Warren Morris ACTION	.25	.11
❑ 341A Warren Morris POR	.25	.11
❑ 342 Todd Ritchie	.15	.07
❑ 343 Jason Schmidt	.15	.07
❑ 344 Ed Sprague	.15	.07
❑ 345 Mike Williams	.15	.07
❑ 346 Kevin Young	.25	.11
❑ 347 Rick Ankiel	3.00	1.35
❑ 348 Ricky Bottalico	.15	.07
❑ 349 Kent Bottenfield	.15	.07
❑ 350 Darren Bragg	.15	.07
❑ 351 Eric Davis	.25	.11
❑ 352 J.D. Drew ACTION	.75	.35
❑ 352A J.D. Drew POR	.75	.35
❑ 353 Adam Kennedy	.25	.11
❑ 354 Ray Lankford	.25	.11
❑ 355 Joe McEwing	.15	.07
❑ 356 Mark McGwire ACTION	3.00	1.35
❑ 356A Mark McGwire POR	3.00	1.35
❑ 357A Matt Morris ACTION	.15	.07
❑ 357B Matt Morris PORT	.15	.07
❑ 358 Darren Oliver	.15	.07
❑ 359 Edgar Renteria	.15	.07
❑ 360 Fernando Tatis	.25	.11
❑ 361 Andy Ashby	.15	.07
❑ 362 Ben Davis	.40	.18
❑ 363 Tony Gwynn ACTION	1.50	.70
❑ 363A Tony Gwynn POR	1.50	.70
❑ 364 Sterling Hitchcock	.15	.07
❑ 365 Trevor Hoffman	.25	.11
❑ 366 Damian Jackson	.15	.07
❑ 367 Wally Joyner	.25	.11
❑ 368 Dave Magadan	.15	.07
❑ 369 Gary Matthews Jr.	.15	.07
❑ 370 Phil Nevin	.15	.07
❑ 371 Eric Owens	.15	.07
❑ 372 Ruben Rivera	.15	.07
❑ 373 Reggie Sanders ACTION	.25	.11
❑ 373A Reggie Sanders POR	.25	.11
❑ 374 Quilvio Veras	.15	.07
❑ 375 Rich Aurilia	.15	.07
❑ 376 Marvin Benard	.15	.07
❑ 377 Barry Bonds ACTION	.75	.35
❑ 377A Barry Bonds POR	.75	.35
❑ 378 Ellis Burks	.25	.11
❑ 379 Shawn Estes	.15	.07
❑ 380 Livan Hernandez	.15	.07
❑ 381 Jeff Kent ACTION	.25	.11
❑ 381A Jeff Kent POR	.25	.11
❑ 382 Brent Mayne	.15	.07
❑ 383 Bill Mueller	.15	.07
❑ 384 Calvin Murray	.15	.07
❑ 385 Robb Nen	.25	.11
❑ 386 Russ Ortiz	.25	.11
❑ 387 Kirk Rueter	.15	.07
❑ 388 J.T. Snow	.25	.11
❑ 389 David Bell	.15	.07
❑ 390 Jay Buhner	.25	.11
❑ 391 Russ Davis	.15	.07
❑ 392 Freddy Garcia ACTION	.75	.35
❑ 392A Freddy Garcia POR	.75	.35
❑ 393 Ken Griffey Jr. ACTION	3.00	1.35
❑ 393A Ken Griffey Jr. POR	3.00	1.35
❑ 394 Carlos Guillen	.15	.07
❑ 395 John Halama	.15	.07
❑ 396 Brian L.Hunter	.15	.07
❑ 397 Ryan Jackson	.15	.07
❑ 398 Edgar Martinez	.25	.11
❑ 399 Gil Meche	.25	.11
❑ 400 Jose Mesa	.15	.07
❑ 401 Jamie Moyer	.15	.07
❑ 402 Alex Rodriguez ACTION	2.00	.90
❑ 402A Alex Rodriguez POR.	2.00	.90
❑ 403 Dan Wilson	.15	.07
❑ 404 Wilson Alvarez	.15	.07
❑ 405 Rolando Arrojo	.15	.07
❑ 406 Wade Boggs ACTION	.60	.25
❑ 406A Wade Boggs POR	.60	.25
❑ 407 Miguel Cairo	.15	.07
❑ 408 Jose Canseco ACTION.	.75	.35
❑ 408A Jose Canseco POR	.75	.35
❑ 409 John Flaherty	.15	.07
❑ 410 Jose Guillen	.25	.11
❑ 411 Roberto Hernandez	.25	.11
❑ 412 Terrell Lowery	.15	.07
❑ 413 Dave Martinez	.15	.07
❑ 414 Quinton McCracken	.15	.07
❑ 415 Fred McGriff ACTION	.40	.18
❑ 415A Fred McGriff POR	.40	.18
❑ 416 Ryan Rupe	.25	.11
❑ 417 Kevin Stocker	.15	.07
❑ 418 Bubba Trammell	.15	.07
❑ 419 Royce Clayton	.15	.07
❑ 420 Juan Gonzalez ACTION	1.25	.55
❑ 420A Juan Gonzalez POR.	1.25	.55
❑ 421 Tom Goodwin	.15	.07
❑ 422 Rusty Greer	.25	.11
❑ 423 Rick Helling	.15	.07
❑ 424 Roberto Kelly	.15	.07
❑ 425 Ruben Mateo	.40	.18
❑ 426 Mark McLemore	.15	.07
❑ 427 Mike Morgan	.15	.07
❑ 428 Rafael Palmeiro	.60	.25
❑ 429 Ivan Rodriguez ACTION	.75	.35
❑ 429A Ivan Rodriguez POR	.75	.35
❑ 430 Aaron Sele	.15	.07
❑ 431 Lee Stevens	.15	.07
❑ 432 John Wetteland	.15	.07
❑ 433 Todd Zeile	.25	.11
❑ 434 Jeff Zimmerman	.25	.11
❑ 435 Tony Batista	.25	.11
❑ 436 Casey Blake	.15	.07
❑ 437 Homer Bush	.25	.11
❑ 438 Chris Carpenter	.25	.11
❑ 439 Jose Cruz Jr.	.25	.11
❑ 440 Carlos Delgado ACTION	.50	.23
❑ 440A Carlos Delgado POR	.50	.23
❑ 441 Tony Fernandez	.25	.11
❑ 442 Darrin Fletcher	.15	.07
❑ 443 Alex Gonzalez	.15	.07
❑ 444 Shawn Green ACTION	.60	.25
❑ 444A Shawn Green POR	.60	.25
❑ 445 Roy Halladay	.15	.07
❑ 446 Billy Koch	.15	.07
❑ 447 David Segui	.15	.07
❑ 448 Shannon Stewart	.25	.11
❑ 449 David Wells	.25	.11
❑ 450 Vernon Wells	.25	.11
❑ SAMP Tony Gwynn Sample	2.00	.90

	MINT	NRMT
COMMON CARD (1-450)	4.00	1.80

*STARS: 10X TO 25X BASIC CARDS
*YNG.STARS: 8X TO 20X BASIC CARDS
*RC'S: 6X TO 15X BASIC CARDS
RANDOM INSERTS IN HOBBY PACKS
STATED PRINT RUN 99 SERIAL #'d SETS
DUAL VERSIONS EXIST IN PARALLEL SET

2000 Pacific Platinum Blue

	MINT	NRMT
COMMON CARD (1-450)	6.00	2.70

*STARS: 15X TO 40X BASIC CARDS
*YNG.STARS: 10X TO 25X BASIC CARDS
*RC'S: 10X TO 25X BASIC CARDS
RANDOM INSERTS IN ALL PACKS
STATED PRINT RUN 75 SERIAL #'d SETS
DUAL VERSIONS EXIST IN PARALLEL SET

2000 Pacific Premiere Date

	MINT	NRMT
COMMON CARD (1-450)	10.00	4.50

*STARS: 25X TO 60X BASIC CARDS
*YNG.STARS: 15X TO 40X BASIC CARDS
*RC'S: 15X TO 40X BASIC CARDS
STATED ODDS 1:24 HOBBY
STATED PRINT RUN 37 SERIAL #'d SETS
DUAL VERSIONS EXIST IN PARALLEL SET

2000 Pacific Cramer's Choice

	MINT	NRMT
COMPLETE SET (10)	600.00	275.00
COMMON CARD (1-10)	50.00	22.00
STATED ODDS 1:721		
❑ 1 Chipper Jones	50.00	22.00
❑ 2 Cal Ripken	80.00	36.00
❑ 3 Nomar Garciaparra	60.00	27.00
❑ 4 Sammy Sosa	60.00	27.00
❑ 5 Mike Piazza	60.00	27.00
❑ 6 Derek Jeter	60.00	27.00
❑ 7 Mark McGwire	100.00	45.00
❑ 8 Tony Gwynn	50.00	22.00

2000 Pacific Copper

		MINT	NRMT
❑ 9	Ken Griffey Jr.	100.00	45.00
❑ 10	Alex Rodriguez	60.00	27.00

2000 Pacific Diamond Leaders

	MINT	NRMT
COMPLETE SET (30)	100.00	45.00
COMMON CARD (1-30)	1.00	.45
STATED ODDS 2:25		

		MINT	NRMT
❑ 1	Garret Anderson	2.00	.90
	Chuck Finley		
	Troy Percival		
	Mo Vaughn		
❑ 2	Albert Belle	2.50	1.10
	Mike Mussina		
	B.J. Surhoff		
❑ 3	Nomar Garciaparra	8.00	3.60
	Pedro Martinez		
	Troy O'Leary		
❑ 4	Ray Durham	5.00	2.20
	Magglio Ordonez		
	Frank Thomas		
❑ 5	Bartolo Colon	3.00	1.35
	Manny Ramirez		
	Omar Vizquel		
❑ 6	Deivi Cruz	1.00	.45
	Dave Mlicki		
	Dean Palmer		
❑ 7	Johnny Damon	1.00	.45
	Jermaine Dye		
	Jose Rosado		
	Mike Sweeney		
❑ 8	Corey Koskie	1.00	.45
	Eric Milton		
	Brad Radke		
❑ 9	Orlando Hernandez	8.00	3.60
	Derek Jeter		
	Mariano Rivera		
	Bernie Williams		
❑ 10	Jason Giambi	2.50	1.10
	Tim Hudson		
	Matt Stairs		
❑ 11	Freddy Garcia	12.00	5.50
	Ken Griffey Jr.		
	Edgar Martinez		
❑ 12	Jose Canseco	3.00	1.35
	Roberto Hernandez		
	Fred McGriff		

		MINT	NRMT
❑ 13	Rafael Palmeiro	3.00	1.35
	Ivan Rodriguez		
	John Wetteland		
❑ 14	Carlos Delgado	2.00	.90
	Shannon Stewart		
	David Wells		
❑ 15	Luis Gonzalez	2.50	1.10
	Randy Johnson		
	Matt Williams		
❑ 16	Chipper Jones	6.00	2.70
	Brian Jordan		
	Greg Maddux		
❑ 17	Mark Grace	8.00	3.60
	Jon Lieber		
	Sammy Sosa		
❑ 18	Sean Casey	2.00	.90
	Pete Harnisch		
	Greg Vaughn		
❑ 19	Pedro Astacio	2.50	1.10
	Dante Bichette		
	Larry Walker		
❑ 20	Luis Castillo	1.00	.45
	Alex Fernandez		
	Preston Wilson		
❑ 21	Jeff Bagwell	3.00	1.35
	Mike Hampton		
	Billy Wagner		
❑ 22	Kevin Brown	1.50	.70
	Mark Grudzielanek		
	Eric Karros		
❑ 23	Jeromy Burnitz	2.00	.90
	Jeff Cirillo		
	Marquis Grissom		
	Hideo Nomo		
❑ 24	Vladimir Guerrero	3.00	1.35
	Dustin Hermanson		
	Ugueth Urbina		
❑ 25	Roger Cedeno	8.00	3.60
	Rickey Henderson		
	Mike Piazza		
❑ 26	Bob Abreu	1.00	.45
	Mike Lieberthal		
	Curt Schilling		
❑ 27	Brian Giles	1.00	.45
	Jason Kendall		
	Kevin Young		
❑ 28	Kent Bottenfield	15.00	6.75
	Ray Lankford		
	Mark McGwire		
❑ 29	Tony Gwynn	6.00	2.70
	Trevor Hoffman		
	Reggie Sanders		
❑ 30	Barry Bonds	3.00	1.35
	Jeff Kent		
	Russ Ortiz		

2000 Pacific Gold Crown Die Cuts

	MINT	NRMT
COMPLETE SET (36)	350.00	160.00
COMMON CARD (1-36)	3.00	1.35
STATED ODDS 1:25		

		MINT	NRMT
❑ 1	Mo Vaughn	5.00	2.20
❑ 2	Matt Williams	5.00	2.20
❑ 3	Andruw Jones	6.00	2.70
❑ 4	Chipper Jones	15.00	6.75

		MINT	NRMT
❑ 5	Greg Maddux	15.00	6.75
❑ 6	Cal Ripken	25.00	11.00
❑ 7	Nomar Garciaparra	20.00	9.00
❑ 8	Pedro Martinez	8.00	3.60
❑ 9	Sammy Sosa	20.00	9.00
❑ 10	Magglio Ordonez	4.00	1.80
❑ 11	Frank Thomas	12.00	5.50
❑ 12	Sean Casey	5.00	2.20
❑ 13	Roberto Alomar	6.00	2.70
❑ 14	Manny Ramirez	8.00	3.60
❑ 15	Larry Walker	6.00	2.70
❑ 16	Jeff Bagwell	8.00	3.60
❑ 17	Craig Biggio	5.00	2.20
❑ 18	Carlos Beltran	5.00	2.20
❑ 19	Vladimir Guerrero	8.00	3.60
❑ 20	Mike Piazza	20.00	9.00
❑ 21	Roger Clemens	15.00	6.75
❑ 22	Derek Jeter	20.00	9.00
❑ 23	Bernie Williams	6.00	2.70
❑ 24	Scott Rolen	8.00	3.60
❑ 25	Warren Morris	3.00	1.35
❑ 26	J.D. Drew	6.00	2.70
❑ 27	Mark McGwire	30.00	13.50
❑ 28	Tony Gwynn	15.00	6.75
❑ 29	Barry Bonds	8.00	3.60
❑ 30	Ken Griffey Jr.	30.00	13.50
❑ 31	Alex Rodriguez	20.00	9.00
❑ 32	Jose Canseco	8.00	3.60
❑ 33	Juan Gonzalez	12.00	5.50
❑ 34	Rafael Palmeiro	6.00	2.70
❑ 35	Ivan Rodriguez	8.00	3.60
❑ 36	Shawn Green	6.00	2.70

2000 Pacific Ornaments

	MINT	NRMT
COMPLETE SET (20)	150.00	70.00
COMMON CARD (1-20)	3.00	1.35
STATED ODDS 2:25		

		MINT	NRMT
❑ 1	Mo Vaughn	3.00	1.35
❑ 2	Chipper Jones	10.00	4.50
❑ 3	Greg Maddux	10.00	4.50
❑ 4	Cal Ripken	15.00	6.75
❑ 5	Nomar Garciaparra	12.00	5.50
❑ 6	Sammy Sosa	12.00	5.50
❑ 7	Frank Thomas	8.00	3.60
❑ 8	Manny Ramirez	5.00	2.20
❑ 9	Larry Walker	4.00	1.80
❑ 10	Jeff Bagwell	5.00	2.20
❑ 11	Mike Piazza	12.00	5.50
❑ 12	Roger Clemens	10.00	4.50
❑ 13	Derek Jeter	12.00	5.50
❑ 14	Scott Rolen	5.00	2.20
❑ 15	J.D. Drew	4.00	1.80
❑ 16	Mark McGwire	20.00	9.00
❑ 17	Tony Gwynn	10.00	4.50
❑ 18	Ken Griffey Jr.	20.00	9.00
❑ 19	Alex Rodriguez	12.00	5.50
❑ 20	Ivan Rodriguez	5.00	2.20

2000 Pacific Past and Present

	MINT	NRMT
COMPLETE SET (20)	250.00	110.00
COMMON CARD (1-20)	6.00	2.70
STATED ODDS 1:49		

PROOFS PRINT RUN 1 SERIAL #'d SET
PROOFS NOT PRICED DUE TO SCARCITY

❏ 1 Chipper Jones	15.00	6.75
❏ 2 Greg Maddux	15.00	6.75
❏ 3 Cal Ripken	25.00	11.00
❏ 4 Nomar Garciaparra	20.00	9.00
❏ 5 Pedro Martinez	8.00	3.60
❏ 6 Sammy Sosa	20.00	9.00
❏ 7 Frank Thomas	12.00	5.50
❏ 8 Manny Ramirez	8.00	3.60
❏ 9 Larry Walker	6.00	2.70
❏ 10 Jeff Bagwell	8.00	3.60
❏ 11 Mike Piazza	20.00	9.00
❏ 12 Roger Clemens	15.00	6.75
❏ 13 Derek Jeter	20.00	9.00
❏ 14 Mark McGwire	30.00	13.50
❏ 15 Tony Gwynn	15.00	6.75
❏ 16 Barry Bonds	8.00	3.60
❏ 17 Ken Griffey Jr.	30.00	13.50
❏ 18 Alex Rodriguez	20.00	9.00
❏ 19 Wade Boggs	6.00	2.70
❏ 20 Ivan Rodriguez	8.00	3.60

2000 Pacific Reflections

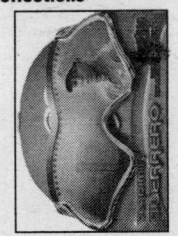

	MINT	NRMT
COMPLETE SET (20)	500.00	220.00
COMMON CARD (1-20)	12.00	5.50
STATED ODDS 1:97		

❏ 1 Andruw Jones	12.00	5.50
❏ 2 Chipper Jones	30.00	13.50
❏ 3 Cal Ripken	50.00	22.00
❏ 4 Nomar Garciaparra	40.00	18.00
❏ 5 Sammy Sosa	40.00	18.00
❏ 6 Frank Thomas	25.00	11.00
❏ 7 Manny Ramirez	15.00	6.75
❏ 8 Jeff Bagwell	15.00	6.75
❏ 9 Vladimir Guerrero	15.00	6.75
❏ 10 Mike Piazza	40.00	18.00
❏ 11 Derek Jeter	40.00	18.00
❏ 12 Bernie Williams	12.00	5.50
❏ 13 Scott Rolen	15.00	6.75
❏ 14 J.D. Drew	12.00	5.50
❏ 15 Mark McGwire	60.00	27.00
❏ 16 Tony Gwynn	30.00	13.50
❏ 17 Ken Griffey Jr.	60.00	27.00
❏ 18 Alex Rodriguez	40.00	18.00

1998 Pacific Aurora

	MINT	NRMT
COMPLETE SET (200)	50.00	22.00
COMMON CARD (1-200)	.20	.09
MINOR STARS	.30	.14
SEMISTARS	.50	.23
UNLISTED STARS	.75	.35

❏ 1 Garret Anderson	.30	.14
❏ 2 Jim Edmonds	.30	.14
❏ 3 Darin Erstad	.50	.23
❏ 4 Cecil Fielder	.30	.14
❏ 5 Chuck Finley	.30	.14
❏ 6 Todd Greene	.20	.09
❏ 7 Ken Hill	.20	.09
❏ 8 Tim Salmon	.50	.23
❏ 9 Roberto Alomar	.75	.35
❏ 10 Brady Anderson	.30	.14
❏ 11 Joe Carter	.30	.14
❏ 12 Mike Mussina	.75	.35
❏ 13 Rafael Palmeiro	.75	.35
❏ 14 Cal Ripken	3.00	1.35
❏ 15 B.J. Surhoff	.30	.14
❏ 16 Steve Avery	.20	.09
❏ 17 Nomar Garciaparra	2.50	1.10
❏ 18 Pedro Martinez	1.00	.45
❏ 19 John Valentin	.30	.14
❏ 20 Jason Varitek	.30	.14
❏ 21 Mo Vaughn	.75	.35
❏ 22 Albert Belle	.75	.35
❏ 23 Ray Durham	.30	.14
❏ 24 Magglio Ordonez	2.50	1.10
❏ 25 Frank Thomas	1.50	.70
❏ 26 Robin Ventura	.30	.14
❏ 27 Sandy Alomar Jr.	.30	.14
❏ 28 Travis Fryman	.30	.14
❏ 29 Dwight Gooden	.20	.09
❏ 30 David Justice	.30	.14
❏ 31 Kenny Lofton	.50	.23
❏ 32 Manny Ramirez	1.00	.45
❏ 33 Jim Thome	.75	.35
❏ 34 Omar Vizquel	.30	.14
❏ 35 Enrique Wilson	.20	.09
❏ 36 Jaret Wright	.30	.14
❏ 37 Tony Clark	.30	.14
❏ 38 Bobby Higginson	.30	.14
❏ 39 Brian Hunter	.20	.09
❏ 40 Bip Roberts	.20	.09
❏ 41 Justin Thompson	.20	.09
❏ 42 Jeff Conine	.20	.09
❏ 43 Johnny Damon	.30	.14
❏ 44 Jermaine Dye	.30	.14
❏ 45 Jeff King	.20	.09
❏ 46 Jeff Montgomery	.20	.09
❏ 47 Hal Morris	.20	.09
❏ 48 Dean Palmer	.30	.14
❏ 49 Terry Pendleton	.30	.14
❏ 50 Rick Aguilera	.20	.09
❏ 51 Marty Cordova	.20	.09
❏ 52 Paul Molitor	.75	.35
❏ 53 Otis Nixon	.20	.09
❏ 54 Brad Radke	.30	.14
❏ 55 Terry Steinbach	.20	.09
❏ 56 Todd Walker	.30	.14
❏ 57 Chili Davis	.30	.14
❏ 58 Derek Jeter	2.50	1.10
❏ 59 Chuck Knoblauch	.30	.14
❏ 60 Tino Martinez	.30	.14
❏ 61 Paul O'Neill	.30	.14
❏ 62 Andy Pettitte	.30	.14
❏ 63 Mariano Rivera	.30	.14
❏ 64 Bernie Williams	.75	.35
❏ 65 Jason Giambi	.30	.14
❏ 66 Ben Grieve	.75	.45
❏ 67 Rickey Henderson	1.00	.45
❏ 68 A.J. Hinch	.20	.09
❏ 69 Kenny Rogers	.20	.09
❏ 70 Jay Buhner	.30	.14
❏ 71 Joey Cora	.20	.09
❏ 72 Ken Griffey Jr.	4.00	1.80
❏ 73 Randy Johnson	.75	.35
❏ 74 Edgar Martinez	.30	.14
❏ 75 Jamie Moyer	.20	.09
❏ 76 Alex Rodriguez	2.50	1.10
❏ 77 David Segui	.20	.09
❏ 78 Rolando Arrojo	.75	.35
❏ 79 Wade Boggs	.75	.35
❏ 80 Roberto Hernandez	.20	.09
❏ 81 Dave Martinez	.20	.09
❏ 82 Fred McGriff	.50	.23
❏ 83 Paul Sorrento	.20	.09
❏ 84 Kevin Stocker	.20	.09
❏ 85 Will Clark	.75	.35
❏ 86 Juan Gonzalez	1.50	.70
❏ 87 Tom Goodwin	.20	.09
❏ 88 Rusty Greer	.30	.14
❏ 89 Ivan Rodriguez	1.00	.45
❏ 90 John Wetteland	.30	.14
❏ 91 Jose Canseco	1.00	.45
❏ 92 Roger Clemens	2.00	.90
❏ 93 Jose Cruz Jr.	.30	.14
❏ 94 Carlos Delgado	.75	.35
❏ 95 Pat Hentgen	.20	.09
❏ 96 Jay Bell	.20	.09
❏ 97 Andy Benes	.20	.09
❏ 98 Karim Garcia	.20	.09
❏ 99 Travis Lee	.50	.23
❏ 100 Devon White	.20	.09
❏ 101 Matt Williams	.75	.35
❏ 102 Andres Galarraga	.50	.23
❏ 103 Tom Glavine	.75	.35
❏ 104 Andruw Jones	.75	.35
❏ 105 Chipper Jones	2.00	.90
❏ 106 Ryan Klesko	.30	.14
❏ 107 Javy Lopez	.30	.14
❏ 108 Greg Maddux	2.00	.90
❏ 109 Walt Weiss	.30	.14
❏ 110 Rod Beck	.20	.09
❏ 111 Jeff Blauser	.20	.09
❏ 112 Mark Grace	.50	.23
❏ 113 Lance Johnson	.20	.09
❏ 114 Mickey Morandini	.20	.09
❏ 115 Henry Rodriguez	.30	.14
❏ 116 Sammy Sosa	2.50	1.10
❏ 117 Kerry Wood	1.00	.45
❏ 118 Lenny Harris	.20	.09
❏ 119 Damian Jackson	.20	.09
❏ 120 Barry Larkin	.75	.35
❏ 121 Reggie Sanders	.20	.09
❏ 122 Brett Tomko	.20	.09
❏ 123 Dante Bichette	.30	.14
❏ 124 Ellis Burks	.30	.14
❏ 125 Vinny Castilla	.30	.14
❏ 126 Todd Helton	1.00	.45
❏ 127 Darryl Kile	.20	.09
❏ 128 Larry Walker	.75	.35
❏ 129 Bobby Bonilla	.30	.14
❏ 130 Livan Hernandez	.20	.09
❏ 131 Charles Johnson	.30	.14
❏ 132 Derrek Lee	.20	.09
❏ 133 Edgar Renteria	.20	.09
❏ 134 Gary Sheffield	.30	.14
❏ 135 Moises Alou	.30	.14
❏ 136 Jeff Bagwell	1.00	.45
❏ 137 Derek Bell	.30	.14
❏ 138 Craig Biggio	.75	.35
❏ 139 John Halama	.30	.14
❏ 140 Mike Hampton	.30	.14
❏ 141 Richard Hidalgo	.30	.14
❏ 142 Wilton Guerrero	.20	.09

❑ 143	Todd Hollandsworth	.20	.09
❑ 144	Eric Karros	.30	.14
❑ 145	Paul Konerko	.30	.14
❑ 146	Raul Mondesi	.30	.14
❑ 147	Hideo Nomo	.75	.35
❑ 148	Chan Ho Park	.30	.14
❑ 149	Mike Piazza	2.50	1.10
❑ 150	Jeromy Burnitz	.30	.14
❑ 151	Todd Dunn	.20	.09
❑ 152	Marquis Grissom	.20	.09
❑ 153	John Jaha	.30	.14
❑ 154	Dave Nilsson	.20	.09
❑ 155	Fernando Vina	.20	.09
❑ 156	Mark Grudzielanek	.20	.09
❑ 157	Vladimir Guerrero	1.00	.45
❑ 158	F.P. Santangelo	.20	.09
❑ 159	Jose Vidro	.20	.09
❑ 160	Rondell White	.30	.14
❑ 161	Edgardo Alfonzo	.50	.23
❑ 162	Carlos Baerga	.30	.14
❑ 163	John Franco	.20	.09
❑ 164	Todd Hundley	.30	.14
❑ 165	Brian McRae	.20	.09
❑ 166	John Olerud	.30	.14
❑ 167	Rey Ordonez	.20	.09
❑ 168	Masato Yoshii	.50	.23
❑ 169	Ricky Bottalico	.20	.09
❑ 170	Doug Glanville	.30	.14
❑ 171	Gregg Jefferies	.20	.09
❑ 172	Desi Relaford	.20	.09
❑ 173	Scott Rolen	1.00	.45
❑ 174	Curt Schilling	.50	.23
❑ 175	Jose Guillen	.30	.14
❑ 176	Jason Kendall	.30	.14
❑ 177	Al Martin	.20	.09
❑ 178	Doug Strange	.20	.09
❑ 179	Kevin Young	.30	.14
❑ 180	Royce Clayton	.20	.09
❑ 181	Delino DeShields	.20	.09
❑ 182	Gary Gaetti	.30	.14
❑ 183	Ron Gant	.30	.14
❑ 184	Brian Jordan	.30	.14
❑ 185	Ray Lankford	.30	.14
❑ 186	Willie McGee	.30	.14
❑ 187	Mark McGwire	5.00	2.20
❑ 188	Kevin Brown	.50	.23
❑ 189	Ken Caminiti	.30	.14
❑ 190	Steve Finley	.30	.14
❑ 191	Tony Gwynn	2.00	.90
❑ 192	Wally Joyner	.30	.14
❑ 193	Ruben Rivera	.20	.09
❑ 194	Quivio Veras	.20	.09
❑ 195	Barry Bonds	1.00	.45
❑ 196	Shawn Estes	.20	.09
❑ 197	Orel Hershiser	.30	.14
❑ 198	Jeff Kent	.30	.14
❑ 199	Robb Nen	.20	.09
❑ 200	J.T. Snow	.30	.14
❑ NNO	Tony Gwynn Sample..	3.00	1.35

1998 Pacific Aurora Cubes

	MINT	NRMT
COMPLETE SET (20)	200.00	90.00
COMMON CARD (1-20)	2.00	.90
SEMISTARS	3.00	1.35
UNLISTED STARS	5.00	2.20

ONE PER HOBBY BOX

❑ 1	Travis Lee	3.00	1.35
❑ 2	Chipper Jones	12.00	5.50
❑ 3	Greg Maddux	12.00	5.50
❑ 4	Cal Ripken	20.00	9.00
❑ 5	Nomar Garciaparra	15.00	6.75
❑ 6	Frank Thomas	10.00	4.50
❑ 7	Manny Ramirez	6.00	2.70
❑ 8	Larry Walker	5.00	2.20
❑ 9	Hideo Nomo	5.00	2.20
❑ 10	Mike Piazza	15.00	6.75
❑ 11	Derek Jeter	15.00	6.75
❑ 12	Ben Grieve	5.00	2.20
❑ 13	Mark McGwire	30.00	13.50
❑ 14	Tony Gwynn	12.00	5.50
❑ 15	Barry Bonds	6.00	2.70
❑ 16	Ken Griffey Jr.	25.00	11.00
❑ 17	Alex Rodriguez	15.00	6.75
❑ 18	Wade Boggs	5.00	2.20
❑ 19	Juan Gonzalez	10.00	4.50
❑ 20	Jose Cruz Jr.	2.00	.90

1998 Pacific Aurora Hardball Cel-Fusions

	MINT	NRMT
COMPLETE SET (20)	600.00	275.00
COMMON CARD (1-20)	5.00	2.20
SEMISTARS	8.00	3.60
UNLISTED STARS	12.00	5.50
STATED ODDS 1:73		

❑ 1	Travis Lee	8.00	3.60
❑ 2	Chipper Jones	30.00	13.50
❑ 3	Greg Maddux	30.00	13.50
❑ 4	Cal Ripken	50.00	22.00
❑ 5	Nomar Garciaparra	40.00	18.00
❑ 6	Frank Thomas	25.00	11.00
❑ 7	David Justice	5.00	2.20
❑ 8	Jeff Bagwell	15.00	6.75
❑ 9	Hideo Nomo	12.00	5.50
❑ 10	Mike Piazza	40.00	18.00
❑ 11	Derek Jeter	40.00	18.00
❑ 12	Ben Grieve	12.00	5.50
❑ 13	Scott Rolen	15.00	6.75
❑ 14	Mark McGwire	80.00	36.00
❑ 15	Tony Gwynn	30.00	13.50
❑ 16	Ken Griffey Jr.	60.00	27.00
❑ 17	Alex Rodriguez	40.00	18.00
❑ 18	Ivan Rodriguez	15.00	6.75
❑ 19	Roger Clemens	30.00	13.50
❑ 20	Jose Cruz Jr.	5.00	2.20

1998 Pacific Aurora Kings of the Major Leagues

	MINT	NRMT
COMPLETE SET (10)	800.00	350.00
COMMON CARD (1-10)	50.00	22.00
STATED ODDS 1:361		

❑ 1	Chipper Jones	60.00	27.00
❑ 2	Greg Maddux	60.00	27.00
❑ 3	Cal Ripken	100.00	45.00

❑ 4	Nomar Garciaparra	80.00	36.00
❑ 5	Frank Thomas	50.00	22.00
❑ 6	Mike Piazza	80.00	36.00
❑ 7	Mark McGwire	150.00	70.00
❑ 8	Tony Gwynn	60.00	27.00
❑ 9	Ken Griffey Jr.	120.00	55.00
❑ 10	Alex Rodriguez	80.00	36.00

1998 Pacific Aurora On Deck Laser Cuts

	MINT	NRMT
COMPLETE SET (20)	100.00	45.00
COMMON CARD (1-20)	1.00	.45
STATED ODDS 4:37 HOBBY		

❑ 1	Travis Lee	1.50	.70
❑ 2	Chipper Jones	6.00	2.70
❑ 3	Greg Maddux	6.00	2.70
❑ 4	Cal Ripken	10.00	4.50
❑ 5	Nomar Garciaparra	8.00	3.60
❑ 6	Frank Thomas	5.00	2.20
❑ 7	Manny Ramirez	3.00	1.35
❑ 8	Larry Walker	2.50	1.10
❑ 9	Hideo Nomo	2.50	1.10
❑ 10	Mike Piazza	8.00	3.60
❑ 11	Derek Jeter	8.00	3.60
❑ 12	Ben Grieve	2.50	1.10
❑ 13	Mark McGwire	15.00	6.75
❑ 14	Tony Gwynn	6.00	2.70
❑ 15	Barry Bonds	3.00	1.35
❑ 16	Ken Griffey Jr.	12.00	5.50
❑ 17	Alex Rodriguez	8.00	3.60
❑ 18	Wade Boggs	2.50	1.10
❑ 19	Juan Gonzalez	5.00	2.20
❑ 20	Jose Cruz Jr.	1.00	.45

1998 Pacific Aurora Pennant Fever

	MINT	NRMT
COMPLETE SET (50)	30.00	13.50
COMMON CARD (1-50)	.30	.14

ONE PER PACK
*RED CARDS: 1.5X TO 4X BASE CARD HI
RED STATED ODDS 1:4 RETAIL
*SILVER CARDS: 12.5X TO 30X BASE CARD HI
SILVER: RANDOM INSERTS IN RETAIL PACKS

SILVER PRINT RUN 250 SERIAL #'d SETS
*PL.BLUE CARDS: 25X TO 60X BASE CARD HI
PLAT.BLUE: RANDOM INSERTS IN ALL PACKS
PLAT.BLUE PRINT RUN 100 SERIAL #'d SETS
*COPPER CARDS: 80X TO 200X BASE CARD HI
COPPER: RANDOM INSERTS IN HOBBY PACKS
COPPER PRINT RUN 20 SERIAL #'d SETS

#	Player	MINT	NRMT
1	Tony Gwynn	2.00	.90
2	Derek Jeter	2.50	1.10
3	Alex Rodriguez	2.50	1.10
4	Paul Molitor	.75	.35
5	Nomar Garciaparra	2.50	1.10
6	Jeff Bagwell	1.00	.45
7	Ivan Rodriguez	1.00	.45
8	Cal Ripken	3.00	1.35
9	Matt Williams	.75	.35
10	Chipper Jones	2.00	.90
11	Edgar Martinez	.30	.14
12	Wade Boggs	.75	.35
13	Paul Konerko	.30	.14
14	Ben Grieve	.75	.35
15	Sandy Alomar Jr.	.30	.14
16	Travis Lee	.50	.23
17	Scott Rolen	1.25	.55
18	Ryan Klesko	.30	.14
19	Juan Gonzalez	1.50	.70
20	Albert Belle	.75	.35
21	Roger Clemens	2.00	.90
22	Javy Lopez	.30	.14
23	Jose Cruz Jr.	.30	.14
24	Ken Griffey Jr.	4.00	1.80
25	Mark McGwire	5.00	2.20
26	Brady Anderson	.30	.14
27	Jaret Wright	.30	.14
28	Roberto Alomar	.75	.35
29	Joe Carter	.30	.14
30	Hideo Nomo	.75	.35
31	Mike Piazza	2.50	1.10
32	Andres Galarraga	.50	.23
33	Larry Walker	.75	.35
34	Tim Salmon	.50	.23
35	Frank Thomas	1.50	.70
36	Moises Alou	.30	.14
37	David Justice	.30	.14
38	Manny Ramirez	1.00	.45
39	Jim Edmonds	.30	.14
40	Barry Bonds	1.00	.45
41	Jim Thome	.75	.35
42	Mo Vaughn	.75	.35
43	Rafael Palmeiro	.75	.35
44	Darin Erstad	.50	.23
45	Pedro Martinez	1.00	.45
46	Greg Maddux	2.00	.90
47	Jose Canseco	1.00	.45
48	Vladimir Guerrero	1.00	.45
49	Bernie Williams	.75	.35
50	Randy Johnson	.75	.35

1999 Pacific Aurora

	MINT	NRMT
COMPLETE SET (200)	60.00	27.00
COMMON CARD (1-200)	.20	.09
MINOR STARS	.30	.14
SEMISTARS	.50	.23
UNLISTED STARS	.75	.35

#	Player	MINT	NRMT
1	Garret Anderson	.30	.14
2	Jim Edmonds	.30	.14
3	Darin Erstad	.50	.23
4	Matt Luke	.20	.09
5	Tim Salmon	.50	.23
6	Mo Vaughn	.75	.35
7	Jay Bell	.30	.14
8	David Dellucci	.20	.09
9	Steve Finley	.30	.14
10	Bernard Gilkey	.20	.09
11	Randy Johnson	.75	.35
12	Travis Lee	.60	.35
13	Matt Williams	.75	.35
14	Andres Galarraga	.50	.23
15	Tom Glavine	.75	.35
16	Andruw Jones	.75	.35
17	Chipper Jones	2.00	.90
18	Brian Jordan	.30	.14
19	Javy Lopez	.30	.14
20	Greg Maddux	2.00	.90
21	Albert Belle	.75	.35
22	Will Clark	.75	.35
23	Scott Erickson	.20	.09
24	Mike Mussina	.75	.35
25	Cal Ripken	3.00	1.35
26	B.J. Surhoff	.20	.14
27	Nomar Garciaparra	2.50	1.10
28	Reggie Jefferson	.20	.09
29	Darren Lewis	.20	.09
30	Pedro Martinez	1.00	.45
31	John Valentin	.30	.14
32	Rod Beck	.20	.09
33	Mark Grace	.50	.23
34	Lance Johnson	.20	.09
35	Mickey Morandini	.20	.09
36	Sammy Sosa	2.50	1.10
37	Kerry Wood	.75	.35
38	James Baldwin	.20	.09
39	Mike Caruso	.20	.09
40	Ray Durham	.30	.14
41	Magglio Ordonez	.75	.35
42	Frank Thomas	1.50	.70
43	Aaron Boone	.20	.09
44	Sean Casey	.75	.35
45	Barry Larkin	.75	.35
46	Hal Morris	.20	.09
47	Denny Neagle	.20	.09
48	Greg Vaughn	.30	.14
49	Pat Watkins	.20	.09
50	Roberto Alomar	.75	.35
51	Sandy Alomar Jr.	.30	.14
52	David Justice	.30	.14
53	Kenny Lofton	.50	.23
54	Manny Ramirez	1.00	.45
55	Richie Sexson	.50	.23
56	Jim Thome	.75	.35
57	Omar Vizquel	.30	.14
58	Dante Bichette	.30	.14
59	Vinny Castilla	.30	.14
60	Edgard Clemente	.20	.09
61	Derrick Gibson	.20	.09
62	Todd Helton	.75	.35
63	Darryl Kile	.20	.09
64	Larry Walker	.75	.35
65	Tony Clark	.30	.14
66	Damion Easley	.30	.14
67	Bob Higginson	.30	.14
68	Brian Hunter	.20	.09
69	Dean Palmer	.30	.14
70	Justin Thompson	.20	.09
71	Craig Counsell	.20	.09
72	Todd Dunwoody	.20	.09
73	Cliff Floyd	.30	.14
74	Alex Gonzalez	.30	.14
75	Livan Hernandez	.20	.09
76	Mark Kotsay	.20	.09
77	Derrek Lee	.20	.09
78	Moises Alou	.30	.14
79	Jeff Bagwell	1.00	.45
80	Derek Bell	.30	.14
81	Craig Biggio	.75	.35
82	Ken Caminiti	.30	.14
83	Richard Hidalgo	.30	.14
84	Shane Reynolds	.30	.14
85	Jeff Conine	.20	.09
86	Johnny Damon	.30	.14
87	Jermaine Dye	.30	.14
88	Jeff King	.20	.09
89	Jeff Montgomery	.20	.09
90	Mike Sweeney	.30	.14
91	Kevin Brown	.50	.23
92	Mark Grudzielanek	.20	.09
93	Eric Karros	.30	.14
94	Raul Mondesi	.30	.14
95	Chan Ho Park	.30	.14
96	Gary Sheffield	.30	.14
97	Jeromy Burnitz	.30	.14
98	Jeff Cirillo	.20	.09
99	Marquis Grissom	.30	.14
100	Geoff Jenkins	.30	.14
101	Dave Nilsson	.20	.09
102	Jose Valentin	.20	.09
103	Fernando Vina	.20	.09
104	Marty Cordova	.20	.09
105	Matt Lawton	.20	.09
106	David Ortiz	.20	.09
107	Brad Radke	.30	.14
108	Todd Walker	.30	.14
109	Shane Andrews	.20	.09
110	Orlando Cabrera	.20	.09
111	Brad Fullmer	.20	.09
112	Vladimir Guerrero	1.00	.45
113	Wilton Guerrero	.20	.09
114	Carl Pavano	.20	.09
115	Fernando Seguignol	.30	.14
116	Ugueth Urbina	.20	.09
117	Edgardo Alfonzo	.50	.23
118	Bobby Bonilla	.30	.14
119	Rickey Henderson	1.00	.45
120	Hideo Nomo	.75	.35
121	John Olerud	.30	.14
122	Rey Ordonez	.30	.14
123	Mike Piazza	2.50	1.10
124	Masato Yoshii	.30	.14
125	Scott Brosius	.30	.14
126	Orlando Hernandez	.75	.35
127	Hideki Irabu	.30	.14
128	Derek Jeter	2.50	1.10
129	Chuck Knoblauch	.30	.14
130	Tino Martinez	.30	.14
131	Jorge Posada	.20	.09
132	Bernie Williams	.75	.35
133	Eric Chavez	.50	.23
134	Ryan Christenson	.20	.09
135	Jason Giambi	.30	.14
136	Ben Grieve	.75	.35
137	A.J. Hinch	.20	.09
138	Matt Stairs	.30	.14
139	Miguel Tejada	.30	.14
140	Bob Abreu	.20	.09
141	Gary Bennett	.20	.09
142	Desi Relaford	.20	.09
143	Scott Rolen	1.00	.45
144	Curt Schilling	.50	.23
145	Kevin Sefcik	.20	.09
146	Brian Giles	.30	.14
147	Jose Guillen	.20	.09
148	Jason Kendall	.30	.14
149	Aramis Ramirez	.50	.23
150	Tony Womack	.30	.14
151	Kevin Young	.30	.14

		MINT	NRMT
❑ 152	Eric Davis	.30	.14
❑ 153	J.D. Drew	1.25	.55
❑ 154	Ray Lankford	.30	.14
❑ 155	Eli Marrero	.20	.09
❑ 156	Mark McGwire	5.00	2.20
❑ 157	Luis Ordaz	.20	.09
❑ 158	Edgar Renteria	.20	.09
❑ 159	Andy Ashby	.20	.09
❑ 160	Tony Gwynn	2.00	.90
❑ 161	Trevor Hoffman	.30	.14
❑ 162	Wally Joyner	.30	.14
❑ 163	Jim Leyritz	.20	.09
❑ 164	Ruben Rivera	.20	.09
❑ 165	Reggie Sanders	.20	.09
❑ 166	Quilvio Veras	.20	.09
❑ 167	Rich Aurilia	.20	.09
❑ 168	Marvin Benard	.20	.09
❑ 169	Barry Bonds	1.00	.45
❑ 170	Ellis Burks	.30	.14
❑ 171	Jeff Kent	.30	.14
❑ 172	Bill Mueller	.20	.09
❑ 173	J.T. Snow	.30	.14
❑ 174	Jay Buhner	.20	.09
❑ 175	Jeff Fassero	.20	.09
❑ 176	Ken Griffey Jr.	4.00	1.80
❑ 177	Carlos Guillen	.20	.09
❑ 178	Edgar Martinez	.30	.14
❑ 179	Alex Rodriguez	2.50	1.10
❑ 180	David Segui	.20	.09
❑ 181	Dan Wilson	.20	.09
❑ 182	Rolando Arrojo	.20	.09
❑ 183	Wade Boggs	.75	.35
❑ 184	Jose Canseco	1.00	.45
❑ 185	Aaron Ledesma	.20	.09
❑ 186	Dave Martinez	.20	.09
❑ 187	Quinton McCracken	.20	.09
❑ 188	Fred McGriff	.50	.23
❑ 189	Juan Gonzalez	1.50	.70
❑ 190	Tom Goodwin	.20	.09
❑ 191	Rusty Greer	.30	.14
❑ 192	Roberto Kelly	.20	.09
❑ 193	Rafael Palmeiro	.75	.35
❑ 194	Ivan Rodriguez	1.00	.45
❑ 195	Roger Clemens	2.00	.90
❑ 196	Jose Cruz Jr.	.30	.14
❑ 197	Carlos Delgado	.75	.35
❑ 198	Alex Gonzalez	.30	.14
❑ 199	Roy Halladay	.30	.14
❑ 200	Pat Hentgen	.20	.09

1999 Pacific Aurora Opening Day

	MINT	NRMT
COMMON CARD (1-200)	12.00	5.50

*STARS: 25X to 60X BASIC CARDS
*YNG.STARS: 20X TO 50X BASIC CARDS
STATED ODDS ONE PER 36 CT.HOBBY BOX
STATED PRINT RUN 31 SERIAL #'d SETS

1999 Pacific Aurora Complete Players

	MINT	NRMT
COMPLETE SET (20)	400.00	180.00
COMMON CARD (1A-10B)	8.00	3.60

RANDOM INSERTS IN HOB/RET PACKS

STATED PRINT RUN 299 SERIAL #'d A CARDS
STATED PRINT RUN 299 SERIAL #'d B CARDS
A AND B CARDS ARE EQUALLY VALUED!
A CARDS LISTED BELOW

		MINT	NRMT
❑ 1A	Cal Ripken	50.00	22.00
❑ 1B	Cal Ripken	50.00	22.00
❑ 2A	Nomar Garciaparra	40.00	18.00
❑ 2B	Nomar Garciaparra	40.00	18.00
❑ 3A	Sammy Sosa	40.00	18.00
❑ 3B	Sammy Sosa	40.00	18.00
❑ 4A	Kerry Wood	12.00	5.50
❑ 4B	Kerry Wood	12.00	5.50
❑ 5A	Frank Thomas	25.00	11.00
❑ 5B	Frank Thomas	25.00	11.00
❑ 6A	Mike Piazza	40.00	18.00
❑ 6B	Mike Piazza	40.00	18.00
❑ 7A	Mark McGwire	80.00	36.00
❑ 7B	Mark McGwire	80.00	36.00
❑ 8A	Tony Gwynn	30.00	13.50
❑ 8B	Tony Gwynn	30.00	13.50
❑ 9A	Ken Griffey Jr.	60.00	27.00
❑ 9B	Ken Griffey Jr.	60.00	27.00
❑ 10A	Alex Rodriguez	40.00	18.00
❑ 10B	Alex Rodriguez	40.00	18.00

1999 Pacific Aurora Kings of the Major Leagues

	MINT	NRMT
COMPLETE SET (10)	1200.00	550.00
COMMON CARD (1-10)	25.00	11.00

STATED ODDS 1:361 HOB/RET

		MINT	NRMT
❑ 1	Cal Ripken	150.00	70.00
❑ 2	Nomar Garciaparra	120.00	55.00
❑ 3	Sammy Sosa	120.00	55.00
❑ 4	Kerry Wood	25.00	11.00
❑ 5	Frank Thomas	80.00	36.00
❑ 6	Mike Piazza	120.00	55.00
❑ 7	Mark McGwire	250.00	110.00
❑ 8	Tony Gwynn	100.00	55.00
❑ 9	Ken Griffey Jr.	200.00	90.00
❑ 10	Alex Rodriguez	120.00	55.00

1999 Pacific Aurora On Deck Laser-Cuts

	MINT	NRMT
COMPLETE SET (20)	120.00	55.00
COMMON CARD (1-20)	2.50	1.10

STATED ODDS 4:37 HOBBY

		MINT	NRMT
❑ 1	Chipper Jones	8.00	3.60
❑ 2	Cal Ripken	12.00	5.50
❑ 3	Nomar Garciaparra	10.00	4.50
❑ 4	Sammy Sosa	10.00	4.50
❑ 5	Frank Thomas	6.00	2.70
❑ 6	Manny Ramirez	4.00	1.80
❑ 7	Todd Helton	3.00	1.35
❑ 8	Larry Walker	2.50	1.10
❑ 9	Jeff Bagwell	4.00	1.80
❑ 10	Vladimir Guerrero	4.00	1.80
❑ 11	Mike Piazza	10.00	4.50
❑ 12	Derek Jeter	10.00	4.50
❑ 13	Bernie Williams	3.00	1.35
❑ 14	J.D. Drew	4.00	1.80
❑ 15	Mark McGwire	20.00	9.00
❑ 16	Tony Gwynn	8.00	3.60
❑ 17	Ken Griffey Jr.	15.00	6.75
❑ 18	Alex Rodriguez	10.00	4.50
❑ 19	Juan Gonzalez	6.00	2.70
❑ 20	Ivan Rodriguez	4.00	1.80

1999 Pacific Aurora Pennant Fever

	MINT	NRMT
COMPLETE SET (20)	120.00	55.00
COMMON CARD (1-20)	1.50	.70

STATED ODDS 4:37 HOB/RET
*SILVER: 1.5X TO 4X HI COLUMN
SILVER: RANDOM INSERTS IN RETAIL PACKS
SILVER PRINT RUN 250 SERIAL #'d SETS
*PLAT.BLUE: 3X TO 8X HI COLUMN
PLAT.BLUE: RANDOM INS.IN HOB/RET.PACKS
PLAT.BLUE PRINT RUN 100 SERIAL #'d SETS
*COPPER: 10X TO 25X HI COLUMN
COPPER: RANDOM INSERTS IN HOBBY PACKS
COPPER PRINT RUN 20 SERIAL #'d SETS
GWYNN SIGNED 97 P.FEVER BASIC CARDS
GWYNN SIGNED 1 P.FEVER COPPER CARD
GWYNN SIGNED 1 P.FEVER P.BLUE CARD
GWYNN SIGNED 1 P.FEVER SILVER CARD

		MINT	NRMT
❑ 1	Chipper Jones	6.00	2.70
❑ 2	Greg Maddux	6.00	2.70
❑ 3	Cal Ripken	10.00	4.50
❑ 4	Nomar Garciaparra	8.00	3.60
❑ 5	Sammy Sosa	8.00	3.60
❑ 6	Kerry Wood	1.50	.70
❑ 7	Frank Thomas	5.00	2.20
❑ 8	Manny Ramirez	3.00	1.35
❑ 9	Todd Helton	2.50	1.10
❑ 10	Jeff Bagwell	3.00	1.35
❑ 11	Mike Piazza	8.00	3.60
❑ 12	Derek Jeter	8.00	3.60
❑ 13	Bernie Williams	2.50	1.10
❑ 14	J.D. Drew	3.00	1.35
❑ 15	Mark McGwire	15.00	6.75
❑ 16	Tony Gwynn	6.00	2.70
❑ 17	Ken Griffey Jr.	12.00	5.50
❑ 18	Alex Rodriguez	8.00	3.60

	MINT	NRMT
□ 19 Juan Gonzalez	5.00	2.20
□ 20 Ivan Rodriguez	3.00	1.35
□ S16 Tony Gwynn AU/97		

1999 Pacific Aurora Styrotechs

	MINT	NRMT
COMPLETE SET (20)	300.00	135.00
COMMON CARD (1-20)	4.00	1.80
UNLISTED STARS	6.00	2.70
STATED ODDS 1:37 HOB/RET		

□ 1 Chipper Jones	15.00	6.75
□ 2 Greg Maddux	15.00	6.75
□ 3 Cal Ripken	25.00	11.00
□ 4 Nomar Garciaparra	20.00	9.00
□ 5 Sammy Sosa	20.00	9.00
□ 6 Kerry Wood	4.00	1.80
□ 7 Frank Thomas	12.00	5.50
□ 8 Manny Ramirez	8.00	3.60
□ 9 Larry Walker	6.00	2.70
□ 10 Jeff Bagwell	8.00	3.60
□ 11 Mike Piazza	20.00	9.00
□ 12 Derek Jeter	20.00	9.00
□ 13 Bernie Williams	6.00	2.70
□ 14 J.D. Drew	8.00	3.60
□ 15 Mark McGwire	40.00	18.00
□ 16 Tony Gwynn	15.00	6.75
□ 17 Ken Griffey Jr.	30.00	13.50
□ 18 Alex Rodriguez	20.00	9.00
□ 19 Juan Gonzalez	12.00	5.50
□ 20 Ivan Rodriguez	8.00	3.60

1999 Pacific Crown Collection

	MINT	NRMT
COMPLETE SET (300)	50.00	22.00
COMMON CARD (1-300)	.15	.07
MINOR STARS	.25	.11
SEMISTARS	.40	.18
UNLISTED STARS	.60	.25

□ 1 Garret Anderson	.25	.11
□ 2 Gary DiSarcina	.15	.07
□ 3 Jim Edmonds	.25	.11
□ 4 Darin Erstad	.40	.18
□ 5 Shigetoshi Hasegawa	.15	.07
□ 6 Norberto Martin	.15	.07
□ 7 Omar Olivares	.15	.07
□ 8 Orlando Palmeiro	.15	.07
□ 9 Tim Salmon	.40	.18
□ 10 Randy Velarde	.15	.07
□ 11 Tony Batista	.15	.07
□ 12 Jay Bell	.25	.11
□ 13 Yamil Benitez	.15	.07
□ 14 Omar Daal	.15	.07
□ 15 David Dellucci	.15	.07
□ 16 Karim Garcia	.15	.07
□ 17 Travis Lee	.40	.18
□ 18 Felix Rodriguez	.15	.07
□ 19 Devon White	.15	.07
□ 20 Matt Williams	.60	.25
□ 21 Andres Galarraga	.40	.18
□ 22 Tom Glavine	.25	.11
□ 23 Ozzie Guillen	.15	.07
□ 24 Andruw Jones	.60	.25
□ 25 Chipper Jones	1.50	.70
□ 26 Ryan Klesko	.25	.11
□ 27 Javy Lopez	.25	.11
□ 28 Greg Maddux	1.50	.70
□ 29 Dennis Martinez	.25	.11
□ 30 Odalis Perez	.15	.07
□ 31 Rudy Seanez	.15	.07
□ 32 John Smoltz	.40	.18
□ 33 Roberto Alomar	.60	.25
□ 34 Armando Benitez	.15	.07
□ 35 Scott Erickson	.15	.07
□ 36 Juan Guzman	.15	.07
□ 37 Mike Mussina	.60	.25
□ 38 Jesse Orosco	.15	.07
□ 39 Rafael Palmeiro	.60	.25
□ 40 Sidney Ponson	.15	.07
□ 41 Cal Ripken	2.50	1.10
□ 42 B.J. Surhoff	.25	.11
□ 43 Lenny Webster	.15	.07
□ 44 Dennis Eckersley	.25	.11
□ 45 Nomar Garciaparra	2.00	.90
□ 46 Darren Lewis	.15	.07
□ 47 Pedro Martinez	.75	.35
□ 48 Troy O'Leary	.15	.07
□ 49 Bret Saberhagen	.25	.11
□ 50 John Valentin	.15	.07
□ 51 Mo Vaughn	.60	.25
□ 52 Tim Wakefield	.15	.07
□ 53 Manny Alexander	.15	.07
□ 54 Rod Beck	.15	.07
□ 55 Gary Gaetti	.25	.11
□ 56 Mark Grace	.40	.18
□ 57 Felix Heredia	.15	.07
□ 58 Jose Hernandez	.15	.07
□ 59 Henry Rodriguez	.25	.11
□ 60 Sammy Sosa	2.00	.90
□ 61 Kevin Tapani	.15	.07
□ 62 Kerry Wood	.60	.25
□ 63 James Baldwin	.15	.07
□ 64 Albert Belle	.60	.25
□ 65 Mike Caruso	.15	.07
□ 66 Carlos Castillo	.15	.07
□ 67 Wil Cordero	.15	.07
□ 68 Jaime Navarro	.15	.07
□ 69 Magglio Ordonez	.60	.25
□ 70 Frank Thomas	1.25	.55
□ 71 Robin Ventura	.25	.11
□ 72 Bret Boone	.25	.11
□ 73 Sean Casey	.60	.25
□ 74 Guillermo Garcia	.15	.07
□ 75 Barry Larkin	.60	.25
□ 76 Melvin Nieves	.15	.07
□ 77 Eduardo Perez	.15	.07
□ 78 Roberto Petagine	.15	.07
□ 79 Reggie Sanders	.15	.07
□ 80 Eddie Taubensee	.15	.07
□ 81 Brett Tomko	.15	.07
□ 82 Sandy Alomar Jr.	.25	.11
□ 83 Bartolo Colon	.25	.11
□ 84 Joey Cora	.15	.07
□ 85 Einar Diaz	.15	.07
□ 86 David Justice	.25	.11
□ 87 Kenny Lofton	.40	.18
□ 88 Manny Ramirez	.75	.35
□ 89 Jim Thome	.60	.25
□ 90 Omar Vizquel	.25	.11
□ 91 Enrique Wilson	.15	.07
□ 92 Pedro Astacio	.15	.07
□ 93 Dante Bichette	.25	.11
□ 94 Vinny Castilla	.25	.11
□ 95 Edgard Clemente	.15	.07
□ 96 Todd Helton	.60	.25
□ 97 Darryl Kile	.15	.07
□ 98 Mike Munoz	.15	.07
□ 99 Neifi Perez	.25	.11
□ 100 Jeff Reed	.15	.07
□ 101 Larry Walker	.60	.25
□ 102 Gabe Alvarez	.15	.07
□ 103 Kimera Bartee	.15	.07
□ 104 Frank Castillo	.15	.07
□ 105 Tony Clark	.25	.11
□ 106 Deivi Cruz	.15	.07
□ 107 Damion Easley	.25	.11
□ 108 Luis Gonzalez	.25	.11
□ 109 Marino Santana	.15	.07
□ 110 Justin Thompson	.15	.07
□ 111 Antonio Alfonseca	.15	.07
□ 112 Alex Fernandez	.25	.11
□ 113 Cliff Floyd	.25	.11
□ 114 Alex Gonzalez	.15	.07
□ 115 Livan Hernandez	.15	.07
□ 116 Mark Kotsay	.15	.07
□ 117 Derrek Lee	.15	.07
□ 118 Edgar Renteria	.15	.07
□ 119 Jesus Sanchez	.15	.07
□ 120 Moises Alou	.25	.11
□ 121 Jeff Bagwell	.75	.35
□ 122 Derek Bell	.25	.11
□ 123 Craig Biggio	.60	.25
□ 124 Tony Eusebio	.15	.07
□ 125 Ricky Gutierrez	.15	.07
□ 126 Richard Hidalgo	.25	.11
□ 127 Randy Johnson	.60	.25
□ 128 Jose Lima	.25	.11
□ 129 Shane Reynolds	.25	.11
□ 130 Johnny Damon	.25	.11
□ 131 Carlos Febles	.25	.11
□ 132 Jeff King	.15	.07
□ 133 Mendy Lopez	.15	.07
□ 134 Hal Morris	.15	.07
□ 135 Jose Offerman	.25	.11
□ 136 Jose Rosado	.15	.07
□ 137 Jose Santiago	.15	.07
□ 138 Bobby Bonilla	.25	.11
□ 139 Roger Cedeno	.15	.07
□ 140 Alex Cora	.15	.07
□ 141 Eric Karros	.25	.11
□ 142 Raul Mondesi	.25	.11
□ 143 Antonio Osuna	.15	.07
□ 144 Chan Ho Park	.25	.11
□ 145 Gary Sheffield	.25	.11
□ 146 Ismael Valdes	.15	.07
□ 147 Jeromy Burnitz	.25	.11
□ 148 Jeff Cirillo	.25	.11
□ 149 Valerio De Los Santos	.15	.07
□ 150 Marquis Grissom	.15	.07
□ 151 Scott Karl	.15	.07
□ 152 Dave Nilsson	.15	.07
□ 153 Al Reyes	.15	.07
□ 154 Rafael Roque	.25	.11
□ 155 Jose Valentin	.15	.07
□ 156 Fernando Vina	.15	.07
□ 157 Rick Aguilera	.15	.07
□ 158 Hector Carrasco	.15	.07
□ 159 Marty Cordova	.15	.07
□ 160 Eddie Guardado	.15	.07
□ 161 Paul Molitor	.60	.25
□ 162 Otis Nixon	.15	.07
□ 163 Alex Ochoa	.15	.07
□ 164 David Ortiz	.15	.07
□ 165 Frank Rodriguez	.15	.07
□ 166 Todd Walker	.25	.11
□ 167 Miguel Batista	.15	.07
□ 168 Orlando Cabrera	.15	.07
□ 169 Vladimir Guerrero	.75	.35
□ 170 Wilton Guerrero	.15	.07
□ 171 Carl Pavano	.15	.07
□ 172 Robert Perez	.15	.07
□ 173 F.P. Santangelo	.15	.07
□ 174 Fernando Seguignol	.25	.11
□ 175 Ugueth Urbina	.15	.07
□ 176 Javier Vazquez	.15	.07
□ 177 Edgard Alfonzo	.40	.18
□ 178 Carlos Baerga	.15	.07

☐ 179 John Franco	.25	.11
☐ 180 Luis Lopez	.15	.07
☐ 181 Hideo Nomo	.60	.25
☐ 182 John Olerud	.25	.11
☐ 183 Rey Ordonez	.25	.11
☐ 184 Mike Piazza	2.00	.90
☐ 185 Armando Reynoso	.15	.07
☐ 186 Masato Yoshii	.25	.11
☐ 187 David Cone	.40	.18
☐ 188 Orlando Hernandez	.60	.25
☐ 189 Hideki Irabu	.25	.11
☐ 190 Derek Jeter	2.00	.90
☐ 191 Ricky Ledee	.25	.11
☐ 192 Tino Martinez	.25	.11
☐ 193 Ramiro Mendoza	.15	.07
☐ 194 Paul O'Neill	.25	.11
☐ 195 Jorge Posada	.15	.07
☐ 196 Mariano Rivera	.25	.11
☐ 197 Luis Sojo	.15	.07
☐ 198 Bernie Williams	.60	.25
☐ 199 Rafael Bournigal	.15	.07
☐ 200 Eric Chavez	.40	.18
☐ 201 Ryan Christenson	.15	.07
☐ 202 Jason Giambi	.25	.11
☐ 203 Ben Grieve	.60	.25
☐ 204 Rickey Henderson	.75	.35
☐ 205 A.J. Hinch	.15	.07
☐ 206 Kenny Rogers	.15	.07
☐ 207 Miguel Tejada	.25	.11
☐ 208 Jorge Velandia	.15	.07
☐ 209 Bobby Abreu	.15	.07
☐ 210 Marlon Anderson	.15	.07
☐ 211 Alex Arias	.15	.07
☐ 212 Bobby Estalella	.25	.11
☐ 213 Doug Glanville	.15	.07
☐ 214 Scott Rolen	.75	.35
☐ 215 Curt Schilling	.40	.18
☐ 216 Kevin Sefcik	.15	.07
☐ 217 Adrian Brown	.15	.07
☐ 218 Francisco Cordova	.15	.07
☐ 219 Freddy Garcia	.15	.07
☐ 220 Jose Guillen	.15	.07
☐ 221 Jason Kendall	.25	.11
☐ 222 Al Martin	.15	.07
☐ 223 Abraham Nunez	.15	.07
☐ 224 Aramis Ramirez	.40	.18
☐ 225 Ricardo Rincon	.15	.07
☐ 226 Kevin Young	.25	.11
☐ 227 J.D. Drew	1.00	.45
☐ 228 Ron Gant	.25	.11
☐ 229 Jose Jimenez	.25	.11
☐ 230 Brian Jordan	.25	.11
☐ 231 Ray Lankford	.25	.11
☐ 232 Eli Marrero	.15	.07
☐ 233 Mark McGwire	4.00	1.80
☐ 234 Luis Ordaz	.15	.07
☐ 235 Placido Polanco	.15	.07
☐ 236 Fernando Tatis	.60	.25
☐ 237 Andy Ashby	.15	.07
☐ 238 Kevin Brown	.40	.18
☐ 239 Ken Caminiti	.25	.11
☐ 240 Steve Finley	.25	.11
☐ 241 Chris Gomez	.15	.07
☐ 242 Tony Gwynn	1.50	.70
☐ 243 Carlos Hernandez	.15	.07
☐ 244 Trevor Hoffman	.25	.11
☐ 245 Wally Joyner	.25	.11
☐ 246 Ruben Rivera	.15	.07
☐ 247 Greg Vaughn	.25	.11
☐ 248 Quilvio Veras	.15	.07
☐ 249 Rich Aurilia	.15	.07
☐ 250 Barry Bonds	.75	.35
☐ 251 Stan Javier	.15	.07
☐ 252 Jeff Kent	.25	.11
☐ 253 Ramon E.Martinez	.15	.07
☐ 254 Jose Mesa	.15	.07
☐ 255 Armando Rios	.15	.07
☐ 256 Rich Rodriguez	.15	.07
☐ 257 Rey Sanchez	.15	.07
☐ 258 J.T. Snow	.25	.11
☐ 259 Julian Tavarez	.15	.07
☐ 260 Jeff Fassero	.15	.07
☐ 261 Ken Griffey Jr.	3.00	1.35
☐ 262 Giomar Guevara	.15	.07
☐ 263 Carlos Guillen	.15	.07
☐ 264 Raul Ibanez	.15	.07

☐ 265 Edgar Martinez	.25	.11
☐ 266 Jamie Moyer	.15	.07
☐ 267 Alex Rodriguez	2.00	.90
☐ 268 David Segui	.15	.07
☐ 269 Makato Suzuki	.15	.07
☐ 270 Wilson Alvarez	.15	.07
☐ 271 Rolando Arrojo	.15	.07
☐ 272 Wade Boggs	.60	.25
☐ 273 Miguel Cairo	.15	.07
☐ 274 Roberto Hernandez	.15	.07
☐ 275 Aaron Ledesma	.15	.07
☐ 276 Albie Lopez	.15	.07
☐ 277 Quinton McCracken	.15	.07
☐ 278 Fred McGriff	.40	.18
☐ 279 Esteban Yan	.15	.07
☐ 280 Luis Alicea	.15	.07
☐ 281 Will Clark	.60	.25
☐ 282 Juan Gonzalez	1.25	.55
☐ 283 Rusty Greer	.25	.11
☐ 284 Rick Helling	.15	.07
☐ 285 Xavier Hernandez	.15	.07
☐ 286 Roberto Kelly	.15	.07
☐ 287 Esteban Loaiza	.15	.07
☐ 288 Ivan Rodriguez	.75	.35
☐ 289 Aaron Sele	.15	.07
☐ 290 John Wetteland	.15	.07
☐ 291 Jose Canseco	.75	.35
☐ 292 Roger Clemens	1.50	.70
☐ 293 Felipe Crespo	.15	.07
☐ 294 Jose Cruz Jr.	.25	.11
☐ 295 Carlos Delgado	.60	.25
☐ 296 Kelvim Escobar	.15	.07
☐ 297 Tony Fernandez	.25	.11
☐ 298 Alex Gonzalez	.15	.07
☐ 299 Tomas Perez	.15	.07
☐ 300 Juan Samuel	.15	.07
☐ NNO Tony Gwynn Sample..	3.00	1.35

1999 Pacific Crown Collection Platinum Blue

	MINT	NRMT
COMMON CARD (1-300)	6.00	2.70

*STARS: 15X TO 40X BASIC CARDS
*YOUNG STARS: 15X TO 40X BASIC CARDS
STATED ODDS 1:73

1999 Pacific Crown Collection In The Cage

	MINT	NRMT
COMPLETE SET (20)	800.00	350.00
COMMON CARD (1-20)	8.00	3.60
SEMISTARS	10.00	4.50
UNLISTED STARS	15.00	6.75
STATED ODDS 1:145		
☐ 1 Chipper Jones	40.00	18.00
☐ 2 Cal Ripken	60.00	27.00
☐ 3 Nomar Garciaparra	50.00	22.00
☐ 4 Sammy Sosa	50.00	22.00
☐ 5 Frank Thomas	30.00	13.50
☐ 6 Manny Ramirez	20.00	9.00
☐ 7 Todd Helton	15.00	6.75
☐ 8 Moises Alou	8.00	3.60
☐ 9 Vladimir Guerrero	20.00	9.00
☐ 10 Mike Piazza	50.00	22.00
☐ 11 Derek Jeter	50.00	22.00
☐ 12 Ben Grieve	15.00	6.75
☐ 13 J.D. Drew	20.00	9.00
☐ 14 Mark McGwire	100.00	45.00
☐ 15 Tony Gwynn	40.00	18.00
☐ 16 Ken Griffey Jr.	80.00	36.00
☐ 17 Edgar Martinez	8.00	3.60
☐ 18 Alex Rodriguez	50.00	22.00
☐ 19 Juan Gonzalez	30.00	13.50
☐ 20 Ivan Rodriguez	20.00	9.00

1999 Pacific Crown Collection Latinos of the Major Leagues

	MINT	NRMT
COMPLETE SET (36)	80.00	36.00
COMMON CARD (1-36)	1.00	.45
MINOR STARS	1.50	.70
SEMISTARS	2.50	1.10
UNLISTED STARS	4.00	1.80
STATED ODDS 2:37		
☐ 1 Roberto Alomar	4.00	1.80
☐ 2 Rafael Palmeiro	4.00	1.80
☐ 3 Nomar Garciaparra	12.00	5.50
☐ 4 Pedro Martinez	5.00	2.20
☐ 5 Magglio Ordonez	4.00	1.80
☐ 6 Sandy Alomar Jr.	1.50	.70
☐ 7 Bartolo Colon	1.50	.70
☐ 8 Manny Ramirez	5.00	2.20
☐ 9 Omar Vizquel	1.50	.70
☐ 10 Enrique Wilson	1.00	.45
☐ 11 David Ortiz	1.00	.45
☐ 12 Orlando Hernandez	4.00	1.80
☐ 13 Tino Martinez	1.50	.70
☐ 14 Mariano Rivera	1.50	.70
☐ 15 Bernie Williams	4.00	1.80
☐ 16 Edgar Martinez	1.50	.70
☐ 17 Alex Rodriguez	12.00	5.50
☐ 18 David Segui	1.00	.45
☐ 19 Rolando Arrojo	1.00	.45
☐ 20 Juan Gonzalez	8.00	3.60
☐ 21 Ivan Rodriguez	5.00	2.20
☐ 22 Jose Canseco	5.00	2.20
☐ 23 Jose Cruz Jr.	1.50	.70
☐ 24 Andres Galarraga	2.50	1.10
☐ 25 Andruw Jones	4.00	1.80
☐ 26 Javy Lopez	1.50	.70
☐ 27 Sammy Sosa	12.00	5.50

□ 28 Vinny Castilla	1.50	.70
□ 29 Alex Gonzalez	1.50	.70
□ 30 Moises Alou	1.50	.70
□ 31 Bobby Bonilla	1.50	.70
□ 32 Raul Mondesi	1.50	.70
□ 33 Fernando Vina	1.00	.45
□ 34 Vladimir Guerrero	5.00	2.20
□ 35 Carlos Baerga	1.00	.45
□ 36 Rey Ordonez	1.50	.70

□ 10 Raul Mondesi	5.00	2.20
□ 11 Vladimir Guerrero	12.00	5.50
□ 12 Mike Piazza	30.00	13.50
□ 13 J.D. Drew	12.00	5.50
□ 14 Mark McGwire	60.00	27.00
□ 15 Greg Vaughn	5.00	2.20
□ 16 Ken Griffey Jr.	50.00	22.00
□ 17 Alex Rodriguez	30.00	13.50
□ 18 Juan Gonzalez	20.00	9.00
□ 19 Ivan Rodriguez	12.00	5.50
□ 20 Jose Canseco	12.00	5.50

1999 Pacific Crown Collection Pacific Cup

	MINT	NRMT
COMPLETE SET (10)	750.00	350.00
COMMON CARD (1-10)	15.00	6.75
STATED ODDS 1:721		

□ 1 Cal Ripken	100.00	45.00
□ 2 Nomar Garciaparra	80.00	36.00
□ 3 Frank Thomas	50.00	22.00
□ 4 Ken Griffey Jr.	120.00	55.00
□ 5 Alex Rodriguez	80.00	36.00
□ 6 Greg Maddux	60.00	27.00
□ 7 Sammy Sosa	80.00	36.00
□ 8 Kerry Wood	20.00	9.00
□ 9 Mark McGwire	150.00	70.00
□ 10 Tony Gwynn	60.00	27.00

1999 Pacific Crown Collection Tape Measure

	MINT	NRMT
COMPLETE SET (20)	400.00	180.00
COMMON CARD (1-20)	5.00	2.20
SEMISTARS	6.00	2.70
UNLISTED STARS	10.00	4.50
STATED ODDS 1:73		

□ 1 Andres Galarraga	6.00	2.70
□ 2 Chipper Jones	25.00	11.00
□ 3 Nomar Garciaparra	30.00	13.50
□ 4 Sammy Sosa	30.00	13.50
□ 5 Frank Thomas	20.00	9.00
□ 6 Manny Ramirez	12.00	5.50
□ 7 Vinny Castilla	5.00	2.20
□ 8 Moises Alou	5.00	2.20
□ 9 Jeff Bagwell	12.00	5.50

1999 Pacific Crown Collection Team Checklists

	MINT	NRMT
COMPLETE SET (30)	300.00	135.00
COMMON CARD (1-30)	1.50	.70
MINOR STARS	2.50	1.10
SEMISTARS	4.00	1.80
UNLISTED STARS	6.00	2.70
STATED ODDS 1:37		

□ 1 Darin Erstad	4.00	1.80
□ 2 Travis Lee	4.00	1.80
□ 3 Chipper Jones	15.00	6.75
□ 4 Cal Ripken	25.00	11.00
□ 5 Nomar Garciaparra	20.00	9.00
□ 6 Sammy Sosa	20.00	9.00
□ 7 Frank Thomas	12.00	5.50
□ 8 Barry Larkin	6.00	2.70
□ 9 Manny Ramirez	8.00	3.60
□ 10 Larry Walker	6.00	2.70
□ 11 Bob Higginson	2.50	1.10
□ 12 Livan Hernandez	1.50	.70
□ 13 Moises Alou	2.50	1.10
□ 14 Jeff King	1.50	.70
□ 15 Raul Mondesi	2.50	1.10
□ 16 Marquis Grissom	1.50	.70
□ 17 David Ortiz	1.50	.70
□ 18 Vladimir Guerrero	8.00	3.60
□ 19 Mike Piazza	20.00	9.00
□ 20 Derek Jeter	20.00	9.00
□ 21 Ben Grieve	6.00	2.70
□ 22 Scott Rolen	8.00	3.60
□ 23 Jason Kendall	2.50	1.10
□ 24 Mark McGwire	40.00	18.00
□ 25 Tony Gwynn	15.00	6.75
□ 26 Barry Bonds	8.00	3.60
□ 27 Ken Griffey Jr.	30.00	13.50
□ 28 Maggio Ordonez	6.00	2.70
□ 29 Juan Gonzalez	12.00	5.50
□ 30 Jose Canseco	8.00	3.60

1998 Pacific Invincible

	MINT	NRMT
COMPLETE SET (150)	180.00	80.00
COMMON CARD (1-150)	.75	.35
MINOR STARS	1.25	.55
SEMISTARS	2.00	.90
UNLISTED STARS	3.00	1.35
COMMON SILVER (1-150)	4.00	1.80
*SILVER STARS: 2X TO 5X HI COLUMN		
SILVER STATED ODDS 2:37 HOB/RET.		

□ 1 Garret Anderson	1.25	.55
□ 2 Jim Edmonds	1.25	.55
□ 3 Darin Erstad	2.00	.90
□ 4 Chuck Finley	1.25	.55
□ 5 Tim Salmon	2.00	.90
□ 6 Roberto Alomar	3.00	1.35
□ 7 Brady Anderson	1.25	.55
□ 8 Geronimo Berroa	.75	.35
□ 9 Eric Davis	1.25	.55
□ 10 Mike Mussina	3.00	1.35
□ 11 Rafael Palmeiro	3.00	1.35
□ 12 Cal Ripken	12.00	5.50
□ 13 Steve Avery	.75	.35
□ 14 Nomar Garciaparra	10.00	4.50
□ 15 John Valentin	1.25	.55
□ 16 Mo Vaughn	3.00	1.35
□ 17 Albert Belle	3.00	1.35
□ 18 Ozzie Guillen	.75	.35
□ 19 Norberto Martin	.75	.35
□ 20 Frank Thomas	6.00	2.70
□ 21 Robin Ventura	1.25	.55
□ 22 Sandy Alomar Jr.	1.25	.55
□ 23 David Justice	1.25	.55
□ 24 Kenny Lofton	2.00	.90
□ 25 Manny Ramirez	4.00	1.80
□ 26 Jim Thome	3.00	1.35
□ 27 Omar Vizquel	1.25	.55
□ 28 Matt Williams	3.00	1.35
□ 29 Jaret Wright	1.25	.55
□ 30 Raul Casanova	1.25	.55
□ 31 Tony Clark	1.25	.55
□ 32 Deivi Cruz	1.25	.55
□ 33 Bobby Higginson	1.25	.55
□ 34 Justin Thompson	.75	.35
□ 35 Yamil Benitez	.75	.35
□ 36 Johnny Damon	1.25	.55
□ 37 Jermaine Dye	1.25	.55
□ 38 Jed Hansen	.75	.35
□ 39 Larry Sutton	.75	.35
□ 40 Jeromy Burnitz	1.25	.55
□ 41 Jeff Cirillo	1.25	.55
□ 42 Dave Nilsson	.75	.35
□ 43 Jose Valentin	.75	.35
□ 44 Fernando Vina	.75	.35
□ 45 Marty Cordova	.75	.35
□ 46 Chuck Knoblauch	1.25	.55
□ 47 Paul Molitor	3.00	1.35
□ 48 Brad Radke	1.25	.55
□ 49 Terry Steinbach	.75	.35
□ 50 Wade Boggs	3.00	1.35
□ 51 Hideki Irabu	1.25	.55
□ 52 Derek Jeter	10.00	4.50
□ 53 Tino Martinez	1.25	.55
□ 54 Andy Pettitte	1.25	.55
□ 55 Mariano Rivera	1.25	.55
□ 56 Bernie Williams	3.00	1.35
□ 57 Jose Canseco	4.00	1.80
□ 58 Jason Giambi	1.25	.55
□ 59 Ben Grieve	3.00	1.35
□ 60 Aaron Small	.75	.35
□ 61 Jay Buhner	1.25	.55
□ 62 Ken Cloude	.75	.35
□ 63 Joey Cora	.75	.35
□ 64 Ken Griffey Jr.	15.00	6.75
□ 65 Randy Johnson	3.00	1.35
□ 66 Edgar Martinez	1.25	.55
□ 67 Alex Rodriguez	10.00	4.50
□ 68 Will Clark	3.00	1.35

		MINT	NRMT
❑ 69	Juan Gonzalez	6.00	2.70
❑ 70	Rusty Greer	1.25	.55
❑ 71	Ivan Rodriguez	4.00	1.80
❑ 72	Joe Carter	1.25	.55
❑ 73	Roger Clemens	8.00	3.60
❑ 74	Jose Cruz Jr.	1.25	.55
❑ 75	Carlos Delgado	3.00	1.35
❑ 76	Andruw Jones	3.00	1.35
❑ 77	Chipper Jones	8.00	3.60
❑ 78	Ryan Klesko	1.25	.55
❑ 79	Javier Lopez	1.25	.55
❑ 80	Greg Maddux	8.00	3.60
❑ 81	Miguel Batista	.75	.35
❑ 82	Jeremi Gonzalez	.75	.35
❑ 83	Mark Grace	2.00	.90
❑ 84	Kevin Orie	.75	.35
❑ 85	Sammy Sosa	10.00	4.50
❑ 86	Barry Larkin	3.00	1.35
❑ 87	Deion Sanders	1.25	.55
❑ 88	Reggie Sanders	.75	.35
❑ 89	Chris Stynes	.75	.35
❑ 90	Dante Bichette	1.25	.55
❑ 91	Vinny Castilla	1.25	.55
❑ 92	Andres Galarraga	2.00	.90
❑ 93	Neifi Perez	1.25	.55
❑ 94	Larry Walker	3.00	1.35
❑ 95	Moises Alou	1.25	.55
❑ 96	Bobby Bonilla	1.25	.55
❑ 97	Kevin Brown	2.00	.90
❑ 98	Craig Counsell	.75	.35
❑ 99	Livan Hernandez	.75	.35
❑ 100	Edgar Renteria	.75	.35
❑ 101	Gary Sheffield	1.25	.55
❑ 102	Jeff Bagwell	4.00	1.80
❑ 103	Craig Biggio	3.00	1.35
❑ 104	Luis Gonzalez	.75	.35
❑ 105	Darryl Kile	.75	.35
❑ 106	Wilton Guerrero	.75	.35
❑ 107	Eric Karros	.75	.35
❑ 108	Ramon Martinez	.75	.35
❑ 109	Raul Mondesi	1.25	.55
❑ 110	Hideo Nomo	3.00	1.35
❑ 111	Chan Ho Park	1.25	.55
❑ 112	Mike Piazza	10.00	4.50
❑ 113	Mark Grudzielanek	.75	.35
❑ 114	Vladimir Guerrero	3.00	1.35
❑ 115	Pedro Martinez	4.00	1.80
❑ 116	Henry Rodriguez	1.25	.55
❑ 117	David Segui	.75	.35
❑ 118	Edgardo Alfonzo	2.00	.90
❑ 119	Carlos Baerga	.75	.35
❑ 120	John Franco	1.25	.55
❑ 121	John Olerud	1.25	.55
❑ 122	Rey Ordonez	1.25	.55
❑ 123	Ricky Bottalico	.75	.35
❑ 124	Gregg Jefferies	.75	.35
❑ 125	Mickey Morandini	.75	.35
❑ 126	Scott Rolen	3.00	1.35
❑ 127	Curt Schilling	2.00	.90
❑ 128	Jose Guillen	.75	.35
❑ 129	Esteban Loaiza	.75	.35
❑ 130	Al Martin	.75	.35
❑ 131	Tony Womack	.75	.35
❑ 132	Dennis Eckersley	1.25	.55
❑ 133	Gary Gaetti	1.25	.55
❑ 134	Curtis King	.75	.35
❑ 135	Ray Lankford	1.25	.55
❑ 136	Mark McGwire	20.00	9.00
❑ 137	Ken Caminiti	1.25	.55
❑ 138	Steve Finley	1.25	.55
❑ 139	Tony Gwynn	8.00	3.60
❑ 140	Carlos Hernandez	.75	.35
❑ 141	Wally Joyner	1.25	.55
❑ 142	Barry Bonds	4.00	1.80
❑ 143	Jacob Cruz	.75	.35
❑ 144	Shawn Estes	.75	.35
❑ 145	Stan Javier	.75	.35
❑ 146	J.T. Snow	1.25	.55
❑ 147	Nomar Garciaparra ROY	5.00	2.20
❑ 148	Scott Rolen ROY	3.00	1.35
❑ 149	Ken Griffey Jr. MVP	8.00	3.60
❑ 150	Larry Walker MVP	1.25	.55

1998 Pacific Invincible Platinum Blue

	MINT	NRMT
COMMON CARD (1-150)	10.00	4.50

*STARS: 5X TO 12X BASIC CARDS
STATED ODDS 1:73

1998 Pacific Invincible Cramer's Choice Green

	MINT	NRMT
COMP.GREEN SET (10)	1500.00	700.00
COMMON GREEN (1-10)	40.00	18.00

*DARK BLUE: .5X TO 1.2X GREEN HI
*LIGHT BLUE: .6X TO 1.5X GREEN HI
*RED: 1X TO 2.5X GREEN HI
*GOLD: 1.5X TO 4X GREEN HI.
*PURPLE: 2.5X TO 6X GREEN HI
GREEN PRINT RUN 99 SERIAL #'d SETS
DARK BLUE PRINT RUN 80 SERIAL #'d SETS
LIGHT BLUE PRINT RUN 50 SERIAL #'d SETS
RED PRINT RUN 25 SERIAL#'d SETS
GOLD PRINT RUN 15 SERIAL #'d SETS
PURPLE PRINT RUN 10 SERIAL #'d SETS
RANDOM INSERTS IN PACKS
GREEN CARDS LISTED BELOW!

		MINT	NRMT
❑ 1	Greg Maddux	120.00	55.00
❑ 2	Roberto Alomar	40.00	18.00
❑ 3	Cal Ripken	200.00	90.00
❑ 4	Nomar Garciaparra	150.00	70.00
❑ 5	Larry Walker	50.00	22.00
❑ 6	Mike Piazza	150.00	70.00
❑ 7	Mark McGwire	300.00	135.00
❑ 8	Tony Gwynn	120.00	55.00
❑ 9	Ken Griffey Jr.	250.00	110.00
❑ 10	Roger Clemens	120.00	55.00

1998 Pacific Invincible Gems of the Diamond

	MINT	NRMT
COMPLETE SET (220)	40.00	18.00
COMMON CARD (1-220)	.15	.07
MINOR STARS	.25	.11
SEMISTARS	.40	.18
UNLISTED STARS	.60	.25

FOUR GEMS OF DIAMOND PER PACK

		MINT	NRMT
❑ 1	Jim Edmonds	.25	.11
❑ 2	Todd Greene	.15	.07
❑ 3	Ken Hill	.15	.07
❑ 4	Mike Holtz	.15	.07
❑ 5	Mike James	.15	.07
❑ 6	Chad Kreuter	.15	.07
❑ 7	Tim Salmon	.40	.18
❑ 8	Roberto Alomar	.60	.25
❑ 9	Brady Anderson	.25	.11
❑ 10	Dave Dellucci	.60	.25
❑ 11	Jeffrey Hammonds	.15	.07
❑ 12	Mike Mussina	.60	.25
❑ 13	Rafael Palmeiro	.60	.25
❑ 14	Arthur Rhodes	.15	.07
❑ 15	Cal Ripken	2.50	1.10
❑ 16	Nerio Rodriguez	.15	.07
❑ 17	Tony Tarasco	.15	.07
❑ 18	Lenny Webster	.15	.07
❑ 19	Mike Benjamin	.15	.07
❑ 20	Rich Garces	.15	.07
❑ 21	Nomar Garciaparra	2.00	.90
❑ 22	Shane Mack	.15	.07
❑ 23	Jose Malave	.15	.07
❑ 24	Jesus Tavarez	.15	.07
❑ 25	Mo Vaughn	.60	.25
❑ 26	John Wasdin	.15	.07
❑ 27	Jeff Abbott	.15	.07
❑ 28	Albert Belle	.60	.25
❑ 29	Mike Cameron	.25	.11
❑ 30	Al Levine	.15	.07
❑ 31	Robert Machado	.15	.07
❑ 32	Greg Norton	.15	.07
❑ 33	Magglio Ordonez	2.00	.90
❑ 34	Mike Sirotka	.15	.07
❑ 35	Frank Thomas	1.25	.55
❑ 36	Mario Valdez	.15	.07
❑ 37	Sandy Alomar Jr.	.25	.11
❑ 38	David Justice	.25	.11
❑ 39	Jack McDowell	.15	.07
❑ 40	Eric Plunk	.15	.07
❑ 41	Manny Ramirez	.75	.35
❑ 42	Kevin Seitzer	.15	.07
❑ 43	Paul Shuey	.15	.07
❑ 44	Omar Vizquel	.25	.11
❑ 45	Kimera Bartee	.15	.07
❑ 46	Glenn Dishman	.15	.07
❑ 47	Orlando Miller	.15	.07
❑ 48	Mike Myers	.15	.07
❑ 49	Phil Nevin	.15	.07
❑ 50	A.J. Sager	.15	.07
❑ 51	Ricky Bones	.15	.07
❑ 52	Scott Cooper	.15	.07
❑ 53	Shane Halter	.15	.07
❑ 54	David Howard	.15	.07
❑ 55	Glendon Rusch	.15	.07
❑ 56	Joe Vitiello	.15	.07
❑ 57	Jeff D'Amico	.15	.07
❑ 58	Mike Fetters	.15	.07
❑ 59	Mike Matheny	.15	.07
❑ 60	Jose Mercedes	.15	.07
❑ 61	Ron Villone	.15	.07
❑ 62	Jack Voigt	.15	.07
❑ 63	Brent Brede	.15	.07
❑ 64	Chuck Knoblauch	.25	.11
❑ 65	Paul Molitor	.60	.25
❑ 66	Todd Ritchie	.15	.07
❑ 67	Frankie Rodriguez	.15	.07
❑ 68	Scott Stahoviak	.15	.07

❑ 69	Greg Swindell	.15	.07
❑ 70	Todd Walker	.25	.11
❑ 71	Wade Boggs	.60	.25
❑ 72	Hideki Irabu	.25	.11
❑ 73	Derek Jeter	2.00	.90
❑ 74	Pat Kelly	.15	.07
❑ 75	Graeme Lloyd	.15	.07
❑ 76	Tino Martinez	.25	.11
❑ 77	Jeff Nelson	.15	.07
❑ 78	Scott Pose	.15	.07
❑ 79	Mike Stanton	.15	.07
❑ 80	Darryl Strawberry	.25	.11
❑ 81	Bernie Williams	.60	.25
❑ 82	Tony Batista	.15	.07
❑ 83	Mark Bellhorn	.15	.07
❑ 84	Ben Grieve	.60	.25
❑ 85	Pat Lennon	.15	.07
❑ 86	Brian Lesher	.15	.07
❑ 87	Miguel Tejada	.25	.11
❑ 88	George Williams	.15	.07
❑ 89	Joey Cora	.15	.07
❑ 90	Rob Ducey	.15	.07
❑ 91	Ken Griffey Jr.	3.00	1.35
❑ 92	Randy Johnson	.60	.25
❑ 93	Edgar Martinez	.25	.11
❑ 94	John Marzano	.15	.07
❑ 95	Greg McCarthy	.15	.07
❑ 96	Alex Rodriguez	2.00	.90
❑ 97	Andy Sheets	.15	.07
❑ 98	Mike Timlin	.15	.07
❑ 99	Lee Tinsley	.15	.07
❑ 100	Damon Buford	.15	.07
❑ 101	Alex Diaz	.15	.07
❑ 102	Benji Gil	.15	.07
❑ 103	Juan Gonzalez	1.25	.55
❑ 104	Eric Gunderson	.15	.07
❑ 105	Danny Patterson	.15	.07
❑ 106	Ivan Rodriguez	.75	.35
❑ 107	Mike Simms	.15	.07
❑ 108	Luis Andujar	.15	.07
❑ 109	Joe Carter	.25	.11
❑ 110	Roger Clemens	1.50	.70
❑ 111	Jose Cruz Jr.	.25	.11
❑ 112	Shawn Green	.60	.25
❑ 113	Robert Perez	.15	.07
❑ 114	Juan Samuel	.15	.07
❑ 115	Ed Sprague	.15	.07
❑ 116	Shannon Stewart	.25	.11
❑ 117	Danny Bautista	.15	.07
❑ 118	Chipper Jones	1.50	.70
❑ 119	Ryan Klesko	.25	.11
❑ 120	Keith Lockhart	.15	.07
❑ 121	Javier Lopez	.25	.11
❑ 122	Greg Maddux	1.50	.70
❑ 123	Kevin Millwood	2.00	.90
❑ 124	Mike Mordecai	.15	.07
❑ 125	Eddie Perez	.15	.07
❑ 126	Randall Simon	.25	.11
❑ 127	Miguel Cairo	.15	.07
❑ 128	Dave Clark	.15	.07
❑ 129	Kevin Foster	.15	.07
❑ 130	Mark Grace	.40	.18
❑ 131	Tyler Houston	.15	.07
❑ 132	Mike Hubbard	.15	.07
❑ 133	Kevin Orie	.15	.07
❑ 134	Ryne Sandberg	.75	.35
❑ 135	Sammy Sosa	2.00	.90
❑ 136	Lenny Harris	.15	.07
❑ 137	Kent Mercker	.15	.07
❑ 138	Mike Morgan	.15	.07
❑ 139	Deion Sanders	.25	.11
❑ 140	Chris Stynes	.15	.07
❑ 141	Gabe White	.15	.07
❑ 142	Jason Bates	.15	.07
❑ 143	Vinny Castilla	.25	.11
❑ 144	Andres Galarraga	.40	.18
❑ 145	Curtis Leskanic	.15	.07
❑ 146	Jeff McCurry	.15	.07
❑ 147	Mike Munoz	.15	.07
❑ 148	Larry Walker	.60	.25
❑ 149	Jamey Wright	.15	.07
❑ 150	Moises Alou	.25	.11
❑ 151	Bobby Bonilla	.25	.11
❑ 152	Kevin Brown	.40	.18
❑ 153	John Cangelosi	.15	.07
❑ 154	Jeff Conine	.15	.07
❑ 155	Cliff Floyd	.25	.11
❑ 156	Jay Powell	.15	.07
❑ 157	Edgar Renteria	.15	.07
❑ 158	Tony Saunders	.15	.07
❑ 159	Gary Sheffield	.25	.11
❑ 160	Jeff Bagwell	.75	.35
❑ 161	Tim Bogar	.15	.07
❑ 162	Tony Eusebio	.15	.07
❑ 163	Chris Holt	.15	.07
❑ 164	Ray Montgomery	.15	.07
❑ 165	Luis Rivera	.15	.07
❑ 166	Eric Anthony	.15	.07
❑ 167	Brett Butler	.25	.11
❑ 168	Juan Castro	.15	.07
❑ 169	Tripp Cromer	.15	.07
❑ 170	Raul Mondesi	.25	.11
❑ 171	Hideo Nomo	.60	.25
❑ 172	Mike Piazza	2.00	.90
❑ 173	Tom Prince	.15	.07
❑ 174	Adam Riggs	.15	.07
❑ 175	Shane Andrews	.15	.07
❑ 176	Shayne Bennett	.15	.07
❑ 177	Raul Chavez	.15	.07
❑ 178	Pedro Martinez	.75	.35
❑ 179	Sherman Obando	.15	.07
❑ 180	Andy Stankiewicz	.15	.07
❑ 181	Alberto Castillo	.15	.07
❑ 182	Shawn Gilbert	.15	.07
❑ 183	Luis Lopez	.15	.07
❑ 184	Roberto Petagine	.15	.07
❑ 185	Armando Reynoso	.15	.07
❑ 186	Midre Cummings	.15	.07
❑ 187	Kevin Jordan	.15	.07
❑ 188	Desi Relaford	.15	.07
❑ 189	Scott Rolen	.75	.35
❑ 190	Ken Ryan	.15	.07
❑ 191	Kevin Sefcik	.15	.07
❑ 192	Emil Brown	.15	.07
❑ 193	Lou Collier	.15	.07
❑ 194	Francisco Cordova	.15	.07
❑ 195	Kevin Elster	.15	.07
❑ 196	Mark Smith	.15	.07
❑ 197	Marc Wilkins	.15	.07
❑ 198	Manny Aybar	.25	.11
❑ 199	Jose Bautista	.15	.07
❑ 200	David Bell	.15	.07
❑ 201	Rigo Beltran	.15	.07
❑ 202	Delino DeShields	.15	.07
❑ 203	Dennis Eckersley	.25	.11
❑ 204	John Mabry	.15	.07
❑ 205	Eli Marrero	.15	.07
❑ 206	Willie McGee	.25	.11
❑ 207	Mark McGwire	4.00	1.80
❑ 208	Ken Caminiti	.25	.11
❑ 209	Tony Gwynn	1.50	.70
❑ 210	Chris Jones	.15	.07
❑ 211	Craig Shipley	.15	.07
❑ 212	Pete Smith	.15	.07
❑ 213	Jorge Velandia	.15	.07
❑ 214	Dario Veras	.15	.07
❑ 215	Rich Aurilia	.15	.07
❑ 216	Damon Berryhill	.15	.07
❑ 217	Barry Bonds	.75	.35
❑ 218	Osvaldo Fernandez	.15	.07
❑ 219	Dante Powell	.15	.07
❑ 220	Rich Rodriguez	.15	.07

1998 Pacific Invincible Interleague Players

		MINT	NRMT
	COMPLETE SET (30)	600.00	275.00
	COMMON CARD (1A-15N)	3.00	1.35
	MINOR STARS	5.00	2.20
	SEMISTARS	8.00	3.60
	UNLISTED STARS	12.00	5.50
	STATED ODDS 1:73		
❑ 1A	Roberto Alomar	12.00	5.50
❑ 1N	Craig Biggio	12.00	5.50
❑ 2A	Cal Ripken	50.00	22.00
❑ 2N	Chipper Jones	30.00	13.50
❑ 3A	Nomar Garciaparra	40.00	18.00
❑ 3N	Scott Rolen	15.00	6.75
❑ 4A	Mo Vaughn	12.00	5.50

❑ 4N	Andres Galarraga	8.00	3.60
❑ 5A	Frank Thomas	25.00	11.00
❑ 5N	Tony Gwynn	30.00	13.50
❑ 6A	Albert Belle	12.00	5.50
❑ 6N	Barry Bonds	15.00	6.75
❑ 7A	Hideki Irabu	5.00	2.20
❑ 7N	Hideo Nomo	12.00	5.50
❑ 8A	Derek Jeter	40.00	18.00
❑ 8N	Rey Ordonez	5.00	2.20
❑ 9A	Tino Martinez	5.00	2.20
❑ 9N	Mark McGwire	80.00	36.00
❑ 10A	Alex Rodriguez	40.00	18.00
❑ 10N	Edgar Renteria	3.00	1.35
❑ 11A	Ken Griffey Jr.	60.00	27.00
❑ 11N	Larry Walker	12.00	5.50
❑ 12A	Randy Johnson	12.00	5.50
❑ 12N	Greg Maddux	30.00	13.50
❑ 13A	Ivan Rodriguez	15.00	6.75
❑ 13N	Mike Piazza	40.00	18.00
❑ 14A	Roger Clemens	30.00	13.50
❑ 14N	Pedro Martinez	15.00	6.75
❑ 15A	Jose Cruz Jr.	5.00	2.20
❑ 15N	Wilton Guerrero	3.00	1.35

1998 Pacific Invincible Moments in Time

		MINT	NRMT
	COMPLETE SET (20)	800.00	350.00
	COMMON CARD (1-20)	5.00	2.20
	MINOR STARS	8.00	3.60
	SEMISTARS	12.00	5.50
	UNLISTED STARS	20.00	9.00
	STATED ODDS 1:145		
❑ 1	Chipper Jones	50.00	22.00
❑ 2	Cal Ripken	80.00	36.00
❑ 3	Frank Thomas	40.00	18.00
❑ 4	David Justice	8.00	3.60
❑ 5	Andres Galarraga	12.00	5.50
❑ 6	Larry Walker	20.00	9.00
❑ 7	Livan Hernandez	5.00	2.20
❑ 8	Wilton Guerrero	5.00	2.20
❑ 9	Hideo Nomo	20.00	9.00
❑ 10	Mike Piazza	60.00	27.00
❑ 11	Pedro Martinez	25.00	11.00
❑ 12	Bernie Williams	20.00	9.00
❑ 13	Ben Grieve	20.00	9.00
❑ 14	Scott Rolen	25.00	11.00
❑ 15	Mark McGwire	120.00	55.00

	MINT	NRMT
❑ 16 Tony Gwynn	50.00	22.00
❑ 17 Ken Griffey Jr.	100.00	45.00
❑ 18 Alex Rodriguez	60.00	27.00
❑ 19 Juan Gonzalez	40.00	18.00
❑ 20 Jose Cruz Jr.	8.00	3.60

1998 Pacific Invincible Photoengravings

	MINT	NRMT
COMPLETE SET (18)	200.00	90.00
COMMON CARD (1-18)	2.00	.90
UNLISTED STARS	5.00	2.20
STATED ODDS 1:37		

	MINT	NRMT
❑ 1 Greg Maddux	12.00	5.50
❑ 2 Cal Ripken	20.00	9.00
❑ 3 Nomar Garciaparra	15.00	6.75
❑ 4 Frank Thomas	10.00	4.50
❑ 5 Larry Walker	5.00	2.20
❑ 6 Mike Piazza	15.00	6.75
❑ 7 Hideo Nomo	5.00	2.20
❑ 8 Pedro Martinez	6.00	2.70
❑ 9 Derek Jeter	15.00	6.75
❑ 10 Tino Martinez	2.00	.90
❑ 11 Mark McGwire	30.00	13.50
❑ 12 Tony Gwynn	12.00	5.50
❑ 13 Barry Bonds	6.00	2.70
❑ 14 Ken Griffey Jr.	25.00	11.00
❑ 15 Alex Rodriguez	15.00	6.75
❑ 16 Ivan Rodriguez	6.00	2.70
❑ 17 Roger Clemens	12.00	5.50
❑ 18 Jose Cruz Jr.	2.00	.90

1998 Pacific Invincible Team Checklists

	MINT	NRMT
COMPLETE SET (30)	200.00	90.00
COMMON CARD (1-30)	1.25	.55
MINOR STARS	2.00	.90
SEMISTARS	3.00	1.35
UNLISTED STARS	5.00	2.20
STATED ODDS 2:37		
FOUR OR FIVE PLAYERS ON EACH CARD		
ONLY TOP STARS LISTED BELOW		

	MINT	NRMT
❑ 1 Anaheim Angels	6.00	2.70
Jim Edmonds		
Tim Salmon		
Darin Erstad		
Garret Anderson		
Rickey Henderson		
❑ 2 Atlanta Braves	12.00	5.50
Greg Maddux		
Chipper Jones		
Javier Lopez		
Ryan Klesko		
Andruw Jones		
❑ 3 Baltimore Orioles	20.00	9.00
Cal Ripken		
Roberto Alomar		
Brady Anderson		
Mike Mussina		
Rafael Palmeiro		
❑ 4 Boston Red Sox	15.00	6.75
Nomar Garciaparra		
Mo Vaughn		
Steve Avery		
John Valentin		
❑ 5 Chicago Cubs	15.00	6.75
Sammy Sosa		
Mark Grace		
Ryne Sandberg		
Jeremi Gonzalez		
Frank Thomas		
❑ 6 Chicago White Sox	10.00	4.50
Albert Belle		
Robin Ventura		
Ozzie Guillen		
❑ 7 Cincinnati Reds	5.00	2.20
Barry Larkin		
Deion Sanders		
Reggie Sanders		
Brett Tomko		
❑ 8 Cleveland Indians	6.00	2.70
Sandy Alomar		
Manny Ramirez		
David Justice		
Jim Thome		
Omar Vizquel		
❑ 9 Colorado Rockies	5.00	2.20
Andres Galarraga		
Larry Walker		
Vinny Castilla		
Dante Bichette		
Ellis Burks		
❑ 10 Detroit Tigers	2.00	.90
Justin Thompson		
Tony Clark		
Deivi Cruz		
Bobby Higginson		
❑ 11 Florida Marlins	2.00	.90
Gary Sheffield		
Edgar Renteria		
Livan Hernandez		
Charles Johnson		
Bobby Bonilla		
❑ 12 Houston Astros	6.00	2.70
Jeff Bagwell		
Craig Biggio		
Richard Hidalgo		
Darryl Kile		
❑ 13 Kansas City Royals	2.00	.90
Johnny Damon		
Jermaine Dye		
Chili Davis		
Jose Rosado		
❑ 14 Los Angeles Dodgers	15.00	6.75
Mike Piazza		
Wilton Guerrero		
Raul Mondesi		
Hideo Nomo		
Ramon Martinez		
❑ 15 Milwaukee Brewers	2.00	.90
Dave Nilsson		
Fernando Vina		
Jeromy Burnitz		
Julio Franco		
Jeff Cirillo		
❑ 16 Minnesota Twins	5.00	2.20
Paul Molitor		
Chuck Knoblauch		
Brad Radke		
Terry Steinbach		
Marty Cordova		
❑ 17 Montreal Expos	6.00	2.70
Henry Rodriguez		
Vladimir Guerrero		
Pedro Martinez		
David Segui		
Mark Grudzielanek		
❑ 18 New York Mets	2.00	.90
Carlos Baerga		
Todd Hundley		
Rey Ordonez		
John Olerud		
Edgardo Alfonzo		
❑ 19 New York Yankees	15.00	6.75
Derek Jeter		
Tino Martinez		
Bernie Williams		
Andy Pettitte		
Mariano Rivera		
❑ 20 Oakland Athletics	8.00	3.60
Jose Canseco		
Ben Grieve		
Jason Giambi		
Matt Stairs		
❑ 21 Philadelphia Phillies	6.00	2.70
Curt Schilling		
Scott Rolen		
Gregg Jefferies		
Len Dykstra		
Ricky Bottalico		
❑ 22 Pittsburgh Pirates	1.25	.55
Al Martin		
Tony Womack		
Jose Guillen		
Esteban Loaiza		
❑ 23 St. Louis Cardinals	30.00	13.50
Mark McGwire		
Dennis Eckersley		
Delino DeShields		
Willie McGee		
Ray Lankford		
❑ 24 San Diego Padres	12.00	5.50
Tony Gwynn		
Ken Caminiti		
Wally Joyner		
Steve Finley		
❑ 25 San Francisco Giants	6.00	2.70
Barry Bonds		
J.T. Snow		
Stan Javier		
Rod Beck		
Jose Vizcaino		
❑ 26 Seattle Mariners	25.00	11.00
Ken Griffey Jr.		
Alex Rodriguez		
Edgar Martinez		
Randy Johnson		
Jay Buhner		
❑ 27 Texas Rangers	10.00	4.50
Juan Gonzalez		
Ivan Rodriguez		
Will Clark		
John Wetteland		
Rusty Greer		
❑ 28 Toronto Blue Jays	12.00	5.50
Jose Cruz Jr.		
Roger Clemens		
Pat Hentgen		
Joe Carter		
❑ 29 Arizona Diamond Backs	5.00	2.20
Yamil Benitez		
Devon White		
Matt Williams		
Jay Bell		
❑ 30 Tampa Bay Devil Rays	5.00	2.20
Wade Boggs		
Paul Sorrento		
Fred McGriff		
Roberto Hernandez		

1999 Pacific Invincible

	MINT	NRMT
COMPLETE SET (150)	180.00	80.00
COMMON CARD (1-150)	.60	.25
MINOR STARS	1.00	.45
SEMISTARS	1.50	.70

UNLISTED STARS 2.50   1.10

☐ 1 Jim Edmonds	1.00	.45
☐ 2 Darin Erstad	1.50	.70
☐ 3 Troy Glaus	2.50	1.10
☐ 4 Tim Salmon	1.50	.70
☐ 5 Mo Vaughn	2.50	1.10
☐ 6 Steve Finley	1.00	.45
☐ 7 Randy Johnson	2.50	1.10
☐ 8 Travis Lee	1.50	.70
☐ 9 Dante Powell	.60	.25
☐ 10 Matt Williams	2.50	1.10
☐ 11 Bret Boone	1.00	.45
☐ 12 Andruw Jones	2.50	1.10
☐ 13 Chipper Jones	6.00	2.70
☐ 14 Brian Jordan	1.00	.45
☐ 15 Ryan Klesko	1.00	.45
☐ 16 Javy Lopez	1.00	.45
☐ 17 Greg Maddux	6.00	2.70
☐ 18 Brady Anderson	1.00	.45
☐ 19 Albert Belle	2.50	1.10
☐ 20 Will Clark	2.50	1.10
☐ 21 Mike Mussina	2.50	1.10
☐ 22 Cal Ripken	10.00	4.50
☐ 23 Nomar Garciaparra	8.00	3.60
☐ 24 Pedro Martinez	3.00	1.35
☐ 25 Trot Nixon	1.00	.45
☐ 26 Jose Offerman	1.00	.45
☐ 27 Donnie Sadler	.60	.25
☐ 28 John Valentin	1.00	.45
☐ 29 Mark Grace	1.50	.70
☐ 30 Lance Johnson	.60	.25
☐ 31 Henry Rodriguez	1.00	.45
☐ 32 Sammy Sosa	8.00	3.60
☐ 33 Kerry Wood	2.50	1.10
☐ 34 McKay Christensen	.60	.25
☐ 35 Ray Durham	1.00	.45
☐ 36 Jeff Liefer	.60	.25
☐ 37 Frank Thomas	5.00	2.20
☐ 38 Mike Cameron	.60	.25
☐ 39 Barry Larkin	2.50	1.10
☐ 40 Greg Vaughn	1.00	.45
☐ 41 Dmitri Young	1.00	.45
☐ 42 Roberto Alomar	2.50	1.10
☐ 43 Sandy Alomar Jr.	1.00	.45
☐ 44 David Justice	1.00	.45
☐ 45 Kenny Lofton	1.50	.70
☐ 46 Manny Ramirez	3.00	1.35
☐ 47 Jim Thome	2.50	1.10
☐ 48 Dante Bichette	1.00	.45
☐ 49 Vinny Castilla	1.00	.45
☐ 50 Darryl Hamilton	.60	.25
☐ 51 Todd Helton	2.50	1.10
☐ 52 Neifi Perez	1.00	.45
☐ 53 Larry Walker	2.50	1.10
☐ 54 Tony Clark	1.00	.45
☐ 55 Damion Easley	1.00	.45
☐ 56 Bob Higginson	1.00	.45
☐ 57 Brian L Hunter	.60	.25
☐ 58 Gabe Kapler	2.50	1.10
☐ 59 Cliff Floyd	1.00	.45
☐ 60 Alex Gonzalez	1.00	.45
☐ 61 Mark Kotsay	.60	.25
☐ 62 Derrek Lee	.60	.25
☐ 63 Braden Looper	.60	.25
☐ 64 Moises Alou	1.00	.45
☐ 65 Jeff Bagwell	3.00	1.35
☐ 66 Craig Biggio	2.50	1.10
☐ 67 Ken Caminiti	1.00	.45
☐ 68 Scott Elarton	.60	.25
☐ 69 Mitch Meluskey	.60	.25
☐ 70 Carlos Beltran	3.00	1.35
☐ 71 Johnny Damon	1.00	.45
☐ 72 Carlos Febles	1.00	.45
☐ 73 Jeremy Giambi	1.00	.45
☐ 74 Kevin Brown	1.50	.70
☐ 75 Todd Hundley	1.00	.45
☐ 76 Paul LoDuca	.60	.45
☐ 77 Raul Mondesi	1.00	.45
☐ 78 Gary Sheffield	1.00	.45
☐ 79 Geoff Jenkins	1.00	.45
☐ 80 Jeromy Burnitz	1.00	.45
☐ 81 Marquis Grissom	.60	.25
☐ 82 Jose Valentin	.60	.25
☐ 83 Fernando Vina	.60	.25
☐ 84 Corey Koskie	.60	.25
☐ 85 Matt Lawton	.60	.25
☐ 86 Christian Guzman	.60	.25
☐ 87 Torii Hunter	.60	.25
☐ 88 Doug Mientkiewicz	1.25	.55
☐ 89 Michael Barrett	1.50	.70
☐ 90 Brad Fullmer	.60	.25
☐ 91 Vladimir Guerrero	3.00	1.35
☐ 92 Fernando Seguignol	1.00	.45
☐ 93 Ugueth Urbina	.60	.25
☐ 94 Bobby Bonilla	1.00	.45
☐ 95 Rickey Henderson	3.00	1.35
☐ 96 Rey Ordonez	1.00	.45
☐ 97 Mike Piazza	8.00	3.60
☐ 98 Robin Ventura	1.00	.45
☐ 99 Roger Clemens	6.00	2.70
☐ 100 Derek Jeter	8.00	3.60
☐ 101 Chuck Knoblauch	1.00	.45
☐ 102 Tino Martinez	1.00	.45
☐ 103 Paul O'Neill	1.00	.45
☐ 104 Bernie Williams	2.50	1.10
☐ 105 Eric Chavez	1.50	.70
☐ 106 Ryan Christenson	.60	.25
☐ 107 Jason Giambi	1.00	.45
☐ 108 Ben Grieve	2.50	1.10
☐ 109 Miguel Tejada	1.00	.45
☐ 110 Marlon Anderson	.60	.25
☐ 111 Doug Glanville	1.00	.45
☐ 112 Scott Rolen	3.00	1.35
☐ 113 Curt Schilling	1.50	.70
☐ 114 Brian Giles	1.00	.45
☐ 115 Warren Morris	1.00	.45
☐ 116 Jason Kendall	1.00	.45
☐ 117 Kris Benson	1.00	.45
☐ 118 J.D. Drew	4.00	1.80
☐ 119 Ray Lankford	1.00	.45
☐ 120 Mark McGwire	15.00	6.75
☐ 121 Matt Clement	1.00	.45
☐ 122 Tony Gwynn	6.00	2.70
☐ 123 Trevor Hoffman	1.00	.45
☐ 124 Wally Joyner	1.00	.45
☐ 125 Reggie Sanders	.60	.25
☐ 126 Barry Bonds	3.00	1.35
☐ 127 Ellis Burks	1.00	.45
☐ 128 Jeff Kent	1.00	.45
☐ 129 Stan Javier	.60	.25
☐ 130 J.T. Snow	1.00	.45
☐ 131 Jay Buhner	1.00	.45
☐ 132 Freddy Garcia	10.00	4.50
☐ 133 Ken Griffey Jr.	12.00	5.50
☐ 134 Russ Davis	.60	.25
☐ 135 Edgar Martinez	1.00	.45
☐ 136 Alex Rodriguez	8.00	3.60
☐ 137 David Segui	.60	.25
☐ 138 Rolando Arrojo	.60	.25
☐ 139 Wade Boggs	2.50	1.10
☐ 140 Jose Canseco	3.00	1.35
☐ 141 Quinton McCracken	.60	.25
☐ 142 Fred McGriff	1.50	.70
☐ 143 Juan Gonzalez	5.00	2.20
☐ 144 Tom Goodwin	.60	.25
☐ 145 Rusty Greer	1.00	.45
☐ 146 Ivan Rodriguez	3.00	1.35
☐ 147 Jose Cruz Jr.	1.00	.45
☐ 148 Carlos Delgado	2.50	1.10
☐ 149 Shawn Green	2.50	1.10
☐ 150 Roy Halladay	1.00	.45

1999 Pacific Invincible Opening Day

	MINT	NRMT
COMMON CARD (1-150)	8.00	3.60
*STARS: 5X TO 12X BASIC CARDS		
*YNG.STARS: 4X TO 10X BASIC CARDS		
*ROOKIES: 3X TO 8X BASIC CARDS		
STATED ODDS 1:25 HOBBY		
STATED PRINT RUN 69 SERIAL #'d SETS		

1999 Pacific Invincible Platinum Blue

	MINT	NRMT
COMMON CARD (1-150)	8.00	3.60
*STARS: 5X TO 12X BASIC CARDS		
*YNG.STARS: 4X TO 10X BASIC CARDS		
*ROOKIES: 3X TO 8X BASIC CARDS		
RANDOM INSERTS IN PACKS		
STATED PRINT RUN 67 SERIAL #'d SETS		

1999 Pacific Invincible Diamond Magic

	MINT	NRMT
COMPLETE SET (10)	150.00	70.00
COMMON CARD (1-10)	8.00	3.60
STATED ODDS 1:49		

☐ 1 Cal Ripken	25.00	11.00
☐ 2 Nomar Garciaparra	20.00	9.00

	MINT	NRMT
3 Sammy Sosa	20.00	9.00
4 Frank Thomas	12.00	5.50
5 Mike Piazza	20.00	9.00
6 J.D. Drew	8.00	3.60
7 Mark McGwire	40.00	18.00
8 Tony Gwynn	15.00	6.75
9 Ken Griffey Jr.	30.00	13.50
10 Alex Rodriguez	20.00	9.00

1999 Pacific Invincible Flash Point

	MINT	NRMT
COMPLETE SET (20)	200.00	90.00
COMMON CARD (1-20)	4.00	1.80
STATED ODDS 1:25		

	MINT	NRMT
1 Mo Vaughn	4.00	1.80
2 Chipper Jones	12.00	5.50
3 Greg Maddux	15.00	6.75
4 Cal Ripken	20.00	9.00
5 Nomar Garciaparra	15.00	6.75
6 Sammy Sosa	15.00	6.75
7 Frank Thomas	10.00	4.50
8 Manny Ramirez	6.00	2.70
9 Vladimir Guerrero	6.00	2.70
10 Mike Piazza	15.00	6.75
11 Roger Clemens	12.00	5.50
12 Derek Jeter	15.00	6.75
13 Ben Grieve	4.00	1.80
14 Scott Rolen	6.00	2.70
15 J.D. Drew	6.00	2.70
16 Mark McGwire	30.00	13.50
17 Tony Gwynn	12.00	5.50
18 Ken Griffey Jr.	25.00	11.00
19 Alex Rodriguez	15.00	6.75
20 Juan Gonzalez	10.00	4.50

1999 Pacific Invincible Giants of the Game

	MINT	NRMT

RANDOM INSERTS IN PACKS
STATED PRINT RUN 10 SERIAL #'d SETS
NO PRICING AVAILABLE DUE TO SCARCITY

- 1 Cal Ripken
- 2 Nomar Garciaparra
- 3 Sammy Sosa
- 4 Frank Thomas
- 5 Mike Piazza
- 6 J.D. Drew
- 7 Mark McGwire
- 8 Tony Gwynn
- 9 Ken Griffey Jr.
- 10 Alex Rodriguez

1999 Pacific Invincible Sandlot Heroes

	MINT	NRMT
COMPLETE SET (40)	30.00	13.50
COMMON CARD (1A-20B)	.30	.14
UNLISTED STARS	.50	.23

ONE PER PACK
TWO VERSIONS OF EACH CARD EXIST

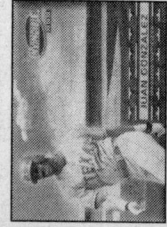

A/B VERSIONS VALUED EQUALLY

	MINT	NRMT
1 Mo Vaughn	.50	.23
1B Mo Vaughn	.50	.23
2 Chipper Jones	1.25	.55
2B Chipper Jones	1.25	.55
3 Greg Maddux	1.25	.55
3B Greg Maddux	1.25	.55
4 Cal Ripken	2.00	.90
4B Cal Ripken	2.00	.90
5 Nomar Garciaparra	1.50	.70
5B Nomar Garciaparra	1.50	.70
6 Sammy Sosa	1.50	.70
6B Sammy Sosa	1.50	.70
7 Frank Thomas	1.00	.45
7B Frank Thomas	1.00	.45
8 Manny Ramirez	.60	.25
8B Manny Ramirez	.60	.25
9 Vladimir Guerrero	.60	.25
9B Vladimir Guerrero	.60	.25
10 Mike Piazza	1.50	.70
10B Mike Piazza	1.50	.70
11 Roger Clemens	1.25	.55
11B Roger Clemens	1.25	.55
12 Derek Jeter	1.50	.70
12B Derek Jeter	1.50	.70
13 Eric Chavez	.30	.14
13B Eric Chavez	.30	.14
14 Ben Grieve	.50	.23
14B Ben Grieve	.50	.23
15 J.D. Drew	.75	.35
15B J.D. Drew	.75	.35
16 Mark McGwire	3.00	1.35
16B Mark McGwire	3.00	1.35
17 Tony Gwynn	1.25	.55
17B Tony Gwynn	1.25	.55
18 Ken Griffey Jr	2.50	1.10
18B Ken Griffey Jr.	2.50	1.10
19 Alex Rodriguez	1.50	.70
19B Alex Rodriguez	1.50	.70
20 Juan Gonzalez	1.00	.45
20B Juan Gonzalez	1.00	.45

1999 Pacific Invincible Seismic Force

	MINT	NRMT
COMPLETE SET (40)	40.00	18.00
COMMON CARD (1A-20B)	.50	.23

ONE PER PACK

**TWO VERSIONS OF EACH CARD EXIST
A/B VERSIONS VALUED EQUALLY**

	MINT	NRMT
1 Mo Vaughn	.50	.23
1B Mo Vaughn	.50	.23
2 Chipper Jones	1.25	.55
2B Chipper Jones	1.25	.55
3 Greg Maddux	1.25	.55
3B Greg Maddux	1.25	.55
4 Cal Ripken	2.00	.90
4B Cal Ripken	2.00	.90
5 Nomar Garciaparra	1.50	.70
5B Nomar Garciaparra	1.50	.70
6 Sammy Sosa	1.50	.70
6B Sammy Sosa	1.50	.70
7 Frank Thomas	1.00	.45
7B Frank Thomas	1.00	.45
8 Manny Ramirez	.60	.25
8B Manny Ramirez	.60	.25
9 Vladimir Guerrero	.60	.25
9B Vladimir Guerrero	.60	.25
10 Mike Piazza	1.50	.70
10B Mike Piazza	1.50	.70
11 Bernie Williams	.50	.23
11B Bernie Williams	.50	.23
12 Derek Jeter	1.50	.70
12B Derek Jeter	1.50	.70
13 Ben Grieve	.50	.23
13B Ben Grieve	.50	.23
14 J.D. Drew	.75	.35
14B J.D. Drew	.75	.35
15 Mark McGwire	3.00	1.35
15B Mark McGwire	3.00	1.35
16 Tony Gwynn	1.25	.55
16B Tony Gwynn	1.25	.55
17 Ken Griffey Jr.	2.50	1.10
17B Ken Griffey Jr.	2.50	1.10
18 Alex Rodriguez	1.50	.70
18B Alex Rodriguez	1.50	.70
19 Juan Gonzalez	1.00	.45
19B Juan Gonzalez	1.00	.45
20 Ivan Rodriguez	.60	.25
20B Ivan Rodriguez	.60	.25

1999 Pacific Invincible Thunder Alley

	MINT	NRMT
COMPLETE SET (20)	750.00	350.00
COMMON CARD (1-20)	12.00	5.50
STATED ODDS 1:121		

	MINT	NRMT
1 Mo Vaughn	12.00	5.50
2 Chipper Jones	40.00	18.00
3 Cal Ripken	60.00	27.00
4 Nomar Garciaparra	50.00	22.00
5 Sammy Sosa	50.00	22.00
6 Frank Thomas	30.00	13.50
7 Manny Ramirez	20.00	9.00
8 Todd Helton	12.00	5.50
9 Vladimir Guerrero	20.00	9.00
10 Mike Piazza	50.00	22.00
11 Derek Jeter	50.00	22.00
12 Ben Grieve	12.00	5.50
13 Scott Rolen	20.00	9.00
14 J.D. Drew	20.00	9.00
15 Mark McGwire	100.00	45.00
16 Tony Gwynn	40.00	18.00

		MINT	NRMT
❑ 17	Ken Griffey Jr.	80.00	36.00
❑ 18	Alex Rodriguez	50.00	22.00
❑ 19	Juan Gonzalez	30.00	13.50
❑ 20	Ivan Rodriguez	20.00	9.00

1998 Pacific Omega

		MINT	NRMT
COMPLETE SET (250)		40.00	18.00
COMMON CARD (1-250)		.15	.07
MINOR STARS		.25	.11
SEMISTARS		.40	.18
UNLISTED STARS		.60	.25

❑ 1	Garret Anderson	.25	.11
❑ 2	Gary DiSarcina	.15	.07
❑ 3	Jim Edmonds	.25	.11
❑ 4	Darin Erstad	.40	.18
❑ 5	Cecil Fielder	.25	.11
❑ 6	Chuck Finley	.15	.07
❑ 7	Shigetoshi Hasegawa	.25	.11
❑ 8	Tim Salmon	.40	.18
❑ 9	Brian Anderson	.15	.07
❑ 10	Jay Bell	.25	.11
❑ 11	Andy Benes	.15	.07
❑ 12	Yamil Benitez	.15	.07
❑ 13	Jorge Fabregas	.15	.07
❑ 14	Travis Lee	.40	.18
❑ 15	Devon White	.15	.07
❑ 16	Matt Williams	.60	.25
❑ 17	Andres Galarraga	.40	.18
❑ 18	Tom Glavine	.60	.25
❑ 19	Andruw Jones	.60	.25
❑ 20	Chipper Jones	1.50	.70
❑ 21	Ryan Klesko	.25	.11
❑ 22	Javy Lopez	.25	.11
❑ 23	Greg Maddux	1.50	.70
❑ 24	Kevin Millwood	2.00	.90
❑ 25	Denny Neagle	.15	.07
❑ 26	John Smoltz	.40	.18
❑ 27	Roberto Alomar	.60	.25
❑ 28	Brady Anderson	.25	.11
❑ 29	Joe Carter	.25	.11
❑ 30	Eric Davis	.15	.07
❑ 31	Jimmy Key	.15	.07
❑ 32	Mike Mussina	.60	.25
❑ 33	Rafael Palmeiro	.60	.25
❑ 34	Cal Ripken	2.50	1.10
❑ 35	B.J. Surhoff	.25	.11
❑ 36	Dennis Eckersley	.25	.11
❑ 37	Nomar Garciaparra	2.00	.90
❑ 38	Reggie Jefferson	.15	.07
❑ 39	Derek Lowe	.15	.07
❑ 40	Pedro Martinez	.75	.35
❑ 41	Brian Rose	.15	.07
❑ 42	John Valentin	.25	.11
❑ 43	Jason Varitek	.25	.11
❑ 44	Mo Vaughn	.60	.25
❑ 45	Jeff Blauser	.15	.07
❑ 46	Jeremi Gonzalez	.15	.07
❑ 47	Mark Grace	.40	.18
❑ 48	Lance Johnson	.15	.07
❑ 49	Kevin Orie	.15	.07
❑ 50	Henry Rodriguez	.15	.07
❑ 51	Sammy Sosa	2.00	.90
❑ 52	Kerry Wood	.75	.35
❑ 53	Albert Belle	.60	.25
❑ 54	Mike Cameron	.25	.11
❑ 55	Mike Caruso	.15	.07
❑ 56	Ray Durham	.25	.11
❑ 57	Jaime Navarro	.15	.07
❑ 58	Greg Norton	.15	.07
❑ 59	Magglio Ordonez	2.00	.90
❑ 60	Frank Thomas	1.25	.55
❑ 61	Robin Ventura	.25	.11
❑ 62	Bret Boone	.25	.11
❑ 63	Willie Greene	.15	.07
❑ 64	Barry Larkin	.60	.25
❑ 65	Jon Nunnally	.15	.07
❑ 66	Eduardo Perez	.15	.07
❑ 67	Reggie Sanders	.15	.07
❑ 68	Brett Tomko	.15	.07
❑ 69	Sandy Alomar Jr.	.25	.11
❑ 70	Travis Fryman	.25	.11
❑ 71	David Justice	.25	.11
❑ 72	Kenny Lofton	.40	.18
❑ 73	Charles Nagy	.15	.07
❑ 74	Manny Ramirez	.75	.35
❑ 75	Jim Thome	.60	.25
❑ 76	Omar Vizquel	.25	.11
❑ 77	Enrique Wilson	.15	.07
❑ 78	Jaret Wright	.25	.11
❑ 79	Dante Bichette	.25	.11
❑ 80	Ellis Burks	.25	.11
❑ 81	Vinny Castilla	.25	.11
❑ 82	Todd Helton	.75	.35
❑ 83	Darryl Kile	.15	.07
❑ 84	Mike Lansing	.15	.07
❑ 85	Neifi Perez	.15	.07
❑ 86	Larry Walker	.60	.25
❑ 87	Raul Casanova	.15	.07
❑ 88	Tony Clark	.25	.11
❑ 89	Luis Gonzalez	.25	.11
❑ 90	Bobby Higginson	.25	.11
❑ 91	Brian Hunter	.15	.07
❑ 92	Bip Roberts	.15	.07
❑ 93	Justin Thompson	.15	.07
❑ 94	Josh Booty	.15	.07
❑ 95	Craig Counsell	.15	.07
❑ 96	Livan Hernandez	.15	.07
❑ 97	Ryan Jackson	.25	.11
❑ 98	Mark Kotsay	.25	.11
❑ 99	Derrek Lee	.15	.07
❑ 100	Mike Piazza	2.00	.90
❑ 101	Edgar Renteria	.25	.11
❑ 102	Cliff Floyd	.25	.11
❑ 103	Moises Alou	.25	.11
❑ 104	Jeff Bagwell	.75	.35
❑ 105	Derek Bell	.25	.11
❑ 106	Sean Berry	.15	.07
❑ 107	Craig Biggio	.60	.25
❑ 108	John Halama	.60	.25
❑ 109	Richard Hidalgo	.25	.11
❑ 110	Shane Reynolds	.25	.11
❑ 111	Tim Belcher	.15	.07
❑ 112	Brian Bevil	.15	.07
❑ 113	Jeff Conine	.15	.07
❑ 114	Johnny Damon	.25	.11
❑ 115	Jeff King	.15	.07
❑ 116	Jeff Montgomery	.15	.07
❑ 117	Dean Palmer	.25	.11
❑ 118	Terry Pendleton	.25	.11
❑ 119	Bobby Bonilla	.15	.07
❑ 120	Wilton Guerrero	.15	.07
❑ 121	Todd Hollandsworth	.15	.07
❑ 122	Charles Johnson	.25	.11
❑ 123	Eric Karros	.25	.11
❑ 124	Paul Konerko	.25	.11
❑ 125	Ramon Martinez	.25	.11
❑ 126	Raul Mondesi	.25	.11
❑ 127	Hideo Nomo	.60	.25
❑ 128	Gary Sheffield	.25	.11
❑ 129	Ismael Valdes	.15	.07
❑ 130	Jeromy Burnitz	.25	.11
❑ 131	Jeff Cirillo	.15	.07
❑ 132	Todd Dunn	.15	.07
❑ 133	Marquis Grissom	.15	.07
❑ 134	John Jaha	.15	.07
❑ 135	Scott Karl	.15	.07
❑ 136	Dave Nilsson	.15	.07
❑ 137	Jose Valentin	.15	.07
❑ 138	Fernando Vina	.15	.07
❑ 139	Rick Aguilera	.15	.07
❑ 140	Marty Cordova	.15	.07
❑ 141	Pat Meares	.15	.07
❑ 142	Paul Molitor	.60	.25
❑ 143	David Ortiz	.15	.07
❑ 144	Brad Radke	.25	.11
❑ 145	Terry Steinbach	.15	.07
❑ 146	Todd Walker	.25	.11
❑ 147	Shane Andrews	.15	.07
❑ 148	Brad Fullmer	.25	.11
❑ 149	Mark Grudzielanek	.15	.07
❑ 150	Vladimir Guerrero	.75	.35
❑ 151	F.P. Santangelo	.15	.07
❑ 152	Jose Vidro	.15	.07
❑ 153	Rondell White	.25	.11
❑ 154	Carlos Baerga	.25	.11
❑ 155	Bernard Gilkey	.15	.07
❑ 156	Todd Hundley	.25	.11
❑ 157	Butch Huskey	.15	.07
❑ 158	Bobby Jones	.15	.07
❑ 159	Brian McRae	.15	.07
❑ 160	John Olerud	.25	.11
❑ 161	Rey Ordonez	.25	.11
❑ 162	Masato Yoshii	.40	.18
❑ 163	David Cone	.40	.18
❑ 164	Hideki Irabu	.25	.11
❑ 165	Derek Jeter	2.00	.90
❑ 166	Chuck Knoblauch	.25	.11
❑ 167	Tino Martinez	.25	.11
❑ 168	Paul O'Neill	.25	.11
❑ 169	Andy Pettitte	.25	.11
❑ 170	Mariano Rivera	.25	.11
❑ 171	Darryl Strawberry	.25	.11
❑ 172	David Wells	.25	.11
❑ 173	Bernie Williams	.60	.25
❑ 174	Ryan Christenson	.25	.11
❑ 175	Jason Giambi	.25	.11
❑ 176	Ben Grieve	.60	.25
❑ 177	Rickey Henderson	.75	.35
❑ 178	A.J. Hinch	.15	.07
❑ 179	Kenny Rogers	.15	.07
❑ 180	Ricky Bottalico	.15	.07
❑ 181	Rico Brogna	.15	.07
❑ 182	Doug Glanville	.25	.11
❑ 183	Gregg Jefferies	.15	.07
❑ 184	Mike Lieberthal	.25	.11
❑ 185	Scott Rolen	.75	.35
❑ 186	Curt Schilling	.40	.18
❑ 187	Jermaine Allensworth	.15	.07
❑ 188	Lou Collier	.15	.07
❑ 189	Jose Guillen	.25	.11
❑ 190	Jason Kendall	.25	.11
❑ 191	Al Martin	.15	.07
❑ 192	Tony Womack	.15	.07
❑ 193	Kevin Young	.25	.11
❑ 194	Royce Clayton	.15	.07
❑ 195	Delino DeShields	.25	.11
❑ 196	Gary Gaetti	.25	.11
❑ 197	Ron Gant	.25	.11
❑ 198	Brian Jordan	.25	.11
❑ 199	Ray Lankford	.25	.11
❑ 200	Mark McGwire	4.00	1.80
❑ 201	Todd Stottlemyre	.15	.07
❑ 202	Kevin Brown	.40	.18
❑ 203	Ken Caminiti	.25	.11
❑ 204	Steve Finley	.15	.07
❑ 205	Tony Gwynn	1.50	.70
❑ 206	Carlos Hernandez	.15	.07
❑ 207	Wally Joyner	.25	.11
❑ 208	Greg Vaughn	.25	.11
❑ 209	Barry Bonds	.75	.35
❑ 210	Shawn Estes	.15	.07
❑ 211	Orel Hershiser	.25	.11
❑ 212	Stan Javier	.15	.07
❑ 213	Jeff Kent	.25	.11
❑ 214	Bill Mueller	.15	.07
❑ 215	Robb Nen	.15	.07
❑ 216	J.T. Snow	.25	.11
❑ 217	Jay Buhner	.25	.11
❑ 218	Ken Cloude	.15	.07
❑ 219	Joey Cora	.15	.07
❑ 220	Ken Griffey Jr.	3.00	1.35
❑ 221	Glenallen Hill	.25	.11
❑ 222	Randy Johnson	.60	.25
❑ 223	Edgar Martinez	.25	.11
❑ 224	Jamie Moyer	.15	.07
❑ 225	Alex Rodriguez	2.00	.90
❑ 226	David Segui	.15	.07

	MINT	NRMT
❏ 227 Dan Wilson	.15	.07
❏ 228 Rolando Arrojo	.60	.25
❏ 229 Wade Boggs	.60	.25
❏ 230 Miguel Cairo	.15	.07
❏ 231 Roberto Hernandez	.15	.07
❏ 232 Quinton McCracken	.15	.07
❏ 233 Fred McGriff	.40	.18
❏ 234 Paul Sorrento	.15	.07
❏ 235 Kevin Stocker	.15	.07
❏ 236 Will Clark	.60	.25
❏ 237 Juan Gonzalez	1.25	.55
❏ 238 Rusty Greer	.25	.11
❏ 239 Rick Helling	.15	.07
❏ 240 Roberto Kelly	.15	.07
❏ 241 Ivan Rodriguez	.75	.35
❏ 242 Aaron Sele	.25	.11
❏ 243 John Wetteland	.25	.11
❏ 244 Jose Canseco	.75	.35
❏ 245 Roger Clemens	1.50	.70
❏ 246 Jose Cruz Jr.	.25	.11
❏ 247 Carlos Delgado	.60	.25
❏ 248 Alex Gonzalez	.15	.07
❏ 249 Ed Sprague	.15	.07
❏ 250 Shannon Stewart	.25	.11
❏ NNO Tony Gwynn Sample..	3.00	1.35

1998 Pacific Omega Red

	MINT	NRMT
COMMON CARD (1-250)	1.50	.70

*STARS: 4X TO 10X BASIC CARDS
*ROOKIES: 2.5X TO 6X BASIC CARDS
STATED ODDS 1:4 RETAIL

1998 Pacific Omega EO Portraits

	MINT	NRMT
COMPLETE SET (20)	400.00	180.00
COMMON CARD (1-20)	6.00	2.70
UNLISTED STARS	10.00	4.50

STATED ODDS 1:73
EO PORTRAIT 1 OF 1 PARALLELS EXIST
EO PORT. 1 OF 1'S TOO SCARCE TO PRICE

	MINT	NRMT
❏ 1 Cal Ripken	40.00	18.00
❏ 2 Nomar Garciaparra	30.00	13.50
❏ 3 Mo Vaughn	10.00	4.50
❏ 4 Frank Thomas	20.00	9.00

	MINT	NRMT
❏ 5 Manny Ramirez	12.00	5.50
❏ 6 Ben Grieve	10.00	4.50
❏ 7 Ken Griffey Jr.	50.00	22.00
❏ 8 Alex Rodriguez	30.00	13.50
❏ 9 Juan Gonzalez	20.00	9.00
❏ 10 Ivan Rodriguez	12.00	5.50
❏ 11 Travis Lee	6.00	2.70
❏ 12 Greg Maddux	25.00	11.00
❏ 13 Chipper Jones	25.00	11.00
❏ 14 Kerry Wood	10.00	4.50
❏ 15 Larry Walker	10.00	4.50
❏ 16 Jeff Bagwell	12.00	5.50
❏ 17 Mike Piazza	30.00	13.50
❏ 18 Mark McGwire	60.00	27.00
❏ 19 Tony Gwynn	25.00	11.00
❏ 20 Barry Bonds	12.00	5.50

1998 Pacific Omega Face To Face

	MINT	NRMT
COMPLETE SET (10)	300.00	135.00
COMMON CARD (1-10)	10.00	4.50

STATED ODDS 1:145

	MINT	NRMT
❏ 1 Alex Rodriguez Nomar Garciaparra	40.00	18.00
❏ 2 Mark McGwire Ken Griffey Jr.	60.00	27.00
❏ 3 Mike Piazza Sandy Alomar Jr.	30.00	13.50
❏ 4 Kerry Wood Roger Clemens	20.00	9.00
❏ 5 Cal Ripken Paul Molitor	40.00	18.00
❏ 6 Tony Gwynn Wade Boggs	25.00	11.00
❏ 7 Frank Thomas Chipper Jones	30.00	13.50
❏ 8 Travis Lee Ben Grieve	10.00	4.50
❏ 9 Hideo Nomo Hideki Irabu	10.00	4.50
❏ 10 Juan Gonzalez Manny Ramirez	20.00	9.00

1998 Pacific Omega Online Inserts

	MINT	NRMT
COMPLETE SET (36)	200.00	90.00
COMMON CARD (1-36)	1.00	.45

STATED ODDS 4:37

	MINT	NRMT
❏ 1 Cal Ripken	15.00	6.75
❏ 2 Nomar Garciaparra	12.00	5.50
❏ 3 Pedro Martinez	5.00	2.20
❏ 4 Mo Vaughn	4.00	1.80
❏ 5 Frank Thomas	8.00	3.60
❏ 6 Sandy Alomar Jr.	1.50	.70
❏ 7 Manny Ramirez	5.00	2.20
❏ 8 Jaret Wright	1.50	.70
❏ 9 Paul Molitor	4.00	1.80
❏ 10 Derek Jeter	12.00	5.50
❏ 11 Bernie Williams	4.00	1.80
❏ 12 Ben Grieve	4.00	1.80
❏ 13 Ken Griffey Jr.	20.00	9.00
❏ 14 Edgar Martinez	1.50	.70
❏ 15 Alex Rodriguez	12.00	5.50
❏ 16 Wade Boggs	4.00	1.80
❏ 17 Juan Gonzalez	8.00	3.60
❏ 18 Ivan Rodriguez	5.00	2.20
❏ 19 Roger Clemens	10.00	4.50
❏ 20 Travis Lee	2.50	1.10
❏ 21 Matt Williams	4.00	1.80
❏ 22 Andres Galarraga	2.50	1.10
❏ 23 Chipper Jones	10.00	4.50
❏ 24 Greg Maddux	10.00	4.50
❏ 25 Sammy Sosa	12.00	5.50
❏ 26 Kerry Wood	4.00	1.80
❏ 27 Barry Larkin	4.00	1.80
❏ 28 Larry Walker	4.00	1.80
❏ 29 Derek Lee	1.00	.45
❏ 30 Jeff Bagwell	5.00	2.20
❏ 31 Hideo Nomo	4.00	1.80
❏ 32 Mike Piazza	12.00	5.50
❏ 33 Scott Rolen	6.00	2.70
❏ 34 Mark McGwire	25.00	11.00
❏ 35 Tony Gwynn	10.00	4.50
❏ 36 Barry Bonds	5.00	2.20

1998 Pacific Omega Prisms

	MINT	NRMT
COMPLETE SET (20)	200.00	90.00
COMMON CARD (1-20)	2.00	.90

STATED ODDS 1:37

	MINT	NRMT
❏ 1 Cal Ripken	20.00	9.00
❏ 2 Nomar Garciaparra	15.00	6.75
❏ 3 Pedro Martinez	6.00	2.70
❏ 4 Frank Thomas	10.00	4.50
❏ 5 Manny Ramirez	6.00	2.70
❏ 6 Brian Giles	2.00	.90
❏ 7 Derek Jeter	15.00	6.75
❏ 8 Ben Grieve	5.00	2.20
❏ 9 Ken Griffey Jr.	25.00	11.00
❏ 10 Alex Rodriguez	15.00	6.75
❏ 11 Juan Gonzalez	10.00	4.50
❏ 12 Travis Lee	3.00	1.35
❏ 13 Chipper Jones	12.00	5.50
❏ 14 Greg Maddux	12.00	5.50
❏ 15 Kerry Wood	5.00	2.20
❏ 16 Larry Walker	5.00	2.20
❏ 17 Hideo Nomo	5.00	2.20
❏ 18 Mike Piazza	15.00	6.75

		MINT	NRMT
❏ 19 Mark McGwire		30.00	13.50
❏ 20 Tony Gwynn		12.00	5.50

1998 Pacific Omega Rising Stars

	MINT	NRMT
COMPLETE SET (30)	50.00	22.00
COMMON CARD (1-30)	1.00	.45
MINOR STARS	1.50	.70
SEMISTARS	2.50	1.10
UNLISTED STARS	3.00	1.35

STATED ODDS 4:37 HOBBY
*TIER 1: 4X TO 10X HI COLUMN
TIER 1 PRINT RUN 100 SERIAL #'d SETS
TIER 1 CARDS ARE 2/10/16/19/20/25
*TIER 2: 5X TO 12X HI COLUMN
TIER 2 PRINT RUN 75 SERIAL #'d SETS
TIER 2 CARDS ARE 3/12/18/23/26/27
*TIER 3: 6X TO 15X HI COLUMN
TIER 3 PRINT RUN 50 SERIAL #'d SETS
TIER 3 CARDS ARE 1/7/15/17/22/28
*TIER 4: 12.5X TO 30X HI COLUMN
TIER 4 PRINT RUN 25 SERIAL #'d SETS
TIER 4 CARDS ARE 6/9/11/14/21/29
TIER 5 STATED PRINT RUN 1 SET
TIER 5 CARDS ARE 4/5/8/13/24/30
TIER 5 NOT PRICED DUE TO SCARCITY

		MINT	NRMT
❏ 1 Nerio Rodriguez		1.50	.70
	Sidney Ponson		
❏ 2 Frank Catalanotto		1.00	.45
	Roberto Duran		
	Sean Runyan		
❏ 3 Kevin L.Brown		1.00	.45
	Carlos Almanzar		
❏ 4 Aaron Boone		1.00	.45
	Pat Watkins		
	Scott Winchester		
❏ 5 Brian Meadows		1.00	.45
	Andy Larkin		
	Antonio Alfonseca		
❏ 6 DaRond Stovall		1.00	.45
	Trey Moore		
	Shayne Bennett		
❏ 7 Felix Martinez		1.00	.45
	Larry Sutton		
	Brian Bevil		
❏ 8 Homer Bush		1.00	.45
	Mike Buddie		
❏ 9 Rich Butler		2.50	1.10
	Esteban Yan		
❏ 10 Dave Hollins		1.00	.45
	Brian Edmondson		
❏ 11 Lou Collier		1.00	.45
	Jose Silva		
	Javier Martinez		
❏ 12 Steve Sinclair		1.00	.45
	Mark Dalesandro		
❏ 13 Jason Varitek		1.50	.70
	Brian Rose		
	Brian Shouse		
❏ 14 Mike Caruso		1.00	.45
	Jeff Abbott		
	Tom Fordham		
❏ 15 Jason Johnson		1.00	.45
	Bobby Smith		
❏ 16 Dave Berg		1.50	.70

		MINT	NRMT
	Mark Kotsay		
	Jesus Sanchez		
❏ 17 Richard Hidalgo		3.00	1.35
	John Halama		
	Trever Miller		
❏ 18 Geoff Jenkins		1.50	.70
	Bobby Hughes		
	Steve Woodard		
❏ 19 Eli Marrero		1.00	.45
	Cliff Politte		
	Mike Busby		
❏ 20 Desi Relaford		1.00	.45
	Darrin Winston		
❏ 21 Todd Helton		5.00	2.20
	Bobby Jones		
❏ 22 Rolando Arrojo		3.00	1.35
	Miguel Cairo		
	Dan Carlson		
❏ 23 David Ortiz		1.00	.45
	Jose Valentin		
	Eric Milton		
❏ 24 Magglio Ordonez		10.00	4.50
	Greg Norton		
❏ 25 Brad Fullmer		1.00	.45
	Javier Vazquez		
	Rick DeHart		
❏ 26 Paul Konerko		1.50	.70
	Matt Luke		
❏ 27 Derrek Lee		3.00	1.35
	Ryan Jackson		
	John Roskos		
❏ 28 Ben Grieve		4.00	1.80
	A.J.Hinch		
	Ryan Christenson		
❏ 29 Travis Lee		2.50	1.10
	Karim Garcia		
	Dave Dellucci		
❏ 30 Kerry Wood		5.00	2.20
	Marc Pisciotta		

1999 Pacific Omega

	MINT	NRMT
COMPLETE SET (250)	40.00	18.00
COMMON CARD (1-250)	.15	.07
MINOR STARS	.25	.11
SEMISTARS	.40	.18
UNLISTED STARS	.60	.25
COMMON DUAL-PLAYER	.50	.23
DUAL MINOR STARS	.75	.35
DUAL SEMISTARS	1.00	.45

		MINT	NRMT
❏ 1 Garret Anderson		.25	.11
❏ 2 Jim Edmonds		.25	.11
❏ 3 Darin Erstad		.40	.18
❏ 4 Chuck Finley		.25	.11
❏ 5 Troy Glaus		.60	.25
❏ 6 Troy Percival		.25	.11
❏ 7 Chris Pritchett		.15	.07
❏ 8 Tim Salmon		.40	.18
❏ 9 Mo Vaughn		.60	.25
❏ 10 Jay Bell		.25	.11
❏ 11 Steve Finley		.25	.11
❏ 12 Luis Gonzalez		.25	.11
❏ 13 Randy Johnson		.60	.25
❏ 14 Byung-Hyun Kim		2.50	1.10
❏ 15 Travis Lee		.40	.18
❏ 16 Matt Williams		.60	.25

		MINT	NRMT
❏ 17 Tony Womack		.15	.07
❏ 18 Bret Boone		.25	.11
❏ 19 Mark DeRosa		.15	.07
❏ 20 Tom Glavine		.60	.25
❏ 21 Andruw Jones		.60	.25
❏ 22 Chipper Jones		1.50	.70
❏ 23 Brian Jordan		.25	.11
❏ 24 Ryan Klesko		.25	.11
❏ 25 Javy Lopez		.25	.11
❏ 26 Greg Maddux		1.50	.70
❏ 27 John Smoltz		.40	.18
❏ 28 Bruce Chen		.75	.35
	Odalis Perez		
❏ 29 Brady Anderson		.25	.11
❏ 30 Harold Baines		.25	.11
❏ 31 Albert Belle		.60	.25
❏ 32 Will Clark		.60	.25
❏ 33 Delino DeShields		.15	.07
❏ 34 Jerry Hairston Jr.		.25	.11
❏ 35 Charles Johnson		.25	.11
❏ 36 Mike Mussina		.60	.25
❏ 37 Cal Ripken		2.50	1.10
❏ 38 B.J. Surhoff		.25	.11
❏ 39 Jin Ho Cho		.25	.11
❏ 40 Nomar Garciaparra		2.00	.90
❏ 41 Pedro Martinez		.75	.35
❏ 42 Jose Offerman		.25	.11
❏ 43 Troy O'Leary		.25	.11
❏ 44 John Valentin		.25	.11
❏ 45 Jason Varitek		.25	.11
❏ 46 Juan Pena		.75	.35
	Brian Rose		
❏ 47 Mark Grace		.40	.18
❏ 48 Glenallen Hill		.15	.07
❏ 49 Tyler Houston		.15	.07
❏ 50 Mickey Morandini		.15	.07
❏ 51 Henry Rodriguez		.25	.11
❏ 52 Sammy Sosa		2.00	.90
❏ 53 Kevin Tapani		.15	.07
❏ 54 Mike Caruso		.15	.07
❏ 55 Ray Durham		.25	.11
❏ 56 Paul Konerko		.25	.11
❏ 57 Carlos Lee		.25	.11
❏ 58 Magglio Ordonez		.60	.25
❏ 59 Mike Sirotka		.15	.07
❏ 60 Frank Thomas		1.25	.55
❏ 61 Mark Johnson		.75	.35
	Chris Singleton		
❏ 62 Mike Cameron		.15	.07
❏ 63 Sean Casey		.60	.25
❏ 64 Pete Harnisch		.15	.07
❏ 65 Barry Larkin		.60	.25
❏ 66 Pokey Reese		.15	.07
❏ 67 Greg Vaughn		.25	.11
❏ 68 Scott Williamson		.25	.11
❏ 69 Dmitri Young		.25	.11
❏ 70 Roberto Alomar		.60	.25
❏ 71 Sandy Alomar Jr.		.25	.11
❏ 72 Travis Fryman		.25	.11
❏ 73 David Justice		.25	.11
❏ 74 Kenny Lofton		.40	.18
❏ 75 Manny Ramirez		.75	.35
❏ 76 Richie Sexson		.40	.18
❏ 77 Jim Thome		.60	.25
❏ 78 Omar Vizquel		.25	.11
❏ 79 Jaret Wright		.25	.11
❏ 80 Dante Bichette		.25	.11
❏ 81 Vinny Castilla		.25	.11
❏ 82 Todd Helton		.60	.25
❏ 83 Darryl Hamilton		.15	.07
❏ 84 Darryl Kile		.15	.07
❏ 85 Neifi Perez		.15	.07
❏ 86 Larry Walker		.60	.25
❏ 87 Tony Clark		.25	.11
❏ 88 Damion Easley		.15	.07
❏ 89 Juan Encarnacion		.25	.11
❏ 90 Bobby Higginson		.25	.11
❏ 91 Gabe Kapler		.60	.25
❏ 92 Dean Palmer		.25	.11
❏ 93 Justin Thompson		.15	.07
❏ 94 Jeff Weaver		1.50	.70
	Masao Kida		
❏ 95 Bruce Aven		.15	.07
❏ 96 Luis Castillo		.15	.07
❏ 97 Alex Fernandez		.15	.07
❏ 98 Cliff Floyd		.25	.11

❏ 99 Alex Gonzalez	.25	.11
❏ 100 Mark Kotsay	.15	.07
❏ 101 Preston Wilson	.25	.11
❏ 102 Moises Alou	.25	.11
❏ 103 Jeff Bagwell	.75	.35
❏ 104 Craig Biggio	.60	.25
❏ 105 Derek Bell	.25	.11
❏ 106 Mike Hampton	.25	.11
❏ 107 Richard Hidalgo	.25	.11
❏ 108 Jose Lima	.25	.11
❏ 109 Billy Wagner	.25	.11
❏ 110 Russ Johnson	.75	.35
Daryle Ward		
❏ 111 Carlos Beltran	.75	.35
❏ 112 Johnny Damon	.25	.11
❏ 113 Jermaine Dye	.25	.11
❏ 114 Carlos Febles	.25	.11
❏ 115 Jeremy Giambi	.25	.11
❏ 116 Joe Randa	.15	.07
❏ 117 Mike Sweeney	.25	.11
❏ 118 Orber Moreno	1.00	.45
Jose Santiago		
❏ 119 Kevin Brown	.40	.18
❏ 120 Todd Hundley	.25	.11
❏ 121 Eric Karros	.25	.11
❏ 122 Raul Mondesi	.25	.11
❏ 123 Chan Ho Park	.25	.11
❏ 124 Angel Pena	.15	.07
❏ 125 Gary Sheffield	.25	.11
❏ 126 Devon White	.15	.07
❏ 127 Eric Young	.15	.07
❏ 128 Ron Belliard	.25	.11
❏ 129 Jeromy Burnitz	.25	.11
❏ 130 Jeff Cirillo	.25	.11
❏ 131 Marquis Grissom	.15	.07
❏ 132 Geoff Jenkins	.25	.11
❏ 133 David Nilsson	.25	.11
❏ 134 Hideo Nomo	.50	.25
❏ 135 Fernando Vina	.15	.07
❏ 136 Ron Coomer	.15	.07
❏ 137 Marty Cordova	.15	.07
❏ 138 Corey Koskie	.15	.07
❏ 139 Brad Radke	.25	.11
❏ 140 Todd Walker	.25	.11
❏ 141 Chad Allen	.75	.35
Torii Hunter		
❏ 142 Cristian Guzman	.75	.35
Jacque Jones		
❏ 143 Michael Barrett	.40	.18
❏ 144 Orlando Cabrera	.15	.07
❏ 145 Vladimir Guerrero	.75	.35
❏ 146 Wilton Guerrero	.15	.07
❏ 147 Ugueth Urbina	.15	.07
❏ 148 Rondell White	.25	.11
❏ 149 Chris Widger	.15	.07
❏ 150 Edgardo Alfonzo	.40	.18
❏ 151 Roger Cedeno	.25	.11
❏ 152 Octavio Dotel	.25	.11
❏ 153 Rickey Henderson	.75	.35
❏ 154 John Olerud	.25	.11
❏ 155 Rey Ordonez	.25	.11
❏ 156 Mike Piazza	2.00	.90
❏ 157 Robin Ventura	.25	.11
❏ 158 Scott Brosius	.25	.11
❏ 159 Roger Clemens	1.50	.70
❏ 160 David Cone	.40	.18
❏ 161 Chili Davis	.25	.11
❏ 162 Orlando Hernandez	.60	.25
❏ 163 Derek Jeter	2.00	.90
❏ 164 Chuck Knoblauch	.25	.11
❏ 165 Tino Martinez	.25	.11
❏ 166 Paul O'Neill	.25	.11
❏ 167 Bernie Williams	.60	.25
❏ 168 Jason Giambi	.25	.11
❏ 169 Ben Grieve	.60	.25
❏ 170 Chad Harville	1.00	.45
❏ 171 Tim Hudson	3.00	1.35
❏ 172 Tony Phillips	.15	.07
❏ 173 Kenny Rogers	.15	.07
❏ 174 Matt Stairs	.25	.11
❏ 175 Miguel Tejada	.25	.11
❏ 176 Eric Chavez	1.00	.45
Olmedo Saenz		
❏ 177 Bobby Abreu	.25	.11
❏ 178 Ron Gant	.25	.11
❏ 179 Doug Glanville	.15	.11

❏ 180 Mike Lieberthal	.25	.11
❏ 181 Desi Relaford	.15	.07
❏ 182 Scott Rolen	.75	.35
❏ 183 Curt Schilling	.40	.18
❏ 184 Marlon Anderson	.75	.35
Randy Wolf		
❏ 185 Brant Brown	.15	.07
❏ 186 Brian Giles	.25	.11
❏ 187 Jason Kendall	.25	.11
❏ 188 Al Martin	.15	.07
❏ 189 Ed Sprague	.15	.07
❏ 190 Kevin Young	.25	.11
❏ 191 Kris Benson	.75	.35
Warren Morris		
❏ 192 Kent Bottenfield	.15	.07
❏ 193 Eric Davis	.25	.11
❏ 194 J.D. Drew	1.00	.45
❏ 195 Ray Lankford	.25	.11
❏ 196 Joe McEwing	2.50	1.10
❏ 197 Mark McGwire	4.00	1.80
❏ 198 Edgar Renteria	.15	.07
❏ 199 Fernando Tatis	.60	.25
❏ 200 Andy Ashby	.15	.07
❏ 201 Ben Davis	.40	.18
❏ 202 Tony Gwynn	1.50	.70
❏ 203 Trevor Hoffman	.25	.11
❏ 204 Wally Joyner	.25	.11
❏ 205 Gary Matthews Jr.	.15	.07
❏ 206 Ruben Rivera	.15	.07
❏ 207 Reggie Sanders	.15	.07
❏ 208 Rich Aurilia	.15	.07
❏ 209 Marvin Benard	.15	.07
❏ 210 Barry Bonds	.75	.35
❏ 211 Ellis Burks	.25	.11
❏ 212 Stan Javier	.15	.07
❏ 213 Jeff Kent	.25	.11
❏ 214 Robb Nen	.15	.07
❏ 215 J.T. Snow	.25	.11
❏ 216 Gil Meche	.25	.11
❏ 217 David Bell	.15	.07
❏ 218 Freddy Garcia	6.00	2.70
❏ 219 Ken Griffey Jr.	3.00	1.35
❏ 220 Brian L.Hunter	.15	.07
❏ 221 John Halama	.15	.07
❏ 222 Edgar Martinez	.25	.11
❏ 223 Jamie Moyer	.15	.07
❏ 224 Alex Rodriguez	2.00	.90
❏ 225 Jay Buhner	.25	.11
❏ 226 Rolando Arrojo	.15	.07
❏ 227 Wade Boggs	.60	.25
❏ 228 Miguel Cairo	.25	.11
❏ 229 Jose Canseco	.75	.35
❏ 230 Dave Martinez	.25	.11
❏ 231 Fred McGriff	.40	.18
❏ 232 Kevin Stocker	.25	.11
❏ 233 Michael Duvall	.75	.35
David Lamb		
❏ 234 Royce Clayton	.15	.07
❏ 235 Juan Gonzalez	1.25	.55
❏ 236 Rusty Greer	.25	.11
❏ 237 Ruben Mateo	.60	.25
❏ 238 Rafael Palmeiro	.60	.25
❏ 239 Ivan Rodriguez	.75	.35
❏ 240 John Wetteland	.25	.11
❏ 241 Todd Zeile	.25	.11
❏ 242 Jeff Zimmerman	1.50	.70
❏ 243 Homer Bush	.15	.07
❏ 244 Jose Cruz Jr.	.25	.11
❏ 245 Carlos Delgado	.60	.25
❏ 246 Tony Fernandez	.25	.11
❏ 247 Shawn Green	.60	.25
❏ 248 Shannon Stewart	.25	.11
❏ 249 David Wells	.25	.11
❏ 250 Roy Halladay	.75	.35
Billy Koch		
❏ S1 Tony Gwynn Sample	3.00	1.35
❏ S1A T.Gwynn Samp. Stamped	6.00	2.70

*RC'S/DUAL: 4X TO 10X BASIC CARDS
RANDOM INSERTS IN HOBBY PACKS
STATED PRINT RUN 99 SERIAL #'d SETS

1999 Pacific Omega Gold

	MINT	NRMT
COMMON CARD (1-250)	2.50	1.10

*STARS: 6X TO 15X BASIC CARDS
*RC'S/DUAL: 2X TO 5X BASIC CARDS
RANDOM INSERTS IN RETAIL PACKS
STATED PRINT RUN 299 SERIAL #'d SETS

1999 Pacific Omega Platinum Blue

	MINT	NRMT
COMMON CARD (1-250)	6.00	2.70

*STARS: 15X TO 40X BASIC CARDS
*RC'S/DUAL: 5X TO 12X BASIC CARDS
RANDOM INSERTS IN ALL PACKS
STATED PRINT RUN 75 SERIAL #'d SETS

1999 Pacific Omega Copper

	MINT	NRMT
COMMON CARD (1-250)	5.00	2.20

*STARS: 12.5X TO 30X BASIC CARDS

1999 Pacific Omega Premiere Date

	MINT	NRMT
COMMON CARD (1-250)	10.00	4.50

*RC'S/DUAL: 8X TO 20X BASIC CARDS
ONE PER HOBBY BOX
STATED PRINT RUN 50 SERIAL #'d SETS

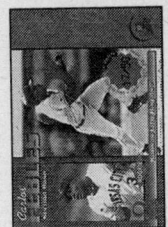

1999 Pacific Omega 5-Tool Talents

	MINT	NRMT
COMPLETE SET (30)	150.00	70.00
COMMON CARD (1-30)	1.50	.70
SEMISTARS	2.00	.90
UNLISTED STARS	3.00	1.35
STATED ODDS 4:37		

		MINT	NRMT
❏ 1	Randy Johnson	3.00	1.35
❏ 2	Greg Maddux	8.00	3.60
❏ 3	Pedro Martinez	4.00	1.80
❏ 4	Kevin Brown	2.00	.90
❏ 5	Roger Clemens	8.00	3.60
❏ 6	Carlos Lee	1.50	.70
❏ 7	Gabe Kapler	3.00	1.35
❏ 8	Carlos Beltran	3.00	1.35
❏ 9	J.D. Drew	4.00	1.80
❏ 10	Ruben Mateo	3.00	1.35
❏ 11	Chipper Jones	8.00	3.60
❏ 12	Sammy Sosa	10.00	4.50
❏ 13	Manny Ramirez	4.00	1.80
❏ 14	Vladimir Guerrero	4.00	1.80
❏ 15	Mark McGwire	20.00	9.00
❏ 16	Ken Griffey Jr.	15.00	6.75
❏ 17	Jose Canseco	4.00	1.80
❏ 18	Nomar Garciaparra	10.00	4.50
❏ 19	Frank Thomas	6.00	2.70
❏ 20	Larry Walker	3.00	1.35
❏ 21	Jeff Bagwell	4.00	1.80
❏ 22	Mike Piazza	10.00	4.50
❏ 23	Tony Gwynn	8.00	3.60
❏ 24	Juan Gonzalez	6.00	2.70
❏ 25	Cal Ripken	12.00	5.50
❏ 26	Derek Jeter	10.00	4.50
❏ 27	Scott Rolen	4.00	1.80
❏ 28	Barry Bonds	4.00	1.80
❏ 29	Alex Rodriguez	10.00	4.50
❏ 30	Ivan Rodriguez	4.00	1.80

1999 Pacific Omega 5-Tool Talents Tiers

	MINT	NRMT
*TIER 1: 2.5X TO 6X BASIC 5-TOOL
TIER 1 CARDS ARE 1/6/11/18/21/28
TIER 1 PRINT RUN 100 SERIAL #'d SETS
TIER 1 CARDS HAVE BLUE FOIL
*TIER 2: 3X TO 6X BASIC 5-TOOL
TIER 2 CARDS ARE 2/7/13/16/19/30
TIER 2 PRINT RUN 75 SERIAL #'d SETS
TIER 2 CARDS HAVE RED FOIL
*TIER 3: 5X TO 12X BASIC 5-TOOL
TIER 3 CARDS ARE 3/8/15/20/25/26
TIER 3 PRINT RUN 50 SERIAL #'d SETS
TIER 3 CARDS HAVE GREEN FOIL
*TIER 4: 8X TO 20X BASIC 5-TOOL
TIER 4 CARDS ARE 4/9/12/17/23/29
TIER 4 PRINT RUN 25 SERIAL #'d SETS
TIER 4 CARDS HAVE PURPLE FOIL
TIER 5 CARDS ARE 5/10/14/22/24/27
TIER 5 PRINT RUN 1 SERIAL #'d SET
TIER 5 CARDS HAVE GOLD FOIL
TIER 5 CARDS TOO SCARCE TO PRICE

1999 Pacific Omega Debut Duos

	MINT	NRMT
COMPLETE SET (10)	250.00	110.00
COMMON CARD (1-10)	10.00	4.50
STATED ODDS 1:145		

		MINT	NRMT
❏ 1	Nomar Garciaparra / Vladimir Guerrero	30.00	13.50
❏ 2	Derek Jeter / Andy Pettitte	30.00	13.50
❏ 3	Garrett Anderson / Alex Rodriguez	30.00	13.50
❏ 4	Chipper Jones / Raul Mondesi	25.00	11.00
❏ 5	Pedro Martinez / Mike Piazza	30.00	13.50
❏ 6	Mo Vaughn / Bernie Williams	10.00	4.50
❏ 7	Juan Gonzalez / Ken Griffey Jr.	50.00	22.00
❏ 8	Sammy Sosa / Larry Walker	30.00	13.50
❏ 9	Barry Bonds	60.00	27.00

Mark McGwire
❏ 10 Wade Boggs 25.00 11.00
Tony Gwynn

1999 Pacific Omega Diamond Masters

	MINT	NRMT
COMPLETE SET (36)	150.00	70.00
COMMON CARD (1-36)	1.50	.70
SEMISTARS	2.00	.90
UNLISTED STARS	3.00	1.35
STATED ODDS 4:37		

		MINT	NRMT
❏ 1	Darin Erstad	2.00	.90
❏ 2	Mo Vaughn	3.00	1.35
❏ 3	Matt Williams	3.00	1.35
❏ 4	Andruw Jones	3.00	1.35
❏ 5	Chipper Jones	8.00	3.60
❏ 6	Greg Maddux	8.00	3.60
❏ 7	Cal Ripken	12.00	5.50
❏ 8	Nomar Garciaparra	10.00	4.50
❏ 9	Pedro Martinez	4.00	1.80
❏ 10	Sammy Sosa	10.00	4.50
❏ 11	Frank Thomas	6.00	2.70
❏ 12	Kenny Lofton	2.00	.90
❏ 13	Manny Ramirez	4.00	1.80
❏ 14	Larry Walker	3.00	1.35
❏ 15	Gabe Kapler	3.00	1.35
❏ 16	Jeff Bagwell	4.00	1.80
❏ 17	Craig Biggio	3.00	1.35
❏ 18	Raul Mondesi	1.50	.70
❏ 19	Vladimir Guerrero	4.00	1.80
❏ 20	Mike Piazza	10.00	4.50
❏ 21	Roger Clemens	8.00	3.60
❏ 22	Derek Jeter	10.00	4.50
❏ 23	Bernie Williams	3.00	1.35
❏ 24	Scott Rolen	4.00	1.80
❏ 25	J.D. Drew	4.00	1.80
❏ 26	Mark McGwire	20.00	9.00
❏ 27	Fernando Tatis	3.00	1.35
❏ 28	Tony Gwynn	8.00	3.60
❏ 29	Barry Bonds	4.00	1.80
❏ 30	Ken Griffey Jr.	15.00	6.75
❏ 31	Alex Rodriguez	10.00	4.50
❏ 32	Jose Canseco	4.00	1.80
❏ 33	Juan Gonzalez	6.00	2.70
❏ 34	Ruben Mateo	3.00	1.35
❏ 35	Ivan Rodriguez	4.00	1.80
❏ 36	Shawn Green	3.00	1.35

1999 Pacific Omega EO Portraits

	MINT	NRMT
COMPLETE SET (20)	400.00	180.00
COMMON CARD (1-20)	8.00	3.60
STATED ODDS 1:73		

EO PORTRAIT 1 OF 1 PARALLELS EXIST
EO PORT.1 OF 1'S TOO SCARCE TO PRICE

		MINT	NRMT
❏ 1	Mo Vaughn	8.00	3.60
❏ 2	Chipper Jones	25.00	11.00
❏ 3	Greg Maddux	25.00	11.00
❏ 4	Cal Ripken	40.00	18.00
❏ 5	Nomar Garciaparra	30.00	13.50
❏ 6	Sammy Sosa	30.00	13.50

		MINT	NRMT
❑ 7	Frank Thomas	20.00	9.00
❑ 8	Manny Ramirez	12.00	5.50
❑ 9	Jeff Bagwell	12.00	5.50
❑ 10	Mike Piazza	30.00	13.50
❑ 11	Roger Clemens	25.00	11.00
❑ 12	Derek Jeter	30.00	13.50
❑ 13	Scott Rolen	12.00	5.50
❑ 14	Mark McGwire	60.00	27.00
❑ 15	Tony Gwynn	25.00	11.00
❑ 16	Barry Bonds	12.00	5.50
❑ 17	Ken Griffey Jr.	50.00	22.00
❑ 18	Alex Rodriguez	30.00	13.50
❑ 19	Jose Canseco	12.00	5.50
❑ 20	Juan Gonzalez	20.00	9.00

1999 Pacific Omega Hit Machine 3000

		MINT	NRMT
COMPLETE SET (20)		200.00	90.00
COMMON CARD (1-20)		10.00	4.50

RANDOM INSERTS IN PACKS
STATED PRINT RUN 3000 SERIAL #'d SETS
CARD 21 DIST.AT '99 SPORTSFEST SHOW

		MINT	NRMT
❑ 1	Tony Gwynn	10.00	4.50
❑ 2	Tony Gwynn	10.00	4.50
❑ 3	Tony Gwynn	10.00	4.50
❑ 4	Tony Gwynn	10.00	4.50
❑ 5	Tony Gwynn	10.00	4.50
❑ 6	Tony Gwynn	10.00	4.50
❑ 7	Tony Gwynn	10.00	4.50
❑ 8	Tony Gwynn	10.00	4.50
❑ 9	Tony Gwynn	10.00	4.50
❑ 10	Tony Gwynn	10.00	4.50
❑ 11	Tony Gwynn	10.00	4.50
❑ 12	Tony Gwynn	10.00	4.50
❑ 13	Tony Gwynn	10.00	4.50
❑ 14	Tony Gwynn	10.00	4.50
❑ 15	Tony Gwynn	10.00	4.50
❑ 16	Tony Gwynn	10.00	4.50
❑ 17	Tony Gwynn	10.00	4.50
❑ 18	Tony Gwynn	25.00	11.00
❑ 19	Tony Gwynn	10.00	4.50
❑ 20	Tony Gwynn	10.00	4.50
❑ 21	T.Gwynn Philly Sportsfest	25.00	11.00

1999 Pacific Omega HR 99

		MINT	NRMT
COMPLETE SET (20)		150.00	70.00
COMMON CARD (1-20)		2.50	1.10
UNLISTED STARS		4.00	1.80

STATED ODDS 1:37

		MINT	NRMT
❑ 1	Mo Vaughn	4.00	1.80
❑ 2	Matt Williams	4.00	1.80
❑ 3	Chipper Jones	12.00	5.50
❑ 4	Albert Belle	4.00	1.80
❑ 5	Nomar Garciaparra	15.00	6.75
❑ 6	Sammy Sosa	15.00	6.75
❑ 7	Frank Thomas	10.00	4.50
❑ 8	Manny Ramirez	6.00	2.70
❑ 9	Jeff Bagwell	6.00	2.70
❑ 10	Raul Mondesi	2.50	1.10
❑ 11	Vladimir Guerrero	6.00	2.70
❑ 12	Mike Piazza	15.00	6.75
❑ 13	Derek Jeter	15.00	6.75
❑ 14	Mark McGwire	30.00	13.50
❑ 15	Fernando Tatis	4.00	1.80
❑ 16	Barry Bonds	6.00	2.70
❑ 17	Ken Griffey Jr.	25.00	11.00
❑ 18	Alex Rodriguez	15.00	6.75
❑ 19	Jose Canseco	6.00	2.70
❑ 20	Juan Gonzalez	10.00	4.50

1998 Pacific Online

		MINT	NRMT
COMPLETE SET (800)		180.00	80.00
COMMON CARD (1-780)		.20	.09
MINOR STARS		.30	.14
SEMISTARS		.50	.23
UNLISTED STARS		.75	.35

DUAL VERSIONS EXIST FOR FOLLOWING:
41/63/67/101/113/157/182/260/311/485/505
530/621/637/655/686/693/704/732/743

		MINT	NRMT
❑ 1	Garret Anderson	.30	.14
❑ 2	Rich DeLucia	.20	.09
❑ 3	Jason Dickson	.20	.09
❑ 4	Gary DiSarcina	.20	.09
❑ 5	Jim Edmonds	.30	.14
❑ 6	Darin Erstad	.50	.23
❑ 7	Cecil Fielder	.30	.14
❑ 8	Chuck Finley	.30	.14
❑ 9	Carlos Garcia	.20	.09
❑ 10	Shigetoshi Hasegawa	.30	.14
❑ 11	Ken Hill	.20	.09
❑ 12	Dave Hollins	.20	.09
❑ 13	Mike Holtz	.20	.09
❑ 14	Mike James	.20	.09
❑ 15	Norberto Martin	.20	.09
❑ 16	Damon Mashore	.20	.09
❑ 17	Jack McDowell	.20	.09
❑ 18	Phil Nevin	.20	.09
❑ 19	Omar Olivares	.20	.09
❑ 20	Troy Percival	.30	.14
❑ 21	Rich Robertson	.20	.09
❑ 22	Tim Salmon	.50	.23
❑ 23	Craig Shipley	.20	.09
❑ 24	Matt Walbeck	.20	.09
❑ 25	Allen Watson	.20	.09
❑ 26	Jim Edmonds TC	.20	.09
❑ 27	Brian Anderson	.20	.09
❑ 28	Tony Batista	.20	.09
❑ 29	Jay Bell	.30	.14
❑ 30	Andy Benes	.20	.09
❑ 31	Yamil Benitez	.20	.09
❑ 32	Willie Blair	.20	.09
❑ 33	Brent Brede	.20	.09
❑ 34	Scott Brow	.20	.09
❑ 35	Omar Daal	.20	.09
❑ 36	Dave Dellucci	.60	.25
❑ 37	Edwin Diaz	.20	.09
❑ 38	Jorge Fabregas	.20	.09
❑ 39	Andy Fox	.20	.09
❑ 40	Karim Garcia	.20	.09
❑ 41	T.Lee Fielding	.50	.23
❑ 41A	T.Lee Hitting	.50	.23
❑ 42	Barry Manuel	.20	.09
❑ 43	Gregg Olson	.20	.09
❑ 44	Felix Rodriguez	.20	.09
❑ 45	Clint Sodowsky	.20	.09
❑ 46	Russ Springer	.20	.09
❑ 47	Andy Stankiewicz	.20	.09
❑ 48	Kelly Stinnett	.20	.09
❑ 49	Jeff Suppan	.20	.09
❑ 50	Devon White	.20	.09
❑ 51	Matt Williams	.75	.35
❑ 52	Travis Lee TC	.30	.14
❑ 53	Danny Bautista	.20	.09
❑ 54	Rafael Belliard	.20	.09
❑ 55	Adam Butler	.30	.14
❑ 56	Mike Cather	.20	.09
❑ 57	Brian Edmondson	.20	.09
❑ 58	Alan Embree	.20	.09
❑ 59	Andres Galarraga	.50	.23
❑ 60	Tom Glavine	.75	.35
❑ 61	Tony Graffanino	.20	.09
❑ 62	Andruw Jones	.75	.35
❑ 63	C.Jones Fielding	2.00	.90
❑ 63A	C.Jones Hitting	2.00	.90
❑ 64	Ryan Klesko	.30	.14
❑ 65	Keith Lockhart	.20	.09
❑ 66	Javy Lopez	.30	.14
❑ 67	G.Maddux Hitting	2.00	.90
❑ 67A	G.Maddux Pitching	2.50	1.10
❑ 68	Dennis Martinez	.30	.14
❑ 69	Kevin Millwood	2.50	1.10
❑ 70	Denny Neagle	.20	.09
❑ 71	Eddie Perez	.20	.09
❑ 72	Curtis Pride	.20	.09
❑ 73	John Smoltz	.50	.23
❑ 74	Michael Tucker	.20	.09
❑ 75	Walt Weiss	.30	.14
❑ 76	Gerald Williams	.20	.09
❑ 77	Mark Wohlers	.20	.09
❑ 78	Chipper Jones TC	1.00	.45
❑ 79	Roberto Alomar	.75	.35
❑ 80	Brady Anderson	.30	.14
❑ 81	Harold Baines	.30	.14
❑ 82	Armando Benitez	.20	.09
❑ 83	Mike Bordick	.20	.09
❑ 84	Joe Carter	.30	.14
❑ 85	Norm Charlton	.20	.09
❑ 86	Eric Davis	.30	.14
❑ 87	Doug Drabek	.20	.09
❑ 88	Scott Erickson	.20	.09
❑ 89	Jeffrey Hammonds	.20	.09
❑ 90	Chris Hoiles	.20	.09
❑ 91	Scott Kamieniecki	.20	.09

92	Jimmy Key	.30	.14
93	Terry Mathews	.20	.09
94	Alan Mills	.20	.09
95	Mike Mussina	.75	.35
96	Jesse Orosco	.20	.09
97	Rafael Palmeiro	.75	.35
98	Sidney Ponson	.30	.14
99	Jeff Reboulet	.20	.09
100	Arthur Rhodes	.20	.09
101	C.Ripken Hitting	3.00	1.35
101A	C.Ripken Hitting Close-Up	3.00	1.35
102	Nerio Rodriguez	.20	.09
103	B.J. Surhoff	.20	.14
104	Lenny Webster	.20	.09
105	Cal Ripken TC	1.50	.70
106	Steve Avery	.20	.09
107	Mike Benjamin	.20	.09
108	Darren Bragg	.20	.09
109	Damon Buford	.20	.09
110	Jim Corsi	.20	.09
111	Dennis Eckersley	.30	.14
112	Rich Garces	.20	.09
113	N.Garciaparra Fielding	2.50	1.10
113A	N.Garciaparra Hitting	2.50	1.10
114	Tom Gordon	.30	.14
115	Scott Hatteberg	.20	.09
116	Butch Henry	.20	.09
117	Reggie Jefferson	.20	.09
118	Mark Lemke	.20	.09
119	Darren Lewis	.20	.09
120	Jim Leyritz	.20	.09
121	Derek Lowe	.20	.09
122	Pedro Martinez	1.00	.45
123	Troy O'Leary	.30	.14
124	Brian Rose	.20	.09
125	Bret Saberhagen	.30	.14
126	Donnie Sadler	.20	.09
127	Brian Shouse	.20	.14
128	John Valentin	.30	.14
129	Jason Varitek	.30	.14
130	Mo Vaughn	.75	.35
131	Tim Wakefield	.20	.09
132	John Wasdin	.20	.09
133	Nomar Garciaparra TC	1.25	.55
134	Terry Adams	.20	.09
135	Manny Alexander	.20	.09
136	Rod Beck	.30	.14
137	Jeff Blauser	.20	.09
138	Brant Brown	.20	.09
139	Mark Clark	.20	.09
140	Jeremi Gonzalez	.20	.09
141	Mark Grace	.50	.23
142	Jose Hernandez	.20	.09
143	Tyler Houston	.20	.09
144	Lance Johnson	.20	.09
145	Sandy Martinez	.20	.09
146	Matt Mieske	.20	.09
147	Mickey Morandini	.20	.09
148	Terry Mulholland	.20	.09
149	Kevin Orie	.20	.09
150	Bob Patterson	.20	.09
151	Marc Pisciotta	.20	.09
152	Henry Rodriguez	.30	.14
153	Scott Servais	.20	.09
154	Sammy Sosa	2.50	1.10
155	Kevin Tapani	.20	.09
156	Steve Trachsel	.20	.09
157	K.Wood Pitching	1.00	.45
157A	K.Wood Pitching Close-Up	.75	.35
158	Kerry Wood TC	.30	.14
159	Jeff Abbott	.20	.09
160	James Baldwin	.20	.09
161	Albert Belle	.75	.35
162	Jason Bere	.20	.09
163	Mike Cameron	.30	.14
164	Mike Caruso	.20	.09
165	Carlos Castillo	.20	.09
166	Tony Castillo	.20	.09
167	Ray Durham	.30	.14
168	Scott Eyre	.20	.09
169	Tom Fordham	.20	.09
170	Keith Foulke	.20	.09
171	Lou Frazier	.20	.09
172	Matt Karchner	.20	.09
173	Chad Kreuter	.20	.09
174	Jaime Navarro	.20	.09
175	Greg Norton	.20	.09
176	Charlie O'Brien	.20	.09
177	Magglio Ordonez	2.50	1.10
178	Ruben Sierra	.20	.09
179	Bill Simas	.20	.09
180	Mike Sirotka	.20	.09
181	Chris Snopek	.20	.09
182	F.Thomas Batter's Box	1.50	.70
182A	F.Thomas Swing Through	2.00	.90
183	Robin Ventura	.30	.14
184	Frank Thomas TC	.75	.35
185	Stan Belinda	.20	.09
186	Aaron Boone	.30	.14
187	Bret Boone	.30	.14
188	Brook Fordyce	.20	.09
189	Willie Greene	.20	.09
190	Pete Harnisch	.20	.09
191	Lenny Harris	.20	.09
192	Mark Hutton	.20	.09
193	Damian Jackson	.20	.09
194	Ricardo Jordan	.20	.09
195	Barry Larkin	.75	.35
196	Eduardo Perez	.20	.09
197	Pokey Reese	.20	.09
198	Mike Remlinger	.20	.09
199	Reggie Sanders	.20	.09
200	Jeff Shaw	.20	.09
201	Chris Stynes	.20	.09
202	Scott Sullivan	.20	.09
203	Eddie Taubensee	.20	.09
204	Brett Tomko	.20	.09
205	Pat Watkins	.20	.09
206	David Weathers	.20	.09
207	Gabe White	.20	.09
208	Scott Winchester	.20	.09
209	Barry Larkin TC	.30	.14
210	Sandy Alomar Jr.	.30	.14
211	Paul Assenmacher	.20	.09
212	Geronimo Berroa	.20	.09
213	Pat Borders	.20	.09
214	Jeff Branson	.20	.09
215	Dave Burba	.20	.09
216	Bartolo Colon	.30	.14
217	Shawon Dunston	.20	.09
218	Travis Fryman	.30	.14
219	Brian Giles	.30	.14
220	Dwight Gooden	.20	.09
221	Mike Jackson	.20	.09
222	David Justice	.30	.14
223	Kenny Lofton	.50	.23
224	Jose Mesa	.20	.09
225	Alvin Morman	.20	.09
226	Charles Nagy	.30	.14
227	Chad Ogea	.20	.09
228	Eric Plunk	.20	.09
229	Manny Ramirez	1.00	.45
230	Paul Shuey	.20	.09
231	Jim Thome	.75	.35
232	Ron Villone	.20	.09
233	Omar Vizquel	.30	.14
234	Enrique Wilson	.20	.09
235	Jaret Wright	.30	.14
236	Manny Ramirez TC	.50	.23
237	Pedro Astacio	.20	.09
238	Jason Bates	.20	.09
239	Dante Bichette	.30	.14
240	Ellis Burks	.30	.14
241	Vinny Castilla	.30	.14
242	Greg Colbrunn	.20	.09
243	Mike DeJean	.20	.09
244	Jerry Dipoto	.20	.09
245	Curtis Goodwin	.20	.09
246	Todd Helton	1.00	.45
247	Bobby Jones	.20	.09
248	Darryl Kile	.20	.09
249	Mike Lansing	.20	.09
250	Curtis Leskanic	.20	.09
251	Nelson Liriano	.20	.09
252	Kirt Manwaring	.20	.09
253	Chuck McElroy	.20	.09
254	Mike Munoz	.20	.09
255	Neifi Perez	.30	.14
256	Jeff Reed	.20	.09
257	Mark Thompson	.20	.09
258	John Vander Wal	.20	.09
259	Dave Veres	.20	.09
260	L.Walker Hitting	.75	.35
260A	L.Walker Hitting Close Up	.75	.35
261	Jamey Wright	.20	.09
262	Larry Walker TC	.30	.14
263	Kimera Bartee	.20	.09
264	Doug Brocail	.20	.09
265	Raul Casanova	.20	.09
266	Frank Castillo	.20	.09
267	Frank Catalanotto	.30	.14
268	Tony Clark	.30	.14
269	Deivi Cruz	.20	.09
270	Roberto Duran	.30	.14
271	Damion Easley	.20	.14
272	Bryce Florie	.20	.09
273	Luis Gonzalez	.30	.14
274	Bobby Higginson	.30	.14
275	Brian Hunter	.20	.09
276	Todd Jones	.20	.09
277	Greg Keagle	.20	.09
278	Jeff Manto	.20	.09
279	Brian Moehler	.20	.09
280	Joe Oliver	.20	.09
281	Joe Randa	.20	.09
282	Bill Ripken	.20	.09
283	Bip Roberts	.20	.09
284	Sean Runyan	.20	.09
285	A.J. Sager	.20	.09
286	Justin Thompson	.20	.09
287	Tony Clark TC	.20	.09
288	Antonio Alfonseca	.20	.09
289	Dave Berg	.20	.09
290	Josh Booty	.20	.09
291	John Cangelosi	.20	.09
292	Craig Counsell	.20	.09
293	Vic Darensbourg	.20	.09
294	Cliff Floyd	.30	.14
295	Oscar Henriquez	.20	.09
296	Felix Heredia	.20	.09
297	Ryan Jackson	.30	.14
298	Mark Kotsay	.30	.14
299	Andy Larkin	.20	.09
300	Derrek Lee	.20	.09
301	Brian Meadows	.20	.09
302	Rafael Medina	.20	.09
303	Jay Powell	.20	.09
304	Edgar Renteria	.20	.09
305	Jesus Sanchez	.50	.23
306	Rob Stanifer	.20	.09
307	Gregg Zaun	.20	.09
308	Derrek Lee TC	.20	.09
309	Moises Alou	.30	.14
310	Brad Ausmus	.20	.09
311	J.Bagwell Fielding	1.00	.45
311A	J.Bagwell Hitting	.75	.35
312	Derek Bell	.30	.14
313	Sean Bergman	.20	.09
314	Sean Berry	.20	.09
315	Craig Biggio	.75	.35
316	Tim Bogar	.20	.09
317	Jose Cabrera	.20	.09
318	Dave Clark	.20	.09
319	Tony Eusebio	.20	.09
320	Carl Everett	.30	.14
321	Ricky Gutierrez	.20	.09
322	John Halama	.75	.35
323	Mike Hampton	.30	.14
324	Doug Henry	.20	.09
325	Richard Hidalgo	.30	.14
326	Jack Howell	.20	.09
327	Jose Lima	.30	.14
328	Mike Magnante	.20	.09
329	Trever Miller	.20	.09
330	C.J. Nitkowski	.20	.09
331	Shane Reynolds	.30	.14
332	Bill Spiers	.20	.09
333	Billy Wagner	.30	.14
334	Jeff Bagwell TC	.50	.23
335	Tim Belcher	.20	.09
336	Brian Bevil	.20	.09
337	Johnny Damon	.30	.14
338	Jermaine Dye	.30	.14
339	Sal Fasano	.20	.09

340	Shane Halter	.20	.09
341	Chris Haney	.20	.09
342	Jed Hansen	.20	.09
343	Jeff King	.20	.09
344	Jeff Montgomery	.20	.09
345	Hal Morris	.20	.09
346	Jose Offerman	.30	.14
347	Dean Palmer	.30	.14
348	Terry Pendleton	.30	.14
349	Hipolito Pichardo	.20	.09
350	Jim Pittsley	.20	.09
351	Pat Rapp	.20	.09
352	Jose Rosado	.20	.09
353	Glendon Rusch	.20	.09
354	Scott Service	.20	.09
355	Larry Sutton	.20	.09
356	Mike Sweeney	.30	.14
357	Joe Vitiello	.20	.09
358	Matt Whisenant	.20	.09
359	Ernie Young	.20	.09
360	Jeff King TC	.20	.09
361	Bobby Bonilla	.30	.14
362	Jim Bruske	.20	.09
363	Juan Castro	.20	.09
364	Roger Cedeno	.30	.14
365	Mike Devereaux	.20	.09
366	Darren Dreifort	.20	.09
367	Jim Eisenreich	.20	.09
368	Wilton Guerrero	.20	.09
369	Mark Guthrie	.20	.09
370	Darren Hall	.20	.09
371	Todd Hollandsworth	.20	.09
372	Thomas Howard	.20	.09
373	Trenidad Hubbard	.20	.09
374	Charles Johnson	.30	.14
375	Eric Karros	.30	.14
376	Paul Konerko	.30	.14
377	Matt Luke	.20	.09
378	Ramon Martinez	.30	.14
379	Raul Mondesi	.30	.14
380	Hideo Nomo	.75	.35
381	Antonio Osuna	.20	.09
382	Chan Ho Park	.30	.14
383	Tom Prince	.20	.09
384	Scott Radinsky	.20	.09
385	Gary Sheffield	.30	.14
386	Ismael Valdes	.20	.09
387	Jose Vizcaino	.20	.09
388	Eric Young	.20	.09
389	Gary Sheffield TC	.20	.09
390	Jeromy Burnitz	.30	.14
391	Jeff Cirillo	.30	.14
392	Cal Eldred	.20	.09
393	Chad Fox	.20	.09
394	Marquis Grissom	.20	.09
395	Bob Hamelin	.20	.09
396	Bobby Hughes	.20	.09
397	Darrin Jackson	.20	.09
398	John Jaha	.30	.14
399	Geoff Jenkins	.30	.14
400	Doug Jones	.20	.09
401	Jeff Juden	.20	.09
402	Scott Karl	.20	.09
403	Jesse Levis	.20	.09
404	Mark Loretta	.20	.09
405	Mike Matheny	.20	.09
406	Jose Mercedes	.20	.09
407	Mike Myers	.20	.09
408	Marc Newfield	.20	.09
409	Dave Nilsson	.20	.09
410	Al Reyes	.20	.09
411	Jose Valentin	.20	.09
412	Fernando Vina	.20	.09
413	Paul Wagner	.20	.09
414	Bob Wickman	.20	.09
415	Steve Woodard	.20	.09
416	Marquis Grissom TC	.20	.09
417	Rick Aguilera	.20	.09
418	Ron Coomer	.20	.09
419	Marty Cordova	.20	.09
420	Brent Gates	.20	.09
421	Eddie Guardado	.20	.09
422	Denny Hocking	.20	.09
423	Matt Lawton	.20	.09
424	Pat Meares	.20	.09
425	Orlando Merced	.20	.09
426	Eric Milton	.20	.09
427	Paul Molitor	.75	.35
428	Mike Morgan	.20	.09
429	Dan Naulty	.20	.09
430	Otis Nixon	.20	.09
431	Alex Ochoa	.20	.09
432	David Ortiz	.20	.09
433	Brad Radke	.30	.14
434	Todd Ritchie	.20	.09
435	Frank Rodriguez	.20	.09
436	Terry Steinbach	.20	.09
437	Greg Swindell	.20	.09
438	Bob Tewksbury	.20	.09
439	Mike Trombley	.20	.09
440	Javier Valentin	.20	.09
441	Todd Walker	.30	.14
442	Paul Molitor TC	.30	.14
443	Shane Andrews	.20	.09
444	Miguel Batista	.20	.09
445	Shayne Bennett	.20	.09
446	Rick DeHart	.20	.09
447	Brad Fullmer	.20	.09
448	Mark Grudzielanek	.20	.09
449	Vladimir Guerrero	1.00	.45
450	Dustin Hermanson	.20	.09
451	Steve Kline	.20	.09
452	Scott Livingstone	.20	.09
453	Mike Maddux	.20	.09
454	Derrick May	.20	.09
455	Ryan McGuire	.20	.09
456	Trey Moore	.20	.09
457	Mike Mordecai	.20	.09
458	Carl Pavano	.20	.09
459	Carlos Perez	.20	.09
460	F.P. Santangelo	.20	.09
461	DaRond Stovall	.20	.09
462	Anthony Telford	.20	.09
463	Ugueth Urbina	.20	.09
464	Marc Valdes	.20	.09
465	Jose Vidro	.20	.09
466	Rondell White	.30	.14
467	Chris Widger	.20	.09
468	Vladimir Guerrero TC	.50	.23
469	Edgardo Alfonzo	.50	.23
470	Carlos Baerga	.20	.09
471	Rich Becker	.20	.09
472	Brian Bohanon	.20	.09
473	Alberto Castillo	.20	.09
474	Dennis Cook	.20	.09
475	John Franco	.30	.14
476	Matt Franco	.20	.09
477	Bernard Gilkey	.20	.09
478	John Hudek	.20	.09
479	Butch Huskey	.20	.09
480	Bobby Jones	.20	.09
481	Al Leiter	.30	.14
482	Luis Lopez	.20	.09
483	Brian McRae	.20	.09
484	Dave Mlicki	.20	.09
485	John Olerud	.30	.14
486	Rey Ordonez	.30	.14
487	Craig Paquette	.20	.09
488	M.Piazza Hitting	2.50	1.10
488A	M.Piazza Hitting Close-Up	2.50	1.10
489	Todd Pratt	.20	.09
490	Mel Rojas	.20	.09
491	Tim Spehr	.20	.09
492	Turk Wendell	.20	.09
493	Masato Yoshii	.50	.23
494	Mike Piazza TC	1.25	.55
495	Willie Banks	.20	.09
496	Scott Brosius	.30	.14
497	Mike Buddie	.20	.09
498	Homer Bush	.20	.09
499	David Cone	.50	.23
500	Chad Curtis	.20	.09
501	Chili Davis	.30	.14
502	Joe Girardi	.20	.09
503	Darren Holmes	.20	.09
504	Hideki Irabu	.30	.14
505	D.Jeter Hitting	2.50	1.10
505A	D.Jeter Hitting	2.00	.90
506	Chuck Knoblauch	.30	.14
507	Graeme Lloyd	.20	.09
508	Tino Martinez	.30	.14
509	Ramiro Mendoza	.20	.09
510	Jeff Nelson	.20	.09
511	Paul O'Neill	.30	.14
512	Andy Pettitte	.30	.14
513	Jorge Posada	.20	.09
514	Tim Raines	.30	.14
515	Mariano Rivera	.30	.14
516	Luis Sojo	.20	.09
517	Mike Stanton	.20	.09
518	Darryl Strawberry	.30	.14
519	Dale Sveum	.20	.09
520	David Wells	.30	.14
521	Bernie Williams	.75	.35
522	Bernie Williams TC	.30	.14
523	Kurt Abbott	.20	.09
524	Mike Blowers	.20	.09
525	Rafael Bournigal	.20	.09
526	Tom Candiotti	.20	.09
527	Ryan Christenson	.30	.14
528	Mike Fetters	.20	.09
529	Jason Giambi	.30	.14
530	B.Grieve Running	1.00	.45
530A	B.Grieve Swinging	1.50	.70
531	Buddy Groom	.20	.09
532	Jimmy Haynes	.20	.09
533	Rickey Henderson	1.00	.45
534	A.J. Hinch	.20	.09
535	Mike Macfarlane	.20	.09
536	Dave Magadan	.20	.09
537	T.J. Mathews	.20	.09
538	Jason McDonald	.20	.09
539	Kevin Mitchell	.20	.09
540	Mike Mohler	.20	.09
541	Mike Oquist	.20	.09
542	Ariel Prieto	.20	.09
543	Kenny Rogers	.20	.09
544	Aaron Small	.20	.09
545	Scott Spiezio	.20	.09
546	Matt Stairs	.30	.14
547	Bill Taylor	.20	.09
548	Dave Telgheder	.20	.09
549	Jack Voigt	.20	.09
550	Ben Grieve TC	.50	.23
551	Bob Abreu	.20	.09
552	Ruben Amaro	.20	.09
553	Alex Arias	.20	.09
554	Matt Beech	.20	.09
555	Ricky Bottalico	.20	.09
556	Billy Brewer	.20	.09
557	Rico Brogna	.30	.14
558	Doug Glanville	.30	.14
559	Wayne Gomes	.20	.09
560	Mike Grace	.20	.09
561	Tyler Green	.20	.09
562	Rex Hudler	.20	.09
563	Gregg Jefferies	.20	.09
564	Kevin Jordan	.20	.09
565	Mark Leiter	.20	.09
566	Mark Lewis	.20	.09
567	Mike Lieberthal	.30	.14
568	Mark Parent	.20	.09
569	Yorkis Perez	.20	.09
570	Desi Relaford	.20	.09
571	Scott Rolen	1.00	.45
572	Curt Schilling	.50	.23
573	Kevin Sefcik	.20	.09
574	Jerry Spradlin	.20	.09
575	Garrett Stephenson	.20	.09
576	Darrin Winston	.20	.09
577	Scott Rolen TC	.75	.35
578	Jermaine Allensworth	.20	.09
579	Jason Christiansen	.20	.09
580	Lou Collier	.20	.09
581	Francisco Cordova	.20	.09
582	Elmer Dessens	.20	.09
583	Freddy Garcia	.20	.09
584	Jose Guillen	.30	.14
585	Jason Kendall	.30	.14
586	Jon Lieber	.20	.09
587	Esteban Loaiza	.20	.09
588	Al Martin	.20	.09
589	Javier Martinez	.50	.23
590	Chris Peters	.20	.09
591	Kevin Polcovich	.20	.09
592	Ricardo Rincon	.20	.09
593	Jason Schmidt	.20	.09

594 Jose Silva	.20	.09
595 Mark Smith	.20	.09
596 Doug Strange	.20	.09
597 Turner Ward	.20	.09
598 Marc Wilkins	.20	.09
599 Mike Williams	.20	.09
600 Tony Womack	.20	.09
601 Kevin Young	.30	.14
602 Tony Womack TC	.20	.09
603 Manny Aybar	.30	.14
604 Kent Bottenfield	.20	.09
605 Jeff Brantley	.20	.09
606 Mike Busby	.20	.09
607 Royce Clayton	.20	.09
608 Delino DeShields	.20	.09
609 John Frascatore	.20	.09
610 Gary Gaetti	.30	.14
611 Ron Gant	.30	.14
612 David Howard	.20	.09
613 Brian Hunter	.20	.09
614 Brian Jordan	.30	.14
615 Tom Lampkin	.20	.09
616 Ray Lankford	.30	.14
617 Braden Looper	.20	.09
618 John Mabry	.20	.09
619 Eli Marrero	.20	.09
620 Willie McGee	.30	.14
621 M.McGwire Fielding	5.00	2.20
621A M.McGwire Hitting	5.00	2.20
622 Kent Mercker	.20	.09
623 Matt Morris	.20	.09
624 Donovan Osborne	.20	.09
625 Tom Pagnozzi	.20	.09
626 Lance Painter	.20	.09
627 Mark Petkovsek	.20	.09
628 Todd Stottlemyre	.20	.09
629 Mark McGwire TC	2.50	1.10
630 Andy Ashby	.20	.09
631 Brian Boehringer	.20	.09
632 Kevin Brown	.50	.23
633 Ken Caminiti	.30	.14
634 Steve Finley	.30	.14
635 Ed Giovanola	.20	.09
636 Chris Gomez	.20	.09
637 T.Gwynn Blue Jersey	2.00	.90
637A T.Gwynn White Jersey	2.00	.90
638 Joey Hamilton	.20	.09
639 Carlos Hernandez	.20	.09
640 Sterling Hitchcock	.20	.09
641 Trevor Hoffman	.30	.14
642 Wally Joyner	.30	.14
643 Dan Miceli	.20	.09
644 James Mouton	.20	.09
645 Greg Myers	.20	.09
646 Carlos Reyes	.20	.09
647 Andy Sheets	.20	.09
648 Pete Smith	.20	.09
649 Mark Sweeney	.20	.09
650 Greg Vaughn	.30	.14
651 Quilvio Veras	.20	.09
652 Tony Gwynn TC	1.00	.45
653 Rich Aurilia	.20	.09
654 Marvin Benard	.20	.09
655 B.Bonds Hitting	1.00	.45
655A B.Bonds Hitting Close-Up	.75	.35
656 Danny Darwin	.20	.09
657 Shawn Estes	.20	.09
658 Mark Gardner	.20	.09
659 Darryl Hamilton	.20	.09
660 Charlie Hayes	.20	.09
661 Orel Hershiser	.30	.14
662 Stan Javier	.20	.09
663 Brian Johnson	.20	.09
664 John Johnstone	.20	.09
665 Jeff Kent	.30	.14
666 Brent Mayne	.20	.09
667 Bill Mueller	.20	.09
668 Robb Nen	.20	.09
669 Jim Poole	.20	.09
670 Steve Reed	.20	.09
671 Rich Rodriguez	.20	.09
672 Kirk Rueter	.20	.09
673 Rey Sanchez	.20	.09
674 J.T. Snow	.30	.14
675 Julian Tavarez	.20	.09
676 Barry Bonds TC	.50	.23
677 Rich Amaral	.20	.09
678 Bobby Ayala	.20	.09
679 Jay Buhner	.30	.14
680 Ken Cloude	.20	.09
681 Joey Cora	.20	.09
682 Russ Davis	.30	.14
683 Rob Ducey	.20	.09
684 Jeff Fassero	.20	.09
685 Tony Fossas	.20	.09
686 K.Griffey Jr. Fielding	4.00	1.80
686A K.Griffey Jr. Hitting	4.00	1.80
687 Glenallen Hill	.20	.09
688 Jeff Huson	.20	.09
689 Randy Johnson	.75	.35
690 Edgar Martinez	.30	.14
691 John Marzano	.20	.09
692 Jamie Moyer	.20	.09
693 A.Rodriguez Fielding	2.50	1.10
693A A.Rodriguez Hitting	2.50	1.10
694 David Segui	.20	.09
695 Heathcliff Slocumb	.20	.09
696 Paul Spoljaric	.20	.09
697 Bill Swift	.20	.09
698 Mike Timlin	.20	.09
699 Bob Wells	.20	.09
700 Dan Wilson	.20	.09
701 Ken Griffey Jr. TC	2.00	.90
702 Wilson Alvarez	.20	.09
703 Rolando Arrojo	.75	.35
704 W.Boggs Fielding	.75	.35
704A W.Boggs Hitting	.75	.35
705 Rich Butler	.50	.23
706 Miguel Cairo	.20	.09
707 Mike Difelice	.20	.09
708 John Flaherty	.20	.09
709 Roberto Hernandez	.20	.09
710 Mike Kelly	.20	.09
711 Aaron Ledesma	.20	.09
712 Albie Lopez	.20	.09
713 Dave Martinez	.20	.09
714 Quinton McCracken	.20	.09
715 Fred McGriff	.50	.23
716 Jim Mecir	.20	.09
717 Tony Saunders	.20	.09
718 Bobby Smith	.20	.09
719 Paul Sorrento	.20	.09
720 Dennis Springer	.20	.09
721 Kevin Stocker	.20	.09
722 Ramon Tatis	.20	.09
723 Bubba Trammell	.20	.09
724 Esteban Yan	.60	.25
725 Wade Boggs TC	.30	.14
726 Luis Alicea	.20	.09
727 Scott Bailes	.20	.09
728 John Burkett	.20	.09
729 Domingo Cedeno	.20	.09
730 Will Clark	.75	.35
731 Kevin Elster	.20	.09
732 J.Gonzalez With Bat	1.50	.70
732A J.Gonzalez Without Bat	2.00	.90
733 Tom Goodwin	.20	.09
734 Rusty Greer	.30	.14
735 Eric Gunderson	.20	.09
736 Bill Haselman	.20	.09
737 Rick Helling	.20	.09
738 Roberto Kelly	.20	.09
739 Mark McLemore	.20	.09
740 Darren Oliver	.20	.09
741 Danny Patterson	.20	.09
742 Roger Pavlik	.20	.09
743 I.Rodriguez Fielding	1.00	.45
743A I.Rodriguez Hitting	1.00	.45
744 Aaron Sele	.30	.14
745 Mike Simms	.20	.09
746 Lee Stevens	.20	.09
747 Fernando Tatis	.75	.35
748 John Wetteland	.30	.14
749 Bobby Witt	.20	.09
750 Juan Gonzalez TC	.75	.35
751 Carlos Almanzar	.20	.09
752 Kevin Brown	.50	.23
753 Jose Canseco	.75	.35
754 Chris Carpenter	.30	.14
755 Roger Clemens	2.00	.90
756 Felipe Crespo	.20	.09
757 Jose Cruz Jr.	.30	.14
758 Mark Dalesandro	.20	.09
759 Carlos Delgado	.75	.35
760 Kelvim Escobar	.30	.14
761 Tony Fernandez	.30	.14
762 Darrin Fletcher	.20	.09
763 Alex Gonzalez	.20	.09
764 Craig Grebeck	.20	.09
765 Shawn Green	.75	.35
766 Juan Guzman	.20	.09
767 Erik Hanson	.20	.09
768 Pat Hentgen	.30	.14
769 Randy Myers	.20	.09
770 Robert Person	.20	.09
771 Dan Plesac	.20	.09
772 Paul Quantrill	.20	.09
773 Bill Risley	.20	.09
774 Juan Samuel	.20	.09
775 Steve Sinclair	.20	.09
776 Ed Sprague	.20	.09
777 Mike Stanley	.20	.09
778 Shannon Stewart	.30	.14
779 Woody Williams	.20	.09
780 Roger Clemens TC	1.00	.45
SAMP Tony Gwynn Sample	3.00	1.35

1998 Pacific Online Red

	MINT	NRMT
COMPLETE SET (800)	180.00	80.00
COMMON CARD (1-780)	.20	.09

*RED CARDS: SAME VALUE AS BASIC CARDS
EIGHT CARDS PER RETAIL PACK

1998 Pacific Online Web Cards

	MINT	NRMT
COMPLETE SET (800)	750.00	350.00
COMMON CARD (1-780)	.50	.23

*STARS: 1.5X TO 4X BASIC CARDS
*YOUNG STARS: 1.25X TO 3X BASIC CARDS
*ROOKIES: .75X TO 2X BASIC CARDS
ONE PER PACK

1998 Pacific Paramount

	MINT	NRMT
COMPLETE SET (250)	30.00	13.50

COMMON CARD (1-250)	.10	.05
MINOR STARS	.15	.07
SEMISTARS	.25	.11
UNLISTED STARS	.40	.18

1	Garret Anderson	.15	.07
2	Gary DiSarcina	.10	.05
3	Jim Edmonds	.15	.07
4	Darin Erstad	.25	.11
5	Cecil Fielder	.15	.07
6	Chuck Finley	.15	.07
7	Todd Greene	.10	.05
8	Shigetoshi Hasegawa	.15	.07
9	Tim Salmon	.25	.11
10	Roberto Alomar	.40	.18
11	Brady Anderson	.15	.07
12	Joe Carter	.15	.07
13	Eric Davis	.15	.07
14	Ozzie Guillen	.10	.05
15	Mike Mussina	.40	.18
16	Rafael Palmeiro	.40	.18
17	Cal Ripken	1.50	.70
18	B.J. Surhoff	.15	.07
19	Steve Avery	.10	.05
20	Nomar Garciaparra	1.25	.55
21	Reggie Jefferson	.10	.05
22	Pedro Martinez	.50	.23
23	Tim Naehring	.10	.05
24	John Valentin	.15	.07
25	Mo Vaughn	.40	.18
26	James Baldwin	.10	.05
27	Albert Belle	.40	.18
28	Ray Durham	.15	.07
29	Benji Gil	.10	.05
30	Jaime Navarro	.10	.05
31	Magglio Ordonez	1.25	.55
32	Frank Thomas	.75	.35
33	Robin Ventura	.15	.07
34	Sandy Alomar Jr.	.15	.07
35	Geronimo Berroa	.10	.05
36	Travis Fryman	.15	.07
37	David Justice	.15	.07
38	Kenny Lofton	.25	.11
39	Charles Nagy	.15	.07
40	Manny Ramirez	.50	.23
41	Jim Thome	.40	.18
42	Omar Vizquel	.15	.07
43	Jaret Wright	.15	.07
44	Raul Casanova	.10	.05
45	Frank Catalanotto	.15	.07
46	Tony Clark	.15	.07
47	Bobby Higginson	.15	.07
48	Brian Hunter	.10	.05
49	Todd Jones	.10	.05
50	Bip Roberts	.10	.05
51	Justin Thompson	.10	.05
52	Kevin Appier	.10	.05
53	Johnny Damon	.15	.07
54	Jermaine Dye	.15	.07
55	Jeff King	.10	.05
56	Jeff Montgomery	.10	.05
57	Dean Palmer	.15	.07
58	Jose Rosado	.10	.05
59	Larry Sutton	.10	.05
60	Rick Aguilera	.10	.05
61	Marty Cordova	.15	.07
62	Pat Meares	.10	.05
63	Paul Molitor	.40	.18
64	Otis Nixon	.10	.05
65	Brad Radke	.15	.07
66	Terry Steinbach	.15	.07
67	Todd Walker	.15	.07
68	Hideki Irabu	.15	.07
69	Derek Jeter	1.25	.55
70	Chuck Knoblauch	.15	.07
71	Tino Martinez	.15	.07
72	Paul O'Neill	.15	.07
73	Andy Pettitte	.15	.07
74	Mariano Rivera	.15	.07
75	Bernie Williams	.40	.18
76	Mark Bellhorn	.10	.05
77	Tom Candiotti	.10	.05
78	Jason Giambi	.15	.07
79	Ben Grieve	.40	.18
80	Rickey Henderson	.50	.23
81	Jason McDonald	.10	.05
82	Aaron Small	.10	.05
83	Miguel Tejada	.15	.07
84	Jay Buhner	.15	.07
85	Joey Cora	.10	.05
86	Jeff Fassero	.10	.05
87	Ken Griffey Jr.	2.00	.90
88	Randy Johnson	.40	.18
89	Edgar Martinez	.15	.07
90	Alex Rodriguez	1.25	.55
91	David Segui	.10	.05
92	Dan Wilson	.10	.05
93	Wilson Alvarez	.10	.05
94	Wade Boggs	.40	.18
95	Miguel Cairo	.10	.05
96	John Flaherty	.10	.05
97	Dave Martinez	.10	.05
98	Quinton McCracken	.10	.05
99	Fred McGriff	.25	.11
100	Paul Sorrento	.10	.05
101	Kevin Stocker	.10	.05
102	John Burkett	.10	.05
103	Will Clark	.40	.18
104	Juan Gonzalez	.75	.35
105	Rusty Greer	.15	.07
106	Roberto Kelly	.10	.05
107	Ivan Rodriguez	.50	.23
108	Fernando Tatis	.40	.18
109	John Wetteland	.15	.07
110	Jose Canseco	.50	.23
111	Roger Clemens	1.00	.45
112	Jose Cruz Jr.	.15	.07
113	Carlos Delgado	.40	.18
114	Alex Gonzalez	.10	.05
115	Pat Hentgen	.10	.05
116	Ed Sprague	.10	.05
117	Shannon Stewart	.15	.07
118	Brian Anderson	.10	.05
119	Jay Bell	.15	.07
120	Andy Benes	.10	.05
121	Yamil Benitez	.10	.05
122	Jorge Fabregas	.10	.05
123	Travis Lee	.25	.11
124	Devon White	.10	.05
125	Matt Williams	.40	.18
126	Bob Wolcott	.10	.05
127	Andres Galarraga	.25	.11
128	Tom Glavine	.40	.18
129	Andruw Jones	.40	.18
130	Chipper Jones	1.00	.45
131	Ryan Klesko	.15	.07
132	Javy Lopez	.15	.07
133	Greg Maddux	1.00	.45
134	Denny Neagle	.15	.07
135	John Smoltz	.25	.11
136	Rod Beck	.10	.05
137	Jeff Blauser	.10	.05
138	Mark Grace	.25	.11
139	Lance Johnson	.10	.05
140	Mickey Morandini	.10	.05
141	Kevin Orie	.10	.05
142	Sammy Sosa	1.25	.55
143	Aaron Boone	.10	.05
144	Bret Boone	.15	.07
145	Dave Burba	.10	.05
146	Lenny Harris	.10	.05
147	Barry Larkin	.40	.18
148	Reggie Sanders	.10	.05
149	Brett Tomko	.10	.05
150	Pedro Astacio	.10	.05
151	Dante Bichette	.15	.07
152	Ellis Burks	.15	.07
153	Vinny Castilla	.15	.07
154	Todd Helton	.50	.23
155	Darryl Kile	.10	.05
156	Jeff Reed	.10	.05
157	Larry Walker	.40	.18
158	Bobby Bonilla	.15	.07
159	Todd Dunwoody	.10	.05
160	Livan Hernandez	.15	.07
161	Charles Johnson	.15	.07
162	Mark Kotsay	.15	.07
163	Derrek Lee	.10	.05
164	Edgar Renteria	.15	.07
165	Gary Sheffield	.15	.07
166	Moises Alou	.15	.07
167	Jeff Bagwell	.50	.23
168	Derek Bell	.10	.05
169	Craig Biggio	.40	.18
170	Mike Hampton	.15	.07
171	Richard Hidalgo	.15	.07
172	Chris Holt	.10	.05
173	Shane Reynolds	.15	.07
174	Wilton Guerrero	.10	.05
175	Eric Karros	.15	.07
176	Paul Konerko	.15	.07
177	Ramon Martinez	.10	.05
178	Raul Mondesi	.15	.07
179	Hideo Nomo	.40	.18
180	Chan Ho Park	.15	.07
181	Mike Piazza	1.25	.55
182	Ismael Valdes	.10	.05
183	Jeromy Burnitz	.15	.07
184	Jeff Cirillo	.15	.07
185	Todd Dunn	.10	.05
186	Marquis Grissom	.10	.05
187	John Jaha	.10	.05
188	Doug Jones	.10	.05
189	Dave Nilsson	.10	.05
190	Jose Valentin	.10	.05
191	Fernando Vina	.10	.05
192	Orlando Cabrera	.10	.05
193	Steve Falteisek	.10	.05
194	Mark Grudzielanek	.10	.05
195	Vladimir Guerrero	.50	.23
196	Carlos Perez	.10	.05
197	F.P. Santangelo	.10	.05
198	Jose Vidro	.10	.05
199	Rondell White	.15	.07
200	Edgardo Alfonzo	.25	.11
201	Carlos Baerga	.10	.05
202	John Franco	.15	.07
203	Bernard Gilkey	.10	.05
204	Todd Hundley	.15	.07
205	Butch Huskey	.10	.05
206	Bobby Jones	.10	.05
207	Brian McRae	.10	.05
208	John Olerud	.15	.07
209	Rey Ordonez	.10	.05
210	Ricky Bottalico	.10	.05
211	Bobby Estalella	.10	.05
212	Doug Glanville	.15	.07
213	Gregg Jefferies	.10	.05
214	Mike Lieberthal	.10	.05
215	Desi Relaford	.10	.05
216	Scott Rolen	.50	.23
217	Curt Schilling	.25	.11
218	Adrian Brown	.10	.05
219	Emil Brown	.10	.05
220	Francisco Cordova	.10	.05
221	Jose Guillen	.15	.07
222	Al Martin	.10	.05
223	Abraham Nunez	.10	.05
224	Tony Womack	.15	.07
225	Kevin Young	.15	.07
226	Alan Benes	.10	.05
227	Royce Clayton	.10	.05
228	Gary Gaetti	.15	.07
229	Ron Gant	.15	.07
230	Brian Jordan	.15	.07
231	Ray Lankford	.15	.07
232	Mark McGwire	2.50	1.10
233	Todd Stottlemyre	.10	.05
234	Kevin Brown	.15	.07
235	Ken Caminiti	.15	.07

		MINT	NRMT
❑ 236 Steve Finley	.15	.07
❑ 237 Tony Gwynn	1.00	.45
❑ 238 Wally Joyner	.15	.07
❑ 239 Ruben Rivera	.10	.05
❑ 240 Greg Vaughn	.15	.07
❑ 241 Quilvio Veras	.10	.05
❑ 242 Barry Bonds	.50	.23
❑ 243 Jacob Cruz	.10	.05
❑ 244 Shawn Estes	.10	.05
❑ 245 Orel Hershiser	.15	.07
❑ 246 Stan Javier	.10	.05
❑ 247 Brian Johnson	.10	.05
❑ 248 Jeff Kent	.15	.07
❑ 249 Robb Nen	.10	.05
❑ 250 J.T. Snow	.15	.07

1998 Pacific Paramount Copper

	MINT	NRMT
COMPLETE SET (250)	120.00	55.00
COMMON CARD (1-250)	.25	.11

*COPPER STARS: 1.25X TO 3X BASIC CARDS
*COPPER ROOKIES: 1X TO 2.5X BASIC CARDS
ONE PER HOBBY PACK

1998 Pacific Paramount Gold

	MINT	NRMT
COMPLETE SET (250)	150.00	70.00
COMMON CARD (1-250)	.30	.14

*STARS: 1.5X TO 4X BASIC CARDS
*ROOKIES: 1.25X TO 3X BASIC CARDS
ONE PER RETAIL PACK

1998 Pacific Paramount Holographic Silver

	MINT	NRMT
COMMON CARD (1-250)	8.00	3.60

*STARS: 30X TO 80X BASIC CARDS
*YNG.STARS: 25X TO 60X BASIC CARDS
*ROOKIES: 20X TO 50X BASIC CARDS
RANDOM INSERTS IN HOBBY PACKS
STATED PRINT RUN 99 SERIAL #'d SETS

1998 Pacific Paramount Platinum Blue

	MINT	NRMT
COMMON CARD (1-250)	5.00	2.20

*STARS: 20X TO 50X BASIC CARDS
*YNG.STARS: 15X TO 40X BASIC CARDS
*ROOKIES: 12.5X TO 30X BASIC CARDS
STATED ODDS 1:73 HOBBY/RETAIL

1998 Pacific Paramount Red

	MINT	NRMT
COMPLETE SET (250)	200.00	90.00
COMMON CARD (1-250)	.40	.18

*STARS: 2X TO 5X BASIC CARDS
*ROOKIES: 1.5X TO 4X BASIC CARDS
ONE PER ANCO PACK

1998 Pacific Paramount Cooperstown Bound

	MINT	NRMT
COMPLETE SET (10)	550.00	250.00
COMMON CARD (1-10)	20.00	9.00

STATED ODDS 1:361
*PACIFIC PROOFS: 3X TO 8X HI COLUMN
PROOFS: RANDOM INSERTS IN HOBBY
PACKS
PAC.PROOFS PRINT RUN 20 SERIAL #'d
SETS

		MINT	NRMT
❑ 1 Greg Maddux		50.00	22.00
❑ 2 Cal Ripken		80.00	36.00
❑ 3 Frank Thomas		40.00	18.00
❑ 4 Mike Piazza		60.00	27.00
❑ 5 Paul Molitor		20.00	9.00
❑ 6 Mark McGwire		120.00	55.00
❑ 7 Tony Gwynn		50.00	22.00
❑ 8 Barry Bonds		25.00	11.00
❑ 9 Ken Griffey Jr.		100.00	45.00
❑ 10 Wade Boggs		20.00	9.00

1998 Pacific Paramount Fielder's Choice

	MINT	NRMT
COMPLETE SET (20)	400.00	180.00
COMMON CARD (1-20)	8.00	3.60
UNLISTED STARS	10.00	4.50

STATED ODDS 1:73

	MINT	NRMT
❑ 1 Chipper Jones	25.00	11.00
❑ 2 Greg Maddux	25.00	11.00
❑ 3 Cal Ripken	40.00	18.00
❑ 4 Nomar Garciaparra	30.00	13.50
❑ 5 Frank Thomas	20.00	9.00
❑ 6 David Justice	8.00	3.60
❑ 7 Larry Walker	10.00	4.50
❑ 8 Jeff Bagwell	12.00	5.50
❑ 9 Hideo Nomo	10.00	4.50
❑ 10 Mike Piazza	30.00	13.50
❑ 11 Derek Jeter	30.00	13.50
❑ 12 Ben Grieve	10.00	4.50
❑ 13 Mark McGwire	60.00	27.00
❑ 14 Tony Gwynn	25.00	11.00
❑ 15 Barry Bonds	12.00	5.50
❑ 16 Ken Griffey Jr.	50.00	22.00
❑ 17 Alex Rodriguez	30.00	13.50
❑ 18 Wade Boggs	10.00	4.50
❑ 19 Ivan Rodriguez	12.00	5.50
❑ 20 Jose Cruz Jr.	8.00	3.60

1998 Pacific Paramount Special Delivery

	MINT	NRMT
COMPLETE SET (20)	200.00	90.00
COMMON CARD (1-20)	2.00	.90

STATED ODDS 1:37

	MINT	NRMT
❑ 1 Chipper Jones	12.00	5.50

		MINT	NRMT
❑ 2	Greg Maddux	12.00	5.50
❑ 3	Cal Ripken	20.00	9.00
❑ 4	Nomar Garciaparra	15.00	6.75
❑ 5	Pedro Martinez	6.00	2.70
❑ 6	Frank Thomas	10.00	4.50
❑ 7	David Justice	2.00	.90
❑ 8	Larry Walker	5.00	2.20
❑ 9	Jeff Bagwell	6.00	2.70
❑ 10	Hideo Nomo	5.00	2.20
❑ 11	Mike Piazza	15.00	6.75
❑ 12	Vladimir Guerrero	6.00	2.70
❑ 13	Derek Jeter	15.00	6.75
❑ 14	Ben Grieve	5.00	2.20
❑ 15	Mark McGwire	30.00	13.50
❑ 16	Tony Gwynn	12.00	5.50
❑ 17	Barry Bonds	6.00	2.70
❑ 18	Ken Griffey Jr.	25.00	11.00
❑ 19	Alex Rodriguez	15.00	6.75
❑ 20	Jose Cruz Jr.	2.00	.90

1998 Pacific Paramount Team Checklists

	MINT	NRMT
COMPLETE SET (30)	150.00	70.00
COMMON CARD (1-30)	1.50	.70
STATED ODDS 2:37		

		MINT	NRMT
❑ 1	Tim Salmon	2.50	1.10
❑ 2	Cal Ripken	15.00	6.75
❑ 3	Nomar Garciaparra	12.00	5.50
❑ 4	Frank Thomas	8.00	3.60
❑ 5	Manny Ramirez	5.00	2.20
❑ 6	Tony Clark	1.50	.70
❑ 7	Dean Palmer	1.50	.70
❑ 8	Paul Molitor	4.00	1.80
❑ 9	Derek Jeter	12.00	5.50
❑ 10	Ben Grieve	4.00	1.80
❑ 11	Ken Griffey Jr.	20.00	9.00
❑ 12	Wade Boggs	4.00	1.80
❑ 13	Ivan Rodriguez	5.00	2.20
❑ 14	Roger Clemens	10.00	4.50
❑ 15	Matt Williams	4.00	1.80
❑ 16	Chipper Jones	10.00	4.50
❑ 17	Sammy Sosa	12.00	5.50
❑ 18	Barry Larkin	4.00	1.80
❑ 19	Larry Walker	4.00	1.80
❑ 20	Livan Hernandez	1.00	.45
❑ 21	Jeff Bagwell	5.00	2.20
❑ 22	Mike Piazza	12.00	5.50
❑ 23	John Jaha	1.50	.70
❑ 24	Vladimir Guerrero	5.00	2.20
❑ 25	Todd Hundley	1.50	.70
❑ 26	Scott Rolen	6.00	2.70
❑ 27	Kevin Young	1.50	.70
❑ 28	Mark McGwire	25.00	11.00
❑ 29	Tony Gwynn	10.00	4.50
❑ 30	Barry Bonds	5.00	2.20

1999 Pacific Paramount

	MINT	NRMT
COMPLETE SET (250)	35.00	16.00
COMMON CARDS (1-250)	.10	.05
MINOR STARS	.15	.07
SEMISTARS	.25	.11
UNLISTED STARS	.40	.18

❑ 1	Garret Anderson	.15	.07
❑ 2	Gary DiSarcina	.10	.05
❑ 3	Jim Edmonds	.15	.07
❑ 4	Darin Erstad	.25	.11
❑ 5	Chuck Finley	.15	.07
❑ 6	Troy Glaus	.40	.18
❑ 7	Troy Percival	.15	.07
❑ 8	Tim Salmon	.25	.11
❑ 9	Mo Vaughn	.40	.18
❑ 10	Tony Batista	.10	.05
❑ 11	Jay Bell	.15	.07
❑ 12	Andy Benes	.10	.05
❑ 13	Steve Finley	.15	.07
❑ 14	Luis Gonzalez	.15	.07
❑ 15	Randy Johnson	.40	.18
❑ 16	Travis Lee	.25	.11
❑ 17	Todd Stottlemyre	.10	.05
❑ 18	Matt Williams	.40	.18
❑ 19	David Dellucci	.10	.05
❑ 20	Bret Boone	.15	.07
❑ 21	Andres Galarraga	.25	.11
❑ 22	Tom Glavine	.25	.11
❑ 23	Andruw Jones	.40	.18
❑ 24	Chipper Jones	1.00	.45
❑ 25	Brian Jordan	.15	.07
❑ 26	Ryan Klesko	.25	.11
❑ 27	Javy Lopez	.15	.07
❑ 28	Greg Maddux	1.00	.45
❑ 29	John Smoltz	.25	.11
❑ 30	Brady Anderson	.15	.07
❑ 31	Albert Belle	.40	.18
❑ 32	Will Clark	.40	.18
❑ 33	Delino DeShields	.10	.05
❑ 34	Charles Johnson	.15	.07
❑ 35	Mike Mussina	.40	.18
❑ 36	Cal Ripken	1.50	.70
❑ 37	B.J. Surhoff	.10	.05
❑ 38	Nomar Garciaparra	1.25	.55
❑ 39	Reggie Jefferson	.10	.05
❑ 40	Darren Lewis	.10	.05
❑ 41	Pedro Martinez	.50	.23
❑ 42	Troy O'Leary	.15	.07
❑ 43	Jose Offerman	.15	.07
❑ 44	Donnie Sadler	.10	.05
❑ 45	John Valentin	.15	.07
❑ 46	Rod Beck	.15	.07
❑ 47	Gary Gaetti	.15	.07
❑ 48	Mark Grace	.25	.11
❑ 49	Lance Johnson	.10	.05
❑ 50	Mickey Morandini	.10	.05
❑ 51	Henry Rodriguez	.15	.07
❑ 52	Sammy Sosa	1.25	.55
❑ 53	Kerry Wood	.40	.18
❑ 54	Mike Caruso	.15	.07
❑ 55	Ray Durham	.15	.07
❑ 56	Paul Konerko	.15	.07
❑ 57	Jaime Navarro	.10	.05
❑ 58	Greg Norton	.10	.05
❑ 59	Magglio Ordonez	.40	.18
❑ 60	Frank Thomas	.75	.35
❑ 61	Aaron Boone	.10	.05
❑ 62	Mike Cameron	.10	.05
❑ 63	Barry Larkin	.40	.18
❑ 64	Hal Morris	.10	.05
❑ 65	Pokey Reese	.10	.05
❑ 66	Brett Tomko	.10	.05
❑ 67	Greg Vaughn	.15	.07
❑ 68	Dmitri Young	.15	.07

❑ 69	Roberto Alomar	.40	.18
❑ 70	Sandy Alomar Jr.	.15	.07
❑ 71	Bartolo Colon	.15	.07
❑ 72	Travis Fryman	.15	.07
❑ 73	David Justice	.15	.07
❑ 74	Kenny Lofton	.25	.11
❑ 75	Manny Ramirez	.50	.23
❑ 76	Richie Sexson	.25	.11
❑ 77	Jim Thome	.40	.18
❑ 78	Omar Vizquel	.15	.07
❑ 79	Dante Bichette	.15	.07
❑ 80	Vinny Castilla	.15	.07
❑ 81	Darryl Hamilton	.10	.05
❑ 82	Todd Helton	.40	.18
❑ 83	Darryl Kile	.10	.05
❑ 84	Mike Lansing	.10	.05
❑ 85	Neifi Perez	.15	.07
❑ 86	Larry Walker	.40	.18
❑ 87	Tony Clark	.15	.07
❑ 88	Damion Easley	.15	.07
❑ 89	Bob Higginson	.15	.07
❑ 90	Brian Hunter	.10	.05
❑ 91	Dean Palmer	.10	.05
❑ 92	Justin Thompson	.10	.05
❑ 93	Todd Dunwoody	.10	.05
❑ 94	Cliff Floyd	.15	.07
❑ 95	Alex Gonzalez	.15	.07
❑ 96	Livan Hernandez	.10	.05
❑ 97	Mark Kotsay	.10	.05
❑ 98	Derek Lee	.10	.05
❑ 99	Kevin Orie	.10	.05
❑ 100	Moises Alou	.15	.07
❑ 101	Jeff Bagwell	.50	.23
❑ 102	Derek Bell	.15	.07
❑ 103	Craig Biggio	.40	.18
❑ 104	Ken Caminiti	.15	.07
❑ 105	Ricky Gutierrez	.10	.05
❑ 106	Richard Hidalgo	.15	.07
❑ 107	Billy Wagner	.15	.07
❑ 108	Jeff Conine	.10	.05
❑ 109	Johnny Damon	.15	.07
❑ 110	Carlos Febles	.15	.07
❑ 111	Jeremy Giambi	.15	.07
❑ 112	Jeff King	.10	.05
❑ 113	Jeff Montgomery	.10	.05
❑ 114	Joe Randa	.10	.05
❑ 115	Kevin Brown	.25	.11
❑ 116	Mark Grudzielanek	.15	.07
❑ 117	Todd Hundley	.15	.07
❑ 118	Eric Karros	.15	.07
❑ 119	Raul Mondesi	.25	.11
❑ 120	Chan Ho Park	.15	.07
❑ 121	Gary Sheffield	.15	.07
❑ 122	Devon White	.10	.05
❑ 123	Eric Young	.10	.05
❑ 124	Jeromy Burnitz	.15	.07
❑ 125	Jeff Cirillo	.15	.07
❑ 126	Marquis Grissom	.15	.07
❑ 127	Geoff Jenkins	.15	.07
❑ 128	Dave Nilsson	.10	.05
❑ 129	Jose Valentin	.10	.05
❑ 130	Fernando Vina	.10	.05
❑ 131	Rick Aguilera	.10	.05
❑ 132	Ron Coomer	.10	.05
❑ 133	Marty Cordova	.10	.05
❑ 134	Matt Lawton	.10	.05
❑ 135	David Ortiz	.10	.05
❑ 136	Brad Radke	.15	.07
❑ 137	Terry Steinbach	.15	.07
❑ 138	Javier Valentin	.10	.05
❑ 139	Todd Walker	.15	.07
❑ 140	Orlando Cabrera	.10	.05
❑ 141	Brad Fullmer	.10	.05
❑ 142	Vladimir Guerrero	.50	.23
❑ 143	Wilton Guerrero	.10	.05
❑ 144	Carl Pavano	.10	.05
❑ 145	Ugueth Urbina	.10	.05
❑ 146	Rondell White	.15	.07
❑ 147	Chris Widger	.10	.05
❑ 148	Edgardo Alfonzo	.25	.11
❑ 149	Bobby Bonilla	.15	.07
❑ 150	Rickey Henderson	.50	.23
❑ 151	Brian McRae	.10	.05
❑ 152	Hideo Nomo	.40	.18
❑ 153	John Olerud	.15	.07
❑ 154	Rey Ordonez	.15	.07

❑ 155 Mike Piazza	1.25	.55
❑ 156 Robin Ventura	.15	.07
❑ 157 Masato Yoshii	.10	.05
❑ 158 Roger Clemens	1.00	.45
❑ 159 David Cone	.25	.11
❑ 160 Orlando Hernandez	.40	.18
❑ 161 Hideki Irabu	.15	.07
❑ 162 Derek Jeter	1.25	.55
❑ 163 Chuck Knoblauch	.15	.07
❑ 164 Tino Martinez	.15	.07
❑ 165 Paul O'Neill	.15	.07
❑ 166 Darryl Strawberry	.15	.07
❑ 167 Bernie Williams	.40	.18
❑ 168 Eric Chavez	.25	.11
❑ 169 Ryan Christenson	.10	.05
❑ 170 Jason Giambi	.15	.07
❑ 171 Ben Grieve	.40	.18
❑ 172 Tony Phillips	.10	.05
❑ 173 Tim Raines	.15	.07
❑ 174 Scott Spiezio	.10	.05
❑ 175 Miguel Tejada	.15	.07
❑ 176 Bobby Abreu	.10	.05
❑ 177 Rico Brogna	.10	.05
❑ 178 Ron Gant	.15	.07
❑ 179 Doug Glanville	.15	.07
❑ 180 Desi Relaford	.10	.05
❑ 181 Scott Rolen	.50	.23
❑ 182 Curt Schilling	.25	.11
❑ 183 Brant Brown	.10	.05
❑ 184 Brian Giles	.10	.05
❑ 185 Jose Guillen	.10	.05
❑ 186 Jason Kendall	.10	.05
❑ 187 Al Martin	.10	.05
❑ 188 Ed Sprague	.10	.05
❑ 189 Kevin Young	.15	.07
❑ 190 Eric Davis	.15	.07
❑ 191 J.D. Drew	.60	.25
❑ 192 Ray Lankford	.15	.07
❑ 193 Eli Marrero	.10	.05
❑ 194 Mark McGwire	2.50	1.10
❑ 195 Edgar Renteria	.10	.05
❑ 196 Fernando Tatis	.40	.18
❑ 197 Andy Ashby	.10	.05
❑ 198 Tony Gwynn	1.00	.45
❑ 199 Carlos Hernandez	.10	.05
❑ 200 Trevor Hoffman	.15	.07
❑ 201 Wally Joyner	.15	.07
❑ 202 Jim Leyritz	.10	.05
❑ 203 Ruben Rivera	.10	.05
❑ 204 Matt Clement	.15	.07
❑ 205 Quilvio Veras	.10	.05
❑ 206 Rich Aurilia	.10	.05
❑ 207 Marvin Benard	.10	.05
❑ 208 Barry Bonds	.50	.23
❑ 209 Ellis Burks	.15	.07
❑ 210 Jeff Kent	.15	.07
❑ 211 Bill Mueller	.15	.05
❑ 212 Robb Nen	.10	.05
❑ 213 J.T. Snow	.15	.07
❑ 214 Jay Buhner	.15	.07
❑ 215 Jeff Fassero	.10	.05
❑ 216 Ken Griffey Jr.	2.00	.90
❑ 217 Carlos Guillen	.10	.05
❑ 218 Butch Huskey	.10	.05
❑ 219 Edgar Martinez	.15	.07
❑ 220 Alex Rodriguez	1.25	.55
❑ 221 David Segui	.10	.05
❑ 222 Dan Wilson	.10	.05
❑ 223 Rolando Arrojo	.10	.05
❑ 224 Wade Boggs	.40	.18
❑ 225 Jose Canseco	.50	.23
❑ 226 Roberto Hernandez	.10	.05
❑ 227 Dave Martinez	.10	.05
❑ 228 Quinton McCracken	.10	.05
❑ 229 Fred McGriff	.25	.11
❑ 230 Kevin Stocker	.10	.05
❑ 231 Randy Winn	.10	.05
❑ 232 Royce Clayton	.10	.05
❑ 233 Juan Gonzalez	.75	.35
❑ 234 Tom Goodwin	.10	.05
❑ 235 Rusty Greer	.10	.05
❑ 236 Rick Helling	.10	.05
❑ 237 Rafael Palmeiro	.40	.18
❑ 238 Ivan Rodriguez	.50	.23
❑ 239 Aaron Sele	.15	.07
❑ 240 John Wetteland	.15	.07

❑ 241 Todd Zeile	.15	.07
❑ 242 Jose Cruz Jr.	.15	.07
❑ 243 Carlos Delgado	.40	.18
❑ 244 Tony Fernandez	.15	.07
❑ 245 Cecil Fielder	.15	.07
❑ 246 Alex Gonzalez	.15	.07
❑ 247 Shawn Green	.40	.18
❑ 248 Roy Halladay	.15	.07
❑ 249 Shannon Stewart	.15	.07
❑ 250 David Wells	.15	.07
❑ NNO Tony Gwynn Sample	3.00	1.35

1999 Pacific Paramount Copper

	MINT	NRMT
COMPLETE SET (250)	100.00	45.00
COMMON CARDS (1-250)	.40	.18

*STARS: 1.5X TO 4X BASIC CARDS
ONE PER HOBBY PACK

1999 Pacific Paramount Gold

	MINT	NRMT
COMPLETE SET (250)	100.00	45.00
COMMON CARDS (1-250)	.40	.18

*STARS: 1.5X TO 4X BASIC CARDS
ONE PER RETAIL PACK

1999 Pacific Paramount Holo-Gold

	MINT	NRMT
COMMON CARDS (1-250)	3.00	1.35

*STARS: 12.5X TO 30X BASIC CARDS
*YNG.STARS: 10X TO 25X BASIC CARDS
RANDOM INSERTS IN PACKS
STATED PRINT RUN 199 SERIAL #'d SETS

1999 Pacific Paramount Holographic Silver

	MINT	NRMT
COMMON CARDS (1-250)	5.00	2.20

*STARS: 20X TO 50X BASIC CARDS
*YNG.STARS: 15X TO 40X BASIC CARDS
RANDOM INSERTS IN HOBBY PACKS
STATED PRINT RUN 99 SERIAL #'d SETS

1999 Pacific Paramount Opening Day

	MINT	NRMT
COMMON CARD (1-250)	6.00	2.70

*STARS: 25X TO 60X BASIC CARDS
*YNG.STARS: 20X TO 50X BASIC CARDS
STATED ODDS 1:36
STATED PRINT RUN 74 SERIAL #'D SETS

1999 Pacific Paramount Platinum Blue

	MINT	NRMT
COMMON CARDS (1-250)	5.00	2.20

*STARS: 20X TO 50X BASIC CARDS
*YNG.STARS: 15X TO 40X BASIC CARDS
STATED ODDS 1:73 HOB/RET

1999 Pacific Paramount Red

	MINT	NRMT
COMPLETE SET (250)	100.00	45.00
COMMON CARDS (1-250)	.40	.18

*STARS: 1.5X TO 4X BASIC CARDS
ONE PER RETAIL PACK

1999 Pacific Paramount Cooperstown Bound

	MINT	NRMT
COMPLETE SET (10)	600.00	275.00
COMMON CARDS (1-10)	40.00	18.00

STATED ODDS 1:361
*PACIFIC PROOFS: 2.5X TO 6X HI COLUMN
PROOFS: RANDOM INSERTS IN HOBBY
PACKS
PAC.PROOFS PRINT RUN 20 SERIAL #'d
SETS

		MINT	NRMT
❑ 1	Greg Maddux	50.00	22.00
❑ 2	Cal Ripken	80.00	36.00
❑ 3	Nomar Garciaparra	60.00	27.00
❑ 4	Sammy Sosa	60.00	27.00
❑ 5	Frank Thomas	40.00	18.00
❑ 6	Mike Piazza	60.00	27.00
❑ 7	Mark McGwire	120.00	55.00
❑ 8	Tony Gwynn	50.00	22.00
❑ 9	Ken Griffey Jr.	100.00	45.00
❑ 10	Alex Rodriguez	60.00	27.00

1999 Pacific Paramount Fielder's Choice

Derek Jeter

	MINT	NRMT
COMPLETE SET (20)	400.00	180.00
COMMON CARDS (1-20)	10.00	4.50

STATED ODDS 1:73

		MINT	NRMT
❑ 1	Chipper Jones	25.00	11.00
❑ 2	Greg Maddux	25.00	11.00
❑ 3	Cal Ripken	40.00	18.00
❑ 4	Nomar Garciaparra	30.00	13.50

		MINT	NRMT
❏ 5	Sammy Sosa	30.00	13.50
❏ 6	Kerry Wood	10.00	4.50
❏ 7	Frank Thomas	20.00	9.00
❏ 8	Manny Ramirez	12.00	5.50
❏ 9	Todd Helton	10.00	4.50
❏ 10	Jeff Bagwell	12.00	5.50
❏ 11	Mike Piazza	30.00	13.50
❏ 12	Derek Jeter	30.00	13.50
❏ 13	Bernie Williams	10.00	4.50
❏ 14	J.D. Drew	12.00	5.50
❏ 15	Mark McGwire	60.00	27.00
❏ 16	Tony Gwynn	25.00	11.00
❏ 17	Ken Griffey Jr.	50.00	22.00
❏ 18	Alex Rodriguez	30.00	13.50
❏ 19	Juan Gonzalez	20.00	9.00
❏ 20	Ivan Rodriguez	12.00	5.50

1999 Pacific Paramount Personal Bests

		MINT	NRMT
COMPLETE SET (36)		500.00	220.00
COMMON CARDS (1-36)		4.00	1.80
SEMISTARS		5.00	2.20
UNLISTED STARS		8.00	3.60
STATED ODDS 1:37			

		MINT	NRMT
❏ 1	Darin Erstad	5.00	2.20
❏ 2	Mo Vaughn	8.00	3.60
❏ 3	Travis Lee	5.00	2.20
❏ 4	Chipper Jones	20.00	9.00
❏ 5	Greg Maddux	20.00	9.00
❏ 6	Albert Belle	8.00	3.60
❏ 7	Cal Ripken	30.00	13.50
❏ 8	Nomar Garciaparra	25.00	11.00
❏ 9	Sammy Sosa	25.00	11.00
❏ 10	Andruw Jones	8.00	3.60
❏ 11	Frank Thomas	15.00	6.75
❏ 12	Roberto Alomar	8.00	3.60
❏ 13	Manny Ramirez	10.00	4.50
❏ 14	Todd Helton	8.00	3.60
❏ 15	Larry Walker	8.00	3.60
❏ 16	Jeff Bagwell	10.00	4.50
❏ 17	Craig Biggio	8.00	3.60
❏ 18	Raul Mondesi	4.00	1.80
❏ 19	Vladimir Guerrero	10.00	4.50
❏ 20	Hideo Nomo	8.00	3.60
❏ 21	Mike Piazza	25.00	11.00
❏ 22	Roger Clemens	20.00	9.00
❏ 23	Derek Jeter	25.00	11.00
❏ 24	Bernie Williams	8.00	3.60
❏ 25	Eric Chavez	5.00	2.20
❏ 26	Ben Grieve	8.00	3.60
❏ 27	Scott Rolen	10.00	4.50
❏ 28	J.D. Drew	10.00	4.50
❏ 29	Mark McGwire	50.00	22.00
❏ 30	Tony Gwynn	20.00	9.00
❏ 31	Barry Bonds	10.00	4.50
❏ 32	Ken Griffey Jr.	40.00	18.00
❏ 33	Alex Rodriguez	25.00	11.00
❏ 34	Wade Boggs	8.00	3.60
❏ 35	Juan Gonzalez	15.00	6.75
❏ 36	Ivan Rodriguez	10.00	4.50

1999 Pacific Paramount Team Checklists

		MINT	NRMT
COMPLETE SET (30)		150.00	70.00
COMMON CARDS (1-30)		1.00	.45
MINOR STARS		1.50	.70
SEMISTARS		2.50	1.10
UNLISTED STARS		4.00	1.80
STATED ODDS 2:37			

		MINT	NRMT
❏ 1	Mo Vaughn	4.00	1.80
❏ 2	Travis Lee	2.50	1.10
❏ 3	Chipper Jones	10.00	4.50
❏ 4	Cal Ripken	15.00	6.75
❏ 5	Nomar Garciaparra	12.00	5.50
❏ 6	Sammy Sosa	12.00	5.50
❏ 7	Frank Thomas	8.00	3.60
❏ 8	Barry Larkin	4.00	1.80
❏ 9	Manny Ramirez	5.00	2.20
❏ 10	Larry Walker	4.00	1.80
❏ 11	Damion Easley	1.50	.70
❏ 12	Mark Kotsay	1.00	.45
❏ 13	Jeff Bagwell	5.00	2.20
❏ 14	Jeremy Giambi	1.50	.70
❏ 15	Raul Mondesi	1.50	.70
❏ 16	Marquis Grissom	1.00	.45
❏ 17	Brad Radke	1.50	.70
❏ 18	Vladimir Guerrero	5.00	2.20
❏ 19	Mike Piazza	12.00	5.50
❏ 20	Roger Clemens	10.00	4.50
❏ 21	Ben Grieve	4.00	1.80
❏ 22	Scott Rolen	5.00	2.20
❏ 23	Jason Kendall	1.50	.70
❏ 24	Mark McGwire	25.00	11.00
❏ 25	Tony Gwynn	10.00	4.50
❏ 26	Barry Bonds	5.00	2.20
❏ 27	Ken Griffey Jr.	20.00	9.00
❏ 28	Wade Boggs	4.00	1.80
❏ 29	Juan Gonzalez	8.00	3.60
❏ 30	Jose Cruz Jr.	1.50	.70

1995 Pacific Prisms

		MINT	NRMT
COMPLETE SET (144)		150.00	70.00
COMMON CARD (1-144)		1.00	.45
SEMISTARS		2.00	.90
UNLISTED STARS		3.00	1.35
COMP.TEAM LOGO SET (28)		5.00	2.20

ONE CL OR TEAM LOGO PER PACK

		MINT	NRMT
❏ 1	David Justice	3.00	1.35
❏ 2	Ryan Klesko	1.50	.70
❏ 3	Javier Lopez	1.50	.70
❏ 4	Greg Maddux	8.00	3.60
❏ 5	Fred McGriff	2.00	.90
❏ 6	Tony Tarasco	1.00	.45
❏ 7	Jeffrey Hammonds	1.50	.70
❏ 8	Mike Mussina	3.00	1.35
❏ 9	Rafael Palmeiro	3.00	1.35
❏ 10	Cal Ripken	12.00	5.50
❏ 11	Lee Smith	1.50	.70
❏ 12	Roger Clemens	8.00	3.60
❏ 13	Scott Cooper	1.00	.45
❏ 14	Mike Greenwell	1.00	.45
❏ 15	Carlos Rodriguez	1.00	.45
❏ 16	Mo Vaughn	3.00	1.35
❏ 17	Chili Davis	1.50	.70
❏ 18	Jim Edmonds UER	2.00	.90
	Card incorrectly numbered 21		
❏ 19	Jorge Fabregas	1.00	.45
❏ 20	Bo Jackson	1.50	.70
❏ 21	Tim Salmon	3.00	1.35
❏ 22	Mark Grace	2.00	.90
❏ 23	Jose Guzman	1.00	.45
❏ 24	Randy Myers	1.00	.45
❏ 25	Rey Sanchez	1.00	.45
❏ 26	Sammy Sosa	10.00	4.50
❏ 27	Wilson Alvarez	1.50	.70
❏ 28	Julio Franco	1.50	.70
❏ 29	Ozzie Guillen	1.00	.45
❏ 30	Jack McDowell	1.50	.70
❏ 31	Frank Thomas	6.00	2.70
❏ 32	Bret Boone	1.50	.70
❏ 33	Barry Larkin	3.00	1.35
❏ 34	Hal Morris	1.00	.45
❏ 35	Jose Rijo	1.00	.45
❏ 36	Deion Sanders	1.50	.70
❏ 37	Carlos Baerga	1.00	.45
❏ 38	Albert Belle	3.00	1.35
❏ 39	Kenny Lofton	2.00	.90
❏ 40	Dennis Martinez	1.00	.45
❏ 41	Manny Ramirez	4.00	1.80
❏ 42	Omar Vizquel	1.50	.70
❏ 43	Dante Bichette	1.50	.70
❏ 44	Marvin Freeman	1.00	.45
❏ 45	Andres Galarraga	3.00	1.35
❏ 46	Mike Kingery	1.00	.45
❏ 47	Danny Bautista	1.00	.45
❏ 48	Cecil Fielder	1.50	.70
❏ 49	Travis Fryman	1.50	.70
❏ 50	Tony Phillips	1.00	.45
❏ 51	Alan Trammell	1.50	.70
❏ 52	Lou Whitaker	1.50	.70
❏ 53	Alex Arias	1.00	.45
❏ 54	Bret Barberie	1.00	.45
❏ 55	Jeff Conine	1.00	.45
❏ 56	Charles Johnson	1.50	.70
❏ 57	Gary Sheffield	1.50	.70
❏ 58	Jeff Bagwell	4.00	1.80
❏ 59	Craig Biggio	3.00	1.35
❏ 60	Doug Drabek	1.00	.45
❏ 61	Tony Eusebio	1.00	.45
❏ 62	Luis Gonzalez	1.00	.45
❏ 63	David Cone	2.00	.90
❏ 64	Bob Hamelin	1.00	.45
❏ 65	Felix Jose	1.00	.45
❏ 66	Wally Joyner	1.50	.70
❏ 67	Brian McRae	1.00	.45
❏ 68	Brett Butler	1.50	.70
❏ 69	Garey Ingram	1.00	.45
❏ 70	Ramon Martinez	1.50	.70
❏ 71	Raul Mondesi	2.00	.90
❏ 72	Mike Piazza	10.00	4.50
❏ 73	Henry Rodriguez	1.50	.70
❏ 74	Ricky Bones	1.00	.45
❏ 75	Pat Listach	1.00	.45
❏ 76	Dave Nilsson	1.00	.45
❏ 77	Jose Valentin	1.00	.45
❏ 78	Rick Aguilera	1.00	.45
❏ 79	Denny Hocking	1.00	.45
❏ 80	Shane Mack	1.00	.45
❏ 81	Pedro Munoz	1.00	.45
❏ 82	Kirby Puckett	5.00	2.20
❏ 83	Dave Winfield	3.00	1.35

		MINT	NRMT
❏ 84	Moises Alou	1.50	.70
❏ 85	Wil Cordero	1.00	.45
❏ 86	Cliff Floyd	1.50	.70
❏ 87	Marquis Grissom	1.50	.70
❏ 88	Pedro Martinez	4.00	1.80
❏ 89	Larry Walker	3.00	1.35
❏ 90	Bobby Bonilla	1.50	.70
❏ 91	Jeromy Burnitz	1.50	.70
❏ 92	John Franco	1.50	.70
❏ 93	Jeff Kent	1.50	.70
❏ 94	Jose Vizcaino	1.00	.45
❏ 95	Wade Boggs	3.00	1.35
❏ 96	Jimmy Key	1.50	.70
❏ 97	Don Mattingly	8.00	3.60
❏ 98	Paul O'Neill	1.50	.70
❏ 99	Luis Polonia	1.00	.45
❏ 100	Danny Tartabull	1.00	.45
❏ 101	Geronimo Berroa	1.00	.45
❏ 102	Rickey Henderson	4.00	1.80
❏ 103	Ruben Sierra	1.00	.45
❏ 104	Terry Steinbach	1.00	.45
❏ 105	Darren Daulton	1.50	.70
❏ 106	Mariano Duncan	1.00	.45
❏ 107	Lenny Dykstra	1.50	.70
❏ 108	Mike Lieberthal	1.00	.45
❏ 109	Tony Longmire	1.00	.45
❏ 110	Tom Marsh	1.00	.45
❏ 111	Jay Bell	1.50	.70
❏ 112	Carlos Garcia	1.00	.45
❏ 113	Orlando Merced	1.00	.45
❏ 114	Andy Van Slyke	1.50	.70
❏ 115	Derek Bell	1.00	.45
❏ 116	Tony Gwynn	8.00	3.60
❏ 117	Luis Lopez	1.00	.45
❏ 118	Bip Roberts	1.00	.45
❏ 119	Rod Beck	1.00	.45
❏ 120	Barry Bonds	4.00	1.80
❏ 121	Darryl Strawberry	1.50	.70
❏ 122	Wm. Van Landingham	1.00	.45
❏ 123	Matt Williams	3.00	1.35
❏ 124	Jay Buhner	1.50	.70
❏ 125	Felix Fermin	1.00	.45
❏ 126	Ken Griffey Jr.	15.00	6.75
❏ 127	Randy Johnson	3.00	1.35
❏ 128	Edgar Martinez	1.50	.70
❏ 129	Alex Rodriguez	12.00	5.50
❏ 130	Rene Arocha	1.00	.45
❏ 131	Gregg Jefferies	1.00	.45
❏ 132	Mike Perez	1.00	.45
❏ 133	Ozzie Smith	4.00	1.80
❏ 134	Jose Canseco	4.00	1.80
❏ 135	Will Clark	3.00	1.35
❏ 136	Juan Gonzalez	6.00	2.70
❏ 137	Ivan Rodriguez	3.00	1.35
❏ 138	Roberto Alomar	3.00	1.35
❏ 139	Joe Carter	1.50	.70
❏ 140	Carlos Delgado	3.00	1.35
❏ 141	Alex Gonzalez	1.00	.45
❏ 142	Juan Guzman	1.00	.45
❏ 143	Paul Molitor	3.00	1.35
❏ 144	John Olerud	1.50	.70
❏ CL1	Checklist	.25	.11
❏ CL2	Checklist	.25	.11

1996 Pacific Prisms

	MINT	NRMT
COMPLETE SET (144)	150.00	70.00
COMMON CARD (1-144)	.75	.35
MINOR STARS	1.25	.55
SEMISTARS	2.00	.90
UNLISTED STARS	3.00	1.35
COMMON GOLD (1-144)	2.50	1.10
*GOLD: 1.25X TO 3X HI COLUMN		
GOLD STATED ODDS 1:18		

❏ P1	Tom Glavine	3.00	1.35
❏ P2	Chipper Jones	8.00	3.60
❏ P3	David Justice	3.00	1.35
❏ P4	Ryan Klesko	1.25	.55
❏ P5	Javy Lopez	1.25	.55
❏ P6	Greg Maddux	8.00	3.60
❏ P7	Fred McGriff	2.00	.90
❏ P8	Frank Castillo	.75	.35
❏ P9	Luis Gonzalez	1.25	.55
❏ P10	Mark Grace	2.00	.90
❏ P11	Brian McRae	.75	.35
❏ P12	Jaime Navarro	.75	.35
❏ P13	Sammy Sosa	10.00	4.50
❏ P14	Bret Boone	1.25	.55
❏ P15	Ron Gant	.75	.35
❏ P16	Barry Larkin	3.00	1.35
❏ P17	Reggie Sanders	1.25	.55
❏ P18	Benito Santiago	.75	.35
❏ P19	Dante Bichette	1.25	.55
❏ P20	Vinny Castilla	2.00	.90
❏ P21	Andres Galarraga	3.00	1.35
❏ P22	Bryan Rekar	.75	.35
❏ P23	Roberto Alomar	3.00	1.35
❏ P24	Jeff Conine	.75	.35
❏ P25	Andre Dawson	2.00	.90
❏ P26	Charles Johnson	1.25	.55
❏ P27	Gary Sheffield	1.25	.55
❏ P28	Quilvio Veras	.75	.35
❏ P29	Jeff Bagwell	4.00	1.80
❏ P30	Derek Bell	1.25	.55
❏ P31	Craig Biggio	3.00	1.35
❏ P32	Tony Eusebio	.75	.35
❏ P33	Karim Garcia	1.25	.55
❏ P34	Eric Karros	1.25	.55
❏ P35	Ramon Martinez	1.25	.55
❏ P36	Raul Mondesi	3.00	1.35
❏ P37	Hideo Nomo	3.00	1.35
❏ P38	Mike Piazza	10.00	4.50
❏ P39	Ismael Valdes	1.25	.55
❏ P40	Moises Alou	1.25	.55
❏ P41	Wil Cordero	.75	.35
❏ P42	Pedro Martinez	4.00	1.80
❏ P43	Mel Rojas	.75	.35
❏ P44	David Segui	1.25	.55
❏ P45	Edgardo Alfonzo	3.00	1.35
❏ P46	Rico Brogna	.75	.35
❏ P47	John Franco	1.25	.55
❏ P48	Jason Isringhausen	.75	.35
❏ P49	Jose Vizcaino	.75	.35
❏ P50	Ricky Bottalico	.75	.35
❏ P51	Darren Daulton	1.25	.55
❏ P52	Lenny Dykstra	1.25	.55
❏ P53	Tyler Green	.75	.35
❏ P54	Gregg Jefferies	.75	.35
❏ P55	Jay Bell	1.25	.55
❏ P56	Jason Christiansen	.75	.35
❏ P57	Carlos Garcia	.75	.35
❏ P58	Esteban Loaiza	.75	.35
❏ P59	Orlando Merced	.75	.35
❏ P60	Andujar Cedeno	.75	.35
❏ P61	Tony Gwynn	8.00	3.60
❏ P62	Melvin Nieves	.75	.35
❏ P63	Phil Plantier	.75	.35
❏ P64	Fernando Valenzuela	1.25	.55
❏ P65	Barry Bonds	4.00	1.80
❏ P66	J.R. Phillips	.75	.35
❏ P67	Deion Sanders	1.25	.55
❏ P68	Matt Williams	3.00	1.35
❏ P69	Bernard Gilkey	.75	.35
❏ P70	Tom Henke	.75	.35
❏ P71	Brian Jordan	1.25	.55
❏ P72	Ozzie Smith	4.00	1.80
❏ P73	Manny Alexander	.75	.35
❏ P74	Bobby Bonilla	1.25	.55
❏ P75	Mike Mussina	3.00	1.35
❏ P76	Rafael Palmeiro	3.00	1.35
❏ P77	Cal Ripken	12.00	5.50
❏ P78	Jose Canseco	4.00	1.80
❏ P79	Roger Clemens	8.00	3.60
❏ P80	John Valentin	1.25	.55
❏ P81	Mo Vaughn	3.00	1.35
❏ P82	Tim Wakefield	.75	.35
❏ P83	Garret Anderson	1.25	.55
❏ P84	Damion Easley	1.25	.55
❏ P85	Jim Edmonds	2.00	.90
❏ P86	Tim Salmon	2.00	.90
❏ P87	Wilson Alvarez	.75	.35
❏ P88	Alex Fernandez	.75	.35
❏ P89	Ozzie Guillen	.75	.35
❏ P90	Roberto Hernandez	.75	.35
❏ P91	Frank Thomas	6.00	2.70
❏ P92	Robin Ventura	1.25	.55
❏ P93	Carlos Baerga	.75	.35
❏ P94	Albert Belle	3.00	1.35
❏ P95	Kenny Lofton	2.00	.90
❏ P96	Dennis Martinez	1.25	.55
❏ P97	Eddie Murray	3.00	1.35
❏ P98	Manny Ramirez	4.00	1.80
❏ P99	Omar Vizquel	1.25	.55
❏ P100	Chad Curtis	.75	.35
❏ P101	Cecil Fielder	1.25	.55
❏ P102	Felipe Lira	.75	.35
❏ P103	Alan Trammell	2.00	.90
❏ P104	Kevin Appier	1.25	.55
❏ P105	Johnny Damon	2.00	.90
❏ P106	Gary Gaetti	1.25	.55
❏ P107	Wally Joyner	1.25	.55
❏ P108	Ricky Bones	.75	.35
❏ P109	John Jaha	.75	.35
❏ P110	B.J. Surhoff	.75	.35
❏ P111	Jose Valentin	.75	.35
❏ P112	Fernando Vina	.75	.35
❏ P113	Marty Cordova	.75	.35
❏ P114	Chuck Knoblauch	3.00	1.35
❏ P115	Scott Leius	.75	.35
❏ P116	Pedro Munoz	.75	.35
❏ P117	Kirby Puckett	5.00	2.20
❏ P118	Wade Boggs	3.00	1.35
❏ P119	Don Mattingly	6.00	2.70
❏ P120	Jack McDowell	1.25	.55
❏ P121	Paul O'Neill	1.25	.55
❏ P122	Ruben Rivera	1.25	.55
❏ P123	Bernie Williams	3.00	1.35
❏ P124	Geronimo Berroa	.75	.35
❏ P125	Rickey Henderson	4.00	1.80
❏ P126	Mark McGwire	15.00	6.75
❏ P127	Terry Steinbach	.75	.35
❏ P128	Danny Tartabull	.75	.35
❏ P129	Jay Buhner	1.25	.55
❏ P130	Joey Cora	.75	.35
❏ P131	Ken Griffey Jr.	15.00	6.75
❏ P132	Randy Johnson	3.00	1.35
❏ P133	Edgar Martinez	1.25	.55
❏ P134	Tino Martinez	3.00	1.35
❏ P135	Will Clark	3.00	1.35
❏ P136	Juan Gonzalez	6.00	2.70
❏ P137	Dean Palmer	1.25	.55
❏ P138	Ivan Rodriguez	4.00	1.80
❏ P139	Mickey Tettleton	.75	.35
❏ P140	Larry Walker	3.00	1.35
❏ P141	Joe Carter	1.25	.55
❏ P142	Carlos Delgado	3.00	1.35
❏ P143	Alex Gonzalez	1.25	.55
❏ P144	Paul Molitor	3.00	1.35

1996 Pacific Prisms Fence Busters

	MINT	NRMT
COMPLETE SET (20)	150.00	70.00
COMMON CARD (FB1-FB20)	2.50	1.10
STATED ODDS 1:37		

❏ FB1	Albert Belle	6.00	2.70
❏ FB2	Dante Bichette	2.50	1.10
❏ FB3	Barry Bonds	8.00	3.60
❏ FB4	Jay Buhner	2.50	1.10
❏ FB5	Jose Canseco	8.00	3.60
❏ FB6	Ken Griffey Jr.	30.00	13.50
❏ FB7	Chipper Jones	15.00	6.75
❏ FB8	Dave Justice	6.00	2.70
❏ FB9	Eric Karros	2.50	1.10
❏ FB10	Edgar Martinez	2.50	1.10

	MINT	NRMT
COMPLETE SET (20)	200.00	90.00
COMMON CARD (1-20)	4.00	1.80
STATED ODDS 1:37		
❑ RH1 Roberto Alomar	6.00	2.70
❑ RH2 Jose Canseco	8.00	3.60
❑ RH3 Chipper Jones	15.00	6.75
❑ RH4 Mike Piazza	20.00	9.00
❑ RH5 Tim Salmon	5.00	2.20
❑ RH6 Jeff Bagwell	6.00	2.70
❑ RH7 Ken Griffey Jr.	30.00	13.50
❑ RH8 Greg Maddux	15.00	6.75
❑ RH9 Kirby Puckett	10.00	4.50
❑ RH10 Frank Thomas	12.00	5.50
❑ RH11 Albert Belle	6.00	2.70
❑ RH12 Tony Gwynn	15.00	6.75
❑ RH13 Edgar Martinez	4.00	1.80
❑ RH14 Manny Ramirez	8.00	3.60
❑ RH15 Barry Bonds	8.00	3.60
❑ RH16 Wade Boggs	6.00	2.70
❑ RH17 Randy Johnson	6.00	2.70
❑ RH18 Don Mattingly	12.00	5.50
❑ RH19 Cal Ripken	30.00	13.50
❑ RH20 Mo Vaughn	6.00	2.70

1997 Pacific Prisms

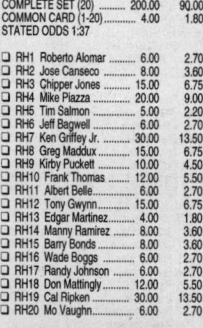

	MINT	NRMT
COMPLETE SET (150)	180.00	80.00
COMMON CARD (1-150)	1.00	.45
SEMISTARS	2.00	.90
UNLISTED STARS	3.00	1.35
*LT.BLUE STARS: 1.25X TO 3X HI COLUMN		
LT.BLUE STAT.ODDS 1:18 WAL-MART/SAM'S		
*PLATINUM STARS: 1.25X TO 3X HI COLUMN		
PLATINUM STATED ODDS 1:18 HOBBY		
❑ 1 Chili Davis	1.50	.70
❑ 2 Jim Edmonds	2.00	.90
❑ 3 Darin Erstad	3.00	1.35
❑ 4 Orlando Palmeiro	1.00	.45
❑ 5 Tim Salmon	3.00	1.35
❑ 6 J.T. Snow	1.50	.70
❑ 7 Roberto Alomar	3.00	1.35
❑ 8 Brady Anderson	1.50	.70
❑ 9 Eddie Murray	3.00	1.35
❑ 10 Mike Mussina	3.00	1.35
❑ 11 Rafael Palmeiro	3.00	1.35
❑ 12 Cal Ripken	12.00	5.50
❑ 13 Jose Canseco	4.00	1.80
❑ 14 Roger Clemens	8.00	3.60
❑ 15 Nomar Garciaparra	10.00	4.50
❑ 16 Reggie Jefferson	1.00	.45
❑ 17 Mo Vaughn	3.00	1.35
❑ 18 Wilson Alvarez	1.50	.70
❑ 19 Harold Baines	1.50	.70
❑ 20 Alex Fernandez	1.00	.45
❑ 21 Danny Tartabull	1.00	.45
❑ 22 Frank Thomas	6.00	2.70
❑ 23 Robin Ventura	1.50	.70
❑ 24 Sandy Alomar Jr.	1.50	.70
❑ 25 Albert Belle	3.00	1.35
❑ 26 Kenny Lofton	2.00	.90
❑ 27 Jim Thome	3.00	1.35
❑ 28 Omar Vizquel	1.50	.70
❑ 29 Raul Casanova	1.00	.45
❑ 30 Tony Clark	2.00	.90

❑ 31 Travis Fryman	1.50	.70
❑ 32 Bobby Higginson	1.50	.70
❑ 33 Melvin Nieves	1.00	.45
❑ 34 Justin Thompson	1.50	.70
❑ 35 Johnny Damon	1.50	.70
❑ 36 Tom Goodwin	1.00	.45
❑ 37 Jeff Montgomery	1.00	.45
❑ 38 Jose Offerman	1.50	.70
❑ 39 John Jaha	1.00	.45
❑ 40 Jeff Cirillo	1.50	.70
❑ 41 Dave Nilsson	1.00	.45
❑ 42 Jose Valentin	1.00	.45
❑ 43 Fernando Vina	1.00	.45
❑ 44 Marty Cordova	1.00	.45
❑ 45 Roberto Kelly	1.00	.45
❑ 46 Chuck Knoblauch	3.00	1.35
❑ 47 Paul Molitor	3.00	1.35
❑ 48 Todd Walker	3.00	1.35
❑ 49 Wade Boggs	3.00	1.35
❑ 50 Cecil Fielder	1.50	.70
❑ 51 Derek Jeter	8.00	3.60
❑ 52 Tino Martinez	3.00	1.35
❑ 53 Andy Pettitte	2.00	.90
❑ 54 Mariano Rivera	1.50	.70
❑ 55 Bernie Williams	3.00	1.35
❑ 56 Tony Batista	2.00	.90
❑ 57 Geronimo Berroa	1.00	.45
❑ 58 Jason Giambi	1.50	.70
❑ 59 Mark McGwire	15.00	6.75
❑ 60 Terry Steinbach	1.00	.45
❑ 61 Jay Buhner	1.50	.70
❑ 62 Joey Cora	1.00	.45
❑ 63 Ken Griffey Jr.	15.00	6.75
❑ 64 Edgar Martinez	1.50	.70
❑ 65 Alex Rodriguez	10.00	4.50
❑ 66 Paul Sorrento	1.00	.45
❑ 67 Will Clark	3.00	1.35
❑ 68 Juan Gonzalez	6.00	2.70
❑ 69 Rusty Greer	1.50	.70
❑ 70 Dean Palmer	1.50	.70
❑ 71 Ivan Rodriguez	4.00	1.80
❑ 72 Joe Carter	1.50	.70
❑ 73 Carlos Delgado	3.00	1.35
❑ 74 Juan Guzman	1.00	.45
❑ 75 Pat Hentgen	1.50	.70
❑ 76 Ed Sprague	1.00	.45
❑ 77 Jermaine Dye	1.50	.70
❑ 78 Andruw Jones	4.00	1.80
❑ 79 Chipper Jones	8.00	3.60
❑ 80 Ryan Klesko	3.00	1.35
❑ 81 Javier Lopez	1.50	.70
❑ 82 Greg Maddux	10.00	4.50
❑ 83 John Smoltz	2.00	.90
❑ 84 Mark Grace	2.00	.90
❑ 85 Luis Gonzalez	1.50	.70
❑ 86 Brooks Kieschnick	1.00	.45
❑ 87 Jaime Navarro	1.00	.45
❑ 88 Ryne Sandberg	4.00	1.80
❑ 89 Sammy Sosa	10.00	4.50
❑ 90 Bret Boone	1.50	.70
❑ 91 Jeff Brantley	1.00	.45
❑ 92 Eric Davis	1.50	.70
❑ 93 Barry Larkin	3.00	1.35
❑ 94 Reggie Sanders	1.50	.70
❑ 95 Ellis Burks	1.50	.70
❑ 96 Dante Bichette	1.50	.70
❑ 97 Vinny Castilla	2.00	.90
❑ 98 Andres Galarraga	3.00	1.35
❑ 99 Eric Young	1.50	.70
❑ 100 Kevin Brown	2.00	.90
❑ 101 Jeff Conine	1.00	.45
❑ 102 Charles Johnson	1.50	.70
❑ 103 Edgar Renteria	1.50	.70
❑ 104 Gary Sheffield	1.50	.70
❑ 105 Jeff Bagwell	4.00	1.80
❑ 106 Derek Bell	1.50	.70
❑ 107 Sean Berry	1.00	.45
❑ 108 Craig Biggio	3.00	1.35
❑ 109 Shane Reynolds	1.50	.70
❑ 110 Karim Garcia	1.50	.70
❑ 111 Todd Hollandsworth	1.00	.45
❑ 112 Ramon Martinez	1.50	.70
❑ 113 Raul Mondesi	1.50	.70
❑ 114 Hideo Nomo	3.00	1.35
❑ 115 Mike Piazza	10.00	4.50
❑ 116 Ismael Valdes	1.50	.70

❑ FB11 Mark McGwire	30.00	13.50
❑ FB12 Eddie Murray	6.00	2.70
❑ FB13 Mike Piazza	20.00	9.00
❑ FB14 Kirby Puckett	10.00	4.50
❑ FB15 Cal Ripken	25.00	11.00
❑ FB16 Tim Salmon	4.00	1.80
❑ FB17 Sammy Sosa	20.00	9.00
❑ FB18 Frank Thomas	12.00	5.50
❑ FB19 Mo Vaughn	6.00	2.70
❑ FB20 Larry Walker	6.00	2.70

1996 Pacific Prisms Flame Throwers

	MINT	NRMT
COMPLETE SET (10)	120.00	55.00
COMMON CARD (1-10)	3.00	1.35
MINOR STARS	5.00	2.20
SEMISTARS	8.00	3.60
STATED ODDS 1:73		
❑ FT1 Randy Johnson	12.00	5.50
❑ FT2 Mike Mussina	12.00	5.50
❑ FT3 Roger Clemens	30.00	13.50
❑ FT4 Tom Glavine	10.00	4.50
❑ FT5 Hideo Nomo	10.00	4.50
❑ FT6 Jose Rijo	3.00	1.35
❑ FT7 Greg Maddux	30.00	13.50
❑ FT8 David Cone	8.00	3.60
❑ FT9 Ramon Martinez	5.00	2.20
❑ FT10 Jose Mesa	3.00	1.35

1996 Pacific Prisms Red Hot Stars

❏ 117 Moises Alou	1.50	.70
❏ 118 Mark Grudzielanek	1.50	.70
❏ 119 Pedro Martinez	4.00	1.80
❏ 120 Henry Rodriguez	1.50	.70
❏ 121 F.P. Santangelo	1.00	.45
❏ 122 Carlos Baerga	1.00	.45
❏ 123 Bernard Gilkey	1.00	.45
❏ 124 Todd Hundley	1.50	.70
❏ 125 Lance Johnson	1.00	.45
❏ 126 Alex Ochoa	1.00	.45
❏ 127 Rey Ordonez	1.50	.70
❏ 128 Lenny Dykstra	1.50	.70
❏ 129 Gregg Jefferies	1.00	.45
❏ 130 Ricky Otero	1.00	.45
❏ 131 Benito Santiago	1.00	.45
❏ 132 Jermaine Allensworth	1.00	.45
❏ 133 Francisco Cordova	1.00	.45
❏ 134 Carlos Garcia	1.00	.45
❏ 135 Jason Kendall	2.00	.90
❏ 136 Al Martin	1.00	.45
❏ 137 Dennis Eckersley	1.50	.70
❏ 138 Ron Gant	1.00	.45
❏ 139 Brian Jordan	1.50	.70
❏ 140 John Mabry	1.00	.45
❏ 141 Ozzie Smith	4.00	1.80
❏ 142 Ken Caminiti	2.00	.90
❏ 143 Steve Finley	1.00	.45
❏ 144 Tony Gwynn	8.00	3.60
❏ 145 Wally Joyner	1.50	.70
❏ 146 Fernando Valenzuela	1.50	.70
❏ 147 Barry Bonds	4.00	1.80
❏ 148 Jacob Cruz	1.00	.45
❏ 149 Osvaldo Fernandez	1.00	.45
❏ 150 Matt Williams	3.00	1.35

1997 Pacific Prisms Gate Attractions

	MINT	NRMT
COMPLETE SET (32)	500.00	220.00
COMMON CARD (GA1-GA32)	2.50	1.10
MINOR STARS	5.00	2.20
UNLISTED STARS	10.00	4.50
STATED ODDS 1:73		

❏ GA1 Roberto Alomar	10.00	4.50
❏ GA2 Brady Anderson	5.00	2.20
❏ GA3 Cal Ripken	40.00	18.00
❏ GA4 Frank Thomas	20.00	9.00
❏ GA5 Kenny Lofton	6.00	2.70
❏ GA6 Omar Vizquel	5.00	2.20
❏ GA7 Paul Molitor	10.00	4.50
❏ GA8 Wade Boggs	10.00	4.50
❏ GA9 Derek Jeter	30.00	13.50
❏ GA10 Andy Pettitte	6.00	2.70
❏ GA11 Bernie Williams	10.00	4.50
❏ GA12 Geronimo Berroa	2.50	1.10
❏ GA13 Mark McGwire	50.00	22.00
❏ GA14 Ken Griffey Jr.	50.00	22.00
❏ GA15 Alex Rodriguez	30.00	13.50
❏ GA16 Juan Gonzalez	20.00	9.00
❏ GA17 Andruw Jones	12.00	5.50
❏ GA18 Chipper Jones	25.00	11.00
❏ GA19 Greg Maddux	25.00	11.00
❏ GA20 Ryne Sandberg	12.00	5.50
❏ GA21 Sammy Sosa	30.00	13.50
❏ GA22 Andres Galarraga	10.00	4.50
❏ GA23 Jeff Bagwell	12.00	5.50

❏ GA24 Todd Hollandsworth	2.50	1.10
❏ GA25 Hideo Nomo	10.00	4.50
❏ GA26 Mike Piazza	30.00	13.50
❏ GA27 Todd Hundley	2.50	1.10
❏ GA28 Lance Johnson	2.50	1.10
❏ GA29 Ozzie Smith	12.00	5.50
❏ GA30 Ken Caminiti	6.00	2.70
❏ GA31 Tony Gwynn	25.00	11.00
❏ GA32 Barry Bonds	12.00	5.50

1997 Pacific Prisms Gems of the Diamond

	MINT	NRMT
COMPLETE SET (220)	60.00	27.00
COMMON CARD (GD1-GD220)	.25	.11
MINOR STARS	.50	.23
UNLISTED STARS	1.00	.45
STATED ODDS 2:1		

❏ GD1 Jim Abbott	.50	.23
❏ GD2 Shawn Boskie	.25	.11
❏ GD3 Gary Disarcina	.25	.11
❏ GD4 Jim Edmonds	.75	.35
❏ GD5 Todd Greene	.25	.11
❏ GD6 Jack Howell	.25	.11
❏ GD7 Jeff Schmidt	.25	.11
❏ GD8 Shad Williams	.25	.11
❏ GD9 Roberto Alomar	1.00	.45
❏ GD10 Cesar Devarez	.25	.11
❏ GD11 Alan Mills	.25	.11
❏ GD12 Eddie Murray	1.00	.45
❏ GD13 Jesse Orosco	.50	.11
❏ GD14 Arthur Rhodes	.25	.11
❏ GD15 Bill Ripken	.25	.11
❏ GD16 Cal Ripken	4.00	1.80
❏ GD17 Mark Smith	.25	.11
❏ GD18 Roger Clemens	2.50	1.10
❏ GD19 Vaughn Eshelman	.25	.11
❏ GD20 Rich Garces	.25	.11
❏ GD21 Bill Haselman	.25	.11
❏ GD22 Dwayne Hosey	.25	.11
❏ GD23 Mike Maddux	.25	.11
❏ GD24 Jose Malave	.25	.11
❏ GD25 Aaron Sele	.50	.23
❏ GD26 James Baldwin	.50	.23
❏ GD27 Pat Borders	.25	.11
❏ GD28 Mike Cameron	.50	.23
❏ GD29 Tony Castillo	.25	.11
❏ GD30 Domingo Cedeno	.25	.11
❏ GD31 Greg Norton	.25	.11
❏ GD32 Frank Thomas	2.00	.90
❏ GD33 Albert Belle	1.00	.45
❏ GD34 Einar Diaz	.25	.11
❏ GD35 Alan Embree	.25	.11
❏ GD36 Albie Lopez	.25	.11
❏ GD37 Chad Ogea	.25	.11
❏ GD38 Tony Pena	.25	.11
❏ GD39 Joe Roa	.25	.11
❏ GD40 Fausto Cruz	.25	.11
❏ GD41 Joey Eischen	.25	.11
❏ GD42 Travis Fryman	.50	.23
❏ GD43 Mike Myers	.25	.11
❏ GD44 A.J. Sager	.25	.11
❏ GD45 Duane Singleton	.25	.11
❏ GD46 Justin Thompson	.50	.23
❏ GD47 Jeff Granger	.25	.11
❏ GD48 Les Norman	.25	.11

❏ GD49 Jon Nunnally	.25	.11
❏ GD50 Craig Paquette	.25	.11
❏ GD51 Michael Tucker	.25	.11
❏ GD52 Julio Valera	.25	.11
❏ GD53 Kevin Young	.25	.11
❏ GD54 Cal Eldred	.25	.11
❏ GD55 Ramon Garcia	.25	.11
❏ GD56 Marc Newfield	.25	.11
❏ GD57 Al Reyes	.25	.11
❏ GD58 Tim Unroe	.25	.11
❏ GD59 Tim Vanegmond	.25	.11
❏ GD60 Turner Ward	.25	.11
❏ GD61 Bob Wickman	.25	.11
❏ GD62 Chuck Knoblauch	1.00	.45
❏ GD63 Paul Molitor	1.00	.45
❏ GD64 Kirby Puckett	1.50	.70
❏ GD65 Tom Quinlan	.25	.11
❏ GD66 Rich Robertson	.25	.11
❏ GD67 Dave Stevens	.25	.11
❏ GD68 Matt Walbeck	.25	.11
❏ GD69 Wade Boggs	1.00	.45
❏ GD70 Tony Fernandez	.50	.23
❏ GD71 Andy Fox	.25	.11
❏ GD72 Joe Girardi	.25	.11
❏ GD73 Charlie Hayes	.25	.11
❏ GD74 Pat Kelly	.25	.11
❏ GD75 Jeff Nelson	.25	.11
❏ GD76 Melido Perez	.25	.11
❏ GD77 Mark Acre	.25	.11
❏ GD78 Allen Battle	.25	.11
❏ GD79 Rafael Bournigal	.25	.11
❏ GD80 Mark McGwire	5.00	2.20
❏ GD81 Pedro Munoz	.25	.11
❏ GD82 Scott Spiezio	.25	.11
❏ GD83 Don Wengert	.25	.11
❏ GD84 Steve Wojciechowski	.25	.11
❏ GD85 Alex Diaz	.25	.11
❏ GD86 Ken Griffey Jr.	5.00	2.20
❏ GD87 Raul Ibanez	.25	.11
❏ GD88 Mike Jackson	.50	.23
❏ GD89 John Marzano	.25	.11
❏ GD90 Greg McCarthy	.25	.11
❏ GD91 Alex Rodriguez	3.00	1.35
❏ GD92 Andy Sheets	.25	.11
❏ GD93 Mac Suzuki	.25	.11
❏ GD94 Benji Gil	.25	.11
❏ GD95 Juan Gonzalez	2.00	.90
❏ GD96 Kevin Gross	.25	.11
❏ GD97 Gil Heredia	.25	.11
❏ GD98 Luis Ortiz	.25	.11
❏ GD99 Jeff Russell	.25	.11
❏ GD100 Dave Valle	.25	.11
❏ GD101 Marty Janzen	.25	.11
❏ GD102 Sandy Martinez	.25	.11
❏ GD103 Julio Mosquera	.25	.11
❏ GD104 Otis Nixon	.25	.11
❏ GD105 Paul Spoljaric	.25	.11
❏ GD106 Shannon Stewart	.50	.23
❏ GD107 Woody Williams	.25	.11
❏ GD108 Steve Avery	.25	.11
❏ GD109 Mike Bielecki	.25	.11
❏ GD110 Pedro Borbon	.25	.11
❏ GD111 Ed Giovanola	.25	.11
❏ GD112 Chipper Jones	2.50	1.10
❏ GD113 Greg Maddux	2.50	1.10
❏ GD114 Mike Mordecai	.25	.11
❏ GD115 Terrell Wade	.25	.11
❏ GD116 Terry Adams	.25	.11
❏ GD117 Brian Dorsett	.25	.11
❏ GD118 Doug Glanville	.75	.35
❏ GD119 Tyler Houston	.25	.11
❏ GD120 Robin Jennings	.25	.11
❏ GD121 Ryne Sandberg	1.25	.55
❏ GD122 Terry Shumpert	.25	.11
❏ GD123 Amaury Telemaco	.25	.11
❏ GD124 Steve Trachsel	.25	.11
❏ GD125 Curtis Goodwin	.25	.11
❏ GD126 Mike Kelly	.25	.11
❏ GD127 Chad Mottola	.25	.11
❏ GD128 Mark Portugal	.25	.11
❏ GD129 Roger Salkeld	.25	.11
❏ GD130 John Smiley	.25	.11
❏ GD131 Lee Smith	.50	.23
❏ GD132 Roger Bailey	.25	.11
❏ GD133 Andres Galarraga	1.00	.45
❏ GD134 Darren Holmes	.25	.11

☐ GD135 Curtis Leskanic	.25	.11
☐ GD136 Mike Munoz	.25	.11
☐ GD137 Jeff Reed	.25	.11
☐ GD138 Mark Thompson	.25	.11
☐ GD139 Jamey Wright	.25	.11
☐ GD140 Andre Dawson	.75	.35
☐ GD141 Craig Grebeck	.25	.11
☐ GD142 Matt Mantei	.25	.11
☐ GD143 Billy McMillon	.25	.11
☐ GD144 Kurt Miller	.25	.11
☐ GD145 Ralph Milliard	.25	.11
☐ GD146 Bob Natal	.25	.11
☐ GD147 Joe Siddall	.25	.11
☐ GD148 Bob Abreu	.75	.35
☐ GD149 Doug Brocail	.25	.11
☐ GD150 Danny Darwin	.25	.11
☐ GD151 Mike Hampton	.50	.23
☐ GD152 Todd Jones	.25	.11
☐ GD153 Kirt Manwaring	.25	.11
☐ GD154 Alvin Morman	.25	.11
☐ GD155 Billy Ashley	.25	.11
☐ GD156 Tom Candiotti	.25	.11
☐ GD157 Darren Dreifort	.50	.23
☐ GD158 Greg Gagne	.25	.11
☐ GD159 Wilton Guerrero	.25	.11
☐ GD160 Hideo Nomo	1.00	
☐ GD161 Mike Piazza	3.00	1.35
☐ GD162 Tom Prince	.25	.11
☐ GD163 Todd Worrell	.25	.11
☐ GD164 Moises Alou	.50	.23
☐ GD165 Shane Andrews	.25	.11
☐ GD166 Derek Aucoin	.25	.11
☐ GD167 Raul Chavez	.25	.11
☐ GD168 Darrin Fletcher	.25	.11
☐ GD169 Mark Leiter	.25	.11
☐ GD170 Henry Rodriguez	.25	.11
☐ GD171 Dave Veres	.25	.11
☐ GD172 Paul Byrd	.25	.11
☐ GD173 Alberto Castillo	.25	.11
☐ GD174 Mark Clark	.25	.11
☐ GD175 Rey Ordonez	.50	.23
☐ GD176 Roberto Petagine	.25	.11
☐ GD177 Andy Tomberlin	.25	.11
☐ GD178 Derek Wallace	.25	.11
☐ GD179 Paul Wilson	.25	.11
☐ GD180 Ruben Amaro Jr.	.25	.11
☐ GD181 Toby Borland	.25	.11
☐ GD182 Rich Hunter	.25	.11
☐ GD183 Tony Longmire	.25	.11
☐ GD184 Wendell Magee	.25	.11
☐ GD185 Bobby Munoz	.25	.11
☐ GD186 Scott Rolen	1.50	.70
☐ GD187 Mike Williams	.25	.11
☐ GD188 Trey Beamon	.25	.11
☐ GD189 Jason Christiansen	.25	.11
☐ GD190 Elmer Dessens	.25	.11
☐ GD191 Angelo Encarnacion	.25	.11
☐ GD192 Carlos Garcia	.25	.11
☐ GD193 Mike Kingery	.25	.11
☐ GD194 Chris Peters	.25	.11
☐ GD195 Tony Womack	1.00	.45
☐ GD196 Brian Barber	.25	.11
☐ GD197 David Bell	.25	.11
☐ GD198 Tony Fossas	.25	.11
☐ GD199 Rick Honeycutt	.25	.11
☐ GD200 T.J. Mathews	.25	.11
☐ GD201 Miguel Mejia	.25	.11
☐ GD202 Donovan Osborne	.25	.11
☐ GD203 Ozzie Smith	1.25	.55
☐ GD204 Andres Berumen	.25	.11
☐ GD205 Ken Caminiti	.75	.35
☐ GD206 Chris Gwynn	.25	.11
☐ GD207 Tony Gwynn	2.50	1.10
☐ GD208 Rickey Henderson	1.25	.55
☐ GD209 Scott Sanders	.25	.11
☐ GD210 Jason Thompson	.25	.11
☐ GD211 Fernando Valenzuela	.50	.23
☐ GD212 Tim Worrell	.25	.11
☐ GD213 Barry Bonds	1.25	.55
☐ GD214 Jay Canizaro	.25	.11
☐ GD215 Doug Creek	.25	.11
☐ GD216 Jacob Cruz	.25	.11
☐ GD217 Gienallen Hill	.25	.11
☐ GD218 Tom Lampkin	.25	.11
☐ GD219 Jim Poole	.25	.11
☐ GD220 Desi Wilson	.25	.11

1997 Pacific Prisms Sizzling Lumber

	MINT	NRMT
COMPLETE SET (36)	300.00	135.00
COMMON CARD (SL1-SL12)	1.50	.70
STATED ODDS 1:37		

☐ SL1A Cal Ripken	25.00	11.00
☐ SL1B Rafael Palmeiro	6.00	2.70
☐ SL1C Roberto Alomar	6.00	2.70
☐ SL2A Frank Thomas	12.00	5.50
☐ SL2B Robin Ventura	3.00	1.35
☐ SL2C Harold Baines	3.00	1.35
☐ SL3A Albert Belle	6.00	2.70
☐ SL3B Manny Ramirez	8.00	3.60
☐ SL3C Kenny Lofton	5.00	2.20
☐ SL4A Derek Jeter	15.00	6.75
☐ SL4B Bernie Williams	6.00	2.70
☐ SL4C Wade Boggs	6.00	2.70
☐ SL5A Mark McGwire	30.00	13.50
☐ SL5B Jason Giambi	3.00	1.35
☐ SL5C Geronimo Berroa	1.50	.70
☐ SL6A Ken Griffey Jr.	30.00	13.50
☐ SL6B Alex Rodriguez	20.00	9.00
☐ SL6C Jay Buhner	3.00	1.35
☐ SL7A Juan Gonzalez	12.00	5.50
☐ SL7B Dean Palmer	3.00	1.35
☐ SL7C Ivan Rodriguez	8.00	3.60
☐ SL8A Ryan Klesko	3.00	1.35
☐ SL8B Chipper Jones	15.00	6.75
☐ SL8C Andruw Jones	6.00	2.70
☐ SL9A Dante Bichette	3.00	1.35
☐ SL9B Andres Galarraga	6.00	2.70
☐ SL9C Vinny Castilla	5.00	2.20
☐ SL10A Jeff Bagwell	8.00	3.60
☐ SL10B Craig Biggio	6.00	2.70
☐ SL10C Derek Bell		1.35
☐ SL11A Mike Piazza	20.00	9.00
☐ SL11B Raul Mondesi	3.00	1.35
☐ SL11C Karim Garcia	3.00	1.35
☐ SL12A Tony Gwynn	15.00	6.75
☐ SL12B Ken Caminiti	5.00	2.20
☐ SL12C Greg Vaughn	3.00	1.35

1997 Pacific Prisms Sluggers and Hurlers

	MINT	NRMT
COMPLETE SET (24)	600.00	275.00

COMMON CARD (SH1A-SH12B)	4.00	1.80
MINOR STARS	6.00	2.70
SEMISTARS	10.00	4.50
UNLISTED STARS	15.00	6.75
STATED ODDS 1:145		

☐ SH1A Cal Ripken	60.00	27.00
☐ SH1B Mike Mussina	15.00	6.75
☐ SH2A Jose Canseco	20.00	9.00
☐ SH2B Roger Clemens	40.00	18.00
☐ SH3A Frank Thomas	30.00	13.50
☐ SH3B Wilson Alvarez	6.00	2.70
☐ SH4A Kenny Lofton	10.00	4.50
☐ SH4B Orel Hershiser	6.00	2.70
☐ SH5A Derek Jeter	50.00	22.00
☐ SH5B Andy Pettitte	10.00	4.50
☐ SH6A Ken Griffey Jr.	80.00	36.00
☐ SH6B Randy Johnson	15.00	6.75
☐ SH7A Alex Rodriguez	50.00	22.00
☐ SH7B Jamie Moyer	4.00	1.80
☐ SH8A Andruw Jones	20.00	9.00
☐ SH8B Greg Maddux	40.00	18.00
☐ SH9A Chipper Jones	40.00	18.00
☐ SH9B John Smoltz	10.00	4.50
☐ SH10A Jeff Bagwell	20.00	9.00
☐ SH10B Shane Reynolds	6.00	2.70
☐ SH11A Mike Piazza	50.00	22.00
☐ SH11B Hideo Nomo	15.00	6.75
☐ SH12A Tony Gwynn	40.00	18.00
☐ SH12B Fernando Valenzuela	6.00	2.70

1999 Pacific Prism

	MINT	NRMT
COMPLETE SET (150)	80.00	36.00
COMMON CARD (1-150)	.30	.14
MINOR STARS	.50	.23
SEMISTARS	.75	.35
UNLISTED STARS	1.25	.55

☐ 1 Garret Anderson	.50	.23
☐ 2 Jim Edmonds	.50	.23
☐ 3 Darin Erstad	.75	.35
☐ 4 Chuck Finley	.50	.23
☐ 5 Tim Salmon	.75	.35
☐ 6 Jay Bell	.50	.23
☐ 7 David Dellucci	.30	.14
☐ 8 Travis Lee	.75	.35
☐ 9 Matt Williams	1.25	.55
☐ 10 Andres Galarraga	.75	.35
☐ 11 Tom Glavine	1.25	.55
☐ 12 Andruw Jones	1.25	.55
☐ 13 Chipper Jones	3.00	1.35
☐ 14 Ryan Klesko	.50	.23
☐ 15 Javy Lopez	.50	.23
☐ 16 Greg Maddux	3.00	1.35
☐ 17 Roberto Alomar	1.25	.55
☐ 18 Ryan Minor	.50	.23
☐ 19 Mike Mussina	1.25	.55
☐ 20 Rafael Palmeiro	1.25	.55
☐ 21 Cal Ripken	5.00	2.20
☐ 22 Nomar Garciaparra	4.00	1.80
☐ 23 Pedro Martinez	1.50	.70
☐ 24 John Valentin	.50	.23
☐ 25 Mo Vaughn	1.25	.55
☐ 26 Tim Wakefield	.30	.14
☐ 27 Rod Beck	.50	.23
☐ 28 Mark Grace	.75	.35
☐ 29 Lance Johnson	.30	.14

#	Player	MINT	NRMT
30	Sammy Sosa	4.00	1.80
31	Kerry Wood	1.25	.55
32	Albert Belle	1.25	.55
33	Mike Caruso	.30	.14
34	Magglio Ordonez	1.25	.55
35	Frank Thomas	2.50	1.10
36	Robin Ventura	.50	.23
37	Aaron Boone	.30	.14
38	Barry Larkin	1.25	.55
39	Reggie Sanders	.30	.14
40	Brett Tomko	.30	.14
41	Sandy Alomar Jr.	.50	.23
42	Bartolo Colon	.50	.23
43	David Justice	.50	.23
44	Kenny Lofton	.75	.35
45	Manny Ramirez	1.50	.70
46	Richie Sexson	.75	.35
47	Jim Thome	1.25	.55
48	Omar Vizquel	.50	.23
49	Dante Bichette	.50	.23
50	Vinny Castilla	.50	.23
51	Edgard Clemente	.30	.14
52	Todd Helton	1.25	.55
53	Quinton McCracken	.30	.14
54	Larry Walker	1.25	.55
55	Tony Clark	.50	.23
56	Damion Easley	.50	.23
57	Luis Gonzalez	.50	.23
58	Bob Higginson	.50	.23
59	Brian Hunter	.30	.14
60	Cliff Floyd	.50	.23
61	Alex Gonzalez	.50	.23
62	Livan Hernandez	.30	.14
63	Derrek Lee	.30	.14
64	Edgar Renteria	.30	.14
65	Moises Alou	.50	.23
66	Jeff Bagwell	1.50	.70
67	Derek Bell	.50	.23
68	Craig Biggio	1.25	.55
69	Randy Johnson	1.25	.55
70	Johnny Damon	.30	.14
71	Jeff King	.30	.14
72	Hal Morris	.30	.14
73	Dean Palmer	.50	.23
74	Eric Karros	.50	.23
75	Raul Mondesi	.50	.23
76	Chan Ho Park	.50	.23
77	Gary Sheffield	.50	.23
78	Jeromy Burnitz	.50	.23
79	Jeff Cirillo	.50	.23
80	Marquis Grissom	.30	.14
81	Jose Valentin	.30	.14
82	Fernando Vina	.30	.14
83	Paul Molitor	1.25	.55
84	Otis Nixon	.30	.14
85	David Ortiz	.50	.23
86	Todd Walker	.50	.23
87	Vladimir Guerrero	1.50	.70
88	Carl Pavano	.30	.14
89	Fernando Seguignol	.30	.14
90	Ugueth Urbina	.30	.14
91	Carlos Baerga	.50	.23
92	Bobby Bonilla	.50	.23
93	Hideo Nomo	1.25	.55
94	John Olerud	.50	.23
95	Rey Ordonez	.50	.23
96	Mike Piazza	4.00	1.80
97	David Cone	.75	.35
98	Orlando Hernandez	1.25	.55
99	Hideki Irabu	.50	.23
100	Derek Jeter	4.00	1.80
101	Tino Martinez	.50	.23
102	Bernie Williams	1.25	.55
103	Eric Chavez	.75	.35
104	Jason Giambi	.50	.23
105	Ben Grieve	1.25	.55
106	Rickey Henderson	1.50	.70
107	Bob Abreu	.50	.23
108	Doug Glanville	.30	.14
109	Scott Rolen	1.50	.70
110	Curt Schilling	.75	.35
111	Emil Brown	.30	.14
112	Jose Guillen	.30	.14
113	Jason Kendall	.50	.23
114	Al Martin	.30	.14
115	Aramis Ramirez	.75	.35
116	Kevin Young	.50	.23
117	J.D. Drew	2.00	.90
118	Ron Gant	.50	.23
119	Brian Jordan	.50	.23
120	Eli Marrero	.30	.14
121	Mark McGwire	8.00	3.60
122	Kevin Brown	.75	.35
123	Tony Gwynn	3.00	1.35
124	Trevor Hoffman	.50	.23
125	Wally Joyner	.50	.23
126	Greg Vaughn	.50	.23
127	Barry Bonds	1.50	.70
128	Ellis Burks	.50	.23
129	Jeff Kent	.50	.23
130	Robb Nen	.30	.14
131	J.T. Snow	.50	.23
132	Jay Buhner	.50	.23
133	Ken Griffey Jr.	6.00	2.70
134	Edgar Martinez	.50	.23
135	Alex Rodriguez	4.00	1.80
136	David Segui	.30	.14
137	Rolando Arrojo	.30	.14
138	Wade Boggs	1.25	.55
139	Aaron Ledesma	.30	.14
140	Fred McGriff	.75	.35
141	Will Clark	1.25	.55
142	Juan Gonzalez	2.50	1.10
143	Rusty Greer	.50	.23
144	Ivan Rodriguez	1.50	.70
145	Aaron Sele	.50	.23
146	Jose Canseco	1.50	.70
147	Roger Clemens	3.00	1.35
148	Jose Cruz Jr.	.50	.23
149	Carlos Delgado	1.25	.55
150	Alex Gonzalez	.50	.23
SA	Tony Gwynn Sample	4.00	1.80
S&H	Tony Gwynn Sample Hawaii/200	8.00	3.60

1999 Pacific Prism Holographic Blue

	MINT	NRMT
COMMON CARD (1-150)	8.00	3.60

*STARS: 10X TO 25X BASIC CARDS
*YNG.STARS: 8X TO 20X BASIC CARDS
RANDOM INSERTS IN PACKS
STATED PRINT RUN 80 SERIAL #'d SETS

1999 Pacific Prism Holographic Gold

	MINT	NRMT
COMMON CARD (1-150)	2.00	.90

*STARS: 2.5X TO 6X BASIC CARDS
*YNG.STARS: 2X TO 5X BASIC CARDS
RANDOM INSERTS IN PACKS
STATED PRINT RUN 480 SERIAL #'d SETS

1999 Pacific Prism Holographic Mirror

	MINT	NRMT
COMMON CARD (1-150)	5.00	2.20

*STARS: 6X TO 15X BASIC CARDS
*YNG.STARS: 5X TO 12X BASIC CARDS
RANDOM INSERTS IN PACKS
STATED PRINT RUN 160 SERIAL #'d SETS

1999 Pacific Prism Holographic Purple

	MINT	NRMT
COMMON CARD (1-150)	2.50	1.10

*STARS: 3X TO 8X BASIC CARDS
*YNG.STARS: 2.5X TO 6X BASIC CARDS
RANDOM INSERTS IN HOBBY PACKS
STATED PRINT RUN 320 SERIAL #'d SETS

1999 Pacific Prism Red

	MINT	NRMT
COMMON CARD (1-150)	1.50	.70

*STARS: 2X TO 5X BASIC CARDS

*YNG.STARS: 1.5X TO 4X BASIC CARDS
STATED ODDS 2:25 RETAIL

1999 Pacific Prism Ahead of the Game

	MINT	NRMT
COMPLETE SET (20)	300.00	135.00
COMMON CARD (1-20)	6.00	2.70
STATED ODDS 1:49		
☐ 1 Darin Erstad	6.00	2.70
☐ 2 Travis Lee	6.00	2.70
☐ 3 Chipper Jones	15.00	6.75
☐ 4 Cal Ripken	25.00	11.00
☐ 5 Nomar Garciaparra	20.00	9.00
☐ 6 Sammy Sosa	20.00	9.00
☐ 7 Kerry Wood	6.00	2.70
☐ 8 Frank Thomas	12.00	5.50
☐ 9 Manny Ramirez	8.00	3.60
☐ 10 Todd Helton	6.00	2.70
☐ 11 Jeff Bagwell	8.00	3.60
☐ 12 Mike Piazza	20.00	9.00
☐ 13 Derek Jeter	20.00	9.00
☐ 14 Bernie Williams	6.00	2.70
☐ 15 J.D. Drew	8.00	3.60
☐ 16 Mark McGwire	40.00	18.00
☐ 17 Tony Gwynn	15.00	6.75
☐ 18 Ken Griffey Jr.	30.00	13.50
☐ 19 Alex Rodriguez	20.00	9.00
☐ 20 Ivan Rodriguez	8.00	3.60

1999 Pacific Prism Ballpark Legends

	MINT	NRMT
COMPLETE SET (10)	400.00	180.00
COMMON CARD (1-10)	8.00	3.60
STATED ODDS 1:193		
☐ 1 Cal Ripken	50.00	22.00
☐ 2 Nomar Garciaparra	40.00	18.00
☐ 3 Frank Thomas	25.00	11.00
☐ 4 Ken Griffey Jr.	60.00	27.00
☐ 5 Alex Rodriguez	40.00	18.00
☐ 6 Greg Maddux	30.00	13.50
☐ 7 Sammy Sosa	40.00	18.00
☐ 8 Kerry Wood	8.00	3.60
☐ 9 Mark McGwire	80.00	36.00
☐ 10 Tony Gwynn	30.00	13.50

1999 Pacific Prism Diamond Glory

	MINT	NRMT
COMPLETE SET (20)	120.00	55.00
COMMON CARD (1-20)	1.50	.70
UNLISTED STARS	2.50	1.10
STATED ODDS 2:25		
☐ 1 Darin Erstad	1.50	.70
☐ 2 Travis Lee	1.50	.70
☐ 3 Chipper Jones	6.00	2.70
☐ 4 Greg Maddux	6.00	2.70
☐ 5 Cal Ripken	10.00	4.50
☐ 6 Nomar Garciaparra	8.00	3.60
☐ 7 Sammy Sosa	8.00	3.60
☐ 8 Kerry Wood	2.50	1.10
☐ 9 Frank Thomas	5.00	2.20
☐ 10 Todd Helton	2.50	1.10
☐ 11 Jeff Bagwell	3.00	1.35
☐ 12 Mike Piazza	8.00	3.60
☐ 13 Derek Jeter	8.00	3.60
☐ 14 Bernie Williams	2.50	1.10
☐ 15 J.D. Drew	3.00	1.35
☐ 16 Mark McGwire	15.00	6.75
☐ 17 Tony Gwynn	6.00	2.70
☐ 18 Ken Griffey Jr.	12.00	5.50
☐ 19 Alex Rodriguez	8.00	3.60
☐ 20 Juan Gonzalez	5.00	2.20

1999 Pacific Prism Epic Performers

	MINT	NRMT
COMPLETE SET (10)	250.00	110.00
COMMON CARD (1-10)	5.00	2.20
STATED ODDS 1:97 HOBBY		
☐ 1 Cal Ripken	30.00	13.50
☐ 2 Nomar Garciaparra	25.00	11.00
☐ 3 Frank Thomas	15.00	6.75
☐ 4 Ken Griffey Jr.	40.00	18.00
☐ 5 Alex Rodriguez	25.00	11.00
☐ 6 Greg Maddux	20.00	9.00
☐ 7 Sammy Sosa	25.00	11.00
☐ 8 Kerry Wood	5.00	2.20
☐ 9 Mark McGwire	50.00	22.00
☐ 10 Tony Gwynn	20.00	9.00

1999 Pacific Private Stock

	MINT	NRMT
COMPLETE SET (150)	80.00	36.00
COMMON CARD (1-150)	.25	.11
MINOR STARS	.40	.18
SEMISTARS	.60	.25
UNLISTED STARS	1.00	.45
☐ 1 Jeff Bagwell	1.25	.55
☐ 2 Roger Clemens	2.50	1.10
☐ 3 J.D. Drew	1.50	.70
☐ 4 Nomar Garciaparra	3.00	1.35
☐ 5 Juan Gonzalez	2.00	.90
☐ 6 Ken Griffey Jr.	5.00	2.20
☐ 7 Tony Gwynn	2.50	1.10
☐ 8 Derek Jeter	3.00	1.35
☐ 9 Chipper Jones	2.50	1.10
☐ 10 Travis Lee	.60	.25
☐ 11 Greg Maddux	2.50	1.10
☐ 12 Mark McGwire	6.00	2.70
☐ 13 Mike Piazza	3.00	1.35
☐ 14 Manny Ramirez	1.25	.55
☐ 15 Cal Ripken	4.00	1.80
☐ 16 Alex Rodriguez	3.00	1.35
☐ 17 Ivan Rodriguez	1.25	.55
☐ 18 Sammy Sosa	3.00	1.35
☐ 19 Frank Thomas	2.00	.90
☐ 20 Kerry Wood	1.00	.45
☐ 21 Roberto Alomar	1.00	.45
☐ 22 Moises Alou	.40	.18
☐ 23 Albert Belle	1.00	.45
☐ 24 Craig Biggio	1.00	.45
☐ 25 Wade Boggs	1.00	.45
☐ 26 Barry Bonds	1.25	.55
☐ 27 Jose Canseco	1.25	.55
☐ 28 Jim Edmonds	.40	.18
☐ 29 Darin Erstad	.60	.25
☐ 30 Andres Galarraga	.60	.25
☐ 31 Tom Glavine	1.00	.45
☐ 32 Ben Grieve	1.00	.45
☐ 33 Vladimir Guerrero	1.25	.55
☐ 34 Wilton Guerrero	.25	.11
☐ 35 Todd Helton	1.00	.45
☐ 36 Andruw Jones	1.00	.45
☐ 37 Ryan Klesko	.40	.18
☐ 38 Kenny Lofton	.60	.25
☐ 39 Javy Lopez	.40	.18
☐ 40 Pedro Martinez	1.25	.55
☐ 41 Paul Molitor	1.00	.45
☐ 42 Raul Mondesi	.40	.18
☐ 43 Rafael Palmeiro	1.00	.45
☐ 44 Tim Salmon	.60	.25
☐ 45 Jim Thome	1.00	.45
☐ 46 Mo Vaughn	1.00	.45
☐ 47 Larry Walker	1.00	.45
☐ 48 David Wells	.40	.18
☐ 49 Bernie Williams	1.00	.45
☐ 50 Jaret Wright	.40	.18
☐ 51 Bob Abreu	.40	.18
☐ 52 Garret Anderson	.40	.18
☐ 53 Rolando Arrojo	.25	.11
☐ 54 Tony Batista	.25	.11
☐ 55 Rod Beck	.25	.11
☐ 56 Derek Bell	.40	.18
☐ 57 Marvin Benard	.25	.11
☐ 58 Dave Berg	.25	.11

❏ 59 Dante Bichette	.40	.18
❏ 60 Aaron Boone	.25	.11
❏ 61 Bret Boone	.40	.18
❏ 62 Scott Brosius	.40	.18
❏ 63 Brant Brown	.25	.11
❏ 64 Kevin Brown	.60	.25
❏ 65 Jeromy Burnitz	.40	.18
❏ 66 Ken Caminiti	.40	.18
❏ 67 Mike Caruso	.25	.11
❏ 68 Sean Casey	1.00	.45
❏ 69 Vinny Castilla	.40	.18
❏ 70 Eric Chavez	.60	.25
❏ 71 Ryan Christenson	.25	.11
❏ 72 Jeff Cirillo	.40	.18
❏ 73 Tony Clark	.40	.18
❏ 74 Will Clark	1.00	.45
❏ 75 Edgard Clemente	.25	.11
❏ 76 David Cone	.60	.25
❏ 77 Marty Cordova	.25	.11
❏ 78 Jose Cruz Jr.	.40	.18
❏ 79 Eric Davis	.40	.18
❏ 80 Carlos Delgado	1.00	.45
❏ 81 David Dellucci	.25	.11
❏ 82 Delino DeShields	.25	.11
❏ 83 Gary DiSarcina	.25	.11
❏ 84 Damion Easley	.40	.18
❏ 85 Dennis Eckersley	.40	.18
❏ 86 Cliff Floyd	.40	.18
❏ 87 Jason Giambi	.40	.18
❏ 88 Doug Glanville	.40	.18
❏ 89 Alex Gonzalez	.40	.18
❏ 90 Mark Grace	.60	.25
❏ 91 Rusty Greer	.40	.18
❏ 92 Jose Guillen	.25	.11
❏ 93 Carlos Guillen	.25	.11
❏ 94 Jeffrey Hammonds	.25	.11
❏ 95 Rick Helling	.25	.11
❏ 96 Bob Henley	.25	.11
❏ 97 Livan Hernandez	.25	.11
❏ 98 Orlando Hernandez	1.00	.45
❏ 99 Bob Higginson	.40	.18
❏ 100 Trevor Hoffman	.40	.18
❏ 101 Randy Johnson	1.00	.45
❏ 102 Brian Jordan	.40	.18
❏ 103 Wally Joyner	.40	.18
❏ 104 Eric Karros	.40	.18
❏ 105 Jason Kendall	.40	.18
❏ 106 Jeff Kent	.40	.18
❏ 107 Jeff King	.25	.11
❏ 108 Mark Kotsay	.40	.18
❏ 109 Ray Lankford	.40	.18
❏ 110 Barry Larkin	1.00	.45
❏ 111 Mark Loretta	.25	.11
❏ 112 Edgar Martinez	.40	.18
❏ 113 Tino Martinez	.40	.18
❏ 114 Quinton McCracken	.25	.11
❏ 115 Fred McGriff	.60	.25
❏ 116 Ryan Minor	.40	.18
❏ 117 Hal Morris	.25	.11
❏ 118 Bill Mueller	.25	.11
❏ 119 Mike Mussina	1.00	.45
❏ 120 Dave Nilsson	.25	.11
❏ 121 Otis Nixon	.25	.11
❏ 122 Hideo Nomo	1.00	.45
❏ 123 Paul O'Neill	.40	.18
❏ 124 Jose Offerman	.40	.18
❏ 125 John Olerud	.40	.18
❏ 126 Rey Ordonez	.40	.18
❏ 127 David Ortiz	.25	.11
❏ 128 Dean Palmer	.40	.18
❏ 129 Chan Ho Park	.40	.18
❏ 130 Aramis Ramirez	.60	.25
❏ 131 Edgar Renteria	.25	.11
❏ 132 Armando Rios	.25	.11
❏ 133 Henry Rodriguez	.40	.18
❏ 134 Scott Rolen	1.25	.55
❏ 135 Curt Schilling	.60	.25
❏ 136 David Segui	.25	.11
❏ 137 Richie Sexson	.60	.25
❏ 138 Gary Sheffield	.40	.18
❏ 139 John Smoltz	.60	.25
❏ 140 Matt Stairs	.25	.11
❏ 141 Justin Thompson	.25	.11
❏ 142 Greg Vaughn	.40	.18
❏ 143 Omar Vizquel	.40	.18
❏ 144 Tim Wakefield	.25	.11
❏ 145 Todd Walker	.40	.18
❏ 146 Devon White	.25	.11
❏ 147 Rondell White	.40	.18
❏ 148 Matt Williams	1.00	.45
❏ 149 Enrique Wilson	.25	.11
❏ 150 Kevin Young	.40	.18

1999 Pacific Private Stock Exclusive

	MINT	NRMT
COMPLETE SET (20)	500.00	220.00
COMMON CARD (1-20)	10.00	4.50

*STARS: 4X TO 10X BASIC CARDS
*YNG.STARS: 4X TO 10X BASIC CARDS
RANDOM INSERTS IN PACKS
STATED PRINT RUN 299 SERIAL #'d SETS

1999 Pacific Private Stock Platinum

	MINT	NRMT
COMMON CARD (1-50)	4.00	1.80

*STARS: 6X TO 15X BASIC CARDS
*YNG.STARS: 5X TO 12X BASIC CARDS
RANDOM INSERTS IN PACKS
STATED PRINT RUN 199 SERIAL #'d SETS

1999 Pacific Private Stock Preferred

	MINT	NRMT
COMPLETE SET (20)	400.00	180.00
COMMON CARD (1-20)	8.00	3.60

*STARS: 3X TO 8X BASIC CARDS
*YNG.STARS: 3X TO 8X BASIC CARDS
RANDOM INSERTS IN PACKS
STATED PRINT RUN 399 SERIAL #'d SETS

1999 Pacific Private Stock Vintage

	MINT	NRMT
COMMON CARD (1-50)	6.00	2.70

*STARS: 10X TO 25X BASIC CARDS
*YNG.STARS: 10X TO 25X BASIC CARDS
RANDOM INSERTS IN PACKS
STATED PRINT RUN 99 SERIAL #'d SETS

1999 Pacific Private Stock PS-206

	MINT	NRMT
COMPLETE SET (150)	250.00	110.00
COMMON CARD (1-150)	.75	.35
MINOR STARS	1.25	.55
SEMISTARS	2.00	.90
UNLISTED STARS	3.00	1.35

ONE BLUE-BACKED CARD PER PACK

1999 Pacific Private Stock PS-206 Red

	MINT	NRMT
COMMON CARD (1-150)	4.00	1.80

*PS-206 RED: 2X TO 5X BASIC PS-206
STATED ODDS 1:25 HOB/1:33 RET

1999 Pacific Private Stock Home Run History

	MINT	NRMT
COMPLETE SET (22)	300.00	135.00
COMMON CARD (1-22)	10.00	4.50

STATED ODDS 1:25 HOB/1:17 RET

		MINT	NRMT
❑ 1	Mark McGwire 61	15.00	6.75
❑ 2	Sammy Sosa 59	10.00	4.50
❑ 3	Mark McGwire 62	20.00	9.00
❑ 4	Sammy Sosa 60	10.00	4.50
❑ 5	Mark McGwire 63	15.00	6.75
❑ 6	Sammy Sosa 61	10.00	4.50
❑ 7	Mark McGwire 64	15.00	6.75
❑ 8	Sammy Sosa 62	10.00	4.50
❑ 9	Mark McGwire 65	15.00	6.75
❑ 10	Sammy Sosa 63	10.00	4.50
❑ 11	Mark McGwire 67	15.00	6.75
❑ 12	Sammy Sosa 64	10.00	4.50
❑ 13	Mark McGwire 66	15.00	6.75
❑ 14	Sammy Sosa 65	10.00	4.50
❑ 15	Mark McGwire 70	30.00	13.50
❑ 16	Sammy Sosa 66	20.00	9.00
❑ 17	Mark McGwire w/J.D. Drew	20.00	9.00
❑ 18	Sammy Sosa A Celebration of Celebration	10.00	4.50
❑ 19	Sammy Sosa Mark McGwire Awesome Power	15.00	6.75
❑ 20	Mark McGwire Sammy Sosa Transcending Sports	15.00	6.75
❑ 21	Mark McGwire Crown Die Cut	40.00	18.00
❑ 22	Cal Ripken Crown Die Cut	25.00	11.00

1992 Pinnacle

	MINT	NRMT
COMPLETE SET (620)	40.00	18.00
COMPLETE SERIES 1 (310)	25.00	11.00
COMPLETE SERIES 2 (310)	15.00	6.75

COMMON CARD (1-620)		.10	.05
MINOR STARS		.20	.09
UNLISTED STARS		.40	.18

SUBSET CARDS HALF VALUE OF BASE CARDS

❑ 1	Frank Thomas	1.00	.45
❑ 2	Benito Santiago	.10	.05
❑ 3	Carlos Baerga	.10	.05
❑ 4	Cecil Fielder	.20	.09
❑ 5	Barry Larkin	.30	.14
❑ 6	Ozzie Smith	.50	.23
❑ 7	Willie McGee	.20	.09
❑ 8	Paul Molitor	.40	.18
❑ 9	Andy Van Slyke	.20	.09
❑ 10	Ryne Sandberg	.50	.23
❑ 11	Kevin Seitzer	.10	.05
❑ 12	Len Dykstra	.20	.09
❑ 13	Edgar Martinez	.30	.14
❑ 14	Ruben Sierra	.20	.09
❑ 15	Howard Johnson	.10	.05
❑ 16	Dave Henderson	.10	.05
❑ 17	Devon White	.10	.05
❑ 18	Terry Pendleton	.10	.05
❑ 19	Steve Finley	.20	.09
❑ 20	Kirby Puckett	.60	.25
❑ 21	Orel Hershiser	.10	.05
❑ 22	Hal Morris	.10	.05
❑ 23	Don Mattingly	.75	.35
❑ 24	Delino DeShields	.20	.09
❑ 25	Dennis Eckersley	.20	.09
❑ 26	Ellis Burks	.10	.05
❑ 27	Jay Buhner	.30	.14
❑ 28	Matt Williams	.30	.14
❑ 29	Lou Whitaker	.20	.09
❑ 30	Alex Fernandez	.20	.09
❑ 31	Albert Belle	.40	.18
❑ 32	Todd Zeile	.10	.05
❑ 33	Tony Pena	.10	.05
❑ 34	Jay Bell	.20	.09
❑ 35	Rafael Palmeiro	.40	.18
❑ 36	Wes Chamberlain	.10	.05
❑ 37	George Bell	.20	.09
❑ 38	Robin Yount	.40	.18
❑ 39	Vince Coleman	.10	.05
❑ 40	Bruce Hurst	.10	.05
❑ 41	Harold Baines	.20	.09
❑ 42	Chuck Finley	.20	.09
❑ 43	Ken Caminiti	.30	.14
❑ 44	Ben McDonald	.20	.09
❑ 45	Roberto Alomar	.40	.18
❑ 46	Chili Davis	.10	.05
❑ 47	Bill Doran	.10	.05
❑ 48	Jerald Clark	.10	.05
❑ 49	Jose Lind	.10	.05
❑ 50	Nolan Ryan	1.50	.70
❑ 51	Phil Plantier	.20	.09
❑ 52	Gary DiSarcina	.10	.05
❑ 53	Kevin Bass	.10	.05
❑ 54	Pat Kelly	.10	.05
❑ 55	Mark Wohlers	.10	.05
❑ 56	Walt Weiss	.10	.05
❑ 57	Lenny Harris	.10	.05
❑ 58	Ivan Calderon	.10	.05
❑ 59	Harold Reynolds	.10	.05
❑ 60	George Brett	.75	.35
❑ 61	Gregg Olson	.10	.05
❑ 62	Orlando Merced	.10	.05
❑ 63	Steve Decker	.10	.05
❑ 64	John Franco	.20	.09
❑ 65	Greg Maddux	1.00	.45
❑ 66	Alex Cole	.10	.05
❑ 67	Dave Hollins	.10	.05
❑ 68	Kent Hrbek	.20	.09
❑ 69	Tom Pagnozzi	.10	.05
❑ 70	Jeff Bagwell	.75	.35
❑ 71	Jim Gantner	.10	.05
❑ 72	Matt Nokes	.10	.05
❑ 73	Brian Harper	.10	.05
❑ 74	Andy Benes	.20	.09
❑ 75	Tom Glavine	.30	.14
❑ 76	Terry Steinbach	.10	.05
❑ 77	Dennis Martinez	.20	.09
❑ 78	John Olerud	.20	.09
❑ 79	Ozzie Guillen	.10	.05
❑ 80	Darryl Strawberry	.20	.09
❑ 81	Gary Gaetti	.20	.09
❑ 82	Dave Righetti	.10	.05
❑ 83	Chris Hoiles	.10	.05
❑ 84	Andujar Cedeno	.10	.05
❑ 85	Jack Clark	.20	.09
❑ 86	David Howard	.10	.05
❑ 87	Bill Gullickson	.10	.05
❑ 88	Bernard Gilkey	.10	.05
❑ 89	Kevin Elster	.10	.05
❑ 90	Kevin Maas	.10	.05
❑ 91	Mark Lewis	.10	.05
❑ 92	Greg Vaughn	.30	.14
❑ 93	Bret Barberie	.10	.05
❑ 94	Dave Smith	.10	.05
❑ 95	Roger Clemens	1.00	.45
❑ 96	Doug Drabek	.10	.05
❑ 97	Omar Vizquel	.20	.09
❑ 98	Jose Guzman	.10	.05
❑ 99	Juan Samuel	.10	.05
❑ 100	Dave Justice	.40	.18
❑ 101	Tom Browning	.10	.05
❑ 102	Mark Gubicza	.10	.05
❑ 103	Mickey Morandini	.10	.05
❑ 104	Ed Whitson	.10	.05
❑ 105	Lance Parrish	.10	.05
❑ 106	Scott Erickson	.20	.09
❑ 107	Jack McDowell	.20	.09
❑ 108	Dave Stieb	.10	.05
❑ 109	Mike Moore	.10	.05
❑ 110	Travis Fryman	.20	.09
❑ 111	Dwight Gooden	.20	.09
❑ 112	Fred McGriff	.30	.14
❑ 113	Alan Trammell	.30	.14
❑ 114	Roberto Kelly	.20	.09
❑ 115	Andre Dawson	.30	.14
❑ 116	Bill Landrum	.10	.05
❑ 117	Brian McRae	.10	.05
❑ 118	B.J. Surhoff	.10	.05
❑ 119	Chuck Knoblauch	.40	.18
❑ 120	Steve Olin	.10	.05
❑ 121	Robin Ventura	.20	.09
❑ 122	Will Clark	.40	.18
❑ 123	Tino Martinez	.40	.18
❑ 124	Dale Murphy	.20	.09
❑ 125	Pete O'Brien	.10	.05
❑ 126	Ray Lankford	.40	.18
❑ 127	Juan Gonzalez	1.00	.45
❑ 128	Ron Gant	.20	.09
❑ 129	Marquis Grissom	.20	.09
❑ 130	Jose Canseco	.50	.23
❑ 131	Mike Greenwell	.10	.05
❑ 132	Mark Langston	.10	.05
❑ 133	Brett Butler	.20	.09
❑ 134	Kelly Gruber	.10	.05
❑ 135	Chris Sabo	.10	.05
❑ 136	Mark Grace	.30	.14
❑ 137	Tony Fernandez	.10	.05
❑ 138	Glenn Davis	.10	.05
❑ 139	Pedro Munoz	.10	.05
❑ 140	Craig Biggio	.40	.18
❑ 141	Pete Schourek	.10	.05
❑ 142	Mike Boddicker	.10	.05
❑ 143	Robby Thompson	.10	.05
❑ 144	Mel Hall	.10	.05
❑ 145	Bryan Harvey	.10	.05
❑ 146	Mike LaValliere	.10	.05
❑ 147	John Kruk	.20	.09
❑ 148	Joe Carter	.20	.09
❑ 149	Greg Olson	.10	.05
❑ 150	Julio Franco	.20	.09
❑ 151	Darryl Hamilton	.10	.05
❑ 152	Felix Fermin	.10	.05
❑ 153	Jose Offerman	.20	.09
❑ 154	Paul O'Neill	.20	.09
❑ 155	Tommy Greene	.10	.05
❑ 156	Ivan Rodriguez	.75	.35
❑ 157	Dave Stewart	.20	.09
❑ 158	Jeff Reardon	.20	.09
❑ 159	Felix Jose	.10	.05
❑ 160	Doug Dascenzo	.10	.05
❑ 161	Tim Wallach	.20	.09
❑ 162	Dan Plesac	.10	.05
❑ 163	Luis Gonzalez	.30	.14
❑ 164	Mike Henneman	.10	.05
❑ 165	Mike Devereaux	.10	.05
❑ 166	Luis Polonia	.10	.05

❑ 167	Mike Sharperson	.10	.05
❑ 168	Chris Donnels	.10	.05
❑ 169	Greg W. Harris	.10	.05
❑ 170	Deion Sanders	.40	.18
❑ 171	Mike Schooler	.10	.05
❑ 172	Jose DeJesus	.10	.05
❑ 173	Jeff Montgomery	.20	.09
❑ 174	Milt Cuyler	.10	.05
❑ 175	Wade Boggs	.40	.18
❑ 176	Kevin Tapani	.10	.05
❑ 177	Bill Spiers	.10	.05
❑ 178	Tim Raines	.20	.09
❑ 179	Randy Milligan	.10	.05
❑ 180	Rob Dibble	.10	.05
❑ 181	Kirt Manwaring	.10	.05
❑ 182	Pascual Perez	.10	.05
❑ 183	Juan Guzman	.10	.05
❑ 184	John Smiley	.10	.05
❑ 185	David Segui	.20	.09
❑ 186	Omar Olivares	.10	.05
❑ 187	Joe Slusarski	.10	.05
❑ 188	Erik Hanson	.10	.05
❑ 189	Mark Portugal	.10	.05
❑ 190	Walt Terrell	.10	.05
❑ 191	John Smoltz	.30	.14
❑ 192	Wilson Alvarez	.20	.09
❑ 193	Jimmy Key	.20	.09
❑ 194	Larry Walker	.40	.18
❑ 195	Lee Smith	.20	.09
❑ 196	Pete Harnisch	.10	.05
❑ 197	Mike Harkey	.10	.05
❑ 198	Frank Tanana	.10	.05
❑ 199	Terry Mulholland	.10	.05
❑ 200	Cal Ripken	1.50	.70
❑ 201	Dave Magadan	.10	.05
❑ 202	Bud Black	.10	.05
❑ 203	Terry Shumpert	.10	.05
❑ 204	Mike Mussina	.60	.25
❑ 205	Mo Vaughn	.50	.23
❑ 206	Steve Farr	.10	.05
❑ 207	Darrin Jackson	.10	.05
❑ 208	Jerry Browne	.10	.05
❑ 209	Jeff Russell	.10	.05
❑ 210	Mike Scioscia	.10	.05
❑ 211	Rick Aguilera	.20	.09
❑ 212	Jaime Navarro	.10	.05
❑ 213	Randy Tomlin	.10	.05
❑ 214	Bobby Thigpen	.10	.05
❑ 215	Mark Gardner	.10	.05
❑ 216	Norm Charlton	.10	.05
❑ 217	Mark McGwire	2.00	.90
❑ 218	Skeeter Barnes	.10	.05
❑ 219	Bob Tewksbury	.10	.05
❑ 220	Junior Felix	.10	.05
❑ 221	Sam Horn	.10	.05
❑ 222	Jody Reed	.10	.05
❑ 223	Luis Sojo	.10	.05
❑ 224	Jerome Walton	.10	.05
❑ 225	Darryl Kile	.20	.09
❑ 226	Mickey Tettleton	.10	.05
❑ 227	Dan Pasqua	.10	.05
❑ 228	Jim Gott	.10	.05
❑ 229	Bernie Williams	.40	.18
❑ 230	Shane Mack	.10	.05
❑ 231	Steve Avery	.10	.05
❑ 232	Dave Valle	.10	.05
❑ 233	Mark Leonard	.10	.05
❑ 234	Spike Owen	.10	.05
❑ 235	Gary Sheffield	.40	.18
❑ 236	Steve Chitren	.10	.05
❑ 237	Zane Smith	.10	.05
❑ 238	Tom Gordon	.10	.05
❑ 239	Jose Oquendo	.10	.05
❑ 240	Todd Stottlemyre	.20	.09
❑ 241	Darren Daulton	.20	.09
❑ 242	Tim Naehring	.10	.05
❑ 243	Tony Phillips	.10	.05
❑ 244	Shawon Dunston	.10	.05
❑ 245	Manuel Lee	.10	.05
❑ 246	Mike Pagliarulo	.10	.05
❑ 247	Jim Thome	1.00	.45
❑ 248	Luis Mercedes	.10	.05
❑ 249	Cal Eldred	.10	.05
❑ 250	Derek Bell	.20	.09
❑ 251	Arthur Rhodes	.10	.05
❑ 252	Scott Cooper	.10	.05
❑ 253	Roberto Hernandez	.30	.14
❑ 254	Mo Sanford	.10	.05
❑ 255	Scott Servais	.10	.05
❑ 256	Eric Karros	.40	.18
❑ 257	Andy Mota	.10	.05
❑ 258	Keith Mitchell	.10	.05
❑ 259	Joel Johnston	.10	.05
❑ 260	John Wehner	.10	.05
❑ 261	Gino Minutelli	.10	.05
❑ 262	Greg Gagne	.10	.05
❑ 263	Stan Royer	.10	.05
❑ 264	Carlos Garcia	.10	.05
❑ 265	Andy Ashby	.20	.09
❑ 266	Kim Batiste	.10	.05
❑ 267	Julio Valera	.10	.05
❑ 268	Royce Clayton	.10	.05
❑ 269	Gary Scott	.10	.05
❑ 270	Kirk Dressendorfer	.10	.05
❑ 271	Sean Berry	.10	.05
❑ 272	Lance Dickson	.10	.05
❑ 273	Rob Maurer	.10	.05
❑ 274	Scott Brosius	.50	.23
❑ 275	Dave Fleming	.10	.05
❑ 276	Lenny Webster	.10	.05
❑ 277	Mike Humphreys	.10	.05
❑ 278	Freddie Benavides	.10	.05
❑ 279	Harvey Pulliam	.10	.05
❑ 280	Jeff Carter	.10	.05
❑ 281	Jim Abbott I	.40	.18
	Nolan Ryan		
❑ 282	Wade Boggs I	.40	.18
	George Brett		
❑ 283	Ken Griffey Jr. I	.75	.35
	Rickey Henderson		
❑ 284	Wally Joyner I	.20	.09
	Dale Murphy		
❑ 285	Chuck Knoblauch I	.40	.18
	Ozzie Smith		
❑ 286	Robin Ventura I	.50	.23
	Lou Gehrig		
❑ 287	Robin Yount SIDE	.20	.09
❑ 288	Bob Tewksbury SIDE	.10	.05
❑ 289	Kirby Puckett SIDE	.40	.18
❑ 290	Kenny Lofton SIDE	.30	.14
❑ 291	Jack McDowell SIDE	.10	.05
❑ 292	John Burkett SIDE	.10	.05
❑ 293	Dwight Smith SIDE	.10	.05
❑ 294	Nolan Ryan SIDE	.75	.35
❑ 295	Manny Ramirez DP	4.00	1.80
❑ 296	Cliff Floyd DP UER	.50	.23
	(Throws right, not left as		
	indicated on back)		
❑ 297	Al Shirley DP	.10	.05
❑ 298	Brian Barber DP	.10	.05
❑ 299	Jon Farrell DP	.10	.05
❑ 300	Scott Ruffcorn DP	.10	.05
❑ 301	Tyrone Hill DP	.10	.05
❑ 302	Benji Gil DP	.10	.05
❑ 303	Tyler Green DP	.10	.05
❑ 304	Allen Watson DP	.10	.05
❑ 305	Jay Buhner SH	.20	.09
❑ 306	Roberto Alomar SH	.20	.09
❑ 307	Chuck Knoblauch SH	.20	.09
❑ 308	Darryl Strawberry SH	.10	.05
❑ 309	Danny Tartabull SH	.10	.05
❑ 310	Bobby Bonilla SH	.10	.05
❑ 311	Mike Felder	.10	.05
❑ 312	Storm Davis	.10	.05
❑ 313	Tim Teufel	.10	.05
❑ 314	Tom Brunansky	.10	.05
❑ 315	Rex Hudler	.10	.05
❑ 316	Dave Otto	.10	.05
❑ 317	Jeff King	.10	.05
❑ 318	Dan Gladden	.10	.05
❑ 319	Bill Pecota	.10	.05
❑ 320	Franklin Stubbs	.10	.05
❑ 321	Gary Carter	.40	.18
❑ 322	Melido Perez	.10	.05
❑ 323	Eric Davis	.20	.09
❑ 324	Greg Myers	.10	.05
❑ 325	Pete Incaviglia	.10	.05
❑ 326	Von Hayes	.10	.05
❑ 327	Greg Swindell	.10	.05
❑ 328	Steve Sax	.10	.05
❑ 329	Chuck McElroy	.10	.05
❑ 330	Gregg Jefferies	.10	.05
❑ 331	Joe Oliver	.10	.05
❑ 332	Paul Faries	.10	.05
❑ 333	David West	.10	.05
❑ 334	Craig Grebeck	.10	.05
❑ 335	Chris Hammond	.10	.05
❑ 336	Billy Ripken	.10	.05
❑ 337	Scott Sanderson	.10	.05
❑ 338	Dick Schofield	.10	.05
❑ 339	Bob Milacki	.10	.05
❑ 340	Kevin Reimer	.10	.05
❑ 341	Jose DeLeon	.10	.05
❑ 342	Henry Cotto	.10	.05
❑ 343	Daryl Boston	.10	.05
❑ 344	Kevin Gross	.10	.05
❑ 345	Milt Thompson	.10	.05
❑ 346	Luis Rivera	.10	.05
❑ 347	Al Osuna	.10	.05
❑ 348	Rob Deer	.10	.05
❑ 349	Tim Leary	.10	.05
❑ 350	Mike Stanton	.10	.05
❑ 351	Dean Palmer	.20	.09
❑ 352	Trevor Wilson	.10	.05
❑ 353	Mark Eichhorn	.10	.05
❑ 354	Scott Aldred	.10	.05
❑ 355	Mark Whiten	.10	.05
❑ 356	Leo Gomez	.10	.05
❑ 357	Rafael Belliard	.10	.05
❑ 358	Carlos Quintana	.10	.05
❑ 359	Mark Davis	.10	.05
❑ 360	Chris Nabholz	.10	.05
❑ 361	Carlton Fisk	.40	.18
❑ 362	Joe Orsulak	.10	.05
❑ 363	Eric Anthony	.10	.05
❑ 364	Greg Hibbard	.10	.05
❑ 365	Scott Leius	.10	.05
❑ 366	Hensley Meulens	.10	.05
❑ 367	Chris Bosio	.10	.05
❑ 368	Brian Drahman	.10	.05
❑ 369	Sammy Sosa	1.25	.55
❑ 370	Stan Belinda	.10	.05
❑ 371	Joe Grahe	.10	.05
❑ 372	Luis Salazar	.10	.05
❑ 373	Lance Johnson	.10	.05
❑ 374	Kal Daniels	.10	.05
❑ 375	Dave Winfield	.40	.18
❑ 376	Brook Jacoby	.10	.05
❑ 377	Mariano Duncan	.10	.05
❑ 378	Ron Darling	.10	.05
❑ 379	Randy Johnson	.40	.18
❑ 380	Chito Martinez	.10	.05
❑ 381	Andres Galarraga	.40	.18
❑ 382	Willie Randolph	.20	.09
❑ 383	Charles Nagy	.20	.09
❑ 384	Tim Belcher	.10	.05
❑ 385	Duane Ward	.10	.05
❑ 386	Vicente Palacios	.10	.05
❑ 387	Mike Gallego	.10	.05
❑ 388	Rich DeLucia	.10	.05
❑ 389	Scott Radinsky	.10	.05
❑ 390	Damon Berryhill	.10	.05
❑ 391	Kirk McCaskill	.10	.05
❑ 392	Pedro Guerrero	.10	.05
❑ 393	Kevin Mitchell	.20	.09
❑ 394	Dickie Thon	.10	.05
❑ 395	Bobby Bonilla	.20	.09
❑ 396	Bill Wegman	.10	.05
❑ 397	Dave Martinez	.10	.05
❑ 398	Rick Sutcliffe	.10	.05
❑ 399	Larry Andersen	.10	.05
❑ 400	Tony Gwynn	1.00	.45
❑ 401	Rickey Henderson	.50	.23
❑ 402	Greg Gagne	.10	.05
❑ 403	Keith Miller	.10	.05
❑ 404	Bip Roberts	.10	.05
❑ 405	Kevin Brown	.30	.14
❑ 406	Mitch Williams	.10	.05
❑ 407	Frank Viola	.10	.05
❑ 408	Darren Lewis	.10	.05
❑ 409	Bob Welch	.10	.05
❑ 410	Bob Walk	.10	.05
❑ 411	Todd Frohwirth	.10	.05
❑ 412	Brian Hunter	.10	.05
❑ 413	Ron Karkovice	.10	.05
❑ 414	Mike Morgan	.10	.05
❑ 415	Joe Hesketh	.10	.05
❑ 416	Don Slaught	.10	.05

❏ 417 Tom Henke	.10	.05
❏ 418 Kurt Stillwell	.10	.05
❏ 419 Hector Villanueva	.10	.05
❏ 420 Glenallen Hill	.10	.05
❏ 421 Pat Borders	.10	.05
❏ 422 Charlie Hough	.20	.09
❏ 423 Charlie Leibrandt	.10	.05
❏ 424 Eddie Murray	.40	.18
❏ 425 Jesse Barfield	.10	.05
❏ 426 Mark Lemke	.10	.05
❏ 427 Kevin McReynolds	.10	.05
❏ 428 Gilberto Reyes	.10	.05
❏ 429 Ramon Martinez	.20	.09
❏ 430 Steve Buechele	.10	.05
❏ 431 David Wells	.20	.09
❏ 432 Kyle Abbott	.10	.05
❏ 433 John Habyan	.10	.05
❏ 434 Kevin Appier	.20	.09
❏ 435 Gene Larkin	.10	.05
❏ 436 Sandy Alomar Jr.	.20	.09
❏ 437 Mike Jackson	.10	.05
❏ 438 Todd Benzinger	.10	.05
❏ 439 Teddy Higuera	.10	.05
❏ 440 Reggie Sanders	.20	.09
❏ 441 Mark Carreon	.10	.05
❏ 442 Bret Saberhagen	.20	.09
❏ 443 Gene Nelson	.10	.05
❏ 444 Jay Howell	.10	.05
❏ 445 Roger McDowell	.10	.05
❏ 446 Sid Bream	.10	.05
❏ 447 Mackey Sasser	.10	.05
❏ 448 Bill Swift	.10	.05
❏ 449 Hubie Brooks	.10	.05
❏ 450 David Cone	.20	.09
❏ 451 Bobby Witt	.10	.05
❏ 452 Brady Anderson	.30	.14
❏ 453 Lee Stevens	.10	.05
❏ 454 Luis Aquino	.10	.05
❏ 455 Carney Lansford	.20	.09
❏ 456 Carlos Hernandez	.10	.05
❏ 457 Danny Jackson	.10	.05
❏ 458 Gerald Young	.10	.05
❏ 459 Tom Candiotti	.10	.05
❏ 460 Billy Hatcher	.10	.05
❏ 461 John Wetteland	.20	.09
❏ 462 Mike Bordick	.10	.05
❏ 463 Don Robinson	.10	.05
❏ 464 Jeff Johnson	.10	.05
❏ 465 Lonnie Smith	.10	.05
❏ 466 Paul Assenmacher	.10	.05
❏ 467 Alvin Davis	.10	.05
❏ 468 Jim Eisenreich	.10	.05
❏ 469 Brent Mayne	.10	.05
❏ 470 Jeff Brantley	.10	.05
❏ 471 Tim Burke	.10	.05
❏ 472 Pat Mahomes	.10	.05
❏ 473 Ryan Bowen	.10	.05
❏ 474 Bryn Smith	.10	.05
❏ 475 Mike Flanagan	.10	.05
❏ 476 Reggie Jefferson	.20	.09
❏ 477 Jeff Blauser	.10	.05
❏ 478 Craig Lefferts	.10	.05
❏ 479 Todd Worrell	.10	.05
❏ 480 Scott Scudder	.10	.05
❏ 481 Kirk Gibson	.20	.09
❏ 482 Kenny Rogers	.10	.05
❏ 483 Jack Morris	.20	.09
❏ 484 Russ Swan	.10	.05
❏ 485 Mike Huff	.10	.05
❏ 486 Ken Hill	.10	.05
❏ 487 Geronimo Pena	.10	.05
❏ 488 Charlie O'Brien	.10	.05
❏ 489 Mike Maddux	.10	.05
❏ 490 Scott Livingstone	.10	.05
❏ 491 Carl Willis	.10	.05
❏ 492 Kelly Downs	.10	.05
❏ 493 Dennis Cook	.10	.05
❏ 494 Joe Magrane	.10	.05
❏ 495 Bob Kipper	.10	.05
❏ 496 Jose Mesa	.10	.05
❏ 497 Charlie Hayes	.10	.05
❏ 498 Joe Girardi	.20	.09
❏ 499 Doug Jones	.10	.05
❏ 500 Barry Bonds	.50	.23
❏ 501 Bill Krueger	.10	.05
❏ 502 Glenn Braggs	.10	.05

❏ 503 Eric King	.10	.05
❏ 504 Frank Castillo	.10	.05
❏ 505 Mike Gardiner	.10	.05
❏ 506 Cory Snyder	.10	.05
❏ 507 Steve Howe	.10	.05
❏ 508 Jose Rijo	.10	.05
❏ 509 Sid Fernandez	.10	.05
❏ 510 Archi Cianfrocco	.10	.05
❏ 511 Mark Guthrie	.10	.05
❏ 512 Bob Ojeda	.10	.05
❏ 513 John Doherty	.10	.05
❏ 514 Dante Bichette	.30	.14
❏ 515 Juan Berenguer	.10	.05
❏ 516 Jeff M. Robinson	.10	.05
❏ 517 Mike Macfarlane	.10	.05
❏ 518 Matt Young	.10	.05
❏ 519 Otis Nixon	.20	.09
❏ 520 Brian Holman	.10	.05
❏ 521 Chris Haney	.10	.05
❏ 522 Jeff Kent	.40	.18
❏ 523 Chad Curtis	.40	.18
❏ 524 Vince Horsman	.10	.05
❏ 525 Rod Nichols	.10	.05
❏ 526 Peter Hoy	.10	.05
❏ 527 Shawn Boskie	.10	.05
❏ 528 Alejandro Pena	.10	.05
❏ 529 Dave Burba	.10	.05
❏ 530 Ricky Jordan	.10	.05
❏ 531 Dave Silvestri	.10	.05
❏ 532 John Patterson UER	.10	.05
(Listed as being born in 1960; should be 1967)		
❏ 533 Jeff Branson	.10	.05
❏ 534 Derrick May	.10	.05
❏ 535 Esteban Beltre	.10	.05
❏ 536 Jose Melendez	.10	.05
❏ 537 Wally Joyner	.20	.09
❏ 538 Eddie Taubensee	.10	.05
❏ 539 Jim Abbott	.20	.09
❏ 540 Brian Williams	.10	.05
❏ 541 Donovan Osborne	.10	.05
❏ 542 Patrick Lennon	.10	.05
❏ 543 Mike Groppuso	.10	.05
❏ 544 Jarvis Brown	.10	.05
❏ 545 Shawn Livsey	.10	.05
❏ 546 Jeff Ware	.10	.05
❏ 547 Danny Tartabull	.10	.05
❏ 548 Bobby Jones	.40	.18
❏ 549 Ken Griffey Jr.	2.50	1.10
❏ 550 Rey Sanchez	.10	.05
❏ 551 Pedro Astacio	.40	.18
❏ 552 Juan Guerrero	.10	.05
❏ 553 Jacob Brumfield	.10	.05
❏ 554 Ben Rivera	.10	.05
❏ 555 Brian Jordan	1.25	.55
❏ 556 Denny Neagle	.30	.14
❏ 557 Cliff Brantley	.10	.05
❏ 558 Anthony Young	.10	.05
❏ 559 John Vander Wal	.10	.05
❏ 560 Monty Fariss	.10	.05
❏ 561 Russ Springer	.10	.05
❏ 562 Pat Listach	.10	.05
❏ 563 Pat Hentgen	.40	.18
❏ 564 Andy Stankiewicz	.10	.05
❏ 565 Mike Perez	.10	.05
❏ 566 Mike Bielecki	.10	.05
❏ 567 Butch Henry	.10	.05
❏ 568 Dave Nilsson	.20	.09
❏ 569 Scott Hatteberg	.10	.05
❏ 570 Ruben Amaro	.10	.05
❏ 571 Todd Hundley	.20	.09
❏ 572 Moises Alou	.40	.18
❏ 573 Hector Fajardo	.10	.05
❏ 574 Todd Van Poppel	.10	.05
❏ 575 Willie Banks	.10	.05
❏ 576 Bob Zupcic	.10	.05
❏ 577 J.J. Johnson	.20	.09
❏ 578 John Burkett	.10	.05
❏ 579 Trever Miller	.10	.05
❏ 580 Scott Bankhead	.10	.05
❏ 581 Rich Amaral	.10	.05
❏ 582 Kenny Lofton	.50	.23
❏ 583 Matt Stairs	.60	.25
❏ 584 Don Mattingly	.40	.18
Rod Carew IDOLS		
❏ 585 Steve Avery	.10	.05

Jack Morris IDOLS		
❏ 586 Roberto Alomar	.30	.14
Sandy Alomar SR. IDOLS		
❏ 587 Scott Sanderson	.20	.09
Catfish Hunter IDOLS		
❏ 588 Dave Justice	.40	.18
Willie Stargell IDOLS		
❏ 589 Rex Hudler	.40	.18
Roger Staubach IDOLS		
❏ 590 David Cone	.40	.18
Jackie Gleason IDOLS		
❏ 591 Tony Gwynn	.40	.18
Willie Davis IDOLS		
❏ 592 Orel Hershiser SIDE	.10	.05
❏ 593 John McDowell SIDE	.10	.05
❏ 594 Tom Glavine SIDE	.20	.09
❏ 595 Randy Johnson SIDE	.20	.09
❏ 596 Jim Gott SIDE	.10	.05
❏ 597 Donald Harris	.10	.05
❏ 598 Shawn Hare	.10	.05
❏ 599 Chris Gardner	.10	.05
❏ 600 Rusty Meacham	.10	.05
❏ 601 Benito Santiago	.10	.05
❏ 602 Eric Davis SHADE	.10	.05
❏ 603 Jose Lind SHADE	.10	.05
❏ 604 Dave Justice SHADE	.20	.09
❏ 605 Tim Raines SHADE	.20	.09
❏ 606 Randy Tomlin GRIP	.10	.05
❏ 607 Jack McDowell GRIP	.10	.05
❏ 608 Greg Maddux GRIP	.50	.23
❏ 609 Charles Nagy GRIP	.10	.05
❏ 610 Tom Candiotti GRIP	.10	.05
❏ 611 David Cone GRIP	.10	.05
❏ 612 Steve Avery GRIP	.10	.05
❏ 613 Rod Beck GRIP	.20	.09
❏ 614 Rickey Henderson TECH	.20	.09
❏ 615 Benito Santiago TECH	.10	.05
❏ 616 Ruben Sierra TECH	.10	.05
❏ 617 Ryne Sandberg TECH	.40	.18
❏ 618 Nolan Ryan TECH	.75	.35
❏ 619 Brett Butler TECH	.10	.05
❏ 620 Dave Justice TECH	.20	.09

1992 Pinnacle Rookie Idols

	MINT	NRMT
COMPLETE SET (18)	120.00	55.00
COMMON PAIR (1-18)	3.00	1.35
UNLISTED STARS	6.00	2.70
RANDOM INSERTS IN SER.2 FOIL PACKS		

❏ 1 Reggie Sanders and Eric Davis	4.00	1.80
❏ 2 Hector Fajardo and Jim Abbott	3.00	1.35
❏ 3 Gary Cooper and George Brett	12.00	5.50
❏ 4 Mark Wohlers and Roger Clemens	15.00	6.75
❏ 5 Luis Mercedes and Julio Franco	3.00	1.35
❏ 6 Willie Banks and Doc Gooden	3.00	1.35
❏ 7 Kenny Lofton and Rickey Henderson	15.00	6.75
❏ 8 Keith Mitchell and Dave Henderson	3.00	1.35

	MINT	NRMT
☐ 9 Kim Batiste and Barry Larkin	5.00	2.20
☐ 10 Todd Hundley and Thurman Munson	8.00	3.60
☐ 11 Eddie Zosky and Cal Ripken	25.00	11.00
☐ 12 Todd Van Poppel and Nolan Ryan	25.00	11.00
☐ 13 Jim Thome and Ryne Sandberg	25.00	11.00
☐ 14 Dave Fleming and Bobby Murcer	3.00	1.35
☐ 15 Royce Clayton and Ozzie Smith	8.00	3.60
☐ 16 Donald Harris and Darryl Strawberry	3.00	1.35
☐ 17 Chad Curtis and Alan Trammell	6.00	2.70
☐ 18 Derek Bell and Dave Winfield	6.00	2.70

1992 Pinnacle Slugfest

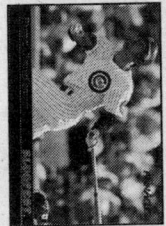

	MINT	NRMT
COMPLETE SET (15)	40.00	18.00
COMMON CARD (1-15)	.50	.23
ONE PER SLUGFEST JUMBO PACK		
☐ 1 Cecil Fielder	.75	.35
☐ 2 Mark McGwire	8.00	3.60
☐ 3 Jose Canseco	2.00	.90
☐ 4 Barry Bonds	2.00	.90
☐ 5 David Justice	1.25	.55
☐ 6 Bobby Bonilla	.75	.35
☐ 7 Ken Griffey Jr.	10.00	4.50
☐ 8 Ron Gant	.75	.35
☐ 9 Ryne Sandberg	2.00	.90
☐ 10 Ruben Sierra	.50	.23
☐ 11 Frank Thomas	4.00	1.80
☐ 12 Will Clark	1.25	.55
☐ 13 Kirby Puckett	2.50	1.10
☐ 14 Cal Ripken	6.00	2.70
☐ 15 Jeff Bagwell	3.00	1.35

1992 Pinnacle Team 2000

	MINT	NRMT
COMPLETE SET (80)	30.00	13.50
COMPLETE SERIES 1 (40)	20.00	9.00
COMPLETE SERIES 2 (40)	10.00	4.50
COMMON CARD (1-80)	.15	.07
THREE PER JUMBO PACK		
☐ 1 Mike Mussina	1.50	.70
☐ 2 Phil Plantier	.15	.07
☐ 3 Frank Thomas	2.50	1.10
☐ 4 Travis Fryman	.25	.11
☐ 5 Kevin Appier	.25	.11
☐ 6 Chuck Knoblauch	.75	.35
☐ 7 Pat Kelly	.15	.07
☐ 8 Ivan Rodriguez	2.00	.90
☐ 9 Dave Justice	.75	.35
☐ 10 Jeff Bagwell	2.00	.90
☐ 11 Marquis Grissom	.25	.11
☐ 12 Andy Benes	.25	.11
☐ 13 Gregg Olson	.15	.07
☐ 14 Kevin Morton	.15	.07
☐ 15 Tim Naehring	.15	.07
☐ 16 Dave Hollins	.25	.11
☐ 17 Sandy Alomar Jr.	.25	.11
☐ 18 Albert Belle	.75	.35
☐ 19 Charles Nagy	.25	.11
☐ 20 Brian McRae	.15	.07
☐ 21 Larry Walker	.75	.35
☐ 22 Delino DeShields	.25	.11
☐ 23 Jeff Johnson	.15	.07
☐ 24 Bernie Williams	.75	.35
☐ 25 Jose Offerman	.25	.11
☐ 26 Juan Gonzalez	2.50	1.10
☐ 27A Juan Guzman (Pinnacle logo at top)	.25	.11
☐ 27B Juan Guzman (Pinnacle logo at bottom)	.25	.11
☐ 28 Eric Anthony	.15	.07
☐ 29 Brian Hunter	.15	.07
☐ 30 John Smoltz	.40	.18
☐ 31 Deion Sanders	.75	.35
☐ 32 Greg Maddux	2.50	1.10
☐ 33 Andujar Cedeno	.15	.07
☐ 34 Royce Clayton	.15	.07
☐ 35 Kenny Lofton	2.50	1.10
☐ 36 Cal Eldred	.15	.07
☐ 37 Jim Thome	2.50	1.10
☐ 38 Gary DiSarcina	.15	.07
☐ 39 Brian Jordan	3.00	1.35
☐ 40 Chad Curtis	.25	.11
☐ 41 Ben McDonald	.15	.07
☐ 42 Jim Abbott	.25	.11
☐ 43 Robin Ventura	.25	.11
☐ 44 Milt Cuyler	.15	.07
☐ 45 Gregg Jefferies	.15	.07
☐ 46 Scott Radinsky	.15	.07
☐ 47 Ken Griffey Jr.	6.00	2.70
☐ 48 Roberto Alomar	.75	.35
☐ 49 Ramon Martinez	.25	.11
☐ 50 Bret Barberie	.15	.07
☐ 51 Ray Lankford	.75	.35
☐ 52 Leo Gomez	.15	.07
☐ 53 Tommy Greene	.15	.07
☐ 54 Mo Vaughn	1.25	.55
☐ 55 Sammy Sosa	3.00	1.35
☐ 56 Carlos Baerga	.15	.07
☐ 57 Mark Lewis	.15	.07
☐ 58 Tom Gordon	.15	.07
☐ 59 Gary Sheffield	.75	.35
☐ 60 Scott Erickson	.25	.11
☐ 61 Pedro Munoz	.25	.11
☐ 62 Tino Martinez	.75	.35
☐ 63 Darren Lewis	.15	.07
☐ 64 Dean Palmer	.25	.11
☐ 65 John Olerud	.25	.11
☐ 66 Steve Avery	.15	.07
☐ 67 Pete Harnisch	.15	.07
☐ 68 Luis Gonzalez	.40	.18
☐ 69 Kim Batiste	.15	.07
☐ 70 Reggie Sanders	.25	.11
☐ 71 Luis Mercedes	.15	.07
☐ 72 Todd Van Poppel	.15	.07
☐ 73 Gary Scott	.15	.07
☐ 74 Monty Fariss	.15	.07
☐ 75 Kyle Abbott	.15	.07
☐ 76 Eric Karros	.75	.35
☐ 77 Mo Sanford	.15	.07
☐ 78 Todd Hundley	.15	.07
☐ 79 Reggie Jefferson	.25	.11
☐ 80 Pat Mahomes	.15	.07

1992 Pinnacle Team Pinnacle

	MINT	NRMT
COMPLETE SET (12)	80.00	36.00
COMMON PAIR (1-12)	3.00	1.35
RANDOM INSERTS IN SER.1 FOIL PACKS		
☐ 1 Roger Clemens and Ramon Martinez	12.00	5.50
☐ 2 Jim Abbott and Steve Avery	3.00	1.35
☐ 3 Ivan Rodriguez and Benito Santiago	8.00	3.60
☐ 4 Frank Thomas and Will Clark	15.00	6.75
☐ 5 Roberto Alomar and Ryne Sandberg	6.00	2.70
☐ 6 Robin Ventura and Matt Williams	4.00	1.80
☐ 7 Cal Ripken and Barry Larkin	20.00	9.00
☐ 8 Danny Tartabull and Barry Bonds	6.00	2.70
☐ 9 Ken Griffey Jr. and Brett Butler	25.00	11.00
☐ 10 Ruben Sierra and Dave Justice	3.00	1.35
☐ 11 Dennis Eckersley and Rob Dibble	3.00	1.35
☐ 12 Scott Radinsky and John Franco	3.00	1.35

1992 Pinnacle Rookies

	MINT	NRMT
COMP.FACT.SET (30)	4.00	1.80
COMMON CARD (1-30)	.15	.07
MINOR STARS	.40	.18
UNLISTED STARS	.75	.35
☐ 1 Luis Mercedes	.15	.07
☐ 2 Scott Cooper	.15	.07
☐ 3 Kenny Lofton	.75	.35
☐ 4 John Doherty	.15	.07
☐ 5 Pat Listach	.15	.07
☐ 6 Andy Stankiewicz	.15	.07
☐ 7 Derek Bell	.40	.18
☐ 8 Gary DiSarcina	.15	.07
☐ 9 Roberto Hernandez	.60	.25

10	Joel Johnston	.15	.07
11	Pat Mahomes	.15	.07
12	Todd Van Poppel	.15	.07
13	Dave Fleming	.15	.07
14	Monty Fariss	.15	.07
15	Gary Scott	.15	.07
16	Moises Alou	.75	.35
17	Todd Hundley	.40	.18
18	Kim Batiste	.15	.07
19	Denny Neagle	.60	.25
20	Donovan Osborne	.15	.07
21	Mark Wohlers	.15	.07
22	Reggie Sanders	.40	.18
23	Brian Williams	.15	.07
24	Eric Karros	.75	.35
25	Frank Seminara	.15	.07
26	Royce Clayton	.15	.07
27	Dave Nilsson	.40	.18
28	Matt Stairs	.75	.35
29	Chad Curtis	.60	.25
30	Carlos Hernandez	.15	.07

1993 Pinnacle

Carlos Baerga

	MINT	NRMT
COMPLETE SET (620)	40.00	18.00
COMPLETE SERIES 1 (310) ..	15.00	6.75
COMPLETE SERIES 2 (310) ..	25.00	11.00
COMMON CARD (1-620)	.15	.07
MINOR STARS	.30	.14
UNLISTED STARS	.30	.25

SUBSET CARDS HALF VALUE OF BASE CARDS

1	Gary Sheffield	.60	.25
2	Cal Eldred	.40	.18
3	Larry Walker	.60	.25
4	Deion Sanders	.40	.18
5	Dave Fleming	.15	.07
6	Carlos Baerga	.15	.07
7	Bernie Williams	.60	.25
8	John Kruk	.30	.14
9	Jimmy Key	.30	.14
10	Jeff Bagwell	.75	.35
11	Jim Abbott	.30	.14
12	Terry Steinbach	.15	.07
13	Bob Tewksbury	.15	.07
14	Eric Karros	.40	.18
15	Ryne Sandberg	.75	.35
16	Will Clark	.60	.25
17	Edgar Martinez	.40	.18
18	Eddie Murray	.60	.25
19	Andy Van Slyke	.30	.14
20	Cal Ripken Jr.	2.50	1.10
21	Ivan Rodriguez	.75	.35
22	Barry Larkin	.25	.10
23	Don Mattingly	1.25	.55
24	Gregg Jefferies	.15	.07
25	Roger Clemens	1.50	.70
26	Cecil Fielder	.30	.14
27	Kent Hrbek	.30	.14
28	Robin Ventura	.30	.14
29	Rickey Henderson	.75	.35
30	Roberto Alomar	.60	.25
31	Luis Polonia	.15	.07
32	Andujar Cedeno	.15	.07
33	Pat Listach	.15	.07
34	Mark Grace	.40	.18
35	Otis Nixon	.15	.07
36	Felix Jose	.15	.07
37	Mike Sharperson	.15	.07
38	Dennis Martinez	.30	.14
39	Willie McGee	.30	.14
40	Kenny Lofton	.60	.25
41	Randy Johnson	.60	.25
42	Andy Benes	.30	.14
43	Bobby Bonilla	.30	.14
44	Mike Mussina	.60	.25
45	Len Dykstra	.30	.14
46	Ellis Burks	.30	.14
47	Chris Sabo	.15	.07
48	Jay Bell	.30	.14
49	Jose Canseco	.75	.35
50	Craig Biggio	.60	.25
51	Wally Joyner	.30	.14
52	Mickey Tettleton	.15	.07
53	Tim Raines	.30	.14
54	Brian Harper	.15	.07
55	Rene Gonzales	.15	.07
56	Mark Langston	.15	.07
57	Jack Morris	.30	.14
58	Mark McGwire	3.00	1.35
59	Ken Caminiti	.40	.18
60	Terry Pendleton	.15	.07
61	Dave Nilsson	.30	.14
62	Tom Pagnozzi	.15	.07
63	Mike Morgan	.15	.07
64	Darryl Strawberry	.30	.14
65	Charles Nagy	.30	.14
66	Ken Hill	.15	.07
67	Matt Williams	.40	.18
68	Jay Buhner	.40	.18
69	Vince Coleman	.15	.07
70	Brady Anderson	.30	.14
71	Fred McGriff	.40	.18
72	Ben McDonald	.15	.07
73	Terry Mulholland	.15	.07
74	Randy Tomlin	.15	.07
75	Nolan Ryan	2.50	1.10
76	Frank Viola UER	.15	.07
	(Card incorrectly states he has a surgically repaired elbow)		
77	Jose Rijo	.15	.07
78	Shane Mack	.15	.07
79	Travis Fryman	.30	.14
80	Jack McDowell	.15	.07
81	Mark Gubicza	.15	.07
82	Matt Nokes	.15	.07
83	Bert Blyleven	.30	.14
84	Eric Anthony	.15	.07
85	Mike Bordick	.15	.07
86	John Olerud	.40	.18
87	B.J. Surhoff	.30	.14
88	Bernard Gilkey	.15	.07
89	Shawon Dunston	.15	.07
90	Tom Glavine	.40	.18
91	Brett Butler	.30	.14
92	Moises Alou	.30	.14
93	Albert Belle	.60	.25
94	Darren Lewis	.15	.07
95	Omar Vizquel	.30	.14
96	Dwight Gooden	.30	.14
97	Gregg Olson	.15	.07
98	Tony Gwynn	1.50	.70
99	Darren Daulton	.30	.14
100	Dennis Eckersley	.30	.14
101	Rob Dibble	.15	.07
102	Mike Greenwell	.15	.07
103	Jose Lind	.15	.07
104	Julio Franco	.15	.07
105	Tom Gordon	.15	.07
106	Scott Livingstone	.15	.07
107	Chuck Knoblauch	.60	.25
108	Frank Thomas	1.25	.55
109	Melido Perez	.15	.07
110	Ken Griffey Jr.	3.00	1.35
111	Harold Baines	.30	.14
112	Gary Gaetti	.30	.14
113	Pete Harnisch	.15	.07
114	David Wells	.30	.14
115	Charlie Leibrandt	.15	.07
116	Ray Lankford	.40	.18
117	Kevin Seitzer	.15	.07
118	Robin Yount	.40	.18
119	Lenny Harris	.15	.07
120	Chris James	.15	.07
121	Delino DeShields	.30	.14
122	Kirt Manwaring	.15	.07
123	Gienallen Hill	.15	.07
124	Hensley Meulens	.15	.07
125	Darrin Jackson	.15	.07
126	Todd Hundley	.40	.18
127	Dave Hollins	.15	.07
128	Sam Horn	.15	.07
129	Roberto Hernandez	.30	.14
130	Vicente Palacios	.15	.07
131	George Brett	1.25	.55
132	Dave Martinez	.15	.07
133	Kevin Appier	.30	.14
134	Pat Kelly	.15	.07
135	Pedro Munoz	.15	.07
136	Mark Carreon	.15	.07
137	Lance Johnson	.15	.07
138	Devon White	.15	.07
139	Julio Valera	.15	.07
140	Eddie Taubensee	.15	.07
141	Willie Wilson	.15	.07
142	Stan Belinda	.15	.07
143	John Smoltz	.40	.18
144	Darryl Hamilton	.15	.07
145	Sammy Sosa	2.00	.90
146	Carlos Hernandez	.15	.07
147	Tom Candiotti	.15	.07
148	Mike Felder	.15	.07
149	Rusty Meacham	.15	.07
150	Ivan Calderon	.15	.07
151	Pete O'Brien	.15	.07
152	Erik Hanson	.15	.07
153	Billy Ripken	.15	.07
154	Kurt Stillwell	.15	.07
155	Jeff Kent	.30	.14
156	Mickey Morandini	.15	.07
157	Randy Milligan	.15	.07
158	Reggie Sanders	.30	.14
159	Luis Rivera	.15	.07
160	Orlando Merced	.15	.07
161	Dean Palmer	.30	.14
162	Mike Perez	.15	.07
163	Scott Erickson	.15	.07
164	Kevin McReynolds	.15	.07
165	Kevin Maas	.15	.07
166	Ozzie Guillen	.15	.07
167	Rob Deer	.15	.07
168	Danny Tartabull	.15	.07
169	Lee Stevens	.30	.14
170	Dave Henderson	.15	.07
171	Derek Bell	.30	.14
172	Steve Finley	.30	.14
173	Greg Olson	.15	.07
174	Geronimo Pena	.15	.07
175	Paul Quantrill	.15	.07
176	Steve Buechele	.15	.07
177	Kevin Gross	.15	.07
178	Tim Wallach	.15	.07
179	Dave Valle	.15	.07
180	Dave Silvestri	.15	.07
181	Bud Black	.15	.07
182	Henry Rodriguez	.30	.14
183	Tim Teufel	.15	.07
184	Mark McLemore	.15	.07
185	Bret Saberhagen	.30	.14
186	Chris Hoiles	.30	.14
187	Ricky Jordan	.15	.07
188	Don Slaught	.15	.07
189	Mo Vaughn	.60	.25
190	Joe Oliver	.15	.07
191	Juan Gonzalez	1.25	.55
192	Scott Leius	.15	.07
193	Milt Cuyler	.15	.07
194	Chris Haney	.15	.07
195	Ron Karkovice	.15	.07
196	Steve Farr	.15	.07
197	John Orton	.15	.07
198	Kelly Gruber	.15	.07
199	Ron Darling	.15	.07
200	Ruben Sierra	.30	.14
201	Chuck Finley	.30	.14
202	Mike Moore	.15	.07
203	Pat Borders	.15	.07
204	Sid Bream	.15	.07

205	Todd Zeile	.15	.07
206	Rick Wilkins	.15	.07
207	Jim Gantner	.15	.07
208	Frank Castillo	.15	.07
209	Dave Hansen	.15	.07
210	Trevor Wilson	.15	.07
211	Sandy Alomar Jr.	.30	.14
212	Sean Berry	.15	.07
213	Tino Martinez	.60	.25
214	Chito Martinez	.15	.07
215	Dan Walters	.15	.07
216	John Franco	.30	.14
217	Glenn Davis	.15	.07
218	Mariano Duncan	.15	.07
219	Mike LaValliere	.15	.07
220	Rafael Palmeiro	.60	.25
221	Jack Clark	.15	.07
222	Hal Morris	.15	.07
223	Ed Sprague	.15	.07
224	John Valentin	.30	.14
225	Sam Militello	.15	.07
226	Bob Wickman	.30	.14
227	Damion Easley	.30	.14
228	John Jaha	.15	.07
229	Bob Ayrault	.15	.07
230	Mo Sanford	.15	.07
231	Walt Weiss	.15	.07
232	Dante Bichette	.30	.14
233	Steve Decker	.15	.07
234	Jerald Clark	.15	.07
235	Bryan Harvey	.15	.07
236	Joe Girardi	.30	.14
237	Dave Magadan	.15	.07
238	David Nied	.15	.07
239	Eric Wedge	.15	.07
240	Rico Brogna	.30	.14
241	J.T.Bruett	.15	.07
242	Jonathan Hurst	.15	.07
243	Bret Boone	.30	.14
244	Manny Alexander	.15	.07
245	Scooter Tucker	.15	.07
246	Troy Neel	.15	.07
247	Eddie Zosky	.15	.07
248	Melvin Nieves	.15	.07
249	Ryan Thompson	.15	.07
250	Shawn Barton	.15	.07
251	Ryan Klesko	.60	.25
252	Mike Piazza	3.00	1.35
253	Steve Hosey	.15	.07
254	Shane Reynolds	.30	.14
255	Dan Wilson	.30	.14
256	Tom Marsh	.15	.07
257	Barry Manuel	.15	.07
258	Paul Miller	.15	.07
259	Pedro Martinez	1.25	.55
260	Steve Cooke	.15	.07
261	Johnny Guzman	.15	.07
262	Mike Butcher	.15	.07
263	Bien Figueroa	.15	.07
264	Rich Rowland	.15	.07
265	Shawn Jeter	.15	.07
266	Gerald Williams	.15	.07
267	Derek Parks	.15	.07
268	Henry Mercedes	.15	.07
269	David Hulse	.15	.07
270	Tim Pugh	.15	.07
271	William Suero	.15	.07
272	Ozzie Canseco	.15	.07
273	Fernando Ramsey	.15	.07
274	Bernardo Brito	.15	.07
275	Dave Mlicki	.15	.07
276	Tim Salmon	.60	.25
277	Mike Raczka	.15	.07
278	Ken Ryan	.15	.07
279	Rafael Bournigal	.15	.07
280	Wil Cordero	.15	.07
281	Billy Ashley	.15	.07
282	Paul Wagner	.15	.07
283	Bias Minor	.15	.07
284	Rick Trlicek	.15	.07
285	Willie Greene	.15	.07
286	Ted Wood	.15	.07
287	Phil Clark	.15	.07
288	Jesse Levis	.15	.07
289	Tony Gwynn NT	.75	.35
290	Nolan Ryan NT	1.25	.55
291	Dennis Martinez NT	.15	.07
292	Eddie Murray NT	.30	.14
293	Robin Yount NT	.30	.14
294	George Brett NT	.60	.25
295	Dave Winfield NT	.30	.14
296	Bert Blyleven NT	.15	.07
297	Jeff Bagwell	.60	.25
	Carl Yastrzemski		
298	John Smoltz	.30	.14
	Jack Morris		
299	Larry Walker	.60	.25
	Mike Bossy		
300	Gary Sheffield	.30	.14
	Barry Larkin		
301	Ivan Rodriguez	.30	.14
	Carlton Fisk		
302	Delino DeShields	.60	.25
	Malcolm X		
303	Tim Salmon	.40	.18
	Dwight Evans		
304	Bernard Gilkey HH	.15	.07
305	Cal Ripken Jr. HH	1.25	.55
306	Barry Larkin HH	.15	.07
307	Kent Hrbek HH	.15	.07
308	Rickey Henderson HH	.30	.14
309	Darryl Strawberry HH	.15	.07
310	John Franco HH	.15	.07
311	Todd Stottlemyre	.15	.07
312	Luis Gonzalez	.30	.14
313	Tommy Greene	.15	.07
314	Randy Velarde	.15	.07
315	Steve Avery	.30	.14
316	Jose Oquendo	.15	.07
317	Rey Sanchez	.15	.07
318	Greg Vaughn	.30	.14
319	Orel Hershiser	.30	.14
320	Paul Sorrento	.15	.07
321	Royce Clayton	.15	.07
322	John Vander Wal	.15	.07
323	Henry Cotto	.15	.07
324	Pete Schourek	.15	.07
325	David Segui	.15	.07
326	Arthur Rhodes	.15	.07
327	Bruce Hurst	.15	.07
328	Wes Chamberlain	.15	.07
329	Ozzie Smith	.75	.35
330	Scott Cooper	.15	.07
331	Felix Fermin	.15	.07
332	Mike Macfarlane	.15	.07
333	Dan Gladden	.15	.07
334	Kevin Tapani	.15	.07
335	Steve Sax	.15	.07
336	Jeff Montgomery	.30	.14
337	Gary DiSarcina	.15	.07
338	Lance Blankenship	.15	.07
339	Brian Williams	.15	.07
340	Duane Ward	.15	.07
341	Chuck McElroy	.15	.07
342	Joe Magrane	.15	.07
343	Jaime Navarro	.15	.07
344	Dave Justice	.60	.25
345	Jose Offerman	.30	.14
346	Marquis Grissom	.30	.14
347	Bill Swift	.15	.07
348	Jim Thome	.75	.35
349	Archi Cianfrocco	.15	.07
350	Anthony Young	.15	.07
351	Leo Gomez	.15	.07
352	Bill Gullickson	.15	.07
353	Alan Trammell	.40	.18
354	Dan Pasqua	.15	.07
355	Jeff King	.15	.07
356	Kevin Brown	.40	.18
357	Tim Belcher	.15	.07
358	Bip Roberts	.15	.07
359	Brent Mayne	.15	.07
360	Rheal Cormier	.15	.07
361	Mark Guthrie	.15	.07
362	Craig Grebeck	.15	.07
363	Andy Stankiewicz	.15	.07
364	Juan Guzman	.15	.07
365	Bobby Witt	.15	.07
366	Mark Portugal	.15	.07
367	Brian McRae	.15	.07
368	Mark Lemke	.15	.07
369	Bill Wegman	.15	.07
370	Donovan Osborne	.15	.07
371	Derrick May	.15	.07
372	Carl Willis	.15	.07
373	Chris Nabholz	.15	.07
374	Mark Lewis	.15	.07
375	John Burkett	.15	.07
376	Luis Mercedes	.15	.07
377	Ramon Martinez	.30	.14
378	Kyle Abbott	.15	.07
379	Mark Wohlers	.15	.07
380	Bob Walk	.15	.07
381	Kenny Rogers	.15	.07
382	Tim Naehring	.15	.07
383	Alex Fernandez	.30	.14
384	Keith Miller	.15	.07
385	Mike Henneman	.15	.07
386	Rick Aguilera	.15	.07
387	George Bell	.15	.07
388	Mike Gallego	.15	.07
389	Howard Johnson	.15	.07
390	Kim Batiste	.15	.07
391	Jerry Browne	.15	.07
392	Damon Berryhill	.15	.07
393	Ricky Bones	.15	.07
394	Omar Olivares	.15	.07
395	Mike Harkey	.15	.07
396	Pedro Astacio	.30	.14
397	John Wetteland	.30	.14
398	Rod Beck	.30	.14
399	Thomas Howard	.15	.07
400	Mike Devereaux	.15	.07
401	Tim Wakefield	.30	.14
402	Curt Schilling	.30	.14
403	Zane Smith	.15	.07
404	Bob Zupcic	.15	.07
405	Tom Browning	.15	.07
406	Tony Phillips	.15	.07
407	John Doherty	.15	.07
408	Pat Mahomes	.15	.07
409	John Habyan	.15	.07
410	Steve Olin	.15	.07
411	Chad Curtis	.30	.14
412	Joe Grahe	.15	.07
413	John Patterson	.15	.07
414	Brian Hunter	.15	.07
415	Doug Henry	.15	.07
416	Lee Smith	.30	.14
417	Bob Scanlan	.15	.07
418	Kent Mercker	.15	.07
419	Mel Rojas	.15	.07
420	Mark Whiten	.15	.07
421	Carlton Fisk	.60	.25
422	Candy Maldonado	.15	.07
423	Doug Drabek	.15	.07
424	Wade Boggs	.60	.25
425	Mark Davis	.15	.07
426	Kirby Puckett	1.00	.45
427	Joe Carter	.30	.14
428	Paul Molitor	.60	.25
429	Eric Davis	.30	.14
430	Darryl Kile	.15	.07
431	Jeff Parrett	.15	.07
432	Jeff Blauser	.15	.07
433	Dan Plesac	.15	.07
434	Andres Galarraga	.60	.25
435	Jim Gott	.15	.07
436	Jose Mesa	.15	.07
437	Ben Rivera	.15	.07
438	Dave Winfield	.40	.18
439	Norm Charlton	.15	.07
440	Chris Bosio	.15	.07
441	Wilson Alvarez	.30	.14
442	Dave Stewart	.30	.14
443	Doug Jones	.15	.07
444	Jeff Russell	.15	.07
445	Ron Gant	.30	.14
446	Paul O'Neill	.30	.14
447	Charlie Hayes	.15	.07
448	Joe Hesketh	.15	.07
449	Chris Hammond	.15	.07
450	Hipolito Pichardo	.15	.07
451	Scott Radinsky	.15	.07
452	Bobby Thigpen	.15	.07
453	Xavier Hernandez	.15	.07
454	Lenny Webster	.15	.07
455	Jamie Arnold DP	.15	.07

☐ 456 B.J. Wallace DP	.15 .07
☐ 457 Derek Jeter DP	15.00 6.75
☐ 458 Jason Kendall DP	2.00 .90
☐ 459 Rick Helling DP	.40 .18
☐ 460 Derek Wallace DP	.15 .07
☐ 461 Sean Lowe DP	.15 .07
☐ 462 Shannon Stewart DP	1.50 .70
☐ 463 Benji Grigsby DP	.15 .07
☐ 464 Todd Steverson DP	.15 .07
☐ 465 Dan Serafini DP	.15 .07
☐ 466 Michael Tucker DP	.60 .25
☐ 467 Chris Roberts DP	.15 .07
☐ 468 Pete Janicki DP	.15 .07
☐ 469 Jeff Schmidt DP	.15 .07
☐ 470 Don Mattingly NT	.60 .25
☐ 471 Cal Ripken Jr. NT	1.25 .55
☐ 472 Jack Morris NT	.15 .07
☐ 473 Terry Pendleton NT	.15 .07
☐ 474 Dennis Eckersley NT	.15 .07
☐ 475 Carlton Fisk NT	.30 .14
☐ 476 Wade Boggs NT	.60 .25
☐ 477 Lenny Dykstra	.30 .14
Ken Stabler	
☐ 478 Danny Tartabull	.15 .07
Jose Tartabull	
☐ 479 Jeff Conine	.30 .14
Dale Murphy	
☐ 480 Gregg Jefferies	.15 .07
Ron Cey	
☐ 481 Paul Molitor	.40 .18
Harmon Killebrew	
☐ 482 John Valentin	.15 .07
Dave Concepcion	
☐ 483 Alex Arias	.30 .14
Dave Winfield	
☐ 484 Barry Bonds HH	.40 .18
☐ 485 Doug Drabek HH	.15 .07
☐ 486 Dave Winfield HH	.30 .14
☐ 487 Brett Butler HH	.15 .07
☐ 488 Harold Baines HH	.15 .07
☐ 489 David Cone HH	.30 .14
☐ 490 Willie McGee HH	.15 .07
☐ 491 Robby Thompson	.15 .07
☐ 492 Pete Incaviglia	.15 .07
☐ 493 Manuel Lee	.15 .07
☐ 494 Rafael Belliard	.15 .07
☐ 495 Scott Fletcher	.15 .07
☐ 496 Jeff Frye	.15 .07
☐ 497 Andre Dawson	.40 .18
☐ 498 Mike Scioscia	.15 .07
☐ 499 Spike Owen	.15 .07
☐ 500 Sid Fernandez	.15 .07
☐ 501 Joe Orsulak	.15 .07
☐ 502 Benito Santiago	.40 .18
☐ 503 Dale Murphy	.40 .18
☐ 504 Barry Bonds	.75 .35
☐ 505 Jose Guzman	.15 .07
☐ 506 Tony Pena	.15 .07
☐ 507 Greg Swindell	.15 .07
☐ 508 Mike Pagliarulo	.15 .07
☐ 509 Lou Whitaker	.30 .14
☐ 510 Greg Gagne	.15 .07
☐ 511 Butch Henry	.15 .07
☐ 512 Jeff Brantley	.15 .07
☐ 513 Jack Armstrong	.15 .07
☐ 514 Danny Jackson	.15 .07
☐ 515 Junior Felix	.15 .07
☐ 516 Milt Thompson	.15 .07
☐ 517 Greg Maddux	1.50 .70
☐ 518 Eric Young	.60 .25
☐ 519 Jody Reed	.15 .07
☐ 520 Roberto Kelly	.15 .07
☐ 521 Darren Holmes	.15 .07
☐ 523 Craig Lefferts	.15 .07
☐ 523 Charlie Hough	.30 .14
☐ 524 Bo Jackson	.30 .14
☐ 525 Bill Spiers	.15 .07
☐ 526 Orestes Destrade	.15 .07
☐ 527 Greg Hibbard	.15 .07
☐ 528 Roger McDowell	.15 .07
☐ 529 Cory Snyder	.15 .07
☐ 530 Harold Reynolds	.15 .07
☐ 531 Kevin Reimer	.15 .07
☐ 532 Rick Sutcliffe	.15 .07
☐ 533 Tony Fernandez	.15 .07
☐ 534 Tom Brunansky	.15 .07

☐ 535 Jeff Reardon	.30 .14
☐ 536 Chili Davis	.30 .14
☐ 537 Bob Ojeda	.15 .07
☐ 538 Greg Colbrunn	.15 .07
☐ 539 Phil Plantier	.15 .07
☐ 540 Brian Jordan	.30 .14
☐ 541 Pete Smith	.15 .07
☐ 542 Frank Tanana	.15 .07
☐ 543 John Smiley	.15 .07
☐ 544 David Cone	.40 .18
☐ 545 Daryl Boston	.15 .07
☐ 546 Tom Henke	.15 .07
☐ 547 Bill Krueger	.15 .07
☐ 548 Freddie Benavides	.15 .07
☐ 549 Randy Myers	.30 .14
☐ 550 Reggie Jefferson	.30 .14
☐ 551 Kevin Mitchell	.30 .14
☐ 552 Dave Stieb	.15 .07
☐ 553 Bret Barberie	.15 .07
☐ 554 Tim Crews	.15 .07
☐ 555 Doug Dascenzo	.15 .07
☐ 556 Alex Cole	.15 .07
☐ 557 Jeff Innis	.15 .07
☐ 558 Carlos Garcia	.15 .07
☐ 559 Steve Howe	.15 .07
☐ 560 Kirk McCaskill	.15 .07
☐ 561 Frank Seminara	.15 .07
☐ 562 Cris Carpenter	.15 .07
☐ 563 Mike Stanley	.15 .07
☐ 564 Carlos Quintana	.15 .07
☐ 565 Mitch Williams	.15 .07
☐ 566 Juan Bell	.15 .07
☐ 567 Eric Fox	.15 .07
☐ 568 Al Leiter	.30 .14
☐ 569 Mike Stanton	.15 .07
☐ 570 Scott Kamieniecki	.15 .07
☐ 571 Ryan Bowen	.15 .07
☐ 572 Andy Ashby	.30 .14
☐ 573 Bob Welch	.15 .07
☐ 574 Scott Sanderson	.15 .07
☐ 575 Joe Kmak	.15 .07
☐ 576 Scott Pose	.15 .07
☐ 577 Ricky Gutierrez	.15 .07
☐ 578 Mike Trombley	.15 .07
☐ 579 Sterling Hitchcock	.50 .23
☐ 580 Rodney Bolton	.15 .07
☐ 581 Tyler Green	.15 .07
☐ 582 Tim Costo	.15 .07
☐ 583 Tim Laker	.15 .07
☐ 584 Steve Reed	.15 .07
☐ 585 Tom Kramer	.15 .07
☐ 586 Robb Nen	.40 .18
☐ 587 Jim Tatum	.15 .07
☐ 588 Frank Bolick	.15 .07
☐ 589 Kevin Young	.30 .14
☐ 590 Matt Whiteside	.15 .07
☐ 591 Cesar Hernandez	.15 .07
☐ 592 Mike Mohler	.15 .07
☐ 593 Alan Embree	.15 .07
☐ 594 Terry Jorgensen	.15 .07
☐ 595 John Cummings	.15 .07
☐ 596 Domingo Martinez	.15 .07
☐ 597 Benji Gil	.15 .07
☐ 598 Todd Pratt	.40 .18
☐ 599 Rene Arocha	.15 .07
☐ 600 Dennis Moeller	.15 .07
☐ 601 Jeff Conine	.15 .07
☐ 602 Trevor Hoffman	.60 .25
☐ 603 Daniel Smith	.15 .07
☐ 604 Lee Tinsley	.15 .07
☐ 605 Dan Peltier	.15 .07
☐ 606 Billy Brewer	.15 .07
☐ 607 Matt Walbeck	.15 .07
☐ 608 Richie Lewis	.15 .07
☐ 609 J.T. Snow	.75 .35
☐ 610 Pat Gomez	.15 .07
☐ 611 Phil Hiatt	.15 .07
☐ 612 Alex Arias	.15 .07
☐ 613 Kevin Rogers	.15 .07
☐ 614 Al Martin	.15 .07
☐ 615 Greg Gohr	.15 .07
☐ 616 Graeme Lloyd	.15 .07
☐ 617 Kent Bottenfield	.15 .07
☐ 618 Chuck Carr	.15 .07
☐ 619 Darrell Sherman	.15 .07
☐ 620 Mike Lansing	.30 .14

1993 Pinnacle Expansion Opening Day

	MINT	NRMT
COMPLETE SET (9)	15.00	6.75
COMMON PAIR (1-9)	1.50	.70
MINOR STARS	4.00	1.80
ONE CARD PER SEALED SER.2 HOBBY BOX		
SETS DISTRIBUTED VIA MAIL-IN OFFER		

☐ 1 Charlie Hough	4.00	1.80
David Nied		
☐ 2 Benito Santiago	1.50	.70
Joe Girardi		
☐ 3 Orestes Destrade	6.00	2.70
Andres Galarraga		
☐ 4 Bret Barberie	4.00	1.80
Eric Young		
☐ 5 Dave Magadan	1.50	.70
Charlie Hayes		
☐ 6 Walt Weiss	1.50	.70
Freddie Benavides		
☐ 7 Jeff Conine	5.00	2.20
Jerald Clark		
☐ 8 Scott Pose	1.50	.70
Alex Cole		
☐ 9 Junior Felix	6.00	2.70
Dante Bichette		

1993 Pinnacle Rookie Team Pinnacle

	MINT	NRMT
COMPLETE SET (10)	100.00	45.00
COMMON PAIR (1-10)	4.00	1.80
SEMISTARS	8.00	3.60
SER.2 STATED ODDS 1:90		

☐ 1 Pedro Martinez	20.00	9.00
Mike Trombley		
☐ 2 Kevin Rogers	4.00	1.80
Sterling Hitchcock		
☐ 3 Mike Piazza	50.00	22.00
Jesse Levis		
☐ 4 Ryan Klesko	8.00	3.60
J.T. Snow		
☐ 5 John Valentin	4.00	1.80
Bret Boone		
☐ 6 Kevin Young	4.00	1.80
Domingo Martinez		

	MINT	NRMT
❏ 7 Wil Cordero	4.00	1.80
Manny Alexander		
❏ 8 Steve Hosey	8.00	3.60
Tim Salmon		
❏ 9 Ryan Thompson	4.00	1.80
Gerald Williams		
❏ 10 Melvin Nieves	6.00	2.70
David Hulse		

1993 Pinnacle Slugfest

DON MATTINGLY

	MINT	NRMT
COMPLETE SET (30)	60.00	27.00
COMMON CARD (1-25)	1.00	.45
ONE PER SER.2 JUMBO PACK		

		MINT	NRMT
❏ 1	Juan Gonzalez	6.00	2.70
❏ 2	Mark McGwire	15.00	6.75
❏ 3	Cecil Fielder	1.50	.70
❏ 4	Joe Carter	1.50	.70
❏ 5	Fred McGriff	2.00	.90
❏ 6	Barry Bonds	4.00	1.80
❏ 7	Gary Sheffield	2.50	1.10
❏ 8	Dave Hollins	1.00	.45
❏ 9	Frank Thomas	6.00	2.70
❏ 10	Danny Tartabull	1.00	.45
❏ 11	Albert Belle	2.50	1.10
❏ 12	Ruben Sierra	1.00	.45
❏ 13	Larry Walker	2.50	1.10
❏ 14	Jeff Bagwell	4.00	1.80
❏ 15	David Justice	2.50	1.10
❏ 16	Kirby Puckett	5.00	2.20
❏ 17	John Kruk	1.00	.70
❏ 18	Howard Johnson	1.00	.45
❏ 19	Darryl Strawberry	1.50	.70
❏ 20	Will Clark	2.50	1.10
❏ 21	Kevin Mitchell	1.50	.70
❏ 22	Mickey Tettleton	1.00	.45
❏ 23	Don Mattingly	6.00	2.70
❏ 24	Jose Canseco	4.00	1.80
❏ 25	George Bell	1.00	.45
❏ 26	Andre Dawson	2.00	.90
❏ 27	Ryne Sandberg	4.00	1.80
❏ 28	Ken Griffey Jr.	15.00	6.75
❏ 29	Carlos Baerga	1.00	.45
❏ 30	Travis Fryman	1.50	.70

1993 Pinnacle Team 2001

	MINT	NRMT
COMPLETE SET (30)	40.00	18.00
COMMON CARD (1-30)	.75	.35
ONE PER SER.1 JUMBO PACK		

		MINT	NRMT
❏ 1	Wil Cordero	.75	.35
❏ 2	Cal Eldred	.75	.35
❏ 3	Mike Mussina	3.00	1.35
❏ 4	Chuck Knoblauch	3.00	1.35
❏ 5	Melvin Nieves	.75	.35
❏ 6	Tim Wakefield	1.25	.55
❏ 7	Carlos Baerga	.75	.35
❏ 8	Bret Boone	1.25	.55
❏ 9	Jeff Bagwell	4.00	1.80
❏ 10	Travis Fryman	1.25	.55
❏ 11	Royce Clayton	.75	.35
❏ 12	Delino DeShields	.75	.35
❏ 13	Juan Gonzalez	6.00	2.70
❏ 14	Pedro Martinez	6.00	2.70
❏ 15	Bernie Williams	3.00	1.35
❏ 16	Billy Ashley	.75	.35
❏ 17	Marquis Grissom	1.25	.55
❏ 18	Kenny Lofton	3.00	1.35
❏ 19	Ray Lankford	1.50	.70
❏ 20	Tim Salmon	3.00	1.35
❏ 21	Steve Hosey	.75	.35
❏ 22	Charles Nagy	1.25	.55
❏ 23	Dave Fleming	.75	.35
❏ 24	Reggie Sanders	1.25	.55
❏ 25	Sam Militello	.75	.35
❏ 26	Eric Karros	1.50	.70
❏ 27	Ryan Klesko	3.00	1.35
❏ 28	Dean Palmer	1.25	.55
❏ 29	Ivan Rodriguez	4.00	1.80
❏ 30	Sterling Hitchcock	1.25	.55

1993 Pinnacle Team Pinnacle

	MINT	NRMT
COMPLETE SET (10)	90.00	40.00
COMMON PAIR (1-10/B11)	3.00	1.35
SEMISTARS	6.00	2.70
UNLISTED STARS	8.00	3.60
RANDOM INSERTS IN SER.1 PACKS		
B11 DISTRIBUTED ONLY BY MAIL		

		MINT	NRMT
❏ 1	Greg Maddux	20.00	9.00
	Mike Mussina		
❏ 2	Tom Glavine	6.00	2.70
	John Smiley		
❏ 3	Darren Daulton	10.00	4.50
	Ivan Rodriguez		
❏ 4	Fred McGriff	15.00	6.75
	Frank Thomas		
❏ 5	Delino DeShields	4.00	1.80
	Carlos Baerga		
❏ 6	Gary Sheffield	8.00	3.60
	Edgar Martinez		
❏ 7	Ozzie Smith	10.00	4.50
	Pat Listach		
❏ 8	Barry Bonds	15.00	6.75
	Juan Gonzalez		
❏ 9	Andy Van Slyke	12.00	5.50
	Kirby Puckett		
❏ 10	Larry Walker	8.00	3.60
	Joe Carter		
❏ B11	Rob Dibble	3.00	1.35
	Rick Aguilera		

1993 Pinnacle Tribute

George Brett   PINNACLE

	MINT	NRMT
COMPLETE SET (10)	75.00	34.00
COMMON BRETT (1-5)	5.00	2.20
COMMON RYAN (6-10)	10.00	4.50
SER.2 STATED ODDS 1:24		

		MINT	NRMT
❏ 1	George Brett	5.00	2.20
	Kansas City Royalty		
❏ 2	George Brett	5.00	2.20
	The Chase for .400		
❏ 3	George Brett	5.00	2.20
	Pine Tar Pandemonium		
❏ 4	George Brett	5.00	2.20
	MVP and a World Series, Too		
❏ 5	George Brett	5.00	2.20
	3,000 or Bust		
❏ 6	Nolan Ryan	10.00	4.50
	The Rookie		
❏ 7	Nolan Ryan	10.00	4.50
	Angel of No Mercy		
❏ 8	Nolan Ryan	10.00	4.50
	Astronomical Success		
❏ 9	Nolan Ryan	10.00	4.50
	5,000 Ks		
❏ 10	Nolan Ryan	10.00	4.50
	No-Hitter No. 7		

1994 Pinnacle

	MINT	NRMT
COMPLETE SET (540)	20.00	9.00
COMPLETE SERIES 1 (270)	10.00	4.50
COMPLETE SERIES 2 (270)	10.00	4.50
COMMON CARD (1-540)	.10	.05
MINOR STARS	.25	.11
UNLISTED STARS	.50	.23
COMMON AP (1-540)	3.00	1.35
*AP STARS: 12.5X TO 30X HI COLUMN		
*AP YOUNG STARS: 10X TO 25X HI		
*AP ROOKIES: 6X TO 15X HI		
AP STATED ODDS 1:26 HOB, 1:22 RET		
COMMON MUSEUM (1-540)	1.00	.45
MUS.TRADE (279/3/3/328)	3.00	1.35
MUS.TRADE (382/387)	3.00	1.35
*MUSEUM STARS: 4X TO 10X HI COLUMN		
*MUSEUM YOUNG STARS: 3X TO 8X HI		
*MUSEUM ROOKIES: 2.5X TO 6X HI		
MUSEUM STAT.ODDS 1:4H, 1:3R, 1:4J		

DELGADO SR STATED ODDS 1:360

☐ 1	Frank Thomas	1.00	.45
☐ 2	Carlos Baerga	.10	.05
☐ 3	Sammy Sosa	2.00	.90
☐ 4	Tony Gwynn	1.25	.55
☐ 5	John Olerud	.25	.11
☐ 6	Ryne Sandberg	.60	.25
☐ 7	Moises Alou	.25	.11
☐ 8	Steve Avery	.10	.05
☐ 9	Tim Salmon	.50	.23
☐ 10	Cecil Fielder	.25	.11
☐ 11	Greg Maddux	1.25	.55
☐ 12	Barry Larkin	.50	.23
☐ 13	Mike Devereaux	.10	.05
☐ 14	Charlie Hayes	.10	.05
☐ 15	Albert Belle	.50	.23
☐ 16	Andy Van Slyke	.25	.11
☐ 17	Mo Vaughn	.50	.23
☐ 18	Brian McRae	.10	.05
☐ 19	Cal Eldred	.10	.05
☐ 20	Craig Biggio	.50	.23
☐ 21	Kirby Puckett	.75	.35
☐ 22	Derek Bell	.25	.11
☐ 23	Don Mattingly	1.00	.45
☐ 24	John Burkett	.10	.05
☐ 25	Roger Clemens	1.25	.55
☐ 26	Barry Bonds	.60	.25
☐ 27	Paul Molitor	.50	.23
☐ 28	Mike Piazza	1.50	.70
☐ 29	Robin Ventura	.25	.11
☐ 30	Jeff Conine	.10	.05
☐ 31	Wade Boggs	.50	.23
☐ 32	Dennis Eckersley	.25	.11
☐ 33	Bobby Bonilla	.25	.11
☐ 34	Lenny Dykstra	.25	.11
☐ 35	Manny Alexander	.10	.05
☐ 36	Ray Lankford	.25	.11
☐ 37	Greg Vaughn	.25	.11
☐ 38	Chuck Finley	.25	.11
☐ 39	Todd Benzinger	.10	.05
☐ 40	Dave Justice	.50	.23
☐ 41	Rob Dibble	.10	.05
☐ 42	Tom Henke	.10	.05
☐ 43	David Nied	.10	.05
☐ 44	Sandy Alomar Jr.	.25	.11
☐ 45	Pete Harnisch	.10	.05
☐ 46	Jeff Russell	.10	.05
☐ 47	Terry Mulholland	.10	.05
☐ 48	Kevin Appier	.25	.11
☐ 49	Randy Tomlin	.10	.05
☐ 50	Cal Ripken Jr.	2.00	.90
☐ 51	Andy Benes	.25	.11
☐ 52	Jimmy Key	.25	.11
☐ 53	Kirt Manwaring	.10	.05
☐ 54	Kevin Tapani	.10	.05
☐ 55	Jose Guzman	.10	.05
☐ 56	Todd Stottlemyre	.10	.05
☐ 57	Jack McDowell	.10	.05
☐ 58	Orel Hershiser	.25	.11
☐ 59	Chris Hammond	.10	.05
☐ 60	Chris Nabholz	.10	.05
☐ 61	Ruben Sierra	.10	.05
☐ 62	Dwight Gooden	.25	.11
☐ 63	John Kruk	.25	.11
☐ 64	Omar Vizquel	.25	.11
☐ 65	Tim Naehring	.10	.05
☐ 66	Dwight Smith	.10	.05
☐ 67	Mickey Tettleton	.10	.05
☐ 68	J.T. Snow	.25	.11
☐ 69	Greg McMichael	.10	.05
☐ 70	Kevin Mitchell	.10	.05
☐ 71	Kevin Brown	.25	.11
☐ 72	Scott Cooper	.10	.05
☐ 73	Jim Thome	.50	.23
☐ 74	Joe Girardi	.10	.05
☐ 75	Eric Anthony	.10	.05
☐ 76	Orlando Merced	.10	.05
☐ 77	Felix Jose	.10	.05
☐ 78	Tommy Greene	.10	.05
☐ 79	Bernard Gilkey	.10	.05
☐ 80	Phil Plantier	.10	.05
☐ 81	Danny Tartabull	.10	.05
☐ 82	Trevor Wilson	.10	.05
☐ 83	Chuck Knoblauch	.50	.23
☐ 84	Rick Wilkins	.10	.05
☐ 85	Devon White	.10	.05
☐ 86	Lance Johnson	.10	.05
☐ 87	Eric Karros	.25	.11
☐ 88	Gary Sheffield	.50	.23
☐ 89	Wil Cordero	.10	.05
☐ 90	Ron Darling	.10	.05
☐ 91	Darren Daulton	.25	.11
☐ 92	Joe Orsulak	.10	.05
☐ 93	Steve Cooke	.10	.05
☐ 94	Darryl Hamilton	.10	.05
☐ 95	Aaron Sele	.25	.11
☐ 96	John Doherty	.10	.05
☐ 97	Gary DiSarcina	.10	.05
☐ 98	Jeff Blauser	.10	.05
☐ 99	John Smiley	.10	.05
☐ 100	Ken Griffey Jr.	2.50	1.10
☐ 101	Dean Palmer	.10	.05
☐ 102	Felix Fermin	.10	.05
☐ 103	Jerald Clark	.10	.05
☐ 104	Doug Drabek	.10	.05
☐ 105	Curt Schilling	.25	.11
☐ 106	Jeff Montgomery	.10	.05
☐ 107	Rene Arocha	.10	.05
☐ 108	Carlos Garcia	.10	.05
☐ 109	Wally Whitehurst	.10	.05
☐ 110	Jim Abbott	.25	.11
☐ 111	Royce Clayton	.10	.05
☐ 112	Chris Hoiles	.10	.05
☐ 113	Mike Morgan	.10	.05
☐ 114	Joe Magrane	.10	.05
☐ 115	Tom Candiotti	.10	.05
☐ 116	Ron Karkovice	.10	.05
☐ 117	Ryan Bowen	.10	.05
☐ 118	Rod Beck	.10	.05
☐ 119	John Wetteland	.25	.11
☐ 120	Terry Steinbach	.10	.05
☐ 121	Dave Hollins	.10	.05
☐ 122	Jeff Kent	.25	.11
☐ 123	Ricky Bones	.10	.05
☐ 124	Brian Jordan	.25	.11
☐ 125	Chad Kreuter	.10	.05
☐ 126	John Valentin	.25	.11
☐ 127	Hilly Hathaway	.10	.05
☐ 128	Wilson Alvarez	.25	.11
☐ 129	Tino Martinez	.50	.23
☐ 130	Rodney Bolton	.10	.05
☐ 131	David Segui	.25	.11
☐ 132	Wayne Kirby	.10	.05
☐ 133	Eric Young	.10	.05
☐ 134	Scott Servais	.10	.05
☐ 135	Scott Radinsky	.10	.05
☐ 136	Bret Barberie	.10	.05
☐ 137	John Roper	.10	.05
☐ 138	Ricky Gutierrez	.10	.05
☐ 139	Bernie Williams	.50	.23
☐ 140	Bud Black	.10	.05
☐ 141	Jose Vizcaino	.10	.05
☐ 142	Gerald Williams	.10	.05
☐ 143	Duane Ward	.10	.05
☐ 144	Danny Jackson	.10	.05
☐ 145	Allen Watson	.10	.05
☐ 146	Scott Fletcher	.10	.05
☐ 147	Delino DeShields	.10	.05
☐ 148	Shane Mack	.10	.05
☐ 149	Jim Eisenreich	.10	.05
☐ 150	Troy Neel	.10	.05
☐ 151	Jay Bell	.25	.11
☐ 152	B.J. Surhoff	.10	.05
☐ 153	Mark Whiten	.10	.05
☐ 154	Mike Henneman	.10	.05
☐ 155	Todd Hundley	.25	.11
☐ 156	Greg Myers	.10	.05
☐ 157	Ryan Klesko	.25	.11
☐ 158	Dave Fleming	.10	.05
☐ 159	Mickey Morandini	.10	.05
☐ 160	Blas Minor	.10	.05
☐ 161	Reggie Jefferson	.10	.05
☐ 162	David Hulse	.10	.05
☐ 163	Greg Swindell	.10	.05
☐ 164	Roberto Hernandez	.10	.05
☐ 165	Brady Anderson	.25	.11
☐ 166	Jack Armstrong	.10	.05
☐ 167	Phil Clark	.10	.05
☐ 168	Melido Perez	.10	.05
☐ 169	Darren Lewis	.10	.05
☐ 170	Sam Horn	.10	.05
☐ 171	Mike Harkey	.10	.05
☐ 172	Juan Guzman	.25	.11
☐ 173	Bob Natal	.10	.05
☐ 174	Deion Sanders	.25	.11
☐ 175	Carlos Quintana	.10	.05
☐ 176	Mel Rojas	.10	.05
☐ 177	Willie Banks	.10	.05
☐ 178	Ben Rivera	.10	.05
☐ 179	Kenny Lofton	.50	.23
☐ 180	Leo Gomez	.10	.05
☐ 181	Roberto Mejia	.10	.05
☐ 182	Mike Perez	.10	.05
☐ 183	Travis Fryman	.25	.11
☐ 184	Ben McDonald	.10	.05
☐ 185	Steve Frey	.10	.05
☐ 186	Kevin Young	.10	.05
☐ 187	Dave Magadan	.10	.05
☐ 188	Bobby Munoz	.10	.05
☐ 189	Pat Rapp	.10	.05
☐ 190	Jose Offerman	.25	.11
☐ 191	Vinny Castilla	.25	.11
☐ 192	Ivan Calderon	.10	.05
☐ 193	Ken Caminiti	.30	.14
☐ 194	Benji Gil	.10	.05
☐ 195	Chuck Carr	.10	.05
☐ 196	Derrick May	.10	.05
☐ 197	Pat Kelly	.10	.05
☐ 198	Jeff Brantley	.10	.05
☐ 199	Jose Lind	.10	.05
☐ 200	Steve Buechele	.10	.05
☐ 201	Wes Chamberlain	.10	.05
☐ 202	Eduardo Perez	.10	.05
☐ 203	Bret Saberhagen	.25	.11
☐ 204	Gregg Jefferies	.10	.05
☐ 205	Darrin Fletcher	.10	.05
☐ 206	Kent Hrbek	.25	.11
☐ 207	Kim Batiste	.10	.05
☐ 208	Jeff King	.10	.05
☐ 209	Donovan Osborne	.10	.05
☐ 210	Dave Nilsson	.10	.05
☐ 211	Al Martin	.10	.05
☐ 212	Mike Moore	.10	.05
☐ 213	Sterling Hitchcock	.25	.11
☐ 214	Geronimo Pena	.10	.05
☐ 215	Kevin Higgins	.10	.05
☐ 216	Norm Charlton	.10	.05
☐ 217	Don Slaught	.10	.05
☐ 218	Mitch Williams	.10	.05
☐ 219	Derek Lilliquist	.10	.05
☐ 220	Armando Reynoso	.10	.05
☐ 221	Kenny Rogers	.10	.05
☐ 222	Doug Jones	.10	.05
☐ 223	Luis Aquino	.10	.05
☐ 224	Mike Oquist	.10	.05
☐ 225	Darryl Scott	.10	.05
☐ 226	Kurt Abbott	.10	.05
☐ 227	Andy Tomberlin	.10	.05
☐ 228	Norberto Martin	.10	.05
☐ 229	Pedro Castellano	.10	.05
☐ 230	Curtis Pride	.10	.05
☐ 231	Jeff McNeely	.10	.05
☐ 232	Scott Lydy	.10	.05
☐ 233	Darren Oliver	.50	.23
☐ 234	Danny Bautista	.10	.05
☐ 235	Butch Huskey	.25	.11
☐ 236	Chipper Jones	1.25	.55
☐ 237	Eddie Zambrano	.10	.05
☐ 238	Domingo Jean	.10	.05
☐ 239	Javier Lopez	.30	.14
☐ 240	Nigel Wilson	.10	.05
☐ 241	Drew Denson	.10	.05
☐ 242	Raul Mondesi	.50	.23
☐ 243	Luis Ortiz	.10	.05
☐ 244	Manny Ramirez	1.00	.45
☐ 245	Greg Blosser	.10	.05
☐ 246	Rondell White	.25	.11
☐ 247	Steve Karsay	.10	.05
☐ 248	Scott Stahoviak	.10	.05
☐ 249	Jose Valentin	.10	.05
☐ 250	Marc Newfield	.10	.05
☐ 251	Keith Kessinger	.10	.05
☐ 252	Carl Everett	.25	.11
☐ 253	John O'Donoghue	.10	.05
☐ 254	Turk Wendell	.10	.05
☐ 255	Scott Ruffcorn	.10	.05
☐ 256	Tony Tarasco	.10	.05

257	Andy Cook	.10	.05
258	Matt Mieske	.10	.05
259	Luis Lopez	.10	.05
260	Ramon Caraballo	.10	.05
261	Salomon Torres	.10	.05
262	Brooks Kieschnick	.10	.05
263	Daron Kirkreit	.10	.05
264	Bill Wagner	.60	.25
265	Matt Drews	.25	.11
266	Scott Christman	.10	.05
267	Torii Hunter	.10	.05
268	Jamey Wright	.25	.11
269	Jeff Granger	.10	.05
270	Trot Nixon	1.00	.45
271	Randy Myers	.10	.05
272	Trevor Hoffman	.25	.11
273	Bob Wickman	.10	.05
274	Willie McGee	.25	.11
275	Hipolito Pichardo	.10	.05
276	Bobby Witt	.10	.05
277	Gregg Olson	.10	.05
278	Randy Johnson	.50	.23
279	Robb Nen	.10	.05
280	Paul O'Neill	.25	.11
281	Lou Whitaker	.25	.11
282	Chad Curtis	.10	.05
283	Doug Henry	.10	.05
284	Tom Glavine	.50	.23
285	Mike Greenwell	.10	.05
286	Roberto Kelly	.10	.05
287	Roberto Alomar	.50	.23
288	Charlie Hough	.10	.05
289	Alex Fernandez	.10	.05
290	Jeff Bagwell	.60	.25
291	Wally Joyner	.25	.11
292	Andujar Cedeno	.10	.05
293	Rick Aguilera	.10	.05
294	Darryl Strawberry	.25	.11
295	Mike Mussina	.50	.23
296	Jeff Gardner	.10	.05
297	Chris Gwynn	.10	.05
298	Matt Williams	.30	.14
299	Brent Gates	.10	.05
300	Mark McGwire	2.50	1.10
301	Jim Deshaies	.10	.05
302	Edgar Martinez	.25	.11
303	Danny Darwin	.10	.05
304	Pat Meares	.10	.05
305	Benito Santiago	.10	.05
306	Jose Canseco	.60	.25
307	Jim Gott	.10	.05
308	Paul Sorrento	.10	.05
309	Scott Kamieniecki	.10	.05
310	Larry Walker	.50	.23
311	Mark Langston	.10	.05
312	John Jaha	.10	.05
313	Stan Javier	.10	.05
314	Hal Morris	.10	.05
315	Robby Thompson	.10	.05
316	Pat Hentgen	.25	.11
317	Tom Gordon	.10	.05
318	Joey Cora	.10	.05
319	Luis Alicea	.10	.05
320	Andre Dawson	.30	.14
321	Darryl Kile	.10	.05
322	Jose Rijo	.10	.05
323	Luis Gonzalez	.25	.11
324	Billy Ashley	.25	.11
325	David Cone	.30	.14
326	Bill Swift	.10	.05
327	Phil Hiatt	.10	.05
328	Craig Paquette	.10	.05
329	Bob Welch	.10	.05
330	Tony Phillips	.10	.05
331	Archi Cianfrocco	.10	.05
332	Dave Winfield	.50	.23
333	David McCarty	.10	.05
334	Al Leiter	.25	.11
335	Tom Browning	.10	.05
336	Mark Grace	.30	.14
337	Jose Mesa	.10	.05
338	Mike Stanley	.10	.05
339	Roger McDowell	.10	.05
340	Damion Easley	.25	.11
341	Angel Miranda	.10	.05
342	John Smoltz	.30	.14
343	Jay Buhner	.25	.11
344	Bryan Harvey	.10	.05
345	Joe Carter	.25	.11
346	Dante Bichette	.25	.11
347	Jason Bere	.10	.05
348	Frank Viola	.10	.05
349	Ivan Rodriguez	.60	.25
350	Juan Gonzalez	1.00	.45
351	Steve Finley	.10	.05
352	Mike Felder	.10	.05
353	Ramon Martinez	.25	.11
354	Greg Gagne	.10	.05
355	Ken Hill	.10	.05
356	Pedro Munoz	.10	.05
357	Todd Van Poppel	.10	.05
358	Marquis Grissom	.25	.11
359	Milt Cuyler	.10	.05
360	Reggie Sanders	.25	.11
361	Scott Erickson	.25	.11
362	Billy Hatcher	.10	.05
363	Gene Harris	.10	.05
364	Rene Gonzales	.10	.05
365	Kevin Rogers	.10	.05
366	Eric Plunk	.10	.05
367	Todd Zeile	.10	.05
368	John Franco	.25	.11
369	Brett Butler	.25	.11
370	Bill Spiers	.10	.05
371	Terry Pendleton	.10	.05
372	Chris Bosio	.10	.05
373	Orestes Destrade	.10	.05
374	Dave Stewart	.25	.11
375	Darren Holmes	.10	.05
376	Doug Strange	.10	.05
377	Brian Turang	.10	.05
378	Carl Willis	.10	.05
379	Mark McLemore	.10	.05
380	Bobby Jones	.10	.05
381	Scott Sanders	.10	.05
382	Kirk Rueter	.10	.05
383	Randy Velarde	.10	.05
384	Fred McGriff	.30	.14
385	Charles Nagy	.25	.11
386	Rich Amaral	.10	.05
387	Geronimo Berroa	.10	.05
388	Eric Davis	.25	.11
389	Ozzie Smith	.60	.25
390	Alex Arias	.10	.05
391	Brad Ausmus	.10	.05
392	Cliff Floyd	.25	.11
393	Roger Salkeld	.10	.05
394	Jim Edmonds	.50	.23
395	Jeromy Burnitz	.25	.11
396	Dave Staton	.10	.05
397	Rob Butler	.10	.05
398	Marcos Armas	.10	.05
399	Darrell Whitmore	.10	.05
400	Ryan Thompson	.10	.05
401	Ross Powell	.10	.05
402	Joe Oliver	.10	.05
403	Paul Carey	.10	.05
404	Chris Sabo	.10	.05
405	Chris Turner	.10	.05
406	Nate Minchey	.10	.05
407	Lonnie Maclin	.10	.05
408	Harold Baines	.25	.11
409	Brian Williams	.10	.05
410	Johnny Ruffin	.10	.05
411	Julian Tavarez	.10	.05
412	Mark Hutton	.10	.05
413	Carlos Delgado	.50	.23
414	Chris Gomez	.10	.05
415	Mike Hampton	.10	.05
416	Alex Diaz	.10	.05
417	Jeffrey Hammonds	.25	.11
418	Jayhawk Owens	.10	.05
419	J.R. Phillips	.10	.05
420	Cory Bailey	.10	.05
421	Denny Hocking	.10	.05
422	Jon Shave	.10	.05
423	Damon Buford	.10	.05
424	Troy O'Leary	.25	.11
425	Tripp Cromer	.10	.05
426	Albie Lopez	.25	.11
427	Tony Fernandez	.25	.11
428	Ozzie Guillen	.10	.05
429	Alan Trammell	.30	.14
430	John Wasdin	.25	.11
431	Marc Valdes	.10	.05
432	Brian Anderson	.30	.14
433	Matt Brunson	.10	.05
434	Wayne Gomes	.10	.05
435	Jay Powell	.30	.14
436	Kirk Presley	.10	.05
437	Jon Ratliff	.10	.05
438	Derrek Lee	.40	.18
439	Tom Pagnozzi	.10	.05
440	Kent Mercker	.10	.05
441	Phil Leftwich	.10	.05
442	Jamie Moyer	.10	.05
443	John Flaherty	.10	.05
444	Mark Wohlers	.10	.05
445	Jose Bautista	.10	.05
446	Andres Galarraga	.50	.23
447	Mark Lemke	.10	.05
448	Tim Wakefield	.25	.11
449	Pat Listach	.10	.05
450	Rickey Henderson	.60	.25
451	Mike Gallego	.10	.05
452	Bob Tewksbury	.10	.05
453	Kirk Gibson	.25	.11
454	Pedro Astacio	.10	.05
455	Mike Lansing	.10	.05
456	Sean Berry	.10	.05
457	Bob Walk	.10	.05
458	Chili Davis	.25	.11
459	Ed Sprague	.10	.05
460	Kevin Stocker	.10	.05
461	Mike Stanton	.10	.05
462	Tim Raines	.25	.11
463	Mike Bordick	.10	.05
464	David Wells	.30	.14
465	Tim Laker	.10	.05
466	Cory Snyder	.10	.05
467	Alex Cole	.10	.05
468	Pete Incaviglia	.10	.05
469	Roger Pavlik	.10	.05
470	Greg W. Harris	.10	.05
471	Xavier Hernandez	.10	.05
472	Erik Hanson	.10	.05
473	Jesse Orosco	.10	.05
474	Greg Colbrunn	.10	.05
475	Harold Reynolds	.10	.05
476	Greg A. Harris	.10	.05
477	Pat Borders	.10	.05
478	Melvin Nieves	.10	.05
479	Mariano Duncan	.10	.05
480	Greg Hibbard	.10	.05
481	Tim Pugh	.10	.05
482	Bobby Ayala	.10	.05
483	Sid Fernandez	.10	.05
484	Tim Wallach	.10	.05
485	Randy Milligan	.10	.05
486	Walt Weiss	.10	.05
487	Matt Walbeck	.10	.05
488	Mike Macfarlane	.10	.05
489	Jerry Browne	.10	.05
490	Chris Sabo	.10	.05
491	Tim Belcher	.10	.05
492	Spike Owen	.10	.05
493	Rafael Palmeiro	.50	.23
494	Brian Harper	.10	.05
495	Eddie Murray	.50	.23
496	Ellis Burks	.25	.11
497	Karl Rhodes	.10	.05
498	Otis Nixon	.10	.05
499	Lee Smith	.25	.11
500	Bip Roberts	.10	.05
501	Pedro Martinez	.60	.25
502	Brian Hunter	.10	.05
503	Tyler Green	.10	.05
504	Bruce Hurst	.10	.05
505	Alex Gonzalez	.10	.05
506	Mark Portugal	.10	.05
507	Bob Ojeda	.10	.05
508	Dave Henderson	.10	.05
509	Bo Jackson	.25	.11
510	Bret Boone	.25	.11
511	Mark Eichhorn	.10	.05
512	Luis Polonia	.10	.05
513	Will Clark	.50	.23
514	Dave Valle	.10	.05

☐ 515 Dan Wilson	.10	.05
☐ 516 Dennis Martinez	.25	.11
☐ 517 Jim Leyritz	.25	.11
☐ 518 Howard Johnson	.10	.05
☐ 519 Jody Reed	.10	.05
☐ 520 Julio Franco	.10	.05
☐ 521 Jeff Reardon	.25	.11
☐ 522 Willie Greene	.10	.05
☐ 523 Shawon Dunston	.10	.05
☐ 524 Keith Mitchell	.10	.05
☐ 525 Rick Helling	.25	.11
☐ 526 Mark Kiefer	.10	.05
☐ 527 Chan Ho Park	.75	.35
☐ 528 Tony Longmire	.10	.05
☐ 529 Rich Becker	.10	.05
☐ 530 Tim Hyers	.10	.05
☐ 531 Darrin Jackson	.10	.05
☐ 532 Jack Morris	.25	.11
☐ 533 Rick White	.10	.05
☐ 534 Mike Kelly	.10	.05
☐ 535 James Mouton	.10	.05
☐ 536 Steve Trachsel	.10	.05
☐ 537 Tony Eusebio	.10	.05
☐ 538 Kelly Stinnett	.10	.05
☐ 539 Paul Spoljaric	.10	.05
☐ 540 Darren Dreifort	.25	.11
☐ SR1 Carlos Delgado	3.00	1.35
Super Rookie		

1994 Pinnacle Rookie Team Pinnacle

	MINT	NRMT
COMPLETE SET (9)	60.00	27.00
COMMON PAIR (1-9)	4.00	1.80
MINOR STARS	6.00	2.70
SER.1 STATED ODDS 1:90 HOB, 1:72 RET		

☐ 1 Carlos Delgado	10.00	4.50
Javier Lopez		
☐ 2 Bob Hamelin	4.00	1.80
J.P. Phillips		
☐ 3 Jon Shave	4.00	1.80
Keith Kessinger		
☐ 4 Luis Ortiz	6.00	2.70
Butch Huskey		
☐ 5 Kurt Abbott	20.00	9.00
Chipper Jones		
☐ 6 Manny Ramirez	15.00	6.75
Rondell White		
☐ 7 Jeffrey Hammonds	6.00	2.70
Cliff Floyd		
☐ 8 Marc Newfield	4.00	1.80
Nigel Wilson		
☐ 9 Mark Hutton	4.00	1.80
Salomon Torres		

1994 Pinnacle Run Creators

	MINT	NRMT
COMPLETE SET (44)	80.00	36.00
COMPLETE SERIES 1 (22)	50.00	22.00
COMPLETE SERIES 2 (22)	30.00	13.50
COMMON CARD (RC1-RC44)	.60	.25
STATED ODDS 1:4 JUMBO		

☐ RC1 John Olerud	1.00	.45
☐ RC2 Frank Thomas	5.00	2.20
☐ RC3 Ken Griffey Jr.	12.00	5.50
☐ RC4 Paul Molitor	2.00	.90
☐ RC5 Rafael Palmeiro	2.00	.90
☐ RC6 Roberto Alomar	2.00	.90
☐ RC7 Juan Gonzalez	5.00	2.20
☐ RC8 Albert Belle	2.00	.90
☐ RC9 Travis Fryman	1.00	.45
☐ RC10 Rickey Henderson	3.00	1.35
☐ RC11 Tony Phillips	.60	.25
☐ RC12 Mo Vaughn	2.00	.90
☐ RC13 Tim Salmon	2.00	.90
☐ RC14 Kenny Lofton	2.00	.90
☐ RC15 Carlos Baerga	.60	.25
☐ RC16 Greg Vaughn	1.00	.45
☐ RC17 Jay Buhner	1.00	.45
☐ RC18 Chris Hoiles	.60	.25
☐ RC19 Mickey Tettleton	.60	.25
☐ RC20 Kirby Puckett	5.00	2.20
☐ RC21 Danny Tartabull	.60	.25
☐ RC22 Devon White	.60	.25
☐ RC23 Barry Bonds	3.00	1.35
☐ RC24 Lenny Dykstra	1.00	.45
☐ RC25 John Kruk	1.00	.45
☐ RC26 Fred McGriff	1.50	.70
☐ RC27 Gregg Jefferies	.60	.25
☐ RC28 Mike Piazza	8.00	3.60
☐ RC29 Jeff Blauser	.60	.25
☐ RC30 Andres Galarraga	2.00	.90
☐ RC31 Darren Daulton	1.00	.45
☐ RC32 Dave Justice	2.00	.90
☐ RC33 Craig Biggio	2.00	.90
☐ RC34 Mark Grace	1.50	.70
☐ RC35 Tony Gwynn	6.00	2.70
☐ RC36 Jeff Bagwell	3.00	1.35
☐ RC37 Jay Bell	1.00	.45
☐ RC38 Marquis Grissom	.60	.25
☐ RC39 Matt Williams	1.50	.70
☐ RC40 Charlie Hayes	.60	.25
☐ RC41 Dante Bichette	1.00	.45
☐ RC42 Bernard Gilkey	1.00	.45
☐ RC43 Brett Butler	1.00	.45
☐ RC44 Rick Wilkins	.60	.25

1994 Pinnacle Team Pinnacle

	MINT	NRMT
COMPLETE SET (9)	120.00	55.00

COMMON PAIR (1-9)	6.00	2.70
SER.2 STATED ODDS 1:90 HOB/RET		

☐ 1 Jeff Bagwell	12.00	5.50
Frank Thomas		
☐ 2 Carlos Baerga	6.00	2.70
Robby Thompson		
☐ 3 Matt Williams	8.00	3.60
Dean Palmer		
☐ 4 Cal Ripken Jr.	25.00	11.00
Jay Bell		
☐ 5 Ivan Rodriguez	20.00	9.00
Mike Piazza		
☐ 6 Lenny Dykstra	30.00	13.50
Ken Griffey Jr.		
☐ 7 Juan Gonzalez	15.00	6.75
Barry Bonds		
☐ 8 Tim Salmon	15.00	6.75
Dave Justice		
☐ 9 Greg Maddux	15.00	6.75
Jack McDowell		

1994 Pinnacle Tribute

	MINT	NRMT
COMPLETE SET (18)	100.00	45.00
COMPLETE SERIES 1 (9)	30.00	13.50
COMPLETE SERIES 2 (9)	70.00	32.00
COMMON CARD (TR1-TR18)	1.00	.45
STATED ODDS 1:18 HOBBY		

☐ TR1 Paul Molitor	4.00	1.80
☐ TR2 Jim Abbott	1.50	.70
☐ TR3 Dave Winfield	4.00	1.80
☐ TR4 Bo Jackson	1.50	.70
☐ TR5 David Justice	4.00	1.80
☐ TR6 Len Dykstra	1.50	.70
☐ TR7 Mike Piazza	12.00	5.50
☐ TR8 Barry Bonds	5.00	2.20
☐ TR9 Randy Johnson	4.00	1.80
☐ TR10 Ozzie Smith	5.00	2.20
☐ TR11 Mark Whiten	1.00	.45
☐ TR12 Greg Maddux	10.00	4.50
☐ TR13 Cal Ripken Jr.	15.00	6.75
☐ TR14 Frank Thomas	10.00	4.50
☐ TR15 Juan Gonzalez	8.00	3.60
☐ TR16 Roberto Alomar	4.00	1.80
☐ TR17 Ken Griffey Jr.	20.00	9.00
☐ TR18 Lee Smith	1.50	.70

1995 Pinnacle

	MINT	NRMT
COMPLETE SET (450)	30.00	13.50
COMPLETE SERIES 1 (225)	15.00	6.75
COMPLETE SERIES 2 (225)	15.00	6.75
COMMON CARD (1-450)	.15	.07
MINOR STARS	.25	.11
UNLISTED STARS	.50	.23
SUBSET CARDS HALF VALUE OF BASE CARDS		
COMMON AP (1-450)	3.00	1.35
*AP STARS: 10X TO 25X HI COLUMN		
*AP RC's/PROSPECTS: 6X TO 15X HI		
AP SER.1 STATED ODDS 1:36 HOB/RET		
AP SER.2 STATED ODDS 1:26 HOB/RET		
COMMON MUSEUM (1-450)	1.00	.45
TRADE (410/413/416/420)	3.00	1.35
TRADE (423/426/444)	3.00	1.35
*MUSEUM STARS: 4X TO 10X HI COLUMN		
*MUSEUM RC's/PROSPECTS: 2.5X TO 6X HI		
MUSEUM STATED ODDS 1:4 H/R/J, 1:3ANCO		

#	Player	MINT	NRMT
1	Jeff Bagwell	.60	.25
2	Roger Clemens	1.25	.55
3	Mark Whiten	.15	.07
4	Shawon Dunston	.15	.07
5	Bobby Bonilla	.25	.11
6	Kevin Tapani	.15	.07
7	Eric Karros	.25	.11
8	Cliff Floyd	.25	.11
9	Pat Kelly	.15	.07
10	Jeffrey Hammonds	.25	.11
11	Jeff Conine	.15	.07
12	Fred McGriff	.40	.18
13	Chris Bosio	.15	.07
14	Mike Mussina	.50	.23
15	Danny Bautista	.15	.07
16	Mickey Morandini	.15	.07
17	Chuck Finley	.25	.11
18	Jim Thome	.50	.23
19	Luis Ortiz	.15	.07
20	Walt Weiss	.15	.07
21	Don Mattingly	1.00	.45
22	Bob Hamelin	.15	.07
23	Melido Perez	.15	.07
24	Keith Mitchell	.15	.07
25	John Smoltz	.40	.18
26	Hector Carrasco	.15	.07
27	Pat Hentgen	.25	.11
28	Derrick May	.15	.07
29	Mike Kingery	.15	.07
30	Chuck Carr	.15	.07
31	Billy Ashley	.25	.11
32	Todd Hundley	.25	.11
33	Luis Gonzalez	.25	.11
34	Marquis Grissom	.25	.11
35	Jeff King	.15	.07
36	Eddie Williams	.15	.07
37	Tom Pagnozzi	.15	.07
38	Chris Hoiles	.25	.11
39	Sandy Alomar Jr.	.25	.11
40	Mike Greenwell	.15	.07
41	Lance Johnson	.15	.07
42	Junior Felix	.15	.07
43	Felix Jose	.15	.07
44	Scott Leius	.15	.07
45	Ruben Sierra	.15	.07
46	Kevin Seitzer	.15	.07
47	Wade Boggs	.50	.23
48	Reggie Jefferson	.15	.07
49	Jose Canseco	.60	.25
50	David Justice	.50	.23
51	John Smiley	.15	.07
52	Joe Carter	.25	.11
53	Rick Wilkins	.15	.07
54	Ellis Burks	.25	.11
55	Dave Weathers	.15	.07
56	Pedro Astacio	.15	.07
57	Ryan Thompson	.15	.07
58	James Mouton	.15	.07
59	Mel Rojas	.15	.07
60	Orlando Merced	.15	.07
61	Matt Williams	.50	.23
62	Bernard Gilkey	.15	.07
63	J.R. Phillips	.15	.07
64	Lee Smith	.25	.11
65	Jim Edmonds	.40	.18
66	Darrin Jackson	.15	.07
67	Scott Cooper	.15	.07
68	Ron Karkovice	.15	.07
69	Chris Gomez	.15	.07
70	Kevin Appier	.25	.11
71	Bobby Jones	.15	.07
72	Doug Drabek	.15	.07
73	Matt Mieske	.15	.07
74	Sterling Hitchcock	.15	.07
75	John Valentin	.25	.11
76	Reggie Sanders	.25	.11
77	Wally Joyner	.25	.11
78	Turk Wendell	.15	.07
79	Charlie Hayes	.15	.07
80	Bret Barberie	.15	.07
81	Troy Neel	.15	.07
82	Ken Caminiti	.40	.18
83	Milt Thompson	.15	.07
84	Paul Sorrento	.15	.07
85	Trevor Hoffman	.25	.11
86	Jay Bell	.25	.11
87	Mark Portugal	.15	.07
88	Sid Fernandez	.15	.07
89	Charles Nagy	.25	.11
90	Jeff Montgomery	.15	.07
91	Chuck Knoblauch	.50	.23
92	Jeff Frye	.15	.07
93	Tony Gwynn	1.25	.55
94	John Olerud	.25	.11
95	David Nied	.15	.07
96	Chris Hammond	.15	.07
97	Edgar Martinez	.25	.11
98	Kevin Stocker	.15	.07
99	Jeff Fassero	.15	.07
100	Curt Schilling	.40	.18
101	Dave Clark	.15	.07
102	Delino DeShields	.15	.07
103	Lou Gomez	.15	.07
104	Dave Hollins	.15	.07
105	Tim Naehring	.15	.07
106	Otis Nixon	.15	.07
107	Ozzie Guillen	.15	.07
108	Jose Lind	.15	.07
109	Stan Javier	.15	.07
110	Greg Vaughn	.25	.11
111	Chipper Jones	1.25	.55
112	Ed Sprague	.15	.07
113	Mike Macfarlane	.15	.07
114	Steve Finley	.25	.11
115	Ken Hill	.15	.07
116	Carlos Garcia	.15	.07
117	Lou Whitaker	.25	.11
118	Todd Zeile	.15	.07
119	Gary Sheffield	.25	.11
120	Ben McDonald	.15	.07
121	Pete Harnisch	.15	.07
122	Ivan Rodriguez	.60	.25
123	Wilson Alvarez	.15	.07
124	Travis Fryman	.25	.11
125	Pedro Munoz	.15	.07
126	Mark Lemke	.15	.07
127	Jose Valentin	.15	.07
128	Ken Griffey Jr.	2.50	1.10
129	Omar Vizquel	.25	.11
130	Milt Cuyler	.15	.07
131	Steve Trachsel	.15	.07
132	Alex Rodriguez	2.00	.90
133	Garret Anderson	.25	.11
134	Armando Benitez	.15	.07
135	Shawn Green	.50	.23
136	Jorge Fabregas	.15	.07
137	Orlando Miller	.15	.07
138	Rikkert Faneyte	.15	.07
139	Ismael Valdes	.25	.11
140	Jose Oliva	.15	.07
141	Aaron Small	.15	.07
142	Tim Davis	.15	.07
143	Ricky Bottalico	.15	.07
144	Mike Matheny	.15	.07
145	Roberto Petagine	.15	.07
146	Fausto Cruz	.15	.07
147	Bryce Florie	.15	.07
148	Jose Lima	.50	.23
149	John Hudek	.15	.07
150	Duane Singleton	.15	.07
151	John Mabry	.15	.07
152	Robert Eenhoorn	.15	.07
153	Jon Lieber	.15	.07
154	Garey Ingram	.15	.07
155	Paul Shuey	.15	.07
156	Mike Lieberthal	.15	.07
157	Steve Dunn	.25	.11
158	Charles Johnson	.25	.11
159	Ernie Young	.15	.07
160	Jose Martinez	.15	.07
161	Kurt Miller	.15	.07
162	Joey Eischen	.15	.07
163	Dave Stevens	.15	.07
164	Brian L. Hunter	.25	.11
165	Jeff Cirillo	.25	.11
166	Mark Smith	.15	.07
167	McKay Christensen	.15	.07
168	C.J. Nitkowski	.15	.07
169	Antone Williamson	.15	.07
170	Paul Konerko	.75	.35
171	Scott Elarton	.75	.35
172	Jacob Shumate	.15	.07
173	Terrence Long	.40	.18
174	Mark Johnson	.15	.07
175	Ben Grieve	1.25	.55
176	Jayson Peterson	.15	.07
177	Checklist	.15	.07
178	Checklist	.15	.07
179	Checklist	.15	.07
180	Checklist	.15	.07
181	Brian Anderson	.25	.11
182	Steve Buechele	.15	.07
183	Mark Clark	.15	.07
184	Cecil Fielder	.25	.11
185	Steve Avery	.15	.07
186	Devon White	.15	.07
187	Craig Shipley	.15	.07
188	Brady Anderson	.25	.11
189	Kenny Lofton	.40	.18
190	Alex Cole	.15	.07
191	Brent Gates	.15	.07
192	Dean Palmer	.25	.11
193	Alex Gonzalez	.15	.07
194	Steve Cooke	.15	.07
195	Ray Lankford	.25	.11
196	Mark McGwire	2.50	1.10
197	Marc Newfield	.15	.07
198	Pat Rapp	.15	.07
199	Darren Lewis	.15	.07
200	Carlos Baerga	.15	.07
201	Rickey Henderson	.60	.25
202	Kurt Abbott	.15	.07
203	Kirt Manwaring	.15	.07
204	Cal Ripken	2.00	.90
205	Darren Daulton	.25	.11
206	Greg Colbrunn	.15	.07
207	Darryl Hamilton	.15	.07
208	Bo Jackson	.25	.11
209	Tony Phillips	.15	.07
210	Geronimo Berroa	.15	.07
211	Rich Becker	.15	.07
212	Tony Tarasco	.15	.07
213	Karl Rhodes	.15	.07
214	Phil Plantier	.15	.07
215	J.T. Snow	.25	.11
216	Mo Vaughn	.50	.23
217	Greg Gagne	.15	.07
218	Ricky Bones	.15	.07
219	Mike Bordick	.15	.07
220	Chad Curtis	.15	.07
221	Royce Clayton	.15	.07
222	Roberto Alomar	.50	.23
223	Jose Rijo	.15	.07
224	Ryan Klesko	.25	.11
225	Mark Langston	.15	.07
226	Frank Thomas	1.00	.45
227	Juan Gonzalez	1.00	.45
228	Ron Gant	.25	.11
229	Javier Lopez	.25	.11
230	Sammy Sosa	1.50	.70
231	Kevin Brown	.40	.18
232	Gary DiSarcina	.15	.07
233	Albert Belle	.50	.23
234	Jay Buhner	.25	.11
235	Pedro Martinez	.60	.25
236	Bob Tewksbury	.15	.07
237	Mike Piazza	1.50	.70

❑ 238	Darryl Kile	.15	.07
❑ 239	Bryan Harvey	.15	.07
❑ 240	Andres Galarraga	.50	.23
❑ 241	Jeff Blauser	.15	.07
❑ 242	Jeff Kent	.25	.11
❑ 243	Bobby Munoz	.15	.07
❑ 244	Greg Maddux	1.25	.55
❑ 245	Paul O'Neill	.25	.11
❑ 246	Lenny Dykstra	.15	.07
❑ 247	Todd Van Poppel	.15	.07
❑ 248	Bernie Williams	.50	.23
❑ 249	Glenallen Hill	.15	.07
❑ 250	Duane Ward	.15	.07
❑ 251	Dennis Eckersley	.25	.11
❑ 252	Pat Mahomes	.15	.07
❑ 253	Rusty Greer	.50	.23
❑ 254	Roberto Kelly	.15	.07
❑ 255	Randy Myers	.15	.07
❑ 256	Scott Ruffcorn	.15	.07
❑ 257	Robin Ventura	.25	.11
❑ 258	Eduardo Perez	.15	.07
❑ 259	Aaron Sele	.25	.11
❑ 260	Paul Molitor	.50	.23
❑ 261	Juan Guzman	.15	.07
❑ 262	Darren Oliver	.15	.07
❑ 263	Mike Stanley	.15	.07
❑ 264	Tom Glavine	.50	.23
❑ 265	Rico Brogna	.15	.07
❑ 266	Craig Biggio	.60	.23
❑ 267	Darryl Whitmore	.15	.07
❑ 268	Jimmy Key	.25	.11
❑ 269	Will Clark	.50	.23
❑ 270	David Cone	.40	.18
❑ 271	Brian Jordan	.25	.11
❑ 272	Barry Bonds	.60	.25
❑ 273	Danny Tartabull	.15	.07
❑ 274	Ramon J.Martinez	.25	.11
❑ 275	Al Martin	.15	.07
❑ 276	Fred McGriff SM	.15	.07
❑ 277	Carlos Delgado SM	.25	.11
❑ 278	Juan Gonzalez SM	.50	.23
❑ 279	Shawn Green SM	.25	.11
❑ 280	Carlos Baerga SM	.15	.07
❑ 281	Cliff Floyd SM	.15	.07
❑ 282	Ozzie Smith SM	.50	.23
❑ 283	Alex Rodriguez SM	1.00	.45
❑ 284	Kenny Lofton SM	.15	.07
❑ 285	Dave Justice SM	.25	.11
❑ 286	Tim Salmon SM	.25	.11
❑ 287	Manny Ramirez SM	.25	.11
❑ 288	Will Clark SM	.25	.11
❑ 289	Garret Anderson SM	.15	.07
❑ 290	Billy Ashley SM	.15	.07
❑ 291	Tony Gwynn SM	.60	.25
❑ 292	Raul Mondesi SM	.15	.07
❑ 293	Rafael Palmeiro SM	.15	.07
❑ 294	Matt Williams SM	.25	.11
❑ 295	Don Mattingly SM	.50	.23
❑ 296	Kirby Puckett SM	.50	.23
❑ 297	Paul Molitor SM	.25	.11
❑ 298	Albert Belle SM	.25	.11
❑ 299	Barry Bonds SM	.40	.18
❑ 300	Mike Piazza SM	.75	.35
❑ 301	Jeff Bagwell SM	.50	.23
❑ 302	Frank Thomas SM	.50	.23
❑ 303	Chipper Jones SM	.60	.25
❑ 304	Ken Griffey Jr. SM	1.25	.55
❑ 305	Cal Ripken Jr. SM	1.00	.45
❑ 306	Eric Anthony	.15	.07
❑ 307	Todd Benzinger	.15	.07
❑ 308	Jacob Brumfield	.15	.07
❑ 309	Wes Chamberlain	.15	.07
❑ 310	Tino Martinez	.50	.23
❑ 311	Roberto Mejia	.15	.07
❑ 312	Jose Offerman	.25	.11
❑ 313	David Segui	.25	.11
❑ 314	Eric Young	.15	.07
❑ 315	Rey Sanchez	.15	.07
❑ 316	Raul Mondesi	.40	.18
❑ 317	Bret Boone	.25	.11
❑ 318	Andre Dawson	.25	.11
❑ 319	Brian McRae	.15	.07
❑ 320	Dave Nilsson	.15	.07
❑ 321	Moises Alou	.25	.11
❑ 322	Don Slaught	.15	.07
❑ 323	Dave McCarty	.15	.07
❑ 324	Mike Huff	.15	.07
❑ 325	Rick Aguilera	.15	.07
❑ 326	Rod Beck	.15	.07
❑ 327	Kenny Rogers	.15	.07
❑ 328	Andy Benes	.25	.11
❑ 329	Allen Watson	.15	.07
❑ 330	Randy Johnson	.50	.23
❑ 331	Willie Greene	.15	.07
❑ 332	Hal Morris	.15	.07
❑ 333	Ozzie Smith	.60	.25
❑ 334	Jason Bere	.15	.07
❑ 335	Scott Erickson	.25	.11
❑ 336	Dante Bichette	.25	.11
❑ 337	Willie Banks	.15	.07
❑ 338	Eric Davis	.25	.11
❑ 339	Rondell White	.25	.11
❑ 340	Kirby Puckett	.75	.35
❑ 341	Deion Sanders	.50	.23
❑ 342	Eddie Murray	.50	.23
❑ 343	Mike Harkey	.15	.07
❑ 344	Joey Hamilton	.25	.11
❑ 345	Roger Salkeld	.15	.07
❑ 346	Wil Cordero	.15	.07
❑ 347	John Wetteland	.25	.11
❑ 348	Geronimo Pena	.15	.07
❑ 349	Kirk Gibson	.25	.11
❑ 350	Manny Ramirez	.60	.25
❑ 351	Wm.VanLandingham	.15	.07
❑ 352	B.J. Surhoff	.25	.11
❑ 353	Ken Ryan	.15	.07
❑ 354	Terry Steinbach	.15	.07
❑ 355	Bret Saberhagen	.25	.11
❑ 356	John Jaha	.15	.07
❑ 357	Joe Girardi	.15	.07
❑ 358	Steve Karsay	.15	.07
❑ 359	Alex Fernandez	.15	.07
❑ 360	Salomon Torres	.15	.07
❑ 361	John Burkett	.15	.07
❑ 362	Derek Bell	.25	.11
❑ 363	Tom Henke	.15	.07
❑ 364	Gregg Jefferies	.15	.07
❑ 365	Jack McDowell	.15	.07
❑ 366	Andujar Cedeno	.15	.07
❑ 367	Dave Winfield	.50	.23
❑ 368	Carl Everett	.15	.07
❑ 369	Danny Jackson	.15	.07
❑ 370	Jeromy Burnitz	.25	.11
❑ 371	Mark Grace	.40	.18
❑ 372	Larry Walker	.50	.23
❑ 373	Bill Swift	.15	.07
❑ 374	Dennis Martinez	.25	.11
❑ 375	Mickey Tettleton	.15	.07
❑ 376	Mel Nieves	.15	.07
❑ 377	Cal Eldred	.25	.11
❑ 378	Orel Hershiser	.25	.11
❑ 379	David Wells	.40	.18
❑ 380	Gary Gaetti	.25	.11
❑ 381	Jeromy Burnitz	.25	.11
❑ 382	Barry Larkin	.50	.23
❑ 383	Jason Jacome	.15	.07
❑ 384	Tim Wallach	.15	.07
❑ 385	Robby Thompson	.15	.07
❑ 386	Frank Viola	.25	.11
❑ 387	Dave Stewart	.25	.11
❑ 388	Bip Roberts	.15	.07
❑ 389	Ron Darling	.15	.07
❑ 390	Carlos Delgado	.50	.23
❑ 391	Tim Salmon	.50	.23
❑ 392	Alan Trammell	.25	.11
❑ 393	Kevin Foster	.15	.07
❑ 394	Jim Abbott	.25	.11
❑ 395	John Kruk	.25	.11
❑ 396	Andy Van Slyke	.25	.11
❑ 397	Dave Magadan	.15	.07
❑ 398	Rafael Palmeiro	.50	.23
❑ 399	Mike Devereaux	.15	.07
❑ 400	Benito Santiago	.15	.07
❑ 401	Brett Butler	.25	.11
❑ 402	John Franco	.15	.07
❑ 403	Matt Walbeck	.15	.07
❑ 404	Terry Pendleton	.15	.07
❑ 405	Chris Sabo	.15	.07
❑ 406	Andrew Lorraine	.15	.07
❑ 407	Dan Wilson	.15	.07
❑ 408	Mike Lansing	.15	.07
❑ 409	Ray McDavid	.15	.07
❑ 410	Shane Andrews	.15	.07
❑ 411	Tom Gordon	.15	.07
❑ 412	Chad Ogea	.15	.07
❑ 413	James Baldwin	.25	.11
❑ 414	Russ Davis	.25	.11
❑ 415	Ray Holbert	.15	.07
❑ 416	Ray Durham	.25	.11
❑ 417	Matt Nokes	.15	.07
❑ 418	Rod Henderson	.15	.07
❑ 419	Gabe White	.15	.07
❑ 420	Todd Hollandsworth	.15	.07
❑ 421	Midre Cummings	.15	.07
❑ 422	Harold Baines	.25	.11
❑ 423	Troy Percival	.15	.07
❑ 424	Joe Vitiello	.15	.07
❑ 425	Andy Ashby	.15	.07
❑ 426	Michael Tucker	.25	.11
❑ 427	Mark Gubicza	.15	.07
❑ 428	Jim Bullinger	.15	.07
❑ 429	Jose Malave	.15	.07
❑ 430	Pete Schourek	.15	.07
❑ 431	Bobby Ayala	.15	.07
❑ 432	Marvin Freeman	.15	.07
❑ 433	Pat Listach	.15	.07
❑ 434	Eddie Taubensee	.15	.07
❑ 435	Steve Howe	.15	.07
❑ 436	Kent Mercker	.15	.07
❑ 437	Hector Fajardo	.15	.07
❑ 438	Scott Kamieniecki	.15	.07
❑ 439	Robb Nen	.15	.07
❑ 440	Mike Kelly	.15	.07
❑ 441	Tom Candiotti	.15	.07
❑ 442	Albie Lopez	.15	.07
❑ 443	Jeff Granger	.15	.07
❑ 444	Rich Aude	.15	.07
❑ 445	Luis Polonia	.15	.07
❑ 446	Frank Thomas CL	.50	.23
❑ 447	Ken Griffey Jr. CL	1.25	.55
❑ 448	Mike Piazza CL	.75	.35
❑ 449	Jeff Bagwell CL	.50	.23
❑ 450	Jeff Bagwell CL	1.00	.45
	Frank Thomas		
	Ken Griffey Jr.		
	Mike Piazza		

1995 Pinnacle ETA

	MINT	NRMT
COMPLETE SET (6)	25.00	11.00
COMMON CARD (1-6)	2.00	.90
SER.1 STATED ODDS 1:24 HOBBY		

❑ 1	Ben Grieve	6.00	2.70
❑ 2	Alex Ochoa	2.00	.90
❑ 3	Joe Vitiello	2.00	.90
❑ 4	Johnny Damon	4.00	1.80
❑ 5	Trey Beamon	2.00	.90
❑ 6	Brooks Kieschnick	2.00	.90

1995 Pinnacle Gate Attractions

	MINT	NRMT
COMPLETE SET (18)	80.00	36.00
COMMON CARD (GA1-GA18)	1.50	.70
SER.2 STATED ODDS 1:12 JUMBO		

❑ GA1	Ken Griffey Jr.	25.00	11.00

❑ GA2	Frank Thomas	10.00	4.50
❑ GA3	Cal Ripken	20.00	9.00
❑ GA4	Jeff Bagwell	6.00	2.70
❑ GA5	Mike Piazza	15.00	6.75
❑ GA6	Barry Bonds	5.00	2.20
❑ GA7	Kirby Puckett	8.00	3.60
❑ GA8	Albert Belle	4.00	1.80
❑ GA9	Tony Gwynn	12.00	5.50
❑ GA10	Raul Mondesi	2.50	1.10
❑ GA11	Will Clark	4.00	1.80
❑ GA12	Don Mattingly	10.00	4.50
❑ GA13	Roger Clemens	12.00	5.50
❑ GA14	Paul Molitor	4.00	1.80
❑ GA15	Matt Williams	4.00	1.80
❑ GA16	Greg Maddux	12.00	5.50
❑ GA17	Kenny Lofton	2.50	1.10
❑ GA18	Cliff Floyd	1.50	.70

1995 Pinnacle New Blood

	MINT	NRMT
COMPLETE SET (9)	80.00	36.00
COMMON CARD (NB1-NB9)	2.50	1.10
SEMISTARS	5.00	2.20
UNLISTED STARS	8.00	3.60
SER.2 STAT.ODDS 1:90 HOB/RET, 1:72 ANCO		

❑ NB1	Alex Rodriguez	30.00	13.50
❑ NB2	Shawn Green	10.00	4.50
❑ NB3	Brian Hunter	4.00	1.80
*❑ NB4	Garret Anderson	4.00	1.80
❑ NB5	Charles Johnson	4.00	1.80
❑ NB6	Chipper Jones	25.00	11.00
❑ NB7	Carlos Delgado	8.00	3.60
❑ NB8	Billy Ashley	2.50	1.10
❑ NB9	J.R. Phillips UER	2.50	1.10

Dodgers logo on back
Phillips played for the Giants

1995 Pinnacle Performers

	MINT	NRMT
COMPLETE SET (18)	100.00	45.00
COMMON CARD (PP1-PP18)	1.50	.70
SER.1 STATED ODDS 1:12 JUMBO		

❑ PP1	Frank Thomas	12.00	5.50
❑ PP2	Albert Belle	6.00	2.70
❑ PP3	Barry Bonds	8.00	3.60
❑ PP4	Juan Gonzalez	12.00	5.50
❑ PP5	Andres Galarraga	6.00	2.70
❑ PP6	Raul Mondesi	4.00	1.80
❑ PP7	Paul Molitor	6.00	2.70
❑ PP8	Tim Salmon	6.00	2.70
❑ PP9	Mike Piazza	20.00	9.00
❑ PP10	Gregg Jefferies	1.50	.70
❑ PP11	Will Clark	6.00	2.70
❑ PP12	Greg Maddux	15.00	6.75
❑ PP13	Manny Ramirez	8.00	3.60
❑ PP14	Kirby Puckett	10.00	4.50
❑ PP15	Shawn Green	6.00	2.70
❑ PP16	Rafael Palmeiro	6.00	2.70
❑ PP17	Paul O'Neill	2.50	1.10
❑ PP18	Jason Bere	1.50	.70

1995 Pinnacle Pin Redemption

	MINT	NRMT
COMPLETE SET (18)	80.00	36.00
COMMON CARD (1-18)	1.50	.70
SER.2 STAT.ODDS 1:48 H/R, 1:36 JUM/ANCO		
COMP.PIN SET (18)	80.00	36.00
*PINS: 2X TO 5X BASE CARD HI		
ONE PIN VIA MAIL PER REDEMPTION CARD		

❑ 1	Greg Maddux	8.00	3.60
❑ 2	Mike Mussina	3.00	1.35
❑ 3	Mike Piazza	10.00	4.50
❑ 4	Carlos Delgado	3.00	1.35
❑ 5	Jeff Bagwell	4.00	1.80
❑ 6	Frank Thomas	6.00	2.70
❑ 7	Craig Biggio	3.00	1.35
❑ 8	Roberto Alomar	3.00	1.35
❑ 9	Ozzie Smith	3.00	1.35
❑ 10	Cal Ripken Jr.	12.00	5.50
❑ 11	Matt Williams	3.00	1.35
❑ 12	Travis Fryman	1.50	.70
❑ 13	Barry Bonds	3.00	1.35
❑ 14	Ken Griffey Jr.	15.00	6.75
❑ 15	Dave Justice	3.00	1.35
❑ 16	Albert Belle	3.00	1.35
❑ 17	Tony Gwynn	8.00	3.60
❑ 18	Kirby Puckett	3.00	1.35

1995 Pinnacle Red Hot

	MINT	NRMT
COMPLETE SET (25)	80.00	36.00

COMMON CARD (RH1-RH25)	1.00	.45
SER.2 STAT.ODDS 1:16 HOB/RET, 1:12 ANCO		
COMP.WHITE SET (25)	300.00	135.00
*WHITE HOT: 8X TO 20X BASE CARD HI		
W.HOT SER.2 STATED ODDS 1:36 HOBBY		

❑ RH1	Cal Ripken Jr.	12.00	5.50
❑ RH2	Ken Griffey Jr.	15.00	6.75
❑ RH3	Frank Thomas	6.00	2.70
❑ RH4	Jeff Bagwell	4.00	1.80
❑ RH5	Mike Piazza	10.00	4.50
❑ RH6	Barry Bonds	3.00	1.35
❑ RH7	Albert Belle	3.00	1.35
❑ RH8	Tony Gwynn	8.00	3.60
❑ RH9	Kirby Puckett	5.00	2.20
❑ RH10	Don Mattingly	6.00	2.70
❑ RH11	Matt Williams	3.00	1.35
❑ RH12	Greg Maddux	8.00	3.60
❑ RH13	Raul Mondesi	2.00	.90
❑ RH14	Paul Molitor	3.00	1.35
❑ RH15	Manny Ramirez	4.00	1.80
❑ RH16	Joe Carter	1.50	.70
❑ RH17	Will Clark	3.00	1.35
❑ RH18	Roger Clemens	8.00	3.60
❑ RH19	Tim Salmon	3.00	1.35
❑ RH20	Dave Justice	3.00	1.35
❑ RH21	Kenny Lofton	2.00	.90
❑ RH22	Deion Sanders	1.50	.70
❑ RH23	Roberto Alomar	3.00	1.35
❑ RH24	Cliff Floyd	1.50	.70
❑ RH25	Carlos Baerga	1.00	.45

1995 Pinnacle Team Pinnacle

	MINT	NRMT
COMPLETE SET (9)	200.00	90.00
COMMON CARD (TP1-TP9)	5.00	2.20
UNLISTED STARS	10.00	4.50
SER.1 STAT.ODDS 1:90 HOB/RET, 1:72 ANCO		

❑ TP1	Mike Mussina Greg Maddux	25.00	11.00
❑ TP2	Carlos Delgado Mike Piazza	30.00	13.50
❑ TP3	Frank Thomas Jeff Bagwell	20.00	9.00
❑ TP4	Roberto Alomar Craig Biggio	10.00	4.50
❑ TP5	Cal Ripken	40.00	18.00

Ozzie Smith

		MINT	NRMT
❏ TP6	Travis Fryman	5.00	2.20
	Matt Williams		
❏ TP7	Ken Griffey Jr.	50.00	22.00
	Barry Bonds		
❏ TP8	Albert Belle	10.00	4.50
	David Justice		
❏ TP9	Kirby Puckett	25.00	11.00
	Tony Gwynn		

1995 Pinnacle Upstarts

		MINT	NRMT
	COMPLETE SET (30)	50.00	22.00
	COMMON CARD (US1-US30)	1.00	.45
	SER.1 STATED ODDS 1:8 HOB/RET, 1:6 ANCO		

❏ US1	Frank Thomas	8.00	3.60
❏ US2	Roberto Alomar	4.00	1.80
❏ US3	Mike Piazza	12.00	5.50
❏ US4	Javier Lopez	1.50	.70
❏ US5	Albert Belle	4.00	1.80
❏ US6	Carlos Delgado	4.00	1.80
❏ US7	Brent Gates	1.00	.45
❏ US8	Tim Salmon	4.00	1.80
❏ US9	Raul Mondesi	2.50	1.10
❏ US10	Juan Gonzalez	8.00	3.60
❏ US11	Manny Ramirez	5.00	2.20
❏ US12	Sammy Sosa	12.00	5.50
❏ US13	Jeff Kent	1.50	.70
❏ US14	Melvin Nieves	1.00	.45
❏ US15	Rondell White	1.50	.70
❏ US16	Shawn Green	4.00	1.80
❏ US17	Bernie Williams	4.00	1.80
❏ US18	Aaron Sele	1.50	.70
❏ US19	Jason Bere	1.00	.45
❏ US20	Joey Hamilton	1.50	.70
❏ US21	Mike Kelly	1.00	.45
❏ US22	Wil Cordero	1.50	.70
❏ US23	Moises Alou	1.50	.70
❏ US24	Roberto Kelly	1.00	.45
❏ US25	Deion Sanders	1.50	.70
❏ US26	Steve Karsay	1.00	.45
❏ US27	Bret Boone	1.50	.70
❏ US28	Willie Greene	1.00	.45
❏ US29	Billy Ashley	1.00	.45
❏ US30	Brian Anderson	1.50	.70

1996 Pinnacle

	MINT	NRMT
COMPLETE SET (400)	30.00	13.50
COMPLETE SERIES 1 (200)	15.00	6.75
COMPLETE SERIES 2 (200)	15.00	6.75
COMMON CARD (1-399)	.10	.05
MINOR STARS	.15	.07
UNLISTED STARS	.40	.18
SUBSET CARDS HALF VALUE OF BASE CARDS		
COMP.FOIL SET (200)	30.00	13.50
COMMON FOIL (201-399)	.25	.11
*FOIL: .75X TO 2X HI COLUMN		
FOIL AVAIL.IN SER.2 RETAIL SUPER PACKS		
COMMON STARBURST (1-200)	.75	.35
*STARBURST ROOKIES: 2X TO 5X HI		
*STARBURST STARS: 3X TO 8X HI COLUMN		
STARB.ODDS 1:7 H/R, 1:6 JUM, 1:10 MAG		
COMMON STAR.AP (1-200)	2.00	.90
*STAR.AP STARS: 8X TO 20X HI COLUMN		
*STAR.AP ROOKIES: 5X TO 12X HI		
STAR.AP ODDS 1:47 H/R,1:39 JUM,1:67 MAG		
RIPKEN TRIB.SER.1 STATED ODDS 1:150		

❏ 1	Greg Maddux	1.00	.45
❏ 2	Bill Pulsipher	.10	.05
❏ 3	Dante Bichette	.15	.07
❏ 4	Mike Piazza	1.25	.55
❏ 5	Garret Anderson	.15	.07
❏ 6	Steve Finley	.15	.07
❏ 7	Andy Benes	.15	.07
❏ 8	Chuck Knoblauch	.40	.18
❏ 9	Tom Gordon	.10	.05
❏ 10	Jeff Bagwell	.50	.23
❏ 11	Wil Cordero	.10	.05
❏ 12	John Mabry	.10	.05
❏ 13	Jeff Frye	.10	.05
❏ 14	Travis Fryman	.15	.07
❏ 15	John Wetteland	.15	.07
❏ 16	Jason Bates	.10	.05
❏ 17	Danny Tartabull	.15	.07
❏ 18	Charles Nagy	.15	.07
❏ 19	Robin Ventura	.15	.07
❏ 20	Reggie Sanders	.15	.07
❏ 21	Dave Clark	.10	.05
❏ 22	Jaime Navarro	.10	.05
❏ 23	Joey Hamilton	.10	.05
❏ 24	Al Leiter	.15	.07
❏ 25	Deion Sanders	.15	.07
❏ 26	Tim Salmon	.30	.14
❏ 27	Tino Martinez	.25	.11
❏ 28	Mike Greenwell	.10	.05
❏ 29	Phil Plantier	.10	.05
❏ 30	Bobby Bonilla	.15	.07
❏ 31	Kenny Rogers	.10	.05
❏ 32	Chili Davis	.15	.07
❏ 33	Joe Carter	.15	.07
❏ 34	Mike Mussina	.40	.18
❏ 35	Matt Mieske	.10	.05
❏ 36	Jose Canseco	.50	.23
❏ 37	Brad Radke	.15	.07
❏ 38	Juan Gonzalez	.75	.35
❏ 39	David Segui	.10	.05
❏ 40	Alex Fernandez	.10	.05
❏ 41	Jeff Kent	.15	.07
❏ 42	Todd Zeile	.15	.07
❏ 43	Darryl Strawberry	.15	.07
❏ 44	Jose Rijo	.10	.05
❏ 45	Ramon Martinez	.15	.07
❏ 46	Manny Ramirez	.50	.23
❏ 47	Gregg Jefferies	.15	.07
❏ 48	Bryan Rekar	.10	.05
❏ 49	Jeff King	.10	.05
❏ 50	John Olerud	.15	.07
❏ 51	Marc Newfield	.10	.05
❏ 52	Charles Johnson	.15	.07
❏ 53	Robby Thompson	.10	.05
❏ 54	Brian L. Hunter	.15	.07
❏ 55	Mike Blowers	.10	.05
❏ 56	Keith Lockhart	.10	.05
❏ 57	Ray Lankford	.15	.07
❏ 58	Tim Wallach	.10	.05
❏ 59	Ivan Rodriguez	.50	.23
❏ 60	Ed Sprague	.10	.05
❏ 61	Paul Molitor	.40	.18
❏ 62	Eric Karros	.15	.07
❏ 63	Glenallen Hill	.10	.05

❏ 64	Jay Bell	.15	.07
❏ 65	Tom Pagnozzi	.10	.05
❏ 66	Greg Colbrunn	.10	.05
❏ 67	Edgar Martinez	.15	.07
❏ 68	Paul Sorrento	.10	.05
❏ 69	Kirt Manwaring	.10	.05
❏ 70	Pete Schourek	.10	.05
❏ 71	Orlando Merced	.10	.05
❏ 72	Shawon Dunston	.10	.05
❏ 73	Ricky Bottalico	.10	.05
❏ 74	Brady Anderson	.15	.07
❏ 75	Steve Ontiveros	.10	.05
❏ 76	Jim Abbott	.15	.07
❏ 77	Carl Everett	.15	.07
❏ 78	Mo Vaughn	.40	.18
❏ 79	Pedro Martinez	.50	.23
❏ 80	Harold Baines	.15	.07
❏ 81	Alan Trammell	.30	.14
❏ 82	Steve Avery	.10	.05
❏ 83	Jeff Cirillo	.15	.07
❏ 84	John Valentin	.10	.05
❏ 85	Bernie Williams	.40	.18
❏ 86	Andre Dawson	.30	.14
❏ 87	Dave Winfield	.40	.18
❏ 88	B.J. Surhoff	.15	.07
❏ 89	Jeff Blauser	.10	.05
❏ 90	Barry Larkin	.40	.18
❏ 91	Cliff Floyd	.15	.07
❏ 92	Sammy Sosa	1.25	.55
❏ 93	Andres Galarraga	.40	.18
❏ 94	Dave Nilsson	.10	.05
❏ 95	James Mouton	.10	.05
❏ 96	Marquis Grissom	.15	.07
❏ 97	Matt Williams	.40	.18
❏ 98	John Jaha	.10	.05
❏ 99	Don Mattingly	.75	.35
❏ 100	Tim Naehring	.10	.05
❏ 101	Kevin Appier	.15	.07
❏ 102	Bobby Higginson	.15	.07
❏ 103	Andy Pettitte	.30	.14
❏ 104	Ozzie Smith	.50	.23
❏ 105	Kenny Lofton	.30	.14
❏ 106	Ken Caminiti	.15	.07
❏ 107	Walt Weiss	.10	.05
❏ 108	Jack McDowell	.10	.05
❏ 109	Brian McRae	.10	.05
❏ 110	Gary Gaetti	.15	.07
❏ 111	Curtis Goodwin	.10	.05
❏ 112	Dennis Martinez	.15	.07
❏ 113	Omar Vizquel	.15	.07
❏ 114	Chipper Jones	1.00	.45
❏ 115	Mark Gubicza	.10	.05
❏ 116	Ruben Sierra	.15	.07
❏ 117	Eddie Murray	.40	.18
❏ 118	Chad Curtis	.10	.05
❏ 119	Hal Morris	.10	.05
❏ 120	Ben McDonald	.10	.05
❏ 121	Marty Cordova	.10	.05
❏ 122	Ken Griffey Jr. UER	2.00	.90
	Card says Ken homered from both sides;He is only a left hitter		
❏ 123	Gary Sheffield	.15	.07
❏ 124	Charlie Hayes	.10	.05
❏ 125	Shawn Green	.40	.18
❏ 126	Jason Giambi	.15	.07
❏ 127	Mark Langston	.10	.05
❏ 128	Mark Whiten	.10	.05
❏ 129	Greg Vaughn	.15	.07
❏ 130	Mark McGwire	2.00	.90
❏ 131	Hideo Nomo	.40	.18
❏ 132	Eric Karros	.40	.18
	Mike Piazza		
	Raul Mondesi		
	Hideo Nomo		
❏ 133	Jason Bere	.10	.05
❏ 134	Ken Griffey Jr. NAT	1.00	.45
❏ 135	Frank Thomas NAT	.40	.18
❏ 136	Cal Ripken NAT	.75	.35
❏ 137	Albert Belle NAT	.15	.07
❏ 138	Mike Piazza NAT	.60	.25
❏ 139	Dante Bichette NAT	.10	.05
❏ 140	Sammy Sosa NAT	.60	.25
❏ 141	Mo Vaughn NAT	.15	.07
❏ 142	Tim Salmon NAT	.10	.05
❏ 143	Reggie Sanders NAT	.10	.05

#	Player	Price 1	Price 2
144	Cecil Fielder NAT	.10	.05
145	Jim Edmonds NAT	.10	.05
146	Rafael Palmeiro NAT	.15	.07
147	Edgar Martinez NAT	.10	.05
148	Barry Bonds NAT	.30	.14
149	Manny Ramirez NAT	.40	.18
150	Larry Walker NAT	.15	.07
151	Jeff Bagwell NAT	.40	.18
152	Ron Gant NAT	.05	.02
153	Andres Galarraga NAT	.15	.07
154	Eddie Murray NAT	.15	.07
155	Kirby Puckett NAT	.40	.18
156	Will Clark NAT	.15	.07
157	Don Mattingly NAT	.40	.18
158	Mark McGwire NAT	1.00	.45
159	Dean Palmer NAT	.10	.05
160	Matt Williams NAT	.15	.07
161	Fred McGriff NAT	.10	.05
162	Joe Carter NAT	.15	.07
163	Juan Gonzalez NAT	.40	.18
164	Alex Ochoa	.10	.05
165	Ruben Rivera	.15	.07
166	Tony Clark	.40	.18
167	Brian Barber	.10	.05
168	Matt Lawton	.50	.23
169	Terrell Wade	.10	.05
170	Johnny Damon	.30	.14
171	Derek Jeter	1.25	.55
172	Phil Nevin	.10	.05
173	Robert Perez	.10	.05
174	C.J. Nitkowski	.10	.05
175	Joe Vitiello	.10	.05
176	Roger Cedeno	.15	.07
177	Ron Coomer	.10	.05
178	Chris Widger	.10	.05
179	Jimmy Haynes	.10	.05
180	Mike Sweeney	.75	.35
181	Howard Battle	.10	.05
182	John Wasdin	.10	.05
183	Jim Pittsley	.10	.05
184	Bob Wolcott	.10	.05
185	LaTroy Hawkins	.10	.05
186	Nigel Wilson	.10	.05
187	Dustin Hermanson	.10	.05
188	Chris Snopek	.10	.05
189	Mariano Rivera	.30	.14
190	Jose Herrera	.10	.05
191	Chris Stynes	.10	.05
192	Larry Thomas	.10	.05
193	David Bell	.10	.05
194	Frank Thomas CL	.40	.18
195	Ken Griffey Jr. CL	1.00	.45
196	Cal Ripken CL	.75	.35
197	Jeff Bagwell CL	.40	.18
198	Mike Piazza CL	.60	.25
199	Barry Bonds CL	.30	.14
200	Garret Anderson CL Chipper Jones	.40	.18
201	Frank Thomas	.75	.35
202	Michael Tucker	.25	.11
203	Kirby Puckett	.60	.25
204	Alex Gonzalez	.10	.05
205	Tony Gwynn	1.00	.45
206	Moises Alou	.15	.07
207	Albert Belle	.40	.18
208	Barry Bonds	.50	.23
209	Fred McGriff	.30	.14
210	Dennis Eckersley	.15	.07
211	Craig Biggio	.40	.18
212	David Cone	.30	.14
213	Will Clark	.40	.18
214	Cal Ripken	1.50	.70
215	Wade Boggs	.40	.18
216	Pete Schourek	.10	.05
217	Darren Daulton	.15	.07
218	Carlos Baerga	.15	.07
219	Larry Walker	.40	.18
220	Denny Neagle	.15	.07
221	Jim Edmonds	.30	.14
222	Lee Smith	.15	.07
223	Jason Isringhausen	.15	.07
224	Jay Buhner	.15	.07
225	John Olerud	.15	.07
226	Jeff Conine	.10	.05
227	Dean Palmer	.15	.07
228	Jim Abbott	.15	.07
229	Raul Mondesi	.15	.07
230	Tom Glavine	.40	.18
231	Kevin Seltzer	.10	.05
232	Lenny Dykstra	.15	.07
233	Brian Jordan	.15	.07
234	Rondell White	.15	.07
235	Bret Boone	.15	.07
236	Randy Johnson	.40	.18
237	Paul O'Neill	.25	.11
238	Jim Thome	.40	.18
239	Edgardo Alfonzo	.40	.18
240	Terry Pendleton	.10	.05
241	Harold Baines	.15	.07
242	Roberto Alomar	.40	.18
243	Mark Grace	.30	.14
244	Derek Bell	.15	.07
245	Vinny Castilla	.30	.14
246	Cecil Fielder	.15	.07
247	Roger Clemens	1.00	.45
248	Orel Hershiser	.15	.07
249	J.T. Snow	.15	.07
250	Rafael Palmeiro	.40	.18
251	Bret Saberhagen	.10	.05
252	Todd Hollandsworth	.10	.05
253	Ryan Klesko	.50	.23
254	Greg Maddux HH	1.00	.45
255	Ken Griffey Jr. HH	1.00	.45
256	Hideo Nomo HH	.15	.07
257	Frank Thomas HH	.40	.18
258	Cal Ripken HH	.75	.35
259	Jeff Bagwell HH	.40	.18
260	Barry Bonds HH	.30	.14
261	Mo Vaughn HH	.15	.07
262	Albert Belle HH	.25	.11
263	Sammy Sosa HH	.60	.25
264	Reggie Sanders HH	.10	.05
265	Mike Piazza HH	.60	.25
266	Chipper Jones HH	.50	.23
267	Tony Gwynn HH	.50	.23
268	Kirby Puckett HH	.40	.18
269	Wade Boggs HH	.15	.07
270	Will Clark HH	.15	.07
271	Gary Sheffield HH	.10	.05
272	Dante Bichette HH	.15	.07
273	Randy Johnson HH	.15	.07
274	Matt Williams HH	.15	.07
275	Alex Rodriguez HH	.60	.25
276	Tim Salmon HH	.10	.05
277	Johnny Damon HH	.10	.05
278	Manny Ramirez HH	.40	.18
279	Derek Jeter HH	.60	.25
280	Eddie Murray HH	.15	.07
281	Ozzie Smith HH	.40	.18
282	Garret Anderson HH	.10	.05
283	Raul Mondesi HH	.10	.05
284	Terry Steinbach	.10	.05
285	Carlos Garcia	.10	.05
286	Dave Justice	.40	.18
287	Eric Anthony	.10	.05
288	Benji Gil	.10	.05
289	Bob Hamelin	.10	.05
290	Dwayne Hosey	.10	.05
291	Andy Pettitte HH	.15	.07
292	Rod Beck	.10	.05
293	Shane Andrews	.10	.05
294	Julian Tavarez	.10	.05
295	Willie Greene	.15	.07
296	Ismael Valdes	.15	.07
297	Glenallen Hill	.10	.05
298	Troy Percival	.15	.07
299	Ray Durham	.15	.07
300	Jeff Conine 300	.10	.05
301	Ken Griffey Jr. 300	1.00	.45
302	Will Clark 300	.15	.07
303	Mike Greenwell 300	.10	.05
304	Carlos Baerga 300	.10	.05
305A	Paul Molitor 300	.15	.07
305B	Jeff Bagwell 300	.40	.18
306	Mark Grace 300	.10	.05
307	Don Mattingly 300	.40	.18
308	Hal Morris 300	.10	.05
309	Butch Huskey 300	.10	.05
310	Ozzie Guillen 300	.10	.05
311	Erik Hanson	.10	.05
312	Kenny Lofton 300	.30	.14
313	Edgar Martinez 300	.10	.05
314	Kurt Abbott	.10	.05
315	John Smoltz	.30	.14
316	Ariel Prieto	.10	.05
317	Mark Carreon	.10	.05
318	Kirby Puckett 300	.40	.18
319	Carlos Perez	.10	.05
320	Gary DiSarcina	.10	.05
321	Trevor Hoffman	.15	.07
322	Mike Piazza 300	.60	.25
323	Frank Thomas 300	.40	.18
324	Juan Acevedo	.10	.05
325	Bip Roberts	.10	.05
326	Javier Lopez	.15	.07
327	Benito Santiago	.10	.05
328	Mark Lewis	.10	.05
329	Royce Clayton	.10	.05
330	Tom Gordon	.10	.05
331	Ben McDonald	.10	.05
332	Dan Wilson	.10	.05
333	Ron Gant	.10	.05
334	Wade Boggs 300	.15	.07
335	Paul Molitor	.40	.18
336	Tony Gwynn 300	.50	.23
337	Sean Berry	.10	.05
338	Rickey Henderson	.50	.23
339	Wil Cordero	.10	.05
340	Kent Mercker	.10	.05
341	Kenny Rogers	.10	.05
342	Ryne Sandberg	.50	.23
343	Charlie Hayes	.10	.05
344	Andy Benes	.15	.07
345	Sterling Hitchcock	.10	.05
346	Bernard Gilkey	.10	.05
347	Julio Franco	.10	.05
348	Ken Hill	.10	.05
349	Russ Davis	.10	.05
350	Mike Blowers	.10	.05
351	B.J. Surhoff	.15	.07
352	Lance Johnson	.10	.05
353	Darryl Hamilton	.10	.05
354	Shawon Dunston	.10	.05
355	Rick Aguilera	.10	.05
356	Danny Tartabull	.10	.05
357	Todd Stottlemyre	.10	.05
358	Mike Bordick	.10	.05
359	Jack McDowell	.10	.05
360	Todd Zeile	.10	.05
361	Tino Martinez	.15	.07
362	Greg Gagne	.10	.05
363	Mike Kelly	.10	.05
364	Tim Raines	.15	.07
365	Ernie Young	.10	.05
366	Mike Stanley	.10	.05
367	Wally Joyner	.15	.07
368	Karim Garcia	.15	.07
369	Paul Wilson	.10	.05
370	Sal Fasano	.10	.05
371	Jason Schmidt	.10	.05
372	Livan Hernandez	.60	.25
373	George Arias	.10	.05
374	Steve Gibralter	.10	.05
375	Jermaine Dye	.15	.07
376	Jason Kendall	.40	.18
377	Brooks Kieschnick	.10	.05
378	Jeff Ware	.10	.05
379	Alan Benes	.15	.07
380	Rey Ordonez	.40	.18
381	Jay Powell	.10	.05
382	Osvaldo Fernandez	.10	.05
383	Wilton Guerrero	.30	.14
384	Eric Owens	.10	.05
385	George Williams	.10	.05
386	Chan Ho Park	.30	.14
387	Jeff Suppan	.10	.05
388	F.P. Santangelo	.10	.05
389	Terry Adams	.10	.05
390	Bob Abreu	.10	.05
391	Quinton McCracken	.10	.05
392	Mike Busby	.10	.05
393	Cal Ripken CL	.75	.35
394	Ken Griffey Jr. CL	1.00	.45
395	Frank Thomas CL	.40	.18
396	Chipper Jones CL	.50	.23
397	Greg Maddux CL	.50	.23
398	Mike Piazza CL	.60	.25
399	Ken Griffey Jr CL	.75	.35

Cal Ripken Jr.
Chipper Jones
Frank Thomas
Greg Maddux
Mike Piazza
❏ CR1 Cal Ripken Tribute 15.00   6.75

1996 Pinnacle Christie Brinkley Collection

	MINT	NRMT
COMPLETE SET (16)	60.00	27.00
COMMON CARD (1-16)	1.50	.70
SER.2 STATED ODDS 1:23H/R, 1:19J, 1:32 M		

		MINT	NRMT
❏ 1	Greg Maddux	15.00	6.75
❏ 2	Ryan Klesko	2.00	.90
❏ 3	Dave Justice	5.00	2.20
❏ 4	Tom Glavine	5.00	2.20
❏ 5	Chipper Jones	15.00	6.75
❏ 6	Fred McGriff	3.00	1.35
❏ 7	Javier Lopez	2.00	.90
❏ 8	Marquis Grissom	1.50	.70
❏ 9	Jason Schmidt	1.50	.70
❏ 10	Albert Belle	5.00	2.20
❏ 11	Manny Ramirez	6.00	2.70
❏ 12	Carlos Baerga	1.50	.70
❏ 13	Sandy Alomar Jr.	2.00	.90
❏ 14	Jim Thome	5.00	2.20
❏ 15	Julio Franco	1.50	.70
❏ 16	Kenny Lofton	3.00	1.35
❏ PCB	Christie Brinkley Promo	6.00	2.70
	On the Beach		

1996 Pinnacle Essence of the Game

	MINT	NRMT
COMPLETE SET (18)	150.00	70.00
COMMON CARD (1-18)	2.00	.90
SER.1 STATED ODDS 1:23 HOBBY		

		MINT	NRMT
❏ 1	Cal Ripken	20.00	9.00
❏ 2	Greg Maddux	12.00	5.50
❏ 3	Frank Thomas	10.00	4.50
❏ 4	Matt Williams	5.00	2.20
❏ 5	Chipper Jones	12.00	5.50
❏ 6	Reggie Sanders	2.00	.90
❏ 7	Ken Griffey Jr.	25.00	11.00
❏ 8	Kirby Puckett	8.00	3.60

		MINT	NRMT
❏ 9	Hideo Nomo	5.00	2.20
❏ 10	Mike Piazza	15.00	6.75
❏ 11	Jeff Bagwell	6.00	2.70
❏ 12	Mo Vaughn	5.00	2.20
❏ 13	Albert Belle	5.00	2.20
❏ 14	Tim Salmon	3.00	1.35
❏ 15	Don Mattingly	10.00	4.50
❏ 16	Will Clark	5.00	2.20
❏ 17	Eddie Murray	5.00	2.20
❏ 18	Barry Bonds	6.00	2.70

1996 Pinnacle First Rate

	MINT	NRMT
COMPLETE SET (18)	120.00	55.00
COMMON CARD (1-18)	2.00	.90
SER.1 STATED ODDS 1:23 RETAIL		

		MINT	NRMT
❏ 1	Ken Griffey Jr.	30.00	13.50
❏ 2	Frank Thomas	12.00	5.50
❏ 3	Mo Vaughn	6.00	2.70
❏ 4	Chipper Jones	15.00	6.75
❏ 5	Alex Rodriguez	20.00	9.00
❏ 6	Kirby Puckett	10.00	4.50
❏ 7	Gary Sheffield	2.00	.90
❏ 8	Matt Williams	2.00	.90
❏ 9	Barry Bonds	8.00	3.60
❏ 10	Craig Biggio	6.00	2.70
❏ 11	Robin Ventura	2.00	.90
❏ 12	Michael Tucker	2.00	.90
❏ 13	Derek Jeter	20.00	9.00
❏ 14	Manny Ramirez	8.00	3.60
❏ 15	Barry Larkin	6.00	2.70
❏ 16	Shawn Green	6.00	2.70
❏ 17	Will Clark	6.00	2.70
❏ 18	Mark McGwire	30.00	13.50

1996 Pinnacle Power

	MINT	NRMT
COMPLETE SET (20)	120.00	55.00
COMMON CARD (1-20)	2.50	1.10
SER.1 STATED ODDS 1:35		

		MINT	NRMT
❏ 1	Frank Thomas	12.00	5.50
❏ 2	Mo Vaughn	6.00	2.70
❏ 3	Ken Griffey Jr.	30.00	13.50
❏ 4	Matt Williams	6.00	2.70
❏ 5	Barry Bonds	8.00	3.60

		MINT	NRMT
❏ 6	Reggie Sanders	2.50	1.10
❏ 7	Mike Piazza	20.00	9.00
❏ 8	Jim Edmonds	3.00	1.35
❏ 9	Dante Bichette	2.50	1.10
❏ 10	Sammy Sosa	20.00	9.00
❏ 11	Jeff Bagwell	8.00	3.60
❏ 12	Fred McGriff	3.00	1.35
❏ 13	Albert Belle	6.00	2.70
❏ 14	Tim Salmon	3.00	1.35
❏ 15	Joe Carter	2.50	1.10
❏ 16	Manny Ramirez	8.00	3.60
❏ 17	Eddie Murray	6.00	2.70
❏ 18	Cecil Fielder	2.00	.90
❏ 19	Larry Walker	6.00	2.70
❏ 20	Juan Gonzalez	12.00	5.50

1996 Pinnacle Project Stardom

	MINT	NRMT
COMPLETE SET (18)	150.00	70.00
COMMON CARD (1-18)	3.00	1.35
SEMISTARS	6.00	2.70
UNLISTED STARS	10.00	4.50
SER.2 STATED ODDS 1:35		

		MINT	NRMT
❏ 1	Paul Wilson	3.00	1.35
❏ 2	Derek Jeter	30.00	13.50
❏ 3	Karim Garcia	4.00	1.80
❏ 4	Johnny Damon	6.00	2.70
❏ 5	Alex Rodriguez	30.00	13.50
❏ 6	Chipper Jones	25.00	11.00
❏ 7	Charles Johnson	4.00	1.80
❏ 8	Bob Abreu	6.00	2.70
❏ 9	Alan Benes	3.00	1.35
❏ 10	Richard Hidalgo	4.00	1.80
❏ 11	Brooks Kieschnick	3.00	1.35
❏ 12	Garret Anderson	4.00	1.80
❏ 13	Livan Hernandez	10.00	4.50
❏ 14	Manny Ramirez	12.00	5.50
❏ 15	Jermaine Dye	4.00	1.80
❏ 16	Todd Hollandsworth	3.00	1.35
❏ 17	Raul Mondesi	4.00	1.80
❏ 18	Ryan Klesko	4.00	1.80

1996 Pinnacle Skylines

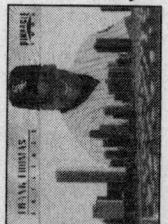

	MINT	NRMT
COMPLETE SET (18)	250.00	110.00
COMMON CARD (1-18)	6.00	2.70

	MINT	NRMT
UNLISTED STARS	10.00	4.50

SER.2 STATED ODDS 1:29 JUM, 1:50 MAG

		MINT	NRMT
❑ 1	Ken Griffey Jr.	50.00	22.00
❑ 2	Frank Thomas	20.00	9.00
❑ 3	Greg Maddux	25.00	11.00
❑ 4	Cal Ripken	40.00	18.00
❑ 5	Albert Belle	10.00	4.50
❑ 6	Mo Vaughn	10.00	4.50
❑ 7	Mike Piazza	30.00	13.50
❑ 8	Wade Boggs	10.00	4.50
❑ 9	Will Clark	10.00	4.50
❑ 10	Barry Bonds	12.00	5.50
❑ 11	Gary Sheffield	6.00	2.70
❑ 12	Hideo Nomo	10.00	4.50
❑ 13	Tony Gwynn	25.00	11.00
❑ 14	Kirby Puckett	15.00	6.75
❑ 15	Chipper Jones	25.00	11.00
❑ 16	Jeff Bagwell	12.00	5.50
❑ 17	Manny Ramirez	12.00	5.50
❑ 18	Raul Mondesi	6.00	2.70

1996 Pinnacle Slugfest

	MINT	NRMT
COMPLETE SET (18)	200.00	90.00
COMMON CARD (1-18)	4.00	1.80

SER.2 RETAIL STATED ODDS 1:35

		MINT	NRMT
❑ 1	Frank Thomas	20.00	9.00
❑ 2	Ken Griffey Jr.	40.00	18.00
❑ 3	Jeff Bagwell	8.00	3.60
❑ 4	Barry Bonds	8.00	3.60
❑ 5	Mo Vaughn	8.00	3.60
❑ 6	Albert Belle	8.00	3.60
❑ 7	Mike Piazza	25.00	11.00
❑ 8	Matt Williams	8.00	3.60
❑ 9	Dante Bichette	4.00	1.80
❑ 10	Sammy Sosa	20.00	9.00
❑ 11	Gary Sheffield	4.00	1.80
❑ 12	Reggie Sanders	4.00	1.80
❑ 13	Manny Ramirez	8.00	3.60
❑ 14	Eddie Murray	8.00	3.60
❑ 15	Juan Gonzalez	20.00	9.00
❑ 16	Dean Palmer	4.00	1.80
❑ 17	Rafael Palmeiro	8.00	3.60
❑ 18	Cecil Fielder	4.00	1.80

1996 Pinnacle Team Pinnacle

	MINT	NRMT
COMPLETE SET (9)	150.00	70.00
COMMON CARD (1-9)	4.00	1.80
UNLISTED STARS	6.00	2.70

SER.1 STATED ODDS 1:72

		MINT	NRMT
❑ 1	Frank Thomas / Jeff Bagwell	12.00	5.50
❑ 2	Chuck Knoblauch / Craig Biggio	6.00	2.70
❑ 3	Jim Thome / Matt Williams	4.00	1.80
❑ 4	Barry Larkin / Cal Ripken	25.00	11.00
❑ 5	Barry Bonds / Tim Salmon	8.00	3.60
❑ 6	Ken Griffey Jr. / Reggie Sanders	30.00	13.50
❑ 7	Albert Belle / Sammy Sosa	20.00	9.00
❑ 8	Ivan Rodriguez / Mike Piazza	20.00	9.00
❑ 9	Greg Maddux / Randy Johnson	15.00	6.75

1996 Pinnacle Team Spirit

	MINT	NRMT
COMPLETE SET (12)	250.00	110.00
COMMON CARD (1-12)	6.00	2.70

SER.2 STAT.ODDS 1:72H/R, 1:60J, 1:103M

		MINT	NRMT
❑ 1	Greg Maddux	25.00	11.00
❑ 2	Ken Griffey Jr.	40.00	18.00
❑ 3	Derek Jeter	20.00	9.00
❑ 4	Mike Piazza	25.00	11.00
❑ 5	Cal Ripken	30.00	13.50
❑ 6	Frank Thomas	20.00	9.00
❑ 7	Jeff Bagwell	8.00	3.60
❑ 8	Mo Vaughn	8.00	3.60
❑ 9	Albert Belle	8.00	3.60
❑ 10	Chipper Jones	20.00	9.00
❑ 11	Johnny Damon	6.00	2.70
❑ 12	Barry Bonds	8.00	3.60

1996 Pinnacle Team Tomorrow

	MINT	NRMT
COMPLETE SET (10)	60.00	27.00
COMMON CARD (1-10)	2.50	1.10
SEMISTARS	5.00	2.20
UNLISTED STARS	6.00	2.70

SER.1 STATED ODDS 1:19 JUMBO

		MINT	NRMT
❑ 1	Ruben Rivera	4.00	1.80
❑ 2	Johnny Damon	5.00	2.20
❑ 3	Raul Mondesi	4.00	1.80
❑ 4	Manny Ramirez	8.00	3.60
❑ 5	Hideo Nomo	6.00	2.70
❑ 6	Chipper Jones	15.00	6.75
❑ 7	Garret Anderson	4.00	1.80
❑ 8	Alex Rodriguez	20.00	9.00
❑ 9	Derek Jeter	20.00	9.00
❑ 10	Karim Garcia	4.00	1.80

1997 Pinnacle

	MINT	NRMT
COMPLETE SET (200)	20.00	9.00
COMMON CARD (1-200)	.15	.07
MINOR STARS	.30	.14
UNLISTED STARS	.60	.25
COM.MUSEUM (PP1-PP200)	1.50	.70

*MUSEUM STARS: 5X TO 12X HI COLUMN
*MUSEUM YOUNG STARS: 4X TO 10X HI
STATED ODDS 1:9 HOB/RET; 1:13 MAG

		MINT	NRMT
❑ 1	Cecil Fielder	.30	.14
❑ 2	Garret Anderson	.30	.14
❑ 3	Charles Nagy	.30	.14
❑ 4	Darryl Hamilton	.15	.07
❑ 5	Greg Myers	.15	.07
❑ 6	Eric Davis	.30	.14
❑ 7	Jeff Frye	.15	.07
❑ 8	Marquis Grissom	.30	.14
❑ 9	Curt Schilling	.40	.18
❑ 10	Jeff Fassero	.15	.07
❑ 11	Alan Benes	.15	.07
❑ 12	Orlando Miller	.15	.07
❑ 13	Alex Fernandez	.15	.07
❑ 14	Andy Pettitte	.40	.18
❑ 15	Andre Dawson	.40	.18
❑ 16	Mark Grudzielanek	.30	.14
❑ 17	Joe Vitiello	.15	.07
❑ 18	Juan Gonzalez	1.25	.55
❑ 19	Mark Whiten	.15	.07
❑ 20	Lance Johnson	.15	.07
❑ 21	Trevor Hoffman	.30	.14
❑ 22	Marc Newfield	.15	.07
❑ 23	Jim Eisenreich	.15	.07
❑ 24	Joe Carter	.30	.14
❑ 25	Jose Canseco	.75	.35
❑ 26	Bill Swift	.15	.07
❑ 27	Ellis Burks	.30	.14
❑ 28	Ben McDonald	.15	.07
❑ 29	Edgar Martinez	.30	.14
❑ 30	Jamie Moyer	.15	.07
❑ 31	Chan Ho Park	.60	.25
❑ 32	Carlos Delgado	.60	.25
❑ 33	Kevin Mitchell	.15	.07
❑ 34	Carlos Garcia	.15	.07
❑ 35	Darryl Strawberry	.30	.14
❑ 36	Jim Thome	.60	.25
❑ 37	Jose Offerman	.30	.14
❑ 38	Ryan Klesko	.30	.14

❑ 39 Ruben Sierra	.15	.07
❑ 40 Devon White	.30	.14
❑ 41 Brian Jordan	.30	.14
❑ 42 Tony Gwynn	1.50	.70
❑ 43 Rafael Palmeiro	.60	.25
❑ 44 Dante Bichette	.30	.14
❑ 45 Scott Stahoviak	.15	.07
❑ 46 Roger Cedeno	.30	.14
❑ 47 Ivan Rodriguez	.75	.35
❑ 48 Bob Abreu	.30	.14
❑ 49 Darryl Kile	.15	.07
❑ 50 Darren Dreifort	.30	.14
❑ 51 Shawon Dunston	.15	.07
❑ 52 Mark McGwire	3.00	1.35
❑ 53 Tim Salmon	.60	.25
❑ 54 Gene Schall	.15	.07
❑ 55 Roger Clemens	1.50	.70
❑ 56 Rondell White	.30	.14
❑ 57 Ed Sprague	.15	.07
❑ 58 Craig Paquette	.15	.07
❑ 59 David Segui	.30	.14
❑ 60 Jaime Navarro	.15	.07
❑ 61 Tom Glavine	.60	.25
❑ 62 Jeff Brantley	.15	.07
❑ 63 Kimera Bartee	.15	.07
❑ 64 Fernando Vina	.15	.07
❑ 65 Eddie Murray	.60	.25
❑ 66 Lenny Dykstra	.30	.14
❑ 67 Kevin Elster	.15	.07
❑ 68 Vinny Castilla	.40	.18
❑ 69 Mike Fetters	.15	.07
❑ 70 Brett Butler	.30	.14
❑ 71 Robby Thompson	.15	.07
❑ 72 Reggie Jefferson	.15	.07
❑ 73 Todd Hundley	.30	.14
❑ 74 Jeff King	.15	.07
❑ 75 Ernie Young	.15	.07
❑ 76 Jeff Bagwell	.75	.35
❑ 77 Dan Wilson	.15	.07
❑ 78 Paul Molitor	.60	.25
❑ 79 Kevin Seitzer	.15	.07
❑ 80 Kevin Brown	.40	.18
❑ 81 Ron Gant	.15	.07
❑ 82 Dwight Gooden	.30	.14
❑ 83 Todd Stottlemyre	.15	.07
❑ 84 Ken Caminiti	.40	.18
❑ 85 James Baldwin	.30	.14
❑ 86 Jermaine Dye	.30	.14
❑ 87 Harold Baines	.30	.14
❑ 88 Pat Hentgen	.15	.07
❑ 89 Frank Rodriguez	.15	.07
❑ 90 Mark Johnson	.40	.18
❑ 91 Jason Kendall	.40	.18
❑ 92 Alex Rodriguez	2.00	.90
❑ 93 Alan Trammell	.30	.14
❑ 94 Scott Brosius	.30	.14
❑ 95 Delino DeShields	.15	.07
❑ 96 Chipper Jones	1.50	.70
❑ 97 Barry Bonds	.75	.35
❑ 98 Brady Anderson	.30	.14
❑ 99 Ryne Sandberg	.75	.35
❑ 100 Albert Belle	.60	.25
❑ 101 Jeff Cirillo	.30	.14
❑ 102 Frank Thomas	1.25	.55
❑ 103 Mike Piazza	2.00	.90
❑ 104 Rickey Henderson	.75	.35
❑ 105 Rey Ordonez	.30	.14
❑ 106 Mark Grace	.40	.18
❑ 107 Terry Steinbach	.15	.07
❑ 108 Ray Durham	.30	.14
❑ 109 Barry Larkin	.60	.25
❑ 110 Tony Clark	.40	.18
❑ 111 Bernie Williams	.60	.25
❑ 112 John Smoltz	.40	.18
❑ 113 Moises Alou	.30	.14
❑ 114 Alex Gonzalez	.15	.07
❑ 115 Rico Brogna	.15	.07
❑ 116 Eric Karros	.30	.14
❑ 117 Jeff Conine	.15	.07
❑ 118 Todd Hollandsworth	.15	.07
❑ 119 Troy Percival	.30	.14
❑ 120 Paul Wilson	.15	.07
❑ 121 Orel Hershiser	.30	.14
❑ 122 Ozzie Smith	.75	.35
❑ 123 Dave Hollins	.15	.07
❑ 124 Ken Hill	.15	.07

❑ 125 Rick Wilkins	.15	.07
❑ 126 Scott Servais	.15	.07
❑ 127 Fernando Valenzuela	.30	.14
❑ 128 Mariano Rivera	.30	.14
❑ 129 Mark Loretta	.15	.07
❑ 130 Shane Reynolds	.30	.14
❑ 131 Darren Oliver	.15	.07
❑ 132 Steve Trachsel	.15	.07
❑ 133 Darren Bragg	.15	.07
❑ 134 Jason Dickson	.15	.07
❑ 135 Darrin Fletcher	.15	.07
❑ 136 Gary Gaetti	.30	.14
❑ 137 Joey Cora	.15	.07
❑ 138 Terry Pendleton	.15	.07
❑ 139 Derek Jeter	2.00	.90
❑ 140 Danny Tartabull	.15	.07
❑ 141 John Flaherty	.15	.07
❑ 142 B.J. Surhoff	.30	.14
❑ 143 Mike Sweeney	.30	.14
❑ 144 Chad Mottola	.15	.07
❑ 145 Andujar Cedeno	.15	.07
❑ 146 Tim Belcher	.15	.07
❑ 147 Mark Thompson	.15	.07
❑ 148 Rafael Bournigal	.15	.07
❑ 149 Marty Cordova	.15	.07
❑ 150 Osvaldo Fernandez	.15	.07
❑ 151 Mike Stanley	.15	.07
❑ 152 Ricky Bottalico	.30	.14
❑ 153 Donne Wall	.15	.07
❑ 154 Omar Vizquel	.30	.14
❑ 155 Mike Mussina	.60	.25
❑ 156 Brant Brown	.15	.07
❑ 157 F.P. Santangelo	.15	.07
❑ 158 Ryan Hancock	.15	.07
❑ 159 Jeff D'Amico	.15	.07
❑ 160 Luis Castillo	.30	.14
❑ 161 Darin Erstad	.60	.25
❑ 162 Ugueth Urbina	.30	.14
❑ 163 Andruw Jones	.75	.35
❑ 164 Steve Gibralter	.15	.07
❑ 165 Robin Jennings	.15	.07
❑ 166 Mike Cameron	.30	.14
❑ 167 George Arias	.15	.07
❑ 168 Chris Stynes	.15	.07
❑ 169 Justin Thompson	.30	.14
❑ 170 Jamey Wright	.15	.07
❑ 171 Todd Walker	.60	.25
❑ 172 Nomar Garciaparra	2.00	.90
❑ 173 Jose Paniagua	.15	.07
❑ 174 Marvin Benard	.15	.07
❑ 175 Rocky Coppinger	.15	.07
❑ 176 Quinton McCracken	.15	.07
❑ 177 Amaury Telemaco	.15	.07
❑ 178 Neifi Perez	.30	.14
❑ 179 Todd Greene	.30	.14
❑ 180 Jason Thompson	.15	.07
❑ 181 Wilton Guerrero	.15	.07
❑ 182 Edgar Renteria	.30	.14
❑ 183 Billy Wagner	.30	.14
❑ 184 Alex Ochoa	.15	.07
❑ 185 Dmitri Young	.30	.14
❑ 186 Kenny Lofton CT	.40	.18
❑ 187 Andres Galarraga CT	.30	.14
❑ 188 Chuck Knoblauch CT	.30	.14
❑ 189 Greg Maddux CT	1.50	.70
❑ 190 Mo Vaughn CT	.60	.25
❑ 191 Cal Ripken CT	2.50	1.10
❑ 192 Hideo Nomo CT	.30	.14
❑ 193 Ken Griffey Jr. CT	3.00	1.35
❑ 194 Sammy Sosa CT	.30	.14
❑ 195 Jay Buhner CT	.15	.07
❑ 196 Manny Ramirez CT	.40	.18
❑ 197 Matt Williams CT	.30	.14
❑ 198 Andruw Jones CL	.40	.18
❑ 199 Darin Erstad CL	.60	.25
❑ 200 Trey Beamon CL	.15	.07

1997 Pinnacle Artist's Proofs

	MINT	NRMT
*BRONZE CARDS: 15X TO 40X BASE CARD HI		
*SILVER CARDS: 20X TO 50X BASE CARD HI		
*GOLD CARDS: 25X TO 60X BASE CARD HI		
STATED ODDS 1:47 HOB/RET, 1:55 MAG		

❑ PP1 Cecil Fielder B	10.00	4.50
❑ PP2 Garret Anderson B	10.00	4.50
❑ PP3 Charles Nagy B	10.00	4.50
❑ PP4 Darryl Hamilton B	6.00	2.70
❑ PP5 Greg Myers B	6.00	2.70
❑ PP6 Eric Davis B	10.00	4.50
❑ PP7 Jeff Frye B	6.00	2.70
❑ PP8 Marquis Grissom S	8.00	3.60
❑ PP9 Curt Schilling B	10.00	4.50
❑ PP10 Jeff Fassero B	6.00	2.70
❑ PP11 Alan Benes S	12.00	5.50
❑ PP12 Orlando Miller B	6.00	2.70
❑ PP13 Alex Fernandez B	6.00	2.70
❑ PP14 Andy Pettitte G	25.00	11.00
❑ PP15 Andre Dawson B	15.00	6.75
❑ PP16 Mark Grudzielanek B	10.00	4.50
❑ PP17 Joe Vitiello B	6.00	2.70
❑ PP18 Juan Gonzalez G	100.00	45.00
❑ PP19 Mark Whiten B	6.00	2.70
❑ PP20 Lance Johnson B	6.00	2.70
❑ PP21 Trevor Hoffman B	10.00	4.50
❑ PP22 Marc Newfield B	6.00	2.70
❑ PP23 Jim Eisenreich B	6.00	2.70
❑ PP24 Joe Carter S	12.00	5.50
❑ PP25 Jose Canseco S	40.00	18.00
❑ PP26 Bill Swift B	6.00	2.70
❑ PP27 Ellis Burks B	10.00	4.50
❑ PP28 Ben McDonald B	6.00	2.70
❑ PP29 Edgar Martinez S	12.00	5.50
❑ PP30 Jamie Moyer B	6.00	2.70
❑ PP31 Chan Ho Park S	30.00	13.50
❑ PP32 Carlos Delgado S	30.00	13.50
❑ PP33 Kevin Mitchell B	6.00	2.70
❑ PP34 Carlos Garcia B	6.00	2.70
❑ PP35 Darryl Strawberry G	15.00	6.75
❑ PP36 Jim Thome G	40.00	18.00
❑ PP37 Jose Offerman B	10.00	4.50
❑ PP38 Ryan Klesko S	12.00	5.50
❑ PP39 Ruben Sierra B	6.00	2.70
❑ PP40 Devon White B	10.00	4.50
❑ PP41 Brian Jordan B	15.00	6.75
❑ PP42 Tony Gwynn S	80.00	36.00
❑ PP43 Rafael Palmeiro S	30.00	13.50
❑ PP44 Dante Bichette B	10.00	4.50
❑ PP45 Scott Stahoviak B	6.00	2.70
❑ PP46 Roger Cedeno B	10.00	4.50
❑ PP47 Ivan Rodriguez G	50.00	22.00
❑ PP48 Bob Abreu S	12.00	5.50
❑ PP49 Darryl Kile B	6.00	2.70
❑ PP50 Darren Dreifort B	6.00	2.70
❑ PP51 Shawon Dunston B	6.00	2.70
❑ PP52 Mark McGwire S	150.00	70.00
❑ PP53 Tim Salmon S	30.00	13.50
❑ PP54 Gene Schall B	6.00	2.70
❑ PP55 Roger Clemens B	60.00	27.00
❑ PP56 Rondell White S	12.00	5.50
❑ PP57 Ed Sprague B	6.00	2.70
❑ PP58 Craig Paquette B	6.00	2.70
❑ PP59 David Segui B	6.00	2.70
❑ PP60 Jaime Navarro B	6.00	2.70
❑ PP61 Tom Glavine S	30.00	13.50
❑ PP62 Jeff Brantley B	6.00	2.70
❑ PP63 Kimera Bartee B	6.00	2.70
❑ PP64 Fernando Vina B	6.00	2.70
❑ PP65 Eddie Murray S	30.00	13.50
❑ PP66 Lenny Dykstra B	10.00	4.50
❑ PP67 Kevin Elster B	6.00	2.70
❑ PP68 Vinny Castilla B	10.00	4.50

		MINT	NRMT
❑ PP69 Mike Fetters S		8.00	3.60
❑ PP70 Brett Butler B		10.00	4.50
❑ PP71 Robby Thompson B		6.00	2.70
❑ PP72 Reggie Jefferson B		6.00	2.70
❑ PP73 Todd Hundley S		12.00	5.50
❑ PP74 Jeff King B		6.00	2.70
❑ PP75 Ernie Young S		8.00	3.60
❑ PP76 Jeff Bagwell G		50.00	22.00
❑ PP77 Dan Wilson B		6.00	2.70
❑ PP78 Paul Molitor G		40.00	18.00
❑ PP79 Kevin Seitzer B		6.00	2.70
❑ PP80 Kevin Brown S		20.00	9.00
❑ PP81 Ron Gant S		8.00	3.60
❑ PP82 Dwight Gooden S		12.00	5.50
❑ PP83 Todd Stottlemyre B		6.00	2.70
❑ PP84 Ken Caminiti G		15.00	6.75
❑ PP85 James Baldwin B		10.00	4.50
❑ PP86 Jermaine Dye S		12.00	5.50
❑ PP87 Harold Baines B		10.00	4.50
❑ PP88 Pat Hentgen B		6.00	2.70
❑ PP89 Frank Rodriguez B		6.00	2.70
❑ PP90 Mark Johnson B		6.00	2.70
❑ PP91 Jason Kendall S		20.00	9.00
❑ PP92 Alex Rodriguez G		120.00	55.00
❑ PP93 Alan Trammell B		10.00	4.50
❑ PP94 Scott Brosius B		10.00	4.50
❑ PP95 Delino DeShields B		6.00	2.70
❑ PP96 Chipper Jones S		80.00	36.00
❑ PP97 Barry Bonds S		40.00	18.00
❑ PP98 Brady Anderson S		12.00	5.50
❑ PP99 Ryne Sandberg S		40.00	18.00
❑ PP100 Albert Belle G		40.00	18.00
❑ PP101 Jeff Cirillo B		10.00	4.50
❑ PP102 Frank Thomas G		80.00	36.00
❑ PP103 Mike Piazza S		100.00	45.00
❑ PP104 Rickey Henderson B		30.00	13.50
❑ PP105 Rey Ordonez S		12.00	5.50
❑ PP106 Mark Grace S		20.00	9.00
❑ PP107 Terry Steinbach B		10.00	4.50
❑ PP108 Ray Durham B		10.00	4.50
❑ PP109 Barry Larkin S		40.00	18.00
❑ PP110 Tony Clark S		20.00	9.00
❑ PP111 Bernie Williams G		40.00	18.00
❑ PP112 John Smoltz G		25.00	11.00
❑ PP113 Moises Alou B		10.00	4.50
❑ PP114 Alex Gonzalez B		6.00	2.70
❑ PP115 Rico Brogna B		6.00	2.70
❑ PP116 Eric Karros B		10.00	4.50
❑ PP117 Jeff Conine S		8.00	3.60
❑ PP118 Todd Hollandsworth G		10.00	4.50
❑ PP119 Troy Percival S		12.00	5.50
❑ PP120 Paul Wilson S		8.00	3.60
❑ PP121 Orel Hershiser B		10.00	4.50
❑ PP122 Ozzie Smith S		40.00	18.00
❑ PP123 Dave Hollins B		6.00	2.70
❑ PP124 Ken Hill B		6.00	2.70
❑ PP125 Rick Wilkins B		6.00	2.70
❑ PP126 Scott Servais B		6.00	2.70
❑ PP127 F. Valenzuela B		10.00	4.50
❑ PP128 Mariano Rivera G		15.00	6.75
❑ PP129 Mark Loretta B		6.00	2.70
❑ PP130 Shane Reynolds S		12.00	5.50
❑ PP131 Darren Oliver B		6.00	2.70
❑ PP132 Steve Trachsel B		6.00	2.70
❑ PP133 Darren Bragg B		6.00	2.70
❑ PP134 Jason Dickson B		6.00	2.70
❑ PP135 Darren Fletcher B		6.00	2.70
❑ PP136 Gary Gaetti B		10.00	4.50
❑ PP137 Joey Cora B		6.00	2.70
❑ PP138 Terry Pendleton B		6.00	2.70
❑ PP139 Derek Jeter G		120.00	55.00
❑ PP140 Danny Tartabull B		6.00	2.70
❑ PP141 John Flaherty B		6.00	2.70
❑ PP142 B.J. Surhoff B		10.00	4.50
❑ PP143 Mark Sweeney B		6.00	2.70
❑ PP144 Chad Mottola B		6.00	2.70
❑ PP145 Andujar Cedeno B		6.00	2.70
❑ PP146 Tim Belcher B		6.00	2.70
❑ PP147 Mark Thompson B		6.00	2.70
❑ PP148 Rafael Bournigal B		6.00	2.70
❑ PP149 Marty Cordova S		8.00	3.60
❑ PP150 Osvaldo Fernandez B		6.00	2.70
❑ PP151 Mike Stanley B		6.00	2.70
❑ PP152 Ricky Bottalico B		10.00	4.50
❑ PP153 Donne Wall B		6.00	2.70
❑ PP154 Omar Vizquel B		10.00	4.50
❑ PP155 Mike Mussina S		30.00	13.50
❑ PP156 Brant Brown B		10.00	4.50
❑ PP157 F.P. Santangelo S		8.00	3.60
❑ PP158 Ryan Hancock B		6.00	2.70
❑ PP159 Jeff D'Amico B		6.00	2.70
❑ PP160 Luis Castillo B		10.00	4.50
❑ PP161 Darin Erstad G		40.00	18.00
❑ PP162 Ugueth Urbina B		10.00	4.50
❑ PP163 Andruw Jones G		40.00	18.00
❑ PP164 Steve Gibralter B		6.00	2.70
❑ PP165 Robin Jennings S		8.00	3.60
❑ PP166 Mike Cameron B		10.00	4.50
❑ PP167 George Arias S		8.00	3.60
❑ PP168 Chris Stynes B		6.00	2.70
❑ PP169 Justin Thompson B		10.00	4.50
❑ PP170 Jamey Wright B		6.00	2.70
❑ PP171 Todd Walker G		15.00	6.75
❑ PP172 Nomar Garciaparra B		80.00	36.00
❑ PP173 Jose Paniagua B		6.00	2.70
❑ PP174 Marvin Benard B		6.00	2.70
❑ PP175 Rocky Coppinger B		6.00	2.70
❑ PP176 Quinton McCracken B		6.00	2.70
❑ PP177 Amaury Telemaco B		6.00	2.70
❑ PP178 Neifi Perez B		10.00	4.50
❑ PP179 Todd Greene B		6.00	2.70
❑ PP180 Jason Thompson B		6.00	2.70
❑ PP181 Wilton Guerrero B		6.00	2.70
❑ PP182 Edgar Renteria S		12.00	5.50
❑ PP183 Billy Wagner S		10.00	4.50
❑ PP184 Alex Ochoa S		10.00	4.50
❑ PP185 Dmitri Young B		10.00	4.50
❑ PP186 Kenny Lofton CT B		25.00	11.00
❑ PP187 A. Galarraga CT B		25.00	11.00
❑ PP188 C. Knoblauch CT G		40.00	18.00
❑ PP189 Greg Maddux CT S		100.00	45.00
❑ PP190 Mo Vaughn CT S		30.00	13.50
❑ PP191 Cal Ripken CT G		150.00	70.00
❑ PP192 Hideo Nomo CT S		30.00	13.50
❑ PP193 Ken Griffey Jr. CT G		200.00	90.00
❑ PP194 Sammy Sosa CT S		100.00	45.00
❑ PP195 Jay Buhner CT S		12.00	5.50
❑ PP196 Manny Ramirez CT G		40.00	18.00
❑ PP197 Matt Williams CT S		10.00	4.50
❑ PP198 Andruw Jones CL B		10.00	4.50
❑ PP199 Darin Erstad CL B		25.00	11.00
❑ PP200 Trey Beamon CL B		6.00	2.70

1997 Pinnacle Cardfrontations

	MINT	NRMT
COMPLETE SET (20)	250.00	110.00
COMMON CARD (1-20)	4.00	1.80
UNLISTED STARS	8.00	3.60
SER.1 STATED ODDS 1:23 HOBBY		
❑ 1 Greg Maddux	30.00	13.50
Mike Piazza		
❑ 2 Tom Glavine	6.00	2.70
Ken Caminiti		
❑ 3 Randy Johnson	30.00	13.50
Cal Ripken		
❑ 4 Kevin Appier	40.00	18.00
Mark McGwire		
❑ 5 Andy Pettitte	15.00	6.75
Juan Gonzalez		
❑ 6 Pat Hentgen	8.00	3.60
Albert Belle		
❑ 7 Hideo Nomo	20.00	9.00
Chipper Jones		
❑ 8 Ismael Valdes	25.00	11.00
Sammy Sosa		
❑ 9 Mike Mussina	10.00	4.50
Manny Ramirez		
❑ 10 David Cone	6.00	2.70
Jay Buhner		
❑ 11 Mark Wohlers	8.00	3.60
Gary Sheffield		
❑ 12 Andy Benes	10.00	4.50
Barry Bonds		
❑ 13 Roger Clemens	20.00	9.00
Ivan Rodriguez		
❑ 14 Mariano Rivera	40.00	18.00
Ken Griffey Jr.		
❑ 15 Dwight Gooden	15.00	6.75
Frank Thomas		
❑ 16 John Wetteland	8.00	3.60
Darin Erstad		
❑ 17 John Smoltz	4.00	1.80
Brian Jordan		
❑ 18 Kevin Brown	10.00	4.50
Jeff Bagwell		
❑ 19 Jack McDowell	25.00	11.00
Alex Rodriguez		
❑ 20 Charles Nagy	8.00	3.60
Bernie Williams		

1997 Pinnacle Home/Away

	MINT	NRMT
COMPLETE SET (24)	400.00	180.00
*AWAY SINGLES: 4X TO 10X BASE CARD HI		
*HOME SINGLES: 6X TO 15X BASE CARD HI		
SER.1 STATED ODDS 1:33 JUMBO		
❑ 1 Chipper Jones Away	15.00	6.75
❑ 2 Chipper Jones Home	20.00	9.00
❑ 3 Ken Griffey Jr. Away	30.00	13.50
❑ 4 Ken Griffey Jr. Home	50.00	22.00
❑ 5 Mike Piazza Away	20.00	9.00
❑ 6 Mike Piazza Home	30.00	13.50
❑ 7 Frank Thomas Away	12.00	5.50
❑ 8 Frank Thomas Home	20.00	9.00
❑ 9 Jeff Bagwell Away	8.00	3.60
❑ 10 Jeff Bagwell Home	12.00	5.50
❑ 11 Alex Rodriguez Away	20.00	9.00
❑ 12 Alex Rodriguez Home	30.00	13.50
❑ 13 Barry Bonds Away	8.00	3.60
❑ 14 Barry Bonds Home	12.00	5.50
❑ 15 Mo Vaughn Away	8.00	3.60
❑ 16 Mo Vaughn Home	12.00	5.50
❑ 17 Derek Jeter Away	15.00	6.75
❑ 18 Derek Jeter Home	20.00	9.00
❑ 19 Mark McGwire Away	30.00	13.50
❑ 20 Mark McGwire Home	50.00	22.00
❑ 21 Cal Ripken Away	25.00	11.00
❑ 22 Cal Ripken Home	40.00	18.00
❑ 23 Albert Belle Away	8.00	3.60
❑ 24 Albert Belle Home	8.00	3.60

1997 Pinnacle Passport to the Majors

	MINT	NRMT
COMPLETE SET (25)	250.00	110.00

COMMON CARD (1-25) .... 1.50 .70
SER.1 STAT.ODDS 1:36 HOB/RET, 1:51 MAG

		MINT	NRMT
❏ 1	Greg Maddux	15.00	6.75
❏ 2	Ken Griffey Jr.	30.00	13.50
❏ 3	Frank Thomas	12.00	5.50
❏ 4	Cal Ripken	25.00	11.00
❏ 5	Mike Piazza	20.00	9.00
❏ 6	Alex Rodriguez	20.00	9.00
❏ 7	Mo Vaughn	6.00	2.70
❏ 8	Chipper Jones	15.00	6.75
❏ 9	Roberto Alomar	6.00	2.70
❏ 10	Edgar Martinez	3.00	1.35
❏ 11	Javier Lopez	3.00	1.35
❏ 12	Ivan Rodriguez	6.00	2.70
❏ 13	Juan Gonzalez	12.00	5.50
❏ 14	Carlos Baerga	1.50	.70
❏ 15	Sammy Sosa	20.00	9.00
❏ 16	Manny Ramirez	8.00	3.60
❏ 17	Raul Mondesi	3.00	1.35
❏ 18	Henry Rodriguez	1.50	.70
❏ 19	Rafael Palmeiro	6.00	2.70
❏ 20	Rey Ordonez	3.00	1.35
❏ 21	Hideo Nomo	6.00	2.70
❏ 22	Mac Suzuki	1.50	.70
❏ 23	Chan Ho Park	6.00	2.70
❏ 24	Larry Walker	6.00	2.70
❏ 25	Ruben Rivera	1.50	.70

1997 Pinnacle Shades

		MINT	NRMT
COMPLETE SET (10)		80.00	36.00
COMMON CARD (1-10)		2.00	.90
SER.1 STATED ODDS 1:23 MAGAZINE			
❏ 1	Ken Griffey Jr.	20.00	9.00
❏ 2	Juan Gonzalez	8.00	3.60
❏ 3	John Smoltz	2.50	1.10
❏ 4	Gary Sheffield	2.00	.90
❏ 5	Cal Ripken	15.00	6.75
❏ 6	Mo Vaughn	3.00	1.35
❏ 7	Brian Jordan	2.00	.90
❏ 8	Mike Piazza	12.00	5.50
❏ 9	Frank Thomas	8.00	3.60
❏ 10	Alex Rodriguez	12.00	5.50

1997 Pinnacle Team Pinnacle

		MINT	NRMT
COMPLETE SET (10)		200.00	90.00
COMMON CARD (1-10)		8.00	3.60
SER.1 STAT.ODDS 1:90 HOB/RET, 1:107 MAG			
❏ 1	Frank Thomas	20.00	9.00
	Jeff Bagwell		
❏ 2	Chuck Knoblauch	10.00	4.50
	Eric Young		
❏ 3	Ken Caminiti	10.00	4.50
	Jim Thome		
❏ 4	Alex Rodriguez	40.00	18.00
	Chipper Jones		
❏ 5	Mike Piazza	30.00	13.50
	Ivan Rodriguez		
❏ 6	Albert Belle	12.00	5.50
	Barry Bonds		
❏ 7	Ken Griffey Jr.	50.00	22.00
	Ellis Burks		
❏ 8	Juan Gonzalez	20.00	9.00
	Gary Sheffield		
❏ 9	John Smoltz	8.00	3.60
	Andy Pettitte		
❏ 10	Frank Thomas	12.00	5.50
	Jeff Bagwell		
	Chuck Knoblauch		
	Eric Young		
	Ken Caminiti		
	Jim Thome		
	Alex Rodriguez		
	Chipper Jones		
	Mike Piazza		
	Ivan Rodriguez		
	Albert Belle		
	Barry Bonds		
	Ken Griffey Jr.		
	Ellis Burks		
	Juan Gonzalez		
	Gary Sheffield		
	John Smoltz		
	Andy Pettit		

1998 Pinnacle

		MINT	NRMT
COMPLETE SET (200)		25.00	11.00
COMMON CARD (1-200)		.15	.07

MINOR STARS		.25	.11
SEMISTARS		.40	.18
UNLISTED STARS		.60	.25
COMMON AP (PP1-PP100)		4.00	1.80

*AP STARS: 10X TO 25X HI COLUMN
*AP YOUNG STARS: 8X TO 20X HI
AP STATED ODDS 1:39
AP NUMBERS DON'T MATCH BASIC CARDS
COMMON MUSEUM (PP1-PP100) 1.50 .70
*MUSEUM STARS: 4X TO 10X HI COLUMN
*MUSEUM YNG.STARS: 3X TO 8X HI
MUSEUM STATED ODDS 1:9
MUS.NUMBERS DON'T MATCH BASIC CARDS

❏ 1	Tony Gwynn	1.50	.70
❏ 2	Pedro Martinez	.75	.35
❏ 3	Kenny Lofton	.40	.18
❏ 4	Curt Schilling	.40	.18
❏ 5	Shawn Estes	.15	.07
❏ 6	Tom Glavine	.60	.25
❏ 7	Mike Piazza	2.00	.90
❏ 8	Ray Lankford	.25	.11
❏ 9	Barry Larkin	.60	.25
❏ 10	Tony Womack	.15	.07
❏ 11	Jeff Blauser	.15	.07
❏ 12	Rod Beck	.25	.11
❏ 13	Larry Walker	.60	.25
❏ 14	Greg Maddux	1.50	.70
❏ 15	Mark Grace	.40	.18
❏ 16	Ken Caminiti	.25	.11
❏ 17	Bobby Jones	.15	.07
❏ 18	Chipper Jones	1.50	.70
❏ 19	Javier Lopez	.25	.11
❏ 20	Moises Alou	.25	.11
❏ 21	Royce Clayton	.15	.07
❏ 22	Darryl Kile	.25	.11
❏ 23	Barry Bonds	.75	.35
❏ 24	Steve Finley	.25	.11
❏ 25	Andres Galarraga	.40	.18
❏ 26	Denny Neagle	.15	.07
❏ 27	Todd Hundley	.25	.11
❏ 28	Jeff Bagwell	.75	.35
❏ 29	Andy Pettitte	.25	.11
❏ 30	Darin Erstad	.40	.18
❏ 31	Carlos Delgado	.60	.25
❏ 32	Matt Williams	.60	.25
❏ 33	Will Clark	.60	.25
❏ 34	Vinny Castilla	.25	.11
❏ 35	Brad Radke	.25	.11
❏ 36	John Olerud	.25	.11
❏ 37	Andruw Jones	.60	.25
❏ 38	Jason Giambi	.25	.11
❏ 39	Scott Rolen	.75	.35
❏ 40	Gary Sheffield	.25	.11
❏ 41	Jimmy Key	.15	.07
❏ 42	Kevin Appier	.25	.11
❏ 43	Wade Boggs	.60	.25
❏ 44	Hideo Nomo	.60	.25
❏ 45	Manny Ramirez	.75	.35
❏ 46	Wilton Guerrero	.15	.07
❏ 47	Travis Fryman	.25	.11
❏ 48	Chili Davis	.15	.07
❏ 49	Jeromy Burnitz	.25	.11
❏ 50	Craig Biggio	.60	.25
❏ 51	Tim Salmon	.40	.18
❏ 52	Jose Cruz Jr.	.25	.11
❏ 53	Sammy Sosa	2.00	.90
❏ 54	Hideki Irabu	.25	.11
❏ 55	Chan Ho Park	.25	.11
❏ 56	Robin Ventura	.25	.11
❏ 57	Jose Guillen	.15	.07
❏ 58	Deion Sanders	.25	.11
❏ 59	Jose Canseco	.75	.35
❏ 60	Jay Buhner	.25	.11
❏ 61	Rafael Palmeiro	.60	.25
❏ 62	Vladimir Guerrero	.75	.35
❏ 63	Mark McGwire	4.00	1.80
❏ 64	Derek Jeter	2.00	.90
❏ 65	Bobby Bonilla	.25	.11
❏ 66	Raul Mondesi	.25	.11
❏ 67	Paul Molitor	.25	.11
❏ 68	Joe Carter	.25	.11
❏ 69	Marquis Grissom	.15	.07
❏ 70	Juan Gonzalez	1.25	.55
❏ 71	Kevin Orie	.15	.07

❏ 72 Rusty Greer .25 .11
❏ 73 Henry Rodriguez .25 .11
❏ 74 Fernando Tatis .60 .25
❏ 75 John Valentin .25 .11
❏ 76 Matt Morris .15 .07
❏ 77 Ray Durham .25 .11
❏ 78 Geronimo Berroa .15 .07
❏ 79 Scott Brosius .15 .07
❏ 80 Willie Greene .15 .07
❏ 81 Rondell White .25 .11
❏ 82 Doug Drabek .25 .11
❏ 83 Derek Bell .25 .11
❏ 84 Butch Huskey .15 .07
❏ 85 Doug Jones .15 .07
❏ 86 Jeff Kent .25 .11
❏ 87 Jim Edmonds .25 .11
❏ 88 Mark McLemore .15 .07
❏ 89 Todd Zeile .25 .11
❏ 90 Edgardo Alfonzo .40 .18
❏ 91 Carlos Baerga .15 .07
❏ 92 Jorge Fabregas .15 .07
❏ 93 Alan Benes .15 .07
❏ 94 Troy Percival .25 .11
❏ 95 Edgar Renteria .15 .07
❏ 96 Jeff Fassero .15 .07
❏ 97 Reggie Sanders .15 .07
❏ 98 Dean Palmer .25 .11
❏ 99 J.T. Snow .25 .11
❏ 100 Dave Nilsson .15 .07
❏ 101 Dan Wilson .15 .07
❏ 102 Rob Nen .15 .07
❏ 103 Damion Easley .25 .11
❏ 104 Kevin Foster .15 .07
❏ 105 Jose Offerman .15 .07
❏ 106 Steve Cooke .15 .07
❏ 107 Matt Stairs .15 .07
❏ 108 Darryl Hamilton .15 .07
❏ 109 Steve Karsay .15 .07
❏ 110 Gary DiSarcina .15 .07
❏ 111 Dante Bichette .25 .11
❏ 112 Billy Wagner .25 .11
❏ 113 David Segui .15 .07
❏ 114 Bobby Higginson .25 .11
❏ 115 Jeffrey Hammonds .15 .07
❏ 116 Kevin Brown .40 .18
❏ 117 Paul Sorrento .15 .07
❏ 118 Mark Leiter .15 .07
❏ 119 Charles Nagy .25 .11
❏ 120 Danny Patterson .15 .07
❏ 121 Brian McRae .15 .07
❏ 122 Jay Bell .25 .11
❏ 123 Jamie Moyer .15 .07
❏ 124 Carl Everett .25 .11
❏ 125 Greg Colbrunn .15 .07
❏ 126 Jason Kendall .25 .11
❏ 127 Luis Sojo .15 .07
❏ 128 Mike Lieberthal .25 .11
❏ 129 Reggie Jefferson .15 .07
❏ 130 Cal Eldred .15 .07
❏ 131 Orel Hershiser .25 .11
❏ 132 Doug Glanville .15 .07
❏ 133 Willie Blair .15 .07
❏ 134 Neifi Perez .15 .07
❏ 135 Sean Berry .15 .07
❏ 136 Chuck Finley .15 .07
❏ 137 Alex Gonzalez .15 .07
❏ 138 Dennis Eckersley .25 .11
❏ 139 Kenny Rogers .15 .07
❏ 140 Troy O'Leary .15 .07
❏ 141 Roger Bailey .15 .07
❏ 142 Yamil Benitez .15 .07
❏ 143 Wally Joyner .25 .11
❏ 144 Bobby Witt .15 .07
❏ 145 Pete Schourek .15 .07
❏ 146 Terry Steinbach .15 .07
❏ 147 B.J. Surhoff .15 .07
❏ 148 Esteban Loaiza .15 .07
❏ 149 Heathcliff Slocumb .15 .07
❏ 150 Ed Sprague .15 .07
❏ 151 Gregg Jefferies .15 .07
❏ 152 Scott Erickson .15 .07
❏ 153 Jaime Navarro .15 .07
❏ 154 David Wells .25 .11
❏ 155 Alex Fernandez .15 .07
❏ 156 Tim Belcher .15 .07
❏ 157 Mark Grudzielanek .15 .07

❏ 158 Scott Hatteberg .15 .07
❏ 159 Paul Konerko .25 .11
❏ 160 Ben Grieve .60 .25
❏ 161 Abraham Nunez .15 .07
❏ 162 Shannon Stewart .25 .11
❏ 163 Jaret Wright .25 .11
❏ 164 Derek Lee .15 .07
❏ 165 Todd Dunwoody .15 .07
❏ 166 Steve Woodard .15 .07
❏ 167 Ryan McGuire .15 .07
❏ 168 Jeremi Gonzalez .15 .07
❏ 169 Mark Kotsay .25 .11
❏ 170 Brett Tomko .15 .07
❏ 171 Bobby Estalella .15 .07
❏ 172 Livan Hernandez .15 .07
❏ 173 Todd Helton .75 .35
❏ 174 Garrett Stephenson .15 .07
❏ 175 Pokey Reese .15 .07
❏ 176 Tony Saunders .15 .07
❏ 177 Antone Williamson .15 .07
❏ 178 Bartolo Colon .25 .11
❏ 179 Karim Garcia .15 .07
❏ 180 Juan Encarnacion .25 .11
❏ 181 Jacob Cruz .15 .07
❏ 182 Alex Rodriguez FV 1.00 .45
❏ 183 Cal Ripken FV 1.00 .45
  Roberto Alomar
❏ 184 Roger Clemens FV .75 .35
❏ 185 Derek Jeter FV 1.00 .45
❏ 186 Frank Thomas FV .60 .25
❏ 187 Ken Griffey Jr. FV 1.50 .70
❏ 188 Mark McGwire GJ 2.00 .90
❏ 189 Tino Martinez GJ .15 .07
❏ 190 Larry Walker GJ .25 .11
❏ 191 Brady Anderson GJ .15 .07
❏ 192 Jeff Bagwell GJ .40 .18
❏ 193 Ken Griffey Jr. GJ 1.50 .70
❏ 194 Chipper Jones GJ .75 .35
❏ 195 Ray Lankford GJ .15 .07
❏ 196 Jim Thome GJ .25 .11
❏ 197 Nomar Garciaparra GJ 1.00 .45
❏ 198 AS HR Contestants .75 .35
  Brady Anderson
  Jeff Bagwell
  Nomar Garciaparra
  Ken Griffey Jr.
  Chipper Jones
  Ray Lankford
  Tino Martinez
  Mark McGwire
  Jim Thome
  Larry Walker
❏ 199 Tino Martinez CL .15 .07
❏ 200 Jacobs Field CL .15 .07

1998 Pinnacle Hit It Here

	MINT	NRMT
COMPLETE SET (10)	40.00	18.00
COMMON CARD (1-10)	.75	.35
UNLISTED STARS	2.00	.90
STATED ODDS 1:17		

❏ 1 Larry Walker 2.00 .90
❏ 2 Ken Griffey Jr. 10.00 4.50
❏ 3 Mike Piazza 6.00 2.70
❏ 4 Frank Thomas 4.00 1.80

❏ 5 Barry Bonds 2.50 1.10
❏ 6 Albert Belle 2.00 .90
❏ 7 Tino Martinez .75 .35
❏ 8 Mark McGwire 12.00 5.50
❏ 9 Juan Gonzalez 4.00 1.80
❏ 10 Jeff Bagwell 2.50 1.10

1998 Pinnacle Power Pack Jumbos

	MINT	NRMT
COMPLETE SET (24)	30.00	13.50
COMMON CARD (1-24)	.40	.18
UNLISTED STARS	.75	.35
ONE PER POWER PACK		

❏ 1 Alex Rodriguez FV 2.50 1.10
❏ 2 Cal Ripken 2.50 1.10
  Roberto Alomar FV
❏ 3 Roger Clemens FV 2.00 .90
❏ 4 Derek Jeter FV 2.50 1.10
❏ 5 Frank Thomas FV 1.50 .70
❏ 6 Ken Griffey Jr. FV 4.00 1.80
❏ 7 Mark McGwire GJ 5.00 2.20
❏ 8 Tino Martinez GJ .40 .18
❏ 9 Larry Walker GJ .75 .35
❏ 10 Brady Anderson GJ .40 .18
❏ 11 Jeff Bagwell GJ 1.00 .45
❏ 12 Ken Griffey Jr. GJ 4.00 1.80
❏ 13 Chipper Jones GJ 2.00 .90
❏ 14 Ray Lankford GJ .40 .18
❏ 15 Jim Thome GJ .75 .35
❏ 16 Nomar Garciaparra GJ 2.50 1.10
❏ 17 Mike Piazza 2.50 1.10
❏ 18 Andruw Jones .75 .35
❏ 19 Greg Maddux 2.00 .90
❏ 20 Tony Gwynn 2.00 .90
❏ 21 Larry Walker .75 .35
❏ 22 Jeff Bagwell 1.00 .45
❏ 23 Chipper Jones 2.00 .90
❏ 24 Scott Rolen 1.00 .45

1998 Pinnacle Spellbound

	MINT	NRMT
COMMON M.MCGWIRE	20.00	9.00
COMMON R.CLEMENS	8.00	3.60
COMMON F.THOMAS	6.00	2.70
COMMON S.ROLEN	5.00	2.20

COMMON K.GRIFFEY	15.00	6.75
COMMON L.WALKER	3.00	1.35
COMMON N.GARCIAPARRA	10.00	4.50
COMMON C.RIPKEN	12.00	5.50
COMMON T.GWYNN	8.00	3.60
STATED ODDS 1:17		

❏ 1	Mark McGwire M	20.00	9.00
❏ 2	Mark McGwire C	20.00	9.00
❏ 3	Mark McGwire W	20.00	9.00
❏ 4	Mark McGwire I	20.00	9.00
❏ 5	Mark McGwire R	20.00	9.00
❏ 6	Mark McGwire H	20.00	9.00
❏ 7	Mark McGwire E	20.00	9.00
❏ 8	Roger Clemens B	8.00	3.60
❏ 9	Roger Clemens O	8.00	3.60
❏ 10	Roger Clemens C	8.00	3.60
❏ 11	Roger Clemens K	8.00	3.60
❏ 12	Roger Clemens E	8.00	3.60
❏ 13	Roger Clemens T	8.00	3.60
❏ 14	Frank Thomas B	6.00	2.70
❏ 15	Frank Thomas G	6.00	2.70
❏ 16	Frank Thomas O	6.00	2.70
❏ 17	Frank Thomas N	6.00	2.70
❏ 18	Frank Thomas A	6.00	2.70
❏ 19	Frank Thomas R	6.00	2.70
❏ 20	Frank Thomas T	6.00	2.70
❏ 21	Scott Rolen R	5.00	2.20
❏ 22	Scott Rolen O	5.00	2.20
❏ 23	Scott Rolen L	5.00	2.20
❏ 24	Scott Rolen E	5.00	2.20
❏ 25	Scott Rolen N	5.00	2.20
❏ 26	Ken Griffey Jr. G	15.00	6.75
❏ 27	Ken Griffey Jr. R	15.00	6.75
❏ 28	Ken Griffey Jr. E	15.00	6.75
❏ 29	Ken Griffey Jr. F	15.00	6.75
❏ 30	Ken Griffey Jr. F	15.00	6.75
❏ 31	Ken Griffey Jr. E	15.00	6.75
❏ 32	Ken Griffey Jr. Y	15.00	6.75
❏ 33	Larry Walker W	3.00	1.35
❏ 34	Larry Walker A	3.00	1.35
❏ 35	Larry Walker L	3.00	1.35
❏ 36	Larry Walker K	3.00	1.35
❏ 37	Larry Walker E	3.00	1.35
❏ 38	Larry Walker R	3.00	1.35
❏ 39	Nomar Garciaparra N	10.00	4.50
❏ 40	Nomar Garciaparra O	10.00	4.50
❏ 41	Nomar Garciaparra M	10.00	4.50
❏ 42	Nomar Garciaparra A	10.00	4.50
❏ 43	Nomar Garciaparra R	10.00	4.50
❏ 44	Cal Ripken C	12.00	5.50
❏ 45	Cal Ripken A	12.00	5.50
❏ 46	Cal Ripken L	12.00	5.50
❏ 47	Tony Gwynn T	8.00	3.60
❏ 48	Tony Gwynn O	8.00	3.60
❏ 49	Tony Gwynn N	8.00	3.60
❏ 50	Tony Gwynn Y	8.00	3.60

1996 Pinnacle Aficionado

	MINT	NRMT
COMPLETE SET (200)	50.00	22.00
COMMON CARD (1-200)	.25	.11
MINOR STARS	.50	.23
UNLISTED STARS	1.00	.45
SUBSET CARDS HALF VALUE OF BASE CARDS		

COMP.AP SET (200)	1500.00	700.00
COMMON ART.PRF. (1-200)	4.00	1.80
*ART.PRF.STARS: 8X TO 20X HI COLUMN		
*ART.PRF.YOUNG STARS: 6X TO 15X HI		
AP STATED ODDS 1:35		

❏ 1	Jack McDowell	.25	.11
❏ 2	Jay Bell	.50	.23
❏ 3	Rafael Palmeiro	1.00	.45
❏ 4	Wally Joyner	.50	.23
❏ 5	Ozzie Smith	1.25	.55
❏ 6	Mark McGwire	5.00	2.20
❏ 7	Kevin Seitzer	.25	.11
❏ 8	Fred McGriff	.75	.35
❏ 9	Roger Clemens	2.50	1.10
❏ 10	Randy Johnson	1.00	.45
❏ 11	Cecil Fielder	.50	.23
❏ 12	David Cone	.75	.35
❏ 13	Chili Davis	.50	.23
❏ 14	Andres Galarraga	1.00	.45
❏ 15	Joe Carter	.50	.23
❏ 16	Ryne Sandberg	1.25	.55
❏ 17	Paul O'Neill	.50	.23
❏ 18	Cal Ripken	4.00	1.80
❏ 19	Wade Boggs	1.00	.45
❏ 20	Greg Gagne	.25	.11
❏ 21	Edgar Martinez	.50	.23
❏ 22	Greg Maddux	2.50	1.10
❏ 23	Ken Caminiti	.50	.23
❏ 24	Kirby Puckett	1.50	.70
❏ 25	Craig Biggio	1.00	.45
❏ 26	Will Clark	1.00	.45
❏ 27	Ron Gant	.25	.11
❏ 28	Eddie Murray	1.00	.45
❏ 29	Lance Johnson	.25	.11
❏ 30	Tony Gwynn	2.50	1.10
❏ 31	Dante Bichette	.50	.23
❏ 32	Darren Daulton	.50	.23
❏ 33	Danny Tartabull	.25	.11
❏ 34	Jeff King	.25	.11
❏ 35	Tom Glavine	1.00	.45
❏ 36	Rickey Henderson	1.25	.55
❏ 37	Jose Canseco	1.25	.55
❏ 38	Barry Larkin	1.00	.45
❏ 39	Dennis Martinez	.50	.23
❏ 40	Ruben Sierra	.25	.11
❏ 41	Bobby Bonilla	.50	.23
❏ 42	Jeff Conine	.25	.11
❏ 43	Lee Smith	.50	.23
❏ 44	Charlie Hayes	.25	.11
❏ 45	Walt Weiss	.25	.11
❏ 46	Jay Buhner	.50	.23
❏ 47	Kenny Rogers	.25	.11
❏ 48	Paul Molitor	1.00	.45
❏ 49	Hal Morris	.25	.11
❏ 50	Todd Stottlemyre	.25	.11
❏ 51	Mike Stanley	.25	.11
❏ 52	Mark Grace	.75	.35
❏ 53	Lenny Dykstra	.50	.23
❏ 54	Andre Dawson	.75	.35
❏ 55	Dennis Eckersley	.50	.23
❏ 56	Ben McDonald	.25	.11
❏ 57	Ray Lankford	.50	.23
❏ 58	Mo Vaughn	1.00	.45
❏ 59	Frank Thomas	2.00	.90
❏ 60	Julio Franco	.25	.11
❏ 61	Jim Abbott	.50	.23
❏ 62	Greg Vaughn	.50	.23
❏ 63	Marquis Grissom	.25	.11
❏ 64	Tino Martinez	.50	.23
❏ 65	Kevin Appier	.50	.23
❏ 66	Matt Williams	1.00	.45
❏ 67	Sammy Sosa	3.00	1.35
❏ 68	Larry Walker	1.00	.45
❏ 69	Ivan Rodriguez	1.25	.55
❏ 70	Eric Karros	.50	.23
❏ 71	Bernie Williams	1.00	.45
❏ 72	Carlos Baerga	.25	.11
❏ 73	Jeff Bagwell	1.25	.55
❏ 74	Pete Schourek	.25	.11
❏ 75	Ken Griffey Jr.	5.00	2.20
❏ 76	Bernard Gilkey	.25	.11
❏ 77	Albert Belle	1.00	.45
❏ 78	Chuck Knoblauch	1.00	.45
❏ 79	John Smoltz	.75	.35
❏ 80	Barry Bonds	1.25	.55
❏ 81	Vinny Castilla	.75	.35
❏ 82	John Olerud	.50	.23
❏ 83	Mike Mussina	1.00	.45
❏ 84	Alex Fernandez	.25	.11
❏ 85	Shawon Dunston	.25	.11
❏ 86	Travis Fryman	.50	.23
❏ 87	Moises Alou	.50	.23
❏ 88	Dean Palmer	.50	.23
❏ 89	Gregg Jefferies	.25	.11
❏ 90	Jim Thome	1.00	.45
❏ 91	Dave Justice	1.00	.45
❏ 92	B.J. Surhoff	.50	.23
❏ 93	Ramon Martinez	.50	.23
❏ 94	Gary Sheffield	.50	.23
❏ 95	Andy Benes	.50	.23
❏ 96	Reggie Sanders	.50	.23
❏ 97	Roberto Alomar	1.00	.45
❏ 98	Omar Vizquel	.50	.23
❏ 99	Juan Gonzalez	2.00	.90
❏ 100	Robin Ventura	.50	.23
❏ 101	Jason Isringhausen	.25	.11
❏ 102	Greg Colbrunn	.25	.11
❏ 103	Brian Jordan	.50	.23
❏ 104	Shawn Green	1.00	.45
❏ 105	Brian Hunter	.25	.11
❏ 106	Rondell White	.50	.23
❏ 107	Ryan Klesko	.50	.23
❏ 108	Sterling Hitchcock	.25	.11
❏ 109	Manny Ramirez	1.25	.55
❏ 110	Bret Boone	.50	.23
❏ 111	Michael Tucker	.25	.11
❏ 112	Julian Tavarez	.25	.11
❏ 113	Benji Gil	.25	.11
❏ 114	Kenny Lofton	.75	.35
❏ 115	Mike Kelly	.25	.11
❏ 116	Ray Durham	.50	.23
❏ 117	Trevor Hoffman	.50	.23
❏ 118	Butch Huskey	.25	.11
❏ 119	Phil Nevin	.25	.11
❏ 120	Pedro Martinez	1.25	.55
❏ 121	Wil Cordero	.25	.11
❏ 122	Tim Salmon	.75	.35
❏ 123	Jim Edmonds	.75	.35
❏ 124	Mike Piazza	3.00	1.35
❏ 125	Rico Brogna	.25	.11
❏ 126	John Mabry	.25	.11
❏ 127	Chipper Jones	1.50	.70
❏ 128	Johnny Damon	.75	.35
❏ 129	Raul Mondesi	.50	.23
❏ 130	Denny Neagle	.50	.23
❏ 131	Marc Newfield	.25	.11
❏ 132	Hideo Nomo	1.00	.45
❏ 133	Joe Vitiello	.25	.11
❏ 134	Garret Anderson	.50	.23
❏ 135	Dave Nilsson	.25	.11
❏ 136	Alex Rodriguez	3.00	1.35
❏ 137	Russ Davis	.25	.11
❏ 138	Frank Rodriguez	.25	.11
❏ 139	Royce Clayton	.25	.11
❏ 140	John Valentin	.50	.23
❏ 141	Marty Cordova	.25	.11
❏ 142	Alex Gonzalez	.25	.11
❏ 143	Carlos Delgado	1.00	.45
❏ 144	Willie Greene	.50	.23
❏ 145	Cliff Floyd	.50	.23
❏ 146	Bobby Higginson	.50	.23
❏ 147	J.T. Snow	.50	.23
❏ 148	Derek Bell	.50	.23
❏ 149	Edgardo Alfonzo	1.00	.45
❏ 150	Charles Johnson	.50	.23
❏ 151	Hideo Nomo GR	.50	.23
❏ 152	Larry Walker GR	.50	.23
❏ 153	Bob Abreu GR	.25	.11
❏ 154	Karim Garcia GR	.25	.11
❏ 155	Dave Nilsson GR	.25	.11
❏ 156	Chan Ho Park GR	.25	.11
❏ 157	Dennis Martinez GR	.25	.11
❏ 158	Sammy Sosa GR	1.50	.70
❏ 159	Rey Ordonez GR	.50	.23
❏ 160	Roberto Alomar GR	.50	.23
❏ 161	George Arias	.25	.11
❏ 162	Jason Schmidt	.25	.11
❏ 163	Derek Jeter	3.00	1.35
❏ 164	Chris Snopek	.25	.11
❏ 165	Todd Hollandsworth	.25	.11
❏ 166	Sal Fasano	.25	.11

		MINT	NRMT
❏ 167	Jay Powell	.25	.11
❏ 168	Paul Wilson	.25	.11
❏ 169	Jim Pittsley	.25	.11
❏ 170	LaTroy Hawkins	.25	.11
❏ 171	Bob Abreu	.75	.35
❏ 172	Mike Grace	.25	.11
❏ 173	Karim Garcia	.50	.23
❏ 174	Richard Hidalgo	.50	.23
❏ 175	Felipe Crespo	.25	.11
❏ 176	Terrell Wade	.25	.11
❏ 177	Steve Gibralter	.25	.11
❏ 178	Jermaine Dye	.50	.23
❏ 179	Alan Benes	.25	.11
❏ 180	Wilton Guerrero	.75	.35
❏ 181	Brooks Kieschnick	.25	.11
❏ 182	Roger Cedeno	.50	.23
❏ 183	Osvaldo Fernandez	.25	.11
❏ 184	Matt Lawton	1.25	.55
❏ 185	George Williams	.25	.11
❏ 186	Jimmy Haynes	.25	.11
❏ 187	Mike Busby	.25	.11
❏ 188	Chan Ho Park	.75	.35
❏ 189	Marc Barcelo	.25	.11
❏ 190	Jason Kendall	1.00	.45
❏ 191	Rey Ordonez	1.00	.45
❏ 192	Tyler Houston	.25	.11
❏ 193	John Wasdin	.25	.11
❏ 194	Jeff Suppan	.25	.11
❏ 195	Jeff Ware	.25	.11
❏ 196	Ken Griffey Jr. CL	2.50	1.10
❏ 197	Albert Belle CL	.50	.23
❏ 198	Mike Piazza CL	1.50	.70
❏ 199	Greg Maddux CL	1.25	.55
❏ 200	Frank Thomas CL	1.00	.45

1996 Pinnacle Aficionado Magic Numbers

		MINT	NRMT
	COMPLETE SET (10)	200.00	90.00
	COMMON CARD (1-10)	8.00	3.60
	STATED ODDS 1:72		
❏ 1	Ken Griffey Jr.	50.00	22.00
❏ 2	Greg Maddux	30.00	13.50
❏ 3	Frank Thomas	25.00	11.00
❏ 4	Mo Vaughn	8.00	3.60
❏ 5	Jeff Bagwell	8.00	3.60
❏ 6	Chipper Jones	25.00	11.00
❏ 7	Albert Belle	8.00	3.60
❏ 8	Cal Ripken	40.00	18.00
❏ 9	Matt Williams	8.00	3.60
❏ 10	Sammy Sosa	25.00	11.00

1996 Pinnacle Aficionado Rivals

		MINT	NRMT
	COMPLETE SET (24)	250.00	110.00
	COMMON CARD (1-24)	8.00	3.60
	STATED ODDS 1:24		
❏ 1	Ken Griffey / Frank Thomas	20.00	9.00
❏ 2	Frank Thomas	15.00	6.75

		MINT	NRMT
❏ 3	Cal Ripken / Mo Vaughn	8.00	3.60
❏ 4	Mo Vaughn / Ken Griffey Jr.	15.00	6.75
❏ 5	Ken Griffey Jr. / Cal Ripken	25.00	11.00
❏ 6	Frank Thomas	8.00	3.60
❏ 7	Cal Ripken / Ken Griffey Jr.	25.00	11.00
❏ 8	Mo Vaughn / Frank Thomas	8.00	3.60
❏ 9	Ken Griffey Jr. / Mo Vaughn	15.00	6.75
❏ 10	Frank Thomas / Ken Griffey Jr.	20.00	9.00
❏ 11	Cal Ripken / Frank Thomas	15.00	6.75
❏ 12	Mo Vaughn / Cal Ripken	10.00	4.50
❏ 13	Mike Piazza / Jeff Bagwell	8.00	3.60
❏ 14	Jeff Bagwell / Barry Bonds	8.00	3.60
❏ 15	Jeff Bagwell / Mike Piazza	8.00	3.60
❏ 16	Tony Gwynn / Mike Piazza	8.00	3.60
❏ 17	Mike Piazza / Barry Bonds	8.00	3.60
❏ 18	Jeff Bagwell / Tony Gwynn	8.00	3.60
❏ 19	Barry Bonds / Mike Piazza	8.00	3.60
❏ 20	Tony Gwynn / Jeff Bagwell	8.00	3.60
❏ 21	Mike Piazza / Jeff Bagwell	8.00	3.60
❏ 22	Barry Bonds / Jeff Bagwell	8.00	3.60
❏ 23	Tony Gwynn / Barry Bonds	8.00	3.60
❏ 24	Barry Bonds / Tony Gwynn	8.00	3.60

1996 Pinnacle Aficionado Slick Picks

		MINT	NRMT
	COMPLETE SET (32)	200.00	90.00
	COMMON CARD (1-32)	2.00	.90
	STATED ODDS 1:10		
❏ 1	Mike Piazza	15.00	6.75
❏ 2	Cal Ripken	20.00	9.00
❏ 3	Ken Griffey Jr.	25.00	11.00
❏ 4	Paul Wilson	2.00	.90
❏ 5	Frank Thomas	10.00	4.50
❏ 6	Mo Vaughn	5.00	2.20
❏ 7	Barry Bonds	6.00	2.70
❏ 8	Albert Belle	5.00	2.20
❏ 9	Jeff Bagwell	6.00	2.70
❏ 10	Dante Bichette	2.50	1.10
❏ 11	Hideo Nomo	5.00	2.20
❏ 12	Raul Mondesi	2.50	1.10
❏ 13	Manny Ramirez	6.00	2.70
❏ 14	Greg Maddux	12.00	5.50
❏ 15	Tony Gwynn	12.00	5.50
❏ 16	Ryne Sandberg	6.00	2.70
❏ 17	Reggie Sanders	2.50	1.10
❏ 18	Derek Jeter	15.00	6.75
❏ 19	Johnny Damon	3.00	1.35
❏ 20	Alex Rodriguez	15.00	6.75
❏ 21	Ryan Klesko	2.50	1.10
❏ 22	Jim Thome	5.00	2.20
❏ 23	Kenny Lofton	3.00	1.35
❏ 24	Tino Martinez	2.50	1.10
❏ 25	Randy Johnson	5.00	2.20
❏ 26	Wade Boggs	5.00	2.20
❏ 27	Juan Gonzalez	10.00	4.50
❏ 28	Kirby Puckett	8.00	3.60
❏ 29	Tim Salmon	3.00	1.35
❏ 30	Chipper Jones	12.00	5.50
❏ 31	Garret Anderson	2.50	1.10
❏ 32	Eddie Murray	5.00	2.20

1997 Pinnacle Certified

		MINT	NRMT
	COMPLETE SET (150)	40.00	18.00
	COMMON CARD (1-150)	.25	.11
	MINOR STARS	.50	.23
	UNLISTED STARS	1.00	.45
	COMP.SET EXCLUDES CRUZ JR. (151)		
	COMMON RED (1-150)	1.50	.70
	*RED STARS: 2.5X TO 6X HI COLUMN		
	*RED YNG.STARS: 2X TO 5X HI		
	RED STATED ODDS 1:5		
	SCARCE MIRROR BLACK PARALLELS EXIST		
❏ 1	Barry Bonds	1.25	.55
❏ 2	Mo Vaughn	1.00	.45
❏ 3	Matt Williams	1.00	.45
❏ 4	Ryne Sandberg	1.25	.55
❏ 5	Jeff Bagwell	1.25	.55
❏ 6	Alan Benes	.25	.11
❏ 7	John Wetteland	.50	.23
❏ 8	Fred McGriff	.75	.35
❏ 9	Craig Biggio	1.00	.45
❏ 10	Bernie Williams	1.00	.45
❏ 11	Brian Hunter	.50	.23
❏ 12	Sandy Alomar Jr.	.50	.23
❏ 13	Ray Lankford	.50	.23
❏ 14	Ryan Klesko	.50	.23
❏ 15	Jermaine Dye	.50	.23
❏ 16	Andy Benes	.50	.23

		MINT	NRMT
17	Albert Belle	1.00	.45
18	Tony Clark	.75	.35
19	Dean Palmer	.50	.23
20	Bernard Gilkey	.25	.11
21	Ken Caminiti	.75	.35
22	Alex Rodriguez	3.00	1.35
23	Tim Salmon	1.00	.45
24	Larry Walker	1.00	.45
25	Barry Larkin	1.00	.45
26	Mike Piazza	3.00	1.35
27	Brady Anderson	.50	.23
28	Cal Ripken	4.00	1.80
29	Charles Nagy	.50	.23
30	Paul Molitor	1.00	.45
31	Darin Erstad	1.00	.45
32	Rey Ordonez	.50	.23
33	Wally Joyner	.50	.23
34	David Cone	.75	.35
35	Sammy Sosa	3.00	1.35
36	Dante Bichette	.50	.23
37	Eric Karros	.50	.23
38	Omar Vizquel	.50	.23
39	Roger Clemens	2.50	1.10
40	Joe Carter	.50	.23
41	Frank Thomas	2.00	.90
42	Javy Lopez	.50	.23
43	Mike Mussina	1.00	.45
44	Gary Sheffield	.50	.23
45	Tony Gwynn	2.50	1.10
46	Jason Kendall	.75	.35
47	Jim Thome	1.00	.45
48	Andres Galarraga	1.00	.45
49	Mark McGwire	5.00	2.20
50	Troy Percival	.50	.23
51	Derek Jeter	3.00	1.35
52	Todd Hollandsworth	.25	.11
53	Ken Griffey Jr.	5.00	2.20
54	Randy Johnson	1.00	.45
55	Pat Hentgen	.50	.23
56	Rusty Greer	.50	.23
57	John Jaha	.25	.11
58	Kenny Lofton	.75	.35
59	Chipper Jones	2.50	1.10
60	Robb Nen	.25	.11
61	Rafael Palmeiro	1.00	.45
62	Mariano Rivera	.50	.23
63	Hideo Nomo	1.00	.45
64	Greg Vaughn	.50	.23
65	Ron Gant	.25	.11
66	Eddie Murray	1.00	.45
67	John Smoltz	.75	.35
68	Manny Ramirez	1.25	.55
69	Juan Gonzalez	2.00	.90
70	F.P. Santangelo	.25	.11
71	Moises Alou	.50	.23
72	Alex Ochoa	.25	.11
73	Chuck Knoblauch	1.00	.45
74	Raul Mondesi	.50	.23
75	J.T. Snow	.50	.23
76	Rickey Henderson	1.25	.55
77	Bobby Bonilla	.50	.23
78	Wade Boggs	1.00	.45
79	Ivan Rodriguez	1.25	.55
80	Brian Jordan	.50	.23
81	Al Leiter	.50	.23
82	Jay Buhner	.50	.23
83	Greg Maddux	2.50	1.10
84	Edgar Martinez	.75	.35
85	Kevin Brown	.75	.35
86	Eric Young	.50	.23
87	Todd Hundley	.50	.23
88	Ellis Burks	.50	.23
89	Marquis Grissom	.50	.23
90	Jose Canseco	1.25	.55
91	Henry Rodriguez	.75	.35
92	Andy Pettitte	.75	.35
93	Mark Grudzielanek	.50	.23
94	Dwight Gooden	.50	.23
95	Roberto Alomar	1.00	.45
96	Paul Wilson	.25	.11
97	Will Clark	1.00	.45
98	Rondell White	.50	.23
99	Charles Johnson	.50	.23
100	Jim Edmonds	.75	.35
101	Jason Giambi	.50	.23
102	Billy Wagner	.50	.23
103	Edgar Renteria	.50	.23
104	Johnny Damon	.50	.23
105	Jason Isringhausen	.25	.11
106	Andruw Jones	1.25	.55
107	Jose Guillen	.75	.35
108	Kevin Orie	.25	.11
109	Brian Giles	5.00	2.20
110	Danny Patterson	.25	.11
111	Vladimir Guerrero	1.50	.70
112	Scott Rolen	1.50	.70
113	Damon Mashore	.25	.11
114	Nomar Garciaparra	3.00	1.35
115	Todd Walker	1.00	.45
116	Wilton Guerrero	.25	.11
117	Bob Abreu	.50	.23
118	Brooks Kieschnick	.25	.11
119	Pokey Reese	.25	.11
120	Todd Greene	.25	.11
121	Dmitri Young	.25	.11
122	Raul Casanova	.25	.11
123	Glendon Rusch	.25	.11
124	Jason Dickson	.25	.11
125	Jorge Posada	.50	.23
126	Rod Myers	.25	.11
127	Bubba Trammell	1.00	.45
128	Scott Spiezio	.25	.11
129	Hideki Irabu	1.50	.70
130	Wendell Magee	.25	.11
131	Bartolo Colon	.50	.23
132	Chris Holt	.25	.11
133	Calvin Maduro	.25	.11
134	Ray Montgomery	.25	.11
135	Shannon Stewart	.50	.23
136	Ken Griffey Jr. CERT	2.50	1.10
137	Vladimir Guerrero CERT	1.00	.45
138	Roger Clemens CERT	1.25	.55
139	Mark McGwire CERT	2.50	1.10
140	Albert Belle CERT	.50	.23
141	Derek Jeter CERT	1.50	.70
142	Juan Gonzalez CERT	1.00	.45
143	Greg Maddux CERT	1.25	.55
144	Alex Rodriguez CERT	1.50	.70
145	Jeff Bagwell CERT	.50	.23
146	Cal Ripken CERT	2.00	.90
147	Tony Gwynn CERT	1.25	.55
148	Frank Thomas CERT	1.00	.45
149	Hideo Nomo CERT	.50	.23
150	Andruw Jones CERT	.75	.35
151	Jose Cruz Jr. Blue Jays	2.50	1.10

*ROOKIES: 20X TO 50X BASIC CARDS
STATED ODDS 1:299

1997 Pinnacle Certified Mirror Red

	MINT	NRMT
COMMON CARD (1-150)	8.00	3.60

*STARS: 12.5X TO 30X BASIC CARDS
*YNG.STARS: 10X TO 25X BASIC CARDS
*ROOKIES: 6X TO 15X BASIC CARDS
STATED ODDS 1:99

1997 Pinnacle Certified Certified Team

	MINT	NRMT
COMPLETE SET (20)	250.00	110.00
COMMON CARD (1-20)	3.00	1.35
UNLISTED STARS	6.00	2.70

STATED ODDS 1:19 HOBBY
*GOLD TEAM: 1X TO 2.5X HI COLUMN
GOLD TEAM STATED ODDS 1:119 HOBBY
GOLD TEAM PRINT RUN 475 SERIAL #'d SETS
*MIRROR GOLD: 6X TO 15X HI
MIR.GOLD: RANDOM INSERTS IN PACKS
MIR.GOLD PRINT RUN 25 SETS

		MINT	NRMT
1	Frank Thomas	12.00	5.50
2	Jeff Bagwell	8.00	3.60
3	Derek Jeter	20.00	9.00

1997 Pinnacle Certified Mirror Blue

	MINT	NRMT
COMMON CARD (1-150)	12.00	5.50

*STARS: 20X TO 50X BASIC CARDS
*YNG.STARS: 15X TO 40X BASIC CARDS
*ROOKIES: 10X TO 25X BASIC CARDS
STATED ODDS 1:299

1997 Pinnacle Certified Mirror Gold

	MINT	NRMT
COMMON CARD (1-150)	25.00	11.00

*STARS: 40X TO 100X BASIC CARDS
*YNG.STARS: 30X TO 80X BASIC CARDS

❏ 4 Chipper Jones	15.00	6.75
❏ 5 Alex Rodriguez	20.00	9.00
❏ 6 Ken Caminiti	5.00	2.20
❏ 7 Cal Ripken	25.00	11.00
❏ 8 Mo Vaughn	6.00	2.70
❏ 9 Ivan Rodriguez	8.00	3.60
❏ 10 Mike Piazza	20.00	9.00
❏ 11 Juan Gonzalez	12.00	5.50
❏ 12 Barry Bonds	8.00	3.60
❏ 13 Ken Griffey Jr.	30.00	13.50
❏ 14 Andruw Jones	8.00	3.60
❏ 15 Albert Belle	6.00	2.70
❏ 16 Gary Sheffield	4.00	1.80
❏ 17 Andy Pettitte	5.00	2.20
❏ 18 Hideo Nomo	6.00	2.70
❏ 19 Greg Maddux	15.00	6.75
❏ 20 John Smoltz	5.00	2.20

1997 Pinnacle Certified Lasting Impressions

	MINT	NRMT
COMPLETE SET (20)	150.00	70.00
COMMON CARD (1-20)	3.00	1.35
SEMISTARS	5.00	2.20
UNLISTED STARS	6.00	2.70
STATED ODDS 1:19 HOBBY		

❏ 1 Cal Ripken	25.00	11.00
❏ 2 Ken Griffey Jr.	30.00	13.50
❏ 3 Mo Vaughn	6.00	2.70
❏ 4 Brian Jordan	4.00	1.80
❏ 5 Mark McGwire	30.00	13.50
❏ 6 Chuck Knoblauch	6.00	2.70
❏ 7 Sammy Sosa	20.00	9.00
❏ 8 Brady Anderson	4.00	1.80
❏ 9 Frank Thomas	12.00	5.50
❏ 10 Tony Gwynn	15.00	6.75
❏ 11 Roger Clemens	15.00	6.75
❏ 12 Alex Rodriguez	20.00	9.00
❏ 13 Paul Molitor	6.00	2.70
❏ 14 Kenny Lofton	5.00	2.20
❏ 15 John Smoltz	5.00	2.20
❏ 16 Roberto Alomar	6.00	2.70
❏ 17 Randy Johnson	6.00	2.70
❏ 18 Ryne Sandberg	8.00	3.60
❏ 19 Manny Ramirez	8.00	3.60
❏ 20 Mike Mussina	6.00	2.70

1997 Pinnacle Inside

	MINT	NRMT
COMPLETE SET (150)	40.00	18.00
COMMON CARD (1-150)	.20	.09
MINOR STARS	.40	.18
UNLISTED STARS	.75	.35
COMMON CLUB EDIT (1-200)	1.25	.55
*CLUB EDIT.STARS: 2.5X TO 6X HI COLUMN		
*CLUB EDIT.YNG.STARS: 2X TO 5X HI		
CLUB EDIT.STATED ODDS 1:7		

❏ 1 David Cone	.50	.23
❏ 2 Sammy Sosa	2.50	1.10
❏ 3 Joe Carter	.40	.18
❏ 4 Juan Gonzalez	1.50	.70
❏ 5 Hideo Nomo	.75	.35
❏ 6 Moises Alou	.40	.18
❏ 7 Marc Newfield	.20	.09
❏ 8 Alex Rodriguez	2.50	1.10
❏ 9 Kimera Bartee	.20	.09
❏ 10 Chuck Knoblauch	.75	.35
❏ 11 Jason Isringhausen	.20	.09
❏ 12 Jermaine Allensworth	.20	.09
❏ 13 Frank Thomas	1.50	.70
❏ 14 Paul Molitor	.75	.35
❏ 15 John Mabry	.20	.09
❏ 16 Greg Maddux	2.00	.90
❏ 17 Rafael Palmeiro	.75	.35
❏ 18 Brian Jordan	.40	.18
❏ 19 Ken Griffey Jr.	4.00	1.80
❏ 20 Brady Anderson	.40	.18
❏ 21 Ruben Sierra	.40	.18
❏ 22 Travis Fryman	.40	.18
❏ 23 Cal Ripken	3.00	1.35
❏ 24 Will Clark	.75	.35
❏ 25 Todd Hollandsworth	.20	.09
❏ 26 Kevin Brown	.50	.23
❏ 27 Mike Piazza	2.50	1.10
❏ 28 Craig Biggio	.75	.35
❏ 29 Paul Wilson	.20	.09
❏ 30 Andres Galarraga	.75	.35
❏ 31 Chipper Jones	2.00	.90
❏ 32 Jason Giambi	.40	.18
❏ 33 Ernie Young	.20	.09
❏ 34 Marty Cordova	.40	.18
❏ 35 Albert Belle	.75	.35
❏ 36 Roger Clemens	2.00	.90
❏ 37 Ryne Sandberg	1.00	.45
❏ 38 Henry Rodriguez	.40	.18
❏ 39 Jay Buhner	.40	.18
❏ 40 Raul Mondesi	.40	.18
❏ 41 Jeff Fassero	.20	.09
❏ 42 Edgar Martinez	.40	.18
❏ 43 Trey Beamon	.20	.09
❏ 44 Mo Vaughn	.75	.35
❏ 45 Gary Sheffield	.40	.18
❏ 46 Ray Durham	.40	.18
❏ 47 Brett Butler	.40	.18
❏ 48 Ivan Rodriguez	1.00	.45
❏ 49 Fred McGriff	.50	.23
❏ 50 Dean Palmer	.40	.18
❏ 51 Rickey Henderson	1.00	.45
❏ 52 Andy Pettitte	.50	.23
❏ 53 Bobby Bonilla	.40	.18
❏ 54 Shawn Green	.75	.35
❏ 55 Tino Martinez	.40	.18
❏ 56 Tony Gwynn	2.00	.90
❏ 57 Tom Glavine	.75	.35
❏ 58 Eric Young	.40	.18
❏ 59 Kevin Appier	.40	.18
❏ 60 Barry Bonds	1.00	.45
❏ 61 Wade Boggs	.75	.35
❏ 62 Jason Kendall	.50	.23
❏ 63 Jeff Bagwell	1.00	.45
❏ 64 Jeff Conine	.20	.09
❏ 65 Greg Maddux	.40	.18
❏ 66 Eric Karros	.40	.18
❏ 67 Manny Ramirez	1.00	.45
❏ 68 John Smoltz	.50	.23
❏ 69 Terrell Wade	.20	.09
❏ 70 John Wetteland	.40	.18
❏ 71 Kenny Lofton	.50	.23
❏ 72 Jim Thome	.75	.35
❏ 73 Bill Pulsipher	.20	.09
❏ 74 Darryl Strawberry	.40	.18
❏ 75 Roberto Alomar	.75	.35
❏ 76 Bobby Higginson	.40	.18

❏ 77 James Baldwin	.40	.18
❏ 78 Mark McGwire	4.00	1.80
❏ 79 Jose Canseco	1.00	.45
❏ 80 Mark Grudzielanek	.40	.18
❏ 81 Ryan Klesko	.40	.18
❏ 82 Javy Lopez	.40	.18
❏ 83 Ken Caminiti	.50	.23
❏ 84 Dave Nilsson	.20	.09
❏ 85 Tim Salmon	.75	.35
❏ 86 Cecil Fielder	.40	.18
❏ 87 Derek Jeter	2.50	1.10
❏ 88 Garret Anderson	.40	.18
❏ 89 Dwight Gooden	.40	.18
❏ 90 Carlos Delgado	.75	.35
❏ 91 Ugueth Urbina	.40	.18
❏ 92 Chan Ho Park	.75	.35
❏ 93 Eddie Murray	.75	.35
❏ 94 Alex Ochoa	.20	.09
❏ 95 Rusty Greer	.40	.18
❏ 96 Mark Grace	.50	.23
❏ 97 Pat Hentgen	.40	.18
❏ 98 John Jaha	.20	.09
❏ 99 Charles Johnson	.40	.18
❏ 100 Jermaine Dye	.40	.18
❏ 101 Quinton McCracken	.20	.09
❏ 102 Troy Percival	.40	.18
❏ 103 Shane Reynolds	.40	.18
❏ 104 Rondell White	.40	.18
❏ 105 Charles Nagy	.40	.18
❏ 106 Alan Benes	.20	.09
❏ 107 Tom Goodwin	.20	.09
❏ 108 Ron Gant	.20	.09
❏ 109 Dan Wilson	.20	.09
❏ 110 Darin Erstad	.75	.35
❏ 111 Matt Williams	.75	.35
❏ 112 Barry Larkin	.75	.35
❏ 113 Mariano Rivera	.40	.18
❏ 114 Larry Walker	.75	.35
❏ 115 Jim Edmonds	.50	.23
❏ 116 Michael Tucker	.20	.09
❏ 117 Todd Hundley	.40	.18
❏ 118 Alex Fernandez	.20	.09
❏ 119 J.T. Snow	.40	.18
❏ 120 Ellis Burks	.40	.18
❏ 121 Steve Finley	.40	.18
❏ 122 Mike Mussina	.75	.35
❏ 123 Curtis Pride	.20	.09
❏ 124 Derek Bell	.40	.18
❏ 125 Dante Bichette	.40	.18
❏ 126 Terry Steinbach	.20	.09
❏ 127 Randy Johnson	.75	.35
❏ 128 Andruw Jones	1.00	.45
❏ 129 Vladimir Guerrero	1.25	.55
❏ 130 Ruben Rivera	.20	.09
❏ 131 Billy Wagner	.40	.18
❏ 132 Scott Rolen	1.25	.55
❏ 133 Rey Ordonez	.40	.18
❏ 134 Karim Garcia	.40	.18
❏ 135 George Arias	.20	.09
❏ 136 Todd Greene	.20	.09
❏ 137 Robin Jennings	.20	.09
❏ 138 Raul Casanova	.20	.09
❏ 139 Steve Gibralter	.20	.09
❏ 140 Edgar Renteria	.40	.18
❏ 141 Chad Mottola	.20	.09
❏ 142 Dmitri Young	.40	.18
❏ 143 Tony Clark	.50	.23
❏ 144 Todd Walker	.75	.35
❏ 145 Kevin Brown	.50	.23
❏ 146 Nomar Garciaparra	2.50	1.10
❏ 147 Neifi Perez	.40	.18
❏ 148 Derek Jeter CL	.75	.35
	Todd Hollandsworth	
❏ 149 Pat Hentgen CL	.20	.09
	John Smoltz	
❏ 150 Juan Gonzalez CL	.75	.35
	Ken Caminiti	

1997 Pinnacle Inside Diamond Edition

	MINT	NRMT
COMMON CARD (1-150)	8.00	3.60
*STARS: 15X TO 40X BASIC CARDS		
*YNG.STARS: 12.5X TO 30X BASIC CARDS		
STATED ODDS 1:63		

1997 Pinnacle Inside 40 Something

	MINT	NRMT
COMPLETE SET (16)	250.00	110.00
COMMON CARD (1-16)	5.00	2.20
SEMISTARS	8.00	3.60
UNLISTED STARS	12.00	5.50
STATED ODDS 1:47		

		MINT	NRMT
❑ 1	Juan Gonzalez	25.00	11.00
❑ 2	Barry Bonds	15.00	6.75
❑ 3	Ken Caminiti	8.00	3.60
❑ 4	Mark McGwire	60.00	27.00
❑ 5	Todd Hundley	5.00	2.20
❑ 6	Albert Belle	12.00	5.50
❑ 7	Ellis Burks	5.00	2.20
❑ 8	Jay Buhner	5.00	2.20
❑ 9	Brady Anderson	5.00	2.20
❑ 10	Vinny Castilla	8.00	3.60
❑ 11	Mo Vaughn	12.00	5.50
❑ 12	Ken Griffey Jr.	60.00	27.00
❑ 13	Sammy Sosa	40.00	18.00
❑ 14	Andres Galarraga	12.00	5.50
❑ 15	Gary Sheffield	5.00	2.20
❑ 16	Frank Thomas	25.00	11.00

1997 Pinnacle Inside Cans

	MINT	NRMT
COMPLETE SET (24)	25.00	11.00
*CANS: .3X TO .8X BASE CARD HI		
COMMON SEALED CAN	3.00	1.35
*SEALED: .75X TO 2X BASE HI ON 1.50+ CANS		

		MINT	NRMT
❑ 1	Kenny Lofton	.40	.18
❑ 2	Frank Thomas	2.00	.90
❑ 3	John Smoltz	.40	.18
❑ 4	Manny Ramirez	.75	.35
❑ 5	Alex Rodriguez	2.00	.90
❑ 6	Barry Bonds	.75	.35
❑ 7	Mo Vaughn	.60	.25
❑ 8	Ken Griffey Jr.	3.00	1.35
❑ 9	Albert Belle	.60	.25
❑ 10	Greg Maddux	1.50	.70
❑ 11	Juan Gonzalez	1.25	.55
❑ 12	Andy Pettitte	.40	.18
❑ 13	Jeff Bagwell	1.00	.45

		MINT	NRMT
❑ 14	Ryan Klesko	.30	.14
❑ 15	Chipper Jones	1.50	.70
❑ 16	Derek Jeter	2.00	.90
❑ 17	Ivan Rodriguez	.75	.35
❑ 18	Andruw Jones	1.25	.55
❑ 19	Mike Piazza	2.00	.90
❑ 20	Hideo Nomo	.60	.25
❑ 21	Ken Caminiti	.40	.18
❑ 22	Cal Ripken	2.50	1.10
❑ 23	Mark McGwire	3.00	1.35
❑ 24	Tony Gwynn	1.50	.70

1997 Pinnacle Inside Dueling Dugouts

	MINT	NRMT
COMPLETE SET (20)	350.00	160.00
COMMON CARD (1-20)	6.00	2.70
UNLISTED STARS	8.00	3.60
STATED ODDS 1:23		

		MINT	NRMT
❑ 1	Alex Rodriguez / Cal Ripken	50.00	22.00
❑ 2	Jeff Bagwell / Ken Caminiti	10.00	4.50
❑ 3	Barry Bonds / Albert Belle	10.00	4.50
❑ 4	Mike Piazza / Ivan Rodriguez	30.00	13.50
❑ 5	Chuck Knoblauch / Roberto Alomar	8.00	3.60
❑ 6	Ken Griffey Jr. / Andruw Jones	50.00	22.00
❑ 7	Chipper Jones / Jim Thome	20.00	9.00
❑ 8	Frank Thomas / Mo Vaughn	20.00	9.00
❑ 9	Fred McGriff / Mark McGwire	40.00	18.00
❑ 10	Brian Jordan / Tony Gwynn	20.00	9.00
❑ 11	Barry Larkin / Derek Jeter	25.00	11.00
❑ 12	Kenny Lofton / Bernie Williams	8.00	3.60
❑ 13	Juan Gonzalez / Manny Ramirez	15.00	6.75
❑ 14	Will Clark / Rafael Palmeiro	8.00	3.60
❑ 15	Greg Maddux / Roger Clemens	30.00	13.50
❑ 16	John Smoltz / Andy Pettitte	8.00	3.60
❑ 17	Mariano Rivera / John Wetteland	8.00	3.60
❑ 18	Hideo Nomo / Mike Mussina	8.00	3.60
❑ 19	Todd Hollandsworth / Darin Erstad	8.00	3.60
❑ 20	Vladimir Guerrero / Karim Garcia	12.00	5.50

1998 Pinnacle Inside

	MINT	NRMT
COMPLETE SET (150)	30.00	13.50
COMMON CARD (1-150)	.20	.09
MINOR STARS	.30	.14

	MINT	NRMT
SEMISTARS	.50	.23
UNLISTED STARS	.75	.35
COMMON CLUB EDIT. (1-150)	2.00	.90
*CLUB EDIT.STARS: 4X TO 10X HI COLUMN		
*CLUB EDIT.YNG.STARS: 3X TO 8X HI		
CLUB EDIT.STATED ODDS 1:7		

		MINT	NRMT
❑ 1	Darin Erstad	.50	.23
❑ 2	Derek Jeter	2.50	1.10
❑ 3	Alex Rodriguez	2.50	1.10
❑ 4	Bobby Higginson	.30	.14
❑ 5	Nomar Garciaparra	2.50	1.10
❑ 6	Kenny Lofton	.50	.23
❑ 7	Ivan Rodriguez	1.00	.45
❑ 8	Cal Ripken	3.00	1.35
❑ 9	Todd Hundley	.30	.14
❑ 10	Chipper Jones	2.00	.90
❑ 11	Barry Larkin	.75	.35
❑ 12	Roberto Alomar	.75	.35
❑ 13	Mo Vaughn	.75	.35
❑ 14	Sammy Sosa	2.50	1.10
❑ 15	Sandy Alomar Jr.	.30	.14
❑ 16	Albert Belle	.75	.35
❑ 17	Scott Rolen	1.00	.45
❑ 18	Pokey Reese	.20	.09
❑ 19	Ryan Klesko	.30	.14
❑ 20	Andres Galarraga	.50	.23
❑ 21	Justin Thompson	.20	.09
❑ 22	Gary Sheffield	.30	.14
❑ 23	David Justice	.30	.14
❑ 24	Ken Griffey Jr.	4.00	1.80
❑ 25	Andruw Jones	.75	.35
❑ 26	Jeff Bagwell	1.00	.45
❑ 27	Vladimir Guerrero	1.00	.45
❑ 28	Mike Piazza	2.50	1.10
❑ 29	Chuck Knoblauch	.30	.14
❑ 30	Rondell White	.30	.14
❑ 31	Greg Maddux	2.00	.90
❑ 32	Andy Pettitte	.30	.14
❑ 33	Larry Walker	.75	.35
❑ 34	Bobby Estalella	.20	.09
❑ 35	Frank Thomas	1.50	.70
❑ 36	Tony Womack	.20	.09
❑ 37	Tony Gwynn	2.00	.90
❑ 38	Barry Bonds	1.00	.45
❑ 39	Randy Johnson	.75	.35
❑ 40	Mark McGwire	5.00	2.20
❑ 41	Juan Gonzalez	1.50	.70
❑ 42	Tim Salmon	.50	.23
❑ 43	John Smoltz	.50	.23
❑ 44	Rafael Palmeiro	.75	.35
❑ 45	Mark Grace	.50	.23
❑ 46	Mike Cameron	.30	.14
❑ 47	Jim Thome	.75	.35
❑ 48	Neifi Perez	.30	.14
❑ 49	Kevin Brown	.50	.23
❑ 50	Craig Biggio	.75	.35
❑ 51	Bernie Williams	.75	.35
❑ 52	Hideo Nomo	.75	.35
❑ 53	Bob Abreu	.30	.14
❑ 54	Edgardo Alfonzo	.50	.23
❑ 55	Wade Boggs	.50	.23
❑ 56	Jose Guillen	.20	.09
❑ 57	Ken Caminiti	.30	.14
❑ 58	Paul Molitor	.75	.35
❑ 59	Shawn Estes	.20	.09
❑ 60	Edgar Martinez	.30	.14
❑ 61	Livan Hernandez	.20	.09

❏ 62 Ray Lankford	.30	.14
❏ 63 Rusty Greer	.30	.14
❏ 64 Jim Edmonds	.30	.14
❏ 65 Tom Glavine	.75	.35
❏ 66 Alan Benes	.20	.09
❏ 67 Will Clark	.75	.35
❏ 68 Garret Anderson	.30	.14
❏ 69 Javier Lopez	.30	.14
❏ 70 Mike Mussina	.75	.35
❏ 71 Kevin Orie	.20	.09
❏ 72 Matt Williams	.75	.35
❏ 73 Bobby Bonilla	.30	.14
❏ 74 Ruben Rivera	.20	.09
❏ 75 Jason Giambi	.30	.14
❏ 76 Todd Walker	.30	.14
❏ 77 Tino Martinez	.30	.14
❏ 78 Matt Morris	.20	.09
❏ 79 Fernando Tatis	.75	.35
❏ 80 Todd Greene	.20	.09
❏ 81 Fred McGriff	.50	.23
❏ 82 Brady Anderson	.30	.14
❏ 83 Mark Kotsay	.30	.14
❏ 84 Raul Mondesi	.30	.14
❏ 85 Moises Alou	.30	.14
❏ 86 Roger Clemens	2.00	.90
❏ 87 Wilton Guerrero	.20	.09
❏ 88 Shannon Stewart	.30	.14
❏ 89 Chan Ho Park	.30	.14
❏ 90 Carlos Delgado	.75	.35
❏ 91 Jose Cruz Jr.	.30	.14
❏ 92 Shawn Green	.75	.35
❏ 93 Robin Ventura	.30	.14
❏ 94 Reggie Sanders	.30	.14
❏ 95 Orel Hershiser	.30	.14
❏ 96 Dante Bichette	.30	.14
❏ 97 Charles Johnson	.30	.14
❏ 98 Pedro Martinez	1.00	.45
❏ 99 Mariano Rivera	.30	.14
❏ 100 Joe Randa	.20	.09
❏ 101 Jeff Kent	.30	.14
❏ 102 Jay Buhner	.30	.14
❏ 103 Brian Jordan	.30	.14
❏ 104 Jason Kendall	.30	.14
❏ 105 Scott Spiezio	.20	.09
❏ 106 Desi Relaford	.20	.09
❏ 107 Bernard Gilkey	.20	.09
❏ 108 Manny Ramirez	1.00	.45
❏ 109 Tony Clark	.30	.14
❏ 110 Eric Young	.20	.09
❏ 111 Johnny Damon	.30	.14
❏ 112 Glendon Rusch	.20	.09
❏ 113 Ben Grieve	.75	.35
❏ 114 Homer Bush	.20	.09
❏ 115 Miguel Tejada	.30	.14
❏ 116 Lou Collier	.20	.09
❏ 117 Derrek Lee	.20	.09
❏ 118 Jacob Cruz	.20	.09
❏ 119 Raul Ibanez	.20	.09
❏ 120 Ryan McGuire	.20	.09
❏ 121 Antone Williamson	.20	.09
❏ 122 Abraham Nunez	.20	.09
❏ 123 Jeff Abbott	.20	.09
❏ 124 Brett Tomko	.20	.09
❏ 125 Richie Sexson	.50	.23
❏ 126 Todd Helton	1.00	.45
❏ 127 Juan Encarnacion	.30	.14
❏ 128 Richard Hidalgo	.30	.14
❏ 129 Paul Konerko	.30	.14
❏ 130 Brad Fullmer	.20	.09
❏ 131 Jeremi Gonzalez	.20	.09
❏ 132 Jaret Wright	.30	.14
❏ 133 Derek Jeter IT	1.25	.55
❏ 134 Frank Thomas IT	.75	.35
❏ 135 Nomar Garciaparra IT	1.25	.55
❏ 136 Kenny Lofton IT	.30	.14
❏ 137 Jeff Bagwell IT	.50	.23
❏ 138 Todd Hundley IT	.20	.09
❏ 139 Alex Rodriguez IT	1.25	.55
❏ 140 Ken Griffey Jr. IT	2.00	.90
❏ 141 Sammy Sosa IT	1.25	.55
❏ 142 Greg Maddux IT	1.00	.45
❏ 143 Albert Belle IT	.30	.14
❏ 144 Cal Ripken IT	1.50	.70
❏ 145 Mark McGwire IT	2.50	1.10
❏ 146 Chipper Jones IT	1.00	.45
❏ 147 Charles Johnson IT	.20	.09

❏ 148 Ken Griffey Jr. CL	2.00	.90
❏ 149 Jose Cruz Jr. CL	.20	.09
❏ 150 Larry Walker CL	.30	.14

1998 Pinnacle Inside Diamond Edition

	MINT	NRMT
COMMON CARD (1-150)	8.00	3.60

*STARS: 15X TO 40X BASIC CARDS
*YNG. STARS: 12.5X TO 30X BASIC CARDS
STATED ODDS 1:67

1998 Pinnacle Inside Behind the Numbers

	MINT	NRMT
COMPLETE SET (20)	300.00	135.00
COMMON CARD (1-20)	3.00	1.35
UNLISTED STARS	8.00	3.60

STATED ODDS 1:23

❏ 1 Ken Griffey Jr.		40.00	18.00
❏ 2 Cal Ripken		30.00	13.50
❏ 3 Alex Rodriguez		25.00	11.00
❏ 4 Jose Cruz Jr.		3.00	1.35
❏ 5 Mike Piazza		25.00	11.00
❏ 6 Nomar Garciaparra		25.00	11.00
❏ 7 Scott Rolen		10.00	4.50
❏ 8 Andruw Jones		8.00	3.60
❏ 9 Frank Thomas		15.00	6.75
❏ 10 Mark McGwire		50.00	22.00
❏ 11 Ivan Rodriguez		10.00	4.50
❏ 12 Greg Maddux		20.00	9.00
❏ 13 Roger Clemens		20.00	9.00
❏ 14 Derek Jeter		25.00	11.00
❏ 15 Tony Gwynn		20.00	9.00
❏ 16 Ben Grieve		8.00	3.60
❏ 17 Jeff Bagwell		10.00	4.50
❏ 18 Chipper Jones		20.00	9.00
❏ 19 Hideo Nomo		8.00	3.60
❏ 20 Sandy Alomar Jr.		3.00	1.35

1998 Pinnacle Inside Cans

	MINT	NRMT
COMPLETE SET (23)	25.00	11.00
COMMON CAN (1-23)	.25	.11

UNLISTED STARS	.60	.25
COMMON SEALED CAN	3.00	1.35

*SEALED: 1X TO 2.5X HI ON 1.50+ CANS
*GOLD CANS: 2.5X TO 6X HI COLUMN
COMMON GOLD SEALED CAN 10.00   4.50
*GOLD SEALED: 3X TO 8X HI ON 1.50+ CANS
GOLD CAN STATED ODDS 1:24 HOBBY

❏ 1 Roger Clemens	1.50	.70
❏ 2 Jose Cruz Jr.	.25	.11
❏ 3 Nomar Garciaparra ROY	2.00	.90
❏ 4 Juan Gonzalez	1.25	.55
❏ 5 Ben Grieve	.60	.25
❏ 6 Ken Griffey Jr.	3.00	1.35
❏ 7 Vladimir Guerrero	.75	.35
❏ 8 Tony Gwynn	1.50	.70
❏ 9 Derek Jeter	2.00	.90
❏ 10 Andruw Jones	.60	.25
❏ 11 Chipper Jones	1.50	.70
❏ 12 Greg Maddux	1.50	.70
❏ 13 Mark McGwire	4.00	1.80
❏ 14 Hideo Nomo	.60	.25
❏ 15 Mike Piazza	2.00	.90
❏ 16 Cal Ripken	2.50	1.10
❏ 17 Alex Rodriguez	2.00	.90
❏ 18 Scott Rolen ROY	.75	.35
❏ 19 Frank Thomas	1.25	.55
❏ 20 Larry Walker MVP	.60	.25
❏ 21 Arizona Diamondbacks	.25	.11
❏ 22 Florida Marlins Champs	.25	.11
❏ 23 Tamps Bay Devil Rays	.25	.11

1998 Pinnacle Inside Stand-Up Guys

	MINT	NRMT
COMPLETE SET (50)	60.00	27.00
COMMON CARD (1AB-25CD)	1.00	.45
UNLISTED STARS	1.25	.55

CD CARDS EQUAL VALUE TO AB CARDS
ONE PER PACK

❏ 1AB Mike Piazza	6.00	2.70
Ken Griffey Jr.		
Tony Gwynn		
Cal Ripken		
❏ 1CD Ken Griffey Jr.	6.00	2.70
Tony Gwynn		
Cal Ripken		
Mike Piazza		

		MINT	NRMT

☐ 2AB Nomar Garciaparra 4.00 1.80
Andruw Jones
Scott Rolen
Alex Rodriguez
☐ 2CD Andruw Jones 4.00 1.80
Scott Rolen
Alex Rodriguez
Nomar Garciaparra
☐ 3AB Chipper Jones 3.00 1.35
Andruw Jones
Javy Lopez
Greg Maddux
☐ 3CD Andruw Jones 3.00 1.35
Javy Lopez
Greg Maddux
Chipper Jones
☐ 4AB Alex Rodriguez 5.00 2.20
Jay Buhner
Ken Griffey Jr.
Randy Johnson
☐ 4CD Jay Buhner 5.00 2.20
Ken Griffey Jr.
Randy Johnson
Alex Rodriguez
☐ 5AB Mo Vaughn 6.00 2.70
Frank Thomas
Mark McGwire
Jeff Bagwell
☐ 5CD Frank Thomas 6.00 2.70
Mark McGwire
Jeff Bagwell
Mo Vaughn
☐ 6AB Barry Larkin 4.00 1.80
Nomar Garciaparra
Alex Rodriguez
Derek Jeter
☐ 6CD Nomar Garciaparra 4.00 1.80
Alex Rodriguez
Derek Jeter
Barry Larkin
☐ 7AB Javy Lopez 2.50 1.10
Mike Piazza
Charles Johnson
Ivan Rodriguez
☐ 7CD Mike Piazza 2.50 1.10
Charles Johnson
Ivan Rodriguez
Javy Lopez
☐ 8AB Scott Rolen 4.00 1.80
Cal Ripken
Ken Caminiti
Chipper Jones
☐ 8CD Cal Ripken 4.00 1.80
Ken Caminiti
Chipper Jones
Scott Rolen
☐ 9AB Jose Guillen 2.00 .90
Jose Cruz Jr.
Andruw Jones
Vladimir Guerrero
☐ 9CD Jose Cruz Jr. 2.00 .90
Andruw Jones
Vladimir Guerrero
Jose Guillen
☐ 10AB Neifi Perez 1.00 .45
Larry Walker
Ellis Burks
Dante Bichette
☐ 10CD Larry Walker 1.00 .45
Ellis Burks
Dante Bichette
Neifi Perez
☐ 11AB Manny Ramirez 2.50 1.10
Juan Gonzalez
Vladimir Guerrero
Sammy Sosa
☐ 11CD Juan Gonzalez 2.50 1.10
Vladimir Guerrero
Sammy Sosa
Manny Ramirez
☐ 12AB Randy Johnson 3.00 1.35
Greg Maddux
Hideo Nomo
Roger Clemens
☐ 12CD Greg Maddux 3.00 1.35
Hideo Nomo

Roger Clemens
Randy Johnson
☐ 13AB Fernando Tatis 2.50 1.10
Ben Grieve
Jose Cruz Jr.
Paul Konerko
☐ 13CD Ben Grieve 2.50 1.10
Jose Cruz Jr.
Paul Konerko
Fernando Tatis
☐ 14AB Craig Biggio 1.50 .70
Ryne Sandberg
Roberto Alomar
Chuck Knoblauch
☐ 14CD Ryne Sandberg 1.50 .70
Roberto Alomar
Chuck Knoblauch
Craig Biggio
☐ 15AB Roberto Alomar 3.00 1.35
Cal Ripken
Rafael Palmeiro
Brady Anderson
☐ 15CD Cal Ripken 3.00 1.35
Rafael Palmeiro
Brady Anderson
Roberto Alomar
☐ 16AB Garret Anderson 1.00 .45
Darin Erstad
Tim Salmon
Jim Edmonds
☐ 16CD Darin Erstad 1.00 .45
Tim Salmon
Jim Edmonds
Garret Anderson
☐ 17AB Eric Karros 3.00 1.35
Mike Piazza
Raul Mondesi
Hideo Nomo
☐ 17CD Mike Piazza 3.00 1.35
Raul Mondesi
Hideo Nomo
Eric Karros
☐ 18AB Rusty Greer 1.50 .70
Ivan Rodriguez
Will Clark
Juan Gonzalez
☐ 18CD Ivan Rodriguez 1.50 .70
Will Clark
Juan Gonzalez
Rusty Greer
☐ 19AB Andy Pettitte 2.00 .90
Derek Jeter
Tino Martinez
Bernie Williams
☐ 19CD Derek Jeter 2.00 .90
Tino Martinez
Bernie Williams
Andy Pettitte
☐ 20AB Bernie Williams 4.00 1.80
Kenny Lofton
Brady Anderson
Ken Griffey Jr.
☐ 20CD Kenny Lofton 4.00 1.80
Brady Anderson
Ken Griffey Jr.
Bernie Williams
☐ 21AB Rickey Henderson 1.50 .70
Paul Molitor
Ryne Sandberg
Eddie Murray
☐ 21CD Paul Molitor 1.50 .70
Ryne Sandberg
Eddie Murray
Rickey Henderson
☐ 22AB Mark McGwire 6.00 2.70
Tony Clark
Jeff Bagwell
Frank Thomas
☐ 22CD Tony Clark 6.00 2.70
Jeff Bagwell
Frank Thomas
Mark McGwire
☐ 23AB Sandy Alomar Jr. 2.00 .90
Manny Ramirez
David Justice
Jim Thome

☐ 23CD Manny Ramirez 2.00 .90
David Justice
Jim Thome
Sandy Alomar
☐ 24AB Dante Bichette 1.50 .70
Barry Bonds
Jeff Bagwell
Albert Belle
☐ 24CD Barry Bonds 1.50 .70
Jeff Bagwell
Albert Belle
Dante Bichette
☐ 25AB Andruw Jones 6.00 2.70
Ken Griffey Jr.
Alex Rodriguez
Frank Thomas
☐ 25CD Ken Griffey Jr. 6.00 2.70
Alex Rodriguez
Frank Thomas
Andruw Jones

1998 Pinnacle Performers

	MINT	NRMT
COMPLETE SET (150)	20.00	9.00
COMMON CARD (1-150)	.10	.05
MINOR STARS	.15	.07
SEMISTARS	.25	.11
UNLISTED STARS	.40	.18
COMP.PEAK SET (150)	200.00	90.00
COMMON PEAK (1-150)	.75	.35

*PEAK STARS: 3X TO 8X HI COLUMN
*PEAK YNG.STARS: 2.5X TO 6X HI
PEAK PERFORMERS STATED ODDS 1:7

☐ 1 Ken Griffey Jr. 2.00 .90
☐ 2 Frank Thomas .75 .35
☐ 3 Cal Ripken 1.50 .70
☐ 4 Alex Rodriguez 1.25 .55
☐ 5 Greg Maddux 1.00 .45
☐ 6 Mike Piazza 1.25 .55
☐ 7 Chipper Jones 1.00 .45
☐ 8 Tony Gwynn 1.00 .45
☐ 9 Derek Jeter 1.25 .55
☐ 10 Jeff Bagwell .50 .23
☐ 11 Juan Gonzalez .75 .35
☐ 12 Nomar Garciaparra 1.25 .55
☐ 13 Andruw Jones .40 .18
☐ 14 Hideo Nomo .40 .18
☐ 15 Roger Clemens 1.00 .45
☐ 16 Mark McGwire 2.50 1.10
☐ 17 Scott Rolen .50 .23
☐ 18 Vladimir Guerrero .50 .23
☐ 19 Barry Bonds .50 .23
☐ 20 Darin Erstad .25 .11
☐ 21 Albert Belle .40 .18
☐ 22 Kenny Lofton .25 .11
☐ 23 Mo Vaughn .40 .18
☐ 24 Tony Clark .15 .07
☐ 25 Ivan Rodriguez .50 .23
☐ 26 Jose Cruz Jr. .15 .07
☐ 27 Larry Walker .15 .07
☐ 28 Jaret Wright .15 .07
☐ 29 Andy Pettitte .15 .07
☐ 30 Roberto Alomar .40 .18
☐ 31 Randy Johnson .40 .18
☐ 32 Manny Ramirez .50 .23

☐ 33 Paul Molitor	.40	.18
☐ 34 Mike Mussina	.40	.18
☐ 35 Jim Thome	.40	.18
☐ 36 Tino Martinez	.15	.07
☐ 37 Gary Sheffield	.15	.07
☐ 38 Chuck Knoblauch	.15	.07
☐ 39 Bernie Williams	.40	.18
☐ 40 Tim Salmon	.25	.11
☐ 41 Sammy Sosa	1.25	.55
☐ 42 Wade Boggs	.40	.18
☐ 43 Will Clark	.40	.18
☐ 44 Andres Galarraga	.25	.11
☐ 45 Raul Mondesi	.15	.07
☐ 46 Rickey Henderson	.50	.23
☐ 47 Jose Canseco	.50	.23
☐ 48 Pedro Martinez	.50	.23
☐ 49 Jay Buhner	.15	.07
☐ 50 Ryan Klesko	.15	.07
☐ 51 Barry Larkin	.40	.18
☐ 52 Charles Johnson	.15	.07
☐ 53 Tom Glavine	.40	.18
☐ 54 Edgar Martinez	.15	.07
☐ 55 Fred McGriff	.25	.11
☐ 56 Moises Alou	.15	.07
☐ 57 Dante Bichette	.15	.07
☐ 58 Jim Edmonds	.15	.07
☐ 59 Mark Grace	.25	.11
☐ 60 Chan Ho Park	.15	.07
☐ 61 Justin Thompson	.10	.05
☐ 62 John Smoltz	.25	.11
☐ 63 Craig Biggio	.40	.18
☐ 64 Ken Caminiti	.15	.07
☐ 65 Richard Hidalgo	.15	.07
☐ 66 Carlos Delgado	.40	.18
☐ 67 David Justice	.15	.07
☐ 68 J.T. Snow	.15	.07
☐ 69 Jason Giambi	.15	.07
☐ 70 Garret Anderson	.15	.07
☐ 71 Rondell White	.15	.07
☐ 72 Matt Williams	.40	.18
☐ 73 Brady Anderson	.15	.07
☐ 74 Eric Karros	.15	.07
☐ 75 Javier Lopez	.15	.07
☐ 76 Pat Hentgen	.10	.05
☐ 77 Todd Hundley	.15	.07
☐ 78 Ray Lankford	.15	.07
☐ 79 Denny Neagle	.10	.05
☐ 80 Sandy Alomar Jr.	.15	.07
☐ 81 Jason Kendall	.15	.07
☐ 82 Omar Vizquel	.15	.07
☐ 83 Kevin Brown	.25	.11
☐ 84 Kevin Appier	.15	.07
☐ 85 Al Martin	.15	.07
☐ 86 Rusty Greer	.15	.07
☐ 87 Bobby Bonilla	.15	.07
☐ 88 Shawn Estes	.10	.05
☐ 89 Rafael Palmeiro	.40	.18
☐ 90 Edgar Renteria	.15	.07
☐ 91 Alan Benes	.10	.05
☐ 92 Bobby Higginson	.10	.05
☐ 93 Mark Grudzielanek	.10	.05
☐ 94 Jose Guillen	.10	.05
☐ 95 Neifi Perez	.10	.05
☐ 96 Jeff Abbott	.10	.05
☐ 97 Todd Walker	.15	.07
☐ 98 Eric Young	.10	.05
☐ 99 Brett Tomko	.10	.05
☐ 100 Mike Cameron	.15	.07
☐ 101 Karim Garcia	.10	.05
☐ 102 Brian Jordan	.15	.07
☐ 103 Jeff Suppan	.10	.05
☐ 104 Robin Ventura	.15	.07
☐ 105 Henry Rodriguez	.15	.07
☐ 106 Shannon Stewart	.15	.07
☐ 107 Kevin Orie	.10	.05
☐ 108 Bartolo Colon	.15	.07
☐ 109 Bob Abreu	.15	.07
☐ 110 Vinny Castilla	.15	.07
☐ 111 Livan Hernandez	.10	.05
☐ 112 Derek Lee	.15	.07
☐ 113 Mark Kotsay	.15	.07
☐ 114 Todd Greene	.10	.05
☐ 115 Edgardo Alfonzo	.25	.11
☐ 116 A.J. Hinch	.15	.07
☐ 117 Paul Konerko	.15	.07
☐ 118 Todd Helton	.50	.23

☐ 119 Miguel Tejada	.15	.07
☐ 120 Fernando Tatis	.40	.18
☐ 121 Ben Grieve	.40	.18
☐ 122 Travis Lee	.25	.11
☐ 123 Kerry Wood	.50	.23
☐ 124 Eli Marrero	.10	.05
☐ 125 David Ortiz	.10	.05
☐ 126 Juan Encarnacion	.15	.07
☐ 127 Brad Fullmer	.25	.11
☐ 128 Richie Sexson	.25	.11
☐ 129 Aaron Boone	.10	.05
☐ 130 Enrique Wilson	.10	.05
☐ 131 Javier Valentin	.10	.05
☐ 132 Abraham Nunez	.10	.05
☐ 133 Ricky Ledee	.15	.07
☐ 134 Carl Pavano	.15	.07
☐ 135 Bobby Estalella	.10	.05
☐ 136 Homer Bush	.10	.05
☐ 137 Brian Rose	.10	.05
☐ 138 Ken Griffey Jr. FA	1.00	.45
☐ 139 Frank Thomas FA	.40	.18
☐ 140 Mike Piazza FA	.75	.35
☐ 141 Alex Rodriguez FA	.60	.25
☐ 142 Greg Maddux FA	.50	.23
☐ 143 Chipper Jones FA	.50	.23
☐ 144 Mike Piazza FA	.50	.23
☐ 145 Tony Gwynn FA	.50	.23
☐ 146 Derek Jeter FA	.60	.25
☐ 147 Jeff Bagwell FA	.25	.11
☐ 148 Checklist	.10	.05
☐ 149 Checklist	.10	.05
☐ 150 Checklist	.10	.05

1998 Pinnacle Performers Big Bang

	MINT	NRMT
COMPLETE SET (20)	200.00	90.00
COMMON CARD (1-20)	2.50	1.10
STATED ODDS 1:45		
STATED PRINT RUN 2500 SERIAL #'d SETS		

☐ 1 Ken Griffey Jr.	30.00	13.50
☐ 2 Frank Thomas	12.00	5.50
☐ 3 Mike Piazza	20.00	9.00
☐ 4 Chipper Jones	15.00	6.75
☐ 5 Alex Rodriguez	20.00	9.00
☐ 6 Nomar Garciaparra	20.00	9.00
☐ 7 Jeff Bagwell	8.00	3.60
☐ 8 Cal Ripken	25.00	11.00
☐ 9 Albert Belle	6.00	2.70
☐ 10 Mark McGwire	40.00	18.00
☐ 11 Juan Gonzalez	12.00	5.50
☐ 12 Larry Walker	6.00	2.70
☐ 13 Tino Martinez	2.50	1.10
☐ 14 Jim Thome	6.00	2.70
☐ 15 Manny Ramirez	8.00	3.60
☐ 16 Barry Bonds	8.00	3.60
☐ 17 Mo Vaughn	6.00	2.70
☐ 18 Jose Cruz Jr.	2.50	1.10
☐ 19 Tony Clark	2.50	1.10
☐ 20 Andruw Jones	6.00	2.70

1998 Pinnacle Performers Big Bang Seasonal Outburst

	MINT	NRMT
COMMON CARD (1-20)	20.00	9.00
RANDOM INSERTS IN PACKS		
PRINT RUNS LISTED BELOW		
THESE CARDS ARE NOT SERIAL #'d		

☐ 1 Ken Griffey Jr./56	200.00	90.00
☐ 2 Frank Thomas/35	100.00	45.00
☐ 3 Mike Piazza/40	120.00	55.00
☐ 4 Chipper Jones/21	250.00	110.00
☐ 5 Alex Rodriguez/23	250.00	110.00
☐ 6 Nomar Garciaparra/30	150.00	70.00
☐ 7 Jeff Bagwell/43	50.00	22.00
☐ 8 Cal Ripken/11	500.00	220.00
☐ 9 Albert Belle/30	40.00	18.00
☐ 10 Mark McGwire/48	250.00	110.00
☐ 11 Juan Gonzalez/42	80.00	36.00
☐ 12 Larry Walker/49	40.00	18.00
☐ 13 Tino Martinez/44	30.00	13.50
☐ 14 Jim Thome/40	30.00	13.50
☐ 15 Manny Ramirez/26	80.00	36.00
☐ 16 Barry Bonds/40	50.00	22.00
☐ 17 Mo Vaughn/35	40.00	18.00
☐ 18 Jose Cruz Jr./26	40.00	18.00
☐ 19 Tony Clark/32	20.00	9.00
☐ 20 Andruw Jones/18	120.00	55.00

1998 Pinnacle Performers Launching Pad

	MINT	NRMT
COMPLETE SET (20)	80.00	36.00
COMMON CARD (1-20)	.75	.35
STATED ODDS 1:9		

☐ 1 Ben Grieve	2.00	.90
☐ 2 Ken Griffey Jr.	10.00	4.50
☐ 3 Derek Jeter	6.00	2.70
☐ 4 Frank Thomas	4.00	1.80
☐ 5 Travis Lee	1.25	.55
☐ 6 Vladimir Guerrero	2.00	.90
☐ 7 Tony Gwynn	5.00	2.20
☐ 8 Jose Cruz Jr.	.75	.35

		MINT	NRMT
❏ 9	Cal Ripken	8.00	3.60
❏ 10	Chipper Jones	5.00	2.20
❏ 11	Scott Rolen	3.00	1.35
❏ 12	Andruw Jones	2.00	.90
❏ 13	Ivan Rodriguez	2.00	.90
❏ 14	Todd Helton	2.00	.90
❏ 15	Nomar Garciaparra	6.00	2.70
❏ 16	Mark McGwire	12.00	5.50
❏ 17	Gary Sheffield	.75	.35
❏ 18	Bernie Williams	2.00	.90
❏ 19	Alex Rodriguez	6.00	2.70
❏ 20	Mike Piazza	6.00	2.70

1998 Pinnacle Performers Power Trip

		MINT	NRMT
COMPLETE SET (10)		60.00	27.00
COMMON CARD (1-10)		3.00	1.35
STATED ODDS 1:21			
STATED PRINT RUN 10,000 SERIAL #'d SETS			
❏ 1	Frank Thomas	5.00	2.20
❏ 2	Alex Rodriguez	8.00	3.60
❏ 3	Nomar Garciaparra	8.00	3.60
❏ 4	Jeff Bagwell	3.00	1.35
❏ 5	Cal Ripken	10.00	4.50
❏ 6	Mike Piazza	8.00	3.60
❏ 7	Chipper Jones	6.00	2.70
❏ 8	Ken Griffey Jr.	12.00	5.50
❏ 9	Mark McGwire	15.00	6.75
❏ 10	Juan Gonzalez	5.00	2.20

1998 Pinnacle Performers Swing for the Fences

		MINT	NRMT
COMPLETE SET (50)		50.00	22.00
COMMON CARD (1-50)		.40	.18
STATED ODDS 1:2			
❏ 1	Brady Anderson	.40	.18
❏ 2	Albert Belle	1.00	.45
❏ 3	Jay Buhner	.40	.18
❏ 4	Jose Canseco	1.25	.55
❏ 5	Tony Clark	.40	.18
❏ 6	Jose Cruz Jr.	.40	.18
❏ 7	Jim Edmonds	.40	.18
❏ 8	Cecil Fielder	.40	.18
❏ 9	Travis Fryman	.40	.18
❏ 10	Nomar Garciaparra	3.00	1.35
❏ 11	Juan Gonzalez	2.00	.90
❏ 12	Ken Griffey Jr.	5.00	2.20
❏ 13	David Justice	.40	.18
❏ 14	Travis Lee	.60	.25
❏ 15	Edgar Martinez	.40	.18
❏ 16	Tino Martinez	.40	.18
❏ 17	Rafael Palmeiro	1.00	.45
❏ 18	Manny Ramirez	1.25	.55
❏ 19	Cal Ripken	4.00	1.80
❏ 20	Alex Rodriguez	3.00	1.35
❏ 21	Tim Salmon	.60	.25
❏ 22	Frank Thomas	2.00	.90
❏ 23	Jim Thome	1.00	.45
❏ 24	Mo Vaughn	1.00	.45
❏ 25	Bernie Williams	1.00	.45
❏ 26	Fred McGriff	.60	.25
❏ 27	Jeff Bagwell	1.25	.55
❏ 28	Dante Bichette	.40	.18
❏ 29	Barry Bonds	1.25	.55
❏ 30	Ellis Burks	.40	.18
❏ 31	Ken Caminiti	.40	.18
❏ 32	Vinny Castilla	.40	.18
❏ 33	Andres Galarraga	.60	.25
❏ 34	Vladimir Guerrero	1.25	.55
❏ 35	Todd Helton	1.25	.55
❏ 36	Todd Hundley	.40	.18
❏ 37	Andruw Jones	1.00	.45
❏ 38	Chipper Jones	2.50	1.10
❏ 39	Eric Karros	.40	.18
❏ 40	Ryan Klesko	.40	.18
❏ 41	Ray Lankford	.40	.18
❏ 42	Mark McGwire	6.00	2.70
❏ 43	Raul Mondesi	.40	.18
❏ 44	Mike Piazza	3.00	1.35
❏ 45	Scott Rolen	1.50	.70
❏ 46	Gary Sheffield	.40	.18
❏ 47	Sammy Sosa	3.00	1.35
❏ 48	Larry Walker	1.00	.45
❏ 49	Matt Williams	1.00	.45
❏ 50	Wild Card	.40	.18

1998 Pinnacle Plus

		MINT	NRMT
COMPLETE SET (200)		30.00	13.50
COMMON CARD (1-200)		.10	.05
MINOR STARS		.20	.09
SEMISTARS		.30	.14
UNLISTED STARS		.50	.23
❏ 1	Roberto Alomar	.50	.23
❏ 2	Sandy Alomar Jr.	.20	.09
❏ 3	Brady Anderson	.20	.09
❏ 4	Albert Belle	.50	.23
❏ 5	Jeff Cirillo	.20	.09
❏ 6	Roger Clemens	1.25	.55
❏ 7	David Cone	.30	.14
❏ 8	Nomar Garciaparra	1.50	.70
❏ 9	Ken Griffey Jr.	2.50	1.10
❏ 10	Jason Dickson	.10	.05
❏ 11	Edgar Martinez	.20	.09
❏ 12	Tino Martinez	.20	.09
❏ 13	Randy Johnson	.50	.23
❏ 14	Mark McGwire	3.00	1.35
❏ 15	David Justice	.20	.09
❏ 16	Mike Mussina	.50	.23
❏ 17	Chuck Knoblauch	.20	.09
❏ 18	Joey Cora	.10	.05
❏ 19	Pat Hentgen	.10	.05
❏ 20	Randy Myers	.20	.09
❏ 21	Cal Ripken	2.00	.90
❏ 22	Mariano Rivera	.20	.09
❏ 23	Jose Rosado	.10	.05
❏ 24	Frank Thomas	1.00	.45
❏ 25	Alex Rodriguez	1.50	.70
❏ 26	Justin Thompson	.10	.05
❏ 27	Ivan Rodriguez	.60	.25
❏ 28	Bernie Williams	.50	.23
❏ 29	Pedro Martinez	.60	.25
❏ 30	Tony Clark	.20	.09
❏ 31	Garret Anderson	.20	.09
❏ 32	Travis Fryman	.20	.09
❏ 33	Mike Piazza	1.50	.70
❏ 34	Carl Pavano	.10	.05
❏ 35	Kevin Millwood	1.50	.70
❏ 36	Miguel Tejada	.20	.09
❏ 37	Willie Blair	.10	.05
❏ 38	Devon White	.10	.05
❏ 39	Andres Galarraga	.30	.14
❏ 40	Barry Larkin	.50	.23
❏ 41	Al Leiter	.20	.09
❏ 42	Moises Alou	.20	.09
❏ 43	Eric Young	.10	.05
❏ 44	John Jaha	.10	.05
❏ 45	Bernard Gilkey	.10	.05
❏ 46	Freddy Garcia	.10	.05
❏ 47	Ruben Rivera	.10	.05
❏ 48	Robb Nen	.10	.05
❏ 49	Ray Lankford	.20	.09
❏ 50	Kenny Lofton	.30	.14
❏ 51	Joe Carter	.20	.09
❏ 52	Jason McDonald	.20	.09
❏ 53	Quinton McCracken	.10	.05
❏ 54	Kerry Wood	.60	.25
❏ 55	Mike Lansing	.10	.05
❏ 56	Chipper Jones	1.25	.55
❏ 57	Barry Bonds	.60	.25
❏ 58	Brad Fullmer	.10	.05
❏ 59	Jeff Bagwell	.60	.25
❏ 60	Rondell White	.20	.09
❏ 61	Geronimo Berroa	.10	.05
❏ 62	Magglio Ordonez	1.50	.70
❏ 63	Dwight Gooden	.10	.05
❏ 64	Brian Hunter	.10	.05
❏ 65	Todd Walker	.20	.09
❏ 66	Frank Catalanotto	.20	.09
❏ 67	Tony Saunders	.10	.05
❏ 68	Travis Lee	.30	.14
❏ 69	Michael Tucker	.10	.05
❏ 70	Reggie Sanders	.10	.05
❏ 71	Derrek Lee	.10	.05
❏ 72	Larry Walker	.50	.23
❏ 73	Marquis Grissom	.10	.05
❏ 74	Craig Biggio	.50	.23
❏ 75	Kevin Brown	.30	.14
❏ 76	J.T. Snow	.20	.09
❏ 77	Eric Davis	.10	.05
❏ 78	Jeff Abbott	.10	.05
❏ 79	Jermaine Dye	.20	.09
❏ 80	Otis Nixon	.10	.05
❏ 81	Curt Schilling	.30	.14
❏ 82	Enrique Wilson	.10	.05
❏ 83	Tony Gwynn	1.25	.55
❏ 84	Orlando Cabrera	.10	.05
❏ 85	Ramon Martinez	.10	.05
❏ 86	Greg Vaughn	.20	.09
❏ 87	Alan Benes	.10	.05
❏ 88	Dennis Eckersley	.20	.09
❏ 89	Jim Thome	.50	.23
❏ 90	Juan Encarnacion	.20	.09
❏ 91	Jeff King	.10	.05
❏ 92	Shannon Stewart	.20	.09
❏ 93	Roberto Hernandez	.10	.05
❏ 94	Raul Ibanez	.10	.05
❏ 95	Darryl Kile	.10	.05
❏ 96	Charles Johnson	.20	.09
❏ 97	Rich Becker	.10	.05
❏ 98	Hal Morris	.10	.05
❏ 99	Ismael Valdes	.10	.05
❏ 100	Orel Hershiser	.20	.09
❏ 101	Mo Vaughn	.50	.23

❑ 102 Aaron Boone	.10	.05
❑ 103 Jeff Conine	.10	.05
❑ 104 Paul O'Neill	.20	.09
❑ 105 Tom Candiotti	.10	.05
❑ 106 Wilson Alvarez	.10	.05
❑ 107 Mike Stanley	.10	.05
❑ 108 Carlos Delgado	.50	.23
❑ 109 Tony Batista	.10	.05
❑ 110 Dante Bichette	.20	.09
❑ 111 Henry Rodriguez	.20	.09
❑ 112 Karim Garcia	.10	.05
❑ 113 Shane Reynolds	.20	.09
❑ 114 Ken Caminiti	.20	.09
❑ 115 Jose Silva	.10	.05
❑ 116 Juan Gonzalez	1.00	.45
❑ 117 Brian Jordan	.20	.09
❑ 118 Jim Leyritz	.10	.05
❑ 119 Manny Ramirez	.60	.25
❑ 120 Fred McGriff	.30	.14
❑ 121 Brooks Kieschnick	.20	.09
❑ 122 Sean Casey	.75	.35
❑ 123 John Smoltz	.30	.14
❑ 124 Rusty Greer	.20	.09
❑ 125 Cecil Fielder	.20	.09
❑ 126 Mike Cameron	.20	.09
❑ 127 Reggie Jefferson	.10	.05
❑ 128 Bobby Higginson	.20	.09
❑ 129 Kevin Appier	.20	.09
❑ 130 Robin Ventura	.20	.09
❑ 131 Ben Grieve	.50	.23
❑ 132 Wade Boggs	.50	.23
❑ 133 Jose Cruz Jr.	.20	.09
❑ 134 Jeff Suppan	.10	.05
❑ 135 Vinny Castilla	.20	.09
❑ 136 Sammy Sosa	1.50	.70
❑ 137 Mark Wohlers	.10	.05
❑ 138 Jay Bell	.10	.05
❑ 139 Brett Tomko	.10	.05
❑ 140 Gary Sheffield	.20	.09
❑ 141 Tim Salmon	.30	.14
❑ 142 Jaret Wright	.20	.09
❑ 143 Kenny Rogers	.10	.05
❑ 144 Brian Anderson	.10	.05
❑ 145 Darrin Fletcher	.10	.05
❑ 146 John Flaherty	.10	.05
❑ 147 Dmitri Young	.20	.09
❑ 148 Andruw Jones	.50	.23
❑ 149 Matt Williams	.50	.23
❑ 150 Bobby Bonilla	.20	.09
❑ 151 Mike Hampton	.20	.09
❑ 152 Al Martin	.10	.05
❑ 153 Mark Grudzielanek	.20	.09
❑ 154 Dave Nilsson	.10	.05
❑ 155 Roger Cedeno	.10	.05
❑ 156 Greg Maddux	1.25	.55
❑ 157 Mark Kotsay	.20	.09
❑ 158 Steve Finley	.20	.09
❑ 159 Wilson Delgado	.20	.09
❑ 160 Ron Gant	.20	.09
❑ 161 Jim Edmonds	.20	.09
❑ 162 Jeff Blauser	.10	.05
❑ 163 Dave Burba	.10	.05
❑ 164 Pedro Astacio	.10	.05
❑ 165 Livan Hernandez	.20	.09
❑ 166 Neifi Perez	.20	.09
❑ 167 Ryan Klesko	.20	.09
❑ 168 Fernando Tatis	.50	.23
❑ 169 Richard Hidalgo	.20	.09
❑ 170 Carlos Perez	.10	.05
❑ 171 Bob Abreu	.20	.09
❑ 172 Francisco Cordova	.10	.05
❑ 173 Todd Hollandsworth	.60	.25
❑ 174 Doug Glanville	.20	.09
❑ 175 Brian Rose	.10	.05
❑ 176 Yamil Benitez	.10	.05
❑ 177 Darin Erstad	.30	.14
❑ 178 Scott Rolen	.60	.25
❑ 179 John Wetteland	.20	.09
❑ 180 Paul Sorrento	.10	.05
❑ 181 Walt Weiss	.20	.09
❑ 182 Vladimir Guerrero	.60	.25
❑ 183 Ken Griffey Jr. NAT	1.25	.55
❑ 184 Alex Rodriguez NAT	.75	.35
❑ 185 Cal Ripken NAT	1.00	.45
❑ 186 Frank Thomas NAT	.50	.23
❑ 187 Chipper Jones NAT	.60	.25

❑ 188 Hideo Nomo NAT	.20	.09
❑ 189 Nomar Garciaparra NAT	.75	.35
❑ 190 Mike Piazza NAT	.75	.35
❑ 191 Greg Maddux NAT	.60	.25
❑ 192 Tony Gwynn NAT	.60	.25
❑ 193 Mark McGwire NAT	1.50	.70
❑ 194 Roger Clemens NAT	.60	.25
❑ 195 Mike Piazza FV	.75	.35
❑ 196 Mark McGwire FV	1.50	.70
❑ 197 Chipper Jones FV	.60	.25
❑ 198 Larry Walker FV	.20	.09
❑ 199 Hideo Nomo FV	.20	.09
❑ 200 Barry Bonds FV	.30	.14

1998 Pinnacle Plus Artist's Proofs

	MINT	NRMT
COMMON CARD (PP1-PP60)	3.00	1.35

*STARS: 10X TO 25X BASIC CARDS
*YNG.STARS: 8X TO 20X BASIC CARDS
STATED ODDS 1:35

	MINT	NRMT
COMMON GOLD AP (PP1-PP60)	10.00	4.50

*GOLD AP STARS: 30X TO 80X BASIC
*GOLD AP YNG.STARS: 25X TO 60X BASIC
GOLD AP RANDOM INSERTS IN PACKS
GOLD AP PRINT RUN 100 SERIAL #'d SETS
ONE OF ONE MIRROR AP'S EXIST

❑ PP1 Roberto Alomar	12.00	5.50
❑ PP2 Albert Belle	12.00	5.50
❑ PP3 Roger Clemens	30.00	13.50
❑ PP4 Nomar Garciaparra	40.00	18.00
❑ PP5 Ken Griffey Jr.	60.00	27.00
❑ PP6 Tino Martinez	5.00	2.20
❑ PP7 Randy Johnson	12.00	5.50
❑ PP8 Mark McGwire	80.00	36.00
❑ PP9 David Justice	5.00	2.20
❑ PP10 Chuck Knoblauch	5.00	2.20
❑ PP11 Cal Ripken	50.00	22.00
❑ PP12 Frank Thomas	25.00	11.00
❑ PP13 Alex Rodriguez	40.00	18.00
❑ PP14 Ivan Rodriguez	15.00	6.75
❑ PP15 Bernie Williams	12.00	5.50
❑ PP16 Pedro Martinez	15.00	6.75
❑ PP17 Tony Clark	5.00	2.20
❑ PP18 Mike Piazza	40.00	18.00
❑ PP19 Miguel Tejada	5.00	2.20
❑ PP20 Andres Galarraga	8.00	3.60
❑ PP21 Barry Larkin	12.00	5.50
❑ PP22 Kenny Lofton	8.00	3.60
❑ PP23 Chipper Jones	30.00	13.50
❑ PP24 Barry Bonds	15.00	6.75
❑ PP25 Brad Fullmer	3.00	1.35
❑ PP26 Jeff Bagwell	15.00	6.75
❑ PP27 Todd Walker	5.00	2.20
❑ PP28 Travis Lee	8.00	3.60
❑ PP29 Larry Walker	5.00	2.20
❑ PP30 Craig Biggio	12.00	5.50
❑ PP31 Tony Gwynn	30.00	13.50
❑ PP32 Jim Thorne	12.00	5.50
❑ PP33 Juan Encarnacion	5.00	2.20
❑ PP34 Mo Vaughn	12.00	5.50
❑ PP35 Karim Garcia	3.00	1.35
❑ PP36 Ken Caminiti	5.00	2.20
❑ PP37 Juan Gonzalez	25.00	11.00
❑ PP38 Manny Ramirez	15.00	6.75
❑ PP39 Fred McGriff	8.00	3.60

❑ PP40 Rusty Greer	5.00	2.20
❑ PP41 Bobby Higginson	5.00	2.20
❑ PP42 Ben Grieve	12.00	5.50
❑ PP43 Wade Boggs	12.00	5.50
❑ PP44 Jose Cruz Jr.	5.00	2.20
❑ PP45 Sammy Sosa	40.00	18.00
❑ PP46 Gary Sheffield	5.00	2.20
❑ PP47 Tim Salmon	8.00	3.60
❑ PP48 Jaret Wright	5.00	2.20
❑ PP49 Andruw Jones	12.00	5.50
❑ PP50 Matt Williams	12.00	5.50
❑ PP51 Greg Maddux	30.00	13.50
❑ PP52 Jim Edmonds	5.00	2.20
❑ PP53 Livan Hernandez	3.00	1.35
❑ PP54 Neifi Perez	5.00	2.20
❑ PP55 Fernando Tatis	12.00	5.50
❑ PP56 Richard Hidalgo	5.00	2.20
❑ PP57 Todd Helton	12.00	5.50
❑ PP58 Darin Erstad	8.00	3.60
❑ PP59 Scott Rolen	20.00	9.00
❑ PP60 Vladimir Guerrero	15.00	6.75

1998 Pinnacle Plus All-Star Epix

	MINT	NRMT
COMPLETE SET (24)	250.00	110.00
COMMON CARD (1-24)	3.00	1.35
UNLISTED STARS	5.00	2.20

*PURPLE CARDS: .6X TO 1.5X ORANGE
*EMERALD CARDS: 1.25X TO 3X ORANGE
STATED ODDS 1:21
ONLY ORANGE CARDS LISTED BELOW!
USE MULTIPLIERS FOR EMERALD/PURPLE
CARDS 1-12 DISTRIBUTED IN SCORE R/T
CARDS 13-24 DISTRIBUTED IN PIN.PLUS

❑ 1 Ken Griffey Jr. MOM	25.00	11.00
❑ 2 Juan Gonzalez MOM	10.00	4.50
❑ 3 Jeff Bagwell MOM	6.00	2.70
❑ 4 Ivan Rodriguez MOM	6.00	2.70
❑ 5 Nomar Garciaparra MOM	15.00	6.75
❑ 6 Ryne Sandberg MOM	10.00	4.50
❑ 7 Frank Thomas MOM	20.00	9.00
❑ 8 Derek Jeter MOM	15.00	6.75
❑ 9 Tony Gwynn MOM	12.00	5.50
❑ 10 Albert Belle MOM	5.00	2.20
❑ 11 Scott Rolen MOM	6.00	2.70
❑ 12 Barry Larkin MOM	5.00	2.20
❑ 13 Alex Rodriguez MOM	15.00	6.75
❑ 14 Cal Ripken MOM	20.00	9.00
❑ 15 Chipper Jones MOM	12.00	5.50
❑ 16 Roger Clemens MOM	12.00	5.50
❑ 17 Mo Vaughn MOM	5.00	2.20
❑ 18 Mark McGwire MOM	30.00	13.50
❑ 19 Mike Piazza MOM	15.00	6.75
❑ 20 Andruw Jones MOM	5.00	2.20
❑ 21 Greg Maddux MOM	12.00	5.50
❑ 22 Barry Bonds MOM	6.00	2.70
❑ 23 Paul Molitor MOM	5.00	2.20
❑ 24 Hideo Nomo MOM	5.00	2.20

1998 Pinnacle Plus Lasting Memories

	MINT	NRMT
COMPLETE SET (30)	60.00	27.00

	MINT	NRMT
COMMON CARD (1-30)	.50	.23
STATED ODDS 1:5		

		MINT	NRMT
❏ 1	Nomar Garciaparra	4.00	1.80
❏ 2	Ken Griffey Jr.	6.00	2.70
❏ 3	Livan Hernandez	.50	.23
❏ 4	Hideo Nomo	1.25	.55
❏ 5	Ben Grieve	1.25	.55
❏ 6	Scott Rolen	2.00	.90
❏ 7	Roger Clemens	3.00	1.35
❏ 8	Cal Ripken	5.00	2.20
❏ 9	Mo Vaughn	1.25	.55
❏ 10	Frank Thomas	2.50	1.10
❏ 11	Mark McGwire	8.00	3.60
❏ 12	Barry Larkin	1.25	.55
❏ 13	Matt Williams	1.25	.55
❏ 14	Jose Cruz Jr.	.50	.23
❏ 15	Andruw Jones	1.25	.55
❏ 16	Mike Piazza	4.00	1.80
❏ 17	Jeff Bagwell	1.50	.70
❏ 18	Chipper Jones	3.00	1.35
❏ 19	Juan Gonzalez	2.50	1.10
❏ 20	Kenny Lofton	.75	.35
❏ 21	Greg Maddux	3.00	1.35
❏ 22	Ivan Rodriguez	1.50	.70
❏ 23	Alex Rodriguez	4.00	1.80
❏ 24	Derek Jeter	4.00	1.80
❏ 25	Albert Belle	1.25	.55
❏ 26	Barry Bonds	1.50	.70
❏ 27	Larry Walker	1.25	.55
❏ 28	Sammy Sosa	4.00	1.80
❏ 29	Tony Gwynn	3.00	1.35
❏ 30	Randy Johnson	1.25	.55

1998 Pinnacle Plus Piece of the Game

	MINT	NRMT
COMPLETE SET (10)	80.00	36.00
COMMON CARD (1-10)	4.00	1.80
STATED ODDS 1:19		

		MINT	NRMT
❏ 1	Ken Griffey Jr.	20.00	9.00
❏ 2	Frank Thomas	8.00	3.60
❏ 3	Alex Rodriguez	12.00	5.50
❏ 4	Chipper Jones	10.00	4.50
❏ 5	Cal Ripken	15.00	6.75
❏ 6	Mike Piazza	12.00	5.50
❏ 7	Greg Maddux	10.00	4.50
❏ 8	Juan Gonzalez	8.00	3.60

		MINT	NRMT
❏ 9	Nomar Garciaparra	12.00	5.50
❏ 10	Larry Walker	4.00	1.80

1998 Pinnacle Plus Team Pinnacle

	MINT	NRMT
COMPLETE SET (15)	400.00	180.00
COMMON CARD (1-15)	12.00	5.50
STATED ODDS 1:71		
*GOLD: 1X TO 2.5X HI COLUMN		
GOLD STATED ODDS 1:199 HOBBY		
*MIRROR: 4X TO 10X HI COLUMN		
MIRROR: RANDOM INSERTS IN PACKS		
MIRROR STATED PRINT RUN 25 SETS		

		MINT	NRMT
❏ 1	Mike Piazza	40.00	18.00
	Ivan Rodriguez		
❏ 2	Mark McGwire	60.00	27.00
	Mo Vaughn		
❏ 3	Roberto Alomar	12.00	5.50
	Craig Biggio		
❏ 4	Alex Rodriguez	40.00	18.00
	Barry Larkin		
❏ 5	Cal Ripken	50.00	22.00
	Chipper Jones		
❏ 6	Ken Griffey Jr.	50.00	22.00
	Larry Walker		
❏ 7	Juan Gonzalez	40.00	18.00
	Tony Gwynn		
❏ 8	Albert Belle	20.00	9.00
	Barry Bonds		
❏ 9	Kenny Lofton	12.00	5.50
	Andruw Jones		
❏ 10	Tino Martinez	20.00	9.00
	Jeff Bagwell		
❏ 11	Frank Thomas	25.00	11.00
	Andres Galarraga		
❏ 12	Roger Clemens	30.00	13.50
	Greg Maddux		
❏ 13	Pedro Martinez	20.00	9.00
	Hideo Nomo		
❏ 14	Nomar Garciaparra	40.00	18.00
	Scott Rolen		
❏ 15	Ben Grieve	12.00	5.50
	Paul Konerko		

1998 Pinnacle Plus Yardwork

	MINT	NRMT
COMPLETE SET (15)	40.00	18.00
COMMON CARD (1-15)	.60	.25
STATED ODDS 1:7		

		MINT	NRMT
❏ 1	Mo Vaughn	1.50	.70
❏ 2	Frank Thomas	3.00	1.35
❏ 3	Albert Belle	1.50	.70
❏ 4	Nomar Garciaparra	5.00	2.20
❏ 5	Tony Clark	.60	.25
❏ 6	Tino Martinez	.60	.25
❏ 7	Ken Griffey Jr.	8.00	3.60
❏ 8	Juan Gonzalez	3.00	1.35
❏ 9	Sammy Sosa	5.00	2.20
❏ 10	Jose Cruz Jr.	.60	.25
❏ 11	Jeff Bagwell	1.50	.70
❏ 12	Mike Piazza	5.00	2.20
❏ 13	Larry Walker	1.50	.70
❏ 14	Mark McGwire	10.00	4.50
❏ 15	Barry Bonds	1.50	.70

1997 Pinnacle Totally Certified Platinum Blue

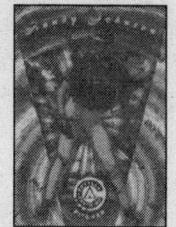

	MINT	NRMT
COMMON CARD (1-150)	2.00	.90
*STARS: .6X TO 1.5X RED		
*ROOKIES: .6X TO 1.5X RED		
STATED ODDS ONE PER PACK		
STATED PRINT RUN 1999 SERIAL #'d SETS		

1997 Pinnacle Totally Certified Platinum Gold

	MINT	NRMT
COMMON CARD (1-150)	30.00	13.50
*STARS: 12.5X TO 30X PLAT. RED		
*ROOKIES: 5X TO 12X PLAT.RED		
STATED ODDS 1:79 PACKS		
STATED PRINT RUN 30 SETS		

1997 Pinnacle Totally Certified Platinum Red

	MINT	NRMT
COMPLETE SET (150)	300.00	135.00
COMMON CARD (1-150)	1.25	.55
MINOR STARS	2.50	1.10
UNLISTED STARS	5.00	2.20

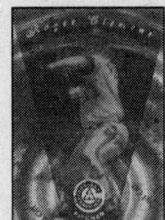

RED PRINT RUN 3,999 SERIAL #'d SETS

❏ 1	Barry Bonds	6.00	2.70
❏ 2	Mo Vaughn	5.00	2.20
❏ 3	Matt Williams	5.00	2.20
❏ 4	Ryne Sandberg	6.00	2.70
❏ 5	Jeff Bagwell	6.00	2.70
❏ 6	Alan Benes	1.25	.55
❏ 7	John Wetteland	2.50	1.10
❏ 8	Fred McGriff	4.00	1.80
❏ 9	Craig Biggio	5.00	2.20
❏ 10	Bernie Williams	5.00	2.20
❏ 11	Brian Hunter	2.50	1.10
❏ 12	Sandy Alomar Jr.	2.50	1.10
❏ 13	Ray Lankford	2.50	1.10
❏ 14	Ryan Klesko	2.50	1.10
❏ 15	Jermaine Dye	2.50	1.10
❏ 16	Andy Benes	2.50	1.10
❏ 17	Albert Belle	5.00	2.20
❏ 18	Tony Clark	4.00	1.80
❏ 19	Dean Palmer	2.50	1.10
❏ 20	Bernard Gilkey	1.25	.55
❏ 21	Ken Caminiti	4.00	1.80
❏ 22	Alex Rodriguez	15.00	6.75
❏ 23	Tim Salmon	5.00	2.20
❏ 24	Larry Walker	5.00	2.20
❏ 25	Barry Larkin	5.00	2.20
❏ 26	Mike Piazza	15.00	6.75
❏ 27	Brady Anderson	2.50	1.10
❏ 28	Cal Ripken	20.00	9.00
❏ 29	Charles Nagy	2.50	1.10
❏ 30	Paul Molitor	5.00	2.20
❏ 31	Darin Erstad	5.00	2.20
❏ 32	Rey Ordonez	2.50	1.10
❏ 33	Wally Joyner	2.50	1.10
❏ 34	David Cone	4.00	1.80
❏ 35	Sammy Sosa	15.00	6.75
❏ 36	Dante Bichette	2.50	1.10
❏ 37	Eric Karros	2.50	1.10
❏ 38	Omar Vizquel	2.50	1.10
❏ 39	Roger Clemens	12.00	5.50
❏ 40	Joe Carter	2.50	1.10
❏ 41	Frank Thomas	10.00	4.50
❏ 42	Javy Lopez	2.50	1.10
❏ 43	Mike Mussina	5.00	2.20
❏ 44	Gary Sheffield	2.50	1.10
❏ 45	Tony Gwynn	12.00	5.50
❏ 46	Jason Kendall	4.00	1.80
❏ 47	Jim Thome	5.00	2.20
❏ 48	Andres Galarraga	5.00	2.20
❏ 49	Mark McGwire	25.00	11.00
❏ 50	Troy Percival	2.50	1.10
❏ 51	Derek Jeter	15.00	6.75
❏ 52	Todd Hollandsworth	1.25	.55
❏ 53	Ken Griffey Jr.	25.00	11.00
❏ 54	Randy Johnson	5.00	2.20
❏ 55	Pat Hentgen	2.50	1.10
❏ 56	Rusty Greer	2.50	1.10
❏ 57	John Jaha	1.25	.55
❏ 58	Kenny Lofton	4.00	1.80
❏ 59	Chipper Jones	12.00	5.50
❏ 60	Robb Nen	1.25	.55
❏ 61	Rafael Palmeiro	5.00	2.20
❏ 62	Mariano Rivera	2.50	1.10
❏ 63	Hideo Nomo	5.00	2.20
❏ 64	Greg Vaughn	2.50	1.10
❏ 65	Ron Gant	1.25	.55
❏ 66	Eddie Murray	5.00	2.20

❏ 67	John Smoltz	4.00	1.80
❏ 68	Manny Ramirez	6.00	2.70
❏ 69	Juan Gonzalez	10.00	4.50
❏ 70	F.P. Santangelo	1.25	.55
❏ 71	Moises Alou	2.50	1.10
❏ 72	Alex Ochoa	1.25	.55
❏ 73	Chuck Knoblauch	5.00	2.20
❏ 74	Raul Mondesi	2.50	1.10
❏ 75	J.T. Snow	2.50	1.10
❏ 76	Rickey Henderson	6.00	2.70
❏ 77	Bobby Bonilla	2.50	1.10
❏ 78	Wade Boggs	5.00	2.20
❏ 79	Ivan Rodriguez	6.00	2.70
❏ 80	Brian Jordan	2.50	1.10
❏ 81	Al Leiter	2.50	1.10
❏ 82	Jay Buhner	2.50	1.10
❏ 83	Greg Maddux	12.00	5.50
❏ 84	Edgar Martinez	2.50	1.10
❏ 85	Kevin Brown	4.00	1.80
❏ 86	Eric Young	2.50	1.10
❏ 87	Todd Hundley	2.50	1.10
❏ 88	Ellis Burks	2.50	1.10
❏ 89	Marquis Grissom	2.50	1.10
❏ 90	Jose Canseco	6.00	2.70
❏ 91	Henry Rodriguez	2.50	1.10
❏ 92	Andy Pettitte	4.00	1.80
❏ 93	Mark Grudzielanek	2.50	1.10
❏ 94	Dwight Gooden	2.50	1.10
❏ 95	Roberto Alomar	5.00	2.20
❏ 96	Paul Wilson	1.25	.55
❏ 97	Will Clark	5.00	2.20
❏ 98	Rondell White	2.50	1.10
❏ 99	Charles Johnson	2.50	1.10
❏ 100	Jim Edmonds	4.00	1.80
❏ 101	Jason Giambi	2.50	1.10
❏ 102	Billy Wagner	2.50	1.10
❏ 103	Edgar Renteria	2.50	1.10
❏ 104	Johnny Damon	2.50	1.10
❏ 105	Jason Isringhausen	1.25	.55
❏ 106	Andruw Jones	6.00	2.70
❏ 107	Jose Guillen	4.00	1.80
❏ 108	Kevin Orie	1.25	.55
❏ 109	Brian Giles	15.00	6.75
❏ 110	Danny Patterson	2.50	1.10
❏ 111	Vladimir Guerrero	8.00	3.60
❏ 112	Scott Rolen	8.00	3.60
❏ 113	Damon Mashore	1.25	.55
❏ 114	Nomar Garciaparra	15.00	6.75
❏ 115	Todd Walker	5.00	2.20
❏ 116	Wilton Guerrero	1.25	.55
❏ 117	Bob Abreu	2.50	1.10
❏ 118	Brooks Kieschnick	1.25	.55
❏ 119	Pokey Reese	2.50	1.10
❏ 120	Todd Greene	1.25	.55
❏ 121	Dmitri Young	2.50	1.10
❏ 122	Raul Casanova	1.25	.55
❏ 123	Glendon Rusch	1.25	.55
❏ 124	Jason Dickson	1.25	.55
❏ 125	Jorge Posada	2.50	1.10
❏ 126	Rod Myers	1.25	.55
❏ 127	Bubba Trammell	5.00	2.20
❏ 128	Scott Spiezio	1.25	.55
❏ 129	Hideki Irabu	8.00	3.60
❏ 130	Wendell Magee	1.25	.55
❏ 131	Bartolo Colon	2.50	1.10
❏ 132	Chris Holt	1.25	.55
❏ 133	Calvin Maduro	1.25	.55
❏ 134	Ray Montgomery	1.25	.55
❏ 135	Shannon Stewart	2.50	1.10
❏ 136	Ken Griffey Jr. CERT	12.00	5.50
❏ 137	Vladimir Guerrero CERT	5.00	2.20
❏ 138	Roger Clemens CERT	5.00	2.20
❏ 139	Mark McGwire CERT	12.00	5.50
❏ 140	Albert Belle CERT	2.50	1.10
❏ 141	Derek Jeter CERT	8.00	3.60
❏ 142	Juan Gonzalez CERT	5.00	2.20
❏ 143	Greg Maddux CERT	6.00	2.70
❏ 144	Alex Rodriguez CERT	8.00	3.60
❏ 145	Jeff Bagwell CERT	5.00	2.20
❏ 146	Cal Ripken CERT	10.00	4.50
❏ 147	Tony Gwynn CERT	6.00	2.70
❏ 148	Frank Thomas CERT	5.00	2.20
❏ 149	Hideo Nomo CERT	2.50	1.10
❏ 150	Andruw Jones CERT	4.00	1.80

1997 Pinnacle X-Press

	MINT	NRMT
COMPLETE SET (150)	15.00	6.75
COMMON CARD (1-150)	.10	.05
MINOR STARS	.20	.09
UNLISTED STARS	.40	.18
SUBSET CARDS HALF VALUE OF BASE CARDS		
COMMON SUMMER (1-150)	1.50	.70

*SUMMER STARS: 6X TO 15X HI COLUMN
*SUMMER ROOKIES: 3X TO 8X HI
MEN OF SUMMER ODDS 1:7 HOBBY
MEN OF SUMMER 1 PER MASTER DECK

❏ 1	Larry Walker	.40	.18
❏ 2	Andy Pettitte	.30	.14
❏ 3	Matt Williams	.40	.18
❏ 4	Juan Gonzalez	.75	.35
❏ 5	Frank Thomas	.75	.35
❏ 6	Kenny Lofton	.30	.14
❏ 7	Ken Griffey Jr.	2.00	.90
❏ 8	Andres Galarraga	.40	.18
❏ 9	Greg Maddux	1.00	.45
❏ 10	Hideo Nomo	.40	.18
❏ 11	Cecil Fielder	.20	.09
❏ 12	Jose Canseco	.50	.23
❏ 13	Tony Gwynn	1.00	.45
❏ 14	Eddie Murray	.40	.18
❏ 15	Alex Rodriguez	1.25	.55
❏ 16	Mike Piazza	1.25	.55
❏ 17	Ken Hill	.10	.05
❏ 18	Chuck Knoblauch	.40	.18
❏ 19	Ellis Burks	.20	.09
❏ 20	Rafael Palmeiro	.40	.18
❏ 21	Vinny Castilla	.30	.14
❏ 22	Rusty Greer	.20	.09
❏ 23	Chipper Jones	1.00	.45
❏ 24	Rey Ordonez	.20	.09
❏ 25	Mariano Rivera	.20	.09
❏ 26	Garret Anderson	.20	.09
❏ 27	Edgar Martinez	.20	.09
❏ 28	Dante Bichette	.20	.09
❏ 29	Todd Hundley	.20	.09
❏ 30	Barry Bonds	.50	.23
❏ 31	Barry Larkin	.40	.18
❏ 32	Derek Jeter	1.25	.55
❏ 33	Marquis Grissom	.20	.09
❏ 34	Dave Justice	.40	.18
❏ 35	Ivan Rodriguez	.50	.23
❏ 36	Jay Buhner	.20	.09
❏ 37	Fred McGriff	.30	.14
❏ 38	Brady Anderson	.20	.09
❏ 39	Tony Clark	.30	.14
❏ 40	Eric Young	.10	.05
❏ 41	Charles Nagy	.20	.09
❏ 42	Mark McGwire	2.00	.90
❏ 43	Paul O'Neill	.40	.18
❏ 44	Tino Martinez	.40	.18
❏ 45	Ryne Sandberg	.50	.23
❏ 46	Bernie Williams	.40	.18
❏ 47	Albert Belle	.40	.18
❏ 48	Jeff Cirillo	.20	.09
❏ 49	Tim Salmon	.40	.18
❏ 50	Steve Finley	.20	.09
❏ 51	Lance Johnson	.10	.05
❏ 52	John Smoltz	.30	.14
❏ 53	Javier Lopez	.20	.09

		MINT	NRMT
❏ 54	Roger Clemens	1.00	.45
❏ 55	Kevin Appier	.20	.09
❏ 56	Ken Caminiti	.30	.14
❏ 57	Cal Ripken	1.50	.70
❏ 58	Moises Alou	.20	.09
❏ 59	Marty Cordova	.10	.05
❏ 60	David Cone	.30	.14
❏ 61	Manny Ramirez	.50	.23
❏ 62	Ray Durham	.20	.09
❏ 63	Jermaine Dye	.20	.09
❏ 64	Craig Biggio	.40	.18
❏ 65	Will Clark	.40	.18
❏ 66	Omar Vizquel	.20	.09
❏ 67	Bernard Gilkey	.10	.05
❏ 68	Greg Vaughn	.20	.09
❏ 69	Wade Boggs	.40	.18
❏ 70	Dave Nilsson	.10	.05
❏ 71	Mark Grace	.30	.14
❏ 72	Dean Palmer	.20	.09
❏ 73	Sammy Sosa	1.25	.55
❏ 74	Mike Mussina	.40	.18
❏ 75	Alex Fernandez	.10	.05
❏ 76	Henry Rodriguez	.20	.09
❏ 77	Travis Fryman	.20	.09
❏ 78	Jeff Bagwell	.50	.23
❏ 79	Pat Hentgen	.20	.09
❏ 80	Gary Sheffield	.20	.09
❏ 81	Jim Edmonds	.30	.14
❏ 82	Darin Erstad	.40	.18
❏ 83	Mark Grudzielanek	.20	.09
❏ 84	Jim Thome	.40	.18
❏ 85	Bobby Higginson	.20	.09
❏ 86	Al Martin	.10	.05
❏ 87	Jason Giambi	.20	.09
❏ 88	Mo Vaughn	.40	.18
❏ 89	Jeff Conine	.10	.05
❏ 90	Edgar Renteria	.20	.09
❏ 91	Andy Ashby	.10	.05
❏ 92	Ryan Klesko	.20	.09
❏ 93	John Jaha	.10	.05
❏ 94	Paul Molitor	.40	.18
❏ 95	Brian Hunter	.20	.09
❏ 96	Randy Johnson	.40	.18
❏ 97	Joey Hamilton	.20	.09
❏ 98	Billy Wagner	.20	.09
❏ 99	John Wetteland	.20	.09
❏ 100	Jeff Fassero	.20	.09
❏ 101	Rondell White	.20	.09
❏ 102	Kevin Brown	.30	.14
❏ 103	Andy Benes	.20	.09
❏ 104	Raul Mondesi	.20	.09
❏ 105	Todd Hollandsworth	.10	.05
❏ 106	Alex Ochoa	.20	.09
❏ 107	Bobby Bonilla	.20	.09
❏ 108	Brian Jordan	.20	.09
❏ 109	Tom Glavine	.40	.18
❏ 110	Ron Gant	.10	.05
❏ 111	Jason Kendall	.30	.14
❏ 112	Roberto Alomar	.40	.18
❏ 113	Troy Percival	.20	.09
❏ 114	Michael Tucker	.10	.05
❏ 115	Joe Carter	.20	.09
❏ 116	Andruw Jones	.50	.23
❏ 117	Nomar Garciaparra	1.25	.55
❏ 118	Todd Walker	.40	.18
❏ 119	Jose Guillen	.30	.14
❏ 120	Bubba Trammell	.40	.18
❏ 121	Wilton Guerrero	.10	.05
❏ 122	Bob Abreu	.20	.09
❏ 123	Vladimir Guerrero	.60	.25
❏ 124	Dmitri Young	.20	.09
❏ 125	Kevin Orie	.10	.05
❏ 126	Jose Cruz Jr.	.75	.35
❏ 127	Brooks Kieschnick	.20	.09
❏ 128	Scott Spiezio	.10	.05
❏ 129	Brian Giles	1.25	.55
❏ 130	Jason Dickson	.10	.05
❏ 131	Damon Mashore	.10	.05
❏ 132	Wendell Magee	.10	.05
❏ 133	Matt Morris	.20	.09
❏ 134	Scott Rolen	.60	.25
❏ 135	Shannon Stewart	.20	.09
❏ 136	Deivi Cruz	.40	.18
❏ 137	Hideki Irabu	.60	.25
❏ 138	Larry Walker PP	.20	.09
❏ 139	Ken Griffey Jr. PP	1.00	.45
❏ 140	Frank Thomas PP	.40	.18
❏ 141	Ivan Rodriguez PP	.30	.14
❏ 142	Randy Johnson PP	.20	.09
❏ 143	Mark McGwire PP	1.00	.45
❏ 144	Tino Martinez PP	.20	.09
❏ 145	Tony Clark PP	.10	.05
❏ 146	Mike Piazza PP	.60	.25
❏ 147	Alex Rodriguez PP	.60	.25
❏ 148	Roger Clemens CL	.50	.23
❏ 149	Greg Maddux CL	.50	.23
❏ 150	Hideo Nomo CL	.20	.09

1997 Pinnacle X-Press Far and Away

		MINT	NRMT
COMPLETE SET (18)		120.00	55.00
COMMON CARD (1-18)		2.50	1.10
STAT.ODDS 1:19 HOB, 1:5 MAST.DECK			

		MINT	NRMT
❏ 1	Albert Belle	4.00	1.80
❏ 2	Mark McGwire	20.00	9.00
❏ 3	Frank Thomas	8.00	3.60
❏ 4	Mo Vaughn	4.00	1.80
❏ 5	Jeff Bagwell	5.00	2.20
❏ 6	Juan Gonzalez	8.00	3.60
❏ 7	Mike Piazza	12.00	5.50
❏ 8	Andruw Jones	5.00	2.20
❏ 9	Chipper Jones	10.00	4.50
❏ 10	Gary Sheffield	2.50	1.10
❏ 11	Sammy Sosa	12.00	5.50
❏ 12	Darin Erstad	4.00	1.80
❏ 13	Jay Buhner	2.50	1.10
❏ 14	Ken Griffey Jr.	20.00	9.00
❏ 15	Ken Caminiti	2.50	1.10
❏ 16	Brady Anderson	2.50	1.10
❏ 17	Manny Ramirez	5.00	2.20
❏ 18	Alex Rodriguez	12.00	5.50

1997 Pinnacle X-Press Melting Pot

		MINT	NRMT
COMPLETE SET (20)		600.00	275.00
COMMON CARD (1-20)		5.00	2.20
MINOR STARS		8.00	3.60
SEMISTARS		12.00	5.50
UNLISTED STARS		20.00	9.00
STAT.ODDS 1:288 HOB, 1:189 MAST.DECK			
STATED PRINT RUN 500 SERIAL #'d SETS			

		MINT	NRMT
❏ 1	Jose Guillen	12.00	5.50
❏ 2	Vladimir Guerrero	30.00	13.50
❏ 3	Andruw Jones	25.00	11.00
❏ 4	Larry Walker	20.00	9.00
❏ 5	Manny Ramirez	25.00	11.00
❏ 6	Ken Griffey Jr.	100.00	45.00
❏ 7	Alex Rodriguez	60.00	27.00
❏ 8	Frank Thomas	40.00	18.00
❏ 9	Juan Gonzalez	40.00	18.00
❏ 10	Ivan Rodriguez	25.00	11.00
❏ 11	Hideo Nomo	20.00	9.00
❏ 12	Rafael Palmeiro	20.00	9.00
❏ 13	Dave Nilsson	5.00	2.20
❏ 14	Nomar Garciaparra	60.00	27.00
❏ 15	Wilton Guerrero	5.00	2.20
❏ 16	Sammy Sosa	60.00	27.00
❏ 17	Edgar Renteria	8.00	3.60
❏ 18	Cal Ripken	80.00	36.00
❏ 19	Derek Jeter	60.00	27.00
❏ 20	Rey Ordonez	8.00	3.60

1997 Pinnacle X-Press Metal Works

		MINT	NRMT
COMP.BRONZE SET (20)		120.00	55.00
COMMON CARD (1-20)		3.00	1.35
ONE BRONZE PER MASTER DECK			
*SILVER SINGLES: 15X TO 40X BASE CARD HI			
SILVER ODDS 1:54 MASTER DECKS			
SILVER REDEMPTION ODDS 1:470 HOBBY			
SILVER PRINT RUN 400 SERIAL #'d SETS			
*GOLD SINGLES: 30X TO 80X BASE CARD HI			
GOLD ODDS 1:108 MASTER DECKS			
GOLD REDEMPTION ODDS 1:950 HOBBY			
GOLD PRINT RUN 200 SERIAL #'d SETS			

		MINT	NRMT
❏ 1	Ken Griffey Jr.	15.00	6.75
❏ 2	Frank Thomas	6.00	2.70
❏ 3	Andruw Jones	3.00	1.35
❏ 4	Alex Rodriguez	10.00	4.50
❏ 5	Derek Jeter	8.00	3.60
❏ 6	Cal Ripken	12.00	5.50
❏ 7	Mike Piazza	10.00	4.50
❏ 8	Chipper Jones	8.00	3.60
❏ 9	Juan Gonzalez	6.00	2.70
❏ 10	Greg Maddux	8.00	3.60
❏ 11	Tony Gwynn	8.00	3.60
❏ 12	Jeff Bagwell	4.00	1.80
❏ 13	Albert Belle	4.00	1.80
❏ 14	Mark McGwire	15.00	6.75
❏ 15	Nomar Garciaparra	10.00	4.50
❏ 16	Mo Vaughn	4.00	1.80
❏ 17	Andy Pettitte	3.00	1.35
❏ 18	Manny Ramirez	5.00	2.20
❏ 19	Kenny Lofton	3.00	1.35
❏ 20	Roger Clemens	8.00	3.60
❏ NNO	Gold Redemption Card	80.00	36.00
❏ NNO	Silver Redemption Card	40.00	18.00

1997 Pinnacle X-Press Swing for the Fences

	MINT	NRMT
COMPLETE SET (60)	60.00	27.00
COMMON CARD	.25	.11

MINOR STARS .... .50 .23
UNLISTED STARS.............. 1.00 .45
STATED ODDS 1:2
COMP.UPGRADE SET (60).. 200.00 90.00
COMMON UPGRADE .... 1.50 .70
*UPG.STARS: 2.5X TO 6X HI COLUMN
*UPG.YOUNG STARS: 2X TO 5X HI
TEN UPGRADES VIA MAIL PER WINNER
UPGRADE EXCH.DEADLINE: 3/1/98
NNO CARDS LISTED IN ALPH.ORDER

		MINT	NRMT
❏ 1	Sandy Alomar Jr.	.50	.23
❏ 2	Moises Alou	.50	.23
❏ 3	Brady Anderson	.50	.23
❏ 4	Jeff Bagwell	1.25	.55
❏ 5	Derek Bell	.50	.23
❏ 6	Jay Bell	.50	.23
❏ 7	Albert Belle	1.00	.45
❏ 8	Geronimo Berroa	.25	.11
❏ 9	Dante Bichette	.50	.23
❏ 10	Barry Bonds	1.25	.55
❏ 11	Bobby Bonilla	.50	.23
❏ 12	Jay Buhner	.50	.23
❏ 13	Ellis Burks	.50	.23
❏ 14	Ken Caminiti	.75	.35
❏ 15	Jose Canseco	1.25	.55
❏ 16	Joe Carter	.50	.23
❏ 17	Vinny Castilla	.75	.35
❏ 18	Tony Clark	.75	.35
❏ 19	Carlos Delgado	1.00	.45
❏ 20	Jim Edmonds	.75	.35
❏ 21	Cecil Fielder	.25	.11
❏ 22	Andres Galarraga	1.00	.45
❏ 23	Ron Gant	.25	.11
❏ 24	Bernard Gilkey	.25	.11
❏ 25	Juan Gonzalez	2.00	.90
❏ 26	Ken Griffey Jr. W.	15.00	6.75
❏ 27	Vladimir Guerrero	1.50	.70
❏ 28	Todd Hundley	.25	.11
❏ 29	John Jaha	.25	.11
❏ 30	Andruw Jones	.75	.35
❏ 31	Chipper Jones	2.50	1.10
❏ 32	David Justice	1.00	.45
❏ 33	Jeff Kent	.50	.23
❏ 34	Ryan Klesko	.50	.23
❏ 35	Barry Larkin	1.00	.45
❏ 36	Mike Lieberthal	.25	.11
❏ 37	Javier Lopez	.50	.23
❏ 38	Edgar Martinez	.50	.23
❏ 39	Tino Martinez	1.00	.45
❏ 40	Fred McGriff	.75	.35
❏ 41	Mark McGwire W	15.00	6.75
❏ 42	Raul Mondesi	.50	.23
❏ 43	Tim Naehring	.25	.11
❏ 44	Dave Nilsson	.25	.11
❏ 45	Rafael Palmeiro	1.00	.45
❏ 46	Dean Palmer	.50	.23
❏ 47	Mike Piazza	3.00	1.35
❏ 48	Cal Ripken	4.00	1.80
❏ 49	Henry Rodriguez	.25	.11
❏ 50	Tim Salmon	1.00	.45
❏ 51	Gary Sheffield	.50	.23
❏ 52	Sammy Sosa	3.00	1.35
❏ 53	Terry Steinbach	.25	.11
❏ 54	Frank Thomas	2.00	.90
❏ 55	Jim Thome	1.00	.45
❏ 56	Mo Vaughn	1.00	.45
❏ 57	Larry Walker W	3.00	1.35

❏ 58	Rondell White	.50	.23
❏ 59	Matt Williams	1.00	.45
❏ 60	Todd Zeile	.25	.11
❏ U26	Ken Griffey Jr. UPG	30.00	13.50
❏ U41	Mark McGwire UPG	30.00	13.50
❏ U57	Larry Walker UPG	6.00	2.70
❏ NNO	A.Jones AU EXCH	30.00	13.50

1998 Revolution

		MINT	NRMT
COMPLETE SET (150)		125.00	55.00
COMMON CARD (1-150)		.50	.23
MINOR STARS		.75	.35
SEMISTARS		1.25	.55
UNLISTED STARS		2.00	.90

❏ 1	Garret Anderson	.75	.35
❏ 2	Jim Edmonds	.75	.35
❏ 3	Darin Erstad	1.25	.55
❏ 4	Chuck Finley	.75	.35
❏ 5	Tim Salmon	1.25	.55
❏ 6	Jay Bell	.75	.35
❏ 7	Travis Lee	1.25	.55
❏ 8	Devon White	.50	.23
❏ 9	Matt Williams	1.25	.55
❏ 10	Andres Galarraga	1.25	.55
❏ 11	Tom Glavine	2.00	.90
❏ 12	Andruw Jones	2.00	.90
❏ 13	Chipper Jones	5.00	2.20
❏ 14	Ryan Klesko	.75	.35
❏ 15	Javy Lopez	.75	.35
❏ 16	Greg Maddux	5.00	2.20
❏ 17	Walt Weiss	.50	.35
❏ 18	Roberto Alomar	2.00	.90
❏ 19	Joe Carter	.75	.35
❏ 20	Mike Mussina	2.00	.90
❏ 21	Rafael Palmeiro	2.00	.90
❏ 22	Cal Ripken	8.00	3.60
❏ 23	B.J. Surhoff	.50	.35
❏ 24	Nomar Garciaparra	6.00	2.70
❏ 25	Reggie Jefferson	.50	.23
❏ 26	Pedro Martinez	2.50	1.10
❏ 27	Troy O'Leary	.75	.35
❏ 28	Mo Vaughn	2.00	.90
❏ 29	Mark Grace	.75	.55
❏ 30	Mickey Morandini	.50	.23
❏ 31	Henry Rodriguez	.75	.35
❏ 32	Sammy Sosa	6.00	2.70
❏ 33	Kerry Wood	2.50	1.10
❏ 34	Albert Belle	2.00	.90
❏ 35	Ray Durham	.75	.35
❏ 36	Magglio Ordonez	6.00	2.70
❏ 37	Frank Thomas	4.00	1.80
❏ 38	Robin Ventura	.75	.35
❏ 39	Bret Boone	.75	.35
❏ 40	Barry Larkin	2.00	.90
❏ 41	Reggie Sanders	.50	.23
❏ 42	Brett Tomko	.50	.23
❏ 43	Sandy Alomar Jr.	.75	.35
❏ 44	David Justice	.75	.35
❏ 45	Kenny Lofton	1.25	.55
❏ 46	Manny Ramirez	2.50	1.10
❏ 47	Jim Thome	2.00	.90
❏ 48	Omar Vizquel	.75	.35
❏ 49	Jaret Wright	.75	.35
❏ 50	Dante Bichette	.75	.35
❏ 51	Ellis Burks	.75	.35

❏ 52	Vinny Castilla	.75	.35
❏ 53	Todd Helton	2.50	1.10
❏ 54	Larry Walker	2.00	.90
❏ 55	Tony Clark	.75	.35
❏ 56	Deivi Cruz	.50	.23
❏ 57	Damion Easley	.75	.35
❏ 58	Bobby Higginson	.75	.35
❏ 59	Brian Hunter	.50	.23
❏ 60	Cliff Floyd	.75	.35
❏ 61	Livan Hernandez	.50	.23
❏ 62	Derek Lee	.50	.23
❏ 63	Edgar Renteria	.50	.23
❏ 64	Moises Alou	.75	.35
❏ 65	Jeff Bagwell	2.50	1.10
❏ 66	Derek Bell	.75	.35
❏ 67	Craig Biggio	2.00	.90
❏ 68	Richard Hidalgo	.75	.35
❏ 69	Johnny Damon	.75	.35
❏ 70	Jeff King	.50	.23
❏ 71	Hal Morris	.50	.23
❏ 72	Dean Palmer	.75	.35
❏ 73	Bobby Bonilla	.75	.35
❏ 74	Charles Johnson	.75	.35
❏ 75	Eric Karros	.75	.35
❏ 76	Raul Mondesi	.75	.35
❏ 77	Gary Sheffield	.75	.35
❏ 78	Jeromy Burnitz	.75	.35
❏ 79	Marquis Grissom	.50	.23
❏ 80	Dave Nilsson	.50	.23
❏ 81	Fernando Vina	.50	.23
❏ 82	Marty Cordova	.50	.23
❏ 83	Pat Meares	.50	.23
❏ 84	Paul Molitor	2.00	.90
❏ 85	Brad Radke	.75	.35
❏ 86	Terry Steinbach	.50	.23
❏ 87	Todd Walker	.75	.35
❏ 88	Brad Fullmer	.50	.23
❏ 89	Vladimir Guerrero	2.50	1.10
❏ 90	Carl Pavano	.50	.23
❏ 91	Rondell White	.75	.35
❏ 92	Bernard Gilkey	.50	.23
❏ 93	Hideo Nomo	2.00	.90
❏ 94	John Olerud	.75	.35
❏ 95	Rey Ordonez	.75	.35
❏ 96	Mike Piazza	6.00	2.70
❏ 97	Masato Yoshii	1.25	.55
❏ 98	Hideki Irabu	.75	.35
❏ 99	Derek Jeter	6.00	2.70
❏ 100	Chuck Knoblauch	.75	.35
❏ 101	Tino Martinez	.75	.35
❏ 102	Paul O'Neill	.75	.35
❏ 103	Darryl Strawberry	.75	.35
❏ 104	Bernie Williams	2.00	.90
❏ 105	Jason Giambi	.75	.35
❏ 106	Ben Grieve	2.00	.90
❏ 107	Rickey Henderson	2.50	1.10
❏ 108	Matt Stairs	.75	.35
❏ 109	Doug Glanville	.75	.35
❏ 110	Desi Relaford	.50	.23
❏ 111	Scott Rolen	2.50	1.10
❏ 112	Curt Schilling	1.25	.55
❏ 113	Jason Kendall	.75	.35
❏ 114	Al Martin	.50	.23
❏ 115	Jason Schmidt	.50	.23
❏ 116	Kevin Young	.75	.35
❏ 117	Delino DeShields	.50	.23
❏ 118	Gary Gaetti	.75	.35
❏ 119	Brian Jordan	.75	.35
❏ 120	Ray Lankford	.75	.35
❏ 121	Mark McGwire	12.00	5.50
❏ 122	Kevin Brown	1.25	.55
❏ 123	Steve Finley	.75	.35
❏ 124	Tony Gwynn	5.00	2.20
❏ 125	Wally Joyner	.75	.35
❏ 126	Greg Vaughn	.75	.35
❏ 127	Barry Bonds	2.50	1.10
❏ 128	Orel Hershiser	.75	.35
❏ 129	Jeff Kent	.75	.35
❏ 130	Bill Mueller	.75	.35
❏ 131	Jay Buhner	.75	.35
❏ 132	Ken Griffey Jr.	10.00	4.50
❏ 133	Randy Johnson	2.00	.90
❏ 134	Edgar Martinez	.75	.35
❏ 135	Alex Rodriguez	6.00	2.70
❏ 136	David Segui	.50	.23
❏ 137	Rolando Arrojo	2.00	.90

		MINT	NRMT
❑ 138	Wade Boggs	2.00	.90
❑ 139	Quinton McCracken	.50	.23
❑ 140	Fred McGriff	1.25	.55
❑ 141	Will Clark	2.00	.90
❑ 142	Juan Gonzalez	4.00	1.80
❑ 143	Tom Goodwin	.50	.23
❑ 144	Ivan Rodriguez	2.50	1.10
❑ 145	Aaron Sele	.75	.35
❑ 146	John Wetteland	.75	.35
❑ 147	Jose Canseco	2.50	1.10
❑ 148	Roger Clemens	5.00	2.20
❑ 149	Jose Cruz Jr.	.75	.35
❑ 150	Carlos Delgado	2.00	.90

1998 Revolution Shadow Series

	MINT	NRMT
COMMON CARD (1-150)	8.00	3.60

*STARS: 6X TO 15X BASIC CARDS
*YOUNG STARS: 5X TO 12X BASIC CARDS
*ROOKIES: 4X TO 10X BASIC CARDS
RANDOM INSERTS IN HOBBY PACKS
STATED PRINT RUN 99 SERIAL #'d SETS

1998 Revolution Foul Pole

	MINT	NRMT
COMPLETE SET (20)	500.00	220.00
COMMON CARD (1-20)	5.00	2.20
SEMISTARS	8.00	3.60
UNLISTED STARS	12.00	5.50

STATED ODDS 1:49

		MINT	NRMT
❑ 1	Cal Ripken	50.00	22.00
❑ 2	Nomar Garciaparra	40.00	18.00
❑ 3	Mo Vaughn	12.00	5.50
❑ 4	Frank Thomas	25.00	11.00
❑ 5	Manny Ramirez	15.00	6.75
❑ 6	Bernie Williams	12.00	5.50
❑ 7	Ben Grieve	12.00	5.50
❑ 8	Ken Griffey Jr.	60.00	27.00
❑ 9	Alex Rodriguez	40.00	18.00
❑ 10	Juan Gonzalez	25.00	11.00
❑ 11	Ivan Rodriguez	15.00	6.75
❑ 12	Travis Lee	8.00	3.60
❑ 13	Chipper Jones	30.00	13.50
❑ 14	Sammy Sosa	40.00	18.00
❑ 15	Vinny Castilla	5.00	2.20

		MINT	NRMT
❑ 16	Moises Alou	5.00	2.20
❑ 17	Gary Sheffield	5.00	2.20
❑ 18	Mike Piazza	40.00	18.00
❑ 19	Mark McGwire	80.00	36.00
❑ 20	Barry Bonds	15.00	6.75

1998 Revolution Major League Icons

	MINT	NRMT
COMPLETE SET (10)	500.00	220.00
COMMON CARD (1-10)	15.00	6.75

STATED ODDS 1:121

		MINT	NRMT
❑ 1	Cal Ripken	60.00	27.00
❑ 2	Nomar Garciaparra	50.00	22.00
❑ 3	Frank Thomas	30.00	13.50
❑ 4	Ken Griffey Jr.	80.00	36.00
❑ 5	Alex Rodriguez	50.00	22.00
❑ 6	Chipper Jones	40.00	18.00
❑ 7	Kerry Wood	15.00	6.75
❑ 8	Mike Piazza	50.00	22.00
❑ 9	Mark McGwire	100.00	45.00
❑ 10	Tony Gwynn	40.00	18.00

1998 Revolution Prime Time Performers

	MINT	NRMT
COMPLETE SET (20)	300.00	135.00
COMMON CARD (1-20)	2.50	1.10

STATED ODDS 1:25

		MINT	NRMT
❑ 1	Cal Ripken	25.00	11.00
❑ 2	Nomar Garciaparra	20.00	9.00
❑ 3	Frank Thomas	12.00	5.50
❑ 4	Jim Thome	6.00	2.70
❑ 5	Hideki Irabu	2.50	1.10
❑ 6	Derek Jeter	20.00	9.00
❑ 7	Ben Grieve	6.00	2.70
❑ 8	Ken Griffey Jr.	30.00	13.50
❑ 9	Alex Rodriguez	20.00	9.00
❑ 10	Juan Gonzalez	12.00	5.50
❑ 11	Ivan Rodriguez	8.00	3.60
❑ 12	Travis Lee	4.00	1.80
❑ 13	Chipper Jones	15.00	6.75
❑ 14	Greg Maddux	15.00	6.75
❑ 15	Kerry Wood	6.00	2.70
❑ 16	Larry Walker	6.00	2.70
❑ 17	Jeff Bagwell	8.00	3.60

		MINT	NRMT
❑ 18	Mike Piazza	20.00	9.00
❑ 19	Mark McGwire	40.00	18.00
❑ 20	Tony Gwynn	15.00	6.75

1998 Revolution Rookies and Hardball Heroes

	MINT	NRMT
COMPLETE SET (30)	120.00	55.00
COMMON CARD (1-30)	.75	.35

STATED ODDS 1:6 HOBBY

		MINT	NRMT
❑ 1	Justin Baughman	1.25	.55
❑ 2	Jarrod Washburn	.75	.35
❑ 3	Travis Lee	2.00	.90
❑ 4	Kerry Wood	3.00	1.35
❑ 5	Magglio Ordonez	6.00	2.70
❑ 6	Todd Helton	3.00	1.35
❑ 7	Derek Lee	.75	.35
❑ 8	Richard Hidalgo	1.25	.55
❑ 9	Mike Caruso	.75	.35
❑ 10	David Ortiz	.75	.35
❑ 11	Brad Fullmer	.75	.35
❑ 12	Masato Yoshii	1.50	.70
❑ 13	Orlando Hernandez	5.00	2.20
❑ 14	Ricky Ledee	1.25	.55
❑ 15	Ben Grieve	3.00	1.35
❑ 16	Carlton Loewer	.75	.35
❑ 17	Desi Relaford	.75	.35
❑ 18	Ruben Rivera	.75	.35
❑ 19	Rolando Arrojo	2.00	.90
❑ 20	Matt Perisho	.75	.35
❑ 21	Chipper Jones	8.00	3.60
❑ 22	Greg Maddux	8.00	3.60
❑ 23	Cal Ripken	12.00	5.50
❑ 24	Nomar Garciaparra	10.00	4.50
❑ 25	Frank Thomas	6.00	2.70
❑ 26	Mark McGwire	20.00	9.00
❑ 27	Tony Gwynn	8.00	3.60
❑ 28	Ken Griffey Jr.	15.00	6.75
❑ 29	Alex Rodriguez	10.00	4.50
❑ 30	Juan Gonzalez	6.00	2.70

1998 Revolution Rookies and Hardball Heroes Gold

	MINT	NRMT
COMMON CARD (1-20)	15.00	6.75

*GOLD: 6X TO 15X BASIC HEROES
RANDOM INSERTS IN HOBBY PACKS
STATED PRINT RUN 50 SERIAL #'d SETS

1998 Revolution Showstoppers

	MINT	NRMT
COMPLETE SET (36)	300.00	135.00
COMMON CARD (1-36)	2.00	.90

STATED ODDS 2:25

		MINT	NRMT
❑ 1	Cal Ripken	20.00	9.00
❑ 2	Nomar Garciaparra	15.00	6.75
❑ 3	Pedro Martinez	6.00	2.70

		MINT	NRMT
❏ 4	Mo Vaughn	5.00	2.20
❏ 5	Frank Thomas	10.00	4.50
❏ 6	Manny Ramirez	6.00	2.70
❏ 7	Jim Thome	5.00	2.20
❏ 8	Jaret Wright	5.00	2.20
❏ 9	Paul Molitor	5.00	2.20
❏ 10	Orlando Hernandez	10.00	4.50
❏ 11	Derek Jeter	15.00	6.75
❏ 12	Bernie Williams	5.00	2.20
❏ 13	Ben Grieve	5.00	2.20
❏ 14	Ken Griffey Jr.	25.00	11.00
❏ 15	Alex Rodriguez	15.00	6.75
❏ 16	Wade Boggs	5.00	2.20
❏ 17	Juan Gonzalez	10.00	4.50
❏ 18	Ivan Rodriguez	6.00	2.70
❏ 19	Jose Canseco	6.00	2.70
❏ 20	Roger Clemens	12.00	5.50
❏ 21	Travis Lee	3.00	1.35
❏ 22	Andres Galarraga	3.00	1.35
❏ 23	Chipper Jones	12.00	5.50
❏ 24	Greg Maddux	12.00	5.50
❏ 25	Sammy Sosa	15.00	6.75
❏ 26	Kerry Wood	5.00	2.20
❏ 27	Vinny Castilla	2.00	.90
❏ 28	Larry Walker	5.00	2.20
❏ 29	Moises Alou	2.00	.90
❏ 30	Raul Mondesi	2.00	.90
❏ 31	Gary Sheffield	2.00	.90
❏ 32	Hideki Irabu	2.00	.90
❏ 33	Mike Piazza	15.00	6.75
❏ 34	Mark McGwire	30.00	13.50
❏ 35	Tony Gwynn	12.00	5.50
❏ 36	Barry Bonds	6.00	2.70

1999 Revolution

	MINT	NRMT
COMPLETE SET (150)	150.00	70.00
COMMON CARD (1-150)	.50	.23
MINOR STARS	.75	.35
SEMISTARS	1.25	.55
UNLISTED STARS	2.00	.90
COMMON SP	1.50	.70
SP STATED ODDS 1:4		

❏ 1	Jim Edmonds	.75	.35
❏ 2	Darin Erstad	1.25	.55
❏ 3	Troy Glaus	2.00	.90
❏ 4	Tim Salmon	1.25	.55
❏ 5	Mo Vaughn	2.00	.90
❏ 6	Steve Finley	.75	.35

❏ 7	Luis Gonzalez	.75	.35
❏ 8	Randy Johnson	2.00	.90
❏ 9	Travis Lee	1.25	.55
❏ 10	Matt Williams	2.00	.90
❏ 11	Andruw Jones	2.00	.90
❏ 12	Chipper Jones	5.00	2.20
❏ 13	Brian Jordan	.75	.35
❏ 14	Javy Lopez	.75	.35
❏ 15	Greg Maddux	5.00	2.20
❏ 16	Kevin McGlinchy SP	.70	
❏ 17	John Smoltz	1.25	.55
❏ 18	Brady Anderson	.75	.35
❏ 19	Albert Belle	2.00	.90
❏ 20	Will Clark	2.00	.90
❏ 21	Willis Otanez SP	2.00	.90
❏ 22	Calvin Pickering SP	1.50	.70
❏ 23	Cal Ripken	8.00	3.60
❏ 24	Nomar Garciaparra	6.00	2.70
❏ 25	Pedro Martinez	2.50	1.10
❏ 26	Troy O'Leary	.75	.35
❏ 27	Jose Offerman	.75	.35
❏ 28	Mark Grace	1.25	.55
❏ 29	Mickey Morandini	.50	.23
❏ 30	Henry Rodriguez	.75	.35
❏ 31	Sammy Sosa	6.00	2.70
❏ 32	Ray Durham	.75	.35
❏ 33	Carlos Lee SP	2.00	.90
❏ 34	Jeff Liefer SP	1.50	.70
❏ 35	Magglio Ordonez	2.00	.90
❏ 36	Frank Thomas	4.00	1.80
❏ 37	Mike Cameron	.50	.23
❏ 38	Sean Casey	2.00	.90
❏ 39	Barry Larkin	2.00	.90
❏ 40	Greg Vaughn	.75	.35
❏ 41	Roberto Alomar	2.00	.90
❏ 42	Sandy Alomar Jr.	.75	.35
❏ 43	David Justice	.75	.35
❏ 44	Kenny Lofton	1.25	.55
❏ 45	Manny Ramirez	2.50	1.10
❏ 46	Richie Sexson	1.25	.55
❏ 47	Jim Thome	2.00	.90
❏ 48	Dante Bichette	.75	.35
❏ 49	Vinny Castilla	.75	.35
❏ 50	Darryl Hamilton	.50	.23
❏ 51	Todd Helton	2.00	.90
❏ 52	Larry Walker	2.00	.90
❏ 53	Tony Clark	.75	.35
❏ 54	Damion Easley	.75	.35
❏ 55	Bob Higginson	.75	.35
❏ 56	Gabe Kapler SP	3.00	1.35
❏ 57	Alex Gonzalez SP	1.50	.70
❏ 58	Mark Kotsay	.50	.23
❏ 59	Kevin Orie	.50	.23
❏ 60	Preston Wilson SP	1.50	.70
❏ 61	Jeff Bagwell	2.50	1.10
❏ 62	Derek Bell	.75	.35
❏ 63	Craig Biggio	2.00	.90
❏ 64	Ken Caminiti	.75	.35
❏ 65	Carlos Beltran SP	5.00	2.20
❏ 66	Johnny Damon	.75	.35
❏ 67	Jermaine Dye	.75	.35
❏ 68	Carlos Febles SP	2.00	.90
❏ 69	Kevin Brown	1.25	.55
❏ 70	Todd Hundley	.75	.35
❏ 71	Eric Karros	.75	.35
❏ 72	Raul Mondesi	.75	.35
❏ 73	Gary Sheffield	.75	.35
❏ 74	Jeromy Burnitz	.75	.35
❏ 75	Jeff Cirillo	.75	.35
❏ 76	Marquis Grissom	.50	.23
❏ 77	Fernando Vina	.50	.23
❏ 78	Chad Allen SP	2.00	.90
❏ 79	Corey Koskie SP	1.50	.70
❏ 80	Doug Mientkiewicz SP	2.00	.90
❏ 81	Brad Radke	.75	.35
❏ 82	Todd Walker	.75	.35
❏ 83	Michael Barrett SP	2.00	.90
❏ 84	Vladimir Guerrero	2.50	1.10
❏ 85	Wilton Guerrero	.50	.23
❏ 86	Guillermo Mota SP	2.00	.90
❏ 87	Rondell White	.75	.35
❏ 88	Edgardo Alfonzo	1.25	.55
❏ 89	Rickey Henderson	2.50	1.10
❏ 90	John Olerud	.75	.35
❏ 91	Mike Piazza	6.00	2.70
❏ 92	Robin Ventura	.75	.35

❏ 93	Roger Clemens	5.00	2.20
❏ 94	Chili Davis	.75	.35
❏ 95	Derek Jeter	6.00	2.70
❏ 96	Chuck Knoblauch	.75	.35
❏ 97	Tino Martinez	.75	.35
❏ 98	Paul O'Neill	.75	.35
❏ 99	Bernie Williams	2.00	.90
❏ 100	Eric Chavez SP	2.00	.90
❏ 101	Jason Giambi	.75	.35
❏ 102	Ben Grieve	2.00	.90
❏ 103	John Jaha	.75	.35
❏ 104	Olmedo Saenz SP	1.50	.70
❏ 105	Bobby Abreu	.75	.35
❏ 106	Doug Glanville	.75	.35
❏ 107	Desi Relaford	.50	.23
❏ 108	Scott Rolen	2.50	1.10
❏ 109	Curt Schilling	1.25	.55
❏ 110	Brian Giles	.75	.35
❏ 111	Jason Kendall	.75	.35
❏ 112	Pat Meares	.50	.23
❏ 113	Kevin Young	.75	.35
❏ 114	J.D. Drew SP	6.00	2.70
❏ 115	Ray Lankford	.75	.35
❏ 116	Eli Marrero	.50	.23
❏ 117	Joe McEwing SP	6.00	2.70
❏ 118	Mark McGwire	12.00	5.50
❏ 119	Fernando Tatis	2.00	.90
❏ 120	Tony Gwynn	5.00	2.20
❏ 121	Trevor Hoffman	.75	.35
❏ 122	Wally Joyner	.75	.35
❏ 123	Reggie Sanders	.50	.23
❏ 124	Barry Bonds	2.50	1.10
❏ 125	Ellis Burks	.75	.35
❏ 126	Jeff Kent	.75	.35
❏ 127	Ramon E.Martinez SP	1.50	.70
❏ 128	Joe Nathan SP	2.00	.90
❏ 129	Freddy Garcia SP	15.00	6.75
❏ 130	Ken Griffey Jr.	10.00	4.50
❏ 131	Brian Hunter	.50	.23
❏ 132	Edgar Martinez	.75	.35
❏ 133	Alex Rodriguez	6.00	2.70
❏ 134	David Segui	.50	.23
❏ 135	Wade Boggs	2.00	.90
❏ 136	Jose Canseco	2.50	1.10
❏ 137	Quinton McCracken	.50	.23
❏ 138	Fred McGriff	1.25	.55
❏ 139	Kelly Dransfeldt SP	2.50	1.10
❏ 140	Juan Gonzalez	4.00	1.80
❏ 141	Rusty Greer	.75	.35
❏ 142	Rafael Palmeiro	2.00	.90
❏ 143	Ivan Rodriguez	2.50	1.10
❏ 144	Lee Stevens	.50	.23
❏ 145	Jose Cruz Jr.	.75	.35
❏ 146	Carlos Delgado	2.00	.90
❏ 147	Shawn Green	2.00	.90
❏ 148	Roy Halladay SP	1.50	.70
❏ 149	Shannon Stewart	.75	.35
❏ 150	Kevin Witt SP	1.50	.70

1999 Revolution Premiere Date

	MINT	NRMT
COMMON CARD (1-150)	10.00	4.50
*STARS: 8X TO 20X BASIC CARDS		
*YNG.STARS: 6X TO 15X BASIC		
*SP'S: 3X TO 8X BASIC SP'S		
*SP RCs: 2.5X TO 6X BASIC SP RC's		

STATED ODDS 1:25 HOBBY
STATED PRINT RUN 49 SERIAL #'d SETS

1999 Revolution Red

	MINT	NRMT
COMMON CARD (1-150)	2.50	1.10

*STARS: 2X TO 5X BASIC CARDS
*YNG.STARS: 1.5X TO 4X BASIC CARDS
*SP'S: .75X TO 2X BASIC SP'S
*SP RC'S: .6X TO 1.5X BASIC SP RC'S
RANDOM INSERTS IN RETAIL PACKS
STATED PRINT RUN 299 SERIAL #'d SETS

1999 Revolution Shadow Series

	MINT	NRMT
COMMON CARD (1-150)	5.00	2.20

*STARS: 4X TO 10X BASIC CARDS
*YNG.STARS: 3X TO 8X BASIC CARDS
*SP'S: 1.5X TO 4X BASIC SP'S
*SP RC'S: 1.25X TO 3X BASIC SP RC'S
RANDOM INSERTS IN HOBBY PACKS
STATED PRINT RUN 99 SERIAL #'d SETS

1999 Revolution Diamond Legacy

	MINT	NRMT
COMPLETE SET (36)	300.00	135.00
COMMON CARD (1-36)	2.50	1.10

		MINT	NRMT
UNLISTED STARS		5.00	2.20
STATED ODDS 2:25			
❏ 1	Troy Glaus	5.00	2.20
❏ 2	Mo Vaughn	5.00	2.20
❏ 3	Matt Williams	5.00	2.20
❏ 4	Chipper Jones	12.00	5.50
❏ 5	Andruw Jones	5.00	2.20
❏ 6	Greg Maddux	12.00	5.50
❏ 7	Albert Belle	5.00	2.20
❏ 8	Cal Ripken	20.00	9.00
❏ 9	Nomar Garciaparra	15.00	6.75
❏ 10	Sammy Sosa	15.00	6.75
❏ 11	Frank Thomas	10.00	4.50
❏ 12	Manny Ramirez	6.00	2.70
❏ 13	Todd Helton	5.00	2.20
❏ 14	Larry Walker	5.00	2.20
❏ 15	Gabe Kapler	5.00	2.20
❏ 16	Jeff Bagwell	6.00	2.70
❏ 17	Craig Biggio	5.00	2.20
❏ 18	Raul Mondesi	2.50	1.10
❏ 19	Vladimir Guerrero	6.00	2.70
❏ 20	Mike Piazza	15.00	6.75
❏ 21	Roger Clemens	12.00	5.50
❏ 22	Derek Jeter	15.00	6.75
❏ 23	Bernie Williams	5.00	2.20
❏ 24	Ben Grieve	5.00	2.20
❏ 25	Scott Rolen	6.00	2.70
❏ 26	J.D. Drew	6.00	2.70
❏ 27	Mark McGwire	30.00	13.50
❏ 28	Fernando Tatis	5.00	2.20
❏ 29	Tony Gwynn	12.00	5.50
❏ 30	Barry Bonds	6.00	2.70
❏ 31	Ken Griffey Jr.	25.00	11.00
❏ 32	Alex Rodriguez	15.00	6.75
❏ 33	Jose Canseco	6.00	2.70
❏ 34	Juan Gonzalez	10.00	4.50
❏ 35	Ivan Rodriguez	6.00	2.70
❏ 36	Shawn Green	5.00	2.20

1999 Revolution Foul Pole

		MINT	NRMT
COMPLETE SET (20)		600.00	275.00
COMMON CARD (1-20)		6.00	2.70
UNLISTED STARS		12.00	5.50
STATED ODDS 1:49			
❏ 1	Chipper Jones	30.00	13.50
❏ 2	Andruw Jones	12.00	5.50
❏ 3	Cal Ripken	50.00	22.00
❏ 4	Nomar Garciaparra	40.00	18.00
❏ 5	Sammy Sosa	40.00	18.00
❏ 6	Frank Thomas	25.00	11.00
❏ 7	Manny Ramirez	15.00	6.75
❏ 8	Jeff Bagwell	15.00	6.75
❏ 9	Raul Mondesi	6.00	2.70
❏ 10	Vladimir Guerrero	15.00	6.75
❏ 11	Mike Piazza	40.00	18.00
❏ 12	Derek Jeter	40.00	18.00
❏ 13	Bernie Williams	12.00	5.50
❏ 14	Scott Rolen	15.00	6.75
❏ 15	J.D. Drew	15.00	6.75
❏ 16	Mark McGwire	80.00	36.00
❏ 17	Tony Gwynn	30.00	13.50
❏ 18	Ken Griffey Jr.	60.00	27.00
❏ 19	Alex Rodriguez	40.00	18.00
❏ 20	Juan Gonzalez	25.00	11.00

1999 Revolution MLB Icons

		MINT	NRMT
COMPLETE SET (10)		500.00	220.00
COMMON CARD (1-10)		30.00	13.50
STATED ODDS 1:121			
❏ 1	Cal Ripken	60.00	27.00
❏ 2	Nomar Garciaparra	50.00	22.00
❏ 3	Sammy Sosa	50.00	22.00
❏ 4	Frank Thomas	30.00	13.50
❏ 5	Mike Piazza	50.00	22.00
❏ 6	Derek Jeter	50.00	22.00
❏ 7	Mark McGwire	100.00	45.00
❏ 8	Tony Gwynn	40.00	18.00
❏ 9	Ken Griffey Jr.	80.00	36.00
❏ 10	Alex Rodriguez	50.00	22.00

1999 Revolution Thorn in the Side

		MINT	NRMT
COMPLETE SET (20)		300.00	135.00
COMMON CARD (1-20)		5.00	2.20
UNLISTED STARS		6.00	2.70
STATED ODDS 1:25			
❏ 1	Mo Vaughn	5.00	2.20
❏ 2	Chipper Jones	15.00	6.75
❏ 3	Greg Maddux	15.00	6.75
❏ 4	Cal Ripken	25.00	11.00
❏ 5	Nomar Garciaparra	20.00	9.00
❏ 6	Sammy Sosa	20.00	9.00
❏ 7	Frank Thomas	12.00	5.50
❏ 8	Manny Ramirez	8.00	3.60
❏ 9	Jeff Bagwell	8.00	3.60
❏ 10	Mike Piazza	20.00	9.00
❏ 11	Derek Jeter	20.00	9.00
❏ 12	Bernie Williams	6.00	2.70
❏ 13	J.D. Drew	8.00	3.60
❏ 14	Mark McGwire	40.00	18.00
❏ 15	Tony Gwynn	15.00	6.75
❏ 16	Barry Bonds	8.00	3.60
❏ 17	Ken Griffey Jr.	30.00	13.50
❏ 18	Alex Rodriguez	20.00	9.00
❏ 19	Juan Gonzalez	12.00	5.50
❏ 20	Ivan Rodriguez	8.00	3.60

1999 Revolution Tripleheader

	MINT	NRMT
COMPLETE SET (30)	150.00	70.00
COMMON CARD (1-30)	1.00	.45
UNLISTED STARS	2.50	1.10
STATED ODDS 4:25 HOBBY		
COMMON TIER 1 (1-10)	40.00	18.00
*TIER 1: 3X TO 8X HI COLUMN		
TIER 1 PRINT RUN 99 SERIAL #'d SETS		
COMMON TIER 2 (11-20)	10.00	4.50
*TIER 2: 2X TO 5X HI COLUMN		
TIER 2 PRINT RUN 199 SERIAL #'d SETS		
COMMON TIER 3 (21-30)	5.00	2.20
*TIER 3: 1.25X TO 3X HI COLUMN		
TIER 3 PRINT RUN 299 SERIAL #'d SETS		
TIER CARDS RANDOM IN HOBBY PACKS		

		MINT	NRMT
❑ 1	Greg Maddux	6.00	2.70
❑ 2	Cal Ripken	10.00	4.50
❑ 3	Nomar Garciaparra	8.00	3.60
❑ 4	Sammy Sosa	8.00	3.60
❑ 5	Frank Thomas	5.00	2.20
❑ 6	Mike Piazza	8.00	3.60
❑ 7	Mark McGwire	15.00	6.75
❑ 8	Tony Gwynn	6.00	2.70
❑ 9	Ken Griffey Jr.	12.00	5.50
❑ 10	Alex Rodriguez	8.00	3.60
❑ 11	Mo Vaughn	2.50	1.10
❑ 12	Chipper Jones	6.00	2.70
❑ 13	Manny Ramirez	3.00	1.35
❑ 14	Larry Walker	2.50	1.10
❑ 15	Jeff Bagwell	3.00	1.35
❑ 16	Vladimir Guerrero	3.00	1.35
❑ 17	Derek Jeter	8.00	3.60
❑ 18	J.D. Drew	3.00	1.35
❑ 19	Barry Bonds	3.00	1.35
❑ 20	Juan Gonzalez	5.00	2.20
❑ 21	Troy Glaus	2.50	1.10
❑ 22	Andruw Jones	2.50	1.10
❑ 23	Matt Williams	2.50	1.10
❑ 24	Craig Biggio	2.50	1.10
❑ 25	Raul Mondesi	1.00	.45
❑ 26	Roger Clemens	6.00	2.70
❑ 27	Bernie Williams	2.50	1.10
❑ 28	Scott Rolen	3.00	1.35
❑ 29	Jose Canseco	3.00	1.35
❑ 30	Ivan Rodriguez	3.00	1.35

1988 Score

		MINT	NRMT
COMPLETE SET (660)		10.00	4.50
COMP.FACT.SET (660)		12.00	5.50
COMMON CARD (1-660)		.05	.02
MINOR STARS		.10	.05
UNLISTED STARS		.20	.09
❑ 1	Don Mattingly	.40	.18
❑ 2	Wade Boggs	.20	.09
❑ 3	Tim Raines	.20	.09
❑ 4	Andre Dawson	.20	.09
❑ 5	Mark McGwire	2.00	.90
❑ 6	Kevin Seitzer	.10	.05
❑ 7	Wally Joyner	.15	.07
❑ 8	Jesse Barfield	.05	.02
❑ 9	Pedro Guerrero	.05	.02
❑ 10	Eric Davis	.40	.18
❑ 11	George Brett	.25	.11
❑ 12	Ozzie Smith	.25	.11
❑ 13	Rickey Henderson	.25	.11
❑ 14	Jim Rice	.10	.05
❑ 15	Matt Nokes	.05	.02
❑ 16	Mike Schmidt	.30	.14
❑ 17	Dave Parker	.10	.05
❑ 18	Eddie Murray	.20	.09
❑ 19	Andres Galarraga	.20	.09
❑ 20	Tony Fernandez	.10	.05
❑ 21	Kevin McReynolds	.05	.02
❑ 22	B.J. Surhoff	.10	.05
❑ 23	Pat Tabler	.05	.02
❑ 24	Kirby Puckett	.30	.14
❑ 25	Benny Santiago	.05	.02
❑ 26	Ryne Sandberg	.25	.11
❑ 27	Kelly Downs (Will Clark in background, out of focus)	.05	.02
❑ 28	Jose Cruz	.05	.02
❑ 29	Pete O'Brien	.05	.02
❑ 30	Mark Langston	.05	.02
❑ 31	Lee Smith	.10	.05
❑ 32	Juan Samuel	.05	.02
❑ 33	Kevin Bass	.05	.02
❑ 34	R.J. Reynolds	.05	.02
❑ 35	Steve Sax	.10	.05
❑ 36	John Kruk	.10	.05
❑ 37	Alan Trammell	.15	.07
❑ 38	Chris Bosio	.05	.02
❑ 39	Brook Jacoby	.05	.02
❑ 40	Willie McGee UER (Excited misspelled as excitd)	.10	.05
❑ 41	Dave Magadan	.05	.02
❑ 42	Fred Lynn	.05	.02
❑ 43	Kent Hrbek	.05	.02
❑ 44	Brian Downing	.05	.02
❑ 45	Jose Canseco	.40	.18
❑ 46	Jim Presley	.05	.02
❑ 47	Mike Stanley	.10	.05
❑ 48	Tony Pena	.05	.02
❑ 49	David Cone	.25	.11
❑ 50	Rick Sutcliffe	.05	.02
❑ 51	Doug Drabek	.05	.02
❑ 52	Bill Doran	.05	.02
❑ 53	Mike Scioscia	.05	.02
❑ 54	Candy Maldonado	.05	.02
❑ 55	Dave Winfield	.20	.09
❑ 56	Lou Whitaker	.05	.02
❑ 57	Tom Henke	.05	.02
❑ 58	Ken Gerhart	.05	.02
❑ 59	Glenn Braggs	.05	.02
❑ 60	Julio Franco	.05	.02
❑ 61	Charlie Leibrandt	.05	.02
❑ 62	Gary Gaetti	.10	.05
❑ 63	Bob Boone	.10	.05
❑ 64	Luis Polonia	.05	.02
❑ 65	Dwight Evans	.10	.05
❑ 66	Phil Bradley	.05	.02
❑ 67	Mike Boddicker	.05	.02
❑ 68	Vince Coleman	.10	.05
❑ 69	Howard Johnson	.10	.05
❑ 70	Tim Wallach	.05	.02
❑ 71	Keith Moreland	.05	.02
❑ 72	Barry Larkin	.20	.09
❑ 73	Alan Ashby	.05	.02
❑ 74	Rick Rhoden	.05	.02
❑ 75	Darrell Evans	.10	.05
❑ 76	Dave Stieb	.05	.02
❑ 77	Dan Plesac	.05	.02
❑ 78	Will Clark UER (Born 3/17/64, should be 3/13/64)	.25	.11
❑ 79	Frank White	.10	.05
❑ 80	Joe Carter	.20	.09
❑ 81	Mike Witt	.05	.02
❑ 82	Terry Steinbach	.10	.05
❑ 83	Alvin Davis	.05	.02
❑ 84	Tommy Herr (Will Clark shown sliding into second)	.10	.05
❑ 85	Vance Law	.05	.02
❑ 86	Kal Daniels	.05	.02
❑ 87	Rick Honeycutt UER (Wrong years for stats on back)	.05	.02
❑ 88	Alfredo Griffin	.05	.02
❑ 89	Bret Saberhagen	.10	.05
❑ 90	Bert Blyleven	.10	.05
❑ 91	Jeff Reardon	.10	.05
❑ 92	Cory Snyder	.05	.02
❑ 93A	Greg Walker ERR (93 of 66)	2.00	.90
❑ 93B	Greg Walker COR (93 of 660)	.05	.02
❑ 94	Joe Magrane	.05	.02
❑ 95	Rob Deer	.05	.02
❑ 96	Ray Knight	.05	.02
❑ 97	Casey Candaele	.05	.02
❑ 98	John Cerutti	.05	.02
❑ 99	Buddy Bell	.10	.05
❑ 100	Jack Clark	.05	.02
❑ 101	Eric Bell	.05	.02
❑ 102	Willie Wilson	.05	.02
❑ 103	Dave Schmidt	.05	.02
❑ 104	Dennis Eckersley UER (Complete games stats are wrong)	.10	.05
❑ 105	Don Sutton	.20	.09
❑ 106	Danny Tartabull	.20	.09
❑ 107	Fred McGriff	.20	.09
❑ 108	Les Straker	.05	.02
❑ 109	Lloyd Moseby	.05	.02
❑ 110	Roger Clemens	.50	.23
❑ 111	Glenn Hubbard	.05	.02
❑ 112	Ken Williams	.05	.02
❑ 113	Ruben Sierra	.05	.02
❑ 114	Stan Jefferson	.05	.02
❑ 115	Milt Thompson	.05	.02
❑ 116	Bobby Bonilla	.15	.07
❑ 117	Wayne Tolleson	.05	.02
❑ 118	Matt Williams	1.00	.45
❑ 119	Chet Lemon	.05	.02
❑ 120	Dale Sveum	.05	.02
❑ 121	Dennis Boyd	.05	.02
❑ 122	Brett Butler	.10	.05
❑ 123	Terry Kennedy	.05	.02
❑ 124	Jack Howell	.05	.02
❑ 125	Curt Young	.05	.02
❑ 126A	Dave Valle ERR (Misspelled Dale on card front)	.10	.05
❑ 126B	Dave Valle COR	.05	.02
❑ 127	Curt Wilkerson	.05	.02
❑ 128	Tim Teufel	.05	.02
❑ 129	Ozzie Virgil	.05	.02
❑ 130	Brian Fisher	.05	.02
❑ 131	Lance Parrish	.05	.02
❑ 132	Tom Browning	.05	.02
❑ 133A	Larry Andersen ERR (Misspelled Anderson on card front)	.10	.05
❑ 133B	Larry Andersen COR	.05	.02
❑ 134A	Bob Brenly ERR (Misspelled Brenley on card front)	.10	.05
❑ 134B	Bob Brenly COR	.05	.02
❑ 135	Mike Marshall	.05	.02
❑ 136	Gerald Perry	.05	.02
❑ 137	Bobby Meacham	.05	.02
❑ 138	Larry Herndon	.05	.02
❑ 139	Fred Manrique	.05	.02
❑ 140	Charlie Hough	.10	.05
❑ 141	Ron Darling	.05	.02

142	Herm Winningham	.05	.02
143	Mike Diaz	.05	.02
144	Mike Jackson	.20	.09
145	Denny Walling	.05	.02
146	Robby Thompson	.05	.02
147	Franklin Stubbs	.05	.02
148	Albert Hall	.05	.02
149	Bobby Witt	.05	.02
150	Lance McCullers	.05	.02
151	Scott Bradley	.05	.02
152	Mark McLemore	.05	.02
153	Tim Laudner	.05	.02
154	Greg Swindell	.05	.02
155	Marty Barrett	.05	.02
156	Mike Heath	.05	.02
157	Gary Ward	.05	.02
158A	Lee Mazzilli ERR	.10	.05
	(Misspelled Mazilli on card front)		
158B	Lee Mazzilli COR	.05	.02
159	Tom Foley	.05	.02
160	Robin Yount	.20	.09
161	Steve Bedrosian	.05	.02
162	Bob Walk	.05	.02
163	Nick Esasky	.05	.02
164	Ken Caminiti	.50	.23
165	Jose Uribe	.05	.02
166	Dave Anderson	.05	.02
167	Ed Whitson	.05	.02
168	Ernie Whitt	.05	.02
169	Cecil Cooper	.10	.05
170	Mike Pagliarulo	.05	.02
171	Pat Sheridan	.05	.02
172	Chris Bando	.05	.02
173	Lee Lacy	.05	.02
174	Steve Lombardozzi	.05	.02
175	Mike Greenwell	.05	.02
176	Greg Minton	.05	.02
177	Moose Haas	.05	.02
178	Mike Kingery	.05	.02
179	Greg A. Harris	.05	.02
180	Bo Jackson	.20	.09
181	Carmelo Martinez	.05	.02
182	Alex Trevino	.05	.02
183	Ron Oester	.05	.02
184	Danny Darwin	.05	.02
185	Mike Krukow	.05	.02
186	Rafael Palmeiro	.40	.18
187	Tim Burke	.05	.02
188	Roger McDowell	.05	.02
189	Garry Templeton	.05	.02
190	Terry Pendleton	.10	.05
191	Larry Parrish	.05	.02
192	Rey Quinones	.05	.02
193	Joaquin Andujar	.05	.02
194	Tom Brunansky	.05	.02
195	Donnie Moore	.05	.02
196	Dan Pasqua	.05	.02
197	Jim Gantner	.05	.02
198	Mark Eichhorn	.05	.02
199	John Grubb	.05	.02
200	Bill Ripken	.05	.02
201	Sam Horn	.05	.02
202	Todd Worrell	.10	.05
203	Terry Leach	.05	.02
204	Garth Iorg	.05	.02
205	Brian Dayett	.05	.02
206	Bo Diaz	.05	.02
207	Craig Reynolds	.05	.02
208	Brian Holton	.05	.02
209	Marvell Wynne UER	.05	.02
	(Misspelled Marvelle on card front)		
210	Dave Concepcion	.10	.05
211	Mike Davis	.05	.02
212	Devon White	.10	.05
213	Mickey Brantley	.05	.02
214	Greg Gagne	.05	.02
215	Oddibe McDowell	.05	.02
216	Jimmy Key	.10	.05
217	Dave Bergman	.05	.02
218	Calvin Schiraldi	.05	.02
219	Larry Sheets	.05	.02
220	Mike Easler	.05	.02
221	Kurt Stillwell	.05	.02
222	Chuck Jackson	.05	.02
223	Dave Martinez	.05	.02
224	Tim Leary	.05	.02
225	Steve Garvey	.15	.07
226	Greg Mathews	.05	.02
227	Doug Sisk	.05	.02
228	Dave Henderson	.05	.02
	(Wearing Red Sox uniform; Red Sox logo on back)		
229	Jimmy Dwyer	.05	.02
230	Larry Owen	.05	.02
231	Andre Thornton	.10	.05
232	Mark Salas	.05	.02
233	Tom Brookens	.05	.02
234	Greg Brock	.05	.02
235	Rance Mulliniks	.05	.02
236	Bob Brower	.05	.02
237	Joe Niekro	.05	.02
238	Scott Bankhead	.05	.02
239	Doug DeCinces	.05	.02
240	Tommy John	.10	.05
241	Rich Gedman	.05	.02
242	Ted Power	.05	.02
243	Dave Meads	.05	.02
244	Jim Sundberg	.05	.02
245	Ken Oberkfell	.05	.02
246	Jimmy Jones	.05	.02
247	Ken Landreaux	.05	.02
248	Jose Oquendo	.05	.02
249	John Mitchell	.05	.02
250	Don Baylor	.10	.05
251	Scott Fletcher	.05	.02
252	Al Newman	.05	.02
253	Carney Lansford	.10	.05
254	Johnny Ray	.05	.02
255	Gary Pettis	.05	.02
256	Ken Phelps	.05	.02
257	Rick Leach	.05	.02
258	Tim Stoddard	.05	.02
259	Ed Romero	.05	.02
260	Sid Bream	.05	.02
261A	Tom Niedenfuer ERR	.10	.05
	(Misspelled Neidenfuer on card front)		
261B	Tom Niedenfuer COR	.05	.02
262	Rick Dempsey	.05	.02
263	Lonnie Smith	.05	.02
264	Bob Forsch	.05	.02
265	Barry Bonds	.50	.23
266	Willie Randolph	.10	.05
267	Mike Ramsey	.05	.02
268	Don Slaught	.05	.02
269	Mickey Tettleton	.10	.05
270	Jerry Reuss	.05	.02
271	Marc Sullivan	.05	.02
272	Jim Morrison	.05	.02
273	Steve Balboni	.05	.02
274	Dick Schofield	.05	.02
275	John Tudor	.05	.02
276	Gene Larkin	.05	.02
277	Harold Reynolds	.10	.05
278	Jerry Browne	.05	.02
279	Willie Upshaw	.05	.02
280	Ted Higuera	.05	.02
281	Terry McGriff	.05	.02
282	Terry Puhl	.05	.02
283	Mark Wasinger	.05	.02
284	Luis Salazar	.05	.02
285	Ted Simmons	.10	.05
286	John Shelby	.05	.02
287	John Smiley	.10	.05
288	Curt Ford	.05	.02
289	Steve Crawford	.05	.02
290	Dan Quisenberry	.05	.02
291	Alan Wiggins	.05	.02
292	Randy Bush	.05	.02
293	John Candelaria	.05	.02
294	Tony Phillips	.05	.02
295	Mike Morgan	.05	.02
296	Bill Wegman	.05	.02
297A	Terry Francona ERR	.10	.05
	(Misspelled Franconia on card front)		
297B	Terry Francona COR	.05	.02
298	Mickey Hatcher	.05	.02
299	Andres Thomas	.05	.02
300	Bob Stanley	.05	.02
301	Al Pedrique	.05	.02
302	Jim Lindeman	.05	.02
303	Wally Backman	.05	.02
304	Paul O'Neill	.15	.07
305	Hubie Brooks	.05	.02
306	Steve Buechele	.05	.02
307	Bobby Thigpen	.05	.02
308	George Hendrick	.05	.02
309	John Moses	.05	.02
310	Ron Guidry	.05	.02
311	Bill Schroeder	.05	.02
312	Jose Nunez	.05	.02
313	Bud Black	.05	.02
314	Joe Sambito	.05	.02
315	Scott McGregor	.05	.02
316	Rafael Santana	.05	.02
317	Frank Williams	.05	.02
318	Mike Fitzgerald	.05	.02
319	Rick Mahler	.05	.02
320	Jim Gott	.05	.02
321	Mariano Duncan	.05	.02
322	Jose Guzman	.05	.02
323	Lee Guetterman	.05	.02
324	Dan Gladden	.05	.02
325	Gary Carter	.15	.07
326	Tracy Jones	.05	.02
327	Floyd Youmans	.05	.02
328	Bill Dawley	.05	.02
329	Paul Noce	.05	.02
330	Angel Salazar	.05	.02
331	Goose Gossage	.15	.07
332	George Frazier	.05	.02
333	Ruppert Jones	.05	.02
334	Billy Joe Robidoux	.05	.02
335	Mike Scott	.05	.02
336	Randy Myers	.15	.07
337	Bob Sebra	.05	.02
338	Eric Show	.05	.02
339	Mitch Williams	.05	.02
340	Paul Molitor	.20	.09
341	Gus Polidor	.05	.02
342	Steve Trout	.05	.02
343	Jerry Don Gleaton	.05	.02
344	Bob Knepper	.05	.02
345	Mitch Webster	.05	.02
346	John Morris	.05	.02
347	Andy Hawkins	.05	.02
348	Dave Leiper	.05	.02
349	Ernest Riles	.05	.02
350	Dwight Gooden	.10	.05
351	Dave Righetti	.05	.02
352	Pat Dodson	.05	.02
353	John Habyan	.05	.02
354	Jim Deshaies	.05	.02
355	Butch Wynegar	.05	.02
356	Bryn Smith	.05	.02
357	Matt Young	.05	.02
358	Tom Pagnozzi	.05	.02
359	Floyd Rayford	.05	.02
360	Darryl Strawberry	.10	.05
361	Sal Butera	.05	.02
362	Domingo Ramos	.05	.02
363	Chris Brown	.05	.02
364	Jose Gonzalez	.05	.02
365	Dave Smith	.05	.02
366	Andy McGaffigan	.05	.02
367	Stan Javier	.05	.02
368	Henry Cotto	.05	.02
369	Mike Birkbeck	.05	.02
370	Len Dykstra	.05	.05
371	Dave Collins	.05	.05
372	Spike Owen	.05	.05
373	Geno Petralli	.05	.05
374	Ron Karkovice	.05	.05
375	Shane Rawley	.05	.05
376	DeWayne Buice	.05	.05
377	Bill Pecota	.05	.05
378	Leon Durham	.05	.05
379	Ed Olwine	.05	.05
380	Bruce Hurst	.05	.05
381	Bob McClure	.05	.05
382	Mark Thurmond	.05	.05
383	Buddy Biancalana	.05	.05
384	Tim Conroy	.05	.02
385	Tony Gwynn	.50	.23
386	Greg Gross	.05	.02

387	Barry Lyons	.05	.02
388	Mike Felder	.05	.02
389	Pat Clements	.05	.02
390	Ken Griffey	.10	.05
391	Mark Davis	.05	.02
392	Jose Rijo	.05	.02
393	Mike Young	.05	.02
394	Willie Fraser	.05	.02
395	Dion James	.05	.02
396	Steve Shields	.05	.02
397	Randy St.Claire	.05	.02
398	Danny Jackson	.05	.02
399	Cecil Fielder	.15	.07
400	Keith Hernandez	.10	.05
401	Don Carman	.05	.02
402	Chuck Crim	.05	.02
403	Rob Woodward	.05	.02
404	Junior Ortiz	.05	.02
405	Glenn Wilson	.05	.02
406	Ken Howell	.05	.02
407	Jeff Kunkel	.05	.02
408	Jeff Reed	.05	.02
409	Chris James	.05	.02
410	Zane Smith	.05	.02
411	Ken Dixon	.05	.02
412	Ricky Horton	.05	.02
413	Frank DiPino	.05	.02
414	Shane Mack	.05	.02
415	Danny Cox	.05	.02
416	Andy Van Slyke	.10	.05
417	Danny Heep	.05	.02
418	John Cangelosi	.05	.02
419A	John Christensen ERR	.10	.05
	(Christiansen on card front)		
419B	John Christensen COR	.05	.02
420	Joey Cora	.20	.09
421	Mike LaValliere	.05	.02
422	Kelly Gruber	.05	.02
423	Bruce Benedict	.05	.02
424	Len Matuszek	.05	.02
425	Kent Tekulve	.05	.02
426	Rafael Ramirez	.05	.02
427	Mike Flanagan	.05	.02
428	Mike Gallego	.05	.02
429	Juan Castillo	.05	.02
430	Neal Heaton	.05	.02
431	Phil Garner	.05	.02
432	Mike Dunne	.05	.02
433	Wallace Johnson	.05	.02
434	Jack O'Connor	.05	.02
435	Steve Jeltz	.05	.02
436	Donell Nixon	.05	.02
437	Jack Lazorko	.05	.02
438	Keith Comstock	.05	.02
439	Jeff D. Robinson	.05	.02
440	Graig Nettles	.10	.05
441	Mel Hall	.05	.02
442	Gerald Young	.05	.02
443	Gary Redus	.05	.02
444	Charlie Moore	.05	.02
445	Bill Madlock	.10	.05
446	Mark Clear	.05	.02
447	Greg Booker	.05	.02
448	Rick Schu	.05	.02
449	Ron Kittle	.05	.02
450	Dale Murphy	.20	.09
451	Bob Dernier	.05	.02
452	Dale Mohorcic	.05	.02
453	Rafael Belliard	.05	.02
454	Charlie Puleo	.05	.02
455	Dwayne Murphy	.05	.02
456	Jim Eisenreich	.20	.09
457	David Palmer	.05	.02
458	Dave Stewart	.10	.05
459	Pascual Perez	.05	.02
460	Glenn Davis	.05	.02
461	Dan Petry	.05	.02
462	Jim Winn	.05	.02
463	Darrell Miller	.05	.02
464	Mike Moore	.05	.02
465	Mike LaCoss	.05	.02
466	Steve Farr	.05	.02
467	Jerry Mumphrey	.05	.02
468	Kevin Gross	.05	.02
469	Bruce Bochy	.05	.02
470	Orel Hershiser	.10	.05
471	Eric King	.05	.02
472	Ellis Burks	.25	.11
473	Darren Daulton	.05	.02
474	Mookie Wilson	.10	.05
475	Frank Viola	.05	.02
476	Ron Robinson	.05	.02
477	Bob Melvin	.05	.02
478	Jeff Musselman	.05	.02
479	Charlie Kerfeld	.05	.02
480	Richard Dotson	.05	.02
481	Kevin Mitchell	.10	.05
482	Gary Roenicke	.05	.02
483	Tim Flannery	.05	.02
484	Rich Yett	.05	.02
485	Pete Incaviglia	.05	.02
486	Rick Cerone	.05	.02
487	Tony Armas	.05	.02
488	Jerry Reed	.05	.02
489	Dave Lopes	.10	.05
490	Frank Tanana	.05	.02
491	Mike Loynd	.05	.02
492	Bruce Ruffin	.05	.02
493	Chris Speier	.05	.02
494	Tom Hume	.05	.02
495	Jesse Orosco	.05	.02
496	Robbie Wine UER	.05	.02
	(Misspelled Robby on card front)		
497	Jeff Montgomery	.20	.09
498	Jeff Dedmon	.05	.02
499	Luis Aguayo	.05	.02
500	Reggie Jackson	.20	.09
	(Oakland A's)		
501	Reggie Jackson	.20	.09
	(Baltimore Orioles)		
502	Reggie Jackson	.20	.09
	(New York Yankees)		
503	Reggie Jackson	.20	.09
	(California Angels)		
504	Reggie Jackson	.20	.09
	(Oakland A's)		
505	Billy Hatcher	.05	.02
506	Ed Lynch	.05	.02
507	Willie Hernandez	.05	.02
508	Jose DeLeon	.05	.02
509	Joel Youngblood	.05	.02
510	Bob Welch	.05	.02
511	Steve Ontiveros	.05	.02
512	Randy Ready	.05	.02
513	Juan Nieves	.05	.02
514	Jeff Russell	.05	.02
515	Von Hayes	.05	.02
516	Mark Gubicza	.05	.02
517	Ken Dayley	.05	.02
518	Don Aase	.05	.02
519	Rick Reuschel	.05	.02
520	Mike Henneman	.10	.05
521	Rick Aguilera	.10	.05
522	Jay Howell	.05	.02
523	Ed Correa	.05	.02
524	Manny Trillo	.05	.02
525	Kirk Gibson	.10	.05
526	Wally Ritchie	.05	.02
527	Al Nipper	.05	.02
528	Atlee Hammaker	.05	.02
529	Shawon Dunston	.05	.02
530	Jim Clancy	.05	.02
531	Tom Paciorek	.10	.05
532	Joel Skinner	.05	.02
533	Scott Garrelts	.05	.02
534	Tom O'Malley	.05	.02
535	John Franco	.05	.02
536	Paul Kilgus	.05	.02
537	Darrell Porter	.05	.02
538	Walt Terrell	.05	.02
539	Bill Long	.05	.02
540	George Bell	.05	.02
541	Jeff Sellers	.05	.02
542	Joe Boever	.05	.02
543	Steve Howe	.05	.02
544	Scott Sanderson	.05	.02
545	Jack Morris	.10	.05
546	Todd Benzinger	.05	.02
547	Steve Henderson	.05	.02
548	Eddie Milner	.05	.02
549	Jeff M. Robinson	.05	.02
550	Cal Ripken	.75	.35
551	Jody Davis	.05	.02
552	Kirk McCaskill	.05	.02
553	Craig Lefferts	.05	.02
554	Darnell Coles	.05	.02
555	Phil Niekro	.20	.09
556	Mike Aldrete	.05	.02
557	Pat Perry	.05	.02
558	Juan Agosto	.05	.02
559	Rob Murphy	.05	.02
560	Dennis Rasmussen	.05	.02
561	Manny Lee	.05	.02
562	Jeff Blauser	.20	.09
563	Bob Ojeda	.05	.02
564	Dave Dravecky	.10	.05
565	Gene Garber	.05	.02
566	Ron Roenicke	.05	.02
567	Tommy Hinzo	.05	.02
568	Eric Nolte	.05	.02
569	Ed Hearn	.05	.02
570	Mark Davidson	.05	.02
571	Jim Walewander	.05	.02
572	Donnie Hill UER	.05	.02
	(84 Stolen Base total listed as 7)		
573	Jamie Moyer	.05	.02
574	Ken Schrom	.05	.02
575	Nolan Ryan	.75	.35
576	Jim Acker	.05	.02
577	Jamie Quirk	.05	.02
578	Jay Aldrich	.05	.02
579	Claudell Washington	.05	.02
580	Jeff Leonard	.05	.02
581	Carmen Castillo	.05	.02
582	Daryl Boston	.05	.02
583	Jeff DeWillis	.05	.02
584	John Marzano	.05	.02
585	Bill Gullickson	.05	.02
586	Andy Allanson	.05	.02
587	Lee Tunnell UER	.05	.02
	(1987 stat line reads .4.84 ERA)		
588	Gene Nelson	.05	.02
589	Dave LaPoint	.05	.02
590	Harold Baines	.10	.05
591	Bill Buckner	.10	.05
592	Carlton Fisk	.20	.09
593	Rick Manning	.05	.02
594	Doug Jones	.20	.09
595	Tom Candiotti	.05	.02
596	Steve Lake	.05	.02
597	Jose Lind	.05	.02
598	Ross Jones	.05	.02
599	Gary Matthews	.05	.02
600	Fernando Valenzuela	.10	.05
601	Dennis Martinez	.10	.05
602	Les Lancaster	.05	.02
603	Ozzie Guillen	.05	.02
604	Tony Bernazard	.05	.02
605	Chili Davis	.15	.07
606	Roy Smalley	.05	.02
607	Ivan Calderon	.05	.02
608	Jay Tibbs	.05	.02
609	Guy Hoffman	.05	.02
610	Doyle Alexander	.05	.02
611	Mike Bielecki	.05	.02
612	Shawn Hillegas	.05	.02
613	Keith Atherton	.05	.02
614	Eric Plunk	.05	.02
615	Sid Fernandez	.05	.02
616	Dennis Lamp	.05	.02
617	Dave Engle	.05	.02
618	Harry Spilman	.05	.02
619	Don Robinson	.05	.02
620	John Farrell	.05	.02
621	Nelson Liriano	.05	.02
622	Floyd Bannister	.05	.02
623	Randy Milligan	.05	.02
624	Kevin Elster	.05	.02
625	Jody Reed	.10	.05
626	Shawn Abner	.05	.02
627	Kirt Manwaring	.05	.02
628	Pete Stanicek	.05	.02
629	Rob Ducey	.05	.02
630	Steve Kiefer	.05	.02

		MINT	NRMT
❑ 631	Gary Thurman	.05	.02
❑ 632	Darrel Akerfelds	.05	.02
❑ 633	Dave Clark	.05	.02
❑ 634	Roberto Kelly	.20	.09
❑ 635	Keith Hughes	.05	.02
❑ 636	John Davis	.05	.02
❑ 637	Mike Devereaux	.10	.05
❑ 638	Tom Glavine	1.00	.45
❑ 639	Keith A. Miller	.05	.02
❑ 640	Chris Gwynn UER (Wrong batting and throwing on back)	.10	.05
❑ 641	Tim Crews	.05	.02
❑ 642	Mackey Sasser	.05	.02
❑ 643	Vicente Palacios	.05	.02
❑ 644	Kevin Romine	.05	.02
❑ 645	Gregg Jefferies	.20	.09
❑ 646	Jeff Treadway	.05	.02
❑ 647	Ron Gant	.25	.11
❑ 648	Mark McGwire Matt Nokes Rookie Sluggers	1.00	.45
❑ 649	Eric Davis Tim Raines Speed and Power	.10	.05
❑ 650	Don Mattingly Jack Clark	.15	.07
❑ 651	Tony Fernandez Alan Trammell Cal Ripken	.25	.11
❑ 652	Vince Coleman HL 100 Stolen Bases	.05	.02
❑ 653	Kirby Puckett HL 10 Hits in a Row	.20	.09
❑ 654	Benito Santiago HL Hitting Streak	.05	.02
❑ 655	Juan Nieves HL No Hitter	.05	.02
❑ 656	Steve Bedrosian HL Saves Record	.05	.02
❑ 657	Mike Schmidt HL 500 Homers	.15	.07
❑ 658	Don Mattingly HL Home Run Streak	.15	.07
❑ 659	Mark McGwire HL Rookie HR Record	1.00	.45
❑ 660	Paul Molitor HL Hitting Streak	.15	.07

1988 Score Glossy

	MINT	NRMT
COMP.FACT.SET (660)	200.00	90.00
COMMON CARD (1-660)	.50	.23

*STARS: 7.5X TO 15X BASIC CARDS
*ROOKIES: 15X TO 30X BASIC CARDS
STATED PRINT RUN 5000 SETS
DISTRIBUTED ONLY IN FACTORY SET FORM

1988 Score Rookie/Traded

	MINT	NRMT
COMP.FACT.SET (110)	40.00	18.00
COMMON CARD (1T-110T)	.25	.11
MINOR STARS	.75	.35
SEMISTARS	1.50	.70
UNLISTED STARS	3.00	1.35

		MINT	NRMT
❑ 1T	Jack Clark	.75	.35
❑ 2T	Danny Jackson	.25	.11
❑ 3T	Brett Butler	.75	.35
❑ 4T	Kurt Stillwell	.25	.11
❑ 5T	Tom Brunansky	.25	.11
❑ 6T	Dennis Lamp	.25	.11
❑ 7T	Jose DeLeon	.25	.11
❑ 8T	Tom Herr	.25	.11
❑ 9T	Keith Moreland	.25	.11
❑ 10T	Kirk Gibson	3.00	1.35
❑ 11T	Bud Black	.25	.11
❑ 12T	Rafael Ramirez	.25	.11
❑ 13T	Luis Salazar	.25	.11
❑ 14T	Goose Gossage	1.50	.70
❑ 15T	Bob Welch	.25	.11
❑ 16T	Vance Law	.25	.11
❑ 17T	Ray Knight	.25	.11
❑ 18T	Dan Quisenberry	.25	.11
❑ 19T	Don Slaught	.25	.11
❑ 20T	Lee Smith	.75	.35
❑ 21T	Rick Cerone	.25	.11
❑ 22T	Pat Tabler	.25	.11
❑ 23T	Larry McWilliams	.25	.11
❑ 24T	Ricky Horton	.25	.11
❑ 25T	Graig Nettles	.75	.35
❑ 26T	Dan Petry	.25	.11
❑ 27T	Jose Rijo	.25	.11
❑ 28T	Chili Davis	1.50	.70
❑ 29T	Dickie Thon	.25	.11
❑ 30T	Mackey Sasser	.25	.11
❑ 31T	Mickey Tettleton	.75	.35
❑ 32T	Rick Dempsey	.25	.11
❑ 33T	Ron Hassey	.25	.11
❑ 34T	Phil Bradley	.25	.11
❑ 35T	Jay Howell	.25	.11
❑ 36T	Bill Buckner	.75	.35
❑ 37T	Alfredo Griffin	.25	.11
❑ 38T	Gary Pettis	.25	.11
❑ 39T	Calvin Schiraldi	.25	.11
❑ 40T	John Candelaria	.25	.11
❑ 41T	Joe Orsulak	.25	.11
❑ 42T	Willie Upshaw	.25	.11
❑ 43T	Herm Winningham	.25	.11
❑ 44T	Ron Kittle	.25	.11
❑ 45T	Bob Dernier	.25	.11
❑ 46T	Steve Balboni	.25	.11
❑ 47T	Steve Shields	.25	.11
❑ 48T	Henry Cotto	.25	.11
❑ 49T	Dave Henderson	.25	.11
❑ 50T	Dave Parker	.75	.35
❑ 51T	Mike Young	.25	.11
❑ 52T	Mark Salas	.25	.11
❑ 53T	Mike Davis	.25	.11
❑ 54T	Rafael Santana	.25	.11
❑ 55T	Don Baylor	.75	.35
❑ 56T	Dan Pasqua	.25	.11
❑ 57T	Ernest Riles	.25	.11
❑ 58T	Glenn Hubbard	.25	.11
❑ 59T	Mike Smithson	.25	.11
❑ 60T	Richard Dotson	.25	.11
❑ 61T	Jerry Reuss	.25	.11
❑ 62T	Mike Jackson	3.00	1.35
❑ 63T	Floyd Bannister	.25	.11
❑ 64T	Jesse Orosco	.25	.11
❑ 65T	Larry Parrish	.25	.11
❑ 66T	Jeff Bittiger	.25	.11
❑ 67T	Ray Hayward	.25	.11
❑ 68T	Ricky Jordan	.75	.35
❑ 69T	Tommy Gregg	.25	.11
❑ 70T	Brady Anderson	4.00	1.80
❑ 71T	Jeff Montgomery	3.00	1.35
❑ 72T	Darryl Hamilton	.75	.35
❑ 73T	Cecil Espy	.25	.11
❑ 74T	Greg Briley	.25	.11
❑ 75T	Joey Meyer	.25	.11
❑ 76T	Mike Macfarlane	.25	.11
❑ 77T	Oswald Peraza	.25	.11
❑ 78T	Jack Armstrong	.25	.11
❑ 79T	Don Heinkel	.25	.11
❑ 80T	Mark Grace	8.00	3.60
❑ 81T	Steve Curry	.25	.11
❑ 82T	Damon Berryhill	.25	.11
❑ 83T	Steve Ellsworth	.25	.11
❑ 84T	Pete Smith	.25	.11
❑ 85T	Jack McDowell	3.00	1.35
❑ 86T	Rob Dibble	.75	.35
❑ 87T	Bryan Harvey UER (Games Pitched 47, Innings 5)	.75	.35
❑ 88T	John Dopson	.25	.11
❑ 89T	Dave Gallagher	.25	.11
❑ 90T	Todd Stottlemyre	2.00	.90
❑ 91T	Mike Schooler	.25	.11
❑ 92T	Don Gordon	.25	.11
❑ 93T	Sil Campusano	.25	.11
❑ 94T	Jeff Pico	.25	.11
❑ 95T	Jay Buhner	4.00	1.80
❑ 96T	Nelson Santovenia	.25	.11
❑ 97T	Al Leiter	3.00	1.35
❑ 98T	Luis Alicea	.75	.35
❑ 99T	Pat Borders	.75	.35
❑ 100T	Chris Sabo	.75	.35
❑ 101T	Tim Belcher	.75	.35
❑ 102T	Walt Weiss	2.00	.90
❑ 103T	Craig Biggio	15.00	6.75
❑ 104T	Don August	.25	.11
❑ 105T	Roberto Alomar	20.00	9.00
❑ 106T	Todd Burns	.25	.11
❑ 107T	John Costello	.25	.11
❑ 108T	Melido Perez	.25	.11
❑ 109T	Darrin Jackson	.25	.11
❑ 110T	Orestes Destrade	.75	.35

1988 Score Rookie/Traded Glossy

	MINT	NRMT
COMP.FACT.SET (110)	200.00	90.00
COMMON CARD (1T-110T)	.50	.23

*STARS: 1.5X TO 3X BASIC CARDS
*ROOKIES: 2X TO 4X BASIC CARDS
STATED PRINT RUN 3000 SETS
DISTRIBUTED ONLY IN FACTORY SET FORM

1989 Score

	MINT	NRMT
COMPLETE SET (660)	8.00	3.60
COMP.FACT.SET (660)	10.00	4.50
COMMON CARD (1-660)	.05	.02
MINOR STARS	.10	.05
UNLISTED STARS	.20	.09

		MINT	NRMT
❑ 1	Jose Canseco	.25	.11
❑ 2	Andre Dawson	.20	.09
❑ 3	Mark McGwire UER	1.25	.55

EDDIE MURRAY

□	4	Benito Santiago	.05	.02
□	5	Rick Reuschel	.05	.02
□	6	Fred McGriff	.20	.09
□	7	Kal Daniels	.05	.02
□	8	Gary Gaetti	.05	.02
□	9	Ellis Burks	.15	.07
□	10	Darryl Strawberry	.10	.05
□	11	Julio Franco	.05	.02
□	12	Lloyd Moseby	.05	.02
□	13	Jeff Pico	.05	.02
□	14	Johnny Ray	.05	.02
□	15	Cal Ripken	.75	.35
□	16	Dick Schofield	.05	.02
□	17	Mel Hall	.05	.02
□	18	Bill Ripken	.05	.02
□	19	Brook Jacoby	.05	.02
□	20	Kirby Puckett	.40	.18
□	21	Bill Doran	.05	.02
□	22	Pete O'Brien	.05	.02
□	23	Matt Nokes	.05	.02
□	24	Brian Fisher	.05	.02
□	25	Jack Clark	.05	.02
□	26	Gary Pettis	.05	.02
□	27	Dave Valle	.05	.02
□	28	Willie Wilson	.05	.02
□	29	Curt Young	.05	.02
□	30	Dale Murphy	.20	.09
□	31	Barry Larkin	.20	.09
□	32	Dave Stewart	.10	.05
□	33	Mike LaValliere	.05	.02
□	34	Glenn Hubbard	.05	.02
□	35	Ryne Sandberg	.25	.11
□	36	Tony Pena	.05	.02
□	37	Greg Walker	.05	.02
□	38	Von Hayes	.05	.02
□	39	Kevin Mitchell	.10	.05
□	40	Tim Raines	.10	.05
□	41	Keith Hernandez	.10	.05
□	42	Keith Moreland	.05	.02
□	43	Ruben Sierra	.05	.02
□	44	Chet Lemon	.05	.02
□	45	Willie Randolph	.10	.05
□	46	Andy Allanson	.05	.02
□	47	Candy Maldonado	.05	.02
□	48	Sid Bream	.05	.02
□	49	Denny Walling	.05	.02
□	50	Dave Winfield	.20	.09
□	51	Alvin Davis	.05	.02
□	52	Cory Snyder	.05	.02
□	53	Hubie Brooks	.05	.02
□	54	Chili Davis	.10	.05
□	55	Kevin Seitzer	.05	.02
□	56	Jose Uribe	.05	.02
□	57	Tony Fernandez	.05	.02
□	58	Tim Teufel	.05	.02
□	59	Oddibe McDowell	.05	.02
□	60	Les Lancaster	.05	.02
□	61	Billy Hatcher	.05	.02
□	62	Dan Gladden	.05	.02
□	63	Marty Barrett	.05	.02
□	64	Nick Esasky	.05	.02
□	65	Wally Joyner	.10	.05
□	66	Mike Greenwell	.05	.02
□	67	Ken Williams	.05	.02
□	68	Bob Horner	.05	.02
□	69	Steve Sax	.05	.02
□	70	Rickey Henderson	.25	.11
□	71	Mitch Webster	.05	.02

□	72	Rob Deer	.05	.02
□	73	Jim Presley	.05	.02
□	74	Albert Hall	.05	.02
□	75	George Brett COR	.40	.18
		(At age 35)		
□	75A	George Brett ERR	.75	.35
		(At age 33)		
□	76	Brian Downing	.05	.02
□	77	Dave Martinez	.05	.02
□	78	Scott Fletcher	.05	.02
□	79	Phil Bradley	.05	.02
□	80	Ozzie Smith	.25	.11
□	81	Larry Sheets	.05	.02
□	82	Mike Aldrete	.05	.02
□	83	Darnell Coles	.05	.02
□	84	Len Dykstra	.10	.05
□	85	Jim Rice	.10	.05
□	86	Jeff Treadway	.05	.02
□	87	Jose Lind	.05	.02
□	88	Willie McGee	.10	.05
□	89	Mickey Brantley	.05	.02
□	90	Tony Gwynn	.50	.23
□	91	R.J. Reynolds	.05	.02
□	92	Milt Thompson	.05	.02
□	93	Kevin McReynolds	.05	.02
□	94	Eddie Murray UER	.20	.09
		('86 batting .205,		
		should be .305)		
□	95	Lance Parrish	.05	.02
□	96	Ron Kittle	.05	.02
□	97	Gerald Young	.05	.02
□	98	Ernie Whitt	.05	.02
□	99	Jeff Reed	.05	.02
□	100	Don Mattingly	.40	.18
□	101	Gerald Perry	.05	.02
□	102	Vance Law	.05	.02
□	103	John Shelby	.05	.02
□	104	Chris Sabo	.05	.02
□	105	Danny Tartabull	.05	.02
□	106	Glenn Wilson	.05	.02
□	107	Mark Davidson	.05	.02
□	108	Dave Parker	.10	.05
□	109	Eric Davis	.10	.05
□	110	Alan Trammell	.15	.07
□	111	Ozzie Virgil	.05	.02
□	112	Frank Tanana	.05	.02
□	113	Rafael Ramirez	.05	.02
□	114	Dennis Martinez	.10	.05
□	115	Jose DeLeon	.05	.02
□	116	Bob Ojeda	.05	.02
□	117	Doug Drabek	.05	.02
□	118	Andy Hawkins	.05	.02
□	119	Greg Maddux	.60	.25
□	120	Cecil Fielder UER	.10	.05
		Reversed Photo on back		
□	121	Mike Scioscia	.05	.02
□	122	Dan Petry	.05	.02
□	123	Terry Kennedy	.05	.02
□	124	Kelly Downs	.05	.02
□	125	Greg Gross UER	.05	.02
		(Gregg on back)		
□	126	Fred Lynn	.05	.02
□	127	Barry Bonds	.40	.18
□	128	Harold Baines	.10	.05
□	129	Doyle Alexander	.05	.02
□	130	Kevin Elster	.05	.02
□	131	Mike Heath	.05	.02
□	132	Teddy Higuera	.05	.02
□	133	Charlie Leibrandt	.05	.02
□	134	Tim Laudner	.05	.02
□	135A	Ray Knight ERR	.20	.09
		(Reverse negative)		
□	135B	Ray Knight COR	.05	.02
□	136	Howard Johnson	.05	.02
□	137	Terry Pendleton	.10	.05
□	138	Andy McGaffigan	.05	.02
□	139	Ken Oberkfell	.05	.02
□	140	Butch Wynegar	.05	.02
□	141	Rob Murphy	.05	.02
□	142	Rich Renteria	.05	.02
□	143	Jose Guzman	.05	.02
□	144	Andres Galarraga	.20	.09
□	145	Ricky Horton	.05	.02
□	146	Frank DiPino	.05	.02
□	147	Glenn Braggs	.05	.02
□	148	John Kruk	.10	.05

□	149	Mike Schmidt	.30	.14
□	150	Lee Smith	.10	.05
□	151	Robin Yount	.20	.09
□	152	Mark Eichhorn	.05	.02
□	153	DeWayne Buice	.05	.02
□	154	B.J. Surhoff	.10	.05
□	155	Vince Coleman	.05	.02
□	156	Tony Phillips	.05	.02
□	157	Willie Fraser	.05	.02
□	158	Lance McCullers	.05	.02
□	159	Greg Gagne	.05	.02
□	160	Jesse Barfield	.05	.02
□	161	Mark Langston	.05	.02
□	162	Kurt Stillwell	.05	.02
□	163	Dion James	.05	.02
□	164	Glenn Davis	.05	.02
□	165	Walt Weiss	.05	.02
□	166	Dave Concepcion	.10	.05
□	167	Alfredo Griffin	.05	.02
□	168	Don Heinkel	.05	.02
□	169	Luis Rivera	.05	.02
□	170	Shane Rawley	.05	.02
□	171	Darrell Evans	.10	.05
□	172	Robby Thompson	.05	.02
□	173	Jody Davis	.05	.02
□	174	Andy Van Slyke	.10	.05
□	175	Wade Boggs UER	.20	.09
		(Bio says .364,		
		should be .356)		
□	176	Garry Templeton	.05	.02
		('85 stats		
		off-centered)		
□	177	Gary Redus	.05	.02
□	178	Craig Lefferts	.05	.02
□	179	Carney Lansford	.10	.05
□	180	Ron Darling	.05	.02
□	181	Kirk McCaskill	.05	.02
□	182	Tony Armas	.05	.02
□	183	Steve Farr	.05	.02
□	184	Tom Brunansky	.05	.02
□	185	Bryan Harvey UER	.05	.02
		('87 games 47,		
		should be 3)		
□	186	Mike Marshall	.05	.02
□	187	Bo Diaz	.05	.02
□	188	Willie Upshaw	.05	.02
□	189	Mike Pagliarulo	.05	.02
□	190	Mike Krukow	.05	.02
□	191	Tommy Herr	.05	.02
□	192	Jim Pankovits	.05	.02
□	193	Dwight Evans	.10	.05
□	194	Kelly Gruber	.05	.02
□	195	Bobby Bonilla	.15	.07
□	196	Wallace Johnson	.05	.02
□	197	Dave Stieb	.05	.02
□	198	Pat Borders	.10	.05
□	199	Rafael Palmeiro	.25	.11
□	200	Dwight Gooden	.10	.05
□	201	Pete Incaviglia	.05	.02
□	202	Chris James	.05	.02
□	203	Marvell Wynne	.05	.02
□	204	Pat Sheridan	.05	.02
□	205	Don Baylor	.10	.05
□	206	Paul O'Neill	.10	.05
□	207	Pete Smith	.05	.02
□	208	Mark McLemore	.05	.02
□	209	Henry Cotto	.05	.02
□	210	Kirk Gibson	.10	.05
□	211	Claudell Washington	.05	.02
□	212	Randy Bush	.05	.02
□	213	Joe Carter	.15	.07
□	214	Bill Buckner	.05	.02
□	215	Bert Blyleven UER	.10	.05
		(Wrong birth year)		
□	216	Brett Butler	.10	.05
□	217	Lee Mazzilli	.05	.02
□	218	Spike Owen	.05	.02
□	219	Bill Swift	.05	.02
□	220	Tim Wallach	.05	.02
□	221	David Cone	.20	.09
□	222	Don Carman	.05	.02
□	223	Rich Gossage	.10	.05
□	224	Bob Walk	.05	.02
□	225	Dave Righetti	.05	.02
□	226	Kevin Bass	.05	.02
□	227	Kevin Gross	.05	.02

❏ 228	Tim Burke	.05	.02
❏ 229	Rick Mahler	.05	.02
❏ 230	Lou Whitaker UER	.10	.05
	(252 games in '85, should be 152)		
❏ 231	Luis Alicea	.05	.02
❏ 232	Roberto Alomar	.30	.14
❏ 233	Bob Boone	.10	.05
❏ 234	Dickie Thon	.05	.02
❏ 235	Shawon Dunston	.05	.02
❏ 236	Pete Stanicek	.05	.02
❏ 237	Craig Biggio	.75	.35
	(Inconsistent design, portrait on front)		
❏ 238	Dennis Boyd	.05	.02
❏ 239	Tom Candiotti	.05	.02
❏ 240	Gary Carter	.15	.07
❏ 241	Mike Stanley	.05	.02
❏ 242	Ken Phelps	.05	.02
❏ 243	Chris Bosio	.05	.02
❏ 244	Les Straker	.05	.02
❏ 245	Dave Smith	.05	.02
❏ 246	John Candelaria	.05	.02
❏ 247	Joe Orsulak	.05	.02
❏ 248	Storm Davis	.05	.02
❏ 249	Floyd Bannister UER	.05	.02
	(ML Batting Record)		
❏ 250	Jack Morris	.10	.05
❏ 251	Bret Saberhagen	.10	.05
❏ 252	Tom Niedenfuer	.05	.02
❏ 253	Neal Heaton	.05	.02
❏ 254	Eric Show	.05	.02
❏ 255	Juan Samuel	.05	.02
❏ 256	Dale Sveum	.05	.02
❏ 257	Jim Gott	.05	.02
❏ 258	Scott Garrelts	.05	.02
❏ 259	Larry McWilliams	.05	.02
❏ 260	Steve Bedrosian	.05	.02
❏ 261	Jack Howell	.05	.02
❏ 262	Jay Tibbs	.05	.02
❏ 263	Jamie Moyer	.05	.02
❏ 264	Doug Sisk	.05	.02
❏ 265	Todd Worrell	.05	.02
❏ 266	John Farrell	.05	.02
❏ 267	Dave Collins	.05	.02
❏ 268	Sid Fernandez	.05	.02
❏ 269	Tom Brookens	.05	.02
❏ 270	Shane Mack	.05	.02
❏ 271	Paul Kilgus	.05	.02
❏ 272	Chuck Crim	.05	.02
❏ 273	Bob Knepper	.05	.02
❏ 274	Mike Moore	.05	.02
❏ 275	Guillermo Hernandez	.05	.02
❏ 276	Dennis Eckersley	.15	.07
❏ 277	Graig Nettles	.10	.05
❏ 278	Rich Dotson	.05	.02
❏ 279	Larry Herndon	.05	.02
❏ 280	Gene Larkin	.05	.02
❏ 281	Roger McDowell	.05	.02
❏ 282	Greg Swindell	.05	.02
❏ 283	Juan Agosto	.05	.02
❏ 284	Jeff M. Robinson	.05	.02
❏ 285	Mike Dunne	.05	.02
❏ 286	Greg Mathews	.05	.02
❏ 287	Kent Tekulve	.05	.02
❏ 288	Jerry Mumphrey	.05	.02
❏ 289	Jack McDowell	.10	.05
❏ 290	Frank Viola	.05	.02
❏ 291	Mark Gubicza	.05	.02
❏ 292	Dave Schmidt	.05	.02
❏ 293	Mike Henneman	.05	.02
❏ 294	Jimmy Jones	.05	.02
❏ 295	Charlie Hough	.10	.05
❏ 296	Rafael Santana	.05	.02
❏ 297	Chris Speier	.05	.02
❏ 298	Mike Witt	.05	.02
❏ 299	Pascual Perez	.05	.02
❏ 300	Nolan Ryan	.75	.35
❏ 301	Mitch Williams	.05	.02
❏ 302	Mookie Wilson	.05	.02
❏ 303	Mackey Sasser	.05	.02
❏ 304	John Cerutti	.05	.02
❏ 305	Jeff Reardon	.10	.05
❏ 306	Randy Myers UER	.10	.05
	(6 hits in '87, should be 61)		
❏ 307	Greg Brock	.05	.02
❏ 308	Bob Welch	.05	.02
❏ 309	Jeff D. Robinson	.05	.02
❏ 310	Harold Reynolds	.05	.02
❏ 311	Jim Walewander	.05	.02
❏ 312	Dave Magadan	.05	.02
❏ 313	Jim Gantner	.05	.02
❏ 314	Walt Terrell	.05	.02
❏ 315	Wally Backman	.05	.02
❏ 316	Luis Salazar	.05	.02
❏ 317	Rick Rhoden	.05	.02
❏ 318	Tom Henke	.05	.02
❏ 319	Mike Macfarlane	.05	.02
❏ 320	Dan Plesac	.05	.02
❏ 321	Calvin Schiraldi	.05	.02
❏ 322	Stan Javier	.05	.02
❏ 323	Devon White	.10	.05
❏ 324	Scott Bradley	.05	.02
❏ 325	Bruce Hurst	.05	.02
❏ 326	Manny Lee	.05	.02
❏ 327	Rick Aguilera	.10	.05
❏ 328	Bruce Ruffin	.05	.02
❏ 329	Ed Whitson	.05	.02
❏ 330	Bo Jackson	.15	.07
❏ 331	Ivan Calderon	.05	.02
❏ 332	Mickey Hatcher	.05	.02
❏ 333	Barry Jones	.05	.02
❏ 334	Ron Hassey	.05	.02
❏ 335	Bill Wegman	.05	.02
❏ 336	Damon Berryhill	.05	.02
❏ 337	Steve Ontiveros	.05	.02
❏ 338	Dan Pasqua	.05	.02
❏ 339	Bill Pecota	.05	.02
❏ 340	Greg Cadaret	.05	.02
❏ 341	Scott Bankhead	.05	.02
❏ 342	Ron Guidry	.10	.05
❏ 343	Danny Heep	.05	.02
❏ 344	Bob Brower	.05	.02
❏ 345	Rich Gedman	.05	.02
❏ 346	Nelson Santovenia	.05	.02
❏ 347	George Bell	.05	.02
❏ 348	Ted Power	.05	.02
❏ 349	Mark Grant	.05	.02
❏ 350	Roger Clemens COR	.50	.23
	(78 career wins)		
❏ 350A	Roger Clemens ERR	2.00	.90
	(78 career wins)		
❏ 351	Bill Long	.05	.02
❏ 352	Jay Bell	.15	.07
❏ 353	Steve Balboni	.05	.02
❏ 354	Bob Kipper	.05	.02
❏ 355	Steve Jeltz	.05	.02
❏ 356	Jesse Orosco	.05	.02
❏ 357	Bob Dernier	.05	.02
❏ 358	Mickey Tettleton	.10	.05
❏ 359	Duane Ward	.05	.02
❏ 360	Darrin Jackson	.05	.02
❏ 361	Rey Quinones	.05	.02
❏ 362	Mark Grace	.20	.09
❏ 363	Steve Lake	.05	.02
❏ 364	Pat Perry	.05	.02
❏ 365	Terry Steinbach	.10	.05
❏ 366	Alan Ashby	.05	.02
❏ 367	Jeff Montgomery	.10	.05
❏ 368	Steve Buechele	.05	.02
❏ 369	Chris Brown	.05	.02
❏ 370	Orel Hershiser	.10	.05
❏ 371	Todd Benzinger	.05	.02
❏ 372	Ron Gant	.20	.09
❏ 373	Paul Assenmacher	.05	.02
❏ 374	Joey Meyer	.05	.02
❏ 375	Neil Allen	.05	.02
❏ 376	Mike Davis	.05	.02
❏ 377	Jeff Parrett	.05	.02
❏ 378	Jay Howell	.05	.02
❏ 379	Rafael Belliard	.05	.02
❏ 380	Luis Polonia UER	.05	.02
	(2 triples in '87, should be 10)		
❏ 381	Keith Atherton	.05	.02
❏ 382	Kent Hrbek	.10	.05
❏ 383	Bob Stanley	.05	.02
❏ 384	Dave LaPoint	.05	.02
❏ 385	Rance Mulliniks	.05	.02
❏ 386	Melido Perez	.05	.02
❏ 387	Doug Jones	.05	.02
❏ 388	Steve Lyons	.05	.02
❏ 389	Alejandro Pena	.05	.02
❏ 390	Frank White	.10	.05
❏ 391	Pat Tabler	.05	.02
❏ 392	Eric Plunk	.05	.02
❏ 393	Mike Maddux	.05	.02
❏ 394	Allan Anderson	.05	.02
❏ 395	Bob Brenly	.05	.02
❏ 396	Rick Cerone	.05	.02
❏ 397	Scott Terry	.05	.02
❏ 398	Mike Jackson	.15	.07
❏ 399	Bobby Thigpen UER	.05	.02
	(Bio says 37 saves in '88, should be 34)		
❏ 400	Don Sutton	.20	.09
❏ 401	Cecil Espy	.05	.02
❏ 402	Junior Ortiz	.05	.02
❏ 403	Mike Smithson	.05	.02
❏ 404	Bud Black	.05	.02
❏ 405	Tom Foley	.05	.02
❏ 406	Andres Thomas	.05	.02
❏ 407	Rick Sutcliffe	.05	.02
❏ 408	Brian Harper	.05	.02
❏ 409	John Smiley	.05	.02
❏ 410	Juan Nieves	.05	.02
❏ 411	Shawn Abner	.05	.02
❏ 412	Wes Gardner	.05	.02
❏ 413	Darren Daulton	.10	.05
❏ 414	Juan Berenguer	.05	.02
❏ 415	Charles Hudson	.05	.02
❏ 416	Rick Honeycutt	.05	.02
❏ 417	Greg Booker	.05	.02
❏ 418	Tim Belcher	.05	.02
❏ 419	Don August	.05	.02
❏ 420	Dale Mohorcic	.05	.02
❏ 421	Steve Lombardozzi	.05	.02
❏ 422	Atlee Hammaker	.05	.02
❏ 423	Jerry Don Gleaton	.05	.02
❏ 424	Scott Bailes	.05	.02
❏ 425	Bruce Sutter	.05	.02
❏ 426	Randy Ready	.05	.02
❏ 427	Jerry Reed	.05	.02
❏ 428	Bryn Smith	.05	.02
❏ 429	Tim Leary	.05	.02
❏ 430	Mark Clear	.05	.02
❏ 431	Terry Leach	.05	.02
❏ 432	John Moses	.05	.02
❏ 433	Ozzie Guillen	.05	.02
❏ 434	Gene Nelson	.05	.02
❏ 435	Gary Ward	.05	.02
❏ 436	Luis Aguayo	.05	.02
❏ 437	Fernando Valenzuela	.10	.05
❏ 438	Jeff Russell UER	.05	.02
	(Saves total does not add up correctly)		
❏ 439	Cecilio Guante	.05	.02
❏ 440	Don Robinson	.05	.02
❏ 441	Rick Anderson	.05	.02
❏ 442	Tom Glavine	.20	.09
❏ 443	Daryl Boston	.05	.02
❏ 444	Joe Price	.05	.02
❏ 445	Stewart Cliburn	.05	.02
❏ 446	Manny Trillo	.05	.02
❏ 447	Joel Skinner	.05	.02
❏ 448	Charlie Puleo	.05	.02
❏ 449	Carlton Fisk	.20	.09
❏ 450	Will Clark	.20	.09
❏ 451	Otis Nixon	.10	.05
❏ 452	Rick Schu	.05	.02
❏ 453	Todd Stottlemyre UER	.15	.07
	(ML Batting Record)		
❏ 454	Tim Birtsas	.05	.02
❏ 455	Dave Gallagher	.05	.02
❏ 456	Barry Lyons	.05	.02
❏ 457	Fred Manrique	.05	.02
❏ 458	Ernest Riles	.05	.02
❏ 459	Doug Jennings	.05	.02
❏ 460	Joe Magrane	.05	.02
❏ 461	Jamie Quirk	.05	.02
❏ 462	Jack Armstrong	.05	.02
❏ 463	Bobby Witt	.05	.02
❏ 464	Keith A. Miller	.05	.02
❏ 465	Todd Burns	.05	.02
❏ 466	John Dopson	.05	.02
❏ 467	Rich Yett	.05	.02
❏ 468	Craig Reynolds	.05	.02

469 Dave Bergman	.05	.02
470 Rex Hudler	.05	.02
471 Eric King	.05	.02
472 Joaquin Andujar	.05	.02
473 Sil Campusano	.05	.02
474 Terry Mulholland	.05	.02
475 Mike Flanagan	.05	.02
476 Greg A. Harris	.05	.02
477 Tommy John	.10	.05
478 Dave Anderson	.05	.02
479 Fred Toliver	.05	.02
480 Jimmy Key	.10	.05
481 Donell Nixon	.05	.02
482 Mark Portugal	.05	.02
483 Tom Pagnozzi	.05	.02
484 Jeff Kunkel	.05	.02
485 Frank Williams	.05	.02
486 Jody Reed	.05	.02
487 Roberto Kelly	.10	.05
488 Shawn Hillegas UER	.05	.02
(165 innings in '87, should be 165.2)		
489 Jerry Reuss	.05	.02
490 Mark Davis	.05	.02
491 Jeff Sellers	.05	.02
492 Zane Smith	.05	.02
493 Al Newman	.05	.02
494 Mike Young	.05	.02
495 Larry Parrish	.05	.02
496 Herm Winningham	.05	.02
497 Carmen Castillo	.05	.02
498 Joe Hesketh	.05	.02
499 Darrell Miller	.05	.02
500 Mike LaCoss	.05	.02
501 Charlie Lea	.05	.02
502 Bruce Benedict	.05	.02
503 Chuck Finley	.10	.05
504 Brad Wellman	.05	.02
505 Tim Crews	.05	.02
506 Ken Gerhart	.05	.02
507A Brian Holton ERR	.05	.02
(Born 1/25/65 Denver, should be 11/29/59 in McKeesport)		
507B Brian Holton COR	2.00	.90
508 Dennis Lamp	.05	.02
509 Bobby Meacham UER	.05	.02
('84 games 099)		
510 Tracy Jones	.05	.02
511 Mike R. Fitzgerald	.05	.02
512 Jeff Bittiger	.05	.02
513 Tim Flannery	.05	.02
514 Ray Hayward	.05	.02
515 Dave Leiper	.05	.02
516 Rod Scurry	.05	.02
517 Carmelo Martinez	.05	.02
518 Curtis Wilkerson	.05	.02
519 Stan Jefferson	.05	.02
520 Dan Quisenberry	.05	.02
521 Lloyd McClendon	.05	.02
522 Steve Trout	.05	.02
523 Larry Andersen	.05	.02
524 Don Aase	.05	.02
525 Bob Forsch	.05	.02
526 Geno Petralli	.05	.02
527 Angel Salazar	.05	.02
528 Mike Schooler	.05	.02
529 Jose Oquendo	.05	.02
530 Jay Buhner UER	.20	.09
(Wearing 43 on front, listed as 34 on back)		
531 Tom Bolton	.05	.02
532 Al Nipper	.05	.02
533 Dave Henderson	.05	.02
534 John Costello	.05	.02
535 Donnie Moore	.05	.02
536 Mike Laga	.05	.02
537 Mike Gallego	.05	.02
538 Jim Clancy	.05	.02
539 Joel Youngblood	.05	.02
540 Rick Leach	.05	.02
541 Kevin Romine	.05	.02
542 Mark Salas	.05	.02
543 Greg Minton	.05	.02
544 Dave Palmer	.05	.02
545 Dwayne Murphy UER	.05	.02

(Game-sinning)		
546 Jim Deshaies	.05	.02
547 Don Gordon	.05	.02
548 Ricky Jordan	.10	.05
549 Mike Boddicker	.05	.02
550 Mike Scott	.05	.02
551 Jeff Ballard	.05	.02
552A Jose Rijo ERR	.20	.09
(Uniform listed as 27 on back)		
552B Jose Rijo COR	.20	.09
(Uniform listed as 24 on back)		
553 Danny Darwin	.05	.02
554 Tom Browning	.05	.02
555 Danny Jackson	.05	.02
556 Rick Dempsey	.05	.02
557 Jeffrey Leonard	.05	.02
558 Jeff Musselman	.05	.02
559 Ron Robinson	.05	.02
560 John Tudor	.05	.02
561 Don Slaught UER	.05	.02
(237 games in 1987)		
562 Dennis Rasmussen	.05	.02
563 Brady Anderson	.40	.18
564 Pedro Guerrero	.05	.02
565 Paul Molitor	.20	.09
566 Terry Clark	.05	.02
567 Terry Puhl	.05	.02
568 Mike Campbell	.05	.02
569 Paul Mirabella	.05	.02
570 Jeff Hamilton	.05	.02
571 Oswald Peraza	.05	.02
572 Bob McClure	.05	.02
573 Jose Bautista	.05	.02
574 Alex Trevino	.05	.02
575 John Franco	.10	.05
576 Mark Parent	.05	.02
577 Nelson Liriano	.05	.02
578 Steve Shields	.05	.02
579 Odell Jones	.05	.02
580 Al Leiter	.20	.09
581 Dave Stapleton	.05	.02
582 World Series '88	.10	.05
Orel Hershiser		
Jose Canseco		
Kirk Gibson		
Dave Stewart		
583 Donnie Hill	.05	.02
584 Chuck Jackson	.05	.02
585 Rene Gonzales	.05	.02
586 Tracy Woodson	.05	.02
587 Jim Adduci	.05	.02
588 Mario Soto	.05	.02
589 Jeff Blauser	.10	.05
590 Jim Traber	.05	.02
591 Jon Perlman	.05	.02
592 Mark Williamson	.05	.02
593 Dave Meads	.05	.02
594 Jim Eisenreich	.05	.02
595A Paul Gibson P1	1.00	.45
595B Paul Gibson P2	.05	.02
(Airbrushed leg on player in background)		
596 Mike Birkbeck	.05	.02
597 Terry Francona	.10	.05
598 Paul Zuvella	.05	.02
599 Franklin Stubbs	.05	.02
600 Gregg Jefferies	.10	.05
601 John Cangelosi	.05	.02
602 Mike Sharperson	.05	.02
603 Mike Diaz	.05	.02
604 Gary Varsho	.05	.02
605 Terry Blocker	.05	.02
606 Charlie O'Brien	.05	.02
607 Jim Eppard	.05	.02
608 John Davis	.05	.02
609 Ken Griffey Sr.	.10	.05
610 Buddy Bell	.10	.05
611 Ted Simmons UER	.10	.05
(78 stats Cardinal)		
612 Matt Williams	.20	.09
613 Danny Cox	.05	.02
614 Al Pedrique	.05	.02
615 Ron Oester	.05	.02
616 John Smoltz	.75	.35

617 Bob Melvin	.05	.02
618 Rob Dibble	.10	.05
619 Kirt Manwaring	.05	.02
620 Felix Fermin	.05	.02
621 Doug Dascenzo	.05	.02
622 Bill Brennan	.05	.02
623 Carlos Quintana	.05	.02
624 Mike Harkey UER	.05	.02
(13 and 31 walks in '88, should be 35 and 33)		
625 Gary Sheffield	.50	.23
626 Tom Prince	.05	.02
627 Steve Searcy	.05	.02
628 Charlie Hayes	.20	.09
(Listed as outfielder)		
629 Felix Jose UER	.05	.02
(Modesto misspelled as Modestoi)		
630 Sandy Alomar Jr.	.25	.11
(Inconsistent design, portrait on front)		
631 Derek Lilliquist	.05	.02
632 Geronimo Berroa	.05	.02
633 Luis Medina	.05	.02
634 Tom Gordon UER	.20	.09
(Height 6'0"		
635 Ramon Martinez	.25	.11
636 Craig Worthington	.05	.02
637 Edgar Martinez	.20	.09
638 Chad Kreuter	.05	.02
639 Ron Jones	.05	.02
640 Van Snider	.05	.02
641 Lance Blankenship	.05	.02
642 Dwight Smith UER	.10	.05
(10 HR's in '87, should be 18)		
643 Cameron Drew	.05	.02
644 Jerald Clark	.05	.02
645 Randy Johnson	1.50	.70
646 Norm Charlton	.10	.05
647 Todd Frohwirth UER	.05	.02
(Southpaw on back)		
648 Luis De Los Santos	.05	.02
649 Tim Jones	.05	.02
650 Dave West UER	.05	.02
ML hits 3 should be 6		
651 Bob Milacki	.05	.02
652 Wrigley Field HL	.10	.05
(Let There Be Lights)		
653 Orel Hershiser HL	.10	.05
(The Streak)		
654A Wade Boggs HL ERR	1.50	.70
(Wade Whacks 'Em)		
"seasaon" on back)		
654B Wade Boggs HL COR	.10	.05
(Wade Whacks 'Em)		
655 Jose Canseco HL	.05	.02
(One of a Kind)		
656 Doug Jones HL	.05	.02
(Doug Sets Saves)		
657 Rickey Henderson HL	.10	.05
(Rickey Rocks 'Em)		
658 Tom Browning HL	.05	.02
(Tom Perfect Pitches)		
659 Mike Greenwell HL	.05	.02
(Greenwell Gamers)		
660 Boston Red Sox HL	.05	.02
(Joe Morgan MG, Sox Sock 'Em)		

1989 Score Rookie/Traded

	MINT	NRMT
COMP.FACT.SET (110)	60.00	27.00
COMMON CARD (1T-110T)	.10	.05
MINOR STARS	.20	.09
UNLISTED STARS	.40	.18

1T Rafael Palmeiro	.50	.23
2T Nolan Ryan	3.00	1.35
3T Jack Clark	.10	.05
4T Dave LaPoint	.10	.05

RAFAEL PALMEIRO

		MINT	NRMT
☐ 5T	Mike Moore	.10	.05
☐ 6T	Pete O'Brien	.10	.05
☐ 7T	Jeffrey Leonard	.10	.05
☐ 8T	Rob Murphy	.10	.05
☐ 9T	Tom Herr	.10	.05
☐ 10T	Claudell Washington	.10	.05
☐ 11T	Mike Pagliarulo	.10	.05
☐ 12T	Steve Lake	.10	.05
☐ 13T	Spike Owen	.10	.05
☐ 14T	Andy Hawkins	.10	.05
☐ 15T	Todd Benzinger	.10	.05
☐ 16T	Mookie Wilson	.20	.09
☐ 17T	Bert Blyleven	.20	.09
☐ 18T	Jeff Treadway	.10	.05
☐ 19T	Bruce Hurst	.10	.05
☐ 20T	Steve Sax	.10	.05
☐ 21T	Juan Samuel	.10	.05
☐ 22T	Jesse Barfield	.10	.05
☐ 23T	Carmen Castillo	.10	.05
☐ 24T	Terry Leach	.10	.05
☐ 25T	Mark Langston	.10	.05
☐ 26T	Eric King	.10	.05
☐ 27T	Steve Balboni	.10	.05
☐ 28T	Len Dykstra	.20	.09
☐ 29T	Keith Moreland	.10	.05
☐ 30T	Terry Kennedy	.10	.05
☐ 31T	Eddie Murray	.40	.18
☐ 32T	Mitch Williams	.10	.05
☐ 33T	Jeff Parrett	.10	.05
☐ 34T	Wally Backman	.10	.05
☐ 35T	Julio Franco	.10	.05
☐ 36T	Lance Parrish	.10	.05
☐ 37T	Nick Esasky	.10	.05
☐ 38T	Luis Polonia	.10	.05
☐ 39T	Kevin Gross	.10	.05
☐ 40T	John Dopson	.10	.05
☐ 41T	Willie Randolph	.20	.09
☐ 42T	Jim Clancy	.10	.05
☐ 43T	Tracy Jones	.10	.05
☐ 44T	Phil Bradley	.10	.05
☐ 45T	Milt Thompson	.10	.05
☐ 46T	Chris James	.10	.05
☐ 47T	Scott Fletcher	.10	.05
☐ 48T	Kal Daniels	.10	.05
☐ 49T	Steve Bedrosian	.10	.05
☐ 50T	Rickey Henderson	.50	.23
☐ 51T	Dion James	.10	.05
☐ 52T	Tim Leary	.10	.05
☐ 53T	Roger McDowell	.10	.05
☐ 54T	Mel Hall	.10	.05
☐ 55T	Dickie Thon	.10	.05
☐ 56T	Zane Smith	.10	.05
☐ 57T	Danny Heep	.10	.05
☐ 58T	Bob McClure	.10	.05
☐ 59T	Brian Holton	.10	.05
☐ 60T	Randy Ready	.10	.05
☐ 61T	Bob Melvin	.10	.05
☐ 62T	Harold Baines	.20	.09
☐ 63T	Lance McCullers	.10	.05
☐ 64T	Jody Davis	.10	.05
☐ 65T	Darrell Evans	.20	.09
☐ 66T	Joel Youngblood	.10	.05
☐ 67T	Frank Viola	.10	.05
☐ 68T	Mike Aldrete	.10	.05
☐ 69T	Greg Cadaret	.10	.05
☐ 70T	John Kruk	.20	.09
☐ 71T	Pat Sheridan	.10	.05
☐ 72T	Oddibe McDowell	.10	.05

☐ 73T	Tom Brookens	.10	.05
☐ 74T	Bob Boone	.20	.09
☐ 75T	Walt Terrell	.10	.05
☐ 76T	Joel Skinner	.10	.05
☐ 77T	Randy Johnson	3.00	1.35
☐ 78T	Felix Fermin	.10	.05
☐ 79T	Rick Mahler	.10	.05
☐ 80T	Richard Dotson	.10	.05
☐ 81T	Cris Carpenter	.10	.05
☐ 82T	Bill Spiers	.10	.05
☐ 83T	Junior Felix	.10	.05
☐ 84T	Joe Girardi	.40	.18
☐ 85T	Jerome Walton	.40	.18
☐ 86T	Greg Litton	.10	.05
☐ 87T	Greg W.Harris	.10	.05
☐ 88T	Jim Abbott	.40	.18
☐ 89T	Kevin Brown	1.00	.45
☐ 90T	John Wetteland	.50	.23
☐ 91T	Gary Wayne	.10	.05
☐ 92T	Rich Monteleone	.10	.05
☐ 93T	Bob Geren	.10	.05
☐ 94T	Clay Parker	.10	.05
☐ 95T	Steve Finley	1.00	.45
☐ 96T	Gregg Olson	.40	.18
☐ 97T	Ken Patterson	.10	.05
☐ 98T	Ken Hill	.40	.18
☐ 99T	Scott Scudder	.10	.05
☐ 100T	Ken Griffey Jr.	40.00	18.00
☐ 101T	Jeff Brantley	.30	.14
☐ 102T	Donn Pall	.10	.05
☐ 103T	Carlos Martinez	.10	.05
☐ 104T	Joe Oliver	.20	.09
☐ 105T	Omar Vizquel	1.25	.55
☐ 106T	Joey Belle	8.00	3.60
☐ 107T	Kenny Rogers	.40	.18
☐ 108T	Mark Carreon	.10	.05
☐ 109T	Rolando Roomes	.10	.05
☐ 110T	Pete Harnisch	.50	.23

1989 Scoremasters

		MINT	NRMT
COMP.FACT.SET (42)		25.00	11.00
COMMON PLAYER (1-42)		.05	.02
MINOR STARS		.10	.05
UNLISTED STARS		.20	.09
☐ 1	Bo Jackson	.15	.07
☐ 2	Jerome Walton	.20	.09
☐ 3	Cal Ripken	.75	.35
☐ 4	Mike Scott	.05	.02
☐ 5	Nolan Ryan	.75	.35
☐ 6	Don Mattingly	.40	.18
☐ 7	Tom Gordon	.20	.09
☐ 8	Jack Morris	.20	.09
☐ 9	Carlton Fisk	.20	.09
☐ 10	Will Clark	.40	.18
☐ 11	George Brett	.40	.18
☐ 12	Kevin Mitchell	.05	.02
☐ 13	Mark Langston	.05	.02
☐ 14	Dave Stewart	.10	.05
☐ 15	Dale Murphy	.20	.09
☐ 16	Gary Gaetti	.05	.02
☐ 17	Wade Boggs	.20	.09
☐ 18	Eric Davis	.10	.05
☐ 19	Kirby Puckett	.40	.18
☐ 20	Roger Clemens	.50	.23
☐ 21	Orel Hershiser	.10	.05

☐ 22	Mark Grace	.20	.09
☐ 23	Ryne Sandberg	.25	.11
☐ 24	Barry Larkin	.20	.09
☐ 25	Ellis Burks	.15	.07
☐ 26	Dwight Gooden	.10	.05
☐ 27	Ozzie Smith	.25	.11
☐ 28	Andre Dawson	.20	.09
☐ 29	Julio Franco	.05	.02
☐ 30	Ken Griffey Jr.	20.00	9.00
☐ 31	Ruben Sierra	.05	.02
☐ 32	Mark McGwire	1.00	.45
☐ 33	Andres Galarraga	.20	.09
☐ 34	Joe Carter	.15	.07
☐ 35	Vince Coleman	.05	.02
☐ 36	Mike Greenwell	.05	.02
☐ 37	Tony Gwynn	.50	.23
☐ 38	Andy Van Slyke	.10	.05
☐ 39	Gregg Jefferies	.10	.05
☐ 40	Jose Canseco	.25	.11
☐ 41	Dave Winfield	.20	.09
☐ 42	Darryl Strawberry	.10	.05

1989 Score Young Superstars I

WALT WEISS SHORTSTOP 7

		MINT	NRMT
COMPLETE SET (42)		8.00	3.60
COMMON PLAYER (1-42)		.15	.07
MINOR STARS		.25	.11
SEMISTARS		.50	.23
ONE PER RACK PACK			
☐ 1	Gregg Jefferies	.25	.11
☐ 2	Jody Reed	.15	.07
☐ 3	Mark Grace	.75	.35
☐ 4	Dave Gallagher	.15	.07
☐ 5	Bo Jackson	.50	.23
☐ 6	Jay Buhner	.60	.25
☐ 7	Melido Perez	.15	.07
☐ 8	Bobby Witt	.15	.07
☐ 9	David Cone	.75	.35
☐ 10	Chris Sabo	.15	.07
☐ 11	Pat Borders	.15	.07
☐ 12	Mark Grant	.15	.07
☐ 13	Mike Macfarlane	.15	.07
☐ 14	Mike Jackson	.50	.23
☐ 15	Ricky Jordan	.15	.07
☐ 16	Ron Gant	.25	.11
☐ 17	Al Leiter	.60	.25
☐ 18	Jeff Parrett	.15	.07
☐ 19	Pete Smith	.15	.07
☐ 20	Walt Weiss	.25	.11
☐ 21	Doug Drabek	.15	.07
☐ 22	Kirt Manwaring	.15	.07
☐ 23	Keith Miller	.15	.07
☐ 24	Damon Berryhill	.15	.07
☐ 25	Gary Sheffield	1.50	.70
☐ 26	Brady Anderson	1.00	.45
☐ 27	Mitch Williams	.15	.07
☐ 28	Roberto Alomar	1.25	.55
☐ 29	Bobby Thigpen	.15	.07
☐ 30	Bryan Harvey UER	.15	.07
	(47 games in '87)		
☐ 31	Jose Rijo	.15	.07
☐ 32	Dave West	.15	.07
☐ 33	Joey Meyer	.15	.07
☐ 34	Allan Anderson	.15	.07
☐ 35	Rafael Palmeiro	1.00	.45

			MINT	NRMT
❑ 36	Tim Belcher	.15	.07
❑ 37	John Smiley	.15	.07
❑ 38	Mackey Sasser	.15	.07
❑ 39	Greg Maddux	2.50	1.10
❑ 40	Ramon Martinez	.60	.25
❑ 41	Randy Myers	.25	.11
❑ 42	Scott Bankhead	.15	.07

1989 Score Young Superstars II

	MINT	NRMT
COMP.FACT.SET (42)	100.00	45.00
COMMON PLAYER (1-42)	.15	.07
MINOR STARS	.25	.11
SEMISTARS	.50	.23
DISTRIBUTED IN FACTORY SET FORM ONLY		

- ❑ 1 Sandy Alomar Jr. 1.00 .45
- ❑ 2 Tom Gordon 1.00 .45
- ❑ 3 Ron Jones .15 .07
- ❑ 4 Todd Burns .15 .07
- ❑ 5 Paul O'Neill .25 .11
- ❑ 6 Gene Larkin .15 .07
- ❑ 7 Eric King .15 .07
- ❑ 8 Jeff M. Robinson .15 .07
- ❑ 9 Bill Wegman .15 .07
- ❑ 10 Cecil Espy .15 .07
- ❑ 11 Jose Guzman .15 .07
- ❑ 12 Kelly Gruber .15 .07
- ❑ 13 Duane Ward .15 .07
- ❑ 14 Mark Gubicza .15 .07
- ❑ 15 Norm Charlton .25 .11
- ❑ 16 Jose Oquendo .15 .07
- ❑ 17 Geronimo Berroa .15 .07
- ❑ 18 Ken Griffey Jr. 80.00 36.00
- ❑ 19 Lance McCullers .15 .07
- ❑ 20 Todd Stottlemyre .50 .23
- ❑ 21 Craig Worthington .15 .07
- ❑ 22 Mike Devereaux .15 .07
- ❑ 23 Tom Glavine 1.25 .55
- ❑ 24 Dale Sveum .15 .07
- ❑ 25 Roberto Kelly .25 .11
- ❑ 26 Luis Medina .15 .07
- ❑ 27 Steve Searcy .15 .07
- ❑ 28 Don August .15 .07
- ❑ 29 Shawn Hillegas .15 .07
- ❑ 30 Mike Campbell .15 .07
- ❑ 31 Mike Harkey .15 .07
- ❑ 32 Randy Johnson 6.00 2.70
- ❑ 33 Craig Biggio 4.00 1.80
- ❑ 34 Mike Schooler .15 .07
- ❑ 35 Andres Thomas .15 .07
- ❑ 36 Jerome Walton .75 .35
- ❑ 37 Cris Carpenter .15 .07
- ❑ 38 Kevin Mitchell .25 .11
- ❑ 39 Eddie Williams .15 .07
- ❑ 40 Chad Kreuter .15 .07
- ❑ 41 Danny Jackson .15 .07
- ❑ 42 Kurt Stillwell .15 .07

1990 Score

	MINT	NRMT
COMPLETE SET (704)	12.00	5.50
COMP.RETAIL SET (704)	12.00	5.50
COMP.HOBBY SET (714)	15.00	6.75
COMMON CARD (1-704)	.05	.02

	MINT	NRMT
MINOR STARS	.10	.05
UNLISTED STARS	.20	.09
SUBSET CARDS HALF VALUE OF BASE CARDS		

- ❑ 1 Don Mattingly .40 .18
- ❑ 2 Cal Ripken .75 .35
- ❑ 3 Dwight Evans .10 .05
- ❑ 4 Barry Bonds .25 .11
- ❑ 5 Kevin McReynolds .05 .02
- ❑ 6 Ozzie Guillen .05 .02
- ❑ 7 Terry Kennedy .05 .02
- ❑ 8 Bryan Harvey .05 .02
- ❑ 9 Alan Trammell .15 .07
- ❑ 10 Cory Snyder .05 .02
- ❑ 11 Jody Reed .05 .02
- ❑ 12 Roberto Alomar .20 .09
- ❑ 13 Pedro Guerrero .05 .02
- ❑ 14 Gary Redus .05 .02
- ❑ 15 Marty Barrett .05 .02
- ❑ 16 Ricky Jordan .05 .02
- ❑ 17 Joe Magrane .05 .02
- ❑ 18 Sid Fernandez .05 .02
- ❑ 19 Richard Dotson .05 .02
- ❑ 20 Jack Clark .10 .05
- ❑ 21 Bob Walk .05 .02
- ❑ 22 Ron Karkovice .05 .02
- ❑ 23 Lenny Harris .05 .02
- ❑ 24 Phil Bradley .05 .02
- ❑ 25 Andres Galarraga .20 .09
- ❑ 26 Brian Downing .05 .02
- ❑ 27 Dave Martinez .05 .02
- ❑ 28 Eric King .05 .02
- ❑ 29 Barry Lyons .05 .02
- ❑ 30 Dave Schmidt .05 .02
- ❑ 31 Mike Boddicker .05 .02
- ❑ 32 Tom Foley .05 .02
- ❑ 33 Brady Anderson .20 .09
- ❑ 34 Jim Presley .05 .02
- ❑ 35 Lance Parrish .05 .02
- ❑ 36 Von Hayes .05 .02
- ❑ 37 Lee Smith .10 .05
- ❑ 38 Herm Winningham .05 .02
- ❑ 39 Alejandro Pena .05 .02
- ❑ 40 Mike Scott .05 .02
- ❑ 41 Joe Orsulak .05 .02
- ❑ 42 Rafael Ramirez .05 .02
- ❑ 43 Gerald Young .05 .02
- ❑ 44 Dick Schofield .05 .02
- ❑ 45 Dave Smith .05 .02
- ❑ 46 Dave Magadan .05 .02
- ❑ 47 Dennis Martinez .10 .05
- ❑ 48 Greg Minton .05 .02
- ❑ 49 Milt Thompson .05 .02
- ❑ 50 Orel Hershiser .10 .05
- ❑ 51 Bip Roberts .05 .02
- ❑ 52 Jerry Browne .05 .02
- ❑ 53 Bob Ojeda .05 .02
- ❑ 54 Fernando Valenzuela .10 .05
- ❑ 55 Matt Nokes .05 .02
- ❑ 56 Brook Jacoby .05 .02
- ❑ 57 Frank Tanana .05 .02
- ❑ 58 Scott Fletcher .05 .02
- ❑ 59 Ron Oester .05 .02
- ❑ 60 Bob Boone .10 .05
- ❑ 61 Dan Gladden .05 .02
- ❑ 62 Darnell Coles .05 .02
- ❑ 63 Gregg Olson .10 .05

- ❑ 64 Todd Burns .05 .02
- ❑ 65 Todd Benzinger .05 .02
- ❑ 66 Dale Murphy .20 .09
- ❑ 67 Mike Flanagan .05 .02
- ❑ 68 Jose Oquendo .05 .02
- ❑ 69 Cecil Espy .05 .02
- ❑ 70 Chris Sabo .05 .02
- ❑ 71 Shane Rawley .05 .02
- ❑ 72 Tom Brunansky .05 .02
- ❑ 73 Vance Law .05 .02
- ❑ 74 B.J. Surhoff .10 .05
- ❑ 75 Lou Whitaker .10 .05
- ❑ 76 Ken Caminiti UER .20 .09
  Euclid and Ohio should be Hanford and California
- ❑ 77 Nelson Liriano .05 .02
- ❑ 78 Tommy Gregg .05 .02
- ❑ 79 Don Slaught .05 .02
- ❑ 80 Eddie Murray .20 .09
- ❑ 81 Joe Boever .05 .02
- ❑ 82 Charlie Leibrandt .05 .02
- ❑ 83 Jose Lind .05 .02
- ❑ 84 Tony Phillips .05 .02
- ❑ 85 Mitch Webster .05 .02
- ❑ 86 Dan Plesac .05 .02
- ❑ 87 Rick Mahler .05 .02
- ❑ 88 Steve Lyons .05 .02
- ❑ 89 Tony Fernandez .05 .02
- ❑ 90 Ryne Sandberg .25 .11
- ❑ 91 Nick Esasky .05 .02
- ❑ 92 Luis Salazar .05 .02
- ❑ 93 Pete Incaviglia .05 .02
- ❑ 94 Ivan Calderon .05 .02
- ❑ 95 Jeff Treadway .05 .02
- ❑ 96 Kurt Stillwell .05 .02
- ❑ 97 Gary Sheffield .20 .09
- ❑ 98 Jeffrey Leonard .05 .02
- ❑ 99 Andres Thomas .05 .02
- ❑ 100 Roberto Kelly .05 .02
- ❑ 101 Alvaro Espinoza .05 .02
- ❑ 102 Greg Gagne .05 .02
- ❑ 103 John Farrell .05 .02
- ❑ 104 Willie Wilson .05 .02
- ❑ 105 Glenn Braggs .05 .02
- ❑ 106 Chet Lemon .05 .02
- ❑ 107A Jamie Moyer ERR .05 .02
  (Scintillating)
- ❑ 107B Jamie Moyer COR .10 .05
  (Scintillating)
- ❑ 108 Chuck Crim .05 .02
- ❑ 109 Dave Valle .05 .02
- ❑ 110 Walt Weiss .05 .02
- ❑ 111 Larry Sheets .05 .02
- ❑ 112 Don Robinson .05 .02
- ❑ 113 Danny Heep .05 .02
- ❑ 114 Carmelo Martinez .05 .02
- ❑ 115 Dave Gallagher .05 .02
- ❑ 116 Mike LaValliere .05 .02
- ❑ 117 Bob McClure .05 .02
- ❑ 118 Rene Gonzales .05 .02
- ❑ 119 Mark Parent .05 .02
- ❑ 120 Wally Joyner .10 .05
- ❑ 121 Mark Gubicza .05 .02
- ❑ 122 Tony Pena .05 .02
- ❑ 123 Carmen Castillo .05 .02
- ❑ 124 Howard Johnson .05 .02
- ❑ 125 Steve Sax .10 .05
- ❑ 126 Tim Belcher .05 .02
- ❑ 127 Tim Burke .05 .02
- ❑ 128 Al Newman .05 .02
- ❑ 129 Dennis Rasmussen .05 .02
- ❑ 130 Doug Jones .05 .02
- ❑ 131 Fred Lynn .05 .02
- ❑ 132 Jeff Hamilton .05 .02
- ❑ 133 German Gonzalez .05 .02
- ❑ 134 John Morris .05 .02
- ❑ 135 Dave Parker .10 .05
- ❑ 136 Gary Pettis .05 .02
- ❑ 137 Dennis Boyd .05 .02
- ❑ 138 Candy Maldonado .05 .02
- ❑ 139 Rick Cerone .05 .02
- ❑ 140 George Brett .40 .18
- ❑ 141 Dave Clark .05 .02
- ❑ 142 Dickie Thon .05 .02
- ❑ 143 Junior Ortiz .05 .02
- ❑ 144 Don August .05 .02

145	Gary Gaetti	.10	
146	Kirt Manwaring	.05	.02
147	Jeff Reed	.05	.02
148	Jose Alvarez	.05	.02
149	Mike Schooler	.05	.02
150	Mark Grace	.20	
151	Geronimo Berroa	.05	.02
152	Barry Jones	.05	.02
153	Geno Petralli	.05	.02
154	Jim Deshaies	.05	.02
155	Barry Larkin	.20	.09
156	Alfredo Griffin	.05	.02
157	Tom Henke	.05	.02
158	Mike Jeffcoat	.05	.02
159	Bob Welch	.05	.02
160	Julio Franco	.05	.02
161	Henry Cotto	.05	.02
162	Terry Steinbach	.05	.02
163	Damon Berryhill	.05	.02
164	Tim Crews	.05	.02
165	Tom Browning	.05	.02
166	Fred Manrique	.05	.02
167	Harold Reynolds	.05	.02
168A	Ron Hassey ERR (27 on back)	.05	.02
168B	Ron Hassey COR (24 on back)	.50	.23
169	Shawon Dunston	.05	.02
170	Bobby Bonilla	.10	.05
171	Tommy Herr	.05	.02
172	Mike Heath	.05	.02
173	Rich Gedman	.05	.02
174	Bill Ripken	.05	.02
175	Pete O'Brien	.05	.02
176A	Lloyd McClendon ERR (Uniform number on back listed as 1)	.50	.23
176B	Lloyd McClendon COR (Uniform number on back listed as 10)	.05	.02
177	Brian Holton	.05	.02
178	Jeff Blauser	.05	.02
179	Jim Eisenreich	.05	.02
180	Bert Blyleven	.10	.05
181	Rob Murphy	.05	.02
182	Bill Doran	.05	.02
183	Curt Ford	.05	.02
184	Mike Henneman	.05	.02
185	Eric Davis	.10	.05
186	Lance McCullers	.05	.02
187	Steve Davis	.05	.02
188	Bill Wegman	.05	.02
189	Brian Harper	.05	.02
190	Mike Moore	.05	.02
191	Dale Mohorcic	.05	.02
192	Tim Wallach	.05	.02
193	Keith Hernandez	.10	.05
194	Dave Righetti	.05	.02
195A	Bret Saberhagen ERR (Joke)	.10	.05
195B	Bret Saberhagen COR (Joke)	.10	.05
196	Paul Kilgus	.05	.02
197	Bud Black	.05	.02
198	Juan Samuel	.05	.02
199	Kevin Seitzer	.05	.02
200	Darryl Strawberry	.10	.05
201	Dave Stieb	.05	.02
202	Charlie Hough	.05	.02
203	Jack Morris	.10	.05
204	Rance Mulliniks	.05	.02
205	Alvin Davis	.05	.02
206	Jack Howell	.05	.02
207	Ken Patterson	.05	.02
208	Terry Pendleton	.05	.02
209	Craig Lefferts	.05	.02
210	Kevin Brown UER (First mention of '89 Rangers should be '88)	.20	.09
211	Dan Petry	.05	.02
212	Dave Leiper	.05	.02
213	Daryl Boston	.05	.02
214	Kevin Hickey	.05	.02
215	Mike Krukow	.05	.02
216	Terry Francona	.05	.02
217	Kirk McCaskill	.05	.02
218	Scott Bailes	.05	.02
219	Bob Forsch	.05	.02
220A	Mike Aldrete ERR (25 on back)	.05	.02
220B	Mike Aldrete COR (24 on back)	.10	.05
221	Steve Buechele	.05	.02
222	Jesse Barfield	.05	.02
223	Juan Berenguer	.05	.02
224	Andy McGaffigan	.05	.02
225	Pete Smith	.05	.02
226	Mike Witt	.05	.02
227	Jay Howell	.05	.02
228	Scott Bradley	.05	.02
229	Jerome Walton	.05	.02
230	Greg Swindell	.05	.02
231	Atlee Hammaker	.05	.02
232A	Mike Devereaux ERR (RF on front)	.05	.02
232B	Mike Devereaux COR (CF on front)	.50	.23
233	Ken Hill	.10	.05
234	Craig Worthington	.05	.02
235	Scott Terry	.05	.02
236	Brett Butler	.10	.05
237	Doyle Alexander	.05	.02
238	Dave Anderson	.05	.02
239	Bob Milacki	.05	.02
240	Dwight Smith	.05	.02
241	Otis Nixon	.10	.05
242	Pat Tabler	.05	.02
243	Derek Lilliquist	.05	.02
244	Danny Tartabull	.05	.02
245	Wade Boggs	.20	.09
246	Scott Garrelts (Should say Relief Pitcher on front)	.05	.02
247	Spike Owen	.05	.02
248	Norm Charlton	.05	.02
249	Gerald Perry	.05	.02
250	Nolan Ryan	.75	.35
251	Kevin Gross	.05	.02
252	Randy Milligan	.05	.02
253	Mike LaCoss	.05	.02
254	Dave Bergman	.05	.02
255	Tony Gwynn	.50	.23
256	Felix Fermin	.05	.02
257	Greg W. Harris	.05	.02
258	Junior Felix	.05	.02
259	Mark Davis	.05	.02
260	Vince Coleman	.05	.02
261	Paul Gibson	.05	.02
262	Mitch Williams	.05	.02
263	Jeff Russell	.05	.02
264	Omar Vizquel	.20	.09
265	Andre Dawson	.20	.09
266	Storm Davis	.05	.02
267	Guillermo Hernandez	.05	.02
268	Mike Felder	.05	.02
269	Tom Candiotti	.05	.02
270	Bruce Hurst	.05	.02
271	Fred McGriff	.20	.09
272	Glenn Davis	.05	.02
273	John Franco	.10	.05
274	Rich Yett	.05	.02
275	Craig Biggio	.20	.09
276	Gene Larkin	.05	.02
277	Rob Dibble	.05	.02
278	Randy Bush	.05	.02
279	Kevin Bass	.05	.02
280A	Bo Jackson ERR (Watham)	.20	.09
280B	Bo Jackson COR (Watham)	.10	.05
281	Wally Backman	.05	.02
282	Larry Andersen	.05	.02
283	Chris Bosio	.05	.02
284	Juan Agosto	.05	.02
285	Ozzie Smith	.25	.11
286	George Bell	.05	.02
287	Rex Hudler	.05	.02
288	Pat Borders	.05	.02
289	Danny Jackson	.05	.02
290	Carlton Fisk	.20	.09
291	Tracy Jones	.05	.02
292	Allan Anderson	.05	.02
293	Johnny Ray	.05	.02
294	Lee Guetterman	.05	.02
295	Paul O'Neill	.10	.05
296	Carney Lansford	.10	.05
297	Tom Brookens	.05	.02
298	Claudell Washington	.05	.02
299	Hubie Brooks	.05	.02
300	Will Clark	.20	.09
301	Kenny Rogers	.10	.05
302	Darrell Evans	.10	.05
303	Greg Briley	.05	.02
304	Donn Pall	.05	.02
305	Teddy Higuera	.05	.02
306	Dan Pasqua	.05	.02
307	Dave Winfield	.20	.09
308	Dennis Powell	.05	.02
309	Jose DeLeon	.05	.02
310	Roger Clemens UER (Dominate, should say dominant)	.50	.23
311	Melido Perez	.05	.02
312	Devon White	.05	.02
313	Dwight Gooden	.10	.05
314	Carlos Martinez	.05	.02
315	Dennis Eckersley	.15	.07
316	Clay Parker UER (Height 6'11")	.05	.02
317	Rick Honeycutt	.05	.02
318	Tim Laudner	.05	.02
319	Joe Carter	.20	.09
320	Robin Yount	.20	.09
321	Felix Jose	.05	.02
322	Mickey Tettleton	.10	.05
323	Mike Gallego	.05	.02
324	Edgar Martinez	.05	.02
325	Dave Henderson	.05	.02
326	Chili Davis	.10	.05
327	Steve Balboni	.05	.02
328	Jody Davis	.05	.02
329	Shawn Hillegas	.05	.02
330	Jim Abbott	.15	.07
331	John Dopson	.05	.02
332	Mark Williamson	.05	.02
333	Jeff D. Robinson	.05	.02
334	John Smiley	.05	.02
335	Bobby Thigpen	.05	.02
336	Garry Templeton	.05	.02
337	Marvell Wynne	.05	.02
338A	Ken Griffey Sr. ERR (Uniform number on back listed as 25)	.10	.05
338B	Ken Griffey Sr. COR (Uniform number on back listed as 30)	.50	.23
339	Steve Finley	.20	.09
340	Ellis Burks	.15	.07
341	Frank Williams	.05	.02
342	Mike Morgan	.05	.02
343	Kevin Mitchell	.05	.02
344	Joel Youngblood	.05	.02
345	Mike Greenwell	.05	.02
346	Glenn Wilson	.05	.02
347	John Costello	.05	.02
348	Wes Gardner	.05	.02
349	Jeff Ballard	.05	.02
350	Mark Thurmond UER (ERA is 192, should be 1.92)	.05	.02
351	Randy Myers	.10	.05
352	Shawn Abner	.05	.02
353	Jesse Orosco	.05	.02
354	Greg Walker	.05	.02
355	Pete Harnisch	.05	.02
356	Steve Farr	.05	.02
357	Dave LaPoint	.05	.02
358	Willie Fraser	.05	.02
359	Mickey Hatcher	.05	.02
360	Rickey Henderson	.25	.11
361	Mike Fitzgerald	.05	.02
362	Bill Schroeder	.05	.02
363	Mark Carreon	.05	.02
364	Ron Jones	.05	.02
365	Jeff Montgomery	.10	.05
366	Bill Krueger	.05	.02
367	John Cangelosi	.05	.02
368	Jose Gonzalez	.05	.02

369	Greg Hibbard	.05	
370	John Smoltz	.20	.09
371	Jeff Brantley	.05	.02
372	Frank White	.10	
373	Ed Whitson	.05	
374	Willie McGee	.10	
375	Jose Canseco	.25	.11
376	Randy Ready	.05	.02
377	Don Aase	.05	.02
378	Tony Armas	.05	.02
379	Steve Bedrosian	.05	.02
380	Chuck Finley	.05	
381	Kent Hrbek	.10	.05
382	Jim Gantner	.05	
383	Mel Hall	.05	.02
384	Mike Marshall	.05	.02
385	Mark McGwire	1.00	.45
386	Wayne Tolleson	.05	.02
387	Brian Holman	.05	
388	John Wetteland	.20	.09
389	Darren Daulton	.10	.05
390	Rob Deer	.05	
391	John Moses	.05	.02
392	Todd Worrell	.05	
393	Chuck Cary	.05	.02
394	Stan Javier	.05	
395	Willie Randolph	.10	.05
396	Bill Buckner	.05	
397	Robby Thompson	.05	
398	Mike Scioscia	.05	.02
399	Lonnie Smith	.05	.02
400	Kirby Puckett	.30	.14
401	Mark Langston	.05	.02
402	Danny Darwin	.05	.02
403	Greg Maddux	.50	.23
404	Lloyd Moseby	.05	
405	Rafael Palmeiro	.20	.09
406	Chad Kreuter	.05	
407	Jimmy Key	.10	.05
408	Tim Birtsas	.05	
409	Tim Raines	.10	.05
410	Dave Stewart	.10	
411	Eric Yelding	.05	.02
412	Kent Anderson	.05	.02
413	Les Lancaster	.05	.02
414	Rick Dempsey	.05	.02
415	Randy Johnson	.30	.14
416	Gary Carter	.20	.09
417	Rolando Roomes	.05	.02
418	Dan Schatzeder	.05	.02
419	Bryn Smith	.05	.02
420	Ruben Sierra	.05	.02
421	Steve Jeltz	.05	
422	Ken Oberkfell	.05	.02
423	Sid Bream	.05	.02
424	Jim Clancy	.05	.02
425	Kelly Gruber	.05	.02
426	Rick Leach	.05	.02
427	Len Dykstra	.10	.05
428	Jeff Pico	.05	
429	John Cerutti	.05	.02
430	David Cone	.20	.09
431	Jeff Kunkel	.05	.02
432	Luis Aquino	.05	.02
433	Ernie Whitt	.05	
434	Bo Diaz	.05	.02
435	Steve Lake	.05	.02
436	Pat Perry	.05	.02
437	Mike Davis	.05	.02
438	Cecilio Guante	.05	.02
439	Duane Ward	.05	.02
440	Andy Van Slyke	.10	.05
441	Gene Nelson	.05	.02
442	Luis Polonia	.05	.02
443	Kevin Elster	.05	.02
444	Keith Moreland	.05	.02
445	Roger McDowell	.05	.02
446	Ron Darling	.05	.02
447	Ernest Riles	.05	.02
448	Mookie Wilson	.10	.05
449A	Billy Spiers ERR (No birth year)	.20	.09
449B	Billy Spiers COR (Born in 1966)	.05	.02
450	Rick Sutcliffe	.05	
451	Nelson Santovenia	.05	.02
452	Andy Allanson	.05	.02
453	Bob Melvin	.05	.02
454	Benito Santiago	.05	.02
455	Jose Uribe	.05	.02
456	Bill Landrum	.05	.02
457	Bobby Witt	.05	.02
458	Kevin Romine	.05	.02
459	Lee Mazzilli	.05	.02
460	Paul Molitor	.20	.09
461	Ramon Martinez	.15	.07
462	Frank DiPino	.05	.02
463	Walt Terrell	.05	.02
464	Bob Geren	.05	.02
465	Rick Reuschel	.05	.02
466	Mark Grant	.05	.02
467	John Kruk	.10	.05
468	Gregg Jefferies	.10	.05
469	R.J. Reynolds	.05	.02
470	Harold Baines	.10	.05
471	Dennis Lamp	.05	.02
472	Tom Gordon	.05	.02
473	Terry Puhl	.05	.02
474	Curt Wilkerson	.05	.02
475	Dan Quisenberry	.05	.02
476	Oddibe McDowell	.05	.02
477A	Zane Smith ERR (Career ERA .393)	.05	.02
477B	Zane Smith COR (career ERA 3.93)	.05	.02
478	Franklin Stubbs	.05	.02
479	Wallace Johnson	.05	.02
480	Jay Tibbs	.05	.02
481	Tom Glavine	.20	.09
482	Manny Lee	.05	.02
483	Joe Hesketh UER (Says Rookiess on back, should say Rookies)	.05	.02
484	Mike Bielecki	.05	.02
485	Greg Brock	.05	.02
486	Pascual Perez	.05	.02
487	Kirk Gibson	.10	.05
488	Scott Sanderson	.05	.02
489	Domingo Ramos	.05	.02
490	Kal Daniels	.05	.02
491A	David Wells ERR (Reverse negative photo on card back)	.75	.35
491B	David Wells COR	.15	.07
492	Jerry Reed	.05	.02
493	Eric Show	.05	.02
494	Mike Pagliarulo	.05	.02
495	Ron Robinson	.05	.02
496	Brad Komminsk	.05	.02
497	Greg Litton	.05	.02
498	Chris James	.05	.02
499	Luis Quinones	.05	.02
500	Frank Viola	.05	.02
501	Tim Teufel UER (Twins '85, the s is lower case, should be upper case)	.05	.02
502	Terry Leach	.05	.02
503	Matt Williams UER (Wearing 10 on front, listed as 9 on back)	.20	.09
504	Tim Leary	.05	.02
505	Doug Drabek	.05	.02
506	Mariano Duncan	.05	.02
507	Charlie Hayes	.05	.02
508	Joey Belle	.75	.35
509	Pat Sheridan	.05	.02
510	Mackey Sasser	.05	.02
511	Jose Rijo	.05	.02
512	Mike Smithson	.05	.02
513	Gary Ward	.05	.02
514	Dion James	.05	.02
515	Jim Gott	.05	.02
516	Drew Hall	.05	.02
517	Doug Bair	.05	.02
518	Scott Scudder	.05	.02
519	Rick Aguilera	.10	.05
520	Rafael Belliard	.05	.02
521	Jay Buhner	.05	.02
522	Jeff Reardon	.10	.05
523	Steve Rosenberg	.05	.02
524	Randy Velarde	.05	.02
525	Jeff Musselman	.05	.02
526	Bill Long	.05	.02
527	Gary Wayne	.05	.02
528	Dave Johnson (P)	.05	.02
529	Ron Kittle	.05	.02
530	Erik Hanson UER (5th line on back says seson, should say season)	.05	.02
531	Steve Wilson	.05	.02
532	Joey Meyer	.05	.02
533	Curt Young	.05	.02
534	Kelly Downs	.05	.02
535	Joe Girardi	.15	.07
536	Lance Blankenship	.05	.02
537	Greg Mathews	.05	.02
538	Donell Nixon	.05	.02
539	Mark Knudson	.05	.02
540	Jeff Wetherby	.05	.02
541	Darrin Jackson	.05	.02
542	Terry Mulholland	.05	.02
543	Eric Hetzel	.05	.02
544	Rick Reed	.25	.11
545	Dennis Cook	.05	.02
546	Mike Jackson	.10	.05
547	Brian Fisher	.05	.02
548	Gene Harris	.05	.02
549	Jeff King	.20	.09
550	Dave Dravecky	.20	.09
551	Randy Kutcher	.05	.02
552	Mark Portugal	.05	.02
553	Jim Corsi	.05	.02
554	Todd Stottlemyre	.10	.05
555	Scott Bankhead	.05	.02
556	Ken Dayley	.05	.02
557	Rick Wrona	.05	.02
558	Sammy Sosa	6.00	2.70
559	Keith Miller	.05	.02
560	Ken Griffey Jr.	2.00	.90
561A	Ryne Sandberg HL ERR (Position on front listed as 3B)	5.00	2.20
561B	Ryne Sandberg HL COR	.20	.09
562	Billy Hatcher	.05	.02
563	Jay Bell	.10	.05
564	Jack Daugherty	.05	.02
565	Rich Monteleone	.05	.02
566	Bo Jackson AS-MVP	.10	.05
567	Tony Fossas	.05	.02
568	Roy Smith	.05	.02
569	Jaime Navarro	.05	.02
570	Lance Johnson	.05	.02
571	Mike Dyer	.05	.02
572	Kevin Ritz	.05	.02
573	Dave West	.05	.02
574	Gary Mielke	.05	.02
575	Scott Lusader	.05	.02
576	Joe Oliver	.05	.02
577	Sandy Alomar Jr.	.10	.05
578	Andy Benes UER (Extra comma between day and year)	.20	.09
579	Tim Jones	.05	.02
580	Randy McCament	.05	.02
581	Curt Schilling	.50	.23
582	John Orton	.05	.02
583A	Milt Cuyler ERR (998 games)	.50	.23
583B	Milt Cuyler COR (98 games; the extra 9 was ghosted out and may still be visible)	.05	.02
584	Eric Anthony	.05	.02
585	Greg Vaughn	.40	.18
586	Deion Sanders	.20	.09
587	Jose DeJesus	.05	.02
588	Chip Hale	.05	.02
589	John Olerud	.80	.25
590	Steve Olin	.10	.05
591	Marquis Grissom	.25	.11
592	Moises Alou	.40	.18
593	Mark Lemke	.05	.02
594	Dean Palmer	.50	.23
595	Robin Ventura	.20	.09
596	Tino Martinez	.25	.11

#	Player	MINT	NRMT
597	Mike Huff	.05	.02
598	Scott Hemond	.05	.02
599	Wally Whitehurst	.05	.02
600	Todd Zeile	.10	.05
601	Glenallen Hill	.05	.02
602	Hal Morris	.05	.02
603	Juan Bell	.05	.02
604	Bobby Rose	.05	.02
605	Matt Merullo	.05	.02
606	Kevin Maas	.10	.05
607	Randy Nosek	.05	.02
608A	Billy Bates (Text mentions 12 triples in tenth line)	.05	.02
608B	Billy Bates (Text has no mention of triples)	.05	.02
609	Mike Stanton	.05	.02
610	Mauro Gozzo	.05	.02
611	Charles Nagy	.20	.09
612	Scott Coolbaugh	.05	.02
613	Jose Vizcaino	.15	.07
614	Greg Smith	.05	.02
615	Jeff Huson	.05	.02
616	Mickey Weston	.05	.02
617	John Pawlowski	.05	.02
618A	Joe Skalski ERR (27 on back)	.05	.02
618B	Joe Skalski COR (67 on back)	.50	.23
619	Bernie Williams	1.25	.55
620	Shawn Holman	.05	.02
621	Gary Eave	.05	.02
622	Darrin Fletcher UER (Elmherst, should be Elmhurst)	.10	.02
623	Pat Combs	.05	.02
624	Mike Blowers	.10	.05
625	Kevin Appier	.15	.07
626	Pat Austin	.05	.02
627	Kelly Mann	.05	.02
628	Matt Kinzer	.05	.02
629	Chris Hammond	.05	.02
630	Dean Wilkins	.05	.02
631	Larry Walker UER (Uniform number 55 on front and 33 on back; Home is Maple Ridge, not Maple River)	1.25	.55
632	Blaine Beatty	.05	.02
633A	Tommy Barrett ERR (29 on back)	.05	.02
633B	Tommy Barrett COR (14 on back)	.50	.23
634	Stan Belinda	.05	.02
635	Mike (Tex) Smith	.05	.02
636	Hensley Meulens	.05	.02
637	Juan Gonzalez UER (Sarasota on back, should be Sarasota)	2.50	1.10
638	Lenny Webster	.05	.02
639	Mark Gardner	.05	.02
640	Tommy Greene	.05	.02
641	Mike Hartley	.05	.02
642	Phil Stephenson	.05	.02
643	Kevin Mmahat	.05	.02
644	Ed Whited	.05	.02
645	Delino DeShields	.20	.09
646	Kevin Blankenship	.05	.02
647	Paul Sorrento	.15	.07
648	Mike Roesler	.05	.02
649	Jason Grimsley	.05	.02
650	Dave Justice	.50	.23
651	Scott Cooper	.05	.02
652	Dave Eiland	.05	.02
653	Mike Munoz	.05	.02
654	Jeff Fischer	.05	.02
655	Terry Jorgensen	.05	.02
656	George Canale	.05	.02
657	Brian DuBois UER (Misspelled Dubois on card)	.05	.02
658	Carlos Quintana	.05	.02
659	Luis de los Santos	.05	.02
660	Jerald Clark	.05	.02
661	Donald Harris DC	.05	.02
662	Paul Coleman DC	.05	.02
663	Frank Thomas DC	2.50	1.10
664	Brent Mayne DC	.05	.02
665	Eddie Zosky DC	.05	.02
666	Steve Hosey DC	.05	.02
667	Scott Bryant DC	.05	.02
668	Tom Goodwin DC	.20	.09
669	Cal Eldred DC	.10	.05
670	Earl Cunningham DC	.05	.02
671	Alan Zinter DC	.05	.02
672	Chuck Knoblauch DC	.50	.23
673	Kyle Abbott DC	.05	.02
674	Roger Salkeld DC	.05	.02
675	Maurice Vaughn DC	1.00	.45
676	Keith(Kiki) Jones DC	.05	.02
677	Tyler Houston DC	.15	.07
678	Jeff Jackson DC	.05	.02
679	Greg Gohr DC	.05	.02
680	Ben McDonald DC	.10	.05
681	Greg Blosser DC	.05	.02
682	Willie Greene DC UER (Name spelled as Green)	.10	.05
683A	Wade Boggs DT ERR (Text says 215 hits in '89, should be 205)	.10	.05
683B	Wade Boggs DT COR (Text says 205 hits in '89)	.10	.05
684	Will Clark DT	.10	.05
685	Tony Gwynn DT UER (Text reads battling instead of batting)	.20	.09
686	Rickey Henderson DT	.10	.05
687	Bo Jackson DT	.10	.05
688	Mark Langston DT	.05	.02
689	Barry Larkin DT	.10	.05
690	Kirby Puckett DT	.20	.09
691	Ryne Sandberg DT	.20	.09
692	Mike Scott DT	.05	.02
693A	Terry Steinbach DT ERR (cathers)	.05	.02
693B	Terry Steinbach DT COR (catchers)	.05	.02
694	Bobby Thigpen DT	.05	.02
695	Mitch Williams DT	.05	.02
696	Nolan Ryan HL	.35	.16
697	Bo Jackson FB/BB	.50	.23
698	Rickey Henderson ALCS-MVP	.10	.05
699	Will Clark NLCS-MVP	.10	.05
700	WS Games 1/2 (Dave Stewart Mike Moore)	.10	.05
701	Lights Out: Candlestick 5:04pm (10/17/89)	.20	.09
702	WS Game 3 (Bashers Blast Giants (Carney Lansford, Rickey Henderson, Jose Canseco, Dave Henderson)	.20	.09
703	WS Game 4/Wrap-up A's Sweep Battle of the Bay (A's Celebrate!)	.05	.02
704	Wade Boggs HL Wade Raps 200	.10	.05

1990 Score Rookie Dream Team

	MINT	NRMT
COMPLETE SET (10)	4.00	1.80
COMMON CARD (B1-B10)	.20	.09
ONE SET PER HOBBY FACTORY SET		

#	Player	MINT	NRMT
B1	A.Bartlett Giamatti COMM MEM	.50	.23
B2	Pat Combs	.20	.09
B3	Todd Zeile	.30	.14
B4	Luis de los Santos	.20	.09
B5	Mark Lemke	.20	.09
B6	Robin Ventura	.50	.23
B7	Jeff Huson	.20	.09
B8	Greg Vaughn	1.50	.70
B9	Marquis Grissom	1.00	.45
B10	Eric Anthony	.25	.11

1990 Score Rookie/Traded

	MINT	NRMT
COMP.FACT.SET (110)	5.00	2.20
COMMON CARD (1T-110T)	.05	.02
MINOR STARS	.10	.05
UNLISTED STARS	.20	.09

#	Player	MINT	NRMT
1T	Dave Winfield	.20	.09
2T	Kevin Bass	.05	.02
3T	Nick Esasky	.05	.02
4T	Mitch Webster	.05	.02
5T	Pascual Perez	.05	.02
6T	Gary Pettis	.05	.02
7T	Tony Pena	.05	.02
8T	Candy Maldonado	.05	.02
9T	Cecil Fielder	.10	.05
10T	Carmelo Martinez	.05	.02
11T	Mark Langston	.05	.02
12T	Dave Parker	.10	.05
13T	Don Slaught	.05	.02
14T	Tony Phillips	.05	.02
15T	John Franco	.10	.05
16T	Randy Myers	.10	.05
17T	Jeff Reardon	.10	.05
18T	Sandy Alomar Jr.	.20	.09
19T	Joe Carter	.10	.05
20T	Fred Lynn	.05	.02
21T	Storm Davis	.05	.02
22T	Craig Lefferts	.05	.02
23T	Pete O'Brien	.05	.02
24T	Dennis Boyd	.05	.02
25T	Lloyd Moseby	.05	.02
26T	Mark Davis	.05	.02
27T	Tim Leary	.05	.02
28T	Gerald Perry	.05	.02
29T	Don Aase	.05	.02
30T	Ernie Whitt	.05	.02
31T	Dale Murphy	.20	.09
32T	Alejandro Pena	.05	.02
33T	Juan Samuel	.05	.02
34T	Hubie Brooks	.05	.02
35T	Gary Carter	.20	.09
36T	Jim Presley	.05	.02
37T	Wally Backman	.05	.02

		MINT	NRMT
❑ 38T	Matt Nokes	.05	.02
❑ 39T	Dan Petry	.05	.02
❑ 40T	Franklin Stubbs	.05	.02
❑ 41T	Jeff Huson	.05	.02
❑ 42T	Billy Hatcher	.05	.02
❑ 43T	Terry Leach	.05	.02
❑ 44T	Phil Bradley	.05	.02
❑ 45T	Claudell Washington	.05	.02
❑ 46T	Luis Polonia	.05	.02
❑ 47T	Daryl Boston	.05	.02
❑ 48T	Lee Smith	.10	.05
❑ 49T	Tom Brunansky	.05	.02
❑ 50T	Mike Witt	.05	.02
❑ 51T	Willie Randolph	.10	.05
❑ 52T	Stan Javier	.05	.02
❑ 53T	Brad Komminsk	.05	.02
❑ 54T	John Candelaria	.05	.02
❑ 55T	Bryn Smith	.05	.02
❑ 56T	Glenn Braggs	.05	.02
❑ 57T	Keith Hernandez	.10	.05
❑ 58T	Ken Oberkfell	.05	.02
❑ 59T	Steve Jeltz	.05	.02
❑ 60T	Chris James	.05	.02
❑ 61T	Scott Sanderson	.05	.02
❑ 62T	Bill Long	.05	.02
❑ 63T	Rick Cerone	.05	.02
❑ 64T	Scott Bailes	.05	.02
❑ 65T	Larry Sheets	.05	.02
❑ 66T	Junior Ortiz	.05	.02
❑ 67T	Francisco Cabrera	.05	.02
❑ 68T	Gary DiSarcina	.15	.07
❑ 69T	Greg Olson	.05	.02
❑ 70T	Beau Allred	.05	.02
❑ 71T	Oscar Azocar	.05	.02
❑ 72T	Kent Mercker	.05	.02
❑ 73T	John Burkett	.05	.02
❑ 74T	Carlos Baerga	.20	.09
❑ 75T	Dave Hollins	.20	.09
❑ 76T	Todd Hundley	.25	.11
❑ 77T	Rick Parker	.05	.02
❑ 78T	Steve Cummings	.05	.02
❑ 79T	Bill Sampen	.05	.02
❑ 80T	Jerry Kutzler	.05	.02
❑ 81T	Derek Bell	.40	.18
❑ 82T	Kevin Tapani	.10	.05
❑ 83T	Jim Leyritz	.25	.11
❑ 84T	Ray Lankford	.40	.18
❑ 85T	Wayne Edwards	.05	.02
❑ 86T	Frank Thomas	2.50	1.10
❑ 87T	Tim Naehring	.10	.05
❑ 88T	Willie Blair	.05	.02
❑ 89T	Alan Mills	.05	.02
❑ 90T	Scott Radinsky	.05	.02
❑ 91T	Howard Farmer	.05	.02
❑ 92T	Julio Machado	.05	.02
❑ 93T	Rafael Valdez	.05	.02
❑ 94T	Shawn Boskie	.05	.02
❑ 95T	David Segui	.25	.11
❑ 96T	Chris Hoiles	.20	.09
❑ 97T	D.J. Dozier	.10	.05
❑ 98T	Hector Villanueva	.05	.02
❑ 99T	Eric Gunderson	.05	.02
❑ 100T	Eric Lindros	1.50	.70
❑ 101T	Dave Otto	.05	.02
❑ 102T	Dana Kiecker	.05	.02
❑ 103T	Tim Drummond	.05	.02
❑ 104T	Mickey Pina	.05	.02
❑ 105T	Craig Grebeck	.05	.02
❑ 106T	Bernard Gilkey	.25	.11
❑ 107T	Tim Layana	.05	.02
❑ 108T	Scott Chiamparino	.05	.02
❑ 109T	Steve Avery	.05	.02
❑ 110T	Terry Shumpert	.05	.02

1990 Score Rising Stars

		MINT	NRMT
COMP.FACT.SET (100)		25.00	11.00
COMMON CARD (1-100)		.05	.02
MINOR STARS		.25	.11
UNLISTED STARS		.50	.23
DISTRIBUTED IN FACTORY SET FORM ONLY			
❑ 1	Tom Gordon	.25	.11
❑ 2	Jerome Walton	.10	.05
❑ 3	Ken Griffey Jr.	10.00	4.50

		MINT	NRMT
❑ 4	Dwight Smith	.10	.05
❑ 5	Jim Abbott	.40	.18
❑ 6	Todd Zeile	.25	.11
❑ 7	Donn Pall	.10	.05
❑ 8	Rick Reed	.75	.35
❑ 9	Joey Belle	2.00	.90
❑ 10	Gregg Jefferies	.25	.11
❑ 11	Kevin Ritz	.10	.05
❑ 12	Charlie Hayes	.10	.05
❑ 13	Kevin Appier	.40	.18
❑ 14	Jeff Huson	.10	.05
❑ 15	Gary Wayne	.10	.05
❑ 16	Eric Yelding	.10	.05
❑ 17	Clay Parker	.10	.05
❑ 18	Junior Felix	.10	.05
❑ 19	Derek Lilliquist	.10	.05
❑ 20	Gary Sheffield	.50	.23
❑ 21	Craig Worthington	.10	.05
❑ 22	Jeff Brantley	.10	.05
❑ 23	Eric Hetzel	.10	.05
❑ 24	Greg W.Harris	.10	.05
❑ 25	John Wetteland	.50	.23
❑ 26	Joe Oliver	.10	.05
❑ 27	Kevin Maas	.25	.11
❑ 28	Kevin Brown	.50	.23
❑ 29	Mike Stanton	.10	.05
❑ 30	Greg Vaughn	1.00	.45
❑ 31	Ron Jones	.10	.05
❑ 32	Gregg Olson	.25	.11
❑ 33	Joe Girardi	.40	.18
❑ 34	Ken Hill	.25	.11
❑ 35	Sammy Sosa	10.00	4.50
❑ 36	Geronimo Berroa	.10	.05
❑ 37	Omar Vizquel	.50	.23
❑ 38	Dean Palmer	.50	.23
❑ 39	John Olerud	1.00	.45
❑ 40	Deion Sanders	.50	.23
❑ 41	Randy Kramer	.10	.05
❑ 42	Scott Lusader	.10	.05
❑ 43	Dave Johnson (P)	.10	.05
❑ 44	Jeff Wetherby	.10	.05
❑ 45	Eric Anthony	.10	.05
❑ 46	Kenny Rogers	.25	.11
❑ 47	Matt Winters	.10	.05
❑ 48	Mauro Gozzo	.10	.05
❑ 49	Carlos Quintana	.10	.05
❑ 50	Bob Geren	.10	.05
❑ 51	Chad Kreuter	.10	.05
❑ 52	Randy Johnson	1.00	.45
❑ 53	Hensley Meulens	.10	.05
❑ 54	Gene Harris	.10	.05
❑ 55	Bill Spiers	.10	.05
❑ 56	Kelly Mann	.10	.05
❑ 57	Tom McCarthy	.10	.05
❑ 58	Steve Finley	.50	.23
❑ 59	Ramon Martinez	.40	.18
❑ 60	Greg Briley	.10	.05
❑ 61	Jack Daugherty	.10	.05
❑ 62	Tim Jones	.10	.05
❑ 63	Doug Strange	.10	.05
❑ 64	John Orton	.10	.05
❑ 65	Scott Scudder	.10	.05
❑ 66	Mark Gardner	.10	.05
❑ 67	Mark Carreon	.10	.05
❑ 68	Bob Milacki	.10	.05
❑ 69	Andy Benes	.50	.23
❑ 70	Carlos Martinez	.10	.05
❑ 71	Jeff King	.10	.05

		MINT	NRMT
❑ 72	Brad Arnsberg	.10	.05
❑ 73	Rick Wrona	.10	.05
❑ 74	Cris Carpenter	.10	.05
❑ 75	Dennis Cook	.10	.05
❑ 76	Pete Harnisch	.10	.05
❑ 77	Greg Hibbard	.10	.05
❑ 78	Ed Whited	.10	.05
❑ 79	Scott Coolbaugh	.10	.05
❑ 80	Billy Bates	.10	.05
❑ 81	German Gonzalez	.10	.05
❑ 82	Lance Blankenship	.10	.05
❑ 83	Lenny Harris	.10	.05
❑ 84	Milt Cuyler	.10	.05
❑ 85	Erik Hanson	.10	.05
❑ 86	Kent Anderson	.10	.05
❑ 87	Hal Morris	.10	.05
❑ 88	Mike Brumley	.10	.05
❑ 89	Ken Patterson	.10	.05
❑ 90	Mike Devereaux	.10	.05
❑ 91	Greg Litton	.10	.05
❑ 92	Rolando Roomes	.10	.05
❑ 93	Ben McDonald	.10	.05
❑ 94	Curt Schilling	2.00	.90
❑ 95	Jose DeJesus	.10	.05
❑ 96	Robin Ventura	.50	.23
❑ 97	Steve Searcy	.10	.05
❑ 98	Chip Hale	.10	.05
❑ 99	Marquis Grissom	.50	.23
❑ 100	Luis de los Santos	.10	.05

1990 Score Young Superstars I

	MINT	NRMT
COMPLETE SET (42)	10.00	4.50
COMMON CARD (1-42)	.15	.07
MINOR STARS	.30	.14
SEMISTARS	.60	.25
UNLISTED STARS	1.00	.45
ONE PER RACK PACK		

		MINT	NRMT
❑ 1	Bo Jackson	.30	.14
❑ 2	Dwight Smith	.15	.07
❑ 3	Albert Belle	4.00	1.80
❑ 4	Gregg Olson	.30	.14
❑ 5	Jim Abbott	.60	.25
❑ 6	Felix Fermin	.15	.07
❑ 7	Brian Holman	.15	.07
❑ 8	Clay Parker	.15	.07
❑ 9	Junior Felix	.15	.07
❑ 10	Joe Oliver	.15	.07
❑ 11	Steve Finley	1.00	.45
❑ 12	Greg Briley	.15	.07
❑ 13	Greg Vaughn	2.00	.90
❑ 14	Bill Spiers	.15	.07
❑ 15	Eric Yelding	.15	.07
❑ 16	Jose Gonzalez	.15	.07
❑ 17	Mark Carreon	.15	.07
❑ 18	Greg W. Harris	.15	.07
❑ 19	Felix Jose	.15	.07
❑ 20	Bob Milacki	.15	.07
❑ 21	Kenny Rogers	.30	.14
❑ 22	Rolando Roomes	.15	.07
❑ 23	Bip Roberts	.15	.07
❑ 24	Jeff Brantley	.15	.07
❑ 25	Jeff Ballard	.15	.07
❑ 26	John Dopson	.15	.07
❑ 27	Ken Patterson	.15	.07

	MINT	NRMT
☐ 28 Omar Vizquel	1.00	.45
☐ 29 Kevin Brown	1.00	.45
☐ 30 Derek Lilliquist	.15	.07
☐ 31 David Wells	.30	.25
☐ 32 Ken Hill	.60	.14
☐ 33 Greg Litton	.15	.07
☐ 34 Rob Ducey	.15	.07
☐ 35 Carlos Martinez	.15	.07
☐ 36 John Smoltz	1.00	.45
☐ 37 Lenny Harris	.15	.07
☐ 38 Charlie Hayes	.15	.07
☐ 39 Tommy Gregg	.15	.07
☐ 40 John Wetteland	1.00	.45
☐ 41 Jeff Huson	.15	.07
☐ 42 Eric Anthony	.15	.07

1990 Score Young Superstars II

	MINT	NRMT
COMP.FACT.SET (42)	60.00	27.00
COMMON CARD (1-42)	.25	.11
MINOR STARS	.50	.23
SEMISTARS	1.00	.45
DISTRIBUTED ONLY IN FACTORY SET FORM		

☐ 1 Todd Zeile	.50	.23
☐ 2 Ben McDonald	.25	.11
☐ 3 Delino DeShields	1.50	.70
☐ 4 Pat Combs	.25	.11
☐ 5 John Olerud	4.00	1.80
☐ 6 Marquis Grissom	1.50	.70
☐ 7 Mike Stanton	.25	.11
☐ 8 Robin Ventura	2.00	.90
☐ 9 Larry Walker	8.00	3.60
☐ 10 Dante Bichette	1.50	.70
☐ 11 Jack Armstrong	.25	.11
☐ 12 Jay Bell	.50	.23
☐ 13 Andy Benes	.50	.23
☐ 14 Joey Cora	.50	.23
☐ 15 Rob Dibble	.25	.11
☐ 16 Jeff King	.25	.11
☐ 17 Jeff Hamilton	.25	.11
☐ 18 Erik Hanson	.25	.11
☐ 19 Pete Harnisch	.25	.11
☐ 20 Greg Hibbard	.25	.11
☐ 21 Stan Javier	.25	.11
☐ 22 Mark Lemke	.25	.11
☐ 23 Steve Olin	.50	.23
☐ 24 Tommy Greene	.25	.11
☐ 25 Sammy Sosa	40.00	18.00
☐ 26 Gary Wayne	.25	.11
☐ 27 Deion Sanders	1.50	.70
☐ 28 Steve Wilson	.25	.11
☐ 29 Joe Girardi	1.00	.45
☐ 30 John Orton	.25	.11
☐ 31 Kevin Tapani	.50	.23
☐ 32 Carlos Baerga	1.50	.70
☐ 33 Glenallen Hill	.25	.11
☐ 34 Mike Blowers	.50	.23
☐ 35 Dave Hollins	1.50	.70
☐ 36 Lance Blankenship	.25	.11
☐ 37 Hal Morris	.25	.11
☐ 38 Lance Johnson	.25	.11
☐ 39 Chris Gwynn	.25	.11
☐ 40 Doug Dascenzo	.25	.11
☐ 41 Jerald Clark	.25	.11
☐ 42 Carlos Quintana	.25	.11

1991 Score

	MINT	NRMT
COMPLETE SET (893)	10.00	4.50
COMP.FACT.SET (900)	20.00	9.00
COMMON CARD (1-893)		
MINOR STARS	.10	.05
UNLISTED STARS	.20	.09
SUBSET CARDS HALF VALUE OF BASE CARDS		

☐ 1 Jose Canseco	.25	.11
☐ 2 Ken Griffey Jr.	1.50	.70
☐ 3 Ryne Sandberg	.25	.11
☐ 4 Nolan Ryan	.75	.35
☐ 5 Bo Jackson	.10	.05
☐ 6 Bret Saberhagen UER	.05	.02
(In bio, missed misspelled as mised)		
☐ 7 Will Clark	.20	.09
☐ 8 Ellis Burks	.10	.05
☐ 9 Joe Carter	.10	.05
☐ 10 Rickey Henderson	.25	.11
☐ 11 Ozzie Guillen	.05	.02
☐ 12 Wade Boggs	.20	.09
☐ 13 Jerome Walton	.05	.02
☐ 14 John Franco	.10	.05
☐ 15 Ricky Jordan UER	.05	.02
(League misspelled as legue)		
☐ 16 Wally Backman	.05	.02
☐ 17 Rob Dibble	.05	.02
☐ 18 Glenn Braggs	.05	.02
☐ 19 Cory Snyder	.05	.02
☐ 20 Kal Daniels	.05	.02
☐ 21 Mark Langston	.05	.02
☐ 22 Kevin Gross	.05	.02
☐ 23 Don Mattingly UER	.40	.18
(First line, 's is missing from Yankee)		
☐ 24 Dave Righetti	.05	.02
☐ 25 Roberto Alomar	.20	.09
☐ 26 Robby Thompson	.05	.02
☐ 27 Jack McDowell	.05	.02
☐ 28 Bip Roberts UER	.05	.02
(Bio reads playd)		
☐ 29 Jay Howell	.05	.02
☐ 30 Dave Stieb UER	.05	.02
(17 wins in bio, 18 in stats)		
☐ 31 Johnny Ray	.05	.02
☐ 32 Steve Sax	.05	.02
☐ 33 Terry Mulholland	.05	.02
☐ 34 Lee Guetterman	.05	.02
☐ 35 Tim Raines	.10	.05
☐ 36 Scott Fletcher	.05	.02
☐ 37 Lance Parrish	.05	.02
☐ 38 Tony Phillips UER	.05	.02
(Born 4/15 should be 4/25)		
☐ 39 Todd Stottlemyre	.05	.02
☐ 40 Alan Trammell	.15	.07
☐ 41 Todd Burns	.05	.02
☐ 42 Mookie Wilson	.10	.05
☐ 43 Chris Bosio	.05	.02
☐ 44 Jeffrey Leonard	.05	.02
☐ 45 Doug Jones	.05	.02
☐ 46 Mike Scott UER	.05	.02

(In first line, dominate should read dominating)		
☐ 47 Andy Hawkins	.05	.02
☐ 48 Harold Reynolds	.05	.02
☐ 49 Paul Molitor	.20	.09
☐ 50 John Farrell	.05	.02
☐ 51 Danny Darwin	.05	.02
☐ 52 Jeff Blauser	.05	.02
☐ 53 John Tudor UER	.05	.02
(41 wins in '81)		
☐ 54 Milt Thompson	.05	.02
☐ 55 Dave Justice	.20	.09
☐ 56 Greg Olson	.05	.02
☐ 57 Willie Blair	.05	.02
☐ 58 Rick Parker	.05	.02
☐ 59 Shawn Boskie	.05	.02
☐ 60 Kevin Tapani	.05	.02
☐ 61 Dave Hollins	.05	.02
☐ 62 Scott Radinsky	.05	.02
☐ 63 Francisco Cabrera	.05	.02
☐ 64 Tim Layana	.05	.02
☐ 65 Jim Leyritz	.10	.05
☐ 66 Wayne Edwards	.05	.02
☐ 67 Lee Stevens	.10	.05
☐ 68 Bill Sampen UER	.05	.02
(Fourth line, long is spelled along)		
☐ 69 Craig Grebeck UER	.05	.02
(Born in Cerritos, not Johnstown)		
☐ 70 John Burkett	.05	.02
☐ 71 Hector Villanueva	.05	.02
☐ 72 Oscar Azocar	.05	.02
☐ 73 Alan Mills	.05	.02
☐ 74 Carlos Baerga	.20	.09
☐ 75 Charles Nagy	.20	.09
☐ 76 Tim Drummond	.05	.02
☐ 77 Dana Kiecker	.05	.02
☐ 78 Tom Edens	.05	.02
☐ 79 Kent Mercker	.05	.02
☐ 80 Steve Avery	.20	.09
☐ 81 Lee Smith	.10	.05
☐ 82 Dave Martinez	.05	.02
☐ 83 Dave Winfield	.20	.09
☐ 84 Bill Spiers	.05	.02
☐ 85 Dan Pasqua	.05	.02
☐ 86 Randy Milligan	.05	.02
☐ 87 Tracy Jones	.05	.02
☐ 88 Greg Myers	.05	.02
☐ 89 Keith Hernandez	.10	.05
☐ 90 Todd Benzinger	.05	.02
☐ 91 Mike Jackson	.05	.02
☐ 92 Mike Stanley	.05	.02
☐ 93 Candy Maldonado	.05	.02
☐ 94 John Kruk UER	.05	.02
(No decimal point before 1990 BA)		
☐ 95 Cal Ripken UER	.75	.35
(Genius spelled genuis)		
☐ 96 Willie Fraser	.05	.02
☐ 97 Mike Felder	.05	.02
☐ 98 Bill Landrum	.05	.02
☐ 99 Chuck Crim	.05	.02
☐ 100 Chuck Finley	.10	.05
☐ 101 Kirt Manwaring	.05	.02
☐ 102 Jaime Navarro	.05	.02
☐ 103 Dickie Thon	.05	.02
☐ 104 Brian Downing	.05	.02
☐ 105 Jim Abbott	.10	.05
☐ 106 Tom Brookens	.05	.02
☐ 107 Darryl Hamilton UER	.05	.02
(Bio info is for Jeff Hamilton)		
☐ 108 Bryan Harvey	.05	.02
☐ 109 Greg A. Harris UER	.05	.02
(Shown pitching lefty, bio says righty)		
☐ 110 Greg Swindell	.05	.02
☐ 111 Juan Berenguer	.05	.02
☐ 112 Mike Heath	.05	.02
☐ 113 Scott Bradley	.05	.02
☐ 114 Jack Morris	.10	.05
☐ 115 Barry Jones	.05	.02
☐ 116 Kevin Romine	.05	.02
☐ 117 Garry Templeton	.05	.02

□			
118	Scott Sanderson	.05	.02
119	Roberto Kelly	.05	.02
120	George Brett	.40	.18
121	Oddibe McDowell	.05	.02
122	Jim Acker	.05	.02
123	Bill Swift UER	.05	.02
	(Born 12/27/61,		
	should be 10/27)		
124	Eric King	.05	.02
125	Jay Buhner	.20	.09
126	Matt Young	.05	.02
127	Alvaro Espinoza	.05	.02
128	Greg Hibbard	.05	.02
129	Jeff M. Robinson	.05	.02
130	Mike Greenwell	.05	.02
131	Dion James	.05	.02
132	Donn Pall UER	.05	.02
	(1988 ERA in stats 0.00)		
133	Lloyd Moseby	.05	.02
134	Randy Velarde	.05	.02
135	Allan Anderson	.05	.02
136	Mark Davis	.05	.02
137	Eric Davis	.10	.05
138	Phil Stephenson	.05	.02
139	Felix Fermin	.05	.02
140	Pedro Guerrero	.05	.02
141	Charlie Hough	.10	.05
142	Mike Henneman	.05	.02
143	Jeff Montgomery	.10	.05
144	Lenny Harris	.05	.02
145	Bruce Hurst	.05	.02
146	Eric Anthony	.05	.02
147	Paul Assenmacher	.05	.02
148	Jesse Barfield	.05	.02
149	Carlos Quintana	.05	.02
150	Dave Stewart	.10	.05
151	Roy Smith	.05	.02
152	Paul Gibson	.05	.02
153	Mickey Hatcher	.05	.02
154	Jim Eisenreich	.05	.02
155	Kenny Rogers	.05	.02
156	Dave Schmidt	.05	.02
157	Lance Johnson	.05	.02
158	Dave West	.05	.02
159	Steve Balboni	.05	.02
160	Jeff Brantley	.05	.02
161	Craig Biggio	.20	.09
162	Brook Jacoby	.05	.02
163	Dan Gladden	.05	.02
164	Jeff Reardon UER	.10	.05
	(Total IP shown as		
	943.2, should be 943.1)		
165	Mark Carreon	.05	.02
166	Mel Hall	.05	.02
167	Gary Mielke	.05	.02
168	Cecil Fielder	.10	.05
169	Darrin Jackson	.05	.02
170	Rick Aguilera	.10	.05
171	Walt Weiss	.05	.02
172	Steve Farr	.05	.02
173	Jody Reed	.05	.02
174	Mike Jeffcoat	.05	.02
175	Mark Grace	.20	.09
176	Larry Sheets	.05	.02
177	Bill Gullickson	.05	.02
178	Chris Gwynn	.05	.02
179	Melido Perez	.05	.02
180	Sid Fernandez UER	.05	.02
	(779 runs in 1990)		
181	Tim Burke	.05	.02
182	Gary Pettis	.05	.02
183	Rob Murphy	.05	.02
184	Craig Lefferts	.05	.02
185	Howard Johnson	.20	.09
186	Ken Caminiti	.20	.09
187	Tim Belcher	.05	.02
188	Greg Cadaret	.05	.02
189	Matt Williams	.20	.09
190	Dave Magadan	.05	.02
191	Geno Petralli	.05	.02
192	Jeff D. Robinson	.05	.02
193	Jim Deshaies	.05	.02
194	Willie Randolph	.10	.05
195	George Bell	.05	.02
196	Hubie Brooks	.05	.02
197	Tom Gordon	.05	.02

□			
198	Mike Fitzgerald	.05	.02
199	Mike Pagliarulo	.05	.02
200	Kirby Puckett	.30	.14
201	Shawon Dunston	.05	.02
202	Dennis Boyd	.05	.02
203	Junior Felix UER	.05	.02
	(Text has him in NL)		
204	Alejandro Pena	.05	.02
205	Pete Smith	.05	.02
206	Tom Glavine UER	.20	.09
	(Lefty spelled leftie)		
207	Luis Salazar	.05	.02
208	John Smoltz	.20	.09
209	Doug Dascenzo	.05	.02
210	Tim Wallach	.05	.02
211	Greg Gagne	.05	.02
212	Mark Gubicza	.05	.02
213	Mark Parent	.05	.02
214	Ken Oberkfell	.05	.02
215	Gary Carter	.20	.09
216	Rafael Palmeiro	.20	.09
217	Tom Niedenfuer	.05	.02
218	Dave LaPoint	.05	.02
219	Jeff Treadway	.05	.02
220	Mitch Williams UER	.05	.02
	('89 ERA shown as 2.76,		
	should be 2.64)		
221	Jose DeLeon	.05	.02
222	Mike LaValliere	.05	.02
223	Darrel Akerfelds	.05	.02
224A	Kent Anderson ERR	.10	.05
	(First line, flachy		
	should read flashy)		
224B	Kent Anderson COR	.10	.05
	(Corrected in		
	factory sets)		
225	Dwight Evans	.10	.05
226	Gary Redus	.05	.02
227	Paul O'Neill	.10	.05
228	Marty Barrett	.05	.02
229	Tom Browning	.05	.02
230	Terry Pendleton	.10	.05
231	Jack Armstrong	.05	.02
232	Mike Boddicker	.05	.02
233	Neal Heaton	.05	.02
234	Marquis Grissom	.20	.09
235	Bert Blyleven	.10	.05
236	Curt Young	.05	.02
237	Don Carman	.05	.02
238	Charlie Hayes	.05	.02
239	Mark Knudson	.05	.02
240	Todd Zeile	.10	.05
241	Larry Walker UER	.30	.14
	(Maple River, should		
	be Maple Ridge)		
242	Jerald Clark	.05	.02
243	Jeff Ballard	.05	.02
244	Jeff King	.05	.02
245	Tom Brunansky	.05	.02
246	Darren Daulton	.10	.05
247	Scott Terry	.05	.02
248	Rob Deer	.05	.02
249	Brady Anderson UER	.05	.02
	(1990 Hagerstown 1 hit,		
	should say 13 hits)		
250	Len Dykstra	.10	.05
251	Greg W. Harris	.05	.02
252	Mike Hartley	.05	.02
253	Joey Cora	.05	.02
254	Ivan Calderon	.05	.02
255	Ted Power	.05	.02
256	Sammy Sosa	1.25	.55
257	Steve Buechele	.05	.02
258	Mike Devereaux UER	.05	.02
	(No comma between		
	city and state)		
259	Brad Komminsk UER	.05	.02
	(Last text line,		
	Ba should be BA)		
260	Ted Higuera	.05	.02
261	Shawn Abner	.05	.02
262	Dave Valle	.05	.02
263	Jeff Huson	.05	.02
264	Edgar Martinez	.20	.09
265	Carlton Fisk	.20	.09
266	Steve Finley	.20	.09

□			
267	John Wetteland	.20	.09
268	Kevin Appier	.10	.05
269	Steve Lyons	.05	.02
270	Mickey Tettleton	.10	.05
271	Luis Rivera	.05	.02
272	Steve Jeltz	.05	.02
273	R.J. Reynolds	.05	.02
274	Carlos Martinez	.05	.02
275	Dan Plesac	.05	.02
276	Mike Morgan UER	.05	.02
	(Total IP shown as		
	1149.1, should be 1149)		
277	Jeff Russell	.05	.02
278	Pete Incaviglia	.05	.02
279	Kevin Seitzer UER	.05	.02
	(Bio has 200 hits twice		
	and .300 four times,		
	should be once and		
	three times)		
280	Bobby Thigpen	.05	.02
281	Stan Javier UER	.05	.02
	(Born 1/9,		
	should say 9/1)		
282	Henry Cotto	.05	.02
283	Gary Wayne	.05	.02
284	Shane Mack	.05	.02
285	Brian Holman	.05	.02
286	Gerald Perry	.05	.02
287	Steve Crawford	.05	.02
288	Nelson Liriano	.05	.02
289	Don Aase	.05	.02
290	Randy Johnson	.25	.11
291	Harold Baines	.10	.05
292	Kent Hrbek	.05	.02
293A	Les Lancaster ERR	.05	.02
	(No comma between		
	Dallas and Texas)		
293B	Les Lancaster COR	.05	.02
	(Corrected in		
	factory sets)		
294	Jeff Musselman	.05	.02
295	Kurt Stillwell	.05	.02
296	Stan Belinda	.05	.02
297	Lou Whitaker	.10	.05
298	Glenn Wilson	.05	.02
299	Omar Vizquel UER	.20	.09
	(Born 5/15, should be		
	4/24, there is a decimal		
	before GP total for '90)		
300	Ramon Martinez	.10	.05
301	Dwight Smith	.05	.02
302	Tim Crews	.05	.02
303	Lance Blankenship	.05	.02
304	Sid Bream	.05	.02
305	Rafael Ramirez	.05	.02
306	Steve Wilson	.05	.02
307	Mackey Sasser	.05	.02
308	Franklin Stubbs	.05	.02
309	Jack Daugherty UER	.05	.02
	(Born 6/3/60,		
	should say July)		
310	Eddie Murray	.20	.09
311	Bob Welch	.05	.02
312	Brian Harper	.05	.02
313	Lance McCullers	.05	.02
314	Dave Smith	.05	.02
315	Bobby Bonilla	.05	.02
316	Jerry Don Gleaton	.05	.02
317	Greg Maddux	.50	.23
318	Keith Miller	.05	.02
319	Mark Portugal	.05	.02
320	Robin Ventura	.20	.09
321	Bob Ojeda	.05	.02
322	Mike Harkey	.05	.02
323	Jay Bell	.10	.05
324	Mark McGwire	1.00	.45
325	Gary Gaetti	.10	.05
326	Jeff Pico	.05	.02
327	Kevin McReynolds	.05	.02
328	Frank Tanana	.05	.02
329	Eric Yelding UER	.05	.02
	(Listed as 6'3"		
	should be 5'11")		
330	Barry Bonds	.25	.11
331	Brian McRae UER	.10	.05
	(No comma between		

(city and state)

332	Pedro Munoz	.05	.02
333	Daryl Irvine	.05	.02
334	Chris Hoiles	.05	.02
335	Thomas Howard	.05	.02
336	Jeff Schulz	.05	.02
337	Jeff Manto	.05	.02
338	Beau Allred	.05	.02
339	Mike Bordick	.20	.09
340	Todd Hundley	.20	.09
341	Jim Vatcher UER	.05	.02
	(Height 6'9", should be 5'9")		
342	Luis Sojo	.05	.02
343	Jose Offerman UER	.15	.07
	(Born 1969, should say 1968)		
344	Pete Coachman	.05	.02
345	Mike Benjamin	.05	.02
346	Ozzie Canseco	.05	.02
347	Tim McIntosh	.05	.02
348	Phil Plantier	.05	.02
349	Terry Shumpert	.05	.02
350	Darren Lewis	.10	.05
351	David Walsh	.05	.02
352A	Scott Chiamparino	.10	.05
	ERR (Bats left, should be right)		
352B	Scott Chiamparino	.10	.05
	COR (corrected in factory sets)		
353	Julio Valera	.05	.02
	UER (Progressed misspelled as progessed)		
354	Anthony Telford	.05	.02
355	Kevin Wickander	.05	.02
356	Tim Naehring	.05	.02
357	Jim Poole	.05	.02
358	Mark Whiten UER	.05	.02
	(Shown hitting lefty, bio says righty)		
359	Terry Wells	.05	.02
360	Rafael Valdez	.05	.02
361	Mel Stottlemyre Jr.	.05	.02
362	David Segui	.10	.05
363	Paul Abbott	.05	.02
364	Steve Howard	.05	.02
365	Karl Rhodes	.05	.02
366	Rafael Novoa	.05	.02
367	Joe Grahe	.05	.02
368	Darren Reed	.05	.02
369	Jeff McKnight	.05	.02
370	Scott Leius	.05	.02
371	Mark Dewey	.05	.02
372	Mark Lee UER	.05	.02
	(Shown hitting lefty, bio says righty, born in Dakota, should say North Dakota)		
373	Rosario Rodriguez	.05	.02
	(Shown hitting lefty, bio says righty) UER		
374	Chuck McElroy	.05	.02
375	Mike Bell	.05	.02
376	Mickey Morandini	.05	.02
377	Bill Haselman	.05	.02
378	Dave Pavlas	.05	.02
379	Derrick May	.05	.02
380	Jeromy Burnitz FDP	.60	.25
381	Donald Peters FDP	.05	.02
382	Alex Fernandez FDP	.10	.05
383	Mike Mussina FDP	1.25	.55
384	Dan Smith FDP	.05	.02
385	Lance Dickson FDP	.05	.02
386	Carl Everett FDP	.50	.23
387	Tom Nevers FDP	.05	.02
388	Adam Hyzdu FDP	.05	.02
389	Todd Van Poppel FDP	.05	.02
390	Rondell White FDP	.40	.18
391	Marc Newfield FDP	.05	.02
392	Julio Franco AS	.05	.02
393	Wade Boggs AS	.10	.05
394	Ozzie Guillen AS	.05	.02
395	Cecil Fielder AS	.05	.02
396	Ken Griffey Jr. AS	.75	.35
397	Rickey Henderson AS	.10	.05
398	Jose Canseco AS	.10	.05
399	Roger Clemens AS	.25	.11
400	Sandy Alomar Jr. AS	.05	.02
401	Bobby Thigpen AS	.05	.02
402	Bobby Bonilla MB	.05	.02
403	Eric Davis MB	.05	.02
404	Fred McGriff MB	.10	.05
405	Glenn Davis MB	.05	.02
406	Kevin Mitchell MB	.05	.02
407	Rob Dibble MB	.05	.02
408	Ramon Martinez KM	.05	.02
409	David Cone KM	.05	.02
410	Bobby Witt KM	.05	.02
411	Mark Langston KM	.05	.02
412	Bo Jackson RIF	.10	.05
413	Shawon Dunston RIF	.05	.02
	UER (In the baseball, should say in baseball)		
414	Jesse Barfield RIF	.05	.02
415	Ken Caminiti RIF	.10	.05
416	Benito Santiago RIF	.05	.02
417	Nolan Ryan HL	.40	.18
418	Bobby Thigpen HL UER	.05	.02
	(Back refers to Hal McRae Jr., should say Brian McRae)		
419	Ramon Martinez HL	.05	.02
420	Bo Jackson HL	.05	.02
421	Carlton Fisk HL	.10	.05
422	Jimmy Key	.05	.02
423	Junior Noboa	.05	.02
424	Al Newman	.05	.02
425	Pat Borders	.05	.02
426	Von Hayes	.05	.02
427	Tim Teufel	.05	.02
428	Eric Plunk UER	.05	.02
	(Text says Eric's had, no apostrophe needed)		
429	John Moses	.05	.02
430	Mike Witt	.05	.02
431	Otis Nixon	.10	.05
432	Tony Fernandez	.05	.02
433	Rance Mulliniks	.05	.02
434	Dan Petry	.05	.02
435	Bob Geren	.05	.02
436	Steve Frey	.05	.02
437	Jamie Moyer	.05	.02
438	Junior Ortiz	.05	.02
439	Tom O'Malley	.05	.02
440	Pat Combs	.05	.02
441	Jose Canseco DT	.25	.11
442	Alfredo Griffin	.05	.02
443	Andres Galarraga	.20	.09
444	Bryn Smith	.05	.02
445	Andre Dawson	.20	.09
446	Juan Samuel	.05	.02
447	Mike Aldrete	.05	.02
448	Ron Gant	.10	.05
449	Fernando Valenzuela	.10	.05
450	Vince Coleman UER	.05	.02
	(Should say topped majors in steals four times, not three times)		
451	Kevin Mitchell	.05	.02
452	Spike Owen	.05	.02
453	Mike Bielecki	.05	.02
454	Dennis Martinez	.05	.02
455	Brett Butler	.10	.05
456	Ron Darling	.05	.02
457	Dennis Rasmussen	.05	.02
458	Ken Howell	.05	.02
459	Steve Bedrosian	.05	.02
460	Frank Viola	.10	.05
461	Jose Lind	.05	.02
462	Chris Sabo	.05	.02
463	Dante Bichette	.20	.09
464	Rick Mahler	.05	.02
465	John Smiley	.05	.02
466	Devon White	.05	.02
467	John Orton	.05	.02
468	Mike Stanton	.05	.02
469	Billy Hatcher	.05	.02
470	Wally Joyner	.10	.05
471	Gene Larkin	.05	.02
472	Doug Drabek	.05	.02
473	Gary Sheffield	.20	.09
474	David Wells	.10	.05
475	Andy Van Slyke	.10	.05
476	Mike Gallego	.05	.02
477	B.J. Surhoff	.05	.02
478	Gene Nelson	.05	.02
479	Mariano Duncan	.05	.02
480	Fred McGriff	.20	.09
481	Jerry Browne	.05	.02
482	Alvin Davis	.05	.02
483	Bill Wegman	.05	.02
484	Dave Parker	.10	.05
485	Dennis Eckersley	.10	.05
486	Erik Hanson UER	.05	.02
	(Basketball misspelled as baseketball)		
487	Bill Ripken	.05	.02
488	Tom Candiotti	.05	.02
489	Mike Schooler	.05	.02
490	Gregg Olson	.05	.02
491	Chris James	.05	.02
492	Pete Harnisch	.05	.02
493	Julio Franco	.05	.02
494	Greg Briley	.05	.02
495	Ruben Sierra	.05	.02
496	Steve Olin	.05	.02
497	Mike Fetters	.05	.02
498	Mark Williamson	.05	.02
499	Bob Tewksbury	.05	.02
500	Tony Gwynn	.50	.23
501	Randy Myers	.10	.05
502	Keith Comstock	.05	.02
503	Craig Worthington UER	.05	.02
	(DeCinces misspelled DeCinces on back)		
504	Mark Eichhorn UER	.05	.02
	(Stats incomplete, doesn't have '89 Braves stint)		
505	Barry Larkin	.20	.09
506	Dave Johnson	.05	.02
507	Bobby Witt	.05	.02
508	Joe Orsulak	.05	.02
509	Pete O'Brien	.05	.02
510	Brad Arnsberg	.05	.02
511	Storm Davis	.05	.02
512	Bob Milacki	.05	.02
513	Bill Pecota	.05	.02
514	Glenallen Hill	.05	.02
515	Danny Tartabull	.10	.05
516	Mike Moore	.05	.02
517	Ron Robinson UER	.05	.02
	(577 K's in 1990)		
518	Mark Gardner	.05	.02
519	Rick Wrona	.05	.02
520	Mike Scioscia	.05	.02
521	Frank Wills	.05	.02
522	Greg Brock	.05	.02
523	Jack Clark	.10	.05
524	Bruce Ruffin	.05	.02
525	Robin Yount	.20	.09
526	Tom Foley	.05	.02
527	Pat Perry	.05	.02
528	Greg Vaughn	.05	.02
529	Wally Whitehurst	.05	.02
530	Norm Charlton	.05	.02
531	Marvell Wynne	.05	.02
532	Jim Gantner	.05	.02
533	Greg Litton	.05	.02
534	Manny Lee	.05	.02
535	Scott Bailes	.05	.02
536	Charlie Leibrandt	.05	.02
537	Roger McDowell	.05	.02
538	Andy Benes	.10	.05
539	Rick Honeycutt	.05	.02
540	Dwight Gooden	.10	.05
541	Scott Garrelts	.05	.02
542	Dave Clark	.05	.02
543	Lonnie Smith	.05	.02
544	Rick Reuschel	.05	.02
545	Delino DeShields UER	.10	.05
	(Rockford misspelled as Rock Ford in '88)		
546	Mike Sharperson	.05	.02
547	Mike Kingery	.05	.02
548	Terry Kennedy	.05	.02
549	David Cone	.10	.05

550	Orel Hershiser	.10	.05
551	Matt Nokes	.05	.02
552	Eddie Williams	.05	.02
553	Frank DiPino	.05	.02
554	Fred Lynn	.05	.02
555	Alex Cole	.05	.02
556	Terry Leach	.05	.02
557	Chet Lemon	.05	.02
558	Paul Mirabella	.05	.02
559	Bill Long	.05	.02
560	Phil Bradley	.05	.02
561	Duane Ward	.05	.02
562	Dave Bergman	.05	.02
563	Eric Show	.05	.02
564	Xavier Hernandez	.05	.02
565	Jeff Parrett	.05	.02
566	Chuck Cary	.05	.02
567	Ken Hill	.05	.02
568	Bob Welch Hand	.05	.02
	(Complement should be compliment) UER		
569	John Mitchell	.05	.02
570	Travis Fryman	.20	.09
571	Derek Lilliquist	.05	.02
572	Steve Lake	.05	.02
573	John Barfield	.05	.02
574	Randy Bush	.05	.02
575	Joe Magrane	.05	.02
576	Eddie Diaz	.05	.02
577	Casey Candaele	.05	.02
578	Jesse Orosco	.05	.02
579	Tom Henke	.05	.02
580	Rick Cerone UER	.05	.02
	(Actually his third go-round with Yankees)		
581	Drew Hall	.05	.02
582	Tony Castillo	.05	.02
583	Jimmy Jones	.05	.02
584	Rick Reed	.05	.02
585	Joe Girardi	.10	.05
586	Jeff Gray	.05	.02
587	Luis Polonia	.05	.02
588	Joe Klink	.05	.02
589	Rex Hudler	.05	.02
590	Kirk McCaskill	.05	.02
591	Juan Agosto	.05	.02
592	Wes Gardner	.05	.02
593	Rich Rodriguez	.05	.02
594	Mitch Webster	.05	.02
595	Kelly Gruber	.05	.02
596	Dale Mohorcic	.05	.02
597	Willie McGee	.10	.05
598	Bill Krueger	.05	.02
599	Bob Walk UER	.05	.02
	(Cards says he's 33, but actually he's 34)		
600	Kevin Maas	.05	.02
601	Danny Jackson	.05	.02
602	Craig McMurtry UER	.05	.02
	(Anonymously misspelled anonimously)		
603	Curtis Wilkerson	.05	.02
604	Adam Peterson	.05	.02
605	Sam Horn	.05	.02
606	Tommy Gregg	.05	.02
607	Ken Dayley	.05	.02
608	Carmelo Castillo	.05	.02
609	John Shelby	.05	.02
610	Don Slaught	.05	.02
611	Calvin Schiraldi	.05	.02
612	Dennis Lamp	.05	.02
613	Andres Thomas	.05	.02
614	Jose Gonzalez	.05	.02
615	Randy Ready	.05	.02
616	Kevin Bass	.05	.02
617	Mike Marshall	.05	.02
618	Daryl Boston	.05	.02
619	Andy McGaffigan	.05	.02
620	Joe Oliver	.05	.02
621	Jim Gott	.05	.02
622	Jose Oquendo	.05	.02
623	Jose DeJesus	.05	.02
624	Mike Brumley	.05	.02
625	John Olerud	.15	.07
626	Ernest Riles	.05	.02
627	Gene Harris	.05	.02
628	Jose Uribe	.05	.02
629	Darnell Coles	.05	.02
630	Carney Lansford	.10	.05
631	Tim Leary	.05	.02
632	Tim Hulett	.05	.02
633	Kevin Elster	.05	.02
634	Tony Fossas	.05	.02
635	Francisco Oliveras	.05	.02
636	Bob Patterson	.05	.02
637	Gary Ward	.05	.02
638	Rene Gonzales	.05	.02
639	Don Robinson	.05	.02
640	Darryl Strawberry	.10	.05
641	Dave Anderson	.05	.02
642	Scott Scudder	.05	.02
643	Reggie Harris UER	.05	.02
	(Hepatitis misspelled as hepititis)		
644	Dave Henderson	.05	.02
645	Ben McDonald	.25	.11
646	Bob Kipper	.05	.02
647	Hal Morris UER	.05	.02
	(It's should be its)		
648	Tim Birtsas	.05	.02
649	Steve Searcy	.05	.02
650	Dale Murphy	.20	.09
651	Ron Oester	.05	.02
652	Mike LaCoss	.05	.02
653	Ron Jones	.05	.02
654	Kelly Downs	.05	.02
655	Roger Clemens	.50	.23
656	Herm Winningham	.05	.02
657	Trevor Wilson	.05	.02
658	Jose Rijo	.05	.02
659	Dann Bilardello UER	.05	.02
	(Bio has 13 games, 1 hit, and 32 AB, stats show 19, 2, and 37)		
660	Gregg Jefferies	.05	.02
661	Doug Drabek AS UER	.05	.02
	(Through is mis-spelled though)		
662	Randy Myers AS	.05	.02
663	Benny Santiago AS	.05	.02
664	Will Clark AS	.10	.05
665	Ryne Sandberg AS	.20	.09
666	Barry Larkin AS UER	.10	.05
	(Line 13, coolly misspelled cooly)		
667	Matt Williams AS	.10	.05
668	Barry Bonds AS	.20	.09
669	Eric Davis AS	.05	.02
670	Bobby Bonilla AS	.05	.02
671	Chipper Jones FDP	4.00	1.80
672	Eric Christopherson FDP	.05	.02
673	Robbie Beckett FDP	.05	.02
674	Shane Andrews FDP	.05	.02
675	Steve Karsay FDP	.25	.11
676	Aaron Holbert FDP	.05	.02
677	Donovan Osborne FDP	.05	.02
678	Todd Ritchie FDP	.05	.02
679	Ron Walden FDP	.05	.02
680	Tim Costo FDP	.20	.09
681	Dan Wilson FDP	.05	.02
682	Kurt Miller FDP	.05	.02
683	Mike Lieberthal FDP	.50	.23
684	Roger Clemens KM	.25	.11
685	Doc Gooden KM	.05	.02
686	Nolan Ryan KM	.40	.18
687	Frank Viola KM	.05	.02
688	Erik Hanson KM	.05	.02
689	Matt Williams MB	.05	.02
690	Jose Canseco MB UER	.10	.05
	(Mammoth misspelled as monmoth)		
691	Darryl Strawberry MB	.05	.02
692	Bo Jackson MB	.10	.05
693	Cecil Fielder MB	.05	.02
694	Sandy Alomar Jr. RF	.05	.02
695	Cory Snyder RF	.05	.02
696	Eric Davis RF	.05	.02
697	Ken Griffey Jr. RF	.75	.35
698	Andy Van Slyke RF UER	.05	.02
	(Line 2, outfielders does not need)		
699	Mark Langston NH / Mike Witt	.05	.02
700	Randy Johnson NH	.20	.09
701	Nolan Ryan NH	.40	.18
702	Dave Stewart NH	.05	.02
703	Fernando Valenzuela NH	.05	.02
704	Andy Hawkins NH	.05	.02
705	Melido Perez NH	.05	.02
706	Terry Mulholland NH	.05	.02
707	Dave Stieb NH	.05	.02
708	Brian Barnes	.05	.02
709	Bernard Gilkey	.10	.05
710	Steve Decker	.05	.02
711	Paul Faries	.05	.02
712	Paul Marak	.05	.02
713	Wes Chamberlain	.05	.02
714	Kevin Belcher	.05	.02
715	Dan Boone UER	.05	.02
	(IP adds up to 101, but card has 101.2)		
716	Steve Adkins	.05	.02
717	Geronimo Pena	.05	.02
718	Howard Farmer	.05	.02
719	Mark Leonard	.05	.02
720	Tom Lampkin	.05	.02
721	Mike Gardiner	.05	.02
722	Jeff Conine	.20	.09
723	Efrain Valdez	.05	.02
724	Chuck Malone	.05	.02
725	Leo Gomez	.05	.02
726	Paul McClellan	.05	.02
727	Mark Leiter	.05	.02
728	Rich DeLucia UER	.05	.02
	(Line 2, all told is written altold)		
729	Mel Rojas	.10	.05
730	Hector Wagner	.05	.02
731	Ray Lankford	.20	.09
732	Turner Ward	.05	.02
733	Gerald Alexander	.05	.02
734	Scott Anderson	.05	.02
735	Tony Perezchica	.05	.02
736	Jimmy Kremers	.05	.02
737	American Flag	.20	.09
	(Pray for Peace)		
738	Mike York	.05	.02
739	Mike Rochford	.05	.02
740	Scott Aldred	.05	.02
741	Rico Brogna	.15	.07
742	Dave Burba	.05	.02
743	Ray Stephens	.05	.02
744	Eric Gunderson	.05	.02
745	Troy Afenir	.05	.02
746	Jeff Shaw	.05	.02
747	Orlando Merced	.05	.02
748	Omar Olivares UER	.05	.02
	(Line 9, league is misspelled legaue)		
749	Jerry Kutzler	.05	.02
750	Mo Vaughn UER	.40	.18
	(44 SB's in 1990)		
751	Matt Stark	.05	.02
752	Randy Hennis	.05	.02
753	Andujar Cedeno	.05	.02
754	Kelvin Torve	.05	.02
755	Joe Kraemer	.05	.02
756	Phil Clark	.05	.02
757	Ed Vosberg	.05	.02
758	Mike Perez	.05	.02
759	Scott Lewis	.05	.02
760	Steve Chitren	.05	.02
761	Ray Young	.05	.02
762	Andres Santana	.05	.02
763	Rodney McCray	.05	.02
764	Sean Berry UER	.10	.05
	(Name misspelled Barry on card front)		
765	Brent Mayne	.05	.02
766	Mike Simms	.05	.02
767	Glenn Sutko	.05	.02
768	Gary DiSarcina	.05	.02
769	George Brett HL	.20	.09
770	Cecil Fielder HL	.05	.02
771	Jim Presley	.05	.02
772	John Dopson	.05	.02
773	Bo Jackson Breaker	.10	.05

❏ 774 Brent Knackert UER ...... .05	.02	
(Born in 1954, shown		
throwing righty, but		
bio says lefty)		
❏ 775 Bill Doran UER .... .05	.02	
(Reds in NL East)		
❏ 776 Dick Schofield .... .05	.02	
❏ 777 Nelson Santovenia .... .05	.02	
❏ 778 Mark Guthrie .... .05	.02	
❏ 779 Mark Lemke .... .05	.02	
❏ 780 Terry Steinbach .... .10	.05	
❏ 781 Tom Bolton .... .05	.02	
❏ 782 Randy Tomlin .... .05	.02	
❏ 783 Jeff Kunkel .... .05	.02	
❏ 784 Felix Jose .... .05	.02	
❏ 785 Rick Sutcliffe .... .05	.02	
❏ 786 John Cerutti .... .05	.02	
❏ 787 Jose Vizcaino UER .... .05	.02	
(Offerman, not Opperman)		
❏ 788 Curt Schilling .... .20	.09	
❏ 789 Ed Whitson .... .05	.02	
❏ 790 Tony Pena .... .05	.02	
❏ 791 John Candelaria .... .05	.02	
❏ 792 Carmelo Martinez .... .05	.02	
❏ 793 Sandy Alomar Jr. UER .. .10	.05	
(Indian's should		
say Indians')		
❏ 794 Jim Neidlinger .... .05	.02	
❏ 795 Barry Larkin WS .... .10	.05	
and Chris Sabo		
❏ 796 Paul Sorrento .... .10	.05	
❏ 797 Tom Pagnozzi .... .05	.02	
❏ 798 Tino Martinez .... .20	.09	
❏ 799 Scott Ruskin UER .... .05	.02	
(Text says first three		
seasons but lists		
averages for four)		
❏ 800 Kirk Gibson .... .10	.05	
❏ 801 Walt Terrell .... .05	.02	
❏ 802 John Russell .... .05	.02	
❏ 803 Chili Davis .... .10	.05	
❏ 804 Chris Nabholz .... .05	.02	
❏ 805 Juan Gonzalez .... .75	.35	
❏ 806 Ron Hassey .... .05	.02	
❏ 807 Todd Worrell .... .05	.02	
❏ 808 Tommy Greene .... .05	.02	
❏ 809 Joel Skinner UER .... .05	.02	
(Joel, not Bob, was		
drafted in 1979)		
❏ 810 Benito Santiago .... .05	.02	
❏ 811 Pat Tabler UER .... .05	.02	
(Line 3, always		
misspelled alway)		
❏ 812 Scott Erickson UER ...... .15	.07	
(Record spelled rcord)		
❏ 813 Moises Alou .... .20	.09	
❏ 814 Dale Sveum .... .05	.02	
❏ 815 Ryne Sandberg MANYR .20	.09	
❏ 816 Rick Dempsey .... .05	.02	
❏ 817 Scott Bankhead .... .05	.02	
❏ 818 Jason Grimsley .... .05	.02	
❏ 819 Doug Jennings .... .05	.02	
❏ 820 Tom Herr .... .05	.02	
❏ 821 Rob Ducey .... .05	.02	
❏ 822 Luis Quinones .... .05	.02	
❏ 823 Greg Minton .... .05	.02	
❏ 824 Mark Grant .... .05	.02	
❏ 825 Ozzie Smith UER .... .25	.11	
(Shortstop misspelled		
shortsop)		
❏ 826 Dave Eiland .... .05	.02	
❏ 827 Danny Heep .... .05	.02	
❏ 828 Hensley Meulens .... .05	.02	
❏ 829 Charlie O'Brien .... .05	.02	
❏ 830 Glenn Davis .... .05	.02	
❏ 831 John Marzano UER ...... .05	.02	
(International mis-		
spelled Internaional)		
❏ 832 Steve Ontiveros .... .05	.02	
❏ 833 Ron Karkovice .... .05	.02	
❏ 834 Jerry Goff .... .05	.02	
❏ 835 Ken Griffey Sr. .... .10	.05	
❏ 836 Kevin Reimer .... .05	.02	
❏ 837 Randy Kutcher UER ..... .05	.02	
(Infectious mis-		
spelled infectous)		

❏ 838 Mike Blowers .... .05	.02	
❏ 839 Mike Macfarlane .... .05	.02	
❏ 840 Frank Thomas UER ...... .75	.35	
(1989 Sarasota stats		
15 games but 188 AB)		
❏ 841 The Griffeys................ .75	.35	
Ken Griffey Jr.		
Ken Griffey Sr.		
❏ 842 Jack Howell .... .05	.02	
❏ 843 Goose Gozzo .... .05	.02	
❏ 844 Gerald Young .... .05	.02	
❏ 845 Zane Smith .... .05	.02	
❏ 846 Kevin Brown .... .15	.07	
❏ 847 Sil Campusano .... .05	.02	
❏ 848 Larry Andersen .... .05	.02	
❏ 849 Cal Ripken FRAN .... .40	.18	
❏ 850 Roger Clemens FRAN .. .25	.11	
❏ 851 Sandy Alomar Jr. FRAN .05	.02	
❏ 852 Alan Trammell FRAN .... .10	.05	
❏ 853 George Brett FRAN ...... .20	.09	
❏ 854 Robin Yount FRAN .... .20	.09	
❏ 855 Kirby Puckett FRAN ..... .20	.09	
❏ 856 Don Mattingly FRAN .... .20	.09	
❏ 857 Rickey Henderson FRAN .10	.05	
❏ 858 Ken Griffey Jr. FRAN ... .75	.35	
❏ 859 Ruben Sierra FRAN ...... .05	.02	
❏ 860 John Olerud FRAN .... .15	.07	
❏ 861 Dave Justice FRAN ...... .20	.09	
❏ 862 Ryne Sandberg FRAN .. .20	.09	
❏ 863 Eric Davis FRAN .... .05	.02	
❏ 864 Darryl Strawberry FRAN .05	.02	
❏ 865 Tim Wallach FRAN .... .05	.02	
❏ 866 Doc Gooden FRAN .... .05	.02	
❏ 867 Len Dykstra FRAN .... .05	.02	
❏ 868 Barry Bonds FRAN ...... .20	.09	
❏ 869 Todd Zeile FRAN UER ... .05	.02	
(Powerful misspelled		
as powerul)		
❏ 870 Benito Santiago FRAN .. .05	.02	
❏ 871 Will Clark FRAN .... .10	.05	
❏ 872 Craig Biggio FRAN ...... .10	.05	
❏ 873 Wally Joyner FRAN ...... .05	.02	
❏ 874 Frank Thomas FRAN .... .40	.18	
❏ 875 Rickey Henderson MVP .05	.02	
❏ 876 Barry Bonds MVP .... .20	.09	
❏ 877 Bob Welch CY .... .05	.02	
❏ 878 Doug Drabek CY .... .05	.02	
❏ 879 Sandy Alomar Jr ROY .. .05	.02	
❏ 880 Dave Justice ROY .... .10	.05	
❏ 881 Damon Berryhill.......... .05	.02	
❏ 882 Frank Viola DT .... .05	.02	
❏ 883 Dave Stewart DT .... .05	.02	
❏ 884 Doug Jones DT .... .05	.02	
❏ 885 Randy Myers DT .... .05	.02	
❏ 886 Will Clark DT .... .10	.05	
❏ 887 Roberto Alomar DT ...... .10	.05	
❏ 888 Barry Larkin DT .... .10	.05	
❏ 889 Wade Boggs DT .... .10	.05	
❏ 890 Rickey Henderson DT .. .25	.11	
❏ 891 Kirby Puckett DT .... .30	.14	
❏ 892 Ken Griffey Jr DT 1.50	.70	
❏ 893 Benny Santiago DT ..... .05	.02	

1991 Score Cooperstown

COOPERSTOWN CARD®

BARRY LARKIN

	MINT	NRMT
COMPLETE SET (7)	10.00	4.50
COMMON CARD (B1-B7)	.50	.23
ONE SET PER FACTORY SET		
❏ B1 Wade Boggs	.50	.23
❏ B2 Barry Larkin	.50	.23
❏ B3 Ken Griffey Jr.	6.00	2.70
❏ B4 Rickey Henderson	1.00	.45
❏ B5 George Brett	.50	.70
❏ B6 Will Clark	.50	.23
❏ B7 Nolan Ryan	3.00	1.35

1991 Score Hot Rookies

HOT ROOKIE

FRANK THOMAS

	MINT	NRMT
COMPLETE SET (10)	12.00	5.50
COMMON CARD (1-10)	.50	.23
SEMISTARS	1.00	.45
UNLISTED STARS	1.50	.70
ONE PER BLISTER PACK		
❏ 1 Dave Justice	1.50	.70
❏ 2 Kevin Maas	.50	.23
❏ 3 Hal Morris	.50	.23
❏ 4 Frank Thomas	5.00	2.20
❏ 5 Jeff Conine	1.50	.70
❏ 6 Sandy Alomar Jr.	.75	.35
❏ 7 Ray Lankford	1.50	.70
❏ 8 Steve Decker	.50	.23
❏ 9 Juan Gonzalez	5.00	2.20
❏ 10 Jose Offerman	1.00	.45

1991 Score Mantle

Triple Crown

	MINT	NRMT
COMPLETE SET (7)	200.00	90.00
COMMON MANTLE (1-7)........	30.00	13.50
RANDOM INSERTS IN SER.2 PACKS		
❏ 1 Mickey Mantle	30.00	13.50
The Rookie		
(With Billy Martin)		
❏ 2 Mickey Mantle	30.00	13.50
Triple Crown		
❏ 3 Mickey Mantle	30.00	13.50
World Series		
❏ 4 Mickey Mantle	30.00	13.50
Going, Going, Gone		
❏ 5 Mickey Mantle	30.00	13.50
Speed and Grace		
❏ 6 Mickey Mantle	30.00	13.50
A True Yankee		

		MINT	NRMT
❑ 7	Mickey Mantle Twilight	30.00	13.50
❑ AU0	Mickey Mantle AU (Autographed with certified signature)	400.00	180.00

1991 Score Rookie/Traded

	MINT	NRMT
COMP.FACT.SET (110)	8.00	3.60
COMMON CARD (1T-110T)	.05	.02
MINOR STARS	.10	.05
UNLISTED STARS	.25	.11

		MINT	NRMT
❑ 1T	Bo Jackson	.10	.05
❑ 2T	Mike Flanagan	.05	.02
❑ 3T	Pete Incaviglia	.05	.02
❑ 4T	Jack Clark	.10	.05
❑ 5T	Hubie Brooks	.05	.02
❑ 6T	Ivan Calderon	.05	.02
❑ 7T	Glenn Davis	.05	.02
❑ 8T	Wally Backman	.05	.02
❑ 9T	Dave Smith	.05	.02
❑ 10T	Tim Raines	.10	.05
❑ 11T	Joe Carter	.10	.05
❑ 12T	Sid Bream	.05	.02
❑ 13T	George Bell	.05	.02
❑ 14T	Steve Bedrosian	.05	.02
❑ 15T	Willie Wilson	.05	.02
❑ 16T	Darryl Strawberry	.10	.05
❑ 17T	Danny Jackson	.05	.02
❑ 18T	Kirk Gibson	.05	.02
❑ 19T	Willie McGee	.10	.05
❑ 20T	Junior Felix	.05	.02
❑ 21T	Steve Farr	.05	.02
❑ 22T	Pat Tabler	.05	.02
❑ 23T	Brett Butler	.10	.05
❑ 24T	Danny Darwin	.05	.02
❑ 25T	Mickey Tettleton	.10	.05
❑ 26T	Gary Carter	.25	.11
❑ 27T	Mitch Williams	.05	.02
❑ 28T	Candy Maldonado	.05	.02
❑ 29T	Otis Nixon	.10	.05
❑ 30T	Brian Downing	.05	.02
❑ 31T	Tom Candiotti	.05	.02
❑ 32T	John Candelaria	.05	.02
❑ 33T	Rob Murphy	.05	.02
❑ 34T	Deion Sanders	.10	.05
❑ 35T	Willie Randolph	.10	.05
❑ 36T	Pete Harnisch	.05	.02
❑ 37T	Dante Bichette	.25	.11
❑ 38T	Garry Templeton	.05	.02
❑ 39T	Gary Gaetti	.10	.05
❑ 40T	John Cerutti	.05	.02
❑ 41T	Rick Cerone	.05	.02
❑ 42T	Mike Pagliarulo	.05	.02
❑ 43T	Ron Hassey	.05	.02
❑ 44T	Roberto Alomar	.25	.11
❑ 45T	Mike Boddicker	.05	.02
❑ 46T	Bud Black	.05	.02
❑ 47T	Rob Deer	.05	.02
❑ 48T	Devon White	.05	.02
❑ 49T	Luis Sojo	.05	.02
❑ 50T	Terry Pendleton	.10	.05
❑ 51T	Kevin Gross	.05	.02
❑ 52T	Mike Huff	.05	.02
❑ 53T	Dave Righetti	.05	.02

		MINT	NRMT
❑ 54T	Matt Young	.05	.02
❑ 55T	Earnest Riles	.05	.02
❑ 56T	Bill Gullickson	.05	.02
❑ 57T	Vince Coleman	.05	.02
❑ 58T	Fred McGriff	.25	.11
❑ 59T	Franklin Stubbs	.05	.02
❑ 60T	Eric King	.05	.02
❑ 61T	Cory Snyder	.05	.02
❑ 62T	Dwight Evans	.10	.05
❑ 63T	Gerald Perry	.05	.02
❑ 64T	Eric Show	.05	.02
❑ 65T	Shawn Hillegas	.05	.02
❑ 66T	Tony Fernandez	.05	.02
❑ 67T	Tim Teufel	.05	.02
❑ 68T	Mitch Webster	.05	.02
❑ 69T	Mike Heath	.05	.02
❑ 70T	Chili Davis	.10	.05
❑ 71T	Larry Andersen	.05	.02
❑ 72T	Gary Varsho	.05	.02
❑ 73T	Juan Berenguer	.05	.02
❑ 74T	Jack Morris	.10	.05
❑ 75T	Barry Jones	.05	.02
❑ 76T	Rafael Belliard	.05	.02
❑ 77T	Steve Buechele	.05	.02
❑ 78T	Scott Sanderson	.05	.02
❑ 79T	Bob Ojeda	.05	.02
❑ 80T	Curt Schilling	.25	.11
❑ 81T	Brian Drahman	.05	.02
❑ 82T	Ivan Rodriguez	4.00	1.80
❑ 83T	David Howard	.05	.02
❑ 84T	Heathcliff Slocumb	.25	.11
❑ 85T	Mike Timlin	.05	.02
❑ 86T	Darryl Kile	.25	.11
❑ 87T	Pete Schourek	.10	.05
❑ 88T	Bruce Walton	.05	.02
❑ 89T	Al Osuna	.05	.02
❑ 90T	Gary Scott	.05	.02
❑ 91T	Doug Simons	.05	.02
❑ 92T	Chris Jones	.05	.02
❑ 93T	Chuck Knoblauch	.25	.11
❑ 94T	Dana Allison	.05	.02
❑ 95T	Erik Pappas	.05	.02
❑ 96T	Jeff Bagwell	4.00	1.80
❑ 97T	Kirk Dressendorfer	.05	.02
❑ 98T	Freddie Benavides	.05	.02
❑ 99T	Luis Gonzalez	.75	.35
❑ 100T	Wade Taylor	.05	.02
❑ 101T	Ed Sprague	.05	.02
❑ 102T	Bob Scanlan	.05	.02
❑ 103T	Rick Wilkins	.05	.02
❑ 104T	Chris Donnels	.05	.02
❑ 105T	Joe Slusarski	.05	.02
❑ 106T	Mark Lewis	.05	.02
❑ 107T	Pat Kelly	.05	.02
❑ 108T	John Briscoe	.05	.02
❑ 109T	Luis Lopez	.05	.02
❑ 110T	Jeff Johnson	.05	.02

1992 Score

	MINT	NRMT
COMPLETE SET (893)	15.00	6.75
COMP.FACT.SET (910)	20.00	9.00
COMPLETE SERIES 1 (442)	8.00	3.60
COMPLETE SERIES 2 (451)	8.00	3.60
COMMON CARD (1-893)	.05	.02
MINOR STARS	.10	.05
UNLISTED STARS	.20	.09

SUBSET CARDS HALF VALUE OF BASE CARDS

		MINT	NRMT
❑ 1	Ken Griffey Jr.	1.25	.55
❑ 2	Nolan Ryan	.75	.35
❑ 3	Will Clark	.20	.09
❑ 4	Dave Justice	.20	.09
❑ 5	Dave Henderson	.05	.02
❑ 6	Bret Saberhagen	.10	.05
❑ 7	Fred McGriff	.15	.07
❑ 8	Erik Hanson	.05	.02
❑ 9	Darryl Strawberry	.10	.05
❑ 10	Dwight Gooden	.10	.05
❑ 11	Juan Gonzalez	.50	.23
❑ 12	Mark Langston	.05	.02
❑ 13	Lonnie Smith	.05	.02
❑ 14	Jeff Montgomery	.10	.05
❑ 15	Roberto Alomar	.20	.09
❑ 16	Delino DeShields	.10	.05
❑ 17	Steve Bedrosian	.05	.02
❑ 18	Terry Pendleton	.05	.02
❑ 19	Mark Carreon	.05	.02
❑ 20	Mark McGwire	1.00	.45
❑ 21	Roger Clemens	.50	.23
❑ 22	Chuck Crim	.05	.02
❑ 23	Don Mattingly	.40	.18
❑ 24	Dickie Thon	.05	.02
❑ 25	Ron Gant	.10	.05
❑ 26	Milt Cuyler	.05	.02
❑ 27	Mike MacFarlane	.05	.02
❑ 28	Dan Gladden	.05	.02
❑ 29	Melido Perez	.05	.02
❑ 30	Willie Randolph	.10	.05
❑ 31	Albert Belle	.20	.09
❑ 32	Dave Winfield	.20	.09
❑ 33	Jimmy Jones	.05	.02
❑ 34	Kevin Gross	.05	.02
❑ 35	Andres Galarraga	.20	.09
❑ 36	Mike Devereaux	.05	.02
❑ 37	Chris Bosio	.05	.02
❑ 38	Mike LaValliere	.05	.02
❑ 39	Gary Gaetti	.10	.05
❑ 40	Felix Jose	.05	.02
❑ 41	Alvaro Espinoza	.05	.02
❑ 42	Rick Aguilera	.05	.02
❑ 43	Mike Gallego	.05	.02
❑ 44	Eric Davis	.10	.05
❑ 45	George Bell	.05	.02
❑ 46	Tom Brunansky	.05	.02
❑ 47	Steve Farr	.05	.02
❑ 48	Duane Ward	.05	.02
❑ 49	David Wells	.05	.02
❑ 50	Cecil Fielder	.10	.05
❑ 51	Walt Weiss	.05	.02
❑ 52	Todd Zeile	.05	.02
❑ 53	Doug Jones	.05	.02
❑ 54	Bob Walk	.05	.02
❑ 55	Rafael Palmeiro	.20	.09
❑ 56	Rob Deer	.05	.02
❑ 57	Paul O'Neill	.10	.05
❑ 58	Jeff Reardon	.10	.05
❑ 59	Randy Ready	.05	.02
❑ 60	Scott Erickson	.10	.05
❑ 61	Paul Molitor	.20	.09
❑ 62	Jack McDowell	.05	.02
❑ 63	Jim Acker	.05	.02
❑ 64	Jay Buhner	.15	.07
❑ 65	Travis Fryman	.10	.05
❑ 66	Marquis Grissom	.10	.05
❑ 67	Mike Harkey	.05	.02
❑ 68	Luis Polonia	.05	.02
❑ 69	Ken Caminiti	.15	.07
❑ 70	Chris Sabo	.05	.02
❑ 71	Gregg Olson	.05	.02
❑ 72	Carlton Fisk	.20	.09
❑ 73	Juan Samuel	.05	.02
❑ 74	Todd Stottlemyre	.05	.02
❑ 75	Andre Dawson	.15	.07
❑ 76	Alvin Davis	.05	.02
❑ 77	Bill Doran	.05	.02
❑ 78	B.J. Surhoff	.05	.02
❑ 79	Kirk McCaskill	.05	.02
❑ 80	Dale Murphy	.20	.09
❑ 81	Jose DeLeon	.05	.02
❑ 82	Alex Fernandez	.10	.05
❑ 83	Ivan Calderon	.05	.02

84	Brent Mayne	.05	.02
85	Jody Reed	.05	.02
86	Randy Tomlin	.05	.02
87	Randy Milligan	.05	.02
88	Pascual Perez	.05	.02
89	Hensley Meulens	.05	.02
90	Joe Carter	.10	.05
91	Mike Moore	.05	.02
92	Ozzie Guillen	.05	.02
93	Shawn Hillegas	.05	.02
94	Chili Davis	.10	.05
95	Vince Coleman	.05	.02
96	Jimmy Key	.10	.05
97	Billy Ripken	.05	.02
98	Dave Smith	.05	.02
99	Tom Bolton	.05	.02
100	Barry Larkin	.15	.07
101	Kenny Rogers	.05	.02
102	Mike Boddicker	.05	.02
103	Kevin Elster	.05	.02
104	Ken Hill	.05	.02
105	Charlie Leibrandt	.05	.02
106	Pat Combs	.05	.02
107	Hubie Brooks	.05	.02
108	Julio Franco	.05	.02
109	Vicente Palacios	.05	.02
110	Kal Daniels	.05	.02
111	Bruce Hurst	.05	.02
112	Willie McGee	.10	.05
113	Ted Power	.05	.02
114	Milt Thompson	.05	.02
115	Doug Drabek	.05	.02
116	Rafael Belliard	.05	.02
117	Scott Garrelts	.05	.02
118	Terry Mulholland	.05	.02
119	Jay Howell	.05	.02
120	Danny Jackson	.05	.02
121	Scott Ruskin	.05	.02
122	Robin Ventura	.10	.05
123	Bip Roberts	.05	.02
124	Jeff Russell	.05	.02
125	Hal Morris	.05	.02
126	Teddy Higuera	.05	.02
127	Luis Sojo	.05	.02
128	Carlos Baerga	.05	.02
129	Jeff Ballard	.05	.02
130	Tom Gordon	.05	.02
131	Sid Bream	.05	.02
132	Rance Mulliniks	.05	.02
133	Andy Benes	.10	.05
134	Mickey Tettleton	.05	.02
135	Rich DeLucia	.05	.02
136	Tom Pagnozzi	.05	.02
137	Harold Baines	.10	.05
138	Danny Darwin	.05	.02
139	Kevin Bass	.05	.02
140	Chris Nabholz	.05	.02
141	Pete O'Brien	.05	.02
142	Jeff Treadway	.05	.02
143	Mickey Morandini	.05	.02
144	Eric King	.05	.02
145	Danny Tartabull	.05	.02
146	Lance Johnson	.05	.02
147	Casey Candaele	.05	.02
148	Felix Fermin	.05	.02
149	Rich Rodriguez	.05	.02
150	Dwight Evans	.10	.05
151	Joe Klink	.05	.02
152	Kevin Reimer	.05	.02
153	Orlando Merced	.10	.05
154	Mel Hall	.05	.02
155	Randy Myers	.10	.05
156	Greg A. Harris	.05	.02
157	Jeff Brantley	.05	.02
158	Jim Eisenreich	.05	.02
159	Luis Rivera	.05	.02
160	Cris Carpenter	.05	.02
161	Bruce Ruffin	.05	.02
162	Omar Vizquel	.10	.05
163	Gerald Alexander	.05	.02
164	Mark Guthrie	.05	.02
165	Scott Lewis	.05	.02
166	Bill Sampen	.05	.02
167	Dave Anderson	.05	.02
168	Kevin McReynolds	.05	.02
169	Jose Vizcaino	.05	.02
170	Bob Geren	.05	.02
171	Mike Morgan	.05	.02
172	Jim Gott	.05	.02
173	Mike Pagliarulo	.05	.02
174	Mike Jeffcoat	.05	.02
175	Craig Lefferts	.05	.02
176	Steve Finley	.10	.05
177	Wally Backman	.05	.02
178	Kent Mercker	.05	.02
179	John Cerutti	.05	.02
180	Jay Bell	.10	.05
181	Dale Sveum	.05	.02
182	Greg Gagne	.05	.02
183	Donnie Hill	.05	.02
184	Rex Hudler	.05	.02
185	Pat Kelly	.05	.02
186	Jeff D. Robinson	.05	.02
187	Jeff Gray	.05	.02
188	Jerry Willard	.05	.02
189	Carlos Quintana	.05	.02
190	Dennis Eckersley	.10	.05
191	Kelly Downs	.05	.02
192	Gregg Jefferies	.05	.02
193	Darrin Fletcher	.05	.02
194	Mike Jackson	.10	.05
195	Eddie Murray	.20	.09
196	Bill Landrum	.05	.02
197	Eric Yelding	.05	.02
198	Devon White	.05	.02
199	Larry Walker	.20	.09
200	Ryne Sandberg	.25	.11
201	Dave Magadan	.05	.02
202	Steve Chitren	.05	.02
203	Scott Fletcher	.05	.02
204	Dwayne Henry	.05	.02
205	Scott Coolbaugh	.05	.02
206	Tracy Jones	.05	.02
207	Von Hayes	.05	.02
208	Bob Melvin	.05	.02
209	Scott Scudder	.05	.02
210	Luis Gonzalez	.15	.07
211	Scott Sanderson	.05	.02
212	Chris Donnels	.05	.02
213	Heathcliff Slocumb	.05	.02
214	Mike Timlin	.05	.02
215	Brian Harper	.05	.02
216	Juan Berenguer UER (Decimal point missing in IP total)	.05	.02
217	Mike Henneman	.05	.02
218	Bill Spiers	.05	.02
219	Scott Terry	.05	.02
220	Frank Viola	.05	.02
221	Mark Eichhorn	.05	.02
222	Ernest Riles	.05	.02
223	Ray Lankford	.20	.09
224	Pete Harnisch	.05	.02
225	Bobby Bonilla	.10	.05
226	Mike Scioscia	.05	.02
227	Joel Skinner	.05	.02
228	Brian Holman	.05	.02
229	Gilberto Reyes	.05	.02
230	Matt Williams	.15	.07
231	Jaime Navarro	.05	.02
232	Jose Rijo	.05	.02
233	Atlee Hammaker	.05	.02
234	Tim Teufel	.05	.02
235	John Kruk	.10	.05
236	Kurt Stillwell	.05	.02
237	Dan Pasqua	.05	.02
238	Tim Crews	.05	.02
239	Dave Gallagher	.05	.02
240	Leo Gomez	.05	.02
241	Steve Avery	.05	.02
242	Bill Gullickson	.05	.02
243	Mark Portugal	.05	.02
244	Lee Guetterman	.05	.02
245	Benito Santiago	.05	.02
246	Jim Gantner	.05	.02
247	Robby Thompson	.05	.02
248	Terry Shumpert	.05	.02
249	Mike Bell	.05	.02
250	Harold Reynolds	.05	.02
251	Mike Felder	.05	.02
252	Bill Pecota	.05	.02
253	Bill Krueger	.05	.02
254	Alfredo Griffin	.05	.02
255	Lou Whitaker	.10	.05
256	Roy Smith	.05	.02
257	Jerald Clark	.05	.02
258	Sammy Sosa	.50	.25
259	Tim Naehring	.05	.02
260	Dave Righetti	.05	.02
261	Paul Gibson	.05	.02
262	Chris James	.05	.02
263	Larry Andersen	.05	.02
264	Storm Davis	.05	.02
265	Jose Lind	.05	.02
266	Greg Hibbard	.05	.02
267	Norm Charlton	.05	.02
268	Paul Kilgus	.05	.02
269	Greg Maddux	.50	.23
270	Ellis Burks	.10	.05
271	Frank Tanana	.05	.02
272	Gene Larkin	.05	.02
273	Ron Hassey	.05	.02
274	Jeff M. Robinson	.05	.02
275	Steve Howe	.05	.02
276	Daryl Boston	.05	.02
277	Mark Lee	.05	.02
278	Jose Segura	.05	.02
279	Lance Blankenship	.05	.02
280	Don Slaught	.05	.02
281	Russ Swan	.05	.02
282	Bob Tewksbury	.05	.02
283	Geno Petralli	.05	.02
284	Shane Mack	.05	.02
285	Bob Scanlan	.05	.02
286	Tim Leary	.05	.02
287	John Smoltz	.15	.07
288	Pat Borders	.05	.02
289	Mark Davidson	.05	.02
290	Sam Horn	.05	.02
291	Lenny Harris	.05	.02
292	Franklin Stubbs	.05	.02
293	Thomas Howard	.05	.02
294	Steve Lyons	.05	.02
295	Francisco Oliveras	.05	.02
296	Terry Leach	.05	.02
297	Barry Jones	.05	.02
298	Lance Parrish	.05	.02
299	Wally Whitehurst	.05	.02
300	Bob Welch	.05	.02
301	Charlie Hayes	.05	.02
302	Charlie Hough	.10	.05
303	Gary Redus	.05	.02
304	Scott Bradley	.05	.02
305	Jose Oquendo	.05	.02
306	Pete Incaviglia	.05	.02
307	Marvin Freeman	.05	.02
308	Gary Pettis	.05	.02
309	Joe Slusarski	.05	.02
310	Kevin Seitzer	.05	.02
311	Jeff Reed	.05	.02
312	Pat Tabler	.05	.02
313	Mike Maddux	.05	.02
314	Bob Milacki	.05	.02
315	Eric Anthony	.05	.02
316	Dante Bichette	.15	.07
317	Steve Decker	.05	.02
318	Jack Clark	.10	.05
319	Doug Dascenzo	.05	.02
320	Scott Leius	.05	.02
321	Jim Lindeman	.05	.02
322	Bryan Harvey	.05	.02
323	Spike Owen	.05	.02
324	Roberto Kelly	.05	.02
325	Stan Belinda	.05	.02
326	Joey Cora	.05	.02
327	Jeff Innis	.05	.02
328	Willie Wilson	.05	.02
329	Juan Agosto	.05	.02
330	Charles Nagy	.10	.05
331	Scott Bailes	.05	.02
332	Pete Schourek	.05	.02
333	Mike Flanagan	.05	.02
334	Omar Olivares	.05	.02
335	Dennis Lamp	.05	.02
336	Tommy Greene	.05	.02
337	Randy Velarde	.05	.02
338	Tom Lampkin	.05	.02
339	John Russell	.05	.02

340	Bob Kipper	.05	.02
341	Todd Burns	.05	.02
342	Ron Jones	.05	.02
343	Dave Valle	.05	.02
344	Mike Heath	.05	.02
345	John Olerud	.10	.05
346	Gerald Young	.05	.02
347	Ken Patterson	.05	.02
348	Les Lancaster	.05	.02
349	Steve Crawford	.05	.02
350	John Candelaria	.05	.02
351	Mike Aldrete	.05	.02
352	Mariano Duncan	.05	.02
353	Julio Machado	.05	.02
354	Ken Williams	.05	.02
355	Walt Terrell	.05	.02
356	Mitch Williams	.05	.02
357	Al Newman	.05	.02
358	Bud Black	.05	.02
359	Joe Hesketh	.05	.02
360	Paul Assenmacher	.05	.02
361	Bo Jackson	.10	.05
362	Jeff Blauser	.05	.02
363	Mike Brumley	.05	.02
364	Jim Deshaies	.05	.02
365	Brady Anderson	.15	.07
366	Chuck McElroy	.05	.02
367	Matt Merullo	.05	.02
368	Tim Belcher	.05	.02
369	Luis Aquino	.05	.02
370	Joe Oliver	.05	.02
371	Greg Swindell	.05	.02
372	Lee Stevens	.10	.05
373	Mark Knudson	.05	.02
374	Bill Wegman	.05	.02
375	Jerry Don Gleaton	.05	.02
376	Pedro Guerrero	.05	.02
377	Randy Bush	.05	.02
378	Greg W. Harris	.05	.02
379	Eric Plunk	.05	.02
380	Jose DeJesus	.05	.02
381	Bobby Witt	.05	.02
382	Curtis Wilkerson	.05	.02
383	Gene Nelson	.05	.02
384	Wes Chamberlain	.05	.02
385	Tom Henke	.05	.02
386	Mark Lemke	.05	.02
387	Greg Briley	.05	.02
388	Rafael Ramirez	.05	.02
389	Tony Fossas	.05	.02
390	Henry Cotto	.05	.02
391	Tim Hulett	.05	.02
392	Dean Palmer	.10	.05
393	Glenn Braggs	.05	.02
394	Mark Salas	.05	.02
395	Rusty Meacham	.05	.02
396	Andy Ashby	.10	.05
397	Jose Melendez	.05	.02
398	Warren Newson	.05	.02
399	Frank Castillo	.05	.02
400	Chito Martinez	.05	.02
401	Bernie Williams	.20	.09
402	Derek Bell	.10	.05
403	Javier Ortiz	.05	.02
404	Tim Sherrill	.05	.02
405	Rob MacDonald	.05	.02
406	Phil Plantier	.15	.07
407	Troy Afenir	.05	.02
408	Gino Minutelli	.05	.02
409	Reggie Jefferson	.10	.05
410	Mike Remlinger	.05	.02
411	Carlos Rodriguez	.05	.02
412	Joe Redfield	.05	.02
413	Alonzo Powell	.05	.02
414	Scott Livingstone UER	.05	.02

(Travis Fryman, not Woody, should be referenced on back)

415	Scott Kamieniecki	.05	.02
416	Tim Spehr	.05	.02
417	Brian Hunter	.05	.02
418	Ced Landrum	.05	.02
419	Bret Barberie	.05	.02
420	Kevin Morton	.05	.02
421	Doug Henry	.05	.02
422	Doug Piatt	.05	.02

423	Pat Rice	.05	.02
424	Juan Guzman	.05	.02
425	Nolan Ryan NH	.40	.18
426	Tommy Greene NH	.05	.02
427	Bob Milacki and	.05	.02

Mike Flanagan NH
(Mark Williamson
and Gregg Olson)

428	Wilson Alvarez NH	.05	.02
429	Otis Nixon HL	.05	.02
430	Rickey Henderson HL	.10	.05
431	Cecil Fielder AS	.05	.02
432	Julio Franco AS	.05	.02
433	Cal Ripken AS	.20	.09
434	Wade Boggs AS	.20	.09
435	Joe Carter AS	.05	.02
436	Ken Griffey Jr. AS	.60	.25
437	Ruben Sierra AS	.05	.02
438	Scott Erickson AS	.05	.02
439	Tom Henke AS	.05	.02
440	Terry Steinbach AS	.05	.02
441	Rickey Henderson DT	.25	.11
442	Ryne Sandberg DT	.25	.11
443	Otis Nixon	.10	.05
444	Scott Radinsky	.05	.02
445	Mark Grace	.15	.07
446	Tony Pena	.05	.02
447	Billy Hatcher	.05	.02
448	Glenallen Hill	.05	.02
449	Chris Gwynn	.05	.02
450	Tom Glavine	.15	.07
451	John Habyan	.05	.02
452	Al Osuna	.05	.02
453	Tony Phillips	.05	.02
454	Greg Cadaret	.05	.02
455	Rob Dibble	.05	.02
456	Rick Honeycutt	.05	.02
457	Jerome Walton	.05	.02
458	Mookie Wilson	.10	.05
459	Mark Gubicza	.05	.02
460	Craig Biggio	.20	.09
461	Dave Cochrane	.05	.02
462	Keith Miller	.05	.02
463	Alex Cole	.05	.02
464	Pete Smith	.05	.02
465	Brett Butler	.10	.05
466	Jeff Huson	.05	.02
467	Steve Lake	.05	.02
468	Lloyd Moseby	.05	.02
469	Tim McIntosh	.05	.02
470	Dennis Martinez	.10	.05
471	Greg Myers	.05	.02
472	Mackey Sasser	.05	.02
473	Junior Ortiz	.05	.02
474	Greg Olson	.05	.02
475	Steve Sax	.05	.02
476	Ricky Jordan	.05	.02
477	Max Venable	.05	.02
478	Brian McRae	.05	.02
479	Doug Simons	.05	.02
480	Rickey Henderson	.25	.11
481	Gary Varsho	.05	.02
482	Carl Willis	.05	.02
483	Rick Wilkins	.05	.02
484	Donn Pall	.05	.02
485	Edgar Martinez	.15	.07
486	Tom Foley	.05	.02
487	Mark Williamson	.05	.02
488	Jack Armstrong	.05	.02
489	Gary Carter	.20	.09
490	Ruben Sierra	.05	.02
491	Gerald Perry	.05	.02
492	Rob Murphy	.05	.02
493	Zane Smith	.05	.02
494	Darryl Kile	.10	.05
495	Kelly Gruber	.05	.02
496	Jerry Browne	.05	.02
497	Darryl Hamilton	.05	.02
498	Mike Stanton	.05	.02
499	Mark Leonard	.05	.02
500	Jose Canseco	.25	.11
501	Dave Martinez	.05	.02
502	Jose Guzman	.05	.02
503	Terry Kennedy	.05	.02
504	Ed Sprague	.05	.02
505	Frank Thomas UER	.50	.23

(His Gulf Coast League stats are wrong)

506	Darren Daulton	.10	.05
507	Kevin Tapani	.05	.02
508	Luis Salazar	.05	.02
509	Paul Faries	.05	.02
510	Sandy Alomar Jr.	.10	.05
511	Jeff King	.05	.02
512	Gary Thurman	.05	.02
513	Chris Hammond	.05	.02
514	Pedro Munoz	.05	.02
515	Alan Trammell	.15	.07
516	Geronimo Pena	.05	.02
517	Rodney McCray UER	.05	.02

(Stole 6 bases in 1990, not 5; career totals are correct at 7)

518	Manny Lee	.05	.02
519	Junior Felix	.05	.02
520	Kirk Gibson	.10	.05
521	Darrin Jackson	.05	.02
522	John Burkett	.05	.02
523	Jeff Johnson	.05	.02
524	Jim Corsi	.05	.02
525	Robin Yount	.20	.09
526	Jamie Quirk	.05	.02
527	Bob Ojeda	.05	.02
528	Mark Lewis	.05	.02
529	Bryn Smith	.05	.02
530	Kent Hrbek	.10	.05
531	Dennis Boyd	.05	.02
532	Ron Karkovice	.05	.02
533	Don August	.05	.02
534	Todd Frohwirth	.05	.02
535	Wally Joyner	.10	.05
536	Dennis Rasmussen	.05	.02
537	Andy Allanson	.05	.02
538	Rich Gossage	.10	.05
539	John Marzano	.05	.02
540	Cal Ripken	.75	.35
541	Bill Swift UER	.05	.02

(Brewers logo on front)

542	Kevin Appier	.10	.05
543	Dave Bergman	.05	.02
544	Bernard Gilkey	.10	.05
545	Mike Greenwell	.05	.02
546	Jose Uribe	.05	.02
547	Jesse Orosco	.05	.02
548	Bob Patterson	.05	.02
549	Mike Stanley	.05	.02
550	Howard Johnson	.05	.02
551	Joe Orsulak	.05	.02
552	Dick Schofield	.05	.02
553	Dave Hollins	.05	.02
554	David Segui	.10	.05
555	Barry Bonds	.25	.11
556	Mo Vaughn	.25	.11
557	Craig Wilson	.05	.02
558	Bobby Rose	.05	.02
559	Rod Nichols	.05	.02
560	Len Dykstra	.10	.05
561	Craig Grebeck	.05	.02
562	Darren Lewis	.05	.02
563	Todd Benzinger	.05	.02
564	Ed Whitson	.05	.02
565	Jesse Barfield	.05	.02
566	Lloyd McClendon	.05	.02
567	Dan Plesac	.05	.02
568	Danny Cox	.05	.02
569	Skeeter Barnes	.05	.02
570	Bobby Thigpen	.05	.02
571	Deion Sanders	.20	.09
572	Chuck Knoblauch	.20	.09
573	Matt Nokes	.05	.02
574	Herm Winningham	.05	.02
575	Tom Candiotti	.05	.02
576	Jeff Bagwell	.40	.18
577	Brook Jacoby	.05	.02
578	Chico Walker	.05	.02
579	Brian Downing	.05	.02
580	Dave Stewart	.10	.05
581	Francisco Cabrera	.05	.02
582	Rene Gonzales	.05	.02
583	Stan Javier	.05	.02
584	Randy Johnson	.20	.09
585	Chuck Finley	.10	.05

❑ 586	Mark Gardner	.05	.02
❑ 587	Mark Whiten	.05	.02
❑ 588	Garry Templeton	.05	.02
❑ 589	Gary Sheffield	.20	.09
❑ 590	Ozzie Smith	.25	.11
❑ 591	Candy Maldonado	.05	.02
❑ 592	Mike Sharperson	.05	.02
❑ 593	Carlos Martinez	.05	.02
❑ 594	Scott Bankhead	.05	.02
❑ 595	Tim Wallach	.05	.02
❑ 596	Tino Martinez	.20	.09
❑ 597	Roger McDowell	.05	.02
❑ 598	Cory Snyder	.05	.02
❑ 599	Andujar Cedeno	.05	.02
❑ 600	Kirby Puckett	.30	.14
❑ 601	Rick Parker	.05	.02
❑ 602	Todd Hundley	.10	.05
❑ 603	Greg Litton	.05	.02
❑ 604	Dave Johnson	.05	.02
❑ 605	John Franco	.10	.05
❑ 606	Mike Fetters	.05	.02
❑ 607	Luis Alicea	.05	.02
❑ 608	Trevor Wilson	.05	.02
❑ 609	Rob Ducey	.05	.02
❑ 610	Ramon Martinez	.10	.05
❑ 611	Dave Burba	.05	.02
❑ 612	Dwight Smith	.05	.02
❑ 613	Kevin Maas	.05	.02
❑ 614	John Costello	.05	.02
❑ 615	Glenn Davis	.05	.02
❑ 616	Shawn Abner	.05	.02
❑ 617	Scott Hemond	.05	.02
❑ 618	Tom Prince	.05	.02
❑ 619	Wally Ritchie	.05	.02
❑ 620	Jim Abbott	.10	.05
❑ 621	Charlie O'Brien	.05	.02
❑ 622	Jack Daugherty	.05	.02
❑ 623	Tommy Gregg	.05	.02
❑ 624	Jeff Shaw	.05	.02
❑ 625	Tony Gwynn	.50	.23
❑ 626	Mark Leiter	.05	.02
❑ 627	Jim Clancy	.05	.02
❑ 628	Tim Layana	.05	.02
❑ 629	Jeff Schaefer	.05	.02
❑ 630	Lee Smith	.10	.05
❑ 631	Wade Taylor	.05	.02
❑ 632	Mike Simms	.05	.02
❑ 633	Terry Steinbach	.05	.02
❑ 634	Shawon Dunston	.05	.02
❑ 635	Tim Raines	.10	.05
❑ 636	Kirt Manwaring	.05	.02
❑ 637	Warren Cromartie	.05	.02
❑ 638	Luis Quinones	.05	.02
❑ 639	Greg Vaughn	.15	.07
❑ 640	Kevin Mitchell	.10	.05
❑ 641	Chris Hoiles	.05	.02
❑ 642	Tom Browning	.05	.02
❑ 643	Mitch Webster	.05	.02
❑ 644	Steve Olin	.05	.02
❑ 645	Tony Fernandez	.05	.02
❑ 646	Juan Bell	.05	.02
❑ 647	Joe Boever	.05	.02
❑ 648	Carney Lansford	.10	.05
❑ 649	Mike Benjamin	.05	.02
❑ 650	George Brett	.40	.18
❑ 651	Tim Burke	.05	.02
❑ 652	Jack Morris	.05	.02
❑ 653	Orel Hershiser	.10	.05
❑ 654	Mike Schooler	.05	.02
❑ 655	Andy Van Slyke	.10	.05
❑ 656	Dave Stieb	.05	.02
❑ 657	Dave Clark	.05	.02
❑ 658	Ben McDonald	.05	.02
❑ 659	John Smiley	.05	.02
❑ 660	Wade Boggs	.20	.09
❑ 661	Eric Bullock	.05	.02
❑ 662	Eric Show	.05	.02
❑ 663	Lenny Webster	.05	.02
❑ 664	Mike Huff	.05	.02
❑ 665	Rick Sutcliffe	.05	.02
❑ 666	Jeff Manto	.05	.02
❑ 667	Mike Fitzgerald	.05	.02
❑ 668	Matt Young	.05	.02
❑ 669	Dave West	.05	.02
❑ 670	Mike Hartley	.05	.02
❑ 671	Curt Schilling	.15	.07
❑ 672	Brian Bohanon	.05	.02
❑ 673	Cecil Espy	.05	.02
❑ 674	Joe Grahe	.05	.02
❑ 675	Sid Fernandez	.05	.02
❑ 676	Edwin Nunez	.05	.02
❑ 677	Hector Villanueva	.05	.02
❑ 678	Sean Berry	.05	.02
❑ 679	Dave Eiland	.05	.02
❑ 680	Dave Cone	.10	.05
❑ 681	Mike Bordick	.05	.02
❑ 682	Tony Castillo	.05	.02
❑ 683	John Barfield	.05	.02
❑ 684	Jeff Hamilton	.05	.02
❑ 685	Ken Dayley	.05	.02
❑ 686	Carmelo Martinez	.05	.02
❑ 687	Mike Capel	.05	.02
❑ 688	Scott Chiamparino	.05	.02
❑ 689	Rich Gedman	.05	.02
❑ 690	Rich Monteleone	.05	.02
❑ 691	Alejandro Pena	.05	.02
❑ 692	Oscar Azocar	.05	.02
❑ 693	Jim Poole	.05	.02
❑ 694	Mike Gardiner	.05	.02
❑ 695	Steve Buechele	.05	.02
❑ 696	Rudy Seanez	.05	.02
❑ 697	Paul Abbott	.05	.02
❑ 698	Steve Searcy	.05	.02
❑ 699	Jose Offerman	.10	.05
❑ 700	Ivan Rodriguez	.40	.18
❑ 701	Joe Girardi	.10	.05
❑ 702	Tony Perezchica	.05	.02
❑ 703	Paul McClellan	.05	.02
❑ 704	David Howard	.05	.02
❑ 705	Dan Petry	.05	.02
❑ 706	Jack Howell	.05	.02
❑ 707	Jose Mesa	.05	.02
❑ 708	Randy St. Claire	.05	.02
❑ 709	Kevin Brown	.15	.07
❑ 710	Ron Darling	.05	.02
❑ 711	Jason Grimsley	.05	.02
❑ 712	John Orton	.05	.02
❑ 713	Shawn Boskie	.05	.02
❑ 714	Pat Clements	.05	.02
❑ 715	Brian Barnes	.05	.02
❑ 716	Luis Lopez	.05	.02
❑ 717	Bob McClure	.05	.02
❑ 718	Mark Davis	.05	.02
❑ 719	Dann Bilardello	.05	.02
❑ 720	Tom Edens	.05	.02
❑ 721	Willie Fraser	.05	.02
❑ 722	Curt Young	.05	.02
❑ 723	Neal Heaton	.05	.02
❑ 724	Craig Worthington	.05	.02
❑ 725	Mel Rojas	.05	.02
❑ 726	Daryl Irvine	.05	.02
❑ 727	Roger Mason	.05	.02
❑ 728	Kirk Dressendorfer	.05	.02
❑ 729	Scott Aldred	.05	.02
❑ 730	Willie Blair	.05	.02
❑ 731	Allan Anderson	.05	.02
❑ 732	Dana Kiecker	.05	.02
❑ 733	Jose Gonzalez	.05	.02
❑ 734	Brian Drahman	.05	.02
❑ 735	Brad Komminsk	.05	.02
❑ 736	Arthur Rhodes	.05	.02
❑ 737	Terry Mathews	.05	.02
❑ 738	Jeff Fassero	.05	.02
❑ 739	Mike Magnante	.05	.02
❑ 740	Kip Gross	.05	.02
❑ 741	Jim Hunter	.05	.02
❑ 742	Jose Mota	.05	.02
❑ 743	Joe Bitker	.05	.02
❑ 744	Tim Mauser	.05	.02
❑ 745	Ramon Garcia	.05	.02
❑ 746	Rod Beck	.20	.09
❑ 747	Jim Austin	.05	.02
❑ 748	Keith Mitchell	.05	.02
❑ 749	Wayne Rosenthal	.05	.02
❑ 750	Bryan Hickerson	.05	.02
❑ 751	Bruce Egloff	.05	.02
❑ 752	John Wehner	.05	.02
❑ 753	Darren Holmes	.05	.02
❑ 754	Dave Hansen	.05	.02
❑ 755	Mike Mussina	.30	.14
❑ 756	Anthony Young	.05	.02
❑ 757	Ron Tingley	.05	.02
❑ 758	Ricky Bones	.05	.02
❑ 759	Mark Wohlers	.05	.02
❑ 760	Wilson Alvarez	.10	.05
❑ 761	Harvey Pulliam	.05	.02
❑ 762	Ryan Bowen	.05	.02
❑ 763	Terry Bross	.05	.02
❑ 764	Joel Johnston	.05	.02
❑ 765	Terry McDaniel	.05	.02
❑ 766	Esteban Beltre	.05	.02
❑ 767	Rob Maurer	.05	.02
❑ 768	Ted Wood	.05	.02
❑ 769	Mo Sanford	.05	.02
❑ 770	Jeff Carter	.05	.02
❑ 771	Gil Heredia	.05	.02
❑ 772	Monty Fariss	.05	.02
❑ 773	Will Clark AS	.10	.05
❑ 774	Ryne Sandberg AS	.20	.09
❑ 775	Barry Larkin AS	.15	.07
❑ 776	Howard Johnson AS	.05	.02
❑ 777	Barry Bonds AS	.20	.09
❑ 778	Brett Butler AS	.05	.02
❑ 779	Tony Gwynn AS	.20	.09
❑ 780	Ramon Martinez AS	.05	.02
❑ 781	Lee Smith AS	.05	.02
❑ 782	Mike Scioscia AS	.05	.02
❑ 783	Dennis Martinez HL UER	.05	.02
	(Card has both 13th and 15th perfect game in Major League history)		
❑ 784	Dennis Martinez NH	.05	.02
❑ 785	Mark Gardner NH	.05	.02
❑ 786	Bret Saberhagen NH	.05	.02
❑ 787	Kent Mercker NH / Mark Wohlers / Alejandro Pena	.05	.02
❑ 788	Cal Ripken MVP	.40	.18
❑ 789	Terry Pendleton MVP	.05	.02
❑ 790	Roger Clemens CY	.20	.09
❑ 791	Tom Glavine CY	.10	.05
❑ 792	Chuck Knoblauch ROY	.10	.05
❑ 793	Jeff Bagwell ROY	.15	.07
❑ 794	Cal Ripken MANYR	.40	.18
❑ 795	David Cone HL	.05	.02
❑ 796	Kirby Puckett HL	.20	.09
❑ 797	Steve Avery HL	.05	.02
❑ 798	Jack Morris HL	.05	.02
❑ 799	Allen Watson DC	.05	.02
❑ 800	Manny Ramirez DC	2.00	.90
❑ 801	Cliff Floyd DC	.25	.11
❑ 802	Al Shirley DC	.05	.02
❑ 803	Brian Barber DC	.05	.02
❑ 804	Jon Farrell DC	.05	.02
❑ 805	Brent Gates DC	.05	.02
❑ 806	Scott Ruffcorn DC	.05	.02
❑ 807	Tyrone Hill DC	.05	.02
❑ 808	Benji Gil DC	.05	.02
❑ 809	Aaron Sele DC	.30	.14
❑ 810	Tyler Green DC	.05	.02
❑ 811	Chris Jones	.05	.02
❑ 812	Steve Wilson	.05	.02
❑ 813	Freddie Benavides	.05	.02
❑ 814	Don Wakamatsu	.05	.02
❑ 815	Mike Humphreys	.05	.02
❑ 816	Scott Servais	.05	.02
❑ 817	Rico Rossy	.05	.02
❑ 818	John Ramos	.05	.02
❑ 819	Rob Mallicoat	.05	.02
❑ 820	Milt Hill	.05	.02
❑ 821	Carlos Garcia	.05	.02
❑ 822	Stan Royer	.05	.02
❑ 823	Jeff Plympton	.05	.02
❑ 824	Braulio Castillo	.05	.02
❑ 825	David Haas	.05	.02
❑ 826	Luis Mercedes	.05	.02
❑ 827	Eric Karros	.20	.09
❑ 828	Shawn Hare	.05	.02
❑ 829	Reggie Sanders	.10	.05
❑ 830	Tom Goodwin	.10	.05
❑ 831	Dan Gakeler	.05	.02
❑ 832	Stacy Jones	.05	.02
❑ 833	Kim Batiste	.05	.02
❑ 834	Cal Eldred	.05	.02
❑ 835	Chris George	.05	.02
❑ 836	Wayne Housie	.05	.02
❑ 837	Mike Ignasiak	.05	.02
❑ 838	Josias Manzanillo	.05	.02

❑ 839	Jim Olander	.05	.02
❑ 840	Gary Cooper	.05	.02
❑ 841	Royce Clayton	.05	.02
❑ 842	Hector Fajardo	.05	.02
❑ 843	Blaine Beatty	.05	.02
❑ 844	Jorge Pedre	.05	.02
❑ 845	Kenny Lofton	.25	.11
❑ 846	Scott Brosius	.25	.11
❑ 847	Chris Cron	.05	.02
❑ 848	Denis Boucher	.05	.02
❑ 849	Kyle Abbott	.05	.02
❑ 850	Bob Zupcic	.05	.02
❑ 851	Rheal Cormier	.05	.02
❑ 852	Jim Lewis	.05	.02
❑ 853	Anthony Telford	.05	.02
❑ 854	Cliff Brantley	.05	.02
❑ 855	Kevin Campbell	.05	.02
❑ 856	Craig Shipley	.05	.02
❑ 857	Chuck Carr	.05	.02
❑ 858	Tony Eusebio	.20	.09
❑ 859	Jim Thome	.50	.23
❑ 860	Vinny Castilla	2.50	1.10
❑ 861	Dann Howitt	.05	.02
❑ 862	Kevin Ward	.05	.02
❑ 863	Steve Wapnick	.05	.02
❑ 864	Rod Brewer	.05	.02
❑ 865	Todd Van Poppel	.05	.02
❑ 866	Jose Hernandez	.05	.02
❑ 867	Amalio Carreno	.05	.02
❑ 868	Calvin Jones	.05	.02
❑ 869	Jeff Gardner	.05	.02
❑ 870	Jarvis Brown	.05	.02
❑ 871	Eddie Taubensee	.10	.05
❑ 872	Andy Mota	.05	.02
❑ 873	Chris Haney	.05	.02
❑ 874	Roberto Hernandez	.15	.07
❑ 875	Laddie Renfroe	.05	.02
❑ 876	Scott Cooper	.05	.02
❑ 877	Armando Reynoso	.05	.02
❑ 878	Ty Cobb MEMO	.25	.11
❑ 879	Babe Ruth MEMO	.40	.18
❑ 880	Honus Wagner MEMO	.20	.09
❑ 881	Lou Gehrig MEMO	.25	.11
❑ 882	Satchel Paige MEMO	.20	.09
❑ 883	Will Clark DT	.10	.05
❑ 884	Cal Ripken DT	2.00	.90
❑ 885	Wade Boggs DT	.10	.05
❑ 886	Kirby Puckett DT	.30	.14
❑ 887	Tony Gwynn DT	.50	.23
❑ 888	Craig Biggio DT	.10	.05
❑ 889	Scott Erickson DT	.05	.02
❑ 890	Tom Glavine DT	.10	.05
❑ 891	Rob Dibble DT	.05	.02
❑ 892	Mitch Williams DT	.05	.02
❑ 893	Frank Thomas DT	.50	.23
❑ X672	Chuck Knoblauch AU	60.00	27.00

(1990 Score card,
autographed with
special hologram on back)

1992 Score DiMaggio

	MINT	NRMT
COMPLETE SET (5)	150.00	70.00
COMMON DIMAGGIO (1-5)	30.00	13.50

RANDOM INSERTS IN SER.1 PACKS

❑ 1	Joe DiMaggio	30.00	13.50

	The Minors		
❑ 2	Joe DiMaggio	30.00	13.50
	The Rookie		
❑ 3	Joe DiMaggio	30.00	13.50
	The MVP		
❑ 4	Joe DiMaggio	30.00	13.50
	The Streak		
❑ 5	Joe DiMaggio	30.00	13.50
	The Legend		
❑ AU	Joe DiMaggio AU	500.00	220.00

(Autographed with certified signature)

1992 Score Factory Inserts

	MINT	NRMT
COMPLETE SET (17)	6.00	2.70
COMMON CARD (B1-B17)	.25	.11

ONE SET PER FACTORY SET

❑ B1	Greg Gagne WS	.25	.11
❑ B2	Scott Leius WS	.25	.11
❑ B3	Mark Lemke WS	.50	.23
❑ B4	Lonnie Smith WS	.25	.11
❑ B5	David Justice WS	1.00	.45
❑ B6	Kirby Puckett WS	2.50	1.10
❑ B7	Gene Larkin WS	.25	.11
❑ B8	Carlton Fisk	1.00	.45
❑ B9	Ozzie Smith	2.00	.90
❑ B10	Dave Winfield	1.00	.45
❑ B11	Robin Yount	1.00	.45
❑ B12	Joe DiMaggio	1.50	.70
❑ B13	Joe DiMaggio	1.50	.70
❑ B14	Joe DiMaggio	1.50	.70
❑ B15	Carl Yastrzemski	.75	.35
❑ B16	Carl Yastrzemski	.75	.35
❑ B17	Carl Yastrzemski	.75	.35

1992 Score Franchise

	MINT	NRMT
COMPLETE SET (4)	30.00	13.50
COMMON CARD (1-4)	4.00	1.80

RANDOM INSERTS IN SER.2 PACKS

❑ 1	Stan Musial	5.00	2.20
❑ 2	Mickey Mantle	12.00	5.50
❑ 3	Carl Yastrzemski	4.00	1.80
❑ 4	The Franchise Players	10.00	4.50
	Stan Musial		
	Mickey Mantle		
	Carl Yastrzemski		
❑ AU1	Stan Musial	150.00	70.00
	(Autographed with certified signature)		
❑ AU2	Mickey Mantle	500.00	220.00
	(Autographed with certified signature)		
❑ AU3	Carl Yastrzemski	120.00	55.00
	(Autographed with certified signature)		
❑ AU4	Franchise Players	1500.00	700.00
	Stan Musial		
	Mickey Mantle		
	Carl Yastrzemski		
	(Autographed with certified signatures of all three)		

1992 Score Hot Rookies

	MINT	NRMT
COMPLETE SET (10)	12.00	5.50
COMMON CARD (1-10)	.50	.23
MINOR STARS	1.00	.45
SEMISTARS	2.00	.90

ONE PER BLISTER PACK

❑ 1	Cal Eldred	.50	.23
❑ 2	Royce Clayton	.50	.23
❑ 3	Kenny Lofton	3.00	1.35
❑ 4	Todd Van Poppel	.50	.23
❑ 5	Scott Cooper	.50	.23
❑ 6	Todd Hundley	1.00	.45
❑ 7	Tino Martinez	3.00	1.35
❑ 8	Anthony Telford	.50	.23
❑ 9	Derek Bell	1.00	.45
❑ 10	Reggie Jefferson	1.00	.45

1992 Score Impact Players

	MINT	NRMT
COMPLETE SET (90)	20.00	9.00

	MINT	NRMT
COMPLETE SERIES 1 (45)	14.00	6.25
COMPLETE SERIES 2 (45)	6.00	2.70
COMMON CARD (1-10)	.10	.05
FIVE PER JUMBO PACK		
1 Chuck Knoblauch	.40	.18
2 Jeff Bagwell	1.25	.55
3 Juan Guzman	.10	.05
4 Milt Cuyler	.10	.05
5 Ivan Rodriguez	1.25	.55
6 Rich DeLucia	.10	.05
7 Orlando Merced	.10	.05
8 Ray Lankford	.40	.18
9 Brian Hunter	.10	.05
10 Roberto Alomar	.40	.18
11 Wes Chamberlain	.10	.05
12 Steve Avery	.10	.05
13 Scott Erickson	.20	.09
14 Jim Abbott	.20	.09
15 Mark Whiten	.10	.05
16 Leo Gomez	.10	.05
17 Doug Henry	.10	.05
18 Brent Mayne	.10	.05
19 Charles Nagy	.20	.09
20 Phil Plantier	.10	.05
21 Mo Vaughn	.75	.35
22 Craig Biggio	.40	.18
23 Derek Bell	.20	.09
24 Royce Clayton	.10	.05
25 Gary Cooper	.10	.05
26 Scott Cooper	.10	.05
27 Juan Gonzalez	1.50	.70
28 Ken Griffey Jr.	4.00	1.80
29 Larry Walker	.40	.18
30 John Smoltz	.30	.14
31 Todd Hundley	.20	.09
32 Kenny Lofton	1.00	.45
33 Andy Mota	.10	.05
34 Todd Zeile	.10	.05
35 Arthur Rhodes	.10	.05
36 Jim Thome	1.50	.70
37 Todd Van Poppel	.10	.05
38 Mark Wohlers	.10	.05
39 Anthony Young	.10	.05
40 Sandy Alomar Jr	.20	.09
41 John Olerud	.20	.09
42 Robin Ventura	.20	.09
43 Frank Thomas	1.50	.70
44 Dave Justice	.40	.18
45 Hal Morris	.10	.05
46 Ruben Sierra	.10	.05
47 Travis Fryman	.20	.09
48 Mike Mussina	1.00	.45
49 Tom Glavine	.30	.14
50 Barry Larkin	.30	.14
51 Will Clark UER	.40	.18
Career Totals spelled To als		
52 Jose Canseco	.75	.35
53 Bo Jackson	.20	.09
54 Dwight Gooden	.20	.09
55 Barry Bonds	.75	.35
56 Fred McGriff	.30	.14
57 Roger Clemens	1.25	.55
58 Benito Santiago	.10	.05
59 Darryl Strawberry	.20	.09
60 Cecil Fielder	.20	.09
61 John Franco	.20	.09
62 Matt Williams	.30	.14
63 Marquis Grissom	.20	.09
64 Danny Tartabull	.20	.05
65 Ron Gant	.20	.09
66 Paul O'Neill	.20	.09
67 Devon White	.10	.05
68 Rafael Palmeiro	.40	.18
69 Tom Gordon	.10	.05
70 Shawon Dunston	.10	.05
71 Rob Dibble	.10	.05
72 Eddie Zosky	.10	.05
73 Jack McDowell	.20	.09
74 Len Dykstra	.20	.09
75 Ramon Martinez	.20	.09
76 Reggie Sanders	.20	.09
77 Greg Maddux	1.50	.70
78 Ellis Burks	.20	.09
79 John Smiley	.10	.05
80 Roberto Kelly	.10	.05
81 Ben McDonald	.10	.05
82 Mark Lewis	.10	.05
83 Jose Rijo	.10	.05
84 Ozzie Guillen	.10	.05
85 Lance Dickson	.10	.05
86 Kim Batiste	.10	.05
87 Gregg Olson	.10	.05
88 Andy Benes	.20	.09
89 Cal Eldred	.10	.05
90 David Cone	.20	.09

1992 Score Rookie/Traded

	MINT	NRMT
COMP.FACT.SET (110)	15.00	6.75
COMMON CARD (1T-110T)	.15	.07
MINOR STARS	.30	.14
SEMISTARS	.50	.23
UNLISTED STARS	.75	.35
1T Gary Sheffield	.75	.35
2T Kevin Seitzer	.15	.07
3T Danny Tartabull	.15	.07
4T Steve Sax	.15	.07
5T Bobby Bonilla	.30	.14
6T Frank Viola	.15	.07
7T Dave Winfield	.75	.35
8T Rick Sutcliffe	.15	.07
9T Jose Canseco	1.00	.45
10T Greg Swindell	.15	.07
11T Eddie Murray	.75	.35
12T Randy Myers	.30	.14
13T Wally Joyner	.30	.14
14T Kenny Lofton	2.50	1.10
15T Jack Morris	.30	.14
16T Charlie Hayes	.15	.07
17T Pete Incaviglia	.15	.07
18T Kevin Mitchell	.30	.14
19T Kurt Stillwell	.15	.07
20T Bret Saberhagen	.30	.14
21T Steve Buechele	.15	.07
22T John Smiley	.15	.07
23T Sammy Sosa	3.00	1.35
24T George Bell	.15	.07
25T Curt Schilling	1.00	.45
26T Dick Schofield	.15	.07
27T David Cone	.30	.14
28T Dan Gladden	.15	.07
29T Kirk McCaskill	.15	.07
30T Mike Gallego	.15	.07
31T Kevin McReynolds	.15	.07
32T Bill Swift	.15	.07
33T Dave Martinez	.15	.07
34T Storm Davis	.15	.07
35T Willie Randolph	.30	.14
36T Melido Perez	.15	.07
37T Mark Carreon	.15	.07
38T Doug Jones	.15	.07
39T Gregg Jefferies	.15	.07
40T Mike Jackson	.30	.14
41T Dickie Thon	.15	.07
42T Eric King	.15	.07
43T Herm Winningham	.15	.07
44T Derek Lilliquist	.15	.07
45T Dave Anderson	.15	.07
46T Jeff Reardon	.30	.14
47T Scott Bankhead	.15	.07
48T Cory Snyder	.15	.07
49T Al Newman	.15	.07
50T Keith Miller	.15	.07
51T Dave Burba	.15	.07
52T Bill Pecota	.15	.07
53T Chuck Crim	.15	.07
54T Mariano Duncan	.15	.07
55T Dave Gallagher	.15	.07
56T Chris Gwynn	.15	.07
57T Scott Ruskin	.15	.07
58T Jack Armstrong	.15	.07
59T Gary Carter	.75	.35
60T Andres Galarraga	.75	.35
61T Ken Hill	.15	.07
62T Eric Davis	.30	.14
63T Ruben Sierra	.15	.07
64T Darrin Fletcher	.15	.07
65T Tim Belcher	.15	.07
66T Mike Morgan	.15	.07
67T Scott Scudder	.15	.07
68T Tom Candiotti	.15	.07
69T Hubie Brooks	.15	.07
70T Kal Daniels	.15	.07
71T Bruce Ruffin	.15	.07
72T Billy Hatcher	.15	.07
73T Bob Melvin	.15	.07
74T Lee Guetterman	.15	.07
75T Rene Gonzales	.15	.07
76T Kevin Bass	.15	.07
77T Tom Bolton	.15	.07
78T John Wetteland	.30	.14
79T Bip Roberts	.15	.07
80T Pat Listach	.15	.07
81T John Doherty	.15	.07
82T Sam Militello	.15	.07
83T Brian Jordan	2.50	1.10
84T Jeff Kent	1.00	.45
85T Dave Fleming	.15	.07
86T Jeff Tackett	.15	.07
87T Chad Curtis	.50	.23
88T Eric Fox	.15	.07
89T Denny Neagle	.50	.23
90T Donovan Osborne	.15	.07
91T Carlos Hernandez	.15	.07
92T Tim Wakefield	1.00	.45
93T Tim Salmon	3.00	1.35
94T Dave Nilsson	.30	.14
95T Mike Perez	.15	.07
96T Pat Hentgen	.75	.35
97T Frank Seminara	.15	.07
98T Ruben Amaro	.15	.07
99T Archi Cianfrocco	.15	.07
100T Andy Stankiewicz	.15	.07
101T Jim Bullinger	.15	.07
102T Pat Mahomes	.15	.07
103T Hipolito Pichardo	.15	.07
104T Bret Boone	.75	.35
105T John Vander Wal	.15	.07
106T Vince Horsman	.15	.07
107T James Austin	.15	.07
108T Brian Williams	.15	.07
109T Dan Walters	.15	.07
110T Wil Cordero	.15	.07

1993 Score

	MINT	NRMT
COMPLETE SET (660)	40.00	18.00

COMMON CARD (1-660)	.10	.05
MINOR STARS	.20	.09
SEMISTARS	.30	.14
UNLISTED STARS	.40	.18
SUBSET CARDS HALF VALUE OF BASE CARDS		

#	Name	Price 1	Price 2
❑ 1	Ken Griffey Jr.	2.00	.90
❑ 2	Gary Sheffield	.40	.18
❑ 3	Frank Thomas	.75	.35
❑ 4	Ryne Sandberg	.50	.23
❑ 5	Larry Walker	.40	.18
❑ 6	Cal Ripken Jr.	1.50	.70
❑ 7	Roger Clemens	1.00	.45
❑ 8	Bobby Bonilla	.20	.09
❑ 9	Carlos Baerga	.10	.05
❑ 10	Darren Daulton	.20	.09
❑ 11	Travis Fryman	.20	.09
❑ 12	Andy Van Slyke	.20	.09
❑ 13	Jose Canseco	.50	.23
❑ 14	Roberto Alomar	.40	.18
❑ 15	Tom Glavine	.30	.14
❑ 16	Barry Larkin	.40	.18
❑ 17	Gregg Jefferies	.10	.05
❑ 18	Craig Biggio	.40	.18
❑ 19	Shane Mack	.10	.05
❑ 20	Brett Butler	.20	.09
❑ 21	Dennis Eckersley	.20	.09
❑ 22	Will Clark	.40	.18
❑ 23	Don Mattingly	.75	.35
❑ 24	Tony Gwynn	1.00	.45
❑ 25	Ivan Rodriguez	.50	.23
❑ 26	Shawon Dunston	.10	.05
❑ 27	Mike Mussina	.40	.18
❑ 28	Marquis Grissom	.20	.09
❑ 29	Charles Nagy	.20	.09
❑ 30	Len Dykstra	.20	.09
❑ 31	Cecil Fielder	.20	.09
❑ 32	Jay Bell	.20	.09
❑ 33	B.J. Surhoff	.20	.09
❑ 34	Bob Tewksbury	.10	.05
❑ 35	Danny Tartabull	.10	.05
❑ 36	Terry Pendleton	.10	.05
❑ 37	Jack Morris	.20	.09
❑ 38	Hal Morris	.10	.05
❑ 39	Luis Polonia	.10	.05
❑ 40	Ken Caminiti	.30	.14
❑ 41	Robin Ventura	.20	.09
❑ 42	Darryl Strawberry	.20	.09
❑ 43	Wally Joyner	.20	.09
❑ 44	Fred McGriff	.30	.14
❑ 45	Kevin Tapani	.10	.05
❑ 46	Matt Williams	.30	.14
❑ 47	Robin Yount	.30	.14
❑ 48	Ken Hill	.10	.05
❑ 49	Edgar Martinez	.10	.05
❑ 50	Mark Grace	.30	.14
❑ 51	Juan Gonzalez	.75	.35
❑ 52	Curt Schilling	.20	.09
❑ 53	Dwight Gooden	.20	.09
❑ 54	Chris Hoiles	.10	.05
❑ 55	Frank Viola	.10	.05
❑ 56	Ray Lankford	.30	.14
❑ 57	George Brett	.75	.35
❑ 58	Kenny Lofton	.40	.18
❑ 59	Nolan Ryan	1.50	.70
❑ 60	Mickey Tettleton	.10	.05
❑ 61	John Smoltz	.30	.14
❑ 62	Howard Johnson	.10	.05
❑ 63	Eric Karros	.30	.14
❑ 64	Rick Aguilera	.10	.05
❑ 65	Steve Finley	.10	.05
❑ 66	Mark Langston	.10	.05
❑ 67	Bill Swift	.10	.05
❑ 68	John Olerud	.30	.14
❑ 69	Kevin McReynolds	.10	.05
❑ 70	Jack McDowell	.10	.05
❑ 71	Rickey Henderson	.50	.23
❑ 72	Brian Harper	.10	.05
❑ 73	Mike Morgan	.10	.05
❑ 74	Rafael Palmeiro	.40	.18
❑ 75	Dennis Martinez	.20	.09
❑ 76	Tino Martinez	.40	.18
❑ 77	Eddie Murray	.40	.18
❑ 78	Ellis Burks	.10	.05
❑ 79	John Kruk	.20	.09
❑ 80	Gregg Olson	.10	.05
❑ 81	Bernard Gilkey	.10	.05
❑ 82	Milt Cuyler	.10	.05
❑ 83	Mike LaValliere	.10	.05
❑ 84	Albert Belle	.40	.18
❑ 85	Bip Roberts	.10	.05
❑ 86	Melido Perez	.10	.05
❑ 87	Otis Nixon	.10	.05
❑ 88	Bill Spiers	.10	.05
❑ 89	Jeff Bagwell	.50	.23
❑ 90	Orel Hershiser	.20	.09
❑ 91	Andy Benes	.20	.09
❑ 92	Devon White	.10	.05
❑ 93	Willie McGee	.20	.09
❑ 94	Ozzie Guillen	.10	.05
❑ 95	Ivan Calderon	.10	.05
❑ 96	Keith Miller	.10	.05
❑ 97	Steve Buechele	.10	.05
❑ 98	Kent Hrbek	.20	.09
❑ 99	Dave Hollins	.20	.09
❑ 100	Mike Bordick	.10	.05
❑ 101	Randy Tomlin	.10	.05
❑ 102	Omar Vizquel	.20	.09
❑ 103	Lee Smith	.20	.09
❑ 104	Leo Gomez	.10	.05
❑ 105	Jose Rijo	.10	.05
❑ 106	Mark Whiten	.10	.05
❑ 107	Dave Justice	.40	.18
❑ 108	Eddie Taubensee	.10	.05
❑ 109	Lance Johnson	.10	.05
❑ 110	Felix Jose	.10	.05
❑ 111	Mike Harvey	.10	.05
❑ 112	Randy Milligan	.10	.05
❑ 113	Anthony Young	.10	.05
❑ 114	Rico Brogna	.20	.09
❑ 115	Bret Saberhagen	.20	.09
❑ 116	Sandy Alomar Jr.	.20	.09
❑ 117	Terry Mulholland	.10	.05
❑ 118	Darryl Hamilton	.10	.05
❑ 119	Todd Zeile	.20	.09
❑ 120	Bernie Williams	.40	.18
❑ 121	Zane Smith	.10	.05
❑ 122	Derek Bell	.20	.09
❑ 123	Deion Sanders	.30	.14
❑ 124	Luis Sojo	.10	.05
❑ 125	Joe Oliver	.10	.05
❑ 126	Craig Grebeck	.10	.05
❑ 127	Andujar Cedeno	.10	.05
❑ 128	Brian McRae	.10	.05
❑ 129	Jose Offerman	.20	.09
❑ 130	Pedro Munoz	.10	.05
❑ 131	Bud Black	.10	.05
❑ 132	Mo Vaughn	.40	.18
❑ 133	Bruce Hurst	.10	.05
❑ 134	Dave Henderson	.10	.05
❑ 135	Tom Pagnozzi	.10	.05
❑ 136	Erik Hanson	.10	.05
❑ 137	Orlando Merced	.10	.05
❑ 138	Dean Palmer	.20	.09
❑ 139	John Franco	.10	.05
❑ 140	Brady Anderson	.20	.09
❑ 141	Ricky Jordan	.10	.05
❑ 142	Jeff Blauser	.10	.05
❑ 143	Sammy Sosa	1.25	.55
❑ 144	Bob Walk	.10	.05
❑ 145	Delino DeShields	.20	.09
❑ 146	Kevin Brown	.30	.14
❑ 147	Mark Lemke	.10	.05
❑ 148	Chuck Knoblauch	.40	.18
❑ 149	Chris Sabo	.10	.05
❑ 150	Bobby Witt	.10	.05
❑ 151	Luis Gonzalez	.20	.09
❑ 152	Ron Karkovice	.10	.05
❑ 153	Jeff Brantley	.10	.05
❑ 154	Kevin Appier	.20	.09
❑ 155	Darrin Jackson	.10	.05
❑ 156	Kelly Gruber	.10	.05
❑ 157	Royce Clayton	.20	.09
❑ 158	Chuck Finley	.20	.09
❑ 159	Jeff King	.10	.05
❑ 160	Greg Vaughn	.20	.09
❑ 161	Geronimo Pena	.10	.05
❑ 162	Steve Farr	.10	.05
❑ 163	Jose Oquendo	.10	.05
❑ 164	Mark Lewis	.10	.05
❑ 165	John Wetteland	.20	.09
❑ 166	Mike Henneman	.10	.05
❑ 167	Todd Hundley	.30	.14
❑ 168	Wes Chamberlain	.10	.05
❑ 169	Steve Avery	.10	.05
❑ 170	Mike Devereaux	.10	.05
❑ 171	Reggie Sanders	.20	.09
❑ 172	Jay Buhner	.30	.14
❑ 173	Eric Anthony	.10	.05
❑ 174	John Burkett	.10	.05
❑ 175	Tom Candiotti	.10	.05
❑ 176	Phil Plantier	.10	.05
❑ 177	Doug Henry	.10	.05
❑ 178	Scott Leius	.10	.05
❑ 179	Kirt Manwaring	.10	.05
❑ 180	Jeff Parrett	.10	.05
❑ 181	Don Slaught	.10	.05
❑ 182	Scott Radinsky	.10	.05
❑ 183	Luis Alicea	.10	.05
❑ 184	Tom Gordon	.10	.05
❑ 185	Rick Wilkins	.10	.05
❑ 186	Todd Stottlemyre	.10	.05
❑ 187	Moises Alou	.20	.09
❑ 188	Joe Grahe	.10	.05
❑ 189	Jeff Kent	.20	.09
❑ 190	Bill Wegman	.10	.05
❑ 191	Kim Batiste	.10	.05
❑ 192	Matt Nokes	.10	.05
❑ 193	Mark Wohlers	.10	.05
❑ 194	Paul Sorrento	.10	.05
❑ 195	Chris Hammond	.10	.05
❑ 196	Scott Livingstone	.10	.05
❑ 197	Doug Jones	.10	.05
❑ 198	Scott Cooper	.10	.05
❑ 199	Ramon Martinez	.20	.09
❑ 200	Dave Valle	.10	.05
❑ 201	Mariano Duncan	.10	.05
❑ 202	Ben McDonald	.10	.05
❑ 203	Darren Lewis	.10	.05
❑ 204	Kenny Rogers	.10	.05
❑ 205	Manuel Lee	.10	.05
❑ 206	Scott Erickson	.10	.05
❑ 207	Dan Gladden	.10	.05
❑ 208	Bob Welch	.10	.05
❑ 209	Greg Olson	.10	.05
❑ 210	Dan Pasqua	.10	.05
❑ 211	Tim Wallach	.10	.05
❑ 212	Jeff Montgomery	.20	.09
❑ 213	Derrick May	.10	.05
❑ 214	Ed Sprague	.10	.05
❑ 215	David Haas	.10	.05
❑ 216	Darrin Fletcher	.10	.05
❑ 217	Brian Jordan	.20	.09
❑ 218	Jaime Navarro	.10	.05
❑ 219	Randy Velarde	.10	.05
❑ 220	Ron Gant	.20	.09
❑ 221	Paul Quantrill	.10	.05
❑ 222	Damion Easley	.20	.09
❑ 223	Charlie Hough	.10	.05
❑ 224	Brad Brink	.10	.05
❑ 225	Barry Manuel	.10	.05
❑ 226	Kevin Koslofski	.10	.05
❑ 227	Ryan Thompson	.20	.09
❑ 228	Mike Munoz	.10	.05
❑ 229	Dan Wilson	.20	.09
❑ 230	Peter Hoy	.10	.05
❑ 231	Pedro Astacio	.20	.09
❑ 232	Matt Stairs	.30	.14
❑ 233	Jeff Reboulet	.10	.05
❑ 234	Manny Alexander	.10	.05
❑ 235	Willie Banks	.10	.05
❑ 236	John Jaha	.10	.05
❑ 237	Scooter Tucker	.10	.05
❑ 238	Russ Springer	.10	.05
❑ 239	Paul Miller	.10	.05
❑ 240	Dan Peltier	.10	.05
❑ 241	Ozzie Canseco	.10	.05
❑ 242	Ben Rivera	.10	.05
❑ 243	John Valentin	.20	.09
❑ 244	Henry Rodriguez	.20	.09
❑ 245	Derek Parks	.10	.05
❑ 246	Carlos Garcia	.10	.05
❑ 247	Tim Pugh	.10	.05
❑ 248	Melvin Nieves	.10	.05
❑ 249	Rich Amaral	.10	.05
❑ 250	Willie Greene	.10	.05
❑ 251	Tim Scott	.10	.05

252	Dave Silvestri	.10	.05
253	Rob Mallicoat	.10	.05
254	Donald Harris	.10	.05
255	Craig Colbert	.10	.05
256	Jose Guzman	.10	.05
257	Domingo Martinez	.10	.05
258	William Suero	.10	.05
259	Juan Guerrero	.10	.05
260	J.T. Snow	.50	.23
261	Tony Pena	.10	.05
262	Tim Fortugno	.10	.05
263	Tom Marsh	.10	.05
264	Kurt Knudsen	.10	.05
265	Tim Costo	.10	.05
266	Steve Shifflett	.10	.05
267	Billy Ashley	.10	.05
268	Jerry Nielsen	.10	.05
269	Pete Young	.10	.05
270	Johnny Guzman	.10	.05
271	Greg Colbrunn	.10	.05
272	Jeff Nelson	.10	.05
273	Kevin Young	.20	.09
274	Jeff Frye	.10	.05
275	J.T. Bruett	.10	.05
276	Todd Pratt	.25	.11
277	Mike Butcher	.10	.05
278	John Flaherty	.10	.05
279	John Patterson	.10	.05
280	Eric Hillman	.10	.05
281	Bien Figueroa	.10	.05
282	Shane Reynolds	.20	.09
283	Rich Rowland	.10	.05
284	Steve Foster	.10	.05
285	Dave Mlicki	.10	.05
286	Mike Piazza	2.00	.90
287	Mike Trombley	.10	.05
288	Jim Pena	.10	.05
289	Bob Ayrault	.10	.05
290	Henry Mercedes	.10	.05
291	Bob Wickman	.10	.05
292	Jacob Brumfield	.10	.05
293	David Hulse	.10	.05
294	Ryan Klesko	.40	.18
295	Doug Linton	.10	.05
296	Steve Cooke	.10	.05
297	Eddie Zosky	.10	.05
298	Gerald Williams	.10	.05
299	Jonathan Hurst	.10	.05
300	Larry Carter	.10	.05
301	William Pennyfeather	.10	.05
302	Cesar Hernandez	.10	.05
303	Steve Hosey	.10	.05
304	Blas Minor	.10	.05
305	Jeff Grotewald	.10	.05
306	Bernardo Brito	.10	.05
307	Rafael Bournigal	.10	.05
308	Jeff Branson	.10	.05
309	Tom Quinlan	.10	.05
310	Pat Gomez	.10	.05
311	Sterling Hitchcock	.40	.18
312	Kent Bottenfield	.10	.05
313	Alan Trammell	.30	.14
314	Cris Colon	.10	.05
315	Paul Wagner	.10	.05
316	Matt Maysey	.10	.05
317	Mike Stanton	.10	.05
318	Rick Trlicek	.10	.05
319	Kevin Rogers	.10	.05
320	Mark Clark	.10	.05
321	Pedro Martinez	.75	.35
322	Al Martin	.10	.05
323	Mike Macfarlane	.10	.05
324	Rey Sanchez	.10	.05
325	Roger Pavlik	.10	.05
326	Troy Neel	.10	.05
327	Kerry Woodson	.10	.05
328	Wayne Kirby	.10	.05
329	Ken Ryan	.10	.05
330	Jesse Levis	.10	.05
331	James Austin	.10	.05
332	Dan Walters	.10	.05
333	Brian Williams	.10	.05
334	Wil Cordero	.10	.05
335	Bret Boone	.20	.09
336	Hipolito Pichardo	.10	.05
337	Pat Mahomes	.10	.05
338	Andy Stankiewicz	.10	.05
339	Jim Bullinger	.10	.05
340	Archi Cianfrocco	.10	.05
341	Ruben Amaro	.10	.05
342	Frank Seminara	.10	.05
343	Pat Hentgen	.30	.14
344	Dave Nilsson	.20	.09
345	Mike Perez	.10	.05
346	Tim Salmon	.40	.18
347	Tim Wakefield	.20	.09
348	Carlos Hernandez	.10	.05
349	Donovan Osborne	.10	.05
350	Denny Neagle	.20	.09
351	Sam Militello	.10	.05
352	Eric Fox	.10	.05
353	John Doherty	.10	.05
354	Chad Curtis	.20	.09
355	Jeff Tackett	.10	.05
356	Dave Fleming	.10	.05
357	Pat Listach	.10	.05
358	Kevin Wickander	.10	.05
359	John Vander Wal	.10	.05
360	Arthur Rhodes	.10	.05
361	Bob Scanlan	.10	.05
362	Bob Zupcic	.10	.05
363	Mel Rojas	.10	.05
364	Jim Thome	.50	.23
365	Bill Pecota	.10	.05
366	Mark Carreon	.10	.05
367	Mitch Williams	.10	.05
368	Cal Eldred	.10	.05
369	Stan Belinda	.10	.05
370	Pat Kelly	.10	.05
371	Rheal Cormier	.10	.05
372	Juan Guzman	.10	.05
373	Damon Berryhill	.10	.05
374	Gary DiSarcina	.10	.05
375	Norm Charlton	.10	.05
376	Roberto Hernandez	.20	.09
377	Scott Kamieniecki	.10	.05
378	Rusty Meacham	.10	.05
379	Kurt Stillwell	.10	.05
380	Lloyd McClendon	.10	.05
381	Mark Leonard	.10	.05
382	Jerry Browne	.10	.05
383	Glenn Davis	.10	.05
384	Randy Johnson	.40	.18
385	Mike Greenwell	.10	.05
386	Scott Chiamparino	.10	.05
387	George Bell	.10	.05
388	Steve Olin	.10	.05
389	Chuck McElroy	.10	.05
390	Mark Gardner	.10	.05
391	Rod Beck	.20	.09
392	Dennis Rasmussen	.10	.05
393	Charlie Leibrandt	.10	.05
394	Julio Franco	.10	.05
395	Pete Harnisch	.10	.05
396	Sid Bream	.10	.05
397	Milt Thompson	.10	.05
398	Gienallen Hill	.10	.05
399	Chico Walker	.10	.05
400	Alex Cole	.10	.05
401	Trevor Wilson	.10	.05
402	Jeff Conine	.10	.05
403	Kyle Abbott	.10	.05
404	Tom Browning	.10	.05
405	Jerald Clark	.10	.05
406	Vince Horsman	.10	.05
407	Kevin Mitchell	.20	.09
408	Pete Smith	.10	.05
409	Jeff Innis	.10	.05
410	Mike Timlin	.10	.05
411	Charlie Hayes	.10	.05
412	Alex Fernandez	.20	.09
413	Jeff Russell	.10	.05
414	Jody Reed	.10	.05
415	Mickey Morandini	.10	.05
416	Darnell Coles	.10	.05
417	Xavier Hernandez	.10	.05
418	Steve Sax	.10	.05
419	Joe Girardi	.20	.09
420	Mike Fetters	.10	.05
421	Danny Jackson	.10	.05
422	Jim Gott	.10	.05
423	Tim Belcher	.10	.05
424	Jose Mesa	.10	.05
425	Junior Felix	.10	.05
426	Thomas Howard	.10	.05
427	Julio Valera	.10	.05
428	Dante Bichette	.20	.09
429	Mike Sharperson	.10	.05
430	Darryl Kile	.10	.05
431	Lonnie Smith	.10	.05
432	Monty Fariss	.10	.05
433	Reggie Jefferson	.20	.09
434	Bob McClure	.10	.05
435	Craig Lefferts	.10	.05
436	Duane Ward	.10	.05
437	Shawn Abner	.10	.05
438	Roberto Kelly	.10	.05
439	Paul O'Neill	.20	.09
440	Alan Mills	.10	.05
441	Roger Mason	.10	.05
442	Gary Pettis	.10	.05
443	Steve Lake	.10	.05
444	Gene Larkin	.10	.05
445	Larry Andersen	.10	.05
446	Doug Dascenzo	.10	.05
447	Daryl Boston	.10	.05
448	John Candelaria	.10	.05
449	Storm Davis	.10	.05
450	Tom Edens	.10	.05
451	Mike Maddux	.10	.05
452	Tim Naehring	.10	.05
453	John Orton	.10	.05
454	Joey Cora	.10	.05
455	Chuck Crim	.10	.05
456	Dan Plesac	.10	.05
457	Mike Bielecki	.10	.05
458	Terry Jorgensen	.10	.05
459	John Habyan	.10	.05
460	Pete O'Brien	.10	.05
461	Jeff Treadway	.10	.05
462	Frank Castillo	.10	.05
463	Jimmy Jones	.10	.05
464	Tommy Greene	.10	.05
465	Tracy Woodson	.10	.05
466	Rich Rodriguez	.10	.05
467	Joe Hesketh	.10	.05
468	Greg Myers	.10	.05
469	Kirk McCaskill	.10	.05
470	Ricky Bones	.10	.05
471	Lenny Webster	.10	.05
472	Francisco Cabrera	.10	.05
473	Turner Ward	.10	.05
474	Dwayne Henry	.10	.05
475	Al Osuna	.10	.05
476	Craig Wilson	.10	.05
477	Chris Nabholz	.10	.05
478	Rafael Belliard	.10	.05
479	Terry Leach	.10	.05
480	Tim Teufel	.10	.05
481	Dennis Eckersley AW	.10	.05
482	Barry Bonds AW	.30	.14
483	Dennis Eckersley AW	.10	.05
484	Greg Maddux AW	.50	.23
485	Pat Listach AW	.10	.05
486	Eric Karros AW	.10	.05
487	Jamie Arnold DP	.10	.05
488	B.J. Wallace DP	.10	.05
489	Derek Jeter DP	12.00	5.50
490	Jason Kendall DP	1.25	.55
491	Rick Helling DP	.30	.14
492	Sean Lowe DP	.10	.05
493	Shannon Stewart DP	1.00	.45
494	Benji Grigsby DP	.10	.05
495	Benji Grigsby DP	.10	.05
496	Todd Steverson DP	.10	.05
497	Dan Serafini DP	.10	.05
498	Michael Tucker DP	.40	.18
499	Chris Roberts DP	.10	.05
500	Pete Janicki DP	.10	.05
501	Jeff Schmidt DP	.10	.05
502	Edgar Martinez AS	.20	.09
503	Omar Vizquel AS	.10	.05
504	Ken Griffey Jr. AS	1.00	.45
505	Kirby Puckett AS	.40	.18
506	Joe Carter AS	.10	.05
507	Ivan Rodriguez AS	.30	.14
508	Jack Morris AS	.10	.05
509	Dennis Eckersley AS	.10	.05

☐ 510 Frank Thomas AS	.40	.18
☐ 511 Roberto Alomar AS	.20	.09
☐ 512 Mickey Morandini AS	.10	.05
☐ 513 Dennis Eckersley HL	.10	.05
☐ 514 Jeff Reardon HL	.10	.05
☐ 515 Danny Tartabull HL	.10	.05
☐ 516 Bip Roberts HL	.10	.05
☐ 517 George Brett HL	.40	.18
☐ 518 Robin Yount HL	.30	.14
☐ 519 Kevin Gross HL	.10	.05
☐ 520 Ed Sprague WS	.10	.05
☐ 521 Dave Winfield WS	.20	.09
☐ 522 Ozzie Smith AS	.30	.14
☐ 523 Barry Bonds AS	.40	.18
☐ 524 Andy Van Slyke AS	.10	.05
☐ 525 Tony Gwynn AS	.50	.23
☐ 526 Darren Daulton AS	.10	.05
☐ 527 Greg Maddux AS	.50	.23
☐ 528 Fred McGriff AS	.30	.14
☐ 529 Lee Smith AS	.10	.05
☐ 530 Ryne Sandberg AS	.30	.14
☐ 531 Gary Sheffield AS	.20	.09
☐ 532 Ozzie Smith DT	.30	.14
☐ 533 Kirby Puckett DT	.40	.18
☐ 534 Gary Sheffield DT	.20	.09
☐ 535 Andy Van Slyke DT	.10	.05
☐ 536 Ken Griffey Jr. DT	1.00	.45
☐ 537 Ivan Rodriguez DT	.30	.14
☐ 538 Charles Nagy DT	.10	.05
☐ 539 Tom Glavine DT	.20	.09
☐ 540 Dennis Eckersley DT	.10	.05
☐ 541 Frank Thomas DT	.40	.18
☐ 542 Roberto Alomar DT	.20	.09
☐ 543 Sean Berry	.10	.05
☐ 544 Mike Schooler	.10	.05
☐ 545 Chuck Carr	.10	.05
☐ 546 Lenny Harris	.10	.05
☐ 547 Gary Scott	.10	.05
☐ 548 Derek Lilliquist	.10	.05
☐ 549 Brian Hunter	.10	.05
☐ 550 Kirby Puckett MOY	.40	.18
☐ 551 Jim Eisenreich	.10	.05
☐ 552 Andre Dawson	.30	.14
☐ 553 David Nied	.10	.05
☐ 554 Spike Owen	.10	.05
☐ 555 Greg Gagne	.10	.05
☐ 556 Sid Fernandez	.10	.05
☐ 557 Mark McGwire	2.00	.90
☐ 558 Bryan Harvey	.10	.05
☐ 559 Harold Reynolds	.10	.05
☐ 560 Barry Bonds	.50	.23
☐ 561 Eric Wedge	.10	.05
☐ 562 Ozzie Smith	.50	.23
☐ 563 Rick Sutcliffe	.10	.05
☐ 564 Jeff Reardon	.20	.09
☐ 565 Alex Arias	.10	.05
☐ 566 Greg Swindell	.10	.05
☐ 567 Brook Jacoby	.10	.05
☐ 568 Pete Incaviglia	.10	.05
☐ 569 Butch Henry	.10	.05
☐ 570 Eric Davis	.20	.09
☐ 571 Kevin Seitzer	.10	.05
☐ 572 Tony Fernandez	.20	.09
☐ 573 Steve Reed	.10	.05
☐ 574 Cory Snyder	.10	.05
☐ 575 Joe Carter	.20	.09
☐ 576 Greg Maddux	1.00	.45
☐ 577 Bert Blyleven UER	.20	.09
(Should say 3701		
career strikeouts)		
☐ 578 Kevin Bass	.10	.05
☐ 579 Carlton Fisk	.40	.18
☐ 580 Doug Drabek	.10	.05
☐ 581 Mark Gubicza	.10	.05
☐ 582 Bobby Thigpen	.10	.05
☐ 583 Chili Davis	.20	.09
☐ 584 Scott Bankhead	.10	.05
☐ 585 Harold Baines	.20	.09
☐ 586 Eric Young	.40	.18
☐ 587 Lance Parrish	.10	.05
☐ 588 Juan Bell	.10	.05
☐ 589 Bob Ojeda	.10	.05
☐ 590 Joe Orsulak	.10	.05
☐ 591 Benito Santiago	.20	.09
☐ 592 Wade Boggs	.40	.18
☐ 593 Robby Thompson	.10	.05

☐ 594 Eric Plunk	.10	.05
☐ 595 Hensley Meulens	.10	.05
☐ 596 Lou Whitaker	.20	.09
☐ 597 Dale Murphy	.30	.14
☐ 598 Paul Molitor	.40	.18
☐ 599 Greg W. Harris	.10	.05
☐ 600 Darren Holmes	.10	.05
☐ 601 Dave Martinez	.10	.05
☐ 602 Tom Henke	.10	.05
☐ 603 Mike Benjamin	.10	.05
☐ 604 Rene Gonzales	.10	.05
☐ 605 Roger McDowell	.10	.05
☐ 606 Kirby Puckett	.60	.25
☐ 607 Randy Myers	.20	.09
☐ 608 Ruben Sierra	.20	.09
☐ 609 Wilson Alvarez	.20	.09
☐ 610 David Segui	.10	.05
☐ 611 Juan Samuel	.10	.05
☐ 612 Tom Brunansky	.10	.05
☐ 613 Willie Randolph	.20	.09
☐ 614 Tony Phillips	.10	.05
☐ 615 Candy Maldonado	.10	.05
☐ 616 Chris Bosio	.10	.05
☐ 617 Bret Barberie	.10	.05
☐ 618 Scott Sanderson	.10	.05
☐ 619 Ron Darling	.10	.05
☐ 620 Dave Winfield	.30	.14
☐ 621 Mike Felder	.10	.05
☐ 622 Greg Harris	.10	.05
☐ 623 Mike Scioscia	.10	.05
☐ 624 John Smiley	.10	.05
☐ 625 Alejandro Pena	.10	.05
☐ 626 Terry Steinbach	.10	.05
☐ 627 Freddie Benavides	.10	.05
☐ 628 Kevin Reimer	.10	.05
☐ 629 Braulio Castillo	.10	.05
☐ 630 Dave Stieb	.10	.05
☐ 631 Dave Magadan	.10	.05
☐ 632 Scott Fletcher	.10	.05
☐ 633 Cris Carpenter	.10	.05
☐ 634 Kevin Maas	.10	.05
☐ 635 Todd Worrell	.10	.05
☐ 636 Rob Deer	.10	.05
☐ 637 Dwight Smith	.10	.05
☐ 638 Chito Martinez	.10	.05
☐ 639 Jimmy Key	.20	.09
☐ 640 Greg A. Harris	.10	.05
☐ 641 Mike Moore	.10	.05
☐ 642 Pat Borders	.10	.05
☐ 643 Bill Gullickson	.10	.05
☐ 644 Gary Gaetti	.20	.09
☐ 645 David Howard	.10	.05
☐ 646 Jim Abbott	.20	.09
☐ 647 Willie Wilson	.10	.05
☐ 648 David Wells	.10	.05
☐ 649 Andres Galarraga	.40	.18
☐ 650 Vince Coleman	.10	.05
☐ 651 Rob Dibble	.10	.05
☐ 652 Frank Tanana	.10	.05
☐ 653 Steve Decker	.10	.05
☐ 654 David Cone	.30	.14
☐ 655 Jack Armstrong	.20	.09
☐ 656 Dave Stewart	.20	.09
☐ 657 Billy Hatcher	.10	.05
☐ 658 Tim Raines	.20	.09
☐ 659 Walt Weiss	.10	.05
☐ 660 Jose Lind	.10	.05

1993 Score Boys of Summer

	MINT	NRMT
COMPLETE SET (30)	50.00	22.00
COMMON CARD (1-30)	1.90	.85
MINOR STARS	2.00	.90
RANDOM INSERTS IN JUMBO PACKS		
☐ 1 Billy Ashley	1.00	.45
☐ 2 Tim Salmon	5.00	2.20
☐ 3 Pedro Martinez	15.00	6.75
☐ 4 Luis Mercedes	1.00	.45
☐ 5 Mike Piazza	30.00	13.50
☐ 6 Troy Neel	1.00	.45
☐ 7 Melvin Nieves	1.00	.45
☐ 8 Ryan Klesko	4.00	1.80

☐ 9 Ryan Thompson	1.00	.45
☐ 10 Kevin Young	2.00	.90
☐ 11 Gerald Williams	1.00	.45
☐ 12 Willie Greene	1.00	.45
☐ 13 John Patterson	1.00	.45
☐ 14 Carlos Garcia	1.00	.45
☐ 15 Ed Zosky	1.00	.45
☐ 16 Sean Berry	1.00	.45
☐ 17 Rico Brogna	2.00	.90
☐ 18 Larry Carter	1.00	.45
☐ 19 Bobby Ayala	1.00	.45
☐ 20 Alan Embree	1.00	.45
☐ 21 Donald Harris	1.00	.45
☐ 22 Sterling Hitchcock	1.50	.70
☐ 23 David Nied	1.00	.45
☐ 24 Henry Mercedes	1.00	.45
☐ 25 Ozzie Canseco	1.00	.45
☐ 26 David Hulse	1.00	.45
☐ 27 Al Martin	1.00	.45
☐ 28 Dan Wilson	2.00	.90
☐ 29 Paul Miller	1.00	.45
☐ 30 Rich Rowland	1.00	.45

1993 Score Franchise

	MINT	NRMT
COMPLETE SET (28)	120.00	55.00
COMMON CARD (1-660)	1.50	.70
STATED ODDS 1:24		
☐ 1 Cal Ripken	25.00	11.00
☐ 2 Roger Clemens	15.00	6.75
☐ 3 Mark Langston	1.50	.70
☐ 4 Frank Thomas	15.00	6.75
☐ 5 Carlos Baerga	1.50	.70
☐ 6 Cecil Fielder	2.50	1.10
☐ 7 Gregg Jefferies	1.50	.70
☐ 8 Robin Yount	4.00	1.80
☐ 9 Kirby Puckett	10.00	4.50
☐ 10 Don Mattingly	10.00	4.50
☐ 11 Dennis Eckersley	2.50	1.10
☐ 12 Ken Griffey Jr.	30.00	13.50
☐ 13 Juan Gonzalez	15.00	6.75
☐ 14 Roberto Alomar	6.00	2.70
☐ 15 Terry Pendleton	1.50	.70
☐ 16 Ryne Sandberg	6.00	2.70
☐ 17 Barry Larkin	6.00	2.70
☐ 18 Jeff Bagwell	6.00	2.70
☐ 19 Brett Butler	2.50	1.10
☐ 20 Larry Walker	6.00	2.70
☐ 21 Bobby Bonilla	2.50	1.10

❏ 22 Darren Daulton	2.50	1.10
❏ 23 Andy Van Slyke	1.50	.70
❏ 24 Ray Lankford	4.00	1.80
❏ 25 Gary Sheffield	6.00	2.70
❏ 26 Will Clark	6.00	2.70
❏ 27 Bryan Harvey	1.50	.70
❏ 28 David Nied	1.50	.70

1993 Score Gold Dream Team

	MINT	NRMT
COMPLETE SET (12)	5.00	2.20
COMMON CARD (1-12)	.20	.09

SETS DISTRIBUTED VIA MAIL-IN OFFER

❏ 1 Ozzie Smith	.50	.23
❏ 2 Kirby Puckett	.60	.25
❏ 3 Gary Sheffield		.18
❏ 4 Andy Van Slyke	.20	.09
❏ 5 Ken Griffey Jr.	2.00	.90
❏ 6 Ivan Rodriguez	.50	.23
❏ 7 Charles Nagy	.20	.09
❏ 8 Tom Glavine	.30	.14
❏ 9 Dennis Eckersley	.20	.09
❏ 10 Frank Thomas	.75	.35
❏ 11 Roberto Alomar	.40	.18
❏ NNO Header Card	1.00	.45

1994 Score

	MINT	NRMT
COMPLETE SET (660)	24.00	11.00
COMPLETE SERIES 1 (330)	12.00	5.50
COMPLETE SERIES 2 (330)	12.00	5.50
COMMON CARD (1-660)	.10	.05
MINOR STARS	.20	.09
UNLISTED STARS	.40	.18

SUBSET CARDS HALF VALUE OF BASE CARDS

COMP.G.RUSH SET (660)	160.00	70.00
COMP.G.RUSH SER.1 (330)	80.00	36.00
COMP.G.RUSH SER.2 (330)	80.00	36.00
COMMON G.RUSH (1-660)	.25	.11
*G.RUSH STARS: 1.5X TO 4X HI COLUMN		
*G.RUSH YOUNG STARS: 1.25X TO 3X HI		
ONE GOLD RUSH PER PACK		

❏ 1 Barry Bonds		.23
❏ 2 John Olerud	.20	.09

❏ 3 Ken Griffey Jr.	2.00	.90
❏ 4 Jeff Bagwell	.50	.23
❏ 5 John Burkett	.10	.05
❏ 6 Jack McDowell	.10	.05
❏ 7 Albert Belle	.40	.18
❏ 8 Andres Galarraga	.40	.18
❏ 9 Mike Mussina	.40	.18
❏ 10 Will Clark	.40	.18
❏ 11 Travis Fryman	.20	.09
❏ 12 Tony Gwynn	1.00	.45
❏ 13 Robin Yount	.40	.18
❏ 14 Dave Magadan	.10	.05
❏ 15 Paul O'Neill	.20	.09
❏ 16 Ray Lankford	.20	.09
❏ 17 Damion Easley	.20	.09
❏ 18 Andy Van Slyke	.20	.09
❏ 19 Brian McRae	.10	.05
❏ 20 Ryne Sandberg	.50	.23
❏ 21 Kirby Puckett	.60	.25
❏ 22 Dwight Gooden	.20	.09
❏ 23 Don Mattingly	.75	.35
❏ 24 Kevin Mitchell	.10	.05
❏ 25 Roger Clemens	1.00	.45
❏ 26 Eric Karros	.20	.09
❏ 27 Juan Gonzalez	.75	.35
❏ 28 John Kruk	.20	.09
❏ 29 Gregg Jefferies	.10	.05
❏ 30 Tom Glavine	.20	.09
❏ 31 Ivan Rodriguez	.50	.23
❏ 32 Jay Bell	.20	.09
❏ 33 Randy Johnson	.40	.18
❏ 34 Darren Daulton	.20	.09
❏ 35 Rickey Henderson	.50	.23
❏ 36 Eddie Murray	.40	.18
❏ 37 Brian Harper	.10	.05
❏ 38 Delino DeShields	.10	.05
❏ 39 Jose Lind	.10	.05
❏ 40 Benito Santiago	.10	.05
❏ 41 Frank Thomas	.75	.35
❏ 42 Mark Grace	.30	.14
❏ 43 Roberto Alomar	.40	.18
❏ 44 Andy Benes	.20	.09
❏ 45 Luis Polonia	.10	.05
❏ 46 Brett Butler	.20	.09
❏ 47 Terry Steinbach	.10	.05
❏ 48 Craig Biggio	.40	.18
❏ 49 Greg Vaughn	.20	.09
❏ 50 Charlie Hayes	.10	.05
❏ 51 Mickey Tettleton	.10	.05
❏ 52 Jose Rijo	.10	.05
❏ 53 Carlos Baerga	.20	.09
❏ 54 Jeff Blauser	.10	.05
❏ 55 Leo Gomez	.10	.05
❏ 56 Bob Tewksbury	.10	.05
❏ 57 Mo Vaughn	.40	.18
❏ 58 Orlando Merced	.10	.05
❏ 59 Tino Martinez	.40	.18
❏ 60 Lenny Dykstra	.20	.09
❏ 61 Jose Canseco	.50	.23
❏ 62 Tony Fernandez	.10	.05
❏ 63 Donovan Osborne	.10	.05
❏ 64 Ken Hill	.10	.05
❏ 65 Kent Hrbek	.20	.09
❏ 66 Bryan Harvey	.10	.05
❏ 67 Wally Joyner	.20	.09
❏ 68 Derrick May	.10	.05
❏ 69 Lance Johnson	.10	.05
❏ 70 Willie McGee	.20	.09
❏ 71 Mark Langston	.10	.05
❏ 72 Terry Pendleton	.10	.05
❏ 73 Joe Carter	.20	.09
❏ 74 Barry Larkin	.40	.18
❏ 75 Jimmy Key	.10	.05
❏ 76 Joe Girardi	.10	.05
❏ 77 B.J. Surhoff	.10	.05
❏ 78 Pete Harnisch	.10	.05
❏ 79 Lou Whitaker UER	.20	.09
(Milt Cuyler pictured on front)		

❏ 80 Cory Snyder	.10	.05
❏ 81 Kenny Lofton	.40	.18
❏ 82 Fred McGriff	.30	.14
❏ 83 Mike Greenwell	.10	.05
❏ 84 Mike Perez	.10	.05
❏ 85 Cal Ripken	1.50	.70
❏ 86 Don Slaught	.10	.05

❏ 87 Omar Vizquel	.20	.09
❏ 88 Curt Schilling	.20	.09
❏ 89 Chuck Knoblauch	.40	.18
❏ 90 Moises Alou	.20	.09
❏ 91 Greg Gagne	.10	.05
❏ 92 Bret Saberhagen	.20	.09
❏ 93 Ozzie Guillen	.10	.05
❏ 94 Matt Williams	.30	.14
❏ 95 Chad Curtis	.10	.05
❏ 96 Mike Harkey	.10	.05
❏ 97 Devon White	.10	.05
❏ 98 Walt Weiss	.10	.05
❏ 99 Kevin Brown	.20	.09
❏ 100 Gary Sheffield	.40	.18
❏ 101 Wade Boggs	.40	.18
❏ 102 Orel Hershiser	.10	.05
❏ 103 Tony Phillips	.10	.05
❏ 104 Andujar Cedeno	.10	.05
❏ 105 Bill Spiers	.10	.05
❏ 106 Otis Nixon	.10	.05
❏ 107 Felix Fermin	.10	.05
❏ 108 Bip Roberts	.10	.05
❏ 109 Dennis Eckersley	.20	.09
❏ 110 Dante Bichette	.20	.09
❏ 111 Ben McDonald	.10	.05
❏ 112 Jim Poole	.10	.05
❏ 113 John Dopson	.10	.05
❏ 114 Rob Dibble	.10	.05
❏ 115 Jeff Treadway	.10	.05
❏ 116 Ricky Jordan	.10	.05
❏ 117 Mike Henneman	.10	.05
❏ 118 Willie Blair	.10	.05
❏ 119 Doug Henry	.10	.05
❏ 120 Gerald Perry	.10	.05
❏ 121 Greg Myers	.10	.05
❏ 122 John Franco	.20	.09
❏ 123 Roger Mason	.10	.05
❏ 124 Chris Hammond	.10	.05
❏ 125 Hubie Brooks	.10	.05
❏ 126 Kent Mercker	.10	.05
❏ 127 Jim Abbott	.20	.09
❏ 128 Kevin Bass	.10	.05
❏ 129 Rick Aguilera	.10	.05
❏ 130 Mitch Webster	.10	.05
❏ 131 Eric Plunk	.10	.05
❏ 132 Mark Carreon	.10	.05
❏ 133 Dave Stewart	.20	.09
❏ 134 Willie Wilson	.10	.05
❏ 135 Dave Fleming	.10	.05
❏ 136 Jeff Tackett	.10	.05
❏ 137 Geno Petralli	.10	.05
❏ 138 Gene Harris	.10	.05
❏ 139 Scott Bankhead	.10	.05
❏ 140 Trevor Wilson	.10	.05
❏ 141 Alvaro Espinoza	.10	.05
❏ 142 Ryan Bowen	.10	.05
❏ 143 Mike Moore	.10	.05
❏ 144 Bill Pecota	.10	.05
❏ 145 Jaime Navarro	.10	.05
❏ 146 Jack Daugherty	.10	.05
❏ 147 Bob Wickman	.10	.05
❏ 148 Chris Jones	.10	.05
❏ 149 Todd Stottlemyre	.10	.05
❏ 150 Brian Williams	.10	.05
❏ 151 Chuck Finley	.20	.09
❏ 152 Lenny Harris	.10	.05
❏ 153 Alex Fernandez	.10	.05
❏ 154 Candy Maldonado	.10	.05
❏ 155 Jeff Montgomery	.10	.05
❏ 156 David West	.10	.05
❏ 157 Mark Williamson	.10	.05
❏ 158 Milt Thompson	.10	.05
❏ 159 Ron Darling	.10	.05
❏ 160 Stan Belinda	.10	.05
❏ 161 Henry Cotto	.10	.05
❏ 162 Mel Rojas	.10	.05
❏ 163 Doug Strange	.10	.05
❏ 164 Rene Arocha	.10	.05
❏ 165 Tim Hulett	.10	.05
❏ 166 Steve Avery	.30	.14
❏ 167 Jim Thome	.40	.18
❏ 168 Tom Browning	.10	.05
❏ 169 Mario Diaz	.10	.05
❏ 170 Steve Reed	.10	.05
❏ 171 Scott Livingstone	.10	.05
❏ 172 Chris Donnels	.10	.05

❏ 173	John Jaha	.10	.05
❏ 174	Carlos Hernandez	.10	.05
❏ 175	Dion James	.10	.05
❏ 176	Bud Black	.10	.05
❏ 177	Tony Castillo	.10	.05
❏ 178	Jose Guzman	.10	.05
❏ 179	Torey Lovullo	.10	.05
❏ 180	John Vander Wal	.10	.05
❏ 181	Mike LaValliere	.10	.05
❏ 182	Sid Fernandez	.10	.05
❏ 183	Brent Mayne	.10	.05
❏ 184	Terry Mulholland	.10	.05
❏ 185	Willie Banks	.10	.05
❏ 186	Steve Cooke	.10	.05
❏ 187	Brent Gates	.10	.05
❏ 188	Erik Pappas	.10	.05
❏ 189	Bill Haselman	.10	.05
❏ 190	Fernando Valenzuela	.20	.09
❏ 191	Gary Redus	.10	.05
❏ 192	Danny Darwin	.10	.05
❏ 193	Mark Portugal	.10	.05
❏ 194	Derek Lilliquist	.10	.05
❏ 195	Charlie O'Brien	.10	.05
❏ 196	Matt Nokes	.10	.05
❏ 197	Danny Sheaffer	.10	.05
❏ 198	Bill Gullickson	.10	.05
❏ 199	Alex Arias	.10	.05
❏ 200	Mike Fetters	.10	.05
❏ 201	Brian Jordan	.20	.09
❏ 202	Joe Grahe	.10	.05
❏ 203	Tom Candiotti	.10	.05
❏ 204	Jeremy Hernandez	.10	.05
❏ 205	Mike Stanton	.10	.05
❏ 206	David Howard	.10	.05
❏ 207	Darren Holmes	.10	.05
❏ 208	Rick Honeycutt	.10	.05
❏ 209	Danny Jackson	.10	.05
❏ 210	Rich Amaral	.10	.05
❏ 211	Blas Minor	.10	.05
❏ 212	Kenny Rogers	.10	.05
❏ 213	Jim Leyritz	.20	.09
❏ 214	Mike Morgan	.10	.05
❏ 215	Dan Gladden	.10	.05
❏ 216	Randy Velarde	.10	.05
❏ 217	Mitch Williams	.10	.05
❏ 218	Hipolito Pichardo	.10	.05
❏ 219	Dave Burba	.10	.05
❏ 220	Wilson Alvarez	.10	.05
❏ 221	Bob Zupcic	.10	.05
❏ 222	Francisco Cabrera	.10	.05
❏ 223	Julio Valera	.10	.05
❏ 224	Paul Assenmacher	.10	.05
❏ 225	Jeff Branson	.10	.05
❏ 226	Todd Frohwirth	.10	.05
❏ 227	Armando Reynoso	.10	.05
❏ 228	Rich Rowland	.10	.05
❏ 229	Freddie Benavides	.10	.05
❏ 230	Wayne Kirby	.10	.05
❏ 231	Darryl Kile	.10	.05
❏ 232	Skeeter Barnes	.10	.05
❏ 233	Ramon Martinez	.20	.09
❏ 234	Tom Gordon	.10	.05
❏ 235	Dave Gallagher	.10	.05
❏ 236	Ricky Bones	.10	.05
❏ 237	Larry Andersen	.10	.05
❏ 238	Pat Meares	.10	.05
❏ 239	Zane Smith	.10	.05
❏ 240	Tim Leary	.10	.05
❏ 241	Phil Clark	.10	.05
❏ 242	Danny Cox	.10	.05
❏ 243	Mike Jackson	.20	.09
❏ 244	Mike Gallego	.10	.05
❏ 245	Lee Smith	.10	.05
❏ 246	Todd Jones	.10	.05
❏ 247	Steve Bedrosian	.10	.05
❏ 248	Troy Neel	.10	.05
❏ 249	Jose Bautista	.10	.05
❏ 250	Steve Frey	.10	.05
❏ 251	Jeff Reardon	.20	.09
❏ 252	Stan Javier	.10	.05
❏ 253	Mo Sanford	.10	.05
❏ 254	Steve Sax	.10	.05
❏ 255	Luis Aquino	.10	.05
❏ 256	Domingo Jean	.10	.05
❏ 257	Scott Servais	.10	.05
❏ 258	Brad Pennington	.10	.05

❏ 259	Dave Hansen	.10	.05
❏ 260	Rich Gossage	.20	.09
❏ 261	Jeff Fassero	.10	.05
❏ 262	Junior Ortiz	.10	.05
❏ 263	Anthony Young	.10	.05
❏ 264	Chris Bosio	.10	.05
❏ 265	Ruben Amaro	.10	.05
❏ 266	Mark Eichhorn	.10	.05
❏ 267	Dave Clark	.10	.05
❏ 268	Gary Thurman	.10	.05
❏ 269	Les Lancaster	.10	.05
❏ 270	Jamie Moyer	.10	.05
❏ 271	Ricky Gutierrez	.10	.05
❏ 272	Greg A. Harris	.10	.05
❏ 273	Mike Benjamin	.10	.05
❏ 274	Gene Nelson	.10	.05
❏ 275	Damon Berryhill	.10	.05
❏ 276	Scott Radinsky	.10	.05
❏ 277	Mike Aldrete	.10	.05
❏ 278	Jerry DiPoto	.10	.05
❏ 279	Chris Haney	.10	.05
❏ 280	Richie Lewis	.10	.05
❏ 281	Jarvis Brown	.10	.05
❏ 282	Juan Bell	.10	.05
❏ 283	Joe Klink	.10	.05
❏ 284	Graeme Lloyd	.10	.05
❏ 285	Casey Candaele	.10	.05
❏ 286	Bob MacDonald	.10	.05
❏ 287	Mike Sharperson	.10	.05
❏ 288	Gene Larkin	.10	.05
❏ 289	Brian Barnes	.10	.05
❏ 290	David McCarty	.10	.05
❏ 291	Jeff Innis	.10	.05
❏ 292	Bob Patterson	.10	.05
❏ 293	Ben Rivera	.10	.05
❏ 294	John Habyan	.10	.05
❏ 295	Rich Rodriguez	.10	.05
❏ 296	Edwin Nunez	.10	.05
❏ 297	Rod Brewer	.10	.05
❏ 298	Mike Timlin	.10	.05
❏ 299	Jesse Orosco	.10	.05
❏ 300	Gary Gaetti	.20	.09
❏ 301	Todd Benzinger	.10	.05
❏ 302	Jeff Nelson	.10	.05
❏ 303	Rafael Belliard	.10	.05
❏ 304	Matt Whiteside	.10	.05
❏ 305	Vinny Castilla	.20	.09
❏ 306	Matt Turner	.10	.05
❏ 307	Eduardo Perez	.10	.05
❏ 308	Joel Johnston	.10	.05
❏ 309	Chris Gomez	.10	.05
❏ 310	Pat Rapp	.10	.05
❏ 311	Jim Tatum	.10	.05
❏ 312	Kirk Rueter	.10	.05
❏ 313	John Flaherty	.10	.05
❏ 314	Tom Kramer	.10	.05
❏ 315	Mark Whiten	.10	.05
❏ 316	Chris Bosio	.10	.05
❏ 317	Baltimore Orioles CL	.10	.05
❏ 318	Boston Red Sox CL UER	.10	.05
	(Viola listed as 316; should be 331)		
❏ 319	California Angels CL	.10	.05
❏ 320	Chicago White Sox CL	.10	.05
❏ 321	Cleveland Indians CL	.10	.05
❏ 322	Detroit Tigers CL	.10	.05
❏ 323	Kansas City Royals CL	.10	.05
❏ 324	Milwaukee Brewers CL	.10	.05
❏ 325	Minnesota Twins CL	.10	.05
❏ 326	New York Yankees CL	.10	.05
❏ 327	Oakland Athletics CL	.10	.05
❏ 328	Seattle Mariners CL	.10	.05
❏ 329	Texas Rangers CL	.10	.05
❏ 330	Toronto Blue Jays CL	.10	.05
❏ 331	Frank Viola	.10	.05
❏ 332	Ron Gant	.20	.09
❏ 333	Charles Nagy	.20	.09
❏ 334	Roberto Kelly	.10	.05
❏ 335	Brady Anderson	.20	.09
❏ 336	Alex Cole	.10	.05
❏ 337	Alan Trammell	.30	.14
❏ 338	Derek Bell	.20	.09
❏ 339	Bernie Williams	.40	.18
❏ 340	Jose Offerman	.10	.05
❏ 341	Bill Wegman	.10	.05
❏ 342	Ken Caminiti	.30	.14

❏ 343	Pat Borders	.10	.05
❏ 344	Kirt Manwaring	.10	.05
❏ 345	Chili Davis	.20	.09
❏ 346	Steve Buechele	.10	.05
❏ 347	Robin Ventura	.20	.09
❏ 348	Teddy Higuera	.10	.05
❏ 349	Jerry Browne	.10	.05
❏ 350	Scott Kamieniecki	.10	.05
❏ 351	Kevin Tapani	.10	.05
❏ 352	Marquis Grissom	.20	.09
❏ 353	Jay Buhner	.20	.09
❏ 354	Dave Hollins	.10	.05
❏ 355	Dan Wilson	.10	.05
❏ 356	Bob Walk	.10	.05
❏ 357	Chris Hoiles	.10	.05
❏ 358	Todd Zeile	.10	.05
❏ 359	Kevin Appier	.20	.09
❏ 360	Chris Sabo	.10	.05
❏ 361	David Segui	.10	.05
❏ 362	Jerald Clark	.10	.05
❏ 363	Tony Pena	.10	.05
❏ 364	Steve Finley	.20	.09
❏ 365	Roger Pavlik	.10	.05
❏ 366	John Smoltz	.30	.14
❏ 367	Scott Fletcher	.10	.05
❏ 368	Jody Reed	.10	.05
❏ 369	David Wells	.30	.14
❏ 370	Jose Vizcaino	.10	.05
❏ 371	Pat Listach	.10	.05
❏ 372	Orestes Destrade	.10	.05
❏ 373	Danny Tartabull	.10	.05
❏ 374	Greg W. Harris	.10	.05
❏ 375	Juan Guzman	.10	.05
❏ 376	Larry Walker	.40	.18
❏ 377	Gary DiSarcina	.10	.05
❏ 378	Bobby Bonilla	.20	.09
❏ 379	Tim Raines	.20	.09
❏ 380	Tommy Greene	.10	.05
❏ 381	Chris Gwynn	.10	.05
❏ 382	Jeff King	.10	.05
❏ 383	Shane Mack	.10	.05
❏ 384	Ozzie Smith	.50	.23
❏ 385	Eddie Zambrano	.10	.05
❏ 386	Mike Devereaux	.10	.05
❏ 387	Erik Hanson	.10	.05
❏ 388	Scott Cooper	.10	.05
❏ 389	Dean Palmer	.20	.09
❏ 390	John Wetteland	.20	.09
❏ 391	Reggie Jefferson	.10	.05
❏ 392	Mark Lemke	.10	.05
❏ 393	Cecil Fielder	.20	.09
❏ 394	Reggie Sanders	.20	.09
❏ 395	Darryl Hamilton	.10	.05
❏ 396	Daryl Boston	.10	.05
❏ 397	Pat Kelly	.10	.05
❏ 398	Joe Orsulak	.10	.05
❏ 399	Ed Sprague	.10	.05
❏ 400	Eric Anthony	.10	.05
❏ 401	Scott Sanderson	.10	.05
❏ 402	Jim Gott	.10	.05
❏ 403	Ron Karkovice	.10	.05
❏ 404	Phil Plantier	.10	.05
❏ 405	David Cone	.30	.14
❏ 406	Robby Thompson	.10	.05
❏ 407	Dave Winfield	.40	.18
❏ 408	Dwight Smith	.10	.05
❏ 409	Ruben Sierra	.20	.09
❏ 410	Jack Armstrong	.10	.05
❏ 411	Mike Felder	.10	.05
❏ 412	Wil Cordero	.10	.05
❏ 413	Julio Franco	.10	.05
❏ 414	Howard Johnson	.10	.05
❏ 415	Mark McLemore	.10	.05
❏ 416	Pete Incaviglia	.10	.05
❏ 417	John Valentin	.20	.09
❏ 418	Tim Wakefield	.20	.09
❏ 419	Jose Mesa	.10	.05
❏ 420	Bernard Gilkey	.10	.05
❏ 421	Kirk Gibson	.20	.09
❏ 422	Dave Justice	.40	.18
❏ 423	Tom Brunansky	.20	.09
❏ 424	John Smiley	.10	.05
❏ 425	Kevin Maas	.10	.05
❏ 426	Doug Drabek	.10	.05
❏ 427	Paul Molitor	.40	.18
❏ 428	Darryl Strawberry	.20	.09

		MINT	NRMT
❏ 429	Tim Naehring	.10	.05
❏ 430	Bill Swift	.10	.05
❏ 431	Ellis Burks	.20	.09
❏ 432	Greg Hibbard	.10	.05
❏ 433	Felix Jose	.10	.05
❏ 434	Bret Barberie	.10	.05
❏ 435	Pedro Munoz	.10	.05
❏ 436	Darrin Fletcher	.10	.05
❏ 437	Bobby Witt	.10	.05
❏ 438	Wes Chamberlain	.10	.05
❏ 439	Mackey Sasser	.05	
❏ 440	Mark Whiten	.10	.05
❏ 441	Harold Reynolds	.10	.05
❏ 442	Greg Olson	.10	.05
❏ 443	Billy Hatcher	.10	.05
❏ 444	Joe Oliver	.10	.05
❏ 445	Sandy Alomar Jr.	.20	.09
❏ 446	Tim Wallach	.10	.05
❏ 447	Karl Rhodes	.10	.05
❏ 448	Royce Clayton	.10	.05
❏ 449	Cal Eldred	.10	.05
❏ 450	Rick Wilkins	.10	.05
❏ 451	Mike Stanley	.10	.05
❏ 452	Charlie Hough	.10	.05
❏ 453	Jack Morris	.20	.09
❏ 454	Jon Ratliff	.10	.05
❏ 455	Rene Gonzales	.10	.05
❏ 456	Eddie Taubensee	.10	.05
❏ 457	Roberto Hernandez	.10	.05
❏ 458	Todd Hundley	.20	.09
❏ 459	Mike Macfarlane	.10	.05
❏ 460	Mickey Morandini	.10	.05
❏ 461	Scott Erickson	.20	.09
❏ 462	Lonnie Smith	.10	.05
❏ 463	Dave Henderson	.10	.05
❏ 464	Ryan Klesko	.20	.09
❏ 465	Edgar Martinez	.20	.09
❏ 466	Tom Pagnozzi	.10	.05
❏ 467	Charlie Leibrandt	.10	.05
❏ 468	Brian Anderson	.30	.14
❏ 469	Harold Baines	.20	.09
❏ 470	Tim Belcher	.10	.05
❏ 471	Andre Dawson	.30	.14
❏ 472	Eric Young	.10	.05
❏ 473	Paul Sorrento	.10	.05
❏ 474	Luis Gonzalez	.20	.09
❏ 475	Rob Deer	.10	.05
❏ 476	Mike Piazza	1.25	.55
❏ 477	Kevin Reimer	.10	.05
❏ 478	Jeff Gardner	.10	.05
❏ 479	Melido Perez	.10	.05
❏ 480	Darren Lewis	.10	.05
❏ 481	Duane Ward	.10	.05
❏ 482	Rey Sanchez	.10	.05
❏ 483	Mark Lewis	.10	.05
❏ 484	Jeff Conine	.10	.05
❏ 485	Joey Cora	.10	.05
❏ 486	Trot Nixon	.75	.35
❏ 487	Kevin McReynolds	.10	.05
❏ 488	Mike Lansing	.20	.09
❏ 489	Mike Pagliarulo	.10	.05
❏ 490	Mariano Duncan	.10	.05
❏ 491	Mike Bordick	.10	.05
❏ 492	Kevin Young	.10	.05
❏ 493	Dave Valle	.10	.05
❏ 494	Wayne Gomes	.10	.05
❏ 495	Rafael Palmeiro	.40	.18
❏ 496	Deion Sanders	.20	.09
❏ 497	Rick Sutcliffe	.10	.05
❏ 498	Randy Milligan	.10	.05
❏ 499	Carlos Quintana	.10	.05
❏ 500	Chris Turner	.10	.05
❏ 501	Thomas Howard	.10	.05
❏ 502	Greg Swindell	.10	.05
❏ 503	Chad Kreuter	.10	.05
❏ 504	Eric Davis	.20	.09
❏ 505	Dickie Thon	.10	.05
❏ 506	Matt Drews	.20	.09
❏ 507	Spike Owen	.10	.05
❏ 508	Rod Beck	.10	.05
❏ 509	Pat Hentgen	.20	.09
❏ 510	Sammy Sosa	1.25	.55
❏ 511	J.T. Snow	.20	.09
❏ 512	Chuck Carr	.10	.05
❏ 513	Bo Jackson	.20	.09
❏ 514	Dennis Martinez	.20	.09
❏ 515	Phil Hiatt	.10	.05
❏ 516	Jeff Kent	.20	.09
❏ 517	Brooks Kieschnick	.10	.05
❏ 518	Kirk Presley	.10	.05
❏ 519	Kevin Seitzer	.10	.05
❏ 520	Carlos Garcia	.10	.05
❏ 521	Mike Blowers	.10	.05
❏ 522	Luis Alicea	.10	.05
❏ 523	David Hulse	.10	.05
❏ 524	Greg Maddux UER	1.00	.45
	(career strikeout totals listed		
	as 113; should be 1134)		
❏ 525	Gregg Olson	.10	.05
❏ 526	Hal Morris	.10	.05
❏ 527	Daron Kirkreit	.10	.05
❏ 528	David Nied	.10	.05
❏ 529	Jeff Russell	.10	.05
❏ 530	Kevin Gross	.10	.05
❏ 531	John Doherty	.10	.05
❏ 532	Matt Brunson	.10	.05
❏ 533	Dave Nilsson	.10	.05
❏ 534	Randy Myers	.10	.05
❏ 535	Steve Farr	.10	.05
❏ 536	Billy Wagner	.50	.23
❏ 537	Darrell Coles	.10	.05
❏ 538	Frank Tanana	.10	.05
❏ 539	Tim Salmon	.40	.18
❏ 540	Kim Batiste	.10	.05
❏ 541	George Bell	.10	.05
❏ 542	Tom Henke	.10	.05
❏ 543	Sam Horn	.10	.05
❏ 544	Doug Jones	.10	.05
❏ 545	Scott Leius	.10	.05
❏ 546	Al Martin	.10	.05
❏ 547	Bob Welch	.10	.05
❏ 548	Scott Christman	.10	.05
❏ 549	Norm Charlton	.10	.05
❏ 550	Mark McGwire	2.00	.90
❏ 551	Greg McMichael	.10	.05
❏ 552	Tim Costo	.10	.05
❏ 553	Rodney Bolton	.10	.05
❏ 554	Pedro Martinez	.50	.23
❏ 555	Marc Valdes	.10	.05
❏ 556	Darrell Whitmore	.10	.05
❏ 557	Tim Bogar	.10	.05
❏ 558	Steve Karsay	.10	.05
❏ 559	Danny Bautista	.10	.05
❏ 560	Jeffrey Hammonds	.20	.09
❏ 561	Aaron Sele	.20	.09
❏ 562	Russ Springer	.10	.05
❏ 563	Jason Bere	.10	.05
❏ 564	Billy Brewer	.10	.05
❏ 565	Sterling Hitchcock	.20	.09
❏ 566	Bobby Munoz	.10	.05
❏ 567	Craig Paquette	.10	.05
❏ 568	Bret Boone	.20	.09
❏ 569	Dan Peltier	.10	.05
❏ 570	Jeromy Burnitz	.20	.09
❏ 571	John Wasdin	.20	.09
❏ 572	Chipper Jones	1.00	.45
❏ 573	Jamey Wright	.20	.09
❏ 574	Jeff Granger	.10	.05
❏ 575	Jay Powell	.30	.14
❏ 576	Ryan Thompson	.10	.05
❏ 577	Lou Frazier	.10	.05
❏ 578	Paul Wagner	.10	.05
❏ 579	Brad Ausmus	.10	.05
❏ 580	Jack Voigt	.10	.05
❏ 581	Kevin Rogers	.10	.05
❏ 582	Damon Buford	.10	.05
❏ 583	Paul Quantrill	.10	.05
❏ 584	Marc Newfield	.10	.05
❏ 585	Derek Lee	.25	.11
❏ 586	Shane Reynolds	.20	.09
❏ 587	Cliff Floyd	.20	.09
❏ 588	Jeff Schwarz	.10	.05
❏ 589	Ross Powell	.10	.05
❏ 590	Gerald Williams	.10	.05
❏ 591	Mike Trombley	.10	.05
❏ 592	Ken Ryan	.10	.05
❏ 593	John O'Donoghue	.10	.05
❏ 594	Rod Correia	.10	.05
❏ 595	Darrell Sherman	.10	.05
❏ 596	Steve Scarsone	.10	.05
❏ 597	Sherman Obando	.10	.05
❏ 598	Kurt Abbott	.10	.05
❏ 599	Dave Telgheder	.10	.05
❏ 600	Rick Trlicek	.10	.05
❏ 601	Carl Everett	.20	.09
❏ 602	Luis Ortiz	.10	.05
❏ 603	Larry Luebbers	.10	.05
❏ 604	Kevin Roberson	.10	.05
❏ 605	Butch Huskey	.20	.09
❏ 606	Benji Gil	.10	.05
❏ 607	Todd Van Poppel	.10	.05
❏ 608	Mark Hutton	.10	.05
❏ 609	Chip Hale	.10	.05
❏ 610	Matt Maysey	.10	.05
❏ 611	Scott Ruffcorn	.10	.05
❏ 612	Hilly Hathaway	.10	.05
❏ 613	Allen Watson	.10	.05
❏ 614	Carlos Delgado	.40	.18
❏ 615	Roberto Mejia	.10	.05
❏ 616	Turk Wendell	.10	.05
❏ 617	Tony Tarasco	.10	.05
❏ 618	Raul Mondesi	.40	.18
❏ 619	Kevin Stocker	.10	.05
❏ 620	Javier Lopez	.30	.14
❏ 621	Keith Kessinger	.10	.05
❏ 622	Bob Hamelin	.10	.05
❏ 623	John Roper	.10	.05
❏ 624	Lenny Dykstra WS	.10	.05
❏ 625	Joe Carter WS	.10	.05
❏ 626	Jim Abbott HL	.10	.05
❏ 627	Lee Smith HL	.10	.05
❏ 628	Ken Griffey Jr. HL	1.00	.45
❏ 629	Dave Winfield HL	.20	.09
❏ 630	Darryl Kile HL	.10	.05
❏ 631	Frank Thomas AL MVP	.40	.18
❏ 632	Barry Bonds NL MVP	.40	.18
❏ 633	Jack McDowell AL CY	.10	.05
❏ 634	Greg Maddux NL CY	.50	.23
❏ 635	Tim Salmon AL ROY	.20	.09
❏ 636	Mike Piazza NL ROY	.60	.25
❏ 637	Brian Turang	.10	.05
❏ 638	Rondell White	.20	.09
❏ 639	Nigel Wilson	.10	.05
❏ 640	Torii Hunter	.10	.05
❏ 641	Salomon Torres	.10	.05
❏ 642	Kevin Higgins	.10	.05
❏ 643	Eric Wedge	.10	.05
❏ 644	Roger Salkeld	.10	.05
❏ 645	Manny Ramirez	.75	.35
❏ 646	Jeff McNeely	.10	.05
❏ 647	Atlanta Braves CL	.10	.05
❏ 648	Chicago Cubs CL	.10	.05
❏ 649	Cincinnati Reds CL	.10	.05
❏ 650	Colorado Rockies CL	.10	.05
❏ 651	Florida Marlins CL	.10	.05
❏ 652	Houston Astros CL	.10	.05
❏ 653	Los Angeles Dodgers CL	.10	.05
❏ 654	Montreal Expos CL	.10	.05
❏ 655	New York Mets CL	.10	.05
❏ 656	Philadelphia Phillies CL	.10	.05
❏ 657	Pittsburgh Pirates CL	.10	.05
❏ 658	St. Louis Cardinals CL	.10	.05
❏ 659	San Diego Padres CL	.10	.05
❏ 660	San Francisco Giants CL	.10	.05

1994 Score Boys of Summer

	MINT	NRMT
COMPLETE SET (60)	60.00	27.00

		MINT	NRMT
COMPLETE SERIES 1 (30)	25.00		11.00
COMPLETE SERIES 2 (30)	35.00		16.00
COMMON CARD (1-60)	1.00		.45
MINOR STARS	2.00		.90

STATED ODDS 1:4 SUPER PACKS

❑ 1 Jeff Conine	1.00		.45
❑ 2 Aaron Sele	2.00		.90
❑ 3 Kevin Stocker	1.00		.45
❑ 4 Pat Meares	1.00		.45
❑ 5 Jeromy Burnitz	2.00		.90
❑ 6 Mike Piazza	15.00		6.75
❑ 7 Allen Watson	1.00		.45
❑ 8 Jeffrey Hammonds	2.00		.90
❑ 9 Kevin Roberson	1.00		.45
❑ 10 Hilly Hathaway	1.00		.45
❑ 11 Kirk Rueter	1.00		.45
❑ 12 Eduardo Perez	1.00		.45
❑ 13 Ricky Gutierrez	1.00		.45
❑ 14 Domingo Jean	1.00		.45
❑ 15 David Nied	1.00		.45
❑ 16 Wayne Kirby	1.00		.45
❑ 17 Mike Lansing	2.00		.90
❑ 18 Jason Bere	1.00		.45
❑ 19 Brent Gates	1.00		.45
❑ 20 Javier Lopez	3.00		1.35
❑ 21 Greg McMichael	1.00		.45
❑ 22 David Hulse	1.00		.45
❑ 23 Roberto Mejia	1.00		.45
❑ 24 Tim Salmon	3.00		1.35
❑ 25 Rene Arocha	1.00		.45
❑ 26 Bret Boone	2.00		.90
❑ 27 David McCarty	1.00		.45
❑ 28 Todd Van Poppel	1.00		.45
❑ 29 Lance Painter	1.00		.45
❑ 30 Erik Pappas	1.00		.45
❑ 31 Chuck Carr	1.00		.45
❑ 32 Mark Hutton	1.00		.45
❑ 33 Jeff McNeely	1.00		.45
❑ 34 Willie Greene	1.00		.45
❑ 35 Nigel Wilson	1.00		.45
❑ 36 Rondell White	2.00		.90
❑ 37 Brian Turang	1.00		.45
❑ 38 Manny Ramirez	10.00		4.50
❑ 39 Salomon Torres	1.00		.45
❑ 40 Melvin Nieves	1.00		.45
❑ 41 Ryan Klesko	2.00		.90
❑ 42 Keith Kessinger	1.00		.45
❑ 43 Brad Ausmus	1.00		.45
❑ 44 Bob Hamelin	1.00		.45
❑ 45 Carlos Delgado	4.00		1.80
❑ 46 Marc Newfield	1.00		.45
❑ 47 Raul Mondesi	2.50		1.10
❑ 48 Tim Costo	1.00		.45
❑ 49 Pedro Martinez	6.00		2.70
❑ 50 Steve Karsay	1.00		.45
❑ 51 Danny Bautista	1.00		.45
❑ 52 Butch Huskey	2.00		.90
❑ 53 Kurt Abbott	1.00		.45
❑ 54 Darrell Sherman	1.00		.45
❑ 55 Damon Buford	1.00		.45
❑ 56 Ross Powell	1.00		.45
❑ 57 Darrell Whitmore	1.00		.45
❑ 58 Chipper Jones	12.00		5.50
❑ 59 Jeff Granger	1.00		.45
❑ 60 Cliff Floyd	2.00		.90

1994 Score Cycle

		MINT	NRMT
COMPLETE SET (20)	150.00		70.00
COMMON CARD (TC1-TC20)	2.50		1.10
MINOR STARS	4.00		1.80
UNLISTED STARS	10.00		4.50

SER.2 STATED ODDS 1:72, 1:36 JUM

❑ TC1 Brett Butler	4.00		1.80
❑ TC2 Kenny Lofton	10.00		4.50
❑ TC3 Paul Molitor	10.00		4.50
❑ TC4 Carlos Baerga	2.50		1.10
❑ TC5 Gregg Jefferies	2.50		1.10
Tony Phillips			
❑ TC6 John Olerud	4.00		1.80
❑ TC7 Charlie Hayes	2.50		1.10
❑ TC8 Lenny Dykstra	4.00		1.80
❑ TC9 Dante Bichette	4.00		1.80
❑ TC10 Devon White	2.50		1.10
❑ TC11 Lance Johnson	2.50		1.10
❑ TC12 Joey Cora	2.50		1.10
Steve Finley			
❑ TC13 Tony Fernandez	2.50		1.10
❑ TC14 David Hulse	2.50		1.10
Brett Butler			
❑ TC15 Jay Bell	2.50		1.10
Brian McRae			
Mickey Morandini			
❑ TC16 Juan Gonzalez	15.00		6.75
Barry Bonds			
❑ TC17 Ken Griffey Jr.	50.00		22.00
❑ TC18 Frank Thomas	20.00		9.00
❑ TC19 Dave Justice	10.00		4.50
❑ TC20 Matt Williams	10.00		4.50
Albert Belle			

1994 Score Dream Team

		MINT	NRMT
COMPLETE SET (10)	60.00		27.00
COMMON CARD (1-10)	2.50		1.10
SEMISTARS	6.00		2.70
UNLISTED STARS	10.00		4.50

SER.1 STATED ODDS 1:72, 1:36 JUM

❑ 1 Mike Mussina	10.00		4.50
❑ 2 Tom Glavine	10.00		4.50
❑ 3 Don Mattingly	20.00		9.00
❑ 4 Carlos Baerga	2.50		1.10
❑ 5 Barry Larkin	10.00		4.50
❑ 6 Matt Williams	6.00		2.70
❑ 7 Juan Gonzalez	20.00		9.00
❑ 8 Andy Van Slyke	4.00		1.80
❑ 9 Larry Walker	10.00		4.50
❑ 10 Mike Stanley	2.50		1.10

1994 Score Gold Stars

		MINT	NRMT
COMPLETE SET (60)	250.00		110.00
COMPLETE NL SERIES (30)	100.00		45.00
COMPLETE AL SERIES (30)	150.00		70.00
COMMON CARD (1-60)	1.50		.70

STATED ODDS 1:18 HOBBY

❑ 1 Barry Bonds	8.00		3.60
❑ 2 Orlando Merced	1.50		.70
❑ 3 Mark Grace	4.00		1.80
❑ 4 Darren Daulton	2.50		1.10

❑ 5 Jeff Blauser	1.50		.70
❑ 6 Deion Sanders	2.50		1.10
❑ 7 John Kruk	2.50		1.10
❑ 8 Jeff Bagwell	6.00		2.70
❑ 9 Gregg Jefferies	1.50		.70
❑ 10 Matt Williams	4.00		1.80
❑ 11 Andres Galarraga	6.00		2.70
❑ 12 Jay Bell	2.50		1.10
❑ 13 Mike Piazza	20.00		9.00
❑ 14 Ron Gant	1.50		.70
❑ 15 Barry Larkin	6.00		2.70
❑ 16 Tom Glavine	6.00		2.70
❑ 17 Lenny Dykstra	2.50		1.10
❑ 18 Fred McGriff	4.00		1.80
❑ 19 Andy Van Slyke	2.50		1.10
❑ 20 Gary Sheffield	6.00		2.70
❑ 21 John Burkett	1.50		.70
❑ 22 Dante Bichette	2.50		1.10
❑ 23 Tony Gwynn	15.00		6.75
❑ 24 Dave Justice	6.00		2.70
❑ 25 Marquis Grissom	1.50		.70
❑ 26 Bobby Bonilla	2.50		1.10
❑ 27 Larry Walker	6.00		2.70
❑ 28 Brett Butler	2.50		1.10
❑ 29 Robby Thompson	1.50		.70
❑ 30 Jeff Conine	1.50		.70
❑ 31 Joe Carter	2.50		1.10
❑ 32 Ken Griffey Jr.	30.00		13.50
❑ 33 Juan Gonzalez	12.00		5.50
❑ 34 Rickey Henderson	8.00		3.60
❑ 35 Bo Jackson	2.50		1.10
❑ 36 Cal Ripken	25.00		11.00
❑ 37 John Olerud	2.50		1.10
❑ 38 Carlos Baerga	1.50		.70
❑ 39 Jack McDowell	1.50		.70
❑ 40 Cecil Fielder	1.50		.70
❑ 41 Kenny Lofton	6.00		2.70
❑ 42 Roberto Alomar	6.00		2.70
❑ 43 Randy Johnson	6.00		2.70
❑ 44 Tim Salmon	6.00		2.70
❑ 45 Frank Thomas	12.00		5.50
❑ 46 Albert Belle	6.00		2.70
❑ 47 Greg Vaughn	2.50		1.10
❑ 48 Travis Fryman	2.50		1.10
❑ 49 Don Mattingly	12.00		5.50
❑ 50 Wade Boggs	6.00		2.70
❑ 51 Mo Vaughn	6.00		2.70
❑ 52 Kirby Puckett	10.00		4.50
❑ 53 Devon White	1.50		.70
❑ 54 Tony Phillips	1.50		.70
❑ 55 Brian Harper	1.50		.70
❑ 56 Chad Curtis	1.50		.70
❑ 57 Paul Molitor	6.00		2.70
❑ 58 Ivan Rodriguez	8.00		3.60
❑ 59 Rafael Palmeiro	6.00		2.70
❑ 60 Brian McRae	1.50		.70

1994 Score Rookie/Traded

	MINT	NRMT
COMPLETE SET (165)	15.00	6.75
COMMON CARD (RT1-RT165)	.15	.07
MINOR STARS	.25	.11
SEMISTARS	.40	.18
UNLISTED STARS	.60	.25

A.ROD CALL UP EXCH.STATED ODDS 1:240

A.ROD CALL-UP VIA MAIL PER EXCH.CARD

❑ RT1 Will Clark	.60	.25
❑ RT2 Lee Smith	.25	.11
❑ RT3 Bo Jackson	.25	.11
❑ RT4 Ellis Burks	.25	.11
❑ RT5 Eddie Murray	.60	.25
❑ RT6 Delino DeShields	.15	.07
❑ RT7 Erik Hanson	.15	.07
❑ RT8 Rafael Palmeiro	.60	.25
❑ RT9 Luis Polonia	.15	.07
❑ RT10 Omar Vizquel	.25	.11
❑ RT11 Kurt Abbott	.15	.07
❑ RT12 Vince Coleman	.15	.07
❑ RT13 Rickey Henderson	.75	.35
❑ RT14 Terry Mulholland	.15	.07
❑ RT15 Greg Hibbard	.15	.07
❑ RT16 Walt Weiss	.15	.07
❑ RT17 Chris Sabo	.15	.07
❑ RT18 Dave Henderson	.15	.07
❑ RT19 Rick Sutcliffe	.15	.07
❑ RT20 Harold Reynolds	.15	.07
❑ RT21 Jack Morris	.25	.11
❑ RT22 Dan Wilson	.15	.07
❑ RT23 Dave Magadan	.15	.07
❑ RT24 Dennis Martinez	.25	.11
❑ RT25 Wes Chamberlain	.15	.07
❑ RT26 Otis Nixon	.15	.07
❑ RT27 Eric Anthony	.15	.07
❑ RT28 Randy Milligan	.15	.07
❑ RT29 Julio Franco	.15	.07
❑ RT30 Kevin McReynolds	.15	.07
❑ RT31 Anthony Young	.15	.07
❑ RT32 Brian Harper	.15	.07
❑ RT33 Gene Harris	.15	.07
❑ RT34 Eddie Taubensee	.15	.07
❑ RT35 David Segui	.25	.11
❑ RT36 Stan Javier	.15	.07
❑ RT37 Felix Fermin	.15	.07
❑ RT38 Darrin Jackson	.15	.07
❑ RT39 Tony Fernandez	.25	.11
❑ RT40 Jose Vizcaino	.15	.07
❑ RT41 Willie Banks	.15	.07
❑ RT42 Brian Hunter	.15	.07
❑ RT43 Reggie Jefferson	.15	.07
❑ RT44 Junior Felix	.15	.07
❑ RT45 Jack Armstrong	.15	.07
❑ RT46 Bip Roberts	.15	.07
❑ RT47 Jerry Browne	.15	.07
❑ RT48 Marvin Freeman	.15	.07
❑ RT49 Jody Reed	.15	.07
❑ RT50 Alex Cole	.15	.07
❑ RT51 Sid Fernandez	.15	.07
❑ RT52 Pete Smith	.15	.07
❑ RT53 Xavier Hernandez	.15	.07
❑ RT54 Scott Sanderson	.15	.07
❑ RT55 Turner Ward	.15	.07
❑ RT56 Rex Hudler	.15	.07
❑ RT57 Deion Sanders	.25	.11
❑ RT58 Sid Bream	.15	.07
❑ RT59 Tony Pena	.15	.07
❑ RT60 Bret Boone	.25	.11
❑ RT61 Bobby Ayala	.15	.07
❑ RT62 Pedro Martinez	.75	.35
❑ RT63 Howard Johnson	.15	.07
❑ RT64 Mark Portugal	.15	.07
❑ RT65 Roberto Kelly	.15	.07
❑ RT66 Spike Owen	.15	.07

❑ RT67 Jeff Treadway	.15	.07
❑ RT68 Mike Harkey	.15	.07
❑ RT69 Doug Jones	.15	.07
❑ RT70 Steve Farr	.15	.07
❑ RT71 Billy Taylor	.15	.07
❑ RT72 Manny Ramirez	1.25	.55
❑ RT73 Bob Hamelin	.15	.07
❑ RT74 Steve Karsay	.15	.07
❑ RT75 Ryan Klesko	.25	.11
❑ RT76 Cliff Floyd	.25	.11
❑ RT77 Jeffrey Hammonds	.25	.11
❑ RT78 Javier Lopez	.40	.18
❑ RT79 Roger Salkeld	.15	.07
❑ RT80 Hector Carrasco	.15	.07
❑ RT81 Gerald Williams	.15	.07
❑ RT82 Raul Mondesi	.60	.25
❑ RT83 Sterling Hitchcock	.15	.07
❑ RT84 Danny Bautista	.15	.07
❑ RT85 Chris Turner	.15	.07
❑ RT86 Shane Reynolds	.25	.11
❑ RT87 Rondell White	.25	.11
❑ RT88 Salomon Torres	.15	.07
❑ RT89 Turk Wendell	.15	.07
❑ RT90 Tony Tarasco	.15	.07
❑ RT91 Shawn Green	1.00	.45
❑ RT92 Greg Colbrunn	.15	.07
❑ RT93 Eddie Zambrano	.15	.07
❑ RT94 Rich Becker	.15	.07
❑ RT95 Chris Gomez	.15	.07
❑ RT96 John Patterson	.15	.07
❑ RT97 Derek Parks	.15	.07
❑ RT98 Rich Rowland	.15	.07
❑ RT99 James Mouton	.15	.07
❑ RT100 Tim Hyers	.15	.07
❑ RT101 Jose Valentin	.15	.07
❑ RT102 Carlos Delgado	.60	.25
❑ RT103 Robert Eenhoorn	.15	.07
❑ RT104 John Hudek	.15	.07
❑ RT105 Domingo Cedeno	.15	.07
❑ RT106 Denny Hocking	.15	.07
❑ RT107 Greg Pirkl	.15	.07
❑ RT108 Mark Smith	.15	.07
❑ RT109 Paul Shuey	.15	.07
❑ RT110 Jorge Fabregas	.15	.07
❑ RT111 Rikkert Faneyte	.15	.07
❑ RT112 Rob Butler	.15	.07
❑ RT113 Darren Oliver	.60	.25
❑ RT114 Troy O'Leary	.25	.11
❑ RT115 Scott Brow	.15	.07
❑ RT116 Tony Eusebio	.15	.07
❑ RT117 Carlos Reyes	.15	.07
❑ RT118 J.R. Phillips	.15	.07
❑ RT119 Alex Diaz	.15	.07
❑ RT120 Charles Johnson	.25	.11
❑ RT121 Nate Minchey	.15	.07
❑ RT122 Scott Sanders	.15	.07
❑ RT123 Daryl Boston	.15	.07
❑ RT124 Joey Hamilton	.40	.18
❑ RT125 Brian Anderson	.40	.18
❑ RT126 Dan Miceli	.15	.07
❑ RT127 Tom Brunansky	.15	.07
❑ RT128 Dave Staton	.15	.07
❑ RT129 Mike Oquist	.15	.07
❑ RT130 John Mabry	.15	.07
❑ RT131 Norberto Martin	.15	.07
❑ RT132 Hector Fajardo	.15	.07
❑ RT133 Mark Hutton	.15	.07
❑ RT134 Fernando Vina	.15	.07
❑ RT135 Lee Tinsley	.15	.07
❑ RT136 Chan Ho Park	1.00	.45
❑ RT137 Paul Spoljaric	.15	.07
❑ RT138 Matias Carrillo	.15	.07
❑ RT139 Mark Kiefer	.15	.07
❑ RT140 Stan Royer	.15	.07
❑ RT141 Bryan Eversgerd	.15	.07
❑ RT142 Brian L. Hunter	.25	.11
❑ RT143 Joe Hall	.15	.07
❑ RT144 Johnny Ruffin	.15	.07
❑ RT145 Alex Gonzalez	.15	.07
❑ RT146 Keith Lockhart	.15	.07
❑ RT147 Tom Marsh	.15	.07
❑ RT148 Tony Longmire	.15	.07
❑ RT149 Keith Mitchell	.15	.07
❑ RT150 Melvin Nieves	.15	.07
❑ RT151 Kelly Stinnett	.15	.07
❑ RT152 Miguel Jimenez	.15	.07

❑ RT153 Jeff Juden	.15	.07
❑ RT154 Matt Walbeck	.15	.07
❑ RT155 Marc Newfield	.15	.07
❑ RT156 Matt Mieske	.15	.07
❑ RT157 Marcus Moore	.15	.07
❑ RT158 Jose Lima SP	10.00	4.50
❑ RT159 Mike Kelly	.15	.07
❑ RT160 Jim Edmonds	.60	.25
❑ RT161 Steve Trachsel	.15	.07
❑ RT162 Greg Blosser	.15	.07
❑ RT163 Marc Acre	.15	.07
❑ RT164 AL Checklist	.15	.07
❑ RT165 NL Checklist	.15	.07
❑ HC1 Alex Rodriguez	450.00	200.00
Call-Up Redemption		

1994 Score Rookie/Traded Gold Rush

	MINT	NRMT
COMPLETE SET (165)	50.00	22.00
COMMON CARD (RT1-RT165)	.25	.11

*STARS: 1X TO 2.5X BASIC CARDS
*ROOKIES: 1X TO 2.5X BASIC CARDS
ONE GOLD RUSH PER PACK

1994 Score Rookie/Traded Changing Places

	MINT	NRMT
COMPLETE SET (10)	30.00	13.50
COMMON CARD (CP1-CP10)	2.50	1.10

STATED ODDS 1:36 HOB/RET

❑ CP1 Will Clark	6.00	2.70
❑ CP2 Rafael Palmeiro	6.00	2.70
❑ CP3 Roberto Kelly	2.50	1.10
❑ CP4 Bo Jackson	4.00	1.80
❑ CP5 Otis Nixon	2.50	1.10
❑ CP6 Rickey Henderson	6.00	2.70
❑ CP7 Ellis Burks	4.00	1.80
❑ CP8 Lee Smith	4.00	1.80
❑ CP9 Delino DeShields	2.50	1.10
❑ CP10 Deion Sanders	4.00	1.80

1994 Score Rookie/Traded Super Rookies

	MINT	NRMT
COMPLETE SET (18)	60.00	27.00
COMMON CARD (SU1-SU18)	2.50	1.10
MINOR STARS	5.00	2.20
STATED ODDS 1:36 HOBBY		

		MINT	NRMT
❏ SU1	Carlos Delgado	8.00	3.60
❏ SU2	Manny Ramirez	20.00	9.00
❏ SU3	Ryan Klesko	5.00	2.20
❏ SU4	Raul Mondesi	8.00	3.60
❏ SU5	Bob Hamelin	2.50	1.10
❏ SU6	Steve Karsay	2.50	1.10
❏ SU7	Jeffrey Hammonds	5.00	2.20
❏ SU8	Cliff Floyd	5.00	2.20
❏ SU9	Kurt Abbott	2.50	1.10
❏ SU10	Marc Newfield	2.50	1.10
❏ SU11	Javier Lopez	6.00	2.70
❏ SU12	Rich Becker	2.50	1.10
❏ SU13	Greg Pirkl	2.50	1.10
❏ SU14	Rondell White	5.00	2.20
❏ SU15	James Mouton	2.50	1.10
❏ SU16	Tony Tarasco	2.50	1.10
❏ SU17	Brian Anderson	6.00	2.70
❏ SU18	Jim Edmonds	8.00	3.60

1995 Score

	MINT	NRMT
COMPLETE SET (605)	24.00	11.00
COMPLETE SERIES 1 (330)	12.00	5.50
COMPLETE SERIES 2 (275)	12.00	5.50
COMMON CARD (1-605)	.10	.05
MINOR STARS	.20	.09
UNLISTED STARS	.40	.18
SUBSET CARDS HALF VALUE OF BASE CARDS		
COMP.G.RUSH SET (605)	120.00	55.00
COMP.G.RUSH SER.1 (330)	60.00	27.00
COMP.G.RUSH SER.2 (275)	60.00	27.00
GOLD RUSH COMMON (1-605)	.25	.11
*G.RUSH STARS: 2X TO 5X HI COLUMN		
ONE GOLD RUSH PER PACK		
COMMON PLATINUM (1-587)	.50	.23
*PLATINUM STARS: 4X TO 10X HI COLUMN		
ONE PLAT.TEAM VIA MAIL PER G.RUSH TEAM		

COMP.YOU TRADE EM SET (11)	1.50		.70
*YTE CARDS: 1X TO 2X HI COLUMN			
ONE YTE SET VIA MAIL PER YTE TRADE CARD			
KLESKO RG1 SER.1 STATED ODDS 1:720 RET			
KLESKO SG1 SER.1 STATED ODDS 1:720 HOB			

❏ 1	Frank Thomas	.75	.35
❏ 2	Roberto Alomar	.40	.18
❏ 3	Cal Ripken	1.50	.70
❏ 4	Jose Canseco	.50	.23
❏ 5	Matt Williams	.40	.18
❏ 6	Esteban Beltre	.10	.05
❏ 7	Domingo Cedeno	.10	.05
❏ 8	John Valentin	.20	.09
❏ 9	Glenallen Hill	.10	.05
❏ 10	Rafael Belliard	.10	.05
❏ 11	Randy Myers	.10	.05
❏ 12	Mo Vaughn	.40	.18
❏ 13	Hector Carrasco	.10	.05
❏ 14	Chili Davis	.20	.09
❏ 15	Dante Bichette	.20	.09
❏ 16	Darrin Jackson	.10	.05
❏ 17	Mike Piazza	1.25	.55
❏ 18	Junior Felix	.10	.05
❏ 19	Moises Alou	.20	.09
❏ 20	Mark Gubicza	.10	.05
❏ 21	Bret Saberhagen	.20	.09
❏ 22	Lenny Dykstra	.20	.09
❏ 23	Steve Howe	.10	.05
❏ 24	Mark Dewey	.10	.05
❏ 25	Brian Harper	.10	.05
❏ 26	Ozzie Smith	.50	.23
❏ 27	Scott Erickson	.20	.09
❏ 28	Tony Gwynn	1.00	.45
❏ 29	Bob Welch	.10	.05
❏ 30	Barry Bonds	.50	.23
❏ 31	Leo Gomez	.10	.05
❏ 32	Greg Maddux	1.00	.45
❏ 33	Mike Greenwell	.10	.05
❏ 34	Sammy Sosa	1.25	.55
❏ 35	Darnell Coles	.10	.05
❏ 36	Tommy Greene	.10	.05
❏ 37	Will Clark	.40	.18
❏ 38	Steve Ontiveros	.10	.05
❏ 39	Stan Javier	.10	.05
❏ 40	Bip Roberts	.10	.05
❏ 41	Paul O'Neill	.20	.09
❏ 42	Bill Haselman	.10	.05
❏ 43	Shane Mack	.10	.05
❏ 44	Orlando Merced	.10	.05
❏ 45	Kevin Seitzer	.10	.05
❏ 46	Trevor Hoffman	.20	.09
❏ 47	Greg Gagne	.10	.05
❏ 48	Jeff Kent	.20	.09
❏ 49	Tony Phillips	.10	.05
❏ 50	Ken Hill	.10	.05
❏ 51	Carlos Baerga	.20	.09
❏ 52	Henry Rodriguez	.20	.09
❏ 53	Scott Sanderson	.10	.05
❏ 54	Jeff Conine	.20	.09
❏ 55	Chris Turner	.10	.05
❏ 56	Ken Caminiti	.30	.14
❏ 57	Harold Baines	.20	.09
❏ 58	Charlie Hayes	.10	.05
❏ 59	Roberto Kelly	.10	.05
❏ 60	John Olerud	.20	.09
❏ 61	Tim Davis	.10	.05
❏ 62	Rich Rowland	.10	.05
❏ 63	Rey Sanchez	.10	.05
❏ 64	Junior Ortiz	.10	.05
❏ 65	Ricky Gutierrez	.10	.05
❏ 66	Rex Hudler	.10	.05
❏ 67	Johnny Ruffin	.10	.05
❏ 68	Jay Buhner	.20	.09
❏ 69	Tom Pagnozzi	.10	.05
❏ 70	Julio Franco	.10	.05
❏ 71	Eric Young	.10	.05
❏ 72	Mike Bordick	.10	.05
❏ 73	Don Slaught	.10	.05
❏ 74	Goose Gossage	.20	.09
❏ 75	Lonnie Smith	.10	.05
❏ 76	Jimmy Key	.10	.05
❏ 77	Dave Hollins	.10	.05

❏ 78	Mickey Tettleton	.10	.05
❏ 79	Luis Gonzalez	.10	.05
❏ 80	Dave Winfield	.40	.18
❏ 81	Ryan Thompson	.10	.05
❏ 82	Felix Jose	.10	.05
❏ 83	Rusty Meacham	.10	.05
❏ 84	Darryl Hamilton	.10	.05
❏ 85	John Wetteland	.20	.09
❏ 86	Tom Brunansky	.10	.05
❏ 87	Mark Lemke	.10	.05
❏ 88	Spike Owen	.10	.05
❏ 89	Shawon Dunston	.10	.05
❏ 90	Wilson Alvarez	.20	.09
❏ 91	Lee Smith	.20	.09
❏ 92	Scott Kamieniecki	.10	.05
❏ 93	Jacob Brumfield	.10	.05
❏ 94	Kirk Gibson	.20	.09
❏ 95	Joe Girardi	.10	.05
❏ 96	Mike Macfarlane	.10	.05
❏ 97	Greg Colbrunn	.10	.05
❏ 98	Ricky Bones	.10	.05
❏ 99	Delino DeShields	.10	.05
❏ 100	Pat Meares	.10	.05
❏ 101	Jeff Fassero	.10	.05
❏ 102	Jim Leyritz	.10	.05
❏ 103	Gary Redus	.10	.05
❏ 104	Terry Steinbach	.10	.05
❏ 105	Kevin McReynolds	.10	.05
❏ 106	Felix Fermin	.10	.05
❏ 107	Danny Jackson	.10	.05
❏ 108	Chris James	.10	.05
❏ 109	Jeff King	.10	.05
❏ 110	Pat Hentgen	.20	.09
❏ 111	Gerald Perry	.10	.05
❏ 112	Tim Raines	.20	.09
❏ 113	Eddie Williams	.10	.05
❏ 114	Jamie Moyer	.10	.05
❏ 115	Bud Black	.10	.05
❏ 116	Chris Gomez	.10	.05
❏ 117	Luis Lopez	.10	.05
❏ 118	Roger Clemens	1.00	.45
❏ 119	Javier Lopez	.20	.09
❏ 120	Dave Nilsson	.10	.05
❏ 121	Karl Rhodes	.10	.05
❏ 122	Rick Aguilera	.10	.05
❏ 123	Tony Fernandez	.20	.09
❏ 124	Bernie Williams	.40	.18
❏ 125	James Mouton	.10	.05
❏ 126	Mark Langston	.10	.05
❏ 127	Mike Lansing	.10	.05
❏ 128	Tino Martinez	.40	.18
❏ 129	Joe Orsulak	.10	.05
❏ 130	David Hulse	.10	.05
❏ 131	Pete Incaviglia	.10	.05
❏ 132	Mark Clark	.10	.05
❏ 133	Tony Eusebio	.10	.05
❏ 134	Chuck Finley	.20	.09
❏ 135	Lou Frazier	.10	.05
❏ 136	Craig Grebeck	.10	.05
❏ 137	Kelly Stinnett	.10	.05
❏ 138	Paul Shuey	.10	.05
❏ 139	David Nied	.10	.05
❏ 140	Billy Brewer	.10	.05
❏ 141	Dave Weathers	.10	.05
❏ 142	Scott Leius	.10	.05
❏ 143	Brian Jordan	.20	.09
❏ 144	Melido Perez	.10	.05
❏ 145	Tony Tarasco	.10	.05
❏ 146	Dan Wilson	.10	.05
❏ 147	Rondell White	.20	.09
❏ 148	Mike Henneman	.10	.05
❏ 149	Brian Johnson	.10	.05
❏ 150	Tom Henke	.10	.05
❏ 151	John Patterson	.10	.05
❏ 152	Bobby Witt	.10	.05
❏ 153	Eddie Taubensee	.10	.05
❏ 154	Pat Borders	.10	.05
❏ 155	Ramon Martinez	.20	.09
❏ 156	Mike Kingery	.10	.05
❏ 157	Zane Smith	.10	.05
❏ 158	Benito Santiago	.10	.05
❏ 159	Matias Carrillo	.10	.05
❏ 160	Scott Brosius	.20	.09
❏ 161	Dave Clark	.10	.05
❏ 162	Mark McLemore	.10	.05
❏ 163	Curt Schilling	.30	.14

#	Player	Val	Val
164	J.T. Snow	.20	.09
165	Rod Beck	.10	.05
166	Scott Fletcher	.10	.05
167	Bob Tewksbury	.10	.05
168	Mike LaValliere	.10	.05
169	Dave Hansen	.10	.05
170	Pedro Martinez	.50	.23
171	Kirk Rueter	.10	.05
172	Jose Lind	.10	.05
173	Luis Alicea	.10	.05
174	Mike Moore	.10	.05
175	Andy Ashby	.10	.05
176	Jody Reed	.10	.05
177	Darryl Kile	.10	.05
178	Carl Willis	.10	.05
179	Jeromy Burnitz	.20	.09
180	Mike Gallego	.10	.05
181	Bill VanLandingham	.10	.05
182	Sid Fernandez	.10	.05
183	Kim Batiste	.10	.05
184	Greg Myers	.10	.05
185	Steve Avery	.10	.05
186	Steve Farr	.10	.05
187	Robb Nen	.10	.05
188	Dan Pasqua	.10	.05
189	Bruce Ruffin	.10	.05
190	Jose Valentin	.10	.05
191	Willie Banks	.10	.05
192	Mike Aldrete	.10	.05
193	Randy Milligan	.10	.05
194	Steve Karsay	.10	.05
195	Mike Stanley	.10	.05
196	Jose Mesa	.10	.05
197	Tom Browning	.10	.05
198	John Vander Wal	.10	.05
199	Kevin Brown	.30	.14
200	Mike Oquist	.10	.05
201	Greg Swindell	.10	.05
202	Eddie Zambrano	.10	.05
203	Joe Boever	.10	.05
204	Gary Varsho	.10	.05
205	Chris Gwynn	.10	.05
206	David Howard	.10	.05
207	Jerome Walton	.10	.05
208	Danny Darwin	.10	.05
209	Darryl Strawberry	.20	.09
210	Todd Van Poppel	.10	.05
211	Scott Livingstone	.10	.05
212	Dave Fleming	.10	.05
213	Todd Worrell	.10	.05
214	Carlos Delgado	.40	.18
215	Bill Pecota	.10	.05
216	Jim Lindeman	.10	.05
217	Rick White	.10	.05
218	Jose Oquendo	.10	.05
219	Tony Castillo	.10	.05
220	Fernando Vina	.10	.05
221	Jeff Bagwell	.50	.23
222	Randy Johnson	.40	.18
223	Albert Belle	.40	.18
224	Chuck Carr	.10	.05
225	Mark Leiter	.10	.05
226	Hal Morris	.10	.05
227	Robin Ventura	.20	.09
228	Mike Munoz	.10	.05
229	Jim Thome	.40	.18
230	Mario Diaz	.10	.05
231	John Doherty	.10	.05
232	Bobby Jones	.10	.05
233	Raul Mondesi	.30	.14
234	Ricky Jordan	.10	.05
235	John Jaha	.10	.05
236	Carlos Garcia	.10	.05
237	Kirby Puckett	.60	.25
238	Orel Hershiser	.20	.09
239	Don Mattingly	.75	.35
240	Sid Bream	.10	.05
241	Brent Gates	.10	.05
242	Tony Longmire	.10	.05
243	Robby Thompson	.10	.05
244	Rick Sutcliffe	.10	.05
245	Dean Palmer	.20	.09
246	Marquis Grissom	.20	.09
247	Paul Molitor	.40	.18
248	Mark Carreon	.10	.05
249	Jack Voigt	.10	.05
250	Greg McMichael UER (photo on front is Mike Stanton)	.10	.05
251	Damon Berryhill	.10	.05
252	Brian Dorsett	.10	.05
253	Jim Edmonds	.30	.14
254	Barry Larkin	.40	.18
255	Jack McDowell	.10	.05
256	Wally Joyner	.20	.09
257	Eddie Murray	.40	.18
258	Lenny Webster	.10	.05
259	Milt Cuyler	.10	.05
260	Todd Benzinger	.10	.05
261	Vince Coleman	.10	.05
262	Todd Stottlemyre	.10	.05
263	Turner Ward	.10	.05
264	Ray Lankford	.20	.09
265	Matt Walbeck	.10	.05
266	Deion Sanders	.20	.09
267	Gerald Williams	.10	.05
268	Jim Gott	.10	.05
269	Jeff Frye	.10	.05
270	Jose Rijo	.10	.05
271	Dave Justice	.40	.18
272	Ismael Valdes	.20	.09
273	Ben McDonald	.10	.05
274	Darren Lewis	.10	.05
275	Graeme Lloyd	.10	.05
276	Luis Ortiz	.10	.05
277	Julian Tavarez	.10	.05
278	Mark Dalesandro	.10	.05
279	Brett Merriman	.10	.05
280	Ricky Bottalico	.10	.05
281	Robert Eenhoorn	.10	.05
282	Rikkert Faneyte	.10	.05
283	Mark Kelly	.10	.05
284	Mark Smith	.10	.05
285	Turk Wendell	.10	.05
286	Greg Blosser	.10	.05
287	Garey Ingram	.10	.05
288	Jorge Fabregas	.10	.05
289	Blaise Ilsley	.10	.05
290	Joe Hall	.10	.05
291	Orlando Miller	.10	.05
292	Jose Lima	.40	.18
293	Greg O'Halloran	.10	.05
294	Mark Kiefer	.10	.05
295	Jose Oliva	.10	.05
296	Rich Becker	.10	.05
297	Brian L. Hunter	.20	.09
298	Dave Silvestri	.10	.05
299	Armando Benitez	.10	.05
300	Darren Dreifort	.20	.09
301	John Mabry	.10	.05
302	Greg Pirkl	.10	.05
303	J.R. Phillips	.10	.05
304	Shawn Green	.40	.18
305	Roberto Petagine	.10	.05
306	Keith Lockhart	.10	.05
307	Jonathan Hurst	.10	.05
308	Paul Spoljaric	.10	.05
309	Mike Lieberthal	.10	.05
310	Garret Anderson	.20	.09
311	John Johnstone	.10	.05
312	Alex Rodriguez	1.50	.70
313	Kent Mercker HL	.10	.05
314	John Valentin HL	.10	.05
315	Kenny Rogers HL	.10	.05
316	Fred McGriff HL	.10	.05
317	Team Checklists	.10	.05
318	Team Checklists	.10	.05
319	Team Checklists	.10	.05
320	Team Checklists	.10	.05
321	Team Checklists	.10	.05
322	Team Checklists	.10	.05
323	Team Checklists	.10	.05
324	Team Checklists	.10	.05
325	Team Checklists	.10	.05
326	Team Checklists	.10	.05
327	Team Checklists	.10	.05
328	Team Checklists	.10	.05
329	Team Checklists	.10	.05
330	Team Checklists	.10	.05
331	Pedro Munoz	.10	.05
332	Ryan Klesko	.20	.09
333	Andre Dawson	.30	.14
334	Derrick May	.10	.05
335	Aaron Sele	.20	.09
336	Kevin Mitchell	.10	.05
337	Steve Trachsel	.10	.05
338	Andres Galarraga	.40	.18
339	Terry Pendleton	.10	.05
340	Gary Sheffield	.20	.09
341	Travis Fryman	.20	.09
342	Bo Jackson	.20	.09
343	Gary Gaetti	.20	.09
344	Brett Butler	.20	.09
345	B.J. Surhoff	.20	.09
346	Larry Walker	.40	.18
347	Kevin Tapani	.10	.05
348	Rick Wilkins	.10	.05
349	Wade Boggs	.40	.18
350	Mariano Duncan	.10	.05
351	Ruben Sierra	.10	.05
352	Andy Van Slyke	.20	.09
353	Reggie Jefferson	.10	.05
354	Gregg Jefferies	.20	.09
355	Tim Naehring	.10	.05
356	John Roper	.10	.05
357	Joe Carter	.20	.09
358	Kurt Abbott	.10	.05
359	Lenny Harris	.10	.05
360	Lance Johnson	.10	.05
361	Brian Anderson	.20	.09
362	Jim Eisenreich	.10	.05
363	Jerry Browne	.10	.05
364	Mark Grace	.30	.14
365	Devon White	.10	.05
366	Reggie Sanders	.20	.09
367	Ivan Rodriguez	.50	.23
368	Kirt Manwaring	.10	.05
369	Pat Kelly	.10	.05
370	Ellis Burks	.20	.09
371	Charles Nagy	.20	.09
372	Kevin Bass	.10	.05
373	Lou Whitaker	.20	.09
374	Rene Arocha	.10	.05
375	Derek Parks	.10	.05
376	Mark Whiten	.10	.05
377	Mark McGwire	2.00	.90
378	Doug Drabek	.10	.05
379	Greg Vaughn	.20	.09
380	Al Martin	.10	.05
381	Ron Darling	.10	.05
382	Tim Wallach	.10	.05
383	Alan Trammell	.20	.09
384	Randy Velarde	.10	.05
385	Chris Sabo	.10	.05
386	Wil Cordero	.10	.05
387	Darrin Fletcher	.10	.05
388	David Segui	.10	.05
389	Steve Buechele	.10	.05
390	Dave Gallagher	.10	.05
391	Thomas Howard	.10	.05
392	Chad Curtis	.10	.05
393	Cal Eldred	.20	.09
394	Jason Bere	.20	.09
395	Bret Barberie	.10	.05
396	Paul Sorrento	.10	.05
397	Steve Finley	.20	.09
398	Cecil Fielder	.20	.09
399	Eric Karros	.20	.09
400	Jeff Montgomery	.10	.05
401	Cliff Floyd	.20	.09
402	Matt Mieske	.10	.05
403	Brian Hunter	.10	.05
404	Alex Cole	.10	.05
405	Kevin Stocker	.10	.05
406	Eric Davis	.20	.09
407	Marvin Freeman	.10	.05
408	Dennis Eckersley	.20	.09
409	Todd Zeile	.10	.05
410	Keith Mitchell	.10	.05
411	Andy Benes	.20	.09
412	Juan Bell	.10	.05
413	Royce Clayton	.10	.05
414	Ed Sprague	.10	.05
415	Mike Mussina	.40	.18
416	Todd Hundley	.20	.09
417	Pat Listach	.10	.05
418	Joe Oliver	.10	.05
419	Rafael Palmeiro	.40	.18
420	Tim Salmon	.40	.18

❑ 421 Brady Anderson	.20	.09	❑ 507 Mark Wohlers	.10	.05	Front Photo is Jim Tatum	
❑ 422 Kenny Lofton	.30	.14	❑ 508 Scott Sanders	.10	.05	❑ 589 Darren Bragg .10	.05
❑ 423 Craig Biggio	.40	.18	❑ 509 Pete Harnisch	.10	.05	❑ 590 Kevin King .10	.05
❑ 424 Bobby Bonilla	.20	.09	❑ 510 Wes Chamberlain	.10	.05	❑ 591 Kurt Miller .10	.05
❑ 425 Kenny Rogers	.10	.05	❑ 511 Tom Candiotti	.10	.05	❑ 592 Aaron Small .10	.05
❑ 426 Derek Bell	.20	.09	❑ 512 Albie Lopez	.10	.05	❑ 593 Troy O'Leary .20	.09
❑ 427 Scott Cooper	.10	.05	❑ 513 Denny Neagle	.20	.09	❑ 594 Phil Stidham .10	.05
❑ 428 Ozzie Guillen	.10	.05	❑ 514 Sean Berry	.10	.05	❑ 595 Steve Dunn .10	.05
❑ 429 Omar Vizquel	.20	.09	❑ 515 Billy Hatcher	.10	.05	❑ 596 Cory Bailey .10	.05
❑ 430 Phil Plantier	.10	.05	❑ 516 Todd Jones	.10	.05	❑ 597 Alex Gonzalez .10	.05
❑ 431 Chuck Knoblauch	.40	.18	❑ 517 Wayne Kirby	.10	.05	❑ 598 Jim Bowie .10	.05
❑ 432 Darren Daulton	.20	.09	❑ 518 Butch Henry	.10	.05	❑ 599 Jeff Cirillo .20	.09
❑ 433 Bob Hamelin	.10	.05	❑ 519 Sandy Alomar Jr.	.20	.09	❑ 600 Mark Hutton .10	.05
❑ 434 Tom Glavine	.40	.18	❑ 520 Kevin Appier	.20	.09	❑ 601 Russ Davis .20	.09
❑ 435 Walt Weiss	.10	.05	❑ 521 Roberto Mejia	.10	.05	❑ 602 Checklist .10	.05
❑ 436 Jose Vizcaino	.10	.05	❑ 522 Steve Cooke	.10	.05	❑ 603 Checklist .10	.05
❑ 437 Ken Griffey Jr.	2.00	.90	❑ 523 Terry Shumpert	.10	.05	❑ 604 Checklist .10	.05
❑ 438 Jay Bell	.10	.05	❑ 524 Mike Jackson	.20	.09	❑ 605 Checklist .10	.05
❑ 439 Juan Gonzalez	.75	.35	❑ 525 Kent Mercker	.10	.05	❑ RG1 R.Klesko Rook.Great. 1.00	.45
❑ 440 Jeff Blauser	.10	.05	❑ 526 David Wells	.30	.14	❑ SG1 Ryan Klesko AU6100 10.00	4.50
❑ 441 Rickey Henderson	.50	.23	❑ 527 Juan Samuel	.10	.05	❑ NNO Trade Hall of Gold 1.00	.45
❑ 442 Bobby Ayala	.10	.05	❑ 528 Salomon Torres	.10	.05		
❑ 443 David Cone	.30	.14	❑ 529 Duane Ward	.10	.05		
❑ 444 Pedro Martinez	.50	.23	❑ 530 Rob Dibble	.10	.05		
❑ 445 Manny Ramirez	.50	.23	❑ 531 Mike Blowers	.10	.05		
❑ 446 Mark Portugal	.10	.05	❑ 532 Mark Eichhorn	.10	.05		
❑ 447 Damion Easley	.10	.05	❑ 533 Alex Diaz	.10	.05		
❑ 448 Gary DiSarcina	.10	.05	❑ 534 Dan Miceli	.10	.05		
❑ 449 Roberto Hernandez	.10	.05	❑ 535 Jeff Branson	.10	.05		
❑ 450 Jeffrey Hammonds	.20	.09	❑ 536 Dave Stevens	.10	.05		
❑ 451 Jeff Treadway	.10	.05	❑ 537 Charlie O'Brien	.10	.05		
❑ 452 Jim Abbott	.20	.09	❑ 538 Shane Reynolds	.20	.09		
❑ 453 Carlos Rodriguez	.10	.05	❑ 539 Rich Amaral	.10	.05		
❑ 454 Joey Cora	.10	.05	❑ 540 Rusty Greer	.40	.18		
❑ 455 Bret Boone	.20	.09	❑ 541 Alex Arias	.10	.05		
❑ 456 Danny Tartabull	.20	.09	❑ 542 Eric Plunk	.10	.05		
❑ 457 John Franco	.10	.05	❑ 543 John Hudek	.10	.05		
❑ 458 Roger Salkeld	.10	.05	❑ 544 Kirk McCaskill	.10	.05		
❑ 459 Fred McGriff	.30	.14	❑ 545 Jeff Reboulet	.10	.05		
❑ 460 Pedro Astacio	.10	.05	❑ 546 Sterling Hitchcock	.10	.05		

1995 Score Airmail | | | | | |

❑ 461 Jon Lieber	.10	.05	❑ 547 Warren Newson	.10 .05
❑ 462 Luis Polonia	.10	.05	❑ 548 Bryan Harvey	.10 .05
❑ 463 Geronimo Pena	.10	.05	❑ 549 Mike Huff	.10 .05
❑ 464 Tom Gordon	.10	.05	❑ 550 Lance Parrish	.10 .05
❑ 465 Brad Ausmus	.10	.05	❑ 551 Ken Griffey Jr. HIT 1.00 .45	
❑ 466 Willie McGee	.20	.09	❑ 552 Matt Williams HIT .20 .09	
❑ 467 Doug Jones	.10	.05	❑ 553 Roberto Alomar HIT UER .20 .09	
❑ 468 John Smoltz	.30	.14	(Card says he's a All-Star	
❑ 469 Troy Neel	.10	.05	He plays in the AL)	
❑ 470 Luis Sojo	.10	.05	❑ 554 Jeff Bagwell HIT .40 .18	
❑ 471 John Smiley	.10	.05	❑ 555 Dave Justice HIT .20 .09	
❑ 472 Rafael Bournigal	.10	.05	❑ 556 Cal Ripken Jr. HIT .75 .35	
❑ 473 Bill Taylor	.10	.05	❑ 557 Albert Belle HIT .20 .09	
❑ 474 Juan Guzman	.10	.05	❑ 558 Mike Piazza HIT .60 .25	
❑ 475 Dave Magadan	.10	.05	❑ 559 Kirby Puckett HIT .40 .18	
❑ 476 Mike Devereaux	.10	.05	❑ 560 Wade Boggs HIT .20 .09	
❑ 477 Andujar Cedeno	.10	.05	❑ 561 Tony Gwynn HIT UER .50 .23	
❑ 478 Edgar Martinez	.20	.09	card has him winning AL batting titles	
❑ 479 Milt Thompson	.10	.05	he's played whole career in the NL	
❑ 480 Allen Watson	.10	.05	❑ 562 Barry Bonds HIT .30 .14	
❑ 481 Ron Karkovice	.10	.05	❑ 563 Mo Vaughn HIT .30 .14	
❑ 482 Joey Hamilton	.20	.09	❑ 564 Don Mattingly HIT .40 .18	
❑ 483 Vinny Castilla	.30	.14	❑ 565 Carlos Baerga HIT .20 .09	
❑ 484 Tim Belcher	.10	.05	❑ 566 Paul Molitor HIT .20 .09	
❑ 485 Bernard Gilkey	.10	.05	❑ 567 Raul Mondesi HIT .10 .05	
❑ 486 Scott Servais	.10	.05	❑ 568 Manny Ramirez HIT .20 .09	
❑ 487 Cory Snyder	.10	.05	❑ 569 Alex Rodriguez HIT .75 .35	
❑ 488 Mel Rojas	.10	.05	❑ 570 Will Clark HIT .20 .09	
❑ 489 Carlos Reyes	.10	.05	❑ 571 Frank Thomas HIT .40 .18	
❑ 490 Chip Hale	.10	.05	❑ 572 Moises Alou HIT .10 .05	
❑ 491 Bill Swift	.10	.05	❑ 573 Jeff Conine HIT .10 .05	
❑ 492 Pat Rapp	.10	.05	❑ 574 Joe Ausanio .10 .05	
❑ 493 Brian McRae	.10	.05	❑ 575 Charles Johnson .20 .09	
❑ 494 Mickey Morandini	.10	.05	❑ 576 Ernie Young .10 .05	
❑ 495 Tony Pena	.10	.05	❑ 577 Jeff Granger .10 .05	
❑ 496 Danny Bautista	.10	.05	❑ 578 Robert Perez .10 .05	
❑ 497 Armando Reynoso	.10	.05	❑ 579 Melvin Nieves .10 .05	
❑ 498 Ken Ryan	.10	.05	❑ 580 Gar Finnvold .10 .05	
❑ 499 Billy Ripken	.10	.05	❑ 581 Duane Singleton .10 .05	
❑ 500 Pat Mahomes	.10	.05	❑ 582 Chan Ho Park .40 .18	
❑ 501 Mark Acre	.10	.05	❑ 583 Fausto Cruz .10 .05	
❑ 502 Geronimo Berroa	.10	.05	❑ 584 Dave Staton .10 .05	
❑ 503 Norberto Martin	.10	.05	❑ 585 Denny Hocking .10 .05	
❑ 504 Chad Kreuter	.10	.05	❑ 586 Nate Minchey .10 .05	
❑ 505 Howard Johnson	.10	.05	❑ 587 Marc Newfield .10 .05	
❑ 506 Eric Anthony	.10	.05	❑ 588 Jayhawk Owens UER .10 .05	

	MINT	NRMT
COMPLETE SET (18)	50.00	22.00
COMMON CARD (AM1-AM18)	2.00	.90
SEMISTARS	4.00	1.80
UNLISTED STARS	6.00	2.70
SER.2 STATED ODDS 1:24 JUMBO		
❑ AM1 Bob Hamelin	2.00	.90
❑ AM2 John Mabry	2.00	.90
❑ AM3 Marc Newfield	2.00	.90
❑ AM4 Jose Oliva	2.00	.90
❑ AM5 Charles Johnson	3.00	1.35
❑ AM6 Russ Davis	3.00	1.35
❑ AM7 Ernie Young	2.00	.90
❑ AM8 Billy Ashley	2.00	.90
❑ AM9 Ryan Klesko	3.00	1.35
❑ AM10 J.R. Phillips	2.00	.90
❑ AM11 Cliff Floyd	3.00	1.35
❑ AM12 Carlos Delgado	6.00	2.70
❑ AM13 Melvin Nieves	2.00	.90
❑ AM14 Raul Mondesi	4.00	1.80
❑ AM15 Manny Ramirez	8.00	3.60
❑ AM16 Mike Kelly	2.00	.90
❑ AM17 Alex Rodriguez	30.00	13.50
❑ AM18 Rusty Greer	6.00	2.70

1995 Score Double Gold Champs

	MINT	NRMT
COMPLETE SET (12)	100.00	45.00
COMMON CARD (GC1-GC12)	2.50	1.10
SER.2 STATED ODDS 1:36 HOBBY		
❑ GC1 Frank Thomas	8.00	3.60
❑ GC2 Ken Griffey Jr.	20.00	9.00
❑ GC3 Barry Bonds	4.00	1.80
❑ GC4 Tony Gwynn	10.00	4.50
❑ GC5 Don Mattingly	8.00	3.60
❑ GC6 Greg Maddux	10.00	4.50
❑ GC7 Roger Clemens	10.00	4.50
❑ GC8 Kenny Lofton	2.50	1.10
❑ GC9 Jeff Bagwell	5.00	2.20
❑ GC10 Matt Williams	4.00	1.80
❑ GC11 Kirby Puckett	6.00	2.70
❑ GC12 Cal Ripken	15.00	6.75

1995 Score Draft Picks

	MINT	NRMT
COMPLETE SET (18)	30.00	13.50
COMMON CARD (DP1-DP18)	1.00	.45
MINOR STARS	1.50	.70
SER.1 STATED ODDS 1:36 HOBBY		
❑ DP1 McKay Christensen	1.00	.45
❑ DP2 Bret Wagner	1.00	.45
❑ DP3 Paul Wilson	1.00	.45
❑ DP4 C.J. Nitkowski	1.00	.45
❑ DP5 Josh Booty	1.00	.45
❑ DP6 Antone Williamson	1.00	.45
❑ DP7 Paul Konerko	5.00	2.20
❑ DP8 Scott Elarton	3.00	1.35
❑ DP9 Jacob Shumate	1.00	.45
❑ DP10 Terrence Long	1.50	.70
❑ DP11 Mark Johnson	1.00	.45
❑ DP12 Ben Grieve	8.00	3.60
❑ DP13 Doug Million	1.00	.45
❑ DP14 Jayson Peterson	1.00	.45
❑ DP15 Dustin Hermanson	1.00	.45
❑ DP16 Matt Smith	1.00	.45
❑ DP17 Kevin Witt	2.00	.90
❑ DP18 Brian Buchanan	1.00	.45

1995 Score Dream Team

	MINT	NRMT
COMPLETE SET (12)	150.00	70.00
COMMON CARD (DG1-DG12)	2.50	1.10
SER.1 STATED ODDS 1:72		

❑ DG1 Frank Thomas	20.00	9.00
❑ DG2 Roberto Alomar	8.00	3.60
❑ DG3 Cal Ripken	30.00	13.50
❑ DG4 Matt Williams	8.00	3.60
❑ DG5 Mike Piazza	25.00	11.00
❑ DG6 Albert Belle	8.00	3.60
❑ DG7 Ken Griffey Jr.	40.00	18.00
❑ DG8 Tony Gwynn	20.00	9.00
❑ DG9 Paul Molitor	8.00	3.60
❑ DG10 Barry Larkin	5.00	2.20
❑ DG11 Greg Maddux	25.00	11.00
❑ DG12 Lee Smith	2.50	1.10

1995 Score Hall of Gold

	MINT	NRMT
COMPLETE SET (110)	80.00	36.00
COMPLETE SERIES 1 (55)	50.00	22.00
COMPLETE SERIES 2 (55)	30.00	13.50
COMMON CARD (HG1-HG110)	.50	.23
STATED ODDS 1:6H/R, 1:4J, 1:3ANCO		
COMP.YOU.TRADE EM SET (5)	4.00	1.80
*YTE CARDS: 2.5X TO 6X BASE CARD HI		
ONE YTE SET VIA MAIL PER YTE TRADE		
CARD		

❑ HG1 Ken Griffey Jr.	12.00	5.50
❑ HG2 Matt Williams	2.00	.90
❑ HG3 Roberto Alomar	2.00	.90
❑ HG4 Jeff Bagwell	3.00	1.35
❑ HG5 Dave Justice	2.00	.90
❑ HG6 Cal Ripken	10.00	4.50
❑ HG7 Randy Johnson	2.00	.90
❑ HG8 Barry Larkin	2.00	.90
❑ HG9 Albert Belle	2.00	.90
❑ HG10 Mike Piazza	8.00	3.60
❑ HG11 Kirby Puckett	2.00	.90
❑ HG12 Moises Alou	1.00	.45
❑ HG13 Jose Canseco	3.00	1.35
❑ HG14 Tony Gwynn	6.00	2.70
❑ HG15 Roger Clemens	6.00	2.70
❑ HG16 Barry Bonds	3.00	1.35
❑ HG17 Mo Vaughn	2.00	.90
❑ HG18 Greg Maddux	6.00	2.70
❑ HG19 Dante Bichette	1.00	.45
❑ HG20 Will Clark	2.00	.90
❑ HG21 Lenny Dykstra	1.00	.45
❑ HG22 Don Mattingly	5.00	2.20
❑ HG23 Carlos Baerga	.50	.23
❑ HG24 Ozzie Smith	3.00	1.35
❑ HG25 Paul Molitor	2.00	.90
❑ HG26 Paul O'Neill	1.00	.45
❑ HG27 Deion Sanders	1.00	.45
❑ HG28 Jeff Conine	.50	.23
❑ HG29 John Olerud	1.00	.45
❑ HG30 Jose Rijo	.50	.23
❑ HG31 Sammy Sosa	8.00	3.60
❑ HG32 Robin Ventura	1.00	.45
❑ HG33 Raul Mondesi	1.50	.70
❑ HG34 Eddie Murray	2.00	.90
❑ HG35 Marquis Grissom	1.00	.45
❑ HG36 Darryl Strawberry	1.00	.45
❑ HG37 Dave Nilsson	.50	.23
❑ HG38 Manny Ramirez	2.50	1.10
❑ HG39 Delino DeShields	.50	.23
❑ HG40 Lee Smith	1.00	.45
❑ HG41 Alex Rodriguez	10.00	4.50
❑ HG42 Julio Franco	.50	.23

❑ HG43 Bret Saberhagen	1.00	.45
❑ HG44 Ken Hill	.50	.23
❑ HG45 Roberto Kelly	.50	.23
❑ HG46 Hal Morris	.50	.23
❑ HG47 Jimmy Key	1.00	.45
❑ HG48 Terry Steinbach	.50	.23
❑ HG49 Mickey Tettleton	.50	.23
❑ HG50 Tony Phillips	.50	.23
❑ HG51 Carlos Garcia	.50	.23
❑ HG52 Jim Edmonds	1.50	.70
❑ HG53 Rod Beck	.50	.23
❑ HG54 Shane Mack	.50	.23
❑ HG55 Ken Caminiti	1.50	.70
❑ HG56 Frank Thomas	6.00	2.70
❑ HG57 Kenny Lofton	1.50	.70
❑ HG58 Juan Gonzalez	5.00	2.20
❑ HG59 Jason Bere	.50	.23
❑ HG60 Joe Carter	1.00	.45
❑ HG61 Gary Sheffield	1.00	.45
❑ HG62 Andres Galarraga	2.00	.90
❑ HG63 Ellis Burks	1.00	.45
❑ HG64 Bobby Bonilla	1.00	.45
❑ HG65 Tom Glavine	2.00	.90
❑ HG66 John Smoltz	1.50	.70
❑ HG67 Fred McGriff	1.50	.70
❑ HG68 Craig Biggio	2.00	.90
❑ HG69 Reggie Sanders	1.00	.45
❑ HG70 Kevin Mitchell	.50	.23
❑ HG71 Larry Walker	2.00	.90
❑ HG72 Carlos Delgado	2.00	.90
❑ HG73 Alex Gonzalez	.50	.23
❑ HG74 Ivan Rodriguez	3.00	1.35
❑ HG75 Ryan Klesko	1.00	.45
❑ HG76 John Kruk	1.00	.45
❑ HG77 Brian McRae	.50	.23
❑ HG78 Tim Salmon	2.00	.90
❑ HG79 Travis Fryman	1.00	.45
❑ HG80 Chuck Knoblauch	2.00	.90
❑ HG81 Jay Bell	1.00	.45
❑ HG82 Cecil Fielder	1.00	.45
❑ HG83 Cliff Floyd	1.00	.45
❑ HG84 Ruben Sierra	.50	.23
❑ HG85 Mike Mussina	2.00	.90
❑ HG86 Mark Grace	1.50	.70
❑ HG87 Dennis Eckersley	1.00	.45
❑ HG88 Dennis Martinez	.50	.23
❑ HG89 Rafael Palmeiro	2.00	.90
❑ HG90 Ben McDonald	.50	.23
❑ HG91 Dave Hollins	.50	.23
❑ HG92 Steve Avery	.50	.23
❑ HG93 David Cone	1.50	.70
❑ HG94 Darren Daulton	1.00	.45
❑ HG95 Bret Boone	1.00	.45
❑ HG96 Wade Boggs	2.00	.90
❑ HG97 Doug Drabek	.50	.23
❑ HG98 Andy Benes	1.00	.45
❑ HG99 Jim Thome	2.00	.90
❑ HG100 Chili Davis	1.00	.45
❑ HG101 Jeffrey Hammonds	1.00	.45
❑ HG102 Rickey Henderson	3.00	1.35
❑ HG103 Brett Butler	1.00	.45
❑ HG104 Tim Wallach	.50	.23
❑ HG105 Wil Cordero	.50	.23
❑ HG106 Mark Whiten	.50	.23
❑ HG107 Bob Hamelin	1.00	.45
❑ HG108 Rondell White	1.00	.45
❑ HG109 Devon White	1.00	.45
❑ HG110 Tony Tarasco	.50	.23

1995 Score Rookie Dream Team

	MINT	NRMT
COMPLETE SET (12)	60.00	27.00
COMMON CARD (RDT1-RDT12)	2.50	1.10
MINOR STARS	4.00	1.80
SER.2 STAT.ODDS 1:72 HOB/RET, 1:43 ANCO		
❑ RDT1 J.R. Phillips	2.50	1.10
❑ RDT2 Alex Gonzalez	2.50	1.10
❑ RDT3 Alex Rodriguez	30.00	13.50
❑ RDT4 Jose Oliva	2.50	1.10
❑ RDT5 Charles Johnson	4.00	1.80
❑ RDT6 Shawn Green	4.00	1.80
❑ RDT7 Brian Hunter	4.00	1.80

		MINT	NRMT
❑ RDT8	Garret Anderson	4.00	1.80
❑ RDT9	Julian Tavarez	2.50	1.10
❑ RDT10	Jose Lima	5.00	2.20
❑ RDT11	Armando Benitez	2.50	1.10
❑ RDT12	Ricky Bottalico	2.50	1.10

1995 Score Rules

		MINT	NRMT
COMPLETE SET (30)		120.00	55.00
COMMON CARD (SR1-SR30)		1.00	.45
SER.1 STATED ODDS 1:8 JUMBO			
❑ SR1	Ken Griffey Jr.	20.00	9.00
❑ SR2	Frank Thomas	8.00	3.60
❑ SR3	Mike Piazza	12.00	5.50
❑ SR4	Jeff Bagwell	4.00	1.80
❑ SR5	Alex Rodriguez	15.00	6.75
❑ SR6	Albert Belle	3.00	1.35
❑ SR7	Matt Williams	3.00	1.35
❑ SR8	Roberto Alomar	3.00	1.35
❑ SR9	Barry Bonds	4.00	1.80
❑ SR10	Raul Mondesi	2.50	1.10
❑ SR11	Jose Canseco	4.00	1.80
❑ SR12	Kirby Puckett	4.00	1.80
❑ SR13	Fred McGriff	2.50	1.10
❑ SR14	Kenny Lofton	2.50	1.10
❑ SR15	Greg Maddux	10.00	4.50
❑ SR16	Juan Gonzalez	8.00	3.60
❑ SR17	Cliff Floyd	2.00	.90
❑ SR18	Cal Ripken Jr.	15.00	6.75
❑ SR19	Will Clark	3.00	1.35
❑ SR20	Tim Salmon	3.00	1.35
❑ SR21	Paul O'Neill	2.00	.90
❑ SR22	Jason Bere	1.00	.45
❑ SR23	Tony Gwynn	10.00	4.50
❑ SR24	Manny Ramirez	4.00	1.80
❑ SR25	Don Mattingly	8.00	3.60
❑ SR26	Dave Justice	3.00	1.35
❑ SR27	Javier Lopez	2.00	.90
❑ SR28	Ryan Klesko	2.00	.90
❑ SR29	Carlos Delgado	3.00	1.35
❑ SR30	Mike Mussina	3.00	1.35

1996 Score

	MINT	NRMT
COMPLETE SET (517)	24.00	11.00
COMPLETE SERIES 1 (275)	12.00	5.50
COMPLETE SERIES 2 (242)	12.00	5.50
COMMON CARD (1-517)	.10	.05

MINOR STARS		.20	.09
UNLISTED STARS		.40	.18
SUBSET CARDS HALF VALUE OF BASE CARDS			
RIPKEN 2131 ODDS 1:300 H/R, 1:150 JUM			
❑ 1	Will Clark	.40	.18
❑ 2	Rich Becker	.10	.05
❑ 3	Ryan Klesko	.20	.09
❑ 4	Jim Edmonds	.30	.14
❑ 5	Barry Larkin	.40	.18
❑ 6	Jim Thome	.40	.18
❑ 7	Raul Mondesi	.20	.09
❑ 8	Don Mattingly	.75	.35
❑ 9	Jeff Conine	.10	.05
❑ 10	Rickey Henderson	.50	.23
❑ 11	Chad Curtis	.10	.05
❑ 12	Darren Daulton	.20	.09
❑ 13	Larry Walker	.40	.18
❑ 14	Carlos Garcia	.10	.05
❑ 15	Carlos Baerga	.10	.05
❑ 16	Tony Gwynn	1.00	.45
❑ 17	Jon Nunnally	.10	.05
❑ 18	Deion Sanders	.20	.09
❑ 19	Mark Grace	.30	.14
❑ 20	Alex Rodriguez	1.25	.55
❑ 21	Frank Thomas	.75	.35
❑ 22	Brian Jordan	.20	.09
❑ 23	J.T. Snow	.20	.09
❑ 24	Shawn Green	.40	.18
❑ 25	Tim Wakefield	.10	.05
❑ 26	Curtis Goodwin	.10	.05
❑ 27	John Smoltz	.30	.14
❑ 28	Devon White	.10	.05
❑ 29	Johnny Damon	.30	.14
❑ 30	Tim Salmon	.30	.14
❑ 31	Rafael Palmeiro	.40	.18
❑ 32	Bernard Gilkey	.10	.05
❑ 33	John Valentin	.20	.09
❑ 34	Randy Johnson	.40	.18
❑ 35	Garret Anderson	.20	.09
❑ 36	Rikkert Faneyte	.10	.05
❑ 37	Ray Durham	.20	.09
❑ 38	Bip Roberts	.10	.05
❑ 39	Jaime Navarro	.10	.05
❑ 40	Mark Johnson	.10	.05
❑ 41	Darren Lewis	.10	.05
❑ 42	Tyler Green	.10	.05
❑ 43	Bill Pulsipher	.10	.05
❑ 44	Jason Giambi	.20	.09
❑ 45	Kevin Ritz	.10	.05
❑ 46	Jack McDowell	.20	.09
❑ 47	Felipe Lira	.10	.05
❑ 48	Rico Brogna	.10	.05
❑ 49	Terry Pendleton	.20	.09
❑ 50	Rondell White	.20	.09
❑ 51	Andre Dawson	.30	.14
❑ 52	Kirby Puckett	.60	.25
❑ 53	Wally Joyner	.20	.09
❑ 54	B.J. Surhoff	.10	.05
❑ 55	Randy Velarde	.10	.05
❑ 56	Greg Vaughn	.20	.09
❑ 57	Roberto Alomar	.40	.18
❑ 58	David Justice	.40	.18
❑ 59	Kevin Seitzer	.10	.05
❑ 60	Cal Ripken	1.50	.70
❑ 61	Ozzie Smith	.50	.23
❑ 62	Mo Vaughn	.40	.18
❑ 63	Ricky Bones	.10	.05
❑ 64	Gary DiSarcina	.10	.05
❑ 65	Matt Williams	.40	.18
❑ 66	Wilson Alvarez	.10	.05
❑ 67	Lenny Dykstra	.20	.09
❑ 68	Brian McRae	.10	.05
❑ 69	Todd Stottlemyre	.10	.05
❑ 70	Bret Boone	.20	.09
❑ 71	Sterling Hitchcock	.10	.05
❑ 72	Albert Belle	.40	.18
❑ 73	Todd Hundley	.20	.09
❑ 74	Vinny Castilla	.30	.14
❑ 75	Moises Alou	.20	.09
❑ 76	Cecil Fielder	.20	.09
❑ 77	Brad Radke	.20	.09
❑ 78	Quilvio Veras	.10	.05
❑ 79	Eddie Murray	.40	.18
❑ 80	James Mouton	.10	.05
❑ 81	Pat Listach	.10	.05
❑ 82	Mark Gubicza	.10	.05
❑ 83	Dave Winfield	.40	.18
❑ 84	Fred McGriff	.30	.14
❑ 85	Darryl Hamilton	.10	.05
❑ 86	Jeffrey Hammonds	.20	.09
❑ 87	Pedro Munoz	.10	.05
❑ 88	Craig Biggio	.40	.18
❑ 89	Cliff Floyd	.20	.09
❑ 90	Tim Naehring	.10	.05
❑ 91	Brett Butler	.20	.09
❑ 92	Kevin Foster	.10	.05
❑ 93	Pat Kelly	.10	.05
❑ 94	John Smiley	.10	.05
❑ 95	Terry Steinbach	.20	.09
❑ 96	Orel Hershiser	.10	.05
❑ 97	Darrin Fletcher	.10	.05
❑ 98	Walt Weiss	.10	.05
❑ 99	John Wetteland	.20	.09
❑ 100	Alan Trammell	.30	.14
❑ 101	Steve Avery	.10	.05
❑ 102	Tony Eusebio	.10	.05
❑ 103	Sandy Alomar Jr.	.20	.09
❑ 104	Joe Girardi	.10	.05
❑ 105	Rick Aguilera	.10	.05
❑ 106	Tony Tarasco	.10	.05
❑ 107	Chris Hammond	.10	.05
❑ 108	Mike Macfarlane	.10	.05
❑ 109	Doug Drabek	.10	.05
❑ 110	Derek Bell	.20	.09
❑ 111	Ed Sprague	.10	.05
❑ 112	Todd Hollandsworth	.20	.09
❑ 113	Otis Nixon	.10	.05
❑ 114	Keith Lockhart	.10	.05
❑ 115	Donovan Osborne	.10	.05
❑ 116	Dave Magadan	.10	.05
❑ 117	Edgar Martinez	.20	.09
❑ 118	Chuck Carr	.10	.05
❑ 119	J.R. Phillips	.10	.05
❑ 120	Sean Bergman	.10	.05
❑ 121	Andujar Cedeno	.10	.05
❑ 122	Eric Young	.10	.05
❑ 123	Al Martin	.10	.05
❑ 124	Mark Lemke	.10	.05
❑ 125	Jim Eisenreich	.10	.05
❑ 126	Benito Santiago	.10	.05
❑ 127	Ariel Prieto	.10	.05
❑ 128	Jim Bullinger	.10	.05
❑ 129	Russ Davis	.10	.05
❑ 130	Jim Abbott	.20	.09
❑ 131	Jason Isringhausen	.20	.09
❑ 132	Carlos Perez	.10	.05
❑ 133	David Segui	.10	.05
❑ 134	Troy O'Leary	.10	.05
❑ 135	Pat Meares	.10	.05
❑ 136	Chris Hoiles	.10	.05
❑ 137	Ismael Valdes	.20	.09
❑ 138	Jose Oliva	.10	.05
❑ 139	Carlos Delgado	.40	.18
❑ 140	Tom Goodwin	.10	.05
❑ 141	Bob Tewksbury	.10	.05
❑ 142	Chris Gomez	.10	.05
❑ 143	Jose Oquendo	.10	.05
❑ 144	Mark Lewis	.10	.05
❑ 145	Salomon Torres	.10	.05
❑ 146	Luis Gonzalez	.20	.09
❑ 147	Mark Carreon	.10	.05
❑ 148	Lance Johnson	.10	.05

❏ 149 Melvin Nieves .10 .05	❏ 234 Ugueth Urbina .20 .09	❏ 318 Erik Hanson .10 .05
❏ 150 Lee Smith .20 .09	❏ 235 Ricky Otero .10 .05	❏ 319 Kenny Rogers .10 .05
❏ 151 Jacob Brumfield .10 .05	❏ 236 Mark Smith .10 .05	❏ 320 Hideo Nomo .40 .18
❏ 152 Armando Benitez .10 .05	❏ 237 Brian Barber .10 .05	❏ 321 Gregg Jefferies .10 .05
❏ 153 Curt Schilling .30 .14	❏ 238 Kevin Flora .10 .05	❏ 322 Chipper Jones 1.00 .45
❏ 154 Javier Lopez .20 .09	❏ 239 Joe Rosselli .10 .05	❏ 323 Jay Buhner .20 .09
❏ 155 Frank Rodriguez .10 .05	❏ 240 Derek Jeter 1.25 .55	❏ 324 Dennis Eckersley .20 .09
❏ 156 Alex Gonzalez .10 .05	❏ 241 Michael Tucker .10 .05	❏ 325 Kenny Lofton .30 .14
❏ 157 Todd Worrell .10 .05	❏ 242 Ben Blomdahl .10 .05	❏ 326 Robin Ventura .20 .09
❏ 158 Benji Gil .10 .05	❏ 243 Joe Vitiello .10 .05	❏ 327 Tom Glavine .40 .18
❏ 159 Greg Gagne .10 .05	❏ 244 Todd Steverson .10 .05	❏ 328 Tim Salmon .30 .14
❏ 160 Tom Henke .10 .05	❏ 245 James Baldwin .10 .05	❏ 329 Andres Galarraga .40 .18
❏ 161 Randy Myers .10 .05	❏ 246 Alan Embree .10 .05	❏ 330 Hal Morris .10 .05
❏ 162 Joey Cora .10 .05	❏ 247 Shannon Penn .10 .05	❏ 331 Brady Anderson .20 .09
❏ 163 Scott Ruffcorn .10 .05	❏ 248 Chris Stynes .10 .05	❏ 332 Chili Davis .20 .09
❏ 164 W. VanLandingham .10 .05	❏ 249 Oscar Munoz .10 .05	❏ 333 Roger Clemens 1.00 .45
❏ 165 Tony Phillips .10 .05	❏ 250 Jose Herrera .10 .05	❏ 334 Marquis Grissom .10 .05
❏ 166 Eddie Williams .10 .05	❏ 251 Scott Sullivan .10 .05	❏ 335 Mike Greenwell UER .10 .05
❏ 167 Bobby Bonilla .20 .09	❏ 252 Reggie Williams .10 .05	Name spelled Jeff on Front
❏ 168 Denny Neagle .20 .09	❏ 253 Mark Grudzielanek .10 .05	❏ 336 Sammy Sosa 1.25 .55
❏ 169 Troy Percival .20 .09	❏ 254 Steve Rodriguez .10 .05	❏ 337 Ron Gant .10 .05
❏ 170 Billy Ashley .10 .05	❏ 255 Terry Bradshaw .10 .05	❏ 338 Ken Caminiti .20 .09
❏ 171 Andy Van Slyke .10 .05	❏ 256 F.P. Santangelo .10 .05	❏ 339 Danny Tartabull .10 .05
❏ 172 Jose Offerman .10 .05	❏ 257 Lyle Mouton .10 .05	❏ 340 Barry Bonds .50 .23
❏ 173 Mark Parent .10 .05	❏ 258 George Williams .10 .05	❏ 341 Ben McDonald .10 .05
❏ 174 Edgardo Alfonzo .40 .18	❏ 259 Larry Thomas .10 .05	❏ 342 Ruben Sierra .10 .05
❏ 175 Trevor Hoffman .20 .09	❏ 260 Rudy Pemberton .10 .05	❏ 343 Bernie Williams .40 .18
❏ 176 David Cone .30 .14	❏ 261 Jim Pittsley .10 .05	❏ 344 Wil Cordero .10 .05
❏ 177 Dan Wilson .10 .05	❏ 262 Les Norman .10 .05	❏ 345 Wade Boggs .40 .18
❏ 178 Steve Ontiveros .10 .05	❏ 263 Ruben Rivera .20 .09	❏ 346 Gary Gaetti .20 .09
❏ 179 Dean Palmer .20 .09	❏ 264 Cesar Devarez .10 .05	❏ 347 Greg Colbrunn .10 .05
❏ 180 Mike Kelly .10 .05	❏ 265 Greg Zaun .10 .05	❏ 348 Juan Gonzalez .75 .35
❏ 181 Jim Leyritz .10 .05	❏ 266 Dustin Hermanson .10 .05	❏ 349 Marc Newfield .10 .05
❏ 182 Ron Karkovice .10 .05	❏ 267 John Frascatore .10 .05	❏ 350 Charles Nagy .20 .09
❏ 183 Kevin Brown .30 .14	❏ 268 Joe Randa .10 .05	❏ 351 Robby Thompson .10 .05
❏ 184 Jose Valentin .10 .05	❏ 269 Jeff Bagwell CL .40 .18	❏ 352 Roberto Petagine .10 .05
❏ 185 Jorge Fabregas .10 .05	❏ 270 Mike Piazza CL .60 .25	❏ 353 Darryl Strawberry .20 .09
❏ 186 Jose Mesa .10 .05	❏ 271 Dante Bichette CL .10 .05	❏ 354 Tino Martinez .20 .09
❏ 187 Brent Mayne .10 .05	❏ 272 Frank Thomas CL .40 .18	❏ 355 Eric Karros .20 .09
❏ 188 Carl Everett .20 .09	❏ 273 Ken Griffey Jr. CL 1.00 .45	❏ 356 Cal Ripken SS .75 .35
❏ 189 Paul Sorrento .10 .05	❏ 274 Cal Ripken CL .75 .35	❏ 357 Cecil Fielder SS .20 .09
❏ 190 Pete Schourek .10 .05	❏ 275 Greg Maddux CL .20 .09	❏ 358 Kirby Puckett SS .40 .18
❏ 191 Scott Kamieniecki .10 .05	Albert Belle	❏ 359 Jim Edmonds SS .10 .05
❏ 192 Roberto Hernandez .10 .05	❏ 276 Greg Maddux 1.00 .45	❏ 360 Matt Williams SS .20 .09
❏ 193 Randy Johnson RR .20 .09	❏ 277 Pedro Martinez .50 .23	❏ 361 Alex Rodriguez SS .60 .25
❏ 194 Greg Maddux RR .50 .23	❏ 278 Bobby Higginson .20 .09	❏ 362 Barry Larkin SS .20 .09
❏ 195 Hideo Nomo RR .20 .09	❏ 279 Ray Lankford .20 .09	❏ 363 Rafael Palmeiro SS .20 .09
❏ 196 David Cone RR .10 .05	❏ 280 Shawon Dunston .10 .05	❏ 364 David Cone SS .10 .05
❏ 197 Mike Mussina RR .20 .09	❏ 281 Gary Sheffield .20 .09	❏ 365 Roberto Alomar SS .20 .09
❏ 198 Andy Benes RR .10 .05	❏ 282 Ken Griffey Jr. 2.00 .90	❏ 366 Eddie Murray SS .20 .09
❏ 199 Kevin Appier RR .10 .05	❏ 283 Paul Molitor .40 .18	❏ 367 Randy Johnson SS .20 .09
❏ 200 John Smoltz RR .10 .05	❏ 284 Kevin Appier .10 .05	❏ 368 Ryan Klesko SS .20 .09
❏ 201 John Wetteland RR .10 .05	❏ 285 Chuck Knoblauch .20 .09	❏ 369 Raul Mondesi SS .10 .05
❏ 202 Mark Wohlers RR .10 .05	❏ 286 Alex Fernandez .10 .05	❏ 370 Mo Vaughn SS .20 .09
❏ 203 Stan Belinda .10 .05	❏ 287 Steve Finley .20 .09	❏ 371 Will Clark SS .20 .09
❏ 204 Brian Anderson .10 .05	❏ 288 Jeff Blauser .10 .05	❏ 372 Carlos Baerga SS .10 .05
❏ 205 Mike Devereaux .10 .05	❏ 289 Charles Johnson .20 .09	❏ 373 Frank Thomas SS .40 .18
❏ 206 Mark Wohlers .10 .05	❏ 290 John Franco .20 .09	❏ 374 Larry Walker SS .20 .09
❏ 207 Omar Vizquel .20 .09	❏ 291 Mark Langston .10 .05	❏ 375 Garret Anderson SS .10 .05
❏ 208 Jose Rijo .10 .05	❏ 292 Bret Saberhagen .10 .05	❏ 376 Edgar Martinez SS .10 .05
❏ 209 Willie Blair .10 .05	❏ 293 John Mabry .10 .05	❏ 377 Don Mattingly SS .40 .18
❏ 210 Jamie Moyer .10 .05	❏ 294 Ramon Martinez .20 .09	❏ 378 Tony Gwynn SS .50 .23
❏ 211 Craig Shipley .10 .05	❏ 295 Mike Blowers .10 .05	❏ 379 Albert Belle SS .20 .09
❏ 212 Shane Reynolds .20 .09	❏ 296 Paul O'Neill .20 .09	❏ 380 Jason Isringhausen SS .10 .05
❏ 213 Chad Fonville .10 .05	❏ 297 Dave Nilsson .10 .05	❏ 381 Ruben Rivera SS .10 .05
❏ 214 Jose Vizcaino .10 .05	❏ 298 Dante Bichette .20 .09	❏ 382 Johnny Damon SS .10 .05
❏ 215 Sid Fernandez .10 .05	❏ 299 Marty Cordova .40 .18	❏ 383 Karim Garcia SS .10 .05
❏ 216 Andy Ashby .10 .05	❏ 300 Jay Bell .20 .09	❏ 384 Derek Jeter SS .60 .25
❏ 217 Frank Castillo .10 .05	❏ 301 Mike Mussina .40 .18	❏ 385 David Justice SS .20 .09
❏ 218 Kevin Tapani .10 .05	❏ 302 Ivan Rodriguez .50 .23	❏ 386 Royce Clayton .20 .09
❏ 219 Kent Mercker .10 .05	❏ 303 Jose Canseco .50 .23	❏ 387 Mark Whiten .10 .05
❏ 220 Karim Garcia .20 .09	❏ 304 Jeff Bagwell .50 .23	❏ 388 Mickey Tettleton .10 .05
❏ 221 Antonio Osuna .10 .05	❏ 305 Manny Ramirez .50 .23	❏ 389 Steve Trachsel .10 .05
❏ 222 Tim Unroe .10 .05	❏ 306 Dennis Martinez .20 .09	❏ 390 Danny Bautista .10 .05
❏ 223 Johnny Damon .30 .14	❏ 307 Charlie Hayes .10 .05	❏ 391 Midre Cummings .10 .05
❏ 224 LaTroy Hawkins .10 .05	❏ 308 Joe Carter .20 .09	❏ 392 Scott Leius .10 .05
❏ 225 Mariano Rivera .30 .14	❏ 309 Travis Fryman .20 .09	❏ 393 Manny Alexander .10 .05
❏ 226 Jose Alberro .10 .05	❏ 310 Mark McGwire 2.00 .90	❏ 394 Brent Gates .10 .05
❏ 227 Angel Martinez .10 .05	❏ 311 Reggie Sanders UER .10 .05	❏ 395 Rey Sanchez .10 .05
❏ 228 Jason Schmidt .10 .05	Photo on front is John Roper	❏ 396 Andy Pettitte .30 .14
❏ 229 Tony Clark .40 .18	❏ 312 Julian Tavarez .10 .05	❏ 397 Jeff Cirillo .20 .09
❏ 230 Kevin Jordan UER .10 .05	❏ 313 Jeff Montgomery .10 .05	❏ 398 Kurt Abbott .10 .05
Ricky Jordan pictured on both sides	❏ 314 Andy Benes .20 .09	❏ 399 Lee Tinsley .10 .05
❏ 231 Mark Thompson .10 .05	❏ 315 John Jaha .10 .05	❏ 400 Paul Assenmacher .10 .05
❏ 232 Jim Dougherty .10 .05	❏ 316 Jeff Kent .20 .09	❏ 401 Scott Erickson .20 .09
❏ 233 Roger Cedeno .20 .09	❏ 317 Mike Piazza 1.25 .55	❏ 402 Todd Zeile .10 .05

❏ 403	Tom Pagnozzi	.10	.05
❏ 404	Ozzie Guillen	.10	.05
❏ 405	Jeff Frye	.10	.05
❏ 406	Kirt Manwaring	.10	.05
❏ 407	Chad Ogea	.10	.05
❏ 408	Harold Baines	.20	.09
❏ 409	Jason Bere	.10	.05
❏ 410	Chuck Finley	.20	.09
❏ 411	Jeff Fassero	.10	.05
❏ 412	Joey Hamilton	.10	.05
❏ 413	John Olerud	.20	.09
❏ 414	Kevin Stocker	.10	.05
❏ 415	Eric Anthony	.10	.05
❏ 416	Aaron Sele	.20	.09
❏ 417	Chris Bosio	.10	.05
❏ 418	Michael Mimbs	.10	.05
❏ 419	Orlando Miller	.10	.05
❏ 420	Stan Javier	.10	.05
❏ 421	Matt Mieske	.10	.05
❏ 422	Jason Bates	.10	.05
❏ 423	Orlando Merced	.10	.05
❏ 424	John Flaherty	.10	.05
❏ 425	Reggie Jefferson	.10	.05
❏ 426	Scott Stahoviak	.10	.05
❏ 427	John Burkett	.10	.05
❏ 428	Rod Beck	.10	.05
❏ 429	Bill Swift	.10	.05
❏ 430	Scott Cooper	.10	.05
❏ 431	Mel Rojas	.10	.05
❏ 432	Todd Van Poppel	.10	.05
❏ 433	Bobby Jones	.10	.05
❏ 434	Mike Harkey	.10	.05
❏ 435	Sean Berry	.10	.05
❏ 436	Glenallen Hill	.10	.05
❏ 437	Ryan Thompson	.10	.05
❏ 438	Luis Alicea	.10	.05
❏ 439	Esteban Loaiza	.10	.05
❏ 440	Jeff Reboulet	.10	.05
❏ 441	Vince Coleman	.10	.05
❏ 442	Ellis Burks	.20	.09
❏ 443	Allen Battle	.10	.05
❏ 444	Jimmy Key	.20	.09
❏ 445	Ricky Bottalico	.10	.05
❏ 446	Delino DeShields	.10	.05
❏ 447	Albie Lopez	.10	.05
❏ 448	Mark Petkovsek	.10	.05
❏ 449	Tim Raines	.20	.09
❏ 450	Bryan Harvey	.10	.05
❏ 451	Pat Hentgen	.20	.09
❏ 452	Tim Laker	.10	.05
❏ 453	Tom Gordon	.10	.05
❏ 454	Phil Plantier	.10	.05
❏ 455	Ernie Young	.10	.05
❏ 456	Pete Harnisch	.10	.05
❏ 457	Roberto Kelly	.10	.05
❏ 458	Mark Portugal	.10	.05
❏ 459	Mark Leiter	.10	.05
❏ 460	Tony Pena	.10	.05
❏ 461	Roger Pavlik	.10	.05
❏ 462	Jeff King	.10	.05
❏ 463	Bryan Rekar	.10	.05
❏ 464	Al Leiter	.20	.09
❏ 465	Phil Nevin	.10	.05
❏ 466	Jose Lima	.30	.14
❏ 467	Mike Stanley	.10	.05
❏ 468	David McCarty	.10	.05
❏ 469	Herb Perry	.10	.05
❏ 470	Geronimo Berroa	.10	.05
❏ 471	David Wells	.30	.14
❏ 472	Vaughn Eshelman	.10	.05
❏ 473	Greg Swindell	.10	.05
❏ 474	Steve Sparks	.10	.05
❏ 475	Luis Sojo	.10	.05
❏ 476	Derrick May	.10	.05
❏ 477	Joe Oliver	.10	.05
❏ 478	Alex Arias	.10	.05
❏ 479	Brad Ausmus	.10	.05
❏ 480	Gabe White	.10	.05
❏ 481	Pat Rapp	.10	.05
❏ 482	Damon Buford	.10	.05
❏ 483	Turk Wendell	.10	.05
❏ 484	Jeff Brantley	.10	.05
❏ 485	Curtis Leskanic	.10	.05
❏ 486	Robb Nen	.10	.05
❏ 487	Lou Whitaker	.20	.09
❏ 488	Melido Perez	.10	.05

❏ 489	Luis Polonia	.10	.05
❏ 490	Scott Brosius	.20	.09
❏ 491	Robert Perez	.10	.05
❏ 492	Mike Sweeney	.75	.35
❏ 493	Mark Loretta	.10	.05
❏ 494	Alex Ochoa	.10	.05
❏ 495	Matt Lawton	.50	.23
❏ 496	Shawn Estes	.20	.09
❏ 497	John Wasdin	.10	.05
❏ 498	Marc Kroon	.10	.05
❏ 499	Chris Snopek	.10	.05
❏ 500	Jeff Suppan	.10	.05
❏ 501	Terrell Wade	.10	.05
❏ 502	Marvin Benard	.10	.05
❏ 503	Chris Widger	.10	.05
❏ 504	Quinton McCracken	.10	.05
❏ 505	Bob Wolcott	.10	.05
❏ 506	C.J. Nitkowski	.10	.05
❏ 507	Aaron Ledesma	.10	.05
❏ 508	Scott Hatteberg	.10	.05
❏ 509	Jimmy Haynes	.10	.05
❏ 510	Howard Battle	.10	.05
❏ 511	Marty Cordova CL	.10	.05
❏ 512	Randy Johnson CL	.20	.09
❏ 513	Mo Vaughn CL	.20	.09
❏ 514	Chan Ho Park CL	.10	.05
❏ 515	Greg Maddux CL	.50	.23
❏ 516	Barry Larkin CL	.10	.05
❏ 517	Tom Glavine CL	.20	.09
❏ NNO	Cal Ripken 2131	20.00	9.00

1996 Score All-Stars

Albert Belle

		MINT	NRMT
COMPLETE SET (20)		60.00	27.00
COMMON CARD (1-20)		1.25	.55
SER.2 STATED ODDS 1:9 JUMBO			

❏ 1	Frank Thomas	6.00	2.70
❏ 2	Albert Belle	2.50	1.10
❏ 3	Ken Griffey Jr.	15.00	6.75
❏ 4	Cal Ripken	12.00	5.50
❏ 5	Mo Vaughn	2.50	1.10
❏ 6	Matt Williams	2.50	1.10
❏ 7	Barry Bonds	4.00	1.80
❏ 8	Dante Bichette	1.25	.55
❏ 9	Tony Gwynn	8.00	3.60
❏ 10	Greg Maddux	8.00	3.60
❏ 11	Randy Johnson	2.50	1.10
❏ 12	Hideo Nomo	2.50	1.10
❏ 13	Tim Salmon	2.00	.90
❏ 14	Jeff Bagwell	4.00	1.80
❏ 15	Edgar Martinez	1.25	.55
❏ 16	Reggie Sanders	1.25	.55
❏ 17	Larry Walker	2.50	1.10
❏ 18	Chipper Jones	8.00	3.60
❏ 19	Manny Ramirez	4.00	1.80
❏ 20	Eddie Murray	2.50	1.10

1996 Score Big Bats

		MINT	NRMT
COMPLETE SET (20)		100.00	45.00
COMMON CARD (1-20)		1.50	.70
SER.1 STATED ODDS 1:31 RETAIL			

❏ 1	Cal Ripken	15.00	6.75
❏ 2	Ken Griffey Jr.	20.00	9.00

BIG BAT Frank Thomas

❏ 3	Frank Thomas	8.00	3.60
❏ 4	Jeff Bagwell	5.00	2.20
❏ 5	Mike Piazza	12.00	5.50
❏ 6	Barry Bonds	5.00	2.20
❏ 7	Matt Williams	4.00	1.80
❏ 8	Raul Mondesi	2.00	.90
❏ 9	Tony Gwynn	10.00	4.50
❏ 10	Albert Belle	4.00	1.80
❏ 11	Manny Ramirez	5.00	2.20
❏ 12	Carlos Baerga	1.50	.70
❏ 13	Mo Vaughn	4.00	1.80
❏ 14	Derek Bell	2.00	.90
❏ 15	Larry Walker	4.00	1.80
❏ 16	Kenny Lofton	2.50	1.10
❏ 17	Edgar Martinez	2.00	.90
❏ 18	Reggie Sanders	2.00	.90
❏ 19	Eddie Murray	4.00	1.80
❏ 20	Chipper Jones	10.00	4.50

1996 Score Diamond Aces

NOMO

		MINT	NRMT
COMPLETE SET (30)		120.00	55.00
COMMON CARD (1-30)		1.50	.70
SER.1 STATED ODDS 1:8 JUMBO			

❏ 1	Hideo Nomo	4.00	1.80
❏ 2	Brian L.Hunter	1.50	.70
❏ 3	Ray Durham	2.00	.90
❏ 4	Frank Thomas	8.00	3.60
❏ 5	Cal Ripken	15.00	6.75
❏ 6	Barry Bonds	5.00	2.20
❏ 7	Greg Maddux	10.00	4.50
❏ 8	Chipper Jones	10.00	4.50
❏ 9	Raul Mondesi	2.00	.90
❏ 10	Mike Piazza	12.00	5.50
❏ 11	Derek Jeter	12.00	5.50
❏ 12	Bill Pulsipher	1.50	.70
❏ 13	Larry Walker	4.00	1.80
❏ 14	Ken Griffey Jr.	20.00	9.00
❏ 15	Alex Rodriguez	12.00	5.50
❏ 16	Manny Ramirez	5.00	2.20
❏ 17	Mo Vaughn	4.00	1.80
❏ 18	Reggie Sanders	2.00	.90
❏ 19	Derek Bell	2.00	.90
❏ 20	Jim Edmonds	2.50	1.10
❏ 21	Albert Belle	4.00	1.80
❏ 22	Eddie Murray	4.00	1.80
❏ 23	Tony Gwynn	10.00	4.50

		MINT	NRMT
☐ 24	Jeff Bagwell	5.00	2.20
☐ 25	Carlos Baerga	1.50	.70
☐ 26	Matt Williams	4.00	1.80
☐ 27	Garret Anderson	2.00	.90
☐ 28	Todd Hollandsworth	1.50	.70
☐ 29	Johnny Damon	2.50	1.10
☐ 30	Tim Salmon	2.50	1.10

1996 Score Dream Team

	MINT	NRMT
COMPLETE SET (9)	80.00	36.00
COMMON CARD (1-9)	1.50	.70
SER.1 STATED ODDS 1:72 HOB/RET		

		MINT	NRMT
☐ 1	Cal Ripken	15.00	6.75
☐ 2	Frank Thomas	8.00	3.60
☐ 3	Carlos Baerga	1.50	.70
☐ 4	Matt Williams	4.00	1.80
☐ 5	Mike Piazza	12.00	5.50
☐ 6	Barry Bonds	5.00	2.20
☐ 7	Ken Griffey Jr.	20.00	9.00
☐ 8	Manny Ramirez	5.00	2.20
☐ 9	Greg Maddux	10.00	4.50

1996 Score Dugout Collection

	MINT	NRMT
COMPLETE SERIES 1 (110)	50.00	22.00
COMPLETE SERIES 2 (110)	50.00	22.00
COMMON CARD (A1-B110)	.40	.18
MINOR STARS	.60	.25
SEMISTARS	1.00	.45
UNLISTED STARS	1.50	.70
STATED ODDS 1:3 HOB/RET		
SUBSET CARDS HALF VALUE OF BASE CARDS		
*AP STARS: 2.5X TO 6X HI COLUMN		
AP STATED ODDS 1:36 HOB/RET		

		MINT	NRMT
☐ A1	Will Clark	1.50	.70
☐ A2	Rich Becker	.40	.18
☐ A3	Ryan Klesko	.60	.25
☐ A4	Jim Edmonds	1.00	.45
☐ A5	Barry Larkin	1.50	.70
☐ A6	Jim Thome	1.50	.70
☐ A7	Raul Mondesi	.60	.25
☐ A8	Don Mattingly	3.00	1.35
☐ A9	Jeff Conine	.40	.18
☐ A10	Rickey Henderson	2.00	.90
☐ A11	Chad Curtis	.40	.18
☐ A12	Darren Daulton	.60	.25
☐ A13	Larry Walker	1.50	.70
☐ A14	Carlos Baerga	.40	.18
☐ A15	Tony Gwynn	4.00	1.80
☐ A16	Jon Nunnally	.40	.18
☐ A17	Deion Sanders	.60	.25
☐ A18	Mark Grace	1.00	.45
☐ A19	Alex Rodriguez	6.00	2.70
☐ A20	Frank Thomas	3.00	1.35
☐ A21	Brian Jordan	.60	.25
☐ A22	J.T. Snow	.60	.25
☐ A23	Shawn Green	1.50	.70
☐ A24	Tim Wakefield	.40	.18
☐ A25	Curtis Goodwin	.40	.18
☐ A26	John Smoltz	1.00	.45
☐ A27	Devon White	.60	.25
☐ A28	Brian L.Hunter	.40	.18
☐ A29	Rusty Greer	.60	.25
☐ A30	Rafael Palmeiro	1.50	.70
☐ A31	Bernard Gilkey	.40	.18
☐ A32	John Valentin	.60	.25
☐ A33	Randy Johnson	1.50	.70
☐ A34	Garret Anderson	.60	.25
☐ A35	Ray Durham	.60	.25
☐ A36	Bip Roberts	.40	.18
☐ A37	Tyler Green	.40	.18
☐ A38	Bill Pulsipher	.40	.18
☐ A39	Jason Giambi	.60	.25
☐ A40	Jack McDowell	.40	.18
☐ A41	Rico Brogna	.40	.18
☐ A42	Terry Pendleton	.40	.18
☐ A43	Rondell White	.60	.25
☐ A44	Andre Dawson	1.00	.45
☐ A45	Kirby Puckett	2.50	1.10
☐ A46	Wally Joyner	.60	.25
☐ A47	B.J. Surhoff	.40	.18
☐ A48	Randy Velarde	.40	.18
☐ A49	Greg Vaughn	.60	.25
☐ A50	Roberto Alomar	1.50	.70
☐ A51	David Justice	1.50	.70
☐ A52	Cal Ripken	6.00	2.70
☐ A53	Ozzie Smith	2.00	.90
☐ A54	Mo Vaughn	1.50	.70
☐ A55	Gary DiSarcina	.40	.18
☐ A56	Matt Williams	1.50	.70
☐ A57	Lenny Dykstra	.60	.25
☐ A58	Bret Boone	.60	.25
☐ A59	Albert Belle	1.50	.70
☐ A60	Vinny Castilla	1.00	.45
☐ A61	Moises Alou	.60	.25
☐ A62	Cecil Fielder	.60	.25
☐ A63	Brad Radke	.60	.25
☐ A64	Quivilio Veras	.40	.18
☐ A65	Eddie Murray	1.50	.70
☐ A66	Dave Winfield	1.50	.70
☐ A67	Fred McGriff	1.00	.45
☐ A68	Craig Biggio	1.50	.70
☐ A69	Cliff Floyd	.60	.25
☐ A70	Tim Naehring	.40	.18
☐ A71	John Wetteland	.60	.25
☐ A72	Alan Trammell	1.00	.45
☐ A73	Steve Avery	.40	.18
☐ A74	Rick Aguilera	.40	.18
☐ A75	Derek Bell	.60	.25
☐ A76	Todd Hollandsworth	.40	.18
☐ A77	Edgar Martinez	.60	.25
☐ A78	Mark Lemke	.40	.18
☐ A79	Ariel Prieto	.40	.18
☐ A80	Russ Davis	.40	.18
☐ A81	Jim Abbott	.60	.25
☐ A82	Jason Isringhausen	.40	.18
☐ A83	Carlos Perez	.40	.18
☐ A84	David Segui	.40	.18
☐ A85	Troy O'Leary	.60	.25
☐ A86	Ismael Valdes	.60	.25
☐ A87	Carlos Delgado	1.50	.70
☐ A88	Lee Smith	.60	.25
☐ A89	Javier Lopez	.60	.25
☐ A90	Frank Rodriguez	.40	.18
☐ A91	Alex Gonzalez	.40	.18
☐ A92	Benji Gil	.40	.18
☐ A93	Greg Gagne	.40	.18
☐ A94	Randy Myers	.40	.18
☐ A95	Bobby Bonilla	.60	.25
☐ A96	Billy Ashley	.40	.18
☐ A97	Andy Van Slyke	.40	.18
☐ A98	Edgardo Alfonzo	1.50	.70
☐ A99	David Cone	1.00	.45
☐ A100	Dean Palmer	.40	.25
☐ A101	Jose Mesa	.40	.18
☐ A102	Karim Garcia	.40	.25
☐ A103	Johnny Damon	1.00	.45
☐ A104	LaTroy Hawkins	.40	.18
☐ A105	Mark Smith	.40	.18
☐ A106	Derek Jeter	5.00	2.20
☐ A107	Michael Tucker	.60	.25
☐ A108	Joe Vitiello	.40	.18
☐ A109	Ruben Rivera	.60	.25
☐ A110	Greg Zaun	.40	.18
☐ B1	Greg Maddux	4.00	1.80
☐ B2	Pedro Martinez	2.00	.90
☐ B3	Bobby Higginson	.60	.25
☐ B4	Ray Lankford	.60	.25
☐ B5	Shawon Dunston	.40	.18
☐ B6	Gary Sheffield	.60	.25
☐ B7	Ken Griffey Jr.	8.00	3.60
☐ B8	Paul Molitor	1.50	.70
☐ B9	Kevin Appier	.60	.25
☐ B10	Chuck Knoblauch	1.50	.70
☐ B11	Alex Fernandez	.40	.18
☐ B12	Steve Finley	.60	.25
☐ B13	Jeff Blauser	.40	.18
☐ B14	Charles Johnson	.60	.25
☐ B15	John Franco	.60	.25
☐ B16	Mark Langston	.40	.18
☐ B17	Bret Saberhagen	.40	.25
☐ B18	John Mabry	.40	.18
☐ B19	Ramon Martinez	.60	.25
☐ B20	Mike Blowers	.40	.18
☐ B21	Paul O'Neill	.60	.25
☐ B22	Dave Nilsson	.40	.18
☐ B23	Dante Bichette	.60	.25
☐ B24	Marty Cordova	.60	.25
☐ B25	Jay Bell	.60	.25
☐ B26	Mike Mussina	1.50	.70
☐ B27	Ivan Rodriguez	2.00	.90
☐ B28	Jose Canseco	2.00	.90
☐ B29	Jeff Bagwell	2.00	.90
☐ B30	Manny Ramirez	2.00	.90
☐ B31	Dennis Martinez	.60	.25
☐ B32	Charlie Hayes	.40	.18
☐ B33	Joe Carter	.60	.25
☐ B34	Travis Fryman	.60	.25
☐ B35	Mark McGwire	8.00	3.60
☐ B36	Reggie Sanders	.40	.18
☐ B37	Julian Tavarez	.40	.18
☐ B38	Jeff Montgomery	.40	.18
☐ B39	Andy Benes	.60	.25
☐ B40	John Jaha	.40	.18
☐ B41	Jeff Kent	.60	.25
☐ B42	Mike Piazza	5.00	2.20
☐ B43	Erik Hanson	.40	.18
☐ B44	Kenny Rogers	.40	.18
☐ B45	Hideo Nomo	1.50	.70
☐ B46	Gregg Jefferies	.40	.18
☐ B47	Chipper Jones	5.00	2.20
☐ B48	Jay Buhner	.60	.25
☐ B49	Dennis Eckersley	.60	.25
☐ B50	Kenny Lofton	1.00	.45
☐ B51	Robin Ventura	.60	.25
☐ B52	Tom Glavine	1.50	.70
☐ B53	Tim Salmon	1.00	.45
☐ B54	Andres Galarraga	1.50	.70
☐ B55	Hal Morris	.60	.25
☐ B56	Brady Anderson	.60	.25
☐ B57	Chili Davis	.60	.25
☐ B58	Roger Clemens	4.00	1.80
☐ B59	Marquis Grissom	.60	.25
☐ B60	Mike Greenwell UER	.40	.18
	(Front says Jeff Greenwell)		
☐ B61	Sammy Sosa	5.00	2.20
☐ B62	Ron Gant	.40	.18
☐ B63	Ken Caminiti	.60	.25
☐ B64	Danny Tartabull	.40	.18
☐ B65	Barry Bonds	2.00	.90
☐ B66	Ben McDonald	.40	.18
☐ B67	Ruben Sierra	.40	.18
☐ B68	Bernie Williams	1.50	.70
☐ B69	Wil Cordero	.40	.18
☐ B70	Wade Boggs	1.50	.70

B71 Gary Gaetti	.60	.25
B72 Greg Colbrunn	.40	.18
B73 Juan Gonzalez	3.00	1.35
B74 Marc Newfield	.40	.18
B75 Charles Nagy	.60	.25
B76 Robby Thompson	.40	.18
B77 Roberto Petagine	.40	.18
B78 Darryl Strawberry	.60	.25
B79 Tino Martinez	.60	.25
B80 Eric Karros	.60	.25
B81 Cal Ripken SS	3.00	1.35
B82 Cecil Fielder SS	.40	.18
B83 Kirby Puckett SS	1.50	.70
B84 Jim Edmonds SS	.40	.25
B85 Matt Williams SS	.60	.25
B86 Alex Rodriguez SS	3.00	1.35
B87 Barry Larkin SS	.40	.18
B88 Rafael Palmeiro SS	.40	.18
B89 David Cone SS	.40	.18
B90 Roberto Alomar SS	.60	.25
B91 Eddie Murray SS	.60	.25
B92 Randy Johnson SS	.60	.25
B93 Ryan Klesko SS	.40	.18
B94 Raul Mondesi SS	.40	.18
B95 Mo Vaughn SS	.60	.25
B96 Will Clark SS	.60	.25
B97 Carlos Baerga SS	.40	.18
B98 Frank Thomas SS	1.50	.70
B99 Larry Walker SS	.60	.25
B100 Garret Anderson SS	.40	.18
B101 Edgar Martinez SS	.40	.18
B102 Don Mattingly SS	1.50	.70
B103 Tony Gwynn SS	2.00	.90
B104 Albert Belle SS	.60	.25
B105 Jason Isringhausen SS	.40	.18
B106 Ruben Rivera SS	.40	.18
B107 Johnny Damon SS	.40	.18
B108 Karim Garcia SS	.40	.18
B109 Derek Jeter SS	2.50	1.10
B110 David Justice SS	.60	.25

1996 Score Future Franchise

	MINT	NRMT
COMPLETE SET (16)	100.00	45.00
COMMON CARD (1-16)	3.00	1.35
SEMISTARS	5.00	2.20
UNLISTED STARS	8.00	3.60
SER.2 STATED ODDS 1:72 HOB/RET		

1 Jason Isringhausen	4.00	1.80
2 Chipper Jones	20.00	9.00
3 Derek Jeter	25.00	11.00
4 Alex Rodriguez	25.00	11.00
5 Alex Ochoa	3.00	1.35
6 Manny Ramirez	10.00	4.50
7 Johnny Damon	5.00	2.20
8 Ruben Rivera	4.00	1.80
9 Karim Garcia	4.00	1.80
10 Garret Anderson	4.00	1.80
11 Marty Cordova	3.00	1.35
12 Bill Pulsipher	3.00	1.35
13 Hideo Nomo	8.00	3.60
14 Marc Newfield	3.00	1.35
15 Charles Johnson	4.00	1.80
16 Raul Mondesi	4.00	1.80

1996 Score Gold Stars

	MINT	NRMT
COMPLETE SET (30)	50.00	22.00
COMMON CARD (1-30)	.50	.23
SER.2 STATED ODDS 1:15 HOB/RET		

1 Ken Griffey Jr.	10.00	4.50
2 Frank Thomas	4.00	1.80
3 Reggie Sanders	1.00	.45
4 Tim Salmon	1.50	.70
5 Mike Piazza	6.00	2.70
6 Tony Gwynn	5.00	2.20
7 Gary Sheffield	1.00	.45
8 Matt Williams	2.00	.90
9 Bernie Williams	2.00	.90
10 Jason Isringhausen	1.00	.45
11 Albert Belle	2.00	.90
12 Chipper Jones	5.00	2.20
13 Edgar Martinez	1.00	.45
14 Barry Larkin	2.00	.90
15 Barry Bonds	2.50	1.10
16 Jeff Bagwell	2.50	1.10
17 Greg Maddux	5.00	2.20
18 Mo Vaughn	2.00	.90
19 Ryan Klesko	1.00	.45
20 Sammy Sosa	6.00	2.70
21 Darren Daulton	1.00	.45
22 Ivan Rodriguez	2.50	1.10
23 Dante Bichette	1.00	.45
24 Hideo Nomo	2.00	.90
25 Cal Ripken	8.00	3.60
26 Rafael Palmeiro	2.00	.90
27 Larry Walker	2.00	.90
28 Carlos Baerga	.50	.23
29 Randy Johnson	2.00	.90
30 Manny Ramirez	2.50	1.10

1996 Score Numbers Game

	MINT	NRMT
COMPLETE SET (30)	60.00	27.00
COMMON CARD (1-30)	1.00	.45
SER.1 STATED ODDS 1:15 HOB/RET		

1 Cal Ripken	8.00	3.60
2 Frank Thomas	5.00	2.20
3 Ken Griffey Jr.	10.00	4.50
4 Mike Piazza	6.00	2.70
5 Barry Bonds	2.50	1.10
6 Greg Maddux	5.00	2.20
7 Jeff Bagwell	2.50	1.10
8 Derek Bell	1.00	.45
9 Tony Gwynn	5.00	2.20
10 Hideo Nomo	2.00	.90
11 Raul Mondesi	1.00	.45
12 Manny Ramirez	2.50	1.10
13 Albert Belle	2.00	.90
14 Matt Williams	2.00	.90
15 Jim Edmonds	1.50	.70
16 Edgar Martinez	1.00	.45
17 Mo Vaughn	2.00	.90
18 Reggie Sanders	1.00	.45
19 Chipper Jones	5.00	2.20
20 Larry Walker	2.00	.90
21 Juan Gonzalez	4.00	1.80
22 Kenny Lofton	1.50	.70
23 Don Mattingly	5.00	2.20
24 Ivan Rodriguez	2.50	1.10
25 Randy Johnson	2.00	.90
26 Derek Jeter	6.00	2.70
27 J.T. Snow	1.00	.45
28 Will Clark	2.00	.90
29 Rafael Palmeiro	2.00	.90
30 Alex Rodriguez	6.00	2.70

1996 Score Power Pace

	MINT	NRMT
COMPLETE SET (18)	60.00	27.00
COMMON CARD (1-18)	1.25	.55
SER.2 STATED ODDS 1:31 RETAIL		

1 Mark McGwire	15.00	6.75
2 Albert Belle	3.00	1.35
3 Jay Buhner	1.25	.55
4 Frank Thomas	6.00	2.70
5 Matt Williams	3.00	1.35
6 Gary Sheffield	1.25	.55
7 Mike Piazza	10.00	4.50
8 Larry Walker	3.00	1.35
9 Mo Vaughn	3.00	1.35
10 Rafael Palmeiro	3.00	1.35
11 Dante Bichette	1.25	.55
12 Ken Griffey Jr.	15.00	6.75
13 Barry Bonds	4.00	1.80
14 Manny Ramirez	4.00	1.80
15 Sammy Sosa	10.00	4.50
16 Tim Salmon	2.00	.90
17 Dave Justice	3.00	1.35
18 Eric Karros	1.25	.55

1996 Score Reflextions

	MINT	NRMT
COMPLETE SET (20)	100.00	45.00
COMMON CARD (1-20)	1.25	.55
UNLISTED STARS	3.00	.55
SER.1 STATED ODDS 1:15 HOBBY		

1 Cal Ripken	15.00	6.75
Chipper Jones		
2 Ken Griffey Jr.	20.00	9.00
Alex Rodriguez		
3 Frank Thomas	6.00	2.70
Mo Vaughn		
4 Kenny Lofton	3.00	1.35

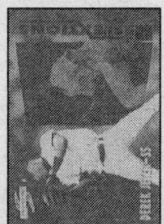

Brian L.Hunter
❏ 5	Don Mattingly	6.00	2.70
	J.T.Snow		
❏ 6	Manny Ramirez	4.00	1.80
	Raul Mondesi		
❏ 7	Tony Gwynn	8.00	3.60
	Garret Anderson		
❏ 8	Roberto Alomar	2.00	.90
	Larry Walker		
❏ 9	Andre Dawson	2.00	.90
❏ 10	Barry Larkin	10.00	4.50
	Derek Jeter		
❏ 11	Barry Bonds	4.00	1.80
	Reggie Sanders		
❏ 12	Mike Piazza	10.00	4.50
	Albert Belle		
❏ 13	Wade Boggs	3.00	1.35
	Edgar Martinez		
❏ 14	David Cone	1.25	.55
	John Smoltz		
❏ 15	Will Clark	4.00	1.80
	Jeff Bagwell		
❏ 16	Mark McGwire	15.00	6.75
	Cecil Fielder		
❏ 17	Greg Maddux	8.00	3.60
	Mike Mussina		
❏ 18	Randy Johnson	4.00	1.80
	Hideo Nomo		
❏ 19	Jim Thome	3.00	1.35
	Dean Palmer		
❏ 20	Chuck Knoblauch	3.00	1.35
	Craig Biggio		

1996 Score Titanic Taters

		MINT	NRMT
	COMPLETE SET (18)	80.00	36.00
	COMMON CARD (1-18)	1.50	.70
	SER.2 STATED ODDS 1:31 HOBBY		
❏ 1	Albert Belle	4.00	1.80
❏ 2	Frank Thomas	8.00	3.60
❏ 3	Mo Vaughn	4.00	1.80
❏ 4	Ken Griffey Jr.	20.00	9.00
❏ 5	Matt Williams	4.00	1.80
❏ 6	Mark McGwire	20.00	9.00
❏ 7	Dante Bichette	2.00	.90
❏ 8	Tim Salmon	2.50	1.10

❏ 9	Jeff Bagwell	5.00	2.20
❏ 10	Rafael Palmeiro	4.00	1.80
❏ 11	Mike Piazza	12.00	5.50
❏ 12	Cecil Fielder	1.50	.70
❏ 13	Larry Walker	4.00	1.80
❏ 14	Sammy Sosa	12.00	5.50
❏ 15	Manny Ramirez	5.00	2.20
❏ 16	Gary Sheffield	2.00	.90
❏ 17	Barry Bonds	5.00	2.20
❏ 18	Jay Buhner	2.00	.90

1997 Score

	MINT	NRMT
COMPLETE SET (551)	40.00	18.00
COMP.FACT.SET (551)	40.00	18.00
COMPLETE SERIES 1 (330)	15.00	6.75
COMPLETE SERIES 2 (221)	25.00	11.00
COMMON CARD (1-551)	.10	.05
MINOR STARS	.20	.09
UNLISTED STARS	.40	.18
SUBSET CARDS HALF VALUE OF BASE CARDS		
IRABU ENGLISH IN FACT.SET/RETAIL PACKS		
COMP.PRM.ST.SET (551)	80.00	36.00
COMP.PRM.ST.SER.1 (330)	40.00	18.00
COMP.PRM.ST.SER.2 (221)	40.00	18.00
COMMON PRM.STOCK (1-551)	.20	.09
*PREM.STOCK: .75X TO 2X HI COLUMN		
*PREM.STOCK IRABU: 4X TO 1X HI		
PRM.STOCK ONLY AVAIL.TO HOBBY		
IRABU JAPANESE IN HOBBY RESERVE PACKS		
PRM.ST.CALLED HOBBY RESERVE IN SER.2		
COMMON RESERVE (331-551) 2.00		.90
*RESERVE STARS: 10X TO 20X HI COL.		
*RESERVE ROOKIES: 4X TO 8X HI		
*RESERVE IRABU: 1.5X TO 3X HI		
SER.2 RESERVE ODDS 1:11 HOBBY		
COMMON SHOWCASE (1-551) .75		.35
*SHOWCASE STARS: 4X TO 8X HI COLUMN		
*SHOWCASE ROOKIES: 2X TO 4X HI		
*SHOWCASE IRABU: .6X TO 1.2X HI		
SER.1 SHOW.ODDS 1:7H/R,1:2JUM,1:4MAG		
SER.2 SHOW.ODDS 1:5 HOBBY, 1:7 RETAIL		
COMMON SHOW AP (1-551) .. 3.00		1.35
*SHOW.AP STARS: 15X TO 30X HI COLUMN		
*SHOW.AP ROOKIES: 5X TO 10X HI		
*SHOW.AP IRABU: 2X TO 4X HI		
SER.2 AP ODDS 1:23 HOBBY, 1:35 RETAIL		
SER.1 AP ODDS 1:35H/R, 1:7JUM, 1:17MAG		

❏ 1	Jeff Bagwell	.50	.23
❏ 2	Mickey Tettleton	.10	.05
❏ 3	Johnny Damon	.20	.09
❏ 4	Jeff Conine	.10	.05
❏ 5	Bernie Williams	.40	.18
❏ 6	Will Clark	.40	.18
❏ 7	Ryan Klesko	.20	.09
❏ 8	Cecil Fielder	.20	.09
❏ 9	Paul Wilson	.10	.05
❏ 10	Gregg Jefferies	.10	.05
❏ 11	Chili Davis	.20	.09
❏ 12	Albert Belle	.40	.18
❏ 13	Ken Hill	.10	.05
❏ 14	Cliff Floyd	.20	.09
❏ 15	Jaime Navarro	.10	.05
❏ 16	Ismael Valdes	.20	.09

❏ 17	Jeff King	.10	.05
❏ 18	Chris Bosio	.10	.05
❏ 19	Reggie Sanders	.20	.09
❏ 20	Darren Daulton	.20	.09
❏ 21	Ken Caminiti	.30	.14
❏ 22	Mike Piazza	1.25	.55
❏ 23	Chad Mottola	.10	.05
❏ 24	Darin Erstad	.40	.18
❏ 25	Dante Bichette	.20	.09
❏ 26	Frank Thomas	.75	.35
❏ 27	Ben McDonald	.10	.05
❏ 28	Raul Casanova	.10	.05
❏ 29	Kevin Ritz	.10	.05
❏ 30	Garret Anderson	.20	.09
❏ 31	Jason Kendall	.30	.14
❏ 32	Billy Wagner	.20	.09
❏ 33	Dave Justice	.40	.18
❏ 34	Marty Cordova	.10	.05
❏ 35	Derek Jeter	1.25	.55
❏ 36	Trevor Hoffman	.20	.09
❏ 37	Geronimo Berroa	.10	.05
❏ 38	Walt Weiss	.10	.05
❏ 39	Kirt Manwaring	.10	.05
❏ 40	Alex Gonzalez	.10	.05
❏ 41	Sean Berry	.10	.05
❏ 42	Kevin Appier	.20	.09
❏ 43	Rusty Greer	.20	.09
❏ 44	Pete Incaviglia	.10	.05
❏ 45	Rafael Palmeiro	.40	.18
❏ 46	Eddie Murray	.40	.18
❏ 47	Moises Alou	.20	.09
❏ 48	Mark Lewis	.10	.05
❏ 49	Hal Morris	.10	.05
❏ 50	Edgar Renteria	.20	.09
❏ 51	Rickey Henderson	.50	.23
❏ 52	Pat Listach	.10	.05
❏ 53	John Wasdin	.10	.05
❏ 54	James Baldwin	.20	.09
❏ 55	Brian Jordan	.20	.09
❏ 56	Edgar Martinez	.20	.09
❏ 57	Wil Cordero	.10	.05
❏ 58	Danny Tartabull	.10	.05
❏ 59	Keith Lockhart	.10	.05
❏ 60	Rico Brogna	.10	.05
❏ 61	Ricky Bottalico	.10	.05
❏ 62	Terry Pendleton	.10	.05
❏ 63	Bret Boone	.20	.09
❏ 64	Charlie Hayes	.10	.05
❏ 65	Marc Newfield	.10	.05
❏ 66	Sterling Hitchcock	.20	.09
❏ 67	Roberto Alomar	.40	.18
❏ 68	John Jaha	.10	.05
❏ 69	Greg Colbrunn	.10	.05
❏ 70	Sal Fasano	.10	.05
❏ 71	Brooks Kieschnick	.10	.05
❏ 72	Pedro Martinez	.50	.23
❏ 73	Kevin Elster	.10	.05
❏ 74	Ellis Burks	.20	.09
❏ 75	Chuck Finley	.20	.09
❏ 76	John Olerud	.20	.09
❏ 77	Jay Bell	.20	.09
❏ 78	Allen Watson	.10	.05
❏ 79	Darryl Strawberry	.20	.09
❏ 80	Orlando Miller	.10	.05
❏ 81	Jose Herrera	.10	.05
❏ 82	Andy Pettitte	.30	.14
❏ 83	Juan Guzman	.10	.05
❏ 84	Alan Benes	.10	.05
❏ 85	Jack McDowell	.10	.05
❏ 86	Ugueth Urbina	.10	.05
❏ 87	Rocky Coppinger	.10	.05
❏ 88	Jeff Cirillo	.20	.09
❏ 89	Tom Glavine	.40	.18
❏ 90	Robby Thompson	.10	.05
❏ 91	Barry Bonds	.50	.23
❏ 92	Carlos Delgado	.40	.18
❏ 93	Mo Vaughn	.40	.18
❏ 94	Ryne Sandberg	.50	.23
❏ 95	Alex Rodriguez	1.25	.55
❏ 96	Brady Anderson	.20	.09
❏ 97	Scott Brosius	.10	.05
❏ 98	Dennis Eckersley	.20	.09
❏ 99	Brian McRae	.10	.05
❏ 100	Rey Ordonez	.20	.09
❏ 101	John Valentin	.10	.05
❏ 102	Brett Butler	.20	.09

#	Player			#	Player			#	Player		
103	Eric Karros	.20	.09	189	Quinton McCracken	.10	.05	275	Ed Sprague	.10	.05
104	Harold Baines	.20	.09	190	Randy Myers	.10	.05	276	F.P. Santangelo	.10	.05
105	Javier Lopez	.20	.09	191	Jeromy Burnitz	.20	.09	277	Todd Greene	.10	.05
106	Alan Trammell	.20	.09	192	Randy Johnson	.40	.18	278	Butch Huskey	.10	.05
107	Jim Thorne	.40	.18	193	Chipper Jones	1.00	.45	279	Steve Finley	.20	.09
108	Frank Rodriguez	.10	.05	194	Greg Vaughn	.20	.09	280	Eric Davis	.20	.09
109	Bernard Gilkey	.10	.05	195	Travis Fryman	.20	.09	281	Shawn Green	.40	.18
110	Reggie Jefferson	.10	.05	196	Tim Naehring	.10	.05	282	Al Martin	.10	.05
111	Scott Stahoviak	.10	.05	197	B.J. Surhoff	.20	.09	283	Michael Tucker	.10	.05
112	Steve Gibralter	.10	.05	198	Juan Gonzalez	.75	.35	284	Shane Reynolds	.20	.09
113	Todd Hollandsworth	.10	.05	199	Terrell Wade	.10	.05	285	Matt Mieske	.10	.05
114	Ruben Rivera	.10	.05	200	Jeff Frye	.10	.05	286	Jose Rosado	.10	.05
115	Dennis Martinez	.20	.09	201	Joey Cora	.10	.05	287	Mark Langston	.20	.09
116	Mariano Rivera	.20	.09	202	Raul Mondesi	.20	.09	288	Ralph Milliard	.10	.05
117	John Smoltz	.30	.14	203	Ivan Rodriguez	.50	.23	289	Mike Lansing	.10	.05
118	John Mabry	.10	.05	204	Armando Reynoso	.10	.05	290	Scott Servais	.10	.05
119	Tom Gordon	.10	.05	205	Jeffrey Hammonds	.20	.09	291	Royce Clayton	.10	.05
120	Alex Ochoa	.10	.05	206	Darren Dreifort	.20	.09	292	Mike Grace	.10	.05
121	Jamey Wright	.10	.05	207	Kevin Seitzer	.10	.05	293	James Mouton	.10	.05
122	Dave Nilsson	.10	.05	208	Tino Martinez	.40	.18	294	Charles Johnson	.20	.09
123	Bobby Bonilla	.20	.09	209	Jim Bruske	.10	.05	295	Gary Gaetti	.20	.09
124	Al Leiter	.20	.09	210	Jeff Suppan	.10	.05	296	Kevin Mitchell	.10	.05
125	Rick Aguilera	.10	.05	211	Mark Carreon	.10	.05	297	Carlos Garcia	.10	.05
126	Jeff Brantley	.10	.05	212	Wilson Alvarez	.20	.09	298	Desi Relaford	.10	.05
127	Kevin Brown	.30	.14	213	John Burkett	.10	.05	299	Jason Thompson	.10	.05
128	George Arias	.10	.05	214	Tony Phillips	.10	.05	300	Osvaldo Fernandez	.10	.05
129	Darren Oliver	.10	.05	215	Greg Maddux	1.00	.45	301	Fernando Vina	.10	.05
130	Bill Pulsipher	.10	.05	216	Mark Whiten	.10	.05	302	Jose Offerman	.20	.09
131	Roberto Hernandez	.10	.05	217	Curtis Pride	.10	.05	303	Yamil Benitez	.10	.05
132	Delino DeShields	.10	.05	218	Lyle Mouton	.10	.05	304	J.T. Snow	.20	.09
133	Mark Grudzielanek	.20	.09	219	Todd Hundley	.20	.09	305	Rafael Bournigal	.10	.05
134	John Wetteland	.20	.09	220	Greg Gagne	.10	.05	306	Jason Isringhausen	.20	.09
135	Carlos Baerga	.10	.05	221	Rich Amaral	.10	.05	307	Bobby Higginson	.20	.09
136	Paul Sorrento	.10	.05	222	Tom Goodwin	.10	.05	308	Nerio Rodriguez	.25	.11
137	Leo Gomez	.10	.05	223	Chris Hoiles	.10	.05	309	Brian Giles	1.25	.55
138	Andy Ashby	.10	.05	224	Jayhawk Owens	.10	.05	310	Andruw Jones	.50	.23
139	Julio Franco	.20	.09	225	Kenny Rogers	.10	.05	311	Tony Graffanino	.10	.05
140	Brian Hunter	.20	.09	226	Mike Greenwell	.10	.05	312	Arquimedez Pozo	.10	.05
141	Jermaine Dye	.20	.09	227	Mark Wohlers	.10	.05	313	Jermaine Allensworth	.10	.05
142	Tony Clark	.30	.14	228	Henry Rodriguez	.20	.09	314	Jeff Darwin	.10	.05
143	Ruben Sierra	.10	.05	229	Robert Perez	.10	.05	315	George Williams	.10	.05
144	Donovan Osborne	.10	.05	230	Jeff Kent	.20	.09	316	Karim Garcia	.20	.09
145	Mark McLemore	.10	.05	231	Darryl Hamilton	.10	.05	317	Trey Beamon	.10	.05
146	Terry Steinbach	.10	.05	232	Alex Fernandez	.10	.05	318	Mac Suzuki	.10	.05
147	Bob Wells	.10	.05	233	Ron Karkovice	.10	.05	319	Robin Jennings	.10	.05
148	Chan Ho Park	.40	.18	234	Jimmy Haynes	.10	.05	320	Danny Patterson	.10	.05
149	Tim Salmon	.40	.18	235	Craig Biggio	.40	.18	321	Damon Mashore	.10	.05
150	Paul O'Neill	.20	.09	236	Ray Lankford	.20	.09	322	Wendell Magee	.10	.05
151	Cal Ripken	1.50	.70	237	Lance Johnson	.10	.05	323	Dax Jones	.10	.05
152	Wally Joyner	.20	.09	238	Matt Williams	.40	.18	324	Kevin Brown	.30	.14
153	Omar Vizquel	.20	.09	239	Chad Curtis	.10	.05	325	Marvin Benard	.10	.05
154	Mike Mussina	.40	.18	240	Mark Thompson	.10	.05	326	Mike Cameron	.20	.09
155	Andres Galarraga	.40	.18	241	Jason Giambi	.20	.09	327	Marcus Jensen	.10	.05
156	Ken Griffey Jr.	2.00	.90	242	Barry Larkin	.40	.18	328	Eddie Murray CL	.20	.09
157	Kenny Lofton	.30	.14	243	Paul Molitor	.40	.18	329	Paul Molitor CL	.20	.09
158	Ray Durham	.20	.09	244	Sammy Sosa	1.25	.55	330	Todd Hundley CL	.10	.05
159	Hideo Nomo	.40	.18	245	Kevin Tapani	.10	.05	331	Norm Charlton	.10	.05
160	Ozzie Guillen	.10	.05	246	Marquis Grissom	.20	.09	332	Bruce Ruffin	.10	.05
161	Roger Pavlik	.10	.05	247	Joe Carter	.20	.09	333	John Wetteland	.20	.09
162	Manny Ramirez	.50	.23	248	Ramon Martinez	.20	.09	334	Marquis Grissom	.20	.09
163	Mark Lemke	.10	.05	249	Tony Gwynn	1.00	.45	335	Sterling Hitchcock	.20	.09
164	Mike Stanley	.10	.05	250	Andy Fox	.10	.05	336	John Olerud	.20	.09
165	Chuck Knoblauch	.40	.18	251	Troy O'Leary	.10	.05	337	David Wells	.20	.09
166	Kimera Bartee	.10	.05	252	Warren Newson	.10	.05	338	Chili Davis	.20	.09
167	Wade Boggs	.40	.18	253	Troy Percival	.20	.09	339	Mark Lewis	.10	.05
168	Jay Buhner	.20	.09	254	Jamie Moyer	.10	.05	340	Kenny Lofton	.30	.14
169	Eric Young	.20	.09	255	Danny Graves	.10	.05	341	Alex Fernandez	.20	.09
170	Jose Canseco	.50	.23	256	David Wells	.10	.05	342	Ruben Sierra	.10	.05
171	Dwight Gooden	.20	.09	257	Todd Zeile	.10	.05	343	Delino DeShields	.10	.05
172	Fred McGriff	.30	.14	258	Raul Ibanez	.10	.05	344	John Wasdin	.10	.05
173	Sandy Alomar Jr.	.20	.09	259	Tyler Houston	.10	.05	345	Dennis Martinez	.20	.09
174	Andy Benes	.20	.09	260	LaTroy Hawkins	.10	.05	346	Kevin Elster	.10	.05
175	Dean Palmer	.20	.09	261	Joey Hamilton	.20	.09	347	Bobby Bonilla	.20	.09
176	Larry Walker	.40	.18	262	Mike Sweeney	.20	.09	348	Jaime Navarro	.10	.05
177	Charles Nagy	.20	.09	263	Brant Brown	.20	.09	349	Chad Curtis	.10	.05
178	David Cone	.30	.14	264	Pat Hentgen	.20	.09	350	Terry Steinbach	.10	.05
179	Mark Grace	.30	.14	265	Mark Johnson	.10	.05	351	Ariel Prieto	.10	.05
180	Robin Ventura	.20	.09	266	Robb Nen	.10	.05	352	Jeff Kent	.20	.09
181	Roger Clemens	1.00	.45	267	Justin Thompson	.20	.09	353	Carlos Garcia	.10	.05
182	Bobby Witt	.10	.05	268	Ron Gant	.20	.09	354	Mark Whiten	.10	.05
183	Vinny Castilla	.30	.14	269	Jeff D'Amico	.10	.05	355	Todd Zeile	.10	.05
184	Gary Sheffield	.20	.09	270	Shawn Estes	.20	.09	356	Eric Davis	.20	.09
185	Dan Wilson	.10	.05	271	Derek Bell	.20	.09	357	Greg Colbrunn	.10	.05
186	Roger Cedeno	.10	.05	272	Fernando Valenzuela	.20	.09	358	Moises Alou	.20	.09
187	Mark McGwire	2.00	.90	273	Tom Pagnozzi	.10	.05	359	Allen Watson	.10	.05
188	Darren Bragg	.10	.05	274	John Burke	.10	.05	360	Jose Canseco	.50	.23

361	Matt Williams	.40	.18
362	Jeff King	.10	.05
363	Darryl Hamilton	.10	.05
364	Mark Clark	.10	.05
365	J.T. Snow	.20	.09
366	Kevin Mitchell	.10	.05
367	Orlando Miller	.10	.05
368	Rico Brogna	.10	.05
369	Mike James	.10	.05
370	Brad Ausmus	.10	.05
371	Darryl Kile	.10	.05
372	Edgardo Alfonzo	.30	.14
373	Julian Tavarez	.10	.05
374	Darren Lewis	.10	.05
375	Steve Karsay	.10	.05
376	Lee Stevens	.20	.09
377	Albie Lopez	.10	.05
378	Orel Hershiser	.20	.09
379	Lee Smith	.20	.09
380	Rick Helling	.10	.05
381	Carlos Perez	.10	.05
382	Tony Tarasco	.10	.05
383	Melvin Nieves	.10	.05
384	Benji Gil	.10	.05
385	Devon White	.20	.09
386	Armando Benitez	.10	.05
387	Bill Swift	.10	.05
388	John Smiley	.10	.05
389	Midre Cummings	.10	.05
390	Tim Belcher	.10	.05
391	Tim Raines	.20	.09
392	Todd Worrell	.10	.05
393	Quilvio Veras	.10	.05
394	Matt Lawton	.20	.09
395	Aaron Sele	.20	.09
396	Bip Roberts	.10	.05
397	Denny Neagle	.20	.09
398	Tyler Green	.10	.05
399	Hipolito Pichardo	.10	.05
400	Scott Erickson	.20	.09
401	Bobby Jones	.10	.05
402	Jim Edmonds	.30	.14
403	Chad Ogea	.10	.05
404	Cal Eldred	.10	.05
405	Pat Listach	.10	.05
406	Todd Stottlemyre	.10	.05
407	Phil Nevin	.10	.05
408	Otis Nixon	.10	.05
409	Billy Ashley	.10	.05
410	Jimmy Key	.20	.09
411	Mike Timlin	.10	.05
412	Joe Vitiello	.10	.05
413	Rondell White	.20	.09
414	Jeff Fassero	.10	.05
415	Rex Hudler	.10	.05
416	Curt Schilling	.30	.14
417	Rich Becker	.10	.05
418	William Van Landingham	.10	.05
419	Chris Snopek	.10	.05
420	David Segui	.20	.09
421	Eddie Murray	.40	.18
422	Shane Andrews	.10	.05
423	Gary DiSarcina	.10	.05
424	Brian Hunter	.20	.09
425	Willie Greene	.10	.05
426	Felipe Crespo	.10	.05
427	Jason Bates	.10	.05
428	Albert Belle	.40	.18
429	Rey Sanchez	.10	.05
430	Roger Clemens	1.00	.45
431	Deion Sanders	.20	.09
432	Ernie Young	.10	.05
433	Jay Bell	.20	.09
434	Jeff Blauser	.10	.05
435	Lenny Dykstra	.20	.09
436	Chuck Carr	.10	.05
437	Russ Davis	.10	.05
438	Carl Everett	.20	.09
439	Damion Easley	.20	.09
440	Pat Kelly	.10	.05
441	Pat Rapp	.10	.05
442	Dave Justice	.40	.18
443	Graeme Lloyd	.10	.05
444	Damon Buford	.10	.05
445	Jose Valentin	.10	.05
446	Jason Schmidt	.10	.05
447	Dave Martinez	.10	.05
448	Danny Tartabull	.10	.05
449	Jose Vizcaino	.10	.05
450	Steve Avery	.10	.05
451	Mike Devereaux	.10	.05
452	Jim Eisenreich	.10	.05
453	Mark Leiter	.10	.05
454	Roberto Kelly	.10	.05
455	Benito Santiago	.10	.05
456	Steve Trachsel	.10	.05
457	Gerald Williams	.10	.05
458	Pete Schourek	.10	.05
459	Esteban Loaiza	.10	.05
460	Mel Rojas	.10	.05
461	Tim Wakefield	.20	.09
462	Tony Fernandez	.20	.09
463	Doug Drabek	.10	.05
464	Joe Girardi	.10	.05
465	Mike Bordick	.10	.05
466	Jim Leyritz	.10	.05
467	Erik Hanson	.10	.05
468	Michael Tucker	.10	.05
469	Tony Womack	.30	.14
470	Doug Glanville	.30	.14
471	Rudy Pemberton	.10	.05
472	Keith Lockhart	.10	.05
473	Nomar Garciaparra	1.25	.55
474	Scott Rolen	.60	.25
475	Jason Dickson	.10	.05
476	Glendon Rusch	.10	.05
477	Todd Walker	.40	.18
478	Dmitri Young	.20	.09
479	Rod Myers	.10	.05
480	Wilton Guerrero	.10	.05
481	Jorge Posada	.20	.09
482	Brant Brown	.20	.09
483	Bubba Trammell	.40	.18
484	Jose Guillen	.30	.14
485	Scott Spiezio	.10	.05
486	Bob Abreu	.20	.09
487	Chris Holt	.10	.05
488	Delvi Cruz	.40	.18
489	Vladimir Guerrero	.60	.25
490	Julio Santana	.10	.05
491	Ray Montgomery	.10	.05
492	Kevin Orie	.10	.05
493	Todd Hundley GY	.10	.05
494	Tim Salmon GY	.20	.09
495	Albert Belle GY	.20	.09
496	Manny Ramirez GY	.30	.14
497	Rafael Palmeiro GY	.20	.09
498	Juan Gonzalez GY	.40	.18
499	Ken Griffey Jr. GY	1.00	.45
500	Andruw Jones GY	.30	.14
501	Mike Piazza GY	.60	.25
502	Jeff Bagwell GY	.20	.09
503	Bernie Williams GY	.20	.09
504	Barry Bonds GY	.20	.09
505	Ken Caminiti GY	.10	.05
506	Darin Erstad GY	.40	.18
507	Alex Rodriguez GY	.60	.25
508	Frank Thomas GY	.40	.18
509	Chipper Jones GY	.50	.23
510	Mo Vaughn GY	.20	.09
511	Mark McGwire GY	1.00	.45
512	Fred McGriff GY	.20	.09
513	Jay Buhner GY	.10	.05
514	Gary Sheffield GY	.20	.09
515	Jim Thome GY	.20	.09
516	Dean Palmer GY	.20	.09
517	Henry Rodriguez GY	.10	.05
518	Andy Pettitte RF	.10	.05
519	Mike Mussina RF	.20	.09
520	Greg Maddux RF	.50	.23
521	John Smoltz RF	.20	.09
522	Hideo Nomo RF	.20	.09
523	Troy Percival RF	.10	.05
524	John Wetteland RF	.10	.05
525	Roger Clemens RF	.50	.23
526	Charles Nagy RF	.10	.05
527	Mariano Rivera RF	.10	.05
528	Tom Glavine RF	.20	.09
529	Randy Johnson RF	.20	.09
530	Jason Isringhausen RF	.10	.05
531	Alex Fernandez RF	.10	.05
532	Kevin Brown RF	.10	.05
533	Chuck Knoblauch TG	.20	.09
534	Rusty Greer TG	.10	.05
535	Tony Gwynn TG	.50	.23
536	Ryan Klesko TG	.10	.05
537	Ryne Sandberg TG	.40	.18
538	Barry Larkin TG	.20	.09
539	Will Clark TG	.40	.18
540	Kenny Lofton TG	.20	.09
541	Paul Molitor TG	.20	.09
542	Roberto Alomar TG	.20	.09
543	Rey Ordonez TG	.10	.05
544	Jason Giambi TG	.10	.05
545	Derek Jeter TG	.60	.25
546	Cal Ripken TG	.75	.35
547	Ivan Rodriguez TG	.30	.14
548	Ken Griffey Jr. CL	1.00	.45
549	Frank Thomas CL	.40	.18
550	Mike Piazza CL	.60	.25
551A	Hideki Irabu SP	8.00	3.60
551B	Hideki Irabu SP	8.00	3.60
	Japenese SP		

1997 Score Blast Masters

	MINT	NRMT
COMPLETE SET (18)	100.00	45.00
COMMON CARD (1-18)	2.00	.90
SER.2 ODDS 1:35 RETAIL, 1:23 HOBBY		

1	Mo Vaughn	4.00	1.80
2	Mark McGwire	20.00	9.00
3	Juan Gonzalez	8.00	3.60
4	Albert Belle	4.00	1.80
5	Barry Bonds	5.00	2.20
6	Ken Griffey Jr.	20.00	9.00
7	Andruw Jones	4.00	1.80
8	Chipper Jones	10.00	4.50
9	Mike Piazza	12.00	5.50
10	Jeff Bagwell	5.00	2.20
11	Dante Bichette	2.00	.90
12	Alex Rodriguez	12.00	5.50
13	Gary Sheffield	2.00	.90
14	Ken Caminiti	3.00	1.35
15	Sammy Sosa	12.00	5.50
16	Vladimir Guerrero	5.00	2.20
17	Brian Jordan	2.00	.90
18	Tim Salmon	4.00	1.80

1997 Score Franchise

	MINT	NRMT
COMPLETE SET (9)	100.00	45.00
COMMON CARD (1-9)	4.00	1.80

SER.1 ODDS 1:72 H/R, 1:17 JUM, 1:35 MAG
*GLOWING: 12.5X TO 30X BASE CARD HI
GLOW.SER.1 ODDS 1:240H/R, 1:79J, 1:120M

		MINT	NRMT
❏ 1	Ken Griffey Jr.	25.00	11.00
❏ 2	John Smoltz	4.00	1.80
❏ 3	Cal Ripken	20.00	9.00
❏ 4	Chipper Jones	12.00	5.50
❏ 5	Mike Piazza	15.00	6.75
❏ 6	Albert Belle	5.00	2.20
❏ 7	Frank Thomas	10.00	4.50
❏ 8	Sammy Sosa	15.00	6.75
❏ 9	Roberto Alomar	5.00	2.20

1997 Score Heart of the Order

	MINT	NRMT
COMPLETE SET (36)	100.00	45.00
COMMON CARD (1-660)	.75	.35

CARDS 1-18 RETAIL, 19-36 HOBBY
STATED ODDS 1:23 RETAIL, 1:15 HOBBY

		MINT	NRMT
❏ 1	Will Clark	3.00	1.35
❏ 2	Ivan Rodriguez	4.00	1.80
❏ 3	Juan Gonzalez	6.00	2.70
❏ 4	Frank Thomas	6.00	2.70
❏ 5	Albert Belle	3.00	1.35
❏ 6	Robin Ventura	1.25	.55
❏ 7	Alex Rodriguez	10.00	4.50
❏ 8	Jay Buhner	1.25	.55
❏ 9	Ken Griffey Jr.	15.00	6.75
❏ 10	Rafael Palmeiro	3.00	1.35
❏ 11	Roberto Alomar	3.00	1.35
❏ 12	Cal Ripken	12.00	5.50
❏ 13	Manny Ramirez	4.00	1.80
❏ 14	Matt Williams	3.00	1.35
❏ 15	Jim Thome	3.00	1.35
❏ 16	Derek Jeter	8.00	3.60
❏ 17	Wade Boggs	3.00	1.35
❏ 18	Bernie Williams	3.00	1.35
❏ 19	Chipper Jones	8.00	3.60
❏ 20	Andruw Jones	3.00	1.35
❏ 21	Ryan Klesko	1.25	.55
❏ 22	Mike Piazza	10.00	4.50
❏ 23	Wilton Guerrero	.75	.35
❏ 24	Paul Molitor	1.25	.55
❏ 25	Tony Gwynn	8.00	3.60
❏ 26	Greg Vaughn	1.25	.55
❏ 27	Ken Caminiti	2.00	.90
❏ 28	Brian Jordan	1.25	.55
❏ 29	Ron Gant	.75	.35
❏ 30	Dmitri Young	1.25	.55
❏ 31	Darin Erstad	3.00	1.35
❏ 32	Tim Salmon	3.00	1.35
❏ 33	Jim Edmonds	2.00	.90
❏ 34	Chuck Knoblauch	3.00	1.35
❏ 35	Paul Molitor	3.00	1.35
❏ 36	Todd Walker	3.00	1.35

1997 Score Highlight Zone

	MINT	NRMT
COMPLETE SET (18)	200.00	90.00

	MINT	NRMT
COMMON CARD (1-18)	4.00	1.80

SER.1 ODDS 1:35 HOBBY, 1:9 JUMBO PS

		MINT	NRMT
❏ 1	Frank Thomas	12.00	5.50
❏ 2	Ken Griffey Jr.	30.00	13.50
❏ 3	Mo Vaughn	6.00	2.70
❏ 4	Albert Belle	6.00	2.70
❏ 5	Mike Piazza	20.00	9.00
❏ 6	Barry Bonds	8.00	3.60
❏ 7	Greg Maddux	15.00	6.75
❏ 8	Sammy Sosa	20.00	9.00
❏ 9	Jeff Bagwell	8.00	3.60
❏ 10	Alex Rodriguez	20.00	9.00
❏ 11	Chipper Jones	15.00	6.75
❏ 12	Brady Anderson	4.00	1.80
❏ 13	Ozzie Smith	8.00	3.60
❏ 14	Edgar Martinez	4.00	1.80
❏ 15	Cal Ripken	25.00	11.00
❏ 16	Ryan Klesko	4.00	1.80
❏ 17	Randy Johnson	6.00	2.70
❏ 18	Eddie Murray	6.00	2.70

1997 Score Pitcher Perfect

	MINT	NRMT
COMPLETE SET (15)	60.00	27.00
COMMON CARD (1-15)	1.00	.45

SER.1 ODDS 1:23 H/R,1:11 MAG,1:15 JUM PS

		MINT	NRMT
❏ 1	Cal Ripken	10.00	4.50
❏ 2	Alex Rodriguez	8.00	3.60
❏ 3	Alex Rodriguez	12.00	5.50
	Cal Ripken		
❏ 4	Edgar Martinez	1.00	.45
❏ 5	Ivan Rodriguez	3.00	1.35
❏ 6	Mark McGwire	12.00	5.50
❏ 7	Tim Salmon	2.50	1.10
❏ 8	Chili Davis	1.00	.45
❏ 9	Joe Carter	1.00	.45
❏ 10	Frank Thomas	5.00	2.20
❏ 11	Will Clark	2.50	1.10
❏ 12	Mo Vaughn	2.50	1.10
❏ 13	Wade Boggs	2.50	1.10
❏ 14	Ken Griffey Jr.	12.00	5.50
❏ 15	Randy Johnson	2.50	1.10

1997 Score Stand and Deliver

	MINT	NRMT
COMPLETE SET (24)	350.00	160.00
COMMON CARD (1-24)	2.50	1.10
MINOR STARS	5.00	2.20
UNLISTED STARS	10.00	4.50

SER.2 ODDS 1:71 RETAIL, 1:41 HOBBY

		MINT	NRMT
❏ 1	Andruw Jones	12.00	5.50
❏ 2	Greg Maddux	25.00	11.00
❏ 3	Chipper Jones	25.00	11.00
❏ 4	John Smoltz	6.00	2.70
❏ 5	Ken Griffey Jr.	50.00	22.00
❏ 6	Alex Rodriguez	30.00	13.50
❏ 7	Jay Buhner	5.00	2.20
❏ 8	Randy Johnson	10.00	4.50
❏ 9	Derek Jeter	30.00	13.50
❏ 10	Andy Pettitte	6.00	2.70
❏ 11	Bernie Williams	10.00	4.50
❏ 12	Mariano Rivera	5.00	2.20
❏ 13	Mike Piazza	30.00	13.50
❏ 14	Hideo Nomo	10.00	4.50
❏ 15	Raul Mondesi	5.00	2.20
❏ 16	Todd Hollandsworth	2.50	1.10
❏ 17	Manny Ramirez	12.00	5.50
❏ 18	Jim Thome	10.00	4.50
❏ 19	Dave Justice	10.00	4.50
❏ 20	Matt Williams	10.00	4.50
❏ 21	Juan Gonzalez W	20.00	9.00
❏ 22	Jeff Bagwell W	12.00	5.50
❏ 23	Cal Ripken W	40.00	18.00
❏ 24	Frank Thomas W	20.00	9.00

1997 Score Stellar Season

	MINT	NRMT
COMPLETE SET (18)	80.00	36.00
COMMON CARD (1-18)	.75	.35

SER.1 STATED ODDS 1:35 MAGAZINE

		MINT	NRMT
❏ 1	Juan Gonzalez	6.00	2.70
❏ 2	Chuck Knoblauch	3.00	1.35
❏ 3	Jeff Bagwell	4.00	1.80
❏ 4	John Smoltz	2.00	.90
❏ 5	Mark McGwire	15.00	6.75
❏ 6	Ken Griffey Jr.	15.00	6.75
❏ 7	Frank Thomas	6.00	2.70

		MINT	NRMT
8	Alex Rodriguez	10.00	4.50
9	Mike Piazza	10.00	4.50
10	Albert Belle	3.00	1.35
11	Roberto Alomar	3.00	1.35
12	Sammy Sosa	10.00	4.50
13	Mo Vaughn	3.00	1.35
14	Brady Anderson	1.50	.70
15	Henry Rodriguez	.75	.35
16	Eric Young	.75	.35
17	Gary Sheffield	1.50	.70
18	Ryan Klesko	1.50	.70

1997 Score Titanic Taters

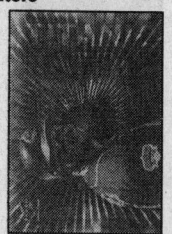

		MINT	NRMT
COMPLETE SET (18)		120.00	55.00
COMMON CARD (1-18)		2.50	1.10
SER.1 STATED ODDS 1:35 RETAIL			
1	Mark McGwire	25.00	11.00
2	Mike Piazza	15.00	6.75
3	Ken Griffey Jr.	25.00	11.00
4	Juan Gonzalez	10.00	4.50
5	Frank Thomas	10.00	4.50
6	Albert Belle	5.00	2.20
7	Sammy Sosa	15.00	6.75
8	Jeff Bagwell	6.00	2.70
9	Todd Hundley	2.50	1.10
10	Ryan Klesko	2.50	1.10
11	Brady Anderson	2.50	1.10
12	Mo Vaughn	5.00	2.20
13	Jay Buhner	2.50	1.10
14	Chipper Jones	12.00	5.50
15	Barry Bonds	6.00	2.70
16	Gary Sheffield	2.50	1.10
17	Alex Rodriguez	15.00	6.75
18	Cecil Fielder	2.50	1.10

1998 Score

		MINT	NRMT
COMPLETE SET (270)		40.00	18.00
COMMON CARD (1-270)		.10	.05
MINOR STARS		.15	.07
SEMISTARS		.25	.11
UNLISTED STARS		.40	.18
COMMON AP (PP1-PP160)		2.00	.90
*AP STARS: 8X TO 20X HI COLUMN			
*AP YOUNG STARS: 6X TO 15X HI			

ARTIST'S PROOFS STATED ODDS 1:35
COMMON SHOW. (PP1-PP160) .50 .23
*SHOWCASE STARS: 2X TO 5X HI COLUMN
*SHOWCASE YOUNG STARS: 1.5X TO 4X HI
SHOWCASE SERIES STATED ODDS 1:7

1	Andruw Jones	.40	.18
2	Dan Wilson	.10	.05
3	Hideo Nomo	.40	.18
4	Chuck Carr	.10	.05
5	Barry Bonds	.50	.23
6	Jack McDowell	.10	.05
7	Albert Belle	.40	.18
8	Francisco Cordova	.10	.05
9	Greg Maddux	1.00	.45
10	Alex Rodriguez	1.25	.55
11	Steve Avery	.10	.05
12	Chuck McElroy	.10	.05
13	Larry Walker	.40	.18
14	Hideki Irabu	.15	.07
15	Roberto Alomar	.40	.18
16	Neifi Perez	.15	.07
17	Jim Thome	.40	.18
18	Rickey Henderson	.50	.23
19	Andres Galarraga	.25	.11
20	Jeff Fassero	.10	.05
21	Kevin Young	.15	.07
22	Derek Jeter	1.25	.55
23	Andy Benes	.10	.05
24	Mike Piazza	1.25	.55
25	Todd Stottlemyre	.10	.05
26	Michael Tucker	.10	.05
27	Denny Neagle	.10	.05
28	Javier Lopez	.15	.07
29	Aaron Sele	.15	.07
30	Ryan Klesko	.15	.07
31	Dennis Eckersley	.15	.07
32	Quinton McCracken	.10	.05
33	Brian Anderson	.10	.05
34	Ken Griffey Jr.	2.00	.90
35	Shawn Estes	.10	.05
36	Tim Wakefield	.10	.05
37	Jimmy Key	.15	.07
38	Jeff Bagwell	.50	.23
39	Edgardo Alfonzo	.25	.11
40	Mike Cameron	.15	.07
41	Mark McGwire	2.50	1.10
42	Tino Martinez	.15	.07
43	Cal Ripken	1.50	.70
44	Curtis Goodwin	.10	.05
45	Bobby Ayala	.10	.05
46	Sandy Alomar Jr.	.15	.07
47	Bobby Jones	.10	.05
48	Omar Vizquel	.15	.07
49	Roger Clemens	1.00	.45
50	Tony Gwynn	1.00	.45
51	Chipper Jones	1.00	.45
52	Ron Coomer	.10	.05
53	Dmitri Young	.10	.05
54	Brian Giles	.15	.07
55	Steve Finley	.15	.07
56	David Cone	.25	.11
57	Andy Pettitte	.15	.07
58	Wilton Guerrero	.10	.05
59	Deion Sanders	.15	.07
60	Carlos Delgado	.40	.18
61	Jason Giambi	.15	.07
62	Ozzie Guillen	.10	.05
63	Jay Bell	.15	.07
64	Barry Larkin	.40	.18
65	Sammy Sosa	1.25	.55
66	Bernie Williams	.40	.18
67	Terry Steinbach	.10	.05
68	Scott Rolen	.50	.23
69	Melvin Nieves	.10	.05
70	Craig Biggio	.40	.18
71	Todd Greene	.10	.05
72	Greg Gagne	.10	.05
73	Shigetoshi Hasegawa	.15	.07
74	Mark McLemore	.10	.05
75	Darren Bragg	.10	.05
76	Brett Butler	.15	.07
77	Ron Gant	.15	.07
78	Mike Difelice	.10	.05
79	Charles Nagy	.15	.07
80	Scott Hatteberg	.10	.05
81	Brady Anderson	.15	.07
82	Jay Buhner	.15	.07
83	Todd Hollandsworth	.10	.05
84	Geronimo Berroa	.10	.05
85	Jeff Suppan	.10	.05
86	Pedro Martinez	.50	.23
87	Roger Cedeno	.15	.07
88	Ivan Rodriguez	.50	.23
89	Jaime Navarro	.10	.05
90	Chris Hoiles	.10	.05
91	Nomar Garciaparra	1.25	.55
92	Rafael Palmeiro	.40	.18
93	Darin Erstad	.25	.11
94	Kenny Lofton	.25	.11
95	Mike Timlin	.10	.05
96	Chris Clemons	.10	.05
97	Vinny Castilla	.15	.07
98	Charlie Hayes	.10	.05
99	Lyle Mouton	.10	.05
100	Jason Dickson	.10	.05
101	Justin Thompson	.10	.05
102	Pat Kelly	.10	.05
103	Chan Ho Park	.15	.07
104	Ray Lankford	.15	.07
105	Frank Thomas	.75	.35
106	Jermaine Allensworth	.10	.05
107	Doug Drabek	.10	.05
108	Todd Hundley	.15	.07
109	Carl Everett	.10	.05
110	Edgar Martinez	.15	.07
111	Robin Ventura	.15	.07
112	John Wetteland	.10	.05
113	Mariano Rivera	.15	.07
114	Jose Rosado	.10	.05
115	Ken Caminiti	.15	.07
116	Paul O'Neill	.15	.07
117	Tim Salmon	.25	.11
118	Eduardo Perez	.10	.05
119	Mike Jackson	.10	.05
120	John Smoltz	.25	.11
121	Brant Brown	.10	.05
122	John Mabry	.10	.05
123	Chuck Knoblauch	.15	.07
124	Reggie Sanders	.15	.07
125	Ken Hill	.10	.05
126	Mike Mussina	.40	.18
127	Chad Curtis	.10	.05
128	Todd Worrell	.10	.05
129	Chris Widger	.10	.05
130	Damon Mashore	.10	.05
131	Kevin Brown	.25	.11
132	Bip Roberts	.10	.05
133	Tim Naehring	.10	.05
134	Dave Martinez	.10	.05
135	Jeff Blauser	.10	.05
136	David Justice	.15	.07
137	Dave Hollins	.10	.05
138	Pat Hentgen	.10	.05
139	Darren Daulton	.15	.07
140	Ramon Martinez	.10	.05
141	Raul Casanova	.10	.05
142	Tom Glavine	.40	.18
143	J.T. Snow	.15	.07
144	Tony Graffanino	.10	.05
145	Randy Johnson	.40	.18
146	Orlando Merced	.10	.05
147	Jeff Juden	.10	.05
148	Darryl Kile	.10	.05
149	Ray Durham	.15	.07
150	Alex Fernandez	.10	.05
151	Joey Cora	.10	.05
152	Royce Clayton	.10	.05
153	Randy Myers	.10	.05
154	Charles Johnson	.15	.07
155	Alan Benes	.10	.05
156	Mike Bordick	.10	.05
157	Heathcliff Slocumb	.10	.05
158	Roger Bailey	.10	.05
159	Reggie Jefferson	.10	.05
160	Ricky Bottalico	.10	.05
161	Scott Erickson	.10	.05
162	Matt Williams	.40	.18
163	Rob Nen	.10	.05
164	Matt Stairs	.15	.07
165	Ismael Valdes	.10	.05
166	Lee Stevens	.10	.05

☐ 167 Gary DiSarcina	.10	.05
☐ 168 Brad Radke	.15	.07
☐ 169 Mike Lansing	.10	.05
☐ 170 Armando Benitez	.10	.05
☐ 171 Mike James	.10	.05
☐ 172 Russ Davis	.10	.07
☐ 173 Lance Johnson	.10	.05
☐ 174 Joey Hamilton	.10	.05
☐ 175 John Valentin	.15	.07
☐ 176 David Segui	.10	.05
☐ 177 David Wells	.15	.07
☐ 178 Delino DeShields	.10	.05
☐ 179 Eric Karros	.15	.07
☐ 180 Jim Leyritz	.10	.05
☐ 181 Paul Mondesi	.15	.07
☐ 182 Travis Fryman	.15	.07
☐ 183 Todd Zeile	.10	.05
☐ 184 Brian Jordan	.15	.07
☐ 185 Rey Ordonez	.15	.07
☐ 186 Jim Edmonds	.15	.07
☐ 187 Terrell Wade	.10	.05
☐ 188 Marquis Grissom	.10	.05
☐ 189 Chris Snopek	.10	.05
☐ 190 Shane Reynolds	.15	.07
☐ 191 Jeff Frye	.10	.05
☐ 192 Paul Sorrento	.10	.05
☐ 193 James Baldwin	.10	.05
☐ 194 Brian McRae	.10	.05
☐ 195 Fred McGriff	.25	.11
☐ 196 Troy Percival	.15	.07
☐ 197 Rich Amaral	.10	.05
☐ 198 Juan Guzman	.10	.05
☐ 199 Cecil Fielder	.15	.07
☐ 200 Willie Blair	.10	.05
☐ 201 Chili Davis	.15	.07
☐ 202 Gary Gaetti	.15	.07
☐ 203 B.J. Surhoff	.10	.05
☐ 204 Steve Cooke	.10	.05
☐ 205 Chuck Finley	.15	.07
☐ 206 Jeff Kent	.15	.07
☐ 207 Ben McDonald	.10	.05
☐ 208 Jeffrey Hammonds	.10	.05
☐ 209 Tom Goodwin	.10	.05
☐ 210 Billy Ashley	.10	.05
☐ 211 Wil Cordero	.10	.05
☐ 212 Shawon Dunston	.10	.05
☐ 213 Tony Phillips	.10	.05
☐ 214 Jamie Moyer	.10	.05
☐ 215 John Jaha	.15	.07
☐ 216 Troy O'Leary	.10	.07
☐ 217 Brad Ausmus	.10	.05
☐ 218 Garret Anderson	.15	.07
☐ 219 Wilson Alvarez	.10	.05
☐ 220 Kent Mercker	.10	.05
☐ 221 Wade Boggs	.40	.18
☐ 222 Mark Wohlers	.10	.05
☐ 223 Kevin Appier	.15	.07
☐ 224 Tony Fernandez	.15	.07
☐ 225 Ugueth Urbina	.10	.05
☐ 226 Gregg Jefferies	.10	.05
☐ 227 Mo Vaughn	.40	.18
☐ 228 Arthur Rhodes	.10	.05
☐ 229 Jorge Fabregas	.10	.05
☐ 230 Mark Gardner	.10	.05
☐ 231 Shane Mack	.10	.05
☐ 232 Jorge Posada	.15	.07
☐ 233 Jose Cruz Jr.	.40	.07
☐ 234 Paul Konerko	.15	.07
☐ 235 Derrek Lee	.10	.05
☐ 236 Steve Woodard	.10	.05
☐ 237 Todd Dunwoody	.10	.05
☐ 238 Fernando Tatis	.40	.18
☐ 239 Jacob Cruz	.10	.05
☐ 240 Pokey Reese	.10	.05
☐ 241 Mark Kotsay	.15	.07
☐ 242 Matt Morris	.10	.05
☐ 243 Antone Williamson	.10	.05
☐ 244 Ben Grieve	.40	.18
☐ 245 Ryan McGuire	.10	.05
☐ 246 Lou Collier	.10	.05
☐ 247 Shannon Stewart	.15	.07
☐ 248 Brett Tomko	.10	.05
☐ 249 Bobby Estalella	.10	.05
☐ 250 Livan Hernandez	.10	.05
☐ 251 Todd Helton	.50	.23
☐ 252 Jaret Wright	.15	.07

☐ 253 Darryl Hamilton IM	.10	.05
☐ 254 Stan Javier IM	.10	.05
☐ 255 Glenallen Hill IM	.10	.05
☐ 256 Mark Gardner IM	.10	.05
☐ 257 Cal Ripken IM	.75	.35
☐ 258 Mike Mussina IM	.15	.07
☐ 259 Mike Piazza IM	.60	.25
☐ 260 Sammy Sosa IM	.60	.25
☐ 261 Todd Hundley IM	.10	.05
☐ 262 Eric Karros IM	.10	.05
☐ 263 Denny Neagle IM	.10	.05
☐ 264 Jeromy Burnitz IM	.10	.05
☐ 265 Greg Maddux IM	.50	.23
☐ 266 Tony Clark IM	.10	.05
☐ 267 Vladimir Guerrero IM	.25	.11
☐ 268 Cal Ripken CL UER	.75	.35
☐ 269 Ken Griffey Jr. CL	.10	.45
☐ 270 Mark McGwire CL	.25	.55
☐ NNO Checklist Regular Issue	.10	.05
☐ NNO Checklist All-Star Edition	.25	.11

1998 Score All Score Team

	MINT	NRMT
COMPLETE SET (20)	120.00	55.00
COMMON CARD (1-20)	1.50	.70
STATED ODDS 1:35		

☐ 1 Mike Piazza	12.00	5.50
☐ 2 Ivan Rodriguez	5.00	2.20
☐ 3 Frank Thomas	8.00	3.60
☐ 4 Mark McGwire	25.00	11.00
☐ 5 Ryne Sandberg	5.00	2.20
☐ 6 Roberto Alomar	4.00	1.80
☐ 7 Cal Ripken	15.00	6.75
☐ 8 Barry Larkin	4.00	1.80
☐ 9 Paul Molitor	4.00	1.80
☐ 10 Travis Fryman	1.50	.70
☐ 11 Kirby Puckett	6.00	2.70
☐ 12 Tony Gwynn	10.00	4.50
☐ 13 Ken Griffey Jr.	20.00	9.00
☐ 14 Juan Gonzalez	8.00	3.60
☐ 15 Barry Bonds	5.00	2.20
☐ 16 Andruw Jones	4.00	1.80
☐ 17 Roger Clemens	10.00	4.50
☐ 18 Randy Johnson	4.00	1.80
☐ 19 Greg Maddux	10.00	4.50
☐ 20 Dennis Eckersley	1.50	.70

1998 Score Complete Players

	MINT	NRMT
COMPLETE SET (30)	200.00	90.00
COMMON CARD (1-10)	2.00	.90
STATED ODDS 1:23		
THREE CARDS PER PLAYER		

☐ 1A Ken Griffey Jr.	15.00	6.75
☐ 1B Ken Griffey Jr.	15.00	6.75
☐ 1C Ken Griffey Jr.	15.00	6.75
☐ 2A Mark McGwire	20.00	9.00
☐ 2B Mark McGwire	20.00	9.00
☐ 2C Mark McGwire	20.00	9.00
☐ 3A Derek Jeter	10.00	4.50
☐ 3B Derek Jeter	10.00	4.50

☐ 3C Derek Jeter	10.00	4.50
☐ 4A Cal Ripken	12.00	5.50
☐ 4B Cal Ripken	12.00	5.50
☐ 4C Cal Ripken	12.00	5.50
☐ 5A Mike Piazza	10.00	4.50
☐ 5B Mike Piazza	10.00	4.50
☐ 5C Mike Piazza	10.00	4.50
☐ 6A Darin Erstad	2.00	.90
☐ 6B Darin Erstad	2.00	.90
☐ 6C Darin Erstad	2.00	.90
☐ 7A Frank Thomas	6.00	2.70
☐ 7B Frank Thomas	6.00	2.70
☐ 7C Frank Thomas	6.00	2.70
☐ 8A Andruw Jones	3.00	1.35
☐ 8B Andruw Jones	3.00	1.35
☐ 8C Andruw Jones	3.00	1.35
☐ 9A Nomar Garciaparra	10.00	4.50
☐ 9B Nomar Garciaparra	10.00	4.50
☐ 9C Nomar Garciaparra	10.00	4.50
☐ 10A Manny Ramirez	4.00	1.80
☐ 10B Manny Ramirez	4.00	1.80
☐ 10C Manny Ramirez	4.00	1.80

1998 Score Epix

	MINT	NRMT
COMMON CARD (E1-E24)	4.00	1.80
*PURPLE CARDS: .6X TO 1.5X ORANGE		
*EMERALD CARDS: 1.25X TO 3X ORANGE		
STATED ODDS 1:61		
LESS THAN 30 EMERALD MOMENTS PRINT-ED		
ONLY ORANGE CARDS LISTED BELOW!		
USE MULTIPLIERS FOR EMERALD/PURPLE		

1998 Score First Pitch

Pitch

	MINT	NRMT
COMPLETE SET (20)	80.00	36.00
COMMON CARD (1-20)	2.00	.90
STATED ODDS 1:11 AS EDIT.		

☐ 1 Ken Griffey Jr.	10.00	4.50
☐ 2 Frank Thomas	4.00	1.80
☐ 3 Alex Rodriguez	6.00	2.70
☐ 4 Cal Ripken	8.00	3.60
☐ 5 Chipper Jones	5.00	2.20
☐ 6 Juan Gonzalez	4.00	1.80
☐ 7 Derek Jeter	6.00	2.70
☐ 8 Mike Piazza	6.00	2.70
☐ 9 Andruw Jones	2.00	.90

		MINT	NRMT
❑ 10	Nomar Garciaparra	6.00	2.70
❑ 11	Barry Bonds	2.50	1.10
❑ 12	Jeff Bagwell	2.50	1.10
❑ 13	Scott Rolen	3.00	1.35
❑ 14	Hideo Nomo	2.00	.90
❑ 15	Roger Clemens	5.00	2.20
❑ 16	Mark McGwire	12.00	5.50
❑ 17	Greg Maddux	5.00	2.20
❑ 18	Albert Belle	2.00	.90
❑ 19	Ivan Rodriguez	2.50	1.10
❑ 20	Mo Vaughn	2.00	.90

1998 Score Loaded Lineup

		MINT	NRMT
COMPLETE SET (10)		80.00	36.00
COMMON CARD (LL1-LL10)		1.50	.70
STATED ODDS 1:45 AS EDIT.			
❑ LL1	Chuck Knoblauch	1.50	.70
❑ LL2	Tony Gwynn	10.00	4.50
❑ LL3	Frank Thomas	8.00	3.60
❑ LL4	Ken Griffey Jr.	20.00	9.00
❑ LL5	Mike Piazza	12.00	5.50
❑ LL6	Barry Bonds	5.00	2.20
❑ LL7	Cal Ripken	15.00	6.75
❑ LL8	Paul Molitor	2.50	1.10
❑ LL9	Nomar Garciaparra	12.00	5.50
❑ LL10	Greg Maddux	10.00	4.50

1998 Score New Season

		MINT	NRMT
COMPLETE SET (15)		80.00	36.00
COMMON CARD (NS1-NS15)		1.25	.55
STATED ODDS 1:23 AS EDIT.			
❑ NS1	Kenny Lofton	2.00	.90
❑ NS2	Nomar Garciaparra	10.00	4.50
❑ NS3	Todd Helton	3.00	1.35
❑ NS4	Miguel Tejada	1.25	.55
❑ NS5	Jaret Wright	1.25	.55
❑ NS6	Alex Rodriguez	10.00	4.50
❑ NS7	Vladimir Guerrero	4.00	1.80
❑ NS8	Ken Griffey Jr.	15.00	6.75
❑ NS9	Ben Grieve	3.00	1.35
❑ NS10	Travis Lee	2.00	.90
❑ NS11	Jose Cruz Jr.	1.25	.55
❑ NS12	Paul Konerko	1.25	.55

		MINT	NRMT
❑ NS13	Frank Thomas	6.00	2.70
❑ NS14	Chipper Jones	8.00	3.60
❑ NS15	Cal Ripken	12.00	5.50

1998 Score Rookie Traded

		MINT	NRMT
COMPLETE SET (270)		30.00	13.50
COMMON SP (1-50)		.25	.11
SP SEMISTARS 1-50		.40	.18
SP UNLISTED STARS 1-50		.60	.25
SP CARDS 1-50 ONE PER PACK			
COMMON CARD (51-270)		.10	.05
MINOR STARS 51-270		.15	.07
SEMISTARS 51-270		.25	.11
UNLISTED STARS 51-270		.40	.18
ONE OF ONE PARALLELS EXIST			
❑ 1	Tony Clark	.30	.14
❑ 2	Juan Gonzalez	1.25	.55
❑ 3	Frank Thomas	1.25	.55
❑ 4	Greg Maddux	1.50	.70
❑ 5	Barry Larkin	.60	.25
❑ 6	Derek Jeter	2.00	.90
❑ 7	Randy Johnson	.60	.25
❑ 8	Roger Clemens	1.50	.70
❑ 9	Tony Gwynn	1.50	.70
❑ 10	Barry Bonds	.75	.35
❑ 11	Jim Edmonds	.30	.14
❑ 12	Bernie Williams	.60	.25
❑ 13	Ken Griffey Jr.	3.00	1.35
❑ 14	Tim Salmon	.40	.18
❑ 15	Mo Vaughn	.60	.25
❑ 16	David Justice	.30	.14
❑ 17	Jose Cruz Jr.	.30	.14
❑ 18	Andruw Jones	.60	.25
❑ 19	Sammy Sosa	2.00	.90
❑ 20	Jeff Bagwell	.75	.35
❑ 21	Scott Rolen	.75	.35
❑ 22	Darin Erstad	.40	.18
❑ 23	Andy Pettitte	.30	.14
❑ 24	Mike Mussina	.60	.25
❑ 25	Mark McGwire	4.00	1.80
❑ 26	Hideo Nomo	.60	.25
❑ 27	Chipper Jones	1.50	.70
❑ 28	Cal Ripken	2.50	1.10
❑ 29	Chuck Knoblauch	.30	.14
❑ 30	Alex Rodriguez	2.00	.90
❑ 31	Jim Thome	.60	.25
❑ 32	Mike Piazza	2.00	.90
❑ 33	Ivan Rodriguez	.75	.35
❑ 34	Roberto Alomar	.60	.25
❑ 35	Nomar Garciaparra	2.00	.90
❑ 36	Albert Belle	.60	.25
❑ 37	Vladimir Guerrero	.75	.35
❑ 38	Raul Mondesi	.30	.14
❑ 39	Larry Walker	.60	.25
❑ 40	Manny Ramirez	.75	.35
❑ 41	Tino Martinez	.40	.18
❑ 42	Craig Biggio	.60	.25
❑ 43	Jay Buhner	.30	.14
❑ 44	Kenny Lofton	.40	.18
❑ 45	Pedro Martinez	.75	.35
❑ 46	Edgar Martinez	.30	.14
❑ 47	Gary Sheffield	.30	.14
❑ 48	Jose Guillen	.25	.11
❑ 49	Ken Caminiti		.14

		MINT	NRMT
❑ 50	Bobby Higginson	.30	.14
❑ 51	Alan Benes	.10	.05
❑ 52	Shawn Green	.40	.18
❑ 53	Ron Coomer	.10	.05
❑ 54	Charles Nagy	.15	.07
❑ 55	Steve Karsay	.10	.05
❑ 56	Matt Morris	.10	.05
❑ 57	Bobby Jones	.10	.05
❑ 58	Jason Kendall	.15	.07
❑ 59	Jeff Conine	.10	.05
❑ 60	Joe Girardi	.10	.05
❑ 61	Mark Kotsay	.15	.07
❑ 62	Eric Karros	.15	.07
❑ 63	Bartolo Colon	.15	.07
❑ 64	Mariano Rivera	.15	.07
❑ 65	Alex Gonzalez	.10	.05
❑ 66	Scott Spiezio	.10	.05
❑ 67	Luis Castillo	.10	.05
❑ 68	Joey Cora	.10	.05
❑ 69	Mark McLemore	.10	.05
❑ 70	Reggie Jefferson	.10	.05
❑ 71	Lance Johnson	.10	.05
❑ 72	Damian Jackson	.10	.05
❑ 73	Jeff D'Amico	.10	.05
❑ 74	David Ortiz	.10	.05
❑ 75	J.T. Snow	.15	.07
❑ 76	Todd Hundley	.15	.07
❑ 77	Billy Wagner	.15	.07
❑ 78	Vinny Castilla	.15	.07
❑ 79	Ismael Valdes	.10	.05
❑ 80	Neifi Perez	.10	.05
❑ 81	Derek Bell	.10	.05
❑ 82	Ryan Klesko	.15	.07
❑ 83	Rey Ordonez	.10	.05
❑ 84	Carlos Garcia	.10	.05
❑ 85	Curt Schilling	.25	.11
❑ 86	Robin Ventura	.15	.07
❑ 87	Pat Hentgen	.10	.05
❑ 88	Glendon Rusch	.10	.05
❑ 89	Hideki Irabu	.15	.07
❑ 90	Antone Williamson	.10	.05
❑ 91	Denny Neagle	.15	.07
❑ 92	Kevin Orie	.10	.05
❑ 93	Reggie Sanders	.10	.05
❑ 94	Brady Anderson	.15	.07
❑ 95	Andy Benes	.15	.07
❑ 96	John Valentin	.10	.05
❑ 97	Bobby Bonilla	.15	.07
❑ 98	Walt Weiss	.10	.05
❑ 99	Robin Jennings	.10	.05
❑ 100	Marty Cordova	.10	.05
❑ 101	Brad Ausmus	.10	.05
❑ 102	Brian Rose	.10	.05
❑ 103	Calvin Williams	.10	.05
❑ 104	Raul Casanova	.10	.05
❑ 105	Jeff King	.10	.05
❑ 106	Sandy Alomar Jr.	.15	.07
❑ 107	Tim Naehring	.10	.05
❑ 108	Mike Cameron	.15	.07
❑ 109	Omar Vizquel	.15	.07
❑ 110	Brad Radke	.15	.07
❑ 111	Jeff Fassero	.10	.05
❑ 112	Deivi Cruz	.10	.05
❑ 113	Dave Hollins	.10	.05
❑ 114	Dean Palmer	.15	.07
❑ 115	Esteban Loaiza	.10	.05
❑ 116	Brian Giles	.15	.07
❑ 117	Steve Finley	.15	.07
❑ 118	Jose Canseco	.50	.23
❑ 119	Al Martin	.10	.05
❑ 120	Eric Young	.10	.05
❑ 121	Curtis Goodwin	.10	.05
❑ 122	Ellis Burks	.15	.07
❑ 123	Mike Hampton	.15	.07
❑ 124	Lou Collier	.10	.05
❑ 125	John Olerud	.15	.07
❑ 126	Ramon Martinez	.10	.05
❑ 127	Todd Dunwoody	.10	.05
❑ 128	Jermaine Allensworth	.10	.05
❑ 129	Eduardo Perez	.10	.05
❑ 130	Dante Bichette	.15	.07
❑ 131	Edgar Renteria	.15	.07
❑ 132	Bob Abreu	.15	.07
❑ 133	Rondell White	.15	.07
❑ 134	Michael Coleman	.10	.05
❑ 135	Jason Giambi	.15	.07

#	Player	MINT	NRMT
136	Brant Brown	.10	.05
137	Michael Tucker	.10	.05
138	Dave Nilsson	.10	.05
139	Benito Santiago	.10	.05
140	Ray Durham	.15	.07
141	Jeff Kent	.15	.07
142	Matt Stairs	.15	.07
143	Kevin Young	.15	.07
144	Eric Davis	.15	.07
145	John Wetteland	.15	.07
146	Esteban Yan	.30	.14
147	Wilton Guerrero	.10	.05
148	Moises Alou	.15	.07
149	Edgardo Alfonzo	.25	.11
150	Andy Ashby	.10	.05
151	Todd Walker	.15	.07
152	Jermaine Dye	.15	.07
153	Brian Hunter	.10	.05
154	Shawn Estes	.10	.05
155	Bernard Gilkey	.10	.05
156	Tony Womack	.15	.07
157	John Smoltz	.25	.11
158	Delino DeShields	.10	.05
159	Jacob Cruz	.10	.05
160	Javier Valentin	.10	.05
161	Chris Hoiles	.10	.05
162	Garret Anderson	.15	.07
163	Dan Wilson	.10	.05
164	Paul O'Neill	.15	.07
165	Matt Williams	.40	.18
166	Travis Fryman	.15	.07
167	Javier Lopez	.15	.07
168	Ray Lankford	.15	.07
169	Bobby Estalella	.10	.05
170	Henry Rodriguez	.10	.05
171	Quinton McCracken	.10	.05
172	Jaret Wright	.15	.07
173	Darryl Kile	.15	.07
174	Wade Boggs	.40	.18
175	Orel Hershiser	.15	.07
176	B.J. Surhoff	.15	.07
177	Fernando Tatis	.40	.18
178	Carlos Delgado	.40	.18
179	Jorge Fabregas	.10	.05
180	Tony Saunders	.10	.05
181	Devon White	.10	.05
182	Dmitri Young	.15	.07
183	Ryan McGuire	.10	.05
184	Mark Bellhorn	.10	.05
185	Joe Carter	.15	.07
186	Kevin Stocker	.10	.05
187	Mike Lansing	.10	.05
188	Jason Dickson	.15	.07
189	Charles Johnson	.15	.07
190	Will Clark	.40	.18
191	Shannon Stewart	.15	.07
192	Johnny Damon	.15	.07
193	Todd Greene	.10	.05
194	Carlos Baerga	.10	.05
195	David Cone	.25	.11
196	Pokey Reese	.10	.05
197	Livan Hernandez	.15	.07
198	Tom Glavine	.40	.18
199	Geronimo Berroa	.10	.05
200	Darryl Hamilton	.10	.05
201	Terry Steinbach	.15	.07
202	Robb Nen	.15	.07
203	Ron Gant	.15	.07
204	Rafael Palmeiro	.40	.18
205	Rickey Henderson	.50	.23
206	Justin Thompson	.10	.05
207	Jeff Suppan	.10	.05
208	Kevin Brown	.25	.11
209	Jimmy Key	.15	.07
210	Brian Jordan	.15	.07
211	Aaron Sele	.15	.07
212	Fred McGriff	.25	.11
213	Jay Bell	.15	.07
214	Andres Galarraga	.25	.11
215	Mark Grace	.25	.11
216	Brett Tomko	.10	.05
217	Francisco Cordova	.10	.05
218	Rusty Greer	.15	.07
219	Bubba Trammell	.10	.05
220	Derrek Lee	.10	.05
221	Brian Anderson	.10	.05
222	Mark Grudzielanek	.10	.05
223	Marquis Grissom	.10	.05
224	Gary DiSarcina	.10	.05
225	Jim Leyritz	.10	.05
226	Jeffrey Hammonds	.10	.05
227	Karim Garcia	.10	.05
228	Chan Ho Park	.15	.07
229	Brooks Kieschnick	.10	.05
230	Trey Beamon	.10	.05
231	Kevin Appier	.15	.07
232	Wally Joyner	.15	.07
233	Richie Sexson	.25	.11
234	Frank Catalanotto	.15	.07
235	Rafael Medina	.10	.05
236	Travis Lee	.40	.18
237	Eli Marrero	.15	.07
238	Carl Pavano	.10	.05
239	Enrique Wilson	.10	.05
240	Richard Hidalgo	.15	.07
241	Todd Helton	.50	.23
242	Ben Grieve	.40	.18
243	Mario Valdez	.10	.05
244	Magglio Ordonez	1.25	.55
245	Juan Encarnacion	.15	.07
246	Russell Branyan	.15	.07
247	Sean Casey	.60	.25
248	Abraham Nunez	.10	.05
249	Brad Fullmer	.10	.05
250	Paul Konerko	.15	.07
251	Miguel Tejada	.15	.07
252	Mike Lowell	.40	.18
253	Ken Griffey Jr. ST	1.00	.45
254	Frank Thomas ST	.60	.25
255	Alex Rodriguez ST	.60	.25
256	Jose Cruz Jr. ST	.10	.05
257	Jeff Bagwell ST	.25	.11
258	Chipper Jones ST	.50	.23
259	Mo Vaughn ST	.15	.07
260	Nomar Garciaparra ST	.60	.25
261	Jim Thome ST	.15	.07
262	Derek Jeter ST	.60	.25
263	Mike Piazza ST	.60	.25
264	Tony Gwynn ST	.50	.23
265	Scott Rolen ST	.40	.18
266	Andruw Jones ST	.15	.07
267	Cal Ripken ST	.75	.35
268	Checklist 1	.10	.05
269	Checklist 2	.10	.05
270	Checklist 3	.10	.05
S250	Paul Konerko AU500	15.00	6.75

1998 Score Rookie Traded Showcase Series

		MINT	NRMT
	COMMON CARD (PP1-PP160)	.50	.23

*STARS 1.50: 1.25X TO 3X BASIC CARDS
*STARS 51-270: 2X TO 5X BASIC CARDS
*ROOKIES 51-270: 1.5X TO 4X BASIC CARDS
STATED ODDS 1:7

#	Player	MINT	NRMT
PP1	Tony Clark	.75	.35
PP2	Juan Gonzalez	4.00	1.80
PP3	Frank Thomas	4.00	1.80
PP4	Greg Maddux	5.00	2.20
PP5	Barry Larkin	2.00	.90
PP6	Derek Jeter	6.00	2.70
PP7	Randy Johnson	2.00	.90
PP8	Roger Clemens	5.00	2.20
PP9	Tony Gwynn	5.00	2.20
PP10	Barry Bonds	2.50	1.10
PP11	Jim Edmonds	.75	.35
PP12	Bernie Williams	2.00	.90
PP13	Ken Griffey Jr.	10.00	4.50
PP14	Tim Salmon	1.25	.55
PP15	Mo Vaughn	2.00	.90
PP16	David Justice	.75	.35
PP17	Jose Cruz Jr.	.75	.35
PP18	Andruw Jones	2.00	.90
PP19	Sammy Sosa	6.00	2.70
PP20	Jeff Bagwell	2.50	1.10
PP21	Scott Rolen	3.00	1.35
PP22	Darin Erstad	1.25	.55
PP23	Andy Pettitte	.75	.35
PP24	Mike Mussina	2.00	.90
PP25	Mark McGwire	12.00	5.50
PP26	Hideo Nomo	2.00	.90
PP27	Chipper Jones	5.00	2.20
PP28	Cal Ripken	8.00	3.60
PP29	Chuck Knoblauch	.75	.35
PP30	Alex Rodriguez	6.00	2.70
PP31	Jim Thome	2.00	.90
PP32	Mike Piazza	6.00	2.70
PP33	Ivan Rodriguez	2.50	1.10
PP34	Roberto Alomar	2.00	.90
PP35	Nomar Garciaparra	6.00	2.70
PP36	Albert Belle	2.00	.90
PP37	Vladimir Guerrero	2.50	1.10
PP38	Raul Mondesi	.75	.35
PP39	Larry Walker	2.00	.90
PP40	Manny Ramirez	2.50	1.10
PP41	Tino Martinez	.75	.35
PP42	Craig Biggio	2.00	.90
PP43	Jay Buhner	.75	.35
PP44	Kenny Lofton	1.25	.55
PP45	Pedro Martinez	2.50	1.10
PP46	Edgar Martinez	.75	.35
PP47	Gary Sheffield	.75	.35
PP48	Jose Guillen	.50	.23
PP49	Ken Caminiti	.75	.35
PP50	Bobby Higginson	.50	.23
PP51	Alan Benes	.50	.23
PP52	Shawn Green	2.00	.90
PP53	Matt Morris	.50	.23
PP54	Jason Kendall	.75	.35
PP55	Mark Kotsay	.75	.35
PP56	Bartolo Colon	.75	.35
PP57	Damian Jackson	.50	.23
PP58	David Ortiz	.50	.23
PP59	J.T. Snow	.75	.35
PP60	Todd Hundley	.75	.35
PP61	Neifi Perez	.50	.23
PP62	Ryan Klesko	.75	.35
PP63	Robin Ventura	.75	.35
PP64	Pat Hentgen	.50	.23
PP65	Antone Williamson	.50	.23
PP66	Kevin Orie	.50	.23
PP67	Brady Anderson	.75	.35
PP68	Bobby Bonilla	.75	.35
PP69	Brian Rose	.50	.23
PP70	Sandy Alomar Jr.	.75	.35
PP71	Mike Cameron	.75	.35
PP72	Omar Vizquel	.75	.35
PP73	Steve Finley	.75	.35
PP74	Jose Canseco	2.50	1.10
PP75	Al Martin	.50	.23
PP76	Eric Young	.50	.23
PP77	Ellis Burks	.75	.35
PP78	Todd Dunwoody	.50	.23
PP79	Dante Bichette	.75	.35
PP80	Edgar Renteria	.50	.23
PP81	Bob Abreu	.75	.35
PP82	Rondell White	.75	.35
PP83	Michael Coleman	.50	.23
PP84	Jason Giambi	.75	.35
PP85	Wilton Guerrero	.50	.23
PP86	Moises Alou	.75	.35
PP87	Todd Walker	.75	.35
PP88	Shawn Estes	.50	.23
PP89	John Smoltz	1.25	.55
PP90	Jacob Cruz	.50	.23
PP91	Javier Valentin	.50	.23
PP92	Garret Anderson	.75	.35
PP93	Paul O'Neill	.75	.35

		MINT	NRMT
❏ PP94	Matt Williams	2.00	.90
❏ PP95	Travis Fryman	.75	.35
❏ PF96	Javier Lopez	.75	.35
❏ PP97	Ray Lankford	.75	.35
❏ PP98	Bobby Estalella	.50	.23
❏ PP99	Jaret Wright	.75	.35
❏ PP100	Wade Boggs	2.00	.90
❏ PP101	Fernando Tatis	2.00	.90
❏ PP102	Carlos Delgado	2.00	.90
❏ PP103	Joe Carter	.75	.35
❏ PP104	Jason Dickson	.50	.23
❏ PP105	Charles Johnson	.75	.35
❏ PP106	Will Clark	2.00	.90
❏ PP107	Shannon Stewart	.75	.35
❏ PP108	Todd Greene	.50	.23
❏ PP109	Pokey Reese	.50	.23
❏ PP110	Livan Hernandez	.50	.23
❏ PP111	Tom Glavine	2.00	.90
❏ PP112	Rafael Palmeiro	2.00	.90
❏ PP113	Justin Thompson	.50	.23
❏ PP114	Jeff Suppan	.50	.23
❏ PP115	Kevin Brown	1.25	.55
❏ PP116	Brian Jordan	.75	.35
❏ PP117	Fred McGriff	1.25	.55
❏ PP118	Andres Galarraga	1.25	.55
❏ PP119	Mark Grace	1.25	.55
❏ PP120	Rusty Greer	.75	.35
❏ PP121	Bubba Trammell	.50	.23
❏ PP122	Derrek Lee	.50	.23
❏ PP123	Brian Anderson	.50	.23
❏ PP124	Karim Garcia	.50	.23
❏ PP125	Chan Ho Park	.75	.35
❏ PP126	Richie Sexson	1.25	.55
❏ PP127	Frank Catalanotto	.75	.35
❏ PP128	Rafael Medina	.50	.23
❏ PP129	Travis Lee	1.25	.55
❏ PP130	Eli Marrero	.50	.23
❏ PP131	Carl Pavano	.50	.23
❏ PP132	Enrique Wilson	.50	.23
❏ PP133	Richard Hidalgo	.75	.35
❏ PP134	Todd Helton	2.00	.90
❏ PP135	Ben Grieve	2.00	.90
❏ PP136	Mario Valdez	.50	.23
❏ PP137	Magglio Ordonez	6.00	2.70
❏ PP138	Juan Encarnacion	.75	.35
❏ PP139	Russell Branyan	.75	.35
❏ PP140	Sean Casey	2.50	1.10
❏ PP141	Abraham Nunez	.50	.23
❏ PP142	Brad Fullmer	.50	.23
❏ PP143	Paul Konerko	.75	.35
❏ PP144	Miguel Tejada	.75	.35
❏ PP145	Mike Lowell	1.50	.70
❏ PP146	Ken Griffey Jr. ST	5.00	2.20
❏ PP147	Frank Thomas ST		.90
❏ PP148	Alex Rodriguez ST	3.00	1.35
❏ PP149	Jose Cruz Jr. ST	.50	.23
❏ PP150	Jeff Bagwell ST	1.25	.55
❏ PP151	Chipper Jones ST	2.50	1.10
❏ PP152	Mo Vaughn ST	.75	.35

❏ PP153 Nomar Garciaparra ST UER162
#(misnumbered as 162 instead of 153 3.00 1.35

❏ PP154	Jim Thome ST	.75	.35
❏ PP155	Derek Jeter ST	3.00	1.35
❏ PP156	Mike Piazza ST	3.00	1.35
❏ PP157	Tony Gwynn ST	2.50	1.10
❏ PP158	Scott Rolen ST	2.00	.90
❏ PP159	Andruw Jones ST		.90
❏ PP160	Cal Ripken ST	4.00	1.80

1998 Score Rookie Traded Showcase Series Artist's Proofs

	MINT	NRMT
COMMON CARD (PP1-PP160)	2.00	.90

*STARS 1-50: 5X TO 12X BASIC CARD
*STARS 51-270: 8X TO 20X BASIC CARD
*YNG.STARS: 6X TO 15X BASIC
CARDS
*ROOKIES 51-270: 4X TO 10X BASIC CARDS
STATED ODDS 1:35

1998 Score Rookie Traded All-Star Epix

	MINT	NRMT

PLEASE SEE 1998 PINNACLE PLUS AS EPIX

1998 Score Rookie Traded Complete Players

	MINT	NRMT
COMPLETE SET (30)	100.00	45.00
COMMON CARD (1-10)	.60	.25

STATED ODDS 1:11
THREE CARDS PER PLAYER

❏ 1A	Ken Griffey Jr.	8.00	3.60
❏ 1B	Ken Griffey Jr.	8.00	3.60
❏ 1C	Ken Griffey Jr.	8.00	3.60
❏ 2A	Larry Walker	1.50	.70
❏ 2B	Larry Walker	1.50	.70
❏ 2C	Larry Walker	1.50	.70
❏ 3A	Alex Rodriguez	5.00	2.20
❏ 3B	Alex Rodriguez	5.00	2.20
❏ 3C	Alex Rodriguez	5.00	2.20
❏ 4A	Jose Cruz Jr.	.60	.25
❏ 4B	Jose Cruz Jr.	.60	.25
❏ 4C	Jose Cruz Jr.	.60	.25
❏ 5A	Jeff Bagwell	2.00	.90
❏ 5B	Jeff Bagwell	2.00	.90
❏ 5C	Jeff Bagwell	2.00	.90
❏ 6A	Greg Maddux	4.00	1.80
❏ 6B	Greg Maddux	4.00	1.80
❏ 6C	Greg Maddux	4.00	1.80
❏ 7A	Ivan Rodriguez	2.00	.90
❏ 7B	Ivan Rodriguez	2.00	.90
❏ 7C	Ivan Rodriguez	2.00	.90
❏ 8A	Roger Clemens	4.00	1.80
❏ 8B	Roger Clemens	4.00	1.80
❏ 8C	Roger Clemens	4.00	1.80
❏ 9A	Chipper Jones	4.00	1.80
❏ 9B	Chipper Jones	4.00	1.80
❏ 9C	Chipper Jones	4.00	1.80
❏ 10A	Hideo Nomo	1.50	.70
❏ 10B	Hideo Nomo	1.50	.70
❏ 10C	Hideo Nomo	1.50	.70

1998 Score Rookie Traded Star Gazing

	MINT	NRMT
COMPLETE SET (20)	150.00	70.00
COMMON CARD (1-20)	1.50	.70

STATED ODDS 1:35

❏ 1	Ken Griffey Jr.	20.00	9.00
❏ 2	Frank Thomas	8.00	3.60
❏ 3	Chipper Jones	10.00	4.50
❏ 4	Mark McGwire	25.00	11.00
❏ 5	Cal Ripken	15.00	6.75
❏ 6	Mike Piazza	12.00	5.50
❏ 7	Nomar Garciaparra	12.00	5.50
❏ 8	Derek Jeter	12.00	5.50
❏ 9	Juan Gonzalez	8.00	3.60
❏ 10	Vladimir Guerrero	5.00	2.20
❏ 11	Alex Rodriguez	12.00	5.50
❏ 12	Tony Gwynn	10.00	4.50
❏ 13	Andruw Jones	4.00	1.80
❏ 14	Scott Rolen	6.00	2.70
❏ 15	Jose Cruz Jr.	1.50	.70
❏ 16	Mo Vaughn	4.00	1.80
❏ 17	Bernie Williams	4.00	1.80
❏ 18	Greg Maddux	10.00	4.50
❏ 19	Tony Clark	1.50	.70
❏ 20	Ben Grieve	4.00	1.80

1993 Select

	MINT	NRMT
COMPLETE SET (405)	20.00	9.00
COMMON CARD (1-405)	.15	.05
MINOR STARS	.15	.07
SEMISTARS	.25	.11
UNLISTED STARS	.40	.18

❏ 1	Barry Bonds	.50	.23
❏ 2	Ken Griffey Jr.	2.00	.90
❏ 3	Will Clark	.40	.18
❏ 4	Kirby Puckett	.60	.25
❏ 5	Tony Gwynn	1.00	.45
❏ 6	Frank Thomas	.75	.35
❏ 7	Tom Glavine	.25	.11
❏ 8	Roberto Alomar	.40	.18
❏ 9	Andre Dawson	.25	.11
❏ 10	Ron Darling	.10	.05
❏ 11	Bobby Bonilla	.15	.07
❏ 12	Danny Tartabull	.10	.05

❑ 13	Darren Daulton	.15	.07
❑ 14	Roger Clemens	1.00	.45
❑ 15	Ozzie Smith	.50	.23
❑ 16	Mark McGwire	2.00	.90
❑ 17	Terry Pendleton	.10	.05
❑ 18	Cal Ripken	1.50	.70
❑ 19	Fred McGriff	.25	.11
❑ 20	Cecil Fielder	.15	.07
❑ 21	Darryl Strawberry	.15	.07
❑ 22	Robin Yount	.25	.11
❑ 23	Barry Larkin	.40	.18
❑ 24	Don Mattingly	.75	.35
❑ 25	Craig Biggio	.40	.18
❑ 26	Sandy Alomar Jr.	.15	.07
❑ 27	Larry Walker	.40	.18
❑ 28	Junior Felix	.10	.05
❑ 29	Eddie Murray	.15	.07
❑ 30	Robin Ventura	.15	.07
❑ 31	Greg Maddux	1.00	.45
❑ 32	Dave Winfield	.25	.11
❑ 33	John Kruk	.15	.07
❑ 34	Wally Joyner	.15	.07
❑ 35	Andy Van Slyke	.15	.07
❑ 36	Chuck Knoblauch	.40	.18
❑ 37	Tom Pagnozzi	.10	.05
❑ 38	Dennis Eckersley	.15	.07
❑ 39	Dave Justice	.40	.18
❑ 40	Juan Gonzalez	.75	.35
❑ 41	Gary Sheffield	.40	.18
❑ 42	Paul Molitor	.40	.18
❑ 43	Delino DeShields	.15	.07
❑ 44	Travis Fryman	.15	.07
❑ 45	Hal Morris	.10	.05
❑ 46	Greg Olson	.10	.05
❑ 47	Ken Caminiti	.25	.11
❑ 48	Wade Boggs	.40	.18
❑ 49	Orel Hershiser	.15	.07
❑ 50	Albert Belle	.40	.18
❑ 51	Bill Swift	.10	.05
❑ 52	Mark Langston	.10	.05
❑ 53	Joe Girardi	.10	.05
❑ 54	Keith Miller	.10	.05
❑ 55	Gary Carter	.25	.11
❑ 56	Brady Anderson	.15	.07
❑ 57	Dwight Gooden	.15	.07
❑ 58	Julio Franco	.10	.05
❑ 59	Lenny Dykstra	.15	.07
❑ 60	Mickey Tettleton	.10	.05
❑ 61	Randy Tomlin	.10	.05
❑ 62	B.J. Surhoff	.15	.07
❑ 63	Todd Zeile	.10	.05
❑ 64	Roberto Kelly	.10	.05
❑ 65	Rob Dibble	.10	.05
❑ 66	Leo Gomez	.10	.05
❑ 67	Doug Jones	.10	.05
❑ 68	Ellis Burks	.15	.07
❑ 69	Mike Scioscia	.10	.05
❑ 70	Charles Nagy	.15	.07
❑ 71	Cory Snyder	.10	.05
❑ 72	Devon White	.10	.05
❑ 73	Mark Grace	.25	.11
❑ 74	Luis Polonia	.10	.05
❑ 75	John Smiley 2X	.10	.05
❑ 76	Carlton Fisk	.40	.18
❑ 77	Luis Sojo	.10	.05
❑ 78	George Brett	.75	.35
❑ 79	Mitch Williams	.10	.05
❑ 80	Kent Hrbek	.15	.07
❑ 81	Jay Bell	.10	.05
❑ 82	Edgar Martinez	.25	.11
❑ 83	Lee Smith	.15	.07
❑ 84	Deion Sanders	.25	.11
❑ 85	Bill Gullickson	.10	.05
❑ 86	Paul O'Neill	.15	.07
❑ 87	Kevin Seitzer	.10	.05
❑ 88	Steve Finley	.15	.07
❑ 89	Mel Hall	.10	.05
❑ 90	Nolan Ryan	1.50	.70
❑ 91	Eric Davis	.15	.07
❑ 92	Mike Mussina	.40	.18
❑ 93	Tony Fernandez	.15	.07
❑ 94	Frank Viola	.10	.05
❑ 95	Matt Williams	.25	.11
❑ 96	Joe Carter	.25	.11
❑ 97	Ryne Sandberg	.50	.23
❑ 98	Jim Abbott	.15	.07

❑ 99	Marquis Grissom	.15	.07
❑ 100	George Bell	.10	.05
❑ 101	Howard Johnson	.10	.05
❑ 102	Kevin Appier	.15	.07
❑ 103	Dale Murphy	.25	.11
❑ 104	Shane Mack	.10	.05
❑ 105	Jose Lind	.10	.05
❑ 106	Rickey Henderson	.50	.23
❑ 107	Bob Tewksbury	.10	.05
❑ 108	Kevin Mitchell	.15	.07
❑ 109	Steve Avery	.15	.07
❑ 110	Candy Maldonado	.10	.05
❑ 111	Bip Roberts	.10	.05
❑ 112	Lou Whitaker	.15	.07
❑ 113	Jeff Bagwell	.50	.23
❑ 114	Dante Bichette	.10	.05
❑ 115	Brett Butler	.15	.07
❑ 116	Melido Perez	.10	.05
❑ 117	Andy Benes	.15	.07
❑ 118	Randy Johnson	.40	.18
❑ 119	Willie McGee	.15	.07
❑ 120	Jody Reed	.10	.05
❑ 121	Shawon Dunston	.10	.05
❑ 122	Carlos Baerga	.25	.11
❑ 123	Bret Saberhagen	.15	.07
❑ 124	John Olerud	.25	.11
❑ 125	Ivan Calderon	.10	.05
❑ 126	Bryan Harvey	.10	.05
❑ 127	Terry Mulholland	.10	.05
❑ 128	Ozzie Guillen	.10	.05
❑ 129	Steve Buechele	.10	.05
❑ 130	Kevin Tapani	.10	.05
❑ 131	Felix Jose	.10	.05
❑ 132	Terry Steinbach	.10	.05
❑ 133	Ron Gant	.15	.07
❑ 134	Harold Reynolds	.10	.05
❑ 135	Chris Sabo	.10	.05
❑ 136	Ivan Rodriguez	.50	.23
❑ 137	Eric Anthony	.10	.05
❑ 138	Mike Henneman	.10	.05
❑ 139	Robby Thompson	.10	.05
❑ 140	Scott Fletcher	.10	.05
❑ 141	Bruce Hurst	.10	.05
❑ 142	Kevin Maas	.10	.05
❑ 143	Tom Candiotti	.10	.05
❑ 144	Chris Hoiles	.10	.05
❑ 145	Mike Morgan	.10	.05
❑ 146	Mark Whiten	.10	.05
❑ 147	Dennis Martinez	.15	.07
❑ 148	Tony Pena	.10	.05
❑ 149	Dave Magadan	.10	.05
❑ 150	Mark Lewis	.10	.05
❑ 151	Mariano Duncan	.10	.05
❑ 152	Gregg Jefferies	.15	.07
❑ 153	Doug Drabek	.15	.07
❑ 154	Brian Harper	.10	.05
❑ 155	Ray Lankford	.25	.11
❑ 156	Carney Lansford	.15	.07
❑ 157	Mike Sharperson	.10	.05
❑ 158	Jack Morris	.15	.07
❑ 159	Otis Nixon	.10	.05
❑ 160	Steve Sax	.10	.05
❑ 161	Mark Lemke	.10	.05
❑ 162	Rafael Palmeiro	.40	.18
❑ 163	Jose Rijo	.10	.05
❑ 164	Omar Vizquel	.15	.07
❑ 165	Sammy Sosa	1.25	.55
❑ 166	Milt Cuyler	.10	.05
❑ 167	Ken Hill	.10	.05
❑ 168	Darryl Hamilton	.10	.05
❑ 169	Ken Hill	.10	.05
❑ 170	Mike Devereaux	.15	.07
❑ 171	Don Slaught	.10	.05
❑ 172	Steve Farr	.10	.05
❑ 173	Bernard Gilkey	.10	.05
❑ 174	Mike Fetters	.10	.05
❑ 175	Vince Coleman	.10	.05
❑ 176	Kevin McReynolds	.10	.05
❑ 177	John Smoltz	.25	.11
❑ 178	Greg Gagne	.10	.05
❑ 179	Greg Swindell	.10	.05
❑ 180	Juan Guzman	.10	.05
❑ 181	Kal Daniels	.10	.05
❑ 182	Rick Sutcliffe	.10	.05
❑ 183	Orlando Merced	.10	.05
❑ 184	Bill Wegman	.10	.05

❑ 185	Mark Gardner	.10	.05
❑ 186	Rob Deer	.10	.05
❑ 187	Dave Hollins	.10	.05
❑ 188	Jack Clark	.10	.05
❑ 189	Brian Hunter	.10	.05
❑ 190	Tim Wallach	.10	.05
❑ 191	Tim Belcher	.10	.05
❑ 192	Walt Weiss	.10	.05
❑ 193	Kurt Stillwell	.10	.05
❑ 194	Charlie Hayes	.10	.05
❑ 195	Willie Randolph	.15	.07
❑ 196	Jack McDowell	.10	.05
❑ 197	Jose Offerman	.15	.07
❑ 198	Chuck Finley	.15	.07
❑ 199	Darrin Jackson	.10	.05
❑ 200	Kelly Gruber	.10	.05
❑ 201	John Wetteland	.15	.07
❑ 202	Jay Buhner	.25	.11
❑ 203	Mike LaValliere	.10	.05
❑ 204	Kevin Brown	.25	.11
❑ 205	Luis Gonzalez	.15	.07
❑ 206	Rick Aguilera	.10	.05
❑ 207	Norm Charlton	.10	.05
❑ 208	Mike Bordick	.10	.05
❑ 209	Charlie Leibrandt	.10	.05
❑ 210	Tom Brunansky	.10	.05
❑ 211	Tom Henke	.10	.05
❑ 212	Randy Milligan	.10	.05
❑ 213	Ramon Martinez	.15	.07
❑ 214	Mo Vaughn	.40	.18
❑ 215	Randy Myers	.15	.07
❑ 216	Greg Hibbard	.10	.05
❑ 217	Wes Chamberlain	.10	.05
❑ 218	Tony Phillips	.10	.05
❑ 219	Pete Harnisch	.10	.05
❑ 220	Mike Gallego	.10	.05
❑ 221	Bud Black	.10	.05
❑ 222	Gregg Olson	.15	.07
❑ 223	Milt Thompson	.10	.05
❑ 224	Ben McDonald	.15	.07
❑ 225	Billy Hatcher	.10	.05
❑ 226	Paul Sorrento	.10	.05
❑ 227	Mark Gubicza	.10	.05
❑ 228	Mike Greenwell	.15	.07
❑ 229	Curt Schilling	.15	.07
❑ 230	Alan Trammell	.25	.11
❑ 231	Zane Smith	.10	.05
❑ 232	Bobby Thigpen	.10	.05
❑ 233	Greg Olson	.10	.05
❑ 234	Joe Orsulak	.10	.05
❑ 235	Joe Oliver	.10	.05
❑ 236	Tim Raines	.15	.07
❑ 237	Juan Samuel	.10	.05
❑ 238	Chili Davis	.15	.07
❑ 239	Spike Owen	.10	.05
❑ 240	Dave Stewart	.15	.07
❑ 241	Jim Eisenreich	.10	.05
❑ 242	Phil Plantier	.15	.07
❑ 243	Sid Fernandez	.10	.05
❑ 244	Dan Gladden	.10	.05
❑ 245	Mickey Morandini	.10	.05
❑ 246	Tino Martinez	.40	.18
❑ 247	Kirt Manwaring	.10	.05
❑ 248	Dean Palmer	.15	.07
❑ 249	Tom Browning	.10	.05
❑ 250	Brian McRae	.15	.07
❑ 251	Scott Leius	.10	.05
❑ 252	Bert Blyleven	.15	.07
❑ 253	Scott Erickson	.10	.05
❑ 254	Bob Welch	.10	.05
❑ 255	Pat Kelly	.10	.05
❑ 256	Felix Fermin	.10	.05
❑ 257	Harold Baines	.15	.07
❑ 258	Duane Ward	.10	.05
❑ 259	Bill Spiers	.10	.05
❑ 260	Jaime Navarro	.10	.05
❑ 261	Scott Sanderson	.10	.05
❑ 262	Gary Gaetti	.15	.07
❑ 263	Bob Ojeda	.10	.05
❑ 264	Jeff Montgomery	.15	.07
❑ 265	Scott Bankhead	.10	.05
❑ 266	Lance Johnson	.10	.05
❑ 267	Rafael Belliard	.10	.05
❑ 268	Kevin Reimer	.10	.05
❑ 269	Benito Santiago	.15	.07
❑ 270	Mike Moore	.10	.05

❑ 271 Dave Fleming	.10	.05
❑ 272 Moises Alou	.15	.07
❑ 273 Pat Listach	.10	.05
❑ 274 Reggie Sanders	.15	.07
❑ 275 Kenny Lofton	.40	.18
❑ 276 Donovan Osborne	.10	.05
❑ 277 Rusty Meacham	.10	.05
❑ 278 Eric Karros	.25	.11
❑ 279 Andy Stankiewicz	.10	.05
❑ 280 Brian Jordan	.15	.07
❑ 281 Gary DiSarcina	.10	.05
❑ 282 Mark Wohlers	.10	.05
❑ 283 Dave Nilsson	.15	.07
❑ 284 Anthony Young	.10	.05
❑ 285 Jim Bullinger	.10	.05
❑ 286 Derek Bell	.15	.07
❑ 287 Brian Williams	.10	.05
❑ 288 Julio Valera	.10	.05
❑ 289 Dan Walters	.10	.05
❑ 290 Chad Curtis	.15	.07
❑ 291 Michael Tucker DP	.40	.18
❑ 292 Bob Zupcic	.10	.05
❑ 293 Todd Hundley	.25	.11
❑ 294 Jeff Tackett	.10	.05
❑ 295 Greg Colbrunn	.10	.05
❑ 296 Cal Eldred	.10	.05
❑ 297 Chris Roberts DP	.10	.05
❑ 298 John Doherty	.10	.05
❑ 299 Denny Neagle	.15	.07
❑ 300 Arthur Rhodes	.10	.05
❑ 301 Mark Clark	.10	.05
❑ 302 Scott Cooper	.10	.05
❑ 303 Jamie Arnold DP	.10	.05
❑ 304 Jim Thome	.50	.23
❑ 305 Frank Seminara	.10	.05
❑ 306 Kurt Knudsen	.10	.05
❑ 307 Tim Wakefield	.15	.07
❑ 308 John Jaha	.10	.05
❑ 309 Pat Hentgen	.25	.11
❑ 310 B.J. Wallace DP	.10	.05
❑ 311 Roberto Hernandez	.15	.07
❑ 312 Hipolito Pichardo	.10	.05
❑ 313 Eric Fox	.10	.05
❑ 314 Willie Banks	.10	.05
❑ 315 Sam Militello	.10	.05
❑ 316 Vince Horsman	.10	.05
❑ 317 Carlos Hernandez	.10	.05
❑ 318 Jeff Kent	.15	.07
❑ 319 Mike Perez	.10	.05
❑ 320 Scott Livingstone	.10	.05
❑ 321 Jeff Conine	.10	.05
❑ 322 James Austin	.10	.05
❑ 323 John Vander Wal	.10	.05
❑ 324 Pat Mahomes	.10	.05
❑ 325 Pedro Astacio	.15	.07
❑ 326 Bret Boone UER	.15	.07
(Misspelled Brett)		
❑ 327 Matt Stairs	.25	.11
❑ 328 Damion Easley	.15	.07
❑ 329 Ben Rivera	.10	.05
❑ 330 Reggie Jefferson	.15	.07
❑ 331 Luis Mercedes	.10	.05
❑ 332 Kyle Abbott	.10	.05
❑ 333 Eddie Taubensee	.10	.05
❑ 334 Tim McIntosh	.10	.05
❑ 335 Phil Clark	.10	.05
❑ 336 Wil Cordero	.10	.05
❑ 337 Russ Springer	.10	.05
❑ 338 Craig Colbert	.10	.05
❑ 339 Tim Salmon	.40	.18
❑ 340 Braulio Castillo	.10	.05
❑ 341 Donald Harris	.10	.05
❑ 342 Eric Young	.40	.18
❑ 343 Bob Wickman	.10	.05
❑ 344 John Valentin	.15	.07
❑ 345 Dan Wilson	.15	.07
❑ 346 Steve Hosey	.10	.05
❑ 347 Mike Piazza	2.00	.90
❑ 348 Willie Greene	.10	.05
❑ 349 Tom Goodwin	.10	.05
❑ 350 Eric Hillman	.10	.05
❑ 351 Steve Reed	.10	.05
❑ 352 Dan Serafini DP	.10	.05
❑ 353 Todd Steverson DP	.10	.05
❑ 354 Benji Grigsby DP	.10	.05
❑ 355 Shannon Stewart DP	1.00	.45

❑ 356 Sean Lowe DP	.10	.05
❑ 357 Derek Wallace DP	.10	.05
❑ 358 Rick Helling DP	.25	.11
❑ 359 Jason Kendall DP	1.25	.55
❑ 360 Derek Jeter DP	10.00	4.50
❑ 361 David Cone	.25	.11
❑ 362 Jeff Reardon	.15	.07
❑ 363 Bobby Witt	.10	.05
❑ 364 Jose Canseco	.50	.23
❑ 365 Jeff Russell	.10	.05
❑ 366 Ruben Sierra	.10	.05
❑ 367 Alan Mills	.10	.05
❑ 368 Matt Nokes	.10	.05
❑ 369 Pat Borders	.10	.05
❑ 370 Pedro Munoz	.10	.05
❑ 371 Danny Jackson	.10	.05
❑ 372 Geronimo Pena	.10	.05
❑ 373 Craig Lefferts	.10	.05
❑ 374 Joe Grahe	.10	.05
❑ 375 Roger McDowell	.10	.05
❑ 376 Jimmy Key	.15	.07
❑ 377 Steve Olin	.10	.05
❑ 378 Glenn Davis	.10	.05
❑ 379 Rene Gonzales	.10	.05
❑ 380 Manuel Lee	.10	.05
❑ 381 Ron Karkovice	.10	.05
❑ 382 Sid Bream	.10	.05
❑ 383 Gerald Williams	.10	.05
❑ 384 Lenny Harris	.10	.05
❑ 385 J.T. Snow	.50	.23
❑ 386 Dave Stieb	.10	.05
❑ 387 Kirk McCaskill	.10	.05
❑ 388 Lance Parrish	.10	.05
❑ 389 Craig Grebeck	.10	.05
❑ 390 Rick Wilkins	.10	.05
❑ 391 Manny Alexander	.10	.05
❑ 392 Mike Schooler	.10	.05
❑ 393 Bernie Williams	.40	.18
❑ 394 Kevin Koslofski	.10	.05
❑ 395 Willie Wilson	.10	.05
❑ 396 Jeff Parrett	.10	.05
❑ 397 Mike Harkey	.10	.05
❑ 398 Frank Tanana	.10	.05
❑ 399 Doug Henry	.10	.05
❑ 400 Royce Clayton	.10	.05
❑ 401 Eric Wedge	.10	.05
❑ 402 Derrick May	.10	.05
❑ 403 Carlos Garcia	.10	.05
❑ 404 Henry Rodriguez	.15	.07
❑ 405 Ryan Klesko	.40	.18

1993 Select Aces

	MINT	NRMT
COMPLETE SET (24)	50.00	22.00
COMMON CARD (1-24)	2.00	.90
STATED ODDS 1:4 JUMBO		

❑ 1 Roger Clemens	15.00	6.75
❑ 2 Tom Glavine	4.00	1.80
❑ 3 Jack McDowell	2.00	.90
❑ 4 Greg Maddux	20.00	9.00
❑ 5 Jack Morris	3.00	1.35
❑ 6 Dennis Martinez	3.00	1.35
❑ 7 Kevin Brown	4.00	1.80
❑ 8 Dwight Gooden	3.00	1.35
❑ 9 Kevin Appier	3.00	1.35
❑ 10 Mike Morgan	2.00	.90
❑ 11 Juan Guzman	2.00	.90
❑ 12 Charles Nagy	3.00	1.35
❑ 13 John Smiley	2.00	.90
❑ 14 Ken Hill	2.00	.90
❑ 15 Bob Tewksbury	2.00	.90
❑ 16 Doug Drabek	2.00	.90
❑ 17 John Smoltz	4.00	1.80
❑ 18 Greg Swindell	2.00	.90
❑ 19 Bruce Hurst	2.00	.90
❑ 20 Mike Mussina	6.00	2.70
❑ 21 Cal Eldred	2.00	.90
❑ 22 Melido Perez	2.00	.90
❑ 23 Dave Fleming	2.00	.90
❑ 24 Kevin Tapani	2.00	.90

1993 Select Chase Rookies

	MINT	NRMT
COMPLETE SET (21)	50.00	22.00
COMMON CARD (1-21)	2.50	1.10
MINOR STARS	5.00	2.20
STATED ODDS 1:18 HOBBY		

❑ 1 Pat Listach	2.50	1.10
❑ 2 Moises Alou	5.00	2.20
❑ 3 Reggie Sanders	5.00	2.20
❑ 4 Kenny Lofton	8.00	3.60
❑ 5 Eric Karros	8.00	3.60
❑ 6 Brian Williams	2.50	1.10
❑ 7 Donovan Osborne	2.50	1.10
❑ 8 Sam Militello	2.50	1.10
❑ 9 Chad Curtis	5.00	2.20
❑ 10 Bob Zupcic	2.50	1.10
❑ 11 Tim Salmon	10.00	4.50
❑ 12 Jeff Conine	2.50	1.10
❑ 13 Pedro Astacio	5.00	2.20
❑ 14 Arthur Rhodes	2.50	1.10
❑ 15 Cal Eldred	2.50	1.10
❑ 16 Tim Wakefield	5.00	2.20
❑ 17 Andy Stankiewicz	2.50	1.10
❑ 18 Wil Cordero	2.50	1.10
❑ 19 Todd Hundley	8.00	3.60
❑ 20 Dave Fleming	2.50	1.10
❑ 21 Bret Boone	5.00	2.20

1993 Select Chase Stars

	MINT	NRMT
COMPLETE SET (24)	100.00	45.00
COMMON CARD (1-24)	1.00	.45
STATED ODDS 1:18 RETAIL		
☐ 1 Fred McGriff	2.50	1.10
☐ 2 Ryne Sandberg	3.00	1.35
☐ 3 Ozzie Smith	3.00	1.35
☐ 4 Gary Sheffield	3.00	1.35
☐ 5 Darren Daulton	1.50	.70
☐ 6 Andy Van Slyke	1.00	.45
☐ 7 Barry Bonds	6.00	2.70
☐ 8 Tony Gwynn	12.00	5.50
☐ 9 Greg Maddux	15.00	6.75
☐ 10 Tom Glavine	2.50	1.10
☐ 11 John Franco	1.50	.70
☐ 12 Lee Smith	1.50	.70
☐ 13 Cecil Fielder	1.50	.70
☐ 14 Roberto Alomar	3.00	1.35
☐ 15 Cal Ripken	20.00	9.00
☐ 16 Edgar Martinez	2.50	1.10
☐ 17 Ivan Rodriguez	3.00	1.35
☐ 18 Kirby Puckett	8.00	3.60
☐ 19 Ken Griffey Jr.	25.00	11.00
☐ 20 Joe Carter	1.50	.70
☐ 21 Roger Clemens	12.00	5.50
☐ 22 Dave Fleming	1.00	.45
☐ 23 Paul Molitor	3.00	1.35
☐ 24 Dennis Eckersley	1.50	.70

1993 Select Stat Leaders

	MINT	NRMT
COMPLETE SET (90)	10.00	4.50
COMMON CARD (1-90)	.10	.05
ONE PER SCORE PACK		
☐ 1 Edgar Martinez	.30	.14
☐ 2 Kirby Puckett	.50	.23
☐ 3 Frank Thomas	.75	.35
☐ 4 Gary Sheffield	.40	.18
☐ 5 Andy Van Slyke	.10	.05
☐ 6 John Kruk	.20	.09
☐ 7 Kirby Puckett	.50	.23
☐ 8 Carlos Baerga	.10	.05
☐ 9 Paul Molitor	.40	.18
☐ 10 Terry Pendleton	.10	.05
Andy Van Slyke		
☐ 11 Ryne Sandberg	.50	.23
☐ 12 Mark Grace	.30	.14
☐ 13 Frank Thomas	.50	.23
Edgar Martinez		
☐ 14 Don Mattingly	.40	.18
Robin Yount		
☐ 15 Ken Griffey	1.25	.55
☐ 16 Andy Van Slyke	.10	.05
☐ 17 Mariano Duncan	.20	.09
Will Clark		
Ray Lankford		
☐ 18 Marquis Grissom	.20	.09
Terry Pendleton		
☐ 19 Lance Johnson	.10	.05
☐ 20 Mike Devereaux	.10	.05
☐ 21 Brady Anderson	.20	.09
☐ 22 Deion Sanders	.30	.14
☐ 23 Steve Finley	.20	.09
☐ 24 Andy Van Slyke	.10	.05

☐ 25 Juan Gonzalez	.60	.25
☐ 26 Mark McGwire	1.25	.55
☐ 27 Cecil Fielder	.20	.09
☐ 28 Fred McGriff	.30	.14
☐ 29 Barry Bonds	.50	.23
☐ 30 Gary Sheffield	.40	.18
☐ 31 Cecil Fielder	.20	.09
☐ 32 Joe Carter	.20	.09
☐ 33 Frank Thomas	.60	.25
☐ 34 Darren Daulton	.20	.09
☐ 35 Terry Pendleton	.10	.05
☐ 36 Fred McGriff	.30	.14
☐ 37 Tony Phillips	.10	.05
☐ 38 Frank Thomas	.60	.25
☐ 39 Roberto Alomar	.40	.18
☐ 40 Barry Bonds	.50	.23
☐ 41 Dave Hollins	.10	.05
☐ 42 Andy Van Slyke	.10	.05
☐ 43 Mark McGwire	1.25	.55
☐ 44 Edgar Martinez	.30	.14
☐ 45 Frank Thomas	.60	.25
☐ 46 Barry Bonds	.50	.23
☐ 47 Gary Sheffield	.40	.18
☐ 48 Fred McGriff	.30	.14
☐ 49 Frank Thomas	.60	.25
☐ 50 Danny Tartabull	.10	.05
☐ 51 Roberto Alomar	.40	.18
☐ 52 Barry Bonds	.50	.23
☐ 53 John Kruk	.20	.09
☐ 54 Brett Butler	.20	.09
☐ 55 Kenny Lofton	.40	.18
☐ 56 Pat Listach	.20	.09
☐ 57 Brady Anderson	.20	.09
☐ 58 Marquis Grissom	.20	.09
☐ 59 Delino DeShields	.10	.05
☐ 60 Bip Roberts	.10	.05
Steve Finley		
☐ 61 Jack McDowell	.10	.05
☐ 62 Kevin Brown	.40	.18
Roger Clemens		
☐ 63 Charles Nagy	.10	.05
Melido Perez		
☐ 64 Terry Mulholland	.10	.05
☐ 65 Curt Schilling	.10	.05
Doug Drabek		
☐ 66 Greg Maddux	.50	.23
John Smoltz		
☐ 67 Dennis Eckersley	.20	.09
☐ 68 Rick Aguilera	.10	.05
☐ 69 Jeff Montgomery	.10	.05
☐ 70 Lee Smith	.20	.09
☐ 71 Randy Myers	.20	.09
☐ 72 John Wetteland	.20	.09
☐ 73 Randy Johnson	.40	.18
☐ 74 Melido Perez	.10	.05
☐ 75 Roger Clemens	.75	.35
☐ 76 John Smoltz	.30	.14
☐ 77 David Cone	.30	.14
☐ 78 Greg Maddux	.75	.35
☐ 79 Roger Clemens	.75	.35
☐ 80 Kevin Appier	.20	.09
☐ 81 Mike Mussina	.40	.18
☐ 82 Bill Swift	.10	.05
☐ 83 Bob Tewksbury	.10	.05
☐ 84 Greg Maddux	.75	.35
☐ 85 Jack Morris	.20	.09
Kevin Brown		
☐ 86 Jack McDowell	.10	.05
☐ 87 Roger Clemens	.40	.18
Mike Mussina		
☐ 88 Tom Glavine	.60	.25
Greg Maddux		
☐ 89 Ken Hill	.10	.05
Bob Tewksbury		
☐ 90 Mike Morgan	.10	.05
Dennis Martinez		

1993 Select Triple Crown

	MINT	NRMT
COMPLETE SET (3)	50.00	22.00
COMMON CARD (1-3)	10.00	4.50
RANDOM INSERTS IN HOBBY PACKS		

	MINT	NRMT
☐ 1 Mickey Mantle	40.00	18.00
☐ 2 Carl Yastrzemski	10.00	4.50
☐ 3 Frank Robinson	10.00	4.50

1993 Select Rookie/Traded

	MINT	NRMT
COMPLETE SET (150)	15.00	6.75
COMMON CARD (1T-150T)	.30	.14
MINOR STARS	.50	.23
SEMISTARS	.75	.35
UNLISTED STARS	1.25	.55
RYAN TRIBUTE STATED ODDS 1:288		
ROY STATED ODDS 1:576		
☐ 1T Rickey Henderson	1.50	.70
☐ 2T Rob Deer	.30	.14
☐ 3T Tim Belcher	.30	.14
☐ 4T Gary Sheffield	1.25	.55
☐ 5T Fred McGriff	.75	.35
☐ 6T Mark Whiten	.30	.14
☐ 7T Jeff Russell	.30	.14
☐ 8T Harold Baines	.50	.23
☐ 9T Dave Winfield	.75	.35
☐ 10T Ellis Burks	.50	.23
☐ 11T Andre Dawson	.75	.35
☐ 12T Gregg Jefferies	.30	.14
☐ 13T Jimmy Key	.50	.23
☐ 14T Harold Reynolds	.30	.14
☐ 15T Tom Henke	.30	.14
☐ 16T Paul Molitor	1.25	.55
☐ 17T Wade Boggs	1.25	.55
☐ 18T David Cone	.75	.35
☐ 19T Tony Fernandez	.30	.14
☐ 20T Roberto Kelly	.30	.14
☐ 21T Paul O'Neill	.50	.23
☐ 22T Jose Lind	.30	.14
☐ 23T Barry Bonds	1.50	.70
☐ 24T Dave Stewart	.50	.23
☐ 25T Randy Myers	.50	.23
☐ 26T Benito Santiago	.30	.14
☐ 27T Tim Wallach	.30	.14
☐ 28T Greg Gagne	.30	.14
☐ 29T Kevin Mitchell	.50	.23
☐ 30T Jim Abbott	.50	.23
☐ 31T Lee Smith	.50	.23
☐ 32T Bobby Munoz	.30	.14
☐ 33T Mo Sanford	.30	.14
☐ 34T John Roper	.30	.14

❑ 35T David Hulse	.30	.14
❑ 36T Pedro Martinez	2.50	1.10
❑ 37T Chuck Carr	.30	.14
❑ 38T Armando Reynoso	.30	.14
❑ 39T Ryan Thompson	.30	.14
❑ 40T Carlos Garcia	.30	.14
❑ 41T Matt Whiteside	.30	.14
❑ 42T Benji Gil	.30	.14
❑ 43T Rodney Bolton	.30	.14
❑ 44T J.T. Snow	1.25	.55
❑ 45T David McCarty	.30	.14
❑ 46T Paul Quantrill	.30	.14
❑ 47T Al Martin	.30	.14
❑ 48T Lance Painter	.30	.14
❑ 49T Lou Frazier	.30	.14
❑ 50T Eduardo Perez	.30	.14
❑ 51T Kevin Young	.50	.23
❑ 52T Mike Trombley	.30	.14
❑ 53T Sterling Hitchcock	2.00	.90
❑ 54T Tim Bogar	.30	.14
❑ 55T Hilly Hathaway	.30	.14
❑ 56T Wayne Kirby	.30	.14
❑ 57T Craig Paquette	.30	.14
❑ 58T Bret Boone	.50	.23
❑ 59T Greg McMichael	.30	.14
❑ 60T Mike Lansing	.50	.23
❑ 61T Brent Gates	.30	.14
❑ 62T Rene Arocha	.30	.14
❑ 63T Ricky Gutierrez	.30	.14
❑ 64T Kevin Rogers	.30	.14
❑ 65T Ken Ryan	.30	.14
❑ 66T Phil Hiatt	.30	.14
❑ 67T Pat Meares	.30	.14
❑ 68T Troy Neel	.30	.14
❑ 69T Steve Cooke	.30	.14
❑ 70T Sherman Obando	.30	.14
❑ 71T Blas Minor	.30	.14
❑ 72T Angel Miranda	.30	.14
❑ 73T Tom Kramer	.30	.14
❑ 74T Chip Hale	.30	.14
❑ 75T Brad Pennington	.30	.14
❑ 76T Graeme Lloyd	.30	.14
❑ 77T Darrell Whitmore	.30	.14
❑ 78T David Nied	.30	.14
❑ 79T Todd Van Poppel	.30	.14
❑ 80T Chris Gomez	.50	.23
❑ 81T Jason Bere	.30	.14
❑ 82T Jeffrey Hammonds	.50	.23
❑ 83T Brad Ausmus	.30	.14
❑ 84T Kevin Stocker	.50	.23
❑ 85T Jeromy Burnitz	.50	.23
❑ 86T Aaron Sele	1.25	.55
❑ 87T Roberto Mejia	.30	.14
❑ 88T Kirk Rueter	1.00	.45
❑ 89T Kevin Roberson	.30	.14
❑ 90T Allen Watson	.30	.14
❑ 91T Charlie Leibrandt	.30	.14
❑ 92T Eric Davis	.50	.23
❑ 93T Jody Reed	.30	.14
❑ 94T Danny Jackson	.30	.14
❑ 95T Gary Gaetti	.50	.23
❑ 96T Norm Charlton	.30	.14
❑ 97T Doug Drabek	.30	.14
❑ 98T Scott Fletcher	.30	.14
❑ 99T Greg Swindell	.30	.14
❑ 100T John Smiley	.30	.14
❑ 101T Kevin Reimer	.30	.14
❑ 102T Andres Galarraga	1.25	.55
❑ 103T Greg Hibbard	.30	.14
❑ 104T Chris Hammond	.30	.14
❑ 105T Darnell Coles	.30	.14
❑ 106T Mike Felder	.30	.14
❑ 107T Jose Guzman	.30	.14
❑ 108T Chris Bosio	.30	.14
❑ 109T Spike Owen	.30	.14
❑ 110T Felix Jose	.30	.14
❑ 111T Cory Snyder	.30	.14
❑ 112T Craig Lefferts	.30	.14
❑ 113T David Wells	.50	.23
❑ 114T Pete Incaviglia	.30	.14
❑ 115T Mike Pagliarulo	.30	.14
❑ 116T Dave Magadan	.30	.14
❑ 117T Charlie Hough	.50	.23
❑ 118T Ivan Calderon	.30	.14
❑ 119T Manuel Lee	.30	.14
❑ 120T Bob Patterson	.30	.14

❑ 121T Bob Ojeda	.30	.14
❑ 122T Scott Bankhead	.30	.14
❑ 123T Greg Maddux	3.00	1.35
❑ 124T Chili Davis	.50	.23
❑ 125T Milt Thompson	.30	.14
❑ 126T Dave Martinez	.30	.14
❑ 127T Frank Tanana	.30	.14
❑ 128T Phil Plantier	.30	.14
❑ 129T Juan Samuel	.30	.14
❑ 130T Eric Young	1.25	.55
❑ 131T Joe Orsulak	.30	.14
❑ 132T Derek Bell	.50	.23
❑ 133T Darrin Jackson	.30	.14
❑ 134T Tom Brunansky	.30	.14
❑ 135T Jeff Reardon	.50	.23
❑ 136T Kevin Higgins	.30	.14
❑ 137T Joel Johnston	.30	.14
❑ 138T Rick Trlicek	.30	.14
❑ 139T Richie Lewis	.30	.14
❑ 140T Jeff Gardner	.30	.14
❑ 141T Jack Voigt	.30	.14
❑ 142T Rod Correia	.30	.14
❑ 143T Billy Brewer	.30	.14
❑ 144T Terry Jorgensen	.30	.14
❑ 145T Rich Amaral	.30	.14
❑ 146T Sean Berry	.30	.14
❑ 147T Dan Peltier	.30	.14
❑ 148T Paul Wagner	.30	.14
❑ 149T Damon Buford	.30	.14
❑ 150T Wil Cordero	.30	.14
❑ NR1 Nolan Ryan Tribute	40.00	18.00
❑ ROY1 Tim Salmon AL ROY	8.00	3.60
❑ ROY2 Mike Piazza NL ROY	40.00	18.00

1993 Select Rookie/Traded All-Star Rookies

RENE AROCHA

	MINT	NRMT
COMPLETE SET (10)	100.00	45.00
COMMON CARD (1-10)	3.00	1.35
MINOR STARS	6.00	2.70
STATED ODDS 1:58		

❑ 1 Jeff Conine	3.00	1.35
❑ 2 Brent Gates	3.00	1.35
❑ 3 Mike Lansing	6.00	2.70
❑ 4 Kevin Stocker	3.00	1.35
❑ 5 Mike Piazza	60.00	27.00
❑ 6 Jeffrey Hammonds	6.00	2.70
❑ 7 David Hulse	3.00	1.35
❑ 8 Tim Salmon	12.00	5.50
❑ 9 Rene Arocha	3.00	1.35
❑ 10 Greg McMichael	3.00	1.35

1994 Select

	MINT	NRMT
COMPLETE SET (420)	25.00	11.00
COMPLETE SERIES 1 (210)	15.00	6.75
COMPLETE SERIES 2 (210)	10.00	4.50
COMMON CARD (1-420)	.15	.07
MINOR STARS	.30	.14
UNLISTED STARS	.60	.25
SER.1 SALUTE STATED ODDS 1:360		
SER.2 MVP/ROY STATED ODDS 1:360		

❑ 1 Ken Griffey Jr.	3.00	1.35
❑ 2 Greg Maddux	1.50	.70
❑ 3 Paul Molitor	.60	.25
❑ 4 Mike Piazza	2.00	.90
❑ 5 Jay Bell	.30	.14
❑ 6 Frank Thomas	1.25	.55
❑ 7 Barry Larkin	.60	.25
❑ 8 Paul O'Neill	.30	.14
❑ 9 Darren Daulton	.30	.14
❑ 10 Mike Greenwell	.15	.07
❑ 11 Chuck Carr	.15	.07
❑ 12 Joe Carter	.30	.14
❑ 13 Lance Johnson	.15	.07
❑ 14 Jeff Blauser	.15	.07
❑ 15 Chris Hoiles	.15	.07
❑ 16 Rick Wilkins	.15	.07
❑ 17 Kirby Puckett	1.00	.45
❑ 18 Larry Walker	.60	.25
❑ 19 Randy Johnson	.60	.25
❑ 20 Bernard Gilkey	.15	.07
❑ 21 Devon White	.15	.07
❑ 22 Randy Myers	.15	.07
❑ 23 Don Mattingly	1.25	.55
❑ 24 John Kruk	.30	.14
❑ 25 Ozzie Guillen	.15	.07
❑ 26 Jeff Conine	.15	.07
❑ 27 Mike Macfarlane	.15	.07
❑ 28 Dave Hollins	.15	.07
❑ 29 Chuck Knoblauch	.60	.25
❑ 30 Ozzie Smith	.75	.35
❑ 31 Harold Baines	.30	.14
❑ 32 Ryne Sandberg	.75	.35
❑ 33 Ron Karkovice	.15	.07
❑ 34 Terry Pendleton	.15	.07
❑ 35 Wally Joyner	.30	.14
❑ 36 Mike Mussina	.60	.25
❑ 37 Felix Jose	.15	.07
❑ 38 Derrick May	.15	.07
❑ 39 Scott Cooper	.15	.07
❑ 40 Jose Rijo	.15	.07
❑ 41 Robin Ventura	.30	.14
❑ 42 Charlie Hayes	.15	.07
❑ 43 Jimmy Key	.15	.07
❑ 44 Eric Karros	.30	.14
❑ 45 Ruben Sierra	.15	.07
❑ 46 Ryan Thompson	.15	.07
❑ 47 Brian McRae	.15	.07
❑ 48 Pat Hentgen	.30	.14
❑ 49 John Valentin	.15	.07
❑ 50 Al Martin	.15	.07
❑ 51 Jose Lind	.15	.07
❑ 52 Kevin Stocker	.15	.07
❑ 53 Mike Gallego	.15	.07
❑ 54 Dwight Gooden	.30	.14
❑ 55 Brady Anderson	.30	.14
❑ 56 Jeff King	.15	.07
❑ 57 Mark McGwire	3.00	1.35
❑ 58 Sammy Sosa	2.00	.90
❑ 59 Ryan Bowen	.15	.07
❑ 60 Mark Lemke	.15	.07
❑ 61 Roger Clemens	1.50	.70
❑ 62 Brian Jordan	.30	.14
❑ 63 Andres Galarraga	.60	.25
❑ 64 Kevin Appier	.15	.07
❑ 65 Don Slaught	.15	.07
❑ 66 Mike Blowers	.15	.07
❑ 67 Wes Chamberlain	.15	.07
❑ 68 Troy Neel	.15	.07

69	John Wetteland	.30	.14
70	Joe Girardi	.15	.07
71	Reggie Sanders	.30	.14
72	Edgar Martinez	.30	.14
73	Todd Hundley	.30	.14
74	Pat Borders	.15	.07
75	Roberto Mejia	.15	.07
76	David Cone	.40	.18
77	Tony Gwynn	1.50	.70
78	Jim Abbott	.30	.14
79	Jay Buhner	.30	.14
80	Mark McLemore	.15	.07
81	Wil Cordero	.15	.07
82	Pedro Astacio	.15	.07
83	Bob Tewksbury	.15	.07
84	Dave Winfield	.60	.25
85	Jeff Kent	.30	.14
86	Todd Van Poppel	.15	.07
87	Steve Avery	.15	.07
88	Mike Lansing	.30	.14
89	Lenny Dykstra	.30	.14
90	Jose Guzman	.15	.07
91	Brian R. Hunter	.15	.07
92	Tim Raines	.30	.14
93	Andre Dawson	.40	.18
94	Joe Orsulak	.15	.07
95	Ricky Jordan	.15	.07
96	Billy Hatcher	.15	.07
97	Jack McDowell	.15	.07
98	Tom Pagnozzi	.15	.07
99	Darryl Strawberry	.30	.14
100	Mike Stanley	.15	.07
101	Bret Saberhagen	.30	.14
102	Willie Greene	.15	.07
103	Bryan Harvey	.15	.07
104	Tim Bogar	.15	.07
105	Jack Voigt	.15	.07
106	Brad Ausmus	.15	.07
107	Ramon Martinez	.30	.14
108	Mike Perez	.15	.07
109	Jeff Montgomery	.15	.07
110	Danny Darwin	.15	.07
111	Wilson Alvarez	.30	.14
112	Kevin Mitchell	.15	.07
113	David Nied	.15	.07
114	Rich Amaral	.15	.07
115	Stan Javier	.15	.07
116	Mo Vaughn	.60	.25
117	Ben McDonald	.15	.07
118	Tom Gordon	.15	.07
119	Carlos Garcia	.15	.07
120	Phil Plantier	.15	.07
121	Mike Morgan	.15	.07
122	Pat Meares	.15	.07
123	Kevin Young	.15	.07
124	Jeff Fassero	.15	.07
125	Gene Harris	.15	.07
126	Bob Welch	.15	.07
127	Walt Weiss	.15	.07
128	Bobby Witt	.15	.07
129	Andy Van Slyke	.30	.14
130	Steve Cooke	.15	.07
131	Mike Devereaux	.15	.07
132	Joey Cora	.15	.07
133	Bret Barberie	.15	.07
134	Orel Hershiser	.30	.14
135	Ed Sprague	.15	.07
136	Shawon Dunston	.15	.07
137	Alex Arias	.15	.07
138	Archi Cianfrocco	.15	.07
139	Tim Wallach	.15	.07
140	Bernie Williams	.60	.25
141	Karl Rhodes	.15	.07
142	Pat Kelly	.15	.07
143	Dave Magadan	.15	.07
144	Kevin Tapani	.15	.07
145	Eric Young	.15	.07
146	Derek Bell	.30	.14
147	Dante Bichette	.30	.14
148	Geronimo Pena	.15	.07
149	Joe Oliver	.15	.07
150	Orestes Destrade	.15	.07
151	Tim Naehring	.15	.07
152	Ray Lankford	.30	.14
153	Phil Clark	.15	.07
154	David McCarty	.15	.07
155	Tommy Greene	.15	.07
156	Wade Boggs	.60	.25
157	Kevin Gross	.15	.07
158	Hal Morris	.15	.07
159	Moises Alou	.30	.14
160	Rick Aguilera	.15	.07
161	Curt Schilling	.30	.14
162	Chip Hale	.15	.07
163	Tino Martinez	.60	.25
164	Mark Whiten	.15	.07
165	Dave Stewart	.30	.14
166	Steve Buechele	.15	.07
167	Bobby Jones	.15	.07
168	Darrin Fletcher	.15	.07
169	John Smiley	.15	.07
170	Cory Snyder	.15	.07
171	Scott Erickson	.30	.14
172	Kirk Rueter	.15	.07
173	Dave Fleming	.15	.07
174	John Smoltz	.40	.18
175	Ricky Gutierrez	.15	.07
176	Mike Bordick	.15	.07
177	Chan Ho Park	.75	.35
178	Alex Gonzalez	.15	.07
179	Steve Karsay	.15	.07
180	Jeffrey Hammonds	.30	.14
181	Manny Ramirez	1.25	.55
182	Salomon Torres	.15	.07
183	Raul Mondesi	.60	.25
184	James Mouton	.15	.07
185	Cliff Floyd	.30	.14
186	Danny Bautista	.15	.07
187	Kurt Abbott	.15	.07
188	Javier Lopez	.40	.18
189	John Patterson	.15	.07
190	Greg Blosser	.15	.07
191	Bob Hamelin	.15	.07
192	Tony Eusebio	.15	.07
193	Carlos Delgado	.60	.25
194	Chris Gomez	.15	.07
195	Kelly Stinnett	.15	.07
196	Shane Reynolds	.30	.14
197	Ryan Klesko	.30	.14
198	Jim Edmonds UER	.60	.25
	Mark Dalesandro pictured on front		
199	James Hurst	.15	.07
200	Dave Staton	.15	.07
201	Rondell White	.30	.14
202	Keith Mitchell	.15	.07
203	Darren Oliver	.60	.25
204	Mike Matheny	.15	.07
205	Chris Turner	.15	.07
206	Matt Mieske	.15	.07
207	NL Team Checklist	.15	.07
208	NL Team Checklist	.15	.07
209	AL Team Checklist	.15	.07
210	AL Team Checklist	.15	.07
211	Barry Bonds	.75	.35
212	Juan Gonzalez	1.25	.55
213	Jim Eisenreich	.15	.07
214	Ivan Rodriguez	.75	.35
215	Tony Phillips	.15	.07
216	John Jaha	.15	.07
217	Lee Smith	.30	.14
218	Bip Roberts	.15	.07
219	Dave Hansen	.15	.07
220	Pat Listach	.15	.07
221	Willie McGee	.30	.14
222	Damion Easley	.15	.07
223	Dean Palmer	.15	.07
224	Mike Moore	.15	.07
225	Brian Harper	.15	.07
226	Gary DiSarcina	.15	.07
227	Delino DeShields	.15	.07
228	Otis Nixon	.15	.07
229	Roberto Alomar	.60	.25
230	Mark Grace	.40	.18
231	Kenny Lofton	.60	.25
232	Gregg Jefferies	.15	.07
233	Cecil Fielder	.30	.14
234	Jeff Bagwell	.75	.35
235	Albert Belle	.60	.25
236	Dave Justice	.60	.25
237	Tom Henke	.15	.07
238	Bobby Bonilla	.30	.14
239	John Olerud	.30	.14
240	Robby Thompson	.15	.07
241	Dave Valle	.15	.07
242	Marquis Grissom	.30	.14
243	Greg Swindell	.15	.07
244	Todd Zeile	.15	.07
245	Dennis Eckersley	.30	.14
246	Jose Offerman	.30	.14
247	Greg McMichael	.15	.07
248	Tim Belcher	.15	.07
249	Cal Ripken Jr.	2.50	1.10
250	Tom Glavine	.60	.25
251	Luis Polonia	.15	.07
252	Bill Swift	.15	.07
253	Juan Guzman	.15	.07
254	Rickey Henderson	.75	.35
255	Terry Mulholland	.15	.07
256	Gary Sheffield	.60	.25
257	Terry Steinbach	.15	.07
258	Brett Butler	.30	.14
259	Jason Bere	.15	.07
260	Doug Strange	.15	.07
261	Kent Hrbek	.30	.14
262	Graeme Lloyd	.15	.07
263	Lou Frazier	.15	.07
264	Charles Nagy	.30	.14
265	Bret Boone	.30	.14
266	Kirk Gibson	.30	.14
267	Kevin Brown	.30	.14
268	Fred McGriff	.40	.18
269	Matt Williams	.40	.18
270	Greg Gagne	.15	.07
271	Mariano Duncan	.15	.07
272	Jeff Russell	.15	.07
273	Eric Davis	.30	.14
274	Shane Mack	.15	.07
275	Jose Vizcaino	.15	.07
276	Jose Canseco	.75	.35
277	Roberto Hernandez	.15	.07
278	Royce Clayton	.15	.07
279	Carlos Baerga	.30	.14
280	Pete Incaviglia	.15	.07
281	Brent Gates	.30	.14
282	Jeromy Burnitz	.30	.14
283	Chili Davis	.15	.07
284	Pete Harnisch	.15	.07
285	Alan Trammell	.40	.18
286	Eric Anthony	.15	.07
287	Ellis Burks	.30	.14
288	Julio Franco	.15	.07
289	Jack Morris	.30	.14
290	Erik Hanson	.15	.07
291	Chuck Finley	.15	.07
292	Reggie Jefferson	.15	.07
293	Kevin McReynolds	.15	.07
294	Greg Hibbard	.15	.07
295	Travis Fryman	.30	.14
296	Craig Biggio	.60	.25
297	Kenny Rogers	.15	.07
298	Dave Henderson	.15	.07
299	Jim Thome	.60	.25
300	Rene Arocha	.15	.07
301	Pedro Munoz	.15	.07
302	David Hulse	.15	.07
303	Greg Vaughn	.30	.14
304	Darren Lewis	.15	.07
305	Deion Sanders	.30	.14
306	Danny Tartabull	.15	.07
307	Darryl Hamilton	.15	.07
308	Andujar Cedeno	.15	.07
309	Tim Salmon	.60	.25
310	Tony Fernandez	.15	.07
311	Alex Fernandez	.15	.07
312	Roberto Kelly	.15	.07
313	Harold Reynolds	.15	.07
314	Chris Sabo	.15	.07
315	Howard Johnson	.15	.07
316	Mark Portugal	.15	.07
317	Rafael Palmeiro	.60	.25
318	Pete Smith	.15	.07
319	Will Clark	.60	.25
320	Henry Rodriguez	.30	.14
321	Omar Vizquel	.30	.14
322	David Segui	.15	.07
323	Lou Whitaker	.30	.14
324	Felix Fermin	.15	.07
325	Spike Owen	.15	.07

❑ 326 Darryl Kile	.15	.07
❑ 327 Chad Kreuter	.15	.07
❑ 328 Rod Beck	.15	.07
❑ 329 Eddie Murray	.60	.25
❑ 330 B.J. Surhoff	.30	.14
❑ 331 Mickey Tettleton	.15	.07
❑ 332 Pedro Martinez	.75	.35
❑ 333 Roger Pavlik	.15	.07
❑ 334 Eddie Taubensee	.15	.07
❑ 335 John Doherty	.15	.07
❑ 336 Jody Reed	.15	.07
❑ 337 Aaron Sele	.30	.14
❑ 338 Leo Gomez	.15	.07
❑ 339 Dave Nilsson	.15	.07
❑ 340 Rob Dibble	.15	.07
❑ 341 John Burkett	.15	.07
❑ 342 Wayne Kirby	.15	.07
❑ 343 Dan Wilson	.15	.07
❑ 344 Armando Reynoso	.15	.07
❑ 345 Chad Curtis	.15	.07
❑ 346 Dennis Martinez	.30	.14
❑ 347 Cal Eldred	.15	.07
❑ 348 Luis Gonzalez	.30	.14
❑ 349 Doug Drabek	.15	.07
❑ 350 Jim Leyritz	.30	.14
❑ 351 Mark Langston	.15	.07
❑ 352 Darrin Jackson	.15	.07
❑ 353 Sid Fernandez	.15	.07
❑ 354 Benito Santiago	.15	.07
❑ 355 Kevin Seitzer	.15	.07
❑ 356 Bo Jackson	.30	.14
❑ 357 David Wells	.15	.07
❑ 358 Paul Sorrento	.15	.18
❑ 359 Ken Caminiti	.40	.18
❑ 360 Eduardo Perez	.15	.07
❑ 361 Orlando Merced	.15	.07
❑ 362 Steve Finley	.30	.14
❑ 363 Andy Benes	.15	.07
❑ 364 Manuel Lee	.15	.07
❑ 365 Todd Benzinger	.15	.07
❑ 366 Sandy Alomar Jr.	.30	.14
❑ 367 Rex Hudler	.15	.07
❑ 368 Mike Henneman	.15	.07
❑ 369 Vince Coleman	.15	.07
❑ 370 Kirt Manwaring	.15	.07
❑ 371 Ken Hill	.15	.07
❑ 372 Glenallen Hill	.15	.07
❑ 373 Sean Berry	.15	.07
❑ 374 Geronimo Berroa	.15	.07
❑ 375 Duane Ward	.15	.07
❑ 376 Allen Watson	.15	.07
❑ 377 Marc Newfield	.15	.07
❑ 378 Dan Miceli	.15	.07
❑ 379 Denny Hocking	.15	.07
❑ 380 Mark Kiefer	.15	.07
❑ 381 Tony Tarasco	.15	.07
❑ 382 Tony Longmire	.15	.07
❑ 383 Brian Anderson	.40	.18
❑ 384 Fernando Vina	.15	.07
❑ 385 Hector Carrasco	.15	.07
❑ 386 Mike Kelly	.15	.07
❑ 387 Greg Colbrunn	.15	.07
❑ 388 Roger Salkeld	.15	.07
❑ 389 Steve Trachsel	.15	.07
❑ 390 Rich Becker	.15	.07
❑ 391 Billy Taylor	.15	.07
❑ 392 Rich Rowland	.15	.07
❑ 393 Carl Everett	.30	.14
❑ 394 Johnny Ruffin	.15	.07
❑ 395 Keith Lockhart	.15	.07
❑ 396 J.R. Phillips	.15	.07
❑ 397 Sterling Hitchcock	.30	.14
❑ 398 Jorge Fabregas	.15	.07
❑ 399 Jeff Granger	.15	.07
❑ 400 Eddie Zambrano	.15	.07
❑ 401 Rikkert Faneyte	.15	.07
❑ 402 Gerald Williams	.15	.07
❑ 403 Joey Hamilton	.60	.25
❑ 404 Joe Hall	.15	.07
❑ 405 John Hudek	.15	.07
❑ 406 Roberto Petagine	.15	.07
❑ 407 Charles Johnson	.30	.14
❑ 408 Mark Smith	.15	.07
❑ 409 Jeff Juden	.15	.07
❑ 410 Carlos Pulido	.15	.07
❑ 411 Paul Shuey	.15	.07

❑ 412 Rob Butler	.15	.07
❑ 413 Mark Acre	.15	.07
❑ 414 Greg Pirkl	.15	.07
❑ 415 Melvin Nieves	.15	.07
❑ 416 Tim Hyers	.15	.07
❑ 417 NL Checklist	.15	.07
❑ 418 NL Checklist	.15	.07
❑ 419 AL Checklist	.15	.07
❑ 420 AL Checklist	.15	.07
❑ RY1 Carlos Delgado	4.00	1.80
❑ SS1 Cal Ripken Jr. Salute	20.00	9.00
❑ SS2 Dave Winfield Salute	4.00	1.80
❑ MVP1 Paul Molitor	5.00	2.20

1994 Select Crown Contenders

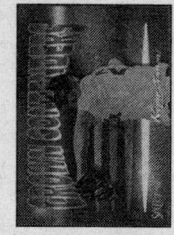

	MINT	NRMT
COMPLETE SET (10)	80.00	36.00
COMMON CARD (CC1-CC10)	1.50	.70
SER.1 STATED ODDS 1:24		

❑ CC1 Lenny Dykstra	1.50	.70
❑ CC2 Greg Maddux	10.00	4.50
❑ CC3 Roger Clemens	10.00	4.50
❑ CC4 Randy Johnson	5.00	2.20
❑ CC5 Frank Thomas	8.00	3.60
❑ CC6 Barry Bonds	5.00	2.20
❑ CC7 Juan Gonzalez	8.00	3.60
❑ CC8 John Olerud	1.50	.70
❑ CC9 Mike Piazza	12.00	5.50
❑ CC10 Ken Griffey Jr.	20.00	9.00

1994 Select Rookie Surge

	MINT	NRMT
COMPLETE SET (18)	80.00	36.00
COMPLETE SERIES 1 (9)	30.00	13.50
COMPLETE SERIES 2 (9)	50.00	22.00
COMMON CARD (RS1-RS18)	4.00	1.80
MINOR STARS	8.00	3.60
STATED ODDS 1:48		

❑ RS1 Cliff Floyd	8.00	3.60
❑ RS2 Bob Hamelin	4.00	1.80
❑ RS3 Ryan Klesko	8.00	3.60
❑ RS4 Carlos Delgado	12.00	5.50

❑ RS5 Jeffrey Hammonds	8.00	3.60
❑ RS6 Rondell White	8.00	3.60
❑ RS7 Salomon Torres	4.00	1.80
❑ RS8 Steve Karsay	4.00	1.80
❑ RS9 Javier Lopez	10.00	4.50
❑ RS10 Manny Ramirez	30.00	13.50
❑ RS11 Tony Tarasco	4.00	1.80
❑ RS12 Kurt Abbott	4.00	1.80
❑ RS13 Chan Ho Park	12.00	5.50
❑ RS14 Rich Becker	4.00	1.80
❑ RS15 James Mouton	4.00	1.80
❑ RS16 Alex Gonzalez	4.00	1.80
❑ RS17 Raul Mondesi	15.00	6.75
❑ RS18 Steve Trachsel	4.00	1.80

1994 Select Skills

	MINT	NRMT
COMPLETE SET (10)	60.00	27.00
COMMON CARD (SK1-SK10)	4.00	1.80
SER.2 STATED ODDS 1:24		

❑ SK1 Randy Johnson	10.00	4.50
❑ SK2 Barry Larkin	10.00	4.50
❑ SK3 Lenny Dykstra	4.00	1.80
❑ SK4 Kenny Lofton	10.00	4.50
❑ SK5 Juan Gonzalez	25.00	11.00
❑ SK6 Barry Bonds	10.00	4.50
❑ SK7 Marquis Grissom	4.00	1.80
❑ SK8 Ivan Rodriguez	10.00	4.50
❑ SK9 Larry Walker	10.00	4.50
❑ SK10 Travis Fryman	4.00	1.80

1995 Select

	MINT	NRMT
COMPLETE SET (250)	15.00	6.75
COMMON CARD (1-250)	.10	.05
MINOR STARS	.20	.09
UNLISTED STARS	.40	.18
SUBSET CARDS HALF VALUE OF BASE CARDS		
COMMON ART.PRF (1-250)	3.00	1.35
*AP STARS: 15X TO 40X HI COLUMN		
AP STATED ODDS 1:24		
NOMO CARD ISSUED DIRECT TO DEALERS		

❑ 1 Cal Ripken Jr.	1.50	.70
❑ 2 Robin Ventura	.20	.09
❑ 3 Al Martin	.10	.05
❑ 4 Jeff Frye	.10	.05

❑ 5	Darryl Strawberry	.20	.09
❑ 6	Chan Ho Park	.40	.18
❑ 7	Steve Avery	.10	.05
❑ 8	Bret Boone	.20	.09
❑ 9	Danny Tartabull	.10	.05
❑ 10	Dante Bichette	.20	.09
❑ 11	Rondell White	.20	.09
❑ 12	Dave McCarty	.05	.05
❑ 13	Bernard Gilkey	.10	.05
❑ 14	Mark McGwire	2.00	.90
❑ 15	Ruben Sierra	.10	.05
❑ 16	Wade Boggs	.40	.18
❑ 17	Mike Piazza	1.25	.55
❑ 18	Jeffrey Hammonds	.20	.09
❑ 19	Mike Mussina	.40	.18
❑ 20	Darryl Kile	.10	.05
❑ 21	Greg Maddux	1.00	.45
❑ 22	Frank Thomas	.75	.35
❑ 23	Kevin Appier	.20	.09
❑ 24	Jay Bell	.20	.09
❑ 25	Kirk Gibson	.20	.09
❑ 26	Pat Hentgen	.20	.09
❑ 27	Joey Hamilton	.20	.09
❑ 28	Bernie Williams	.40	.18
❑ 29	Aaron Sele	.20	.09
❑ 30	Delino DeShields	.10	.05
❑ 31	Danny Bautista	.10	.05
❑ 32	Jim Thome	.40	.18
❑ 33	Rikkert Faneyte	.10	.05
❑ 34	Roberto Alomar	.40	.18
❑ 35	Paul Molitor	.40	.18
❑ 36	Allen Watson	.10	.05
❑ 37	Jeff Bagwell	.50	.23
❑ 38	Jay Buhner	.20	.09
❑ 39	Marquis Grissom	.20	.09
❑ 40	Jim Edmonds	.30	.14
❑ 41	Ryan Klesko	.20	.09
❑ 42	Fred McGriff	.30	.14
❑ 43	Tony Tarasco	.10	.05
❑ 44	Darren Daulton	.20	.09
❑ 45	Marc Newfield	.10	.05
❑ 46	Barry Bonds	.50	.23
❑ 47	Bobby Bonilla	.20	.09
❑ 48	Greg Pirkl	.10	.05
❑ 49	Steve Karsay	.10	.05
❑ 50	Bob Hamelin	.10	.05
❑ 51	Javier Lopez	.20	.09
❑ 52	Barry Larkin	.40	.18
❑ 53	Kevin Young	.10	.05
❑ 54	Sterling Hitchcock	.10	.05
❑ 55	Tom Glavine	.40	.18
❑ 56	Carlos Delgado	.40	.18
❑ 57	Darren Oliver	.20	.09
❑ 58	Cliff Floyd	.20	.09
❑ 59	Tim Salmon	.40	.18
❑ 60	Albert Belle	.40	.18
❑ 61	Salomon Torres	.10	.05
❑ 62	Gary Sheffield	.50	.23
❑ 63	Ivan Rodriguez	.50	.23
❑ 64	Charles Nagy	.20	.09
❑ 65	Eduardo Perez	.10	.05
❑ 66	Terry Steinbach	.10	.05
❑ 67	Dave Justice	.40	.18
❑ 68	Jason Bere	.10	.05
❑ 69	Dave Nilsson	.20	.09
❑ 70	Brian Anderson	.20	.09
❑ 71	Billy Ashley	.10	.05
❑ 72	Roger Clemens	1.00	.45
❑ 73	Jimmy Key	.20	.09
❑ 74	Wally Joyner	.20	.09
❑ 75	Andy Benes	.20	.09
❑ 76	Ray Lankford	.20	.09
❑ 77	Jeff Kent	.20	.09
❑ 78	Moises Alou	.20	.09
❑ 79	Kirby Puckett	.60	.25
❑ 80	Joe Carter	.40	.18
❑ 81	Manny Ramirez	.50	.23
❑ 82	J.R. Phillips	.10	.05
❑ 83	Matt Mieske	.10	.05
❑ 84	John Olerud	.20	.09
❑ 85	Andres Galarraga	.40	.18
❑ 86	Juan Gonzalez	.75	.35
❑ 87	Pedro Martinez	.50	.23
❑ 88	Dean Palmer	.20	.09
❑ 89	Ken Griffey Jr.	2.00	.90
❑ 90	Brian Jordan	.20	.09
❑ 91	Hal Morris	.10	.05
❑ 92	Lenny Dykstra	.20	.09
❑ 93	Wil Cordero	.10	.05
❑ 94	Tony Gwynn	1.00	.45
❑ 95	Alex Gonzalez	.10	.05
❑ 96	Cecil Fielder	.20	.09
❑ 97	Mo Vaughn	.40	.18
❑ 98	John Valentin	.20	.09
❑ 99	Will Clark	.40	.18
❑ 100	Geronimo Pena	.10	.05
❑ 101	Don Mattingly	.75	.35
❑ 102	Charles Johnson	.20	.09
❑ 103	Raul Mondesi	.30	.14
❑ 104	Reggie Sanders	.20	.09
❑ 105	Royce Clayton	.10	.05
❑ 106	Reggie Jefferson	.10	.05
❑ 107	Craig Biggio	.40	.18
❑ 108	Jack McDowell	.10	.05
❑ 109	James Mouton	.10	.05
❑ 110	Mike Greenwell	.10	.05
❑ 111	David Cone	.30	.14
❑ 112	Matt Williams	.40	.18
❑ 113	Garret Anderson	.20	.09
❑ 114	Carlos Garcia	.10	.05
❑ 115	Alex Fernandez	.10	.05
❑ 116	Deion Sanders	.20	.09
❑ 117	Chili Davis	.20	.09
❑ 118	Mike Kelly	.10	.05
❑ 119	Jeff Conine	.10	.05
❑ 120	Kenny Lofton	.30	.14
❑ 121	Rafael Palmeiro	.40	.18
❑ 122	Chuck Knoblauch	.40	.18
❑ 123	Ozzie Smith	.50	.23
❑ 124	Carlos Baerga	.10	.05
❑ 125	Brett Butler	.20	.09
❑ 126	Sammy Sosa	1.25	.55
❑ 127	Ellis Burks	.20	.09
❑ 128	Bret Saberhagen	.20	.09
❑ 129	Doug Drabek	.10	.05
❑ 130	Dennis Martinez	.20	.09
❑ 131	Paul O'Neill	.20	.09
❑ 132	Travis Fryman	.20	.09
❑ 133	Brent Gates	.10	.05
❑ 134	Rickey Henderson	.50	.23
❑ 135	Randy Johnson	.40	.18
❑ 136	Mark Langston	.10	.05
❑ 137	Greg Colbrunn	.10	.05
❑ 138	Jose Rijo	.10	.05
❑ 139	Bryan Harvey	.10	.05
❑ 140	Dennis Eckersley	.20	.09
❑ 141	Ron Gant	.20	.09
❑ 142	Carl Everett	.10	.05
❑ 143	Jeff Granger	.10	.05
❑ 144	Ben McDonald	.10	.05
❑ 145	Kurt Abbott UER	.10	.05
	(Mariners logo on front)		
❑ 146	Jim Abbott	.20	.09
❑ 147	Jason Jacome	.10	.05
❑ 148	Rico Brogna	.20	.09
❑ 149	Cal Eldred	.10	.05
❑ 150	Rich Becker	.10	.05
❑ 151	Pete Harnisch	.10	.05
❑ 152	Roberto Petagine	.10	.05
❑ 153	Jacob Brumfield	.10	.05
❑ 154	Todd Hundley	.20	.09
❑ 155	Roger Cedeno	.10	.05
❑ 156	Harold Baines	.20	.09
❑ 157	Steve Dunn	.10	.05
❑ 158	Tim Belk	.10	.05
❑ 159	Marty Cordova	.20	.09
❑ 160	Russ Davis	.20	.09
❑ 161	Jose Malave	.10	.05
❑ 162	Brian Hunter	.20	.09
❑ 163	Andy Pettitte	.40	.18
❑ 164	Brooks Kieschnick	.20	.09
❑ 165	Midre Cummings	.10	.05
❑ 166	Frank Rodriguez	.10	.05
❑ 167	Chad Mottola	.10	.05
❑ 168	Brian Barber	.10	.05
❑ 169	Tim Unroe	.10	.05
❑ 170	Shane Andrews	.10	.05
❑ 171	Jose Flora	.10	.05
❑ 172	Ray Durham	.20	.09
❑ 173	Chipper Jones	1.00	.45
❑ 174	Butch Huskey	.10	.05
❑ 175	Ray McDavid	.10	.05
❑ 176	Jeff Cirillo	.20	.09
❑ 177	Terry Pendleton	.10	.05
❑ 178	Scott Ruffcorn	.10	.05
❑ 179	Ray Holbert	.10	.05
❑ 180	Joe Randa	.10	.05
❑ 181	Jose Oliva	.10	.05
❑ 182	Andy Van Slyke	.20	.09
❑ 183	Albie Lopez	.10	.05
❑ 184	Chad Curtis	.10	.05
❑ 185	Ozzie Guillen	.10	.05
❑ 186	Chad Ogea	.10	.05
❑ 187	Dan Wilson	.10	.05
❑ 188	Tony Fernandez	.20	.09
❑ 189	John Smoltz	.30	.14
❑ 190	Willie Greene	.10	.05
❑ 191	Darren Lewis	.10	.05
❑ 192	Orlando Miller	.10	.05
❑ 193	Kurt Miller	.10	.05
❑ 194	Andrew Lorraine	.10	.05
❑ 195	Ernie Young	.10	.05
❑ 196	Jimmy Haynes	.10	.05
❑ 197	Raul Casanova	.10	.05
❑ 198	Joe Vitiello	.10	.05
❑ 199	Brad Woodall	.10	.05
❑ 200	Juan Acevedo	.10	.05
❑ 201	Michael Tucker	.20	.09
❑ 202	Shawn Green	.40	.18
❑ 203	Alex Rodriguez	1.50	.70
❑ 204	Julian Tavarez	.10	.05
❑ 205	Jose Lima	.10	.05
❑ 206	Wilson Alvarez	.20	.09
❑ 207	Rich Aude	.10	.05
❑ 208	Armando Benitez	.10	.05
❑ 209	Dwayne Hosey	.10	.05
❑ 210	Gabe White	.10	.05
❑ 211	Joey Eischen	.10	.05
❑ 212	Bill Pulsipher	.20	.09
❑ 213	Robby Thompson	.10	.05
❑ 214	Toby Borland	.10	.05
❑ 215	Rusty Greer	.40	.18
❑ 216	Fausto Cruz	.10	.05
❑ 217	Luis Ortiz	.10	.05
❑ 218	Duane Singleton	.10	.05
❑ 219	Troy Percival	.20	.09
❑ 220	Gregg Jefferies	.20	.09
❑ 221	Mark Grace	.30	.14
❑ 222	Mickey Tettleton	.10	.05
❑ 223	Phil Plantier	.10	.05
❑ 224	Larry Walker	.40	.18
❑ 225	Ken Caminiti	.30	.14
❑ 226	Dave Winfield	.40	.18
❑ 227	Brady Anderson	.20	.09
❑ 228	Kevin Brown	.30	.14
❑ 229	Andujar Cedeno	.10	.05
❑ 230	Roberto Kelly	.10	.05
❑ 231	Jose Canseco	.50	.23
❑ 232	Scott Ruffcorn ST	.10	.05
❑ 233	Billy Ashley ST	.10	.05
❑ 234	J.R. Phillips ST	.10	.05
❑ 235	Chipper Jones ST	.50	.23
❑ 236	Charles Johnson ST	.10	.05
❑ 237	Midre Cummings ST	.10	.05
❑ 238	Brian I. Hunter ST	.10	.05
❑ 239	Garret Anderson ST	.10	.05
❑ 240	Shawn Green ST	.20	.09
❑ 241	Alex Rodriguez ST	.75	.35
❑ 242	Frank Thomas CL	.40	.18
❑ 243	Ken Griffey Jr. CL	1.00	.45
❑ 244	Albert Belle CL	.20	.09
❑ 245	Cal Ripken Jr. CL	.75	.35
❑ 246	Barry Bonds CL	.30	.14
❑ 247	Raul Mondesi CL	.10	.05
❑ 248	Mike Piazza CL	.60	.25
❑ 249	Jeff Bagwell CL	.40	.18
❑ 250	Jeff Bagwell CL	1.00	.45
	Ken Griffey Jr.		
	Frank Thomas		
	Mike Piazza CL		
❑ 251S	Hideo Nomo	1.00	.45

1995 Select Big Sticks

	MINT	NRMT
COMPLETE SET (12)	150.00	70.00
COMMON CARD (BS1-BS12)	6.00	2.70
STATED ODDS 1:48		

	MINT	NRMT
☐ BS1 Frank Thomas	12.00	5.50
☐ BS2 Ken Griffey Jr.	30.00	13.50
☐ BS3 Cal Ripken Jr.	25.00	11.00
☐ BS4 Mike Piazza	20.00	9.00
☐ BS5 Don Mattingly	12.00	5.50
☐ BS6 Will Clark	6.00	2.70
☐ BS7 Tony Gwynn	15.00	6.75
☐ BS8 Jeff Bagwell	8.00	3.60
☐ BS9 Barry Bonds	8.00	3.60
☐ BS10 Paul Molitor	6.00	2.70
☐ BS11 Matt Williams	6.00	2.70
☐ BS12 Albert Belle	6.00	2.70

1995 Select Can't Miss

	MINT	NRMT
COMPLETE SET (12)	50.00	22.00
COMMON CARD (CM1-CM12)	2.00	.90
SEMISTARS	3.00	1.35
UNLISTED STARS	5.00	2.20
STATED ODDS 1:24		
☐ CM1 Cliff Floyd	2.50	1.10
☐ CM2 Ryan Klesko	2.50	1.10
☐ CM3 Charles Johnson	2.50	1.10
☐ CM4 Raul Mondesi	3.00	1.35
☐ CM5 Manny Ramirez	8.00	3.60
☐ CM6 Billy Ashley	2.00	.90
☐ CM7 Alex Gonzalez	2.00	.90
☐ CM8 Carlos Delgado	5.00	2.20
☐ CM9 Garret Anderson	2.50	1.10
☐ CM10 Alex Rodriguez	20.00	9.00
☐ CM11 Chipper Jones	15.00	6.75
☐ CM12 Shawn Green	2.00	.90

1995 Select Sure Shots

	MINT	NRMT
COMPLETE SET (10)	50.00	22.00
COMMON CARD (SS1-SS10)	2.00	.90
MINOR STARS	3.00	1.35
STATED ODDS 1:90		
☐ SS1 Ben Grieve	12.00	5.50
☐ SS2 Kevin Witt	6.00	2.70
☐ SS3 Mark Farris	2.00	.90
☐ SS4 Paul Konerko	8.00	3.60
☐ SS5 Dustin Hermanson	2.00	.90
☐ SS6 Ramon Castro	3.00	1.35
☐ SS7 McKay Christensen	2.00	.90
☐ SS8 Brian Buchanan	2.00	.90

	MINT	NRMT
☐ SS9 Paul Wilson	2.00	.90
☐ SS10 Terrence Long	4.00	1.80

1996 Select

	MINT	NRMT
COMPLETE SET (200)	15.00	6.75
COMMON CARD (1-200)	.10	.05
MINOR STARS	.20	.09
UNLISTED STARS	.40	.18
SUBSET CARDS HALF VALUE OF BASE CARDS		
COMMON ART.PRF. (1-200)	3.00	1.35
*ART.PRF.STARS: 12.5X TO 30X HI COLUMN		
*ART.PRF.ROOKIES: 8X TO 20X HI		
AP STATED ODDS 1:35		
☐ 1 Wade Boggs	.40	.18
☐ 2 Shawn Green	.40	.18
☐ 3 Andres Galarraga	.40	.18
☐ 4 Bill Pulsipher	.10	.05
☐ 5 Chuck Knoblauch	.20	.09
☐ 6 Ken Griffey Jr.	2.00	.90
☐ 7 Greg Maddux	1.00	.45
☐ 8 Manny Ramirez	.50	.23
☐ 9 Ivan Rodriguez	.50	.23
☐ 10 Tim Salmon	.30	.14
☐ 11 Frank Thomas	.75	.35
☐ 12 Jeff Bagwell	.50	.23
☐ 13 Travis Fryman	.20	.09
☐ 14 Kenny Lofton	.30	.14
☐ 15 Matt Williams	.40	.18
☐ 16 Jay Bell	.20	.09
☐ 17 Ken Caminiti	.20	.09
☐ 18 Ray Lankford	.20	.09
☐ 19 Cal Ripken	1.50	.70
☐ 20 Roger Clemens	1.00	.45
☐ 21 Carlos Baerga	.10	.05
☐ 22 Mike Piazza	1.25	.55
☐ 23 Gregg Jefferies	.10	.05
☐ 24 Reggie Sanders	.20	.09
☐ 25 Rondell White	.20	.09
☐ 26 Sammy Sosa	1.25	.55
☐ 27 Kevin Appier	.20	.09
☐ 28 Kevin Seitzer	.10	.05
☐ 29 Gary Sheffield	.40	.18
☐ 30 Mike Mussina	.40	.18
☐ 31 Mark McGwire	2.00	.90
☐ 32 Barry Larkin	.40	.18
☐ 33 Marc Newfield	.10	.05
☐ 34 Ismael Valdes	.20	.09

☐ 35 Marty Cordova	.10	.05
☐ 36 Albert Belle	.40	.18
☐ 37 Johnny Damon	.30	.14
☐ 38 Garret Anderson	.20	.09
☐ 39 Cecil Fielder	.20	.09
☐ 40 John Mabry	.10	.05
☐ 41 Chipper Jones	1.00	.45
☐ 42 Omar Vizquel	.20	.09
☐ 43 Jose Rijo	.10	.05
☐ 44 Charles Johnson	.20	.09
☐ 45 Alex Rodriguez	1.25	.55
☐ 46 Rico Brogna	.10	.05
☐ 47 Joe Carter	.20	.09
☐ 48 Mo Vaughn	.40	.18
☐ 49 Moises Alou	.20	.09
☐ 50 Raul Mondesi	.20	.09
☐ 51 Robin Ventura	.20	.09
☐ 52 Jim Thome	.40	.18
☐ 53 David Justice	.40	.18
☐ 54 Jeff King	.10	.05
☐ 55 Brian L.Hunter	.20	.09
☐ 56 Juan Gonzalez	.75	.35
☐ 57 John Olerud	.20	.09
☐ 58 Rafael Palmeiro	.40	.18
☐ 59 Tony Gwynn	1.00	.45
☐ 60 Eddie Murray	.40	.18
☐ 61 Jason Isringhausen	.20	.09
☐ 62 Dante Bichette	.20	.09
☐ 63 Randy Johnson	.40	.18
☐ 64 Kirby Puckett	.60	.25
☐ 65 Jim Edmonds	.30	.14
☐ 66 David Cone	.20	.09
☐ 67 Ozzie Smith	.50	.23
☐ 68 Fred McGriff	.30	.14
☐ 69 Darren Daulton	.20	.09
☐ 70 Edgar Martinez	.20	.09
☐ 71 J.T. Snow	.20	.09
☐ 72 Butch Huskey	.10	.05
☐ 73 Hideo Nomo	.50	.23
☐ 74 Pedro Martinez	.50	.23
☐ 75 Bobby Bonilla	.20	.09
☐ 76 Jeff Conine	.10	.05
☐ 77 Ryan Klesko	.20	.09
☐ 78 Bernie Williams	.40	.18
☐ 79 Andre Dawson	.30	.14
☐ 80 Trevor Hoffman	.20	.09
☐ 81 Mark Grace	.30	.14
☐ 82 Benji Gil	.10	.05
☐ 83 Eric Karros	.20	.09
☐ 84 Pete Schourek	.10	.05
☐ 85 Edgardo Alfonzo	.40	.18
☐ 86 Jay Buhner	.20	.09
☐ 87 Vinny Castilla	.30	.14
☐ 88 Bret Boone	.20	.09
☐ 89 Ray Durham	.20	.09
☐ 90 Brian Jordan	.20	.09
☐ 91 Jose Canseco	.50	.23
☐ 92 Paul O'Neill	.20	.09
☐ 93 Chili Davis	.20	.09
☐ 94 Tom Glavine	.40	.18
☐ 95 Julian Tavarez	.10	.05
☐ 96 Derek Bell	.20	.09
☐ 97 Will Clark	.40	.18
☐ 98 Larry Walker	.40	.18
☐ 99 Denny Neagle	.20	.09
☐ 100 Alex Fernandez	.10	.05
☐ 101 Barry Bonds	.50	.23
☐ 102 Ben McDonald	.10	.05
☐ 103 Andy Pettitte	.30	.14
☐ 104 Tino Martinez	.20	.09
☐ 105 Sterling Hitchcock	.10	.05
☐ 106 Royce Clayton	.10	.05
☐ 107 Jim Abbott	.20	.09
☐ 108 Rickey Henderson	.50	.23
☐ 109 Ramon Martinez	.20	.09
☐ 110 Paul Molitor	.40	.18
☐ 111 Dennis Eckersley	.20	.09
☐ 112 Alex Gonzalez	.10	.05
☐ 113 Marquis Grissom	.10	.05
☐ 114 Greg Vaughn	.20	.09
☐ 115 Lance Johnson	.10	.05
☐ 116 Todd Stottlemyre	.10	.05
☐ 117 Jack McDowell	.10	.05
☐ 118 Ruben Sierra	.20	.09
☐ 119 Brady Anderson	.20	.09
☐ 120 Julio Franco	.10	.05

❑ 121 Brooks Kieschnick	.10	.05
❑ 122 Roberto Alomar	.40	.18
❑ 123 Greg Gagne	.10	.05
❑ 124 Wally Joyner	.20	.09
❑ 125 John Smoltz	.30	.14
❑ 126 John Valentin	.20	.09
❑ 127 Russ Davis	.10	.05
❑ 128 Joe Vitiello	.10	.05
❑ 129 Shawon Dunston	.10	.05
❑ 130 Frank Rodriguez	.10	.05
❑ 131 Charlie Hayes	.10	.05
❑ 132 Andy Benes	.20	.09
❑ 133 B.J. Surhoff	.20	.09
❑ 134 Dave Nilsson	.10	.05
❑ 135 Carlos Delgado	.40	.18
❑ 136 Walt Weiss	.10	.05
❑ 137 Mike Stanley	.10	.05
❑ 138 Greg Colbrunn	.10	.05
❑ 139 Mike Kelly	.10	.05
❑ 140 Ryne Sandberg	.50	.23
❑ 141 Lee Smith	.20	.09
❑ 142 Dennis Martinez	.20	.09
❑ 143 Bernard Gilkey	.10	.05
❑ 144 Lenny Dykstra	.20	.09
❑ 145 Danny Tartabull	.10	.05
❑ 146 Dean Palmer	.20	.09
❑ 147 Craig Biggio	.40	.18
❑ 148 Juan Acevedo	.10	.05
❑ 149 Michael Tucker	.10	.05
❑ 150 Bobby Higginson	.20	.09
❑ 151 Ken Griffey Jr. LUL	1.00	.45
❑ 152 Frank Thomas LUL	.40	.18
❑ 153 Cal Ripken LUL	.75	.35
❑ 154 Albert Belle LUL	.20	.09
❑ 155 Mike Piazza LUL	.60	.25
❑ 156 Barry Bonds LUL	.30	.14
❑ 157 Sammy Sosa LUL	.60	.25
❑ 158 Mo Vaughn LUL	.20	.09
❑ 159 Greg Maddux LUL	.50	.23
❑ 160 Jeff Bagwell LUL	.40	.18
❑ 161 Derek Jeter	1.25	.55
❑ 162 Paul Wilson	.10	.05
❑ 163 Chris Snopek	.10	.05
❑ 164 Jason Schmidt	.10	.05
❑ 165 Jimmy Haynes	.10	.05
❑ 166 George Arias	.10	.05
❑ 167 Steve Gibralter	.10	.05
❑ 168 Bob Wolcott	.10	.05
❑ 169 Jason Kendall	.40	.18
❑ 170 Greg Zaun	.10	.05
❑ 171 Quinton McCracken	.10	.05
❑ 172 Alan Benes	.10	.05
❑ 173 Rey Ordonez	.40	.18
❑ 174 Livan Hernandez	.60	.25
❑ 175 Osvaldo Fernandez	.10	.05
❑ 176 Marc Barcelo	.10	.05
❑ 177 Sal Fasano	.10	.05
❑ 178 Mike Grace	.10	.05
❑ 179 Chan Ho Park	.30	.14
❑ 180 Robert Perez	.10	.05
❑ 181 Todd Hollandsworth	.10	.05
❑ 182 Wilton Guerrero	.30	.14
❑ 183 John Wasdin	.10	.05
❑ 184 Jim Pittsley	.10	.05
❑ 185 LaTroy Hawkins	.10	.05
❑ 186 Jay Powell	.10	.05
❑ 187 Felipe Crespo	.10	.05
❑ 188 Jermaine Dye	.20	.09
❑ 189 Bob Abreu	.30	.14
❑ 190 Matt Luke	.10	.05
❑ 191 Richard Hidalgo	.20	.09
❑ 192 Karim Garcia	.20	.09
❑ 193 Marvin Benard	.10	.05
❑ 194 Andy Fox	.10	.05
❑ 195 Terrell Wade	.10	.05
❑ 196 Frank Thomas CL	.40	.18
❑ 197 Ken Griffey Jr. CL	1.00	.45
❑ 198 Greg Maddux CL	.50	.23
❑ 199 Mike Piazza CL	.60	.25
❑ 200 Cal Ripken CL	.75	.35

1996 Select Claim To Fame

	MINT	NRMT
COMPLETE SET (20)	250.00	110.00

COMMON CARD (1-20)	3.00	1.35
SEMISTARS	5.00	2.20
UNLISTED STARS	8.00	3.60
STATED ODDS 1:72		
❑ 1 Cal Ripken	30.00	13.50
❑ 2 Greg Maddux	20.00	9.00
❑ 3 Ken Griffey Jr.	40.00	18.00
❑ 4 Frank Thomas	15.00	6.75
❑ 5 Mo Vaughn	8.00	3.60
❑ 6 Albert Belle	8.00	3.60
❑ 7 Jeff Bagwell	10.00	4.50
❑ 8 Sammy Sosa	25.00	11.00
❑ 9 Reggie Sanders	4.00	1.80
❑ 10 Hideo Nomo	8.00	3.60
❑ 11 Chipper Jones	20.00	9.00
❑ 12 Mike Piazza	25.00	11.00
❑ 13 Matt Williams	8.00	3.60
❑ 14 Tony Gwynn	20.00	9.00
❑ 15 Johnny Damon	5.00	2.20
❑ 16 Dante Bichette	4.00	1.80
❑ 17 Kirby Puckett	12.00	5.50
❑ 18 Barry Bonds	10.00	4.50
❑ 19 Randy Johnson	8.00	3.60
❑ 20 Eddie Murray	8.00	3.60

1996 Select En Fuego

	MINT	NRMT
COMPLETE SET (25)	250.00	110.00
COMMON CARD (1-25)	3.00	1.35
STATED ODDS 1:48		
❑ 1 Ken Griffey Jr.	30.00	13.50
❑ 2 Frank Thomas	12.00	5.50
❑ 3 Cal Ripken	25.00	11.00
❑ 4 Greg Maddux	15.00	6.75
❑ 5 Jeff Bagwell	8.00	3.60
❑ 6 Barry Bonds	8.00	3.60
❑ 7 Mo Vaughn	6.00	2.70
❑ 8 Albert Belle	6.00	2.70
❑ 9 Sammy Sosa	20.00	9.00
❑ 10 Reggie Sanders	3.00	1.35
❑ 11 Mike Piazza	20.00	9.00
❑ 12 Chipper Jones	15.00	6.75
❑ 13 Tony Gwynn	6.00	2.70
❑ 14 Kirby Puckett	10.00	4.50
❑ 15 Wade Boggs	6.00	2.70
❑ 16 Dan Patrick ANN	6.00	2.70
❑ 17 Gary Sheffield	3.00	1.35
❑ 18 Dante Bichette	3.00	1.35

❑ 19 Randy Johnson	6.00	2.70
❑ 20 Matt Williams	6.00	2.70
❑ 21 Alex Rodriguez	20.00	9.00
❑ 22 Tim Salmon	4.00	1.80
❑ 23 Johnny Damon	4.00	1.80
❑ 24 Manny Ramirez	8.00	3.60
❑ 25 Hideo Nomo	6.00	2.70

1996 Select Team Nucleus

	MINT	NRMT
COMPLETE SET (28)	80.00	36.00
COMMON CARD (1-28)	2.00	.90
UNLISTED STARS	3.00	1.35
STATED ODDS 1:18		
❑ 1 Albert Belle Manny Ramirez Carlos Baerga	4.00	1.80
❑ 2 Ray Lankford Brian Jordan Ozzie Smith	3.00	1.35
❑ 3 Jay Bell Jeff King Denny Neagle	2.00	.90
❑ 4 Dante Bichette Andres Galarraga Larry Walker	3.00	1.35
❑ 5 Mark McGwire Mike Bordick Terry Steinbach	15.00	6.75
❑ 6 Bernie Williams Wade Boggs David Cone	3.00	1.35
❑ 7 Joe Carter Alex Gonzalez Shawn Green	2.00	.90
❑ 8 Roger Clemens Mo Vaughn Jose Canseco	8.00	3.60
❑ 9 Ken Griffey Jr. Edgar Martinez Randy Johnson	15.00	6.75
❑ 10 Gregg Jefferies Darren Daulton Len Dykstra	2.00	.90
❑ 11 Mike Piazza Raul Mondesi Hideo Nomo	10.00	4.50
❑ 12 Greg Maddux Chipper Jones Ryan Klesko	10.00	4.50
❑ 13 Cecil Fielder Travis Fryman Phil Nevin	2.00	.90
❑ 14 Ivan Rodriguez Will Clark Juan Gonzalez	6.00	2.70
❑ 15 Ryne Sandberg Sammy Sosa Mark Grace	10.00	4.50
❑ 16 Gary Sheffield Charles Johnson Andre Dawson	3.00	1.35
❑ 17 Johnny Damon Michael Tucker Kevin Appier	2.00	.90

□ 18 Barry Bonds .... 3.00 ... 1.35
  Matt Williams
  Rod Beck
□ 19 Kirby Puckett .... 6.00 ... 2.70
  Chuck Knoblauch
  Marty Cordova
□ 20 Cal Ripken .... 12.00 ... 5.50
  Barry Bonilla
  Mike Mussina
□ 21 Jason Isringhausen .... 2.00 ... .90
  Bill Pulsipher
  Rico Brogna
□ 22 Tony Gwynn .... 8.00 ... 3.60
  Ken Caminiti
  Mark Newfield
□ 23 Tim Salmon .... 3.00 ... 1.35
  Garret Anderson
  Jim Edmonds
□ 24 Moises Alou .... 2.00 ... .90
  Rondell White
  Cliff Floyd
□ 25 Barry Larkin .... 2.50 ... 1.10
  Reggie Sanders
  Bret Boone
□ 26 Jeff Bagwell .... 4.00 ... 1.80
  Craig Biggio
  Derek Bell
□ 27 Frank Thomas .... 6.00 ... 2.70
  Robin Ventura
  Alex Fernandez
□ 28 John Jaha .... 2.00 ... .90
  Greg Vaughn
  Kevin Seitzer

1997 Select

	MINT	NRMT
COMPLETE SET (200)	80.00	36.00
COMPLETE SERIES 1 (150)	50.00	22.00
COMMON RED (1-150)	.15	.07
RED MINOR STARS	.30	.14
RED UNLISTED STAR	.60	.25
COMMON BLUE (1-150)	.30	.14
BLUE MINOR STARS	.60	.25
BLUE UNLISTED STAR	1.25	.55
COMPLETE HI SERIES (50) ..	30.00	13.50
COMMON HI SERIES (151-200)	.30	.14
HI SERIES MINOR STARS	.60	.25
HI SERIES UNLISTED STARS	1.25	.55

SUBSET CARDS HALF VALUE OF BASE CARDS
ALL HI SERIES FRONTS ERRONEOUSLY HAVE "SELECT COMPANY" TEXT ON THEM

COMMON AP RED (1-150)	4.00	1.80
COMMON AP BLUE (1-150) ..	10.00	4.50

*AP STARS: 12.5X TO 30X HI COLUMN
*AP YOUNG STARS: 10X TO 25X HI
AP STATED ODDS 1:71 RED, 1:355 BLUE

COMMON COMPANY (1-200) ..	.50	.23

*CMPY.RED STARS: 1.25X TO 3X HI COLUMN
*CMPY.BLUE STARS: .6X TO 1.5X HI
*CMPY.HI SERIES STARS: .6X TO 1.5X HI
ONE COMPANY PER HI SERIES PACK
COMPANY FRONTS HAVE COARSE FINISH

COMMON RG RED (1-150)	1.00	.45
COMMON RG BLUE (1-150)	.60	.90

*REG.GOLD: 2.5X TO 6X HI COLUMN
*REG.GOLD YNG.STARS: 2X TO 5X HI

REG.GOLD ODDS 1:11 RED, 1:47 BLUE

#	Player	MINT	NRMT
□ 1	Juan Gonzalez B	2.50	1.10
□ 2	Mo Vaughn B	1.25	.55
□ 3	Tony Gwynn R	1.50	.70
□ 4	Manny Ramirez B	1.50	.70
□ 5	Jose Canseco R	.75	.35
□ 6	David Cone R	.40	.18
□ 7	Chan Ho Park R	.60	.25
□ 8	Frank Thomas B	2.50	1.10
□ 9	Todd Hollandsworth R	.15	.07
□ 10	Marty Cordova R	.15	.07
□ 11	Gary Sheffield B	.60	.25
□ 12	John Smoltz R	.75	.35
□ 13	Mark Grudzielanek R	.30	.14
□ 14	Sammy Sosa B	4.00	1.80
□ 15	Paul Molitor R	.60	.25
□ 16	Kevin Brown R	.40	.18
□ 17	Eric Young R	.30	.14
□ 18	John Wetteland R	.30	.14
□ 19	Ryan Klesko B	.60	.25
□ 20	Joe Carter R	.30	.14
□ 21	Alex Ochoa R	.15	.07
□ 22	Alex Ochoa R	.15	.07
□ 23	Greg Maddux B	3.00	1.35
□ 24	Roger Clemens B	3.00	1.35
□ 25	Ivan Rodriguez B	1.50	.70
□ 26	Barry Bonds B	1.50	.70
□ 27	Kenny Lofton B	.75	.35
□ 28	Javy Lopez R	.30	.14
□ 29	Hideo Nomo B	1.25	.55
□ 30	Rusty Greer R	.30	.14
□ 31	Rafael Palmeiro R	.60	.25
□ 32	Mike Piazza B	4.00	1.80
□ 33	Ryne Sandberg R	.75	.35
□ 34	Wade Boggs R	.60	.25
□ 35	Jim Thome B	1.25	.55
□ 36	Ken Caminiti R	.75	.35
□ 37	Mark Grace R	.40	.18
□ 38	Brian Jordan R	.30	.14
□ 39	Craig Biggio R	.60	.25
□ 40	Henry Rodriguez R	.30	.14
□ 41	Dean Palmer R	.30	.14
□ 42	Jason Kendall R	.40	.18
□ 43	Bill Pulsipher R	.15	.07
□ 44	Tim Salmon B	1.25	.55
□ 45	Marc Newfield R	.15	.07
□ 46	Pat Hentgen R	.30	.14
□ 47	Ken Griffey Jr. B	6.00	2.70
□ 48	Paul Wilson R	.15	.07
□ 49	Jay Buhner R	.60	.25
□ 50	Rickey Henderson R	.75	.35
□ 51	Jeff Bagwell B	1.50	.70
□ 52	Cecil Fielder R	.30	.14
□ 53	Alex Rodriguez B	4.00	1.80
□ 54	John Jaha R	.15	.07
□ 55	Brady Anderson R	.60	.25
□ 56	Andres Galarraga R	.60	.25
□ 57	Raul Mondesi R	.30	.14
□ 58	Andy Pettitte R	.40	.18
□ 59	Roberto Alomar B	1.25	.55
□ 60	Derek Jeter B	4.00	1.80
□ 61	Charles Johnson R	.30	.14
□ 62	Travis Fryman R	.30	.14
□ 63	Chipper Jones B	3.00	1.35
□ 64	Edgar Martinez R	.30	.14
□ 65	Bobby Bonilla R	.30	.14
□ 66	Greg Vaughn R	.30	.14
□ 67	Bobby Higginson R	.30	.14
□ 68	Garret Anderson R	.30	.14
□ 69	Chuck Knoblauch B	1.25	.55
□ 70	Jermaine Dye R	.15	.07
□ 71	Cal Ripken B	5.00	2.20
□ 72	Jason Giambi R	.30	.14
□ 73	Trey Beamon R	.15	.07
□ 74	Shawn Green R	.60	.25
□ 75	Mark McGwire B	6.00	2.70
□ 76	Carlos Delgado R	.30	.14
□ 77	Jason Isringhausen R	.15	.07
□ 78	Randy Johnson B	1.25	.55
□ 79	Troy Percival R	.30	.14
□ 80	Ron Gant R	.15	.07
□ 81	Ellis Burks R	.30	.14
□ 82	Mike Mussina B	1.25	.55
□ 83	Todd Hundley R	.30	.14
□ 84	Jim Edmonds R	.40	.18
□ 85	Charles Nagy R	.30	.14
□ 86	Dante Bichette B	.60	.25
□ 87	Mariano Rivera R	.30	.14
□ 88	Matt Williams B	1.25	.55
□ 89	Rondell White R	.30	.14
□ 90	Steve Finley R	.30	.14
□ 91	Alex Fernandez R	.15	.07
□ 92	Barry Larkin R	.30	.14
□ 93	Tom Goodwin R	.15	.07
□ 94	Will Clark R	.60	.25
□ 95	Michael Tucker R	.15	.07
□ 96	Derek Bell R	.30	.14
□ 97	Larry Walker R	.60	.25
□ 98	Alan Benes R	.15	.07
□ 99	Tom Glavine R	.60	.25
□ 100	Darin Erstad B	.60	.25
□ 101	Andruw Jones B	1.50	.70
□ 102	Scott Rolen R	1.00	.45
□ 103	Todd Walker B	1.25	.55
□ 104	Dmitri Young R	.30	.14
□ 105	Vladimir Guerrero B	2.00	.90
□ 106	Nomar Garciaparra R	2.00	.90
□ 107	Danny Patterson R	.15	.07
□ 108	Karim Garcia R	.30	.14
□ 109	Todd Greene R	.15	.07
□ 110	Ruben Rivera R	.15	.07
□ 111	Raul Casanova R	.15	.07
□ 112	Mike Cameron R	.30	.14
□ 113	Bartolo Colon R	.30	.14
□ 114	Rod Myers R	.15	.07
□ 115	Todd Dunn R	.15	.07
□ 116	Torii Hunter R	.15	.07
□ 117	Jason Dickson R	.15	.07
□ 118	Eugene Kingsale R	.30	.14
□ 119	Rafael Medina R	.15	.07
□ 120	Raul Ibanez R	.15	.07
□ 121	Bobby Henley R	.15	.07
□ 122	Scott Spiezio R	.15	.07
□ 123	Bobby Smith R	.15	.07
□ 124	J.J. Johnson R	.15	.07
□ 125	Bubba Trammell R	.60	.25
□ 126	Jeff Abbott R	.15	.07
□ 127	Neifi Perez R	.30	.14
□ 128	Derek Lee R	.40	.18
□ 129	Kevin Brown C R	.15	.07
□ 130	Mendy Lopez R	.15	.07
□ 131	Kevin Orie R	.15	.07
□ 132	Ryan Jones R	.15	.07
□ 133	Juan Encarnacion R	.30	.14
□ 134	Jose Guillen B	.40	.18
□ 135	Greg Norton R	.15	.07
□ 136	Richie Sexson R	.60	.25
□ 137	Jay Payton R	.15	.07
□ 138	Bob Abreu R	.30	.14
□ 139	Ron Belliard R	.30	.14
□ 140	Wilton Guerrero B	.30	.14
□ 141	Alex Rodriguez SS B	2.00	.90
□ 142	Juan Gonzalez SS B	.60	.25
□ 143	Ken Caminiti SS B	.30	.14
□ 144	Frank Thomas SS B	1.25	.55
□ 145	Ken Griffey Jr. SS B	3.00	1.35
□ 146	John Smoltz SS B	2.00	.90
□ 147	Mike Piazza SS B	2.00	.90
□ 148	Derek Jeter SS B	2.00	.90
□ 149	Frank Thomas CL R	.60	.25
□ 150	Ken Griffey Jr. CL R	1.50	.70
□ 151	Jose Cruz Jr.	4.00	1.80
□ 152	Moises Alou	.60	.25
□ 153	Hideki Irabu	2.50	1.10
□ 154	Glendon Rusch	.30	.14
□ 155	Ron Coomer	.30	.14
□ 156	Jeremi Gonzalez	.75	.35
□ 157	Fernando Tatis	8.00	3.60
□ 158	John Olerud	.60	.25
□ 159	Rickey Henderson	1.50	.70
□ 160	Shannon Stewart	.30	.14
□ 161	Kevin Polcovich	.30	.14
□ 162	Jose Rosado	.30	.14
□ 163	Ray Lankford	.60	.25
□ 164	David Justice	1.25	.55
□ 165	Mark Kotsay	2.00	.90
□ 166	Delvi Cruz	1.25	.55
□ 167	Billy Wagner	.60	.25
□ 168	Jacob Cruz	.30	.14
□ 169	Matt Morris	.60	.25
□ 170	Brian Banks	.30	.14

		MINT	NRMT
❏ 171	Brett Tomko	.60	.25
❏ 172	Todd Helton	2.50	1.10
❏ 173	Eric Young	.60	.25
❏ 174	Bernie Williams	1.25	.55
❏ 175	Jeff Fassero	.30	.14
❏ 176	Ryan McGuire	.30	.14
❏ 177	Darryl Kile	.30	.14
❏ 178	Kelvim Escobar	1.50	.70
❏ 179	Dave Nilsson	.30	.14
❏ 180	Geronimo Berroa	.30	.14
❏ 181	Livan Hernandez	.60	.25
❏ 182	Tony Womack	1.25	.55
❏ 183	Deion Sanders	.60	.25
❏ 184	Jeff Kent	.60	.25
❏ 185	Brian Hunter	.60	.25
❏ 186	Jose Malave	.30	.14
❏ 187	Steve Woodard	1.50	.70
❏ 188	Brad Radke	.60	.25
❏ 189	Todd Dunwoody	.60	.25
❏ 190	Joey Hamilton	.60	.25
❏ 191	Denny Neagle	.60	.25
❏ 192	Bobby Jones	.30	.14
❏ 193	Tony Clark	.75	.35
❏ 194	Jaret Wright	4.00	1.80
❏ 195	Matt Stairs	.60	.25
❏ 196	Francisco Cordova	.30	.14
❏ 197	Justin Thompson	.60	.25
❏ 198	Pokey Reese	.60	.25
❏ 199	Garrett Stephenson	.30	.14
❏ 200	Carl Everett	.60	.25

1997 Select Rookie Autographs

		MINT	NRMT
COMPLETE SET (4)		50.00	22.00
COMMON CARD		8.00	3.60
3000 OF EACH EXCEPT A.JONES (2500)			
❏ 1	Jose Guillen	10.00	4.50
❏ 2	Wilton Guerrero	8.00	3.60
❏ 3	Andruw Jones	30.00	13.50
❏ 4	Todd Walker	10.00	4.50

1997 Select Rookie Revolution

	MINT	NRMT
COMPLETE SET (20)	100.00	45.00
COMMON CARD (1-20)	2.00	.90

MINOR STARS		4.00	1.80
SEMISTARS		6.00	2.70
STATED ODDS 1:56			
❏ 1	Andruw Jones	12.00	5.50
❏ 2	Derek Jeter	30.00	13.50
❏ 3	Todd Hollandsworth	2.00	.90
❏ 4	Edgar Renteria	4.00	1.80
❏ 5	Jason Kendall	6.00	2.70
❏ 6	Rey Ordonez	4.00	1.80
❏ 7	F.P. Santangelo	2.00	.90
❏ 8	Jermaine Dye	4.00	1.80
❏ 9	Alex Ochoa	2.00	.90
❏ 10	Vladimir Guerrero	15.00	6.75
❏ 11	Dmitri Young	4.00	1.80
❏ 12	Todd Walker	15.00	6.75
❏ 13	Scott Rolen	15.00	6.75
❏ 14	Nomar Garciaparra	25.00	11.00
❏ 15	Ruben Rivera	2.00	.90
❏ 16	Darin Erstad	15.00	6.75
❏ 17	Todd Greene	2.00	.90
❏ 18	Mariano Rivera	4.00	1.80
❏ 19	Trey Beamon	2.00	.90
❏ 20	Karim Garcia	4.00	1.80

1997 Select Tools of the Trade

		MINT	NRMT
COMPLETE SET (25)		120.00	55.00
COMMON CARD (1-25)		1.25	.55
UNLISTED STARS		2.50	1.10
STATED ODDS 1:9			
COMP.MIRROR BLUE (25)		800.00	350.00
*MIRROR BLUE: 2.5X TO 6X HI COLUMN			
MIRROR BLUE STATED ODDS 1:240			
❏ 1	Ken Griffey Jr.	15.00	6.75
	Andruw Jones		
❏ 2	Greg Maddux	6.00	2.70
	Andy Pettitte		
❏ 3	Cal Ripken	12.00	5.50
	Chipper Jones		
❏ 4	Mike Piazza	8.00	3.60
	Jason Kendall		
❏ 5	Albert Belle	2.50	1.10
	Karim Garcia		
❏ 6	Mo Vaughn	2.50	1.10
	Dmitri Young		
❏ 7	Juan Gonzalez	6.00	2.70
	Vladimir Guerrero		
❏ 8	Tony Gwynn	6.00	2.70
	Jermaine Dye		
❏ 9	Barry Bonds	3.00	1.35
	Alex Ochoa		
❏ 10	Jeff Bagwell	3.00	1.35
	Jason Giambi		
❏ 11	Kenny Lofton	2.50	1.10
	Darin Erstad		
❏ 12	Gary Sheffield	3.00	1.35
	Manny Ramirez		
❏ 13	Tim Salmon	2.50	1.10
	Todd Hollandsworth		
❏ 14	Sammy Sosa	8.00	3.60
	Ruben Rivera		
❏ 15	Paul Molitor	2.50	1.10
	George Arias		
❏ 16	Jim Thome	2.50	1.10
	Todd Walker		
❏ 17	Wade Boggs	4.00	1.80
	Scott Rolen		
❏ 18	Ryne Sandberg	3.00	1.35
	Chuck Knoblauch		
❏ 19	Mark McGwire	12.00	5.50
	Frank Thomas		
❏ 20	Ivan Rodriguez	3.00	1.35
	Charles Johnson		
❏ 21	Brian Jordan	1.25	.55
	Rusty Greer		
❏ 22	Roger Clemens	6.00	2.70
	Troy Percival		
❏ 23	John Smoltz	2.50	1.10
	Mike Mussina		
❏ 24	Alex Rodriguez	8.00	3.60
	Rey Ordonez		
❏ 25	Derek Jeter	10.00	4.50
	Nomar Garciaparra		

1995 Select Certified

	MINT	NRMT
COMPLETE SET (135)	40.00	18.00
COMMON CARD (1-135)	.25	.11
MINOR STARS	.50	.23
UNLISTED STARS	1.00	.45
SET INCLUDES CARD 2131		
CARD NUMBER 18 DOES NOT EXIST		
COMP. CHECKLIST SET (7)	4.00	1.80
CL: RANDOM INSERTS IN PACKS		
❏ 1	Barry Bonds	1.25	.55
❏ 2	Reggie Sanders	.50	.23
❏ 3	Terry Steinbach	.25	.11
❏ 4	Eduardo Perez	.25	.11
❏ 5	Frank Thomas	2.00	.90
❏ 6	Wil Cordero	.25	.11
❏ 7	John Olerud	.50	.23
❏ 8	Deion Sanders	.50	.23
❏ 9	Mike Mussina	1.00	.45
❏ 10	Mo Vaughn	1.00	.45
❏ 11	Will Clark	1.00	.45
❏ 12	Chili Davis	.50	.23
❏ 13	Jimmy Key	.50	.23
❏ 14	Eddie Murray	1.00	.45
❏ 15	Bernard Gilkey	.25	.11
❏ 16	David Cone	.75	.35
❏ 17	Tim Salmon	1.00	.45
❏ 19	Steve Ontiveros	.25	.11
❏ 20	Andres Galarraga	1.00	.45
❏ 21	Don Mattingly	2.00	.90
❏ 22	Kevin Appier	.50	.23
❏ 23	Paul Molitor	1.00	.45
❏ 24	Edgar Martinez	.50	.23
❏ 25	Andy Benes	.50	.23
❏ 26	Rafael Palmeiro	1.00	.45
❏ 27	Barry Larkin	1.00	.45
❏ 28	Gary Sheffield	.50	.23
❏ 29	Wally Joyner	.50	.23
❏ 30	Wade Boggs	1.00	.45
❏ 31	Rico Brogna	.25	.11
❏ 32	Eddie Murray 3000th Hit	.50	.23
❏ 33	Kirby Puckett	1.50	.70
❏ 34	Bobby Bonilla	.50	.23
❏ 35	Hal Morris	.25	.11
❏ 36	Moises Alou	.50	.23
❏ 37	Javier Lopez	.50	.23

☐ 38 Chuck Knoblauch	1.00	.45
☐ 39 Mike Piazza	3.00	1.35
☐ 40 Travis Fryman	.50	.23
☐ 41 Rickey Henderson	1.25	.55
☐ 42 Jim Thome	1.00	.45
☐ 43 Carlos Baerga	.25	.11
☐ 44 Dean Palmer	.50	.23
☐ 45 Kirk Gibson	.50	.23
☐ 46 Bret Saberhagen	.50	.23
☐ 47 Cecil Fielder	.50	.23
☐ 48 Manny Ramirez	1.25	.55
☐ 49 Derek Bell	.50	.23
☐ 50 Mark McGwire	5.00	2.20
☐ 51 Jim Edmonds	.75	.35
☐ 52 Robin Ventura	.50	.23
☐ 53 Ryan Klesko	.50	.23
☐ 54 Jeff Bagwell	1.25	.55
☐ 55 Ozzie Smith	1.25	.55
☐ 56 Albert Belle	1.00	.45
☐ 57 Darren Daulton	.50	.23
☐ 58 Jeff Conine	.25	.11
☐ 59 Greg Maddux	2.50	1.10
☐ 60 Lenny Dykstra	.50	.23
☐ 61 Randy Johnson	1.00	.45
☐ 62 Fred McGriff	.75	.35
☐ 63 Ray Lankford	.50	.23
☐ 64 David Justice	1.00	.45
☐ 65 Paul O'Neill	.50	.23
☐ 66 Tony Gwynn	2.50	1.10
☐ 67 Matt Williams	1.00	.45
☐ 68 Dante Bichette	.50	.23
☐ 69 Craig Biggio	1.00	.45
☐ 70 Ken Griffey Jr.	5.00	2.20
☐ 71 J.T. Snow	.50	.23
☐ 72 Cal Ripken	4.00	1.80
☐ 73 Jay Bell	.50	.23
☐ 74 Joe Carter	.50	.23
☐ 75 Roberto Alomar	1.00	.45
☐ 76 Benji Gil	.25	.11
☐ 77 Ivan Rodriguez	1.25	.55
☐ 78 Raul Mondesi	.75	.35
☐ 79 Cliff Floyd	.50	.23
☐ 80 Eric Karros	1.00	.45
Mike Piazza		
Raul Mondesi		
☐ 81 Royce Clayton	.25	.11
☐ 82 Billy Ashley	.25	.11
☐ 83 Joey Hamilton	.50	.23
☐ 84 Sammy Sosa	3.00	1.35
☐ 85 Jason Bere	.25	.11
☐ 86 Dennis Martinez	.50	.23
☐ 87 Greg Vaughn	.50	.23
☐ 88 Roger Clemens	2.50	1.10
☐ 89 Larry Walker	1.00	.45
☐ 90 Mark Grace	.75	.35
☐ 91 Kenny Lofton	.75	.35
☐ 92 Carlos Perez	.50	.23
☐ 93 Roger Cedeno	.25	.11
☐ 94 Scott Ruffcorn	.25	.11
☐ 95 Jim Pittsley	.25	.11
☐ 96 Andy Pettitte	1.00	.45
☐ 97 James Baldwin	.50	.23
☐ 98 Hideo Nomo	2.50	1.10
☐ 99 Ismael Valdes	.50	.23
☐ 100 Armando Benitez	.25	.11
☐ 101 Jose Malave	.25	.11
☐ 102 Bob Higginson	1.50	.70
☐ 103 LaTroy Hawkins	.25	.11
☐ 104 Russ Davis	.25	.11
☐ 105 Shawn Green	1.00	.45
☐ 106 Jose Vitiello	.25	.11
☐ 107 Chipper Jones	2.50	1.10
☐ 108 Shane Andrews	.25	.11
☐ 109 Jose Oliva	.25	.11
☐ 110 Ray Durham	.50	.23
☐ 111 Jon Nunnally	.25	.11
☐ 112 Alex Gonzalez	.25	.11
☐ 113 Vaughn Eshelman	.25	.11
☐ 114 Marty Cordova	.25	.11
☐ 115 Mark Grudzielanek	.75	.35
☐ 116 Brian L.Hunter	.50	.23
☐ 117 Charles Johnson	.50	.23
☐ 118 Alex Rodriguez	4.00	1.80
☐ 119 David Bell	.25	.11
☐ 120 Todd Hollandsworth	.25	.11
☐ 121 Joe Randa	.25	.11

☐ 122 Derek Jeter	3.00	1.35
☐ 123 Frank Rodriguez	.25	.11
☐ 124 Curtis Goodwin	.25	.11
☐ 125 Bill Pulsipher	.25	.11
☐ 126 John Mabry	.25	.11
☐ 127 Julian Tavarez	.25	.11
☐ 128 Edgardo Alfonzo	1.00	.45
☐ 129 Orlando Miller	.25	.11
☐ 130 Juan Acevedo	.25	.11
☐ 131 Jeff Cirillo	.50	.23
☐ 132 Roberto Petagine	.25	.11
☐ 133 Antonio Osuna	.25	.11
☐ 134 Michael Tucker	.50	.23
☐ 135 Garret Anderson	.50	.23
☐ 2131 Cal Ripken TRIB	4.00	1.80

1995 Select Certified Mirror Gold

	MINT	NRMT
COMPLETE SET (135)	1000.00	450.00
COMMON CARD (1-135)	3.00	1.35
*STARS: 5X TO 12X BASIC CARDS		
*ROOKIES: 3X TO 8X BASIC CARDS		
STATED ODDS 1:5		

1995 Select Certified Future

Ray Durham

	MINT	NRMT
COMPLETE SET (10)	60.00	27.00
COMMON CARD (1-10)	2.00	.90
UNLISTED STARS	5.00	2.20
STATED ODDS 1:19		

☐ 1 Chipper Jones	15.00	6.75
☐ 2 Curtis Goodwin	2.00	.90
☐ 3 Hideo Nomo	8.00	3.60
☐ 4 Shawn Green	5.00	2.20
☐ 5 Ray Durham	3.00	1.35
☐ 6 Todd Hollandsworth	2.00	.90
☐ 7 Brian L.Hunter	3.00	1.35
☐ 8 Carlos Delgado	5.00	2.20
☐ 9 Michael Tucker UER	3.00	1.35
(Front photo is Jon Nunnally)		
☐ 10 Alex Rodriguez	20.00	9.00

1995 Select Certified Gold Team

	MINT	NRMT
COMPLETE SET (12)	300.00	135.00
COMMON CARD (1-12)	8.00	3.60
STATED ODDS 1:41		

☐ 1 Ken Griffey Jr.	60.00	27.00
☐ 2 Frank Thomas	25.00	11.00
☐ 3 Cal Ripken	50.00	22.00
☐ 4 Jeff Bagwell	15.00	6.75
☐ 5 Mike Piazza	40.00	18.00
☐ 6 Barry Bonds	15.00	6.75
☐ 7 Matt Williams	8.00	3.60
☐ 8 Don Mattingly	25.00	11.00
☐ 9 Will Clark	8.00	3.60
☐ 10 Tony Gwynn	30.00	13.50
☐ 11 Kirby Puckett	20.00	9.00
☐ 12 Jose Canseco	15.00	6.75

1995 Select Certified Potential Unlimited 1975

ALEX GONZALEZ

	MINT	NRMT
COMPLETE SET (20)	250.00	110.00
COMMON CARD (1-20)	5.00	2.20
SEMISTARS	10.00	4.50
STATED ODDS 1:32		
STATED PRINT RUN 1975 SETS		
COMP.903 SET (20)	300.00	135.00
*903 CARDS: .5X TO 1.2X HI COLUMN		
ONE 903 CARD PER SEALED BOX		
STATED PRINT RUN 903 SETS		

☐ 1 Cliff Floyd	8.00	3.60
☐ 2 Manny Ramirez	20.00	9.00
☐ 3 Raul Mondesi	10.00	4.50
☐ 4 Scott Ruffcorn	5.00	2.20
☐ 5 Billy Ashley	5.00	2.20
☐ 6 Alex Gonzalez	5.00	2.20
☐ 7 Midre Cummings	5.00	2.20
☐ 8 Charles Johnson	8.00	3.60
☐ 9 Garret Anderson	8.00	3.60
☐ 10 Hideo Nomo	25.00	11.00
☐ 11 Chipper Jones	50.00	22.00
☐ 12 Curtis Goodwin	5.00	2.20
☐ 13 Frank Rodriguez	5.00	2.20

		MINT	NRMT
❏ 14	Shawn Green	12.00	5.50
❏ 15	Ray Durham	8.00	3.60
❏ 16	Todd Hollandsworth	5.00	2.20
❏ 17	Brian L. Hunter	8.00	3.60
❏ 18	Carlos Delgado	12.00	5.50
❏ 19	Michael Tucker	8.00	3.60
❏ 20	Alex Rodriguez	60.00	27.00

1996 Select Certified

	MINT	NRMT
COMPLETE SET (144)	40.00	18.00
COMMON CARD (1-144)	.25	.11
MINOR STARS	.50	.23
UNLISTED STARS	1.00	.45
COMMON ART.PRF. (1-144)	3.00	1.35

*AP STARS: 6X TO 15X HI COLUMN
*AP ROOKIES: 2.5X TO 6X HI
AP STATED ODDS 1:18

	MINT	NRMT
COMMON BLUE (1-144)	6.00	2.70

*BLUE STARS: 15X TO 40X HI COLUMN
*BLUE ROOKIES: 6X TO 15X HI
BLUE STATED ODDS 1:50

	MINT	NRMT
COMMON RED (1-144)	1.00	.45

*RED STARS: 2.5X TO 6X HI COLUMN
*RED ROOKIES: 1X TO 2.5X HI
RED STATED ODDS 1:5

❏ 1	Frank Thomas	2.00	.90
❏ 2	Tino Martinez	.50	.23
❏ 3	Gary Sheffield	.50	.23
❏ 4	Kenny Lofton	.75	.35
❏ 5	Joe Carter	.50	.23
❏ 6	Alex Rodriguez	3.00	1.35
❏ 7	Chipper Jones	2.50	1.10
❏ 8	Roger Clemens	2.50	1.10
❏ 9	Jay Bell	.50	.23
❏ 10	Eddie Murray	1.00	.45
❏ 11	Will Clark	1.00	.45
❏ 12	Mike Mussina	1.00	.45
❏ 13	Hideo Nomo	1.00	.45
❏ 14	Andres Galarraga	1.00	.45
❏ 15	Marc Newfield	.25	.11
❏ 16	Jason Isringhausen	.50	.23
❏ 17	Randy Johnson	1.00	.45
❏ 18	Chuck Knoblauch	1.00	.45
❏ 19	J.T. Snow	.50	.23
❏ 20	Mark McGwire	5.00	2.20
❏ 21	Tony Gwynn	2.50	1.10
❏ 22	Albert Belle	1.00	.45
❏ 23	Gregg Jefferies	.25	.11
❏ 24	Reggie Sanders	.50	.23
❏ 25	Bernie Williams	1.00	.45
❏ 26	Ray Lankford	.50	.23
❏ 27	Johnny Damon	.75	.35
❏ 28	Ryne Sandberg	1.25	.55
❏ 29	Rondell White	.50	.23
❏ 30	Mike Piazza	3.00	1.35
❏ 31	Barry Bonds	1.25	.55
❏ 32	Greg Maddux	2.50	1.10
❏ 33	Craig Biggio	1.00	.45
❏ 34	John Valentin	.50	.23
❏ 35	Ivan Rodriguez	1.25	.55
❏ 36	Rico Brogna	.25	.11
❏ 37	Tim Salmon	.75	.35
❏ 38	Sterling Hitchcock	.25	.11
❏ 39	Charles Johnson	.50	.23
❏ 40	Travis Fryman	.50	.23
❏ 41	Barry Larkin	1.00	.45
❏ 42	Tom Glavine	1.00	.45
❏ 43	Marty Cordova	.25	.11
❏ 44	Shawn Green	1.00	.45
❏ 45	Ben McDonald	.25	.11
❏ 46	Robin Ventura	.50	.23
❏ 47	Ken Griffey Jr.	5.00	2.20
❏ 48	Orlando Merced	.25	.11
❏ 49	Paul O'Neill	.50	.23
❏ 50	Ozzie Smith	1.25	.55
❏ 51	Manny Ramirez	1.25	.55
❏ 52	Ismael Valdes	.50	.23
❏ 53	Cal Ripken	4.00	1.80
❏ 54	Jeff Bagwell	1.25	.55
❏ 55	Greg Vaughn	.50	.23
❏ 56	Juan Gonzalez	2.00	.90
❏ 57	Raul Mondesi	.50	.23
❏ 58	Carlos Baerga	.25	.11
❏ 59	Sammy Sosa	3.00	1.35
❏ 60	Mike Kelly	.25	.11
❏ 61	Edgar Martinez	.50	.23
❏ 62	Kirby Puckett	1.50	.70
❏ 63	Cecil Fielder	.50	.23
❏ 64	David Cone	.75	.35
❏ 65	Moises Alou	.50	.23
❏ 66	Fred McGriff	.75	.35
❏ 67	Mo Vaughn	1.00	.45
❏ 68	Edgardo Alfonzo	1.00	.45
❏ 69	Jim Thome	1.00	.45
❏ 70	Rickey Henderson	1.25	.55
❏ 71	Dante Bichette	.50	.23
❏ 72	Lenny Dykstra	.50	.23
❏ 73	Benji Gil	.25	.11
❏ 74	Wade Boggs	.75	.35
❏ 75	Jim Edmonds	.75	.35
❏ 76	Michael Tucker	.25	.11
❏ 77	Carlos Delgado	1.00	.45
❏ 78	Butch Huskey	.25	.11
❏ 79	Billy Ashley	.25	.11
❏ 80	Dean Palmer	.50	.23
❏ 81	Paul Molitor	1.00	.45
❏ 82	Ryan Klesko	.50	.23
❏ 83	Brian Jordan	.25	.11
❏ 84	Jay Buhner	.50	.23
❏ 85	Larry Walker	1.00	.45
❏ 86	Mike Bordick	.25	.11
❏ 87	Matt Williams	1.00	.45
❏ 88	Jack McDowell	.25	.11
❏ 89	Hal Morris	.25	.11
❏ 90	Brian Jordan	.50	.23
❏ 91	Andy Pettitte	.75	.35
❏ 92	Melvin Nieves	.25	.11
❏ 93	Pedro Martinez	1.25	.55
❏ 94	Mark Grace	.75	.35
❏ 95	Garret Anderson	.50	.23
❏ 96	Andre Dawson	.75	.35
❏ 97	Ray Durham	.25	.11
❏ 98	Jose Canseco	1.25	.55
❏ 99	Roberto Alomar	1.00	.45
❏ 100	Derek Jeter	3.00	1.35
❏ 101	Alan Benes	.25	.11
❏ 102	Karim Garcia	.50	.23
❏ 103	Robin Jennings	.25	.11
❏ 104	Bob Abreu	.75	.35
❏ 105	Sal Fasano UER	.25	.11
	(Name on front is Livan Hernandez)		
❏ 106	Steve Gibralter	.25	.11
❏ 107	Jermaine Dye	.50	.23
❏ 108	Jason Kendall	1.00	.45
❏ 109	Mike Grace	.25	.11
❏ 110	Jason Schmidt	.25	.11
❏ 111	Paul Wilson	.25	.11
❏ 112	Rey Ordonez	1.00	.45
❏ 113	Wilton Guerrero	.75	.35
❏ 114	Brooks Kieschnick	.25	.11
❏ 115	George Arias	.25	.11
❏ 116	Osvaldo Fernandez	.25	.11
❏ 117	Todd Hollandsworth	.25	.11
❏ 118	John Wasdin	.25	.11
❏ 119	Eric Owens	.25	.11
❏ 120	Chan Ho Park	.75	.35
❏ 121	Mark Loretta	.25	.11
❏ 122	Richard Hidalgo	.50	.23
❏ 123	Jeff Suppan	.25	.11
❏ 124	Jim Pittsley	.25	.11
❏ 125	LaTroy Hawkins	.25	.11
❏ 126	Chris Snopek	.25	.11
❏ 127	Justin Thompson	.50	.23
❏ 128	Jay Powell	.25	.11
❏ 129	Alex Ochoa	.25	.11
❏ 130	Felipe Crespo	.25	.11
❏ 131	Matt Lawton	1.25	.55
❏ 132	Jimmy Haynes	.25	.11
❏ 133	Terrell Wade	.25	.11
❏ 134	Ruben Rivera	.50	.23
❏ 135	Frank Thomas PP	1.00	.45
❏ 136	Ken Griffey Jr. PP	2.50	1.10
❏ 137	Greg Maddux PP	1.25	.55
❏ 138	Mike Piazza PP	1.50	.70
❏ 139	Cal Ripken PP	2.00	.90
❏ 140	Albert Belle PP	.50	.23
❏ 141	Mo Vaughn PP	.50	.23
❏ 142	Chipper Jones PP	1.25	.55
❏ 143	Hideo Nomo PP	.50	.23
❏ 144	Ryan Klesko PP	.25	.11

1996 Select Certified Mirror Blue

	MINT	NRMT
COMMON CARD (1-144)	25.00	11.00

*STARS: 40X TO 100X BASIC CARDS
*PP STARS 135-144: 30X TO 80X BASIC CARDS
*ROOKIES: 20X TO 50X BASIC CARDS
STATED ODDS 1:200
STATED PRINT RUN 45 SETS

1996 Select Certified Mirror Gold

	MINT	NRMT
COMMON CARD (1-144)	60.00	27.00

*STARS: 100X TO 250X BASIC CARDS
*PP STARS 135-144: 80X TO 200X BASIC
*ROOKIES: 40X TO 100X BASIC CARDS
STATED ODDS 1:300
STATED PRINT RUN 30 SETS

1996 Select Certified Mirror Red

	MINT	NRMT
COMMON CARD (1-144)	15.00	6.75

*STARS: 25X TO 60X BASIC CARDS

*ROOKIES: 12.5X TO 30X BASIC CARDS
STATED ODDS 1:100
STATED PRINT RUN 90 SETS

1996 Select Certified Interleague Preview

	MINT	NRMT
COMPLETE SET (25)	300.00	135.00
COMMON CARD (1-25)	6.00	2.70
UNLISTED STARS	8.00	3.60
STATED ODDS 1:42		

		MINT	NRMT
❑ 1	Ken Griffey Jr.	40.00	18.00
	Hideo Nomo		
❑ 2	Greg Maddux	20.00	9.00
	Mo Vaughn		
❑ 3	Frank Thomas	40.00	18.00
	Sammy Sosa		
❑ 4	Mike Piazza	25.00	11.00
	Jim Edmonds		
❑ 5	Ryan Klesko	20.00	9.00
	Roger Clemens		
❑ 6	Derek Jeter	25.00	11.00
	Rey Ordonez		
❑ 7	Johnny Damon	6.00	2.70
	Ray Lankford		
❑ 8	Manny Ramirez	10.00	4.50
	Reggie Sanders		
❑ 9	Barry Bonds	10.00	4.50
	Jay Buhner		
❑ 10	Jason Isringhausen	6.00	2.70
	Wade Boggs		
❑ 11	David Cone	20.00	9.00
	Chipper Jones		
❑ 12	Jeff Bagwell	10.00	4.50
	Will Clark		
❑ 13	Tony Gwynn	20.00	9.00
	Randy Johnson		
❑ 14	Cal Ripken	30.00	13.50
	Tom Glavine		
❑ 15	Kirby Puckett	12.00	5.50
	Andy Benes		
❑ 16	Gary Sheffield	8.00	3.60
	Mike Mussina		
❑ 17	Raul Mondesi	8.00	3.60
	Tim Salmon		
❑ 18	Rondell White	6.00	2.70
	Carlos Delgado		
❑ 19	Cecil Fielder	10.00	4.50
	Ryne Sandberg		
❑ 20	Kenny Lofton	8.00	3.60
	Brian L.Hunter		
❑ 21	Paul Wilson	6.00	2.70
	Paul O'Neill		
❑ 22	Ismael Valdes	6.00	2.70
	Edgar Martinez		
❑ 23	Matt Williams	40.00	18.00
	Mark McGwire		
❑ 24	Albert Belle	8.00	3.60
	Barry Larkin		
❑ 25	Brady Anderson	8.00	3.60
	Marquis Grissom		

1996 Select Certified Select Few

	MINT	NRMT
COMPLETE SET (18)	250.00	110.00
COMMON CARD (1-18)	5.00	2.20
UNLISTED STARS	8.00	3.60
STATED ODDS 1:60		

		MINT	NRMT
❑ 1	Sammy Sosa	25.00	11.00
❑ 2	Derek Jeter	25.00	11.00
❑ 3	Ken Griffey Jr.	40.00	18.00
❑ 4	Albert Belle	8.00	3.60
❑ 5	Cal Ripken	30.00	13.50
❑ 6	Greg Maddux	20.00	9.00
❑ 7	Frank Thomas	15.00	6.75
❑ 8	Mo Vaughn	8.00	3.60
❑ 9	Chipper Jones	20.00	9.00
❑ 10	Mike Piazza	25.00	11.00
❑ 11	Ryan Klesko	5.00	2.20
❑ 12	Hideo Nomo	8.00	3.60
❑ 13	Alan Benes	5.00	2.20
❑ 14	Manny Ramirez	10.00	4.50
❑ 15	Gary Sheffield	5.00	2.20
❑ 16	Barry Bonds	10.00	4.50
❑ 17	Matt Williams	8.00	3.60
❑ 18	Johnny Damon	6.00	2.70

1998 SkyBox Dugout Axcess

	MINT	NRMT
COMPLETE SET (150)	15.00	6.75
COMMON CARD (1-150)	.10	.05
MINOR STARS	.15	.07
SEMISTARS	.25	.11
UNLISTED STARS	.40	.18

❑ 1	Travis Lee	.75	.35
❑ 2	Matt Williams	.15	.07
❑ 3	Andy Benes	.15	.07
❑ 4	Chipper Jones	1.00	.45
❑ 5	Ryan Klesko	.15	.07
❑ 6	Greg Maddux	1.00	.45
❑ 7	Sammy Sosa	1.25	.55
❑ 8	Henry Rodriguez	.15	.07
❑ 9	Mark Grace	.25	.11
❑ 10	Barry Larkin	.25	.11
❑ 11	Bret Boone	.15	.07
❑ 12	Reggie Sanders	.15	.07

❑ 13	Vinny Castilla	.25	.11
❑ 14	Larry Walker	.40	.18
❑ 15	Darryl Kile	.15	.07
❑ 16	Charles Johnson	.15	.07
❑ 17	Edgar Renteria	.15	.07
❑ 18	Gary Sheffield	.25	.11
❑ 19	Jeff Bagwell	.50	.23
❑ 20	Craig Biggio	.40	.18
❑ 21	Moises Alou	.25	.11
❑ 22	Mike Piazza	1.25	.55
❑ 23	Hideo Nomo	.40	.18
❑ 24	Raul Mondesi	.25	.11
❑ 25	John Jaha	.10	.05
❑ 26	Jeff Cirillo	.15	.07
❑ 27	Jeromy Burnitz	.15	.07
❑ 28	Mark Grudzielanek	.15	.07
❑ 29	Vladimir Guerrero	.50	.23
❑ 30	Rondell White	.15	.07
❑ 31	Edgardo Alfonzo	.15	.07
❑ 32	Rey Ordonez	.15	.07
❑ 33	Bernard Gilkey	.10	.05
❑ 34	Scott Rolen	.50	.23
❑ 35	Curt Schilling	.15	.07
❑ 36	Ricky Bottalico	.15	.07
❑ 37	Tony Womack	.15	.07
❑ 38	Al Martin	.10	.05
❑ 39	Jason Kendall	.15	.07
❑ 40	Ron Gant	.10	.05
❑ 41	Mark McGwire	2.50	1.10
❑ 42	Ray Lankford	.15	.07
❑ 43	Tony Gwynn	1.00	.45
❑ 44	Ken Caminiti	.25	.11
❑ 45	Kevin Brown	.25	.11
❑ 46	Barry Bonds	.50	.23
❑ 47	J.T. Snow	.15	.07
❑ 48	Shawn Estes	.15	.07
❑ 49	Jim Edmonds	.25	.11
❑ 50	Tim Salmon	.40	.18
❑ 51	Jason Dickson	.15	.07
❑ 52	Cal Ripken	1.50	.70
❑ 53	Mike Mussina	.40	.18
❑ 54	Roberto Alomar	.40	.18
❑ 55	Mo Vaughn	.40	.18
❑ 56	Pedro Martinez	.50	.23
❑ 57	Nomar Garciaparra	1.25	.55
❑ 58	Albert Belle	.40	.18
❑ 59	Frank Thomas	.75	.35
❑ 60	Robin Ventura	.15	.07
❑ 61	Jim Thome	.40	.18
❑ 62	Sandy Alomar Jr.	.15	.07
❑ 63	Jaret Wright	.40	.18
❑ 64	Bobby Higginson	.25	.11
❑ 65	Tony Clark	.25	.11
❑ 66	Justin Thompson	.15	.07
❑ 67	Dean Palmer	.15	.07
❑ 68	Kevin Appier	.15	.07
❑ 69	Johnny Damon	.15	.07
❑ 70	Paul Molitor	.40	.18
❑ 71	Marty Cordova	.10	.05
❑ 72	Brad Radke	.15	.07
❑ 73	Derek Jeter	1.25	.55
❑ 74	Bernie Williams	.40	.18
❑ 75	Andy Pettitte	.25	.11
❑ 76	Matt Stairs	.15	.07
❑ 77	Ben Grieve	.75	.35
❑ 78	Jason Giambi	.15	.07
❑ 79	Randy Johnson	.40	.18
❑ 80	Ken Griffey Jr.	2.00	.90
❑ 81	Alex Rodriguez	1.25	.55
❑ 82	Fred McGriff	.25	.11
❑ 83	Wade Boggs	.40	.18
❑ 84	Wilson Alvarez	.15	.07
❑ 85	Juan Gonzalez	.75	.35
❑ 86	Ivan Rodriguez	.50	.23
❑ 87	Fernando Tatis	.15	.07
❑ 88	Roger Clemens	1.00	.45
❑ 89	Jose Cruz Jr.	.40	.18
❑ 90	Shawn Green	.15	.07
❑ 91	Jeff Suppan	.15	.07
❑ 92	Eli Marrero	.15	.07
❑ 93	Mike Lowell	.40	.18
❑ 94	Ben Grieve	.75	.35
❑ 95	Cliff Politte	.15	.07
❑ 96	Rolando Arrojo	.40	.18
❑ 97	Mike Caruso	.15	.07
❑ 98	Miguel Tejada	.15	.07

☐ 99 Rod Myers	.10	.05
☐ 100 Juan Encarnacion	.15	.07
☐ 101 Enrique Wilson	.15	.07
☐ 102 Brian Giles	.15	.07
☐ 103 Magglio Ordonez	1.25	.55
☐ 104 Brian Rose	.15	.07
☐ 105 Ryan Jackson	.25	.11
☐ 106 Mark Kotsay	.25	.11
☐ 107 Desi Relaford	.10	.05
☐ 108 A.J. Hinch	.15	.07
☐ 109 Eric Milton	.15	.07
☐ 110 Ricky Ledee	.15	.07
☐ 111 Karim Garcia	.15	.07
☐ 112 Derrek Lee	.15	.07
☐ 113 Brad Fullmer	.15	.07
☐ 114 Travis Lee	.75	.35
☐ 115 Greg Norton	.10	.05
☐ 116 Rich Butler	.25	.11
☐ 117 Masato Yoshii	.40	.18
☐ 118 Paul Konerko	.40	.18
☐ 119 Richard Hidalgo	.15	.07
☐ 120 Todd Helton	.50	.23
☐ 121 Nomar Garciaparra 7TH	.60	.25
☐ 122 Scott Rolen 7TH	.40	.18
☐ 123 Cal Ripken 7TH	.75	.35
☐ 124 Derek Jeter 7TH	.60	.25
☐ 125 Mike Piazza 7TH	.60	.25
☐ 126 Tony Gwynn 7TH	.50	.23
☐ 127 Mark McGwire 7TH	1.25	.55
☐ 128 Kenny Lofton 7TH	.15	.07
☐ 129 Greg Maddux 7TH	.50	.23
☐ 130 Jeff Bagwell 7TH	.40	.18
☐ 131 Randy Johnson 7TH	.15	.07
☐ 132 Alex Rodriguez 7TH	.60	.25
☐ 133 Mo Vaughn NAME	.25	.11
☐ 134 Chipper Jones NAME	.50	.23
☐ 135 Juan Gonzalez NAME	.40	.18
☐ 136 Tony Clark NAME	.10	.05
☐ 137 Fred McGriff NAME	.10	.05
☐ 138 Roger Clemens NAME	.50	.23
☐ 139 Ken Griffey Jr. NAME	1.00	.45
☐ 140 Ivan Rodriguez NAME	.25	.11
☐ 141 Vinny Castilla TRIV	.10	.05
☐ 142 Livan Hernandez TRIV	.10	.05
☐ 143 Jose Cruz Jr. TRIV	.25	.11
☐ 144 Andruw Jones TRIV	.25	.11
☐ 145 Rafael Palmeiro TRIV	.10	.05
☐ 146 Chuck Knoblauch TRIV	.15	.07
☐ 147 Jay Buhner TRIV	.10	.05
☐ 148 Andres Galarraga TRIV	.15	.07
☐ 149 Frank Thomas TRIV	.50	.23
☐ 150 Todd Hundley TRIV	.10	.05
☐ NNO Alex Rodriguez Sample	3.00	1.35

1998 SkyBox Dugout Axcess Inside Axcess

	MINT	NRMT
COMMON CARD (1-150)	12.00	5.50

*STARS: 50X TO 120X BASIC CARDS
*YNG.STARS: 40X TO 100X BASIC CARDS
*ROOKIES: 25X TO 60X BASIC
RANDOM INSERTS IN ALL PACKS
STATED PRINT RUN 50 SERIAL #'d SETS

1998 SkyBox Dugout Axcess Autograph Redemptions

	MINT	NRMT

STATED ODDS 1:96 HOBBY
EXPIRATION DATE 3/31/99

☐ 1 Jay Buhner Ball	15.00	6.75
☐ 2 Roger Clemens Ball	120.00	55.00
☐ 3 Jose Cruz Jr. Ball	30.00	13.50
☐ 4 Darin Erstad Glove		
☐ 5 Nomar Garciaparra Ball	120.00	55.00
☐ 6 Tony Gwynn Ball	100.00	45.00
☐ 7 Roberto Hernandez Ball		
☐ 8 Todd Hollandsworth Glove		
☐ 9 Greg Maddux Ball	150.00	70.00
☐ 10 Alex Ochoa Glove		
☐ 11 Alex Rodriguez Ball	150.00	70.00
☐ 12 Scott Rolen Ball	80.00	36.00
☐ 13 Scott Rolen Glove		
☐ 14 Todd Walker Glove		
☐ 15 Tony Womack Ball	15.00	6.75

1998 SkyBox Dugout Axcess Dishwashers

	MINT	NRMT
COMPLETE SET (10)	12.00	5.50
COMMON CARD (D1-D10)	.15	.07

STATED ODDS 1:8

☐ D1 Greg Maddux	4.00	1.80
☐ D2 Kevin Brown	.75	.35
☐ D3 Pedro Martinez	1.25	.55
☐ D4 Randy Johnson	1.25	.55
☐ D5 Curt Schilling	.50	.23
☐ D6 John Smoltz	.50	.23
☐ D7 Darryl Kile	.50	.23
☐ D8 Roger Clemens	3.00	1.35
☐ D9 Andy Pettitte	.75	.35
☐ D10 Mike Mussina	1.25	.55

1998 SkyBox Dugout Axcess Double Header

	MINT	NRMT
COMPLETE SET (20)	5.00	2.20

	MINT	NRMT
COMMON CARD (DH1-DH20)	.05	.02

TWO PER PACK

☐ DH1 Jeff Bagwell	.25	.11
☐ DH2 Albert Belle	.20	.09
☐ DH3 Barry Bonds	.20	.09
☐ DH4 Derek Jeter	.50	.23
☐ DH5 Tony Clark	.15	.07
☐ DH6 Nomar Garciaparra	.60	.25
☐ DH7 Juan Gonzalez	.50	.23
☐ DH8 Ken Griffey Jr.	1.00	.45
☐ DH9 Chipper Jones	.50	.23
☐ DH10 Kenny Lofton	.20	.09
☐ DH11 Mark McGwire	1.25	.55
☐ DH12 Mo Vaughn	.20	.09
☐ DH13 Mike Piazza	.60	.25
☐ DH14 Cal Ripken	.75	.35
☐ DH15 Ivan Rodriguez	.20	.09
☐ DH16 Scott Rolen	.50	.23
☐ DH17 Frank Thomas	.50	.23
☐ DH18 Tony Gwynn	.50	.23
☐ DH19 Travis Lee	.40	.18
☐ DH20 Jose Cruz Jr.	.20	.09

1998 SkyBox Dugout Axcess Frequent Flyers

	MINT	NRMT
COMPLETE SET (10)	4.00	1.80
COMMON CARD (FF1-FF10)	.20	.09

STATED ODDS 1:4

☐ FF1 Brian Hunter	.30	.14
☐ FF2 Kenny Lofton	.60	.25
☐ FF3 Chuck Knoblauch	.60	.25
☐ FF4 Tony Womack	.30	.14
☐ FF5 Marquis Grissom	.30	.14
☐ FF6 Craig Biggio	.60	.25
☐ FF7 Barry Bonds	1.00	.45
☐ FF8 Tom Goodwin	.20	.09
☐ FF9 Delino DeShields	.20	.09
UER front DeShields		
☐ FF10 Eric Young	.30	.14

1998 SkyBox Dugout Axcess Gronks

	MINT	NRMT
COMPLETE SET (10)	120.00	55.00
COMMON CARD (G1-G10)	4.00	1.80

STATED ODDS 1:72 HOBBY

		MINT	NRMT
☐	G1 Jeff Bagwell	6.00	2.70
☐	G2 Albert Belle	6.00	2.70
☐	G3 Juan Gonzalez	15.00	6.75
☐	G4 Ken Griffey Jr.	30.00	13.50
☐	G5 Mark McGwire	40.00	18.00
☐	G6 Mike Piazza	20.00	9.00
☐	G7 Frank Thomas	15.00	6.75
☐	G8 Mo Vaughn	6.00	2.70
☐	G9 Ken Caminiti	4.00	1.80
☐	G10 Tony Clark	4.00	1.80

1998 SkyBox Dugout Axcess SuperHeroes

	MINT	NRMT
COMPLETE SET (10)	40.00	18.00
COMMON CARD (SH1-SH10)	2.00	.90
STATED ODDS 1:20		

		MINT	NRMT
☐	SH1 Barry Bonds	2.00	.90
☐	SH2 Andres Galarraga	2.00	.90
☐	SH3 Ken Griffey Jr.	12.00	5.50
☐	SH4 Chipper Jones	6.00	2.70
☐	SH5 Andruw Jones	2.00	.90
☐	SH6 Hideo Nomo	2.00	.90
☐	SH7 Cal Ripken	10.00	4.50
☐	SH8 Alex Rodriguez	8.00	3.60
☐	SH9 Frank Thomas	6.00	2.70
☐	SH10 Mo Vaughn	2.00	.90

1999 SkyBox Molten Metal

	MINT	NRMT
COMPLETE SET (150)	100.00	45.00
COMMON CARD (1-100)	.25	.11
MINOR STARS 1-100	.40	.18
SEMISTARS 1-100	.60	.25
UNLISTED STARS 1-100	1.00	.45
METALSMITHS 1-100 STATED ODDS 4:1		
COMMON CARD (101-130)	.30	.14
MINOR STARS 101-130	.50	.23
SEMISTARS 101-130	.75	.35
UNLISTED STARS 101-130	1.25	.55
HEAVY METAL 101-130 STATED ODDS 1:1		
COMMON CARD (131-150)	1.25	.55
UNLISTED STARS 131-150	1.50	.70
SUPERNATURAL 131-150 STATED ODDS 1:2		

☐	1 Larry Walker MS	1.00	.45
☐	2 Jose Canseco MS	1.25	.55
☐	3 Brian Jordan MS	.40	.18
☐	4 Rafael Palmeiro MS	1.00	.45
☐	5 Edgar Renteria MS	.25	.11
☐	6 Dante Bichette MS	.40	.18
☐	7 Mark Kotsay MS	.25	.11
☐	8 Denny Neagle MS	.25	.11
☐	9 Ellis Burks MS	.40	.18
☐	10 Paul O'Neill MS	.40	.18
☐	11 Miguel Tejada MS	.40	.18
☐	12 Ken Caminiti MS	.40	.18
☐	13 David Cone MS	.60	.25
☐	14 Jason Kendall MS	.40	.18
☐	15 Ruben Rivera MS	.25	.11
☐	16 Todd Walker MS	.40	.18
☐	17 Bobby Higginson MS	.40	.18
☐	18 Derek Lee MS	.25	.11
☐	19 Rondell White MS	.40	.18
☐	20 Pedro Martinez MS	1.25	.55
☐	21 Jeff Kent MS	.40	.18
☐	22 Randy Johnson MS	1.00	.45
☐	23 Matt Williams MS	1.00	.45
☐	24 Sean Casey MS	.40	.18
☐	25 Eric Davis MS	.40	.18
☐	26 Ryan Klesko MS	.40	.18
☐	27 Curt Schilling MS	.60	.25
☐	28 Geoff Jenkins MS	.40	.18
☐	29 Bob Abreu MS	.40	.18
☐	30 Vinny Castilla MS	.40	.18
☐	31 Will Clark MS	1.00	.45
☐	32 Ray Durham MS	.40	.18
☐	33 Ray Lankford MS	.40	.18
☐	34 Richie Sexson MS	.60	.25
☐	35 Derrick Gibson MS	.40	.18
☐	36 Mark Grace MS	.60	.25
☐	37 Greg Vaughn MS	.40	.18
☐	38 Bartolo Colon MS	.40	.18
☐	39 Steve Finley MS	.40	.18
☐	40 Chuck Knoblauch MS	.40	.18
☐	41 Ricky Ledee MS	.40	.18
☐	42 John Smoltz MS	.60	.25
☐	43 Moises Alou MS	.40	.18
☐	44 Jim Edmonds MS	.40	.18
☐	45 Cliff Floyd MS	.40	.18
☐	46 Javy Lopez MS	.40	.18
☐	47 Jim Thome MS	1.00	.45
☐	48 J.T. Snow MS	.40	.18
☐	49 Sandy Alomar Jr. MS	.40	.18
☐	50 Andy Pettitte MS	.40	.18
☐	51 Juan Encarnacion MS	.40	.18
☐	52 Travis Fryman MS	.40	.18
☐	53 Eli Marrero MS	.25	.11
☐	54 Jeff Cirillo MS	.40	.18
☐	55 Brady Anderson MS	.40	.18
☐	56 Jose Cruz Jr. MS	.40	.18
☐	57 Edgar Martinez MS	.40	.18
☐	58 Garret Anderson MS	.40	.18
☐	59 Paul Konerko MS	.40	.18
☐	60 Eric Milton MS	.25	.11
☐	61 Jason Giambi MS	.40	.18
☐	62 Tom Glavine MS	1.00	.45
☐	63 Justin Thompson MS	.25	.11
☐	64 Brad Fullmer MS	.25	.11
☐	65 Marquis Grissom MS	.25	.11
☐	66 Fernando Tatis MS	1.00	.45
☐	67 Carlos Beltran MS	1.25	.55
☐	68 Charles Johnson MS	.40	.18

☐	69 Raul Mondesi MS	.40	.18
☐	70 Richard Hildago MS	.40	.18
☐	71 Barry Larkin MS	1.00	.45
☐	72 David Wells MS	.40	.18
☐	73 Jay Buhner MS	.40	.18
☐	74 Matt Clement MS	.40	.18
☐	75 Eric Karros MS	.40	.18
☐	76 Carl Pavano MS	.25	.11
☐	77 Mariano Rivera MS	.40	.18
☐	78 Livan Hernandez MS	.25	.11
☐	79 A.J. Hinch MS	.25	.11
☐	80 Tino Martinez MS	.40	.18
☐	81 Rusty Greer MS	.40	.18
☐	82 Jose Guillen MS	.25	.11
☐	83 Robin Ventura MS	.40	.18
☐	84 Kevin Brown MS	.60	.25
☐	85 Chan Ho Park MS	.40	.18
☐	86 John Olerud MS	.40	.18
☐	87 Johnny Damon MS	.40	.18
☐	88 Todd Hundley MS	.40	.18
☐	89 Fred McGriff MS	.60	.25
☐	90 Wade Boggs MS	1.00	.45
☐	91 Mike Cameron MS	.25	.11
☐	92 Gary Sheffield MS	.40	.18
☐	93 Rickey Henderson MS	1.25	.55
☐	94 Pat Hentgen MS	.25	.11
☐	95 Omar Vizquel MS	.40	.18
☐	96 Craig Biggio MS	1.00	.45
☐	97 Mike Caruso MS	.25	.11
☐	98 Neifi Perez MS	.40	.18
☐	99 Mike Mussina MS	1.00	.45
☐	100 Carlos Delgado MS	1.00	.45
☐	101 Andruw Jones HM	1.25	.55
☐	102 Pat Burrell HM	5.00	2.20
☐	103 Orlando Hernandez HM	1.25	.55
☐	104 Darin Erstad HM	.75	.35
☐	105 Roberto Alomar HM	.75	.35
☐	106 Tim Salmon HM	.75	.35
☐	107 Albert Belle HM	1.25	.55
☐	108 Chad Allen HM	.60	.25
☐	109 Travis Lee HM	.75	.35
☐	110 Jesse Garcia HM	.50	.23
☐	111 Tony Clark HM	.50	.23
☐	112 Ivan Rodriguez HM	1.50	.70
☐	113 Troy Glaus HM	1.25	.55
☐	114 A.J. Burnett HM	1.25	.55
☐	115 David Justice HM	.50	.23
☐	116 Adrian Beltre HM	1.25	.55
☐	117 Eric Chavez HM	.75	.35
☐	118 Kenny Lofton HM	.75	.35
☐	119 Michael Barrett HM	.75	.35
☐	120 Jeff Weaver HM	1.25	.55
☐	121 Manny Ramirez HM	1.50	.70
☐	122 Barry Bonds HM	1.50	.70
☐	123 Bernie Williams HM	1.25	.55
☐	124 Freddy Garcia HM	5.00	2.20
☐	125 Scott Hunter HM	.60	.25
☐	126 Jeremy Giambi HM	.50	.23
☐	127 Masao Kida HM	1.00	.45
☐	128 Todd Helton HM	1.25	.55
☐	129 Mike Figga HM	.30	.14
☐	130 Mo Vaughn HM	1.25	.55
☐	131 J.D. Drew SN	2.50	1.10
☐	132 Cal Ripken SN	6.00	2.70
☐	133 Ken Griffey Jr. SN	8.00	3.60
☐	134 Mark McGwire SN	10.00	4.50
☐	135 Nomar Garciaparra SN	5.00	2.20
☐	136 Greg Maddux SN	4.00	1.80
☐	137 Mike Piazza SN	5.00	2.20
☐	138 Alex Rodriguez SN	5.00	2.20
☐	139 Frank Thomas SN	3.00	1.35
☐	140 Juan Gonzalez SN	3.00	1.35
☐	141 Tony Gwynn SN	4.00	1.80
☐	142 Derek Jeter SN	5.00	2.20
☐	143 Chipper Jones SN	4.00	1.80
☐	144 Scott Rolen SN	2.00	.90
☐	145 Sammy Sosa SN	5.00	2.20
☐	146 Kerry Wood SN	1.25	.55
☐	147 Roger Clemens SN	4.00	1.80
☐	148 Jeff Bagwell SN	2.00	.90
☐	149 Vladimir Guerrero SN	2.00	.90
☐	150 Ben Grieve SN	1.50	.70

1999 SkyBox Molten Metal Xplosion

	MINT	NRMT
COMPLETE SET (150)	600.00	275.00
COMMON CARD (1-150)	1.50	.70

*METALSMITHS 1-100: 2.5X TO 6X BASIC
*HEAVY METAL 101-130: 2X TO 5X BASIC
*HVY.MTL RC'S 101-130: 1.25X TO 3X BASIC
*S'NATURAL 131-150: 1.5X TO 4X BASIC
XPLOSION STATED ODDS 1:2

☐ NNO Kerry Wood Sample .. 2.00 .90

1999 SkyBox Molten Metal Fusion

	MINT	NRMT
COMPLETE SET (50)	600.00	275.00
COMMON CARD (1-30)	2.50	1.10
SEMISTARS 1-30	4.00	1.80
UNLISTED STARS 1-30	6.00	2.70
HEAVY METAL 1-30 STATED ODDS 1:12		
COMMON CARD (31-50)	6.00	2.70
UNLISTED STARS 31-50	8.00	3.60
SUPERNATURAL 31-50 STATED ODDS 1:24		

1999 SkyBox Molten Metal Fusion Sterling

	MINT	NRMT
COMPLETE SET (50)	1000.00	450.00

COMMON CARD (1-50)	5.00	2.20

*HEAVY METAL 1-30: .6X TO 1.5X FUSION
*S'NATURAL 31-50: .6X TO 1.5X FUSION
STATED PRINT RUN 500 SERIAL #'d SETS

1999 SkyBox Molten Metal Fusion Titanium

	MINT	NRMT
COMMON CARD (1-50)	20.00	9.00

*HEAVY METAL 1-30: 3X TO 8X FUSION
*HVY.MTL RC'S 1-30: 3X TO 8X FUSION
*S'NATURAL 31-50: 2.5X TO 6X FUSION
STATED PRINT RUN 50 SERIAL #'d SETS

1999 SkyBox Molten Metal Oh Atlanta

	MINT	NRMT
COMPLETE SET (30)	100.00	45.00
COMMON CARD (1-30)	1.50	.70
MINOR STARS	2.50	1.10
SEMISTARS	4.00	1.80

ONE PER NATIONAL EDITION PACK

☐ 1 Kenny Lofton	4.00	1.80
☐ 2 Kevin Millwood	5.00	2.20
☐ 3 Bret Boone	2.50	1.10
☐ 4 Otis Nixon	1.50	.70
☐ 5 Vinny Castilla	2.50	1.10
☐ 6 Brian Jordan	2.50	1.10
☐ 7 Chipper Jones	15.00	6.75
☐ 8 David Justice	2.50	1.10
☐ 9 Micah Bowie	4.00	1.80
☐ 10 Fred McGriff	4.00	1.80
☐ 11 Ron Gant	2.50	1.10
☐ 12 Andruw Jones	6.00	2.70
☐ 13 Kent Mercker	1.50	.70
☐ 14 Greg McMichael	1.50	.70
☐ 15 Steve Avery	1.50	.70
☐ 16 Marquis Grissom	1.50	.70
☐ 17 Jason Schmidt	1.50	.70
☐ 18 Ryan Klesko	2.50	1.10
☐ 19 Charlie O'Brien	1.50	.70
☐ 20 Terry Pendleton	2.50	1.10
☐ 21 Denny Neagle	1.50	.70
☐ 22 Greg Maddux	15.00	6.75
☐ 23 Tom Glavine	5.00	2.20
☐ 24 Javy Lopez	2.50	1.10
☐ 25 John Rocker	5.00	2.20

☐ 26 Walt Weiss	1.50	.70
☐ 27 John Smoltz	4.00	1.80
☐ 28 Michael Tucker	1.50	.70
☐ 29 Odalis Perez	1.50	.70
☐ 30 Andres Galarraga	4.00	1.80

1999 SkyBox Premium

	MINT	NRMT
COMP.MASTER SET (350)	400.00	180.00
COMP.SET w/o SP's (300)	50.00	22.00
COMMON (1-222/274-300)	.15	.07
MINOR STARS 1-222/274-300	.25	.11
SEMISTARS 1-222/274-300	.40	.18
UNLISTED 1-222/274-300	.60	.25
COMMON (223-272)	.25	.11
MINOR STARS 223-272	.40	.18
SEMISTARS 223-272	.60	.25
UNLISTED STARS 223-272	1.00	.45
COMMON SP (223-272)	2.00	.90
SP MINOR STARS	3.00	1.35
SP SEMISTARS	5.00	2.20
SP UNLISTED STARS	8.00	3.60

SP STATED ODDS 1:8
223-272: TWO VERSIONS OF EACH EXIST
SP CARDS FEATURE FULL BODY SHOTS
BASIC CARDS FEATURE CLOSE UP SHOTS

☐ 1 Alex Rodriguez	2.00	.90
☐ 2 Sidney Ponson	.15	.07
☐ 3 Shawn Green	.60	.25
☐ 4 Dan Wilson	.15	.07
☐ 5 Rolando Arrojo	.15	.07
☐ 6 Roberto Alomar	.60	.25
☐ 7 Matt Anderson	.15	.07
☐ 8 David Segui	.15	.07
☐ 9 Alex Gonzalez	.25	.11
☐ 10 Edgar Renteria	.15	.07
☐ 11 Benito Santiago	.15	.07
☐ 12 Todd Stottlemyre	.15	.07
☐ 13 Rico Brogna	.15	.07
☐ 14 Troy Glaus	.60	.25
☐ 15 Al Leiter	.25	.11
☐ 16 Pedro Martinez	.75	.35
☐ 17 Paul O'Neill	.25	.11
☐ 18 Manny Ramirez	.75	.35
☐ 19 Scott Rolen	.75	.35
☐ 20 Curt Schilling	.40	.18
☐ 21 Bobby Abreu	.25	.11
☐ 22 Robb Nen	.15	.07
☐ 23 Andy Pettitte	.25	.11
☐ 24 John Wetteland	.25	.11
☐ 25 Bobby Bonilla	.25	.11
☐ 26 Darin Erstad	.40	.18
☐ 27 Shawn Estes	.15	.07
☐ 28 John Franco	.25	.11
☐ 29 Nomar Garciaparra	2.00	.90
☐ 30 Rick Helling	.15	.07
☐ 31 David Justice	.25	.11
☐ 32 Chuck Knoblauch	.25	.11
☐ 33 Quinton McCracken	.15	.07
☐ 34 Kenny Rogers	.15	.07
☐ 35 Brian Giles	.25	.11
☐ 36 Armando Benitez	.15	.07
☐ 37 Trevor Hoffman	.25	.11
☐ 38 Charles Johnson	.25	.11
☐ 39 Travis Lee	.40	.18
☐ 40 Tom Glavine	.60	.25

41	Rondell White	.25	.11
42	Orlando Hernandez	.60	.25
43	Mickey Morandini	.15	.07
44	Darryl Kile	.15	.07
45	Greg Vaughn	.25	.11
46	Gregg Jefferies	.15	.07
47	Mark McGwire	4.00	1.80
48	Kerry Wood	.25	.11
49	Jeromy Burnitz	.25	.11
50	Ron Gant	.25	.11
51	Vinny Castilla	.25	.11
52	Doug Glanville	.15	.07
53	Juan Guzman	.15	.07
54	Dustin Hermanson	.15	.07
55	Jose Hernandez	.15	.07
56	Bobby Higginson	.25	.11
57	A.J. Hinch	.15	.07
58	Randy Johnson	.60	.25
59	Eli Marrero	.15	.07
60	Rafael Palmeiro	.60	.25
61	Carl Pavano	.15	.07
62	Brett Tomko	.15	.07
63	Jose Guillen	.25	.11
64	Mike Lieberthal	.25	.11
65	Jim Abbott	.25	.11
66	Dante Bichette	.25	.11
67	Jeff Cirillo	.25	.11
68	Eric Davis	.25	.11
69	Delino DeShields	.15	.07
70	Steve Finley	.25	.11
71	Mark Grace	.40	.18
72	Jason Kendall	.25	.11
73	Jeff Kent	.25	.11
74	Desi Relaford	.15	.07
75	Ivan Rodriguez	.75	.35
76	Shannon Stewart	.25	.11
77	Geoff Jenkins	.25	.11
78	Ben Grieve	.60	.25
79	Cliff Floyd	.25	.11
80	Jason Giambi	.25	.11
81	Rod Beck	.25	.11
82	Derek Bell	.25	.11
83	Will Clark	.60	.25
84	David Dellucci	.15	.07
85	Joey Hamilton	.15	.07
86	Livan Hernandez	.15	.07
87	Barry Larkin	.60	.25
88	Matt Mantei	.25	.11
89	Dean Palmer	.25	.11
90	Chan Ho Park	.25	.11
91	Jim Thome	.60	.25
92	Miguel Tejada	.25	.11
93	Justin Thompson	.15	.07
94	David Wells	.25	.11
95	Bernie Williams	.60	.25
96	Jeff Bagwell	.75	.35
97	Derrek Lee	.25	.11
98	Devon White	.15	.07
99	Jeff Shaw	.15	.07
100	Brad Radke	.25	.11
101	Mark Grudzielanek	.15	.07
102	Javy Lopez	.25	.11
103	Mike Sirotka	.15	.07
104	Robin Ventura	.25	.11
105	Andy Ashby	.15	.07
106	Juan Gonzalez	1.25	.55
107	Albert Belle	.60	.25
108	Andy Benes	.15	.07
109	Jay Buhner	.25	.11
110	Ken Caminiti	.25	.11
111	Roger Clemens	1.50	.70
112	Mike Hampton	.25	.11
113	Pete Harnisch	.15	.07
114	Mike Piazza	2.00	.90
115	J.T. Snow	.25	.11
116	John Olerud	.25	.11
117	Tony Womack	.15	.07
118	Todd Zeile	.15	.07
119	Tony Gwynn	1.50	.70
120	Brady Anderson	.25	.11
121	Sean Casey	.60	.25
122	Jose Cruz Jr.	.25	.11
123	Carlos Delgado	.60	.25
124	Edgar Martinez	.25	.11
125	Jose Mesa	.15	.07
126	Shane Reynolds	.25	.11
127	John Valentin	.25	.11
128	Mo Vaughn	.60	.25
129	Kevin Young	.25	.11
130	Jay Bell	.25	.11
131	Aaron Boone	.15	.07
132	John Smoltz	.40	.18
133	Mike Stanley	.15	.07
134	Bret Saberhagen	.25	.11
135	Tim Salmon	.40	.18
136	Mariano Rivera	.25	.11
137	Ken Griffey Jr.	3.00	1.35
138	Jose Offerman	.25	.11
139	Troy Percival	.25	.11
140	Greg Maddux	1.50	.70
141	Frank Thomas	1.25	.55
142	Steve Avery	.15	.07
143	Kevin Millwood	.40	.18
144	Sammy Sosa	2.00	.90
145	Larry Walker	.60	.25
146	Matt Williams	.60	.25
147	Mike Caruso	.15	.07
148	Todd Helton	.60	.25
149	Andruw Jones	.60	.25
150	Ray Lankford	.25	.11
151	Craig Biggio	.60	.25
152	Ugueth Urbina	.15	.07
153	Wade Boggs	.60	.25
154	Derek Jeter	2.00	.90
155	Wally Joyner	.25	.11
156	Mike Mussina	.60	.25
157	Gregg Olson	.15	.07
158	Henry Rodriguez	.25	.11
159	Reggie Sanders	.25	.11
160	Fernando Tatis	.60	.25
161	Dmitri Young	.25	.11
162	Rick Aguilera	.15	.07
163	Marty Cordova	.15	.07
164	Johnny Damon	.25	.11
165	Ray Durham	.25	.11
166	Brad Fullmer	.15	.07
167	Chipper Jones	1.50	.70
168	Bobby Smith	.15	.07
169	Omar Vizquel	.25	.11
170	Todd Hundley	.25	.11
171	David Cone	.40	.18
172	Royce Clayton	.15	.07
173	Ryan Klesko	.25	.11
174	Jeff Montgomery	.15	.07
175	Magglio Ordonez	.60	.25
176	Billy Wagner	.25	.11
177	Masato Yoshii	.25	.11
178	Jason Christiansen	.15	.07
179	Chuck Finley	.25	.11
180	Tom Gordon	.25	.11
181	Wilton Guerrero	.15	.07
182	Rickey Henderson	.75	.35
183	Sterling Hitchcock	.15	.07
184	Kenny Lofton	.40	.18
185	Tino Martinez	.25	.11
186	Fred McGriff	.40	.18
187	Matt Stairs	.25	.11
188	Neifi Perez	.25	.11
189	Bob Wickman	.15	.07
190	Barry Bonds	.75	.35
191	Jose Canseco	.75	.35
192	Damion Easley	.25	.11
193	Jim Edmonds	.25	.11
194	Juan Encarnacion	.25	.11
195	Travis Fryman	.25	.11
196	Tom Goodwin	.15	.07
197	Rusty Greer	.25	.11
198	Roberto Hernandez	.15	.07
199	B.J. Surhoff	.25	.11
200	Scott Brosius	.25	.11
201	Brian Jordan	.25	.11
202	Paul Konerko	.25	.11
203	Ismael Valdes	.15	.07
204	Eric Milton	.15	.07
205	Adrian Beltre	.60	.25
206	Tony Clark	.25	.11
207	Bartolo Colon	.25	.11
208	Cal Ripken	2.50	1.10
209	Moises Alou	.25	.11
210	Wilson Alvarez	.15	.07
211	Kevin Brown	.40	.18
212	Orlando Cabrera	.15	.07
213	Vladimir Guerrero	.75	.35
214	Jose Rosado	.15	.07
215	Raul Mondesi	.25	.11
216	David Nilsson	.15	.07
217	Carlos Perez	.15	.07
218	Jason Schmidt	.15	.07
219	Richie Sexson	.40	.18
220	Gary Sheffield	.25	.11
221	Fernando Vina	.15	.07
222	Todd Walker	.25	.11
223	Scott Sauerbeck SP	.15	.07
223S	Scott Sauerbeck SP	3.00	1.35
224	Pascual Matos	.25	.11
224S	Pascual Matos SP	3.00	1.35
225	Kyle Farnsworth	1.00	.45
225S	Kyle Farnsworth SP	5.00	2.20
226	Freddy Garcia	4.00	1.80
226S	Freddy Garcia SP	20.00	9.00
227	David Lundquist	.15	.07
227S	David Lundquist SP	2.00	.90
228	Jolbert Cabrera	.15	.07
228S	Jolbert Cabrera SP	2.00	.90
229	Dan Perkins	.15	.07
229S	Dan Perkins SP	2.00	.90
230	Warren Morris	.25	.11
230S	Warren Morris SP	3.00	1.35
231	Carlos Febles	.25	.11
231S	Carlos Febles SP	3.00	1.35
232	Brett Hinchliffe	.50	.23
232S	Brett Hinchliffe SP	2.50	1.10
233	Jason Phillips	.15	.07
233S	Jason Phillips SP	2.00	.90
234	Glen Barker	.15	.07
234S	Glen Barker SP	2.00	.90
235	Jose Macias	.25	.11
235S	Jose Macias SP	3.00	1.35
236	Joe Mays	1.25	.55
236S	Joe Mays SP	6.00	2.70
237	Chad Allen	.50	.23
237S	Chad Allen SP	2.50	1.10
238	Miguel Del Toro	.15	.07
238S	Miguel Del Toro SP	2.00	.90
239	Chris Singleton	.25	.11
239S	Chris Singleton SP	3.00	1.35
240	Jesse Garcia	.15	.07
240S	Jesse Garcia SP	2.00	.90
241	Kris Benson	.25	.11
241S	Kris Benson SP	3.00	1.35
242	Clay Bellinger	.15	.07
242S	Clay Bellinger SP	2.00	.90
243	Scott Williamson	.25	.11
243S	Scott Williamson SP	3.00	1.35
244	Masao Kida	.60	.25
244S	Masao Kida SP	3.00	1.35
245	Guillermo Garcia	.15	.07
245S	Guillermo Garcia SP	2.00	.90
246	A.J. Burnett	1.00	.45
246S	A.J. Burnett SP	5.00	2.20
247	Bo Porter	.15	.07
247S	Bo Porter SP	2.00	.90
248	Pat Burrell	4.00	1.80
248S	Pat Burrell SP	20.00	9.00
249	Carlos Lee	.25	.11
249S	Carlos Lee SP	3.00	1.35
250	Jeff Weaver	1.00	.45
250S	Jeff Weaver SP	5.00	2.20
251	Ruben Mateo	.60	.25
251S	Ruben Mateo SP	8.00	3.60
252	J.D. Drew	1.50	.70
252S	J.D. Drew SP	12.00	5.50
253	Jeremy Giambi	.25	.11
253S	Jeremy Giambi SP	3.00	1.35
254	Gary Bennett	.25	.11
254S	Gary Bennett SP	2.00	.90
255	Edwards Guzman	.50	.23
255S	Edwards Guzman SP	2.50	1.10
256	Ramon E.Martinez	.15	.07
256S	Ramon E.Martinez SP	2.00	.90
257	Giomar Guevara	.15	.07
257S	Giomar Guevara SP	2.00	.90
258	Joe McEwing	1.50	.70
258S	Joe McEwing SP	8.00	3.60
259	Tom Davey	.15	.07
259S	Tom Davey SP	2.00	.90
260	Gabe Kapler	.60	.25
260S	Gabe Kapler SP	8.00	3.60

	MINT	NRMT
☐ 261 Ryan Rupe .60	.25
☐ 261S Ryan Rupe SP 3.00	1.35
☐ 262 Kelly Dransfeldt .60	.25
☐ 262S Kelly Dransfeldt SP 3.00	1.35
☐ 263 Michael Barrett .40	.18
☐ 263S Michael Barrett SP 5.00	2.20
☐ 264 Eric Chavez .40	.18
☐ 264S Eric Chavez SP 5.00	2.20
☐ 265 Orber Moreno .60	.25
☐ 265S Orber Moreno SP 3.00	1.35
☐ 266 Marlon Anderson .15	.07
☐ 266S Marlon Anderson SP 2.00	.90
☐ 267 Carlos Beltran 1.25	.55
☐ 267S Carlos Beltran SP 10.00	4.50
☐ 268 Doug Mientkiewicz .50	.23
☐ 268S Doug Mientkiewicz SP 2.50	1.10
☐ 269 Roy Halladay .25	.11
☐ 269S Roy Halladay SP 3.00	1.35
☐ 270 Torii Hunter .15	.07
☐ 270S Torii Hunter SP 2.00	.90
☐ 271 Stan Spencer .15	.07
☐ 271S Stan Spencer SP 2.00	.90
☐ 272 Alex Gonzalez .25	.11
☐ 272S Alex Gonzalez SP 3.00	1.35
☐ 273 Mark McGwire SF 2.00	.90
☐ 274 Scott Rolen SF .60	.25
☐ 275 Jeff Bagwell SF .40	.18
☐ 276 Derek Jeter SF 1.00	.45
☐ 277 Tony Gwynn SF .75	.35
☐ 278 Frank Thomas SF .60	.25
☐ 279 Sammy Sosa SF 1.00	.45
☐ 280 Nomar Garciaparra SF 1.00	.45
☐ 281 Cal Ripken SF 1.25	.55
☐ 282 Albert Belle SF .25	.11
☐ 283 Kerry Wood SF .25	.11
☐ 284 Greg Maddux SF .75	.35
☐ 285 Barry Bonds SF .40	.18
☐ 286 Juan Gonzalez SF .60	.25
☐ 287 Ken Griffey Jr. SF 1.50	.70
☐ 288 Alex Rodriguez SF 1.00	.45
☐ 289 Ben Grieve SF .25	.11
☐ 290 Travis Lee SF .25	.11
☐ 291 Mo Vaughn SF .25	.11
☐ 292 Mike Piazza SF 1.00	.45
☐ 293 Roger Clemens SF .75	.35
☐ 294 J.D. Drew SF .60	.25
☐ 295 Randy Johnson SF .25	.11
☐ 296 Chipper Jones SF .75	.35
☐ 297 Vladimir Guerrero SF .40	.18
☐ 298 Nomar Garciaparra CL 1.00	.45
☐ 299 Ken Griffey Jr. CL 1.50	.70
☐ 300 Mark McGwire CL 2.00	.90
☐ S83 Ben Grieve Sample 3.00	1.35

1999 SkyBox Premium Star Rubies

	MINT	NRMT
COMMON CARD (1-300) 10.00	4.50

*STARS: 25X TO 60X BASIC CARDS
*YNG.STARS: 20X TO 50X BASIC CARDS
*PROSPECTS 223-272: 12.5X TO 30X BASIC
*ROOKIES 223-272: 12.5X TO 30X BASIC RC'S
STATED PRINT RUN 50 SERIAL #'d SETS
COMMON SP (223-272) 25.00 | 11.00
*SP PROSP.223-272: 5X TO 12X BASIC SP'S
*SP RC'S 223-272: 5X TO 12X BASIC SP RC'S
SP PRINT RUN 15 SERIAL #'d SETS
RANDOM INSERTS IN PACKS

1999 SkyBox Premium Autographics

	MINT	NRMT
COMMON CARD 10.00	4.50

STATED ODDS 1:68
UNNUMBERED CARDS LISTED IN
ALPH.ORDER

☐ 1 Roberto Alomar 50.00	22.00
☐ 2 Paul Bako 10.00	4.50
☐ 3 Michael Barrett 15.00	6.75
☐ 4 Kris Benson 15.00	6.75
☐ 5 Micah Bowie 25.00	11.00
☐ 6 Roosevelt Brown 15.00	6.75
☐ 7 A.J. Burnett 15.00	6.75
☐ 8 Pat Burrell 60.00	27.00
☐ 9 Ken Caminiti 20.00	9.00
☐ 10 Royce Clayton 10.00	4.50
☐ 11 Edgard Clemente 10.00	4.50
☐ 12 Bartolo Colon 20.00	9.00
☐ 13 J.D. Drew 50.00	22.00
☐ 14 Damion Easley 15.00	6.75
☐ 15 Derrin Ebert 25.00	11.00
☐ 16 Mario Encarnacion 20.00	9.00
☐ 17 Juan Encarnacion 15.00	6.75
☐ 18 Troy Glaus 30.00	13.50
☐ 19 Tom Glavine 40.00	18.00
☐ 20 Juan Gonzalez	
☐ 21 Shawn Green 40.00	18.00
☐ 22 Wilton Guerrero 10.00	4.50
☐ 23 Jose Guillen 10.00	4.50
☐ 24 Tony Gwynn 120.00	55.00
☐ 25 Mark Harriger 10.00	4.50
☐ 26 Todd Hollandsworth 10.00	4.50
☐ 27 Scott Hunter 15.00	6.75
☐ 28 Gabe Kapler 25.00	11.00
☐ 29 Scott Karl 10.00	4.50
☐ 30 Mike Kinkade 15.00	6.75
☐ 31 Ray Lankford 15.00	6.75
☐ 32 Barry Larkin	
☐ 33 Matt Lawton 10.00	4.50
☐ 34 Ricky Ledee 15.00	6.75
☐ 35 Travis Lee 15.00	6.75
☐ 36 Eli Marrero 10.90	4.50
☐ 37 Ruben Mateo 25.00	11.00
☐ 38 Joe McEwing 25.00	11.00
☐ 39 Doug Mientkiewicz 15.00	6.75
☐ 40 Russ Ortiz 10.00	4.50
☐ 41 Jim Parque 10.00	4.50
☐ 42 Robert Person 10.00	4.50
☐ 43 Alex Rodriguez 150.00	70.00
☐ 44 Scott Rolen 50.00	22.00
☐ 45 Benj Sampson 10.00	4.50
☐ 46 Luis Saturria 15.00	6.75
☐ 47 Curt Schilling 25.00	11.00
☐ 48 David Segui 10.00	4.50
☐ 49 Fernando Tatis 20.00	9.00
☐ 50 Peter Tucci 10.00	4.50
☐ 51 Javier Vazquez 10.00	4.50
☐ 52 Robin Ventura 30.00	13.50

1999 SkyBox Premium Autographics Blue Ink

	MINT	NRMT
COMMON CARD 25.00	11.00

*BLUE INK STARS: 1.25X TO 3X BASIC AU'S
*BLUE INK ROOKIES: 1X TO 2.5X BASIC AU'S
RANDOM INSERTS IN PACKS
BLUE INK PRINT RUN 50 SERIAL #'d SETS
UNNUMBERED CARDS LISTED IN
ALPH.ORDER

1999 SkyBox Premium Diamond Debuts

JOE McEWING

	MINT	NRMT
COMPLETE SET (15) 100.00	45.00
COMMON CARD (1-15) 5.00	2.20
SEMISTARS 8.00	3.60

STATED ODDS 1:49

☐ 1 Eric Chavez 8.00	3.60
☐ 2 Kyle Farnsworth 10.00	4.50
☐ 3 Ryan Rupe 8.00	3.60
☐ 4 Jeremy Giambi 6.00	2.70
☐ 5 Marlon Anderson 5.00	2.20
☐ 6 J.D. Drew 20.00	9.00
☐ 7 Carlos Febles 6.00	2.70
☐ 8 Joe McEwing 12.00	5.50
☐ 9 Jeff Weaver 8.00	3.60
☐ 10 Alex Gonzalez 6.00	2.70
☐ 11 Chad Allen 6.00	2.70
☐ 12 Michael Barrett 8.00	3.60
☐ 13 Gabe Kapler 10.00	4.50
☐ 14 Carlos Lee 6.00	2.70
☐ 15 Edwards Guzman 8.00	3.60

1999 SkyBox Premium Intimidation Nation

	MINT	NRMT
COMPLETE SET (15) 1200.00	550.00
COMMON CARD (1-15) 40.00	18.00

RANDOM INSERTS IN PACKS
STATED PRINT RUN 99 SERIAL #'d SETS

☐ 1 Cal Ripken 120.00	55.00
☐ 2 Tony Gwynn 80.00	36.00
☐ 3 Nomar Garciaparra 100.00	45.00
☐ 4 Frank Thomas 60.00	27.00
☐ 5 Mike Piazza 100.00	45.00
☐ 6 Mark McGwire 200.00	90.00
☐ 7 Scott Rolen 40.00	18.00
☐ 8 Chipper Jones 80.00	36.00
☐ 9 Greg Maddux 80.00	36.00

		MINT	NRMT
□ 10	Ken Griffey Jr.	150.00	70.00
□ 11	Juan Gonzalez	60.00	27.00
□ 12	Derek Jeter	100.00	45.00
□ 13	J.D. Drew	40.00	18.00
□ 14	Roger Clemens	80.00	36.00
□ 15	Alex Rodriguez	100.00	45.00

1999 SkyBox Premium Live Bats

	MINT	NRMT
COMPLETE SET (15)	30.00	13.50
COMMON CARD (1-15)	.50	.23
UNLISTED STARS	.75	.35
STATED ODDS 1:7		

		MINT	NRMT
□ 1	Juan Gonzalez	2.00	.90
□ 2	Mark McGwire	6.00	2.70
□ 3	Jeff Bagwell	1.25	.55
□ 4	Frank Thomas	2.00	.90
□ 5	Mike Piazza	3.00	1.35
□ 6	Nomar Garciaparra	3.00	1.35
□ 7	Alex Rodriguez	3.00	1.35
□ 8	Scott Rolen	1.25	.55
□ 9	Travis Lee	.50	.23
□ 10	Tony Gwynn	2.50	1.10
□ 11	Derek Jeter	3.00	1.35
□ 12	Ben Grieve	.75	.35
□ 13	Chipper Jones	2.50	1.10
□ 14	Ken Griffey Jr.	5.00	2.20
□ 15	Cal Ripken	4.00	1.80

1999 SkyBox Premium Show Business

	MINT	NRMT
COMPLETE SET (15)	250.00	110.00
COMMON CARD (1-15)	5.00	2.20
STATED ODDS 1:70		

		MINT	NRMT
□ 1	Mark McGwire	40.00	18.00
□ 2	Tony Gwynn	15.00	6.75
□ 3	Nomar Garciaparra	20.00	9.00
□ 4	Juan Gonzalez	12.00	5.50
□ 5	Roger Clemens	15.00	6.75
□ 6	Chipper Jones	15.00	6.75
□ 7	Cal Ripken	20.00	9.00
□ 8	Alex Rodriguez	20.00	9.00
□ 9	Orlando Hernandez	5.00	2.20
□ 10	Greg Maddux	15.00	6.75

		MINT	NRMT
□ 11	Mike Piazza	20.00	9.00
□ 12	Frank Thomas	12.00	5.50
□ 13	Ken Griffey Jr.	30.00	13.50
□ 14	Scott Rolen	8.00	3.60
□ 15	Derek Jeter	20.00	9.00

1999 SkyBox Premium Soul of the Game

	MINT	NRMT
COMPLETE SET (15)	60.00	27.00
COMMON CARD (1-15)	2.50	1.10
STATED ODDS 1:14		

		MINT	NRMT
□ 1	Alex Rodriguez	6.00	2.70
□ 2	Vladimir Guerrero	2.50	1.10
□ 3	Chipper Jones	5.00	2.20
□ 4	Derek Jeter	6.00	2.70
□ 5	Tony Gwynn	5.00	2.20
□ 6	Scott Rolen	2.50	1.10
□ 7	Juan Gonzalez	4.00	1.80
□ 8	Mark McGwire	12.00	5.50
□ 9	Ken Griffey Jr.	10.00	4.50
□ 10	Jeff Bagwell	2.50	1.10
□ 11	Cal Ripken	8.00	3.60
□ 12	Frank Thomas	4.00	1.80
□ 13	Mike Piazza	6.00	2.70
□ 14	Nomar Garciaparra	6.00	2.70
□ 15	Sammy Sosa	6.00	2.70

1999 SkyBox Thunder

	MINT	NRMT
COMPLETE SET (300)	40.00	18.00
COMMON CARD (1-140)	.10	.05
MINOR STARS 1-140	.15	.07
SEMISTARS 1-140	.25	.11
UNLISTED STARS 1-140	.40	.18
CARDS 1-140 FOUR TO FIVE PER PACK		
COMMON CARD (141-240)	.15	.07
MINOR STARS 141-240	.25	.11
SEMISTARS 141-240	.40	.18
UNLISTED STARS 141-240	.60	.25
CARDS 141-240 TWO PER PACK		
COMMON CARD (241-300)	.20	.09
MINOR STARS 241-300	.30	.14
SEMISTARS 241-300	.50	.23
UNLISTED STARS 241-300	.75	.35
CARDS 241-300 ONE PER PACK		

□ 1	John Smoltz	.25	.11
□ 2	Garret Anderson	.15	.07
□ 3	Matt Williams	.40	.18
□ 4	Daryle Ward	.15	.07
□ 5	Andy Ashby	.15	.07
□ 6	Miguel Tejada	.15	.07
□ 7	Dmitri Young	.15	.07
□ 8	Roberto Alomar	.40	.18
□ 9	Kevin Brown	.25	.11
□ 10	Eric Young	.10	.05
□ 11	Odalis Perez	.10	.07
□ 12	Preston Wilson	.10	.07
□ 13	Jeff Abbott	.10	.05
□ 14	Bret Boone	.10	.07
□ 15	Mendy Lopez	.10	.05
□ 16	B.J. Surhoff	.10	.07
□ 17	Steve Woodard	.10	.05
□ 18	Ron Coomer	.10	.05
□ 19	Rondell White	.10	.07
□ 20	Edgardo Alfonzo	.25	.11
□ 21	Kevin Millwood	.25	.11
□ 22	Jose Canseco	.50	.23
□ 23	Blake Stein	.10	.05
□ 24	Quilvio Veras	.10	.05
□ 25	Chuck Knoblauch	.15	.07
□ 26	David Segui	.10	.07
□ 27	Eric Davis	.15	.07
□ 28	Francisco Cordova	.10	.05
□ 29	Randy Winn	.10	.05
□ 30	Will Clark	.40	.18
□ 31	Billy Wagner	.10	.05
□ 32	Kevin Witt	.10	.05
□ 33	Jim Edmonds	.15	.07
□ 34	Todd Stottlemyre	.10	.05
□ 35	Shane Andrews	.10	.05
□ 36	Michael Tucker	.10	.05
□ 37	Sandy Alomar Jr.	.15	.07
□ 38	Neifi Perez	.10	.05
□ 39	Jaret Wright	.15	.07
□ 40	Devon White	.10	.05
□ 41	Edgar Renteria	.15	.07
□ 42	Shane Reynolds	.10	.05
□ 43	Jeff King	.10	.05
□ 44	Darren Dreifort	.10	.05
□ 45	Fernando Vina	.10	.05
□ 46	Marty Cordova	.10	.05
□ 47	Ugueth Urbina	.10	.07
□ 48	Bobby Bonilla	.15	.07
□ 49	Omar Vizquel	.15	.07
□ 50	Tom Gordon	.15	.07
□ 51	Ryan Christenson	.10	.05
□ 52	Aaron Boone	.10	.05
□ 53	Jamie Moyer	.10	.05
□ 54	Brian Giles	.10	.05
□ 55	Kevin Tapani	.10	.05
□ 56	Scott Brosius	.10	.07
□ 57	Ellis Burks	.15	.07
□ 58	Al Leiter	.15	.07
□ 59	Royce Clayton	.10	.05
□ 60	Chris Carpenter	.10	.05
□ 61	Bubba Trammell	.15	.07
□ 62	Tom Glavine	.40	.18
□ 63	Shannon Stewart	.15	.07
□ 64	Todd Zeile	.15	.07
□ 65	J.T. Snow	.15	.07
□ 66	Matt Clement	.10	.05
□ 67	Matt Stairs	.15	.07
□ 68	Ismael Valdes	.15	.07
□ 69	Todd Walker	.15	.07
□ 70	Jose Lima	.15	.07
□ 71	Mike Caruso	.10	.05
□ 72	Brett Tomko	.10	.05
□ 73	Mike Lansing	.10	.05
□ 74	Justin Thompson	.15	.07
□ 75	Damion Easley	.10	.05
□ 76	Derrek Lee	.15	.07
□ 77	Derek Bell	.15	.07
□ 78	Brady Anderson	.15	.07
□ 79	Charles Johnson	.15	.07
□ 80	Rafael Roque	.10	.05
□ 81	Corey Koskie	.15	.07
□ 82	Fernando Seguignol	.15	.07
□ 83	Jay Tessmer	.10	.05
□ 84	Jason Giambi	.15	.07
□ 85	Mike Lieberthal	.15	.07
□ 86	Jose Guillen	.10	.05

❏ 87 Jim Leyritz	.10	.05
❏ 88 Shawn Estes	.10	.05
❏ 89 Ray Lankford	.15	.07
❏ 90 Paul Sorrento	.10	.05
❏ 91 Javy Lopez	.15	.07
❏ 92 John Wetteland	.10	.07
❏ 93 Sean Casey	.40	.18
❏ 94 Chuck Finley	.15	.07
❏ 95 Trot Nixon	.15	.07
❏ 96 Ray Durham	.15	.07
❏ 97 Reggie Sanders	.10	.05
❏ 98 Bartolo Colon	.15	.07
❏ 99 Henry Rodriguez	.15	.07
❏ 100 Rolando Arrojo	.10	.05
❏ 101 Geoff Jenkins	.15	.07
❏ 102 Darryl Kile	.10	.05
❏ 103 Mark Kotsay	.10	.07
❏ 104 Craig Biggio	.40	.18
❏ 105 Omar Daal	.10	.05
❏ 106 Carlos Febles	.15	.07
❏ 107 Eric Karros	.15	.07
❏ 108 Matt Lawton	.10	.05*
❏ 109 Carl Pavano	.10	.05
❏ 110 Brian McRae	.10	.05
❏ 111 Mariano Rivera	.15	.07
❏ 112 Jay Buhner	.15	.07
❏ 113 Doug Glanville	.15	.07
❏ 114 Jason Kendall	.15	.07
❏ 115 Wally Joyner	.15	.07
❏ 116 Jeff Kent	.15	.07
❏ 117 Shane Monahan	.10	.05
❏ 118 Eli Marrero	.10	.05
❏ 119 Bobby Smith	.10	.05
❏ 120 Shawn Green	.40	.18
❏ 121 Kirk Rueter	.10	.05
❏ 122 Tom Goodwin	.10	.05
❏ 123 Andy Benes	.10	.05
❏ 124 Ed Sprague	.10	.05
❏ 125 Mike Mussina	.40	.18
❏ 126 Jose Offerman	.15	.07
❏ 127 Mickey Morandini	.10	.05
❏ 128 Paul Konerko	.15	.07
❏ 129 Denny Neagle	.15	.07
❏ 130 Travis Fryman	.25	.07
❏ 131 John Rocker	.25	.11
❏ 132 Robert Fick	.15	.07
❏ 133 Livan Hernandez	.10	.05
❏ 134 Ken Caminiti	.25	.11
❏ 135 Johnny Damon	.15	.07
❏ 136 Jeff Kubenka	.10	.05
❏ 137 Marquis Grissom	.10	.05
❏ 138 Doug Mientkiewicz	.25	.11
❏ 139 Dustin Hermanson	.10	.05
❏ 140 Carl Everett	.15	.07
❏ 141 Hideo Nomo	.60	.25
❏ 142 Jorge Posada	.25	.11
❏ 143 Rickey Henderson	.75	.35
❏ 144 Robb Nen	.15	.07
❏ 145 Ron Gant	.25	.11
❏ 146 Aramis Ramirez	.40	.18
❏ 147 Trevor Hoffman	.25	.11
❏ 148 Bill Mueller	.15	.07
❏ 149 Edgar Martinez	.25	.11
❏ 150 Fred McGriff	.40	.18
❏ 151 Rusty Greer	.25	.11
❏ 152 Tom Evans	.15	.07
❏ 153 Todd Greene	.15	.07
❏ 154 Jay Bell	.15	.07
❏ 155 Mike Lowell	.15	.07
❏ 156 Orlando Cabrera	.15	.07
❏ 157 Troy O'Leary	.25	.11
❏ 158 Jose Hernandez	.15	.07
❏ 159 Magglio Ordonez	.25	.25
❏ 160 Barry Larkin	.60	.25
❏ 161 David Justice	.25	.11
❏ 162 Derrick Gibson	.25	.11
❏ 163 Luis Castillo	.25	.11
❏ 164 Alex Gonzalez	.25	.11
❏ 165 Scott Elarton	.25	.11
❏ 166 Dermal Brown	.25	.11
❏ 167 Eric Milton	.15	.07
❏ 168 Raul Mondesi	.25	.11
❏ 169 Jeff Cirillo	.25	.11
❏ 170 Benj Sampson	.15	.07
❏ 171 John Olerud	.25	.11
❏ 172 Andy Pettitte	.25	.11
❏ 173 A.J. Hinch	.15	.07
❏ 174 Rico Brogna	.15	.07
❏ 175 Jason Schmidt	.15	.07
❏ 176 Dean Palmer	.25	.11
❏ 177 Matt Morris	.15	.07
❏ 178 Quinton McCracken	.15	.07
❏ 179 Rick Helling	.15	.07
❏ 180 Walt Weiss	.15	.07
❏ 181 Troy Percival	.25	.11
❏ 182 Tony Batista	.25	.11
❏ 183 Brian Jordan	.25	.11
❏ 184 Jerry Hairston Jr.	.25	.11
❏ 185 Bret Saberhagen	.25	.11
❏ 186 Mark Grace	.40	.18
❏ 187 Brian Simmons	.15	.07
❏ 188 Pete Harnisch	.15	.07
❏ 189 Kenny Lofton	.40	.18
❏ 190 Vinny Castilla	.25	.11
❏ 191 Bobby Higginson	.25	.11
❏ 192 Joey Hamilton	.15	.07
❏ 193 Cliff Floyd	.25	.11
❏ 194 Andres Galarraga	.40	.18
❏ 195 Chan Ho Park	.25	.11
❏ 196 Jeromy Burnitz	.25	.11
❏ 197 David Ortiz	.15	.07
❏ 198 Wilton Guerrero	.15	.07
❏ 199 Rey Ordonez	.25	.11
❏ 200 Paul O'Neill	.25	.11
❏ 201 Kenny Rogers	.15	.07
❏ 202 Marlon Anderson	.15	.07
❏ 203 Tony Womack	.25	.11
❏ 204 Robin Ventura	.25	.11
❏ 205 Russ Ortiz	.15	.07
❏ 206 Mike Frank	.15	.07
❏ 207 Fernando Tatis	.60	.25
❏ 208 Miguel Cairo	.15	.07
❏ 209 Ivan Rodriguez	.75	.35
❏ 210 Carlos Delgado	.60	.25
❏ 211 Tim Salmon	.40	.18
❏ 212 Brian Anderson	.15	.07
❏ 213 Ryan Klesko	.25	.11
❏ 214 Scott Erickson	.15	.07
❏ 215 Mike Stanley	.15	.07
❏ 216 Brant Brown	.15	.05
❏ 217 Rod Beck	.25	.11
❏ 218 Guillermo Garcia	.15	.07
❏ 219 David Wells	.25	.11
❏ 220 Dante Bichette	.25	.07
❏ 221 Armando Benitez	.15	.07
❏ 222 Todd Dunwoody	.15	.07
❏ 223 Kelvim Escobar	.15	.07
❏ 224 Richard Hidalgo	.25	.11
❏ 225 Angel Pena	.15	.07
❏ 226 Ronnie Belliard	.25	.11
❏ 227 Brad Radke	.25	.11
❏ 228 Brad Fullmer	.15	.07
❏ 229 Jay Payton	.15	.07
❏ 230 Tino Martinez	.25	.11
❏ 231 Scott Spiezio	.15	.07
❏ 232 Bobby Abreu	.25	.11
❏ 233 John Valentin	.25	.11
❏ 234 Kevin Young	.25	.11
❏ 235 Steve Finley	.25	.11
❏ 236 David Cone	.40	.18
❏ 237 Armando Rios	.15	.07
❏ 238 Russ Davis	.15	.07
❏ 239 Wade Boggs	.60	.25
❏ 240 Aaron Sele	.25	.11
❏ 241 Jose Cruz Jr.	.30	.14
❏ 242 George Lombard	.30	.14
❏ 243 Todd Helton	.75	.35
❏ 244 Andruw Jones	.75	.35
❏ 245 Troy Glaus	.75	.35
❏ 246 Manny Ramirez	1.00	.45
❏ 247 Ben Grieve	.75	.35
❏ 248 Richie Sexson	.50	.23
❏ 249 Juan Encarnacion	.30	.14
❏ 250 Randy Johnson	.75	.35
❏ 251 Gary Sheffield	.30	.14
❏ 252 Rafael Palmeiro	.35	.14
❏ 253 Roy Halladay	.30	.14
❏ 254 Mike Piazza	2.50	1.10
❏ 255 Tony Gwynn	2.00	.90
❏ 256 Juan Gonzalez	1.50	.70
❏ 257 Jeremy Giambi	.30	.14
❏ 258 Ben Davis	.50	.23
❏ 259 Russ Branyan	.30	.14
❏ 260 Pedro Martinez	1.00	.45
❏ 261 Frank Thomas	1.50	.70
❏ 262 Calvin Pickering	.30	.14
❏ 263 Chipper Jones	2.00	.90
❏ 264 Ryan Minor	.30	.14
❏ 265 Roger Clemens	2.00	.90
❏ 266 Sammy Sosa	2.50	1.10
❏ 267 Mo Vaughn	.75	.35
❏ 268 Carlos Beltran	.75	.35
❏ 269 Jim Thome	.75	.35
❏ 270 Mark McGwire	5.00	2.20
❏ 271 Travis Lee	.50	.23
❏ 272 Darin Erstad	.50	.23
❏ 273 Derek Jeter	2.50	1.10
❏ 274 Greg Maddux	2.00	.90
❏ 275 Ricky Ledee	.30	.14
❏ 276 Alex Rodriguez	2.50	1.10
❏ 277 Vladimir Guerrero	1.00	.45
❏ 278 Greg Vaughn	.30	.14
❏ 279 Scott Rolen	1.00	.45
❏ 280 Carlos Guillen	.20	.09
❏ 281 Jeff Bagwell	1.00	.45
❏ 282 Bruce Chen	.30	.14
❏ 283 Tony Clark	.30	.14
❏ 284 Albert Belle	.75	.35
❏ 285 Cal Ripken	3.00	1.35
❏ 286 Barry Bonds	1.00	.45
❏ 287 Curt Schilling	.50	.23
❏ 288 Eric Chavez	.50	.23
❏ 289 Larry Walker	.75	.35
❏ 290 Orlando Hernandez	.75	.35
❏ 291 Moises Alou	.30	.14
❏ 292 Ken Griffey Jr.	4.00	1.80
❏ 293 Kerry Wood	.75	.35
❏ 294 Nomar Garciaparra	2.50	1.10
❏ 295 Gabe Kapler	.75	.35
❏ 296 Bernie Williams	.75	.35
❏ 297 Matt Anderson	.20	.09
❏ 298 Adrian Beltre	.75	.35
❏ 299 J.D. Drew	1.25	.55
❏ 300 Ryan Bradley	.30	.14
❏ S247 Ben Grieve Sample	2.00	.90

1999 SkyBox Thunder Rant

	MINT	NRMT
COMPLETE SET (300)	300.00	135.00
COMMON CARD (1-300)	.50	.23

*RANT 1-140: 4X TO 10X BASIC 1-140
*RANT 141-240: 2.5X TO 6X BASIC 141-240
*RANT 241-300: 2X TO 5X BASIC 241-300
STATED ODDS 1:2 RETAIL

1999 SkyBox Thunder Rave

	MINT	NRMT
COMMON CARD (1-300)	6.00	2.70

*RAVE 1-140: 25X TO 60X BASIC 1-140
*RAVE 141-240: 15X TO 40X BASIC 141-240
*RAVE 241-300: 12.5X TO 30X BASIC 241-300
RANDOM INSERTS IN HOBBY PACKS
STATED PRINT RUN 150 SERIAL #'d SETS

1999 SkyBox Thunder Super Rave

	MINT	NRMT
COMMON CARD (1-300)	25.00	11.00

*SUP.RAVE 1-140: 100X TO 250X BASIC 1-140
*S.RAVE 141-240: 60X TO 150X BASIC 141-240
*S.RAVE 241-300: 50X TO 125X BASIC 241-300
RANDOM INSERTS IN HOBBY PACKS
STATED PRINT RUN 25 SERIAL #'d SETS

1999 SkyBox Thunder Dial 1

	MINT	NRMT
COMPLETE SET (10)	500.00	220.00
COMMON CARD (D1-D10)	15.00	6.75

STATED ODDS 1:300

		MINT	NRMT
❑ D1	Nomar Garciaparra	60.00	27.00
❑ D2	Juan Gonzalez	40.00	18.00
❑ D3	Ken Griffey Jr.	100.00	45.00
❑ D4	Chipper Jones	50.00	22.00
❑ D5	Mark McGwire	120.00	55.00
❑ D6	Mike Piazza	60.00	27.00
❑ D7	Manny Ramirez	25.00	11.00
❑ D8	Alex Rodriguez	60.00	27.00
❑ D9	Sammy Sosa	60.00	27.00
❑ D10	Mo Vaughn	15.00	6.75

1999 SkyBox Thunder Hip-No-Tized

	MINT	NRMT
COMPLETE SET (15)	150.00	70.00
COMMON CARD (H1-H15)	4.00	1.80

STATED ODDS 1:36

		MINT	NRMT
❑ H1	J.D. Drew	5.00	2.20
❑ H2	Nomar Garciaparra	12.00	5.50
❑ H3	Juan Gonzalez	8.00	3.60
❑ H4	Ken Griffey Jr.	20.00	9.00
❑ H5	Derek Jeter	12.00	5.50
❑ H6	Randy Johnson	4.00	1.80
❑ H7	Chipper Jones	10.00	4.50
❑ H8	Mark McGwire	25.00	11.00
❑ H9	Mike Piazza	12.00	5.50

		MINT	NRMT
❑ H10	Cal Ripken	15.00	6.75
❑ H11	Alex Rodriguez	12.00	5.50
❑ H12	Sammy Sosa	12.00	5.50
❑ H13	Frank Thomas	8.00	3.60
❑ H14	Jim Thome	4.00	1.80
❑ H15	Kerry Wood	4.00	1.80

1999 SkyBox Thunder In Depth

		MINT	NRMT
COMPLETE SET (10)		60.00	27.00
COMMON CARD (ID1-ID10)		2.50	1.10

STATED ODDS 1:24

		MINT	NRMT
❑ ID1	Albert Belle	2.50	1.10
❑ ID2	Barry Bonds	3.00	1.35
❑ ID3	Roger Clemens	6.00	2.70
❑ ID4	Juan Gonzalez	5.00	2.20
❑ ID5	Ken Griffey Jr.	12.00	5.50
❑ ID6	Mark McGwire	15.00	6.75
❑ ID7	Mike Piazza	8.00	3.60
❑ ID8	Sammy Sosa	8.00	3.60
❑ ID9	Mo Vaughn	2.50	1.10
❑ ID10	Kerry Wood	2.50	1.10

1999 SkyBox Thunder Turbo-Charged

	MINT	NRMT
COMPLETE SET (10)	120.00	55.00
COMMON CARD (TC1-TC10)	4.00	1.80

STATED ODDS 1:72

		MINT	NRMT
❑ TC1	Jose Canseco	6.00	2.70
❑ TC2	Juan Gonzalez	10.00	4.50
❑ TC3	Ken Griffey Jr.	25.00	11.00
❑ TC4	Vladimir Guerrero	6.00	2.70
❑ TC5	Mark McGwire	30.00	13.50
❑ TC6	Mike Piazza	15.00	6.75
❑ TC7	Manny Ramirez	6.00	2.70
❑ TC8	Alex Rodriguez	15.00	6.75
❑ TC9	Sammy Sosa	15.00	6.75
❑ TC10	Mo Vaughn	4.00	1.80

1999 SkyBox Thunder Unleashed

	MINT	NRMT
COMPLETE SET (15)	20.00	9.00
COMMON CARD (U1-U15)	1.00	.45
SEMISTARS	1.50	.70
UNLISTED STARS	2.50	1.10

STATED ODDS 1:6

		MINT	NRMT
❑ U1	Carlos Beltran	3.00	1.35
❑ U2	Adrian Beltre	2.50	1.10
❑ U3	Eric Chavez	1.50	.70
❑ U4	J.D. Drew	4.00	1.80
❑ U5	Juan Encarnacion	1.00	.45
❑ U6	Jeremy Giambi	1.00	.45
❑ U7	Troy Glaus	2.50	1.10
❑ U8	Ben Grieve	2.50	1.10
❑ U9	Todd Helton	2.50	1.10
❑ U10	Orlando Hernandez	2.50	1.10
❑ U11	Gabe Kapler	2.50	1.10
❑ U12	Travis Lee	1.50	.70
❑ U13	Calvin Pickering	1.00	.45
❑ U14	Richie Sexson	1.50	.70
❑ U15	Kerry Wood	2.50	1.10

1999 SkyBox Thunder www.batterz.com

	MINT	NRMT
COMPLETE SET (10)	60.00	27.00
COMMON CARD (WB1-WB10)	2.00	.90

STATED ODDS 1:18

		MINT	NRMT
❑ WB1	J.D. Drew	2.50	1.10
❑ WB2	Nomar Garciaparra	6.00	2.70
❑ WB3	Ken Griffey Jr.	10.00	4.50

	MINT	NRMT
❏ WB4 Tony Gwynn	5.00	2.20
❏ WB5 Derek Jeter	6.00	2.70
❏ WB6 Mark McGwire	12.00	5.50
❏ WB7 Alex Rodriguez	6.00	2.70
❏ WB8 Scott Rolen	2.50	1.10
❏ WB9 Sammy Sosa	6.00	2.70
❏ WB10 Bernie Williams	2.00	.90

1993 SP

Bill Clark

	MINT	NRMT
COMPLETE SET (290)	125.00	55.00
COMMON CARD (1-270)	.25	.11
FOIL PROSPECTS (271-290)	.50	.23
MINOR STARS	.50	.23
SEMISTARS	1.00	.45
UNLISTED STARS	1.50	.70
FOIL CARDS ARE CONDITION SENSITIVE		

		MINT	NRMT
❏ 1	Roberto Alomar AS	1.50	.70
❏ 2	Wade Boggs AS	1.50	.70
❏ 3	Joe Carter AS	.25	.11
❏ 4	Ken Griffey Jr. AS	8.00	3.60
❏ 5	Mark Langston AS	.25	.11
❏ 6	John Olerud AS	1.00	.45
❏ 7	Kirby Puckett AS	2.50	1.10
❏ 8	Cal Ripken Jr. AS	6.00	2.70
❏ 9	Ivan Rodriguez AS	.50	.90
❏ 10	Barry Bonds AS	2.00	.90
❏ 11	Darren Daulton AS	.50	.23
❏ 12	Marquis Grissom AS	.50	.23
❏ 13	David Justice AS	1.50	.70
❏ 14	John Kruk AS	.50	.23
❏ 15	Barry Larkin AS	1.50	.70
❏ 16	Terry Mulholland AS	.25	.11
❏ 17	Ryne Sandberg AS	2.00	.90
❏ 18	Gary Sheffield AS	.50	.23
❏ 19	Chad Curtis	.25	.11
❏ 20	Chili Davis	.50	.23
❏ 21	Gary DiSarcina	.25	.11
❏ 22	Damion Easley	.50	.23
❏ 23	Chuck Finley	.25	.11
❏ 24	Luis Polonia	.25	.11
❏ 25	Tim Salmon	1.50	.70
❏ 26	J.T. Snow	2.00	.90
❏ 27	Russ Springer	.25	.11
❏ 28	Jeff Bagwell	2.00	.90
❏ 29	Craig Biggio	1.50	.70
❏ 30	Ken Caminiti	1.00	.45
❏ 31	Andujar Cedeno	.25	.11
❏ 32	Doug Drabek	.25	.11
❏ 33	Steve Finley	.50	.23
❏ 34	Luis Gonzalez	.50	.23
❏ 35	Pete Harnisch	.25	.11
❏ 36	Darryl Kile	.25	.11
❏ 37	Mike Bordick	.25	.11
❏ 38	Dennis Eckersley	.50	.23
❏ 39	Brent Gates	.25	.11
❏ 40	Rickey Henderson	2.00	.90
❏ 41	Mark McGwire	8.00	3.60
❏ 42	Craig Paquette	.25	.11
❏ 43	Ruben Sierra	.25	.11
❏ 44	Terry Steinbach	.25	.11
❏ 45	Todd Van Poppel	.25	.11
❏ 46	Pat Borders	.25	.11
❏ 47	Tony Fernandez	.50	.23
❏ 48	Juan Guzman	.25	.11
❏ 49	Pat Hentgen	1.00	.45

		MINT	NRMT
❏ 50	Paul Molitor	1.50	.70
❏ 51	Jack Morris	.50	.23
❏ 52	Ed Sprague	.25	.11
❏ 53	Duane Ward	.25	.11
❏ 54	Devon White	.25	.11
❏ 55	Steve Avery	.25	.11
❏ 56	Jeff Blauser	.25	.11
❏ 57	Ron Gant	.50	.23
❏ 58	Tom Glavine	1.00	.45
❏ 59	Greg Maddux	4.00	1.80
❏ 60	Fred McGriff	1.00	.45
❏ 61	Terry Pendleton	.25	.11
❏ 62	Deion Sanders	1.00	.45
❏ 63	John Smoltz	1.00	.45
❏ 64	Cal Eldred	.25	.11
❏ 65	Darryl Hamilton	.25	.11
❏ 66	John Jaha	.25	.11
❏ 67	Pat Listach	.25	.11
❏ 68	Jaime Navarro	.25	.11
❏ 69	Kevin Reimer	.25	.11
❏ 70	B.J. Surhoff	.50	.23
❏ 71	Greg Vaughn	.50	.23
❏ 72	Robin Yount	1.00	.45
❏ 73	Rene Arocha	.25	.11
❏ 74	Bernard Gilkey	.25	.11
❏ 75	Gregg Jefferies	.25	.11
❏ 76	Ray Lankford	1.00	.45
❏ 77	Tom Pagnozzi	.25	.11
❏ 78	Lee Smith	.50	.23
❏ 79	Ozzie Smith	2.00	.90
❏ 80	Bob Tewksbury	.25	.11
❏ 81	Mark Whiten	.25	.11
❏ 82	Steve Buechele	.25	.11
❏ 83	Mark Grace	1.00	.45
❏ 84	Jose Guzman	.25	.11
❏ 85	Derrick May	.25	.11
❏ 86	Mike Morgan	.25	.11
❏ 87	Randy Myers	.50	.23
❏ 88	Kevin Roberson	.25	.11
❏ 89	Sammy Sosa	5.00	2.20
❏ 90	Rick Wilkins	.25	.11
❏ 91	Brett Butler	.50	.23
❏ 92	Eric Davis	.50	.23
❏ 93	Orel Hershiser	.50	.23
❏ 94	Eric Karros	1.00	.45
❏ 95	Ramon Martinez	.50	.23
❏ 96	Raul Mondesi	1.50	.70
❏ 97	Jose Offerman	.50	.23
❏ 98	Mike Piazza	8.00	3.60
❏ 99	Darryl Strawberry	.50	.23
❏ 100	Moises Alou	.50	.23
❏ 101	Wil Cordero	.25	.11
❏ 102	Delino DeShields	.50	.23
❏ 103	Darrin Fletcher	.25	.11
❏ 104	Ken Hill	.25	.11
❏ 105	Mike Lansing	.50	.23
❏ 106	Dennis Martinez	.50	.23
❏ 107	Larry Walker	1.50	.70
❏ 108	John Wetteland	.50	.23
❏ 109	Rod Beck	.50	.23
❏ 110	John Burkett	.25	.11
❏ 111	Will Clark	1.50	.70
❏ 112	Royce Clayton	.25	.11
❏ 113	Darren Lewis	.25	.11
❏ 114	Willie McGee	.50	.23
❏ 115	Bill Swift	.25	.11
❏ 116	Robby Thompson	.25	.11
❏ 117	Matt Williams	1.00	.45
❏ 118	Sandy Alomar Jr.	.50	.23
❏ 119	Carlos Baerga	.25	.11
❏ 120	Albert Belle	1.50	.70
❏ 121	Reggie Jefferson	.50	.23
❏ 122	Wayne Kirby	.25	.11
❏ 123	Kenny Lofton	1.50	.70
❏ 124	Carlos Martinez	.25	.11
❏ 125	Charles Nagy	.50	.23
❏ 126	Paul Sorrento	.25	.11
❏ 127	Rich Amaral	.25	.11
❏ 128	Jay Buhner	1.00	.45
❏ 129	Norm Charlton	.25	.11
❏ 130	Dave Fleming	.25	.11
❏ 131	Erik Hanson	.25	.11
❏ 132	Randy Johnson	1.50	.70
❏ 133	Edgar Martinez	1.00	.45
❏ 134	Tino Martinez	1.50	.70
❏ 135	Omar Vizquel	.50	.23

		MINT	NRMT
❏ 136	Bret Barberie	.25	.11
❏ 137	Chuck Carr	.25	.11
❏ 138	Jeff Conine	.25	.11
❏ 139	Orestes Destrade	.25	.11
❏ 140	Chris Hammond	.25	.11
❏ 141	Bryan Harvey	.25	.11
❏ 142	Benito Santiago	.25	.11
❏ 143	Walt Weiss	.25	.11
❏ 144	Darrell Whitmore	.25	.11
❏ 145	Tim Bogar	.25	.11
❏ 146	Bobby Bonilla	.50	.23
❏ 147	Jeromy Burnitz	.50	.23
❏ 148	Vince Coleman	.25	.11
❏ 149	Dwight Gooden	.50	.23
❏ 150	Todd Hundley	1.00	.45
❏ 151	Howard Johnson	.25	.11
❏ 152	Eddie Murray	1.50	.70
❏ 153	Bret Saberhagen	.50	.23
❏ 154	Brady Anderson	.50	.23
❏ 155	Mike Devereaux	.25	.11
❏ 156	Jeffrey Hammonds	.50	.23
❏ 157	Chris Hoiles	.25	.11
❏ 158	Ben McDonald	.25	.11
❏ 159	Mark McLemore	.25	.11
❏ 160	Mike Mussina	1.50	.70
❏ 161	Gregg Olson	.25	.11
❏ 162	David Segui	.25	.11
❏ 163	Derek Bell	.50	.23
❏ 164	Andy Benes	.50	.23
❏ 165	Archi Cianfrocco	.25	.11
❏ 166	Ricky Gutierrez	.25	.11
❏ 167	Tony Gwynn	4.00	1.80
❏ 168	Gene Harris	.25	.11
❏ 169	Trevor Hoffman	1.50	.70
❏ 170	Ray McDavid	.25	.11
❏ 171	Phil Plantier	.25	.11
❏ 172	Mariano Duncan	.25	.11
❏ 173	Len Dykstra	.50	.23
❏ 174	Tommy Greene	.25	.11
❏ 175	Dave Hollins	.25	.11
❏ 176	Pete Incaviglia	.25	.11
❏ 177	Mickey Morandini	.25	.11
❏ 178	Curt Schilling	.50	.23
❏ 179	Kevin Stocker	.25	.11
❏ 180	Mitch Williams	.25	.11
❏ 181	Stan Belinda	.25	.11
❏ 182	Jay Bell	.50	.23
❏ 183	Steve Cooke	.25	.11
❏ 184	Carlos Garcia	.25	.11
❏ 185	Jeff King	.25	.11
❏ 186	Orlando Merced	.25	.11
❏ 187	Don Slaught	.25	.11
❏ 188	Andy Van Slyke	.50	.23
❏ 189	Kevin Young	.50	.23
❏ 190	Kevin Brown	1.00	.45
❏ 191	Jose Canseco	2.00	.90
❏ 192	Julio Franco	.25	.11
❏ 193	Benji Gil	.25	.11
❏ 194	Juan Gonzalez	3.00	1.35
❏ 195	Tom Henke	.25	.11
❏ 196	Rafael Palmeiro	1.50	.70
❏ 197	Dean Palmer	.50	.23
❏ 198	Nolan Ryan	6.00	2.70
❏ 199	Roger Clemens	4.00	1.80
❏ 200	Scott Cooper	.25	.11
❏ 201	Andre Dawson	1.00	.45
❏ 202	Mike Greenwell	.25	.11
❏ 203	Carlos Quintana	.25	.11
❏ 204	Jeff Russell	.25	.11
❏ 205	Aaron Sele	1.50	.70
❏ 206	Mo Vaughn	1.50	.70
❏ 207	Frank Viola	.25	.11
❏ 208	Rob Dibble	.25	.11
❏ 209	Roberto Kelly	.25	.11
❏ 210	Kevin Mitchell	.50	.23
❏ 211	Hal Morris	.25	.11
❏ 212	Joe Oliver	.25	.11
❏ 213	Jose Rijo	.25	.11
❏ 214	Bip Roberts	.25	.11
❏ 215	Chris Sabo	.25	.11
❏ 216	Reggie Sanders	.50	.23
❏ 217	Dante Bichette	.50	.23
❏ 218	Jerald Clark	.25	.11
❏ 219	Alex Cole	.25	.11
❏ 220	Andres Galarraga	1.50	.70
❏ 221	Joe Girardi	.50	.23

❏ 222 Charlie Hayes	.25	.11
❏ 223 Roberto Mejia	.25	.11
❏ 224 Armando Reynoso	.25	.11
❏ 225 Eric Young	1.50	.70
❏ 226 Kevin Appier	.50	.23
❏ 227 George Brett	3.00	1.35
❏ 228 David Cone	1.00	.45
❏ 229 Phil Hiatt	.25	.11
❏ 230 Felix Jose	.25	.11
❏ 231 Wally Joyner	.50	.23
❏ 232 Mike Macfarlane	.25	.11
❏ 233 Brian McRae	.25	.11
❏ 234 Jeff Montgomery	.50	.23
❏ 235 Rob Deer	.25	.11
❏ 236 Cecil Fielder	.50	.23
❏ 237 Travis Fryman	.50	.23
❏ 238 Mike Henneman	.25	.11
❏ 239 Tony Phillips	.25	.11
❏ 240 Mickey Tettleton	.25	.11
❏ 241 Alan Trammell	1.00	.45
❏ 242 David Wells	.50	.23
❏ 243 Lou Whitaker	.50	.23
❏ 244 Rick Aguilera	.25	.11
❏ 245 Scott Erickson	.25	.11
❏ 246 Brian Harper	.25	.11
❏ 247 Kent Hrbek	.50	.23
❏ 248 Chuck Knoblauch	1.50	.70
❏ 249 Shane Mack	.50	.23
❏ 250 David McCarty	.25	.11
❏ 251 Pedro Munoz	.25	.11
❏ 252 Dave Winfield	1.00	.45
❏ 253 Alex Fernandez	.25	.11
❏ 254 Ozzie Guillen	.25	.11
❏ 255 Bo Jackson	.50	.23
❏ 256 Lance Johnson	.25	.11
❏ 257 Ron Karkovice	.25	.11
❏ 258 Jack McDowell	.25	.11
❏ 259 Tim Raines	.50	.23
❏ 260 Frank Thomas	3.00	1.35
❏ 261 Robin Ventura	.50	.23
❏ 262 Jim Abbott	.50	.23
❏ 263 Steve Farr	.25	.11
❏ 264 Jimmy Key	.50	.23
❏ 265 Don Mattingly	3.00	1.35
❏ 266 Paul O'Neill	.50	.23
❏ 267 Mike Stanley	.25	.11
❏ 268 Danny Tartabull	.25	.11
❏ 269 Bob Wickman	.25	.11
❏ 270 Bernie Williams	1.50	.70
❏ 271 Jason Bere FOIL	.50	.23
❏ 272 Roger Cedeno FOIL	8.00	3.60
❏ 273 Johnny Damon FOIL	5.00	2.20
❏ 274 Russ Davis FOIL	.50	.23
❏ 275 Carlos Delgado FOIL	3.00	1.35
❏ 276 Carl Everett FOIL	1.00	.45
❏ 277 Cliff Floyd FOIL	.50	.23
❏ 278 Alex Gonzalez FOIL	.50	.23
❏ 279 Derek Jeter FOIL	100.00	45.00
❏ 280 Chipper Jones FOIL	8.00	3.60
❏ 281 Javier Lopez FOIL	1.50	.70
❏ 282 Chad Mottola FOIL	.50	.23
❏ 283 Marc Newfield FOIL	.50	.23
❏ 284 Eduardo Perez FOIL	.50	.23
❏ 285 Manny Ramirez FOIL	8.00	3.60
❏ 286 Todd Steverson FOIL	.50	.23
❏ 287 Michael Tucker FOIL	1.50	.70
❏ 288 Allen Watson FOIL	.50	.23
❏ 289 Rondell White FOIL	1.00	.45
❏ 290 Dmitri Young FOIL	2.00	.90

1993 SP Platinum Power

	MINT	NRMT
COMPLETE SET (20)	100.00	45.00
COMMON CARD (PP1-PP20)	1.25	.55
STATED ODDS 1:9		

❏ PP1 Albert Belle	5.00	2.20
❏ PP2 Barry Bonds	5.00	2.20
❏ PP3 Joe Carter	2.00	.90
❏ PP4 Will Clark	5.00	2.20
❏ PP5 Darren Daulton	2.00	.90
❏ PP6 Cecil Fielder	2.00	.90
❏ PP7 Ron Gant	2.00	.90

❏ PP8 Juan Gonzalez	12.00	5.50
❏ PP9 Ken Griffey Jr.	25.00	11.00
❏ PP10 Dave Hollins	1.25	.55
❏ PP11 David Justice	5.00	2.20
❏ PP12 Fred McGriff	3.00	1.35
❏ PP13 Mark McGwire	25.00	11.00
❏ PP14 Dean Palmer	2.00	.90
❏ PP15 Mike Piazza	20.00	9.00
❏ PP16 Tim Salmon	5.00	2.20
❏ PP17 Ryne Sandberg	5.00	2.20
❏ PP18 Gary Sheffield	5.00	2.20
❏ PP19 Frank Thomas	12.00	5.50
❏ PP20 Matt Williams	3.00	1.35

1994 SP Previews

	MINT	NRMT
COMPLETE SET (15)	180.00	80.00
COMPLETE CENTRAL (5)	80.00	36.00
COMPLETE EAST (5)	40.00	18.00
COMMON CARD	1.50	.70
COMPLETE WEST (5)	60.00	27.00
STATED ODDS 1:35 REG'L SER.2 UD HOBBY		

❏ CR1 Jeff Bagwell	6.00	2.70
❏ CR2 Michael Jordan	40.00	18.00
❏ CR3 Kirby Puckett	10.00	4.50
❏ CR4 Manny Ramirez	6.00	2.70
❏ CR5 Frank Thomas	15.00	6.75
❏ ER1 Roberto Alomar	6.00	2.70
❏ ER2 Cliff Floyd	1.50	.70
❏ ER3 Javier Lopez	4.00	1.80
❏ ER4 Don Mattingly	10.00	4.50
❏ ER5 Cal Ripken	25.00	11.00
❏ WR1 Barry Bonds	6.00	2.70
❏ WR2 Juan Gonzalez	15.00	6.75
❏ WR3 Ken Griffey Jr.	30.00	13.50
❏ WR4 Mike Piazza	20.00	9.00
❏ WR5 Tim Salmon	6.00	2.70

1994 SP

	MINT	NRMT
COMPLETE SET (200)	110.00	50.00
COMMON FOIL (1-20)	.50	.23
COMMON CARD (21-200)	.20	.09
MINOR STARS	.40	.18
UNLISTED STARS	.75	.35
FOIL CARDS CONDITION SENSITIVE		

❏ 1 Mike Bell FOIL	.50	.23

❏ 2 D.J. Boston FOIL	.50	.23
❏ 3 Johnny Damon FOIL	.75	.35
❏ 4 Brad Fullmer FOIL	2.00	.90
❏ 5 Joey Hamilton FOIL	.75	.35
❏ 6 Todd Hollandsworth FOIL	.60	.25
❏ 7 Brian L. Hunter FOIL	.60	.25
❏ 8 LaTroy Hawkins FOIL	.60	.25
❏ 9 Brooks Kieschnick FOIL	.50	.23
❏ 10 Derrek Lee FOIL	1.25	.55
❏ 11 Trot Nixon FOIL	4.00	1.80
❏ 12 Alex Ochoa FOIL	.50	.23
❏ 13 Chan Ho Park FOIL	2.50	1.10
❏ 14 Kirk Presley FOIL	.50	.23
❏ 15 Alex Rodriguez FOIL	85.00	38.00
❏ 16 Jose Silva FOIL	.50	.23
❏ 17 Terrell Wade FOIL	.50	.23
❏ 18 Billy Wagner FOIL	2.00	.90
❏ 19 Glenn Williams FOIL	.75	.35
❏ 20 Preston Wilson FOIL	2.00	.90
❏ 21 Brian Anderson	1.00	.45
❏ 22 Chad Curtis	.20	.09
❏ 23 Chili Davis	.40	.18
❏ 24 Bo Jackson	.40	.18
❏ 25 Mark Langston	.20	.09
❏ 26 Tim Salmon	.75	.35
❏ 27 Jeff Bagwell	1.00	.45
❏ 28 Craig Biggio	.75	.35
❏ 29 Ken Caminiti	.20	.09
❏ 30 Doug Drabek	.20	.09
❏ 31 John Hudek	.20	.09
❏ 32 Greg Swindell	.20	.09
❏ 33 Brent Gates	.20	.09
❏ 34 Rickey Henderson	1.00	.45
❏ 35 Steve Karsay	.20	.09
❏ 36 Mark McGwire	4.00	1.80
❏ 37 Ruben Sierra	.40	.18
❏ 38 Terry Steinbach	.20	.09
❏ 39 Roberto Alomar	.75	.35
❏ 40 Joe Carter	.40	.18
❏ 41 Carlos Delgado	.75	.35
❏ 42 Alex Gonzalez	.20	.09
❏ 43 Juan Guzman	.20	.09
❏ 44 Paul Molitor	.75	.35
❏ 45 John Olerud	.75	.35
❏ 46 Devon White	.20	.09
❏ 47 Steve Avery	.20	.09
❏ 48 Jeff Blauser	.20	.09
❏ 49 Tom Glavine	.75	.35
❏ 50 David Justice	.75	.35
❏ 51 Roberto Kelly	.20	.09
❏ 52 Ryan Klesko	.40	.18
❏ 53 Javier Lopez	.60	.25
❏ 54 Greg Maddux	2.00	.90
❏ 55 Fred McGriff	.60	.25
❏ 56 Ricky Bones	.20	.09
❏ 57 Cal Eldred	.20	.09
❏ 58 Brian Harper	.20	.09
❏ 59 Pat Listach	.20	.09
❏ 60 B.J. Surhoff	.20	.09
❏ 61 Greg Vaughn	.40	.18
❏ 62 Bernard Gilkey	.40	.18
❏ 63 Gregg Jefferies	.40	.18
❏ 64 Ray Lankford	.40	.18
❏ 65 Ozzie Smith	1.00	.45
❏ 66 Bob Tewksbury	.20	.09
❏ 67 Mark Whiten	.20	.09
❏ 68 Todd Zeile	.20	.09
❏ 69 Mark Grace	.60	.25

❏ 70	Randy Myers	.20	.09
❏ 71	Ryne Sandberg	1.00	.45
❏ 72	Sammy Sosa	2.50	1.10
❏ 73	Steve Trachsel	.20	.09
❏ 74	Rick Wilkins	.20	.09
❏ 75	Brett Butler	.40	.18
❏ 76	Delino DeShields	.20	.09
❏ 77	Orel Hershiser	.40	.18
❏ 78	Eric Karros	.40	.18
❏ 79	Raul Mondesi	.75	.35
❏ 80	Mike Piazza	2.50	1.10
❏ 81	Tim Wallach	.20	.09
❏ 82	Moises Alou	.40	.18
❏ 83	Cliff Floyd	.40	.18
❏ 84	Marquis Grissom	.40	.18
❏ 85	Pedro Martinez	1.00	.45
❏ 86	Larry Walker	.75	.35
❏ 87	John Wetteland	.40	.18
❏ 88	Rondell White	.40	.18
❏ 89	Rod Beck	.20	.09
❏ 90	Barry Bonds	1.00	.45
❏ 91	John Burkett	.20	.09
❏ 92	Royce Clayton	.20	.09
❏ 93	Billy Swift	.20	.09
❏ 94	Robby Thompson	.20	.09
❏ 95	Matt Williams	.60	.25
❏ 96	Carlos Baerga	.40	.18
❏ 97	Albert Belle	.75	.35
❏ 98	Kenny Lofton	.75	.35
❏ 99	Dennis Martinez	.40	.18
❏ 100	Eddie Murray	.75	.35
❏ 101	Manny Ramirez	1.50	.70
❏ 102	Eric Anthony	.20	.09
❏ 103	Chris Bosio	.20	.09
❏ 104	Jay Buhner	.40	.18
❏ 105	Ken Griffey Jr.	4.00	1.80
❏ 106	Randy Johnson	.75	.35
❏ 107	Edgar Martinez	.40	.18
❏ 108	Chuck Carr	.20	.09
❏ 109	Jeff Conine	.40	.18
❏ 110	Carl Everett	.40	.18
❏ 111	Chris Hammond	.20	.09
❏ 112	Bryan Harvey	.20	.09
❏ 113	Charles Johnson	.40	.18
❏ 114	Gary Sheffield	.75	.35
❏ 115	Bobby Bonilla	.40	.18
❏ 116	Dwight Gooden	.40	.18
❏ 117	Todd Hundley	.40	.18
❏ 118	Bobby Jones	.20	.09
❏ 119	Jeff Kent	.40	.18
❏ 120	Bret Saberhagen	.40	.18
❏ 121	Jeffrey Hammonds	.40	.18
❏ 122	Chris Hoiles	.20	.09
❏ 123	Ben McDonald	.20	.09
❏ 124	Mike Mussina	.75	.35
❏ 125	Rafael Palmeiro	.75	.35
❏ 126	Cal Ripken Jr.	3.00	1.35
❏ 127	Lee Smith	.40	.18
❏ 128	Derek Bell	.40	.18
❏ 129	Andy Benes	.40	.18
❏ 130	Tony Gwynn	2.00	.90
❏ 131	Trevor Hoffman	.40	.18
❏ 132	Phil Plantier	.20	.09
❏ 133	Bip Roberts	.20	.09
❏ 134	Darren Daulton	.40	.18
❏ 135	Lenny Dykstra	.40	.18
❏ 136	Dave Hollins	.20	.09
❏ 137	Danny Jackson	.20	.09
❏ 138	John Kruk	.40	.18
❏ 139	Kevin Stocker	.20	.09
❏ 140	Jay Bell	.40	.18
❏ 141	Carlos Garcia	.20	.09
❏ 142	Jeff King	.20	.09
❏ 143	Orlando Merced	.20	.09
❏ 144	Andy Van Slyke	.40	.18
❏ 145	Rick White	.20	.09
❏ 146	Jose Canseco	1.00	.45
❏ 147	Will Clark	.75	.35
❏ 148	Juan Gonzalez	1.50	.70
❏ 149	Rick Helling	.40	.18
❏ 150	Dean Palmer	.20	.09
❏ 151	Ivan Rodriguez	1.00	.45
❏ 152	Roger Clemens	2.00	.90
❏ 153	Scott Cooper	.20	.09
❏ 154	Andre Dawson	.60	.25
❏ 155	Mike Greenwell	.20	.09

❏ 156	Aaron Sele	.40	.18
❏ 157	Mo Vaughn	.75	.35
❏ 158	Bret Boone	.40	.18
❏ 159	Barry Larkin	.75	.35
❏ 160	Kevin Mitchell	.20	.09
❏ 161	Jose Rijo	.20	.09
❏ 162	Deion Sanders	.40	.18
❏ 163	Reggie Sanders	.40	.18
❏ 164	Dante Bichette	.40	.18
❏ 165	Ellis Burks	.40	.18
❏ 166	Andres Galarraga	.75	.35
❏ 167	Charlie Hayes	.20	.09
❏ 168	David Nied	.20	.09
❏ 169	Walt Weiss	.20	.09
❏ 170	Kevin Appier	.40	.18
❏ 171	David Cone	.60	.25
❏ 172	Jeff Granger	.20	.09
❏ 173	Felix Jose	.20	.09
❏ 174	Wally Joyner	.40	.18
❏ 175	Brian McRae	.20	.09
❏ 176	Cecil Fielder	.40	.18
❏ 177	Travis Fryman	.40	.18
❏ 178	Mike Henneman	.20	.09
❏ 179	Tony Phillips	.20	.09
❏ 180	Mickey Tettleton	.20	.09
❏ 181	Alan Trammell	.60	.25
❏ 182	Rick Aguilera	.20	.09
❏ 183	Rich Becker	.20	.09
❏ 184	Scott Erickson	.40	.18
❏ 185	Chuck Knoblauch	.75	.35
❏ 186	Kirby Puckett	1.25	.55
❏ 187	Dave Winfield	.75	.35
❏ 188	Wilson Alvarez	.40	.18
❏ 189	Jason Bere	.20	.09
❏ 190	Alex Fernandez	.20	.09
❏ 191	Julio Franco	.20	.09
❏ 192	Jack McDowell	.20	.09
❏ 193	Frank Thomas	1.50	.70
❏ 194	Robin Ventura	.40	.18
❏ 195	Jim Abbott	.40	.18
❏ 196	Wade Boggs	.75	.35
❏ 197	Jimmy Key	.40	.18
❏ 198	Don Mattingly	1.50	.70
❏ 199	Paul O'Neil	.40	.18
❏ 200	Danny Tartabull	.20	.09
❏ P24	Ken Griffey Jr. Promo	3.00	1.35

1994 SP Die Cuts

	MINT	NRMT
COMPLETE SET (200)	150.00	70.00
COMMON CARD (1-200)	.40	.18

*STARS: .75X TO 2X BASIC CARDS
*ROOKIES: .4X TO 1X BASIC CARDS
ONE DIE CUT PER PACK
DIE CUTS HAVE SILVER HOLOGRAMS

1994 SP Holoviews

	MINT	NRMT
COMPLETE SET (38)	150.00	70.00
COMMON CARD (1-38)	1.00	.45
SEMISTARS	2.50	1.10
UNLISTED STARS	4.00	1.80
STATED ODDS 1:5		

❏ 1	Roberto Alomar	4.00	1.80
❏ 2	Kevin Appier	1.50	.70

❏ 3	Jeff Bagwell	5.00	2.20
❏ 4	Jose Canseco	5.00	2.20
❏ 5	Roger Clemens	10.00	4.50
❏ 6	Carlos Delgado	4.00	1.80
❏ 7	Cecil Fielder	1.00	.45
❏ 8	Cliff Floyd	1.50	.70
❏ 9	Travis Fryman	1.50	.70
❏ 10	Andres Galarraga	4.00	1.80
❏ 11	Juan Gonzalez	8.00	3.60
❏ 12	Ken Griffey Jr.	20.00	9.00
❏ 13	Tony Gwynn	10.00	4.50
❏ 14	Jeffrey Hammonds	1.50	.70
❏ 15	Bo Jackson	1.50	.70
❏ 16	Michael Jordan	20.00	9.00
❏ 17	David Justice	4.00	1.80
❏ 18	Steve Karsay	1.00	.45
❏ 19	Jeff Kent	1.50	.70
❏ 20	Brooks Kieschnick	1.00	.45
❏ 21	Ryan Klesko	1.50	.70
❏ 22	John Kruk	1.50	.70
❏ 23	Barry Larkin	4.00	1.80
❏ 24	Pat Listach	1.00	.45
❏ 25	Don Mattingly	8.00	3.60
❏ 26	Mark McGwire	20.00	9.00
❏ 27	Raul Mondesi	4.00	1.80
❏ 28	Trot Nixon	5.00	2.20
❏ 29	Mike Piazza	12.00	5.50
❏ 30	Kirby Puckett	6.00	2.70
❏ 31	Manny Ramirez	8.00	3.60
❏ 32	Cal Ripken	15.00	6.75
❏ 33	Alex Rodriguez	40.00	18.00
❏ 34	Tim Salmon	4.00	1.80
❏ 35	Gary Sheffield	4.00	1.80
❏ 36	Ozzie Smith	5.00	2.20
❏ 37	Sammy Sosa	12.00	5.50
❏ 38	Andy Van Slyke	1.50	.70

1994 SP Holoviews Die Cuts

	MINT	NRMT
COMPLETE SET (38)	1200.00	550.00
COMMON CARD (1-38)	5.00	2.20

*HOLO DIE CUTS: 2X TO 5X BASIC HOLO
STATED ODDS 1:75

1995 SP

	MINT	NRMT
COMPLETE SET (207)	40.00	18.00

COMMON CARD (1-207) .... .20 .09
FOIL PROSPECTS (5-24) .... .25 .11
MINOR STARS .... .40 .18
UNLISTED STARS .... .75 .35
COMP. SILVER SET (207) 100.00 45.00
COMMON SILVER (1-207) ...... .25 .11
*SILVER STARS: 1X TO 2.5X HI COLUMN
*SILVER ROOKIES: .6X TO 1.5X HI
ONE SILVER PER PACK

❏ 1 Cal Ripken Salute	3.00	1.35
❏ 2 Nolan Ryan Salute	3.00	1.35
❏ 3 George Brett Salute	1.50	.70
❏ 4 Mike Schmidt Salute	1.25	.55
❏ 5 Dustin Hermanson FOIL	.20	.09
❏ 6 Antonio Osuna FOIL	.25	.11
❏ 7 Mark Grudzielanek FOIL	.60	.25
❏ 8 Ray Durham FOIL	.40	.18
❏ 9 Ugueth Urbina FOIL	.40	.18
❏ 10 Ruben Rivera FOIL	.40	.18
❏ 11 Curtis Goodwin FOIL	.25	.11
❏ 12 Jimmy Hurst FOIL	.25	.11
❏ 13 Jose Malave FOIL	.25	.11
❏ 14 Hideo Nomo FOIL	2.00	.90
❏ 15 Juan Acevedo FOIL	.25	.11
❏ 16 Tony Clark FOIL	.75	.35
❏ 17 Jim Pittsley FOIL	.25	.11
❏ 18 Freddy Garcia FOIL	.25	.11
❏ 19 Carlos Perez FOIL	.40	.18
❏ 20 Raul Casanova FOIL	.25	.11
❏ 21 Quilvio Veras FOIL	.40	.18
❏ 22 Edgardo Alfonzo FOIL	.75	.35
❏ 23 Marty Cordova FOIL	.25	.11
❏ 24 C.J. Nitkowski FOIL	.25	.11
❏ 25 Wade Boggs CL	.40	.18
❏ 26 Dave Winfield CL	.40	.18
❏ 27 Eddie Murray CL	.40	.18
❏ 28 David Justice	.75	.35
❏ 29 Marquis Grissom	.40	.18
❏ 30 Fred McGriff	.60	.25
❏ 31 Greg Maddux	2.00	.90
❏ 32 Tom Glavine	.75	.35
❏ 33 Steve Avery	.20	.09
❏ 34 Chipper Jones	2.00	.90
❏ 35 Sammy Sosa	2.50	1.10
❏ 36 Jaime Navarro	.20	.09
❏ 37 Randy Myers	.20	.09
❏ 38 Mark Grace	.60	.25
❏ 39 Todd Zeile	.40	.18
❏ 40 Brian McRae	.20	.09
❏ 41 Reggie Sanders	.40	.18
❏ 42 Ron Gant	.40	.18
❏ 43 Deion Sanders	.40	.18
❏ 44 Bret Boone	.40	.18
❏ 45 Barry Larkin	.75	.35
❏ 46 Jose Rijo	.20	.09
❏ 47 Jason Bates	.20	.09
❏ 48 Andres Galarraga	.75	.35
❏ 49 Bill Swift	.20	.09
❏ 50 Larry Walker	.75	.35
❏ 51 Vinny Castilla	.60	.25
❏ 52 Dante Bichette	.40	.18
❏ 53 Jeff Conine	.20	.09
❏ 54 John Burkett	.20	.09
❏ 55 Gary Sheffield	.40	.18
❏ 56 Andre Dawson	.20	.09
❏ 57 Terry Pendleton	.20	.09
❏ 58 Charles Johnson	.40	.18

❏ 59 Brian L. Hunter	.40	.18
❏ 60 Jeff Bagwell	1.00	.45
❏ 61 Craig Biggio	.75	.35
❏ 62 Phil Nevin	.20	.09
❏ 63 Doug Drabek	.20	.09
❏ 64 Derek Bell	.40	.18
❏ 65 Raul Mondesi	.60	.25
❏ 66 Eric Karros	.40	.18
❏ 67 Roger Cedeno	.20	.09
❏ 68 Delino DeShields	.20	.09
❏ 69 Ramon Martinez	.40	.18
❏ 70 Mike Piazza	2.50	1.10
❏ 71 Billy Ashley	.20	.09
❏ 72 Jeff Fassero	.20	.09
❏ 73 Shane Andrews	.20	.09
❏ 74 Wil Cordero	.20	.09
❏ 75 Tony Tarasco	.20	.09
❏ 76 Rondell White	.40	.18
❏ 77 Pedro Martinez	1.00	.45
❏ 78 Moises Alou	.40	.18
❏ 79 Rico Brogna	.20	.09
❏ 80 Bobby Bonilla	.40	.18
❏ 81 Jeff Kent	.20	.09
❏ 82 Brett Butler	.40	.18
❏ 83 Bobby Jones	.20	.09
❏ 84 Bill Pulsipher	.60	.09
❏ 85 Bret Saberhagen	.20	.09
❏ 86 Gregg Jefferies	.20	.09
❏ 87 Lenny Dykstra	.20	.09
❏ 88 Dave Hollins	.20	.09
❏ 89 Charlie Hayes	.20	.09
❏ 90 Darren Daulton	.40	.18
❏ 91 Curt Schilling	.60	.25
❏ 92 Heathcliff Slocumb	.20	.09
❏ 93 Carlos Garcia	.20	.09
❏ 94 Denny Neagle	.40	.18
❏ 95 Jay Bell	.40	.18
❏ 96 Orlando Merced	.20	.09
❏ 97 Dave Clark	.20	.09
❏ 98 Bernard Gilkey	.20	.09
❏ 99 Scott Cooper	.20	.09
❏ 100 Ozzie Smith	1.00	.45
❏ 101 Tom Henke	.20	.09
❏ 102 Ken Hill	.20	.09
❏ 103 Brian Jordan	.40	.18
❏ 104 Ray Lankford	.40	.18
❏ 105 Tony Gwynn	2.00	.90
❏ 106 Andy Benes	.40	.18
❏ 107 Ken Caminiti	.60	.25
❏ 108 Steve Finley	.40	.18
❏ 109 Joey Hamilton	.40	.18
❏ 110 Bip Roberts	.20	.09
❏ 111 Eddie Williams	.20	.09
❏ 112 Rod Beck	.20	.09
❏ 113 Matt Williams	.75	.35
❏ 114 Glenallen Hill	.20	.09
❏ 115 Barry Bonds	1.00	.45
❏ 116 Robby Thompson	.20	.09
❏ 117 Mark Portugal	.20	.09
❏ 118 Brady Anderson	.40	.18
❏ 119 Mike Mussina	.75	.35
❏ 120 Rafael Palmeiro	.75	.35
❏ 121 Chris Hoiles	.20	.09
❏ 122 Harold Baines	.40	.18
❏ 123 Jeffrey Hammonds	.40	.18
❏ 124 Tim Naehring	.20	.09
❏ 125 Mo Vaughn	.75	.35
❏ 126 Mike Macfarlane	.20	.09
❏ 127 Roger Clemens	2.00	.90
❏ 128 John Valentin	.40	.18
❏ 129 Aaron Sele	.40	.18
❏ 130 Jose Canseco	1.00	.45
❏ 131 J.T. Snow	.40	.18
❏ 132 Mark Langston	.20	.09
❏ 133 Chili Davis	.40	.18
❏ 134 Chuck Finley	.40	.18
❏ 135 Tim Salmon	.75	.35
❏ 136 Tony Phillips	.20	.09
❏ 137 Jason Bere	.20	.09
❏ 138 Robin Ventura	.40	.18
❏ 139 Tim Raines	.40	.18
❏ 140 Frank Thomas COR	1.50	.70
❏ 140A Frank Thomas ERR	8.00	3.60
❏ 141 Alex Fernandez	.20	.09
❏ 142 Jim Abbott	.40	.18
❏ 143 Wilson Alvarez	.40	.18

❏ 144 Carlos Baerga	.20	.09
❏ 145 Albert Belle	.75	.35
❏ 146 Jim Thome	.75	.35
❏ 147 Dennis Martinez	.40	.18
❏ 148 Eddie Murray	.75	.35
❏ 149 Dave Winfield	.75	.35
❏ 150 Kenny Lofton	.60	.25
❏ 151 Manny Ramirez	1.00	.45
❏ 152 Chad Curtis	.20	.09
❏ 153 Lou Whitaker	.40	.18
❏ 154 Alan Trammell	.40	.18
❏ 155 Cecil Fielder	.40	.18
❏ 156 Kirk Gibson	.40	.18
❏ 157 Michael Tucker	.40	.18
❏ 158 Jon Nunnally	.20	.09
❏ 159 Wally Joyner	.40	.18
❏ 160 Kevin Appier	.40	.18
❏ 161 Jeff Montgomery	.20	.09
❏ 162 Greg Gagne	.20	.09
❏ 163 Ricky Bones	.20	.09
❏ 164 Cal Eldred	.20	.09
❏ 165 Greg Vaughn	.40	.18
❏ 166 Kevin Seitzer	.20	.09
❏ 167 Jose Valentin	.20	.09
❏ 168 Joe Oliver	.20	.09
❏ 169 Rick Aguilera	.20	.09
❏ 170 Kirby Puckett	1.25	.55
❏ 171 Scott Stahoviak	.20	.09
❏ 172 Kevin Tapani	.20	.09
❏ 173 Chuck Knoblauch	.75	.35
❏ 174 Rich Becker	.20	.09
❏ 175 Don Mattingly	1.50	.70
❏ 176 Jack McDowell	.20	.09
❏ 177 Jimmy Key	.40	.18
❏ 178 Paul O'Neill	.40	.18
❏ 179 John Wetteland	.20	.09
❏ 180 Wade Boggs	.75	.35
❏ 181 Derek Jeter	2.50	1.10
❏ 182 Rickey Henderson	1.00	.45
❏ 183 Terry Steinbach	.20	.09
❏ 184 Ruben Sierra	.20	.09
❏ 185 Mark McGwire	4.00	1.80
❏ 186 Todd Stottlemyre	.20	.09
❏ 187 Dennis Eckersley	.40	.18
❏ 188 Alex Rodriguez	3.00	1.35
❏ 189 Randy Johnson	.75	.35
❏ 190 Ken Griffey Jr.	4.00	1.80
❏ 191 Tino Martinez UER	.40	.18

Mike Blowers pictured on back

❏ 192 Jay Buhner	.40	.18
❏ 193 Edgar Martinez	.40	.18
❏ 194 Mickey Tettleton	.20	.09
❏ 195 Juan Gonzalez	1.50	.70
❏ 196 Benji Gil	.20	.09
❏ 197 Dean Palmer	.40	.18
❏ 198 Ivan Rodriguez	1.00	.45
❏ 199 Kenny Rogers	.20	.09
❏ 200 Will Clark	.75	.35
❏ 201 Roberto Alomar	.75	.35
❏ 202 David Cone	.60	.25
❏ 203 Paul Molitor	.75	.35
❏ 204 Shawn Green	.75	.35
❏ 205 Joe Carter	.40	.18
❏ 206 Alex Gonzalez	.20	.09
❏ 207 Pat Hentgen	.40	.18
❏ P100 Ken Griffey Jr. Promo	3.00	1.35
❏ AU190 Ken Griffey Jr. AU	200.00	90.00

1995 SP Platinum Power

	MINT	NRMT
COMPLETE SET (20)	20.00	9.00
COMMON CARD (PP1-PP20)	.25	.11
STATED ODDS 1:5		
❏ PP1 Jeff Bagwell	1.25	.55
❏ PP2 Barry Bonds	1.25	.55
❏ PP3 Ron Gant	.25	.11
❏ PP4 Fred McGriff	.75	.35
❏ PP5 Raul Mondesi	.75	.35
❏ PP6 Mike Piazza	3.00	1.35
❏ PP7 Larry Walker	1.00	.45
❏ PP8 Matt Williams	1.00	.45
❏ PP9 Albert Belle	1.00	.45

		MINT	NRMT
PP10	Cecil Fielder	.50	.23
PP11	Juan Gonzalez	2.00	.90
PP12	Ken Griffey Jr.	5.00	2.20
PP13	Mark McGwire	5.00	2.20
PP14	Eddie Murray	1.00	.45
PP15	Manny Ramirez	1.25	.55
PP16	Cal Ripken	4.00	1.80
PP17	Tim Salmon	1.00	.45
PP18	Frank Thomas	2.00	.90
PP19	Jim Thome	1.00	.45
PP20	Mo Vaughn	1.00	.45

1995 SP Special FX

		MINT	NRMT
	COMPLETE SET (48)	500.00	220.00
	COMMON CARD (1-48)	4.00	1.80
	SEMISTARS	8.00	3.60
	UNLISTED STARS	12.00	5.50
	STATED ODDS 1:75		
1	Jose Canseco	15.00	6.75
2	Roger Clemens	30.00	13.50
3	Mo Vaughn	12.00	5.50
4	Tim Salmon	12.00	5.50
5	Chuck Finley	6.00	2.70
6	Robin Ventura	6.00	2.70
7	Jason Bere	4.00	1.80
8	Carlos Baerga	4.00	1.80
9	Albert Belle	12.00	5.50
10	Kenny Lofton	8.00	3.60
11	Manny Ramirez	15.00	6.75
12	Jeff Montgomery	4.00	1.80
13	Kirby Puckett	20.00	9.00
14	Wade Boggs	12.00	5.50
15	Don Mattingly	25.00	11.00
16	Cal Ripken	50.00	22.00
17	Ruben Sierra	4.00	1.80
18	Ken Griffey Jr.	60.00	27.00
19	Randy Johnson	12.00	5.50
20	Alex Rodriguez	50.00	22.00
21	Will Clark	12.00	5.50
22	Juan Gonzalez	25.00	11.00
23	Roberto Alomar	12.00	5.50
24	Joe Carter	6.00	2.70
25	Alex Gonzalez	4.00	1.80
26	Paul Molitor	12.00	5.50
27	Ryan Klesko	6.00	2.70
28	Fred McGriff	8.00	3.60
29	Greg Maddux	30.00	13.50
30	Sammy Sosa	40.00	18.00
31	Bret Boone	6.00	2.70
32	Barry Larkin	12.00	5.50
33	Reggie Sanders	6.00	2.70
34	Dante Bichette	6.00	2.70
35	Andres Galarraga	12.00	5.50
36	Charles Johnson	6.00	2.70
37	Gary Sheffield	6.00	2.70
38	Jeff Bagwell	15.00	6.75
39	Craig Biggio	12.00	5.50
40	Eric Karros	6.00	2.70
41	Billy Ashley	4.00	1.80
42	Raul Mondesi	12.00	5.50
43	Mike Piazza	40.00	18.00
44	Rondell White	6.00	2.70
45	Bret Saberhagen	6.00	2.70
46	Tony Gwynn	30.00	13.50
47	Melvin Nieves	4.00	1.80
48	Matt Williams	12.00	5.50

1996 SP

		MINT	NRMT
	COMPLETE SET (188)	40.00	18.00
	COMMON CARDS (1-188)	.20	.09
	MINOR STARS	.40	.18
	UNLISTED STARS	.75	.35
	SUBSET CARDS HALF VALUE OF BASE CARDS		
1	Rey Ordonez FOIL	.75	.35
2	George Arias FOIL	.20	.09
3	Osvaldo Fernandez FOIL	.20	.09
4	Darin Erstad FOIL	10.00	4.50
5	Paul Wilson FOIL	.40	.18
6	Richard Hidalgo FOIL	.40	.18
7	Justin Thompson FOIL	.20	.09
8	Jimmy Haynes FOIL	.20	.09
9	Edgar Renteria FOIL	.40	.18
10	Ruben Rivera FOIL	.40	.18
11	Chris Snopek FOIL	.20	.09
12	Billy Wagner FOIL	.60	.25
13	Mike Grace FOIL	.20	.09
14	Todd Greene FOIL	.20	.09
15	Karim Garcia FOIL	.40	.18
16	John Wasdin FOIL	.20	.09
17	Jason Kendall FOIL	.75	.35
18	Bob Abreu FOIL	.60	.25
19	Jermaine Dye FOIL	.40	.18
20	Jason Schmidt FOIL	.20	.09
21	Jay Lopez FOIL	.40	.18
22	Ryan Klesko FOIL	.40	.18
23	Tom Glavine FOIL	.75	.35
24	John Smoltz FOIL	.60	.25
25	Greg Maddux FOIL	2.00	.90
26	Chipper Jones FOIL	2.00	.90
27	Fred McGriff FOIL	.60	.25
28	David Justice FOIL	.75	.35
29	Roberto Alomar FOIL	.75	.35
30	Cal Ripken FOIL	3.00	1.35
31	B.J. Surhoff FOIL	.40	.18
32	Bobby Bonilla FOIL	.40	.18
33	Mike Mussina FOIL	.75	.35
34	Randy Myers FOIL	.20	.09
35	Rafael Palmeiro FOIL	.75	.35
36	Brady Anderson FOIL	.40	.18
37	Tim Naehring FOIL	.20	.09
38	Jose Canseco FOIL	1.00	.45
39	Roger Clemens FOIL	2.00	.90
40	Mo Vaughn FOIL	.75	.35
41	Jose Valentin	.20	.09
42	Kevin Mitchell	.20	.09
43	Chili Davis	.40	.18
44	Garret Anderson	.40	.18
45	Tim Salmon	.60	.25
46	Chuck Finley	.40	.18
47	Troy Percival	.40	.18
48	Jim Abbott	.40	.18
49	J.T. Snow	.40	.18
50	Jim Edmonds	.60	.25
51	Sammy Sosa	2.50	1.10
52	Brian McRae	.20	.09
53	Ryne Sandberg	1.00	.45
54	Jaime Navarro	.20	.09
55	Mark Grace	.60	.25
56	Harold Baines	.40	.18
57	Robin Ventura	.40	.18
58	Tony Phillips	.20	.09
59	Alex Fernandez	.20	.09
60	Frank Thomas	1.50	.70
61	Ray Durham	.40	.18
62	Bret Boone	.40	.18
63	Reggie Sanders	.40	.18
64	Pete Schourek	.20	.09
65	Barry Larkin	.75	.35
66	John Smiley	.20	.09
67	Carlos Baerga	.20	.09
68	Jim Thome	.75	.35
69	Eddie Murray	.75	.35
70	Albert Belle	.75	.35
71	Dennis Martinez	.40	.18
72	Jack McDowell	.20	.09
73	Kenny Lofton	.60	.25
74	Manny Ramirez	1.00	.45
75	Dante Bichette	.40	.18
76	Vinny Castilla	.60	.25
77	Andres Galarraga	.75	.35
78	Walt Weiss	.20	.09
79	Ellis Burks	.40	.18
80	Larry Walker	.75	.35
81	Cecil Fielder	.40	.18
82	Melvin Nieves	.20	.09
83	Travis Fryman	.40	.18
84	Chad Curtis	.20	.09
85	Alan Trammell	.60	.25
86	Gary Sheffield	.40	.18
87	Charles Johnson	.40	.18
88	Andre Dawson	.60	.25
89	Jeff Conine	.20	.09
90	Greg Colbrunn	.20	.09
91	Derek Bell	.40	.18
92	Brian L.Hunter	.20	.09
93	Doug Drabek	.20	.09
94	Craig Biggio	.75	.35
95	Jeff Bagwell	1.00	.45
96	Kevin Appier	.20	.09
97	Jeff Montgomery	.20	.09
98	Michael Tucker	.20	.09
99	Bip Roberts	.20	.09
100	Johnny Damon	.60	.25
101	Eric Karros	.40	.18
102	Raul Mondesi	.40	.18
103	Ramon Martinez	.40	.18
104	Ismael Valdes	.40	.18
105	Mike Piazza	2.50	1.10
106	Hideo Nomo	.75	.35
107	Chan Ho Park	.60	.25
108	Ben McDonald	.20	.09
109	Kevin Seitzer	.20	.09
110	Greg Vaughn	.40	.18
111	Jose Valentin	.20	.09
112	Rick Aguilera	.20	.09
113	Marty Cordova	.20	.09
114	Brad Radke	.40	.18
115	Kirby Puckett	1.25	.55
116	Chuck Knoblauch	.75	.35
117	Paul Molitor	.75	.35
118	Pedro Martinez	1.00	.45
119	Mike Lansing	.20	.09
120	Rondell White	.40	.18
121	Moises Alou	.40	.18
122	Mark Grudzielanek	.20	.09
123	Jeff Fassero	.20	.09
124	Rico Brogna	.20	.09
125	Jason Isringhausen	.40	.18
126	Jeff Kent	.40	.18

❏ 127	Bernard Gilkey	.20	.09
❏ 128	Todd Hundley	.40	.18
❏ 129	David Cone	.60	.25
❏ 130	Andy Pettitte	.60	.25
❏ 131	Wade Boggs	.75	.35
❏ 132	Paul O'Neill	.40	.18
❏ 133	Ruben Sierra	.20	.09
❏ 134	John Wetteland	.40	.18
❏ 135	Derek Jeter	2.50	1.10
❏ 136	Geronimo Berroa	.20	.09
❏ 137	Terry Steinbach	.20	.09
❏ 138	Ariel Prieto	.20	.09
❏ 139	Scott Brosius	.40	.18
❏ 140	Mark McGwire	4.00	1.80
❏ 141	Lenny Dykstra	.40	.18
❏ 142	Todd Zeile	.20	.09
❏ 143	Benito Santiago	.20	.09
❏ 144	Mickey Morandini	.20	.09
❏ 145	Gregg Jefferies	.20	.09
❏ 146	Denny Neagle	.40	.18
❏ 147	Orlando Merced	.20	.09
❏ 148	Charlie Hayes	.20	.09
❏ 149	Carlos Garcia	.20	.09
❏ 150	Jay Bell	.40	.18
❏ 151	Ray Lankford	.40	.18
❏ 152	Alan Benes Andy Benes	.40	.18
❏ 153	Dennis Eckersley	.40	.18
❏ 154	Gary Gaetti	.20	.09
❏ 155	Ozzie Smith	1.00	.45
❏ 156	Ron Gant	.20	.09
❏ 157	Brian Jordan	.40	.18
❏ 158	Ken Caminiti	.40	.18
❏ 159	Rickey Henderson	1.00	.45
❏ 160	Tony Gwynn	1.50	.70
❏ 161	Wally Joyner	.40	.18
❏ 162	Andy Ashby	.20	.09
❏ 163	Steve Finley	.40	.18
❏ 164	Glenallen Hill	.20	.09
❏ 165	Matt Williams	.75	.35
❏ 166	Barry Bonds	1.00	.45
❏ 167	William VanLandingham	.20	.09
❏ 168	Rod Beck	.20	.09
❏ 169	Randy Johnson	.75	.35
❏ 170	Kevin Brown	4.00	1.80
❏ 171	Alex Rodriguez	2.50	1.10
❏ 172	Edgar Martinez	.40	.18
❏ 173	Jay Buhner	.40	.18
❏ 174	Russ Davis	.20	.09
❏ 175	Juan Gonzalez	1.50	.70
❏ 176	Mickey Tettleton	.20	.09
❏ 177	Will Clark	.75	.35
❏ 178	Ken Hill	.20	.09
❏ 179	Dean Palmer	.40	.18
❏ 180	Ivan Rodriguez	1.00	.45
❏ 181	Carlos Delgado	.75	.35
❏ 182	Alex Gonzalez	.20	.09
❏ 183	Shawn Green	.75	.35
❏ 184	Juan Guzman	.20	.09
❏ 185	Joe Carter	.40	.18
❏ 186	Hideo Nomo CL UER	.40	.18
	Checklist lists Livan Hernandez as #4		
❏ 187	Cal Ripken CL	1.50	.70
❏ 188	Ken Griffey Jr. CL	2.00	.90

1996 SP Baseball Heroes

	MINT	NRMT
COMPLETE SET (10)	250.00	110.00
COMMON CARD (81-90)	10.00	4.50
STATED ODDS 1:96		

❏ 82	Frank Thomas	25.00	11.00
❏ 83	Albert Belle	10.00	4.50
❏ 84	Barry Bonds	10.00	4.50
❏ 85	Chipper Jones	25.00	11.00
❏ 86	Hideo Nomo	10.00	4.50
❏ 87	Mike Piazza	30.00	13.50
❏ 88	Manny Ramirez	10.00	4.50
❏ 89	Greg Maddux	30.00	13.50
❏ 90	Ken Griffey Jr.	50.00	22.00
❏ NNO	Ken Griffey Jr. HDR	50.00	22.00

1996 SP Marquee Matchups

	MINT	NRMT
COMPLETE SET (20)	40.00	18.00
COMMON CARD (MM1-MM20)	1.00	.45
STATED ODDS 1:5		
*DIE CUT STARS: 4X TO 10X BASE CARD HI		
DC STATED ODDS 1:61		

❏ MM1	Ken Griffey Jr.	8.00	3.60
❏ MM2	Hideo Nomo	1.50	.70
❏ MM3	Derek Jeter	5.00	2.20
❏ MM4	Rey Ordonez	1.50	.70
❏ MM5	Tim Salmon	1.00	.45
❏ MM6	Mike Piazza	5.00	2.20
❏ MM7	Mark McGwire	8.00	3.60
❏ MM8	Barry Bonds	2.00	.90
❏ MM9	Cal Ripken	6.00	2.70
❏ MM10	Greg Maddux	4.00	1.80
❏ MM11	Albert Belle	1.50	.70
❏ MM12	Barry Larkin	1.50	.70
❏ MM13	Jeff Bagwell	2.00	.90
❏ MM14	Juan Gonzalez	3.00	1.35
❏ MM15	Frank Thomas	4.00	1.80
❏ MM16	Sammy Sosa	5.00	2.20
❏ MM17	Mike Mussina	1.50	.70
❏ MM18	Chipper Jones	4.00	1.80
❏ MM19	Roger Clemens	4.00	1.80
❏ MM20	Fred McGriff	1.00	.45

1996 SP Special FX

	MINT	NRMT
COMPLETE SET (48)	150.00	70.00
COMMON CARD (1-48)	1.50	.70
STATED ODDS 1:5		
*DIE CUTS: 10X TO 25X BASE CARD HI		
DIE CUTS STATED ODDS 1:75		

❏ 1	Greg Maddux	10.00	4.50
❏ 2	Eric Karros	2.00	.90
❏ 3	Mike Piazza	12.00	5.50
❏ 4	Raul Mondesi	2.00	.90
❏ 5	Hideo Nomo	4.00	1.80
❏ 6	Jim Edmonds	2.50	1.10
❏ 7	Jason Isringhausen	2.00	.90
❏ 8	Jay Buhner	2.00	.90
❏ 9	Barry Larkin	4.00	1.80
❏ 10	Ken Griffey Jr.	20.00	9.00
❏ 11	Gary Sheffield	2.00	.90
❏ 12	Craig Biggio	4.00	1.80
❏ 13	Paul Wilson	1.50	.70
❏ 14	Rondell White	2.00	.90
❏ 15	Chipper Jones	10.00	4.50
❏ 16	Kirby Puckett	6.00	2.70
❏ 17	Ron Gant	1.50	.70
❏ 18	Wade Boggs	4.00	1.80
❏ 19	Fred McGriff	2.50	1.10
❏ 20	Cal Ripken	15.00	6.75
❏ 21	Jason Kendall	4.00	1.80
❏ 22	Johnny Damon	2.50	1.10
❏ 23	Kenny Lofton	2.50	1.10
❏ 24	Roberto Alomar	4.00	1.80
❏ 25	Barry Bonds	5.00	2.20
❏ 26	Dante Bichette	2.00	.90
❏ 27	Mark McGwire	20.00	9.00
❏ 28	Rafael Palmeiro	4.00	1.80
❏ 29	Juan Gonzalez	8.00	3.60
❏ 30	Albert Belle	4.00	1.80
❏ 31	Randy Johnson	4.00	1.80
❏ 32	Jose Canseco	5.00	2.20
❏ 33	Sammy Sosa	12.00	5.50
❏ 34	Eddie Murray	4.00	1.80
❏ 35	Frank Thomas	8.00	3.60
❏ 36	Tom Glavine	4.00	1.80
❏ 37	Matt Williams	4.00	1.80
❏ 38	Roger Clemens	10.00	4.50
❏ 39	Paul Molitor	4.00	1.80
❏ 40	Tony Gwynn	10.00	4.50
❏ 41	Mo Vaughn	4.00	1.80
❏ 42	Tim Salmon	2.50	1.10
❏ 43	Manny Ramirez	5.00	2.20
❏ 44	Jeff Bagwell	4.00	1.80
❏ 45	Edgar Martinez	2.00	.90
❏ 46	Rey Ordonez	4.00	1.80
❏ 47	Osvaldo Fernandez	1.50	.70
❏ 48	Derek Jeter	12.00	5.50

1997 SP

	MINT	NRMT
COMPLETE SET (184)	60.00	27.00
COMMON (1-159/181-184)	.20	.09
MINOR STARS	.40	.18
UNLISTED STARS	.75	.35
COMMON SP (160-180)	.30	.14
SP MINOR STARS	.50	.23
SP SEMISTARS	.75	.35
SP UNLISTED STARS	1.25	.55

❑ 1 Andruw Jones FOIL	1.00	.45
❑ 2 Kevin Orie FOIL	.20	.09
❑ 3 Nomar Garciaparra FOIL	2.50	1.10
❑ 4 Jose Guillen FOIL	.50	.23
❑ 5 Todd Walker FOIL	.75	.35
❑ 6 Derrick Gibson FOIL	.50	.23
❑ 7 Aaron Boone FOIL	.20	.09
❑ 8 Bartolo Colon FOIL	.40	.18
❑ 9 Derrek Lee FOIL	.50	.23
❑ 10 Vladimir Guerrero FOIL	1.25	.55
❑ 11 Wilton Guerrero FOIL	.20	.09
❑ 12 Luis Castillo FOIL	.40	.18
❑ 13 Jason Dickson FOIL	.20	.09
❑ 14 Bubba Trammell FOIL	.75	.35
❑ 15 Jose Cruz Jr. FOIL	1.50	.70
❑ 16 Eddie Murray	.75	.35
❑ 17 Darin Erstad	.75	.35
❑ 18 Garret Anderson	.40	.18
❑ 19 Jim Edmonds	.50	.23
❑ 20 Tim Salmon	.75	.35
❑ 21 Chuck Finley	.40	.18
❑ 22 John Smoltz	.50	.23
❑ 23 Greg Maddux	2.00	.90
❑ 24 Kenny Lofton	.50	.23
❑ 25 Chipper Jones	2.00	.90
❑ 26 Ryan Klesko	.40	.18
❑ 27 Javier Lopez	.40	.18
❑ 28 Fred McGriff	.50	.23
❑ 29 Roberto Alomar	.75	.35
❑ 30 Rafael Palmeiro	.75	.35
❑ 31 Mike Mussina	.75	.35
❑ 32 Brady Anderson	.40	.18
❑ 33 Rocky Coppinger	.20	.09
❑ 34 Cal Ripken	3.00	1.35
❑ 35 Mo Vaughn	.75	.35
❑ 36 Steve Avery	.20	.09
❑ 37 Tom Gordon	.20	.09
❑ 38 Tim Naehring	.20	.09
❑ 39 Troy O'Leary	.20	.09
❑ 40 Sammy Sosa	2.50	1.10
❑ 41 Brian McRae	.20	.09
❑ 42 Mel Rojas	.20	.09
❑ 43 Ryne Sandberg	1.00	.45
❑ 44 Mark Grace	.50	.23
❑ 45 Albert Belle	.75	.35
❑ 46 Robin Ventura	.40	.18
❑ 47 Roberto Hernandez	.20	.09
❑ 48 Ray Durham	.40	.18
❑ 49 Harold Baines	.40	.18
❑ 50 Frank Thomas	1.50	.70
❑ 51 Bret Boone	.40	.18
❑ 52 Reggie Sanders	.40	.18
❑ 53 Deion Sanders	.40	.18
❑ 54 Hal Morris	.20	.09
❑ 55 Barry Larkin	.75	.35
❑ 56 Jim Thome	.75	.35
❑ 57 Marquis Grissom	.40	.18
❑ 58 David Justice	.75	.35
❑ 59 Charles Nagy	.40	.18
❑ 60 Manny Ramirez	1.00	.45
❑ 61 Matt Williams	.75	.35
❑ 62 Jack McDowell	.20	.09
❑ 63 Vinny Castilla	.50	.23
❑ 64 Dante Bichette	.40	.18
❑ 65 Andres Galarraga	.75	.35
❑ 66 Ellis Burks	.40	.18
❑ 67 Larry Walker	.75	.35
❑ 68 Eric Young	.40	.18
❑ 69 Brian L. Hunter	.40	.18
❑ 70 Travis Fryman	.40	.18
❑ 71 Tony Clark	.50	.23
❑ 72 Bobby Higginson	.40	.18
❑ 73 Melvin Nieves	.20	.09
❑ 74 Jeff Conine	.20	.09
❑ 75 Gary Sheffield	.75	.35
❑ 76 Moises Alou	.40	.18
❑ 77 Edgar Renteria	.40	.18
❑ 78 Alex Fernandez	.20	.09
❑ 79 Charles Johnson	.40	.18
❑ 80 Bobby Bonilla	.40	.18
❑ 81 Darryl Kile	.20	.09
❑ 82 Derek Bell	.40	.18
❑ 83 Shane Reynolds	.40	.18
❑ 84 Craig Biggio	.75	.35
❑ 85 Jeff Bagwell	1.00	.45
❑ 86 Billy Wagner	.40	.18
❑ 87 Chili Davis	.40	.18
❑ 88 Kevin Appier	.40	.18
❑ 89 Jay Bell	.40	.18
❑ 90 Johnny Damon	.40	.18
❑ 91 Jeff King	.20	.09
❑ 92 Hideo Nomo	.75	.35
❑ 93 Todd Hollandsworth	.20	.09
❑ 94 Eric Karros	.40	.18
❑ 95 Mike Piazza	2.50	1.10
❑ 96 Ramon Martinez	.40	.18
❑ 97 Todd Worrell	.20	.09
❑ 98 Raul Mondesi	.40	.18
❑ 99 Dave Nilsson	.20	.09
❑ 100 John Jaha	.20	.09
❑ 101 Jose Valentin	.20	.09
❑ 102 Jeff Cirillo	.40	.18
❑ 103 Jeff D'Amico	.20	.09
❑ 104 Ben McDonald	.20	.09
❑ 105 Paul Molitor	.75	.35
❑ 106 Rich Becker	.20	.09
❑ 107 Frank Rodriguez	.20	.09
❑ 108 Marty Cordova	.20	.09
❑ 109 Terry Steinbach	.20	.09
❑ 110 Chuck Knoblauch	.75	.35
❑ 111 Mark Grudzielanek	.40	.18
❑ 112 Mike Lansing	.20	.09
❑ 113 Pedro Martinez	1.00	.45
❑ 114 Henry Rodriguez	.40	.18
❑ 115 Rondell White	.40	.18
❑ 116 Rey Ordonez	.40	.18
❑ 117 Carlos Baerga	.20	.09
❑ 118 Lance Johnson	.20	.09
❑ 119 Bernard Gilkey	.20	.09
❑ 120 Todd Hundley	.40	.18
❑ 121 John Franco	.20	.09
❑ 122 Bernie Williams	.75	.35
❑ 123 David Cone	.50	.23
❑ 124 Cecil Fielder	.40	.18
❑ 125 Derek Jeter	2.50	1.10
❑ 126 Tino Martinez	.75	.35
❑ 127 Mariano Rivera	.40	.18
❑ 128 Andy Pettitte	.50	.23
❑ 129 Wade Boggs	.75	.35
❑ 130 Mark McGwire	4.00	1.80
❑ 131 Jose Canseco	1.00	.45
❑ 132 Geronimo Berroa	.20	.09
❑ 133 Jason Giambi	.40	.18
❑ 134 Ernie Young	.20	.09
❑ 135 Scott Rolen	1.25	.55
❑ 136 Ricky Bottalico	.40	.18
❑ 137 Curt Schilling	.50	.23
❑ 138 Gregg Jefferies	.20	.09
❑ 139 Mickey Morandini	.20	.09
❑ 140 Jason Kendall	.50	.23
❑ 141 Kevin Elster	.20	.09
❑ 142 Al Martin	.20	.09
❑ 143 Joe Randa	.20	.09
❑ 144 Jason Schmidt	.20	.09
❑ 145 Ray Lankford	.40	.18
❑ 146 Brian Jordan	.40	.18
❑ 147 Andy Benes	.40	.18
❑ 148 Alan Benes	.40	.18
❑ 149 Gary Gaetti	.40	.18
❑ 150 Ron Gant	.20	.09
❑ 151 Dennis Eckersley	.40	.18
❑ 152 Rickey Henderson	1.00	.45
❑ 153 Joey Hamilton	.40	.18
❑ 154 Ken Caminiti	.50	.23
❑ 155 Tony Gwynn	2.00	.90
❑ 156 Steve Finley	.40	.18
❑ 157 Trevor Hoffman	.40	.18
❑ 158 Greg Vaughn	.40	.18
❑ 159 J.T. Snow	.40	.18
❑ 160 Barry Bonds SP	1.50	.70
❑ 161 Glenallen Hill SP	.30	.14
❑ 162 Bill VanLandingham SP	.30	.14
❑ 163 Jeff Kent SP	.50	.23
❑ 164 Jay Buhner SP	.50	.23
❑ 165 Ken Griffey Jr. SP	6.00	2.70
❑ 166 Alex Rodriguez SP	4.00	1.80
❑ 167 Randy Johnson SP	1.25	.55
❑ 168 Edgar Martinez SP	.50	.23
❑ 169 Dan Wilson SP	.30	.14
❑ 170 Ivan Rodriguez SP	1.50	.70
❑ 171 Roger Pavlik SP	.30	.14
❑ 172 Will Clark SP	1.25	.55
❑ 173 Dean Palmer SP	.50	.23
❑ 174 Rusty Greer SP	.50	.23
❑ 175 Juan Gonzalez SP	2.50	1.10
❑ 176 John Wetteland SP	.50	.23
❑ 177 Joe Carter SP	.50	.23
❑ 178 Ed Sprague SP	.30	.14
❑ 179 Carlos Delgado SP	.50	.23
❑ 180 Roger Clemens SP	3.00	1.35
❑ 181 Juan Guzman	.30	.14
❑ 182 Pat Hentgen	.50	.23
❑ 183 Ken Griffey Jr. CL	3.00	1.35
❑ 184 Hideki Irabu	1.25	.55

1997 SP Game Film

	MINT	NRMT
COMPLETE SET (10)	600.00	275.00
COMMON CARD (GF1-GF10)	25.00	11.00
RANDOM INSERTS IN PACKS		
STATED PRINT RUN 500 SERIAL #'d SETS		
❑ GF1 Alex Rodriguez	60.00	27.00
❑ GF2 Frank Thomas	40.00	18.00
❑ GF3 Andruw Jones	25.00	11.00
❑ GF4 Cal Ripken	80.00	36.00
❑ GF5 Mike Piazza	60.00	27.00
❑ GF6 Derek Jeter	60.00	27.00
❑ GF7 Mark McGwire	100.00	45.00
❑ GF8 Chipper Jones	50.00	22.00
❑ GF9 Barry Bonds	25.00	11.00
❑ GF10 Ken Griffey Jr.	100.00	45.00

1997 SP Griffey Heroes

	MINT	NRMT
COMPLETE SET (10)	200.00	90.00
COMMON CARD (91-100)	20.00	9.00
RANDOM INSERTS IN PACKS		
STATED PRINT RUN 2000 SERIAL #'d SETS		
CONDITION SENSITIVE SET		
❑ 91 Ken Griffey Jr.	20.00	9.00
❑ 92 Ken Griffey Jr.	20.00	9.00
❑ 93 Ken Griffey Jr.	20.00	9.00
❑ 94 Ken Griffey Jr.	20.00	9.00
❑ 95 Ken Griffey Jr.	20.00	9.00
❑ 96 Ken Griffey Jr.	20.00	9.00
❑ 97 Ken Griffey Jr.	20.00	9.00
❑ 98 Ken Griffey Jr.	20.00	9.00
❑ 99 Ken Griffey Jr.	20.00	9.00
❑ 100 Ken Griffey Jr.	20.00	9.00

1997 SP Inside Info

	MINT	NRMT
COMPLETE SET (25)	250.00	110.00
COMMON CARD (1-25)	2.50	1.10
UNLISTED STARS	5.00	2.20
ONE PER SEALED BOX		

		MINT	NRMT
☐ 1	Ken Griffey Jr.	25.00	11.00
☐ 2	Mark McGwire	25.00	11.00
☐ 3	Kenny Lofton	2.50	1.10
☐ 4	Paul Molitor	5.00	2.20
☐ 5	Frank Thomas	10.00	4.50
☐ 6	Greg Maddux	12.00	5.50
☐ 7	Mo Vaughn	5.00	2.20
☐ 8	Cal Ripken	20.00	9.00
☐ 9	Jeff Bagwell	6.00	2.70
☐ 10	Alex Rodriguez	15.00	6.75
☐ 11	John Smoltz	2.50	1.10
☐ 12	Manny Ramirez	6.00	2.70
☐ 13	Sammy Sosa	15.00	6.75
☐ 14	Vladimir Guerrero	8.00	3.60
☐ 15	Albert Belle	5.00	2.20
☐ 16	Mike Piazza	15.00	6.75
☐ 17	Derek Jeter	15.00	6.75
☐ 18	Scott Rolen	8.00	3.60
☐ 19	Tony Gwynn	12.00	5.50
☐ 20	Barry Bonds	6.00	2.70
☐ 21	Ken Caminiti	2.50	1.10
☐ 22	Chipper Jones	12.00	5.50
☐ 23	Juan Gonzalez	10.00	4.50
☐ 24	Roger Clemens	12.00	5.50
☐ 25	Andruw Jones	6.00	2.70

1997 SP Marquee Matchups

	MINT	NRMT
COMPLETE SET (20)	50.00	22.00
COMMON CARD (MM1-MM20)	1.00	.45
STATED ODDS 1:5		

		MINT	NRMT
☐ MM1	Ken Griffey Jr.	8.00	3.60
☐ MM2	Andres Galarraga	1.50	.70
☐ MM3	Barry Bonds	2.00	.90
☐ MM4	Mark McGwire	8.00	3.60
☐ MM5	Mike Piazza	5.00	2.20
☐ MM6	Tim Salmon	1.50	.70
☐ MM7	Tony Gwynn	4.00	1.80
☐ MM8	Alex Rodriguez	5.00	2.20
☐ MM9	Chipper Jones	4.00	1.80
☐ MM10	Derek Jeter	5.00	2.20
☐ MM11	Manny Ramirez	2.00	.90
☐ MM12	Jeff Bagwell	2.00	.90
☐ MM13	Greg Maddux	4.00	1.80
☐ MM14	Cal Ripken	6.00	2.70
☐ MM15	Mo Vaughn	1.50	.70
☐ MM16	Gary Sheffield	1.00	.45
☐ MM17	Jim Thome	1.50	.70
☐ MM18	Barry Larkin	1.50	.70
☐ MM19	Frank Thomas	4.00	1.80
☐ MM20	Sammy Sosa	5.00	2.20

1997 SP Special FX

	MINT	NRMT
COMPLETE SET (48)	250.00	110.00
COMMON CARD (1-47/49)	2.00	.90
UNLISTED STARS	4.00	1.80
STATED ODDS 1:9		

		MINT	NRMT
☐ 1	Ken Griffey Jr.	20.00	9.00
☐ 2	Frank Thomas	8.00	3.60
☐ 3	Barry Bonds	5.00	2.20
☐ 4	Albert Belle	4.00	1.80
☐ 5	Mike Piazza	12.00	5.50
☐ 6	Greg Maddux	10.00	4.50
☐ 7	Chipper Jones	10.00	4.50
☐ 8	Cal Ripken	15.00	6.75
☐ 9	Jeff Bagwell	5.00	2.20
☐ 10	Alex Rodriguez	12.00	5.50
☐ 11	Mark McGwire	20.00	9.00
☐ 12	Kenny Lofton	3.00	1.35
☐ 13	Juan Gonzalez	8.00	3.60
☐ 14	Mo Vaughn	4.00	1.80
☐ 15	John Smoltz	3.00	1.35
☐ 16	Derek Jeter	12.00	5.50
☐ 17	Tony Gwynn	10.00	4.50
☐ 18	Ivan Rodriguez	5.00	2.20
☐ 19	Barry Larkin	4.00	1.80
☐ 20	Sammy Sosa	12.00	5.50
☐ 21	Mike Mussina	4.00	1.80
☐ 22	Gary Sheffield	2.00	.90
☐ 23	Brady Anderson	2.00	.90
☐ 24	Roger Clemens	10.00	4.50
☐ 25	Ken Caminiti	3.00	1.35
☐ 26	Roberto Alomar	4.00	1.80
☐ 27	Hideo Nomo	4.00	1.80
☐ 28	Bernie Williams	4.00	1.80
☐ 29	Todd Hundley	2.00	.90
☐ 30	Manny Ramirez	5.00	2.20
☐ 31	Eric Karros	2.00	.90
☐ 32	Tim Salmon	4.00	1.80
☐ 33	Jay Buhner	2.00	.90
☐ 34	Andy Pettitte	3.00	1.35
☐ 35	Jim Thome	4.00	1.80
☐ 36	Ryne Sandberg	5.00	2.20
☐ 37	Matt Williams	4.00	1.80
☐ 38	Ryan Klesko	4.00	1.80
☐ 39	Jose Canseco	5.00	2.20
☐ 40	Paul Molitor	4.00	1.80
☐ 41	Eddie Murray	4.00	1.80
☐ 42	Darin Erstad	4.00	1.80
☐ 43	Todd Walker	4.00	1.80
☐ 44	Wade Boggs	4.00	1.80
☐ 45	Andruw Jones	5.00	2.20
☐ 46	Scott Rolen	6.00	2.70
☐ 47	Vladimir Guerrero	6.00	2.70
☐ 49	Alex Rodriguez '96	15.00	6.75

1997 SP SPx Force

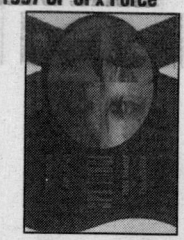

	MINT	NRMT
COMPLETE SET (10)	350.00	160.00
COMMON CARD (1-10)	25.00	11.00
RANDOM INSERTS IN PACKS		
STATED PRINT RUN 500 SERIAL #'d SETS		

		MINT	NRMT
☐ 1	Ken Griffey Jr.	60.00	27.00
	Jay Buhner		
	Andres Galarraga		
	Dante Bichette		
☐ 2	Albert Belle	60.00	27.00
	Brady Anderson		
	Mark McGwire		
	Cecil Fielder		
☐ 3	Mo Vaughn	25.00	11.00
	Ken Caminiti		
	Frank Thomas		
	Jeff Bagwell		
☐ 4	Gary Sheffield	40.00	18.00
	Sammy Sosa		
	Barry Bonds		
	Jose Canseco		
☐ 5	Greg Maddux	30.00	13.50
	Roger Clemens		
	John Smoltz		
	Randy Johnson		
☐ 6	Alex Rodriguez	40.00	18.00
	Derek Jeter		
	Chipper Jones		
	Rey Ordonez		
☐ 7	Todd Hollandsworth	40.00	18.00
	Mike Piazza		
	Raul Mondesi		
	Hideo Nomo		
☐ 8	Juan Gonzalez	25.00	11.00
	Manny Ramirez		
	Roberto Alomar		
	Ivan Rodriguez		
☐ 9	Tony Gwynn	30.00	13.50
	Wade Boggs		
	Eddie Murray		
	Paul Molitor		
☐ 10	Andruw Jones	25.00	11.00
	Vladimir Guerrero		
	Todd Walker		
	Scott Rolen		

1997 SP SPx Force Autographs

	MINT	NRMT
RANDOM INSERTS IN PACKS		
STATED PRINT RUN 100 SERIAL #'d SETS		

		MINT	NRMT
☐ 1	Ken Griffey Jr. AU	600.00	275.00
☐ 2	Albert Belle AU	100.00	45.00
☐ 3	Mo Vaughn AU EXCH.	100.00	45.00
☐ 4	Gary Sheffield AU	60.00	27.00
☐ 5	Greg Maddux AU	300.00	135.00
☐ 6	Alex Rodriguez AU	400.00	180.00
☐ 7	Todd Hollandsworth AU	50.00	22.00
☐ 8	Roberto Alomar AU	100.00	45.00
☐ 9	Tony Gwynn AU	250.00	110.00
☐ 10	Andruw Jones AU	120.00	55.00

1997 SP Vintage Autographs

	MINT	NRMT

RANDOM INSERTS IN PACKS
PRINT RUNS LISTED AFTER YEAR BELOW

		MINT	NRMT
❑ 1	Jeff Bagwell '93/7		
❑ 2	Jeff Bagwell '95/173	80.00	36.00
❑ 3	Jeff Bagwell '96/292	60.00	27.00
❑ 4	Jeff Bagwell '96 MM/23	300.00	135.00
❑ 5	Jay Buhner '95/57	50.00	22.00
❑ 6	Jay Buhner '96/79	40.00	18.00
❑ 7	Jay Buhner '96 FX/27	40.00	18.00
❑ 8	Ken Griffey Jr. '93/16	2000.00	900.00
❑ 9	Ken Griffey Jr. '93 PP/5		
❑ 10	Ken Griffey Jr. '94/103	800.00	350.00
❑ 11	Ken Griffey Jr. '95/38	1000.00	450.00
❑ 12	Ken Griffey Jr. '96/312	400.00	180.00
❑ 13	Tony Gwynn '93/17	600.00	275.00
❑ 14	Tony Gwynn '94/367	120.00	55.00
❑ 15	Tony Gwynn '94 HV/31	400.00	180.00
❑ 16	Tony Gwynn '95/64	300.00	135.00
❑ 17	Tony Gwynn '96/20	500.00	220.00
❑ 18	T. Hollandsworth '94/167	15.00	6.75
❑ 19	Chipper Jones '93/34	400.00	180.00
❑ 20	Chipper Jones '95/60	300.00	135.00
❑ 21	Chipper Jones '96/102	250.00	110.00
❑ 22	R.Ordonez '96/111	50.00	22.00
❑ 23	Rey Ordonez '96 MM/40	80.00	36.00
❑ 24	Alex Rodriguez '94/94	600.00	275.00
❑ 25	Alex Rodriguez '95/63	400.00	180.00
❑ 26	Alex Rodriguez '96/73	400.00	180.00
❑ 27	Gary Sheffield '94/130	50.00	22.00
❑ 28	Gary Sheffield '94 HVDC/4		
❑ 29	Gary Sheffield '95/221	30.00	13.50
❑ 30	Gary Sheffield '96/58	60.00	27.00
❑ 31	Mo Vaughn '97/293	50.00	22.00

1998 SP Authentic

	MINT	NRMT
COMPLETE SET (198)	80.00	36.00
COMMON CARD (1-198)	.25	.11
MINOR STARS	.40	.18
SEMISTARS	.60	.25
UNLISTED STARS	1.00	.45

		MINT	NRMT
❑ 1	Travis Lee FOIL	.60	.25
❑ 2	Mike Caruso FOIL	.25	.11

❑ 3	Kerry Wood FOIL	1.25	.55
❑ 4	Mark Kotsay FOIL	.40	.18
❑ 5	Magglio Ordonez FOIL	10.00	4.50
❑ 6	Scott Elarton FOIL	.25	.11
❑ 7	Carl Pavano FOIL	.25	.11
❑ 8	A.J. Hinch FOIL	.25	.11
❑ 9	Rolando Arrojo FOIL	1.50	.70
❑ 10	Ben Grieve FOIL	1.00	.45
❑ 11	Gabe Alvarez FOIL	.25	.11
❑ 12	Mike Kinkade FOIL	.75	.35
❑ 13	Bruce Chen FOIL	.40	.18
❑ 14	Juan Encarnacion FOIL	1.25	.55
❑ 15	Todd Helton FOIL	1.25	.55
❑ 16	Aaron Boone FOIL	.25	.11
❑ 17	Sean Casey FOIL	1.50	.70
❑ 18	Ramon Hernandez FOIL	.25	.11
❑ 19	Daryle Ward FOIL	.40	.18
❑ 20	Paul Konerko FOIL	.40	.18
❑ 21	David Ortiz FOIL	.25	.11
❑ 22	Derrek Lee FOIL	.25	.11
❑ 23	Brad Fullmer FOIL	.25	.11
❑ 24	Javier Vazquez FOIL	.25	.11
❑ 25	Miguel Tejada FOIL	.40	.18
❑ 26	Dave Dellucci FOIL	1.25	.55
❑ 27	Alex Gonzalez FOIL	.25	.11
❑ 28	Matt Clement FOIL	.40	.18
❑ 29	Masato Yoshii FOIL	1.25	.55
❑ 30	Russell Branyan FOIL	.40	.18
❑ 31	Chuck Finley	.40	.18
❑ 32	Jim Edmonds	.40	.18
❑ 33	Darin Erstad	.60	.25
❑ 34	Jason Dickson	.25	.11
❑ 35	Tim Salmon	.60	.25
❑ 36	Cecil Fielder	.40	.18
❑ 37	Todd Greene	.25	.11
❑ 38	Andy Benes	.25	.11
❑ 39	Jay Bell	.40	.18
❑ 40	Matt Williams	1.00	.45
❑ 41	Brian Anderson	.25	.11
❑ 42	Karim Garcia	.25	.11
❑ 43	Javy Lopez	.40	.18
❑ 44	Tom Glavine	1.00	.45
❑ 45	Greg Maddux	2.50	1.10
❑ 46	Andruw Jones	1.00	.45
❑ 47	Chipper Jones	2.50	1.10
❑ 48	Ryan Klesko	.40	.18
❑ 49	John Smoltz	.60	.25
❑ 50	Andres Galarraga	.60	.25
❑ 51	Rafael Palmeiro	1.00	.45
❑ 52	Mike Mussina	1.00	.45
❑ 53	Roberto Alomar	1.00	.45
❑ 54	Joe Carter	.40	.18
❑ 55	Cal Ripken	4.00	1.80
❑ 56	Brady Anderson	.40	.18
❑ 57	Mo Vaughn	1.00	.45
❑ 58	John Valentin	.40	.18
❑ 59	Dennis Eckersley	.40	.18
❑ 60	Nomar Garciaparra	3.00	1.35
❑ 61	Pedro Martinez	1.25	.55
❑ 62	Jeff Blauser	.25	.11
❑ 63	Kevin Orie	.25	.11
❑ 64	Henry Rodriguez	.40	.18
❑ 65	Mark Grace	.60	.25
❑ 66	Albert Belle	1.00	.45
❑ 67	Mike Cameron	.40	.18
❑ 68	Robin Ventura	.40	.18
❑ 69	Frank Thomas	2.00	.90
❑ 70	Barry Larkin	1.00	.45
❑ 71	Brett Tomko	.25	.11
❑ 72	Willie Greene	.25	.11
❑ 73	Reggie Sanders	.25	.11
❑ 74	Sandy Alomar Jr.	.40	.18
❑ 75	Kenny Lofton	.60	.25
❑ 76	Jaret Wright	.40	.18
❑ 77	David Justice	.40	.18
❑ 78	Omar Vizquel	.40	.18
❑ 79	Manny Ramirez	1.25	.55
❑ 80	Jim Thome	1.00	.45
❑ 81	Travis Fryman	.40	.18
❑ 82	Neifi Perez	.40	.18
❑ 83	Mike Lansing	.25	.11
❑ 84	Vinny Castilla	.40	.18
❑ 85	Larry Walker	1.00	.45
❑ 86	Dante Bichette	.60	.25
❑ 87	Darryl Kile	.40	.18
❑ 88	Justin Thompson	.25	.11

❑ 89	Damion Easley	.40	.18
❑ 90	Tony Clark	.40	.18
❑ 91	Bobby Higginson	.40	.18
❑ 92	Brian Hunter	.25	.11
❑ 93	Edgar Renteria	.25	.11
❑ 94	Craig Counsell	.25	.11
❑ 95	Mike Piazza	3.00	1.35
❑ 96	Livan Hernandez	.25	.11
❑ 97	Todd Zeile	.40	.18
❑ 98	Richard Hidalgo	.40	.18
❑ 99	Moises Alou	.40	.18
❑ 100	Jeff Bagwell	1.25	.55
❑ 101	Mike Hampton	.40	.18
❑ 102	Craig Biggio	1.00	.45
❑ 103	Dean Palmer	.40	.18
❑ 104	Tim Belcher	.25	.11
❑ 105	Jeff King	.25	.11
❑ 106	Jeff Conine	.25	.11
❑ 107	Johnny Damon	.40	.18
❑ 108	Hideo Nomo	1.00	.45
❑ 109	Raul Mondesi	.40	.18
❑ 110	Gary Sheffield	.40	.18
❑ 111	Ramon Martinez	.25	.11
❑ 112	Chan Ho Park	.40	.18
❑ 113	Eric Young	.25	.11
❑ 114	Charles Johnson	.40	.18
❑ 115	Eric Karros	.40	.18
❑ 116	Bobby Bonilla	.40	.18
❑ 117	Jeromy Burnitz	.40	.18
❑ 118	Cal Eldred	.25	.11
❑ 119	Jeff D'Amico	.25	.11
❑ 120	Marquis Grissom	.25	.11
❑ 121	Dave Nilsson	.25	.11
❑ 122	Brad Radke	.40	.18
❑ 123	Marty Cordova	.25	.11
❑ 124	Ron Coomer	.25	.11
❑ 125	Paul Molitor	1.00	.45
❑ 126	Todd Walker	.40	.18
❑ 127	Rondell White	.40	.18
❑ 128	Mark Grudzielanek	.25	.11
❑ 129	Carlos Perez	.25	.11
❑ 130	Vladimir Guerrero	1.25	.55
❑ 131	Dustin Hermanson	.25	.11
❑ 132	Butch Huskey	.25	.11
❑ 133	John Franco	.40	.18
❑ 134	Rey Ordonez	.40	.18
❑ 135	Todd Hundley	.40	.18
❑ 136	Edgardo Alfonzo	.60	.25
❑ 137	Bobby Jones	.25	.11
❑ 138	John Olerud	.40	.18
❑ 139	Chili Davis	.40	.18
❑ 140	Tino Martinez	.40	.18
❑ 141	Andy Pettitte	.40	.18
❑ 142	Chuck Knoblauch	.40	.18
❑ 143	Bernie Williams	1.00	.45
❑ 144	David Cone	.60	.25
❑ 145	Derek Jeter	3.00	1.35
❑ 146	Paul O'Neill	.40	.18
❑ 147	Rickey Henderson	1.25	.55
❑ 148	Jason Giambi	.40	.18
❑ 149	Kenny Rogers	.25	.11
❑ 150	Scott Rolen	1.25	.55
❑ 151	Curt Schilling	.60	.25
❑ 152	Ricky Bottalico	.25	.11
❑ 153	Mike Lieberthal	.25	.11
❑ 154	Francisco Cordova	.25	.11
❑ 155	Jose Guillen	.25	.11
❑ 156	Jason Schmidt	.25	.11
❑ 157	Jason Kendall	.40	.18
❑ 158	Kevin Young	.40	.18
❑ 159	Delino DeShields	.25	.11
❑ 160	Mark McGwire	6.00	2.70
❑ 161	Ray Lankford	.40	.18
❑ 162	Brian Jordan	.40	.18
❑ 163	Ron Gant	.40	.18
❑ 164	Todd Stottlemyre	.25	.11
❑ 165	Ken Caminiti	.40	.18
❑ 166	Kevin Brown	.60	.25
❑ 167	Trevor Hoffman	.40	.18
❑ 168	Steve Finley	.40	.18
❑ 169	Wally Joyner	.40	.18
❑ 170	Tony Gwynn	2.50	1.10
❑ 171	Shawn Estes	.25	.11
❑ 172	J.T. Snow	.40	.18
❑ 173	Jeff Kent	.40	.18
❑ 174	Robb Nen	.25	.11

		MINT	NRMT
❑ 175	Barry Bonds	1.25	.55
❑ 176	Randy Johnson	1.00	.45
❑ 177	Edgar Martinez	.40	.18
❑ 178	Jay Buhner	.40	.18
❑ 179	Alex Rodriguez	3.00	1.35
❑ 180	Ken Griffey Jr.	5.00	2.20
❑ 181	Ken Cloude	.25	.11
❑ 182	Wade Boggs	1.00	.45
❑ 183	Tony Saunders	.25	.11
❑ 184	Wilson Alvarez	.25	.11
❑ 185	Fred McGriff	.60	.25
❑ 186	Roberto Hernandez	.25	.11
❑ 187	Kevin Stocker	.25	.11
❑ 188	Fernando Tatis	1.00	.45
❑ 189	Will Clark	1.00	.45
❑ 190	Juan Gonzalez	2.00	.90
❑ 191	Rusty Greer	.40	.18
❑ 192	Ivan Rodriguez	1.25	.55
❑ 193	Jose Canseco	1.25	.55
❑ 194	Carlos Delgado	1.00	.45
❑ 195	Roger Clemens	2.50	1.10
❑ 196	Pat Hentgen	.25	.11
❑ 197	Randy Myers	.40	.18
❑ 198	Ken Griffey Jr. CL	2.50	1.10
❑ S123	Ken Griffey Jr. Sample	5.00	2.20

1998 SP Authentic Chirography

	MINT	NRMT
COMPLETE SET (30)	1500.00	700.00
COMMON CARD	15.00	6.75

STATED ODDS 1:25
1000 OR MORE OF EACH UNLESS STATED
SP PRINT RUNS STATED BELOW
GRIFFEY EXCH.DEADLINE 7/27/99

❑ AJ	Andruw Jones	40.00	18.00
❑ AR	Alex Rodriguez SP800	150.00	70.00
❑ BG	Ben Grieve	30.00	13.50
❑ CJ	Charles Johnson	15.00	6.75
❑ CP	Chipper Jones SP800	100.00	45.00
❑ DE	Darin Erstad	20.00	9.00
❑ GS	Gary Sheffield	15.00	6.75
❑ IR	Ivan Rodriguez	50.00	22.00
❑ JC	Jose Cruz Jr.	15.00	6.75
❑ JW	Jaret Wright	15.00	6.75
❑ KG	K.Griffey Jr. SP400 EXCH	400.00	180.00
❑ LH	Livan Hernandez	15.00	6.75
❑ MK	Mark Kotsay	15.00	6.75
❑ MM	Mike Mussina	40.00	18.00
❑ MT	Miguel Tejada	15.00	6.75
❑ MV	Mo Vaughn SP800	30.00	13.50
❑ NG	N. Garciaparra SP400	200.00	90.00
❑ PK	Paul Konerko	15.00	6.75
❑ PM	Paul Molitor SP800	50.00	22.00
❑ RA	Roberto Alomar SP800	50.00	22.00
❑ RB	Russell Branyan	15.00	6.75
❑ RC	Roger Clemens SP400	200.00	90.00
❑ RL	Ray Lankford	15.00	6.75
❑ SC	Sean Casey	50.00	22.00
❑ SR	Scott Rolen	50.00	22.00
❑ TC	Tony Clark	15.00	6.75
❑ TG	Tony Gwynn SP850	100.00	45.00
❑ TH	Todd Helton	30.00	13.50
❑ TL	Travis Lee	25.00	11.00
❑ VG	Vladimir Guerrero	50.00	22.00

1998 SP Authentic Sheer Dominance

	MINT	NRMT
COMPLETE SET (42)	150.00	70.00
COMMON CARD (SD1-SD42)	1.00	.45

STATED ODDS 1:3
*GOLD CARDS: 3X TO 8X BASE CARD HI
GOLD: RANDOM INSERTS IN PACKS
GOLD PRINT RUN 2000 SERIAL #'d SETS
*TITANIUM: 15X TO 40X BASE CARD HI
TITANIUM: RANDOM INSERTS IN PACKS
TITANIUM PRINT RUN 100 SERIAL #'d SETS

❑ SD1	Ken Griffey Jr.	12.00	5.50
❑ SD2	Rickey Henderson	3.00	1.35
❑ SD3	Jaret Wright	1.00	.45
❑ SD4	Craig Biggio	2.50	1.10
❑ SD5	Travis Lee	1.50	.70
❑ SD6	Kenny Lofton	1.50	.70
❑ SD7	Raul Mondesi	1.00	.45
❑ SD8	Cal Ripken	10.00	4.50
❑ SD9	Matt Williams	2.50	1.10
❑ SD10	Mark McGwire	15.00	6.75
❑ SD11	Alex Rodriguez	8.00	3.60
❑ SD12	Fred McGriff	1.50	.70
❑ SD13	Scott Rolen	4.00	1.80
❑ SD14	Paul Molitor	2.50	1.10
❑ SD15	Nomar Garciaparra	8.00	3.60
❑ SD16	Vladimir Guerrero	3.00	1.35
❑ SD17	Andruw Jones	2.50	1.10
❑ SD18	Manny Ramirez	3.00	1.35
❑ SD19	Tony Gwynn	6.00	2.70
❑ SD20	Barry Bonds	3.00	1.35
❑ SD21	Ben Grieve	2.50	1.10
❑ SD22	Ivan Rodriguez	3.00	1.35
❑ SD23	Jose Cruz Jr.	1.00	.45
❑ SD24	Pedro Martinez	3.00	1.35
❑ SD25	Chipper Jones	6.00	2.70
❑ SD26	Albert Belle	2.50	1.10
❑ SD27	Todd Helton	2.50	1.10
❑ SD28	Paul Konerko	1.00	.45
❑ SD29	Sammy Sosa	8.00	3.60
❑ SD30	Frank Thomas	5.00	2.20
❑ SD31	Greg Maddux	6.00	2.70
❑ SD32	Randy Johnson	2.50	1.10
❑ SD33	Larry Walker	2.50	1.10
❑ SD34	Roberto Alomar	2.50	1.10
❑ SD35	Roger Clemens	6.00	2.70
❑ SD36	Mo Vaughn	2.50	1.10
❑ SD37	Jim Thome	2.50	1.10
❑ SD38	Jeff Bagwell	3.00	1.35
❑ SD39	Tino Martinez	1.00	.45
❑ SD40	Mike Piazza	8.00	3.60
❑ SD41	Derek Jeter	8.00	3.60
❑ SD42	Juan Gonzalez	5.00	2.20

1998 SP Authentic Trade Cards

	MINT	NRMT

STATED ODDS 1:291
PRINT RUNS LISTED BELOW
EXCHANGE DEADLINE WAS 8/1/99
GRIFFEY GLOVE/JERS.TOO SCARCE TO
PRICE

❑ 1	Roberto Alomar	25.00	11.00
	Ball 100		
❑ 2	Albert Belle	25.00	11.00
	Ball 100		
❑ 3	Jay Buhner	10.00	4.50
	Jersey Card 125		
❑ 4	Ken Griffey Jr.	25.00	11.00
	300 Card 1000 made		
❑ 5	Ken Griffey Jr.		
	Auto Glove 30		
❑ 6	Ken Griffey Jr.		
	Auto Jersey 30		
❑ 7	Ken Griffey Jr.	120.00	55.00
	Jersey Card 125		
❑ 8	Ken Griffey Jr.	80.00	36.00
	Standee 200		
❑ 9	Tony Gwynn	25.00	11.00
	Jersey Card 415		
❑ 10	Brian Jordan	25.00	11.00
	Ball 50		
❑ 11	Greg Maddux	60.00	27.00
	Jersey Card 125		
❑ 12	Raul Mondesi	15.00	6.75
	Ball 100		
❑ 13	Alex Rodriguez	80.00	36.00
	Jersey Card 125		
❑ 14	Gary Sheffield	10.00	4.50
	Jersey Card 125		
❑ 15	Robin Ventura	30.00	13.50
	Ball 50		

1999 SP Authentic

	MINT	NRMT
COMPLETE SET (135)	300.00	135.00
COMP.SET w/o SP's (90)	40.00	18.00
COMMON CARD (1-90)	.20	.09
MINOR STARS	.30	.14
SEMISTARS	.50	.23
UNLISTED STARS	.75	.35
COMMON FW (91-120)	3.00	1.35
FW MINOR STARS	5.00	2.20
FW SEMISTARS	8.00	3.60

FW PRINT RUN 2700 SERIAL #'d SUBSETS

COMMON STR (121-135)	4.00	1.80
STR UNLISTED STARS	6.00	2.70

STR PRINT RUN 2700 SERIAL #'d SUBSETS
E.BANKS BAT LISTED W/UD APH 500 CLUB

❑ 1	Mo Vaughn	.75	.35
❑ 2	Jim Edmonds	.30	.14

3	Darin Erstad	.50	.23
4	Travis Lee	.50	.23
5	Matt Williams	.75	.35
6	Randy Johnson	.75	.35
7	Chipper Jones	2.00	.90
8	Greg Maddux	2.00	.90
9	Andruw Jones	.75	.35
10	Andres Galarraga	.50	.23
11	Tom Glavine	.75	.35
12	Cal Ripken	3.00	1.35
13	Brady Anderson	.30	.14
14	Albert Belle	.75	.35
15	Nomar Garciaparra	2.50	1.10
16	Donnie Sadler	.20	.09
17	Pedro Martinez	1.00	.45
18	Sammy Sosa	2.50	1.10
19	Kerry Wood	.75	.35
20	Mark Grace	.50	.23
21	Mike Caruso	.20	.09
22	Frank Thomas	1.50	.70
23	Paul Konerko	.30	.14
24	Sean Casey	.75	.35
25	Barry Larkin	.75	.35
26	Kenny Lofton	.50	.23
27	Manny Ramirez	1.00	.45
28	Jim Thome	.75	.35
29	Bartolo Colon	.30	.14
30	Jaret Wright	.30	.14
31	Larry Walker	.75	.35
32	Todd Helton	.75	.35
33	Tony Clark	.30	.14
34	Dean Palmer	.30	.14
35	Mark Kotsay	.20	.09
36	Cliff Floyd	.30	.14
37	Ken Caminiti	.30	.14
38	Craig Biggio	.75	.35
39	Jeff Bagwell	1.00	.45
40	Moises Alou	.30	.14
41	Johnny Damon	.30	.14
42	Larry Sutton	.20	.09
43	Kevin Brown	.50	.23
44	Gary Sheffield	.50	.23
45	Raul Mondesi	.30	.14
46	Jeromy Burnitz	.30	.14
47	Jeff Cirillo	.30	.14
48	Todd Walker	.30	.14
49	David Ortiz	.20	.09
50	Brad Radke	.30	.14
51	Vladimir Guerrero	1.00	.45
52	Rondell White	.30	.14
53	Brad Fullmer	.20	.09
54	Mike Piazza	2.50	1.10
55	Robin Ventura	.30	.14
56	John Olerud	.30	.14
57	Derek Jeter	2.50	1.10
58	Tino Martinez	.30	.14
59	Bernie Williams	.75	.35
60	Roger Clemens	2.00	.90
61	Ben Grieve	.75	.35
62	Miguel Tejada	.30	.14
63	A.J. Hinch	.20	.09
64	Scott Rolen	1.00	.45
65	Curt Schilling	.50	.23
66	Doug Glanville	.30	.14
67	Aramis Ramirez	.50	.23
68	Tony Womack	.30	.14
69	Jason Kendall	.30	.14
70	Tony Gwynn	2.00	.90
71	Wally Joyner	.30	.14
72	Greg Vaughn	.30	.14
73	Barry Bonds	1.00	.45
74	Ellis Burks	.30	.14
75	Jeff Kent	.30	.14
76	Ken Griffey Jr.	4.00	1.80
77	Alex Rodriguez	2.50	1.10
78	Edgar Martinez	.30	.14
79	Mark McGwire	5.00	2.20
80	Eli Marrero	.20	.09
81	Matt Morris	.20	.09
82	Rolando Arrojo	.20	.09
83	Quinton McCracken	.20	.09
84	Jose Canseco	1.00	.45
85	Ivan Rodriguez	1.00	.45
86	Juan Gonzalez	1.50	.70
87	Royce Clayton	.20	.09
88	Shawn Green	.75	.35
89	Jose Cruz Jr.	.30	.14
90	Carlos Delgado	.75	.35
91	Troy Glaus FW	12.00	5.50
92	George Lombard FW	5.00	2.20
93	Ryan Minor FW	5.00	2.20
94	Calvin Pickering FW	5.00	2.20
95	Jin Ho Cho FW	5.00	2.20
96	Russ Branyan FW	5.00	2.20
97	Derrick Gibson FW	5.00	2.20
98	Gabe Kapler FW	10.00	4.50
99	Matt Anderson FW	3.00	1.35
100	Preston Wilson FW	5.00	2.20
101	Alex Gonzalez FW	5.00	2.20
102	Carlos Beltran FW	15.00	6.75
103	Dee Brown FW	5.00	2.20
104	Jeremy Giambi FW	5.00	2.20
105	Angel Pena FW	3.00	1.35
106	Geoff Jenkins FW	5.00	2.20
107	Corey Koskie FW	3.00	1.35
108	A.J. Pierzynski FW	3.00	1.35
109	Michael Barrett FW	8.00	3.60
110	Fernando Seguignol FW	5.00	2.20
111	Mike Kinkade FW	3.00	1.35
112	Ricky Ledee FW	5.00	2.20
113	Mike Lowell FW	3.00	1.35
114	Eric Chavez FW	8.00	3.60
115	Matt Clement FW	5.00	2.20
116	Shane Monahan FW	3.00	1.35
117	J.D. Drew FW	20.00	9.00
118	Bubba Trammell FW	3.00	1.35
119	Kevin Witt FW	3.00	1.35
120	Roy Halladay FW	5.00	2.20
121	Mark McGwire STR	40.00	18.00
122	Mark McGwire STR / Sammy Sosa	30.00	13.50
123	Sammy Sosa STR	20.00	9.00
124	Ken Griffey Jr. STR	30.00	13.50
125	Cal Ripken STR	25.00	11.00
126	Juan Gonzalez STR	12.00	5.50
127	Kerry Wood STR	6.00	2.70
128	Trevor Hoffman STR	4.00	1.80
129	Barry Bonds STR	8.00	3.60
130	Alex Rodriguez STR	20.00	9.00
131	Ben Grieve STR	6.00	2.70
132	Tom Glavine STR	6.00	2.70
133	David Wells STR	4.00	1.80
134	Mike Piazza STR	20.00	9.00
135	Scott Brosius STR	4.00	1.80

1999 SP Authentic Chirography

	MINT	NRMT
COMMON CARD	10.00	4.50
MINOR STARS	15.00	6.75
STATED ODDS 1:24		
AG Alex Gonzalez	15.00	6.75
BC Bruce Chen	15.00	6.75
BF Brad Fullmer	10.00	4.50
BG Ben Grieve	30.00	13.50
CB Carlos Beltran	40.00	18.00
CJ Chipper Jones	100.00	45.00
CK Corey Koskie	10.00	4.50
CP Calvin Pickering	15.00	6.75
CR Cal Ripken EXCH	250.00	110.00
EC Eric Chavez	20.00	9.00
GK Gabe Kapler	25.00	11.00
GL George Lombard	15.00	6.75
GM Greg Maddux	150.00	70.00
GV Greg Vaughn	25.00	11.00
IR Ivan Rodriguez	60.00	27.00
JD J.D. Drew	50.00	22.00
JG Jeremy Giambi	15.00	6.75
JK Ken Griffey Jr. EXCH	300.00	135.00
JT Jim Thome	40.00	18.00
KW Kevin Witt	10.00	4.50
KW Kerry Wood	30.00	13.50
MA Matt Anderson	10.00	4.50
MK Mike Kinkade	10.00	4.50
ML Mike Lowell	10.00	4.50
NG Nomar Garciaparra	150.00	70.00
RB Russ Branyan	15.00	6.75
RH Richard Hidalgo	15.00	6.75
RL Ricky Ledee	15.00	6.75
RM Ryan Minor	15.00	6.75
RR Ruben Rivera EXCH	10.00	4.50
SM Shane Monahan	10.00	4.50
SR Scott Rolen EXCH	50.00	22.00
TG Tony Gwynn	100.00	45.00
TH Todd Helton	30.00	13.50
TL Travis Lee	25.00	11.00
TW Todd Walker	15.00	6.75
VG Vladimir Guerrero	50.00	22.00
GMJ Gary Matthews Jr.	10.00	4.50
TGI Troy Glaus	30.00	13.50

1999 SP Authentic Chirography Gold

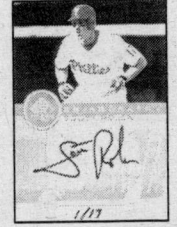

RANDOM INSERTS IN PACKS
CARDS SERIAL #'d TO PLAYER'S JERSEY

	MINT	NRMT
AG Alex Gonzalez/22	60.00	27.00
BC Bruce Chen/48	60.00	27.00
BF Brad Fullmer/20	60.00	27.00
BG Ben Grieve/14	200.00	90.00
CB Carlos Beltran/36	150.00	70.00
CJ Chipper Jones/10		
CK Corey Koskie/47	50.00	22.00
CP Calvin Pickering/6		
CR Cal Ripken/8		
EC Eric Chavez/30	100.00	45.00
GK Gabe Kapler/51	100.00	45.00
GL George Lombard/26	80.00	36.00
GM Greg Maddux/31	500.00	220.00
GV Greg Vaughn/23	60.00	27.00
IR Ivan Rodriguez/7		
JD J.D. Drew/8		
JG Jeremy Giambi/15	100.00	45.00
JK Ken Griffey Jr./24	1500.00	700.00
JT Jim Thome/25	200.00	90.00
KW Kerry Wood/34	120.00	55.00
KW Kevin Witt/6		
MA Matt Anderson/14		
MK Mike Kinkade/33	50.00	22.00
ML Mike Lowell/60	50.00	22.00
NG Nomar Garciaparra/5		
RB Russ Branyan/66	60.00	27.00
RH Richard Hidalgo/18	60.00	27.00
RL Ricky Ledee/38	60.00	27.00
RM Ryan Minor/10		
RR Ruben Rivera/28	40.00	18.00
SM Shane Monahan/12		
SR Scott Rolen/17	300.00	135.00

	MINT	NRMT
❏ TG Tony Gwynn/19	600.00	275.00
❏ TH Todd Helton/17	200.00	90.00
❏ TL Travis Lee/16	120.00	55.00
❏ TW Todd Walker/12		
❏ VG Vladimir Guerrero/27	200.00	90.00
❏ GMJ Gary Matthews Jr./68	40.00	18.00
❏ TGI Troy Glaus/14		

1999 SP Authentic Epic Figures

	MINT	NRMT
COMPLETE SET (30)	150.00	70.00
COMMON CARD (1-30)	1.50	.70
UNLISTED STARS	3.00	1.35
STATED ODDS 1:7		
❏ E1 Mo Vaughn		1.35
❏ E2 Travis Lee	2.00	.90
❏ E3 Andres Galarraga	2.00	.90
❏ E4 Andruw Jones	3.00	1.35
❏ E5 Chipper Jones	8.00	3.60
❏ E6 Greg Maddux	8.00	3.60
❏ E7 Cal Ripken	12.00	5.50
❏ E8 Nomar Garciaparra	10.00	4.50
❏ E9 Sammy Sosa	10.00	4.50
❏ E10 Frank Thomas	6.00	2.70
❏ E11 Kerry Wood	3.00	1.35
❏ E12 Kenny Lofton	2.00	.90
❏ E13 Manny Ramirez	4.00	1.80
❏ E14 Larry Walker	3.00	1.35
❏ E15 Jeff Bagwell	4.00	1.80
❏ E16 Paul Molitor	3.00	1.35
❏ E17 Vladimir Guerrero	4.00	1.80
❏ E18 Derek Jeter	10.00	4.50
❏ E19 Tino Martinez	1.50	.70
❏ E20 Mike Piazza	10.00	4.50
❏ E21 Ben Grieve	3.00	1.35
❏ E22 Scott Rolen	4.00	1.80
❏ E23 Mark McGwire	20.00	9.00
❏ E24 Tony Gwynn	8.00	3.60
❏ E25 Barry Bonds	4.00	1.80
❏ E26 Ken Griffey Jr.	15.00	6.75
❏ E27 Alex Rodriguez	10.00	4.50
❏ E28 J.D. Drew	4.00	1.80
❏ E29 Juan Gonzalez	6.00	2.70
❏ E30 Kevin Brown	2.00	.90

1999 SP Authentic Home Run Chronicles

	MINT	NRMT
COMPLETE SET (70)	120.00	55.00
COMMON CARD (1-70)	.40	.18
SEMISTARS	.50	.23
UNLISTED STARS	.75	.35
ONE PER PACK		

*DIE CUTS: 8X TO 20X HI COLUMN
DIE CUTS RANDOM INSERTS IN PACKS
DIE CUT PRINT RUN 70 SERIAL #'d SETS

	MINT	NRMT
❏ HR1 Mark McGwire	8.00	3.60
❏ HR2 Sammy Sosa	2.50	1.10
❏ HR3 Ken Griffey Jr.	4.00	1.80
❏ HR4 Mark McGwire	5.00	2.20
❏ HR5 Mark McGwire	5.00	2.20
❏ HR6 Albert Belle	.75	.35
❏ HR7 Jose Canseco	1.00	.45
❏ HR8 Juan Gonzalez	1.50	.70
❏ HR9 Manny Ramirez	1.00	.45
❏ HR10 Rafael Palmeiro	.75	.35
❏ HR11 Mo Vaughn	.75	.35
❏ HR12 Carlos Delgado	.75	.35
❏ HR13 Nomar Garciaparra	2.50	1.10
❏ HR14 Barry Bonds	1.00	.45
❏ HR15 Alex Rodriguez	2.50	1.10
❏ HR16 Tony Clark	.40	.18
❏ HR17 Jim Thome	.75	.35
❏ HR18 Edgar Martinez	.40	.18
❏ HR19 Frank Thomas	1.50	.70
❏ HR20 Greg Vaughn	.40	.18
❏ HR21 Vinny Castilla	.40	.18
❏ HR22 Andres Galarraga	.50	.23
❏ HR23 Moises Alou	.40	.18
❏ HR24 Jeromy Burnitz	.40	.18
❏ HR25 Vladimir Guerrero	1.00	.45
❏ HR26 Jeff Bagwell	1.00	.45
❏ HR27 Chipper Jones	2.00	.90
❏ HR28 Javier Lopez	.40	.18
❏ HR29 Mike Piazza	2.50	1.10
❏ HR30 Andruw Jones	.75	.35
❏ HR31 Henry Rodriguez	.40	.18
❏ HR32 Jeff Kent	.40	.18
❏ HR33 Ray Lankford	.40	.18
❏ HR34 Scott Rolen	1.00	.45
❏ HR35 Raul Mondesi	.40	.18
❏ HR36 Ken Caminiti	.40	.18
❏ HR37 J.D. Drew	1.25	.55
❏ HR38 Troy Glaus	.75	.35
❏ HR39 Gabe Kapler	.75	.35
❏ HR40 Alex Rodriguez	2.50	1.10
❏ HR41 Ken Griffey Jr.	4.00	1.80
❏ HR42 Sammy Sosa	2.50	1.10
❏ HR43 Mark McGwire	5.00	2.20
❏ HR44 Sammy Sosa	2.50	1.10
❏ HR45 Mark McGwire	5.00	2.20
❏ HR46 Vinny Castilla	.40	.18
❏ HR47 Sammy Sosa	2.50	1.10
❏ HR48 Mark McGwire	5.00	2.20
❏ HR49 Sammy Sosa	2.50	1.10
❏ HR50 Greg Vaughn	.40	.18
❏ HR51 Sammy Sosa	2.50	1.10
❏ HR52 Mark McGwire	5.00	2.20
❏ HR53 Sammy Sosa	2.50	1.10
❏ HR54 Mark McGwire	5.00	2.20
❏ HR55 Sammy Sosa	2.50	1.10
❏ HR56 Ken Griffey Jr.	4.00	1.80
❏ HR57 Sammy Sosa	2.50	1.10
❏ HR58 Mark McGwire	5.00	2.20
❏ HR59 Sammy Sosa	2.50	1.10
❏ HR60 Mark McGwire	5.00	2.20
❏ HR61 Mark McGwire	8.00	3.60
❏ HR62 Mark McGwire	10.00	4.50
❏ HR63 Mark McGwire	5.00	2.20
❏ HR64 Mark McGwire	5.00	2.20
❏ HR65 Mark McGwire	5.00	2.20
❏ HR66 Sammy Sosa	12.00	5.50
❏ HR67 Mark McGwire	5.00	2.20
❏ HR68 Mark McGwire	5.00	2.20
❏ HR69 Mark McGwire	5.00	2.20
❏ HR70 Mark McGwire	20.00	9.00

1999 SP Authentic Redemption Cards

	MINT	NRMT
STATED ODDS 1:864		

EXPIRATION DATE: 3/1/2000
PRICES BELOW REFER ONLY TO TRADE CARDS

	MINT	NRMT
❏ 1 K.Griffey Jr. AU Jersey/25		
❏ 2 K.Griffey Jr. AU Baseball/75		
❏ 3 K.Griffey Jr. AU SI Cover/75		
❏ 4 K.Griffey Jr. AU Mini Helmet/75		
❏ 5 M.McGwire AU 62 Ticket/1		
❏ 6 M.McGwire AU 70 Ticket/3		
❏ 7 K.Griffey Jr. Standee/300	25.00	11.00
❏ 8 K.Griffey Jr. Glove Card/200	60.00	27.00
❏ 9 K.Griffey Jr. HE Cel Card/346	50.00	22.00
❏ 10 K.Griffey Jr. SI Cover/200	30.00	13.50

1999 SP Authentic Reflections

	MINT	NRMT
COMPLETE SET (30)	300.00	135.00
COMMON CARD (1-30)	3.00	1.35
SEMISTARS	4.00	1.80
UNLISTED STARS	6.00	2.70
STATED ODDS 1:23		
❏ R1 Mo Vaughn	6.00	2.70
❏ R2 Travis Lee	4.00	1.80
❏ R3 Andres Galarraga	4.00	1.80
❏ R4 Andruw Jones	6.00	2.70
❏ R5 Chipper Jones	15.00	6.75
❏ R6 Greg Maddux	15.00	6.75
❏ R7 Cal Ripken	25.00	11.00
❏ R8 Nomar Garciaparra	20.00	9.00
❏ R9 Sammy Sosa	20.00	9.00
❏ R10 Frank Thomas	12.00	5.50
❏ R11 Kerry Wood	6.00	2.70
❏ R12 Kenny Lofton	4.00	1.80
❏ R13 Manny Ramirez	8.00	3.60
❏ R14 Larry Walker	6.00	2.70
❏ R15 Jeff Bagwell	8.00	3.60
❏ R16 Paul Molitor	6.00	2.70
❏ R17 Vladimir Guerrero	8.00	3.60
❏ R18 Derek Jeter	20.00	9.00
❏ R19 Tino Martinez	3.00	1.35
❏ R20 Mike Piazza	20.00	9.00
❏ R21 Ben Grieve	6.00	2.70
❏ R22 Scott Rolen	8.00	3.60
❏ R23 Mark McGwire	40.00	18.00
❏ R24 Tony Gwynn	15.00	6.75

	MINT	NRMT
❑ R25 Barry Bonds	8.00	3.60
❑ R26 Ken Griffey Jr	30.00	13.50
❑ R27 Alex Rodriguez	20.00	9.00
❑ R28 J.D. Drew	8.00	3.60
❑ R29 Juan Gonzalez	12.00	5.50
❑ R30 Roger Clemens	15.00	6.75

1995 SP Championship

	MINT	NRMT
COMPLETE SET (200)	40.00	18.00
COMMON CARD (1-200)	.20	.09
MINOR STARS	.40	.18
UNLISTED STARS	.75	.35

SUBSET CARDS HALF VALUE OF BASE CARDS

COMP.DIE CUT SET (200)	120.00	55.00
COMMON DIE CUT (1-200)	.30	.14

*DIE CUT STARS: 1X TO 2.5X HI COLUMN
*DIE CUT ROOKIES: .6X TO 1.5X HI
ONE DIE CUT PER PACK

	MINT	NRMT
❑ 1 Hideo Nomo	2.00	.90
❑ 2 Roger Cedeno	.20	.09
❑ 3 Curtis Goodwin	.20	.09
❑ 4 Jon Nunnally	.20	.09
❑ 5 Bill Pulsipher	.20	.09
❑ 6 Garret Anderson	.40	.18
❑ 7 Dustin Hermanson	.20	.09
❑ 8 Marty Cordova	.40	.18
❑ 9 Ruben Rivera	.40	.18
❑ 10 Ariel Prieto	.20	.09
❑ 11 Edgardo Alfonzo	.75	.35
❑ 12 Ray Durham	.40	.18
❑ 13 Quilvio Veras	.20	.09
❑ 14 Ugueth Urbina	.20	.09
❑ 15 Carlos Perez	.40	.18
❑ 16 Glenn Dishman	.40	.18
❑ 17 Jeff Suppan	.40	.18
❑ 18 Jason Bates	.20	.09
❑ 19 Jason Isringhausen	.40	.18
❑ 20 Derek Jeter	2.50	1.10
❑ 21 Fred McGriff CL	.20	.09
❑ 22 Marquis Grissom	.40	.18
❑ 23 Fred McGriff	.60	.25
❑ 24 Tom Glavine	.75	.35
❑ 25 Greg Maddux	2.00	.90
❑ 26 Chipper Jones	2.00	.90
❑ 27 Sammy Sosa MLP	1.25	.55
❑ 28 Randy Myers	.20	.09
❑ 29 Mark Grace	.60	.25
❑ 30 Sammy Sosa	2.50	1.10
❑ 31 Todd Zeile	.20	.09
❑ 32 Brian McRae	.20	.09
❑ 33 Ron Gant MLP	.20	.09
❑ 34 Reggie Sanders	.40	.18
❑ 35 Ron Gant	.20	.09
❑ 36 Barry Larkin	.75	.35
❑ 37 Bret Boone	.40	.18
❑ 38 John Smiley	.20	.09
❑ 39 Larry Walker MLP	.40	.18
❑ 40 Andres Galarraga	.75	.35
❑ 41 Bill Swift	.20	.09
❑ 42 Larry Walker	.75	.35
❑ 43 Vinny Castilla	.60	.25
❑ 44 Dante Bichette	.40	.18
❑ 45 Jeff Conine MLP	.20	.09
❑ 46 Charles Johnson	.40	.18
❑ 47 Gary Sheffield	.40	.18
❑ 48 Andre Dawson	.60	.25
❑ 49 Jeff Conine	.20	.09
❑ 50 Jeff Bagwell MLP	.40	.18
❑ 51 Phil Nevin	.20	.09
❑ 52 Craig Biggio	.75	.35
❑ 53 Brian L. Hunter	.20	.09
❑ 54 Doug Drabek	.20	.09
❑ 55 Jeff Bagwell	1.00	.45
❑ 56 Derek Bell	.40	.18
❑ 57 Mike Piazza MLP	1.25	.55
❑ 58 Raul Mondesi	.60	.25
❑ 59 Eric Karros	.40	.18
❑ 60 Mike Piazza	2.50	1.10
❑ 61 Ramon Martinez	.20	.09
❑ 62 Billy Ashley	.20	.09
❑ 63 Rondell White MLP	.20	.09
❑ 64 Jeff Fassero	.20	.09
❑ 65 Moises Alou	.40	.18
❑ 66 Tony Tarasco	.20	.09
❑ 67 Rondell White	.40	.18
❑ 68 Pedro Martinez	1.00	.45
❑ 69 Bobby Jones MLP	.20	.09
❑ 70 Bobby Bonilla	.40	.18
❑ 71 Bobby Jones	.20	.09
❑ 72 Bret Saberhagen	.40	.18
❑ 73 Darren Daulton MLP	.20	.09
❑ 74 Darren Daulton	.20	.09
❑ 75 Gregg Jefferies	.20	.09
❑ 76 Tyler Green	.20	.09
❑ 77 Heathcliff Slocumb	.20	.09
❑ 78 Lenny Dykstra	.40	.18
❑ 79 Jay Bell MLP	.40	.18
❑ 80 Denny Neagle	.40	.18
❑ 81 Orlando Merced	.20	.09
❑ 82 Jay Bell	.20	.09
❑ 83 Ozzie Smith MLP	.75	.35
❑ 84 Ken Hill	.20	.09
❑ 85 Ozzie Smith	1.00	.45
❑ 86 Bernard Gilkey	.20	.09
❑ 87 Ray Lankford	.40	.18
❑ 88 Tony Gwynn MLP	1.00	.45
❑ 89 Ken Caminiti	.60	.25
❑ 90 Tony Gwynn	2.00	.90
❑ 91 Joey Hamilton	.40	.18
❑ 92 Bip Roberts	.20	.09
❑ 93 Deion Sanders MLP	.40	.18
❑ 94 Glenallen Hill	.20	.09
❑ 95 Matt Williams	.75	.35
❑ 96 Barry Bonds	1.00	.45
❑ 97 Rod Beck	.20	.09
❑ 98 Eddie Murray CL	.40	.18
❑ 99 Cal Ripken Jr. CL	1.50	.70
❑ 100 Roberto Alomar CL	.75	.35
❑ 101 George Brett OL	1.50	.70
❑ 102 Joe Carter OL	.20	.09
❑ 103 Will Clark OL	.40	.18
❑ 104 Dennis Eckersley OL	.20	.09
❑ 105 Whitey Ford OL	.75	.35
❑ 106 Steve Garvey OL	.40	.18
❑ 107 Kirk Gibson OL	.20	.09
❑ 108 Orel Hershiser OL	.20	.09
❑ 109 Reggie Jackson OL	1.00	.45
❑ 110 Paul Molitor OL	.40	.18
❑ 111 Kirby Puckett OL	1.25	.55
❑ 112 Mike Schmidt OL	1.25	.55
❑ 113 Dave Stewart OL	.20	.09
❑ 114 Alan Trammell OL	.40	.18
❑ 115 Cal Ripken Jr. MLP	1.50	.70
❑ 116 Brady Anderson	.40	.18
❑ 117 Mike Mussina	.75	.35
❑ 118 Rafael Palmeiro	.75	.35
❑ 119 Chris Hoiles	.20	.09
❑ 120 Cal Ripken Jr.	3.00	1.35
❑ 121 Mo Vaughn MLP	.60	.25
❑ 122 Roger Clemens	2.00	.90
❑ 123 Tim Naehring	.20	.09
❑ 124 John Valentin	.40	.18
❑ 125 Mo Vaughn	.75	.35
❑ 126 Tim Wakefield	.40	.18
❑ 127 Jose Canseco	1.00	.45
❑ 128 Rick Aguilera	.20	.09
❑ 129 Chili Davis MLP	.20	.09
❑ 130 Lee Smith	.40	.18
❑ 131 Jim Edmonds	.60	.25
❑ 132 Chuck Finley	.20	.18
❑ 133 Chili Davis	.40	.18
❑ 134 J.T. Snow	.40	.18
❑ 135 Tim Salmon	.75	.35
❑ 136 Frank Thomas MLP	.75	.35
❑ 137 Jason Bere	.20	.09
❑ 138 Robin Ventura	.40	.18
❑ 139 Tim Raines	.40	.18
❑ 140 Frank Thomas	1.50	.70
❑ 141 Alex Fernandez	.20	.09
❑ 142 Eddie Murray MLP	.40	.18
❑ 143 Carlos Baerga	.20	.09
❑ 144 Eddie Murray	.75	.35
❑ 145 Albert Belle	.75	.35
❑ 146 Jim Thome	.75	.35
❑ 147 Dennis Martinez	.40	.18
❑ 148 Dave Winfield	.75	.35
❑ 149 Kenny Lofton	.60	.25
❑ 150 Manny Ramirez	1.00	.45
❑ 151 Cecil Fielder MLP	.20	.09
❑ 152 Lou Whitaker	.40	.18
❑ 153 Alan Trammell	.40	.18
❑ 154 Kirk Gibson	.20	.09
❑ 155 Cecil Fielder	.40	.18
❑ 156 Bobby Higginson	1.25	.55
❑ 157 Kevin Appier MLP	.20	.09
❑ 158 Wally Joyner	.40	.18
❑ 159 Jeff Montgomery	.20	.09
❑ 160 Kevin Appier	.40	.18
❑ 161 Gary Gaetti	.40	.18
❑ 162 Greg Gagne	.20	.09
❑ 163 Ricky Bones MLP	.20	.09
❑ 164 Greg Vaughn	.40	.18
❑ 165 Kevin Seitzer	.40	.18
❑ 166 Ricky Bones	.20	.09
❑ 167 Kirby Puckett MLP	.75	.35
❑ 168 Pedro Munoz	.20	.09
❑ 169 Chuck Knoblauch	.75	.35
❑ 170 Kirby Puckett	1.25	.55
❑ 171 Don Mattingly MLP	.75	.35
❑ 172 Wade Boggs	.75	.35
❑ 173 Paul O'Neill	.40	.18
❑ 174 John Wetteland	.20	.09
❑ 175 Don Mattingly	1.50	.70
❑ 176 Jack McDowell	.20	.09
❑ 177 Mark McGwire MLP	2.00	.90
❑ 178 Rickey Henderson	1.00	.45
❑ 179 Terry Steinbach	.20	.09
❑ 180 Ruben Sierra	.20	.09
❑ 181 Mark McGwire	4.00	1.80
❑ 182 Dennis Eckersley	.40	.18
❑ 183 Ken Griffey Jr. MLP	2.00	.90
❑ 184 Alex Rodriguez	3.00	1.35
❑ 185 Ken Griffey Jr.	4.00	1.80
❑ 186 Randy Johnson	.75	.35
❑ 187 Jay Buhner	.40	.18
❑ 188 Edgar Martinez	.40	.18
❑ 189 Will Clark MLP	.40	.18
❑ 190 Juan Gonzalez	1.50	.70
❑ 191 Benji Gil	.20	.09
❑ 192 Ivan Rodriguez	1.00	.45
❑ 193 Kenny Rogers	.20	.09
❑ 194 Will Clark	.75	.35
❑ 195 Paul Molitor MLP	.40	.18
❑ 196 Roberto Alomar	.75	.35
❑ 197 David Cone	.60	.25
❑ 198 Paul Molitor	.75	.35
❑ 199 Shawn Green	.75	.35
❑ 200 Joe Carter	.40	.18
❑ CR1 Cal Ripken, Jr. Tribute	15.00	6.75
❑ CR1 Cal Ripken 2131 DC	50.00	22.00

1995 SP Championship Classic Performances

	MINT	NRMT
COMPLETE SET (10)	40.00	18.00
COMMON CARD (CP1-CP10)	2.00	.90
UNLISTED STARS	4.00	1.80
COMP.DIE CUT SET (10)	200.00	90.00

*DIE CUTS: 2X TO 5X HI COLUMN
DC STATED ODDS 1:75

❑ CP1 Reggie Jackson	5.00	2.20
❑ CP2 Nolan Ryan	15.00	6.75
❑ CP3 Kirk Gibson	2.00	.90

		MINT	NRMT
❑ CP4	Joe Carter	2.00	.90
❑ CP5	George Brett	8.00	3.60
❑ CP6	Roberto Alomar	4.00	1.80
❑ CP7	Ozzie Smith	5.00	2.20
❑ CP8	Kirby Puckett	6.00	2.70
❑ CP9	Bret Saberhagen	2.00	.90
❑ CP10	Steve Garvey	2.00	.90

1995 SP Championship Fall Classic

		MINT	NRMT
	COMPLETE SET (9)	120.00	55.00
	COMMON CARD (1-9)	4.00	1.80
	STATED ODDS 1:40		
	*DIE CUTS: 5X TO 12X BASE CARD HI		
	DC STATED ODDS 1:75		

❑ 1	Ken Griffey Jr.	30.00	13.50
❑ 2	Frank Thomas	12.00	5.50
❑ 3	Albert Belle	6.00	2.70
❑ 4	Mike Piazza	20.00	9.00
❑ 5	Don Mattingly	12.00	5.50
❑ 6	Hideo Nomo	10.00	4.50
❑ 7	Greg Maddux	15.00	6.75
❑ 8	Fred McGriff	4.00	1.80
❑ 9	Barry Bonds	8.00	3.60

1999 SP Signature

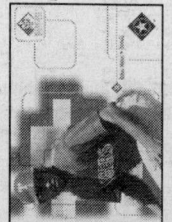

		MINT	NRMT
	COMPLETE SET (180)	250.00	110.00
	COMMON CARD (1-180)	.50	.23

	MINOR STARS	.75	.35
	SEMISTARS	1.25	.55
	UNLISTED STARS	2.00	.90
	MEL OTT BAT LISTED W/UD APH 500 CLUB		
❑ 1	Nomar Garciaparra	6.00	2.70
❑ 2	Ken Griffey Jr.	10.00	4.50
❑ 3	J.D. Drew	3.00	1.35
❑ 4	Alex Rodriguez	6.00	2.70
❑ 5	Juan Gonzalez	4.00	1.80
❑ 6	Mo Vaughn	2.00	.90
❑ 7	Greg Maddux	5.00	2.20
❑ 8	Chipper Jones	5.00	2.20
❑ 9	Frank Thomas	4.00	1.80
❑ 10	Vladimir Guerrero	2.50	1.10
❑ 11	Mike Piazza	6.00	2.70
❑ 12	Eric Chavez	1.25	.55
❑ 13	Tony Gwynn	5.00	2.20
❑ 14	Orlando Hernandez	2.00	.90
❑ 15	Pat Burrell	25.00	11.00
❑ 16	Darin Erstad	1.25	.55
❑ 17	Greg Vaughn	.75	.35
❑ 18	Russ Branyan	.75	.35
❑ 19	Gabe Kapler	2.00	.90
❑ 20	Craig Biggio	2.00	.90
❑ 21	Troy Glaus	.75	.35
❑ 22	Pedro Martinez	2.50	1.10
❑ 23	Carlos Beltran	2.50	1.10
❑ 24	Derrek Lee	.50	.23
❑ 25	Manny Ramirez	2.50	1.10
❑ 26	Shea Hillenbrand	2.50	1.10
❑ 27	Carlos Lee	.75	.35
❑ 28	Angel Pena	.50	.23
❑ 29	Rafael Roque	1.00	.45
❑ 30	Octavio Dotel	.75	.35
❑ 31	Jeromy Burnitz	.75	.35
❑ 32	Jeremy Giambi	.75	.35
❑ 33	Andruw Jones	2.00	.90
❑ 34	Todd Helton	2.00	.90
❑ 35	Scott Rolen	2.50	1.10
❑ 36	Jason Kendall	.75	.35
❑ 37	Trevor Hoffman	.75	.35
❑ 38	Barry Bonds	2.50	1.10
❑ 39	Ivan Rodriguez	2.50	1.10
❑ 40	Roy Halladay	.75	.35
❑ 41	Rickey Henderson	2.50	1.10
❑ 42	Ryan Minor	.75	.35
❑ 43	Brian Jordan	.75	.35
❑ 44	Alex Gonzalez	.75	.35
❑ 45	Raul Mondesi	.75	.35
❑ 46	Corey Koskie	.75	.35
❑ 47	Paul O'Neill	.75	.35
❑ 48	Todd Walker	.75	.35
❑ 49	Carlos Febles	.75	.35
❑ 50	Travis Fryman	.75	.35
❑ 51	Albert Belle	2.00	.90
❑ 52	Travis Lee	1.25	.55
❑ 53	Bruce Chen	.50	.23
❑ 54	Reggie Taylor	.50	.23
❑ 55	Jerry Hairston Jr.	.75	.35
❑ 56	Carlos Guillen	.50	.23
❑ 57	Michael Barrett	1.25	.55
❑ 58	Jason Conti	.50	.23
❑ 59	Joe Lawrence	.50	.23
❑ 60	Jeff Cirillo	.75	.35
❑ 61	Juan Melo	.50	.23
❑ 62	Chad Hermansen	.75	.35
❑ 63	Ruben Mateo	2.00	.90
❑ 64	Ben Davis	1.25	.55
❑ 65	Mike Caruso	.50	.23
❑ 66	Jason Giambi	.75	.35
❑ 67	Jose Canseco	2.50	1.10
❑ 68	Chad Hutchinson	6.00	2.70
❑ 69	Mitch Meluskey	.50	.23
❑ 70	Adrian Beltre	2.00	.90
❑ 71	Mark Kotsay	.75	.35
❑ 72	Juan Encarnacion	.75	.35
❑ 73	Dermal Brown	.75	.35
❑ 74	Kevin Witt	.50	.23
❑ 75	Vinny Castilla	.75	.35
❑ 76	Aramis Ramirez	1.25	.55
❑ 77	Marlon Anderson	.50	.23
❑ 78	Mike Kinkade	.50	.23
❑ 79	Kevin Barker	.75	.35
❑ 80	Ron Belliard	.75	.35
❑ 81	Chris Haas	.50	.23
❑ 82	Bob Henley	.50	.23
❑ 83	Fernando Seguignol	.75	.23
❑ 84	Damon Minor	.50	.23
❑ 85	A.J. Burnett	4.00	1.80
❑ 86	Calvin Pickering	.75	.35
❑ 87	Mike Darr	.75	.35
❑ 88	Cesar King	.50	.23
❑ 89	Rob Bell	.50	.23
❑ 90	Derrick Gibson	.75	.35
❑ 91	Orber Moreno	2.50	1.10
❑ 92	Robert Fick	.75	.35
❑ 93	Doug Mientkiewicz	2.00	.90
❑ 94	A.J. Pierzynski	.50	.23
❑ 95	Orlando Palmeiro	.50	.23
❑ 96	Sidney Ponson	.50	.23
❑ 97	Ivanon Coffie	1.00	.45
❑ 98	Juan Pena	2.00	.90
❑ 99	Matt Karchner	.50	.23
❑ 100	Carlos Castillo	.50	.23
❑ 101	Bryan Ward	1.00	.45
❑ 102	Mario Valdez	.50	.23
❑ 103	Billy Wagner	.75	.35
❑ 104	Miguel Tejada	.75	.35
❑ 105	Jose Cruz Jr.	.75	.35
❑ 106	George Lombard	.75	.35
❑ 107	Geoff Jenkins	.75	.35
❑ 108	Ray Lankford	.75	.35
❑ 109	Todd Stottlemyre	.50	.23
❑ 110	Mike Lowell	.50	.23
❑ 111	Matt Clement	.50	.23
❑ 112	Scott Brosius	.75	.35
❑ 113	Preston Wilson	.75	.35
❑ 114	Bartolo Colon	.75	.35
❑ 115	Rolando Arrojo	.50	.23
❑ 116	Jose Guillen	.50	.23
❑ 117	Ron Gant	.50	.23
❑ 118	Ricky Ledee	.50	.23
❑ 119	Carlos Delgado	2.00	.90
❑ 120	Abraham Nunez	.50	.23
❑ 121	John Olerud	.75	.35
❑ 122	Chan Ho Park	.75	.35
❑ 123	Brad Radke	.75	.35
❑ 124	Al Leiter	.75	.35
❑ 125	Gary Matthews Jr.	.50	.23
❑ 126	F.P. Santangelo	.50	.23
❑ 127	Brad Fullmer	.50	.23
❑ 128	Matt Anderson	.50	.23
❑ 129	A.J. Hinch	.50	.23
❑ 130	Sterling Hitchcock	.50	.23
❑ 131	Edgar Martinez	.75	.35
❑ 132	Fernando Tatis	2.00	.90
❑ 133	Bobby Smith	.50	.23
❑ 134	Paul Konerko	.50	.23
❑ 135	Sean Casey	2.00	.90
❑ 136	Donnie Sadler	.50	.23
❑ 137	Denny Neagle	.50	.23
❑ 138	Sandy Alomar Jr.	.75	.35
❑ 139	Mariano Rivera	.75	.35
❑ 140	Emil Brown	.50	.23
❑ 141	J.T. Snow	.50	.23
❑ 142	Eli Marrero	.50	.23
❑ 143	Rusty Greer	.75	.35
❑ 144	Johnny Damon	.75	.35
❑ 145	Damion Easley	.50	.23
❑ 146	Eric Milton	.50	.23
❑ 147	Rico Brogna	.50	.23
❑ 148	Ray Durham	.75	.35
❑ 149	Wally Joyner	.75	.35
❑ 150	Royce Clayton	.50	.23
❑ 151	David Ortiz	.50	.23
❑ 152	Wade Boggs	2.00	.90
❑ 153	Ugueth Urbina	.50	.23
❑ 154	Richard Hidalgo	.75	.35
❑ 155	Bobby Abreu	.75	.35
❑ 156	Robb Nen	.50	.23
❑ 157	David Segui	.50	.23
❑ 158	Sean Berry	.50	.23
❑ 159	Kevin Tapani	.50	.23
❑ 160	Jason Varitek	.75	.35
❑ 161	Fernando Vina	.50	.23
❑ 162	Jim Leyritz	.50	.23
❑ 163	Enrique Wilson	.50	.23
❑ 164	Jim Parque	.50	.23
❑ 165	Doug Glanville	.75	.35
❑ 166	Jesus Sanchez	.50	.23
❑ 167	Nolan Ryan	12.00	5.50

168	Robin Yount	2.50	1.10
169	Stan Musial	5.00	2.20
170	Tom Seaver	4.00	1.80
171	Mike Schmidt	5.00	2.20
172	Willie Stargell	2.00	.90
173	Rollie Fingers	1.25	.55
174	Willie McCovey	2.50	1.10
175	Harmon Killebrew	2.50	1.10
176	Eddie Mathews	2.50	1.10
177	Reggie Jackson	5.00	2.20
178	Frank Robinson	2.50	1.10
179	Ken Griffey Sr.	.75	.35
180	Eddie Murray	3.00	1.35
S1	Ken Griffey Jr. Sample	5.00	2.20

1999 SP Signature Autographs

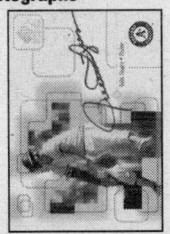

	MINT	NRMT
COMMON CARD	10.00	4.50
MINOR STARS	15.00	6.75

ONE PER PACK
EXCHANGE DEADLINE 5/12/2000

Code	Player	MINT	NRMT
AB	Albert Belle	50.00	22.00
AG	Alex Gonzalez	15.00	6.75
AJ	Andruw Jones	40.00	18.00
AL	Al Leiter	15.00	6.75
AN	Abraham Nunez	10.00	4.50
AP	Angel Pena	10.00	4.50
AR	Alex Rodriguez	200.00	90.00
BA	Bobby Abreu	25.00	11.00
BB	Barry Bonds	80.00	36.00
BC	Bruce Chen	15.00	6.75
BD	Ben Davis	25.00	11.00
BF	Brad Fullmer	10.00	4.50
BH	Bob Henley	15.00	6.75
BR	Brad Radke	15.00	6.75
BS	Bobby Smith	10.00	4.50
BW	Bryan Ward	15.00	6.75
CC	Carlos Castillo	10.00	4.50
CD	Carlos Delgado	30.00	13.50
CF	Carlos Febles	15.00	6.75
CH	Chad Hermansen	15.00	6.75
CJ	Chipper Jones	100.00	45.00
CK	Corey Koskie	10.00	4.50
CL	Carlos Lee	15.00	6.75
CP	Calvin Pickering	10.00	4.50
DB	Dermal Brown	15.00	6.75
DE	Darin Erstad	20.00	9.00
DG	Derrick Gibson	15.00	6.75
DL	Derrek Lee	10.00	4.50
DO	Darel Ortiz	10.00	4.50
DS	Donnie Sadler	10.00	4.50
EB	Emil Brown	10.00	4.50
EC	Eric Chavez	15.00	6.75
ED	Orlando Hernandez	50.00	22.00
EM	Edgar Martinez	25.00	11.00
EW	Enrique Wilson	10.00	4.50
FR	Frank Robinson	40.00	18.00
FS	Fernando Seguignol	15.00	6.75
FT	Frank Thomas	120.00	55.00
FV	Fernando Vina	10.00	4.50
GJ	Geoff Jenkins	15.00	6.75
GK	Gabe Kapler	20.00	9.00
GM	Greg Maddux	150.00	70.00
GV	Greg Vaughn	30.00	13.50
HK	Harmon Killebrew	40.00	18.00
IC	Ivanon Coffie	15.00	6.75
JC	Jason Conti	10.00	4.50
JD	J.D. Drew	50.00	22.00
JE	Juan Encarnacion	15.00	6.75
JG	Jose Guillen	10.00	4.50
JK	Jason Kendall	20.00	9.00
JM	Juan Melo	10.00	4.50
JO	John Olerud	20.00	9.00
JP	Jim Parque EXCH	10.00	4.50
JR	Ken Griffey Jr.	300.00	135.00
JS	Jesus Sanchez	10.00	4.50
JT	J.T. Snow EXCH	15.00	6.75
JV	Jason Varitek	15.00	6.75
KB	Kevin Barker	10.00	4.50
KW	Kevin Witt	10.00	4.50
MA	Marlon Anderson	10.00	4.50
MB	Michael Barrett	25.00	11.00
MC	Mike Caruso	10.00	4.50
MK	Mark Kotsay	10.00	4.50
MO	Mo Vaughn	50.00	22.00
MP	Mike Piazza EXCH	250.00	110.00
MR	Manny Ramirez	60.00	27.00
MS	Mike Schmidt	100.00	45.00
MT	Miguel Tejada	15.00	6.75
MV	Mario Valdez	10.00	4.50
NG	Nomar Garciaparra	150.00	70.00
NR	Nolan Ryan	300.00	135.00
OD	Octavio Dotel	15.00	6.75
OP	Orlando Palmeiro	10.00	4.50
PB	Pat Burrell	50.00	22.00
PG	Ivan Rodriguez	60.00	27.00
PK	Paul Konerko	15.00	6.75
PM	Pedro Martinez EXCH	100.00	45.00
PO	Paul O'Neill	20.00	9.00
RB	Russ Branyan	10.00	4.50
RC	Royce Clayton	10.00	4.50
RD	Ray Durham	15.00	6.75
RH	Roy Halladay	15.00	6.75
RJ	Reggie Jackson	250.00	110.00
RL	Ray Lankford	15.00	6.75
RM	Ryan Minor	15.00	6.75
RN	Robb Nen	10.00	4.50
RR	Rafael Roque	15.00	6.75
RT	Reggie Taylor	10.00	4.50
RY	Robin Yount	80.00	36.00
SA	Sandy Alomar Jr.	15.00	6.75
SB	Scott Brosius	20.00	9.00
SC	Sean Casey EXCH	30.00	13.50
SM	Stan Musial	120.00	55.00
SP	Sidney Ponson	10.00	4.50
SR	Ken Griffey Sr.	25.00	11.00
SR	Scott Rolen EXCH	50.00	22.00
TG	Tony Gwynn	80.00	36.00
TW	Todd Walker	15.00	6.75
VC	Vinny Castilla EXCH	25.00	11.00
VG	Vladimir Guerrero	50.00	22.00
WJ	Wally Joyner	15.00	6.75
ABE	Adrian Beltre	20.00	9.00
AJB	A.J. Burnett EXCH	15.00	6.75
AJP	A.J. Pierzynski	10.00	4.50
ARA	Aramis Ramirez	25.00	11.00
BCO	Bartolo Colon EXCH	20.00	9.00
BWA	Billy Wagner	15.00	6.75
CBE	Carlos Beltran	30.00	13.50
CHA	Chris Haas	10.00	4.50
CHU	Chad Hutchinson	25.00	11.00
CKI	Cesar King	10.00	4.50
DAM	Damon Minor	10.00	4.50
DEA	Damion Easley	10.00	4.50
DGI	Doug Glanville	15.00	6.75
DOM	Doug Mientkiewicz	15.00	6.75
DSE	David Segui	10.00	4.50
ELI	Eli Marrero	10.00	4.50
EMA	Eddie Mathews	40.00	18.00
EMI	Eric Milton	10.00	4.50
FTA	Fernando Tatis	15.00	6.75
GMJ	Gary Matthews Jr.	10.00	4.50
JAG	Jason Giambi	15.00	6.75
JCI	Jeff Cirillo	15.00	6.75
JDA	Johnny Damon	15.00	6.75
JEG	Jeremy Giambi	15.00	6.75
JHJ	Jerry Hairston Jr.	15.00	6.75
JLA	Joe Lawrence	10.00	4.50
JLE	Jim Leyritz	10.00	4.50
JOC	Jose Canseco	150.00	70.00
MCI	Matt Clement	15.00	6.75
MKA	Matt Karchner	10.00	4.50
MKI	Mike Kinkade	10.00	4.50
MME	Mitch Meluskey	10.00	4.50
MRI	Mariano Rivera	30.00	13.50
POP	Willie Stargell EXCH	40.00	18.00
RBE	Ron Belliard	15.00	6.75
RGA	Ron Gant	25.00	11.00
RGR	Rusty Greer	20.00	9.00
RMA	Ruben Mateo EXCH	20.00	9.00
ROB	Rob Bell	10.00	4.50
ROB	Robert Fick	15.00	6.75
ROL	Rollie Fingers	25.00	11.00
SHH	Shea Hillenbrand	25.00	11.00
STH	Sterling Hitchcock	10.00	4.50
TGL	Troy Glaus	25.00	11.00
THE	Todd Helton	30.00	13.50
THO	Trevor Hoffman	15.00	6.75
TSE	Tom Seaver	100.00	45.00
TST	Todd Stottlemyre	10.00	4.50
WMC	Willie McCovey	40.00	18.00

1999 SP Signature Autographs Gold

	MINT	NRMT
COMMON NO AU CARD	15.00	6.75
COMMON AU CARD	25.00	11.00
MINOR STARS	40.00	18.00

RANDOM INSERTS IN PACKS
STATED PRINT RUN 50 SERIAL #'d SETS
11 PLAYERS DID NOT SIGN THEIR CARDS
UNSIGNED CARDS MARKED AS NO AU
EXCHANGE DEADLINE 5/12/2000

Code	Player	MINT	NRMT
AB	Albert Belle	100.00	45.00
AG	Alex Gonzalez	40.00	18.00
AJ	Andruw Jones	120.00	55.00
AP	Angel Pena	15.00	6.75
AR	Alex Rodriguez	500.00	220.00
BB	Barry Bonds	200.00	90.00
BC	Bruce Chen	40.00	18.00
BD	Ben Davis	50.00	22.00
BH	Bob Henley	15.00	6.75
BJ	Brian Jordan NO AU	20.00	9.00
CB	Craig Biggio NO AU	40.00	18.00
CF	Carlos Febles	40.00	18.00
CG	Carlos Guillen NO AU	15.00	6.75
CH	Chad Hermansen	40.00	18.00
CJ	Chipper Jones	400.00	180.00
CK	Corey Koskie	15.00	6.75
CL	Carlos Lee	50.00	22.00
CP	Calvin Pickering	50.00	22.00
DB	Dermal Brown	40.00	18.00
DE	Darin Erstad	80.00	36.00
DG	Derrick Gibson	40.00	18.00
DL	Derrek Lee	15.00	6.75
EC	Eric Chavez	60.00	27.00
ED	Orlando Hernandez	100.00	45.00
FS	Fernando Seguignol	40.00	18.00
FT	Frank Thomas	300.00	135.00
GK	Gabe Kapler	80.00	36.00
GM	Greg Maddux	400.00	180.00
GV	Greg Vaughn	80.00	36.00
JB	Jeromy Burnitz NO AU	20.00	9.00
JC	Jason Conti	15.00	6.75
JD	J.D. Drew	150.00	70.00
JE	Juan Encarnacion	40.00	18.00
JK	Jason Kendall	80.00	36.00

☐ JM	Juan Melo	15.00	6.75
☐ JR	Ken Griffey Jr.	800.00	350.00
☐ KB	Kevin Barker	15.00	6.75
☐ KW	Kevin Witt	15.00	6.75
☐ MA	Marlon Anderson	15.00	6.75
☐ MB	Michael Barrett	40.00	18.00
☐ MC	Mike Caruso	15.00	6.75
☐ MD	Mike Darr NO AU	40.00	18.00
☐ MK	Mark Kotsay	15.00	6.75
☐ MO	Mo Vaughn	120.00	55.00
☐ MP	Mike Piazza EXCH	500.00	220.00
☐ MR	Manny Ramirez	200.00	90.00
☐ NG	Nomar Garciaparra	400.00	180.00
☐ OD	Octavio Dotel	50.00	22.00
☐ PB	Pat Burrell	200.00	90.00
☐ PG	Ivan Rodriguez	200.00	90.00
☐ PM	Pedro Martinez EXCH	200.00	90.00
☐ PO	Paul O'Neill	80.00	36.00
☐ RB	Russ Branyan	50.00	22.00
☐ RH	Roy Halladay	40.00	18.00
☐ RM	Ryan Minor	40.00	18.00
☐ RR	Rafael Roque	40.00	18.00
☐ RT	Reggie Taylor	15.00	6.75
☐ SR	Scott Rolen EXCH	150.00	70.00
☐ TF	Travis Fryman NO AU	40.00	18.00
☐ TG	Tony Gwynn	300.00	135.00
☐ TL	Travis Lee NO AU	20.00	9.00
☐ TW	Todd Walker	40.00	18.00
☐ VC	Vinny Castilla EXCH	80.00	36.00
☐ VG	Vladimir Guerrero	150.00	70.00
☐ ABE	Adrian Beltre	80.00	36.00
☐ AJB	A.J. Burnett EXCH	50.00	22.00
☐ ARA	Aramis Ramirez	50.00	22.00
☐ CBE	Carlos Beltran	120.00	55.00
☐ CHA	Chris Haas	15.00	6.75
☐ CHU	Chad Hutchinson	60.00	27.00
☐ CKI	Cesar King	15.00	6.75
☐ DAM	Damon Minor	15.00	6.75
☐ JAG	Jason Giambi	60.00	27.00
☐ JCI	Jeff Cirillo	40.00	18.00
☐ JEG	Jeremy Giambi NO AU	40.00	18.00
☐ JHJ	Jerry Hairston Jr.	40.00	18.00
☐ JLA	Joe Lawrence	15.00	6.75
☐ JOC	Jose Canseco	300.00	135.00
☐ JUG	Juan Gonzalez NO AU	100.00	45.00
☐ MKI	Mike Kinkade	15.00	6.75
☐ MME	Mitch Meluskey	15.00	6.75
☐ RBE	Ron Belliard	40.00	18.00
☐ RHE	R. Henderson NO AU	60.00	27.00
☐ RMA	Ruben Mateo EXCH	80.00	36.00
☐ RMO	Raul Mondesi NO AU	20.00	9.00
☐ ROB	Rob Bell	15.00	6.75
☐ SHH	Shea Hillenbrand	15.00	6.75
☐ TGL	Troy Glaus	100.00	45.00
☐ THE	Todd Helton	100.00	45.00
☐ THO	Trevor Hoffman	50.00	22.00

1999 SP Signature Legendary Cuts

		MINT	NRMT
RANDOM INSERTS IN PACKS			
ONE OF ONE AUTO CARDS			
☐ ROY	Roy Campanella		
☐ XX	Jimmie Foxx		
☐ LG	Lefty Grove		
☐ W	Walter Johnson		

☐ MEL1	Mel Ott	
☐ MEL2	Mel Ott	
☐ BR	Babe Ruth	
☐ CY	Cy Young	

1986 Sportflics Rookies

	MINT	NRMT
COMP.FACT.SET (50)	15.00	6.75
COMMON PLAYER (1-50)	.10	.05
MINOR STARS	.15	.07
SEMISTARS	.25	.11
UNLISTED STARS	.50	.23

			MINT	NRMT
☐ 1	John Kruk		.60	.25
☐ 2	Edwin Correa		.10	.05
☐ 3	Pete Incaviglia		.15	.07
☐ 4	Dale Sveum		.10	.05
☐ 5	Juan Nieves		.10	.05
☐ 6	Will Clark		1.25	.55
☐ 7	Wally Joyner		1.00	.45
☐ 8	Lance McCullers		.10	.05
☐ 9	Scott Bailes		.10	.05
☐ 10	Dan Plesac		.10	.05
☐ 11	Jose Canseco		5.00	2.20
☐ 12	Bobby Witt		.15	.07
☐ 13	Barry Bonds		8.00	3.60
☐ 14	Andres Thomas		.10	.05
☐ 15	Jim Deshaies		.10	.05
☐ 16	Ruben Sierra		.50	.23
☐ 17	Steve Lombardozzi		.10	.05
☐ 18	Cory Snyder		.10	.05
☐ 19	Reggie Williams		.10	.05
☐ 20	Mitch Williams		.15	.07
☐ 21	Glenn Braggs		.10	.05
☐ 22	Danny Tartabull		.15	.07
☐ 23	Charlie Kerfeld		.10	.05
☐ 24	Paul Assenmacher		.10	.05
☐ 25	Bobby Thompson		.10	.05
☐ 26	Bobby Bonilla		.60	.25
☐ 27	Andres Galarraga		1.00	.45
☐ 28	Billy Joe Robidoux		.10	.05
☐ 29	Bruce Ruffin		.10	.05
☐ 30	Greg Swindell		.15	.07
☐ 31	John Cangelosi		.10	.05
☐ 32	Jim Traber		.10	.05
☐ 33	Russ Morman		.10	.05
☐ 34	Barry Larkin		2.00	.90
☐ 35	Todd Worrell		.50	.23
☐ 36	John Cerutti		.10	.05
☐ 37	Mike Kingery		.10	.05
☐ 38	Mark Eichhorn		.10	.05
☐ 39	Scott Bankhead		.10	.05
☐ 40	Bo Jackson		1.00	.45
☐ 41	Greg Mathews		.10	.05
☐ 42	Eric King		.10	.05
☐ 43	Kal Daniels		.10	.05
☐ 44	Calvin Schiraldi		.10	.05
☐ 45	Mickey Brantley		.10	.05
☐ 46	Tri-Stars		.75	.35
	Willie Mays			
	Pete Rose			
	Fred Lynn			
☐ 47	Tri-Stars		.50	.23
	Tom Seaver			
	Fernando Valenzuela			
	Dwight Gooden			
☐ 48	Big Six		1.00	.45

		MINT	NRMT
	Eddie Murray		
	Lou Whitaker		
	Dave Righetti		
	Steve Sax		
	Cal Ripken		
	Darryl Strawberry		
☐ 49	Kevin Mitchell	.25	.11
☐ 50	Mike Diaz	.10	.05

1994 Sportflics

	MINT	NRMT
COMPLETE SET (193)	25.00	11.00
COMMON CARD (1-193)	.15	.07
MINOR STARS	.30	.14
UNLISTED STARS	.60	.25
SUBSET CARDS HALF VALUE OF BASE CARDS		
SPECIAL CARDS STATED ODDS 1:360		

		MINT	NRMT
☐ 1	Lenny Dykstra	.30	.14
☐ 2	Mike Stanley	.15	.07
☐ 3	Alex Fernandez	.15	.07
☐ 4	Mark McGwire UER	3.00	1.35
	(Name spelled McGuire on front)		
☐ 5	Eric Karros	.30	.14
☐ 6	Dave Justice	.60	.25
☐ 7	Jeff Bagwell	.75	.35
☐ 8	Darren Lewis	.15	.07
☐ 9	David McCarty	.15	.07
☐ 10	Albert Belle	.60	.25
☐ 11	Ben McDonald	.15	.07
☐ 12	Joe Carter	.30	.14
☐ 13	Benito Santiago	.15	.07
☐ 14	Rob Dibble	.15	.07
☐ 15	Roger Clemens	1.50	.70
☐ 16	Travis Fryman	.30	.14
☐ 17	Doug Drabek	.15	.07
☐ 18	Jay Buhner	.30	.14
☐ 19	Orlando Merced	.15	.07
☐ 20	Ryan Klesko	.30	.14
☐ 21	Chuck Finley	.15	.07
☐ 22	Dante Bichette	.30	.14
☐ 23	Wally Joyner	.30	.14
☐ 24	Robin Yount	.60	.25
☐ 25	Tony Gwynn	1.50	.70
☐ 26	Allen Watson	.15	.07
☐ 27	Rick Wilkins	.15	.07
☐ 28	Gary Sheffield	.60	.25
☐ 29	John Burkett	.15	.07
☐ 30	Randy Johnson	.60	.25
☐ 31	Roberto Alomar	.60	.25
☐ 32	Fred McGriff	.40	.18
☐ 33	Ozzie Guillen	.15	.07
☐ 34	Jimmy Key	.30	.14
☐ 35	Juan Gonzalez	1.25	.55
☐ 36	Wil Cordero	.15	.07
☐ 37	Aaron Sele	.30	.14
☐ 38	Mark Langston	.15	.07
☐ 39	David Cone	.40	.18
☐ 40	John Jaha	.15	.07
☐ 41	Ozzie Smith	.75	.35
☐ 42	Kirby Puckett	1.00	.45
☐ 43	Kenny Lofton	.60	.25
☐ 44	Mike Mussina	.60	.25
☐ 45	Ryne Sandberg	.75	.35
☐ 46	Robby Thompson	.15	.07
☐ 47	Bryan Harvey	.15	.07

❏ 48	Marquis Grissom	.30	.14
❏ 49	Bobby Bonilla	.30	.14
❏ 50	Dennis Eckersley	.30	.14
❏ 51	Curt Schilling	.30	.14
❏ 52	Andy Benes	.30	.14
❏ 53	Greg Maddux	1.50	.70
❏ 54	Bill Swift	.15	.07
❏ 55	Andres Galarraga	.60	.25
❏ 56	Tony Phillips	.15	.07
❏ 57	Darryl Hamilton	.15	.07
❏ 58	Duane Ward	.15	.07
❏ 59	Bernie Williams	.60	.25
❏ 60	Steve Avery	.15	.07
❏ 61	Eduardo Perez	.15	.07
❏ 62	Jeff Conine	.15	.07
❏ 63	Dave Winfield	.60	.25
❏ 64	Phil Plantier	.15	.07
❏ 65	Ray Lankford	.30	.14
❏ 66	Robin Ventura	.30	.14
❏ 67	Mike Piazza	2.00	.90
❏ 68	Jason Bere	.15	.07
❏ 69	Cal Ripken	2.50	1.10
❏ 70	Frank Thomas	1.25	.55
❏ 71	Carlos Baerga	.30	.14
❏ 72	Darryl Kile	.15	.07
❏ 73	Ruben Sierra	.15	.07
❏ 74	Gregg Jefferies UER	.15	.07
	Name spelled Jeffries on front		
❏ 75	John Olerud	.30	.14
❏ 76	Andy Van Slyke	.30	.14
❏ 77	Larry Walker	.30	.14
❏ 78	Cecil Fielder	.30	.14
❏ 79	Andre Dawson	.40	.18
❏ 80	Tom Glavine	.60	.25
❏ 81	Sammy Sosa	2.00	.90
❏ 82	Charlie Hayes	.15	.07
❏ 83	Chuck Knoblauch	.60	.25
❏ 84	Kevin Appier	.30	.14
❏ 85	Dean Palmer	.30	.14
❏ 86	Royce Clayton	.15	.07
❏ 87	Moises Alou	.30	.14
❏ 88	Ivan Rodriguez	.75	.35
❏ 89	Tim Salmon	.60	.25
❏ 90	Ron Gant	.30	.14
❏ 91	Barry Bonds	.75	.35
❏ 92	Jack McDowell	.15	.07
❏ 93	Alan Trammell	.40	.18
❏ 94	Dwight Gooden	.30	.14
❏ 95	Jay Bell	.30	.14
❏ 96	Devon White	.15	.07
❏ 97	Wilson Alvarez	.30	.14
❏ 98	Jim Thome	.60	.25
❏ 99	Ramon Martinez	.30	.14
❏ 100	Kent Hrbek	.30	.14
❏ 101	John Kruk	.30	.14
❏ 102	Wade Boggs	.60	.25
❏ 103	Greg Vaughn	.30	.14
❏ 104	Tom Henke	.15	.07
❏ 105	Brian Jordan	.30	.14
❏ 106	Paul Molitor	.60	.25
❏ 107	Cal Eldred	.15	.07
❏ 108	Deion Sanders	.30	.14
❏ 109	Barry Larkin	.60	.25
❏ 110	Mike Greenwell	.15	.07
❏ 111	Jeff Blauser	.15	.07
❏ 112	Jose Rijo	.15	.07
❏ 113	Pete Harnisch	.15	.07
❏ 114	Chris Hoiles	.15	.07
❏ 115	Edgar Martinez	.30	.14
❏ 116	Juan Guzman	.15	.07
❏ 117	Todd Zeile	.15	.07
❏ 118	Danny Tartabull	.15	.07
❏ 119	Chad Curtis	.15	.07
❏ 120	Mark Grace	.40	.18
❏ 121	J.T. Snow	.30	.14
❏ 122	Mo Vaughn	.60	.25
❏ 123	Lance Johnson	.15	.07
❏ 124	Eric Davis	.30	.14
❏ 125	Orel Hershiser	.30	.14
❏ 126	Kevin Mitchell	.15	.07
❏ 127	Don Mattingly	1.25	.55
❏ 128	Darren Daulton	.30	.14
❏ 129	Rod Beck	.15	.07
❏ 130	Charles Nagy	.30	.14
❏ 131	Mickey Tettleton	.15	.07
❏ 132	Kevin Brown	.30	.14

❏ 133	Pat Hentgen	.30	.14
❏ 134	Terry Mulholland	.15	.07
❏ 135	Steve Finley	.15	.07
❏ 136	John Smoltz	.40	.18
❏ 137	Frank Viola	.15	.07
❏ 138	Jim Abbott	.30	.14
❏ 139	Matt Williams	.40	.18
❏ 140	Bernard Gilkey	.15	.07
❏ 141	Jose Canseco	.75	.35
❏ 142	Mark Whiten	.15	.07
❏ 143	Ken Griffey Jr.	3.00	1.35
❏ 144	Rafael Palmeiro	.60	.25
❏ 145	Dave Hollins	.15	.07
❏ 146	Will Clark	.60	.25
❏ 147	Paul O'Neill	.30	.14
❏ 148	Bobby Jones	.15	.07
❏ 149	Butch Huskey	.15	.07
❏ 150	Jeffrey Hammonds	.30	.14
❏ 151	Manny Ramirez	1.25	.55
❏ 152	Bob Hamelin	.15	.07
❏ 153	Kurt Abbott	.15	.07
❏ 154	Scott Stahoviak	.15	.07
❏ 155	Steve Hosey	.15	.07
❏ 156	Salomon Torres	.15	.07
❏ 157	Sterling Hitchcock	.30	.14
❏ 158	Nigel Wilson	.15	.07
❏ 159	Luis Lopez	.15	.07
❏ 160	Chipper Jones	1.50	.70
❏ 161	Norberto Martin	.15	.07
❏ 162	Raul Mondesi	.60	.25
❏ 163	Steve Karsay	.15	.07
❏ 164	J.R. Phillips	.15	.07
❏ 165	Marc Newfield	.15	.07
❏ 166	Mark Hutton	.15	.07
❏ 167	Curtis Pride	.15	.07
❏ 168	Carl Everett	.30	.14
❏ 169	Scott Ruffcorn	.15	.07
❏ 170	Turk Wendell	.15	.07
❏ 171	Jeff McNeely	.15	.07
❏ 172	Javier Lopez	.40	.18
❏ 173	Cliff Floyd	.30	.14
❏ 174	Rondell White	.30	.14
❏ 175	Scott Lydy	.15	.07
❏ 176	Frank Thomas AS	.60	.25
❏ 177	Roberto Alomar AS	.30	.14
❏ 178	Travis Fryman AS	.15	.07
❏ 179	Cal Ripken AS	1.25	.55
❏ 180	Chris Hoiles AS	.15	.07
❏ 181	Ken Griffey Jr. AS	1.50	.70
❏ 182	Juan Gonzalez AS	.60	.25
❏ 183	Joe Carter AS	.15	.07
❏ 184	Jack McDowell AS	.15	.07
❏ 185	Fred McGriff AS	.30	.14
❏ 186	Robby Thompson AS	.15	.07
❏ 187	Matt Williams AS	.15	.07
❏ 188	Jay Bell AS	.15	.07
❏ 189	Mike Piazza AS	1.00	.45
❏ 190	Barry Bonds AS	.60	.25
❏ 191	Lenny Dykstra AS	.15	.07
❏ 192	Dave Justice AS	.30	.14
❏ 193	Greg Maddux AS	.75	.35
❏ NNO	Cliff Floyd Special	2.00	.90
❏ NNO	Paul Molitor Special	8.00	3.60

1994 Sportflics Movers

	MINT	NRMT
COMPLETE SET (12)	50.00	22.00

COMMON CARD (MM1-MM12)	1.00	.45
STATED ODDS 1:24 RETAIL		
❏ MM1 Gregg Jefferies	1.00	.45
❏ MM2 Ryne Sandberg	8.00	3.60
❏ MM3 Cecil Fielder	1.00	.45
❏ MM4 Kirby Puckett	8.00	3.60
❏ MM5 Tony Gwynn	12.00	5.50
❏ MM6 Andres Galarraga	5.00	2.20
❏ MM7 Sammy Sosa	12.00	5.50
❏ MM8 Rickey Henderson	6.00	2.70
❏ MM9 Don Mattingly	8.00	3.60
❏ MM10 Joe Carter	2.00	.90
❏ MM11 Carlos Baerga	1.00	.45
❏ MM12 Lenny Dykstra	2.00	.90

1994 Sportflics Shakers

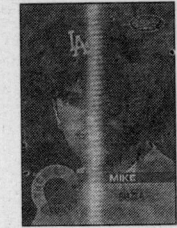

	MINT	NRMT
COMPLETE SET (12)	70.00	32.00
COMMON CARD (SH1-SH12)	1.50	.70
STATED ODDS 1:24 HOBBY		
❏ SH1 Kenny Lofton	6.00	2.70
❏ SH2 Tim Salmon	6.00	2.70
❏ SH3 Jeff Bagwell	6.00	2.70
❏ SH4 Jason Bere	1.50	.70
❏ SH5 Salomon Torres	1.50	.70
❏ SH6 Rondell White	2.50	1.10
❏ SH7 Javier Lopez	4.00	1.80
❏ SH8 Dean Palmer	2.50	1.10
❏ SH9 Jim Thome	6.00	2.70
❏ SH10 J.T. Snow	2.50	1.10
❏ SH11 Mike Piazza	20.00	9.00
❏ SH12 Manny Ramirez	12.00	5.50

1994 Sportflics Rookie/Traded

	MINT	NRMT
COMPLETE SET (150)	25.00	11.00
COMMON CARD (1-150)	.25	.11
MINOR STARS	.50	.23
UNLISTED STARS	1.00	.45
ROY STATED ODDS 1:360		
❏ 1 Will Clark	1.00	.45
❏ 2 Sid Fernandez	.25	.11
❏ 3 Joe Magrane	.25	.11
❏ 4 Pete Smith	.25	.11

❏ 5	Roberto Kelly	.25	.11
❏ 6	Delino DeShields	.25	.11
❏ 7	Brian Harper	.25	.11
❏ 8	Darrin Jackson	.25	.11
❏ 9	Omar Vizquel	.50	.23
❏ 10	Luis Polonia	.25	.11
❏ 11	Reggie Jefferson	.25	.11
❏ 12	Geronimo Berroa	.25	.11
❏ 13	Mike Harkey	.25	.11
❏ 14	Bret Boone	.50	.23
❏ 15	Dave Henderson	.25	.11
❏ 16	Pedro Martinez	1.25	.55
❏ 17	Jose Vizcaino	.25	.11
❏ 18	Xavier Hernandez	.25	.11
❏ 19	Eddie Taubensee	.25	.11
❏ 20	Ellis Burks	.50	.23
❏ 21	Turner Ward	.25	.11
❏ 22	Terry Mulholland	.25	.11
❏ 23	Howard Johnson	.25	.11
❏ 24	Vince Coleman	.25	.11
❏ 25	Deion Sanders	.50	.23
❏ 26	Rafael Palmeiro	1.00	.45
❏ 27	Dave Weathers	.25	.11
❏ 28	Kent Mercker	.25	.11
❏ 29	Gregg Olson	.25	.11
❏ 30	Cory Bailey	.25	.11
❏ 31	Brian L. Hunter	.50	.23
❏ 32	Garey Ingram	.25	.11
❏ 33	Daniel Smith	.25	.11
❏ 34	Denny Hocking	.25	.11
❏ 35	Charles Johnson	.50	.23
❏ 36	Otis Nixon	.25	.11
❏ 37	Hector Fajardo	.25	.11
❏ 38	Lee Smith	.50	.23
❏ 39	Phil Stidham	.25	.11
❏ 40	Melvin Nieves	.25	.11
❏ 41	Julio Franco	.25	.11
❏ 42	Greg Gohr	.25	.11
❏ 43	Steve Dunn	.25	.11
❏ 44	Tony Fernandez	.50	.23
❏ 45	Toby Borland	.25	.11
❏ 46	Paul Shuey	.25	.11
❏ 47	Shawn Hare	.25	.11
❏ 48	Shawn Green	1.50	.70
❏ 49	Julian Tavarez	.25	.11
❏ 50	Ernie Young	.25	.11
❏ 51	Chris Sabo	.25	.11
❏ 52	Greg O'Halloran	.25	.11
❏ 53	Donnie Elliott	.25	.11
❏ 54	Jim Converse	.25	.11
❏ 55	Ray Holbert	.25	.11
❏ 56	Keith Lockhart	.25	.11
❏ 57	Tony Longmire	.25	.11
❏ 58	Jorge Fabregas	.25	.11
❏ 59	Ravelo Manzanillo	.25	.11
❏ 60	Marcus Moore	.25	.11
❏ 61	Carlos Rodriguez	.25	.11
❏ 62	Mark Portugal	.25	.11
❏ 63	Yorkis Perez	.25	.11
❏ 64	Dan Miceli	.25	.11
❏ 65	Chris Turner	.25	.11
❏ 66	Mike Oquist	.25	.11
❏ 67	Tom Quinlan	.25	.11
❏ 68	Matt Walbeck	.25	.11
❏ 69	Dave Staton	.25	.11
❏ 70	Wm. VanLandingham	.25	.11
❏ 71	Dave Stevens	.25	.11
❏ 72	Domingo Cedeno	.25	.11
❏ 73	Alex Diaz	.25	.11
❏ 74	Darren Bragg	.25	.11
❏ 75	James Hurst	.25	.11
❏ 76	Alex Gonzalez	.50	.23
❏ 77	Steve Dreyer	.25	.11
❏ 78	Robert Eenhoorn	.25	.11
❏ 79	Derek Parks	.25	.11
❏ 80	Jose Valentin	.25	.11
❏ 81	Wes Chamberlain	.25	.11
❏ 82	Tony Tarasco	.25	.11
❏ 83	Steve Traschel	.25	.11
❏ 84	Willie Banks	.25	.11
❏ 85	Rob Butler	.25	.11
❏ 86	Miguel Jimenez	.25	.11
❏ 87	Gerald Williams	.25	.11
❏ 88	Aaron Small	.25	.11
❏ 89	Matt Mieske	.25	.11
❏ 90	Tim Hyers	.25	.11

❏ 91	Eddie Murray	1.00	.45
❏ 92	Dennis Martinez	.50	.23
❏ 93	Tony Eusebio	.25	.11
❏ 94	Brian Anderson	.75	.35
❏ 95	Blaise Ilsley	.25	.11
❏ 96	Johnny Ruffin	.25	.11
❏ 97	Carlos Reyes	.25	.11
❏ 98	Greg Pirkl	.25	.11
❏ 99	Jack Morris	.50	.23
❏ 100	John Mabry	.25	.11
❏ 101	Mike Kelly	.25	.11
❏ 102	Rich Becker	.25	.11
❏ 103	Chris Gomez	.25	.11
❏ 104	Jim Edmonds	1.00	.45
❏ 105	Rich Rowland	.25	.11
❏ 106	Damon Buford	.25	.11
❏ 107	Mark Kiefer	.25	.11
❏ 108	Matias Carrillo	.25	.11
❏ 109	James Mouton	.25	.11
❏ 110	Kelly Stinnett	.25	.11
❏ 111	Billy Ashley	.25	.11
❏ 112	Fausto Cruz	.25	.11
❏ 113	Roberto Petagine	.25	.11
❏ 114	Joe Hall	.25	.11
❏ 115	Brian Johnson	.25	.11
❏ 116	Kevin Jarvis	.25	.11
❏ 117	Tim Davis	.25	.11
❏ 118	John Patterson	.25	.11
❏ 119	Stan Royer	.25	.11
❏ 120	Jeff Juden	.25	.11
❏ 121	Bryan Eversgerd	.25	.11
❏ 122	Chan Ho Park	1.25	.55
❏ 123	Shane Reynolds	.50	.23
❏ 124	Danny Bautista	.25	.11
❏ 125	Rikkert Faneyte	.25	.11
❏ 126	Carlos Pulido	.25	.11
❏ 127	Mike Matheny	.25	.11
❏ 128	Hector Carrasco	.25	.11
❏ 129	Eddie Zambrano	.25	.11
❏ 130	Lee Tinsley	.25	.11
❏ 131	Roger Salkeld	.25	.11
❏ 132	Carlos Delgado	1.00	.45
❏ 133	Troy O'Leary	.50	.23
❏ 134	Keith Mitchell	.25	.11
❏ 135	Lance Painter	.25	.11
❏ 136	Nate Minchey	.25	.11
❏ 137	Eric Anthony	.25	.11
❏ 138	Rafael Bournigal	.25	.11
❏ 139	Joey Hamilton	1.00	.45
❏ 140	Bobby Munoz	.25	.11
❏ 141	Rex Hudler	.25	.11
❏ 142	Alex Cole	.25	.11
❏ 143	Stan Javier	.25	.11
❏ 144	Jose Oliva	.25	.11
❏ 145	Tom Brunansky	.25	.11
❏ 146	Greg Colbrunn	.25	.11
❏ 147	Luis S.Lopez	.25	.11
❏ 148	Alex Rodriguez	15.00	6.75
❏ 149	Darryl Strawberry	.50	.23
❏ 150	Bo Jackson	.50	.23
❏ RO1	R.Klesko ROY	8.00	3.60
	M.Ramirez		

1994 Sportflics Rookie/Traded Artist's Proofs

	MINT	NRMT
COMPLETE SET (150)	1500.00	700.00
COMMON CARD (1-150)	10.00	4.50
*STARS: 20X TO 50X HI COLUMN		
STATED ODDS 1:24		

1994 Sportflics Rookie/Traded Going Going Gone

	MINT	NRMT
COMPLETE SET (12)	90.00	40.00
COMMON CARD (GG1-GG12)	2.00	.90
STATED ODDS 1:18		

❏ GG1	Gary Sheffield	5.00	2.20
❏ GG2	Matt Williams	4.00	1.80
❏ GG3	Juan Gonzalez	10.00	4.50
❏ GG4	Ken Griffey Jr.	25.00	11.00
❏ GG5	Mike Piazza	15.00	6.75
❏ GG6	Frank Thomas	10.00	4.50
❏ GG7	Tim Salmon	5.00	2.20
❏ GG8	Barry Bonds	6.00	2.70
❏ GG9	Fred McGriff	4.00	1.80
❏ GG10	Cecil Fielder	2.00	.90
❏ GG11	Albert Belle	5.00	2.20
❏ GG12	Joe Carter	3.00	1.35

1994 Sportflics Rookie/Traded Rookie Starflics

	MINT	NRMT
COMPLETE SET (18)	150.00	70.00
COMMON CARD (TR1-TR18)	5.00	2.20
MINOR STARS	10.00	4.50
STATED ODDS 1:36		

❏ TR1	John Hudek	5.00	2.20
❏ TR2	Manny Ramirez	25.00	11.00
❏ TR3	Jeffrey Hammonds	10.00	4.50
❏ TR4	Carlos Delgado	15.00	6.75
❏ TR5	Javier Lopez	12.00	5.50
❏ TR6	Alex Gonzalez	5.00	2.20
❏ TR7	Raul Mondesi	15.00	6.75
❏ TR8	Bob Hamelin	5.00	2.20
❏ TR9	Ryan Klesko	10.00	4.50
❏ TR10	Brian Anderson	12.00	5.50

		MINT	NRMT
❑ TR11	Alex Rodriguez	60.00	27.00
❑ TR12	Cliff Floyd	10.00	4.50
❑ TR13	Chan Ho Park	12.00	5.50
❑ TR14	Steve Karsay	5.00	2.20
❑ TR15	Rondell White	10.00	4.50
❑ TR16	Shawn Green	20.00	9.00
❑ TR17	Rich Becker	5.00	2.20
❑ TR18	Charles Johnson	10.00	4.50

1995 Sportflix

	MINT	NRMT
COMPLETE SET (170)	20.00	9.00
COMMON CARD (1-170)	.15	.07
MINOR STARS	.30	.14
UNLISTED STARS	.60	.25
SUBSET CARDS HALF VALUE OF BASE CARDS		
COMP.AP SET (170)	1000.00	450.00
COMMON ART.PRF. (1-170)	3.00	1.35

*ART.PRF.STARS: 10X TO 20X HI COLUMN
*ART.PRF.YOUNG STARS: 7.5X TO 15X HI
AP STATED ODDS 1:36

❑ 1	Ken Griffey Jr.	3.00	1.35
❑ 2	Jeffrey Hammonds	.30	.14
❑ 3	Fred McGriff	.40	.18
❑ 4	Rickey Henderson	.75	.35
❑ 5	Derrick May	.15	.07
❑ 6	Robin Ventura	.30	.14
❑ 7	Royce Clayton	.15	.07
❑ 8	Paul Molitor	.60	.25
❑ 9	Charlie Hayes	.15	.07
❑ 10	David Nied	.15	.07
❑ 11	Ellis Burks	.30	.14
❑ 12	Bernard Gilkey	.15	.07
❑ 13	Don Mattingly	1.25	.55
❑ 14	Albert Belle	.60	.25
❑ 15	Doug Drabek	.15	.07
❑ 16	Tony Gwynn	1.50	.70
❑ 17	Delino DeShields	.15	.07
❑ 18	Bobby Bonilla	.30	.14
❑ 19	Cliff Floyd	.30	.14
❑ 20	Frank Thomas	1.25	.55
❑ 21	Raul Mondesi	.40	.18
❑ 22	Dave Nilsson	.15	.07
❑ 23	Todd Zeile	.15	.07
❑ 24	Bernie Williams	.60	.25
❑ 25	Kirby Puckett	1.00	.45
❑ 26	David Cone	.40	.18
❑ 27	Darren Daulton	.30	.14
❑ 28	Marquis Grissom	.30	.14
❑ 29	Randy Johnson	.60	.25
❑ 30	Jeff Kent	.15	.07
❑ 31	Orlando Merced	.15	.07
❑ 32	Dave Justice	.60	.25
❑ 33	Ivan Rodriguez	.75	.35
❑ 34	Kirk Gibson	.15	.07
❑ 35	Alex Fernandez	.15	.07
❑ 36	Rick Wilkins	.15	.07
❑ 37	Andy Benes	.15	.07
❑ 38	Bret Saberhagen	.30	.14
❑ 39	Billy Ashley	.15	.07
❑ 40	Jose Rijo	.15	.07
❑ 41	Matt Williams	.60	.25
❑ 42	Lenny Dykstra	.30	.14
❑ 43	Jay Bell	.30	.14
❑ 44	Reggie Jefferson	.15	.07
❑ 45	Greg Maddux	1.50	.70
❑ 46	Gary Sheffield	.30	.14
❑ 47	Bret Boone	.30	.14
❑ 48	Jeff Bagwell	.75	.35
❑ 49	Ben McDonald	.15	.07
❑ 50	Eric Karros	.30	.14
❑ 51	Roger Clemens	1.50	.70
❑ 52	Sammy Sosa	2.00	.90
❑ 53	Barry Bonds	.75	.35
❑ 54	Joey Hamilton	.30	.14
❑ 55	Brian Jordan	.30	.14
❑ 56	Wil Cordero	.15	.07
❑ 57	Aaron Sele	.30	.14
❑ 58	Paul O'Neill	.30	.14
❑ 59	Carlos Garcia	.15	.07
❑ 60	Mike Mussina	.60	.25
❑ 61	John Olerud	.30	.14
❑ 62	Kevin Appier	.30	.14
❑ 63	Matt Mieske	.15	.07
❑ 64	Carlos Baerga	.15	.07
❑ 65	Ryan Klesko	.30	.14
❑ 66	Jimmy Key	.30	.14
❑ 67	James Mouton	.15	.07
❑ 68	Tim Salmon	.60	.25
❑ 69	Hal Morris	.15	.07
❑ 70	Albie Lopez	.15	.07
❑ 71	Dave Hollins	.15	.07
❑ 72	Greg Colbrunn	.15	.07
❑ 73	Juan Gonzalez	1.25	.55
❑ 74	Wally Joyner	.30	.14
❑ 75	Bob Hamelin	.15	.07
❑ 76	Brady Anderson	.30	.14
❑ 77	Deion Sanders	.30	.14
❑ 78	Javier Lopez	.15	.07
❑ 79	Brian McRae	.15	.07
❑ 80	Craig Biggio	.60	.25
❑ 81	Kenny Lofton	.40	.18
❑ 82	Cecil Fielder	.30	.14
❑ 83	Mike Piazza	2.00	.90
❑ 84	Rafael Palmeiro	.60	.25
❑ 85	Jim Thome	.60	.25
❑ 86	Ruben Sierra	.15	.07
❑ 87	Mark Langston	.15	.07
❑ 88	John Valentin	.30	.14
❑ 89	Shawon Dunston	.15	.07
❑ 90	Travis Fryman	.30	.14
❑ 91	Chuck Knoblauch	.30	.14
❑ 92	Dean Palmer	.30	.14
❑ 93	Robby Thompson	.15	.07
❑ 94	Barry Larkin	.60	.25
❑ 95	Darren Lewis	.15	.07
❑ 96	Andres Galarraga	.60	.25
❑ 97	Tony Phillips	.15	.07
❑ 98	Mo Vaughn	.60	.25
❑ 99	Pedro Martinez	.75	.35
❑ 100	Chad Curtis	.15	.07
❑ 101	Brent Gates	.15	.07
❑ 102	Pat Hentgen	.30	.14
❑ 103	Rico Brogna	.15	.07
❑ 104	Carlos Delgado	.60	.25
❑ 105	Manny Ramirez	.75	.35
❑ 106	Mike Greenwell	.15	.07
❑ 107	Wade Boggs	.60	.25
❑ 108	Ozzie Smith	.75	.35
❑ 109	Rusty Greer	.60	.25
❑ 110	Willie Greene	.15	.07
❑ 111	Chili Davis	.15	.07
❑ 112	Reggie Sanders	.30	.14
❑ 113	Roberto Kelly	.15	.07
❑ 114	Tom Glavine	.60	.25
❑ 115	Moises Alou	.30	.14
❑ 116	Dennis Eckersley	.30	.14
❑ 117	Danny Tartabull	.15	.07
❑ 118	Jeff Conine	.15	.07
❑ 119	Will Clark	.60	.25
❑ 120	Joe Carter	.30	.14
❑ 121	Mark McGwire	3.00	1.35
❑ 122	Cal Ripken Jr.	2.50	1.10
❑ 123	Danny Jackson	.15	.07
❑ 124	Phil Plantier	.15	.07
❑ 125	Dante Bichette	.30	.14
❑ 126	Jack McDowell	.15	.07
❑ 127	Jose Canseco	.75	.35
❑ 128	Roberto Alomar	.60	.25
❑ 129	Rondell White	.30	.14
❑ 130	Ray Lankford	.15	.07
❑ 131	Ryan Thompson	.15	.07
❑ 132	Ken Caminiti	.40	.18
❑ 133	Gregg Jefferies	.30	.14
❑ 134	Omar Vizquel	.15	.07
❑ 135	Mark Grace	.40	.18
❑ 136	Derek Bell	.30	.14
❑ 137	Mickey Tettleton	.15	.07
❑ 138	Wilson Alvarez	.30	.14
❑ 139	Larry Walker	.60	.25
❑ 140	Bo Jackson	.30	.14
❑ 141	Alex Rodriguez	2.50	1.10
❑ 142	Orlando Miller	.15	.07
❑ 143	Shawn Green	.60	.25
❑ 144	Steve Dunn	.15	.07
❑ 145	Midre Cummings	.15	.07
❑ 146	Chan Ho Park	.60	.25
❑ 147	Jose Oliva	.15	.07
❑ 148	Armando Benitez	.15	.07
❑ 149	J.R. Phillips	.15	.07
❑ 150	Charles Johnson	.30	.14
❑ 151	Garret Anderson	.30	.14
❑ 152	Russ Davis	.15	.07
❑ 153	Brian L.Hunter	.30	.14
❑ 154	Ernie Young	.15	.07
❑ 155	Marc Newfield	.15	.07
❑ 156	Greg Pirkl	.15	.07
❑ 157	Scott Ruffcorn	.15	.07
❑ 158	Rikkert Faneyte	.15	.07
❑ 159	Duane Singleton	.15	.07
❑ 160	Gabe White	.15	.07
❑ 161	Alex Gonzalez	.15	.07
❑ 162	Chipper Jones	1.50	.70
❑ 163	Mike Kelly	.15	.07
❑ 164	Kurt Miller	.15	.07
❑ 165	Roberto Petagine	.15	.07
❑ 166	Jeff Bagwell CL	.60	.25
❑ 167	Mike Piazza CL	1.00	.45
❑ 168	Ken Griffey Jr. CL	1.50	.70
❑ 169	Frank Thomas CL	.60	.25
❑ 170	Barry Bonds CL	1.25	.55
	Cal Ripken		

1995 Sportflix Detonators

	MINT	NRMT
COMPLETE SET (9)	30.00	13.50
COMMON CARD (DE1-DE9)	1.00	.45
STATED ODDS 1:16		

❑ DE1	Jeff Bagwell	2.50	1.10
❑ DE2	Matt Williams	2.00	.90
❑ DE3	Ken Griffey Jr.	10.00	4.50
❑ DE4	Frank Thomas	4.00	1.80
❑ DE5	Mike Piazza	6.00	2.70
❑ DE6	Barry Bonds	2.50	1.10
❑ DE7	Albert Belle	2.00	.90
❑ DE8	Cliff Floyd	1.00	.45
❑ DE9	Juan Gonzalez	4.00	1.80

1995 Sportflix Double Take

	MINT	NRMT
COMPLETE SET (12)	120.00	55.00
COMMON CARD (1-12)	4.00	1.80
STATED ODDS 1:48		

		MINT	
❑ 1	Jeff Bagwell	12.00	5.50
	Frank Thomas		
❑ 2	Will Clark	4.00	1.80
	Fred McGriff		
❑ 3	Roberto Alomar	4.00	1.80
	Jeff Kent		
❑ 4	Matt Williams	4.00	1.80
	Wade Boggs		
❑ 5	Cal Ripken Jr.	20.00	9.00
	Ozzie Smith		
❑ 6	Alex Rodriguez	20.00	9.00
	Wil Cordero		
❑ 7	Mike Piazza	15.00	6.75
	Carlos Delgado		
❑ 8	Kenny Lofton	4.00	1.80
	Dave Justice		
❑ 9	Barry Bonds	25.00	11.00
	Ken Griffey Jr.		
❑ 10	Albert Belle	4.00	1.80
	Raul Mondesi		
❑ 11	Tony Gwynn	15.00	6.75
	Kirby Puckett		
❑ 12	Jimmy Key	10.00	4.50
	Greg Maddux		

1995 Sportflix Hammer Team

MANNY RAMIREZ

		MINT	NRMT
COMPLETE SET (18)		25.00	11.00
COMMON CARD (HT1-HT18)		.75	.35
STATED ODDS 1:4			

❑ HT1	Ken Griffey Jr.	5.00	2.20
❑ HT2	Frank Thomas	2.00	.90
❑ HT3	Jeff Bagwell	1.25	.55
❑ HT4	Mike Piazza	3.00	1.35
❑ HT5	Cal Ripken Jr.	4.00	1.80
❑ HT6	Albert Belle	1.00	.45
❑ HT7	Barry Bonds	1.25	.55
❑ HT8	Don Mattingly	2.00	.90
❑ HT9	Will Clark	1.00	.45
❑ HT10	Tony Gwynn	2.50	1.10
❑ HT11	Matt Williams	1.00	.45
❑ HT12	Kirby Puckett	1.50	.70
❑ HT13	Manny Ramirez	1.25	.55
❑ HT14	Fred McGriff	.75	.35
❑ HT15	Juan Gonzalez	2.00	.90
❑ HT16	Kenny Lofton	.75	.35
❑ HT17	Raul Mondesi	.75	.35
❑ HT18	Tim Salmon	1.00	.45

1995 Sportflix ProMotion

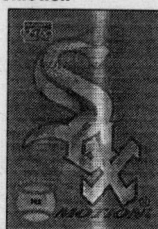

	MINT	NRMT
COMPLETE SET (12)	120.00	55.00
COMMON CARD (PM1-PM12)	6.00	2.70
STATED ODDS 1:18 JUMBO		

❑ PM1	Ken Griffey Jr.	30.00	13.50
❑ PM2	Frank Thomas	12.00	5.50
❑ PM3	Cal Ripken Jr.	25.00	11.00
❑ PM4	Jeff Bagwell	8.00	3.60
❑ PM5	Mike Piazza	20.00	9.00
❑ PM6	Matt Williams	6.00	2.70
❑ PM7	Albert Belle	6.00	2.70
❑ PM8	Jose Canseco	8.00	3.60
❑ PM9	Don Mattingly	12.00	5.50
❑ PM10	Barry Bonds	8.00	3.60
❑ PM11	Will Clark	6.00	2.70
❑ PM12	Kirby Puckett	6.00	2.70

1996 Sportflix

	MINT	NRMT
COMPLETE SET (144)	25.00	11.00
COMMON CARD (1-144)	.15	.07
MINOR STARS	.30	.14
UNLISTED STARS	.60	.25
SUBSET CARDS HALF VALUE OF BASE CARDS		
COMMON ART.PRF. (1-144)	4.00	1.80
*AP STARS: 10X TO 25X HI COLUMN		
*AP ROOKIES: 6X TO 15X HI		
AP STATED ODDS 1:48		

❑ 1	Wade Boggs	.60	.25
❑ 2	Tim Salmon	.40	.18
❑ 3	Will Clark	.60	.25
❑ 4	Dante Bichette	.30	.14
❑ 5	Barry Bonds	.75	.35
❑ 6	Kirby Puckett	1.00	.45
❑ 7	Albert Belle	.60	.25
❑ 8	Greg Maddux	1.50	.70
❑ 9	Tony Gwynn	1.50	.70
❑ 10	Mike Piazza	2.00	.90
❑ 11	Ivan Rodriguez	.75	.35
❑ 12	Marty Cordova	.15	.07
❑ 13	Frank Thomas	1.25	.55
❑ 14	Raul Mondesi	.30	.14
❑ 15	Johnny Damon	.40	.18

❑ 16	Mark McGwire	3.00	1.35
❑ 17	Len Dykstra	.30	.14
❑ 18	Ken Griffey Jr.	3.00	1.35
❑ 19	Chipper Jones	1.50	.70
❑ 20	Alex Rodriguez	2.00	.90
❑ 21	Jeff Bagwell	.75	.35
❑ 22	Jim Edmonds	.40	.18
❑ 23	Edgar Martinez	.30	.14
❑ 24	David Cone	.40	.18
❑ 25	Tom Glavine	.60	.25
❑ 26	Eddie Murray	.60	.25
❑ 27	Paul Molitor	.60	.25
❑ 28	Ryan Klesko	.30	.14
❑ 29	Rafael Palmeiro	.60	.25
❑ 30	Manny Ramirez	.75	.35
❑ 31	Mo Vaughn	.60	.25
❑ 32	Rico Brogna	.15	.07
❑ 33	Marc Newfield	.15	.07
❑ 34	J.T. Snow	.30	.14
❑ 35	Reggie Sanders	.30	.14
❑ 36	Fred McGriff	.40	.18
❑ 37	Craig Biggio	.60	.25
❑ 38	Jeff King	.15	.07
❑ 39	Kenny Lofton	.40	.18
❑ 40	Gary Gaetti	.30	.14
❑ 41	Eric Karros	.30	.14
❑ 42	Jason Isringhausen	.30	.14
❑ 43	B.J. Surhoff	.30	.14
❑ 44	Michael Tucker	.15	.07
❑ 45	Gary Sheffield	.30	.14
❑ 46	Chili Davis	.30	.14
❑ 47	Bobby Bonilla	.30	.14
❑ 48	Hideo Nomo	.60	.25
❑ 49	Ray Durham	.30	.14
❑ 50	Phil Nevin	.15	.07
❑ 51	Randy Johnson	.60	.25
❑ 52	Bill Pulsipher	.15	.07
❑ 53	Ozzie Smith	.75	.35
❑ 54	Cal Ripken	2.50	1.10
❑ 55	Cecil Fielder	.30	.14
❑ 56	Matt Williams	.60	.25
❑ 57	Sammy Sosa	2.00	.90
❑ 58	Roger Clemens	1.50	.70
❑ 59	Brian L.Hunter	.15	.07
❑ 60	Barry Larkin	.60	.25
❑ 61	Charles Johnson	.30	.14
❑ 62	David Justice	.60	.25
❑ 63	Garret Anderson	.30	.14
❑ 64	Rondell White	.30	.14
❑ 65	Derek Bell	.30	.14
❑ 66	Andres Galarraga	.60	.25
❑ 67	Moises Alou	.30	.14
❑ 68	Travis Fryman	.30	.14
❑ 69	Pedro Martinez	.75	.35
❑ 70	Carlos Baerga	.15	.07
❑ 71	John Valentin	.30	.14
❑ 72	Larry Walker	.60	.25
❑ 73	Roberto Alomar	.60	.25
❑ 74	Mike Mussina	.60	.25
❑ 75	Kevin Appier	.30	.14
❑ 76	Bernie Williams	.60	.25
❑ 77	Ray Lankford	.30	.14
❑ 78	Gregg Jefferies	.15	.07
❑ 79	Robin Ventura	.30	.14
❑ 80	Kenny Rogers	.15	.07
❑ 81	Paul O'Neill	.30	.14
❑ 82	Mark Grace	.40	.18
❑ 83	Deion Sanders	.30	.14
❑ 84	Tino Martinez	.30	.14
❑ 85	Joe Carter	.30	.14
❑ 86	Pete Schourek	.15	.07
❑ 87	Jack McDowell	.15	.07
❑ 88	John Mabry	.15	.07
❑ 89	Darren Daulton	.30	.14
❑ 90	Jim Thome	.60	.25
❑ 91	Jay Buhner	.30	.14
❑ 92	Jay Bell	.30	.14
❑ 93	Kevin Seitzer	.15	.07
❑ 94	Jose Canseco	.75	.35
❑ 95	Juan Gonzalez	1.25	.55
❑ 96	Jeff Conine	.15	.07
❑ 97	Chipper Jones UC3	.75	.35
❑ 98	Ken Griffey Jr. UC3	1.50	.70
❑ 99	Frank Thomas UC3	.60	.25
❑ 100	Cal Ripken UC3	1.25	.55
❑ 101	Albert Belle UC3	.30	.14

		MINT	NRMT
❏ 102	Mike Piazza UC3	1.00	.45
❏ 103	Dante Bichette UC3	.15	.07
❏ 104	Sammy Sosa UC3	1.00	.45
❏ 105	Mo Vaughn UC3	.30	.14
❏ 106	Tim Salmon UC3	.15	.07
❏ 107	Reggie Sanders UC3	.15	.07
❏ 108	Gary Sheffield UC3	.15	.07
❏ 109	Ruben Rivera UC3	.15	.07
❏ 110	Rafael Palmeiro UC3	.15	.07
❏ 111	Edgar Martinez UC3	.15	.07
❏ 112	Barry Bonds UC3	.40	.18
❏ 113	Manny Ramirez UC3	.60	.25
❏ 114	Larry Walker UC3	.30	.14
❏ 115	Jeff Bagwell UC3	.60	.25
❏ 116	Matt Williams UC3	.30	.14
❏ 117	Mark McGwire UC3	1.50	.70
❏ 118	Johnny Damon UC3	.15	.07
❏ 119	Eddie Murray UC3	.30	.14
❏ 120	Jay Buhner UC3	.15	.07
❏ 121	Tim Unroe	.15	.07
❏ 122	Todd Hollandsworth	.15	.07
❏ 123	Tony Clark	.60	.25
❏ 124	Roger Cedeno	.30	.14
❏ 125	Jim Pittsley	.15	.07
❏ 126	Ruben Rivera	.30	.14
❏ 127	Bob Wolcott	.15	.07
❏ 128	Chan Ho Park	.40	.18
❏ 129	Chris Snopek	.15	.07
❏ 130	Alex Ochoa	.15	.07
❏ 131	Yamil Benitez	.15	.07
❏ 132	Jimmy Haynes	.15	.07
❏ 133	Dustin Hermanson	.15	.07
❏ 134	Shawn Estes	.30	.14
❏ 135	Howard Battle	.15	.07
❏ 136	Matt Lawton	.75	.35
❏ 137	Terrell Wade	.15	.07
❏ 138	Jason Schmidt	.15	.07
❏ 139	Derek Jeter	2.00	.90
❏ 140	Shannon Stewart	.30	.14
❏ 141	Chris Stynes	.15	.07
❏ 142	Ken Griffey Jr. CL	1.50	.70
❏ 143	Greg Maddux CL	.75	.35
❏ 144	Cal Ripken CL	1.25	.55

1996 Sportflix Double Take

	MINT	NRMT
COMPLETE SET (12)	100.00	45.00
COMMON CARD (1-12)	4.00	1.80
STATED ODDS 1:22 JUMBO		

		MINT	NRMT
❏ 1	Barry Larkin Cal Ripken	12.00	5.50
❏ 2	Roberto Alomar Craig Biggio	4.00	1.80
❏ 3	Chipper Jones Matt Williams	8.00	3.60
❏ 4	Ken Griffey Ruben Rivera	15.00	6.75
❏ 5	Greg Maddux Hideo Nomo	8.00	3.60
❏ 6	Frank Thomas Mo Vaughn	6.00	2.70
❏ 7	Ivan Rodriguez Mike Piazza	10.00	4.50
❏ 8	Albert Belle Barry Bonds	4.00	1.80
❏ 9	Alex Rodriguez Derek Jeter	15.00	6.75
❏ 10	Kirby Puckett Tony Gwynn	10.00	4.50
❏ 11	Sammy Sosa Manny Ramirez	10.00	4.50
❏ 12	Jeff Bagwell Rico Brogna	4.00	1.80

1996 Sportflix Hit Parade

	MINT	NRMT
COMPLETE SET (16)	80.00	36.00
COMMON CARD (1-16)	2.00	.90
STATED ODDS 1:35		

		MINT	NRMT
❏ 1	Ken Griffey Jr.	15.00	6.75
❏ 2	Cal Ripken	12.00	5.50
❏ 3	Frank Thomas	6.00	2.70
❏ 4	Mike Piazza	10.00	4.50
❏ 5	Mo Vaughn	3.00	1.35
❏ 6	Albert Belle	3.00	1.35
❏ 7	Jeff Bagwell	4.00	1.80
❏ 8	Matt Williams	3.00	1.35
❏ 9	Sammy Sosa	10.00	4.50
❏ 10	Kirby Puckett	5.00	2.20
❏ 11	Dante Bichette	2.00	.90
❏ 12	Gary Sheffield	2.00	.90
❏ 13	Tony Gwynn	8.00	3.60
❏ 14	Wade Boggs	3.00	1.35
❏ 15	Chipper Jones	8.00	3.60
❏ 16	Barry Bonds	4.00	1.80

1996 Sportflix Power Surge

	MINT	NRMT
COMPLETE SET (24)	120.00	55.00
COMMON CARD (1-24)	2.00	.90
STATED ODDS 1:35 RETAIL		

		MINT	NRMT
❏ 1	Chipper Jones	12.00	5.50
❏ 2	Ken Griffey Jr.	25.00	11.00
❏ 3	Frank Thomas	10.00	4.50
❏ 4	Cal Ripken	20.00	9.00
❏ 5	Albert Belle	5.00	2.20
❏ 6	Mike Piazza	15.00	6.75
❏ 7	Dante Bichette	2.00	.90
❏ 8	Sammy Sosa	15.00	6.75
❏ 9	Mo Vaughn	5.00	2.20
❏ 10	Tim Salmon	3.00	1.35
❏ 11	Reggie Sanders	2.00	.90
❏ 12	Gary Sheffield	2.00	.90
❏ 13	Ruben Rivera	2.00	.90
❏ 14	Rafael Palmeiro	5.00	2.20
❏ 15	Edgar Martinez	2.00	.90
❏ 16	Barry Bonds	6.00	2.70
❏ 17	Manny Ramirez	6.00	2.70
❏ 18	Larry Walker	5.00	2.20
❏ 19	Jeff Bagwell	6.00	2.70
❏ 20	Matt Williams	5.00	2.20
❏ 21	Mark McGwire	25.00	11.00
❏ 22	Johnny Damon	3.00	1.35
❏ 23	Eddie Murray	5.00	2.20
❏ 24	Jay Buhner	2.00	.90

1996 Sportflix ProMotion

	MINT	NRMT
COMPLETE SET (20)	60.00	27.00
COMMON CARD (1-20)	1.25	.55
STATED ODDS 1:17		

		MINT	NRMT
❏ 1	Cal Ripken	10.00	4.50
❏ 2	Greg Maddux	6.00	2.70
❏ 3	Mo Vaughn	2.50	1.10
❏ 4	Albert Belle	2.50	1.10
❏ 5	Mike Piazza	8.00	3.60
❏ 6	Ken Griffey Jr.	12.00	5.50
❏ 7	Frank Thomas	5.00	2.20
❏ 8	Jeff Bagwell	3.00	1.35
❏ 9	Hideo Nomo	2.50	1.10
❏ 10	Chipper Jones	6.00	2.70
❏ 11	Tony Gwynn	6.00	2.70
❏ 12	Don Mattingly	5.00	2.20
❏ 13	Dante Bichette	1.25	.55
❏ 14	Matt Williams	2.50	1.10
❏ 15	Manny Ramirez	3.00	1.35
❏ 16	Barry Bonds	3.00	1.35
❏ 17	Reggie Sanders	1.25	.55
❏ 18	Tim Salmon	1.50	.70
❏ 19	Ruben Rivera	1.25	.55
❏ 20	Garret Anderson	1.25	.55

1997 Sports Illustrated

	MINT	NRMT
COMPLETE SET (180)	40.00	18.00

COMMON CARD (1-180)	.15	.07
MINOR STARS	.30	.14
UNLISTED STARS	.60	.25

SUBSET CARDS HALF VALUE OF BASE CARDS

❑ 1 Bob Abreu	.30		.14
❑ 2 Jaime Bluma	.15		.07
❑ 3 Emil Brown	.40		.18
❑ 4 Jose Cruz Jr.	1.25		.55
❑ 5 Jason Dickson	.15		.07
❑ 6 Nomar Garciaparra	2.00		.90
❑ 7 Todd Greene	.15		.07
❑ 8 Vladimir Guerrero	1.00		.45
❑ 9 Wilton Guerrero	.30		.14
❑ 10 Jose Guillen	.40		.18
❑ 11 Hideki Irabu	1.00		.45
❑ 12 Russ Johnson	.15		.07
❑ 13 Andruw Jones	.75		.35
❑ 14 Damon Mashore	.15		.07
❑ 15 Jason McDonald	.15		.07
❑ 16 Ryan McGuire	.15		.07
❑ 17 Matt Morris	.30		.14
❑ 18 Kevin Orie	.15		.07
❑ 19 Dante Powell	.15		.07
❑ 20 Pokey Reese	.30		.14
❑ 21 Joe Roa	.15		.07
❑ 22 Scott Rolen	1.00		.45
❑ 23 Glendon Rusch	.15		.07
❑ 24 Scott Spiezio	.15		.07
❑ 25 Bubba Trammell	.60		.25
❑ 26 Todd Walker	.60		.25
❑ 27 Jamey Wright	.15		.07
❑ 28 Ken Griffey Jr. SH	1.50		.70
❑ 29 Tino Martinez SH	.30		.14
❑ 30 Roger Clemens SH	.75		.35
❑ 31 Hideki Irabu SH	.60		.25
❑ 32 Kevin Brown SH	.15		.07
❑ 33 Chipper Jones SH	1.50		.70
Cal Ripken			
❑ 34 Sandy Alomar SH	.15		.07
❑ 35 Ken Caminiti SH	.15		.07
❑ 36 Randy Johnson SH	.30		.14
❑ 37 Andy Ashby IB	.15		.07
❑ 38 Jay Buhner IB	.15		.07
❑ 39 Joe Carter IB	.15		.07
❑ 40 Darren Daulton IB	.15		.07
❑ 41 Jeff Fassero IB	.15		.07
❑ 42 Andres Galarraga IB	.30		.14
❑ 43 Rusty Greer IB	.15		.07
❑ 44 Marquis Grissom IB	.15		.07
❑ 45 Joey Hamilton IB	.15		.07
❑ 46 Jimmy Key IB	.15		.07
❑ 47 Ryan Klesko IB	.15		.07
❑ 48 Eddie Murray IB	.30		.14
❑ 49 Charles Nagy IB	.15		.07
❑ 50 Dave Nilsson IB	.15		.07
❑ 51 Ricardo Rincon IB	.15		.07
❑ 52 Billy Wagner IB	.15		.07
❑ 53 Dan Wilson IB	.15		.07
❑ 54 Dmitri Young IB	.15		.07
❑ 55 Roberto Alomar SIV	.30		.14
❑ 56 Sandy Alomar Jr. SIV	.15		.07
❑ 57 Scott Brosius SIV	.15		.07
❑ 58 Tony Clark SIV	.30		.14
❑ 59 Carlos Delgado SIV	.30		.14
❑ 60 Jermaine Dye SIV	.15		.07
❑ 61 Darin Erstad SIV	.60		.25
❑ 62 Derek Jeter SIV	1.00		.45
❑ 63 Jason Kendall SIV	.15		.07
❑ 64 Hideo Nomo SIV	.60		.25
❑ 65 Rey Ordonez SIV	.15		.07
❑ 66 Andy Pettitte SIV	.15		.07
❑ 67 Manny Ramirez SIV	.30		.14
❑ 68 Edgar Renteria SIV	.15		.07
❑ 69 Shane Reynolds SIV	.15		.07
❑ 70 Alex Rodriguez SIV	1.00		.45
❑ 71 Ivan Rodriguez SIV	.40		.18
❑ 72 Jose Rosado SIV	.15		.07
❑ 73 John Smoltz	.40		.18
❑ 74 Tom Glavine	.40		.25
❑ 75 Greg Maddux	1.50		.70
❑ 76 Chipper Jones	1.50		.70
❑ 77 Kenny Lofton	.40		.18
❑ 78 Fred McGriff	.40		.18
❑ 79 Kevin Brown	.40		.18

❑ 80 Alex Fernandez	.15		.07
❑ 81 Al Leiter	.30		.14
❑ 82 Bobby Bonilla	.30		.14
❑ 83 Gary Sheffield	.30		.14
❑ 84 Moises Alou	.30		.14
❑ 85 Henry Rodriguez	.30		.14
❑ 86 Mark Grudzielanek	.30		.14
❑ 87 Pedro Martinez	.75		.35
❑ 88 Todd Hundley	.30		.14
❑ 89 Bernard Gilkey	.15		.07
❑ 90 Bobby Jones	.15		.07
❑ 91 Curt Schilling	.40		.18
❑ 92 Ricky Bottalico	.30		.14
❑ 93 Mike Lieberthal	.15		.07
❑ 94 Sammy Sosa	2.00		.90
❑ 95 Ryne Sandberg	.75		.35
❑ 96 Mark Grace	.40		.18
❑ 97 Deion Sanders	.30		.14
❑ 98 Reggie Sanders	.30		.14
❑ 99 Barry Larkin	.60		.25
❑ 100 Craig Biggio	.60		.25
❑ 101 Jeff Bagwell	.75		.35
❑ 102 Derek Bell	.30		.14
❑ 103 Brian Jordan	.30		.14
❑ 104 Ray Lankford	.30		.14
❑ 105 Ron Gant	.30		.14
❑ 106 Al Martin	.15		.07
❑ 107 Kevin Elster	.15		.07
❑ 108 Jermaine Allensworth	.15		.07
❑ 109 Vinny Castilla	.40		.18
❑ 110 Dante Bichette	.30		.14
❑ 111 Larry Walker	.60		.25
❑ 112 Mike Piazza	2.00		.90
❑ 113 Eric Karros	.30		.14
❑ 114 Todd Hollandsworth	.15		.07
❑ 115 Raul Mondesi	.30		.14
❑ 116 Hideo Nomo	.60		.25
❑ 117 Ramon Martinez	.30		.14
❑ 118 Ken Caminiti	.40		.18
❑ 119 Tony Gwynn	1.50		.70
❑ 120 Steve Finley	.15		.07
❑ 121 Barry Bonds	.75		.35
❑ 122 J.T. Snow	.30		.14
❑ 123 Rod Beck	.15		.07
❑ 124 Cal Ripken	2.50		1.10
❑ 125 Mike Mussina	.60		.25
❑ 126 Brady Anderson	.30		.14
❑ 127 Bernie Williams	.60		.25
❑ 128 Derek Jeter	2.00		.90
❑ 129 Tino Martinez	.60		.25
❑ 130 Andy Pettitte	.40		.18
❑ 131 David Cone	.30		.14
❑ 132 Mariano Rivera	.30		.14
❑ 133 Roger Clemens	1.50		.70
❑ 134 Pat Hentgen	.15		.07
❑ 135 Juan Guzman	.15		.07
❑ 136 Bob Higginson	.30		.14
❑ 137 Tony Clark	.40		.18
❑ 138 Travis Fryman	.30		.14
❑ 139 Mo Vaughn	.60		.25
❑ 140 Tim Naehring	.15		.07
❑ 141 John Valentin	.15		.07
❑ 142 Matt Williams	.60		.25
❑ 143 David Justice	.60		.25
❑ 144 Jim Thome	.60		.25
❑ 145 Chuck Knoblauch	.60		.25
❑ 146 Paul Molitor	.60		.25
❑ 147 Marty Cordova	.30		.14
❑ 148 Frank Thomas	1.25		.55
❑ 149 Albert Belle	.60		.25
❑ 150 Robin Ventura	.30		.14
❑ 151 John Jaha	.15		.07
❑ 152 Jeff Cirillo	.30		.14
❑ 153 Jose Valentin	.15		.07
❑ 154 Jay Bell	.30		.14
❑ 155 Jeff King	.15		.07
❑ 156 Kevin Appier	.15		.07
❑ 157 Ken Griffey Jr.	3.00		1.35
❑ 158 Alex Rodriguez	2.00		.90
❑ 159 Randy Johnson	.60		.25
❑ 160 Juan Gonzalez	1.25		.55
❑ 161 Will Clark	.60		.25
❑ 162 Dean Palmer	.30		.14
❑ 163 Tim Salmon	.60		.25
❑ 164 Jim Edmonds	.40		.18
❑ 165 Jim Leyritz	.15		.07

❑ 166 Jose Canseco	.75		.35
❑ 167 Jason Giambi	.30		.14
❑ 168 Mark McGwire	3.00		1.35
❑ 169 Barry Bonds CC	.30		.14
❑ 170 Alex Rodriguez CC	1.00		.45
❑ 171 Roger Clemens CC	.75		.35
❑ 172 Ken Griffey Jr. CC	1.50		.70
❑ 173 Greg Maddux CC	.75		.35
❑ 174 Mike Piazza CC	1.00		.45
❑ 175 Will Clark CC	1.00		.45
Mark McGwire			
❑ 176 Hideo Nomo CC	.30		.14
❑ 177 Cal Ripken CC	1.25		.55
❑ 178 Ken Griffey Jr. CC	1.50		.70
Frank Thomas			
❑ 179 Alex Rodriguez CC	1.25		.55
Derek Jeter			
❑ 180 John Wetteland CC	.15		.07
❑ P158 Alex Rodriguez Promo	1.00		.45
❑ NNO Jose Cruz Jr. CL	.25		.11

1997 Sports Illustrated Extra Edition

	MINT	NRMT
COMPLETE SET (180)	2500.00	1100.00
COMMON CARD (1-180)	5.00	2.20

*STARS: 15X TO 30X HI COLUMN
*YOUNG STARS: 12.5X TO 25X HI
*ROOKIES: 7.5X TO 15X HI
RANDOM INSERTS IN PACKS
STATED PRINT RUN 500 SERIAL #'d SETS

1997 Sports Illustrated Autographed Mini-Covers

	MINT	NRMT
RANDOM INSERTS IN PACKS		
STATED PRINT RUN 250 SETS		
❑ 1 Alex Rodriguez	250.00	110.00
❑ 2 Cal Ripken	300.00	135.00
❑ 3 Kirby Puckett	120.00	55.00
❑ 4 Willie Mays	200.00	90.00
❑ 5 Frank Robinson	80.00	36.00
❑ 6 Hank Aaron	150.00	70.00

1997 Sports Illustrated Cooperstown Collection

	MINT	NRMT
COMPLETE SET (12)	60.00	27.00
COMMON CARD (1-12)	5.00	2.20
STATED ODDS 1:12		
☐ 1 Hank Aaron	10.00	4.50
☐ 2 Yogi Berra	6.00	2.70
☐ 3 Lou Brock	5.00	2.20
☐ 4 Rod Carew	5.00	2.20
☐ 5 Juan Marichal	5.00	2.20
☐ 6 Al Kaline	6.00	2.70
☐ 7 Joe Morgan	5.00	2.20
☐ 8 Brooks Robinson	5.00	2.20
☐ 9 Willie Stargell	5.00	2.20
☐ 10 Kirby Puckett	8.00	3.60
☐ 11 Willie Mays	12.00	5.50
☐ 12 Frank Robinson	5.00	2.20

1997 Sports Illustrated Great Shots

	MINT	NRMT
COMPLETE SET (25)	8.00	3.60
COMMON CARD (1-25)	.20	.09
STATED ODDS ONE PER PACK		
☐ 1 Chipper Jones	1.00	.45
☐ 2 Ryan Klesko	.20	.09
☐ 3 Kenny Lofton	.30	.14
☐ 4 Greg Maddux	1.00	.45
☐ 5 John Smoltz	.30	.14
☐ 6 Roberto Alomar	.40	.18
☐ 7 Cal Ripken	1.50	.70
☐ 8 Mo Vaughn	.40	.18
☐ 9 Albert Belle	1.00	.45
☐ 10 Frank Thomas	1.00	.45
☐ 11 Ryne Sandberg	.40	.18
☐ 12 Deion Sanders	.20	.09
☐ 13 Vinny Castilla	.30	.14
Andres Galarraga		
☐ 14 Eric Karros	.20	.09
☐ 15 Mike Piazza	1.25	.55
☐ 16 Derek Jeter	1.50	.70
☐ 17 Mark McGwire	2.00	.90
☐ 18 Darren Dreifort	.20	.09
☐ 19 Andy Ashby	.20	.09
☐ 20 Barry Bonds	.50	.23
☐ 21 Jay Buhner	.20	.09
☐ 22 Randy Johnson	.40	.18
☐ 23 Alex Rodriguez	1.25	.55
☐ 24 Juan Gonzalez	.75	.35
☐ 25 Ken Griffey Jr.	2.00	.90

1998 Sports Illustrated

	MINT	NRMT
COMPLETE SET (200)	40.00	18.00
COMMON CARD (1-200)	.15	.07
MINOR STARS	.25	.11
SEMISTARS	.40	.18
UNLISTED STARS	.60	.25
COMPLETE SET DOES NOT INCLUDE SP #201		
☐ 1 Edgardo Alfonzo	.40	.18
☐ 2 Roberto Alomar	.60	.25
☐ 3 Sandy Alomar Jr.	.25	.11
☐ 4 Moises Alou	.25	.11

☐ 5 Brady Anderson	.25	.11
☐ 6 Garret Anderson	.25	.11
☐ 7 Kevin Appier	.25	.11
☐ 8 Jeff Bagwell	.75	.35
☐ 9 Jay Bell	.25	.11
☐ 10 Albert Belle	.60	.25
☐ 11 Dante Bichette	.25	.11
☐ 12 Craig Biggio	.60	.25
☐ 13 Barry Bonds	.75	.35
☐ 14 Bobby Bonilla	.25	.11
☐ 15 Kevin Brown	.40	.18
☐ 16 Jay Buhner	.25	.11
☐ 17 Ellis Burks	.25	.11
☐ 18 Mike Cameron	.25	.11
☐ 19 Ken Caminiti	.25	.11
☐ 20 Jose Canseco	.75	.35
☐ 21 Joe Carter	.25	.11
☐ 22 Vinny Castilla	.25	.11
☐ 23 Jeff Cirillo	.25	.11
☐ 24 Tony Clark	.25	.11
☐ 25 Will Clark	.60	.25
☐ 26 Roger Clemens	1.50	.70
☐ 27 David Cone	.40	.18
☐ 28 Jose Cruz Jr.	.25	.11
☐ 29 Carlos Delgado	.60	.25
☐ 30 Jason Dickson	.15	.07
☐ 31 Dennis Eckersley	.25	.11
☐ 32 Jim Edmonds	.25	.11
☐ 33 Scott Erickson	.15	.07
☐ 34 Darin Erstad	.40	.18
☐ 35 Shawn Estes	.15	.07
☐ 36 Jeff Fassero	.15	.07
☐ 37 Alex Fernandez	.15	.07
☐ 38 Chuck Finley	.25	.11
☐ 39 Steve Finley	.25	.11
☐ 40 Travis Fryman	.25	.11
☐ 41 Andres Galarraga	.40	.18
☐ 42 Ron Gant	.25	.11
☐ 43 Nomar Garciaparra	2.00	.90
☐ 44 Jason Giambi	.25	.11
☐ 45 Tom Glavine	.60	.25
☐ 46 Juan Gonzalez	1.25	.55
☐ 47 Mark Grace	.40	.18
☐ 48 Willie Greene	.15	.07
☐ 49 Rusty Greer	.25	.11
☐ 50 Ben Grieve	.60	.25
☐ 51 Ken Griffey Jr.	3.00	1.35
☐ 52 Mark Grudzielanek	.15	.07
☐ 53 Vladimir Guerrero	.75	.35
☐ 54 Juan Guzman	.15	.07
☐ 55 Tony Gwynn	1.50	.70
☐ 56 Joey Hamilton	.15	.07
☐ 57 Rickey Henderson	.75	.35
☐ 58 Pat Hentgen	.15	.07
☐ 59 Livan Hernandez	.25	.11
☐ 60 Bobby Higginson	.25	.11
☐ 61 Todd Hundley	.25	.11
☐ 62 Hideki Irabu	.25	.11
☐ 63 John Jaha	.15	.07
☐ 64 Derek Jeter	2.00	.90
☐ 65 Charles Johnson	.25	.11
☐ 66 Randy Johnson	.60	.25
☐ 67 Andruw Jones	.60	.25
☐ 68 Bobby Jones	.15	.07
☐ 69 Chipper Jones	1.50	.70
☐ 70 Brian Jordan	.25	.11
☐ 71 David Justice	.40	.18
☐ 72 Eric Karros	.25	.11

☐ 73 Jeff Kent	.25	.11
☐ 74 Jimmy Key	.25	.11
☐ 75 Darryl Kile	.15	.07
☐ 76 Jeff King	.15	.07
☐ 77 Ryan Klesko	.25	.11
☐ 78 Chuck Knoblauch	.25	.11
☐ 79 Ray Lankford	.25	.11
☐ 80 Barry Larkin	.60	.25
☐ 81 Kenny Lofton	.40	.18
☐ 82 Greg Maddux	1.50	.70
☐ 83 Al Martin	.15	.07
☐ 84 Edgar Martinez	.25	.11
☐ 85 Pedro Martinez	.75	.35
☐ 86 Tino Martinez	.25	.11
☐ 87 Mark McGwire	4.00	1.80
☐ 88 Paul Molitor	.60	.25
☐ 89 Raul Mondesi	.25	.11
☐ 90 Jamie Moyer	.15	.07
☐ 91 Mike Mussina	.60	.25
☐ 92 Tim Naehring	.15	.07
☐ 93 Charles Nagy	.15	.07
☐ 94 Denny Neagle	.15	.07
☐ 95 Dave Nilsson	.15	.07
☐ 96 Hideo Nomo	.60	.25
☐ 97 Rey Ordonez	.25	.11
☐ 98 Dean Palmer	.25	.11
☐ 99 Rafael Palmeiro	.60	.25
☐ 100 Andy Pettitte	.25	.11
☐ 101 Mike Piazza	2.00	.90
☐ 102 Brad Radke	.25	.11
☐ 103 Manny Ramirez	.75	.35
☐ 104 Edgar Renteria	.15	.07
☐ 105 Cal Ripken	2.50	1.10
☐ 106 Alex Rodriguez	2.00	.90
☐ 107 Henry Rodriguez	.25	.11
☐ 108 Ivan Rodriguez	.75	.35
☐ 109 Scott Rolen	.75	.35
☐ 110 Tim Salmon	.40	.18
☐ 111 Curt Schilling	.40	.18
☐ 112 Gary Sheffield	.25	.11
☐ 113 John Smoltz	.40	.18
☐ 114 J.T. Snow	.25	.11
☐ 115 Sammy Sosa	2.00	.90
☐ 116 Matt Stairs	.25	.11
☐ 117 Shannon Stewart	.25	.11
☐ 118 Frank Thomas	1.25	.55
☐ 119 Jim Thome	.60	.25
☐ 120 Justin Thompson	.15	.07
☐ 121 Mo Vaughn	.60	.25
☐ 122 Robin Ventura	.25	.11
☐ 123 Larry Walker	.60	.25
☐ 124 Rondell White	.25	.11
☐ 125 Bernie Williams	.60	.25
☐ 126 Matt Williams	.60	.25
☐ 127 Tony Womack	.15	.07
☐ 128 Jaret Wright	.25	.11
☐ 129 Edgar Renteria BB	.15	.07
☐ 130 Kenny Lofton BB	.25	.11
☐ 131 Tony Gwynn BB	.75	.35
☐ 132 Mark McGwire BB	2.00	.90
☐ 133 Craig Biggio BB	.25	.11
☐ 134 Charles Johnson BB	.15	.07
☐ 135 J.T. Snow BB	.15	.07
☐ 136 Ken Caminiti BB	.15	.07
☐ 137 Vladimir Guerrero BB	.40	.18
☐ 138 Jim Edmonds BB	.15	.07
☐ 139 Randy Johnson BB	.25	.11
☐ 140 Darryl Kile BB	.15	.07
☐ 141 John Smoltz BB	.25	.11
☐ 142 Greg Maddux BB	.75	.35
☐ 143 Andy Pettitte BB	.15	.07
☐ 144 Ken Griffey Jr. BB	1.50	.70
☐ 145 Mike Piazza BB	1.00	.45
☐ 146 Todd Greene RB	.15	.07
☐ 147 Vinny Castilla BB	.15	.07
☐ 148 Derek Jeter BB	1.00	.45
☐ 149 Robert Machado OW	.15	.07
☐ 150 Mike Gulan OW	.15	.07
☐ 151 Randall Simon OW	.25	.11
☐ 152 Michael Coleman OW	.25	.11
☐ 153 Brian Rose OW	.15	.07
☐ 154 Scott Eyre OW	.15	.07
☐ 155 Magglio Ordonez OW	2.00	.90
☐ 156 Todd Helton OW	.75	.35
☐ 157 Juan Encarnacion OW	.25	.11
☐ 158 Mark Kotsay OW	.25	.11

		MINT	NRMT
❑ 159	Josh Booty OW	.15	.07
❑ 160	Melvin Rosario OW	.15	.07
❑ 161	Shane Halter OW	.15	.07
❑ 162	Paul Konerko OW	.25	.11
❑ 163	Henry Blanco OW	.15	.07
❑ 164	Antone Williamson OW	.15	.07
❑ 165	Brad Fullmer OW	.15	.07
❑ 166	Ricky Ledee OW	.25	.11
❑ 167	Ben Grieve OW	.60	.25
❑ 168	Frank Catalanotto OW	.25	.11
❑ 169	Bobby Estalella OW	.15	.07
❑ 170	Dennis Reyes OW	.15	.07
❑ 171	Kevin Polcovich OW	.15	.07
❑ 172	Jacob Cruz OW	.15	.07
❑ 173	Ken Cloude OW	.15	.07
❑ 174	Eli Marrero OW	.15	.07
❑ 175	Fernando Tatis OW	.60	.25
❑ 176	Tom Evans OW	.15	.07
❑ 177	Rafael Palmeiro OW	.60	.25
	Chipper Jones '97		
❑ 178	Eric Davis	.15	.07
	'97 Returns From Cancer		
❑ 179	Roger Clemens	.75	.35
	'97 Triple Crown/200 Wins		
❑ 180	Brett Butler	.25	.11
	Eddie Murray		
	'97 Retirees		
❑ 181	Frank Thomas	.60	.25
	'97 Batting Title		
❑ 182	Curt Schilling	.25	.11
	'97 Sets Strikeout Record		
❑ 183	Jeff Bagwell	.40	.18
	'97 1B Goes 30-30		
❑ 184	Mark McGwire	2.00	.90
	Ken Griffey Jr.		
	'97 Chase Maris		
❑ 185	Kevin Brown	.25	.11
	'97 No-Hitter		
❑ 186	Francisco Cordova	.15	.07
	Ricardo Rincon		
	'97 No-Hitter		
❑ 187	Charles Johnson	.15	.07
	'97 Errorless Streak		
❑ 188	Hideki Irabu	.15	.07
	'97 Debuts		
❑ 189	Tony Gwynn	.75	.35
	'97 8th Batting Title		
❑ 190	Sandy Alomar Jr.	.15	.07
	'97 All-Star MVP		
❑ 191	Ken Griffey Jr.	1.50	.70
	'97 AL MVP		
❑ 192	Larry Walker	.25	.11
	'97 NL MVP		
❑ 193	Roger Clemens	.75	.35
	'97 AL Cy Young Award		
❑ 194	Pedro Martinez	.40	.18
	'97 NL Cy Young Award		
❑ 195	Nomar Garciaparra	1.00	.45
	'97 AL ROY		
❑ 196	Scott Rolen	.60	.25
	'97 NL ROY		
❑ 197	Brian Anderson	.15	.07
	'97 Arizona 1st Draft Pick		
❑ 198	Tony Saunders	.15	.07
	'97 TB 1st Draft Pick		
❑ 199	Florida Celebration	.15	.07
	'97 World Series Champs		
❑ 200	Livan Hernandez	.15	.07
	'97 World Series MVP		
❑ 201	Travis Lee OW SP	5.00	2.20
❑ P106	Alex Rodriguez PROMO	3.00	1.35
❑ NNO	Alex Rodriguez CL	.50	.23

1998 Sports Illustrated Extra Edition

	MINT	NRMT
COMMON CARD (1-201)	5.00	2.20

*STARS: 12.5X TO 30X BASIC CARDS
*YNG.STARS: 10X TO 25X BASIC CARDS
*ROOKIES: 6X TO 15X BASIC CARDS
RANDOM INSERTS IN PACKS
STATED PRINT RUN 250 SERIAL #'d SETS

FIRST EDITION 1 OF 1 PARALLELS EXIST

		MINT	NRMT
❑ 201	Travis Lee OW	15.00	6.75

1998 Sports Illustrated Autographs

Rollie Fingers

	MINT	NRMT

RANDOM INSERTS IN PACKS
SERIAL #'d PRINT RUNS LISTED BELOW
EXCHANGE DEADLINE: 11/1/99

		MINT	NRMT
❑ 1	Lou Brock/500	80.00	36.00
❑ 2	Jose Cruz Jr./250	20.00	9.00
❑ 3	Rollie Fingers/500	40.00	18.00
❑ 4	Ben Grieve EXCH/250	60.00	27.00
❑ 5	Paul Konerko EXCH/250	30.00	13.50
❑ 6	Brooks Robinson/500	80.00	36.00

1998 Sports Illustrated Covers

	MINT	NRMT
COMPLETE SET (10)	30.00	13.50
COMMON CARD (C1-C10)	1.00	.45

STATED ODDS 1:9

		MINT	NRMT
❑ C1	Ken Griffey	8.00	3.60
	Mike Piazza		
❑ C2	Derek Jeter	6.00	2.70
❑ C3	Ken Griffey Jr.	10.00	4.50
❑ C4	Cal Ripken	8.00	3.60

		MINT	NRMT
❑ C5	Manny Ramirez	2.50	1.10
❑ C6	Jay Buhner	1.00	.45
❑ C7	Matt Williams	2.00	.90
❑ C8	Randy Johnson	2.00	.90
❑ C9	Deion Sanders	1.00	.45
❑ C10	Jose Canseco	2.50	1.10

1998 Sports Illustrated Editor's Choice

	MINT	NRMT
COMPLETE SET (10)	120.00	55.00
COMMON CARD (EC1-EC10)	2.00	.90

STATED ODDS 1:24

		MINT	NRMT
❑ EC1	Ken Griffey Jr.	25.00	11.00
❑ EC2	Alex Rodriguez	15.00	6.75
❑ EC3	Frank Thomas	10.00	4.50
❑ EC4	Mark McGwire	30.00	13.50
❑ EC5	Greg Maddux	12.00	5.50
❑ EC6	Derek Jeter	15.00	6.75
❑ EC7	Cal Ripken	20.00	9.00
❑ EC8	Nomar Garciaparra	15.00	6.75
❑ EC9	Jeff Bagwell	6.00	2.70
❑ EC10	Jose Cruz Jr.	2.00	.90

1998 Sports Illustrated Opening Day Mini Posters

	MINT	NRMT
COMPLETE SET (30)	10.00	4.50
COMMON CARD (OD1-OD30)	.10	.05

ONE PER PACK

		MINT	NRMT
❑ OD1	Tim Salmon	.25	.70
❑ OD2	Matt Williams	.40	.18
❑ OD3	John Smoltz	.75	.35
	Greg Maddux		
❑ OD4	Cal Ripken	1.50	.70
❑ OD5	Nomar Garciaparra	1.25	.55
❑ OD6	Sammy Sosa	1.25	.55
❑ OD7	Frank Thomas	.75	.35
❑ OD8	Barry Larkin	.40	.18
❑ OD9	David Justice	.15	.07
❑ OD10	Larry Walker	.40	.18
❑ OD11	Tony Clark	.15	.07
❑ OD12	Livan Hernandez	.10	.05
❑ OD13	Jeff Bagwell	.50	.23

		MINT	NRMT
❏ OD14	Kevin Appier	.15	.07
❏ OD15	Mike Piazza	1.25	.55
❏ OD16	Fernando Vina	.10	.05
❏ OD17	Paul Molitor	.40	.18
❏ OD18	Vladimir Guerrero	.50	.23
❏ OD19	Rey Ordonez	.15	.07
❏ OD20	Bernie Williams	.40	.18
❏ OD21	Matt Stairs	.15	.07
❏ OD22	Curt Schilling	.25	.11
❏ OD23	Tony Womack	.10	.05
❏ OD24	Mark McGwire	2.50	1.10
❏ OD25	Tony Gwynn	1.00	.45
❏ OD26	Barry Bonds	.50	.23
❏ OD27	Ken Griffey Jr.	2.00	.90
❏ OD28	Fred McGriff	.25	.11
❏ OD29	Juan Gonzalez	.60	.25
	Ivan Rodriguez		
❏ OD30	Roger Clemens	1.00	.45

1999 Sports Illustrated

OMAR VIZQUEL

	MINT	NRMT
COMPLETE SET (180)	50.00	22.00
COMMON CARD (1-180)	.15	.07
MINOR STARS	.25	.11
SEMISTARS	.40	.18
UNLISTED STARS	.60	.25

		MINT	NRMT
❏ 1	Yankees POST	.25	.11
❏ 2	Scott Brosius POST	.15	.07
❏ 3	David Wells POST	.15	.07
❏ 4	Sterling Hitchcock POST	.15	.07
❏ 5	David Justice POST	.25	.11
❏ 6	David Cone POST	.25	.11
❏ 7	Greg Maddux POST	.75	.35
❏ 8	Jim Leyritz POST	.15	.07
❏ 9	Gary Gaetti POST	.15	.07
❏ 10	Mark McGwire	1.50	.70
	Ken Griffey Jr. AW		
❏ 11	Sammy Sosa	1.00	.45
	Juan Gonzalez AW		
❏ 12	Larry Walker	.25	.11
	Bernie Williams AW		
❏ 13	Tony Womack	.40	.18
	Rickey Henderson AW		
❏ 14	Tom Glavine	.25	.11
	Roger Clemens		
	David Cone		
	Rick Helling AW		
❏ 15	Curt Schilling	2.00	.11
	Roger Clemens AW		
❏ 16	Greg Maddux	.75	.35
	Roger Clemens AW		
❏ 17	Trevor Hoffman	.15	.07
	Tom Gordon AW		
❏ 18	Kerry Wood	.60	.25
	Ben Glavine AW		
❏ 19	Tom Glavine	.25	.11
	Roger Clemens AW		
❏ 20	Sammy Sosa	1.00	.45
	Juan Gonzalez AW		
❏ 21	Travis Lee SH	.25	.11
❏ 22	Roberto Alomar SH	.25	.11
❏ 23	Roger Clemens SH	.75	.35
❏ 24	Barry Bonds SH	.40	.18
❏ 25	Paul Molitor SH	.25	.11
❏ 26	Todd Stottlemyre SH	.15	.07
❏ 27	Chris Hoiles SH	.15	.07

		MINT	NRMT
❏ 28	Albert Belle SH	.25	.11
❏ 29	Tony Clark SH	.15	.07
❏ 30	Kerry Wood SH	.25	.11
❏ 31	David Wells SH	.15	.07
❏ 32	Dennis Eckersley SH	.15	.07
❏ 33	Mark McGwire SH	2.00	.90
❏ 34	Cal Ripken SH	1.25	.55
❏ 35	Ken Griffey Jr. SH	1.50	.70
❏ 36	Alex Rodriguez SH	1.00	.45
❏ 37	Craig Biggio SH	.25	.11
❏ 38	Sammy Sosa SH	1.00	.45
❏ 39	Dennis Martinez SH	.15	.07
❏ 40	Curt Schilling SH	.25	.11
❏ 41	Orlando Hernandez SH	.25	.11
❏ 42	Troy Glaus	.60	.25
	Ben Molina		
	Todd Greene		
❏ 43	Mitch Meluskey	.25	.11
	Daryle Ward		
	Mike Grzanich		
❏ 44	Eric Chavez	.40	.18
	Blake Stein		
	Mike Neill		
❏ 45	Roy Halladay	.25	.11
	Tom Evans		
	Kevin Witt		
❏ 46	George Lombard	.25	.11
	Adam Butler		
	Bruce Chen		
❏ 47	Rafael Roque	.25	.11
	Ron Belliard		
	Valerio de los Santos		
❏ 48	J.D.Drew	1.25	.55
	Placido Polanco		
	Mark Little		
❏ 49	Jason Maxwell	.40	.18
	Jose Nieves		
	Jeremi Gonzalez		
❏ 50	Scott McClain	.25	.11
	Kerry Robinson		
	Mike Duvall		
❏ 51	Ben Ford	.25	.11
	Bryan Corey		
	Danny Klassen		
❏ 52	Angel Pena	.15	.07
	Jeff Kubenka		
	Paul LoDuca		
❏ 53	Fernando Seguignol	.25	.11
	Kirk Bullinger		
	Tim Young		
❏ 54	Ramon E. Martinez	.15	.07
	Wilson Delgado		
	Armando Rios		
❏ 55	Jolbert Cabrera	.25	.11
	Russell Branyan		
	Jason Rakers		
❏ 56	Carlos Guillen	.15	.07
	Dave Holdridge		
	Giomar Guevara		
❏ 57	Alex Gonzalez	.25	.11
	Joe Fontenot		
	Preston Wilson		
❏ 58	Mike Kinkade	.25	.11
	Jay Payton		
	Masato Yoshii		
❏ 59	Calvin Pickering	.25	.11
	Ryan Minor		
	Willis Otanez		
❏ 60	Ben Davis	.25	.11
	Matt Clement		
	Stan Spencer		
❏ 61	Marlon Anderson	.25	.11
	Mike Welch		
	Gary Bennett		
❏ 62	Abraham Nunez	.15	.07
	Sean Lawrence		
	Aramis Ramirez		
❏ 63	Jonathan Johnson	.25	.11
	Robert Sasser		
	Scott Sheldon		
❏ 64	Keith Glauber	.15	.07
	Guillermo Garcia		
	Eddie Priest		
❏ 65	Brian Barkley	.25	.11
	Jin Ho Cho		
	Donnie Sadler		

		MINT	NRMT
❏ 66	Derrick Gibson	.25	.11
	Mark Strittmatter		
	Edgard Clemente		
❏ 67	Jeremy Giambi	.25	.11
	Dermal Brown		
	Chris Hatcher		
❏ 68	Gabe Kapler	.60	.25
	Robert Fick		
	Marino Santana		
❏ 69	Corey Koskie	.15	.07
	A.J.Pierzynski		
	Benji Sampson		
❏ 70	Brian Simmons	.15	.07
	Mark Johnson		
	Craig Wilson		
❏ 71	Ryan Bradley	.25	.11
	Mike Lowell		
	Jay Tessmer		
❏ 72	Ben Grieve	.60	.25
❏ 73	Shawn Green	.60	.25
❏ 74	Rafael Palmeiro	.60	.25
❏ 75	Juan Gonzalez	1.25	.55
❏ 76	Mike Piazza	2.00	.90
❏ 77	Devon White	.15	.07
❏ 78	Jim Thome	.60	.25
❏ 79	Barry Larkin	.60	.25
❏ 80	Scott Rolen	.75	.35
❏ 81	Raul Mondesi	.25	.11
❏ 82	Jason Giambi	.25	.11
❏ 83	Jose Canseco	.75	.35
❏ 84	Tony Gwynn	1.50	.70
❏ 85	Cal Ripken	2.50	1.10
❏ 86	Andy Pettitte	.25	.11
❏ 87	Carlos Delgado	.60	.25
❏ 88	Jeff Cirillo	.25	.11
❏ 89	Bret Saberhagen	.25	.11
❏ 90	John Olerud	.25	.11
❏ 91	Ron Coomer	.15	.07
❏ 92	Todd Helton	.60	.25
❏ 93	Ray Lankford	.25	.11
❏ 94	Tim Salmon	.40	.18
❏ 95	Fred McGriff	.40	.18
❏ 96	Matt Stairs	.25	.11
❏ 97	Ken Griffey Jr.	3.00	1.35
❏ 98	Chipper Jones	1.50	.70
❏ 99	Mark Grace	.40	.18
❏ 100	Ivan Rodriguez	.75	.35
❏ 101	Jeromy Burnitz	.25	.11
❏ 102	Kenny Rogers	.15	.07
❏ 103	Kevin Millwood	.40	.18
❏ 104	Vinny Castilla	.25	.11
❏ 105	Jim Edmonds	.25	.11
❏ 106	Craig Biggio	.60	.25
❏ 107	Andres Galarraga	.40	.18
❏ 108	Sammy Sosa	2.00	.90
❏ 109	Juan Encarnacion	.25	.11
❏ 110	Larry Walker	.25	.11
❏ 111	John Smoltz	.40	.18
❏ 112	Randy Johnson	.60	.25
❏ 113	Bobby Higginson	.25	.11
❏ 114	Albert Belle	.60	.25
❏ 115	Jaret Wright	.25	.11
❏ 116	Edgar Renteria	.15	.07
❏ 117	Andruw Jones	.60	.25
❏ 118	Barry Bonds	.75	.35
❏ 119	Rondell White	.25	.11
❏ 120	Jamie Moyer	.15	.07
❏ 121	Darin Erstad	.25	.11
❏ 122	Al Leiter	.25	.11
❏ 123	Mark McGwire	4.00	1.80
❏ 124	Mo Vaughn	.60	.25
❏ 125	Livan Hernandez	.15	.07
❏ 126	Jason Kendall	.25	.11
❏ 127	Frank Thomas	1.25	.55
❏ 128	Denny Neagle	.15	.07
❏ 129	Johnny Damon	.25	.11
❏ 130	Derek Bell	.25	.11
❏ 131	Jeff Kent	.25	.11
❏ 132	Tony Womack	.15	.07
❏ 133	Trevor Hoffman	.25	.11
❏ 134	Gary Sheffield	.25	.11
❏ 135	Tino Martinez	.25	.11
❏ 136	Travis Fryman	.25	.11
❏ 137	Rolando Arrojo	.15	.07
❏ 138	Dante Bichette	.25	.11
❏ 139	Nomar Garciaparra	2.00	.90

❏ 140 Moises Alou	.25	.11
❏ 141 Chuck Knoblauch	.25	.11
❏ 142 Robin Ventura	.25	.11
❏ 143 Scott Erickson	.15	.07
❏ 144 David Cone	.40	.18
❏ 145 Greg Vaughn	.25	.11
❏ 146 Wade Boggs	.60	.25
❏ 147 Mike Mussina	.60	.25
❏ 148 Tony Clark	.25	.11
❏ 149 Alex Rodriguez	2.00	.90
❏ 150 Javy Lopez	.25	.11
❏ 151 Bartolo Colon	.25	.11
❏ 152 Derek Jeter	2.00	.90
❏ 153 Greg Maddux	1.50	.70
❏ 154 Kevin Brown	.40	.18
❏ 155 Curt Schilling	.40	.18
❏ 156 Jeff King	.15	.07
❏ 157 Bernie Williams	.60	.25
❏ 158 Roberto Alomar	.60	.25
❏ 159 Travis Lee	.40	.18
❏ 160 Kerry Wood	.60	.25
❏ 161 Jeff Bagwell	.75	.35
❏ 162 Roger Clemens	1.50	.70
❏ 163 Matt Williams	.60	.25
❏ 164 Chan Ho Park	.25	.11
❏ 165 Damion Easley	.25	.11
❏ 166 Manny Ramirez	.75	.35
❏ 167 Quinton McCracken	.15	.07
❏ 168 Todd Walker	.25	.11
❏ 169 Eric Karros	.25	.11
❏ 170 Will Clark	.60	.25
❏ 171 Edgar Martinez	.25	.11
❏ 172 Cliff Floyd	.25	.11
❏ 173 Vladimir Guerrero	.75	.35
❏ 174 Tom Glavine	.60	.25
❏ 175 Pedro Martinez	.75	.35
❏ 176 Chuck Finley	.25	.11
❏ 177 Dean Palmer	.25	.11
❏ 178 Omar Vizquel	.25	.11
❏ 179 Checklist	.15	.07
❏ 180 Checklist	.15	.07
❏ S160 Kerry Wood Sample	2.00	.90

1999 Sports Illustrated Diamond Dominators

	MINT	NRMT
COMPLETE SET (10)	400.00	180.00
COMMON CARD (1-10)	6.00	2.70
UNLISTED STARS	10.00	4.50
STATED ODDS 1:90 PITCHER/1:180 HITTER		

❏ 1 Kerry Wood	6.00	2.70
❏ 2 Roger Clemens	25.00	11.00
❏ 3 Randy Johnson	10.00	4.50
❏ 4 Greg Maddux	25.00	11.00
❏ 5 Pedro Martinez	12.00	5.50
❏ 6 Ken Griffey Jr.	80.00	36.00
❏ 7 Sammy Sosa	50.00	22.00
❏ 8 Nomar Garciaparra	50.00	22.00
❏ 9 Mark McGwire	100.00	45.00
❏ 10 Alex Rodriguez	50.00	22.00

1999 Sports Illustrated Fabulous 40's

	MINT	NRMT
COMPLETE SET (13)	80.00	36.00

COMMON CARD (1-13)	2.00	.90
SEMISTARS	2.50	1.10
UNLISTED STARS	4.00	1.80
STATED ODDS 1:20		

❏ 1 Mark McGwire	25.00	11.00
❏ 2 Sammy Sosa	12.00	5.50
❏ 3 Ken Griffey Jr	20.00	9.00
❏ 4 Greg Vaughn	2.00	.90
❏ 5 Albert Belle	4.00	1.80
❏ 6 Jose Canseco	5.00	2.20
❏ 7 Vinny Castilla	2.00	.90
❏ 8 Juan Gonzalez	8.00	3.60
❏ 9 Manny Ramirez	5.00	2.20
❏ 10 Andres Galarraga	2.50	1.10
❏ 11 Rafael Palmeiro	4.00	1.80
❏ 12 Alex Rodriguez	12.00	5.50
❏ 13 Mo Vaughn	4.00	1.80

1999 Sports Illustrated Fabulous 40's Extra

	MINT	NRMT
COMMON CARD (1-13)	20.00	9.00
RANDOM INSERTS IN PACKS		
PRINT RUNS LISTED BELOW		

❏ 1 Mark McGwire/70	250.00	110.00
❏ 2 Sammy Sosa/66	120.00	55.00
❏ 3 Ken Griffey Jr./56	200.00	90.00
❏ 4 Greg Vaughn/50	20.00	9.00
❏ 5 Albert Belle/49	30.00	13.50
❏ 6 Jose Canseco/48	50.00	22.00
❏ 7 Vinny Castilla/46	20.00	9.00
❏ 8 Juan Gonzalez/45	80.00	36.00
❏ 9 Manny Ramirez/45	50.00	22.00
❏ 10 Andres Galarraga/44	20.00	9.00
❏ 11 Rafael Palmeiro/43	40.00	18.00
❏ 12 Alex Rodriguez/42	120.00	55.00
❏ 13 Mo Vaughn/40	30.00	13.50

1999 Sports Illustrated Headliners

	MINT	NRMT
COMPLETE SET (25)	40.00	18.00
COMMON CARD (1-25)	.75	.35
UNLISTED STARS	1.25	.55
STATED ODDS 1:4		

❏ 1 Vladimir Guerrero	1.50	.70
❏ 2 Randy Johnson	1.25	.55
❏ 3 Mo Vaughn	1.25	.55
❏ 4 Chipper Jones	3.00	1.35
❏ 5 Jeff Bagwell	1.50	.70
❏ 6 Juan Gonzalez	2.50	1.10
❏ 7 Mark McGwire	8.00	3.60
❏ 8 Cal Ripken	5.00	2.20
❏ 9 Frank Thomas	2.50	1.10
❏ 10 Manny Ramirez	1.50	.70
❏ 11 Ken Griffey Jr.	6.00	2.70
❏ 12 Scott Rolen	1.50	.70
❏ 13 Alex Rodriguez	4.00	1.80
❏ 14 Barry Bonds	1.50	.70
❏ 15 Roger Clemens	3.00	1.35
❏ 16 Darin Erstad	.75	.35
❏ 17 Nomar Garciaparra	4.00	1.80
❏ 18 Mike Piazza	4.00	1.80
❏ 19 Greg Maddux	3.00	1.35
❏ 20 Ivan Rodriguez	1.50	.70
❏ 21 Derek Jeter	4.00	1.80
❏ 22 Sammy Sosa	4.00	1.80
❏ 23 Andruw Jones	1.25	.55
❏ 24 Pedro Martinez	1.50	.70
❏ 25 Kerry Wood	1.25	.55

1999 Sports Illustrated One's To Watch

	MINT	NRMT
COMPLETE SET (15)	20.00	9.00
COMMON CARD (1-15)	.75	.35
MINOR STARS	1.25	.55
SEMISTARS	2.00	.90
UNLISTED STARS	3.00	1.35
STATED ODDS 1:12		

❏ 1 J.D. Drew	5.00	2.20
❏ 2 Marlon Anderson	.75	.35
❏ 3 Roy Halladay	1.25	.55
❏ 4 Ben Grieve	3.00	1.35
❏ 5 Todd Helton	3.00	1.35
❏ 6 Gabe Kapler	1.25	.55
❏ 7 Troy Glaus	3.00	1.35
❏ 8 Ben Davis	2.00	.90
❏ 9 Eric Chavez	2.00	.90
❏ 10 Richie Sexson	2.00	.90
❏ 11 Fernando Seguignol	1.25	.55
❏ 12 Kerry Wood	3.00	1.35
❏ 13 Bobby Smith	.75	.35
❏ 14 Ryan Minor	1.25	.55
❏ 15 Jeremy Giambi	1.25	.55
❏ NNO J.D. Drew AU/250	80.00	36.00

1999 Sports Illustrated Greats of the Game

	MINT	NRMT
COMPLETE SET (90)	75.00	34.00
COMMON CARD (1-90)	.25	.11
MINOR STARS	.50	.23
SEMISTARS	.75	.35
UNLISTED STARS	1.25	.55

❏ 1 Jimmie Foxx	2.00	.90
❏ 2 Red Schoendienst	.75	.35
❏ 3 Babe Ruth	5.00	2.20

Maury Wills

❏ 4 Lou Gehrig	4.00	1.80
❏ 5 Mel Ott	1.50	.70
❏ 6 Stan Musial	2.00	.90
❏ 7 Mickey Mantle	5.00	2.20
❏ 8 Carl Yastrzemski	2.00	.90
❏ 9 Enos Slaughter	.75	.35
❏ 10 Andre Dawson	1.25	.55
❏ 11 Luis Aparicio	1.25	.55
❏ 12 Ferguson Jenkins	1.25	.55
❏ 13 Christy Mathewson	1.25	.55
❏ 14 Ernie Banks	1.50	.70
❏ 15 Johnny Podres	.50	.23
❏ 16 George Foster	.50	.23
❏ 17 Jerry Koosman	.50	.23
❏ 18 Curt Simmons	.25	.11
❏ 19 Bob Feller	1.25	.55
❏ 20 Frank Robinson	1.50	.70
❏ 21 Gary Carter	.75	.35
❏ 22 Frank Thomas	.25	.11
❏ 23 Bill Lee	.50	.23
❏ 24 Willie Mays	3.00	1.35
❏ 25 Tommie Agee	.50	.23
❏ 26 Boog Powell	.75	.35
❏ 27 Jim Wynn	.50	.23
❏ 28 Sparky Lyle	.50	.23
❏ 29 Bo Belinsky	.25	.11
❏ 30 Maury Wills	.50	.23
❏ 31 Bill Buckner	.50	.23
❏ 32 Steve Carlton	2.00	.90
❏ 33 Harmon Killebrew	1.25	.55
❏ 34 Nolan Ryan	5.00	2.20
❏ 35 Randy Jones	.25	.11
❏ 36 Robin Roberts	1.25	.55
❏ 37 Al Oliver	.50	.23
❏ 38 Rico Petrocelli	.25	.11
❏ 39 Dave Parker	.50	.23
❏ 40 Eddie Mathews	1.50	.70
❏ 41 Earl Weaver	.75	.35
❏ 42 Jackie Robinson	4.00	1.80
❏ 43 Lou Brock	1.25	.55
❏ 44 Reggie Jackson	2.00	.90
❏ 45 Bob Gibson	1.25	.55
❏ 46 Jeff Burroughs	.25	.11
❏ 47 Jim Bouton	.50	.23
❏ 48 Bob Forsch	.25	.11
❏ 49 Ron Guidry	.50	.23
❏ 50 Ty Cobb	3.00	1.35
❏ 51 Roy White	.50	.23
❏ 52 Joe Rudi	.50	.23
❏ 53 Moose Skowron	.50	.23
❏ 54 Goose Gossage	.50	.23
❏ 55 Ed Kranepool	.25	.11
❏ 56 Paul Blair	.25	.11
❏ 57 Kent Hrbek	.50	.23
❏ 58 Orlando Cepeda	.75	.35
❏ 59 Buck O'Neill	.50	.23
❏ 60 Al Kaline	1.50	.70
❏ 61 Vida Blue	.50	.23
❏ 62 Sam McDowell	.25	.11
❏ 63 Jesse Barfield	.25	.11
❏ 64 Dave Kingman	.50	.23
❏ 65 Ron Santo	.75	.35
❏ 66 Steve Garvey	.75	.35
❏ 67 Gaylord Perry	1.25	.55
❏ 68 Darrell Evans	.50	.23
❏ 69 Rollie Fingers	.75	.35
❏ 70 Walter Johnson	1.50	.70
❏ 71 Al Hrabosky	.50	.23

❏ 72 Mickey Rivers	.25	.11
❏ 73 Mike Torrez	.25	.11
❏ 74 Hank Bauer	.50	.23
❏ 75 Tug McGraw	.50	.23
❏ 76 David Clyde	.25	.11
❏ 77 Jim Lonborg	.25	.11
❏ 78 Clete Boyer	.50	.23
❏ 79 Harry Walker	.50	.23
❏ 80 Cy Young	2.00	.90
❏ 81 Bud Harrelson	.25	.11
❏ 82 Paul Splittorff	.25	.11
❏ 83 Bert Campaneris	.50	.23
❏ 84 Joe Niekro	.50	.23
❏ 85 Bob Horner	.50	.23
❏ 86 Jerry Royster	.25	.11
❏ 87 Tommy John	.50	.23
❏ 88 Mark Fidrych	.50	.23
❏ 89 Dick Williams	.50	.23
❏ 90 Graig Nettles	.50	.23

1999 Sports Illustrated Greats of the Game Autographs

Autograph Collection

	MINT	NRMT
COMMON CARD	8.00	3.60
MINOR STARS	15.00	6.75

ONE CARD PER PACK
NNO CARDS LISTED IN ALPHABETICAL ORDER

❏ 1 Tommie Agee	15.00	6.75
❏ 2 Luis Aparicio	30.00	13.50
❏ 3 Ernie Banks	40.00	18.00
❏ 4 Jesse Barfield	8.00	3.60
❏ 5 Hank Bauer	15.00	6.75
❏ 6 Bo Belinsky	8.00	3.60
❏ 7 Paul Blair	8.00	3.60
❏ 8 Vida Blue	15.00	6.75
❏ 9 Jim Bouton	15.00	6.75
❏ 10 Clete Boyer	15.00	6.75
❏ 11 Lou Brock	20.00	9.00
❏ 12 Bill Buckner	15.00	6.75
❏ 13 Jeff Burroughs	8.00	3.60
❏ 14 Bert Campaneris	15.00	6.75
❏ 15 Steve Carlton	40.00	18.00
❏ 16 Gary Carter	25.00	11.00
❏ 17 Orlando Cepeda	30.00	13.50
❏ 18 David Clyde	8.00	3.60
❏ 19 Andre Dawson	25.00	11.00
❏ 20 Darrell Evans	15.00	6.75
❏ 21 Bob Feller	30.00	13.50
❏ 22 Mark Fidrych	15.00	6.75
❏ 23 Rollie Fingers	20.00	9.00
❏ 24 Bob Forsch	8.00	3.60
❏ 25 George Foster	15.00	6.75
❏ 26 Steve Garvey	20.00	9.00
❏ 27 Bob Gibson	20.00	9.00
❏ 28 Goose Gossage	20.00	9.00
❏ 29 Ron Guidry	25.00	11.00
❏ 30 Bud Harrelson	8.00	3.60
❏ 31 Bob Horner	15.00	6.75
❏ 32 Al Hrabosky	15.00	6.75
❏ 33 Kent Hrbek	15.00	6.75
❏ 34A Reggie Jackson	250.00	110.00
❏ 34B R.Jackson "Mr. October"	400.00	180.00
❏ 34C R.Jackson "HOF 93"	400.00	180.00

❏ 35 Ferguson Jenkins	20.00	9.00
❏ 36 Tommy John	15.00	6.75
❏ 37 Randy Jones	8.00	3.60
❏ 38 Al Kaline	30.00	13.50
❏ 39 Harmon Killebrew	40.00	18.00
❏ 40 Dave Kingman	15.00	6.75
❏ 41 Jerry Koosman	15.00	6.75
❏ 42 Ed Kranepool	8.00	3.60
❏ 43 Bill Lee	15.00	6.75
❏ 44 Jim Lonborg	8.00	3.60
❏ 45 Sparky Lyle	15.00	6.75
❏ 46 Eddie Mathews	40.00	18.00
❏ 47 Willie Mays	250.00	110.00
❏ 48 Sam McDowell	8.00	3.60
❏ 49 Tug McGraw	15.00	6.75
❏ 50 Stan Musial	200.00	90.00
❏ 51 Graig Nettles	25.00	11.00
❏ 52 Joe Niekro	15.00	6.75
❏ 53 Buck O'Neill	15.00	6.75
❏ 54 Al Oliver	15.00	6.75
❏ 55 Dave Parker	25.00	11.00
❏ 56 Gaylord Perry	25.00	11.00
❏ 57 Rico Petrocelli	8.00	3.60
❏ 58 Johnny Podres	25.00	11.00
❏ 59 Boog Powell	20.00	9.00
❏ 60 Mickey Rivers	8.00	3.60
❏ 61 Robin Roberts	25.00	11.00
❏ 62 Frank Robinson	40.00	18.00
❏ 63 Jerry Royster	8.00	3.60
❏ 64 Joe Rudi	15.00	6.75
❏ 65 Nolan Ryan	300.00	135.00
❏ 66 Ron Santo	25.00	11.00
❏ 67 Red Schoendienst	20.00	9.00
❏ 68 Curt Simmons	8.00	3.60
❏ 69 Moose Skowron	25.00	11.00
❏ 70 Enos Slaughter	30.00	13.50
❏ 71 Paul Splittorff	8.00	3.60
❏ 72 Frank Thomas	8.00	3.60
❏ 73 Mike Torrez	8.00	3.60
❏ 74 Harry Walker	8.00	3.60
❏ 75 Earl Weaver	20.00	9.00
❏ 76 Roy White	15.00	6.75
❏ 77 Dick Williams	15.00	6.75
❏ 78 Maury Wills	20.00	9.00
❏ 79 Jim Wynn	15.00	6.75
❏ 80 Carl Yastrzemski	125.00	55.00

1999 Sports Illustrated Greats of the Game Cover Collection

Sports Illustrated

	MINT	NRMT
COMPLETE SET (50)	60.00	27.00
COMMON CARD (1-50)	.30	.14
MINOR STARS	.50	.23
SEMISTARS	.75	.35
UNLISTED STARS	1.25	.55

ONE PER PACK

❏ 1 Johnny Podres	.50	.23
❏ 2 Mickey Mantle	8.00	3.60
❏ 3 Stan Musial	2.00	.90
❏ 4 Eddie Mathews	1.50	.70
❏ 5 Frank Thomas	.30	.14
❏ 6 Willie Mays	3.00	1.35
❏ 7 Red Schoendienst	.75	.35
❏ 8 Luis Aparicio	1.25	.55

❏ 9 Mickey Mantle	8.00	3.60
❏ 10 Al Kaline	1.50	.70
❏ 11 Maury Wills	.50	.23
❏ 12 Sam McDowell	.30	.14
❏ 13 Harry Walker	.30	.14
❏ 14 Carl Yastrzemski	1.50	.70
❏ 15 Carl Yastrzemski	1.50	.70
❏ 16 Lou Brock	1.50	.70
❏ 17 Ron Santo	.75	.35
❏ 18 Reggie Jackson	2.00	.90
❏ 19 Frank Robinson	1.50	.70
❏ 20 Jerry Koosman	.50	.23
❏ 21 Bud Harrelson	.30	.14
❏ 22 Vida Blue	.50	.23
❏ 23 Ferguson Jenkins	1.25	.55
❏ 24 Sparky Lyle	.50	.23
❏ 25 Steve Carlton	1.50	.70
❏ 26 Bert Campaneris	.50	.23
❏ 27 Jim Wynn	.50	.23
❏ 28 Steve Garvey	.75	.35
❏ 29 Nolan Ryan	6.00	2.70
❏ 30 Randy Jones	.30	.14
❏ 31 Reggie Jackson	2.00	.90
❏ 32 Joe Rudi	.50	.23
❏ 33 Reggie Jackson	2.00	.90
❏ 34 Dave Parker	.50	.23
❏ 35 Mark Fidrych	.50	.23
❏ 36 Earl Weaver	.75	.35
❏ 37 Nolan Ryan	6.00	2.70
❏ 38 Steve Carlton	1.50	.70
❏ 39 Reggie Jackson	2.00	.90
❏ 40 Rollie Fingers	.75	.35
❏ 41 Gary Carter	.75	.35
❏ 42 Graig Nettles	.50	.23
❏ 43 Gaylord Perry	1.25	.55
❏ 44 Kent Hrbek	.50	.23
❏ 45 Gary Carter	.75	.35
❏ 46 Steve Garvey	.75	.35
❏ 47 Steve Carlton	1.50	.70
❏ 48 Nolan Ryan	6.00	2.70
❏ 49 Nolan Ryan	6.00	2.70
❏ 50 Mickey Mantle	8.00	3.60

1999 Sports Illustrated Greats of the Game Record Breakers

	MINT	NRMT
COMPLETE SET (10)	120.00	55.00
COMMON CARD (1-10)	5.00	2.20
STATED ODDS 1:12		
*GOLD: 2X TO 5X HI COLUMN		
GOLD STATED ODDS 1:120		

❏ 1 Mickey Mantle	30.00	13.50
❏ 2 Stan Musial	10.00	4.50
❏ 3 Babe Ruth	25.00	11.00
❏ 4 Christy Mathewson	5.00	2.20
❏ 5 Cy Young	8.00	3.60
❏ 6 Nolan Ryan	20.00	9.00
❏ 7 Jackie Robinson	20.00	9.00
❏ 8 Lou Gehrig	20.00	9.00
❏ 9 Ty Cobb	10.00	4.50
❏ 10 Walter Johnson	5.00	2.20

1998 Sports Illustrated Then and Now

	MINT	NRMT
COMPLETE SET (150)	40.00	18.00
COMMON CARD (1-150)	.15	.07
MINOR STARS	.30	.14
UNLISTED STARS	.60	.25

❏ 1 Luis Aparicio	.40	.18
❏ 2 Richie Ashburn	.40	.18
❏ 3 Ernie Banks	.75	.35
❏ 4 Yogi Berra	.75	.35
❏ 5 Lou Boudreau	.30	.14
❏ 6 Lou Brock	.60	.25
❏ 7 Jim Bunning	.30	.14
❏ 8 Rod Carew	.60	.25
❏ 9 Bob Feller	.60	.25
❏ 10 Rollie Fingers	.30	.14
❏ 11 Bob Gibson	.60	.25
❏ 12 Ferguson Jenkins	.40	.18
❏ 13 Al Kaline	.75	.35
❏ 14 George Kell	.30	.14
❏ 15 Harmon Killebrew	.30	.14
❏ 16 Ralph Kiner	.30	.14
❏ 17 Tommy Lasorda	.30	.14
❏ 18 Juan Marichal	.60	.25
❏ 19 Eddie Mathews	.60	.25
❏ 20 Willie Mays	1.50	.70
❏ 21 Willie McCovey	.60	.25
❏ 22 Joe Morgan	.60	.25
❏ 23 Gaylord Perry	.40	.18
❏ 24 Kirby Puckett	1.00	.45
❏ 25 Pee Wee Reese	.40	.18
❏ 26 Phil Rizzuto	.40	.18
❏ 27 Robin Roberts	.30	.14
❏ 28 Brooks Robinson	.60	.25
❏ 29 Frank Robinson	.60	.25
❏ 30 Red Schoendienst	.30	.14
❏ 31 Enos Slaughter	.30	.14
❏ 32 Warren Spahn	.60	.25
❏ 33 Willie Stargell	.40	.18
❏ 34 Earl Weaver	.30	.14
❏ 35 Billy Williams	.40	.18
❏ 36 Early Wynn	.30	.14
❏ 37 Rickey Henderson HIST	.40	.18
❏ 38 Greg Maddux HIST	.75	.35
❏ 39 Mike Mussina HIST	.30	.14
❏ 40 Cal Ripken HIST	1.25	.55
❏ 41 Albert Belle HIST	.30	.14
❏ 42 Frank Thomas HIST	.60	.25
❏ 43 Jeff Bagwell HIST	.40	.18
❏ 44 Paul Molitor HIST	.30	.14
❏ 45 Chuck Knoblauch HIST	.15	.07
❏ 46 Todd Hundley HIST	.15	.07
❏ 47 Bernie Williams HIST	.30	.14
❏ 48 Tony Gwynn HIST	.75	.35
❏ 49 Barry Bonds HIST	.40	.18
❏ 50 Ken Griffey Jr. HIST	1.50	.70
❏ 51 Randy Johnson HIST	.30	.14
❏ 52 Mark McGwire HIST	2.00	.90
❏ 53 Roger Clemens HIST	.75	.35
❏ 54 Jose Cruz Jr. HIST	.15	.07
❏ 55 Roberto Alomar	.60	.25
❏ 56 Sandy Alomar Jr.	.30	.14
❏ 57 Brady Anderson	.30	.14
❏ 58 Kevin Appier	.30	.14
❏ 59 Jeff Bagwell	.75	.35

❏ 60 Albert Belle	.60	.25
❏ 61 Dante Bichette	.30	.14
❏ 62 Craig Biggio	.60	.25
❏ 63 Barry Bonds	.75	.35
❏ 64 Kevin Brown	.40	.18
❏ 65 Jay Buhner	.30	.14
❏ 66 Ellis Burks	.30	.14
❏ 67 Ken Caminiti	.30	.14
❏ 68 Jose Canseco	.75	.35
❏ 69 Joe Carter	.30	.14
❏ 70 Vinny Castilla	.30	.14
❏ 71 Tony Clark	.30	.14
❏ 72 Roger Clemens	1.50	.70
❏ 73 David Cone	.40	.18
❏ 74 Jose Cruz Jr.	.30	.14
❏ 75 Jason Dickson	.15	.07
❏ 76 Jim Edmonds	.30	.14
❏ 77 Scott Erickson	.15	.07
❏ 78 Darin Erstad	.40	.18
❏ 79 Alex Fernandez	.15	.07
❏ 80 Steve Finley	.30	.14
❏ 81 Travis Fryman	.30	.14
❏ 82 Andres Galarraga	.40	.18
❏ 83 Nomar Garciaparra	2.00	.90
❏ 84 Tom Glavine	.60	.25
❏ 85 Juan Gonzalez	1.25	.55
❏ 86 Mark Grace	.40	.18
❏ 87 Willie Greene	.15	.07
❏ 88 Ken Griffey Jr.	3.00	1.35
❏ 89 Vladimir Guerrero	.75	.35
❏ 90 Tony Gwynn	1.50	.70
❏ 91 Livan Hernandez	.15	.07
❏ 92 Bobby Higginson	.30	.14
❏ 93 Derek Jeter	2.00	.90
❏ 94 Charles Johnson	.30	.14
❏ 95 Randy Johnson	.60	.25
❏ 96 Andruw Jones	.60	.25
❏ 97 Chipper Jones	1.50	.70
❏ 98 David Justice	.30	.14
❏ 99 Eric Karros	.30	.14
❏ 100 Jason Kendall	.30	.14
❏ 101 Jimmy Key	.30	.14
❏ 102 Darryl Kile	.15	.07
❏ 103 Chuck Knoblauch	.30	.14
❏ 104 Ray Lankford	.30	.14
❏ 105 Barry Larkin	.60	.25
❏ 106 Kenny Lofton	.40	.18
❏ 107 Greg Maddux	1.50	.70
❏ 108 Al Martin	.15	.07
❏ 109 Edgar Martinez	.30	.14
❏ 110 Pedro Martinez	.75	.35
❏ 111 Ramon Martinez	.15	.07
❏ 112 Tino Martinez	.30	.14
❏ 113 Mark McGwire	4.00	1.80
❏ 114 Raul Mondesi	.30	.14
❏ 115 Matt Morris	.15	.07
❏ 116 Charles Nagy	.30	.14
❏ 117 Denny Neagle	.15	.07
❏ 118 Hideo Nomo	.60	.25
❏ 119 Dean Palmer	.15	.07
❏ 120 Andy Pettitte	.30	.14
❏ 121 Mike Piazza	2.00	.90
❏ 122 Manny Ramirez	.75	.35
❏ 123 Edgar Renteria	.15	.07
❏ 124 Cal Ripken	2.50	1.10
❏ 125 Alex Rodriguez	2.00	.90
❏ 126 Henry Rodriguez	.30	.14
❏ 127 Ivan Rodriguez	.75	.35
❏ 128 Scott Rolen	.75	.35
❏ 129 Tim Salmon	.40	.18
❏ 130 Curt Schilling	.40	.18
❏ 131 Gary Sheffield	.30	.14
❏ 132 John Smoltz	.40	.18
❏ 133 Sammy Sosa	2.00	.90
❏ 134 Frank Thomas	1.25	.55
❏ 135 Jim Thome	.60	.25
❏ 136 Mo Vaughn	.60	.25
❏ 137 Robin Ventura	.30	.14
❏ 138 Larry Walker	.60	.25
❏ 139 Bernie Williams	.60	.25
❏ 140 Matt Williams	.60	.25
❏ 141 Jaret Wright	.30	.14
❏ 142 Michael Coleman	.30	.14
❏ 143 Juan Encarnacion	.30	.14
❏ 144 Brad Fullmer	.15	.07
❏ 145 Ben Grieve	.60	.25

		MINT	NRMT
☐ 146	Todd Helton	.75	.35
☐ 147	Paul Konerko	.30	.14
☐ 148	Derrek Lee	.15	.07
☐ 149	Magglio Ordonez	2.00	.90
☐ 150	Enrique Wilson	.15	.07
☐ P125	Alex Rodriguez PROMO	3.00	1.35
☐ NNO	Alex Rodriguez CL	.50	.23

1998 Sports Illustrated Then and Now Extra Edition

	MINT	NRMT
COMMON CARD (1-150)	4.00	1.80

*STARS: 10X TO 25X BASIC CARDS
*YNG.STARS: 8X TO 20X BASIC CARDS
*ROOKIES: 5X TO 12X BASIC CARDS
RANDOM INSERTS IN PACKS
STATED PRINT RUN 500 SERIAL #'d SETS

1998 Sports Illustrated Then and Now Art of the Game

	MINT	NRMT
COMPLETE SET (8)	25.00	11.00
COMMON CARD (AG1-AG8)	.50	.23
STATED ODDS 1:9		

		MINT	NRMT
☐ AG1	Ken Griffey Jr.	8.00	3.60
☐ AG2	Alex Rodriguez	5.00	2.20
☐ AG3	Mike Piazza	5.00	2.20
☐ AG4	Brooks Robinson	1.50	.70
☐ AG5	David Justice	.75	.35
☐ AG6	Cal Ripken	6.00	2.70
☐ AG7	Prospect 'n Prospector..	.50	.23
☐ AG8	Barry Bonds	1.50	.70

1998 Sports Illustrated Then and Now Autographs

	MINT	NRMT
COMPLETE SET (6)	750.00	350.00
COMMON CARD (1-6)	80.00	36.00

ONE CARD VIA MAIL PER RDMP CARD
SERIAL #'d PRINT RUNS LISTED BELOW

Bob Gibson

*EXCHANGE CARDS: 1X TO .25X HI COLUMN
EXCHANGE DEADLINE: 11/1/99

		MINT	NRMT
☐ 1	Roger Clemens/250	150.00	70.00
☐ 2	Bob Gibson/500	80.00	36.00
☐ 3	Tony Gwynn/250	150.00	70.00
☐ 4	Harmon Killebrew/500	80.00	36.00
☐ 5	Willie Mays/200	200.00	90.00
☐ 6	Scott Rolen/250	100.00	45.00

1998 Sports Illustrated Then and Now Covers

	MINT	NRMT
COMPLETE SET (12)	80.00	36.00
COMMON CARD (C1-C12)	4.00	1.80
STATED ODDS 1:18		

		MINT	NRMT
☐ C1	Lou Brock	4.00	1.80
☐ C2	Kirby Puckett	6.00	2.70
☐ C3	Harmon Killebrew	4.00	1.80
☐ C4	Eddie Mathews	4.00	1.80
☐ C5	Willie Mays	10.00	4.50
☐ C6	Frank Robinson	4.00	1.80
☐ C7	Cal Ripken	15.00	6.75
☐ C8	Roger Clemens	10.00	4.50
☐ C9	Ken Griffey Jr.	20.00	9.00
☐ C10	Mark McGwire	25.00	11.00
☐ C11	Tony Gwynn	10.00	4.50
☐ C12	Ivan Rodriguez	5.00	2.20

1998 Sports Illustrated Then and Now Great Shots

	MINT	NRMT
COMPLETE SET (25)	10.00	4.50
COMMON CARD (1-25)	.15	.07

ONE PER PACK

		MINT	NRMT
☐ 1	Ken Griffey Jr.	2.00	.90
☐ 2	Frank Thomas	.75	.35
☐ 3	Alex Rodriguez	1.25	.55
☐ 4	Andruw Jones	.40	.18
☐ 5	Chipper Jones	1.00	.45
☐ 6	Cal Ripken	1.50	.70
☐ 7	Mark McGwire	2.50	1.10
☐ 8	Derek Jeter	1.25	.55
☐ 9	Greg Maddux	1.00	.45

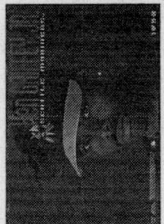

		MINT	NRMT
☐ 10	Jeff Bagwell	.50	.23
☐ 11	Mike Piazza	1.25	.55
☐ 12	Scott Rolen	.60	.25
☐ 13	Nomar Garciaparra	1.25	.55
☐ 14	Jose Cruz Jr.	.15	.07
☐ 15	Charles Johnson	.15	.07
☐ 16	Fergie Jenkins	.25	.11
☐ 17	Lou Brock	.40	.18
☐ 18	Bob Gibson	.40	.18
☐ 19	Harmon Killebrew	.40	.18
☐ 20	Juan Marichal	.40	.18
☐ 21	Brooks Robinson	.40	.18
	Frank Robinson		
☐ 22	Rod Carew	.40	.18
☐ 23	Yogi Berra	.50	.23
☐ 24	Willie Mays	1.00	.45
☐ 25	Kirby Puckett	.60	.25

1998 Sports Illustrated Then and Now Road to Cooperstown

	MINT	NRMT
COMPLETE SET (10)	100.00	45.00
COMMON CARD (RC1-RC10)	5.00	2.20
STATED ODDS 1:24		

		MINT	NRMT
☐ RC1	Barry Bonds	6.00	2.70
☐ RC2	Roger Clemens	12.00	5.50
☐ RC3	Ken Griffey Jr.	25.00	11.00
☐ RC4	Tony Gwynn	12.00	5.50
☐ RC5	Rickey Henderson	6.00	2.70
☐ RC6	Greg Maddux	12.00	5.50
☐ RC7	Paul Molitor	5.00	2.20
☐ RC8	Mike Piazza	15.00	6.75
☐ RC9	Cal Ripken	20.00	9.00
☐ RC10	Frank Thomas	10.00	4.50

1998 Sports Illustrated World Series Fever

	MINT	NRMT
COMPLETE SET (150)	45.00	20.00
COMMON CARD (1-150)	.15	.07
MINOR STARS	.25	.11
SEMISTARS	.40	.18
UNLISTED STARS	.60	.25

FIRST EDITION 1 OF 1 PARALLELS EXIST

☐ 1 Mickey Mantle COV	3.00	1.35
☐ 2 W.S. Preview COV	.15	.07
☐ 3 W.S. Preview COV	.15	.07
☐ 4 Chicago (AL) COV	.15	.07
☐ 5 W.S. Preview COV	.15	.07
☐ 6 Lou Brock COV	.60	.25
☐ 7 Brooks Robinson COV	.60	.25
☐ 8 Frank Robinson COV	.60	.25
☐ 9 L.A. Oakland COV	.15	.07
☐ 10 Reggie Jackson COV	.75	.35
☐ 11 Kansas City COV	.15	.07
☐ 12 Minnesota COV	.15	.07
☐ 13 Orel Hershiser COV	.25	.11
☐ 14 Rickey Henderson COV	.75	.35
☐ 15 Minnesota COV	.15	.07
☐ 16 Toronto COV	.15	.07
☐ 17 Joe Carter COV	.25	.11
☐ 18 Atlanta COV	.15	.07
☐ 19 New York Yankees COV	.15	.07
☐ 20 Edgar Renteria COV	.15	.07
☐ 21 Bill Mazeroski MM	.25	.11
☐ 22 Joe Carter MM	.25	.11
☐ 23 Carlton Fisk MM	.40	.18
☐ 24 Bucky Dent MM	.25	.11
☐ 25 Mookie Wilson MM	.25	.11
☐ 26 Enos Slaughter MM	.25	.11
☐ 27 Mickey Lolich MM	.15	.07
☐ 28 Bobby Richardson MM	.15	.07
☐ 29 Kirk Gibson MM	.25	.11
☐ 30 Edgar Renteria MM	.15	.07
☐ 31 Albert Belle	.60	.25
☐ 32 Kevin Brown	.60	.18
☐ 33 Brian Rose	.15	.07
☐ 34 Ron Gant	.25	.11
☐ 35 Jeromy Burnitz	.25	.11
☐ 36 Andres Galarraga	.40	.18
☐ 37 Jim Edmonds	.25	.11
☐ 38 Jose Cruz Jr.	.25	.11
☐ 39 Mark Grudzielanek	.15	.07
☐ 40 Shawn Estes	.15	.07
☐ 41 Mark Grace	.40	.18
☐ 42 Nomar Garciaparra	2.00	.90
☐ 43 Juan Gonzalez	1.25	.55
☐ 44 Tom Glavine	.60	.25
☐ 45 Brady Anderson	.25	.11
☐ 46 Tony Clark	.25	.11
☐ 47 Jeff Cirillo	.25	.11
☐ 48 Dante Bichette	.25	.11
☐ 49 Ben Grieve	.60	.25
☐ 50 Ken Griffey Jr.	3.00	1.35
☐ 51 Edgard Alfonzo	.40	.18
☐ 52 Roger Clemens	1.50	.70
☐ 53 Pat Hentgen	.15	.07
☐ 54 Todd Helton	.75	.35
☐ 55 Andy Benes	.15	.07
☐ 56 Tony Gwynn	1.50	.70
☐ 57 Andruw Jones	.60	.25
☐ 58 Bobby Higginson	.25	.11
☐ 59 Bobby Jones	.15	.07
☐ 60 Darryl Kile	.15	.07
☐ 61 Chan Ho Park	.25	.11
☐ 62 Charles Johnson	.25	.11
☐ 63 Rusty Greer	.25	.11
☐ 64 Travis Fryman	.25	.11
☐ 65 Derek Jeter	2.00	.90
☐ 66 Jay Buhner	.25	.11
☐ 67 Chuck Knoblauch	.25	.11
☐ 68 David Justice	.25	.11

☐ 69 Brian Hunter	.15	.07
☐ 70 Eric Karros	.25	.11
☐ 71 Edgar Martinez	.25	.11
☐ 72 Chipper Jones	1.50	.70
☐ 73 Barry Larkin	.60	.25
☐ 74 Mike Lansing	.15	.07
☐ 75 Craig Biggio	.60	.25
☐ 76 Al Martin	.15	.07
☐ 77 Barry Bonds	.75	.35
☐ 78 Randy Johnson	.60	.25
☐ 79 Ryan Klesko	.25	.11
☐ 80 Mark McGwire	4.00	1.80
☐ 81 Fred McGriff	.40	.18
☐ 82 Javy Lopez	.25	.11
☐ 83 Kenny Lofton	.40	.18
☐ 84 Sandy Alomar Jr.	.25	.11
☐ 85 Matt Morris	.15	.07
☐ 86 Paul Konerko	.25	.11
☐ 87 Ray Lankford	.25	.11
☐ 88 Kerry Wood	.75	.35
☐ 89 Roberto Alomar	.25	.11
☐ 90 Greg Maddux	1.50	.70
☐ 91 Travis Lee	.40	.18
☐ 92 Moises Alou	.25	.11
☐ 93 Dean Palmer	.15	.07
☐ 94 Hideo Nomo	.60	.25
☐ 95 Ken Caminiti	.25	.11
☐ 96 Pedro Martinez	.75	.35
☐ 97 Raul Mondesi	.25	.11
☐ 98 Denny Neagle	.15	.07
☐ 99 Tino Martinez	.25	.11
☐ 100 Mike Mussina	.60	.25
☐ 101 Kevin Appier	.15	.07
☐ 102 Vinny Castilla	.25	.11
☐ 103 Jeff Bagwell	.75	.35
☐ 104 Paul O'Neill	.25	.11
☐ 105 Rey Ordonez	.15	.07
☐ 106 Vladimir Guerrero	.75	.35
☐ 107 Rafael Palmeiro	.60	.25
☐ 108 Alex Rodriguez	2.00	.90
☐ 109 Andy Pettitte	.25	.11
☐ 110 Carl Pavano	.15	.07
☐ 111 Henry Rodriguez	.25	.11
☐ 112 Gary Sheffield	.25	.11
☐ 113 Curt Schilling	.40	.18
☐ 114 John Smoltz	.40	.18
☐ 115 Reggie Sanders	.15	.07
☐ 116 Scott Rolen	.75	.35
☐ 117 Mike Piazza	2.00	.90
☐ 118 Manny Ramirez	.75	.35
☐ 119 Cal Ripken	2.50	1.10
☐ 120 Brad Radke	.25	.11
☐ 121 Tim Salmon	.40	.18
☐ 122 Brett Tomko	.15	.07
☐ 123 Robin Ventura	.25	.11
☐ 124 Mo Vaughn	.60	.25
☐ 125 A.J. Hinch	.15	.07
☐ 126 Derrek Lee	.15	.07
☐ 127 Orlando Hernandez	1.50	.70
☐ 128 Aramis Ramirez	.60	.25
☐ 129 Frank Thomas	1.25	.55
☐ 130 J.T. Snow	.25	.11
☐ 131 Magglio Ordonez	2.00	.90
☐ 132 Bobby Bonilla	.25	.11
☐ 133 Marquis Grissom	.15	.07
☐ 134 Jim Thome	.25	.11
☐ 135 Justin Thompson	.15	.07
☐ 136 Matt Williams	.60	.25
☐ 137 Matt Stairs	.15	.07
☐ 138 Wade Boggs	.60	.25
☐ 139 Chuck Finley	.15	.07
☐ 140 Jaret Wright	.25	.11
☐ 141 Ivan Rodriguez	.75	.35
☐ 142 Brad Fullmer	.25	.11
☐ 143 Bernie Williams	.60	.25
☐ 144 Jason Giambi	.25	.11
☐ 145 Larry Walker	.60	.25
☐ 146 Tony Womack	.15	.07
☐ 147 Sammy Sosa	2.00	.90
☐ 148 Rondell White	.25	.11
☐ 149 Todd Stottlemyre	.15	.07
☐ 150 Shane Reynolds	.25	.11
☐ P8 Cal Ripken Promo	3.00	1.35

1998 Sports Illustrated World Series Fever Extra Edition

	MINT	NRMT
COMMON CARD (1-150)	10.00	4.50

*STARS: 25X TO 60X BASIC CARDS
*YNG.STARS: 20X TO 50X BASIC CARDS
*ROOKIES: 12.5X TO 30X BASIC CARDS
RANDOM INSERTS IN PACKS
STATED PRINT RUN 98 SERIAL #'d SETS

1998 Sports Illustrated World Series Fever Autumn Excellence

	MINT	NRMT
COMPLETE SET (10)	80.00	36.00
COMMON CARD (1-10)	2.00	.90
UNLISTED STARS	5.00	2.20

STATED ODDS 1:24
*GOLD STARS: 1.5X TO 4X HI COLUMN
GOLD STATED ODDS 1:240

☐ 1 Willie Mays	12.00	5.50
☐ 2 Kirby Puckett	8.00	3.60
☐ 3 Babe Ruth	20.00	9.00
☐ 4 Reggie Jackson	6.00	2.70
☐ 5 Whitey Ford	5.00	2.20
☐ 6 Lou Brock	5.00	2.20
☐ 7 Mickey Mantle	25.00	11.00
☐ 8 Yogi Berra	8.00	3.60
☐ 9 Bob Gibson	5.00	2.20
☐ 10 Don Larsen	2.00	.90

1998 Sports Illustrated World Series Fever MVP Collection

	MINT	NRMT
COMPLETE SET (10)	8.00	3.60
COMMON CARD (1-10)	.50	.23
MINOR STARS	.75	.35
SEMISTARS	1.25	.55
UNLISTED STARS	2.00	.90

STATED ODDS 1:4

❑ 1 Frank Robinson	2.00	.90
❑ 2 Brooks Robinson	2.00	.90
❑ 3 Willie Stargell	1.25	.55
❑ 4 Bret Saberhagen	.75	.35
❑ 5 Rollie Fingers	.75	.35
❑ 6 Orel Hershiser	.75	.35
❑ 7 Paul Molitor	2.00	.90
❑ 8 Tom Glavine	2.00	.90
❑ 9 John Wetteland	.75	.35
❑ 10 Livan Hernandez	.50	.23

1998 Sports Illustrated World Series Fever Reggie Jackson's Picks

	MINT	NRMT
COMPLETE SET (15)	60.00	27.00
COMMON CARD (1-15)	1.25	.55
STATED ODDS 1:12		

❑ 1 Paul O'Neill	1.00	.45
❑ 2 Barry Bonds	2.50	1.10
❑ 3 Ken Griffey Jr.	10.00	4.50
❑ 4 Juan Gonzalez	4.00	1.80
❑ 5 Greg Maddux	5.00	2.20
❑ 6 Mike Piazza	6.00	2.70
❑ 7 Larry Walker	2.00	.90
❑ 8 Mo Vaughn	2.00	.90
❑ 9 Roger Clemens	5.00	2.20
❑ 10 John Smoltz	1.25	.55
❑ 11 Alex Rodriguez	6.00	2.70
❑ 12 Frank Thomas	4.00	1.80
❑ 13 Mark McGwire	12.00	5.50
❑ 14 Jeff Bagwell	2.50	1.10
❑ 15 Randy Johnson	2.00	.90

1996 SPx

	MINT	NRMT
COMPLETE SET (60)	80.00	36.00
COMMON CARD (1-60)	1.00	.45
SEMISTARS	1.50	.70
UNLISTED STARS	2.00	.90
COMMON GOLD (1-60)	4.00	1.80
*GOLD STARS: 1.5X TO 4X HI COLUMN		
GOLD STATED ODDS 1:7		
GRIFFEY KG1 STATED ODDS 1:75		
PIAZZA MP1 STATED ODDS 1:95		
GRIFFEY AUTO STATED ODDS 1:2000		
PIAZZA AUTO STATED ODDS 1:2000.		

❑ 1 Greg Maddux	5.00	2.20
❑ 2 Chipper Jones	5.00	2.20
❑ 3 Fred McGriff	1.50	.70
❑ 4 Tom Glavine	2.00	.90
❑ 5 Cal Ripken	8.00	3.60
❑ 6 Roberto Alomar	2.00	.90
❑ 7 Rafael Palmeiro	2.00	.90
❑ 8 Jose Canseco	2.50	1.10
❑ 9 Roger Clemens	5.00	2.20
❑ 10 Mo Vaughn	2.00	.90
❑ 11 Jim Edmonds	1.50	.70
❑ 12 Tim Salmon	1.50	.70
❑ 13 Sammy Sosa	6.00	2.70
❑ 14 Ryne Sandberg	2.50	1.10
❑ 15 Mark Grace	1.50	.70
❑ 16 Frank Thomas	4.00	1.80
❑ 17 Barry Larkin	2.00	.90
❑ 18 Kenny Lofton	1.50	.70
❑ 19 Albert Belle	2.50	1.10
❑ 20 Eddie Murray	2.00	.90
❑ 21 Manny Ramirez	2.50	1.10
❑ 22 Dante Bichette	1.25	.55
❑ 23 Larry Walker	2.00	.90
❑ 24 Vinny Castilla	1.50	.70
❑ 25 Andres Galarraga	2.00	.90
❑ 26 Cecil Fielder	1.25	.55
❑ 27 Gary Sheffield	2.00	.90
❑ 28 Craig Biggio	1.25	.55
❑ 29 Jeff Bagwell	2.50	1.10
❑ 30 Derek Bell	1.25	.55
❑ 31 Johnny Damon	1.25	.55
❑ 32 Eric Karros	1.25	.55
❑ 33 Mike Piazza	6.00	2.70
❑ 34 Raul Mondesi	1.25	.55
❑ 35 Hideo Nomo	2.00	.90
❑ 36 Kirby Puckett	3.00	1.35
❑ 37 Paul Molitor	2.00	.90
❑ 38 Marty Cordova	1.00	.45
❑ 39 Rondell White	1.25	.55
❑ 40 Jason Isringhausen	1.25	.55
❑ 41 Paul Wilson	1.00	.45
❑ 42 Rey Ordonez	2.00	.90
❑ 43 Derek Jeter	6.00	2.70
❑ 44 Wade Boggs	2.00	.90
❑ 45 Mark McGwire	10.00	4.50
❑ 46 Jason Kendall	2.00	.90
❑ 47 Ron Gant	1.00	.45
❑ 48 Ozzie Smith	2.50	1.10
❑ 49 Tony Gwynn	5.00	2.20
❑ 50 Ken Caminiti	1.25	.55
❑ 51 Barry Bonds	2.50	1.10
❑ 52 Matt Williams	2.00	.90
❑ 53 Osvaldo Fernandez	1.00	.45
❑ 54 Jay Buhner	1.25	.55
❑ 55 Ken Griffey Jr.	10.00	4.50
❑ 56 Randy Johnson	2.00	.90
❑ 57 Alex Rodriguez	6.00	2.70
❑ 58 Juan Gonzalez	4.00	1.80
❑ 59 Joe Carter	1.25	.55
❑ 60 Carlos Delgado	2.00	.90
❑ KG1 Ken Griffey Jr. Comm.	15.00	6.75
❑ MP1 Mike Piazza Trib.	8.00	3.60
❑ KGAU Ken Griffey Jr. Auto.	300.00	135.00
❑ MPAU Mike Piazza Auto.	225.00	100.00

1996 SPx Bound for Glory

	MINT	NRMT
COMPLETE SET (10)	100.00	45.00
COMMON CARD (1-10)	5.00	2.20
STATED ODDS 1:24		

❑ 1 Ken Griffey Jr.	25.00	11.00
❑ 2 Frank Thomas	10.00	4.50
❑ 3 Barry Bonds	6.00	2.70
❑ 4 Cal Ripken	20.00	9.00
❑ 5 Greg Maddux	12.00	5.50
❑ 6 Chipper Jones	12.00	5.50
❑ 7 Roberto Alomar	5.00	2.20
❑ 8 Manny Ramirez	6.00	2.70
❑ 9 Tony Gwynn	12.00	5.50
❑ 10 Mike Piazza	15.00	6.75

1997 SPx

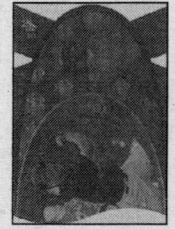

	MINT	NRMT
COMPLETE SET (50)	60.00	27.00
COMMON CARD (1-50)	.50	.23
SEMISTARS	.75	.35
UNLISTED STARS	1.25	.55
COMP.STEEL SET (50)	100.00	45.00
COMMON STEEL (1-50)	.75	.35
*STEEL CARDS: .6X TO 1.5X HI COLUMN		
*STEEL ROOKIES: .5X TO 1.2X HI		
STEEL RANDOM INSERTS IN PACKS		
COMP.BRONZE SET (50)	150.00	70.00
COMMON BRONZE (1-50)	1.25	.55
*BRONZE CARDS: 1X TO 2.5X HI COLUMN		
*BRONZE ROOKIES: .6X TO 1.5X HI		
BRONZE RANDOM INSERTS IN PACKS		
COMMON SILVER (1-50)	2.00	.90
*SILVER CARDS: 1.5X TO 4X HI COLUMN		
*SILVER ROOKIES: 1X TO 2.5X HI		
SILVER RANDOM INSERTS IN PACKS		
COMMON GOLD (1-50)	4.00	1.80
*GOLD STARS: 3X TO 8X HI COLUMN		
*GOLD ROOKIES: 2X TO 5X HI		
GOLD STATED ODDS 1:17		
GOLD: SILVER HOLOVIEW IMAGE ON FRONT		

❑ 1 Eddie Murray	1.25	.55
❑ 2 Darin Erstad	1.25	.55
❑ 3 Tim Salmon	1.25	.55
❑ 4 Andruw Jones	1.50	.70

		MINT	NRMT
❑ 5	Chipper Jones	3.00	1.35
❑ 6	John Smoltz	.75	.35
❑ 7	Greg Maddux	3.00	1.35
❑ 8	Kenny Lofton	.75	.35
❑ 9	Roberto Alomar	1.25	.55
❑ 10	Rafael Palmeiro	1.25	.55
❑ 11	Brady Anderson	.50	.23
❑ 12	Cal Ripken	5.00	2.20
❑ 13	Nomar Garciaparra	4.00	1.80
❑ 14	Mo Vaughn	1.25	.55
❑ 15	Ryne Sandberg	1.50	.70
❑ 16	Sammy Sosa	4.00	1.80
❑ 17	Frank Thomas	2.50	1.10
❑ 18	Albert Belle	1.25	.55
❑ 19	Barry Larkin	1.25	.55
❑ 20	Deion Sanders	.50	.23
❑ 21	Manny Ramirez	1.50	.70
❑ 22	Jim Thome	1.25	.55
❑ 23	Dante Bichette	.50	.23
❑ 24	Andres Galarraga	1.25	.55
❑ 25	Larry Walker	1.25	.55
❑ 26	Gary Sheffield	.50	.23
❑ 27	Jeff Bagwell	1.50	.70
❑ 28	Raul Mondesi	.50	.23
❑ 29	Hideo Nomo	1.25	.55
❑ 30	Mike Piazza	4.00	1.80
❑ 31	Paul Molitor	1.25	.55
❑ 32	Todd Walker	1.25	.55
❑ 33	Vladimir Guerrero	2.00	.90
❑ 34	Todd Hundley	.50	.23
❑ 35	Andy Pettitte	.75	.35
❑ 36	Derek Jeter	4.00	1.80
❑ 37	Jose Canseco	1.50	.70
❑ 38	Mark McGwire	6.00	2.70
❑ 39	Scott Rolen	2.00	.90
❑ 40	Ron Gant	.50	.23
❑ 41	Ken Caminiti	.75	.35
❑ 42	Tony Gwynn	3.00	1.35
❑ 43	Barry Bonds	1.50	.70
❑ 44	Jay Buhner	.50	.23
❑ 45	Ken Griffey Jr.	6.00	2.70
❑ 46	Alex Rodriguez	4.00	1.80
❑ 47	Jose Cruz Jr.	2.50	1.10
❑ 48	Juan Gonzalez	2.50	1.10
❑ 49	Ivan Rodriguez	1.50	.70
❑ 50	Roger Clemens	3.00	1.35
❑ S45	Ken Griffey Jr. SAMPLE	3.00	1.35

1997 SPx Grand Finale

	MINT	NRMT
COMMON CARD (1-50)	15.00	6.75

*STARS: 20X TO 50X BASIC CARDS
*ROOKIES: 10X TO 25X BASIC CARDS
RANDOM INSERTS IN PACKS
STATED PRINT RUN 50 SETS
GOLD HOLOVIEW IMAGE ON FRONT

1997 SPx Bound for Glory

	MINT	NRMT
COMPLETE SET (20)	400.00	180.00
COMMON CARD (1-20)	8.00	3.60
UNLISTED STARS	10.00	4.50

RANDOM INSERTS IN PACKS
STATED PRINT RUN 1500 SERIAL #'d SETS

		MINT	NRMT
❑ 1	Andruw Jones	12.00	5.50
❑ 2	Chipper Jones	25.00	11.00
❑ 3	Greg Maddux	25.00	11.00
❑ 4	Kenny Lofton	8.00	3.60
❑ 5	Cal Ripken	40.00	18.00
❑ 6	Mo Vaughn	10.00	4.50
❑ 7	Frank Thomas	20.00	9.00
❑ 8	Albert Belle	10.00	4.50
❑ 9	Manny Ramirez	12.00	5.50
❑ 10	Gary Sheffield	8.00	3.60
❑ 11	Jeff Bagwell	12.00	5.50
❑ 12	Mike Piazza	30.00	13.50
❑ 13	Derek Jeter	30.00	13.50
❑ 14	Mark McGwire	50.00	22.00
❑ 15	Tony Gwynn	25.00	11.00
❑ 16	Ken Caminiti	8.00	3.60
❑ 17	Barry Bonds	12.00	5.50
❑ 18	Alex Rodriguez	30.00	13.50
❑ 19	Ken Griffey Jr.	50.00	22.00
❑ 20	Juan Gonzalez	20.00	9.00

1997 SPx Bound for Glory Supreme Signatures

	MINT	NRMT
COMPLETE SET (5)	1200.00	550.00
COMMON CARD (1-5)	60.00	27.00

RANDOM INSERTS IN PACKS
STATED PRINT RUN 250 SERIAL #'d SETS

		MINT	NRMT
❑ 1	Jeff Bagwell	120.00	55.00
❑ 2	Ken Griffey Jr.	500.00	220.00
❑ 3	Andruw Jones	120.00	55.00
❑ 4	Alex Rodriguez	300.00	135.00
❑ 5	Gary Sheffield	60.00	27.00

1997 SPx Cornerstones of the Game

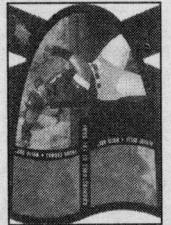

	MINT	NRMT
COMPLETE SET (10)	350.00	160.00
COMMON CARD (1-10)	25.00	11.00

RANDOM INSERTS IN PACKS
STATED PRINT RUN 500 SERIAL #'d SETS

		MINT	NRMT
❑ 1	Ken Griffey Jr.	100.00	45.00
	Barry Bonds		
❑ 2	Frank Thomas	40.00	18.00

		MINT	NRMT
	Albert Belle		
❑ 3	Chipper Jones	50.00	22.00
	Greg Maddux		
❑ 4	Tony Gwynn	50.00	22.00
	Paul Molitor		
❑ 5	Andruw Jones	30.00	13.50
	Vladimir Guerrero		
❑ 6	Jeff Bagwell	25.00	11.00
	Ryne Sandberg		
❑ 7	Mike Piazza	60.00	27.00
	Ivan Rodriguez		
❑ 8	Cal Ripken	80.00	36.00
	Eddie Murray		
❑ 9	Mo Vaughn	100.00	45.00
	Mark McGwire		
❑ 10	Alex Rodriguez	60.00	27.00
	Derek Jeter		

1998 SPx Finite

	MINT	NRMT
COMP.YM SER.1 (30)	60.00	27.00
COMMON YM (1-30)	.75	.35
YM MINOR STARS 1-30	1.25	.55
YM SEMISTARS 1-30	2.00	.90
YM UNLISTED STARS 1-30	3.00	1.35
YM 1-30 PRINT RUN 5000 SERIAL #'d SETS		
COMP.PE SER.1 (20)	150.00	70.00
COMMON PE (31-50)	2.00	.90
PE SEMISTARS 31-50	3.00	1.35
PE UNLISTED STARS 31-50	5.00	2.20
PE 31-50 PRINT RUN 4000 SERIAL #'d SETS		
COMP.BASIC SER.1 (90)	100.00	45.00
COMMON CARD (51-140)	.50	.23
MINOR STARS 51-140	.75	.35
SEMISTARS 51-140	1.25	.55
UNLISTED STARS 51-140	2.00	.90
BASIC 51-140 PR.RUN 9000 SERIAL #'d SETS		
COMP.SF SER.1 (30)	120.00	55.00
COMMON SF (141-170)	1.00	.45
SF SEMISTARS 141-170	1.50	.70
SF UNLISTED STARS 141-170	2.50	1.10
SF 141-170 PRINT RUN 7000 SERIAL #'d SETS		
COMP.HG SER.1 (10)	200.00	90.00
COMMON HG (171-180)	10.00	4.50
HG 171-180 PRINT RUN 2000 SERIAL #'d SETS		
COMP.YM SER.2 (30)	60.00	27.00
COMMON YM (181-210)	.75	.35
YM MINOR STARS 181-210	1.25	.55
YM SEMISTARS 181-210	2.00	.90
YM UNLISTED STARS 181-210	3.00	1.35
YM 181-210 PRINT RUN 5000 SERIAL #'d SETS		
COMP.PP SER.2 (30)	100.00	45.00
COMMON PP (211-240)	1.00	.45
PP SEMISTARS 211-240	1.50	.70
PP UNLISTED STARS 211-240	2.50	1.10
PP 211-240 PRINT RUN 7000 SERIAL #'d SETS		
COMP.BASIC SER.2 (90)	60.00	27.00
COMMON CARD (241-330)	.50	.23
MINOR STARS 241-330	.75	.35
SEMISTARS 241-330	1.25	.55
UNLISTED STARS 241-330	2.00	.90
BASIC 241-330 PR.RUN 9000 SERIAL #'d SETS		

COMP.TW SER.2 (20)	40.00	18.00
COMMON TW (331-350)	1.25	.55
TW MINOR STARS 331-350	2.00	.90
TW SEMISTARS 331-350	3.00	1.35
TW UNLISTED STARS 331-350	5.00	2.20
TW 331-350 PRINT RUN 4000 SERIAL #'d SETS		
COMP.CG SER.2 (10)	200.00	90.00
COMMON CG (351-360)	10.00	4.50
CG 351-360 PRINT RUN 2000 SERIAL #'d SETS		

1	Nomar Garciaparra YM	10.00	4.50
2	Miguel Tejada YM	1.25	.55
3	Mike Cameron YM	1.25	.55
4	Ken Cloude YM	.75	.35
5	Jaret Wright YM	1.25	.55
6	Mark Kotsay YM	1.25	.55
7	Craig Counsell YM	.75	.35
8	Jose Guillen YM	.75	.35
9	Neifi Perez YM	1.25	.55
10	Jose Cruz Jr. YM	1.25	.55
11	Brett Tomko YM	.75	.35
12	Matt Morris YM	.75	.35
13	Justin Thompson YM	.75	.35
14	Jeremi Gonzalez YM	.75	.35
15	Scott Rolen YM	4.00	1.80
16	Vladimir Guerrero YM	4.00	1.80
17	Brad Fullmer YM	.75	.35
18	Brian Giles YM	1.25	.55
19	Todd Dunwoody YM	.75	.35
20	Ben Grieve YM	3.00	1.35
21	Juan Encarnacion YM	1.25	.55
22	Aaron Boone YM	.75	.35
23	Richie Sexson YM	2.00	.90
24	Richard Hidalgo YM	1.25	.55
25	Andruw Jones YM	3.00	1.35
26	Todd Helton YM	3.00	1.35
27	Paul Konerko YM	1.25	.55
28	Dante Powell YM	.75	.35
29	Eli Marrero YM	.75	.35
30	Derek Jeter YM	10.00	4.50
31	Mike Piazza PE	15.00	6.75
32	Tony Clark PE	2.00	.90
33	Larry Walker PE	5.00	2.20
34	Jim Thome PE	5.00	2.20
35	Juan Gonzalez PE	10.00	4.50
36	Jeff Bagwell PE	6.00	2.70
37	Jay Buhner PE	2.00	.90
38	Tim Salmon PE	3.00	1.35
39	Albert Belle PE	5.00	2.20
40	Mark McGwire PE	30.00	13.50
41	Sammy Sosa PE	15.00	6.75
42	Mo Vaughn PE	5.00	2.20
43	Manny Ramirez PE	6.00	2.70
44	Tino Martinez PE	2.00	.90
45	Frank Thomas PE	10.00	4.50
46	Nomar Garciaparra PE	15.00	6.75
47	Alex Rodriguez PE	15.00	6.75
48	Chipper Jones PE	12.00	5.50
49	Barry Bonds PE	5.00	2.20
50	Ken Griffey Jr. PE	25.00	11.00
51	Jason Dickson	.50	.23
52	Jim Edmonds	.75	.35
53	Darin Erstad	1.25	.55
54	Tim Salmon	1.25	.55
55	Chipper Jones	5.00	2.20
56	Ryan Klesko	.75	.35
57	Tom Glavine	2.00	.90
58	Denny Neagle	.50	.23
59	John Smoltz	1.25	.55
60	Javy Lopez	.75	.35
61	Roberto Alomar	2.00	.90
62	Rafael Palmeiro	2.00	.90
63	Mike Mussina	2.00	.90
64	Cal Ripken	8.00	3.60
65	Mo Vaughn	2.00	.90
66	Tim Naehring	.50	.23
67	John Valentin	.75	.35
68	Mark Grace	1.25	.55
69	Kevin Orie	.50	.23
70	Sammy Sosa	6.00	2.70
71	Albert Belle	2.00	.90
72	Frank Thomas	4.00	1.80
73	Robin Ventura	.75	.35
74	David Justice	.75	.35
75	Kenny Lofton	1.25	.55
76	Omar Vizquel	.75	.35
77	Manny Ramirez	2.50	1.10
78	Jim Thome	2.00	.90
79	Dante Bichette	.75	.35
80	Larry Walker	2.00	.90
81	Vinny Castilla	.75	.35
82	Ellis Burks	.75	.35
83	Bobby Higginson	.75	.35
84	Brian Hunter	.50	.23
85	Tony Clark	.75	.35
86	Mike Hampton	.75	.35
87	Jeff Bagwell	2.50	1.10
88	Craig Biggio	2.00	.90
89	Derek Bell	.75	.35
90	Mike Piazza	6.00	2.70
91	Ramon Martinez	.50	.23
92	Raul Mondesi	.75	.35
93	Hideo Nomo	2.00	.90
94	Eric Karros	.75	.35
95	Paul Molitor	2.00	.90
96	Marty Cordova	.50	.23
97	Brad Radke	.75	.35
98	Mark Grudzielanek	.50	.23
99	Carlos Perez	.50	.23
100	Rondell White	.75	.35
101	Todd Hundley	.75	.35
102	Edgardo Alfonzo	1.25	.55
103	John Franco	.75	.35
104	John Olerud	.75	.35
105	Tino Martinez	.75	.35
106	David Cone	1.25	.55
107	Paul O'Neill	.75	.35
108	Andy Pettitte	.75	.35
109	Bernie Williams	2.00	.90
110	Rickey Henderson	2.50	1.10
111	Jason Giambi	.75	.35
112	Matt Stairs	.75	.35
113	Gregg Jefferies	.50	.23
114	Rico Brogna	.50	.23
115	Curt Schilling	1.25	.55
116	Jason Schmidt	.50	.23
117	Jose Guillen	.50	.23
118	Kevin Young	.75	.35
119	Ray Lankford	.75	.35
120	Mark McGwire	12.00	5.50
121	Delino DeShields	.50	.23
122	Ken Caminiti	.75	.35
123	Tony Gwynn	5.00	2.20
124	Trevor Hoffman	.75	.35
125	Barry Bonds	2.50	1.10
126	Jeff Kent	.75	.35
127	Shawn Estes	.50	.23
128	J.T. Snow	.75	.35
129	Jay Buhner	.75	.35
130	Ken Griffey Jr.	10.00	4.50
131	Dan Wilson	.50	.23
132	Edgar Martinez	.75	.35
133	Alex Rodriguez	6.00	2.70
134	Rusty Greer	.75	.35
135	Juan Gonzalez	4.00	1.80
136	Fernando Tatis	.50	.23
137	Ivan Rodriguez	2.50	1.10
138	Carlos Delgado	2.00	.90
139	Pat Hentgen	.50	.23
140	Roger Clemens	5.00	2.20
141	Chipper Jones SF	6.00	2.70
142	Greg Maddux SF	6.00	2.70
143	Rafael Palmeiro SF	2.50	1.10
144	Mike Mussina SF	2.50	1.10
145	Cal Ripken SF	10.00	4.50
146	Nomar Garciaparra SF	8.00	3.60
147	Mo Vaughn SF	2.50	1.10
148	Sammy Sosa SF	8.00	3.60
149	Albert Belle SF	2.50	1.10
150	Frank Thomas SF	5.00	2.20
151	Jim Thome SF	2.50	1.10
152	Kenny Lofton SF	1.50	.70
153	Manny Ramirez SF	3.00	1.35
154	Larry Walker SF	2.50	1.10
155	Jeff Bagwell SF	3.00	1.35
156	Craig Biggio SF	2.50	1.10
157	Mike Piazza SF	8.00	3.60
158	Paul Molitor SF	2.50	1.10
159	Derek Jeter SF	8.00	3.60
160	Tino Martinez SF	1.00	.45
161	Curt Schilling SF	1.50	.70
162	Mark McGwire SF	15.00	6.75
163	Tony Gwynn SF	6.00	2.70
164	Barry Bonds SF	3.00	1.35
165	Ken Griffey Jr. SF	12.00	5.50
166	Randy Johnson SF	2.50	1.10
167	Alex Rodriguez SF	8.00	3.60
168	Juan Gonzalez SF	5.00	2.20
169	Ivan Rodriguez SF	3.00	1.35
170	Roger Clemens SF	6.00	2.70
171	Greg Maddux HG	20.00	9.00
172	Cal Ripken HG	30.00	13.50
173	Frank Thomas HG	15.00	6.75
174	Jeff Bagwell HG	10.00	4.50
175	Mike Piazza HG	25.00	11.00
176	Mark McGwire HG	50.00	22.00
177	Barry Bonds HG	10.00	4.50
178	Ken Griffey Jr. HG	40.00	18.00
179	Alex Rodriguez HG	25.00	11.00
180	Roger Clemens HG	20.00	9.00
181	Mike Caruso YM	.75	.35
182	David Ortiz YM	.75	.35
183	Gabe Alvarez YM	.75	.35
184	Gary Matthews Jr. YM	2.00	.90
185	Kerry Wood YM	4.00	1.80
186	Carl Pavano YM	.75	.35
187	Alex Gonzalez YM	1.25	.55
188	Masato Yoshii YM	2.50	1.10
189	Larry Sutton YM	.75	.35
190	Russell Branyan YM	1.25	.55
191	Bruce Chen YM	1.25	.55
192	Rolando Arrojo YM	3.00	1.35
193	Ryan Christenson YM	1.25	.55
194	Cliff Politte YM	.75	.35
195	A.J. Hinch YM	.75	.35
196	Kevin Witt YM	.75	.35
197	Daryle Ward YM	1.25	.55
198	Corey Koskie YM	3.00	1.35
199	Mike Lowell YM	3.00	1.35
200	Travis Lee YM	4.00	1.80
201	Kevin Millwood YM	10.00	4.50
202	Robert Smith YM	.75	.35
203	Magglio Ordonez YM	10.00	4.50
204	Eric Milton YM	.75	.35
205	Geoff Jenkins YM	1.25	.55
206	Rich Butler YM	2.00	.90
207	Mike Kinkade YM	2.00	.90
208	Braden Looper YM	.75	.35
209	Matt Clement YM	1.25	.55
210	Derrek Lee YM	.75	.35
211	Ramon Johnson PP	2.50	1.10
212	John Smoltz PP	1.50	.70
213	Roger Clemens PP	6.00	2.70
214	Curt Schilling PP	1.50	.70
215	Pedro Martinez PP	3.00	1.35
216	Vinny Castilla PP	1.00	.45
217	Jose Cruz Jr. PP	1.00	.45
218	Jim Thome PP	2.50	1.10
219	Alex Rodriguez PP	8.00	3.60
220	Frank Thomas PP	5.00	2.20
221	Tim Salmon PP	1.00	.45
222	Larry Walker PP	2.50	1.10
223	Albert Belle PP	2.50	1.10
224	Manny Ramirez PP	3.00	1.35
225	Mark McGwire PP	15.00	6.75
226	Mo Vaughn PP	2.50	1.10
227	Andres Galarraga PP	1.50	.70
228	Scott Rolen PP	3.00	1.35
229	Travis Lee PP	1.50	.70
230	Mike Piazza PP	8.00	3.60
231	Nomar Garciaparra PP	8.00	3.60
232	Andruw Jones PP	2.50	1.10
233	Barry Bonds PP	3.00	1.35
234	Jeff Bagwell PP	3.00	1.35
235	Juan Gonzalez PP	5.00	2.20
236	Tino Martinez PP	1.00	.45
237	Vladimir Guerrero PP	3.00	1.35
238	Rafael Palmeiro PP	2.50	1.10
239	Russell Branyan PP	1.00	.45
240	Ken Griffey Jr. PP	12.00	5.50
241	Cecil Fielder	.75	.35
242	Chuck Finley	.75	.35
243	Jay Bell	.75	.35
244	Andy Benes	.50	.23
245	Matt Williams	2.00	.90
246	Brian Anderson	.50	.23

❑ 247 Dave Dellucci	1.50	.70
❑ 248 Andres Galarraga	1.25	.55
❑ 249 Andruw Jones	2.00	.90
❑ 250 Greg Maddux	5.00	2.20
❑ 251 Brady Anderson	.75	.35
❑ 252 Joe Carter	.75	.35
❑ 253 Eric Davis	.75	.35
❑ 254 Pedro Martinez	2.50	1.10
❑ 255 Nomar Garciaparra	6.00	2.70
❑ 256 Dennis Eckersley	.75	.35
❑ 257 Henry Rodriguez	.75	.35
❑ 258 Jeff Blauser	.50	.23
❑ 259 Jaime Navarro	.50	.23
❑ 260 Ray Durham	.75	.35
❑ 261 Chris Stynes	.50	.23
❑ 262 Willie Greene	.50	.23
❑ 263 Reggie Sanders	.50	.23
❑ 264 Bret Boone	.75	.35
❑ 265 Barry Larkin	2.00	.90
❑ 266 Travis Fryman	.75	.35
❑ 267 Charles Nagy	.75	.35
❑ 268 Sandy Alomar Jr.	.75	.35
❑ 269 Darryl Kile	.50	.23
❑ 270 Mike Lansing	.50	.23
❑ 271 Pedro Astacio	.50	.23
❑ 272 Damion Easley	.75	.35
❑ 273 Joe Randa	.75	.35
❑ 274 Luis Gonzalez	.75	.35
❑ 275 Mike Piazza	6.00	2.70
❑ 276 Todd Zeile	.75	.35
❑ 277 Edgar Renteria	.50	.23
❑ 278 Livan Hernandez	.50	.23
❑ 279 Cliff Floyd	.75	.35
❑ 280 Moises Alou	.75	.35
❑ 281 Billy Wagner	.75	.35
❑ 282 Jeff King	.50	.23
❑ 283 Hal Morris	.50	.23
❑ 284 Johnny Damon	.75	.35
❑ 285 Dean Palmer	.75	.35
❑ 286 Tim Belcher	.50	.23
❑ 287 Eric Young	.50	.23
❑ 288 Bobby Bonilla	.75	.35
❑ 289 Gary Sheffield	.75	.35
❑ 290 Chan Ho Park	.75	.35
❑ 291 Charles Johnson	.75	.35
❑ 292 Jeff Cirillo	.75	.35
❑ 293 Jeromy Burnitz	.75	.35
❑ 294 Jose Valentin	.50	.23
❑ 295 Marquis Grissom	.50	.23
❑ 296 Todd Walker	.75	.35
❑ 297 Terry Steinbach	.50	.23
❑ 298 Rick Aguilera	.50	.23
❑ 299 Vladimir Guerrero	2.50	1.10
❑ 300 Rey Ordonez	.75	.35
❑ 301 Butch Huskey	.50	.23
❑ 302 Bernard Gilkey	.50	.23
❑ 303 Mariano Rivera	.75	.35
❑ 304 Chuck Knoblauch	.75	.35
❑ 305 Derek Jeter	6.00	2.70
❑ 306 Ricky Bottalico	.50	.23
❑ 307 Bob Abreu	.75	.35
❑ 308 Scott Rolen	2.50	1.10
❑ 309 Al Martin	.50	.23
❑ 310 Jason Kendall	.75	.35
❑ 311 Brian Jordan	.75	.35
❑ 312 Ron Gant	.75	.35
❑ 313 Todd Stottlemyre	.50	.23
❑ 314 Greg Vaughn	.75	.35
❑ 315 Kevin Brown	1.25	.35
❑ 316 Wally Joyner	.75	.35
❑ 317 Robb Nen	.50	.23
❑ 318 Orel Hershiser	.75	.35
❑ 319 Russ Davis	.75	.35
❑ 320 Randy Johnson	2.00	.90
❑ 321 Quinton McCracken	.50	.23
❑ 322 Tony Saunders	.50	.23
❑ 323 Wilson Alvarez	.50	.23
❑ 324 Wade Boggs	2.00	.90
❑ 325 Fred McGriff	1.25	.55
❑ 326 Lee Stevens	.50	.23
❑ 327 John Wetteland	.75	.35
❑ 328 Jose Canseco	2.50	1.10
❑ 329 Randy Myers	.75	.35
❑ 330 Jose Cruz Jr.	.75	.35
❑ 331 Matt Williams TW	5.00	2.20
❑ 332 Andres Galarraga TW	3.00	1.35

❑ 333 Walt Weiss TW	2.00	.90
❑ 334 Joe Carter TW	2.00	.90
❑ 335 Pedro Martinez TW	6.00	2.70
❑ 336 Henry Rodriguez TW	2.00	.90
❑ 337 Travis Fryman TW	2.00	.90
❑ 338 Darryl Kile TW	1.25	.55
❑ 339 Mike Lansing TW	1.25	.55
❑ 340 Mike Piazza TW	15.00	6.75
❑ 341 Moises Alou TW	2.00	.90
❑ 342 Charles Johnson TW	2.00	.90
❑ 343 Chuck Knoblauch TW	2.00	.90
❑ 344 Rickey Henderson TW	6.00	2.70
❑ 345 Kevin Brown TW	3.00	1.35
❑ 346 Orel Hershiser TW	2.00	.90
❑ 347 Wade Boggs TW	5.00	2.20
❑ 348 Fred McGriff TW	3.00	1.35
❑ 349 Jose Canseco TW	5.00	2.20
❑ 350 Gary Sheffield TW	2.00	.90
❑ 351 Travis Lee CG	5.00	2.20
❑ 352 Nomar Garciaparra CG	25.00	11.00
❑ 353 Frank Thomas CG	15.00	6.75
❑ 354 Cal Ripken CG	30.00	13.50
❑ 355 Mark McGwire CG	50.00	22.00
❑ 356 Mike Piazza CG	25.00	11.00
❑ 357 Alex Rodriguez CG	25.00	11.00
❑ 358 Barry Bonds CG	10.00	4.50
❑ 359 Tony Gwynn CG	20.00	9.00
❑ 360 Ken Griffey Jr. CG	40.00	18.00

1998 SPx Finite Radiance

	MINT	NRMT
*YM RADIANCE: .75X TO 2X BASIC YM		
YM 1-30 PRINT RUN 2500 SERIAL #'d SETS		
*PE RADIANCE: 1.25X TO 3X BASIC PE		
PE 31-50 PRINT RUN 1000 SERIAL #'d SETS		
EXCH.CARDS MADE FOR #'s 39/40/41/46		
EXCHANGE DEADLINE WAS 6/2/99		
*BASIC RADIANCE: .75X TO 2X BASIC CARDS		
BASIC 51-140 PR.RUN 4500 SERIAL #'d SETS		
*SF RADIANCE: .75X TO 2X BASIC SF		
SF 141-170 PRINT RUN 3500 SERIAL #'d SETS		
*HG RADIANCE: 3X TO 8X BASIC HG		
HG 171-180 PRINT RUN 100 SERIAL #'d SETS		
*YM RADIANCE: .75X TO 2X BASIC YM		
YM 181-210 PRINT RUN 2500 SERIAL #'d SETS		
*PP RADIANCE: .6X TO 1.5X BASIC PP		
PP 211-240 PRINT RUN 3500 SERIAL #'d SETS		
*BASIC RADIANCE: .75X TO 2X BASIC CARDS		
BASIC 241-330 PR.RUN 4500 SERIAL #'d SETS		
*TW RADIANCE: 1.25X TO 3X BASIC TW		
TW 331-350 PRINT RUN 1000 SERIAL #'d SETS		
*CG RADIANCE: 3X TO 8X BASIC CG		
CG 351-360 PRINT RUN 100 SERIAL #'d SETS		
RANDOM INSERTS IN PACKS		

1998 SPx Finite Spectrum

	MINT	NRMT
*YM SPECTRUM: 1.25X TO 3X BASIC YM		

	MINT	NRMT
YM 1-30 PRINT RUN 1250 SERIAL #'d SETS		
*PE SPECTRUM: 8X TO 20X BASIC PE		
PE 31-50 PRINT RUN 50 SERIAL #'d SETS		
*BASIC SPECTRUM: 1.25X TO 3X BASIC CARDS		
BASIC 51-140 PR.RUN 2250 SERIAL #'d SETS		
*SF SPECTRUM: 1.25X TO 3X BASIC SF		
SF 141-170 PRINT RUN 1750 SERIAL #'d SETS		
*YM SPECTRUM: 1X TO 2.5X BASIC YM		
YM 181-210 PRINT RUN 1250 SERIAL #'d SETS		
*PP SPECTRUM: 1.25X TO 3X BASIC PP		
PP 211-240 PRINT RUN 1750 SERIAL #'d SETS		
*BASIC SPECTRUM: 1.25X TO 3X BASIC CARDS		
BASIC 241-330 PR.RUN 2250 SERIAL #'d SETS		
*TW SPECTRUM: 8X TO 20X BASIC TW		
TW 331-350 PRINT RUN 50 SERIAL #'d SETS		
COMMON CG (351-360)		
CG 351-360 PRINT RUN 1 SERIAL #'d SET		
CG NOT PRICED DUE TO SCARCITY		
RANDOM INSERTS IN PACKS		

1998 SPx Finite Home Run Hysteria

	MINT	NRMT
COMPLETE SET (10)	1500.00	700.00
COMMON CARD (HR1-HR10)	30.00	13.50
RANDOM INSERTS IN SER.2 PACKS		
STATED PRINT RUN 62 SERIAL #'d SETS		

❑ HR1 Ken Griffey Jr.	300.00	135.00
❑ HR2 Mark McGwire	400.00	180.00
❑ HR3 Sammy Sosa	200.00	90.00
❑ HR4 Albert Belle	50.00	22.00
❑ HR5 Alex Rodriguez	200.00	90.00
❑ HR6 Greg Vaughn	30.00	13.50
❑ HR7 Andres Galarraga	40.00	18.00
❑ HR8 Vinny Castilla	30.00	13.50
❑ HR9 Juan Gonzalez	120.00	55.00
❑ HR10 Chipper Jones	150.00	70.00

1999 SPx

	MINT	NRMT
COMPLETE SET (120)	600.00	275.00
COMP.SET w/o SP's (80)	75.00	34.00
COMMON MCGWIRE (1-10)	6.00	2.70
COMMON CARD (11-80)	.40	.18
MINOR STARS 11-80	.60	.25
SEMISTARS 11-80	1.00	.45
UNLISTED STARS 11-80	1.50	.70
COMMON SP (81-120)	5.00	2.20
SP MINOR STARS 81-120	8.00	3.60
SP SEMISTARS 81-120	10.00	4.50

SP CARDS RANDOM INSERTS IN PACKS
SP PRINT RUN 1999 SERIAL #'d SUBSETS
W.MAYS BAT LISTED W/UD APH 500 CLUB

❏ 1	Mark McGwire 61	8.00	3.60
❏ 2	Mark McGwire 62	8.00	3.60
❏ 3	Mark McGwire 63	6.00	2.70
❏ 4	Mark McGwire 64	6.00	2.70
❏ 5	Mark McGwire 65	6.00	2.70
❏ 6	Mark McGwire 66	6.00	2.70
❏ 7	Mark McGwire 67	6.00	2.70
❏ 8	Mark McGwire 68	6.00	2.70
❏ 9	Mark McGwire 69	6.00	2.70
❏ 10	Mark McGwire 70	10.00	4.50
❏ 11	Mo Vaughn	1.50	.70
❏ 12	Darin Erstad	1.00	.45
❏ 13	Travis Lee	1.00	.45
❏ 14	Randy Johnson	1.50	.70
❏ 15	Matt Williams	1.50	.70
❏ 16	Chipper Jones	4.00	1.80
❏ 17	Greg Maddux	4.00	1.80
❏ 18	Andruw Jones	1.50	.70
❏ 19	Andres Galarraga	1.00	.45
❏ 20	Cal Ripken	6.00	2.70
❏ 21	Albert Belle	1.50	.70
❏ 22	Mike Mussina	1.50	.70
❏ 23	Nomar Garciaparra	5.00	2.28
❏ 24	Pedro Martinez	2.00	.90
❏ 25	John Valentin	.60	.25
❏ 26	Kerry Wood	1.50	.70
❏ 27	Sammy Sosa	5.00	2.20
❏ 28	Mark Grace	1.00	.45
❏ 29	Frank Thomas	3.00	1.35
❏ 30	Mike Caruso	.40	.18
❏ 31	Barry Larkin	1.50	.70
❏ 32	Sean Casey	1.50	.70
❏ 33	Jim Thome	1.50	.70
❏ 34	Kenny Lofton	1.00	.45
❏ 35	Manny Ramirez	2.00	.90
❏ 36	Larry Walker	1.50	.70
❏ 37	Todd Helton	1.50	.70
❏ 38	Vinny Castilla	.60	.25
❏ 39	Tony Clark	.60	.25
❏ 40	Derrek Lee	.40	.18
❏ 41	Mark Kotsay	.40	.18
❏ 42	Jeff Bagwell	2.00	.90
❏ 43	Craig Biggio	1.50	.70
❏ 44	Moises Alou	.60	.25
❏ 45	Larry Sutton	.40	.18
❏ 46	Johnny Damon	.60	.25
❏ 47	Gary Sheffield	.60	.25
❏ 48	Raul Mondesi	.60	.25
❏ 49	Jeromy Burnitz	.60	.25
❏ 50	Todd Walker	.60	.25
❏ 51	David Ortiz	.40	.18

❏ 52	Vladimir Guerrero	2.00	.90
❏ 53	Rondell White	.60	.25
❏ 54	Mike Piazza	5.00	2.20
❏ 55	Derek Jeter	5.00	2.20
❏ 56	Tino Martinez	.60	.25
❏ 57	Roger Clemens	4.00	1.80
❏ 58	Ben Grieve	1.50	.70
❏ 59	A.J. Hinch	.40	.18
❏ 60	Scott Rolen	2.00	.90
❏ 61	Doug Glanville	.60	.25
❏ 62	Aramis Ramirez	1.00	.45
❏ 63	Jose Guillen	.40	.18
❏ 64	Tony Gwynn	4.00	1.80
❏ 65	Greg Vaughn	.60	.25
❏ 66	Ruben Rivera	.40	.18
❏ 67	Barry Bonds	2.00	.90
❏ 68	J.T. Snow	.60	.25
❏ 69	Alex Rodriguez	5.00	2.20
❏ 70	Ken Griffey Jr.	8.00	3.60
❏ 71	Jay Buhner	.60	.25
❏ 72	Mark McGwire	10.00	4.50
❏ 73	Fernando Tatis	1.50	.70
❏ 74	Quinton McCracken	.40	.18
❏ 75	Wade Boggs	1.50	.70
❏ 76	Ivan Rodriguez	2.00	.90
❏ 77	Juan Gonzalez	3.00	1.35
❏ 78	Rafael Palmeiro	1.50	.70
❏ 79	Jose Cruz Jr.	.60	.25
❏ 80	Carlos Delgado	1.50	.70
❏ 81	Troy Glaus SP	15.00	6.75
❏ 82	Vladimir Nunez SP	5.00	2.20
❏ 83	George Lombard SP	8.00	3.60
❏ 84	Bruce Chen SP	8.00	3.60
❏ 85	Ryan Minor SP	8.00	3.60
❏ 86	Calvin Pickering SP	8.00	3.60
❏ 87	Jin Ho Cho SP	8.00	3.60
❏ 88	Russ Branyan SP	8.00	3.60
❏ 89	Derrick Gibson SP	8.00	3.60
❏ 90	Gabe Kapler SP AU	30.00	13.50
❏ 91	Matt Anderson SP	5.00	2.20
❏ 92	Robert Fick SP	8.00	3.60
❏ 93	Juan Encarnacion SP	8.00	3.60
❏ 94	Preston Wilson SP	8.00	3.60
❏ 95	Alex Gonzalez SP	8.00	3.60
❏ 96	Carlos Beltran SP	20.00	9.00
❏ 97	Jeremy Giambi SP	8.00	3.60
❏ 98	Dee Brown SP	8.00	3.60
❏ 99	Adrian Beltre SP	15.00	6.75
❏ 100	Alex Cora SP	5.00	2.20
❏ 101	Angel Pena SP	5.00	2.20
❏ 102	Geoff Jenkins SP	8.00	3.60
❏ 103	Ronnie Belliard SP	8.00	3.60
❏ 104	Corey Koskie SP	5.00	2.20
❏ 105	A.J. Pierzynski SP	5.00	2.20
❏ 106	Michael Barrett SP	10.00	4.50
❏ 107	Fernando Seguignol SP	8.00	3.60
❏ 108	Mike Kinkade SP	5.00	2.20
❏ 109	Mike Lowell SP	5.00	2.20
❏ 110	Ricky Ledee SP	8.00	3.60
❏ 111	Eric Chavez SP	10.00	4.50
❏ 112	Abraham Nunez SP	5.00	2.20
❏ 113	Matt Clement SP	8.00	3.60
❏ 114	Ben Davis SP	10.00	4.50
❏ 115	Mike Darr SP	8.00	3.60
❏ 116	Ramon E.Martinez SP	5.00	2.20
❏ 117	Carlos Guillen SP	5.00	2.20
❏ 118	Shane Monahan SP	5.00	2.20
❏ 119	J.D. Drew SP AU	60.00	27.00
❏ 120	Kevin Witt SP	5.00	2.20
❏ 24EAST	K. Griffey Jr. Sample	5.00	2.20

1999 SPx Finite Radiance

	MINT	NRMT
COMMON CARD (1-120)	10.00	4.50
*RADIANCE 1-10: 6X TO 15X BASIC 1-10		
*RADIANCE 11-80: 8X TO 20X BASIC 11-80		
*RADIANCE 81-120: 1.25X TO 3X BASIC 81-120		

THREE CARDS PER RADIANCE HOT PACK
STATED PRINT RUN 100 SERIAL #'D SETS

1999 SPx Finite Spectrum

	MINT	NRMT
THREE CARDS PER HOT PACK
STATED PRINT RUN 1 SERIAL #'d SET
NO PRICING DUE TO SCARCITY

1999 SPx Dominance

	MINT	NRMT
COMPLETE SET (20)	200.00	90.00
COMMON CARD (FB1-FB20)	4.00	1.80
STATED ODDS 1:17		

❏ FB1	Chipper Jones	12.00	5.50
❏ FB2	Greg Maddux	12.00	5.50
❏ FB3	Cal Ripken	20.00	9.00
❏ FB4	Nomar Garciaparra	15.00	6.75
❏ FB5	Mo Vaughn	4.00	1.80
❏ FB6	Sammy Sosa	15.00	6.75
❏ FB7	Albert Belle	4.00	1.80
❏ FB8	Frank Thomas	10.00	4.50
❏ FB9	Jim Thome	4.00	1.80
❏ FB10	Jeff Bagwell	6.00	2.70
❏ FB11	Vladimir Guerrero	6.00	2.70
❏ FB12	Mike Piazza	15.00	6.75
❏ FB13	Derek Jeter	15.00	6.75
❏ FB14	Tony Gwynn	12.00	5.50
❏ FB15	Barry Bonds	6.00	2.70
❏ FB16	Ken Griffey Jr.	25.00	11.00
❏ FB17	Alex Rodriguez	15.00	6.75
❏ FB18	Mark McGwire	30.00	13.50
❏ FB19	J.D. Drew	6.00	2.70
❏ FB20	Juan Gonzalez	10.00	4.50

1999 SPx Power Explosion

	MINT	NRMT
COMPLETE SET (30)	60.00	27.00
COMMON CARD (PE1-PE30)	.60	.25
SEMISTARS	1.00	.45
UNLISTED STARS	1.50	.70
STATED ODDS 1:3		

❏ PE1	Troy Glaus	1.50	.70
❏ PE2	Mo Vaughn	1.50	.70
❏ PE3	Travis Lee	1.00	.45

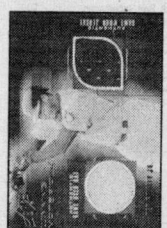

		MINT	NRMT
❏ PS15	Chipper Jones	15.00	6.75
❏ PS16	Nomar Garciaparra	20.00	9.00
❏ PS17	Greg Maddux	15.00	6.75
❏ PS18	Scott Rolen	8.00	3.60
❏ PS19	Vladimir Guerrero	8.00	3.60
❏ PS20	Albert Belle	6.00	2.70
❏ PS21	Ken Griffey Jr.	30.00	13.50
❏ PS22	Alex Rodriguez	20.00	9.00
❏ PS23	Ben Grieve	6.00	2.70
❏ PS24	Juan Gonzalez	12.00	5.50
❏ PS25	Barry Bonds	8.00	3.60
❏ PS26	Roger Clemens	15.00	6.75
❏ PS27	Tony Gwynn	15.00	6.75
❏ PS28	Randy Johnson	6.00	2.70
❏ PS29	Travis Lee	4.00	1.80
❏ PS30	Mo Vaughn	6.00	2.70

❏ PE4	Chipper Jones	4.00	1.80
❏ PE5	Andres Galarraga	1.00	.45
❏ PE6	Brady Anderson	.60	.25
❏ PE7	Albert Belle	1.50	.70
❏ PE8	Nomar Garciaparra	5.00	2.20
❏ PE9	Sammy Sosa	5.00	2.20
❏ PE10	Frank Thomas	3.00	1.35
❏ PE11	Jim Thome	1.50	.70
❏ PE12	Manny Ramirez	1.50	.70
❏ PE13	Larry Walker	1.50	.70
❏ PE14	Tony Clark	.60	.25
❏ PE15	Jeff Bagwell	2.00	.90
❏ PE16	Moises Alou	.60	.25
❏ PE17	Ken Caminiti	.60	.25
❏ PE18	Vladimir Guerrero	2.00	.90
❏ PE19	Mike Piazza	5.00	2.20
❏ PE20	Tino Martinez	.60	.25
❏ PE21	Ben Grieve	1.50	.70
❏ PE22	Scott Rolen	2.50	1.10
❏ PE23	Greg Vaughn	.60	.25
❏ PE24	Barry Bonds	2.00	.90
❏ PE25	Ken Griffey Jr.	8.00	3.60
❏ PE26	Alex Rodriguez	5.00	2.20
❏ PE27	Mark McGwire	10.00	4.50
❏ PE28	J.D. Drew	2.00	.90
❏ PE29	Juan Gonzalez	3.00	1.35
❏ PE30	Ivan Rodriguez	2.00	.90

1999 SPx Premier Stars

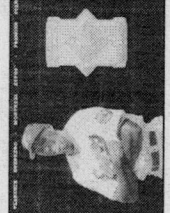

	MINT	NRMT
COMMON CARD (30)	400.00	180.00
COMPLETE SET (PS1-PS30)	2.50	1.10
SEMISTARS	4.00	1.80
UNLISTED STARS	6.00	2.70
STATED ODDS 1:17		

		MINT	NRMT
❏ PS1	Mark McGwire	40.00	18.00
❏ PS2	Sammy Sosa	20.00	9.00
❏ PS3	Frank Thomas	12.00	5.50
❏ PS4	J.D. Drew	8.00	3.60
❏ PS5	Kerry Wood	6.00	2.70
❏ PS6	Moises Alou	2.50	1.10
❏ PS7	Kenny Lofton	4.00	1.80
❏ PS8	Jeff Bagwell	8.00	3.60
❏ PS9	Tony Clark	2.50	1.10
❏ PS10	Roberto Alomar	6.00	2.70
❏ PS11	Cal Ripken	25.00	11.00
❏ PS12	Derek Jeter	20.00	9.00
❏ PS13	Mike Piazza	20.00	9.00
❏ PS14	Jose Cruz Jr.	2.50	1.10

1999 SPx Star Focus

	MINT	NRMT
COMPLETE SET (30)	200.00	90.00
COMMON CARD (SF1-SF30)	2.00	.90
SEMISTARS	2.50	1.10
UNLISTED STARS	4.00	1.80
STATED ODDS 1:8		

		MINT	NRMT
❏ SF1	Chipper Jones	10.00	4.50
❏ SF2	Greg Maddux	10.00	4.50
❏ SF3	Cal Ripken	15.00	6.75
❏ SF4	Nomar Garciaparra	12.00	5.50
❏ SF5	Mo Vaughn	4.00	1.80
❏ SF6	Sammy Sosa	12.00	5.50
❏ SF7	Albert Belle	4.00	1.80
❏ SF8	Frank Thomas	8.00	3.60
❏ SF9	Jim Thome	4.00	1.80
❏ SF10	Kenny Lofton	2.50	1.10
❏ SF11	Manny Ramirez	5.00	2.20
❏ SF12	Larry Walker	4.00	1.80
❏ SF13	Jeff Bagwell	5.00	2.20
❏ SF14	Craig Biggio	4.00	1.80
❏ SF15	Randy Johnson	4.00	1.80
❏ SF16	Vladimir Guerrero	5.00	2.20
❏ SF17	Mike Piazza	12.00	5.50
❏ SF18	Derek Jeter	12.00	5.50
❏ SF19	Tino Martinez	2.00	.90
❏ SF20	Bernie Williams	4.00	1.80
❏ SF21	Curt Schilling	2.50	1.10
❏ SF22	Tony Gwynn	10.00	4.50
❏ SF23	Barry Bonds	5.00	2.20
❏ SF24	Ken Griffey Jr.	20.00	9.00
❏ SF25	Alex Rodriguez	12.00	5.50
❏ SF26	Mark McGwire	25.00	11.00
❏ SF27	J.D. Drew	5.00	2.20
❏ SF28	Juan Gonzalez	8.00	3.60
❏ SF29	Ivan Rodriguez	5.00	2.20
❏ SF30	Ben Grieve	4.00	1.80

1999 SPx Winning Materials

	MINT	NRMT
COMMON CARD (1-8)	50.00	22.00
STATED ODDS 1:251		

		MINT	NRMT
❏ IR	Ivan Rodriguez	120.00	55.00
❏ JD	J.D. Drew	150.00	70.00
❏ JR	Ken Griffey Jr	500.00	220.00
❏ TG	Tony Gwynn	200.00	90.00

		MINT	NRMT
❏ TH	Todd Helton	80.00	36.00
❏ TL	Travis Lee	50.00	22.00
❏ VC	Vinny Castilla	50.00	22.00
❏ VG	Vladimir Guerrero	120.00	55.00

1991 Stadium Club

	MINT	NRMT
COMPLETE SET (600)	80.00	36.00
COMPLETE SERIES 1 (300)	50.00	22.00
COMPLETE SERIES 2 (300)	30.00	13.50
COMMON CARD (1-600)	.25	.11
MINOR STARS	.50	.23
UNLISTED STARS	1.00	.45

		MINT	NRMT
❏ 1	Dave Stewart TUX	1.00	.45
❏ 2	Wally Joyner	.50	.23
❏ 3	Shawon Dunston	.25	.11
❏ 4	Darren Daulton	.50	.23
❏ 5	Will Clark	1.00	.45
❏ 6	Sammy Sosa	6.00	2.70
❏ 7	Dan Plesac	.25	.11
❏ 8	Marquis Grissom	1.00	.45
❏ 9	Erik Hanson	.25	.11
❏ 10	Geno Petralli	.25	.11
❏ 11	Jose Rijo	.25	.11
❏ 12	Carlos Quintana	.25	.11
❏ 13	Junior Ortiz	.25	.11
❏ 14	Bob Walk	.25	.11
❏ 15	Mike Macfarlane	.25	.11
❏ 16	Eric Yelding	.25	.11
❏ 17	Bryn Smith	.25	.11
❏ 18	Bip Roberts	.25	.11
❏ 19	Mike Scioscia	.25	.11
❏ 20	Mark Williamson	.25	.11
❏ 21	Don Mattingly	2.00	.90
❏ 22	John Franco	.50	.23
❏ 23	Chet Lemon	.25	.11
❏ 24	Tom Henke	.25	.11
❏ 25	Jerry Browne	.25	.11
❏ 26	Dave Justice	1.00	.45
❏ 27	Mark Langston	.25	.11
❏ 28	Damon Berryhill	.25	.11
❏ 29	Kevin Bass	.25	.11
❏ 30	Scott Fletcher	.25	.11
❏ 31	Moises Alou	1.50	.70
❏ 32	Dave Valle	.25	.11
❏ 33	Jody Reed	.25	.11
❏ 34	Dave West	.25	.11
❏ 35	Kevin McReynolds	.25	.11
❏ 36	Pat Combs	.25	.11
❏ 37	Eric Davis	.50	.23

38	Bret Saberhagen	.50	.23
39	Stan Javier	.25	.11
40	Chuck Cary	.25	.11
41	Tony Phillips	.25	.11
42	Lee Smith	.50	.23
43	Tim Teufel	.25	.11
44	Lance Dickson	.25	.11
45	Greg Litton	.25	.11
46	Ted Higuera	.25	.11
47	Edgar Martinez	1.00	.45
48	Steve Avery	.25	.11
49	Walt Weiss	.25	.11
50	David Segui	.50	.23
51	Andy Benes	.50	.23
52	Karl Rhodes	.25	.11
53	Neal Heaton	.25	.11
54	Danny Gladden	.25	.11
55	Luis Rivera	.25	.11
56	Kevin Brown	.75	.35
57	Frank Thomas	4.00	1.80
58	Terry Mulholland	.25	.11
59	Dick Schofield	.25	.11
60	Ron Darling	.25	.11
61	Sandy Alomar Jr.	.50	.23
62	Dave Stieb	.25	.11
63	Alan Trammell	.75	.35
64	Matt Nokes	.25	.11
65	Lenny Harris	.25	.11
66	Milt Thompson	.25	.11
67	Storm Davis	.25	.11
68	Joe Oliver	.25	.11
69	Andres Galarraga	1.00	.45
70	Ozzie Guillen	.25	.11
71	Ken Howell	.25	.11
72	Garry Templeton	.25	.11
73	Derrick May	.25	.11
74	Xavier Hernandez	.25	.11
75	Dave Parker	.50	.23
76	Rick Aguilera	.50	.23
77	Robby Thompson	.25	.11
78	Pete Incaviglia	.25	.11
79	Bob Welch	.25	.11
80	Randy Milligan	.25	.11
81	Chuck Finley	.50	.23
82	Alvin Davis	.25	.11
83	Tim Naehring	.25	.11
84	Jay Bell	.50	.23
85	Joe Magrane	.25	.11
86	Howard Johnson	.25	.11
87	Jack McDowell	.25	.11
88	Kevin Seitzer	.25	.11
89	Bruce Ruffin	.25	.11
90	Fernando Valenzuela	.50	.23
91	Terry Kennedy	.25	.11
92	Barry Larkin	1.00	.45
93	Larry Walker	1.50	.70
94	Luis Salazar	.25	.11
95	Gary Sheffield	1.00	.45
96	Bobby Witt	.25	.11
97	Lonnie Smith	.25	.11
98	Bryan Harvey	.25	.11
99	Mookie Wilson	.25	.11
100	Dwight Gooden	.50	.23
101	Lou Whitaker	.50	.23
102	Ron Karkovice	.25	.11
103	Jesse Barfield	.25	.11
104	Jose DeJesus	.25	.11
105	Benito Santiago	.25	.11
106	Brian Holman	.25	.11
107	Rafael Ramirez	.25	.11
108	Ellis Burks	.50	.23
109	Mike Bielecki	.25	.11
110	Kirby Puckett	1.50	.70
111	Terry Shumpert	.25	.11
112	Chuck Crim	.25	.11
113	Todd Benzinger	.25	.11
114	Brian Barnes	.25	.11
115	Carlos Baerga	.50	.23
116	Kal Daniels	.25	.11
117	Dave Johnson	.25	.11
118	Andy Van Slyke	.50	.23
119	John Burkett	.25	.11
120	Rickey Henderson	1.25	.55
121	Tim Jones	.25	.11
122	Daryl Irvine	.25	.11
123	Ruben Sierra	.25	.11
124	Jim Abbott	.50	.23
125	Daryl Boston	.25	.11
126	Greg Maddux	2.50	1.10
127	Von Hayes	.25	.11
128	Mike Fitzgerald	.25	.11
129	Wayne Edwards	.25	.11
130	Greg Briley	.25	.11
131	Rob Dibble	.25	.11
132	Gene Larkin	.25	.11
133	David Wells	.50	.23
134	Steve Balboni	.25	.11
135	Greg Vaughn	1.00	.45
136	Mark Davis	.25	.11
137	Dave Rhode	.25	.11
138	Eric Show	.25	.11
139	Bobby Bonilla	.50	.23
140	Dana Kiecker	.25	.11
141	Gary Pettis	.25	.11
142	Dennis Boyd	.25	.11
143	Mike Benjamin	.25	.11
144	Luis Polonia	.25	.11
145	Doug Jones	.25	.11
146	Al Newman	.25	.11
147	Alex Fernandez	.50	.23
148	Bill Doran	.25	.11
149	Kevin Elster	.25	.11
150	Len Dykstra	.50	.23
151	Mike Gallego	.25	.11
152	Tim Belcher	.25	.11
153	Jay Buhner	1.00	.45
154	Ozzie Smith UER	1.25	.55
	(Rookie card is 1979, but card back says '78)		
155	Jose Canseco	1.25	.55
156	Gregg Olson	.25	.11
157	Charlie O'Brien	.25	.11
158	Frank Tanana	.25	.11
159	George Brett	2.00	.90
160	Jeff Huson	.25	.11
161	Kevin Tapani	.25	.11
162	Jerome Walton	.25	.11
163	Charlie Hayes	.25	.11
164	Chris Bosio	.25	.11
165	Chris Sabo	.25	.11
166	Lance Parrish	.25	.11
167	Don Robinson	.25	.11
168	Manny Lee	.25	.11
169	Dennis Rasmussen	.25	.11
170	Wade Boggs	1.00	.45
171	Bob Geren	.25	.11
172	Mackey Sasser	.25	.11
173	Julio Franco	.25	.11
174	Otis Nixon	.50	.23
175	Bert Blyleven	.50	.23
176	Craig Biggio	1.00	.45
177	Eddie Murray	1.00	.45
178	Randy Tomlin	.25	.11
179	Tino Martinez	1.00	.45
180	Carlton Fisk	1.00	.45
181	Dwight Smith	.25	.11
182	Scott Garrelts	.25	.11
183	Jim Gantner	.25	.11
184	Dickie Thon	.25	.11
185	John Farrell	.25	.11
186	Cecil Fielder	.50	.23
187	Glenn Braggs	.25	.11
188	Allan Anderson	.25	.11
189	Kurt Stillwell	.25	.11
190	Jose Oquendo	.25	.11
191	Joe Orsulak	.25	.11
192	Ricky Jordan	.25	.11
193	Kelly Downs	.25	.11
194	Delino DeShields	.50	.23
195	Omar Vizquel	1.00	.45
196	Mark Carreon	.25	.11
197	Mike Harkey	.25	.11
198	Jack Howell	.25	.11
199	Lance Johnson	.25	.11
200	Nolan Ryan TUX	4.00	1.80
201	John Marzano	.25	.11
202	Doug Drabek	.25	.11
203	Mark Lemke	.25	.11
204	Steve Sax	.25	.11
205	Greg Harris	.25	.11
206	B.J. Surhoff	.50	.23
207	Todd Burns	.25	.11
208	Jose Gonzalez	.25	.11
209	Mike Scott	.25	.11
210	Dave Magadan	.25	.11
211	Dante Bichette	1.00	.45
212	Trevor Wilson	.25	.11
213	Hector Villanueva	.25	.11
214	Dan Pasqua	.25	.11
215	Greg Colbrunn	.25	.11
216	Mike Jeffcoat	.25	.11
217	Harold Reynolds	.25	.11
218	Paul O'Neill	.50	.23
219	Mark Guthrie	.25	.11
220	Barry Bonds	1.25	.55
221	Jimmy Key	.50	.23
222	Billy Ripken	.25	.11
223	Tom Pagnozzi	.25	.11
224	Bo Jackson	.50	.23
225	Sid Fernandez	.25	.11
226	Mike Marshall	.25	.11
227	John Kruk	.50	.23
228	Mike Fetters	.25	.11
229	Eric Anthony	.25	.11
230	Ryne Sandberg	1.25	.55
231	Carney Lansford	.50	.23
232	Melido Perez	.25	.11
233	Jose Lind	.25	.11
234	Darryl Hamilton	.25	.11
235	Tom Browning	.25	.11
236	Spike Owen	.25	.11
237	Juan Gonzalez	6.00	2.70
238	Felix Fermin	.25	.11
239	Keith Miller	.25	.11
240	Mark Gubicza	.25	.11
241	Kent Anderson	.25	.11
242	Alvaro Espinoza	.25	.11
243	Dale Murphy	1.00	.45
244	Orel Hershiser	.50	.23
245	Paul Molitor	1.00	.45
246	Eddie Whitson	.25	.11
247	Joe Girardi	.50	.23
248	Kent Hrbek	.50	.23
249	Bill Sampen	.25	.11
250	Kevin Mitchell	.25	.11
251	Mariano Duncan	.25	.11
252	Scott Bradley	.25	.11
253	Mike Greenwell	.25	.11
254	Tom Gordon	.25	.11
255	Todd Zeile	.50	.23
256	Bobby Thigpen	.25	.11
257	Gregg Jefferies	.25	.11
258	Kenny Rogers	.25	.11
259	Shane Mack	.25	.11
260	Zane Smith	.25	.11
261	Mitch Williams	.25	.11
262	Jim Deshaies	.25	.11
263	Dave Winfield	1.00	.45
264	Ben McDonald	.25	.11
265	Randy Ready	.25	.11
266	Pat Borders	.25	.11
267	Jose Uribe	.25	.11
268	Derek Lilliquist	.25	.11
269	Greg Brock	.25	.11
270	Ken Griffey Jr.	8.00	3.60
271	Jeff Gray	.25	.11
272	Danny Tartabull	.50	.23
273	Dennis Martinez	.25	.23
274	Robin Ventura	1.00	.45
275	Randy Myers	.50	.23
276	Jack Daugherty	.25	.11
277	Greg Gagne	.25	.11
278	Jay Howell	.25	.11
279	Mike LaValliere	.25	.11
280	Rex Hudler	.25	.11
281	Mike Simms	.25	.11
282	Kevin Maas	.25	.11
283	Jeff Ballard	.25	.11
284	Dave Henderson	.25	.11
285	Pete O'Brien	.25	.11
286	Brook Jacoby	.25	.11
287	Mike Henneman	.25	.11
288	Greg Olson	.25	.11
289	Greg Myers	.25	.11
290	Mark Grace	1.00	.45
291	Shawn Abner	.25	.11
292	Frank Viola	.25	.11
293	Lee Stevens	.50	.23

294	Jason Grimsley	.25	.11
295	Matt Williams	1.00	.45
296	Ron Robinson	.25	.11
297	Tom Brunansky	.25	.11
298	Checklist 1-100	.25	.11
299	Checklist 101-200	.25	.11
300	Checklist 201-300	.25	.11
301	Darryl Strawberry	.50	.23
302	Bud Black	.25	.11
303	Harold Baines	.50	.23
304	Roberto Alomar	1.00	.45
305	Norm Charlton	.25	.11
306	Gary Thurman	.25	.11
307	Mike Felder	.25	.11
308	Tony Gwynn	2.50	1.10
309	Roger Clemens	2.50	1.10
310	Andre Dawson	1.00	.45
311	Scott Radinsky	.25	.11
312	Bob Melvin	.25	.11
313	Kirk McCaskill	.25	.11
314	Pedro Guerrero	.25	.11
315	Walt Terrell	.25	.11
316	Sam Horn	.25	.11
317	Wes Chamberlain UER (Card listed as 1989 Debut card, should be 1990)	.25	.11
318	Pedro Munoz	.25	.11
319	Roberto Kelly	.25	.11
320	Mark Portugal	.25	.11
321	Tim McIntosh	.25	.11
322	Jesse Orosco	.25	.11
323	Gary Green	.25	.11
324	Greg Harris	.25	.11
325	Hubie Brooks	.25	.11
326	Chris Nabholz	.25	.11
327	Terry Pendleton	.50	.23
328	Eric King	.25	.11
329	Chili Davis	.50	.23
330	Anthony Telford	.25	.11
331	Kelly Gruber	.25	.11
332	Dennis Eckersley	.50	.23
333	Mel Hall	.25	.11
334	Bob Kipper	.25	.11
335	Willie McGee	.50	.23
336	Steve Olin	.25	.11
337	Steve Buechele	.25	.11
338	Scott Leius	.25	.11
339	Hal Morris	.25	.11
340	Jose Offerman	.75	.35
341	Kent Mercker	.25	.11
342	Ken Griffey Sr.	.50	.23
343	Pete Harnisch	.25	.11
344	Kirk Gibson	.50	.23
345	Dave Smith	.25	.11
346	Dave Martinez	.25	.11
347	Atlee Hammaker	.25	.11
348	Brian Downing	.25	.11
349	Todd Hundley	1.50	.70
350	Candy Maldonado	.25	.11
351	Dwight Evans	.50	.23
352	Steve Searcy	.25	.11
353	Gary Gaetti	.50	.23
354	Jeff Reardon	.50	.23
355	Travis Fryman	1.00	.45
356	Dave Righetti	.25	.11
357	Fred McGriff	1.00	.45
358	Don Slaught	.25	.11
359	Gene Nelson	.25	.11
360	Billy Spiers	.25	.11
361	Lee Guetterman	.25	.11
362	Darren Lewis	.50	.23
363	Duane Ward	.25	.11
364	Lloyd Moseby	.25	.11
365	John Smoltz	1.00	.45
366	Felix Jose	.25	.11
367	David Cone	.50	.23
368	Wally Backman	.25	.11
369	Jeff Montgomery	.50	.23
370	Rich Garces	.25	.11
371	Billy Hatcher	.25	.11
372	Bill Swift	.25	.11
373	Jim Eisenreich	.25	.11
374	Rob Ducey	.25	.11
375	Tim Crews	.25	.11
376	Steve Finley	1.00	.45
377	Jeff Blauser	.25	.11
378	Willie Wilson	.25	.11
379	Gerald Perry	.25	.11
380	Jose Mesa	.25	.11
381	Pat Kelly	.25	.11
382	Matt Merullo	.25	.11
383	Ivan Calderon	.25	.11
384	Scott Chiamparino	.25	.11
385	Lloyd McClendon	.25	.11
386	Dave Bergman	.25	.11
387	Ed Sprague	.25	.11
388	Jeff Bagwell	8.00	3.60
389	Brett Butler	.50	.23
390	Larry Andersen	.25	.11
391	Glenn Davis	.25	.11
392	Alex Cole UER (Front photo actually Otis Nixon)	.25	.11
393	Mike Heath	.25	.11
394	Danny Darwin	.25	.11
395	Steve Lake	.25	.11
396	Tim Layana	.25	.11
397	Terry Leach	.25	.11
398	Bill Wegman	.25	.11
399	Mark McGwire	5.00	2.20
400	Mike Boddicker	.25	.11
401	Steve Howe	.25	.11
402	Bernard Gilkey	.50	.23
403	Thomas Howard	.25	.11
404	Rafael Belliard	.25	.11
405	Tom Candiotti	.25	.11
406	Rene Gonzales	.25	.11
407	Chuck McElroy	.25	.11
408	Paul Sorrento	.50	.23
409	Randy Johnson	1.25	.55
410	Brady Anderson	1.00	.45
411	Dennis Cook	.25	.11
412	Mickey Tettleton	.50	.23
413	Mike Stanton	.25	.11
414	Ken Oberkfell	.25	.11
415	Rick Honeycutt	.25	.11
416	Nelson Santovenia	.25	.11
417	Bob Tewksbury	.25	.11
418	Brent Mayne	.25	.11
419	Steve Farr	.25	.11
420	Phil Stephenson	.25	.11
421	Jeff Russell	.25	.11
422	Chris James	.25	.11
423	Tim Leary	.25	.11
424	Gary Carter	1.00	.45
425	Glenallen Hill	.25	.11
426	Matt Young UER (Card mentions 83T/Tr as RC, but 84T shown)	.25	.11
427	Sid Bream	.25	.11
428	Greg Swindell	.25	.11
429	Scott Aldred	.25	.11
430	Cal Ripken	4.00	1.80
431	Bill Landrum	.25	.11
432	Earnest Riles	.25	.11
433	Danny Jackson	.25	.11
434	Casey Candaele	.25	.11
435	Ken Hill	.25	.11
436	Jaime Navarro	.25	.11
437	Lance Blankenship	.25	.11
438	Randy Velarde	.25	.11
439	Frank DiPino	.25	.11
440	Carl Nichols	.25	.11
441	Jeff M. Robinson	.25	.11
442	Deion Sanders	.50	.23
443	Vicente Palacios	.25	.11
444	Devon White	.25	.11
445	John Cerutti	.25	.11
446	Tracy Jones	.25	.11
447	Jack Morris	.50	.23
448	Mitch Webster	.25	.11
449	Bob Ojeda	.25	.11
450	Oscar Azocar	.25	.11
451	Luis Aquino	.25	.11
452	Mark Whiten	.25	.11
453	Stan Belinda	.25	.11
454	Ron Gant	.50	.23
455	Jose DeLeon	.25	.11
456	Mark Salas UER (Back has 85T photo, but calls it 86T)	.25	.11
457	Junior Felix	.25	.11
458	Wally Whitehurst	.25	.11
459	Phil Plantier	.25	.11
460	Juan Berenguer	.25	.11
461	Franklin Stubbs	.25	.11
462	Joe Boever	.25	.11
463	Tim Wallach	.25	.11
464	Mike Moore	.25	.11
465	Albert Belle	1.25	.55
466	Mike Witt	.25	.11
467	Craig Worthington	.25	.11
468	Jerald Clark	.25	.11
469	Scott Terry	.25	.11
470	Milt Cuyler	.25	.11
471	John Smiley	.25	.11
472	Charles Nagy	1.00	.45
473	Alan Mills	.25	.11
474	John Russell	.25	.11
475	Bruce Hurst	.25	.11
476	Andujar Cedeno	.25	.11
477	Dave Eiland	.25	.11
478	Brian McRae	.50	.23
479	Mike LaCoss	.25	.11
480	Chris Gwynn	.25	.11
481	Jamie Moyer	.25	.11
482	John Olerud	.75	.35
483	Efrain Valdez	.25	.11
484	Sil Campusano	.25	.11
485	Pascual Perez	.25	.11
486	Gary Redus	.25	.11
487	Andy Hawkins	.25	.11
488	Cory Snyder	.25	.11
489	Chris Hoiles	.25	.11
490	Ron Hassey	.25	.11
491	Gary Wayne	.25	.11
492	Mark Lewis	.25	.11
493	Scott Coolbaugh	.25	.11
494	Gerald Young	.25	.11
495	Juan Samuel	.25	.11
496	Willie Fraser	.25	.11
497	Jeff Treadway	.25	.11
499	Cris Carpenter	.25	.11
500	Jack Clark	.50	.23
501	Kevin Appier	.25	.11
502	Rafael Palmeiro	1.00	.45
503	Hensley Meulens	.25	.11
504	George Bell	.25	.11
505	Tony Pena	.25	.11
506	Roger McDowell	.25	.11
507	Luis Sojo	.25	.11
508	Mike Schooler	.25	.11
509	Robin Yount	1.00	.45
510	Jack Armstrong	.25	.11
511	Rick Cerone	.25	.11
512	Curt Wilkerson	.25	.11
513	Joe Carter	.50	.23
514	Tim Burke	.25	.11
515	Tony Fernandez	.50	.23
516	Ramon Martinez	.50	.23
517	Tim Hulett	.25	.11
518	Terry Steinbach	.50	.23
519	Pete Smith	.25	.11
520	Ken Caminiti	1.00	.45
521	Shawn Boskie	.25	.11
522	Mike Pagliarulo	.25	.11
523	Tim Raines	.50	.23
524	Alfredo Griffin	.25	.11
525	Henry Cotto	.25	.11
526	Mike Stanley	.25	.11
527	Charlie Leibrandt	.25	.11
528	Jeff King	.25	.11
529	Eric Plunk	.25	.11
530	Tom Lampkin	.25	.11
531	Steve Bedrosian	.25	.11
532	Tom Herr	.25	.11
533	Craig Lefferts	.25	.11
534	Jeff Reed	.25	.11
535	Mickey Morandini	.25	.11
536	Greg Cadaret	.25	.11
537	Ray Lankford	2.00	.90
538	John Candelaria	.25	.11
539	Rob Deer	.25	.11
540	Brad Arnsberg	.25	.11
541	Mike Sharperson	.25	.11
542	Jeff D. Robinson	.25	.11
543	Mo Vaughn	4.00	1.80

#	Player	MINT	NRMT
☐ 544	Jeff Parrett	.25	.11
☐ 545	Willie Randolph	.50	.23
☐ 546	Herm Winningham	.25	.11
☐ 547	Jeff Innis	.25	.11
☐ 548	Chuck Knoblauch	1.25	.55
☐ 549	Tommy Greene UER	.25	.11
	(Born in North Carolina, not South Carolina)		
☐ 550	Jeff Hamilton	.25	.11
☐ 551	Barry Jones	.25	.11
☐ 552	Ken Dayley	.25	.11
☐ 553	Rick Dempsey	.25	.11
☐ 554	Greg Smith	.25	.11
☐ 555	Mike Devereaux	.25	.11
☐ 556	Keith Comstock	.25	.11
☐ 557	Paul Faries	.25	.11
☐ 558	Tom Glavine	1.00	.45
☐ 559	Craig Grebeck	.25	.11
☐ 560	Scott Erickson	.75	.35
☐ 561	Joel Skinner	.25	.11
☐ 562	Mike Morgan	.25	.11
☐ 563	Dave Gallagher	.25	.11
☐ 564	Todd Stottlemyre	.50	.23
☐ 565	Rich Rodriguez	.25	.11
☐ 566	Craig Wilson	.25	.11
☐ 567	Jeff Brantley	.25	.11
☐ 568	Scott Kamieniecki	.25	.11
☐ 569	Steve Decker	.25	.11
☐ 570	Juan Agosto	.25	.11
☐ 571	Tommy Gregg	.25	.11
☐ 572	Kevin Wickander	.25	.11
☐ 573	Jamie Quirk UER	.25	.11
	(Rookie card is 1976, but card back is 1990)		
☐ 574	Jerry Don Gleaton	.25	.11
☐ 575	Chris Hammond	.25	.11
☐ 576	Luis Gonzalez	1.50	.70
☐ 577	Russ Swan	.25	.11
☐ 578	Jeff Conine	1.00	.45
☐ 579	Charlie Hough	.50	.23
☐ 580	Jeff Kunkel	.25	.11
☐ 581	Darrel Akerfelds	.25	.11
☐ 582	Jeff Manto	.25	.11
☐ 583	Alejandro Pena	.25	.11
☐ 584	Mark Davidson	.25	.11
☐ 585	Bob MacDonald	.25	.11
☐ 586	Paul Assenmacher	.25	.11
☐ 587	Dan Wilson	1.00	.45
☐ 588	Tom Bolton	.25	.11
☐ 589	Brian Harper	.25	.11
☐ 590	John Habyan	.25	.11
☐ 591	John Orton	.25	.11
☐ 592	Mark Gardner	.25	.11
☐ 593	Turner Ward	.25	.11
☐ 594	Bob Patterson	.25	.11
☐ 595	Ed Nunez	.25	.11
☐ 596	Gary Scott UER	.25	.11
	(Major League Batting Record should be Minor League)		
☐ 597	Scott Bankhead	.25	.11
☐ 598	Checklist 301-400	.25	.11
☐ 599	Checklist 401-500	.25	.11
☐ 600	Checklist 501-600	.25	.11

1992 Stadium Club Dome

		MINT	NRMT
	COMP.FACT.SET (200)	40.00	18.00
	COMMON CARD (1-200)	.10	.05
	MINOR STARS	.20	.09
	UNLISTED STARS	.40	.18
	ORIGINALLY INTENDED AS A 1991 RELEASE		
☐ 1	Terry Adams	.30	.14
☐ 2	Tommy Adams	.10	.05
☐ 3	Rick Aguilera	.20	.09
☐ 4	Ron Allen	.10	.05
☐ 5	Roberto Alomar	.40	.18
☐ 6	Sandy Alomar Jr.	.20	.09
☐ 7	Greg Anthony	.10	.05
☐ 8	James Austin	.10	.05
☐ 9	Steve Avery	.10	.05
☐ 10	Harold Baines	.20	.09
☐ 11	Brian Barber	.10	.05
☐ 12	Jon Barnes	.10	.05
☐ 13	George Bell	.10	.05
☐ 14	Doug Bennett	.10	.05
☐ 15	Sean Bergman	.10	.05
☐ 16	Craig Biggio	.40	.18
☐ 17	Bill Bliss	.10	.05
☐ 18	Wade Boggs	.40	.18
☐ 19	Bobby Bonilla	.20	.09
☐ 20	Russell Brock	.10	.05
☐ 21	Tarrik Brock	.10	.05
☐ 22	Tom Browning	.10	.05
☐ 23	Brett Butler	.20	.09
☐ 24	Ivan Calderon	.10	.05
☐ 25	Joe Carter	.20	.09
☐ 26	Joe Caruso	.10	.05
☐ 27	Dan Cholowsky	.10	.05
☐ 28	Will Clark	.40	.18
☐ 29	Roger Clemens	1.00	.45
☐ 30	Shawn Curran	.10	.05
☐ 31	Chris Curtis	.10	.05
☐ 32	Chili Davis	.20	.09
☐ 33	Andre Dawson	.30	.14
☐ 34	Joe DeBerry	.10	.05
☐ 35	John Dettmer	.10	.05
☐ 36	Rob Dibble	.10	.05
☐ 37	John Donati	.10	.05
☐ 38	Dave Doornweerd	.10	.05
☐ 39	Darren Dreifort	.20	.09
☐ 40	Mike Durant	.10	.05
☐ 41	Chris Durkin	.10	.05
☐ 42	Dennis Eckersley	.20	.09
☐ 43	Brian Edmondson	.10	.05
☐ 44	Vaughn Eshelman	.10	.05
☐ 45	Shawn Estes	.50	.23
☐ 46	Jorge Fabregas	.10	.05
☐ 47	Jon Farrell	.10	.05
☐ 48	Cecil Fielder	.20	.09
☐ 49	Carlton Fisk	.40	.18
☐ 50	Tim Flannelly	.10	.05
☐ 51	Cliff Floyd	1.25	.55
☐ 52	Julio Franco	.10	.05
☐ 53	Greg Gagne	.10	.05
☐ 54	Chris Gambs	.10	.05
☐ 55	Ron Gant	.20	.09
☐ 56	Brent Gates	.10	.05
☐ 57	Dwayne Gerald	.10	.05
☐ 58	Jason Giambi	1.00	.45
☐ 59	Benji Gil	.10	.05
☐ 60	Mark Gipner	.10	.05
☐ 61	Danny Gladden	.10	.05
☐ 62	Tom Glavine	.30	.14
☐ 63	Jimmy Gonzalez	.10	.05
☐ 64	Jeff Granger	.10	.05
☐ 65	Dan Grapenthien	.10	.05
☐ 66	Dennis Gray	.10	.05
☐ 67	Shawn Green	20.00	9.00
☐ 68	Tyler Green	.10	.05
☐ 69	Todd Greene	.10	.05
☐ 70	Ken Griffey Jr.	2.00	.90
☐ 71	Kelly Gruber	.10	.05
☐ 72	Ozzie Guillen	.10	.05
☐ 73	Tony Gwynn	1.00	.45
☐ 74	Shane Halter	.10	.05
☐ 75	Jeffrey Hammonds	.40	.18
☐ 76	Larry Hanlon	.10	.05
☐ 77	Pete Harnisch	.10	.05
☐ 78	Mike Harrison	.10	.05
☐ 79	Bryan Harvey	.10	.05
☐ 80	Scott Hatteberg	.10	.05
☐ 81	Rick Helling	.40	.18
☐ 82	Dave Henderson	.10	.05
☐ 83	Rickey Henderson	.50	.23
☐ 84	Tyrone Hill	.10	.05
☐ 85	Todd Hollandsworth	.40	.18
☐ 86	Brian Holliday	.10	.05
☐ 87	Terry Horn	.10	.05
☐ 88	Jeff Hostetler	.10	.05
☐ 89	Kent Hrbek	.20	.09
☐ 90	Mark Hubbard	.10	.05
☐ 91	Charles Johnson	.75	.35
☐ 92	Howard Johnson	.10	.05
☐ 93	Todd Johnson	.10	.05
☐ 94	Bobby Jones	.40	.18
☐ 95	Dan Jones	.10	.05
☐ 96	Felix Jose	.10	.05
☐ 97	David Justice	.40	.18
☐ 98	Jimmy Key	.20	.09
☐ 99	Marc Kroon	.10	.05
☐ 100	John Kruk	.20	.09
☐ 101	Mark Langston	.10	.05
☐ 102	Barry Larkin	.30	.14
☐ 103	Mike LaValliere	.10	.05
☐ 104	Scott Leius	.10	.05
☐ 105	Mark Lemke	.10	.05
☐ 106	Donnie Leshnock	.10	.05
☐ 107	Jimmy Lewis	.10	.05
☐ 108	Shane Livesy	.10	.05
☐ 109	Ryan Long	.10	.05
☐ 110	Trevor Mallory	.10	.05
☐ 111	Dennis Martinez	.20	.09
☐ 112	Justin Mashore	.10	.05
☐ 113	Jason McDonald	.10	.05
☐ 114	Jack McDowell	.20	.09
☐ 115	Tom McKinnon	.10	.05
☐ 116	Billy McMillon	.10	.05
☐ 117	Buck McNabb	.20	.09
☐ 118	Jim Meier	.10	.05
☐ 119	Dan Melendez	.10	.05
☐ 120	Shawn Miller	.10	.05
☐ 121	Trever Miller	.10	.05
☐ 122	Paul Molitor	.40	.18
☐ 123	Vincent Moore	.10	.05
☐ 124	Mike Morgan	.10	.05
☐ 125	Jack Morris WS	.10	.05
☐ 126	Jack Morris AS	.10	.05
☐ 127	Sean Mulligan	.10	.05
☐ 128	Eddie Murray AS	.40	.18
☐ 129	Mike Neill	.10	.05
☐ 130	Phil Nevin	.40	.18
☐ 131	Mark O'Brien	.10	.05
☐ 132	Alex Ochoa	.50	.23
☐ 133	Chad Ogea	.30	.14
☐ 134	Greg Olson	.10	.05
☐ 135	Paul O'Neill	.20	.09
☐ 136	Jared Osentowski	.10	.05
☐ 137	Mike Pagliarulo	.10	.05
☐ 138	Rafael Palmeiro	.40	.18
☐ 139	Rodney Pedraza	.10	.05
☐ 140	Tony Phillips (P)	.10	.05
☐ 141	Scott Pisciotta	.10	.05
☐ 142	Christopher Pritchett	.10	.05
☐ 143	Jason Pruitt	.10	.05
☐ 144	Kirby Puckett WS UER	.60	.25
	(Championship series AB and BA is wrong)		
☐ 145	Kirby Puckett AS	.60	.25
☐ 146	Manny Ramirez	15.00	6.75
☐ 147	Eddie Ramos	.10	.05
☐ 148	Mark Ratekin	.10	.05
☐ 149	Jeff Reardon	.20	.09
☐ 150	Sean Rees	.10	.05
☐ 151	Calvin Reese	.40	.18
☐ 152	Desmond Relaford	.40	.18
☐ 153	Eric Richardson	.10	.05
☐ 154	Cal Ripken	1.50	.70
☐ 155	Chris Roberts	.10	.05
☐ 156	Mike Robertson	.10	.05
☐ 157	Steve Rodriguez	.10	.05
☐ 158	Mike Rossiter	.10	.05
☐ 159	Scott Ruffcorn	.10	.05
☐ 160	Chris Sabo	.10	.05
☐ 161	Juan Samuel	.10	.05
☐ 162	Ryne Sandberg	.50	.23
	(On 5th line, prior		

misspelled as prilor)

		MINT	NRMT
❑ 163	Scott Sanderson	.10	.05
❑ 164	Benny Santiago	.10	.05
❑ 165	Gene Schall	.10	.05
❑ 166	Chad Schoenvogel	.10	.05
❑ 167	Chris Seelbach	.10	.05
❑ 168	Aaron Sele	1.25	.55
❑ 169	Basil Shabazz	.10	.05
❑ 170	Al Shirley	.10	.05
❑ 171	Paul Shuey	.10	.05
❑ 172	Ruben Sierra	.10	.05
❑ 173	John Smiley	.10	.05
❑ 174	Lee Smith	.20	.09
❑ 175	Ozzie Smith	.50	.23
❑ 176	Tim Smith	.10	.05
❑ 177	Zane Smith	.10	.05
❑ 178	John Smoltz	.30	.14
❑ 179	Scott Stahoviak	.10	.05
❑ 180	Kennie Steenstra	.10	.05
❑ 181	Kevin Stocker	.10	.05
❑ 182	Chris Stynes	.40	.18
❑ 183	Danny Tartabull	.10	.05
❑ 184	Brien Taylor	.10	.05
❑ 185	Todd Taylor	.10	.05
❑ 186	Larry Thomas	.10	.05
❑ 187	Ozzie Timmons	.20	.09
	(See also 188)		
❑ 188	David Tuttle UER	.10	.05
	(Mistakenly numbered as 187 on card)		
❑ 189	Andy Van Slyke	.20	.09
❑ 190	Frank Viola	.10	.05
❑ 191	Michael Walkden	.10	.05
❑ 192	Jeff Ware	.10	.05
❑ 193	Allen Watson	.10	.05
❑ 194	Steve Whitaker	.10	.05
❑ 195	Jerry Willard	.10	.05
❑ 196	Craig Wilson	.10	.05
❑ 197	Chris Wimmer	.10	.05
❑ 198	Steve Wojciechowski	.10	.05
❑ 199	Joel Wolfe	.10	.05
❑ 200	Ivan Zweig	.10	.05

1992 Stadium Club

	MINT	NRMT
COMPLETE SET (900)	50.00	22.00
COMPLETE SERIES 1 (300)	18.00	8.00
COMPLETE SERIES 2 (300)	18.00	8.00
COMPLETE SERIES 3 (300)	18.00	8.00
COMMON CARD (1-900)	.10	.05
MINOR STARS	.20	.09
UNLISTED STARS	.40	.18
SUBSET CARDS HALF VALUE OF BASE CARDS		

❑ 1	Cal Ripken UER	1.50	.70
	(Misspelled Ripkin on card back)		
❑ 2	Eric Yelding	.10	.05
❑ 3	Geno Petralli	.10	.05
❑ 4	Wally Backman	.10	.05
❑ 5	Milt Cuyler	.10	.05
❑ 6	Kevin Bass	.10	.05
❑ 7	Dante Bichette	.30	.14
❑ 8	Ray Lankford	.40	.18
❑ 9	Mel Hall	.10	.05
❑ 10	Joe Carter	.20	.09

❑ 11	Juan Samuel	.10	.05
❑ 12	Jeff Montgomery	.20	.09
❑ 13	Glenn Braggs	.10	.05
❑ 14	Henry Cotto	.10	.05
❑ 15	Deion Sanders	.40	.18
❑ 16	Dick Schofield	.10	.05
❑ 17	David Cone	.20	.09
❑ 18	Chili Davis	.10	.05
❑ 19	Tom Foley	.10	.05
❑ 20	Ozzie Guillen	.10	.05
❑ 21	Luis Salazar	.10	.05
❑ 22	Terry Steinbach	.10	.05
❑ 23	Chris James	.10	.05
❑ 24	Jeff King	.10	.05
❑ 25	Carlos Quintana	.10	.05
❑ 26	Mike Maddux	.10	.05
❑ 27	Tommy Greene	.10	.05
❑ 28	Jeff Russell	.10	.05
❑ 29	Steve Finley	.20	.09
❑ 30	Mike Flanagan	.10	.05
❑ 31	Darren Lewis	.10	.05
❑ 32	Mark Lee	.10	.05
❑ 33	Willie Fraser	.10	.05
❑ 34	Bom Henneman	.10	.05
	(Born Tampa, not Tamps)		
❑ 35	Kevin Maas	.10	.05
❑ 36	Dave Hansen	.10	.05
❑ 37	Erik Hanson	.10	.05
❑ 38	Bill Doran	.10	.05
❑ 39	Mike Boddicker	.10	.05
❑ 40	Vince Coleman	.10	.05
❑ 41	Devon White	.10	.05
❑ 42	Mark Gardner	.10	.05
❑ 43	Scott Lewis	.10	.05
❑ 44	Juan Berenguer	.10	.05
❑ 45	Carney Lansford	.20	.09
❑ 46	Curt Wilkerson	.10	.05
❑ 47	Shane Mack	.10	.05
❑ 48	Bip Roberts	.10	.05
❑ 49	Greg A. Harris	.10	.05
❑ 50	Ryne Sandberg	.50	.23
❑ 51	Mark Whiten	.10	.05
❑ 52	Jack McDowell	.10	.05
❑ 53	Jimmy Jones	.10	.05
❑ 54	Steve Lake	.10	.05
❑ 55	Bud Black	.10	.05
❑ 56	Dave Valle	.10	.05
❑ 57	Kevin Reimer	.10	.05
❑ 58	Rich Gedman UER	.10	.05
	(Wrong BARS chart used)		
❑ 59	Travis Fryman	.20	.09
❑ 60	Steve Avery	.10	.05
❑ 61	Francisco de la Rosa	.10	.05
❑ 62	Scott Hemond	.10	.05
❑ 63	Hal Morris	.10	.05
❑ 64	Hensley Meulens	.10	.05
❑ 65	Frank Castillo	.10	.05
❑ 66	Gene Larkin	.10	.05
❑ 67	Jose DeLeon	.10	.05
❑ 68	Al Osuna	.10	.05
❑ 69	Dave Cochrane	.10	.05
❑ 70	Robin Ventura	.20	.09
❑ 71	John Cerutti	.10	.05
❑ 72	Kevin Gross	.10	.05
❑ 73	Ivan Calderon	.10	.05
❑ 74	Mike Macfarlane	.10	.05
❑ 75	Stan Belinda	.10	.05
❑ 76	Shawn Hillegas	.10	.05
❑ 77	Pat Borders	.10	.05
❑ 78	Jim Vatcher	.10	.05
❑ 79	Bobby Rose	.10	.05
❑ 80	Roger Clemens	1.00	.45
❑ 81	Craig Worthington	.10	.05
❑ 82	Jeff Treadway	.10	.05
❑ 83	Jamie Quirk	.10	.05
❑ 84	Randy Bush	.10	.05
❑ 85	Anthony Young	.10	.05
❑ 86	Trevor Wilson	.10	.05
❑ 87	Jaime Navarro	.10	.05
❑ 88	Les Lancaster	.10	.05
❑ 89	Pat Kelly	.10	.05
❑ 90	John Davis	.10	.05
❑ 91	Larry Andersen	.10	.05
❑ 92	Rob Deer	.10	.05
❑ 93	Mike Sharperson	.10	.05
❑ 94	Lance Parrish	.10	.05
❑ 95	Cecil Espy	.10	.05

❑ 96	Tim Spehr	.10	.05
❑ 97	Dave Stieb	.10	.05
❑ 98	Terry Mulholland	.10	.05
❑ 99	Dennis Boyd	.10	.05
❑ 100	Barry Larkin	.30	.14
❑ 101	Ryan Bowen	.10	.05
❑ 102	Felix Fermin	.10	.05
❑ 103	Luis Alicea	.10	.05
❑ 104	Tim Hulett	.10	.05
❑ 105	Rafael Belliard	.10	.05
❑ 106	Mike Gallego	.10	.05
❑ 107	Dave Righetti	.10	.05
❑ 108	Jeff Schaefer	.10	.05
❑ 109	Ricky Bones	.10	.05
❑ 110	Scott Erickson	.20	.09
❑ 111	Matt Nokes	.10	.05
❑ 112	Bob Scanlan	.10	.05
❑ 113	Tom Candiotti	.10	.05
❑ 114	Sean Berry	.10	.05
❑ 115	Kevin Morton	.10	.05
❑ 116	Scott Fletcher	.10	.05
❑ 117	B.J. Surhoff	.20	.09
❑ 118	Dave Magadan UER	.10	.05
❑ 119	Bill Gullickson	.10	.05
❑ 120	Marquis Grissom	.20	.09
❑ 121	Lenny Harris	.10	.05
❑ 122	Wally Joyner	.20	.09
❑ 123	Kevin Brown	.30	.14
❑ 124	Braulio Castillo	.10	.05
❑ 125	Eric King	.10	.05
❑ 126	Mark Portugal	.10	.05
❑ 127	Calvin Jones	.10	.05
❑ 128	Mike Heath	.10	.05
❑ 129	Todd Van Poppel	.10	.05
❑ 130	Benny Santiago	.10	.05
❑ 131	Gary Thurman	.10	.05
❑ 132	Joe Girardi	.20	.09
❑ 133	Dave Eiland	.10	.05
❑ 134	Orlando Merced	.10	.05
❑ 135	Joe Orsulak	.10	.05
❑ 136	John Burkett	.10	.05
❑ 137	Ken Dayley	.10	.05
❑ 138	Ken Hill	.10	.05
❑ 139	Walt Terrell	.10	.05
❑ 140	Mike Scioscia	.10	.05
❑ 141	Junior Felix	.10	.05
❑ 142	Ken Caminiti	.30	.14
❑ 143	Carlos Baerga	.10	.05
❑ 144	Tony Fossas	.10	.05
❑ 145	Craig Grebeck	.10	.05
❑ 146	Scott Bradley	.10	.05
❑ 147	Kent Mercker	.10	.05
❑ 148	Derrick May	.10	.05
❑ 149	Jerald Clark	.10	.05
❑ 150	George Brett	.75	.35
❑ 151	Luis Quinones	.10	.05
❑ 152	Mike Pagliarulo	.10	.05
❑ 153	Jose Guzman	.10	.05
❑ 154	Charlie O'Brien	.10	.05
❑ 155	Darren Holmes	.10	.05
❑ 156	Joe Boever	.10	.05
❑ 157	Rich Monteleone	.10	.05
❑ 158	Reggie Harris	.10	.05
❑ 159	Roberto Alomar	.40	.18
❑ 160	Robby Thompson	.10	.05
❑ 161	Chris Hoiles	.10	.05
❑ 162	Tom Pagnozzi	.10	.05
❑ 163	Omar Vizquel	.20	.09
❑ 164	John Candelaria	.10	.05
❑ 165	Terry Shumpert	.10	.05
❑ 166	Andy Mota	.10	.05
❑ 167	Scott Bailes	.10	.05
❑ 168	Jeff Blauser	.10	.05
❑ 169	Steve Olin	.10	.05
❑ 170	Doug Drabek	.10	.05
❑ 171	Dave Bergman	.10	.05
❑ 172	Eddie Whitson	.10	.05
❑ 173	Gilberto Reyes	.10	.05
❑ 174	Mark Grace	.30	.14
❑ 175	Paul O'Neill	.20	.09
❑ 176	Greg Cadaret	.10	.05
❑ 177	Mark Williamson	.10	.05
❑ 178	Casey Candaele	.10	.05
❑ 179	Candy Maldonado	.10	.05
❑ 180	Lee Smith	.20	.09

181	Harold Reynolds	.10	.05
182	David Justice	.40	.18
183	Lenny Webster	.10	.05
184	Donn Pall	.10	.05
185	Gerald Alexander	.10	.05
186	Jack Clark	.20	.09
187	Stan Javier	.10	.05
188	Ricky Jordan	.10	.05
189	Franklin Stubbs	.10	.05
190	Dennis Eckersley	.20	.09
191	Danny Tartabull	.10	.05
192	Pete O'Brien	.10	.05
193	Mark Lewis	.10	.05
194	Mike Felder	.10	.05
195	Mickey Tettleton	.10	.05
196	Dwight Smith	.10	.05
197	Shawn Abner	.10	.05
198	Jim Leyritz UER (Career totals less than 1991 totals)	.10	.05
199	Mike Devereaux	.10	.05
200	Craig Biggio	.40	.18
201	Kevin Elster	.10	.05
202	Rance Mulliniks	.10	.05
203	Tony Fernandez	.10	.05
204	Allan Anderson	.10	.05
205	Herm Winningham	.10	.05
206	Tim Jones	.10	.05
207	Ramon Martinez	.20	.09
208	Teddy Higuera	.10	.05
209	John Kruk	.20	.09
210	Jim Abbott	.20	.09
211	Dean Palmer	.20	.09
212	Mark Davis	.10	.05
213	Jay Buhner	.30	.14
214	Jesse Barfield	.10	.05
215	Kevin Mitchell	.20	.09
216	Mike LaValliere	.10	.05
217	Mark Wohlers	.10	.05
218	Dave Henderson	.10	.05
219	Dave Smith	.10	.05
220	Albert Belle	.40	.18
221	Spike Owen	.10	.05
222	Jeff Gray	.10	.05
223	Paul Gibson	.10	.05
224	Bobby Thigpen	.10	.05
225	Mike Mussina	.60	.25
226	Darrin Jackson	.10	.05
227	Luis Gonzalez	.30	.14
228	Greg Briley	.10	.05
229	Brent Mayne	.10	.05
230	Paul Molitor	.40	.18
231	Al Leiter	.20	.09
232	Andy Van Slyke	.20	.09
233	Ron Tingley	.10	.05
234	Bernard Gilkey	.20	.09
235	Kent Hrbek	.20	.09
236	Eric Karros	.40	.18
237	Randy Velarde	.10	.05
238	Andy Allanson	.10	.05
239	Willie McGee	.20	.09
240	Juan Gonzalez	1.00	.45
241	Karl Rhodes	.10	.05
242	Luis Mercedes	.10	.05
243	Bill Swift	.10	.05
244	Tommy Gregg	.10	.05
245	David Howard	.10	.05
246	Dave Hollins	.10	.05
247	Kip Gross	.10	.05
248	Walt Weiss	.10	.05
249	Mackey Sasser	.10	.05
250	Cecil Fielder	.20	.09
251	Jerry Browne	.10	.05
252	Doug Dascenzo	.10	.05
253	Darryl Hamilton	.10	.05
254	Dann Bilardello	.10	.05
255	Luis Rivera	.10	.05
256	Larry Walker	.40	.18
257	Ron Karkovice	.10	.05
258	Bob Tewksbury	.10	.05
259	Jimmy Key	.10	.05
260	Bernie Williams	.40	.18
261	Gary Wayne	.10	.05
262	Mike Simms UER (Reversed negative)	.10	.05
263	John Orton	.10	.05
264	Marvin Freeman	.10	.05
265	Mike Jeffcoat	.10	.05
266	Roger Mason	.10	.05
267	Edgar Martinez	.30	.14
268	Henry Rodriguez	.40	.18
269	Sam Horn	.10	.05
270	Brian McRae	.10	.05
271	Kirt Manwaring	.10	.05
272	Mike Bordick	.10	.05
273	Chris Sabo	.10	.05
274	Jim Olander	.10	.05
275	Greg W. Harris	.10	.05
276	Dan Gakeler	.10	.05
277	Bill Sampen	.10	.05
278	Joel Skinner	.10	.05
279	Curt Schilling	.30	.14
280	Dale Murphy	.40	.18
281	Lee Stevens	.20	.09
282	Lonnie Smith	.10	.05
283	Manuel Lee	.10	.05
284	Shawn Boskie	.10	.05
285	Kevin Seitzer	.10	.05
286	Stan Royer	.10	.05
287	John Dopson	.10	.05
288	Scott Bullett	.10	.05
289	Ken Patterson	.10	.05
290	Todd Hundley	.20	.09
291	Tim Leary	.10	.05
292	Brett Butler	.20	.09
293	Gregg Olson	.10	.05
294	Jeff Brantley	.10	.05
295	Brian Holman	.10	.05
296	Brian Harper	.10	.05
297	Brian Bohanon	.10	.05
298	Checklist 1-100	.10	.05
299	Checklist 101-200	.10	.05
300	Checklist 201-300	.10	.05
301	Frank Thomas	1.00	.45
302	Lloyd McClendon	.10	.05
303	Brady Anderson	.30	.14
304	Julio Valera	.10	.05
305	Mike Aldrete	.10	.05
306	Joe Oliver	.10	.05
307	Todd Stottlemyre	.20	.09
308	Rey Sanchez	.10	.05
309	Gary Sheffield UER (Listed as 5'1", should be 5'11")	.40	.18
310	Andujar Cedeno	.10	.05
311	Kenny Rogers	.10	.05
312	Bruce Hurst	.10	.05
313	Mike Schooler	.10	.05
314	Mike Benjamin	.10	.05
315	Chuck Finley	.20	.09
316	Mark Lemke	.10	.05
317	Scott Livingstone	.10	.05
318	Chris Nabholz	.10	.05
319	Mike Humphreys	.10	.05
320	Pedro Guerrero	.10	.05
321	Willie Banks	.10	.05
322	Tom Goodwin	.20	.09
323	Hector Wagner	.10	.05
324	Wally Ritchie	.10	.05
325	Mo Vaughn	.50	.23
326	Joe Klink	.10	.05
327	Cal Eldred	.10	.05
328	Daryl Boston	.10	.05
329	Mike Huff	.10	.05
330	Jeff Bagwell	.75	.35
331	Bob Milacki	.10	.05
332	Tom Prince	.10	.05
333	Pat Tabler	.10	.05
334	Ced Landrum	.10	.05
335	Reggie Jefferson	.20	.09
336	Mo Sanford	.10	.05
337	Kevin Ritz	.10	.05
338	Gerald Perry	.10	.05
339	Jeff Hamilton	.10	.05
340	Tim Wallach	.10	.05
341	Jeff Huson	.10	.05
342	Jose Melendez	.10	.05
343	Willie Wilson	.10	.05
344	Mike Stanton	.10	.05
345	Joel Johnston	.10	.05
346	Lee Guetterman	.10	.05
347	Francisco Oliveras	.10	.05
348	Dave Burba	.10	.05
349	Tim Crews	.10	.05
350	Scott Leius	.10	.05
351	Danny Cox	.10	.05
352	Wayne Housie	.10	.05
353	Chris Donnels	.10	.05
354	Chris George	.10	.05
355	Gerald Young	.10	.05
356	Roberto Hernandez	.30	.14
357	Neal Heaton	.10	.05
358	Todd Frohwirth	.10	.05
359	Jose Vizcaino	.10	.05
360	Jim Thome	1.00	.45
361	Craig Wilson	.10	.05
362	Dave Haas	.10	.05
363	Billy Hatcher	.10	.05
364	John Barfield	.10	.05
365	Luis Aquino	.10	.05
366	Charlie Leibrandt	.10	.05
367	Howard Farmer	.10	.05
368	Bryn Smith	.10	.05
369	Mickey Morandini	.10	.05
370	Jose Canseco (See also 597)	.50	.23
371	Jose Uribe	.10	.05
372	Bob MacDonald	.10	.05
373	Luis Sojo	.10	.05
374	Craig Shipley	.10	.05
375	Scott Bankhead	.10	.05
376	Greg Gagne	.10	.05
377	Scott Cooper	.10	.05
378	Jose Offerman	.20	.09
379	Bill Spiers	.10	.05
380	John Smiley	.10	.05
381	Jeff Carter	.10	.05
382	Heathcliff Slocumb	.10	.05
383	Jeff Tackett	.10	.05
384	John Kiely	.10	.05
385	John Vander Wal	.10	.05
386	Omar Olivares	.10	.05
387	Ruben Sierra	.10	.05
388	Tom Gordon	.10	.05
389	Charles Nagy	.20	.09
390	Dave Stewart	.20	.09
391	Pete Harnisch	.10	.05
392	Tim Burke	.10	.05
393	Roberto Kelly	.10	.05
394	Freddie Benavides	.10	.05
395	Tom Glavine	.30	.14
396	Wes Chamberlain	.10	.05
397	Eric Gunderson	.10	.05
398	Dave West	.10	.05
399	Ellis Burks	.20	.09
400	Ken Griffey Jr.	2.50	1.10
401	Thomas Howard	.10	.05
402	Juan Guzman	.10	.05
403	Mitch Webster	.10	.05
404	Matt Merullo	.10	.05
405	Steve Buechele	.10	.05
406	Danny Jackson	.10	.05
407	Felix Jose	.10	.05
408	Doug Piatt	.10	.05
409	Jim Eisenreich	.10	.05
410	Bryan Harvey	.10	.05
411	Jim Austin	.10	.05
412	Jim Poole	.10	.05
413	Glenallen Hill	.10	.05
414	Gene Nelson	.10	.05
415	Ivan Rodriguez	.75	.35
416	Frank Tanana	.10	.05
417	Steve Decker	.10	.05
418	Jason Grimsley	.10	.05
419	Tim Layana	.10	.05
420	Don Mattingly	.75	.35
421	Jerome Walton	.10	.05
422	Rob Ducey	.10	.05
423	Andy Benes	.20	.09
424	John Marzano	.10	.05
425	Gene Harris	.10	.05
426	Tim Raines	.20	.09
427	Bret Barberie	.10	.05
428	Harvey Pulliam	.10	.05
429	Cris Carpenter	.10	.05
430	Howard Johnson	.10	.05
431	Orel Hershiser	.20	.09
432	Brian Hunter	.10	.05

433	Kevin Tapani	.10	.05
434	Rick Reed	.10	.05
435	Ron Witmeyer	.10	.05
436	Gary Gaetti	.20	.09
437	Alex Cole	.10	.05
438	Chito Martinez	.10	.05
439	Greg Litton	.10	.05
440	Julio Franco	.10	.05
441	Mike Munoz	.10	.05
442	Erik Pappas	.10	.05
443	Pat Combs	.10	.05
444	Lance Johnson	.10	.05
445	Ed Sprague	.10	.05
446	Mike Greenwell	.10	.05
447	Milt Thompson	.10	.05
448	Mike Magnante	.10	.05
449	Chris Haney	.10	.05
450	Robin Yount	.40	.18
451	Rafael Ramirez	.10	.05
452	Gino Minutelli	.10	.05
453	Tom Lampkin	.10	.05
454	Tony Perezchica	.10	.05
455	Dwight Gooden	.20	.09
456	Mark Guthrie	.10	.05
457	Jay Howell	.10	.05
458	Gary DiSarcina	.10	.05
459	John Smoltz	.30	.14
460	Will Clark	.40	.18
461	Dave Otto	.10	.05
462	Rob Maurer	.10	.05
463	Dwight Evans	.20	.09
464	Tom Brunansky	.10	.05
465	Shawn Hare	.10	.05
466	Geronimo Pena	.10	.05
467	Alex Fernandez	.20	.09
468	Greg Myers	.10	.05
469	Jeff Fassero	.10	.05
470	Len Dykstra	.20	.09
471	Jeff Johnson	.10	.05
472	Russ Swan	.10	.05
473	Archie Corbin	.10	.05
474	Chuck McElroy	.10	.05
475	Mark McGwire	2.00	.90
476	Wally Whitehurst	.10	.05
477	Tim McIntosh	.10	.05
478	Sid Bream	.10	.05
479	Jeff Juden	.10	.05
480	Carlton Fisk	.40	.18
481	Jeff Plympton	.10	.05
482	Carlos Martinez	.10	.05
483	Jim Gott	.10	.05
484	Bob McClure	.10	.05
485	Tim Teufel	.10	.05
486	Vicente Palacios	.10	.05
487	Jeff Reed	.10	.05
488	Tony Phillips	.10	.05
489	Mel Rojas	.10	.05
490	Ben McDonald	.10	.05
491	Andres Santana	.10	.05
492	Chris Beasley	.10	.05
493	Mike Timlin	.10	.05
494	Brian Downing	.10	.05
495	Kirk Gibson	.20	.09
496	Scott Sanderson	.10	.05
497	Nick Esasky	.10	.05
498	Johnny Guzman	.10	.05
499	Mitch Williams	.10	.05
500	Kirby Puckett	.60	.25
501	Mike Harkey	.10	.05
502	Jim Gantner	.10	.05
503	Bruce Egloff	.10	.05
504	Josias Manzanillo	.10	.05
505	Delino DeShields	.20	.09
506	Rheal Cormier	.10	.05
507	Jay Bell	.20	.09
508	Rich Rowland	.10	.05
509	Scott Servais	.10	.05
510	Terry Pendleton	.10	.05
511	Rich DeLucia	.10	.05
512	Warren Newson	.10	.05
513	Paul Faries	.10	.05
514	Kal Daniels	.10	.05
515	Jarvis Brown	.10	.05
516	Rafael Palmeiro	.40	.18
517	Kelly Downs	.10	.05
518	Steve Chitren	.10	.05
519	Moises Alou	.40	.18
520	Wade Boggs	.40	.18
521	Pete Schourek	.10	.05
522	Scott Terry	.10	.05
523	Kevin Appier	.20	.09
524	Gary Redus	.10	.05
525	George Bell	.10	.05
526	Jeff Kaiser	.10	.05
527	Alvaro Espinoza	.10	.05
528	Luis Polonia	.10	.05
529	Darren Daulton	.20	.09
530	Norm Charlton	.10	.05
531	John Olerud	.20	.09
532	Dan Plesac	.10	.05
533	Billy Ripken	.10	.05
534	Rod Nichols	.10	.05
535	Joey Cora	.10	.05
536	Harold Baines	.20	.09
537	Bob Ojeda	.10	.05
538	Mark Leonard	.10	.05
539	Danny Darwin	.10	.05
540	Shawon Dunston	.10	.05
541	Pedro Munoz	.10	.05
542	Mark Gubicza	.10	.05
543	Kevin Baez	.10	.05
544	Todd Zeile	.10	.05
545	Don Slaught	.10	.05
546	Tony Eusebio	.40	.18
547	Alonzo Powell	.10	.05
548	Gary Pettis	.10	.05
549	Brian Barnes	.10	.05
550	Lou Whitaker	.20	.09
551	Keith Mitchell	.10	.05
552	Oscar Azocar	.10	.05
553	Stu Cole	.10	.05
554	Steve Wapnick	.10	.05
555	Derek Bell	.20	.09
556	Luis Lopez	.10	.05
557	Anthony Telford	.10	.05
558	Tim Mauser	.10	.05
559	Glen Sutko	.10	.05
560	Darryl Strawberry	.20	.09
561	Tom Bolton	.10	.05
562	Cliff Young	.10	.05
563	Bruce Walton	.10	.05
564	Chico Walker	.10	.05
565	John Franco	.20	.09
566	Paul McClellan	.10	.05
567	Paul Abbott	.10	.05
568	Gary Varsho	.10	.05
569	Carlos Maldonado	.10	.05
570	Kelly Gruber	.10	.05
571	Jose Oquendo	.10	.05
572	Steve Frey	.10	.05
573	Tino Martinez	.40	.18
574	Bill Haselman	.10	.05
575	Eric Anthony	.10	.05
576	John Habyan	.10	.05
577	Jeff McNeely	.10	.05
578	Chris Nabholz	.10	.05
579	Joe Grahe	.10	.05
580	Fred McGriff	.30	.14
581	Rick Honeycutt	.10	.05
582	Matt Williams	.30	.14
583	Cliff Brantley	.10	.05
584	Rob Dibble	.10	.05
585	Skeeter Barnes	.10	.05
586	Greg Hibbard	.10	.05
587	Randy Milligan	.10	.05
588	Checklist 301-400	.10	.05
589	Checklist 401-500	.10	.05
590	Checklist 501-600	.10	.05
591	Frank Thomas MC	.50	.23
592	David Justice MC	.20	.09
593	Roger Clemens MC	.40	.18
594	Steve Avery MC	.10	.05
595	Cal Ripken MC	1.25	.55
596	Barry Larkin MC UER (Ranked in AL, should be NL)	.20	.09
597	Jose Canseco MC UER (Mistakenly numbered 370 on card back)	.20	.09
598	Will Clark MC	.20	.09
599	Cecil Fielder MC	.10	.05
600	Ryne Sandberg MC	.40	.18
601	Chuck Knoblauch MC	.20	.09
602	Dwight Gooden MC	.10	.05
603	Ken Griffey Jr. MC	1.25	.55
604	Barry Bonds MC	.40	.18
605	Nolan Ryan MC	.75	.35
606	Jeff Bagwell MC	.30	.14
607	Robin Yount MC	.20	.09
608	Bobby Bonilla MC	.10	.05
609	George Brett MC	.40	.18
610	Howard Johnson MC	.10	.05
611	Esteban Beltre	.10	.05
612	Mike Christopher	.10	.05
613	Troy Afenir	.10	.05
614	Mariano Duncan	.10	.05
615	Doug Henry	.10	.05
616	Doug Jones	.10	.05
617	Alvin Davis	.10	.05
618	Craig Lefferts	.10	.05
619	Kevin McReynolds	.10	.05
620	Barry Bonds	.50	.23
621	Turner Ward	.10	.05
622	Joe Magrane	.10	.05
623	Mark Parent	.10	.05
624	Tom Browning	.10	.05
625	John Smiley	.10	.05
626	Steve Wilson	.10	.05
627	Mike Gallego	.10	.05
628	Sammy Sosa	1.25	.55
629	Rico Rossy	.10	.05
630	Royce Clayton	.10	.05
631	Clay Parker	.10	.05
632	Pete Smith	.10	.05
633	Jeff McKnight	.10	.05
634	Jack Daugherty	.10	.05
635	Steve Sax	.10	.05
636	Joe Hesketh	.10	.05
637	Vince Horsman	.10	.05
638	Eric King	.10	.05
639	Joe Boever	.10	.05
640	Jack Morris	.20	.09
641	Arthur Rhodes	.10	.05
642	Bob Melvin	.10	.05
643	Rick Wilkins	.10	.05
644	Scott Scudder	.10	.05
645	Bip Roberts	.10	.05
646	Julio Valera	.10	.05
647	Kevin Campbell	.10	.05
648	Steve Searcy	.10	.05
649	Scott Kamieniecki	.10	.05
650	Kurt Stillwell	.10	.05
651	Bob Welch	.10	.05
652	Andres Galarraga	.40	.18
653	Mike Jackson	.20	.09
654	Bo Jackson	.20	.09
655	Sid Fernandez	.10	.05
656	Mike Bielecki	.10	.05
657	Jeff Reardon	.20	.09
658	Wayne Rosenthal	.10	.05
659	Eric Bullock	.10	.05
660	Eric Davis	.20	.09
661	Randy Tomlin	.10	.05
662	Tom Edens	.10	.05
663	Rob Murphy	.10	.05
664	Leo Gomez	.10	.05
665	Greg Maddux	1.00	.45
666	Greg Vaughn	.30	.14
667	Wade Taylor	.10	.05
668	Brad Arnsberg	.10	.05
669	Mike Moore	.10	.05
670	Mark Langston	.10	.05
671	Barry Jones	.10	.05
672	Bill Landrum	.10	.05
673	Greg Swindell	.10	.05
674	Wayne Edwards	.10	.05
675	Greg Olson	.10	.05
676	Bill Pulsipher	.10	.05
677	Bobby Witt	.10	.05
678	Mark Carreon	.10	.05
679	Patrick Lennon	.10	.05
680	Ozzie Smith	.50	.23
681	John Briscoe	.10	.05
682	Matt Young	.10	.05
683	Jeff Conine	.10	.05
684	Phil Stephenson	.10	.05
685	Ron Darling	.10	.05
686	Bryan Hickerson	.10	.05

687	Dale Sveum	.10	.05	773	Denis Boucher	.10	.05	858	Hector Villanueva	.10	.05

☐	#	Player	MINT	NRMT
☐	687	Dale Sveum	.10	.05
☐	688	Kirk McCaskill	.10	.05
☐	689	Rich Amaral	.10	.05
☐	690	Danny Tartabull	.10	.05
☐	691	Donald Harris	.10	.05
☐	692	Doug Davis	.10	.05
☐	693	John Farrell	.10	.05
☐	694	Paul Gibson	.10	.05
☐	695	Kenny Lofton	.50	.23
☐	696	Mike Fetters	.10	.05
☐	697	Rosario Rodriguez	.10	.05
☐	698	Chris Jones	.10	.05
☐	699	Jeff Manto	.10	.05
☐	700	Rick Sutcliffe	.10	.05
☐	701	Scott Bankhead	.10	.05
☐	702	Donnie Hill	.10	.05
☐	703	Todd Worrell	.10	.05
☐	704	Rene Gonzales	.10	.05
☐	705	Rick Cerone	.10	.05
☐	706	Tony Pena	.10	.05
☐	707	Paul Sorrento	.10	.05
☐	708	Gary Scott	.10	.05
☐	709	Junior Noboa	.10	.05
☐	710	Wally Joyner	.20	.09
☐	711	Charlie Hayes	.10	.05
☐	712	Rich Rodriguez	.10	.05
☐	713	Rudy Seanez	.10	.05
☐	714	Jim Bullinger	.10	.05
☐	715	Jeff M. Robinson	.10	.05
☐	716	Jeff Branson	.10	.05
☐	717	Andy Ashby	.20	.09
☐	718	Dave Burba	.10	.05
☐	719	Rich Gossage	.20	.09
☐	720	Randy Johnson	.40	.18
☐	721	David Wells	.20	.09
☐	722	Paul Kilgus	.10	.05
☐	723	Dave Martinez	.10	.05
☐	724	Denny Neagle	.30	.14
☐	725	Andy Stankiewicz	.10	.05
☐	726	Rick Aguilera	.20	.09
☐	727	Junior Ortiz	.10	.05
☐	728	Storm Davis	.10	.05
☐	729	Don Robinson	.10	.05
☐	730	Ron Gant	.20	.09
☐	731	Paul Assenmacher	.10	.05
☐	732	Mike Gardiner	.10	.05
☐	733	Milt Hill	.10	.05
☐	734	Jeremy Hernandez	.10	.05
☐	735	Ken Hill	.10	.05
☐	736	Xavier Hernandez	.10	.05
☐	737	Gregg Jefferies	.10	.05
☐	738	Dick Schofield	.10	.05
☐	739	Ron Robinson	.10	.05
☐	740	Sandy Alomar Jr	.20	.09
☐	741	Mike Stanley	.10	.05
☐	742	Butch Henry	.10	.05
☐	743	Floyd Bannister	.10	.05
☐	744	Brian Drahman	.10	.05
☐	745	Dave Winfield	.40	.18
☐	746	Bob Walk	.10	.05
☐	747	Chris James	.10	.05
☐	748	Don Prybylinski	.10	.05
☐	749	Dennis Rasmussen	.10	.05
☐	750	Rickey Henderson	.50	.23
☐	751	Chris Hammond	.10	.05
☐	752	Bob Kipper	.10	.05
☐	753	Dave Rohde	.10	.05
☐	754	Hubie Brooks	.10	.05
☐	755	Bret Saberhagen	.20	.09
☐	756	Jeff D. Robinson	.10	.05
☐	757	Pat Listach	.10	.05
☐	758	Bill Wegman	.10	.05
☐	759	John Wetteland	.20	.09
☐	760	Phil Plantier	.10	.05
☐	761	Wilson Alvarez	.20	.09
☐	762	Scott Aldred	.10	.05
☐	763	Armando Reynoso	.10	.05
☐	764	Todd Benzinger	.10	.05
☐	765	Kevin Mitchell	.20	.09
☐	766	Gary Sheffield	.40	.18
☐	767	Allan Anderson	.10	.05
☐	768	Rusty Meacham	.10	.05
☐	769	Rick Parker	.10	.05
☐	770	Nolan Ryan	1.50	.70
☐	771	Jeff Ballard	.10	.05
☐	772	Cory Snyder	.10	.05
☐	773	Denis Boucher	.10	.05
☐	774	Jose Gonzalez	.10	.05
☐	775	Juan Guerrero	.10	.05
☐	776	Ed Nunez	.10	.05
☐	777	Scott Ruskin	.10	.05
☐	778	Terry Leach	.10	.05
☐	779	Carl Willis	.10	.05
☐	780	Bobby Bonilla	.20	.09
☐	781	Duane Ward	.10	.05
☐	782	Joe Slusarski	.10	.05
☐	783	David Segui	.20	.09
☐	784	Kirk Gibson	.20	.09
☐	785	Frank Viola	.10	.05
☐	786	Keith Miller	.10	.05
☐	787	Mike Morgan	.10	.05
☐	788	Kim Batiste	.10	.05
☐	789	Sergio Valdez	.10	.05
☐	790	Eddie Taubensee	.20	.09
☐	791	Jack Armstrong	.10	.05
☐	792	Scott Fletcher	.10	.05
☐	793	Steve Farr	.10	.05
☐	794	Dan Pasqua	.10	.05
☐	795	Eddie Murray	.40	.18
☐	796	John Morris	.10	.05
☐	797	Francisco Cabrera	.10	.05
☐	798	Mike Perez	.10	.05
☐	799	Ted Wood	.10	.05
☐	800	Jose Rijo	.10	.05
☐	801	Danny Gladden	.10	.05
☐	802	Archi Cianfrocco	.10	.05
☐	803	Monty Fariss	.10	.05
☐	804	Roger McDowell	.10	.05
☐	805	Randy Myers	.20	.09
☐	806	Kirk Dressendorfer	.10	.05
☐	807	Zane Smith	.10	.05
☐	808	Glenn Davis	.10	.05
☐	809	Torey Lovullo	.10	.05
☐	810	Andre Dawson	.30	.14
☐	811	Bill Pecota	.10	.05
☐	812	Ted Power	.10	.05
☐	813	Willie Blair	.10	.05
☐	814	Dave Fleming	.10	.05
☐	815	Chris Gwynn	.10	.05
☐	816	Jody Reed	.10	.05
☐	817	Mark Dewey	.10	.05
☐	818	Kyle Abbott	.10	.05
☐	819	Tom Henke	.10	.05
☐	820	Kevin Seitzer	.10	.05
☐	821	Al Newman	.10	.05
☐	822	Tim Sherrill	.10	.05
☐	823	Chuck Crim	.10	.05
☐	824	Darren Reed	.10	.05
☐	825	Tony Gwynn	1.00	.45
☐	826	Steve Foster	.10	.05
☐	827	Steve Howe	.10	.05
☐	828	Brook Jacoby	.10	.05
☐	829	Rodney McCray	.10	.05
☐	830	Chuck Knoblauch	.40	.18
☐	831	John Wehner	.10	.05
☐	832	Scott Garrelts	.10	.05
☐	833	Alejandro Pena	.10	.05
☐	834	Jeff Parrett UER (Kentucky)	.10	.05
☐	835	Juan Bell	.10	.05
☐	836	Lance Dickson	.10	.05
☐	837	Darryl Kile	.20	.09
☐	838	Efrain Valdez	.10	.05
☐	839	Bob Zupcic	.10	.05
☐	840	George Bell	.10	.05
☐	841	Dave Gallagher	.10	.05
☐	842	Tim Belcher	.10	.05
☐	843	Jeff Shaw	.10	.05
☐	844	Mike Fitzgerald	.10	.05
☐	845	Gary Carter	.40	.18
☐	846	John Russell	.10	.05
☐	847	Eric Hillman	.10	.05
☐	848	Mike Witt	.10	.05
☐	849	Curt Wilkerson	.10	.05
☐	850	Alan Trammell	.30	.14
☐	851	Rex Hudler	.10	.05
☐	852	Mike Walkden	.10	.05
☐	853	Kevin Ward	.10	.05
☐	854	Tim Naehring	.10	.05
☐	855	Bill Swift	.10	.05
☐	856	Damon Berryhill	.10	.05
☐	857	Mark Eichhorn	.10	.05
☐	858	Hector Villanueva	.10	.05
☐	859	Jose Lind	.10	.05
☐	860	Dennis Martinez	.20	.09
☐	861	Bill Krueger	.10	.05
☐	862	Mike Kingery	.10	.05
☐	863	Jeff Innis	.10	.05
☐	864	Derek Lilliquist	.10	.05
☐	865	Reggie Sanders	.20	.09
☐	866	Ramon Garcia	.10	.05
☐	867	Bruce Ruffin	.10	.05
☐	868	Dickie Thon	.10	.05
☐	869	Melido Perez	.10	.05
☐	870	Ruben Amaro	.10	.05
☐	871	Alan Mills	.10	.05
☐	872	Matt Sinatro	.10	.05
☐	873	Eddie Zosky	.10	.05
☐	874	Pete Incaviglia	.10	.05
☐	875	Tom Candiotti	.10	.05
☐	876	Bob Patterson	.10	.05
☐	877	Neal Heaton	.10	.05
☐	878	Terrel Hansen	.10	.05
☐	879	Dave Eiland	.10	.05
☐	880	Von Hayes	.10	.05
☐	881	Tim Scott	.10	.05
☐	882	Otis Nixon	.20	.09
☐	883	Herm Winningham	.10	.05
☐	884	Dion James	.10	.05
☐	885	Dave Wainhouse	.10	.05
☐	886	Frank DiPino	.10	.05
☐	887	Dennis Cook	.10	.05
☐	888	Jose Mesa	.10	.05
☐	889	Mark Leiter	.10	.05
☐	890	Willie Randolph	.20	.09
☐	891	Craig Colbert	.10	.05
☐	892	Dwayne Henry	.10	.05
☐	893	Jim Lindeman	.10	.05
☐	894	Charlie Hough	.20	.09
☐	895	Gil Heredia	.10	.05
☐	896	Scott Chiamparino	.10	.05
☐	897	Lance Blankenship	.10	.05
☐	898	Checklist 601-700	.10	.05
☐	899	Checklist 701-800	.10	.05
☐	900	Checklist 801-900	.10	.05

1992 Stadium Club First Draft Picks

	MINT	NRMT
COMPLETE SET (3)	16.00	7.25
COMMON CARD (1-3)	1.00	.45
RANDOM INSERTS IN SER.3 PACKS		
ONE CARD SENT TO EACH ST.CLUB MEMBER		

☐	#	Player	MINT	NRMT
☐	1	Chipper Jones	15.00	6.75
☐	2	Brien Taylor	1.00	.45
☐	3	Phil Nevin	2.00	.90

1993 Stadium Club Murphy

	MINT	NRMT
COMP.FACT.SET (212)	120.00	55.00
COMMON CARD (1-200)	.15	.07
MINOR STARS	.30	.14
UNLISTED STARS	.60	.25

❑ 1 Dave Winfield .40	.18
❑ 2 Juan Guzman .15	.07
❑ 3 Tony Gwynn 1.50	.70
❑ 4 Chris Roberts .15	.07
❑ 5 Benny Santiago .15	.07
❑ 6 Sherard Clinkscales .15	.07
❑ 7 Jon Nunnally .30	.14
❑ 8 Chuck Knoblauch .60	.25
❑ 9 Bob Wolcott .30	.14
❑ 10 Steve Rodriguez .15	.07
❑ 11 Mark Williams .15	.07
❑ 12 Danny Clyburn .15	.07
❑ 13 Darren Dreifort .15	.07
❑ 14 Andy Van Slyke .30	.14
❑ 15 Wade Boggs .60	.25
❑ 16 Scott Patton .15	.07
❑ 17 Gary Sheffield .60	.25
❑ 18 Ron Villone .15	.07
❑ 19 Roberto Alomar .60	.25
❑ 20 Marc Valdes .15	.07
❑ 21 Daron Kirkreit .15	.07
❑ 22 Jeff Granger .15	.07
❑ 23 Levon Largusa .15	.07
❑ 24 Jimmy Key .30	.14
❑ 25 Kevin Pearson .15	.07
❑ 26 Michael Moore .15	.07
❑ 27 Preston Wilson 8.00	3.60
❑ 28 Kirby Puckett 1.00	.45
❑ 29 Tim Crabtree .15	.07
❑ 30 Bip Roberts .15	.07
❑ 31 Kelly Gruber .15	.07
❑ 32 Tony Fernandez .30	.14
❑ 33 Jason Angel .15	.07
❑ 34 Calvin Murray .15	.07
❑ 35 Chad McConnell .15	.07
❑ 36 Jason Moler .15	.07
❑ 37 Mark Lemke .15	.07
❑ 38 Tom Knauss .15	.07
❑ 39 Larry Mitchell .15	.07
❑ 40 Doug Mirabelli .15	.07
❑ 41 Everett Stull II .15	.07
❑ 42 Chris Wimmer .15	.07
❑ 43 Dan Serafini .15	.07
❑ 44 Ryne Sandberg .75	.35
❑ 45 Steve Lyons .15	.07
❑ 46 Ryan Freeburg .15	.07
❑ 47 Ruben Sierra .15	.07
❑ 48 David Mysel .15	.07
❑ 49 Joe Hamilton .15	.07
❑ 50 Steve Rodriguez .15	.07
❑ 51 Tim Wakefield .30	.14
❑ 52 Scott Gentile .15	.07
❑ 53 Doug Jones .15	.07
❑ 54 Willie Brown .15	.07
❑ 55 Chad Mottola .15	.07
❑ 56 Ken Griffey Jr. 3.00	1.35
❑ 57 Jon Lieber .15	.07
❑ 58 Dennis Martinez .30	.14
❑ 59 Joe Petcka .15	.07
❑ 60 Benji Simonton .15	.07
❑ 61 Brett Backlund .15	.07
❑ 62 Damon Berryhill .15	.07
❑ 63 Juan Guzman .15	.07
❑ 64 Doug Hecker .15	.07
❑ 65 Jamie Arnold .15	.07
❑ 66 Bob Tewksbury .15	.07
❑ 67 Tim Leger .15	.07
❑ 68 Todd Etler .15	.07

❑ 69 Lloyd McClendon .15	.07
❑ 70 Kurt Ehmann .15	.07
❑ 71 Rick Magdaleno .15	.07
❑ 72 Tom Pagnozzi .15	.07
❑ 73 Jeffrey Hammonds .30	.14
❑ 74 Joe Carter .30	.14
❑ 75 Chris Holt .15	.07
❑ 76 Charles Johnson 1.00	.45
❑ 77 Bob Walk .15	.07
❑ 78 Fred McGriff .40	.18
❑ 79 Tom Evans 1.00	.45
❑ 80 Scott Klingenbeck .15	.07
❑ 81 Chad McConnell .15	.07
❑ 82 Chris Eddy .15	.07
❑ 83 Phil Nevin .15	.07
❑ 84 John Kruk .15	.07
❑ 85 Tony Sheffield .15	.07
❑ 86 John Smoltz .40	.18
❑ 87 Trevor Humphry .15	.07
❑ 88 Charles Nagy .30	.14
❑ 89 Sean Runyan .15	.07
❑ 90 Mike Gulan .15	.07
❑ 91 Darren Daulton .30	.14
❑ 92 Otis Nixon .15	.07
❑ 93 Nomar Garciaparra 30.00	13.50
❑ 94 Larry Walker .60	.25
❑ 95 Hut Smith .15	.07
❑ 96 Rick Helling .40	.18
❑ 97 Roger Clemens 1.50	.70
❑ 98 Ron Gant .30	.14
❑ 99 Kenny Felder .15	.07
❑ 100 Steve Murphy .15	.07
❑ 101 Mike Smith .15	.07
❑ 102 Terry Pendleton .15	.07
❑ 103 Tim Davis .15	.07
❑ 104 Jeff Patzke .30	.14
❑ 105 Craig Wilson .15	.07
❑ 106 Tom Glavine .40	.18
❑ 107 Mark Langston .15	.07
❑ 108 Mark Thompson .15	.07
❑ 109 Eric Owens 2.00	.90
❑ 110 Keith Johnson .15	.07
❑ 111 Robin Ventura .30	.14
❑ 112 Ed Sprague .15	.07
❑ 113 Jeff Schmidt .15	.07
❑ 114 Don Wengert .15	.07
❑ 115 Craig Biggio .60	.25
❑ 116 Kenny Carlyle .15	.07
❑ 117 Derek Jeter 60.00	27.00
❑ 118 Manuel Lee .15	.07
❑ 119 Jeff Haas .15	.07
❑ 120 Roger Bailey .15	.07
❑ 121 Sean Lowe .15	.07
❑ 122 Rick Aguilera .15	.07
❑ 123 Sandy Alomar Jr. .30	.14
❑ 124 Derek Wallace .15	.07
❑ 125 B.J. Wallace .15	.07
❑ 126 Greg Maddux 1.50	.70
❑ 127 Tim Moore .15	.07
❑ 128 Lee Smith .30	.14
❑ 129 Todd Steverson .15	.07
❑ 130 Chris Widger 1.00	.45
❑ 131 Paul Molitor .60	.25
❑ 132 Chris Smith .15	.07
❑ 133 Chris Gomez .30	.14
❑ 134 Jimmy Baron .15	.07
❑ 135 John Smoltz .40	.18
❑ 136 Pat Borders .15	.07
❑ 137 Donnie Leshnock .15	.07
❑ 138 Gus Gandarillos .15	.07
❑ 139 Will Clark .60	.25
❑ 140 Ryan Luzinski .15	.07
❑ 141 Cal Ripken 2.50	1.10
❑ 142 B.J. Wallace .15	.07
❑ 143 Trey Beamon .30	.14
❑ 144 Norm Charlton .15	.07
❑ 145 Mike Mussina .60	.25
❑ 146 Billy Owens .15	.07
❑ 147 Ozzie Smith .75	.35
❑ 148 Jason Kendall 12.00	5.50
❑ 149 Mike Matthews .15	.07
❑ 150 David Spykstra .15	.07
❑ 151 Benji Grigsby .15	.07
❑ 152 Sean Smith .15	.07
❑ 153 Mark McGwire 3.00	1.35
❑ 154 David Cone .40	.18

❑ 155 Shon Walker .15	.07
❑ 156 Jason Giambi .60	.25
❑ 157 Jack McDowell .15	.07
❑ 158 Paxton Briley .15	.07
❑ 159 Edgar Martinez .40	.18
❑ 160 Brian Sackinsky .15	.07
❑ 161 Barry Bonds .75	.35
❑ 162 Roberto Kelly .15	.07
❑ 163 Jeff Alkire .15	.07
❑ 164 Mike Sharperson .15	.07
❑ 165 Jarnie Taylor .15	.07
❑ 166 John Saffer .15	.07
❑ 167 Jerry Browne .15	.07
❑ 168 Travis Fryman .30	.14
❑ 169 Brady Anderson .30	.14
❑ 170 Chris Roberts .15	.07
❑ 171 Lloyd Peever .15	.07
❑ 172 Francisco Cabrera .15	.07
❑ 173 Ramiro Martinez .15	.07
❑ 174 Jeff Alkire .15	.07
❑ 175 Ivan Rodriguez .75	.35
❑ 176 Kevin Brown .40	.18
❑ 177 Chad Roper .15	.07
❑ 178 Rod Henderson .15	.07
❑ 179 Dennis Eckersley .30	.14
❑ 180 Shannon Stewart 10.00	4.50
❑ 181 DeShawn Warren .15	.07
❑ 182 Lonnie Smith .15	.07
❑ 183 Willie Adams .15	.07
❑ 184 Jeff Montgomery .30	.14
❑ 185 Damon Hollins .15	.07
❑ 186 Byron Mathews .15	.07
❑ 187 Harold Baines .30	.14
❑ 188 Rick Greene .15	.07
❑ 189 Carlos Baerga .15	.07
❑ 190 Brandon Cromer .15	.07
❑ 191 Roberto Alomar .60	.25
❑ 192 Rich Ireland .15	.07
❑ 193 Steve Montgomery .15	.07
❑ 194 Brant Brown 2.00	.90
❑ 195 Ritchie Moody .15	.07
❑ 196 Michael Tucker .60	.25
❑ 197 Jason Varitek 1.50	.70
❑ 198 David Manning .15	.07
❑ 199 Marquis Riley .15	.07
❑ 200 Jason Giambi .60	.25

1993 Stadium Club Murphy Master Photos

	MINT	NRMT
COMPLETE SET (12)	5.00	2.20
*MASTER PHOTOS: .5X TO 1X BASIC CARDS		
UNNUMBERED LARGE CARDS		
ONE MP SET PER MURPHY FACTORY SET		

❑ 1 Sandy Alomar Jr. AS .25	.11
❑ 2 Tom Glavine AS .40	.18
❑ 3 Ken Griffey Jr. AS 5.00	2.20
❑ 4 Tony Gwynn AS 2.00	.90
❑ 5 Chuck Knoblauch AS .75	.35
❑ 6 Chad Mottola '92 .10	.05
❑ 7 Kirby Puckett AS 1.50	.70
❑ 8 Chris Roberts USA .10	.05
❑ 9 Ryne Sandberg AS 1.00	.45
❑ 10 Gary Sheffield AS .75	.35
❑ 11 Larry Walker AS .75	.35
❑ 12 Preston Wilson '92 2.00	.90

1993 Stadium Club

	MINT	NRMT
COMPLETE SET (750)	60.00	27.00
COMPLETE SERIES 1 (300)	20.00	9.00
COMPLETE SERIES 2 (300)	25.00	11.00
COMPLETE SERIES 3 (150)	15.00	6.75
COMMON CARD (1-750)	.15	.07
MINOR STARS	.30	.14
UNLISTED STARS	.60	.25
SUBSET CARDS HALF VALUE OF BASE CARDS		
COMP.1ST DAY SET (750)	2000.00	900.00
COMP.1ST DAY SER.1 (300)	700.00	325.00
COMP.1ST DAY SER.2 (300)	800.00	350.00
COMP.1ST DAY SER.3 (150)	500.00	220.00
COMMON 1ST DAY (1-750)	2.00	.90

*1ST DAY STARS: 10X TO 25X HI COLUMN
1ST DAY STAT.ODDS 1:24 H/R, 1:15 JUM

❑ 1	Pat Borders	.15	.07
❑ 2	Greg Maddux	1.50	.70
❑ 3	Daryl Boston	.15	.07
❑ 4	Bob Ayrault	.15	.07
❑ 5	Tony Phillips IF	.15	.07
❑ 6	Damion Easley	.30	.14
❑ 7	Kip Gross	.15	.07
❑ 8	Jim Thome	.75	.35
❑ 9	Tim Belcher	.15	.07
❑ 10	Gary Wayne	.15	.07
❑ 11	Sam Militello	.15	.07
❑ 12	Mike Magnante	.15	.07
❑ 13	Tim Wakefield	.30	.14
❑ 14	Tim Hulett	.15	.07
❑ 15	Rheal Cormier	.15	.07
❑ 16	Juan Guerrero	.15	.07
❑ 17	Rich Gossage	.30	.14
❑ 18	Tim Laker	.15	.07
❑ 19	Darrin Jackson	.15	.07
❑ 20	Jack Clark	.15	.07
❑ 21	Roberto Hernandez	.30	.14
❑ 22	Dean Palmer	.30	.14
❑ 23	Harold Reynolds	.15	.07
❑ 24	Dan Plesac	.15	.07
❑ 25	Brent Mayne	.15	.07
❑ 26	Pat Hentgen	.40	.18
❑ 27	Luis Sojo	.15	.07
❑ 28	Ron Gant	.30	.14
❑ 29	Paul Gibson	.15	.07
❑ 30	Bip Roberts	.15	.07
❑ 31	Mickey Tettleton	.15	.07
❑ 32	Randy Velarde	.15	.07
❑ 33	Brian McRae	.15	.07
❑ 34	Wes Chamberlain	.15	.07
❑ 35	Wayne Kirby	.15	.07
❑ 36	Rey Sanchez	.15	.07
❑ 37	Jesse Orosco	.15	.07
❑ 38	Mike Stanton	.15	.07
❑ 39	Royce Clayton	.15	.07
❑ 40	Cal Ripken UER	2.50	1.10

Place Hof of birth Havre de Grave; should be Havre de Grace)

❑ 41	John Dopson	.15	.07
❑ 42	Gene Larkin	.15	.07
❑ 43	Tim Raines	.30	.14
❑ 44	Randy Myers	.15	.07
❑ 45	Clay Parker	.15	.07
❑ 46	Mike Scioscia	.15	.07
❑ 47	Pete Incaviglia	.15	.07
❑ 48	Todd Van Poppel	.15	.07
❑ 49	Ray Lankford	.40	.18
❑ 50	Eddie Murray	.60	.25
❑ 51	Barry Bonds COR	.75	.35
❑ 51A	Barry Bonds ERR	.75	.35

(Missing four stars over name to indicate NL MVP)

❑ 52	Gary Thurman	.15	.07
❑ 53	Bob Wickman	.15	.07
❑ 54	Joey Cora	.15	.07
❑ 55	Kenny Rogers	.15	.07
❑ 56	Mike Devereaux	.15	.07
❑ 57	Kevin Seitzer	.15	.07
❑ 58	Rafael Belliard	.15	.07
❑ 59	David Wells	.30	.14
❑ 60	Mark Clark	.15	.07
❑ 61	Carlos Baerga	.15	.07
❑ 62	Scott Brosius	.30	.14
❑ 63	Jeff Grotewold	.15	.07
❑ 64	Rick Wrona	.15	.07
❑ 65	Kurt Knudsen	.15	.07
❑ 66	Lloyd McClendon	.15	.07
❑ 67	Omar Vizquel	.30	.14
❑ 68	Jose Vizcaino	.15	.07
❑ 69	Rob Ducey	.15	.07
❑ 70	Casey Candaele	.15	.07
❑ 71	Ramon Martinez	.30	.14
❑ 72	Todd Hundley	.40	.18
❑ 73	John Marzano	.15	.07
❑ 74	Derek Parks	.15	.07
❑ 75	Jack McDowell	.15	.07
❑ 76	Tim Scott	.15	.07
❑ 77	Mike Mussina	.60	.25
❑ 78	Delino DeShields	.30	.14
❑ 79	Chris Bosio	.15	.07
❑ 80	Mike Bordick	.15	.07
❑ 81	Rod Beck	.30	.14
❑ 82	Ted Power	.15	.07
❑ 83	John Kruk	.30	.14
❑ 84	Steve Shifflett	.15	.07
❑ 85	Danny Tartabull	.15	.07
❑ 86	Mike Greenwell	.15	.07
❑ 87	Jose Melendez	.15	.07
❑ 88	Craig Wilson	.15	.07
❑ 89	Melvin Nieves	.15	.07
❑ 90	Ed Sprague	.15	.07
❑ 91	Willie McGee	.30	.14
❑ 92	Joe Orsulak	.15	.07
❑ 93	Jeff King	.15	.07
❑ 94	Dan Pasqua	.15	.07
❑ 95	Brian Harper	.15	.07
❑ 96	Joe Oliver	.15	.07
❑ 97	Shane Turner	.15	.07
❑ 98	Lenny Harris	.15	.07
❑ 99	Jeff Parrett	.15	.07
❑ 100	Luis Polonia	.15	.07
❑ 101	Kent Bottenfield	.15	.07
❑ 102	Albert Belle	.60	.25
❑ 103	Mike Maddux	.15	.07
❑ 104	Randy Tomlin	.15	.07
❑ 105	Andy Stankiewicz	.15	.07
❑ 106	Rico Rossy	.15	.07
❑ 107	Joe Hesketh	.15	.07
❑ 108	Dennis Powell	.15	.07
❑ 109	Derrick May	.15	.07
❑ 110	Pete Harnisch	.15	.07
❑ 111	Kent Mercker	.15	.07
❑ 112	Scott Fletcher	.15	.07
❑ 113	Rex Hudler	.15	.07
❑ 114	Chico Walker	.15	.07
❑ 115	Rafael Palmeiro	.60	.25
❑ 116	Mark Leiter	.15	.07
❑ 117	Pedro Munoz	.15	.07
❑ 118	Jim Bullinger	.15	.07
❑ 119	Ivan Calderon	.15	.07
❑ 120	Mike Timlin	.15	.07
❑ 121	Rene Gonzales	.15	.07
❑ 122	Greg Vaughn	.30	.14
❑ 123	Mike Flanagan	.15	.07
❑ 124	Mike Hartley	.15	.07
❑ 125	Jeff Montgomery	.30	.14
❑ 126	Mike Gallego	.15	.07
❑ 127	Don Slaught	.15	.07
❑ 128	Charlie O'Brien	.15	.07
❑ 129	Jose Offerman	.30	.14

(Can be found with home town missing on back)

❑ 130	Mark Wohlers	.15	.07
❑ 131	Eric Fox	.15	.07
❑ 132	Doug Strange	.15	.07
❑ 133	Jeff Frye	.15	.07
❑ 134	Wade Boggs UER	.60	.25

(Redundantly lists lefty breakdown)

❑ 135	Lou Whitaker	.30	.14
❑ 136	Craig Grebeck	.15	.07
❑ 137	Rich Rodriguez	.15	.07
❑ 138	Jay Bell	.30	.14
❑ 139	Felix Fermin	.15	.07
❑ 140	Dennis Martinez	.30	.14
❑ 141	Eric Anthony	.15	.07
❑ 142	Roberto Alomar	.60	.25
❑ 143	Darren Lewis	.15	.07
❑ 144	Mike Blowers	.15	.07
❑ 145	Scott Bankhead	.15	.07
❑ 146	Jeff Reboulet	.15	.07
❑ 147	Frank Viola	.15	.07
❑ 148	Bill Pecota	.15	.07
❑ 149	Carlos Hernandez	.15	.07
❑ 150	Bobby Witt	.15	.07
❑ 151	Sid Bream	.15	.07
❑ 152	Todd Zeile	.15	.07
❑ 153	Dennis Cook	.15	.07
❑ 154	Brian Bohanon	.15	.07
❑ 155	Pat Kelly	.15	.07
❑ 156	Milt Cuyler	.15	.07
❑ 157	Juan Bell	.15	.07
❑ 158	Randy Milligan	.15	.07
❑ 159	Mark Gardner	.15	.07
❑ 160	Pat Tabler	.15	.07
❑ 161	Jeff Reardon	.30	.14
❑ 162	Ken Patterson	.15	.07
❑ 163	Bobby Bonilla	.30	.14
❑ 164	Tony Pena	.15	.07
❑ 165	Greg Swindell	.15	.07
❑ 166	Kirk McCaskill	.15	.07
❑ 167	Doug Drabek	.15	.07
❑ 168	Franklin Stubbs	.15	.07
❑ 169	Ron Tingley	.15	.07
❑ 170	Willie Banks	.15	.07
❑ 171	Sergio Valdez	.15	.07
❑ 172	Mark Lemke	.15	.07
❑ 173	Robin Yount	.40	.18
❑ 174	Storm Davis	.15	.07
❑ 175	Dan Walters	.15	.07
❑ 176	Steve Farr	.15	.07
❑ 177	Curt Wilkerson	.15	.07
❑ 178	Luis Alicea	.15	.07
❑ 179	Russ Swan	.15	.07
❑ 180	Mitch Williams	.15	.07
❑ 181	Wilson Alvarez	.30	.14
❑ 182	Carl Willis	.15	.07
❑ 183	Craig Biggio	.60	.25
❑ 184	Sean Berry	.15	.07
❑ 185	Trevor Wilson	.15	.07
❑ 186	Jeff Tackett	.15	.07
❑ 187	Ellis Burks	.30	.14
❑ 188	Jeff Branson	.15	.07
❑ 189	Matt Nokes	.15	.07
❑ 190	John Smiley	.15	.07
❑ 191	Danny Gladden	.15	.07
❑ 192	Mike Boddicker	.15	.07
❑ 193	Roger Pavlik	.15	.07
❑ 194	Paul Sorrento	.15	.07
❑ 195	Vince Coleman	.15	.07
❑ 196	Gary DiSarcina	.15	.07
❑ 197	Rafael Bournigal	.15	.07
❑ 198	Mike Schooler	.15	.07
❑ 199	Scott Ruskin	.15	.07
❑ 200	Frank Thomas	1.25	.55
❑ 201	Kyle Abbott	.15	.07
❑ 202	Mike Perez	.15	.07
❑ 203	Andre Dawson	.40	.18
❑ 204	Bill Swift	.15	.07
❑ 205	Alejandro Pena	.15	.07
❑ 206	Dave Winfield	.40	.18
❑ 207	Andujar Cedeno	.15	.07
❑ 208	Terry Steinbach	.15	.07
❑ 209	Chris Hammond	.15	.07
❑ 210	Todd Burns	.15	.07
❑ 211	Hipolito Pichardo	.15	.07

❑ 212	John Kiely	.15	.07
❑ 213	Tim Teufel	.15	.07
❑ 214	Lee Guetterman	.15	.07
❑ 215	Geronimo Pena	.15	.07
❑ 216	Brett Butler	.30	.14
❑ 217	Bryan Hickerson	.15	.07
❑ 218	Rick Trlicek	.15	.07
❑ 219	Lee Stevens	.30	.14
❑ 220	Roger Clemens	1.50	.70
❑ 221	Carlton Fisk	.60	.25
❑ 222	Chili Davis	.30	.14
❑ 223	Walt Terrell	.15	.07
❑ 224	Jim Eisenreich	.15	.07
❑ 225	Ricky Bones	.15	.07
❑ 226	Henry Rodriguez	.30	.14
❑ 227	Ken Hill	.15	.07
❑ 228	Rick Wilkins	.15	.07
❑ 229	Ricky Jordan	.15	.07
❑ 230	Bernard Gilkey	.15	.07
❑ 231	Tim Fortugno	.15	.07
❑ 232	Geno Petralli	.15	.07
❑ 233	Jose Rijo	.15	.07
❑ 234	Jim Leyritz	.15	.07
❑ 235	Kevin Campbell	.15	.07
❑ 236	Al Osuna	.15	.07
❑ 237	Pete Smith	.15	.07
❑ 238	Pete Schourek	.15	.07
❑ 239	Moises Alou	.30	.14
❑ 240	Donn Pall	.15	.07
❑ 241	Denny Neagle	.30	.14
❑ 242	Dan Peltier	.15	.07
❑ 243	Scott Scudder	.15	.07
❑ 244	Juan Guzman	.15	.07
❑ 245	Dave Burba	.15	.07
❑ 246	Rick Sutcliffe	.15	.07
❑ 247	Tony Fossas	.15	.07
❑ 248	Mike Munoz	.15	.07
❑ 249	Tim Salmon	.60	.25
❑ 250	Rob Murphy	.15	.07
❑ 251	Roger McDowell	.15	.07
❑ 252	Lance Parrish	.15	.07
❑ 253	Cliff Brantley	.15	.07
❑ 254	Scott Leius	.15	.07
❑ 255	Carlos Martinez	.15	.07
❑ 256	Vince Horsman	.15	.07
❑ 257	Oscar Azocar	.15	.07
❑ 258	Craig Shipley	.15	.07
❑ 259	Ben McDonald	.15	.07
❑ 260	Jeff Brantley	.15	.07
❑ 261	Damon Berryhill	.15	.07
❑ 262	Joe Grahe	.15	.07
❑ 263	Dave Hansen	.15	.07
❑ 264	Rich Amaral	.15	.07
❑ 265	Tim Pugh	.15	.07
❑ 266	Dion James	.15	.07
❑ 267	Frank Tanana	.15	.07
❑ 268	Stan Belinda	.15	.07
❑ 269	Jeff Kent	.30	.14
❑ 270	Bruce Ruffin	.15	.07
❑ 271	Xavier Hernandez	.15	.07
❑ 272	Darrin Fletcher	.15	.07
❑ 273	Tino Martinez	.60	.25
❑ 274	Benny Santiago	.15	.07
❑ 275	Scott Radinsky	.15	.07
❑ 276	Mariano Duncan	.15	.07
❑ 277	Kenny Lofton	.60	.25
❑ 278	Dwight Smith	.15	.07
❑ 279	Joe Carter	.30	.14
❑ 280	Tim Jones	.15	.07
❑ 281	Jeff Huson	.15	.07
❑ 282	Phil Plantier	.15	.07
❑ 283	Kirby Puckett	1.00	.45
❑ 284	Johnny Guzman	.15	.07
❑ 285	Mike Morgan	.15	.07
❑ 286	Chris Sabo	.15	.07
❑ 287	Matt Williams	.40	.18
❑ 288	Checklist 1-100	.15	.07
❑ 289	Checklist 101-200	.15	.07
❑ 290	Checklist 201-300	.15	.07
❑ 291	Dennis Eckersley MC	.15	.07
❑ 292	Eric Karros MC	.15	.07
❑ 293	Pat Listach MC	.15	.07
❑ 294	Andy Van Slyke MC	.15	.07
❑ 295	Robin Ventura MC	.30	.14
❑ 296	Tom Glavine MC	.30	.14
❑ 297	Juan Gonzalez MC UER	.60	.25
	(Misspelled Gonzales)		
❑ 298	Travis Fryman MC	.15	.07
❑ 299	Larry Walker MC	.30	.14
❑ 300	Gary Sheffield MC	.30	.14
❑ 301	Chuck Finley	.30	.14
❑ 302	Luis Gonzalez	.30	.14
❑ 303	Darryl Hamilton	.15	.07
❑ 304	Bien Figueroa	.15	.07
❑ 305	Ron Darling	.15	.07
❑ 306	Jonathan Hurst	.15	.07
❑ 307	Mike Sharperson	.15	.07
❑ 308	Mike Christopher	.15	.07
❑ 309	Marvin Freeman	.15	.07
❑ 310	Jay Buhner	.40	.18
❑ 311	Butch Henry	.15	.07
❑ 312	Greg W. Harris	.15	.07
❑ 313	Darren Daulton	.30	.14
❑ 314	Chuck Knoblauch	.60	.25
❑ 315	Greg A. Harris	.15	.07
❑ 316	John Franco	.30	.14
❑ 317	John Wehner	.15	.07
❑ 318	Donald Harris	.15	.07
❑ 319	Benny Santiago	.15	.07
❑ 320	Larry Walker	.60	.25
❑ 321	Randy Knorr	.15	.07
❑ 322	Ramon Martinez	.30	.14
❑ 323	Mike Stanley	.15	.07
❑ 324	Bill Wegman	.15	.07
❑ 325	Tom Candiotti	.15	.07
❑ 326	Glenn Davis	.15	.07
❑ 327	Chuck Crim	.15	.07
❑ 328	Scott Livingstone	.15	.07
❑ 329	Eddie Taubensee	.15	.07
❑ 330	George Bell	.15	.07
❑ 331	Edgar Martinez	.40	.18
❑ 332	Paul Assenmacher	.15	.07
❑ 333	Steve Hosey	.15	.07
❑ 334	Mo Vaughn	.60	.25
❑ 335	Bret Saberhagen	.30	.14
❑ 336	Mike Trombley	.15	.07
❑ 337	Mark Lewis	.15	.07
❑ 338	Terry Pendleton	.15	.07
❑ 339	Dave Hollins	.15	.07
❑ 340	Jeff Conine	.15	.07
❑ 341	Bob Tewksbury	.15	.07
❑ 342	Billy Ashley	.15	.07
❑ 343	Zane Smith	.15	.07
❑ 344	John Wetteland	.30	.14
❑ 345	Chris Holles	.15	.07
❑ 346	Frank Castillo	.15	.07
❑ 347	Bruce Hurst	.15	.07
❑ 348	Kevin McReynolds	.15	.07
❑ 349	Dave Henderson	.15	.07
❑ 350	Ryan Bowen	.15	.07
❑ 351	Sid Fernandez	.15	.07
❑ 352	Mark Whiten	.15	.07
❑ 353	Nolan Ryan	2.50	1.10
❑ 354	Rick Aguilera	.15	.07
❑ 355	Mark Langston	.15	.07
❑ 356	Jack Morris	.30	.14
❑ 357	Rob Deer	.15	.07
❑ 358	Dave Fleming	.15	.07
❑ 359	Lance Johnson	.15	.07
❑ 360	Joe Millette	.15	.07
❑ 361	Wil Cordero	.15	.07
❑ 362	Chito Martinez	.15	.07
❑ 363	Scott Servais	.15	.07
❑ 364	Bernie Williams	.60	.25
❑ 365	Pedro Martinez	1.25	.55
❑ 366	Ryne Sandberg	.75	.35
❑ 367	Brad Ausmus	.15	.07
❑ 368	Scott Cooper	.15	.07
❑ 369	Rob Dibble	.15	.07
❑ 370	Walt Weiss	.15	.07
❑ 371	Mark Davis	.15	.07
❑ 372	Orlando Merced	.15	.07
❑ 373	Mike Jackson	.30	.14
❑ 374	Kevin Appier	.30	.14
❑ 375	Esteban Beltre	.15	.07
❑ 376	Joe Slusarski	.15	.07
❑ 377	William Suero	.15	.07
❑ 378	Pete O'Brien	.15	.07
❑ 379	Alan Embree	.15	.07
❑ 380	Lenny Webster	.15	.07
❑ 381	Eric Davis	.30	.14
❑ 382	Duane Ward	.15	.07
❑ 383	John Habyan	.15	.07
❑ 384	Jeff Bagwell	.75	.35
❑ 385	Ruben Amaro	.15	.07
❑ 386	Julio Valera	.15	.07
❑ 387	Robin Ventura	.30	.14
❑ 388	Archi Cianfrocco	.15	.07
❑ 389	Skeeter Barnes	.15	.07
❑ 390	Tim Costo	.15	.07
❑ 391	Luis Mercedes	.15	.07
❑ 392	Jeremy Hernandez	.15	.07
❑ 393	Shawon Dunston	.15	.07
❑ 394	Andy Van Slyke	.30	.14
❑ 395	Kevin Maas	.15	.07
❑ 396	Kevin Brown	.40	.18
❑ 397	J.T. Bruett	.15	.07
❑ 398	Darryl Strawberry	.30	.14
❑ 399	Tom Pagnozzi	.15	.07
❑ 400	Sandy Alomar Jr.	.30	.14
❑ 401	Keith Miller	.15	.07
❑ 402	Rich DeLucia	.15	.07
❑ 403	Shawn Abner	.15	.07
❑ 404	Howard Johnson	.15	.07
❑ 405	Mike Benjamin	.15	.07
❑ 406	Roberto Mejia	.15	.07
❑ 407	Mike Butcher	.15	.07
❑ 408	Deion Sanders UER	.40	.18
	(Braves on front and Yankees on back)		
❑ 409	Todd Stottlemyre	.15	.07
❑ 410	Scott Kamieniecki	.15	.07
❑ 411	Doug Jones	.15	.07
❑ 412	John Burkett	.15	.07
❑ 413	Lance Blankenship	.15	.07
❑ 414	Jeff Parrett	.15	.07
❑ 415	Barry Larkin	.60	.25
❑ 416	Alan Trammell	.40	.18
❑ 417	Mark Kiefer	.15	.07
❑ 418	Gregg Olson	.15	.07
❑ 419	Mark Grace	.40	.18
❑ 420	Shane Mack	.15	.07
❑ 421	Bob Walk	.15	.07
❑ 422	Curt Schilling	.30	.14
❑ 423	Erik Hanson	.15	.07
❑ 424	George Brett	1.25	.55
❑ 425	Reggie Jefferson	.30	.14
❑ 426	Mark Portugal	.15	.07
❑ 427	Ron Karkovice	.15	.07
❑ 428	Matt Young	.15	.07
❑ 429	Troy Neel	.15	.07
❑ 430	Hector Fajardo	.15	.07
❑ 431	Dave Righetti	.15	.07
❑ 432	Pat Listach	.15	.07
❑ 433	Jeff Innis	.15	.07
❑ 434	Bob MacDonald	.15	.07
❑ 435	Brian Jordan	.30	.14
❑ 436	Jeff Blauser	.15	.07
❑ 437	Mike Myers	.15	.07
❑ 438	Frank Seminara	.15	.07
❑ 439	Rusty Meacham	.15	.07
❑ 440	Greg Briley	.15	.07
❑ 441	Derek Lilliquist	.15	.07
❑ 442	John Vander Wal	.15	.07
❑ 443	Scott Erickson	.15	.07
❑ 444	Bob Scanlan	.15	.07
❑ 445	Todd Frohwirth	.15	.07
❑ 446	Tom Goodwin	.15	.07
❑ 447	William Pennyfeather	.15	.07
❑ 448	Travis Fryman	.30	.14
❑ 449	Mickey Morandini	.15	.07
❑ 450	Greg Olson	.15	.07
❑ 451	Trevor Hoffman	.60	.25
❑ 452	Dave Magadan	.15	.07
❑ 453	Shawn Jeter	.15	.07
❑ 454	Andres Galarraga	.60	.25
❑ 455	Ted Wood	.15	.07
❑ 456	Freddie Benavides	.15	.07
❑ 457	Junior Felix	.15	.07
❑ 458	Alex Cole	.15	.07
❑ 459	John Orton	.15	.07
❑ 460	Eddie Zosky	.15	.07
❑ 461	Dennis Eckersley	.30	.14
❑ 462	Lee Smith	.30	.14
❑ 463	John Smoltz	.40	.18
❑ 464	Ken Caminiti	.40	.18
❑ 465	Melido Perez	.15	.07
❑ 466	Tom Marsh	.15	.07

467	Jeff Nelson	.15	.07
468	Jesse Levis	.15	.07
469	Chris Nabholz	.15	.07
470	Mike Macfarlane	.30	.14
471	Reggie Sanders	.30	.14
472	Chuck McElroy	.15	.07
473	Kevin Gross	.15	.07
474	Matt Whiteside	.15	.07
475	Cal Eldred	.15	.07
476	Dave Gallagher	.15	.07
477	Len Dykstra	.30	.14
478	Mark McGwire	3.00	1.35
479	David Segui	.15	.07
480	Mike Henneman	.15	.07
481	Bret Barberie	.15	.07
482	Steve Sax	.15	.07
483	Dave Valle	.15	.07
484	Danny Darwin	.15	.07
485	Devon White	.15	.07
486	Eric Plunk	.15	.07
487	Jim Gott	.15	.07
488	Scooter Tucker	.15	.07
489	Omar Olivares	.15	.07
490	Greg Myers	.15	.07
491	Brian Hunter	.15	.07
492	Kevin Tapani	.15	.07
493	Rich Monteleone	.15	.07
494	Steve Buechele	.15	.07
495	Bo Jackson	.30	.14
496	Mike LaValliere	.15	.07
497	Mark Leonard	.15	.07
498	Daryl Boston	.15	.07
499	Jose Canseco	.75	.35
500	Brian Barnes	.15	.07
501	Randy Johnson	.60	.25
502	Tim McIntosh	.15	.07
503	Cecil Fielder	.30	.14
504	Derek Bell	.30	.14
505	Kevin Koslofski	.15	.07
506	Darren Holmes	.15	.07
507	Brady Anderson	.30	.14
508	John Valentin	.30	.14
509	Jerry Browne	.15	.07
510	Fred McGriff	.40	.18
511	Pedro Astacio	.30	.14
512	Gary Gaetti	.15	.07
513	John Burke	.15	.07
514	Dwight Gooden	.30	.14
515	Thomas Howard	.15	.07
516	Darrell Whitmore UER	.15	.07
	(11 games played in 1992; should be 121)		
517	Ozzie Guillen	.15	.07
518	Darryl Kile	.15	.07
519	Rich Rowland	.15	.07
520	Carlos Delgado	.60	.25
521	Doug Henry	.15	.07
522	Greg Colbrunn	.15	.07
523	Tom Gordon	.15	.07
524	Ivan Rodriguez	.75	.35
525	Kent Hrbek	.30	.14
526	Eric Young	.60	.25
527	Rod Brewer	.15	.07
528	Eric Karros	.40	.18
529	Marquis Grissom	.30	.14
530	Rico Brogna	.15	.07
531	Sammy Sosa	2.00	.90
532	Bret Boone	.30	.14
533	Luis Rivera	.15	.07
534	Hal Morris	.15	.07
535	Monty Fariss	.15	.07
536	Leo Gomez	.30	.14
537	Wally Joyner	.30	.14
538	Tony Gwynn	1.50	.70
539	Mike Williams	.15	.07
540	Juan Gonzalez	1.25	.55
541	Ryan Klesko	.60	.25
542	Ryan Thompson	.15	.07
543	Chad Curtis	.30	.14
544	Orel Hershiser	.30	.14
545	Carlos Garcia	.15	.07
546	Bob Welch	.15	.07
547	Vinny Castilla	.75	.35
548	Ozzie Smith	.75	.35
549	Luis Salazar	.15	.07
550	Mark Guthrie	.15	.07
551	Charles Nagy	.30	.14
552	Alex Fernandez	.30	.14
553	Mel Rojas	.15	.07
554	Orestes Destrade	.15	.07
555	Mark Gubicza	.15	.07
556	Steve Finley	.30	.14
557	Don Mattingly	1.25	.55
558	Rickey Henderson	.75	.35
559	Tommy Greene	.15	.07
560	Arthur Rhodes	.15	.07
561	Alfredo Griffin	.15	.07
562	Will Clark	.60	.25
563	Bob Zupcic	.15	.07
564	Chuck Carr	.15	.07
565	Henry Cotto	.15	.07
566	Billy Spiers	.15	.07
567	Jack Armstrong	.15	.07
568	Kurt Stillwell	.15	.07
569	David McCarty	.15	.07
570	Joe Vitiello	.15	.07
571	Gerald Williams	.15	.07
572	Dale Murphy	.40	.18
573	Scott Aldred	.15	.07
574	Bill Gullickson	.15	.07
575	Bobby Thigpen	.15	.07
576	Glenallen Hill	.15	.07
577	Dwayne Henry	.15	.07
578	Calvin Jones	.15	.07
579	Al Martin	.15	.07
580	Ruben Sierra	.15	.07
581	Andy Benes	.30	.14
582	Anthony Young	.15	.07
583	Shawn Boskie	.15	.07
584	Scott Pose	.15	.07
585	Mike Piazza	3.00	1.35
586	Donovan Osborne	.15	.07
587	James Austin	.15	.07
588	Checklist 301-400	.15	.07
589	Checklist 401-500	.15	.07
590	Checklist 501-600	.15	.07
591	Ken Griffey Jr. MC	1.50	.70
592	Ivan Rodriguez MC	.40	.18
593	Carlos Baerga MC	.15	.07
594	Fred McGriff MC	.30	.14
595	Mark McGwire MC	1.50	.70
596	Roberto Alomar MC	.30	.14
597	Kirby Puckett MC	.60	.25
598	Marquis Grissom MC	.15	.07
599	John Smoltz MC	.30	.14
600	Ryne Sandberg MC	.40	.18
601	Wade Boggs	.60	.25
602	Jeff Reardon	.30	.14
603	Billy Ripken	.15	.07
604	Bryan Harvey	.15	.07
605	Carlos Quintana	.15	.07
606	Greg Hibbard	.15	.07
607	Ellis Burks	.30	.14
608	Greg Swindell	.15	.07
609	Dave Winfield	.40	.18
610	Charlie Hough	.30	.14
611	Chili Davis	.30	.14
612	Jody Reed	.15	.07
613	Mark Williamson	.15	.07
614	Phil Plantier	.15	.07
615	Jim Abbott	.30	.14
616	Dante Bichette	.30	.14
617	Mark Eichhorn	.15	.07
618	Gary Sheffield	.60	.25
619	Richie Lewis	.15	.07
620	Joe Girardi	.30	.14
621	Jaime Navarro	.15	.07
622	Willie Wilson	.15	.07
623	Scott Fletcher	.15	.07
624	Bud Black	.15	.07
625	Tom Brunansky	.15	.07
626	Steve Avery	.30	.14
627	Paul Molitor	.60	.25
628	Gregg Jefferies	.15	.07
629	Dave Stewart	.30	.14
630	Javier Lopez	.60	.25
631	Greg Gagne	.15	.07
632	Roberto Kelly	.15	.07
633	Mike Fetters	.15	.07
634	Ozzie Canseco	.15	.07
635	Jeff Russell	.15	.07
636	Pete Incaviglia	.15	.07
637	Tom Henke	.15	.07
638	Chipper Jones	2.00	.90
639	Jimmy Key	.30	.14
640	Dave Martinez	.15	.07
641	Dave Stieb	.15	.07
642	Milt Thompson	.15	.07
643	Alan Mills	.15	.07
644	Tony Fernandez	.30	.14
645	Randy Bush	.15	.07
646	Joe Magrane	.15	.07
647	Ivan Calderon	.15	.07
648	Jose Guzman	.15	.07
649	John Olerud	.40	.18
650	Tom Glavine	.40	.18
651	Julio Franco	.15	.07
652	Armando Reynoso	.15	.07
653	Felix Jose	.15	.07
654	Ben Rivera	.15	.07
655	Andre Dawson	.40	.18
656	Mike Harkey	.15	.07
657	Kevin Seitzer	.15	.07
658	Lonnie Smith	.15	.07
659	Norm Charlton	.15	.07
660	David Justice	.60	.25
661	Fernando Valenzuela	.30	.14
662	Dan Wilson	.30	.14
663	Mark Gardner	.15	.07
664	Doug Dascenzo	.15	.07
665	Greg Maddux	1.50	.70
666	Harold Baines	.30	.14
667	Randy Myers	.30	.14
668	Harold Reynolds	.15	.07
669	Candy Maldonado	.15	.07
670	Al Leiter	.30	.14
671	Jerald Clark	.15	.07
672	Doug Drabek	.15	.07
673	Kirk Gibson	.30	.14
674	Steve Reed	.15	.07
675	Mike Felder	.15	.07
676	Ricky Gutierrez	.15	.07
677	Spike Owen	.15	.07
678	Otis Nixon	.15	.07
679	Scott Sanderson	.15	.07
680	Mark Carreon	.15	.07
681	Terry Pendleton	.40	.18
682	Kevin Stocker	.15	.07
683	Jim Converse	.15	.07
684	Barry Bonds	.75	.35
685	Greg Gohr	.15	.07
686	Tim Wallach	.15	.07
687	Matt Mieske	.15	.07
688	Robby Thompson	.15	.07
689	Brien Taylor	.15	.07
690	Kirt Manwaring	.15	.07
691	Mike Lansing	.30	.14
692	Steve Decker	.15	.07
693	Mike Moore	.15	.07
694	Kevin Mitchell	.30	.14
695	Phil Hiatt	.15	.07
696	Tony Tarasco	.15	.07
697	Benji Gil	.15	.07
698	Jeff Juden	.15	.07
699	Kevin Reimer	.15	.07
700	Andy Ashby	.30	.14
701	John Jaha	.15	.07
702	Tim Bogar	.15	.07
703	David Cone	.40	.18
704	Willie Greene	.15	.07
705	David Hulse	.15	.07
706	Cris Carpenter	.15	.07
707	Ken Griffey Jr.	3.00	1.35
708	Steve Bedrosian	.15	.07
709	Dave Nilsson	.30	.14
710	Paul Wagner	.15	.07
711	B.J. Surhoff	.30	.14
712	Rene Arocha	.15	.07
713	Manuel Lee	.15	.07
714	Brian Williams	.15	.07
715	Sherman Obando	.15	.07
716	Terry Mulholland	.15	.07
717	Paul O'Neill	.30	.14
718	David Nied	.15	.07
719	J.T. Snow	.75	.35
720	Nigel Wilson	.15	.07
721	Mike Bielecki	.15	.07
722	Kevin Young	.30	.14

		MINT	NRMT
☐ 723	Charlie Leibrandt	.15	.07
☐ 724	Frank Bolick	.15	.07
☐ 725	Jon Shave	.15	.07
☐ 726	Steve Cooke	.15	.07
☐ 727	Domingo Martinez	.15	.07
☐ 728	Todd Worrell	.15	.07
☐ 729	Jose Lind	.15	.07
☐ 730	Jim Tatum	.15	.07
☐ 731	Mike Hampton	.60	.25
☐ 732	Mike Draper	.15	.07
☐ 733	Henry Mercedes	.15	.07
☐ 734	John Johnstone	.15	.07
☐ 735	Mitch Webster	.15	.07
☐ 736	Russ Springer	.15	.07
☐ 737	Rob Natal	.15	.07
☐ 738	Steve Howe	.15	.07
☐ 739	Darrell Sherman	.15	.07
☐ 740	Pat Mahomes	.15	.07
☐ 741	Alex Arias	.15	.07
☐ 742	Damon Buford	.15	.07
☐ 743	Charlie Hayes	.15	.07
☐ 744	Guillermo Velasquez	.15	.07
☐ 745	Checklist 601-750 UER	.15	.07
	(650 Tom Glavine)		
☐ 746	Frank Thomas MC	.60	.25
☐ 747	Barry Bonds MC	.40	.18
☐ 748	Roger Clemens MC	.75	.35
☐ 749	Joe Carter MC	.15	.07
☐ 750	Greg Maddux MC	.75	.35

1993 Stadium Club Inserts

	MINT	NRMT
COMPLETE SET (10)	16.00	7.25
COMPLETE SERIES 1 (4)	5.00	2.20
COMPLETE SERIES 2 (4)	10.00	4.50
COMPLETE SERIES 3 (2)	2.00	.90
COMMON CARD (A1-C2)	.50	.23

A1-A4 SER.1 STATED ODDS 1:15
B1-B4 SER.2 STATED ODDS 1:15
C1-C2 SER.3 STATED ODDS 1:15

		MINT	NRMT
☐ A1	Robin Yount	1.00	.45
	3000 Hit Club		
☐ A2	George Brett	4.00	1.80
	3000 Hit Club		
☐ A3	David Nied	.50	.23
	First Draft Pick		
	of the Rockies		
☐ A4	Nigel Wilson	.50	.23
	1st DP Marlins		
☐ B1	Will Clark	4.00	1.80
	Mark McGwire		
	Pacific Terrific		
☐ B2	Dwight Gooden	1.25	.55
	Don Mattingly		
	Broadway Stars NY		
☐ B3	Ryne Sandberg	2.00	.90
	Frank Thomas		
	Second City Sluggers		
☐ B4	Darryl Strawberry	4.00	1.80
	Ken Griffey Jr.		
	Pacific Terrific		
☐ C1	David Nied	.50	.23
	Colorado Rockies Firsts		
	(Misspelled pitch-		
	hitter on back)		
☐ C2	Charlie Hough	.50	.23
	Florida Marlins Firsts		

1993 Stadium Club Master Photos

	MINT	NRMT
COMPLETE SET (30)	24.00	11.00
COMPLETE SERIES 1 (12)	6.00	2.70
COMPLETE SERIES 2 (12)	8.00	3.60
COMPLETE SERIES 3 (6)	10.00	4.50
COMMON CARD (1-3)	.25	.11

STATED ODDS 1:24 HOB/RET, 1:15 JUM
COMP.JUMBO SET (30) 24.00 11.00
*JUMBOS: .6X TO 1.5X BASE CARD HI
THREE JUMBOS VIA MAIL PER WINNER
CARD
ONE JUMBO PER HOBBY BOX

		MINT	NRMT
☐ 1	Carlos Baerga	.25	.11
☐ 2	Delino DeShields	.25	.11
☐ 3	Brian McRae	.25	.11
☐ 4	Sam Militello	.25	.11
☐ 5	Joe Oliver	.25	.11
☐ 6	Kirby Puckett	1.50	.70
☐ 7	Cal Ripken	4.00	1.80
☐ 8	Bip Roberts	.25	.11
☐ 9	Mike Scioscia	.25	.11
☐ 10	Rick Sutcliffe	.25	.11
☐ 11	Danny Tartabull	.25	.11
☐ 12	Tim Wakefield	.50	.23
☐ 13	George Brett	2.00	.90
☐ 14	Jose Canseco	1.25	.55
☐ 15	Will Clark	1.00	.45
☐ 16	Travis Fryman	.50	.23
☐ 17	Dwight Gooden	.50	.23
☐ 18	Mark Grace	.75	.35
☐ 19	Rickey Henderson	1.25	.55
☐ 20	Mark McGwire MC	2.00	.90
☐ 21	Nolan Ryan	4.00	1.80
☐ 22	Ruben Sierra	.25	.11
☐ 23	Darryl Strawberry	.50	.23
☐ 24	Larry Walker	1.00	.45
☐ 25	Barry Bonds	1.25	.55
☐ 26	Ken Griffey Jr.	5.00	2.20
☐ 27	Greg Maddux	2.50	1.10
☐ 28	David Nied	.25	.11
☐ 29	J.T. Snow	1.00	.45
☐ 30	Brien Taylor	.25	.11

1994 Stadium Club

		MINT	NRMT
COMPLETE SET (720)	55.00	25.00	
COMPLETE SERIES 1 (270)	20.00	9.00	
COMPLETE SERIES 2 (270)	20.00	9.00	
COMPLETE SERIES 3 (180)	15.00	6.75	
COMMON CARD (1-720)	.15	.07	
MINOR STARS	.30	.14	
UNLISTED STARS	.60	.25	

SUBSET CARDS HALF VALUE OF BASE
CARDS
COMMON 1ST DAY (1-720) .... 2.00 .90
*1ST DAY STARS: 10X TO 25X HI COLUMN
*1ST DAY YOUNG STARS: 8X TO 20X HI
*1ST DAY ROOKIES: 6X TO 15X HI
1ST DAY ODDS 1:24 H/R, 1:15 JUM
COMP.RAINBOW (720) 170.00 75.00
COMP.RAINBOW SER.1 (270) 65.00 29.00
COMP.RAINBOW SER.2 (270) 65.00 29.00
COMP.RAINBOW SER.3 (180) 40.00 18.00
COMMON RAINBOW (1-720) ... .25 .11
*RAINBOW STARS: 1.5X TO 4X HI COLUMN
*RAINBOW YOUNG STARS: 1.25X TO 3X HI
ONE RAINBOW PER PACK

		MINT	NRMT
☐ 1	Robin Yount	.60	.25
☐ 2	Rick Wilkins	.15	.07
☐ 3	Steve Scarsone	.15	.07
☐ 4	Gary Sheffield	.60	.25
☐ 5	George Brett UER	1.25	.55
	(Birthdate listed as 1963;		
	should be 1953)		
☐ 6	Al Martin	.15	.07
☐ 7	Joe Oliver	.15	.07
☐ 8	Stan Belinda	.15	.07
☐ 9	Denny Hocking	.15	.07
☐ 10	Roberto Alomar	.60	.25
☐ 11	Luis Polonia	.15	.07
☐ 12	Scott Hemond	.15	.07
☐ 13	Jody Reed	.15	.07
☐ 14	Mel Rojas	.15	.07
☐ 15	Junior Ortiz	.15	.07
☐ 16	Harold Baines	.30	.14
☐ 17	Brad Pennington	.15	.07
☐ 18	Jay Bell	.15	.14
☐ 19	Tom Henke	.15	.07
☐ 20	Jeff Branson	.15	.07
☐ 21	Roberto Mejia	.15	.07
☐ 22	Pedro Munoz	.15	.07
☐ 23	Matt Nokes	.15	.07
☐ 24	Jack McDowell	.15	.07
☐ 25	Cecil Fielder	.30	.14
☐ 26	Tony Fossas	.15	.07
☐ 27	Jim Eisenreich	.15	.07
☐ 28	Anthony Young	.15	.07
☐ 29	Chuck Carr	.15	.07
☐ 30	Jeff Treadway	.15	.07
☐ 31	Chris Nabholz	.15	.07
☐ 32	Tom Candiotti	.15	.07
☐ 33	Mike Maddux	.15	.07
☐ 34	Nolan Ryan	2.50	1.10
☐ 35	Luis Gonzalez	.30	.14
☐ 36	Tim Salmon	.60	.25
☐ 37	Mark Whiten	.15	.07
☐ 38	Roger McDowell	.15	.07
☐ 39	Royce Clayton	.15	.07
☐ 40	Troy Neel	.15	.07
☐ 41	Mike Harkey	.15	.07
☐ 42	Darrin Fletcher	.15	.07
☐ 43	Wayne Kirby	.15	.07
☐ 44	Rich Amaral	.15	.07
☐ 45	Robb Nen UER	.15	.07
	(Nenn on back)		
☐ 46	Tim Teufel	.15	.07
☐ 47	Steve Cooke	.15	.07
☐ 48	Jeff McNeely	.15	.07
☐ 49	Jeff Montgomery	.15	.07
☐ 50	Skeeter Barnes	.15	.07
☐ 51	Scott Stahoviak	.15	.07
☐ 52	Pat Kelly	.15	.07
☐ 53	Brady Anderson	.30	.14
☐ 54	Mariano Duncan	.15	.07
☐ 55	Brian Bohanon	.15	.07
☐ 56	Jerry Spradlin	.15	.07
☐ 57	Ron Karkovice	.15	.07
☐ 58	Jeff Gardner	.15	.07
☐ 59	Bobby Bonilla	.30	.14

60	Tino Martinez	.60	.25
61	Todd Benzinger	.15	.07
62	Steve Trachsel	.15	.07
63	Brian Jordan	.30	.14
64	Steve Bedrosian	.15	.07
65	Brent Gates	.15	.07
66	Shawn Green	1.00	.45
67	Sean Berry	.15	.07
68	Joe Klink	.15	.07
69	Fernando Valenzuela	.30	.14
70	Andy Tomberlin	.15	.07
71	Tony Pena	.15	.07
72	Eric Young	.15	.07
73	Chris Gomez	.15	.07
74	Paul O'Neill	.30	.14
75	Ricky Gutierrez	.15	.07
76	Brad Holman	.15	.07
77	Lance Painter	.15	.07
78	Mike Butcher	.15	.07
79	Sid Bream	.15	.07
80	Sammy Sosa	2.00	.90
81	Felix Fermin	.15	.07
82	Todd Hundley	.30	.14
83	Kevin Higgins	.15	.07
84	Todd Pratt	.15	.07
85	Ken Griffey Jr.	3.00	1.35
86	John O'Donoghue	.15	.07
87	Rick Renteria	.15	.07
88	John Burkett	.15	.07
89	Jose Vizcaino	.15	.07
90	Kevin Seitzer	.15	.07
91	Bobby Witt	.15	.07
92	Chris Turner	.15	.07
93	Omar Vizquel	.30	.14
94	David Justice	.60	.25
95	David Segui	.30	.14
96	Dave Hollins	.15	.07
97	Doug Strange	.15	.07
98	Jerald Clark	.15	.07
99	Mike Moore	.15	.07
100	Joey Cora	.15	.07
101	Scott Kamieniecki	.15	.07
102	Andy Benes	.30	.14
103	Chris Bosio	.15	.07
104	Rey Sanchez	.15	.07
105	John Jaha	.15	.07
106	Otis Nixon	.15	.07
107	Rickey Henderson	.75	.35
108	Jeff Bagwell	.75	.35
109	Gregg Jefferies	.15	.07
110	Roberto Alomar Paul Molitor John Olerud	.40	.18
111	Ron Gant David Justice Fred McGriff	.30	.14
112	Juan Gonzalez Rafael Palmeiro Dean Palmer	.40	.18
113	Greg Swindell	.15	.07
114	Bill Haselman	.15	.07
115	Phil Plantier	.15	.07
116	Ivan Rodriguez	.75	.35
117	Kevin Tapani	.15	.07
118	Mike LaValliere	.15	.07
119	Tim Costo	.15	.07
120	Mickey Morandini	.15	.07
121	Brett Butler	.30	.14
122	Tom Pagnozzi	.15	.07
123	Ron Gant	.30	.14
124	Damion Easley	.15	.07
125	Dennis Eckersley	.30	.14
126	Matt Mieske	.15	.07
127	Cliff Floyd	.30	.14
128	Julian Tavarez	.15	.07
129	Arthur Rhodes	.15	.07
130	Dave West	.15	.07
131	Tim Naehring	.15	.07
132	Freddie Benavides	.15	.07
133	Paul Assenmacher	.15	.07
134	Ben McCarty	.15	.07
135	Jose Lind	.15	.07
136	Reggie Sanders	.30	.14
137	Don Slaught	.15	.07
138	Andujar Cedeno	.15	.07
139	Rob Deer	.15	.07
140	Mike Piazza UER (listed as outfielder)	2.00	.90
141	Moises Alou	.30	.14
142	Tom Foley	.15	.07
143	Benito Santiago	.15	.07
144	Sandy Alomar Jr.	.30	.14
145	Carlos Hernandez	.15	.07
146	Luis Alicea	.15	.07
147	Tom Lampkin	.15	.07
148	Ryan Klesko	.30	.14
149	Juan Guzman	.15	.07
150	Scott Servais	.15	.07
151	Tony Gwynn	1.50	.70
152	Tim Wakefield	.30	.14
153	David Nied	.15	.07
154	Chris Haney	.15	.07
155	Danny Bautista	.15	.07
156	Randy Velarde	.15	.07
157	Darrin Jackson	.15	.07
158	J.R. Phillips	.15	.07
159	Greg Gagne	.15	.07
160	Luis Aquino	.15	.07
161	John Vander Wal	.15	.07
162	Randy Myers	.15	.07
163	Ted Power	.15	.07
164	Scott Brosius	.30	.14
165	Len Dykstra	.30	.14
166	Jacob Brumfield	.15	.07
167	Bo Jackson	.30	.14
168	Eddie Taubensee	.15	.07
169	Carlos Baerga	.30	.14
170	Tim Bogar	.15	.07
171	Jose Canseco	.75	.35
172	Greg Blosser UER (Gregg on front)	.15	.07
173	Chili Davis	.30	.14
174	Randy Knorr	.15	.07
175	Mike Perez	.15	.07
176	Henry Rodriguez	.30	.14
177	Brian Turang	.15	.07
178	Roger Pavlik	.15	.07
179	Aaron Sele	.30	.14
180	Fred McGriff Gary Sheffield	.40	.18
181	J.T. Snow Tim Salmon	.60	.25
182	Roberto Hernandez	.15	.07
183	Jeff Reboulet	.15	.07
184	John Doherty	.15	.07
185	Danny Sheaffer	.15	.07
186	Bip Roberts	.15	.07
187	Dennis Martinez	.30	.14
188	Darryl Hamilton	.15	.07
189	Eduardo Perez	.15	.07
190	Pete Harnisch	.15	.07
191	Rich Gossage	.30	.14
192	Mickey Tettleton	.15	.07
193	Lenny Webster	.15	.07
194	Lance Johnson	.15	.07
195	Don Mattingly	1.25	.55
196	Gregg Olson	.15	.07
197	Mark Gubicza	.15	.07
198	Scott Fletcher	.15	.07
199	Jon Shave	.15	.07
200	Tim Mauser	.15	.07
201	Jeromy Burnitz	.30	.14
202	Rob Dibble	.15	.07
203	Will Clark	.60	.25
204	Steve Buechele	.15	.07
205	Brian Williams	.15	.07
206	Carlos Garcia	.15	.07
207	Mark Clark	.15	.07
208	Rafael Palmeiro	.60	.25
209	Eric Davis	.30	.14
210	Pat Meares	.15	.07
211	Chuck Finley	.30	.14
212	Jason Bere	.15	.07
213	Gary DiSarcina	.15	.07
214	Tony Fernandez	.30	.14
215	B.J. Surhoff	.30	.14
216	Lee Guetterman	.15	.07
217	Tim Wallach	.15	.07
218	Kirt Manwaring	.15	.07
219	Albert Belle	.60	.25
220	Dwight Gooden	.30	.14
221	Archi Cianfrocco	.15	.07
222	Terry Mulholland	.15	.07
223	Hipolito Pichardo	.15	.07
224	Kent Hrbek	.30	.14
225	Craig Grebeck	.15	.07
226	Todd Jones	.15	.07
227	Mike Bordick	.15	.07
228	John Olerud	.30	.14
229	Jeff Blauser	.15	.07
230	Alex Arias	.15	.07
231	Bernard Gilkey	.15	.07
232	Denny Neagle	.15	.07
233	Pedro Borbon	.15	.07
234	Dick Schofield	.15	.07
235	Matias Carrillo	.15	.07
236	Juan Bell	.15	.07
237	Mike Hampton	.15	.07
238	Barry Bonds	.75	.35
239	Cris Carpenter	.15	.07
240	Eric Karros	.30	.14
241	Greg McMichael	.15	.07
242	Pat Hentgen	.30	.14
243	Tim Pugh	.15	.07
244	Vinny Castilla	.30	.14
245	Charlie Hough	.15	.07
246	Bobby Munoz	.15	.07
247	Kevin Baez	.15	.07
248	Todd Frohwirth	.15	.07
249	Charlie Hayes	.15	.07
250	Mike Macfarlane	.15	.07
251	Danny Darwin	.15	.07
252	Ben Rivera	.15	.07
253	Dave Henderson	.15	.07
254	Steve Avery	.15	.07
255	Tim Belcher	.15	.07
256	Dan Plesac	.15	.07
257	Jim Thome	.60	.25
258	Albert Belle HR	.30	.14
259	Barry Bonds HR	.60	.25
260	Ron Gant HR	.15	.07
261	Juan Gonzalez HR	.60	.25
262	Ken Griffey Jr. HR	1.50	.70
263	David Justice HR	.30	.14
264	Fred McGriff HR	.15	.07
265	Rafael Palmeiro HR	.30	.14
266	Mike Piazza HR	1.00	.45
267	Frank Thomas HR	.60	.25
268	Matt Williams HR	.15	.07
269	Checklist 1-135	.15	.07
270	Checklist 136-270	.15	.07
271	Mike Stanley	.15	.07
272	Tony Tarasco	.15	.07
273	Teddy Higuera	.15	.07
274	Ryan Thompson	.15	.07
275	Rick Aguilera	.15	.07
276	Ramon Martinez	.30	.14
277	Orlando Merced	.15	.07
278	Guillermo Velasquez	.15	.07
279	Mark Hutton	.15	.07
280	Larry Walker	.60	.25
281	Kevin Gross	.15	.07
282	Jose Offerman	.30	.14
283	Jim Leyritz	.30	.14
284	Jamie Moyer	.15	.07
285	Frank Thomas	1.25	.55
286	Derek Bell	.30	.14
287	Derrick May	.15	.07
288	Dave Winfield	.60	.25
289	Curt Schilling	.30	.14
290	Carlos Quintana	.15	.07
291	Bob Natal	.15	.07
292	David Cone	.40	.18
293	Al Osuna	.15	.07
294	Bob Hamelin	.15	.07
295	Chad Curtis	.15	.07
296	Danny Jackson	.15	.07
297	Bob Welch	.15	.07
298	Felix Jose	.15	.07
299	Jay Buhner	.30	.14
300	Joe Carter	.60	.25
301	Kenny Lofton	.60	.25
302	Kirk Rueter	.15	.07
303	Kim Batiste	.15	.07
304	Mike Morgan	.15	.07
305	Pat Borders	.15	.07
306	Rene Arocha	.15	.07
307	Ruben Sierra	.15	.07

❑ 308	Steve Finley	.30	.14
❑ 309	Travis Fryman	.30	-.14
❑ 310	Zane Smith	.15	.07
❑ 311	Willie Wilson	.15	.07
❑ 312	Trevor Hoffman	.30	.14
❑ 313	Terry Pendleton	.15	.07
❑ 314	Salomon Torres	.15	.07
❑ 315	Robin Ventura	.30	.14
❑ 316	Randy Tomlin	.15	.07
❑ 317	Dave Stewart	.30	.14
❑ 318	Mike Benjamin	.15	.07
❑ 319	Matt Turner	.15	.07
❑ 320	Manny Ramirez	1.25	.55
❑ 321	Kevin Young	.15	.07
❑ 322	Ken Caminiti	.40	.18
❑ 323	Joe Girardi	.15	.07
❑ 324	Jeff McKnight	.15	.07
❑ 325	Gene Harris	.15	.07
❑ 326	Devon White	.15	.07
❑ 327	Darryl Kile	.15	.07
❑ 328	Craig Paquette	.15	.07
❑ 329	Cal Eldred	.15	.07
❑ 330	Bill Swift	.15	.07
❑ 331	Alan Trammell	.40	.18
❑ 332	Armando Reynoso	.15	.07
❑ 333	Brent Mayne	.15	.07
❑ 334	Chris Donnels	.15	.07
❑ 335	Darryl Strawberry	.30	.14
❑ 336	Dean Palmer	.30	.14
❑ 337	Frank Castillo	.15	.07
❑ 338	Jeff King	.15	.07
❑ 339	John Franco	.30	.14
❑ 340	Kevin Appier	.30	.14
❑ 341	Lance Blankenship	.15	.07
❑ 342	Mark McLemore	.15	.07
❑ 343	Pedro Astacio	.15	.07
❑ 344	Rich Batchelor	.15	.07
❑ 345	Ryan Bowen	.15	.07
❑ 346	Terry Steinbach	.15	.07
❑ 347	Troy O'Leary	.30	.14
❑ 348	Willie Blair	.15	.07
❑ 349	Wade Boggs	.60	.25
❑ 350	Tim Raines	.30	.14
❑ 351	Scott Livingstone	.15	.07
❑ 352	Rod Correia	.15	.07
❑ 353	Ray Lankford	.30	.14
❑ 354	Pat Listach	.15	.07
❑ 355	Milt Thompson	.15	.07
❑ 356	Miguel Jimenez	.15	.07
❑ 357	Marc Newfield	.15	.07
❑ 358	Mark McGwire	3.00	1.35
❑ 359	Kirby Puckett	1.00	.45
❑ 360	Kent Mercker	.15	.07
❑ 361	John Kruk	.30	.14
❑ 362	Jeff Kent	.30	.14
❑ 363	Hal Morris	.15	.07
❑ 364	Edgar Martinez	.30	.14
❑ 365	Dave Magadan	.15	.07
❑ 366	Dante Bichette	.30	.14
❑ 367	Chris Hammond	.15	.07
❑ 368	Bret Saberhagen	.30	.14
❑ 369	Billy Ripken	.15	.07
❑ 370	Bill Gullickson	.15	.07
❑ 371	Andre Dawson	.40	.18
❑ 372	Roberto Kelly	.15	.07
❑ 373	Cal Ripken	2.50	1.10
❑ 374	Craig Biggio	.60	.25
❑ 375	Dan Pasqua	.15	.07
❑ 376	Dave Nilsson	.15	.07
❑ 377	Duane Ward	.15	.07
❑ 378	Greg Vaughn	.30	.14
❑ 379	Jeff Fassero	.15	.07
❑ 380	Jerry DiPoto	.15	.07
❑ 381	John Patterson	.15	.07
❑ 382	Kevin Brown	.30	.14
❑ 383	Kevin Roberson	.15	.07
❑ 384	Joe Orsulak	.15	.07
❑ 385	Hilly Hathaway	.15	.07
❑ 386	Mike Greenwell	.15	.07
❑ 387	Orestes Destrade	.15	.07
❑ 388	Mike Gallego	.15	.07
❑ 389	Ozzie Guillen	.15	.07
❑ 390	Raul Mondesi	.60	.25
❑ 391	Scott Lydy	.15	.07
❑ 392	Tom Urbani	.15	.07
❑ 393	Wil Cordero	.15	.07
❑ 394	Tony Longmire	.15	.07
❑ 395	Todd Zeile	.15	.07
❑ 396	Scott Cooper	.15	.07
❑ 397	Ryne Sandberg	.75	.35
❑ 398	Ricky Bones	.15	.07
❑ 399	Phil Clark	.15	.07
❑ 400	Orel Hershiser	.30	.14
❑ 401	Mike Henneman	.15	.07
❑ 402	Mark Lemke	.15	.07
❑ 403	Mark Grace	.40	.18
❑ 404	Ken Ryan	.15	.07
❑ 405	John Smoltz	.40	.18
❑ 406	Jeff Conine	.15	.07
❑ 407	Greg Harris	.15	.07
❑ 408	Doug Drabek	.15	.07
❑ 409	Dave Fleming	.15	.07
❑ 410	Danny Tartabull	.15	.07
❑ 411	Chad Kreuter	.15	.07
❑ 412	Brad Ausmus	.15	.07
❑ 413	Ben McDonald	.15	.07
❑ 414	Barry Larkin	.60	.25
❑ 415	Bret Barberie	.15	.07
❑ 416	Chuck Knoblauch	.60	.25
❑ 417	Ozzie Smith	.75	.35
❑ 418	Ed Sprague	.15	.07
❑ 419	Matt Williams	.40	.18
❑ 420	Jeremy Hernandez	.15	.07
❑ 421	Jose Bautista	.15	.07
❑ 422	Kevin Mitchell	.15	.07
❑ 423	Manuel Lee	.15	.07
❑ 424	Mike Devereaux	.15	.07
❑ 425	Omar Olivares	.15	.07
❑ 426	Rafael Belliard	.15	.07
❑ 427	Richie Lewis	.15	.07
❑ 428	Ron Darling	.15	.07
❑ 429	Shane Mack	.15	.07
❑ 430	Tim Hulett	.15	.07
❑ 431	Wally Joyner	.30	.14
❑ 432	Wes Chamberlain	.15	.07
❑ 433	Tom Browning	.15	.07
❑ 434	Scott Radinsky	.15	.07
❑ 435	Rondell White	.30	.14
❑ 436	Rod Beck	.15	.07
❑ 437	Rheal Cormier	.15	.07
❑ 438	Randy Johnson	.60	.25
❑ 439	Pete Schourek	.15	.07
❑ 440	Mo Vaughn	.60	.25
❑ 441	Mike Timlin	.15	.07
❑ 442	Mark Langston	.15	.07
❑ 443	Lou Whitaker	.30	.14
❑ 444	Kevin Stocker	.15	.07
❑ 445	Ken Hill	.15	.07
❑ 446	John Wetteland	.30	.14
❑ 447	J.T. Snow	.30	.14
❑ 448	Erik Pappas	.15	.07
❑ 449	David Hulse	.15	.07
❑ 450	Darren Daulton	.30	.14
❑ 451	Chris Hoiles	.15	.07
❑ 452	Bryan Harvey	.15	.07
❑ 453	Darren Lewis	.15	.07
❑ 454	Andres Galarraga	.60	.25
❑ 455	Joe Hesketh	.15	.07
❑ 456	Jose Valentin	.15	.07
❑ 457	Dan Peltier	.15	.07
❑ 458	Joe Beaver	.15	.07
❑ 459	Kevin Rogers	.15	.07
❑ 460	Eddie Murray	.30	.14
❑ 461	Alvaro Espinoza	.15	.07
❑ 462	Mike Alvarez	.30	.14
❑ 463	Cory Snyder	.15	.07
❑ 464	Carlos Maldonado	.15	.07
❑ 465	Bias Minor	.15	.07
❑ 466	Rod Bolton	.15	.07
❑ 467	Kenny Rogers	.15	.07
❑ 468	Greg Myers	.15	.07
❑ 469	Jimmy Key	.30	.14
❑ 470	Tony Castillo	.15	.07
❑ 471	Mike Stanton	.15	.07
❑ 472	Deion Sanders	.30	.14
❑ 473	Tito Navarro	.15	.07
❑ 474	Mike Gardiner	.15	.07
❑ 475	Steve Reed	.15	.07
❑ 476	John Roper	.15	.07
❑ 477	Mike Trombley	.30	.14
❑ 478	Charles Nagy	.30	.14
❑ 479	Larry Casian	.15	.07
❑ 480	Eric Hillman	.15	.07
❑ 481	Bill Wertz	.15	.07
❑ 482	Jeff Schwarz	.15	.07
❑ 483	John Valentin	.30	.14
❑ 484	Carl Willis	.15	.07
❑ 485	Gary Gaetti	.30	.14
❑ 486	Bill Pecota	.15	.07
❑ 487	John Smiley	.15	.07
❑ 488	Mike Mussina	.60	.25
❑ 489	Mike Ignasiak	.15	.07
❑ 490	Billy Brewer	.15	.07
❑ 491	Jack Voigt	.15	.07
❑ 492	Mike Munoz	.15	.07
❑ 493	Lee Tinsley	.15	.07
❑ 494	Bob Wickman	.15	.07
❑ 495	Roger Salkeld	.15	.07
❑ 496	Thomas Howard	.15	.07
❑ 497	Mark Davis	.15	.07
❑ 498	Dave Clark	.15	.07
❑ 499	Turk Wendell	.15	.07
❑ 500	Rafael Bournigal	.15	.07
❑ 501	Chip Hale	.15	.07
❑ 502	Matt Whiteside	.15	.07
❑ 503	Brian Koelling	.15	.07
❑ 504	Jeff Reed	.15	.07
❑ 505	Paul Wagner	.15	.07
❑ 506	Torey Lovullo	.15	.07
❑ 507	Curt Leskanic	.15	.07
❑ 508	Derek Lilliquist	.15	.07
❑ 509	Joe Magrane	.15	.07
❑ 510	Mackey Sasser	.15	.07
❑ 511	Lloyd McClendon	.15	.07
❑ 512	Jayhawk Owens	.15	.07
❑ 513	Woody Williams	.15	.07
❑ 514	Gary Redus	.15	.07
❑ 515	Tim Spehr	.15	.07
❑ 516	Jim Abbott	.30	.14
❑ 517	Lou Frazier	.15	.07
❑ 518	Erik Plantenberg	.15	.07
❑ 519	Tim Worrell	.15	.07
❑ 520	Brian McRae	.15	.07
❑ 521	Chan Ho Park	1.00	.45
❑ 522	Mark Wohlers	.15	.07
❑ 523	Geronimo Pena	.15	.07
❑ 524	Andy Ashby	.15	.07
❑ 525	Tim Raines TALE	.15	.07
❑ 526	Paul Molitor TALE	.30	.14
❑ 527	Joe Carter DL	.15	.07
❑ 528	Frank Thomas DL UER	.60	.25

(listed as third in RBI in
1993; was actually second)

❑ 529	Ken Griffey Jr. DL	1.50	.70
❑ 530	David Justice DL	.30	.14
❑ 531	Gregg Jefferies DL	.15	.07
❑ 532	Barry Bonds DL	.60	.25
❑ 533	John Kruk QS	.15	.07
❑ 534	Roger Clemens QS	.75	.35
❑ 535	Cecil Fielder QS	.15	.07
❑ 536	Ruben Sierra QS	.15	.07
❑ 537	Tony Gwynn QS	.75	.35
❑ 538	Tom Glavine QS	.30	.14
❑ 539	Checklist 271-405 UER	.15	.07

(Number on back is 269)

❑ 540	Checklist 406-540 UER	.15	.07

(Numbered 270 on back)

❑ 541	Ozzie Smith ATL	.60	.25
❑ 542	Eddie Murray ATL	.30	.14
❑ 543	Lee Smith ATL	.15	.07
❑ 544	Greg Maddux	1.50	.70
❑ 545	Denis Boucher	.15	.07
❑ 546	Mark Gardner	.15	.07
❑ 547	Bo Jackson	.30	.14
❑ 548	Eric Anthony	.15	.07
❑ 549	Delino DeShields	.15	.07
❑ 550	Turner Ward	.15	.07
❑ 551	Scott Sanderson	.15	.07
❑ 552	Hector Carrasco	.15	.07
❑ 553	Tony Phillips	.15	.07
❑ 554	Melido Perez	.15	.07
❑ 555	Mike Felder	.15	.07
❑ 556	Jack Morris	.30	.14
❑ 557	Rafael Palmeiro	.60	.25
❑ 558	Shane Reynolds	.30	.14
❑ 559	Pete Incaviglia	.15	.07
❑ 560	Greg Harris	.15	.07
❑ 561	Matt Walbeck	.15	.07

❑ 562 Todd Van Poppel	.15	.07
❑ 563 Todd Stottlemyre	.15	.07
❑ 564 Ricky Bones	.15	.07
❑ 565 Mike Jackson	.30	.14
❑ 566 Kevin McReynolds	.15	.07
❑ 567 Melvin Nieves	.15	.07
❑ 568 Juan Gonzalez	1.25	.55
❑ 569 Frank Viola	.15	.07
❑ 570 Vince Coleman	.15	.07
❑ 571 Brian Anderson	.40	.18
❑ 572 Omar Vizquel	.30	.14
❑ 573 Bernie Williams	.60	.25
❑ 574 Tom Glavine	.60	.25
❑ 575 Mitch Williams	.15	.07
❑ 576 Shawon Dunston	.15	.07
❑ 577 Mike Lansing	.30	.14
❑ 578 Greg Pirkl	.15	.07
❑ 579 Sid Fernandez	.15	.07
❑ 580 Doug Jones	.15	.07
❑ 581 Walt Weiss	.15	.07
❑ 582 Tim Belcher	.15	.07
❑ 583 Alex Fernandez	.15	.07
❑ 584 Alex Cole	.15	.07
❑ 585 Greg Cadaret	.15	.07
❑ 586 Bob Tewksbury	.15	.07
❑ 587 Dave Hansen	.15	.07
❑ 588 Kurt Abbott	.15	.07
❑ 589 Rick White	.15	.07
❑ 590 Kevin Bass	.15	.07
❑ 591 Geronimo Berroa	.15	.07
❑ 592 Jaime Navarro	.15	.07
❑ 593 Steve Farr	.15	.07
❑ 594 Jack Armstrong	.15	.07
❑ 595 Steve Howe	.15	.07
❑ 596 Jose Rijo	.15	.07
❑ 597 Otis Nixon	.15	.07
❑ 598 Robby Thompson	.15	.07
❑ 599 Kelly Stinnett	.15	.07
❑ 600 Carlos Delgado	.60	.25
❑ 601 Brian Johnson	.15	.07
❑ 602 Gregg Olson	.15	.07
❑ 603 Jim Edmonds	.60	.25
❑ 604 Mike Blowers	.15	.07
❑ 605 Lee Smith	.30	.14
❑ 606 Pat Rapp	.15	.07
❑ 607 Mike Magnante	.15	.07
❑ 608 Karl Rhodes	.15	.07
❑ 609 Jeff Juden	.15	.07
❑ 610 Rusty Meacham	.15	.07
❑ 611 Pedro Martinez	.15	.07
❑ 612 Todd Worrell	.15	.07
❑ 613 Stan Javier	.15	.07
❑ 614 Mike Hampton	.15	.07
❑ 615 Jose Guzman	.15	.07
❑ 616 Xavier Hernandez	.15	.07
❑ 617 David Wells	.40	.18
❑ 618 John Habyan	.15	.07
❑ 619 Chris Nabholz	.15	.07
❑ 620 Bobby Jones	.15	.07
❑ 621 Chris James	.15	.07
❑ 622 Ellis Burks	.30	.14
❑ 623 Erik Hanson	.15	.07
❑ 624 Pat Meares	.15	.07
❑ 625 Harold Reynolds	.15	.07
❑ 626 Bob Hamelin RR	.15	.07
❑ 627 Manny Ramirez RR	.40	.18
❑ 628 Ryan Klesko RR	.15	.07
❑ 629 Carlos Delgado RR	.60	.25
❑ 630 Javier Lopez RR	.40	.18
❑ 631 Steve Karsay RR	.15	.07
❑ 632 Rick Helling RR	.30	.14
❑ 633 Steve Trachsel RR	.15	.07
❑ 634 Hector Carrasco RR	.15	.07
❑ 635 Andy Stankiewicz	.15	.07
❑ 636 Paul Sorrento	.15	.07
❑ 637 Scott Erickson	.30	.14
❑ 638 Chipper Jones	1.50	.70
❑ 639 Luis Polonia	.15	.07
❑ 640 Howard Johnson	.15	.07
❑ 641 John Dopson	.15	.07
❑ 642 Jody Reed	.15	.07
❑ 643 Lonnie Smith UER	.15	.07
Card numbered 543		
❑ 644 Mark Portugal	.15	.07
❑ 645 Paul Molitor	.60	.25
❑ 646 Paul Assenmacher	.15	.07

❑ 647 Hubie Brooks	.15	.07
❑ 648 Gary Wayne	.15	.07
❑ 649 Sean Berry	.15	.07
❑ 650 Roger Clemens	1.50	.70
❑ 651 Brian L. Hunter	.30	.14
❑ 652 Wally Whitehurst	.15	.07
❑ 653 Allen Watson	.15	.07
❑ 654 Rickey Henderson	.75	.35
❑ 655 Sid Bream	.15	.07
❑ 656 Dan Wilson	.15	.07
❑ 657 Ricky Jordan	.15	.07
❑ 658 Sterling Hitchcock	.30	.14
❑ 659 Darrin Jackson	.15	.07
❑ 660 Junior Felix	.15	.07
❑ 661 Tom Brunansky	.15	.07
❑ 662 Jose Vizcaino	.15	.07
❑ 663 Mark Leiter	.15	.07
❑ 664 Gil Heredia	.15	.07
❑ 665 Fred McGriff	.40	.18
❑ 666 Will Clark	.60	.25
❑ 667 Al Leiter	.30	.14
❑ 668 James Mouton	.15	.07
❑ 669 Billy Bean	.15	.07
❑ 670 Scott Leius	.15	.07
❑ 671 Bret Boone	.30	.14
❑ 672 Darren Holmes	.15	.07
❑ 673 Dave Weathers	.15	.07
❑ 674 Eddie Murray	.60	.25
❑ 675 Felix Fermin	.15	.07
❑ 676 Chris Sabo	.15	.07
❑ 677 Billy Spiers	.15	.07
❑ 678 Aaron Sele	.30	.14
❑ 679 Juan Samuel	.15	.07
❑ 680 Julio Franco	.15	.07
❑ 681 Heathcliff Slocumb	.15	.07
❑ 682 Dennis Martinez	.30	.14
❑ 683 Jerry Browne	.15	.07
❑ 684 Pedro Martinez	.15	.07
❑ 685 Rex Hudler	.15	.07
❑ 686 Willie McGee	.30	.14
❑ 687 Andy Van Slyke	.30	.14
❑ 688 Pat Mahomes	.15	.07
❑ 689 Dave Henderson	.15	.07
❑ 690 Tony Eusebio	.15	.07
❑ 691 Rick Sutcliffe	.15	.07
❑ 692 Willie Banks	.15	.07
❑ 693 Alan Mills	.15	.07
❑ 694 Jeff Treadway	.15	.07
❑ 695 Alex Gonzalez	.15	.07
❑ 696 David Segui	.30	.14
❑ 697 Rick Helling	.30	.14
❑ 698 Bip Roberts	.15	.07
❑ 699 Jeff Cirillo	.75	.35
❑ 700 Terry Mulholland	.15	.07
❑ 701 Marvin Freeman	.15	.07
❑ 702 Jason Bere	.15	.07
❑ 703 Javier Lopez	.40	.18
❑ 704 Greg Hibbard	.15	.07
❑ 705 Tommy Greene	.15	.07
❑ 706 Marquis Grissom	.30	.14
❑ 707 Brian Harper	.15	.07
❑ 708 Steve Karsay	.15	.07
❑ 709 Jeff Brantley	.15	.07
❑ 710 Jeff Russell	.15	.07
❑ 711 Bryan Hickerson	.15	.07
❑ 712 Jim Pittsley	.15	.07
❑ 713 Bobby Ayala	.15	.07
❑ 714 John Smoltz	.40	.18
❑ 715 Jose Rijo	.15	.07
❑ 716 Greg Maddux	.75	.35
❑ 717 Matt Williams	.40	.18
❑ 718 Frank Thomas	2.00	.25
❑ 719 Ryne Sandberg	.60	.25
❑ 720 Checklist	.15	.07

1994 Stadium Club Dugout Dirt

	MINT	NRMT
COMPLETE SET (12)	10.00	4.50
COMPLETE SERIES 1 (4)	5.00	2.20
COMPLETE SERIES 2 (4)	2.00	1.35
COMPLETE SERIES 3 (4)	3.00	1.35
COMMON CARD (DD1-DD12)	.15	.07
STATED ODDS 1:6 H/R, 1:3 JUM		

❑ DD1 Mike Piazza	2.00	.90
❑ DD2 Dave Winfield	.60	.25
❑ DD3 John Kruk	.15	.07
❑ DD4 Cal Ripken	2.50	1.10
❑ DD5 Jack McDowell	.15	.07
❑ DD6 Barry Bonds	.75	.35
❑ DD7 Ken Griffey Jr.	3.00	1.35
❑ DD8 Tim Salmon	.60	.25
❑ DD9 Frank Thomas	1.25	.55
❑ DD10 Jeff Kent	.25	.11
❑ DD11 Randy Johnson	.60	.25
❑ DD12 Darren Daulton	.25	.11

1994 Stadium Club Finest

	MINT	NRMT
COMPLETE SET (10)	30.00	13.50
COMMON CARD (F1-F10)	1.00	.45
SER.3 STATED ODDS 1:6		

❑ F1 Jeff Bagwell	2.50	1.10
❑ F2 Albert Belle	2.00	.90
❑ F3 Barry Bonds	2.50	1.10
❑ F4 Juan Gonzalez	4.00	1.80
❑ F5 Ken Griffey Jr.	10.00	4.50
❑ F6 Marquis Grissom	1.00	.45
❑ F7 David Justice	2.00	.90
❑ F8 Mike Piazza	6.00	2.70
❑ F9 Tim Salmon	2.00	.90
❑ F10 Frank Thomas	4.00	1.80

1994 Stadium Club Super Teams

	MINT	NRMT
COMPLETE SET (28)	50.00	22.00
COMMON TEAM (1-28)	1.00	.45
SEMISTARS	1.50	.70
UNLISTED STARS	2.00	.90
SER.1 STAT.ODDS 1:24 HOB/RET, 1:15 JUM		
CONTEST APPLIED TO 1995 SEASON		

❑ ST1 Atlanta Braves (Jeff Blauser Terry Pendleton)	10.00	4.50
❑ ST2 Chicago Cubs (Sammy Sosa Derrick May)	1.00	.45
❑ ST3 Cincinnati Reds	2.00	.90

(Reggie Sanders
Barry Larkin)
❑ ST4 Colorado Rockies .... 1.00 .45
(Vinny Castilla
Eric Young)
❑ ST5 Florida Marlins .... 1.00 .45
(Alex Arias)
❑ ST6 Houston Astros .... 1.00 .45
(Eric Anthony
Steve Finley)
❑ ST7 Los Angeles Dodgers .. 6.00 2.70
(Mike Piazza)
❑ ST8 Montreal Expos .... 1.00 .45
(Marquis Grissom)
❑ ST9 New York Mets .... 1.00 .45
(Bobby Bonilla)
❑ ST10 Philadelphia Phillies .. 1.00 .45
(Mickey Morandini)
❑ ST11 Pittsburgh Pirates .... 1.00 .45
(Andy Van Slyke
Jay Bell)
❑ ST12 St. Louis Cardinals ... 1.00 .45
(Todd Zeile
Gregg Jefferies)
❑ ST13 San Diego Padres .... 1.00 .45
(Ricky Gutierrez)
❑ ST14 San Francisco Giants 2.00 .90
(Matt Williams
Kirt Manwaring)
❑ ST15 Baltimore Orioles 8.00 3.60
(Cal Ripken)
❑ ST16 Boston Red Sox ...... 2.00 .90
(Luis Rivera
John Valentin)
❑ ST17 California Angels ...... 1.00 .45
(Tim Salmon)
❑ ST18 Chicago White Sox ... 1.00 .45
(Joey Cora)
❑ ST19 Cleveland Indians 3.00 1.35
(Kenny Lofton
Carlos Baerga
Albert Belle)
❑ ST20 Detroit Tigers .... 1.00 .45
(Alan Trammell
Tony Phillips)
❑ ST21 Kansas City Royals .. 1.00 .45
(Jose Lind
Curt Wilkerson)
❑ ST22 Milwaukee Brewers .. 1.00 .45
(Pat Listach
John Jaha
Cal Eldred)
❑ ST23 Minnesota Twins 4.00 1.80
(Kirby Puckett
Kent Hrbek)
❑ ST24 New York Yankees 4.00 1.80
(Don Mattingly
Bernie Williams)
❑ ST25 Oakland Athletics ..... 1.00 .45
(Mike Bordick
Brent Gates)
❑ ST26 Seattle Mariners ...... 2.00 .90
(Jay Buhner
Mike Blowers)
❑ ST27 Texas Rangers 4.00 1.80
(Ivan Rodriguez
Dean Palmer
Jose Canseco)

Juan Gonzalez)
❑ ST28 Toronto Blue Jays...... 1.00 .45
(John Olerud)

1995 Stadium Club

	MINT	NRMT
COMPLETE SET (630)	60.00	27.00
COMPLETE SERIES 1 (270) ..	25.00	11.00
COMPLETE SERIES 2 (225) ..	20.00	9.00
COMPLETE SERIES 3 (135) ..	15.00	6.75
COMMON CARD (1-630)	.15	.07
MINOR STARS	.30	.14
UNLISTED STARS	.60	.25

SUBSET CARDS HALF VALUE OF BASE
CARDS
COMP.1ST DAY SET (270) ... 275.00 125.00
COMMON 1ST DAY (1-270) .... 1.00 .45
*1ST DAY STARS: 6X TO 12X HI COLUMN
*1ST DAY YOUNG STARS: 5X TO 10X HI
*1ST DAY DP STARS: 1.5X TO 3X HI
1ST DAY: RANDOM INS.IN TOPPS SER.2
1ST DAY DP'S ALSO IN TOPPS SER.1
TEN 1ST DAY PER TOPPS FACTORY SET
COMP.SUP.TM.SET (585) 100.00 45.00
COMP.SUP.TM.EC/TA SET (45) 15.00 6.75
*SUP.TM.STARS: .75X TO 2X HI COLUMN
*SUP.TM.YOUNG STARS: .6X TO 1.5X HI
ONE SET VIA MAIL PER 94 BRAVES SUP.TM
SER.3 EC/TA SUBSETS SHIPPED LATER
COMP.VI.REAL.SET (270) 100.00 45.00
COMP.VI.REAL.SER.1 (135) .. 50.00 22.00
COMP.VI.REAL.SER.2 (135) .. 50.00 22.00
*VIRT.REAL.STARS: .75X TO 2X HI COLUMN
*VIRT.REAL.YOUNG STARS: .6X TO 1.5X HI
ONE VIRTUAL REALITY CARD PER PACK

❑ 1 Cal Ripken	2.50	1.10
❑ 2 Bo Jackson	.30	.14
❑ 3 Bryan Harvey	.15	.07
❑ 4 Curt Schilling	.40	.18
❑ 5 Bruce Ruffin	.15	.07
❑ 6 Travis Fryman	.30	.14
❑ 7 Jim Abbott	.30	.14
❑ 8 David McCarty	.15	.07
❑ 9 Gary Gaetti	.30	.14
❑ 10 Roger Clemens	1.50	.70
❑ 11 Carlos Garcia	.15	.07
❑ 12 Lee Smith	.30	.14
❑ 13 Bobby Ayala	.15	.07
❑ 14 Charles Nagy	.30	.14
❑ 15 Lou Frazier	.15	.07
❑ 16 Rene Arocha	.15	.07
❑ 17 Carlos Delgado	.60	.25
❑ 18 Steve Finley	.30	.14
❑ 19 Ryan Klesko	.30	.14
❑ 20 Cal Eldred	.15	.07
❑ 21 Rey Sanchez	.15	.07
❑ 22 Ken Hill	.30	.14
❑ 23 Benito Santiago	.15	.07
❑ 24 Julian Tavarez	.15	.07
❑ 25 Jose Vizcaino	.15	.07
❑ 26 Andy Benes	.30	.14
❑ 27 Mariano Duncan	.15	.07
❑ 28 Checklist A	.15	.07
❑ 29 Shawon Dunston	.15	.07
❑ 30 Rafael Palmeiro	.60	.25
❑ 31 Dean Palmer	.30	.14

❑ 32 Andres Galarraga	.60	.25
❑ 33 Joey Cora	.15	.07
❑ 34 Mickey Tettleton	.15	.07
❑ 35 Barry Larkin	.60	.25
❑ 36 Carlos Baerga	.15	.07
❑ 37 Orel Hershiser	.30	.14
❑ 38 Jody Reed	.15	.07
❑ 39 Paul Molitor	.60	.25
❑ 40 Jim Edmonds	.40	.18
❑ 41 Bob Tewksbury	.15	.07
❑ 42 John Patterson	.15	.07
❑ 43 Ray McDavid	.15	.07
❑ 44 Zane Smith	.15	.07
❑ 45 Bret Saberhagen SE .	.30	.14
❑ 46 Greg Maddux SE	.75	.35
❑ 47 Frank Thomas SE	.60	.25
❑ 48 Carlos Baerga SE	.15	.07
❑ 49 Billy Spiers	.15	.07
❑ 50 Stan Javier	.15	.07
❑ 51 Rex Hudler	.15	.07
❑ 52 Denny Hocking	.15	.07
❑ 53 Todd Worrell	.15	.07
❑ 54 Mark Clark	.15	.07
❑ 55 Hipolito Pichardo	.15	.07
❑ 56 Bob Wickman	.15	.07
❑ 57 Raul Mondesi	.40	.18
❑ 58 Steve Cooke	.15	.07
❑ 59 Rod Beck	.15	.07
❑ 60 Tim Davis	.15	.07
❑ 61 Jeff Kent	.30	.14
❑ 62 John Valentin	.30	.14
❑ 63 Alex Arias	.15	.07
❑ 64 Steve Reed	.15	.07
❑ 65 Ozzie Smith	.75	.35
❑ 66 Terry Pendleton	.15	.07
❑ 67 Kenny Rogers	.15	.07
❑ 68 Vince Coleman	.15	.07
❑ 69 Tom Pagnozzi	.15	.07
❑ 70 Roberto Alomar	.60	.25
❑ 71 Darrin Jackson	.15	.07
❑ 72 Dennis Eckersley	.30	.14
❑ 73 Jay Buhner	.30	.14
❑ 74 Darren Lewis	.15	.07
❑ 75 Dave Weathers	.15	.07
❑ 76 Matt Walbeck	.15	.07
❑ 77 Brad Ausmus	.15	.07
❑ 78 Danny Bautista	.15	.07
❑ 79 Bob Hamelin	.15	.07
❑ 80 Steve Trachsel	.15	.07
❑ 81 Ken Ryan	.15	.07
❑ 82 Chris Turner	.15	.07
❑ 83 David Segui	.30	.14
❑ 84 Ben McDonald	.15	.07
❑ 85 Wade Boggs	.60	.25
❑ 86 John VanderWal	.15	.07
❑ 87 Sandy Alomar Jr	.30	.14
❑ 88 Ron Karkovice	.15	.07
❑ 89 Doug Jones	.15	.07
❑ 90 Gary Sheffield	.30	.14
❑ 91 Ken Caminiti	.40	.18
❑ 92 Chris Bosio	.15	.07
❑ 93 Kevin Tapani	.15	.07
❑ 94 Walt Weiss	.15	.07
❑ 95 Erik Hanson	.15	.07
❑ 96 Ruben Sierra	.15	.07
❑ 97 Nomar Garciaparra ...	3.00	1.35
❑ 98 Terrence Long	.40	.18
❑ 99 Jacob Shumate	.15	.07
❑ 100 Paul Wilson	.15	.07
❑ 101 Kevin Witt	.60	.25
❑ 102 Paul Konerko	1.00	.45
❑ 103 Ben Grieve	1.50	.70
❑ 104 Mark Johnson	.15	.07
❑ 105 Cade Gaspar	.30	.14
❑ 106 Mark Farris	.15	.07
❑ 107 Dustin Hermanson .	.15	.07
❑ 108 Scott Elarton	1.00	.45
❑ 109 Doug Million	.15	.07
❑ 110 Matt Smith	.15	.07
❑ 111 Brian Buchanan	.30	.14
❑ 112 Jayson Peterson	.15	.07
❑ 113 Bret Wagner	.15	.07
❑ 114 C.J. Nitkowski	.15	.07
❑ 115 Ramon Castro	.30	.14
❑ 116 Rafael Bournigal	.15	.07
❑ 117 Jeff Fassero	.15	.07

#	Player				#	Player				#	Player		
118	Bobby Bonilla	.30	.14		204	David Cone	.40	.18		290	Bernie Williams	.60	.25
119	Ricky Gutierrez	.15	.07		205	Todd Hundley	.30	.14		291	Mickey Morandini	.15	.07
120	Roger Pavlik	.15	.07		206	Ozzie Guillen	.15	.07		292	Scott Leius	.15	.07
121	Mike Greenwell	.15	.07		207	Alex Cole	.15	.07		293	David Hulse	.15	.07
122	Deion Sanders	.30	.14		208	Tony Phillips	.15	.07		294	Greg Gagne	.15	.07
123	Charlie Hayes	.15	.07		209	Jim Eisenreich	.15	.07		295	Moises Alou	.30	.14
124	Paul O'Neill	.30	.14		210	Greg Vaughn BES	.15	.07		296	Geronimo Berroa	.15	.07
125	Jay Bell	.30	.14		211	Barry Larkin BES	.30	.14		297	Eddie Zambrano	.15	.07
126	Royce Clayton	.15	.07		212	Don Mattingly BES	.60	.25		298	Alan Trammell	.30	.14
127	Willie Banks	.15	.07		213	Mark Grace BES	.15	.07		299	Don Slaught	.15	.07
128	Mark Wohlers	.15	.07		214	Jose Canseco BES	.30	.14		300	Jose Rijo	.15	.07
129	Todd Jones	.15	.07		215	Joe Carter BES	.15	.07		301	Joe Ausanio	.15	.07
130	Todd Stottlemyre	.15	.07		216	David Cone BES	.15	.07		302	Tim Raines	.30	.14
131	Will Clark	.60	.25		217	Sandy Alomar Jr. BES	.15	.07		303	Melido Perez	.15	.07
132	Wilson Alvarez	.30	.14		218	Al Martin BES	.15	.07		304	Kent Mercker	.15	.07
133	Chili Davis	.30	.14		219	Roberto Kelly BES	.15	.07		305	James Mouton	.15	.07
134	Dave Burba	.15	.07		220	Paul Sorrento	.15	.07		306	Luis Lopez	.15	.07
135	Chris Hoiles	.15	.07		221	Tony Fernandez	.30	.14		307	Mike Kingery	.15	.07
136	Jeff Blauser	.15	.07		222	Stan Belinda	.15	.07		308	Willie Greene	.15	.07
137	Jeff Reboulet	.15	.07		223	Mike Stanley	.15	.07		309	Cecil Fielder	.30	.14
138	Bret Saberhagen	.30	.14		224	Doug Drabek	.15	.07		310	Scott Kamieniecki	.15	.07
139	Kirk Rueter	.15	.07		225	Todd Van Poppel	.15	.07		311	Mike Greenwell BES	.15	.07
140	Dave Nilsson	.15	.07		226	Matt Mieske	.15	.07		312	Bobby Bonilla BES	.15	.07
141	Pat Borders	.15	.07		227	Tino Martinez	.60	.25		313	Andres Galarraga BES	.60	.25
142	Ron Darling	.15	.07		228	Andy Ashby	.15	.07		314	Cal Ripken BES	1.25	.55
143	Derek Bell	.30	.14		229	Midre Cummings	.15	.07		315	Matt Williams BES	.30	.14
144	Dave Hollins	.15	.07		230	Jeff Frye	.15	.07		316	Tom Pagnozzi BES	.15	.07
145	Juan Gonzalez	1.25	.55		231	Hal Morris	.15	.07		317	Len Dykstra BES	.15	.07
146	Andre Dawson	.40	.18		232	Jose Lind	.15	.07		318	Frank Thomas BES	.60	.25
147	Jim Thome	.60	.25		233	Shawn Green	.60	.25		319	Kirby Puckett BES	.60	.25
148	Larry Walker	.60	.25		234	Rafael Belliard	.15	.07		320	Mike Piazza BES	1.00	.45
149	Mike Piazza	2.00	.90		235	Randy Myers	.15	.07		321	Jason Jacome	.15	.07
150	Mike Perez	.15	.07		236	Frank Thomas CE	.60	.25		322	Brian Hunter	.15	.07
151	Steve Avery	.15	.07		237	Darren Daulton CE	.15	.07		323	Brent Gates	.15	.07
152	Dan Wilson	.15	.07		238	Sammy Sosa CE	1.00	.45		324	Jim Converse	.15	.07
153	Andy Van Slyke	.30	.14		239	Cal Ripken CE	1.25	.55		325	Damion Easley	.30	.14
154	Junior Felix	.15	.07		240	Jeff Bagwell CE	.60	.25		326	Dante Bichette	.30	.14
155	Jack McDowell	.15	.07		241	Ken Griffey Jr. CE	3.00	1.35		327	Kurt Abbott	.15	.07
156	Danny Tartabull	.15	.07		242	Brett Butler	.30	.14		328	Scott Cooper	.15	.07
157	Willie Blair	.15	.07		243	Derrick May	.15	.07		329	Mike Henneman	.15	.07
158	Wm.VanLandingham	.15	.07		244	Pat Listach	.15	.07		330	Orlando Miller	.15	.07
159	Robb Nen	.15	.07		245	Mike Bordick	.15	.07		331	John Kruk	.30	.14
160	Lee Tinsley	.15	.07		246	Mark Langston	.15	.07		332	Jose Oliva	.15	.07
161	Ismael Valdes	.30	.14		247	Randy Velarde	.15	.07		333	Reggie Sanders	.30	.14
162	Juan Guzman	.15	.07		248	Julio Franco	.15	.07		334	Omar Vizquel	.30	.14
163	Scott Servais	.15	.07		249	Chuck Knoblauch	.60	.25		335	Devon White	.30	.14
164	Cliff Floyd	.30	.14		250	Bill Gullickson	.15	.07		336	Mike Morgan	.15	.07
165	Allen Watson	.15	.07		251	Dave Henderson	.15	.07		337	J.R. Phillips	.15	.07
166	Eddie Taubensee	.15	.07		252	Bret Boone	.30	.14		338	Gary DiSarcina	.15	.07
167	Scott Hemond	.15	.07		253	Al Martin	.15	.07		339	Joey Hamilton	.30	.14
168	Jeff Tackett	.15	.07		254	Armando Benitez	.15	.07		340	Randy Johnson	.60	.25
169	Chad Curtis	.15	.07		255	Wil Cordero	.15	.07		341	Jim Leyritz	.15	.07
170	Rico Brogna	.15	.07		256	Al Leiter	.30	.14		342	Bobby Jones	.15	.07
171	Luis Polonia	.15	.07		257	Luis Gonzalez	.15	.07		343	Jaime Navarro	.15	.07
172	Checklist B	.15	.07		258	Charlie O'Brien	.15	.07		344	Bip Roberts	.15	.07
173	Lance Johnson	.15	.07		259	Tim Wallach	.15	.07		345	Steve Karsay	.15	.07
174	Sammy Sosa	2.00	.90		260	Scott Sanders	.15	.07		346	Kevin Stocker	.15	.07
175	Mike Macfarlane	.15	.07		261	Tom Henke	.15	.07		347	Jose Canseco	.75	.35
176	Darryl Hamilton	.15	.07		262	Otis Nixon	.15	.07		348	Bill Wegman	.15	.07
177	Rick Aguilera	.15	.07		263	Darren Daulton	.30	.14		349	Rondell White	.30	.14
178	Dave West	.15	.07		264	Manny Ramirez	.75	.35		350	Mo Vaughn	.60	.25
179	Mike Gallego	.15	.07		265	Bret Barberie	.15	.07		351	Joe Orsulak	.15	.07
180	Marc Newfield	.15	.07		266	Mel Rojas	.15	.07		352	Pat Meares	.15	.07
181	Steve Buechele	.15	.07		267	John Burkett	.15	.07		353	Albie Lopez	.15	.07
182	David Wells	.40	.18		268	Brady Anderson	.30	.14		354	Edgar Martinez	.30	.14
183	Tom Glavine	.60	.25		269	John Roper	.15	.07		355	Brian Jordan	.30	.14
184	Joe Girardi	.15	.07		270	Shane Reynolds	.30	.14		356	Tommy Greene	.15	.07
185	Craig Biggio	.60	.25		271	Barry Bonds	.75	.35		357	Chuck Carr	.15	.07
186	Eddie Murray	.60	.25		272	Alex Fernandez	.15	.07		358	Pedro Astacio	.15	.07
187	Kevin Gross	.15	.07		273	Brian McRae	.15	.07		359	Russ Davis	.30	.14
188	Sid Fernandez	.15	.07		274	Todd Zeile	.15	.07		360	Chris Hammond	.15	.07
189	John Franco	.30	.14		275	Greg Swindell	.15	.07		361	Gregg Jefferies	.15	.07
190	Bernard Gilkey	.15	.07		276	Johnny Ruffin	.15	.07		362	Shane Mack	.15	.07
191	Matt Williams	.60	.25		277	Troy Neel	.15	.07		363	Fred McGriff	.40	.18
192	Darrin Fletcher	.15	.07		278	Eric Karros	.30	.14		364	Pat Rapp	.15	.07
193	Jeff Conine	.15	.07		279	John Hudek	.15	.07		365	Bill Swift	.15	.07
194	Ed Sprague	.15	.07		280	Thomas Howard	.15	.07		366	Checklist	.15	.07
195	Eduardo Perez	.15	.07		281	Joe Carter	.30	.14		367	Robin Ventura	.30	.14
196	Scott Livingstone	.15	.07		282	Mike Devereaux	.15	.07		368	Bobby Witt	.15	.07
197	Ivan Rodriguez	.75	.35		283	Butch Henry	.15	.07		369	Karl Rhodes	.15	.07
198	Orlando Merced	.15	.07		284	Reggie Jefferson	.15	.07		370	Eddie Williams	.15	.07
199	Ricky Bones	.15	.07		285	Mark Lemke	.15	.07		371	John Jaha	.15	.07
200	Javier Lopez	.30	.14		286	Jeff Montgomery	.15	.07		372	Steve Howe	.15	.07
201	Miguel Jimenez	.15	.07		287	Ryan Thompson	.15	.07		373	Leo Gomez	.15	.07
202	Terry McGriff	.15	.07		288	Paul Shuey	.15	.07		374	Hector Fajardo	.15	.07
203	Mike Lieberthal	.15	.07		289	Mark McGwire	3.00	1.35		375	Jeff Bagwell	.75	.35

376	Mark Acre	.15	.07
377	Wayne Kirby	.15	.07
378	Mark Portugal	.15	.07
379	Jesus Tavarez	.15	.07
380	Jim Lindeman	.15	.07
381	Don Mattingly	1.25	.55
382	Trevor Hoffman	.30	.14
383	Chris Gomez	.15	.07
384	Garret Anderson	.30	.14
385	Bobby Munoz	.15	.07
386	Jon Lieber	.15	.07
387	Rick Helling	.30	.14
388	Marvin Freeman	.15	.07
389	Juan Castillo	.15	.07
390	Jeff Cirillo	.30	.14
391	Sean Berry	.15	.07
392	Hector Carrasco	.15	.07
393	Mark Grace	.40	.18
394	Pat Kelly	.15	.07
395	Tim Naehring	.15	.07
396	Greg Pirkl	.15	.07
397	John Smoltz	.40	.18
398	Robby Thompson	.15	.07
399	Rick White	.15	.07
400	Frank Thomas	1.25	.55
401	Jeff Conine CS	.15	.07
402	Jose Valentin CS	.15	.07
403	Carlos Baerga CS	.15	.07
404	Rick Aguilera CS	.15	.07
405	Wilson Alvarez CS	.15	.07
406	Juan Gonzalez CS	.60	.25
407	Barry Larkin CS	.30	.14
408	Ken Hill CS	.15	.07
409	Chuck Carr CS	.15	.07
410	Tim Raines CS	.15	.07
411	Bryan Eversgerd	.15	.07
412	Phil Plantier	.15	.07
413	Josias Manzanillo	.15	.07
414	Roberto Kelly	.15	.07
415	Rickey Henderson	.75	.35
416	John Smiley	.15	.07
417	Kevin Brown	.40	.18
418	Jimmy Key	.30	.14
419	Wally Joyner	.15	.07
420	Roberto Hernandez	.15	.07
421	Felix Fermin	.15	.07
422	Checklist	.15	.07
423	Greg Vaughn	.30	.14
424	Ray Lankford	.30	.14
425	Greg Maddux	1.50	.70
426	Mike Mussina	.60	.25
427	Geronimo Pena	.15	.07
428	David Nied	.15	.07
429	Scott Erickson	.30	.14
430	Kevin Mitchell	.15	.07
431	Mike Lansing	.30	.14
432	Brian Anderson	.30	.14
433	Jeff King	.15	.07
434	Ramon Martinez	.30	.14
435	Kevin Seitzer	.15	.07
436	Salomon Torres	.15	.07
437	Brian L.Hunter	.30	.14
438	Melvin Nieves	.15	.07
439	Mike Kelly	.15	.07
440	Marquis Grissom	.30	.14
441	Chuck Finley	.30	.14
442	Len Dykstra	.15	.07
443	Ellis Burks	.30	.14
444	Harold Baines	.30	.14
445	Kevin Appier	.30	.14
446	David Justice	.60	.25
447	Darryl Kile	.15	.07
448	John Olerud	.30	.14
449	Greg McMichael	.15	.07
450	Kirby Puckett	1.00	.45
451	Jose Valentin	.15	.07
452	Rick Wilkins	.15	.07
453	Arthur Rhodes	.15	.07
454	Pat Hentgen	.30	.14
455	Tom Gordon	.15	.07
456	Tom Candiotti	.15	.07
457	Jason Bere	.15	.07
458	Wes Chamberlain	.15	.07
459	Greg Colbrunn	.15	.07
460	John Doherty	.15	.07
461	Kevin Foster	.15	.07
462	Mark Whiten	.15	.07
463	Terry Steinbach	.15	.07
464	Aaron Sele	.30	.14
465	Kirt Manwaring	.15	.07
466	Darren Hall	.15	.07
467	Delino DeShields	.15	.07
468	Andujar Cedeno	.15	.07
469	Billy Ashley	.15	.07
470	Kenny Lofton	.40	.18
471	Pedro Munoz	.15	.07
472	John Wetteland	.30	.14
473	Tim Salmon	.60	.25
474	Denny Neagle	.30	.14
475	Tony Gwynn	1.50	.70
476	Vinny Castilla	.40	.18
477	Steve Dreyer	.15	.07
478	Jeff Shaw	.15	.07
479	Chad Ogea	.15	.07
480	Scott Ruffcorn	.15	.07
481	Lou Whitaker	.30	.14
482	J.T. Snow	.30	.14
483	Rich Rowland	.15	.07
484	Denny Martinez	.30	.14
485	Pedro Martinez	.75	.35
486	Rusty Greer	.60	.25
487	Dave Fleming	.15	.07
488	John Dettmer	.15	.07
489	Albert Belle	.60	.25
490	Ravelo Manzanillo	.15	.07
491	Henry Rodriguez	.30	.14
492	Andrew Lorraine	.15	.07
493	Dwayne Hosey	.15	.07
494	Mike Blowers	.15	.07
495	Turner Ward	.15	.07
496	Fred McGriff EC	.15	.07
497	Sammy Sosa EC	1.00	.45
498	Barry Larkin EC	.30	.14
499	Andres Galarraga EC	.60	.25
500	Gary Sheffield EC	.15	.07
501	Jeff Bagwell EC	.60	.25
502	Mike Piazza EC	1.00	.45
503	Moises Alou EC	.15	.07
504	Bobby Bonilla EC	.15	.07
505	Darren Daulton EC	.15	.07
506	Jeff King EC	.15	.07
507	Ray Lankford EC	.15	.07
508	Tony Gwynn EC	.75	.35
509	Barry Bonds EC	.40	.18
510	Cal Ripken EC	1.25	.55
511	Mo Vaughn EC	.40	.18
512	Tim Salmon EC	.30	.14
513	Frank Thomas EC	.60	.25
514	Albert Belle EC	.30	.14
515	Cecil Fielder EC	.15	.07
516	Kevin Appier EC	.15	.07
517	Greg Vaughn EC	.15	.07
518	Kirby Puckett EC	.60	.25
519	Paul O'Neill EC	.15	.07
520	Ruben Sierra EC	.15	.07
521	Ken Griffey Jr. EC	1.50	.70
522	Will Clark EC	.30	.14
523	Joe Carter EC	.15	.07
524	Antonio Osuna	.15	.07
525	Glenallen Hill	.15	.07
526	Alex Gonzalez	.15	.07
527	Dave Stewart	.30	.14
528	Ron Gant	.30	.14
529	Jason Bates	.15	.07
530	Mike Macfarlane	.15	.07
531	Esteban Loaiza	.15	.07
532	Joe Randa	.15	.07
533	Dave Winfield	.60	.25
534	Danny Darwin	.15	.07
535	Pete Harnisch	.15	.07
536	Joey Cora	.15	.07
537	Jaime Navarro	.15	.07
538	Marty Cordova	.15	.07
539	Andujar Cedeno	.15	.07
540	Mickey Tettleton	.15	.07
541	Andy Van Slyke	.30	.14
542	Carlos Perez	.30	.14
543	Chipper Jones	1.50	.70
544	Tony Fernandez	.30	.14
545	Tom Henke	.15	.07
546	Pat Borders	.15	.07
547	Chad Curtis	.15	.07
548	Ray Durham	.30	.14
549	Joe Oliver	.15	.07
550	Jose Mesa	.15	.07
551	Steve Finley	.30	.14
552	Otis Nixon	.15	.07
553	Jacob Brumfield	.15	.07
554	Bill Swift	.15	.07
555	Quilvio Veras	.15	.07
556	Hideo Nomo UER	1.50	.70
	Wins and IP totals reversed		
557	Joe Vitiello	.15	.07
558	Mike Perez	.15	.07
559	Charlie Hayes	.15	.07
560	Brad Radke	1.00	.45
561	Darren Bragg	.15	.07
562	Orel Hershiser	.30	.14
563	Edgardo Alfonzo	.60	.25
564	Doug Jones	.15	.07
565	Andy Pettitte	.60	.25
566	Benito Santiago	.15	.07
567	John Burkett	.15	.07
568	Brad Clontz	.15	.07
569	Jim Abbott	.30	.14
570	Joe Rosselli	.15	.07
571	Mark Grudzielanek	.40	.18
572	Dustin Hermanson	.15	.07
573	Benji Gil	.15	.07
574	Mark Whiten	.15	.07
575	Mike Ignasiak	.15	.07
576	Kevin Ritz	.15	.07
577	Paul Quantrill	.15	.07
578	Andre Dawson	.40	.18
579	Jerald Clark	.15	.07
580	Frank Rodriguez	.15	.07
581	Mark Kiefer	.15	.07
582	Trevor Wilson	.15	.07
583	Gary Wilson	.15	.07
584	Andy Stankiewicz	.15	.07
585	Felipe Lira	.15	.07
586	Mike Mimbs	.15	.07
587	Jon Nunnally	.15	.07
588	Tomas Perez	.30	.14
589	Checklist	.15	.07
590	Todd Hollandsworth	.15	.07
591	Roberto Petagine	.15	.07
592	Mariano Rivera	.60	.25
593	Mark McLemore	.15	.07
594	Bobby Witt	.15	.07
595	Jose Offerman	.30	.14
596	Jason Christiansen	.15	.07
597	Jeff Manto	.15	.07
598	Jim Dougherty	.15	.07
599	Juan Acevedo	.15	.07
600	Troy O'Leary	.30	.14
601	Ron Villone	.15	.07
602	Tripp Cromer	.15	.07
603	Steve Scarsone	.15	.07
604	Lance Parrish	.15	.07
605	Ozzie Timmons	.15	.07
606	Ray Holbert	.15	.07
607	Tony Phillips	.15	.07
608	Phil Plantier	.15	.07
609	Shane Andrews	.15	.07
610	Heathcliff Slocumb	.15	.07
611	Bobby Higginson	1.00	.45
612	Bob Tewksbury	.15	.07
613	Terry Pendleton	.15	.07
614	Scott Cooper TA	.15	.07
615	John Wetteland TA	.15	.07
616	Ken Hill TA	.15	.07
617	Marquis Grissom TA	.15	.07
618	Larry Walker TA	.30	.14
619	Derek Bell TA	.15	.07
620	David Cone TA	.15	.07
621	Ken Caminiti TA	.15	.07
622	Jack McDowell TA	.15	.07
623	Vaughn Eshelman TA	.15	.07
624	Brian McRae TA	.15	.07
625	Gregg Jefferies TA	.15	.07
626	Kevin Brown TA	.15	.07
627	Lee Smith TA	.15	.07
628	Tony Tarasco TA	.15	.07
629	Brett Butler TA	.15	.07
630	Jose Canseco TA	.30	.14

1995 Stadium Club Clear Cut

	MINT	NRMT
COMPLETE SET (28)	80.00	36.00
COMPLETE SERIES 1 (14)	40.00	18.00
COMPLETE SERIES 2 (14)	40.00	18.00
COMMON CARD (CC1-CC28)	1.50	.70
STATED ODDS 1:24 HOB/RET,1:10 RACK		

		MINT	NRMT
❏ CC1	Mike Piazza	15.00	6.75
❏ CC2	Ruben Sierra	1.50	.70
❏ CC3	Tony Gwynn	12.00	5.50
❏ CC4	Frank Thomas	10.00	4.50
❏ CC5	Fred McGriff	4.00	1.80
❏ CC6	Rafael Palmeiro	5.00	2.20
❏ CC7	Bobby Bonilla	2.50	1.10
❏ CC8	Chili Davis	2.50	1.10
❏ CC9	Hal Morris	1.50	.70
❏ CC10	Jose Canseco	6.00	2.70
❏ CC11	Jay Bell	2.50	1.10
❏ CC12	Kirby Puckett	8.00	3.60
❏ CC13	Gary Sheffield	2.50	1.10
❏ CC14	Bob Hamelin	1.50	.70
❏ CC15	Jeff Bagwell	6.00	2.70
❏ CC16	Albert Belle	5.00	2.20
❏ CC17	Sammy Sosa	15.00	6.75
❏ CC18	Ken Griffey Jr.	25.00	11.00
❏ CC19	Todd Zeile	1.50	.70
❏ CC20	Mo Vaughn	5.00	2.20
❏ CC21	Moises Alou	2.50	1.10
❏ CC22	Paul O'Neill	2.50	1.10
❏ CC23	Andres Galarraga	5.00	2.20
❏ CC24	Greg Vaughn	2.50	1.10
❏ CC25	Len Dykstra	2.50	1.10
❏ CC26	Joe Carter	2.50	1.10
❏ CC27	Barry Bonds	6.00	2.70
❏ CC28	Cecil Fielder	2.50	1.10

1995 Stadium Club Crunch Time

	MINT	NRMT
COMPLETE SET (20)	40.00	18.00
COMMON CARD (1-20)	.50	.23
ONE PER SER.1 RACK PACK		

		MINT	NRMT
❏ 1	Jeff Bagwell	2.50	1.10
❏ 2	Kirby Puckett	2.00	.90
❏ 3	Frank Thomas	4.00	1.80

		MINT	NRMT
❏ 4	Albert Belle	2.00	.90
❏ 5	Julio Franco	.50	.23
❏ 6	Jose Canseco	2.50	1.10
❏ 7	Paul Molitor	2.00	.90
❏ 8	Joe Carter	1.00	.45
❏ 9	Ken Griffey Jr.	10.00	4.50
❏ 10	Larry Walker	2.00	.90
❏ 11	Dante Bichette	1.00	.45
❏ 12	Carlos Baerga	.50	.23
❏ 13	Fred McGriff	1.50	.70
❏ 14	Ruben Sierra	.50	.23
❏ 15	Will Clark	2.00	.90
❏ 16	Moises Alou	1.00	.45
❏ 17	Rafael Palmeiro	2.00	.90
❏ 18	Travis Fryman	1.00	.45
❏ 19	Barry Bonds	2.00	.90
❏ 20	Cal Ripken	8.00	3.60

1995 Stadium Club Crystal Ball

	MINT	NRMT
COMPLETE SET (15)	60.00	27.00
COMMON CARD (CB1-CB15)	2.00	.90
MINOR STARS	4.00	1.80
SER.3 STATED ODDS 1:24		

		MINT	NRMT
❏ CB1	Chipper Jones	25.00	11.00
❏ CB2	Dustin Hermanson	2.00	.90
❏ CB3	Ray Durham	4.00	1.80
❏ CB4	Phil Nevin	2.00	.90
❏ CB5	Billy Ashley	2.00	.90
❏ CB6	Shawn Green	10.00	4.50
❏ CB7	Jason Bates	2.00	.90
❏ CB8	Benji Gil	2.00	.90
❏ CB9	Marty Cordova	2.00	.90
❏ CB10	Quilvio Veras	2.00	.90
❏ CB11	Mark Grudzielanek	4.00	1.80
❏ CB12	Ruben Rivera	4.00	1.80
❏ CB13	Bill Pulsipher	2.00	.90
❏ CB14	Derek Jeter	30.00	13.50
❏ CB15	LaTroy Hawkins	2.00	.90

1995 Stadium Club Power Zone

	MINT	NRMT
COMPLETE SET (12)	80.00	36.00
COMMON CARD (PZ1-PZ12)	2.50	1.10
SER.3 STATED ODDS 1:24		

		MINT	NRMT
❏ PZ1	Jeff Bagwell	8.00	3.60
❏ PZ2	Albert Belle	6.00	2.70
❏ PZ3	Barry Bonds	8.00	3.60
❏ PZ4	Joe Carter	2.50	1.10
❏ PZ5	Cecil Fielder	2.50	1.10
❏ PZ6	Andres Galarraga	6.00	2.70
❏ PZ7	Ken Griffey Jr.	30.00	13.50
❏ PZ8	Paul Molitor	6.00	2.70
❏ PZ9	Fred McGriff	4.00	1.80
❏ PZ10	Rafael Palmeiro	6.00	2.70
❏ PZ11	Frank Thomas	12.00	5.50
❏ PZ12	Matt Williams	6.00	2.70

1995 Stadium Club Ring Leaders

	MINT	NRMT
COMPLETE SET (40)	160.00	70.00
COMPLETE SERIES 1 (20)	80.00	36.00
COMPLETE SERIES 2 (20)	80.00	36.00
COMMON CARD (RL1-RL40)	1.50	.70
STATED ODDS 1:24 HOB/RET,1:10 RACK		
ONE SET VIA MAIL PER PHONE WINNER		

		MINT	NRMT
❏ RL1	Jeff Bagwell	8.00	3.60
❏ RL2	Mark McGwire	30.00	13.50
❏ RL3	Ozzie Smith	10.00	4.50
❏ RL4	Paul Molitor	6.00	2.70
❏ RL5	Darryl Strawberry	2.50	1.10
❏ RL6	Eddie Murray	6.00	2.70
❏ RL7	Tony Gwynn	15.00	6.75
❏ RL8	Jose Canseco	8.00	3.60
❏ RL9	Howard Johnson	1.50	.70
❏ RL10	Andre Dawson	4.00	1.80
❏ RL11	Matt Williams	6.00	2.70
❏ RL12	Tim Raines	2.50	1.10
❏ RL13	Fred McGriff	4.00	1.80
❏ RL14	Ken Griffey Jr.	30.00	13.50
❏ RL15	Gary Sheffield	2.50	1.10
❏ RL16	Dennis Eckersley	2.50	1.10
❏ RL17	Kevin Mitchell	1.50	.70
❏ RL18	Will Clark	6.00	2.70
❏ RL19	Darren Daulton	2.50	1.10
❏ RL20	Paul O'Neill	2.50	1.10
❏ RL21	Julio Franco	1.50	.70
❏ RL22	Albert Belle	6.00	2.70
❏ RL23	Juan Gonzalez	12.00	5.50
❏ RL24	Kirby Puckett	10.00	4.50
❏ RL25	Joe Carter	2.50	1.10
❏ RL26	Frank Thomas	12.00	5.50
❏ RL27	Cal Ripken	25.00	11.00
❏ RL28	John Olerud	2.50	1.10
❏ RL29	Ruben Sierra	1.50	.70
❏ RL30	Barry Bonds	8.00	3.60
❏ RL31	Cecil Fielder	2.50	1.10
❏ RL32	Roger Clemens	15.00	6.75
❏ RL33	Don Mattingly	12.00	5.50
❏ RL34	Terry Pendleton	1.50	.70
❏ RL35	Rickey Henderson	8.00	3.60
❏ RL36	Dave Sheffield	6.00	2.70
❏ RL37	Edgar Martinez	2.50	1.10
❏ RL38	Wade Boggs	6.00	2.70
❏ RL39	Willie McGee	2.50	1.10
❏ RL40	Andres Galarraga	6.00	2.70

1995 Stadium Club Super Skills

	MINT	NRMT
COMPLETE SET (20)	70.00	32.00
COMPLETE SERIES 1 (9)	30.00	13.50
COMPLETE SERIES 2 (11)	40.00	18.00
COMMON CARD (SS1-SS20)	1.50	.70
STATED ODDS 1:24 HOBBY		

		MINT	NRMT
❏ SS1	Roberto Alomar	5.00	2.20
❏ SS2	Barry Bonds	6.00	2.70
❏ SS3	Jay Buhner	2.50	1.10
❏ SS4	Chuck Carr	1.50	.70
❏ SS5	Don Mattingly	10.00	4.50
❏ SS6	Raul Mondesi	4.00	1.80
❏ SS7	Tim Salmon	5.00	2.20
❏ SS8	Deion Sanders	2.50	1.10
❏ SS9	Devon White	2.50	1.10
❏ SS10	Mark Whiten	1.50	.70
❏ SS11	Ken Griffey Jr.	25.00	11.00
❏ SS12	Marquis Grissom	2.50	1.10
❏ SS13	Paul O'Neill	2.50	1.10
❏ SS14	Kenny Lofton	4.00	1.80
❏ SS15	Larry Walker	5.00	2.20
❏ SS16	Scott Cooper	1.50	.70
❏ SS17	Barry Larkin	5.00	2.20
❏ SS18	Matt Williams	5.00	2.20
❏ SS19	John Wetteland	2.50	1.10
❏ SS20	Randy Johnson	5.00	2.20

1995 Stadium Club Virtual Extremists

	MINT	NRMT
COMPLETE SET (10)	120.00	55.00
COMMON CARD (VRE1-VRE10)	2.50	1.10
SER.2 STATED ODDS 1:10 RACK		

		MINT	NRMT
❏ VRE1	Barry Bonds	8.00	3.60
❏ VRE2	Ken Griffey Jr.	40.00	18.00
❏ VRE3	Jeff Bagwell	8.00	3.60
❏ VRE4	Albert Belle	8.00	3.60
❏ VRE5	Frank Thomas	20.00	9.00
❏ VRE6	Tony Gwynn	20.00	9.00
❏ VRE7	Kenny Lofton	5.00	2.20
❏ VRE8	Deion Sanders	4.00	1.80
❏ VRE9	Ken Hill	2.50	1.10
❏ VRE10	Jimmy Key	4.00	1.80

1996 Stadium Club

	MINT	NRMT
COMPLETE SET (450)	80.00	36.00
COMP.CEREAL SET (454)	80.00	36.00
COMPLETE SERIES 1 (225)	40.00	18.00
COMPLETE SERIES 2 (225)	40.00	18.00
COMMON (1-180/271-450)	.15	.07
MINOR STARS	.30	.14
UNLISTED STARS	.60	.25
COMMON TSC SP (181-270)	.25	.11
TSC SP SEMISTARS	.50	.23
TSC SP UNLISTED STARS	.75	.35

		MINT	NRMT
❏ 1	Hideo Nomo	.60	.25
❏ 2	Paul Molitor	.60	.25
❏ 3	Garret Anderson	.30	.14
❏ 4	Jose Mesa	.15	.07
❏ 5	Vinny Castilla	.40	.18
❏ 6	Mike Mussina	.60	.25
❏ 7	Ray Durham	.30	.14
❏ 8	Jack McDowell	.15	.07
❏ 9	Juan Gonzalez	1.25	.55
❏ 10	Chipper Jones	1.50	.70
❏ 11	Deion Sanders	.30	.14
❏ 12	Rondell White	.30	.14
❏ 13	Tom Henke	.15	.07
❏ 14	Derek Bell	.30	.14
❏ 15	Randy Myers	.15	.07
❏ 16	Randy Johnson	.60	.25
❏ 17	Len Dykstra	.30	.14
❏ 18	Bill Pulsipher	.15	.07
❏ 19	Greg Colbrunn	.15	.07
❏ 20	David Wells	.40	.18
❏ 21	Chad Curtis	.15	.07
❏ 22	Roberto Hernandez	.15	.07
❏ 23	Kirby Puckett	1.00	.45
❏ 24	Joe Vitiello	.15	.07
❏ 25	Roger Clemens	1.50	.70
❏ 26	Al Martin	.15	.07
❏ 27	Chad Ogea	.15	.07
❏ 28	David Segui	.30	.14
❏ 29	Joey Hamilton	.15	.07
❏ 30	Dan Wilson	.15	.07
❏ 31	Chad Fonville	.15	.07
❏ 32	Bernard Gilkey	.15	.07
❏ 33	Kevin Seitzer	.15	.07
❏ 34	Shawn Green	.60	.25
❏ 35	Rick Aguilera	.15	.07
❏ 36	Gary DiSarcina	.15	.07
❏ 37	Jaime Navarro	.15	.07
❏ 38	Doug Jones	.15	.07
❏ 39	Brent Gates	.15	.07
❏ 40	Dean Palmer	.30	.14
❏ 41	Pat Rapp	.15	.07
❏ 42	Tony Clark	.60	.25
❏ 43	Bill Swift	.15	.07
❏ 44	Randy Velarde	.15	.07
❏ 45	Matt Williams	.60	.25
❏ 46	John Mabry	.15	.07
❏ 47	Mike Fetters	.15	.07
❏ 48	Orlando Miller	.15	.07
❏ 49	Tom Glavine	.60	.25
❏ 50	Delino DeShields	.15	.07
❏ 51	Scott Erickson	.30	.14
❏ 52	Andy Van Slyke	.30	.14
❏ 53	Jim Bullinger	.15	.07
❏ 54	Lyle Mouton	.15	.07

		MINT	NRMT
❏ 55	Bret Saberhagen	.30	.14
❏ 56	Benito Santiago	.15	.07
❏ 57	Dan Miceli	.15	.07
❏ 58	Carl Everett	.30	.14
❏ 59	Rod Beck	.15	.07
❏ 60	Phil Nevin	.30	.14
❏ 61	Jason Giambi	.30	.14
❏ 62	Paul Menhart	.15	.07
❏ 63	Eric Karros	.30	.14
❏ 64	Allen Watson	.15	.07
❏ 65	Jeff Cirillo	.30	.14
❏ 66	Lee Smith	.30	.14
❏ 67	Sean Berry	.15	.07
❏ 68	Luis Sojo	.15	.07
❏ 69	Jeff Montgomery	.15	.07
❏ 70	Todd Hundley	.30	.14
❏ 71	John Burkett	.15	.07
❏ 72	Mark Gubicza	.15	.07
❏ 73	Don Mattingly	1.25	.55
❏ 74	Jeff Brantley	.15	.07
❏ 75	Matt Walbeck	.15	.07
❏ 76	Steve Parris	.15	.07
❏ 77	Ken Caminiti	.30	.14
❏ 78	Kirt Manwaring	.15	.07
❏ 79	Greg Vaughn	.30	.14
❏ 80	Pedro Martinez	.75	.35
❏ 81	Benji Gil	.15	.07
❏ 82	Heathcliff Slocumb	.15	.07
❏ 83	Joe Girardi	.15	.07
❏ 84	Sean Bergman	.15	.07
❏ 85	Matt Karchner	.15	.07
❏ 86	Butch Huskey	.15	.07
❏ 87	Mike Morgan	.15	.07
❏ 88	Todd Worrell	.15	.07
❏ 89	Mike Bordick	.15	.07
❏ 90	Bip Roberts	.15	.07
❏ 91	Mike Hampton	.30	.14
❏ 92	Troy O'Leary	.15	.07
❏ 93	Wally Joyner	.30	.14
❏ 94	Steve Stevens	.15	.07
❏ 95	Cecil Fielder	.30	.14
❏ 96	Wade Boggs	.60	.25
❏ 97	Hal Morris	.15	.07
❏ 98	Mickey Tettleton	.15	.07
❏ 99	Jeff Kent	.15	.07
❏ 100	Denny Martinez	.30	.14
❏ 101	Luis Gonzalez	.30	.14
❏ 102	John Jaha	.15	.07
❏ 103	Javier Lopez	.30	.14
❏ 104	Mark McGwire	3.00	1.35
❏ 105	Ken Griffey Jr.	3.00	1.35
❏ 106	Darren Daulton	.30	.14
❏ 107	Bryan Rekar	.15	.07
❏ 108	Mike Macfarlane	.15	.07
❏ 109	Gary Gaetti	.30	.14
❏ 110	Shane Reynolds	.15	.07
❏ 111	Pat Meares	.15	.07
❏ 112	Jason Schmidt	.15	.07
❏ 113	Otis Nixon	.15	.07
❏ 114	John Franco	.30	.14
❏ 115	Marc Newfield	.15	.07
❏ 116	Andy Benes	.30	.14
❏ 117	Ozzie Guillen	.15	.07
❏ 118	Brian Jordan	.30	.14
❏ 119	Terry Pendleton	.15	.07
❏ 120	Chuck Finley	.30	.14
❏ 121	Scott Stahoviak	.15	.07
❏ 122	Sid Fernandez	.15	.07
❏ 123	Derek Jeter	2.00	.90
❏ 124	John Smiley	.15	.07
❏ 125	David Bell	.15	.07
❏ 126	Brett Butler	.30	.14
❏ 127	Doug Drabek	.15	.07
❏ 128	J.T. Snow	.30	.14
❏ 129	Joe Carter	.30	.14
❏ 130	Dennis Eckersley	.30	.14
❏ 131	Marty Cordova	.30	.14
❏ 132	Greg Maddux	1.50	.70
❏ 133	Tom Goodwin	.15	.07
❏ 134	Andy Ashby	.15	.07
❏ 135	Paul Sorrento	.15	.07
❏ 136	Ricky Bones	.15	.07
❏ 137	Shawon Dunston	.15	.07
❏ 138	Moises Alou	.30	.14
❏ 139	Mickey Morandini	.15	.07
❏ 140	Ramon Martinez	.30	.14

141	Royce Clayton	.15	.07
142	Brad Ausmus	.15	.07
143	Kenny Rogers	.15	.07
144	Tim Naehring	.15	.07
145	Chris Gomez	.15	.07
146	Bobby Bonilla	.30	.14
147	Wilson Alvarez	.15	.07
148	Johnny Damon	.40	.18
149	Pat Hentgen	.30	.14
150	Andres Galarraga	.60	.25
151	David Cone	.40	.18
152	Lance Johnson	.15	.07
153	Carlos Garcia	.15	.07
154	Doug Johns	.15	.07
155	Midre Cummings	.15	.07
156	Steve Sparks	.15	.07
157	Sandy Martinez	.15	.07
158	Wm. Van Landingham	.15	.07
159	David Justice	.60	.25
160	Mark Grace	.40	.18
161	Robb Nen	.15	.07
162	Mike Greenwell	.15	.07
163	Brad Radke	.30	.14
164	Edgardo Alfonzo	.60	.25
165	Mark Leiter	.15	.07
166	Walt Weiss	.15	.07
167	Mel Rojas	.15	.07
168	Bret Boone	.30	.14
169	Ricky Bottalico	.15	.07
170	Bobby Higginson	.30	.14
171	Trevor Hoffman	.30	.14
172	Jay Bell	.30	.14
173	Gabe White	.15	.07
174	Curtis Goodwin	.15	.07
175	Tyler Green	.15	.07
176	Roberto Alomar	.60	.25
177	Sterling Hitchcock	.15	.07
178	Ryan Klesko	.30	.14
179	Donne Wall	.15	.07
180	Brian McRae	.15	.07
181	Will Clark TSC SP	.75	.35
182	Frank Thomas TSC SP	1.50	.70
183	Jeff Bagwell TSC SP	1.00	.45
184	Mo Vaughn TSC SP	.75	.35
185	Tino Martinez TSC SP	.40	.18
186	Craig Biggio TSC SP	.75	.35
187	C. Knoblauch TSC SP	.75	.35
188	Carlos Baerga TSC SP	.25	.11
189	Quilvio Veras TSC SP	.25	.11
190	Luis Alicea TSC SP	.25	.11
191	Jim Thome TSC SP	.75	.35
192	Mike Blowers TSC SP	.25	.11
193	Robin Ventura TSC SP	.40	.18
194	Jeff King TSC SP	.25	.11
195	Tony Phillips TSC SP	.25	.11
196	John Valentin TSC SP	.40	.18
197	Barry Larkin TSC SP	.75	.35
198	Cal Ripken TSC SP	3.00	1.35
199	Omar Vizquel TSC SP	.40	.18
200	Kurt Abbott TSC SP	.25	.11
201	Albert Belle TSC SP	.40	.18
202	Barry Bonds TSC SP	1.00	.45
203	Ron Gant TSC SP	.25	.11
204	Dante Bichette TSC SP	.40	.18
205	Jeff Conine TSC SP	.40	.18
206	Jim Edmonds TSC SP UER	.50	.23
	Greg Myers pictured on front		
207	Stan Javier TSC SP	.25	.11
208	Kenny Lofton TSC SP	.50	.23
209	Ray Lankford TSC SP	.40	.18
210	Bernie Williams TSC SP	.75	.35
211	Jay Buhner TSC SP	.40	.18
212	Paul O'Neill TSC SP	.40	.18
213	Tim Salmon TSC SP	.50	.23
214	Reggie Sanders TSC SP	.40	.18
215	Manny Ramirez TSC SP	1.00	.45
216	Mike Piazza TSC SP	2.50	1.10
217	Mike Stanley TSC SP	.25	.11
218	Tony Eusebio TSC SP	.25	.11
219	Chris Hoiles TSC SP	.25	.11
220	Ron Karkovice TSC SP	.25	.11
221	Edgar Martinez TSC SP	.40	.18
222	Chili Davis TSC SP	.40	.18
223	Jose Canseco TSC SP	1.00	.45
224	Eddie Murray TSC SP	.75	.35
225	Geronimo Berroa TSC SP	.25	.11
226	Chipper Jones TSC SP	2.00	.90
227	Garret Anderson TSC SP	.40	.18
228	Marty Cordova TSC SP	.25	.11
229	Jon Nunnally TSC SP	.25	.11
230	Brian L. Hunter TSC SP	.25	.11
231	Shawn Green TSC SP	.75	.35
232	Ray Durham TSC SP	.40	.18
233	Alex Gonzalez TSC SP	.25	.11
234	Bobby Higginson TSC SP	.40	.18
235	Randy Johnson TSC SP	.75	.35
236	Al Leiter TSC SP	.40	.18
237	Tom Glavine TSC SP	.75	.35
238	Kenny Rogers TSC SP	.25	.11
239	Mike Hampton TSC SP	.40	.18
240	David Wells TSC SP	.50	.23
241	Jim Abbott TSC SP	.40	.18
242	Denny Neagle TSC SP	.40	.18
243	Wilson Alvarez TSC SP	.25	.11
244	John Smiley TSC SP	.25	.11
245	Greg Maddux TSC SP	2.00	.90
246	Andy Ashby TSC SP	.25	.11
247	Hideo Nomo TSC SP	.75	.35
248	Pat Rapp TSC SP	.25	.11
249	Tim Wakefield TSC SP	.25	.11
250	John Smoltz TSC SP	.50	.23
251	Joey Hamilton TSC SP	.25	.11
252	Frank Castillo TSC SP	.25	.11
253	Denny Martinez TSC SP	.40	.18
254	Jaime Navarro TSC SP	.25	.11
255	Karim Garcia TSC SP	.40	.18
256	Bob Abreu TSC SP	.50	.23
257	Butch Huskey TSC SP	.25	.11
258	Ruben Rivera TSC SP	.40	.18
259	Johnny Damon TSC SP	.50	.23
260	Derek Jeter TSC SP	2.50	1.10
261	D. Eckersley TSC SP	.40	.18
262	Jose Mesa TSC SP	.25	.11
263	Tom Henke TSC SP	.25	.11
264	Rick Aguilera TSC SP	.25	.11
265	Randy Myers TSC SP	.25	.11
266	John Franco TSC SP	.40	.18
267	Jeff Brantley TSC SP	.25	.11
268	John Wetteland TSC SP	.40	.18
269	Mark Wohlers TSC SP	.25	.11
270	Rod Beck TSC SP	.25	.11
271	Barry Larkin	.40	.25
272	Paul O'Neill	.30	.14
273	Bobby Jones	.15	.07
274	Will Clark	.60	.25
275	Steve Avery	.15	.07
276	Jim Edmonds	.40	.18
277	John Olerud	.30	.14
278	Carlos Perez	.15	.07
279	Chris Hoiles	.15	.07
280	Jeff Conine	.15	.07
281	Jim Eisenreich	.15	.07
282	Jason Jacome	.15	.07
283	Ray Lankford	.30	.14
284	John Wasdin	.15	.07
285	Frank Thomas	1.25	.55
286	Jason Isringhausen	.30	.14
287	Glenallen Hill	.15	.07
288	Esteban Loaiza	.15	.07
289	Bernie Williams	.60	.25
290	Curtis Leskanic	.15	.07
291	Scott Cooper	.15	.07
292	Curt Schilling	.40	.18
293	Eddie Murray	.60	.25
294	Rick Krivda	.15	.07
295	Domingo Cedeno	.15	.07
296	Jeff Fassero	.15	.07
297	Albert Belle	.60	.25
298	Craig Biggio	.60	.25
299	Fernando Vina	.15	.07
300	Edgar Martinez	.30	.14
301	Tony Gwynn	1.50	.70
302	Felipe Lira	.15	.07
303	Mo Vaughn	.60	.25
304	Alex Fernandez	.15	.07
305	Keith Lockhart	.15	.07
306	Roger Pavlik	.15	.07
307	Lee Tinsley	.15	.07
308	Omar Vizquel	.30	.14
309	Scott Servais	.15	.07
310	Danny Tartabull	.15	.07
311	Chili Davis	.30	.14
312	Cal Eldred	.15	.07
313	Roger Cedeno	.30	.14
314	Chris Hammond	.15	.07
315	Rusty Greer	.30	.14
316	Brady Anderson	.30	.14
317	Ron Villone	.15	.07
318	Mark Carreon	.15	.07
319	Larry Walker	.60	.25
320	Pete Harnisch	.15	.07
321	Robin Ventura	.30	.14
322	Tim Belcher	.15	.07
323	Tony Tarasco	.15	.07
324	Juan Guzman	.15	.07
325	Kenny Lofton	.40	.18
326	Kevin Foster	.15	.07
327	Wil Cordero	.15	.07
328	Troy Percival	.30	.14
329	Turk Wendell	.15	.07
330	Thomas Howard	.15	.07
331	Carlos Baerga	.15	.07
332	B.J. Surhoff	.30	.14
333	Jay Buhner	.30	.14
334	Andujar Cedeno	.15	.07
335	Jeff King	.15	.07
336	Dante Bichette	.30	.14
337	Alan Trammell	.40	.18
338	Scott Leius	.15	.07
339	Chris Snopek	.15	.07
340	Roger Bailey	.15	.07
341	Jacob Brumfield	.15	.07
342	Jose Canseco	.75	.35
343	Rafael Palmeiro	.60	.25
344	Quilvio Veras	.15	.07
345	Darrin Fletcher	.15	.07
346	Carlos Delgado	.60	.25
347	Tony Eusebio	.15	.07
348	Ismael Valdes	.30	.14
349	Terry Steinbach	.15	.07
350	Orel Hershiser	.30	.14
351	Kurt Abbott	.15	.07
352	Jody Reed	.15	.07
353	David Howard	.15	.07
354	Ruben Sierra	.30	.14
355	John Ericks	.15	.07
356	Buck Showalter MG	.15	.07
357	Jim Thome	.60	.25
358	Geronimo Berroa	.15	.07
359	Robby Thompson	.15	.07
360	Jose Vizcaino	.15	.07
361	Jeff Frye	.15	.07
362	Kevin Appier	.30	.14
363	Pat Kelly	.15	.07
364	Ron Gant	.30	.14
365	Luis Alicea	.15	.07
366	Armando Benitez	.15	.07
367	Rico Brogna	.15	.07
368	Manny Ramirez	.75	.35
369	Mike Lansing	.15	.07
370	Sammy Sosa	2.00	.90
371	Don Wengert	.15	.07
372	Dave Nilsson	.15	.07
373	Sandy Alomar Jr.	.30	.14
374	Joey Cora	.15	.07
375	Larry Thomas	.15	.07
376	John Valentin	.30	.14
377	Kevin Ritz	.15	.07
378	Steve Finley	.30	.14
379	Frank Rodriguez	.15	.07
380	Ivan Rodriguez	.75	.35
381	Alex Ochoa	.15	.07
382	Mark Lemke	.15	.07
383	Scott Brosius	.30	.14
384	James Hanson	.15	.07
385	Mark Langston	.15	.07
386	Ed Sprague	.15	.07
387	Joe Oliver	.15	.07
388	Steve Ontiveros	.15	.07
389	Rey Sanchez	.15	.07
390	Mike Henneman	.15	.07
391	Jose Valentin	.15	.07
392	Tom Candiotti	.15	.07
393	Damon Buford	.15	.07
394	Erik Hanson	.15	.07
395	Mark Smith	.15	.07
396	Pete Schourek	.15	.07

	MINT	NRMT
❑ 397 John Flaherty	.15	.07
❑ 398 Dave Martinez	.15	.07
❑ 399 Tommy Greene	.15	.07
❑ 400 Gary Sheffield	.30	.14
❑ 401 Glenn Dishman	.15	.07
❑ 402 Barry Bonds	.75	.35
❑ 403 Tom Pagnozzi	.15	.07
❑ 404 Todd Stottlemyre	.15	.07
❑ 405 Tim Salmon	.40	.18
❑ 406 John Hudek	.15	.07
❑ 407 Fred McGriff	.40	.18
❑ 408 Orlando Merced	.15	.07
❑ 409 Brian Barber	.15	.07
❑ 410 Ryan Thompson	.15	.07
❑ 411 Mariano Rivera	.40	.18
❑ 412 Eric Young	.15	.07
❑ 413 Chris Bosio	.15	.07
❑ 414 Chuck Knoblauch	.60	.25
❑ 415 Jamie Moyer	.15	.07
❑ 416 Chan Ho Park	.40	.18
❑ 417 Mark Portugal	.15	.07
❑ 418 Tim Raines	.30	.14
❑ 419 Antonio Osuna	.15	.07
❑ 420 Todd Zeile	.15	.07
❑ 421 Steve Wojciechowski	.15	.07
❑ 422 Marquis Grissom	.15	.07
❑ 423 Norm Charlton	.15	.07
❑ 424 Cal Ripken	2.50	1.10
❑ 425 Gregg Jefferies	.15	.07
❑ 426 Mike Stanton	.15	.07
❑ 427 Tony Fernandez	.15	.07
❑ 428 Jose Rijo	.15	.07
❑ 429 Jeff Bagwell	.75	.35
❑ 430 Raul Mondesi	.30	.14
❑ 431 Travis Fryman	.30	.14
❑ 432 Ron Karkovice	.15	.07
❑ 433 Alan Benes	.15	.07
❑ 434 Tony Phillips	.15	.07
❑ 435 Reggie Sanders	.30	.14
❑ 436 Andy Pettitte	.40	.18
❑ 437 Matt Lawton	.75	.35
❑ 438 Jeff Blauser	.15	.07
❑ 439 Michael Tucker	.15	.07
❑ 440 Mark Loretta	.15	.07
❑ 441 Charlie Hayes	.15	.07
❑ 442 Mike Piazza	2.00	.90
❑ 443 Shane Andrews	.15	.07
❑ 444 Jeff Suppan	.15	.07
❑ 445 Steve Rodriguez	.15	.07
❑ 446 Mike Matheny	.15	.07
❑ 447 Trenidad Hubbard	.15	.07
❑ 448 Denny Hocking	.15	.07
❑ 449 Mark Grudzielanek	.15	.07
❑ 450 Joe Randa	.15	.07

1996 Stadium Club Bash and Burn

	MINT	NRMT
COMPLETE SET (10)	30.00	13.50
COMMON CARD (BB1-BB10) ..	1.25	.55
SER.2 STATED ODDS 1:48 HOB, 1:24 RET		
❑ BB1 Sammy Sosa	20.00	9.00
❑ BB2 Barry Bonds	8.00	3.60
❑ BB3 Reggie Sanders	2.00	.90
❑ BB4 Craig Biggio	5.00	2.20
❑ BB5 Raul Mondesi	2.00	.90

	MINT	NRMT
❑ BB6 Ron Gant	1.25	.55
❑ BB7 Ray Lankford	2.00	.90
❑ BB8 Glenallen Hill	1.25	.55
❑ BB9 Chad Curtis	1.25	.55
❑ BB10 John Valentin	2.00	.90

1996 Stadium Club Extreme Players Bronze

	MINT	NRMT
COMP.BRONZE SET (179) ..	250.00	110.00
COMP.BRONZE SER.1 (90)	125.00	55.00
COMP.BRONZE SER.2 (89)	125.00	55.00
COMMON CARD (1-179)	.75	.35
BRONZE STATED ODDS 1:12		
*SILVER SINGLES: 4X TO 10X BASE CARD HI		
*SILVER WIN: .6X TO 1.5X BRONZE WIN		
SILVER STATED ODDS 1:24		
*GOLD SINGLES: 8X TO 20X BASE CARD HI		
*GOLD WIN: 1.25X TO 3X BRONZE WIN		
GOLD STATED ODDS 1:48		
SKIP-NUMBERED SET		
❑ 1 Hideo Nomo	3.00	1.35
❑ 3 Garret Anderson	1.25	.55
❑ 4 Jose Mesa	.75	.35
❑ 5 Vinny Castilla	2.00	.90
❑ 6 Mike Mussina	3.00	1.35
❑ 7 Ray Durham	1.25	.55
❑ 8 Jack McDowell	.75	.35
❑ 9 Juan Gonzalez	8.00	3.60
❑ 10 Chipper Jones	10.00	4.50
❑ 11 Deion Sanders	1.25	.55
❑ 12 Rondell White	1.25	.55
❑ 13 Tom Henke	.75	.35
❑ 14 Derek Bell	1.25	.55
❑ 15 Randy Myers	.75	.35
❑ 16 Randy Johnson	3.00	1.35
❑ 17 Len Dykstra	1.25	.55
❑ 18 Bill Pulsipher	.75	.35
❑ 21 Chad Curtis	.75	.35
❑ 22 Roberto Hernandez	.75	.35
❑ 23 Kirby Puckett	5.00	2.20
❑ 25 Roger Clemens	8.00	3.60
❑ 31 Chad Fonville	.75	.35
❑ 32 Bernard Gilkey	.75	.35
❑ 34 Shawn Green	3.00	1.35
❑ 35 Rick Aguilera	.75	.35
❑ 40 Dean Palmer	1.25	.55
❑ 45 Matt Williams	3.00	1.35
❑ 49 Tom Glavine	3.00	1.35
❑ 50 Delino DeShields	.75	.35
❑ 56 Benito Santiago	.75	.35
❑ 59 Rod Beck	.75	.35
❑ 63 Eric Karros	1.25	.55
❑ 66 Lee Smith	1.25	.55
❑ 69 Jeff Montgomery	.75	.35
❑ 70 Todd Hundley	1.25	.55
❑ 73 Don Mattingly	5.00	2.20
❑ 77 Ken Caminiti W	4.00	1.80
❑ 80 Pedro Martinez	3.00	1.35
❑ 82 Heathcliff Slocumb	.75	.35
❑ 83 Joe Girardi	.75	.35
❑ 88 Todd Worrell W	1.50	.70
❑ 90 Bip Roberts	.75	.35
❑ 95 Cecil Fielder	1.25	.55
❑ 96 Wade Boggs	3.00	1.35
❑ 98 Mickey Tettleton	.75	.35

	MINT	NRMT
❑ 99 Jeff Kent	1.25	.55
❑ 100 Denny Martinez	1.25	.55
❑ 101 Luis Gonzalez	1.25	.55
❑ 103 Javy Lopez	1.25	.55
❑ 104 Mark McGwire	15.00	6.75
❑ 105 Ken Griffey Jr. W	30.00	13.50
❑ 106 Darren Daulton	1.25	.55
❑ 108 Mike Macfarlane	.75	.35
❑ 110 Shane Reynolds	1.25	.55
❑ 114 John Franco	1.25	.55
❑ 116 Andy Benes	1.25	.55
❑ 118 Brian Jordan	1.25	.55
❑ 120 Chuck Finley	.75	.35
❑ 123 Derek Jeter	8.00	3.60
❑ 124 John Smiley	.75	.35
❑ 126 Brett Butler	1.25	.55
❑ 127 Doug Drabek	.75	.35
❑ 128 J.T. Snow	1.25	.55
❑ 129 Joe Carter	1.25	.55
❑ 130 Dennis Eckersley	1.25	.55
❑ 131 Marty Cordova	.75	.35
❑ 132 Greg Maddux W	15.00	6.75
❑ 135 Paul Sorrento	.75	.35
❑ 137 Shawon Dunston	.75	.35
❑ 138 Moises Alou	1.25	.55
❑ 140 Ramon Martinez	1.25	.55
❑ 141 Royce Clayton	.75	.35
❑ 143 Kenny Rogers	.75	.35
❑ 144 Tim Naehring	.75	.35
❑ 145 Chris Gomez	.75	.35
❑ 148 Bobby Bonilla	1.25	.55
❑ 150 Andres Galarraga W	4.00	1.80
❑ 151 David Cone	2.00	.90
❑ 152 Lance Johnson	.75	.35
❑ 159 David Justice	3.00	1.35
❑ 160 Mark Grace	2.00	.90
❑ 161 Robb Nen	.75	.35
❑ 162 Mike Greenwell	.75	.35
❑ 167 Mel Rojas	.75	.35
❑ 168 Bret Boone	1.25	.55
❑ 172 Jay Bell	1.25	.55
❑ 176 Roberto Alomar	3.00	1.35
❑ 178 Ryan Klesko	1.25	.55
❑ 271 Barry Larkin W	4.00	1.80
❑ 272 Paul O'Neill	1.25	.55
❑ 274 Will Clark	3.00	1.35
❑ 275 Steve Avery	.75	.35
❑ 276 Jim Edmonds	2.00	.90
❑ 277 John Olerud	1.25	.55
❑ 279 Chris Hoiles	.75	.35
❑ 280 Jeff Conine	.75	.35
❑ 283 Ray Lankford	1.25	.55
❑ 285 Frank Thomas	8.00	3.60
❑ 286 Jason Isringhausen	.75	.35
❑ 287 Glenallen Hill	.75	.35
❑ 289 Bernie Williams	3.00	1.35
❑ 290 Eddie Murray	3.00	1.35
❑ 296 Jeff Fassero	.75	.35
❑ 297 Albert Belle	3.00	1.35
❑ 298 Craig Biggio	3.00	1.35
❑ 300 Edgar Martinez	1.25	.55
❑ 301 Tony Gwynn	3.00	1.35
❑ 303 Mo Vaughn	3.00	1.35
❑ 304 Alex Fernandez	.75	.35
❑ 308 Omar Vizquel	1.25	.55
❑ 310 Danny Tartabull	.75	.35
❑ 316 Brady Anderson	1.25	.55
❑ 319 Larry Walker	3.00	1.35
❑ 321 Robin Ventura	1.25	.55
❑ 325 Kenny Lofton	2.00	.90
❑ 327 Wil Cordero	.75	.35
❑ 328 Troy Percival	1.25	.55
❑ 331 Carlos Baerga	1.25	.55
❑ 333 Jay Buhner	.75	.35
❑ 335 Jeff King	.75	.35
❑ 336 Dante Bichette	1.25	.55
❑ 337 Alan Trammell	2.00	.90
❑ 342 Jose Canseco	3.00	1.35
❑ 343 Rafael Palmeiro	3.00	1.35
❑ 344 Quilvio Veras	.75	.35
❑ 345 Darrin Fletcher	.75	.35
❑ 347 Tony Eusebio	.75	.35
❑ 348 Ismael Valdes	1.25	.55
❑ 349 Terry Steinbach	.75	.35

	MINT	NRMT
☐ 350 Orel Hershiser	1.25	.55
☐ 351 Kurt Abbott	.75	.35
☐ 354 Ruben Sierra	.75	.35
☐ 357 Jim Thome	3.00	1.35
☐ 358 Geronimo Berroa	.75	.35
☐ 359 Robby Thompson	.75	.35
☐ 360 Jose Vizcaino	.75	.35
☐ 362 Kevin Appier	1.25	.55
☐ 364 Ron Gant	.75	.35
☐ 367 Rico Brogna	.75	.35
☐ 368 Manny Ramirez	3.00	1.35
☐ 370 Sammy Sosa	8.00	3.60
☐ 373 Sandy Alomar Jr.	1.25	.55
☐ 378 Steve Finley	1.25	.55
☐ 380 Ivan Rodriguez	3.00	1.35
☐ 382 Mark Lemke	.75	.35
☐ 385 Mark Langston	.75	.35
☐ 386 Ed Sprague	.75	.35
☐ 388 Steve Ontiveros	.75	.35
☐ 392 Tom Candiotti	.75	.35
☐ 394 Erik Hanson	.75	.35
☐ 396 Pete Schourek	.75	.35
☐ 400 Gary Sheffield W	4.00	1.80
☐ 402 Barry Bonds W	8.00	3.60
☐ 403 Tom Pagnozzi	.75	.35
☐ 404 Todd Stottlemyre	.75	.35
☐ 405 Tim Salmon	2.00	.90
☐ 407 Fred McGriff	2.00	.90
☐ 408 Orlando Merced	.75	.35
☐ 412 Eric Young	.75	.35
☐ 414 Chuck Knoblauch W	5.00	2.20
☐ 417 Mark Portugal	.75	.35
☐ 418 Tim Raines	1.25	.55
☐ 420 Todd Zeile	.75	.35
☐ 422 Marquis Grissom	.75	.35
☐ 423 Norm Charlton	.75	.35
☐ 424 Cal Ripken	12.00	5.50
☐ 425 Gregg Jefferies	.75	.35
☐ 428 Jose Rijo	.75	.35
☐ 429 Jeff Bagwell	3.00	1.35
☐ 430 Raul Mondesi	1.25	.55
☐ 431 Travis Fryman	1.25	.55
☐ 434 Tony Phillips	.75	.35
☐ 435 Reggie Sanders	1.25	.55
☐ 436 Andy Pettitte	2.00	.90
☐ 438 Jeff Blauser	.75	.35
☐ 441 Charlie Hayes	.75	.35
☐ 442 Mike Piazza W	20.00	9.00

1996 Stadium Club Extreme Winners Bronze

	MINT	NRMT
COMPLETE SET (10)	25.00	11.00
COMMON CARD (EW1-EW10)	.50	.23
MINOR STARS	.75	.35
UNLISTED STARS	1.50	.70
ONE SET VIA MAIL PER BRONZE WINNER		
COMP.SILVER SET (10)	80.00	36.00
*SILVER SINGLES: 1.25X TO 3X HI COLUMN		
ONE SILV.SET VIA MAIL PER SILV.WINNER		
*GOLD SINGLES: 5X TO 12X HI COLUMN		
ONE GOLD CARD VIA MAIL PER GOLD WNR.		

	MINT	NRMT
☐ EW1 Greg Maddux	5.00	2.20
☐ EW2 Mike Piazza	6.00	2.70
☐ EW3 Andres Galarraga	1.50	.70
☐ EW4 Chuck Knoblauch	1.50	.70
☐ EW5 Ken Caminiti	.75	.35
☐ EW6 Barry Larkin	1.50	.70
☐ EW7 Barry Bonds	2.50	1.10
☐ EW8 Ken Griffey Jr.	10.00	4.50
☐ EW9 Gary Sheffield	.75	.35
☐ EW10 Todd Worrell	.50	.23

1996 Stadium Club Mantle

	MINT	NRMT
COMPLETE SET (19)	170.00	75.00
COMPLETE SERIES 1 (9)	110.00	50.00
COMPLETE SERIES 2 (10)	60.00	27.00
COMMON CARD (MM1-MM9)	15.00	6.75
COMMON CARD (MM10-MM19)	8.00	3.60
SER.1 STATED ODDS 1:24		
SER.2 STATED ODDS 1:12		

	MINT	NRMT
☐ MM1 Mickey Mantle	15.00	6.75
Batting Follow Through, 1950		
☐ MM2 Mickey Mantle	15.00	6.75
☐ MM3 Mickey Mantle	15.00	6.75
Locker room shot, 1965		
☐ MM4 Mickey Mantle	15.00	6.75
☐ MM5 Mickey Mantle	15.00	6.75
☐ MM6 Mickey Mantle	15.00	6.75
☐ MM7 Mickey Mantle	15.00	6.75
☐ MM8 Mickey Mantle	15.00	6.75
☐ MM9 Mickey Mantle	15.00	6.75
Batting both ways, 1959		
☐ MM10 Mickey Mantle	8.00	3.60
☐ MM11 Mickey Mantle	8.00	3.60
Beating out hit, 1961		
☐ MM12 Mickey Mantle	8.00	3.60
Roger Maris, 1961		
☐ MM13 Mickey Mantle	8.00	3.60
☐ MM14 Mickey Mantle	8.00	3.60
☐ MM15 Mickey Mantle	8.00	3.60
Smiling Pose, 1964		
☐ MM16 Mickey Mantle	8.00	3.60
☐ MM17 Mickey Mantle	8.00	3.60
☐ MM18 Mickey Mantle	8.00	3.60
☐ MM19 Mickey Mantle	8.00	3.60

1996 Stadium Club Megaheroes

	MINT	NRMT
COMPLETE SET (10)	50.00	22.00
COMMON CARD (MH1-MH10)	1.00	.45
SER.1 STATED ODDS 1:48 HOB, 1:24 RET		

	MINT	NRMT
☐ MH1 Frank Thomas	8.00	3.60
☐ MH2 Ken Griffey Jr.	20.00	9.00
☐ MH3 Hideo Nomo	4.00	1.80
☐ MH4 Ozzie Smith	5.00	2.20
☐ MH5 Will Clark	4.00	1.80
☐ MH6 Jack McDowell	1.00	.45
☐ MH7 Andres Galarraga	4.00	1.80
☐ MH8 Roger Clemens	10.00	4.50
☐ MH9 Deion Sanders	2.00	.90
☐ MH10 Mo Vaughn	4.00	1.80

1996 Stadium Club Metalists

	MINT	NRMT
COMPLETE SET (8)	40.00	18.00
COMMON CARD (M1-M8)	1.50	.70
SER.2 STATED ODDS 1:48 HOB, 1:96 RET		

	MINT	NRMT
☐ M1 Jeff Bagwell	4.00	1.80
☐ M2 Barry Bonds	4.00	1.80
☐ M3 Jose Canseco	4.00	1.80
☐ M4 Roger Clemens	8.00	3.60
☐ M5 Dennis Eckersley	1.50	.70
☐ M6 Greg Maddux	8.00	3.60
☐ M7 Cal Ripken	12.00	5.50
☐ M8 Frank Thomas	6.00	2.70

1996 Stadium Club Midsummer Matchups

	MINT	NRMT
COMPLETE SET (10)	60.00	27.00
COMMON CARD (M1-M10)	2.00	.90
UNLISTED STARS	4.00	1.80
SER.1 STATED ODDS 1:48 HOB, 1:24 RET		

	MINT	NRMT
☐ MM1 Hideo Nomo	4.00	1.80
Randy Johnson		
☐ MM2 Mike Piazza	12.00	5.50
Ivan Rodriguez		
☐ MM3 Fred McGriff	8.00	3.60
Frank Thomas		
☐ MM4 Craig Biggio	2.00	.90
Carlos Baerga		
☐ MM5 Vinny Castilla	4.00	1.80
Wade Boggs		

		MINT	NRMT
❏ MM6	Barry Larkin	15.00	6.75
	Cal Ripken		
❏ MM7	Barry Bonds	5.00	2.20
	Albert Belle		
❏ MM8	Len Dykstra	5.00	2.20
	Kenny Lofton		
❏ MM9	Tony Gwynn	12.00	5.50
	Kirby Puckett		
❏ MM10	Ron Gant	2.50	1.10
	Edgar Martinez		

1996 Stadium Club Power Packed

	MINT	NRMT
COMPLETE SET (15)	80.00	36.00
COMMON CARD (PP1-PP15)	2.00	.90
SER.2 STATED ODDS 1:48 RETAIL		

❏ PP1	Albert Belle	5.00	2.20
❏ PP2	Mark McGwire	25.00	11.00
❏ PP3	Jose Canseco	6.00	2.70
❏ PP4	Mike Piazza	15.00	6.75
❏ PP5	Ron Gant	2.00	.90
❏ PP6	Ken Griffey Jr.	25.00	11.00
❏ PP7	Mo Vaughn	5.00	2.20
❏ PP8	Cecil Fielder	2.50	1.10
❏ PP9	Tim Salmon	3.00	1.35
❏ PP10	Frank Thomas	10.00	4.50
❏ PP11	Juan Gonzalez	10.00	4.50
❏ PP12	Andres Galarraga	5.00	2.20
❏ PP13	Fred McGriff	3.00	1.35
❏ PP14	Jay Buhner	2.50	1.10
❏ PP15	Dante Bichette	2.50	1.10

1996 Stadium Club Power Streak

	MINT	NRMT
COMPLETE SET (15)	60.00	27.00
COMMON CARD (PS1-PS15)	1.25	.55
SER.1 STATED ODDS 1:24 HOB, 1:48 RET		

❏ PS1	Randy Johnson	5.00	2.20
❏ PS2	Hideo Nomo	5.00	2.20
❏ PS3	Albert Belle	5.00	2.20
❏ PS4	Dante Bichette	2.00	.90
❏ PS5	Jay Buhner	2.00	.90
❏ PS6	Frank Thomas	10.00	4.50
❏ PS7	Mark McGwire	25.00	11.00

❏ PS8	Rafael Palmeiro	5.00	2.20
❏ PS9	Mo Vaughn	5.00	2.20
❏ PS10	Sammy Sosa	15.00	6.75
❏ PS11	Larry Walker	5.00	2.20
❏ PS12	Gary Gaetti	1.25	.55
❏ PS13	Tim Salmon	3.00	1.35
❏ PS14	Barry Bonds	6.00	2.70
❏ PS15	Jim Edmonds	3.00	1.35

1996 Stadium Club Prime Cuts

	MINT	NRMT
COMPLETE SET (8)	60.00	27.00
COMMON CARD (PC1-PC8)	2.50	1.10
SER.1 STATED ODDS 1:36 HOB, 1:72 RET		

❏ PC1	Albert Belle	4.00	1.80
❏ PC2	Barry Bonds	5.00	2.20
❏ PC3	Ken Griffey Jr.	20.00	9.00
❏ PC4	Tony Gwynn	10.00	4.50
❏ PC5	Edgar Martinez	2.50	1.10
❏ PC6	Rafael Palmeiro	4.00	1.80
❏ PC7	Mike Piazza	12.00	5.50
❏ PC8	Frank Thomas	8.00	3.60

1996 Stadium Club TSC Awards

	MINT	NRMT
COMPLETE SET (10)	40.00	18.00
COMMON CARD (1-10)	1.00	.45
SER.2 STATED ODDS 1:48 HOB, 1:24 RET		

❏ 1	Cal Ripken	12.00	5.50
❏ 2	Albert Belle	3.00	1.35
❏ 3	Tom Glavine	3.00	1.35
❏ 4	Jeff Conine	1.00	.45
❏ 5	Ken Griffey Jr.	15.00	6.75
❏ 6	Hideo Nomo	3.00	1.35
❏ 7	Greg Maddux	8.00	3.60
❏ 8	Chipper Jones	8.00	3.60
❏ 9	Randy Johnson	3.00	1.35
❏ 10	Jose Mesa	1.00	.45

1997 Stadium Club

	MINT	NRMT
COMPLETE SET (390)	80.00	36.00
COMPLETE SERIES 1 (195)	40.00	18.00

		MINT	NRMT
COMPLETE SERIES 2 (195)		40.00	18.00
COMMON (1-180/196-375)		.15	.07
MINOR STARS		.30	.14
UNLISTED STARS		.60	.25
COM.SP (181-195/376-390)		.30	.14
SP MINOR STARS		.50	.23
SP SEMISTARS		.75	.35
SP UNLISTED STARS		1.25	.55
CARDS 361 AND 374 DON'T EXIST			
SWEENEY AND PAGNOZZI NUMBERED 274			
J.DYE AND B.BROWN NUMBERED 351			
COM.MATRIX (1-60/196-255)		1.50	.70
*MATRIX STARS: 5X TO 12X HI COLUMN			
*MATRIX YOUNG STARS: 4X TO 10X HI			
MATRIX ODDS:1:12H/R, 1:18ANCO, 1:6HCP			

❏ 1	Chipper Jones	1.50	.70
❏ 2	Gary Sheffield	.30	.14
❏ 3	Kenny Lofton	.40	.18
❏ 4	Brian Jordan	.30	.14
❏ 5	Mark McGwire	3.00	1.35
❏ 6	Charles Nagy	.30	.14
❏ 7	Tim Salmon	.60	.25
❏ 8	Cal Ripken	2.50	1.10
❏ 9	Jeff Conine	.15	.07
❏ 10	Paul Molitor	.60	.25
❏ 11	Mariano Rivera	.30	.14
❏ 12	Pedro Martinez	.75	.35
❏ 13	Jeff Bagwell	.75	.35
❏ 14	Bobby Bonilla	.30	.14
❏ 15	Barry Bonds	.75	.35
❏ 16	Ryan Klesko	.60	.25
❏ 17	Barry Larkin	.60	.25
❏ 18	Jim Thome	.60	.25
❏ 19	Jay Buhner	.30	.14
❏ 20	Juan Gonzalez	1.25	.55
❏ 21	Mike Mussina	.60	.25
❏ 22	Kevin Appier	.30	.14
❏ 23	Eric Karros	.30	.14
❏ 24	Steve Finley	.30	.14
❏ 25	Ed Sprague	.15	.07
❏ 26	Bernard Gilkey	.15	.07
❏ 27	Tony Phillips	.15	.07
❏ 28	Henry Rodriguez	.30	.14
❏ 29	John Smoltz	.40	.18
❏ 30	Dante Bichette	.30	.14
❏ 31	Mike Piazza	2.00	.90
❏ 32	Paul O'Neill	.30	.14
❏ 33	Billy Wagner	.30	.14
❏ 34	Reggie Sanders	.30	.14
❏ 35	John Jaha	.15	.07
❏ 36	Eddie Murray	.60	.25
❏ 37	Eric Young	.30	.14
❏ 38	Roberto Hernandez	.15	.07
❏ 39	Pat Hentgen	.30	.14
❏ 40	Sammy Sosa	2.00	.90
❏ 41	Todd Hundley	.30	.14
❏ 42	Mo Vaughn	.60	.25
❏ 43	Robin Ventura	.30	.14
❏ 44	Mark Grudzielanek	.30	.14
❏ 45	Shane Reynolds	.30	.14
❏ 46	Andy Pettitte	.40	.18
❏ 47	Fred McGriff	.40	.18
❏ 48	Rey Ordonez	.30	.14
❏ 49	Will Clark	.60	.25
❏ 50	Ken Griffey Jr.	3.00	1.35
❏ 51	Todd Worrell	.15	.07
❏ 52	Rusty Greer	.30	.14

53	Mark Grace	.40	.18
54	Tom Glavine	.60	.25
55	Derek Jeter	2.00	.90
56	Rafael Palmeiro	.60	.25
57	Bernie Williams	.60	.25
58	Marty Cordova	.15	.07
59	Andres Galarraga	.25	.14
60	Ken Caminiti	.40	.18
61	Garret Anderson	.30	.14
62	Denny Martinez	.30	.14
63	Mike Greenwell	.15	.07
64	David Segui	.15	.07
65	Julio Franco	.30	.14
66	Rickey Henderson	.75	.35
67	Ozzie Guillen	.15	.07
68	Pete Harnisch	.15	.07
69	Chan Ho Park	.60	.25
70	Harold Baines	.30	.14
71	Mark Clark	.15	.07
72	Steve Avery	.15	.07
73	Brian Hunter	.30	.14
74	Pedro Astacio	.15	.07
75	Jack McDowell	.15	.07
76	Gregg Jefferies	.15	.07
77	Jason Kendall	.40	.18
78	Todd Walker	.60	.25
79	B.J. Surhoff	.30	.14
80	Moises Alou	.30	.14
81	Fernando Vina	.15	.07
82	Darryl Strawberry	.30	.14
83	Jose Rosado	.15	.07
84	Chris Gomez	.15	.07
85	Chili Davis	.30	.14
86	Alan Benes	.15	.07
87	Todd Hollandsworth	.15	.07
88	Jose Vizcaino	.15	.07
89	Edgardo Alfonzo	.40	.18
90	Ruben Rivera	.15	.07
91	Donovan Osborne	.15	.07
92	Doug Glanville	.40	.18
93	Gary DiSarcina	.15	.07
94	Brooks Kieschnick	.15	.07
95	Bobby Jones	.15	.07
96	Raul Casanova	.15	.07
97	Jermaine Allensworth	.15	.07
98	Kenny Rogers	.15	.07
99	Mark McLemore	.15	.07
100	Jeff Fassero	.15	.07
101	Sandy Alomar Jr.	.30	.14
102	Chuck Finley	.30	.14
103	Eric Owens	.15	.07
104	Billy McMillon	.15	.07
105	Dwight Gooden	.30	.14
106	Sterling Hitchcock	.30	.14
107	Doug Drabek	.15	.07
108	Paul Wilson	.15	.07
109	Chris Snopek	.15	.07
110	Al Leiter	.30	.14
111	Bob Tewksbury	.15	.07
112	Todd Greene	.15	.07
113	Jose Valentin	.15	.07
114	Delino DeShields	.15	.07
115	Mike Bordick	.15	.07
116	Pat Meares	.15	.07
117	Mariano Duncan	.15	.07
118	Steve Trachsel	.15	.07
119	Luis Castillo	.30	.14
120	Andy Benes	.30	.14
121	Donne Wall	.15	.07
122	Alex Gonzalez	.15	.07
123	Dan Wilson	.15	.07
124	Omar Vizquel	.30	.14
125	Devon White	.30	.14
126	Darryl Hamilton	.15	.07
127	Orlando Merced	.15	.07
128	Royce Clayton	.15	.07
129	William VanLandingham	.15	.07
130	Terry Steinbach	.15	.07
131	Jeff Blauser	.15	.07
132	Jeff Cirillo	.30	.14
133	Roger Pavlik	.15	.07
134	Danny Tartabull	.15	.07
135	Jeff Montgomery	.15	.07
136	Bobby Higginson	.30	.14
137	Mike Grace	.15	.07
138	Kevin Elster	.15	.07
139	Brian Giles	2.00	.90
140	Rod Beck	.15	.07
141	Ismael Valdes	.30	.14
142	Scott Brosius	.30	.14
143	Mike Fetters	.15	.07
144	Gary Gaetti	.30	.14
145	Mike Lansing	.15	.07
146	Glenallen Hill	.15	.07
147	Shawn Green	.60	.25
148	Mel Rojas	.15	.07
149	Joey Cora	.15	.07
150	John Smiley	.15	.07
151	Marvin Benard	.15	.07
152	Curt Schilling	.40	.18
153	Dave Nilsson	.15	.07
154	Edgar Renteria	.30	.14
155	Joey Hamilton	.30	.14
156	Carlos Garcia	.15	.07
157	Nomar Garciaparra	2.00	.90
158	Kevin Ritz	.15	.07
159	Keith Lockhart	.15	.07
160	Justin Thompson	.30	.14
161	Terry Adams	.15	.07
162	Jamey Wright	.15	.07
163	Otis Nixon	.15	.07
164	Michael Tucker	.15	.07
165	Mike Stanley	.15	.07
166	Ben McDonald	.15	.07
167	John Mabry	.15	.07
168	Troy O'Leary	.30	.14
169	Mel Nieves	.15	.07
170	Bret Boone	.30	.14
171	Mike Timlin	.15	.07
172	Scott Rolen	1.00	.45
173	Reggie Jefferson	.15	.07
174	Neifi Perez	.30	.14
175	Brian McRae	.15	.07
176	Tom Goodwin	.15	.07
177	Aaron Sele	.30	.14
178	Benito Santiago	.15	.07
179	Frank Rodriguez	.15	.07
180	Eric Davis	.30	.14
181	Andruw Jones 2000 SP	2.00	.90
182	Todd Walker 2000 SP	1.25	.55
183	Wes Helms 2000 SP	.30	.14
184	Nelson Figueroa 2000 SP	.50	.23
185	V. Guerrero 2000 SP	2.50	1.10
186	Billy McMillon 2000 SP	.30	.14
187	Todd Helton 2000 SP	2.50	1.10
188	N. Garciaparra 2000 SP	4.00	1.80
189	K. Maeda 2000 SP	.50	.23
190	Russell Branyan 2000 SP	1.50	.70
191	Glendon Rusch 2000 SP	.30	.14
192	Bartolo Colon 2000 SP	.50	.23
193	Scott Rolen 2000 SP	2.50	1.10
194	A. Echevarria 2000 SP	.30	.14
195	Bob Abreu 2000 SP	.50	.23
196	Greg Maddux	1.50	.70
197	Joe Carter	.30	.14
198	Alex Ochoa	.15	.07
199	Ellis Burks	.30	.14
200	Ivan Rodriguez	.75	.35
201	Marquis Grissom	.30	.14
202	Trevor Hoffman	.30	.14
203	Matt Williams	.60	.25
204	Carlos Delgado	.60	.25
205	Ramon Martinez	.30	.14
206	Chuck Knoblauch	.60	.25
207	Juan Guzman	.15	.07
208	Derek Bell	.30	.14
209	Roger Clemens	1.50	.70
210	Vladimir Guerrero	1.00	.45
211	Cecil Fielder	.30	.14
212	Hideo Nomo	.60	.25
213	Frank Thomas	1.25	.55
214	Greg Vaughn	.30	.14
215	Javy Lopez	.30	.14
216	Raul Mondesi	.30	.14
217	Wade Boggs	.60	.25
218	Carlos Baerga	.15	.07
219	Tony Gwynn	1.50	.70
220	Tino Martinez	.60	.25
221	Vinny Castilla	.40	.18
222	Lance Johnson	.15	.07
223	David Justice	.60	.25
224	Rondell White	.30	.14
225	Dean Palmer	.30	.14
226	Jim Edmonds	.40	.18
227	Albert Belle	.60	.25
228	Alex Fernandez	.15	.07
229	Ryne Sandberg	.75	.35
230	Jose Mesa	.15	.07
231	David Cone	.40	.18
232	Troy Percival	.30	.14
233	Edgar Martinez	.30	.14
234	Jose Canseco	.75	.35
235	Kevin Brown	.40	.18
236	Ray Lankford	.30	.14
237	Karim Garcia	.30	.14
238	J.T. Snow	.30	.14
239	Dennis Eckersley	.30	.14
240	Roberto Alomar	.60	.25
241	John Valentin	.30	.14
242	Ron Gant	.15	.07
243	Geronimo Berroa	.15	.07
244	Manny Ramirez	.75	.35
245	Travis Fryman	.30	.14
246	Denny Neagle	.30	.14
247	Randy Johnson	.60	.25
248	Darin Erstad	.60	.25
249	Mark Wohlers	.15	.07
250	Ken Hill	.15	.07
251	Larry Walker	.60	.25
252	Craig Biggio	.60	.25
253	Brady Anderson	.30	.14
254	John Wetteland	.30	.14
255	Andruw Jones	.75	.35
256	Turk Wendell	.15	.07
257	Jason Isringhausen	.15	.07
258	Jaime Navarro	.15	.07
259	Sean Berry	.15	.07
260	Mike Lopez	.15	.07
261	Jay Bell	.30	.14
262	Bobby Witt	.15	.07
263	Tony Clark	.40	.18
264	Tim Wakefield	.30	.14
265	Brad Radke	.30	.14
266	Tim Belcher	.15	.07
267	Nerio Rodriguez	.50	.23
268	Roger Cedeno	.30	.14
269	Tim Naehring	.15	.07
270	Kevin Tapani	.15	.07
271	Joe Randa	.15	.07
272	Randy Myers	.15	.07
273	Dave Burba	.15	.07
274	Mike Sweeney	.30	.14
275	Danny Graves	.30	.14
276	Scott Radinsky	.15	.07
277	Ruben Sierra	.15	.07
278	Norm Charlton	.15	.07
279	Scott Sanders	.15	.07
280	Jacob Cruz	.15	.07
281	Mike Macfarlane	.15	.07
282	Rich Becker	.15	.07
283	Shannon Stewart	.30	.14
284	Gerald Williams	.15	.07
285	Jody Reed	.15	.07
286	Jeff D'Amico	.15	.07
287	Walt Weiss	.15	.07
288	Jim Leyritz	.15	.07
289	Francisco Cordova	.15	.07
290	F.P. Santangelo	.15	.07
291	Scott Erickson	.30	.14
292	Hal Morris	.15	.07
293	Ray Durham	.30	.14
294	Andy Ashby	.15	.07
295	Darryl Kile	.30	.14
296	Jose Paniagua	.15	.07
297	Mickey Tettleton	.15	.07
298	Joe Girardi	.15	.07
299	Rocky Coppinger	.15	.07
300	Bob Abreu	.30	.14
301	John Olerud	.30	.14
302	Paul Shuey	.15	.07
303	Jeff Brantley	.15	.07
304	Bob Wells	.15	.07
305	Kevin Seitzer	.15	.07
306	Shawon Dunston	.15	.07
307	Jose Herrera	.15	.07
308	Butch Huskey	.15	.07
309	Jose Offerman	.30	.14
310	Rick Aguilera	.15	.07

❑ 311 Greg Gagne	.15	.07
❑ 312 John Burkett	.15	.07
❑ 313 Mark Thompson	.15	.07
❑ 314 Alvaro Espinoza	.15	.07
❑ 315 Todd Stottlemyre	.15	.07
❑ 316 Al Martin	.15	.07
❑ 317 James Baldwin	.30	.14
❑ 318 Cal Eldred	.15	.07
❑ 319 Sid Fernandez	.15	.07
❑ 320 Mickey Morandini	.15	.07
❑ 321 Robb Nen	.15	.07
❑ 322 Mark Lemke	.15	.07
❑ 323 Pete Schourek	.15	.07
❑ 324 Marcus Jensen	.15	.07
❑ 325 Rich Aurilia	.15	.14
❑ 326 Jeff King	.15	.07
❑ 327 Scott Stahoviak	.15	.07
❑ 328 Ricky Otero	.15	.07
❑ 329 Antonio Osuna	.15	.07
❑ 330 Chris Hoiles	.15	.07
❑ 331 Luis Gonzalez	.30	.14
❑ 332 Wil Cordero	.15	.07
❑ 333 Johnny Damon	.30	.14
❑ 334 Mark Langston	.30	.14
❑ 335 Orlando Miller	.15	.07
❑ 336 Jason Giambi	.30	.14
❑ 337 Damian Jackson	.15	.07
❑ 338 David Wells	.30	.14
❑ 339 Bip Roberts	.15	.07
❑ 340 Matt Ruebel	.15	.07
❑ 341 Tom Candiotti	.15	.07
❑ 342 Wally Joyner	.30	.14
❑ 343 Jimmy Key	.30	.14
❑ 344 Tony Batista	.40	.18
❑ 345 Paul Sorrento	.15	.07
❑ 346 Ron Karkovice	.15	.07
❑ 347 Wilson Alvarez	.30	.14
❑ 348 John Flaherty	.15	.07
❑ 349 Rey Sanchez	.15	.07
❑ 350 John Vander Wal	.15	.07
❑ 351 Jermaine Dye	.30	.14
❑ 352 Mike Hampton	.30	.14
❑ 353 Greg Colbrunn	.15	.07
❑ 354 Heathcliff Slocumb	.15	.07
❑ 355 Ricky Bottalico	.30	.14
❑ 356 Marty Janzen	.15	.07
❑ 357 Orel Hershiser	.30	.14
❑ 358 Rex Hudler	.15	.07
❑ 359 Amaury Telemaco	.15	.07
❑ 360 Darrin Fletcher	.15	.07
❑ 361 Brant Brown UER	.30	.14
Card numbered 351		
❑ 362 Russ Davis	.30	.14
❑ 363 Allen Watson	.15	.07
❑ 364 Mike Lieberthal	.15	.07
❑ 365 Dave Stevens	.15	.07
❑ 366 Jay Powell	.15	.07
❑ 367 Tony Fossas	.15	.07
❑ 368 Bob Wolcott	.15	.07
❑ 369 Mark Loretta	.15	.07
❑ 370 Shawn Estes	.30	.14
❑ 371 Sandy Martinez	.15	.07
❑ 372 Wendell Magee Jr.	.15	.07
❑ 373 John Franco	.30	.14
❑ 374 Tom Pagnozzi UER	.15	.07
misnumbered as 274		
❑ 375 Willie Adams	.15	.07
❑ 376 Chipper Jones SS SP	3.00	1.35
❑ 377 Mo Vaughn SS SP	1.25	.55
❑ 378 Frank Thomas SS SP	2.50	1.10
❑ 379 Albert Belle SS SP	1.25	.55
❑ 380 Andres Galarraga SS SP	1.25	.55
❑ 381 Gary Sheffield SS SP	.50	.23
❑ 382 Jeff Bagwell SS SP	1.50	.70
❑ 383 Mike Piazza SS SP	4.00	1.80
❑ 384 Mark McGwire SS SP	6.00	2.70
❑ 385 Ken Griffey Jr. SS SP	6.00	2.70
❑ 386 Barry Bonds SS SP	1.50	.70
❑ 387 Juan Gonzalez SS SP	2.50	1.10
❑ 388 Brady Anderson SS SP	.75	.35
❑ 389 Ken Caminiti SS SP	.75	.35
❑ 390 Jay Buhner SS SP	.50	.23

1997 Stadium Club Co-Signers

	MINT	NRMT
COMPLETE SET (10)	500.00	220.00
COMPLETE SERIES 1 (5)	250.00	110.00
COMPLETE SERIES 2 (5)	250.00	110.00
COMMON CARD (CO1-CO10)	10.00	4.50
STATED ODDS 1:168 HOBBY, 1:96 HCP		

❑ CO1 Andy Pettitte	100.00	45.00
Derek Jeter		
❑ CO2 Paul Wilson	10.00	4.50
Todd Hundley		
❑ CO3 Jermaine Dye	15.00	6.75
Mark Wohlers		
❑ CO4 Scott Rolen	60.00	27.00
Gregg Jefferies		
❑ CO5 Todd Hollandsworth	20.00	9.00
Jason Kendall		
❑ CO6 Alan Benes	25.00	11.00
Robin Ventura		
❑ CO7 Eric Karros	25.00	11.00
Raul Mondesi		
❑ CO8 Rey Ordonez	100.00	45.00
Nomar Garciaparra		
❑ CO9 Rondell White	15.00	6.75
Marty Cordova		
❑ CO10 Tony Gwynn	80.00	36.00
Karim Garcia		

1997 Stadium Club Firebrand Redemption

	MINT	NRMT
COMPLETE SET (12)	150.00	70.00
COMMON CARD (F1-F12)	3.00	1.35
SER.1 STAT.ODDS 1:24 HOB/RET,1:36 ANCO		
*WOOD SINGLES: 5X TO 12X BASE CARD HI		
ONE WOOD CARD VIA MAIL PER		
EXCH.CARD		

❑ F1 Jeff Bagwell	8.00	3.60
❑ F2 Albert Belle	6.00	2.70
❑ F3 Barry Bonds	8.00	3.60
❑ F4 Andres Galarraga	6.00	2.70
❑ F5 Ken Griffey Jr.	30.00	13.50
❑ F6 Brady Anderson	3.00	1.35
❑ F7 Mark McGwire	30.00	13.50
❑ F8 Chipper Jones	15.00	6.75
❑ F9 Frank Thomas	12.00	5.50
❑ F10 Mike Piazza	20.00	9.00
❑ F11 Mo Vaughn	6.00	2.70
❑ F12 Juan Gonzalez	12.00	5.50

1997 Stadium Club Instavision

	MINT	NRMT
COMPLETE SET (22)	50.00	22.00
COMPLETE SERIES 1 (10)	25.00	11.00
COMPLETE SERIES 2 (12)	25.00	11.00
COMMON CARD (I1-I22)	1.50	.70
STATED ODDS 1:24 HOB/RET, 1:36 ANCO		

❑ I1 Eddie Murray	3.00	1.35
❑ I2 Paul Molitor	3.00	1.35
❑ I3 Todd Hundley	1.50	.70
❑ I4 Roger Clemens	8.00	3.60
❑ I5 Barry Bonds	4.00	1.80
❑ I6 Mark McGwire	15.00	6.75
❑ I7 Brady Anderson	2.00	.90
❑ I8 Barry Larkin	3.00	1.35
❑ I9 Ken Caminiti	3.00	1.35
❑ I10 Hideo Nomo	3.00	1.35
❑ I11 Bernie Williams	3.00	1.35
❑ I12 Juan Gonzalez	6.00	2.70
❑ I13 Andy Pettitte	3.00	1.35
❑ I14 Albert Belle	3.00	1.35
❑ I15 John Smoltz	3.00	1.35
❑ I16 Brian Jordan	2.00	.90
❑ I17 Derek Jeter	8.00	3.60
❑ I18 Ken Caminiti	2.00	.90
❑ I19 John Wetteland	2.00	.90
❑ I20 Brady Anderson	2.00	.90
❑ I21 Andruw Jones	3.00	1.35
❑ I22 Jim Leyritz	1.50	.70

1997 Stadium Club Millennium

	MINT	NRMT
COMPLETE SET (40)	200.00	90.00
COMPLETE SERIES 1 (20)	80.00	36.00
COMPLETE SERIES 2 (20)	120.00	55.00
COMMON CARD (M1-M40)	1.50	.70
MINOR STARS	3.00	1.35
UNLISTED STARS	6.00	2.70
STATED ODDS 1:24H/R, 1:36ANCO, 1:12HCP		

		MINT	NRMT
❑ M1	Derek Jeter	20.00	9.00
❑ M2	Mark Grudzielanek	3.00	1.35
❑ M3	Jacob Cruz	1.50	.70
❑ M4	Ray Durham	3.00	1.35
❑ M5	Tony Clark	5.00	2.20
❑ M6	Chipper Jones	15.00	6.75
❑ M7	Luis Castillo	3.00	1.35
❑ M8	Carlos Delgado	6.00	2.70
❑ M9	Brant Brown	3.00	1.35
❑ M10	Jason Kendall	5.00	2.20
❑ M11	Alan Benes	1.50	.70
❑ M12	Rey Ordonez	3.00	1.35
❑ M13	Justin Thompson	3.00	1.35
❑ M14	Jermaine Allensworth	1.50	.70
❑ M15	Brian Hunter	3.00	1.35
❑ M16	Marty Cordova	1.50	.70
❑ M17	Edgar Renteria	3.00	1.35
❑ M18	Karim Garcia	3.00	1.35
❑ M19	Todd Greene	1.50	.70
❑ M20	Paul Wilson	1.50	.70

1997 Stadium Club
Patent Leather

	MINT	NRMT
COMPLETE SET (13)	120.00	55.00
COMMON CARD (PL1-PL13)	2.00	.90
MINOR STARS	4.00	1.80
UNLISTED STARS	8.00	3.60
SER.2 STATED ODDS 1:36 RETAIL		

		MINT	NRMT
❑ PL1	Ivan Rodriguez	10.00	4.50
❑ PL2	Ken Caminiti	5.00	2.20
❑ PL3	Barry Bonds	10.00	4.50
❑ PL4	Ken Griffey Jr.	40.00	18.00
❑ PL5	Greg Maddux	20.00	9.00
❑ PL6	Craig Biggio	8.00	3.60
❑ PL7	Andres Galarraga	8.00	3.60
❑ PL8	Kenny Lofton	5.00	2.20
❑ PL9	Barry Larkin	8.00	3.60
❑ PL10	Mark Grace	5.00	2.20
❑ PL11	Rey Ordonez	4.00	1.80
❑ PL12	Roberto Alomar	8.00	3.60
❑ PL13	Derek Jeter	25.00	11.00

1997 Stadium Club Pure
Gold

	MINT	NRMT
COMPLETE SET (20)	350.00	160.00

		MINT	NRMT
COMPLETE SERIES 1 (10)		150.00	70.00
COMPLETE SERIES 2 (10)		200.00	90.00
COMMON CARD (PG1-PG20)		5.00	2.20
UNLISTED STARS		10.00	4.50
STATED ODDS 1:72H/R, 1:108ANCO, 1:36HCP			

		MINT	NRMT
❑ PG1	Brady Anderson	5.00	2.20
❑ PG2	Albert Belle	10.00	4.50
❑ PG3	Dante Bichette	5.00	2.20
❑ PG4	Barry Bonds	12.00	5.50
❑ PG5	Jay Buhner	5.00	2.20
❑ PG6	Tony Gwynn	25.00	11.00
❑ PG7	Chipper Jones	25.00	11.00
❑ PG8	Mark McGwire	50.00	22.00
❑ PG9	Gary Sheffield	10.00	4.50
❑ PG10	Frank Thomas	20.00	9.00
❑ PG11	Juan Gonzalez	20.00	9.00
❑ PG12	Ken Caminiti	6.00	2.70
❑ PG13	Kenny Lofton	6.00	2.70
❑ PG14	Jeff Bagwell	12.00	5.50
❑ PG15	Ken Griffey Jr.	50.00	22.00
❑ PG16	Cal Ripken	40.00	18.00
❑ PG17	Mo Vaughn	10.00	4.50
❑ PG18	Mike Piazza	30.00	13.50
❑ PG19	Derek Jeter	30.00	13.50
❑ PG20	Andres Galarraga	10.00	4.50

1998 Stadium Club

	MINT	NRMT
COMPLETE SET (400)	80.00	36.00
COMPLETE SERIES 1 (200)	40.00	18.00
COMPLETE SERIES 2 (200)	40.00	18.00
COMMON CARD (1-400)	.15	.07
MINOR STARS	.25	.11
SEMISTARS	.40	.18
UNLISTED STARS	.60	.25
ODD CARDS DISTRIBUTED IN SER.1 PACKS		
EVEN CARDS DISTRIBUTED IN SER.2 PACKS		
ONE RIPKEN SOUND CHIP PER HTA BOX		

		MINT	NRMT
❑ 1	Chipper Jones	1.50	.70
❑ 2	Frank Thomas	1.25	.55
❑ 3	Vladimir Guerrero	.75	.35
❑ 4	Ellis Burks	.25	.11
❑ 5	John Franco	.25	.11
❑ 6	Paul Molitor	.60	.25
❑ 7	Rusty Greer	.25	.11
❑ 8	Todd Hundley	.25	.11
❑ 9	Brett Tomko	.15	.07
❑ 10	Eric Karros	.25	.11
❑ 11	Mike Cameron	.25	.11
❑ 12	Jim Edmonds	.25	.11
❑ 13	Bernie Williams	.60	.25
❑ 14	Denny Neagle	.15	.07
❑ 15	Jason Dickson	.15	.07
❑ 16	Sammy Sosa	2.00	.90
❑ 17	Brian Jordan	.25	.11
❑ 18	Jose Vidro	.25	.11
❑ 19	Scott Spiezio	.15	.07
❑ 20	Jay Buhner	.25	.11
❑ 21	Jim Thome	.60	.25
❑ 22	Sandy Alomar Jr.	.25	.11
❑ 23	Livan Hernandez	.15	.07
❑ 24	Roberto Alomar	.60	.25
❑ 25	Chris Gomez	.15	.07
❑ 26	John Wetteland	.25	.11
❑ 27	Willie Greene	.15	.07
❑ 28	Gregg Jefferies	.15	.07
❑ 29	Johnny Damon	.25	.11
❑ 30	Barry Larkin	.60	.25
❑ 31	Chuck Knoblauch	.25	.11
❑ 32	Mo Vaughn	.60	.25
❑ 33	Tony Clark	.25	.11
❑ 34	Marty Cordova	.15	.07
❑ 35	Vinny Castilla	.25	.11
❑ 36	Jeff King	.15	.07
❑ 37	Reggie Jefferson	.15	.07
❑ 38	Mariano Rivera	.25	.11
❑ 39	Jermaine Allensworth	.15	.07
❑ 40	Livan Hernandez	.15	.07
❑ 41	Heathcliff Slocumb	.15	.07
❑ 42	Jacob Cruz	.15	.07
❑ 43	Barry Bonds	.75	.35
❑ 44	Dave Magadan	.15	.07
❑ 45	Chan Ho Park	.25	.11
❑ 46	Jeremi Gonzalez	.15	.07
❑ 47	Jeff Cirillo	.25	.11
❑ 48	Delino DeShields	.15	.07
❑ 49	Craig Biggio	.60	.25
❑ 50	Benito Santiago	.15	.07
❑ 51	Mark Clark	.15	.07
❑ 52	Fernando Vina	.15	.07
❑ 53	F.P. Santangelo	.15	.07
❑ 54	Pep Harris	.15	.07
❑ 55	Edgar Renteria	.15	.07
❑ 56	Jeff Bagwell	.75	.35
❑ 57	Jimmy Key	.15	.07
❑ 58	Bartolo Colon	.25	.11
❑ 59	Curt Schilling	.40	.18
❑ 60	Steve Finley	.25	.11
❑ 61	Andy Ashby	.15	.07
❑ 62	John Burkett	.15	.07
❑ 63	Orel Hershiser	.25	.11
❑ 64	Pokey Reese	.15	.07
❑ 65	Scott Servais	.15	.07
❑ 66	Todd Jones	.15	.07
❑ 67	Javy Lopez	.25	.11
❑ 68	Robin Ventura	.25	.11
❑ 69	Miguel Tejada	.25	.11
❑ 70	Raul Casanova	.15	.07
❑ 71	Reggie Sanders	.15	.07
❑ 72	Edgardo Alfonzo	.40	.18
❑ 73	Dean Palmer	.25	.11
❑ 74	Todd Stottlemyre	.15	.07
❑ 75	David Wells	.25	.11
❑ 76	Troy Percival	.25	.11
❑ 77	Albert Belle	.60	.25
❑ 78	Pat Hentgen	.15	.07
❑ 79	Brian Hunter	.15	.07
❑ 80	Richard Hidalgo	.25	.11
❑ 81	Darren Oliver	.15	.07
❑ 82	Mark Wohlers	.15	.07
❑ 83	Cal Ripken	2.50	1.10
❑ 84	Hideo Nomo	.60	.25
❑ 85	Derrek Lee	.15	.07
❑ 86	Stan Javier	.15	.07
❑ 87	Rey Ordonez	.25	.11
❑ 88	Randy Johnson	.60	.25
❑ 89	Jeff Kent	.25	.11
❑ 90	Brian McRae	.15	.07
❑ 91	Manny Ramirez	.75	.35
❑ 92	Trevor Hoffman	.25	.11
❑ 93	Doug Glanville	.25	.11
❑ 94	Todd Walker	.25	.11
❑ 95	Andy Benes	.15	.07
❑ 96	Jason Schmidt	.15	.07
❑ 97	Mike Matheny	.15	.07
❑ 98	Tim Naehring	.15	.07
❑ 99	Keith Lockhart	.15	.07
❑ 100	Jose Rosado	.15	.07
❑ 101	Roger Clemens	1.50	.70
❑ 102	Pedro Astacio	.15	.07
❑ 103	Mark Bellhorn	.15	.07
❑ 104	Paul O'Neill	.25	.11
❑ 105	Darin Erstad	.40	.18
❑ 106	Mike Lieberthal	.15	.07
❑ 107	Wilson Alvarez	.15	.07
❑ 108	Mike Mussina	.60	.25
❑ 109	George Williams	.15	.07
❑ 110	Cliff Floyd	.25	.11
❑ 111	Shawn Estes	.15	.07
❑ 112	Mark Grudzielanek	.15	.07
❑ 113	Tony Gwynn	1.50	.70

114	Alan Benes	.15	.07
115	Terry Steinbach	.15	.07
116	Greg Maddux	1.50	.70
117	Andy Pettitte	.25	.11
118	Dave Nilsson	.15	.07
119	Deivi Cruz	.15	.07
120	Carlos Delgado	.60	.25
121	Scott Hatteberg	.15	.07
122	John Olerud	.25	.11
123	Todd Dunwoody	.15	.07
124	Garret Anderson	.25	.11
125	Royce Clayton	.15	.07
126	Dante Powell	.15	.07
127	Tom Glavine	.60	.25
128	Gary DiSarcina	.15	.07
129	Terry Adams	.15	.07
130	Raul Mondesi	.25	.11
131	Dan Wilson	.15	.07
132	Al Martin	.15	.07
133	Mickey Morandini	.15	.07
134	Rafael Palmeiro	.60	.25
135	Juan Encarnacion	.25	.11
136	Jim Pittsley	.15	.07
137	Magglio Ordonez	2.00	.90
138	Will Clark	.60	.25
139	Todd Helton	.75	.35
140	Kelvim Escobar	.25	.11
141	Esteban Loaiza	.15	.07
142	John Jaha	.25	.11
143	Jeff Fassero	.15	.07
144	Harold Baines	.25	.11
145	Butch Huskey	.15	.07
146	Pat Meares	.15	.07
147	Brian Giles	.25	.11
148	Ramiro Mendoza	.15	.07
149	John Smoltz	.40	.18
150	Felix Martinez	.15	.07
151	Jose Valentin	.15	.07
152	Brad Rigby	.15	.07
153	Ed Sprague	.15	.07
154	Mike Hampton	.25	.11
155	Carlos Perez	.15	.07
156	Ray Lankford	.25	.11
157	Bobby Bonilla	.25	.11
158	Bill Mueller	.15	.07
159	Jeffrey Hammonds	.15	.07
160	Charles Nagy	.25	.11
161	Rich Loiselle	.40	.18
162	Al Leiter	.25	.11
163	Larry Walker	.60	.25
164	Chris Hoiles	.15	.07
165	Jeff Montgomery	.15	.07
166	Francisco Cordova	.15	.07
167	James Baldwin	.15	.07
168	Mark McLemore	.15	.07
169	Kevin Appier	.25	.11
170	Jamey Wright	.15	.07
171	Nomar Garciaparra	2.00	.90
172	Matt Franco	.15	.07
173	Armando Benitez	.15	.07
174	Jeromy Burnitz	.25	.11
175	Ismael Valdes	.15	.07
176	Lance Johnson	.15	.07
177	Paul Sorrento	.15	.07
178	Rondell White	.25	.11
179	Kevin Elster	.15	.07
180	Jason Giambi	.25	.11
181	Carlos Baerga	.15	.07
182	Russ Davis	.15	.07
183	Ryan McGuire	.15	.07
184	Eric Young	.15	.07
185	Ron Gant	.25	.11
186	Manny Alexander	.15	.07
187	Scott Karl	.15	.07
188	Brady Anderson	.25	.11
189	Randall Simon	.25	.11
190	Tim Belcher	.15	.07
191	Jaret Wright	.25	.11
192	Dante Bichette	.25	.11
193	John Valentin	.25	.11
194	Darren Bragg	.15	.07
195	Mike Sweeney	.25	.11
196	Craig Counsell	.15	.07
197	Jaime Navarro	.15	.07
198	Todd Dunn	.15	.07
199	Ken Griffey Jr.	3.00	1.35
200	Juan Gonzalez	1.25	.55
201	Billy Wagner	.25	.11
202	Tino Martinez	.25	.11
203	Mark McGwire	4.00	1.80
204	Jeff D'Amico	.15	.07
205	Rico Brogna	.15	.07
206	Todd Hollandsworth	.15	.07
207	Chad Curtis	.15	.07
208	Tom Goodwin	.15	.07
209	Neifi Perez	.25	.11
210	Derek Bell	.25	.11
211	Quilvio Veras	.15	.07
212	Greg Vaughn	.25	.11
213	Kirk Rueter	.15	.07
214	Arthur Rhodes	.15	.07
215	Cal Eldred	.15	.07
216	Bill Taylor	.15	.07
217	Todd Greene	.15	.07
218	Mario Valdez	.15	.07
219	Ricky Bottalico	.15	.07
220	Frank Rodriguez	.15	.07
221	Rich Becker	.15	.07
222	Roberto Duran	.25	.11
223	Ivan Rodriguez	.75	.35
224	Mike Jackson	.15	.07
225	Deion Sanders	.25	.11
226	Tony Womack	.25	.11
227	Mark Kotsay	.25	.11
228	Steve Trachsel	.15	.07
229	Ryan Klesko	.25	.11
230	Ken Cloude	.15	.07
231	Luis Gonzalez	.25	.11
232	Gary Gaetti	.25	.11
233	Michael Tucker	.15	.07
234	Shawn Green	.60	.25
235	Ariel Prieto	.15	.07
236	Kirt Manwaring	.15	.07
237	Omar Vizquel	.25	.11
238	Matt Beech	.15	.07
239	Justin Thompson	.15	.07
240	Bret Boone	.25	.11
241	Derek Jeter	2.00	.90
242	Ken Caminiti	.25	.11
243	Jose Offerman	.25	.11
244	Kevin Tapani	.15	.07
245	Jason Kendall	.25	.11
246	Jose Guillen	.25	.11
247	Mike Bordick	.15	.07
248	Dustin Hermanson	.15	.07
249	Darrin Fletcher	.15	.07
250	Dave Hollins	.15	.07
251	Ramon Martinez	.25	.11
252	Hideki Irabu	.25	.11
253	Mark Grace	.40	.18
254	Jason Isringhausen	.15	.07
255	Jose Cruz Jr.	.25	.11
256	Brian Johnson	.15	.07
257	Brad Ausmus	.15	.07
258	Andruw Jones	.60	.25
259	Doug Jones	.15	.07
260	Jeff Shaw	.15	.07
261	Chuck Finley	.15	.07
262	Gary Sheffield	.25	.11
263	David Segui	.15	.07
264	John Smiley	.15	.07
265	Tim Salmon	.40	.18
266	J.T. Snow	.25	.11
267	Alex Fernandez	.25	.11
268	Matt Stairs	.25	.11
269	B.J. Surhoff	.25	.11
270	Keith Foulke	.15	.07
271	Edgar Martinez	.25	.11
272	Shannon Stewart	.25	.11
273	Eduardo Perez	.15	.07
274	Wally Joyner	.25	.11
275	Kevin Young	.15	.07
276	Eli Marrero	.15	.07
277	Brad Radke	.25	.11
278	Jamie Moyer	.15	.07
279	Joe Girardi	.15	.07
280	Troy O'Leary	.15	.07
281	Jeff Frye	.15	.07
282	Jose Offerman	.25	.11
283	Scott Erickson	.15	.07
284	Sean Berry	.15	.07
285	Shigetoshi Hasegawa	.25	.11
286	Felix Heredia	.15	.07
287	Willie McGee	.25	.11
288	Alex Rodriguez	2.00	.90
289	Ugueth Urbina	.15	.07
290	Jon Lieber	.15	.07
291	Fernando Tatis	.60	.25
292	Chris Stynes	.15	.07
293	Bernard Gilkey	.15	.07
294	Joey Hamilton	.15	.07
295	Matt Karchner	.15	.07
296	Paul Wilson	.15	.07
297	Damion Easley	.25	.11
298	Kevin Millwood	2.00	.90
299	Ellis Burks	.25	.11
300	Jerry DiPoto	.15	.07
301	Jermaine Dye	.25	.11
302	Travis Lee	.40	.18
303	Ron Coomer	.15	.07
304	Matt Williams	.60	.25
305	Bobby Higginson	.25	.11
306	Jorge Fabregas	.15	.07
307	Jon Nunnally	.15	.07
308	Jay Bell	.25	.11
309	Jason Schmidt	.15	.07
310	Andy Benes	.25	.11
311	Sterling Hitchcock	.15	.07
312	Jeff Suppan	.15	.07
313	Shane Reynolds	.25	.11
314	Willie Blair	.15	.07
315	Scott Rolen	.75	.35
316	Wilson Alvarez	.15	.07
317	David Justice	.25	.11
318	Fred McGriff	.40	.18
319	Bobby Jones	.15	.07
320	Wade Boggs	.60	.25
321	Tim Wakefield	.15	.07
322	Tony Saunders	.15	.07
323	David Cone	.40	.18
324	Roberto Hernandez	.15	.07
325	Jose Canseco	.75	.35
326	Kevin Stocker	.15	.07
327	Gerald Williams	.15	.07
328	Quinton McCracken	.15	.07
329	Mark Gardner	.15	.07
330	Ben Grieve	.60	.25
331	Kevin Brown	.40	.18
332	Mike Lowell	.60	.25
333	Jed Hansen	.15	.07
334	Abraham Nunez	.15	.07
335	John Thomson	.15	.07
336	Masato Yoshii	.40	.18
337	Mike Piazza	2.00	.90
338	Brad Fullmer	.15	.07
339	Ray Durham	.25	.11
340	Kerry Wood	.75	.35
341	Kevin Polcovich	.15	.07
342	Russ Johnson	.15	.07
343	Darryl Hamilton	.15	.07
344	David Ortiz	.25	.11
345	Kevin Orie	.15	.07
346	Mike Caruso	.25	.11
347	Juan Guzman	.15	.07
348	Ruben Rivera	.25	.11
349	Rick Aguilera	.15	.07
350	Bobby Estalella	.15	.07
351	Bobby Witt	.15	.07
352	Paul Konerko	.25	.11
353	Matt Morris	.15	.07
354	Carl Pavano	.15	.07
355	Todd Zeile	.25	.11
356	Kevin Brown TR	.40	.18
357	Alex Gonzalez	.15	.07
358	Chuck Knoblauch TR	.25	.11
359	Joey Cora	.15	.07
360	Mike Lansing TR	.15	.07
361	Adrian Beltre	.60	.25
362	Dennis Eckersley TR	.25	.11
363	A.J. Hinch	.15	.07
364	Kenny Lofton TR	.40	.18
365	Alex Gonzalez	.25	.11
366	Henry Rodriguez TR	.25	.11
367	Mike Stoner	.40	.18
368	Darryl Kile TR	.15	.07
369	Keith McGlinchy	.15	.07
370	Walt Weiss TR	.15	.07
371	Kris Benson	.25	.11

		MINT	NRMT
❏ 372	Cecil Fielder TR	.25	.11
❏ 373	Dermal Brown TR	.25	.11
❏ 374	Rod Beck TR	.25	.11
❏ 375	Eric Milton	.15	.07
❏ 376	Travis Fryman TR	.25	.11
❏ 377	Preston Wilson TR	.25	.11
❏ 378	Chili Davis TR	.25	.11
❏ 379	Travis Lee	.40	.18
❏ 380	Jim Leyritz TR	.15	.07
❏ 381	Vernon Wells	.40	.18
❏ 382	Joe Carter TR	.25	.11
❏ 383	J.J. Davis	.25	.11
❏ 384	Marquis Grissom TR	.15	.07
❏ 385	Mike Cuddyer	1.00	.45
❏ 386	Rickey Henderson TR	.75	.35
❏ 387	Chris Enochs	.40	.18
❏ 388	Andres Galarraga TR	.40	.18
❏ 389	Jason Dellaero	.15	.07
❏ 390	Robb Nen TR	.15	.07
❏ 391	Mark Mangum	.15	.07
❏ 392	Jeff Blauser TR	.15	.07
❏ 393	Adam Kennedy	.25	.11
❏ 394	Bob Abreu TR	.25	.11
❏ 395	Jack Cust	1.25	.55
❏ 396	Jose Vizcaino TR	.15	.07
❏ 397	Jon Garland	.15	.07
❏ 398	Pedro Martinez TR	.75	.35
❏ 399	Aaron Akin	.15	.07
❏ 400	Jeff Conine TR	.15	.07
❏ NNO	C. Ripken Sound Chip 1	15.00	6.75
❏ NNO	C. Ripken Sound Chip 2	15.00	6.75

1998 Stadium Club First Day Issue

	MINT	NRMT
COMMON CARD (1-400)	8.00	3.60

*STARS: 20X TO 50X BASIC CARDS
*YNG.STARS: 15X TO 40X BASIC CARDS
*ROOKIES: 10X TO 25X BASIC CARDS
SER.1 STATED ODDS 1:42 RETAIL PACKS
SER.2 STATED ODDS 1:47 RETAIL PACKS
STATED PRINT RUN 200 SERIAL #'d SETS

1998 Stadium Club One Of A Kind

	MINT	NRMT
COMMON CARD (1-400)	10.00	4.50

*STARS: 25X TO 60X BASIC CARDS

*YOUNG STARS: 20X TO 50X BASIC CARDS
*ROOKIES: 12.5X TO 30X BASIC CARDS
SER.1 STATED ODDS 1:21 HOB, 1:13 HTA
SER.2 STATED ODDS 1:24 HOB, 1:14 HTA
STATED PRINT RUN 150 SERIAL #'d SETS

1998 Stadium Club Bowman Previews

	MINT	NRMT
COMPLETE SET (10)	40.00	18.00
COMMON CARD (BP1-BP10)	.75	.35

SER.1 STATED ODDS 1:12 H/R, 1:4 HTA

		MINT	NRMT
❏ BP1	Nomar Garciaparra	6.00	2.70
❏ BP2	Scott Rolen	3.00	1.35
❏ BP3	Ken Griffey Jr.	10.00	4.50
❏ BP4	Frank Thomas	4.00	1.80
❏ BP5	Larry Walker	2.00	.90
❏ BP6	Mike Piazza	6.00	2.70
❏ BP7	Chipper Jones	5.00	2.20
❏ BP8	Tino Martinez	.75	.35
❏ BP9	Mark McGwire	12.00	5.50
❏ BP10	Barry Bonds	2.50	1.10

1998 Stadium Club Bowman Prospect Previews

	MINT	NRMT
COMPLETE SET (10)	15.00	6.75
COMMON CARD (BP1-BP10)	1.00	.45
SEMISTARS	1.50	.70
UNLISTED STARS	2.50	1.10

SER.2 STATED ODDS 1:12 H/R, 1:4 HTA

		MINT	NRMT
❏ BP1	Ben Grieve	2.50	1.10
❏ BP2	Brad Fullmer	1.00	.45
❏ BP3	Ryan Anderson	4.00	1.80
❏ BP4	Mark Kotsay	1.00	.45
❏ BP5	Bobby Estalella	1.00	.45
❏ BP6	Juan Encarnacion	1.00	.45
❏ BP7	Todd Helton	3.00	1.35
❏ BP8	Mike Lowell	2.50	1.10
❏ BP9	A.J. Hinch	1.00	.45
❏ BP10	Richard Hidalgo	1.00	.45

1998 Stadium Club Co-Signers

	MINT	NRMT
COMMON CARD (CS1-CS36)	15.00	6.75

SER.1 A ODDS 1:4372 HOB, 1:2623 HTA
SER.2 A ODDS 1:4702 HOB, 1:2821 HTA
SER.1 B ODDS 1:1457 HOB, 1:874 HTA
SER.2 B ODDS 1:1567 HOB, 1:940 HTA
SER.1 C ODDS 1:121 HOB, 1:73 HTA
SER.2 C ODDS 1:131 HOB, 1:78 HTA

		MINT	NRMT
❏ CS1	Nomar Garciaparra A Scott Rolen	800.00	350.00
❏ CS2	Nomar Garciaparra B Derek Jeter	300.00	135.00
❏ CS3	Nomar Garciaparra C Eric Karros	120.00	55.00
❏ CS4	Scott Rolen C Derek Jeter	150.00	70.00
❏ CS5	Scott Rolen B Eric Karros	120.00	55.00
❏ CS6	Derek Jeter A Eric Karros	600.00	275.00
❏ CS7	Travis Lee B Jose Cruz Jr.	30.00	13.50
❏ CS8	Travis Lee C Mark Kotsay	15.00	6.75
❏ CS9	Travis Lee A Paul Konerko	80.00	36.00
❏ CS10	Jose Cruz Jr. A Mark Kotsay	100.00	45.00
❏ CS11	Jose Cruz Jr. C Paul Konerko	15.00	6.75
❏ CS12	Mark Kotsay B Paul Konerko	50.00	22.00
❏ CS13	Tony Gwynn A Larry Walker	600.00	275.00
❏ CS14	Tony Gwynn C Mark Grudzielanek	100.00	45.00
❏ CS15	Tony Gwynn B Andres Galarraga	250.00	110.00
❏ CS16	Larry Walker B Mark Grudzielanek	100.00	45.00
❏ CS17	Larry Walker C Andres Galarraga	50.00	22.00
❏ CS18	Mark Grudzielanek A Andres Galarraga	120.00	55.00
❏ CS19	Sandy Alomar A Roberto Alomar	500.00	220.00
❏ CS20	Sandy Alomar C Andy Pettitte	25.00	11.00
❏ CS21	Sandy Alomar B Tino Martinez	80.00	36.00
❏ CS22	Roberto Alomar B Andy Pettitte	120.00	55.00
❏ CS23	Roberto Alomar C Tino Martinez	50.00	22.00
❏ CS24	Andy Pettitte A Tino Martinez	200.00	90.00
❏ CS25	Tony Clark A Todd Hundley	100.00	45.00
❏ CS26	Tony Clark B Tim Salmon	60.00	27.00
❏ CS27	Tony Clark C Robin Ventura	25.00	11.00
❏ CS28	Todd Hundley C Tim Salmon	25.00	11.00

		MINT	NRMT
☐ CS29	Todd Hundley B ..... Robin Ventura	50.00	22.00
☐ CS30	Tim Salmon A .... Robin Ventura	150.00	70.00
☐ CS31	Roger Clemens B.. Randy Johnson	250.00	110.00
☐ CS32	Roger Clemens A. Jaret Wright	500.00	220.00
☐ CS33	Roger Clemens C. Matt Morris	100.00	45.00
☐ CS34	Randy Johnson C... Jaret Wright	50.00	22.00
☐ CS35	Randy Johnson A.. Matt Morris	200.00	90.00
☐ CS36	Jaret Wright B	40.00	18.00

1998 Stadium Club In The Wings

		MINT	NRMT
COMPLETE SET (15)		50.00	22.00
COMMON CARD (W1-W15)		2.00	.90
MINOR STARS		3.00	1.35
SEMISTARS		5.00	2.20
SER.1 STATED ODDS 1:36 H/R, 1:12 HTA			

☐ W1	Juan Encarnacion	3.00	1.35
☐ W2	Brad Fullmer	2.00	.90
☐ W3	Ben Grieve	8.00	3.60
☐ W4	Todd Helton	10.00	4.50
☐ W5	Richard Hidalgo	3.00	1.35
☐ W6	Russ Johnson	2.00	.90
☐ W7	Paul Konerko	3.00	1.35
☐ W8	Mark Kotsay	3.00	1.35
☐ W9	Derrek Lee	2.00	.90
☐ W10	Travis Lee	5.00	2.20
☐ W11	Eli Marrero	2.00	.90
☐ W12	David Ortiz	2.00	.90
☐ W13	Randall Simon	3.00	1.35
☐ W14	Shannon Stewart	3.00	1.35
☐ W15	Fernando Tatis	8.00	3.60

1998 Stadium Club Never Compromise

	MINT	NRMT
COMPLETE SET (20)	100.00	45.00
COMMON CARD (NC1-NC20)..	1.25	.55

☐ NC1	Cal Ripken	12.00	5.50
☐ NC2	Ivan Rodriguez	4.00	1.80
☐ NC3	Ken Griffey Jr.	15.00	6.75
☐ NC4	Frank Thomas	6.00	2.70
☐ NC5	Tony Gwynn	8.00	3.60
☐ NC6	Mike Piazza	10.00	4.50
☐ NC7	Randy Johnson	3.00	1.35
☐ NC8	Greg Maddux	8.00	3.60
☐ NC9	Roger Clemens	8.00	3.60
☐ NC10	Derek Jeter	10.00	4.50
☐ NC11	Chipper Jones	8.00	3.60
☐ NC12	Barry Bonds	4.00	1.80
☐ NC13	Larry Walker	3.00	1.35
☐ NC14	Jeff Bagwell	4.00	1.80
☐ NC15	Barry Larkin	3.00	1.35
☐ NC16	Ken Caminiti	1.25	.55
☐ NC17	Mark McGwire	20.00	9.00
☐ NC18	Manny Ramirez	4.00	1.80
☐ NC19	Tim Salmon	2.00	.90
☐ NC20	Paul Molitor	3.00	1.35

1998 Stadium Club Playing With Passion

	MINT	NRMT
COMPLETE SET (10)	30.00	13.50
COMMON CARD (P1-P10)	.75	.35
SER.2 STATED ODDS 1:12 H/R, 1:4 HTA		

☐ P1	Bernie Williams	2.00	.90
☐ P2	Jim Edmonds	.75	.35
☐ P3	Chipper Jones	5.00	2.20
☐ P4	Cal Ripken	8.00	3.60
☐ P5	Craig Biggio	2.00	.90
☐ P6	Juan Gonzalez	4.00	1.80
☐ P7	Alex Rodriguez	6.00	2.70
☐ P8	Tino Martinez	.75	.35
☐ P9	Mike Piazza	6.00	2.70
☐ P10	Ken Griffey Jr.	10.00	4.50

1998 Stadium Club Royal Court

	MINT	NRMT
COMPLETE SET (15)	200.00	90.00
COMMON CARD (RC1-RC15).	2.50	1.10
SER.2 STATED ODDS 1:36 H/R, 1:12 HTA		

☐ RC1	Ken Griffey Jr.	30.00	13.50
☐ RC2	Frank Thomas	12.00	5.50
☐ RC3	Mike Piazza	20.00	9.00
☐ RC4	Chipper Jones	15.00	6.75
☐ RC5	Mark McGwire	40.00	18.00
☐ RC6	Cal Ripken	25.00	11.00
☐ RC7	Jeff Bagwell	8.00	3.60
☐ RC8	Barry Bonds	8.00	3.60
☐ RC9	Juan Gonzalez	12.00	5.50
☐ RC10	Alex Rodriguez	20.00	9.00
☐ RC11	Travis Lee	4.00	1.80
☐ RC12	Paul Konerko	2.50	1.10
☐ RC13	Todd Helton	6.00	2.70
☐ RC14	Ben Grieve	6.00	2.70
☐ RC15	Mark Kotsay	2.50	1.10

1998 Stadium Club Triumvirate Luminous

	MINT	NRMT
COMPLETE SET (54)	1000.00	450.00
COMPLETE SERIES 1 (24)	400.00	180.00
COMPLETE SERIES 2 (30)	600.00	275.00
COMMON CARD (T1A-T18C) .	5.00	2.20
SEMISTARS	8.00	3.60
UNLISTED STARS	12.00	5.50
STATED ODDS 1:48 RETAIL		
*LUMINESCENT: 1.25X TO 3X HI COLUMN		
LUMINESCENT STATED ODDS 1:192 RETAIL		
*ILLUMINATOR: 2X TO 5X HI COLUMN		
ILLUMINATOR STATED ODDS 1:384 RETAIL		

☐ T1A	Chipper Jones	30.00	13.50
☐ T1B	Andruw Jones	12.00	5.50
☐ T1C	Kenny Lofton	8.00	3.60
☐ T2A	Derek Jeter	40.00	18.00
☐ T2B	Bernie Williams	12.00	5.50
☐ T2C	Tino Martinez	5.00	2.20
☐ T3A	Jay Buhner	5.00	2.20
☐ T3B	Edgar Martinez	5.00	2.20
☐ T3C	Ken Griffey Jr.	60.00	27.00
☐ T4A	Albert Belle	12.00	5.50
☐ T4B	Robin Ventura	5.00	2.20
☐ T4C	Frank Thomas	25.00	11.00
☐ T5A	Brady Anderson	5.00	2.20
☐ T5B	Cal Ripken	50.00	22.00
☐ T5C	Rafael Palmeiro	12.00	5.50
☐ T6A	Mike Piazza	40.00	18.00
☐ T6B	Raul Mondesi	5.00	2.20
☐ T6C	Eric Karros	5.00	2.20
☐ T7A	Vinny Castilla	5.00	2.20
☐ T7B	Andres Galarraga	8.00	3.60
☐ T7C	Larry Walker	12.00	5.50
☐ T8A	Jim Thome	12.00	5.50
☐ T8B	Manny Ramirez	15.00	6.75
☐ T8C	David Justice	5.00	2.20
☐ T9A	Mike Mussina	12.00	5.50
☐ T9B	Greg Maddux	30.00	13.50
☐ T9C	Randy Johnson	12.00	5.50
☐ T10A	Mike Piazza	40.00	18.00
☐ T10B	Sandy Alomar Jr.	5.00	2.20
☐ T10C	Ivan Rodriguez	15.00	6.75
☐ T11A	Mark McGwire	80.00	36.00
☐ T11B	Tino Martinez	5.00	2.20
☐ T11C	Frank Thomas	25.00	11.00
☐ T12A	Roberto Alomar	12.00	5.50
☐ T12B	Chuck Knoblauch	5.00	2.20
☐ T12C	Craig Biggio	12.00	5.50

		MINT	NRMT
❏ T13A	Cal Ripken	50.00	22.00
❏ T13B	Chipper Jones	30.00	13.50
❏ T13C	Ken Caminiti	5.00	2.20
❏ T14A	Derek Jeter	30.00	13.50
❏ T14B	Nomar Garciaparra	40.00	18.00
❏ T14C	Alex Rodriguez	40.00	18.00
❏ T15A	Barry Bonds	15.00	6.75
❏ T15B	David Justice	5.00	2.20
❏ T15C	Albert Belle	12.00	5.50
❏ T16A	Bernie Williams	12.00	5.50
❏ T16B	Ken Griffey Jr.	60.00	27.00
❏ T16C	Ray Lankford	5.00	2.20
❏ T17A	Tim Salmon	8.00	3.60
❏ T17B	Larry Walker	12.00	5.50
❏ T17C	Tony Gwynn	25.00	11.00
❏ T18A	Paul Molitor	12.00	5.50
❏ T18B	Edgar Martinez	5.00	2.20
❏ T18C	Juan Gonzalez	25.00	11.00

1999 Stadium Club

	MINT	NRMT
COMPLETE SET (355)	125.00	55.00
COMPLETE SERIES 1 (170)	65.00	29.00
COMP.SER.1 w/o SP's (150)	25.00	11.00
COMPLETE SERIES 2 (185)	60.00	27.00
COMP.SER.2 w/o SP's (165)	25.00	11.00
COMMON CARD (1-140/161-170)	.15	.07
COMMON CARD (171-335)	.15	.07
MINOR STARS	.25	.11
SEMISTARS	.40	.18
UNLISTED STARS	.60	.25
COMM.SP (141-160/336-355)	1.00	.45
SP ODDS 1:3 HOB/RET, 1 PER HTA		

#	Player	MINT	NRMT
❏ 1	Alex Rodriguez	2.00	.90
❏ 2	Chipper Jones	1.50	.70
❏ 3	Rusty Greer	.25	.11
❏ 4	Jim Edmonds	.25	.11
❏ 5	Ron Gant	.25	.11
❏ 6	Kevin Polcovich	.15	.07
❏ 7	Darryl Strawberry	.25	.11
❏ 8	Bill Mueller	.15	.07
❏ 9	Vinny Castilla	.25	.11
❏ 10	Wade Boggs	.60	.25
❏ 11	Jose Lima	.25	.11
❏ 12	Darren Dreifort	.15	.07
❏ 13	Jay Bell	.25	.11
❏ 14	Ben Grieve	.60	.25
❏ 15	Shawn Green	.60	.25
❏ 16	Andres Galarraga	.40	.18
❏ 17	Bartolo Colon	.25	.11
❏ 18	Francisco Cordova	.15	.07
❏ 19	Paul O'Neill	.25	.11
❏ 20	Trevor Hoffman	.25	.11
❏ 21	Darren Oliver	.15	.07
❏ 22	John Franco	.25	.11
❏ 23	Eli Marrero	.15	.07
❏ 24	Roberto Hernandez	.15	.07
❏ 25	Craig Biggio	.60	.25
❏ 26	Brad Fullmer	.25	.11
❏ 27	Scott Erickson	.15	.07
❏ 28	Tom Gordon	.25	.11
❏ 29	Brian Hunter	.15	.07
❏ 30	Raul Mondesi	.25	.11
❏ 31	Rick Reed	.15	.07
❏ 32	Jose Canseco	.75	.35
❏ 33	Robb Nen	.15	.07
❏ 34	Turner Ward	.15	.07
❏ 35	Orlando Hernandez	.60	.25
❏ 36	Jeff Shaw	.15	.07
❏ 37	Matt Lawton	.15	.07
❏ 38	David Wells	.25	.11
❏ 39	Bob Abreu	.25	.11
❏ 40	Jeromy Burnitz	.25	.11
❏ 41	Delvi Cruz	.15	.07
❏ 42	Derek Bell	.25	.11
❏ 43	Rico Brogna	.15	.07
❏ 44	Dmitri Young	.25	.11
❏ 45	Chuck Knoblauch	.25	.11
❏ 46	Johnny Damon	.25	.11
❏ 47	Brian Meadows	.15	.07
❏ 48	Jeremi Gonzalez	.15	.07
❏ 49	Gary DiSarcina	.15	.07
❏ 50	Frank Thomas	1.25	.55
❏ 51	F.P. Santangelo	.15	.07
❏ 52	Tom Candiotti	.15	.07
❏ 53	Shane Reynolds	.25	.11
❏ 54	Rod Beck	.25	.11
❏ 55	Rey Ordonez	.25	.11
❏ 56	Todd Helton	.60	.25
❏ 57	Mickey Morandini	.15	.07
❏ 58	Jorge Posada	.15	.07
❏ 59	Mike Mussina	.60	.25
❏ 60	Al Leiter	.25	.11
❏ 61	David Segui	.15	.07
❏ 62	Brian McRae	.15	.07
❏ 63	Fred McGriff	.40	.18
❏ 64	Brett Tomko	.15	.07
❏ 65	Derek Jeter	2.00	.90
❏ 66	Sammy Sosa	2.00	.90
❏ 67	Kenny Rogers	.15	.07
❏ 68	Dave Nilsson	.15	.07
❏ 69	Eric Young	.15	.07
❏ 70	Mark McGwire	4.00	1.80
❏ 71	Kenny Lofton	.40	.18
❏ 72	Tom Glavine	.60	.25
❏ 73	Jose Hamilton	.15	.07
❏ 74	John Valentin	.25	.11
❏ 75	Mariano Rivera	.25	.11
❏ 76	Ray Durham	.25	.11
❏ 77	Tony Clark	.25	.11
❏ 78	Livan Hernandez	.15	.07
❏ 79	Rickey Henderson	.75	.35
❏ 80	Vladimir Guerrero	.75	.35
❏ 81	J.T. Snow	.25	.11
❏ 82	Juan Guzman	.15	.07
❏ 83	Darryl Hamilton	.15	.07
❏ 84	Matt Anderson	.15	.07
❏ 85	Travis Lee	.40	.18
❏ 86	Joe Randa	.15	.07
❏ 87	Dave Dellucci	.15	.07
❏ 88	Moises Alou	.25	.11
❏ 89	Alex Gonzalez	.25	.11
❏ 90	Tony Womack	.25	.11
❏ 91	Neifi Perez	.25	.11
❏ 92	Travis Fryman	.25	.11
❏ 93	Masato Yoshii	.15	.07
❏ 94	Woody Williams	.15	.07
❏ 95	Ray Lankford	.25	.11
❏ 96	Roger Clemens	1.00	.45
❏ 97	Dustin Hermanson	.15	.07
❏ 98	Joe Carter	.25	.11
❏ 99	Jason Schmidt	.15	.07
❏ 100	Greg Maddux	1.50	.70
❏ 101	Kevin Tapani	.15	.07
❏ 102	Charles Johnson	.25	.11
❏ 103	Derek Lee	.15	.07
❏ 104	Pete Harnisch	.15	.07
❏ 105	Dante Bichette	.25	.11
❏ 106	Scott Brosius	.15	.07
❏ 107	Mike Caruso	.15	.07
❏ 108	Eddie Taubensee	.15	.07
❏ 109	Jeff Fassero	.15	.07
❏ 110	Marquis Grissom	.15	.07
❏ 111	Jose Hernandez	.15	.07
❏ 112	Chan Ho Park	.25	.11
❏ 113	Wally Joyner	.25	.11
❏ 114	Bobby Estalella	.15	.07
❏ 115	Pedro Martinez	.75	.35
❏ 116	Shawn Estes	.15	.07
❏ 117	Walt Weiss	.15	.07
❏ 118	John Mabry	.15	.07
❏ 119	Brian Johnson	.15	.07
❏ 120	Jim Thome	.60	.25
❏ 121	Bill Spiers	.15	.07
❏ 122	John Olerud	.25	.11
❏ 123	Jeff King	.15	.07
❏ 124	Tim Belcher	.15	.07
❏ 125	John Wetteland	.25	.11
❏ 126	Tony Gwynn	1.50	.70
❏ 127	Brady Anderson	.25	.11
❏ 128	Randy Winn	.15	.07
❏ 129	Andy Fox	.15	.07
❏ 130	Eric Karros	.25	.11
❏ 131	Kevin Millwood	.40	.18
❏ 132	Andy Benes	.15	.07
❏ 133	Andy Ashby	.15	.07
❏ 134	Ron Coomer	.15	.07
❏ 135	Juan Gonzalez	1.25	.55
❏ 136	Randy Johnson	.60	.25
❏ 137	Aaron Sele	.25	.11
❏ 138	Edgardo Alfonzo	.40	.18
❏ 139	B.J. Surhoff	.25	.11
❏ 140	Jose Vizcaino	.15	.07
❏ 141	Chad Moeller SP	1.50	.70
❏ 142	Mike Zywica SP	1.25	.55
❏ 143	Angel Pena SP	1.00	.45
❏ 144	Nick Johnson SP	8.00	3.60
❏ 145	G. Chiaramonte SP	1.50	.70
❏ 146	Kit Pellow SP	2.00	.90
❏ 147	Clayton Andrews SP	1.25	.55
❏ 148	Jerry Hairston Jr. SP	1.00	.45
❏ 149	Jason Tyner SP	1.50	.70
❏ 150	Chip Ambres SP	2.00	.90
❏ 151	Pat Burrell SP	10.00	4.50
❏ 152	Josh McKinley SP	1.25	.55
❏ 153	Choo Freeman SP	2.00	.90
❏ 154	Rick Elder SP	2.50	1.10
❏ 155	Eric Valent SP	3.00	1.35
❏ 156	Jeff Winchester SP	1.25	.55
❏ 157	Mike Nannini SP	1.25	.55
❏ 158	Mamon Tucker SP	1.50	.70
❏ 159	Nate Bump SP	1.25	.55
❏ 160	Andy Brown SP	1.50	.70
❏ 161	Troy Glaus	.60	.25
❏ 162	Adrian Beltre	.60	.25
❏ 163	Mitch Meluskey	.15	.07
❏ 164	Alex Gonzalez	.25	.11
❏ 165	George Lombard	.25	.11
❏ 166	Bruce Chavez	.40	.18
❏ 167	Ruben Mateo	.60	.25
❏ 168	Calvin Pickering	.25	.11
❏ 169	Gabe Kapler	.60	.25
❏ 170	Bruce Chen	.25	.11
❏ 171	Darin Erstad	.40	.18
❏ 172	Sandy Alomar Jr.	.25	.11
❏ 173	Miguel Cairo	.15	.07
❏ 174	Jason Kendall	.25	.11
❏ 175	Cal Ripken	2.50	1.10
❏ 176	Darryl Kyle	.25	.11
❏ 177	David Cone	.40	.18
❏ 178	Mike Sweeney	.25	.11
❏ 179	Royce Clayton	.15	.07
❏ 180	Curt Schilling	.40	.18
❏ 181	Barry Larkin	.60	.25
❏ 182	Eric Milton	.15	.07
❏ 183	Ellis Burks	.25	.11
❏ 184	A.J. Hinch	.25	.11
❏ 185	Garret Anderson	.25	.11
❏ 186	Sean Bergman	.15	.07
❏ 187	Shannon Stewart	.25	.11
❏ 188	Bernard Gilkey	.15	.07
❏ 189	Jeff Blauser	.15	.07
❏ 190	Andruw Jones	.60	.25
❏ 191	Omar Daal	.15	.07
❏ 192	Jeff Kent	.25	.11
❏ 193	Mark Kotsay	.25	.11
❏ 194	Dave Burba	.15	.07
❏ 195	Bobby Higginson	.25	.11
❏ 196	Hideki Irabu	.25	.11
❏ 197	Jamie Moyer	.15	.07
❏ 198	Doug Glanville	.25	.11
❏ 199	Quinton McCracken	.15	.07
❏ 200	Ken Griffey Jr.	3.00	1.35
❏ 201	Mike Lieberthal	.25	.11
❏ 202	Carl Everett	.25	.11
❏ 203	Omar Vizquel	.25	.11
❏ 204	Mike Lansing	.15	.07
❏ 205	Manny Ramirez	.75	.35

❑ 206 Ryan Klesko	.25	.11
❑ 207 Jeff Montgomery	.15	.07
❑ 208 Chad Curtis	.15	.07
❑ 209 Rick Helling	.15	.07
❑ 210 Justin Thompson	.15	.07
❑ 211 Tom Goodwin	.15	.07
❑ 212 Todd Dunwoody	.15	.07
❑ 213 Kevin Young	.25	.11
❑ 214 Tony Saunders	.15	.07
❑ 215 Gary Sheffield	.25	.11
❑ 216 Jaret Wright	.25	.11
❑ 217 Quivilo Veras	.15	.07
❑ 218 Marty Cordova	.15	.07
❑ 219 Tino Martinez	.25	.11
❑ 220 Scott Rolen	.75	.35
❑ 221 Fernando Tatis	.60	.25
❑ 222 Damion Easley	.25	.11
❑ 223 Aramis Ramirez	.40	.18
❑ 224 Brad Radke	.25	.11
❑ 225 Nomar Garciaparra	3.00	1.35
❑ 226 Magglio Ordonez	.60	.25
❑ 227 Andy Pettitte	.25	.11
❑ 228 David Ortiz	.15	.07
❑ 229 Todd Jones	.15	.07
❑ 230 Larry Walker	.60	.25
❑ 231 Tim Wakefield	.25	.11
❑ 232 Jose Guillen	.15	.07
❑ 233 Gregg Olson	.15	.07
❑ 234 Ricky Gutierrez	.15	.07
❑ 235 Todd Walker	.25	.11
❑ 236 Abraham Nunez	.15	.07
❑ 237 Sean Casey	.25	.11
❑ 238 Greg Norton	.15	.07
❑ 239 Bret Saberhagen	.25	.11
❑ 240 Bernie Williams	.60	.25
❑ 241 Tim Salmon	.40	.18
❑ 242 Jason Giambi	.25	.11
❑ 243 Fernando Vina	.15	.07
❑ 244 Darrin Fletcher	.15	.07
❑ 245 Greg Vaughn	.25	.11
❑ 246 Dennis Reyes	.15	.07
❑ 247 Hideo Nomo	.60	.25
❑ 248 Kevin Stocker	.15	.07
❑ 249 Mike Hampton	.25	.11
❑ 250 Kerry Wood	.60	.25
❑ 251 Ismael Valdes	.15	.07
❑ 252 Pat Hentgen	.25	.11
❑ 253 Scott Spiezio	.15	.07
❑ 254 Chuck Finley	.25	.11
❑ 255 Troy Glaus	.60	.25
❑ 256 Bobby Jones	.25	.07
❑ 257 Wayne Gomes	.15	.07
❑ 258 Rondell White	.25	.11
❑ 259 Todd Zeile	.25	.11
❑ 260 Matt Williams	.60	.25
❑ 261 Henry Rodriguez	.15	.07
❑ 262 Matt Stairs	.15	.07
❑ 263 Jose Valentin	.15	.07
❑ 264 David Justice	.25	.11
❑ 265 Javy Lopez	.25	.11
❑ 266 Matt Morris	.15	.07
❑ 267 Steve Trachsel	.15	.07
❑ 268 Edgar Martinez	.25	.11
❑ 269 Al Martin	.15	.07
❑ 270 Ivan Rodriguez	.75	.35
❑ 271 Carlos Delgado	.60	.25
❑ 272 Mark Grace	.40	.18
❑ 273 Ugueth Urbina	.15	.07
❑ 274 Jay Buhner	.25	.11
❑ 275 Mike Piazza	2.00	.90
❑ 276 Rick Aguilera	.15	.07
❑ 277 Javier Valentin	.15	.07
❑ 278 Brian Anderson	.15	.07
❑ 279 Cliff Floyd	.25	.11
❑ 280 Barry Bonds	.75	.35
❑ 281 Troy O'Leary	.15	.07
❑ 282 Seth Greisinger	.15	.07
❑ 283 Mark Grudzielanek	.15	.07
❑ 284 Jose Cruz Jr.	.25	.11
❑ 285 Jeff Bagwell	.75	.35
❑ 286 John Smoltz	.40	.18
❑ 287 Jeff Cirillo	.25	.11
❑ 288 Richie Sexson	.40	.18
❑ 289 Charles Nagy	.25	.11
❑ 290 Pedro Martinez	.75	.35
❑ 291 Juan Encarnacion	.25	.11
❑ 292 Phil Nevin	.15	.07
❑ 293 Terry Steinbach	.15	.07
❑ 294 Miguel Tejada	.25	.11
❑ 295 Dan Wilson	.15	.07
❑ 296 Chris Peters	.15	.07
❑ 297 Brian Moehler	.15	.07
❑ 298 Jason Christiansen	.15	.07
❑ 299 Kelly Stinnett	.15	.07
❑ 300 Dwight Gooden	.25	.11
❑ 301 Randy Velarde	.15	.07
❑ 302 Kirt Manwaring	.15	.07
❑ 303 Jeff Abbott	.15	.07
❑ 304 Dave Hollins	.15	.07
❑ 305 Kerry Ligtenberg	.25	.11
❑ 306 Aaron Boone	.15	.07
❑ 307 Carlos Hernandez	.15	.07
❑ 308 Mike DiFelice	.15	.07
❑ 309 Brian Meadows	.15	.07
❑ 310 Tim Bogar	.15	.07
❑ 311 Greg Vaughn TR	.25	.11
❑ 312 Brant Brown TR	.15	.07
❑ 313 Steve Finley TR	.25	.11
❑ 314 Bret Boone TR	.25	.11
❑ 315 Albert Belle TR	.60	.25
❑ 316 Robin Ventura TR	.25	.11
❑ 317 Eric Davis TR	.25	.11
❑ 318 Todd Hundley TR	.25	.11
❑ 319 Roger Clemens TR	.75	.35
❑ 320 Kevin Brown TR	.40	.18
❑ 321 Jose Offerman TR	.15	.07
❑ 322 Brian Jordan TR	.25	.11
❑ 323 Mike Cameron TR	.15	.07
❑ 324 Bobby Bonilla TR	.25	.11
❑ 325 Roberto Alomar TR	.60	.25
❑ 326 Ken Caminiti TR	.25	.11
❑ 327 Todd Stottlemyre TR	.15	.07
❑ 328 Randy Johnson TR	.60	.25
❑ 329 Luis Gonzalez TR	.25	.11
❑ 330 Rafael Palmeiro TR	.60	.25
❑ 331 Devon White TR	.15	.07
❑ 332 Will Clark TR	.60	.25
❑ 333 Dean Palmer TR	.25	.11
❑ 334 Gregg Jefferies TR	.15	.07
❑ 335 Mo Vaughn TR	.60	.25
❑ 336 Brad Lidge SP	1.50	.70
❑ 337 Chris George SP	1.50	.70
❑ 338 Austin Kearns SP	2.50	1.10
❑ 339 Matt Belisle SP	1.25	.55
❑ 340 Nate Cornejo SP	1.50	.70
❑ 341 Matt Holliday SP	2.50	1.10
❑ 342 J.M. Gold SP	1.50	.70
❑ 343 Matt Roney SP	1.50	.70
❑ 344 Seth Etherton SP	1.25	.55
❑ 345 Adam Everett SP	2.00	.90
❑ 346 Marlon Anderson SP	1.00	.45
❑ 347 Ron Belliard SP	1.00	.45
❑ 348 Fernando Seguignol SP	1.00	.45
❑ 349 Michael Barrett SP	1.50	.70
❑ 350 Dernell Stenson SP	1.00	.45
❑ 351 Ryan Anderson SP	1.00	.45
❑ 352 Ramon Hernandez SP	1.00	.45
❑ 353 Jeremy Giambi SP	1.00	.45
❑ 354 Ricky Ledee SP	1.00	.45
❑ 355 Carlos Lee SP	1.00	.45

	MINT	NRMT
COMMON CARD (1-355)	4.00	1.80

*STARS: 10X TO 25X BASIC CARDS
*YNG.STARS: 8X TO 20X BASIC CARDS
*SP'S 141-160/336-355: 2X TO 5X BASIC SP'S
SER.1 STATED ODDS 1:75 RETAIL
SER.2 STATED ODDS 1:60 RETAIL
SER.1 PRINT RUN 170 SERIAL #'d SETS
SER.2 PRINT RUN 200 SERIAL #'d SETS

1999 Stadium Club One of a Kind

	MINT	NRMT
COMMON CARD (1-355)	4.00	1.80

*STARS: 10X TO 25X BASIC CARDS
*YNG.STARS: 8X TO 20X BASIC CARDS
*SP'S 141-160/336-355: 2X TO 5X BASIC
SER.1 STATED ODDS 1:53 HOBBY, 1:21 HTA
SER.2 STATED ODDS 1:48 HOBBY, 1:19 HTA
STATED PRINT RUN 150 SERIAL #'d SETS

1999 Stadium Club Printing Plates

	MINT	NRMT

SER.1 STATED ODDS 1:190 HTA
SER.2 STATED ODDS 1:175 HTA
STATED PRINT RUN 4 DIFT.COLOR SETS
NO PRICING DUE TO SCARCITY

1999 Stadium Club First Day Issue

1999 Stadium Club Autographs

	MINT	NRMT
COMPLETE SET (10)	600.00	275.00
COMMON CARD (SCA1-SCA10)	25.00	11.00
SER.1 STATED ODDS 1:1107 RETAIL		
SER.2 STATED ODDS 1:877 RETAIL		
CARDS 1-5 IN SER.1, 6-10 IN SER.2		
☐ SCA1 Alex Rodriguez	150.00	70.00
☐ SCA2 Chipper Jones	120.00	55.00
☐ SCA3 Barry Bonds	60.00	27.00
☐ SCA4 Tino Martinez	25.00	11.00
☐ SCA5 Ben Grieve	40.00	18.00
☐ SCA6 Juan Gonzalez	100.00	45.00
☐ SCA7 Vladimir Guerrero	60.00	27.00
☐ SCA8 Albert Belle	40.00	18.00
☐ SCA9 Kerry Wood	40.00	18.00
☐ SCA10 Todd Helton	40.00	18.00

1999 Stadium Club Chrome

	MINT	NRMT
COMPLETE SET (40)	120.00	55.00
COMPLETE SERIES 1 (20)	60.00	27.00
COMPLETE SERIES 2 (20)	60.00	27.00
COMMON CARD (SCC1-SCC40)	.75	.35
MINOR STARS	1.25	.55
SEMISTARS	2.00	.90
UNLISTED STARS	3.00	1.35
STATED ODDS 1:24 HOB/RET, 1:6 HTA		
*REFRACTORS: 1.25X TO 3X BASIC CHROME		
REFRACTOR ODDS 1:96 HOB/RET, 1:24 HTA		
☐ SCC1 Nomar Garciaparra	10.00	4.50
☐ SCC2 Kerry Wood	3.00	1.35
☐ SCC3 Jeff Bagwell	4.00	1.80
☐ SCC4 Ivan Rodriguez	4.00	1.80
☐ SCC5 Albert Belle	3.00	1.35
☐ SCC6 Gary Sheffield	1.25	.55
☐ SCC7 Andruw Jones	3.00	1.35
☐ SCC8 Kevin Brown	2.00	.90
☐ SCC9 David Cone	2.00	.90
☐ SCC10 Darin Erstad	2.00	.90
☐ SCC11 Manny Ramirez	4.00	1.80
☐ SCC12 Larry Walker	3.00	1.35
☐ SCC13 Mike Piazza	10.00	4.50
☐ SCC14 Cal Ripken	12.00	5.50
☐ SCC15 Pedro Martinez	4.00	1.80
☐ SCC16 Greg Vaughn	1.25	.55
☐ SCC17 Barry Bonds	4.00	1.80
☐ SCC18 Mo Vaughn	3.00	1.35
☐ SCC19 Bernie Williams	3.00	1.35
☐ SCC20 Ken Griffey Jr.	15.00	6.75
☐ SCC21 Alex Rodriguez	10.00	4.50
☐ SCC22 Chipper Jones	8.00	3.60
☐ SCC23 Ben Grieve	3.00	1.35
☐ SCC24 Frank Thomas	6.00	2.70
☐ SCC25 Derek Jeter	10.00	4.50
☐ SCC26 Sammy Sosa	10.00	4.50
☐ SCC27 Mark McGwire	20.00	9.00
☐ SCC28 Vladimir Guerrero	3.00	1.35
☐ SCC29 Greg Maddux	8.00	3.60
☐ SCC30 Juan Gonzalez	6.00	2.70
☐ SCC31 Troy Glaus	3.00	1.35
☐ SCC32 Adrian Beltre	3.00	1.35
☐ SCC33 Mitch Meluskey	.75	.35
☐ SCC34 Alex Gonzalez	1.25	.55
☐ SCC35 George Lombard	1.25	.55
☐ SCC36 Eric Chavez	2.00	.90
☐ SCC37 Ruben Mateo	3.00	1.35
☐ SCC38 Calvin Pickering	1.25	.55
☐ SCC39 Gabe Kapler	3.00	1.35
☐ SCC40 Bruce Chen	1.25	.55

1999 Stadium Club Co-Signers

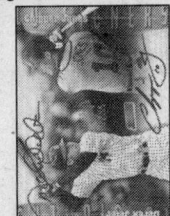

	MINT	NRMT
COMMON CARD (CS1-CS42)	15.00	6.75
SER.1 A ODDS 1:45213 HOB, 1:18085 HTA		
SER.2 A ODDS 1:43639 HOB, 1:18171 HTA		
SER.1 B ODDS 1:9043 HOB, 1:3617 HTA		
SER.2 B ODDS 1:8984 HOB, 1:3533 HTA		
SER.1 C ODDS 1:3104 HOB, 1:1006 HTA		
SER.2 C ODDS 1:2975 HOB, 1:1189 HTA		
SER.1 D ODDS 1:254 HOB, 1:102 HTA		
SER.2 D ODDS 1:251 HOB, 1:100 HTA		
☐ CS1 Ben Grieve	40.00	18.00
Richie Sexson D		
☐ CS2 Todd Helton	40.00	18.00
Troy Glaus D		
☐ CS3 Alex Rodriguez	150.00	70.00
Scott Rolen D		
☐ CS4 Derek Jeter	250.00	110.00
Chipper Jones D		
☐ CS5 Cliff Floyd	15.00	6.75
Eli Marrero D		
☐ CS6 Jay Buhner	25.00	11.00
Kevin Young D		
☐ CS7 Ben Grieve	100.00	45.00
Troy Glaus C		
☐ CS8 Todd Helton	80.00	36.00
Richie Sexson C		
☐ CS9 Alex Rodriguez	300.00	135.00
Chipper Jones C		
☐ CS10 Derek Jeter	250.00	110.00
Scott Rolen C		
☐ CS11 Cliff Floyd	30.00	13.50
Kevin Young C		
☐ CS12 Jay Buhner	60.00	27.00
Eli Marrero B		
☐ CS13 Ben Grieve	150.00	70.00
Todd Helton B		
☐ CS14 Richie Sexson	120.00	55.00
Troy Glaus B		
☐ CS15 Alex Rodriguez	500.00	220.00
Derek Jeter B		
☐ CS16 Chipper Jones	400.00	180.00
Scott Rolen B		
☐ CS17 Cliff Floyd	60.00	27.00
Jay Buhner B		
☐ CS18 Eli Marrero	40.00	18.00
Kevin Young B		
☐ CS19 Ben Grieve		
Todd Helton		
Richie Sexson		
Troy Glaus A		
☐ CS20 Alex Rodriguez		
Derek Jeter		
Chipper Jones		
☐ CS21 Cliff Floyd		
Jay Buhner		
Eli Marrero		
Kevin Young A		
☐ CS22 Edgardo Alfonzo	30.00	13.50
Jose Guillen D		
☐ CS23 Mike Lowell	15.00	6.75
Ricardo Rincon D		
☐ CS24 Juan Gonzalez	60.00	27.00
Vinny Castilla D		
☐ CS25 Moises Alou	80.00	36.00
Roger Clemens D		
☐ CS26 Scott Spiezio	15.00	6.75
Tony Womack D		
☐ CS27 Fernando Vina	15.00	6.75
Quilvio Veras D		
☐ CS28 Edgardo Alfonzo		
Ricardo Rincon C		
☐ CS29 Jose Guillen		
Mike Lowell C		
☐ CS30 Juan Gonzalez		
Moises Alou C		
☐ CS31 Roger Clemens		
Vinny Castilla C		
☐ CS32 Scott Spiezio		
Fernando Vina C		
☐ CS33 Tony Womack		
Quilvio Veras B		
☐ CS34 Edgardo Alfonzo		
Mike Lowell B		
☐ CS35 Jose Guillen		
Ricardo Rincon B		
☐ CS36 Juan Gonzalez		
Roger Clemens B		
☐ CS37 Moises Alou		
Vinny Castilla B		
☐ CS38 Scott Spiezio		
Quilvio Veras B		
☐ CS39 Tony Womack		
Fernando Vina B		
☐ CS40 Edgardo Alfonzo		
Jose Guillen		
Mike Lowell		
Ricardo Rincon A		
☐ CS41 Juan Gonzalez		
Moises Alou		
Roger Clemens		
Vinny Castilla A		
☐ CS42 Scott Spiezio		
Tony Womack		
Fernando Vina		
Quilvio Veras A		

1999 Stadium Club Never Compromise

	MINT	NRMT
COMPLETE SET (20)	65.00	29.00
COMPLETE SERIES 1 (10)	40.00	18.00
COMPLETE SERIES 2 (10)	25.00	11.00
COMMON CARD (NC1-NC20)	1.00	.45
SEMISTARS	1.25	.55
UNLISTED STARS	2.00	.90
STATED ODDS 1:12 HOB/RET, 1:4 HTA		
☐ NC1 Mark McGwire	12.00	5.50
☐ NC2 Sammy Sosa	6.00	2.70
☐ NC3 Ken Griffey Jr.	10.00	4.50
☐ NC4 Greg Maddux	5.00	2.20
☐ NC5 Barry Bonds	2.50	1.10
☐ NC6 Alex Rodriguez	6.00	2.70
☐ NC7 Darin Erstad	1.25	.55

❏ NC8 Roger Clemens	5.00	2.20
❏ NC9 Nomar Garciaparra	6.00	2.70
❏ NC10 Derek Jeter	6.00	2.70
❏ NC11 Cal Ripken	8.00	3.60
❏ NC12 Mike Piazza	6.00	2.70
❏ NC13 Kerry Wood	2.00	.90
❏ NC14 Andres Galarraga	1.25	.55
❏ NC15 Vinny Castilla	1.00	.45
❏ NC16 Jeff Bagwell	2.50	1.10
❏ NC17 Chipper Jones	5.00	2.20
❏ NC18 Eric Chavez	1.25	.55
❏ NC19 Orlando Hernandez	2.00	.90
❏ NC20 Troy Glaus	2.00	.90

1999 Stadium Club Triumvirate Luminous

	MINT	NRMT
COMPLETE SET (48)	270.00	120.00
COMPLETE SERIES 1 (24)	120.00	55.00
COMPLETE SERIES 2 (24)	150.00	70.00
COMMON CARD (T1A-T16C)	1.50	.70
SEMISTARS	2.50	1.10
UNLISTED STARS	4.00	1.80

STATED ODDS 1:36 H, 1:48 R, 1:18 HTA
*ILLUMINATOR: 2X to 5X LUMINOUS
ILLUM.ODDS 1:288 H, 1:384 R, 1:144 HTA
*LUMINESCENT: 1.25X TO 3X LUMINOUS
L'SCENT.ODDS 1:144 H, 1:192 R, 1:72 HTA

❏ T1A Greg Vaughn	2.00	.90
❏ T1B Ken Caminiti	2.00	.90
❏ T1C Tony Gwynn	10.00	4.50
❏ T2A Andruw Jones	4.00	1.80
❏ T2B Chipper Jones	10.00	4.50
❏ T2C Andres Galarraga	2.50	1.10
❏ T3A Jay Buhner	2.00	.90
❏ T3B Ken Griffey Jr.	20.00	9.00
❏ T3C Alex Rodriguez	12.00	5.50
❏ T4A Derek Jeter	12.00	5.50
❏ T4B Tino Martinez	2.00	.90
❏ T4C Bernie Williams	4.00	1.80
❏ T5A Brian Jordan	2.00	.90
❏ T5B Ray Lankford	2.00	.90
❏ T5C Mark McGwire	25.00	11.00
❏ T6A Jeff Bagwell	5.00	2.20
❏ T6B Craig Biggio	4.00	1.80
❏ T6C Randy Johnson	4.00	1.80
❏ T7A Nomar Garciaparra	12.00	5.50
❏ T7B Pedro Martinez	5.00	2.20
❏ T7C Mo Vaughn	4.00	1.80
❏ T8A Sammy Sosa	12.00	5.50
❏ T8B Mark Grace	2.50	1.10
❏ T8C Kerry Wood	4.00	1.80
❏ T9A Alex Rodriguez	12.00	5.50
❏ T9B Nomar Garciaparra	12.00	5.50
❏ T9C Derek Jeter	12.00	5.50
❏ T10A Todd Helton	4.00	1.80
❏ T10B Travis Lee	2.50	1.10
❏ T10C Pat Burrell	8.00	3.60
❏ T11A Greg Maddux	10.00	4.50
❏ T11B Kerry Wood	4.00	1.80
❏ T11C Tom Glavine	4.00	1.80
❏ T12A Chipper Jones	10.00	4.50
❏ T12B Vinny Castilla	2.00	.90
❏ T12C Scott Rolen	6.00	2.70
❏ T13A Juan Gonzalez	8.00	3.60
❏ T13B Ken Griffey Jr.	20.00	9.00

❏ T13C Ben Grieve	4.00	1.80
❏ T14A Sammy Sosa	12.00	5.50
❏ T14B Larry Walker	4.00	1.80
❏ T14C Barry Bonds	5.00	2.20
❏ T15A Frank Thomas	8.00	3.60
❏ T15B Jim Thome	4.00	1.80
❏ T15C Tino Martinez	2.00	.90
❏ T16A Mark McGwire	25.00	11.00
❏ T16B Andres Galarraga	2.50	1.10
❏ T16C Jeff Bagwell	5.00	2.20

1999 Stadium Club Video Replay

	MINT	NRMT
COMPLETE SET (5)	20.00	9.00
COMMON CARD (VR1-VR5)	.75	.35

SER.2 STATED ODDS 1:12 HOB/RET, 1:4 HTA

❏ VR1 Mark McGwire	8.00	3.60
❏ VR2 Sammy Sosa	4.00	1.80
❏ VR3 Ken Griffey Jr.	6.00	2.70
❏ VR4 Kerry Wood	.75	.35
❏ VR5 Alex Rodriguez	4.00	1.80

1991 Studio Previews

	MINT	NRMT
COMPLETE SET (18)	25.00	11.00
COMMON CARD (1-17)	1.00	.45
MINOR STARS	2.00	.90
SEMISTARS	3.00	1.35

FOUR PER DONRUSS RETAIL FACTORY SET

❏ 1 Juan Bell	1.00	.45
❏ 2 Roger Clemens	12.00	5.50
❏ 3 Dave Parker	2.00	.90
❏ 4 Tim Raines	2.00	.90
❏ 5 Kevin Seitzer	1.00	.45
❏ 6 Ted Higuera	1.00	.45
❏ 7 Bernie Williams	10.00	4.50
❏ 8 Harold Baines	2.00	.90
❏ 9 Gary Pettis	1.00	.45
❏ 10 Dave Justice	3.00	1.35
❏ 11 Eric Davis	2.00	.90
❏ 12 Andujar Cedeno	1.00	.45
❏ 13 Tom Foley	1.00	.45
❏ 14 Dwight Gooden	2.00	.90
❏ 15 Doug Drabek	1.00	.45
❏ 16 Steve Decker	1.00	.45

❏ 17 Joe Torre MG	2.00	.90
❏ NNO Title card	1.00	.45

1991 Studio

	MINT	NRMT
COMPLETE SET (264)	15.00	6.75
COMMON CARD (1-263)	.10	.09
MINOR STARS	.20	.09
UNLISTED STARS	.40	.18

❏ 1 Glenn Davis	.20	.05
❏ 2 Dwight Evans	.20	.09
❏ 3 Leo Gomez	.10	.05
❏ 4 Chris Hoiles	.10	.05
❏ 5 Sam Horn	.10	.05
❏ 6 Ben McDonald	.10	.05
❏ 7 Randy Milligan	.10	.05
❏ 8 Gregg Olson	.10	.05
❏ 9 Cal Ripken	1.50	.70
❏ 10 David Segui	.20	.09
❏ 11 Wade Boggs	.40	.18
❏ 12 Ellis Burks	.20	.09
❏ 13 Jack Clark	.20	.09
❏ 14 Roger Clemens	1.00	.45
❏ 15 Mike Greenwell	.10	.05
❏ 16 Tim Naehring	.10	.05
❏ 17 Tony Pena	.10	.05
❏ 18 Phil Plantier	.10	.05
❏ 19 Jeff Reardon	.20	.09
❏ 20 Mo Vaughn	.75	.35
❏ 21 Jimmie Reese CO	.20	.09
❏ 22 Jim Abbott UER	.20	.09
(Born in 1967, not 1969)		
❏ 23 Bert Blyleven	.20	.09
❏ 24 Chuck Finley	.20	.09
❏ 25 Gary Gaetti	.20	.09
❏ 26 Wally Joyner	.20	.09
❏ 27 Mark Langston	.10	.05
❏ 28 Kirk McCaskill	.10	.05
❏ 29 Lance Parrish	.10	.05
❏ 30 Dave Winfield	.40	.18
❏ 31 Alex Fernandez	.20	.09
❏ 32 Carlton Fisk	.40	.18
❏ 33 Scott Fletcher	.10	.05
❏ 34 Greg Hibbard	.10	.05
❏ 35 Charlie Hough	.20	.09
❏ 36 Jack McDowell	.10	.05
❏ 37 Tim Raines	.20	.09
❏ 38 Sammy Sosa	2.50	1.10
❏ 39 Bobby Thigpen	.10	.05
❏ 40 Frank Thomas	1.50	.70
❏ 41 Sandy Alomar Jr.	.20	.09
❏ 42 John Farrell	.10	.05
❏ 43 Glenallen Hill	.10	.05
❏ 44 Brook Jacoby	.10	.05
❏ 45 Chris James	.10	.05
❏ 46 Doug Jones	.10	.05
❏ 47 Eric King	.10	.05
❏ 48 Mark Lewis	.10	.05
❏ 49 Greg Swindell UER	.10	.05
(Photo actually Turner Ward)		
❏ 50 Mark Whiten	.10	.05
❏ 51 Milt Cuyler	.10	.05
❏ 52 Rob Deer	.20	.09
❏ 53 Cecil Fielder	.20	.09
❏ 54 Travis Fryman	.40	.18

❑ 55	Bill Gullickson	.10	.05
❑ 56	Lloyd Moseby	.10	.05
❑ 57	Frank Tanana	.10	.05
❑ 58	Mickey Tettleton	.20	.09
❑ 59	Alan Trammell	.30	.14
❑ 60	Lou Whitaker	.20	.09
❑ 61	Mike Boddicker	.10	.05
❑ 62	George Brett	.75	.35
❑ 63	Jeff Conine	.40	.18
❑ 64	Warren Cromartie	.10	.05
❑ 65	Storm Davis	.10	.05
❑ 66	Kirk Gibson	.20	.09
❑ 67	Mark Gubicza	.10	.05
❑ 68	Brian McRae	.20	.09
❑ 69	Bret Saberhagen	.20	.09
❑ 70	Kurt Stillwell	.10	.05
❑ 71	Tim McIntosh	.10	.05
❑ 72	Candy Maldonado	.10	.05
❑ 73	Paul Molitor	.40	.18
❑ 74	Willie Randolph	.20	.09
❑ 75	Ron Robinson	.10	.05
❑ 76	Gary Sheffield	.40	.18
❑ 77	Franklin Stubbs	.10	.05
❑ 78	B.J. Surhoff	.20	.09
❑ 79	Greg Vaughn	.20	.09
❑ 80	Robin Yount	.40	.18
❑ 81	Rick Aguilera	.20	.09
❑ 82	Steve Bedrosian	.10	.05
❑ 83	Scott Erickson	.30	.14
❑ 84	Greg Gagne	.10	.05
❑ 85	Dan Gladden	.10	.05
❑ 86	Brian Harper	.10	.05
❑ 87	Kent Hrbek	.20	.09
❑ 88	Shane Mack	.10	.05
❑ 89	Jack Morris	.20	.09
❑ 90	Kirby Puckett	.60	.25
❑ 91	Jesse Barfield	.10	.05
❑ 92	Steve Farr	.10	.05
❑ 93	Steve Howe	.10	.05
❑ 94	Roberto Kelly	.10	.05
❑ 95	Tim Leary	.10	.05
❑ 96	Kevin Maas	.10	.05
❑ 97	Don Mattingly	.75	.35
❑ 98	Hensley Meulens	.10	.05
❑ 99	Scott Sanderson	.10	.05
❑ 100	Steve Sax	.10	.05
❑ 101	Jose Canseco	.50	.23
❑ 102	Dennis Eckersley	.20	.09
❑ 103	Dave Henderson	.10	.05
❑ 104	Rickey Henderson	.50	.23
❑ 105	Rick Honeycutt	.10	.05
❑ 106	Mark McGwire	2.00	.90
❑ 107	Dave Stewart UER	.10	.05
	(No-hitter against		
	Toronto, not Texas)		
❑ 108	Eric Show	.10	.05
❑ 109	Todd Van Poppel	.10	.05
❑ 110	Bob Welch	.10	.05
❑ 111	Alvin Davis	.10	.05
❑ 112	Ken Griffey Jr.	3.00	1.35
❑ 113	Ken Griffey Sr.	.20	.09
❑ 114	Erik Hanson UER	.10	.05
	(Misspelled Eric)		
❑ 115	Brian Holman	.10	.05
❑ 116	Randy Johnson	.50	.23
❑ 117	Edgar Martinez	.40	.18
❑ 118	Tino Martinez	.40	.18
❑ 119	Harold Reynolds	.10	.05
❑ 120	David Valle	.10	.05
❑ 121	Kevin Belcher	.10	.05
❑ 122	Scott Chiamparino	.10	.05
❑ 123	Julio Franco	.20	.09
❑ 124	Juan Gonzalez	1.50	.70
❑ 125	Rich Gossage	.20	.09
❑ 126	Jeff Kunkel	.10	.05
❑ 127	Rafael Palmeiro	.40	.18
❑ 128	Nolan Ryan	1.50	.70
❑ 129	Ruben Sierra	.40	.18
❑ 130	Bobby Witt	.10	.05
❑ 131	Roberto Alomar	.40	.18
❑ 132	Tom Candiotti	.10	.05
❑ 133	Joe Carter	.20	.09
❑ 134	Ken Dayley	.10	.05
❑ 135	Kelly Gruber	.10	.05
❑ 136	John Olerud	.30	.14
❑ 137	Dave Stieb	.10	.05

❑ 138	Turner Ward	.10	.05
❑ 139	Devon White	.10	.05
❑ 140	Mookie Wilson	.20	.09
❑ 141	Steve Avery	.10	.05
❑ 142	Sid Bream	.10	.05
❑ 143	Nick Esasky UER	.10	.05
	(Homers abbreviated RH)		
❑ 144	Ron Gant	.20	.09
❑ 145	Tom Glavine	.40	.18
❑ 146	David Justice	.40	.18
❑ 147	Kelly Mann	.10	.05
❑ 148	Terry Pendleton	.20	.09
❑ 149	John Smoltz	.40	.18
❑ 150	Jeff Treadway	.10	.05
❑ 151	George Bell	.10	.05
❑ 152	Shawn Boskie	.10	.05
❑ 153	Andre Dawson	.40	.18
❑ 154	Lance Dickson	.10	.05
❑ 155	Shawon Dunston	.10	.05
❑ 156	Joe Girardi	.20	.09
❑ 157	Mark Grace	.40	.18
❑ 158	Ryne Sandberg	.50	.23
❑ 159	Gary Scott	.10	.05
❑ 160	Dave Smith	.10	.05
❑ 161	Tom Browning	.10	.05
❑ 162	Eric Davis	.20	.09
❑ 163	Rob Dibble	.10	.05
❑ 164	Mariano Duncan	.10	.05
❑ 165	Chris Hammond	.10	.05
❑ 166	Billy Hatcher	.10	.05
❑ 167	Barry Larkin	.40	.18
❑ 168	Hal Morris	.10	.05
❑ 169	Paul O'Neill	.20	.09
❑ 170	Chris Sabo	.10	.05
❑ 171	Eric Anthony	.10	.05
❑ 172	Jeff Bagwell	3.00	1.35
❑ 173	Craig Biggio	.40	.18
❑ 174	Ken Caminiti	.40	.18
❑ 175	Jim Deshaies	.10	.05
❑ 176	Steve Finley	.40	.18
❑ 177	Pete Harnisch	.10	.05
❑ 178	Darryl Kile	.10	.05
❑ 179	Curt Schilling	.40	.18
❑ 180	Mike Scott	.10	.05
❑ 181	Brett Butler	.20	.09
❑ 182	Gary Carter	.40	.18
❑ 183	Orel Hershiser	.20	.09
❑ 184	Ramon Martinez	.20	.09
❑ 185	Eddie Murray	.40	.18
❑ 186	Jose Offerman	.30	.14
❑ 187	Bob Ojeda	.10	.05
❑ 188	Juan Samuel	.10	.05
❑ 189	Mike Scioscia	.10	.05
❑ 190	Darryl Strawberry	.20	.09
❑ 191	Moises Alou	.40	.18
❑ 192	Brian Barnes	.10	.05
❑ 193	Oil Can Boyd	.10	.05
❑ 194	Ivan Calderon	.10	.05
❑ 195	Delino DeShields	.20	.09
❑ 196	Mike Fitzgerald	.10	.05
❑ 197	Andres Galarraga	.40	.18
❑ 198	Marquis Grissom	.40	.18
❑ 199	Bill Sampen	.10	.05
❑ 200	Tim Wallach	.10	.05
❑ 201	Daryl Boston	.10	.05
❑ 202	Vince Coleman	.10	.05
❑ 203	John Franco	.20	.09
❑ 204	Dwight Gooden	.20	.09
❑ 205	Tom Herr	.10	.05
❑ 206	Gregg Jefferies	.10	.05
❑ 207	Howard Johnson	.10	.05
❑ 208	Dave Magadan UER	.10	.05
	(Born 1862,		
	should be 1962)		
❑ 209	Kevin McReynolds	.10	.05
❑ 210	Frank Viola	.10	.05
❑ 211	Wes Chamberlain	.10	.05
❑ 212	Darren Daulton	.20	.09
❑ 213	Len Dykstra	.20	.09
❑ 214	Charlie Hayes	.10	.05
❑ 215	Ricky Jordan	.10	.05
❑ 216	Steve Lake	.20	.09
	(Pictured with parrot		
	on his shoulder)		
❑ 217	Roger McDowell	.10	.05
❑ 218	Mickey Morandini	.10	.05

❑ 219	Terry Mulholland	.10	.05
❑ 220	Dale Murphy	.40	.18
❑ 221	Jay Bell	.20	.09
❑ 222	Barry Bonds	.50	.23
❑ 223	Bobby Bonilla	.20	.09
❑ 224	Doug Drabek	.10	.05
❑ 225	Bill Landrum	.10	.05
❑ 226	Mike LaValliere	.10	.05
❑ 227	Jose Lind	.10	.05
❑ 228	Don Slaught	.10	.05
❑ 229	John Smiley	.10	.05
❑ 230	Andy Van Slyke	.20	.09
❑ 231	Bernard Gilkey	.20	.09
❑ 232	Pedro Guerrero	.10	.05
❑ 233	Rex Hudler	.10	.05
❑ 234	Ray Lankford	.40	.18
❑ 235	Joe Magrane	.10	.05
❑ 236	Jose Oquendo	.10	.05
❑ 237	Lee Smith	.20	.09
❑ 238	Ozzie Smith	.50	.23
❑ 239	Milt Thompson	.10	.05
❑ 240	Todd Zeile	.20	.09
❑ 241	Larry Andersen	.10	.05
❑ 242	Andy Benes	.20	.09
❑ 243	Paul Faries	.10	.05
❑ 244	Tony Fernandez	.10	.05
❑ 245	Tony Gwynn	1.00	.45
❑ 246	Atlee Hammaker	.10	.05
❑ 247	Fred McGriff	.40	.18
❑ 248	Bip Roberts	.10	.05
❑ 249	Benito Santiago	.10	.05
❑ 250	Ed Whitson	.10	.05
❑ 251	Dave Anderson	.10	.05
❑ 252	Mike Benjamin	.10	.05
❑ 253	John Burkett UER	.10	.05
	(Front photo actually		
	Trevor Wilson)		
❑ 254	Will Clark	.40	.18
❑ 255	Scott Garrelts	.10	.05
❑ 256	Willie McGee	.20	.09
❑ 257	Kevin Mitchell	.10	.05
❑ 258	Dave Righetti	.10	.05
❑ 259	Matt Williams	.40	.18
❑ 260	Bud Black	.10	.05
	Steve Decker		
❑ 261	Sparky Anderson MG CL	.20	.09
❑ 262	Tom Lasorda MG CL	.30	.14
❑ 263	Tony LaRussa MG CL	.20	.09
❑ NNO	Title Card	.10	.05

1992 Studio

	MINT	NRMT
COMPLETE SET (264)	15.00	6.75
COMMON CARD (1-264)	.05	.02
MINOR STARS	.10	.05
UNLISTED STARS	.30	.14

❑ 1	Steve Avery	.05	.02
❑ 2	Sid Bream	.05	.02
❑ 3	Ron Gant	.10	.05
❑ 4	Tom Glavine	.20	.09
❑ 5	David Justice	.30	.14
❑ 6	Mark Lemke	.05	.02
❑ 7	Greg Olson	.05	.02
❑ 8	Terry Pendleton	.05	.02
❑ 9	Deion Sanders	.30	.14
❑ 10	John Smoltz	.20	.09

11	Doug Dascenzo	.05	.02
12	Andre Dawson	.20	.09
13	Joe Girardi	.10	.05
14	Mark Grace	.20	.09
15	Greg Maddux	.75	.35
16	Chuck McElroy	.05	.02
17	Mike Morgan	.05	.02
18	Ryne Sandberg	.40	.18
19	Gary Scott	.05	.02
20	Sammy Sosa	1.00	.45
21	Norm Charlton	.05	.02
22	Rob Dibble	.05	.02
23	Barry Larkin	.20	.09
24	Hal Morris	.05	.02
25	Paul O'Neill	.10	.05
26	Jose Rijo	.05	.02
27	Bip Roberts	.05	.02
28	Chris Sabo	.05	.02
29	Reggie Sanders	.10	.05
30	Greg Swindell	.05	.02
31	Jeff Bagwell	.60	.25
32	Craig Biggio	.30	.14
33	Ken Caminiti	.20	.09
34	Andujar Cedeno	.05	.02
35	Steve Finley	.10	.05
36	Pete Harnisch	.05	.02
37	Butch Henry	.05	.02
38	Doug Jones	.05	.02
39	Darryl Kile	.10	.05
40	Eddie Taubensee	.05	.02
41	Brett Butler	.10	.05
42	Tom Candiotti	.05	.02
43	Eric Davis	.10	.05
44	Orel Hershiser	.10	.05
45	Eric Karros	.30	.14
46	Ramon Martinez	.10	.05
47	Jose Offerman	.10	.05
48	Mike Scioscia	.05	.02
49	Mike Sharperson	.05	.02
50	Darryl Strawberry	.10	.05
51	Bret Barberie	.05	.02
52	Ivan Calderon	.05	.02
53	Gary Carter	.30	.14
54	Delino DeShields	.10	.05
55	Marquis Grissom	.10	.05
56	Ken Hill	.05	.02
57	Dennis Martinez	.05	.02
58	Spike Owen	.05	.02
59	Larry Walker	.30	.14
60	Tim Wallach	.05	.02
61	Bobby Bonilla	.10	.05
62	Tim Burke	.05	.02
63	Vince Coleman	.10	.05
64	John Franco	.10	.05
65	Dwight Gooden	.10	.05
66	Todd Hundley	.10	.05
67	Howard Johnson	.05	.02
68	Eddie Murray UER	.30	.14
	(he's not all-time switch homer leader, but he has most games with homers from both sides)		
69	Bret Saberhagen	.10	.05
70	Anthony Young	.05	.02
71	Kim Batiste	.05	.02
72	Wes Chamberlain	.05	.02
73	Darren Daulton	.10	.05
74	Mariano Duncan	.05	.02
75	Len Dykstra	.10	.05
76	John Kruk	.10	.05
77	Mickey Morandini	.05	.02
78	Terry Mulholland	.05	.02
79	Dale Murphy	.30	.14
80	Mitch Williams	.05	.02
81	Jay Bell	.10	.05
82	Barry Bonds	.40	.18
83	Steve Buechele	.05	.02
84	Doug Drabek	.05	.02
85	Mike LaValliere	.05	.02
86	Jose Lind	.05	.02
87	Denny Neagle	.20	.09
88	Randy Tomlin	.05	.02
89	Andy Van Slyke	.10	.05
90	Gary Varsho	.05	.02
91	Pedro Guerrero	.05	.02
92	Rex Hudler	.05	.02
93	Brian Jordan	1.00	.45
94	Felix Jose	.05	.02
95	Donovan Osborne	.05	.02
96	Tom Pagnozzi	.05	.02
97	Lee Smith	.10	.05
98	Ozzie Smith	.40	.18
99	Todd Worrell	.05	.02
100	Todd Zeile	.05	.02
101	Andy Benes	.10	.05
102	Jerald Clark	.05	.02
103	Tony Fernandez	.05	.02
104	Tony Gwynn	.75	.35
105	Greg W. Harris	.05	.02
106	Fred McGriff	.20	.09
107	Benito Santiago	.05	.02
108	Gary Sheffield	.30	.14
109	Kurt Stillwell	.05	.02
110	Tim Teufel	.05	.02
111	Kevin Bass	.05	.02
112	Jeff Brantley	.05	.02
113	John Burkett	.05	.02
114	Will Clark	.30	.14
115	Royce Clayton	.05	.02
116	Mike Jackson	.10	.05
117	Darren Lewis	.05	.02
118	Bill Swift	.05	.02
119	Robby Thompson	.05	.02
120	Matt Williams	.20	.09
121	Brady Anderson	.20	.09
122	Glenn Davis	.05	.02
123	Mike Devereaux	.05	.02
124	Chris Hoiles	.05	.02
125	Sam Horn	.05	.02
126	Ben McDonald	.05	.02
127	Mike Mussina	.50	.23
128	Gregg Olson	.05	.02
129	Cal Ripken Jr.	1.25	.55
130	Rick Sutcliffe	.05	.02
131	Wade Boggs	.30	.14
132	Roger Clemens	.75	.35
133	Greg A. Harris	.05	.02
134	Tim Naehring	.05	.02
135	Tony Pena	.05	.02
136	Phil Plantier	.05	.02
137	Jeff Reardon	.10	.05
138	Jody Reed	.05	.02
139	Mo Vaughn	.40	.18
140	Frank Viola	.05	.02
141	Jim Abbott	.10	.05
142	Hubie Brooks	.05	.02
143	Chad Curtis	.40	.18
144	Gary DiSarcina	.05	.02
145	Chuck Finley	.10	.05
146	Bryan Harvey	.05	.02
147	Von Hayes	.05	.02
148	Mark Langston	.05	.02
149	Lance Parrish	.05	.02
150	Lee Stevens	.10	.05
151	George Bell	.05	.02
152	Alex Fernandez	.10	.05
153	Greg Hibbard	.05	.02
154	Lance Johnson	.05	.02
155	Kirk McCaskill	.05	.02
156	Tim Raines	.10	.05
157	Steve Sax	.05	.02
158	Bobby Thigpen	.05	.02
159	Frank Thomas	.75	.35
160	Robin Ventura	.10	.05
161	Sandy Alomar Jr.	.10	.05
162	Jack Armstrong	.05	.02
163	Carlos Baerga	.20	.09
164	Albert Belle	.30	.14
165	Alex Cole	.05	.02
166	Glenallen Hill	.05	.02
167	Mark Lewis	.05	.02
168	Kenny Lofton	.40	.18
169	Paul Sorrento	.05	.02
170	Mark Whiten	.05	.02
171	Milt Cuyler	.05	.02
172	Rob Deer	.05	.02
173	Cecil Fielder	.10	.05
174	Travis Fryman	.10	.05
175	Mike Henneman	.05	.02
176	Tony Phillips	.05	.02
177	Frank Tanana	.05	.02
178	Mickey Tettleton	.05	.02
179	Alan Trammell	.20	.09
180	Lou Whitaker	.10	.05
181	George Brett	.60	.25
182	Tom Gordon	.05	.02
183	Mark Gubicza	.05	.02
184	Gregg Jefferies	.05	.02
185	Wally Joyner	.10	.05
186	Brent Mayne	.05	.02
187	Brian McRae	.05	.02
188	Kevin McReynolds	.05	.02
189	Keith Miller	.05	.02
190	Jeff Montgomery	.10	.05
191	Dante Bichette	.20	.09
192	Ricky Bones	.05	.02
193	Scott Fletcher	.05	.02
194	Paul Molitor	.30	.14
195	Jaime Navarro	.05	.02
196	Franklin Stubbs	.05	.02
197	B.J. Surhoff	.10	.05
198	Greg Vaughn	.20	.09
199	Bill Wegman	.05	.02
200	Robin Yount	.30	.14
201	Rick Aguilera	.10	.05
202	Scott Erickson	.10	.05
203	Greg Gagne	.05	.02
204	Brian Harper	.05	.02
205	Kent Hrbek	.05	.02
206	Scott Leius	.05	.02
207	Shane Mack	.05	.02
208	Pat Mahomes	.05	.02
209	Kirby Puckett	.50	.23
210	John Smiley	.05	.02
211	Mike Gallego	.05	.02
212	Charlie Hayes	.05	.02
213	Pat Kelly	.05	.02
214	Roberto Kelly	.05	.02
215	Kevin Maas	.05	.02
216	Don Mattingly	.60	.25
217	Matt Nokes	.05	.02
218	Melido Perez	.05	.02
219	Scott Sanderson	.05	.02
220	Danny Tartabull	.05	.02
221	Harold Baines	.05	.02
222	Jose Canseco	.40	.18
223	Dennis Eckersley	.10	.05
224	Dave Henderson	.05	.02
225	Carney Lansford	.05	.02
226	Mark McGwire	1.50	.70
227	Mike Moore	.05	.02
228	Randy Ready	.05	.02
229	Terry Steinbach	.05	.02
230	Dave Stewart	.10	.05
231	Jay Buhner	.20	.09
232	Ken Griffey Jr.	2.00	.90
233	Erik Hanson	.05	.02
234	Randy Johnson	.30	.14
235	Edgar Martinez	.20	.09
236	Tino Martinez	.30	.14
237	Kevin Mitchell	.05	.02
238	Pete O'Brien	.05	.02
239	Harold Reynolds	.05	.02
240	David Valle	.05	.02
241	Julio Franco	.05	.02
242	Juan Gonzalez	.75	.35
243	Jose Guzman	.05	.02
244	Rafael Palmeiro	.30	.14
245	Dean Palmer	.10	.05
246	Ivan Rodriguez	.60	.25
247	Jeff Russell	.05	.02
248	Nolan Ryan	1.25	.55
249	Ruben Sierra	.30	.14
250	Dickie Thon	.05	.02
251	Roberto Alomar	.30	.14
252	Derek Bell	.10	.05
253	Pat Borders	.05	.02
254	Joe Carter	.10	.05
255	Kelly Gruber	.05	.02
256	Juan Guzman	.20	.09
257	Jack Morris	.10	.05
258	John Olerud	.05	.02
259	Devon White	.05	.02
260	Dave Winfield	.30	.14
261	Checklist	.05	.02
262	Checklist	.05	.02
263	Checklist	.05	.02
264	History Card	.05	.02

1992 Studio Heritage

RYNE SANDBERG

	MINT	NRMT
COMPLETE SET (14)	25.00	11.00
COMP.FOIL SET (8)	15.00	6.75
COMP.JUMBO SET (6)	10.00	4.50
COMMON CARD (BC1-BC14)	.75	.35
FOIL: RAND.INSERTS IN FOIL PACKS		
JUMBO'S: ONE PER JUMBO PACK		

❑ BC1 Ryne Sandberg	2.00	.90
❑ BC2 Carlton Fisk	1.50	.70
❑ BC3 Wade Boggs	1.50	.70
❑ BC4 Jose Canseco	2.00	.90
❑ BC5 Don Mattingly	3.00	1.35
❑ BC6 Darryl Strawberry	1.00	.45
❑ BC7 Cal Ripken	6.00	2.70
❑ BC8 Will Clark	1.50	.70
❑ BC9 Andre Dawson	1.25	.55
❑ BC10 Andy Van Slyke	.75	.35
❑ BC11 Paul Molitor	1.50	.70
❑ BC12 Jeff Bagwell	3.00	1.35
❑ BC13 Darren Daulton	1.00	.45
❑ BC14 Kirby Puckett	2.50	1.10

1993 Studio

	MINT	NRMT
COMPLETE SET (220)	20.00	9.00
COMMON CARD (1-220)	.10	.05
MINOR STARS	.25	.11
UNLISTED STARS	.50	.23

❑ 1 Dennis Eckersley	.25	.11
❑ 2 Chad Curtis	.25	.11
❑ 3 Eric Anthony	.10	.05
❑ 4 Roberto Alomar	.50	.23
❑ 5 Steve Avery	.25	.11
❑ 6 Cal Eldred	.10	.05
❑ 7 Bernard Gilkey	.10	.05
❑ 8 Steve Buechele	.10	.05
❑ 9 Brett Butler	.25	.11
❑ 10 Terry Mulholland	.10	.05
❑ 11 Moises Alou	.25	.11
❑ 12 Barry Bonds	.60	.25
❑ 13 Sandy Alomar Jr.	.25	.11
❑ 14 Chris Bosio	.10	.05
❑ 15 Scott Sanderson	.10	.05
❑ 16 Bobby Bonilla	.25	.11
❑ 17 Brady Anderson	.25	.11
❑ 18 Derek Bell	.25	.11
❑ 19 Wes Chamberlain	.10	.05
❑ 20 Jay Bell	.25	.11
❑ 21 Kevin Brown	.35	.16
❑ 22 Roger Clemens	1.25	.55
❑ 23 Roberto Kelly	.10	.05
❑ 24 Dante Bichette	.25	.11
❑ 25 George Brett	1.00	.45
❑ 26 Rob Deer	.10	.05
❑ 27 Brian Harper	.10	.05
❑ 28 George Bell	.10	.05
❑ 29 Jim Abbott	.25	.11
❑ 30 Dave Henderson	.10	.05
❑ 31 Wade Boggs	.50	.23
❑ 32 Chili Davis	.25	.11
❑ 33 Ellis Burks	.25	.11
❑ 34 Jeff Bagwell	.60	.25
❑ 35 Kent Hrbek	.25	.11
❑ 36 Pat Borders	.10	.05
❑ 37 Cecil Fielder	.25	.11
❑ 38 Sid Bream	.10	.05
❑ 39 Greg Gagne	.10	.05
❑ 40 Darryl Hamilton	.10	.05
❑ 41 Jerald Clark	.10	.05
❑ 42 Mark Grace	.35	.16
❑ 43 Barry Larkin	.50	.23
❑ 44 John Burkett	.10	.05
❑ 45 Scott Cooper	.10	.05
❑ 46 Mike Lansing	.25	.11
❑ 47 Jose Canseco	.60	.25
❑ 48 Will Clark	.50	.23
❑ 49 Carlos Garcia	.10	.05
❑ 50 Carlos Baerga	.25	.11
❑ 51 Darren Daulton	.25	.11
❑ 52 Jay Buhner	.35	.16
❑ 53 Andy Benes	.25	.11
❑ 54 Jeff Conine	.10	.05
❑ 55 Mike Devereaux	.10	.05
❑ 56 Vince Coleman	.10	.05
❑ 57 Terry Steinbach	.10	.05
❑ 58 J.T. Snow	.60	.25
❑ 59 Greg Swindell	.10	.05
❑ 60 Devon White	.10	.05
❑ 61 John Smoltz	.35	.16
❑ 62 Todd Zeile	.10	.05
❑ 63 Rick Wilkins	.10	.05
❑ 64 Tim Wallach	.10	.05
❑ 65 John Wetteland	.25	.11
❑ 66 Matt Williams	.35	.16
❑ 67 Paul Sorrento	.10	.05
❑ 68 David Valle	.10	.05
❑ 69 Walt Weiss	.10	.05
❑ 70 John Franco	.25	.11
❑ 71 Nolan Ryan	2.00	.90
❑ 72 Frank Viola	.10	.05
❑ 73 Chris Sabo	.10	.05
❑ 74 David Nied	.10	.05
❑ 75 Kevin McReynolds	.10	.05
❑ 76 Lou Whitaker	.25	.11
❑ 77 Dave Winfield	.35	.16
❑ 78 Robin Ventura	.25	.11
❑ 79 Spike Owen	.10	.05
❑ 80 Cal Ripken Jr.	2.00	.90
❑ 81 Dan Walters	.10	.05
❑ 82 Mitch Williams	.10	.05
❑ 83 Tim Wakefield	.25	.11
❑ 84 Rickey Henderson	.60	.25
❑ 85 Gary DiSarcina	.10	.05
❑ 86 Craig Biggio	.50	.23
❑ 87 Joe Carter	.25	.11
❑ 88 Ron Gant	.25	.11
❑ 89 Dan Jaha	.10	.05
❑ 90 Gregg Jefferies	.25	.11
❑ 91 Jose Guzman	.10	.05
❑ 92 Eric Karros	.35	.16
❑ 93 Wil Cordero	.25	.11
❑ 94 Royce Clayton	.10	.05
❑ 95 Albert Belle	.50	.23
❑ 96 Ken Griffey Jr.	2.50	1.10
❑ 97 Orestes Destrade	.10	.05
❑ 98 Tony Fernandez	.25	.11
❑ 99 Leo Gomez	.10	.05
❑ 100 Tony Gwynn	1.25	.55
❑ 101 Len Dykstra	.25	.11
❑ 102 Jeff King	.10	.05
❑ 103 Julio Franco	.10	.05
❑ 104 Andre Dawson	.35	.16
❑ 105 Randy Milligan	.10	.05
❑ 106 Alex Cole	.10	.05
❑ 107 Phil Hiatt	.10	.05
❑ 108 Travis Fryman	.25	.11
❑ 109 Chuck Knoblauch	.50	.23
❑ 110 Bo Jackson	.25	.11
❑ 111 Pat Kelly	.10	.05
❑ 112 Bret Saberhagen	.25	.11
❑ 113 Ruben Sierra	.10	.05
❑ 114 Tim Salmon	.50	.23
❑ 115 Doug Jones	.10	.05
❑ 116 Ed Sprague	.10	.05
❑ 117 Terry Pendleton	.25	.11
❑ 118 Robin Yount	.35	.16
❑ 119 Mark Whiten	.10	.05
❑ 120 Checklist 1-110	.10	.05
❑ 121 Sammy Sosa	1.50	.70
❑ 122 Darryl Strawberry	.25	.11
❑ 123 Larry Walker	.50	.23
❑ 124 Robby Thompson	.10	.05
❑ 125 Carlos Martinez	.10	.05
❑ 126 Edgar Martinez	.35	.16
❑ 127 Benito Santiago	.25	.11
❑ 128 Howard Johnson	.10	.05
❑ 129 Harold Reynolds	.10	.05
❑ 130 Craig Shipley	.10	.05
❑ 131 Curt Schilling	.25	.11
❑ 132 Andy Van Slyke	.25	.11
❑ 133 Ivan Rodriguez	.60	.25
❑ 134 Mo Vaughn	.50	.23
❑ 135 Bip Roberts	.10	.05
❑ 136 Charlie Hayes	.10	.05
❑ 137 Brian McRae	.10	.05
❑ 138 Mickey Tettleton	.10	.05
❑ 139 Frank Thomas	1.00	.45
❑ 140 Paul O'Neill	.25	.11
❑ 141 Mark McGwire	2.50	1.10
❑ 142 Damion Easley	.25	.11
❑ 143 Ken Caminiti	.35	.16
❑ 144 Juan Guzman	.10	.05
❑ 145 Tom Glavine	.35	.16
❑ 146 Pat Listach	.10	.05
❑ 147 Lee Smith	.25	.11
❑ 148 Derrick May	.10	.05
❑ 149 Ramon Martinez	.25	.11
❑ 150 Delino DeShields	.25	.11
❑ 151 Kirt Manwaring	.10	.05
❑ 152 Reggie Jefferson	.25	.11
❑ 153 Randy Johnson	.50	.23
❑ 154 Dave Magadan	.10	.05
❑ 155 Dwight Gooden	.25	.11
❑ 156 Chris Hoiles	.10	.05
❑ 157 Fred McGriff	.35	.16
❑ 158 Dave Hollins	.10	.05
❑ 159 Al Martin	.10	.05
❑ 160 Juan Gonzalez	1.00	.45
❑ 161 Mike Greenwell	.10	.05
❑ 162 Kevin Mitchell	.25	.11
❑ 163 Andres Galarraga	.50	.23
❑ 164 Wally Joyner	.25	.11
❑ 165 Kirk Gibson	.10	.05
❑ 166 Pedro Munoz	.10	.05
❑ 167 Ozzie Guillen	.10	.05
❑ 168 Jimmy Key	.25	.11
❑ 169 Kevin Seitzer	.10	.05
❑ 170 Luis Polonia	.10	.05
❑ 171 Luis Gonzalez	.25	.11
❑ 172 Paul Molitor	.50	.23
❑ 173 David Justice	.50	.23
❑ 174 B.J. Surhoff	.10	.05
❑ 175 Ray Lankford	.35	.16
❑ 176 Wayne Berland	.60	.25
❑ 177 Jody Reed	.10	.05
❑ 178 Marquis Grissom	.25	.11
❑ 179 Willie McGee	.10	.05
❑ 180 Kenny Lofton	.50	.23
❑ 181 Junior Felix	.10	.05
❑ 182 Jose Offerman	.25	.11
❑ 183 John Kruk	.25	.11
❑ 184 Orlando Merced	.10	.05
❑ 185 Rafael Palmeiro	.50	.23
❑ 186 Billy Hatcher	.10	.05
❑ 187 Joe Oliver	.10	.05
❑ 188 Joe Girardi	.25	.11
❑ 189 Jose Lind	.10	.05
❑ 190 Harold Baines	.25	.11

☐ 191 Mike Pagliarulo	.10	.05
☐ 192 Lance Johnson	.10	.05
☐ 193 Don Mattingly	1.00	.45
☐ 194 Doug Drabek	.10	.05
☐ 195 John Olerud	.35	.16
☐ 196 Greg Maddux	1.25	.55
☐ 197 Greg Vaughn	.25	.11
☐ 198 Tom Pagnozzi	.10	.05
☐ 199 Willie Wilson	.10	.05
☐ 200 Jack McDowell	.10	.05
☐ 201 Mike Piazza	2.50	1.10
☐ 202 Mike Mussina	.50	.23
☐ 203 Charles Nagy	.25	.11
☐ 204 Tino Martinez	.50	.23
☐ 205 Charlie Hough	.25	.11
☐ 206 Todd Hundley	.35	.16
☐ 207 Gary Sheffield	.50	.23
☐ 208 Mickey Morandini	.10	.05
☐ 209 Don Slaught	.10	.05
☐ 210 Dean Palmer	.25	.11
☐ 211 Jose Rijo	.10	.05
☐ 212 Vinny Castilla	.60	.25
☐ 213 Tony Phillips	.10	.05
☐ 214 Kirby Puckett	.75	.35
☐ 215 Tim Raines	.25	.11
☐ 216 Otis Nixon	.10	.05
☐ 217 Ozzie Smith	.60	.25
☐ 218 Jose Vizcaino	.10	.05
☐ 219 Randy Tomlin	.10	.05
☐ 220 Checklist 111-220	.10	.05

1993 Studio Heritage

	MINT	NRMT
COMPLETE SET (12)	30.00	13.50
COMMON CARD (1-12)	1.00	.45
RANDOM INSERTS IN ALL PACKS		

☐ 1 George Brett	6.00	2.70
☐ 2 Juan Gonzalez	6.00	2.70
☐ 3 Roger Clemens	8.00	3.60
☐ 4 Mark McGwire	15.00	6.75
☐ 5 Mark Grace	2.00	.90
☐ 6 Ozzie Smith	4.00	1.80
☐ 7 Barry Larkin	3.00	1.35
☐ 8 Frank Thomas	6.00	2.70
☐ 9 Carlos Baerga	1.00	.45
☐ 10 Eric Karros	2.00	.90
☐ 11 J.T. Snow	3.00	1.35
☐ 12 John Kruk	1.50	.70

1993 Studio Silhouettes

	MINT	NRMT
COMPLETE SET (10)	25.00	11.00
COMMON CARD (1-10)	.50	.23
ONE PER JUMBO PACK		

☐ 1 Frank Thomas	3.00	1.35
☐ 2 Barry Bonds	2.00	.90
☐ 3 Jeff Bagwell	2.00	.90
☐ 4 Juan Gonzalez	3.00	1.35
☐ 5 Travis Fryman	.75	.35
☐ 6 J.T. Snow	1.50	.70
☐ 7 John Kruk	.75	.35
☐ 8 Jeff Blauser	.50	.23

SILHOUETTES

☐ 9 Mike Piazza	8.00	3.60
☐ 10 Nolan Ryan	6.00	2.70

1993 Studio Superstars on Canvas

SUPERSTARS ON CANVAS

	MINT	NRMT
COMPLETE SET (10)	35.00	16.00
COMMON CARD (1-10)	1.50	.70
RANDOM INSERTS IN HOBBY/RETAIL PACKS		

☐ 1 Ken Griffey Jr.	15.00	6.75
☐ 2 Jose Canseco	4.00	1.80
☐ 3 Mark McGwire	15.00	6.75
☐ 4 Mike Mussina	3.00	1.35
☐ 5 Joe Carter	1.50	.70
☐ 6 Frank Thomas	6.00	2.70
☐ 7 Darren Daulton	1.50	.70
☐ 8 Mark Grace	2.00	.90
☐ 9 Andres Galarraga	3.00	1.35
☐ 10 Barry Bonds	4.00	1.80

1993 Studio Thomas

FRANK THOMAS COLLECTION

	MINT	NRMT
COMPLETE SET (5)	30.00	13.50
COMMON THOMAS (1-5)	6.00	2.70
RANDOM INSERTS IN ALL PACKS		

☐ 1 Frank Thomas	6.00	2.70
Childhood		
☐ 2 Frank Thomas	6.00	2.70
Baseball Memories		
☐ 3 Frank Thomas	6.00	2.70
Family		
☐ 4 Frank Thomas	6.00	2.70
Performance		
☐ 5 Frank Thomas	6.00	2.70
Role Model		

1994 Studio

	MINT	NRMT
COMPLETE SET (220)	15.00	6.75
COMMON CARD (1-220)	.15	.07
MINOR STARS	.30	.14
UNLISTED STARS	.60	.25

☐ 1 Dennis Eckersley	.30	.14
☐ 2 Brent Gates	.15	.07
☐ 3 Rickey Henderson	.75	.35
☐ 4 Mark McGwire	3.00	1.35
☐ 5 Troy Neel	.15	.07
☐ 6 Ruben Sierra	.15	.07
☐ 7 Terry Steinbach	.15	.07
☐ 8 Chad Curtis	.15	.07
☐ 9 Chili Davis	.30	.14
☐ 10 Gary DiSarcina	.15	.07
☐ 11 Damion Easley	.30	.14
☐ 12 Bo Jackson	.30	.14
☐ 13 Mark Langston	.15	.07
☐ 14 Eduardo Perez	.15	.07
☐ 15 Tim Salmon	.60	.25
☐ 16 Jeff Bagwell	.75	.35
☐ 17 Craig Biggio	.60	.25
☐ 18 Ken Caminiti	.40	.18
☐ 19 Andujar Cedeno	.15	.07
☐ 20 Doug Drabek	.15	.07
☐ 21 Steve Finley	.30	.14
☐ 22 Luis Gonzalez	.30	.14
☐ 23 Darryl Kile	.15	.07
☐ 24 Roberto Alomar	.60	.25
☐ 25 Pat Borders	.15	.07
☐ 26 Joe Carter	.30	.14
☐ 27 Carlos Delgado	.60	.25
☐ 28 Pat Hentgen	.30	.14
☐ 29 Paul Molitor	.60	.25
☐ 30 John Olerud	.30	.14
☐ 31 Ed Sprague	.15	.07
☐ 32 Devon White	.15	.07
☐ 33 Steve Avery	.15	.07
☐ 34 Tom Glavine	.60	.25
☐ 35 David Justice	.60	.25
☐ 36 Roberto Kelly	.15	.07
☐ 37 Ryan Klesko	.30	.14
☐ 38 Javier Lopez	.40	.18
☐ 39 Greg Maddux	1.50	.70
☐ 40 Fred McGriff	.40	.18
☐ 41 Terry Pendleton	.15	.07
☐ 42 Ricky Bones	.15	.07
☐ 43 Darryl Hamilton	.15	.07
☐ 44 Brian Harper	.15	.07
☐ 45 John Jaha	.15	.07
☐ 46 Dave Nilsson	.15	.07
☐ 47 Kevin Seitzer	.15	.07
☐ 48 Greg Vaughn	.30	.14
☐ 49 Turner Ward	.15	.07
☐ 50 Bernard Gilkey	.15	.07
☐ 51 Gregg Jefferies	.15	.07
☐ 52 Ray Lankford	.30	.14
☐ 53 Tom Pagnozzi	.15	.07
☐ 54 Ozzie Smith	.75	.35
☐ 55 Bob Tewksbury	.15	.07

❏ 56 Mark Whiten	.15	.07
❏ 57 Todd Zeile	.15	.07
❏ 58 Steve Buechele	.15	.07
❏ 59 Shawon Dunston	.15	.07
❏ 60 Mark Grace	.40	.18
❏ 61 Derrick May	.15	.07
❏ 62 Karl Rhodes	.15	.07
❏ 63 Ryne Sandberg	.75	.35
❏ 64 Sammy Sosa	2.00	.90
❏ 65 Rick Wilkins	.15	.07
❏ 66 Brett Butler	.30	.14
❏ 67 Delino DeShields	.15	.07
❏ 68 Orel Hershiser	.30	.14
❏ 69 Eric Karros	.30	.14
❏ 70 Raul Mondesi	.60	.25
❏ 71 Jose Offerman	.30	.14
❏ 72 Mike Piazza	2.00	.90
❏ 73 Tim Wallach	.15	.07
❏ 74 Moises Alou	.30	.14
❏ 75 Sean Berry	.15	.07
❏ 76 Wil Cordero	.15	.07
❏ 77 Cliff Floyd	.30	.14
❏ 78 Marquis Grissom	.30	.14
❏ 79 Ken Hill	.15	.07
❏ 80 Larry Walker	.60	.25
❏ 81 John Wetteland	.30	.14
❏ 82 Rod Beck	.15	.07
❏ 83 Barry Bonds	.75	.35
❏ 84 Royce Clayton	.15	.07
❏ 85 Darren Lewis	.15	.07
❏ 86 Willie McGee	.30	.14
❏ 87 Bill Swift	.15	.07
❏ 88 Robby Thompson	.15	.07
❏ 89 Matt Williams	.40	.18
❏ 90 Sandy Alomar Jr.	.30	.14
❏ 91 Carlos Baerga	.30	.14
❏ 92 Albert Belle	.60	.25
❏ 93 Kenny Lofton	.60	.25
❏ 94 Eddie Murray	.60	.25
❏ 95 Manny Ramirez	1.25	.55
❏ 96 Paul Sorrento	.15	.07
❏ 97 Jim Thome	.60	.25
❏ 98 Rich Amaral	.15	.07
❏ 99 Eric Anthony	.15	.07
❏ 100 Jay Buhner	.30	.14
❏ 101 Ken Griffey Jr.	3.00	1.35
❏ 102 Randy Johnson	.60	.25
❏ 103 Edgar Martinez	.30	.14
❏ 104 Tino Martinez	.60	.25
❏ 105 Kurt Abbott	.15	.07
❏ 106 Bret Barberie	.15	.07
❏ 107 Chuck Carr	.15	.07
❏ 108 Jeff Conine	.15	.07
❏ 109 Chris Hammond	.15	.07
❏ 110 Bryan Harvey	.15	.07
❏ 111 Benito Santiago	.15	.07
❏ 112 Gary Sheffield	.60	.25
❏ 113 Bobby Bonilla	.30	.14
❏ 114 Dwight Gooden	.30	.14
❏ 115 Todd Hundley	.15	.07
❏ 116 Bobby Jones	.30	.14
❏ 117 Jeff Kent	.30	.14
❏ 118 Kevin McReynolds	.15	.07
❏ 119 Bret Saberhagen	.15	.07
❏ 120 Ryan Thompson	.15	.07
❏ 121 Harold Baines	.30	.14
❏ 122 Mike Devereaux	.15	.07
❏ 123 Jeffrey Hammonds	.30	.14
❏ 124 Ben McDonald	.15	.07
❏ 125 Mike Mussina	.60	.25
❏ 126 Rafael Palmeiro	.60	.25
❏ 127 Cal Ripken Jr.	2.50	1.10
❏ 128 Lee Smith	.15	.07
❏ 129 Brad Ausmus	.15	.07
❏ 130 Derek Bell	.30	.14
❏ 131 Andy Benes	.30	.14
❏ 132 Tony Gwynn	1.50	.70
❏ 133 Trevor Hoffman	.30	.14
❏ 134 Scott Livingstone	.15	.07
❏ 135 Phil Plantier	.15	.07
❏ 136 Darren Daulton	.30	.14
❏ 137 Mariano Duncan	.15	.07
❏ 138 Lenny Dykstra	.30	.14
❏ 139 Dave Hollins	.15	.07
❏ 140 Pete Incaviglia	.15	.07
❏ 141 Danny Jackson	.15	.07

❏ 142 John Kruk	.30	.14
❏ 143 Kevin Stocker	.15	.07
❏ 144 Jay Bell	.30	.14
❏ 145 Carlos Garcia	.15	.07
❏ 146 Jeff King	.15	.07
❏ 147 Al Martin	.15	.07
❏ 148 Orlando Merced	.15	.07
❏ 149 Don Slaught	.15	.07
❏ 150 Andy Van Slyke	.30	.14
❏ 151 Kevin Brown	.30	.14
❏ 152 Jose Canseco	.75	.35
❏ 153 Will Clark	.60	.25
❏ 154 Juan Gonzalez	1.25	.55
❏ 155 David Hulse	.15	.07
❏ 156 Dean Palmer	.30	.14
❏ 157 Ivan Rodriguez	.75	.35
❏ 158 Kenny Rogers	.15	.07
❏ 159 Roger Clemens	1.50	.70
❏ 160 Scott Cooper	.15	.07
❏ 161 Andre Dawson	.40	.18
❏ 162 Mike Greenwell	.15	.07
❏ 163 Otis Nixon	.15	.07
❏ 164 Aaron Sele	.30	.14
❏ 165 John Valentin	.30	.14
❏ 166 Mo Vaughn	.60	.25
❏ 167 Bret Boone	.30	.14
❏ 168 Barry Larkin	.60	.25
❏ 169 Kevin Mitchell	.15	.07
❏ 170 Hal Morris	.15	.07
❏ 171 Jose Rijo	.15	.07
❏ 172 Deion Sanders	.30	.14
❏ 173 Reggie Sanders	.30	.14
❏ 174 John Smiley	.15	.07
❏ 175 Dante Bichette	.30	.14
❏ 176 Ellis Burks	.30	.14
❏ 177 Andres Galarraga	.60	.25
❏ 178 Joe Girardi	.15	.07
❏ 179 Charlie Hayes	.15	.07
❏ 180 Roberto Mejia	.15	.07
❏ 181 Walt Weiss	.15	.07
❏ 182 David Cone	.40	.18
❏ 183 Gary Gaetti	.30	.14
❏ 184 Greg Gagne	.15	.07
❏ 185 Felix Jose	.15	.07
❏ 186 Wally Joyner	.30	.14
❏ 187 Mike Macfarlane	.15	.07
❏ 188 Brian McRae	.15	.07
❏ 189 Eric Davis	.30	.14
❏ 190 Cecil Fielder	.30	.14
❏ 191 Travis Fryman	.30	.14
❏ 192 Tony Phillips	.15	.07
❏ 193 Mickey Tettleton	.15	.07
❏ 194 Alan Trammell	.40	.18
❏ 195 Lou Whitaker	.30	.14
❏ 196 Kent Hrbek	.30	.14
❏ 197 Chuck Knoblauch	.60	.25
❏ 198 Shane Mack	.15	.07
❏ 199 Pat Meares	.15	.07
❏ 200 Kirby Puckett	1.00	.45
❏ 201 Matt Walbeck	.15	.07
❏ 202 Dave Winfield	.60	.25
❏ 203 Wilson Alvarez	.30	.14
❏ 204 Alex Fernandez	.15	.07
❏ 205 Julio Franco	.15	.07
❏ 206 Ozzie Guillen	.15	.07
❏ 207 Jack McDowell	.30	.14
❏ 208 Tim Raines	.30	.14
❏ 209 Frank Thomas	1.25	.55
❏ 210 Robin Ventura	.30	.14
❏ 211 Jim Abbott	.30	.14
❏ 212 Wade Boggs	.60	.25
❏ 213 Pat Kelly	.15	.07
❏ 214 Jimmy Key	.30	.14
❏ 215 Don Mattingly	1.25	.55
❏ 216 Paul O'Neill	.30	.14
❏ 217 Mike Stanley	.15	.07
❏ 218 Danny Tartabull	.15	.07
❏ 219 Checklist	.15	.07
❏ 220 Checklist	.15	.07

1994 Studio Editor's Choice

	MINT	NRMT
COMPLETE SET (8)	40.00	18.00

	MINT	NRMT
COMMON CARD (1-8)	1.50	.70
STATED ODDS 1:36		

❏ 1 Barry Bonds	4.00	1.80
❏ 2 Frank Thomas	6.00	2.70
❏ 3 Ken Griffey Jr.	15.00	6.75
❏ 4 Andres Galarraga	3.00	1.35
❏ 5 Juan Gonzalez	6.00	2.70
❏ 6 Tim Salmon	3.00	1.35
❏ 7 Paul O'Neill	1.50	.70
❏ 8 Mike Piazza	10.00	4.50

1994 Studio Heritage

	MINT	NRMT
COMPLETE SET (8)	15.00	6.75
COMMON CARD (1-8)	.50	.23
STATED ODDS 1:36		

❏ 1 Barry Bonds	2.00	.90
❏ 2 Frank Thomas	3.00	1.35
❏ 3 Joe Carter	.75	.35
❏ 4 Don Mattingly	3.00	1.35
❏ 5 Ryne Sandberg	2.00	.90
❏ 6 Javier Lopez	1.00	.45
❏ 7 Gregg Jefferies	.50	.23
❏ 8 Mike Mussina	1.50	.70

1994 Studio Series Stars

	MINT	NRMT
COMPLETE SET (10)	150.00	70.00

COMMON CARD (1-10)	3.00	1.35
SILVER STATED ODDS 1:60		
SILVER STATED PRINT RUN 10,000 SETS		
COMP.GOLD SET (10)	300.00	135.00
*GOLD: 8X TO 20X BASE CARD HI		
GOLD STATED ODDS 1:120		
GOLD PRINT RUN 5000 SERIAL #'d SETS		

❏ 1	Tony Gwynn	15.00	6.75
❏ 2	Barry Bonds	6.00	2.70
❏ 3	Frank Thomas	15.00	6.75
❏ 4	Ken Griffey Jr.	30.00	13.50
❏ 5	Joe Carter	3.00	1.35
❏ 6	Mike Piazza	20.00	9.00
❏ 7	Cal Ripken Jr.	25.00	11.00
❏ 8	Greg Maddux	20.00	9.00
❏ 9	Juan Gonzalez	15.00	6.75
❏ 10	Don Mattingly	10.00	4.50

1995 Studio

	MINT	NRMT
COMPLETE SET (200)	60.00	27.00
COMMON CARD (1-200)	.20	.09
MINOR STARS	.40	.18
UNLISTED STARS	.75	.35
COMP.GOLD SET (50)	30.00	13.50
COMMON GOLD (1-50)	.50	.23
*GOLD STARS: .5X TO 1.2X HI COLUMN		
ONE GOLD PER PACK		
COMMON PLATINUM (1-25)	2.00	.90
*PLAT.STARS: 2.5X TO 6X HI COLUMN		
PLATINUM STATED ODDS 1:10		

❏ 1	Frank Thomas	1.50	.70
❏ 2	Jeff Bagwell	1.00	.45
❏ 3	Don Mattingly	1.50	.70
❏ 4	Mike Piazza	2.50	1.10
❏ 5	Ken Griffey Jr.	4.00	1.80
❏ 6	Greg Maddux	2.00	.90
❏ 7	Barry Bonds	1.00	.45
❏ 8	Cal Ripken Jr.	3.00	1.35
❏ 9	Jose Canseco	1.00	.45
❏ 10	Paul Molitor	.75	.35
❏ 11	Kenny Lofton	.60	.25
❏ 12	Will Clark	.75	.35
❏ 13	Tim Salmon	.75	.35
❏ 14	Joe Carter	.40	.18
❏ 15	Albert Belle	.75	.35
❏ 16	Roger Clemens	2.00	.90
❏ 17	Roberto Alomar	.75	.35
❏ 18	Alex Rodriguez	3.00	1.35
❏ 19	Raul Mondesi	.60	.25
❏ 20	Deion Sanders	.40	.18
❏ 21	Juan Gonzalez	1.50	.70
❏ 22	Kirby Puckett	1.25	.55
❏ 23	Fred McGriff	.60	.25
❏ 24	Matt Williams	.75	.35
❏ 25	Tony Gwynn	2.00	.90
❏ 26	Cliff Floyd	.40	.18
❏ 27	Travis Fryman	.40	.18
❏ 28	Shawn Green	.75	.35
❏ 29	Mike Mussina	.75	.35
❏ 30	Bob Hamelin	.20	.09
❏ 31	David Justice	.75	.35
❏ 32	Manny Ramirez	1.00	.45
❏ 33	David Cone	.60	.25
❏ 34	Marquis Grissom	.40	.18
❏ 35	Moises Alou	.40	.18
❏ 36	Carlos Baerga	.20	.09
❏ 37	Barry Larkin	.75	.35
❏ 38	Robin Ventura	.40	.18
❏ 39	Mo Vaughn	.75	.35
❏ 40	Jeffrey Hammonds	.40	.18
❏ 41	Ozzie Smith	1.00	.45
❏ 42	Andres Galarraga	.75	.35
❏ 43	Carlos Delgado	.75	.35
❏ 44	Lenny Dykstra	.40	.18
❏ 45	Cecil Fielder	.40	.18
❏ 46	Wade Boggs	.75	.35
❏ 47	Gregg Jefferies	.20	.09
❏ 48	Randy Johnson	.75	.35
❏ 49	Rafael Palmeiro	.75	.35
❏ 50	Craig Biggio	.75	.35
❏ 51	Steve Avery	.20	.09
❏ 52	Ricky Bottalico	.20	.09
❏ 53	Chris Gomez	.20	.09
❏ 54	Carlos Garcia	.20	.09
❏ 55	Brian Anderson	.40	.18
❏ 56	Wilson Alvarez	.20	.09
❏ 57	Roberto Kelly	.20	.09
❏ 58	Larry Walker	.75	.35
❏ 59	Dean Palmer	.40	.18
❏ 60	Rick Aguilera	.20	.09
❏ 61	Javier Lopez	.40	.18
❏ 62	Shawon Dunston	.20	.09
❏ 63	Wm. VanLandingham	.20	.09
❏ 64	Jeff Kent	.40	.18
❏ 65	David McCarty	.20	.09
❏ 66	Armando Benitez	.20	.09
❏ 67	Brett Butler	.40	.18
❏ 68	Bernard Gilkey	.20	.09
❏ 69	Joey Hamilton	.40	.18
❏ 70	Chad Curtis	.20	.09
❏ 71	Dante Bichette	.40	.18
❏ 72	Chuck Carr	.20	.09
❏ 73	Pedro Martinez	1.00	.45
❏ 74	Ramon Martinez	.40	.18
❏ 75	Rondell White	.40	.18
❏ 76	Alex Fernandez	.20	.09
❏ 77	Dennis Martinez	.40	.18
❏ 78	Sammy Sosa	2.50	1.10
❏ 79	Bernie Williams	.75	.35
❏ 80	Lou Whitaker	.40	.18
❏ 81	Kurt Abbott	.20	.09
❏ 82	Tino Martinez	.75	.35
❏ 83	Willie Greene	.20	.09
❏ 84	Garret Anderson	.40	.18
❏ 85	Jose Rijo	.20	.09
❏ 86	Jeff Montgomery	.20	.09
❏ 87	Mark Langston	.20	.09
❏ 88	Reggie Sanders	.40	.18
❏ 89	Rusty Greer	.75	.35
❏ 90	Delino DeShields	.20	.09
❏ 91	Jason Bere	.20	.09
❏ 92	Lee Smith	.40	.18
❏ 93	Devon White	.40	.18
❏ 94	John Wetteland	.20	.09
❏ 95	Luis Gonzalez	.20	.09
❏ 96	Greg Vaughn	.40	.18
❏ 97	Lance Johnson	.20	.09
❏ 98	Alan Trammell	.40	.18
❏ 99	Bret Saberhagen	.40	.18
❏ 100	Jack McDowell	.20	.09
❏ 101	Trevor Hoffman	.20	.09
❏ 102	Dave Nilsson	.20	.09
❏ 103	Bryan Harvey	.20	.09
❏ 104	Chuck Knoblauch	.75	.35
❏ 105	Bobby Bonilla	.40	.18
❏ 106	Hal Morris	.20	.09
❏ 107	Mark Whiten	.20	.09
❏ 108	Phil Plantier	.20	.09
❏ 109	Ryan Klesko	.40	.18
❏ 110	Greg Gagne	.20	.09
❏ 111	Ruben Sierra	.20	.09
❏ 112	J.R. Phillips	.20	.09
❏ 113	Terry Steinbach	.20	.09
❏ 114	Jay Buhner	.40	.18
❏ 115	Ken Caminiti	.60	.25
❏ 116	Gary DiSarcina	.20	.09
❏ 117	Ivan Rodriguez	1.00	.45
❏ 118	Bip Roberts	.20	.09
❏ 119	Jay Bell	.40	.18
❏ 120	Ken Hill	.20	.09
❏ 121	Mike Greenwell	.20	.09
❏ 122	Rick Wilkins	.20	.09
❏ 123	Rickey Henderson	1.00	.45
❏ 124	Dave Hollins	.20	.09
❏ 125	Terry Pendleton	.20	.09
❏ 126	Rich Becker	.20	.09
❏ 127	Billy Ashley	.20	.09
❏ 128	Derek Bell	.40	.18
❏ 129	Dennis Eckersley	.40	.18
❏ 130	Andujar Cedeno	.20	.09
❏ 131	John Jaha	.20	.09
❏ 132	Chuck Finley	.40	.18
❏ 133	Steve Finley	.40	.18
❏ 134	Danny Tartabull	.20	.09
❏ 135	Jeff Conine	.40	.18
❏ 136	Jon Lieber	.20	.09
❏ 137	Jim Abbott	.40	.18
❏ 138	Steve Trachsel	.20	.09
❏ 139	Bret Boone	.40	.18
❏ 140	Charles Johnson	.40	.18
❏ 141	Mark McGwire	4.00	1.80
❏ 142	Eddie Murray	.75	.35
❏ 143	Doug Drabek	.20	.09
❏ 144	Steve Cooke	.20	.09
❏ 145	Kevin Seitzer	.20	.09
❏ 146	Rod Beck	.20	.09
❏ 147	Eric Karros	.40	.18
❏ 148	Tim Raines	.40	.18
❏ 149	Joe Girardi	.20	.09
❏ 150	Aaron Sele	.40	.18
❏ 151	Robby Thompson	.20	.09
❏ 152	Chan Ho Park	.75	.35
❏ 153	Ellis Burks	.40	.18
❏ 154	Brian McRae	.20	.09
❏ 155	Jimmy Key	.40	.18
❏ 156	Rico Brogna	.20	.09
❏ 157	Ozzie Guillen	.20	.09
❏ 158	Chili Davis	.40	.18
❏ 159	Darren Daulton	.40	.18
❏ 160	Chipper Jones	2.00	.90
❏ 161	Walt Weiss	.20	.09
❏ 162	Paul O'Neill	.40	.18
❏ 163	Al Martin	.20	.09
❏ 164	John Valentin	.40	.18
❏ 165	Tim Wallach	.20	.09
❏ 166	Scott Erickson	.40	.18
❏ 167	Ryan Thompson	.20	.09
❏ 168	Todd Zeile	.20	.09
❏ 169	Scott Cooper	.20	.09
❏ 170	Matt Mieske	.20	.09
❏ 171	Allen Watson	.20	.09
❏ 172	Brian L.Hunter	.40	.18
❏ 173	Kevin Stocker	.20	.09
❏ 174	Cal Eldred	.20	.09
❏ 175	Tony Phillips	.20	.09
❏ 176	Ben McDonald	.20	.09
❏ 177	Mark Grace	.60	.25
❏ 178	Midre Cummings	.20	.09
❏ 179	Orlando Merced	.20	.09
❏ 180	Jeff King	.20	.09
❏ 181	Gary Sheffield	.40	.18
❏ 182	Tom Glavine	.75	.35
❏ 183	Edgar Martinez	.40	.18
❏ 184	Steve Karsay	.20	.09
❏ 185	Pat Listach	.20	.09
❏ 186	Wil Cordero	.20	.09
❏ 187	Brady Anderson	.40	.18
❏ 188	Bobby Jones	.20	.09
❏ 189	Andy Benes	.40	.18
❏ 190	Ray Lankford	.40	.18
❏ 191	John Doherty	.20	.09
❏ 192	Wally Joyner	.40	.18
❏ 193	Jim Thome	.75	.35
❏ 194	Royce Clayton	.20	.09
❏ 195	John Olerud	.40	.18
❏ 196	Steve Buechele	.20	.09
❏ 197	Harold Baines	.40	.18
❏ 198	Geronimo Berroa	.20	.09
❏ 199	Checklist	.20	.09
❏ 200	Checklist	.20	.09

1996 Studio

	MINT	NRMT
COMPLETE SET (150)	15.00	6.75
COMMON CARD (1-150)	.15	.07

MINOR STARS	.25	.11
UNLISTED STARS	.50	.23
COMMON BRZ.PP (1-150)	1.00	.45
*BRONZE PP STARS: 5X TO 12X HI COLUMN		
BRONZE PP STATED ODDS 1:6		
BRONZE PP STATED PRINT RUN 2000 SETS		
COMMON GOLD PP (1-150)	3.00	1.35
*GOLD PP STARS: 15X TO 40X HI COLUMN		
GOLD PP STATED ODDS 1:24		
GOLD PP STATED PRINT RUN 500 SETS		
COMMON SILV.PP (1-150)	10.00	4.50
*SILVER PP STARS: 40X TO 100X HI COLUMN		
SILVER: RANDOM INS.IN MAGAZINE PACKS		
SILVER STATED PRINT RUN 100 SETS		

❏ 1 Cal Ripken	2.00	.90
❏ 2 Alex Gonzalez	.15	.07
❏ 3 Roger Cedeno	.25	.11
❏ 4 Todd Hollandsworth	.15	.07
❏ 5 Gregg Jefferies	.15	.07
❏ 6 Ryne Sandberg	.60	.25
❏ 7 Eric Karros	.25	.11
❏ 8 Jeff Conine	.15	.07
❏ 9 Rafael Palmeiro	.50	.23
❏ 10 Bip Roberts	.15	.07
❏ 11 Roger Clemens	1.25	.55
❏ 12 Tom Glavine	.50	.23
❏ 13 Jason Giambi	.25	.11
❏ 14 Rey Ordonez	.50	.23
❏ 15 Chan Ho Park	.40	.18
❏ 16 Vinny Castilla	.40	.18
❏ 17 Butch Huskey	.15	.07
❏ 18 Greg Maddux	1.25	.55
❏ 19 Bernard Gilkey	.15	.07
❏ 20 Marquis Grissom	.25	.11
❏ 21 Chuck Knoblauch	.50	.23
❏ 22 Ozzie Smith	.60	.25
❏ 23 Garret Anderson	.25	.11
❏ 24 J.T. Snow	.25	.11
❏ 25 John Valentin	.25	.11
❏ 26 Barry Larkin	.50	.23
❏ 27 Bobby Bonilla	.25	.11
❏ 28 Todd Zeile	.15	.07
❏ 29 Roberto Alomar	.50	.23
❏ 30 Ramon Martinez	.25	.11
❏ 31 Jeff King	.15	.07
❏ 32 Dennis Eckersley	.25	.11
❏ 33 Derek Jeter	1.50	.70
❏ 34 Edgar Martinez	.25	.11
❏ 35 Geronimo Berroa	.15	.07
❏ 36 Hal Morris	.15	.07
❏ 37 Troy Percival	.25	.11
❏ 38 Jason Isringhausen	.25	.11
❏ 39 Greg Vaughn	.25	.11
❏ 40 Robin Ventura	.25	.11
❏ 41 Craig Biggio	.50	.23
❏ 42 Will Clark	.50	.23
❏ 43 Sammy Sosa	1.50	.70
❏ 44 Bernie Williams	.50	.23
❏ 45 Kenny Lofton	.40	.18
❏ 46 Wade Boggs	.50	.23
❏ 47 Javy Lopez	.25	.11
❏ 48 Reggie Sanders	.25	.11
❏ 49 Jeff Bagwell	.60	.25
❏ 50 Fred McGriff	.40	.18
❏ 51 Charles Johnson	.25	.11
❏ 52 Darren Daulton	.25	.11
❏ 53 Jose Canseco	.60	.25

❏ 54 Cecil Fielder	.25	.11
❏ 55 Hideo Nomo	.50	.23
❏ 56 Tim Salmon	.40	.18
❏ 57 Carlos Delgado	.50	.23
❏ 58 David Cone	.40	.18
❏ 59 Tim Raines	.25	.11
❏ 60 Lyle Mouton	.15	.07
❏ 61 Wally Joyner	.25	.11
❏ 62 Bret Boone	.25	.11
❏ 63 Raul Mondesi	.25	.11
❏ 64 Gary Sheffield	.25	.11
❏ 65 Alex Rodriguez	1.50	.70
❏ 66 Russ Davis	.15	.07
❏ 67 Checklist	.15	.07
❏ 68 Marty Cordova	.15	.07
❏ 69 Ruben Sierra	.15	.07
❏ 70 Jose Mesa	.15	.07
❏ 71 Matt Williams	.50	.23
❏ 72 Chipper Jones	1.25	.55
❏ 73 Randy Johnson	.50	.23
❏ 74 Kirby Puckett	.75	.35
❏ 75 Jim Edmonds	.40	.18
❏ 76 Barry Bonds	.40	.18
❏ 77 David Segui	.25	.11
❏ 78 Larry Walker	.50	.23
❏ 79 Jason Kendall	.50	.23
❏ 80 Mike Piazza	1.50	.70
❏ 81 Brian L.Hunter	.15	.07
❏ 82 Julio Franco	.25	.11
❏ 83 Jay Bell	.25	.11
❏ 84 Kevin Seltzer	.15	.07
❏ 85 John Smoltz	.40	.18
❏ 86 Joe Carter	.25	.11
❏ 87 Ray Durham	.25	.11
❏ 88 Carlos Baerga	.15	.07
❏ 89 Ron Gant	.25	.11
❏ 90 Orlando Merced	.15	.07
❏ 91 Lee Smith	.15	.07
❏ 92 Pedro Martinez	.60	.25
❏ 93 Frank Thomas	1.00	.45
❏ 94 Al Martin	.15	.07
❏ 95 Chad Curtis	.15	.07
❏ 96 Eddie Murray	.50	.23
❏ 97 Rusty Greer	.25	.11
❏ 98 Jay Buhner	.25	.11
❏ 99 Rico Brogna	.15	.07
❏ 100 Todd Hundley	.25	.11
❏ 101 Moises Alou	.25	.11
❏ 102 Chili Davis	.15	.07
❏ 103 Ismael Valdes	.25	.11
❏ 104 Mo Vaughn	.50	.23
❏ 105 Juan Gonzalez	1.00	.45
❏ 106 Mark Grudzielanek	.15	.07
❏ 107 Derek Bell	.25	.11
❏ 108 Shawn Green	.50	.23
❏ 109 David Justice	.50	.23
❏ 110 Paul O'Neill	.25	.11
❏ 111 Kevin Appier	.25	.11
❏ 112 Ray Lankford	.25	.11
❏ 113 Travis Fryman	.25	.11
❏ 114 Manny Ramirez	.60	.25
❏ 115 Brooks Kieschnick	.15	.07
❏ 116 Ken Griffey Jr.	2.50	1.10
❏ 117 Jeffrey Hammonds	.25	.11
❏ 118 Mark McGwire	2.50	1.10
❏ 119 Denny Neagle	.25	.11
❏ 120 Quilvio Veras	.15	.07
❏ 121 Alan Benes	.15	.07
❏ 122 Rondell White	.25	.11
❏ 123 Osvaldo Fernandez	.15	.07
❏ 124 Andres Galarraga	.50	.23
❏ 125 Johnny Damon	.40	.18
❏ 126 Lenny Dykstra	.25	.11
❏ 127 Jason Schmidt	.25	.11
❏ 128 Mike Mussina	.50	.23
❏ 129 Ken Caminiti	.25	.11
❏ 130 Michael Tucker	.25	.11
❏ 131 LaTroy Hawkins	.15	.07
❏ 132 Checklist	.15	.07
❏ 133 Delino DeShields	.15	.07
❏ 134 Dave Nilsson	.15	.07
❏ 135 Jack McDowell	.15	.07
❏ 136 Joey Hamilton	.25	.11
❏ 137 Dante Bichette	.25	.11
❏ 138 Paul Molitor	.50	.23
❏ 139 Ivan Rodriguez	.60	.25

❏ 140 Mark Grace	.40	.18
❏ 141 Paul Wilson	.15	.07
❏ 142 Orel Hershiser	.25	.11
❏ 143 Albert Belle	.50	.23
❏ 144 Tino Martinez	.25	.11
❏ 145 Tony Gwynn	1.25	.55
❏ 146 George Arias	.15	.07
❏ 147 Brian Jordan	.25	.11
❏ 148 Brian McRae	.15	.07
❏ 149 Rickey Henderson	.60	.25
❏ 150 Ryan Klesko	.25	.11

1996 Studio Hit Parade

	MINT	NRMT
COMPLETE SET (10)	100.00	45.00
COMMON CARD (1-10)	4.00	1.80
STATED ODDS 1:48 HOBBY		
STATED PRINT RUN 5000 SERIAL #'d SETS		

❏ 1 Tony Gwynn	4.00	1.80
❏ 2 Ken Griffey Jr.	25.00	11.00
❏ 3 Frank Thomas	12.00	5.50
❏ 4 Jeff Bagwell	4.00	1.80
❏ 5 Kirby Puckett	8.00	3.60
❏ 6 Mike Piazza	15.00	6.75
❏ 7 Barry Bonds	4.00	1.80
❏ 8 Albert Belle	4.00	1.80
❏ 9 Tim Salmon	4.00	1.80
❏ 10 Mo Vaughn	4.00	1.80

1996 Studio Masterstrokes

	MINT	NRMT
COMPLETE SET (8)	150.00	70.00
COMMON CARD (1-8)	8.00	3.60
STATED ODDS 1:96		
STATED PRINT RUN 5000 SERIAL #'d SETS		

❏ 1 Tony Gwynn	20.00	9.00
❏ 2 Mike Piazza	25.00	11.00
❏ 3 Jeff Bagwell	8.00	3.60
❏ 4 Manny Ramirez	8.00	3.60
❏ 5 Cal Ripken	30.00	13.50
❏ 6 Frank Thomas	20.00	9.00
❏ 7 Ken Griffey Jr.	40.00	18.00
❏ 8 Greg Maddux	25.00	11.00
❏ P2 Mike Piazza Promo	5.00	2.20

1996 Studio Stained Glass Stars

	MINT	NRMT
COMPLETE SET (12)	100.00	45.00
COMMON CARD (1-12)	3.00	1.35
STATED ODDS 1:24		

		MINT	NRMT
❑ 1	Cal Ripken	12.00	5.50
❑ 2	Ken Griffey Jr.	15.00	6.75
❑ 3	Frank Thomas	6.00	2.70
❑ 4	Greg Maddux	8.00	3.60
❑ 5	Chipper Jones	8.00	3.60
❑ 6	Mike Piazza	10.00	4.50
❑ 7	Albert Belle	3.00	1.35
❑ 8	Jeff Bagwell	5.00	2.20
❑ 9	Hideo Nomo	3.00	1.35
❑ 10	Barry Bonds	5.00	2.20
❑ 11	Manny Ramirez	4.00	1.80
❑ 12	Kenny Lofton	3.00	1.35

1997 Studio

	MINT	NRMT
COMPLETE SET (165)	50.00	22.00
COMMON CARD (1-165)	.15	.07
SP's (112,133,137,147,161)	2.00	.90
MINOR STARS	.30	.14
UNLISTED STARS	.60	.25
SUBSET CARDS HALF VALUE OF BASE CARDS		

❑ 1	Frank Thomas	1.25	.55
❑ 2	Gary Sheffield	.30	.14
❑ 3	Jason Isringhausen	.15	.07
❑ 4	Ron Gant	.15	.07
❑ 5	Andy Pettitte	.40	.18
❑ 6	Todd Hollandsworth	.15	.07
❑ 7	Troy Percival	.30	.14
❑ 8	Mark McGwire	3.00	1.35
❑ 9	Barry Larkin	.60	.25
❑ 10	Ken Caminiti	.40	.18
❑ 11	Paul Molitor	.60	.25
❑ 12	Travis Fryman	.30	.14
❑ 13	Kevin Brown	.40	.18
❑ 14	Robin Ventura	.30	.14
❑ 15	Andres Galarraga	.60	.25
❑ 16	Ken Griffey Jr.	3.00	1.35
❑ 17	Roger Clemens	1.50	.70
❑ 18	Alan Benes	.15	.07
❑ 19	Dave Justice	.60	.25
❑ 20	Damon Buford	.15	.07
❑ 21	Mike Piazza	2.00	.90
❑ 22	Ray Durham	.30	.14
❑ 23	Billy Wagner	.30	.14
❑ 24	Dean Palmer	.30	.14
❑ 25	David Cone	.40	.18
❑ 26	Ruben Sierra	.15	.07
❑ 27	Henry Rodriguez	.30	.14
❑ 28	Ray Lankford	.30	.14
❑ 29	Jamey Wright	.15	.07
❑ 30	Brady Anderson	.30	.14
❑ 31	Tino Martinez	.60	.25
❑ 32	Manny Ramirez	.75	.35
❑ 33	Jeff Conine	.15	.07
❑ 34	Dante Bichette	.30	.14
❑ 35	Jose Canseco	.75	.35
❑ 36	Mo Vaughn	.60	.25
❑ 37	Sammy Sosa	2.00	.90
❑ 38	Mark Grudzielanek	.30	.14
❑ 39	Mike Mussina	.60	.25
❑ 40	Bill Pulsipher	.15	.07
❑ 41	Ryne Sandberg	.75	.35
❑ 42	Rickey Henderson	.75	.35
❑ 43	Alex Rodriguez	2.00	.90
❑ 44	Eddie Murray	.60	.25
❑ 45	Ernie Young	.15	.07
❑ 46	Joey Hamilton	.30	.14
❑ 47	Wade Boggs	.60	.25
❑ 48	Rusty Greer	.30	.14
❑ 49	Carlos Delgado	.60	.25
❑ 50	Ellis Burks	.30	.14
❑ 51	Cal Ripken	2.50	1.10
❑ 52	Alex Fernandez	.15	.07
❑ 53	Wally Joyner	.30	.14
❑ 54	James Baldwin	.30	.14
❑ 55	Juan Gonzalez	1.25	.55
❑ 56	John Smoltz	.40	.18
❑ 57	Omar Vizquel	.30	.14
❑ 58	Shane Reynolds	.30	.14
❑ 59	Barry Bonds	.75	.35
❑ 60	Jason Kendall	.40	.18
❑ 61	Marty Cordova	.15	.07
❑ 62	Charles Johnson	.30	.14
❑ 63	John Jaha	.15	.07
❑ 64	Chan Ho Park	.60	.25
❑ 65	Jermaine Allensworth	.15	.07
❑ 66	Mark Grace	.60	.25
❑ 67	Tim Salmon	.60	.25
❑ 68	Edgar Martinez	.30	.14
❑ 69	Marquis Grissom	.30	.14
❑ 70	Craig Biggio	.60	.25
❑ 71	Bobby Higginson	.30	.14
❑ 72	Kevin Seitzer	.15	.07
❑ 73	Hideo Nomo	.60	.25
❑ 74	Dennis Eckersley	.30	.14
❑ 75	Bobby Bonilla	.30	.14
❑ 76	Dwight Gooden	.30	.14
❑ 77	Jeff Cirillo	.30	.14
❑ 78	Brian McRae	.15	.07
❑ 79	Chipper Jones	1.50	.70
❑ 80	Jeff Fassero	.15	.07
❑ 81	Fred McGriff	.40	.18
❑ 82	Garret Anderson	.30	.14
❑ 83	Eric Karros	.30	.14
❑ 84	Derek Bell	.30	.14
❑ 85	Kenny Lofton	.40	.18
❑ 86	John Mabry	.15	.07
❑ 87	Pat Hentgen	.30	.14
❑ 88	Greg Maddux	1.50	.70
❑ 89	Jason Giambi	.30	.14
❑ 90	Al Martin	.15	.07
❑ 91	Derek Jeter	2.00	.90
❑ 92	Rey Ordonez	.30	.14
❑ 93	Will Clark	.60	.25
❑ 94	Kevin Appier	.30	.14
❑ 95	Roberto Alomar	.60	.25
❑ 96	Joe Carter	.30	.14
❑ 97	Bernie Williams	.60	.25
❑ 98	Albert Belle	.60	.25
❑ 99	Greg Vaughn	.30	.14
❑ 100	Tony Clark	.40	.18
❑ 101	Matt Williams	.60	.25
❑ 102	Jeff Bagwell	.75	.35
❑ 103	Reggie Sanders	.30	.14
❑ 104	Mariano Rivera	.30	.14
❑ 105	Larry Walker	.60	.25
❑ 106	Shawn Green	.60	.25
❑ 107	Alex Ochoa	.15	.07
❑ 108	Ivan Rodriguez	.75	.35
❑ 109	Eric Young	.30	.14
❑ 110	Javier Lopez	.30	.14
❑ 111	Brian Hunter	.30	.14
❑ 112	Raul Mondesi SP	2.50	1.10
❑ 113	Randy Johnson	.60	.25
❑ 114	Tony Phillips	.15	.07
❑ 115	Carlos Garcia	.15	.07
❑ 116	Moises Alou	.30	.14
❑ 117	Paul O'Neill	.30	.14
❑ 118	Jim Thome	.60	.25
❑ 119	Jermaine Dye	.30	.14
❑ 120	Wilson Alvarez	.30	.14
❑ 121	Rondell White	.30	.14
❑ 122	Michael Tucker	.15	.07
❑ 123	Mike Lansing	.15	.07
❑ 124	Tony Gwynn	1.50	.70
❑ 125	Ryan Klesko	.30	.14
❑ 126	Jim Edmonds	.40	.18
❑ 127	Chuck Knoblauch	.60	.25
❑ 128	Rafael Palmeiro	.60	.25
❑ 129	Jay Buhner	.30	.14
❑ 130	Tom Glavine	.30	.14
❑ 131	Julio Franco	.30	.14
❑ 132	Cecil Fielder	.30	.14
❑ 133	Paul Wilson SP	2.00	.90
❑ 134	Deion Sanders	.60	.25
❑ 135	Alex Gonzalez	.15	.07
❑ 136	Charles Nagy	.30	.14
❑ 137	Andy Ashby SP	2.00	.90
❑ 138	Edgar Renteria	.30	.14
❑ 139	Pedro Martinez	.75	.35
❑ 140	Brian Jordan	.30	.14
❑ 141	Todd Hundley	.30	.14
❑ 142	Marc Newfield	.15	.07
❑ 143	Darryl Strawberry	.30	.14
❑ 144	Dan Wilson	.15	.07
❑ 145	Brian Giles	2.00	.90
❑ 146	F.P. Santangelo	.15	.07
❑ 147	Shannon Stewart SP	2.00	.90
❑ 148	Scott Spiezio	.15	.07
❑ 149	Andruw Jones	.75	.35
❑ 150	Karim Garcia	.30	.14
❑ 151	Vladimir Guerrero	1.00	.45
❑ 152	George Arias	.15	.07
❑ 153	Brooks Kieschnick	.15	.07
❑ 154	Todd Walker	.60	.25
❑ 155	Scott Rolen	1.00	.45
❑ 156	Todd Greene	.15	.07
❑ 157	Dmitri Young	.30	.14
❑ 158	Ruben Rivera	.15	.07
❑ 159	Bartolo Colon	.30	.14
❑ 160	Nomar Garciaparra	2.00	.90
❑ 161	Bob Abreu SP	2.00	.90
❑ 162	Darin Erstad	.60	.25
❑ 163	Ken Griffey Jr. CL	1.50	.70
❑ 164	Frank Thomas CL	.60	.25
❑ 165	Alex Rodriguez CL	1.00	.45

1997 Studio Gold Press Proofs

	MINT	NRMT
COMMON CARD (1-165)	4.00	1.80
*STARS: 10X TO 25X BASIC CARDS		

*ROOKIES: 5X TO 12X BASIC CARDS
RANDOM INSERTS IN PACKS
STATED PRINT RUN 500 SETS

1997 Studio Silver Press Proofs

	MINT	NRMT
COMMON CARD (1-165)	2.00	.90

*STARS: 5X TO 12X BASIC CARDS
*ROOKIES: 2.5X TO 6X BASIC CARDS
STATED PRINT RUN 1500 SETS

1997 Studio Autographs

	MINT	NRMT

RANDOM INSERTS IN PACKS
SKIP-NUMBERED SET

		MINT	NRMT
❑ 12	Todd Walker/1250	20.00	9.00
❑ 21	Vladimir Guerrero/500	100.00	45.00
❑ 24	Scott Rolen/1000	80.00	36.00

1997 Studio Hard Hats

	MINT	NRMT
COMPLETE SET (24)	150.00	70.00
COMMON CARD (1-24)	2.00	.90
UNLISTED STARS	5.00	2.20

RANDOM INSERTS IN PACKS
STATED PRINT RUN 5000 SERIAL #'d SETS

		MINT	NRMT
❑ 1	Ivan Rodriguez	6.00	2.70

		MINT	NRMT
❑ 2	Albert Belle	5.00	2.20
❑ 3	Ken Griffey Jr.	25.00	11.00
❑ 4	Chuck Knoblauch	5.00	2.20
❑ 5	Frank Thomas	10.00	4.50
❑ 6	Cal Ripken	20.00	9.00
❑ 7	Todd Walker	5.00	2.20
❑ 8	Alex Rodriguez	15.00	6.75
❑ 9	Jim Thome	5.00	2.20
❑ 10	Mike Piazza	15.00	6.75
❑ 11	Barry Larkin	5.00	2.20
❑ 12	Chipper Jones	12.00	5.50
❑ 13	Derek Jeter	15.00	6.75
❑ 14	Matt Williams	5.00	2.20
❑ 15	Jason Giambi	2.50	1.10
❑ 16	Tim Salmon	5.00	2.20
❑ 17	Brady Anderson	2.50	1.10
❑ 18	Rondell White	2.50	1.10
❑ 19	Bernie Williams	5.00	2.20
❑ 20	Juan Gonzalez	10.00	4.50
❑ 21	Karim Garcia	2.00	.90
❑ 22	Scott Rolen	10.00	4.50
❑ 23	Darin Erstad	5.00	2.20
❑ 24	Brian Jordan	2.50	1.10

1997 Studio Master Strokes

	MINT	NRMT
COMPLETE SET (24)	600.00	275.00
COMMON CARD (1-24)	10.00	4.50
UNLISTED STARS	12.00	5.50

RANDOM INSERTS IN PACKS
STATED PRINT RUN 2000 SERIAL #'d SETS

	MINT	NRMT
COMP. 8 X 10 SET (24)	250.00	110.00
COMMON 8 X 10 (1-24)	4.00	1.80

*8 X 10'S: .15X TO .4X HI COLUMN
8 X 10: RANDOM INSERTS IN PACKS
8 X 10 PRINT RUN 5000 SERIAL #'d SETS

		MINT	NRMT
❑ 1	Derek Jeter	40.00	18.00
❑ 2	Jeff Bagwell	15.00	6.75
❑ 3	Ken Griffey Jr.	60.00	27.00
❑ 4	Barry Bonds	15.00	6.75
❑ 5	Frank Thomas	25.00	11.00
❑ 6	Andy Pettitte	10.00	4.50
❑ 7	Mo Vaughn	12.00	5.50
❑ 8	Alex Rodriguez	40.00	18.00
❑ 9	Andruw Jones	15.00	6.75
❑ 10	Kenny Lofton	10.00	4.50
❑ 11	Cal Ripken	50.00	22.00
❑ 12	Greg Maddux	30.00	13.50
❑ 13	Manny Ramirez	15.00	6.75
❑ 14	Mike Piazza	40.00	18.00
❑ 15	Vladimir Guerrero	20.00	9.00
❑ 16	Albert Belle	12.00	5.50
❑ 17	Chipper Jones	30.00	13.50
❑ 18	Hideo Nomo	12.00	5.50
❑ 19	Sammy Sosa	40.00	18.00
❑ 20	Tony Gwynn	30.00	13.50
❑ 21	Gary Sheffield	10.00	4.50
❑ 22	Mark McGwire	60.00	27.00
❑ 23	Juan Gonzalez	25.00	11.00
❑ 24	Paul Molitor	12.00	5.50

1997 Studio Portraits 8x10

	MINT	NRMT
COMPLETE SET (24)	25.00	11.00
COMMON CARD (1-24)	.50	.23

ONE PER PACK

		MINT	NRMT
❑ 1	Ken Griffey Jr.	6.00	2.70
❑ 2	Frank Thomas	2.50	1.10
❑ 3	Alex Rodriguez	4.00	1.80
❑ 4	Andruw Jones	1.50	.70
❑ 5	Cal Ripken	5.00	2.20
❑ 6	Greg Maddux	3.00	1.35
❑ 7	Mike Piazza	4.00	1.80
❑ 8	Chipper Jones	3.00	1.35
❑ 9	Albert Belle	1.25	.55
❑ 10	Derek Jeter	4.00	1.80
❑ 11	Juan Gonzalez	2.50	1.10
❑ 12	Todd Walker	1.25	.55
❑ 13	Mark McGwire	6.00	2.70
❑ 14	Barry Bonds	1.50	.70
❑ 15	Jeff Bagwell	1.50	.70
❑ 16	Manny Ramirez	1.50	.70
❑ 17	Kenny Lofton	1.50	.70
❑ 18	Mo Vaughn	1.25	.55
❑ 19	Hideo Nomo	1.25	.55
❑ 20	Tony Gwynn	3.00	1.35
❑ 21	Vladimir Guerrero	2.00	.90
❑ 22	Gary Sheffield	.50	.23
❑ 23	Ryne Sandberg	1.50	.70
❑ 24	Scott Rolen	2.50	1.10

1998 Studio

	MINT	NRMT
COMPLETE SET (220)	50.00	22.00
COMMON (1-214/CL1-CL6)	.15	.07
MINOR STARS	.25	.11
SEMISTARS	.40	.18
UNLISTED STARS	.60	.25

		MINT	NRMT
❑ 1	Tony Clark	.25	.11
❑ 2	Jose Cruz Jr.	.25	.11
❑ 3	Ivan Rodriguez	.75	.35
❑ 4	Mo Vaughn	.60	.25
❑ 5	Kenny Lofton	.40	.18
❑ 6	Will Clark	.60	.25
❑ 7	Barry Larkin	.60	.25
❑ 8	Jay Bell	.25	.11

❑ 9 Kevin Young	.25	.11
❑ 10 Francisco Cordova	.15	.07
❑ 11 Justin Thompson	.15	.07
❑ 12 Paul Molitor	.25	.11
❑ 13 Jeff Bagwell	.75	.35
❑ 14 Jose Canseco	.75	.35
❑ 15 Scott Rolen	.75	.35
❑ 16 Wilton Guerrero	.15	.07
❑ 17 Shannon Stewart	.25	.11
❑ 18 Hideki Irabu	.25	.11
❑ 19 Michael Tucker	.15	.07
❑ 20 Joe Carter	.25	.11
❑ 21 Gabe Alvarez	.15	.07
❑ 22 Ricky Ledee	.25	.11
❑ 23 Karim Garcia	.15	.07
❑ 24 Eli Marrero	.15	.07
❑ 25 Scott Elarton	.15	.07
❑ 26 Mario Valdes	.15	.07
❑ 27 Ben Grieve	.60	.25
❑ 28 Paul Konerko	.25	.11
❑ 29 Esteban Yan	.50	.23
❑ 30 Esteban Loaiza	.15	.07
❑ 31 Delino DeShields	.15	.07
❑ 32 Bernie Williams	.60	.25
❑ 33 Joe Randa	.15	.07
❑ 34 Randy Johnson	.60	.25
❑ 35 Brett Tomko	.15	.07
❑ 36 Todd Erdos	.25	.11
❑ 37 Bobby Higginson	.25	.11
❑ 38 Jason Kendall	.25	.11
❑ 39 Ray Lankford	.25	.11
❑ 40 Mark Grace	.40	.18
❑ 41 Andy Pettitte	.25	.11
❑ 42 Alex Rodriguez	2.00	.90
❑ 43 Hideo Nomo	.60	.25
❑ 44 Sammy Sosa	2.00	.90
❑ 45 J.T. Snow	.25	.11
❑ 46 Jason Varitek	.25	.11
❑ 47 Vinny Castilla	.25	.11
❑ 48 Neifi Perez	.25	.11
❑ 49 Todd Walker	.25	.11
❑ 50 Mike Cameron	.25	.11
❑ 51 Jeffrey Hammonds	.15	.07
❑ 52 Deivi Cruz	.15	.07
❑ 53 Brian Hunter	.15	.07
❑ 54 Al Martin	.15	.07
❑ 55 Ron Coomer	.15	.07
❑ 56 Chan Ho Park	.25	.11
❑ 57 Pedro Martinez	.75	.35
❑ 58 Darin Erstad	.40	.18
❑ 59 Albert Belle	.60	.25
❑ 60 Nomar Garciaparra	2.00	.90
❑ 61 Tony Gwynn	1.50	.70
❑ 62 Mike Piazza	2.00	.90
❑ 63 Todd Helton	.75	.35
❑ 64 David Ortiz	.25	.11
❑ 65 Todd Dunwoody	.15	.07
❑ 66 Orlando Cabrera	.15	.07
❑ 67 Ken Cloude	.15	.07
❑ 68 Andy Benes	.15	.07
❑ 69 Mariano Rivera	.25	.11
❑ 70 Cecil Fielder	.25	.11
❑ 71 Brian Jordan	.25	.11
❑ 72 Darryl Kile	.15	.07
❑ 73 Reggie Jefferson	.15	.07
❑ 74 Shawn Estes	.15	.07
❑ 75 Bobby Bonilla	.25	.11
❑ 76 Denny Neagle	.15	.07
❑ 77 Robin Ventura	.25	.11
❑ 78 Omar Vizquel	.25	.11
❑ 79 Craig Biggio	.60	.25
❑ 80 Moises Alou	.25	.11
❑ 81 Garret Anderson	.25	.11
❑ 82 Eric Karros	.25	.11
❑ 83 Dante Bichette	.25	.11
❑ 84 Charles Johnson	.25	.11
❑ 85 Rusty Greer	.25	.11
❑ 86 Travis Fryman	.25	.11
❑ 87 Fernando Tatis	.60	.25
❑ 88 Wilson Alvarez	.15	.07
❑ 89 Carl Pavano	.15	.07
❑ 90 Brian Rose	.15	.07
❑ 91 Geoff Jenkins	.25	.11
❑ 92 Magglio Ordonez	2.00	.90
❑ 93 David Segui	.15	.07
❑ 94 David Cone	.40	.18
❑ 95 John Smoltz	.40	.18
❑ 96 Jim Thome	.60	.25
❑ 97 Gary Sheffield	.25	.11
❑ 98 Barry Bonds	.75	.35
❑ 99 Andres Galarraga	.40	.18
❑ 100 Brad Fullmer	.15	.07
❑ 101 Bobby Estalella	.15	.07
❑ 102 Enrique Wilson	.15	.07
❑ 103 Frank Catalanotto	.25	.11
❑ 104 Mike Lowell	.60	.25
❑ 105 Kevin Orie	.15	.07
❑ 106 Matt Morris	.15	.07
❑ 107 Pokey Reese	.15	.07
❑ 108 Shawn Green	.60	.25
❑ 109 Tony Womack	.15	.07
❑ 110 Ken Caminiti	.25	.11
❑ 111 Roberto Alomar	.60	.25
❑ 112 Ken Griffey Jr.	3.00	1.35
❑ 113 Cal Ripken Jr.	2.50	1.10
❑ 114 Lou Collier	.15	.07
❑ 115 Larry Walker	.60	.25
❑ 116 Fred McGriff	.40	.18
❑ 117 Jim Edmonds	.25	.11
❑ 118 Edgar Martinez	.25	.11
❑ 119 Matt Williams	.60	.25
❑ 120 Ismael Valdes	.15	.07
❑ 121 Bartolo Colon	.25	.11
❑ 122 Jeff Cirillo	.25	.11
❑ 123 Steve Woodard	.15	.07
❑ 124 Kevin Millwood	2.00	.90
❑ 125 Derrick Gibson	.25	.11
❑ 126 Jacob Cruz	.15	.07
❑ 127 Russell Branyan	.25	.11
❑ 128 Sean Casey	1.00	.45
❑ 129 Derek Lee	.15	.07
❑ 130 Paul O'Neill	.25	.11
❑ 131 Brad Radke	.25	.11
❑ 132 Kevin Appier	.25	.11
❑ 133 John Olerud	.25	.11
❑ 134 Alan Benes	.15	.07
❑ 135 Todd Greene	.15	.07
❑ 136 Carlos Mendoza	.25	.11
❑ 137 Wade Boggs	.60	.25
❑ 138 Jose Guillen	.25	.11
❑ 139 Tino Martinez	.25	.11
❑ 140 Aaron Boone	.15	.07
❑ 141 Abraham Nunez	.15	.07
❑ 142 Preston Wilson	.25	.11
❑ 143 Randall Simon	.25	.11
❑ 144 Dennis Reyes	.15	.07
❑ 145 Mark Kotsay	.25	.11
❑ 146 Richard Hidalgo	.25	.11
❑ 147 Travis Lee	.40	.18
❑ 148 Hanley Frias	.15	.07
❑ 149 Ruben Rivera	.15	.07
❑ 150 Rafael Medina	.15	.07
❑ 151 Dave Nilsson	.15	.07
❑ 152 Curt Schilling	.25	.11
❑ 153 Brady Anderson	.25	.11
❑ 154 Carlos Delgado	.60	.25
❑ 155 Jason Giambi	.25	.11
❑ 156 Pat Hentgen	.15	.07
❑ 157 Tom Glavine	.60	.25
❑ 158 Ryan Klesko	.25	.11
❑ 159 Chipper Jones	1.50	.70
❑ 160 Juan Gonzalez	1.25	.55
❑ 161 Mark McGwire	4.00	1.80
❑ 162 Vladimir Guerrero	.75	.35
❑ 163 Derek Jeter	2.00	.90
❑ 164 Manny Ramirez	.75	.35
❑ 165 Mike Mussina	.60	.25
❑ 166 Rafael Palmeiro	.60	.25
❑ 167 Henry Rodriguez	.25	.11
❑ 168 Jeff Suppan	.15	.07
❑ 169 Eric Milton	.15	.07
❑ 170 Scott Spiezio	.15	.07
❑ 171 Wilson Delgado	.15	.07
❑ 172 Bubba Trammell	.15	.07
❑ 173 Ellis Burks	.25	.11
❑ 174 Jason Dickson	.15	.07
❑ 175 Butch Huskey	.15	.07
❑ 176 Edgardo Alfonzo	.40	.18
❑ 177 Eric Young	.15	.07
❑ 178 Marquis Grissom	.15	.07
❑ 179 Lance Johnson	.15	.07
❑ 180 Kevin Brown	.40	.18
❑ 181 Sandy Alomar Jr.	.25	.11
❑ 182 Todd Hundley	.25	.11
❑ 183 Rondell White	.25	.11
❑ 184 Javier Lopez	.25	.11
❑ 185 Damian Jackson	.15	.07
❑ 186 Raul Mondesi	.25	.11
❑ 187 Rickey Henderson	.75	.35
❑ 188 David Justice	.25	.11
❑ 189 Jay Buhner	.25	.11
❑ 190 Jaret Wright	.25	.11
❑ 191 Miguel Tejada	.25	.11
❑ 192 Ron Wright	.15	.07
❑ 193 Livan Hernandez	.25	.11
❑ 194 A.J. Hinch	.15	.07
❑ 195 Richie Sexson	.40	.18
❑ 196 Bob Abreu	.25	.11
❑ 197 Louis Castillo	.15	.07
❑ 198 Michael Coleman	.25	.11
❑ 199 Greg Maddux	1.50	.70
❑ 200 Frank Thomas	1.25	.55
❑ 201 Andruw Jones	.60	.25
❑ 202 Roger Clemens	1.50	.70
❑ 203 Tim Salmon	.40	.18
❑ 204 Chuck Knoblauch	.25	.11
❑ 205 Wes Helms	.15	.07
❑ 206 Juan Encarnacion	.25	.11
❑ 207 Russ Davis	.25	.11
❑ 208 John Valentin	.25	.11
❑ 209 Tony Saunders	.15	.07
❑ 210 Mike Sweeney	.25	.11
❑ 211 Steve Finley	.25	.11
❑ 212 Dave Dellucci	.50	.23
❑ 213 Edgar Renteria	.15	.07
❑ 214 Jeremi Gonzalez	.25	.11
❑ CL1 Jeff Bagwell CL	.60	.25
❑ CL2 Mike Piazza CL	1.00	.45
❑ CL3 Greg Maddux CL	.75	.35
❑ CL4 Cal Ripken CL	1.25	.55
❑ CL5 Frank Thomas CL	.60	.25
❑ CL6 Ken Griffey Jr. CL	1.50	.70

1998 Studio Gold Press Proofs

	MINT	NRMT
COMMON (1-214/CL1-CL6)	5.00	2.20

*STARS: 12.5X TO 30X BASIC CARDS
*YNG.STARS 10X TO 25X BASIC CARDS
*ROOKIES: 6X TO 15X BASIC CARDS
RANDOM INSERTS IN PACKS
STATED PRINT RUN 300 SETS

1998 Studio Silver Press Proofs

	MINT	NRMT
COMMON (1-214/CL1-CL6)	2.00	.90

*STARS: 5X TO 12X BASIC CARDS
*YNG.STARS: 3X TO 8X BASIC CARDS
*ROOKIES: 3X TO 8X BASIC CARDS
RANDOM INSERTS IN PACKS
STATED PRINT RUN 1000 SETS

1998 Studio Autographs 8 x 10

	MINT	NRMT
COMPLETE SET (3)	120.00	55.00
COMMON CARD (1-3)	40.00	18.00
RANDOM INSERTS IN PACKS		
PRINT RUNS LISTED BELOW		

		MINT	NRMT
☐ 1 Travis Lee/500		40.00	18.00
☐ 2 Todd Helton/1000		50.00	22.00
☐ 3 Ben Grieve/1000		40.00	18.00

1998 Studio Freeze Frame

	MINT	NRMT
COMPLETE SET (30)	250.00	110.00
COMMON CARD (1-30)	1.25	.55
STATED PRINT RUN 4000 SERIAL #'d SETS		
*DIE CUTS: 8X TO 20X BASE CARD HI		
DIE CUT PRINT RUN 500 SERIAL #'d SETS		
RANDOM INSERTS IN PACKS		

		MINT	NRMT
☐ 1 Ken Griffey Jr.		25.00	11.00
☐ 2 Derek Jeter		15.00	6.75
☐ 3 Ben Grieve		5.00	2.20
☐ 4 Cal Ripken		20.00	9.00
☐ 5 Alex Rodriguez		15.00	6.75
☐ 6 Greg Maddux		12.00	5.50
☐ 7 David Justice		2.00	.90
☐ 8 Mike Piazza		15.00	6.75
☐ 9 Chipper Jones		12.00	5.50
☐ 10 Randy Johnson		5.00	2.20
☐ 11 Jeff Bagwell		6.00	2.70
☐ 12 Nomar Garciaparra		15.00	6.75
☐ 13 Andruw Jones		5.00	2.20
☐ 14 Frank Thomas		10.00	4.50
☐ 15 Scott Rolen		8.00	3.60
☐ 16 Barry Bonds		6.00	2.70
☐ 17 Kenny Lofton		3.00	1.35
☐ 18 Ivan Rodriguez		6.00	2.70
☐ 19 Chuck Knoblauch		2.00	.90
☐ 20 Jose Cruz Jr.		2.00	.90
☐ 21 Bernie Williams		5.00	2.20
☐ 22 Tony Gwynn		12.00	5.50
☐ 23 Juan Gonzalez		10.00	4.50
☐ 24 Gary Sheffield		2.00	.90
☐ 25 Roger Clemens		12.00	5.50

		MINT	NRMT
☐ 26 Travis Lee		3.00	1.35
☐ 27 Brad Fullmer		1.25	.55
☐ 28 Tim Salmon		3.00	1.35
☐ 29 Raul Mondesi		2.00	.90
☐ 30 Roberto Alomar		5.00	2.20

1998 Studio Hit Parade

	MINT	NRMT
COMPLETE SET (20)	120.00	55.00
COMMON CARD (1-20)	2.00	.90
RANDOM INSERTS IN PACKS		
STATED PRINT RUN 5000 SERIAL #'d SETS		

		MINT	NRMT
☐ 1 Tony Gwynn		12.00	5.50
☐ 2 Larry Walker		5.00	2.20
☐ 3 Mike Piazza		15.00	6.75
☐ 4 Frank Thomas		10.00	4.50
☐ 5 Manny Ramirez		6.00	2.70
☐ 6 Ken Griffey Jr.		25.00	11.00
☐ 7 Todd Helton		5.00	2.20
☐ 8 Vladimir Guerrero		6.00	2.70
☐ 9 Albert Belle		5.00	2.20
☐ 10 Jeff Bagwell		6.00	2.70
☐ 11 Juan Gonzalez		10.00	4.50
☐ 12 Jim Thome		5.00	2.20
☐ 13 Scott Rolen		8.00	3.60
☐ 14 Tino Martinez		2.00	.90
☐ 15 Mark McGwire		30.00	13.50
☐ 16 Barry Bonds		6.00	2.70
☐ 17 Tony Clark		2.00	.90
☐ 18 Mo Vaughn		5.00	2.20
☐ 19 Darin Erstad		3.00	1.35
☐ 20 Paul Konerko		2.00	.90

1998 Studio Masterstrokes

	MINT	NRMT
COMPLETE SET (20)	800.00	350.00
COMMON CARD (1-20)	10.00	4.50
UNLISTED STARS	15.00	6.75
RANDOM INSERTS IN PACKS		
STATED PRINT RUN 1000 SERIAL #'d SETS		

		MINT	NRMT
☐ 1 Travis Lee		10.00	4.50
☐ 2 Kenny Lofton		10.00	4.50
☐ 3 Mo Vaughn		15.00	6.75
☐ 4 Ivan Rodriguez		20.00	9.00
☐ 5 Roger Clemens		40.00	18.00

		MINT	NRMT
☐ 6 Mark McGwire		100.00	45.00
☐ 7 Hideo Nomo		15.00	6.75
☐ 8 Andruw Jones		15.00	6.75
☐ 9 Nomar Garciaparra		50.00	22.00
☐ 10 Juan Gonzalez		30.00	13.50
☐ 11 Jeff Bagwell		20.00	9.00
☐ 12 Derek Jeter		50.00	22.00
☐ 13 Tony Gwynn		40.00	18.00
☐ 14 Chipper Jones		40.00	18.00
☐ 15 Mike Piazza		50.00	22.00
☐ 16 Greg Maddux		40.00	18.00
☐ 17 Alex Rodriguez		50.00	22.00
☐ 18 Cal Ripken		60.00	27.00
☐ 19 Frank Thomas		30.00	13.50
☐ 20 Ken Griffey Jr.		80.00	36.00

1998 Studio Portraits 8 x 10

	MINT	NRMT
COMPLETE SET (36)	40.00	18.00
COMMON CARD (1-36)	.40	.18
ONE PER PACK		
*GOLD: 10X TO 25X BASE CARD HI		
GOLD: RANDOM INSERTS IN PACKS		
GOLD PRINT RUN 300 SERIAL #'d SETS		

		MINT	NRMT
☐ 1 Travis Lee		.60	.25
☐ 2 Todd Helton		1.00	.45
☐ 3 Ben Grieve		1.00	.45
☐ 4 Paul Konerko		.40	.18
☐ 5 Jeff Bagwell		1.25	.55
☐ 6 Derek Jeter		3.00	1.35
☐ 7 Ivan Rodriguez		1.25	.55
☐ 8 Cal Ripken		4.00	1.80
☐ 9 Mike Piazza		3.00	1.35
☐ 10 Chipper Jones		2.50	1.10
☐ 11 Frank Thomas		2.00	.90
☐ 12 Tony Gwynn		2.50	1.10
☐ 13 Nomar Garciaparra		3.00	1.35
☐ 14 Juan Gonzalez		2.00	.90
☐ 15 Greg Maddux		2.50	1.10
☐ 16 Hideo Nomo		1.00	.45
☐ 17 Scott Rolen		1.50	.70
☐ 18 Barry Bonds		1.25	.55
☐ 19 Ken Griffey Jr.		5.00	2.20
☐ 20 Alex Rodriguez		3.00	1.35
☐ 21 Roger Clemens		2.50	1.10
☐ 22 Mark McGwire		6.00	2.70
☐ 23 Jose Cruz Jr.		.40	.18
☐ 24 Andruw Jones		1.00	.45
☐ 25 Tino Martinez		.40	.18
☐ 26 Mo Vaughn		1.00	.45
☐ 27 Vladimir Guerrero		1.25	.55
☐ 28 Tony Clark		.40	.18
☐ 29 Andy Pettitte		.40	.18
☐ 30 Jaret Wright		.40	.18
☐ 31 Paul Molitor		1.00	.45
☐ 32 Darin Erstad		.60	.25
☐ 33 Larry Walker		1.00	.45
☐ 34 Chuck Knoblauch		.40	.18
☐ 35 Barry Larkin		1.00	.45
☐ 36 Kenny Lofton		.60	.25

1998 Studio MLB 99

	MINT	NRMT
PLEASE SEE 1998 DONRUSS MLB 99		

1995 Summit

	MINT	NRMT
COMPLETE SET (200)	20.00	9.00
COMMON CARD (1-200)	.10	.05
MINOR STARS	.25	.11
UNLISTED STARS	.50	.23
SUBSET CARDS HALF VALUE OF BASE CARDS		
COMMON NTH DEGREE (1-200)	1.00	.45

*NTH DEGREE STARS: 4X TO 10X HI COLUMN
*NTH DEGREE YOUNG STARS: 3X TO 8X HI
NTH DEGREE STATED ODDS 1:4

❑ 1 Ken Griffey Jr.	2.50	1.10
❑ 2 Alex Fernandez	.10	.05
❑ 3 Fred McGriff	.40	.18
❑ 4 Ben McDonald	.10	.05
❑ 5 Rafael Palmeiro	.50	.23
❑ 6 Tony Gwynn	1.25	.55
❑ 7 Jim Thome	.50	.23
❑ 8 Ken Hill	.10	.05
❑ 9 Barry Bonds	.60	.25
❑ 10 Barry Larkin	.50	.23
❑ 11 Albert Belle	.50	.23
❑ 12 Billy Ashley	.10	.05
❑ 13 Matt Williams	.50	.23
❑ 14 Andy Benes	.25	.11
❑ 15 Midre Cummings	.10	.05
❑ 16 J.R. Phillips	.10	.05
❑ 17 Edgar Martinez	.25	.11
❑ 18 Manny Ramirez	.60	.25
❑ 19 Jose Canseco	.60	.25
❑ 20 Chili Davis	.25	.11
❑ 21 Don Mattingly	1.00	.45
❑ 22 Bernie Williams	.50	.23
❑ 23 Tom Glavine	.50	.23
❑ 24 Robin Ventura	.25	.11
❑ 25 Jeff Conine	.10	.05
❑ 26 Mark Grace	.40	.18
❑ 27 Mark McGwire	2.50	1.10
❑ 28 Carlos Delgado	.50	.23
❑ 29 Greg Colbrunn	.10	.05
❑ 30 Greg Maddux	1.25	.55
❑ 31 Craig Biggio	.50	.23

❑ 32 Kirby Puckett	.75	.35
❑ 33 Derek Bell	.25	.11
❑ 34 Lenny Dykstra	.25	.11
❑ 35 Tim Salmon	.50	.23
❑ 36 Deion Sanders	.25	.11
❑ 37 Moises Alou	.25	.11
❑ 38 Ray Lankford	.25	.11
❑ 39 Willie Greene	.10	.05
❑ 40 Ozzie Smith	.60	.25
❑ 41 Roger Clemens	1.25	.55
❑ 42 Andres Galarraga	.50	.23
❑ 43 Gary Sheffield	.25	.11
❑ 44 Sammy Sosa	1.50	.70
❑ 45 Larry Walker	.50	.23
❑ 46 Kevin Appier	.25	.11
❑ 47 Raul Mondesi	.40	.18
❑ 48 Kenny Lofton	.40	.18
❑ 49 Darryl Hamilton	.10	.05
❑ 50 Roberto Alomar	.50	.23
❑ 51 Hal Morris	.10	.05
❑ 52 Cliff Floyd	.25	.11
❑ 53 Brent Gates	.10	.05
❑ 54 Rickey Henderson	.60	.25
❑ 55 John Olerud	.25	.11
❑ 56 Gregg Jefferies	.10	.05
❑ 57 Cecil Fielder	.25	.11
❑ 58 Paul Molitor	.50	.23
❑ 59 Bret Boone	.25	.11
❑ 60 Greg Vaughn	.25	.11
❑ 61 Wally Joyner	.25	.11
❑ 62 Jeffrey Hammonds	.25	.11
❑ 63 James Mouton	.10	.05
❑ 64 Omar Vizquel	.25	.11
❑ 65 Wade Boggs	.50	.23
❑ 66 Terry Steinbach	.10	.05
❑ 67 Wil Cordero	.10	.05
❑ 68 Joey Hamilton	.25	.11
❑ 69 Rico Brogna	.10	.05
❑ 70 Darren Daulton	.25	.11
❑ 71 Chuck Knoblauch	.50	.23
❑ 72 Bob Hamelin	.10	.05
❑ 73 Carl Everett	.10	.05
❑ 74 Joe Carter	.25	.11
❑ 75 Dave Winfield	.50	.23
❑ 76 Bobby Bonilla	.25	.11
❑ 77 Paul O'Neill	.25	.11
❑ 78 Javier Lopez	.25	.11
❑ 79 Cal Ripken	2.00	.90
❑ 80 David Cone	.40	.18
❑ 81 Bernard Gilkey	.10	.05
❑ 82 Ivan Rodriguez	.60	.25
❑ 83 Dean Palmer	.25	.11
❑ 84 Jason Bere	.10	.05
❑ 85 Will Clark	.50	.23
❑ 86 Scott Cooper	.10	.05
❑ 87 Royce Clayton	.10	.05
❑ 88 Mike Piazza	1.50	.70
❑ 89 Ryan Klesko	.25	.11
❑ 90 Juan Gonzalez	1.00	.45
❑ 91 Travis Fryman	.25	.11
❑ 92 Frank Thomas	1.00	.45
❑ 93 Eduardo Perez	.10	.05
❑ 94 Mo Vaughn	.50	.23
❑ 95 Jay Bell	.25	.11
❑ 96 Jeff Bagwell	.60	.25
❑ 97 Randy Johnson	.50	.23
❑ 98 Jimmy Key	.25	.11
❑ 99 Dennis Eckersley	.25	.11
❑ 100 Carlos Baerga	.10	.05
❑ 101 Eddie Murray	.50	.23
❑ 102 Mike Mussina	.50	.23
❑ 103 Brian Anderson	.25	.11
❑ 104 Jeff Cirillo	.25	.11
❑ 105 Dante Bichette	.25	.11
❑ 106 Bret Saberhagen	.25	.11
❑ 107 Jeff Kent	.25	.11
❑ 108 Ruben Sierra	.25	.11
❑ 109 Kirk Gibson	.25	.11
❑ 110 Steve Karsay	.10	.05
❑ 111 David Justice	.50	.23
❑ 112 Benji Gil	.10	.05
❑ 113 Vaughn Eshelman	.10	.05
❑ 114 Carlos Perez	.10	.05
❑ 115 Chipper Jones	1.25	.55
❑ 116 Shane Andrews	.10	.05
❑ 117 Orlando Miller	.10	.05

❑ 118 Scott Ruffcorn	.10	.05
❑ 119 Jose Oliva	.10	.05
❑ 120 Joe Vitiello	.10	.05
❑ 121 Jon Nunnally	.10	.05
❑ 122 Garret Anderson	.25	.11
❑ 123 Curtis Goodwin	.10	.05
❑ 124 Mark Grudzielanek	.40	.18
❑ 125 Alex Gonzalez	.10	.05
❑ 126 David Bell	.10	.05
❑ 127 Dustin Hermanson	.10	.05
❑ 128 Dave Nilsson	.10	.05
❑ 129 Wilson Heredia	.10	.05
❑ 130 Charles Johnson	.25	.11
❑ 131 Frank Rodriguez	.10	.05
❑ 132 Alex Ochoa	.10	.05
❑ 133 Alex Rodriguez	2.00	.90
❑ 134 Bobby Higginson	.75	.35
❑ 135 Edgardo Alfonzo	.50	.23
❑ 136 Armando Benitez	.10	.05
❑ 137 Rich Aude	.10	.05
❑ 138 Tim Naehring	.10	.05
❑ 139 Joe Randa	.10	.05
❑ 140 Quilvio Veras	.10	.05
❑ 141 Hideo Nomo	1.25	.55
❑ 142 Ray Holbert	.10	.05
❑ 143 Michael Tucker	.25	.11
❑ 144 Chad Mottola	.10	.05
❑ 145 John Valentin	.25	.11
❑ 146 James Baldwin	.25	.11
❑ 147 Esteban Loaiza	.10	.05
❑ 148 Marty Cordova	.10	.05
❑ 149 Juan Acevedo	.10	.05
❑ 150 Tim Unroe UER	.10	.05
Cardinals logo		
❑ 151 Brad Clontz UER	.10	.05
A's logo		
❑ 152 Steve Rodriguez UER	.10	.05
Yankees logo		
❑ 153 Rudy Pemberton UER	.10	.05
Dodgers logo		
❑ 154 Ozzie Timmons UER	.10	.05
Tigers logo		
❑ 155 Ricky Otero	.10	.05
❑ 156 Allen Battle	.10	.05
❑ 157 Joe Rosselli	.10	.05
❑ 158 Roberto Petagine	.10	.05
❑ 159 Todd Hollandsworth	.10	.05
❑ 160 Shannon Penn UER	.10	.05
Cubs logo		
❑ 161 Antonio Osuna UER	.10	.05
Tigers logo		
❑ 162 Russ Davis UER	.25	.11
Red Sox logo		
❑ 163 Jason Giambi UER	.25	.11
two errors: front photo actually Brent Gates		
also Braves logo		
❑ 164 Terry Bradshaw UER	.10	.05
Brewers logo		
❑ 165 Ray Durham	.25	.11
❑ 166 Todd Steverson	.10	.05
❑ 167 Tim Belk	.10	.05
❑ 168 Andy Pettitte	.50	.23
❑ 169 Roger Cedeno	.10	.05
❑ 170 Jose Parra	.10	.05
❑ 171 Scott Sullivan	.10	.05
❑ 172 LaTroy Hawkins	.10	.05
❑ 173 Jeff McCurry	.10	.05
❑ 174 Ken Griffey Jr. BS	1.25	.55
❑ 175 Frank Thomas BS	.50	.23
❑ 176 Cal Ripken Jr. BS	1.00	.45
❑ 177 Jeff Bagwell BS	.50	.23
❑ 178 Mike Piazza BS	.75	.35
❑ 179 Barry Bonds BS	.40	.18
❑ 180 Matt Williams BS	.25	.11
❑ 181 Don Mattingly BS	.50	.23
❑ 182 Will Clark BS	.25	.11
❑ 183 Tony Gwynn BS	.60	.25
❑ 184 Kirby Puckett BS	.50	.23
❑ 185 Jose Canseco BS	.25	.11
❑ 186 Paul Molitor BS	.25	.11
❑ 187 Albert Belle BS	.25	.11
❑ 188 Joe Carter BS	.10	.05
❑ 189 Greg Maddux SD	.60	.25
❑ 190 Roger Clemens SD	.60	.25
❑ 191 David Cone SD	.10	.05

	MINT	NRMT
192 Mike Mussina SD	.25	.11
193 Randy Johnson SD	.25	.11
194 Frank Thomas CL	.50	.23
195 Ken Griffey Jr. CL	1.25	.55
196 Cal Ripken CL	1.00	.45
197 Jeff Bagwell CL	.25	.11
198 Mike Piazza CL	.75	.35
199 Barry Bonds CL	.40	.18
200 Mo Vaughn CL	.40	.18
Matt Williams		

1995 Summit Big Bang

	MINT	NRMT
COMPLETE SET (20)	250.00	110.00
COMMON CARD (BB1-BB20)	5.00	2.20
SEMISTARS	6.00	2.70
UNLISTED STARS	10.00	4.50
STATED ODDS 1:72		
BB1 Ken Griffey Jr.	50.00	22.00
BB2 Frank Thomas	20.00	9.00
BB3 Cal Ripken	40.00	18.00
BB4 Jeff Bagwell	12.00	5.50
BB5 Mike Piazza	30.00	13.50
BB6 Barry Bonds	12.00	5.50
BB7 Matt Williams	10.00	4.50
BB8 Don Mattingly	20.00	9.00
BB9 Will Clark	10.00	4.50
BB10 Tony Gwynn	25.00	11.00
BB11 Kirby Puckett	15.00	6.75
BB12 Jose Canseco	12.00	5.50
BB13 Paul Molitor	10.00	4.50
BB14 Albert Belle	10.00	4.50
BB15 Joe Carter	5.00	2.20
BB16 Rafael Palmeiro	10.00	4.50
BB17 Fred McGriff	6.00	2.70
BB18 David Justice	10.00	4.50
BB19 Tim Salmon	10.00	4.50
BB20 Mo Vaughn	10.00	4.50

1995 Summit New Age

	MINT	NRMT
COMPLETE SET (15)	60.00	27.00
COMMON CARD (NA1-NA15)	1.50	.70
SEMISTARS	3.00	1.35
UNLISTED STARS	6.00	2.70
STATED ODDS 1:18		
NA1 Cliff Floyd	2.00	.90
NA2 Manny Ramirez	8.00	3.60
NA3 Raul Mondesi	3.00	1.35
NA4 Alex Rodriguez	25.00	11.00
NA5 Billy Ashley	1.50	.70
NA6 Alex Gonzalez	1.50	.70
NA7 Michael Tucker	2.00	.90
NA8 Charles Johnson	2.00	.90
NA9 Carlos Delgado	6.00	2.70
NA10 Benji Gil	1.50	.70
NA11 Chipper Jones	20.00	9.00
NA12 Todd Hollandsworth	1.50	.70
NA13 Frankie Rodriguez	1.50	.70
NA14 Shawn Green	6.00	2.70
NA15 Ray Durham	2.00	.90

1995 Summit 21 Club

	MINT	NRMT
COMPLETE SET (9)	25.00	11.00
COMMON CARD (TC1-TC9)	3.00	1.35
STATED ODDS 1:36		
TC1 Bob Abreu	6.00	2.70
TC2 Pokey Reese	4.00	1.80
TC3 Edgardo Alfonzo	5.00	2.20
TC4 Jim Pittsley	3.00	1.35
TC5 Ruben Rivera	4.00	1.80
TC6 Chan Ho Park	4.00	1.80
TC7 Julian Tavarez	3.00	1.35
TC8 Ismael Valdes	4.00	1.80
TC9 Dmitri Young	4.00	1.80

1996 Summit

	MINT	NRMT
COMPLETE SET (200)	25.00	11.00
COMMON CARD (1-200)	.15	.07
MINOR STARS	.30	.14
UNLISTED STARS	.60	.25
SUBSET CARDS HALF VALUE OF BASE CARDS		
COMMON ABV/BYND (1-200)	1.50	.70
*ABV/BYND.STARS: 4X TO 10X HI COLUMN		
*ABV/BYND.ROOKIES: 2.5X TO 6X HI		
ABV.BYND.STATED ODDS 1:4		
COMMON AP (1-200)	4.00	1.80
*AP STARS: 12.5X TO 30X HI COLUMN		
*AP ROOKIES: 8X TO 20X HI		
AP STATED ODDS 1:36		
COMP.FOIL SET (200)	50.00	22.00
COMMON FOIL (1-200)	.15	.07

*FOIL: .6X TO 1.5X HI COLUMN
FOIL CARDS AVAIL.IN RETAIL SUPER PACKS

1 Mike Piazza	2.00	.90
2 Matt Williams	.60	.25
3 Tino Martinez	.30	.14
4 Reggie Sanders	.30	.14
5 Ray Durham	.30	.14
6 Brad Radke	.30	.14
7 Jeff Bagwell	.75	.35
8 Ron Gant	.15	.07
9 Lance Johnson	.15	.07
10 Kevin Seitzer	.15	.07
11 Dante Bichette	.30	.14
12 Ivan Rodriguez	.75	.35
13 Jim Abbott	.30	.14
14 Greg Colbrunn	.15	.07
15 Rondell White	.30	.14
16 Shawn Green	.60	.25
17 Gregg Jefferies	.15	.07
18 Omar Vizquel	.30	.14
19 Cal Ripken	2.50	1.10
20 Mark McGwire	3.00	1.35
21 Wally Joyner	.30	.14
22 Chili Davis	.30	.14
23 Jose Canseco	.75	.35
24 Royce Clayton	.15	.07
25 Jay Bell	.30	.14
26 Travis Fryman	.30	.14
27 Jeff King	.15	.07
28 Todd Hundley	.30	.14
29 Joe Vitiello	.15	.07
30 Russ Davis	.15	.07
31 Mo Vaughn	.60	.25
32 Raul Mondesi	.30	.14
33 Ray Lankford	.30	.14
34 Mike Stanley	.15	.07
35 B.J. Surhoff	.15	.07
36 Greg Vaughn	.30	.14
37 Todd Stottlemyre	.15	.07
38 Carlos Delgado	.60	.25
39 Kenny Lofton	.40	.18
40 Hideo Nomo	.60	.25
41 Sterling Hitchcock	.15	.07
42 Pete Schourek	.15	.07
43 Edgardo Alfonzo	.60	.25
44 Ken Hill	.15	.07
45 Ken Caminiti	.30	.14
46 Bobby Higginson	.30	.14
47 Michael Tucker	.15	.07
48 David Cone	.40	.18
49 Cecil Fielder	.30	.14
50 Brian L. Hunter	.15	.07
51 Charles Johnson	.30	.14
52 Bobby Bonilla	.30	.14
53 Eddie Murray	.60	.25
54 Kenny Rogers	.15	.07
55 Jim Edmonds	.40	.18
56 Trevor Hoffman	.30	.14
57 Kevin Mitchell UER	.15	.07
58 Ruben Sierra	.15	.07
59 Benji Gil	.15	.07
60 Juan Gonzalez	1.25	.55
61 Larry Walker	.60	.25
62 Jack McDowell	.15	.07
63 Shawon Dunston	.15	.07
64 Andy Benes	.30	.14
65 Jay Buhner	.30	.14
66 Rickey Henderson	.75	.35
67 Alex Gonzalez	.15	.07
68 Mike Kelly	.15	.07
69 Fred McGriff	.40	.18
70 Ryne Sandberg	.75	.35
71 Ernie Young	.15	.07
72 Kevin Appier	.30	.14
73 Moises Alou	.30	.14
74 John Jaha	.15	.07
75 J.T. Snow	.30	.14
76 Jim Thome	.60	.25
77 Kirby Puckett	1.00	.45
78 Hal Morris	.15	.07
79 Robin Ventura	.30	.14
80 Ben McDonald	.15	.07
81 Tim Salmon	.40	.18
82 Albert Belle	.60	.25
83 Marquis Grissom	.15	.07

		MINT	NRMT
❏ 84 Alex Rodriguez	2.00		.90
❏ 85 Manny Ramirez	.75		.35
❏ 86 Ken Griffey Jr.	3.00		1.35
❏ 87 Sammy Sosa	2.00		.90
❏ 88 Frank Thomas	1.25		.55
❏ 89 Lee Smith	.30		.14
❏ 90 Marty Cordova	.15		.07
❏ 91 Greg Maddux	1.50		.70
❏ 92 Lenny Dykstra	.30		.14
❏ 93 Butch Huskey	.15		.07
❏ 94 Garret Anderson	.30		.14
❏ 95 Mike Bordick	.15		.07
❏ 96 Dave Justice	.60		.25
❏ 97 Chad Curtis	.15		.07
❏ 98 Carlos Baerga	.15		.07
❏ 99 Jason Isringhausen	.30		.14
❏ 100 Gary Sheffield	.30		.14
❏ 101 Roger Clemens	1.50		.70
❏ 102 Ozzie Smith	.75		.35
❏ 103 Ramon Martinez	.30		.14
❏ 104 Paul O'Neill	.30		.14
❏ 105 Will Clark	.60		.25
❏ 106 Tom Glavine	.60		.25
❏ 107 Barry Bonds	.75		.35
❏ 108 Barry Larkin	.60		.25
❏ 109 Derek Bell	.30		.14
❏ 110 Randy Johnson	.60		.25
❏ 111 Jeff Conine	.15		.07
❏ 112 John Mabry	.15		.07
❏ 113 Julian Tavarez	.15		.07
❏ 114 Gary DiSarcina	.15		.07
❏ 115 Andres Galarraga	.60		.25
❏ 116 Marc Newfield	.15		.07
❏ 117 Frank Rodriguez	.15		.07
❏ 118 Brady Anderson	.30		.14
❏ 119 Mike Mussina	.60		.25
❏ 120 Orlando Merced	.15		.07
❏ 121 Melvin Nieves	.15		.07
❏ 122 Brian Jordan	.30		.14
❏ 123 Rafael Palmeiro	.60		.25
❏ 124 Johnny Damon	.40		.18
❏ 125 Wil Cordero	.15		.07
❏ 126 Chipper Jones	1.50		.70
❏ 127 Eric Karros	.30		.14
❏ 128 Darren Daulton	.30		.14
❏ 129 Vinny Castilla	.40		.18
❏ 130 Joe Carter	.30		.14
❏ 131 Bernie Williams	.60		.25
❏ 132 Bernard Gilkey	.15		.07
❏ 133 Bret Boone	.15		.07
❏ 134 Tony Gwynn	1.50		.70
❏ 135 Dave Nilsson	.15		.07
❏ 136 Ryan Klesko	.30		.14
❏ 137 Paul Molitor	.60		.25
❏ 138 John Olerud	.30		.14
❏ 139 Craig Biggio	.60		.25
❏ 140 John Valentin	.30		.14
❏ 141 Chuck Knoblauch	.60		.25
❏ 142 Edgar Martinez	.30		.14
❏ 143 Rico Brogna	.15		.07
❏ 144 Dean Palmer	.30		.14
❏ 145 Mark Grace	.40		.18
❏ 146 Roberto Alomar	.60		.25
❏ 147 Alex Fernandez	.15		.07
❏ 148 Andre Dawson	.40		.18
❏ 149 Wade Boggs	.60		.25
❏ 150 Mark Lewis	.15		.07
❏ 151 Gary Gaetti	.30		.14
❏ 152 Paul Wilson	.40		.18
Roger Clemens			
❏ 153 Rey Ordonez	.30		.14
Ozzie Smith			
❏ 154 Derek Jeter	1.00		.45
Cal Ripken			
❏ 155 Andy Benes	.15		.07
Alan Benes			
❏ 156 Jason Kendall	.60		.25
Mike Piazza			
❏ 157 Ryan Klesko	.60		.25
Frank Thomas			
❏ 158 Johnny Damon	1.00		.45
Ken Griffey Jr.			
❏ 159 Karim Garcia	1.00		.45
Sammy Sosa			
❏ 160 Raul Mondesi	.30		.14
Tim Salmon			

		MINT	NRMT
❏ 161 Chipper Jones	.60		.25
Matt Williams			
❏ 162 Rey Ordonez	.60		.25
❏ 163 Bob Wolcott	.15		.07
❏ 164 Brooks Kieschnick	.15		.07
❏ 165 Steve Gibralter	.15		.07
❏ 166 Bob Abreu	.40		.18
❏ 167 Greg Zaun	.15		.07
❏ 168 Tavo Alvarez	.15		.07
❏ 169 Sal Fasano	.15		.07
❏ 170 George Arias	.15		.07
❏ 171 Derek Jeter	2.00		.90
❏ 172 Livan Hernandez	1.00		.45
❏ 173 Alan Benes	.15		.07
❏ 174 George Williams	.15		.07
❏ 175 John Wasdin	.15		.07
❏ 176 Chan Ho Park	.40		.18
❏ 177 Paul Wilson	.15		.07
❏ 178 Jeff Suppan	.15		.07
❏ 179 Quinton McCracken	.15		.07
❏ 180 Wilton Guerrero	.50		.23
❏ 181 Eric Owens	.15		.07
❏ 182 Felipe Crespo	.15		.07
❏ 183 LaTroy Hawkins	.30		.14
❏ 184 Jason Schmidt	.15		.07
❏ 185 Terrell Wade	.15		.07
❏ 186 Mike Grace	.15		.07
❏ 187 Chris Snopek	.15		.07
❏ 188 Jason Kendall	.60		.25
❏ 189 Todd Hollandsworth	.15		.07
❏ 190 Jim Pittsley	.15		.07
❏ 191 Jermaine Dye	.30		.14
❏ 192 Mike Busby	.15		.07
❏ 193 Richard Hidalgo	.30		.14
❏ 194 Tyler Houston	.15		.07
❏ 195 Jimmy Haynes	.15		.07
❏ 196 Karim Garcia	.30		.14
❏ 197 Ken Griffey Jr. CL	1.50		.70
❏ 198 Frank Thomas CL	.60		.25
❏ 199 Greg Maddux CL	.75		.35
❏ 200 Cal Ripken CL	1.25		.55

1996 Summit Ballparks

	MINT	NRMT
COMPLETE SET (18)	150.00	70.00
COMMON CARD (1-18)	1.25	.55
STATED ODDS 1:18		
STATED PRINT RUN 8000 SERIAL #'d SETS		

		MINT	NRMT
❏ 1 Cal Ripken	20.00		9.00
❏ 2 Albert Belle	5.00		2.20
❏ 3 Dante Bichette	2.00		.90
❏ 4 Mo Vaughn	5.00		2.20
❏ 5 Ken Griffey Jr.	25.00		11.00
❏ 6 Derek Jeter	12.00		5.50
❏ 7 Juan Gonzalez	12.00		5.50
❏ 8 Greg Maddux	15.00		6.75
❏ 9 Frank Thomas	12.00		5.50
❏ 10 Ryne Sandberg	5.00		2.20
❏ 11 Mike Piazza	15.00		6.75
❏ 12 Johnny Damon	4.00		1.80
❏ 13 Barry Bonds	5.00		2.20
❏ 14 Jeff Bagwell	5.00		2.20
❏ 15 Paul Wilson	1.25		.55
❏ 16 Tim Salmon	4.00		1.80
❏ 17 Kirby Puckett	8.00		3.60
❏ 18 Tony Gwynn	5.00		2.20

1996 Summit Big Bang

	MINT	NRMT
COMPLETE SET (16)	500.00	220.00
COMMON CARD (1-16)	8.00	3.60
SEMISTARS	12.00	5.50
UNLISTED STARS	20.00	9.00
STATED ODDS 1:72		
STATED PRINT RUN 600 SERIAL #'d SETS		
*MIRAGE: 1X BASIC BIG BANG		
MIRAGE STATED ODDS 1:72		
MIRAGE PRINT RUN 600 SERIAL #'d SETS		

❏ 1 Frank Thomas	40.00	18.00
❏ 2 Ken Griffey Jr.	100.00	45.00
❏ 3 Albert Belle	20.00	9.00
❏ 4 Mo Vaughn	20.00	9.00
❏ 5 Barry Bonds	25.00	11.00
❏ 6 Cal Ripken	80.00	36.00
❏ 7 Jeff Bagwell	25.00	11.00
❏ 8 Mike Piazza	60.00	27.00
❏ 9 Ryan Klesko	8.00	3.60
❏ 10 Manny Ramirez	25.00	11.00
❏ 11 Tim Salmon	12.00	5.50
❏ 12 Dante Bichette	8.00	3.60
❏ 13 Sammy Sosa	60.00	27.00
❏ 14 Raul Mondesi	8.00	3.60
❏ 15 Chipper Jones	50.00	22.00
❏ 16 Garret Anderson	8.00	3.60

1996 Summit Hitters Inc.

	MINT	NRMT
COMPLETE SET (16)	250.00	110.00
COMMON CARD (1-16)	5.00	2.20
STATED ODDS 1:36		
STATED PRINT RUN 4000 SERIAL #'d SETS		

❏ 1 Tony Gwynn	20.00	9.00
❏ 2 Mo Vaughn	8.00	3.60
❏ 3 Tim Salmon	6.00	2.70
❏ 4 Ken Griffey Jr.	40.00	18.00
❏ 5 Sammy Sosa	20.00	9.00
❏ 6 Frank Thomas	20.00	9.00
❏ 7 Wade Boggs	8.00	3.60
❏ 8 Albert Belle	8.00	3.60
❏ 9 Cal Ripken	30.00	13.50
❏ 10 Manny Ramirez	8.00	3.60
❏ 11 Ryan Klesko	5.00	2.20

☐ 12 Dante Bichette	5.00	2.20
☐ 13 Mike Piazza	25.00	11.00
☐ 14 Chipper Jones	20.00	9.00
☐ 15 Ryne Sandberg	8.00	3.60
☐ 16 Matt Williams	8.00	3.60

1996 Summit Positions

	MINT	NRMT
COMPLETE SET (9)	350.00	160.00
COMMON CARD (1-9)	15.00	6.75
STATED ODDS 1:50 MAGAZINE		

☐ 1 Jeff Bagwell Mo Vaughn Frank Thomas	40.00	18.00
☐ 2 Roberto Alomar Craig Biggio Chuck Knoblauch	15.00	6.75
☐ 3 Matt Williams Jim Thome Chipper Jones	40.00	18.00
☐ 4 Barry Larkin Cal Ripken Alex Rodriguez	80.00	36.00
☐ 5 Mike Piazza Ivan Rodriguez Charles Johnson	40.00	18.00
☐ 6 Hideo Nomo Greg Maddux Randy Johnson	40.00	18.00
☐ 7 Barry Bonds Albert Belle Ryan Klesko	20.00	9.00
☐ 8 Johnny Damon Jim Edmonds Ken Griffey Jr.	60.00	27.00
☐ 9 Manny Ramirez Gary Sheffield Sammy Sosa	40.00	18.00

1952 Topps

	NRMT	VG-E
COMPLETE SET (407)	65000.00	29200.00
COMMON CARD (1-80)	60.00	27.00
MINOR STARS 1-80	70.00	32.00
SEMISTARS 1-80	80.00	36.00
*RED/BLACK BACKS 1-80 SAME VALUE		
COMMON CARD (81-250)	40.00	18.00
MINOR STARS 81-250	50.00	22.00
SEMISTARS 81-250	60.00	27.00
UNLISTED STARS 81-250	80.00	36.00
COMMON CARD (251-310)	50.00	22.00
MINOR STARS 251-310	60.00	27.00
SEMISTARS 251-310	75.00	34.00
COMMON CARD (311-407)	250.00	110.00
MINOR STARS 311-407	300.00	135.00
*UNLISTED DODGER/YANKEE: 1.25X VALUE		
CARDS PRICED IN NM CONDITION !		

☐ 1 Andy Pafko	2500.00	250.00
☐ 2 Pete Runnels	125.00	55.00
☐ 3 Hank Thompson	70.00	32.00
☐ 4 Don Lenhardt	60.00	27.00
☐ 5 Larry Jansen	70.00	32.00
☐ 6 Grady Hatton	60.00	27.00
☐ 7 Wayne Terwilliger	60.00	27.00
☐ 8 Fred Marsh	60.00	27.00
☐ 9 Robert Hogue	60.00	27.00
☐ 10 Al Rosen	70.00	32.00
☐ 11 Phil Rizzuto	300.00	135.00
☐ 12 Monty Basgall	60.00	27.00
☐ 13 Johnny Wyrostek	60.00	27.00
☐ 14 Bob Elliott	70.00	32.00
☐ 15 Johnny Pesky	70.00	32.00
☐ 16 Gene Hermanski	60.00	27.00
☐ 17 Jim Hegan	70.00	32.00
☐ 18 Merrill Combs	60.00	27.00
☐ 19 Johnny Bucha	60.00	27.00
☐ 20 Billy Loes	125.00	55.00
☐ 21 Ferris Fain	70.00	32.00
☐ 22 Dom DiMaggio	90.00	40.00
☐ 23 Billy Goodman	70.00	32.00
☐ 24 Luke Easter	70.00	32.00
☐ 25 Johnny Groth	60.00	27.00
☐ 26 Monte Irvin	125.00	55.00
☐ 27 Sam Jethroe	70.00	32.00
☐ 28 Jerry Priddy	60.00	27.00
☐ 29 Ted Kluszewski	100.00	45.00
☐ 30 Mel Parnell	70.00	32.00
☐ 31 Gus Zernial	80.00	36.00
Posed with seven baseballs		
☐ 32 Eddie Robinson	60.00	27.00
☐ 33 Warren Spahn	250.00	110.00
☐ 34 Elmer Valo	60.00	27.00
☐ 35 Hank Sauer	70.00	32.00
☐ 36 Gil Hodges	250.00	110.00
☐ 37 Duke Snider	400.00	180.00
☐ 38 Wally Westlake	60.00	27.00
☐ 39 Dizzy Trout	70.00	32.00
☐ 40 Irv Noren	60.00	27.00
☐ 41 Bob Wellman	60.00	27.00
☐ 42 Lou Kretlow	60.00	27.00
☐ 43 Ray Scarborough	60.00	27.00
☐ 44 Con Dempsey	60.00	27.00
☐ 45 Eddie Joost	60.00	27.00
☐ 46 Gordon Goldsberry	60.00	27.00
☐ 47 Willie Jones	70.00	32.00
☐ 48A Joe Page COR	100.00	45.00
☐ 48B Joe Page ERR	300.00	135.00
(Bio for Sain)		
☐ 49A Johnny Sain COR	80.00	36.00
☐ 49B Johnny Sain ERR	275.00	125.00
(Bio for Page)		
☐ 50 Marv Rickert	60.00	27.00
☐ 51 Jim Russell	60.00	27.00
☐ 52 Don Mueller	70.00	32.00
☐ 53 Chris Van Cuyk	60.00	27.00
☐ 54 Leo Kiely	60.00	27.00
☐ 55 Ray Boone	70.00	32.00
☐ 56 Tommy Glaviano	60.00	27.00
☐ 57 Ed Lopat	90.00	40.00
☐ 58 Bob Mahoney	60.00	27.00
☐ 59 Robin Roberts	175.00	80.00
☐ 60 Sid Hudson	60.00	27.00
☐ 61 Tookie Gilbert	60.00	27.00
☐ 62 Chuck Stobbs	60.00	27.00
☐ 63 Howie Pollet	60.00	27.00
☐ 64 Roy Sievers	70.00	32.00
☐ 65 Enos Slaughter	175.00	80.00
☐ 66 Preacher Roe	90.00	40.00
☐ 67 Allie Reynolds	90.00	40.00
☐ 68 Cliff Chambers	60.00	27.00
☐ 69 Virgil Stallcup	60.00	27.00
☐ 70 Al Zarilla	60.00	27.00
☐ 71 Tom Upton	60.00	27.00
☐ 72 Karl Olson	60.00	27.00
☐ 73 Bill Werle	60.00	27.00
☐ 74 Andy Hansen	60.00	27.00
☐ 75 Wes Westrum	70.00	32.00
☐ 76 Eddie Stanky	70.00	32.00
☐ 77 Bob Kennedy	70.00	32.00
☐ 78 Ellis Kinder	60.00	27.00
☐ 79 Gerry Staley	60.00	27.00
☐ 80 Herman Wehmeier	60.00	27.00
☐ 81 Vernon Law	50.00	22.00
☐ 82 Duane Pillette	40.00	18.00
☐ 83 Billy Johnson	40.00	18.00
☐ 84 Vern Stephens	50.00	22.00
☐ 85 Bob Kuzava	50.00	22.00
☐ 86 Ted Gray	40.00	18.00
☐ 87 Dale Coogan	40.00	18.00
☐ 88 Bob Feller	250.00	110.00
☐ 89 Johnny Lipon	40.00	18.00
☐ 90 Mickey Grasso	40.00	18.00
☐ 91 Red Schoendienst	80.00	36.00
☐ 92 Dale Mitchell	50.00	22.00
☐ 93 Al Sima	40.00	18.00
☐ 94 Sam Mele	40.00	18.00
☐ 95 Ken Holcombe	40.00	18.00
☐ 96 Willard Marshall	40.00	18.00
☐ 97 Earl Torgeson	40.00	18.00
☐ 98 Billy Pierce	50.00	22.00
☐ 99 Gene Woodling	60.00	27.00
☐ 100 Del Rice	40.00	18.00
☐ 101 Max Lanier	40.00	18.00
☐ 102 Bill Kennedy	40.00	18.00
☐ 103 Cliff Mapes	50.00	22.00
☐ 104 Don Kolloway	40.00	18.00
☐ 105 Johnny Pramesa	40.00	18.00
☐ 106 Mickey Vernon	60.00	27.00
☐ 107 Connie Ryan	40.00	18.00
☐ 108 Jim Konstanty	60.00	27.00
☐ 109 Ted Wilks	40.00	18.00
☐ 110 Dutch Leonard	40.00	18.00
☐ 111 Peanuts Lowrey	40.00	18.00
☐ 112 Hank Majeski	40.00	18.00
☐ 113 Dick Sisler	50.00	22.00
☐ 114 Willard Ramsdell	40.00	18.00
☐ 115 Red Munger	40.00	18.00
☐ 116 Carl Scheib	40.00	18.00
☐ 117 Sherm Lollar	50.00	22.00
☐ 118 Ken Raffensberger	40.00	18.00
☐ 119 Mickey McDermott	40.00	18.00
☐ 120 Bob Chakales	40.00	18.00
☐ 121 Gus Niarhos	40.00	18.00
☐ 122 Jackie Jensen	80.00	36.00
☐ 123 Eddie Yost	50.00	22.00
☐ 124 Monte Kennedy	40.00	18.00
☐ 125 Bill Rigney	50.00	22.00
☐ 126 Fred Hutchinson	50.00	22.00
☐ 127 Paul Minner	40.00	18.00
☐ 128 Don Bollweg	40.00	18.00
☐ 129 Johnny Mize	150.00	70.00
☐ 130 Sheldon Jones	40.00	18.00
☐ 131 Morrie Martin	40.00	18.00
☐ 132 Clyde Kluttz	40.00	18.00
☐ 133 Al Widmar	40.00	18.00
☐ 134 Joe Tipton	40.00	18.00
☐ 135 Dixie Howell	40.00	18.00
☐ 136 Johnny Schmitz	40.00	18.00
☐ 137 Roy McMillan	50.00	22.00
☐ 138 Bill MacDonald	40.00	18.00
☐ 139 Ken Wood	40.00	18.00
☐ 140 Johnny Antonelli	50.00	22.00
☐ 141 Clint Hartung	40.00	18.00
☐ 142 Harry Perkowski	40.00	18.00
☐ 143 Les Moss	40.00	18.00
☐ 144 Ed Blake	40.00	18.00
☐ 145 Joe Haynes	40.00	18.00
☐ 146 Frank House	40.00	18.00
☐ 147 Bob Young	40.00	18.00
☐ 148 Johnny Klippstein	40.00	18.00
☐ 149 Dick Kryhoski	40.00	18.00
☐ 150 Ted Beard	40.00	18.00
☐ 151 Wally Post	50.00	22.00
☐ 152 Al Evans	40.00	18.00
☐ 153 Bob Rush	40.00	18.00
☐ 154 Joe Muir	40.00	18.00
☐ 155 Frank Overmire	40.00	18.00
☐ 156 Frank Hiller	40.00	18.00
☐ 157 Bob Usher	40.00	18.00

		NRMT	VG-E
☐ 158	Eddie Waitkus	40.00	18.00
☐ 159	Saul Rogovin	40.00	18.00
☐ 160	Owen Friend	40.00	18.00
☐ 161	Bud Byerly	40.00	18.00
☐ 162	Del Crandall	50.00	22.00
☐ 163	Stan Rojek	40.00	18.00
☐ 164	Walt Dubiel	40.00	18.00
☐ 165	Eddie Kazak	40.00	18.00
☐ 166	Paul LaPalme	40.00	18.00
☐ 167	Bill Howerton	40.00	18.00
☐ 168	Charlie Silvera	60.00	27.00
☐ 169	Howie Judson	40.00	18.00
☐ 170	Gus Bell	50.00	22.00
☐ 171	Ed Erautt	40.00	18.00
☐ 172	Eddie Miksis	40.00	18.00
☐ 173	Roy Smalley	40.00	18.00
☐ 174	Clarence Marshall	40.00	18.00
☐ 175	Billy Martin	375.00	170.00
☐ 176	Hank Edwards	40.00	18.00
☐ 177	Bill Wight	40.00	18.00
☐ 178	Cass Michaels	40.00	18.00
☐ 179	Frank Smith	40.00	18.00
☐ 180	Charlie Maxwell	50.00	22.00
☐ 181	Bob Swift	40.00	18.00
☐ 182	Billy Hitchcock	40.00	18.00
☐ 183	Erv Dusak	40.00	18.00
☐ 184	Bob Ramazzotti	40.00	18.00
☐ 185	Bill Nicholson	50.00	22.00
☐ 186	Walt Masterson	40.00	18.00
☐ 187	Bob Miller	40.00	18.00
☐ 188	Clarence Podbielan	40.00	18.00
☐ 189	Pete Reiser	60.00	27.00
☐ 190	Don Johnson	40.00	18.00
☐ 191	Yogi Berra	500.00	220.00
☐ 192	Myron Ginsberg	40.00	18.00
☐ 193	Harry Simpson	50.00	22.00
☐ 194	Joe Hatton	40.00	18.00
☐ 195	Minnie Minoso	150.00	70.00
☐ 196	Solly Hemus	40.00	18.00
☐ 197	George Strickland	40.00	18.00
☐ 198	Phil Haugstad	40.00	18.00
☐ 199	George Zuverink	40.00	18.00
☐ 200	Ralph Houk	80.00	36.00
☐ 201	Alex Kellner	40.00	18.00
☐ 202	Joe Collins	60.00	27.00
☐ 203	Curt Simmons	60.00	27.00
☐ 204	Ron Northey	40.00	18.00
☐ 205	Clyde King	60.00	27.00
☐ 206	Joe Ostrowski	40.00	18.00
☐ 207	Mickey Harris	40.00	18.00
☐ 208	Marlin Stuart	40.00	18.00
☐ 209	Howie Fox	40.00	18.00
☐ 210	Dick Fowler	40.00	18.00
☐ 211	Ray Coleman	40.00	18.00
☐ 212	Ned Garver	40.00	18.00
☐ 213	Nippy Jones	40.00	18.00
☐ 214	Johnny Hopp	50.00	22.00
☐ 215	Hank Bauer	100.00	45.00
☐ 216	Richie Ashburn	200.00	90.00
☐ 217	Snuffy Stirnweiss	50.00	22.00
☐ 218	Clyde McCullough	40.00	18.00
☐ 219	Bobby Shantz	60.00	27.00
☐ 220	Joe Presko	40.00	18.00
☐ 221	Granny Hamner	40.00	18.00
☐ 222	Hoot Evers	40.00	18.00
☐ 223	Del Ennis	50.00	22.00
☐ 224	Bruce Edwards	40.00	18.00
☐ 225	Frank Baumholtz	40.00	18.00
☐ 226	Dave Philley	40.00	18.00
☐ 227	Joe Garagiola	80.00	36.00
☐ 228	Al Brazle	40.00	18.00
☐ 229	Gene Bearden UER	40.00	18.00
	(Misspelled Beardon)		
☐ 230	Matt Batts	40.00	18.00
☐ 231	Sam Zoldak	40.00	18.00
☐ 232	Billy Cox	50.00	22.00
☐ 233	Bob Friend	60.00	27.00
☐ 234	Steve Souchock	40.00	18.00
☐ 235	Walt Dropo	40.00	18.00
☐ 236	Ed Fitzgerald	40.00	18.00
☐ 237	Jerry Coleman	60.00	27.00
☐ 238	Art Houtteman	40.00	18.00
☐ 239	Rocky Bridges	50.00	22.00
☐ 240	Jack Phillips	40.00	18.00
☐ 241	Tommy Byrne	40.00	18.00
☐ 242	Tom Poholsky	40.00	18.00
☐ 243	Larry Doby	100.00	45.00
☐ 244	Vic Wertz	40.00	18.00
☐ 245	Sherry Robertson	40.00	18.00
☐ 246	George Kell	80.00	36.00
☐ 247	Randy Gumpert	40.00	18.00
☐ 248	Frank Shea	40.00	18.00
☐ 249	Bobby Adams	40.00	18.00
☐ 250	Carl Erskine	100.00	45.00
☐ 251	Chico Carrasquel	50.00	22.00
☐ 252	Vern Bickford	50.00	22.00
☐ 253	Johnny Berardino	75.00	34.00
☐ 254	Joe Dobson	50.00	22.00
☐ 255	Clyde Vollmer	50.00	22.00
☐ 256	Pete Suder	50.00	22.00
☐ 257	Bobby Avila	60.00	27.00
☐ 258	Steve Gromek	50.00	22.00
☐ 259	Bob Addis	50.00	22.00
☐ 260	Pete Castiglione	50.00	22.00
☐ 261	Willie Mays	2500.00	1100.00
☐ 262	Virgil Trucks	60.00	27.00
☐ 263	Harry Brecheen	60.00	27.00
☐ 264	Roy Hartsfield	50.00	22.00
☐ 265	Chuck Diering	50.00	22.00
☐ 266	Murry Dickson	50.00	22.00
☐ 267	Sid Gordon	60.00	27.00
☐ 268	Bob Lemon	150.00	70.00
☐ 269	Willard Nixon	50.00	22.00
☐ 270	Lou Brissie	50.00	22.00
☐ 271	Jim Delsing	50.00	22.00
☐ 272	Mike Garcia	60.00	27.00
☐ 273	Erv Palica	50.00	22.00
☐ 274	Ralph Branca	125.00	55.00
☐ 275	Pat Mullin	50.00	22.00
☐ 276	Jim Wilson	50.00	22.00
☐ 277	Early Wynn	150.00	70.00
☐ 278	Allie Clark	50.00	22.00
☐ 279	Eddie Stewart	50.00	22.00
☐ 280	Cloyd Boyer	60.00	27.00
☐ 281	Tommy Brown SP	60.00	27.00
☐ 282	Birdie Tebbetts SP	75.00	34.00
☐ 283	Phil Masi SP	60.00	27.00
☐ 284	Hank Arft SP	60.00	27.00
☐ 285	Cliff Fannin SP	60.00	27.00
☐ 286	Joe DeMaestri SP	60.00	27.00
☐ 287	Steve Bilko SP	60.00	27.00
☐ 288	Chet Nichols SP	60.00	27.00
☐ 289	Tommy Holmes SP	75.00	34.00
☐ 290	Joe Astroth SP	60.00	27.00
☐ 291	Gil Coan SP	60.00	27.00
☐ 292	Floyd Baker SP	60.00	27.00
☐ 293	Sibby Sisti SP	60.00	27.00
☐ 294	Walker Cooper SP	60.00	27.00
☐ 295	Phil Cavarretta SP	75.00	34.00
☐ 296	Red Rolfe MG SP	60.00	27.00
☐ 297	Andy Seminick SP	60.00	27.00
☐ 298	Bob Ross SP	60.00	27.00
☐ 299	Ray Murray SP	60.00	27.00
☐ 300	Barney McCosky SP	60.00	27.00
☐ 301	Bob Porterfield	50.00	22.00
☐ 302	Max Surkont	50.00	22.00
☐ 303	Harry Dorish	50.00	22.00
☐ 304	Sam Dente	50.00	22.00
☐ 305	Paul Richards MG	60.00	27.00
☐ 306	Lou Sleater	50.00	22.00
☐ 307	Frank Campos	50.00	22.00
☐ 308	Luis Aloma	50.00	22.00
☐ 309	Jim Busby	50.00	22.00
☐ 310	George Metkovich	60.00	27.00
☐ 311	Mickey Mantle	18000.00	8100.00
☐ 312	Jackie Robinson DP	1500.00	700.00
☐ 313	Bobby Thomson DP	300.00	135.00
☐ 314	Roy Campanella DP	2200.00	1000.00
☐ 315	Leo Durocher MG	400.00	180.00
☐ 316	Dave Williams	300.00	135.00
☐ 317	Conrado Marrero	300.00	135.00
☐ 318	Harold Gregg	250.00	110.00
☐ 319	Al Walker	250.00	110.00
☐ 320	John Rutherford	300.00	135.00
☐ 321	Joe Black	350.00	160.00
☐ 322	Randy Jackson	250.00	110.00
☐ 323	Bubba Church	250.00	110.00
☐ 324	Warren Hacker	250.00	110.00
☐ 325	Bill Serena	250.00	110.00
☐ 326	George Shuba	400.00	180.00
☐ 327	Al Wilson	250.00	110.00
☐ 328	Bob Borkowski	250.00	110.00
☐ 329	Ike Delock	250.00	110.00
☐ 330	Turk Lown	250.00	110.00
☐ 331	Tom Morgan	250.00	110.00
☐ 332	Anthony Bartirome	250.00	110.00
☐ 333	Pee Wee Reese	1600.00	700.00
☐ 334	Wilmer Mizell	300.00	135.00
☐ 335	Ted Lepcio	250.00	110.00
☐ 336	Dave Koslo	250.00	110.00
☐ 337	Jim Hearn	250.00	110.00
☐ 338	Sal Yvars	250.00	110.00
☐ 339	Russ Meyer	250.00	110.00
☐ 340	Bob Hooper	250.00	110.00
☐ 341	Hal Jeffcoat	250.00	110.00
☐ 342	Clem Labine	400.00	180.00
☐ 343	Dick Gernert	250.00	110.00
☐ 344	Ewell Blackwell	300.00	135.00
☐ 345	Sammy White	250.00	110.00
☐ 346	George Spencer	250.00	110.00
☐ 347	Joe Adcock	300.00	135.00
☐ 348	Robert Kelly	250.00	110.00
☐ 349	Bob Cain	250.00	110.00
☐ 350	Cal Abrams	250.00	110.00
☐ 351	Alvin Dark	300.00	135.00
☐ 352	Karl Drews	250.00	110.00
☐ 353	Bobby Del Greco	250.00	110.00
☐ 354	Fred Hatfield	250.00	110.00
☐ 355	Bobby Morgan	250.00	110.00
☐ 356	Toby Atwell	250.00	110.00
☐ 357	Smoky Burgess	300.00	135.00
☐ 358	John Kucab	250.00	110.00
☐ 359	Dee Fondy	250.00	110.00
☐ 360	George Crowe	300.00	135.00
☐ 361	William Posedel CO	250.00	110.00
☐ 362	Ken Heintzelman	250.00	110.00
☐ 363	Dick Rozek	250.00	110.00
☐ 364	Clyde Sukeforth CO	250.00	110.00
☐ 365	Cookie Lavagetto CO	375.00	170.00
☐ 366	Dave Madison	250.00	110.00
☐ 367	Ben Thorpe	250.00	110.00
☐ 368	Ed Wright	250.00	110.00
☐ 369	Dick Groat	350.00	160.00
☐ 370	Billy Hoeft	300.00	135.00
☐ 371	Bobby Hofman	250.00	110.00
☐ 372	Gil McDougald	400.00	180.00
☐ 373	Jim Turner CO	400.00	180.00
☐ 374	John Benton	250.00	110.00
☐ 375	John Merson	250.00	110.00
☐ 376	Faye Throneberry	250.00	110.00
☐ 377	Chuck Dressen MG	375.00	170.00
☐ 378	Leroy Fusselman	250.00	110.00
☐ 379	Joe Rossi	250.00	110.00
☐ 380	Clem Koshorek	250.00	110.00
☐ 381	Milton Stock CO	250.00	110.00
☐ 382	Sam Jones	350.00	160.00
☐ 383	Del Wilber	250.00	110.00
☐ 384	Frank Crosetti CO	400.00	180.00
☐ 385	Herman Franks CO	250.00	110.00
☐ 386	John Yuhas	250.00	110.00
☐ 387	Billy Meyer MG	250.00	110.00
☐ 388	Bob Chipman	250.00	110.00
☐ 389	Ben Wade	250.00	110.00
☐ 390	Glenn Nelson	250.00	110.00
☐ 391	Ben Chapman UER CO	250.00	110.00
	(Photo actually Sam Chapman)		
☐ 392	Hoyt Wilhelm	750.00	350.00
☐ 393	Ebba St.Claire	250.00	110.00
☐ 394	Billy Herman CO	400.00	180.00
☐ 395	Jake Pitler CO	325.00	145.00
☐ 396	Dick Williams	400.00	180.00
☐ 397	Forrest Main	250.00	110.00
☐ 398	Hal Rice	250.00	110.00
☐ 399	Jim Fridley	250.00	110.00
☐ 400	Bill Dickey CO	800.00	350.00
☐ 401	Bob Schultz	250.00	110.00
☐ 402	Earl Harrist	250.00	110.00
☐ 403	Bill Miller	250.00	110.00
☐ 404	Dick Brodowski	250.00	110.00
☐ 405	Eddie Pellagrini	250.00	110.00
☐ 406	Joe Nuxhall	400.00	180.00
☐ 407	Eddie Mathews	4500.00	1100.00

1953 Topps

	NRMT	VG-E
COMPLETE SET (274)	13500.00	6100.00

BOB FELLER
CLEVELAND INDIANS

COMMON CARD (1-165)	30.00	13.50
COMMON CARD (166-220)	25.00	11.00
COMMON DP (1-220)	15.00	6.75
MINOR STARS 1-220	40.00	18.00
SEMISTARS 1-220	60.00	27.00
UNLISTED STARS 1-220	80.00	36.00
COMMON CARD (221-280)	100.00	45.00
COMMON DP (221-280)	50.00	22.00
MINOR STARS 221-280	120.00	55.00
SEMISTARS 221-280	150.00	70.00
NOT ISSUED (253/261/267)		
NOT ISSUED (268/271/275)		
*UNLISTED DODGER/YANKEE: 1.25X VALUE		
CARDS PRICED IN NM CONDITION !		

❏ 1	Jackie Robinson	550.00	150.00
❏ 2	Luke Easter DP	20.00	9.00
❏ 3	George Crowe	30.00	13.50
❏ 4	Ben Wade	30.00	13.50
❏ 5	Joe Dobson	30.00	13.50
❏ 6	Sam Jones	40.00	18.00
❏ 7	Bob Borkowski DP	15.00	6.75
❏ 8	Clem Koshorek DP	15.00	6.75
❏ 9	Joe Collins	40.00	18.00
❏ 10	Smoky Burgess SP	70.00	32.00
❏ 11	Sal Yvars	30.00	13.50
❏ 12	Howie Judson DP	15.00	6.75
❏ 13	Conrado Marrero DP	15.00	6.75
❏ 14	Clem Labine DP	20.00	9.00
❏ 15	Bobo Newsom DP	30.00	13.50
❏ 16	Peanuts Lowrey DP	15.00	6.75
❏ 17	Billy Hitchcock	30.00	13.50
❏ 18	Ted Lepcio DP	15.00	6.75
❏ 19	Mel Parnell DP	15.00	6.75
❏ 20	Hank Thompson	40.00	18.00
❏ 21	Billy Johnson	30.00	13.50
❏ 22	Howie Fox	30.00	13.50
❏ 23	Toby Atwell DP	15.00	6.75
❏ 24	Ferris Fain	40.00	18.00
❏ 25	Ray Boone	40.00	18.00
❏ 26	Dale Mitchell DP	40.00	18.00
❏ 27	Roy Campanella DP	175.00	80.00
❏ 28	Eddie Pellagrini	30.00	13.50
❏ 29	Hal Jeffcoat	30.00	13.50
❏ 30	Willard Nixon	30.00	13.50
❏ 31	Ewell Blackwell	60.00	27.00
❏ 32	Clyde Vollmer	30.00	13.50
❏ 33	Bob Kennedy DP	15.00	6.75
❏ 34	George Shuba	40.00	18.00
❏ 35	Irv Noren DP	15.00	6.75
❏ 36	Johnny Groth DP	15.00	6.75
❏ 37	Eddie Mathews DP	110.00	50.00
❏ 38	Jim Hearn DP	15.00	6.75
❏ 39	Eddie Miksis	30.00	13.50
❏ 40	John Lipon	30.00	13.50
❏ 41	Enos Slaughter	80.00	36.00
❏ 42	Gus Zernial DP	30.00	13.50
❏ 43	Gil McDougald	60.00	27.00
❏ 44	Ellis Kinder SP	35.00	16.00
❏ 45	Grady Hatton DP	15.00	6.75
❏ 46	Johnny Klippstein DP	15.00	6.75
❏ 47	Bubba Church DP	15.00	6.75
❏ 48	Bob Del Greco DP	15.00	6.75
❏ 49	Faye Throneberry DP	15.00	6.75
❏ 50	Chuck Dressen MG DP	25.00	11.00
❏ 51	Frank Campos DP	15.00	6.75
❏ 52	Ted Gray DP	15.00	6.75
❏ 53	Sherm Lollar DP	30.00	13.50

❏ 54	Bob Feller DP	125.00	55.00
❏ 55	Maurice McDermott DP	15.00	6.75
❏ 56	Gerry Staley DP	15.00	6.75
❏ 57	Carl Scheib	30.00	13.50
❏ 58	George Metkovich	30.00	13.50
❏ 59	Karl Drews DP	15.00	6.75
❏ 60	Cloyd Boyer DP	15.00	6.75
❏ 61	Early Wynn SP	110.00	50.00
❏ 62	Monte Irvin DP	35.00	16.00
❏ 63	Gus Niarhos DP	15.00	6.75
❏ 64	Dave Philley	30.00	13.50
❏ 65	Earl Harrist	30.00	13.50
❏ 66	Minnie Minoso	60.00	27.00
❏ 67	Roy Sievers DP	30.00	13.50
❏ 68	Del Rice	30.00	13.50
❏ 69	Dick Brodowski	30.00	13.50
❏ 70	Ed Yuhas	30.00	13.50
❏ 71	Tony Bartirome	30.00	13.50
❏ 72	Fred Hutchinson MG SP	50.00	22.00
❏ 73	Eddie Robinson	30.00	13.50
❏ 74	Joe Rossi	30.00	13.50
❏ 75	Mike Garcia	40.00	18.00
❏ 76	Pee Wee Reese	160.00	70.00
❏ 77	Johnny Mize DP	80.00	36.00
❏ 78	Red Schoendienst	60.00	27.00
❏ 79	Johnny Wyrostek	30.00	13.50
❏ 80	Jim Hegan	40.00	18.00
❏ 81	Joe Black SP	70.00	32.00
❏ 82	Mickey Mantle	3000.00	1350.00
❏ 83	Howie Pollet	30.00	13.50
❏ 84	Bob Hooper DP	15.00	6.75
❏ 85	Bobby Morgan DP	15.00	6.75
❏ 86	Billy Martin	125.00	55.00
❏ 87	Ed Lopat	50.00	22.00
❏ 88	Willie Jones DP	15.00	6.75
❏ 89	Chuck Stobbs DP	15.00	6.75
❏ 90	Hank Edwards DP	15.00	6.75
❏ 91	Ebba St.Claire DP	15.00	6.75
❏ 92	Paul Minner DP	15.00	6.75
❏ 93	Hal Rice DP	15.00	6.75
❏ 94	Bill Kennedy DP	15.00	6.75
❏ 95	Willard Marshall DP	15.00	6.75
❏ 96	Virgil Trucks	40.00	18.00
❏ 97	Don Kolloway DP	15.00	6.75
❏ 98	Cal Abrams DP	15.00	6.75
❏ 99	Dave Madison	30.00	13.50
❏ 100	Bill Miller	30.00	13.50
❏ 101	Ted Wilks	30.00	13.50
❏ 102	Connie Ryan DP	15.00	6.75
❏ 103	Joe Astroth DP	15.00	6.75
❏ 104	Yogi Berra	225.00	100.00
❏ 105	Joe Nuxhall DP	30.00	13.50
❏ 106	Johnny Antonelli	40.00	18.00
❏ 107	Danny O'Connell DP	15.00	6.75
❏ 108	Bob Porterfield DP	15.00	6.75
❏ 109	Alvin Dark	40.00	18.00
❏ 110	Herman Wehmeier DP	15.00	6.75
❏ 111	Hank Sauer DP	20.00	9.00
❏ 112	Ned Garver DP	15.00	6.75
❏ 113	Jerry Priddy	30.00	13.50
❏ 114	Phil Rizzuto	175.00	80.00
❏ 115	George Spencer	30.00	13.50
❏ 116	Frank Smith DP	15.00	6.75
❏ 117	Sid Gordon DP	15.00	6.75
❏ 118	Gus Bell DP	20.00	9.00
❏ 119	Johnny Sain SP	50.00	22.00
❏ 120	Davey Williams	40.00	18.00
❏ 121	Walt Dropo	40.00	18.00
❏ 122	Elmer Valo	30.00	13.50
❏ 123	Tommy Byrne DP	15.00	6.75
❏ 124	Sibby Sisti DP	15.00	6.75
❏ 125	Dick Williams DP	22.50	10.00
❏ 126	Bill Connelly DP	15.00	6.75
❏ 127	Clint Courtney DP	15.00	6.75
❏ 128	Wilmer Mizell DP	20.00	9.00
	(Inconsistent design, logo on front with black birds)		
❏ 129	Keith Thomas	30.00	13.50
❏ 130	Turk Lown DP	15.00	6.75
❏ 131	Harry Byrd DP	15.00	6.75
❏ 132	Tom Morgan	30.00	13.50
❏ 133	Gil Coan	30.00	13.50
❏ 134	Rube Walker	40.00	18.00
❏ 135	Al Rosen DP	25.00	11.00
❏ 136	Ken Heintzelman DP	15.00	6.75

❏ 137	John Rutherford DP	15.00	6.75
❏ 138	George Keil	60.00	27.00
❏ 139	Sammy White	30.00	13.50
❏ 140	Tommy Glaviano	30.00	13.50
❏ 141	Allie Reynolds DP	25.00	11.00
❏ 142	Vic Wertz	40.00	18.00
❏ 143	Billy Pierce !	60.00	27.00
❏ 144	Bob Schultz DP	15.00	6.75
❏ 145	Harry Dorish DP	15.00	6.75
❏ 146	Granny Hamner	30.00	13.50
❏ 147	Warren Spahn	150.00	70.00
❏ 148	Mickey Grasso	30.00	13.50
❏ 149	Dom DiMaggio DP	35.00	16.00
❏ 150	Harry Simpson DP	15.00	6.75
❏ 151	Hoyt Wilhelm	80.00	36.00
❏ 152	Bob Adams DP	15.00	6.75
❏ 153	Andy Seminick DP	15.00	6.75
❏ 154	Dick Groat	40.00	18.00
❏ 155	Dutch Leonard	30.00	13.50
❏ 156	Jim Rivera DP	30.00	13.50
❏ 157	Bob Addis DP	15.00	6.75
❏ 158	Johnny Logan	35.00	16.00
❏ 159	Wayne Terwilliger DP	15.00	6.75
❏ 160	Bob Young	30.00	13.50
❏ 161	Vern Bickford DP	15.00	6.75
❏ 162	Ted Kluszewski	60.00	27.00
❏ 163	Fred Hatfield DP	15.00	6.75
❏ 164	Frank Shea DP	15.00	6.75
❏ 165	Billy Hoeft	30.00	13.50
❏ 166	Billy Hunter	25.00	11.00
❏ 167	Art Schult	25.00	11.00
❏ 168	Willard Schmidt	25.00	11.00
❏ 169	Dizzy Trout	40.00	18.00
❏ 170	Bill Werle	25.00	11.00
❏ 171	Bill Glynn	25.00	11.00
❏ 172	Rip Repulski	25.00	11.00
❏ 173	Preston Ward	25.00	11.00
❏ 174	Billy Loes	40.00	18.00
❏ 175	Ron Kline	25.00	11.00
❏ 176	Don Hoak	40.00	18.00
❏ 177	Jim Dyck	25.00	11.00
❏ 178	Jim Waugh	25.00	11.00
❏ 179	Gene Hermanski	25.00	11.00
❏ 180	Virgil Stallcup	25.00	11.00
❏ 181	Al Zarilla	25.00	11.00
❏ 182	Bobby Hofman	25.00	11.00
❏ 183	Stu Miller	40.00	18.00
❏ 184	Hal Brown	25.00	11.00
❏ 185	Jim Pendleton	25.00	11.00
❏ 186	Charlie Bishop	25.00	11.00
❏ 187	Jim Fridley	25.00	11.00
❏ 188	Andy Carey	40.00	18.00
❏ 189	Ray Jablonski	25.00	11.00
❏ 190	Dixie Walker CO	40.00	18.00
❏ 191	Ralph Kiner	80.00	36.00
❏ 192	Wally Westlake	25.00	11.00
❏ 193	Mike Clark	25.00	11.00
❏ 194	Eddie Kazak	25.00	11.00
❏ 195	Ed McGhee	25.00	11.00
❏ 196	Bob Keegan	25.00	11.00
❏ 197	Del Crandall	25.00	11.00
❏ 198	Forrest Main	25.00	11.00
❏ 199	Marion Fricano	25.00	11.00
❏ 200	Gordon Goldsberry	25.00	11.00
❏ 201	Paul LaPalme	25.00	11.00
❏ 202	Carl Sawatski	25.00	11.00
❏ 203	Cliff Fannin	25.00	11.00
❏ 204	Dick Bokelman	25.00	11.00
❏ 205	Vern Benson	25.00	11.00
❏ 206	Ed Bailey	25.00	11.00
❏ 207	Whitey Ford	175.00	80.00
❏ 208	Jim Wilson	25.00	11.00
❏ 209	Jim Greengrass	25.00	11.00
❏ 210	Bob Cerv	40.00	18.00
❏ 211	J.W. Porter	25.00	11.00
❏ 212	Jack Dittmer	25.00	11.00
❏ 213	Ray Scarborough	25.00	11.00
❏ 214	Bill Bruton	40.00	18.00
❏ 215	Gene Conley	40.00	18.00
❏ 216	Jim Hughes	25.00	11.00
❏ 217	Murray Wall	25.00	11.00
❏ 218	Les Fusselman	25.00	11.00
❏ 219	Pete Runnels UER	40.00	18.00
	(Photo actually Don Johnson)		
❏ 220	Satchel Paige UER	500.00	220.00

(Misspelled Satchell on card front)

#	Player	NRMT	VG-E
☐ 221	Bob Milliken	100.00	45.00
☐ 222	Vic Janowicz DP	60.00	27.00
☐ 223	Johnny O'Brien DP	50.00	45.00
☐ 224	Lou Sleater DP	100.00	45.00
☐ 225	Bobby Shantz	120.00	55.00
☐ 226	Ed Erautt	100.00	45.00
☐ 227	Morrie Martin	100.00	45.00
☐ 228	Hal Newhouser	150.00	70.00
☐ 229	Rocky Krsnich	100.00	45.00
☐ 230	Johnny Lindell DP	50.00	22.00
☐ 231	Solly Hemus DP	50.00	22.00
☐ 232	Dick Kokos	100.00	45.00
☐ 233	Al Aber	100.00	45.00
☐ 234	Ray Murray DP	50.00	22.00
☐ 235	John Hetki DP	50.00	22.00
☐ 236	Harry Perkowski DP	50.00	22.00
☐ 237	Bud Podbielan DP	50.00	22.00
☐ 238	Cal Hogue DP	50.00	22.00
☐ 239	Jim Delsing	100.00	45.00
☐ 240	Fred Marsh	100.00	45.00
☐ 241	Al Sima DP	50.00	22.00
☐ 242	Charlie Silvera	120.00	55.00
☐ 243	Carlos Bernier DP	50.00	22.00
☐ 244	Willie Mays	2700.00	1200.00
☐ 245	Bill Norman CO	100.00	45.00
☐ 246	Roy Face DP	80.00	36.00
☐ 247	Mike Sandlock DP	50.00	22.00
☐ 248	Gene Stephens DP	50.00	22.00
☐ 249	Eddie O'Brien	50.00	22.00
☐ 250	Bob Wilson	100.00	45.00
☐ 251	Sid Hudson	100.00	45.00
☐ 252	Hank Foiles	100.00	45.00
☐ 253	Does not exist		
☐ 254	Preacher Roe DP	80.00	36.00
☐ 255	Dixie Howell	100.00	45.00
☐ 256	Les Peden	100.00	45.00
☐ 257	Bob Boyd	100.00	45.00
☐ 258	Jim Gilliam	300.00	135.00
☐ 259	Roy McMillan DP	100.00	45.00
☐ 260	Sam Calderone	100.00	45.00
☐ 261	Does not exist		
☐ 262	Bob Oldis	100.00	45.00
☐ 263	Johnny Podres	300.00	135.00
☐ 264	Gene Woodling DP	100.00	45.00
☐ 265	Jackie Jensen	120.00	55.00
☐ 266	Bob Cain	100.00	45.00
☐ 267	Does not exist		
☐ 268	Does not exist		
☐ 269	Duane Pillette	100.00	45.00
☐ 270	Vern Stephens	120.00	55.00
☐ 271	Does not exist		
☐ 272	Bill Antonello	100.00	45.00
☐ 273	Harvey Haddix	120.00	55.00
☐ 274	John Riddle CO	100.00	45.00
☐ 275	Does not exist		
☐ 276	Ken Raffensberger	100.00	45.00
☐ 277	Don Lund	100.00	45.00
☐ 278	Willie Miranda	100.00	45.00
☐ 279	Joe Coleman DP	50.00	22.00
☐ 280	Milt Bolling	350.00	57.50

1954 Topps

RICHIE ASHBURN outfield PHILADELPHIA PHILLIES

	NRMT	VG-E
COMPLETE SET (250)	7500.00	3400.00
COMMON (1-50/76-250)	15.00	6.75

	NRMT	VG-E
MINOR STARS 1-50/76-250	25.00	11.00
SEMISTARS 1-50/76-250	40.00	18.00
UNL. STARS 1-50/76-250	50.00	22.00
COMMON CARD (51-75)	25.00	11.00
MINOR STARS 51-75	30.00	13.50
SEMISTARS 51-75	50.00	22.00
UNLISTED STARS 51-75	60.00	27.00

*UNLISTED DODGER/YANKEE: 1.25X VALUE
CARDS PRICED IN NM CONDITION !

#	Player	NRMT	VG-E
☐ 1	Ted Williams	750.00	275.00
☐ 2	Gus Zernial	25.00	11.00
☐ 3	Monte Irvin	40.00	18.00
☐ 4	Hank Sauer	25.00	11.00
☐ 5	Ed Lopat	25.00	11.00
☐ 6	Pete Runnels	25.00	11.00
☐ 7	Ted Kluszewski	40.00	18.00
☐ 8	Bob Young	15.00	6.75
☐ 9	Harvey Haddix	25.00	11.00
☐ 10	Jackie Robinson	300.00	135.00
☐ 11	Paul Leslie Smith	15.00	6.75
☐ 12	Del Crandall	15.00	6.75
☐ 13	Billy Martin	80.00	36.00
☐ 14	Preacher Roe	25.00	11.00
☐ 15	Al Rosen	25.00	11.00
☐ 16	Vic Janowicz	25.00	11.00
☐ 17	Phil Rizzuto	100.00	45.00
☐ 18	Walt Dropo	15.00	6.75
☐ 19	Johnny Lipon	15.00	6.75
☐ 20	Warren Spahn	75.00	34.00
☐ 21	Bobby Shantz	25.00	11.00
☐ 22	Jim Greengrass	15.00	6.75
☐ 23	Luke Easter	25.00	11.00
☐ 24	Granny Hamner	15.00	6.75
☐ 25	Harvey Kuenn	40.00	18.00
☐ 26	Ray Jablonski	15.00	6.75
☐ 27	Ferris Fain	25.00	11.00
☐ 28	Paul Minner	15.00	6.75
☐ 29	Jim Hegan	25.00	11.00
☐ 30	Eddie Mathews	80.00	36.00
☐ 31	Johnny Klippstein	15.00	6.75
☐ 32	Duke Snider	175.00	80.00
☐ 33	Johnny Schmitz	15.00	6.75
☐ 34	Jim Rivera	15.00	6.75
☐ 35	Jim Gilliam	40.00	18.00
☐ 36	Hoyt Wilhelm	50.00	22.00
☐ 37	Whitey Ford	100.00	45.00
☐ 38	Eddie Stanky MG	25.00	11.00
☐ 39	Sherm Lollar	25.00	11.00
☐ 40	Mel Parnell	25.00	11.00
☐ 41	Willie Jones	15.00	6.75
☐ 42	Don Mueller	25.00	11.00
☐ 43	Dick Groat	25.00	11.00
☐ 44	Ned Garver	15.00	6.75
☐ 45	Richie Ashburn	70.00	32.00
☐ 46	Ken Raffensberger	15.00	6.75
☐ 47	Ellis Kinder	15.00	6.75
☐ 48	Billy Hunter	25.00	11.00
☐ 49	Ray Murray	15.00	6.75
☐ 50	Yogi Berra	200.00	90.00
☐ 51	Johnny Lindell	25.00	11.00
☐ 52	Vic Power	30.00	13.50
☐ 53	Jack Dittmer	25.00	11.00
☐ 54	Vern Stephens	30.00	13.50
☐ 55	Phil Cavarretta MG	30.00	13.50
☐ 56	Willie Miranda	25.00	11.00
☐ 57	Luis Aloma	25.00	11.00
☐ 58	Bob Wilson	25.00	11.00
☐ 59	Gene Conley	30.00	13.50
☐ 60	Frank Baumholtz	25.00	11.00
☐ 61	Bob Cain	25.00	11.00
☐ 62	Eddie Robinson	25.00	11.00
☐ 63	Johnny Pesky	30.00	13.50
☐ 64	Hank Thompson	25.00	11.00
☐ 65	Bob Swift CO	25.00	11.00
☐ 66	Ted Lepcio	25.00	11.00
☐ 67	Jim Willis	25.00	11.00
☐ 68	Sam Calderone	25.00	11.00
☐ 69	Bud Podbielan	25.00	11.00
☐ 70	Larry Doby	50.00	22.00
☐ 71	Frank Smith	25.00	11.00
☐ 72	Preston Ward	25.00	11.00
☐ 73	Wayne Terwilliger	25.00	11.00
☐ 74	Bill Taylor	25.00	11.00
☐ 75	Fred Haney MG	25.00	11.00
☐ 76	Bob Scheffing CO	15.00	6.75

#	Player	NRMT	VG-E
☐ 77	Ray Boone	25.00	11.00
☐ 78	Ted Kazanski	15.00	6.75
☐ 79	Andy Pafko	25.00	11.00
☐ 80	Jackie Jensen	25.00	11.00
☐ 81	Dave Hoskins	15.00	6.75
☐ 82	Milt Bolling	15.00	6.75
☐ 83	Joe Collins	25.00	11.00
☐ 84	Dick Cole	15.00	6.75
☐ 85	Bob Turley	40.00	18.00
☐ 86	Billy Herman CO	25.00	11.00
☐ 87	Roy Face	25.00	11.00
☐ 88	Matt Batts	15.00	6.75
☐ 89	Howie Pollet	15.00	6.75
☐ 90	Willie Mays	500.00	220.00
☐ 91	Bob Oldis	15.00	6.75
☐ 92	Wally Westlake	15.00	6.75
☐ 93	Sid Hudson	15.00	6.75
☐ 94	Ernie Banks	750.00	350.00
☐ 95	Hal Rice	15.00	6.75
☐ 96	Charlie Silvera	25.00	11.00
☐ 97	Jerald Hal Lane	15.00	6.75
☐ 98	Joe Black	40.00	18.00
☐ 99	Bobby Hofman	15.00	6.75
☐ 100	Bob Keegan	15.00	6.75
☐ 101	Gene Woodling	25.00	11.00
☐ 102	Gil Hodges	75.00	34.00
☐ 103	Jim Lemon	15.00	6.75
☐ 104	Mike Sandlock	15.00	6.75
☐ 105	Andy Carey	25.00	11.00
☐ 106	Dick Kokos	15.00	6.75
☐ 107	Duane Pillette	15.00	6.75
☐ 108	Thornton Kipper	15.00	6.75
☐ 109	Bill Bruton	25.00	11.00
☐ 110	Harry Dorish	15.00	6.75
☐ 111	Jim Delsing	15.00	6.75
☐ 112	Bill Renna	15.00	6.75
☐ 113	Bob Boyd	15.00	6.75
☐ 114	Dean Stone	15.00	6.75
☐ 115	Rip Repulski	15.00	6.75
☐ 116	Steve Bilko	15.00	6.75
☐ 117	Solly Hemus	15.00	6.75
☐ 118	Carl Scheib	15.00	6.75
☐ 119	Johnny Antonelli	25.00	11.00
☐ 120	Roy McMillan	15.00	6.75
☐ 121	Clem Labine	25.00	11.00
☐ 122	Johnny Logan	25.00	11.00
☐ 123	Bobby Adams	15.00	6.75
☐ 124	Marion Fricano	15.00	6.75
☐ 125	Harry Perkowski	15.00	6.75
☐ 126	Ben Wade	15.00	6.75
☐ 127	Steve O'Neill MG	15.00	6.75
☐ 128	Hank Aaron	1500.00	700.00
☐ 129	Forrest Jacobs	15.00	6.75
☐ 130	Hank Bauer	25.00	11.00
☐ 131	Reno Bertoia	15.00	6.75
☐ 132	Tommy Lasorda	200.00	90.00
☐ 133	Del Baker CO	15.00	6.75
☐ 134	Cal Hogue	15.00	6.75
☐ 135	Joe Presko	15.00	6.75
☐ 136	Connie Ryan	15.00	6.75
☐ 137	Wally Moon	40.00	18.00
☐ 138	Bob Borkowski	15.00	6.75
☐ 139	The O'Briens Johnny O'Brien Eddie O'Brien	40.00	18.00
☐ 140	Tom Wright	15.00	6.75
☐ 141	Joey Jay	25.00	11.00
☐ 142	Tom Poholsky	15.00	6.75
☐ 143	Rollie Hemsley CO	15.00	6.75
☐ 144	Bill Werle	15.00	6.75
☐ 145	Elmer Valo	15.00	6.75
☐ 146	Don Johnson	15.00	6.75
☐ 147	Johnny Riddle CO	15.00	6.75
☐ 148	Bob Trice	15.00	6.75
☐ 149	Al Robertson	15.00	6.75
☐ 150	Dick Kryhoski	15.00	6.75
☐ 151	Alex Grammas	15.00	6.75
☐ 152	Michael Blyzka	15.00	6.75
☐ 153	Al Walker	15.00	6.75
☐ 154	Mike Fornieles	15.00	6.75
☐ 155	Bob Kennedy	25.00	11.00
☐ 156	Joe Coleman	15.00	6.75
☐ 157	Don Lenhardt	15.00	6.75
☐ 158	Peanuts Lowrey	15.00	6.75
☐ 159	Dave Philley	15.00	6.75
☐ 160	Ralph Kress CO	15.00	6.75

	NRMT	VG-E
161 John Hetki	15.00	6.75
162 Herman Wehmeier	15.00	6.75
163 Frank House	15.00	6.75
164 Stu Miller	25.00	11.00
165 Jim Pendleton	15.00	6.75
166 Johnny Podres	40.00	18.00
167 Don Lund	15.00	6.75
168 Morrie Martin	15.00	6.75
169 Jim Hughes	25.00	11.00
170 James(Dusty) Rhodes	25.00	11.00
171 Leo Kiely	15.00	6.75
172 Harold Brown	15.00	6.75
173 Jack Harshman	15.00	6.75
174 Tom Qualters	15.00	6.75
175 Frank Leja	25.00	11.00
176 Robert Keely CO	15.00	6.75
177 Bob Milliken	15.00	6.75
178 Bill Glynn	15.00	6.75
179 Gair Allie	15.00	6.75
180 Wes Westrum	25.00	11.00
181 Mel Roach	15.00	6.75
182 Chuck Harmon	15.00	6.75
183 Earle Combs CO	25.00	11.00
184 Ed Bailey	15.00	6.75
185 Chuck Stobbs	15.00	6.75
186 Karl Olson	15.00	6.75
187 Heinie Manush CO	25.00	11.00
188 Dave Jolly	15.00	6.75
189 Bob Ross	15.00	6.75
190 Ray Herbert	15.00	6.75
191 John(Dick) Schofield	25.00	11.00
192 Ellis Deal CO	15.00	6.75
193 Johnny Hopp CO	15.00	6.75
194 Bill Sarni	15.00	6.75
195 Billy Consolo	15.00	6.75
196 Stan Jok	15.00	6.75
197 Lynwood Rowe CO ("Schoolboy")	25.00	11.00
198 Carl Swatskit	15.00	6.75
199 Glenn(Rocky) Nelson	15.00	6.75
200 Larry Jansen	25.00	11.00
201 Al Kaline	750.00	350.00
202 Bob Purkey	25.00	11.00
203 Harry Brecheen CO	25.00	11.00
204 Angel Scull	15.00	6.75
205 Johnny Sain	40.00	18.00
206 Ray Crone	15.00	6.75
207 Tom Oliver CO	15.00	6.75
208 Grady Hatton	15.00	6.75
209 Chuck Thompson	15.00	6.75
210 Bob Buhl	25.00	11.00
211 Don Hoak	25.00	11.00
212 Bob Micelotta	15.00	6.75
213 Johnny Fitzpatrick CO	15.00	6.75
214 Arnie Portocarrero	15.00	6.75
215 Ed McGhee	15.00	6.75
216 Al Sima	15.00	6.75
217 Paul Schreiber CO	15.00	6.75
218 Fred Marsh	15.00	6.75
219 Chuck Kress	15.00	6.75
220 Ruben Gomez	25.00	11.00
221 Dick Brodowski	15.00	6.75
222 Bill Wilson	15.00	6.75
223 Joe Haynes CO	15.00	6.75
224 Dick Welk	15.00	6.75
225 Don Liddle	15.00	6.75
226 Jehosie Heard	15.00	6.75
227 Colonel Mills CO	15.00	6.75
228 Gene Hermanski	15.00	6.75
229 Bob Talbot	15.00	6.75
230 Bob Kuzava	25.00	11.00
231 Roy Smalley	15.00	6.75
232 Lou Limmer	15.00	6.75
233 Augie Galan CO	15.00	6.75
234 Jerry Lynch	15.00	6.75
235 Vern Law	25.00	11.00
236 Paul Penson	15.00	6.75
237 Mike Ryba CO	15.00	6.75
238 Al Aber	15.00	6.75
239 Bill Skowron	100.00	45.00
240 Sam Mele	25.00	11.00
241 Robert Miller	15.00	6.75
242 Curt Roberts	15.00	6.75
243 Ray Blades CO	15.00	6.75
244 Leroy Wheat	15.00	6.75
245 Roy Sievers	25.00	11.00
246 Howie Fox	15.00	6.75
247 Ed Mayo CO	15.00	6.75
248 Al Smith	25.00	11.00
249 Wilmer Mizell	25.00	11.00
250 Ted Williams	800.00	325.00

1955 Topps

	NRMT	VG-E
COMPLETE SET (206)	7200.00	3200.00
COMMON CARD (1-150)	12.00	5.50
MINOR STARS 1-150	15.00	6.75
SEMISTARS 1-150	25.00	11.00
UNLISTED STARS 1-150	40.00	18.00
COMMON CARD (151-160)	20.00	9.00
MINOR STARS 151-160	25.00	11.00
SEMISTARS 151-160	40.00	18.00
COMMON CARD (161-210)	30.00	13.50
DP (170/172/184/188)	15.00	6.75
MINOR STARS 161-210	40.00	18.00
SEMISTARS 161-210	60.00	27.00

NOT ISSUED (175/186/203/209)
*UNLISTED DODGER/YANKEE: 1.25X VALUE
CARDS PRICED IN NM CONDITION !

	NRMT	VG-E
1 Dusty Rhodes	75.00	15.00
2 Ted Williams	500.00	220.00
3 Art Fowler	15.00	6.75
4 Al Kaline	150.00	70.00
5 Jim Gilliam	25.00	11.00
6 Stan Hack MG	18.00	8.00
7 Jim Hegan	15.00	6.75
8 Harold Smith	12.00	5.50
9 Robert Miller	15.00	6.75
10 Bob Keegan	12.00	5.50
11 Ferris Fain	15.00	6.75
12 Vernon(Jake) Thies	12.00	5.50
13 Fred Marsh	12.00	5.50
14 Jim Finigan	12.00	5.50
15 Jim Pendleton	12.00	5.50
16 Roy Sievers	15.00	6.75
17 Bobby Hofman	12.00	5.50
18 Russ Kemmerer	12.00	5.50
19 Billy Herman CO	18.00	8.00
20 Andy Carey	15.00	6.75
21 Alex Grammas	12.00	5.50
22 Bill Skowron	20.00	9.00
23 Jack Parks	12.00	5.50
24 Hal Newhouser	18.00	8.00
25 Johnny Podres	20.00	9.00
26 Dick Groat	18.00	8.00
27 Billy Gardner	15.00	6.75
28 Ernie Banks	175.00	80.00
29 Herman Wehmeier	12.00	5.50
30 Vic Power	15.00	6.75
31 Warren Spahn	100.00	45.00
32 Warren McGhee	12.00	5.50
33 Tom Qualters	12.00	5.50
34 Wayne Terwilliger	12.00	5.50
35 Dave Jolly	12.00	5.50
36 Leo Kiely	12.00	5.50
37 Joe Cunningham	15.00	6.75
38 Bob Turley	18.00	8.00
39 Bill Glynn	12.00	5.50
40 Don Hoak	15.00	6.75
41 Chuck Stobbs	12.00	5.50
42 John(Windy) McCall	12.00	5.50
43 Harvey Haddix	18.00	8.00
44 Harold Valentine	12.00	5.50
45 Hank Sauer	18.00	8.00
46 Ted Kazanski	12.00	5.50
47 Hank Aaron UER	350.00	160.00
(Birth incorrectly listed as 2/10)		
48 Bob Kennedy	15.00	6.75
49 J.W. Porter	12.00	5.50
50 Jackie Robinson	300.00	135.00
51 Jim Hughes	15.00	6.75
52 Bill Tremel	12.00	5.50
53 Bill Taylor	12.00	5.50
54 Lou Limmer	12.00	5.50
55 Rip Repulski	12.00	5.50
56 Ray Jablonski	12.00	5.50
57 Billy O'Dell	12.00	5.50
58 Jim Rivera	12.00	5.50
59 Gair Allie	12.00	5.50
60 Dean Stone	12.00	5.50
61 Forrest Jacobs	12.00	5.50
62 Thornton Kipper	12.00	5.50
63 Joe Collins	15.00	6.75
64 Gus Triandos	18.00	8.00
65 Ray Boone	18.00	8.00
66 Ron Jackson	12.00	5.50
67 Wally Moon	18.00	8.00
68 Jim Davis	12.00	5.50
69 Ed Bailey	15.00	6.75
70 Al Rosen	18.00	8.00
71 Ruben Gomez	12.00	5.50
72 Karl Olson	12.00	5.50
73 Jack Shepard	12.00	5.50
74 Bob Borkowski	12.00	5.50
75 Sandy Amoros	30.00	13.50
76 Howie Pollet	12.00	5.50
77 Arnie Portocarrero	12.00	5.50
78 Gordon Jones	12.00	5.50
79 Clyde(Danny) Schell	12.00	5.50
80 Bob Grim	18.00	8.00
81 Gene Conley	15.00	6.75
82 Chuck Harmon	12.00	5.50
83 Tom Brewer	12.00	5.50
84 Camilo Pascual	18.00	8.00
85 Don Mossi	20.00	9.00
86 Bill Wilson	12.00	5.50
87 Frank House	12.00	5.50
88 Bob Skinner	18.00	8.00
89 Joe Frazier	15.00	6.75
90 Karl Spooner	15.00	6.75
91 Milt Bolling	12.00	5.50
92 Don Zimmer	30.00	13.50
93 Steve Bilko	12.00	5.50
94 Reno Bertoia	12.00	5.50
95 Preston Ward	12.00	5.50
96 Chuck Bishop	12.00	5.50
97 Carlos Paula	12.00	5.50
98 John Riddle CO	12.00	5.50
99 Frank Leja	12.00	5.50
100 Monte Irvin	35.00	16.00
101 Johnny Gray	12.00	5.50
102 Wally Westlake	12.00	5.50
103 Chuck White	12.00	5.50
104 Jack Harshman	12.00	5.50
105 Chuck Diering	12.00	5.50
106 Frank Sullivan	12.00	5.50
107 Curt Roberts	12.00	5.50
108 Al Walker	15.00	6.75
109 Ed Lopat	18.00	8.00
110 Gus Zernial	15.00	6.75
111 Bob Milliken	15.00	6.75
112 Nelson King	12.00	5.50
113 Harry Brecheen CO	15.00	6.75
114 Louis Ortiz	12.00	5.50
115 Ellis Kinder	12.00	5.50
116 Tom Hurd	12.00	5.50
117 Mel Roach	12.00	5.50
118 Bob Purkey	12.00	5.50
119 Bob Lennon	12.00	5.50
120 Ted Kluszewski	60.00	27.00
121 Bill Renna	12.00	5.50
122 Carl Sawatski	12.00	5.50
123 Sandy Koufax	800.00	350.00
124 Harmon Killebrew	250.00	110.00
125 Ken Boyer	60.00	27.00
126 Dick Hall	12.00	5.50
127 Dale Long	18.00	8.00

❏ 128 Ted Lepcio	12.00	5.50
❏ 129 Elvin Tappe	12.00	5.50
❏ 130 Mayo Smith MG	12.00	5.50
❏ 131 Grady Hatton	12.00	5.50
❏ 132 Bob Trice	12.00	5.50
❏ 133 Dave Hoskins	12.00	5.50
❏ 134 Joey Jay	15.00	6.75
❏ 135 Johnny O'Brien	15.00	6.75
❏ 136 Veston(Bunky) Stewart	12.00	5.50
❏ 137 Harry Elliott	12.00	5.50
❏ 138 Ray Herbert	12.00	5.50
❏ 139 Steve Kraly	12.00	5.50
❏ 140 Mel Parnell	15.00	6.75
❏ 141 Tom Wright	12.00	5.50
❏ 142 Jerry Lynch	15.00	6.75
❏ 143 John(Dick) Schofield	15.00	6.75
❏ 144 John(Joe) Amalfitano	12.00	5.50
❏ 145 Elmer Valo	12.00	5.50
❏ 146 Dick Donovan	12.00	5.50
❏ 147 Hugh Pepper	12.00	5.50
❏ 148 Hector Brown	12.00	5.50
❏ 149 Ray Crone	12.00	5.50
❏ 150 Mike Higgins MG	12.00	5.50
❏ 151 Ralph Kress CO	20.00	9.00
❏ 152 Harry Agganis	80.00	36.00
❏ 153 Bud Podbielan	20.00	9.00
❏ 154 Willie Miranda	20.00	9.00
❏ 155 Eddie Mathews	100.00	45.00
❏ 156 Joe Black	40.00	18.00
❏ 157 Robert Miller	20.00	9.00
❏ 158 Tommy Carroll	20.00	9.00
❏ 159 Johnny Schmitz	20.00	9.00
❏ 160 Ray Narleski	20.00	9.00
❏ 161 Chuck Tanner	35.00	16.00
❏ 162 Joe Coleman	30.00	13.50
❏ 163 Faye Throneberry	20.00	9.00
❏ 164 Roberto Clemente	2000.00	900.00
❏ 165 Don Johnson	30.00	13.50
❏ 166 Hank Bauer	50.00	22.00
❏ 167 Thomas Casagrande	30.00	13.50
❏ 168 Duane Pillette	30.00	13.50
❏ 169 Bob Oldis	30.00	13.50
❏ 170 Jim Pearce DP	15.00	6.75
❏ 171 Dick Brodowski	30.00	13.50
❏ 172 Frank Baumholtz DP	15.00	6.75
❏ 173 Bob Kline	30.00	13.50
❏ 174 Rudy Minarcin	30.00	13.50
❏ 175 Does not exist		
❏ 176 Norm Zauchin	30.00	13.50
❏ 177 Al Robertson	30.00	13.50
❏ 178 Bobby Adams	30.00	13.50
❏ 179 Jim Bolger	30.00	13.50
❏ 180 Clem Labine	45.00	20.00
❏ 181 Roy McMillan	40.00	18.00
❏ 182 Humberto Robinson	30.00	13.50
❏ 183 Anthony Jacobs	30.00	13.50
❏ 184 Harry Perkowski DP	15.00	6.75
❏ 185 Don Ferrarese	30.00	13.50
❏ 186 Does not exist		
❏ 187 Gil Hodges	150.00	70.00
❏ 188 Charlie Silvera DP	15.00	6.75
❏ 189 Phil Rizzuto	150.00	70.00
❏ 190 Gene Woodling	40.00	18.00
❏ 191 Eddie Stanky MG	40.00	18.00
❏ 192 Jim Delsing	30.00	13.50
❏ 193 Johnny Sain	45.00	20.00
❏ 194 Willie Mays	400.00	180.00
❏ 195 Ed Roebuck	45.00	20.00
❏ 196 Gale Wade	30.00	13.50
❏ 197 Al Smith	40.00	18.00
❏ 198 Yogi Berra	200.00	90.00
❏ 199 Odbert Hamric	40.00	18.00
❏ 200 Jackie Jensen	35.00	16.00
❏ 201 Sherman Lollar I	20.00	9.00
❏ 202 Jim Owens	30.00	13.50
❏ 203 Does not exist		
❏ 204 Frank Smith	30.00	13.50
❏ 205 Gene Freese	30.00	13.50
❏ 206 Pete Daley	30.00	13.50
❏ 207 Billy Consolo	30.00	13.50
❏ 208 Ray Moore	30.00	13.50
❏ 209 Does not exist		
❏ 210 Duke Snider	500.00	150.00

1956 Topps

	NRMT	VG-E
COMPLETE SET (340)	7000.00	3200.00
COMMON CARD (1-100)	10.00	4.50
COMMON CARD (101-180)	12.00	5.50
COMMON CARD (261-340)	12.00	5.50
DP (9/21/46/60/75/80/86)	9.00	4.00
MINOR STARS 1-180/261-340	15.00	6.75
SEMISTARS 1-180/261-340	25.00	11.00
UNL.STARS 1-180/261-340	40.00	18.00
COMMON CARD (181-260)	15.00	6.75
MINOR STARS 181-260	20.00	9.00
SEMISTARS 181-260	30.00	13.50
UNLISTED STARS 181-260	50.00	22.00
*UNLISTED DODGER/YANKEE: 1.25X VALUE		
CARDS PRICED IN NM CONDITION !		

❏ 1 William Harridge PRES	100.00	28.00
❏ 2 Warren Giles PRES	30.00	13.50
❏ 3 Elmer Valo	10.00	4.50
❏ 4 Carlos Paula	10.00	4.50
❏ 5 Ted Williams	350.00	160.00
❏ 6 Ray Boone	15.00	6.75
❏ 7 Ron Negray	10.00	4.50
❏ 8 Walter Alston MG	40.00	18.00
❏ 9 Ruben Gomez DP	9.00	4.00
❏ 10 Warren Spahn	75.00	34.00
❏ 11A Chicago Cubs	30.00	13.50
(Centered)		
❏ 11B Cubs Team	80.00	36.00
(Dated 1955)		
❏ 11C Cubs Team	30.00	13.50
(Name at far left)		
❏ 12 Andy Carey	15.00	6.75
❏ 13 Roy Face	15.00	6.75
❏ 14 Ken Boyer DP	15.00	6.75
❏ 15 Ernie Banks DP	80.00	36.00
❏ 16 Hector Lopez	15.00	6.75
❏ 17 Gene Conley	15.00	6.75
❏ 18 Dick Donovan	10.00	4.50
❏ 19 Chuck Diering	10.00	4.50
❏ 20 Al Kaline	100.00	45.00
❏ 21 Joe Collins DP	15.00	6.75
❏ 22 Jim Finigan	10.00	4.50
❏ 23 Fred Marsh	10.00	4.50
❏ 24 Dick Groat	15.00	6.75
❏ 25 Ted Kluszewski	60.00	27.00
❏ 26 Grady Hatton	10.00	4.50
❏ 27 Nelson Burbrink	10.00	4.50
❏ 28 Bobby Hofman	10.00	4.50
❏ 29 Jack Harshman	10.00	4.50
❏ 30 Jackie Robinson DP	200.00	90.00
❏ 31 Hank Aaron UER	300.00	135.00
(Small photo		
actually Willie Mays)		
❏ 32 Frank House	10.00	4.50
❏ 33 Roberto Clemente	375.00	170.00
❏ 34 Tom Brewer	10.00	4.50
❏ 35 Al Rosen	15.00	6.75
❏ 36 Rudy Minarcin	10.00	4.50
❏ 37 Alex Grammas	10.00	4.50
❏ 38 Bob Kennedy	15.00	6.75
❏ 39 Don Mossi	15.00	6.75
❏ 40 Bob Turley	15.00	6.75
❏ 41 Hank Sauer	15.00	6.75
❏ 42 Sandy Amoros	20.00	9.00
❏ 43 Ray Moore	10.00	4.50

❏ 44 Windy McCall	10.00	4.50
❏ 45 Gus Zernial	15.00	6.75
❏ 46 Gene Freese DP	9.00	4.00
❏ 47 Art Fowler	10.00	4.50
❏ 48 Jim Hegan	15.00	6.75
❏ 49 Pedro Ramos	10.00	4.50
❏ 50 Dusty Rhodes	15.00	6.75
❏ 51 Ernie Oravetz	10.00	4.50
❏ 52 Bob Grim	15.00	6.75
❏ 53 Arnie Portocarrero	10.00	4.50
❏ 54 Bob Keegan	10.00	4.50
❏ 55 Wally Moon	15.00	6.75
❏ 56 Dale Long	15.00	6.75
❏ 57 Duke Maas	10.00	4.50
❏ 58 Ed Roebuck	15.00	6.75
❏ 59 Jose Santiago	10.00	4.50
❏ 60 Mayo Smith MG DP	9.00	4.00
❏ 61 Bill Skowron	20.00	9.00
❏ 62 Hal Smith	10.00	4.50
❏ 63 Roger Craig	25.00	11.00
❏ 64 Luis Arroyo	15.00	6.75
❏ 65 Johnny O'Brien	15.00	6.75
❏ 66 Bob Speake	10.00	4.50
❏ 67 Vic Power	15.00	6.75
❏ 68 Chuck Stobbs	10.00	4.50
❏ 69 Chuck Tanner	15.00	6.75
❏ 70 Jim Rivera	10.00	4.50
❏ 71 Frank Sullivan	10.00	4.50
❏ 72A Phillies Team	30.00	13.50
(Centered)		
❏ 72B Phillies Team	80.00	36.00
(Dated 1955)		
❏ 72C Phillies Team	30.00	13.50
(Name at far left)		
❏ 73 Wayne Terwilliger	10.00	4.50
❏ 74 Jim King	10.00	4.50
❏ 75 Roy Sievers DP	15.00	6.75
❏ 76 Ray Crone	10.00	4.50
❏ 77 Harvey Haddix	15.00	6.75
❏ 78 Herman Wehmeier	10.00	4.50
❏ 79 Sandy Koufax	350.00	100.00
❏ 80 Gus Triandos DP	10.00	4.50
❏ 81 Wally Westlake	10.00	4.50
❏ 82 Bill Renna	10.00	4.50
❏ 83 Karl Spooner	15.00	6.75
❏ 84 Babe Birrer	10.00	4.50
❏ 85A Cleveland Indians	30.00	13.50
(Centered)		
❏ 85B Indians Team	80.00	36.00
(Dated 1955)		
❏ 85C Indians Team	30.00	13.50
(Name at far left)		
❏ 86 Ray Jablonski DP	9.00	4.00
❏ 87 Dean Stone	10.00	4.50
❏ 88 Johnny Kucks	15.00	6.75
❏ 89 Norm Zauchin	10.00	4.50
❏ 90A Cincinnati Redlegs	30.00	13.50
Team (Centered)		
❏ 90B Reds Team	80.00	36.00
(Dated 1955)		
❏ 90C Reds Team	30.00	13.50
(Name at far left)		
❏ 91 Gail Harris	10.00	4.50
❏ 92 Bob(Red) Wilson	10.00	4.50
❏ 93 George Susce	10.00	4.50
❏ 94 Ron Kline	10.00	4.50
❏ 95A Milwaukee Braves	42.00	19.00
Team (Centered)		
❏ 95B Braves Team	80.00	36.00
(Dated 1955)		
❏ 95C Braves Team	42.00	19.00
(Name at far left)		
❏ 96 Bill Tremel	10.00	4.50
❏ 97 Jerry Lynch	15.00	6.75
❏ 98 Camilo Pascual	15.00	6.75
❏ 99 Don Zimmer	15.00	6.75
❏ 100A Baltimore Orioles	35.00	16.00
Team (centered)		
❏ 100B Orioles Team	80.00	36.00
(Dated 1955)		
❏ 100C Orioles Team	35.00	16.00
(Name at far left)		
❏ 101 Roy Campanella	150.00	70.00
❏ 102 Jim Davis	12.00	5.50
❏ 103 Willie Miranda	12.00	5.50
❏ 104 Bob Lennon	12.00	5.50

No.	Name	NRMT	VG-E
105	Al Smith	12.00	5.50
106	Joe Astroth	12.00	5.50
107	Eddie Mathews	75.00	34.00
108	Laurin Pepper	12.00	5.50
109	Enos Slaughter	40.00	18.00
110	Yogi Berra	150.00	70.00
111	Boston Red Sox Team Card	40.00	18.00
112	Dee Fondy	12.00	5.50
113	Phil Rizzuto	125.00	55.00
114	Jim Owens	12.00	5.50
115	Jackie Jensen	15.00	6.75
116	Eddie O'Brien	12.00	5.50
117	Virgil Trucks	15.00	6.75
118	Nellie Fox	50.00	22.00
119	Larry Jackson	12.00	6.75
120	Richie Ashburn	50.00	22.00
121	Pittsburgh Pirates Team Card	25.00	11.00
122	Willard Nixon	12.00	5.50
123	Roy McMillan	15.00	6.75
124	Don Kaiser	12.00	5.50
125	Minnie Minoso	40.00	18.00
126	Jim Brady	12.00	5.50
127	Willie Jones	15.00	6.75
128	Eddie Yost	15.00	6.75
129	Jake Martin	12.00	5.50
130	Willie Mays	300.00	135.00
131	Bob Roselli	12.00	5.50
132	Bobby Avila	12.00	5.50
133	Ray Narleski	12.00	5.50
134	St. Louis Cardinals Team Card	25.00	11.00
135	Mickey Mantle	1400.00	650.00
136	Johnny Logan	15.00	6.75
137	Al Silvera	12.00	5.50
138	Johnny Antonelli	15.00	6.75
139	Tommy Carroll	12.00	5.50
140	Herb Score	60.00	27.00
141	Joe Frazier	12.00	5.50
142	Gene Baker	12.00	5.50
143	Jim Piersall	15.00	6.75
144	Leroy Powell	12.00	5.50
145	Gil Hodges	50.00	22.00
146	Washington Nationals Team Card	25.00	11.00
147	Earl Torgeson	12.00	5.50
148	Alvin Dark	15.00	6.75
149	Dixie Howell	12.00	5.50
150	Duke Snider	125.00	55.00
151	Spook Jacobs	15.00	6.75
152	Billy Hoeft	15.00	6.75
153	Frank Thomas	15.00	6.75
154	Dave Pope	12.00	5.50
155	Harvey Kuenn	15.00	6.75
156	Wes Westrum	15.00	6.75
157	Dick Brodowski	12.00	5.50
158	Wally Post	15.00	6.75
159	Clint Courtney	12.00	5.50
160	Billy Pierce	15.00	6.75
161	Joe DeMaestri	12.00	5.50
162	Dave(Gus) Bell	15.00	6.75
163	Gene Woodling	15.00	6.75
164	Harmon Killebrew	100.00	45.00
165	Red Schoendienst	40.00	18.00
166	Brooklyn Dodgers Team Card	200.00	90.00
167	Harry Dorish	12.00	5.50
168	Sammy White	12.00	5.50
169	Bob Nelson	12.00	5.50
170	Bill Virdon	18.00	8.00
171	Jim Wilson	12.00	5.50
172	Frank Torre	15.00	6.75
173	Johnny Podres	25.00	11.00
174	Glen Gorbous	12.00	5.50
175	Del Crandall	15.00	6.75
176	Alex Kellner	12.00	5.50
177	Hank Bauer	25.00	11.00
178	Joe Black	15.00	6.75
179	Harry Chiti	12.00	5.50
180	Robin Roberts	50.00	22.00
181	Billy Martin	60.00	27.00
182	Paul Minner	15.00	6.75
183	Stan Lopata	15.00	6.75
184	Don Bessent	15.00	6.75
185	Bill Bruton	20.00	9.00
186	Ron Jackson	15.00	6.75
187	Early Wynn	50.00	22.00
188	Chicago White Sox Team Card	50.00	22.00
189	Ned Garver	15.00	6.75
190	Carl Furillo	30.00	13.50
191	Frank Lary	20.00	9.00
192	Smoky Burgess	20.00	9.00
193	Wilmer Mizell	20.00	9.00
194	Monte Irvin	30.00	13.50
195	George Kell	30.00	13.50
196	Tom Poholsky	15.00	6.75
197	Granny Hamner	15.00	6.75
198	Ed Fitzgerald	15.00	6.75
199	Hank Thompson	20.00	9.00
200	Bob Feller	100.00	45.00
201	Rip Repulski	15.00	6.75
202	Jim Hearn	15.00	6.75
203	Bill Tuttle	15.00	6.75
204	Art Swanson	15.00	6.75
205	Whitey Lockman	20.00	9.00
206	Erv Palica	15.00	6.75
207	Jim Small	15.00	6.75
208	Elston Howard	60.00	27.00
209	Max Surkont	15.00	6.75
210	Mike Garcia	20.00	9.00
211	Murry Dickson	15.00	6.75
212	Johnny Temple	15.00	6.75
213	Detroit Tigers Team Card	60.00	27.00
214	Bob Rush	15.00	6.75
215	Tommy Byrne	20.00	9.00
216	Jerry Schoonmaker	15.00	6.75
217	Billy Klaus	15.00	6.75
218	Joe Nuxhall UER (Misspelled Nuxall)	20.00	9.00
219	Lew Burdette	20.00	9.00
220	Del Ennis	20.00	9.00
221	Bob Friend	15.00	6.75
222	Dave Philley	15.00	6.75
223	Randy Jackson	15.00	6.75
224	Bud Podbielan	15.00	6.75
225	Gil McDougald	40.00	18.00
226	New York Giants Team Card	80.00	36.00
227	Russ Meyer	15.00	6.75
228	Mickey Vernon	20.00	9.00
229	Harry Brecheen CO	20.00	9.00
230	Chico Carrasquel	15.00	6.75
231	Bob Hale	15.00	6.75
232	Toby Atwell	15.00	6.75
233	Carl Erskine	30.00	13.50
234	Pete Runnels	15.00	6.75
235	Don Newcombe	50.00	22.00
236	Kansas City Athletics Team Card	30.00	13.50
237	Jose Valdivielso	15.00	6.75
238	Walt Dropo	20.00	9.00
239	Harry Simpson	15.00	6.75
240	Whitey Ford	125.00	55.00
241	Don Mueller UER (6'- tall)	20.00	9.00
242	Hershell Freeman	15.00	6.75
243	Sherm Lollar	20.00	9.00
244	Bob Buhl	20.00	9.00
245	Billy Goodman	15.00	6.75
246	Tom Gorman	15.00	6.75
247	Bill Sarni	15.00	6.75
248	Bob Porterfield	15.00	6.75
249	Johnny Klippstein	15.00	6.75
250	Larry Doby	30.00	13.50
251	New York Yankees Team Card UER (Don Larsen misspelled as Larson on front)	250.00	110.00
252	Vern Law	20.00	9.00
253	Irv Noren	15.00	6.75
254	George Crowe	15.00	6.75
255	Bob Lemon	30.00	13.50
256	Tom Hurd	15.00	6.75
257	Bobby Thomson	30.00	13.50
258	Art Ditmar	15.00	6.75
259	Sam Jones	15.00	6.75
260	Pee Wee Reese	120.00	55.00
261	Bobby Shantz	20.00	9.00
262	Howie Pollet	12.00	5.50
263	Bob Miller	12.00	5.50
264	Ray Monzant	12.00	5.50
265	Sandy Consuegra	12.00	5.50
266	Don Ferrarese	12.00	5.50
267	Bob Nieman	12.00	5.50
268	Dale Mitchell	15.00	6.75
269	Jack Meyer	12.00	5.50
270	Billy Loes	15.00	6.75
271	Foster Castleman	12.00	5.50
272	Danny O'Connell	12.00	5.50
273	Walker Cooper	12.00	5.50
274	Frank Baumholtz	12.00	5.50
275	Jim Greengrass	12.00	5.50
276	George Zuverink	12.00	5.50
277	Daryl Spencer	12.00	5.50
278	Chet Nichols	12.00	5.50
279	Johnny Groth	12.00	5.50
280	Jim Gilliam	40.00	18.00
281	Art Houtteman	12.00	5.50
282	Warren Hacker	12.00	5.50
283	Hal Smith	12.00	5.50
284	Ike Delock	12.00	5.50
285	Eddie Miksis	12.00	5.50
286	Bill Wight	12.00	5.50
287	Bobby Adams	12.00	5.50
288	Bob Cerv	40.00	18.00
289	Hal Jeffcoat	12.00	5.50
290	Curt Simmons	15.00	6.75
291	Frank Kellert	12.00	5.50
292	Luis Aparicio	150.00	70.00
293	Stu Miller	15.00	6.75
294	Ernie Johnson	15.00	6.75
295	Clem Labine	15.00	6.75
296	Andy Seminick	12.00	5.50
297	Bob Skinner	15.00	6.75
298	Johnny Schmitz	12.00	5.50
299	Charlie Neal	40.00	18.00
300	Vic Wertz	15.00	6.75
301	Marv Grissom	12.00	5.50
302	Eddie Robinson	12.00	5.50
303	Jim Dyck	12.00	5.50
304	Frank Malzone	15.00	6.75
305	Brooks Lawrence	12.00	5.50
306	Curt Roberts	12.00	5.50
307	Hoyt Wilhelm	40.00	18.00
308	Chuck Harmon	12.00	5.50
309	Don Blasingame	15.00	6.75
310	Steve Gromek	12.00	5.50
311	Hal Naragon	12.00	5.50
312	Andy Pafko	15.00	6.75
313	Gene Stephens	12.00	5.50
314	Hobie Landrith	12.00	5.50
315	Milt Bolling	12.00	5.50
316	Jerry Coleman	15.00	6.75
317	Al Aber	12.00	5.50
318	Fred Hatfield	12.00	5.50
319	Jack Crimian	12.00	5.50
320	Joe Adcock	15.00	6.75
321	Jim Konstanty	15.00	6.75
322	Karl Olson	12.00	5.50
323	Willard Schmidt	12.00	5.50
324	Rocky Bridges	15.00	6.75
325	Don Liddle	12.00	5.50
326	Connie Johnson	12.00	5.50
327	Bob Wiesler	12.00	5.50
328	Preston Ward	12.00	5.50
329	Lou Berberet	12.00	5.50
330	Jim Busby	12.00	5.50
331	Dick Hall	12.00	5.50
332	Don Larsen	60.00	27.00
333	Rube Walker	12.00	5.50
334	Bob Miller	12.00	5.50
335	Don Hoak	15.00	6.75
336	Ellis Kinder	12.00	5.50
337	Bobby Morgan	12.00	5.50
338	Jim Delsing	12.00	5.50
339	Rance Pless	12.00	5.50
340	Mickey McDermott	60.00	12.00
NNO	Checklist 2/4	275.00	90.00
NNO	Checklist 1/3	275.00	90.00

1957 Topps

	NRMT	VG-E
COMPLETE SET (407)	7000.00	3200.00
COMMON CARD (1-88)	10.00	4.50

RICHIE ASHBURN
PHILADELPHIA PHILLIES O.F.

COMMON CARD (89–176)	8.00	3.60
COMMON CARD (177–264)	8.00	3.60
COMMON CARD (265–352)	20.00	9.00
COMMON CARD (353–407)	8.00	3.60
MINOR STARS 1–264/353–407	15.00	6.75
SEMISTARS 1–264/353–407	20.00	9.00
UNL. STARS 1–264/353–407	30.00	13.50
COMMON DP	14.00	6.25
MINOR STARS 265–352	30.00	13.50
SEMISTARS 265–352	40.00	18.00

*UNLISTED DODGER/YANKEE: 1.25X VALUE
CARDS PRICED IN NM CONDITION

❏ 1	Ted Williams	500.00	150.00
❏ 2	Yogi Berra	135.00	60.00
❏ 3	Dale Long	15.00	6.75
❏ 4	Johnny Logan	15.00	6.75
❏ 5	Sal Maglie	20.00	9.00
❏ 6	Hector Lopez	15.00	6.75
❏ 7	Luis Aparicio	40.00	18.00
❏ 8	Don Mossi	15.00	6.75
❏ 9	Johnny Temple	15.00	6.75
❏ 10	Willie Mays	225.00	100.00
❏ 11	George Zuverink	10.00	4.50
❏ 12	Dick Groat	15.00	6.75
❏ 13	Wally Burnette	10.00	4.50
❏ 14	Bob Nieman	10.00	4.50
❏ 15	Robin Roberts	30.00	13.50
❏ 16	Walt Moryn	10.00	4.50
❏ 17	Billy Gardner	10.00	4.50
❏ 18	Don Drysdale	225.00	100.00
❏ 19	Bob Wilson	10.00	4.50
❏ 20	Hank Aaron UER	200.00	90.00
	(Reverse negative photo on front)		
❏ 21	Frank Sullivan	10.00	4.50
❏ 22	Jerry Snyder UER	10.00	4.50
	(Photo actually Ed Fitzgerald)		
❏ 23	Sherm Lollar	15.00	6.75
❏ 24	Bill Mazeroski	70.00	32.00
❏ 25	Whitey Ford	75.00	34.00
❏ 26	Bob Boyd	10.00	4.50
❏ 27	Ted Kazanski	10.00	4.50
❏ 28	Gene Conley	15.00	6.75
❏ 29	Whitey Herzog	30.00	13.50
❏ 30	Pee Wee Reese	75.00	34.00
❏ 31	Ron Northey	10.00	4.50
❏ 32	Hershell Freeman	10.00	4.50
❏ 33	Jim Small	10.00	4.50
❏ 34	Tom Sturdivant	15.00	6.75
❏ 35	Frank Robinson	200.00	90.00
❏ 36	Bob Grim	10.00	4.50
❏ 37	Frank Torre	10.00	4.50
❏ 38	Nellie Fox	45.00	20.00
❏ 39	Al Worthington	10.00	4.50
❏ 40	Early Wynn	30.00	13.50
❏ 41	Hal W. Smith	10.00	4.50
❏ 42	Dee Fondy	10.00	4.50
❏ 43	Connie Johnson	10.00	4.50
❏ 44	Joe DeMaestri	10.00	4.50
❏ 45	Carl Furillo	25.00	11.00
❏ 46	Robert J. Miller	10.00	4.50
❏ 47	Don Blasingame	10.00	4.50
❏ 48	Bill Bruton	15.00	6.75
❏ 49	Daryl Spencer	10.00	4.50
❏ 50	Herb Score	25.00	11.00
❏ 51	Clint Courtney	10.00	4.50

❏ 52	Lee Walls	10.00	4.50
❏ 53	Clem Labine	20.00	9.00
❏ 54	Elmer Valo	10.00	4.50
❏ 55	Ernie Banks	120.00	55.00
❏ 56	Dave Sisler	10.00	4.50
❏ 57	Jim Lemon	15.00	6.75
❏ 58	Ruben Gomez	10.00	4.50
❏ 59	Dick Williams	15.00	6.75
❏ 60	Billy Hoeft	10.00	6.75
❏ 61	Dusty Rhodes	15.00	6.75
❏ 62	Billy Martin	45.00	20.00
❏ 63	Ike Delock	10.00	4.50
❏ 64	Pete Runnels	15.00	6.75
❏ 65	Wally Moon	15.00	6.75
❏ 66	Brooks Lawrence	10.00	4.50
❏ 67	Chico Carrasquel	10.00	4.50
❏ 68	Ray Crone	10.00	4.50
❏ 69	Roy McMillan	15.00	6.75
❏ 70	Richie Ashburn	50.00	22.00
❏ 71	Murry Dickson	10.00	4.50
❏ 72	Bill Tuttle	10.00	4.50
❏ 73	George Crowe	10.00	4.50
❏ 74	Vito Valentinetti	10.00	4.50
❏ 75	Jimmy Piersall	15.00	6.75
❏ 76	Roberto Clemente	300.00	135.00
❏ 77	Paul Foytack	10.00	4.50
❏ 78	Vic Wertz	15.00	6.75
❏ 79	Lindy McDaniel	15.00	6.75
❏ 80	Gil Hodges	50.00	22.00
❏ 81	Herman Wehmeier	10.00	4.50
❏ 82	Elston Howard	25.00	11.00
❏ 83	Lou Skizas	10.00	4.50
❏ 84	Moe Drabowsky	15.00	6.75
❏ 85	Larry Doby	25.00	11.00
❏ 86	Bill Sarni	10.00	4.50
❏ 87	Tom Gorman	10.00	4.50
❏ 88	Harvey Kuenn	15.00	6.75
❏ 89	Roy Sievers	15.00	6.75
❏ 90	Warren Spahn	70.00	32.00
❏ 91	Mack Burk	8.00	3.60
❏ 92	Mickey Vernon	15.00	6.75
❏ 93	Hal Jeffcoat	8.00	3.60
❏ 94	Bobby Del Greco	8.00	3.60
❏ 95	Mickey Mantle	1000.00	450.00
❏ 96	Hank Aguirre	8.00	3.60
❏ 97	New York Yankees	80.00	36.00
	Team Card		
❏ 98	Alvin Dark	15.00	6.75
❏ 99	Bob Keegan	8.00	3.60
❏ 100	League Presidents	15.00	6.75
	Warren Giles		
	Will Harridge		
❏ 101	Chuck Stobbs	8.00	3.60
❏ 102	Ray Boone	15.00	6.75
❏ 103	Joe Nuxhall	15.00	6.75
❏ 104	Hank Foiles	8.00	3.60
❏ 105	Johnny Antonelli	15.00	6.75
❏ 106	Ray Moore	8.00	3.60
❏ 107	Jim Rivera	8.00	3.60
❏ 108	Tommy Byrne	8.00	6.75
❏ 109	Hank Thompson	8.00	3.60
❏ 110	Bill Virdon	15.00	6.75
❏ 111	Hal R. Smith	8.00	3.60
❏ 112	Tom Brewer	8.00	3.60
❏ 113	Wilmer Mizell	15.00	6.75
❏ 114	Milwaukee Braves	20.00	9.00
	Team Card		
❏ 115	Jim Gilliam	15.00	6.75
❏ 116	Mike Fornieles	8.00	3.60
❏ 117	Joe Adcock	15.00	6.75
❏ 118	Bob Porterfield	8.00	3.60
❏ 119	Stan Lopata	8.00	3.60
❏ 120	Bob Lemon	30.00	13.50
❏ 121	Clete Boyer	25.00	11.00
❏ 122	Ken Boyer	20.00	9.00
❏ 123	Steve Ridzik	8.00	3.60
❏ 124	Dave Philley	8.00	3.60
❏ 125	Al Kaline	100.00	45.00
❏ 126	Bob Wiesler	8.00	3.60
❏ 127	Bob Buhl	15.00	6.75
❏ 128	Ed Bailey	15.00	6.75
❏ 129	Saul Rogovin	8.00	3.60
❏ 130	Don Newcombe	20.00	9.00
❏ 131	Milt Bolling	8.00	3.60
❏ 132	Art Ditmar	15.00	6.75
❏ 133	Del Crandall	15.00	6.75

❏ 134	Don Kaiser	8.00	3.60
❏ 135	Bill Skowron	20.00	9.00
❏ 136	Jim Hegan	15.00	6.75
❏ 137	Bob Rush	8.00	3.60
❏ 138	Minnie Minoso	20.00	9.00
❏ 139	Lou Kretlow	8.00	3.60
❏ 140	Frank Thomas	15.00	6.75
❏ 141	Al Aber	8.00	3.60
❏ 142	Charley Thompson	8.00	3.60
❏ 143	Andy Pafko	15.00	6.75
❏ 144	Ray Narleski	8.00	3.60
❏ 145	Al Smith	8.00	3.60
❏ 146	Don Ferrarese	8.00	3.60
❏ 147	Al Walker	8.00	3.60
❏ 148	Don Mueller	15.00	6.75
❏ 149	Bob Kennedy	15.00	6.75
❏ 150	Bob Friend	15.00	6.75
❏ 151	Willie Miranda	8.00	3.60
❏ 152	Jack Harshman	8.00	3.60
❏ 153	Karl Olson	8.00	3.60
❏ 154	Red Schoendienst	30.00	13.50
❏ 155	Jim Brosnan	15.00	6.75
❏ 156	Gus Triandos	15.00	6.75
❏ 157	Wally Post	15.00	6.75
❏ 158	Curt Simmons	15.00	6.75
❏ 159	Solly Drake	8.00	3.60
❏ 160	Billy Pierce	15.00	6.75
❏ 161	Pittsburgh Pirates	20.00	9.00
	Team Card		
❏ 162	Jack Meyer	8.00	3.60
❏ 163	Sammy White	8.00	3.60
❏ 164	Tommy Carroll	8.00	3.60
❏ 165	Ted Kluszewski	60.00	27.00
❏ 166	Roy Face	15.00	6.75
❏ 167	Vic Power	15.00	6.75
❏ 168	Frank Lary	15.00	6.75
❏ 169	Herb Plews	8.00	3.60
❏ 170	Duke Snider	125.00	55.00
❏ 171	Boston Red Sox	20.00	9.00
	Team Card		
❏ 172	Gene Woodling	15.00	6.75
❏ 173	Roger Craig	15.00	6.75
❏ 174	Willie Jones	8.00	3.60
❏ 175	Don Larsen	30.00	13.50
❏ 176A	Gene Baker ERR	350.00	160.00
	(Misspelled Bakep on card back)		
❏ 176B	Gene Baker COR	15.00	6.75
❏ 177	Eddie Yost	15.00	6.75
❏ 178	Don Bessent	8.00	3.60
❏ 179	Ernie Oravetz	8.00	3.60
❏ 180	Gus Bell	15.00	6.75
❏ 181	Dick Donovan	8.00	3.60
❏ 182	Hobie Landrith	8.00	3.60
❏ 183	Chicago Cubs	20.00	9.00
	Team Card		
❏ 184	Tito Francona	15.00	3.60
❏ 185	Johnny Kucks	15.00	6.75
❏ 186	Jim King	8.00	3.60
❏ 187	Virgil Trucks	15.00	6.75
❏ 188	Felix Mantilla	15.00	6.75
❏ 189	Willard Nixon	8.00	3.60
❏ 190	Randy Jackson	8.00	3.60
❏ 191	Joe Margoneri	8.00	3.60
❏ 192	Jerry Coleman	15.00	6.75
❏ 193	Del Rice	8.00	3.60
❏ 194	Hal Brown	8.00	3.60
❏ 195	Bobby Avila	15.00	6.75
❏ 196	Larry Jackson	15.00	6.75
❏ 197	Hank Sauer	15.00	6.75
❏ 198	Detroit Tigers	20.00	9.00
	Team Card		
❏ 199	Vern Law	15.00	6.75
❏ 200	Gil McDougald	15.00	6.75
❏ 201	Sandy Amoros	15.00	6.75
❏ 202	Dick Gernert	8.00	3.60
❏ 203	Hoyt Wilhelm	30.00	13.50
❏ 204	Kansas City Athletics	20.00	9.00
	Team Card		
❏ 205	Charlie Maxwell	15.00	6.75
❏ 206	Willard Schmidt	8.00	3.60
❏ 207	Gordon(Billy) Hunter	8.00	3.60
❏ 208	Lou Burdette	15.00	6.75
❏ 209	Bob Skinner	15.00	6.75
❏ 210	Roy Campanella	125.00	55.00
❏ 211	Camilo Pascual	15.00	6.75

No.	Player	NRMT	VG-E
212	Rocky Colavito	150.00	70.00
213	Les Moss	8.00	3.60
214	Philadelphia Phillies Team Card	20.00	9.00
215	Enos Slaughter	30.00	13.50
216	Marv Grissom	8.00	3.60
217	Gene Stephens	8.00	3.60
218	Ray Jablonski	8.00	3.60
219	Tom Acker	8.00	3.60
220	Jackie Jensen	15.00	6.75
221	Dixie Howell	8.00	3.60
222	Alex Grammas	8.00	3.60
223	Frank House	8.00	3.60
224	Marv Blaylock	8.00	3.60
225	Harry Simpson	8.00	3.60
226	Preston Ward	8.00	3.60
227	Gerry Staley	8.00	3.60
228	Smoky Burgess UER (Misspelled Smokey on card back)	15.00	6.75
229	George Susce	8.00	3.60
230	George Kell	30.00	13.50
231	Solly Hemus	8.00	3.60
232	Whitey Lockman	15.00	6.75
233	Art Fowler	8.00	3.60
234	Dick Cole	8.00	3.60
235	Tom Poholsky	8.00	3.60
236	Joe Ginsberg	8.00	3.60
237	Foster Castleman	8.00	3.60
238	Eddie Robinson	8.00	3.60
239	Tom Morgan	8.00	3.60
240	Hank Bauer	15.00	6.75
241	Joe Lonnett	8.00	3.60
242	Charlie Neal	15.00	6.75
243	St. Louis Cardinals Team Card	20.00	9.00
244	Billy Loes	15.00	6.75
245	Rip Repulski	8.00	3.60
246	Jose Valdivielso	8.00	3.60
247	Turk Lown	8.00	3.60
248	Jim Finigan	8.00	3.60
249	Dave Pope	8.00	3.60
250	Eddie Mathews	45.00	20.00
251	Baltimore Orioles Team Card	15.00	6.75
252	Carl Erskine	15.00	6.75
253	Gus Zernial	15.00	6.75
254	Ron Negray	8.00	3.60
255	Charlie Silvera	15.00	6.75
256	Ron Kline	8.00	3.60
257	Walt Dropo	8.00	3.60
258	Steve Gromek	8.00	3.60
259	Eddie O'Brien	8.00	3.60
260	Del Ennis	15.00	6.75
261	Bob Chakales	8.00	3.60
262	Bobby Thomson	15.00	6.75
263	George Strickland	8.00	3.60
264	Bob Turley	15.00	6.75
265	Harvey Haddix DP	14.00	6.25
266	Ken Kuhn DP	14.00	6.25
267	Danny Kravitz	20.00	9.00
268	Jack Collum	20.00	9.00
269	Bob Cerv	30.00	13.50
270	Washington Senators Team Card	50.00	22.00
271	Danny O'Connell DP	14.00	6.25
272	Bobby Shantz	30.00	13.50
273	Jim Davis	20.00	9.00
274	Don Hoak	20.00	9.00
275	Cleveland Indians Team Card UER (Text on back credits Tribe with winning AL title in '28. The Yankees won that year.)	50.00	22.00
276	Jim Pyburn	20.00	9.00
277	Johnny Podres DP	45.00	20.00
278	Fred Hatfield DP	14.00	6.25
279	Bob Thurman	20.00	9.00
280	Alex Kellner	20.00	9.00
281	Gail Harris	20.00	9.00
282	Jack Dittmer DP	14.00	6.25
283	Wes Covington DP	14.00	6.25
284	Don Zimmer	40.00	18.00
285	Ned Garver	20.00	9.00
286	Bobby Richardson	125.00	55.00
287	Sam Jones	8.00	3.60
288	Ted Lepcio	20.00	9.00
289	Jim Bolger DP	14.00	6.25
290	Andy Carey DP	30.00	13.50
291	Windy McCall	20.00	9.00
292	Billy Klaus	20.00	9.00
293	Ted Abernathy	20.00	9.00
294	Rocky Bridges DP	14.00	6.25
295	Joe Collins DP	30.00	13.50
296	Johnny Klippstein	20.00	9.00
297	Jack Crimian	20.00	9.00
298	Irv Noren DP	14.00	6.25
299	Chuck Harmon	20.00	9.00
300	Mike Garcia	30.00	13.50
301	Sammy Esposito DP	14.00	6.25
302	Sandy Koufax DP	300.00	135.00
303	Billy Goodman	30.00	13.50
304	Joe Cunningham	30.00	13.50
305	Chico Fernandez	20.00	9.00
306	Darrell Johnson DP	14.00	6.25
307	Jack D. Phillips DP	14.00	6.25
308	Dick Hall	20.00	9.00
309	Jim Busby DP	14.00	6.25
310	Max Surkont DP	14.00	6.25
311	Al Pilarcik DP	14.00	6.25
312	Tony Kubek DP	75.00	34.00
313	Mel Parnell	15.00	6.75
314	Ed Bouchee DP	14.00	6.25
315	Lou Berberet DP	14.00	6.25
316	Billy O'Dell	20.00	9.00
317	New York Giants Team Card	75.00	34.00
318	Mickey McDermott	20.00	9.00
319	Gino Cimoli	20.00	9.00
320	Neil Chrisley	20.00	9.00
321	John(Red) Murff	20.00	9.00
322	Cincinnati Reds Team Card	75.00	34.00
323	Wes Westrum	30.00	13.50
324	Brooklyn Dodgers Team Card	125.00	55.00
325	Frank Bolling	20.00	9.00
326	Pedro Ramos	20.00	9.00
327	Jim Pendleton	20.00	9.00
328	Brooks Robinson	400.00	180.00
329	Chicago White Sox Team Card	50.00	22.00
330	Jim Wilson	20.00	9.00
331	Ray Katt	20.00	9.00
332	Bob Bowman	20.00	9.00
333	Ernie Johnson	20.00	9.00
334	Jerry Schoonmaker	20.00	9.00
335	Granny Hamner	20.00	9.00
336	Haywood Sullivan	30.00	13.50
337	Rene Valdes	20.00	9.00
338	Jim Bunning	125.00	55.00
339	Bob Speake	20.00	9.00
340	Bill Wight	20.00	9.00
341	Don Gross	20.00	9.00
342	Gene Mauch	30.00	13.50
343	Taylor Phillips	20.00	9.00
344	Paul LaPalme	20.00	9.00
345	Paul Smith	20.00	9.00
346	Dick Littlefield	20.00	9.00
347	Hal Naragon	20.00	9.00
348	Jim Hearn	20.00	9.00
349	Nellie King	20.00	9.00
350	Eddie Miksis	20.00	9.00
351	Dave Hillman	20.00	9.00
352	Ellis Kinder	20.00	9.00
353	Cal Neeman	8.00	3.60
354	W. (Rip) Coleman	8.00	3.60
355	Frank Malzone	15.00	6.75
356	Faye Throneberry	8.00	3.60
357	Earl Torgeson	8.00	3.60
358	Jerry Lynch	15.00	6.75
359	Tom Cheney	8.00	3.60
360	Johnny Groth	8.00	3.60
361	Curt Barclay	8.00	3.60
362	Roman Mejias	15.00	6.75
363	Eddie Kasko	8.00	3.60
364	Cal McLish	15.00	6.75
365	Ozzie Virgil	8.00	3.60
366	Ken Lehman	8.00	3.60
367	Ed Fitzgerald	8.00	3.60
368	Bob Purkey	8.00	3.60
369	Milt Graff	8.00	3.60
370	Warren Hacker	8.00	3.60
371	Bob Lennon	8.00	3.60
372	Norm Zauchin	8.00	3.60
373	Pete Whisenant	8.00	3.60
374	Don Cardwell	8.00	3.60
375	Jim Landis	15.00	6.75
376	Don Elston	8.00	3.60
377	Andre Rodgers	8.00	3.60
378	Elmer Singleton	8.00	3.60
379	Don Lee	8.00	3.60
380	Walker Cooper	8.00	3.60
381	Dean Stone	8.00	3.60
382	Jim Brideweser	8.00	3.60
383	Juan Pizarro	8.00	3.60
384	Bobby G. Smith	8.00	3.60
385	Art Houtteman	8.00	3.60
386	Lyle Luttrell	8.00	3.60
387	Jack Sanford	15.00	6.75
388	Pete Daley	8.00	3.60
389	Dave Jolly	8.00	3.60
390	Ron Bertoia	8.00	3.60
391	Ralph Terry	15.00	6.75
392	Chuck Tanner	15.00	6.75
393	Raul Sanchez	8.00	3.60
394	Luis Arroyo	15.00	6.75
395	Bubba Phillips	8.00	3.60
396	Casey Wise	8.00	3.60
397	Roy Smalley	8.00	3.60
398	Al Cicotte	15.00	6.75
399	Billy Consolo	8.00	3.60
400	Dodgers' Sluggers — Carl Furillo, Gil Hodges, Roy Campanella, Duke Snider	250.00	110.00
401	Earl Battey	15.00	6.75
402	Jim Pisoni	8.00	3.60
403	Dick Hyde	8.00	3.60
404	Harry Anderson	8.00	3.60
405	Duke Maas	8.00	3.60
406	Bob Hale	8.00	3.60
407	Yankee Power Hitters — Mickey Mantle, Yogi Berra	500.00	150.00
NNO	Checklist 1/2	250.00	75.00
NNO	Checklist 2/3	400.00	100.00
NNO	Checklist 3/4	750.00	170.00
NNO	Checklist 4/5	900.00	200.00
NNO	Contest Card — Saturday, May 4th, Boston Red Sox vs. Cleveland Indians, Cincinnati Redlegs vs. New York Giants	90.00	22.00
NNO	Contest Card — Saturday, May 25th, Detroit Tigers vs. Kansas City Athletics, Pittsburgh Pirates vs. Philadelphia Phillies	90.00	22.00
NNO	Contest Card — Saturday, June 22nd, Brooklyn Dodgers vs. St. Louis Cardinals, Chicago White Sox vs. New York Yankees	120.00	30.00
NNO	Contest Card — Saturday, July 19th, Milwaukee Braves vs. New York Giants, Baltimore Orioles vs. Kansas City Athletics	120.00	30.00
NNO	Lucky Penny Charm and Key Chain offer card	100.00	45.00

1958 Topps

	NRMT	VG-E
COMPLETE SET (494)	4800.00	2200.00
COMMON CARD (1-110)	12.00	5.50
YELLOW LETTER 1-110	45.00	20.00
YELLOW TEAM 1-110	45.00	20.00
MINOR STARS 1-110	15.00	6.75
SEMISTARS 1-110	20.00	9.00
UNLISTED STARS 1-110	30.00	13.50

Bob Clemente
PITTSBURGH PIRATES

COMMON CARD (111-495)	8.00	3.60
MINOR STARS 111-495	10.00	4.50
SEMISTARS 111-495	15.00	6.75
UNLISTED STARS 111-495	25.00	11.00
NOT ISSUED (145)		

*UNLISTED DODGER/YANKEE: 1.25X VALUE
CARDS PRICED IN NM CONDITION

☐ 1 Ted Williams	425.00	150.00
☐ 2A Bob Lemon	30.00	13.50
☐ 2B Bob Lemon YT	60.00	27.00
☐ 3 Alex Kellner	12.00	5.50
☐ 4 Hank Foiles	12.00	5.50
☐ 5 Willie Mays	225.00	100.00
☐ 6 George Zuverink	12.00	5.50
☐ 7 Dale Long	15.00	6.75
☐ 8A Eddie Kasko	12.00	5.50
☐ 8B Eddie Kasko YL	45.00	20.00
☐ 9 Hank Bauer	15.00	6.75
☐ 10 Lou Burdette	15.00	6.75
☐ 11A Jim Rivera	12.00	5.50
☐ 11B Jim Rivera YT	45.00	20.00
☐ 12 George Crowe	12.00	5.50
☐ 13A Billy Hoeft	12.00	5.50
☐ 13B Billy Hoeft YL	45.00	20.00
☐ 14 Rip Repulski	12.00	5.50
☐ 15 Jim Lemon	12.00	5.50
☐ 16 Charlie Neal	15.00	6.75
☐ 17 Felix Mantilla	12.00	5.50
☐ 18 Frank Sullivan	12.00	5.50
☐ 19 New York Giants Team Card	40.00	8.00
(Checklist on back)		
☐ 20A Gil McDougald	20.00	9.00
☐ 20B Gil McDougald YL	60.00	27.00
☐ 21 Curt Barclay	12.00	5.50
☐ 22 Hal Naragon	12.00	5.50
☐ 23A Bill Tuttle	12.00	5.50
☐ 23B Bill Tuttle YL	45.00	20.00
☐ 24A Hobie Landrith	12.00	5.50
☐ 24B Hobie Landrith YL	45.00	20.00
☐ 25 Don Drysdale	75.00	34.00
☐ 26 Ron Jackson	12.00	5.50
☐ 27 Bud Freeman	12.00	5.50
☐ 28 Jim Busby	12.00	5.50
☐ 29 Ted Lepcio	12.00	5.50
☐ 30A Hank Aaron	200.00	90.00
☐ 30B Hank Aaron YL	450.00	200.00
☐ 31 Tex Clevenger	12.00	5.50
☐ 32A J.W. Porter	12.00	5.50
☐ 32B J.W. Porter YL	45.00	20.00
☐ 33A Cal Neeman	12.00	5.50
☐ 33B Cal Neeman YT	45.00	20.00
☐ 34 Bob Thurman	12.00	5.50
☐ 35A Don Mossi	15.00	6.75
☐ 35B Don Mossi YT	45.00	20.00
☐ 36 Ted Kazanski	12.00	5.50
☐ 37 Mike McCormick UER	15.00	6.75
(Photo actually Ray Monzant)		
☐ 38 Dick Gernert	12.00	5.50
☐ 39 Bob Martyn	12.00	5.50
☐ 40 George Kell	20.00	9.00
☐ 41 Dave Hillman	12.00	5.50
☐ 42 John Roseboro	30.00	13.50
☐ 43 Sal Maglie	15.00	6.75
☐ 44 Washington Senators Team Card	20.00	4.00

(Checklist on back)		
☐ 45 Dick Groat	15.00	6.75
☐ 46A Lou Sleater	12.00	5.50
☐ 46B Lou Sleater YL	45.00	20.00
☐ 47 Roger Maris	400.00	180.00
☐ 48 Chuck Harmon	12.00	5.50
☐ 49 Smoky Burgess	15.00	6.75
☐ 50A Billy Pierce	15.00	6.75
☐ 50B Billy Pierce YT	50.00	22.00
☐ 51 Del Rice	12.00	5.50
☐ 52A Roberto Clemente	300.00	135.00
☐ 52B Roberto Clemente	450.00	200.00
☐ 53A Morrie Martin	12.00	5.50
☐ 53B Morrie Martin YL	45.00	20.00
☐ 54 Norm Siebern	20.00	9.00
☐ 55 Chico Carrasquel	12.00	5.50
☐ 56 Bill Fischer	12.00	5.50
☐ 57A Tim Thompson	12.00	5.50
☐ 57B Tim Thompson YL	45.00	20.00
☐ 58A Art Schult	12.00	5.50
☐ 58B Art Schult YL	45.00	20.00
☐ 59 Dave Sisler	12.00	5.50
☐ 60A Del Ennis	15.00	6.75
☐ 60B Del Ennis YL	50.00	22.00
☐ 61A Darrell Johnson	12.00	5.50
☐ 61B Darrell Johnson YL	45.00	20.00
☐ 62 Joe DeMaestri	12.00	5.50
☐ 63 Joe Nuxhall	15.00	6.75
☐ 64 Joe Lonnett	12.00	5.50
☐ 65A Von McDaniel	12.00	5.50
☐ 65B Von McDaniel YL	45.00	20.00
☐ 66 Lee Walls	12.00	5.50
☐ 67 Joe Ginsberg	12.00	5.50
☐ 68 Daryl Spencer	12.00	5.50
☐ 69 Wally Burnette	12.00	5.50
☐ 70A Al Kaline	100.00	45.00
☐ 70B Al Kaline YL	200.00	90.00
☐ 71 Dodgers Team	60.00	12.00
(Checklist on back)		
☐ 72 Bud Byerly	12.00	5.50
☐ 73 Pete Daley	12.00	5.50
☐ 74 Roy Face	15.00	6.75
☐ 75 Gus Bell	15.00	6.75
☐ 76A Dick Farrell	12.00	5.50
☐ 76B Dick Farrell YT	45.00	20.00
☐ 77A Don Zimmer	15.00	6.75
☐ 77B Don Zimmer YT	50.00	22.00
☐ 78A Ernie Johnson	15.00	6.75
☐ 78B Ernie Johnson YL	50.00	22.00
☐ 79A Dick Williams	15.00	6.75
☐ 79B Dick Williams YT	50.00	22.00
☐ 80 Dick Drott	12.00	5.50
☐ 81A Steve Boros	12.00	5.50
☐ 81B Steve Boros YT	45.00	20.00
☐ 82 Ron Kline	12.00	5.50
☐ 83 Bob Hazle	12.00	5.50
☐ 84 Billy O'Dell	12.00	5.50
☐ 85A Luis Aparicio	30.00	13.50
☐ 85B Luis Aparicio YT	70.00	32.00
☐ 86 Valmy Thomas	12.00	5.50
☐ 87 Johnny Kucks	12.00	5.50
☐ 88 Duke Snider	75.00	34.00
☐ 89 Billy Klaus	12.00	5.50
☐ 90 Robin Roberts	30.00	13.50
☐ 91 Chuck Tanner	15.00	6.75
☐ 92A Clint Courtney	12.00	5.50
☐ 92B Clint Courtney YL	45.00	20.00
☐ 93 Sandy Amoros	15.00	6.75
☐ 94 Bob Skinner	15.00	6.75
☐ 95 Frank Bolling	12.00	5.50
☐ 96 Joe Durham	12.00	5.50
☐ 97A Larry Jackson	12.00	5.50
☐ 97B Larry Jackson YL	45.00	20.00
☐ 98A Billy Hunter	12.00	5.50
☐ 98B Billy Hunter YL	45.00	20.00
☐ 99 Bobby Adams	12.00	5.50
☐ 100A Early Wynn	40.00	18.00
☐ 100B Early Wynn YT	60.00	27.00
☐ 101A Bobby Richardson	30.00	13.50
☐ 101B Bobby Richardson YL	60.00	27.00
☐ 102 George Strickland	12.00	5.50
☐ 103 Jerry Lynch	15.00	6.75
☐ 104 Jim Pendleton	12.00	5.50
☐ 105 Billy Gardner	12.00	5.50
☐ 106 Dick Schofield	15.00	6.75
☐ 107 Ossie Virgil	12.00	5.50

☐ 108A Jim Landis	12.00	5.50
☐ 108B Jim Landis YT	45.00	20.00
☐ 109 Herb Plews	12.00	5.50
☐ 110 Johnny Logan	15.00	6.75
☐ 111 Stu Miller	10.00	4.50
☐ 112 Gus Zernial	10.00	4.50
☐ 113 Jerry Walker	8.00	3.60
☐ 114 Irv Noren	8.00	3.60
☐ 115 Jim Bunning	25.00	11.00
☐ 116 Dave Philley	8.00	3.60
☐ 117 Frank Torre	10.00	4.50
☐ 118 Harvey Haddix	10.00	4.50
☐ 119 Harry Chiti	8.00	3.60
☐ 120 Johnny Podres	10.00	4.50
☐ 121 Eddie Miksis	8.00	3.60
☐ 122 Walt Moryn	8.00	3.60
☐ 123 Dick Tomanek	8.00	3.60
☐ 124 Bobby Usher	8.00	3.60
☐ 125 Alvin Dark	10.00	4.50
☐ 126 Stan Palys	8.00	3.60
☐ 127 Tom Sturdivant	10.00	4.50
☐ 128 Willie Kirkland	8.00	3.60
☐ 129 Jim Derrington	8.00	3.60
☐ 130 Jackie Jensen	10.00	4.50
☐ 131 Bob Henrich	8.00	3.60
☐ 132 Vern Law	10.00	4.50
☐ 133 Russ Nixon	8.00	3.60
☐ 134 Philadelphia Phillies	15.00	3.00
Team Card		
(Checklist on back)		
☐ 135 Mike(Moe) Drabowsky	10.00	4.50
☐ 136 Jim Finigan	8.00	3.60
☐ 137 Russ Kemmerer	8.00	3.60
☐ 138 Earl Torgeson	8.00	3.60
☐ 139 George Brunet	8.00	3.60
☐ 140 Wes Covington	10.00	4.50
☐ 141 Ken Lehman	8.00	3.60
☐ 142 Enos Slaughter	25.00	11.00
☐ 143 Billy Muffett	8.00	3.60
☐ 144 Bobby Morgan	8.00	3.60
☐ 145 Never issued		
☐ 146 Dick Gray		3.60
☐ 147 Don McMahon	8.00	3.60
☐ 148 Billy Consolo	8.00	3.60
☐ 149 Tom Acker	8.00	3.60
☐ 150 Mickey Mantle	800.00	350.00
☐ 151 Buddy Pritchard	8.00	3.60
☐ 152 Johnny Antonelli	10.00	4.50
☐ 153 Les Moss	8.00	3.60
☐ 154 Harry Byrd	8.00	3.60
☐ 155 Hector Lopez	10.00	4.50
☐ 156 Dick Hyde	8.00	3.60
☐ 157 Dee Fondy	8.00	3.60
☐ 158 Cleveland Indians	15.00	3.00
Team Card		
(Checklist on back)		
☐ 159 Taylor Phillips	8.00	3.60
☐ 160 Don Hoak	10.00	4.50
☐ 161 Don Larsen	15.00	6.75
☐ 162 Gil Hodges	40.00	18.00
☐ 163 Jim Wilson	8.00	3.60
☐ 164 Bob Taylor	8.00	3.60
☐ 165 Bob Nieman	8.00	3.60
☐ 166 Danny O'Connell	8.00	3.60
☐ 167 Frank Baumann	8.00	3.60
☐ 168 Joe Cunningham	8.00	3.60
☐ 169 Ralph Terry	10.00	4.50
☐ 170 Vic Wertz	10.00	4.50
☐ 171 Harry Anderson	8.00	3.60
☐ 172 Don Gross	8.00	3.60
☐ 173 Eddie Yost	8.00	3.60
☐ 174 Athletics Team	15.00	3.00
(Checklist on back)		
☐ 175 Marv Throneberry	15.00	6.75
☐ 176 Bob Buhl	10.00	4.50
☐ 177 Al Smith	8.00	3.60
☐ 178 Ted Kluszewski	25.00	11.00
☐ 179 Willie Miranda	8.00	3.60
☐ 180 Lindy McDaniel	10.00	4.50
☐ 181 Willie Jones	8.00	3.60
☐ 182 Joe Caffie	8.00	3.60
☐ 183 Dave Jolly	8.00	3.60
☐ 184 Elvin Tappe	8.00	3.60
☐ 185 Ray Boone	10.00	4.50
☐ 186 Jack Meyer	8.00	3.60
☐ 187 Sandy Koufax	225.00	100.00

188	Milt Bolling UER (Photo actually Lou Berberet)	8.00	3.60
189	George Susce	8.00	3.60
190	Red Schoendienst	25.00	11.00
191	Art Ceccarelli	8.00	3.60
192	Milt Graff	8.00	3.60
193	Jerry Lumpe	8.00	3.60
194	Roger Craig	10.00	4.50
195	Whitey Lockman	10.00	4.50
196	Mike Garcia	10.00	4.50
197	Haywood Sullivan	10.00	4.50
198	Bill Virdon	10.00	4.50
199	Don Blasingame	8.00	3.60
200	Bob Keegan	8.00	3.60
201	Jim Bolger	8.00	3.60
202	Woody Held	8.00	3.60
203	Al Walker	8.00	3.60
204	Leo Kiely	8.00	3.60
205	Johnny Temple	10.00	4.50
206	Bob Shaw	8.00	3.60
207	Solly Hemus	8.00	3.60
208	Cal McLish	8.00	3.60
209	Bob Anderson	8.00	3.60
210	Wally Moon	10.00	4.50
211	Pete Burnside	8.00	3.60
212	Bubba Phillips	8.00	3.60
213	Red Wilson	8.00	3.60
214	Willard Schmidt	8.00	3.60
215	Jim Gilliam	15.00	6.75
216	St. Louis Cardinals Team Card (Checklist on back)	15.00	3.00
217	Jack Harshman	8.00	3.60
218	Dick Rand	8.00	3.60
219	Camilo Pascual	10.00	4.50
220	Tom Brewer	8.00	3.60
221	Jerry Kindall	8.00	3.60
222	Bud Daley	8.00	3.60
223	Andy Pafko	10.00	4.50
224	Bob Grim	10.00	4.50
225	Billy Goodman	10.00	4.50
226	Bob Smith	8.00	3.60
227	Gene Stephens	8.00	3.60
228	Duke Maas	8.00	3.60
229	Frank Zupo	8.00	3.60
230	Richie Ashburn	30.00	13.50
231	Lloyd Merritt	8.00	3.60
232	Reno Bertoia	8.00	3.60
233	Mickey Vernon	10.00	4.50
234	Carl Sawatski	8.00	3.60
235	Tom Gorman	8.00	3.60
236	Ed Fitzgerald	8.00	3.60
237	Bill Wight	8.00	3.60
238	Bill Mazeroski	25.00	11.00
239	Chuck Stobbs	8.00	3.60
240	Bill Skowron	15.00	6.75
241	Dick Littlefield	8.00	3.60
242	Johnny Klippstein	8.00	3.60
243	Larry Raines	8.00	3.60
244	Don Demeter	8.00	3.60
245	Frank Lary	10.00	4.50
246	New York Yankees Team Card (Checklist on back)	100.00	20.00
247	Casey Wise	8.00	3.60
248	Herman Wehmeier	8.00	3.60
249	Ray Moore	8.00	3.60
250	Roy Sievers	10.00	4.50
251	Warren Hacker	8.00	3.60
252	Bob Trowbridge	8.00	3.60
253	Don Mueller	10.00	4.50
254	Alex Grammas	8.00	3.60
255	Bob Turley	10.00	4.50
256	Chicago White Sox Team Card (Checklist on back)	15.00	3.00
257	Hal Smith	8.00	3.60
258	Carl Erskine	15.00	6.75
259	Al Pilarcik	8.00	3.60
260	Frank Malzone	10.00	4.50
261	Turk Lown	8.00	3.60
262	Johnny Groth	8.00	3.60
263	Eddie Bressoud	10.00	4.50
264	Jack Sanford	10.00	4.50
265	Pete Runnels	10.00	4.50
266	Connie Johnson	8.00	3.60
267	Sherm Lollar	10.00	4.50
268	Granny Hamner	8.00	3.60
269	Paul Smith	8.00	3.60
270	Warren Spahn	60.00	27.00
271	Billy Martin	30.00	13.50
272	Ray Crone	8.00	3.60
273	Hal Smith	8.00	3.60
274	Rocky Bridges	8.00	3.60
275	Elston Howard	15.00	6.75
276	Bobby Avila	8.00	3.60
277	Virgil Trucks	10.00	4.50
278	Mack Burk	8.00	3.60
279	Bob Boyd	8.00	3.60
280	Jim Piersall	10.00	4.50
281	Sammy Taylor	8.00	3.60
282	Paul Foytack	8.00	3.60
283	Ray Shearer	8.00	3.60
284	Ray Katt	8.00	3.60
285	Frank Robinson	100.00	45.00
286	Gino Cimoli	8.00	3.60
287	Sam Jones	10.00	4.50
288	Harmon Killebrew	85.00	38.00
289	Lou Burdette Bobby Shantz	10.00	4.50
290	Dick Donovan	8.00	3.60
291	Don Landrum	8.00	3.60
292	Ned Garver	8.00	3.60
293	Gene Freese	8.00	3.60
294	Hal Jeffcoat	8.00	3.60
295	Minnie Minoso	15.00	6.75
296	Ryne Duren	15.00	6.75
297	Don Buddin	8.00	3.60
298	Jim Hearn	8.00	3.60
299	Harry Simpson	8.00	3.60
300	Will Harridge PRES Warren Giles	15.00	6.75
301	Randy Jackson	8.00	3.60
302	Mike Baxes	8.00	3.60
303	Neil Chrisley	8.00	3.60
304	Harvey Kuenn Al Kaline	15.00	6.75
305	Clem Labine	10.00	4.50
306	Whammy Douglas	8.00	3.60
307	Brooks Robinson	100.00	45.00
308	Paul Giel	10.00	4.50
309	Gail Harris	8.00	3.60
310	Ernie Banks	100.00	45.00
311	Bob Purkey	8.00	3.60
312	Boston Red Sox Team Card (Checklist on back)	15.00	3.00
313	Bob Rush	8.00	3.60
314	Duke Snider Walt Alston MG	30.00	13.50
315	Bob Friend	10.00	4.50
316	Tito Francona	10.00	4.50
317	Albie Pearson	10.00	4.50
318	Frank House	8.00	3.60
319	Lou Skizas	8.00	3.60
320	Whitey Ford	60.00	27.00
321	Sluggers Supreme Ted Kluszewski Ted Williams	70.00	32.00
322	Harding Peterson	10.00	4.50
323	Elmer Valo	8.00	3.60
324	Hoyt Wilhelm	25.00	11.00
325	Joe Adcock	10.00	4.50
326	Bob Miller	8.00	3.60
327	Chicago Cubs Team Card (Checklist on back)	15.00	3.00
328	Ike Delock	8.00	3.60
329	Bob Cerv	10.00	4.50
330	Ed Bailey	10.00	4.50
331	Pedro Ramos	8.00	3.60
332	Jim King	8.00	3.60
333	Andy Carey	10.00	4.50
334	Bob Friend Billy Pierce	10.00	4.50
335	Ruben Gomez	8.00	3.60
336	Bert Hamric	8.00	3.60
337	Hank Aguirre	8.00	3.60
338	Walt Dropo	10.00	4.50
339	Fred Hatfield	8.00	3.60
340	Don Newcombe	15.00	6.75
341	Pittsburgh Pirates Team Card (Checklist on back)	15.00	3.00
342	Jim Brosnan	10.00	4.50
343	Orlando Cepeda	90.00	40.00
344	Bob Porterfield	8.00	3.60
345	Jim Hegan	10.00	4.50
346	Steve Bilko	8.00	3.60
347	Don Rudolph	8.00	3.60
348	Chico Fernandez	8.00	3.60
349	Murry Dickson	8.00	3.60
350	Ken Boyer	15.00	6.75
351	Braves Fence Busters Del Crandall Eddie Mathews Hank Aaron Joe Adcock	40.00	18.00
352	Herb Score	15.00	6.75
353	Stan Lopata	8.00	3.60
354	Art Ditmar	10.00	4.50
355	Bill Bruton	10.00	4.50
356	Bob Malkmus	8.00	3.60
357	Danny McDevitt	8.00	3.60
358	Gene Baker	8.00	3.60
359	Billy Loes	10.00	4.50
360	Roy McMillan	10.00	4.50
361	Mike Fornieles	8.00	3.60
362	Ray Jablonski	8.00	3.60
363	Don Elston	8.00	3.60
364	Earl Battey	8.00	3.60
365	Tom Morgan	8.00	3.60
366	Gene Green	8.00	3.60
367	Jack Urban	8.00	3.60
368	Rocky Colavito	50.00	22.00
369	Ralph Lumenti	8.00	3.60
370	Yogi Berra	100.00	45.00
371	Marty Keough	8.00	3.60
372	Don Cardwell	8.00	3.60
373	Joe Pignatano	8.00	3.60
374	Brooks Lawrence	8.00	3.60
375	Pee Wee Reese	60.00	27.00
376	Charley Rabe	8.00	3.60
377A	Milwaukee Braves Team Card (Alphabetical)	15.00	6.75
377B	Milwaukee Team numerical checklist	100.00	20.00
378	Hank Sauer	10.00	4.50
379	Ray Herbert	8.00	3.60
380	Charlie Maxwell	10.00	4.50
381	Hal Brown	8.00	3.60
382	Al Cicotte	8.00	3.60
383	Lou Berberet	8.00	3.60
384	John Goryl	8.00	3.60
385	Wilmer Mizell	10.00	4.50
386	Birdie's Sluggers Ed Bailey Birdie Tebbetts MG Frank Robinson	15.00	6.75
387	Wally Post	10.00	4.50
388	Billy Moran	8.00	3.60
389	Bill Taylor	8.00	3.60
390	Del Crandall	10.00	4.50
391	Dave Melton	8.00	3.60
392	Bennie Daniels	8.00	3.60
393	Tony Kubek	20.00	9.00
394	Jim Grant	8.00	3.60
395	Willard Nixon	8.00	3.60
396	Dutch Dotterer	8.00	3.60
397A	Detroit Tigers (Alphabetical)	15.00	6.75
397B	Detroit Team numerical checklist	100.00	20.00
398	Gene Woodling	10.00	4.50
399	Marv Grissom	8.00	3.60
400	Nellie Fox	30.00	13.50
401	Don Bessent	8.00	3.60
402	Bobby Gene Smith	8.00	3.60
403	Steve Korcheck	8.00	3.60
404	Curt Simmons	10.00	4.50
405	Ken Aspromonte	8.00	3.60
406	Vic Power	10.00	4.50
407	Carlton Willey	8.00	3.60
408A	Baltimore Orioles Team Card	15.00	6.75

(Alphabetical)

	NRMT	VG-E
408B Baltimore Team ... 100.00		20.00
numerical checklist		
409 Frank Thomas	10.00	4.50
410 Murray Wall	8.00	3.60
411 Tony Taylor	10.00	4.50
412 Gerry Staley	8.00	3.60
413 Jim Davenport	8.00	3.60
414 Sammy White	8.00	3.60
415 Bob Bowman	8.00	3.60
416 Foster Castleman	8.00	3.60
417 Carl Furillo	15.00	6.75
418 Mickey Mantle	275.00	125.00
Hank Aaron		
419 Bobby Shantz	10.00	4.50
420 Vada Pinson	40.00	18.00
421 Dixie Howell	8.00	3.60
422 Norm Zauchin	8.00	3.60
423 Phil Clark	8.00	3.60
424 Larry Doby	15.00	6.75
425 Sammy Esposito	8.00	3.60
426 Johnny O'Brien	10.00	4.50
427 Al Worthington	8.00	3.60
428A Cincinnati Reds	15.00	6.75
Team Card		
(Alphabetical)		
428B Cincinnati Team ... 100.00		20.00
numerical checklist		
429 Gus Triandos	10.00	4.50
430 Bobby Thomson	10.00	4.50
431 Gene Conley	10.00	4.50
432 John Powers	8.00	3.60
433A Pancho Herrer ERR	650.00	300.00
433B Pancho Herrera COR	10.00	4.50
434 Harvey Kuenn	10.00	4.50
435 Ed Roebuck	10.00	4.50
436 Willie Mays	75.00	34.00
Duke Snider		
437 Bob Speake	8.00	3.60
438 Whitey Herzog	10.00	4.50
439 Ray Narleski	8.00	3.60
440 Eddie Mathews	40.00	18.00
441 Jim Marshall	8.00	3.60
442 Phil Paine	8.00	3.60
443 Billy Harrell SP	20.00	9.00
444 Danny Kravitz	8.00	3.60
445 Bob Smith	8.00	3.60
446 Carroll Hardy SP	20.00	9.00
447 Ray Monzant	8.00	3.60
448 Charlie Lau	10.00	4.50
449 Gene Fodge	8.00	3.60
450 Preston Ward SP	20.00	9.00
451 Joe Taylor	8.00	3.60
452 Roman Mejias	8.00	3.60
453 Tom Qualters	8.00	3.60
454 Harry Hanebrink	8.00	3.60
455 Hal Griggs	8.00	3.60
456 Dick Brown	8.00	3.60
457 Milt Pappas	10.00	4.50
458 Julio Becquer	8.00	3.60
459 Ron Blackburn	8.00	3.60
460 Chuck Essegian	8.00	3.60
461 Ed Mayer	8.00	3.60
462 Gary Geiger SP	20.00	9.00
463 Vito Valentinetti	8.00	3.60
464 Curt Flood	30.00	13.50
465 Arnie Portocarrero	8.00	3.60
466 Pete Whisenant	8.00	3.60
467 Glen Hobbie	8.00	3.60
468 Bob Schmidt	8.00	3.60
469 Don Ferrarese	8.00	3.60
470 R.C. Stevens	8.00	3.60
471 Lenny Green	8.00	3.60
472 Joey Jay	10.00	4.50
473 Bill Renna	8.00	3.60
474 Roman Semproch	8.00	3.60
475 Fred Haney AS MG and	25.00	7.50
Casey Stengel AS MG		
(Checklist back)		
476 Stan Musial AS TP	40.00	18.00
477 Bill Skowron AS	8.00	3.60
478 Johnny Temple AS	8.00	3.60
479 Nellie Fox AS	15.00	6.75
480 Eddie Mathews AS	25.00	11.00
481 Frank Malzone AS	8.00	3.60
482 Ernie Banks AS	35.00	16.00
483 Luis Aparicio AS	15.00	6.75
484 Frank Robinson AS	35.00	16.00
485 Ted Williams AS	125.00	55.00
486 Willie Mays AS	50.00	22.00
487 Mickey Mantle AS TP	175.00	80.00
488 Hank Aaron AS	50.00	22.00
489 Jackie Jensen AS	10.00	4.50
490 Ed Bailey AS	8.00	3.60
491 Sherm Lollar AS	8.00	3.60
492 Bob Friend AS	8.00	3.60
493 Bob Turley AS	10.00	4.50
494 Warren Spahn AS	25.00	11.00
495 Herb Score AS	20.00	4.00
xx Contest Cards	70.00	32.00

1959 Topps

yogi berra
NEW YORK YANKEES CATCHER

	NRMT	VG-E
COMPLETE SET (572)	4500.00	2000.00
COMMON CARD (1-110)	6.00	2.70
COMMON CARD (111-506)	4.00	1.80
MINOR STARS 1-506	8.00	3.60
SEMISTARS 1-506	12.00	5.50
UNLISTED STARS 1-506	20.00	9.00
COMMON CARD (507-572)	16.00	7.25
MINOR STARS 507-572	20.00	9.00
SEMISTARS 507-572	30.00	13.50

*UNLISTED DODGER/YANKEE: 1.25X VALUE
CARDS PRICED IN NM CONDITION

	NRMT	VG-E
1 Ford Frick COMM	50.00	13.50
2 Eddie Yost	8.00	3.60
3 Don McMahon	8.00	3.60
4 Albie Pearson	8.00	3.60
5 Dick Donovan	6.00	2.70
6 Alex Grammas	6.00	2.70
7 Al Pilarcik	6.00	2.70
8 Phillies Team	75.00	15.00
(Checklist on back)		
9 Paul Giel	8.00	3.60
10 Mickey Mantle	600.00	275.00
11 Billy Hunter	8.00	3.60
12 Vern Law	8.00	3.60
13 Dick Gernert	6.00	2.70
14 Pete Whisenant	6.00	2.70
15 Dick Drott	6.00	2.70
16 Joe Pignatano	6.00	2.70
17 Frank Thomas	8.00	3.60
Danny Murtaugh MG		
Ted Kluszewski		
18 Jack Urban	6.00	2.70
19 Eddie Bressoud	6.00	2.70
20 Duke Snider	50.00	22.00
21 Connie Johnson	6.00	2.70
22 Al Smith	8.00	3.60
23 Murry Dickson	8.00	3.60
24 Red Wilson	6.00	2.70
25 Don Hoak	8.00	3.60
26 Chuck Stobbs	6.00	2.70
27 Andy Pafko	8.00	3.60
28 Al Worthington	6.00	2.70
29 Jim Bolger	6.00	2.70
30 Nellie Fox	30.00	13.50
31 Ken Lehman	6.00	2.70
32 Don Buddin	6.00	2.70
33 Ed Fitzgerald	6.00	2.70
34 Al Kaline	20.00	9.00
Charley Maxwell		
35 Ted Kluszewski	12.00	5.50
36 Hank Aguirre	6.00	2.70
37 Gene Green	6.00	2.70
38 Morrie Martin	6.00	2.70
39 Ed Bouchee	6.00	2.70
40A Warren Spahn ERR ..	75.00	34.00
(Born 1931)		
40B Warren Spahn ERR	100.00	45.00
(Born 1931, but three		
is partially obscured)		
40C Warren Spahn COR ..	50.00	22.00
(Born 1921)		
41 Bob Martyn	6.00	2.70
42 Murray Wall	6.00	2.70
43 Steve Bilko	6.00	2.70
44 Vito Valentinetti	6.00	2.70
45 Andy Carey	6.00	3.60
46 Bill R. Henry	6.00	2.70
47 Jim Finigan	6.00	2.70
48 Orioles Team	24.00	4.80
(Checklist on back)		
49 Bill Hall	6.00	2.70
50 Willie Mays	125.00	55.00
51 Rip Coleman	6.00	2.70
52 Coot Veal	6.00	2.70
53 Stan Williams	8.00	3.60
54 Mel Roach	6.00	2.70
55 Tom Brewer	6.00	2.70
56 Carl Sawatski	6.00	2.70
57 Al Cicotte	6.00	2.70
58 Eddie Miksis	6.00	2.70
59 Irv Noren	8.00	3.60
60 Bob Turley	8.00	3.60
61 Dick Brown	6.00	2.70
62 Tony Taylor	8.00	3.60
63 Jim Hearn	6.00	2.70
64 Joe DeMaestri	6.00	2.70
65 Frank Torre	8.00	3.60
66 Joe Ginsberg	6.00	2.70
67 Brooks Lawrence	6.00	2.70
68 Dick Schofield	8.00	3.60
69 Giants Team	24.00	4.80
(Checklist on back)		
70 Harvey Kuenn	8.00	3.60
71 Don Bessent	6.00	2.70
72 Bill Renna	6.00	2.70
73 Ron Jackson	6.00	2.70
74 Jim Lemon	8.00	3.60
Cookie Lavagetto MG		
Roy Sievers		
75 Sam Jones	8.00	3.60
76 Bobby Richardson	20.00	9.00
77 John Goryl	6.00	2.70
78 Pedro Ramos	6.00	2.70
79 Harry Chiti	6.00	2.70
80 Minnie Minoso	12.00	5.50
81 Hal Jeffcoat	6.00	2.70
82 Bob Boyd	6.00	2.70
83 Bob Smith	6.00	2.70
84 Reno Bertoia	6.00	2.70
85 Harry Anderson	6.00	2.70
86 Bob Keegan	6.00	3.60
87 Danny O'Connell	6.00	2.70
88 Herb Score	12.00	5.50
89 Billy Gardner	6.00	2.70
90 Bill Skowron	12.00	5.50
91 Herb Moford	6.00	2.70
92 Dave Philley	6.00	2.70
93 Julio Becquer	6.00	2.70
94 White Sox Team	40.00	8.00
(Checklist on back)		
95 Carl Willey	6.00	2.70
96 Lou Berberet	6.00	2.70
97 Jerry Lynch	8.00	3.60
98 Arnie Portocarrero	6.00	2.70
99 Ted Kazanski	6.00	2.70
100 Bob Cerv	8.00	3.60
101 Alex Kellner	6.00	2.70
102 Felipe Alou	30.00	13.50
103 Billy Goodman	8.00	3.60
104 Del Rice	6.00	2.70
105 Lee Walls	6.00	2.70
106 Hal Woodeshick	6.00	2.70
107 Norm Larker	8.00	3.60
108 Zack Monroe	6.00	3.60
109 Bob Schmidt	6.00	2.70

❑ 110 George Witt	8.00	3.60
❑ 111 Redlegs Team	15.00	3.00
(Checklist on back)		
❑ 112 Billy Consolo	4.00	1.80
❑ 113 Taylor Phillips	4.00	1.80
❑ 114 Earl Battey	8.00	3.60
❑ 115 Mickey Vernon	8.00	3.60
❑ 116 Bob Allison RP	12.00	3.60
❑ 117 John Blanchard RP	8.00	3.60
❑ 118 John Buzhardt RP	5.00	2.20
❑ 119 John Callison RP	12.00	5.50
❑ 120 Chuck Coles RP	5.00	2.20
❑ 121 Bob Conley RP	5.00	2.20
❑ 122 Bennie Daniels RP	5.00	2.20
❑ 123 Don Dillard RP	5.00	2.20
❑ 124 Dan Dobbek RP	5.00	2.20
❑ 125 Ron Fairly RP	12.00	5.50
❑ 126 Ed Haas RP	5.00	2.20
❑ 127 Kent Hadley RP	5.00	2.20
❑ 128 Bob Hartman RP	5.00	2.20
❑ 129 Frank Herrera RP	5.00	2.20
❑ 130 Lou Jackson RP	5.00	2.20
❑ 131 Deron Johnson RP	12.00	5.50
❑ 132 Don Lee RP	5.00	2.20
❑ 133 Bob Lillis RP	5.00	2.20
❑ 134 Jim McDaniel RP	5.00	2.20
❑ 135 Gene Oliver RP	5.00	2.20
❑ 136 Jim O'Toole RP	5.00	2.20
❑ 137 Dick Ricketts RP	5.00	2.20
❑ 138 John Romano RP	5.00	2.20
❑ 139 Ed Sadowski RP	5.00	2.20
❑ 140 Charlie Secrest RP	5.00	2.20
❑ 141 Joe Shipley RP	5.00	2.20
❑ 142 Dick Stigman RP	5.00	2.20
❑ 143 Willie Tasby RP	5.00	2.20
❑ 144 Jerry Walker RP	5.00	2.20
❑ 145 Dom Zanni RP	5.00	2.20
❑ 146 Jerry Zimmerman RP	5.00	2.20
❑ 147 Cubs Clubbers	30.00	13.50
Dale Long		
Ernie Banks		
Walt Moryn		
❑ 148 Mike McCormick	8.00	3.60
❑ 149 Jim Bunning	20.00	9.00
❑ 150 Stan Musial	125.00	55.00
❑ 151 Bob Malkmus	4.00	1.80
❑ 152 Johnny Klippstein	4.00	1.80
❑ 153 Jim Marshall	4.00	1.80
❑ 154 Ray Herbert	4.00	1.80
❑ 155 Enos Slaughter	20.00	9.00
❑ 156 Ace Hurlers	12.00	5.50
Billy Pierce		
Robin Roberts		
❑ 157 Felix Mantilla	4.00	1.80
❑ 158 Walt Dropo	4.00	1.80
❑ 159 Bob Shaw	8.00	3.60
❑ 160 Dick Groat	8.00	3.60
❑ 161 Frank Baumann	4.00	1.80
❑ 162 Bobby G. Smith	4.00	1.80
❑ 163 Sandy Koufax	150.00	70.00
❑ 164 Johnny Groth	4.00	1.80
❑ 165 Bill Bruton	4.00	1.80
❑ 166 Destruction Crew	30.00	13.50
Minnie Minoso		
Rocky Colavito		
(Misspelled Colovito		
on card back)		
Larry Doby		
❑ 167 Duke Maas	4.00	1.80
❑ 168 Carroll Hardy	4.00	1.80
❑ 169 Ted Abernathy	4.00	1.80
❑ 170 Gene Woodling	8.00	3.60
❑ 171 Willard Schmidt	4.00	1.80
❑ 172 Athletics Team	15.00	3.00
(Checklist on back)		
❑ 173 Bill Monbouquette	8.00	3.60
❑ 174 Jim Pendleton	4.00	1.80
❑ 175 Dick Farrell	8.00	3.60
❑ 176 Preston Ward	4.00	1.80
❑ 177 John Briggs	4.00	1.80
❑ 178 Ruben Amaro	8.00	3.60
❑ 179 Don Rudolph	4.00	1.80
❑ 180 Yogi Berra	75.00	34.00
❑ 181 Bob Porterfield	4.00	1.80
❑ 182 Milt Graff	4.00	1.80
❑ 183 Stu Miller	8.00	3.60

❑ 184 Harvey Haddix	8.00	3.60
❑ 185 Jim Busby	4.00	1.80
❑ 186 Mudcat Grant	8.00	3.60
❑ 187 Bubba Phillips	8.00	3.60
❑ 188 Juan Pizarro	4.00	1.80
❑ 189 Neil Chrisley	4.00	1.80
❑ 190 Bill Virdon	8.00	3.60
❑ 191 Russ Kemmerer	4.00	1.80
❑ 192 Charlie Beamon	4.00	1.80
❑ 193 Sammy Taylor	4.00	1.80
❑ 194 Jim Brosnan	8.00	3.60
❑ 195 Rip Repulski	4.00	1.80
❑ 196 Billy Moran	4.00	1.80
❑ 197 Ray Semproch	4.00	1.80
❑ 198 Jim Davenport	8.00	3.60
❑ 199 Leo Kiely	4.00	1.80
❑ 200 Warren Giles NL PRES	8.00	3.60
❑ 201 Tom Acker	4.00	1.80
❑ 202 Roger Maris	125.00	55.00
❑ 203 Ossie Virgil	4.00	1.80
❑ 204 Casey Wise	4.00	1.80
❑ 205 Don Larsen	8.00	3.60
❑ 206 Carl Furillo	8.00	3.60
❑ 207 George Strickland	4.00	1.80
❑ 208 Willie Jones	4.00	1.80
❑ 209 Lenny Green	4.00	1.80
❑ 210 Ed Bailey	4.00	1.80
❑ 211 Bob Blaylock	4.00	1.80
❑ 212 Hank Aaron	75.00	34.00
Eddie Mathews		
❑ 213 Jim Rivera	8.00	3.60
❑ 214 Marcelino Solis	4.00	1.80
❑ 215 Jim Lemon	8.00	3.60
❑ 216 Andre Rodgers	4.00	1.80
❑ 217 Carl Erskine	8.00	3.60
❑ 218 Roman Mejias	4.00	1.80
❑ 219 George Zuverink	4.00	1.80
❑ 220 Frank Malzone	8.00	3.60
❑ 221 Bob Bowman	4.00	1.80
❑ 222 Bobby Shantz	4.00	1.80
❑ 223 Cardinals Team	15.00	3.00
(Checklist on back)		
❑ 224 Claude Osteen	8.00	3.60
❑ 225 Johnny Logan	8.00	3.60
❑ 226 Art Ceccarelli	4.00	1.80
❑ 227 Hal W. Smith	4.00	1.80
❑ 228 Don Gross	4.00	1.80
❑ 229 Vic Power	8.00	3.60
❑ 230 Bill Fischer	4.00	1.80
❑ 231 Ellis Burton	4.00	1.80
❑ 232 Eddie Kasko	4.00	1.80
❑ 233 Paul Foytack	4.00	1.80
❑ 234 Chuck Tanner	8.00	3.60
❑ 235 Valmy Thomas	4.00	1.80
❑ 236 Ted Bowsfield	4.00	1.80
❑ 237 Run Preventers	12.00	5.50
Gil McDougald		
Bob Turley		
Bobby Richardson		
❑ 238 Gene Baker	4.00	1.80
❑ 239 Bob Trowbridge	4.00	1.80
❑ 240 Hank Bauer	8.00	3.60
❑ 241 Billy Muffett	4.00	1.80
❑ 242 Ron Samford	4.00	1.80
❑ 243 Marv Grissom	4.00	1.80
❑ 244 Ted Gray	4.00	1.80
❑ 245 Ned Garver	4.00	1.80
❑ 246 J.W. Porter	4.00	1.80
❑ 247 Don Ferrarese	4.00	1.80
❑ 248 Red Sox Team	15.00	3.00
(Checklist on back)		
❑ 249 Bobby Adams	4.00	1.80
❑ 250 Billy O'Dell	4.00	1.80
❑ 251 Clete Boyer	8.00	3.60
❑ 252 Ray Boone	8.00	3.60
❑ 253 Seth Morehead	4.00	1.80
❑ 254 Zeke Bella	4.00	1.80
❑ 255 Del Ennis	8.00	3.60
❑ 256 Jerry Davie	4.00	1.80
❑ 257 Leon Wagner	8.00	3.60
❑ 258 Fred Kipp	4.00	1.80
❑ 259 Jim Pisoni	4.00	1.80
❑ 260 Early Wynn UER	20.00	9.00
(1957 Cleevland)		
❑ 261 Gene Stephens	4.00	1.80
❑ 262 Johnny Podres	12.00	5.50

Clem Labine		
Don Drysdale		
❑ 263 Bud Daley	4.00	1.80
❑ 264 Chico Carrasquel	4.00	1.80
❑ 265 Ron Kline	4.00	1.80
❑ 266 Woody Held	4.00	1.80
❑ 267 John Romonosky	4.00	1.80
❑ 268 Tito Francona	8.00	3.60
❑ 269 Jack Meyer	4.00	1.80
❑ 270 Gil Hodges	25.00	11.00
❑ 271 Orlando Pena	4.00	1.80
❑ 272 Jerry Lumpe	4.00	1.80
❑ 273 Joey Jay	8.00	3.60
❑ 274 Jerry Kindall	8.00	3.60
❑ 275 Jack Sanford	8.00	3.60
❑ 276 Pete Daley	4.00	1.80
❑ 277 Turk Lown	8.00	3.60
❑ 278 Chuck Essegian	4.00	1.80
❑ 279 Ernie Johnson	4.00	1.80
❑ 280 Frank Bolling	4.00	1.80
❑ 281 Walt Craddock	4.00	1.80
❑ 282 R.C. Stevens	4.00	1.80
❑ 283 Russ Heman	4.00	1.80
❑ 284 Steve Korcheck	4.00	1.80
❑ 285 Joe Cunningham	4.00	1.80
❑ 286 Dean Stone	4.00	1.80
❑ 287 Don Zimmer	8.00	3.60
❑ 288 Dutch Dotterer	4.00	1.80
❑ 289 Johnny Kucks	8.00	3.60
❑ 290 Wes Covington	4.00	1.80
❑ 291 Pedro Ramos	4.00	1.80
Camilo Pascual		
❑ 292 Dick Williams	8.00	3.60
❑ 293 Ray Moore	4.00	1.80
❑ 294 Hank Foiles	4.00	1.80
❑ 295 Billy Martin	25.00	11.00
❑ 296 Ernie Broglio	4.00	1.80
❑ 297 Jackie Brandt	4.00	1.80
❑ 298 Tex Clevenger	4.00	1.80
❑ 299 Billy Klaus	4.00	1.80
❑ 300 Richie Ashburn	25.00	11.00
❑ 301 Earl Averill	4.00	1.80
❑ 302 Don Mossi	8.00	3.60
❑ 303 Marty Keough	4.00	1.80
❑ 304 Cubs Team	15.00	3.00
(Checklist on back)		
❑ 305 Curt Raydon	4.00	1.80
❑ 306 Jim Gilliam	8.00	3.60
❑ 307 Curt Barclay	4.00	1.80
❑ 308 Norm Siebern	4.00	1.80
❑ 309 Sal Maglie	8.00	3.60
❑ 310 Luis Aparicio	25.00	11.00
❑ 311 Norm Zauchin	4.00	1.80
❑ 312 Don Newcombe	8.00	3.60
❑ 313 Frank House	4.00	1.80
❑ 314 Don Cardwell	4.00	1.80
❑ 315 Joe Adcock	8.00	3.60
❑ 316A Ralph Lumenti UER	4.00	1.80
(Option)		
(Photo actually		
Camilo Pascual)		
❑ 316B Ralph Lumenti UER	80.00	36.00
(No option)		
(Photo actually		
Camilo Pascual)		
❑ 317 Willie Mays	70.00	32.00
Richie Ashburn		
❑ 318 Rocky Bridges	4.00	1.80
❑ 319 Dave Hillman	4.00	1.80
❑ 320 Bob Skinner	8.00	3.60
❑ 321A Bob Giallombardo	4.00	1.80
(Option)		
❑ 321B Bob Giallombardo	80.00	36.00
(No option)		
❑ 322A Harry Hanebrink	4.00	1.80
(Traded)		
❑ 322B Harry Hanebrink	80.00	36.00
(No trade)		
❑ 323 Frank Sullivan	4.00	1.80
❑ 324 Don Demeter	4.00	1.80
❑ 325 Ken Boyer	12.00	5.50
❑ 326 Marv Throneberry	8.00	3.60
❑ 327 Gary Bell	4.00	1.80
❑ 328 Lou Skizas	4.00	1.80
❑ 329 Tigers Team	15.00	3.00
(Checklist on back)		

330	Gus Triandos	8.00	3.60
331	Steve Boros	4.00	1.80
332	Ray Monzant	4.00	1.80
333	Harry Simpson	4.00	1.80
334	Glen Hobbie	4.00	1.80
335	Johnny Temple	8.00	3.60
336A	Billy Loes	8.00	3.60
	(With traded line)		
336B	Billy Loes	80.00	36.00
	(No trade)		
337	George Crowe	4.00	1.80
338	Sparky Anderson	60.00	27.00
339	Roy Face	8.00	3.60
340	Roy Sievers	8.00	3.60
341	Tom Qualters	4.00	1.80
342	Ray Jablonski	4.00	1.80
343	Billy Hoeft	4.00	1.80
344	Russ Nixon	4.00	1.80
345	Gil McDougald	8.00	3.60
346	Dave Sisler	4.00	1.80
	Tom Brewer		
347	Bob Buhl	4.00	1.80
348	Ted Lepcio	4.00	1.80
349	Hoyt Wilhelm	20.00	9.00
350	Ernie Banks	75.00	34.00
351	Earl Torgeson	4.00	1.80
352	Robin Roberts	20.00	9.00
353	Curt Flood	8.00	3.60
354	Pete Burnside	4.00	1.80
355	Jimmy Piersall	8.00	3.60
356	Bob Mabe	4.00	1.80
357	Dick Stuart	8.00	3.60
358	Ralph Terry	8.00	3.60
359	Bill White	20.00	9.00
360	Al Kaline	60.00	27.00
361	Willard Nixon	4.00	1.80
362A	Dolan Nichols	4.00	1.80
	(With option line)		
362B	Dolan Nichols	80.00	36.00
	(No option)		
363	Bobby Avila	4.00	1.80
364	Danny McDevitt	4.00	1.80
365	Gus Bell	8.00	3.60
366	Humberto Robinson	4.00	1.80
367	Cal Neeman	4.00	1.80
368	Don Mueller	8.00	3.60
369	Dick Tomanek	4.00	1.80
370	Pete Runnels	8.00	3.60
371	Dick Brodowski	4.00	1.80
372	Jim Hegan	8.00	3.60
373	Herb Plews	4.00	1.80
374	Art Ditmar	8.00	3.60
375	Bob Nieman	4.00	1.80
376	Hal Naragon	4.00	1.80
377	John Antonelli	8.00	3.60
378	Gail Harris	4.00	1.80
379	Bob Miller	4.00	1.80
380	Hank Aaron	125.00	55.00
381	Mike Baxes	4.00	1.80
382	Curt Simmons	8.00	3.60
383	Words of Wisdom	12.00	5.50
	Don Larsen		
	Casey Stengel MG		
384	Dave Sisler	4.00	1.80
385	Sherm Lollar	8.00	3.60
386	Jim Delsing	4.00	1.80
387	Don Drysdale	40.00	18.00
388	Bob Will	4.00	1.80
389	Joe Nuxhall	8.00	3.60
390	Orlando Cepeda	20.00	9.00
391	Milt Pappas	8.00	3.60
392	Whitey Herzog	8.00	3.60
393	Frank Lary	8.00	3.60
394	Randy Jackson	4.00	1.80
395	Elston Howard	12.00	5.50
396	Bob Rush	4.00	1.80
397	Senators Team	15.00	3.00
	(Checklist on back)		
398	Wally Post	8.00	3.60
399	Larry Jackson	4.00	1.80
400	Jackie Jensen	8.00	3.60
401	Ron Blackburn	4.00	1.80
402	Hector Lopez	8.00	3.60
403	Clem Labine	4.00	1.80
404	Hank Sauer	8.00	3.60
405	Roy McMillan	8.00	3.60
406	Solly Drake	4.00	1.80
407	Moe Drabowsky	8.00	3.60
408	Nellie Fox	35.00	16.00
	Luis Aparicio		
409	Gus Zernial	8.00	3.60
410	Billy Pierce	8.00	3.60
411	Whitey Lockman	8.00	3.60
412	Stan Lopata	4.00	1.80
413	Camilo Pascual UER	8.00	3.60
	(Listed as Camillo		
	on front and Pasqual		
	on back)		
414	Dale Long	8.00	3.60
415	Bill Mazeroski	12.00	5.50
416	Haywood Sullivan	8.00	3.60
417	Virgil Trucks	8.00	3.60
418	Gino Cimoli	4.00	1.80
419	Braves Team	15.00	3.00
	(Checklist on back)		
420	Rocky Colavito	30.00	13.50
421	Herman Wehmeier	4.00	1.80
422	Hobie Landrith	4.00	1.80
423	Bob Grim	8.00	3.60
424	Ken Aspromonte	4.00	1.80
425	Del Crandall	8.00	3.60
426	Gerry Staley	8.00	3.60
427	Charlie Neal	8.00	3.60
428	Ron Kline	4.00	1.80
	Bob Friend		
	Vernon Law		
	Roy Face		
429	Bobby Thomson	8.00	3.60
430	Whitey Ford	60.00	27.00
431	Whammy Douglas	4.00	1.80
432	Smoky Burgess	8.00	3.60
433	Billy Harrell	4.00	1.80
434	Hal Griggs	4.00	1.80
435	Frank Robinson	50.00	22.00
436	Granny Hamner	4.00	1.80
437	Ike Delock	4.00	1.80
438	Sammy Esposito	4.00	1.80
439	Brooks Robinson	50.00	22.00
440	Lou Burdette	8.00	3.60
	(Posing as if		
	lefthanded)		
441	John Roseboro	8.00	3.60
442	Ray Narleski	4.00	1.80
443	Daryl Spencer	4.00	1.80
444	Ron Hansen	8.00	3.60
445	Cal McLish	4.00	1.80
446	Rocky Nelson	4.00	1.80
447	Bob Anderson	4.00	1.80
448	Vada Pinson UER	12.00	5.50
	(Born: 8/8/38		
	should be 8/11/38)		
449	Tom Gorman	4.00	1.80
450	Eddie Mathews	35.00	16.00
451	Jimmy Constable	4.00	1.80
452	Chico Fernandez	4.00	1.80
453	Les Moss	4.00	1.80
454	Phil Clark	4.00	1.80
455	Larry Doby	8.00	3.60
456	Jerry Casale	4.00	1.80
457	Dodgers Team	30.00	6.00
	(Checklist on back)		
458	Gordon Jones	4.00	1.80
459	Bill Tuttle	4.00	1.80
460	Bob Friend	8.00	3.60
461	Mickey Mantle HL	125.00	55.00
462	Rocky Colavito HL	12.00	5.50
463	Al Kaline HL	25.00	11.00
464	Willie Mays HL	40.00	18.00
	54 World Series Catch		
465	Roy Sievers HL	8.00	3.60
466	Billy Pierce HL	8.00	3.60
467	Hank Aaron HL	40.00	18.00
468	Duke Snider HL	20.00	9.00
469	Ernie Banks HL	20.00	9.00
470	Stan Musial HL	25.00	11.00
	3,000 Hits		
471	Tom Sturdivant	4.00	1.80
472	Gene Freese	4.00	1.80
473	Mike Fornieles	4.00	1.80
474	Moe Thacker	4.00	1.80
475	Jack Harshman	4.00	1.80
476	Indians Team	15.00	3.00
	(Checklist on back)		
477	Barry Latman	4.00	1.80
478	Roberto Clemente	225.00	100.00
479	Lindy McDaniel	8.00	3.60
480	Red Schoendienst	12.00	5.50
481	Charlie Maxwell	8.00	3.60
482	Russ Meyer	4.00	1.80
483	Clint Courtney	4.00	1.80
484	Willie Kirkland	4.00	1.80
485	Ryne Duren	8.00	3.60
486	Sammy White	4.00	1.80
487	Hal Brown	4.00	1.80
488	Walt Moryn	4.00	1.80
489	John Powers	4.00	1.80
490	Frank Thomas	8.00	3.60
491	Don Blasingame	4.00	1.80
492	Gene Conley	8.00	3.60
493	Jim Landis	8.00	3.60
494	Don Pavletich	4.00	1.80
495	Johnny Podres	8.00	3.60
496	Wayne Terwilliger UER	4.00	1.80
	(Athltics on front)		
497	Hal R. Smith	4.00	1.80
498	Dick Hyde	4.00	1.80
499	Johnny O'Brien	4.00	1.80
500	Vic Wertz	8.00	3.60
501	Bob Tiefenauer	4.00	1.80
502	Alvin Dark	8.00	3.60
503	Jim Owens	4.00	1.80
504	Ossie Alvarez	4.00	1.80
505	Tony Kubek	12.00	5.50
506	Bob Purkey	4.00	1.80
507	Bob Hale	16.00	7.25
508	Art Fowler	16.00	7.25
509	Norm Cash	75.00	34.00
510	Yankees Team	125.00	25.00
	(Checklist on back)		
511	George Susce	16.00	7.25
512	George Altman	10.00	7.25
513	Tommy Carroll	16.00	7.25
514	Bob Gibson	250.00	110.00
515	Harmon Killebrew	125.00	55.00
516	Mike Garcia	20.00	9.00
517	Joe Koppe	16.00	7.25
518	Mike Cueller UER	30.00	13.50
	(Sic, Cuellar)		
519	Pete Runnels	20.00	9.00
	Dick Gernert		
	Frank Malzone		
520	Don Elston	16.00	7.25
521	Gary Geiger	16.00	7.25
522	Gene Snyder	16.00	7.25
523	Harry Bright	16.00	7.25
524	Larry Osborne	16.00	7.25
525	Jim Coates	20.00	9.00
526	Bob Speake	16.00	7.25
527	Solly Hemus	16.00	7.25
528	Pirates Team	70.00	14.00
	(Checklist on back)		
529	George Bamberger	20.00	9.00
530	Wally Moon	20.00	9.00
531	Ray Webster	16.00	7.25
532	Mark Freeman	16.00	7.25
533	Darrell Johnson	20.00	9.00
534	Faye Throneberry	16.00	7.25
535	Ruben Gomez	16.00	7.25
536	Danny Kravitz	16.00	7.25
537	Rudolph Arias	16.00	7.25
538	Chick King	16.00	7.25
539	Gary Blaylock	16.00	7.25
540	Willie Miranda	16.00	7.25
541	Bob Thurman	16.00	7.25
542	Jim Perry	30.00	13.50
543	Bob Skinner	150.00	70.00
	Bill Virdon		
	Roberto Clemente		
544	Lee Tate	16.00	7.25
545	Tom Morgan	16.00	7.25
546	Al Schroll	16.00	7.25
547	Jim Baxes	16.00	7.25
548	Elmer Singleton	16.00	7.25
549	Howie Nunn	16.00	7.25
550	Roy Campanella	150.00	70.00
	(Symbol of Courage)		
551	Fred Haney AS MG	16.00	7.25
552	Casey Stengel AS MG	30.00	13.50

		NRMT	VG-E
☐ 553	Orlando Cepeda AS ..	30.00	13.50
☐ 554	Bill Skowron AS	20.00	9.00
☐ 555	Bill Mazeroski AS ...	30.00	13.50
☐ 556	Nellie Fox AS	40.00	18.00
☐ 557	Ken Boyer AS	30.00	13.50
☐ 558	Frank Malzone AS ...	16.00	7.25
☐ 559	Ernie Banks AS	60.00	27.00
☐ 560	Luis Aparicio AS	30.00	13.50
☐ 561	Hank Aaron AS	125.00	55.00
☐ 562	Al Kaline AS	60.00	27.00
☐ 563	Willie Mays AS	125.00	55.00
☐ 564	Mickey Mantle AS ...	250.00	110.00
☐ 565	Wes Covington AS ...	16.00	7.25
☐ 566	Roy Sievers AS	16.00	7.25
☐ 567	Del Crandall AS	16.00	7.25
☐ 568	Gus Triandos AS	16.00	7.25
☐ 569	Bob Friend AS	16.00	7.25
☐ 570	Bob Turley AS	16.00	7.25
☐ 571	Warren Spahn AS ...	40.00	18.00
☐ 572	Billy Pierce AS	30.00	9.50

1960 Topps

	NRMT	VG-E
COMPLETE SET (572)	3500.00	1600.00
COMMON CARD (1-440) .	4.00	1.80
MINOR STARS 1-440	6.00	2.70
SEMISTARS 1-440	10.00	4.50
UNLISTED STARS 1-440 .	15.00	6.75
COMMON CARD (441-506)	7.00	3.10
MINOR STARS 441-506 .	10.00	4.50
SEMISTARS 441-506 ...	15.00	6.75
UNLISTED STARS 441-506.	25.00	11.00
COMMON CARD (507-572)	16.00	7.25
MINOR STARS 507-572 .	20.00	9.00
SEMISTARS 507-572 ...	25.00	11.00

*UNLISTED DODGER/YANKEE: 1.25X VALUE
CARDS PRICED IN NM CONDITION

		NRMT	VG-E
☐ 1	Early Wynn	35.00	8.75
☐ 2	Roman Mejias	4.00	1.80
☐ 3	Joe Adcock	6.00	2.70
☐ 4	Bob Purkey	4.00	1.80
☐ 5	Wally Moon	6.00	2.70
☐ 6	Lou Berberet	4.00	1.80
☐ 7	Master and Mentor ..	25.00	11.00
	Willie Mays		
	Bill Rigney MG		
☐ 8	Bud Daley	4.00	1.80
☐ 9	Faye Throneberry ...	4.00	1.80
☐ 10	Ernie Banks	50.00	22.00
☐ 11	Norm Siebern	4.00	1.80
☐ 12	Milt Pappas	6.00	2.70
☐ 13	Wally Post	6.00	2.70
☐ 14	Jim Grant	6.00	2.70
☐ 15	Pete Runnels	6.00	2.70
☐ 16	Ernie Broglio	6.00	2.70
☐ 17	Johnny Callison	6.00	2.70
☐ 18	Dodgers Team	50.00	10.00
	(Checklist on back)		
☐ 19	Felix Mantilla	4.00	1.80
☐ 20	Roy Face	6.00	2.70
☐ 21	Dutch Dotterer	4.00	1.80
☐ 22	Rocky Bridges	4.00	1.80
☐ 23	Eddie Fisher	4.00	1.80
☐ 24	Dick Gray	4.00	1.80
☐ 25	Roy Sievers	6.00	2.70
☐ 26	Wayne Terwilliger ..	4.00	1.80
☐ 27	Dick Drott	4.00	1.80
☐ 28	Brooks Robinson ...	50.00	22.00
☐ 29	Clem Labine	6.00	2.70
☐ 30	Tito Francona	4.00	1.80
☐ 31	Sammy Esposito	4.00	1.80
☐ 32	Sophomore Stalwarts	4.00	1.80
	Jim O'Toole		
	Vada Pinson		
☐ 33	Tom Morgan	4.00	1.80
☐ 34	Sparky Anderson ...	15.00	6.75
☐ 35	Whitey Ford	50.00	22.00
☐ 36	Russ Nixon	4.00	1.80
☐ 37	Bill Bruton	4.00	1.80
☐ 38	Jerry Casale	4.00	1.80
☐ 39	Earl Averill	6.00	1.90
☐ 40	Joe Cunningham ...	4.00	1.80
☐ 41	Barry Latman	4.00	1.80
☐ 42	Hobie Landrith ...	4.00	1.80
☐ 43	Senators Team	10.00	2.00
	(Checklist on back)		
☐ 44	Bobby Locke	4.00	1.80
☐ 45	Roy McMillan	6.00	2.70
☐ 46	Jerry Fisher	4.00	1.80
☐ 47	Don Zimmer	6.00	2.70
☐ 48	Hal W. Smith	4.00	1.80
☐ 49	Curt Raydon	4.00	1.80
☐ 50	Al Kaline	50.00	22.00
☐ 51	Jim Coates	4.00	1.80
☐ 52	Dave Philley	4.00	1.80
☐ 53	Jackie Brandt	4.00	1.80
☐ 54	Mike Fornieles ...	4.00	1.80
☐ 55	Bill Mazeroski ...	10.00	4.50
☐ 56	Steve Korcheck ...	4.00	1.80
☐ 57	Win Savers	4.00	1.80
	Turk Lown		
	Gerry Staley		
☐ 58	Gino Cimoli	4.00	1.80
☐ 59	Juan Pizarro	4.00	1.80
☐ 60	Gus Triandos	6.00	2.70
☐ 61	Eddie Kasko	4.00	1.80
☐ 62	Roger Craig	6.00	2.70
☐ 63	George Strickland .	4.00	1.80
☐ 64	Jack Meyer	4.00	1.80
☐ 65	Elston Howard	6.00	2.70
☐ 66	Bob Trowbridge ...	4.00	1.80
☐ 67	Jose Pagan	4.00	1.80
☐ 68	Dave Hillman	4.00	1.80
☐ 69	Billy Goodman	6.00	2.70
☐ 70	Lew Burdette	6.00	2.70
☐ 71	Marty Keough	4.00	1.80
☐ 72	Tigers Team	25.00	5.00
	(Checklist on back)		
☐ 73	Bob Gibson	50.00	22.00
☐ 74	Walt Moryn	4.00	1.80
☐ 75	Vic Power	6.00	2.70
☐ 76	Bill Fischer	4.00	1.80
☐ 77	Hank Foiles	4.00	1.80
☐ 78	Bob Grim	4.00	1.80
☐ 79	Walt Dropo	4.00	1.80
☐ 80	Johnny Antonelli ..	6.00	2.70
☐ 81	Russ Snyder	4.00	1.80
☐ 82	Ruben Gomez	4.00	1.80
☐ 83	Tony Kubek	6.00	2.70
☐ 84	Hal R. Smith	4.00	1.80
☐ 85	Frank Lary	6.00	2.70
☐ 86	Dick Gernert	4.00	1.80
☐ 87	John Romonosky ..	4.00	1.80
☐ 88	John Roseboro ...	6.00	2.70
☐ 89	Hal Brown	4.00	1.80
☐ 90	Bobby Avila	4.00	1.80
☐ 91	Bennie Daniels ..	4.00	1.80
☐ 92	Whitey Herzog ...	6.00	2.70
☐ 93	Art Schult	4.00	1.80
☐ 94	Leo Kiely	4.00	1.80
☐ 95	Frank Thomas ...	6.00	2.70
☐ 96	Ralph Terry	6.00	2.70
☐ 97	Ted Lepcio	4.00	1.80
☐ 98	Gordon Jones	4.00	1.80
☐ 99	Lenny Green	4.00	1.80
☐ 100	Nellie Fox	20.00	9.00
☐ 101	Bob Miller	4.00	1.80
☐ 102	Kent Hadley	4.00	1.80
☐ 103	Dick Farrell	6.00	2.70
☐ 104	Dick Schofield ..	6.00	2.70
☐ 105	Larry Sherry	6.00	2.70
☐ 106	Billy Gardner ...	4.00	1.80
☐ 107	Carlton Willey ...	4.00	1.80
☐ 108	Pete Daley	4.00	1.80
☐ 109	Clete Boyer	6.00	2.70
☐ 110	Cal McLish	4.00	1.80
☐ 111	Vic Wertz	6.00	2.70
☐ 112	Jack Harshman ..	4.00	1.80
☐ 113	Bob Skinner	4.00	1.80
☐ 114	Ken Aspromonte .	4.00	1.80
☐ 115	Fork and Knuckler	6.00	2.70
	Roy Face		
	Hoyt Wilhelm		
☐ 116	Jim Rivera	4.00	1.80
☐ 117	Tom Borland RP .	4.00	1.80
☐ 118	Bob Bruce RP ...	4.00	1.80
☐ 119	Chico Cardenas RP	6.00	2.70
☐ 120	Duke Carmel RP .	4.00	1.80
☐ 121	Camilo Carreon RP	4.00	1.80
☐ 122	Don Dillard RP ..	4.00	1.80
☐ 123	Dan Dobbek RP .	4.00	1.80
☐ 124	Jim Donohue RP .	4.00	1.80
☐ 125	Dick Ellsworth RP	6.00	2.70
☐ 126	Chuck Estrada RP	6.00	2.70
☐ 127	Ron Hansen RP .	6.00	2.70
☐ 128	Bill Harris RP ..	4.00	1.80
☐ 129	Bob Hartman RP	4.00	1.80
☐ 130	Frank Herrera RP	4.00	1.80
☐ 131	Ed Hobaugh RP .	4.00	1.80
☐ 132	Frank Howard RP	25.00	11.00
☐ 133	Manual Javier RP	6.00	2.70
	(Sic, Julian)		
☐ 134	Deron Johnson RP	6.00	2.70
☐ 135	Ken Johnson RP .	4.00	1.80
☐ 136	Jim Kaat RP	40.00	18.00
☐ 137	Lou Klimchock RP	4.00	1.80
☐ 138	Art Mahaffey RP .	4.00	1.80
☐ 139	Carl Mathias RP .	4.00	1.80
☐ 140	Julio Navarro RP .	4.00	1.80
☐ 141	Jim Proctor RP ..	4.00	1.80
☐ 142	Bill Short RP ...	4.00	1.80
☐ 143	Al Spangler RP .	4.00	1.80
☐ 144	Al Stieglitz RP ..	4.00	1.80
☐ 145	Jim Umbricht RP	4.00	1.80
☐ 146	Ted Wieand RP .	4.00	1.80
☐ 147	Bob Will RP	4.00	1.80
☐ 148	Carl Yastrzemski RP	140.00	65.00
☐ 149	Bob Nieman	4.00	1.80
☐ 150	Billy Pierce	6.00	2.70
☐ 151	Giants Team ...	10.00	2.00
	(Checklist on back)		
☐ 152	Gail Harris	4.00	1.80
☐ 153	Bobby Thomson .	6.00	2.70
☐ 154	Jim Davenport ..	6.00	2.70
☐ 155	Charlie Neal ...	6.00	2.70
☐ 156	Art Ceccarelli ..	4.00	1.80
☐ 157	Rocky Nelson ..	6.00	2.70
☐ 158	Wes Covington .	6.00	2.70
☐ 159	Jim Piersall ...	6.00	2.70
☐ 160	Rival All-Stars .	140.00	65.00
	Mickey Mantle		
	Ken Boyer		
☐ 161	Ray Narleski ...	4.00	1.80
☐ 162	Sammy Taylor ..	4.00	1.80
☐ 163	Hector Lopez ...	6.00	2.70
☐ 164	Reds Team	10.00	2.00
	(Checklist on back)		
☐ 165	Jack Sanford ...	6.00	2.70
☐ 166	Chuck Essegian .	4.00	1.80
☐ 167	Valmy Thomas ..	4.00	1.80
☐ 168	Alex Grammas ..	4.00	1.80
☐ 169	Jake Striker ...	4.00	1.80
☐ 170	Del Crandall ...	6.00	2.70
☐ 171	Johnny Groth ...	4.00	1.80
☐ 172	Willie Kirkland ..	4.00	1.80
☐ 173	Billy Martin	20.00	9.00
☐ 174	Indians Team ...	10.00	2.00
	(Checklist on back)		
☐ 175	Pedro Ramos ...	4.00	1.80
☐ 176	Vada Pinson ...	6.00	2.70
☐ 177	Johnny Kucks ..	4.00	1.80
☐ 178	Woody Held	4.00	1.80
☐ 179	Rip Coleman ...	4.00	1.80
☐ 180	Harry Simpson .	4.00	1.80
☐ 181	Billy Loes	6.00	2.70
☐ 182	Glen Hobbie ...	4.00	1.80
☐ 183	Eli Grba	4.00	1.80
☐ 184	Gary Geiger ...	4.00	1.80

185	Jim Owens	4.00	1.80
186	Dave Sisler	4.00	1.80
187	Jay Hook	4.00	1.80
188	Dick Williams	6.00	2.70
189	Don McMahon	4.00	1.80
190	Gene Woodling	6.00	2.70
191	Johnny Klippstein	4.00	1.80
192	Danny O'Connell	4.00	1.80
193	Dick Hyde	4.00	1.80
194	Bobby Gene Smith	4.00	1.80
195	Lindy McDaniel	6.00	2.70
196	Andy Carey	6.00	2.70
197	Ron Kline	4.00	1.80
198	Jerry Lynch	6.00	2.70
199	Dick Donovan	6.00	2.70
200	Willie Mays	100.00	45.00
201	Larry Osborne	4.00	1.80
202	Fred Kipp	4.00	1.80
203	Sammy White	4.00	1.80
204	Ryne Duren	6.00	2.70
205	Johnny Logan	6.00	2.70
206	Claude Osteen	6.00	2.70
207	Bob Boyd	4.00	1.80
208	White Sox Team	10.00	2.00
	(Checklist on back)		
209	Ron Blackburn	4.00	1.80
210	Harmon Killebrew	25.00	11.00
211	Taylor Phillips	4.00	1.80
212	Walter Alston MG	10.00	4.50
213	Chuck Dressen MG	6.00	2.70
214	Jimmy Dykes MG	6.00	2.70
215	Bob Elliott MG	6.00	2.70
216	Joe Gordon MG	6.00	2.70
217	Charlie Grimm MG	6.00	2.70
218	Solly Hemus MG	4.00	1.80
219	Fred Hutchinson MG	6.00	2.70
220	Billy Jurges MG	4.00	1.80
221	Cookie Lavagetto MG	4.00	1.80
222	Al Lopez MG	6.00	2.70
223	Danny Murtaugh MG	6.00	2.70
224	Paul Richards MG	6.00	2.70
225	Bill Rigney MG	4.00	1.80
226	Eddie Sawyer MG	4.00	1.80
227	Casey Stengel MG	15.00	6.75
228	Ernie Johnson	6.00	2.70
229	Joe M. Morgan	4.00	1.80
230	Mound Magicians	10.00	4.50
	Lou Burdette		
	Warren Spahn		
	Bob Buhl		
231	Hal Naragon	4.00	1.80
232	Jim Busby	4.00	1.80
233	Don Elston	4.00	1.80
234	Don Demeter	4.00	1.80
235	Gus Bell	6.00	2.70
236	Dick Ricketts	4.00	1.80
237	Elmer Valo	4.00	1.80
238	Danny Kravitz	4.00	1.80
239	Joe Shipley	4.00	1.80
240	Luis Aparicio	15.00	6.75
241	Albie Pearson	6.00	2.70
242	Cardinals Team	10.00	2.00
	(Checklist on back)		
243	Bubba Phillips	4.00	1.80
244	Hal Griggs	4.00	1.80
245	Eddie Yost	6.00	2.70
246	Lee Maye	6.00	2.70
247	Gil McDougald	6.00	2.70
248	Del Rice	4.00	1.80
249	Earl Wilson	6.00	2.70
250	Stan Musial	100.00	45.00
251	Bob Malkmus	4.00	1.80
252	Ray Herbert	4.00	1.80
253	Eddie Bressoud	4.00	1.80
254	Arnie Portocarrero	4.00	1.80
255	Jim Gilliam	6.00	2.70
256	Dick Brown	4.00	1.80
257	Gordy Coleman	4.00	1.80
258	Dick Groat	6.00	2.70
259	George Altman	4.00	1.80
260	Power Plus	15.00	6.75
	Rocky Colavito		
	Tito Francona		
261	Pete Burnside	4.00	1.80
262	Hank Bauer	6.00	2.70
263	Darrell Johnson	4.00	1.80
264	Robin Roberts	15.00	6.75
265	Rip Repulski	4.00	1.80
266	Joey Jay	6.00	2.70
267	Jim Marshall	4.00	1.80
268	Al Worthington	4.00	1.80
269	Gene Green	4.00	1.80
270	Bob Turley	6.00	2.70
271	Julio Becquer	4.00	1.80
272	Fred Green	6.00	2.70
273	Neil Chrisley	4.00	1.80
274	Tom Acker	4.00	1.80
275	Curt Flood	6.00	2.70
276	Ken McBride	4.00	1.80
277	Harry Bright	4.00	1.80
278	Stan Williams	6.00	2.70
279	Chuck Tanner	6.00	2.70
280	Frank Sullivan	4.00	1.80
281	Ray Boone	6.00	2.70
282	Joe Nuxhall	6.00	2.70
283	John Blanchard	6.00	2.70
284	Don Gross	4.00	1.80
285	Harry Anderson	4.00	1.80
286	Ray Semproch	4.00	1.80
287	Felipe Alou	6.00	2.70
288	Bob Mabe	4.00	1.80
289	Willie Jones	4.00	1.80
290	Jerry Lumpe	4.00	1.80
291	Bob Keegan	4.00	1.80
292	Dodger Backstops	6.00	2.70
	Joe Pignatano		
	John Roseboro		
293	Gene Conley	6.00	2.70
294	Tony Taylor	6.00	2.70
295	Gil Hodges	25.00	11.00
296	Nelson Chittum	4.00	1.80
297	Reno Bertoia	4.00	1.80
298	George Witt	4.00	1.80
299	Earl Torgeson	4.00	1.80
300	Hank Aaron	80.00	36.00
301	Jerry Davis	4.00	1.80
302	Phillies Team	10.00	2.00
	(Checklist on back)		
303	Billy O'Dell	4.00	1.80
304	Joe Ginsberg	4.00	1.80
305	Richie Ashburn	20.00	9.00
306	Frank Baumann	4.00	1.80
307	Gene Oliver	4.00	1.80
308	Dick Hall	4.00	1.80
309	Bob Hale	4.00	1.80
310	Frank Malzone	6.00	2.70
311	Raul Sanchez	4.00	1.80
312	Charley Lau	6.00	2.70
313	Turk Lown	4.00	1.80
314	Chico Fernandez	4.00	1.80
315	Bobby Shantz	6.00	2.70
316	Willie McCovey	115.00	52.50
317	Pumpsie Green	6.00	2.70
318	Jim Baxes	6.00	2.70
319	Joe Koppe	4.00	1.80
320	Bob Allison	6.00	2.70
321	Ron Fairly	6.00	2.70
322	Willie Tasby	4.00	1.80
323	John Romano	6.00	2.70
324	Jim Perry	6.00	2.70
325	Jim O'Toole	6.00	2.70
326	Roberto Clemente	175.00	80.00
327	Ray Sadecki	4.00	1.80
328	Earl Battey	4.00	1.80
329	Zack Monroe	4.00	1.80
330	Harvey Kuenn	6.00	2.70
331	Henry Mason	4.00	1.80
332	Yankees Team	75.00	15.00
	(Checklist on back)		
333	Danny McDevitt	4.00	1.80
334	Ted Abernathy	4.00	1.80
335	Red Schoendienst	15.00	6.75
336	Ike Delock	4.00	1.80
337	Cal Neeman	4.00	1.80
338	Ray Monzant	4.00	1.80
339	Harry Chiti	4.00	1.80
340	Harvey Haddix	6.00	2.70
341	Carroll Hardy	4.00	1.80
342	Casey Wise	4.00	1.80
343	Sandy Koufax	125.00	55.00
344	Clint Courtney	4.00	1.80
345	Don Newcombe	6.00	2.70
346	J.C. Martin UER	6.00	2.70
	(Face actually		
	Gary Peters)		
347	Ed Bouchee	4.00	1.80
348	Barry Shetrone	4.00	1.80
349	Moe Drabowsky	6.00	2.70
350	Mickey Mantle	450.00	200.00
351	Don Nottebart	4.00	1.80
352	Cincy Clouters	10.00	4.50
	Gus Bell		
	Frank Robinson		
	Jerry Lynch		
353	Don Larsen	6.00	2.70
354	Bob Lillis	4.00	1.80
355	Bill White	6.00	2.70
356	Joe Amalfitano	4.00	1.80
357	Al Schroll	4.00	1.80
358	Joe DeMaestri	4.00	1.80
359	Buddy Gilbert	4.00	1.80
360	Herb Score	6.00	2.70
361	Bob Oldis	4.00	1.80
362	Russ Kemmerer	4.00	1.80
363	Gene Stephens	4.00	1.80
364	Paul Foytack	4.00	1.80
365	Minnie Minoso	6.00	2.70
366	Dallas Green	10.00	4.50
367	Bill Tuttle	4.00	1.80
368	Daryl Spencer	4.00	1.80
369	Billy Hoeft	4.00	1.80
370	Bill Skowron	6.00	2.70
371	Bud Byerly	4.00	1.80
372	Frank House	4.00	1.80
373	Don Hoak	6.00	2.70
374	Bob Buhl	6.00	2.70
375	Dale Long	6.00	2.70
376	John Briggs	4.00	1.80
377	Roger Maris	90.00	40.00
378	Stu Miller	6.00	2.70
379	Red Wilson	4.00	1.00
380	Bob Shaw	4.00	1.80
381	Braves Team	10.00	2.00
	(Checklist on back)		
382	Ted Bowsfield	4.00	1.80
383	Leon Wagner	4.00	1.80
384	Don Cardwell	4.00	1.80
385	Charlie Neal WS	6.00	2.70
386	Charlie Neal WS	6.00	2.70
387	Carl Furillo WS	6.00	2.70
388	Gil Hodges WS	10.00	4.50
389	Luis Aparicio WS	12.00	5.50
	Maury Wills		
390	World Series Game 6	6.00	2.70
391	World Series Summary	6.00	2.70
	The Champs Celebrate		
392	Tex Clevenger	4.00	1.80
393	Smoky Burgess	6.00	2.70
394	Norm Larker	4.00	1.80
395	Hoyt Wilhelm	15.00	6.75
396	Steve Bilko	4.00	1.80
397	Don Blasingame	4.00	1.80
398	Mike Cuellar	6.00	2.70
399	Young Hit Stars	6.00	2.70
	Milt Pappas		
	Jack Fisher		
	Jerry Walker		
400	Rocky Colavito	20.00	9.00
401	Bob Duliba	4.00	1.80
402	Dick Stuart	6.00	2.70
403	Ed Sadowski	4.00	1.80
404	Bob Rush	4.00	1.80
405	Bobby Richardson	15.00	6.75
406	Billy Klaus	4.00	1.80
407	Gary Peters UER	6.00	2.70
	(Face actually		
	J.C. Martin)		
408	Carl Furillo	6.00	2.70
409	Ron Samford	4.00	1.80
410	Sam Jones	6.00	2.70
411	Ed Bailey	4.00	1.80
412	Bob Anderson	4.00	1.80
413	Athletics Team	10.00	2.00
	(Checklist on back)		
414	Don Williams	4.00	1.80
415	Bob Cerv	6.00	2.70
416	Humberto Robinson	4.00	1.80
417	Chuck Cottier	4.00	1.80

❑ 418 Don Mossi	6.00	2.70
❑ 419 George Crowe	4.00	1.80
❑ 420 Eddie Mathews	35.00	16.00
❑ 421 Duke Maas	4.00	1.80
❑ 422 John Powers	4.00	1.80
❑ 423 Ed Fitzgerald	4.00	1.80
❑ 424 Pete Whisenant	4.00	1.80
❑ 425 Johnny Podres	6.00	2.70
❑ 426 Ron Jackson	4.00	1.80
❑ 427 Al Grunwald	4.00	1.80
❑ 428 Al Smith	4.00	1.80
❑ 429 AL Kings	10.00	4.50
Nellie Fox		
Harvey Kuenn		
❑ 430 Art Ditmar	4.00	1.80
❑ 431 Andre Rodgers	4.00	1.80
❑ 432 Chuck Stobbs	4.00	1.80
❑ 433 Irv Noren	4.00	1.80
❑ 434 Brooks Lawrence	4.00	1.80
❑ 435 Gene Freese	4.00	1.80
❑ 436 Marv Throneberry	6.00	2.70
❑ 437 Bob Friend	6.00	2.70
❑ 438 Jim Coker	4.00	1.80
❑ 439 Tom Brewer	4.00	1.80
❑ 440 Jim Lemon	6.00	2.70
❑ 441 Gary Bell	7.00	3.10
❑ 442 Joe Pignatano	7.00	3.10
❑ 443 Charlie Maxwell	7.00	3.10
❑ 444 Jerry Kindall	7.00	3.10
❑ 445 Warren Spahn	50.00	22.00
❑ 446 Ellis Burton	7.00	3.10
❑ 447 Ray Moore	7.00	3.10
❑ 448 Jim Gentile	15.00	6.75
❑ 449 Jim Brosnan	7.00	3.10
❑ 450 Orlando Cepeda	25.00	11.00
❑ 451 Curt Simmons	7.00	3.10
❑ 452 Ray Webster	7.00	3.10
❑ 453 Vern Law	10.00	4.50
❑ 454 Hal Woodeshick	7.00	3.10
❑ 455 Baltimore Coaches	7.00	3.10
Eddie Robinson		
Harry Brecheen		
Luman Harris		
❑ 456 Red Sox Coaches	10.00	4.50
Rudy York		
Billy Herman		
Sal Maglie		
Del Baker		
❑ 457 Cubs Coaches	7.00	3.10
Charlie Root		
Lou Klein		
Elvin Tappe		
❑ 458 White Sox Coaches	7.00	3.10
Johnny Cooney		
Don Gutteridge		
Tony Cuccinello		
Ray Berres		
❑ 459 Reds Coaches	7.00	3.10
Reggie Otero		
Cot Deal		
Wally Moses		
❑ 460 Indians Coaches	10.00	4.50
Mel Harder		
Jo-Jo White		
Bob Lemon		
Ralph(Red) Kress		
❑ 461 Tigers Coaches	10.00	4.50
Tom Ferrick		
Luke Appling		
Billy Hitchcock		
❑ 462 Athletics Coaches	3.00	3.10
Fred Fitzsimmons		
Don Heffner		
Walker Cooper		
❑ 463 Dodgers Coaches	7.00	3.10
Bobby Bragan		
Pete Reiser		
Joe Becker		
Greg Mulleavy		
❑ 464 Braves Coaches	7.00	3.10
Bob Scheffing		
Whitlow Wyatt		
Andy Pafko		
George Myatt		
❑ 465 Yankees Coaches	15.00	6.75
Bill Dickey		

Ralph Houk		
Frank Crosetti		
Ed Lopat		
❑ 466 Phillies Coaches	7.00	3.10
Ken Silvestri		
Dick Carter		
Andy Cohen		
❑ 467 Pirates Coaches	7.00	3.10
Mickey Vernon		
Frank Oceak		
Sam Narron		
Bill Burwell		
❑ 468 Cardinals Coaches	7.00	3.10
Johnny Keane		
Howie Pollet		
Ray Katt		
Harry Walker		
❑ 469 Giants Coaches	7.00	3.10
Wes Westrum		
Salty Parker		
Bill Posedel		
❑ 470 Senators Coaches	7.00	3.10
Bob Swift		
Ellis Clary		
Sam Mele		
❑ 471 Ned Garver	7.00	3.10
❑ 472 Alvin Dark	7.00	3.10
❑ 473 Al Cicotte	7.00	3.10
❑ 474 Haywood Sullivan	7.00	3.10
❑ 475 Don Drysdale	40.00	18.00
❑ 476 Lou Johnson	7.00	3.10
❑ 477 Don Ferrarese	7.00	3.10
❑ 478 Frank Torre	7.00	3.10
❑ 479 Georges Maranda	7.00	3.10
❑ 480 Yogi Berra	70.00	32.00
❑ 481 Wes Stock	7.00	3.10
❑ 482 Frank Bolling	7.00	3.10
❑ 483 Camilo Pascual	7.00	3.10
❑ 484 Pirates Team	40.00	8.00
(Checklist on back)		
❑ 485 Ken Boyer	15.00	6.75
❑ 486 Bobby Del Greco	7.00	3.10
❑ 487 Tom Sturdivant	7.00	3.10
❑ 488 Norm Cash	25.00	11.00
❑ 489 Steve Ridzik	7.00	3.10
❑ 490 Frank Robinson	50.00	22.00
❑ 491 Mel Roach	7.00	3.10
❑ 492 Larry Jackson	7.00	3.10
❑ 493 Duke Snider	50.00	22.00
❑ 494 Orioles Team	25.00	5.00
(Checklist on back)		
❑ 495 Sherm Lollar	7.00	3.10
❑ 496 Bill Virdon	10.00	4.50
❑ 497 John Tsitouris	7.00	3.10
❑ 498 Al Pilarcik	7.00	3.10
❑ 499 Johnny James	7.00	3.10
❑ 500 Johnny Temple	7.00	3.10
❑ 501 Bob Schmidt	7.00	3.10
❑ 502 Jim Bunning	25.00	11.00
❑ 503 Don Lee	7.00	3.10
❑ 504 Seth Morehead	7.00	3.10
❑ 505 Ted Kluszewski	25.00	11.00
❑ 506 Lee Walls	7.00	3.10
❑ 507 Dick Stigman	16.00	7.25
❑ 508 Billy Consolo	16.00	7.25
❑ 509 Tommy Davis	25.00	11.00
❑ 510 Gerry Staley	16.00	7.25
❑ 511 Ken Walters	16.00	7.25
❑ 512 Joe Gibbon	16.00	7.25
❑ 513 Chicago Cubs	30.00	6.00
Team Card		
(Checklist on back)		
❑ 514 Steve Barber	16.00	7.25
❑ 515 Stan Lopata	16.00	7.25
❑ 516 Marty Kutyna	16.00	7.25
❑ 517 Charlie James	16.00	7.25
❑ 518 Tony Gonzalez	16.00	7.25
❑ 519 Ed Roebuck	16.00	7.25
❑ 520 Don Buddin	16.00	7.25
❑ 521 Mike Lee	16.00	7.25
❑ 522 Ken Hunt	20.00	7.25
❑ 523 Clay Dalrymple	16.00	7.25
❑ 524 Bill Henry	16.00	7.25
❑ 525 Marv Breeding	16.00	7.25
❑ 526 Paul Giel	16.00	7.25
❑ 527 Jose Valdivielso	16.00	7.25

❑ 528 Ben Johnson	16.00	7.25
❑ 529 Norm Sherry	20.00	9.00
❑ 530 Mike McCormick	16.00	7.25
❑ 531 Sandy Amoros	16.00	7.25
❑ 532 Mike Garcia	16.00	7.25
❑ 533 Lu Clinton	16.00	7.25
❑ 534 Ken MacKenzie	16.00	7.25
❑ 535 Whitey Lockman	16.00	7.25
❑ 536 Wynn Hawkins	16.00	7.25
❑ 537 Boston Red Sox	30.00	6.00
Team Card		
(Checklist on back)		
❑ 538 Frank Barnes	16.00	7.25
❑ 539 Gene Baker	16.00	7.25
❑ 540 Jerry Walker	16.00	7.25
❑ 541 Tony Curry	16.00	7.25
❑ 542 Ken Hamlin	16.00	7.25
❑ 543 Elio Chacon	16.00	7.25
❑ 544 Bill Monbouquette	16.00	7.25
❑ 545 Carl Sawatski	16.00	7.25
❑ 546 Hank Aguirre	16.00	7.25
❑ 547 Bob Aspromonte	16.00	7.25
❑ 548 Don Mincher	16.00	7.25
❑ 549 John Buzhardt	16.00	7.25
❑ 550 Jim Landis	16.00	7.25
❑ 551 Ed Rakow	16.00	7.25
❑ 552 Walt Bond	16.00	7.25
❑ 553 Bill Skowron AS	20.00	9.00
❑ 554 Willie McCovey AS	30.00	13.50
❑ 555 Nellie Fox AS	30.00	13.50
❑ 556 Charlie Neal AS	16.00	7.25
❑ 557 Frank Malzone AS	16.00	7.25
❑ 558 Eddie Mathews AS	30.00	13.50
❑ 559 Luis Aparicio AS	30.00	13.50
❑ 560 Ernie Banks AS	60.00	27.00
❑ 561 Al Kaline AS	60.00	27.00
❑ 562 Joe Cunningham AS	16.00	7.25
❑ 563 Mickey Mantle AS	250.00	110.00
❑ 564 Willie Mays AS	100.00	45.00
❑ 565 Roger Maris AS	90.00	40.00
❑ 566 Hank Aaron AS	100.00	45.00
❑ 567 Sherm Lollar AS	16.00	7.25
❑ 568 Del Crandall AS	16.00	7.25
❑ 569 Camilo Pascual AS	16.00	7.25
❑ 570 Don Drysdale AS	30.00	13.50
❑ 571 Billy Pierce AS	16.00	7.25
❑ 572 Johnny Antonelli AS	30.00	9.00
❑ NNO Iron-on team transfer	4.00	1.80

1961 Topps

GIL HODGES — Los Angeles Dodgers

	NRMT	VG-E
COMPLETE SET (587)	4800.00	2200.00
COMMON CARD (1-370)	3.00	1.35
COMMON CARD (371-446)	4.00	1.80
MINOR STARS 1-446	6.00	2.70
SEMISTARS 1-446	8.00	3.60
UNLISTED STARS 1-446	12.00	5.50
COMMON CARD (447-522)	7.00	3.10
MINOR STARS 447-522	10.00	4.50
SEMISTARS 447-522	15.00	6.75
UNLSTED STARS 447-522	25.00	11.00
COMMON CARD (523-589)	30.00	13.50
MINOR STARS 523-589	40.00	18.00
NOT ISSUED (587/588)		

*UNLISTED DODGER/YANKEE: 1.25X VALUE
CARDS PRICED IN NM CONDITION

#	Card	Price	Price
1	Dick Groat	30.00	6.00
2	Roger Maris	175.00	80.00
3	John Buzhardt	3.00	1.35
4	Lenny Green	3.00	1.35
5	John Romano	3.00	1.35
6	Ed Roebuck	3.00	1.35
7	White Sox Team	8.00	3.60
8	Dick Williams	6.00	2.70
9	Bob Purkey	3.00	1.35
10	Brooks Robinson	40.00	18.00
11	Curt Simmons	6.00	2.70
12	Moe Thacker	3.00	1.35
13	Chuck Cottier	3.00	1.35
14	Don Mossi	6.00	2.70
15	Willie Kirkland	3.00	1.35
16	Billy Muffett	3.00	1.35
17	Checklist 1	12.00	2.40
18	Jim Grant	6.00	2.70
19	Clete Boyer	8.00	3.60
20	Robin Roberts	12.00	5.50
21	Zorro Versalles UER (First name should be Zoilo)	8.00	3.60
22	Clem Labine	6.00	2.70
23	Don Demeter	3.00	1.35
24	Ken Johnson	3.00	1.35
25	Reds' Heavy Artillery / Vada Pinson / Gus Bell / Frank Robinson	8.00	3.60
26	Wes Stock	3.00	1.35
27	Jerry Kindall	3.00	1.35
28	Hector Lopez	6.00	2.70
29	Don Nottebart	3.00	1.35
30	Nellie Fox	15.00	6.75
31	Bob Schmidt	3.00	1.35
32	Ray Sadecki	3.00	1.35
33	Gary Geiger	3.00	1.35
34	Wynn Hawkins	3.00	1.35
35	Ron Santo	40.00	18.00
36	Jack Kralick	3.00	1.35
37	Charley Maxwell	6.00	2.70
38	Bob Lillis	3.00	1.35
39	Leo Posada	3.00	1.35
40	Bob Turley	6.00	2.70
41	NL Batting Leaders / Dick Groat / Norm Larker / Willie Mays / Roberto Clemente	35.00	16.00
42	AL Batting Leaders / Pete Runnels / Al Smith / Minnie Minoso / Bill Skowron	8.00	3.60
43	NL Home Run Leaders / Ernie Banks / Hank Aaron / Ed Mathews / Ken Boyer	30.00	13.50
44	AL Home Run Leaders / Mickey Mantle / Roger Maris / Jim Lemon / Rocky Colavito	80.00	36.00
45	NL ERA Leaders / Mike McCormick / Ernie Broglio / Don Drysdale / Bob Friend / Stan Williams	8.00	3.60
46	AL ERA Leaders / Frank Baumann / Jim Bunning / Art Ditmar / Hal Brown	8.00	3.60
47	NL Pitching Leaders / Ernie Broglio / Warren Spahn / Vern Law / Lou Burdette	8.00	3.60
48	AL Pitching Leaders / Chuck Estrada / Jim Perry UER (Listed as an Oriole) / Bud Daley / Art Ditmar / Frank Lary / Milt Pappas	8.00	3.60
49	NL Strikeout Leaders / Don Drysdale / Sandy Koufax / Sam Jones / Ernie Broglio	20.00	9.00
50	AL Strikeout Leaders / Jim Bunning / Pedro Ramos / Early Wynn / Frank Lary	8.00	3.60
51	Detroit Tigers Team Card	8.00	3.60
52	George Crowe	3.00	1.35
53	Russ Nixon	3.00	1.35
54	Earl Francis	3.00	1.35
55	Jim Davenport	6.00	2.70
56	Russ Kemmerer	3.00	1.35
57	Marv Throneberry	6.00	2.70
58	Joe Schaffernoth	3.00	1.35
59	Jim Woods	3.00	1.35
60	Woody Held	3.00	1.35
61	Ron Piche	3.00	1.35
62	Al Pilarcik	3.00	1.65
63	Jim Kaat	8.00	3.60
64	Alex Grammas	3.00	1.35
65	Ted Kluszewski	8.00	3.60
66	Bill Henry	3.00	1.35
67	Ossie Virgil	3.00	1.35
68	Deron Johnson	6.00	2.70
69	Earl Wilson	6.00	2.70
70	Bill Virdon	6.00	2.70
71	Jerry Adair	3.00	1.35
72	Stu Miller	6.00	2.70
73	Al Spangler	3.00	1.35
74	Joe Pignatano	3.00	1.35
75	Lindy Shows Larry / Lindy McDaniel / Larry Jackson	6.00	2.70
76	Harry Anderson	3.00	1.35
77	Dick Stigman	3.00	1.35
78	Lee Walls	3.00	1.35
79	Joe Ginsberg	3.00	1.35
80	Harmon Killebrew	20.00	9.00
81	Tracy Stallard	3.00	1.35
82	Joe Christopher	3.00	1.35
83	Bob Bruce	3.00	1.35
84	Lee Maye	3.00	1.35
85	Jerry Walker	3.00	1.35
86	Los Angeles Dodgers Team Card	8.00	3.60
87	Joe Amalfitano	3.00	1.35
88	Richie Ashburn	15.00	6.75
89	Billy Martin	15.00	6.75
90	Gerry Staley	3.00	1.35
91	Walt Moryn	3.00	1.35
92	Hal Naragon	3.00	1.35
93	Tony Gonzalez	3.00	1.35
94	Johnny Kucks	3.00	1.35
95	Norm Cash	8.00	3.60
96	Billy O'Dell	3.00	1.35
97	Jerry Lynch	6.00	2.70
98A	Checklist 2 (Red "Checklist" 98 black on white)	10.00	2.00
98B	Checklist 2 (Yellow "Checklist" 98 black on white)	10.00	2.00
98C	Checklist 2 (Yellow "Checklist" 98 white on black no copyright)	10.00	2.00
99	Don Buddin UER (66 HR's)	3.00	1.35
100	Harvey Haddix	6.00	2.70
101	Bubba Phillips	3.00	1.35
102	Gene Stephens	3.00	1.35
103	Ruben Amaro	3.00	1.35
104	John Blanchard	6.00	2.70
105	Carl Willey	3.00	1.35
106	Whitey Herzog	6.00	2.70
107	Seth Morehead	3.00	1.35
108	Dan Dobbek	3.00	1.35
109	Johnny Podres	6.00	2.70
110	Vada Pinson	6.00	2.70
111	Jack Meyer	3.00	1.35
112	Chico Fernandez	3.00	1.35
113	Mike Fornieles	3.00	1.35
114	Hobie Landrith	3.00	1.35
115	Johnny Antonelli	6.00	2.70
116	Joe DeMaestri	3.00	1.35
117	Dale Long	6.00	2.70
118	Chris Cannizzaro	3.00	1.35
119	A's Big Armor / Norm Siebern / Hank Bauer / Jerry Lumpe	6.00	2.70
120	Eddie Mathews	30.00	13.50
121	Eli Grba	6.00	2.70
122	Chicago Cubs Team Card	8.00	3.60
123	Billy Gardner	3.00	1.35
124	J.C. Martin	3.00	1.35
125	Steve Barber	3.00	1.35
126	Dick Stuart	6.00	2.70
127	Ron Kline	3.00	1.35
128	Rip Repulski	3.00	1.35
129	Ed Hobaugh	3.00	1.35
130	Norm Larker	6.00	2.70
131	Paul Richards MG	6.00	2.70
132	Al Lopez MG	6.00	2.70
133	Ralph Houk MG	6.00	2.70
134	Mickey Vernon MG	6.00	2.70
135	Fred Hutchinson MG	6.00	2.70
136	Walter Alston MG	6.00	2.70
137	Chuck Dressen MG	6.00	2.70
138	Danny Murtaugh MG	6.00	2.70
139	Solly Hemus MG	6.00	2.70
140	Gus Triandos	6.00	2.70
141	Billy Williams	60.00	27.00
142	Luis Arroyo	6.00	2.70
143	Russ Snyder	3.00	1.35
144	Jim Coker	3.00	1.35
145	Bob Buhl	6.00	2.70
146	Marty Keough	3.00	1.35
147	Ed Rakow	3.00	1.35
148	Julian Javier	6.00	2.70
149	Bob Olds	3.00	1.35
150	Willie Mays	100.00	45.00
151	Jim Donohue	3.00	1.35
152	Earl Torgeson	3.00	1.35
153	Don Lee	3.00	1.35
154	Bobby Del Greco	3.00	1.35
155	Johnny Temple	6.00	2.70
156	Ken Hunt	6.00	2.70
157	Cal McLish	3.00	1.35
158	Pete Daley	3.00	1.35
159	Orioles Team	8.00	3.60
160	Whitey Ford UER (Incorrectly listed as 5'0'' tall)	40.00	18.00
161	Sherman Jones UER (Photo actually Eddie Fisher)	3.00	1.35
162	Jay Hook	3.00	1.35
163	Ed Sadowski	3.00	1.35
164	Felix Mantilla	3.00	1.35
165	Gino Cimoli	3.00	1.35
166	Danny Kravitz	3.00	1.35
167	San Francisco Giants Team Card	8.00	3.60
168	Tommy Davis	8.00	3.60
169	Don Elston	3.00	1.35
170	Al Smith	3.00	1.35
171	Paul Foytack	3.00	1.35
172	Don Dillard	3.00	1.35
173	Beantown Bombers / Frank Malzone / Vic Wertz / Jackie Jensen	6.00	2.70
174	Ray Semproch	3.00	1.35
175	Gene Freese	3.00	1.35
176	Ken Aspromonte	3.00	1.35
177	Don Larsen	6.00	2.70
178	Bob Nieman	3.00	1.35
179	Joe Koppe	3.00	1.35
180	Bobby Richardson	12.00	5.50
181	Fred Green	3.00	1.35
182	Dave Nicholson	3.00	1.35
183	Andre Rodgers	3.00	1.35

#	Player	Price 1	Price 2
184	Steve Bilko	6.00	2.70
185	Herb Score	6.00	2.70
186	Elmer Valo	6.00	2.70
187	Billy Klaus	3.00	1.35
188	Jim Marshall	3.00	1.35
189A	Checklist 3 (Copyright symbol almost adjacent to 263 Ken Hamlin)	10.00	2.00
189B	Checklist 3 (Copyright symbol adjacent to 264 Glen Hobbie)	10.00	2.00
190	Stan Williams	6.00	2.70
191	Mike de la Hoz	3.00	1.35
192	Dick Brown	3.00	1.35
193	Gene Conley	6.00	2.70
194	Gordy Coleman	6.00	2.70
195	Jerry Casale	3.00	1.35
196	Ed Bouchee	3.00	1.35
197	Dick Hall	3.00	1.35
198	Carl Sawatski	3.00	1.35
199	Bob Boyd	3.00	1.35
200	Warren Spahn	30.00	13.50
201	Pete Whisenant	3.00	1.35
202	Al Neiger	3.00	1.35
203	Eddie Bressoud	3.00	1.35
204	Bob Skinner	6.00	2.70
205	Billy Pierce	6.00	2.70
206	Gene Green	3.00	1.35
207	Dodger Southpaws Sandy Koufax Johnny Podres	30.00	13.50
208	Larry Osborne	3.00	1.35
209	Ken McBride	3.00	1.35
210	Pete Runnels	3.00	1.35
211	Bob Gibson	40.00	18.00
212	Haywood Sullivan	6.00	2.70
213	Bill Stafford	3.00	1.35
214	Danny Murphy	3.00	1.35
215	Gus Bell	6.00	2.70
216	Ted Bowsfield	3.00	1.35
217	Mel Roach	3.00	1.35
218	Hal Brown	3.00	1.35
219	Gene Mauch MG	6.00	2.70
220	Alvin Dark MG	6.00	2.70
221	Mike Higgins MG	3.00	1.35
222	Jimmy Dykes MG	6.00	2.70
223	Bob Scheffing MG	3.00	1.35
224	Joe Gordon MG	6.00	2.70
225	Bill Rigney MG	6.00	2.70
226	Cookie Lavagetto MG	6.00	2.70
227	Juan Pizarro	3.00	1.35
228	New York Yankees Team Card	60.00	27.00
229	Rudy Hernandez	3.00	1.35
230	Don Hoak	6.00	2.70
231	Dick Drott	3.00	1.35
232	Bill White	6.00	2.70
233	Joey Jay	3.00	1.35
234	Ted Lepcio	3.00	1.35
235	Camilo Pascual	6.00	2.70
236	Don Gile	3.00	1.35
237	Billy Loes	6.00	2.70
238	Jim Gilliam	6.00	2.70
239	Dave Sisler	3.00	1.35
240	Ron Hansen	3.00	1.35
241	Al Cicotte	3.00	1.35
242	Hal Smith	3.00	1.35
243	Frank Lary	6.00	2.70
244	Chico Cardenas	6.00	2.70
245	Joe Adcock	6.00	2.70
246	Bob Davis	3.00	1.35
247	Billy Goodman	3.00	1.35
248	Ed Keegan	3.00	1.35
249	Cincinnati Reds Team Card	8.00	3.60
250	Buc Hill Aces Vern Law Roy Face	6.00	2.70
251	Bill Bruton	3.00	1.35
252	Bill Short	3.00	1.35
253	Sammy Taylor	3.00	1.35
254	Ted Sadowski	3.00	1.35
255	Vic Power	6.00	2.70
256	Billy Hoeft	3.00	1.35
257	Carroll Hardy	3.00	1.35
258	Jack Sanford	6.00	2.70
259	John Schaive	3.00	1.35
260	Don Drysdale	30.00	13.50
261	Charlie Lau	6.00	2.70
262	Tony Curry	3.00	1.35
263	Ken Hamlin	3.00	1.35
264	Glen Hobbie	3.00	1.35
265	Tony Kubek	8.00	3.60
266	Lindy McDaniel	6.00	2.70
267	Norm Siebern	3.00	1.35
268	Ike Delock	3.00	1.35
269	Harry Chiti	3.00	1.35
270	Bob Friend	6.00	2.70
271	Jim Landis	3.00	1.35
272	Tom Morgan	3.00	1.35
273A	Checklist 4 (Copyright symbol adjacent to 336 Don Mincher)	10.00	2.00
273B	Checklist 4 (Copyright symbol adjacent to 339 Gene Baker)	10.00	2.00
274	Gary Bell	3.00	1.35
275	Gene Woodling	6.00	2.70
276	Ray Rippelmeyer	3.00	1.35
277	Hank Foiles	3.00	1.35
278	Don McMahon	3.00	1.35
279	Jose Pagan	3.00	1.35
280	Frank Howard	8.00	3.60
281	Frank Sullivan	3.00	1.35
282	Faye Throneberry	3.00	1.35
283	Bob Anderson	3.00	1.35
284	Dick Gernert	3.00	1.35
285	Sherm Lollar	6.00	2.70
286	George Witt	3.00	1.35
287	Carl Yastrzemski	50.00	22.00
288	Albie Pearson	3.00	1.35
289	Ray Moore	3.00	1.35
290	Stan Musial	100.00	45.00
291	Tex Clevenger	3.00	1.35
292	Jim Baumer	3.00	1.35
293	Tom Sturdivant	3.00	1.35
294	Don Blasingame	3.00	1.35
295	Milt Pappas	6.00	2.70
296	Wes Covington	6.00	2.70
297	Athletics Team	8.00	3.60
298	Jim Golden	3.00	1.35
299	Clay Dalrymple	3.00	1.35
300	Mickey Mantle	400.00	180.00
301	Chet Nichols	3.00	1.35
302	Al Heist	3.00	1.35
303	Gary Peters	6.00	2.70
304	Rocky Nelson	3.00	1.35
305	Mike McCormick	6.00	2.70
306	Bill Virdon WS	8.00	3.60
307	Mickey Mantle WS	80.00	36.00
308	Bobby Richardson WS	12.00	5.50
309	Gino Cimoli WS	9.00	4.00
310	Roy Face WS	9.00	4.00
311	Whitey Ford WS	16.00	7.25
312	Bill Mazeroski WS	20.00	9.00
313	World Series Summary Pirates Celebrate	16.00	7.25
314	Bob Miller	3.00	1.35
315	Earl Battey	6.00	2.70
316	Bobby Gene Smith	3.00	1.35
317	Jim Brewer	3.00	1.35
318	Danny O'Connell	3.00	1.35
319	Valmy Thomas	3.00	1.35
320	Lou Burdette	6.00	2.70
321	Marv Breeding	3.00	1.35
322	Bill Kunkel	3.00	1.35
323	Sammy Esposito	3.00	1.35
324	Hank Aguirre	3.00	1.35
325	Wally Moon	6.00	2.70
326	Dave Hillman	3.00	1.35
327	Matty Alou	12.00	5.50
328	Jim O'Toole	6.00	2.70
329	Julio Becquer	3.00	1.35
330	Rocky Colavito	20.00	9.00
331	Ned Garver	3.00	1.35
332	Dutch Dotterer UER (Photo actually Tommy Dotterer Dutch's brother)	3.00	1.35
333	Fritz Brickell	3.00	1.35
334	Walt Bond	3.00	1.35
335	Frank Bolling	3.00	1.35
336	Don Mincher	6.00	2.70
337	Al's Aces Early Wynn Al Lopez Herb Score	8.00	3.60
338	Don Landrum	3.00	1.35
339	Gene Baker	3.00	1.35
340	Vic Wertz	6.00	2.70
341	Jim Owens	3.00	1.35
342	Clint Courtney	3.00	1.35
343	Earl Robinson	3.00	1.35
344	Sandy Koufax	100.00	45.00
345	Jimmy Piersall	6.00	2.70
346	Howie Nunn	3.00	1.35
347	St. Louis Cardinals Team Card	8.00	3.60
348	Steve Boros	3.00	1.35
349	Danny McDevitt	3.00	1.35
350	Ernie Banks	45.00	20.00
351	Jim King	3.00	1.35
352	Bob Shaw	3.00	1.35
353	Howie Bedell	3.00	1.35
354	Billy Harrell	3.00	1.35
355	Bob Allison	8.00	3.60
356	Ryne Duren	3.00	1.35
357	Daryl Spencer	3.00	1.35
358	Earl Averill	6.00	2.70
359	Dallas Green	3.00	1.35
360	Frank Robinson	40.00	18.00
361A	Checklist 5 (No ad on back)	16.00	3.20
361B	Checklist 5 (Special features ad on back)	16.00	3.20
362	Frank Funk	3.00	1.35
363	John Roseboro	6.00	2.70
364	Moe Drabowsky	3.00	1.35
365	Jerry Lumpe	3.00	1.35
366	Eddie Fisher	3.00	1.35
367	Jim Rivera	3.00	1.35
368	Bennie Daniels	3.00	1.35
369	Dave Philley	3.00	1.35
370	Roy Face	6.00	2.70
371	Bill Skowron SP	50.00	22.00
372	Bob Hendley	4.00	1.80
373	Boston Red Sox Team Card	8.00	3.60
374	Paul Giel	4.00	1.80
375	Ken Boyer	12.00	5.50
376	Mike Roarke	4.00	1.80
377	Ruben Gomez	4.00	1.80
378	Wally Post	4.00	2.70
379	Bobby Shantz	4.00	1.80
380	Minnie Minoso	8.00	3.60
381	Dave Wickersham	4.00	1.80
382	Frank Thomas	6.00	2.70
383	Frisco First Liners Mike McCormick Jack Sanford Billy O'Dell	6.00	2.70
384	Chuck Essegian	4.00	1.80
385	Jim Perry	6.00	2.70
386	Joe Hicks	4.00	1.80
387	Duke Maas	4.00	1.80
388	Roberto Clemente	135.00	60.00
389	Ralph Terry	6.00	2.70
390	Del Crandall	6.00	2.70
391	Winston Brown	4.00	1.80
392	Reno Bertoia	4.00	1.80
393	Batter Bafflers Don Cardwell Glen Hobbie	4.00	1.80
394	Ken Walters	4.00	1.80
395	Chuck Estrada	6.00	2.00
396	Bob Aspromonte	4.00	1.80
397	Hal Woodeshick	4.00	1.80
398	Hank Bauer	6.00	2.70
399	Cliff Cook	4.00	1.80
400	Vern Law	6.00	2.70
401	Babe Ruth HL 60th HR	50.00	22.00

Card	NRMT	VG-E
402 Don Larsen HL SP .... WS Perfect Game	25.00	11.00
403 Joe Oeschger HL .... Leon Cadore 26 Inning Tie	7.00	3.10
404 Rogers Hornsby HL.... .424 Season BA	12.00	5.50
405 Lou Gehrig HL............ Consecutive Game Streak	75.00	34.00
406 Mickey Mantle HL .... 565 foot HR	100.00	45.00
407 Jack Chesbro HL........ 41 victories	7.00	3.10
408 C. Mathewson HL SP 267 Strikeouts	20.00	9.00
409 Walter Johnson SL .... 3 Shutouts in 4 days	12.00	5.50
410 Harvey Haddix HL ...... 12 Perfect Innings	7.00	3.10
411 Tony Taylor	6.00	2.70
412 Larry Sherry	6.00	2.70
413 Eddie Yost	6.00	2.70
414 Dick Donovan	6.00	2.70
415 Hank Aaron	90.00	40.00
416 Dick Howser	8.00	3.60
417 Juan Marichal SP	100.00	45.00
418 Ed Bailey	6.00	2.70
419 Tom Borland	4.00	1.80
420 Ernie Broglio	6.00	2.70
421 Ty Cline SP	18.00	8.00
422 Bud Daley	4.00	1.80
423 Charlie Neal SP	18.00	8.00
424 Turk Lown	4.00	1.80
425 Yogi Berra	80.00	36.00
426 Milwaukee Braves .... Team Card (Back numbered 463)	12.00	5.50
427 Dick Ellsworth	6.00	2.70
428 Ray Barker SP	18.00	8.00
429 Al Kaline	45.00	20.00
430 Bill Mazeroski SP	50.00	22.00
431 Chuck Stobbs	4.00	1.80
432 Coot Veal	6.00	2.70
433 Art Mahaffey	4.00	1.80
434 Tom Brewer	4.00	1.80
435 Orlando Cepeda UER (San Francis on card front)	12.00	5.50
436 Jim Maloney SP	20.00	9.00
437A Checklist 6 .... 440 Louis Aparicio	16.00	3.20
437B Checklist 6 .... 440 Louis Aparicio	16.00	3.20
438 Curt Flood	8.00	3.60
439 Phil Regan	6.00	2.70
440 Luis Aparicio	12.00	5.50
441 Dick Bertell	4.00	1.80
442 Gordon Jones	4.00	1.80
443 Duke Snider	40.00	18.00
444 Joe Nuxhall	6.00	2.70
445 Frank Malzone	6.00	2.70
446 Bob Taylor	4.00	1.80
447 Harry Bright	7.00	3.10
448 Del Rice	7.00	3.10
449 Bob Bolin	7.00	3.10
450 Jim Lemon	7.00	3.10
451 Power for Ernie .... Daryl Spencer Bill White Ernie Broglio	7.00	3.10
452 Bob Allen	7.00	3.10
453 Dick Schofield	7.00	3.10
454 Pumpsie Green	7.00	3.10
455 Early Wynn	15.00	6.75
456 Hal Bevan	7.00	3.10
457 Johnny James .... (Listed as Angel, but wearing Yankee uniform and cap)	7.00	3.10
458 Willie Tasby	7.00	3.10
459 Terry Fox	7.00	3.10
460 Gil Hodges	25.00	11.00
461 Smoky Burgess	10.00	4.50
462 Lou Klimchock	7.00	3.10
463 Jack Fisher .... (See also 426)	7.00	3.10
464 Lee Thomas .... (Pictured with Yankee cap but listed as Los Angeles Angel)	10.00	4.50
465 Roy McMillan	7.00	3.10
466 Ron Moeller	7.00	3.10
467 Cleveland Indians ..... Team Card	12.00	5.50
468 John Callison	10.00	4.50
469 Ralph Lumenti	7.00	3.10
470 Roy Sievers	10.00	4.50
471 Phil Rizzuto MVP	25.00	11.00
472 Yogi Berra MVP	50.00	22.00
473 Bob Shantz MVP	10.00	4.50
474 Al Rosen MVP	10.00	4.50
475 Mickey Mantle MVP ...	175.00	80.00
476 Jackie Jensen MVP	10.00	4.50
477 Nellie Fox MVP	15.00	6.75
478 Roger Maris MVP	60.00	27.00
479 Jim Konstanty MVP	7.00	3.10
480 Roy Campanella MVP	40.00	18.00
481 Hank Sauer MVP	7.00	3.10
482 Willie Mays MVP	50.00	22.00
483 Don Newcombe MVP ...	10.00	4.50
484 Hank Aaron MVP	50.00	22.00
485 Ernie Banks MVP	35.00	16.00
486 Dick Groat MVP	10.00	4.50
487 Gene Oliver	7.00	3.10
488 Joe McClain	7.00	3.10
489 Walt Dropo	7.00	3.10
490 Jim Bunning	15.00	6.75
491 Philadelphia Phillies .. Team Card	12.00	5.50
492 Ron Fairly	10.00	4.50
493 Don Zimmer UER .... (Brooklyn A.L.)	10.00	4.50
494 Tom Cheney	7.00	3.10
495 Elston Howard	10.00	4.50
496 Ken MacKenzie	7.00	3.10
497 Willie Jones	7.00	3.10
498 Ray Herbert	7.00	3.10
499 Chuck Schilling	7.00	3.10
500 Harvey Kuenn	10.00	4.50
501 John DeMerit	7.00	3.10
502 Clarence Coleman	10.00	4.50
503 Tito Francona	7.00	3.10
504 Billy Consolo	7.00	3.10
505 Red Schoendienst	15.00	6.75
506 Willie Davis	15.00	6.75
507 Pete Burnside	7.00	3.10
508 Rocky Bridges	7.00	3.10
509 Camilo Carreon	7.00	3.10
510 Art Ditmar	7.00	3.10
511 Joe M. Morgan	7.00	3.10
512 Bob Will	7.00	3.10
513 Jim Brosnan	7.00	3.10
514 Jake Wood	7.00	3.10
515 Jackie Brandt	7.00	3.10
516 Checklist 7	16.00	3.20
517 Willie McCovey	40.00	18.00
518 Andy Carey	7.00	3.10
519 Jim Pagliaroni	7.00	3.10
520 Joe Cunningham	7.00	3.10
521 Brother Battery .... Norm Sherry Larry Sherry	7.00	3.10
522 Dick Farrell UER ...... (Phillies cap but listed on Dodgers)	7.00	3.10
523 Joe Gibbon	30.00	13.50
524 Johnny Logan	30.00	13.50
525 Ron Perranoski	40.00	18.00
526 R.C. Stevens	30.00	13.50
527 Gene Leek	30.00	13.50
528 Pedro Ramos	30.00	13.50
529 Bob Roselli	30.00	13.50
530 Bob Malkmus	30.00	13.50
531 Jim Coates	40.00	18.00
532 Bob Hale	30.00	13.50
533 Jack Curtis	30.00	13.50
534 Eddie Kasko	30.00	13.50
535 Larry Jackson	30.00	13.50
536 Bill Tuttle	30.00	13.50
537 Bobby Locke	30.00	13.50
538 Chuck Hiller	30.00	13.50
539 Johnny Klippstein	30.00	13.50
540 Jackie Jensen	40.00	18.00
541 Roland Sheldon	40.00	18.00
542 Minnesota Twins .... Team Card	60.00	27.00
543 Roger Craig	40.00	18.00
544 George Thomas	30.00	13.50
545 Hoyt Wilhelm	50.00	22.00
546 Marty Kutyna	30.00	13.50
547 Leon Wagner	30.00	13.50
548 Ted Wills	30.00	13.50
549 Hal R. Smith	30.00	13.50
550 Frank Baumann	30.00	13.50
551 George Altman	30.00	13.50
552 Jim Archer	30.00	13.50
553 Bill Fischer	30.00	13.50
554 Pittsburgh Pirates .... Team Card	70.00	32.00
555 Sam Jones	30.00	13.50
556 Ken R. Hunt	30.00	13.50
557 Jose Valdivielso	30.00	13.50
558 Don Ferrarese	30.00	13.50
559 Jim Gentile	60.00	27.00
560 Barry Latman	30.00	13.50
561 Charley James	30.00	13.50
562 Bill Monbouquette	30.00	13.50
563 Bob Cerv	50.00	22.00
564 Don Cardwell	30.00	13.50
565 Felipe Alou	50.00	22.00
566 Paul Richards AS MG ..	30.00	13.50
567 Danny Murtaugh AS MG	30.00	13.50
568 Bill Skowron AS	50.00	22.00
569 Frank Herrera AS	30.00	13.50
570 Nellie Fox AS	50.00	22.00
571 Bill Mazeroski AS	40.00	18.00
572 Brooks Robinson AS	80.00	36.00
573 Ken Boyer AS	40.00	18.00
574 Luis Aparicio AS	50.00	22.00
575 Ernie Banks AS	80.00	36.00
576 Roger Maris AS	175.00	80.00
577 Hank Aaron AS	150.00	70.00
578 Mickey Mantle AS	400.00	180.00
579 Willie Mays AS	150.00	70.00
580 Al Kaline AS	80.00	36.00
581 Frank Robinson AS	80.00	36.00
582 Earl Battey AS	30.00	13.50
583 Del Crandall AS	30.00	13.50
584 Jim Perry AS	30.00	13.50
585 Bob Friend AS	30.00	13.50
586 Whitey Ford AS	90.00	40.00
589 Warren Spahn AS	100.00	30.00

1962 Topps

	NRMT	VG-E
COMPLETE SET (598)	4600.00	2100.00
COMMON CARD (1-370)	5.00	2.20
COMMON CARD (371-446)	6.00	2.70
B. RUTH STORY (135-144)	20.00	9.00
MINOR STARS 1-446	8.00	3.60
SEMISTARS 1-446	10.00	4.50
UNLISTED STARS 1-446	15.00	6.75
COMMON CARD (447-522)	12.00	5.50
MINOR STARS (447-522)	15.00	6.75
SEMISTARS 447-522	20.00	9.00
COMMON CARD (523-598)	20.00	9.00
COMMON SP (523-598)	35.00	16.00
MINOR STARS 523-598	30.00	13.50
SEMISTARS 523-598	40.00	18.00

COMMON POSE VAR. 25.00 11.00
*UNLISTED DODG/MET/YANK: 1.25X VALUE
CARDS PRICED IN NM CONDITION !

❑ 1 Roger Maris 250.00 60.00
❑ 2 Jim Brosnan 5.00 2.20
❑ 3 Pete Runnels 5.00 2.20
❑ 4 John DeMerit 8.00 3.60
❑ 5 Sandy Koufax UER 135.00 60.00
(Struck ou 18)
❑ 6 Marv Breeding 5.00 2.20
❑ 7 Frank Thomas 10.00 4.50
❑ 8 Ray Herbert 5.00 2.20
❑ 9 Jim Davenport 8.00 3.60
❑ 10 Roberto Clemente 175.00 80.00
❑ 11 Tom Morgan 5.00 2.20
❑ 12 Harry Craft MG 8.00 3.60
❑ 13 Dick Howser 8.00 3.60
❑ 14 Bill White 8.00 3.60
❑ 15 Dick Donovan 5.00 2.20
❑ 16 Darrell Johnson 5.00 2.20
❑ 17 Johnny Callison 8.00 3.60
❑ 18 Managers' Dream 175.00 80.00
Mickey Mantle
Willie Mays
❑ 19 Ray Washburn 5.00 2.20
❑ 20 Rocky Colavito 15.00 6.75
❑ 21 Jim Kaat 8.00 3.60
❑ 22A Checklist 1 ERR 12.00 2.40
(121-176 on back)
❑ 22B Checklist 1 COR 12.00 2.40
❑ 23 Norm Larker 5.00 2.20
❑ 24 Tigers Team 10.00 4.50
❑ 25 Ernie Banks 45.00 20.00
❑ 26 Chris Cannizzaro 8.00 3.60
❑ 27 Chuck Cottier 5.00 2.20
❑ 28 Minnie Minoso 10.00 4.50
❑ 29 Casey Stengel MG 20.00 9.00
❑ 30 Eddie Mathews 30.00 13.50
❑ 31 Tom Tresh 15.00 6.75
❑ 32 John Roseboro 8.00 3.60
❑ 33 Don Larsen 8.00 3.60
❑ 34 Johnny Temple 8.00 3.60
❑ 35 Don Schwall 8.00 3.60
❑ 36 Don Leppert 5.00 2.20
❑ 37 Tribe Hill Trio 5.00 2.20
Barry Latman
Dick Stigman
Jim Perry
❑ 38 Gene Stephens 5.00 2.20
❑ 39 Joe Koppe 5.00 2.20
❑ 40 Orlando Cepeda 15.00 6.75
❑ 41 Cliff Cook 5.00 2.20
❑ 42 Jim King 5.00 2.20
❑ 43 Los Angeles Dodgers .. 10.00 4.50
Team Card
❑ 44 Don Taussig 5.00 2.20
❑ 45 Brooks Robinson 45.00 20.00
❑ 46 Jack Baldschun 5.00 2.20
❑ 47 Bob Will 5.00 2.20
❑ 48 Ralph Terry 8.00 3.60
❑ 49 Hal Jones 5.00 2.20
❑ 50 Stan Musial 100.00 45.00
❑ 51 AL Batting Leaders 8.00 3.60
Norm Cash
Jim Piersall
Al Kaline
Elston Howard
❑ 52 NL Batting Leaders 20.00 9.00
Roberto Clemente
Vada Pinson
Ken Boyer
Wally Moon
❑ 53 AL Home Run Leaders 100.00 45.00
Roger Maris
Mickey Mantle
Jim Gentile
Harmon Killebrew
❑ 54 NL Home Run Leaders 20.00 9.00
Orlando Cepeda
Willie Mays
Frank Robinson
❑ 55 AL ERA Leaders 8.00 3.60
Dick Donovan
Bill Stafford
Don Mossi
Milt Pappas
❑ 56 NL ERA Leaders 8.00 3.60
Warren Spahn
Jim O'Toole
Curt Simmons
Mike McCormick
❑ 57 AL Wins Leaders 8.00 3.60
Whitey Ford
Frank Lary
Steve Barber
Jim Bunning
❑ 58 NL Wins Leaders 8.00 3.60
Warren Spahn
Joe Jay
Jim O'Toole
❑ 59 AL Strikeout Leaders 8.00 3.60
Camilo Pascual
Whitey Ford
Jim Bunning
Juan Pizzaro
❑ 60 NL Strikeout Leaders .. 20.00 9.00
Sandy Koufax
Stan Williams
Don Drysdale
Jim O'Toole
❑ 61 Cardinals Team 10.00 4.50
❑ 62 Steve Boros 5.00 2.20
❑ 63 Tony Cloninger 8.00 3.60
❑ 64 Russ Snyder 5.00 2.20
❑ 65 Bobby Richardson 10.00 4.50
❑ 66 Cuno Barragan 5.00 2.20
❑ 67 Harvey Haddix 8.00 3.60
❑ 68 Ken Hunt 5.00 2.20
❑ 69 Phil Ortega 5.00 2.20
❑ 70 Harmon Killebrew 25.00 11.00
❑ 71 Dick LeMay 5.00 2.20
❑ 72 Bob's Pupils 5.00 2.20
Steve Boros
Bob Scheffing MG
Jake Wood
❑ 73 Nellie Fox 20.00 9.00
❑ 74 Bob Lillis 8.00 3.60
❑ 75 Milt Pappas 8.00 3.60
❑ 76 Howie Bedell 5.00 2.20
❑ 77 Tony Taylor 8.00 3.60
❑ 78 Gene Green 5.00 2.20
❑ 79 Ed Hobaugh 5.00 2.20
❑ 80 Vada Pinson 8.00 3.60
❑ 81 Jim Pagliaroni 5.00 2.20
❑ 82 Deron Johnson 8.00 3.60
❑ 83 Larry Jackson 5.00 2.20
❑ 84 Lenny Green 5.00 2.20
❑ 85 Gil Hodges 20.00 9.00
❑ 86 Donn Clendenon 8.00 3.60
❑ 87 Mike Roarke 5.00 2.20
❑ 88 Ralph Houk MG 8.00 3.60
(Berra in background)
❑ 89 Barney Schultz 5.00 2.20
❑ 90 Jimmy Piersall 8.00 3.60
❑ 91 J.C. Martin 5.00 2.20
❑ 92 Sam Jones 5.00 2.20
❑ 93 John Blanchard 8.00 3.60
❑ 94 Jay Hook 8.00 3.60
❑ 95 Don Hoak 8.00 3.60
❑ 96 Eli Grba 5.00 2.20
❑ 97 Tito Francona 5.00 2.20
❑ 98 Checklist 2 .... 12.00 2.40
❑ 99 John (Boog) Powell 30.00 13.50
❑ 100 Warren Spahn 35.00 16.00
❑ 101 Carroll Hardy 5.00 2.20
❑ 102 Al Schroll 5.00 2.20
❑ 103 Don Blasingame 5.00 2.20
❑ 104 Ted Savage 5.00 2.20
❑ 105 Don Mossi 8.00 3.60
❑ 106 Carl Sawatski 5.00 2.20
❑ 107 Mike McCormick 8.00 3.60
❑ 108 Willie Davis 8.00 3.60
❑ 109 Bob Shaw 5.00 2.20
❑ 110 Bill Skowron 8.00 3.60
❑ 111 Dallas Green 8.00 3.60
❑ 112 Hank Foiles 5.00 2.20
❑ 113 Chicago White Sox 10.00 4.50
Team Card
❑ 114 Howie Koplitz 5.00 2.20
❑ 115 Bob Skinner 8.00 3.60
❑ 116 Herb Score 8.00 3.60
❑ 117 Gary Geiger 5.00 2.20
❑ 118 Julian Javier 8.00 3.60
❑ 119 Danny Murphy 5.00 2.20
❑ 120 Bob Purkey 5.00 2.20
❑ 121 Billy Hitchcock MG 5.00 2.20
❑ 122 Norm Bass 5.00 2.20
❑ 123 Mike de la Hoz 5.00 2.20
❑ 124 Bill Pleis 5.00 2.20
❑ 125 Gene Woodling 8.00 3.60
❑ 126 Al Cicotte 5.00 2.20
❑ 127 Pride of A's 5.00 2.20
Norm Siebern
Hank Bauer MG
Jerry Lumpe
❑ 128 Art Fowler 5.00 2.20
❑ 129A Lee Walls 5.00 2.20
(Facing right)
❑ 129B Lee Walls 30.00 13.50
(Facing left)
❑ 130 Frank Bolling 5.00 2.20
❑ 131 Pete Richert 5.00 2.20
❑ 132A Angels Team 10.00 4.50
(Without photo)
❑ 132B Angels Team 30.00 13.50
(With photo)
❑ 133 Felipe Alou 8.00 3.60
❑ 134A Billy Hoeft 5.00 2.20
(Facing right)
❑ 134B Billy Hoeft 30.00 13.50
(Facing straight)
❑ 135 Babe Ruth Special 1 .. 20.00 9.00
Babe as a Boy
❑ 136 Babe Ruth Special 2 .. 20.00 9.00
Babe Joins Yanks
❑ 137 Babe Ruth Special 3 .. 20.00 9.00
With Miller Huggins
❑ 138 Babe Ruth Special 4 .. 20.00 9.00
Famous Slugger
❑ 139A Babe Ruth Special 5 30.00 13.50
Babe Hits 60
❑ 139B Hal Reniff PORT 15.00 6.75
❑ 139C Hal Reniff 65.00 29.00
(Pitching)
❑ 140 Babe Ruth Special 6 .. 50.00 22.00
With Lou Gehrig
❑ 141 Babe Ruth Special 7 .. 20.00 9.00
Twilight Years
❑ 142 Babe Ruth Special 8 .. 20.00 9.00
Coaching Dodgers
❑ 143 Babe Ruth Special 9 .. 20.00 9.00
Greatest Sports Hero
❑ 144 Babe Ruth Special 10 20.00 9.00
Farewell Speech
❑ 145 Barry Latman 5.00 2.20
❑ 146 Don Demeter 5.00 2.20
❑ 147A Bill Kunkel PORT 5.00 2.20
❑ 147B Bill Kunkel 30.00 13.50
(Pitching pose)
❑ 148 Wally Post 5.00 2.20
❑ 149 Bob Duliba 5.00 2.20
❑ 150 Al Kaline 50.00 22.00
❑ 151 Johnny Klippstein 5.00 2.20
❑ 152 Mickey Vernon MG 8.00 3.60
❑ 153 Pumpsie Green 6.00 2.70
❑ 154 Lee Thomas 6.00 2.70
❑ 155 Stu Miller 6.00 2.70
❑ 156 Merritt Ranew 5.00 2.20
❑ 157 Wes Covington 8.00 3.60
❑ 158 Braves Team 10.00 4.50
❑ 159 Hal Reniff 8.00 3.60
❑ 160 Dick Stuart 8.00 3.60
❑ 161 Frank Baumann 5.00 2.20
❑ 162 Sammy Drake 5.00 2.20
❑ 163 Hot Corner Guard 8.00 3.60
Billy Gardner
Cletis Boyer
❑ 164 Hal Naragon 5.00 2.20
❑ 165 Jackie Brandt 5.00 2.20
❑ 166 Don Lee 5.00 2.20
❑ 167 Tim McCarver 30.00 13.50
❑ 168 Leo Posada 5.00 2.20
❑ 169 Bob Cerv 8.00 3.60
❑ 170 Ron Santo 15.00 6.75
❑ 171 Dave Sisler 5.00 2.20
❑ 172 Fred Hutchinson MG 8.00 3.60
❑ 173 Chico Fernandez 5.00 2.20

174A Carl Willey (Capless)	5.00	2.20
174B Carl Willey (With cap)	30.00	13.50
175 Frank Howard	8.00	3.60
176A Eddie Yost PORT	5.00	2.20
176B Eddie Yost BATTING	30.00	13.50
177 Bobby Shantz	8.00	3.60
178 Camilo Carreon	5.00	2.20
179 Tom Sturdivant	5.00	2.20
180 Bob Allison	8.00	3.60
181 Paul Brown	5.00	2.20
182 Bob Nieman	5.00	2.20
183 Roger Craig	8.00	3.60
184 Haywood Sullivan	8.00	3.60
185 Roland Sheldon	8.00	3.60
186 Mack Jones	5.00	2.20
187 Gene Conley	5.00	2.20
188 Chuck Hiller	5.00	2.20
189 Dick Hall	5.00	2.20
190A Wally Moon PORT	5.00	2.20
190B Wally Moon BATTING	30.00	13.50
191 Jim Brewer	5.00	2.20
192A Checklist 3 (Without comma)	12.00	2.40
192B Checklist 3 (Comma after Checklist)	16.00	3.20
193 Eddie Kasko	5.00	2.20
194 Dean Chance	8.00	3.60
195 Joe Cunningham	5.00	2.20
196 Terry Fox	5.00	2.20
197 Daryl Spencer	5.00	2.20
198 Johnny Keane MG	5.00	2.20
199 Gaylord Perry	80.00	36.00
200 Mickey Mantle	450.00	200.00
201 Ike Delock	5.00	2.20
202 Carl Warwick	5.00	2.20
203 Jack Fisher	5.00	2.20
204 Johnny Weekly	5.00	2.20
205 Gene Freese	5.00	2.20
206 Senators Team	10.00	4.50
207 Pete Burnside	5.00	2.20
208 Billy Martin	20.00	9.00
209 Jim Fregosi	15.00	6.75
210 Roy Face	8.00	3.60
211 Midway Masters Frank Bolling Roy McMillan	5.00	2.20
212 Jim Owens	5.00	2.20
213 Richie Ashburn	20.00	9.00
214 Dom Zanni	5.00	2.20
215 Woody Held	5.00	2.20
216 Ron Kline	5.00	2.20
217 Walter Alston MG	8.00	3.60
218 Joe Torre	40.00	18.00
219 Al Downing	8.00	3.60
220 Roy Sievers	8.00	3.60
221 Bill Short	5.00	2.20
222 Jerry Zimmerman	5.00	2.20
223 Alex Grammas	5.00	2.20
224 Don Rudolph	5.00	2.20
225 Frank Malzone	8.00	3.60
226 San Francisco Giants Team Card	10.00	4.50
227 Bob Tiefenauer	5.00	2.20
228 Dale Long	8.00	3.60
229 Jesus McFarlane	5.00	2.20
230 Camilo Pascual	8.00	3.60
231 Ernie Bowman	5.00	2.20
232 World Series Game 1 Yanks win opener	10.00	4.50
233 Joey Jay WS	10.00	4.50
234 Roger Maris WS	25.00	11.00
235 Whitey Ford WS sets new mark	10.00	4.50
236 World Series Game 5 Yanks crush Reds	8.00	3.60
237 World Series Summary Yanks celebrate	8.00	3.60
238 Norm Sherry	5.00	2.20
239 Cecil Butler	5.00	2.20
240 George Altman	5.00	2.20
241 Johnny Kucks	5.00	2.20
242 Mel McGaha MG	5.00	2.20
243 Robin Roberts	15.00	6.75
244 Don Gile	5.00	2.20
245 Ron Hansen	5.00	2.20
246 Art Ditmar	5.00	2.20
247 Joe Pignatano	5.00	2.20
248 Bob Aspromonte	8.00	3.60
249 Ed Keegan	5.00	2.20
250 Norm Cash	8.00	3.60
251 New York Yankees Team Card	50.00	22.00
252 Earl Francis	5.00	2.20
253 Harry Chiti MG	5.00	2.20
254 Gordon Windhorn	5.00	2.20
255 Juan Pizarro	5.00	2.20
256 Elio Chacon	8.00	3.60
257 Jack Spring	5.00	2.20
258 Marty Keough	5.00	2.20
259 Lou Klimchock	5.00	2.20
260 Billy Pierce	8.00	3.60
261 George Alusik	5.00	2.20
262 Bob Schmidt	5.00	2.20
263 The Right Pitch Bob Purkey Jim Turner CO Joe Jay	5.00	2.20
264 Dick Ellsworth	8.00	3.60
265 Joe Adcock	8.00	3.60
266 John Anderson	5.00	2.20
267 Dan Dobbek	5.00	2.20
268 Ken McBride	5.00	2.20
269 Bob Oldis	5.00	2.20
270 Dick Groat	8.00	3.60
271 Ray Rippelmeyer	5.00	2.20
272 Earl Robinson	5.00	2.20
273 Gary Bell	5.00	2.20
274 Sammy Taylor	5.00	2.20
275 Norm Siebern	5.00	2.20
276 Hal Kolstad	5.00	2.20
277 Checklist 4	16.00	3.20
278 Ken Johnson	8.00	3.60
279 Hobie Landrith UER (Wrong birthdate)	8.00	3.60
280 Johnny Podres	8.00	3.60
281 Jake Gibbs	8.00	3.60
282 Dave Hillman	5.00	2.20
283 Charlie Smith	5.00	2.20
284 Ruben Amaro	5.00	2.20
285 Curt Simmons	8.00	3.60
286 Al Lopez MG	8.00	3.60
287 George Witt	5.00	2.20
288 Billy Williams	30.00	13.50
289 Mike Krsnich	5.00	2.20
290 Jim Gentile	8.00	3.60
291 Hal Stowe	5.00	2.20
292 Jerry Kindall	5.00	2.20
293 Bob Miller	8.00	3.60
294 Phillies Team	10.00	4.50
295 Vern Law	8.00	3.60
296 Ken Hamlin	5.00	2.20
297 Ron Perranoski	8.00	3.60
298 Bill Tuttle	5.00	2.20
299 Don Wert	5.00	2.20
300 Willie Mays	150.00	70.00
301 Galen Cisco	5.00	2.20
302 Johnny Edwards	5.00	2.20
303 Frank Torre	8.00	3.60
304 Dick Farrell	8.00	3.60
305 Jerry Lumpe	5.00	2.20
306 Redbird Rippers Lindy McDaniel Larry Jackson	5.00	2.20
307 Jim Grant	8.00	3.60
308 Neil Chrisley	5.00	2.20
309 Moe Morhardt	5.00	2.20
310 Whitey Ford	45.00	20.00
311 Tony Kubek IA	8.00	3.60
312 Warren Spahn IA	15.00	6.75
313 Roger Maris IA Blasts 61th	40.00	18.00
314 Rocky Colavito IA	8.00	3.60
315 Whitey Ford IA	15.00	6.75
316 Harmon Killebrew IA	15.00	6.75
317 Stan Musial IA	20.00	9.00
318 Mickey Mantle IA	125.00	55.00
319 Mike McCormick IA	5.00	2.20
320 Hank Aaron	150.00	70.00
321 Lee Stange	5.00	2.20
322 Alvin Dark MG	8.00	3.60
323 Don Landrum	5.00	2.20
324 Joe McClain	5.00	2.20
325 Luis Aparicio	15.00	6.75
326 Tom Parsons	5.00	2.20
327 Ozzie Virgil	5.00	2.20
328 Ken Walters	5.00	2.20
329 Bob Bolin	5.00	2.20
330 John Romano	5.00	2.20
331 Moe Drabowsky	8.00	3.60
332 Don Buddin	5.00	2.20
333 Frank Cipriani	5.00	2.20
334 Boston Red Sox Team Card	10.00	4.50
335 Bill Bruton	5.00	2.20
336 Billy Muffett	5.00	2.20
337 Jim Marshall	8.00	3.60
338 Billy Gardner	5.00	2.20
339 Jose Valdivielso	5.00	2.20
340 Don Drysdale	45.00	20.00
341 Mike Hershberger	5.00	2.20
342 Ed Rakow	5.00	2.20
343 Albie Pearson	8.00	3.60
344 Ed Bauta	5.00	2.20
345 Chuck Schilling	5.00	2.20
346 Jack Kralick	5.00	2.20
347 Chuck Hinton	5.00	2.20
348 Larry Burright	8.00	3.60
349 Paul Foytack	5.00	2.20
350 Frank Robinson	45.00	20.00
351 Braves' Backstops Joe Torre Del Crandall	8.00	3.60
352 Frank Sullivan	5.00	2.20
353 Bill Mazeroski	10.00	4.50
354 Roman Mejias	8.00	3.60
355 Steve Barber	5.00	2.20
356 Tom Haller	5.00	2.20
357 Jerry Walker	5.00	2.20
358 Tommy Davis	8.00	3.60
359 Bobby Locke	5.00	2.20
360 Yogi Berra	75.00	34.00
361 Bob Hendley	5.00	2.20
362 Ty Cline	5.00	2.20
363 Bob Roselli	5.00	2.20
364 Ken Hunt	5.00	2.20
365 Charlie Neal	8.00	3.60
366 Phil Regan	8.00	3.60
367 Checklist 5	16.00	3.20
368 Bob Tillman	5.00	2.20
369 Ted Bowsfield	5.00	2.20
370 Ken Boyer	8.00	3.60
371 Earl Battey	6.00	2.70
372 Jack Curtis	6.00	2.70
373 Al Heist	6.00	2.70
374 Gene Mauch MG	10.00	4.50
375 Ron Fairly	10.00	4.50
376 Bud Daley	8.00	3.60
377 John Orsino	6.00	2.70
378 Bennie Daniels	6.00	2.70
379 Chuck Essegian	6.00	2.70
380 Lou Burdette	10.00	4.50
381 Chico Cardenas	10.00	4.50
382 Dick Williams	8.00	3.60
383 Ray Sadecki	6.00	2.70
384 K.C. Athletics Team Card	10.00	4.50
385 Early Wynn	15.00	6.75
386 Don Mincher	8.00	3.60
387 Lou Brock	125.00	55.00
388 Ryne Duren	8.00	3.60
389 Smoky Burgess	10.00	4.50
390 Orlando Cepeda AS	10.00	4.50
391 Bill Mazeroski AS	10.00	4.50
392 Ken Boyer AS	8.00	3.60
393 Roy McMillan AS	6.00	2.70
394 Hank Aaron AS	50.00	22.00
395 Willie Mays AS	50.00	22.00
396 Frank Robinson AS	15.00	6.75
397 John Roseboro AS	6.00	2.70
398 Don Drysdale AS	15.00	6.75
399 Warren Spahn AS	15.00	6.75
400 Elston Howard	10.00	4.50
401 AL/NL Homer Kings Roger Maris Orlando Cepeda	60.00	27.00

No.	Player	Price 1	Price 2
402	Gino Cimoli	6.00	2.70
403	Chet Nichols	6.00	2.70
404	Tim Harkness	8.00	3.60
405	Jim Perry	8.00	3.60
406	Bob Taylor	6.00	2.70
407	Hank Aguirre	6.00	2.70
408	Gus Bell	8.00	3.60
409	Pittsburgh Pirates Team Card	10.00	4.50
410	Al Smith	6.00	2.70
411	Danny O'Connell	6.00	2.70
412	Charlie James	6.00	2.70
413	Matty Alou	10.00	4.50
414	Joe Gaines	6.00	2.70
415	Bill Virdon	10.00	4.50
416	Bob Scheffing MG	6.00	2.70
417	Joe Azcue	6.00	2.70
418	Andy Carey	6.00	2.70
419	Bob Bruce	8.00	3.60
420	Gus Triandos	8.00	3.60
421	Ken MacKenzie	8.00	3.60
422	Steve Bilko	6.00	2.70
423	Rival League Relief Aces: Roy Face Hoyt Wilhelm	10.00	4.50
424	Al McBean	6.00	2.70
425	Carl Yastrzemski	125.00	55.00
426	Bob Farley	6.00	2.70
427	Jake Wood	6.00	2.70
428	Joe Hicks	6.00	2.70
429	Billy O'Dell	6.00	2.70
430	Tony Kubek	10.00	4.50
431	Bob Rodgers	8.00	3.60
432	Jim Pendleton	6.00	2.70
433	Jim Archer	6.00	2.70
434	Clay Dalrymple	6.00	2.70
435	Larry Sherry	8.00	3.60
436	Felix Mantilla	8.00	3.60
437	Ray Moore	6.00	2.70
438	Dick Brown	6.00	2.70
439	Jerry Buchek	6.00	2.70
440	Joey Jay	6.00	2.70
441	Checklist 6	16.00	7.25
442	Wes Stock	6.00	2.70
443	Del Crandall	8.00	3.60
444	Ted Wills	6.00	2.70
445	Vic Power	8.00	3.60
446	Don Elston	6.00	2.70
447	Willie Kirkland	12.00	5.50
448	Joe Gibbon	12.00	5.50
449	Jerry Adair	12.00	5.50
450	Jim O'Toole	15.00	6.75
451	Jose Tartabull	15.00	6.75
452	Earl Averill Jr.	12.00	5.50
453	Cal McLish	12.00	5.50
454	Floyd Robinson	12.00	5.50
455	Luis Arroyo	15.00	6.75
456	Joe Amalfitano	15.00	6.75
457	Lou Clinton	12.00	5.50
458A	Bob Buhl (Braves emblem on cap)	15.00	6.75
458B	Bob Buhl (No emblem on cap)	50.00	22.00
459	Ed Bailey	12.00	5.50
460	Jim Bunning	20.00	9.00
461	Ken Hubbs	35.00	16.00
462A	Willie Tasby (Senators emblem on cap)	12.00	5.50
462B	Willie Tasby (No emblem on cap)	50.00	22.00
463	Hank Bauer MG	15.00	6.75
464	Al Jackson	12.00	5.50
465	Reds Team	20.00	9.00
466	Norm Cash AS	15.00	6.75
467	Chuck Schilling AS	14.00	6.25
468	Brooks Robinson AS	25.00	11.00
469	Luis Aparicio AS	15.00	6.75
470	Al Kaline AS	25.00	11.00
471	Mickey Mantle AS	200.00	90.00
472	Rocky Colavito AS	15.00	6.75
473	Elston Howard AS	15.00	6.75
474	Frank Lary AS	14.00	6.25
475	Whitey Ford AS	15.00	6.75
476	Orioles Team	20.00	9.00
477	Andre Rodgers	12.00	5.50
478	Don Zimmer (Shown with Mets cap, but listed as with Cincinnati)	20.00	9.00
479	Joel Horlen	12.00	5.50
480	Harvey Kuenn	15.00	6.75
481	Vic Wertz	15.00	6.75
482	Sam Mele MG	12.00	5.50
483	Don McMahon	12.00	5.50
484	Dick Schofield	12.00	5.50
485	Pedro Ramos	12.00	5.50
486	Jim Gilliam	15.00	6.75
487	Jerry Lynch	12.00	5.50
488	Hal Brown	12.00	5.50
489	Julio Gotay	12.00	5.50
490	Clete Boyer UER Reversed Negative	15.00	6.75
491	Leon Wagner	12.00	5.50
492	Hal W. Smith	12.00	5.50
493	Danny McDevitt	12.00	5.50
494	Sammy White	12.00	5.50
495	Don Cardwell	12.00	5.50
496	Wayne Causey	12.00	5.50
497	Ed Bouchee	15.00	6.75
498	Jim Donohue	12.00	5.50
499	Zoilo Versalles	15.00	6.75
500	Duke Snider	50.00	22.00
501	Claude Osteen	15.00	6.75
502	Hector Lopez	15.00	6.75
503	Danny Murtaugh MG	15.00	6.75
504	Eddie Bressoud	12.00	5.50
505	Juan Marichal	40.00	18.00
506	Charlie Maxwell	15.00	6.75
507	Ernie Broglio	15.00	6.75
508	Gordy Coleman	15.00	6.75
509	Dave Giusti	15.00	6.75
510	Jim Lemon	12.00	5.50
511	Bubba Phillips	12.00	5.50
512	Mike Fornieles	12.00	5.50
513	Whitey Herzog	15.00	6.75
514	Sherm Lollar	15.00	6.75
515	Stan Williams	15.00	6.75
516	Checklist 7	16.00	3.20
517	Dave Wickersham	12.00	5.50
518	Lee Maye	12.00	5.50
519	Bob Johnson	12.00	5.50
520	Bob Friend	16.00	7.25
521	Jacke Davis UER (Listed as OF on front and P on back)	12.00	5.50
522	Lindy McDaniel	15.00	6.75
523	Russ Nixon SP	12.00	5.50
524	Howie Nunn SP	12.00	5.50
525	George Thomas	20.00	9.00
526	Hal Woodeshick SP	12.00	5.50
527	Dick McAuliffe	30.00	13.50
528	Turk Lown	20.00	9.00
529	John Schaive SP	12.00	5.50
530	Bob Gibson SP	125.00	55.00
531	Bobby G. Smith	20.00	9.00
532	Dick Stigman	20.00	9.00
533	Charley Lau SP	35.00	16.00
534	Tony Gonzalez SP	20.00	9.00
535	Ed Roebuck	20.00	9.00
536	Dick Gernert	20.00	9.00
537	Cleveland Indians Team Card	50.00	22.00
538	Jack Sanford	20.00	9.00
539	Billy Moran	20.00	9.00
540	Jim Landis SP	20.00	9.00
541	Don Nottebart SP	20.00	9.00
542	Dave Philley	20.00	9.00
543	Bob Allen SP	20.00	9.00
544	Willie McCovey SP	100.00	45.00
545	Hoyt Wilhelm SP	50.00	22.00
546	Moe Thacker SP	20.00	9.00
547	Don Ferrarese	20.00	9.00
548	Bobby Del Greco	20.00	9.00
549	Bill Rigney MG SP	40.00	18.00
550	Art Mahaffey SP	40.00	18.00
551	Harry Bright	20.00	9.00
552	Chicago Cubs SP Team Card	50.00	22.00
553	Jim Coates	20.00	9.00
554	Bubba Morton SP	40.00	18.00
555	John Buzhardt SP	40.00	18.00
556	Al Spangler	20.00	9.00
557	Bob Anderson SP	40.00	18.00
558	John Goryl	20.00	9.00
559	Mike Higgins MG	20.00	9.00
560	Chuck Estrada SP	30.00	13.50
561	Gene Oliver SP	30.00	13.50
562	Bill Henry	20.00	9.00
563	Ken Aspromonte	20.00	9.00
564	Bob Grim	20.00	9.00
565	Jose Pagan	20.00	9.00
566	Marty Kutyna SP	30.00	13.50
567	Tracy Stallard SP	30.00	13.50
568	Jim Golden	20.00	9.00
569	Ed Sadowski SP	30.00	13.50
570	Bill Stafford SP	30.00	13.50
571	Billy Klaus SP	35.00	16.00
572	Bob G. Miller SP	20.00	9.00
573	Johnny Logan	20.00	9.00
574	Dean Stone	20.00	9.00
575	Red Schoendienst SP	50.00	22.00
576	Russ Kemmerer SP	30.00	13.50
577	Dave Nicholson SP	30.00	13.50
578	Jim Duffalo	20.00	9.00
579	Jim Schaffer SP	30.00	13.50
580	Bill Monbouquette	20.00	9.00
581	Mel Roach	20.00	9.00
582	Ron Piche	20.00	9.00
583	Larry Osborne	20.00	9.00
584	Minnesota Twins SP Team Card	60.00	27.00
585	Glen Hobbie SP	30.00	13.50
586	Sammy Esposito SP	30.00	13.50
587	Frank Funk SP	30.00	13.50
588	Birdie Tebbetts MG	20.00	9.00
589	Bob Turley	30.00	13.50
590	Curt Flood	30.00	13.50
591	Rookie Pitchers SP Sam McDowell Ron Taylor Ron Nischwitz Art Quirk Dick Radatz	70.00	32.00
592	Rookie Pitchers SP Dan Pfister Bo Belinsky Dave Stenhouse Jim Bouton Joe Bonikowski	70.00	32.00
593	Rookie Pitchers SP Jack Lamabe Craig Anderson Jack Hamilton Bob Moorhead Bob Veale	40.00	18.00
594	Rookie Catchers SP Doc Edwards Ken Retzer Bob Uecker Doug Camilli Don Pavletich	75.00	34.00
595	Rookie Infielders SP Bob Sadowski Felix Torres Marlan Coughtry Ed Charles	40.00	18.00
596	Rookie Infielders SP Bernie Allen Joe Pepitone Phil Linz Rich Rollins	70.00	32.00
597	Rookie Infielders SP Jim McKnight Rod Kanehl Amado Samuel Denis Menke	40.00	18.00
598	Rookie Outfielders SP Al Luplow Manny Jimenez Howie Goss Jim Hickman Ed Olivares	80.00	23.00

1963 Topps

	NRMT	VG-E
COMPLETE SET (576)	5000.00	2200.00
COMMON CARD (1-196)	4.00	1.80
COMMON CARD (197-283)	5.00	2.20
COMMON CARD (284-370)	5.00	2.20
COMMON CARD (371-446)	5.00	2.20
MINOR STARS 1-446	8.00	3.60
SEMISTARS 1-446	10.00	4.50
UNLISTED STARS 1-446	15.00	6.75
COMMON CARD (447-522)	25.00	11.00
MINOR STARS 447-522	30.00	13.50
SEMISTARS 447-522	40.00	18.00
COMMON CARD (523-576)	15.00	6.75
MINOR STARS 523-576	20.00	9.00
SEMISTARS 523-576	30.00	13.50

*UNLISTED DODGER/YANKEE: 1.25X VALUE
CARDS PRICED IN NM CONDITION !

☐ 1	NL Batting Leaders	40.00	8.00
	Tommy Davis		
	Frank Robinson		
	Stan Musial		
	Hank Aaron		
	Bill White		
☐ 2	AL Batting Leaders	50.00	22.00
	Pete Runnels		
	Mickey Mantle		
	Floyd Robinson		
	Norm Siebern		
	Chuck Hinton		
☐ 3	NL Home Run Leaders	30.00	13.50
	Willie Mays		
	Hank Aaron		
	Frank Robinson		
	Orlando Cepeda		
	Ernie Banks		
☐ 4	AL Home Run Leaders	20.00	9.00
	Harmon Killebrew		
	Norm Cash		
	Rocky Colavito		
	Roger Maris		
	Jim Gentile		
	Leon Wagner		
☐ 5	NL ERA Leaders	20.00	9.00
	Sandy Koufax		
	Bob Shaw		
	Bob Purkey		
	Don Drysdale		
☐ 6	AL ERA Leaders	10.00	4.50
	Hank Aguirre		
	Robin Roberts		
	Whitey Ford		
	Eddie Fisher		
	Dean Chance		
☐ 7	NL Pitching Leaders	10.00	4.50
	Don Drysdale		
	Jack Sanford		
	Bob Purkey		
	Billy O'Dell		
	Art Mahaffey		
	Joe Jay		
☐ 8	AL Pitching Leaders	8.00	3.60
	Ralph Terry		
	Dick Donovan		
	Ray Herbert		

	Jim Bunning		
	Camilo Pascual		
☐ 9	NL Strikeout Leaders	25.00	11.00
	Don Drysdale		
	Sandy Koufax		
	Bob Gibson		
	Billy O'Dell		
	Dick Farrell		
☐ 10	AL Strikeout Leaders	8.00	3.60
	Camilo Pascual		
	Jim Bunning		
	Ralph Terry		
	Juan Pizarro		
	Jim Kaat		
☐ 11	Lee Walls	4.00	1.80
☐ 12	Steve Barber	4.00	1.80
☐ 13	Philadelphia Phillies	8.00	3.60
	Team Card		
☐ 14	Pedro Ramos	4.00	1.80
☐ 15	Ken Hubbs UER	10.00	4.50
	(No position listed		
	on front of card)		
☐ 16	Al Smith	4.00	1.80
☐ 17	Ryne Duren	8.00	3.60
☐ 18	Buc Blasters	70.00	32.00
	Smoky Burgess		
	Dick Stuart		
	Bob Clemente		
	Bob Skinner		
☐ 19	Pete Burnside	4.00	1.80
☐ 20	Tony Kubek	8.00	3.60
☐ 21	Marty Keough	4.00	1.80
☐ 22	Curt Simmons	4.00	1.80
☐ 23	Ed Lopat MG	8.00	3.60
☐ 24	Bob Bruce	4.00	1.80
☐ 25	Al Kaline	45.00	20.00
☐ 26	Ray Moore	4.00	1.80
☐ 27	Choo Choo Coleman	8.00	3.60
☐ 28	Mike Fornieles	4.00	1.80
☐ 29A	1962 Rookie Stars	8.00	3.60
	Sammy Ellis		
	Ray Culp		
	John Boozer		
	Jesse Gonder		
☐ 29B	1963 Rookie Stars	4.00	1.80
	Sammy Ellis		
	Ray Culp		
	John Boozer		
	Jesse Gonder		
☐ 30	Harvey Kuenn	8.00	3.60
☐ 31	Cal Koonce	4.00	1.80
☐ 32	Tony Gonzalez	4.00	1.80
☐ 33	Bo Belinsky	8.00	3.60
☐ 34	Dick Schofield	4.00	1.80
☐ 35	John Buzhardt	4.00	1.80
☐ 36	Jerry Kindall	4.00	1.80
☐ 37	Jerry Lynch	4.00	1.80
☐ 38	Bud Daley	8.00	3.60
☐ 39	Angels Team	8.00	3.60
☐ 40	Vic Power	8.00	3.60
☐ 41	Charley Lau	8.00	3.60
☐ 42	Stan Williams	8.00	3.60
	(Listed as Yankee on		
	card but LA cap)		
☐ 43	Veteran Masters	8.00	3.60
	Casey Stengel MG		
	Gene Woodling		
☐ 44	Terry Fox	4.00	1.80
☐ 45	Bob Aspromonte	4.00	1.80
☐ 46	Tommie Aaron	8.00	3.60
☐ 47	Don Lock	4.00	1.80
☐ 48	Birdie Tebbetts MG	8.00	3.60
☐ 49	Dal Maxvill	8.00	3.60
☐ 50	Billy Pierce	8.00	3.60
☐ 51	George Alusik	4.00	1.80
☐ 52	Chuck Schilling	4.00	1.80
☐ 53	Joe Moeller	8.00	3.60
☐ 54A	1962 Rookie Stars	15.00	6.75
	Nelson Mathews		
	Harry Fanok		
	Jack Cullen		
	Dave DeBusschere		
☐ 54B	1963 Rookie Stars	8.00	3.60
	Nelson Mathews		
	Harry Fanok		
	Jack Cullen		

	Dave DeBusschere		
☐ 55	Bill Virdon	8.00	3.60
☐ 56	Dennis Bennett	4.00	1.80
☐ 57	Billy Moran	4.00	1.80
☐ 58	Bob Will	4.00	1.80
☐ 59	Craig Anderson	4.00	1.80
☐ 60	Elston Howard	8.00	3.60
☐ 61	Ernie Bowman	4.00	1.80
☐ 62	Bob Hendley	4.00	1.80
☐ 63	Reds Team	8.00	3.60
☐ 64	Dick McAuliffe	8.00	3.60
☐ 65	Jackie Brandt	4.00	1.80
☐ 66	Mike Joyce	4.00	1.80
☐ 67	Ed Charles	4.00	1.80
☐ 68	Friendly Foes	25.00	11.00
	Duke Snider		
	Gil Hodges		
☐ 69	Bud Zipfel	4.00	1.80
☐ 70	Jim O'Toole	8.00	3.60
☐ 71	Bobby Wine	8.00	3.60
☐ 72	Johnny Romano	4.00	1.80
☐ 73	Bobby Bragan MG	8.00	3.60
☐ 74	Denny Lemaster	4.00	1.80
☐ 75	Bob Allison	8.00	3.60
☐ 76	Earl Wilson	8.00	3.60
☐ 77	Al Spangler	4.00	1.80
☐ 78	Marv Throneberry	8.00	3.60
☐ 79	Checklist 1	12.00	2.40
☐ 80	Jim Gilliam	8.00	3.60
☐ 81	Jim Schaffer	4.00	1.80
☐ 82	Ed Rakow	4.00	1.80
☐ 83	Charley James	4.00	1.80
☐ 84	Ron Kline	4.00	1.80
☐ 85	Tom Haller	8.00	3.60
☐ 86	Charley Maxwell	8.00	3.60
☐ 87	Bob Veale	8.00	3.60
☐ 88	Ron Hansen	4.00	1.80
☐ 89	Dick Stigman	4.00	1.80
☐ 90	Gordy Coleman	8.00	3.60
☐ 91	Dallas Green	8.00	3.60
☐ 92	Hector Lopez	8.00	3.60
☐ 93	Galen Cisco	4.00	1.80
☐ 94	Bob Schmidt	4.00	1.80
☐ 95	Larry Jackson	4.00	1.80
☐ 96	Lou Clinton	4.00	1.80
☐ 97	Bob Duliba	4.00	1.80
☐ 98	George Thomas	4.00	1.80
☐ 99	Jim Umbricht	4.00	1.80
☐ 100	Joe Cunningham	4.00	1.80
☐ 101	Joe Gibbon	4.00	1.80
☐ 102A	Checklist 2	12.00	2.40
	(Red on yellow)		
☐ 102B	Checklist 2	12.00	2.40
	(White on red)		
☐ 103	Chuck Essegian	4.00	1.80
☐ 104	Lew Krausse	4.00	1.80
☐ 105	Ron Fairly	8.00	3.60
☐ 106	Bobby Bolin	4.00	1.80
☐ 107	Jim Hickman	8.00	3.60
☐ 108	Hoyt Wilhelm	10.00	4.50
☐ 109	Lee Maye	4.00	1.80
☐ 110	Rich Rollins	8.00	3.60
☐ 111	Al Jackson	4.00	1.80
☐ 112	Dick Brown	4.00	1.80
☐ 113	Don Landrum UER	4.00	1.80
	(Photo actually		
	Ron Santo)		
☐ 114	Dan Osinski	4.00	1.80
☐ 115	Carl Yastrzemski	40.00	18.00
☐ 116	Jim Brosnan	8.00	3.60
☐ 117	Jacke Davis	4.00	1.80
☐ 118	Sherm Lollar	4.00	1.80
☐ 119	Bob Lillis	4.00	1.80
☐ 120	Roger Maris	50.00	22.00
☐ 121	Jim Hannan	4.00	1.80
☐ 122	Julio Gotay	4.00	1.80
☐ 123	Frank Howard	8.00	3.60
☐ 124	Dick Howser	8.00	3.60
☐ 125	Robin Roberts	15.00	6.75
☐ 126	Bob Uecker	15.00	6.75
☐ 127	Bill Tuttle	4.00	1.80
☐ 128	Matty Alou	8.00	3.60
☐ 129	Gary Bell	4.00	1.80
☐ 130	Dick Groat	8.00	3.60
☐ 131	Washington Senators	8.00	3.60
	Team Card		

132	Jack Hamilton	4.00	1.80
133	Gene Freese	4.00	1.80
134	Bob Scheffing MG	4.00	1.80
135	Richie Ashburn	20.00	9.00
136	Ike Delock	4.00	1.80
137	Mack Jones	4.00	1.80
138	Pride of NL	70.00	32.00
	Willie Mays		
	Stan Musial		
139	Earl Averill	4.00	1.80
140	Frank Lary	8.00	3.60
141	Manny Mota	8.00	3.60
142	Whitey Ford WS	10.00	4.50
143	Jack Sanford WS	8.00	3.60
144	Roger Maris WS	15.00	6.75
145	Chuck Hiller WS	8.00	3.60
146	Tom Tresh WS	8.00	3.60
147	Billy Pierce WS	8.00	3.60
148	Ralph Terry WS	8.00	3.60
149	Marv Breeding	4.00	1.80
150	Johnny Podres	8.00	3.60
151	Pirates Team	8.00	3.60
152	Ron Nischwitz	4.00	1.80
153	Hal Smith	4.00	1.80
154	Walter Alston MG	8.00	3.60
155	Bill Stafford	4.00	1.80
156	Roy McMillan	4.00	1.80
157	Diego Segui	8.00	3.60
158	Rookie Stars	8.00	3.60
	Rogelio Alvares		
	Dave Roberts		
	Tommy Harper		
	Bob Saverine		
159	Jim Pagliaroni	4.00	1.80
160	Juan Pizarro	4.00	1.80
161	Frank Torre	8.00	3.60
162	Twins Team	8.00	3.60
163	Don Larsen	8.00	3.60
164	Bubba Morton	4.00	1.80
165	Jim Kaat	8.00	3.60
166	Johnny Keane MG	4.00	1.80
167	Jim Fregosi	8.00	3.60
168	Russ Nixon	4.00	1.80
169	Rookie Stars	25.00	11.00
	Dick Egan		
	Julio Navarro		
	Tommie Sisk		
	Gaylord Perry		
170	Joe Adcock	8.00	3.60
171	Steve Hamilton	4.00	1.80
172	Gene Oliver	4.00	1.80
173	Bombers' Best	150.00	70.00
	Tom Tresh		
	Mickey Mantle		
	Bobby Richardson		
174	Larry Burright	4.00	1.80
175	Bob Buhl	8.00	3.60
176	Jim King	4.00	1.80
177	Bubba Phillips	4.00	1.80
178	Johnny Edwards	4.00	1.80
179	Ron Piche	4.00	1.80
180	Bill Skowron	8.00	3.60
181	Sammy Esposito	4.00	1.80
182	Albie Pearson	4.00	1.80
183	Joe Pepitone	8.00	3.60
184	Vern Law	4.00	1.80
185	Chuck Hiller	4.00	1.80
186	Jerry Zimmerman	4.00	1.80
187	Willie Kirkland	4.00	1.80
188	Eddie Bressoud	4.00	1.80
189	Dave Giusti	8.00	3.60
190	Minnie Minoso	8.00	3.60
191	Checklist 3	12.00	2.40
192	Clay Dalrymple	4.00	1.80
193	Andre Rodgers	4.00	1.80
194	Joe Nuxhall	4.00	1.80
195	Manny Jimenez	4.00	1.80
196	Doug Camilli	4.00	1.80
197	Roger Craig	8.00	3.60
198	Lenny Green	5.00	2.20
199	Joe Amalfitano	5.00	2.20
200	Mickey Mantle	500.00	220.00
201	Cecil Butler	5.00	2.20
202	Boston Red Sox	8.00	3.60
	Team Card		
203	Chico Cardenas	8.00	3.60
204	Don Nottebart	5.00	2.20
205	Luis Aparicio	15.00	6.75
206	Ray Washburn	5.00	2.20
207	Ken Hunt	5.00	2.20
208	Rookie Stars	5.00	2.20
	Ron Herbel		
	John Miller		
	Wally Wolf		
	Ron Taylor		
209	Hobie Landrith	5.00	2.20
210	Sandy Koufax I	150.00	70.00
211	Fred Whitfield	5.00	2.20
212	Glen Hobbie	5.00	2.20
213	Billy Hitchcock MG	5.00	2.20
214	Orlando Pena	5.00	2.20
215	Bob Skinner	8.00	3.60
216	Gene Conley	8.00	3.60
217	Joe Christopher	5.00	2.20
218	Tiger Twirlers	8.00	3.60
	Frank Lary		
	Don Mossi		
	Jim Bunning		
219	Chuck Cottier	5.00	2.20
220	Camilo Pascual	8.00	3.60
221	Cookie Rojas	8.00	3.60
222	Cubs Team	8.00	3.60
223	Eddie Fisher	5.00	2.20
224	Mike Roarke	5.00	2.20
225	Joey Jay	5.00	2.20
226	Julian Javier	8.00	3.60
227	Jim Grant	8.00	3.60
228	Rookie Stars	40.00	18.00
	Max Alvis		
	Bob Bailey		
	Tony Oliva		
	(Listed as Pedro)		
	Ed Kranepool		
229	Willie Davis	8.00	3.60
230	Pete Runnels	8.00	3.60
231	Eli Grba UER	5.00	2.20
	(Large photo is		
	Ryne Duren)		
232	Frank Malzone	8.00	3.60
233	Casey Stengel MG	20.00	9.00
234	Dave Nicholson	5.00	2.20
235	Billy O'Dell	5.00	2.20
236	Bill Bryan	5.00	2.20
237	Jim Coates	8.00	3.60
238	Lou Johnson	5.00	2.20
239	Harvey Haddix	8.00	3.60
240	Rocky Colavito	15.00	6.75
241	Bob Smith	5.00	2.20
242	Power Plus	60.00	27.00
	Ernie Banks		
	Hank Aaron		
243	Don Leppert	5.00	2.20
244	John Tsitouris	5.00	2.20
245	Gil Hodges	20.00	9.00
246	Lee Stange	5.00	2.20
247	Yankees Team	40.00	18.00
248	Tito Francona	5.00	2.20
249	Leo Burke	5.00	2.20
250	Stan Musial	100.00	45.00
251	Jack Lamabe	5.00	2.20
252	Ron Santo	10.00	4.50
253	Rookie Stars	5.00	2.20
	Len Gabrielson		
	Pete Jernigan		
	John Wojcik		
	Deacon Jones		
254	Mike Hershberger	5.00	2.20
255	Bob Shaw	5.00	2.20
256	Jerry Lumpe	5.00	2.20
257	Hank Aguirre	5.00	2.20
258	Alvin Dark MG	8.00	3.60
259	Johnny Logan	8.00	3.60
260	Jim Gentile	8.00	3.60
261	Bob Miller	5.00	2.20
262	Ellis Burton	5.00	2.20
263	Dave Stenhouse	5.00	2.20
264	Phil Linz	8.00	3.60
265	Vada Pinson	8.00	3.60
266	Bob Allen	5.00	2.20
267	Carl Sawatski	5.00	2.20
268	Don Demeter	5.00	2.20
269	Don Mincher	5.00	2.20
270	Felipe Alou	8.00	3.60
271	Dean Stone	5.00	2.20
272	Danny Murphy	5.00	2.20
273	Sammy Taylor	5.00	2.20
274	Checklist 4	12.00	2.40
275	Eddie Mathews	25.00	11.00
276	Barry Shetrone	5.00	2.20
277	Dick Farrell	5.00	2.20
278	Chico Fernandez	5.00	2.20
279	Wally Moon	8.00	3.60
280	Bob Rodgers	5.00	2.20
281	Tom Sturdivant	5.00	2.20
282	Bobby Del Greco	5.00	2.20
283	Roy Sievers	8.00	3.60
284	Dave Sisler	5.00	2.20
285	Dick Stuart	8.00	3.60
286	Stu Miller	8.00	3.60
287	Dick Bertell	5.00	2.20
288	Chicago White Sox	10.00	4.50
	Team Card		
289	Hal Brown	5.00	2.20
290	Bill White	8.00	3.60
291	Don Rudolph	5.00	2.20
292	Pumpsie Green	8.00	3.60
293	Bill Pleis	5.00	2.20
294	Bill Rigney MG	5.00	2.20
295	Ed Roebuck	5.00	2.20
296	Doc Edwards	5.00	2.20
297	Jim Golden	5.00	2.20
298	Don Dillard	5.00	2.20
299	Rookie Stars	8.00	3.60
	Dave Morehead		
	Bob Dustal		
	Tom Butters		
	Dan Schneider		
300	Willie Mays	150.00	70.00
301	Bill Fischer	5.00	2.20
302	Whitey Herzog	8.00	3.60
303	Earl Francis	5.00	2.20
304	Harry Bright	5.00	2.20
305	Don Hoak	5.00	2.20
306	Star Receivers	8.00	3.60
	Earl Battey		
	Elston Howard		
307	Chet Nichols	5.00	2.20
308	Camilo Carreon	5.00	2.20
309	Jim Brewer	5.00	2.20
310	Tommy Davis	8.00	3.60
311	Joe McClain	5.00	2.20
312	Houston Colts	25.00	11.00
	Team Card		
313	Ernie Broglio	5.00	2.20
314	John Goryl	5.00	2.20
315	Ralph Terry	8.00	3.60
316	Norm Sherry	5.00	2.20
317	Sam McDowell	8.00	3.60
318	Gene Mauch MG	8.00	3.60
319	Joe Gaines	5.00	2.20
320	Warren Spahn	50.00	22.00
321	Gino Cimoli	5.00	2.20
322	Bob Turley	8.00	3.60
323	Bill Mazeroski	10.00	4.50
324	Rookie Stars	8.00	3.60
	George Williams		
	Pete Ward		
	Phil Roof		
	Vic Davalillo		
325	Jack Sanford	5.00	2.20
326	Hank Foiles	5.00	2.20
327	Paul Foytack	5.00	2.20
328	Dick Williams	8.00	3.60
329	Lindy McDaniel	5.00	2.20
330	Chuck Hinton	5.00	2.20
331	Series Foes	8.00	3.60
	Bill Stafford		
	Bill Pierce		
332	Joel Horlen	8.00	3.60
333	Carl Warwick	5.00	2.20
334	Wynn Hawkins	5.00	2.20
335	Leon Wagner	5.00	2.20
336	Ed Bauta	5.00	2.20
337	Dodgers Team	25.00	11.00
338	Russ Kemmerer	5.00	2.20
339	Ted Bowsfield	5.00	2.20
340	Yogi Berra P/CO	70.00	32.00
341	Jack Baldschun	5.00	2.20

#			
❑ 342	Gene Woodling	8.00	3.60
❑ 343	Johnny Pesky MG	8.00	3.60
❑ 344	Don Schwall	5.00	2.20
❑ 345	Brooks Robinson	60.00	27.00
❑ 346	Billy Hoeft	5.00	2.20
❑ 347	Joe Torre	15.00	6.75
❑ 348	Vic Wertz	8.00	3.60
❑ 349	Zoilo Versalles	8.00	3.60
❑ 350	Bob Purkey	5.00	2.20
❑ 351	Al Luplow	5.00	2.20
❑ 352	Ken Johnson	5.00	2.20
❑ 353	Billy Williams	30.00	13.50
❑ 354	Dom Zanni	5.00	2.20
❑ 355	Dean Chance	8.00	3.60
❑ 356	John Schaive	5.00	2.20
❑ 357	George Altman	5.00	2.20
❑ 358	Milt Pappas	8.00	3.60
❑ 359	Haywood Sullivan	8.00	3.60
❑ 360	Don Drysdale	40.00	18.00
❑ 361	Clete Boyer	8.00	3.60
❑ 362	Checklist 5	12.00	2.40
❑ 363	Dick Radatz	8.00	3.60
❑ 364	Howie Goss	5.00	2.20
❑ 365	Jim Bunning	15.00	6.75
❑ 366	Tony Taylor	8.00	3.60
❑ 367	Tony Cloninger	5.00	2.20
❑ 368	Ed Bailey	5.00	2.20
❑ 369	Jim Lemon	5.00	2.20
❑ 370	Dick Donovan	5.00	2.20
❑ 371	Rod Kanehl	8.00	3.60
❑ 372	Don Lee	5.00	2.20
❑ 373	Jim Campbell	5.00	2.20
❑ 374	Claude Osteen	8.00	3.60
❑ 375	Ken Boyer	8.00	3.60
❑ 376	John Wyatt	5.00	2.20
❑ 377	Baltimore Orioles Team Card	10.00	4.50
❑ 378	Bill Henry	5.00	2.20
❑ 379	Bob Anderson	5.00	2.20
❑ 380	Ernie Banks UER (Back has career Major but he never played in Minors)	75.00	34.00
❑ 381	Frank Baumann	5.00	2.20
❑ 382	Ralph Houk MG	8.00	3.60
❑ 383	Pete Richert	5.00	2.20
❑ 384	Bob Tillman	5.00	2.20
❑ 385	Art Mahaffey	5.00	2.20
❑ 386	Rookie Stars	5.00	2.20
	Ed Kirkpatrick		
	John Bateman		
	Larry Bearnarth		
	Garry Roggenburk		
❑ 387	Al McBean	5.00	2.20
❑ 388	Jim Davenport	8.00	3.60
❑ 389	Frank Sullivan	5.00	2.20
❑ 390	Hank Aaron	125.00	55.00
❑ 391	Bill Dailey	5.00	2.20
❑ 392	Tribe Thumpers	5.00	2.20
	Johnny Romano		
	Tito Francona		
❑ 393	Ken MacKenzie	8.00	3.60
❑ 394	Tim McCarver	15.00	6.75
❑ 395	Don McMahon	5.00	2.20
❑ 396	Joe Koppe	5.00	2.20
❑ 397	Kansas City Athletics Team Card	10.00	4.50
❑ 398	Boog Powell	25.00	11.00
❑ 399	Dick Ellsworth	5.00	2.20
❑ 400	Frank Robinson	60.00	27.00
❑ 401	Jim Bouton	15.00	6.75
❑ 402	Mickey Vernon MG	8.00	3.60
❑ 403	Ron Perranoski	8.00	3.60
❑ 404	Bob Oldis	5.00	2.20
❑ 405	Floyd Robinson	5.00	2.20
❑ 406	Howie Koplitz	5.00	2.20
❑ 407	Rookie Stars	5.00	2.20
	Frank Kostro		
	Chico Ruiz		
	Larry Elliot		
	Dick Simpson		
❑ 408	Billy Gardner	5.00	2.20
❑ 409	Roy Face	8.00	3.60
❑ 410	Earl Battey	5.00	2.20
❑ 411	Jim Constable	5.00	2.20
❑ 412	Dodger Big Three	40.00	18.00
	Johnny Podres		
	Don Drysdale		
	Sandy Koufax		
❑ 413	Jerry Walker	5.00	2.20
❑ 414	Ty Cline	5.00	2.20
❑ 415	Bob Gibson	60.00	27.00
❑ 416	Alex Grammas	5.00	2.20
❑ 417	Giants Team	10.00	4.50
❑ 418	John Orsino	5.00	2.20
❑ 419	Tracy Stallard	5.00	2.20
❑ 420	Bobby Richardson	15.00	6.75
❑ 421	Tom Morgan	5.00	2.20
❑ 422	Fred Hutchinson MG	8.00	3.60
❑ 423	Ed Hobaugh	5.00	2.20
❑ 424	Charlie Smith	5.00	2.20
❑ 425	Smoky Burgess	8.00	3.60
❑ 426	Barry Latman	5.00	2.20
❑ 427	Bernie Allen	5.00	2.20
❑ 428	Carl Boles	5.00	2.20
❑ 429	Lou Burdette	8.00	3.60
❑ 430	Norm Siebern	5.00	2.20
❑ 431A	Checklist 6 (White on red)	12.00	2.40
❑ 431B	Checklist 6 (Black on orange)	30.00	6.00
❑ 432	Roman Mejias	5.00	2.20
❑ 433	Denis Menke	5.00	2.20
❑ 434	John Callison	8.00	3.60
❑ 435	Woody Held	5.00	2.20
❑ 436	Tim Harkness	8.00	3.60
❑ 437	Bill Bruton	5.00	2.20
❑ 438	Wes Stock	5.00	2.20
❑ 439	Don Zimmer	8.00	3.60
❑ 440	Juan Marichal	30.00	13.50
❑ 441	Lee Thomas	8.00	3.60
❑ 442	J.C. Hartman	5.00	2.20
❑ 443	Jimmy Piersall	8.00	3.60
❑ 444	Jim Maloney	8.00	3.60
❑ 445	Norm Cash	8.00	3.60
❑ 446	Whitey Ford	50.00	22.00
❑ 447	Felix Mantilla	25.00	11.00
❑ 448	Jack Kralick	25.00	11.00
❑ 449	Jose Tartabull	25.00	11.00
❑ 450	Bob Friend	30.00	13.50
❑ 451	Indians Team	40.00	18.00
❑ 452	Barney Schultz	25.00	11.00
❑ 453	Jake Wood	25.00	11.00
❑ 454A	Art Fowler (Card number on white background)	25.00	11.00
❑ 454B	Art Fowler (Card number on orange background)	30.00	13.50
❑ 455	Ruben Amaro	25.00	11.00
❑ 456	Jim Coker	25.00	11.00
❑ 457	Tex Clevenger	25.00	11.00
❑ 458	Al Lopez MG	30.00	13.50
❑ 459	Dick LeMay	25.00	11.00
❑ 460	Del Crandall	30.00	13.50
❑ 461	Norm Bass	25.00	11.00
❑ 462	Wally Post	25.00	11.00
❑ 463	Joe Schaffernoth	25.00	11.00
❑ 464	Ken Aspromonte	25.00	11.00
❑ 465	Chuck Estrada	25.00	11.00
❑ 466	Rookie Stars SP	60.00	27.00
	Nate Oliver		
	Tony Martinez		
	Bill Freehan		
	Jerry Robinson		
❑ 467	Phil Ortega	25.00	11.00
❑ 468	Carroll Hardy	30.00	13.50
❑ 469	Jay Hook	30.00	13.50
❑ 470	Tom Tresh SP	60.00	27.00
❑ 471	Ken Retzer	25.00	11.00
❑ 472	Lou Brock	80.00	36.00
❑ 473	New York Mets Team Card	100.00	45.00
❑ 474	Jack Fisher	25.00	11.00
❑ 475	Gus Triandos	30.00	13.50
❑ 476	Frank Funk	25.00	11.00
❑ 477	Donn Clendenon	30.00	13.50
❑ 478	Paul Brown	25.00	11.00
❑ 479	Ed Brinkman	25.00	11.00
❑ 480	Bill Monbouquette	25.00	11.00
❑ 481	Bob Taylor	25.00	11.00
❑ 482	Felix Torres	25.00	11.00
❑ 483	Jim Owens UER (Stat column for Wins has an R instead)	25.00	11.00
❑ 484	Dale Long SP	30.00	13.50
❑ 485	Jim Landis	25.00	11.00
❑ 486	Ray Sadecki	25.00	11.00
❑ 487	John Roseboro	30.00	13.50
❑ 488	Jerry Adair	25.00	11.00
❑ 489	Paul Toth	25.00	11.00
❑ 490	Willie McCovey	125.00	55.00
❑ 491	Harry Craft MG	25.00	11.00
❑ 492	Dave Wickersham	25.00	11.00
❑ 493	Walt Bond	25.00	11.00
❑ 494	Phil Regan	25.00	11.00
❑ 495	Frank Thomas SP	30.00	13.50
❑ 496	Rookie Stars	30.00	13.50
	Steve Dalkowski		
	Fred Newman		
	Jack Smith		
	Carl Bouldin		
❑ 497	Bennie Daniels	25.00	11.00
❑ 498	Eddie Kasko	25.00	11.00
❑ 499	J.C. Martin	25.00	11.00
❑ 500	Harmon Killebrew SP	150.00	70.00
❑ 501	Joe Azcue	25.00	11.00
❑ 502	Daryl Spencer	25.00	11.00
❑ 503	Braves Team	40.00	18.00
❑ 504	Bob Johnson	25.00	11.00
❑ 505	Curt Flood	30.00	13.50
❑ 506	Gene Green	25.00	11.00
❑ 507	Roland Sheldon	30.00	13.50
❑ 508	Ted Savage	25.00	11.00
❑ 509A	Checklist 7 (Checklist centered)	30.00	6.00
❑ 509B	Checklist 7 (Copyright to right)	30.00	6.00
❑ 510	Ken McBride	25.00	11.00
❑ 511	Charlie Neal	30.00	13.50
❑ 512	Cal McLish	25.00	11.00
❑ 513	Gary Geiger	25.00	11.00
❑ 514	Larry Osborne	25.00	11.00
❑ 515	Don Elston	25.00	11.00
❑ 516	Purnell Goldy	25.00	11.00
❑ 517	Hal Woodeshick	25.00	11.00
❑ 518	Don Blasingame	25.00	11.00
❑ 519	Claude Raymond	25.00	11.00
❑ 520	Orlando Cepeda	30.00	13.50
❑ 521	Dan Pfister	25.00	11.00
❑ 522	Rookie Stars	30.00	13.50
	Mel Nelson		
	Gary Peters		
	Jim Roland		
	Art Quirk		
❑ 523	Bill Kunkel	15.00	6.75
❑ 524	Cardinals Team	30.00	13.50
❑ 525	Nellie Fox	50.00	22.00
❑ 526	Dick Hall	15.00	6.75
❑ 527	Ed Sadowski	15.00	6.75
❑ 528	Carl Willey	15.00	6.75
❑ 529	Wes Covington	15.00	6.75
❑ 530	Don Mossi	20.00	9.00
❑ 531	Sam Mele MG	15.00	6.75
❑ 532	Steve Boros	15.00	6.75
❑ 533	Bobby Shantz	20.00	9.00
❑ 534	Ken Walters	15.00	6.75
❑ 535	Jim Perry	20.00	9.00
❑ 536	Norm Larker	15.00	6.75
❑ 537	Rookie Stars	850.00	375.00
	Pedro Gonzalez		
	Ken McMullen		
	Al Weis		
	Pete Rose		
❑ 538	George Brunet	15.00	6.75
❑ 539	Wayne Causey	15.00	6.75
❑ 540	Roberto Clemente	300.00	135.00
❑ 541	Ron Moeller	15.00	6.75
❑ 542	Lou Klimchock	15.00	6.75
❑ 543	Russ Snyder	15.00	6.75
❑ 544	Rookie Stars	40.00	18.00
	Duke Carmel		
	Bill Haas		
	Rusty Staub		
	Dick Phillips		
❑ 545	Jose Pagan	15.00	6.75
❑ 546	Hal Reniff	20.00	9.00
❑ 547	Gus Bell	15.00	6.75

		NRMT	VG-E
☐ 548	Tom Satriano	15.00	6.75
☐ 549	Rookie Stars	15.00	6.75
	Marcelino Lopez		
	Pete Lovrich		
	Paul Ratliff		
	Elmo Plaskett		
☐ 550	Duke Snider	75.00	34.00
☐ 551	Billy Klaus	15.00	6.75
☐ 552	Detroit Tigers	50.00	22.00
	Team Card		
☐ 553	Rookie Stars	125.00	55.00
	Brock Davis		
	Jim Gosger		
	Willie Stargell		
	John Herrnstein		
☐ 554	Hank Fischer	15.00	6.75
☐ 555	John Blanchard	20.00	9.00
☐ 556	Al Worthington	15.00	6.75
☐ 557	Cuno Barragan	15.00	6.75
☐ 558	Rookie Stars	20.00	9.00
	Bill Faul		
	Ron Hunt		
	Al Moran		
	Bob Lipski		
☐ 559	Danny Murtaugh MG	15.00	6.75
☐ 560	Ray Herbert	15.00	6.75
☐ 561	Mike De La Hoz	15.00	6.75
☐ 562	Rookie Stars	30.00	13.50
	Randy Cardinal		
	Dave McNally		
	Ken Rowe		
	Don Rowe		
☐ 563	Mike McCormick	15.00	6.75
☐ 564	George Banks	15.00	6.75
☐ 565	Larry Sherry	15.00	6.75
☐ 566	Cliff Cook	15.00	6.75
☐ 567	Jim Duffalo	15.00	6.75
☐ 568	Bob Sadowski	15.00	6.75
☐ 569	Luis Arroyo	20.00	9.00
☐ 570	Frank Bolling	15.00	6.75
☐ 571	Johnny Klippstein	15.00	6.75
☐ 572	Jack Spring	15.00	6.75
☐ 573	Coot Veal	15.00	6.75
☐ 574	Hal Kolstad	15.00	6.75
☐ 575	Don Cardwell	15.00	6.75
☐ 576	Johnny Temple	30.00	11.00

1964 Topps

	NRMT	VG-E
COMPLETE SET (587)	3000.00	1350.00
COMMON CARD (1-196)	3.00	1.35
COMMON CARD (197-370)	4.00	1.80
MINOR STARS 1-370	6.00	2.70
SEMISTARS 1-370	8.00	3.60
UNLISTED STARS 1-370	12.00	5.50
COMMON CARD (371-522)	7.00	3.10
MINOR STARS 371-522	10.00	4.50
SEMISTARS 371-522	15.00	6.75
UNLISTED STARS 371-522	25.00	11.00
COMMON CARD (523-587)	15.00	7.25
MINOR STARS 523-587	20.00	9.00
SEMISTARS 523-587	30.00	13.50

*UNLISTED DODGER/YANKEE: 1.25X VALUE
CARDS PRICED IN NM CONDITION

☐ 1	NL ERA Leaders	30.00	9.00
	Sandy Koufax		
	Dick Ellsworth		
	Bob Friend		
☐ 2	AL ERA Leaders	7.50	3.40
	Gary Peters		
	Juan Pizarro		
	Camilo Pascual		
☐ 3	NL Pitching Leaders	20.00	9.00
	Sandy Koufax		
	Juan Marichal		
	Warren Spahn		
	Jim Maloney		
☐ 4	AL Pitching Leaders	8.00	3.60
	Whitey Ford		
	Camilo Pascual		
	Jim Bouton		
☐ 5	NL Strikeout Leaders	15.00	6.75
	Sandy Koufax		
	Jim Maloney		
	Don Drysdale		
☐ 6	AL Strikeout Leaders	7.50	3.40
	Camilo Pascual		
	Jim Bunning		
	Dick Stigman		
☐ 7	NL Batting Leaders	20.00	9.00
	Tommy Davis		
	Roberto Clemente		
	Dick Groat		
	Hank Aaron		
☐ 8	AL Batting Leaders	15.00	6.75
	Carl Yastrzemski		
	Al Kaline		
	Rich Rollins		
☐ 9	NL Home Run Leaders	30.00	13.50
	Hank Aaron		
	Willie McCovey		
	Willie Mays		
	Orlando Cepeda		
☐ 10	AL Home Run Leaders	8.00	3.60
	Harmon Killebrew		
	Dick Stuart		
	Bob Allison		
☐ 11	NL RBI Leaders	15.00	6.75
	Hank Aaron		
	Ken Boyer		
	Bill White		
☐ 12	AL RBI Leaders	8.00	3.60
	Dick Stuart		
	Al Kaline		
	Harmon Killebrew		
☐ 13	Hoyt Wilhelm	8.00	3.60
☐ 14	Dodgers Rookies	3.00	1.35
	Dick Nen		
	Nick Willhite		
☐ 15	Zoilo Versalles	6.00	2.70
☐ 16	John Boozer	3.00	1.35
☐ 17	Willie Kirkland	3.00	1.35
☐ 18	Billy O'Dell	3.00	1.35
☐ 19	Don Wert	3.00	1.35
☐ 20	Bob Friend	6.00	2.70
☐ 21	Yogi Berra MG	30.00	13.50
☐ 22	Jerry Adair	3.00	1.35
☐ 23	Chris Zachary	3.00	1.35
☐ 24	Carl Sawatski	3.00	1.35
☐ 25	Bill Monbouquette	3.00	1.35
☐ 26	Gino Cimoli	3.00	1.35
☐ 27	New York Mets	8.00	3.60
	Team Card		
☐ 28	Claude Osteen	6.00	2.70
☐ 29	Lou Brock	35.00	16.00
☐ 30	Ron Perranoski	6.00	2.70
☐ 31	Dave Nicholson	3.00	1.35
☐ 32	Dean Chance	6.00	2.70
☐ 33	Reds Rookies	6.00	2.70
	Sammy Ellis		
	Mel Queen		
☐ 34	Jim Perry	6.00	2.70
☐ 35	Eddie Mathews	20.00	9.00
☐ 36	Hal Reniff	3.00	1.35
☐ 37	Smoky Burgess	6.00	2.70
☐ 38	Jim Wynn	8.00	3.60
☐ 39	Hank Aguirre	3.00	1.35
☐ 40	Dick Groat	6.00	2.70
☐ 41	Friendly Foes	8.00	3.60
	Willie McCovey		
	Leon Wagner		
☐ 42	Moe Drabowsky	6.00	2.70
☐ 43	Roy Sievers	6.00	2.70
☐ 44	Duke Carmel	3.00	1.35
☐ 45	Milt Pappas	6.00	2.70
☐ 46	Ed Brinkman	3.00	1.35
☐ 47	Giants Rookies	6.00	2.70
	Jesus Alou		
	Ron Herbel		
☐ 48	Bob Perry	3.00	1.35
☐ 49	Bill Henry	3.00	1.35
☐ 50	Mickey Mantle	300.00	135.00
☐ 51	Pete Richert	3.00	1.35
☐ 52	Chuck Hinton	3.00	1.35
☐ 53	Denis Menke	3.00	1.35
☐ 54	Sam Mele MG	3.00	1.35
☐ 55	Ernie Banks	35.00	16.00
☐ 56	Hal Brown	3.00	1.35
☐ 57	Tim Harkness	3.00	1.35
☐ 58	Don Demeter	3.00	1.35
☐ 59	Ernie Broglio	3.00	1.35
☐ 60	Frank Malzone	6.00	2.70
☐ 61	Angel Backstops	6.00	2.70
	Bob Rodgers		
	Ed Sadowski		
☐ 62	Ted Savage	3.00	1.35
☐ 63	John Orsino	3.00	1.35
☐ 64	Ted Abernathy	3.00	1.35
☐ 65	Felipe Alou	6.00	2.70
☐ 66	Eddie Fisher	3.00	1.35
☐ 67	Tigers Team	8.00	3.60
☐ 68	Willie Davis	6.00	2.70
☐ 69	Clete Boyer	6.00	2.70
☐ 70	Joe Torre	8.00	3.60
☐ 71	Jack Spring	3.00	1.35
☐ 72	Chico Cardenas	3.00	1.35
☐ 73	Jimmie Hall	6.00	2.70
☐ 74	Pirates Rookies	3.00	1.35
	Bob Priddy		
	Tom Butters		
☐ 75	Wayne Causey	3.00	1.35
☐ 76	Checklist 1	10.00	2.00
☐ 77	Jerry Walker	3.00	1.35
☐ 78	Merritt Ranew	3.00	1.35
☐ 79	Bob Heffner	3.00	1.35
☐ 80	Vada Pinson	6.00	2.70
☐ 81	All-Star Vets	12.00	5.50
	Nellie Fox		
	Harmon Killebrew		
☐ 82	Jim Davenport	6.00	2.70
☐ 83	Gus Triandos	6.00	2.70
☐ 84	Carl Willey	3.00	1.35
☐ 85	Pete Ward	3.00	1.35
☐ 86	Al Downing	6.00	2.70
☐ 87	St. Louis Cardinals	6.00	2.70
	Team Card		
☐ 88	John Roseboro	6.00	2.70
☐ 89	Boog Powell	6.00	2.70
☐ 90	Earl Battey	3.00	1.35
☐ 91	Bob Bailey	6.00	2.70
☐ 92	Steve Ridzik	3.00	1.35
☐ 93	Gary Geiger	3.00	1.35
☐ 94	Braves Rookies	3.00	1.35
	Jim Britton		
	Larry Maxie		
☐ 95	George Altman	3.00	1.35
☐ 96	Bob Buhl	6.00	2.70
☐ 97	Jim Fregosi	6.00	2.70
☐ 98	Bill Bruton	3.00	1.35
☐ 99	Al Stanek	3.00	1.35
☐ 100	Elston Howard	6.00	2.70
☐ 101	Walt Alston MG	6.00	2.70
☐ 102	Checklist 2	10.00	2.00
☐ 103	Curt Flood	6.00	2.70
☐ 104	Art Mahaffey	6.00	2.70
☐ 105	Woody Held	3.00	1.35
☐ 106	Joe Nuxhall	6.00	2.70
☐ 107	White Sox Rookies	3.00	1.35
	Bruce Howard		
	Frank Kreutzer		
☐ 108	John Wyatt	3.00	1.35
☐ 109	Rusty Staub	6.00	2.70
☐ 110	Albie Pearson	3.00	1.35
☐ 111	Don Elston	3.00	1.35
☐ 112	Bob Tillman	3.00	1.35
☐ 113	Grover Powell	3.00	1.35
☐ 114	Don Lock	3.00	1.35
☐ 115	Frank Bolling	3.00	1.35

#	Player	NM	
❑ 116	Twins Rookies	12.00	5.50
	Jay Ward		
	Tony Oliva		
❑ 117	Earl Francis	3.00	1.35
❑ 118	John Blanchard	6.00	2.70
❑ 119	Gary Kolb	3.00	1.35
❑ 120	Don Drysdale	20.00	9.00
❑ 121	Pete Runnels	6.00	2.70
❑ 122	Don McMahon	3.00	1.35
❑ 123	Jose Pagan	3.00	1.35
❑ 124	Orlando Pena	3.00	1.35
❑ 125	Pete Rose	125.00	55.00
❑ 126	Russ Snyder	3.00	1.35
❑ 127	Angels Rookies	3.00	1.35
	Aubrey Gatewood		
	Dick Simpson		
❑ 128	Mickey Lolich	20.00	9.00
❑ 129	Amado Samuel	3.00	1.35
❑ 130	Gary Peters	6.00	2.70
❑ 131	Steve Boros	3.00	1.35
❑ 132	Braves Team	6.00	2.70
❑ 133	Jim Grant	6.00	2.70
❑ 134	Don Zimmer	6.00	2.70
❑ 135	Johnny Callison	6.00	2.70
❑ 136	Sandy Koufax WS	20.00	9.00
	strikes out 15		
❑ 137	Tommy Davis WS	8.00	3.60
❑ 138	Ron Fairly WS	8.00	3.60
❑ 139	Frank Howard WS	8.00	3.60
❑ 140	World Series Summary	7.50	3.40
	Dodgers celebrate		
❑ 141	Danny Murtaugh MG	6.00	2.70
❑ 142	John Bateman	3.00	1.35
❑ 143	Bubba Phillips	3.00	1.35
❑ 144	Al Worthington	3.00	1.35
❑ 145	Norm Siebern	3.00	1.35
❑ 146	Indians Rookies	30.00	13.50
	Tommy John		
	Bob Chance		
❑ 147	Ray Sadecki	3.00	1.35
❑ 148	J.C. Martin	3.00	1.35
❑ 149	Paul Foytack	3.00	1.35
❑ 150	Willie Mays	100.00	45.00
❑ 151	Athletics Team	6.00	2.70
❑ 152	Denny Lemaster	3.00	1.35
❑ 153	Dick Williams	6.00	2.70
❑ 154	Dick Tracewski	6.00	2.70
❑ 155	Duke Snider	30.00	13.50
❑ 156	Bill Dailey	3.00	1.35
❑ 157	Gene Mauch MG	6.00	2.70
❑ 158	Ken Johnson	3.00	1.35
❑ 159	Charlie Dees	3.00	1.35
❑ 160	Ken Boyer	6.00	2.70
❑ 161	Dave McNally	6.00	2.70
❑ 162	Hitting Area	6.00	2.70
	Dick Sisler CO		
	Vada Pinson		
❑ 163	Donn Clendenon	6.00	2.70
❑ 164	Bud Daley	3.00	1.35
❑ 165	Jerry Lumpe	3.00	1.35
❑ 166	Marty Keough	3.00	1.35
❑ 167	Senators Rookies	30.00	13.50
	Mike Brumley		
	Lou Piniella		
❑ 168	Al Weis	3.00	1.35
❑ 169	Del Crandall	6.00	2.70
❑ 170	Dick Radatz	6.00	2.70
❑ 171	Ty Cline	3.00	1.35
❑ 172	Indians Team	6.00	2.70
❑ 173	Ryne Duren	6.00	2.70
❑ 174	Doc Edwards	3.00	1.35
❑ 175	Billy Williams	12.00	5.50
❑ 176	Tracy Stallard	3.00	1.35
❑ 177	Harmon Killebrew	20.00	9.00
❑ 178	Hank Bauer MG	6.00	2.70
❑ 179	Carl Warwick	3.00	1.35
❑ 180	Tommy Davis	6.00	2.70
❑ 181	Dave Wickersham	3.00	1.35
❑ 182	Sox Sockers	15.00	6.75
	Carl Yastrzemski		
	Chuck Schilling		
❑ 183	Ron Taylor	3.00	1.35
❑ 184	Al Luplow	3.00	1.35
❑ 185	Jim O'Toole	6.00	2.70
❑ 186	Roman Mejias	3.00	1.35
❑ 187	Ed Roebuck	3.00	1.35
❑ 188	Checklist 3	10.00	2.00
❑ 189	Bob Hendley	3.00	1.35
❑ 190	Bobby Richardson	8.00	3.60
❑ 191	Clay Dalrymple	6.00	2.70
❑ 192	Cubs Rookies	3.00	1.35
	John Boccabella		
	Billy Cowan		
❑ 193	Jerry Lynch	3.00	1.35
❑ 194	John Goryl	3.00	1.35
❑ 195	Floyd Robinson	3.00	1.35
❑ 196	Jim Gentile	3.00	1.35
❑ 197	Frank Lary	6.00	2.70
❑ 198	Len Gabrielson	4.00	1.80
❑ 199	Joe Azcue	4.00	1.80
❑ 200	Sandy Koufax	100.00	45.00
❑ 201	Orioles Rookies	6.00	2.70
	Sam Bowens		
	Wally Bunker		
❑ 202	Galen Cisco	6.00	2.70
❑ 203	John Kennedy	6.00	2.70
❑ 204	Matty Alou	6.00	2.70
❑ 205	Nellie Fox	12.00	5.50
❑ 206	Steve Hamilton	4.00	1.80
❑ 207	Fred Hutchinson MG	6.00	2.70
❑ 208	Wes Covington	6.00	2.70
❑ 209	Bob Allen	4.00	1.80
❑ 210	Carl Yastrzemski	35.00	16.00
❑ 211	Jim Coker	4.00	1.80
❑ 212	Pete Lovrich	4.00	1.80
❑ 213	Angels Team	6.00	2.70
❑ 214	Ken McMullen	6.00	2.70
❑ 215	Ray Herbert	4.00	1.80
❑ 216	Mike de la Hoz	4.00	1.80
❑ 217	Jim King	4.00	1.80
❑ 218	Hank Fischer	4.00	1.80
❑ 219	Young Aces	6.00	2.70
	Al Downing		
	Jim Bouton		
❑ 220	Dick Ellsworth	6.00	2.70
❑ 221	Bob Saverine	4.00	1.80
❑ 222	Billy Pierce	6.00	2.70
❑ 223	George Banks	4.00	1.80
❑ 224	Tommie Sisk	4.00	1.80
❑ 225	Roger Maris	60.00	27.00
❑ 226	Colts Rookies	6.00	2.70
	Jerry Grote		
	Larry Yellen		
❑ 227	Barry Latman	4.00	1.80
❑ 228	Felix Mantilla	4.00	1.80
❑ 229	Charley Lau	6.00	2.70
❑ 230	Brooks Robinson	35.00	16.00
❑ 231	Dick Calmus	4.00	1.80
❑ 232	Al Lopez MG	6.00	2.70
❑ 233	Hal Smith	4.00	1.80
❑ 234	Gary Bell	4.00	1.80
❑ 235	Ron Hunt	4.00	1.80
❑ 236	Bill Faul	4.00	1.80
❑ 237	Cubs Team	6.00	2.70
❑ 238	Roy McMillan	6.00	2.70
❑ 239	Herm Starrette	4.00	1.80
❑ 240	Bill White	6.00	2.70
❑ 241	Jim Owens	4.00	1.80
❑ 242	Harvey Kuenn	6.00	2.70
❑ 243	Phillies Rookies	30.00	13.50
	Richie Allen		
	John Hermstein		
❑ 244	Tony LaRussa	30.00	13.50
❑ 245	Dick Stigman	4.00	1.80
❑ 246	Manny Mota	6.00	2.70
❑ 247	Dave DeBusschere	6.00	2.70
❑ 248	Johnny Pesky MG	6.00	2.70
❑ 249	Doug Camilli	4.00	1.80
❑ 250	Al Kaline	40.00	18.00
❑ 251	Choo Choo Coleman	4.00	1.80
❑ 252	Ken Aspromonte	4.00	1.80
❑ 253	Wally Post	6.00	2.70
❑ 254	Don Hoak	6.00	2.70
❑ 255	Lee Thomas	4.00	1.80
❑ 256	Johnny Weekly	4.00	1.80
❑ 257	San Francisco Giants	6.00	2.70
	Team Card		
❑ 258	Garry Roggenburk	4.00	1.80
❑ 259	Harry Bright	4.00	1.80
❑ 260	Frank Robinson	35.00	16.00
❑ 261	Jim Hannan	4.00	1.80
❑ 262	Cards Rookies	8.00	3.60
	Mike Shannon		
	Harry Fanok		
❑ 263	Chuck Estrada	4.00	1.80
❑ 264	Jim Landis	4.00	1.80
❑ 265	Jim Bunning	12.00	5.50
❑ 266	Gene Freese	4.00	1.80
❑ 267	Wilbur Wood	6.00	2.70
❑ 268	Bill's Got It	6.00	2.70
	Danny Murtaugh MG		
	Bill Virdon		
❑ 269	Ellis Burton	4.00	1.80
❑ 270	Rich Rollins	6.00	2.70
❑ 271	Bob Sadowski	4.00	1.80
❑ 272	Jake Wood	4.00	1.80
❑ 273	Mel Nelson	4.00	1.80
❑ 274	Checklist 4	10.00	2.00
❑ 275	John Tsitouris	4.00	1.80
❑ 276	Jose Tartabull	6.00	2.70
❑ 277	Ken Retzer	4.00	1.80
❑ 278	Bobby Shantz	6.00	2.70
❑ 279	Joe Koppe UER	4.00	1.80
	(Glove on wrong hand)		
❑ 280	Juan Marichal	12.00	5.50
❑ 281	Yankees Rookies	6.00	2.70
	Jake Gibbs		
	Tom Metcalf		
❑ 282	Bob Bruce	4.00	1.80
❑ 283	Tom McCraw	4.00	1.80
❑ 284	Dick Schofield	4.00	1.80
❑ 285	Robin Roberts	12.00	5.50
❑ 286	Don Landrum	4.00	1.80
❑ 287	Red Sox Rookies	50.00	22.00
	Tony Conigliaro		
	Bill Spanswick		
❑ 288	Al Moran	4.00	1.80
❑ 289	Frank Funk	4.00	1.80
❑ 290	Bob Allison	6.00	2.70
❑ 291	Phil Ortega	4.00	1.80
❑ 292	Mike Roarke	4.00	1.80
❑ 293	Phillies Team	6.00	2.70
❑ 294	Ken L. Hunt	4.00	1.80
❑ 295	Roger Craig	6.00	2.70
❑ 296	Ed Kirkpatrick	4.00	1.80
❑ 297	Ken MacKenzie	4.00	1.80
❑ 298	Harry Craft MG	6.00	2.70
❑ 299	Bill Stafford	4.00	1.80
❑ 300	Hank Aaron	90.00	40.00
❑ 301	Larry Brown	4.00	1.80
❑ 302	Dan Pfister	4.00	1.80
❑ 303	Jim Campbell	4.00	1.80
❑ 304	Bob Johnson	4.00	1.80
❑ 305	Jack Lamabe	4.00	1.80
❑ 306	Giant Gunners	40.00	18.00
	Willie Mays		
	Orlando Cepeda		
❑ 307	Joe Gibbon	4.00	1.80
❑ 308	Gene Stephens	4.00	1.80
❑ 309	Paul Toth	4.00	1.80
❑ 310	Jim Gilliam	6.00	2.70
❑ 311	Tom Brown	6.00	2.70
❑ 312	Tigers Rookies	4.00	1.80
	Fritz Fisher		
	Fred Gladding		
❑ 313	Chuck Hiller	4.00	1.80
❑ 314	Jerry Buchek	4.00	1.80
❑ 315	Bo Belinsky	6.00	2.70
❑ 316	Gene Oliver	4.00	1.80
❑ 317	Al Smith	4.00	1.80
❑ 318	Minnesota Twins	6.00	2.70
	Team Card		
❑ 319	Paul Brown	4.00	1.80
❑ 320	Rocky Colavito	12.00	5.50
❑ 321	Bob Lillis	4.00	1.80
❑ 322	George Brunet	4.00	1.80
❑ 323	John Buzhardt	4.00	1.80
❑ 324	Casey Stengel MG	15.00	6.75
❑ 325	Hector Lopez	6.00	2.70
❑ 326	Ron Brand	4.00	1.80
❑ 327	Don Blasingame	4.00	1.80
❑ 328	Bob Shaw	4.00	1.80
❑ 329	Russ Nixon	4.00	1.80
❑ 330	Tommy Harper	6.00	2.70
❑ 331	AL Bombers	150.00	70.00
	Roger Maris		
	Norm Cash		
	Mickey Mantle		

	Al Kaline		
332	Ray Washburn	4.00	1.80
333	Billy Moran	4.00	1.80
334	Lew Krausse	4.00	1.80
335	Don Mossi	6.00	2.70
336	Andre Rodgers	4.00	1.80
337	Dodgers Rookies	6.00	2.70
	Al Ferrara		
	Jeff Torborg		
338	Jack Kralick	4.00	1.80
339	Walt Bond	4.00	1.80
340	Joe Cunningham	4.00	1.80
341	Jim Roland	4.00	1.80
342	Willie Stargell	30.00	13.50
343	Senators Team	6.00	2.70
344	Phil Linz	6.00	2.70
345	Frank Thomas	6.00	2.70
346	Joey Jay	4.00	1.80
347	Bobby Wine	6.00	2.70
348	Ed Lopat MG	6.00	2.70
349	Art Fowler	4.00	1.80
350	Willie McCovey	20.00	9.00
351	Dan Schneider	4.00	1.80
352	Eddie Bressoud	4.00	1.80
353	Wally Moon	6.00	2.70
354	Dave Giusti	4.00	1.80
355	Vic Power	6.00	2.70
356	Reds Rookies	6.00	2.70
	Bill McCool		
	Chico Ruiz		
357	Charley James	4.00	1.80
358	Ron Kline	4.00	1.80
359	Jim Schaffer	4.00	1.80
360	Joe Pepitone	8.00	3.60
361	Jay Hook	4.00	1.80
362	Checklist 5	10.00	2.00
363	Dick McAuliffe	6.00	2.70
364	Joe Gaines	4.00	1.80
365	Cal McLish	6.00	2.70
366	Nelson Mathews	4.00	1.80
367	Fred Whitfield	4.00	1.80
368	White Sox Rookies	6.00	2.70
	Fritz Ackley		
	Don Buford		
369	Jerry Zimmerman	4.00	1.80
370	Hal Woodeshick	4.00	1.80
371	Frank Howard	8.00	3.60
372	Howie Koplitz	7.00	3.10
373	Pirates Team	12.00	5.50
374	Bobby Bolin	7.00	3.10
375	Ron Santo	10.00	4.50
376	Dave Morehead	7.00	3.10
377	Bob Skinner	7.00	3.10
378	Braves Rookies	10.00	4.50
	Woody Woodward		
	Jack Smith		
379	Tony Gonzalez	7.00	3.10
380	Whitey Ford	35.00	16.00
381	Bob Taylor	7.00	3.10
382	Wes Stock	7.00	3.10
383	Bill Rigney MG	7.00	3.10
384	Ron Hansen	7.00	3.10
385	Curt Simmons	10.00	4.50
386	Lenny Green	7.00	3.10
387	Terry Fox	7.00	3.10
388	A's Rookies	10.00	4.50
	John O'Donoghue		
	George Williams		
389	Jim Umbricht	10.00	4.50
	(Card back mentions his death)		
390	Orlando Cepeda	10.00	4.50
391	Sam McDowell	10.00	4.50
392	Jim Pagliaroni	7.00	3.10
393	Casey Teaches	10.00	4.50
	Casey Stengel MG		
	Ed Kranepool		
394	Bob Miller	7.00	3.10
395	Tom Tresh	10.00	4.50
396	Dennis Bennett	7.00	3.10
397	Chuck Cottier	7.00	3.10
398	Mets Rookies	7.00	3.10
	Bill Haas		
	Dick Smith		
399	Jackie Brandt	7.00	3.10
400	Warren Spahn	40.00	18.00
401	Charlie Maxwell	7.00	3.10
402	Tom Sturdivant	7.00	3.10
403	Reds Team	12.00	5.50
404	Tony Martinez	7.00	3.10
405	Ken McBride	7.00	3.10
406	Al Spangler	7.00	3.10
407	Bill Freehan	10.00	4.50
408	Cubs Rookies	7.00	3.10
	Jim Stewart		
	Fred Burdette		
409	Bill Fischer	7.00	3.10
410	Dick Stuart	10.00	4.50
411	Lee Walls	7.00	3.10
412	Ray Culp	10.00	4.50
413	Johnny Keane MG	7.00	3.10
414	Jack Sanford	7.00	3.10
415	Tony Kubek	10.00	4.50
416	Lee Maye	7.00	3.10
417	Don Cardwell	7.00	3.10
418	Orioles Rookies	10.00	4.50
	Darold Knowles		
	Les Narum		
419	Ken Harrelson	15.00	6.75
420	Jim Maloney	10.00	4.50
421	Camilo Carreon	7.00	3.10
422	Jack Fisher	7.00	3.10
423	Tops in NL	125.00	55.00
	Hank Aaron		
	Willie Mays		
424	Dick Bertell	7.00	3.10
425	Norm Cash	10.00	4.50
426	Bob Rodgers	7.00	3.10
427	Don Rudolph	7.00	3.10
428	Red Sox Rookies	7.00	3.10
	Archie Skeen		
	Pete Smith		
	(Back states Archie he retired)		
429	Tim McCarver	10.00	4.50
430	Juan Pizarro	7.00	3.10
431	George Alusik	7.00	3.10
432	Ruben Amaro	10.00	4.50
433	Yankees Team	40.00	18.00
434	Don Nottebart	7.00	3.10
435	Vic Davalillo	7.00	3.10
436	Charlie Neal	10.00	4.50
437	Ed Bailey	7.00	3.10
438	Checklist 6	16.00	3.20
439	Harvey Haddix	10.00	4.50
440	Roberto Clemente UER	225.00	100.00
	1960 Pittsburgh		
441	Bob Duliba	7.00	3.10
442	Pumpsie Green	10.00	4.50
443	Chuck Dressen MG	10.00	4.50
444	Larry Jackson	7.00	3.10
445	Bill Skowron	10.00	4.50
446	Julian Javier	7.00	3.10
447	Ted Bowsfield	7.00	3.10
448	Cookie Rojas	10.00	4.50
449	Deron Johnson	10.00	4.50
450	Steve Barber	7.00	3.10
451	Joe Amalfitano	7.00	3.10
452	Giants Rookies	10.00	4.50
	Gil Garrido		
	Jim Ray Hart		
453	Frank Baumann	7.00	3.10
454	Tommie Aaron	10.00	4.50
455	Bernie Allen	7.00	3.10
456	Dodgers Rookies	10.00	4.50
	Wes Parker		
	John Werhas		
457	Jesse Gonder	7.00	3.10
458	Ralph Terry	10.00	4.50
459	Red Sox Rookies	7.00	3.10
	Pete Charton		
	Dalton Jones		
460	Bob Gibson	35.00	16.00
461	George Thomas	7.00	3.10
462	Birdie Tebbetts MG	7.00	3.10
463	Don Leppert	7.00	3.10
464	Dallas Green	10.00	4.50
465	Mike Hershberger	7.00	3.10
466	A's Rookies	10.00	4.50
	Dick Green		
	Aurelio Monteagudo		
467	Bob Aspromonte	7.00	3.10
468	Gaylord Perry	40.00	18.00
469	Cubs Rookies	10.00	4.50
	Fred Norman		
	Sterling Slaughter		
470	Jim Bouton	10.00	4.50
471	Gates Brown	10.00	4.50
472	Vern Law	10.00	4.50
473	Baltimore Orioles	12.00	5.50
	Team Card		
474	Larry Sherry	10.00	4.50
475	Ed Charles	7.00	3.10
476	Braves Rookies	15.00	6.75
	Rico Carty		
	Dick Kelley		
477	Mike Joyce	7.00	3.10
478	Dick Howser	10.00	4.50
479	Cardinals Rookies	7.00	3.10
	Dave Bakenhaster		
	Johnny Lewis		
480	Bob Purkey	7.00	3.10
481	Chuck Schilling	7.00	3.10
482	Phillies Rookies	10.00	4.50
	John Briggs		
	Danny Cater		
483	Fred Valentine	7.00	3.10
484	Bill Pleis	7.00	3.10
485	Tom Haller	7.00	3.10
486	Bob Kennedy MG	7.00	3.10
487	Mike McCormick	7.00	3.10
488	Yankees Rookies	10.00	4.50
	Pete Mikkelsen		
	Bob Meyer		
489	Julio Navarro	7.00	3.10
490	Ron Fairly	10.00	4.50
491	Ed Rakow	7.00	3.10
492	Colts Rookies	7.00	3.10
	Jim Beauchamp		
	Mike White		
493	Don Lee	7.00	3.10
494	Al Jackson	7.00	3.10
495	Bill Virdon	10.00	4.50
496	White Sox Team	12.00	5.50
497	Jeoff Long	7.00	3.10
498	Dave Stenhouse	7.00	3.10
499	Indians Rookies	7.00	3.10
	Chico Salmon		
	Gordon Seyfried		
500	Camilo Pascual	10.00	4.50
501	Bob Veale	10.00	4.50
502	Angels Rookies	7.00	3.10
	Bobby Knoop		
	Bob Lee		
503	Earl Wilson	7.00	3.10
504	Claude Raymond	7.00	3.10
505	Stan Williams	7.00	3.10
506	Bobby Bragan MG	7.00	3.10
507	Johnny Edwards	7.00	3.10
508	Diego Segui	7.00	3.10
509	Pirates Rookies	10.00	4.50
	Gene Alley		
	Orlando McFarlane		
510	Lindy McDaniel	10.00	4.50
511	Lou Jackson	7.00	3.10
512	Tigers Rookies	15.00	6.75
	Willie Horton		
	Joe Sparma		
513	Don Larsen	10.00	4.50
514	Jim Hickman	10.00	4.50
515	Johnny Romano	7.00	3.10
516	Twins Rookies	7.00	3.10
	Jerry Arrigo		
	Dwight Siebler		
517A	Checklist 7 ERR	25.00	5.00
	(Incorrect numbering sequence on back)		
517B	Checklist 7 COR	16.00	3.20
	(Correct numbering on back)		
518	Carl Bouldin	7.00	3.10
519	Charlie Smith	7.00	3.10
520	Jack Baldschun	10.00	4.50
521	Tom Satriano	7.00	3.10
522	Bob Tiefenauer	7.00	3.10
523	Lou Burdette UER	20.00	9.00
	(Pitching lefty)		
524	Reds Rookies	16.00	7.25

Jim Dickson		
Bobby Klaus		
❑ 525 Al McBean	16.00	7.25
❑ 526 Lou Clinton	16.00	7.25
❑ 527 Larry Bearnarth	16.00	7.25
❑ 528 A's Rookies	20.00	9.00
Dave Duncan		
Tommie Reynolds		
❑ 529 Alvin Dark MG	20.00	9.00
❑ 530 Leon Wagner	16.00	7.25
❑ 531 Los Angeles Dodgers	25.00	11.00
Team Card		
❑ 532 Twins Rookies	16.00	7.25
Bud Bloomfield		
(Bloomfield photo		
actually Jay Ward)		
Joe Nossek		
❑ 533 Johnny Klippstein	16.00	7.25
❑ 534 Gus Bell	16.00	7.25
❑ 535 Phil Regan	16.00	7.25
❑ 536 Mets Rookies	16.00	7.25
Larry Elliot		
John Stephenson		
❑ 537 Dan Osinski	16.00	7.25
❑ 538 Minnie Minoso	20.00	9.00
❑ 539 Roy Face	20.00	9.00
❑ 540 Luis Aparicio	30.00	13.50
❑ 541 Braves Rookies	80.00	36.00
Phil Roof		
Phil Niekro		
❑ 542 Don Mincher	16.00	7.25
❑ 543 Bob Uecker	40.00	18.00
❑ 544 Colts Rookies	16.00	7.25
Steve Hertz		
Joe Hoerner		
❑ 545 Max Alvis	16.00	7.25
❑ 546 Joe Christopher	16.00	7.25
❑ 547 Gil Hodges MG	30.00	13.50
❑ 548 NL Rookies	16.00	7.25
Wayne Schurr		
Paul Speckenbach		
❑ 549 Joe Moeller	16.00	7.25
❑ 550 Ken Hubbs MEM	35.00	16.00
❑ 551 Billy Hoeft	16.00	7.25
❑ 552 Indians Rookies	16.00	7.25
Tom Kelley		
Sonny Siebert		
❑ 553 Jim Brewer	16.00	7.25
❑ 554 Hank Foiles	16.00	7.25
❑ 555 Lee Stange	16.00	7.25
❑ 556 Mets Rookies	16.00	7.25
Steve Dillon		
Ron Locke		
❑ 557 Leo Burke	16.00	7.25
❑ 558 Don Schwall	16.00	7.25
❑ 559 Dick Phillips	16.00	7.25
❑ 560 Dick Farrell	16.00	7.25
❑ 561 Phillies Rookies UER	20.00	9.00
Dave Bennett		
(19 ... is 18)		
Rick Wise		
❑ 562 Pedro Ramos	16.00	7.25
❑ 563 Dal Maxvill	16.00	7.25
❑ 564 AL Rookies	16.00	7.25
Joe McCabe		
Jerry McNertney		
❑ 565 Stu Miller	16.00	7.25
❑ 566 Ed Kranepool	20.00	9.00
❑ 567 Jim Kaat	20.00	9.00
❑ 568 NL Rookies	16.00	7.25
Phil Gagliano		
Cap Peterson		
❑ 569 Fred Newman	16.00	7.25
❑ 570 Bill Mazeroski	20.00	9.00
❑ 571 Gene Conley	16.00	7.25
❑ 572 AL Rookies	16.00	7.25
Dave Gray		
Dick Egan		
❑ 573 Jim Duffalo	16.00	7.25
❑ 574 Manny Jimenez	16.00	7.25
❑ 575 Tony Cloninger	16.00	7.25
❑ 576 Mets Rookies	16.00	7.25
Jerry Hinsley		
Bill Wakefield		
❑ 577 Gordy Coleman	16.00	7.25
❑ 578 Glen Hobbie	16.00	7.25

❑ 579 Red Sox Team	25.00	11.00
❑ 580 Johnny Podres	20.00	9.00
❑ 581 Yankees Rookies	20.00	9.00
Pedro Gonzalez		
Archie Moore		
❑ 582 Rod Kanehl	20.00	9.00
❑ 583 Tito Francona	16.00	7.25
❑ 584 Joel Horlen	16.00	7.25
❑ 585 Tony Taylor	20.00	9.00
❑ 586 Jimmy Piersall	20.00	9.00
❑ 587 Bennie Daniels !	20.00	8.00

1965 Topps

	NRMT	VG-E
COMPLETE SET (598)	3500.00	1600.00
COMMON CARD (1-196)	2.00	.90
COMMON CARD (197-283)	2.50	1.10
MINOR STARS 1-283	4.00	1.80
SEMISTARS 1-283.	6.00	2.70
UNLISTED STARS 1-283.	10.00	4.50
COMMON CARD (284-370)	4.00	1.80
MINOR STARS 284-370	6.00	2.70
SEMISTARS 284-370.	10.00	4.50
UNLISTED STARS 284-370.	15.00	6.75
COMMON SP (371-598)	7.00	3.10
COMMON SP (371-598)	12.00	5.50
MINOR STARS 371-598	15.00	6.75
SEMISTARS 371-598.	25.00	11.00

*UNLISTED DODGER/YANKEE: 1.25X VALUE
CARDS PRICED IN NM CONDITION

❑ 1 AL Batting Leaders	20.00	6.00
Tony Oliva		
Elston Howard		
Brooks Robinson		
❑ 2 NL Batting Leaders	25.00	11.00
Roberto Clemente		
Hank Aaron		
Rico Carty		
❑ 3 AL Home Run Leaders	40.00	18.00
Harmon Killebrew		
Mickey Mantle		
Boog Powell		
❑ 4 NL Home Run Leaders	15.00	6.75
Willie Mays		
Billy Williams		
Jim Ray Hart		
Orlando Cepeda		
Johnny Callison		
❑ 5 AL RBI Leaders	40.00	18.00
Brooks Robinson		
Harmon Killebrew		
Dick Stuart		
❑ 6 NL RBI Leaders	12.00	5.50
Ken Boyer		
Willie Mays		
Ron Santo		
❑ 7 AL ERA Leaders	5.00	2.20
Dean Chance		
Joel Horlen		
❑ 8 NL ERA Leaders	20.00	9.00
Sandy Koufax		
Don Drysdale		
❑ 9 AL Pitching Leaders	5.00	2.20
Dean Chance		
Gary Peters		

Dave Wickersham		
Juan Pizarro		
Wally Bunker		
❑ 10 NL Pitching Leaders	5.00	2.20
Larry Jackson		
Ray Sadecki		
Juan Marichal		
❑ 11 AL Strikeout Leaders	5.00	2.20
Al Downing		
Dean Chance		
Camilo Pascual		
❑ 12 NL Strikeout Leaders	10.00	4.50
Bob Veale		
Don Drysdale		
Bob Gibson		
❑ 13 Pedro Ramos	4.00	1.80
❑ 14 Len Gabrielson	2.00	.90
❑ 15 Robin Roberts	10.00	4.50
❑ 16 Houston Rookie DP	60.00	27.00
Joe Morgan		
Sonny Jackson		
❑ 17 Johnny Romano	2.00	.90
❑ 18 Bill McCool	2.00	.90
❑ 19 Gates Brown	4.00	1.80
❑ 20 Jim Bunning	10.00	4.50
❑ 21 Don Blasingame	2.00	.90
❑ 22 Charlie Smith	2.00	.90
❑ 23 Bob Tiefenauer	2.00	.90
❑ 24 Minnesota Twins	6.00	2.70
Team Card		
❑ 25 Al McBean	2.00	.90
❑ 26 Bobby Knoop	2.00	.90
❑ 27 Dick Bertell	2.00	.90
❑ 28 Barney Schultz	2.00	.90
❑ 29 Felix Mantilla	2.00	.90
❑ 30 Jim Bouton	6.00	2.70
❑ 31 Mike White	2.00	.90
❑ 32 Herman Franks MG	2.00	.90
❑ 33 Jackie Brandt	2.00	.90
❑ 34 Cal Koonce	2.00	.90
❑ 35 Ed Charles	2.00	.90
❑ 36 Bobby Wine	2.00	.90
❑ 37 Fred Gladding	2.00	.90
❑ 38 Jim King	2.00	.90
❑ 39 Gerry Arrigo	2.00	.90
❑ 40 Frank Howard	6.00	2.70
❑ 41 White Sox Rookies	2.00	.90
Bruce Howard		
Marv Staehle		
❑ 42 Earl Wilson	4.00	1.80
❑ 43 Mike Shannon	4.00	1.80
(Name in red, other		
Cardinals in yellow)		
❑ 44 Wade Blasingame	2.00	.90
❑ 45 Roy McMillan	4.00	1.80
❑ 46 Bob Lee	2.00	.90
❑ 47 Tommy Harper	4.00	1.80
❑ 48 Claude Raymond	2.00	.90
❑ 49 Orioles Rookies	4.00	1.80
Curt Blefary		
John Miller		
❑ 50 Juan Marichal	10.00	4.50
❑ 51 Bill Bryan	2.00	.90
❑ 52 Ed Roebuck	2.00	.90
❑ 53 Dick McAuliffe	4.00	1.80
❑ 54 Joe Gibbon	2.00	.90
❑ 55 Tony Conigliaro	15.00	6.75
❑ 56 Ron Kline	2.00	.90
❑ 57 Cardinals Team	6.00	2.70
❑ 58 Fred Talbot	2.00	.90
❑ 59 Nate Oliver	2.00	.90
❑ 60 Jim O'Toole	4.00	1.80
❑ 61 Chris Cannizzaro	2.00	.90
❑ 62 Jim Kaat UER DP	6.00	2.70
(Misspelled Katt)		
❑ 63 Ty Cline	2.00	.90
❑ 64 Lou Burdette	4.00	1.80
❑ 65 Tony Kubek	4.00	1.80
❑ 66 Bill Rigney MG	2.00	.90
❑ 67 Harvey Haddix	4.00	1.80
❑ 68 Del Crandall	4.00	1.80
❑ 69 Bill Virdon	4.00	1.80
❑ 70 Bill Skowron	6.00	2.70
❑ 71 John O'Donoghue	2.00	.90
❑ 72 Tony Gonzalez	2.00	.90
❑ 73 Dennis Ribant	2.00	.90

#	Card	Price 1	Price 2
74	Red Sox Rookies	10.00	4.50
	Rico Petrocelli		
	Jerry Stephenson		
75	Deron Johnson	4.00	1.80
76	Sam McDowell	4.00	1.80
77	Doug Camilli	2.00	.90
78	Dal Maxvill	2.00	.90
79A	Checklist 1	10.00	2.00
	(61 Cannizzaro)		
79B	Checklist 1	10.00	2.00
	(61 C. Cannizzaro)		
80	Turk Farrell	2.00	.90
81	Don Buford	4.00	1.80
82	Braves Rookies	6.00	2.70
	Santos Alomar		
	John Braun		
83	George Thomas	2.00	.90
84	Ron Herbel	2.00	.90
85	Willie Smith	2.00	.90
86	Les Narum	2.00	.90
87	Nelson Mathews	2.00	.90
88	Jack Lamabe	2.00	.90
89	Mike Hershberger	2.00	.90
90	Rich Rollins	4.00	1.80
91	Cubs Team	6.00	2.70
92	Dick Howser	4.00	1.80
93	Jack Fisher	2.00	.90
94	Charlie Lau	4.00	1.80
95	Bill Mazeroski DP	6.00	2.70
96	Sonny Siebert	4.00	1.80
97	Pedro Gonzalez	2.00	.90
98	Bob Miller	2.00	.90
99	Gil Hodges MG	6.00	2.70
100	Ken Boyer	4.00	1.80
101	Fred Newman	2.00	.90
102	Steve Boros	2.00	.90
103	Harvey Kuenn	4.00	1.80
104	Checklist 2	10.00	2.00
105	Chico Salmon	2.00	.90
106	Gene Oliver	2.00	.90
107	Phillies Rookies	4.00	1.80
	Pat Corrales		
	Costen Shockley		
108	Don Mincher	2.00	.90
109	Walt Bond	2.00	.90
110	Ron Santo	6.00	2.70
111	Lee Thomas	4.00	1.80
112	Derrell Griffith	2.00	.90
113	Steve Barber	2.00	.90
114	Jim Hickman	4.00	1.80
115	Bobby Richardson	6.00	2.70
116	Cardinals Rookies	4.00	1.80
	Dave Dowling		
	Bob Tolan		
117	Wes Stock	2.00	.90
118	Hal Lanier	4.00	1.80
119	John Kennedy	2.00	.90
120	Frank Robinson	35.00	16.00
121	Gene Alley	4.00	1.80
122	Bill Pleis	2.00	.90
123	Frank Thomas	4.00	1.80
124	Tom Satriano	2.00	.90
125	Juan Pizarro	2.00	.90
126	Dodgers Team	6.00	2.70
127	Frank Lary	2.00	.90
128	Vic Davalillo	2.00	.90
129	Bennie Daniels	2.00	.90
130	Al Kaline	35.00	16.00
131	Johnny Keane MG	2.00	.90
132	Mike Shannon WS	6.00	2.70
133	Mel Stottlemyre WS	6.00	2.70
134	Mickey Mantle WS	75.00	34.00
	Mantle's Clutch HR		
135	Ken Boyer WS	6.00	2.70
136	Tim McCarver WS	6.00	2.70
137	Jim Bouton WS	6.00	2.70
138	Bob Gibson WS	12.00	5.50
139	World Series Summary	4.00	1.80
	Cards celebrate		
140	Dean Chance	4.00	1.80
141	Charlie James	2.00	.90
142	Bill Monbouquette	2.00	.90
143	Pirates Rookies	2.00	.90
	John Gelnar		
	Jerry May		
144	Ed Kranepool	4.00	1.80
145	Luis Tiant	10.00	4.50
146	Ron Hansen	2.00	.90
147	Dennis Bennett	2.00	.90
148	Willie Kirkland	2.00	.90
149	Wayne Schurr	2.00	.90
150	Brooks Robinson	40.00	18.00
151	Athletics Team	6.00	2.70
152	Phil Ortega	2.00	.90
153	Norm Cash	4.00	1.80
154	Bob Humphreys	2.00	.90
155	Roger Maris	60.00	27.00
156	Bob Sadowski	2.00	.90
157	Zoilo Versalles	4.00	1.80
158	Dick Sisler	2.00	.90
159	Jim Duffalo	2.00	.90
160	Roberto Clemente UER	160.00	70.00
	1960 Pittsburth		
161	Frank Baumann	2.00	.90
162	Russ Nixon	2.00	.90
163	Johnny Briggs	2.00	.90
164	Al Spangler	2.00	.90
165	Dick Ellsworth	2.00	.90
166	Indians Rookies	4.00	1.80
	George Culver		
	Tommie Agee		
167	Bill Wakefield	2.00	.90
168	Dick Green	2.00	.90
169	Dave Vineyard	2.00	.90
170	Hank Aaron	90.00	40.00
171	Jim Roland	2.00	.90
172	Jimmy Piersall	6.00	2.70
173	Detroit Tigers	6.00	2.70
	Team Card		
174	Joey Jay	2.00	.90
175	Bob Aspromonte	2.00	.90
176	Willie McCovey	20.00	9.00
177	Pete Mikkelsen	2.00	.90
178	Dalton Jones	2.00	.90
179	Hal Woodeshick	2.00	.90
180	Bob Allison	4.00	1.80
181	Senators Rookies	2.00	.90
	Don Loun		
	Joe McCabe		
182	Mike de la Hoz	2.00	.90
183	Dave Nicholson	2.00	.90
184	John Boozer	2.00	.90
185	Max Alvis	2.00	.90
186	Billy Cowan	2.00	.90
187	Casey Stengel MG	15.00	6.75
188	Sam Bowens	2.00	.90
189	Checklist 3	10.00	2.00
190	Bill White	6.00	2.70
191	Phil Regan	4.00	1.80
192	Jim Coker	2.00	.90
193	Gaylord Perry	15.00	6.75
194	Rookie Stars	2.00	.90
	Bill Kelso		
	Rick Reichardt		
195	Bob Veale	4.00	1.80
196	Ron Fairly	4.00	1.80
197	Diego Segui	2.50	1.10
198	Smoky Burgess	4.00	1.80
199	Bob Heffner	2.50	1.10
200	Joe Torre	6.00	2.70
201	Twins Rookies	4.00	1.80
	Sandy Valdespino		
	Cesar Tovar		
202	Leo Burke	2.50	1.10
203	Dallas Green	4.00	1.80
204	Russ Snyder	2.50	1.10
205	Warren Spahn	30.00	13.50
206	Willie Horton	4.00	1.80
207	Pete Rose	125.00	55.00
208	Tommy John	6.00	2.70
209	Pirates Team	6.00	2.70
210	Jim Fregosi	4.00	1.80
211	Steve Ridzik	2.50	1.10
212	Ron Brand	2.50	1.10
213	Jim Davenport	2.50	1.10
214	Bob Purkey	2.50	1.10
215	Pete Ward	2.50	1.10
216	Al Worthington	2.50	1.10
217	Walter Alston MG	4.00	1.80
218	Dick Schofield	2.50	1.10
219	Bob Meyer	2.50	1.10
220	Billy Williams	10.00	4.50
221	John Tsitouris	2.50	1.10
222	Bob Tillman	2.50	1.10
223	Dan Osinski	2.50	1.10
224	Bob Chance	2.50	1.10
225	Bo Belinsky	4.00	1.80
226	Yankees Rookies	4.00	1.80
	Elvio Jimenez		
	Jake Gibbs		
227	Bobby Klaus	2.50	1.10
228	Jack Sanford	2.50	1.10
229	Lou Clinton	2.50	1.10
230	Ray Sadecki	2.50	1.10
231	Jerry Adair	2.50	1.10
232	Steve Blass	4.00	1.80
233	Don Zimmer	4.00	1.80
234	White Sox Team	6.00	2.70
235	Chuck Hinton	2.50	1.10
236	Denny McLain	25.00	11.00
237	Bernie Allen	2.50	1.10
238	Joe Moeller	2.50	1.10
239	Doc Edwards	2.50	1.10
240	Bob Bruce	2.50	1.10
241	Mack Jones	2.50	1.10
242	George Brunet	2.50	1.10
243	Reds Rookies	4.00	1.80
	Ted Davidson		
	Tommy Helms		
244	Lindy McDaniel	4.00	1.80
245	Joe Pepitone	4.00	1.80
246	Tom Butters	4.00	1.80
247	Wally Moon	4.00	1.80
248	Gus Triandos	4.00	1.80
249	Dave McNally	4.00	1.80
250	Willie Mays	100.00	45.00
251	Billy Herman MG	4.00	1.80
252	Pete Richert	2.50	1.10
253	Danny Cater	2.50	1.10
254	Roland Sheldon	2.50	1.10
255	Camilo Pascual	4.00	1.80
256	Tito Francona	2.50	1.10
257	Jim Wynn	4.00	1.80
258	Larry Bearnarth	2.50	1.10
259	Tigers Rookies	6.00	2.70
	Jim Northrup		
	Ray Oyler		
260	Don Drysdale	20.00	9.00
261	Duke Carmel	2.50	1.10
262	Bud Daley	2.50	1.10
263	Marty Keough	2.50	1.10
264	Bob Buhl	4.00	1.80
265	Jim Pagliaroni	2.50	1.10
266	Bert Campaneris	10.00	4.50
267	Senators Team	6.00	2.70
268	Ken McBride	2.50	1.10
269	Frank Bolling	2.50	1.10
270	Milt Pappas	4.00	1.80
271	Don Wert	2.50	1.10
272	Chuck Schilling	2.50	1.10
273	Checklist 4	10.00	2.00
274	Lum Harris MG	2.50	1.10
275	Dick Groat	6.00	2.70
276	Hoyt Wilhelm	10.00	4.50
277	Johnny Lewis	2.50	1.10
278	Ken Retzer	2.50	1.10
279	Dick Tracewski	2.50	1.10
280	Dick Stuart	4.00	1.80
281	Bill Stafford	2.50	1.10
282	Giants Rookies	40.00	18.00
	Dick Estelle		
	Masanori Murakami		
283	Fred Whitfield	2.50	1.10
284	Nick Willhite	2.50	1.10
285	Ron Hunt	4.00	1.80
286	Athletics Rookies	4.00	1.80
	Jim Dickson		
	Aurelio Monteagudo		
287	Gary Kolb	4.00	1.80
288	Jack Hamilton	4.00	1.80
289	Gordy Coleman	6.00	2.70
290	Wally Bunker	6.00	2.70
291	Jerry Lynch	4.00	1.80
292	Larry Yellen	4.00	1.80
293	Angels Team	6.00	2.70
294	Tim McCarver	10.00	4.50
295	Dick Radatz	6.00	2.70
296	Tony Taylor	6.00	2.70

#	Player	Price	Price
297	Dave DeBusschere	10.00	4.50
298	Jim Stewart	4.00	1.80
299	Jerry Zimmerman	4.00	1.80
300	Sandy Koufax	100.00	45.00
301	Birdie Tebbetts MG	6.00	2.70
302	Al Stanek	4.00	1.80
303	John Orsino	4.00	1.80
304	Dave Stenhouse	4.00	1.80
305	Rico Carty	6.00	2.70
306	Bubba Phillips	4.00	1.80
307	Barry Latman	4.00	1.80
308	Mets Rookies	6.00	2.70
	Cleon Jones		
	Tom Parsons		
309	Steve Hamilton	6.00	2.70
310	Johnny Callison	6.00	2.70
311	Orlando Pena	4.00	1.80
312	Joe Nuxhall	4.00	1.80
313	Jim Schaffer	4.00	1.80
314	Sterling Slaughter	4.00	1.80
315	Frank Malzone	6.00	2.70
316	Reds Team	6.00	2.70
317	Don McMahon	4.00	1.80
318	Matty Alou	6.00	2.70
319	Ken McMullen	4.00	1.80
320	Bob Gibson	40.00	18.00
321	Rusty Staub	10.00	4.50
322	Rick Wise	6.00	2.70
323	Hank Bauer MG	6.00	2.70
324	Bobby Locke	4.00	1.80
325	Donn Clendenon	6.00	2.70
326	Dwight Siebler	4.00	1.80
327	Denis Menke	4.00	1.80
328	Eddie Fisher	4.00	1.80
329	Hawk Taylor	4.00	1.80
330	Whitey Ford	35.00	16.00
331	Dodgers Rookies	6.00	2.70
	Al Ferrara		
	John Purdin		
332	Ted Abernathy	4.00	1.80
333	Tom Reynolds	4.00	1.80
334	Vic Roznovsky	4.00	1.80
335	Mickey Lolich	6.00	2.70
336	Woody Held	4.00	1.80
337	Mike Cuellar	6.00	2.70
338	Philadelphia Phillies	6.00	2.70
	Team Card		
339	Ryne Duren	6.00	2.70
340	Tony Oliva	20.00	9.00
341	Bob Bolin	4.00	1.80
342	Bob Rodgers	6.00	2.70
343	Mike McCormick	6.00	2.70
344	Wes Parker	6.00	2.70
345	Floyd Robinson	4.00	1.80
346	Bobby Bragan MG	4.00	1.80
347	Roy Face	6.00	2.70
348	George Banks	4.00	1.80
349	Larry Miller	4.00	1.80
350	Mickey Mantle	450.00	200.00
351	Jim Perry	6.00	2.70
352	Alex Johnson	6.00	2.70
353	Jerry Lumpe	4.00	1.80
354	Cubs Rookies	4.00	1.80
	Billy Ott		
	Jack Warner		
355	Vada Pinson	10.00	4.50
356	Bill Spanswick	4.00	1.80
357	Carl Warwick	4.00	1.80
358	Albie Pearson	6.00	2.70
359	Ken Johnson	4.00	1.80
360	Orlando Cepeda	10.00	4.50
361	Checklist 5	12.00	2.40
362	Don Schwall	4.00	1.80
363	Bob Johnson	4.00	1.80
364	Galen Cisco	4.00	1.80
365	Jim Gentile	6.00	2.70
366	Dan Schneider	4.00	1.80
367	Leon Wagner	4.00	1.80
368	White Sox Rookies	6.00	2.70
	Ken Berry		
	Joel Gibson		
369	Phil Linz	6.00	2.70
370	Tommy Davis	6.00	2.70
371	Frank Kreutzer	7.00	3.10
372	Clay Dalrymple	7.00	3.10
373	Curt Simmons	7.00	3.10
374	Angels Rookies	7.00	3.10
	Jose Cardenal		
	Dick Simpson		
375	Dave Wickersham	7.00	3.10
376	Jim Landis	7.00	3.10
377	Willie Stargell	25.00	11.00
378	Chuck Estrada	7.00	3.10
379	Giants Team	7.00	3.10
380	Rocky Colavito	30.00	13.50
381	Al Jackson	7.00	3.10
382	J.C. Martin	7.00	3.10
383	Felipe Alou	15.00	6.75
384	Johnny Klippstein	7.00	3.10
385	Carl Yastrzemski	60.00	27.00
386	Cubs Rookies	7.00	3.10
	Paul Jaeckel		
	Fred Norman		
387	Johnny Podres	15.00	6.75
388	John Blanchard	15.00	6.75
389	Don Larsen	15.00	6.75
390	Bill Freehan	15.00	6.75
391	Mel McGaha MG	7.00	3.10
392	Bob Friend	15.00	6.75
393	Ed Kirkpatrick	7.00	3.10
394	Jim Hannan	7.00	3.10
395	Jim Ray Hart	7.00	3.10
396	Frank Bertaina	7.00	3.10
397	Jerry Buchek	7.00	3.10
398	Reds Rookies	15.00	6.75
	Dan Neville		
	Art Shamsky		
399	Ray Herbert	7.00	3.10
400	Harmon Killebrew	40.00	18.00
401	Carl Willey	7.00	3.10
402	Joe Amalfitano	7.00	3.10
403	Boston Red Sox	7.00	3.10
	Team Card		
404	Stan Williams	7.00	3.10
	(Listed as Indian but Yankee cap)		
405	John Roseboro	15.00	6.75
406	Ralph Terry	15.00	6.75
407	Lee Maye	7.00	3.10
408	Larry Sherry	7.00	3.10
409	Astros Rookies	15.00	6.75
	Jim Beauchamp		
	Larry Dierker		
410	Luis Aparicio	15.00	6.75
411	Roger Craig	15.00	6.75
412	Bob Bailey	7.00	3.10
413	Hal Reniff	7.00	3.10
414	Al Lopez MG	15.00	6.75
415	Curt Flood	15.00	6.75
416	Jim Brewer	7.00	3.10
417	Ed Brinkman	7.00	3.10
418	Johnny Edwards	7.00	3.10
419	Ruben Amaro	7.00	3.10
420	Larry Jackson	7.00	3.10
421	Twins Rookies	7.00	3.10
	Gary Dotter		
	Jay Ward		
422	Aubrey Gatewood	7.00	3.10
423	Jesse Gonder	7.00	3.10
424	Gary Bell	7.00	3.10
425	Wayne Causey	7.00	3.10
426	Braves Team	7.00	3.10
427	Bob Saverine	7.00	3.10
428	Bob Shaw	7.00	3.10
429	Don Demeter	7.00	3.10
430	Gary Peters	7.00	3.10
431	Cards Rookies	15.00	6.75
	Nelson Briles		
	Wayne Spiezio		
432	Jim Grant	15.00	6.75
433	John Bateman	7.00	3.10
434	Dave Morehead	7.00	3.10
435	Willie Davis	15.00	6.75
436	Don Elston	7.00	3.10
437	Chico Cardenas	15.00	6.75
438	Harry Walker MG	7.00	3.10
439	Moe Drabowsky	15.00	6.75
440	Tom Tresh	15.00	6.75
441	Denny Lemaster	7.00	3.10
442	Vic Power	7.00	3.10
443	Checklist 6	12.00	2.40
444	Bob Hendley	7.00	3.10
445	Don Lock	7.00	3.10
446	Art Mahaffey	7.00	3.10
447	Julian Javier	15.00	6.75
448	Lee Stange	7.00	3.10
449	Mets Rookies	7.00	3.10
	Jerry Hinsley		
	Gary Kroll		
450	Elston Howard	15.00	6.75
451	Jim Owens	7.00	3.10
452	Gary Geiger	7.00	3.10
453	Dodgers Rookies	15.00	6.75
	Willie Crawford		
	John Werhas		
454	Ed Rakow	7.00	3.10
455	Norm Siebern	7.00	3.10
456	Bill Henry	7.00	3.10
457	Bob Kennedy MG	15.00	6.75
458	John Buzhardt	7.00	3.10
459	Frank Kostro	7.00	3.10
460	Richie Allen	40.00	18.00
461	Braves Rookies	50.00	22.00
	Clay Carroll		
	Phil Niekro		
462	Lew Krausse UER	7.00	3.10
	(Photo actually Pete Lovrich)		
463	Manny Mota	15.00	6.75
464	Ron Piche	7.00	3.10
465	Tom Haller	15.00	6.75
466	Senators Rookies	7.00	3.10
	Pete Craig		
	Dick Nen		
467	Ray Washburn	7.00	3.10
468	Larry Brown	7.00	3.10
469	Don Nottebart	7.00	3.10
470	Yogi Berra P/CO	50.00	22.00
471	Billy Hoeft	7.00	3.10
472	Don Pavletich UER	7.00	3.10
	Listed as a pitcher		
473	Orioles Rookies	15.00	6.75
	Paul Blair		
	Dave Johnson		
474	Cookie Rojas	15.00	6.75
475	Clete Boyer	15.00	6.75
476	Billy O'Dell	7.00	3.10
477	Cards Rookies	175.00	80.00
	Fritz Ackley		
	Steve Carlton		
478	Wilbur Wood	15.00	6.75
479	Ken Harrelson	15.00	6.75
480	Joel Horlen	7.00	3.10
481	Cleveland Indians	10.00	4.50
	Team Card		
482	Bob Priddy	7.00	3.10
483	George Smith	7.00	3.10
484	Ron Perranoski	15.00	6.75
485	Nellie Fox P/CO	15.00	6.75
486	Angels Rookies	7.00	3.10
	Tom Egan		
	Pat Rogan		
487	Woody Woodward	15.00	6.75
488	Ted Wills	7.00	3.10
489	Gene Mauch MG	15.00	6.75
490	Earl Battey	15.00	6.75
491	Tracy Stallard	7.00	3.10
492	Gene Freese	7.00	3.10
493	Tigers Rookies	7.00	3.10
	Bill Roman		
	Bruce Brubaker		
494	Jay Ritchie	7.00	3.10
495	Joe Christopher	7.00	3.10
496	Joe Cunningham	7.00	3.10
497	Giants Rookies	15.00	6.75
	Ken Henderson		
	Jack Hiatt		
498	Gene Stephens	7.00	3.10
499	Stu Miller	15.00	6.75
500	Eddie Mathews	35.00	16.00
501	Indians Rookies	7.00	3.10
	Ralph Gagliano		
	Jim Rittwage		
502	Don Cardwell	7.00	3.10
503	Phil Gagliano	7.00	3.10
504	Jerry Grote	15.00	6.75
505	Ray Culp	7.00	3.10
506	Sam Mele MG	7.00	3.10

❏ 507 Sammy Ellis	7.00	3.10
❏ 508 Checklist 7	12.00	2.40
❏ 509 Red Sox Rookies	7.00	3.10
Bob Guindon		
Gerry Vezendy		
❏ 510 Ernie Banks	80.00	36.00
❏ 511 Ron Locke	7.00	3.10
❏ 512 Cap Peterson	7.00	3.10
❏ 513 New York Yankees	40.00	18.00
Team Card		
❏ 514 Joe Azcue	7.00	3.10
❏ 515 Vern Law	15.00	6.75
❏ 516 Al Weis	7.00	3.10
❏ 517 Angels Rookies	15.00	6.75
Paul Schaal		
Jack Warner		
❏ 518 Ken Rowe	7.00	3.10
❏ 519 Bob Uecker UER	30.00	13.50
(Posing as a left-handed batter)		
❏ 520 Tony Cloninger	7.00	3.10
❏ 521 Phillies Rookies	7.00	3.10
Dave Bennett		
Morrie Stevens		
❏ 522 Hank Aguirre	7.00	3.10
❏ 523 Mike Brumley SP	12.00	5.50
❏ 524 Dave Giusti SP	12.00	5.50
❏ 525 Eddie Bressoud	7.00	3.10
❏ 526 Athletics Rookies SP	80.00	36.00
Rene Lachemann		
Johnny Odom		
Jim Hunter UER		
(Tim on back)		
Skip Lockwood		
❏ 527 Jeff Torborg SP	15.00	6.75
❏ 528 George Altman	7.00	3.10
❏ 529 Jerry Fosnow SP	12.00	5.50
❏ 530 Jim Maloney	15.00	6.75
❏ 531 Chuck Hiller	7.00	3.10
❏ 532 Hector Lopez	15.00	6.75
❏ 533 Mets Rookies SP	25.00	11.00
Dan Napoleon		
Ron Swoboda		
Tug McGraw		
Jim Bethke		
❏ 534 John Herrnstein	7.00	3.10
❏ 535 Jack Kralick SP	12.00	5.50
❏ 536 Andre Rodgers SP	12.00	5.50
❏ 537 Angels Rookies	7.00	3.10
Marcelino Lopez		
Phil Roof		
Rudy May		
❏ 538 Chuck Dressen SP MG	12.00	5.50
❏ 539 Herm Starrette	7.00	3.10
❏ 540 Lou Brock SP	50.00	22.00
❏ 541 White Sox Rookies	7.00	3.10
Greg Bollo		
Bob Locker		
❏ 542 Lou Klimchock	7.00	3.10
❏ 543 Ed Connolly SP	12.00	5.50
❏ 544 Howie Reed	7.00	3.10
❏ 545 Jesus Alou SP	14.00	6.25
❏ 546 Indians Rookies	7.00	3.10
Bill Davis		
Mike Hedlund		
Ray Barker		
Floyd Weaver		
❏ 547 Jake Wood SP	12.00	5.50
❏ 548 Dick Stigman	7.00	3.10
❏ 549 Cubs Rookies SP	20.00	9.00
Roberto Pena		
Glenn Beckert		
❏ 550 Mel Stottlemyre SP	30.00	13.50
❏ 551 New York Mets SP	30.00	13.50
Team Card		
❏ 552 Julio Gotay	7.00	3.10
❏ 553 Astros Rookies	7.00	3.10
Dan Coombs		
Gene Ratliff		
Jack McClure		
❏ 554 Chico Ruiz SP	12.00	5.50
❏ 555 Jack Baldschun SP	12.00	5.50
❏ 556 Red Schoendienst SP MG	24.00	11.00
❏ 557 Jose Santiago	7.00	3.10
❏ 558 Tommie Sisk	7.00	3.10

❏ 559 Ed Bailey SP	12.00	5.50
❏ 560 Boog Powell SP	24.00	11.00
❏ 561 Dodgers Rookies	10.00	4.50
Dennis Daboll		
Mike Kekich		
Hector Valle		
Jim Lefebvre		
❏ 562 Billy Moran	7.00	3.10
❏ 563 Julio Navarro	7.00	3.10
❏ 564 Mel Nelson	7.00	3.10
❏ 565 Ernie Broglio SP	12.00	5.50
❏ 566 Yankees Rookies SP	12.00	5.50
Gil Blanco		
Ross Moschitto		
Art Lopez		
❏ 567 Tommie Aaron	7.00	3.10
❏ 568 Ron Taylor SP	12.00	5.50
❏ 569 Gino Cimoli SP	12.00	5.50
❏ 570 Claude Osteen SP	15.00	6.75
❏ 571 Ossie Virgil SP	12.00	5.50
❏ 572 Baltimore Orioles SP	25.00	11.00
Team Card		
❏ 573 Red Sox Rookies SP	24.00	11.00
Jim Lonborg		
Gerry Moses		
Bill Schlesinger		
Mike Ryan		
❏ 574 Roy Sievers	15.00	6.75
❏ 575 Jose Pagan	7.00	3.10
❏ 576 Terry Fox SP	12.00	5.50
❏ 577 AL Rookie Stars SP	12.00	5.50
Darold Knowles		
Don Buschhorn		
Richie Scheinblum		
❏ 578 Camilo Carreon SP	12.00	5.50
❏ 579 Dick Smith SP	12.00	5.50
❏ 580 Jimmie Hall SP	12.00	5.50
❏ 581 NL Rookie Stars SP	80.00	36.00
Tony Perez		
Dave Ricketts		
Kevin Collins		
❏ 582 Bob Schmidt SP	12.00	5.50
❏ 583 Wes Covington SP	12.00	5.50
❏ 584 Harry Bright	15.00	6.75
❏ 585 Hank Fischer	7.00	3.10
❏ 586 Tom McCraw SP	12.00	5.50
❏ 587 Joe Sparma	7.00	3.10
❏ 588 Lenny Green	7.00	3.10
❏ 589 Giants Rookies SP	12.00	5.50
Frank Linzy		
Bob Schroder		
❏ 590 John Wyatt	7.00	3.10
❏ 591 Bob Skinner SP	12.00	5.50
❏ 592 Frank Bork SP	12.00	5.50
❏ 593 Tigers Rookies SP	12.00	5.50
Jackie Moore		
John Sullivan		
❏ 594 Joe Gaines	7.00	3.10
❏ 595 Don Lee	7.00	3.10
❏ 596 Don Landrum SP	12.00	5.50
❏ 597 Twins Rookies	7.00	3.10
Joe Nossek		
John Sevcik		
Dick Reese		
❏ 598 Al Downing SP	24.00	7.25

1966 Topps

PHIL NIEKRO pitcher

	NRMT	VG-E
COMPLETE SET (598)	4000.00	1800.00
COMMON CARD (1-109)	1.50	.70
COMMON CARD (110-283)	2.00	.90
MINOR STARS 1-283	4.00	1.80
SEMISTARS 1-283	6.00	2.70
UNLISTED STARS 1-283	8.00	3.60
COMMON CARD (284-370)	3.00	1.35
MINOR STARS 284-370	5.00	2.20
SEMISTARS 284-370	8.00	3.60
UNLISTED STARS 284-370	12.00	5.50
COMMON CARD (371-446)	5.00	2.20
MINOR STARS 371-446	8.00	3.60
SEMISTARS 371-446	10.00	4.50
UNLISTED STARS 371-446	15.00	6.75
COMMON CARD (447-522)	9.00	4.00
MINOR STARS 447-522	15.00	6.75
SEMISTARS 447-522	25.00	11.00
COMMON CARD (523-598)	15.00	6.75
COMMON SP (523-598)	30.00	13.50
MINOR STARS 523-598	25.00	11.00

*UNLISTED DODGER/YANKEE: 1.25X VALUE
CARDS PRICED IN NM CONDITION
LAST SERIES CONDITION SENSITIVE

❏ 1 Willie Mays	150.00	47.50
❏ 2 Ted Abernathy	1.50	.70
❏ 3 Sam Mele MG	1.50	.70
❏ 4 Ray Culp	1.50	.70
❏ 5 Jim Fregosi	4.00	1.80
❏ 6 Chuck Schilling	1.50	.70
❏ 7 Tracy Stallard	1.50	.70
❏ 8 Floyd Robinson	1.50	.70
❏ 9 Clete Boyer	4.00	1.80
❏ 10 Tony Cloninger	1.50	.70
❏ 11 Senators Rookies	1.50	.70
Brant Alyea		
Pete Craig		
❏ 12 John Tsitouris	1.50	.70
❏ 13 Lou Johnson	4.00	1.80
❏ 14 Norm Siebern	1.50	.70
❏ 15 Vern Law	4.00	1.80
❏ 16 Larry Brown	1.50	.70
❏ 17 John Stephenson	1.50	.70
❏ 18 Roland Sheldon	1.50	.70
❏ 19 San Francisco Giants	5.00	2.20
Team Card		
❏ 20 Willie Horton	4.00	1.80
❏ 21 Don Nottebart	1.50	.70
❏ 22 Joe Nossek	1.50	.70
❏ 23 Jack Sanford	1.50	.70
❏ 24 Don Kessinger	6.00	2.70
❏ 25 Pete Ward	1.50	.70
❏ 26 Ray Sadecki	1.50	.70
❏ 27 Orioles Rookies	1.50	.70
Darold Knowles		
Andy Etchebarren		
❏ 28 Phil Niekro	20.00	9.00
❏ 29 Mike Brumley	1.50	.70
❏ 30 Pete Rose DP	35.00	16.00
❏ 31 Jack Cullen	4.00	1.80
❏ 32 Adolfo Phillips	1.50	.70
❏ 33 Jim Pagliaroni	1.50	.70
❏ 34 Checklist 1	8.00	1.60
❏ 35 Ron Swoboda	4.00	1.80
❏ 36 Jim Hunter UER	20.00	9.00
(Stats say 1963 and 1964, should be 1964 and 1965)		
❏ 37 Billy Herman MG	4.00	1.80
❏ 38 Ron Nischwitz	1.50	.70
❏ 39 Ken Henderson	1.50	.70
❏ 40 Jim Grant	1.50	.70
❏ 41 Don LeJohn	1.50	.70
❏ 42 Aubrey Gatewood	1.50	.70
❏ 43A Don Landrum	4.00	1.80
(Dark button on pants showing)		
❏ 43B Don Landrum	20.00	9.00
(Button on pants partially airbrushed)		
❏ 43C Don Landrum	4.00	1.80
(Button on pants not showing)		
❏ 44 Indians Rookies	1.50	.70
Bill Davis		

Tom Kelley		
❑ 45 Jim Gentile 4.00		1.80
❑ 46 Howie Koplitz 1.50		.70
❑ 47 J.C. Martin 1.50		.70
❑ 48 Paul Blair 4.00		1.80
❑ 49 Woody Woodward ... 4.00		1.80
❑ 50 Mickey Mantle DP .. 200.00		90.00
❑ 51 Gordon Richardson .. 1.50		.70
❑ 52 Power Plus 4.00		1.80
Wes Covington		
Johnny Callison		
❑ 53 Bob Duliba 1.50		.70
❑ 54 Jose Pagan 1.50		.70
❑ 55 Ken Harrelson 4.00		1.80
❑ 56 Sandy Valdespino ... 1.50		.70
❑ 57 Jim Lefebvre 4.00		1.80
❑ 58 Dave Wickersham ... 1.50		.70
❑ 59 Reds Team 5.00		2.20
❑ 60 Curt Flood 4.00		1.80
❑ 61 Bob Bolin 1.50		.70
❑ 62A Merritt Ranew 4.00		1.80
(With sold line)		
❑ 62B Merritt Ranew 30.00		13.50
(Without sold line)		
❑ 63 Jim Stewart 1.50		.70
❑ 64 Bob Bruce 1.50		.70
❑ 65 Leon Wagner 1.50		.70
❑ 66 Al Weis 1.50		.70
❑ 67 Mets Rookies 4.00		1.80
Cleon Jones		
Dick Selma		
❑ 68 Hal Reniff 1.50		.70
❑ 69 Ken Hamlin 1.50		.70
❑ 70 Carl Yastrzemski 25.00		11.00
❑ 71 Frank Carpin 1.50		.70
❑ 72 Tony Perez 25.00		11.00
❑ 73 Jerry Zimmerman 1.50		.70
❑ 74 Don Mossi 4.00		1.80
❑ 75 Tommy Davis 4.00		1.80
❑ 76 Red Schoendienst MG .. 4.00		1.80
❑ 77 John Orsino 1.50		.70
❑ 78 Frank Linzy 1.50		.70
❑ 79 Joe Pepitone 4.00		1.80
❑ 80 Richie Allen 6.00		2.70
❑ 81 Ray Oyler 1.50		.70
❑ 82 Bob Hendley 1.50		.70
❑ 83 Albie Pearson 4.00		1.80
❑ 84 Braves Rookies 1.50		.70
Jim Beauchamp		
Dick Kelley		
❑ 85 Eddie Fisher 1.50		.70
❑ 86 John Bateman 1.50		.70
❑ 87 Dan Napoleon 1.50		.70
❑ 88 Fred Whitfield 1.50		.70
❑ 89 Ted Davidson 1.50		.70
❑ 90 Luis Aparicio 8.00		3.60
❑ 91A Bob Uecker TR 10.00		4.50
❑ 91B Bob Uecker NTR 40.00		18.00
❑ 92 Yankees Team 14.00		6.25
❑ 93 Jim Lonborg 4.00		1.80
❑ 94 Matty Alou 4.00		1.80
❑ 95 Pete Richert 1.50		.70
❑ 96 Felipe Alou 4.00		1.80
❑ 97 Jim Merritt 1.50		.70
❑ 98 Don Demeter 1.50		.70
❑ 99 Buc Belters 6.00		2.70
Willie Stargell		
Donn Clendenon		
❑ 100 Sandy Koufax 75.00		34.00
❑ 101A Checklist 2 .... 16.00		3.20
(115 W. Spahn) ERR		
❑ 101B Checklist 2 .... 10.00		2.00
(115 Bill Henry) COR		
❑ 102 Ed Kirkpatrick 1.50		.70
❑ 103A Dick Groat TR 4.00		1.80
❑ 103B Dick Groat NTR 40.00		18.00
❑ 104A Alex Johnson TR 4.00		1.80
❑ 104B Alex Johnson NTR ... 30.00		13.50
❑ 105 Milt Pappas 4.00		1.80
❑ 106 Rusty Staub 4.00		1.80
❑ 107 A's Rookies 1.50		.70
Larry Stahl		
Ron Tompkins		
❑ 108 Bobby Klaus 1.50		.70
❑ 109 Ralph Terry 4.00		1.80
❑ 110 Ernie Banks 30.00		13.50

❑ 111 Gary Peters 2.00		.90
❑ 112 Manny Mota 4.00		1.80
❑ 113 Hank Aguirre 2.00		.90
❑ 114 Jim Gosger 2.00		.90
❑ 115 Bill Henry 2.00		.90
❑ 116 Walter Alston MG ... 4.00		1.80
❑ 117 Jake Gibbs 4.00		1.80
❑ 118 Mike McCormick 4.00		1.80
❑ 119 Art Shamsky 2.00		.90
❑ 120 Harmon Killebrew .. 15.00		6.75
❑ 121 Ray Herbert 2.00		.90
❑ 122 Joe Gaines 2.00		.90
❑ 123 Pirates Rookies 2.00		.90
Frank Bork		
Jerry May		
❑ 124 Tug McGraw 4.00		1.80
❑ 125 Lou Brock 20.00		9.00
❑ 126 Jim Palmer UER ... 100.00		45.00
(Described as a		
lefthander on		
card back)		
❑ 127 Ken Berry 2.00		.90
❑ 128 Jim Landis 2.00		.90
❑ 129 Jack Kralick 2.00		.90
❑ 130 Joe Torre 4.00		1.80
❑ 131 Angels Team 5.00		2.20
❑ 132 Orlando Cepeda 8.00		3.60
❑ 133 Don McMahon 2.00		.90
❑ 134 Wes Parker 4.00		1.80
❑ 135 Dave Morehead 2.00		.90
❑ 136 Woody Held 2.00		.90
❑ 137 Pat Corrales 4.00		1.80
❑ 138 Roger Repoz 2.00		.90
❑ 139 Cubs Rookies 2.00		.90
Byron Browne		
Don Young		
❑ 140 Jim Maloney 4.00		1.80
❑ 141 Tom McCraw 2.00		.90
❑ 142 Don Dennis 2.00		.90
❑ 143 Jose Tartabull 4.00		1.80
❑ 144 Don Schwall 2.00		.90
❑ 145 Bill Freehan 4.00		1.80
❑ 146 George Altman 2.00		.90
❑ 147 Lum Harris MG 2.00		.90
❑ 148 Bob Johnson 2.00		.90
❑ 149 Dick Nen 2.00		.90
❑ 150 Rocky Colavito 8.00		3.60
❑ 151 Gary Wagner 2.00		.90
❑ 152 Frank Malzone 4.00		1.80
❑ 153 Rico Carty 4.00		1.80
❑ 154 Chuck Hiller 2.00		.90
❑ 155 Marcelino Lopez 2.00		.90
❑ 156 Double Play Combo .. 2.00		.90
Dick Schofield		
Hal Lanier		
❑ 157 Rene Lachemann ... 2.00		.90
❑ 158 Jim Brewer 2.00		.90
❑ 159 Chico Ruiz 2.00		.90
❑ 160 Whitey Ford 25.00		11.00
❑ 161 Jerry Lumpe 2.00		.90
❑ 162 Lee Maye 2.00		.90
❑ 163 Tito Francona 2.00		.90
❑ 164 White Sox Rookies .. 4.00		1.80
Tommie Agee		
Marv Staehle		
❑ 165 Don Lock 2.00		.90
❑ 166 Chris Krug 2.00		.90
❑ 167 Boog Powell 6.00		2.70
❑ 168 Dan Osinski 2.00		.90
❑ 169 Duke Sims 2.00		.90
❑ 170 Cookie Rojas 4.00		1.80
❑ 171 Nick Willhite 2.00		.90
❑ 172 Mets Team 5.00		2.20
❑ 173 Al Spangler 2.00		.90
❑ 174 Ron Taylor 2.00		.90
❑ 175 Bert Campaneris ... 4.00		1.80
❑ 176 Jim Davenport 2.00		.90
❑ 177 Hector Lopez 2.00		.90
❑ 178 Bob Tillman 2.00		.90
❑ 179 Cards Rookies 4.00		1.80
Dennis Aust		
Bob Tolan		
❑ 180 Vada Pinson 4.00		1.80
❑ 181 Al Worthington 2.00		.90
❑ 182 Jerry Lynch 2.00		.90
❑ 183A Checklist 3 .... 8.00		1.60

(Large print		
on front)		
❑ 183B Checklist 3 .... 8.00		1.60
(Small print		
on front)		
❑ 184 Denis Menke 2.00		.90
❑ 185 Bob Buhl 4.00		1.80
❑ 186 Ruben Amaro 2.00		.90
❑ 187 Chuck Dressen MG .. 4.00		1.80
❑ 188 Al Luplow 2.00		.90
❑ 189 John Roseboro 4.00		1.80
❑ 190 Jimmie Hall 2.00		.90
❑ 191 Darrell Sutherland ... 2.00		.90
❑ 192 Vic Power 4.00		1.80
❑ 193 Dave McNally 4.00		1.80
❑ 194 Senators Team 5.00		2.20
❑ 195 Joe Morgan 14.00		6.25
❑ 196 Don Pavletich 2.00		.90
❑ 197 Sonny Siebert 2.00		.90
❑ 198 Mickey Stanley 4.00		1.80
❑ 199 Chisox Clubbers 4.00		1.80
Bill Skowron		
Johnny Romano		
Floyd Robinson		
❑ 200 Eddie Mathews 15.00		6.75
❑ 201 Jim Dickson 2.00		.90
❑ 202 Clay Dalrymple 2.00		.90
❑ 203 Jose Santiago 2.00		.90
❑ 204 Cubs Team 5.00		2.20
❑ 205 Tom Tresh 4.00		1.80
❑ 206 Al Jackson 2.00		.90
❑ 207 Frank Quilici 2.00		.90
❑ 208 Bob Miller 2.00		.90
❑ 209 Tigers Rookies 4.00		1.80
Fritz Fisher		
John Hiller		
❑ 210 Bill Mazeroski 6.00		2.70
❑ 211 Frank Kreutzer 2.00		.90
❑ 212 Ed Kranepool 4.00		1.80
❑ 213 Fred Newman 2.00		.90
❑ 214 Tommy Harper 4.00		1.80
❑ 215 NL Batting Leaders .. 50.00		22.00
Bob Clemente		
Hank Aaron		
Willie Mays		
❑ 216 AL Batting Leaders .. 5.00		2.20
Tony Oliva		
Carl Yastrzemski		
Vic Davalillo		
❑ 217 NL Home Run Leaders 20.00		9.00
Willie Mays		
Willie McCovey		
Billy Williams		
❑ 218 AL Home Run Leaders 5.00		2.20
Tony Conigliaro		
Norm Cash		
Willie Horton		
❑ 219 NL RBI Leaders 12.00		5.50
Deron Johnson		
Frank Robinson		
Willie Mays		
❑ 220 AL RBI Leaders 5.00		2.20
Rocky Colavito		
Willie Horton		
Tony Oliva		
❑ 221 NL ERA Leaders 12.00		5.50
Sandy Koufax		
Juan Marichal		
Vern Law		
❑ 222 AL ERA Leaders 5.00		2.20
Sam McDowell		
Eddie Fisher		
Sonny Siebert		
❑ 223 NL Pitching Leaders .. 12.00		5.50
Sandy Koufax		
Tony Cloninger		
Don Drysdale		
❑ 224 AL Pitching Leaders .. 5.00		2.20
Jim Grant		
Mel Stottlemyre		
Jim Kaat		
❑ 225 NL Strikeout Leaders 12.00		5.50
Sandy Koufax		
Bob Veale		
Bob Gibson		
❑ 226 AL Strikeout Leaders .. 5.00		2.20

	Sam McDowell		
	Mickey Lolich		
	Dennis McLain		
	Sonny Siebert		
227	Russ Nixon	2.00	.90
228	Larry Dierker	4.00	1.80
229	Hank Bauer MG	4.00	1.80
230	Johnny Callison	4.00	1.80
231	Floyd Weaver	2.00	.90
232	Glenn Beckert	4.00	1.80
233	Dom Zanni	2.00	.90
234	Yankees Rookies	8.00	3.60
	Rich Beck		
	Roy White		
235	Don Cardwell	2.00	.90
236	Mike Hershberger	2.00	.90
237	Billy O'Dell	2.00	.90
238	Dodgers Team	5.00	2.20
239	Orlando Pena	2.00	.90
240	Earl Battey	2.00	.90
241	Dennis Ribant	2.00	.90
242	Jesus Alou	2.00	.90
243	Nelson Briles	4.00	1.80
244	Astros Rookies	2.00	.90
	Chuck Harrison		
	Sonny Jackson		
245	Jon Buzhardt	2.00	.90
246	Ed Bailey	2.00	.90
247	Carl Warwick	2.00	.90
248	Pete Mikkelsen	2.00	.90
249	Bill Rigney MG	2.00	.90
250	Sammy Ellis	2.00	.90
251	Ed Brinkman	2.00	.90
252	Denny Lemaster	2.00	.90
253	Don Wert	2.00	.90
254	Phillies Rookies	70.00	32.00
	Ferguson Jenkins		
	Bill Sorrell		
255	Willie Stargell	20.00	9.00
256	Lew Krausse	2.00	.90
257	Jeff Torborg	4.00	1.80
258	Dave Giusti	2.00	.90
259	Boston Red Sox	5.00	2.20
	Team Card		
260	Bob Shaw	2.00	.90
261	Ron Hansen	2.00	.90
262	Jack Hamilton	2.00	.90
263	Tom Egan	2.00	.90
264	Twins Rookies	2.00	.90
	Andy Kosco		
	Ted Uhlaender		
265	Stu Miller	4.00	1.80
266	Pedro Gonzalez UER	2.00	.90
	(Misspelled Gonzales on card back)		
267	Joe Sparma	2.00	.90
268	John Blanchard	2.00	.90
269	Don Heffner MG	2.00	.90
270	Claude Osteen	4.00	1.80
271	Hal Lanier	2.00	.90
272	Jack Baldschun	2.00	.90
273	Astro Aces	4.00	1.80
	Bob Aspromonte		
	Rusty Staub		
274	Buster Narum	2.00	.90
275	Tim McCarver	4.00	1.80
276	Jim Bouton	4.00	1.80
277	George Thomas	2.00	.90
278	Cal Koonce	2.00	.90
279A	Checklist 4	8.00	1.60
	(Player's cap black)		
279B	Checklist 4	8.00	1.60
	(Player's cap red)		
280	Bobby Knoop	2.00	.90
281	Bruce Howard	2.00	.90
282	Johnny Lewis	2.00	.90
283	Jim Perry	4.00	1.80
284	Bobby Wine	3.00	1.35
285	Luis Tiant	5.00	2.20
286	Gary Geiger	3.00	1.35
287	Jack Aker	3.00	1.35
288	Dodgers Rookies	50.00	22.00
	Bill Singer		
	Don Sutton		
289	Larry Sherry	3.00	1.35
290	Ron Santo	5.00	2.20
291	Moe Drabowsky	5.00	2.20
292	Jim Coker	3.00	1.35
293	Mike Shannon	5.00	2.20
294	Steve Ridzik	3.00	1.35
295	Jim Ray Hart	5.00	2.20
296	Johnny Keane MG	5.00	2.20
297	Jim Owens	3.00	1.35
298	Rico Petrocelli	5.00	2.20
299	Lou Burdette	5.00	2.20
300	Bob Clemente	150.00	70.00
301	Greg Bollo	3.00	1.35
302	Ernie Bowman	3.00	1.35
303	Cleveland Indians	5.00	2.20
	Team Card		
304	John Herrnstein	3.00	1.35
305	Camilo Pascual	5.00	2.20
306	Ty Cline	3.00	1.35
307	Clay Carroll	5.00	2.20
308	Tom Haller	5.00	2.20
309	Diego Segui	3.00	1.35
310	Frank Robinson	30.00	13.50
311	Reds Rookies	5.00	2.20
	Tommy Helms		
	Dick Simpson		
312	Bob Saverine	3.00	1.35
313	Chris Zachary	3.00	1.35
314	Hector Valle	3.00	1.35
315	Norm Cash	5.00	2.20
316	Jack Fisher	3.00	1.35
317	Dalton Jones	3.00	1.35
318	Harry Walker MG	3.00	1.35
319	Gene Freese	3.00	1.35
320	Bob Gibson	25.00	11.00
321	Rich Reichardt	3.00	1.35
322	Bill Faul	3.00	1.35
323	Ray Barker	3.00	1.35
324	John Boozer	3.00	1.35
325	Vic Davalillo	3.00	1.35
326	Braves Team	5.00	2.20
327	Bernie Allen	3.00	1.35
328	Jerry Grote	5.00	2.20
329	Pete Charton	3.00	1.35
330	Ron Fairly	5.00	2.20
331	Ron Herbel	3.00	1.35
332	Bill Bryan	3.00	1.35
333	Senators Rookies	3.00	1.35
	Joe Coleman		
	Jim French		
334	Marty Keough	3.00	1.35
335	Juan Pizarro	3.00	1.35
336	Gene Alley	5.00	2.20
337	Fred Gladding	3.00	1.35
338	Dal Maxvill	5.00	2.20
339	Del Crandall	5.00	2.20
340	Dean Chance	5.00	2.20
341	Wes Westrum MG	5.00	2.20
342	Bob Humphreys	3.00	1.35
343	Joe Christopher	3.00	1.35
344	Steve Blass	5.00	2.20
345	Bob Allison	5.00	2.20
346	Mike de la Hoz	3.00	1.35
347	Phil Regan	5.00	2.20
348	Orioles Team	8.00	3.60
349	Cap Peterson	3.00	1.35
350	Mel Stottlemyre	5.00	2.20
351	Fred Valentine	3.00	1.35
352	Bob Aspromonte	3.00	1.35
353	Al McBean	3.00	1.35
354	Smoky Burgess	5.00	2.20
355	Wade Blasingame	3.00	1.35
356	Red Sox Rookies	3.00	1.35
	Owen Johnson		
	Ken Sanders		
357	Gerry Arrigo	3.00	1.35
358	Charlie Smith	3.00	1.35
359	Johnny Briggs	3.00	1.35
360	Ron Hunt	3.00	1.35
361	Tom Satriano	3.00	1.35
362	Gates Brown	5.00	2.20
363	Checklist 5	10.00	2.00
364	Nate Oliver	3.00	1.35
365	Roger Maris	40.00	18.00
366	Wayne Causey	3.00	1.35
367	Mel Nelson	3.00	1.35
368	Charlie Lau	5.00	2.20
369	Jim King	3.00	1.35
370	Chico Cardenas	3.00	1.35
371	Lee Stange	5.00	2.20
372	Harvey Kuenn	8.00	3.60
373	Giants Rookies	8.00	3.60
	Jack Hiatt		
	Dick Estelle		
374	Bob Locker	5.00	2.20
375	Donn Clendenon	8.00	3.60
376	Paul Schaal	5.00	2.20
377	Turk Farrell	5.00	2.20
378	Dick Tracewski	5.00	2.20
379	Cardinal Team	10.00	4.50
380	Tony Conigliaro	10.00	4.50
381	Hank Fischer	5.00	2.20
382	Phil Roof	5.00	2.20
383	Jackie Brandt	5.00	2.20
384	Al Downing	8.00	3.60
385	Ken Boyer	8.00	3.60
386	Gil Hodges MG	8.00	3.60
387	Howie Reed	5.00	2.20
388	Don Mincher	5.00	2.20
389	Jim O'Toole	8.00	3.60
390	Brooks Robinson	45.00	20.00
391	Chuck Hinton	5.00	2.20
392	Cubs Rookies	8.00	3.60
	Bill Hands		
	Randy Hundley		
393	George Brunet	5.00	2.20
394	Ron Brand	5.00	2.20
395	Len Gabrielson	5.00	2.20
396	Jerry Stephenson	5.00	2.20
397	Bill White	8.00	3.60
398	Danny Cater	5.00	2.20
399	Ray Washburn	5.00	2.20
400	Zoilo Versalles	8.00	3.60
401	Ken McMullen	5.00	2.20
402	Jim Hickman	5.00	2.20
403	Fred Talbot	5.00	2.20
404	Pittsburgh Pirates	10.00	4.50
	Team Card		
405	Elston Howard	8.00	3.60
406	Joey Jay	5.00	2.20
407	John Kennedy	5.00	2.20
408	Lee Thomas	8.00	3.60
409	Billy Hoeft	5.00	2.20
410	Al Kaline	35.00	16.00
411	Gene Mauch MG	5.00	2.20
412	Sam Bowens	5.00	2.20
413	Johnny Romano	5.00	2.20
414	Dan Coombs	5.00	2.20
415	Max Alvis	5.00	2.20
416	Phil Ortega	5.00	2.20
417	Angels Rookies	5.00	2.20
	Jim McGlothlin		
	Ed Sukla		
418	Phil Gagliano	5.00	2.20
419	Mike Ryan	5.00	2.20
420	Juan Marichal	10.00	4.50
421	Roy McMillan	8.00	3.60
422	Ed Charles	5.00	2.20
423	Ernie Broglio	5.00	2.20
424	Reds Rookies	10.00	4.50
	Lee May		
	Darrell Osteen		
425	Bob Veale	8.00	3.60
426	White Sox Team	10.00	4.50
427	John Miller	5.00	2.20
428	Sandy Alomar	5.00	2.20
429	Bill Monbouquette	5.00	2.20
430	Don Drysdale	20.00	9.00
431	Walt Bond	5.00	2.20
432	Bob Heffner	5.00	2.20
433	Alvin Dark MG	8.00	3.60
434	Willie Kirkland	5.00	2.20
435	Jim Bunning	15.00	6.75
436	Julian Javier	8.00	3.60
437	Al Stanek	5.00	2.20
438	Willie Smith	5.00	2.20
439	Pedro Ramos	5.00	2.20
440	Deron Johnson	8.00	3.60
441	Tommie Sisk	5.00	2.20
442	Orioles Rookies	5.00	2.20
	Ed Barnowski		
	Eddie Watt		
443	Bill Wakefield	5.00	2.20
444	Checklist 6	10.00	2.00

❑ 445 Jim Kaat	10.00	4.50
❑ 446 Mack Jones	5.00	2.20
❑ 447 Dick Ellsworth UER	15.00	6.75
(Photo actually		
Ken Hubbs)		
❑ 448 Eddie Stanky MG	9.00	4.00
❑ 449 Joe Moeller	9.00	4.00
❑ 450 Tony Oliva	12.00	5.50
❑ 451 Barry Latman	9.00	4.00
❑ 452 Joe Azcue	9.00	4.00
❑ 453 Ron Kline	9.00	4.00
❑ 454 Jerry Buchek	9.00	4.00
❑ 455 Mickey Lolich	15.00	6.75
❑ 456 Red Sox Rookies	9.00	4.00
Darrell Brandon		
Joe Foy		
❑ 457 Joe Gibbon	9.00	4.00
❑ 458 Manny Jimenez	9.00	4.00
❑ 459 Bill McCool	9.00	4.00
❑ 460 Curt Blefary	9.00	4.00
❑ 461 Roy Face	15.00	6.75
❑ 462 Bob Rodgers	9.00	4.00
❑ 463 Philadelphia Phillies	15.00	6.75
Team Card		
❑ 464 Larry Bearnarth	9.00	4.00
❑ 465 Don Buford	9.00	4.00
❑ 466 Ken Johnson	9.00	4.00
❑ 467 Vic Roznovsky	9.00	4.00
❑ 468 Johnny Podres	15.00	6.75
❑ 469 Yankees Rookies	25.00	11.00
Bobby Murcer		
Dooley Womack		
❑ 470 Sam McDowell	15.00	6.75
❑ 471 Bob Skinner	9.00	4.00
❑ 472 Terry Fox	9.00	4.00
❑ 473 Rich Rollins	9.00	4.00
❑ 474 Dick Schofield	9.00	4.00
❑ 475 Dick Radatz	9.00	4.00
❑ 476 Bobby Bragan MG	9.00	4.00
❑ 477 Steve Barber	9.00	4.00
❑ 478 Tony Gonzalez	9.00	4.00
❑ 479 Jim Hannan	9.00	4.00
❑ 480 Dick Stuart	9.00	4.00
❑ 481 Bob Lee	9.00	4.00
❑ 482 Cubs Rookies	9.00	4.00
John Boccabella		
Dave Dowling		
❑ 483 Joe Nuxhall	9.00	4.00
❑ 484 Wes Covington	9.00	4.00
❑ 485 Bob Bailey	9.00	4.00
❑ 486 Tommy John	15.00	6.75
❑ 487 Al Ferrara	9.00	4.00
❑ 488 George Banks	9.00	4.00
❑ 489 Curt Simmons	9.00	4.00
❑ 490 Bobby Richardson	15.00	6.75
❑ 491 Dennis Bennett	9.00	4.00
❑ 492 Athletics Team	15.00	6.75
❑ 493 Johnny Klippstein	9.00	4.00
❑ 494 Gordy Coleman	9.00	4.00
❑ 495 Dick McAuliffe	15.00	6.75
❑ 496 Lindy McDaniel	9.00	4.00
❑ 497 Chris Cannizzaro	9.00	4.00
❑ 498 Pirates Rookies	9.00	4.00
Luke Walker		
Woody Fryman		
❑ 499 Wally Bunker	9.00	4.00
❑ 500 Hank Aaron	125.00	55.00
❑ 501 John O'Donoghue	9.00	4.00
❑ 502 Lenny Green UER	9.00	4.00
(Born: aJn. 6, 1933)		
❑ 503 Steve Hamilton	15.00	6.75
❑ 504 Grady Hatton MG	9.00	4.00
❑ 505 Jose Cardenal	9.00	4.00
❑ 506 Bo Belinsky	15.00	6.75
❑ 507 Johnny Edwards	9.00	4.00
❑ 508 Steve Hargan	9.00	4.00
❑ 509 Jake Wood	9.00	4.00
❑ 510 Hoyt Wilhelm	15.00	6.75
❑ 511 Giants Rookies	9.00	4.00
Bob Barton		
Tito Fuentes		
❑ 512 Dick Stigman	9.00	4.00
❑ 513 Camilo Carreon	9.00	4.00
❑ 514 Hal Woodeshick	9.00	4.00
❑ 515 Frank Howard	14.00	6.25
❑ 516 Eddie Bressoud	9.00	4.00

❑ 517A Checklist 7	16.00	3.20
529 White Sox Rookies		
544 Cardinals Rookies		
❑ 517B Checklist 7	16.00	3.20
529 W. Sox Rookies		
544 Cards Rookies		
❑ 518 Braves Rookies	9.00	4.00
Herb Hippauf		
Arnie Umbach		
❑ 519 Bob Friend	15.00	6.75
❑ 520 Jim Wynn	15.00	6.75
❑ 521 John Wyatt	9.00	4.00
❑ 522 Phil Linz	9.00	4.00
❑ 523 Bob Sadowski	15.00	6.75
❑ 524 Giants Rookies SP	30.00	13.50
Ollie Brown		
Don Mason		
❑ 525 Gary Bell SP	30.00	13.50
❑ 526 Twins Team SP	100.00	45.00
❑ 527 Julio Navarro	15.00	6.75
❑ 528 Jesse Gonder SP	30.00	13.50
❑ 529 White Sox Rookies	15.00	6.75
Lee Elia		
Dennis Higgins		
Bill Voss		
❑ 530 Robin Roberts	50.00	22.00
❑ 531 Joe Cunningham	15.00	6.75
❑ 532 Aurelio Monteagudo SP	30.00	13.50
❑ 533 Jerry Adair SP	30.00	13.50
❑ 534 Mets Rookies	15.00	6.75
Dave Eilers		
Rob Gardner		
❑ 535 Willie Davis SP	40.00	18.00
❑ 536 Dick Egan	15.00	6.75
❑ 537 Herman Franks MG	15.00	6.75
❑ 538 Bob Allen SP	30.00	13.50
❑ 539 Astros Rookies	15.00	6.75
Bill Heath		
Carroll Sembera		
❑ 540 Denny McLain SP	60.00	27.00
❑ 541 Gene Oliver SP	30.00	13.50
❑ 542 George Smith	15.00	6.75
❑ 543 Roger Craig SP	30.00	13.50
❑ 544 Cardinals Rookies SP	30.00	13.50
Joe Hoerner		
George Kernek		
Jimy Williams UER		
(Misspelled Jimmy		
on card)		
❑ 545 Dick Green SP	30.00	13.50
❑ 546 Dwight Siebler	15.00	6.75
❑ 547 Horace Clarke SP	40.00	18.00
❑ 548 Gary Kroll SP	30.00	13.50
❑ 549 Senators Rookies	15.00	6.75
Al Closter		
Casey Cox		
❑ 550 Willie McCovey SP	90.00	40.00
❑ 551 Bob Purkey SP	30.00	13.50
❑ 552 Birdie Tebbetts	30.00	13.50
MG SP		
❑ 553 Rookie Stars	15.00	6.75
Pat Garrett		
Jackie Warner		
❑ 554 Jim Northrup SP	30.00	13.50
❑ 555 Ron Perranoski SP	30.00	13.50
❑ 556 Mel Queen SP	30.00	13.50
❑ 557 Felix Mantilla SP	30.00	13.50
❑ 558 Red Sox Rookies	20.00	9.00
Guido Grilli		
Pete Magrini		
George Scott		
❑ 559 Roberto Pena SP	30.00	13.50
❑ 560 Joel Horlen	8.00	3.60
❑ 561 ChoiChoo Coleman SP	30.00	13.50
❑ 562 Russ Snyder	15.00	6.75
❑ 563 Twins Rookies	15.00	6.75
Pete Cimino		
Cesar Tovar		
❑ 564 Bob Chance SP	30.00	13.50
❑ 565 Jimmy Piersall SP	40.00	18.00
❑ 566 Mike Cuellar SP	30.00	13.50
❑ 567 Dick Howser SP	40.00	18.00
❑ 568 Athletics Rookies	15.00	6.75
Paul Lindblad		
Ron Stone		
❑ 569 Orlando McFarlane SP	30.00	13.50

❑ 570 Art Mahaffey SP	30.00	13.50
❑ 571 Dave Roberts SP	30.00	13.50
❑ 572 Bob Priddy	15.00	6.75
❑ 573 Derrell Griffith	15.00	6.75
❑ 574 Mets Rookies	15.00	6.75
Bill Hepler		
Bill Murphy		
❑ 575 Earl Wilson	15.00	6.75
❑ 576 Dave Nicholson SP	30.00	13.50
❑ 577 Jack Lamabe SP	30.00	13.50
❑ 578 Chi Chi Olivo SP	30.00	13.50
❑ 579 Orioles Rookies	20.00	9.00
Frank Bertaina		
Gene Brabender		
Dave Johnson		
❑ 580 Billy Williams SP	60.00	27.00
❑ 581 Tony Martinez	15.00	6.75
❑ 582 Garry Roggenburk	15.00	6.75
❑ 583 Tigers Team SP UER	125.00	55.00
(Text on back states Tigers		
finished third in 1966 instead		
of fourth.)		
❑ 584 Yankees Rookies	15.00	6.75
Frank Fernandez		
Fritz Peterson		
❑ 585 Tony Taylor	25.00	11.00
❑ 586 Claude Raymond SP	30.00	13.50
❑ 587 Dick Bertell	15.00	6.75
❑ 588 Athletics Rookies	15.00	6.75
Chuck Dobson		
Ken Suarez		
❑ 589 Lou Klimchock SP	35.00	16.00
❑ 590 Bill Skowron SP	40.00	18.00
❑ 591 NL Rookies SP	40.00	18.00
Bart Shirley		
Grant Jackson		
❑ 592 Andre Rodgers	15.00	6.75
❑ 593 Doug Camilli SP	30.00	13.50
❑ 594 Chico Salmon	15.00	6.75
❑ 595 Larry Jackson	15.00	6.75
❑ 596 Astros Rookies SP	30.00	13.50
Nate Colbert		
Greg Sims		
❑ 597 John Sullivan	15.00	6.75
❑ 598 Gaylord Perry SP	175.00	50.00

1967 Topps

CURT FLOOD • OUTFIELD

CARDS

	NRMT	VG-E
COMPLETE SET (609)	4600.00	2100.00
COMMON CARD (1-109)	1.50	.70
COMMON CARD (110-283)	2.00	.90
MINOR STARS 1-283	4.00	1.80
SEMISTARS 1-283	6.00	2.70
UNLISTED STARS 1-283	8.00	3.60
COMMON CARD (284-370)	2.50	1.10
MINOR STARS 284-370	5.00	2.20
SEMISTARS 284-370	8.00	3.60
UNLISTED STARS 284-370	10.00	4.50
COMMON CARD (371-457)	4.00	1.80
MINOR STARS 371-457	8.00	3.60
SEMISTARS 371-457	12.00	5.50
UNLISTED STARS 371-457	15.00	6.75
COMMON CARD (458-533)	6.00	2.70
MINOR STARS 458-533	12.00	5.50
SEMISTARS 458-533	20.00	9.00
COMMON CARD (534-609)	16.00	7.25
COMMON DP (534-609)	9.00	4.00

MINOR STARS 534-609 ...... 25.00   11.00
SEMISTARS 534-609 .... 40.00   18.00
*UNLISTED DODGER/YANKEE: 1.25X VALUE
CARDS PRICED IN NM CONDITION

No.	Card	Value	Value2
❑ 1	The Champs DP	25.00	7.50
	Frank Robinson		
	Hank Bauer MG		
	Brooks Robinson		
❑ 2	Jack Hamilton	1.50	.70
❑ 3	Duke Sims	1.50	.70
❑ 4	Hal Lanier	1.50	.70
❑ 5	Whitey Ford UER	20.00	9.00
	1953 listed as		
	1933 in stats on back		
❑ 6	Dick Simpson	1.50	.70
❑ 7	Don McMahon	1.50	.70
❑ 8	Chuck Harrison	1.50	.70
❑ 9	Ron Hansen	1.50	.70
❑ 10	Matty Alou	4.00	1.80
❑ 11	Barry Moore	1.50	.70
❑ 12	Dodgers Rookies	4.00	1.80
	Jim Campanis		
	Bill Singer		
❑ 13	Joe Sparma	1.50	.70
❑ 14	Phil Linz	4.00	1.80
❑ 15	Earl Battey	1.50	.70
❑ 16	Bill Hands	1.50	.70
❑ 17	Jim Gosger	1.50	.70
❑ 18	Gene Oliver	1.50	.70
❑ 19	Jim McGlothlin	1.50	.70
❑ 20	Orlando Cepeda	6.00	2.70
❑ 21	Dave Bristol MG	1.50	.70
❑ 22	Gene Brabender	1.50	.70
❑ 23	Larry Elliot	1.50	.70
❑ 24	Bob Allen	1.50	.70
❑ 25	Elston Howard	4.00	1.80
❑ 26A	Bob Priddy NTR	30.00	13.50
❑ 26B	Bob Priddy TR	4.00	1.80
❑ 27	Bob Saverine	1.50	.70
❑ 28	Barry Latman	1.50	.70
❑ 29	Tom McCraw	1.50	.70
❑ 30	Al Kaline DP	15.00	6.75
❑ 31	Jim Brewer	1.50	.70
❑ 32	Bob Bailey	4.00	1.80
❑ 33	Athletic Rookies	6.00	2.70
	Sal Bando		
	Randy Schwartz		
❑ 34	Pete Cimino	1.50	.70
❑ 35	Rico Carty	4.00	1.80
❑ 36	Bob Tillman	1.50	.70
❑ 37	Rick Wise	4.00	1.80
❑ 38	Bob Johnson	1.50	.70
❑ 39	Curt Simmons	4.00	1.80
❑ 40	Rick Reichardt	1.50	.70
❑ 41	Joe Hoerner	1.50	.70
❑ 42	Mets Team	10.00	4.50
❑ 43	Chico Salmon	1.50	.70
❑ 44	Joe Nuxhall	4.00	1.80
❑ 45	Roger Maris	35.00	16.00
❑ 46	Lindy McDaniel	4.00	1.80
❑ 47	Ken McMullen	1.50	.70
❑ 48	Bill Freehan	4.00	1.80
❑ 49	Roy Face	4.00	1.80
❑ 50	Tony Oliva	6.00	2.70
❑ 51	Astros Rookies	1.50	.70
	Dave Adlesh		
	Wes Bales		
❑ 52	Dennis Higgins	1.50	.70
❑ 53	Clay Dalrymple	1.50	.70
❑ 54	Dick Green	1.50	.70
❑ 55	Don Drysdale	16.00	7.25
❑ 56	Jose Tartabull	1.50	.70
❑ 57	Pat Jarvis	1.50	.70
❑ 58A	Paul Schaal	1.50	.70
	Green Bat		
❑ 58B	Paul Schaal	1.50	.70
	Normal Colored Bat		
❑ 59	Ralph Terry	4.00	1.80
❑ 60	Luis Aparicio	6.00	2.70
❑ 61	Gordy Coleman	4.00	1.80
❑ 62	Frank Robinson CL	8.00	1.60
❑ 63	Cards' Clubbers	8.00	3.60
	Lou Brock		
	Curt Flood		
❑ 64	Fred Valentine	1.50	.70
❑ 65	Tom Haller	4.00	1.80
❑ 66	Manny Mota	4.00	1.80
❑ 67	Ken Berry	1.50	.70
❑ 68	Bob Buhl	4.00	1.80
❑ 69	Vic Davalillo	1.50	.70
❑ 70	Ron Santo	4.00	1.80
❑ 71	Camilo Pascual	4.00	1.80
❑ 72	Tigers Rookies	1.50	.70
	George Korince		
	(Photo actually		
	James Murray Brown)		
	John (Tom) Matchick		
❑ 73	Rusty Staub	4.00	1.80
❑ 74	Wes Stock	1.50	.70
❑ 75	George Scott	4.00	1.80
❑ 76	Jim Barbieri	1.50	.70
❑ 77	Dooley Womack	4.00	1.80
❑ 78	Pat Corrales	4.00	1.80
❑ 79	Bubba Morton	1.50	.70
❑ 80	Jim Maloney	4.00	1.80
❑ 81	Eddie Stanky MG	4.00	1.80
❑ 82	Steve Barber	1.50	.70
❑ 83	Ollie Brown	1.50	.70
❑ 84	Tommie Sisk	1.50	.70
❑ 85	Johnny Callison	4.00	1.80
❑ 86A	Mike McCormick NTR	30.00	13.50
	(Senators on front		
	and Senators on back)		
❑ 86B	Mike McCormick TR	4.00	1.80
	(Traded line		
	at end of bio;		
	Senators on front,		
	but Giants on back)		
❑ 87	George Altman	1.50	.70
❑ 88	Mickey Lolich	4.00	1.80
❑ 89	Felix Millan	4.00	1.80
❑ 90	Jim Nash	1.50	.70
❑ 91	Johnny Lewis	1.50	.70
❑ 92	Ray Washburn	1.50	.70
❑ 93	Yankees Rookies	4.00	1.80
	Stan Bahnsen		
	Bobby Murcer		
❑ 94	Ron Fairly	4.00	1.80
❑ 95	Sonny Siebert	1.50	.70
❑ 96	Art Shamsky	1.50	.70
❑ 97	Mike Cuellar	4.00	1.80
❑ 98	Rich Rollins	1.50	.70
❑ 99	Lee Stange	1.50	.70
❑ 100	Frank Robinson DP	14.00	6.25
❑ 101	Ken Johnson	1.50	.70
❑ 102	Philadelphia Phillies	8.00	3.60
	Team Card		
❑ 103	Mickey Mantle CL	20.00	4.00
❑ 104	Minnie Rojas	1.50	.70
❑ 105	Ken Boyer	4.00	1.80
❑ 106	Randy Hundley	4.00	1.80
❑ 107	Joel Horlen	1.50	.70
❑ 108	Alex Johnson	4.00	1.80
❑ 109	Tribe Thumpers	6.00	2.70
	Rocky Colavito		
	Leon Wagner		
❑ 110	Jack Aker	4.00	1.80
❑ 111	John Kennedy	2.00	.90
❑ 112	Dave Wickersham	2.00	.90
❑ 113	Dave Nicholson	2.00	.90
❑ 114	Jack Baldschun	2.00	.90
❑ 115	Paul Casanova	2.00	.90
❑ 116	Herman Franks MG	2.00	.90
❑ 117	Darrell Brandon	2.00	.90
❑ 118	Bernie Allen	2.00	.90
❑ 119	Wade Blasingame	2.00	.90
❑ 120	Floyd Robinson	2.00	.90
❑ 121	Eddie Bressoud	2.00	.90
❑ 122	George Brunet	2.00	.90
❑ 123	Pirates Rookies	2.00	.90
	Jim Price		
	Luke Walker		
❑ 124	Jim Stewart	2.00	.90
❑ 125	Moe Drabowsky	4.00	1.80
❑ 126	Tony Taylor	2.00	.90
❑ 127	John O'Donoghue	2.00	.90
❑ 128	Ed Spiezio	2.00	.90
❑ 129	Phil Roof	2.00	.90
❑ 130	Phil Regan	4.00	1.80
❑ 131	Yankees Team	10.00	4.50
❑ 132	Ozzie Virgil	2.00	.90
❑ 133	Ron Kline	2.00	.90
❑ 134	Gates Brown	4.00	1.80
❑ 135	Deron Johnson	4.00	1.80
❑ 136	Carroll Sembera	2.00	.90
❑ 137	Twins Rookies	2.00	.90
	Ron Clark		
	Jim Ollum		
❑ 138	Dick Kelley	2.00	.90
❑ 139	Dalton Jones	2.00	1.80
❑ 140	Willie Stargell	20.00	9.00
❑ 141	John Miller	2.00	.90
❑ 142	Jackie Brandt	2.00	.90
❑ 143	Sox Sockers	2.00	.90
	Pete Ward		
	Don Buford		
❑ 144	Bill Hepler	2.00	.90
❑ 145	Larry Brown	2.00	.90
❑ 146	Steve Carlton	50.00	22.00
❑ 147	Tom Egan	2.00	.90
❑ 148	Adolfo Phillips	2.00	.90
❑ 149	Joe Moeller	2.00	.90
❑ 150	Mickey Mantle	250.00	110.00
❑ 151	Moe Drabowsky WS	4.00	1.80
❑ 152	Jim Palmer WS	8.00	3.60
❑ 153	Paul Blair WS	4.00	1.80
❑ 154	Brooks Robinson WS	4.00	1.80
	Dave McNally		
❑ 155	World Series Summary	4.00	1.80
	Winners celebrate		
❑ 156	Ron Herbel	2.00	.90
❑ 157	Danny Cater	2.00	.90
❑ 158	Jimmie Coker	2.00	.90
❑ 159	Bruce Howard	2.00	.90
❑ 160	Willie Davis	4.00	1.80
❑ 161	Dick Williams MG	4.00	1.80
❑ 162	Billy O'Dell	2.00	.90
❑ 163	Vic Roznovsky	2.00	.90
❑ 164	Dwight Siebler UER	2.00	.90
	(Last line of stats		
	shows 1960 Minnesota)		
❑ 165	Cleon Jones	4.00	1.80
❑ 166	Eddie Mathews	15.00	6.75
❑ 167	Senators Rookies	2.00	.90
	Joe Coleman		
	Tim Cullen		
❑ 168	Ray Culp	2.00	.90
❑ 169	Horace Clarke	4.00	1.80
❑ 170	Dick McAuliffe	4.00	1.80
❑ 171	Cal Koonce	2.00	.90
❑ 172	Bill Heath	2.00	.90
❑ 173	St. Louis Cardinals	4.00	1.80
	Team Card		
❑ 174	Dick Radatz	4.00	1.80
❑ 175	Bobby Knoop	2.00	.90
❑ 176	Sammy Ellis	2.00	.90
❑ 177	Tito Fuentes	2.00	.90
❑ 178	John Buzhardt	2.00	.90
❑ 179	Braves Rookies	2.00	.90
	Charles Vaughan		
	Cecil Upshaw		
❑ 180	Curt Blefary	2.00	.90
❑ 181	Terry Fox	2.00	.90
❑ 182	Ed Charles	2.00	.90
❑ 183	Jim Pagliaroni	2.00	.90
❑ 184	George Thomas	2.00	.90
❑ 185	Ken Holtzman	4.00	1.80
❑ 186	Mets Maulers	4.00	1.80
	Ed Kranepool		
	Ron Swoboda		
❑ 187	Pedro Ramos	2.00	.90
❑ 188	Ken Harrelson	4.00	1.80
❑ 189	Chuck Hinton	2.00	.90
❑ 190	Turk Farrell	2.00	.90
❑ 191A	Willie Mays CL	10.00	2.00
	214 Tom Kelley		
❑ 191B	Willie Mays CL	12.00	2.40
	214 Dick Kelley		
❑ 192	Fred Gladding	2.00	.90
❑ 193	Jose Cardenal	4.00	1.80
❑ 194	Bob Allison	4.00	1.80
❑ 195	Al Jackson	2.00	.90
❑ 196	Johnny Romano	2.00	.90
❑ 197	Ron Perranoski	4.00	1.80
❑ 198	Chuck Hiller	2.00	.90
❑ 199	Billy Hitchcock MG	2.00	.90
❑ 200	Willie Mays UER	80.00	36.00

('63 Sna Francisco on card back stats)

201 Hal Reniff	4.00	1.80
202 Johnny Edwards	2.00	.90
203 Al McBean	2.00	.90
204 Orioles Rookies	4.00	1.80
Mike Epstein		
Tom Phoebus		
205 Dick Groat	4.00	1.80
206 Dennis Bennett	2.00	.90
207 John Orsino	2.00	.90
208 Jack Lamabe	2.00	.90
209 Joe Nossek	2.00	.90
210 Bob Gibson	20.00	9.00
211 Twins Team	4.00	1.80
212 Chris Zachary	2.00	.90
213 Jay Johnstone	4.00	1.80
214 Dick Kelley	2.00	.90
215 Ernie Banks	20.00	9.00
216 Bengal Belters	8.00	3.60
Norm Cash		
Al Kaline		
217 Rob Gardner	2.00	.90
218 Wes Parker	4.00	1.80
219 Clay Carroll	4.00	1.80
220 Jim Ray Hart	4.00	1.80
221 Woody Fryman	4.00	1.80
222 Reds Rookies	4.00	1.80
Darrell Osteen		
Lee May		
223 Mike Ryan	4.00	1.80
224 Walt Bond	2.00	.90
225 Mel Stottlemyre	4.00	1.80
226 Julian Javier	4.00	1.80
227 Paul Lindblad	2.00	.90
228 Gil Hodges MG	6.00	2.70
229 Larry Jackson	2.00	.90
230 Boog Powell	6.00	2.70
231 John Bateman	2.00	.90
232 Don Buford	2.00	.90
233 AL ERA Leaders	4.00	1.80
Gary Peters		
Joel Horlen		
Steve Hargan		
234 NL ERA Leaders	15.00	6.75
Sandy Koufax		
Mike Cuellar		
Juan Marichal		
235 AL Pitching Leaders	6.00	2.70
Jim Kaat		
Denny McLain		
Earl Wilson		
236 NL Pitching Leaders	25.00	11.00
Sandy Koufax		
Juan Marichal		
Bob Gibson		
Gaylord Perry		
237 AL Strikeout Leaders	6.00	2.70
Sam McDowell		
Jim Kaat		
Earl Wilson		
238 NL Strikeout Leaders	12.00	5.50
Sandy Koufax		
Jim Bunning		
Bob Veale		
239 AL Batting Leaders	9.00	4.00
Frank Robinson		
Tony Oliva		
Al Kaline		
240 NL Batting Leaders	6.00	2.70
Matty Alou		
Felipe Alou		
Rico Carty		
241 AL RBI Leaders	9.00	4.00
Frank Robinson		
Harmon Killebrew		
Boog Powell		
242 NL RBI Leaders	25.00	11.00
Hank Aaron		
Bob Clemente		
Richie Allen		
243 AL Home Run Leaders	9.00	4.00
Frank Robinson		
Harmon Killebrew		
Boog Powell		
244 NL Home Run Leaders	20.00	9.00
Hank Aaron		
Richie Allen		
Willie Mays		
245 Curt Flood	4.00	1.80
246 Jim Perry	4.00	1.80
247 Jerry Lumpe	2.00	.90
248 Gene Mauch MG	4.00	1.80
249 Nick Willhite	2.00	.90
250 Hank Aaron UER	80.00	36.00
(Second 1961 in stats		
should be 1962)		
251 Woody Held	2.00	.90
252 Bob Bolin	2.00	.90
253 Indians Rookies	2.00	.90
Bill Davis		
Gus Gil		
254 Milt Pappas	4.00	1.80
(No facsimile auto-		
graph on card front)		
255 Frank Howard	4.00	1.80
256 Bob Hendley	2.00	.90
257 Charlie Smith	2.00	.90
258 Lee Maye	2.00	.90
259 Don Dennis	2.00	.90
260 Jim Lefebvre	4.00	1.80
261 John Wyatt	2.00	.90
262 Athletics Team	4.00	1.80
263 Hank Aguirre	2.00	.90
264 Ron Swoboda	4.00	1.80
265 Lou Burdette	4.00	1.80
266 Pitt Power	4.00	1.80
Willie Stargell		
Donn Clendenon		
267 Don Schwall	2.00	.90
268 Johnny Briggs	2.00	.90
269 Don Nottebart	2.00	.90
270 Zoilo Versalles	2.00	.90
271 Eddie Watt	2.00	.90
272 Cubs Rookies	4.00	1.80
Bill Connors		
Dave Dowling		
273 Dick Lines	2.00	.90
274 Bob Aspromonte	2.00	.90
275 Fred Whitfield	2.00	.90
276 Bruce Brubaker	2.00	.90
277 Steve Whitaker	4.00	1.80
278 Jim Kaat CL	7.00	1.40
279 Frank Linzy	2.00	.90
280 Tony Conigliaro	8.00	3.60
281 Bob Rodgers	2.00	.90
282 John Odom	2.00	.90
283 Gene Alley	4.00	1.80
284 Johnny Podres	4.00	1.80
285 Lou Brock	20.00	9.00
286 Wayne Causey	2.50	1.10
287 Mets Rookies	2.50	1.10
Greg Goossen		
Bart Shirley		
288 Denny Lemaster	2.50	1.10
289 Tom Tresh	4.00	2.20
290 Bill White	5.00	2.20
291 Jim Hannan	2.50	1.10
292 Don Pavletich	2.50	1.10
293 Ed Kirkpatrick	2.50	1.10
294 Walter Alston MG	5.00	2.20
295 Sam McDowell	5.00	2.20
296 Glenn Beckert	5.00	2.20
297 Dave Morehead	5.00	2.20
298 Ron Davis	2.50	1.10
299 Norm Siebern	2.50	1.10
300 Jim Kaat	5.00	2.20
301 Jesse Gonder	2.50	1.10
302 Orioles Team	6.00	2.70
303 Gil Blanco	2.50	1.10
304 Phil Gagliano	2.50	1.10
305 Earl Wilson	5.00	2.20
306 Bud Harrelson	5.00	2.20
307 Jim Beauchamp	2.50	1.10
308 Al Downing	5.00	2.20
309 Hurlers Beware	5.00	2.20
Johnny Callison		
Richie Allen		
310 Gary Peters	2.50	1.10
311 Ed Brinkman	2.50	1.10
312 Don Mincher	2.50	1.10
313 Bob Lee	2.50	1.10
314 Red Sox Rookies	8.00	3.60
Mike Andrews		
Reggie Smith		
315 Billy Williams	10.00	4.50
316 Jack Kralick	2.50	1.10
317 Cesar Tovar	2.50	1.10
318 Dave Giusti	2.50	1.10
319 Paul Blair	5.00	2.20
320 Gaylord Perry	15.00	6.75
321 Mayo Smith MG	2.50	1.10
322 Jose Pagan	2.50	1.10
323 Mike Hershberger	2.50	1.10
324 Hal Woodeshick	2.50	1.10
325 Chico Cardenas	5.00	2.20
326 Bob Uecker	10.00	4.50
327 California Angels	6.00	2.70
Team Card		
328 Clete Boyer UER	5.00	2.20
(Stats only go up		
through 1965)		
329 Charlie Lau	5.00	2.20
330 Claude Osteen	5.00	2.20
331 Joe Foy	5.00	2.20
332 Jesus Alou	2.50	1.10
333 Ferguson Jenkins	20.00	9.00
334 Twin Terrors	8.00	3.60
Bob Allison		
Harmon Killebrew		
335 Bob Veale	5.00	2.20
336 Joe Azcue	2.50	1.10
337 Joe Morgan	15.00	6.75
338 Bob Locker	2.50	1.10
339 Chico Ruiz	2.50	1.10
340 Joe Pepitone	5.00	2.20
341 Giants Rookies	2.50	1.10
Dick Dietz		
Bill Sorrell		
342 Hank Fischer	2.50	1.10
343 Tom Satriano	2.50	1.10
344 Ossie Chavarria	2.50	1.10
345 Stu Miller	5.00	2.20
346 Jim Hickman	2.50	1.10
347 Grady Hatton MG	2.50	1.10
348 Tug McGraw	5.00	2.20
349 Bob Chance	2.50	1.10
350 Joe Torre	5.00	2.20
351 Vern Law	5.00	2.20
352 Ray Oyler	2.50	1.10
353 Bill McCool	2.50	1.10
354 Cubs Team	6.00	2.70
355 Carl Yastrzemski	50.00	22.00
356 Larry Jaster	2.50	1.10
357 Bill Skowron	5.00	2.20
358 Ruben Amaro	2.50	1.10
359 Dick Ellsworth	2.50	1.10
360 Leon Wagner	2.50	1.10
361 Roberto Clemente CL	15.00	3.00
362 Darold Knowles	2.50	1.10
363 Dave Johnson	5.00	2.20
364 Claude Raymond	2.50	1.10
365 John Roseboro	5.00	2.20
366 Andy Kosco	2.50	1.10
367 Angels Rookies	2.50	1.10
Bill Kelso		
Don Wallace		
368 Jack Hiatt	2.50	1.10
369 Jim Hunter	15.00	6.75
370 Tommy Davis	5.00	2.20
371 Jim Lonborg	8.00	3.60
372 Mike de la Hoz	4.00	1.80
373 White Sox Rookies DP	4.00	1.80
Duane Josephson		
Fred Klages		
374A Mel Queen ERR DP	20.00	9.00
(Incomplete stat		
line on back)		
374B Mel Queen COR DP	4.00	1.80
(Complete stat		
line on back)		
375 Jake Gibbs	8.00	3.60
376 Don Lock DP	4.00	1.80
377 Luis Tiant	8.00	3.60
378 Detroit Tigers	8.00	3.60
Team Card UER		
(Willie Horton with		
262 RBI's in 1966)		

Card	Price	Price
❑ 379 Jerry May DP	4.00	1.80
❑ 380 Dean Chance DP	4.00	1.80
❑ 381 Dick Schofield DP	4.00	1.80
❑ 382 Dave McNally	8.00	3.60
❑ 383 Ken Henderson DP	4.00	1.80
❑ 384 Cardinals Rookies	4.00	1.80
Jim Cosman		
Dick Hughes		
❑ 385 Jim Fregosi	8.00	3.60
(Batting wrong)		
❑ 386 Dick Selma DP	4.00	1.80
❑ 387 Cap Peterson DP	4.00	1.80
❑ 388 Arnold Earley DP	4.00	1.80
❑ 389 Alvin Dark MG DP	8.00	3.60
❑ 390 Jim Wynn DP	8.00	3.60
❑ 391 Wilbur Wood DP	8.00	3.60
❑ 392 Tommy Harper DP	8.00	3.60
❑ 393 Jim Bouton DP	8.00	3.60
❑ 394 Jake Wood DP	4.00	1.80
❑ 395 Chris Short	8.00	3.60
❑ 396 Atlanta Aces	4.00	1.80
Denis Menke		
Tony Cloninger		
❑ 397 Willie Smith DP	4.00	1.80
❑ 398 Jeff Torborg	8.00	3.60
❑ 399 Al Worthington DP	4.00	1.80
❑ 400 Bob Clemente DP	100.00	45.00
❑ 401 Jim Coates	4.00	1.80
❑ 402A Phillies Rookies DP	20.00	9.00
Grant Jackson		
Billy Wilson		
Incomplete stat line		
❑ 402B Phillies Rookies DP	8.00	3.60
Grant Jackson		
Billy Wilson		
❑ 403 Dick Nen	4.00	1.80
❑ 404 Nelson Briles	8.00	3.60
❑ 405 Russ Snyder	4.00	1.80
❑ 406 Lee Elia DP	4.00	1.80
❑ 407 Reds Team	8.00	3.60
❑ 408 Jim Northrup DP	8.00	3.60
❑ 409 Ray Sadecki	4.00	1.80
❑ 410 Lou Johnson DP	4.00	1.80
❑ 411 Dick Howser DP	4.00	1.80
❑ 412 Astros Rookies	8.00	3.60
Norm Miller		
Doug Rader		
❑ 413 Jerry Grote	4.00	1.80
❑ 414 Casey Cox	4.00	1.80
❑ 415 Sonny Jackson	4.00	1.80
❑ 416 Roger Repoz	4.00	1.80
❑ 417A Bob Bruce ERR DP	30.00	13.50
(RBAVES on back)		
❑ 417B Bob Bruce COR DP	4.00	1.80
❑ 418 Sam Mele MG	4.00	1.80
❑ 419 Don Kessinger DP	8.00	3.60
❑ 420 Denny McLain	8.00	3.60
❑ 421 Dal Maxvill DP	4.00	1.80
❑ 422 Hoyt Wilhelm	12.00	5.50
❑ 423 Fence Busters DP	25.00	11.00
Willie Mays		
Willie McCovey		
❑ 424 Pedro Gonzalez	4.00	1.80
❑ 425 Pete Mikkelsen	4.00	1.80
❑ 426 Lou Clinton	4.00	1.80
❑ 427A Ruben Gomez ERR DP	20.00	9.00
(Incomplete stat line on back)		
❑ 427B Ruben Gomez COR DP	4.00	1.80
(Complete stat line on back)		
❑ 428 Dodgers Rookies DP	8.00	3.60
Tom Hutton		
Gene Michael		
❑ 429 Garry Roggenburk DP	4.00	1.80
❑ 430 Pete Rose	75.00	34.00
❑ 431 Ted Uhlaender	4.00	1.80
❑ 432 Jimmie Hall DP	4.00	1.80
❑ 433 Al Luplow DP	4.00	1.80
❑ 434 Eddie Fisher DP	4.00	1.80
❑ 435 Mack Jones DP	4.00	1.80
❑ 436 Pete Ward	4.00	1.80
❑ 437 Senators Team	8.00	3.60
❑ 438 Chuck Dobson	4.00	1.80
❑ 439 Byron Browne	4.00	1.80
❑ 440 Steve Hargan	4.00	1.80
❑ 441 Jim Davenport	4.00	1.80
❑ 442 Yankees Rookies DP	8.00	3.60
Bill Robinson		
Joe Verbanic		
❑ 443 Tito Francona DP	4.00	1.80
❑ 444 George Smith	4.00	1.80
❑ 445 Don Sutton	25.00	11.00
❑ 446 Russ Nixon DP	4.00	1.80
❑ 447A Bo Belinsky ERR DP	5.00	2.20
(Incomplete stat line on back)		
❑ 447B Bo Belinsky COR DP	8.00	3.60
(Complete stat line on back)		
❑ 448 Harry Walker DP MG	4.00	1.80
❑ 449 Orlando Pena	4.00	1.80
❑ 450 Richie Allen	8.00	3.60
❑ 451 Fred Newman DP	4.00	1.80
❑ 452 Ed Kranepool	8.00	3.60
❑ 453 Aurelio Monteagudo DP	4.00	1.80
❑ 454A Juan Marichal CL	8.00	1.60
Missing left ear		
❑ 454B Juan Marichal CL	8.00	1.60
left ear showing		
❑ 455 Tommie Agee	8.00	3.60
❑ 456 Phil Niekro	15.00	6.75
❑ 457 Andy Etchebarren DP	8.00	3.60
❑ 458 Lee Thomas	6.00	2.70
❑ 459 Senators Rookies	6.00	2.70
Dick Bosman		
Pete Craig		
❑ 460 Harmon Killebrew	60.00	27.00
❑ 461 Bob Miller	6.00	2.70
❑ 462 Bob Barton	6.00	2.70
❑ 463 Hill Aces	12.00	5.50
Sam McDowell		
Sonny Siebert		
❑ 464 Dan Coombs	6.00	2.70
❑ 465 Willie Horton	12.00	5.50
❑ 466 Bobby Wine	6.00	2.70
❑ 467 Jim O'Toole	6.00	2.70
❑ 468 Ralph Houk MG	6.00	2.70
❑ 469 Len Gabrielson	6.00	2.70
❑ 470 Bob Shaw	6.00	2.70
❑ 471 Rene Lachemann	6.00	2.70
❑ 472 Rookies Pirates	6.00	2.70
John Gelnar		
George Spriggs		
❑ 473 Jose Santiago	6.00	2.70
❑ 474 Bob Tolan	6.00	2.70
❑ 475 Jim Palmer	75.00	34.00
❑ 476 Tony Perez SP	60.00	27.00
❑ 477 Braves Team	15.00	6.75
❑ 478 Bob Humphreys	6.00	2.70
❑ 479 Gary Bell	6.00	2.70
❑ 480 Willie McCovey	35.00	16.00
❑ 481 Leo Durocher MG	20.00	9.00
❑ 482 Bill Monbouquette	6.00	2.70
❑ 483 Jim Landis	6.00	2.70
❑ 484 Jerry Adair	6.00	2.70
❑ 485 Tim McCarver	20.00	9.00
❑ 486 Twins Rookies	6.00	2.70
Rich Reese		
Bill Whitby		
❑ 487 Tommie Reynolds	6.00	2.70
❑ 488 Gerry Arrigo	6.00	2.70
❑ 489 Doug Clemens	6.00	2.70
❑ 490 Tony Cloninger	6.00	2.70
❑ 491 Sam Bowens	6.00	2.70
❑ 492 Pittsburgh Pirates	15.00	6.75
Team Card		
❑ 493 Phil Ortega	6.00	2.70
❑ 494 Bill Rigney MG	6.00	2.70
❑ 495 Fritz Peterson	6.00	2.70
❑ 496 Orlando McFarlane	6.00	2.70
❑ 497 Ron Campbell	6.00	2.70
❑ 498 Larry Dierker	12.00	5.50
❑ 499 Indians Rookies	6.00	2.70
George Culver		
Jose Vidal		
❑ 500 Juan Marichal	25.00	11.00
❑ 501 Jerry Zimmerman	6.00	2.70
❑ 502 Derrell Griffith	6.00	2.70
❑ 503 Los Angeles Dodgers	20.00	9.00
Team Card		
❑ 504 Orlando Martinez	6.00	2.70
❑ 505 Tommy Helms	12.00	5.50
❑ 506 Smoky Burgess	6.00	2.70
❑ 507 Orioles Rookies	6.00	2.70
Ed Barnowski		
Larry Haney		
❑ 508 Dick Hall	6.00	2.70
❑ 509 Jim King	6.00	2.70
❑ 510 Bill Mazeroski	20.00	9.00
❑ 511 Don Wert	6.00	2.70
❑ 512 Red Schoendienst MG	20.00	9.00
❑ 513 Marcelino Lopez	6.00	2.70
❑ 514 John Werhas	6.00	2.70
❑ 515 Bert Campaneris	12.00	5.50
❑ 516 Giants Team	15.00	6.75
❑ 517 Fred Talbot	6.00	2.70
❑ 518 Denis Menke	6.00	2.70
❑ 519 Ted Davidson	6.00	2.70
❑ 520 Max Alvis	6.00	2.70
❑ 521 Bird Bombers	12.00	5.50
Boog Powell		
Curt Blefary		
❑ 522 John Stephenson	6.00	2.70
❑ 523 Jim Merritt	6.00	2.70
❑ 524 Felix Mantilla	6.00	2.70
❑ 525 Ron Hunt	6.00	2.70
❑ 526 Tigers Rookies	6.00	2.70
Pat Dobson		
George Korince		
(See 67T-72)		
❑ 527 Dennis Ribant	6.00	2.70
❑ 528 Rico Petrocelli	12.00	5.50
❑ 529 Gary Wagner	6.00	2.70
❑ 530 Felipe Alou	12.00	5.50
❑ 531 Brooks Robinson CL	14.00	2.80
❑ 532 Jim Hicks	6.00	2.70
❑ 533 Jack Fisher	6.00	2.70
❑ 534 Hank Bauer MG DP	9.00	4.00
❑ 535 Donn Clendenon	18.00	8.00
❑ 536 Cubs Rookies	40.00	18.00
Joe Niekro		
Paul Popovich		
❑ 537 Chuck Estrada DP	9.00	4.00
❑ 538 J.C. Martin	16.00	7.25
❑ 539 Dick Egan DP	9.00	4.00
❑ 540 Norm Cash	50.00	22.00
❑ 541 Joe Gibbon	16.00	7.25
❑ 542 Athletics Rookies DP	15.00	6.75
Rick Monday		
Tony Pierce		
❑ 543 Dan Schneider	16.00	7.25
❑ 544 Cleveland Indians	30.00	13.50
Team Card		
❑ 545 Jim Grant	16.00	7.25
❑ 546 Woody Woodward	16.00	7.25
❑ 547 Red Sox Rookies DP	9.00	4.00
Russ Gibson		
Bill Rohr		
❑ 548 Tony Gonzalez DP	9.00	4.00
❑ 549 Jack Sanford	16.00	7.25
❑ 550 Vada Pinson DP	10.00	4.50
❑ 551 Doug Camilli DP	9.00	4.00
❑ 552 Ted Savage	16.00	7.25
❑ 553 Yankees Rookies	40.00	18.00
Mike Hegan		
Thad Tillotson		
❑ 554 Andre Rodgers DP	9.00	4.00
❑ 555 Don Cardwell	25.00	11.00
❑ 556 Al Weis DP	9.00	4.00
❑ 557 Al Ferrara	16.00	7.25
❑ 558 Orioles Rookies	50.00	22.00
Mark Belanger		
Bill Dillman		
❑ 559 Dick Tracewski DP	9.00	4.00
❑ 560 Jim Bunning	60.00	27.00
❑ 561 Sandy Alomar	25.00	11.00
❑ 562 Steve Blass DP	9.00	4.00
❑ 563 Joe Adcock	25.00	11.00
❑ 564 Astros Rookies DP	9.00	4.00
Alonzo Harris		
Aaron Pointer		
❑ 565 Lew Krausse	16.00	7.25
❑ 566 Gary Geiger DP	9.00	4.00
❑ 567 Steve Hamilton	25.00	11.00
❑ 568 John Sullivan	25.00	11.00
❑ 569 AL Rookies	200.00	90.00
Rod Carew		

Hank Allen
- □ 570 Maury Wills 90.00 40.00
- □ 571 Larry Sherry 16.00 7.25
- □ 572 Don Demeter 16.00 7.25
- □ 573 Chicago White Sox .. 30.00 13.50
  Team Card UER
  (Indians team
  stats on back)
- □ 574 Jerry Buchek 16.00 7.25
- □ 575 Dave Boswell 16.00 7.25
- □ 576 NL Rookies 25.00 11.00
  Ramon Hernandez
  Norm Gigon
- □ 577 Bill Short 16.00 7.25
- □ 578 John Boccabella 16.00 7.25
- □ 579 Bill Henry 16.00 7.25
- □ 580 Rocky Colavito 100.00 45.00
- □ 581 Mets Rookies 500.00 220.00
  Bill Denehy
  Tom Seaver
- □ 582 Jim Owens DP 9.00 4.00
- □ 583 Ray Barker 25.00 11.00
- □ 584 Jimmy Piersall 40.00 18.00
- □ 585 Wally Bunker 16.00 7.25
- □ 586 Manny Jimenez 16.00 7.25
- □ 587 NL Rookies 40.00 18.00
  Don Shaw
  Gary Sutherland
- □ 588 Johnny Klippstein DP .. 9.00 4.00
- □ 589 Dave Ricketts DP 9.00 4.00
- □ 590 Pete Richert 16.00 7.25
- □ 591 Ty Cline 16.00 7.25
- □ 592 NL Rookies 25.00 11.00
  Jim Shellenback
  Ron Willis
- □ 593 Wes Westrum MG 25.00 11.00
- □ 594 Dan Osinski 25.00 11.00
- □ 595 Cookie Rojas 25.00 11.00
- □ 596 Galen Cisco DP 10.00 4.50
- □ 597 Ted Abernathy 16.00 7.25
- □ 598 White Sox Rookies 16.00 7.25
  Walt Williams
  Ed Stroud
- □ 599 Bob Duliba DP 9.00 4.00
- □ 600 Brooks Robinson 250.00 110.00
- □ 601 Bill Bryan DP 9.00 4.00
- □ 602 Juan Pizarro 25.00 11.00
- □ 603 Athletics Rookies 25.00 11.00
  Tim Talton
  Ramon Webster
- □ 604 Red Sox Team 125.00 55.00
- □ 605 Mike Shannon 50.00 22.00
- □ 606 Ron Taylor 16.00 7.25
- □ 607 Mickey Stanley 40.00 18.00
- □ 608 Cubs Rookies DP 9.00 4.00
  Rich Nye
  John Upham
- □ 609 Tommy John 70.00 23.00

1968 Topps

	NRMT	VG-E
COMPLETE SET (598)	3000.00	1350.00
COMMON CARD (1-457)	1.75	.80
MINOR STAR 1-457	4.00	1.80
SEMISTARS 1-457	6.00	2.70
UNLISTED STARS 1-457	8.00	3.60
COMMON CARD (458-598)	3.50	1.55

- MINOR STARS 458-598 .... 6.00 2.70
- SEMISTARS 458-598 .... 10.00 4.50
- UNLISTED STARS 458-598 .... 12.00 5.50
- *UNLISTED DODGER/YANKEE: 1.25X VALUE
- CARDS PRICED IN NM CONDITION

- □ 1 NL Batting Leaders 30.00 12.00
  Roberto Clemente
  Tony Gonzalez
  Matty Alou
- □ 2 AL Batting Leaders 14.00 6.25
  Carl Yastrzemski
  Frank Robinson
  Al Kaline
- □ 3 NL RBI Leaders 20.00 9.00
  Orlando Cepeda
  Roberto Clemente
  Hank Aaron
- □ 4 AL RBI Leaders 14.00 6.25
  Carl Yastrzemski
  Harmon Killebrew
  Frank Robinson
- □ 5 NL Home Run Leaders .. 8.00 3.60
  Hank Aaron
  Jim Wynn
  Ron Santo
  Willie McCovey
- □ 6 AL Home Run Leaders .. 8.00 3.60
  Carl Yastrzemski
  Harmon Killebrew
  Frank Howard
- □ 7 NL ERA Leaders 4.00 1.80
  Phil Niekro
  Jim Bunning
  Chris Short
- □ 8 AL ERA Leaders 4.00 1.80
  Joel Horlen
  Gary Peters
  Sonny Siebert
- □ 9 NL Pitching Leaders .. 5.00 2.20
  Mike McCormick
  Ferguson Jenkins
  Jim Bunning
  Claude Osteen
- □ 10A AL Pitching Leaders .. 4.00 1.80
  Jim Lonborg ERR
  (Misspelled Lonberg
  on card back)
  Earl Wilson
  Dean Chance
- □ 10B AL Pitching Leaders .. 4.00 1.80
  Jim Lonborg COR
  Earl Wilson
  Dean Chance
- □ 11 NL Strikeout Leaders .. 6.00 2.70
  Jim Bunning
  Ferguson Jenkins
  Gaylord Perry
- □ 12 AL Strikeout Leaders .. 3.50 1.55
  Jim Lonborg UER
  (Misspelled Longberg
  on card back)
  Sam McDowell
  Dean Chance
- □ 13 Chuck Hartenstein .... 1.75 .80
- □ 14 Jerry McNertney .... 1.75 .80
- □ 15 Ron Hunt .... 1.75 .80
- □ 16 Indians Rookies 6.00 2.70
  Lou Piniella
  Richie Scheinblum
- □ 17 Dick Hall .... 1.75 .80
- □ 18 Mike Hershberger .... 1.75 .80
- □ 19 Juan Pizarro .... 1.75 .80
- □ 20 Brooks Robinson 25.00 11.00
- □ 21 Ron Davis .... 1.75 .80
- □ 22 Pat Dobson 4.00 1.80
- □ 23 Chico Cardenas 4.00 1.80
- □ 24 Bobby Locke .... 1.75 .80
- □ 25 Julian Javier 4.00 1.80
- □ 26 Darrell Brandon .... 1.75 .80
- □ 27 Gil Hodges MG 8.00 3.60
- □ 28 Ted Uhlaender .... 1.75 .80
- □ 29 Joe Verbanic .... 1.75 .80
- □ 30 Joe Torre 6.00 2.70
- □ 31 Ed Stroud .... 1.75 .80
- □ 32 Joe Gibbon .... 1.75 .80

- □ 33 Pete Ward .... 1.75 .80
- □ 34 Al Ferrara .... 1.75 .80
- □ 35 Steve Hargan .... 1.75 .80
- □ 36 Pirates Rookies 4.00 1.80
  Bob Moose
  Bob Robertson
- □ 37 Billy Williams 8.00 3.60
- □ 38 Tony Pierce .... 1.75 .80
- □ 39 Cookie Rojas 4.00 1.80
- □ 40 Denny McLain 8.00 3.60
- □ 41 Julio Gotay .... 1.75 .80
- □ 42 Larry Haney .... 1.75 .80
- □ 43 Gary Bell .... 1.75 .80
- □ 44 Frank Kostro .... 1.75 .80
- □ 45 Tom Seaver 50.00 22.00
- □ 46 Dave Ricketts .... 1.75 .80
- □ 47 Ralph Houk MG 4.00 1.80
- □ 48 Ted Davidson .... 1.75 .80
- □ 49A Eddie Brinkman .... 1.75 .80
  (White team name)
- □ 49B Eddie Brinkman 50.00 22.00
  (Yellow team name)
- □ 50 Willie Mays 60.00 27.00
- □ 51 Bob Locker .... 1.75 .80
- □ 52 Hawk Taylor .... 1.75 .80
- □ 53 Gene Alley 4.00 1.80
- □ 54 Stan Williams 4.00 1.80
- □ 55 Felipe Alou 4.00 1.80
- □ 56 Orioles Rookies .... 1.75 .80
  Dave Leonhard
  Dave May
- □ 57 Dan Schneider .... 1.75 .80
- □ 58 Eddie Mathews 15.00 6.75
- □ 59 Don Lock .... 1.75 .80
- □ 60 Ken Holtzman 4.00 1.80
- □ 61 Reggie Smith 4.00 1.80
- □ 62 Chuck Dobson .... 1.75 .80
- □ 63 Dick Kenworthy .... 1.75 .80
- □ 64 Jim Merritt .... 1.75 .80
- □ 65 John Roseboro 4.00 1.80
- □ 66A Casey Cox .... 1.75 .80
  (White team name)
- □ 66B Casey Cox 100.00 45.00
  (Yellow team name)
- □ 67 Jim Kaat CL 6.00 1.20
- □ 68 Ron Willis .... 1.75 .80
- □ 69 Tom Tresh 4.00 1.80
- □ 70 Bob Veale 4.00 1.80
- □ 71 Vern Fuller .... 1.75 .80
- □ 72 Tommy John 6.00 2.70
- □ 73 Jim Ray Hart 4.00 1.80
- □ 74 Milt Pappas 4.00 1.80
- □ 75 Don Mincher 4.00 1.80
- □ 76 Braves Rookies 4.00 1.80
  Jim Britton
  Ron Reed
- □ 77 Don Wilson 4.00 1.80
- □ 78 Jim Northrup 6.00 2.70
- □ 79 Ted Kubiak .... 1.75 .80
- □ 80 Rod Carew 50.00 22.00
- □ 81 Larry Jackson .... 1.75 .80
- □ 82 Sam Bowens .... 1.75 .80
- □ 83 John Stephenson .... 1.75 .80
- □ 84 Bob Tolan 4.00 1.80
- □ 85 Gaylord Perry 8.00 3.60
- □ 86 Willie Stargell 8.00 3.60
- □ 87 Dick Williams MG 4.00 1.80
- □ 88 Phil Regan 4.00 1.80
- □ 89 Jake Gibbs 4.00 1.80
- □ 90 Vada Pinson 4.00 1.80
- □ 91 Jim Ollom .... 1.75 .80
- □ 92 Ed Kranepool 4.00 1.80
- □ 93 Tony Cloninger .... 1.75 .80
- □ 94 Lee Maye .... 1.75 .80
- □ 95 Bob Aspromonte .... 1.75 .80
- □ 96 Senator Rookies .... 1.75 .80
  Frank Coggins
  Dick Nold
- □ 97 Tom Phoebus .... 1.75 .80
- □ 98 Gary Sutherland .... 1.75 .80
- □ 99 Rocky Colavito 8.00 3.60
- □ 100 Bob Gibson 25.00 11.00
- □ 101 Glenn Beckert 4.00 1.80
- □ 102 Jose Cardenal 4.00 1.80
- □ 103 Don Sutton 6.00 2.70
- □ 104 Dick Dietz .... 1.75 .80

❏ 105	Al Downing	4.00	1.80
❏ 106	Dalton Jones	1.75	.80
❏ 107A	Juan Marichal CL	6.00	1.20
	Tan wide mesh		
❏ 107B	Juan Marichal CL	6.00	1.20
	Brown fine mesh		
❏ 108	Don Pavletich	1.75	.80
❏ 109	Bert Campaneris	4.00	1.80
❏ 110	Hank Aaron	60.00	27.00
❏ 111	Rich Reese	1.75	.80
❏ 112	Woody Fryman	1.75	.80
❏ 113	Tigers Rookies	4.00	1.80
	Tom Matchick		
	Daryl Patterson		
❏ 114	Ron Swoboda	4.00	1.80
❏ 115	Sam McDowell	4.00	1.80
❏ 116	Ken McMullen	1.75	.80
❏ 117	Larry Jaster	1.75	.80
❏ 118	Mark Belanger	4.00	1.80
❏ 119	Ted Savage	1.75	.80
❏ 120	Mel Stottlemyre	4.00	1.80
❏ 121	Jimmie Hall	1.75	.80
❏ 122	Gene Mauch MG	4.00	1.80
❏ 123	Jose Santiago	1.75	.80
❏ 124	Nate Oliver	1.75	.80
❏ 125	Joel Horlen	1.75	.80
❏ 126	Bobby Etheridge	1.75	.80
❏ 127	Paul Lindblad	1.75	.80
❏ 128	Astros Rookies	1.75	.80
	Tom Dukes		
	Alonzo Harris		
❏ 129	Mickey Stanley	6.00	2.70
❏ 130	Tony Perez	8.00	3.60
❏ 131	Frank Bertaina	1.75	.80
❏ 132	Bud Harrelson	4.00	1.80
❏ 133	Fred Whitfield	1.75	.80
❏ 134	Pat Jarvis	1.75	.80
❏ 135	Paul Blair	1.75	1.80
❏ 136	Randy Hundley	4.00	1.80
❏ 137	Twins Team	1.75	1.80
❏ 138	Ruben Amaro	1.75	.80
❏ 139	Chris Short	1.75	.80
❏ 140	Tony Conigliaro	8.00	3.60
❏ 141	Dal Maxvill	1.75	.80
❏ 142	White Sox Rookies	1.75	.80
	Buddy Bradford		
	Bill Voss		
❏ 143	Pete Cimino	1.75	.80
❏ 144	Joe Morgan	12.00	5.50
❏ 145	Don Drysdale	12.00	5.50
❏ 146	Sal Bando	4.00	1.80
❏ 147	Frank Linzy	1.75	.80
❏ 148	Dave Bristol MG	1.75	.80
❏ 149	Bob Saverine	1.75	.80
❏ 150	Roberto Clemente	75.00	34.00
❏ 151	Lou Brock WS	10.00	4.50
❏ 152	Carl Yastrzemski WS	10.00	4.50
❏ 153	Nellie Briles WS	5.00	2.20
❏ 154	Bob Gibson WS	10.00	4.50
❏ 155	Jim Lonborg WS	5.00	2.20
❏ 156	Rico Petrocelli WS	5.00	2.20
❏ 157	World Series Game 7	5.00	2.20
	St. Louis wins 3		
❏ 158	World Series Summary	5.00	2.20
	Cardinals celebrate		
❏ 159	Don Kessinger	4.00	1.80
❏ 160	Earl Wilson	4.00	1.80
❏ 161	Norm Miller	1.75	.80
❏ 162	Cards Rookies	1.75	.80
	Hal Gilson		
	Mike Torrez		
❏ 163	Gene Brabender	1.75	.80
❏ 164	Ramon Webster	1.75	.80
❏ 165	Tony Oliva	6.00	2.70
❏ 166	Claude Raymond	1.75	.80
❏ 167	Elston Howard	6.00	2.70
❏ 168	Dodgers Team	4.00	1.80
❏ 169	Bob Bolin	1.75	.80
❏ 170	Jim Fregosi	4.00	1.80
❏ 171	Don Nottebart	1.75	.80
❏ 172	Walt Williams	1.75	.80
❏ 173	John Boozer	1.75	.80
❏ 174	Bob Tillman	1.75	.80
❏ 175	Maury Wills	6.00	2.70
❏ 176	Bob Allen	1.75	.80
❏ 177	Mets Rookies	800.00	350.00
	Jerry Koosman		
	Nolan Ryan		
❏ 178	Don Wert	4.00	1.80
❏ 179	Bill Stoneman	1.75	.80
❏ 180	Curt Flood	4.00	1.80
❏ 181	Jerry Zimmerman	1.75	.80
❏ 182	Dave Giusti	1.75	.80
❏ 183	Bob Kennedy MG	4.00	1.80
❏ 184	Lou Johnson	4.00	1.80
❏ 185	Tom Haller	1.75	.80
❏ 186	Eddie Watt	1.75	.80
❏ 187	Sonny Jackson	1.75	.80
❏ 188	Cap Peterson	1.75	.80
❏ 189	Bill Landis	1.75	.80
❏ 190	Bill White	4.00	1.80
❏ 191	Dan Frisella	1.75	.80
❏ 192A	Carl Yastrzemski CL	8.00	1.60
	Special Baseball Playing Card		
❏ 192B	Carl Yastrzemski CL	8.00	1.60
	Special Baseball Playing Card Game		
❏ 193	Jack Hamilton	1.75	.80
❏ 194	Don Buford	1.75	.80
❏ 195	Joe Pepitone	4.00	1.80
❏ 196	Gary Nolan	4.00	1.80
❏ 197	Larry Brown	1.75	.80
❏ 198	Roy Face	4.00	1.80
❏ 199	A's Rookies	1.75	.80
	Roberto Rodriquez		
❏ 200	Orlando Cepeda	6.00	2.70
❏ 201	Mike Marshall	4.00	1.80
❏ 202	Adolfo Phillips	1.75	.80
❏ 203	Dick Kelley	1.75	.80
❏ 204	Andy Etchebarren	1.75	.80
❏ 205	Juan Marichal	8.00	3.60
❏ 206	Cal Ermer MG	1.75	.80
❏ 207	Carroll Sembera	1.75	.80
❏ 208	Willie Davis	4.00	1.80
❏ 209	Tim Cullen	1.75	.80
❏ 210	Gary Peters	1.75	.80
❏ 211	J.C. Martin	1.75	.80
❏ 212	Dave Morehead	1.75	.80
❏ 213	Chico Ruiz	1.75	.80
❏ 214	Yankees Rookies	4.00	1.80
	Stan Bahnsen		
	Frank Fernandez		
❏ 215	Jim Bunning	8.00	3.60
❏ 216	Bubba Morton	1.75	.80
❏ 217	Dick Farrell	1.75	.80
❏ 218	Ken Suarez	1.75	.80
❏ 219	Rob Gardner	1.75	.80
❏ 220	Harmon Killebrew	15.00	6.75
❏ 221	Braves Team	4.00	1.80
❏ 222	Jim Hardin	1.75	.80
❏ 223	Ollie Brown	1.75	.80
❏ 224	Jack Aker	1.75	.80
❏ 225	Richie Allen	6.00	2.70
❏ 226	Jimmie Price	1.75	.80
❏ 227	Joe Hoerner	1.75	.80
❏ 228	Dodgers Rookies	4.00	1.80
	Jack Billingham		
	Jim Fairey		
❏ 229	Fred Klages	1.75	.80
❏ 230	Pete Rose	35.00	16.00
❏ 231	Dave Baldwin	1.75	.80
❏ 232	Denis Menke	1.75	.80
❏ 233	George Scott	4.00	1.80
❏ 234	Bill Monbouquette	1.75	.80
❏ 235	Ron Santo	6.00	2.70
❏ 236	Tug McGraw	6.00	2.70
❏ 237	Alvin Dark MG	4.00	1.80
❏ 238	Tom Satriano	1.75	.80
❏ 239	Bill Henry	1.75	.80
❏ 240	Al Kaline	25.00	11.00
❏ 241	Felix Millan	1.75	.80
❏ 242	Moe Drabowsky	4.00	1.80
❏ 243	Rich Rollins	1.75	.80
❏ 244	John Donaldson	1.75	.80
❏ 245	Tony Gonzalez	1.75	.80
❏ 246	Fritz Peterson	4.00	1.80
❏ 247	Reds Rookies	125.00	55.00
	Johnny Bench		
	Ron Tompkins		
❏ 248	Fred Valentine	1.75	.80
❏ 249	Bill Singer	1.75	.80
❏ 250	Carl Yastrzemski	25.00	11.00
❏ 251	Manny Sanguillen	6.00	2.70
❏ 252	Angels Team	4.00	1.80
❏ 253	Dick Hughes	1.75	.80
❏ 254	Cleon Jones	4.00	1.80
❏ 255	Dean Chance	4.00	1.80
❏ 256	Norm Cash	6.00	2.70
❏ 257	Phil Niekro	8.00	3.60
❏ 258	Cubs Rookies	1.75	.80
	Jose Arcia		
	Bill Schlesinger		
❏ 259	Ken Boyer	4.00	1.80
❏ 260	Jim Wynn	4.00	1.80
❏ 261	Dave Duncan	4.00	1.80
❏ 262	Rick Wise	4.00	1.80
❏ 263	Horace Clarke	4.00	1.80
❏ 264	Ted Abernathy	1.75	.80
❏ 265	Tommy Davis	4.00	1.80
❏ 266	Paul Popovich	1.75	.80
❏ 267	Herman Franks MG	1.75	.80
❏ 268	Bob Humphreys	1.75	.80
❏ 269	Bob Tiefenauer	1.75	.80
❏ 270	Matty Alou	4.00	1.80
❏ 271	Bobby Knoop	1.75	.80
❏ 272	Ray Culp	1.75	.80
❏ 273	Dave Johnson	4.00	1.80
❏ 274	Mike Cuellar	4.00	1.80
❏ 275	Tim McCarver	6.00	2.70
❏ 276	Jim Roland	1.75	.80
❏ 277	Jerry Buchek	1.75	.80
❏ 278	Orlando Cepeda CL	6.00	1.20
❏ 279	Bill Hands	1.75	.80
❏ 280	Mickey Mantle	250.00	110.00
❏ 281	Jim Campanis	1.75	.80
❏ 282	Rick Monday	4.00	1.80
❏ 283	Mel Queen	1.75	.80
❏ 284	Johnny Briggs	1.75	.80
❏ 285	Dick McAuliffe	4.00	1.80
❏ 286	Cecil Upshaw	1.75	.80
❏ 287	White Sox Rookies	1.75	.80
	Mickey Abarbanel		
	Cisco Carlos		
❏ 288	Dave Wickersham	1.75	.80
❏ 289	Woody Held	1.75	.80
❏ 290	Willie McCovey	12.00	5.50
❏ 291	Dick Lines	1.75	.80
❏ 292	Art Shamsky	1.75	.80
❏ 293	Bruce Howard	1.75	.80
❏ 294	Red Schoendienst MG	6.00	2.70
❏ 295	Sonny Siebert	1.75	.80
❏ 296	Byron Browne	1.75	.80
❏ 297	Russ Gibson	1.75	.80
❏ 298	Jim Brewer	1.75	.80
❏ 299	Gene Michael	4.00	1.80
❏ 300	Rusty Staub	4.00	1.80
❏ 301	Twins Rookies	1.75	.80
	George Mitterwald		
	Rick Renick		
❏ 302	Gerry Arrigo	1.75	.80
❏ 303	Dick Green	4.00	1.80
❏ 304	Sandy Valdespino	1.75	.80
❏ 305	Minnie Rojas	1.75	.80
❏ 306	Mike Ryan	1.75	.80
❏ 307	John Hiller	4.00	1.80
❏ 308	Pirates Team	4.00	1.80
❏ 309	Ken Henderson	1.75	.80
❏ 310	Luis Aparicio	8.00	3.60
❏ 311	Jack Lamabe	1.75	.80
❏ 312	Curt Blefary	1.75	.80
❏ 313	Al Weis	1.75	.80
❏ 314	Red Sox Rookies	1.75	.80
	Bill Rohr		
	George Spriggs		
❏ 315	Zoilo Versalles	1.75	.80
❏ 316	Steve Barber	1.75	.80
❏ 317	Ron Brand	1.75	.80
❏ 318	Chico Salmon	1.75	.80
❏ 319	George Culver	1.75	.80
❏ 320	Frank Howard	4.00	1.80
❏ 321	Leo Durocher MG	6.00	2.70
❏ 322	Dave Boswell	1.75	.80
❏ 323	Deron Johnson	4.00	1.80
❏ 324	Jim Nash	1.75	.80
❏ 325	Manny Mota	4.00	1.80
❏ 326	Dennis Ribant	1.75	.80
❏ 327	Tony Taylor	4.00	1.80

328	Angels Rookies	1.75	.80
	Chuck Vinson		
	Jim Weaver		
329	Duane Josephson	1.75	.80
330	Roger Maris	35.00	16.00
331	Dan Osinski	1.75	.80
332	Doug Rader	4.00	1.80
333	Ron Herbel	1.75	.80
334	Orioles Team	4.00	1.80
335	Bob Allison	4.00	1.80
336	John Purdin	1.75	.80
337	Bill Robinson	4.00	1.80
338	Bob Johnson	1.75	.80
339	Rich Nye	1.75	.80
340	Max Alvis	1.75	.80
341	Jim Lemon MG	1.75	.80
342	Ken Johnson	1.75	.80
343	Jim Gosger	1.75	.80
344	Donn Clendenon	4.00	1.80
345	Bob Hendley	1.75	.80
346	Jerry Adair	1.75	.80
347	George Brunet	1.75	.80
348	Phillies Rookies	1.75	.80
	Larry Colton		
	Dick Thoenen		
349	Ed Spiezio	1.75	.80
350	Hoyt Wilhelm	8.00	3.60
351	Bob Barton	1.75	.80
352	Jackie Hernandez	1.75	.80
353	Mack Jones	1.75	.80
354	Pete Richert	1.75	.80
355	Ernie Banks	25.00	11.00
356A	Ken Holtzman CL	6.00	1.20
	Head centered within circle		
356B	Ken Holtzman	6.00	1.20
	Head shifted right within circle		
357	Len Gabrielson	1.75	.80
358	Mike Epstein	1.75	.80
359	Joe Moeller	1.75	.80
360	Willie Horton	6.00	2.70
361	Harmon Killebrew AS	8.00	3.60
362	Orlando Cepeda AS	6.00	2.70
363	Rod Carew AS	8.00	3.60
364	Joe Morgan AS	8.00	3.60
365	Brooks Robinson AS	8.00	3.60
366	Ron Santo AS	6.00	2.70
367	Jim Fregosi AS	5.00	2.20
368	Gene Alley AS	5.00	2.20
369	Carl Yastrzemski AS	10.00	4.50
370	Hank Aaron AS	20.00	9.00
371	Tony Oliva AS	5.00	2.20
372	Lou Brock AS	8.00	3.60
373	Frank Robinson AS	8.00	3.60
374	Bob Clemente AS	30.00	13.50
375	Bill Freehan AS	5.00	2.20
376	Tim McCarver AS	6.00	2.70
377	Joel Horlen AS	5.00	2.20
378	Bob Gibson AS	8.00	3.60
379	Gary Peters AS	5.00	2.20
380	Ken Holtzman AS	5.00	2.20
381	Boog Powell	4.00	1.80
382	Ramon Hernandez	1.75	.80
383	Steve Whitaker	1.75	.80
384	Reds Rookies	6.00	2.70
	Bill Henry		
	Hal McRae		
385	Jim Hunter	10.00	4.50
386	Greg Goossen	1.75	.80
387	Joe Foy	1.75	.80
388	Ray Washburn	1.75	.80
389	Jay Johnstone	4.00	1.80
390	Bill Mazeroski	6.00	2.70
391	Bob Priddy	1.75	.80
392	Grady Hatton MG	1.75	.80
393	Jim Perry	4.00	1.80
394	Tommie Aaron	4.00	1.80
395	Camilo Pascual	4.00	1.80
396	Bobby Wine	1.75	.80
397	Vic Davalillo	1.75	.80
398	Jim Grant	1.75	.80
399	Ray Oyler	1.75	.80
400A	Mike McCormick (Yellow letters)	4.00	1.80
400B	Mike McCormick (Team name in white letters)	150.00	70.00
401	Mets Team	4.00	1.80
402	Mike Hegan	4.00	1.80
403	John Buzhardt	1.75	.80
404	Floyd Robinson	1.75	.80
405	Tommy Helms	4.00	1.80
406	Dick Ellsworth	1.75	.80
407	Gary Kolb	1.75	.80
408	Steve Carlton	30.00	13.50
409	Orioles Rookies	1.75	.80
	Frank Peters		
	Ron Stone		
410	Ferguson Jenkins	10.00	4.50
411	Ron Hansen	1.75	.80
412	Clay Carroll	4.00	1.80
413	Tom McCraw	1.75	.80
414	Mickey Lolich	8.00	3.60
415	Johnny Callison	4.00	1.80
416	Bill Rigney MG	1.75	.80
417	Willie Crawford	1.75	.80
418	Eddie Fisher	1.75	.80
419	Jack Hiatt	1.75	.80
420	Cesar Tovar	1.75	.80
421	Ron Taylor	1.75	.80
422	Rene Lachemann	1.75	.80
423	Fred Gladding	1.75	.80
424	Chicago White Sox	4.00	1.80
	Team Card		
425	Jim Maloney	4.00	1.80
426	Hank Allen	1.75	.80
427	Dick Calmus	1.75	.80
428	Vic Roznovsky	1.75	.80
429	Tommie Sisk	1.75	.80
430	Rico Petrocelli	4.00	1.80
431	Dooley Womack	1.75	.80
432	Indians Rookies	1.75	.80
	Bill Davis		
	Jose Vidal		
433	Bob Rodgers	1.75	.80
434	Ricardo Joseph	1.75	.80
435	Ron Perranoski	4.00	1.80
436	Hal Lanier	1.75	.80
437	Don Cardwell	1.75	.80
438	Lee Thomas	4.00	1.80
439	Lum Harris MG	1.75	.80
440	Claude Osteen	4.00	1.80
441	Alex Johnson	4.00	1.80
442	Dick Bosman	1.75	.80
443	Joe Azcue	1.75	.80
444	Jack Fisher	1.75	.80
445	Mike Shannon	4.00	1.80
446	Ron Kline	1.75	.80
447	Tigers Rookies	1.75	.80
	George Korince		
	Fred Lasher		
448	Gary Wagner	1.75	.80
449	Gene Oliver	1.75	.80
450	Jim Kaat	6.00	2.70
451	Al Spangler	1.75	.80
452	Jesus Alou	1.75	.80
453	Sammy Ellis	1.75	.80
454A	Frank Robinson CL	8.00	1.60
	Cap complete within circle		
454B	Frank Robinson CL	8.00	1.60
	Cap partially within circle		
455	Rico Carty	4.00	1.80
456	John O'Donoghue	1.75	.80
457	Jim Lefebvre	4.00	1.80
458	Lew Krausse	6.00	2.70
459	Dick Simpson	3.50	1.55
460	Jim Lonborg	6.00	2.70
461	Chuck Hiller	3.50	1.55
462	Barry Moore	3.50	1.55
463	Jim Schaffer	3.50	1.55
464	Don McMahon	3.50	1.55
465	Tommie Agee	6.00	2.70
466	Bill Dillman	3.50	1.55
467	Dick Howser	6.00	2.70
468	Larry Sherry	3.50	1.55
469	Ty Cline	3.50	1.55
470	Bill Freehan	6.00	2.70
471	Orlando Pena	3.50	1.55
472	Walter Alston MG	6.00	2.70
473	Al Worthington	3.50	1.55
474	Paul Schaal	3.50	1.55
475	Joe Niekro	6.00	2.70
476	Woody Woodward	3.50	1.55
477	Philadelphia Phillies	6.00	2.70
	Team Card		
478	Dave McNally	7.00	3.10
479	Phil Gagliano	3.50	1.55
480	Manager's Dream	80.00	36.00
	Tony Oliva		
	Chico Cardenas		
	Bob Clemente		
481	John Wyatt	3.50	1.55
482	Jose Pagan	3.50	1.55
483	Darold Knowles	3.50	1.55
484	Phil Roof	3.50	1.55
485	Ken Berry	3.50	1.55
486	Cal Koonce	3.50	1.55
487	Lee May	6.00	2.70
488	Dick Tracewski	6.00	2.70
489	Wally Bunker	3.50	1.55
490	Super Stars	175.00	80.00
	Harmon Killebrew		
	Willie Mays		
	Mickey Mantle		
491	Denny Lemaster	3.50	1.55
492	Jeff Torborg	6.00	2.70
493	Jim McGlothlin	3.50	1.55
494	Ray Sadecki	3.50	1.55
495	Leon Wagner	3.50	1.55
496	Steve Hamilton	6.00	2.70
497	Cardinals Team	7.00	3.10
498	Bill Bryan	3.50	1.55
499	Steve Blass	6.00	2.70
500	Frank Robinson	30.00	13.50
501	John Odom	6.00	2.70
502	Mike Andrews	3.50	1.55
503	Al Jackson	3.50	1.55
504	Russ Snyder	3.50	1.55
505	Joe Sparma	10.00	4.50
506	Clarence Jones	3.50	1.55
507	Wade Blasingame	3.50	1.55
508	Duke Sims	3.50	1.55
509	Dennis Higgins	3.50	1.55
510	Ron Fairly	6.00	2.70
511	Bill Kelso	3.50	1.55
512	Grant Jackson	3.50	1.55
513	Hank Bauer MG	6.00	2.70
514	Al McBean	3.50	1.55
515	Russ Nixon	3.50	1.55
516	Pete Mikkelsen	3.50	1.55
517	Diego Segui	6.00	2.70
518A	Clete Boyer CL ERR	12.00	2.40
	539 AL Rookies		
518B	Clete Boyer CL COR	12.00	2.40
	539 ML Rookies		
519	Jerry Stephenson	3.50	1.55
520	Lou Brock	25.00	11.00
521	Don Shaw	3.50	1.55
522	Wayne Causey	3.50	1.55
523	John Tsitouris	3.50	1.55
524	Andy Kosco	3.50	1.55
525	Jim Davenport	3.50	1.55
526	Bill Denehy	3.50	1.55
527	Tito Francona	3.50	1.55
528	Tigers Team	60.00	27.00
529	Bruce Von Hoff	3.50	1.55
530	Bird Belters	40.00	18.00
	Brooks Robinson		
	Frank Robinson		
531	Chuck Hinton	3.50	1.55
532	Luis Tiant	6.00	2.70
533	Wes Parker	6.00	2.70
534	Bob Miller	3.50	1.55
535	Danny Cater	6.00	2.70
536	Bill Short	3.50	1.55
537	Norm Siebern	3.50	1.55
538	Manny Jimenez	3.50	1.55
539	Major League Rookies	3.50	1.55
	Jim Ray		
	Mike Ferraro		
540	Nelson Briles	6.00	2.70
541	Sandy Alomar	6.00	2.70
542	John Boccabella	3.50	1.55
543	Bob Lee	3.50	1.55
544	Mayo Smith MG	10.00	4.50
545	Lindy McDaniel	6.00	2.70
546	Roy White	6.00	2.70
547	Dan Coombs	3.50	1.55

		NRMT	VG-E
❏ 548	Bernie Allen	3.50	1.55
❏ 549	Orioles Rookies	3.50	1.55
	Curt Motton		
	Roger Nelson		
❏ 550	Clete Boyer	6.00	2.70
❏ 551	Darrell Sutherland	3.50	1.55
❏ 552	Ed Kirkpatrick	3.50	1.55
❏ 553	Hank Aguirre	3.50	1.55
❏ 554	A's Team	10.00	4.50
❏ 555	Jose Tartabull	6.00	2.70
❏ 556	Dick Selma	3.50	1.55
❏ 557	Frank Quilici	3.50	1.55
❏ 558	Johnny Edwards	3.50	1.55
❏ 559	Pirates Rookies	3.50	1.55
	Carl Taylor		
	Luke Walker		
❏ 560	Paul Casanova	3.50	1.55
❏ 561	Lee Elia	3.50	1.55
❏ 562	Jim Bouton	6.00	2.70
❏ 563	Ed Charles	3.50	1.55
❏ 564	Eddie Stanky MG	3.50	1.55
❏ 565	Larry Dierker	6.00	2.70
❏ 566	Ken Harrelson	6.00	2.70
❏ 567	Clay Dalrymple	3.50	1.55
❏ 568	Willie Smith	3.50	1.55
❏ 569	NL Rookies	3.50	1.55
	Ivan Murrell		
	Les Rohr		
❏ 570	Rick Reichardt	3.50	1.55
❏ 571	Tony LaRussa	12.00	5.50
❏ 572	Don Bosch	3.50	1.55
❏ 573	Joe Coleman	3.50	1.55
❏ 574	Cincinnati Reds	10.00	4.50
	Team Card		
❏ 575	Jim Palmer	35.00	16.00
❏ 576	Dave Adlesh	3.50	1.55
❏ 577	Fred Talbot	3.50	1.55
❏ 578	Orlando Martinez	3.50	1.55
❏ 579	NL Rookies	6.00	2.70
	Larry Hisle		
	Mike Lum		
❏ 580	Bob Bailey	3.50	1.55
❏ 581	Garry Roggenburk	3.50	1.55
❏ 582	Jerry Grote	6.00	2.70
❏ 583	Gates Brown	6.00	2.70
❏ 584	Larry Shepard MG	3.50	1.55
❏ 585	Wilbur Wood	6.00	2.70
❏ 586	Jim Pagliaroni	6.00	2.70
❏ 587	Roger Repoz	3.50	1.55
❏ 588	Dick Schofield	3.50	1.55
❏ 589	Twins Rookies	3.50	1.55
	Ron Clark		
	Moe Ogier		
❏ 590	Tommy Harper	6.00	2.70
❏ 591	Dick Nen	3.50	1.55
❏ 592	John Bateman	3.50	1.55
❏ 593	Lee Stange	3.50	1.55
❏ 594	Phil Linz	6.00	2.70
❏ 595	Phil Ortega	3.50	1.55
❏ 596	Charlie Smith	3.50	1.55
❏ 597	Bill McCool	3.50	1.55
❏ 598	Jerry May	6.00	1.85

1969 Topps

	NRMT	VG-E
COMPLETE SET (664)	2200.00	1000.00
COMMON (1-218/328-512)	1.50	.70

MNR.STARS 1-218/328-512		2.50	1.10
SEMISTARS 1-218/328-512		4.00	1.80
UNL.STARS 1-218/328-512		6.00	2.70
COMMON CARD (219-327)		2.50	1.10
MINOR STARS 219-327		4.00	1.80
SEMISTARS 219-327		6.00	2.70
UNLISTED STARS 219-327		10.00	4.50
COMMON CARD (513-588)		2.00	.90
MINOR STARS 513-588		3.00	1.35
SEMISTARS 513-588		5.00	2.20
UNLISTED STARS 513-588		8.00	3.60
COMMON CARD (589-664)		3.00	1.35
MINOR STARS 589-664		5.00	2.20
SEMISTARS 589-664		8.00	3.60
UNLISTED STARS 589-664		12.00	5.50
COMMON WHITE LTR		20.00	9.00

*UNLISTED DODGER/YANKEE: 1.25X VALUE
CARDS PRICED IN NM CONDITION

❏ 1	AL Batting Leaders	15.00	5.25
	Carl Yastrzemski		
	Danny Cater		
	Tony Oliva		
❏ 2	NL Batting Leaders	7.00	3.10
	Pete Rose		
	Matty Alou		
	Felipe Alou		
❏ 3	AL RBI Leaders	3.50	1.55
	Ken Harrelson		
	Frank Howard		
	Jim Northrup		
❏ 4	NL RBI Leaders	6.00	2.70
	Willie McCovey		
	Ron Santo		
	Billy Williams		
❏ 5	AL Home Run Leaders	3.50	1.55
	Frank Howard		
	Willie Horton		
	Ken Harrelson		
❏ 6	NL Home Run Leaders	6.00	2.70
	Willie McCovey		
	Richie Allen		
	Ernie Banks		
❏ 7	AL ERA Leaders	3.50	1.55
	Luis Tiant		
	Sam McDowell		
	Dave McNally		
❏ 8	NL ERA Leaders	6.00	2.70
	Bob Gibson		
	Bobby Bolin		
	Bob Veale		
❏ 9	AL Pitching Leaders	3.50	1.55
	Denny McLain		
	Dave McNally		
	Luis Tiant		
	Mel Stottlemyre		
❏ 10	NL Pitching Leaders	7.00	3.10
	Juan Marichal		
	Bob Gibson		
	Fergie Jenkins		
❏ 11	AL Strikeout Leaders	3.50	1.55
	Sam McDowell		
	Denny McLain		
	Luis Tiant		
❏ 12	NL Strikeout Leaders	4.00	1.80
	Bob Gibson		
	Fergie Jenkins		
	Bill Singer		
❏ 13	Mickey Stanley	2.50	1.10
❏ 14	Al McBean	1.50	.70
❏ 15	Boog Powell	4.00	1.80
❏ 16	Giants Rookies	1.50	.70
	Cesar Gutierrez		
	Rich Robertson		
❏ 17	Mike Marshall	2.50	1.10
❏ 18	Dick Schofield	1.50	.70
❏ 19	Ken Suarez	1.50	.70
❏ 20	Ernie Banks	20.00	9.00
❏ 21	Jose Santiago	1.50	.70
❏ 22	Jesus Alou	2.50	1.10
❏ 23	Lew Krausse	1.50	.70
❏ 24	Walt Alston MG	4.00	1.80
❏ 25	Roy White	2.50	1.10
❏ 26	Clay Carroll	2.50	1.10
❏ 27	Bernie Allen	1.50	.70
❏ 28	Mike Ryan	1.50	.70

❏ 29	Dave Morehead	1.50	.70
❏ 30	Bob Allison	2.50	1.10
❏ 31	Mets Rookies	1.50	1.10
	Gary Gentry		
	Amos Otis		
❏ 32	Sammy Ellis	1.50	.70
❏ 33	Wayne Causey	1.50	.70
❏ 34	Gary Peters	1.50	.70
❏ 35	Joe Morgan	10.00	4.50
❏ 36	Luke Walker	1.50	.70
❏ 37	Curt Motton	1.50	.70
❏ 38	Zoilo Versalles	2.50	1.10
❏ 39	Dick Hughes	1.50	.70
❏ 40	Mayo Smith MG	1.50	.70
❏ 41	Bob Barton	1.50	.70
❏ 42	Tommy Harper	2.50	1.10
❏ 43	Joe Niekro	2.50	1.10
❏ 44	Danny Cater	1.50	.70
❏ 45	Maury Wills	2.50	1.10
❏ 46	Fritz Peterson	2.50	1.10
❏ 47A	Paul Popovich	1.50	.70
	(No helmet emblem)		
❏ 47B	Paul Popovich	25.00	11.00
	(C emblem on helmet)		
❏ 48	Brant Alyea	1.50	.70
❏ 49A	Royals Rookies ERR	25.00	11.00
	Steve Jones		
	E. Rodriquez		
❏ 49B	Royals Rookies COR	1.50	.70
	Steve Jones		
	E. Rodriquez		
❏ 50	Roberto Clemente UER	50.00	22.00
	Bats Right listed twice		
❏ 51	Woody Fryman	1.50	.70
❏ 52	Mike Andrews	1.50	.70
❏ 53	Sonny Jackson	1.50	.70
❏ 54	Cisco Carlos	1.50	.70
❏ 55	Jerry Grote	2.50	1.10
❏ 56	Rich Reese	1.50	.70
❏ 57	Denny McLain CL	6.00	1.20
❏ 58	Fred Gladding	1.50	.70
❏ 59	Jay Johnstone	2.50	1.10
❏ 60	Nelson Briles	2.50	1.10
❏ 61	Jimmie Hall	1.50	.70
❏ 62	Chico Salmon	1.50	.70
❏ 63	Jim Hickman	2.50	1.10
❏ 64	Bill Monbouquette	1.50	.70
❏ 65	Willie Davis	2.50	1.10
❏ 66	Orioles Rookies	1.50	.70
	Mike Adamson		
	Merv Rettenmund		
❏ 67	Bill Stoneman	2.50	1.10
❏ 68	Dave Duncan	2.50	1.10
❏ 69	Steve Hamilton	2.50	1.10
❏ 70	Tommy Helms	2.50	1.10
❏ 71	Steve Whitaker	1.50	.70
❏ 72	Ron Taylor	1.50	.70
❏ 73	Johnny Briggs	1.50	.70
❏ 74	Preston Gomez MG	2.50	1.10
❏ 75	Luis Aparicio	6.00	2.70
❏ 76	Norm Miller	1.50	.70
❏ 77A	Ron Perranoski	2.50	1.10
	(No emblem on cap)		
❏ 77B	Ron Perranoski	25.00	11.00
	(LA on cap)		
❏ 78	Tom Satriano	1.50	.70
❏ 79	Milt Pappas	2.50	1.10
❏ 80	Norm Cash	2.50	1.10
❏ 81	Mel Queen	1.50	.70
❏ 82	Pirates Rookies	8.00	3.60
	Rich Hebner		
	Al Oliver		
❏ 83	Mike Ferraro	2.50	1.10
❏ 84	Bob Humphreys	1.50	.70
❏ 85	Lou Brock	20.00	9.00
❏ 86	Pete Richert	1.50	.70
❏ 87	Horace Clarke	2.50	1.10
❏ 88	Rich Nye	1.50	.70
❏ 89	Russ Gibson	1.50	.70
❏ 90	Jerry Koosman	2.50	1.10
❏ 91	Alvin Dark MG	2.50	1.10
❏ 92	Jack Billingham	2.50	1.10
❏ 93	Joe Foy	2.50	1.10
❏ 94	Hank Aguirre	1.50	.70
❏ 95	Johnny Bench	45.00	20.00
❏ 96	Denny Lemaster	1.50	.70

❑ 97	Buddy Bradford	1.50	.70
❑ 98	Dave Giusti	1.50	.70
❑ 99A	Twins Rookies	15.00	6.75
	Danny Morris		
	Graig Nettles		
	(No loop)		
❑ 99B	Twins Rookies	15.00	6.75
	Danny Morris		
	Graig Nettles		
	(Errant loop in		
	upper left corner		
	of obverse)		
❑ 100	Hank Aaron	35.00	16.00
❑ 101	Daryl Patterson	1.50	.70
❑ 102	Jim Davenport	1.50	.70
❑ 103	Roger Repoz	1.50	.70
❑ 104	Steve Blass	2.50	1.10
❑ 105	Rick Monday	2.50	1.10
❑ 106	Jim Hannan	1.50	.70
❑ 107A	Bob Gibson CL ERR.	6.00	1.20
	161 Jim Purdin		
❑ 107B	Bob Gibson CL COR	7.50	1.50
	161 John Purdin		
❑ 108	Tony Taylor	2.50	1.10
❑ 109	Jim Lonborg	2.50	1.10
❑ 110	Mike Shannon	2.50	1.10
❑ 111	Johnny Morris	1.50	.70
❑ 112	J.C. Martin	1.50	.70
❑ 113	Dave May	1.50	.70
❑ 114	Yankees Rookies	2.50	1.10
	Alan Closter		
	John Cumberland		
❑ 115	Bill Hands	1.50	.70
❑ 116	Chuck Harrison	1.50	.70
❑ 117	Jim Fairey	1.50	.70
❑ 118	Stan Williams	1.50	.70
❑ 119	Doug Rader	2.50	1.10
❑ 120	Pete Rose	20.00	9.00
❑ 121	Joe Grzenda	1.50	.70
❑ 122	Ron Fairly	2.50	1.10
❑ 123	Wilbur Wood	2.50	1.10
❑ 124	Hank Bauer MG	2.50	1.10
❑ 125	Ray Sadecki	1.50	.70
❑ 126	Dick Tracewski	1.50	.70
❑ 127	Kevin Collins	2.50	1.10
❑ 128	Tommie Aaron	2.50	1.10
❑ 129	Bill McCool	1.50	.70
❑ 130	Carl Yastrzemski	20.00	9.00
❑ 131	Chris Cannizzaro	1.50	.70
❑ 132	Dave Baldwin	1.50	.70
❑ 133	Johnny Callison	2.50	1.10
❑ 134	Jim Weaver	1.50	.70
❑ 135	Tommy Davis	2.50	1.10
❑ 136	Cards Rookies	1.50	.70
	Steve Huntz		
	Mike Torrez		
❑ 137	Wally Bunker	1.50	.70
❑ 138	John Bateman	1.50	.70
❑ 139	Andy Kosco	1.50	.70
❑ 140	Jim Lefebvre	2.50	1.10
❑ 141	Bill Dillman	1.50	.70
❑ 142	Woody Woodward	2.50	1.10
❑ 143	Joe Nossek	1.50	.70
❑ 144	Bob Hendley	2.50	1.10
❑ 145	Max Alvis	1.50	.70
❑ 146	Jim Perry	2.50	1.10
❑ 147	Leo Durocher MG	4.00	1.80
❑ 148	Lee Stange	1.50	.70
❑ 149	Ollie Brown	2.50	1.10
❑ 150	Denny McLain	4.00	1.80
❑ 151A	Clay Dalrymple	1.50	.70
	Portrait, Orioles		
❑ 151B	Clay Dalrymple	15.00	6.75
	Catching, Phillies		
❑ 152	Tommie Sisk	1.50	.70
❑ 153	Ed Brinkman	1.50	.70
❑ 154	Jim Britton	1.50	.70
❑ 155	Pete Ward	1.50	.70
❑ 156	Houston Rookies	1.50	.70
	Hal Gilson		
	Leon McFadden		
❑ 157	Bob Rodgers	2.50	1.10
❑ 158	Joe Gibbon	1.50	.70
❑ 159	Jerry Adair	1.50	.70
❑ 160	Vada Pinson	2.50	1.10
❑ 161	John Purdin	1.50	.70
❑ 162	Bob Gibson WS	8.00	3.60
	Fans 17		
❑ 163	Willie Horton WS	6.00	2.70
❑ 164	Tim McCarver WS	12.00	5.50
	Roger Maris		
❑ 165	Lou Brock WS	8.00	3.60
❑ 166	Al Kaline WS	8.00	3.60
❑ 167	Jim Northrup WS	6.00	2.70
❑ 168	Mickey Lolich WS	8.00	3.60
	Bob Gibson		
❑ 169	Dick McAuliffe WS	6.00	2.70
	Denny McLain		
	Willie Horton		
❑ 170	Frank Howard	2.50	1.10
❑ 171	Glenn Beckert	2.50	1.10
❑ 172	Jerry Stephenson	1.50	.70
❑ 173	White Sox Rookies	1.50	.70
	Bob Christian		
	Gerry Nyman		
❑ 174	Grant Jackson	1.50	.70
❑ 175	Jim Bunning	6.00	2.70
❑ 176	Joe Azcue	1.50	.70
❑ 177	Ron Reed	1.50	.70
❑ 178	Ray Oyler	2.50	1.10
❑ 179	Don Pavletich	1.50	.70
❑ 180	Willie Horton	2.50	1.10
❑ 181	Mel Nelson	1.50	.70
❑ 182	Bill Rigney MG	1.50	.70
❑ 183	Don Shaw	1.50	.70
❑ 184	Roberto Pena	1.50	.70
❑ 185	Tom Phoebus	1.50	.70
❑ 186	Johnny Edwards	1.50	.70
❑ 187	Leon Wagner	1.50	.70
❑ 188	Rick Wise	2.50	1.10
❑ 189	Red Sox Rookies	1.50	.70
	Joe Lahoud		
	John Thibodeau		
❑ 190	Willie Mays	45.00	20.00
❑ 191	Lindy McDaniel	2.50	1.10
❑ 192	Jose Pagan	1.50	.70
❑ 193	Don Cardwell	1.50	.70
❑ 194	Ted Uhlaender	1.50	.70
❑ 195	John Odom	1.50	.70
❑ 196	Lum Harris MG	1.50	.70
❑ 197	Dick Selma	1.50	.70
❑ 198	Willie Smith	1.50	.70
❑ 199	Jim French	1.50	.70
❑ 200	Bob Gibson	12.00	5.50
❑ 201	Russ Snyder	1.50	.70
❑ 202	Don Wilson	2.50	1.10
❑ 203	Dave Johnson	2.50	1.10
❑ 204	Jack Hiatt	1.50	.70
❑ 205	Rick Reichardt	1.50	.70
❑ 206	Phillies Rookies	2.50	1.10
	Larry Hisle		
	Barry Lersch		
❑ 207	Roy Face	2.50	1.10
❑ 208A	Donn Clendenon	2.50	1.10
	Houston		
❑ 208B	Donn Clendenon	15.00	6.75
	Expos		
❑ 209	Larry Haney UER	1.50	.70
	(Reverse negative)		
❑ 210	Felix Millan	1.50	.70
❑ 211	Galen Cisco	1.50	.70
❑ 212	Tom Tresh	2.50	1.10
❑ 213	Gerry Arrigo	1.50	.70
❑ 214	Checklist 3	6.00	1.20
	With 69T deckle CL		
	no player)		
❑ 215	Rico Petrocelli	2.50	1.10
❑ 216	Don Sutton	6.00	2.70
❑ 217	John Donaldson	1.50	.70
❑ 218	John Roseboro	2.50	1.10
❑ 219	Freddie Patek	4.00	1.80
❑ 220	Sam McDowell	4.00	1.80
❑ 221	Art Shamsky	2.50	1.10
❑ 222	Duane Josephson	2.50	1.10
❑ 223	Tom Dukes	4.00	1.80
❑ 224	Angels Rookies	2.50	1.10
	Bill Harrelson		
	Steve Kealey		
❑ 225	Don Kessinger	4.00	1.80
❑ 226	Bruce Howard	2.50	1.10
❑ 227	Frank Johnson	2.50	1.10
❑ 228	Dave Leonhard	2.50	1.10
❑ 229	Don Lock	2.50	1.10
❑ 230	Rusty Staub UER	4.00	1.80
	For 1966 stats, Houston spelled		
	Houston		
❑ 231	Pat Dobson	4.00	1.80
❑ 232	Dave Ricketts	2.50	1.10
❑ 233	Steve Barber	4.00	1.80
❑ 234	Dave Bristol MG	2.50	1.10
❑ 235	Jim Hunter	10.00	4.50
❑ 236	Manny Mota	4.00	1.80
❑ 237	Bobby Cox	10.00	4.50
❑ 238	Ken Johnson	2.50	1.10
❑ 239	Bob Taylor	4.00	1.80
❑ 240	Ken Harrelson	4.00	1.80
❑ 241	Jim Brewer	2.50	1.10
❑ 242	Frank Kostro	2.50	1.10
❑ 243	Ron Kline	2.50	1.10
❑ 244	Indians Rookies	4.00	1.80
	Ray Fosse		
	George Woodson		
❑ 245	Ed Charles	4.00	1.80
❑ 246	Joe Coleman	2.50	1.10
❑ 247	Gene Oliver	2.50	1.10
❑ 248	Bob Priddy	2.50	1.10
❑ 249	Ed Spiezio	4.00	1.80
❑ 250	Frank Robinson	20.00	9.00
❑ 251	Ron Herbel	2.50	1.10
❑ 252	Chuck Cottier	2.50	1.10
❑ 253	Jerry Johnson	2.50	1.10
❑ 254	Joe Schultz MG	4.00	1.80
❑ 255	Steve Carlton	30.00	13.50
❑ 256	Gates Brown	4.00	1.80
❑ 257	Jim Ray	2.50	1.10
❑ 258	Jackie Hernandez	4.00	1.80
❑ 259	Bill Short	2.50	1.10
❑ 260	Reggie Jackson	250.00	110.00
❑ 261	Bob Johnson	2.50	1.10
❑ 262	Mike Andrews	4.00	1.80
❑ 263	Jerry May	2.50	1.10
❑ 264	Bill Landis	2.50	1.10
❑ 265	Chico Cardenas	2.50	1.10
❑ 266	Dodger Rookies	4.00	1.80
	Tom Hutton		
	Alan Foster		
❑ 267	Vicente Romo	2.50	1.10
❑ 268	Al Spangler	2.50	1.10
❑ 269	Al Weis	4.00	1.80
❑ 270	Mickey Lolich	4.00	1.80
❑ 271	Larry Stahl	2.50	1.10
❑ 272	Ed Stroud	2.50	1.10
❑ 273	Ron Willis	2.50	1.10
❑ 274	Clyde King MG	2.50	1.10
❑ 275	Vic Davalillo	2.50	1.10
❑ 276	Gary Wagner	2.50	1.10
❑ 277	Elrod Hendricks	2.50	1.10
❑ 278	Gary Geiger UER	2.50	1.10
	(Batting wrong)		
❑ 279	Roger Nelson	4.00	1.80
❑ 280	Alex Johnson	4.00	1.80
❑ 281	Ted Kubiak	2.50	1.10
❑ 282	Pat Jarvis	2.50	1.10
❑ 283	Sandy Alomar	4.00	1.80
❑ 284	Expos Rookies	4.00	1.80
	Jerry Robertson		
	Mike Wegener		
❑ 285	Don Mincher	4.00	1.80
❑ 286	Dock Ellis	4.00	1.80
❑ 287	Jose Tartabull	4.00	1.80
❑ 288	Ken Holtzman	2.50	1.10
❑ 289	Bart Shirley	2.50	1.10
❑ 290	Jim Kaat	4.00	1.80
❑ 291	Vern Fuller	2.50	1.10
❑ 292	Al Downing	4.00	1.80
❑ 293	Dick Dietz	2.50	1.10
❑ 294	Jim Lemon MG	2.50	1.10
❑ 295	Tony Perez	12.00	5.50
❑ 296	Andy Messersmith	4.00	1.80
❑ 297	Deron Johnson	2.50	1.10
❑ 298	Dave Nicholson	4.00	1.80
❑ 299	Mark Belanger	4.00	1.80
❑ 300	Felipe Alou	4.00	1.80
❑ 301	Darrell Brandon	4.00	1.80
❑ 302	Jim Pagliaroni	2.50	1.10
❑ 303	Cal Koonce	4.00	1.80
❑ 304	Padres Rookies	6.00	2.70
	Bill Davis		

Clarence Gaston

305	Dick McAuliffe	4.00	1.80
306	Jim Grant	4.00	1.80
307	Gary Kolb	2.50	1.10
308	Wade Blasingame	2.50	1.10
309	Walt Williams	2.50	1.10
310	Tom Haller	2.50	1.10
311	Sparky Lyle	10.00	4.50
312	Lee Elia	2.50	1.10
313	Bill Robinson	4.00	1.80
314	Don Drysdale CL	6.00	1.20
315	Eddie Fisher	2.50	1.10
316	Hal Lanier	2.50	1.10
317	Bruce Look	2.50	1.10
318	Jack Fisher	2.50	1.10
319	Ken McMullen UER	2.50	1.10
	(Headings on back are for a pitcher)		
320	Dal Maxvill	2.50	1.10
321	Jim McAndrew	4.00	1.80
322	Jose Vidal	2.50	1.10
323	Larry Miller	2.50	1.10
324	Tiger Rookies	4.00	1.80
	Les Cain		
	Dave Campbell		
325	Jose Cardenal	4.00	1.80
326	Gary Sutherland	4.00	1.80
327	Willie Crawford	2.50	1.10
328	Joel Horlen	1.50	.70
329	Rick Joseph	1.50	.70
330	Tony Conigliaro	4.00	1.80
331	Braves Rookies	2.50	1.10
	Gil Garrido		
	Tom House		
332	Fred Talbot	1.50	.70
333	Ivan Murrell	1.50	.70
334	Phil Roof	1.50	.70
335	Bill Mazeroski	4.00	1.80
336	Jim Roland	1.50	.70
337	Marty Martinez	1.50	.70
338	Del Unser	1.50	.70
339	Reds Rookies	1.50	.70
	Steve Mingori		
	Jose Pena		
340	Dave McNally	2.50	1.10
341	Dave Adlesh	1.50	.70
342	Bubba Morton	1.50	.70
343	Dan Frisella	1.50	.70
344	Tom Matchick	1.50	.70
345	Frank Linzy	1.50	.70
346	Wayne Comer	1.50	.70
347	Randy Hundley	2.50	1.10
348	Steve Hargan	1.50	.70
349	Dick Williams MG	2.50	1.10
350	Richie Allen	4.00	1.80
351	Carroll Sembera	1.50	.70
352	Paul Schaal	1.50	.70
353	Jeff Torborg	2.50	1.10
354	Nate Oliver	1.50	.70
355	Phil Niekro	6.00	2.70
356	Frank Quilici	1.50	.70
357	Carl Taylor	1.50	.70
358	Athletics Rookies	1.50	.70
	George Lauzerique		
	Roberto Rodriguez		
359	Dick Kelley	1.50	.70
360	Jim Wynn	2.50	1.10
361	Gary Holman	1.50	.70
362	Jim Maloney	2.50	1.10
363	Russ Nixon	1.50	.70
364	Tommie Agee	4.00	1.80
365	Jim Fregosi	2.50	1.10
366	Bo Belinsky	2.50	1.10
367	Lou Johnson	2.50	1.10
368	Vic Roznovsky	1.50	.70
369	Bob Skinner MG	2.50	1.10
370	Juan Marichal	8.00	3.60
371	Sal Bando	2.50	1.10
372	Adolfo Phillips	1.50	.70
373	Fred Lasher	1.50	.70
374	Bob Tillman	1.50	.70
375	Harmon Killebrew	15.00	6.75
376	Royals Rookies	1.50	.70
	Mike Fiore		
	Jim Rooker		
377	Gary Bell	2.50	1.10
378	Jose Herrera	1.50	.70
379	Ken Boyer	2.50	1.10
380	Stan Bahnsen	2.50	1.10
381	Ed Kranepool	2.50	1.10
382	Pat Corrales	2.50	1.10
383	Casey Cox	1.50	.70
384	Larry Shepard MG	1.50	.70
385	Orlando Cepeda	4.00	1.80
386	Jim McGlothlin	1.50	.70
387	Bobby Klaus	1.50	.70
388	Tom McCraw	1.50	.70
389	Dan Coombs	1.50	.70
390	Bill Freehan	2.50	1.10
391	Ray Culp	1.50	.70
392	Bob Burda	1.50	.70
393	Gene Brabender	2.50	1.10
394	Pilots Rookies	6.00	2.70
	Lou Piniella		
	Marv Staehle		
395	Chris Short	1.50	.70
396	Jim Campanis	1.50	.70
397	Chuck Dobson	1.50	.70
398	Tito Francona	1.50	.70
399	Bob Bailey	2.50	1.10
400	Don Drysdale	16.00	7.25
401	Jake Gibbs	2.50	1.10
402	Ken Boswell	2.50	1.10
403	Bob Miller	1.50	.70
404	Cubs Rookies	2.50	1.10
	Vic LaRose		
	Gary Ross		
405	Lee May	2.50	1.10
406	Phil Ortega	1.50	.70
407	Tom Egan	1.50	.70
408	Nate Colbert	1.50	.70
409	Bob Moose	1.50	.70
410	Al Kaline	25.00	11.00
411	Larry Dierker	2.50	1.10
412	Mickey Mantle CL DP	15.00	3.00
413	Roland Sheldon	2.50	1.10
414	Duke Sims	1.50	.70
415	Ray Washburn	1.50	.70
416	Willie McCovey AS	7.00	3.10
417	Ken Harrelson AS	3.50	1.55
418	Tommy Helms AS	3.50	1.55
419	Rod Carew AS	10.00	4.50
420	Ron Santo AS	4.00	1.80
421	Brooks Robinson AS	7.00	3.10
422	Don Kessinger AS	3.50	1.55
423	Bert Campaneris AS	4.00	1.80
424	Pete Rose AS	14.00	6.25
425	Carl Yastrzemski AS	10.00	4.50
426	Curt Flood AS	4.00	1.80
427	Tony Oliva AS	4.00	1.80
428	Lou Brock AS	6.00	2.70
429	Willie Horton AS	3.50	1.55
430	Johnny Bench AS	10.00	4.50
431	Bill Freehan AS	4.00	1.80
432	Bob Gibson AS	6.00	2.70
433	Denny McLain AS	3.50	1.55
434	Jerry Koosman AS	3.00	1.35
435	Sam McDowell AS	2.50	1.10
436	Gene Alley	2.50	1.10
437	Luis Alcaraz	1.50	.70
438	Gary Waslewski	1.50	.70
439	White Sox Rookies	1.50	.70
	Ed Herrmann		
	Dan Lazar		
440A	Willie McCovey	15.00	6.75
440B	Willie McCovey WL	100.00	45.00
	(McCovey white)		
441A	Dennis Higgins	1.50	.70
441B	Dennis Higgins WL	20.00	9.00
	(Higgins white)		
442	Ty Cline	1.50	.70
443	Don Wert	1.50	.70
444A	Joe Moeller	1.50	.70
444B	Joe Moeller WL	20.00	9.00
	(Moeller white)		
445	Bobby Knoop	1.50	.70
446	Claude Raymond	1.50	.70
447A	Ralph Houk MG	2.50	1.10
447B	Ralph Houk WL MG (Houk white)	22.00	10.00
448	Bob Tolan	2.50	1.10
449	Paul Lindblad	1.50	.70
450	Billy Williams	7.00	3.10
451A	Rich Rollins	2.50	1.10
451B	Rich Rollins WL	20.00	9.00
	(Rich and 3B white)		
452A	Al Ferrara	1.50	.70
452B	Al Ferrara WL	20.00	9.00
	(Al and OF white)		
453	Mike Cuellar	2.50	1.10
454A	Phillies Rookies	2.50	1.10
	Larry Colton		
	Don Money		
454B	Phillies Rookies WL	22.00	10.00
	Larry Colton		
	Don Money		
	(Names in white)		
455	Sonny Siebert	1.50	.70
456	Bud Harrelson	2.50	1.10
457	Dalton Jones	1.50	.70
458	Curt Blefary	1.50	.70
459	Dave Boswell	1.50	.70
460	Joe Torre	4.00	1.80
461A	Mike Epstein	1.50	.70
461B	Mike Epstein WL	20.00	9.00
	(Epstein white)		
462	Red Schoendienst MG	2.50	1.10
463	Dennis Ribant	1.50	.70
464A	Dave Marshall	1.50	.70
464B	Dave Marshall WL	20.00	9.00
	(Marshall white)		
465	Tommy John	4.00	1.80
466	John Boccabella	2.50	1.10
467	Tommie Reynolds	1.50	.70
468A	Pirates Rookies	1.50	.70
	Bruce Del Canton		
	Bob Robertson		
468B	Pirates Rookies WL	20.00	9.00
	Bruce Del Canton		
	Bob Robertson		
	(Names in white)		
469	Chico Ruiz	1.50	.70
470A	Mel Stottlemyre	2.50	1.10
470B	Mel Stottlemyre WL	30.00	13.50
	(Stottlemyre white)		
471A	Ted Savage	1.50	.70
471B	Ted Savage WL	20.00	9.00
	(Savage white)		
472	Jim Price	1.50	.70
473A	Jose Arcia	1.50	.70
473B	Jose Arcia WL	20.00	9.00
	(Jose and 2B white)		
474	Tom Murphy	1.50	.70
475	Tim McCarver	4.00	1.80
476A	Boston Rookies	3.00	1.35
	Ken Brett		
	Gerry Moses		
476B	Boston Rookies WL	30.00	13.50
	Ken Brett		
	Gerry Moses		
477	Jeff James	1.50	.70
478	Don Buford	1.50	.70
479	Richie Scheinblum	1.50	.70
480	Tom Seaver	70.00	32.00
481	Bill Melton	2.50	1.10
482A	Jim Gosger	1.50	.70
482B	Jim Gosger WL	20.00	9.00
	(Jim and OF white)		
483	Ted Abernathy	1.50	.70
484	Joe Gordon MG	2.50	1.10
485A	Gaylord Perry	10.00	4.50
485B	Gaylord Perry WL	85.00	38.00
	(Perry white)		
486A	Paul Casanova	1.50	.70
486B	Paul Casanova WL	20.00	9.00
	(Casanova white)		
487	Denis Menke	1.50	.70
488	Joe Sparma	1.50	.70
489	Clete Boyer	2.50	1.10
490	Matty Alou	2.50	1.10
491A	Twins Rookies	1.50	.70
	Jerry Crider		
	George Mitterwald		
491B	Twins Rookies WL	20.00	9.00
	Jerry Crider		
	George Mitterwald		

(Names in white)

	Card	Price	
❑ 492	Tony Cloninger	1.50	.70
❑ 493A	Wes Parker	2.50	1.10
❑ 493B	Wes Parker WL	22.00	10.00
	(Parker white)		
❑ 494	Ken Berry	1.50	.70
❑ 495	Bert Campaneris	2.50	1.10
❑ 496	Larry Jaster	1.50	.70
❑ 497	Julian Javier	2.50	1.10
❑ 498	Juan Pizarro	2.50	1.10
❑ 499	Astro Rookies	1.50	.70
	Don Bryant		
	Steve Shea		
❑ 500A	Mickey Mantle UER	300.00	135.00
	(No Topps copy-right on card back)		
❑ 500B	Mickey Mantle WL	1000.00	450.00
	(Mantle in white; no Topps copyright on card back) UER		
❑ 501A	Tony Gonzalez	2.50	1.10
❑ 501B	Tony Gonzalez WL	22.00	10.00
	(Tony and OF white)		
❑ 502	Minnie Rojas	1.50	.70
❑ 503	Larry Brown	1.50	.70
❑ 504	Brooks Robinson CL	7.00	1.40
❑ 505A	Bobby Bolin	1.50	.70
❑ 505B	Bobby Bolin WL	22.00	10.00
	(Bolin white)		
❑ 506	Paul Blair	2.50	1.10
❑ 507	Cookie Rojas	2.50	1.10
❑ 508	Moe Drabowsky	2.50	1.10
❑ 509	Manny Sanguillen	2.50	1.10
❑ 510	Rod Carew	35.00	16.00
❑ 511A	Diego Segui	2.50	1.10
❑ 511B	Diego Segui WL	22.00	10.00
	(Diego and P white)		
❑ 512	Cleon Jones	2.50	1.10
❑ 513	Camilo Pascual	3.00	1.35
❑ 514	Mike Lum	2.00	.90
❑ 515	Dick Green	2.00	.90
❑ 516	Earl Weaver MG	20.00	9.00
❑ 517	Mike McCormick	3.00	1.35
❑ 518	Fred Whitfield	2.00	.90
❑ 519	Yankees Rookies	2.00	.90
	Jerry Kenney		
	Len Boehmer		
❑ 520	Bob Veale	3.00	1.35
❑ 521	George Thomas	2.00	.90
❑ 522	Joe Hoerner	2.00	.90
❑ 523	Bob Chance	2.00	.90
❑ 524	Expos Rookies	3.00	1.35
	Jose Laboy		
	Floyd Wicker		
❑ 525	Earl Wilson	3.00	1.35
❑ 526	Hector Torres	2.00	.90
❑ 527	Al Lopez MG	5.00	2.20
❑ 528	Claude Osteen	3.00	1.35
❑ 529	Ed Kirkpatrick	3.00	1.35
❑ 530	Cesar Tovar	2.00	.90
❑ 531	Dick Farrell	2.00	.90
❑ 532	Bird Hill Aces	3.00	1.35
	Tom Phoebus		
	Jim Hardin		
	Dave McNally		
	Mike Cuellar		
❑ 533	Nolan Ryan	300.00	135.00
❑ 534	Jerry McNertney	3.00	1.35
❑ 535	Phil Regan	3.00	1.35
❑ 536	Padres Rookies	2.00	.90
	Danny Breeden		
	Dave Roberts		
❑ 537	Mike Paul	2.00	.90
❑ 538	Charlie Smith	2.00	.90
❑ 539	Ted Shows How	12.00	5.50
	Mike Epstein		
	Ted Williams MG		
❑ 540	Curt Flood	3.00	1.35
❑ 541	Joe Verbanic	2.00	.90
❑ 542	Bob Aspromonte	2.00	.90
❑ 543	Fred Newman	2.00	.90
❑ 544	Tigers Rookies	2.00	.90
	Mike Kilkenny		
	Ron Woods		
❑ 545	Willie Stargell	12.00	5.50
❑ 546	Jim Nash	2.00	.90

	Card	Price	
❑ 547	Billy Martin MG	5.00	2.20
❑ 548	Bob Locker	2.00	.90
❑ 549	Ron Brand	2.00	.90
❑ 550	Brooks Robinson	30.00	13.50
❑ 551	Wayne Granger	2.00	.90
❑ 552	Dodgers Rookies	3.00	1.35
	Ted Sizemore		
	Bill Sudakis		
❑ 553	Ron Davis	2.00	.90
❑ 554	Frank Bertaina	2.00	.90
❑ 555	Jim Ray Hart	3.00	1.35
❑ 556	A's Stars	3.00	1.35
	Sal Bando		
	Bert Campaneris		
	Danny Cater		
❑ 557	Frank Fernandez	2.00	.90
❑ 558	Tom Burgmeier	3.00	1.35
❑ 559	Cardinals Rookies	2.00	.90
	Joe Hague		
	Jim Hicks		
❑ 560	Luis Tiant	3.00	1.35
❑ 561	Ron Clark	2.00	.90
❑ 562	Bob Watson	8.00	3.60
❑ 563	Marty Pattin	3.00	1.35
❑ 564	Gil Hodges MG	10.00	4.50
❑ 565	Hoyt Wilhelm	8.00	3.60
❑ 566	Ron Hansen	2.00	.90
❑ 567	Pirates Rookies	2.00	.90
	Elvio Jimenez		
	Jim Shellenback		
❑ 568	Cecil Upshaw	2.00	.90
❑ 569	Billy Harris	2.00	.90
❑ 570	Ron Santo	8.00	3.60
❑ 571	Cap Peterson	2.00	.90
❑ 572	Giants Heroes	16.00	7.25
	Willie McCovey		
	Juan Marichal		
❑ 573	Jim Palmer	30.00	13.50
❑ 574	George Scott	3.00	1.35
❑ 575	Bill Singer	3.00	1.35
❑ 576	Phillies Rookies	2.00	.90
	Ron Stone		
	Bill Wilson		
❑ 577	Mike Hegan	3.00	1.35
❑ 578	Don Bosch	2.00	.90
❑ 579	Dave Nelson	2.00	.90
❑ 580	Jim Northrup	3.00	1.35
❑ 581	Gary Nolan	3.00	1.35
❑ 582A	Tony Oliva CL	6.00	1.20
	White circle on back		
❑ 582B	Tony Oliva CL	7.50	1.50
	Red circle on back		
❑ 583	Clyde Wright	2.00	.90
❑ 584	Don Mason	2.00	.90
❑ 585	Ron Swoboda	3.00	1.35
❑ 586	Tim Cullen	2.00	.90
❑ 587	Joe Rudi	8.00	3.60
❑ 588	Bill White	3.00	1.35
❑ 589	Joe Pepitone	5.00	2.20
❑ 590	Rico Carty	5.00	2.20
❑ 591	Mike Hedlund	3.00	1.35
❑ 592	Padres Rookies	5.00	2.20
	Rafael Robles		
	Al Santorini		
❑ 593	Don Nottebart	3.00	1.35
❑ 594	Dooley Womack	3.00	1.35
❑ 595	Lee Maye	3.00	1.35
❑ 596	Chuck Hartenstein	3.00	1.35
❑ 597	A.L. Rookies	35.00	16.00
	Bob Floyd		
	Larry Burchart		
	Rollie Fingers		
❑ 598	Ruben Amaro	3.00	1.35
❑ 599	John Boozer	3.00	1.35
❑ 600	Tony Oliva	5.00	2.20
❑ 601	Tug McGraw	8.00	3.60
❑ 602	Cubs Rookies	5.00	2.20
	Alec Distaso		
	Don Young		
	Jim Qualls		
❑ 603	Joe Keough	3.00	1.35
❑ 604	Bobby Etheridge	3.00	1.35
❑ 605	Dick Ellsworth	3.00	1.35
❑ 606	Gene Mauch MG	5.00	2.20
❑ 607	Dick Bosman	3.00	1.35
❑ 608	Dick Simpson	3.00	1.35

	Card	Price	
❑ 609	Phil Gagliano	3.00	1.35
❑ 610	Jim Hardin	3.00	1.35
❑ 611	Braves Rookies	5.00	2.20
	Bob Didier		
	Walt Hriniak		
	Gary Neibauer		
❑ 612	Jack Aker	5.00	2.20
❑ 613	Jim Beauchamp	3.00	1.35
❑ 614	Houston Rookies	3.00	1.35
	Tom Griffin		
	Skip Guinn		
❑ 615	Len Gabrielson	3.00	1.35
❑ 616	Don McMahon	3.00	1.35
❑ 617	Jesse Gonder	3.00	1.35
❑ 618	Ramon Webster	3.00	1.35
❑ 619	Royals Rookies	5.00	2.20
	Bill Butler		
	Pat Kelly		
	Juan Rios		
❑ 620	Dean Chance	5.00	2.20
❑ 621	Bill Voss	3.00	1.35
❑ 622	Dan Osinski	3.00	1.35
❑ 623	Hank Allen	3.00	1.35
❑ 624	NL Rookies	5.00	2.20
	Darrel Chaney		
	Duffy Dyer		
	Terry Harmon		
❑ 625	Mack Jones UER	5.00	2.20
	(Batting wrong)		
❑ 626	Gene Michael	5.00	2.20
❑ 627	George Stone	3.00	1.35
❑ 628	Red Sox Rookies	5.00	2.20
	Bill Conigliaro		
	Syd O'Brien		
	Fred Wenz		
❑ 629	Jack Hamilton	3.00	1.35
❑ 630	Bobby Bonds	30.00	13.50
❑ 631	John Kennedy	5.00	2.20
❑ 632	Jon Warden	3.00	1.35
❑ 633	Harry Walker MG	3.00	1.35
❑ 634	Andy Etchebarren	3.00	1.35
❑ 635	George Culver	3.00	1.35
❑ 636	Woody Held	3.00	1.35
❑ 637	Padres Rookies	5.00	2.20
	Jerry DaVanon		
	Frank Reberger		
	Clay Kirby		
❑ 638	Ed Sprague	3.00	1.35
❑ 639	Barry Moore	3.00	1.35
❑ 640	Ferguson Jenkins	20.00	9.00
❑ 641	NL Rookies	5.00	2.20
	Bobby Darwin		
	John Miller		
	Tommy Dean		
❑ 642	John Hiller	3.00	1.35
❑ 643	Billy Cowan	3.00	1.35
❑ 644	Chuck Hinton	3.00	1.35
❑ 645	George Brunet	3.00	1.35
❑ 646	Expos Rookies	5.00	2.20
	Dan McGinn		
	Carl Morton		
❑ 647	Dave Wickersham	3.00	1.35
❑ 648	Bobby Wine	5.00	2.20
❑ 649	Al Jackson	3.00	1.35
❑ 650	Ted Williams MG	20.00	9.00
❑ 651	Gus Gil	5.00	2.20
❑ 652	Eddie Watt	3.00	1.35
❑ 653	Aurelio Rodriguez UER	5.00	2.20
	(Photo actually Angels' batboy)		
❑ 654	White Sox Rookies	5.00	2.20
	Carlos May		
	Don Secrist		
	Rich Morales		
❑ 655	Mike Hershberger	3.00	1.35
❑ 656	Dan Schneider	3.00	1.35
❑ 657	Bobby Murcer	8.00	3.60
❑ 658	AL Rookies	3.00	1.35
	Tom Hall		
	Bill Burbach		
	Jim Miles		
❑ 659	Johnny Podres	5.00	2.20
❑ 660	Reggie Smith	5.00	2.20
❑ 661	Jim Merritt	3.00	1.35
❑ 662	Royals Rookies	5.00	2.20
	Dick Drago		

George Spriggs
Bob Oliver
- ❏ 663 Dick Radatz .... 5.00 — 2.20
- ❏ 664 Ron Hunt .... 5.00 — 1.35

1970 Topps

	NRMT	VG-E
COMPLETE SET (720)	1800.00	800.00
COMMON CARD (1-372)	1.00	.45
COMMON CARD (373-459)	1.50	.70
MINOR STARS 1-459	2.00	.90
SEMISTARS 1-459	4.00	1.80
UNLISTED STARS 1-459	6.00	2.70
COMMON CARD (460-546)	2.00	.90
MINOR STARS 460-546	3.00	1.35
SEMISTARS 460-546	5.00	2.20
UNLISTED STARS 460-546	8.00	3.60
COMMON CARD (547-633)	4.00	1.80
MINOR STARS 547-633	6.00	2.70
SEMISTARS 547-633	8.00	3.60
UNLISTED STARS 547-633	12.00	5.50
COMMON CARD (634-720)	10.00	4.50
MINOR STARS 634-720	15.00	6.75
SEMISTARS 634-720		9.00

CARDS PRICED IN NM CONDITION !

- ❏ 1 New York Mets .... 25.00 — 7.75
  Team Card
- ❏ 2 Diego Segui .... 2.00 — .90
- ❏ 3 Darrel Chaney .... 1.00 — .45
- ❏ 4 Tom Egan .... 2.00 — .90
- ❏ 5 Wes Parker .... 2.00 — .90
- ❏ 6 Grant Jackson .... 1.00 — .45
- ❏ 7 Indians Rookies .... 1.00 — .45
  Gary Boyd
  Russ Nagelson
- ❏ 8 Jose Martinez .... 1.00 — .45
- ❏ 9 Checklist 1 .... 12.00 — 2.40
- ❏ 10 Carl Yastrzemski ..... 15.00 — 6.75
- ❏ 11 Nate Colbert .... 1.00 — .45
- ❏ 12 John Hiller .... 1.00 — .45
- ❏ 13 Jack Hiatt .... 1.00 — .45
- ❏ 14 Hank Allen .... 1.00 — .45
- ❏ 15 Larry Dierker .... 1.00 — .45
- ❏ 16 Charlie Metro MG ..... 1.00 — .45
- ❏ 17 Hoyt Wilhelm .... 6.00 — 2.70
- ❏ 18 Carlos May .... 1.00 — .45
- ❏ 19 John Boccabella ...... 1.00 — .45
- ❏ 20 Dave McNally .... 1.00 — .45
- ❏ 21 A's Rookies .... 6.00 — 2.70
  Vida Blue
  Gene Tenace
- ❏ 22 Ray Washburn .... 1.00 — .45
- ❏ 23 Bill Robinson .... 2.00 — .90
- ❏ 24 Dick Selma .... 1.00 — .45
- ❏ 25 Cesar Tovar .... 1.00 — .45
- ❏ 26 Tug McGraw .... 2.00 — .90
- ❏ 27 Chuck Hinton .... 1.00 — .45
- ❏ 28 Billy Wilson .... 1.00 — .45
- ❏ 29 Sandy Alomar .... 2.00 — .90
- ❏ 30 Matty Alou .... 2.00 — .90
- ❏ 31 Marty Pattin .... 2.00 — .90
- ❏ 32 Harry Walker MG ...... 1.00 — .45
- ❏ 33 Don Wert .... 1.00 — .45
- ❏ 34 Willie Crawford ...... 1.00 — .45
- ❏ 35 Joel Horlen .... 1.00 — .45
- ❏ 36 Red Rookies .... 2.00 — .90
  Danny Breeden
  Bernie Carbo
- ❏ 37 Dick Drago .... 1.00 — .45
- ❏ 38 Mack Jones .... 1.00 — .45
- ❏ 39 Mike Nagy .... 1.00 — .45
- ❏ 40 Rich Allen .... 2.00 — .90
- ❏ 41 George Lauzerique .... 1.00 — .45
- ❏ 42 Tito Fuentes .... 1.00 — .45
- ❏ 43 Jack Aker .... 1.00 — .45
- ❏ 44 Roberto Pena .... 1.00 — .45
- ❏ 45 Dave Johnson .... 2.00 — .90
- ❏ 46 Ken Rudolph .... 1.00 — .45
- ❏ 47 Bob Miller .... 1.00 — .45
- ❏ 48 Gil Garrido .... 1.00 — .45
- ❏ 49 Tim Cullen .... 1.00 — .45
- ❏ 50 Tommie Agee .... 2.00 — .90
- ❏ 51 Bob Christian .... 1.00 — .45
- ❏ 52 Bruce Dal Canton ..... 1.00 — .45
- ❏ 53 John Kennedy .... 1.00 — .45
- ❏ 54 Jeff Torborg .... 2.00 — .90
- ❏ 55 John Odom .... 1.00 — .45
- ❏ 56 Phillies Rookies ..... 1.00 — .45
  Joe Lis
  Scott Reid
- ❏ 57 Pat Kelly .... 1.00 — .45
- ❏ 58 Dave Marshall .... 1.00 — .45
- ❏ 59 Dick Ellsworth .... 1.00 — .45
- ❏ 60 Jim Wynn .... 2.00 — .90
- ❏ 61 NL Batting Leaders ... 12.00 — 5.50
  Pete Rose
  Bob Clemente
  Cleon Jones
- ❏ 62 AL Batting Leaders ... 4.00 — 1.80
  Rod Carew
  Reggie Smith
  Tony Oliva
- ❏ 63 NL RBI Leaders .... 4.00 — 1.80
  Willie McCovey
  Ron Santo
  Tony Perez
- ❏ 64 AL RBI Leaders .... 6.00 — 2.70
  Harmon Killebrew
  Boog Powell
  Reggie Jackson
- ❏ 65 NL Home Run Leaders .. 6.00 — 2.70
  Willie McCovey
  Hank Aaron
  Lee May
- ❏ 66 AL Home Run Leaders .. 6.00 — 2.70
  Harmon Killebrew
  Frank Howard
  Reggie Jackson
- ❏ 67 NL ERA Leaders .... 6.00 — 2.70
  Juan Marichal
  Steve Carlton
  Bob Gibson
- ❏ 68 AL ERA Leaders .... 2.00 — .90
  Dick Bosman
  Jim Palmer
  Mike Cuellar
- ❏ 69 NL Pitching Leaders .. 6.00 — 2.70
  Tom Seaver
  Phil Niekro
  Fergie Jenkins
  Juan Marichal
- ❏ 70 AL Pitching Leaders .. 2.00 — .90
  Dennis McLain
  Mike Cuellar
  Dave Boswell
  Dave McNally
  Jim Perry
  Mel Stottlemyre
- ❏ 71 NL Strikeout Leaders . 4.00 — 1.80
  Fergie Jenkins
  Bob Gibson
  Bill Singer
- ❏ 72 AL Strikeout Leaders . 2.00 — .90
  Sam McDowell
  Mickey Lolich
  Andy Messersmith
- ❏ 73 Wayne Granger .... 1.00 — .45
- ❏ 74 Angels Rookies .... 1.00 — .45
  Greg Washburn
  Wally Wolf
- ❏ 75 Jim Kaat .... 2.00 — .90
- ❏ 76 Carl Taylor .... 1.00 — .45
- ❏ 77 Frank Linzy .... 1.00 — .45
- ❏ 78 Joe Lahoud .... 1.00 — .45
- ❏ 79 Clay Kirby .... 1.00 — .45
- ❏ 80 Don Kessinger .... 2.00 — .90
- ❏ 81 Dave May .... 1.00 — .45
- ❏ 82 Frank Fernandez ...... 1.00 — .45
- ❏ 83 Don Cardwell .... 1.00 — .45
- ❏ 84 Paul Casanova .... 1.00 — .45
- ❏ 85 Max Alvis .... 1.00 — .45
- ❏ 86 Lum Harris MG .... 1.00 — .45
- ❏ 87 Steve Renko .... 1.00 — .45
- ❏ 88 Pilots Rookies .... 2.00 — .90
  Miguel Fuentes
  Dick Baney
- ❏ 89 Juan Rios .... 1.00 — .45
- ❏ 90 Tim McCarver .... 2.00 — .90
- ❏ 91 Rich Morales .... 1.00 — .45
- ❏ 92 George Culver .... 1.00 — .45
- ❏ 93 Rick Renick .... 1.00 — .45
- ❏ 94 Freddie Patek .... 2.00 — .90
- ❏ 95 Earl Wilson .... 2.00 — .90
- ❏ 96 Cardinals Rookies .... 2.00 — .90
  Leron Lee
  Jerry Reuss
- ❏ 97 Joe Moeller .... 1.00 — .45
- ❏ 98 Gates Brown .... 2.00 — .90
- ❏ 99 Bobby Pfeil .... 1.00 — .45
- ❏ 100 Mel Stottlemyre ..... 2.00 — .90
- ❏ 101 Bobby Floyd .... 1.00 — .45
- ❏ 102 Joe Rudi .... 2.00 — .90
- ❏ 103 Frank Reberger ...... 1.00 — .45
- ❏ 104 Gerry Moses .... 1.00 — .45
- ❏ 105 Tony Gonzalez .... 1.00 — .45
- ❏ 106 Darold Knowles ...... 1.00 — .45
- ❏ 107 Bobby Etheridge ..... 1.00 — .45
- ❏ 108 Tom Burgmeier .... 1.00 — .45
- ❏ 109 Expos Rookies .... 1.00 — .45
  Garry Jestadt
  Carl Morton
- ❏ 110 Bob Moose .... 1.00 — .45
- ❏ 111 Mike Hegan .... 2.00 — .90
- ❏ 112 Dave Nelson .... 1.00 — .45
- ❏ 113 Jim Ray .... 1.00 — .45
- ❏ 114 Gene Michael .... 1.00 — .45
- ❏ 115 Alex Johnson .... 2.00 — .90
- ❏ 116 Sparky Lyle .... 2.00 — .90
- ❏ 117 Don Young .... 1.00 — .45
- ❏ 118 George Mitterwald ... 1.00 — .45
- ❏ 119 Chuck Taylor .... 1.00 — .45
- ❏ 120 Sal Bando .... 2.00 — .90
- ❏ 121 Orioles Rookies ..... 1.00 — .45
  Fred Beene
  Terry Crowley
- ❏ 122 George Stone .... 1.00 — .45
- ❏ 123 Don Gutteridge MG ... 1.00 — .45
- ❏ 124 Larry Jaster .... 1.00 — .45
- ❏ 125 Deron Johnson .... 1.00 — .45
- ❏ 126 Marty Martinez ...... 1.00 — .45
- ❏ 127 Joe Coleman .... 1.00 — .45
- ❏ 128A Checklist 2 ERR .... 6.00 — 1.20
  (226 R Perranoski)
- ❏ 128B Checklist 2 COR .... 6.00 — 1.20
  (226 R. Perranoski)
- ❏ 129 Jimmie Price .... 1.00 — .45
- ❏ 130 Ollie Brown .... 1.00 — .45
- ❏ 131 Dodgers Rookies ..... 1.00 — .45
  Ray Lamb
  Bob Stinson
- ❏ 132 Jim McGlothlin ...... 1.00 — .45
- ❏ 133 Clay Carroll .... 1.00 — .45
- ❏ 134 Danny Walton .... 1.00 — .45
- ❏ 135 Dick Dietz .... 1.00 — .45
- ❏ 136 Steve Hargan .... 1.00 — .45
- ❏ 137 Art Shamsky .... 2.00 — .90
- ❏ 138 Joe Foy .... 1.00 — .45
- ❏ 139 Rich Nye .... 1.00 — .45
- ❏ 140 Reggie Jackson ...... 50.00 — 22.00
- ❏ 141 Pirates Rookies ..... 2.00 — .90
  Dave Cash
  Johnny Jeter
- ❏ 142 Fritz Peterson ...... 1.00 — .45
- ❏ 143 Phil Gagliano .... 1.00 — .45
- ❏ 144 Ray Culp .... 1.00 — .45
- ❏ 145 Rico Carty .... 2.00 — .90
- ❏ 146 Danny Murphy .... 1.00 — .45
- ❏ 147 Angel Hermoso .... 1.00 — .45

148	Earl Weaver MG	4.00	1.80
149	Billy Champion	1.00	.45
150	Harmon Killebrew	8.00	3.60
151	Dave Roberts	1.00	.45
152	Ike Brown	1.00	.45
153	Gary Gentry	1.00	.45
154	Senators Rookies	1.00	.45
	Jim Miles		
	Jan Dukes		
155	Denis Menke	1.00	.45
156	Eddie Fisher	1.00	.45
157	Manny Mota	2.00	.90
158	Jerry McNertney	2.00	.90
159	Tommy Helms	2.00	.90
160	Phil Niekro	6.00	2.70
161	Richie Scheinblum	1.00	.45
162	Jerry Johnson	1.00	.45
163	Syd O'Brien	1.00	.45
164	Ty Cline	1.00	.45
165	Ed Kirkpatrick	1.00	.45
166	Al Oliver	2.00	.90
167	Bill Burbach	1.00	.45
168	Dave Watkins	1.00	.45
169	Tom Hall	1.00	.45
170	Billy Williams	6.00	2.70
171	Jim Nash	1.00	.45
172	Braves Rookies	2.00	.90
	Garry Hill		
	Ralph Garr		
173	Jim Hill		.45
174	Ted Sizemore	2.00	.90
175	Dick Bosman	1.00	.45
176	Jim Ray Hart	2.00	.90
177	Jim Northrup	2.00	.90
178	Denny Lemaster	1.00	.45
179	Ivan Murrell	1.00	.45
180	Tommy John	2.00	.90
181	Sparky Anderson MG	6.00	2.70
182	Dick Hall	1.00	.45
183	Jerry Grote	1.00	.45
184	Ray Fosse	1.00	.45
185	Don Mincher	2.00	.90
186	Rick Joseph	1.00	.45
187	Mike Hedlund	1.00	.45
188	Manny Sanguillen	2.00	.90
189	Yankees Rookies	50.00	22.00
	Thurman Munson		
	Dave McDonald		
190	Joe Torre	2.00	.90
191	Vicente Romo	1.00	.45
192	Jim Qualls	1.00	.45
193	Mike Wegener	1.00	.45
194	Chuck Manuel	1.00	.45
195	Tom Seaver NLCS	15.00	6.75
196	Ken Boswell NLCS	2.00	.90
197	Nolan Ryan NLCS	30.00	13.50
198	NL Playoff Summary	15.00	6.75
	Mets celebrate		
	(Nolan Ryan)		
199	Mike Cuellar ALCS	2.00	.90
200	Boog Powell ALCS	4.00	1.80
201	Boog Powell ALCS	2.00	.90
	Andy Etchebarren		
202	AL Playoff Summary	2.00	.90
	Orioles celebrate		
203	Rudy May	1.00	.45
204	Len Gabrielson	1.00	.45
205	Bert Campaneris	2.00	.90
206	Clete Boyer	2.00	.90
207	Tigers Rookies	1.00	.45
	Norman McRae		
	Bob Reed		
208	Fred Gladding	1.00	.45
209	Ken Suarez	1.00	.45
210	Juan Marichal	6.00	2.70
211	Ted Williams MG	12.00	5.50
212	Al Santorini	1.00	.45
213	Andy Etchebarren	1.00	.45
214	Ken Boswell	1.00	.45
215	Reggie Smith	2.00	.90
216	Chuck Hartenstein	1.00	.45
217	Ron Hansen	1.00	.45
218	Ron Stone	1.00	.45
219	Jerry Kenney	1.00	.45
220	Steve Carlton	15.00	6.75
221	Ron Brand	1.00	.45
222	Jim Rooker	2.00	.90
223	Nate Oliver	1.00	.45
224	Steve Barber	2.00	.90
225	Lee May	2.00	.90
226	Ron Perranoski	2.00	.90
227	Astros Rookies	2.00	.90
	John Mayberry		
	Bob Watkins		
228	Aurelio Rodriguez	1.00	.45
229	Rich Robertson	1.00	.45
230	Brooks Robinson	15.00	6.75
231	Luis Tiant	2.00	.90
232	Bob Didier	1.00	.45
233	Lew Krausse	1.00	.45
234	Tommy Dean	1.00	.45
235	Mike Epstein	1.00	.45
236	Bob Veale	1.00	.45
237	Russ Gibson	1.00	.45
238	Jose Laboy	1.00	.45
239	Ken Berry	1.00	.45
240	Ferguson Jenkins	6.00	2.70
241	Royals Rookies	1.00	.45
	Al Fitzmorris		
	Scott Northey		
242	Walter Alston MG	2.00	.90
243	Joe Sparma	1.00	.45
244A	Checklist 3	6.00	1.20
	(Red bat on front)		
244B	Checklist 3	6.00	1.20
	(Brown bat on front)		
245	Leo Cardenas	1.00	.45
246	Jim McAndrew	1.00	.45
247	Lou Klimchock	1.00	.45
248	Jesus Alou	1.00	.45
249	Bob Locker	1.00	.45
250	Willie McCovey UER	10.00	4.50
	(1963 San Francisco)		
251	Dick Schofield	1.00	.45
252	Lowell Palmer	1.00	.45
253	Ron Woods	1.00	.45
254	Camilo Pascual	1.00	.45
255	Jim Spencer	1.00	.45
256	Vic Davalillo	1.00	.45
257	Dennis Higgins	1.00	.45
258	Paul Popovich	1.00	.45
259	Tommie Reynolds	1.00	.45
260	Claude Osteen	1.00	.45
261	Curt Motton	1.00	.45
262	Padres Rookies	1.00	.45
	Jerry Morales		
	Jim Williams		
263	Duane Josephson	1.00	.45
264	Rich Hebner	1.00	.45
265	Randy Hundley	1.00	.45
266	Wally Bunker	1.00	.45
267	Twins Rookies	1.00	.45
	Herman Hill		
	Paul Ratliff		
268	Claude Raymond	1.00	.45
269	Cesar Gutierrez	1.00	.45
270	Chris Short	1.00	.45
271	Greg Goossen	1.00	.45
272	Hector Torres	1.00	.45
273	Ralph Houk MG	2.00	.90
274	Gerry Arrigo	1.00	.45
275	Duke Sims	1.00	.45
276	Ron Hunt	1.00	.45
277	Paul Doyle	1.00	.45
278	Tommie Aaron	1.00	.45
279	Bill Lee	2.00	.90
280	Donn Clendenon	2.00	.90
281	Casey Cox	1.00	.45
282	Steve Huntz	1.00	.45
283	Angel Bravo	1.00	.45
284	Jack Baldschun	1.00	.45
285	Paul Blair	2.00	.90
286	Dodgers Rookies	6.00	2.70
	Jack Jenkins		
	Bill Buckner		
287	Fred Talbot	1.00	.45
288	Larry Hisle	1.00	.45
289	Gene Brabender	1.00	.45
290	Rod Carew	18.00	8.00
291	Leo Durocher MG	4.00	1.80
292	Eddie Leon	1.00	.45
293	Bob Bailey	1.00	.45
294	Jose Azcue	1.00	.45
295	Cecil Upshaw	1.00	.45
296	Woody Woodward	1.00	.45
297	Curt Blefary	1.00	.45
298	Ken Henderson	1.00	.45
299	Buddy Bradford	1.00	.45
300	Tom Seaver	30.00	13.50
301	Chico Salmon	1.00	.45
302	Jeff James	1.00	.45
303	Brant Alyea	1.00	.45
304	Bill Russell	6.00	2.70
305	Don Buford WS	4.00	1.80
306	Donn Clendenon WS	4.00	1.80
307	Tommie Agee WS	4.00	1.80
308	J.C. Martin WS	4.00	1.80
309	Jerry Koosman WS	4.00	1.80
310	World Series Summary	6.00	2.70
	Mets whoop it up		
311	Dick Green	1.00	.45
312	Mike Torrez	1.00	.45
313	Mayo Smith MG	1.00	.45
314	Bill McCool	1.00	.45
315	Luis Aparicio	6.00	2.70
316	Skip Guinn	1.00	.45
317	Red Sox Rookies	1.00	.45
	Billy Conigliaro		
	Luis Alvarado		
318	Willie Smith	1.00	.45
319	Clay Dalrymple	1.00	.45
320	Jim Maloney	1.00	.45
321	Lou Piniella	2.00	.90
322	Luke Walker	1.00	.45
323	Wayne Comer	1.00	.45
324	Tony Taylor	1.00	.45
325	Dave Boswell	1.00	.45
326	Bill Voss	1.00	.45
327	Hal King	1.00	.45
328	George Brunet	1.00	.45
329	Chris Cannizzaro	1.00	.45
330	Lou Brock	10.00	4.50
331	Chuck Dobson	1.00	.45
332	Bobby Wine	1.00	.45
333	Bobby Murcer	2.00	.90
334	Phil Regan	1.00	.45
335	Bill Freehan	2.00	.90
336	Del Unser	1.00	.45
337	Mike McCormick	1.00	.45
338	Paul Schaal	1.00	.45
339	Johnny Edwards	1.00	.45
340	Tony Conigliaro	4.00	1.80
341	Bill Sudakis	1.00	.45
342	Wilbur Wood	2.00	.90
343A	Checklist 4	6.00	1.20
	(Red bat on front)		
343B	Checklist 4	6.00	1.20
	(Brown bat on front)		
344	Marcelino Lopez	1.00	.45
345	Al Ferrara	1.00	.45
346	Red Schoendienst MG	2.00	.90
347	Russ Snyder	1.00	.45
348	Mets Rookies	2.00	.90
	Mike Jorgensen		
	Jesse Hudson		
349	Steve Hamilton	1.00	.45
350	Roberto Clemente	60.00	27.00
351	Tom Murphy	1.00	.45
352	Bob Barton	1.00	.45
353	Stan Williams	1.00	.45
354	Amos Otis	1.50	.70
355	Doug Rader	1.00	.45
356	Fred Lasher	1.00	.45
357	Bob Burda	1.00	.45
358	Pedro Borbon	2.00	.90
359	Phil Roof	1.00	.45
360	Curt Flood	2.00	.90
361	Ray Jarvis	1.00	.45
362	Joe Hague	1.00	.45
363	Tom Shopay	1.00	.45
364	Dan McGinn	1.00	.45
365	Zoilo Versalles	1.00	.45
366	Barry Moore	1.00	.45
367	Mike Lum	1.00	.45
368	Ed Herrmann	1.00	.45
369	Alan Foster	1.00	.45
370	Tommy Harper	2.00	.90
371	Rod Gaspar	1.00	.45

❑ 372	Dave Giusti	1.50	.70
❑ 373	Roy White	2.00	.90
❑ 374	Tommie Sisk	1.50	.70
❑ 375	Johnny Callison	2.00	.90
❑ 376	Lefty Phillips MG	1.50	.70
❑ 377	Bill Butler	1.00	.45
❑ 378	Jim Davenport	1.50	.70
❑ 379	Tom Tischinski	1.50	.70
❑ 380	Tony Perez	6.00	2.70
❑ 381	Athletics Rookies	1.50	.70
	Bobby Brooks		
	Mike Olivo		
❑ 382	Jack DiLauro	1.50	.70
❑ 383	Mickey Stanley	2.00	.90
❑ 384	Gary Neibauer	1.50	.70
❑ 385	George Scott	2.00	.90
❑ 386	Bill Dillman	1.50	.70
❑ 387	Baltimore Orioles	3.00	1.35
	Team Card		
❑ 388	Byron Browne	1.50	.70
❑ 389	Jim Shellenback	1.50	.70
❑ 390	Willie Davis	2.00	.90
❑ 391	Larry Brown	1.50	.70
❑ 392	Walt Hriniak	2.00	.90
❑ 393	John Gelnar	1.50	.70
❑ 394	Gil Hodges MG	4.00	1.80
❑ 395	Walt Williams	1.50	.70
❑ 396	Steve Blass	2.00	.90
❑ 397	Roger Repoz	1.50	.70
❑ 398	Bill Stoneman	1.50	.70
❑ 399	New York Yankees	3.00	1.35
	Team Card		
❑ 400	Denny McLain	2.00	.90
❑ 401	Giants Rookies	1.50	.70
	John Harrell		
	Bernie Williams		
❑ 402	Ellie Rodriguez	1.50	.70
❑ 403	Jim Bunning	6.00	2.70
❑ 404	Rich Reese	1.50	.70
❑ 405	Bill Hands	1.50	.70
❑ 406	Mike Andrews	1.50	.70
❑ 407	Bob Watson	2.00	.90
❑ 408	Paul Lindblad	1.50	.70
❑ 409	Bob Tolan	2.00	.90
❑ 410	Boog Powell	4.00	1.80
❑ 411	Los Angeles Dodgers	3.00	1.35
	Team Card		
❑ 412	Larry Burchart	1.50	.70
❑ 413	Sonny Jackson	1.50	.70
❑ 414	Paul Edmondson	1.50	.70
❑ 415	Julian Javier	2.00	.90
❑ 416	Joe Verbanic	1.50	.70
❑ 417	John Bateman	1.50	.70
❑ 418	John Donaldson	1.50	.70
❑ 419	Ron Taylor	1.50	.70
❑ 420	Ken McMullen	2.00	.90
❑ 421	Pat Dobson	2.00	.90
❑ 422	Royals Team	3.00	1.35
❑ 423	Jerry May	1.50	.70
❑ 424	Mike Kilkenny	1.50	.70
	(Inconsistent design card number in white circle)		
❑ 425	Bobby Bonds	6.00	2.70
❑ 426	Bill Rigney MG	1.50	.70
❑ 427	Fred Norman	1.50	.70
❑ 428	Don Buford	1.50	.70
❑ 429	Cubs Rookies	1.50	.70
	Randy Bobb		
	Jim Cosman		
❑ 430	Andy Messersmith	2.00	.90
❑ 431	Ron Swoboda	2.00	.90
❑ 432A	Checklist 5	6.00	1.20
	(Baseball in yellow letters)		
❑ 432B	Checklist 5	6.00	1.20
	(Baseball in white letters)		
❑ 433	Ron Bryant	1.50	.70
❑ 434	Felipe Alou	2.00	.90
❑ 435	Nelson Briles	2.00	.90
❑ 436	Philadelphia Phillies	3.00	1.35
	Team Card		
❑ 437	Danny Cater	1.50	.70
❑ 438	Pat Jarvis	1.50	.70
❑ 439	Lee Maye	1.50	.70
❑ 440	Bill Mazeroski	4.00	1.80
❑ 441	John O'Donoghue	1.50	.70
❑ 442	Gene Mauch MG	2.00	.90
❑ 443	Al Jackson	1.50	.70
❑ 444	White Sox Rookies	1.50	.70
	Billy Farmer		
	John Matias		
❑ 445	Vada Pinson	2.00	.90
❑ 446	Billy Grabarkewitz	1.50	.70
❑ 447	Lee Stange	1.50	.70
❑ 448	Houston Astros	3.00	1.35
	Team Card		
❑ 449	Jim Palmer	12.00	5.50
❑ 450	Willie McCovey AS	6.00	2.70
❑ 451	Boog Powell AS	4.00	1.80
❑ 452	Felix Millan AS	2.00	.90
❑ 453	Rod Carew AS	6.00	2.70
❑ 454	Ron Santo AS	4.00	1.80
❑ 455	Brooks Robinson AS	6.00	2.70
❑ 456	Don Kessinger AS	2.00	.90
❑ 457	Rico Petrocelli AS	4.00	1.80
❑ 458	Pete Rose AS	14.00	6.25
❑ 459	Reggie Jackson AS	12.00	5.50
❑ 460	Matty Alou AS	3.00	1.35
❑ 461	Carl Yastrzemski AS	10.00	4.50
❑ 462	Hank Aaron AS	15.00	6.75
❑ 463	Frank Robinson AS	7.00	3.10
❑ 464	Johnny Bench AS	15.00	6.75
❑ 465	Bill Freehan AS	3.00	1.35
❑ 466	Juan Marichal AS	5.00	2.20
❑ 467	Denny McLain AS	3.00	1.35
❑ 468	Jerry Koosman AS	3.00	1.35
❑ 469	Sam McDowell AS	3.00	1.35
❑ 470	Willie Stargell	10.00	4.50
❑ 471	Chris Zachary	2.00	.90
❑ 472	Braves Team	3.50	1.55
❑ 473	Don Bryant	2.00	.90
❑ 474	Dick Kelley	2.00	.90
❑ 475	Dick McAuliffe	3.00	1.35
❑ 476	Don Shaw	2.00	.90
❑ 477	Orioles Rookies	2.00	.90
	Al Severinsen		
	Roger Freed		
❑ 478	Bobby Heise	2.00	.90
❑ 479	Dick Woodson	2.00	.90
❑ 480	Glenn Beckert	3.00	1.35
❑ 481	Jose Tartabull	3.00	1.35
❑ 482	Tom Hilgendorf	2.00	.90
❑ 483	Gail Hopkins	2.00	.90
❑ 484	Gary Nolan	3.00	1.35
❑ 485	Jay Johnstone	3.00	1.35
❑ 486	Terry Harmon	2.00	.90
❑ 487	Cisco Carlos	2.00	.90
❑ 488	J.C. Martin	2.00	.90
❑ 489	Eddie Kasko MG	2.00	.90
❑ 490	Bill Singer	3.00	1.35
❑ 491	Graig Nettles	5.00	2.20
❑ 492	Astros Rookies	2.00	.90
	Keith Lampard		
	Scipio Spinks		
❑ 493	Lindy McDaniel	3.00	1.35
❑ 494	Larry Stahl	2.00	.90
❑ 495	Dave Morehead	2.00	.90
❑ 496	Steve Whitaker	2.00	.90
❑ 497	Eddie Watt	2.00	.90
❑ 498	Al Weis	2.00	.90
❑ 499	Skip Lockwood	3.00	1.35
❑ 500	Hank Aaron	50.00	22.00
❑ 501	Chicago White Sox	3.50	1.55
	Team Card		
❑ 502	Rollie Fingers	10.00	4.50
❑ 503	Dal Maxvill	2.00	.90
❑ 504	Don Pavletich	2.00	.90
❑ 505	Ken Holtzman	3.00	1.35
❑ 506	Ed Stroud	2.00	.90
❑ 507	Pat Corrales	3.00	1.35
❑ 508	Joe Niekro	3.00	1.35
❑ 509	Montreal Expos	3.50	1.55
	Team Card		
❑ 510	Tony Oliva	3.00	1.35
❑ 511	Joe Hoerner	2.00	.90
❑ 512	Billy Harris	2.00	.90
❑ 513	Preston Gomez MG	2.00	.90
❑ 514	Steve Hovley	2.00	.90
❑ 515	Don Wilson	3.00	1.35
❑ 516	Yankees Rookies	2.00	.90
	John Ellis		
	Jim Lyttle		
❑ 517	Joe Gibbon	2.00	.90
❑ 518	Bill Melton	2.00	.90
❑ 519	Don McMahon	2.00	.90
❑ 520	Willie Horton	3.00	1.35
❑ 521	Cal Koonce	2.00	.90
❑ 522	Angels Team	3.50	1.55
❑ 523	Jose Pena	2.00	.90
❑ 524	Alvin Dark MG	3.00	1.35
❑ 525	Jerry Adair	2.00	.90
❑ 526	Ron Herbel	2.00	.90
❑ 527	Don Bosch	2.00	.90
❑ 528	Elrod Hendricks	2.00	.90
❑ 529	Bob Aspromonte	2.00	.90
❑ 530	Bob Gibson	14.00	6.25
❑ 531	Ron Clark	2.00	.90
❑ 532	Danny Murtaugh MG	3.00	1.35
❑ 533	Buzz Stephen	2.00	.90
❑ 534	Minnesota Twins	3.50	1.55
	Team Card		
❑ 535	Andy Kosco	2.00	.90
❑ 536	Mike Kekich	2.00	.90
❑ 537	Joe Morgan	10.00	4.50
❑ 538	Bob Humphreys	2.00	.90
❑ 539	Phillies Rookies	8.00	3.60
	Denny Doyle		
	Larry Bowa		
❑ 540	Gary Peters	2.00	.90
❑ 541	Bill Heath	2.00	.90
❑ 542	Checklist 6	6.00	1.20
❑ 543	Clyde Wright	2.00	.90
❑ 544	Cincinnati Reds	3.50	1.55
	Team Card		
❑ 545	Ken Harrelson	3.00	1.35
❑ 546	Ron Reed	2.00	.90
❑ 547	Rick Monday	6.00	2.70
❑ 548	Howie Reed	4.00	1.80
❑ 549	St. Louis Cardinals	6.00	2.70
	Team Card		
❑ 550	Frank Howard	6.00	2.70
❑ 551	Dock Ellis	6.00	2.70
❑ 552	Royals Rookies	4.00	1.80
	Don O'Riley		
	Dennis Paepke		
	Fred Rico		
❑ 553	Jim Lefebvre	6.00	2.70
❑ 554	Tom Timmermann	4.00	1.80
❑ 555	Orlando Cepeda	6.00	2.70
❑ 556	Dave Bristol MG	4.00	1.80
❑ 557	Ed Kranepool	4.00	1.80
❑ 558	Vern Fuller	4.00	1.80
❑ 559	Tommy Davis	6.00	2.70
❑ 560	Gaylord Perry	12.00	5.50
❑ 561	Tom McCraw	4.00	1.80
❑ 562	Ted Abernathy	4.00	1.80
❑ 563	Boston Red Sox	6.00	2.70
	Team Card		
❑ 564	Johnny Briggs	4.00	1.80
❑ 565	Jim Hunter	12.00	5.50
❑ 566	Gene Alley	6.00	2.70
❑ 567	Bob Oliver	4.00	1.80
❑ 568	Stan Bahnsen	4.00	1.80
❑ 569	Cookie Rojas	6.00	2.70
❑ 570	Jim Fregosi	6.00	2.70
	White Chevy Pick-Up in Background		
❑ 571	Jim Brewer	4.00	1.80
❑ 572	Frank Quilici MG	4.00	1.80
❑ 573	Padres Rookies	4.00	1.80
	Mike Corkins		
	Rafael Robles		
	Ron Slocum		
❑ 574	Bobby Bolin	6.00	2.70
❑ 575	Cleon Jones	6.00	2.70
❑ 576	Milt Pappas	6.00	2.70
❑ 577	Bernie Allen	4.00	1.80
❑ 578	Tom Griffin	4.00	1.80
❑ 579	Detroit Tigers	6.00	2.70
	Team Card		
❑ 580	Pete Rose	45.00	20.00
❑ 581	Tom Satriano	4.00	1.80
❑ 582	Mike Paul	4.00	1.80
❑ 583	Hal Lanier	4.00	1.80
❑ 584	Al Downing	6.00	2.70
❑ 585	Rusty Staub	8.00	3.60
❑ 586	Rickey Clark	4.00	1.80

☐ 587	Jose Arcia	4.00	1.80
☐ 588A	Checklist 7 ERR	8.00	1.60
	(666 Adolfo)		
☐ 588B	Checklist 7 COR	6.00	1.20
	(666 Adolpho)		
☐ 589	Joe Keough	4.00	1.80
☐ 590	Mike Cuellar	6.00	2.70
☐ 591	Mike Ryan UER	4.00	1.80
	(Pitching Record header on card back)		
☐ 592	Daryl Patterson	4.00	1.80
☐ 593	Chicago Cubs	8.00	3.60
	Team Card		
☐ 594	Jake Gibbs	4.00	1.80
☐ 595	Maury Wills	8.00	3.60
☐ 596	Mike Hershberger	6.00	2.70
☐ 597	Sonny Siebert	4.00	1.80
☐ 598	Joe Pepitone	6.00	2.70
☐ 599	Senators Rookies	4.00	1.80
	Dick Stelmaszek		
	Gene Martin		
	Dick Such		
☐ 600	Willie Mays	70.00	32.00
☐ 601	Pete Richert	4.00	1.80
☐ 602	Ted Savage	4.00	1.80
☐ 603	Ray Oyler	4.00	1.80
☐ 604	Clarence Gaston	6.00	2.70
☐ 605	Rick Wise	6.00	2.70
☐ 606	Chico Ruiz	4.00	1.80
☐ 607	Gary Waslewski	4.00	1.80
☐ 608	Pittsburgh Pirates	6.00	2.70
	Team Card		
☐ 609	Buck Martinez	6.00	2.70
	(Inconsistent design card number in white circle)		
☐ 610	Jerry Koosman	8.00	3.60
☐ 611	Norm Cash	6.00	2.70
☐ 612	Jim Hickman	6.00	2.70
☐ 613	Dave Baldwin	6.00	2.70
☐ 614	Mike Shannon	6.00	2.70
☐ 615	Mark Belanger	6.00	2.70
☐ 616	Jim Merritt	4.00	1.80
☐ 617	Jim French	4.00	1.80
☐ 618	Billy Wynne	4.00	1.80
☐ 619	Norm Miller	4.00	1.80
☐ 620	Jim Perry	6.00	2.70
☐ 621	Braves Rookies	12.00	5.50
	Mike McQueen		
	Darrell Evans		
	Rick Kester		
☐ 622	Don Sutton	12.00	5.50
☐ 623	Horace Clarke	6.00	2.70
☐ 624	Clyde King MG	4.00	1.80
☐ 625	Dean Chance	4.00	1.80
☐ 626	Dave Ricketts	4.00	1.80
☐ 627	Gary Wagner	4.00	1.80
☐ 628	Wayne Garrett	4.00	1.80
☐ 629	Merv Rettenmund	4.00	1.80
☐ 630	Ernie Banks	50.00	22.00
☐ 631	Oakland Athletics	6.00	2.70
	Team Card		
☐ 632	Gary Sutherland	4.00	1.80
☐ 633	Roger Nelson	4.00	1.80
☐ 634	Bud Harrelson	15.00	6.75
☐ 635	Bob Allison	15.00	6.75
☐ 636	Jim Stewart	10.00	4.50
☐ 637	Cleveland Indians	12.00	5.50
	Team Card		
☐ 638	Frank Bertaina	10.00	4.50
☐ 639	Dave Campbell	10.00	4.50
☐ 640	Al Kaline	50.00	22.00
☐ 641	Al McBean	10.00	4.50
☐ 642	Angels Rookies	10.00	4.50
	Greg Garrett		
	Gordon Lund		
	Jarvis Tatum		
☐ 643	Jose Pagan	10.00	4.50
☐ 644	Gerry Nyman	10.00	4.50
☐ 645	Don Money	15.00	6.75
☐ 646	Jim Britton	10.00	4.50
☐ 647	Tom Matchick	10.00	4.50
☐ 648	Larry Haney	10.00	4.50
☐ 649	Jimmie Hall	10.00	4.50
☐ 650	Sam McDowell	15.00	6.75
☐ 651	Jim Gosger	10.00	4.50
☐ 652	Rich Rollins	15.00	6.75
☐ 653	Moe Drabowsky	10.00	4.50
☐ 654	NL Rookies	15.00	6.75
	Oscar Gamble		
	Boots Day		
	Angel Mangual		
☐ 655	John Roseboro	15.00	6.75
☐ 656	Jim Hardin	10.00	4.50
☐ 657	San Diego Padres	12.00	5.50
	Team Card		
☐ 658	Ken Tatum	10.00	4.50
☐ 659	Pete Ward	10.00	4.50
☐ 660	Johnny Bench	80.00	36.00
☐ 661	Jerry Robertson	10.00	4.50
☐ 662	Frank Lucchesi MG	10.00	4.50
☐ 663	Tito Francona	10.00	4.50
☐ 664	Bob Robertson	10.00	4.50
☐ 665	Jim Lonborg	15.00	6.75
☐ 666	Adolpho Phillips	10.00	4.50
☐ 667	Bob Meyer	15.00	6.75
☐ 668	Bill Stillman	10.00	4.50
☐ 669	White Sox Rookies	10.00	4.50
	Bart Johnson		
	Dan Lazar		
	Mickey Scott		
☐ 670	Ron Santo	15.00	6.75
☐ 671	Jim Campanis	10.00	4.50
☐ 672	Leon McFadden	10.00	4.50
☐ 673	Ted Uhlaender	10.00	4.50
☐ 674	Dave Leonhard	10.00	4.50
☐ 675	Jose Cardenal	15.00	6.75
☐ 676	Washington Senators	12.00	5.50
	Team Card		
☐ 677	Woodie Fryman	10.00	4.50
☐ 678	Dave Duncan	15.00	6.75
☐ 679	Ray Sadecki	10.00	4.50
☐ 680	Rico Petrocelli	15.00	6.75
☐ 681	Bob Garibaldi	10.00	4.50
☐ 682	Dalton Jones	10.00	4.50
☐ 683	Reds Rookies	15.00	6.75
	Vern Geishert		
	Hal McRae		
	Wayne Simpson		
☐ 684	Jack Fisher	10.00	4.50
☐ 685	Tom Haller	10.00	4.50
☐ 686	Jackie Hernandez	10.00	4.50
☐ 687	Bob Priddy	10.00	4.50
☐ 688	Ted Kubiak	15.00	6.75
☐ 689	Ron Fairly	15.00	6.75
☐ 690	Joe Grzenda	10.00	4.50
☐ 691	Duffy Dyer	10.00	4.50
☐ 692	Bob Johnson	10.00	4.50
☐ 693	Gary Ross	10.00	4.50
☐ 694	Bobby Knoop	10.00	4.50
☐ 695	San Francisco Giants	12.00	5.50
	Team Card		
☐ 696	Jim Hannan	10.00	4.50
☐ 697	Tom Tresh	15.00	6.75
☐ 698	Hank Aguirre	10.00	4.50
☐ 699	Frank Robinson	50.00	22.00
☐ 700	Jack Billingham	10.00	4.50
☐ 701	AL Rookies	10.00	4.50
☐ 702	Bob Johnson		
	Ron Klimkowski		
	Bill Zepp		
☐ 703	Lou Marone	10.00	4.50
☐ 704	Frank Baker	10.00	4.50
☐ 705	Tony Cloninger UER	10.00	4.50
	(Batter headings on card back)		
☐ 706	John McNamara MG	10.00	4.50
☐ 707	Kevin Collins	10.00	4.50
☐ 708	Jose Santiago	10.00	4.50
☐ 709	Mike Fiore	10.00	4.50
☐ 710	Felix Millan	10.00	4.50
☐ 711	Ed Brinkman	10.00	4.50
☐ 712	Nolan Ryan	250.00	110.00
☐ 713	Seattle Pilots	25.00	11.00
	Team Card		
☐ 714	Al Spangler	10.00	4.50
☐ 715	Mickey Lolich	15.00	6.75
☐ 716	Cardinals Rookies	15.00	4.50
	Sal Campisi		
	Reggie Cleveland		
	Santiago Guzman		
☐ 717	Tom Phoebus	10.00	4.50
☐ 718	Ed Spiezio	10.00	4.50
☐ 719	Jim Roland	10.00	4.50
☐ 720	Rick Reichardt	15.00	5.00

1971 Topps

	NRMT	VG-E
COMPLETE SET (752)	2000.00	900.00
COMMON CARD (1-393)	1.50	.70
MINOR STARS 1-393	2.00	.90
SEMISTARS 1-393	4.00	1.80
UNLISTED STARS 1-393	6.00	2.70
COMMON CARD (394-523)	2.50	1.10
MINOR STARS 394-523	4.00	1.80
SEMISTARS 394-523	6.00	2.70
UNLISTED STARS 394-523	10.00	4.50
COMMON CARD (524-643)	4.00	1.80
MINOR STARS 524-643	6.00	2.70
SEMISTARS 524-643	8.00	3.60
UNLISTED STARS 524-643	12.00	5.50
COMMON CARD (644-752)	8.00	3.60
COMMON SP (644-752)	12.00	5.50
MINOR STARS 644-752	12.00	5.50
SEMISTARS 644-752	15.00	6.75
CARDS PRICED IN NM CONDITION !		

☐ 1	Baltimore Orioles	15.00	5.00
	Team Card		
☐ 2	Dock Ellis	1.50	.70
☐ 3	Dick McAuliffe	1.50	.70
☐ 4	Vic Davalillo	1.50	.70
☐ 5	Thurman Munson	18.00	8.00
☐ 6	Ed Spiezio	1.50	.70
☐ 7	Jim Holt	1.50	.70
☐ 8	Mike McQueen	1.50	.70
☐ 9	George Scott	2.00	.90
☐ 10	Claude Osteen	1.50	.70
☐ 11	Elliott Maddox	2.00	.90
☐ 12	Johnny Callison	2.00	.90
☐ 13	White Sox Rookies	1.50	.70
	Charlie Brinkman		
	Dick Moloney		
☐ 14	Dave Concepcion	15.00	6.75
☐ 15	Andy Messersmith	2.00	.90
☐ 16	Ken Singleton	4.00	1.80
☐ 17	Billy Sorrell	1.50	.70
☐ 18	Norm Miller	1.50	.70
☐ 19	Skip Pitlock	1.50	.70
☐ 20	Reggie Jackson	25.00	11.00
☐ 21	Dan McGinn	1.50	.70
☐ 22	Phil Roof	1.50	.70
☐ 23	Oscar Gamble	1.50	.70
☐ 24	Rich Hand	1.50	.70
☐ 25	Clarence Gaston	2.00	.90
☐ 26	Bert Blyleven	8.00	3.60
☐ 27	Pirates Rookies	1.50	.70
	Fred Cambria		
	Gene Clines		
☐ 28	Ron Klimkowski	1.50	.70
☐ 29	Don Buford	1.50	.70
☐ 30	Phil Niekro	6.00	2.70
☐ 31	Eddie Kasko MG	1.50	.70
☐ 32	Jerry DaVanon	1.50	.70
☐ 33	Del Unser	1.50	.70
☐ 34	Sandy Vance	1.50	.70
☐ 35	Lou Piniella	2.00	.90
☐ 36	Dean Chance	1.50	.70

37	Rich McKinney	1.50	.70
38	Jim Colborn	1.50	.70
39	Tiger Rookies	1.50	.70
	Lerrin LaGrow		
	Gene Lamont		
40	Lee May	2.00	.90
41	Rick Austin	1.50	.70
42	Boots Day	1.50	.70
43	Steve Kealey	1.50	.70
44	Johnny Edwards	1.50	.70
45	Jim Hunter	6.00	2.70
46	Dave Campbell	1.50	.70
47	Johnny Jeter	1.50	.70
48	Dave Baldwin	1.50	.70
49	Don Money	1.50	.70
50	Willie McCovey	8.00	3.60
51	Steve Kline	1.50	.70
52	Braves Rookies	1.50	.70
	Oscar Brown		
	Earl Williams		
53	Paul Blair	2.00	.90
54	Checklist 1	11.00	2.20
55	Steve Carlton	15.00	6.75
56	Duane Josephson	1.50	.70
57	Von Joshua	1.50	.70
58	Bill Lee	2.00	.90
59	Gene Mauch MG	2.00	.90
60	Dick Dosman	1.50	.70
61	AL Batting Leaders	4.00	1.80
	Alex Johnson		
	Carl Yastrzemski		
	Tony Oliva		
62	NL Batting Leaders	2.00	.90
	Rico Carty		
	Joe Torre		
	Manny Sanguillen		
63	AL RBI Leaders	4.00	1.80
	Frank Howard		
	Tony Conigliaro		
	Boog Powell		
64	NL RBI Leaders	6.00	2.70
	Johnny Bench		
	Tony Perez		
	Billy Williams		
65	AL HR Leaders	4.00	1.80
	Frank Howard		
	Harmon Killebrew		
	Carl Yastrzemski		
66	NL HR Leaders	6.00	2.70
	Johnny Bench		
	Billy Williams		
	Tony Perez		
67	AL ERA Leaders	4.00	1.80
	Diego Segui		
	Jim Palmer		
	Clyde Wright		
68	NL ERA Leaders	4.00	1.80
	Tom Seaver		
	Wayne Simpson		
	Luke Walker		
69	AL Pitching Leaders	2.00	.90
	Mike Cuellar		
	Dave McNally		
	Jim Perry		
70	NL Pitching Leaders	6.00	2.70
	Bob Gibson		
	Gaylord Perry		
	Fergie Jenkins		
71	AL Strikeout Leaders	2.00	.90
	Sam McDowell		
	Mickey Lolich		
	Bob Johnson		
72	NL Strikeout Leaders	6.00	2.70
	Tom Seaver		
	Bob Gibson		
	Fergie Jenkins		
73	George Brunet	1.50	.70
74	Twins Rookies	1.50	.70
	Pete Hamm		
	Jim Nettles		
75	Gary Nolan	2.00	.90
76	Ted Savage	1.50	.70
77	Mike Compton	1.50	.70
78	Jim Spencer	1.50	.70
79	Wade Blasingame	1.50	.70
80	Bill Melton	1.50	.70
81	Felix Millan	1.50	.70
82	Casey Cox	1.50	.70
83	Met Rookies	1.50	.70
	Tim Foli		
	Randy Bobb		
84	Marcel Lachemann	1.50	.70
85	Billy Grabarkewitz	1.50	.70
86	Mike Kilkenny	1.50	.70
87	Jack Heidemann	1.50	.70
88	Hal King	1.50	.70
89	Ken Brett	1.50	.70
90	Joe Pepitone	2.00	.90
91	Bob Lemon MG	2.00	.90
92	Fred Wenz	1.50	.70
93	Senators Rookies	1.50	.70
	Norm McRae		
	Denny Riddleberger		
94	Don Hahn	1.50	.70
95	Luis Tiant	2.00	.90
96	Joe Hague	1.50	.70
97	Floyd Wicker	1.50	.70
98	Joe Decker	1.50	.70
99	Mark Belanger	2.00	.90
100	Pete Rose	25.00	11.00
101	Les Cain	1.50	.70
102	Astros Rookies	2.00	.90
	Ken Forsch		
	Larry Howard		
103	Rich Severson	1.50	.70
104	Dan Frisella	1.50	.70
105	Tony Conigliaro	2.00	.90
106	Tom Dukes	1.50	.70
107	Roy Foster	1.50	.70
108	John Cumberland	1.50	.70
109	Steve Hovley	1.50	.70
110	Bill Mazeroski	2.00	.90
111	Yankee Rookies	1.50	.70
	Loyd Colson		
	Bobby Mitchell		
112	Manny Mota	2.00	.90
113	Jerry Crider	1.50	.70
114	Billy Conigliaro	2.00	.90
115	Donn Clendenon	2.00	.90
116	Ken Sanders	1.50	.70
117	Ted Simmons	8.00	3.60
118	Cookie Rojas	2.00	.90
119	Frank Lucchesi MG	1.50	.70
120	Willie Horton	2.00	.90
121	Cubs Rookies	1.50	.70
	Jim Dunegan		
	Roe Skidmore		
122	Eddie Watt	1.50	.70
123A	Checklist 2	11.00	2.20
	(Card number at bottom right)		
123B	Checklist 2	11.00	2.20
	(Card number centered)		
124	Don Gullett	2.00	.90
125	Ray Fosse	2.00	.90
126	Danny Coombs	1.50	.70
127	Danny Thompson	2.00	.90
128	Frank Johnson	1.50	.70
129	Aurelio Monteagudo	1.50	.70
130	Denis Menke	1.50	.70
131	Curt Blefary	1.50	.70
132	Jose Laboy	1.50	.70
133	Mickey Lolich	2.00	.90
134	Jose Arcia	1.50	.70
135	Rick Monday	2.00	.90
136	Duffy Dyer	1.50	.70
137	Marcelino Lopez	1.50	.70
138	Phillies Rookies	2.00	.90
	Joe Lis		
	Willie Montanez		
139	Paul Casanova	1.50	.70
140	Gaylord Perry	6.00	2.70
141	Frank Quilici	1.50	.70
142	Mack Jones	1.50	.70
143	Steve Blass	2.00	.90
144	Jackie Hernandez	1.50	.70
145	Bill Singer	2.00	.90
146	Ralph Houk MG	2.00	.90
147	Bob Priddy	1.50	.70
148	John Mayberry	2.00	.90
149	Mike Hershberger	1.50	.70
150	Sam McDowell	2.00	.90
151	Tommy Davis	2.00	.90
152	Angels Rookies	1.50	.70
	Lloyd Allen		
	Winston Llenas		
153	Gary Ross	1.50	.70
154	Cesar Gutierrez	1.50	.70
155	Ken Henderson	1.50	.70
156	Bart Johnson	1.50	.70
157	Bob Bailey	1.50	.70
158	Jerry Reuss	2.00	.90
159	Jarvis Tatum	1.50	.70
160	Tom Seaver	20.00	9.00
161	Coin Checklist	11.00	2.20
162	Jack Billingham	1.50	.70
163	Buck Martinez	2.00	.90
164	Reds Rookies	2.00	.90
	Frank Duffy		
	Milt Wilcox		
165	Cesar Tovar	1.50	.70
166	Joe Hoerner	1.50	.70
167	Tom Grieve	2.00	.90
168	Bruce Dal Canton	1.50	.70
169	Ed Herrmann	1.50	.70
170	Mike Cuellar	2.00	.90
171	Bobby Wine	1.50	.70
172	Duke Sims	1.50	.70
173	Gil Garrido	1.50	.70
174	Dave LaRoche	1.50	.70
175	Jim Hickman	1.50	.70
176	Red Sox Rookies	2.00	.90
	Bob Montgomery		
	Doug Griffin		
177	Hal McRae	2.00	.90
178	Dave Duncan	1.50	.70
179	Mike Corkins	1.50	.70
180	Al Kaline UER	20.00	9.00
	(Home instead of Birth)		
181	Hal Lanier	2.00	.70
182	Al Downing	2.00	.90
183	Gil Hodges MG	4.00	1.80
184	Stan Bahnsen	1.50	.70
185	Julian Javier	2.00	.90
186	Bob Spence	1.50	.70
187	Ted Abernathy	1.50	.70
188	Dodgers Rookies	4.00	1.80
	Bob Valentine		
	Mike Strahler		
189	George Mitterwald	1.50	.70
190	Bob Tolan	2.00	.90
191	Mike Andrews	1.50	.70
192	Billy Wilson	1.50	.70
193	Bob Grich	4.00	1.80
194	Mike Lum	1.50	.70
195	Boog Powell ALCS	2.00	.90
196	Dave McNally ALCS	2.00	.90
197	Jim Palmer ALCS	4.00	1.80
198	AL Playoff Summary	2.00	.90
	Orioles celebrate		
199	Ty Cline NLCS	2.00	.90
200	Bobby Tolan NLCS	2.00	.90
201	Ty Cline NLCS	2.00	.90
202	NL Playoff Summary	2.00	.90
	Reds celebrate		
203	Larry Gura	2.00	.90
204	Brewers Rookies	1.50	.70
	Bernie Smith		
	George Kopacz		
205	Gerry Moses	1.50	.70
206	Checklist 3	11.00	2.20
207	Alan Foster	1.50	.70
208	Billy Martin MG	4.00	1.80
209	Steve Renko	1.50	.70
210	Rod Carew	15.00	6.75
211	Phil Hennigan	1.50	.70
212	Rich Hebner	2.00	.90
213	Frank Baker	1.50	.70
214	Al Ferrara	1.50	.70
215	Diego Segui	1.50	.70
216	Cards Rookies	1.50	.70
	Reggie Cleveland		
	Luis Melendez		
217	Ed Stroud	1.50	.70
218	Tony Cloninger	1.50	.70
219	Elrod Hendricks	1.50	.70

❑ 220	Ron Santo	2.00	.90
❑ 221	Dave Morehead	1.50	.70
❑ 222	Bob Watson	2.00	.90
❑ 223	Cecil Upshaw	1.50	.70
❑ 224	Alan Gallagher	1.50	.70
❑ 225	Gary Peters	1.50	.70
❑ 226	Bill Russell	2.00	.90
❑ 227	Floyd Weaver	1.50	.70
❑ 228	Wayne Garrett	1.50	.70
❑ 229	Jim Hannan	1.50	.70
❑ 230	Willie Stargell	8.00	3.60
❑ 231	Indians Rookies	1.50	.70
	Vince Colbert		
	John Lowenstein		
❑ 232	John Strohmayer	1.50	.70
❑ 233	Larry Bowa	2.00	.90
❑ 234	Jim Lyttle	1.50	.70
❑ 235	Nate Colbert	1.50	.70
❑ 236	Bob Humphreys	1.50	.70
❑ 237	Cesar Cedeno	2.00	.90
❑ 238	Chuck Dobson	1.50	.70
❑ 239	Red Schoendienst MG	2.00	.90
❑ 240	Clyde Wright	1.50	.70
❑ 241	Dave Nelson	1.50	.70
❑ 242	Jim Ray	1.50	.70
❑ 243	Carlos May	2.00	.90
❑ 244	Bob Tillman	1.50	.70
❑ 245	Jim Kaat	2.00	.90
❑ 246	Tony Taylor	1.50	.90
❑ 247	Royals Rookies	2.00	.90
	Jerry Cram		
	Paul Splittorff		
❑ 248	Hoyt Wilhelm	4.00	1.80
❑ 249	Chico Salmon	1.50	.70
❑ 250	Johnny Bench	20.00	9.00
❑ 251	Frank Reberger	1.50	.70
❑ 252	Eddie Leon	1.50	.70
❑ 253	Bill Sudakis	1.50	.70
❑ 254	Cal Koonce	1.50	.70
❑ 255	Bob Robertson	2.00	.90
❑ 256	Tony Gonzalez	1.50	.70
❑ 257	Nelson Briles	1.50	.70
❑ 258	Dick Green	1.50	.70
❑ 259	Dave Marshall	1.50	.70
❑ 260	Tommy Harper	2.00	.90
❑ 261	Darold Knowles	1.50	.70
❑ 262	Padres Rookies	1.50	.70
	Jim Williams		
	Dave Robinson		
❑ 263	John Ellis	1.50	.70
❑ 264	Joe Morgan	8.00	3.60
❑ 265	Jim Northrup	2.00	.90
❑ 266	Bill Stoneman	1.50	.70
❑ 267	Rich Morales	1.50	.70
❑ 268	Philadelphia Phillies	4.00	1.80
	Team Card		
❑ 269	Gail Hopkins	1.50	.70
❑ 270	Rico Carty	2.00	.90
❑ 271	Bill Zepp	1.50	.70
❑ 272	Tommy Helms	2.00	.90
❑ 273	Pete Richert	1.50	.70
❑ 274	Ron Slocum	1.50	.70
❑ 275	Vada Pinson	2.00	.90
❑ 276	Giants Rookies	8.00	3.60
	Mike Davison		
	George Foster		
❑ 277	Gary Waslewski	1.50	.70
❑ 278	Jerry Grote	1.50	.70
❑ 279	Lefty Phillips MG	1.50	.70
❑ 280	Ferguson Jenkins	6.00	2.70
❑ 281	Danny Walton	1.50	.70
❑ 282	Jose Pagan	1.50	.70
❑ 283	Dick Such	1.50	.70
❑ 284	Jim Grosger	1.50	.70
❑ 285	Sal Bando	2.00	.90
❑ 286	Jerry McNertney	1.50	.70
❑ 287	Mike Fiore	1.50	.70
❑ 288	Joe Moeller	1.50	.70
❑ 289	Chicago White Sox	2.00	.90
	Team Card		
❑ 290	Tony Oliva	2.00	.90
❑ 291	George Culver	1.50	.70
❑ 292	Jay Johnstone	2.00	.90
❑ 293	Pat Corrales	1.50	.70
❑ 294	Steve Dunning	1.50	.70
❑ 295	Bobby Bonds	4.00	1.80
❑ 296	Tom Timmermann	1.50	.70
❑ 297	Johnny Briggs	1.50	.70
❑ 298	Jim Nelson	1.50	.70
❑ 299	Ed Kirkpatrick	1.50	.70
❑ 300	Brooks Robinson	20.00	9.00
❑ 301	Earl Wilson	1.50	.70
❑ 302	Phil Gagliano	1.50	.70
❑ 303	Lindy McDaniel	2.00	.90
❑ 304	Ron Brand	1.50	.70
❑ 305	Reggie Smith	2.00	.90
❑ 306	Jim Nash	1.50	.70
❑ 307	Don Wert	1.50	.70
❑ 308	St. Louis Cardinals	2.00	.90
	Team Card		
❑ 309	Dick Ellsworth	1.50	.70
❑ 310	Tommie Agee	2.00	.90
❑ 311	Lee Stange	1.50	.70
❑ 312	Harry Walker MG	1.50	.70
❑ 313	Tom Hall	1.50	.70
❑ 314	Jeff Torborg	2.00	.90
❑ 315	Ron Fairly	2.00	.90
❑ 316	Fred Scherman	1.50	.70
❑ 317	Athletic Rookies	1.50	.70
	Jim Driscoll		
	Angel Mangual		
❑ 318	Rudy May	1.50	.70
❑ 319	Ty Cline	1.50	.70
❑ 320	Dave McNally	2.00	.90
❑ 321	Tom Matchick	1.50	.70
❑ 322	Jim Beauchamp	1.50	.70
❑ 323	Billy Champion	1.50	.70
❑ 324	Graig Nettles	2.00	.90
❑ 325	Juan Marichal	6.00	2.70
❑ 326	Richie Scheinblum	1.50	.70
❑ 327	Boog Powell WS	2.00	.90
❑ 328	Don Buford WS	1.50	.70
❑ 329	Frank Robinson WS	4.00	1.80
❑ 330	World Series Game 4	2.00	.90
	Reds stay alive		
❑ 331	Brooks Robinson WS	6.00	2.70
	commits robbery		
❑ 332	World Series Summary	2.00	.90
	Orioles celebrate		
❑ 333	Clay Kirby	1.50	.70
❑ 334	Roberto Pena	1.50	.70
❑ 335	Jerry Koosman	2.00	.90
❑ 336	Detroit Tigers	2.00	.90
	Team Card		
❑ 337	Jesus Alou	1.50	.70
❑ 338	Gene Tenace	2.00	.90
❑ 339	Wayne Simpson	1.50	.70
❑ 340	Rico Petrocelli	2.00	.90
❑ 341	Steve Garvey	30.00	13.50
❑ 342	Frank Tepedino	1.50	.70
❑ 343	Pirates Rookies	1.50	.70
	Ed Acosta		
	Milt May		
❑ 344	Ellie Rodriguez	1.50	.70
❑ 345	Joel Horlen	1.50	.70
❑ 346	Lum Harris MG	1.50	.70
❑ 347	Ted Uhlaender	1.50	.70
❑ 348	Fred Norman	1.50	.70
❑ 349	Rich Reese	1.50	.70
❑ 350	Billy Williams	6.00	2.70
❑ 351	Jim Shellenback	1.50	.70
❑ 352	Denny Doyle	1.50	.70
❑ 353	Carl Taylor	1.50	.70
❑ 354	Don McMahon	1.50	.70
❑ 355	Bud Harrelson	4.00	1.80
	(Nolan Ryan in photo)		
❑ 356	Bob Locker	1.50	.70
❑ 357	Cincinnati Reds	2.00	.90
	Team Card		
❑ 358	Danny Cater	1.50	.70
❑ 359	Ron Reed	1.50	.70
❑ 360	Jim Fregosi	2.00	.90
❑ 361	Don Sutton	6.00	2.70
❑ 362	Orioles Rookies	1.50	.70
	Mike Adamson		
	Roger Freed		
❑ 363	Mike Nagy	1.50	.70
❑ 364	Tommy Dean	1.50	.70
❑ 365	Bob Johnson	1.50	.70
❑ 366	Ron Stone	1.50	.70
❑ 367	Dalton Jones	1.50	.70
❑ 368	Bob Veale	2.00	.90
❑ 369	Checklist 4	11.00	2.20
❑ 370	Joe Torre	2.00	.90
❑ 371	Jack Hiatt	1.50	.70
❑ 372	Lew Krausse	1.50	.70
❑ 373	Tom McCraw	1.50	.70
❑ 374	Clete Boyer	2.00	.90
❑ 375	Steve Hargan	1.50	.70
❑ 376	Expos Rookies	1.50	.70
	Clyde Mashore		
	Ernie McAnally		
❑ 377	Greg Garrett	1.50	.70
❑ 378	Tito Fuentes	1.50	.70
❑ 379	Wayne Granger	1.50	.70
❑ 380	Ted Williams MG	12.00	5.50
❑ 381	Fred Gladding	1.50	.70
❑ 382	Jake Gibbs	1.50	.70
❑ 383	Rod Gaspar	1.50	.70
❑ 384	Rollie Fingers	6.00	2.70
❑ 385	Maury Wills	2.00	.90
❑ 386	Boston Red Sox	2.00	.90
	Team Card		
❑ 387	Ron Herbel	1.50	.70
❑ 388	Al Oliver	2.00	.90
❑ 389	Ed Brinkman	1.50	.70
❑ 390	Glenn Beckert	2.00	.90
❑ 391	Twins Rookies	2.00	.90
	Steve Brye		
	Cotton Nash		
❑ 392	Grant Jackson	1.50	.70
❑ 393	Merv Rettenmund	2.00	.90
❑ 394	Clay Carroll	2.50	1.10
❑ 395	Roy White	4.00	1.80
❑ 396	Dick Schofield	2.50	1.10
❑ 397	Alvin Dark MG	4.00	1.80
❑ 398	Howie Reed	2.50	1.10
❑ 399	Jim French	2.50	1.10
❑ 400	Hank Aaron	50.00	22.00
❑ 401	Tom Murphy	2.50	1.10
❑ 402	Los Angeles Dodgers	5.00	2.20
	Team Card		
❑ 403	Joe Coleman	2.50	1.10
❑ 404	Astros Rookies	2.50	1.10
	Buddy Harris		
	Roger Metzger		
❑ 405	Leo Cardenas	2.50	1.10
❑ 406	Ray Sadecki	2.50	1.10
❑ 407	Joe Rudi	4.00	1.80
❑ 408	Rafael Robles	2.50	1.10
❑ 409	Don Pavletich	2.50	1.10
❑ 410	Ken Holtzman	4.00	1.80
❑ 411	George Spriggs	2.50	1.10
❑ 412	Jerry Johnson	2.50	1.10
❑ 413	Pat Kelly	2.50	1.10
❑ 414	Woodie Fryman	2.50	1.10
❑ 415	Mike Hegan	2.50	1.10
❑ 416	Gene Alley	2.50	1.10
❑ 417	Dick Hall	2.50	1.10
❑ 418	Adolfo Phillips	2.50	1.10
❑ 419	Ron Hansen	2.50	1.10
❑ 420	Jim Merritt	2.50	1.10
❑ 421	John Stephenson	2.50	1.10
❑ 422	Frank Bertaina	2.50	1.10
❑ 423	Tigers Rookies	2.50	1.10
	Dennis Saunders		
	Tim Marting		
❑ 424	Roberto Rodriquez	2.50	1.10
❑ 425	Doug Rader	2.50	1.10
❑ 426	Chris Cannizzaro	2.50	1.10
❑ 427	Bernie Allen	2.50	1.10
❑ 428	Jim McAndrew	2.50	1.10
❑ 429	Chuck Hinton	2.50	1.10
❑ 430	Wes Parker	2.50	1.10
❑ 431	Tom Burgmeier	2.50	1.10
❑ 432	Bob Didier	2.50	1.10
❑ 433	Skip Lockwood	2.50	1.10
❑ 434	Gary Sutherland	2.50	1.10
❑ 435	Jose Cardenal	4.00	1.80
❑ 436	Wilbur Wood	2.50	1.10
❑ 437	Danny Murtaugh MG	4.00	1.80
❑ 438	Mike McCormick	4.00	1.80
❑ 439	Phillies Rookies	6.00	2.70
	Greg Luzinski		
	Scott Reid		
❑ 440	Bert Campaneris	4.00	1.80
❑ 441	Milt Pappas	4.00	1.80
❑ 442	California Angels	4.00	1.80

Card		
Team Card		
❑ 443 Rich Robertson	2.50	1.10
❑ 444 Jimmie Price	2.50	1.10
❑ 445 Art Shamsky	2.50	1.10
❑ 446 Bobby Bolin	2.50	1.10
❑ 447 Cesar Geronimo	4.00	1.80
❑ 448 Dave Roberts	2.50	1.10
❑ 449 Brant Alyea	2.50	1.10
❑ 450 Bob Gibson	15.00	6.75
❑ 451 Joe Keough	2.50	1.10
❑ 452 John Boccabella	2.50	1.10
❑ 453 Terry Crowley	2.50	1.10
❑ 454 Mike Paul	2.50	1.10
❑ 455 Don Kessinger	4.00	1.80
❑ 456 Bob Meyer	2.50	1.10
❑ 457 Willie Smith	2.50	1.10
❑ 458 White Sox Rookies	2.50	1.10
Ron Lolich		
Dave Lemonds		
❑ 459 Jim Lefebvre	2.50	1.10
❑ 460 Fritz Peterson	2.50	1.10
❑ 461 Jim Ray Hart	2.50	1.10
❑ 462 Washington Senators	6.00	2.70
Team Card		
❑ 463 Tom Kelley	2.50	1.10
❑ 464 Aurelio Rodriguez	2.50	1.10
❑ 465 Tim McCarver	6.00	2.70
❑ 466 Ken Berry	2.50	1.10
❑ 467 Al Santorini	2.50	1.10
❑ 468 Frank Fernandez	2.50	1.10
❑ 469 Bob Aspromonte	2.50	1.10
❑ 470 Bob Oliver	2.50	1.10
❑ 471 Tom Griffin	2.50	1.10
❑ 472 Ken Rudolph	2.50	1.10
❑ 473 Gary Wagner	2.50	1.10
❑ 474 Jim Fairey	2.50	1.10
❑ 475 Ron Perranoski	2.50	1.10
❑ 476 Dal Maxvill	2.50	1.10
❑ 477 Earl Weaver MG	6.00	2.70
❑ 478 Bernie Carbo	2.50	1.10
❑ 479 Dennis Higgins	2.50	1.10
❑ 480 Manny Sanguillen	4.00	1.80
❑ 481 Daryl Patterson	2.50	1.10
❑ 482 San Diego Padres	6.00	2.70
Team Card		
❑ 483 Gene Michael	4.00	1.80
❑ 484 Don Wilson	2.50	1.10
❑ 485 Ken McMullen	2.50	1.10
❑ 486 Steve Huntz	2.50	1.10
❑ 487 Paul Schaal	2.50	1.10
❑ 488 Jerry Stephenson	2.50	1.10
❑ 489 Luis Alvarado	2.50	1.10
❑ 490 Deron Johnson	4.00	1.80
❑ 491 Jim Hardin	2.50	1.10
❑ 492 Ken Boswell	2.50	1.10
❑ 493 Dave May	2.50	1.10
❑ 494 Braves Rookies	4.00	1.80
Ralph Garr		
Rick Kester		
❑ 495 Felipe Alou	4.00	1.80
❑ 496 Woody Woodward	2.50	1.10
❑ 497 Horacio Pina	2.50	1.10
❑ 498 John Kennedy	2.50	1.10
❑ 499 Checklist 5	11.00	2.20
❑ 500 Jim Perry	4.00	1.80
❑ 501 Andy Etchebarren	2.50	1.10
❑ 502 Chicago Cubs	5.00	2.20
Team Card		
❑ 503 Gates Brown	4.00	1.80
❑ 504 Ken Wright	2.50	1.10
❑ 505 Ollie Brown	2.50	1.10
❑ 506 Bobby Knoop	2.50	1.10
❑ 507 George Stone	2.50	1.10
❑ 508 Roger Repoz	2.50	1.10
❑ 509 Jim Grant	2.50	1.10
❑ 510 Ken Harrelson	4.00	1.80
❑ 511 Chris Short	4.00	1.80
(Pete Rose leading off second)		
❑ 512 Red Sox Rookies	2.50	1.10
Dick Mills		
Mike Garman		
❑ 513 Nolan Ryan	150.00	70.00
❑ 514 Ron Woods	2.50	1.10
❑ 515 Carl Morton	2.50	1.10
❑ 516 Ted Kubiak	2.50	1.10
❑ 517 Charlie Fox MG	2.50	1.10
❑ 518 Joe Grzenda	2.50	1.10
❑ 519 Willie Crawford	2.50	1.10
❑ 520 Tommy John	6.00	2.70
❑ 521 Leron Lee	2.50	1.10
❑ 522 Minnesota Twins	6.00	2.70
Team Card		
❑ 523 John Odom	2.50	1.10
❑ 524 Mickey Stanley	4.00	1.80
❑ 525 Ernie Banks	50.00	22.00
❑ 526 Ray Jarvis	4.00	1.80
❑ 527 Cleon Jones	4.00	1.80
❑ 528 Wally Bunker	4.00	1.80
❑ 529 NL Rookie Infielders	6.00	2.70
Enzo Hernandez		
Bill Buckner		
Marty Perez		
❑ 530 Carl Yastrzemski	30.00	13.50
❑ 531 Mike Torrez	4.00	1.80
❑ 532 Bill Rigney MG	4.00	1.80
❑ 533 Mike Ryan	4.00	1.80
❑ 534 Luke Walker	4.00	1.80
❑ 535 Curt Flood	6.00	2.70
❑ 536 Claude Raymond	6.00	2.70
❑ 537 Tom Egan	4.00	1.80
❑ 538 Angel Bravo	4.00	1.80
❑ 539 Larry Brown	4.00	1.80
❑ 540 Larry Dierker	6.00	2.70
❑ 541 Bob Burda	4.00	1.80
❑ 542 Bob Miller	4.00	1.80
❑ 543 New York Yankees	10.00	4.50
Team Card		
❑ 544 Vida Blue	6.00	2.70
❑ 545 Dick Dietz	4.00	1.80
❑ 546 John Matias	4.00	1.80
❑ 547 Pat Dobson	6.00	2.70
❑ 548 Don Mason	4.00	1.80
❑ 549 Jim Brewer	6.00	2.70
❑ 550 Harmon Killebrew	25.00	11.00
❑ 551 Frank Linzy	4.00	1.80
❑ 552 Buddy Bradford	4.00	1.80
❑ 553 Kevin Collins	4.00	1.80
❑ 554 Lowell Palmer	4.00	1.80
❑ 555 Walt Williams	4.00	1.80
❑ 556 Jim McGlothlin	4.00	1.80
❑ 557 Tom Satriano	4.00	1.80
❑ 558 Hector Torres	4.00	1.80
❑ 559 AL Rookie Pitchers	4.00	1.80
Terry Cox		
Bill Gogolewski		
Gary Jones		
❑ 560 Rusty Staub	6.00	2.70
❑ 561 Syd O'Brien	4.00	1.80
❑ 562 Dave Giusti	4.00	1.80
❑ 563 San Francisco Giants	8.00	3.60
Team Card		
❑ 564 Al Fitzmorris	4.00	1.80
❑ 565 Jim Wynn	6.00	2.70
❑ 566 Tim Cullen	4.00	1.80
❑ 567 Walt Alston MG	6.00	2.70
❑ 568 Sal Campisi	4.00	1.80
❑ 569 Ivan Murrell	4.00	1.80
❑ 570 Jim Palmer	30.00	13.50
❑ 571 Ted Sizemore	4.00	1.80
❑ 572 Jerry Kenney	4.00	1.80
❑ 573 Ed Kranepool	6.00	2.70
❑ 574 Jim Bunning	8.00	3.60
❑ 575 Bill Freehan	6.00	2.70
❑ 576 Cubs Rookies	4.00	1.80
Adrian Garrett		
Brock Davis		
Garry Jestadt		
❑ 577 Jim Lonborg	6.00	2.70
❑ 578 Ron Hunt	4.00	1.80
❑ 579 Marty Pattin	4.00	1.80
❑ 580 Tony Perez	20.00	9.00
❑ 581 Roger Nelson	4.00	1.80
❑ 582 Dave Cash	6.00	2.70
❑ 583 Ron Cook	4.00	1.80
❑ 584 Cleveland Indians	8.00	3.60
Team Card		
❑ 585 Willie Davis	6.00	2.70
❑ 586 Dick Woodson	4.00	1.80
❑ 587 Sonny Jackson	4.00	1.80
❑ 588 Tom Bradley	4.00	1.80
❑ 589 Bob Barton	4.00	1.80
❑ 590 Alex Johnson	6.00	2.70
❑ 591 Jackie Brown	4.00	1.80
❑ 592 Randy Hundley	6.00	2.70
❑ 593 Jack Aker	4.00	1.80
❑ 594 Cards Rookies	6.00	2.70
Bob Chlupsa		
Bob Stinson		
Al Hrabosky		
❑ 595 Dave Johnson	6.00	2.70
❑ 596 Mike Jorgensen	4.00	1.80
❑ 597 Ken Suarez	4.00	1.80
❑ 598 Rick Wise	6.00	2.70
❑ 599 Norm Cash	6.00	2.70
❑ 600 Willie Mays	100.00	45.00
❑ 601 Ken Tatum	4.00	1.80
❑ 602 Marty Martinez	4.00	1.80
❑ 603 Pittsburgh Pirates	8.00	3.60
Team Card		
❑ 604 John Gelnar	4.00	1.80
❑ 605 Orlando Cepeda	8.00	3.60
❑ 606 Chuck Taylor	4.00	1.80
❑ 607 Paul Ratliff	4.00	1.80
❑ 608 Mike Wegener	4.00	1.80
❑ 609 Leo Durocher MG	8.00	3.60
❑ 610 Amos Otis	6.00	2.70
❑ 611 Tom Phoebus	4.00	1.80
❑ 612 Indians Rookies	4.00	1.80
Lou Camilli		
Ted Ford		
Steve Mingori		
❑ 613 Pedro Borbon	4.00	1.80
❑ 614 Billy Cowan	4.00	1.80
❑ 615 Mel Stottlemyre	6.00	2.70
❑ 616 Larry Hisle	6.00	2.70
❑ 617 Clay Dalrymple	4.00	1.80
❑ 618 Tug McGraw	6.00	2.70
❑ 619A Checklist 6 ERR	11.00	2.20
(No copyright)		
❑ 619B Checklist 6 COR	4.00	1.20
(Copyright on back)		
❑ 620 Frank Howard	6.00	2.70
❑ 621 Ron Bryant	4.00	1.80
❑ 622 Joe Lahoud	4.00	1.80
❑ 623 Pat Jarvis	4.00	1.80
❑ 624 Oakland Athletics	8.00	3.60
Team Card		
❑ 625 Lou Brock	30.00	13.50
❑ 626 Freddie Patek	6.00	2.70
❑ 627 Steve Hamilton	4.00	1.80
❑ 628 John Bateman	4.00	1.80
❑ 629 John Hiller	6.00	2.70
❑ 630 Roberto Clemente	100.00	45.00
❑ 631 Eddie Fisher	4.00	1.80
❑ 632 Darrel Chaney	4.00	1.80
❑ 633 AL Rookie Outfielders	4.00	1.80
Bobby Brooks		
Pete Koegel		
Scott Northey		
❑ 634 Phil Regan	6.00	2.70
❑ 635 Bobby Murcer	6.00	2.70
❑ 636 Denny Lemaster	4.00	1.80
❑ 637 Dave Bristol MG	4.00	1.80
❑ 638 Stan Williams	4.00	1.80
❑ 639 Tom Haller	4.00	1.80
❑ 640 Frank Robinson	40.00	18.00
❑ 641 New York Mets	15.00	6.75
Team Card		
❑ 642 Jim Roland	4.00	1.80
❑ 643 Rick Reichardt	4.00	1.80
❑ 644 Jim Stewart SP	12.00	5.50
❑ 645 Jim Maloney SP	15.00	6.75
❑ 646 Bobby Floyd SP	12.00	5.50
❑ 647 Juan Pizarro	8.00	3.60
❑ 648 Mets Rookies SP	25.00	11.00
Rich Folkers		
Ted Martinez		
John Matlack		
❑ 649 Sparky Lyle SP	15.00	6.75
❑ 650 Rich Allen SP	30.00	13.50
❑ 651 Jerry Robertson SP	12.00	5.50
❑ 652 Atlanta Braves	8.00	3.60
Team Card		
❑ 653 Russ Snyder SP	12.00	5.50
❑ 654 Don Shaw SP	12.00	5.50
❑ 655 Mike Epstein SP	12.00	5.50
❑ 656 Gerry Nyman SP	12.00	5.50
❑ 657 Jose Azcue	8.00	3.60

658 Paul Lindblad SP	12.00	5.50
659 Byron Browne SP	12.00	5.50
660 Ray Culp	8.00	3.60
661 Chuck Tanner MG SP	15.00	6.75
662 Mike Hedlund SP	8.00	3.60
663 Marv Staehle	8.00	3.60
664 Rookie Pitchers SP	15.00	6.75
Archie Reynolds		
Bob Reynolds		
Ken Reynolds		
665 Ron Swoboda SP	15.00	6.75
666 Gene Brabender SP	8.00	3.60
667 Pete Ward	8.00	3.60
668 Gary Neibauer	8.00	3.60
669 Ike Brown SP	15.00	6.75
670 Bill Hands	8.00	3.60
671 Bill Voss SP	12.00	5.50
672 Ed Crosby SP	12.00	5.50
673 Gerry Janeski SP	12.00	5.50
674 Montreal Expos SP	12.00	5.50
Team Card		
675 Dave Boswell	8.00	3.60
676 Tommie Reynolds	8.00	3.60
677 Jack DiLauro SP	12.00	5.50
678 George Thomas	8.00	3.60
679 Don O'Riley	8.00	3.60
680 Don Mincher SP	12.00	5.50
681 Bill Butler	8.00	3.60
682 Terry Harmon	8.00	3.60
683 Bill Burbach SP	12.00	5.50
684 Curt Motton	8.00	3.60
685 Moe Drabowsky	8.00	3.60
686 Chico Ruiz SP	12.00	5.50
687 Ron Taylor SP	12.00	5.50
688 Sparky Anderson MG SP	30.00	13.50
689 Frank Baker	8.00	3.60
690 Bob Moose	8.00	3.60
691 Bobby Heise	8.00	3.60
692 AL Rookie Pitchers SP	12.00	5.50
Hal Haydel		
Rogelio Moret		
Wayne Twitchell		
693 Jose Pena SP	12.00	5.50
694 Rick Renick SP	12.00	5.50
695 Joe Niekro SP	12.00	5.50
696 Jerry Morales	8.00	3.60
697 Rickey Clark SP	12.00	5.50
698 M. Brewers SP	20.00	9.00
Team Card		
699 Jim Britton	8.00	3.60
700 Boog Powell SP	25.00	11.00
701 Bob Garibaldi	8.00	3.60
702 Milt Ramirez	8.00	3.60
703 Mike Kekich	8.00	3.60
704 J.C. Martin SP	12.00	5.50
705 Dick Selma SP	12.00	5.50
706 Joe Foy SP	12.00	5.50
707 Fred Lasher	8.00	3.60
708 Russ Nagelson SP	12.00	5.50
709 Rookie Outfielders SP	80.00	36.00
Dusty Baker		
Don Baylor		
Tom Paciorek		
710 Sonny Siebert	8.00	3.60
711 Larry Stahl SP	12.00	5.50
712 Jose Martinez	8.00	3.60
713 Mike Marshall SP	15.00	6.75
714 Dick Williams MG SP	15.00	6.75
715 Horace Clarke SP	15.00	6.75
716 Dave Leonhard	8.00	3.60
717 Tommie Aaron SP	12.00	5.50
718 Billy Wynne	8.00	3.60
719 Jerry May SP	12.00	5.50
720 Matty Alou	12.00	5.50
721 John Morris	8.00	3.60
722 Houston Astros SP	20.00	9.00
Team Card		
723 Vicente Romo SP	12.00	5.50
724 Tom Tischinski SP	12.00	5.50
725 Gary Gentry SP	12.00	5.50
726 Paul Popovich	8.00	3.60
727 Ray Lamb SP	12.00	5.50
728 NL Rookie Outfielders	8.00	3.60
Wayne Redmond		
Keith Lampard		
Bernie Williams		

729 Dick Billings	8.00	3.60
730 Jim Rooker	8.00	3.60
731 Jim Qualls SP	12.00	5.50
732 Bob Reed	8.00	3.60
733 Lee Maye SP	12.00	5.50
734 Rob Gardner SP	12.00	5.50
735 Mike Shannon SP	15.00	6.75
736 Mel Queen SP	12.00	5.50
737 Preston Gomez SP MG	12.00	5.50
738 Russ Gibson SP	12.00	5.50
739 Barry Lersch SP	12.00	5.50
740 Luis Aparicio SP UER	30.00	13.50
(Led AL in steals		
from 1965 to 1964,		
should be 1956 to 1964)		
741 Skip Guinn	8.00	3.60
742 Kansas City Royals	12.00	5.50
Team Card		
743 John O'Donoghue SP	12.00	5.50
744 Chuck Manuel SP	12.00	5.50
745 Sandy Alomar SP	12.00	5.50
746 Andy Kosco	8.00	3.60
747 NL Rookie Pitchers	8.00	3.60
Al Severinsen		
Scipio Spinks		
Balor Moore		
748 John Purdin SP	12.00	5.50
749 Ken Szotkiewicz	8.00	3.60
750 Denny McLain SP	25.00	11.00
751 Al Weis SP	15.00	6.75
752 Dick Drago	12.00	2.90

1972 Topps

BOB GIBSON / CARDINALS

	NRMT	VG-E
COMPLETE SET (787)	1600.00	700.00
COMMON CARD (1-132)	.60	.25
CUB VR (18B/29B/45B/117B)	5.00	2.20
MINOR STARS 1-132	1.25	.55
SEMISTARS 1-132	2.50	1.10
UNLISTED STARS 1-132	4.00	1.80
COMMON CARD (133-263)	1.00	.45
COMMON CARD (264-394)	1.25	.55
COMMON CARD (395-525)	1.50	.70
MINOR STARS 133-525	2.00	.90
SEMISTARS 133-525	4.00	1.80
UNLISTED STARS 133-525	6.00	2.70
COMMON CARD (526-656)	4.00	1.80
MINOR STARS 526-656	6.00	2.70
SEMISTARS 526-656	8.00	3.60
UNLISTED STARS 526-656	12.00	5.50
COMMON CARD (657-787)	12.00	5.50
MINOR STARS 657-787	15.00	6.75
SEMISTARS 657-787	20.00	9.00
CARDS PRICED IN NM CONDITION		
LAST SERIES CONDITION SENSITIVE		

1 Pittsburgh Pirates	8.00	2.90
Team Card		
2 Ray Culp	.60	.25
3 Bob Tolan	.60	.25
4 Checklist 1-132	6.00	1.20
5 John Bateman	.60	.25
6 Fred Scherman	.60	.25
7 Enzo Hernandez	.60	.25
8 Ron Swoboda	1.25	.55
9 Stan Williams	.60	.25
10 Amos Otis	1.25	.55

11 Bobby Valentine	1.25	.55
12 Jose Cardenal	.60	.25
13 Joe Grzenda	.60	.25
14 Phillies Rookies	.60	.25
Pete Koegel		
Mike Anderson		
Wayne Twitchell		
15 Walt Williams	.60	.25
16 Mike Jorgensen	.60	.25
17 Dave Duncan	.60	.25
18A Juan Pizarro	.60	.25
(Yellow underline		
C and S of Cubs)		
18B Juan Pizarro	5.00	2.20
(Green underline		
C and S of Cubs)		
19 Billy Cowan	.60	.25
20 Don Wilson	.60	.25
21 Atlanta Braves	1.50	.70
Team Card		
22 Rob Gardner	.60	.25
23 Ted Kubiak	.60	.25
24 Ted Ford	.60	.25
25 Bill Singer	.60	.25
26 Andy Etchebarren	.60	.25
27 Bob Johnson	.60	.25
28 Twins Rookies	.60	.25
Bob Gebhard		
Steve Brye		
Hal Haydel		
29A Bill Bonham	.60	.25
(Yellow underline		
C and S of Cubs)		
29B Bill Bonham	5.00	2.20
(Green underline		
C and S of Cubs)		
30 Rico Petrocelli	1.25	.55
31 Cleon Jones	1.25	.55
32 Cleon Jones IA	.60	.25
33 Billy Martin MG	4.00	1.80
34 Billy Martin IA	2.50	1.10
35 Jerry Johnson	.60	.25
36 Jerry Johnson IA	.60	.25
37 Carl Yastrzemski	10.00	4.50
38 Carl Yastrzemski IA	6.00	2.70
39 Bob Barton	.60	.25
40 Bob Barton IA	.60	.25
41 Tommy Davis	1.25	.55
42 Tommy Davis IA	.60	.25
43 Rick Wise	1.25	.55
44 Rick Wise IA	.60	.25
45A Glenn Beckert	1.25	.55
(Yellow underline		
C and S of Cubs)		
45B Glenn Beckert	5.00	2.20
(Green underline		
C and S of Cubs)		
46 Glenn Beckert IA	.60	.25
47 John Ellis	.60	.25
48 John Ellis IA	.60	.25
49 Willie Mays	25.00	11.00
50 Willie Mays IA	14.00	6.25
51 Harmon Killebrew	7.00	3.10
52 Harmon Killebrew IA	4.00	1.80
53 Bud Harrelson	1.25	.55
54 Bud Harrelson IA	.60	.25
55 Clyde Wright	.60	.25
56 Rich Chiles	.60	.25
57 Bob Oliver	.60	.25
58 Ernie McAnally	.60	.25
59 Fred Stanley	.60	.25
60 Manny Sanguillen	1.25	.55
61 Cubs Rookies	1.25	.55
Burt Hooton		
Gene Hiser		
Earl Stephenson		
62 Angel Mangual	.60	.25
63 Duke Sims	.60	.25
64 Pete Broberg	.60	.25
65 Cesar Cedeno	1.25	.55
66 Ray Corbin	.60	.25
67 Red Schoendienst MG	1.25	.55
68 Jim York	.60	.25
69 Roger Freed	.60	.25
70 Mike Cuellar	1.25	.55
71 California Angels	1.50	.70

Card		
Team Card		
72 Bruce Kison	.60	.25
73 Steve Huntz	.60	.25
74 Cecil Upshaw	.60	.25
75 Bert Campaneris	1.25	.55
76 Don Carrithers	.60	.25
77 Ron Theobald	.60	.25
78 Steve Arlin	.60	.25
79 Red Sox Rookies	50.00	22.00
Mike Garman		
Cecil Cooper		
Carlton Fisk		
80 Tony Perez	4.00	1.80
81 Mike Hedlund	.60	.25
82 Ron Woods	.60	.25
83 Dalton Jones	.60	.25
84 Vince Colbert	.60	.25
85 NL Batting Leaders	2.50	1.10
Joe Torre		
Ralph Garr		
Glenn Beckert		
86 AL Batting Leaders	2.50	1.10
Tony Oliva		
Bobby Murcer		
Merv Rettenmund		
87 NL RBI Leaders	4.00	1.80
Joe Torre		
Willie Stargell		
Hank Aaron		
88 AL RBI Leaders	4.00	1.80
Harmon Killebrew		
Frank Robinson		
Reggie Smith		
89 NL Home Run Leaders	2.50	1.10
Willie Stargell		
Hank Aaron		
Lee May		
90 AL Home Run Leaders	2.50	1.10
Bill Melton		
Norm Cash		
Reggie Jackson		
91 NL ERA Leaders	2.50	1.10
Tom Seaver		
Dave Roberts UER		
(Photo actually		
Danny Coombs)		
Don Wilson		
92 AL ERA Leaders	2.50	1.10
Vida Blue		
Wilbur Wood		
Jim Palmer		
93 NL Pitching Leaders	4.00	1.80
Fergie Jenkins		
Steve Carlton		
Al Downing		
Tom Seaver		
94 AL Pitching Leaders	2.50	1.10
Mickey Lolich		
Vida Blue		
Wilbur Wood		
95 NL Strikeout Leaders	4.00	1.80
Tom Seaver		
Fergie Jenkins		
Bill Stoneman		
96 AL Strikeout Leaders	2.50	1.10
Mickey Lolich		
Vida Blue		
Joe Coleman		
97 Tom Kelley	.60	.25
98 Chuck Tanner MG	1.25	.55
99 Ross Grimsley	.60	.25
100 Frank Robinson	8.00	3.60
101 Astros Rookies	1.50	.70
Bill Greif		
J.R. Richard		
Ray Busse		
102 Lloyd Allen	.60	.25
103 Checklist 133-263	6.00	1.20
104 Toby Harrah	1.25	.55
105 Gary Gentry	.60	.25
106 Milwaukee Brewers	1.50	.70
Team Card		
107 Jose Cruz	1.25	.55
108 Gary Waslewski	.60	.25
109 Jerry May	.60	.25
110 Ron Hunt	.60	.25
111 Jim Grant	.60	.25
112 Greg Luzinski	1.25	.55
113 Rogelio Moret	.60	.25
114 Bill Buckner	1.25	.55
115 Jim Fregosi	1.25	.55
116 Ed Farmer	.60	.25
117A Cleo James	.60	.25
(Yellow underline		
C and S of Cubs)		
117B Cleo James	5.00	2.20
(Green underline		
C and S of Cubs)		
118 Skip Lockwood	.60	.25
119 Marty Perez	.60	.25
120 Bill Freehan	1.25	.55
121 Ed Sprague	.60	.25
122 Larry Biittner	.60	.25
123 Ed Acosta	.60	.25
124 Yankees Rookies	.60	.25
Alan Closter		
Rusty Torres		
Roger Hambright		
125 Dave Cash	1.25	.55
126 Bart Johnson	.60	.25
127 Duffy Dyer	.60	.25
128 Eddie Watt	.60	.25
129 Charlie Fox MG	.60	.25
130 Bob Gibson	8.00	3.60
131 Jim Nettles	.60	.25
132 Joe Morgan	6.00	2.70
133 Joe Keough	1.00	.45
134 Carl Morton	1.00	.45
135 Vada Pinson	2.00	.90
136 Darrel Chaney	1.00	.45
137 Dick Williams MG	2.00	.90
138 Mike Kekich	1.00	.45
139 Tim McCarver	2.00	.90
140 Pat Dobson	2.00	.90
141 Mets Rookies	2.00	.90
Buzz Capra		
Lee Stanton		
Jon Matlack		
142 Chris Chambliss	4.00	1.80
143 Garry Jestadt	1.00	.45
144 Marty Pattin	1.00	.45
145 Don Kessinger	2.00	.90
146 Steve Kealey	1.00	.45
147 Dave Kingman	6.00	2.70
148 Dick Billings	1.00	.45
149 Gary Neibauer	1.00	.45
150 Norm Cash	2.00	.90
151 Jim Brewer	1.00	.45
152 Gene Clines	1.00	.45
153 Rick Auerbach	1.00	.45
154 Ted Simmons	4.00	1.80
155 Larry Dierker	2.00	.90
156 Minnesota Twins	2.00	.90
Team Card		
157 Don Gullett	1.00	.45
158 Jerry Kenney	1.00	.45
159 Don Boccabella	1.00	.45
160 Andy Messersmith	2.00	.90
161 Brock Davis	1.00	.45
162 Brewers Rookies UER	2.00	.90
Jerry Bell		
Darrell Porter		
Bob Reynolds		
(Porter and Bell		
photos switched)		
163 Tug McGraw	2.00	.90
164 Tug McGraw IA	2.00	.90
165 Chris Speier	2.00	.90
166 Chris Speier IA	1.00	.45
167 Deron Johnson	1.00	.45
168 Deron Johnson IA	1.00	.45
169 Vida Blue	2.00	.90
170 Vida Blue IA	2.00	.90
171 Darrell Evans	2.00	.90
172 Darrell Evans IA	2.00	.90
173 Clay Kirby	1.00	.45
174 Clay Kirby IA	1.00	.45
175 Tom Haller	1.00	.45
176 Tom Haller IA	1.00	.45
177 Paul Schaal	1.00	.45
178 Paul Schaal IA	1.00	.45
179 Dock Ellis	1.00	.45
180 Dock Ellis IA	1.00	.45
181 Ed Kranepool	1.00	.45
182 Ed Kranepool IA	1.00	.45
183 Bill Melton	1.00	.45
184 Bill Melton IA	1.00	.45
185 Ron Bryant	1.00	.45
186 Ron Bryant IA	1.00	.45
187 Gates Brown	1.00	.45
188 Frank Lucchesi MG	1.00	.45
189 Gene Tenace	2.00	.90
190 Dave Giusti	1.00	.45
191 Jeff Burroughs	2.00	.90
192 Chicago Cubs	2.00	.90
Team Card		
193 Kurt Bevacqua	1.00	.45
194 Fred Norman	1.00	.45
195 Orlando Cepeda	4.00	1.80
196 Mel Queen	1.00	.45
197 Johnny Briggs	1.00	.45
198 Dodgers Rookies	4.00	1.80
Charlie Hough		
Bob O'Brien		
Mike Strahler		
199 Mike Fiore	1.00	.45
200 Lou Brock	7.00	3.10
201 Phil Roof	1.00	.45
202 Scipio Spinks	1.00	.45
203 Ron Blomberg	1.00	.45
204 Tommy Helms	1.00	.45
205 Dick Drago	1.00	.45
206 Dal Maxvill	1.00	.45
207 Tom Egan	1.00	.45
208 Milt Pappas	2.00	.90
209 Joe Rudi	2.00	.90
210 Denny McLain	2.00	.90
211 Gary Sutherland	1.00	.45
212 Grant Jackson	1.00	.45
213 Angels Rookies	1.00	.45
Billy Parker		
Art Kusnyer		
Tom Silverio		
214 Mike McQueen	1.00	.45
215 Alex Johnson	2.00	.90
216 Joe Niekro	2.00	.90
217 Roger Metzger	1.00	.45
218 Eddie Kasko MG	2.00	.90
219 Rennie Stennett	2.00	.90
220 Jim Perry	2.00	.90
221 NL Playoffs	2.00	.90
Bucs champs		
222 Brooks Robinson ALCS	4.00	1.80
223 Dave McNally WS	2.00	.90
224 Dave Johnson WS	2.00	.90
Mark Belanger		
225 Manny Sanguillen WS	2.00	.90
226 Roberto Clemente WS	8.00	3.60
227 Nellie Briles WS	2.00	.90
228 Frank Robinson WS	2.00	.90
Manny Sanguillen		
229 Steve Blass WS	2.00	.90
230 World Series Summary	2.00	.90
(Pirates celebrate)		
231 Casey Cox	1.00	.45
232 Giants Rookies	1.00	.45
Chris Arnold		
Jim Barr		
Dave Rader		
233 Jay Johnstone	2.00	.90
234 Ron Taylor	1.00	.45
235 Merv Rettenmund	2.00	.90
236 Jim McGlothlin	1.00	.45
237 New York Yankees	2.00	.90
Team Card		
238 Leron Lee	1.00	.45
239 Tom Timmermann	1.00	.45
240 Rich Allen	2.00	.90
241 Rollie Fingers	6.00	2.70
242 Don Mincher	1.00	.45
243 Frank Linzy	1.00	.45
244 Steve Braun	1.00	.45
245 Tommie Agee	2.00	.90
246 Tom Burgmeier	1.00	.45
247 Milt May	1.00	.45
248 Tom Bradley	1.00	.45
249 Harry Walker MG	1.00	.45
250 Boog Powell	2.00	.90

No.	Card	Price 1	Price 2
❏ 251	Checklist 264-394	6.00	1.20
❏ 252	Ken Reynolds	1.00	.45
❏ 253	Sandy Alomar	2.00	.90
❏ 254	Boots Day	1.00	.45
❏ 255	Jim Lonborg	2.00	.90
❏ 256	George Foster	2.00	.90
❏ 257	Tigers Rookies	1.00	.45
	Jim Foor		
	Tim Hosley		
	Paul Jata		
❏ 258	Randy Hundley	2.00	.90
❏ 259	Sparky Lyle	2.00	.90
❏ 260	Ralph Garr	2.00	.90
❏ 261	Steve Mingori	1.00	.45
❏ 262	San Diego Padres	2.00	.90
	Team Card		
❏ 263	Felipe Alou	2.00	.90
❏ 264	Tommy John	2.00	.90
❏ 265	Wes Parker	2.00	.90
❏ 266	Bobby Bolin	1.25	.55
❏ 267	Dave Concepcion	4.00	1.80
❏ 268	A's Rookies	1.25	.55
	Dwain Anderson		
	Chris Floethe		
❏ 269	Don Hahn	1.25	.55
❏ 270	Jim Palmer	8.00	3.60
❏ 271	Ken Rudolph	1.25	.55
❏ 272	Mickey Rivers	2.00	.90
❏ 273	Bobby Floyd	1.25	.55
❏ 274	Al Severinsen	1.25	.55
❏ 275	Cesar Tovar	1.25	.55
❏ 276	Gene Mauch MG	2.00	.90
❏ 277	Elliott Maddox	1.25	.55
❏ 278	Dennis Higgins	1.25	.55
❏ 279	Larry Brown	1.25	.55
❏ 280	Willie McCovey	7.00	3.10
❏ 281	Bill Parsons	1.25	.55
❏ 282	Houston Astros	2.00	.90
	Team Card		
❏ 283	Darrell Brandon	1.25	.55
❏ 284	Ike Brown	1.25	.55
❏ 285	Gaylord Perry	6.00	2.70
❏ 286	Gene Alley	2.00	.90
❏ 287	Jim Hardin	1.25	.55
❏ 288	Johnny Jeter	1.25	.55
❏ 289	Syd O'Brien	1.25	.55
❏ 290	Sonny Siebert	1.25	.55
❏ 291	Hal McRae	2.00	.90
❏ 292	Hal McRae IA	2.00	.90
❏ 293	Dan Frisella	1.25	.55
❏ 294	Dan Frisella IA	1.25	.55
❏ 295	Dick Dietz	1.25	.55
❏ 296	Dick Dietz IA	1.25	.55
❏ 297	Claude Osteen	2.00	.90
❏ 298	Claude Osteen IA	1.25	.55
❏ 299	Hank Aaron	40.00	18.00
❏ 300	Hank Aaron	20.00	9.00
❏ 301	George Mitterwald	1.25	.55
❏ 302	George Mitterwald IA	1.25	.55
❏ 303	Joe Pepitone	2.00	.90
❏ 304	Joe Pepitone IA	1.25	.55
❏ 305	Ken Boswell	1.25	.55
❏ 306	Ken Boswell IA	1.25	.55
❏ 307	Steve Renko	1.25	.55
❏ 308	Steve Renko IA	1.25	.55
❏ 309	Roberto Clemente	50.00	22.00
❏ 310	Roberto Clemente IA	25.00	11.00
❏ 311	Clay Carroll	1.25	.55
❏ 312	Clay Carroll IA	1.25	.55
❏ 313	Luis Aparicio	4.00	1.80
❏ 314	Luis Aparicio IA	2.00	.90
❏ 315	Paul Splittorff	1.25	.55
❏ 316	Cardinals Rookies	2.00	.90
	Jim Bibby		
	Jorge Roque		
	Santiago Guzman		
❏ 317	Rich Hand	1.25	.55
❏ 318	Sonny Jackson	1.25	.55
❏ 319	Aurelio Rodriguez	1.25	.55
❏ 320	Steve Blass	2.00	.90
❏ 321	Joe Lahoud	1.25	.55
❏ 322	Jose Pena	1.25	.55
❏ 323	Earl Weaver MG	4.00	1.80
❏ 324	Mike Ryan	1.25	.55
❏ 325	Mel Stottlemyre	2.00	.90
❏ 326	Pat Kelly	1.25	.55
❏ 327	Steve Stone	2.00	.90
❏ 328	Boston Red Sox	2.00	.90
	Team Card		
❏ 329	Roy Foster	1.25	.55
❏ 330	Jim Hunter	4.00	1.80
❏ 331	Stan Swanson	1.25	.55
❏ 332	Buck Martinez	1.25	.55
❏ 333	Steve Barber	1.25	.55
❏ 334	Rangers Rookies	1.25	.55
	Bill Fahey		
	Jim Mason		
	Tom Ragland		
❏ 335	Bill Hands	1.25	.55
❏ 336	Marty Martinez	1.25	.55
❏ 337	Mike Kilkenny	1.25	.55
❏ 338	Bob Grich	2.00	.90
❏ 339	Ron Cook	1.25	.55
❏ 340	Roy White	2.00	.90
❏ 341	Joe Torre KP	1.25	.55
❏ 342	Wilbur Wood KP	1.25	.55
❏ 343	Willie Stargell KP	2.00	.90
❏ 344	Dave McNally KP	1.25	.55
❏ 345	Rick Wise KP	1.25	.55
❏ 346	Jim Fregosi KP	1.25	.55
❏ 347	Tom Seaver KP	4.00	1.80
❏ 348	Sal Bando KP	1.25	.55
❏ 349	Al Fitzmorris	1.25	.55
❏ 350	Frank Howard	2.00	.90
❏ 351	Braves Rookies	1.00	.90
	Tom House		
	Rick Kester		
	Jimmy Britton		
❏ 352	Dave LaRoche	1.25	.55
❏ 353	Art Shamsky	1.25	.55
❏ 354	Tom Murphy	1.25	.55
❏ 355	Bob Watson	2.00	.90
❏ 356	Gerry Moses	1.25	.55
❏ 357	Woody Fryman	1.25	.55
❏ 358	Sparky Anderson MG	4.00	1.80
❏ 359	Don Pavletich	1.25	.55
❏ 360	Dave Roberts	1.25	.55
❏ 361	Mike Andrews	2.00	.90
❏ 362	New York Mets	2.00	.90
	Team Card		
❏ 363	Ron Klimkowski	1.25	.55
❏ 364	Johnny Callison	2.00	.90
❏ 365	Dick Bosman	2.00	.90
❏ 366	Jimmy Rosario	1.25	.55
❏ 367	Ron Perranoski	2.00	.90
❏ 368	Danny Thompson	1.25	.55
❏ 369	Jim Lefebvre	2.00	.90
❏ 370	Don Buford	1.25	.55
❏ 371	Denny Lemaster	1.25	.55
❏ 372	Royals Rookies	1.25	.55
	Lance Clemons		
	Monty Montgomery		
❏ 373	John Mayberry	2.00	.90
❏ 374	Jack Heidemann	1.25	.55
❏ 375	Reggie Cleveland	1.25	.55
❏ 376	Andy Kosco	1.25	.55
❏ 377	Terry Harmon	1.25	.55
❏ 378	Checklist 395-525	6.00	1.20
❏ 379	Ken Berry	1.25	.55
❏ 380	Earl Williams	1.25	.55
❏ 381	Chicago White Sox	2.00	.90
	Team Card		
❏ 382	Joe Gibbon	1.25	.55
❏ 383	Brant Alyea	1.25	.55
❏ 384	Dave Campbell	1.25	.55
❏ 385	Mickey Stanley	2.00	.90
❏ 386	Jim Colborn	1.25	.55
❏ 387	Horace Clarke	2.00	.90
❏ 388	Charlie Williams	1.25	.55
❏ 389	Bill Rigney MG	1.25	.55
❏ 390	Willie Davis	2.00	.90
❏ 391	Ken Sanders	1.25	.55
❏ 392	Pirates Rookies	2.00	.90
	Fred Cambria		
	Richie Zisk		
❏ 393	Curt Motton	1.25	.55
❏ 394	Ken Forsch	2.00	.90
❏ 395	Matty Alou	2.00	.90
❏ 396	Paul Lindblad	1.50	.70
❏ 397	Philadelphia Phillies	2.00	.90
	Team Card		
❏ 398	Larry Hisle	2.00	.90
❏ 399	Milt Wilcox	1.50	.70
❏ 400	Tony Oliva	2.00	.90
❏ 401	Jim Nash	1.50	.70
❏ 402	Bobby Heise	1.50	.70
❏ 403	John Cumberland	1.50	.70
❏ 404	Jeff Torborg	2.00	.90
❏ 405	Ron Fairly	2.00	.90
❏ 406	George Hendrick	2.00	.90
❏ 407	Chuck Taylor	1.00	.45
❏ 408	Jim Northrup	2.00	.90
❏ 409	Frank Baker	1.00	.45
❏ 410	Ferguson Jenkins	6.00	2.70
❏ 411	Bob Montgomery	1.00	.45
❏ 412	Dick Kelley	1.00	.45
❏ 413	White Sox Rookies	1.00	.45
	Don Eddy		
	Dave Lemonds		
❏ 414	Bob Miller	1.00	.45
❏ 415	Cookie Rojas	2.00	.90
❏ 416	Johnny Edwards	1.00	.45
❏ 417	Tom Hall	1.00	.45
❏ 418	Tom Shopay	1.00	.45
❏ 419	Jim Spencer	1.00	.45
❏ 420	Steve Carlton	18.00	8.00
❏ 421	Ellie Rodriguez	1.00	.45
❏ 422	Ray Lamb	1.00	.45
❏ 423	Oscar Gamble	2.00	.90
❏ 424	Bill Gogolewski	1.00	.45
❏ 425	Ken Singleton	2.00	.90
❏ 426	Ken Singleton IA	1.00	.45
❏ 427	Tito Fuentes	1.00	.45
❏ 428	Tito Fuentes IA	1.00	.45
❏ 429	Bob Robertson	1.00	.45
❏ 430	Bob Robertson IA	1.00	.45
❏ 431	Clarence Gaston	2.00	.90
❏ 432	Clarence Gaston IA	2.00	.90
❏ 433	Johnny Bench	25.00	11.00
❏ 434	Johnny Bench IA	15.00	6.75
❏ 435	Reggie Jackson	25.00	11.00
❏ 436	Reggie Jackson IA	12.00	5.50
❏ 437	Maury Wills	2.00	.90
❏ 438	Maury Wills IA	2.00	.90
❏ 439	Billy Williams	6.00	2.70
❏ 440	Billy Williams IA	4.00	1.80
❏ 441	Thurman Munson	15.00	6.75
❏ 442	Thurman Munson IA	8.00	3.60
❏ 443	Ken Henderson	1.50	.70
❏ 444	Ken Henderson IA	1.50	.70
❏ 445	Tom Seaver	30.00	13.50
❏ 446	Tom Seaver IA	15.00	6.75
❏ 447	Willie Stargell	8.00	3.60
❏ 448	Willie Stargell IA	4.00	1.80
❏ 449	Bob Lemon MG	2.00	.90
❏ 450	Mickey Lolich	2.00	.90
❏ 451	Tony LaRussa	4.00	1.80
❏ 452	Ed Herrmann	1.50	.70
❏ 453	Barry Lersch	1.50	.70
❏ 454	Oakland A's	2.00	.90
	Team Card		
❏ 455	Tommy Harper	2.00	.90
❏ 456	Mark Belanger	2.00	.90
❏ 457	Padres Rookies	1.50	.70
	Darcy Fast		
	Derrel Thomas		
	Mike Ivie		
❏ 458	Aurelio Monteagudo	1.50	.70
❏ 459	Rick Renick	1.50	.70
❏ 460	Al Downing	1.50	.70
❏ 461	Tim Cullen	1.50	.70
❏ 462	Rickey Clark	1.50	.70
❏ 463	Bernie Carbo	1.50	.70
❏ 464	Jim Roland	1.50	.70
❏ 465	Gil Hodges MG	4.00	1.80
❏ 466	Norm Miller	1.50	.70
❏ 467	Steve Kline	1.50	.70
❏ 468	Richie Scheinblum	1.50	.70
❏ 469	Ron Herbel	1.50	.70
❏ 470	Ray Fosse	1.50	.70
❏ 471	Luke Walker	1.50	.70
❏ 472	Phil Gagliano	1.50	.70
❏ 473	Dan McGinn	1.50	.70
❏ 474	Orioles Rookies	15.00	6.75
	Don Baylor		
	Roric Harrison		
	Johnny Oates		
❏ 475	Gary Nolan	2.00	.90

No.	Player	Price 1	Price 2
476	Lee Richard	1.50	.70
477	Tom Phoebus	1.50	.70
478	Checklist 526-656	6.00	1.20
479	Don Shaw	1.50	.70
480	Lee May	2.00	.90
481	Billy Conigliaro	2.00	.90
482	Joe Hoerner	1.50	.70
483	Ken Suarez	1.50	.70
484	Lum Harris MG	1.50	.70
485	Phil Regan	2.00	.90
486	John Lowenstein	1.50	.70
487	Detroit Tigers Team Card	2.00	.90
488	Mike Nagy	1.50	.70
489	Expos Rookies Terry Humphrey Keith Lampard	1.50	.70
490	Dave McNally	2.00	.90
491	Lou Piniella KP	2.00	.90
492	Mel Stottlemyre KP	2.00	.90
493	Bob Bailey KP	2.00	.90
494	Willie Horton KP	2.00	.90
495	Bill Melton KP	2.00	.90
496	Bud Harrelson KP	2.00	.90
497	Jim Perry KP	2.00	.90
498	Brooks Robinson KP	4.00	1.80
499	Vicente Romo	1.50	.70
500	Joe Torre	2.00	.90
501	Pete Hamm	1.50	.70
502	Jackie Hernandez	1.50	.70
503	Gary Peters	1.50	.70
504	Ed Spiezio	1.50	.70
505	Mike Marshall	2.00	.90
506	Indians Rookies Terry Ley Jim Moyer Dick Tidrow	1.50	.70
507	Fred Gladding	1.50	.70
508	Elrod Hendricks	1.50	.70
509	Don McMahon	1.50	.70
510	Ted Williams MG	12.00	5.50
511	Tony Taylor	2.00	.90
512	Paul Popovich	1.50	.70
513	Lindy McDaniel	2.00	.90
514	Ted Sizemore	1.50	.70
515	Bert Blyleven	4.00	1.80
516	Oscar Brown	1.00	.45
517	Ken Brett	1.00	.45
518	Wayne Garrett	1.00	.45
519	Ted Abernathy	1.00	.45
520	Larry Bowa	2.00	.90
521	Alan Foster	1.00	.45
522	Los Angeles Dodgers Team Card	2.00	.90
523	Chuck Dobson	1.00	.45
524	Reds Rookies Ed Armbrister Mel Behney	1.00	.45
525	Carlos May	2.00	.90
526	Bob Bailey	6.00	2.70
527	Dave Leonhard	4.00	1.80
528	Ron Stone	4.00	1.80
529	Dave Nelson	6.00	2.70
530	Don Sutton	8.00	3.60
531	Freddie Patek	4.00	2.70
532	Fred Kendall	4.00	1.80
533	Ralph Houk MG	6.00	2.70
534	Jim Hickman	6.00	2.70
535	Ed Brinkman	4.00	1.80
536	Doug Rader	6.00	2.70
537	Bob Locke	4.00	1.80
538	Charlie Sands	4.00	1.80
539	Terry Forster	6.00	2.70
540	Felix Millan	4.00	1.80
541	Roger Repoz	4.00	1.80
542	Jack Billingham	4.00	1.80
543	Duane Josephson	4.00	1.80
544	Ted Martinez	4.00	1.80
545	Wayne Granger	4.00	1.80
546	Joe Hague	4.00	1.80
547	Cleveland Indians Team Card	8.00	3.60
548	Frank Reberger	4.00	1.80
549	Dave May	4.00	1.80
550	Brooks Robinson	25.00	11.00
551	Ollie Brown	4.00	1.80
552	Ollie Brown IA	4.00	1.80
553	Wilbur Wood	6.00	2.70
554	Wilbur Wood IA	4.00	1.80
555	Ron Santo	6.00	2.70
556	Ron Santo IA	4.00	1.80
557	John Odom	4.00	1.80
558	John Odom IA	4.00	1.80
559	Pete Rose	35.00	16.00
560	Pete Rose IA	20.00	9.00
561	Leo Cardenas	4.00	1.80
562	Leo Cardenas IA	4.00	1.80
563	Ray Sadecki	4.00	1.80
564	Ray Sadecki IA	4.00	1.80
565	Reggie Smith	6.00	2.70
566	Reggie Smith IA	4.00	1.80
567	Juan Marichal	12.00	5.50
568	Juan Marichal IA	6.00	2.70
569	Ed Kirkpatrick	4.00	1.80
570	Ed Kirkpatrick IA	4.00	1.80
571	Nate Colbert	4.00	1.80
572	Nate Colbert IA	4.00	1.80
573	Fritz Peterson	4.00	1.80
574	Fritz Peterson IA	4.00	1.80
575	Al Oliver	6.00	2.70
576	Leo Durocher MG	6.00	2.70
577	Mike Paul	4.00	1.80
578	Billy Grabarkewitz	4.00	1.80
579	Doyle Alexander	6.00	2.70
580	Lou Piniella	6.00	2.70
581	Wade Blasingame	4.00	1.80
582	Montreal Expos Team Card	8.00	3.60
583	Darold Knowles	4.00	1.80
584	Jerry McNertney	4.00	1.80
585	George Scott	6.00	2.70
586	Denis Menke	4.00	1.80
587	Billy Wilson	4.00	1.80
588	Jim Holt	4.00	1.80
589	Hal Lanier	4.00	1.80
590	Graig Nettles	6.00	2.70
591	Paul Casanova	4.00	1.80
592	Lew Krausse	4.00	1.80
593	Rich Morales	4.00	1.80
594	Jim Beauchamp	4.00	1.80
595	Nolan Ryan	150.00	70.00
596	Manny Mota	4.50	2.00
597	Jim Magnuson	4.00	1.80
598	Hal King	6.00	2.70
599	Billy Champion	4.00	1.80
600	Al Kaline	25.00	11.00
601	George Stone	4.00	1.80
602	Dave Bristol MG	4.00	1.80
603	Jim Ray	4.00	1.80
604A	Checklist 657-787 (Copyright on back bottom right)	12.00	2.40
604B	Checklist 657-787 (Copyright on back bottom left)	12.00	2.40
605	Nelson Briles	6.00	2.70
606	Luis Melendez	4.00	1.80
607	Frank Duffy	4.00	1.80
608	Mike Corkins	4.00	1.80
609	Tom Grieve	6.00	2.70
610	Bill Stoneman	6.00	2.70
611	Rich Reese	4.00	1.80
612	Joe Decker	4.00	1.80
613	Mike Ferraro	4.00	1.80
614	Ted Uhlaender	4.00	1.80
615	Steve Hargan	4.00	1.80
616	Joe Ferguson	6.00	2.70
617	Kansas City Royals Team Card	8.00	3.60
618	Rich Robertson	4.00	1.80
619	Rich McKinney	4.00	1.80
620	Phil Niekro	12.00	5.50
621	Commissioners Award	8.00	3.60
622	MVP Award	8.00	3.60
623	Cy Young Award	8.00	3.60
624	Minor League Player of the Year	8.00	3.60
625	Rookie of the Year	8.00	3.60
626	Babe Ruth Award	8.00	3.60
627	Moe Drabowsky	4.00	1.80
628	Terry Crowley	4.00	1.80
629	Paul Doyle	4.00	1.80
630	Rich Hebner	6.00	2.70
631	John Strohmayer	4.00	1.80
632	Mike Hegan	4.00	1.80
633	Jack Hiatt	4.00	1.80
634	Dick Woodson	4.00	1.80
635	Don Money	6.00	2.70
636	Bill Lee	6.00	2.70
637	Preston Gomez MG	4.00	1.80
638	Ken Wright	4.00	1.80
639	J.C. Martin	4.00	1.80
640	Joe Coleman	4.00	1.80
641	Mike Lum	4.00	1.80
642	Dennis Riddleberger	4.00	1.80
643	Russ Gibson	4.00	1.80
644	Bernie Allen	4.00	1.80
645	Jim Maloney	6.00	2.70
646	Chico Salmon	4.00	1.80
647	Bob Moose	4.00	1.80
648	Jim Lyttle	4.00	1.80
649	Pete Richert	4.00	1.80
650	Sal Bando	6.00	2.70
651	Cincinnati Reds Team Card	8.00	3.60
652	Marcelino Lopez	4.00	1.80
653	Jim Fairey	4.00	1.80
654	Horacio Pina	6.00	2.70
655	Jerry Grote	4.00	1.80
656	Rudy May	4.00	1.80
657	Bobby Wine	12.00	5.50
658	Steve Dunning	12.00	5.50
659	Bob Aspromonte	12.00	5.50
660	Paul Blair	15.00	6.75
661	Bill Virdon MG	12.00	5.50
662	Stan Bahnsen	12.00	5.50
663	Fran Healy	15.00	6.75
664	Bobby Knoop	12.00	5.50
665	Chris Short	12.00	5.50
666	Hector Torres	12.00	5.50
667	Ray Newman	12.00	5.50
668	Texas Rangers Team Card	30.00	13.50
669	Willie Crawford	12.00	5.50
670	Ken Holtzman	15.00	6.75
671	Donn Clendenon	15.00	6.75
672	Archie Reynolds	12.00	5.50
673	Dave Marshall	12.00	5.50
674	John Kennedy	12.00	5.50
675	Pat Jarvis	12.00	5.50
676	Danny Cater	12.00	5.50
677	Ivan Murrell	12.00	5.50
678	Steve Luebber	12.00	5.50
679	Astros Rookies Bob Fenwick Bob Stinson	12.00	5.50
680	Dave Johnson	15.00	6.75
681	Bobby Pfeil	12.00	5.50
682	Mike McCormick	15.00	6.75
683	Steve Hovley	12.00	5.50
684	Hal Breeden	12.00	5.50
685	Joel Horlen	12.00	5.50
686	Steve Garvey	40.00	18.00
687	Del Unser	12.00	5.50
688	St. Louis Cardinals Team Card	20.00	9.00
689	Eddie Fisher	12.00	5.50
690	Willie Montanez	15.00	6.75
691	Curt Blefary	12.00	5.50
692	Curt Blefary IA	12.00	5.50
693	Alan Gallagher	12.00	5.50
694	Alan Gallagher IA	12.00	5.50
695	Rod Carew	50.00	22.00
696	Rod Carew IA	30.00	13.50
697	Jerry Koosman	15.00	6.75
698	Jerry Koosman IA	15.00	6.75
699	Bobby Murcer	15.00	6.75
700	Bobby Murcer IA	15.00	6.75
701	Jose Pagan	12.00	5.50
702	Jose Pagan IA	12.00	5.50
703	Doug Griffin	12.00	5.50
704	Doug Griffin IA	12.00	5.50
705	Pat Corrales	15.00	6.75
706	Pat Corrales IA	12.00	5.50
707	Tim Foli	12.00	5.50
708	Tim Foli IA	12.00	5.50
709	Jim Kaat	15.00	6.75
710	Jim Kaat IA	15.00	6.75

	NRMT	VG-E
☐ 711 Bobby Bonds	20.00	9.00
☐ 712 Bobby Bonds IA	15.00	6.75
☐ 713 Gene Michael	20.00	9.00
☐ 714 Gene Michael IA	15.00	6.75
☐ 715 Mike Epstein	12.00	5.50
☐ 716 Jesus Alou	12.00	5.50
☐ 717 Bruce Dal Canton	12.00	5.50
☐ 718 Del Rice MG	12.00	5.50
☐ 719 Cesar Geronimo	12.00	5.50
☐ 720 Sam McDowell	15.00	6.75
☐ 721 Eddie Leon	12.00	5.50
☐ 722 Bill Sudakis	12.00	5.50
☐ 723 Al Santorini	12.00	5.50
☐ 724 AL Rookie Pitchers	12.00	5.50
John Curtis		
Rich Hinton		
Mickey Scott		
☐ 725 Dick McAuliffe	15.00	6.75
☐ 726 Dick Selma	12.00	5.50
☐ 727 Jose Laboy	12.00	5.50
☐ 728 Gail Hopkins	12.00	5.50
☐ 729 Bob Veale	12.00	5.50
☐ 730 Rick Monday	15.00	6.75
☐ 731 Baltimore Orioles	20.00	9.00
Team Card		
☐ 732 George Culver	12.00	5.50
☐ 733 Jim Ray Hart	15.00	6.75
☐ 734 Bob Burda	12.00	5.50
☐ 735 Diego Segui	12.00	5.50
☐ 736 Bill Russell	15.00	6.75
☐ 737 Len Randle	15.00	6.75
☐ 738 Jim Merritt	12.00	5.50
☐ 739 Don Mason	12.00	5.50
☐ 740 Rico Carty	15.00	6.75
☐ 741 Rookie First Basemen	15.00	6.75
Tom Hutton		
John Milner		
Rick Miller		
☐ 742 Jim Rooker	12.00	5.50
☐ 743 Cesar Gutierrez	12.00	5.50
☐ 744 Jim Slaton	12.00	5.50
☐ 745 Julian Javier	15.00	6.75
☐ 746 Lowell Palmer	12.00	5.50
☐ 747 Jim Stewart	12.00	5.50
☐ 748 Phil Hennigan	12.00	5.50
☐ 749 Walter Alston MG	15.00	6.75
☐ 750 Willie Horton	12.00	5.50
☐ 751 Steve Carlton	40.00	18.00
☐ 752 Joe Morgan TR	45.00	20.00
☐ 753 Denny McLain TR	20.00	9.00
☐ 754 Frank Robinson TR	45.00	20.00
☐ 755 Jim Fregosi TR	15.00	6.75
☐ 756 Rick Wise TR	15.00	6.75
☐ 757 Jose Cardenal TR	15.00	6.75
☐ 758 Gil Garrido	12.00	5.50
☐ 759 Chris Cannizzaro	12.00	5.50
☐ 760 Bill Mazeroski	15.00	6.75
☐ 761 Rookie Outfielders	25.00	11.00
Ben Oglivie		
Ron Cey		
Bernie Williams		
☐ 762 Wayne Simpson	12.00	5.50
☐ 763 Ron Hansen	12.00	5.50
☐ 764 Dusty Baker	20.00	9.00
☐ 765 Ken McMullen	12.00	5.50
☐ 766 Steve Hamilton	12.00	5.50
☐ 767 Tom McCraw	15.00	6.75
☐ 768 Denny Doyle	12.00	5.50
☐ 769 Jack Aker	12.00	5.50
☐ 770 Jim Wynn	15.00	6.75
☐ 771 San Francisco Giants	20.00	9.00
Team Card		
☐ 772 Ken Tatum	12.00	5.50
☐ 773 Ron Brand	12.00	5.50
☐ 774 Luis Alvarado	12.00	5.50
☐ 775 Jerry Reuss	15.00	6.75
☐ 776 Bill Voss	12.00	5.50
☐ 777 Hoyt Wilhelm	20.00	9.00
☐ 778 Twins Rookies	20.00	9.00
Vic Albury		
Rick Dempsey		
Jim Strickland		
☐ 779 Tony Cloninger	12.00	5.50
☐ 780 Dick Green	12.00	5.50
☐ 781 Jim McAndrew	12.00	5.50
☐ 782 Larry Stahl	12.00	5.50
☐ 783 Les Cain	12.00	5.50
☐ 784 Ken Aspromonte	12.00	5.50
☐ 785 Vic Davalillo	12.00	5.50
☐ 786 Chuck Brinkman	12.00	5.50
☐ 787 Ron Reed	15.00	5.25

1973 Topps

AL KALINE
DETROIT TIGERS — OUTFIELDER

	NRMT	VG-E
COMPLETE SET (660)	700.00	325.00
COMMON CARD (1-264)	.50	.23
COMMON CARD (265-396)	.75	.35
MINOR STARS 1-396	1.50	.70
SEMISTARS 1-396	2.50	1.10
UNLISTED STARS 1-396	4.00	1.80
COMMON CARD (397-528)	1.25	.55
MINOR STARS 397-528	2.00	.90
SEMISTARS 397-528	3.00	1.35
UNLISTED STARS 397-528	5.00	2.20
COMMON CARD (529-660)	3.50	1.55
MINOR STARS 529-660	5.00	2.20
SEMISTARS 529-660	8.00	3.60
BLUE TEAM CL !	8.00	2.40

		NRMT	VG-E
☐ 1	All-Time HR Leaders	40.00	11.50
	Babe Ruth 714		
	Hank Aaron 673		
	Willie Mays 654		
☐ 2	Rich Hebner	1.50	.70
☐ 3	Jim Lonborg	1.50	.70
☐ 4	John Milner	.50	.23
☐ 5	Ed Brinkman	.50	.23
☐ 6	Mac Scarce	.50	.23
☐ 7	Texas Rangers	2.00	.90
	Team Card		
☐ 8	Tom Hall	.50	.23
☐ 9	Johnny Oates	.50	.23
☐ 10	Don Sutton	2.50	1.10
☐ 11	Chris Chambliss	1.50	.70
☐ 12A	Padres Leaders	3.00	1.35
	Don Zimmer MG		
	Dave Garcia CO		
	Johnny Podres CO		
	Bob Skinner CO		
	Whitey Wietelmann CO		
	(Podres no right ear)		
☐ 12B	Padres Leaders	.75	.35
	(Podres has right ear)		
☐ 13	George Hendrick	1.50	.70
☐ 14	Sonny Siebert	.50	.23
☐ 15	Ralph Garr	.50	.23
☐ 16	Steve Braun	.50	.23
☐ 17	Fred Gladding	.50	.23
☐ 18	Leroy Stanton	.50	.23
☐ 19	Tim Foli	.50	.23
☐ 20	Stan Bahnsen	.50	.23
☐ 21	Randy Hundley	1.50	.70
☐ 22	Ted Abernathy	.50	.23
☐ 23	Dave Kingman	1.50	.70
☐ 24	Al Santorini	.50	.23
☐ 25	Roy White	1.50	.70
☐ 26	Pittsburgh Pirates	2.00	.90
	Team Card		
☐ 27	Bill Gogolewski	.50	.23
☐ 28	Hal McRae	1.50	.70
☐ 29	Tony Taylor	1.50	.70
☐ 30	Tug McGraw	1.50	.70
☐ 31	Buddy Bell	2.50	1.10
☐ 32	Fred Norman	.50	.23
☐ 33	Jim Breazeale	.50	.23
☐ 34	Pat Dobson	.50	.23
☐ 35	Willie Davis	1.50	.70
☐ 36	Steve Barber	.50	.23
☐ 37	Bill Robinson	1.50	.70
☐ 38	Mike Epstein	.50	.23
☐ 39	Dave Roberts	.50	.23
☐ 40	Reggie Smith	1.50	.70
☐ 41	Tom Walker	.50	.23
☐ 42	Mike Andrews	.50	.23
☐ 43	Randy Moffitt	.50	.23
☐ 44	Rick Monday	1.50	.70
☐ 45	Ellie Rodriguez UER	.50	.23
	(Photo actually		
	John Felske)		
☐ 46	Lindy McDaniel	1.50	.70
☐ 47	Luis Melendez	.50	.23
☐ 48	Paul Splittorff	.50	.23
☐ 49A	Twins Leaders	3.00	1.35
	Frank Quilici MG		
	Vern Morgan CO		
	Bob Rodgers CO		
	Ralph Rowe CO		
	Al Worthington CO		
	(Solid backgrounds)		
☐ 49B	Twins Leaders	.75	.35
	(Natural backgrounds)		
☐ 50	Roberto Clemente	70.00	32.00
☐ 51	Chuck Seelbach	.50	.23
☐ 52	Denis Menke	.50	.23
☐ 53	Steve Dunning	.50	.23
☐ 54	Checklist 1-132	3.00	.60
☐ 55	Jon Matlack	1.50	.70
☐ 56	Merv Rettenmund	.50	.23
☐ 57	Derrel Thomas	.50	.23
☐ 58	Mike Paul	.50	.23
☐ 59	Steve Yeager	1.50	.70
☐ 60	Ken Holtzman	1.50	.70
☐ 61	Batting Leaders	2.50	1.10
	Billy Williams		
	Rod Carew		
☐ 62	Home Run Leaders	2.50	1.10
	Johnny Bench		
	Dick Allen		
☐ 63	RBI Leaders	2.50	1.10
	Johnny Bench		
	Dick Allen		
☐ 64	Stolen Base Leaders	1.50	.70
	Lou Brock		
	Bert Campaneris		
☐ 65	ERA Leaders	1.50	.70
	Steve Carlton		
	Luis Tiant		
☐ 66	Victory Leaders	1.50	.70
	Steve Carlton		
	Gaylord Perry		
	Wilbur Wood		
☐ 67	Strikeout Leaders	30.00	13.50
	Steve Carlton		
	Nolan Ryan		
☐ 68	Leading Firemen	1.50	.70
	Clay Carroll		
	Sparky Lyle		
☐ 69	Phil Gagliano	.50	.23
☐ 70	Milt Pappas	1.50	.70
☐ 71	Johnny Briggs	.50	.23
☐ 72	Ron Reed	.50	.23
☐ 73	Ed Herrmann	.50	.23
☐ 74	Billy Champion	.50	.23
☐ 75	Vada Pinson	1.50	.70
☐ 76	Doug Rader	.50	.23
☐ 77	Mike Torrez	1.50	.70
☐ 78	Richie Scheinblum	.50	.23
☐ 79	Jim Willoughby	.50	.23
☐ 80	Tony Oliva UER	1.50	.70
	(Minnesota on front)		
☐ 81A	Cubs Leaders	1.50	.70
	Whitey Lockman MG		
	Hank Aguirre CO		
	Ernie Banks CO		
	Larry Jansen CO		
	Pete Reiser CO		
	(Solid backgrounds)		
☐ 81B	Cubs Leaders	1.50	.70
	(Natural backgrounds)		

☐ 82 Fritz Peterson	.50	.23
☐ 83 Leron Lee	.50	.23
☐ 84 Rollie Fingers	4.00	1.80
☐ 85 Ted Simmons	1.50	.70
☐ 86 Tom McCraw	.50	.23
☐ 87 Ken Boswell	.50	.23
☐ 88 Mickey Stanley	.50	.70
☐ 89 Jack Billingham	.50	.23
☐ 90 Brooks Robinson	7.00	3.10
☐ 91 Los Angeles Dodgers	2.00	.90
Team Card		
☐ 92 Jerry Bell	.50	.23
☐ 93 Jesus Alou	.50	.23
☐ 94 Dick Billings	.50	.23
☐ 95 Steve Blass	1.50	.70
☐ 96 Doug Griffin	.50	.23
☐ 97 Willie Montanez	1.50	.70
☐ 98 Dick Woodson	.50	.23
☐ 99 Carl Taylor	.50	.23
• ☐ 100 Hank Aaron	25.00	11.00
☐ 101 Ken Henderson	.50	.23
☐ 102 Rudy May	.50	.23
☐ 103 Celerino Sanchez	.50	.23
☐ 104 Reggie Cleveland	.50	.23
☐ 105 Carlos May	.50	.23
☐ 106 Terry Humphrey	.50	.23
☐ 107 Phil Hennigan	.50	.23
☐ 108 Bill Russell	.50	.70
☐ 109 Doyle Alexander	1.50	.70
☐ 110 Bob Watson	.50	.70
☐ 111 Dave Nelson	.50	.23
☐ 112 Gary Ross	.50	.23
☐ 113 Jerry Grote	.50	.23
☐ 114 Lynn McGlothen	.50	.23
☐ 115 Ron Santo	1.50	.70
☐ 116A Yankees Leaders	3.00	1.35
Ralph Houk MG		
Jim Hegan CO		
Elston Howard CO		
Dick Howser CO		
Jim Turner CO		
(Solid backgrounds)		
☐ 116B Yankees Leaders	.75	.35
(Natural backgrounds)		
☐ 117 Ramon Hernandez	.50	.23
☐ 118 John Mayberry	1.50	.70
☐ 119 Larry Bowa	1.50	.70
☐ 120 Joe Coleman	.50	.23
☐ 121 Dave Rader	.50	.23
☐ 122 Jim Strickland	.50	.23
☐ 123 Sandy Alomar	1.50	.70
☐ 124 Jim Hardin	.50	.23
☐ 125 Ron Fairly	.50	.70
☐ 126 Jim Brewer	.50	.23
☐ 127 Milwaukee Brewers	2.00	.90
Team Card		
☐ 128 Ted Sizemore	.50	.23
☐ 129 Terry Forster	1.50	.70
☐ 130 Pete Rose	14.00	6.25
☐ 131A Red Sox Leaders	3.00	1.35
Eddie Kasko MG		
Doug Camilli CO		
Don Lenhardt CO		
Eddie Popowski CO		
(No right ear)		
Lee Stange CO		
☐ 131B Red Sox Leaders	1.50	.70
(Popowski has right ear showing)		
☐ 132 Matty Alou	1.50	.70
☐ 133 Dave Roberts	.50	.23
☐ 134 Milt Wilcox	.50	.23
☐ 135 Lee May UER	1.50	.70
(Career average .000)		
☐ 136A Orioles Leaders	2.00	.90
Earl Weaver MG		
George Bamberger CO		
Jim Frey CO		
Billy Hunter CO		
George Staller CO		
(Orange backgrounds)		
☐ 136B Orioles Leaders	3.00	1.35
(Dark pale backgrounds)		
☐ 137 Jim Beauchamp	.50	.23
☐ 138 Horacio Pina	.50	.23
☐ 139 Carmen Fanzone	.50	.23
☐ 140 Lou Piniella	1.50	.70
☐ 141 Bruce Kison	.50	.23
☐ 142 Thurman Munson	6.00	2.70
☐ 143 John Curtis	.50	.23
☐ 144 Marty Perez	.50	.23
☐ 145 Bobby Bonds	1.50	.70
☐ 146 Woodie Fryman	.50	.23
☐ 147 Mike Anderson	.50	.23
☐ 148 Dave Goltz	.50	.23
☐ 149 Ron Hunt	.50	.23
☐ 150 Wilbur Wood	1.50	.70
☐ 151 Wes Parker	1.50	.70
☐ 152 Dave May	.50	.23
☐ 153 Al Hrabosky	1.50	.70
☐ 154 Jeff Torborg	.50	.23
☐ 155 Sal Bando	1.50	.70
☐ 156 Cesar Geronimo	.50	.23
☐ 157 Denny Riddleberger	.50	.23
☐ 158 Houston Astros	2.00	.90
Team Card		
☐ 159 Clarence Gaston	1.50	.70
☐ 160 Jim Palmer	7.00	3.10
☐ 161 Ted Martinez	.50	.23
☐ 162 Pete Broberg	.50	.23
☐ 163 Vic Davalillo	.50	.23
☐ 164 Monty Montgomery	.50	.23
☐ 165 Luis Aparicio	4.00	1.80
☐ 166 Terry Harmon	.50	.23
☐ 167 Steve Stone	1.50	.70
☐ 168 Jim Northrup	1.50	.70
☐ 169 Ron Schueler	.50	.23
☐ 170 Harmon Killebrew	5.00	2.20
☐ 171 Bernie Carbo	.50	.23
☐ 172 Steve Kline	.50	.23
☐ 173 Hal Breeden	.50	.23
☐ 174 Rich Gossage	6.00	2.70
☐ 175 Frank Robinson	7.00	3.10
☐ 176 Chuck Taylor	.50	.23
☐ 177 Bill Plummer	.50	.23
☐ 178 Don Rose	.50	.23
☐ 179A A's Leaders	4.00	1.80
Dick Williams MG		
Jerry Adair CO		
Vern Hoscheit CO		
Irv Noren CO		
Wes Stock CO		
(Hoscheit left ear showing)		
☐ 179B A's Leaders	1.50	.70
(Hoscheit left ear not showing)		
☐ 180 Ferguson Jenkins	4.00	1.80
☐ 181 Jack Brohamer	.50	.23
☐ 182 Mike Caldwell	1.50	.70
☐ 183 Don Buford	.50	.23
☐ 184 Jerry Koosman	1.50	.70
☐ 185 Jim Wynn	1.50	.70
☐ 186 Bill Fahey	.50	.23
☐ 187 Luke Walker	.50	.23
☐ 188 Cookie Rojas	.50	.23
☐ 189 Greg Luzinski	1.50	.70
☐ 190 Bob Gibson	7.00	3.10
☐ 191 Detroit Tigers	2.50	1.10
Team Card		
☐ 192 Pat Jarvis	.50	.23
☐ 193 Carlton Fisk	7.00	3.10
☐ 194 Jorge Orta	.50	.23
☐ 195 Clay Carroll	.50	.23
☐ 196 Ken McMullen	.50	.23
☐ 197 Ed Goodson	.50	.23
☐ 198 Horace Clarke	.50	.23
☐ 199 Bert Blyleven	1.50	.70
☐ 200 Billy Williams	4.00	1.80
☐ 201 George Hendrick ALCS	1.50	.70
☐ 202 George Foster NLCS	1.50	.70
☐ 203 Gene Tenace WS	1.50	.70
☐ 204 World Series Game 2	1.50	.70
A's two straight		
☐ 205 Tony Perez WS	2.50	1.10
☐ 206 Gene Tenace WS	1.50	.70
☐ 207 Blue Moon Odom WS	1.50	.70
☐ 208 Johnny Bench WS6	5.00	2.20
☐ 209 Bert Campaneris WS	1.50	.70
☐ 210 World Series Summary	.50	.23
World champions:		
A's Win		
☐ 211 Balor Moore	.50	.23
☐ 212 Joe Lahoud	.50	.23
☐ 213 Steve Garvey	5.00	2.20
☐ 214 Steve Hamilton	.50	.23
☐ 215 Dusty Baker	1.50	.70
☐ 216 Toby Harrah	1.50	.70
☐ 217 Don Wilson	.50	.23
☐ 218 Aurelio Rodriguez	.50	.23
☐ 219 St. Louis Cardinals	2.50	1.10
☐ 220 Nolan Ryan	75.00	34.00
☐ 221 Fred Kendall	.50	.23
☐ 222 Rob Gardner	.50	.23
☐ 223 Bud Harrelson	1.50	.70
☐ 224 Bill Lee	1.50	.70
☐ 225 Al Oliver	1.50	.70
☐ 226 Ray Fosse	.50	.23
☐ 227 Wayne Twitchell	.50	.23
☐ 228 Bobby Darwin	.50	.23
☐ 229 Roric Harrison	.50	.23
☐ 230 Joe Morgan	6.00	2.70
☐ 231 Bill Parsons	.50	.23
☐ 232 Ken Singleton	1.50	.70
☐ 233 Ed Kirkpatrick	.50	.23
☐ 234 Bill North	.50	.23
☐ 235 Jim Hunter	4.00	1.80
☐ 236 Tito Fuentes	.50	.23
☐ 237A Braves Leaders	1.50	.70
Eddie Mathews MG		
Lew Burdette CO		
Jim Busby CO		
Roy Hartsfield CO		
Ken Silvestri CO		
(Burdette right ear showing)		
☐ 237B Braves Leaders	3.00	1.35
(Burdette right ear not showing)		
☐ 238 Tony Muser	.50	.23
☐ 239 Pete Richert	.50	.23
☐ 240 Bobby Murcer	1.50	.70
☐ 241 Dwain Anderson	.50	.23
☐ 242 George Culver	.50	.23
☐ 243 California Angels	2.50	1.10
Team Card		
☐ 244 Ed Acosta	.50	.23
☐ 245 Carl Yastrzemski	8.00	3.60
☐ 246 Ken Sanders	.50	.23
☐ 247 Del Unser	.50	.23
☐ 248 Jerry Johnson	.50	.23
☐ 249 Larry Biittner	.50	.23
☐ 250 Manny Sanguillen	1.50	.70
☐ 251 Roger Nelson	.50	.23
☐ 252A Giants Leaders	4.00	1.80
Charlie Fox MG		
Joe Amalfitano CO		
Andy Gilbert CO		
Don McMahon CO		
John McNamara CO		
(Orange backgrounds)		
☐ 252B Giants Leaders	1.50	.70
(Dark pale backgrounds)		
☐ 253 Mark Belanger	1.50	.70
☐ 254 Bill Stoneman	.50	.23
☐ 255 Reggie Jackson	12.00	5.50
☐ 256 Chris Zachary	.50	.23
☐ 257A Mets Leaders	2.50	1.10
Yogi Berra MG		
Roy McMillan CO		
Joe Pignatano CO		
Rube Walker CO		
Eddie Yost CO		
(Orange backgrounds)		
☐ 257B Mets Leaders	5.00	2.20
(Dark pale backgrounds)		
☐ 258 Tommy John	1.50	.70
☐ 259 Jim Holt	.50	.23
☐ 260 Gary Nolan	1.50	.70
☐ 261 Pat Kelly	.50	.23
☐ 262 Jack Aker	.50	.23
☐ 263 George Scott	1.50	.70
☐ 264 Checklist 133-264	3.00	.60
☐ 265 Gene Michael	1.50	.70

266 Mike Lum	.50	.23
267 Lloyd Allen	.50	.23
268 Jerry Morales	.50	.23
269 Tim McCarver	1.50	.70
270 Luis Tiant	1.50	.70
271 Tom Hutton	.50	.23
272 Ed Farmer	.50	.23
273 Chris Speier	.50	.23
274 Darold Knowles	.50	.23
275 Tony Perez	4.00	1.80
276 Joe Lovitto	.50	.23
277 Bob Miller	.50	.23
278 Baltimore Orioles	1.50	.70
Team Card		
279 Mike Strahler	.50	.23
280 Al Kaline	7.00	3.10
281 Mike Jorgensen	.50	.23
282 Steve Hovley	.50	.23
283 Ray Sadecki	.50	.23
284 Glenn Borgmann	.50	.23
285 Don Kessinger	.50	.23
286 Frank Linzy	.50	.23
287 Eddie Leon	.50	.23
288 Gary Gentry	.50	.23
289 Bob Oliver	.50	.23
290 Cesar Cedeno	1.50	.70
291 Rogelio Moret	.50	.23
292 Jose Cruz	1.50	.70
293 Bernie Allen	.50	.23
294 Steve Arlin	.50	.23
295 Bert Campaneris	1.50	.70
296 Reds Leaders	2.50	1.10
Sparky Anderson CO		
Alex Grammas CO		
Ted Kluszewski CO		
George Scherger CO		
Larry Shepard CO		
297 Walt Williams	.50	.23
298 Ron Bryant	.50	.23
299 Ted Ford	.50	.23
300 Steve Carlton	10.00	4.50
301 Billy Grabarkewitz	.50	.23
302 Terry Crowley	.50	.23
303 Nelson Briles	.50	.23
304 Duke Sims	.50	.23
305 Willie Mays	35.00	16.00
306 Tom Burgmeier	.50	.23
307 Boots Day	.50	.23
308 Skip Lockwood	.50	.23
309 Paul Popovich	.50	.23
310 Dick Allen	1.50	.70
311 Joe Decker	.50	.23
312 Oscar Brown	.50	.23
313 Jim Ray	.50	.23
314 Ron Swoboda	.50	.23
315 John Odom	.50	.23
316 San Diego Padres	1.50	.70
Team Card		
317 Danny Cater	.50	.23
318 Jim McGlothlin	.50	.23
319 Jim Spencer	.50	.23
320 Lou Brock	6.00	2.70
321 Rich Hinton	.50	.23
322 Garry Maddox	1.50	.70
323 Tigers Leaders	1.50	.70
Billy Martin MG		
Art Fowler CO		
Charlie Silvera CO		
Dick Tracewski CO		
324 Al Downing	.50	.23
325 Boog Powell	1.50	.70
326 Darrell Brandon	.50	.23
327 John Lowenstein	.50	.23
328 Bill Bonham	.50	.23
329 Ed Kranepool	.50	.23
330 Rod Carew	7.00	3.10
331 Carl Morton	.50	.23
332 John Felske	.50	.23
333 Gene Clines	.50	.23
334 Freddie Patek	.50	.23
335 Bob Tolan	.50	.23
336 Tom Bradley	.50	.23
337 Dave Duncan	.50	.23
338 Checklist 265-396	3.00	.60
339 Dick Tidrow	.50	.23
340 Nate Colbert	.50	.23
341 Jim Palmer KP	1.50	.70
342 Sam McDowell KP	.50	.23
343 Bobby Murcer KP	.50	.23
344 Jim Hunter KP	1.50	.70
345 Chris Speier KP	.50	.23
346 Gaylord Perry KP	1.50	.70
347 Kansas City Royals	1.50	.70
Team Card		
348 Rennie Stennett	.50	.23
349 Dick McAuliffe	.50	.23
350 Tom Seaver	12.00	5.50
351 Jimmy Stewart	.50	.23
352 Don Stanhouse	.50	.23
353 Steve Brye	.50	.23
354 Billy Parker	.50	.23
355 Mike Marshall	1.50	.70
356 White Sox Leaders	.50	.23
Chuck Tanner MG		
Joe Lonnett CO		
Jim Mahoney CO		
Al Monchak CO		
Johnny Sain CO		
357 Ross Grimsley	.50	.23
358 Jim Nettles	.50	.23
359 Cecil Upshaw	.50	.23
360 Joe Rudi UER	1.50	.70
(Photo actually		
Gene Tenace)		
361 Fran Healy	.50	.23
362 Eddie Watt	.50	.23
363 Jackie Hernandez	.50	.23
364 Rick Wise	.50	.23
365 Rico Petrocelli	1.50	.70
366 Brock Davis	.50	.23
367 Burt Hooton	.50	.23
368 Bill Buckner	1.50	.70
369 Lerrin LaGrow	.50	.23
370 Willie Stargell	5.00	2.20
371 Mike Kekich	.50	.23
372 Oscar Gamble	.50	.23
373 Clyde Wright	.50	.23
374 Darrell Evans	1.50	.70
375 Larry Dierker	1.50	.70
376 Frank Duffy	.50	.23
377 Expos Leaders	.50	.23
Gene Mauch MG		
Dave Bristol CO		
Larry Doby CO		
Cal McLish CO		
Jerry Zimmerman CO		
378 Len Randle	.50	.23
379 Cy Acosta	.50	.23
380 Johnny Bench	12.00	5.50
381 Vicente Romo	.50	.23
382 Mike Hegan	.50	.23
383 Diego Segui	.50	.23
384 Don Baylor	4.00	1.80
385 Jim Perry	1.50	.70
386 Don Money	.50	.23
387 Jim Barr	.50	.23
388 Ben Oglivie	1.50	.70
389 New York Mets	4.00	1.80
Team Card		
390 Mickey Lolich	1.50	.70
391 Lee Lacy	.50	.23
392 Dick Drago	.50	.23
393 Jose Cardenal	.50	.23
394 Sparky Lyle	1.50	.70
395 Roger Metzger	.50	.23
396 Grant Jackson	.50	.23
397 Dave Cash	1.25	.55
398 Rich Hand	1.25	.55
399 George Foster	2.00	.90
400 Gaylord Perry	5.00	2.20
401 Clyde Mashore	1.25	.55
402 Jack Hiatt	1.25	.55
403 Sonny Jackson	1.25	.55
404 Chuck Brinkman	1.25	.55
405 Cesar Tovar	1.25	.55
406 Paul Lindblad	1.25	.55
407 Felix Millan	1.25	.55
408 Jim Colborn	1.25	.55
409 Ivan Murrell	1.25	.55
410 Willie McCovey	6.00	2.70
(Bench behind plate)		
411 Ray Corbin	1.25	.55
412 Manny Mota	2.00	.90
413 Tom Timmermann	1.25	.55
414 Ken Rudolph	1.25	.55
415 Marty Pattin	1.25	.55
416 Paul Schaal	1.25	.55
417 Scipio Spinks	1.25	.55
418 Bob Grich	2.00	.90
419 Casey Cox	1.25	.55
420 Tommie Agee	1.25	.55
421A Angels Leaders	1.50	.70
Bobby Winkles MG		
Tom Morgan CO		
Salty Parker CO		
Jimmie Reese CO		
(Orange backgrounds)		
421B Angels Leaders	1.50	.70
(Dark pale		
backgrounds)		
422 Bob Robertson	1.25	.55
423 Johnny Jeter	1.25	.55
424 Denny Doyle	1.25	.55
425 Alex Johnson	1.25	.55
426 Dave LaRoche	1.25	.55
427 Rick Auerbach	1.25	.55
428 Wayne Simpson	1.25	.55
429 Jim Fairey	1.25	.55
430 Vida Blue	2.00	.90
431 Gerry Moses	1.25	.55
432 Dan Frisella	1.25	.55
433 Willie Horton	2.00	.90
434 San Francisco Giants	3.00	1.35
Team Card		
435 Rico Carty	2.00	.90
436 Jim McAndrew	1.25	.55
437 John Kennedy	1.25	.55
438 Enzo Hernandez	1.25	.55
439 Eddie Fisher	1.25	.55
440 Glenn Beckert	1.25	.55
441 Gail Hopkins	1.25	.55
442 Dick Dietz	1.25	.55
443 Danny Thompson	1.25	.55
444 Ken Brett	1.25	.55
445 Ken Berry	1.25	.55
446 Jerry Reuss	2.00	.90
447 Joe Hague	1.25	.55
448 John Hiller	1.25	.55
449A Indians Leaders	4.00	1.80
Ken Aspromonte MG		
Rocky Colavito CO		
Joe Lutz CO		
Warren Spahn CO		
(Spahn's right		
ear pointed)		
449B Indians Leaders	4.00	1.80
(Spahn's right		
ear round)		
450 Joe Torre	2.00	.90
451 John Vukovich	1.25	.55
452 Paul Casanova	1.25	.55
453 Checklist 397-528	3.00	.60
454 Tom Haller	1.25	.55
455 Bill Melton	1.25	.55
456 Dick Green	1.25	.55
457 John Strohmayer	1.25	.55
458 Jim Mason	1.25	.55
459 Jimmy Howarth	1.25	.55
460 Bill Freehan	2.00	.90
461 Mike Corkins	1.25	.55
462 Ron Blomberg	1.25	.55
463 Ken Tatum	1.25	.55
464 Chicago Cubs	3.00	1.35
Team Card		
465 Dave Giusti	1.25	.55
466 Jose Arcia	1.25	.55
467 Mike Ryan	1.25	.55
468 Tom Griffin	1.25	.55
469 Dan Monzon	1.25	.55
470 Mike Cuellar	2.00	.90
471 Ty Cobb ATL	10.00	4.50
4191 Hits		
472 Lou Gehrig ATL	15.00	6.75
23 Grand Slams		
473 Hank Aaron ATL	10.00	4.50
6172 Total Bases		
474 Babe Ruth ATL	20.00	9.00

	2209 RBI		
☐ 475	Ty Cobb ATL	8.00	3.60
	.367 Batting Average		
☐ 476	Walter Johnson ATL	3.00	1.35
	113 Shutouts		
☐ 477	Cy Young ATL	3.00	1.35
	511 Victories		
☐ 478	Walter Johnson ATL	3.00	1.35
	3508 Strikeouts		
☐ 479	Hal Lanier	1.25	.55
☐ 480	Juan Marichal	5.00	2.20
☐ 481	Chicago White Sox	3.00	1.35
	Team Card		
☐ 482	Rick Reuschel	3.00	1.35
☐ 483	Dal Maxvill	1.25	.55
☐ 484	Ernie McAnally	1.25	.55
☐ 485	Norm Cash	2.00	.90
☐ 486A	Phillies Leaders	1.50	.70
	Danny Ozark MG		
	Carroll Beringer CO		
	Billy DeMars CO		
	Ray Rippelmeyer CO		
	Bob Wine CO		
	(Orange backgrounds)		
☐ 486B	Phillies Leaders	1.50	.70
	(Dark pale backgrounds)		
☐ 487	Bruce Dal Canton	1.25	.55
☐ 488	Dave Campbell	2.00	.90
☐ 489	Jeff Burroughs	2.00	.90
☐ 490	Claude Osteen	1.25	.55
☐ 491	Bob Montgomery	1.25	.55
☐ 492	Pedro Borbon	1.25	.55
☐ 493	Duffy Dyer	1.25	.55
☐ 494	Rich Morales	1.25	.55
☐ 495	Tommy Helms	1.25	.55
☐ 496	Ray Lamb	1.25	.55
☐ 497A	Cardinals Leaders	2.00	.90
	Red Schoendienst MG		
	Vern Benson CO		
	George Kissell CO		
	Barney Schultz CO		
	(Orange backgrounds)		
☐ 497B	Cardinals Leaders	3.00	1.35
	(Dark pale backgrounds)		
☐ 498	Graig Nettles	3.00	1.35
☐ 499	Bob Moose	1.25	.55
☐ 500	Oakland A's	3.00	1.35
	Team Card		
☐ 501	Larry Gura	1.25	.55
☐ 502	Bobby Valentine	3.00	1.35
☐ 503	Phil Niekro	5.00	2.20
☐ 504	Earl Williams	1.25	.55
☐ 505	Bob Bailey	1.25	.55
☐ 506	Bart Johnson	1.25	.55
☐ 507	Darrel Chaney	1.25	.55
☐ 508	Gates Brown	1.25	.55
☐ 509	Jim Nash	1.25	.55
☐ 510	Amos Otis	2.00	.90
☐ 511	Sam McDowell	2.00	.90
☐ 512	Dalton Jones	1.25	.55
☐ 513	Dave Marshall	1.25	.55
☐ 514	Jerry Kenney	1.25	.55
☐ 515	Andy Messersmith	2.00	.90
☐ 516	Danny Walton	1.25	.55
☐ 517A	Pirates Leaders	1.50	.70
	Bill Virdon MG		
	Don Leppert CO		
	Bill Mazeroski CO		
	Dave Ricketts CO		
	Mel Wright CO		
	(Mazeroski has no right ear)		
☐ 517B	Pirates Leaders	1.50	.70
	(Mazeroski has right ear)		
☐ 518	Bob Veale	1.25	.55
☐ 519	Johnny Edwards	1.25	.55
☐ 520	Mel Stottlemyre	2.00	.90
☐ 521	Atlanta Braves	3.00	1.35
	Team Card		
☐ 522	Leo Cardenas	1.25	.55
☐ 523	Wayne Granger	1.25	.55
☐ 524	Gene Tenace	2.00	.90
☐ 525	Jim Fregosi	2.00	.90
☐ 526	Ollie Brown	1.25	.55
☐ 527	Dan McGinn	1.25	.55
☐ 528	Paul Blair	1.25	.55
☐ 529	Milt May	3.50	1.55
☐ 530	Jim Kaat	5.00	2.20
☐ 531	Ron Woods	3.50	1.55
☐ 532	Steve Mingori	3.50	1.55
☐ 533	Larry Stahl	3.50	1.55
☐ 534	Dave Lemonds	3.50	1.55
☐ 535	Johnny Callison	5.00	2.20
☐ 536	Philadelphia Phillies	6.00	2.70
	Team Card		
☐ 537	Bill Slayback	3.50	1.55
☐ 538	Jim Ray Hart	5.00	2.20
☐ 539	Tom Murphy	3.50	1.55
☐ 540	Cleon Jones	5.00	2.20
☐ 541	Bob Bolin	3.50	1.55
☐ 542	Pat Corrales	5.00	2.20
☐ 543	Alan Foster	3.50	1.55
☐ 544	Von Joshua	3.50	1.55
☐ 545	Orlando Cepeda	5.00	2.20
☐ 546	Jim York	3.50	1.55
☐ 547	Bobby Heise	3.50	1.55
☐ 548	Don Durham	3.50	1.55
☐ 549	Rangers Leaders	5.00	2.20
	Whitey Herzog MG		
	Chuck Estrada CO		
	Chuck Hiller CO		
	Jackie Moore CO		
☐ 550	Dave Johnson	5.00	2.20
☐ 551	Mike Kilkenny	3.50	1.55
☐ 552	J.C. Martin	3.50	1.55
☐ 553	Mickey Scott	3.50	1.55
☐ 554	Dave Concepcion	5.00	2.20
☐ 555	Bill Hands	3.50	1.55
☐ 556	New York Yankees	8.00	3.60
	Team Card		
☐ 557	Bernie Williams	3.50	1.55
☐ 558	Jerry May	3.50	1.55
☐ 559	Barry Lersch	3.50	1.55
☐ 560	Frank Howard	5.00	2.20
☐ 561	Jim Geddes	3.50	1.55
☐ 562	Wayne Garrett	3.50	1.55
☐ 563	Larry Haney	3.50	1.55
☐ 564	Mike Thompson	3.50	1.55
☐ 565	Jim Hickman	3.50	1.55
☐ 566	Lew Krausse	3.50	1.55
☐ 567	Bob Fenwick	3.50	1.55
☐ 568	Ray Newman	3.50	1.55
☐ 569	Dodgers Leaders	5.00	2.20
	Walt Alston MG		
	Red Adams CO		
	Monty Basgall CO		
	Jim Gilliam CO		
	Tom Lasorda CO		
☐ 570	Bill Singer	5.00	2.20
☐ 571	Rusty Torres	3.50	1.55
☐ 572	Gary Sutherland	3.50	1.55
☐ 573	Fred Beene	3.50	1.55
☐ 574	Bob Didier	3.50	1.55
☐ 575	Dock Ellis	5.00	2.20
☐ 576	Montreal Expos	6.00	2.70
	Team Card		
☐ 577	Eric Soderholm	3.50	1.55
☐ 578	Ken Wright	3.50	1.55
☐ 579	Tom Grieve	5.00	2.20
☐ 580	Joe Pepitone	5.00	2.20
☐ 581	Steve Kealey	3.50	1.55
☐ 582	Darrell Porter	5.00	2.20
☐ 583	Bill Grief	3.50	1.55
☐ 584	Chris Arnold	3.50	1.55
☐ 585	Joe Niekro	5.00	2.20
☐ 586	Bill Sudakis	3.50	1.55
☐ 587	Rich McKinney	3.50	1.55
☐ 588	Checklist 529-660	20.00	4.00
☐ 589	Ken Forsch	3.50	1.55
☐ 590	Deron Johnson	5.00	2.20
☐ 591	Mike Hedlund	3.50	1.55
☐ 592	John Boccabella	3.50	1.55
☐ 593	Royals Leaders	3.50	1.55
	Jack McKeon MG		
	Galen Cisco CO		
	Harry Dunlop CO		
	Charlie Lau CO		
☐ 594	Vic Harris	3.50	1.55
☐ 595	Don Gullett	5.00	2.20
☐ 596	Boston Red Sox	6.00	2.70
	Team Card		
☐ 597	Mickey Rivers	5.00	2.20
☐ 598	Phil Roof	3.50	1.55
☐ 599	Ed Crosby	3.50	1.55
☐ 600	Dave McNally	5.00	2.20
☐ 601	Rookie Catchers	5.00	2.20
	Sergio Robles		
	George Pena		
	Rick Stelmaszek		
☐ 602	Rookie Pitchers	5.00	2.20
	Mel Behney		
	Ralph Garcia		
	Doug Rau		
☐ 603	Rookie 3rd Basemen	5.00	2.20
	Terry Hughes		
	Bill McNulty		
	Ken Reitz		
☐ 604	Rookie Pitchers	5.00	2.20
	Jesse Jefferson		
	Dennis O'Toole		
	Bob Strampe		
☐ 605	Rookie 1st Basemen	5.00	2.20
	Enos Cabell		
	Pat Bourque		
	Gonzalo Marquez		
☐ 606	Rookie Outfielders	5.00	2.20
	Gary Matthews		
	Tom Paciorek		
	Jorge Roque		
☐ 607	Rookie Shortstops	5.00	2.20
	Pepe Frias		
	Ray Busse		
	Mario Guerrero		
☐ 608	Rookie Pitchers	5.00	2.20
	Steve Busby		
	Dick Colpaert		
	George Medich		
☐ 609	Rookie 2nd Basemen	5.00	2.20
	Larvell Blanks		
	Pedro Garcia		
	Dave Lopes		
☐ 610	Rookie Pitchers	5.00	2.20
	Jimmy Freeman		
	Charlie Hough		
	Hank Webb		
☐ 611	Rookie Outfielders	5.00	2.20
	Rich Coggins		
	Jim Wohlford		
	Richie Zisk		
☐ 612	Rookie Pitchers	5.00	2.20
	Steve Lawson		
	Bob Reynolds		
	Brent Strom		
☐ 613	Rookie Catchers	15.00	6.75
	Bob Boone		
	Skip Jutze		
	Mike Ivie		
☐ 614	Rookie Outfielders	18.00	8.00
	Al Bumbry		
	Dwight Evans		
	Charlie Spikes		
☐ 615	Rookie 3rd Basemen	200.00	90.00
	Ron Cey		
	John Hilton		
	Mike Schmidt		
☐ 616	Rookie Pitchers	5.00	2.20
	Norm Angelini		
	Steve Blateric		
	Mike Garman		
☐ 617	Rich Chiles	3.50	1.55
☐ 618	Andy Etchebarren	3.50	1.55
☐ 619	Billy Wilson	3.50	1.55
☐ 620	Tommy Harper	5.00	2.20
☐ 621	Joe Ferguson	5.00	2.20
☐ 622	Larry Hisle	5.00	2.20
☐ 623	Steve Renko	3.50	1.55
☐ 624	Astros Leaders	5.00	2.20
	Leo Durocher MG		
	Preston Gomez CO		
	Grady Hatton CO		
	Hub Kittle CO		
	Jim Owens CO		
☐ 625	Angel Mangual	3.50	1.55
☐ 626	Bob Barton	3.50	1.55
☐ 627	Luis Alvarado	3.50	1.55

#	Player	NRMT	VG-E
628	Jim Slaton	3.50	1.55
629	Cleveland Indians Team Card	6.00	2.70
630	Denny McLain	8.00	3.60
631	Tom Matchick	3.50	1.55
632	Dick Selma	3.50	1.55
633	Ike Brown	3.50	1.55
634	Alan Closter	3.50	1.55
635	Gene Alley	5.00	2.20
636	Rickey Clark	3.50	1.55
637	Norm Miller	3.50	1.55
638	Ken Reynolds	3.50	1.55
639	Willie Crawford	3.50	1.55
640	Dick Bosman	3.50	1.55
641	Cincinnati Reds Team Card	6.00	2.70
642	Jose Laboy	3.50	1.55
643	Al Fitzmorris	3.50	1.55
644	Jack Heidemann	3.50	1.55
645	Bob Locker	3.50	1.55
646	Brewers Leaders Del Crandall MG Harvey Kuenn CO Joe Nossek CO Bob Shaw CO Jim Walton CO	3.50	1.55
647	George Stone	3.50	1.55
648	Tom Egan	3.50	1.55
649	Rich Folkers	3.50	1.55
650	Felipe Alou	5.00	2.20
651	Don Carrithers	3.50	1.55
652	Ted Kubiak	3.50	1.55
653	Joe Hoerner	3.50	1.55
654	Minnesota Twins Team Card	6.00	2.70
655	Clay Kirby	3.50	1.55
656	John Ellis	3.50	1.55
657	Bob Johnson	3.50	1.55
658	Elliott Maddox	3.50	1.55
659	Jose Pagan	3.50	1.55
660	Fred Scherman	5.00	1.95

1974 Topps

	NRMT	VG-E
COMPLETE SET (660)	600.00	275.00
COMP.FACT.SET (660)	600.00	275.00
COMMON CARD (1-660)	.50	.23
AARON SPECIALS (2-6)	6.00	2.70
WASH.VARIATIONS	4.00	1.80
MINOR STARS	1.00	.45
SEMISTARS	2.00	.90
UNLISTED STARS	3.00	1.35
CARDS PRICED IN NM CONDITION		

#	Player	NRMT	VG-E
1	Hank Aaron All-Time Home Run King (Complete ML record)	40.00	12.00
2	Aaron Special 54-57 (Records on back)	6.00	2.70
3	Aaron Special 58-61 (Memorable homers)	6.00	2.70
4	Aaron Special 62-65 (Life in ML's 1954-63)	6.00	2.70
5	Aaron Special 66-69 (Life in ML's 1964-73)	6.00	2.70
6	Aaron Special 70-73 (Milestone homers)	6.00	2.70
7	Jim Hunter	4.00	1.80
8	George Theodore	.50	.23
9	Mickey Lolich	1.00	.45
10	Johnny Bench	12.00	5.50
11	Jim Bibby	.50	.23
12	Dave May	.50	.23
13	Tom Hilgendorf	.50	.23
14	Paul Popovich	.50	.23
15	Joe Torre	2.00	.90
16	Baltimore Orioles Team Card	1.00	.45
17	Doug Bird	.50	.23
18	Gary Thomasson	.50	.23
19	Gerry Moses	.50	.23
20	Nolan Ryan	60.00	27.00
21	Bob Gallagher	.50	.23
22	Cy Acosta	.50	.23
23	Craig Robinson	.50	.23
24	John Hiller	1.00	.45
25	Ken Singleton	1.00	.45
26	Bill Campbell	.50	.23
27	George Scott	1.00	.45
28	Manny Sanguillen	1.00	.45
29	Phil Niekro	3.00	1.35
30	Bobby Bonds	2.00	.90
31	Astros Leaders Preston Gomez MG Roger Craig CO Hub Kittle CO Grady Hatton CO Bob Lillis CO	1.00	.45
32A	Johnny Grubb SD	1.00	.45
32B	Johnny Grubb WASH	4.00	1.80
33	Don Newhauser	.50	.23
34	Andy Kosco	.50	.23
35	Gaylord Perry	3.00	1.35
36	St. Louis Cardinals Team Card	1.00	.45
37	Dave Sells	.50	.23
38	Don Kessinger	1.00	.45
39	Ken Suarez	.50	.23
40	Jim Palmer	6.00	2.70
41	Bobby Floyd	.50	.23
42	Claude Osteen	1.00	.45
43	Jim Wynn	1.00	.45
44	Mel Stottlemyre	1.00	.45
45	Dave Johnson	1.00	.45
46	Pat Kelly	.50	.23
47	Dick Ruthven	.50	.23
48	Dick Sharon	.50	.23
49	Steve Renko	.50	.23
50	Rod Carew	6.00	2.70
51	Bobby Heise	.50	.23
52	Al Oliver	.50	.23
53A	Fred Kendall SD	1.00	.45
53B	Fred Kendall WASH	4.00	1.80
54	Elias Sosa	.50	.23
55	Frank Robinson	6.00	2.70
56	New York Mets Team Card	1.00	.45
57	Darold Knowles	.50	.23
58	Charlie Spikes	.50	.23
59	Ross Grimsley	.50	.23
60	Lou Brock	6.00	2.70
61	Luis Aparicio	3.00	1.35
62	Bob Locker	.50	.23
63	Bill Sudakis	.50	.23
64	Doug Rau	.50	.23
65	Amos Otis	1.00	.45
66	Sparky Lyle	1.00	.45
67	Tommy Helms	.50	.23
68	Grant Jackson	.50	.23
69	Del Unser	.50	.23
70	Dick Allen	2.00	.90
71	Dan Frisella	.50	.23
72	Aurelio Rodriguez	.50	.23
73	Mike Marshall	2.00	.90
74	Minnesota Twins Team Card	1.00	.45
75	Jim Colborn	.50	.23
76	Mickey Rivers	1.00	.45
77A	Rich Troedson SD	1.00	.45
77B	Rich Troedson WASH	1.00	.45
78	Giants Leaders Charlie Fox MG John McNamara CO Joe Amalfitano CO Andy Gilbert CO Don McMahon CO	1.00	.45
79	Gene Tenace	1.00	.45
80	Tom Seaver	12.00	5.50
81	Frank Duffy	.50	.23
82	Dave Giusti	.50	.23
83	Orlando Cepeda	3.00	1.35
84	Rick Wise	.50	.23
85	Joe Morgan	6.00	2.70
86	Joe Ferguson	1.00	.45
87	Fergie Jenkins	3.00	1.35
88	Freddie Patek	1.00	.45
89	Jackie Brown	.50	.23
90	Bobby Murcer	1.00	.45
91	Ken Forsch	.50	.23
92	Paul Blair	1.00	.45
93	Rod Gilbreath	.50	.23
94	Detroit Tigers Team Card	1.00	.45
95	Steve Carlton	6.00	2.70
96	Jerry Hairston	.50	.23
97	Bob Bailey	.50	.23
98	Bert Blyleven	2.00	.90
99	Brewers Leaders Del Crandall MG Harvey Kuenn CO Joe Nossek CO Jim Walton CO Al Widmar CO	1.00	.45
100	Willie Stargell	4.00	1.80
101	Bobby Valentine	1.00	.45
102A	Bill Greif SD	1.00	.45
102B	Bill Greif WASH	4.00	1.80
103	Sal Bando	1.00	.45
104	Ron Bryant	.50	.23
105	Carlton Fisk	8.00	3.60
106	Harry Parker	.50	.23
107	Alex Johnson	.50	.23
108	Al Hrabosky	1.00	.45
109	Bob Grich	1.00	.45
110	Billy Williams	3.00	1.35
111	Clay Carroll	.50	.23
112	Dave Lopes	2.00	.90
113	Dick Drago	.50	.23
114	Angels Team	1.00	.45
115	Willie Horton	1.00	.45
116	Jerry Reuss	1.00	.45
117	Ron Blomberg	.50	.23
118	Bill Lee	1.00	.45
119	Phillies Leaders Danny Ozark MG Ray Rippelmeyer CO Bobby Wine CO Carroll Beringer CO Billy DeMars CO	1.00	.45
120	Wilbur Wood	.50	.23
121	Larry Lintz	.50	.23
122	Jim Holt	.50	.23
123	Nelson Briles	1.00	.45
124	Bobby Coluccio	.50	.23
125A	Nate Colbert SD	1.00	.45
125B	Nate Colbert WASH	4.00	1.80
126	Checklist 1-132	3.00	.60
127	Tom Paciorek	1.00	.45
128	John Ellis	.50	.23
129	Chris Speier	.50	.23
130	Reggie Jackson	15.00	6.75
131	Bob Boone	2.00	.90
132	Felix Millan	.50	.23
133	David Clyde	1.00	.45
134	Denis Menke	.50	.23
135	Roy White	1.00	.45
136	Rick Reuschel	1.00	.45
137	Al Bumbry	1.00	.45
138	Eddie Brinkman	.50	.23
139	Aurelio Monteagudo	.50	.23
140	Darrell Evans	2.00	.90
141	Pat Bourque	.50	.23
142	Pedro Garcia	.50	.23
143	Dick Woodson	.50	.23
144	Dodgers Leaders Walter Alston MG Tom Lasorda CO Jim Gilliam CO Red Adams CO	2.00	.90

Monty Basgall CO
- □ 145 Dock Ellis .50 .23
- □ 146 Ron Fairly 1.00 .45
- □ 147 Bart Johnson .50 .23
- □ 148A Dave Hilton SD 1.00 .45
- □ 148B Dave Hilton WASH 4.00 1.80
- □ 149 Mac Scarce .50 .23
- □ 150 John Mayberry 1.00 .45
- □ 151 Diego Segui .50 .23
- □ 152 Oscar Gamble 1.00 .45
- □ 153 Jon Matlack 1.00 .45
- □ 154 Houston Astros 1.00 .45
  Team Card
- □ 155 Bert Campaneris 1.00 .45
- □ 156 Randy Moffitt .50 .23
- □ 157 Vic Harris .50 .23
- □ 158 Jack Billingham .50 .23
- □ 159 Jim Ray Hart 1.00 .45
- □ 160 Brooks Robinson 6.00 2.70
- □ 161 Ray Burris UER 1.00 .45
  (Card number is
  printed sideways)
- □ 162 Bill Freehan 1.00 .45
- □ 163 Ken Berry .50 .23
- □ 164 Tom House .50 .23
- □ 165 Willie Davis 1.00 .45
- □ 166 Royals Leaders 1.00 .45
  Jack McKeon MG
  Charlie Lau CO
  Harry Dunlop CO
  Galen Cisco CO
- □ 167 Luis Tiant 2.00 .90
- □ 168 Danny Thompson .50 .23
- □ 169 Steve Rogers 2.00 .90
- □ 170 Bill Melton .50 .23
- □ 171 Eduardo Rodriguez .50 .23
- □ 172 Gene Clines .50 .23
- □ 173A Randy Jones SD 2.00 .90
- □ 173B Randy Jones WASH 6.00 2.70
- □ 174 Bill Robinson 1.00 .45
- □ 175 Reggie Cleveland .50 .23
- □ 176 John Lowenstein .50 .23
- □ 177 Dave Roberts .50 .23
- □ 178 Garry Maddox 1.00 .45
- □ 179 Mets Leaders 4.00 1.80
  Yogi Berra MG
  Rube Walker CO
  Eddie Yost CO
  Roy McMillan CO
  Joe Pignatano CO
- □ 180 Ken Holtzman 1.00 .45
- □ 181 Cesar Geronimo .50 .23
- □ 182 Lindy McDaniel 1.00 .45
- □ 183 Johnny Oates 1.00 .45
- □ 184 Texas Rangers 1.00 .45
  Team Card
- □ 185 Jose Cardenal .50 .23
- □ 186 Fred Scherman .50 .23
- □ 187 Don Baylor 2.00 .90
- □ 188 Rudy Meoli .50 .23
- □ 189 Jim Brewer .50 .23
- □ 190 Tony Oliva 2.00 .90
- □ 191 Al Fitzmorris .50 .23
- □ 192 Mario Guerrero .50 .23
- □ 193 Tom Walker .50 .23
- □ 194 Darrell Porter 1.00 .45
- □ 195 Carlos May .50 .23
- □ 196 Jim Fregosi 1.00 .45
- □ 197A Vicente Romo SD 1.00 .45
- □ 197B Vicente Romo WASH 4.00 1.80
- □ 198 Dave Cash .50 .23
- □ 199 Mike Kekich .50 .23
- □ 200 Cesar Cedeno 1.00 .45
- □ 201 Batting Leaders 5.00 2.20
  Rod Carew
  Pete Rose
- □ 202 Home Run Leaders 5.00 2.20
  Reggie Jackson
  Willie Stargell
- □ 203 RBI Leaders 5.00 2.20
  Reggie Jackson
  Willie Stargell
- □ 204 Stolen Base Leaders 2.00 .90
  Tommy Harper
  Lou Brock
- □ 205 Victory Leaders 1.00 .45

Wilbur Wood
Ron Bryant
- □ 206 ERA Leaders 5.00 2.20
  Jim Palmer
  Tom Seaver
- □ 207 Strikeout Leaders 20.00 9.00
  Nolan Ryan
  Tom Seaver
- □ 208 Firemen Leaders 1.00 .45
  John Hiller
  Mike Marshall
- □ 209 Ted Sizemore .50 .23
- □ 210 Bill Singer .50 .23
- □ 211 Chicago Cubs 1.00 .45
  Team Card
- □ 212 Rollie Fingers 3.00 1.35
- □ 213 Dave Rader .50 .23
- □ 214 Billy Grabarkewitz .50 .23
- □ 215 Al Kaline UER 6.00 2.70
  (No copyright on back)
- □ 216 Ray Sadecki .50 .23
- □ 217 Tim Foli .50 .23
- □ 218 Johnny Briggs .50 .23
- □ 219 Doug Griffin .50 .23
- □ 220 Don Sutton 3.00 1.35
- □ 221 White Sox Leaders 1.00 .45
  Chuck Tanner MG
  Jim Mahoney CO
  Alex Monchak CO
  Johnny Sain CO
  Joe Lonnett CO
- □ 222 Ramon Hernandez .50 .23
- □ 223 Jeff Burroughs 2.00 .90
- □ 224 Roger Metzger .50 .23
- □ 225 Paul Splittorff .50 .23
- □ 226A San Diego Padres .. 2.00 .90
  Team Card San Diego
- □ 226B San Diego Padres .. 8.00 3.60
  Team Card Washington Variation
- □ 227 Mike Lum .50 .23
- □ 228 Ted Kubiak .50 .23
- □ 229 Fritz Peterson .50 .23
- □ 230 Tony Perez 3.00 1.35
- □ 231 Dick Tidrow .50 .23
- □ 232 Steve Brye .50 .23
- □ 233 Jim Barr .50 .23
- □ 234 John Milner .50 .23
- □ 235 Dave McNally 1.00 .45
- □ 236 Cardinals Leaders 2.00 .90
  Red Schoendienst MG
  Barney Schultz CO
  George Kissell CO
  Johnny Lewis CO
  Vern Benson CO
- □ 237 Ken Brett .50 .23
- □ 238 Fran Healy HOR 2.00 .90
  (Munson sliding
  in background)
- □ 239 Bill Russell 1.00 .45
- □ 240 Joe Coleman .50 .23
- □ 241A Glenn Beckett SD 1.00 .45
- □ 241B Glenn Beckett WASH 4.00 1.80
- □ 242 Bill Gogolewski .50 .23
- □ 243 Bob Oliver .50 .23
- □ 244 Carl Morton .50 .23
- □ 245 Cleon Jones .50 .23
- □ 246 Oakland Athletics 2.00 .90
  Team Card
- □ 247 Rick Miller .50 .23
- □ 248 Tom Hall .50 .23
- □ 249 George Mitterwald .50 .23
- □ 250A Willie McCovey SD 6.00 2.70
- □ 250B Willie McCovey WASH 30.00 13.50
- □ 251 Graig Nettles 2.00 .90
- □ 252 Dave Parker 10.00 4.50
- □ 253 John Boccabella .50 .23
- □ 254 Stan Bahnsen .50 .23
- □ 255 Larry Bowa 1.00 .45
- □ 256 Tom Griffin .50 .23
- □ 257 Buddy Bell 2.00 .90
- □ 258 Jerry Morales .50 .23
- □ 259 Bob Reynolds .50 .23
- □ 260 Ted Simmons 2.00 .90
- □ 261 Jerry Bell .50 .23
- □ 262 Ed Kirkpatrick .50 .23
- □ 263 Checklist 133-264 3.00 .60

- □ 264 Joe Rudi 1.00 .45
- □ 265 Tug McGraw 2.00 .90
- □ 266 Jim Northrup 1.00 .45
- □ 267 Andy Messersmith 1.00 .45
- □ 268 Tom Grieve 1.00 .45
- □ 269 Bob Johnson .50 .23
- □ 270 Ron Santo 2.00 .90
- □ 271 Bill Hands .50 .23
- □ 272 Paul Casanova .50 .23
- □ 273 Checklist 265-396 3.00 .60
- □ 274 Fred Beene .50 .23
- □ 275 Ron Hunt .50 .23
- □ 276 Angels Leaders 1.00 .45
  Bobby Winkles MG
  John Roseboro CO
  Tom Morgan CO
  Jimmie Reese CO
  Salty Parker CO
- □ 277 Gary Nolan 1.00 .45
- □ 278 Cookie Rojas 1.00 .45
- □ 279 Jim Crawford .50 .23
- □ 280 Carl Yastrzemski 8.00 3.60
- □ 281 San Francisco Giants 1.00 .45
  Team Card
- □ 282 Doyle Alexander 1.00 .45
- □ 283 Mike Schmidt 30.00 13.50
- □ 284 Dave Duncan 1.00 .45
- □ 285 Reggie Smith 1.00 .45
- □ 286 Tony Muser .50 .23
- □ 287 Clay Kirby .50 .23
- □ 288 Gorman Thomas 2.00 .90
- □ 289 Rick Auerbach .50 .23
- □ 290 Vida Blue 1.00 .45
- □ 291 Don Hahn .50 .23
- □ 292 Chuck Seelbach .50 .23
- □ 293 Milt May .50 .23
- □ 294 Steve Foucault .50 .23
- □ 295 Rick Monday 1.00 .45
- □ 296 Ray Corbin .50 .23
- □ 297 Hal Breeden .50 .23
- □ 298 Roric Harrison .50 .23
- □ 299 Gene Michael 1.00 .45
- □ 300 Pete Rose 20.00 9.00
- □ 301 Bob Montgomery .50 .23
- □ 302 Rudy May .50 .23
- □ 303 George Hendrick 1.00 .45
- □ 304 Don Wilson 1.00 .45
- □ 305 Tito Fuentes .50 .23
- □ 306 Orioles Leaders 2.00 .90
  Earl Weaver MG
  Jim Frey CO
  George Bamberger CO
  Billy Hunter CO
  George Staller CO
- □ 307 Luis Melendez .50 .23
- □ 308 Bruce Dal Canton .50 .23
- □ 309A Dave Roberts SD 1.00 .45
- □ 309B Dave Roberts WASH 6.00 2.70
- □ 310 Terry Forster 1.00 .45
- □ 311 Jerry Grote .50 .23
- □ 312 Deron Johnson 1.00 .45
- □ 313 Barry Lersch .50 .23
- □ 314 Milwaukee Brewers 1.00 .45
  Team Card
- □ 315 Ron Cey 2.00 .90
- □ 316 Jim Perry .50 .23
- □ 317 Richie Zisk 1.00 .45
- □ 318 Jim Merritt .50 .23
- □ 319 Randy Hundley 1.00 .45
- □ 320 Dusty Baker 2.00 .90
- □ 321 Steve Braun .50 .23
- □ 322 Ernie McAnally .50 .23
- □ 323 Richie Scheinblum .50 .23
- □ 324 Steve Kline .50 .23
- □ 325 Tommy Harper 2.00 .90
- □ 326 Reds Leaders 3.00 1.35
  Sparky Anderson MG
  Larry Shepard CO
  George Scherger CO
  Alex Grammas CO
  Ted Kluszewski CO
- □ 327 Tom Timmermann .50 .23
- □ 328 Skip Jutze .50 .23
- □ 329 Mark Belanger 1.00 .45
- □ 330 Juan Marichal 4.00 1.80
- □ 331 All-Star Catchers 5.00 2.20

	Carlton Fisk		
	Johnny Bench		
332	All-Star 1B	8.00	3.60
	Dick Allen		
	Hank Aaron		
333	All-Star 2B	4.00	1.80
	Rod Carew		
	Joe Morgan		
334	All-Star 3B	3.00	1.35
	Brooks Robinson		
	Ron Santo		
335	All-Star SS	1.00	.45
	Bert Campaneris		
	Chris Speier		
336	All-Star LF	5.00	2.20
	Bobby Murcer		
	Pete Rose		
337	All-Star CF	1.00	.45
	Amos Otis		
	Cesar Cedeno		
338	All-Star RF	5.00	2.20
	Reggie Jackson		
	Billy Williams		
339	All-Star Pitchers	3.00	1.35
	Jim Hunter		
	Rick Wise		
340	Thurman Munson	6.00	2.70
341	Dan Driessen	1.00	.45
342	Jim Lonborg	1.00	.45
343	Royals Team	1.00	.45
344	Mike Caldwell	.50	.23
345	Bill North	.50	.23
346	Ron Reed	.50	.23
347	Sandy Alomar	1.00	.45
348	Pete Richert	.50	.23
349	John Vukovich	.50	.23
350	Bob Gibson	6.00	2.70
351	Dwight Evans	3.00	1.35
352	Bill Stoneman	.50	.23
353	Rich Coggins	.50	.23
354	Cubs Leaders	1.00	.45
	Whitey Lockman MG		
	J.C. Martin CO		
	Hank Aguirre CO		
	Al Spangler CO		
	Jim Marshall CO		
355	Dave Nelson	.50	.23
356	Jerry Koosman	1.00	.45
357	Buddy Bradford	.50	.23
358	Dal Maxvill	.50	.23
359	Brent Strom	.50	.23
360	Greg Luzinski	2.00	.90
361	Don Carrithers	.50	.23
362	Hal King	.50	.23
363	New York Yankees	2.00	.90
	Team Card		
364A	Cito Gaston CO	2.00	.90
364B	Cito Gaston WASH.	6.00	2.70
365	Steve Busby	.50	.23
366	Larry Hisle	1.00	.45
367	Norm Cash	2.00	.90
368	Manny Mota	1.00	.45
369	Paul Lindblad	.50	.23
370	Bob Watson	.50	.23
371	Jim Slaton	.50	.23
372	Ken Reitz	.50	.23
373	John Curtis	.50	.23
374	Marty Perez	.50	.23
375	Earl Williams	.50	.23
376	Jorge Orta	.50	.23
377	Ron Woods	.50	.23
378	Burt Hooton	1.00	.45
379	Rangers Leaders	2.00	.90
	Billy Martin MG		
	Frank Lucchesi CO		
	Art Fowler CO		
	Charlie Silvera CO		
	Jackie Moore CO		
380	Bud Harrelson	1.00	.45
381	Charlie Sands	.50	.23
382	Bob Moose	.50	.23
383	Philadelphia Phillies	1.00	.45
	Team Card		
384	Chris Chambliss	1.00	.45
385	Don Gullett	.50	.23
386	Gary Matthews	2.00	.90
387A	Rich Morales SD	1.00	.45
387B	Rich Morales WASH.	6.00	2.70
388	Phil Roof	.50	.23
389	Gates Brown	.50	.23
390	Lou Piniella	2.00	.90
391	Billy Champion	.50	.23
392	Dick Green	.50	.23
393	Orlando Pena	.50	.23
394	Ken Henderson	.50	.23
395	Doug Rader	.50	.23
396	Tommy Davis	1.00	.45
397	George Stone	.50	.23
398	Duke Sims	.50	.23
399	Mike Paul	.50	.23
400	Harmon Killebrew	6.00	2.70
401	Elliott Maddox	.50	.23
402	Jim Rooker	.50	.23
403	Red Sox Leaders	1.00	.45
	Darrell Johnson MG		
	Eddie Popowski CO		
	Lee Stange CO		
	Don Zimmer CO		
	Don Bryant CO		
404	Jim Howarth	.50	.23
405	Ellie Rodriguez	.50	.23
406	Steve Arlin	.50	.23
407	Jim Wohlford	.50	.23
408	Charlie Hough	2.00	.90
409	Ike Brown	.50	.23
410	Pedro Borbon	.50	.23
411	Frank Baker	.50	.23
412	Chuck Taylor	.50	.23
413	Don Money	1.00	.45
414	Checklist 397-528	3.00	.60
415	Gary Gentry	.50	.23
416	Chicago White Sox	1.00	.45
	Team Card		
417	Rich Folkers	.50	.23
418	Walt Williams	.50	.23
419	Wayne Twitchell	.50	.23
420	Ray Fosse	.50	.23
421	Dan Fife	.50	.23
422	Gonzalo Marquez	.50	.23
423	Fred Stanley	.50	.23
424	Jim Beauchamp	.50	.23
425	Pete Broberg	.50	.23
426	Rennie Stennett	.50	.23
427	Bobby Bolin	.50	.23
428	Gary Sutherland	.50	.23
429	Dick Lange	.50	.23
430	Matty Alou	1.00	.45
431	Gene Garber	1.00	.45
432	Chris Arnold	.50	.23
433	Lerrin LaGrow	.50	.23
434	Ken McMullen	.50	.23
435	Dave Concepcion	2.00	.90
436	Don Hood	.50	.23
437	Jim Lyttle	.50	.23
438	Ed Herrmann	.50	.23
439	Norm Miller	.50	.23
440	Jim Kaat	2.00	.90
441	Tom Ragland	.50	.23
442	Alan Foster	.50	.23
443	Tom Hutton	.50	.23
444	Vic Davalillo	.50	.23
445	George Medich	.50	.23
446	Len Randle	.50	.23
447	Twins Leaders	1.00	.45
	Frank Quilici MG		
	Ralph Rowe CO		
	Bob Rodgers CO		
	Vern Morgan CO		
448	Ron Hodges	.50	.23
449	Tom McCraw	.50	.23
450	Rich Hebner	1.00	.45
451	Tommy John	2.00	.90
452	Gene Hiser	.50	.23
453	Balor Moore	.50	.23
454	Kurt Bevacqua	.50	.23
455	Tom Bradley	.50	.23
456	Dave Winfield	60.00	27.00
457	Chuck Goggin	.50	.23
458	Jim Ray	.50	.23
459	Cincinnati Reds	2.00	.90
	Team Card		
460	Boog Powell	2.00	.90
461	John Odom	.50	.23
462	Luis Alvarado	.50	.23
463	Pat Dobson	.50	.23
464	Jose Cruz	2.00	.90
465	Dick Bosman	.50	.23
466	Dick Billings	.50	.23
467	Winston Llenas	.50	.23
468	Pepe Frias	.50	.23
469	Joe Decker	.50	.23
470	Reggie Jackson ALCS	6.00	2.70
471	Jon Matlack NLCS	1.00	.45
472	Darold Knowles WS1	1.00	.45
473	Willie Mays WS	8.00	3.60
474	Bert Campaneris WS3	1.00	.45
475	Rusty Staub WS4	1.00	.45
476	Cleon Jones WS5	1.00	.45
477	Reggie Jackson WS	6.00	2.70
478	Bert Campaneris WS7	1.00	.45
479	World Series Summary	1.00	.45
	A's celebrate; win		
	2nd consecutive		
	championship		
480	Willie Crawford	.50	.23
481	Jerry Terrell	.50	.23
482	Bob Didier	.50	.23
483	Atlanta Braves	1.00	.45
	Team Card		
484	Carmen Fanzone	.50	.23
485	Felipe Alou	2.00	.90
486	Steve Stone	.50	.23
487	Ted Martinez	.50	.23
488	Andy Etchebarren	.50	.23
489	Pirates Leaders	1.00	.45
	Danny Murtaugh MG		
	Don Osborn CO		
	Don Leppert CO		
	Bill Mazeroski CO		
	Bob Skinner CO		
490	Vada Pinson	2.00	.90
491	Roger Nelson	.50	.23
492	Mike Rogodzinski	.50	.23
493	Joe Hoerner	.50	.23
494	Ed Goodson	.50	.23
495	Dick McAuliffe	1.00	.45
496	Tom Murphy	.50	.23
497	Bobby Mitchell	.50	.23
498	Pat Corrales	.50	.23
499	Rusty Torres	.50	.23
500	Lee May	1.00	.45
501	Eddie Leon	.50	.23
502	Dave LaRoche	.50	.23
503	Eric Soderholm	.50	.23
504	Joe Niekro	1.00	.45
505	Bill Buckner	1.00	.45
506	Ed Farmer	.50	.23
507	Larry Stahl	.50	.23
508	Montreal Expos	1.00	.45
	Team Card		
509	Jesse Jefferson	.50	.23
510	Wayne Garrett	.50	.23
511	Toby Harrah	1.00	.45
512	Joe Lahoud	.50	.23
513	Jim Campanis	.50	.23
514	Paul Schaal	.50	.23
515	Willie Montanez	.50	.23
516	Horacio Pina	.50	.23
517	Mike Hegan	.50	.23
518	Derrel Thomas	.50	.23
519	Bill Sharp	.50	.23
520	Tim McCarver	2.00	.90
521	Indians Leaders	1.00	.45
	Ken Aspromonte MG		
	Clay Bryant CO		
	Tony Pacheco CO		
522	J.R. Richard	2.00	.90
523	Cecil Cooper	2.00	.90
524	Bill Plummer	.50	.23
525	Clyde Wright	.50	.23
526	Frank Tepedino	.50	.23
527	Bobby Darwin	.50	.23
528	Bill Bonham	.50	.23
529	Horace Clarke	1.00	.45
530	Mickey Stanley	1.00	.45
531	Expos Leaders	1.00	.45
	Gene Mauch MG		
	Dave Bristol CO		

Cal McLish CO
Larry Doby CO
Jerry Zimmerman CO

❑ 532	Skip Lockwood	.50	.23
❑ 533	Mike Phillips	.50	.23
❑ 534	Eddie Watt	.50	.23
❑ 535	Bob Tolan	.50	.23
❑ 536	Duffy Dyer	.50	.23
❑ 537	Steve Mingori	.50	.23
❑ 538	Cesar Tovar	.50	.23
❑ 539	Lloyd Allen	.50	.23
❑ 540	Bob Robertson	.50	.23
❑ 541	Cleveland Indians Team Card	1.00	.45
❑ 542	Rich Gossage	2.00	.90
❑ 543	Danny Cater	.50	.23
❑ 544	Ron Schueler	.50	.23
❑ 545	Billy Conigliaro	1.00	.45
❑ 546	Mike Corkins	.50	.23
❑ 547	Glenn Borgmann	.50	.23
❑ 548	Sonny Siebert	.50	.23
❑ 549	Mike Jorgensen	.50	.23
❑ 550	Sam McDowell	1.00	.45
❑ 551	Von Joshua	.50	.23
❑ 552	Denny Doyle	.50	.23
❑ 553	Jim Willoughby	.50	.23
❑ 554	Tim Johnson	.50	.23
❑ 555	Woodie Fryman	.50	.23
❑ 556	Dave Campbell	.50	.23
❑ 557	Jim McGlothlin	.50	.23
❑ 558	Bill Fahey	.50	.23
❑ 559	Darrel Chaney	.50	.23
❑ 560	Mike Cuellar	1.00	.45
❑ 561	Ed Kranepool	1.00	.45
❑ 562	Jack Aker	.50	.23
❑ 563	Hal McRae	1.00	.45
❑ 564	Mike Ryan	.50	.23
❑ 565	Milt Wilcox	.50	.23
❑ 566	Jackie Hernandez	.50	.23
❑ 567	Boston Red Sox Team Card	1.00	.45
❑ 568	Mike Torrez	1.00	.45
❑ 569	Rick Dempsey	1.00	.45
❑ 570	Ralph Garr	1.00	.45
❑ 571	Rich Hand	.50	.23
❑ 572	Enzo Hernandez	.50	.23
❑ 573	Mike Adams	.50	.23
❑ 574	Bill Parsons	.50	.23
❑ 575	Steve Garvey	3.00	1.35
❑ 576	Scipio Spinks	.50	.23
❑ 577	Mike Sadek	.50	.23
❑ 578	Ralph Houk MG	1.00	.45
❑ 579	Cecil Upshaw	.50	.23
❑ 580	Jim Spencer	.50	.23
❑ 581	Fred Norman	.50	.23
❑ 582	Bucky Dent	4.00	1.80
❑ 583	Marty Pattin	.50	.23
❑ 584	Ken Rudolph	.50	.23
❑ 585	Merv Rettenmund	.50	.23
❑ 586	Jack Brohamer	.50	.23
❑ 587	Larry Christenson	.50	.23
❑ 588	Hal Lanier	.50	.23
❑ 589	Boots Day	.50	.23
❑ 590	Roger Moret	.50	.23
❑ 591	Sonny Jackson	.50	.23
❑ 592	Ed Bane	.50	.23
❑ 593	Steve Yeager	1.00	.45
❑ 594	Leroy Stanton	.50	.23
❑ 595	Steve Blass	.50	.23
❑ 596	Rookie Pitchers Wayne Garland Fred Holdsworth Mark Littell Dick Pole	.50	.23
❑ 597	Rookie Shortstops Dave Chalk John Gamble Pete MacKanin Manny Trillo	1.00	.45
❑ 598	Rookie Outfielders Dave Augustine Ken Griffey Steve Ontiveros Jim Tyrone	12.00	5.50
❑ 599A	Rookie Pitchers WAS Ron Diorio	2.00	.90

Dave Freisleben
Frank Riccelli
Greg Shanahan

❑ 599B	Rookie Pitchers SD (SD in large print)	3.00	1.35
❑ 599C	Rookie Pitchers SD (SD in small print)	5.00	2.20
❑ 600	Rookie Infielders Ron Cash Jim Cox Bill Madlock Reggie Sanders	5.00	2.20
❑ 601	Rookie Outfielders Ed Armbrister Rich Bladt Brian Downing Bake McBride	3.00	1.35
❑ 602	Rookie Pitchers Glen Abbott Rick Henninger Craig Swan Dan Vossler	1.00	.45
❑ 603	Rookie Catchers Barry Foote Tom Lundstedt Charlie Moore Sergio Robles	1.00	.45
❑ 604	Rookie Infielders Terry Hughes John Knox Andre Thornton Frank White	5.00	2.20
❑ 605	Rookie Pitchers Vic Albury Ken Frailing Kevin Kobel Frank Tanana	4.00	1.80
❑ 606	Rookie Outfielders Jim Fuller Wilbur Howard Tommy Smith Otto Velez	1.00	.45
❑ 607	Rookie Shortstops Leo Foster Tom Heintzelman Dave Rosello Frank Taveras	1.00	.45
❑ 608A	Rookie Pitchers: ERR Bob Apodaca (sic) Dick Baney John D'Acquisto Mike Wallace	2.00	.90
❑ 608B	Rookie Pitchers: COR Bob Apodaca Dick Baney John D'Acquisto Mike Wallace	1.00	.45
❑ 609	Rico Petrocelli	1.00	.45
❑ 610	Dave Kingman	2.00	.90
❑ 611	Rich Stelmaszek	.50	.23
❑ 612	Luke Walker	.50	.23
❑ 613	Dan Monzon	.50	.23
❑ 614	Adrian Devine	.50	.23
❑ 615	Johnny Jeter UER (Misspelled Johnnie on card back)	.50	.23
❑ 616	Larry Gura	.50	.23
❑ 617	Ted Ford	.50	.23
❑ 618	Jim Mason	.50	.23
❑ 619	Mike Anderson	.50	.23
❑ 620	Al Downing	.50	.23
❑ 621	Bernie Carbo	.50	.23
❑ 622	Phil Gagliano	.50	.23
❑ 623	Celerino Sanchez	.50	.23
❑ 624	Bob Miller	.50	.23
❑ 625	Ollie Brown	.50	.23
❑ 626	Pittsburgh Pirates Team Card	1.00	.45
❑ 627	Carl Taylor	.50	.23
❑ 628	Ivan Murrell	.50	.23
❑ 629	Rusty Staub	2.00	.90
❑ 630	Tommie Agee	1.00	.45
❑ 631	Steve Barber	.50	.23
❑ 632	George Culver	.50	.23
❑ 633	Dave Hamilton	.50	.23
❑ 634	Braves Leaders	2.00	.90

Eddie Mathews MG
Herm Starrette CO
Connie Ryan CO
Jim Busby CO
Ken Silvestri CO

❑ 635	Johnny Edwards	.50	.23
❑ 636	Dave Goltz	.50	.23
❑ 637	Checklist 529-660	3.00	.60
❑ 638	Ken Sanders	.50	.23
❑ 639	Joe Lovitto	.50	.23
❑ 640	Milt Pappas	1.00	.45
❑ 641	Chuck Brinkman	.50	.23
❑ 642	Terry Harmon	.50	.23
❑ 643	Dodgers Team	1.00	.45
❑ 644	Wayne Granger	.50	.23
❑ 645	Ken Boswell	.50	.23
❑ 646	George Foster	2.00	.90
❑ 647	Juan Beniquez	.50	.23
❑ 648	Terry Crowley	.50	.23
❑ 649	Fernando Gonzalez	.50	.23
❑ 650	Mike Epstein	.50	.23
❑ 651	Leron Lee	.50	.23
❑ 652	Gail Hopkins	.50	.23
❑ 653	Bob Stinson	.50	.23
❑ 654A	Jesus Alou ERR (No position)	1.00	.45
❑ 654B	Jesus Alou COR (Outfield)	4.00	1.80
❑ 655	Mike Tyson	.50	.23
❑ 656	Adrian Garrett	.50	.23
❑ 657	Jim Shellenback	.50	.23
❑ 658	Lee Lacy	.50	.23
❑ 659	Joe Lis	.50	.23
❑ 660	Larry Dierker	2.00	.50

1974 Topps Traded

	NRMT	VG-E
COMPLETE SET (44)	15.00	6.75
COMMON CARD		.23
MINOR STARS	.75	.35
SEMISTARS	1.00	.45

INCLUDED IN ALL LATE PACKS
CARDS PRICED IN NM CONDITION

❑ 23T	Craig Robinson	.50	.23
❑ 42T	Claude Osteen	.75	.35
❑ 43T	Jim Wynn	.75	.35
❑ 51T	Bobby Heise	.50	.23
❑ 59T	Ross Grimsley	.75	.35
❑ 62T	Bob Locker	.50	.23
❑ 63T	Bill Sudakis	.50	.23
❑ 73T	Mike Marshall	.75	.35
❑ 123T	Nelson Briles	.75	.35
❑ 139T	Aurelio Monteagudo	.50	.23
❑ 151T	Diego Segui	.50	.23
❑ 165T	Willie Davis	.75	.35
❑ 175T	Reggie Cleveland	.50	.23
❑ 182T	Lindy McDaniel	.50	.23
❑ 186T	Fred Scherman	.50	.23
❑ 249T	George Mitterwald	.50	.23
❑ 262T	Ed Kirkpatrick	.50	.23
❑ 269T	Bob Johnson	.50	.23
❑ 270T	Ron Santo	1.00	.45
❑ 313T	Barry Lersch	.50	.23
❑ 319T	Randy Hundley	.75	.35
❑ 330T	Juan Marichal	2.00	.90
❑ 348T	Pete Richert	.50	.23

	NRMT	VG-E
373T John Curtis	.50	.23
390T Lou Piniella	1.00	.45
428T Gary Sutherland	.50	.23
454T Kurt Bevacqua	.50	.23
458T Jim Ray	.50	.23
485T Felipe Alou	1.00	.45
486T Steve Stone	.75	.35
496T Tom Murphy	.50	.23
516T Horacio Pina	.50	.23
534T Eddie Watt	.50	.23
538T Cesar Tovar	.50	.23
544T Ron Schueler	.50	.23
579T Cecil Upshaw	.50	.23
585T Merv Rettenmund	.50	.23
612T Luke Walker	.50	.23
616T Larry Gura	.75	.35
618T Jim Mason	.50	.23
630T Tommie Agee	.75	.35
648T Terry Crowley	.50	.23
649T Fernando Gonzalez	.50	.23
NNO Traded Checklist	1.50	.30

1975 Topps

CARL YASTRZEMSKI

	NRMT	VG-E
COMPLETE SET (660)	750.00	350.00
COMMON CARD (1-660)	.50	.23
MINOR STARS	1.00	.45
SEMISTARS	2.00	.90
UNLISTED STARS	3.00	1.35

CONDITION SENSITIVE SET
CARDS PRICED IN NM CONDITION

1	Hank Aaron RB Sets Homer Mark	30.00	10.00
2	Lou Brock RB 118 Stolen Bases	3.00	1.35
3	Bob Gibson RB 3000th Strikeout	3.00	1.35
4	Al Kaline RB 3000 Hit Club	5.00	2.20
5	Nolan Ryan RB Fans 300 for 3rd Year in a Row	30.00	13.50
6	Mike Marshall HL Hurls 106 Games	1.00	.45
7	Steve Busby HL Dick Bosman Nolan Ryan	12.00	5.50
8	Rogelio Moret	.50	.23
9	Frank Tepedino	.50	.23
10	Willie Davis	1.00	.45
11	Bill Melton	.50	.23
12	David Clyde	.50	.23
13	Gene Locklear	1.00	.45
14	Milt Wilcox	.50	.23
15	Jose Cardenal	1.00	.45
16	Frank Tanana	2.00	.90
17	Dave Concepcion	2.00	.90
18	Tigers: Team/Mgr. Ralph Houk (Checklist back)	2.00	.40
19	Jerry Koosman	1.00	.45
20	Thurman Munson	6.00	2.70
21	Rollie Fingers	3.00	1.35
22	Dave Cash	.50	.23
23	Bill Russell	1.00	.45
24	Al Fitzmorris	.50	.23
25	Lee May	1.00	.45
26	Dave McNally	1.00	.45
27	Ken Reitz	.50	.23
28	Tom Murphy	.50	.23
29	Dave Parker	3.00	1.35
30	Bert Blyleven	2.00	.90
31	Dave Rader	.50	.23
32	Reggie Cleveland	.50	.23
33	Dusty Baker	2.00	.90
34	Steve Renko	.50	.23
35	Ron Santo	1.00	.45
36	Joe Lovitto	.50	.23
37	Dave Freisleben	.50	.23
38	Buddy Bell	2.00	.90
39	Andre Thornton	1.00	.45
40	Bill Singer	.50	.23
41	Cesar Geronimo	1.00	.45
42	Joe Coleman	.50	.23
43	Cleon Jones	.50	.23
44	Pat Dobson	.50	.23
45	Joe Rudi	1.00	.45
46	Phillies: Team/Mgr. Danny Ozark UER (Checklist back) (Terry Harmon listed as 339 instead of 399)	2.00	.40
47	Tommy John	2.00	.90
48	Freddie Patek	1.00	.45
49	Larry Dierker	1.00	.45
50	Brooks Robinson	6.00	2.70
51	Bob Forsch	1.00	.45
52	Darrell Porter	1.00	.45
53	Dave Giusti	.50	.23
54	Eric Soderholm	.50	.23
55	Bobby Bonds	2.00	.90
56	Rick Wise	1.00	.45
57	Dave Johnson	1.00	.45
58	Chuck Taylor	.50	.23
59	Ken Henderson	.50	.23
60	Fergie Jenkins	3.00	1.35
61	Dave Winfield	25.00	11.00
62	Fritz Peterson	.50	.23
63	Steve Swisher	.50	.23
64	Dave Chalk	.50	.23
65	Don Gullett	1.00	.45
66	Willie Horton	1.00	.45
67	Tug McGraw	1.00	.45
68	Ron Blomberg	.50	.23
69	John Odom	.50	.23
70	Mike Schmidt	30.00	13.50
71	Charlie Hough	1.00	.45
72	Royals: Team/Mgr. Jack McKeon (Checklist back)	2.00	.40
73	J.R. Richard	1.00	.45
74	Mark Belanger	1.00	.45
75	Ted Simmons	2.00	.90
76	Ed Sprague	.50	.23
77	Richie Zisk	1.00	.45
78	Ray Corbin	.50	.23
79	Gary Matthews	1.00	.45
80	Carlton Fisk	6.00	2.70
81	Ron Reed	.50	.23
82	Pat Kelly	.50	.23
83	Jim Merritt	.50	.23
84	Enzo Hernandez	.50	.23
85	Bill Bonham	.50	.23
86	Joe Lis	.50	.23
87	George Foster	2.00	.90
88	Tom Egan	.50	.23
89	Jim Ray	.50	.23
90	Rusty Staub	2.00	.90
91	Dick Green	.50	.23
92	Cecil Upshaw	.50	.23
93	Dave Lopes	2.00	.90
94	Jim Lonborg	1.00	.45
95	John Mayberry	1.00	.45
96	Mike Cosgrove	.50	.23
97	Earl Williams	.50	.23
98	Rich Folkers	.50	.23
99	Mike Hegan	.50	.23
100	Willie Stargell	4.00	1.80
101	Expos: Team/Mgr. Gene Mauch (Checklist back)	2.00	.40
102	Joe Decker	.50	.23
103	Rick Miller	.50	.23
104	Bill Madlock	2.00	.90
105	Buzz Capra	.50	.23
106	Mike Hargrove	3.00	1.35
107	Jim Barr	.50	.23
108	Tom Hall	.50	.23
109	George Hendrick	1.00	.45
110	Wilbur Wood	.50	.23
111	Wayne Garrett	.50	.23
112	Larry Hardy	.50	.23
113	Elliott Maddox	.50	.23
114	Dick Lange	.50	.23
115	Joe Ferguson	.50	.23
116	Lerrin LaGrow	.50	.23
117	Orioles: Team/Mgr. Earl Weaver (Checklist back)	3.00	.60
118	Mike Anderson	.50	.23
119	Tommy Helms	.50	.23
120	Steve Busby UER (Photo actually Fran Healy)	1.00	.45
121	Bill North	.50	.23
122	Al Hrabosky	1.00	.45
123	Johnny Briggs	.50	.23
124	Jerry Reuss	1.00	.45
125	Ken Singleton	1.00	.45
126	Checklist 1-132	3.00	.60
127	Glenn Borgmann	.50	.23
128	Bill Lee	1.00	.45
129	Rick Monday	1.00	.45
130	Phil Niekro	3.00	1.35
131	Toby Harrah	1.00	.45
132	Randy Moffitt	.50	.23
133	Dan Driessen	1.00	.45
134	Ron Hodges	.50	.23
135	Charlie Spikes	.50	.23
136	Jim Mason	.50	.23
137	Terry Forster	1.00	.45
138	Del Unser	.50	.23
139	Horacio Pina	.50	.23
140	Steve Garvey	3.00	1.35
141	Mickey Stanley	1.00	.45
142	Bob Reynolds	.50	.23
143	Cliff Johnson	.50	.23
144	Jim Wohlford	.50	.23
145	Ken Holtzman	1.00	.45
146	Padres: Team/Mgr. John McNamara (Checklist back)	2.00	.40
147	Pedro Garcia	.50	.23
148	Jim Rooker	.50	.23
149	Tim Foli	.50	.23
150	Bob Gibson	6.00	2.70
151	Steve Brye	.50	.23
152	Mario Guerrero	.50	.23
153	Rick Reuschel	1.00	.45
154	Mike Lum	.50	.23
155	Jim Bibby	.50	.23
156	Dave Kingman	2.00	.90
157	Pedro Borbon	1.00	.45
158	Jerry Grote	.50	.23
159	Steve Arlin	.50	.23
160	Graig Nettles	2.00	.90
161	Stan Bahnsen	.50	.23
162	Willie Montanez	.50	.23
163	Jim Brewer	.50	.23
164	Mickey Rivers	1.00	.45
165	Doug Rader	1.00	.45
166	Woodie Fryman	.50	.23
167	Rich Coggins	.50	.23
168	Bill Greif	.50	.23
169	Cookie Rojas	1.00	.45
170	Bert Campaneris	1.00	.45
171	Ed Kirkpatrick	.50	.23
172	Red Sox: Team/Mgr. Darrell Johnson (Checklist back)	3.00	.60
173	Steve Rogers	1.00	.45
174	Bake McBride	1.00	.45
175	Don Money	1.00	.45
176	Burt Hooton	1.00	.45
177	Vic Correll	.50	.23
178	Cesar Tovar	.50	.23
179	Tom Bradley	.50	.23
180	Joe Morgan	6.00	2.70

☐ 181	Fred Beene	.50	.23	☐ 214	Harry Parker	.50	.23	☐ 292 Ron Schueler .50 .23
☐ 182	Don Hahn	.50	.23	☐ 215	Bobby Valentine	1.00	.45	☐ 293 Dick Sharon .50 .23
☐ 183	Mel Stottlemyre	1.00	.45	☐ 216	Giants: Team/Mgr.	2.00	.40	☐ 294 Geoff Zahn .50 .23

☐ 181 Fred Beene .50 .23
☐ 182 Don Hahn .50 .23
☐ 183 Mel Stottlemyre 1.00 .45
☐ 184 Jorge Orta .50 .23
☐ 185 Steve Carlton 8.00 3.60
☐ 186 Willie Crawford .50 .23
☐ 187 Denny Doyle .50 .23
☐ 188 Tom Griffin .50 .23
☐ 189 1951 MVP's 4.00 1.80
   Larry (Yogi) Berra
   Roy Campanella
   (Campy never issued)
☐ 190 1952 MVP's 2.00 .90
   Bobby Shantz
   Hank Sauer
☐ 191 1953 MVP's 2.00 .90
   Al Rosen
   Roy Campanella
☐ 192 1954 MVP's 4.00 1.80
   Yogi Berra
   Willie Mays
☐ 193 1955 MVP's UER 3.00 1.35
   Yogi Berra
   Roy Campanella
   (Campy can never
   issued, pictured
   with LA cap)
☐ 194 1956 MVP's 15.00 6.75
   Mickey Mantle
   Don Newcombe
☐ 195 1957 MVP's 20.00 9.00
   Mickey Mantle
   Hank Aaron
☐ 196 1958 MVP's 2.00 .90
   Jackie Jensen
   Ernie Banks
☐ 197 1959 MVP's 2.00 .90
   Nellie Fox
   Ernie Banks
☐ 198 1960 MVP's 2.00 .90
   Roger Maris
   Dick Groat
☐ 199 1961 MVP's 3.00 1.35
   Roger Maris
   Frank Robinson
☐ 200 1962 MVP's 15.00 6.75
   Mickey Mantle
   Maury Wills
   (Wills never issued)
☐ 201 1963 MVP's 2.00 .90
   Elston Howard
   Sandy Koufax
☐ 202 1964 MVP's 2.00 .90
   Brooks Robinson
   Ken Boyer
☐ 203 1965 MVP's 2.00 .90
   Zollo Versalles
   Willie Mays
☐ 204 1966 MVP's 8.00 3.60
   Frank Robinson
   Bob Clemente
☐ 205 1967 MVP's 2.00 .90
   Carl Yastrzemski
   Orlando Cepeda
☐ 206 1968 MVP's 2.00 .90
   Denny McLain
   Bob Gibson
☐ 207 1969 MVP's 2.00 .90
   Harmon Killebrew
   Willie McCovey
☐ 208 1970 MVP's 2.00 .90
   Boog Powell
   Johnny Bench
☐ 209 1971 MVP's 2.00 .90
   Vida Blue
   Joe Torre
☐ 210 1972 MVP's 2.00 .90
   Rich Allen
   Johnny Bench
☐ 211 1973 MVP's 6.00 2.70
   Reggie Jackson
   Pete Rose
☐ 212 1974 MVP's 2.00 .90
   Jeff Burroughs
   Steve Garvey
☐ 213 Oscar Gamble 1.00 .45

☐ 214 Harry Parker .50 .23
☐ 215 Bobby Valentine 1.00 .45
☐ 216 Giants: Team/Mgr. 2.00 .40
   Wes Westrum
   (Checklist back)
☐ 217 Lou Piniella 2.00 .90
☐ 218 Jerry Johnson .50 .23
☐ 219 Ed Herrmann .50 .23
☐ 220 Don Sutton 3.00 1.35
☐ 221 Aurelio Rodriguez .50 .23
☐ 222 Dan Spillner .50 .23
☐ 223 Robin Yount 60.00 27.00
☐ 224 Ramon Hernandez .50 .23
☐ 225 Bob Grich 1.00 .45
☐ 226 Bill Campbell .50 .23
☐ 227 Bob Watson 1.00 .45
☐ 228 George Brett 100.00 45.00
☐ 229 Barry Foote .50 .23
☐ 230 Jim Hunter 4.00 1.80
☐ 231 Mike Tyson .50 .23
☐ 232 Diego Segui .50 .23
☐ 233 Billy Grabarkewitz .50 .23
☐ 234 Tom Grieve 1.00 .45
☐ 235 Jack Billingham 1.00 .45
☐ 236 Angels: Team/Mgr. 2.00 .40
   Dick Williams
   (Checklist back)
☐ 237 Carl Morton .50 .23
☐ 238 Dave Duncan .50 .23
☐ 239 George Stone .50 .23
☐ 240 Garry Maddox 1.00 .45
☐ 241 Dick Tidrow .50 .23
☐ 242 Jay Johnstone 1.00 .45
☐ 243 Jim Kaat 2.00 .90
☐ 244 Bill Buckner 1.00 .45
☐ 245 Mickey Lolich 2.00 .90
☐ 246 Cardinals: Team/Mgr. 2.00 .40
   Red Schoendienst
   (Checklist back)
☐ 247 Enos Cabell .50 .23
☐ 248 Randy Jones 2.00 .90
☐ 249 Danny Thompson .50 .23
☐ 250 Ken Brett .50 .23
☐ 251 Fran Healy .50 .23
☐ 252 Fred Scherman .50 .23
☐ 253 Jesus Alou .50 .23
☐ 254 Mike Torrez 1.00 .45
☐ 255 Dwight Evans 2.00 .90
☐ 256 Billy Champion .50 .23
☐ 257 Checklist: 133-264 3.00 .60
☐ 258 Dave LaRoche .50 .23
☐ 259 Len Randle .50 .23
☐ 260 Johnny Bench 12.00 5.50
☐ 261 Andy Hassler .50 .23
☐ 262 Rowland Office .50 .23
☐ 263 Jim Perry 1.00 .45
☐ 264 John Milner .50 .23
☐ 265 Ron Bryant .50 .23
☐ 266 Sandy Alomar 1.00 .45
☐ 267 Dick Ruthven .50 .23
☐ 268 Hal McRae 1.00 .45
☐ 269 Doug Rau .50 .23
☐ 270 Ron Fairly 1.00 .45
☐ 271 Gerry Moses .50 .23
☐ 272 Lynn McGlothen .50 .23
☐ 273 Steve Braun .50 .23
☐ 274 Vicente Romo .50 .23
☐ 275 Paul Blair 1.00 .45
☐ 276 White Sox Team/Mgr. 2.00 .40
   Chuck Tanner
   (Checklist back)
☐ 277 Frank Tavaras .50 .23
☐ 278 Paul Lindblad .50 .23
☐ 279 Milt May .50 .23
☐ 280 Carl Yastrzemski 8.00 3.60
☐ 281 Jim Slaton .50 .23
☐ 282 Jerry Morales .50 .23
☐ 283 Steve Foucault .50 .23
☐ 284 Ken Griffey 4.00 1.80
☐ 285 Ellie Rodriguez .50 .23
☐ 286 Mike Jorgensen .50 .23
☐ 287 Roric Harrison .50 .23
☐ 288 Bruce Ellingsen .50 .23
☐ 289 Ken Rudolph .50 .23
☐ 290 Jon Matlack .50 .23
☐ 291 Bill Sudakis .50 .23

☐ 292 Ron Schueler .50 .23
☐ 293 Dick Sharon .50 .23
☐ 294 Geoff Zahn .50 .23
☐ 295 Vada Pinson 2.00 .90
☐ 296 Alan Foster .50 .23
☐ 297 Craig Kusick .50 .23
☐ 298 Johnny Grubb .50 .23
☐ 299 Bucky Dent 2.00 .90
☐ 300 Reggie Jackson 15.00 6.75
☐ 301 Dave Roberts .50 .23
☐ 302 Rick Burleson 1.00 .45
☐ 303 Grant Jackson .50 .23
☐ 304 Pirates: Team/Mgr. 2.00 .40
   Danny Murtaugh
   (Checklist back)
☐ 305 Jim Colborn .50 .23
☐ 306 Batting Leaders 2.00 .90
   Rod Carew
   Ralph Garr
☐ 307 Home Run Leaders 4.00 1.80
   Dick Allen
   Mike Schmidt
☐ 308 RBI Leaders 2.00 .90
   Jeff Burroughs
   Johnny Bench
☐ 309 Stolen Base Leaders 2.00 .90
   Bill North
   Lou Brock
☐ 310 Victory Leaders 2.00 .90
   Jim Hunter
   Fergie Jenkins
   Andy Messersmith
   Phil Niekro
☐ 311 ERA Leaders 2.00 .90
   Jim Hunter
   Buzz Capra
☐ 312 Strikeout Leaders 20.00 9.00
   Nolan Ryan
   Steve Carlton
☐ 313 Firemen Leaders 1.00 .45
   Terry Forster
   Mike Marshall
☐ 314 Buck Martinez .50 .23
☐ 315 Don Kessinger 1.00 .45
☐ 316 Jackie Brown .50 .23
☐ 317 Joe Lahoud .50 .23
☐ 318 Ernie McAnally .50 .23
☐ 319 Johnny Oates 1.00 .45
☐ 320 Pete Rose 20.00 9.00
☐ 321 Rudy May .50 .23
☐ 322 Ed Goodson .50 .23
☐ 323 Fred Holdsworth .50 .23
☐ 324 Ed Kranepool 1.00 .45
☐ 325 Tony Oliva 2.00 .90
☐ 326 Wayne Twitchell .50 .23
☐ 327 Jerry Hairston .50 .23
☐ 328 Sonny Siebert .50 .23
☐ 329 Ted Kubiak .50 .23
☐ 330 Mike Marshall 1.00 .45
☐ 331 Indians: Team/Mgr. 2.00 .40
   Frank Robinson
   (Checklist back)
☐ 332 Fred Kendall .50 .23
☐ 333 Dick Drago .50 .23
☐ 334 Greg Gross .50 .23
☐ 335 Jim Palmer 6.00 2.70
☐ 336 Rennie Stennett .50 .23
☐ 337 Kevin Kobel .50 .23
☐ 338 Rich Stelmaszek .50 .23
☐ 339 Jim Fregosi 1.00 .45
☐ 340 Paul Splittorff .50 .23
☐ 341 Hal Breeden .50 .23
☐ 342 Leroy Stanton .50 .23
☐ 343 Danny Frisella .50 .23
☐ 344 Ben Oglivie 1.00 .45
☐ 345 Clay Carroll 1.00 .45
☐ 346 Bobby Darwin .50 .23
☐ 347 Mike Caldwell .50 .23
☐ 348 Tony Muser .50 .23
☐ 349 Ray Sadecki .50 .23
☐ 350 Bobby Murcer 1.00 .45
☐ 351 Bob Boone 2.00 .90
☐ 352 Darold Knowles .50 .23
☐ 353 Luis Melendez .50 .23
☐ 354 Dick Bosman .50 .23
☐ 355 Chris Cannizzaro .50 .23

356	Rico Petrocelli	1.00	.45
357	Ken Forsch	.50	.23
358	Al Bumbry	1.00	.45
359	Paul Popovich	.50	.23
360	George Scott	1.00	.45
361	Dodgers: Team/Mgr.	2.00	.40
	Walter Alston		
	(Checklist back)		
362	Steve Hargan	.50	.23
363	Carmen Fanzone	.50	.23
364	Doug Bird	.50	.23
365	Bob Bailey	.50	.23
366	Ken Sanders	.50	.23
367	Craig Robinson	.50	.23
368	Vic Albury	.50	.23
369	Merv Rettenmund	.50	.23
370	Tom Seaver	12.00	5.50
371	Gates Brown	.50	.23
372	John D'Acquisto	.50	.23
373	Bill Sharp	.50	.23
374	Eddie Watt	.50	.23
375	Roy White	1.00	.45
376	Steve Yeager	1.00	.45
377	Tom Hilgendorf	.50	.23
378	Derrel Thomas	.50	.23
379	Bernie Carbo	.50	.23
380	Sal Bando	1.00	.45
381	John Curtis	.50	.23
382	Don Baylor	2.00	.90
383	Jim York	.50	.23
384	Brewers: Team/Mgr.	2.00	.40
	Del Crandall		
	(Checklist back)		
385	Dock Ellis	.50	.23
386	Checklist: 265-396	3.00	.60
387	Jim Spencer	.50	.23
388	Steve Stone	1.00	.45
389	Tony Solaita	.50	.23
390	Ron Cey	2.00	.90
391	Don DeMola	.50	.23
392	Bruce Bochte	1.00	.45
393	Gary Gentry	.50	.23
394	Larvell Blanks	.50	.23
395	Bud Harrelson	1.00	.45
396	Fred Norman	.50	.23
397	Bill Freehan	1.00	.45
398	Elias Sosa	.50	.23
399	Terry Harmon	.50	.23
400	Dick Allen	2.00	.90
401	Mike Wallace	.50	.23
402	Bob Tolan	.50	.23
403	Tom Buskey	.50	.23
404	Ted Sizemore	.50	.23
405	John Montague	.50	.23
406	Bob Gallagher	.50	.23
407	Herb Washington	2.00	.90
408	Clyde Wright	.50	.23
409	Bob Robertson	.50	.23
410	Mike Cuellar UER	1.00	.45
	(Sic, Cuellar)		
411	George Mitterwald	.50	.23
412	Bill Hands	.50	.23
413	Marty Pattin	.50	.23
414	Manny Mota	1.00	.45
415	John Hiller	1.00	.45
416	Larry Lintz	.50	.23
417	Skip Lockwood	.50	.23
418	Leo Foster	.50	.23
419	Dave Goltz	.50	.23
420	Larry Bowa	2.00	.90
421	Mets: Team/Mgr.	3.00	.60
	Yogi Berra		
	(Checklist back)		
422	Brian Downing	1.00	.45
423	Clay Kirby	.50	.23
424	John Lowenstein	.50	.23
425	Tito Fuentes	.50	.23
426	George Medich	.50	.23
427	Clarence Gaston	1.00	.45
428	Dave Hamilton	.50	.23
429	Jim Dwyer	.50	.23
430	Luis Tiant	2.00	.90
431	Rod Gilbreath	.50	.23
432	Ken Berry	.50	.23
433	Larry Demery	.50	.23
434	Bob Locker	.50	.23
435	Dave Nelson	.50	.23
436	Ken Frailing	.50	.23
437	Al Cowens	1.00	.45
438	Don Carrithers	.50	.23
439	Ed Brinkman	.50	.23
440	Andy Messersmith	1.00	.45
441	Bobby Heise	.50	.23
442	Maximino Leon	.50	.23
443	Twins: Team/Mgr.	2.00	.40
	Frank Quilici		
	(Checklist back)		
444	Gene Garber	1.00	.45
445	Felix Millan	.50	.23
446	Bart Johnson	.50	.23
447	Terry Crowley	.50	.23
448	Frank Duffy	.50	.23
449	Charlie Williams	.50	.23
450	Willie McCovey	6.00	2.70
451	Rick Dempsey	1.00	.45
452	Angel Mangual	.50	.23
453	Claude Osteen	1.00	.45
454	Doug Griffin	.50	.23
455	Don Wilson	.50	.23
456	Bob Coluccio	.50	.23
457	Mario Mendoza	.50	.23
458	Ross Grimsley	.50	.23
459	1974 AL Champs	1.00	.45
	A's over Orioles		
	(Second base action		
	pictured)		
460	Steve Garvey NLCS	2.00	.90
	Frank Taveras		
461	Reggie Jackson WS	5.00	2.20
462	World Series Game 2	1.00	.45
	(Dodger dugout)		
463	Rollie Fingers WS	.50	.23
464	World Series Game 4	1.00	.45
	(A's batter)		
465	Joe Rudi WS	1.00	.45
466	World Series Summary	2.00	.90
	A's do it again;		
	win third straight		
	(A's group picture)		
467	Ed Halicki	.50	.23
468	Bobby Mitchell	.50	.23
469	Tom Dettore	.50	.23
470	Jeff Burroughs	1.00	.45
471	Bob Stinson	.50	.23
472	Bruce Dal Canton	.50	.23
473	Ken McMullen	.50	.23
474	Luke Walker	.50	.23
475	Darrell Evans	1.00	.45
476	Ed Figueroa	.50	.23
477	Tom Hutton	.50	.23
478	Tom Burgmeier	.50	.23
479	Ken Boswell	.50	.23
480	Carlos May	.50	.23
481	Will McEnaney	1.00	.45
482	Tom McCraw	.50	.23
483	Steve Ontiveros	.50	.23
484	Glenn Beckert	1.00	.45
485	Sparky Lyle	1.00	.45
486	Ray Fosse	.50	.23
487	Astros: Team/Mgr.	2.00	.40
	Preston Gomez		
	(Checklist back)		
488	Bill Travers	.50	.23
489	Cecil Cooper	2.00	.90
490	Reggie Smith	1.00	.45
491	Doyle Alexander	1.00	.45
492	Rich Hebner	1.00	.45
493	Don Stanhouse	.50	.23
494	Pete LaCock	.50	.23
495	Nelson Briles	1.00	.45
496	Pepe Frias	.50	.23
497	Jim Nettles	.50	.23
498	Al Downing	.50	.23
499	Marty Perez	.50	.23
500	Nolan Ryan	60.00	27.00
501	Bill Robinson	1.00	.45
502	Pat Bourque	.50	.23
503	Fred Stanley	.50	.23
504	Buddy Bradford	.50	.23
505	Chris Speier	.50	.23
506	Leron Lee	.50	.23
507	Tom Carroll	.50	.23
508	Bob Hansen	.50	.23
509	Dave Hilton	.50	.23
510	Vida Blue	1.00	.45
511	Rangers: Team/Mgr.	2.00	.40
	Billy Martin		
	(Checklist back)		
512	Larry Milbourne	.50	.23
513	Dick Pole	.50	.23
514	Jose Cruz	2.00	.90
515	Manny Sanguillen	1.00	.45
516	Don Hood	.50	.23
517	Checklist: 397-528	3.00	.60
518	Leo Cardenas	.50	.23
519	Jim Todd	.50	.23
520	Amos Otis	1.00	.45
521	Dennis Blair	.50	.23
522	Gary Sutherland	.50	.23
523	Tom Paciorek	1.00	.45
524	John Doherty	.50	.23
525	Tom House	.50	.23
526	Larry Hisle	1.00	.45
527	Mac Scarce	.50	.23
528	Eddie Leon	.50	.23
529	Gary Thomasson	.50	.23
530	Gaylord Perry	3.00	1.35
531	Reds: Team/Mgr.	5.00	1.00
	Sparky Anderson		
	(Checklist back)		
532	Gorman Thomas	1.00	.45
533	Rudy Meoli	.50	.23
534	Alex Johnson	.50	.23
535	Gene Tenace	1.00	.45
536	Bob Moose	.50	.23
537	Tommy Harper	1.00	.45
538	Duffy Dyer	.50	.23
539	Jesse Jefferson	.50	.23
540	Lou Brock	6.00	2.70
541	Roger Metzger	.50	.23
542	Pete Broberg	.50	.23
543	Larry Biittner	.50	.23
544	Steve Mingori	.50	.23
545	Billy Williams	3.00	1.35
546	John Knox	.50	.23
547	Von Joshua	.50	.23
548	Charlie Sands	.50	.23
549	Bill Butler	.50	.23
550	Ralph Garr	1.00	.45
551	Larry Christenson	.50	.23
552	Jack Brohamer	.50	.23
553	John Boccabella	.50	.23
554	Rich Gossage	2.00	.90
555	Al Oliver	2.00	.90
556	Tim Johnson	.50	.23
557	Larry Gura	.50	.23
558	Dave Roberts	.50	.23
559	Bob Montgomery	.50	.23
560	Tony Perez	3.00	1.35
561	A's: Team/Mgr.	2.00	.40
	Alvin Dark		
	(Checklist back)		
562	Gary Nolan	1.00	.45
563	Wilbur Howard	.50	.23
564	Tommy Davis	1.00	.45
565	Joe Torre	2.00	.90
566	Ray Burris	.50	.23
567	Jim Sundberg	2.00	.90
568	Dale Murray	.50	.23
569	Frank White	1.00	.45
570	Jim Wynn	1.00	.45
571	Dave Lemanczyk	.50	.23
572	Roger Nelson	.50	.23
573	Orlando Pena	.50	.23
574	Tony Taylor	1.00	.45
575	Gene Clines	.50	.23
576	Phil Roof	.50	.23
577	John Morris	.50	.23
578	Dave Tomlin	.50	.23
579	Skip Pitlock	.50	.23
580	Frank Robinson	6.00	2.70
581	Darrel Chaney	.50	.23
582	Eduardo Rodriguez	.50	.23
583	Andy Etchebarren	.50	.23
584	Mike Garman	.50	.23
585	Chris Chambliss	1.00	.45
586	Tim McCarver	2.00	.90
587	Chris Ward	.50	.23

588 Rick Auerbach .50 .23
589 Braves: Team/Mgr. 2.00 .40
 Clyde King
 (Checklist back)
590 Cesar Cedeno 1.00 .45
591 Glenn Abbott .50 .23
592 Balor Moore .50 .23
593 Gene Lamont .50 .23
594 Jim Fuller .50 .23
595 Joe Niekro 1.00 .45
596 Ollie Brown .50 .23
597 Winston Llenas .50 .23
598 Bruce Kison .50 .23
599 Nate Colbert .50 .23
600 Rod Carew 6.00 2.70
601 Juan Beniquez .50 .23
602 John Vukovich .50 .23
603 Lew Krausse .50 .23
604 Oscar Zamora .50 .23
605 John Ellis .50 .23
606 Bruce Miller .50 .23
607 Jim Holt .50 .23
608 Gene Michael 1.00 .45
609 Elrod Hendricks .50 .23
610 Ron Hunt .50 .23
611 Yankees: Team/Mgr. 2.00 .40
 Bill Virdon
 (Checklist back)
612 Terry Hughes .50 .23
613 Bill Parsons .50 .23
614 Rookie Pitchers 1.00 .45
 Jack Kucek
 Dyar Miller
 Vern Ruhle
 Paul Siebert
615 Rookie Pitchers 2.00 .90
 Pat Darcy
 Dennis Leonard
 Tom Underwood
 Hank Webb
616 Rookie Outfielders 12.00 5.50
 Dave Augustine
 Pepe Mangual
 Jim Rice
 John Scott
617 Rookie Infielders 2.00 .90
 Mike Cubbage
 Doug DeCinces
 Reggie Sanders
 Manny Trillo
618 Rookie Pitchers 1.00 .45
 Jamie Easterly
 Tom Johnson
 Scott McGregor
 Rick Rhoden
619 Rookie Outfielders 1.00 .45
 Benny Ayala
 Nyls Nyman
 Tommy Smith
 Jerry Turner
620 Rookie Catcher/OF 20.00 9.00
 Gary Carter
 Marc Hill
 Danny Meyer
 Leon Roberts
621 Rookie Pitchers 2.00 .90
 John Denny
 Rawly Eastwick
 Jim Kern
 Juan Veintidos
622 Rookie Outfielders 6.00 2.70
 Ed Armbrister
 Fred Lynn
 Tom Poquette
 Terry Whitfield UER
 (Listed as Ney York)
623 Rookie Infielders 6.00 2.70
 Phil Garner
 Keith Hernandez UER
 (Sic, bats right)
 Bob Sheldon
 Tom Veryzer
624 Rookie Pitchers 1.00 .45
 Doug Konieczny
 Gary Lavelle
 Jim Otten
 Eddie Solomon
625 Boog Powell 2.00 .90
626 Larry Haney UER .50 .23
 (Photo actually
 Dave Duncan)
627 Tom Walker .50 .23
628 Ron LeFlore 1.00 .45
629 Joe Hoerner .50 .23
630 Greg Luzinski 2.00 .90
631 Lee Lacy .50 .23
632 Morris Nettles .50 .23
633 Paul Casanova .50 .23
634 Cy Acosta .50 .23
635 Chuck Dobson .50 .23
636 Charlie Moore .50 .23
637 Ted Martinez .50 .23
638 Cubs: Team/Mgr. 2.00 .40
 Jim Marshall
 (Checklist back)
639 Steve Kline .50 .23
640 Harmon Killebrew 6.00 2.70
641 Jim Northrup .50 .23
642 Mike Phillips .50 .23
643 Brent Strom .50 .23
644 Bill Fahey .50 .23
645 Danny Cater .50 .23
646 Checklist: 529-660 3.00 .60
647 Claudell Washington 2.00 .90
648 Dave Pagan .50 .23
649 Jack Heidemann .50 .23
650 Dave May .50 .23
651 John Morlan .50 .23
652 Lindy McDaniel 1.00 .45
653 Lee Richard UER .50 .23
 (Listed as Richards
 on card front)
654 Jerry Terrell .50 .23
655 Rico Carty 1.00 .45
656 Bill Plummer .50 .23
657 Bob Oliver .50 .23
658 Vic Harris .50 .23
659 Bob Apodaca .50 .23
660 Hank Aaron 30.00 .

1975 Topps Mini

	NRMT	VG-E
COMPLETE SET (660)	1000.00	450.00
COMMON CARD (1-660)	.75	.35

*MINI STARS: .75X TO 1.5X BASIC CARDS
*MINI RC'S: .5X TO 1X BASIC RC'S
CONDITION SENSITIVE SET
CARDS PRICED IN NM CONDITION

1976 Topps

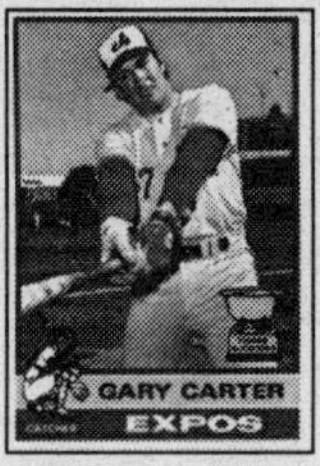

	NRMT	VG-E
COMPLETE SET (660)	300.00	135.00
COMMON CARD (1-660)	.40	.18
MINOR STARS	.75	.35
SEMISTARS	1.50	.70
UNLISTED STARS	2.50	1.10

CARDS PRICED IN NM CONDITION

1 Hank Aaron RB 15.00 4.70
 2262 Career RBIs
2 Bobby Bonds RB 1.50 .70
 Most leadoff HR's 32;
 plus three seasons
 30 homers/30 steals
3 Mickey Lolich RB .75 .35
 Most Lefthanded Strikeouts: 2679
4 Dave Lopes RB .75 .35
 Most Consecutive SB's: 38
5 Tom Seaver RB 5.00 2.20
 Most Consecutive seasons
 with 200 Strikeouts
6 Rennie Stennett RB .75 .35
 7 Hits in a 9 inning game
7 Jim Umbarger .40 .18
8 Tito Fuentes .40 .18
9 Paul Lindblad .40 .18
10 Lou Brock 5.00 2.20
11 Jim Hughes .40 .18
12 Richie Zisk .75 .35
13 John Wockenfuss .40 .18
14 Gene Garber .75 .35
15 George Scott .75 .35
16 Bob Apodaca .40 .18
17 New York Yankees 1.50 .30
 Team Card;
 Billy Martin MG
 (Checklist back)
18 Dale Murray .40 .18
19 George Brett 40.00 18.00
20 Bob Watson .75 .35
21 Dave LaRoche .40 .18
22 Bill Russell .75 .35
23 Brian Downing .40 .18
24 Cesar Geronimo .75 .35
25 Mike Torrez .75 .35
26 Andre Thornton .75 .35
27 Ed Figueroa .40 .18
28 Dusty Baker 1.50 .70
29 Rick Burleson .75 .35
30 John Montefusco .75 .35
31 Len Randle .40 .18
32 Danny Frisella .40 .18
33 Bill North .40 .18
34 Mike Garman .40 .18
35 Tony Oliva 1.50 .70
36 Frank Taveras .40 .18
37 John Hiller .75 .35
38 Garry Maddox .75 .35
39 Pete Broberg .40 .18
40 Dave Kingman 1.50 .70
41 Tippy Martinez .75 .35
42 Barry Foote .40 .18
43 Paul Splittorff .40 .18
44 Doug Rader .75 .35
45 Boog Powell 1.50 .70
46 Los Angeles Dodgers 1.50 .30
 Team Card;
 Walter Alston MG
 (Checklist back)
47 Jesse Jefferson .40 .18
48 Dave Concepcion 1.50 .70
49 Dave Duncan .40 .18
50 Fred Lynn 1.50 .70
51 Ray Burris .40 .18
52 Dave Chalk .40 .18
53 Mike Beard .40 .18
54 Dave Bell FS .40 .18
55 Gaylord Perry 2.50 1.10
56 Bob Tolan .40 .18
57 Phil Garner .75 .35
58 Ron Reed .40 .18
59 Larry Hisle .75 .35
60 Jerry Reuss .75 .35
61 Ron LeFlore .75 .35
62 Johnny Oates .75 .35
63 Bobby Darwin .40 .18
64 Jerry Koosman .75 .35
65 Chris Chambliss .75 .35
66 Gus Bell FS .75 .35
 Buddy Bell
67 Ray Boone FS .75 .35
 Bob Boone
68 Joe Coleman FS .40 .18
 Joe Coleman Jr.
69 Jim Hegan FS .40 .18
 Mike Hegan
70 Roy Smalley FS .75 .35
 Roy Smalley Jr.

№	Player	Price 1	Price 2
71	Steve Rogers	.75	.35
72	Hal McRae	.75	.35
73	Baltimore Orioles; Team Card; Earl Weaver MG (Checklist back)	1.50	.30
74	Oscar Gamble	.75	.35
75	Larry Dierker	.75	.35
76	Willie Crawford	.40	.18
77	Pedro Borbon	.75	.35
78	Cecil Cooper	.75	.35
79	Jerry Morales	.40	.18
80	Jim Kaat	1.50	.70
81	Darrell Evans	.75	.35
82	Von Joshua	.40	.18
83	Jim Spencer	.40	.18
84	Brent Strom	.40	.18
85	Mickey Rivers	.75	.35
86	Mike Tyson	.40	.18
87	Tom Burgmeier	.40	.18
88	Duffy Dyer	.40	.18
89	Vern Ruhle	.40	.18
90	Sal Bando	.75	.35
91	Tom Hutton	.40	.18
92	Eduardo Rodriguez	.40	.18
93	Mike Phillips	.40	.18
94	Jim Dwyer	.40	.18
95	Brooks Robinson	5.00	2.20
96	Doug Bird	.40	.18
97	Wilbur Howard	.40	.18
98	Dennis Eckersley	40.00	18.00
99	Lee Lacy	.40	.18
100	Jim Hunter	3.00	1.35
101	Pete LaCock	.40	.18
102	Jim Willoughby	.40	.18
103	Biff Pocoroba	.40	.18
104	Cincinnati Reds; Team Card; Sparky Anderson MG (Checklist back)	2.50	.50
105	Gary Lavelle	.40	.18
106	Tom Grieve	.40	.18
107	Dave Roberts	.40	.18
108	Don Kirkwood	.40	.18
109	Larry Lintz	.40	.18
110	Carlos May	.40	.18
111	Danny Thompson	.40	.18
112	Kent Tekulve	1.50	.70
113	Gary Sutherland	.40	.18
114	Jay Johnstone	.75	.35
115	Ken Holtzman	.75	.35
116	Charlie Moore	.40	.18
117	Mike Jorgensen	.40	.18
118	Boston Red Sox; Team Card; Darrell Johnson MG (Checklist back)	1.50	.30
119	Checklist 1-132	1.50	.30
120	Rusty Staub	.75	.35
121	Tony Solaita	.40	.18
122	Mike Cosgrove	.40	.18
123	Walt Williams	.40	.18
124	Doug Rau	.40	.18
125	Don Baylor	1.50	.70
126	Tom Dettore	.40	.18
127	Larvell Blanks	.40	.18
128	Ken Griffey Sr.	2.50	1.10
129	Andy Etchebarren	.40	.18
130	Luis Tiant	1.50	.70
131	Bill Stein	.40	.18
132	Don Hood	.40	.18
133	Gary Matthews	.75	.35
134	Mike Ivie	.40	.18
135	Bake McBride	.75	.35
136	Dave Goltz	.40	.18
137	Bill Robinson	.75	.35
138	Lerrin LaGrow	.40	.18
139	Gorman Thomas	.75	.35
140	Vida Blue	.75	.35
141	Larry Parrish	1.50	.70
142	Dick Drago	.40	.18
143	Jerry Grote	.40	.18
144	Al Fitzmorris	.40	.18
145	Larry Bowa	.75	.35
146	George Medich	.40	.18
147	Houston Astros; Team Card; Bill Virdon MG (Checklist back)	1.50	
148	Stan Thomas	.40	.18
149	Tommy Davis	.75	.35
150	Steve Garvey	2.50	1.10
151	Bill Bonham	.40	.18
152	Leroy Stanton	.40	.18
153	Buzz Capra	.40	.18
154	Bucky Dent	.75	.35
155	Jack Billingham	.40	.18
156	Rico Carty	.75	.35
157	Mike Caldwell	.40	.18
158	Ken Reitz	.40	.18
159	Jerry Terrell	.40	.18
160	Dave Winfield	10.00	4.50
161	Bruce Kison	.40	.18
162	Jack Pierce	.40	.18
163	Jim Slaton	.40	.18
164	Pepe Mangual	.40	.18
165	Gene Tenace	.75	.35
166	Skip Lockwood	.40	.18
167	Freddie Patek	.75	.35
168	Tom Hilgendorf	.40	.18
169	Graig Nettles		.70
170	Rick Wise	.40	.18
171	Greg Gross	.40	.18
172	Texas Rangers; Team Card; Frank Lucchesi MG (Checklist back)	1.50	
173	Steve Swisher	.40	.18
174	Charlie Hough	.75	.35
175	Ken Singleton	.75	.35
176	Dick Lange	.40	.18
177	Marty Perez	.40	.18
178	Tom Buskey	.40	.18
179	George Foster	1.50	.70
180	Rich Gossage	1.50	.70
181	Willie Montanez	.40	.18
182	Harry Rasmussen	.40	.18
183	Steve Braun	.40	.18
184	Bill Greif	.40	.18
185	Dave Parker	1.50	.70
186	Tom Walker	.40	.18
187	Pedro Garcia	.40	.18
188	Fred Scherman	.40	.18
189	Claudell Washington	.75	.35
190	Jon Matlack	.75	.35
191	NL Batting Leaders; Bill Madlock; Ted Simmons; Manny Sanguillen	.75	.35
192	AL Batting Leaders; Rod Carew; Fred Lynn; Thurman Munson	2.50	1.10
193	NL Home Run Leaders; Mike Schmidt; Dave Kingman; Greg Luzinski	3.00	
194	AL Home Run Leaders; Reggie Jackson; George Scott; John Mayberry	3.00	1.35
195	NL RBI Leaders; Greg Luzinski; Johnny Bench; Tony Perez	1.50	.70
196	AL RBI Leaders; George Scott; John Mayberry; Fred Lynn	.75	.35
197	NL Stolen Base Leaders; Dave Lopes; Joe Morgan; Lou Brock	1.50	.70
198	AL Stolen Base Leaders; Mickey Rivers; Claudell Washington; Amos Otis	.75	.35
199	NL Victory Leaders; Tom Seaver; Randy Jones; Andy Messersmith	2.50	1.10
200	AL Victory Leaders; Jim Hunter; Jim Palmer; Vida Blue	1.50	.70
201	NL ERA Leaders; Randy Jones; Andy Messersmith; Tom Seaver	1.50	.70
202	AL ERA Leaders; Jim Palmer; Jim Hunter; Dennis Eckersley	3.00	1.35
203	NL Strikeout Leaders; Tom Seaver; John Montefusco; Andy Messersmith	2.50	1.10
204	AL Strikeout Leaders; Frank Tanana; Bert Blyleven; Gaylord Perry	.75	.35
205	Leading Firemen; Al Hrabosky; Rich Gossage	.75	.35
206	Manny Trillo	.40	.18
207	Andy Hassler	.40	.18
208	Mike Lum	.40	.18
209	Alan Ashby	.75	.35
210	Lee May	.75	.35
211	Clay Carroll	.75	.35
212	Pat Kelly	.40	.18
213	Dave Heaverlo	.40	.18
214	Eric Soderholm	.40	.18
215	Reggie Smith	.75	.35
216	Montreal Expos; Team Card; Karl Kuehl MG (Checklist back)	1.50	.30
217	Dave Freisleben	.40	.18
218	John Knox	.40	.18
219	Tom Murphy	.40	.18
220	Manny Sanguillen	.75	.35
221	Jim Todd	.40	.18
222	Wayne Garrett	.40	.18
223	Ollie Brown	.40	.18
224	Jim York	.40	.18
225	Roy White	.75	.35
226	Jim Sundberg	.75	.35
227	Oscar Zamora	.40	.18
228	John Hale	.40	.18
229	Jerry Remy	.40	.18
230	Carl Yastrzemski	6.00	2.70
231	Tom House	.40	.18
232	Frank Duffy	.40	.18
233	Grant Jackson	.40	.18
234	Mike Sadek	.40	.18
235	Bert Blyleven	1.50	.70
236	Kansas City Royals; Team Card; Whitey Herzog MG (Checklist back)	1.50	.30
237	Dave Hamilton	.40	.18
238	Larry Biittner	.40	.18
239	John Curtis	.40	.18
240	Pete Rose	15.00	6.75
241	Hector Torres	.40	.18
242	Dan Meyer	.40	.18
243	Jim Rooker	.40	.18
244	Bill Sharp	.40	.18
245	Felix Millan	.40	.18
246	Cesar Tovar	.40	.18
247	Terry Harmon	.40	.18
248	Dick Tidrow	.40	.18
249	Cliff Johnson	.75	.35
250	Fergie Jenkins	2.50	1.10
251	Rick Monday	.75	.35
252	Tim Nordbrook	.40	.18
253	Bill Buckner	.75	.35
254	Rudy Meoli	.40	.18
255	Fritz Peterson	.40	.18
256	Rowland Office	.40	.18
257	Ross Grimsley	.40	.18
258	Nyls Nyman	.40	.18
259	Darrel Chaney	.40	.18
260	Steve Busby	.40	.18
261	Gary Thomasson	.40	.18
262	Checklist 133-264	1.50	.30
263	Lyman Bostock	1.50	.70

264	Steve Renko	.40	.18
265	Willie Davis	.75	.35
266	Alan Foster	.40	.18
267	Aurelio Rodriguez	.40	.18
268	Del Unser	.40	.18
269	Rick Austin	.40	.18
270	Willie Stargell	3.00	1.35
271	Jim Lonborg	.75	.35
272	Rick Dempsey	.75	.35
273	Joe Niekro	.75	.35
274	Tommy Harper	.75	.35
275	Rick Manning	.40	.18
276	Mickey Scott	.40	.18
277	Chicago Cubs Team Card; Jim Marshall MG (Checklist back)	1.50	.30
278	Bernie Carbo	.40	.18
279	Roy Howell	.40	.18
280	Burt Hooton	.75	.35
281	Dave May	.40	.18
282	Dan Osborn	.40	.18
283	Merv Rettenmund	.40	.18
284	Steve Ontiveros	.40	.18
285	Mike Cuellar	.75	.35
286	Jim Wohlford	.40	.18
287	Pete Mackanin	.40	.18
288	Bill Campbell	.40	.18
289	Enzo Hernandez	.40	.18
290	Ted Simmons	.75	.35
291	Ken Sanders	.40	.18
292	Leon Roberts	.40	.18
293	Bill Castro	.40	.18
294	Ed Kirkpatrick	.40	.18
295	Dave Cash	.40	.18
296	Pat Dobson	.40	.18
297	Roger Metzger	.40	.18
298	Dick Bosman	.40	.18
299	Champ Summers	.40	.18
300	Johnny Bench	10.00	4.50
301	Jackie Brown	.40	.18
302	Rick Miller	.40	.18
303	Steve Foucault	.40	.18
304	California Angels Team Card; Dick Williams MG (Checklist back)	1.50	.30
305	Andy Messersmith	.75	.35
306	Rod Gilbreath	.40	.18
307	Al Bumbry	.75	.35
308	Jim Barr	.40	.18
309	Bill Melton	.40	.18
310	Randy Jones	.75	.35
311	Cookie Rojas	.75	.35
312	Don Carrithers	.40	.18
313	Dan Ford	.40	.18
314	Ed Kranepool	.40	.18
315	Al Hrabosky	.75	.35
316	Robin Yount	15.00	6.75
317	John Candelaria	1.50	.70
318	Bob Boone	1.50	.70
319	Larry Gura	.40	.18
320	Willie Horton	.75	.35
321	Jose Cruz	1.50	.70
322	Glenn Abbott	.40	.18
323	Bob Sperring	.40	.18
324	Jim Bibby	.40	.18
325	Tony Perez	2.50	1.10
326	Dick Pole	.40	.18
327	Dave Moates	.40	.18
328	Carl Morton	.40	.18
329	Joe Ferguson	.40	.18
330	Nolan Ryan	50.00	22.00
331	San Diego Padres Team Card; John McNamara MG (Checklist back)	1.50	.30
332	Charlie Williams	.40	.18
333	Bob Coluccio	.40	.18
334	Dennis Leonard	.75	.35
335	Bob Grich	.75	.35
336	Vic Albury	.40	.18
337	Bud Harrelson	.75	.35
338	Bob Bailey	.40	.18
339	John Denny	.75	.35
340	Jim Rice	2.50	1.10
341	Lou Gehrig ATG	12.00	5.50
342	Rogers Hornsby ATG	3.00	1.35
343	Pie Traynor ATG	1.50	.70
344	Honus Wagner ATG	5.00	2.20
345	Babe Ruth ATG	15.00	6.75
346	Ty Cobb ATG	10.00	4.50
347	Ted Williams ATG	12.00	5.50
348	Mickey Cochrane ATG	1.50	.70
349	Walter Johnson ATG	3.00	1.35
350	Lefty Grove ATG	1.50	.70
351	Randy Hundley	.75	.35
352	Dave Giusti	.40	.18
353	Sixto Lezcano	.75	.35
354	Ron Blomberg	.40	.18
355	Steve Carlton	6.00	2.70
356	Ted Martinez	.40	.18
357	Ken Forsch	.40	.18
358	Buddy Bell	.75	.35
359	Rick Reuschel	.75	.35
360	Jeff Burroughs	.75	.35
361	Detroit Tigers Team Card; Ralph Houk MG (Checklist back)	1.50	.30
362	Will McEnaney	.75	.35
363	Dave Collins	.75	.35
364	Elias Sosa	.40	.18
365	Carlton Fisk	5.00	2.20
366	Bobby Valentine	.75	.35
367	Bruce Miller	.40	.18
368	Wilbur Wood	.40	.18
369	Frank White	.75	.35
370	Ron Cey	.75	.35
371	Elrod Hendricks	.40	.18
372	Rick Baldwin	.40	.18
373	Johnny Briggs	.40	.18
374	Dan Warthen	.40	.18
375	Ron Fairly	.75	.35
376	Rich Hebner	.40	.18
377	Mike Hegan	.40	.18
378	Steve Stone	.75	.35
379	Ken Boswell	.40	.18
380	Bobby Bonds	1.50	.70
381	Denny Doyle	.40	.18
382	Matt Alexander	.40	.18
383	John Ellis	.40	.18
384	Philadelphia Phillies Team Card; Danny Ozark MG (Checklist back)	1.50	.30
385	Mickey Lolich	.75	.35
386	Ed Goodson	.40	.18
387	Mike Miley	.40	.18
388	Stan Perzanowski	.40	.18
389	Glenn Adams	.40	.18
390	Don Gullett	.75	.35
391	Jerry Hairston	.40	.18
392	Checklist 265-396	1.50	.30
393	Paul Mitchell	.40	.18
394	Fran Healy	.40	.18
395	Jim Wynn	.75	.35
396	Bill Lee	.75	.35
397	Tim Foli	.40	.18
398	Dave Tomlin	.40	.18
399	Luis Melendez	.40	.18
400	Rod Carew	5.00	2.20
401	Ken Brett	.40	.18
402	Don Money	.75	.35
403	Geoff Zahn	.40	.18
404	Enos Cabell	.40	.18
405	Rollie Fingers	2.50	1.10
406	Ed Herrmann	.40	.18
407	Tom Underwood	.40	.18
408	Charlie Spikes	.40	.18
409	Dave Lemanczyk	.40	.18
410	Ralph Garr	.75	.35
411	Bill Singer	.40	.18
412	Toby Harrah	.75	.35
413	Pete Varney	.40	.18
414	Wayne Garland	.40	.18
415	Vada Pinson	1.50	.70
416	Tommy John	1.50	.70
417	Gene Clines	.40	.18
418	Jose Morales	.40	.18
419	Reggie Cleveland	.40	.18
420	Joe Morgan	5.00	2.20
421	Oakland A's Team Card; (No MG on front; checklist back)	1.50	.30
422	Johnny Grubb	.40	.18
423	Ed Halicki	.40	.18
424	Phil Roof	.40	.18
425	Rennie Stennett	.40	.18
426	Bob Forsch	.40	.18
427	Kurt Bevacqua	.40	.18
428	Jim Crawford	.40	.18
429	Fred Stanley	.40	.18
430	Jose Cardenal	.75	.35
431	Dick Ruthven	.40	.18
432	Tom Veryzer	.40	.18
433	Rick Waits	.40	.18
434	Morris Nettles	.40	.18
435	Phil Niekro	2.50	1.10
436	Bill Fahey	.40	.18
437	Terry Forster	.40	.18
438	Doug DeCinces	.75	.35
439	Rick Rhoden	.75	.35
440	John Mayberry	.75	.35
441	Gary Carter	4.00	1.80
442	Hank Webb	.40	.18
443	San Francisco Giants Team Card; (No MG on front; checklist back)	1.50	.30
444	Gary Nolan	.75	.35
445	Rico Petrocelli	.75	.35
446	Larry Haney	.40	.18
447	Gene Locklear	.40	.18
448	Tom Johnson	.40	.18
449	Bob Robertson	.40	.18
450	Jim Palmer	5.00	2.20
451	Buddy Bradford	.40	.18
452	Tom Hausman	.40	.18
453	Lou Piniella	1.50	.70
454	Tom Griffin	.40	.18
455	Dick Allen	1.50	.70
456	Joe Coleman	.40	.18
457	Ed Crosby	.40	.18
458	Earl Williams	.40	.18
459	Jim Brewer	.40	.18
460	Cesar Cedeno	.75	.35
461	NL and AL Champs Reds sweep Bucs, Bosox surprise A's	.75	.35
462	'75 World Series Reds Champs	.75	.35
463	Steve Hargan	.40	.18
464	Ken Henderson	.40	.18
465	Mike Marshall	.75	.35
466	Bob Stinson	.40	.18
467	Woodie Fryman	.40	.18
468	Jesus Alou	.40	.18
469	Rawly Eastwick	.75	.35
470	Bobby Murcer	.75	.35
471	Jim Burton	.40	.18
472	Bob Davis	.40	.18
473	Paul Blair	.75	.35
474	Ray Corbin	.40	.18
475	Joe Rudi	.75	.35
476	Bob Moose	1.50	.70
477	Cleveland Indians Team Card; Frank Robinson MG (Checklist back)	1.50	.30
478	Lynn McGlothen	.40	.18
479	Bobby Mitchell	.40	.18
480	Mike Schmidt	15.00	6.75
481	Rudy May	.40	.18
482	Tim Hosley	.40	.18
483	Mickey Stanley	.40	.18
484	Eric Raich	.40	.18
485	Mike Hargrove	.75	.35
486	Bruce Dal Canton	.40	.18
487	Leron Lee	.40	.18
488	Claude Osteen	.75	.35
489	Skip Jutze	.40	.18
490	Frank Tanana	.75	.35
491	Terry Crowley	.40	.18
492	Marty Pattin	.40	.18
493	Derrel Thomas	.40	.18
494	Craig Swan	.75	.35

❏ 495 Nate Colbert	.40	.18
❏ 496 Juan Beniquez	.40	.18
❏ 497 Joe McIntosh	.40	.18
❏ 498 Glenn Borgmann	.40	.18
❏ 499 Mario Guerrero	.40	.18
❏ 500 Reggie Jackson	15.00	6.75
❏ 501 Billy Champion	.40	.18
❏ 502 Tim McCarver	1.50	.70
❏ 503 Elliott Maddox	.40	.18
❏ 504 Pittsburgh Pirates	1.50	.30
Team Card;		
Danny Murtaugh MG		
(Checklist back)		
❏ 505 Mark Belanger	.75	.35
❏ 506 George Mitterwald	.40	.18
❏ 507 Ray Bare	.40	.18
❏ 508 Duane Kuiper	.40	.18
❏ 509 Bill Hands	.40	.18
❏ 510 Amos Otis	.75	.35
❏ 511 Jamie Easterley	.40	.18
❏ 512 Ellie Rodriguez	.40	.18
❏ 513 Bart Johnson	.40	.18
❏ 514 Dan Driessen	.75	.35
❏ 515 Steve Yeager	.75	.35
❏ 516 Wayne Granger	.40	.18
❏ 517 John Milner	.40	.18
❏ 518 Doug Flynn	.40	.18
❏ 519 Steve Brye	.40	.18
❏ 520 Willie McCovey	5.00	2.20
❏ 521 Jim Colborn	.40	.18
❏ 522 Ted Sizemore	.40	.18
❏ 523 Bob Montgomery	.40	.18
❏ 524 Pete Falcone	.40	.18
❏ 525 Billy Williams	2.50	1.10
❏ 526 Checklist 397-528	1.50	.30
❏ 527 Mike Anderson	.40	.18
❏ 528 Dock Ellis	.40	.18
❏ 529 Deron Johnson	.75	.35
❏ 530 Don Sutton	2.50	1.10
❏ 531 New York Mets	1.50	.30
Team Card;		
Joe Frazier MG		
(Checklist back)		
❏ 532 Milt May	.40	.18
❏ 533 Lee Richard	.40	.18
❏ 534 Stan Bahnsen	.40	.18
❏ 535 Dave Nelson	.40	.18
❏ 536 Mike Thompson	.40	.18
❏ 537 Tony Muser	.40	.18
❏ 538 Pat Darcy	.40	.18
❏ 539 John Balaz	.75	.35
❏ 540 Bill Freehan	.75	.35
❏ 541 Steve Mingori	.40	.18
❏ 542 Keith Hernandez	1.50	.70
❏ 543 Wayne Twitchell	.40	.18
❏ 544 Pepe Frias	.40	.18
❏ 545 Sparky Lyle	.75	.35
❏ 546 Dave Rosello	.40	.18
❏ 547 Horace Harrison	.40	.18
❏ 548 Manny Mota	.75	.35
❏ 549 Randy Tate	.40	.18
❏ 550 Hank Aaron	25.00	11.00
❏ 551 Jerry DaVanon	.40	.18
❏ 552 Terry Humphrey	.40	.18
❏ 553 Randy Moffitt	.40	.18
❏ 554 Ray Fosse	.40	.18
❏ 555 Dyar Miller	.40	.18
❏ 556 Minnesota Twins	1.50	.30
Team Card;		
Gene Mauch MG		
(Checklist back)		
❏ 557 Dan Spillner	.40	.18
❏ 558 Clarence Gaston	.75	.35
❏ 559 Clyde Wright	.40	.18
❏ 560 Jorge Orta	.40	.18
❏ 561 Tom Carroll	.40	.18
❏ 562 Adrian Garrett	.40	.18
❏ 563 Larry Demery	.40	.18
❏ 564 Bubble Gum Champ	1.50	.70
Kurt Bevacqua		
❏ 565 Tug McGraw	.75	.35
❏ 566 Ken McMullen	.40	.18
❏ 567 George Stone	.40	.18
❏ 568 Rob Andrews	.40	.18
❏ 569 Nelson Briles	.75	.35
❏ 570 George Hendrick	.75	.35

❏ 571 Don DeMola	.40	.18
❏ 572 Rich Coggins	.40	.18
❏ 573 Bill Travers	.40	.18
❏ 574 Don Kessinger	.75	.35
❏ 575 Dwight Evans	1.50	.70
❏ 576 Maximino Leon	.40	.18
❏ 577 Marc Hill	.40	.18
❏ 578 Ted Kubiak	.40	.18
❏ 579 Clay Kirby	.40	.18
❏ 580 Bert Campaneris	.75	.35
❏ 581 St. Louis Cardinals	1.50	.30
Team Card;		
Red Schoendienst MG		
(Checklist back)		
❏ 582 Mike Kekich	.40	.18
❏ 583 Tommy Helms	.40	.18
❏ 584 Stan Wall	.40	.18
❏ 585 Joe Torre	1.50	.70
❏ 586 Ron Schueler	.40	.18
❏ 587 Leo Cardenas	.40	.18
❏ 588 Kevin Kobel	.40	.18
❏ 589 Rookie Pitchers	1.50	.70
Santo Alcala		
Mike Flanagan		
Joe Pactwa		
Pablo Torrealba		
❏ 590 Rookie Outfielders	.75	.35
Henry Cruz		
Chet Lemon		
Ellis Valentine		
Terry Whitfield		
❏ 591 Rookie Pitchers	.75	.35
Steve Grilli		
Craig Mitchell		
Jose Sosa		
George Throop		
❏ 592 Rookie Infielders	6.00	2.70
Willie Randolph		
Dave McKay		
Jerry Royster		
Roy Staiger		
❏ 593 Rookie Pitchers	.75	.35
Larry Anderson		
Ken Crosby		
Mark Littell		
Butch Metzger		
❏ 594 Rookie Catchers/OF	.75	.35
Andy Merchant		
Ed Ott		
Royle Stillman		
Jerry White		
❏ 595 Rookie Pitchers	.75	.35
Art DeFilippis		
Randy Lerch		
Sid Monge		
Steve Barr		
❏ 596 Rookie Infielders	.75	.35
Craig Reynolds		
Lamar Johnson		
Johnnie LeMaster		
Jerry Manuel		
❏ 597 Rookie Pitchers	.75	.35
Don Aase		
Jack Kucek		
Frank LaCorte		
Mike Pazik		
❏ 598 Rookie Outfielders	.75	.35
Hector Cruz		
Jamie Quirk		
Jerry Turner		
Joe Wallis		
❏ 599 Rookie Pitchers	6.00	2.70
Rob Dressler		
Ron Guidry		
Bob McClure		
Pat Zachry		
❏ 600 Tom Seaver	10.00	4.50
❏ 601 Ken Rudolph	.40	.18
❏ 602 Doug Konieczny	.40	.18
❏ 603 Jim Holt	.40	.18
❏ 604 Joe Lovitto	.40	.18
❏ 605 Al Downing	.40	.18
❏ 606 Milwaukee Brewers	1.50	.30
Team Card;		
Alex Grammas MG		
(Checklist back)		

❏ 607 Rich Hinton	.40	.18
❏ 608 Vic Correll	.40	.18
❏ 609 Fred Norman	.75	.35
❏ 610 Greg Luzinski	1.50	.70
❏ 611 Rich Folkers	.40	.18
❏ 612 Joe Lahoud	.40	.18
❏ 613 Tim Johnson	.40	.18
❏ 614 Fernando Arroyo	.40	.18
❏ 615 Mike Cubbage	.40	.18
❏ 616 Buck Martinez	.40	.18
❏ 617 Darold Knowles	.40	.18
❏ 618 Jack Brohamer	.40	.18
❏ 619 Bill Butler	.40	.18
❏ 620 Al Oliver	.75	.35
❏ 621 Tom Hall	.40	.18
❏ 622 Rick Auerbach	.40	.18
❏ 623 Bob Allietta	.40	.18
❏ 624 Tony Taylor	.75	.35
❏ 625 J.R. Richard	.75	.35
❏ 626 Bob Sheldon	.40	.18
❏ 627 Bill Plummer	.40	.18
❏ 628 John D'Acquisto	.40	.18
❏ 629 Sandy Alomar	.75	.35
❏ 630 Chris Speier	.40	.18
❏ 631 Atlanta Braves	1.50	.30
Team Card;		
Dave Bristol MG		
(Checklist back)		
❏ 632 Rogelio Morel	.40	.18
❏ 633 John Stearns	.75	.35
❏ 634 Larry Christenson	.40	.18
❏ 635 Jim Fregosi	.75	.35
❏ 636 Joe Decker	.40	.18
❏ 637 Bruce Bochte	.40	.18
❏ 638 Doyle Alexander	.75	.35
❏ 639 Fred Kendall	.40	.18
❏ 640 Bill Madlock	1.50	.70
❏ 641 Tom Paciorek	.75	.35
❏ 642 Dennis Blair	.40	.18
❏ 643 Checklist 529-660	1.50	.30
❏ 644 Tom Bradley	.40	.18
❏ 645 Darrell Porter	.75	.35
❏ 646 John Lowenstein	.40	.18
❏ 647 Ramon Hernandez	.40	.18
❏ 648 Al Cowens	.40	.18
❏ 649 Dave Roberts	.40	.18
❏ 650 Thurman Munson	5.00	2.20
❏ 651 John Odom	.40	.18
❏ 652 Ed Armbrister	.40	.18
❏ 653 Mike Norris	.75	.35
❏ 654 Doug Griffin	.40	.18
❏ 655 Mike Vail	.40	.18
❏ 656 Chicago White Sox	1.50	.30
Team Card;		
Chuck Tanner MG		
(Checklist back)		
❏ 657 Roy Smalley	.75	.35
❏ 658 Jerry Johnson	.40	.18
❏ 659 Ben Oglivie	.75	.35
❏ 660 Dave Lopes	1.50	.30

1976 Topps Traded

	NRMT	VG-E
COMPLETE SET (44)	30.00	13.50
COMMON CARD	.40	.18
MINOR STARS	.75	.35
SEMISTARS	1.50	.70

INCLUDED IN ALL LATE PACKS
CARDS PRICED IN NM CONDITION

		NM	VG-E
❑ 27T	Ed Figueroa	.40	.18
❑ 28T	Dusty Baker	1.50	.70
❑ 44T	Doug Rader	.75	.35
❑ 58T	Ron Reed	.40	.18
❑ 74T	Oscar Gamble	1.50	.70
❑ 80T	Jim Kaat	1.50	.70
❑ 83T	Jim Spencer	.40	.18
❑ 85T	Mickey Rivers	.75	.35
❑ 99T	Lee Lacy	.40	.18
❑ 120T	Rusty Staub	.75	.35
❑ 127T	Larvell Blanks	.40	.18
❑ 146T	George Medich	.40	.18
❑ 158T	Ken Reitz	.40	.18
❑ 208T	Mike Lum	.40	.18
❑ 211T	Clay Carroll	.40	.18
❑ 231T	Tom House	.40	.18
❑ 250T	Fergie Jenkins	3.00	1.35
❑ 259T	Darrel Chaney	.40	.18
❑ 292T	Leon Roberts	.40	.18
❑ 296T	Pat Dobson	.40	.18
❑ 309T	Bill Melton	.40	.18
❑ 338T	Bob Bailey	.40	.18
❑ 380T	Bobby Bonds	1.50	.70
❑ 383T	John Ellis	.40	.18
❑ 385T	Mickey Lolich	.75	.18
❑ 401T	Ken Brett	.40	.18
❑ 410T	Ralph Garr	.40	.18
❑ 411T	Bill Singer	.40	.18
❑ 428T	Jim Crawford	.40	.18
❑ 434T	Morris Nettles	.40	.18
❑ 464T	Ken Henderson	.40	.18
❑ 497T	Joe McIntosh	.40	.18
❑ 524T	Pete Falcone	.40	.18
❑ 527T	Mike Anderson	.40	.18
❑ 528T	Dock Ellis	.40	.18
❑ 532T	Milt May	.40	.18
❑ 554T	Ray Fosse	.40	.18
❑ 579T	Clay Kirby	.40	.18
❑ 583T	Tommy Helms	.40	.18
❑ 592T	Willie Randolph	5.00	2.20
❑ 618T	Jack Brohamer	.40	.18
❑ 632T	Rogelio Moret	.40	.18
❑ 649T	Dave Roberts	.40	.18
❑ NNO	Traded Checklist	2.00	.40

1977 Topps

	NRMT	VG-E
COMPLETE SET (660)	250.00	110.00
COMMON CARD (1-660)	.30	.14
MINOR STARS	.75	.35
SEMISTARS	1.50	.70
UNLISTED STARS	2.50	1.10

CARDS PRICED IN NM CONDITION

		NM	VG-E
❑ 1	Batting Leaders	8.00	2.30
	George Brett		
	Bill Madlock		
❑ 2	Home Run Leaders	2.50	1.10
	Graig Nettles		
	Mike Schmidt		
❑ 3	RBI Leaders	1.50	.70
	Lee May		
	George Foster		
❑ 4	Stolen Base Leaders	.75	.35
❑ 5	Victory Leaders	1.50	.70
	Jim Palmer		
	Randy Jones		
❑ 6	Strikeout Leaders	15.00	6.75
	Nolan Ryan		
	Tom Seaver		
❑ 7	ERA Leaders	.75	.35
	Mark Fidrych		
	John Denny		
❑ 8	Firemen Leaders	.75	.35
	Bill Campbell		
	Rawly Eastwick		
❑ 9	Doug Rader	.30	.14
❑ 10	Reggie Jackson	12.00	5.50
❑ 11	Rob Dressler	.30	.14
❑ 12	Larry Haney	.30	.14
❑ 13	Luis Gomez	.30	.14
❑ 14	Tommy Smith	.30	.14
❑ 15	Don Gullett	.75	.35
❑ 16	Bob Jones	.30	.14
❑ 17	Steve Stone	.75	.35
❑ 18	Indians Team/Mgr.	1.50	.30
	Frank Robinson		
	(Checklist back)		
❑ 19	John D'Acquisto	.30	.14
❑ 20	Graig Nettles	1.50	.70
❑ 21	Ken Forsch	.30	.14
❑ 22	Bill Freehan	.75	.35
❑ 23	Dan Driessen	.30	.14
❑ 24	Carl Morton	.30	.14
❑ 25	Dwight Evans	1.50	.70
❑ 26	Ray Sadecki	.30	.14
❑ 27	Bill Buckner	.75	.35
❑ 28	Woodie Fryman	.30	.14
❑ 29	Bucky Dent	.75	.35
❑ 30	Greg Luzinski	1.50	.70
❑ 31	Jim Todd	.30	.14
❑ 32	Checklist 1-132	1.50	.30
❑ 33	Wayne Garland	.30	.14
❑ 34	Angels Team/Mgr.	1.50	.30
	Norm Sherry		
	(Checklist back)		
❑ 35	Rennie Stennett	.30	.14
❑ 36	John Ellis	.30	.14
❑ 37	Steve Hargan	.30	.14
❑ 38	Craig Kusick	.30	.14
❑ 39	Tom Griffin	.30	.14
❑ 40	Bobby Murcer	.75	.35
❑ 41	Jim Kern	.30	.14
❑ 42	Jose Cruz	.75	.35
❑ 43	Ray Bare	.30	.14
❑ 44	Bud Harrelson	.75	.35
❑ 45	Rawly Eastwick	.30	.14
❑ 46	Buck Martinez	.30	.14
❑ 47	Lynn McGlothen	.30	.14
❑ 48	Tom Paciorek	.75	.35
❑ 49	Grant Jackson	.30	.14
❑ 50	Ron Cey	.75	.35
❑ 51	Brewers Team/Mgr.	1.50	.30
	Alex Grammas		
	(Checklist back)		
❑ 52	Ellis Valentine	.30	.14
❑ 53	Paul Mitchell	.30	.14
❑ 54	Sandy Alomar	.75	.35
❑ 55	Jeff Burroughs	.75	.35
❑ 56	Rudy May	.30	.14
❑ 57	Marc Hill	.30	.14
❑ 58	Chet Lemon	.75	.35
❑ 59	Larry Christenson	.30	.14
❑ 60	Jim Rice	2.50	1.10
❑ 61	Manny Sanguillen	.75	.35
❑ 62	Eric Raich	.30	.14
❑ 63	Tito Fuentes	.30	.14
❑ 64	Larry Biittner	.30	.14
❑ 65	Skip Lockwood	.30	.14
❑ 66	Roy Smalley	.75	.35
❑ 67	Joaquin Andujar	.75	.35
❑ 68	Bruce Bochte	.30	.14
❑ 69	Jim Crawford	.30	.14
❑ 70	Johnny Bench	8.00	3.60
❑ 71	Dock Ellis	.30	.14
❑ 72	Mike Anderson	.30	.14
❑ 73	Charlie Williams	.30	.14
❑ 74	A's Team/Mgr.	1.50	.30
	Jack McKeon		
	(Checklist back)		
❑ 75	Dennis Leonard	.75	.35
❑ 76	Tim Foli	.30	.14
❑ 77	Dyar Miller	.30	.14
❑ 78	Bob Davis	.30	.14
❑ 79	Don Money	.75	.35
❑ 80	Andy Messersmith	.75	.35
❑ 81	Juan Beniquez	.30	.14
❑ 82	Jim Rooker	.30	.14
❑ 83	Kevin Bell	.30	.14
❑ 84	Ollie Brown	.30	.14
❑ 85	Duane Kuiper	.30	.14
❑ 86	Pat Zachry	.30	.14
❑ 87	Glenn Borgmann	.30	.14
❑ 88	Stan Wall	.30	.14
❑ 89	Butch Hobson	.75	.35
❑ 90	Cesar Cedeno	.75	.35
❑ 91	John Verhoeven	.30	.14
❑ 92	Dave Rosello	.30	.14
❑ 93	Tom Poquette	.30	.14
❑ 94	Craig Swan	.30	.14
❑ 95	Keith Hernandez	.75	.35
❑ 96	Lou Piniella	.75	.35
❑ 97	Dave Heaverlo	.30	.14
❑ 98	Milt May	.30	.14
❑ 99	Tom Hausman	.30	.14
❑ 100	Joe Morgan	4.00	1.80
❑ 101	Dick Bosman	.30	.14
❑ 102	Jose Morales	.30	.14
❑ 103	Mike Bacsik	.30	.14
❑ 104	Omar Moreno	.75	.35
❑ 105	Steve Yeager	.75	.35
❑ 106	Mike Flanagan	.75	.35
❑ 107	Bill Melton	.30	.14
❑ 108	Alan Foster	.30	.14
❑ 109	Jorge Orta	.30	.14
❑ 110	Steve Carlton	5.00	2.20
❑ 111	Rico Petrocelli	.75	.35
❑ 112	Bill Greif	.30	.14
❑ 113	Blue Jays Leaders	1.50	.30
	Roy Hartsfield MG		
	Don Leppert CO		
	Bob Miller CO		
	Jackie Moore CO		
	Harry Warner CO		
	(Checklist back)		
❑ 114	Bruce Dal Canton	.30	.14
❑ 115	Rick Manning	.30	.14
❑ 116	Joe Niekro	.75	.35
❑ 117	Frank White	.75	.35
❑ 118	Rick Jones	.30	.14
❑ 119	John Stearns	.30	.14
❑ 120	Rod Carew	4.00	1.80
❑ 121	Gary Nolan	.30	.14
❑ 122	Ben Oglivie	.75	.35
❑ 123	Fred Stanley	.30	.14
❑ 124	George Mitterwald	.30	.14
❑ 125	Bill Travers	.30	.14
❑ 126	Rod Gilbreath	.30	.14
❑ 127	Ron Fairly	.75	.35
❑ 128	Tommy John	1.50	.70
❑ 129	Mike Sadek	.30	.14
❑ 130	Al Oliver	.75	.35
❑ 131	Orlando Ramirez	.30	.14
❑ 132	Chip Lang	.30	.14
❑ 133	Ralph Garr	.75	.35
❑ 134	Padres Team/Mgr.	1.50	.30
	John McNamara		
	(Checklist back)		
❑ 135	Mark Belanger	.75	.35
❑ 136	Jerry Mumphrey	.75	.35
❑ 137	Jeff Terpko	.30	.14
❑ 138	Bob Stinson	.30	.14
❑ 139	Fred Norman	.30	.14
❑ 140	Mike Schmidt	12.00	5.50
❑ 141	Mark Littell	.30	.14
❑ 142	Steve Dillard	.30	.14
❑ 143	Ed Herrmann	.30	.14
❑ 144	Bruce Sutter	3.00	1.35
❑ 145	Tom Veryzer	.30	.14
❑ 146	Dusty Baker	1.50	.70
❑ 147	Jackie Brown	.30	.14
❑ 148	Fran Healy	.30	.14
❑ 149	Mike Cubbage	.30	.14
❑ 150	Tom Seaver	8.00	3.60

☐ 151	Johnny LeMaster	.30	.14
☐ 152	Gaylord Perry	2.50	1.10
☐ 153	Ron Jackson	.30	.14
☐ 154	Dave Giusti	.30	.14
☐ 155	Joe Rudi	.75	.35
☐ 156	Pete Mackanin	.30	.14
☐ 157	Ken Brett	.30	.14
☐ 158	Ted Kubiak	.30	.14
☐ 159	Bernie Carbo	.30	.14
☐ 160	Will McEnaney	.30	.14
☐ 161	Garry Templeton	1.50	.70
☐ 162	Mike Cuellar	.75	.35
☐ 163	Dave Hilton	.30	.14
☐ 164	Tug McGraw	.75	.35
☐ 165	Jim Wynn	.75	.35
☐ 166	Bill Campbell	.75	.35
☐ 167	Rich Hebner	.75	.35
☐ 168	Charlie Spikes	.30	.14
☐ 169	Darold Knowles	.30	.14
☐ 170	Thurman Munson	4.00	1.80
☐ 171	Ken Sanders	.30	.14
☐ 172	John Milner	.30	.14
☐ 173	Chuck Scrivener	.30	.14
☐ 174	Nelson Briles	.75	.35
☐ 175	Butch Wynegar	.75	.35
☐ 176	Bob Robertson	.30	.14
☐ 177	Bart Johnson	.30	.14
☐ 178	Bombo Rivera	.30	.14
☐ 179	Paul Hartzell	.30	.14
☐ 180	Dave Lopes	.75	.35
☐ 181	Ken McMullen	.30	.14
☐ 182	Dan Spillner	.30	.14
☐ 183	Cardinals Team/Mgr.	1.50	.30
	Vern Rapp		
	(Checklist back)		
☐ 184	Bo McLaughlin	.30	.14
☐ 185	Sixto Lezcano	.30	.14
☐ 186	Doug Flynn	.30	.14
☐ 187	Dick Pole	.30	.14
☐ 188	Bob Tolan	.30	.14
☐ 189	Rick Dempsey	.75	.35
☐ 190	Ray Burris	.30	.14
☐ 191	Doug Griffin	.30	.14
☐ 192	Clarence Gaston	.75	.35
☐ 193	Larry Gura	.30	.14
☐ 194	Gary Matthews	.75	.35
☐ 195	Ed Figueroa	.30	.14
☐ 196	Len Randle	.30	.14
☐ 197	Ed Ott	.30	.14
☐ 198	Wilbur Wood	.30	.14
☐ 199	Pepe Frias	.30	.14
☐ 200	Frank Tanana	.75	.35
☐ 201	Ed Kranepool	.30	.14
☐ 202	Tom Johnson	.30	.14
☐ 203	Ed Armbrister	.30	.14
☐ 204	Jeff Newman	.30	.14
☐ 205	Pete Falcone	.30	.14
☐ 206	Boog Powell	1.50	.70
☐ 207	Glenn Abbott	.30	.14
☐ 208	Checklist 133-264	1.50	.30
☐ 209	Rob Andrews	.30	.14
☐ 210	Fred Lynn	.75	.15
☐ 211	Giants Team/Mgr.	1.50	.70
	Joe Altobelli		
	(Checklist back)		
☐ 212	Jim Mason	.30	.14
☐ 213	Maximino Leon	.30	.14
☐ 214	Darrell Porter	.75	.35
☐ 215	Butch Metzger	.30	.14
☐ 216	Doug DeCinces	.75	.35
☐ 217	Tom Underwood	.30	.14
☐ 218	John Wathan	.30	.14
☐ 219	Joe Coleman	.30	.14
☐ 220	Chris Chambliss	.75	.35
☐ 221	Bob Bailey	.30	.14
☐ 222	Francisco Barrios	.30	.14
☐ 223	Earl Williams	.30	.14
☐ 224	Rusty Torres	.30	.14
☐ 225	Bob Apodaca	.30	.14
☐ 226	Leroy Stanton	.75	.14
☐ 227	Joe Sambito	.30	.14
☐ 228	Twins Team/Mgr.	1.50	.30
	Gene Mauch		
	(Checklist back)		
☐ 229	Don Kessinger	.75	.35
☐ 230	Vida Blue	.75	.35
☐ 231	George Brett RB	8.00	3.60
	Most consecutive games		
	3 or more hits		
☐ 232	Minnie Minoso RB	.75	.35
	Oldest to hit safely		
☐ 233	Jose Morales RB	.30	.14
	Most pinch-hits season		
☐ 234	Nolan Ryan RB	15.00	6.75
	Most seasons, 300 strikeouts		
☐ 235	Cecil Cooper	.75	.35
☐ 236	Tom Buskey	.30	.14
☐ 237	Gene Clines	.30	.14
☐ 238	Tippy Martinez	.30	.14
☐ 239	Bill Plummer	.30	.14
☐ 240	Ron LeFlore	.75	.35
☐ 241	Dave Tomlin	.30	.14
☐ 242	Ken Henderson	.30	.14
☐ 243	Ron Reed	.30	.14
☐ 244	John Mayberry	.75	.35
	(Cartoon mentions		
	T206 Wagner)		
☐ 245	Rick Rhoden	.75	.35
☐ 246	Mike Vail	.30	.14
☐ 247	Chris Knapp	.30	.14
☐ 248	Wilbur Howard	.30	.14
☐ 249	Pete Redfern	.30	.14
☐ 250	Bill Madlock	.75	.35
☐ 251	Tony Muser	.30	.14
☐ 252	Dale Murray	.30	.14
☐ 253	John Hale	.30	.14
☐ 254	Doyle Alexander	.30	.14
☐ 255	George Scott	.75	.35
☐ 256	Joe Hoerner	.30	.14
☐ 257	Mike Miley	.30	.14
☐ 258	Luis Tiant	.75	.35
☐ 259	Mets Team/Mgr.	1.50	.30
	Joe Frazier		
	(Checklist back)		
☐ 260	J.R. Richard	.75	.35
☐ 261	Phil Garner	.75	.35
☐ 262	Al Cowens	.30	.14
☐ 263	Mike Marshall	.75	.35
☐ 264	Tom Hutton	.30	.14
☐ 265	Mark Fidrych	3.00	1.35
☐ 266	Derrel Thomas	.30	.14
☐ 267	Ray Fosse	.30	.14
☐ 268	Rick Sawyer	.30	.14
☐ 269	Joe Lis	.30	.14
☐ 270	Dave Parker	1.50	.70
☐ 271	Terry Forster	.30	.14
☐ 272	Lee Lacy	.30	.14
☐ 273	Eric Soderholm	.30	.14
☐ 274	Don Stanhouse	.30	.14
☐ 275	Mike Hargrove	.75	.35
☐ 276	Chris Chambliss ALCS	1.50	.70
	homer decides it.		
☐ 277	Pete Rose NLCS	3.00	1.35
☐ 278	Danny Frisella	.30	.14
☐ 279	Joe Wallis	.30	.14
☐ 280	Jim Hunter	2.50	1.10
☐ 281	Roy Staiger	.30	.14
☐ 282	Sid Monge	.30	.14
☐ 283	Jerry DaVanon	.30	.14
☐ 284	Mike Norris	.30	.14
☐ 285	Brooks Robinson	4.00	1.80
☐ 286	Johnny Grubb	.30	.06
☐ 287	Reds Team/Mgr.	1.50	.70
	Sparky Anderson		
	(Checklist back)		
☐ 288	Bob Montgomery	.30	.14
☐ 289	Gene Garber	.75	.35
☐ 290	Amos Otis	.75	.35
☐ 291	Jason Thompson	.75	.35
☐ 292	Rogelio Moret	.30	.14
☐ 293	Jack Brohamer	.30	.14
☐ 294	George Medich	.30	.14
☐ 295	Gary Carter	2.50	1.10
☐ 296	Don Hood	.30	.14
☐ 297	Ken Reitz	.30	.14
☐ 298	Charlie Hough	.75	.35
☐ 299	Otto Velez	.30	.14
☐ 300	Jerry Koosman	.75	.35
☐ 301	Toby Harrah	.75	.35
☐ 302	Mike Garman	.30	.14
☐ 303	Gene Tenace	.75	.35
☐ 304	Jim Hughes	.30	.14
☐ 305	Mickey Rivers	.75	.35
☐ 306	Rick Waits	.30	.14
☐ 307	Gary Sutherland	.30	.14
☐ 308	Gene Pentz	.30	.14
☐ 309	Red Sox Team/Mgr.	1.50	.30
	Don Zimmer		
	(Checklist back)		
☐ 310	Larry Bowa	.75	.35
☐ 311	Vern Ruhle	.30	.14
☐ 312	Rob Belloir	.30	.14
☐ 313	Paul Blair	.75	.35
☐ 314	Steve Mingori	.30	.14
☐ 315	Dave Chalk	.30	.14
☐ 316	Steve Rogers	.30	.14
☐ 317	Kurt Bevacqua	.30	.14
☐ 318	Duffy Dyer	.30	.14
☐ 319	Rich Gossage	1.50	.70
☐ 320	Ken Griffey	1.50	.70
☐ 321	Dave Goltz	.30	.14
☐ 322	Bill Russell	.75	.35
☐ 323	Larry Lintz	.30	.14
☐ 324	John Curtis	.30	.14
☐ 325	Mike Ivie	.30	.14
☐ 326	Jesse Jefferson	.30	.14
☐ 327	Astros Team/Mgr.	1.50	.30
	Bill Virdon		
	(Checklist back)		
☐ 328	Tommy Boggs	.30	.14
☐ 329	Ron Hodges	.30	.14
☐ 330	George Hendrick	.75	.35
☐ 331	Jim Colborn	.30	.14
☐ 332	Elliott Maddox	.30	.14
☐ 333	Paul Reuschel	.30	.14
☐ 334	Bill Stein	.30	.14
☐ 335	Bill Robinson	.75	.35
☐ 336	Denny Doyle	.30	.14
☐ 337	Ron Schueler	.30	.14
☐ 338	Dave Duncan	.30	.14
☐ 339	Adrian Devine	.30	.14
☐ 340	Hal McRae	.75	.35
☐ 341	Joe Kerrigan	.30	.14
☐ 342	Jerry Remy	.30	.14
☐ 343	Ed Halicki	.30	.14
☐ 344	Brian Downing	.75	.35
☐ 345	Reggie Smith	.75	.35
☐ 346	Bill Singer	.30	.14
☐ 347	George Foster	1.50	.70
☐ 348	Brent Strom	.30	.14
☐ 349	Jim Holt	.30	.14
☐ 350	Larry Dierker	.75	.35
☐ 351	Jim Sundberg	.75	.35
☐ 352	Mike Phillips	.30	.14
☐ 353	Stan Thomas	.30	.14
☐ 354	Pirates Team/Mgr.	1.50	.30
	Chuck Tanner		
	(Checklist back)		
☐ 355	Lou Brock	4.00	1.80
☐ 356	Checklist 265-396	1.50	.30
☐ 357	Tim McCarver	1.50	.70
☐ 358	Tom House	.30	.14
☐ 359	Willie Randolph	1.50	.70
☐ 360	Rick Monday	.75	.35
☐ 361	Eduardo Rodriguez	.30	.14
☐ 362	Tommy Davis	.75	.35
☐ 363	Dave Roberts	.30	.14
☐ 364	Vic Correll	.30	.14
☐ 365	Mike Torrez	.75	.35
☐ 366	Ted Sizemore	.30	.14
☐ 367	Dave Hamilton	.30	.14
☐ 368	Mike Jorgensen	.30	.14
☐ 369	Terry Humphrey	.30	.14
☐ 370	John Montefusco	.30	.14
☐ 371	Royals Team/Mgr.	1.50	.30
	Whitey Herzog		
	(Checklist back)		
☐ 372	Rich Folkers	.30	.14
☐ 373	Bert Campaneris	.75	.35
☐ 374	Kent Tekulve	.75	.35
☐ 375	Larry Hisle	.75	.35
☐ 376	Nino Espinosa	.30	.14
☐ 377	Dave McKay	.30	.14
☐ 378	Jim Umbarger	.30	.14
☐ 379	Larry Cox	.30	.14
☐ 380	Lee May	.75	.35
☐ 381	Bob Forsch	.30	.14
☐ 382	Charlie Moore	.30	.14

❏ 383	Stan Bahnsen	.30	.14
❏ 384	Darrel Chaney	.30	.14
❏ 385	Dave LaRoche	.30	.14
❏ 386	Manny Mota	.75	.35
❏ 387	Yankees Team/Mgr.	2.50	.50
	Billy Martin		
	(Checklist back)		
❏ 388	Terry Harmon	.30	.14
❏ 389	Ken Kravec	.30	.14
❏ 390	Dave Winfield	6.00	2.70
❏ 391	Dan Warthen	.30	.14
❏ 392	Phil Roof	.30	.14
❏ 393	John Lowenstein	.30	.14
❏ 394	Bill Laxton	.30	.14
❏ 395	Manny Trillo	.30	.14
❏ 396	Tom Murphy	.30	.14
❏ 397	Larry Herndon	.75	.35
❏ 398	Tom Burgmeier	.30	.14
❏ 399	Bruce Boisclair	.30	.14
❏ 400	Steve Garvey	2.50	1.10
❏ 401	Mickey Scott	.30	.14
❏ 402	Tommy Helms	.30	.14
❏ 403	Tom Grieve	.75	.35
❏ 404	Eric Rasmussen	.30	.14
❏ 405	Claudell Washington	.75	.35
❏ 406	Tim Johnson	.30	.14
❏ 407	Dave Freisleben	.30	.14
❏ 408	Cesar Tovar	.30	.14
❏ 409	Pete Broberg	.30	.14
❏ 410	Willie Montanez	.30	.14
❏ 411	Joe Morgan WS	2.50	1.10
	Johnny Bench		
❏ 412	Johnny Bench WS	2.50	1.10
❏ 413	World Series Summary	.75	.35
	Cincy wins 2nd		
	straight series		
❏ 414	Tommy Harper	.75	.35
❏ 415	Jay Johnstone	.75	.35
❏ 416	Chuck Hartenstein	.30	.14
❏ 417	Wayne Garrett	.30	.14
❏ 418	White Sox Team/Mgr.	1.50	.30
	Bob Lemon		
	(Checklist back)		
❏ 419	Steve Swisher	.30	.14
❏ 420	Rusty Staub	1.50	.70
❏ 421	Doug Rau	.30	.14
❏ 422	Freddie Patek	.75	.35
❏ 423	Gary Lavelle	.30	.14
❏ 424	Steve Brye	.30	.14
❏ 425	Joe Torre	1.50	.70
❏ 426	Dick Drago	.30	.14
❏ 427	Dave Rader	.30	.14
❏ 428	Rangers Team/Mgr.	1.50	.30
	Frank Lucchesi		
	(Checklist back)		
❏ 429	Ken Boswell	.30	.14
❏ 430	Fergie Jenkins	2.50	1.10
❏ 431	Dave Collins UER	.75	.35
	(Photo actually		
	Bobby Jones)		
❏ 432	Buzz Capra	.30	.14
❏ 433	Nate Colbert TBC	.30	.14
	(5 HR, 13 RBI)		
❏ 434	Carl Yastrzemski TBC	1.50	.70
	'67 Triple Crown		
❏ 435	Maury Wills TBC	.75	.35
	104 steals		
❏ 436	Bob Keegan TBC	.30	.14
	Majors' only no-hitter		
❏ 437	Ralph Kiner TBC	1.50	.70
	Leads NL in HR's		
	7th straight year		
❏ 438	Marty Perez	.30	.14
❏ 439	Gorman Thomas	.75	.35
❏ 440	Jon Matlack	.30	.14
❏ 441	Larvell Blanks	.30	.14
❏ 442	Braves Team/Mgr.	1.50	.30
	Dave Bristol		
	(Checklist back)		
❏ 443	Lamar Johnson	.30	.14
❏ 444	Wayne Twitchell	.30	.14
❏ 445	Ken Singleton	.75	.35
❏ 446	Bill Bonham	.30	.14
❏ 447	Jerry Turner	.30	.14
❏ 448	Ellie Rodriguez	.30	.14
❏ 449	Al Fitzmorris	.30	.14
❏ 450	Pete Rose	12.00	5.50
❏ 451	Checklist 397-528	1.50	.30
❏ 452	Mike Caldwell	.30	.14
❏ 453	Pedro Garcia	.30	.14
❏ 454	Andy Etchebarren	.30	.14
❏ 455	Rick Wise	.30	.14
❏ 456	Leon Roberts	.30	.14
❏ 457	Steve Luebber	.30	.14
❏ 458	Leo Foster	.30	.14
❏ 459	Steve Foucault	.30	.14
❏ 460	Willie Stargell	2.50	1.10
❏ 461	Dick Tidrow	.30	.14
❏ 462	Don Baylor	1.50	.70
❏ 463	Jamie Quirk	.30	.14
❏ 464	Randy Moffitt	.30	.14
❏ 465	Rico Carty	.75	.35
❏ 466	Fred Holdsworth	.30	.14
❏ 467	Phillies Team/Mgr.	1.50	.30
	Danny Ozark		
	(Checklist back)		
❏ 468	Ramon Hernandez	.30	.14
❏ 469	Pat Kelly	.30	.14
❏ 470	Ted Simmons	.75	.35
❏ 471	Del Unser	.30	.14
❏ 472	Rookie Pitchers	.30	.14
	Don Aase		
	Bob McClure		
	Gil Patterson		
	Dave Wehrmeister		
❏ 473	Rookie Outfielders	30.00	13.50
	Andre Dawson		
	Gene Richards		
	John Scott		
	Denny Walling		
❏ 474	Rookie Shortstops	.75	.35
	Bob Bailor		
	Kiko Garcia		
	Craig Reynolds		
	Alex Taveras		
❏ 475	Rookie Pitchers	.75	.35
	Chris Batton		
	Rick Camp		
	Scott McGregor		
	Manny Sarmiento		
❏ 476	Rookie Catchers	25.00	11.00
	Gary Alexander		
	Rick Cerone		
	Dale Murphy		
	Kevin Pasley		
❏ 477	Rookie Infielders	.75	.35
	Doug Ault		
	Rich Dauer		
	Orlando Gonzalez		
	Phil Mankowski		
❏ 478	Rookie Pitchers	.75	.35
	Jim Gideon		
	Leon Hooten		
	Dave Johnson		
	Mark Lemongello		
❏ 479	Rookie Outfielders	.75	.35
	Brian Asselstine		
	Wayne Gross		
	Sam Mejias		
	Alvis Woods		
❏ 480	Carl Yastrzemski	5.00	2.20
❏ 481	Roger Metzger	.30	.14
❏ 482	Tony Solaita	.30	.14
❏ 483	Richie Zisk	.30	.14
❏ 484	Burt Hooton	.75	.35
❏ 485	Roy White	.75	.35
❏ 486	Ed Bane	.30	.14
❏ 487	Rookie Pitchers	.75	.35
	Larry Anderson		
	Ed Glynn		
	Joe Henderson		
	Greg Terlecky		
❏ 488	Rookie Outfielders	3.00	1.35
	Jack Clark		
	Ruppert Jones		
	Lee Mazzilli		
	Dan Thomas		
❏ 489	Rookie Pitchers	.75	.35
	Len Barker		
	Randy Lerch		
	Greg Minton		
	Mike Overy		
❏ 490	Rookie Shortstops	.75	.35
	Billy Almon		
	Mickey Klutts		
	Tommy McMillan		
	Mark Wagner		
❏ 491	Rookie Pitchers	5.00	2.20
	Mike Dupree		
	Dennis Martinez		
	Craig Mitchell		
	Bob Sykes		
❏ 492	Rookie Outfielders	.75	.35
	Tony Armas		
	Steve Kemp		
	Carlos Lopez		
	Gary Woods		
❏ 493	Rookie Pitchers	.75	.35
	Mike Krukow		
	Jim Otten		
	Gary Wheelock		
	Mike Willis		
❏ 494	Rookie Infielders	1.50	.70
	Juan Bernhardt		
	Mike Champion		
	Jim Gantner		
	Bump Wills		
❏ 495	Al Hrabosky	.30	.14
❏ 496	Gary Thomasson	.30	.14
❏ 497	Clay Carroll	.30	.14
❏ 498	Sal Bando	.75	.35
❏ 499	Pablo Torrealba	.30	.14
❏ 500	Dave Kingman	1.50	.70
❏ 501	Jim Bibby	.30	.14
❏ 502	Randy Hundley	.30	.14
❏ 503	Bill Lee	.30	.14
❏ 504	Dodgers Team/Mgr.	1.50	.30
	Tom Lasorda		
	(Checklist back)		
❏ 505	Oscar Gamble	.75	.35
❏ 506	Steve Grilli	.30	.14
❏ 507	Mike Hegan	.30	.14
❏ 508	Dave Pagan	.30	.14
❏ 509	Cookie Rojas	.75	.35
❏ 510	John Candelaria	.30	.14
❏ 511	Bill Fahey	.30	.14
❏ 512	Jack Billingham	.30	.14
❏ 513	Jerry Terrell	.30	.14
❏ 514	Cliff Johnson	.30	.14
❏ 515	Chris Speier	.30	.14
❏ 516	Bake McBride	.75	.35
❏ 517	Pete Vuckovich	.75	.35
❏ 518	Cubs Team/Mgr.	1.50	.30
	Herman Franks		
	(Checklist back)		
❏ 519	Don Kirkwood	.30	.14
❏ 520	Garry Maddox	.75	.14
❏ 521	Bob Grich	.75	.35
❏ 522	Enzo Hernandez	.30	.14
❏ 523	Rollie Fingers	2.50	1.10
❏ 524	Rowland Office	.30	.14
❏ 525	Dennis Eckersley	5.00	2.20
❏ 526	Larry Parrish	.75	.35
❏ 527	Dan Meyer	.75	.35
❏ 528	Bill Castro	.30	.14
❏ 529	Jim Essian	.30	.14
❏ 530	Rick Reuschel	.75	.35
❏ 531	Lyman Bostock	.75	.35
❏ 532	Jim Willoughby	.30	.14
❏ 533	Mickey Stanley	.30	.14
❏ 534	Paul Splittorff	.30	.14
❏ 535	Cesar Geronimo	.30	.14
❏ 536	Vic Albury	.30	.14
❏ 537	Dave Roberts	.30	.14
❏ 538	Frank Taveras	.30	.14
❏ 539	Mike Wallace	.30	.14
❏ 540	Bob Watson	.75	.35
❏ 541	John Denny	.75	.35
❏ 542	Frank Duffy	.30	.14
❏ 543	Ron Blomberg	.30	.14
❏ 544	Gary Ross	.30	.14
❏ 545	Bob Boone	.75	.35
❏ 546	Orioles Team/Mgr.	1.50	.30
	Earl Weaver		
	(Checklist back)		
❏ 547	Willie McCovey	4.00	1.80
❏ 548	Joel Youngblood	.30	.14
❏ 549	Jerry Royster	.30	.14

	#	Player		
❏	550	Randy Jones	.30	.14
❏	551	Bill North	.30	.14
❏	552	Pepe Mangual	.30	.14
❏	553	Jack Heidemann	.30	.14
❏	554	Bruce Kimm	.30	.14
❏	555	Dan Ford	.30	.14
❏	556	Doug Bird	.30	.14
❏	557	Jerry White	.30	.14
❏	558	Elias Sosa	.30	.14
❏	559	Alan Bannister	.30	.14
❏	560	Dave Concepcion	1.50	.70
❏	561	Pete LaCock	.30	.14
❏	562	Checklist 529-660	1.50	.30
❏	563	Bruce Kison	.30	.14
❏	564	Alan Ashby	.75	.35
❏	565	Mickey Lolich	.75	.35
❏	566	Rick Miller	.30	.14
❏	567	Enos Cabell	.30	.14
❏	568	Carlos May	.30	.14
❏	569	Jim Lonborg	.75	.35
❏	570	Bobby Bonds	1.50	.70
❏	571	Darrell Evans	.75	.35
❏	572	Ross Grimsley	.30	.14
❏	573	Joe Ferguson	.30	.14
❏	574	Aurelio Rodriguez	.30	.14
❏	575	Dick Ruthven	.30	.14
❏	576	Fred Kendall	.30	.14
❏	577	Jerry Augustine	.30	.14
❏	578	Bob Randall	.30	.14
❏	579	Don Carrithers	.30	.14
❏	580	George Brett	15.00	6.75
❏	581	Pedro Borbon	.30	.14
❏	582	Ed Kirkpatrick	.30	.14
❏	583	Paul Lindblad	.30	.14
❏	584	Ed Goodson	.30	.14
❏	585	Rick Burleson	.75	.35
❏	586	Steve Renko	.30	.14
❏	587	Rick Baldwin	.30	.14
❏	588	Dave Moates	.30	.14
❏	589	Mike Cosgrove	.30	.14
❏	590	Buddy Bell	.75	.35
❏	591	Chris Arnold	.30	.14
❏	592	Dan Briggs	.30	.14
❏	593	Dennis Blair	.30	.14
❏	594	Biff Pocoroba	.30	.14
❏	595	John Hiller	.30	.14
❏	596	Jerry Martin	.30	.14
❏	597	Mariners Leaders	1.50	.30
		Darrell Johnson MG		
		Don Bryant CO		
		Jim Busby CO		
		Vada Pinson CO		
		Wes Stock CO		
		(Checklist back)		
❏	598	Sparky Lyle	.75	.35
❏	599	Mike Tyson	.30	.14
❏	600	Jim Palmer	4.00	1.80
❏	601	Mike Lum	.30	.14
❏	602	Andy Hassler	.30	.14
❏	603	Willie Davis	.75	.35
❏	604	Jim Slaton	.30	.14
❏	605	Felix Millan	.30	.14
❏	606	Steve Braun	.30	.14
❏	607	Larry Demery	.30	.14
❏	608	Roy Howell	.30	.14
❏	609	Jim Barr	.30	.14
❏	610	Jose Cardenal	.75	.35
❏	611	Dave Lemanczyk	.30	.14
❏	612	Barry Foote	.30	.14
❏	613	Reggie Cleveland	.30	.14
❏	614	Greg Gross	.30	.14
❏	615	Phil Niekro	2.50	1.10
❏	616	Tommy Sandt	.30	.14
❏	617	Bobby Darwin	.30	.14
❏	618	Pat Dobson	.30	.14
❏	619	Johnny Oates	.75	.35
❏	620	Don Sutton	2.50	1.10
❏	621	Tigers Team/Mgr.	1.50	.30
		Ralph Houk		
		(Checklist back)		
❏	622	Jim Wohlford	.30	.14
❏	623	Jack Kucek	.30	.14
❏	624	Hector Cruz	.30	.14
❏	625	Ken Holtzman	.75	.35
❏	626	Al Bumbry	.75	.35
❏	627	Bob Myrick	.30	.14

	#	Player		
❏	628	Mario Guerrero	.30	.14
❏	629	Bobby Valentine	.30	.14
❏	630	Bert Blyleven	1.50	.70
❏	631	George Brett	6.00	2.70
		Ken Brett		
❏	632	Bob Forsch	.75	.35
		Ken Forsch		
❏	633	Lee May	.75	.35
		Carlos May		
❏	634	Paul Reuschel	.75	.35
		Rick Reuschel UER		
		(Photos switched)		
❏	635	Robin Yount	8.00	3.60
❏	636	Santo Alcala	.30	.14
❏	637	Alex Johnson	.30	.14
❏	638	Jim Kaat	1.50	.70
❏	639	Jerry Morales	.30	.14
❏	640	Carlton Fisk	4.00	1.80
❏	641	Dan Larson	.30	.14
❏	642	Willie Crawford	.30	.14
❏	643	Mike Pazik	.30	.14
❏	644	Matt Alexander	.30	.14
❏	645	Jerry Reuss	.75	.35
❏	646	Andres Mora	.30	.14
❏	647	Expos Team/Mgr.	1.50	.30
		Dick Williams		
		(Checklist back)		
❏	648	Jim Spencer	.30	.14
❏	649	Dave Cash	.30	.14
❏	650	Nolan Ryan	40.00	18.00
❏	651	Von Joshua	.30	.14
❏	652	Tom Walker	.30	.14
❏	653	Diego Segui	.75	.35
❏	654	Ron Pruitt	.30	.14
❏	655	Tony Perez	2.50	1.10
❏	656	Ron Guidry	1.50	.70
❏	657	Mick Kelleher	.30	.14
❏	658	Marty Pattin	.30	.14
❏	659	Merv Rettenmund	.30	.14
❏	660	Willie Horton	1.50	.30

1978 Topps

BRUCE SUTTER

	NRMT	VG-E
COMPLETE SET (726)	250.00	110.00
COMMON CARD (1-726)	.25	.11
MINOR STARS	.60	.25
SEMISTARS	1.25	.55
UNLISTED STARS	2.50	1.10

1978-1990 PRICED IN NMMT CONDITION

	#	Player		
❏	1	Lou Brock RB	3.00	.90
		Most lifetime steals		
❏	2	Sparky Lyle RB	.60	.25
		Most career games pure relief		
❏	3	Willie McCovey RB	2.50	1.10
		Most times 2 HR's in inning		
❏	4	Brooks Robinson RB	2.50	1.10
		Most consecutive		
		seasons with one club		
❏	5	Pete Rose RB	4.00	1.80
		Most lifetime switch-hitter hits		
❏	6	Nolan Ryan RB	15.00	5.00
		Most games 10 or more strikeouts		
❏	7	Reggie Jackson RB	4.00	1.80
		Most homers,		
		one World Series		
❏	8	Mike Sadek	.25	.11

	#	Player		
❏	9	Doug DeCinces	.60	.25
❏	10	Phil Niekro	2.50	1.10
❏	11	Rick Manning	.25	.11
❏	12	Don Aase	.25	.11
❏	13	Art Howe	.60	.25
❏	14	Lerrin LaGrow	.25	.11
❏	15	Tony Perez DP	1.25	.55
❏	16	Roy White	.60	.25
❏	17	Mike Krukow	.25	.11
❏	18	Bob Grich	.60	.25
❏	19	Darrell Porter	.25	.11
❏	20	Pete Rose DP	8.00	3.60
❏	21	Steve Kemp	.25	.11
❏	22	Charlie Hough	.60	.25
❏	23	Bump Wills	.25	.11
❏	24	Don Money DP	.15	.07
❏	25	Jon Matlack	.25	.11
❏	26	Rich Hebner	.60	.25
❏	27	Geoff Zahn	.25	.11
❏	28	Ed Ott	.25	.11
❏	29	Bob Lacey	.25	.11
❏	30	George Hendrick	.60	.25
❏	31	Glenn Abbott	.25	.11
❏	32	Garry Templeton	.60	.25
❏	33	Dave Lemanczyk	.25	.11
❏	34	Willie McCovey	3.00	1.35
❏	35	Sparky Lyle	.60	.25
❏	36	Eddie Murray	80.00	36.00
❏	37	Rick Waits	.25	.11
❏	38	Willie Montanez	.25	.11
❏	39	Floyd Bannister	.25	.11
❏	40	Carl Yastrzemski	4.00	1.80
❏	41	Burt Hooton	.60	.25
❏	42	Jorge Orta	.25	.11
❏	43	Bill Atkinson	.25	.11
❏	44	Toby Harrah	.60	.25
❏	45	Mark Fidrych	2.50	1.10
❏	46	Al Cowens	.25	.11
❏	47	Jack Billingham	.25	.11
❏	48	Don Baylor	1.25	.55
❏	49	Ed Kranepool	.60	.25
❏	50	Rick Reuschel	.60	.25
❏	51	Charlie Moore DP	.15	.07
❏	52	Jim Lonborg	.25	.11
❏	53	Phil Garner DP	.25	.11
❏	54	Tom Johnson	.25	.11
❏	55	Mitchell Page	.25	.11
❏	56	Randy Jones	.25	.11
❏	57	Dan Meyer	.25	.11
❏	58	Bob Forsch	.25	.11
❏	59	Otto Velez	.25	.11
❏	60	Thurman Munson	3.00	1.35
❏	61	Larvell Blanks	.25	.11
❏	62	Jim Barr	.25	.11
❏	63	Don Zimmer MG	.60	.25
❏	64	Gene Pentz	.25	.11
❏	65	Ken Singleton	.60	.25
❏	66	Chicago White Sox	1.25	.25
		Team Card		
		(Checklist back)		
❏	67	Claudell Washington	.60	.25
❏	68	Steve Foucault DP	.15	.07
❏	69	Mike Vail	.25	.11
❏	70	Rich Gossage	1.25	.55
❏	71	Terry Humphrey	.25	.11
❏	72	Andre Dawson	6.00	2.70
❏	73	Andy Hassler	.25	.11
❏	74	Checklist 1-121	1.25	.25
❏	75	Dick Ruthven	.25	.11
❏	76	Steve Ontiveros	.25	.11
❏	77	Ed Kirkpatrick	.25	.11
❏	78	Pablo Torrealba	.25	.11
❏	79	Darrell Johnson DP MG	.15	.07
❏	80	Ken Griffey Sr.	1.25	.55
❏	81	Pete Redfern	.25	.11
❏	82	San Francisco Giants	1.25	.25
		Team Card		
		(Checklist back)		
❏	83	Bob Montgomery	.25	.11
❏	84	Kent Tekulve	.60	.25
❏	85	Ron Fairly	.60	.25
❏	86	Dave Tomlin	.25	.11
❏	87	John Lowenstein	.25	.11
❏	88	Mike Phillips	.25	.11
❏	89	Ken Clay	.25	.11
❏	90	Larry Bowa	1.25	.55

#	Player		
❑ 91	Oscar Zamora	.25	.11
❑ 92	Adrian Devine	.25	.11
❑ 93	Bobby Cox DP	.25	.11
❑ 94	Chuck Scrivener	.25	.11
❑ 95	Jamie Quirk	.25	.11
❑ 96	Baltimore Orioles	1.25	.25
	Team Card		
	(Checklist back)		
❑ 97	Stan Bahnsen	.25	.11
❑ 98	Jim Essian	.60	.25
❑ 99	Willie Hernandez	1.25	.55
❑ 100	George Brett	15.00	6.75
❑ 101	Sid Monge	.25	.11
❑ 102	Matt Alexander	.25	.11
❑ 103	Tom Murphy	.25	.11
❑ 104	Lee Lacy	.25	.11
❑ 105	Reggie Cleveland	.25	.11
❑ 106	Bill Plummer	.25	.11
❑ 107	Ed Halicki	.25	.11
❑ 108	Von Joshua	.25	.11
❑ 109	Joe Torre MG	.60	.25
❑ 110	Richie Zisk	.25	.11
❑ 111	Mike Tyson	.25	.11
❑ 112	Houston Astros	1.25	.25
	Team Card		
	(Checklist back)		
❑ 113	Don Carrithers	.25	.11
❑ 114	Paul Blair	.60	.25
❑ 115	Gary Nolan	.25	.11
❑ 116	Tucker Ashford	.25	.11
❑ 117	John Montague	.25	.11
❑ 118	Terry Harmon	.25	.11
❑ 119	Dennis Martinez	2.50	1.10
❑ 120	Gary Carter	2.50	1.10
❑ 121	Alvis Woods	.25	.11
❑ 122	Dennis Eckersley	4.00	1.80
❑ 123	Manny Trillo	.25	.11
❑ 124	Dave Rozema	.25	.11
❑ 125	George Scott	.60	.25
❑ 126	Paul Moskau	.25	.11
❑ 127	Chet Lemon	.60	.25
❑ 128	Bill Russell	.60	.25
❑ 129	Jim Colborn	.25	.11
❑ 130	Jeff Burroughs	.60	.25
❑ 131	Bert Blyleven	1.25	.55
❑ 132	Enos Cabell	.25	.11
❑ 133	Jerry Augustine	.25	.11
❑ 134	Steve Henderson	.25	.11
❑ 135	Ron Guidry DP	1.25	.55
❑ 136	Ted Sizemore	.25	.11
❑ 137	Craig Kusick	.25	.11
❑ 138	Larry Demery	.25	.11
❑ 139	Wayne Gross	.25	.11
❑ 140	Rollie Fingers	2.50	1.10
❑ 141	Ruppert Jones	.25	.11
❑ 142	John Montefusco	.25	.11
❑ 143	Keith Hernandez	.60	.25
❑ 144	Jesse Jefferson	.25	.11
❑ 145	Rick Monday	.60	.25
❑ 146	Doyle Alexander	.25	.11
❑ 147	Lee Mazzilli	.25	.11
❑ 148	Andre Thornton	.60	.25
❑ 149	Dale Murray	.25	.11
❑ 150	Bobby Bonds	1.25	.55
❑ 151	Milt Wilcox	.25	.11
❑ 152	Ivan DeJesus	.25	.11
❑ 153	Steve Stone	.60	.25
❑ 154	Cecil Cooper DP	.25	.11
❑ 155	Butch Hobson	.25	.11
❑ 156	Andy Messersmith	.60	.25
❑ 157	Pete LaCock DP	.15	.07
❑ 158	Joaquin Andujar	.60	.25
❑ 159	Lou Piniella	.60	.25
❑ 160	Jim Palmer	3.00	1.35
❑ 161	Bob Boone	.25	.55
❑ 162	Paul Thormodsgard	.25	.11
❑ 163	Bill North	.25	.11
❑ 164	Bob Owchinko	.25	.11
❑ 165	Rennie Stennett	.25	.11
❑ 166	Carlos Lopez	.25	.11
❑ 167	Tim Foli	.25	.11
❑ 168	Reggie Smith	.60	.25
❑ 169	Jerry Johnson	.25	.11
❑ 170	Lou Brock	3.00	1.35
❑ 171	Pat Zachry	.25	.11
❑ 172	Mike Hargrove	.60	.25
❑ 173	Robin Yount UER	6.00	2.70
	(Played for Newark		
	in 1973, not 1971)		
❑ 174	Wayne Garland	.25	.11
❑ 175	Jerry Morales	.25	.11
❑ 176	Milt May	.25	.11
❑ 177	Gene Garber DP	.25	.11
❑ 178	Dave Chalk	.25	.11
❑ 179	Dick Tidrow	.25	.11
❑ 180	Dave Concepcion	1.25	.55
❑ 181	Ken Forsch	.25	.11
❑ 182	Jim Spencer	.25	.11
❑ 183	Doug Bird	.25	.11
❑ 184	Checklist 122-242	1.25	.25
❑ 185	Ellis Valentine	.25	.11
❑ 186	Bob Stanley DP	.25	.11
❑ 187	Jerry Royster DP	.15	.07
❑ 188	Al Bumbry	.60	.25
❑ 189	Tom Lasorda MG	2.50	1.10
❑ 190	John Candelaria	.25	.25
❑ 191	Rodney Scott	.25	.11
❑ 192	San Diego Padres	1.25	.55
	Team Card		
	(Checklist back)		
❑ 193	Rich Chiles	.25	.11
❑ 194	Derrel Thomas	.25	.11
❑ 195	Larry Dierker	.60	.25
❑ 196	Bob Bailor	.25	.11
❑ 197	Nino Espinosa	.25	.11
❑ 198	Ron Pruitt	.25	.11
❑ 199	Craig Reynolds	.25	.11
❑ 200	Reggie Jackson	10.00	4.50
❑ 201	Batting Leaders	1.25	.55
	Dave Parker		
	Rod Carew		
❑ 202	Home Run Leaders DP	.60	.25
	George Foster		
	Jim Rice		
❑ 203	RBI Leaders	.60	.25
	George Foster		
	Larry Hisle		
❑ 204	Stolen Base Leaders DP	.25	.11
	Frank Taveras		
	Freddie Patek		
❑ 205	Victory Leaders	2.50	1.10
	Steve Carlton		
	Dave Goltz		
	Dennis Leonard		
	Jim Palmer		
❑ 206	Strikeout Leaders DP	6.00	2.70
	Phil Niekro		
	Nolan Ryan		
❑ 207	ERA Leaders DP	.60	.25
	John Candelaria		
	Frank Tanana		
❑ 208	Firemen Leaders	1.25	.55
	Rollie Fingers		
	Bill Campbell		
❑ 209	Dock Ellis	.25	.11
❑ 210	Jose Cardenal	.25	.11
❑ 211	Earl Weaver MG DP	1.25	.55
❑ 212	Mike Caldwell	.25	.11
❑ 213	Alan Bannister	.25	.11
❑ 214	California Angels	1.25	.25
	Team Card		
	(Checklist back)		
❑ 215	Darrell Evans	.60	.25
❑ 216	Mike Paxton	.25	.11
❑ 217	Rod Gilbreath	.25	.11
❑ 218	Marty Pattin	.25	.11
❑ 219	Mike Cubbage	.25	.11
❑ 220	Pedro Borbon	.25	.11
❑ 221	Chris Speier	.25	.11
❑ 222	Jerry Martin	.25	.11
❑ 223	Bruce Kison	.25	.11
❑ 224	Jerry Tabb	.25	.11
❑ 225	Don Gullett DP	.25	.11
❑ 226	Joe Ferguson	.25	.11
❑ 227	Al Fitzmorris	.25	.11
❑ 228	Manny Mota DP	.25	.11
❑ 229	Leo Foster	.25	.11
❑ 230	Al Hrabosky	.25	.11
❑ 231	Wayne Nordhagen	.25	.11
❑ 232	Mickey Stanley	.25	.11
❑ 233	Dick Pole	.25	.11
❑ 234	Herman Franks MG	.25	.11
❑ 235	Tim McCarver	.60	.25
❑ 236	Terry Whitfield	.25	.11
❑ 237	Rich Dauer	.25	.11
❑ 238	Juan Beniquez	.25	.11
❑ 239	Dyar Miller	.25	.11
❑ 240	Gene Tenace	.60	.25
❑ 241	Pete Vuckovich	.60	.25
❑ 242	Barry Bonnell DP	.15	.07
❑ 243	Bob McClure	.25	.11
❑ 244	Montreal Expos	.60	.12
	Team Card DP		
	(Checklist back)		
❑ 245	Rick Burleson	.60	.25
❑ 246	Dan Driessen	.25	.11
❑ 247	Larry Christenson	.25	.11
❑ 248	Frank White DP	.60	.25
❑ 249	Dave Goltz DP	.15	.07
❑ 250	Graig Nettles DP	.60	.25
❑ 251	Don Kirkwood	.25	.11
❑ 252	Steve Swisher DP	.15	.07
❑ 253	Jim Kern	.25	.11
❑ 254	Dave Collins	.60	.25
❑ 255	Jerry Reuss	.60	.25
❑ 256	Joe Altobelli MG	.25	.11
❑ 257	Hector Cruz	.25	.11
❑ 258	John Hiller	.25	.11
❑ 259	Los Angeles Dodgers	1.25	.25
	Team Card		
	(Checklist back)		
❑ 260	Bert Campaneris	.60	.25
❑ 261	Tim Hosley	.25	.11
❑ 262	Rudy May	.25	.11
❑ 263	Danny Walton	.25	.11
❑ 264	Jamie Easterly	.25	.11
❑ 265	Sal Bando DP	.60	.25
❑ 266	Bob Shirley	.25	.11
❑ 267	Doug Ault	.25	.11
❑ 268	Gil Flores	.25	.11
❑ 269	Wayne Twitchell	.25	.11
❑ 270	Carlton Fisk	3.00	1.35
❑ 271	Randy Lerch DP	.15	.07
❑ 272	Royle Stillman	.25	.11
❑ 273	Fred Norman	.25	.11
❑ 274	Freddie Patek	.60	.25
❑ 275	Dan Ford	.25	.11
❑ 276	Bill Bonham DP	.15	.07
❑ 277	Bruce Boisclair	.25	.11
❑ 278	Enrique Romo	.25	.11
❑ 279	Bill Virdon MG	.25	.11
❑ 280	Buddy Bell	.60	.25
❑ 281	Eric Rasmussen DP	.15	.07
❑ 282	New York Yankees	2.50	.50
	Team Card		
	(Checklist back)		
❑ 283	Omar Moreno	.25	.11
❑ 284	Randy Moffitt	.25	.11
❑ 285	Steve Yeager DP	.60	.25
❑ 286	Ben Oglivie	.60	.25
❑ 287	Kiko Garcia	.25	.11
❑ 288	Dave Hamilton	.25	.11
❑ 289	Checklist 243-363	1.25	.25
❑ 290	Willie Horton	.60	.25
❑ 291	Gary Ross	.25	.11
❑ 292	Gene Richards	.25	.11
❑ 293	Mike Willis	.25	.11
❑ 294	Larry Parrish	.60	.25
❑ 295	Bill Lee	.25	.11
❑ 296	Biff Pocoroba	.25	.11
❑ 297	Warren Brusstar DP	.15	.07
❑ 298	Tony Armas	.60	.25
❑ 299	Whitey Herzog MG	.60	.25
❑ 300	Joe Morgan	3.00	1.35
❑ 301	Buddy Schultz	.25	.11
❑ 302	Chicago Cubs	1.25	.25
	Team Card		
	(Checklist back)		
❑ 303	Sam Hinds	.25	.11
❑ 304	John Milner	.25	.11
❑ 305	Rico Carty	.60	.25
❑ 306	Joe Niekro	.60	.25
❑ 307	Glenn Borgmann	.25	.11
❑ 308	Jim Rooker	.25	.11
❑ 309	Cliff Johnson	.25	.11
❑ 310	Don Sutton	2.50	1.10
❑ 311	Jose Baez DP	.15	.07
❑ 312	Greg Minton	.25	.11

☐ 313	Andy Etchebarren	.25	.11	☐ 393	Tippy Martinez	.60	.25	☐ 470	J.R. Richard
☐ 314	Paul Lindblad	.25	.11	☐ 394	Roy Howell DP	.15	.07	☐ 471	Roy Smalley

☐ 313 Andy Etchebarren .25 .11
☐ 314 Paul Lindblad .25 .11
☐ 315 Mark Belanger .60 .25
☐ 316 Henry Cruz DP .15 .07
☐ 317 Dave Johnson .25 .11
☐ 318 Tom Griffin .25 .11
☐ 319 Alan Ashby .25 .11
☐ 320 Fred Lynn .60 .25
☐ 321 Santo Alcala .25 .11
☐ 322 Tom Paciorek .25 .11
☐ 323 Jim Fregosi DP .25 .11
☐ 324 Vern Rapp MG .25 .11
☐ 325 Bruce Sutter 1.25 .55
☐ 326 Mike Lum DP .15 .07
☐ 327 Rick Langford DP .15 .07
☐ 328 Milwaukee Brewers 1.25 .25
 Team Card
 (Checklist back)
☐ 329 John Verhoeven .25 .11
☐ 330 Bob Watson .60 .25
☐ 331 Mark Littell .25 .11
☐ 332 Duane Kuiper .25 .11
☐ 333 Jim Todd .25 .11
☐ 334 John Stearns .25 .11
☐ 335 Bucky Dent .60 .25
☐ 336 Steve Busby .25 .11
☐ 337 Tom Grieve .60 .25
☐ 338 Dave Heaverlo .25 .11
☐ 339 Mario Guerrero .25 .11
☐ 340 Bake McBride .60 .25
☐ 341 Mike Flanagan .60 .25
☐ 342 Aurelio Rodriguez .25 .11
☐ 343 John Wathan DP .15 .07
☐ 344 Sam Ewing .25 .11
☐ 345 Luis Tiant .60 .25
☐ 346 Larry Biittner .25 .11
☐ 347 Terry Forster .25 .11
☐ 348 Del Unser .25 .11
☐ 349 Rick Camp DP .15 .07
☐ 350 Steve Garvey 2.50 1.10
☐ 351 Jeff Torborg .60 .25
☐ 352 Tony Scott .25 .11
☐ 353 Doug Bair .25 .11
☐ 354 Cesar Geronimo .25 .11
☐ 355 Bill Travers .25 .11
☐ 356 New York Mets 1.25 .25
 Team Card
 (Checklist back)
☐ 357 Tom Poquette .25 .11
☐ 358 Mark Lemongello .25 .11
☐ 359 Marc Hill .25 .11
☐ 360 Mike Schmidt 10.00 4.50
☐ 361 Chris Knapp .25 .11
☐ 362 Dave May .25 .11
☐ 363 Bob Randall .25 .11
☐ 364 Jerry Turner .25 .11
☐ 365 Ed Figueroa .25 .11
☐ 366 Larry Milbourne DP .15 .07
☐ 367 Rick Dempsey .60 .25
☐ 368 Balor Moore .25 .11
☐ 369 Tim Nordbrook .25 .11
☐ 370 Rusty Staub 1.25 .55
☐ 371 Ray Burris .25 .11
☐ 372 Brian Asselstine .25 .11
☐ 373 Jim Willoughby .25 .11
☐ 374 Jose Morales .25 .11
☐ 375 Tommy John .25 .55
☐ 376 Jim Wohlford .25 .11
☐ 377 Manny Sarmiento .25 .11
☐ 378 Bobby Winkles MG .25 .11
☐ 379 Skip Lockwood .25 .11
☐ 380 Ted Simmons .25 .25
☐ 381 Philadelphia Phillies 1.25 .25
 Team Card
 (Checklist back)
☐ 382 Joe Lahoud .25 .11
☐ 383 Mario Mendoza .25 .11
☐ 384 Jack Clark 1.25 .55
☐ 385 Tito Fuentes .25 .11
☐ 386 Bob Gorinski .25 .11
☐ 387 Ken Holtzman .25 .11
☐ 388 Bill Fahey DP .15 .07
☐ 389 Julio Gonzalez .25 .11
☐ 390 Oscar Gamble .60 .25
☐ 391 Larry Haney .25 .11
☐ 392 Billy Almon .25 .11

☐ 393 Tippy Martinez .60 .25
☐ 394 Roy Howell DP .15 .07
☐ 395 Jim Hughes .25 .11
☐ 396 Bob Stinson DP .15 .07
☐ 397 Greg Gross .25 .11
☐ 398 Don Hood .25 .11
☐ 399 Pete Mackanin .25 .11
☐ 400 Nolan Ryan 40.00 18.00
☐ 401 Sparky Anderson MG .60 .25
☐ 402 Dave Campbell .25 .11
☐ 403 Bud Harrelson .60 .25
☐ 404 Detroit Tigers 1.25 .25
 Team Card
 (Checklist back)
☐ 405 Rawly Eastwick .25 .11
☐ 406 Mike Jorgensen .25 .11
☐ 407 Odell Jones .25 .11
☐ 408 Joe Zdeb .25 .11
☐ 409 Ron Schueler .25 .11
☐ 410 Bill Madlock .60 .25
☐ 411 AL Champs .60 .25
 Willie Randolph
☐ 412 NL Champs .60 .25
 Davey Lopes
☐ 413 World Series 4.00 1.80
 Reggie Jackson
☐ 414 Darold Knowles DP .15 .07
☐ 415 Ray Fosse .25 .11
☐ 416 Jack Brohamer .25 .11
☐ 417 Mike Garman DP .15 .07
☐ 418 Tony Muser .25 .11
☐ 419 Jerry Garvin .25 .11
☐ 420 Greg Luzinski 1.25 .55
☐ 421 Junior Moore .25 .11
☐ 422 Steve Braun .25 .11
☐ 423 Dave Rosello .25 .11
☐ 424 Boston Red Sox 1.25 .25
 Team Card
 (Checklist back)
☐ 425 Steve Rogers DP .25 .11
☐ 426 Fred Kendall .25 .11
☐ 427 Mario Soto .60 .25
☐ 428 Joel Youngblood .25 .11
☐ 429 Mike Barlow .25 .11
☐ 430 Al Oliver .60 .25
☐ 431 Butch Metzger .25 .11
☐ 432 Terry Bulling .25 .11
☐ 433 Fernando Gonzalez .25 .11
☐ 434 Mike Norris .25 .11
☐ 435 Checklist 364-484 1.25 .25
☐ 436 Vic Harris DP .15 .07
☐ 437 Bo McLaughlin .25 .11
☐ 438 John Ellis .25 .11
☐ 439 Ken Kravec .25 .11
☐ 440 Dave Lopes .60 .25
☐ 441 Larry Gura .25 .11
☐ 442 Elliott Maddox .25 .11
☐ 443 Darrel Chaney .25 .11
☐ 444 Roy Hartsfield MG .25 .11
☐ 445 Mike Ivie .25 .11
☐ 446 Tug McGraw .60 .25
☐ 447 Leroy Stanton .25 .11
☐ 448 Bill Castro .25 .11
☐ 449 Tim Blackwell DP .15 .07
☐ 450 Tom Seaver 6.00 2.70
☐ 451 Minnesota Twins 1.25 .25
 Team Card
 (Checklist back)
☐ 452 Jerry Mumphrey .25 .11
☐ 453 Doug Flynn .25 .11
☐ 454 Dave LaRoche .25 .11
☐ 455 Bill Robinson .60 .25
☐ 456 Vern Ruhle .25 .11
☐ 457 Bob Bailey .25 .11
☐ 458 Jeff Newman .25 .11
☐ 459 Charlie Spikes .25 .11
☐ 460 Jim Hunter 2.50 1.10
☐ 461 Rob Andrews DP .15 .07
☐ 462 Rogelio Moret .25 .11
☐ 463 Kevin Bell .25 .11
☐ 464 Jerry Grote .25 .11
☐ 465 Hal McRae .60 .25
☐ 466 Dennis Blair .25 .11
☐ 467 Alvin Dark MG .25 .11
☐ 468 Warren Cromartie .60 .25
☐ 469 Rick Cerone .60 .25

☐ 470 J.R. Richard .60 .25
☐ 471 Roy Smalley .60 .25
☐ 472 Ron Reed .25 .11
☐ 473 Bill Buckner .60 .25
☐ 474 Jim Slaton .25 .11
☐ 475 Gary Matthews .60 .25
☐ 476 Bill Stein .25 .11
☐ 477 Doug Capilla .25 .11
☐ 478 Jerry Remy .25 .11
☐ 479 St. Louis Cardinals 1.25 .25
 Team Card
 (Checklist back)
☐ 480 Ron LeFlore .60 .25
☐ 481 Jackson Todd .25 .11
☐ 482 Rick Miller .25 .11
☐ 483 Ken Macha .25 .11
☐ 484 Jim Norris .25 .11
☐ 485 Chris Chambliss .60 .25
☐ 486 John Curtis .25 .11
☐ 487 Jim Tyrone .25 .11
☐ 488 Dan Spillner .25 .11
☐ 489 Rudy Meoli .25 .11
☐ 490 Amos Otis .60 .25
☐ 491 Scott McGregor .60 .25
☐ 492 Jim Sundberg .60 .25
☐ 493 Steve Renko .25 .11
☐ 494 Chuck Tanner MG .60 .25
☐ 495 Dave Cash .25 .11
☐ 496 Jim Clancy DP .15 .07
☐ 497 Glenn Adams .25 .11
☐ 498 Joe Sambito .25 .11
☐ 499 Seattle Mariners 1.25 .25
 Team Card
 (Checklist back)
☐ 500 George Foster 1.25 .55
☐ 501 Dave Roberts .25 .11
☐ 502 Pat Rockett .25 .11
☐ 503 Ike Hampton .25 .11
☐ 504 Roger Freed .25 .11
☐ 505 Felix Millan .25 .11
☐ 506 Ron Blomberg .25 .11
☐ 507 Willie Crawford .25 .11
☐ 508 Johnny Oates .60 .25
☐ 509 Brent Strom .25 .11
☐ 510 Willie Stargell 2.50 1.10
☐ 511 Frank Duffy .25 .11
☐ 512 Larry Herndon .25 .11
☐ 513 Barry Foote .25 .11
☐ 514 Rob Sperring .25 .11
☐ 515 Tim Corcoran .25 .11
☐ 516 Gary Beare .25 .11
☐ 517 Andres Mora .25 .11
☐ 518 Tommy Boggs DP .15 .07
☐ 519 Brian Downing .25 .11
☐ 520 Larry Hisle .25 .11
☐ 521 Steve Staggs .25 .11
☐ 522 Dick Williams MG .60 .25
☐ 523 Donnie Moore .25 .11
☐ 524 Bernie Carbo .25 .11
☐ 525 Jerry Terrell .25 .11
☐ 526 Cincinnati Reds 1.25 .25
 Team Card
 (Checklist back)
☐ 527 Vic Correll .25 .11
☐ 528 Rob Picciolo .25 .11
☐ 529 Paul Hartzell .25 .11
☐ 530 Dave Winfield 5.00 2.20
☐ 531 Tom Underwood .25 .11
☐ 532 Skip Jutze .25 .11
☐ 533 Sandy Alomar .60 .25
☐ 534 Wilbur Howard .25 .11
☐ 535 Checklist 485-605 1.25 .25
☐ 536 Roric Harrison .25 .11
☐ 537 Bruce Bochte .25 .11
☐ 538 Johnny LeMaster .25 .11
☐ 539 Vic Davalillo DP .15 .07
☐ 540 Steve Carlton 4.00 1.80
☐ 541 Larry Cox .25 .11
☐ 542 Tim Johnson .25 .11
☐ 543 Larry Harlow DP .15 .07
☐ 544 Len Randle DP .15 .07
☐ 545 Bill Campbell .25 .11
☐ 546 Ted Martinez .25 .11
☐ 547 John Scott .25 .11
☐ 548 Billy Hunter DP MG .15 .07
☐ 549 Joe Kerrigan .25 .11

#	Name	NRMT	VG-E
550	John Mayberry	.60	.25
551	Atlanta Braves Team Card (Checklist back)	1.25	.25
552	Francisco Barrios	.25	.11
553	Terry Puhl	.60	.25
554	Joe Coleman	.25	.11
555	Butch Wynegar	.25	.11
556	Ed Armbrister	.25	.11
557	Tony Solaita	.25	.11
558	Paul Mitchell	.25	.11
559	Phil Mankowski	.25	.11
560	Dave Parker	1.25	.55
561	Charlie Williams	.25	.11
562	Glenn Burke	.25	.11
563	Dave Rader	.25	.11
564	Mick Kelleher	.25	.11
565	Jerry Koosman	.60	.25
566	Merv Rettenmund	.25	.11
567	Dick Drago	.25	.11
568	Tom Hutton	.25	.11
569	Lary Sorensen	.25	.11
570	Dave Kingman	1.25	.55
571	Buck Martinez	.25	.11
572	Rick Wise	.25	.11
573	Luis Gomez	.25	.11
574	Bob Lemon MG	1.25	.55
575	Pat Dobson	.25	.11
576	Sam Mejias	.25	.11
577	Oakland A's Team Card (Checklist back)	1.25	.25
578	Buzz Capra	.25	.11
579	Rance Mulliniks	.25	.11
580	Rod Carew	3.00	1.35
581	Lynn McGlothen	.25	.11
582	Fran Healy	.25	.11
583	George Medich	.25	.11
584	John Hale	.25	.11
585	Woodie Fryman DP	.15	.07
586	Ed Goodson	.25	.11
587	John Urrea	.25	.11
588	Jim Mason	.25	.11
589	Bob Knepper	.25	.11
590	Bobby Murcer	.60	.25
591	George Zeber	.25	.11
592	Bob Apodaca	.25	.11
593	Dave Skaggs	.25	.11
594	Dave Freisleben	.25	.11
595	Sixto Lezcano	.25	.11
596	Gary Wheelock	.25	.11
597	Steve Dillard	.25	.11
598	Eddie Solomon	.25	.11
599	Gary Woods	.25	.11
600	Frank Tanana	.60	.25
601	Gene Mauch MG	.60	.25
602	Eric Soderholm	.25	.11
603	Will McEnaney	.25	.11
604	Earl Williams	.25	.11
605	Rick Rhoden	.60	.25
606	Pittsburgh Pirates Team Card (Checklist back)	1.25	.25
607	Fernando Arroyo	.25	.11
608	Johnny Grubb	.25	.11
609	John Denny	.25	.11
610	Garry Maddox	.60	.25
611	Pat Scanlon	.25	.11
612	Ken Henderson	.25	.11
613	Marty Perez	.25	.11
614	Joe Wallis	.25	.11
615	Clay Carroll	.25	.11
616	Pat Kelly	.25	.11
617	Joe Nolan	.25	.11
618	Tommy Helms	.25	.11
619	Thad Bosley DP	.15	.07
620	Willie Randolph	1.25	.55
621	Craig Swan DP	.15	.07
622	Champ Summers	.25	.11
623	Eduardo Rodriguez	.25	.11
624	Gary Alexander DP	.15	.07
625	Jose Cruz	.60	.25
626	Toronto Blue Jays Team Card DP (Checklist back)	1.25	.25
627	David Johnson	.25	.11
628	Ralph Garr	.60	.25
629	Don Stanhouse	.25	.11
630	Ron Cey	1.25	.55
631	Danny Ozark MG	.25	.11
632	Rowland Office	.25	.11
633	Tom Veryzer	.25	.11
634	Len Barker	.25	.11
635	Joe Rudi	.60	.25
636	Jim Bibby	.25	.11
637	Duffy Dyer	.25	.11
638	Paul Splittorff	.25	.11
639	Gene Clines	.25	.11
640	Lee May DP	.25	.11
641	Doug Rau	.25	.11
642	Denny Doyle	.25	.11
643	Tom House	.25	.11
644	Jim Dwyer	.25	.11
645	Mike Torrez	.60	.25
646	Rick Auerbach DP	.15	.07
647	Steve Dunning	.25	.11
648	Gary Thomasson	.25	.11
649	Moose Haas	.25	.11
650	Cesar Cedeno	.60	.25
651	Doug Rader	.25	.11
652	Checklist 606-726	1.25	.25
653	Ron Hodges DP	.15	.07
654	Pepe Frias	.25	.11
655	Lyman Bostock	.60	.25
656	Dave Garcia MG	.25	.11
657	Bombo Rivera	.25	.11
658	Manny Sanguillen	.60	.25
659	Texas Rangers Team Card (Checklist back)	1.25	.25
660	Jason Thompson	.60	.25
661	Grant Jackson	.25	.11
662	Paul Dade	.25	.11
663	Paul Reuschel	.25	.11
664	Fred Stanley	.25	.11
665	Dennis Leonard	.25	.11
666	Billy Smith	.25	.11
667	Jeff Byrd	.25	.11
668	Dusty Baker	1.25	.55
669	Pete Falcone	.25	.11
670	Jim Rice	1.25	.55
671	Gary Lavelle	.25	.11
672	Don Kessinger	.60	.25
673	Steve Brye	.25	.11
674	Ray Knight	2.50	1.10
675	Jay Johnstone	.60	.25
676	Bob Myrick	.25	.11
677	Ed Herrmann	.25	.11
678	Tom Burgmeier	.25	.11
679	Wayne Garrett	.25	.11
680	Vida Blue	.60	.25
681	Rob Belloir	.25	.11
682	Ken Brett	.25	.11
683	Mike Champion	.25	.11
684	Ralph Houk MG	.60	.25
685	Frank Taveras	.25	.11
686	Gaylord Perry	2.50	1.10
687	Julio Cruz	.25	.11
688	George Mitterwald	.25	.11
689	Cleveland Indians Team Card (Checklist back)	1.25	.25
690	Mickey Rivers	.60	.25
691	Ross Grimsley	.25	.11
692	Ken Reitz	.25	.11
693	Lamar Johnson	.25	.11
694	Elias Sosa	.25	.11
695	Dwight Evans	1.25	.55
696	Steve Mingori	.25	.11
697	Roger Metzger	.25	.11
698	Juan Bernhardt	.25	.11
699	Jackie Brown	.25	.11
700	Johnny Bench	6.00	2.70
701	Rookie Pitchers — Tom Hume, Larry Landreth, Steve McCatty, Bruce Taylor	.60	.25
702	Rookie Catchers — Bill Nahorodny, Kevin Pasley, Rick Sweet, Don Werner	.60	.25
703	Rookie Pitchers DP — Larry Andersen, Tim Jones, Mickey Mahler, Jack Morris	5.00	2.20
704	Rookie 2nd Basemen — Garth Iorg, Dave Oliver, Sam Perlozzo, Lou Whitaker	8.00	3.60
705	Rookie Outfielders — Dave Bergman, Miguel Dilone, Clint Hurdle, Willie Norwood	1.25	.55
706	Rookie 1st Basemen — Wayne Cage, Ted Cox, Pat Putnam, Dave Revering	.60	.25
707	Rookie Shortstops — Mickey Klutts, Paul Molitor, Alan Trammell, U.L. Washington	80.00	36.00
708	Rookie Catchers — Bo Diaz, Dale Murphy, Lance Parrish, Ernie Whitt	5.00	2.20
709	Rookie Pitchers — Steve Burke, Matt Keough, Lance Rautzhan, Dan Schatzeder	.60	.25
710	Rookie Outfielders — Dell Alston, Rick Bosetti, Mike Easler, Keith Smith	1.25	.55
711	Rookie Pitchers DP — Cardell Camper, Dennis Lamp, Craig Mitchell, Roy Thomas	.25	.11
712	Bobby Valentine	.60	.25
713	Bob Davis	.25	.11
714	Mike Anderson	.25	.11
715	Jim Kaat	1.25	.55
716	Clarence Gaston	.60	.25
717	Nelson Briles	.25	.11
718	Ron Jackson	.25	.11
719	Randy Elliott	.25	.11
720	Fergie Jenkins	2.50	1.10
721	Billy Martin MG	1.25	.55
722	Pete Broberg	.25	.11
723	John Wockenfuss	.25	.11
724	Kansas City Royals Team Card (Checklist back)	1.25	.25
725	Kurt Bevacqua	.25	.11
726	Wilbur Wood	1.25	.30

1979 Topps

JACK MORRIS P TIGERS

	NRMT	VG-E
COMPLETE SET (726)	180.00	80.00

COMMON CARD (1-726)	.25	.11
MINOR STARS	.50	.23
SEMISTARS	1.00	.45
UNLISTED STARS	2.00	.90
☐ 1 Batting Leaders	2.50	.50
Rod Carew		
Dave Parker		
☐ 2 Home Run Leaders	1.00	.45
Jim Rice		
George Foster		
☐ 3 RBI Leaders	1.00	.45
Jim Rice		
George Foster		
☐ 4 Stolen Base Leaders	.50	.23
Ron LeFlore		
Omar Moreno		
☐ 5 Victory Leaders	.50	.23
Ron Guidry		
Gaylord Perry		
☐ 6 Strikeout Leaders	6.00	2.70
Nolan Ryan		
J.R. Richard		
☐ 7 ERA Leaders	.50	.23
Ron Guidry		
Craig Swan		
☐ 8 Leading Firemen	1.00	.45
Rich Gossage		
Rollie Fingers		
☐ 9 Dave Campbell	.25	.11
☐ 10 Lee May	.50	.23
☐ 11 Marc Hill	.25	.11
☐ 12 Dick Drago	.25	.11
☐ 13 Paul Dade	.25	.11
☐ 14 Rafael Landestoy	.25	.11
☐ 15 Ross Grimsley	.25	.11
☐ 16 Fred Stanley	.25	.11
☐ 17 Donnie Moore	.25	.11
☐ 18 Tony Solaita	.25	.11
☐ 19 Larry Gura DP	.10	.05
☐ 20 Joe Morgan DP	2.00	.90
☐ 21 Kevin Kobel	.25	.11
☐ 22 Mike Jorgensen	.25	.11
☐ 23 Terry Forster	.25	.11
☐ 24 Paul Molitor	20.00	9.00
☐ 25 Steve Carlton	3.00	1.35
☐ 26 Jamie Quirk	.25	.11
☐ 27 Dave Goltz	.25	.11
☐ 28 Steve Brye	.25	.11
☐ 29 Rick Langford	.25	.11
☐ 30 Dave Winfield	4.00	1.80
☐ 31 Tom House DP	.10	.05
☐ 32 Jerry Mumphrey	.25	.11
☐ 33 Dave Rozema	.25	.11
☐ 34 Rob Andrews	.25	.11
☐ 35 Ed Figueroa	.25	.11
☐ 36 Alan Ashby	.25	.11
☐ 37 Joe Kerrigan DP	.10	.05
☐ 38 Bernie Carbo	.25	.11
☐ 39 Dale Murphy	3.00	1.35
☐ 40 Dennis Eckersley	2.00	.90
☐ 41 Twins Team/Mgr.	1.00	.20
Gene Mauch		
(Checklist back)		
☐ 42 Ron Blomberg	.25	.11
☐ 43 Wayne Twitchell	.25	.11
☐ 44 Kurt Bevacqua	.25	.11
☐ 45 Al Hrabosky	.25	.11
☐ 46 Ron Hodges	.25	.11
☐ 47 Fred Norman	.25	.11
☐ 48 Merv Rettenmund	.25	.11
☐ 49 Vern Ruhle	.25	.11
☐ 50 Steve Garvey DP	1.00	.45
☐ 51 Ray Fosse DP	.10	.05
☐ 52 Randy Lerch	.25	.11
☐ 53 Mick Kelleher	.25	.11
☐ 54 Dell Alston DP	.10	.05
☐ 55 Willie Stargell	2.00	.90
☐ 56 John Hale	.25	.11
☐ 57 Eric Rasmussen	.25	.11
☐ 58 Bob Randall DP	.10	.05
☐ 59 John Denny DP	.25	.11
☐ 60 Mickey Rivers	.50	.23
☐ 61 Bo Diaz	.25	.11
☐ 62 Randy Moffitt	.25	.11
☐ 63 Jack Brohamer	.25	.11
☐ 64 Tom Underwood	.25	.11
☐ 65 Mark Belanger	.50	.23
☐ 66 Tigers Team/Mgr.	1.00	.20
Les Moss		
(Checklist back)		
☐ 67 Jim Mason DP	.10	.05
☐ 68 Joe Niekro DP	.25	.11
☐ 69 Elliott Maddox	.25	.11
☐ 70 John Candelaria	.50	.23
☐ 71 Brian Downing	.50	.23
☐ 72 Steve Mingori	.25	.11
☐ 73 Ken Henderson	.25	.11
☐ 74 Shane Rawley	.25	.11
☐ 75 Steve Yeager	.50	.23
☐ 76 Warren Cromartie	.50	.23
☐ 77 Dan Briggs DP	.10	.05
☐ 78 Elias Sosa	.25	.11
☐ 79 Ted Cox	.25	.11
☐ 80 Jason Thompson	.50	.23
☐ 81 Roger Erickson	.25	.11
☐ 82 Mets Team/Mgr.	1.00	.20
Joe Torre		
(Checklist back)		
☐ 83 Fred Kendall	.25	.11
☐ 84 Greg Minton	.25	.11
☐ 85 Gary Matthews	.50	.23
☐ 86 Rodney Scott	.25	.11
☐ 87 Pete Falcone	.25	.11
☐ 88 Bob Molinaro	.25	.11
☐ 89 Dick Tidrow	.25	.11
☐ 90 Bob Boone	1.00	.45
☐ 91 Terry Crowley	.25	.11
☐ 92 Jim Bibby	.25	.11
☐ 93 Phil Mankowski	.25	.11
☐ 94 Len Barker	.25	.11
☐ 95 Robin Yount	5.00	2.20
☐ 96 Indians Team/Mgr.	1.00	.20
Jeff Torborg		
(Checklist back)		
☐ 97 Sam Mejias	.25	.11
☐ 98 Ray Burris	.25	.11
☐ 99 John Wathan	.50	.23
☐ 100 Tom Seaver DP	4.00	1.80
☐ 101 Roy Howell	.25	.11
☐ 102 Mike Anderson	.25	.11
☐ 103 Jim Todd	.25	.11
☐ 104 Johnny Oates DP	.25	.11
☐ 105 Rick Camp DP	.10	.05
☐ 106 Frank Duffy	.25	.11
☐ 107 Jesus Alou DP	.10	.05
☐ 108 Eduardo Rodriguez	.25	.11
☐ 109 Joel Youngblood	.25	.11
☐ 110 Vida Blue	.50	.23
☐ 111 Roger Freed	.25	.11
☐ 112 Phillies Team/Mgr.	1.00	.20
Danny Ozark		
(Checklist back)		
☐ 113 Pete Redfern	.25	.11
☐ 114 Cliff Johnson	.25	.11
☐ 115 Nolan Ryan	30.00	13.50
☐ 116 Ozzie Smith	80.00	36.00
☐ 117 Grant Jackson	.25	.11
☐ 118 Bud Harrelson	.50	.23
☐ 119 Don Stanhouse	.25	.11
☐ 120 Jim Sundberg	.50	.23
☐ 121 Checklist 1-121 DP	.25	.10
☐ 122 Mike Paxton	.25	.11
☐ 123 Lou Whitaker	2.50	1.10
☐ 124 Dan Schatzeder	.25	.11
☐ 125 Rick Burleson	.25	.11
☐ 126 Doug Bair	.25	.11
☐ 127 Thad Bosley	.25	.11
☐ 128 Ted Martinez	.25	.11
☐ 129 Marty Pattin DP	.10	.05
☐ 130 Bob Watson DP	.25	.11
☐ 131 Jim Clancy	.25	.11
☐ 132 Rowland Office	.25	.11
☐ 133 Bill Castro	.25	.11
☐ 134 Alan Bannister	.25	.11
☐ 135 Bobby Murcer	.50	.23
☐ 136 Jim Kaat	.50	.23
☐ 137 Larry Wolfe DP	.10	.05
☐ 138 Mark Lee	.25	.11
☐ 139 Luis Pujols	.25	.11
☐ 140 Don Gullett	.25	.11
☐ 141 Tom Paciorek	.50	.23
☐ 142 Charlie Williams	.25	.11
☐ 143 Tony Scott	.25	.11
☐ 144 Sandy Alomar	.25	.11
☐ 145 Rick Rhoden	.25	.11
☐ 146 Duane Kuiper	.25	.11
☐ 147 Dave Hamilton	.25	.11
☐ 148 Bruce Boisclair	.25	.11
☐ 149 Manny Sarmiento	.25	.11
☐ 150 Wayne Cage	.25	.11
☐ 151 John Hiller	.25	.11
☐ 152 Rick Cerone	.25	.11
☐ 153 Dennis Lamp	.25	.11
☐ 154 Jim Gantner DP	.25	.11
☐ 155 Dwight Evans	1.00	.45
☐ 156 Buddy Solomon	.25	.11
☐ 157 U.L. Washington UER	.25	.11
(Sic, bats left,		
should be right)		
☐ 158 Joe Sambito	.25	.11
☐ 159 Roy White	.50	.23
☐ 160 Mike Flanagan	1.00	.45
☐ 161 Barry Foote	.25	.11
☐ 162 Tom Johnson	.25	.11
☐ 163 Glenn Burke	.25	.11
☐ 164 Mickey Lolich	.50	.23
☐ 165 Frank Taveras	.25	.11
☐ 166 Leon Roberts	.25	.11
☐ 167 Roger Metzger DP	.10	.05
☐ 168 Dave Freisleben	.25	.11
☐ 169 Bill Nahorodny	.25	.11
☐ 170 Don Sutton	2.00	.90
☐ 171 Gene Clines	.25	.11
☐ 172 Mike Bruhert	.25	.11
☐ 173 John Lowenstein	.25	.11
☐ 174 Rick Auerbach	.25	.11
☐ 175 George Hendrick	1.00	.45
☐ 176 Aurelio Rodriguez	.25	.11
☐ 177 Ron Reed	.25	.11
☐ 178 Alvis Woods	.25	.11
☐ 179 Jim Beattie DP	.25	.11
☐ 180 Larry Hisle	.25	.11
☐ 181 Mike Garman	.25	.11
☐ 182 Tim Johnson	.25	.11
☐ 183 Paul Splittorff	.25	.11
☐ 184 Darrel Chaney	.25	.11
☐ 185 Mike Torrez	.50	.23
☐ 186 Eric Soderholm	.25	.11
☐ 187 Mark Lemongello	.25	.11
☐ 188 Pat Kelly	.25	.11
☐ 189 Eddie Whitson	.25	.11
☐ 190 Ron Cey	.50	.23
☐ 191 Mike Norris	.25	.11
☐ 192 Cardinals Team/Mgr.	1.00	.20
Ken Boyer		
(Checklist back)		
☐ 193 Glenn Adams	.25	.11
☐ 194 Randy Jones	.25	.11
☐ 195 Bill Madlock	.50	.23
☐ 196 Steve Kemp DP	.25	.11
☐ 197 Bob Apodaca	.25	.11
☐ 198 Johnny Grubb	.25	.11
☐ 199 Larry Milbourne	.25	.11
☐ 200 Johnny Bench DP	4.00	1.80
☐ 201 RB: Mike Edwards	.25	.11
Most unassisted DP's,		
second base		
☐ 202 RB: Ron Guidry, Most	1.00	.45
strikeouts, lefthander,		
nine innings		
☐ 203 RB: J.R. Richard	.25	.11
Most strikeouts,		
season, righthander		
☐ 204 Pete Rose RB	3.00	1.35
Most hits NL season		
☐ 205 RB: John Stearns	.25	.11
Most SB's by		
catcher, season		
☐ 206 RB: Sammy Stewart	.25	.11
7 straight SO's,		
first ML game		
☐ 207 Dave Lemanczyk	.25	.11
☐ 208 Clarence Gaston	.25	.11
☐ 209 Reggie Cleveland	.25	.11
☐ 210 Larry Bowa	.50	.23
☐ 211 Denny Martinez	2.00	.90
☐ 212 Carney Lansford	1.00	.45

#	Player		
❑ 213	Bill Travers	.25	.11
❑ 214	Red Sox Team/Mgr.	1.00	.20
	Don Zimmer		
	(Checklist back)		
❑ 215	Willie McCovey	2.50	1.10
❑ 216	Wilbur Wood	.25	.11
❑ 217	Steve Dillard	.25	.11
❑ 218	Dennis Leonard	.25	.23
❑ 219	Roy Smalley	.50	.23
❑ 220	Cesar Geronimo	.25	.11
❑ 221	Jesse Jefferson	.25	.11
❑ 222	Bob Beall	.25	.11
❑ 223	Kent Tekulve	.50	.23
❑ 224	Dave Revering	.25	.11
❑ 225	Rich Gossage	1.00	.45
❑ 226	Ron Pruitt	.25	.11
❑ 227	Steve Stone	.50	.23
❑ 228	Vic Davalillo	.25	.11
❑ 229	Doug Flynn	.25	.11
❑ 230	Bob Forsch	.25	.11
❑ 231	John Wockenfuss	.25	.11
❑ 232	Jimmy Sexton	.25	.11
❑ 233	Paul Mitchell	.25	.11
❑ 234	Toby Harrah	.50	.23
❑ 235	Steve Rogers	.25	.11
❑ 236	Jim Dwyer	.25	.11
❑ 237	Billy Smith	.25	.11
❑ 238	Balor Moore	.25	.11
❑ 239	Willie Horton	.50	.23
❑ 240	Rick Reuschel	.50	.23
❑ 241	Checklist 122-242 DP	.50	.10
❑ 242	Pablo Torrealba	.25	.11
❑ 243	Buck Martinez DP	.10	.05
❑ 244	Pirates Team/Mgr.	1.00	.20
	Chuck Tanner		
	(Checklist back)		
❑ 245	Jeff Burroughs	.50	.23
❑ 246	Darrell Jackson	.25	.11
❑ 247	Tucker Ashford DP	.10	.05
❑ 248	Pete LaCock	.25	.11
❑ 249	Paul Thormodsgard	.25	.11
❑ 250	Willie Randolph	.50	.23
❑ 251	Jack Morris	2.00	.90
❑ 252	Bob Stinson	.25	.11
❑ 253	Rick Wise	.25	.11
❑ 254	Luis Gomez	.25	.11
❑ 255	Tommy John	1.00	.45
❑ 256	Mike Sadek	.25	.11
❑ 257	Adrian Devine	.25	.11
❑ 258	Mike Phillips	.25	.11
❑ 259	Reds Team/Mgr.	1.00	.20
	Sparky Anderson		
	(Checklist back)		
❑ 260	Richie Zisk	.25	.11
❑ 261	Mario Guerrero	.25	.11
❑ 262	Nelson Briles	.25	.11
❑ 263	Oscar Gamble	.50	.23
❑ 264	Don Robinson	.25	.11
❑ 265	Don Money	.25	.11
❑ 266	Jim Willoughby	.25	.11
❑ 267	Joe Rudi	.50	.23
❑ 268	Julio Gonzalez	.25	.11
❑ 269	Woodie Fryman	.25	.11
❑ 270	Butch Hobson	.50	.23
❑ 271	Rawly Eastwick	.25	.11
❑ 272	Tim Corcoran	.25	.11
❑ 273	Jerry Terrell	.25	.11
❑ 274	Willie Norwood	.25	.11
❑ 275	Junior Moore	.25	.11
❑ 276	Jim Colborn	.25	.11
❑ 277	Tom Grieve	.50	.23
❑ 278	Andy Messersmith	.50	.23
❑ 279	Jerry Grote DP	.10	.05
❑ 280	Andre Thornton	.50	.23
❑ 281	Vic Correll DP	.10	.05
❑ 282	Blue Jays Team/Mgr.	.50	.10
	Roy Hartsfield		
	(Checklist back)		
❑ 283	Ken Kravec	.25	.11
❑ 284	Johnnie LeMaster	.25	.11
❑ 285	Bobby Bonds	1.00	.45
❑ 286	Duffy Dyer	.25	.11
❑ 287	Andres Mora	.25	.11
❑ 288	Milt Wilcox	.25	.11
❑ 289	Jose Cruz	1.00	.45
❑ 290	Dave Lopes	.50	.23
❑ 291	Tom Griffin	.25	.11
❑ 292	Don Reynolds	.25	.11
❑ 293	Jerry Garvin	.25	.11
❑ 294	Pepe Frias	.25	.11
❑ 295	Mitchell Page	.25	.11
❑ 296	Preston Hanna	.25	.11
❑ 297	Ted Sizemore	.25	.11
❑ 298	Rich Gale	.25	.11
❑ 299	Steve Ontiveros	.25	.11
❑ 300	Rod Carew	2.50	1.10
❑ 301	Tom Hume	.25	.11
❑ 302	Braves Team/Mgr.	1.00	.20
	Bobby Cox		
	(Checklist back)		
❑ 303	Lary Sorensen DP	.10	.05
❑ 304	Steve Swisher	.25	.11
❑ 305	Willie Montanez	.25	.11
❑ 306	Floyd Bannister	.25	.11
❑ 307	Larvell Blanks	.25	.11
❑ 308	Bert Blyleven	1.00	.45
❑ 309	Ralph Garr	.50	.23
❑ 310	Thurman Munson	2.50	1.10
❑ 311	Gary Lavelle	.25	.11
❑ 312	Bob Robertson	.25	.11
❑ 313	Dyar Miller	.25	.11
❑ 314	Larry Harlow	.25	.11
❑ 315	Jon Matlack	.25	.11
❑ 316	Milt May	.25	.11
❑ 317	Jose Cardenal	.50	.23
❑ 318	Bob Welch	2.00	.90
❑ 319	Wayne Garrett	.25	.11
❑ 320	Carl Yastrzemski	3.00	1.35
❑ 321	Gaylord Perry	2.00	.90
❑ 322	Danny Goodwin	.25	.11
❑ 323	Lynn McGlothen	.25	.11
❑ 324	Mike Tyson	.25	.11
❑ 325	Cecil Cooper	.50	.23
❑ 326	Pedro Borbon	.25	.11
❑ 327	Art Howe DP	.25	.11
❑ 328	Oakland A's Team/Mgr.	1.00	.20
	Jack McKeon		
	(Checklist back)		
❑ 329	Joe Coleman	.25	.11
❑ 330	George Brett	12.00	5.50
❑ 331	Mickey Mahler	.25	.11
❑ 332	Gary Alexander	.25	.11
❑ 333	Chet Lemon	.50	.23
❑ 334	Craig Swan	.25	.11
❑ 335	Chris Chambliss	.50	.23
❑ 336	Bobby Thompson	.25	.11
❑ 337	John Montague	.25	.11
❑ 338	Vic Harris	.25	.11
❑ 339	Ron Jackson	.25	.11
❑ 340	Jim Palmer	2.50	1.10
❑ 341	Willie Upshaw	.50	.23
❑ 342	Dave Roberts	.25	.11
❑ 343	Ed Glynn	.25	.11
❑ 344	Jerry Royster	.25	.11
❑ 345	Tug McGraw	.50	.23
❑ 346	Bill Buckner	.50	.23
❑ 347	Doug Rau	.25	.11
❑ 348	Andre Dawson	4.00	1.80
❑ 349	Jim Wright	.25	.11
❑ 350	Garry Templeton	.50	.23
❑ 351	Wayne Nordhagen DP	.10	.05
❑ 352	Steve Renko	.25	.11
❑ 353	Checklist 243-363	1.00	.20
❑ 354	Bill Bonham	.25	.11
❑ 355	Lee Mazzilli	.25	.11
❑ 356	Giants Team/Mgr.	1.00	.20
	Joe Altobelli		
	(Checklist back)		
❑ 357	Jerry Augustine	.25	.11
❑ 358	Alan Trammell	3.00	1.35
❑ 359	Dan Spillner DP	.10	.05
❑ 360	Amos Otis	.50	.23
❑ 361	Tom Dixon	.25	.11
❑ 362	Mike Cubbage	.25	.11
❑ 363	Craig Skok	.25	.11
❑ 364	Gene Richards	.25	.11
❑ 365	Sparky Lyle	.50	.23
❑ 366	Juan Bernhardt	.25	.11
❑ 367	Dave Skaggs	.25	.11
❑ 368	Don Aase	.50	.23
❑ 369A	Bump Wills ERR	3.00	1.35
	(Blue Jays)		
❑ 369B	Bump Wills COR	3.00	1.35
	(Rangers)		
❑ 370	Dave Kingman	1.00	.45
❑ 371	Jeff Holly	.25	.11
❑ 372	Lamar Johnson	.25	.11
❑ 373	Lance Rautzhan	.25	.11
❑ 374	Ed Herrmann	.25	.11
❑ 375	Bill Campbell	.25	.11
❑ 376	Gorman Thomas	.50	.23
❑ 377	Paul Moskau	.25	.11
❑ 378	Rob Picciolo DP	.10	.05
❑ 379	Dale Murray	.25	.11
❑ 380	John Mayberry	.50	.23
❑ 381	Astros Team/Mgr.	1.00	.20
	Bill Virdon		
	(Checklist back)		
❑ 382	Jerry Martin	.25	.11
❑ 383	Phil Garner	.50	.23
❑ 384	Tommy Boggs	.25	.11
❑ 385	Dan Ford	.25	.11
❑ 386	Francisco Barrios	.25	.11
❑ 387	Gary Thomasson	.25	.11
❑ 388	Jack Billingham	.25	.11
❑ 389	Joe Zdeb	.25	.11
❑ 390	Rollie Fingers	2.00	.90
❑ 391	Al Oliver	.50	.23
❑ 392	Doug Ault	.25	.11
❑ 393	Scott McGregor	.50	.23
❑ 394	Randy Stein	.25	.11
❑ 395	Dave Cash	.25	.11
❑ 396	Bill Plummer	.25	.11
❑ 397	Sergio Ferrer	.25	.11
❑ 398	Ivan DeJesus	.25	.11
❑ 399	David Clyde	.25	.11
❑ 400	Jim Rice	1.00	.45
❑ 401	Ray Knight	.50	.23
❑ 402	Paul Hartzell	.25	.11
❑ 403	Tim Foli	.25	.11
❑ 404	White Sox Team/Mgr.	1.00	.20
	Don Kessinger		
	(Checklist back)		
❑ 405	Butch Wynegar DP	.10	.05
❑ 406	Joe Wallis DP	.10	.05
❑ 407	Pete Vuckovich	.50	.23
❑ 408	Charlie Moore DP	.10	.05
❑ 409	Willie Wilson	1.00	.45
❑ 410	Darrell Evans	.50	.45
❑ 411	George Sisler ATL	2.50	1.10
	Ty Cobb		
❑ 412	Hack Wilson ATL	2.50	1.10
	Hank Aaron		
❑ 413	Roger Maris ATL	2.50	1.10
	Ty Cobb		
❑ 414	Rogers Hornsby ATL	2.50	1.10
	Ty Cobb		
❑ 415	Lou Brock ATL	1.00	.45
❑ 416	Jack Chesbro ATL	.50	.23
	Cy Young		
❑ 417	Nolan Ryan ATL DP	5.00	2.20
	Walter Johnson		
❑ 418	Dutch Leonard ATL DP	.25	.11
	Walter Johnson		
❑ 419	Dick Tidrow	.25	.11
❑ 420	Ken Griffey Sr.	.50	.23
❑ 421	Doug DeCinces	.50	.23
❑ 422	Ruppert Jones	.25	.11
❑ 423	Bob Montgomery	.25	.11
❑ 424	Angels Team/Mgr.	1.00	.20
	Jim Fregosi		
	(Checklist back)		
❑ 425	Rick Manning	.25	.11
❑ 426	Chris Speier	.25	.11
❑ 427	Andy Replogle	.25	.11
❑ 428	Bobby Valentine	.50	.23
❑ 429	John Urrea DP	.10	.05
❑ 430	Dave Parker	.25	.11
❑ 431	Glenn Borgmann	.25	.11
❑ 432	Dave Heaverlo	.25	.11
❑ 433	Larry Biittner	.25	.11
❑ 434	Ken Clay	.25	.11
❑ 435	Gene Tenace	.50	.23
❑ 436	Hector Cruz	.25	.11
❑ 437	Rick Williams	.25	.11
❑ 438	Horace Speed	.25	.11
❑ 439	Frank White	.50	.23
❑ 440	Rusty Staub	1.00	.45

#	Player	Price	Price
441	Lee Lacy	.25	.11
442	Doyle Alexander	.25	.11
443	Bruce Bochte	.25	.11
444	Aurelio Lopez	.25	.11
445	Steve Henderson	.25	.11
446	Jim Lonborg	.50	.23
447	Manny Sanguillen	.50	.23
448	Moose Haas	.25	.11
449	Bombo Rivera	.25	.11
450	Dave Concepcion	1.00	.45
451	Royals Team/Mgr. Whitey Herzog (Checklist back)	1.00	.20
452	Jerry Morales	.25	.11
453	Chris Knapp	.25	.11
454	Len Randle	.25	.11
455	Bill Lee DP	.10	.05
456	Chuck Baker	.25	.11
457	Bruce Sutter	.50	.23
458	Jim Essian	.25	.11
459	Sid Monge	.25	.11
460	Graig Nettles	1.00	.45
461	Jim Barr DP	.10	.05
462	Otto Velez	.25	.11
463	Steve Comer	.25	.11
464	Joe Nolan	.25	.11
465	Reggie Smith	.50	.23
466	Mark Littell	.25	.11
467	Don Kessinger DP	.25	.11
468	Stan Bahnsen DP	.10	.05
469	Lance Parrish	1.00	.45
470	Garry Maddox DP	.25	.11
471	Joaquin Andujar	.50	.23
472	Craig Kusick	.25	.11
473	Dave Roberts	.25	.11
474	Dick Davis	.25	.11
475	Dan Driessen	.25	.11
476	Tom Poquette	.25	.11
477	Bob Grich	.50	.23
478	Juan Beniquez	.25	.11
479	Padres Team/Mgr. Roger Craig (Checklist back)	1.00	.20
480	Fred Lynn	.50	.23
481	Skip Lockwood	.25	.11
482	Craig Reynolds	.25	.11
483	Checklist 364-484 DP	.50	.10
484	Rick Waits	.25	.11
485	Bucky Dent	.50	.23
486	Bob Knepper	.25	.11
487	Miguel Dilone	.25	.11
488	Bob Owchinko	.25	.11
489	Larry Cox UER (Photo actually Dave Rader)	.25	.11
490	Al Cowens	.25	.11
491	Tippy Martinez	.25	.11
492	Bob Bailor	.25	.11
493	Larry Christenson	.25	.11
494	Jerry White	.25	.11
495	Tony Perez	2.00	.90
496	Barry Bonnell DP	.10	.05
497	Glenn Abbott	.25	.11
498	Rich Chiles	.25	.11
499	Rangers Team/Mgr. Pat Corrales (Checklist back)	1.00	.20
500	Ron Guidry	.50	.23
501	Junior Kennedy	.25	.11
502	Steve Braun	.25	.11
503	Terry Humphrey	.25	.11
504	Larry McWilliams	.25	.11
505	Ed Kranepool	.25	.11
506	John D'Acquisto	.25	.11
507	Tony Armas	.50	.23
508	Charlie Hough	.50	.23
509	Mario Mendoza UER (Career BA .278, should say .204)	.25	.11
510	Ted Simmons	1.00	.45
511	Paul Reuschel DP	.10	.05
512	Jack Clark	.50	.23
513	Dave Johnson	.25	.11
514	Mike Proly	.25	.11
515	Enos Cabell	.25	.11
516	Champ Summers DP	.10	.05
517	Al Bumbry	.50	.23
518	Jim Umbarger	.25	.11
519	Ben Oglivie	.50	.23
520	Gary Carter	2.00	.90
521	Sam Ewing	.25	.11
522	Ken Holtzman	.50	.23
523	John Milner	.25	.11
524	Tom Burgmeier	.25	.11
525	Freddie Patek	.25	.11
526	Dodgers Team/Mgr. Tom Lasorda (Checklist back)	1.00	.20
527	Lerrin LaGrow	.25	.11
528	Wayne Gross DP	.10	.05
529	Brian Asselstine	.25	.11
530	Frank Tanana	.50	.23
531	Fernando Gonzalez	.25	.11
532	Buddy Schultz	.25	.11
533	Leroy Stanton	.25	.11
534	Ken Forsch	.25	.11
535	Ellis Valentine	.25	.11
536	Jerry Reuss	.50	.23
537	Tom Veryzer	.25	.11
538	Mike Ivie DP	.10	.05
539	John Ellis	.25	.11
540	Greg Luzinski	.50	.23
541	Jim Slaton	.25	.11
542	Rick Bosetti	.25	.11
543	Kiko Garcia	.25	.11
544	Fergie Jenkins	2.00	.90
545	John Stearns	.25	.11
546	Bill Russell	.50	.23
547	Clint Hurdle	.25	.11
548	Enrique Romo	.25	.11
549	Bob Bailey	.25	.11
550	Sal Bando	.50	.23
551	Cubs Team/Mgr. Herman Franks (Checklist back)	1.00	.20
552	Jose Morales	.25	.11
553	Denny Walling	.25	.11
554	Matt Keough	.25	.11
555	Biff Pocoroba	.25	.11
556	Mike Lum	.25	.11
557	Ken Brett	.25	.11
558	Jay Johnstone	.50	.23
559	Greg Pryor	.25	.11
560	John Montefusco	.25	.11
561	Ed Ott	.25	.11
562	Dusty Baker	1.00	.45
563	Roy Thomas	.25	.11
564	Jerry Turner	.25	.11
565	Rico Carty	.50	.23
566	Nino Espinosa	.25	.11
567	Richie Hebner	.50	.23
568	Carlos Lopez	.25	.11
569	Bob Sykes	.25	.11
570	Cesar Cedeno	.50	.23
571	Darrell Porter	.50	.23
572	Rod Gilbreath	.25	.11
573	Jim Kern	.25	.11
574	Claudell Washington	.50	.23
575	Luis Tiant	.50	.23
576	Mike Parrott	.25	.11
577	Brewers Team/Mgr. George Bamberger (Checklist back)	1.00	.20
578	Pete Broberg	.25	.11
579	Greg Gross	.25	.11
580	Ron Fairly	.50	.23
581	Darold Knowles	.25	.11
582	Paul Blair	.50	.23
583	Julio Cruz	.25	.11
584	Jim Rooker	.25	.11
585	Hal McRae	1.00	.45
586	Bob Horner	1.00	.45
587	Ken Reitz	.25	.11
588	Tom Murphy	.25	.11
589	Terry Whitfield	.25	.11
590	J.R. Richard	.50	.23
591	Mike Hargrove	.50	.23
592	Mike Krukow	.25	.11
593	Rick Dempsey	.50	.23
594	Bob Shirley	.25	.11
595	Phil Niekro	2.00	.90
596	Jim Wohlford	.25	.11
597	Bob Stanley	.25	.11
598	Mark Wagner	.25	.11
599	Jim Spencer	.25	.11
600	George Foster	.50	.23
601	Dave LaRoche	.25	.11
602	Checklist 485-605	1.00	.20
603	Rudy May	.25	.11
604	Jeff Newman	.25	.11
605	Rick Monday DP	.25	.11
606	Expos Team/Mgr. Dick Williams (Checklist back)	1.00	.20
607	Omar Moreno	.25	.11
608	Dave McKay	.25	.11
609	Silvio Martinez	.25	.11
610	Mike Schmidt	6.00	2.70
611	Jim Norris	.25	.11
612	Rick Honeycutt	.50	.23
613	Mike Edwards	.25	.11
614	Willie Hernandez	.50	.23
615	Ken Singleton	.50	.23
616	Billy Almon	.25	.11
617	Terry Puhl	.25	.11
618	Jerry Remy	.25	.11
619	Ken Landreaux	.50	.23
620	Bert Campaneris	.50	.23
621	Pat Zachry	.25	.11
622	Dave Collins	.50	.23
623	Bob McClure	.25	.11
624	Larry Herndon	.25	.11
625	Mark Fidrych	2.00	.90
626	Yankees Team/Mgr. Bob Lemon (Checklist back)	1.00	.20
627	Gary Serum	.25	.11
628	Del Unser	.25	.11
629	Gene Garber	.50	.23
630	Bake McBride	.50	.23
631	Jorge Orta	.25	.11
632	Don Kirkwood	.25	.11
633	Rob Wilfong DP	.10	.05
634	Paul Lindblad	.25	.11
635	Don Baylor	1.00	.45
636	Wayne Garland	.25	.11
637	Bill Robinson	.50	.23
638	Al Fitzmorris	.25	.11
639	Manny Trillo	.25	.11
640	Eddie Murray	20.00	9.00
641	Bobby Castillo	.25	.11
642	Wilbur Howard DP	.10	.05
643	Tom Hausman	.25	.11
644	Manny Mota	.50	.23
645	George Scott DP	.25	.11
646	Rick Sweet	.25	.11
647	Bob Lacey	.25	.11
648	Lou Piniella	.50	.23
649	John Curtis	.25	.11
650	Pete Rose	8.00	3.60
651	Mike Caldwell	.25	.11
652	Stan Papi	.25	.11
653	Warren Brusstar DP	.10	.05
654	Rick Miller	.25	.11
655	Jerry Koosman	.50	.23
656	Hosken Powell	.25	.11
657	George Medich	.25	.11
658	Taylor Duncan	.25	.11
659	Mariners Team/Mgr. Darrell Johnson (Checklist back)	1.00	.20
660	Ron LeFlore DP	.25	.11
661	Bruce Kison	.25	.11
662	Kevin Bell	.25	.11
663	Mike Vail	.25	.11
664	Doug Bird	.25	.11
665	Lou Brock	2.50	1.10
666	Rich Dauer	.25	.11
667	Don Hood	.25	.11
668	Bill North	.25	.11
669	Checklist 606-726	1.00	.20
670	Jim Hunter DP	1.00	.45
671	Joe Ferguson DP	.10	.05
672	Ed Halicki	.25	.11
673	Tom Hutton	.25	.11
674	Dave Tomlin	.25	.11
675	Tim McCarver	1.00	.45
676	Johnny Sutton	.25	.11

No.	Player	NRMT	VG-E
677	Larry Parrish	.50	.23
678	Geoff Zahn	.25	.11
679	Derrel Thomas	.25	.11
680	Carlton Fisk	2.50	1.10
681	John Henry Johnson	.25	.11
682	Dave Chalk	.25	.11
683	Dan Meyer DP	.10	.05
684	Jamie Easterly DP	.10	.05
685	Sixto Lezcano	.25	.11
686	Ron Schueler DP	.10	.05
687	Rennie Stennett	.25	.11
688	Mike Willis	.25	.11
689	Orioles Team/Mgr. — Earl Weaver (Checklist back)	1.00	.20
690	Buddy Bell	.25	.11
691	Dock Ellis DP	.10	.05
692	Mickey Stanley	.25	.11
693	Dave Rader	.25	.11
694	Burt Hooton	.50	.23
695	Keith Hernandez	1.00	.45
696	Andy Hassler	.25	.11
697	Dave Bergman	.25	.11
698	Bill Stein	.25	.11
699	Hal Dues	.25	.11
700	Reggie Jackson DP	5.00	2.20
701	Orioles Prospects — Mark Corey, John Flinn, Sammy Stewart	.50	.23
702	Red Sox Prospects — Joel Finch, Garry Hancock, Allen Ripley	.50	.23
703	Angels Prospects — Jim Anderson, Dave Frost, Bob Slater	.50	.23
704	White Sox Prospects — Ross Baumgarten, Mike Colbern, Mike Squires	.50	.23
705	Indians Prospects — Alfredo Griffin, Tim Norrid, Dave Oliver	1.00	.45
706	Tigers Prospects — Dave Stegman, Dave Tobik, Kip Young	.50	.23
707	Royals Prospects — Randy Bass, Jim Gaudet, Randy McGilberry	1.00	.45
708	Brewers Prospects — Kevin Bass, Eddie Romero, Ned Yost	1.00	.45
709	Twins Prospects — Sam Perlozzo, Rick Sofield, Kevin Stanfield	.50	.23
710	Yankees Prospects — Brian Doyle, Mike Heath, Dave Rajsich	.50	.23
711	A's Prospects — Dwayne Murphy, Bruce Robinson, Alan Wirth	.50	.45
712	Mariners Prospects — Bud Anderson, Greg Biercevicz, Byron McLaughlin	.50	.23
713	Rangers Prospects — Danny Darwin, Pat Putnam, Billy Sample	.50	.23
714	Blue Jays Prospects — Victor Cruz, Pat Kelly, Ernie Whitt	.50	.23
715	Braves Prospects — Bruce Benedict, Glenn Hubbard, Larry Whisenton	1.00	.45
716	Cubs Prospects — Dave Geisel, Karl Pagel, Scot Thompson	.50	.23
717	Reds Prospects — Mike LaCoss, Ron Oester, Harry Spilman	.50	.23
718	Astros Prospects — Bruce Bochy, Mike Fischlin, Don Pisker	.50	.23
719	Dodgers Prospects — Pedro Guerrero, Rudy Law, Joe Simpson	1.00	.45
720	Expos Prospects — Jerry Fry, Jerry Pirtle, Scott Sanderson	1.00	.45
721	Mets Prospects — Juan Berenguer, Dwight Bernard, Dan Norman	.50	.23
722	Phillies Prospects — Jim Morrison, Lonnie Smith, Jim Wright	1.00	.45
723	Pirates Prospects — Dale Berra, Eugenio Cotes, Ben Wiltbank	.50	.23
724	Cardinals Prospects — Tom Bruno, George Frazier, Terry Kennedy	1.00	.45
725	Padres Prospects — Jim Beswick, Steve Mura, Broderick Perkins	.50	.23
726	Giants Prospects — Greg Johnston, Joe Strain, John Tamargo	.50	.10

1980 Topps

	NRMT	VG-E
COMPLETE SET (726)	150.00	70.00
COMMON CARD (1-726)	.25	.11
MINOR STARS	.50	.23
SEMISTARS	1.00	.45
UNLISTED STARS	1.50	.70

No.	Player	NRMT	VG-E
1	Lou Brock HL — Carl Yastrzemski — Enter 3000 hit circle	3.00	.60
2	Willie McCovey HL — 512th homer sets new mark for NL lefties	1.00	.45
3	Manny Mota HL — All-time pinch-hits, 145	.25	.11
4	Pete Rose HL — Career Record 10th season with 200 or more hits	2.50	1.10
5	Garry Templeton HL — First with 100 hits from each side of plate	.25	.23
6	Del Unser HL — 3 consecutive pinch homers	.50	.23
7	Mike Lum	.25	.11
8	Craig Swan	.25	.11
9	Steve Braun	.25	.11
10	Dennis Martinez	1.50	.70
11	Jimmy Sexton	.25	.11
12	John Curtis DP	.10	.05
13	Ron Pruitt	.25	.11
14	Dave Cash	.25	.11
15	Bill Campbell	.25	.11
16	Jerry Narron	.25	.11
17	Bruce Sutter	1.00	.45
18	Ron Jackson	.25	.11
19	Balor Moore	.25	.11
20	Dan Ford	.25	.11
21	Manny Sarmiento	.25	.11
22	Pat Putnam	.25	.11
23	Derrel Thomas	.25	.11
24	Jim Slaton	.25	.11
25	Lee Mazzilli	.50	.23
26	Marty Pattin	.25	.11
27	Del Unser	.25	.11
28	Bruce Kison	.25	.11
29	Mark Wagner	.25	.11
30	Vida Blue	1.00	.45
31	Jay Johnstone	.50	.23
32	Julio Cruz DP	.10	.05
33	Tony Scott	.25	.11
34	Jeff Newman DP	.10	.05
35	Luis Tiant	.50	.23
36	Rusty Torres	.25	.11
37	Kiko Garcia	.25	.11
38	Dan Spillner DP	.10	.05
39	Rowland Office	.25	.11
40	Carlton Fisk	2.00	.90
41	Rangers Team/Mgr. — Pat Corrales (Checklist back)	1.00	.20
42	David Palmer	.25	.11
43	Bombo Rivera	.25	.11
44	Bill Fahey	.25	.11
45	Frank White	1.00	.45
46	Rico Carty	.50	.23
47	Bill Bonham DP	.10	.05
48	Rick Miller	.25	.11
49	Mario Guerrero	.25	.11
50	J.R. Richard	.50	.23
51	Joe Ferguson DP	.10	.05
52	Warren Brusstar	.25	.11
53	Ben Oglivie	.50	.23
54	Dennis Lamp	.25	.11
55	Bill Madlock	.50	.23
56	Bobby Valentine	.50	.23
57	Pete Vuckovich	.25	.11
58	Doug Flynn	.25	.11
59	Eddy Putman	.25	.11
60	Bucky Dent	.50	.23
61	Gary Serum	.25	.11
62	Mike Ivie	.25	.11
63	Bob Stanley	.25	.11
64	Joe Nolan	.25	.11
65	Al Bumbry	.50	.23
66	Royals Team/Mgr. — Jim Frey (Checklist back)	1.00	.20
67	Doyle Alexander	.25	.11
68	Larry Harlow	.25	.11
69	Rick Williams	.25	.11
70	Gary Carter	1.50	.70
71	John Milner DP	.10	.05
72	Fred Howard DP	.10	.05
73	Dave Collins	.25	.11
74	Sid Monge	.25	.11
75	Bill Russell	.50	.23
76	John Stearns	.25	.11
77	Dave Stieb	1.50	.70
78	Ruppert Jones	.25	.11
79	Bob Owchinko	.25	.11
80	Ron LeFlore	.50	.23
81	Ted Sizemore	.25	.11
82	Astros Team/Mgr. — Bill Virdon (Checklist back)	1.00	.20
83	Steve Trout	.25	.11

#	Player	Price 1	Price 2
84	Gary Lavelle	.25	.11
85	Ted Simmons	.50	.23
86	Dave Hamilton	.25	.11
87	Pepe Frias	.25	.11
88	Ken Landreaux	.25	.11
89	Don Hood	.25	.11
90	Manny Trillo	.50	.23
91	Rick Dempsey	.50	.23
92	Rick Rhoden	.25	.11
93	Dave Roberts DP	.10	.05
94	Neil Allen	.50	.23
95	Cecil Cooper	.50	.23
96	A's Team/Mgr.	1.00	.20
	Jim Marshall (Checklist back)		
97	Bill Lee	.50	.23
98	Jerry Terrell	.25	.11
99	Victor Cruz	.25	.11
100	Johnny Bench	4.00	1.80
101	Aurelio Lopez	.25	.11
102	Rich Dauer	.25	.11
103	Bill Caudill	.25	.11
104	Manny Mota	.50	.23
105	Frank Tanana	.50	.23
106	Jeff Leonard	1.00	.45
107	Francisco Barrios	.25	.11
108	Bob Horner	.50	.23
109	Bill Travers	.25	.11
110	Fred Lynn DP	.50	.23
111	Bob Knepper	.25	.11
112	White Sox Team/Mgr.	1.00	.20
	Tony LaRussa (Checklist back)		
113	Geoff Zahn	.25	.11
114	Juan Beniquez	.25	.11
115	Sparky Lyle	.50	.23
116	Larry Cox	.25	.11
117	Dock Ellis	.25	.11
118	Phil Garner	.50	.23
119	Sammy Stewart	.25	.11
120	Greg Luzinski	.50	.23
121	Checklist 1-121	1.00	.20
122	Dave Rosello DP	.10	.05
123	Lynn Jones	.25	.11
124	Dave Lemanczyk	.25	.11
125	Tony Perez	1.50	.70
126	Dave Tomlin	.25	.11
127	Gary Thomasson	.25	.11
128	Tom Burgmeier	.25	.11
129	Craig Reynolds	.25	.11
130	Amos Otis	.50	.23
131	Paul Mitchell	.25	.11
132	Biff Pocoroba	.25	.11
133	Jerry Turner	.25	.11
134	Matt Keough	.25	.11
135	Bill Buckner	.50	.23
136	Dick Ruthven	.25	.11
137	John Castino	.25	.11
138	Ross Baumgarten	.25	.11
139	Dane Iorg	.25	.11
140	Rich Gossage	1.00	.45
141	Gary Alexander	.25	.11
142	Phil Huffman	.25	.11
143	Bruce Bochte DP	.10	.05
144	Steve Comer	.25	.11
145	Darrell Evans	.50	.23
146	Bob Welch	.50	.23
147	Terry Puhl	.25	.11
148	Manny Sanguillen	.50	.23
149	Tom Hume	.25	.11
150	Jason Thompson	.25	.11
151	Tom Hausman DP	.10	.05
152	John Fulgham	.25	.11
153	Tim Blackwell	.25	.11
154	Lary Sorensen	.25	.11
155	Jerry Remy	.25	.11
156	Tony Brizzolara	.25	.11
157	Willie Wilson DP	.25	.23
158	Rob Picciolo DP	.10	.05
159	Ken Clay	.25	.11
160	Eddie Murray	10.00	4.50
161	Larry Christenson	.25	.11
162	Bob Randall	.25	.11
163	Steve Swisher	.25	.11
164	Greg Pryor	.25	.11
165	Omar Moreno	.25	.11
166	Glenn Abbott	.25	.11
167	Jack Clark	.50	.23
168	Rick Waits	.25	.11
169	Luis Gomez	.25	.11
170	Burt Hooton	.25	.11
171	Fernando Gonzalez	.25	.11
172	Ron Hodges	.25	.11
173	John Henry Johnson	.25	.11
174	Ray Knight	.50	.23
175	Rick Reuschel	.50	.23
176	Champ Summers	.25	.11
177	Dave Heaverlo	.25	.11
178	Tim McCarver	1.00	.45
179	Ron Davis	.25	.11
180	Warren Cromartie	.25	.11
181	Moose Haas	.25	.11
182	Ken Reitz	.25	.11
183	Jim Anderson DP	.10	.05
184	Steve Renko DP	.10	.05
185	Hal McRae	.50	.23
186	Junior Moore	.25	.11
187	Alan Ashby	.25	.11
188	Terry Crowley	.25	.11
189	Kevin Kobel	.25	.11
190	Buddy Bell	.50	.23
191	Ted Martinez	.25	.11
192	Braves Team/Mgr.	1.00	.20
	Bobby Cox (Checklist back)		
193	Dave Goltz	.25	.11
194	Mike Easler	.25	.11
195	John Montefusco	.25	.11
196	Lance Parrish	.50	.23
197	Byron McLaughlin	.25	.11
198	Dell Alston DP	.10	.05
199	Mike LaCoss	.25	.11
200	Jim Rice	.50	.23
201	Batting Leaders	1.00	.45
	Keith Hernandez		
	Fred Lynn		
202	Home Run Leaders		.45
	Dave Kingman		
	Gorman Thomas		
203	RBI Leaders	1.50	.70
	Dave Winfield		
	Don Baylor		
204	Stolen Base Leaders	.50	.23
	Omar Moreno		
	Willie Wilson		
205	Victory Leaders	1.00	.45
	Joe Niekro		
	Phil Niekro		
	Mike Flanagan		
206	Strikeout Leaders	6.00	2.70
	J.R. Richard		
	Nolan Ryan		
207	ERA Leaders	1.00	.45
	J.R. Richard		
	Ron Guidry		
208	Wayne Cage	.25	.11
209	Von Joshua	.25	.11
210	Steve Carlton	2.50	1.10
211	Dave Skaggs DP	.10	.05
212	Dave Roberts	.25	.11
213	Mike Jorgensen DP	.10	.05
214	Angels Team/Mgr.	1.00	.20
	Jim Fregosi (Checklist back)		
215	Sixto Lezcano	.25	.11
216	Phil Mankowski	.25	.11
217	Ed Halicki	.25	.11
218	Jose Morales	.25	.11
219	Steve Mingori	.25	.11
220	Dave Concepcion	1.00	.45
221	Joe Cannon	.25	.11
222	Ron Hassey	.25	.11
223	Bob Sykes	.25	.11
224	Willie Montanez	.25	.11
225	Lou Piniella	1.00	.45
226	Bill Stein	.25	.11
227	Len Barker	.25	.11
228	Johnny Oates	.50	.23
229	Jim Bibby	.25	.11
230	Dave Winfield	4.00	1.80
231	Steve McCatty	.25	.11
232	Alan Trammell	1.50	.70
233	LaRue Washington	.25	.11
234	Vern Ruhle	.25	.11
235	Andre Dawson	2.50	1.10
236	Marc Hill	.25	.11
237	Scott McGregor	.25	.11
238	Rob Wilfong	.25	.11
239	Don Aase	.25	.11
240	Dave Kingman	1.00	.45
241	Checklist 122-242	1.00	.20
242	Lamar Johnson	.25	.11
243	Jerry Augustine	.25	.11
244	Cardinals Team/Mgr.	1.00	.20
	Ken Boyer (Checklist back)		
245	Phil Niekro	1.50	.70
246	Tim Foli DP	.10	.05
247	Frank Riccelli	.25	.11
248	Jamie Quirk	.25	.11
249	Jim Clancy	.25	.11
250	Jim Kaat	1.00	.45
251	Kip Young	.25	.11
252	Ted Cox	.25	.11
253	John Montague	.25	.11
254	Paul Dade DP	.10	.05
255	Dusty Baker DP	.50	.23
256	Roger Erickson	.25	.11
257	Larry Herndon	.25	.11
258	Paul Moskau	.25	.11
259	Mets Team/Mgr.	1.00	.20
	Joe Torre (Checklist back)		
260	Al Oliver	1.00	.45
261	Dave Chalk	.25	.11
262	Benny Ayala	.25	.11
263	Dave LaRoche DP	.10	.05
264	Bill Robinson	.25	.11
265	Robin Yount	5.00	2.20
266	Bernie Carbo	.25	.11
267	Dan Schatzeder	.25	.11
268	Rafael Landestoy	.25	.11
269	Dave Tobik	.25	.11
270	Mike Schmidt DP	4.00	1.80
271	Dick Drago DP	.10	.05
272	Ralph Garr	.50	.23
273	Eduardo Rodriguez	.25	.11
274	Dale Murphy	1.50	.70
275	Jerry Koosman	.50	.23
276	Tom Veryzer	.25	.11
277	Rick Bosetti	.25	.11
278	Jim Spencer	.25	.11
279	Rob Andrews	.25	.11
280	Gaylord Perry	1.50	.70
281	Paul Blair	.50	.23
282	Mariners Team/Mgr.	1.00	.20
	Darrell Johnson (Checklist back)		
283	John Ellis	.25	.11
284	Larry Murray DP	.10	.05
285	Don Baylor	1.00	.45
286	Darold Knowles DP	.10	.05
287	John Lowenstein	.25	.11
288	Dave Rozema	.25	.11
289	Bruce Bochy	.25	.11
290	Steve Garvey	1.50	.70
291	Randy Scarberry	.25	.11
292	Dale Berra	.25	.11
293	Elias Sosa	.25	.11
294	Charlie Spikes	.25	.11
295	Larry Gura	.25	.11
296	Dave Rader	.25	.11
297	Tim Johnson	.25	.11
298	Ken Holtzman	.50	.23
299	Steve Henderson	.25	.11
300	Ron Guidry	.50	.23
301	Mike Edwards	.25	.11
302	Dodgers Team/Mgr.	1.00	.20
	Tom Lasorda (Checklist back)		
303	Bill Castro	.25	.11
304	Butch Wynegar	.25	.11
305	Randy Jones	.25	.11
306	Denny Walling	.25	.11
307	Rick Honeycutt	.25	.11
308	Mike Hargrove	.50	.23
309	Larry McWilliams	.25	.11
310	Dave Parker	1.00	.45

311	Roger Metzger	.25	.11
312	Mike Barlow	.25	.11
313	Johnny Grubb	.25	.11
314	Tim Stoddard	.25	.11
315	Steve Kemp	.25	.11
316	Bob Lacey	.25	.11
317	Mike Anderson DP	.10	.05
318	Jerry Reuss	.50	.23
319	Chris Speier	.25	.11
320	Dennis Eckersley	1.00	.45
321	Keith Hernandez	.50	.23
322	Claudell Washington	.50	.23
323	Mick Kelleher	.25	.11
324	Tom Underwood	.25	.11
325	Dan Driessen	.25	.11
326	Bo McLaughlin	.25	.11
327	Ray Fosse DP	.10	.05
328	Twins Team/Mgr. Gene Mauch (Checklist back)	1.00	.20
329	Bert Roberge	.25	.11
330	Al Cowens	.25	.11
331	Richie Hebner	.50	.23
332	Enrique Romo	.25	.11
333	Jim Norris DP	.10	.05
334	Jim Beattie	.25	.11
335	Willie McCovey	2.00	.90
336	George Medich	.25	.11
337	Carney Lansford	.50	.23
338	John Wockenfuss	.25	.11
339	John D'Acquisto	.25	.11
340	Ken Singleton	.50	.23
341	Jim Essian	.25	.11
342	Odell Jones	.25	.11
343	Mike Vail	.25	.11
344	Randy Lerch	.25	.11
345	Larry Parrish	.50	.23
346	Buddy Solomon	.25	.11
347	Harry Chappas	.25	.11
348	Checklist 243-363	1.00	.20
349	Jack Brohamer	.25	.11
350	George Hendrick	.50	.23
351	Bob Davis	.25	.11
352	Dan Briggs	.25	.11
353	Andy Hassler	.25	.11
354	Rick Auerbach	.25	.11
355	Gary Matthews	.50	.23
356	Padres Team/Mgr. Jerry Coleman (Checklist back)	1.00	.20
357	Bob McClure	.25	.11
358	Lou Whitaker	1.50	.70
359	Randy Moffitt	.25	.11
360	Darrell Porter DP	.25	.11
361	Wayne Garland	.25	.11
362	Danny Goodwin	.25	.11
363	Wayne Gross	.25	.11
364	Ray Burris	.25	.11
365	Bobby Murcer	.50	.23
366	Rob Dressler	.25	.11
367	Billy Smith	.25	.11
368	Willie Aikens	.25	.11
369	Jim Kern	.25	.11
370	Cesar Cedeno	.50	.23
371	Jack Morris	1.00	.45
372	Joel Youngblood	.25	.11
373	Dan Petry DP	.25	.11
374	Jim Gantner	.50	.23
375	Ross Grimsley	.25	.11
376	Gary Allenson	.25	.11
377	Junior Kennedy	.25	.11
378	Jerry Mumphrey	.25	.11
379	Kevin Bell	.25	.11
380	Garry Maddox	.50	.23
381	Cubs Team/Mgr. Preston Gomez	1.00	.20
382	Dave Freisleben	.25	.11
383	Ed Ott	.25	.11
384	Joey McLaughlin	.25	.11
385	Enos Cabell	.25	.11
386	Darrell Jackson	.25	.11
387A	Fred Stanley YL	5.00	2.20
387B	Fred Stanley (Red name on front)	.25	.11
388	Mike Paxton	.25	.11
389	Pete LaCock	.25	.11
390	Fergie Jenkins	1.50	.70
391	Tony Armas DP	.25	.11
392	Milt Wilcox	.25	.11
393	Ozzie Smith	20.00	9.00
394	Reggie Cleveland	.25	.11
395	Ellis Valentine	.25	.11
396	Dan Meyer	.25	.11
397	Roy Thomas DP	.10	.05
398	Barry Foote	.25	.11
399	Mike Proly DP	.10	.05
400	George Foster	.50	.23
401	Pete Falcone	.25	.11
402	Merv Rettenmund	.25	.11
403	Pete Redfern DP	.10	.05
404	Orioles Team/Mgr. Earl Weaver (Checklist back)	1.00	.20
405	Dwight Evans	.50	.23
406	Paul Molitor	10.00	4.50
407	Tony Solaita	.25	.11
408	Bill North	.25	.11
409	Paul Splittorff	.25	.11
410	Bobby Bonds	1.00	.45
411	Frank LaCorte	.25	.11
412	Thad Bosley	.25	.11
413	Allen Ripley	.25	.11
414	George Scott	.50	.23
415	Bill Atkinson	.25	.11
416	Tom Brookens	.25	.11
417	Craig Chamberlain DP	.10	.05
418	Roger Freed DP	.10	.05
419	Vic Correll	.25	.11
420	Butch Hobson	.25	.11
421	Doug Bird	.25	.11
422	Larry Milbourne	.25	.11
423	Dave Frost	.25	.11
424	Yankees Team/Mgr. Dick Howser (Checklist back)	1.00	.20
425	Mark Belanger	.50	.23
426	Grant Jackson	.25	.11
427	Tom Hutton DP	.10	.05
428	Pat Zachry	.25	.11
429	Duane Kuiper	.25	.11
430	Larry Hisle DP	.10	.05
431	Mike Krukow	.25	.11
432	Willie Norwood	.25	.11
433	Rich Gale	.25	.11
434	Johnnie LeMaster	.25	.11
435	Don Gullett	.50	.23
436	Billy Almon	.25	.11
437	Joe Niekro	.50	.23
438	Dave Revering	.25	.11
439	Mike Phillips	.25	.11
440	Don Sutton	1.50	.70
441	Eric Soderholm	.25	.11
442	Jorge Orta	.25	.11
443	Mike Parrott	.25	.11
444	Alvis Woods	.25	.11
445	Mark Fidrych	1.50	.70
446	Duffy Dyer	.25	.11
447	Nino Espinosa	.25	.11
448	Jim Wohlford	.25	.11
449	Doug Bair	.25	.11
450	George Brett	12.00	5.50
451	Indians Team/Mgr. Dave Garcia (Checklist back)	.50	.10
452	Steve Dillard	.25	.11
453	Mike Bacsik	.25	.11
454	Tom Donohue	.25	.11
455	Mike Torrez	.25	.11
456	Frank Taveras	.25	.11
457	Bert Blyleven	1.00	.45
458	Billy Sample	.25	.11
459	Mickey Lolich DP	.25	.11
460	Willie Randolph	.50	.23
461	Dwayne Murphy	.25	.11
462	Mike Sadek DP	.10	.05
463	Jerry Royster	.25	.11
464	John Denny	.25	.11
465	Rick Monday	.25	.11
466	Mike Squires	.25	.11
467	Jesse Jefferson	.25	.11
468	Aurelio Rodriguez	.25	.11
469	Randy Niemann DP	.10	.05
470	Bob Boone	1.00	.45
471	Hosken Powell DP	.10	.05
472	Willie Hernandez	.50	.23
473	Bump Wills	.25	.11
474	Steve Busby	.25	.11
475	Cesar Geronimo	.25	.11
476	Bob Shirley	.25	.11
477	Buck Martinez	.25	.11
478	Gil Flores	.25	.11
479	Expos Team/Mgr. Dick Williams (Checklist back)	1.00	.20
480	Bob Watson	.50	.23
481	Tom Paciorek	.50	.23
482	Rickey Henderson UER (7 steals at Modesto, should be at Fresno)	70.00	32.00
483	Bo Diaz	.25	.11
484	Checklist 364-484	1.00	.20
485	Mickey Rivers	.50	.23
486	Mike Tyson DP	.10	.05
487	Wayne Nordhagen	.25	.11
488	Roy Howell	.25	.11
489	Preston Hanna DP	.10	.05
490	Lee May	.50	.23
491	Steve Mura DP	.10	.05
492	Todd Cruz	.25	.11
493	Jerry Martin	.25	.11
494	Craig Minetto	.25	.11
495	Bake McBride	.25	.11
496	Silvio Martinez	.25	.11
497	Jim Mason	.25	.11
498	Danny Darwin	.25	.11
499	Giants Team/Mgr. Dave Bristol	.25	.20
500	Tom Seaver	4.00	1.80
501	Rennie Stennett	.25	.11
502	Rich Wortham DP	.10	.05
503	Mike Cubbage	.25	.11
504	Gene Garber	.50	.23
505	Bert Campaneris	.50	.23
506	Tom Buskey	.25	.11
507	Leon Roberts	.25	.11
508	U.L. Washington	.25	.11
509	Ed Glynn	.25	.11
510	Ron Cey	1.00	.45
511	Eric Wilkins	.25	.11
512	Jose Cardenal	.25	.11
513	Tom Dixon DP	.10	.05
514	Steve Ontiveros	.25	.11
515	Mike Caldwell UER 1979 loss total reads 96 instead of 6#	.25	.11
516	Hector Cruz	.25	.11
517	Don Stanhouse	.25	.11
518	Nelson Norman	.25	.11
519	Steve Nicosia	.25	.11
520	Steve Rogers	.25	.11
521	Ken Brett	.25	.11
522	Jim Morrison	.25	.11
523	Ken Henderson	.25	.11
524	Jim Wright DP	.10	.05
525	Clint Hurdle	.25	.11
526	Phillies Team/Mgr. Dallas Green (Checklist back)	1.00	.20
527	Doug Rau DP	.10	.05
528	Adrian Devine	.25	.11
529	Jim Barr	.25	.11
530	Jim Sundberg DP	.25	.11
531	Eric Rasmussen	.25	.11
532	Willie Horton	.50	.23
533	Checklist 485-605	1.00	.20
534	Andre Thornton	.50	.23
535	Bob Forsch	.25	.11
536	Lee Lacy	.25	.11
537	Alex Trevino	.25	.11
538	Joe Strain	.25	.11
539	Rudy May	.25	.11
540	Pete Rose	6.00	2.70
541	Miguel Dilone	.25	.11
542	Joe Coleman	.25	.11
543	Pat Kelly	.25	.11
544	Rick Sutcliffe	1.00	.45

545	Jeff Burroughs	.50	.23
546	Rick Langford	.25	.11
547	John Wathan	.25	.11
548	Dave Rajsich	.25	.11
549	Larry Wolfe	.25	.11
550	Ken Griffey Sr.	1.00	.45
551	Pirates Team/Mgr.	1.00	.20
	Chuck Tanner (Checklist back)		
552	Bill Nahorodny	.25	.11
553	Dick Davis	.25	.11
554	Art Howe	.50	.23
555	Ed Figueroa	.25	.11
556	Joe Rudi	.50	.23
557	Mark Lee	.25	.11
558	Alfredo Griffin	.25	.11
559	Dale Murray	.25	.11
560	Dave Lopes	.50	.23
561	Eddie Whitson	.25	.11
562	Joe Wallis	.25	.11
563	Will McEnaney	.25	.11
564	Rick Manning	.25	.11
565	Dennis Leonard	.50	.23
566	Bud Harrelson	.50	.23
567	Skip Lockwood	.25	.11
568	Gary Roenicke	.50	.23
569	Terry Kennedy	.50	.23
570	Roy Smalley	.25	.11
571	Joe Sambito	.25	.11
572	Jerry Morales DP	.10	.05
573	Kent Tekulve	.50	.23
574	Scot Thompson	.25	.11
575	Ken Kravec	.25	.11
576	Jim Dwyer	.25	.11
577	Blue Jays Team/Mgr.	1.00	.20
	Bobby Mattick (Checklist back)		
578	Scott Sanderson	.50	.23
579	Charlie Moore	.25	.11
580	Nolan Ryan	20.00	9.00
581	Bob Bailor	.25	.11
582	Brian Doyle	.25	.11
583	Bob Stinson	.25	.11
584	Kurt Bevacqua	.25	.11
585	Al Hrabosky	.25	.11
586	Mitchell Page	.25	.11
587	Garry Templeton	.50	.23
588	Greg Minton	.25	.11
589	Chet Lemon	.50	.23
590	Jim Palmer	2.00	.90
591	Rick Cerone	.25	.11
592	Jon Matlack	.25	.11
593	Jesus Alou	.25	.11
594	Dick Tidrow	.25	.11
595	Don Money	.25	.11
596	Rick Matula	.25	.11
597	Tom Poquette	.25	.11
598	Fred Kendall DP	.10	.05
599	Mike Norris	.25	.11
600	Reggie Jackson	5.00	2.20
601	Buddy Schultz	.25	.11
602	Brian Downing	.25	.11
603	Jack Billingham DP	.10	.05
604	Glenn Adams	.25	.11
605	Terry Forster	.25	.11
606	Reds Team/Mgr.	1.00	.20
	John McNamara (Checklist back)		
607	Woodie Fryman	.25	.11
608	Alan Bannister	.25	.11
609	Ron Reed	.25	.11
610	Willie Stargell	1.50	.70
611	Jerry Garvin DP	.10	.05
612	Cliff Johnson	.25	.11
613	Randy Stein	.25	.11
614	John Hiller	.25	.11
615	Doug DeCinces	.50	.23
616	Gene Richards	.25	.11
617	Joaquin Andujar	.50	.23
618	Bob Montgomery DP	.10	.05
619	Sergio Ferrer	.25	.11
620	Richie Zisk	.25	.11
621	Bob Grich	.50	.23
622	Mario Soto	.25	.11
623	Gorman Thomas	.50	.23
624	Lerrin LaGrow	.25	.11
625	Chris Chambliss	.50	.23
626	Tigers Team/Mgr.	1.00	.20
	Sparky Anderson (Checklist back)		
627	Pedro Borbon	.25	.11
628	Doug Capilla	.25	.11
629	Jim Todd	.25	.11
630	Larry Bowa	.50	.23
631	Mark Littell	.25	.11
632	Barry Bonnell	.25	.11
633	Bob Apodaca	.25	.11
634	Glenn Borgmann DP	.10	.05
635	John Candelaria	.50	.23
636	Toby Harrah	.50	.23
637	Joe Simpson	.25	.11
638	Mark Clear	.25	.11
639	Larry Biittner	.25	.11
640	Mike Flanagan	.50	.23
641	Ed Kranepool	.25	.11
642	Ken Forsch DP	.10	.05
643	John Mayberry	.50	.23
644	Charlie Hough	.50	.23
645	Rick Burleson	.25	.11
646	Checklist 606-726	1.00	.20
647	Milt May	.25	.11
648	Roy White	.25	.11
649	Tom Griffin	.25	.11
650	Joe Morgan	2.00	.90
651	Rollie Fingers	1.50	.70
652	Mario Mendoza	.25	.11
653	Stan Bahnsen	.25	.11
654	Bruce Boisclair DP	.10	.05
655	Tug McGraw	.50	.23
656	Larvell Blanks	.25	.11
657	Dave Edwards	.25	.11
658	Chris Knapp	.25	.11
659	Brewers Team/Mgr.	1.00	.20
	George Bamberger (Checklist back)		
660	Rusty Staub	.50	.23
661	Orioles Rookies	.50	.23
	Mark Corey / Dave Ford / Wayne Krenchicki		
662	Red Sox Rookies	.50	.23
	Joel Finch / Mike O'Berry / Chuck Rainey		
663	Angels Rookies	1.00	.45
	Ralph Botting / Bob Clark / Dickie Thon		
664	White Sox Rookies	.50	.23
	Mike Colbern / Guy Hoffman / Dewey Robinson		
665	Indians Rookies	1.00	.45
	Larry Andersen / Bobby Cuellar / Sandy Wihtol		
666	Tigers Rookies	.50	.23
	Mike Chris / Al Greene / Bruce Robbins		
667	Royals Rookies	1.00	.45
	Renie Martin / Bill Paschall / Dan Quisenberry		
668	Brewers Rookies	.50	.23
	Danny Boitano / Willie Mueller / Lenn Sakata		
669	Twins Rookies	.50	.23
	Dan Graham / Rick Sofield / Gary Ward		
670	Yankees Rookies	.50	.23
	Bobby Brown / Brad Gulden / Darryl Jones		
671	A's Rookies	1.50	.70
	Derek Bryant / Brian Kingman / Mike Morgan		
672	Mariners Rookies	.50	.23
	Charlie Beamon / Rodney Craig / Rafael Vasquez		
673	Rangers Rookies	.50	.23
	Brian Allard / Jerry Don Gleaton / Greg Mahlberg		
674	Blue Jays Rookies	.50	.23
	Butch Edge / Pat Kelly / Ted Wilborn		
675	Braves Rookies	.50	.23
	Bruce Benedict / Larry Bradford / Eddie Miller		
676	Cubs Rookies	.50	.23
	Dave Geisel / Steve Macko / Karl Pagel		
677	Reds Rookies	.50	.23
	Art DeFreites / Frank Pastore / Harry Spilman		
678	Astros Rookies	.50	.23
	Reggie Baldwin / Alan Knicely / Pete Ladd		
679	Dodgers Rookies	1.00	.45
	Joe Beckwith / Mickey Hatcher / Dave Patterson		
680	Expos Rookies	1.00	.45
	Tony Bernazard / Randy Miller / John Tamargo		
681	Mets Rookies	1.50	.70
	Dan Norman / Jesse Orosco / Mike Scott		
682	Phillies Rookies	.50	.23
	Ramon Aviles / Dickie Noles / Kevin Saucier		
683	Pirates Rookies	.50	.23
	Dorian Boyland / Alberto Lois / Harry Saferight		
684	Cardinals Rookies	1.00	.45
	George Frazier / Tom Herr / Dan O'Brien		
685	Padres Rookies	.50	.23
	Tim Flannery / Brian Greer / Jim Wilhelm		
686	Giants Rookies	.50	.23
	Greg Johnston / Dennis Littlejohn / Phil Nastu		
687	Mike Heath DP	.10	.05
688	Steve Stone	.50	.23
689	Red Sox Team/Mgr.	1.00	.20
	Don Zimmer (Checklist back)		
690	Tommy John	1.00	.45
691	Ivan DeJesus	.25	.11
692	Rawly Eastwick DP	.10	.05
693	Craig Kusick	.25	.11
694	Jim Rooker	.25	.11
695	Reggie Smith	.50	.23
696	Julio Gonzalez	.25	.11
697	David Clyde	.25	.11
698	Oscar Gamble	.50	.23
699	Floyd Bannister	.25	.11
700	Rod Carew DP	1.50	.70
701	Ken Oberkfell	.25	.11
702	Ed Farmer	.25	.11
703	Otto Velez	.25	.11
704	Gene Tenace	.50	.23
705	Freddie Patek	.25	.11
706	Tippy Martinez	.25	.11
707	Elliott Maddox	.25	.11
708	Bob Tolan	.25	.11
709	Pat Underwood	.25	.11
710	Graig Nettles	1.00	.45
711	Bob Galasso	.25	.11
712	Rodney Scott	.25	.11

❏ 713	Terry Whitfield	.25	.11
❏ 714	Fred Norman	.25	.11
❏ 715	Sal Bando	.50	.23
❏ 716	Lynn McGlothen	.25	.11
❏ 717	Mickey Klutts DP	.10	.05
❏ 718	Greg Gross	.25	.11
❏ 719	Don Robinson	.50	.23
❏ 720	Carl Yastrzemski DP	2.00	.90
❏ 721	Paul Hartzell	.25	.11
❏ 722	Jose Cruz	.50	.23
❏ 723	Shane Rawley	.25	.11
❏ 724	Jerry White	.25	.11
❏ 725	Rick Wise	.25	.11
❏ 726	Steve Yeager	1.00	.20

1981 Topps

	NRMT	VG-E
COMPLETE SET (726)	50.00	22.00
COMMON CARD (1-726)	.15	.07
MINOR STARS	.40	.18
SEMISTARS	.75	.35
UNLISTED STARS	1.50	.70

❏ 1	Batting Leaders	2.50	1.10
	George Brett		
	Bill Buckner		
❏ 2	Home Run Leaders	1.50	.70
	Reggie Jackson		
	Ben Oglivie		
	Mike Schmidt		
❏ 3	RBI Leaders	1.50	.70
	Cecil Cooper		
	Mike Schmidt		
❏ 4	Stolen Base Leaders	2.00	.90
	Rickey Henderson		
	Ron LeFlore		
❏ 5	Victory Leaders	1.50	.70
	Steve Stone		
	Steve Carlton		
❏ 6	Strikeout Leaders	1.50	.70
	Len Barker		
	Steve Carlton		
❏ 7	ERA Leaders	.75	.35
	Rudy May		
	Don Sutton		
❏ 8	Leading Firemen	.75	.35
	Dan Quisenberry		
	Rollie Fingers		
	Tom Hume		
❏ 9	Pete LaCock DP	.10	.05
❏ 10	Mike Flanagan	.40	.18
❏ 11	Jim Wohlford DP	.10	.05
❏ 12	Mark Clear	.15	.07
❏ 13	Joe Charboneau	1.50	.70
❏ 14	John Tudor	.40	.18
❏ 15	Larry Parrish	.15	.07
❏ 16	Ron Davis	.15	.07
❏ 17	Cliff Johnson	.15	.07
❏ 18	Glenn Adams	.15	.07
❏ 19	Jim Clancy	.15	.07
❏ 20	Jeff Burroughs	.15	.07
❏ 21	Ron Oester	.15	.07
❏ 22	Danny Darwin	.15	.07
❏ 23	Alex Trevino	.15	.07
❏ 24	Don Stanhouse	.15	.07
❏ 25	Sixto Lezcano	.15	.07
❏ 26	U.L. Washington	.15	.07
❏ 27	Champ Summers DP	.10	.05
❏ 28	Enrique Romo	.15	.07
❏ 29	Gene Tenace	.40	.18
❏ 30	Jack Clark	.40	.18
❏ 31	Checklist 1-121 DP	.15	.07
❏ 32	Ken Oberkfell	.15	.07
❏ 33	Rick Honeycutt	.15	.07
❏ 34	Aurelio Rodriguez	.15	.07
❏ 35	Mitchell Page	.15	.07
❏ 36	Ed Farmer	.15	.07
❏ 37	Gary Roenicke	.15	.07
❏ 38	Win Remmerswaal	.15	.07
❏ 39	Tom Veryzer	.15	.07
❏ 40	Tug McGraw	.40	.18
❏ 41	Ranger Rookies	.15	.07
	Bob Babcock		
	John Butcher		
	Jerry Don Gleaton		
❏ 42	Jerry White DP	.10	.05
❏ 43	Jose Morales	.15	.07
❏ 44	Larry McWilliams	.15	.07
❏ 45	Enos Cabell	.15	.07
❏ 46	Rick Bosetti	.15	.07
❏ 47	Ken Brett	.15	.07
❏ 48	Dave Skaggs	.15	.07
❏ 49	Bob Shirley	.15	.07
❏ 50	Dave Lopes	.40	.18
❏ 51	Bill Robinson DP	.15	.07
❏ 52	Hector Cruz	.15	.07
❏ 53	Kevin Saucier	.15	.07
❏ 54	Ivan DeJesus	.15	.07
❏ 55	Mike Norris	.15	.07
❏ 56	Buck Martinez	.15	.07
❏ 57	Dave Roberts	.15	.07
❏ 58	Joel Youngblood	.15	.07
❏ 59	Dan Petry	.15	.07
❏ 60	Willie Randolph	.40	.18
❏ 61	Butch Wynegar	.15	.07
❏ 62	Joe Pettini	.15	.07
❏ 63	Steve Renko DP	.10	.05
❏ 64	Brian Asselstine	.15	.07
❏ 65	Scott McGregor	.15	.07
❏ 66	Royals Rookies	.15	.07
	Manny Castillo		
	Tim Ireland		
	Mike Jones		
❏ 67	Ken Kravec	.15	.07
❏ 68	Matt Alexander DP	.10	.05
❏ 69	Ed Halicki	.15	.07
❏ 70	Al Oliver DP	.40	.18
❏ 71	Hal Dues	.15	.07
❏ 72	Barry Evans DP	.10	.05
❏ 73	Doug Bair	.15	.07
❏ 74	Mike Hargrove	.40	.18
❏ 75	Reggie Smith	.40	.18
❏ 76	Mario Mendoza	.15	.07
❏ 77	Mike Barlow	.15	.07
❏ 78	Steve Dillard	.15	.07
❏ 79	Bruce Robbins	.15	.07
❏ 80	Rusty Staub	.40	.18
❏ 81	Dave Stapleton	.15	.07
❏ 82	Astros Rookies DP	.15	.07
	Danny Heep		
	Alan Knicely		
	Bobby Sprowl		
❏ 83	Mike Proly	.15	.07
❏ 84	Johnnie LeMaster	.15	.07
❏ 85	Mike Caldwell	.15	.07
❏ 86	Wayne Gross	.15	.07
❏ 87	Rick Camp	.15	.07
❏ 88	Joe Lefebvre	.15	.07
❏ 89	Darrell Jackson	.15	.07
❏ 90	Bake McBride	.15	.07
❏ 91	Tim Stoddard DP	.10	.05
❏ 92	Mike Easler	.15	.07
❏ 93	Ed Glynn DP	.10	.05
❏ 94	Harry Spilman DP	.10	.05
❏ 95	Jim Sundberg	.40	.18
❏ 96	A's Rookies	.15	.07
	Dave Beard		
	Ernie Camacho		
	Pat Dempsey		
❏ 97	Chris Speier	.15	.07
❏ 98	Clint Hurdle	.15	.07
❏ 99	Eric Wilkins	.15	.07
❏ 100	Rod Carew	1.50	.70
❏ 101	Benny Ayala	.15	.07
❏ 102	Dave Tobik	.15	.07
❏ 103	Jerry Martin	.15	.07
❏ 104	Terry Forster	.15	.07
❏ 105	Jose Cruz	.40	.18
❏ 106	Don Money	.15	.07
❏ 107	Rich Wortham	.15	.07
❏ 108	Bruce Benedict	.15	.07
❏ 109	Mike Scott	.40	.18
❏ 110	Carl Yastrzemski	1.50	.70
❏ 111	Greg Minton	.15	.07
❏ 112	White Sox Rookies	.15	.07
	Rusty Kuntz		
	Fran Mullins		
	Leo Sutherland		
❏ 113	Mike Phillips	.15	.07
❏ 114	Tom Underwood	.15	.07
❏ 115	Roy Smalley	.15	.07
❏ 116	Joe Simpson	.15	.07
❏ 117	Pete Falcone	.15	.07
❏ 118	Kurt Bevacqua	.15	.07
❏ 119	Tippy Martinez	.15	.07
❏ 120	Larry Bowa	.40	.18
❏ 121	Larry Harlow	.15	.07
❏ 122	John Denny	.15	.07
❏ 123	Al Cowens	.15	.07
❏ 124	Jerry Garvin	.15	.07
❏ 125	Andre Dawson	1.50	.70
❏ 126	Charlie Leibrandt	.75	.35
❏ 127	Rudy Law	.15	.07
❏ 128	Gary Allenson DP	.10	.05
❏ 129	Art Howe	.15	.07
❏ 130	Larry Gura	.15	.07
❏ 131	Keith Moreland	.40	.18
❏ 132	Tommy Boggs	.15	.07
❏ 133	Jeff Cox	.15	.07
❏ 134	Steve Mura	.15	.07
❏ 135	Gorman Thomas	.40	.18
❏ 136	Doug Capilla	.15	.07
❏ 137	Hosken Powell	.15	.07
❏ 138	Rich Dotson DP	.15	.07
❏ 139	Oscar Gamble	.15	.07
❏ 140	Bob Forsch	.15	.07
❏ 141	Miguel Dilone	.15	.07
❏ 142	Jackson Todd	.15	.07
❏ 143	Dan Meyer	.15	.07
❏ 144	Allen Ripley	.15	.07
❏ 145	Mickey Rivers	.40	.18
❏ 146	Bobby Castillo	.15	.07
❏ 147	Dale Berra	.15	.07
❏ 148	Randy Niemann	.15	.07
❏ 149	Joe Nolan	.15	.07
❏ 150	Mark Fidrych	1.50	.70
❏ 151	Claudell Washington	.15	.07
❏ 152	John Urrea	.15	.07
❏ 153	Tom Poquette	.15	.07
❏ 154	Rick Langford	.15	.07
❏ 155	Chris Chambliss	.40	.18
❏ 156	Bob McClure	.15	.07
❏ 157	John Wathan	.15	.07
❏ 158	Fergie Jenkins	1.50	.70
❏ 159	Brian Doyle	.15	.07
❏ 160	Garry Maddox	.15	.07
❏ 161	Dan Graham	.15	.07
❏ 162	Doug Corbett	.15	.07
❏ 163	Bill Almon	.15	.07
❏ 164	LaMarr Hoyt	.40	.18
❏ 165	Tony Scott	.15	.07
❏ 166	Floyd Bannister	.15	.07
❏ 167	Terry Whitfield	.15	.07
❏ 168	Don Robinson DP	.10	.05
❏ 169	John Mayberry	.15	.07
❏ 170	Ross Grimsley	.15	.07
❏ 171	Gene Richards	.15	.07
❏ 172	Gary Woods	.15	.07
❏ 173	Bump Wills	.15	.07
❏ 174	Doug Rau	.15	.07
❏ 175	Dave Collins	.15	.07
❏ 176	Mike Krukow	.15	.07
❏ 177	Rick Peters	.15	.07
❏ 178	Jim Essian DP	.10	.05
❏ 179	Rudy May	.15	.07
❏ 180	Pete Rose	3.00	1.35
❏ 181	Elias Sosa	.15	.07
❏ 182	Bob Grich	.40	.18
❏ 183	Dick Davis DP	.10	.05

184	Jim Dwyer	.15	.07
185	Dennis Leonard	.15	.07
186	Wayne Nordhagen	.15	.07
187	Mike Parrott	.15	.07
188	Doug DeCinces	.40	.18
189	Craig Swan	.15	.07
190	Cesar Cedeno	.40	.18
191	Rick Sutcliffe	.40	.18
192	Braves Rookies	.40	.18
	Terry Harper		
	Ed Miller		
	Rafael Ramirez		
193	Pete Vuckovich	.40	.18
194	Rod Scurry	.15	.07
195	Rich Murray	.15	.07
196	Duffy Dyer	.15	.07
197	Jim Kern	.15	.07
198	Jerry Dybzinski	.15	.07
199	Chuck Rainey	.15	.07
200	George Foster	.40	.18
201	Johnny Bench RB	.75	.35
	Most homers catchers		
202	Steve Carlton RB	.75	.35
	Most strikeouts,		
	lefthander, lifetime		
203	Bill Gullickson RB	.75	.35
	Most SO's, game, rookie		
204	Ron LeFlore RB	.40	.18
	Rodney Scott RB		
	Most stolen bases		
	teammates, season		
205	Pete Rose RB	1.50	.70
	Most cons. seasons		
	600 or more at-bats		
206	Mike Schmidt RB	.75	.35
	Most homers, 3rd baseman, season		
207	Ozzie Smith RB	2.00	.90
	Most assists,		
	season, shortstop		
208	Willie Wilson RB	.40	.18
	Most AB's season		
209	Dickie Thon DP	.40	.18
210	Jim Palmer	1.50	.70
211	Derrel Thomas	.15	.07
212	Steve Nicosia	.15	.07
213	Al Holland	.15	.07
214	Angels Rookies	.15	.07
	Ralph Botting		
	Jim Dorsey		
	John Harris		
215	Larry Hisle	.15	.07
216	John Henry Johnson	.15	.07
217	Rich Hebner	.15	.07
218	Paul Splittorff	.15	.07
219	Ken Landreaux	.15	.07
220	Tom Seaver	2.00	.90
221	Bob Davis	.15	.07
222	Jorge Orta	.15	.07
223	Roy Lee Jackson	.15	.07
224	Pat Zachry	.15	.07
225	Ruppert Jones	.15	.07
226	Manny Sanguillen DP	.10	.05
227	Fred Martinez	.15	.07
228	Tom Paciorek	.40	.18
229	Rollie Fingers	1.50	.70
230	George Hendrick	.40	.18
231	Joe Beckwith	.15	.07
232	Mickey Klutts	.15	.07
233	Skip Lockwood	.15	.07
234	Lou Whitaker	1.50	.70
235	Scott Sanderson	.15	.07
236	Mike Ivie	.15	.07
237	Charlie Moore	.15	.07
238	Willie Hernandez	.40	.18
239	Rick Miller DP	.10	.05
240	Nolan Ryan	8.00	3.60
241	Checklist 122-242 DP	.15	.07
242	Chet Lemon	.15	.07
243	Sal Butera	.15	.07
244	Cardinals Rookies	.15	.07
	Tito Landrum		
	Al Olmsted		
	Andy Rincon		
245	Ed Figueroa	.15	.07
246	Ed Ott DP	.10	.05
247	Glenn Hubbard DP	.10	.05
248	Joey McLaughlin	.15	.07
249	Larry Cox	.15	.07
250	Ron Guidry	.40	.18
251	Tom Brookens	.15	.07
252	Victor Cruz	.15	.07
253	Dave Bergman	.15	.07
254	Ozzie Smith	5.00	2.20
255	Mark Littell	.15	.07
256	Bombo Rivera	.15	.07
257	Rennie Stennett	.15	.07
258	Joe Price	.15	.07
259	Mets Rookies	1.50	.70
	Juan Berenguer		
	Hubie Brooks		
	Mookie Wilson		
260	Ron Cey	.40	.18
261	Rickey Henderson	6.00	2.70
262	Sammy Stewart	.15	.07
263	Brian Downing	.40	.18
264	Jim Norris	.15	.07
265	John Candelaria	.40	.18
266	Tom Herr	.15	.07
267	Stan Bahnsen	.15	.07
268	Jerry Royster	.15	.07
269	Ken Forsch	.15	.07
270	Greg Luzinski	.40	.18
271	Bill Castro	.15	.07
272	Bruce Kimm	.15	.07
273	Stan Papi	.15	.07
274	Craig Chamberlain	.15	.07
275	Dwight Evans	.75	.35
276	Dan Spillner	.15	.07
277	Alfredo Griffin	.15	.07
278	Rick Sofield	.15	.07
279	Bob Knepper	.15	.07
280	Ken Griffey	.75	.35
281	Fred Stanley	.15	.07
282	Mariners Rookies	.15	.07
	Rick Anderson		
	Greg Biercevicz		
	Rodney Craig		
283	Billy Sample	.15	.07
284	Brian Kingman	.15	.07
285	Jerry Turner	.15	.07
286	Dave Frost	.15	.07
287	Lenn Sakata	.15	.07
288	Bob Clark	.15	.07
289	Mickey Hatcher	.40	.18
290	Bob Boone DP	.40	.18
291	Aurelio Lopez	.15	.07
292	Mike Squires	.15	.07
293	Charlie Lea	.15	.07
294	Mike Tyson DP	.10	.05
295	Hal McRae	.40	.18
296	Bill Nahorodny DP	.10	.05
297	Bob Bailor	.15	.07
298	Buddy Solomon	.15	.07
299	Elliott Maddox	.15	.07
300	Paul Molitor	3.00	1.35
301	Matt Keough	.15	.07
302	Dodgers Rookies	3.00	1.35
	Jack Perconte		
	Mike Scioscia		
	Fernando Valenzuela		
303	Johnny Oates	.40	.18
304	John Castino	.15	.07
305	Ken Clay	.15	.07
306	Juan Beniquez DP	.10	.05
307	Gene Garber	.15	.07
308	Rick Manning	.15	.07
309	Luis Salazar	.15	.07
310	Vida Blue DP	.15	.07
311	Freddie Patek	.15	.07
312	Rick Rhoden	.15	.07
313	Luis Pujols	.15	.07
314	Rich Dauer	.15	.07
315	Kirk Gibson	3.00	1.35
316	Craig Minetto	.15	.07
317	Lonnie Smith	.40	.18
318	Steve Yeager	.15	.07
319	Rowland Office	.15	.07
320	Tom Burgmeier	.15	.07
321	Leon Durham	.40	.18
322	Neil Allen	.15	.07
323	Jim Morrison DP	.10	.05
324	Mike Willis	.15	.07
325	Ray Knight	.40	.18
326	Biff Pocoroba	.15	.07
327	Moose Haas	.15	.07
328	Twins Rookies	.15	.07
	Dave Engle		
	Greg Johnston		
	Gary Ward		
329	Joaquin Andujar	.40	.18
330	Frank White	.40	.18
331	Dennis Lamp	.15	.07
332	Lee Lacy DP	.10	.05
333	Sid Monge	.15	.07
334	Dane Iorg	.15	.07
335	Rick Cerone	.15	.07
336	Eddie Whitson	.15	.07
337	Lynn Jones	.15	.07
338	Checklist 243-363	.75	.35
339	John Ellis	.15	.07
340	Bruce Kison	.15	.07
341	Dwayne Murphy	.15	.07
342	Eric Rasmussen DP	.10	.05
343	Frank Taveras	.15	.07
344	Byron McLaughlin	.15	.07
345	Warren Cromartie	.15	.07
346	Larry Christenson DP	.10	.05
347	Harold Baines	8.00	3.60
348	Bob Sykes	.15	.07
349	Glenn Hoffman	.15	.07
350	J.R. Richard	.40	.18
351	Otto Velez	.15	.07
352	Dick Tidrow DP	.10	.05
353	Terry Kennedy	.15	.07
354	Mario Soto	.15	.07
355	Bob Horner	.40	.18
356	Padres Rookies	.15	.07
	George Stablein		
	Craig Stimac		
	Tom Tellmann		
357	Jim Slaton	.15	.07
358	Mark Wagner	.15	.07
359	Tom Hausman	.15	.07
360	Willie Wilson	.40	.18
361	Joe Strain	.15	.07
362	Bo Diaz	.15	.07
363	Geoff Zahn	.15	.07
364	Mike Davis	.15	.07
365	Graig Nettles DP	.40	.18
366	Mike Ramsey	.15	.07
367	Dennis Martinez	.75	.35
368	Leon Roberts	.15	.07
369	Frank Tanana	.40	.18
370	Dave Winfield	1.50	.70
371	Charlie Hough	.40	.18
372	Jay Johnstone	.15	.07
373	Pat Underwood	.15	.07
374	Tommy Hutton	.15	.07
375	Dave Concepcion	.40	.18
376	Ron Reed	.15	.07
377	Jerry Morales	.15	.07
378	Dave Rader	.15	.07
379	Lary Sorensen	.15	.07
380	Willie Stargell	1.50	.70
381	Cubs Rookies	.15	.07
	Carlos Lezcano		
	Steve Macko		
	Randy Martz		
382	Paul Mirabella	.15	.07
383	Eric Soderholm DP	.10	.05
384	Mike Sadek	.15	.07
385	Joe Sambito	.15	.07
386	Dave Edwards	.15	.07
387	Phil Niekro	1.50	.70
388	Andre Thornton	.40	.18
389	Marty Pattin	.15	.07
390	Cesar Geronimo	.15	.07
391	Dave Lemanczyk DP	.10	.05
392	Lance Parrish	.40	.18
393	Broderick Perkins	.15	.07
394	Woodie Fryman	.15	.07
395	Scot Thompson	.15	.07
396	Bill Campbell	.15	.07
397	Julio Cruz	.15	.07
398	Ross Baumgarten	.15	.07
399	Orioles Rookies	1.50	.70
	Mike Boddicker		
	Mark Corey		

Floyd Rayford

#	Card	Price	Price
❏ 400	Reggie Jackson WS	2.00	.90
❏ 401	George Brett ALCS	2.00	.90
❏ 402	NL Champs	.75	.35
	Phillies squeak		
	past Astros		
	(Phillies celebrating)		
❏ 403	Larry Bowa WS	.75	.35
❏ 404	Tug McGraw WS	.75	.35
❏ 405	Nino Espinosa	.15	.07
❏ 406	Dickie Noles	.15	.07
❏ 407	Ernie Whitt	.15	.07
❏ 408	Fernando Arroyo	.15	.07
❏ 409	Larry Herndon	.15	.07
❏ 410	Bert Campaneris	.40	.18
❏ 411	Terry Puhl	.15	.07
❏ 412	Britt Burns	.15	.07
❏ 413	Tony Bernazard	.15	.07
❏ 414	John Pacella DP	.15	.07
❏ 415	Ben Oglivie	.40	.18
❏ 416	Gary Alexander	.15	.07
❏ 417	Dan Schatzeder	.15	.07
❏ 418	Bobby Brown	.15	.07
❏ 419	Tom Hume	.15	.07
❏ 420	Keith Hernandez	.40	.18
❏ 421	Bob Stanley	.15	.07
❏ 422	Dan Ford	.15	.07
❏ 423	Shane Rawley	.15	.07
❏ 424	Yankees Rookies	.15	.07
	Tim Lollar		
	Bruce Robinson		
	Dennis Werth		
❏ 425	Al Bumbry	.40	.18
❏ 426	Warren Brusstar	.15	.07
❏ 427	John D'Acquisto	.15	.07
❏ 428	John Stearns	.15	.07
❏ 429	Mick Kelleher	.15	.07
❏ 430	Jim Bibby	.15	.07
❏ 431	Dave Roberts	.15	.07
❏ 432	Len Barker	.15	.07
❏ 433	Rance Mulliniks	.15	.07
❏ 434	Roger Erickson	.15	.07
❏ 435	Jim Spencer	.15	.07
❏ 436	Gary Lucas	.15	.07
❏ 437	Mike Heath DP	.10	.05
❏ 438	John Montefusco	.15	.07
❏ 439	Denny Walling	.15	.07
❏ 440	Jerry Reuss	.40	.18
❏ 441	Ken Reitz	.15	.07
❏ 442	Ron Pruitt	.15	.07
❏ 443	Jim Beattie DP	.10	.05
❏ 444	Garth Iorg	.15	.07
❏ 445	Ellis Valentine	.15	.07
❏ 446	Checklist 364-484	.75	.35
❏ 447	Junior Kennedy DP	.10	.05
❏ 448	Tim Corcoran	.15	.07
❏ 449	Paul Mitchell	.15	.07
❏ 450	Dave Kingman DP	.40	.18
❏ 451	Indians Rookies	.15	.07
	Chris Bando		
	Tom Brennan		
	Sandy Wihtol		
❏ 452	Renie Martin	.15	.07
❏ 453	Rob Wilfong DP	.10	.05
❏ 454	Andy Hassler	.15	.07
❏ 455	Rick Burleson	.15	.07
❏ 456	Jeff Reardon	1.50	.70
❏ 457	Mike Lum	.15	.07
❏ 458	Randy Jones	.15	.07
❏ 459	Greg Gross	.15	.07
❏ 460	Rich Gossage	.75	.35
❏ 461	Dave McKay	.15	.07
❏ 462	Jack Brohamer	.15	.07
❏ 463	Milt May	.15	.07
❏ 464	Adrian Devine	.15	.07
❏ 465	Bill Russell	.40	.18
❏ 466	Bob Molinaro	.15	.07
❏ 467	Dave Stieb	.40	.18
❏ 468	John Wockenfuss	.15	.07
❏ 469	Jeff Leonard	.40	.18
❏ 470	Manny Trillo	.15	.07
❏ 471	Mike Vail	.15	.07
❏ 472	Dyar Miller DP	.10	.05
❏ 473	Jose Cardenal	.15	.07
❏ 474	Mike LaCoss	.15	.07
❏ 475	Buddy Bell	.40	.18
❏ 476	Jerry Koosman	.40	.18
❏ 477	Luis Gomez	.15	.07
❏ 478	Juan Eichelberger	.15	.07
❏ 479	Expos Rookies	3.00	1.35
	Tim Raines		
	Roberto Ramos		
	Bobby Pate		
❏ 480	Carlton Fisk	1.50	.70
❏ 481	Bob Lacey DP	.10	.05
❏ 482	Jim Gantner	.40	.18
❏ 483	Mike Griffin	.15	.07
❏ 484	Max Venable DP	.10	.05
❏ 485	Garry Templeton	.15	.07
❏ 486	Marc Hill	.15	.07
❏ 487	Dewey Robinson	.15	.07
❏ 488	Damaso Garcia	.15	.07
❏ 489	John Littlefield	.15	.07
❏ 490	Eddie Murray	3.00	1.35
❏ 491	Gordy Pladson	.15	.07
❏ 492	Barry Foote	.15	.07
❏ 493	Dan Quisenberry	.40	.18
❏ 494	Bob Walk	.40	.18
❏ 495	Dusty Baker	.75	.35
❏ 496	Paul Dade	.15	.07
❏ 497	Fred Norman	.15	.07
❏ 498	Pat Putnam	.15	.07
❏ 499	Frank Pastore	.15	.07
❏ 500	Jim Rice	.40	.18
❏ 501	Tim Foli DP	.15	.05
❏ 502	Giants Rookies	.15	.07
	Chris Bourjos		
	Al Hargesheimer		
	Mike Rowland		
❏ 503	Steve McCatty	.15	.07
❏ 504	Dale Murphy	1.50	.70
❏ 505	Jason Thompson	.15	.07
❏ 506	Phil Huffman	.15	.07
❏ 507	Jamie Quirk	.15	.07
❏ 508	Rob Dressler	.15	.07
❏ 509	Pete Mackanin	.15	.07
❏ 510	Lee Mazzilli	.15	.07
❏ 511	Wayne Garland	.15	.07
❏ 512	Gary Thomasson	.15	.07
❏ 513	Frank LaCorte	.15	.07
❏ 514	George Riley	.15	.07
❏ 515	Robin Yount	1.50	.70
❏ 516	Doug Bird	.15	.07
❏ 517	Richie Zisk	.15	.07
❏ 518	Grant Jackson	.15	.07
❏ 519	John Tamargo DP	.10	.05
❏ 520	Steve Stone	.40	.18
❏ 521	Sam Mejias	.15	.07
❏ 522	Mike Colbern	.15	.07
❏ 523	John Fulgham	.15	.07
❏ 524	Willie Aikens	.15	.07
❏ 525	Mike Torrez	.15	.07
❏ 526	Phillies Rookies	.15	.07
	Marty Bystrom		
	Jay Loviglio		
	Jim Wright		
❏ 527	Danny Goodwin	.15	.07
❏ 528	Gary Matthews	.40	.18
❏ 529	Dave LaRoche	.15	.07
❏ 530	Steve Garvey	.75	.35
❏ 531	John Curtis	.15	.07
❏ 532	Bill Stein	.15	.07
❏ 533	Jesus Figueroa	.15	.07
❏ 534	Dave Smith	.40	.18
❏ 535	Omar Moreno	.15	.07
❏ 536	Bob Owchinko DP	.10	.05
❏ 537	Ron Hodges	.15	.07
❏ 538	Tom Griffin	.15	.07
❏ 539	Rodney Scott	.15	.07
❏ 540	Mike Schmidt DP	2.00	.90
❏ 541	Steve Swisher	.15	.07
❏ 542	Larry Bradford DP	.10	.05
❏ 543	Terry Crowley	.15	.07
❏ 544	Rich Gale	.15	.07
❏ 545	Johnny Grubb	.15	.07
❏ 546	Paul Moskau	.15	.07
❏ 547	Mario Guerrero	.15	.07
❏ 548	Dave Goltz	.15	.07
❏ 549	Jerry Remy	.15	.07
❏ 550	Tommy John	.75	.35
❏ 551	Pirates Rookies	1.50	.70
	Vance Law		
	Tony Pena		
	Pascual Perez		
❏ 552	Steve Trout	.15	.07
❏ 553	Tim Blackwell	.15	.07
❏ 554	Bert Blyleven UER	.75	.35
	(1 is missing from		
	1980 on card back)		
❏ 555	Cecil Cooper	.40	.18
❏ 556	Jerry Mumphrey	.15	.07
❏ 557	Chris Knapp	.15	.07
❏ 558	Barry Bonnell	.15	.07
❏ 559	Willie Montanez	.15	.07
❏ 560	Joe Morgan	1.50	.70
❏ 561	Dennis Littlejohn	.15	.07
❏ 562	Checklist 485-605	.75	.35
❏ 563	Jim Kaat	.40	.18
❏ 564	Ron Hassey DP	.10	.05
❏ 565	Burt Hooton	.15	.07
❏ 566	Del Unser	.15	.07
❏ 567	Mark Bomback	.15	.07
❏ 568	Dave Revering	.15	.07
❏ 569	Al Williams DP	.10	.05
❏ 570	Ken Singleton	.40	.18
❏ 571	Todd Cruz	.15	.07
❏ 572	Jack Morris	1.50	.70
❏ 573	Phil Garner	.40	.18
❏ 574	Bill Caudill	.15	.07
❏ 575	Tony Perez	1.50	.70
❏ 576	Reggie Cleveland	.15	.07
❏ 577	Blue Jays Rookies	.15	.07
	Luis Leal		
	Brian Milner		
	Ken Schrom		
❏ 578	Bill Gullickson	.75	.35
❏ 579	Tim Flannery	.15	.07
❏ 580	Don Baylor	.75	.35
❏ 581	Roy Howell	.15	.07
❏ 582	Gaylord Perry	1.50	.70
❏ 583	Larry Milbourne	.15	.07
❏ 584	Randy Lerch	.15	.07
❏ 585	Amos Otis	.40	.18
❏ 586	Silvio Martinez	.15	.07
❏ 587	Jeff Newman	.15	.07
❏ 588	Gary Lavelle	.15	.07
❏ 589	Lamar Johnson	.15	.07
❏ 590	Bruce Sutter	.40	.18
❏ 591	John Lowenstein	.15	.07
❏ 592	Steve Comer	.15	.07
❏ 593	Steve Kemp	.15	.07
❏ 594	Preston Hanna DP	.10	.05
❏ 595	Butch Hobson	.15	.07
❏ 596	Jerry Augustine	.15	.07
❏ 597	Rafael Landestoy	.15	.07
❏ 598	George Vukovich DP	.10	.05
❏ 599	Dennis Kinney	.15	.07
❏ 600	Johnny Bench	2.00	.90
❏ 601	Don Aase	.15	.07
❏ 602	Bobby Murcer	.40	.18
❏ 603	John Verhoeven	.15	.07
❏ 604	Rob Picciolo	.15	.07
❏ 605	Don Sutton	1.50	.70
❏ 606	Reds Rookies DP	.15	.07
	Bruce Berenyi		
	Geoff Combe		
	Paul Householder		
❏ 607	David Palmer	.15	.07
❏ 608	Greg Pryor	.15	.07
❏ 609	Lynn McGlothen	.15	.07
❏ 610	Darrell Porter	.15	.07
❏ 611	Rick Matula DP	.10	.05
❏ 612	Duane Kuiper	.15	.07
❏ 613	Jim Anderson	.15	.07
❏ 614	Dave Rozema	.15	.07
❏ 615	Rick Dempsey	.40	.18
❏ 616	Rick Wise	.15	.07
❏ 617	Craig Reynolds	.15	.07
❏ 618	John Milner	.15	.07
❏ 619	Steve Henderson	.15	.07
❏ 620	Dennis Eckersley	1.50	.70
❏ 621	Tom Donohue	.15	.07
❏ 622	Randy Moffitt	.15	.07
❏ 623	Sal Bando	.40	.18
❏ 624	Bob Welch	.40	.18
❏ 625	Bill Buckner	.40	.18
❏ 626	Tigers Rookies	.15	.07
	Dave Steffen		

		NRMT	VG-E
	Jerry Ujdur		
	Roger Weaver		
❑ 627	Luis Tiant	.40	.18
❑ 628	Vic Correll	.15	.07
❑ 629	Tony Armas	.40	.18
❑ 630	Steve Carlton	1.50	.70
❑ 631	Ron Jackson	.15	.07
❑ 632	Alan Bannister	.15	.07
❑ 633	Bill Lee	.40	.18
❑ 634	Doug Flynn	.15	.07
❑ 635	Bobby Bonds	.40	.18
❑ 636	Al Hrabosky	.15	.07
❑ 637	Jerry Narron	.15	.07
❑ 638	Checklist 606-726	.75	.35
❑ 639	Carney Lansford	.40	.18
❑ 640	Dave Parker	.40	.18
❑ 641	Mark Belanger	.15	.07
❑ 642	Vern Ruhle	.15	.07
❑ 643	Lloyd Moseby	.40	.18
❑ 644	Ramon Aviles DP	.10	.05
❑ 645	Rick Reuschel	.40	.18
❑ 646	Marvis Foley	.15	.07
❑ 647	Dick Drago	.15	.07
❑ 648	Darrell Evans	.40	.18
❑ 649	Manny Sarmiento	.15	.07
❑ 650	Bucky Dent	.40	.18
❑ 651	Pedro Guerrero	.75	.35
❑ 652	John Montague	.15	.07
❑ 653	Bill Fahey	.15	.07
❑ 654	Ray Burris	.15	.07
❑ 655	Dan Driessen	.15	.07
❑ 656	Jon Matlack	.15	.07
❑ 657	Mike Cubbage DP	.10	.05
❑ 658	Milt Wilcox	.15	.07
❑ 659	Brewers Rookies	.15	.07
	John Flinn		
	Ed Romero		
	Ned Yost		
❑ 660	Gary Carter	1.50	.70
❑ 661	Orioles Team/Mgr.	.75	.35
	Earl Weaver		
❑ 662	Red Sox Team/Mgr.	.75	.35
	Ralph Houk		
❑ 663	Angels Team/Mgr.	.75	.35
	Jim Fregosi		
❑ 664	White Sox Team/Mgr.	.75	.35
	Tony LaRussa		
❑ 665	Indians Team/Mgr.	.75	.35
	Dave Garcia		
❑ 666	Tigers Team/Mgr.	.75	.35
	Sparky Anderson		
❑ 667	Royals Team/Mgr.	.75	.35
	Jim Frey		
❑ 668	Brewers Team/Mgr.	.75	.35
	Bob Rodgers		
❑ 669	Twins Team/Mgr.	.75	.35
	John Goryl		
❑ 670	Yankees Team/Mgr.	.75	.35
	Gene Michael		
❑ 671	A's Team/Mgr.	.75	.35
	Billy Martin		
❑ 672	Mariners Team/Mgr.	.75	.35
	Maury Wills		
❑ 673	Rangers Team/Mgr.	.75	.35
	Don Zimmer		
❑ 674	Blue Jays Team/Mgr.	.75	.35
	Bobby Mattick		
❑ 675	Braves Team/Mgr.	.75	.35
	Bobby Cox		
❑ 676	Cubs Team/Mgr.	.75	.35
	Joe Amalfitano		
❑ 677	Reds Team/Mgr.	.75	.35
	John McNamara		
❑ 678	Astros Team/Mgr.	.75	.35
	Bill Virdon		
❑ 679	Dodgers Team/Mgr.	.75	.35
	Tom Lasorda		
❑ 680	Expos Team/Mgr.	.75	.35
	Dick Williams		
❑ 681	Mets Team/Mgr.	.75	.35
	Joe Torre		
❑ 682	Phillies Team/Mgr.	.75	.35
	Dallas Green		
❑ 683	Pirates Team/Mgr.	.75	.35
	Chuck Tanner		
❑ 684	Cardinals Team/Mgr.	.75	.35

		NRMT	VG-E
	Whitey Herzog		
❑ 685	Padres Team/Mgr.	.75	.35
	Frank Howard		
❑ 686	Giants Team/Mgr.	.75	.35
	Dave Bristol		
❑ 687	Jeff Jones	.15	.07
❑ 688	Kiko Garcia	.15	.07
❑ 689	Red Sox Rookies	1.50	.70
	Bruce Hurst		
	Keith MacWhorter		
	Reid Nichols		
❑ 690	Bob Watson	.40	.18
❑ 691	Dick Ruthven	.15	.07
❑ 692	Lenny Randle	.15	.07
❑ 693	Steve Howe	.40	.18
❑ 694	Bud Harrelson DP	.15	.07
❑ 695	Kent Tekulve	.40	.18
❑ 696	Alan Ashby	.15	.07
❑ 697	Rick Waits	.15	.07
❑ 698	Mike Jorgensen	.15	.07
❑ 699	Glenn Abbott	.15	.07
❑ 700	George Brett	4.00	1.80
❑ 701	Joe Rudi	.40	.18
❑ 702	George Medich	.15	.07
❑ 703	Alvis Woods	.15	.07
❑ 704	Bill Travers DP	.10	.05
❑ 705	Ted Simmons	.40	.18
❑ 706	Dave Ford	.15	.07
❑ 707	Dave Cash	.15	.07
❑ 708	Doyle Alexander	.15	.07
❑ 709	Alan Trammell DP	1.50	.70
❑ 710	Ron LeFlore DP	.15	.07
❑ 711	Joe Ferguson	.15	.07
❑ 712	Bill Bonham	.15	.07
❑ 713	Bill North	.15	.07
❑ 714	Pete Redfern	.15	.07
❑ 715	Bill Madlock	.40	.18
❑ 716	Glenn Borgmann	.15	.07
❑ 717	Jim Barr DP	.10	.05
❑ 718	Larry Biittner	.15	.07
❑ 719	Sparky Lyle	.40	.18
❑ 720	Fred Lynn	.40	.18
❑ 721	Toby Harrah	.40	.18
❑ 722	Joe Niekro	.40	.18
❑ 723	Bruce Bochte	.15	.07
❑ 724	Lou Piniella	.40	.18
❑ 725	Steve Rogers	.15	.07
❑ 726	Rick Monday	.15	.07

1981 Topps Traded

		NRMT	VG-E
COMP.FACT.SET (132)		30.00	13.50
COMMON CARD (727-858)		.25	.11
MINOR STARS		1.00	.45
SEMISTARS		3.00	1.35
❑ 727	Danny Ainge	5.00	2.20
❑ 728	Doyle Alexander	.25	.11
❑ 729	Gary Alexander	.25	.11
❑ 730	Bill Almon	.25	.11
❑ 731	Joaquin Andujar	1.00	.45
❑ 732	Bob Bailor	.25	.11
❑ 733	Juan Beniquez	.25	.11
❑ 734	Dave Bergman	.25	.11
❑ 735	Tony Bernazard	.25	.11
❑ 736	Larry Biittner	.25	.11
❑ 737	Doug Bird	.25	.11

		NRMT	VG-E
❑ 738	Bert Blyleven	3.00	1.35
❑ 739	Mark Bomback	.25	.11
❑ 740	Bobby Bonds	1.00	.45
❑ 741	Rich Bosetti	.25	.11
❑ 742	Hubie Brooks	1.00	.45
❑ 743	Rick Burleson	.25	.11
❑ 744	Ray Burris	.25	.11
❑ 745	Jeff Burroughs	.25	.11
❑ 746	Enos Cabell	.25	.11
❑ 747	Ken Clay	.25	.11
❑ 748	Mark Clear	.25	.11
❑ 749	Larry Cox	.25	.11
❑ 750	Hector Cruz	.25	.11
❑ 751	Victor Cruz	.25	.11
❑ 752	Mike Cubbage	.25	.11
❑ 753	Dick Davis	.25	.11
❑ 754	Brian Doyle	.25	.11
❑ 755	Dick Drago	.25	.11
❑ 756	Leon Durham	1.00	.45
❑ 757	Jim Dwyer	.25	.11
❑ 758	Dave Edwards UER	.25	.11
	No birthdate on card		
❑ 759	Jim Essian	.25	.11
❑ 760	Bill Fahey	.25	.11
❑ 761	Rollie Fingers	4.00	1.80
❑ 762	Carlton Fisk	5.00	2.20
❑ 763	Barry Foote	.25	.11
❑ 764	Ken Forsch	.25	.11
❑ 765	Kiko Garcia	.25	.11
❑ 766	Cesar Geronimo	.25	.11
❑ 767	Gary Gray	.25	.11
❑ 768	Mickey Hatcher	1.00	.45
❑ 769	Steve Henderson	.25	.11
❑ 770	Marc Hill	.25	.11
❑ 771	Butch Hobson	.25	.11
❑ 772	Rick Honeycutt	.25	.11
❑ 773	Roy Howell	.25	.11
❑ 774	Mike Ivie	.25	.11
❑ 775	Roy Lee Jackson	.25	.11
❑ 776	Cliff Johnson	.25	.11
❑ 777	Randy Jones	.25	.11
❑ 778	Ruppert Jones	.25	.11
❑ 779	Mick Kelleher	.25	.11
❑ 780	Terry Kennedy	.25	.11
❑ 781	Dave Kingman	3.00	1.35
❑ 782	Bob Knepper	.25	.11
❑ 783	Ken Kravec	.25	.11
❑ 784	Bob Lacey	.25	.11
❑ 785	Dennis Lamp	.25	.11
❑ 786	Rafael Landestoy	.25	.11
❑ 787	Ken Landreaux	.25	.11
❑ 788	Carney Lansford	1.00	.45
❑ 789	Dave LaRoche	.25	.11
❑ 790	Joe Lefebvre	.25	.11
❑ 791	Ron LeFlore	1.00	.45
❑ 792	Randy Lerch	.25	.11
❑ 793	Sixto Lezcano	.25	.11
❑ 794	John Littlefield	.25	.11
❑ 795	Mike Lum	.25	.11
❑ 796	Greg Luzinski	1.00	.45
❑ 797	Fred Lynn	1.00	.45
❑ 798	Jerry Martin	.25	.11
❑ 799	Buck Martinez	.25	.11
❑ 800	Gary Matthews	1.00	.45
❑ 801	Mario Mendoza	.25	.11
❑ 802	Larry Milbourne	.25	.11
❑ 803	Rick Miller	.25	.11
❑ 804	John Montefusco	.25	.11
❑ 805	Jerry Morales	.25	.11
❑ 806	Jose Morales	.25	.11
❑ 807	Joe Morgan	4.00	1.80
❑ 808	Jerry Mumphrey	.25	.11
❑ 809	Gene Nelson	.25	.11
❑ 810	Ed Ott	.25	.11
❑ 811	Bob Owchinko	.25	.11
❑ 812	Gaylord Perry	4.00	1.80
❑ 813	Mike Phillips	.25	.11
❑ 814	Darrell Porter	.25	.11
❑ 815	Mike Proly	.25	.11
❑ 816	Tim Raines	6.00	2.70
❑ 817	Lenny Randle	.25	.11
❑ 818	Doug Rau	.25	.11
❑ 819	Jeff Reardon	4.00	1.80
❑ 820	Ken Reitz	.25	.11
❑ 821	Steve Renko	.25	.11
❑ 822	Rick Reuschel	1.00	.45

		NRMT	VG-E
❑ 823	Dave Revering	.25	.11
❑ 824	Dave Roberts	.25	.11
❑ 825	Leon Roberts	.25	.11
❑ 826	Joe Rudi	1.00	.45
❑ 827	Kevin Saucier	.25	.11
❑ 828	Tony Scott	.25	.11
❑ 829	Bob Shirley	.25	.11
❑ 830	Ted Simmons	1.00	.45
❑ 831	Lary Sorensen	.25	.11
❑ 832	Jim Spencer	.25	.11
❑ 833	Harry Spilman	.25	.11
❑ 834	Fred Stanley	.25	.11
❑ 835	Rusty Staub	1.00	.45
❑ 836	Bill Stein	.25	.11
❑ 837	Joe Strain	.25	.11
❑ 838	Bruce Sutter	1.00	.45
❑ 839	Don Sutton	4.00	1.80
❑ 840	Steve Swisher	.25	.11
❑ 841	Frank Tanana	1.00	.45
❑ 842	Gene Tenace	1.00	.45
❑ 843	Jason Thompson	.25	.11
❑ 844	Dickie Thon	1.00	.45
❑ 845	Bill Travers	.25	.11
❑ 846	Tom Underwood	.25	.11
❑ 847	John Urrea	.25	.11
❑ 848	Mike Vail	.25	.11
❑ 849	Ellis Valentine	.25	.11
❑ 850	Fernando Valenzuela	6.00	2.70
❑ 851	Pete Vuckovich	1.25	.55
❑ 852	Mark Wagner	.25	.11
❑ 853	Bob Walk	1.00	.45
❑ 854	Claudell Washington	.25	.11
❑ 855	Dave Winfield	5.00	2.20
❑ 856	Geoff Zahn	.25	.11
❑ 857	Richie Zisk	.25	.11
❑ 858	Checklist 727-858	.25	.11

1982 Topps

	NRMT	VG-E
COMPLETE SET (792)	100.00	45.00
COMMON CARD (1-792)	.15	.07
MINOR STARS	.30	.14
SEMISTARS	.60	.25
UNLISTED STARS	1.25	.55
SUBSET CARDS HALF VALUE OF BASE CARDS		
BEWARE RIPKEN BLANK-BACK FAKES		

		NRMT	VG-E
❑ 1	Steve Carlton HL	1.25	.55
	Sets new NL strikeout record		
❑ 2	Ron Davis HL	.15	.07
	Fans 8 straight in relief		
❑ 3	Tim Raines HL	.60	.25
	71 steals as rookie		
❑ 4	Pete Rose HL	.60	.25
	Sets NL hit mark		
❑ 5	Nolan Ryan HL	3.00	1.35
	Pitches fifth no-hitter		
❑ 6	Fernando Valenzuela HL	.60	.25
	8 shutouts as rookie		
❑ 7	Scott Sanderson	.15	.07
❑ 8	Rich Dauer	.15	.07
❑ 9	Ron Guidry	.30	.14
❑ 10	Ron Guidry SA	.15	.07
❑ 11	Gary Alexander	.15	.07
❑ 12	Moose Haas	.15	.07
❑ 13	Lamar Johnson	.15	.07
❑ 14	Steve Howe	.15	.07
❑ 15	Ellis Valentine	.15	.07
❑ 16	Steve Comer	.15	.07
❑ 17	Darrell Evans	.30	.14
❑ 18	Fernando Arroyo	.15	.07
❑ 19	Ernie Whitt	.15	.07
❑ 20	Garry Maddox	.15	.07
❑ 21	Orioles Rookies	70.00	32.00
	Bob Bonner		
	Cal Ripken		
	Jeff Schneider		
❑ 22	Jim Beattie	.15	.07
❑ 23	Willie Hernandez	.30	.14
❑ 24	Dave Frost	.15	.07
❑ 25	Jerry Remy	.15	.07
❑ 26	Jorge Orta	.15	.07
❑ 27	Tom Herr	.30	.14
❑ 28	John Urrea	.15	.07
❑ 29	Dwayne Murphy	.15	.07
❑ 30	Tom Seaver	1.50	.70
❑ 31	Tom Seaver SA	.60	.25
❑ 32	Gene Garber	.15	.07
❑ 33	Jerry Morales	.15	.07
❑ 34	Joe Sambito	.15	.07
❑ 35	Willie Aikens	.15	.07
❑ 36	Rangers TL	.60	.25
	BA: Al Oliver		
	Pitching: Doc Medich		
❑ 37	Dan Graham	.15	.07
❑ 38	Charlie Lea	.15	.07
❑ 39	Lou Whitaker	1.25	.55
❑ 40	Dave Parker	.30	.14
❑ 41	Dave Parker SA	.15	.07
❑ 42	Rick Sofield	.15	.07
❑ 43	Mike Cubbage	.15	.07
❑ 44	Britt Burns	.15	.07
❑ 45	Rick Cerone	.15	.07
❑ 46	Jerry Augustine	.15	.07
❑ 47	Jeff Leonard	.15	.07
❑ 48	Bobby Castillo	.15	.07
❑ 49	Alvis Woods	.15	.07
❑ 50	Buddy Bell	.30	.14
❑ 51	Cubs Rookies	.60	.25
	Jay Howell		
	Carlos Lezcano		
	Ty Waller		
❑ 52	Larry Andersen	.15	.07
❑ 53	Greg Gross	.15	.07
❑ 54	Ron Hassey	.15	.07
❑ 55	Rick Burleson	.15	.07
❑ 56	Mark Littell	.15	.07
❑ 57	Craig Reynolds	.15	.07
❑ 58	John D'Acquisto	.15	.07
❑ 59	Rich Gedman	.30	.14
❑ 60	Tony Armas	.15	.07
❑ 61	Tommy Boggs	.15	.07
❑ 62	Mike Tyson	.15	.07
❑ 63	Mario Soto	.15	.07
❑ 64	Lynn Jones	.15	.07
❑ 65	Terry Kennedy	.15	.07
❑ 66	Astros TL	2.00	.90
	BA: Art Howe		
	Pitching: Nolan Ryan		
❑ 67	Rich Gale	.15	.07
❑ 68	Roy Howell	.15	.07
❑ 69	Al Williams	.15	.07
❑ 70	Tim Raines	1.25	.55
❑ 71	Roy Lee Jackson	.15	.07
❑ 72	Rick Auerbach	.15	.07
❑ 73	Buddy Solomon	.15	.07
❑ 74	Bob Clark	.15	.07
❑ 75	Tommy John	.60	.25
❑ 76	Greg Pryor	.15	.07
❑ 77	Miguel Dilone	.15	.07
❑ 78	George Medich	.15	.07
❑ 79	Bob Bailor	.15	.07
❑ 80	Jim Palmer	1.25	.55
❑ 81	Jim Palmer SA	.60	.25
❑ 82	Bob Welch	.30	.14
❑ 83	Yankees Rookies	.60	.25
	Steve Balboni		
	Andy McGaffigan		
	Andre Robertson		
❑ 84	Rennie Stennett	.15	.07
❑ 85	Lynn McGlothen	.15	.07
❑ 86	Dane Iorg	.15	.07
❑ 87	Matt Keough	.15	.07
❑ 88	Biff Pocoroba	.15	.07
❑ 89	Steve Henderson	.15	.07
❑ 90	Nolan Ryan	6.00	2.70
❑ 91	Carney Lansford	.30	.14
❑ 92	Brad Havens	.15	.07
❑ 93	Larry Hisle	.15	.07
❑ 94	Andy Hassler	.15	.07
❑ 95	Ozzie Smith	2.50	1.10
❑ 96	Royals TL	1.25	.55
	BA: George Brett		
	Pitching: Larry Gura		
❑ 97	Paul Moskau	.15	.07
❑ 98	Terry Bulling	.15	.07
❑ 99	Barry Bonnell	.15	.07
❑ 100	Mike Schmidt	2.00	.90
❑ 101	Mike Schmidt SA	.60	.25
❑ 102	Dan Briggs	.15	.07
❑ 103	Bob Lacey	.15	.07
❑ 104	Rance Mulliniks	.15	.07
❑ 105	Kirk Gibson	1.25	.55
❑ 106	Enrique Romo	.15	.07
❑ 107	Wayne Krenchicki	.15	.07
❑ 108	Bob Sykes	.15	.07
❑ 109	Dave Revering	.15	.07
❑ 110	Carlton Fisk	1.25	.55
❑ 111	Carlton Fisk SA	.60	.25
❑ 112	Billy Sample	.15	.07
❑ 113	Steve McCatty	.15	.07
❑ 114	Ken Landreaux	.15	.07
❑ 115	Gaylord Perry	1.25	.55
❑ 116	Jim Wohlford	.15	.07
❑ 117	Rawly Eastwick	.15	.07
❑ 118	Expos Rookies	.30	.14
	Terry Francona		
	Brad Mills		
	Bryn Smith		
❑ 119	Joe Pittman	.15	.07
❑ 120	Gary Lucas	.15	.07
❑ 121	Ed Lynch	.15	.07
❑ 122	Jamie Easterly UER	.15	.07
	(Photo actually		
	Reggie Cleveland)		
❑ 123	Danny Goodwin	.15	.07
❑ 124	Reid Nichols	.15	.07
❑ 125	Danny Ainge	1.50	.70
❑ 126	Braves TL	.60	.25
	BA: Claudell Washington		
	Pitching: Rick Mahler		
❑ 127	Lonnie Smith	.30	.14
❑ 128	Frank Pastore	.15	.07
❑ 129	Checklist 1-132	.60	.25
❑ 130	Julio Cruz	.15	.07
❑ 131	Stan Bahnsen	.15	.07
❑ 132	Lee May	.30	.14
❑ 133	Pat Underwood	.15	.07
❑ 134	Dan Ford	.15	.07
❑ 135	Andy Rincon	.15	.07
❑ 136	Lenn Sakata	.15	.07
❑ 137	George Cappuzzello	.15	.07
❑ 138	Tony Pena	.30	.14
❑ 139	Jeff Jones	.15	.07
❑ 140	Ron LeFlore	.30	.14
❑ 141	Indians Rookies	.30	.14
	Chris Bando		
	Tom Brennan		
	Von Hayes		
❑ 142	Dave LaRoche	.15	.07
❑ 143	Mookie Wilson	.30	.14
❑ 144	Fred Breining	.15	.07
❑ 145	Bob Horner	.30	.14
❑ 146	Mike Griffin	.15	.07
❑ 147	Denny Walling	.15	.07
❑ 148	Mickey Klutts	.15	.07
❑ 149	Pat Putnam	.15	.07
❑ 150	Ted Simmons	.30	.14
❑ 151	Dave Edwards	.15	.07
❑ 152	Ramon Aviles	.15	.07
❑ 153	Roger Erickson	.15	.07
❑ 154	Dennis Werth	.15	.07
❑ 155	Otto Velez	.15	.07
❑ 156	Oakland A's TL	.60	.25
	BA: Rickey Henderson		
	Pitching: Steve McCatty		
❑ 157	Steve Crawford	.15	.07
❑ 158	Brian Downing	.15	.07

159	Larry Biittner	.15	.07
160	Luis Tiant	.30	.14
161	Batting Leaders	.30	.14
	Bill Madlock		
	Carney Lansford		
162	Home Run Leaders	1.25	.55
	Mike Schmidt		
	Tony Armas		
	Dwight Evans		
	Bobby Grich		
	Eddie Murray		
163	RBI Leaders	1.25	.55
	Mike Schmidt		
	Eddie Murray		
164	Stolen Base Leaders	1.25	.55
	Tim Raines		
	Rickey Henderson		
165	Victory Leaders	.60	.25
	Tom Seaver		
	Denny Martinez		
	Steve McCatty		
	Jack Morris		
	Pete Vuckovich		
166	Strikeout Leaders	.30	.14
	Fernando Valenzuela		
	Len Barker		
167	ERA Leaders	2.00	.90
	Nolan Ryan		
	Steve McCatty		
168	Leading Firemen	.60	.25
	Bruce Sutter		
	Rollie Fingers		
169	Charlie Leibrandt	.15	.07
170	Jim Bibby	.15	.07
171	Giants Rookies	3.00	1.35
	Bob Brenly		
	Chili Davis		
	Bob Tufts		
172	Bill Gullickson	.15	.07
173	Jamie Quirk	.15	.07
174	Dave Ford	.15	.07
175	Jerry Mumphrey	.15	.07
176	Dewey Robinson	.15	.07
177	John Ellis	.15	.07
178	Dyar Miller	.15	.07
179	Steve Garvey	.60	.25
180	Steve Garvey SA	.30	.14
181	Silvio Martinez	.15	.07
182	Larry Herndon	.15	.07
183	Mike Proly	.15	.07
184	Mick Kelleher	.15	.07
185	Phil Niekro	1.25	.55
186	Cardinals TL	.60	.25
	BA: Keith Hernandez		
	Pitching: Bob Forsch		
187	Jeff Newman	.15	.07
188	Randy Martz	.15	.07
189	Glenn Hoffman	.15	.07
190	J.R. Richard	.30	.14
191	Tim Wallach	.60	.25
192	Broderick Perkins	.15	.07
193	Darrell Jackson	.15	.07
194	Mike Vail	.15	.07
195	Paul Molitor	1.50	.70
196	Willie Upshaw	.15	.07
197	Shane Rawley	.15	.07
198	Chris Speier	.15	.07
199	Don Aase	.15	.07
200	George Brett	2.50	1.10
201	George Brett SA	1.25	.55
202	Rick Manning	.15	.07
203	Blue Jays Rookies	.60	.25
	Jesse Barfield		
	Brian Milner		
	Boomer Wells		
204	Gary Roenicke	.15	.07
205	Neil Allen	.15	.07
206	Tony Bernazard	.15	.07
207	Rod Scurry	.15	.07
208	Bobby Murcer	.30	.14
209	Gary Lavelle	.15	.07
210	Keith Hernandez	.30	.14
211	Dan Petry	.15	.07
212	Mario Mendoza	.15	.07
213	Dave Stewart	1.50	.70
214	Brian Asselstine	.15	.07
215	Mike Krukow	.15	.07
216	White Sox TL	.60	.25
	BA: Chet Lemon		
	Pitching: Dennis Lamp		
217	Bo McLaughlin	.15	.07
218	Dave Roberts	.15	.07
219	John Curtis	.15	.07
220	Manny Trillo	.15	.07
221	Jim Slaton	.15	.07
222	Butch Wynegar	.15	.07
223	Lloyd Moseby	.15	.07
224	Bruce Bochte	.15	.07
225	Mike Torrez	.15	.07
226	Checklist 133-264	.60	.25
227	Ray Burris	.15	.07
228	Sam Mejias	.15	.07
229	Geoff Zahn	.15	.07
230	Willie Wilson	.30	.14
231	Phillies Rookies	.60	.25
	Mark Davis		
	Bob Dernier		
	Ozzie Virgil		
232	Terry Crowley	.15	.07
233	Duane Kuiper	.15	.07
234	Ron Hodges	.15	.07
235	Mike Easler	.15	.07
236	John Martin	.15	.07
237	Rusty Kuntz	.15	.07
238	Kevin Saucier	.15	.07
239	Jon Matlack	.15	.07
240	Bucky Dent	.30	.14
241	Bucky Dent SA	.15	.07
242	Milt May	.15	.07
243	Bob Owchinko	.15	.07
244	Rufino Linares	.15	.07
245	Ken Reitz	.15	.07
246	New York Mets TL	.60	.25
	BA: Hubie Brooks		
	Pitching: Mike Scott		
247	Pedro Guerrero	.30	.14
248	Frank LaCorte	.15	.07
249	Tim Flannery	.15	.07
250	Tug McGraw	.30	.14
251	Fred Lynn	.30	.14
252	Fred Lynn SA	.15	.07
253	Chuck Baker	.15	.07
254	Jorge Bell	1.25	.55
255	Tony Perez	1.25	.55
256	Tony Perez SA	.60	.25
257	Larry Harlow	.15	.07
258	Bo Diaz	.15	.07
259	Rodney Scott	.15	.07
260	Bruce Sutter	.30	.14
261	Tigers Rookies UER	.15	.07
	Howard Bailey		
	Marty Castillo		
	Dave Rucker		
	(Rucker photo actually Roger Weaver)		
262	Doug Bair	.15	.07
263	Victor Cruz	.15	.07
264	Dan Quisenberry	.30	.14
265	Al Bumbry	.15	.07
266	Rick Leach	.15	.07
267	Kurt Bevacqua	.15	.07
268	Rickey Keeton	.15	.07
269	Jim Essian	.15	.07
270	Rusty Staub	.30	.14
271	Larry Bradford	.15	.07
272	Bump Wills	.15	.07
273	Doug Bird	.15	.07
274	Bob Ojeda	.60	.25
275	Bob Watson	.30	.14
276	Angels TL	.60	.25
	BA: Rod Carew		
	Pitching: Ken Forsch		
277	Terry Puhl	.15	.07
278	John Littlefield	.15	.07
279	Bill Russell	.15	.07
280	Ben Oglivie	.30	.14
281	John Verhoeven	.15	.07
282	Ken Macha	.15	.07
283	Brian Allard	.15	.07
284	Bob Grich	.30	.14
285	Sparky Lyle	.30	.14
286	Bill Fahey	.15	.07
287	Alan Bannister	.15	.07
288	Garry Templeton	.15	.07
289	Bob Stanley	.15	.07
290	Ken Singleton	.30	.14
291	Pirates Rookies	.30	.14
	Vance Law		
	Bob Long		
	Johnny Ray		
292	David Palmer	.15	.07
293	Rob Picciolo	.15	.07
294	Mike LaCoss	.15	.07
295	Jason Thompson	.15	.07
296	Bob Walk	.15	.07
297	Clint Hurdle	.15	.07
298	Danny Darwin	.15	.07
299	Steve Trout	.15	.07
300	Reggie Jackson	1.50	.70
301	Reggie Jackson SA	.60	.25
302	Doug Flynn	.15	.07
303	Bill Caudill	.15	.07
304	Johnnie LeMaster	.15	.07
305	Don Sutton	1.25	.55
306	Don Sutton SA	.60	.25
307	Randy Bass	.15	.07
308	Charlie Moore	.15	.07
309	Pete Redfern	.15	.07
310	Mike Hargrove	.30	.14
311	Dodgers TL	.60	.25
	BA: Dusty Baker		
	Pitching: Burt Hooton		
312	Lenny Randle	.15	.07
313	John Harris	.15	.07
314	Buck Martinez	.15	.07
315	Burt Hooton	.15	.07
316	Steve Braun	.15	.07
317	Dick Ruthven	.15	.07
318	Mike Heath	.15	.07
319	Dave Rozema	.15	.07
320	Chris Chambliss	.30	.14
321	Chris Chambliss SA	.15	.07
322	Garry Hancock	.15	.07
323	Bill Lee	.30	.14
324	Steve Dillard	.15	.07
325	Jose Cruz	.30	.14
326	Pete Falcone	.15	.07
327	Joe Nolan	.15	.07
328	Ed Farmer	.15	.07
329	U.L. Washington	.15	.07
330	Rick Wise	.15	.07
331	Benny Ayala	.15	.07
332	Don Robinson	.15	.07
333	Brewers Rookies	.15	.07
	Frank DiPino		
	Marshall Edwards		
	Chuck Porter		
334	Aurelio Rodriguez	.15	.07
335	Jim Sundberg	.15	.07
336	Mariners TL	.60	.25
	BA: Tom Paciorek		
	Pitching: Glenn Abbott		
337	Pete Rose AS	.60	.25
338	Dave Lopes AS	.15	.07
339	Mike Schmidt AS	.60	.25
340	Dave Concepcion AS	.15	.07
341	Andre Dawson AS	.60	.25
342A	George Foster AS	.30	.14
	(With autograph)		
342B	George Foster AS	1.25	.55
	(W/o autograph)		
343	Dave Parker AS	.15	.07
344	Gary Carter AS	.30	.14
345	Fernando Valenzuela AS	.60	.25
346	Tom Seaver AS ERR	1.25	.55
	("t ed")		
346B	Tom Seaver AS COR	1.25	.55
	("tied")		
347	Bruce Sutter AS	.15	.07
348	Derrel Thomas	.15	.07
349	George Frazier	.15	.07
350	Thad Bosley	.15	.07
351	Reds Rookies	.15	.07
	Scott Brown		
	Geoff Combe		
	Paul Householder		
352	Dick Davis	.15	.07
353	Jack O'Connor	.15	.07

354	Roberto Ramos	.15	.07
355	Dwight Evans	.60	.25
356	Denny Lewallyn	.15	.07
357	Butch Hobson	.15	.07
358	Mike Parrott	.15	.07
359	Jim Dwyer	.15	.07
360	Len Barker	.15	.07
361	Rafael Landestoy	.15	.07
362	Jim Wright UER (Wrong Jim Wright pictured)	.15	.07
363	Bob Molinaro	.15	.07
364	Doyle Alexander	.15	.07
365	Bill Madlock	.30	.14
366	Padres TL BA: Luis Salazar Pitching: Juan Eichelberger	.60	.25
367	Jim Kaat	.30	.14
368	Alex Trevino	.15	.07
369	Champ Summers	.15	.07
370	Mike Norris	.15	.07
371	Jerry Don Gleaton	.15	.07
372	Luis Gomez	.15	.07
373	Gene Nelson	.15	.07
374	Tim Blackwell	.15	.07
375	Dusty Baker	.60	.25
376	Chris Welsh	.15	.07
377	Kiko Garcia	.15	.07
378	Mike Caldwell	.15	.07
379	Rob Wilfong	.15	.07
380	Dave Stieb	.30	.14
381	Red Sox Rookies Bruce Hurst Dave Schmidt Julio Valdez	.30	.14
382	Joe Simpson	.15	.07
383A	Pascual Perez ERR (No position on front)	5.00	2.20
383B	Pascual Perez COR	.30	.14
384	Keith Moreland	.15	.07
385	Ken Forsch	.15	.07
386	Jerry White	.15	.07
387	Tom Veryzer	.15	.07
388	Joe Rudi	.15	.07
389	George Vukovich	.15	.07
390	Eddie Murray	1.50	.70
391	Dave Tobik	.15	.07
392	Rick Bosetti	.15	.07
393	Al Hrabosky	.15	.07
394	Checklist 265-396	.60	.25
395	Omar Moreno	.15	.07
396	Twins TL BA: John Castino Fernando Arroyo	.60	.25
397	Ken Brett	.15	.07
398	Mike Squires	.15	.07
399	Pat Zachry	.15	.07
400	Johnny Bench	1.50	.70
401	Johnny Bench SA	.60	.25
402	Bill Stein	.15	.07
403	Jim Tracy	.15	.07
404	Dickie Thon	.15	.07
405	Rick Reuschel	.30	.14
406	Al Holland	.15	.07
407	Danny Boone	.15	.07
408	Ed Romero	.15	.07
409	Don Cooper	.15	.07
410	Ron Cey	.30	.14
411	Ron Cey SA	.15	.07
412	Luis Leal	.15	.07
413	Dan Meyer	.15	.07
414	Elias Sosa	.15	.07
415	Don Baylor	.60	.25
416	Marty Bystrom	.15	.07
417	Pat Kelly	.15	.07
418	Rangers Rookies John Butcher Bobby Johnson Dave Schmidt	.15	.07
419	Steve Stone	.30	.14
420	George Hendrick	.15	.07
421	Mark Clear	.15	.07
422	Cliff Johnson	.15	.07
423	Stan Papi	.15	.07
424	Bruce Benedict	.15	.07
425	John Candelaria	.15	.07
426	Orioles TL BA: Eddie Murray Pitching: Sammy Stewart	.60	.25
427	Ron Oester	.15	.07
428	LaMarr Hoyt	.15	.07
429	John Wathan	.15	.07
430	Vida Blue	.30	.14
431	Vida Blue SA	.15	.07
432	Mike Scott	.30	.14
433	Alan Ashby	.15	.07
434	Joe Lefebvre	.15	.07
435	Robin Yount	1.25	.55
436	Joe Strain	.15	.07
437	Juan Berenguer	.15	.07
438	Pete Mackanin	.15	.07
439	Dave Righetti	1.25	.55
440	Jeff Burroughs	.15	.07
441	Astros Rookies Danny Heep Billy Smith Bobby Sprowl	.15	.07
442	Bruce Kison	.15	.07
443	Mark Wagner	.15	.07
444	Terry Forster	.15	.07
445	Larry Parrish	.15	.07
446	Wayne Garland	.15	.07
447	Darrell Porter	.30	.14
448	Darrell Porter SA	.15	.07
449	Luis Aguayo	.15	.07
450	Jack Morris	.30	.14
451	Ed Miller	.15	.07
452	Lee Smith	3.00	1.35
453	Art Howe	.30	.14
454	Rick Langford	.15	.07
455	Tom Burgmeier	.15	.07
456	Chicago Cubs TL BA: Bill Buckner Pitching: Randy Martz	.60	.25
457	Tim Stoddard	.15	.07
458	Willie Montanez	.15	.07
459	Bruce Berenyi	.15	.07
460	Jack Clark	.30	.14
461	Rich Dotson	.15	.07
462	Dave Chalk	.15	.07
463	Jim Kern	.15	.07
464	Juan Bonilla	.15	.07
465	Lee Mazzilli	.15	.07
466	Randy Lerch	.15	.07
467	Mickey Hatcher	.15	.07
468	Floyd Bannister	.15	.07
469	Ed Ott	.15	.07
470	John Mayberry	.15	.07
471	Royals Rookies Atlee Hammaker Mike Jones Darryl Motley	.15	.07
472	Oscar Gamble	.15	.07
473	Mike Stanton	.15	.07
474	Ken Oberkfell	.15	.07
475	Alan Trammell	1.25	.55
476	Brian Kingman	.15	.07
477	Steve Yeager	.15	.07
478	Ray Searage	.15	.07
479	Rowland Office	.15	.07
480	Steve Carlton	1.25	.55
481	Steve Carlton SA	.60	.25
482	Glenn Hubbard	.15	.07
483	Gary Woods	.15	.07
484	Ivan DeJesus	.15	.07
485	Kent Tekulve	.30	.14
486	Yankees TL BA: Jerry Mumphrey Pitching: Tommy John	.15	.07
487	Bob McClure	.15	.07
488	Ron Jackson	.15	.07
489	Rick Dempsey	.30	.14
490	Dennis Eckersley	1.25	.55
491	Checklist 397-528	.60	.25
492	Joe Price	.15	.07
493	Chet Lemon	.15	.07
494	Hubie Brooks	.30	.14
495	Dennis Leonard	.15	.07
496	Johnny Grubb	.15	.07
497	Jim Anderson	.15	.07
498	Dave Bergman	.15	.07
499	Paul Mirabella	.15	.07
500	Rod Carew	1.25	.55
501	Rod Carew SA	.60	.25
502	Braves Rookies Steve Bedrosian UER (Photo actually Larry Owen) Brett Butler Larry Owen	1.50	.70
503	Julio Gonzalez	.15	.07
504	Rick Peters	.15	.07
505	Graig Nettles	.30	.14
506	Graig Nettles SA	.15	.07
507	Terry Harper	.15	.07
508	Jody Davis	.15	.07
509	Harry Spilman	.15	.07
510	Fernando Valenzuela	1.25	.55
511	Ruppert Jones	.15	.07
512	Jerry Dybzinski	.15	.07
513	Rick Rhoden	.15	.07
514	Joe Ferguson	.15	.07
515	Larry Bowa	.30	.14
516	Larry Bowa SA	.15	.07
517	Mark Brouhard	.15	.07
518	Garth Iorg	.15	.07
519	Glenn Adams	.15	.07
520	Mike Flanagan	.30	.14
521	Bill Almon	.15	.07
522	Chuck Rainey	.15	.07
523	Gary Gray	.15	.07
524	Tom Hausman	.15	.07
525	Ray Knight	.30	.14
526	Expos TL BA: Warren Cromartie Pitching: Bill Gullickson	.60	.25
527	John Henry Johnson	.15	.07
528	Matt Alexander	.15	.07
529	Allen Ripley	.15	.07
530	Dickie Noles	.15	.07
531	A's Rookies Rich Bordi Mark Budaska Kelvin Moore	.15	.07
532	Toby Harrah	.30	.14
533	Joaquin Andujar	.30	.14
534	Dave McKay	.15	.07
535	Lance Parrish	.60	.25
536	Rafael Ramirez	.15	.07
537	Doug Capilla	.15	.07
538	Lou Piniella	.30	.14
539	Vern Ruhle	.15	.07
540	Andre Dawson	1.25	.55
541	Barry Evans	.15	.07
542	Ned Yost	.15	.07
543	Bill Robinson	.15	.07
544	Larry Christenson	.15	.07
545	Reggie Smith	.30	.14
546	Reggie Smith SA	.15	.07
547	Rod Carew AS	1.25	.55
548	Willie Randolph AS	.30	.14
549	George Brett AS	1.25	.55
550	Bucky Dent AS	.15	.07
551	Reggie Jackson AS	.60	.25
552	Ken Singleton AS	.15	.07
553	Dave Winfield AS	.60	.25
554	Carlton Fisk AS	.60	.25
555	Scott McGregor AS	.15	.07
556	Jack Morris AS	.15	.07
557	Rich Gossage AS	.30	.14
558	John Tudor	.30	.14
559	Indians TL BA: Mike Hargrove Pitching: Bert Blyleven	.15	.07
560	Doug Corbett	.15	.07
561	Cardinals Rookies Glenn Brummer Luis DeLeon Gene Roof	.15	.07
562	Mike O'Berry	.15	.07
563	Ross Baumgarten	.15	.07
564	Doug DeCinces	.30	.14
565	Jackson Todd	.15	.07
566	Mike Jorgensen	.15	.07
567	Bob Babcock	.15	.07
568	Joe Pettini	.15	.07

#	Player	Price 1	Price 2
569	Willie Randolph	.30	.14
570	Willie Randolph SA	.30	.14
571	Glenn Abbott	.15	.07
572	Juan Beniquez	.15	.07
573	Rick Waits	.15	.07
574	Mike Ramsey	.15	.07
575	Al Cowens	.15	.07
576	Giants TL	.60	.25
	BA: Milt May		
	Pitching: Vida Blue		
577	Rick Monday	.15	.07
578	Shooty Babitt	.15	.07
579	Rick Mahler	.15	.07
580	Bobby Bonds	.30	.14
581	Ron Reed	.15	.07
582	Luis Pujols	.15	.07
583	Tippy Martinez	.15	.07
584	Hosken Powell	.15	.07
585	Rollie Fingers	1.25	.55
586	Rollie Fingers SA	.60	.25
587	Tim Lollar	.15	.07
588	Dale Berra	.15	.07
589	Dave Stapleton	.15	.07
590	Al Oliver	.30	.14
591	Al Oliver SA	.15	.07
592	Craig Swan	.15	.07
593	Billy Smith	.15	.07
594	Renie Martin	.15	.07
595	Dave Collins	.15	.07
596	Damaso Garcia	.15	.07
597	Wayne Nordhagen	.15	.07
598	Bob Galasso	.15	.07
599	White Sox Rookies	.15	.07
	Jay Loviglio		
	Reggie Patterson		
	Leo Sutherland		
600	Dave Winfield	1.25	.55
601	Sid Monge	.15	.07
602	Freddie Patek	.15	.07
603	Rich Hebner	.30	.14
604	Orlando Sanchez	.15	.07
605	Steve Rogers	.15	.07
606	Blue Jays TL	.60	.25
	BA: John Mayberry		
	Pitching: Dave Stieb		
607	Leon Durham	.15	.07
608	Jerry Royster	.15	.07
609	Rick Sutcliffe	.30	.14
610	Rickey Henderson	3.00	1.35
611	Joe Nolan	.30	.14
612	Gary Ward	.15	.07
613	Jim Gantner	.30	.14
614	Juan Eichelberger	.15	.07
615	Bob Boone	.30	.14
616	Bob Boone SA	.15	.07
617	Scott McGregor	.15	.07
618	Tim Foli	.15	.07
619	Bill Campbell	.15	.07
620	Ken Griffey	.30	.14
621	Ken Griffey SA	.15	.07
622	Dennis Lamp	.15	.07
623	Mets Rookies	.60	.25
	Ron Gardenhire		
	Terry Leach		
	Tim Leary		
624	Fergie Jenkins	1.25	.55
625	Hal McRae	.30	.14
626	Randy Jones	.15	.07
627	Enos Cabell	.15	.07
628	Bill Travers	.15	.07
629	John Wockenfuss	.15	.07
630	Joe Charboneau	.30	.14
631	Gene Tenace	.15	.14
632	Bryan Clark	.15	.07
633	Mitchell Page	.15	.07
634	Checklist 529-660	.60	.25
635	Ron Davis	.15	.07
636	Phillies TL	1.25	.55
	BA: Pete Rose		
	Pitching: Steve Carlton		
637	Rick Camp	.15	.07
638	John Milner	.15	.07
639	Ken Kravec	.15	.07
640	Cesar Cedeno	.30	.14
641	Steve Mura	.15	.07
642	Mike Scioscia	.30	.14
643	Pete Vuckovich	.15	.07
644	John Castino	.15	.07
645	Frank White	.30	.14
646	Frank White SA	.15	.07
647	Warren Brusstar	.15	.07
648	Jose Morales	.15	.07
649	Ken Clay	.15	.07
650	Carl Yastrzemski	1.25	.55
651	Carl Yastrzemski SA	.60	.25
652	Steve Nicosia	.15	.07
653	Angels Rookies	.60	.25
	Tom Brunansky		
	Luis Sanchez		
	Daryl Sconiers		
654	Jim Morrison	.15	.07
655	Joel Youngblood	.15	.07
656	Eddie Whitson	.15	.07
657	Tom Poquette	.15	.07
658	Tito Landrum	.15	.07
659	Fred Martinez	.15	.07
660	Dave Concepcion	.30	.14
661	Dave Concepcion SA	.15	.07
662	Luis Salazar	.15	.07
663	Hector Cruz	.15	.07
664	Dan Spillner	.15	.07
665	Jim Clancy	.15	.07
666	Tigers TL	.60	.25
	BA: Steve Kemp		
	Pitching: Dan Petry		
667	Jeff Reardon	.60	.25
668	Dale Murphy	1.25	.55
669	Larry Milbourne	.15	.07
670	Steve Kemp	.15	.07
671	Mike Davis	.15	.07
672	Bob Knepper	.15	.07
673	Keith Drumwright	.15	.07
674	Dave Goltz	.15	.07
675	Cecil Cooper	.30	.14
676	Sal Butera	.15	.07
677	Alfredo Griffin	.15	.07
678	Tom Paciorek	.30	.14
679	Sammy Stewart	.15	.07
680	Gary Matthews	.30	.14
681	Dodgers Rookies	1.25	.55
	Mike Marshall		
	Ron Roenicke		
	Steve Sax		
682	Jesse Jefferson	.15	.07
683	Phil Garner	.30	.14
684	Harold Baines	1.25	.55
685	Bert Blyleven	.60	.25
686	Gary Allenson	.15	.07
687	Greg Minton	.15	.07
688	Leon Roberts	.15	.07
689	Lary Sorensen	.15	.07
690	Dave Kingman	.30	.14
691	Dan Schatzeder	.15	.07
692	Wayne Gross	.15	.07
693	Cesar Geronimo	.15	.07
694	Dave Wehrmeister	.15	.07
695	Warren Cromartie	.15	.07
696	Pirates TL	.60	.25
	BA: Bill Madlock		
	Pitching: Eddie Solomon		
697	John Montefusco	.15	.07
698	Tony Scott	.15	.07
699	Dick Tidrow	.15	.07
700	George Foster	.30	.14
701	George Foster SA	.15	.07
702	Steve Renko	.15	.07
703	Brewers TL	.60	.25
	BA: Cecil Cooper		
	Pitching: Pete Vuckovich		
704	Mickey Rivers	.15	.07
705	Mickey Rivers SA	.15	.07
706	Barry Foote	.15	.07
707	Mark Bomback	.15	.07
708	Gene Richards	.15	.07
709	Don Money	.15	.07
710	Jerry Reuss	.30	.14
711	Mariners Rookies	.60	.25
	Dave Edler		
	Dave Henderson		
	Reggie Walton		
712	Dennis Martinez	.60	.25
713	Del Unser	.15	.07
714	Jerry Koosman	.30	.14
715	Willie Stargell	1.25	.55
716	Willie Stargell SA	.60	.25
717	Rick Miller	.15	.07
718	Charlie Hough	.30	.14
719	Jerry Narron	.15	.07
720	Greg Luzinski	.30	.14
721	Greg Luzinski SA	.15	.07
722	Jerry Martin	.15	.07
723	Junior Kennedy	.15	.07
724	Dave Rosello	.15	.07
725	Amos Otis	.30	.14
726	Amos Otis SA	.15	.07
727	Sixto Lezcano	.15	.07
728	Aurelio Lopez	.15	.07
729	Jim Spencer	.15	.07
730	Gary Carter	1.25	.55
731	Padres Rookies	.15	.07
	Mike Armstrong		
	Doug Gwosdz		
	Fred Kuhaulua		
732	Mike Lum	.15	.07
733	Larry McWilliams	.15	.07
734	Mike Ivie	.15	.07
735	Rudy May	.15	.07
736	Jerry Turner	.15	.07
737	Reggie Cleveland	.15	.07
738	Dave Engle	.15	.07
739	Joey McLaughlin	.15	.07
740	Dave Lopes	.30	.14
741	Dave Lopes SA	.15	.07
742	Dick Drago	.15	.07
743	John Stearns	.15	.07
744	Mike Witt	.30	.14
745	Bake McBride	.15	.07
746	Andre Thornton	.15	.07
747	John Lowenstein	.15	.07
748	Marc Hill	.15	.07
749	Bob Shirley	.15	.07
750	Jim Rice	.30	.14
751	Rick Honeycutt	.15	.07
752	Lee Lacy	.15	.07
753	Tom Brookens	.15	.07
754	Joe Morgan	1.25	.55
755	Joe Morgan SA	.60	.25
756	Reds TL	.60	.25
	BA: Ken Griffey		
	Pitching: Tom Seaver		
757	Tom Underwood	.15	.07
758	Claudell Washington	.15	.07
759	Paul Splittorff	.15	.07
760	Bill Buckner	.30	.14
761	Dave Smith	.15	.07
762	Mike Phillips	.15	.07
763	Tom Hume	.15	.07
764	Steve Swisher	.15	.07
765	Gorman Thomas	.30	.14
766	Twins Rookies	1.50	.70
	Lenny Faedo		
	Kent Hrbek		
	Tim Laudner		
767	Roy Smalley	.15	.07
768	Jerry Garvin	.15	.07
769	Richie Zisk	.15	.07
770	Rich Gossage	.60	.25
771	Rich Gossage SA	.30	.14
772	Bert Campaneris	.30	.14
773	John Denny	.15	.07
774	Jay Johnstone	.30	.14
775	Bob Forsch	.15	.07
776	Mark Belanger	.15	.07
777	Tom Griffin	.15	.07
778	Kevin Hickey	.15	.07
779	Grant Jackson	.15	.07
780	Pete Rose	2.50	1.10
781	Pete Rose SA	.60	.25
782	Frank Taveras	.15	.07
783	Greg Harris	.15	.07
784	Milt Wilcox	.15	.07
785	Dan Driessen	.15	.07
786	Red Sox TL	.60	.25
	BA: Carney Lansford		
	Pitching: Mike Torrez		
787	Fred Stanley	.15	.07
788	Woodie Fryman	.15	.07
789	Checklist 661-792	.60	.25

❏ 790 Larry Gura ...... .15 .07
❏ 791 Bobby Brown ...... .15 .07
❏ 792 Frank Tanana ...... .30 .14

1982 Topps Traded

CUBS
FERGIE JENKINS

	NRMT	VG-E
COMP.FACT.SET (132)	250.00	110.00
COMMON CARD (1T-132T)	.50	.23
MINOR STARS	1.00	.45
SEMISTARS	2.00	.90
UNLISTED STARS	4.00	1.80

❏ 1T Doyle Alexander	.50	.23
❏ 2T Jesse Barfield	1.00	.45
❏ 3T Ross Baumgarten	.50	.23
❏ 4T Steve Bedrosian	1.00	.45
❏ 5T Mark Belanger	1.00	.45
❏ 6T Kurt Bevacqua	.50	.23
❏ 7T Tim Blackwell	.50	.23
❏ 8T Vida Blue	1.00	.45
❏ 9T Bob Boone	1.00	.45
❏ 10T Larry Bowa	1.00	.45
❏ 11T Dan Briggs	.50	.23
❏ 12T Bobby Brown	.50	.23
❏ 13T Tom Brunansky	1.00	.45
❏ 14T Jeff Burroughs	.50	.23
❏ 15T Enos Cabell	.50	.23
❏ 16T Bill Campbell	.50	.23
❏ 17T Bobby Castillo	.50	.23
❏ 18T Bill Caudill	.50	.23
❏ 19T Cesar Cedeno	1.00	.45
❏ 20T Dave Collins	.50	.23
❏ 21T Doug Corbett	.50	.23
❏ 22T Al Cowens	.50	.23
❏ 23T Chili Davis	8.00	3.60
❏ 24T Dick Davis	.50	.23
❏ 25T Ron Davis	.50	.23
❏ 26T Doug DeCinces	1.00	.45
❏ 27T Ivan DeJesus	.50	.23
❏ 28T Bob Dernier	.50	.23
❏ 29T Bo Diaz	.50	.23
❏ 30T Roger Erickson	.50	.23
❏ 31T Jim Essian	.50	.23
❏ 32T Ed Farmer	.50	.23
❏ 33T Doug Flynn	.50	.23
❏ 34T Tim Foli	.50	.23
❏ 35T Dan Ford	.50	.23
❏ 36T George Foster	1.00	.45
❏ 37T Dave Frost	.50	.23
❏ 38T Rich Gale	.50	.23
❏ 39T Ron Gardenhire	.50	.23
❏ 40T Ken Griffey	1.00	.45
❏ 41T Greg Harris	1.00	.45
❏ 42T Von Hayes	1.00	.45
❏ 43T Larry Herndon	.50	.23
❏ 44T Kent Hrbek	2.00	.90
❏ 45T Mike Ivie	.50	.23
❏ 46T Grant Jackson	.50	.23
❏ 47T Reggie Jackson	8.00	3.60
❏ 48T Ron Jackson	.50	.23
❏ 49T Fergie Jenkins	4.00	1.80
❏ 50T Lamar Johnson	.50	.23
❏ 51T Randy Johnson	.50	.23
❏ 52T Jay Johnstone	1.00	.45
❏ 53T Mick Kelleher	.50	.23
❏ 54T Steve Kemp	.50	.23
❏ 55T Junior Kennedy	.50	.23

❏ 56T Jim Kern	.50	.23
❏ 57T Ray Knight	1.00	.45
❏ 58T Wayne Krenchicki	.50	.23
❏ 59T Mike Krukow	.50	.23
❏ 60T Duane Kuiper	.50	.23
❏ 61T Mike LaCoss	.50	.23
❏ 62T Chet Lemon	.50	.23
❏ 63T Sixto Lezcano	.50	.23
❏ 64T Dave Lopes	1.00	.45
❏ 65T Jerry Martin	.50	.23
❏ 66T Renie Martin	.50	.23
❏ 67T John Mayberry	.50	.23
❏ 68T Lee Mazzilli	.50	.23
❏ 69T Bake McBride	.50	.23
❏ 70T Dan Meyer	.50	.23
❏ 71T Larry Milbourne	.50	.23
❏ 72T Eddie Milner	.50	.23
❏ 73T Sid Monge	.50	.23
❏ 74T John Montefusco	.50	.23
❏ 75T Jose Morales	.50	.23
❏ 76T Keith Moreland	.50	.23
❏ 77T Jim Morrison	.50	.23
❏ 78T Rance Mulliniks	.50	.23
❏ 79T Steve Mura	.50	.23
❏ 80T Gene Nelson	.50	.23
❏ 81T Joe Nolan	.50	.23
❏ 82T Dickie Noles	.50	.23
❏ 83T Al Oliver	1.00	.45
❏ 84T Jorge Orta	.50	.23
❏ 85T Tom Paciorek	1.00	.45
❏ 86T Larry Parrish	.50	.23
❏ 87T Jack Perconte	.50	.23
❏ 88T Gaylord Perry	4.00	1.80
❏ 89T Rob Picciolo	.50	.23
❏ 90T Joe Pittman	.50	.23
❏ 91T Hosken Powell	.50	.23
❏ 92T Mike Proly	.50	.23
❏ 93T Greg Pryor	.50	.23
❏ 94T Charlie Puleo	.50	.23
❏ 95T Shane Rawley	.50	.23
❏ 96T Johnny Ray	1.00	.45
❏ 97T Dave Revering	.50	.23
❏ 98T Cal Ripken	200.00	90.00
❏ 99T Allen Ripley	.50	.23
❏ 100T Bill Robinson	.50	.23
❏ 101T Aurelio Rodriguez	.50	.23
❏ 102T Joe Rudi	.50	.23
❏ 103T Steve Sax	4.00	1.80
❏ 104T Dan Schatzeder	.50	.23
❏ 105T Bob Shirley	.50	.23
❏ 106T Eric Show	1.00	.45
❏ 107T Roy Smalley	.50	.23
❏ 108T Lonnie Smith	1.00	.45
❏ 109T Ozzie Smith	15.00	6.75
❏ 110T Reggie Smith	1.00	.45
❏ 111T Lary Sorensen	.50	.23
❏ 112T Elias Sosa	.50	.23
❏ 113T Mike Stanton	.50	.23
❏ 114T Steve Stroughter	.50	.23
❏ 115T Champ Summers	.50	.23
❏ 116T Rick Sutcliffe	1.00	.45
❏ 117T Frank Tanana	1.00	.45
❏ 118T Frank Taveras	.50	.23
❏ 119T Garry Templeton	1.00	.45
❏ 120T Alex Trevino	.50	.23
❏ 121T Jerry Turner	.50	.23
❏ 122T Ed VandeBerg	.50	.23
❏ 123T Tom Veryzer	.50	.23
❏ 124T Ron Washington	.50	.23
❏ 125T Bob Watson	1.00	.45
❏ 126T Dennis Werth	.50	.23
❏ 127T Eddie Whitson	.50	.23
❏ 128T Rob Wilfong	.50	.23
❏ 129T Bump Wills	.50	.23
❏ 130T Gary Woods	.50	.23
❏ 131T Butch Wynegar	.50	.23
❏ 132T Checklist: 1-132	.50	.23

1983 Topps

	NRMT	VG-E
COMPLETE SET (792)	120.00	55.00
COMMON CARD (1-792)	.15	.07
MINOR STARS	.30	.14
SEMISTARS	.60	.23
UNLISTED STARS	1.25	.55

SUBSET CARDS HALF VALUE OF BASE CARDS

❏ 1 Tony Armas RB	.30	.14
❏ 2 Rickey Henderson RB	.60	.25
Sets modern SB record		
❏ 3 Greg Minton RB	.15	.07
269 1/3 homerless innings streak		
❏ 4 Lance Parrish RB	.15	.07
❏ 5 Manny Trillo RB	.15	.07
479 consecutive errorless chances, second baseman		
❏ 6 John Wathan RB	.15	.07
ML catcher steals, season		
❏ 7 Gene Richards	.15	.07
❏ 8 Steve Balboni	.15	.07
❏ 9 Joey McLaughlin	.15	.07
❏ 10 Gorman Thomas	.15	.07
❏ 11 Billy Gardner MG	.15	.07
❏ 12 Paul Mirabella	.15	.07
❏ 13 Larry Herndon	.15	.07
❏ 14 Frank LaCorte	.15	.07
❏ 15 Ron Cey	.30	.14
❏ 16 George Vukovich	.15	.07
❏ 17 Kent Tekulve	.30	.14
❏ 18 Kent Tekulve SV	.15	.07
❏ 19 Oscar Gamble	.15	.07
❏ 20 Carlton Fisk	1.25	.55
❏ 21 Baltimore Orioles TL	.60	.25
BA: Eddie Murray		
ERA: Jim Palmer		
❏ 22 Randy Martz	.15	.07
❏ 23 Mike Heath	.15	.07
❏ 24 Steve Mura	.15	.07
❏ 25 Hal McRae	.30	.14
❏ 26 Jerry Royster	.15	.07
❏ 27 Doug Corbett	.15	.07
❏ 28 Bruce Bochte	.15	.07
❏ 29 Randy Jones	.15	.07
❏ 30 Jim Rice	.30	.14
❏ 31 Bill Gullickson	.15	.07
❏ 32 Dave Bergman	.15	.07
❏ 33 Jack O'Connor	.15	.07
❏ 34 Paul Householder	.15	.07
❏ 35 Rollie Fingers	1.25	.55
❏ 36 Rollie Fingers SV	.60	.25
❏ 37 Darrell Johnson MG	.15	.07
❏ 38 Tim Flannery	.15	.07
❏ 39 Terry Puhl	.15	.07
❏ 40 Fernando Valenzuela	.60	.25
❏ 41 Jerry Turner	.15	.07
❏ 42 Dale Murray	.15	.07
❏ 43 Bob Dernier	.15	.07
❏ 44 Don Robinson	.15	.07
❏ 45 John Mayberry	.15	.07
❏ 46 Richard Dotson	.15	.07
❏ 47 Dave McKay	.15	.07
❏ 48 Lary Sorensen	.15	.07
❏ 49 Willie McGee	3.00	1.35
❏ 50 Bob Horner UER	.15	.07
('82 RBI total 7)		
❏ 51 Chicago Cubs TL	.30	.14
BA: Leon Durham		
ERA: Fergie Jenkins		
❏ 52 Onix Concepcion	.15	.07
❏ 53 Mike Witt	.15	.07

❏ 54	Jim Maler	.15	.07
❏ 55	Mookie Wilson	.30	.14
❏ 56	Chuck Rainey	.15	.07
❏ 57	Tim Blackwell	.15	.07
❏ 58	Al Holland	.15	.07
❏ 59	Benny Ayala	.15	.07
❏ 60	Johnny Bench	1.50	.70
❏ 61	Johnny Bench SV	.60	.25
❏ 62	Bob McClure	.15	.07
❏ 63	Rick Monday	.15	.07
❏ 64	Bill Stein	.15	.07
❏ 65	Jack Morris	.30	.14
❏ 66	Bob Lillis MG	.15	.07
❏ 67	Sal Butera	.15	.07
❏ 68	Eric Show	.15	.07
❏ 69	Lee Lacy	.15	.07
❏ 70	Steve Carlton	1.25	.55
❏ 71	Steve Carlton SV	.60	.25
❏ 72	Tom Paciorek	.30	.14
❏ 73	Allen Ripley	.15	.07
❏ 74	Julio Gonzalez	.15	.07
❏ 75	Amos Otis	.30	.14
❏ 76	Rick Mahler	.15	.07
❏ 77	Hosken Powell	.15	.07
❏ 78	Bill Caudill	.15	.07
❏ 79	Mick Kelleher	.15	.07
❏ 80	George Foster	.30	.14
❏ 81	Yankees TL	.30	.14
	BA: Jerry Mumphrey		
	ERA: Dave Righetti		
❏ 82	Bruce Hurst	.15	.07
❏ 83	Ryne Sandberg	20.00	9.00
❏ 84	Milt May	.15	.07
❏ 85	Ken Singleton	.15	.07
❏ 86	Tom Hume	.15	.07
❏ 87	Joe Rudi	.15	.07
❏ 88	Jim Gantner	.15	.07
❏ 89	Leon Roberts	.15	.07
❏ 90	Jerry Reuss	.30	.14
❏ 91	Larry Milbourne	.15	.07
❏ 92	Mike LaCoss	.15	.07
❏ 93	John Castino	.15	.07
❏ 94	Dave Edwards	.15	.07
❏ 95	Alan Trammell	1.25	.55
❏ 96	Dick Howser MG	.15	.07
❏ 97	Ross Baumgarten	.15	.07
❏ 98	Vance Law	.15	.07
❏ 99	Dickie Noles	.15	.07
❏ 100	Pete Rose	2.00	.90
❏ 101	Pete Rose SV	.60	.25
❏ 102	Dave Beard	.15	.07
❏ 103	Darrell Porter	.15	.07
❏ 104	Bob Walk	.15	.07
❏ 105	Don Baylor	.60	.25
❏ 106	Gene Nelson	.15	.07
❏ 107	Mike Jorgensen	.15	.07
❏ 108	Glenn Hoffman	.15	.07
❏ 109	Luis Leal	.15	.07
❏ 110	Ken Griffey	.30	.14
❏ 111	Montreal Expos TL	.30	.14
	BA: Al Oliver		
	ERA: Steve Rogers		
❏ 112	Bob Shirley	.15	.07
❏ 113	Ron Roenicke	.15	.07
❏ 114	Jim Slaton	.15	.07
❏ 115	Chili Davis	1.25	.55
❏ 116	Dave Schmidt	.15	.07
❏ 117	Alan Knicely	.15	.07
❏ 118	Chris Welsh	.15	.07
❏ 119	Tom Brookens	.15	.07
❏ 120	Len Barker	.15	.07
❏ 121	Mickey Hatcher	.15	.07
❏ 122	Jimmy Smith	.15	.07
❏ 123	George Frazier	.15	.07
❏ 124	Marc Hill	.15	.07
❏ 125	Leon Durham	.30	.14
❏ 126	Joe Torre MG	.30	.14
❏ 127	Preston Hanna	.15	.07
❏ 128	Mike Ramsey	.15	.07
❏ 129	Checklist: 1-132	.15	.07
❏ 130	Dave Stieb	.30	.14
❏ 131	Ed Ott	.15	.07
❏ 132	Todd Cruz	.15	.07
❏ 133	Jim Barr	.15	.07
❏ 134	Hubie Brooks	.30	.14
❏ 135	Dwight Evans	.30	.14
❏ 136	Willie Aikens	.15	.07
❏ 137	Woodie Fryman	.15	.07
❏ 138	Rick Dempsey	.30	.14
❏ 139	Bruce Berenyi	.15	.07
❏ 140	Willie Randolph	.30	.14
❏ 141	Indians TL	.30	.14
	BA: Toby Harrah		
	ERA: Rick Sutcliffe		
❏ 142	Mike Caldwell	.15	.07
❏ 143	Joe Pettini	.15	.07
❏ 144	Mark Wagner	.15	.07
❏ 145	Don Sutton	1.25	.55
❏ 146	Don Sutton SV	.60	.25
❏ 147	Rick Leach	.15	.07
❏ 148	Dave Roberts	.15	.07
❏ 149	Johnny Ray	.15	.07
❏ 150	Bruce Sutter	.30	.14
❏ 151	Bruce Sutter SV	.15	.07
❏ 152	Jay Johnstone	.30	.14
❏ 153	Jerry Koosman	.30	.14
❏ 154	Johnnie LeMaster	.15	.07
❏ 155	Dan Quisenberry	.30	.14
❏ 156	Billy Martin MG	.30	.14
❏ 157	Steve Bedrosian	.30	.14
❏ 158	Rob Wilfong	.15	.07
❏ 159	Mike Stanton	.15	.07
❏ 160	Dave Kingman	.60	.25
❏ 161	Dave Kingman SV	.30	.14
❏ 162	Mark Clear	.15	.07
❏ 163	Cal Ripken	12.00	5.50
❏ 164	David Palmer	.15	.07
❏ 165	Dan Driessen	.15	.07
❏ 166	John Pacella	.15	.07
❏ 167	Mark Brouhard	.15	.07
❏ 168	Juan Eichelberger	.15	.07
❏ 169	Doug Flynn	.15	.07
❏ 170	Steve Howe	.15	.07
❏ 171	Giants TL	.60	.25
	BA: Joe Morgan		
	ERA: Bill Laskey		
❏ 172	Vern Ruhle	.15	.07
❏ 173	Jim Morrison	.15	.07
❏ 174	Jerry Ujdur	.15	.07
❏ 175	Bo Diaz	.15	.07
❏ 176	Dave Righetti	.30	.14
❏ 177	Harold Baines	1.25	.55
❏ 178	Luis Tiant	.30	.14
❏ 179	Luis Tiant SV	.15	.07
❏ 180	Rickey Henderson	2.00	.90
❏ 181	Terry Felton	.15	.07
❏ 182	Mike Fischlin	.15	.07
❏ 183	Ed VandeBerg	.15	.07
❏ 184	Bob Clark	.15	.07
❏ 185	Tim Lollar	.15	.07
❏ 186	Whitey Herzog MG	.30	.14
❏ 187	Terry Leach	.15	.07
❏ 188	Rick Miller	.15	.07
❏ 189	Dan Schatzeder	.15	.07
❏ 190	Cecil Cooper	.30	.14
❏ 191	Joe Price	.15	.07
❏ 192	Floyd Rayford	.15	.07
❏ 193	Harry Spilman	.15	.07
❏ 194	Cesar Geronimo	.15	.07
❏ 195	Bob Stoddard	.15	.07
❏ 196	Bill Fahey	.15	.07
❏ 197	Jim Eisenreich	1.25	.55
❏ 198	Kiko Garcia	.15	.07
❏ 199	Marty Bystrom	.15	.07
❏ 200	Rod Carew	1.25	.55
❏ 201	Rod Carew SV	.60	.25
❏ 202	Blue Jays TL	.30	.14
	BA: Damaso Garcia		
	ERA: Dave Stieb		
❏ 203	Mike Morgan	.15	.07
❏ 204	Junior Kennedy	.15	.07
❏ 205	Dave Parker	.30	.14
❏ 206	Ken Oberkfell	.15	.07
❏ 207	Rick Camp	.15	.07
❏ 208	Dan Meyer	.15	.07
❏ 209	Mike Moore	.30	.14
❏ 210	Jack Clark	.30	.14
❏ 211	John Denny	.15	.07
❏ 212	John Stearns	.15	.07
❏ 213	Tom Burgmeier	.15	.07
❏ 214	Jerry White	.15	.07
❏ 215	Mario Soto	.15	.07
❏ 216	Tony LaRussa MG	.30	.14
❏ 217	Tim Stoddard	.15	.07
❏ 218	Roy Howell	.15	.07
❏ 219	Mike Armstrong	.15	.07
❏ 220	Dusty Baker	.30	.14
❏ 221	Joe Niekro	.30	.14
❏ 222	Damaso Garcia	.15	.07
❏ 223	John Montefusco	.15	.07
❏ 224	Mickey Rivers	.15	.07
❏ 225	Enos Cabell	.15	.07
❏ 226	Enrique Romo	.15	.07
❏ 227	Chris Bando	.15	.07
❏ 228	Joaquin Andujar	.15	.07
❏ 229	Phillies TL	.60	.25
	BA: Bo Diaz		
	ERA: Steve Carlton		
❏ 230	Fergie Jenkins	1.25	.55
❏ 231	Fergie Jenkins SV	.60	.25
❏ 232	Tom Brunansky	.30	.14
❏ 233	Wayne Gross	.15	.07
❏ 234	Larry Andersen	.15	.07
❏ 235	Claudell Washington	.15	.07
❏ 236	Steve Renko	.15	.07
❏ 237	Dan Norman	.15	.07
❏ 238	Bud Black	.30	.14
❏ 239	Dave Stapleton	.15	.07
❏ 240	Rich Gossage	.60	.25
❏ 241	Rich Gossage SV	.30	.14
❏ 242	Joe Nolan	.15	.07
❏ 243	Duane Walker	.15	.07
❏ 244	Dwight Bernard	.15	.07
❏ 245	Steve Sax	.30	.14
❏ 246	George Bamberger MG	.15	.07
❏ 247	Dave Smith	.15	.07
❏ 248	Bake McBride	.15	.07
❏ 249	Checklist: 133-264	.30	.14
❏ 250	Bill Buckner	.30	.14
❏ 251	Alan Wiggins	.15	.07
❏ 252	Luis Aguayo	.15	.07
❏ 253	Larry McWilliams	.15	.07
❏ 254	Rick Cerone	.15	.07
❏ 255	Gene Garber	.15	.07
❏ 256	Gene Garber SV	.15	.07
❏ 257	Jesse Barfield	.30	.14
❏ 258	Manny Castillo	.15	.07
❏ 259	Jeff Jones	.15	.07
❏ 260	Steve Kemp	.15	.07
❏ 261	Tigers TL	.30	.14
	BA: Larry Herndon		
	ERA: Dan Petry		
❏ 262	Ron Jackson	.15	.07
❏ 263	Renie Martin	.15	.07
❏ 264	Jamie Quirk	.15	.07
❏ 265	Joel Youngblood	.15	.07
❏ 266	Paul Boris	.15	.07
❏ 267	Terry Francona	.15	.07
❏ 268	Storm Davis	.15	.07
❏ 269	Ron Oester	.15	.07
❏ 270	Dennis Eckersley	1.25	.55
❏ 271	Ed Romero	.15	.07
❏ 272	Frank Tanana	.30	.14
❏ 273	Mark Belanger	.15	.07
❏ 274	Terry Kennedy	.15	.07
❏ 275	Ray Knight	.30	.14
❏ 276	Gene Mauch MG	.15	.07
❏ 277	Rance Mulliniks	.15	.07
❏ 278	Kevin Hickey	.15	.07
❏ 279	Greg Gross	.15	.07
❏ 280	Bert Blyleven	.60	.25
❏ 281	Andre Robertson	.15	.07
❏ 282	Reggie Smith	1.25	.55
	(Ryne Sandberg ducking back)		
❏ 283	Reggie Smith SV	.15	.07
❏ 284	Jeff Lahti	.15	.07
❏ 285	Lance Parrish	.30	.14
❏ 286	Rick Langford	.15	.07
❏ 287	Bobby Brown	.15	.07
❏ 288	Joe Cowley	.15	.07
❏ 289	Jerry Dybzinski	.15	.07
❏ 290	Jeff Reardon	.30	.14
❏ 291	Pirates TL	.30	.14
	BA: Bill Madlock		
	ERA: John Candelaria		
❏ 292	Craig Swan	.15	.07
❏ 293	Glenn Gulliver	.15	.07

294	Dave Engle	.15	.07
295	Jerry Remy	.15	.07
296	Greg Harris	.15	.07
297	Ned Yost	.15	.07
298	Floyd Chiffer	.15	.07
299	George Wright	.15	.07
300	Mike Schmidt	2.00	.90
301	Mike Schmidt SV	.60	.25
302	Ernie Whitt	.15	.07
303	Miguel Dilone	.15	.07
304	Dave Rucker	.15	.07
305	Larry Bowa	.30	.14
306	Tom Lasorda MG	.60	.25
307	Lou Piniella	.30	.14
308	Jesus Vega	.15	.07
309	Jeff Leonard	.15	.07
310	Greg Luzinski	.30	.14
311	Glenn Brummer	.15	.07
312	Brian Kingman	.15	.07
313	Gary Gray	.15	.07
314	Ken Dayley	.15	.07
315	Rick Burleson	.15	.07
316	Paul Splittorff	.15	.07
317	Gary Rajsich	.15	.07
318	John Tudor	.15	.07
319	Lenn Sakata	.15	.07
320	Steve Rogers	.15	.07
321	Brewers TL	.60	.25
	BA: Robin Yount		
	ERA: Pete Vuckovich		
322	Dave Van Gorder	.15	.07
323	Luis DeLeon	.15	.07
324	Mike Marshall	.15	.07
325	Von Hayes	.30	.14
326	Garth Iorg	.15	.07
327	Bobby Castillo	.15	.07
328	Craig Reynolds	.15	.07
329	Randy Niemann	.15	.07
330	Buddy Bell	.30	.14
331	Mike Krukow	.15	.07
332	Glenn Wilson	.30	.14
333	Dave LaRoche	.15	.07
334	Dave LaRoche SV	.15	.07
335	Steve Henderson	.15	.07
336	Rene Lachemann MG	.15	.07
337	Tito Landrum	.15	.07
338	Bob Owchinko	.15	.07
339	Terry Harper	.15	.07
340	Larry Gura	.15	.07
341	Doug DeCinces	.30	.14
342	Atlee Hammaker	.15	.07
343	Bob Bailor	.15	.07
344	Roger LaFrancois	.15	.07
345	Jim Clancy	.15	.07
346	Joe Pittman	.15	.07
347	Sammy Stewart	.15	.07
348	Alan Bannister	.15	.07
349	Checklist: 265-396	.30	.14
350	Robin Yount	1.25	.55
351	Reds TL	.30	.14
	BA: Cesar Cedeno		
	ERA: Mario Soto		
352	Mike Scioscia	.30	.14
353	Steve Comer	.15	.07
354	Randy Johnson	.15	.07
355	Jim Bibby	.15	.07
356	Gary Woods	.15	.07
357	Len Matuszek	.15	.07
358	Jerry Garvin	.15	.07
359	Dave Collins	.15	.07
360	Nolan Ryan	6.00	2.70
361	Nolan Ryan SV	3.00	1.35
362	Bill Almon	.15	.07
363	John Stuper	.15	.07
364	Brett Butler	1.25	.55
365	Dave Lopes	.30	.14
366	Dick Williams MG	.15	.07
367	Bud Anderson	.15	.07
368	Richie Zisk	.15	.07
369	Jesse Orosco	.30	.14
370	Gary Carter	1.25	.55
371	Mike Richardt	.15	.07
372	Terry Crowley	.15	.07
373	Kevin Saucier	.15	.07
374	Wayne Krenchicki	.15	.07
375	Pete Vuckovich	.15	.07
376	Ken Landreaux	.15	.07
377	Lee May	.30	.14
378	Lee May SV	.15	.07
379	Guy Sularz	.15	.07
380	Ron Davis	.15	.07
381	Red Sox TL	.30	.14
	BA: Jim Rice		
	ERA: Bob Stanley		
382	Bob Knepper	.15	.07
383	Ozzie Virgil	.15	.07
384	Dave Dravecky	1.25	.55
385	Mike Easler	.15	.07
386	Rod Carew AS	.60	.25
387	Bob Grich AS	.15	.07
388	George Brett AS	1.25	.55
389	Robin Yount AS	.60	.25
390	Reggie Jackson AS	.60	.25
391	Rickey Henderson AS	.60	.25
392	Fred Lynn AS	.15	.07
393	Carlton Fisk AS	.60	.25
394	Pete Vuckovich AS	.15	.07
395	Larry Gura AS	.15	.07
396	Dan Quisenberry AS	.15	.07
397	Pete Rose AS	.60	.25
398	Manny Trillo AS	.15	.07
399	Mike Schmidt AS	.60	.25
400	Dave Concepcion AS	.15	.07
401	Dale Murphy AS	.60	.25
402	Andre Dawson AS	.60	.25
403	Tim Raines AS	.30	.14
404	Gary Carter AS	.60	.25
405	Steve Rogers AS	.15	.07
406	Steve Carlton AS	.60	.25
407	Bruce Sutter AS	.15	.07
408	Rudy May	.15	.07
409	Marvis Foley	.15	.07
410	Phil Niekro	1.25	.55
411	Phil Niekro SV	.60	.25
412	Rangers TL	.30	.14
	BA: Buddy Bell		
	ERA: Charlie Hough		
413	Matt Keough	.15	.07
414	Julio Cruz	.15	.07
415	Bob Forsch	.15	.07
416	Joe Ferguson	.15	.07
417	Tom Hausman	.15	.07
418	Greg Pryor	.15	.07
419	Steve Crawford	.15	.07
420	Al Oliver	.30	.14
421	Al Oliver SV	.15	.07
422	George Cappuzzello	.15	.07
423	Tom Lawless	.15	.07
424	Jerry Augustine	.15	.07
425	Pedro Guerrero	.30	.14
426	Earl Weaver MG	.60	.25
427	Roy Lee Jackson	.15	.07
428	Champ Summers	.15	.07
429	Eddie Whitson	.15	.07
430	Kirk Gibson	1.25	.55
431	Gary Gaetti	1.25	.55
432	Porfirio Altamirano	.15	.07
433	Dale Berra	.15	.07
434	Dennis Lamp	.15	.07
435	Tony Armas	.15	.07
436	Bill Campbell	.15	.07
437	Rick Sweet	.15	.07
438	Dave LaPoint	.15	.07
439	Rafael Ramirez	.15	.07
440	Ron Guidry	.30	.14
441	Astros TL	.30	.14
	BA: Ray Knight		
	ERA: Joe Niekro		
442	Brian Downing	.15	.07
443	Don Hood	.15	.07
444	Wally Backman	.30	.14
445	Mike Flanagan	.30	.14
446	Reid Nichols	.15	.07
447	Bryn Smith	.15	.07
448	Darrell Evans	.30	.14
449	Eddie Milner	.15	.07
450	Ted Simmons	.30	.14
451	Ted Simmons SV	.15	.07
452	Lloyd Moseby	.15	.07
453	Lamar Johnson	.15	.07
454	Bob Welch	.30	.14
455	Sixto Lezcano	.15	.07
456	Lee Elia MG	.15	.07
457	Milt Wilcox	.15	.07
458	Ron Washington	.15	.07
459	Ed Farmer	.15	.07
460	Roy Smalley	.15	.07
461	Steve Trout	.15	.07
462	Steve Nicosia	.15	.07
463	Gaylord Perry	1.25	.55
464	Gaylord Perry SV	.60	.25
465	Lonnie Smith	.15	.07
466	Tom Underwood	.15	.07
467	Rufino Linares	.15	.07
468	Dave Goltz	.15	.07
469	Ron Gardenhire	.15	.07
470	Greg Minton	.15	.07
471	Kansas City Royals TL	.30	.14
	BA: Willie Wilson		
	ERA: Vida Blue		
472	Gary Allenson	.15	.07
473	John Lowenstein	.15	.07
474	Ray Burris	.15	.07
475	Cesar Cedeno	.30	.14
476	Rob Picciolo	.15	.07
477	Tom Niedenfuer	.15	.07
478	Phil Garner	.30	.14
479	Charlie Hough	.30	.14
480	Toby Harrah	.15	.07
481	Scot Thompson	.15	.07
482	Tony Gwynn UER	60.00	27.00
	(No Topps logo under		
	card number on back)		
483	Lynn Jones	.15	.07
484	Dick Ruthven	.15	.07
485	Omar Moreno	.15	.07
486	Clyde King MG	.15	.07
487	Jerry Hairston	.15	.07
488	Alfredo Griffin	.15	.07
489	Tom Herr	.30	.14
490	Jim Palmer	1.25	.55
491	Jim Palmer SV	.60	.25
492	Paul Serna	.15	.07
493	Steve McCatty	.15	.07
494	Bob Brenly	.15	.07
495	Warren Cromartie	.15	.07
496	Tom Veryzer	.15	.07
497	Rick Sutcliffe	.30	.14
498	Wade Boggs	25.00	11.00
499	Jeff Little	.15	.07
500	Reggie Jackson	1.50	.70
501	Reggie Jackson SV	.60	.25
502	Atlanta Braves TL	.30	.14
	BA: Dale Murphy		
	ERA: Phil Niekro		
503	Moose Haas	.15	.07
504	Don Werner	.15	.07
505	Garry Templeton	.15	.07
506	Jim Gott	.15	.07
507	Tony Scott	.15	.07
508	Tom Filer	.15	.07
509	Lou Whitaker	.60	.25
510	Tug McGraw	.30	.14
511	Tug McGraw SV	.15	.07
512	Doyle Alexander	.15	.07
513	Fred Stanley	.15	.07
514	Rudy Law	.15	.07
515	Gene Tenace	.30	.14
516	Bill Virdon MG	.15	.07
517	Gary Ward	.15	.07
518	Bill Laskey	.15	.07
519	Terry Bulling	.15	.07
520	Fred Lynn	.30	.14
521	Bruce Benedict	.15	.07
522	Pat Zachry	.15	.07
523	Carney Lansford	.30	.14
524	Tom Brennan	.15	.07
525	Frank White	.30	.14
526	Checklist: 397-528	.30	.14
527	Larry Biittner	.15	.07
528	Jamie Easterly	.15	.07
529	Tim Laudner	.15	.07
530	Eddie Murray	1.50	.70
531	Oakland A's TL	.60	.25
	BA: Rickey Henderson		
	ERA: Rick Langford		
532	Dave Stewart	.30	.14
533	Luis Salazar	.15	.07

534	John Butcher	.15	.07
535	Manny Trillo	.15	.07
536	John Wockenfuss	.15	.07
537	Rod Scurry	.15	.07
538	Danny Heep	.15	.07
539	Roger Erickson	.15	.07
540	Ozzie Smith	2.00	.90
541	Britt Burns	.15	.07
542	Jody Davis	.15	.07
543	Alan Fowlkes	.15	.07
544	Larry Whisenton	.15	.07
545	Floyd Bannister	.15	.07
546	Dave Garcia MG	.15	.07
547	Geoff Zahn	.15	.07
548	Brian Giles	.15	.07
549	Charlie Puleo	.15	.07
550	Carl Yastrzemski	1.25	.55
551	Carl Yastrzemski SV	.60	.25
552	Tim Wallach	.30	.14
553	Dennis Martinez	.30	.14
554	Mike Vail	.15	.07
555	Steve Yeager	.15	.07
556	Willie Upshaw	.15	.07
557	Rick Honeycutt	.15	.07
558	Dickie Thon	.15	.07
559	Pete Redfern	.15	.07
560	Ron LeFlore	.15	.07
561	Cardinals TL	.30	.14
	BA: Lonnie Smith		
	ERA: Joaquin Andujar		
562	Dave Rozema	.15	.07
563	Juan Bonilla	.15	.07
564	Sid Monge	.15	.07
565	Bucky Dent	.30	.14
566	Manny Sarmiento	.15	.07
567	Joe Simpson	.15	.07
568	Willie Hernandez	.30	.14
569	Jack Perconte	.15	.07
570	Vida Blue	.30	.14
571	Mickey Klutts	.15	.07
572	Bob Watson	.30	.14
573	Andy Hassler	.15	.07
574	Glenn Adams	.15	.07
575	Neil Allen	.15	.07
576	Frank Robinson MG	.60	.25
577	Luis Aponte	.15	.07
578	David Green	.15	.07
579	Rich Dauer	.15	.07
580	Tom Seaver	1.50	.70
581	Tom Seaver SV	.60	.25
582	Marshall Edwards	.15	.07
583	Terry Forster	.15	.07
584	Dave Hostetler	.15	.07
585	Jose Cruz	.30	.14
586	Frank Viola	1.25	.55
587	Ivan DeJesus	.15	.07
588	Pat Underwood	.15	.07
589	Alvis Woods	.15	.07
590	Tony Pena	.15	.07
591	White Sox TL	.30	.14
	BA: Greg Luzinski		
	ERA: LaMarr Hoyt		
592	Shane Rawley	.15	.07
593	Broderick Perkins	.15	.07
594	Eric Rasmussen	.15	.07
595	Tim Raines	1.25	.55
596	Randy Johnson	.15	.07
597	Mike Proly	.15	.07
598	Dwayne Murphy	.15	.07
599	Don Aase	.15	.07
600	George Brett	2.50	1.10
601	Ed Lynch	.15	.07
602	Rich Gedman	.15	.07
603	Joe Morgan	1.25	.55
604	Joe Morgan SV	.60	.25
605	Gary Roenicke	.15	.07
606	Bobby Cox MG	.30	.14
607	Charlie Leibrandt	.15	.07
608	Don Money	.15	.07
609	Danny Darwin	.15	.07
610	Steve Garvey	.60	.25
611	Bert Roberge	.15	.07
612	Steve Swisher	.15	.07
613	Mike Ivie	.15	.07
614	Ed Glynn	.15	.07
615	Garry Maddox	.15	.07
616	Bill Nahorodny	.15	.07
617	Butch Wynegar	.15	.07
618	LaMarr Hoyt	.30	.14
619	Keith Moreland	.15	.07
620	Mike Norris	.15	.07
621	New York Mets TL	.30	.14
	BA: Mookie Wilson		
	ERA: Craig Swan		
622	Dave Edler	.15	.07
623	Luis Sanchez	.15	.07
624	Glenn Hubbard	.15	.07
625	Ken Forsch	.15	.07
626	Jerry Martin	.15	.07
627	Doug Bair	.15	.07
628	Julio Valdez	.15	.07
629	Charlie Lea	.15	.07
630	Paul Molitor	1.50	.70
631	Tippy Martinez	.15	.07
632	Alex Trevino	.15	.07
633	Vicente Romo	.15	.07
634	Max Venable	.15	.07
635	Graig Nettles	.30	.14
636	Graig Nettles SV	.15	.07
637	Pat Corrales MG	.15	.07
638	Dan Petry	.15	.07
639	Art Howe	.30	.14
640	Andre Thornton	.15	.07
641	Billy Sample	.15	.07
642	Checklist: 529-660	.30	.14
643	Bump Wills	.15	.07
644	Joe Lefebvre	.15	.07
645	Bill Madlock	.30	.14
646	Jim Essian	.15	.07
647	Bobby Mitchell	.15	.07
648	Jeff Burroughs	.15	.07
649	Tommy Boggs	.15	.07
650	George Hendrick	.15	.07
651	Angels TL	.60	.25
	BA: Rod Carew		
	ERA: Mike Witt		
652	Butch Hobson	.15	.07
653	Ellis Valentine	.15	.07
654	Bob Ojeda	.15	.07
655	Al Bumbry	.15	.07
656	Dave Frost	.15	.07
657	Mike Gates	.15	.07
658	Frank Pastore	.15	.07
659	Charlie Moore	.15	.07
660	Mike Hargrove	.30	.14
661	Bill Russell	.15	.07
662	Joe Sambito	.15	.07
663	Tom O'Malley	.15	.07
664	Bob Molinaro	.15	.07
665	Jim Sundberg	.30	.14
666	Sparky Anderson MG	.30	.14
667	Dick Davis	.15	.07
668	Larry Christenson	.15	.07
669	Mike Squires	.15	.07
670	Jerry Mumphrey	.15	.07
671	Lenny Faedo	.15	.07
672	Jim Kaat	.30	.14
673	Jim Kaat SV	.15	.07
674	Kurt Bevacqua	.15	.07
675	Jim Beattie	.15	.07
676	Biff Pocoroba	.15	.07
677	Dave Revering	.15	.07
678	Juan Beniquez	.15	.07
679	Mike Scott	.30	.14
680	Andre Dawson	1.25	.55
681	Dodgers Leaders	.30	.14
	BA: Pedro Guerrero		
	ERA: Fernando Valenzuela		
682	Bob Stanley	.15	.07
683	Dan Ford	.15	.07
684	Rafael Landestoy	.15	.07
685	Lee Mazzilli	.15	.07
686	Randy Lerch	.15	.07
687	U.L. Washington	.15	.07
688	Jim Wohlford	.15	.07
689	Ron Hassey	.15	.07
690	Kent Hrbek	.30	.14
691	Dave Tobik	.15	.07
692	Denny Walling	.15	.07
693	Sparky Lyle	.30	.14
694	Sparky Lyle SV	.15	.07
695	Ruppert Jones	.15	.07
696	Chuck Tanner MG	.15	.07
697	Barry Foote	.15	.07
698	Tony Bernazard	.15	.07
699	Lee Smith	1.25	.55
700	Keith Hernandez	.30	.14
701	Batting Leaders	.30	.14
	AL: Willie Wilson		
	NL: Al Oliver		
702	Home Run Leaders	.60	.25
	AL: Reggie Jackson		
	Gorman Thomas		
	NL: Dave Kingman		
703	RBI Leaders	.30	.14
	AL: Hal McRae		
	NL: Dale Murphy		
	NL: Al Oliver		
704	SB Leaders	1.25	.55
	AL: Rickey Henderson		
	NL: Tim Raines		
705	Victory Leaders	.60	.25
	AL: LaMarr Hoyt		
	NL: Steve Carlton		
706	Strikeout Leaders	.60	.25
	AL: Floyd Bannister		
	NL: Steve Carlton		
707	ERA Leaders	.30	.14
	AL: Rick Sutcliffe		
	NL: Steve Rogers		
708	Leading Firemen	.30	.14
	AL: Dan Quisenberry		
	NL: Bruce Sutter		
709	Jimmy Sexton	.15	.07
710	Willie Wilson	.30	.14
711	Mariners TL	.30	.14
	BA: Bruce Bochte		
	ERA: Jim Beattie		
712	Bruce Kison	.15	.07
713	Ron Hodges	.15	.07
714	Wayne Nordhagen	.15	.07
715	Tony Perez	1.25	.55
716	Tony Perez SV	.60	.25
717	Scott Sanderson	.15	.07
718	Jim Dwyer	.15	.07
719	Rich Gale	.15	.07
720	Dave Concepcion	.30	.14
721	John Martin	.15	.07
722	Jorge Orta	.15	.07
723	Randy Moffitt	.15	.07
724	Johnny Grubb	.15	.07
725	Dan Spillner	.15	.07
726	Harvey Kuenn MG	.15	.07
727	Chet Lemon	.15	.07
728	Ron Reed	.15	.07
729	Jerry Morales	.15	.07
730	Jason Thompson	.15	.07
731	Al Williams	.15	.07
732	Dave Henderson	.15	.07
733	Buck Martinez	.15	.07
734	Steve Braun	.15	.07
735	Tommy John	.60	.25
736	Tommy John SV	.30	.14
737	Mitchell Page	.15	.07
738	Tim Foli	.15	.07
739	Rick Ownbey	.15	.07
740	Rusty Staub	.30	.14
741	Rusty Staub SV	.15	.07
742	Padres TL	.30	.14
	BA: Terry Kennedy		
	ERA: Tim Lollar		
743	Mike Torrez	.15	.07
744	Brad Mills	.15	.07
745	Scott McGregor	.15	.07
746	John Wathan	.15	.07
747	Fred Breining	.15	.07
748	Derrel Thomas	.15	.07
749	Jon Matlack	.15	.07
750	Ben Oglivie	.15	.07
751	Brad Havens	.15	.07
752	Luis Pujols	.15	.07
753	Elias Sosa	.15	.07
754	Bill Robinson	.15	.07
755	John Candelaria	.15	.07
756	Russ Nixon MG	.15	.07
757	Rick Manning	.15	.07
758	Aurelio Rodriguez	.15	.07
759	Doug Bird	.15	.07

760	Dale Murphy	1.25	.55
761	Gary Lucas	.15	.07
762	Cliff Johnson	.15	.07
763	Al Cowens	.15	.07
764	Pete Falcone	.15	.07
765	Bob Boone	.30	.14
766	Barry Bonnell	.15	.07
767	Duane Kuiper	.15	.07
768	Chris Speier	.15	.07
769	Checklist: 661-792	.30	.14
770	Dave Winfield	1.25	.55
771	Twins TL	.30	.14
	BA: Kent Hrbek		
	ERA: Bobby Castillo		
772	Jim Kern	.15	.07
773	Larry Hisle	.15	.07
774	Alan Ashby	.15	.07
775	Burt Hooton	.15	.07
776	Larry Parrish	.15	.07
777	John Curtis	.15	.07
778	Rich Hebner	.30	.14
779	Rick Waits	.15	.07
780	Gary Matthews	.30	.14
781	Rick Rhoden	.15	.07
782	Bobby Murcer	.30	.14
783	Bobby Murcer SV	.15	.07
784	Jeff Newman	.15	.07
785	Dennis Leonard	.15	.07
786	Ralph Houk MG	.15	.07
787	Dick Tidrow	.15	.07
788	Dane Iorg	.15	.07
789	Bryan Clark	.15	.07
790	Bob Grich	.30	.14
791	Gary Lavelle	.15	.07
792	Chris Chambliss	.30	.14
XX	Game Insert Card	.10	.05

1983 Topps Traded

		NRMT	VG-E
COMP.FACT.SET (132)		25.00	11.00
COMMON CARD (1T-132T)		.25	.11
MINOR STARS		1.00	.45
SEMISTARS		2.00	.90

1T	Neil Allen	.25	.11
2T	Bill Almon	.25	.11
3T	Joe Altobelli MG	.25	.11
4T	Tony Armas	.25	.11
5T	Doug Bair	.25	.11
6T	Steve Baker	.25	.11
7T	Floyd Bannister	.25	.11
8T	Don Baylor	2.00	.90
9T	Tony Bernazard	.25	.11
10T	Larry Biittner	.25	.11
11T	Dann Bilardello	.25	.11
12T	Doug Bird	.25	.11
13T	Steve Boros MG	.25	.11
14T	Greg Brock	.25	.11
15T	Mike C. Brown	.25	.11
16T	Tom Burgmeier	.25	.11
17T	Randy Bush	.25	.11
18T	Bert Campaneris	1.00	.45
19T	Ron Cey	1.00	.45
20T	Chris Codiroli	.25	.11
21T	Dave Collins	.25	.11
22T	Terry Crowley	.25	.11
23T	Julio Cruz	.25	.11

24T	Mike Davis	.25	.11
25T	Frank DiPino	.25	.11
26T	Bill Doran	1.00	.45
27T	Jerry Dybzinski	.25	.11
28T	Jamie Easterly	.25	.11
29T	Juan Eichelberger	.25	.11
30T	Jim Essian	.25	.11
31T	Pete Falcone	.25	.11
32T	Mike Ferraro MG	.25	.11
33T	Terry Forster	.25	.11
34T	Julio Franco	4.00	1.80
35T	Rich Gale	.25	.11
36T	Kiko Garcia	.25	.11
37T	Steve Garvey	2.00	.90
38T	Johnny Grubb	.25	.11
39T	Mel Hall	1.00	.45
40T	Von Hayes	.25	.11
41T	Danny Heep	.25	.11
42T	Steve Henderson	.25	.11
43T	Keith Hernandez	2.00	.90
44T	Leo Hernandez	.25	.11
45T	Willie Hernandez	1.00	.45
46T	Al Holland	.25	.11
47T	Frank Howard MG	1.00	.45
48T	Bobby Johnson	.25	.11
49T	Cliff Johnson	.25	.11
50T	Odell Jones	.25	.11
51T	Mike Jorgensen	.25	.11
52T	Bob Kearney	.25	.11
53T	Steve Kemp	.25	.11
54T	Matt Keough	.25	.11
55T	Ron Kittle	2.00	.90
56T	Mickey Klutts	.25	.11
57T	Alan Knicely	.25	.11
58T	Mike Krukow	.25	.11
59T	Rafael Landestoy	.25	.11
60T	Carney Lansford	1.00	.45
61T	Joe Lefebvre	.25	.11
62T	Bryan Little	.25	.11
63T	Aurelio Lopez	.25	.11
64T	Mike Madden	.25	.11
65T	Rick Manning	.25	.11
66T	Billy Martin MG	1.00	.45
67T	Lee Mazzilli	.25	.11
68T	Andy McGaffigan	.25	.11
69T	Craig McMurtry	.25	.11
70T	John McNamara MG	.25	.11
71T	Orlando Mercado	.25	.11
72T	Larry Milbourne	.25	.11
73T	Randy Moffitt	.25	.11
74T	Sid Monge	.25	.11
75T	Jose Morales	.25	.11
76T	Omar Moreno	.25	.11
77T	Joe Morgan	3.00	1.35
78T	Mike Morgan	.25	.11
79T	Dale Murray	.25	.11
80T	Jeff Newman	.25	.11
81T	Pete O'Brien	1.00	.45
82T	Jorge Orta	.25	.11
83T	Alejandro Pena	1.00	.45
84T	Pascual Perez	.25	.11
85T	Tony Perez	3.00	1.35
86T	Broderick Perkins	.25	.11
87T	Tony Phillips	3.00	1.35
88T	Charlie Puleo	.25	.11
89T	Pat Putnam	.25	.11
90T	Jamie Quirk	.25	.11
91T	Doug Rader MG	.25	.11
92T	Chuck Rainey	.25	.11
93T	Bobby Ramos	.25	.11
94T	Gary Redus	1.00	.45
95T	Steve Renko	.25	.11
96T	Leon Roberts	.25	.11
97T	Aurelio Rodriguez	.25	.11
98T	Dick Ruthven	.25	.11
99T	Daryl Sconiers	.25	.11
100T	Mike Scott	1.00	.45
101T	Tom Seaver	5.00	2.20
102T	John Shelby	.25	.11
103T	Bob Shirley	.25	.11
104T	Joe Simpson	.25	.11
105T	Doug Sisk	.25	.11
106T	Mike Smithson	.25	.11
107T	Elias Sosa	.25	.11
108T	Darryl Strawberry	12.00	5.50
109T	Tom Tellmann	.25	.11

110T	Gene Tenace	1.00	.45
111T	Gorman Thomas	.25	.11
112T	Dick Tidrow	.25	.11
113T	Dave Tobik	.25	.11
114T	Wayne Tolleson	.25	.11
115T	Mike Torrez	.25	.11
116T	Manny Trillo	.25	.11
117T	Steve Trout	.25	.11
118T	Lee Tunnell	.25	.11
119T	Mike Vail	.25	.11
120T	Ellis Valentine	.25	.11
121T	Tom Veryzer	.25	.11
122T	George Vukovich	.25	.11
123T	Rick Waits	.25	.11
124T	Greg Walker	1.00	.45
125T	Chris Welsh	.25	.11
126T	Len Whitehouse	.25	.11
127T	Eddie Whitson	.25	.11
128T	Jim Wohlford	.25	.11
129T	Matt Young	.25	.11
130T	Joel Youngblood	.25	.11
131T	Pat Zachry	.25	.11
132T	Checklist 1T-132T	.25	.11

1984 Topps

	NRMT	VG-E
COMPLETE SET (792)	40.00	18.00
COMMON CARD (1-792)	.10	.05
MINOR STARS	.20	.09
SEMISTARS	.40	.18
UNLISTED STARS	.60	.25
SUBSET CARDS HALF VALUE OF BASE CARDS		

1	Steve Carlton HL	.60	.25
	300th win and all-time SO king		
2	Rickey Henderson HL	.40	.18
	100 stolen bases three times		
3	Dan Quisenberry HL	.10	.05
	Sets save record		
4	Nolan Ryan HL	1.00	.45
	Steve Carlton Gaylord Perry All surpass Johnson		
5	Dave Righetti HL	.20	.09
	Bob Forsch Mike Warren All pitch no-hitters		
6	Johnny Bench HL	.60	.25
	Gaylord Perry Carl Yastrzemski Superstars retire		
7	Gary Lucas	.10	.05
8	Don Mattingly	8.00	3.60
9	Jim Gott	.10	.05
10	Robin Yount	.60	.25
11	Minnesota Twins TL	.20	.09
	Kent Hrbek Ken Schrom		
12	Billy Sample	.10	.05
13	Scott Holman	.10	.05
14	Tom Brookens	.20	.09
15	Burt Hooton	.10	.05
16	Omar Moreno	.10	.05
17	John Denny	.10	.05

❑ 18	Dale Berra	.10	.05
❑ 19	Ray Fontenot	.10	.05
❑ 20	Greg Luzinski	.20	.09
❑ 21	Joe Altobelli MG	.10	.05
❑ 22	Bryan Clark	.10	.05
❑ 23	Keith Moreland	.10	.05
❑ 24	John Martin	.10	.05
❑ 25	Glenn Hubbard	.10	.05
❑ 26	Bud Black	.10	.05
❑ 27	Daryl Sconiers	.10	.05
❑ 28	Frank Viola	.40	.18
❑ 29	Danny Heep	.10	.05
❑ 30	Wade Boggs	1.25	.55
❑ 31	Andy McGaffigan	.10	.05
❑ 32	Bobby Ramos	.10	.05
❑ 33	Tom Burgmeier	.10	.05
❑ 34	Eddie Milner	.10	.05
❑ 35	Don Sutton	.60	.25
❑ 36	Denny Walling	.10	.05
❑ 37	Texas Rangers TL	.20	.09
	Buddy Bell		
	Rick Honeycutt		
❑ 38	Luis DeLeon	.10	.05
❑ 39	Garth Iorg	.10	.05
❑ 40	Dusty Baker	.20	.09
❑ 41	Tony Bernazard	.10	.05
❑ 42	Johnny Grubb	.10	.05
❑ 43	Ron Reed	.10	.05
❑ 44	Jim Morrison	.10	.05
❑ 45	Jerry Mumphrey	.10	.05
❑ 46	Ray Smith	.10	.05
❑ 47	Rudy Law	.10	.05
❑ 48	Julio Franco	.40	.18
❑ 49	John Stuper	.10	.05
❑ 50	Chris Chambliss	.20	.09
❑ 51	Jim Frey MG	.10	.05
❑ 52	Paul Splittorff	.10	.05
❑ 53	Juan Beniquez	.10	.05
❑ 54	Jesse Orosco	.20	.09
❑ 55	Dave Concepcion	.20	.09
❑ 56	Gary Allenson	.10	.05
❑ 57	Dan Schatzeder	.10	.05
❑ 58	Max Venable	.10	.05
❑ 59	Sammy Stewart	.10	.05
❑ 60	Paul Molitor UER	.60	.25
	('83 stats .272, 613, 167; should be .270, 608, 164)		
❑ 61	Chris Codiroli	.10	.05
❑ 62	Dave Hostetler	.10	.05
❑ 63	Ed VandeBerg	.10	.05
❑ 64	Mike Scioscia	.10	.05
❑ 65	Kirk Gibson	.60	.25
❑ 66	Houston Astros TL	1.00	.45
	Jose Cruz		
	Nolan Ryan		
❑ 67	Gary Ward	.10	.05
❑ 68	Luis Salazar	.10	.05
❑ 69	Rod Scurry	.10	.05
❑ 70	Gary Matthews	.20	.09
❑ 71	Leo Hernandez	.10	.05
❑ 72	Mike Squires	.10	.05
❑ 73	Jody Davis	.10	.05
❑ 74	Jerry Martin	.10	.05
❑ 75	Bob Forsch	.10	.05
❑ 76	Alfredo Griffin	.10	.05
❑ 77	Brett Butler	.40	.18
❑ 78	Mike Torrez	.10	.05
❑ 79	Rob Wilfong	.10	.05
❑ 80	Steve Rogers	.10	.05
❑ 81	Billy Martin MG	.20	.09
❑ 82	Doug Bird	.10	.05
❑ 83	Richie Zisk	.10	.05
❑ 84	Lenny Faedo	.10	.05
❑ 85	Atlee Hammaker	.10	.05
❑ 86	John Shelby	.10	.05
❑ 87	Frank Pastore	.10	.05
❑ 88	Rob Picciolo	.10	.05
❑ 89	Mike Smithson	.10	.05
❑ 90	Pedro Guerrero	.20	.09
❑ 91	Dan Spillner	.10	.05
❑ 92	Lloyd Moseby	.10	.05
❑ 93	Bob Knepper	.10	.05
❑ 94	Mario Ramirez	.10	.05
❑ 95	Aurelio Lopez	.20	.09
❑ 96	Kansas City Royals TL	.20	.09
	Hal McRae		
	Larry Gura		
❑ 97	LaMarr Hoyt	.10	.05
❑ 98	Steve Nicosia	.10	.05
❑ 99	Craig Lefferts	.10	.05
❑ 100	Reggie Jackson	.75	.35
❑ 101	Porfirio Altamirano	.10	.05
❑ 102	Ken Oberkfell	.10	.05
❑ 103	Dwayne Murphy	.10	.05
❑ 104	Ken Dayley	.10	.05
❑ 105	Tony Armas	.10	.05
❑ 106	Tim Stoddard	.10	.05
❑ 107	Ned Yost	.10	.05
❑ 108	Randy Moffitt	.10	.05
❑ 109	Brad Wellman	.10	.05
❑ 110	Ron Guidry	.20	.09
❑ 111	Bill Virdon MG	.10	.05
❑ 112	Tom Niedenfuer	.10	.05
❑ 113	Kelly Paris	.10	.05
❑ 114	Checklist 1-132	.20	.09
❑ 115	Andre Thornton	.10	.05
❑ 116	George Bjorkman	.10	.05
❑ 117	Tom Veryzer	.10	.05
❑ 118	Charlie Hough	.20	.09
❑ 119	John Wockenfuss	.10	.05
❑ 120	Keith Hernandez	.20	.09
❑ 121	Pat Sheridan	.10	.05
❑ 122	Cecilio Guante	.10	.05
❑ 123	Butch Wynegar	.10	.05
❑ 124	Damaso Garcia	.10	.05
❑ 125	Britt Burns	.10	.05
❑ 126	Atlanta Braves TL	.40	.18
	Dale Murphy		
	Craig McMurtry		
❑ 127	Mike Madden	.10	.05
❑ 128	Rick Manning	.10	.05
❑ 129	Bill Laskey	.10	.05
❑ 130	Ozzie Smith	.75	.35
❑ 131	Batting Leaders	.60	.25
	Bill Madlock		
	Wade Boggs		
❑ 132	Home Run Leaders	.60	.25
	Mike Schmidt		
	Jim Rice		
❑ 133	RBI Leaders	.60	.25
	Dale Murphy		
	Cecil Cooper		
	Jim Rice		
❑ 134	Stolen Base Leaders	.60	.25
	Tim Raines		
	Rickey Henderson		
❑ 135	Victory Leaders	.60	.25
	John Denny		
	LaMarr Hoyt		
❑ 136	Strikeout Leaders	.60	.25
	Steve Carlton		
	Jack Morris		
❑ 137	ERA Leaders	.20	.09
	Atlee Hammaker		
	Rick Honeycutt		
❑ 138	Leading Firemen	.20	.09
	Al Holland		
	Dan Quisenberry		
❑ 139	Bert Campaneris	.20	.09
❑ 140	Storm Davis	.10	.05
❑ 141	Pat Corrales MG	.10	.05
❑ 142	Rich Gale	.10	.05
❑ 143	Jose Morales	.10	.05
❑ 144	Brian Harper	.20	.09
❑ 145	Gary Lavelle	.10	.05
❑ 146	Ed Romero	.10	.05
❑ 147	Dan Petry	.20	.09
❑ 148	Joe Lefebvre	.10	.05
❑ 149	Jon Matlack	.10	.05
❑ 150	Dale Murphy	.60	.25
❑ 151	Steve Trout	.10	.05
❑ 152	Glenn Brummer	.10	.05
❑ 153	Dick Tidrow	.10	.05
❑ 154	Dave Henderson	.20	.09
❑ 155	Frank White	.20	.09
❑ 156	Oakland A's TL	.60	.25
	Rickey Henderson		
	Tim Conroy		
❑ 157	Gary Gaetti	.40	.18
❑ 158	John Curtis	.10	.05
❑ 159	Darryl Cias	.10	.05
❑ 160	Mario Soto	.10	.05
❑ 161	Junior Ortiz	.10	.05
❑ 162	Bob Ojeda	.10	.05
❑ 163	Lorenzo Gray	.10	.05
❑ 164	Scott Sanderson	.10	.05
❑ 165	Ken Singleton	.10	.05
❑ 166	Jamie Nelson	.10	.05
❑ 167	Marshall Edwards	.10	.05
❑ 168	Juan Bonilla	.10	.05
❑ 169	Larry Parrish	.10	.05
❑ 170	Jerry Reuss	.10	.05
❑ 171	Frank Robinson MG	.40	.18
❑ 172	Frank DiPino	.10	.05
❑ 173	Marvell Wynne	.10	.05
❑ 174	Juan Berenguer	.10	.05
❑ 175	Graig Nettles	.20	.09
❑ 176	Lee Smith	.60	.25
❑ 177	Jerry Hairston	.10	.05
❑ 178	Bill Krueger	.10	.05
❑ 179	Buck Martinez	.10	.05
❑ 180	Manny Trillo	.10	.05
❑ 181	Roy Thomas	.10	.05
❑ 182	Darryl Strawberry	2.00	.90
❑ 183	Al Williams	.10	.05
❑ 184	Mike O'Berry	.10	.05
❑ 185	Sixto Lezcano	.10	.05
❑ 186	Cardinal TL	.20	.09
	Lonnie Smith		
	John Stuper		
❑ 187	Luis Aponte	.10	.05
❑ 188	Bryan Little	.10	.05
❑ 189	Tim Conroy	.10	.05
❑ 190	Ben Oglivie	.10	.05
❑ 191	Mike Boddicker	.10	.05
❑ 192	Nick Esasky	.10	.05
❑ 193	Darrell Brown	.10	.05
❑ 194	Domingo Ramos	.10	.05
❑ 195	Jack Morris	.60	.25
❑ 196	Don Slaught	.20	.09
❑ 197	Garry Hancock	.10	.05
❑ 198	Bill Doran	.20	.09
❑ 199	Willie Hernandez	.20	.09
❑ 200	Andre Dawson	.60	.25
❑ 201	Bruce Kison	.10	.05
❑ 202	Bobby Cox MG	.20	.09
❑ 203	Matt Keough	.10	.05
❑ 204	Bobby Meacham	.10	.05
❑ 205	Greg Minton	.10	.05
❑ 206	Andy Van Slyke	.60	.25
❑ 207	Donnie Moore	.10	.05
❑ 208	Jose Oquendo	.20	.09
❑ 209	Manny Sarmiento	.10	.05
❑ 210	Joe Morgan	.60	.25
❑ 211	Rick Sweet	.10	.05
❑ 212	Broderick Perkins	.10	.05
❑ 213	Bruce Hurst	.10	.05
❑ 214	Paul Householder	.10	.05
❑ 215	Tippy Martinez	.10	.05
❑ 216	White Sox TL	.20	.09
	Carlton Fisk		
	Richard Dotson		
❑ 217	Alan Ashby	.10	.05
❑ 218	Rick Waits	.10	.05
❑ 219	Joe Simpson	.10	.05
❑ 220	Fernando Valenzuela	.20	.09
❑ 221	Cliff Johnson	.10	.05
❑ 222	Rick Honeycutt	.10	.05
❑ 223	Wayne Krenchicki	.10	.05
❑ 224	Sid Monge	.10	.05
❑ 225	Lee Mazzilli	.10	.05
❑ 226	Juan Eichelberger	.10	.05
❑ 227	Steve Braun	.10	.05
❑ 228	John Rabb	.10	.05
❑ 229	Paul Owens MG	.10	.05
❑ 230	Rickey Henderson	.75	.35
❑ 231	Gary Woods	.10	.05
❑ 232	Tim Wallach	.20	.09
❑ 233	Checklist 133-264	.20	.09
❑ 234	Rafael Ramirez	.10	.05
❑ 235	Matt Young	.10	.05
❑ 236	Ellis Valentine	.10	.05
❑ 237	John Castino	.10	.05
❑ 238	Reid Nichols	.10	.05
❑ 239	Jay Howell	.10	.05
❑ 240	Eddie Murray	.60	.25
❑ 241	Bill Almon	.10	.05

242	Alex Trevino	.10	.05
243	Pete Ladd	.10	.05
244	Candy Maldonado	.10	.05
245	Rick Sutcliffe	.20	.09
246	New York Mets TL	.60	.25
	Mookie Wilson		
	Tom Seaver		
247	Onix Concepcion	.10	.05
248	Bill Dawley	.10	.05
249	Jay Johnstone	.20	.09
250	Bill Madlock	.20	.09
251	Tony Gwynn	4.00	1.80
252	Larry Christenson	.10	.05
253	Jim Wohlford	.10	.05
254	Shane Rawley	.10	.05
255	Bruce Benedict	.10	.05
256	Dave Geisel	.10	.05
257	Julio Cruz	.10	.05
258	Luis Sanchez	.10	.05
259	Sparky Anderson MG	.40	.18
260	Scott McGregor	.10	.05
261	Bobby Brown	.10	.05
262	Tom Candiotti	.60	.25
263	Jack Fimple	.10	.05
264	Doug Frobel	.10	.05
265	Donnie Hill	.10	.05
266	Steve Lubratich	.10	.05
267	Carmelo Martinez	.10	.05
268	Jack O'Connor	.10	.05
269	Aurelio Rodriguez	.10	.05
270	Jeff Russell	.20	.09
271	Moose Haas	.10	.05
272	Rick Dempsey	.10	.05
273	Charlie Puleo	.10	.05
274	Rick Monday	.10	.05
275	Len Matuszek	.10	.05
276	Angels TL	.60	.25
	Rod Carew		
	Geoff Zahn		
277	Eddie Whitson	.10	.05
278	Jorge Bell	.40	.18
279	Ivan DeJesus	.10	.05
280	Floyd Bannister	.10	.05
281	Larry Milbourne	.10	.05
282	Jim Barr	.10	.05
283	Larry Biittner	.10	.05
284	Howard Bailey	.10	.05
285	Darrell Porter	.10	.05
286	Lary Sorensen	.10	.05
287	Warren Cromartie	.10	.05
288	Jim Beattie	.10	.05
289	Randy Johnson	.10	.05
290	Dave Dravecky	.20	.09
291	Chuck Tanner MG	.10	.05
292	Tony Scott	.10	.05
293	Ed Lynch	.10	.05
294	U.L. Washington	.10	.05
295	Mike Flanagan	.10	.05
296	Jeff Newman	.10	.05
297	Bruce Berenyi	.10	.05
298	Jim Gantner	.10	.05
299	John Butcher	.10	.05
300	Pete Rose	1.25	.55
301	Frank LaCorte	.10	.05
302	Barry Bonnell	.10	.05
303	Marty Castillo	.10	.05
304	Warren Brusstar	.10	.05
305	Roy Smalley	.10	.05
306	Dodgers TL	.20	.09
	Pedro Guerrero		
	Bob Welch		
307	Bobby Mitchell	.10	.05
308	Ron Hassey	.10	.05
309	Tony Phillips	.60	.25
310	Willie McGee	.40	.18
311	Jerry Koosman	.20	.09
312	Jorge Orta	.10	.05
313	Mike Jorgensen	.10	.05
314	Orlando Mercado	.10	.05
315	Bobby Grich	.20	.09
316	Mark Bradley	.10	.05
317	Greg Pryor	.10	.05
318	Bill Gullickson	.10	.05
319	Al Bumbry	.10	.05
320	Bob Stanley	.10	.05
321	Harvey Kuenn MG	.20	.09
322	Ken Schrom	.10	.05
323	Alan Knicely	.10	.05
324	Alejandro Pena	.20	.05
325	Darrell Evans	.20	.09
326	Bob Kearney	.10	.05
327	Ruppert Jones	.10	.05
328	Vern Ruhle	.10	.05
329	Pat Tabler	.10	.05
330	John Candelaria	.10	.05
331	Bucky Dent	.20	.09
332	Kevin Gross	.10	.05
333	Larry Herndon	.20	.09
334	Chuck Rainey	.10	.05
335	Don Baylor	.40	.18
336	Seattle Mariners TL	.20	.09
	Pat Putnam		
	Matt Young		
337	Kevin Hagen	.10	.05
338	Mike Warren	.10	.05
339	Roy Lee Jackson	.10	.05
340	Hal McRae	.20	.09
341	Dave Tobik	.10	.05
342	Tim Foli	.10	.05
343	Mark Davis	.10	.05
344	Rick Miller	.10	.05
345	Kent Hrbek	.20	.09
346	Kurt Bevacqua	.10	.05
347	Allan Ramirez	.10	.05
348	Toby Harrah	.10	.09
349	Bob L. Gibson	.10	.05
350	George Foster	.20	.09
351	Russ Nixon MG	.10	.05
352	Dave Stewart	.20	.09
353	Jim Anderson	.10	.05
354	Jeff Burroughs	.10	.05
355	Jason Thompson	.10	.05
356	Glenn Abbott	.10	.05
357	Ron Cey	.20	.09
358	Bob Dernier	.10	.05
359	Jim Acker	.10	.05
360	Willie Randolph	.20	.09
361	Dave Smith	.10	.05
362	David Green	.10	.05
363	Tim Laudner	.10	.05
364	Scott Fletcher	.10	.05
365	Steve Bedrosian	.10	.05
366	Padres TL	.20	.09
	Terry Kennedy		
	Dave Dravecky		
367	Jamie Easterly	.10	.05
368	Hubie Brooks	.10	.05
369	Steve McCatty	.10	.05
370	Tim Raines	.40	.18
371	Dave Gumpert	.10	.05
372	Gary Roenicke	.10	.05
373	Bill Scherrer	.10	.05
374	Don Money	.10	.05
375	Dennis Leonard	.10	.05
376	Dave Anderson	.10	.05
377	Danny Darwin	.10	.05
378	Bob Brenly	.10	.05
379	Checklist 265-396	.20	.09
380	Steve Garvey	.40	.18
381	Ralph Houk MG	.20	.09
382	Chris Nyman	.10	.05
383	Terry Puhl	.10	.05
384	Lee Tunnell	.10	.05
385	Tony Perez	.60	.25
386	George Hendrick AS	.10	.05
387	Johnny Ray AS	.10	.05
388	Mike Schmidt AS	.40	.18
389	Ozzie Smith AS	.60	.25
390	Tim Raines AS	.20	.09
391	Dale Murphy AS	.40	.18
392	Andre Dawson AS	.40	.18
393	Gary Carter AS	.40	.18
394	Steve Rogers AS	.10	.05
395	Steve Carlton AS	.40	.18
396	Jesse Orosco AS	.10	.05
397	Eddie Murray AS	.40	.18
398	Lou Whitaker AS	.20	.09
399	George Brett AS	.60	.25
400	Cal Ripken AS	2.00	.90
401	Jim Rice AS	.40	.18
402	Dave Winfield AS	.40	.18
403	Lloyd Moseby AS	.10	.05
404	Ted Simmons AS	.10	.05
405	LaMarr Hoyt AS	.10	.05
406	Ron Guidry AS	.10	.05
407	Dan Quisenberry AS	.10	.05
408	Lou Piniella	.20	.09
409	Juan Agosto	.10	.05
410	Claudell Washington	.10	.05
411	Houston Jimenez	.10	.05
412	Doug Rader MG	.10	.05
413	Spike Owen	.20	.09
414	Mitchell Page	.10	.05
415	Tommy John	.40	.18
416	Dane Iorg	.10	.05
417	Mike Armstrong	.10	.05
418	Ron Hodges	.10	.05
419	John Henry Johnson	.10	.05
420	Cecil Cooper	.20	.09
421	Charlie Lea	.10	.05
422	Jose Cruz	.20	.09
423	Mike Morgan	.10	.05
424	Dann Bilardello	.10	.05
425	Steve Howe	.10	.05
426	Orioles TL	1.50	.70
	Cal Ripken,		
	Mike Boddicker		
427	Rick Leach	.10	.05
428	Fred Breining	.10	.05
429	Randy Bush	.10	.05
430	Rusty Staub	.20	.09
431	Chris Bando	.10	.05
432	Charles Hudson	.10	.05
433	Rich Hebner	.10	.05
434	Harold Baines	.60	.25
435	Neil Allen	.10	.05
436	Rick Peters	.10	.05
437	Mike Proly	.10	.05
438	Biff Pocoroba	.10	.05
439	Bob Stoddard	.10	.05
440	Steve Kemp	.10	.05
441	Bob Lillis MG	.10	.05
442	Byron McLaughlin	.10	.05
443	Benny Ayala	.10	.05
444	Steve Renko	.10	.05
445	Jerry Remy	.10	.05
446	Luis Pujols	.10	.05
447	Tom Brunansky	.20	.09
448	Ben Hayes	.10	.05
449	Joe Pettini	.10	.05
450	Gary Carter	.60	.25
451	Bob Jones	.10	.05
452	Chuck Porter	.10	.05
453	Willie Upshaw	.10	.05
454	Joe Beckwith	.10	.05
455	Terry Kennedy	.10	.05
456	Chicago Cubs TL	.40	.18
	Keith Moreland		
	Fergie Jenkins		
457	Dave Rozema	.10	.05
458	Kiko Garcia	.10	.05
459	Kevin Hickey	.10	.05
460	Dave Winfield	.60	.25
461	Jim Maler	.10	.05
462	Lee Lacy	.10	.05
463	Dave Engle	.10	.05
464	Jeff A. Jones	.10	.05
465	Mookie Wilson	.20	.09
466	Gene Garber	.10	.05
467	Mike Ramsey	.10	.05
468	Geoff Zahn	.10	.05
469	Tom O'Malley	.10	.05
470	Nolan Ryan	4.00	1.80
471	Dick Howser MG	.10	.05
472	Mike Scioscia	.10	.05
473	Jim Dwyer	.10	.05
474	Greg Bargar	.10	.05
475	Gary Redus	.10	.05
476	Tom Tellmann	.10	.05
477	Rafael Landestoy	.10	.05
478	Alan Bannister	.10	.05
479	Frank Tanana	.20	.09
480	Ron Kittle	.10	.05
481	Mark Thurmond	.10	.05
482	Enos Cabell	.10	.05
483	Fergie Jenkins	.60	.25
484	Ozzie Virgil	.10	.05
485	Rick Rhoden	.10	.05

Card	Price 1	Price 2
486 N.Y. Yankees TL	.60	.25
Don Baylor		
Ron Guidry		
487 Ricky Adams	.10	.05
488 Jesse Barfield	.20	.09
489 Dave Von Ohlen	.10	.05
490 Cal Ripken	4.00	1.80
491 Bobby Castillo	.10	.05
492 Tucker Ashford	.10	.05
493 Mike Norris	.10	.05
494 Chili Davis	.40	.18
495 Rollie Fingers	.60	.25
496 Terry Francona	.10	.05
497 Bud Anderson	.10	.05
498 Rich Gedman	.10	.05
499 Mike Witt	.10	.05
500 George Brett	1.25	.55
501 Steve Henderson	.10	.05
502 Joe Torre MG	.20	.09
503 Elias Sosa	.10	.05
504 Mickey Rivers	.10	.05
505 Pete Vuckovich	.10	.05
506 Ernie Whitt	.10	.05
507 Mike LaCoss	.10	.05
508 Mel Hall	.20	.09
509 Brad Havens	.10	.05
510 Alan Trammell	.60	.25
511 Marty Bystrom	.10	.05
512 Oscar Gamble	.10	.05
513 Dave Beard	.10	.05
514 Floyd Rayford	.10	.05
515 Gorman Thomas	.10	.05
516 Montreal Expos TL	.20	.09
Al Oliver		
Charlie Lea		
517 John Moses	.10	.05
518 Greg Walker	.20	.09
519 Ron Davis	.10	.05
520 Bob Boone	.20	.09
521 Pete Falcone	.10	.05
522 Dave Bergman	.10	.05
523 Glenn Hoffman	.10	.05
524 Carlos Diaz	.10	.05
525 Willie Wilson	.10	.05
526 Ron Oester	.10	.05
527 Checklist 397-528	.20	.09
528 Mark Brouhard	.10	.05
529 Keith Atherton	.10	.05
530 Dan Ford	.10	.05
531 Steve Boros MG	.10	.05
532 Eric Show	.10	.05
533 Ken Landreaux	.10	.05
534 Pete O'Brien	.20	.09
535 Bo Diaz	.10	.05
536 Doug Bair	.10	.05
537 Johnny Ray	.10	.05
538 Kevin Bass	.10	.05
539 George Frazier	.10	.05
540 George Hendrick	.10	.05
541 Dennis Lamp	.10	.05
542 Duane Kuiper	.10	.05
543 Craig McMurtry	.10	.05
544 Cesar Geronimo	.10	.05
545 Bill Buckner	.20	.09
546 Indians TL	.20	.09
Mike Hargrove		
Lary Sorensen		
547 Mike Moore	.10	.05
548 Ron Jackson	.10	.05
549 Walt Terrell	.10	.05
550 Jim Rice	.20	.09
551 Scott Ulger	.10	.05
552 Ray Burris	.10	.05
553 Joe Nolan	.10	.05
554 Ted Power	.10	.05
555 Greg Brock	.10	.05
556 Joey McLaughlin	.10	.05
557 Wayne Tolleson	.10	.05
558 Mike Davis	.10	.05
559 Mike Scott	.20	.09
560 Carlton Fisk	.60	.25
561 Whitey Herzog MG	.20	.09
562 Manny Castillo	.10	.05
563 Glenn Wilson	.10	.05
564 Al Holland	.10	.05
565 Leon Durham	.10	.05
566 Jim Bibby	.10	.05
567 Mike Heath	.10	.05
568 Pete Filson	.10	.05
569 Bake McBride	.10	.05
570 Dan Quisenberry	.10	.05
571 Bruce Bochy	.10	.05
572 Jerry Royster	.10	.05
573 Dave Kingman	.40	.18
574 Brian Downing	.10	.05
575 Jim Gantry	.10	.05
576 Giants TL	.20	.09
Jeff Leonard		
Atlee Hammaker		
577 Mark Clear	.10	.05
578 Lenn Sakata	.10	.05
579 Bob James	.10	.05
580 Lonnie Smith	.10	.05
581 Jose DeLeon	.10	.05
582 Bob McClure	.10	.05
583 Derrel Thomas	.10	.05
584 Dave Schmidt	.10	.05
585 Dan Driessen	.10	.05
586 Joe Niekro	.10	.09
587 Von Hayes	.10	.05
588 Milt Wilcox	.10	.05
589 Mike Easler	.10	.05
590 Dave Stieb	.10	.05
591 Tony LaRussa MG	.20	.09
592 Andre Robertson	.10	.05
593 Jeff Lahti	.10	.05
594 Gene Richards	.10	.05
595 Jeff Reardon	.20	.09
596 Ryne Sandberg	2.00	.90
597 Rick Camp	.10	.05
598 Rusty Kuntz	.10	.05
599 Doug Sisk	.10	.05
600 Rod Carew	.60	.25
601 John Tudor	.20	.09
602 John Wathan	.10	.05
603 Renie Martin	.10	.05
604 John Lowenstein	.10	.05
605 Mike Caldwell	.10	.05
606 Blue Jays TL	.20	.09
Lloyd Moseby		
Dave Stieb		
607 Tom Hume	.10	.05
608 Bobby Johnson	.10	.05
609 Dan Meyer	.10	.05
610 Steve Sax	.20	.09
611 Chet Lemon	.10	.05
612 Harry Spilman	.10	.05
613 Greg Gross	.10	.05
614 Len Barker	.10	.05
615 Garry Templeton	.10	.05
616 Don Robinson	.10	.05
617 Rick Cerone	.10	.05
618 Dickie Noles	.10	.05
619 Jerry Dybzinski	.10	.05
620 Al Oliver	.20	.09
621 Frank Howard MG	.20	.09
622 Al Cowens	.10	.05
623 Ron Washington	.10	.05
624 Terry Harper	.10	.05
625 Larry Gura	.10	.05
626 Bob Clark	.10	.05
627 Dave LaPoint	.10	.05
628 Ed Jurak	.10	.05
629 Rick Langford	.10	.05
630 Ted Simmons	.20	.09
631 Dennis Martinez	.20	.09
632 Tom Foley	.10	.05
633 Mike Krukow	.10	.05
634 Mike Marshall	.20	.09
635 Dave Righetti	.20	.09
636 Pat Putnam	.10	.05
637 Phillies TL	.20	.09
Gary Matthews		
John Denny		
638 George Vukovich	.10	.05
639 Rick Lysander	.10	.05
640 Lance Parrish	.40	.18
641 Mike Richardt	.10	.05
642 Tom Underwood	.10	.05
643 Mike C. Brown	.10	.05
644 Tim Lollar	.10	.05
645 Tony Pena	.10	.05
646 Checklist 529-660	.20	.09
647 Ron Roenicke	.10	.05
648 Len Whitehouse	.10	.05
649 Tom Herr	.20	.09
650 Phil Niekro	.60	.25
651 John McNamara MG	.10	.05
652 Rudy May	.10	.05
653 Dave Stapleton	.10	.05
654 Bob Bailor	.10	.05
655 Amos Otis	.20	.09
656 Bryn Smith	.10	.05
657 Thad Bosley	.10	.05
658 Jerry Augustine	.10	.05
659 Duane Walker	.10	.05
660 Ray Knight	.20	.09
661 Steve Yeager	.10	.05
662 Tom Brennan	.10	.05
663 Johnnie LeMaster	.10	.05
664 Dave Stegman	.10	.05
665 Buddy Bell	.20	.09
666 Detroit Tigers TL	.60	.25
Lou Whitaker		
Jack Morris		
667 Vance Law	.10	.05
668 Larry McWilliams	.10	.05
669 Dave Lopes	.20	.09
670 Rich Gossage	.40	.18
671 Jamie Quirk	.10	.05
672 Ricky Nelson	.10	.05
673 Mike Walters	.10	.05
674 Tim Flannery	.10	.05
675 Pascual Perez	.10	.05
676 Brian Giles	.10	.05
677 Doyle Alexander	.10	.05
678 Chris Speier	.10	.05
679 Art Howe	.20	.09
680 Fred Lynn	.20	.09
681 Tom Lasorda MG	.40	.18
682 Dan Morogiello	.10	.05
683 Marty Barrett	.20	.09
684 Bob Shirley	.10	.05
685 Willie Aikens	.10	.05
686 Joe Price	.10	.05
687 Roy Howell	.10	.05
688 George Wright	.10	.05
689 Mike Flanagan	.10	.05
690 Jack Clark	.20	.09
691 Steve Lake	.10	.05
692 Dickie Thon	.10	.05
693 Alan Wiggins	.10	.05
694 Mike Stanton	.10	.05
695 Lou Whitaker	.60	.25
696 Pirates TL	.20	.09
Bill Madlock		
Rick Rhoden		
697 Dale Murray	.10	.05
698 Marc Hill	.10	.05
699 Dave Rucker	.10	.05
700 Mike Schmidt	1.00	.45
701 NL Active Batting	.60	.25
Bill Madlock		
Pete Rose		
Dave Parker		
702 NL Active Hits	.60	.25
Pete Rose		
Rusty Staub		
Tony Perez		
703 NL Active Home Run	.60	.25
Mike Schmidt		
Tony Perez		
Dave Kingman		
704 NL Active RBI	.60	.25
Tony Perez		
Rusty Staub		
Al Oliver		
705 NL Active Steals	.60	.25
Joe Morgan		
Cesar Cedeno		
Larry Bowa		
706 NL Active Victory	.60	.25
Steve Carlton		
Fergie Jenkins		
Tom Seaver		
707 NL Active Strikeout	1.50	.70
Steve Carlton		
Nolan Ryan		

Tom Seaver
☐ 708 NL Active ERA .... .60 .25
  Tom Seaver
  Steve Carlton
  Steve Rogers
☐ 709 NL Active Save ...... .20 .09
  Bruce Sutter
  Tug McGraw
  Gene Garber
☐ 710 AL Active Batting ...... .60 .25
  Rod Carew
  George Brett
  Cecil Cooper
☐ 711 AL Active Hits ...... .60 .25
  Rod Carew
  Bert Campaneris
  Reggie Jackson
☐ 712 AL Active Home Run ...... .60 .25
  Reggie Jackson
  Graig Nettles
  Greg Luzinski
☐ 713 AL Active RBI ...... .60 .25
  Reggie Jackson
  Ted Simmons
  Graig Nettles
☐ 714 AL Active Steals ...... .20 .09
  Bert Campaneris
  Dave Lopes
  Omar Moreno
☐ 715 AL Active Victory ...... .60 .25
  Jim Palmer
  Don Sutton
  Tommy John
☐ 716 AL Active Strikeout ...... .60 .25
  Don Sutton
  Bert Blyleven
  Jerry Koosman
☐ 717 AL Active ERA ...... .60 .25
  Jim Palmer
  Rollie Fingers
  Ron Guidry
☐ 718 AL Active Save ...... .60 .25
  Rollie Fingers
  Rich Gossage
  Dan Quisenberry
☐ 719 Andy Hassler ...... .20 .05
☐ 720 Dwight Evans ...... .20 .09
☐ 721 Del Crandall MG ...... .10 .05
☐ 722 Bob Welch ...... .10 .05
☐ 723 Rich Dauer ...... .10 .05
☐ 724 Eric Rasmussen ...... .10 .05
☐ 725 Cesar Cedeno ...... .20 .09
☐ 726 Brewers TL ...... .20 .09
  Ted Simmons
  Moose Haas
☐ 727 Joel Youngblood ...... .10 .05
☐ 728 Tug McGraw ...... .20 .09
☐ 729 Gene Tenace ...... .20 .09
☐ 730 Bruce Sutter ...... .20 .09
☐ 731 Lynn Jones ...... .10 .05
☐ 732 Terry Crowley ...... .10 .05
☐ 733 Dave Collins ...... .10 .05
☐ 734 Odell Jones ...... .10 .05
☐ 735 Rick Burleson ...... .10 .05
☐ 736 Dick Ruthven ...... .10 .05
☐ 737 Jim Essian ...... .10 .05
☐ 738 Bill Schroeder ...... .10 .05
☐ 739 Bob Watson ...... .20 .09
☐ 740 Tom Seaver ...... .75 .35
☐ 741 Wayne Gross ...... .10 .05
☐ 742 Dick Williams MG ...... .20 .09
☐ 743 Don Hood ...... .10 .05
☐ 744 Jamie Allen ...... .10 .05
☐ 745 Dennis Eckersley ...... .60 .25
☐ 746 Mickey Hatcher ...... .10 .05
☐ 747 Pat Zachry ...... .10 .05
☐ 748 Jeff Leonard ...... .10 .05
☐ 749 Doug Flynn ...... .10 .05
☐ 750 Jim Palmer ...... .60 .25
☐ 751 Charlie Moore ...... .10 .05
☐ 752 Phil Garner ...... .20 .09
☐ 753 Doug Gwosdz ...... .10 .05
☐ 754 Kent Tekulve ...... .20 .09
☐ 755 Garry Maddox ...... .10 .05
☐ 756 Reds TL ...... .20 .09
  Ron Oester

Mario Soto
☐ 757 Larry Bowa ...... .20 .09
☐ 758 Bill Stein ...... .10 .05
☐ 759 Richard Dotson ...... .10 .05
☐ 760 Bob Horner ...... .10 .05
☐ 761 John Montefusco ...... .10 .05
☐ 762 Rance Mulliniks ...... .10 .05
☐ 763 Craig Swan ...... .10 .05
☐ 764 Mike Hargrove ...... .10 .05
☐ 765 Ken Forsch ...... .10 .05
☐ 766 Mike Vail ...... .10 .05
☐ 767 Carney Lansford ...... .20 .09
☐ 768 Champ Summers ...... .10 .05
☐ 769 Bill Caudill ...... .10 .05
☐ 770 Ken Griffey ...... .20 .09
☐ 771 Billy Gardner MG ...... .10 .05
☐ 772 Jim Slaton ...... .10 .05
☐ 773 Todd Cruz ...... .10 .05
☐ 774 Tom Gorman ...... .10 .05
☐ 775 Dave Parker ...... .20 .09
☐ 776 Craig Reynolds ...... .10 .05
☐ 777 Tom Paciorek ...... .10 .05
☐ 778 Andy Hawkins ...... .10 .05
☐ 779 Jim Sundberg ...... .20 .09
☐ 780 Steve Carlton ...... .60 .25
☐ 781 Checklist 661-792 ...... .20 .05
☐ 782 Steve Balboni ...... .10 .05
☐ 783 Luis Leal ...... .10 .05
☐ 784 Leon Roberts ...... .10 .05
☐ 785 Joaquin Andujar ...... .10 .05
☐ 786 Red Sox TL ...... .60 .25
  Wade Boggs
  Bob Ojeda
☐ 787 Bill Campbell ...... .10 .05
☐ 788 Milt May ...... .10 .05
☐ 789 Bert Blyleven ...... .20 .09
☐ 790 Doug DeCinces ...... .10 .05
☐ 791 Terry Forster ...... .10 .05
☐ 792 Bill Russell ...... .10 .05

1984 Topps Tiffany

	NRMT	VG-E
COMP. FACT SET (792)	175.00	80.00
COMMON CARD (1-792)	.40	.18

*STARS: 4X TO 8X BASIC CARDS
*ROOKIES: 4X TO 8X BASIC CARDS
DISTRIBUTED ONLY IN FACTORY SET FORM

1984 Topps Traded

	NRMT	VG-E
COMP. FACT. SET (132)	30.00	13.50
COMMON CARD (1T-132T)	.40	.18
MINOR STARS	1.00	.45

☐ 1T Willie Aikens ...... .40 .18
☐ 2T Luis Aponte ...... .40 .18
☐ 3T Mike Armstrong ...... .40 .18
☐ 4T Bob Bailor ...... .40 .18
☐ 5T Dusty Baker ...... 1.00 .45
☐ 6T Steve Balboni ...... .40 .18
☐ 7T Alan Bannister ...... .40 .18
☐ 8T Dave Beard ...... .40 .18
☐ 9T Joe Beckwith ...... .40 .18
☐ 10T Bruce Berenyi ...... .40 .18
☐ 11T Dave Bergman ...... .40 .18
☐ 12T Tony Bernazard ...... .40 .18
☐ 13T Yogi Berra MG ...... 2.00 .90
☐ 14T Barry Bonnell ...... .40 .18
☐ 15T Phil Bradley ...... 1.00 .45
☐ 16T Fred Breining ...... .40 .18
☐ 17T Bill Buckner ...... 1.00 .45
☐ 18T Ray Burris ...... .40 .18
☐ 19T John Butcher ...... .40 .18
☐ 20T Brett Butler ...... 1.25 .55
☐ 21T Enos Cabell ...... .40 .18
☐ 22T Bill Campbell ...... .40 .18
☐ 23T Bill Caudill ...... .40 .18
☐ 24T Bob Clark ...... .40 .18
☐ 25T Bryan Clark ...... .40 .18
☐ 26T Jaime Cocanower ...... .40 .18
☐ 27T Ron Darling ...... 1.25 .55
☐ 28T Alvin Davis ...... 1.00 .45
☐ 29T Ken Dayley ...... .40 .18
☐ 30T Jeff Dedmon ...... .40 .18
☐ 31T Bob Dernier ...... .40 .18
☐ 32T Carlos Diaz ...... .40 .18
☐ 33T Mike Easler ...... .40 .18
☐ 34T Dennis Eckersley ...... 1.50 .70
☐ 35T Jim Essian ...... .40 .18
☐ 36T Darrell Evans ...... 1.00 .45
☐ 37T Mike Fitzgerald ...... .40 .18
☐ 38T Tim Foli ...... .40 .18
☐ 39T George Frazier ...... .40 .18
☐ 40T Rich Gale ...... .40 .18
☐ 41T Barbaro Garbey ...... .40 .18
☐ 42T Dwight Gooden 5.00 2.20
☐ 43T Rich Gossage ...... 1.25 .55
☐ 44T Wayne Gross ...... .40 .18
☐ 45T Mark Gubicza ...... 1.00 .45
☐ 46T Jackie Gutierrez ...... .40 .18
☐ 47T Mel Hall ...... 1.00 .45
☐ 48T Toby Harrah ...... .40 .18
☐ 49T Ron Hassey ...... .40 .18
☐ 50T Rich Hebner ...... .40 .18
☐ 51T Willie Hernandez ...... 1.00 .45
☐ 52T Ricky Horton ...... .40 .18
☐ 53T Art Howe ...... 1.00 .45
☐ 54T Dane Iorg ...... .40 .18
☐ 55T Brook Jacoby ...... 1.00 .45
☐ 56T Mike Jeffcoat ...... .40 .18
☐ 57T Dave Johnson MG ...... 1.00 .45
☐ 58T Lynn Jones ...... .40 .18
☐ 59T Ruppert Jones ...... .40 .18
☐ 60T Mike Jorgensen ...... .40 .18
☐ 61T Bob Kearney ...... .40 .18
☐ 62T Jimmy Key 2.50 1.10
☐ 63T Dave Kingman ...... 1.25 .55
☐ 64T Jerry Koosman ...... 1.00 .45
☐ 65T Wayne Krenchicki ...... .40 .18
☐ 66T Rusty Kuntz ...... .40 .18
☐ 67T Rene Lachemann MG ...... .40 .18
☐ 68T Frank LaCorte ...... .40 .18
☐ 69T Dennis Lamp ...... .40 .18
☐ 70T Mark Langston ...... 1.50 .70
☐ 71T Rick Leach ...... .40 .18
☐ 72T Craig Lefferts ...... 1.00 .45
☐ 73T Gary Lucas ...... .40 .18
☐ 74T Jerry Martin ...... .40 .18
☐ 75T Carmelo Martinez ...... .40 .18
☐ 76T Mike Mason ...... .40 .18
☐ 77T Gary Matthews ...... 1.00 .45
☐ 78T Andy McGaffigan ...... .40 .18
☐ 79T Larry Milbourne ...... .40 .18
☐ 80T Sid Monge ...... .40 .18
☐ 81T Jackie Moore MG ...... .40 .18

		NRMT	VG-E

☐ 82T Joe Morgan .... 2.00 .90
☐ 83T Graig Nettles .... 1.00 .45
☐ 84T Phil Niekro .... 1.50 .70
☐ 85T Ken Oberkfell .... .40 .18
☐ 86T Mike O'Berry .... .40 .18
☐ 87T Al Oliver .... 1.00 .45
☐ 88T Jorge Orta .... .40 .18
☐ 89T Amos Otis .... 1.00 .45
☐ 90T Dave Parker .... 1.00 .45
☐ 91T Tony Perez .... 1.50 .70
☐ 92T Gerald Perry .... 1.00 .45
☐ 93T Gary Pettis .... .40 .18
☐ 94T Rob Picciolo .... .40 .18
☐ 95T Vern Rapp MG .... .40 .18
☐ 96T Floyd Rayford .... .40 .18
☐ 97T Randy Ready .... 1.00 .45
☐ 98T Ron Reed .... .40 .18
☐ 99T Gene Richards .... .40 .18
☐ 100T Jose Rijo .... 1.50 .70
☐ 101T Jeff D. Robinson ..... .40 .18
☐ 102T Ron Romanick .... .40 .18
☐ 103T Pete Rose 4.00 1.80
☐ 104T Bret Saberhagen 4.00 1.80
☐ 105T Juan Samuel .... 1.25 .55
☐ 106T Scott Sanderson ..... .40 .18
☐ 107T Dick Schofield .... 1.00 .45
☐ 108T Tom Seaver 4.00 1.80
☐ 109T Jim Slaton .... .40 .18
☐ 110T Mike Smithson .... .40 .18
☐ 111T Lary Sorensen .... .40 .18
☐ 112T Tim Stoddard .... .40 .18
☐ 113T Champ Summers .... .40 .18
☐ 114T Jim Sundberg .... 1.00 .45
☐ 115T Rick Sutcliffe .... 1.25 .55
☐ 116T Craig Swan .... .40 .18
☐ 117T Tim Teufel .... .40 .18
☐ 118T Derrel Thomas .... .40 .18
☐ 119T Gorman Thomas ..... .40 .18
☐ 120T Alex Trevino .... .40 .18
☐ 121T Manny Trillo .... .40 .18
☐ 122T John Tudor .... .40 .18
☐ 123T Tom Underwood ..... .40 .18
☐ 124T Mike Vail .... .40 .18
☐ 125T Tom Waddell .... .40 .18
☐ 126T Gary Ward .... .40 .18
☐ 127T Curtis Wilkerson .... .40 .18
☐ 128T Frank Williams ...... .40 .18
☐ 129T Glenn Wilson .... .40 .18
☐ 130T John Wockenfuss .. .40 .18
☐ 131T Ned Yost .... .40 .18
☐ 132T Checklist 1T-132T .. .40 .18

1984 Topps Traded Tiffany

	NRMT	VG-E
COMP.FACT.SET (132)	50.00	22.00
COMMON CARD (1T-132T)	.40	.18

*STARS: .75X TO 1.5X BASIC CARDS
*ROOKIES: 1.25X TO 2.5X BASIC CARDS
DISTRIBUTED ONLY IN FACTORY SET FORM

1985 Topps

	NRMT	VG-E
COMPLETE SET (792)	250.00	110.00
COMP.FACT.SET (792)	350.00	160.00
COMMON CARD (1-792)	.10	.05

MINOR STARS .... .20 .09
SEMISTARS .... .40 .18
UNLISTED STARS .... .60 .25
SUBSET CARDS HALF VALUE OF BASE
CARDS
BEWARE OF COUNTERFEIT MCGWIRE RC'S

☐ 1 Carlton Fisk RB .... .20 .09
Longest game
by catcher
☐ 2 Steve Garvey RB .... .20 .09
Consecutive error-
less games, 1B
☐ 3 Dwight Gooden RB .... .60 .25
Most rookie strikeouts
☐ 4 Cliff Johnson RB .... .10 .05
Most pinch-hit homers
☐ 5 Joe Morgan RB .... .20 .09
Most homers 2B, lifetime
☐ 6 Pete Rose RB .... .40 .18
Most career singles
☐ 7 Nolan Ryan RB .... 1.50 .70
Most career strikeouts
☐ 8 Juan Samuel RB .... .10 .05
Most SB's, rookie season
☐ 9 Bruce Sutter RB .... .10 .05
Most NL season saves
☐ 10 Don Sutton RB .... .20 .09
Most seasons 100 or more K's
☐ 11 Ralph Houk MG .... .10 .05
☐ 12 Dave Lopes .... .20 .09
(Now with Cubs
on card front)
☐ 13 Tim Lollar .... .10 .05
☐ 14 Chris Bando .... .10 .05
☐ 15 Jerry Koosman .... .20 .09
☐ 16 Bobby Meacham .... .10 .05
☐ 17 Mike Scott .... .10 .05
☐ 18 Mickey Hatcher .... .10 .05
☐ 19 George Frazier .... .10 .05
☐ 20 Chet Lemon .... .10 .05
☐ 21 Lee Tunnell .... .10 .05
☐ 22 Duane Kuiper .... .10 .05
☐ 23 Bret Saberhagen ...... .60 .25
☐ 24 Jesse Barfield .... .20 .09
☐ 25 Steve Bedrosian ...... .10 .05
☐ 26 Roy Smalley .... .10 .05
☐ 27 Bruce Berenyi .... .10 .05
☐ 28 Dann Bilardello .... .10 .05
☐ 29 Odell Jones .... .10 .05
☐ 30 Cal Ripken 3.00 1.35
☐ 31 Terry Whitfield .... .10 .05
☐ 32 Chuck Porter .... .10 .05
☐ 33 Tito Landrum .... .10 .05
☐ 34 Ed Nunez .... .10 .05
☐ 35 Graig Nettles .... .20 .09
☐ 36 Fred Breining .... .10 .05
☐ 37 Reid Nichols .... .10 .05
☐ 38 Jackie Moore MG ...... .10 .05
☐ 39 John Wockenfuss ..... .10 .05
☐ 40 Phil Niekro .... .60 .25
☐ 41 Mike Fischlin .... .10 .05
☐ 42 Luis Sanchez .... .10 .05
☐ 43 Andre David .... .10 .05
☐ 44 Dickie Thon .... .10 .05
☐ 45 Greg Minton .... .10 .05
☐ 46 Gary Woods .... .10 .05
☐ 47 Dave Rozema .... .10 .05

☐ 48 Tony Fernandez .... .40 .18
☐ 49 Butch Davis .... .10 .05
☐ 50 John Candelaria .... .20 .09
☐ 51 Bob Watson .... .20 .09
☐ 52 Jerry Dybzinski .... .10 .05
☐ 53 Tom Gorman .... .10 .05
☐ 54 Cesar Cedeno .... .20 .09
☐ 55 Frank Tanana .... .20 .09
☐ 56 Jim Dwyer .... .10 .05
☐ 57 Pat Zachry .... .10 .05
☐ 58 Orlando Mercado ..... .10 .05
☐ 59 Rick Waits .... .10 .05
☐ 60 George Hendrick ...... .10 .05
☐ 61 Curt Kaufman .... .10 .05
☐ 62 Mike Ramsey .... .10 .05
☐ 63 Steve McCatty .... .10 .05
☐ 64 Mark Bailey .... .10 .05
☐ 65 Bill Buckner .... .20 .09
☐ 66 Dick Williams MG ..... .20 .09
☐ 67 Rafael Santana .... .10 .05
☐ 68 Von Hayes .... .10 .05
☐ 69 Jim Winn .... .10 .05
☐ 70 Don Baylor .... .20 .09
☐ 71 Tim Laudner .... .10 .05
☐ 72 Rick Sutcliffe .... .10 .05
☐ 73 Rusty Kuntz .... .10 .05
☐ 74 Mike Krukow .... .10 .05
☐ 75 Willie Upshaw .... .10 .05
☐ 76 Alan Bannister .... .10 .05
☐ 77 Joe Beckwith .... .10 .05
☐ 78 Scott Fletcher .... .10 .05
☐ 79 Rick Mahler .... .10 .05
☐ 80 Keith Hernandez ...... .20 .09
☐ 81 Lenn Sakata .... .10 .05
☐ 82 Joe Price .... .10 .05
☐ 83 Charlie Moore .... .10 .05
☐ 84 Spike Owen .... .10 .05
☐ 85 Mike Marshall .... .10 .05
☐ 86 Don Aase .... .10 .05
☐ 87 David Green .... .10 .05
☐ 88 Bryn Smith .... .10 .05
☐ 89 Jackie Gutierrez ...... .10 .05
☐ 90 Rich Gossage .... .20 .09
☐ 91 Jeff Burroughs .... .10 .05
☐ 92 Paul Owens MG .... .10 .05
☐ 93 Don Schulze .... .10 .05
☐ 94 Toby Harrah .... .10 .05
☐ 95 Jose Cruz .... .20 .09
☐ 96 Johnny Ray .... .10 .05
☐ 97 Pete Filson .... .10 .05
☐ 98 Steve Lake .... .10 .05
☐ 99 Milt Wilcox .... .10 .05
☐ 100 George Brett .... 1.25 .55
☐ 101 Jim Acker .... .10 .05
☐ 102 Tommy Dunbar .... .10 .05
☐ 103 Randy Lerch .... .10 .05
☐ 104 Mike Fitzgerald ...... .10 .05
☐ 105 Ron Kittle .... .10 .05
☐ 106 Pascual Perez .... .10 .05
☐ 107 Tom Foley .... .10 .05
☐ 108 Darnell Coles .... .10 .05
☐ 109 Gary Roenicke .... .10 .05
☐ 110 Alejandro Pena .... .10 .05
☐ 111 Doug DeCinces ...... .10 .05
☐ 112 Tom Tellmann .... .10 .05
☐ 113 Tom Herr .... .10 .05
☐ 114 Bob James .... .10 .05
☐ 115 Rickey Henderson .. .75 .35
☐ 116 Dennis Boyd .... .10 .05
☐ 117 Greg Gross .... .10 .05
☐ 118 Eric Show .... .10 .05
☐ 119 Pat Corrales MG ..... .10 .05
☐ 120 Steve Kemp .... .10 .05
☐ 121 Checklist: 1-132 ..... .10 .05
☐ 122 Tom Brunansky ...... .20 .09
☐ 123 Dave Smith .... .10 .05
☐ 124 Rich Hebner .... .10 .05
☐ 125 Kent Tekulve .... .10 .05
☐ 126 Ruppert Jones .... .10 .05
☐ 127 Mark Gubicza .... .20 .09
☐ 128 Ernie Whitt .... .10 .05
☐ 129 Gene Garber .... .10 .05
☐ 130 Al Oliver .... .20 .09
☐ 131 Buddy Bell FS .... .20 .09
Gus Bell
☐ 132 Dale Berra FS .... .20 .09

	Yogi Berra		
❏ 133	Bob Boone FS	.10	.05
	Ray Boone		
❏ 134	Terry Francona FS	.10	.05
	Tito Francona		
❏ 135	Terry Kennedy FS	.10	.05
	Bob Kennedy		
❏ 136	Jeff Kunkel FS	.10	.05
	Bill Kunkel		
❏ 137	Vance Law FS	.20	.09
	Vern Law		
❏ 138	Dick Schofield FS	.10	.05
	Dick Schofield		
❏ 139	Joel Skinner FS	.10	.05
	Bob Skinner		
❏ 140	Roy Smalley Jr. FS	.10	.05
	Roy Smalley		
❏ 141	Mike Stenhouse FS	.10	.05
	Dave Stenhouse		
❏ 142	Steve Trout FS	.10	.05
	Dizzy Trout		
❏ 143	Ozzie Virgil FS	.10	.05
	Ossie Virgil		
❏ 144	Ron Gardenhire	.10	.05
❏ 145	Alvin Davis	.20	.09
❏ 146	Gary Redus	.10	.05
❏ 147	Bill Swaggerty	.10	.05
❏ 148	Steve Yeager	.10	.05
❏ 149	Dickie Noles	.10	.05
❏ 150	Jim Rice	.20	.09
❏ 151	Moose Haas	.10	.05
❏ 152	Steve Braun	.10	.05
❏ 153	Frank LaCorte	.10	.05
❏ 154	Argenis Salazar	.10	.05
❏ 155	Yogi Berra MG	.40	.18
❏ 156	Craig Reynolds	.10	.05
❏ 157	Tug McGraw	.20	.09
❏ 158	Pat Tabler	.10	.05
❏ 159	Carlos Diaz	.10	.05
❏ 160	Lance Parrish	.20	.09
❏ 161	Ken Schrom	.10	.05
❏ 162	Benny Distefano	.10	.05
❏ 163	Dennis Eckersley	.60	.25
❏ 164	Jorge Orta	.10	.05
❏ 165	Dusty Baker	.20	.09
❏ 166	Keith Atherton	.10	.05
❏ 167	Rufino Linares	.10	.05
❏ 168	Garth Iorg	.10	.05
❏ 169	Dan Spilliner	.10	.05
❏ 170	George Foster	.20	.09
❏ 171	Bill Stein	.10	.05
❏ 172	Jack Perconte	.10	.05
❏ 173	Mike Young	.10	.05
❏ 174	Rick Honeycutt	.10	.05
❏ 175	Dave Parker	.20	.09
❏ 176	Bill Schroeder	.10	.05
❏ 177	Dave Von Ohlen	.10	.05
❏ 178	Miguel Dilone	.10	.05
❏ 179	Tommy John	.40	.18
❏ 180	Dave Winfield	.60	.25
❏ 181	Roger Clemens	25.00	11.00
❏ 182	Tim Flannery	.10	.05
❏ 183	Larry McWilliams	.10	.05
❏ 184	Carmen Castillo	.10	.05
❏ 185	Al Holland	.10	.05
❏ 186	Bob Lillis MG	.10	.05
❏ 187	Mike Walters	.10	.05
❏ 188	Greg Pryor	.10	.05
❏ 189	Warren Brusstar	.10	.05
❏ 190	Rusty Staub	.20	.09
❏ 191	Steve Nicosia	.10	.05
❏ 192	Howard Johnson	.20	.09
❏ 193	Jimmy Key	.60	.25
❏ 194	Dave Stegman	.10	.05
❏ 195	Glenn Hubbard	.10	.05
❏ 196	Pete O'Brien	.10	.05
❏ 197	Mike Warren	.10	.05
❏ 198	Eddie Milner	.10	.05
❏ 199	Dennis Martinez	.20	.09
❏ 200	Reggie Jackson	.75	.35
❏ 201	Burt Hooton	.10	.05
❏ 202	Gorman Thomas	.10	.05
❏ 203	Bob McClure	.10	.05
❏ 204	Art Howe	.10	.05
❏ 205	Steve Rogers	.10	.05
❏ 206	Phil Garner	.20	.09
❏ 207	Mark Clear	.10	.05
❏ 208	Champ Summers	.10	.05
❏ 209	Bill Campbell	.10	.05
❏ 210	Gary Matthews	.10	.05
❏ 211	Clay Christiansen	.10	.05
❏ 212	George Vukovich	.10	.05
❏ 213	Billy Gardner MG	.20	.05
❏ 214	John Tudor	.10	.05
❏ 215	Bob Brenly	.10	.05
❏ 216	Jerry Don Gleaton	.10	.05
❏ 217	Leon Roberts	.10	.05
❏ 218	Doug Alexander	.10	.05
❏ 219	Gerald Perry	.10	.05
❏ 220	Fred Lynn	.20	.09
❏ 221	Ron Reed	.10	.05
❏ 222	Hubie Brooks	.10	.05
❏ 223	Tom Hume	.10	.05
❏ 224	Al Cowens	.10	.05
❏ 225	Mike Boddicker	.10	.05
❏ 226	Juan Beniquez	.10	.05
❏ 227	Danny Darwin	.10	.05
❏ 228	Dion James	.10	.05
❏ 229	Dave LaPoint	.10	.05
❏ 230	Gary Carter	.60	.25
❏ 231	Dwayne Murphy	.10	.05
❏ 232	Dave Beard	.10	.05
❏ 233	Ed Jurak	.10	.05
❏ 234	Jerry Narron	.10	.05
❏ 235	Garry Maddox	.10	.05
❏ 236	Mark Thurmond	.10	.05
❏ 237	Julio Franco	.40	.18
❏ 238	Jose Rijo	.40	.18
❏ 239	Tim Teufel	.10	.05
❏ 240	Dave Stieb	.20	.09
❏ 241	Jim Frey MG	.10	.05
❏ 242	Greg Harris	.10	.05
❏ 243	Barbaro Garbey	.10	.05
❏ 244	Mike Jones	.10	.05
❏ 245	Chili Davis	.20	.09
❏ 246	Mike Norris	.10	.05
❏ 247	Wayne Tolleson	.10	.05
❏ 248	Terry Forster	.10	.05
❏ 249	Harold Baines	.20	.09
❏ 250	Jesse Orosco	.10	.05
❏ 251	Brad Gulden	.10	.05
❏ 252	Dan Ford	.10	.05
❏ 253	Sid Bream	.20	.09
❏ 254	Pete Vuckovich	.10	.05
❏ 255	Lonnie Smith	.10	.05
❏ 256	Mike Stanton	.10	.05
❏ 257	Bryan Little UER	.10	.05
	Name spelled Brian on front		
❏ 258	Mike C. Brown	.10	.05
❏ 259	Gary Allenson	.10	.05
❏ 260	Dave Righetti	.20	.09
❏ 261	Checklist: 133-264	.10	.05
❏ 262	Greg Booker	.10	.05
❏ 263	Mel Hall	.20	.09
❏ 264	Joe Sambito	.10	.05
❏ 265	Juan Samuel	.20	.09
❏ 266	Frank Viola	.20	.09
❏ 267	Henry Cotto	.10	.05
❏ 268	Chuck Tanner MG	.10	.05
❏ 269	Doug Baker	.10	.05
❏ 270	Dan Quisenberry	.20	.09
❏ 271	Tim Foli FDP68	.10	.05
❏ 272	Jeff Burroughs FDP69	.10	.05
❏ 273	Bill Almon FDP74	.10	.05
❏ 274	Floyd Bannister FDP76	.10	.05
❏ 275	Harold Baines FDP77	.10	.05
❏ 276	Bob Horner FDP78	.10	.05
❏ 277	Al Chambers FDP79	.10	.05
❏ 278	Darryl Strawberry FDP80	.20	.09
❏ 279	Mike Moore FDP81	.10	.05
❏ 280	Shawon Dunston FDP82	.40	.18
❏ 281	Tim Belcher FDP83	.60	.25
❏ 282	Shawn Abner FDP84	.10	.05
❏ 283	Fran Mullins	.10	.05
❏ 284	Marty Bystrom	.10	.05
❏ 285	Dan Driessen	.10	.05
❏ 286	Rudy Law	.10	.05
❏ 287	Walt Terrell	.10	.05
❏ 288	Jeff Kunkel	.10	.05
❏ 289	Tom Underwood	.10	.05
❏ 290	Cecil Cooper	.20	.09
❏ 291	Bob Welch	.10	.05
❏ 292	Brad Komminsk	.10	.05
❏ 293	Curt Young	.10	.05
❏ 294	Tom Nieto	.10	.05
❏ 295	Joe Niekro	.10	.05
❏ 296	Ricky Nelson	.10	.05
❏ 297	Gary Lucas	.10	.05
❏ 298	Marty Barrett	.10	.05
❏ 299	Andy Hawkins	.10	.05
❏ 300	Rod Carew	.60	.25
❏ 301	John Montefusco	.10	.05
❏ 302	Tim Corcoran	.10	.05
❏ 303	Mike Jeffcoat	.10	.05
❏ 304	Gary Gaetti	.20	.09
❏ 305	Dale Berra	.10	.05
❏ 306	Rick Reuschel	.10	.05
❏ 307	Sparky Anderson MG	.20	.09
❏ 308	John Wathan	.10	.05
❏ 309	Mike Witt	.10	.05
❏ 310	Manny Trillo	.10	.05
❏ 311	Jim Gott	.10	.05
❏ 312	Marc Hill	.10	.05
❏ 313	Dave Schmidt	.10	.05
❏ 314	Ron Oester	.10	.05
❏ 315	Doug Sisk	.10	.05
❏ 316	John Lowenstein	.10	.05
❏ 317	Jack Lazorko	.10	.05
❏ 318	Ted Simmons	.20	.09
❏ 319	Jeff Jones	.10	.05
❏ 320	Dale Murphy	.60	.25
❏ 321	Ricky Horton	.10	.05
❏ 322	Dave Stapleton	.10	.05
❏ 323	Andy McGaffigan	.10	.05
❏ 324	Bruce Bochy	.10	.05
❏ 325	John Denny	.10	.05
❏ 326	Kevin Bass	.10	.05
❏ 327	Brook Jacoby	.10	.05
❏ 328	Bob Shirley	.10	.05
❏ 329	Ron Washington	.10	.05
❏ 330	Leon Durham	.10	.05
❏ 331	Bill Laskey	.10	.05
❏ 332	Brian Harper	.10	.05
❏ 333	Willie Hernandez	.10	.05
❏ 334	Dick Howser MG	.20	.09
❏ 335	Bruce Benedict	.10	.05
❏ 336	Rance Mulliniks	.10	.05
❏ 337	Billy Sample	.10	.05
❏ 338	Britt Burns	.10	.05
❏ 339	Danny Heep	.10	.05
❏ 340	Robin Yount	.60	.25
❏ 341	Floyd Rayford	.10	.05
❏ 342	Ted Power	.10	.05
❏ 343	Bill Russell	.10	.05
❏ 344	Dave Henderson	.10	.05
❏ 345	Charlie Lea	.10	.05
❏ 346	Terry Pendleton	.60	.25
❏ 347	Rick Langford	.10	.05
❏ 348	Bob Boone	.20	.09
❏ 349	Domingo Ramos	.10	.05
❏ 350	Wade Boggs	.75	.35
❏ 351	Juan Agosto	.10	.05
❏ 352	Joe Morgan	.60	.25
❏ 353	Julio Solano	.10	.05
❏ 354	Andre Robertson	.10	.05
❏ 355	Bert Blyleven	.20	.09
❏ 356	Dave Meier	.10	.05
❏ 357	Rich Bordi	.10	.05
❏ 358	Tony Pena	.10	.05
❏ 359	Pat Sheridan	.10	.05
❏ 360	Steve Carlton	.60	.25
❏ 361	Alfredo Griffin	.10	.05
❏ 362	Craig McMurtry	.10	.05
❏ 363	Ron Hodges	.10	.05
❏ 364	Richard Dotson	.10	.05
❏ 365	Danny Ozark MG	.10	.05
❏ 366	Todd Cruz	.10	.05
❏ 367	Keefe Cato	.10	.05
❏ 368	Dave Bergman	.10	.05
❏ 369	R.J. Reynolds	.10	.05
❏ 370	Bruce Sutter	.20	.09
❏ 371	Mickey Rivers	.10	.05
❏ 372	Roy Howell	.10	.05
❏ 373	Mike Moore	.10	.05
❏ 374	Brian Downing	.10	.05
❏ 375	Jeff Reardon	.20	.09
❏ 376	Jeff Newman	.10	.05

377	Checklist: 265-396	.10	.05
378	Alan Wiggins	.10	.05
379	Charles Hudson	.10	.05
380	Ken Griffey	.20	.09
381	Roy Smith	.10	.05
382	Denny Walling	.10	.05
383	Rick Lysander	.10	.05
384	Jody Davis	.10	.05
385	Jose DeLeon	.10	.05
386	Dan Gladden	.20	.09
387	Buddy Biancalana	.10	.05
388	Bert Roberge	.10	.05
389	Rod Dedeaux OLY CO	.20	.09
390	Sid Akins OLY	.10	.05
391	Flavio Alfaro OLY	.10	.05
392	Don August OLY	.10	.05
393	Scott Bankhead OLY	.10	.05
394	Bob Caffrey OLY	.10	.05
395	Mike Dunne OLY	.20	.09
396	Gary Green OLY	.10	.05
397	John Hoover OLY	.10	.05
398	Shane Mack OLY	.60	.25
399	John Marzano OLY	.20	.09
400	Oddibe McDowell OLY	.20	.09
401	Mark McGwire OLY	175.00	80.00
402	Pat Pacillo OLY	.20	.09
403	Cory Snyder OLY	.40	.18
404	Billy Swift OLY	.40	.18
405	Tom Veryzer	.10	.05
406	Len Whitehouse	.10	.05
407	Bobby Ramos	.10	.05
408	Sid Monge	.10	.05
409	Brad Wellman	.10	.05
410	Bob Horner	.10	.05
411	Bobby Cox MG	.10	.05
412	Bud Black	.10	.05
413	Vance Law	.10	.05
414	Gary Ward	.10	.05
415	Ron Darling UER	.20	.09
	(No trivia answer)		
416	Wayne Gross	.10	.05
417	John Franco	.60	.25
418	Ken Landreaux	.10	.05
419	Mike Caldwell	.10	.05
420	Andre Dawson	.60	.25
421	Dave Rucker	.10	.05
422	Carney Lansford	.20	.09
423	Barry Bonnell	.10	.05
424	Al Nipper	.10	.05
425	Mike Hargrove	.20	.09
426	Vern Ruhle	.10	.05
427	Mario Ramirez	.10	.05
428	Larry Andersen	.10	.05
429	Rick Cerone	.10	.05
430	Ron Davis	.10	.05
431	U.L. Washington	.10	.05
432	Thad Bosley	.10	.05
433	Jim Morrison	.10	.05
434	Gene Richards	.10	.05
435	Dan Petry	.10	.05
436	Willie Aikens	.10	.05
437	Al Jones	.10	.05
438	Joe Torre MG	.40	.18
439	Junior Ortiz	.10	.05
440	Fernando Valenzuela	.20	.09
441	Duane Walker	.10	.05
442	Ken Forsch	.10	.05
443	George Wright	.10	.05
444	Tony Phillips	.10	.05
445	Tippy Martinez	.10	.05
446	Jim Sundberg	.10	.05
447	Jeff Lahti	.10	.05
448	Derrel Thomas	.10	.05
449	Phil Bradley	.20	.09
450	Steve Garvey	.40	.18
451	Bruce Hurst	.10	.05
452	John Castino	.10	.05
453	Tom Waddell	.10	.05
454	Glenn Wilson	.10	.05
455	Bob Knepper	.10	.05
456	Tim Foli	.10	.05
457	Cecilio Guante	.10	.05
458	Randy Johnson	.10	.05
459	Charlie Leibrandt	.10	.05
460	Ryne Sandberg	1.25	.55
461	Marty Castillo	.10	.05
462	Gary Lavelle	.10	.05
463	Dave Collins	.10	.05
464	Mike Mason	.10	.05
465	Bobby Grich	.20	.09
466	Tony LaRussa MG	.40	.18
467	Ed Lynch	.10	.05
468	Wayne Krenchicki	.10	.05
469	Sammy Stewart	.10	.05
470	Steve Sax	.10	.05
471	Pete Ladd	.10	.05
472	Jim Essian	.10	.05
473	Tim Wallach	.20	.09
474	Kurt Kepshire	.10	.05
475	Andre Thornton	.10	.05
476	Jeff Stone	.10	.05
477	Bob Ojeda	.10	.05
478	Kurt Bevacqua	.10	.05
479	Mike Madden	.10	.05
480	Lou Whitaker	.40	.18
481	Dale Murray	.10	.05
482	Harry Spilman	.10	.05
483	Mike Smithson	.10	.05
484	Larry Bowa	.20	.09
485	Matt Young	.10	.05
486	Steve Balboni	.10	.05
487	Frank Williams	.10	.05
488	Joel Skinner	.10	.05
489	Bryan Clark	.10	.05
490	Jason Thompson	.10	.05
491	Rick Camp	.10	.05
492	Dave Johnson MG	.20	.09
493	Orel Hershiser	.75	.35
494	Rich Dauer	.10	.05
495	Mario Soto	.10	.05
496	Donnie Scott	.10	.05
497	Gary Pettis UER	.10	.05
	(Photo actually		
	Gary's little		
	brother Lynn)		
498	Ed Romero	.10	.05
499	Danny Cox	.10	.05
500	Mike Schmidt	1.00	.45
501	Dan Schatzeder	.10	.05
502	Rick Miller	.10	.05
503	Tim Conroy	.10	.05
504	Jerry Willard	.10	.05
505	Jim Beattie	.10	.05
506	Franklin Stubbs	.10	.05
507	Ray Fontenot	.10	.05
508	John Shelby	.10	.05
509	Milt May	.10	.05
510	Kent Hrbek	.20	.09
511	Lee Smith	.40	.18
512	Tom Brookens	.10	.05
513	Lynn Jones	.10	.05
514	Jeff Cornell	.10	.05
515	Dave Concepcion	.20	.09
516	Roy Lee Jackson	.10	.05
517	Jerry Martin	.10	.05
518	Chris Chambliss	.20	.09
519	Doug Rader MG	.10	.05
520	LaMarr Hoyt	.10	.05
521	Rick Dempsey	.10	.05
522	Paul Molitor	.60	.25
523	Candy Maldonado	.10	.05
524	Rob Wilfong	.10	.05
525	Darrell Porter	.10	.05
526	David Palmer	.10	.05
527	Checklist: 397-528	.10	.05
528	Bill Krueger	.10	.05
529	Rich Gedman	.10	.05
530	Dave Dravecky	.20	.09
531	Joe Lefebvre	.10	.05
532	Frank DiPino	.10	.05
533	Tony Bernazard	.10	.05
534	Brian Dayett	.10	.05
535	Pat Putnam	.10	.05
536	Kirby Puckett	8.00	3.60
537	Don Robinson	.05	
538	Keith Moreland	.10	.05
539	Aurelio Lopez	.10	.05
540	Claudell Washington	.10	.05
541	Mark Davis	.10	.05
542	Don Slaught	.10	.05
543	Mike Squires	.10	.05
544	Bruce Kison	.10	.05
545	Lloyd Moseby	.10	.05
546	Brent Gaff	.10	.05
547	Pete Rose MG	.40	.18
548	Larry Parrish	.10	.05
549	Mike Scioscia	.10	.05
550	Scott McGregor	.10	.05
551	Andy Van Slyke	.40	.18
552	Chris Codiroli	.10	.05
553	Bob Clark	.10	.05
554	Doug Flynn	.10	.05
555	Bob Stanley	.10	.05
556	Sixto Lezcano	.10	.05
557	Len Barker	.10	.05
558	Carmelo Martinez	.10	.05
559	Jay Howell	.10	.05
560	Bill Madlock	.20	.09
561	Darryl Motley	.10	.05
562	Houston Jimenez	.10	.05
563	Dick Ruthven	.10	.05
564	Alan Ashby	.10	.05
565	Kirk Gibson	.20	.09
566	Ed VandeBerg	.10	.05
567	Joel Youngblood	.10	.05
568	Cliff Johnson	.10	.05
569	Ken Oberkfell	.10	.05
570	Darryl Strawberry	.60	.25
571	Charlie Hough	.20	.09
572	Tom Paciorek	.20	.09
573	Jay Tibbs	.10	.05
574	Joe Altobelli MG	.10	.05
575	Pedro Guerrero	.20	.09
576	Jaime Cocanower	.10	.05
577	Chris Speier	.10	.05
578	Terry Francona	.10	.05
579	Ron Romanick	.10	.05
580	Dwight Evans	.20	.09
581	Mark Wagner	.10	.05
582	Ken Phelps	.10	.05
583	Bobby Brown	.10	.05
584	Kevin Gross	.10	.05
585	Butch Wynegar	.10	.05
586	Bill Scherrer	.10	.05
587	Doug Frobel	.10	.05
588	Bobby Castillo	.10	.05
589	Bob Dernier	.10	.05
590	Ray Knight	.10	.05
591	Larry Herndon	.10	.05
592	Jeff D. Robinson	.10	.05
593	Rick Leach	.10	.05
594	Curt Wilkerson	.10	.05
595	Larry Gura	.10	.05
596	Jerry Hairston	.10	.05
597	Brad Lesley	.10	.05
598	Jose Oquendo	.10	.05
599	Storm Davis	.10	.05
600	Pete Rose	1.25	.55
601	Tom Lasorda MG	.40	.18
602	Jeff Dedmon	.10	.05
603	Rick Manning	.10	.05
604	Daryl Sconiers	.10	.05
605	Ozzie Smith	.75	.35
606	Rich Gale	.10	.05
607	Bill Almon	.10	.05
608	Craig Lefferts	.10	.05
609	Broderick Perkins	.10	.05
610	Jack Morris	.20	.09
611	Ozzie Virgil	.10	.05
612	Mike Armstrong	.10	.05
613	Terry Puhl	.10	.05
614	Al Williams	.10	.05
615	Marvell Wynne	.10	.05
616	Scott Sanderson	.10	.05
617	Willie Wilson	.10	.05
618	Pete Falcone	.10	.05
619	Jeff Leonard	.10	.05
620	Dwight Gooden	.75	.35
621	Marvis Foley	.10	.05
622	Luis Leal	.10	.05
623	Greg Walker	.10	.05
624	Benny Ayala	.10	.05
625	Mark Langston	.40	.18
626	German Rivera	.10	.05
627	Eric Davis	1.25	.55
628	Rene Lachemann MG	.10	.05
629	Dick Schofield	.10	.05
630	Tim Raines	.20	.09

		NRMT	VG-E
❏ 631	Bob Forsch	.10	.05
❏ 632	Bruce Bochte	.10	.05
❏ 633	Glenn Hoffman	.10	.05
❏ 634	Bill Dawley	.10	.05
❏ 635	Terry Kennedy	.10	.05
❏ 636	Shane Rawley	.10	.05
❏ 637	Brett Butler	.20	.09
❏ 638	Mike Pagliarulo	.10	.05
❏ 639	Ed Hodge	.10	.05
❏ 640	Steve Henderson	.10	.05
❏ 641	Rod Scurry	.10	.05
❏ 642	Dave Owen	.10	.05
❏ 643	Johnny Grubb	.10	.05
❏ 644	Mark Huismann	.10	.05
❏ 645	Damaso Garcia	.10	.05
❏ 646	Scot Thompson	.10	.05
❏ 647	Rafael Ramirez	.10	.05
❏ 648	Bob Jones	.10	.05
❏ 649	Sid Fernandez	.20	.09
❏ 650	Greg Luzinski	.20	.09
❏ 651	Jeff Russell	.10	.05
❏ 652	Joe Nolan	.10	.05
❏ 653	Mark Brouhard	.10	.05
❏ 654	Dave Anderson	.10	.05
❏ 655	Joaquin Andujar	.10	.05
❏ 656	Chuck Cottier MG	.10	.05
❏ 657	Jim Slaton	.10	.05
❏ 658	Mike Stenhouse	.10	.05
❏ 659	Checklist: 529-660	.10	.05
❏ 660	Tony Gwynn	2.50	1.10
❏ 661	Steve Crawford	.10	.05
❏ 662	Mike Heath	.10	.05
❏ 663	Luis Aguayo	.10	.05
❏ 664	Steve Farr	.20	.09
❏ 665	Don Mattingly	1.50	.70
❏ 666	Mike LaCoss	.10	.05
❏ 667	Dave Engle	.10	.05
❏ 668	Steve Trout	.10	.05
❏ 669	Lee Lacy	.10	.05
❏ 670	Tom Seaver	.75	.35
❏ 671	Dane Iorg	.10	.05
❏ 672	Juan Berenguer	.10	.05
❏ 673	Buck Martinez	.10	.05
❏ 674	Atlee Hammaker	.10	.05
❏ 675	Tony Perez	.60	.25
❏ 676	Albert Hall	.10	.05
❏ 677	Wally Backman	.10	.05
❏ 678	Joey McLaughlin	.10	.05
❏ 679	Bob Kearney	.10	.05
❏ 680	Jerry Reuss	.10	.05
❏ 681	Ben Ogilvie	.10	.05
❏ 682	Doug Corbett	.10	.05
❏ 683	Whitey Herzog MG	.20	.09
❏ 684	Bill Doran	.10	.05
❏ 685	Bill Caudill	.10	.05
❏ 686	Mike Easler	.10	.05
❏ 687	Bill Gullickson	.10	.05
❏ 688	Len Matuszek	.10	.05
❏ 689	Luis DeLeon	.10	.05
❏ 690	Alan Trammell	.40	.18
❏ 691	Dennis Rasmussen	.10	.05
❏ 692	Randy Bush	.10	.05
❏ 693	Tim Stoddard	.10	.05
❏ 694	Joe Carter	.60	.25
❏ 695	Rick Rhoden	.10	.05
❏ 696	John Rabb	.10	.05
❏ 697	Onix Concepcion	.10	.05
❏ 698	Jorge Bell	.20	.09
❏ 699	Donnie Moore	.10	.05
❏ 700	Eddie Murray	.60	.25
❏ 701	Eddie Murray AS	.20	.09
❏ 702	Damaso Garcia AS	.10	.05
❏ 703	George Brett AS	.60	.25
❏ 704	Cal Ripken AS	1.50	.70
❏ 705	Dave Winfield AS	.20	.09
❏ 706	Rickey Henderson AS	.20	.09
❏ 707	Tony Armas AS	.10	.05
❏ 708	Lance Parrish AS	.10	.05
❏ 709	Mike Boddicker AS	.10	.05
❏ 710	Frank Viola AS	.10	.05
❏ 711	Dan Quisenberry AS	.10	.05
❏ 712	Keith Hernandez AS	.10	.05
❏ 713	Ryne Sandberg AS	.60	.25
❏ 714	Mike Schmidt AS	.40	.18
❏ 715	Ozzie Smith AS	.40	.18
❏ 716	Dale Murphy AS	.20	.09

❏ 717	Tony Gwynn AS	1.25	.55
❏ 718	Jeff Leonard AS	.10	.05
❏ 719	Gary Carter AS	.20	.09
❏ 720	Rick Sutcliffe AS	.10	.05
❏ 721	Bob Knepper AS	.10	.05
❏ 722	Bruce Sutter AS	.10	.05
❏ 723	Dave Stewart	.20	.09
❏ 724	Oscar Gamble	.10	.05
❏ 725	Floyd Bannister	.10	.05
❏ 726	Al Bumbry	.10	.05
❏ 727	Frank Pastore	.10	.05
❏ 728	Bob Bailor	.10	.05
❏ 729	Don Sutton	.60	.25
❏ 730	Dave Kingman	.20	.09
❏ 731	Neil Allen	.10	.05
❏ 732	John McNamara MG	.10	.05
❏ 733	Tony Scott	.10	.05
❏ 734	John Henry Johnson	.10	.05
❏ 735	Garry Templeton	.10	.05
❏ 736	Jerry Mumphrey	.10	.05
❏ 737	Bo Diaz	.10	.05
❏ 738	Omar Moreno	.10	.05
❏ 739	Ernie Camacho	.10	.05
❏ 740	Jack Clark	.20	.09
❏ 741	John Butcher	.10	.05
❏ 742	Ron Hassey	.10	.05
❏ 743	Frank White	.20	.09
❏ 744	Doug Bair	.10	.05
❏ 745	Buddy Bell	.20	.09
❏ 746	Jim Clancy	.10	.05
❏ 747	Alex Trevino	.10	.05
❏ 748	Lee Mazzilli	.10	.05
❏ 749	Julio Cruz	.10	.05
❏ 750	Rollie Fingers	.60	.25
❏ 751	Kelvin Chapman	.10	.05
❏ 752	Bob Owchinko	.10	.05
❏ 753	Greg Brock	.10	.05
❏ 754	Larry Milbourne	.10	.05
❏ 755	Ken Singleton	.10	.05
❏ 756	Rob Picciolo	.10	.05
❏ 757	Willie McGee	.20	.09
❏ 758	Ray Burris	.10	.05
❏ 759	Jim Fanning MG	.10	.05
❏ 760	Nolan Ryan	3.00	1.35
❏ 761	Jerry Remy	.10	.05
❏ 762	Eddie Whitson	.10	.05
❏ 763	Kiko Garcia	.10	.05
❏ 764	Jamie Easterly	.10	.05
❏ 765	Willie Randolph	.20	.09
❏ 766	Paul Mirabella	.10	.05
❏ 767	Darrell Brown	.10	.05
❏ 768	Ron Cey	.20	.09
❏ 769	Joe Cowley	.10	.05
❏ 770	Carlton Fisk	.60	.25
❏ 771	Geoff Zahn	.10	.05
❏ 772	Johnnie LeMaster	.10	.05
❏ 773	Hal McRae	.20	.09
❏ 774	Dennis Lamp	.10	.05
❏ 775	Mookie Wilson	.20	.09
❏ 776	Jerry Royster	.10	.05
❏ 777	Ned Yost	.10	.05
❏ 778	Mike Davis	.10	.05
❏ 779	Nick Esasky	.10	.05
❏ 780	Mike Flanagan	.10	.05
❏ 781	Jim Gantner	.10	.05
❏ 782	Tom Niedenfuer	.10	.05
❏ 783	Mike Jorgensen	.10	.05
❏ 784	Checklist: 661-792	.10	.05
❏ 785	Tony Armas	.10	.05
❏ 786	Enos Cabell	.10	.05
❏ 787	Jim Wohlford	.10	.05
❏ 788	Steve Comer	.10	.05
❏ 789	Luis Salazar	.10	.05
❏ 790	Ron Guidry	.20	.09
❏ 791	Ivan DeJesus	.10	.05
❏ 792	Darrell Evans	.20	.09

1985 Topps Tiffany

	NRMT	VG-E
COMP.FACT.SET (792)	1350.00	600.00
COMMON CARD (1-792)	.40	.18

*STARS: 4X TO 8X BASIC CARDS
*ROOKIES: 4X TO 8X BASIC CARDS
STATED PRINT RUN 5000 SETS
DISTRIBUTED ONLY IN FACTORY SET FORM

1985 Topps Traded

	NRMT	VG-E
COMP.FACT.SET (132)	10.00	4.50
COMMON CARD (1T-132T)	.15	.07
MINOR STARS	.40	.18
SEMISTARS	.75	.35

❏ 1T	Don Aase	.15	.07
❏ 2T	Bill Almon	.15	.07
❏ 3T	Benny Ayala	.15	.07
❏ 4T	Dusty Baker	.40	.18
❏ 5T	George Bamberger MG	.15	.07
❏ 6T	Dale Berra	.15	.07
❏ 7T	Rich Bordi	.15	.07
❏ 8T	Daryl Boston	.15	.07
❏ 9T	Hubie Brooks	.15	.07
❏ 10T	Chris Brown	.15	.07
❏ 11T	Tom Browning	.40	.18
❏ 12T	Al Bumbry	.15	.07
❏ 13T	Ray Burris	.15	.07
❏ 14T	Jeff Burroughs	.15	.07
❏ 15T	Bill Campbell	.15	.07
❏ 16T	Don Carman	.15	.07
❏ 17T	Gary Carter	1.00	.45
❏ 18T	Bobby Castillo	.15	.07
❏ 19T	Bill Caudill	.15	.07
❏ 20T	Rick Cerone	.15	.07
❏ 21T	Bryan Clark	.15	.07
❏ 22T	Jack Clark	.40	.18
❏ 23T	Pat Clements	.15	.07
❏ 24T	Vince Coleman	1.00	.45
❏ 25T	Dave Collins	.15	.07
❏ 26T	Danny Darwin	.15	.07
❏ 27T	Jim Davenport MG	.15	.07
❏ 28T	Jerry Davis	.15	.07
❏ 29T	Brian Dayett	.15	.07
❏ 30T	Ivan DeJesus	.15	.07
❏ 31T	Ken Dixon	.15	.07
❏ 32T	Mariano Duncan	1.00	.45
❏ 33T	John Felske MG	.15	.07
❏ 34T	Mike Fitzgerald	.15	.07
❏ 35T	Ray Fontenot	.15	.07
❏ 36T	Greg Gagne	.40	.18
❏ 37T	Oscar Gamble	.15	.07
❏ 38T	Scott Garrelts	.15	.07
❏ 39T	Bob L. Gibson	.15	.07
❏ 40T	Jim Gott	.15	.07
❏ 41T	David Green	.15	.07
❏ 42T	Alfredo Griffin	.15	.07
❏ 43T	Ozzie Guillen	1.00	.45
❏ 44T	Eddie Haas MG	.15	.07
❏ 45T	Terry Harper	.15	.07
❏ 46T	Toby Harrah	.15	.07
❏ 47T	Greg Harris	.15	.07
❏ 48T	Ron Hassey	.15	.07
❏ 49T	Rickey Henderson	2.00	.90
❏ 50T	Steve Henderson	.15	.07
❏ 51T	George Hendrick	.15	.07
❏ 52T	Joe Hesketh	.15	.07
❏ 53T	Teddy Higuera	.40	.18
❏ 54T	Donnie Hill	.15	.07
❏ 55T	Al Holland	.15	.07
❏ 56T	Burt Hooton	.15	.07
❏ 57T	Jay Howell	.15	.07
❏ 58T	Ken Howell	.15	.07
❏ 59T	LaMarr Hoyt	.15	.07
❏ 60T	Tim Hulett	.15	.07

Below card 660 area: TOM BROWNING / REDS (card image caption)

❑ 61T Bob James	.15	.07
❑ 62T Steve Jeltz	.15	.07
❑ 63T Cliff Johnson	.15	.07
❑ 64T Howard Johnson	.40	.18
❑ 65T Ruppert Jones	.15	.07
❑ 66T Steve Kemp	.15	.07
❑ 67T Bruce Kison	.15	.07
❑ 68T Alan Knicely	.15	.07
❑ 69T Mike LaCoss	.15	.07
❑ 70T Lee Lacy	.15	.07
❑ 71T Dave LaPoint	.15	.07
❑ 72T Gary Lavelle	.15	.07
❑ 73T Vance Law	.15	.07
❑ 74T Johnnie LeMaster	.15	.07
❑ 75T Sixto Lezcano	.15	.07
❑ 76T Tim Lollar	.15	.07
❑ 77T Fred Lynn	.40	.18
❑ 78T Billy Martin MG	.40	.18
❑ 79T Ron Mathis	.15	.07
❑ 80T Len Matuszek	.15	.07
❑ 81T Gene Mauch MG	.40	.18
❑ 82T Oddibe McDowell	.40	.18
❑ 83T Roger McDowell	.40	.18
❑ 84T John McNamara MG	.15	.07
❑ 85T Donnie Moore	.15	.07
❑ 86T Gene Nelson	.15	.07
❑ 87T Steve Nicosia	.15	.07
❑ 88T Al Oliver	.40	.18
❑ 89T Joe Orsulak	.40	.18
❑ 90T Rob Picciolo	.15	.07
❑ 91T Chris Pittaro	.15	.07
❑ 92T Jim Presley	.40	.18
❑ 93T Rick Reuschel	.15	.07
❑ 94T Bert Roberge	.15	.07
❑ 95T Bob Rodgers MG	.15	.07
❑ 96T Jerry Royster	.15	.07
❑ 97T Dave Rozema	.15	.07
❑ 98T Dave Rucker	.15	.07
❑ 99T Vern Ruhle	.15	.07
❑ 100T Paul Runge	.15	.07
❑ 101T Mark Salas	.15	.07
❑ 102T Luis Salazar	.15	.07
❑ 103T Joe Sambito	.15	.07
❑ 104T Rick Schu	.15	.07
❑ 105T Donnie Scott	.15	.07
❑ 106T Larry Sheets	.15	.07
❑ 107T Don Slaught	.15	.07
❑ 108T Roy Smalley	.15	.07
❑ 109T Lonnie Smith	.15	.07
❑ 110T Nate Snell UER	.15	.07

(Headings on back
for a batter)

❑ 111T Chris Speier	.15	.07
❑ 112T Mike Stenhouse	.15	.07
❑ 113T Tim Stoddard	.15	.07
❑ 114T Jim Sundberg	.15	.07
❑ 115T Bruce Sutter	.40	.18
❑ 116T Don Sutton	1.00	.45
❑ 117T Kent Tekulve	.15	.07
❑ 118T Tom Tellmann	.15	.07
❑ 119T Walt Terrell	.15	.07
❑ 120T Mickey Tettleton	1.00	.45
❑ 121T Derrel Thomas	.15	.07
❑ 122T Rich Thompson	.15	.07
❑ 123T Alex Trevino	.15	.07
❑ 124T John Tudor	.15	.07
❑ 125T Jose Uribe	.15	.07
❑ 126T Bobby Valentine MG	.15	.07
❑ 127T Dave Von Ohlen	.15	.07
❑ 128T U.L. Washington	.15	.07
❑ 129T Earl Weaver MG	.75	.35
❑ 130T Eddie Whitson	.15	.07
❑ 131T Herm Winningham	.15	.07
❑ 132T Checklist 1-132	.15	.07

1985 Topps Traded Tiffany

	NRMT	VG-E
COMP.FACT.SET (132)	50.00	22.00
COMMON CARD (1T-132T)	.40	.18

*STARS: 2X TO 4X BASIC CARDS
*ROOKIES: 2X TO 4X BASIC CARDS
STATED PRINT RUN 5000 SETS
DISTRIBUTED ONLY IN FACTORY SET FORM

1986 Topps

VINCE COLEMAN

	MINT	NRMT
COMPLETE SET (792)	20.00	9.00
COMP.FACT.SET (792)	30.00	13.50
COMMON CARD (1-792)	.05	.02
PETE ROSE SPECIALS (2-7)	.25	.11
MINOR STARS	.10	.05
SEMISTARS	.20	.09
UNLISTED STARS	.40	.18
SUBSET CARDS HALF VALUE OF BASE CARDS		

❑ 1 Pete Rose	1.00	.45
❑ 2 Rose Special: '63-'66	.25	.11
❑ 3 Rose Special: '67-'70	.25	.11
❑ 4 Rose Special: '71-'74	.25	.11
❑ 5 Rose Special: '75-'78	.25	.11
❑ 6 Rose Special: '79-'82	.25	.11
❑ 7 Rose Special: '83-'85	.25	.11
❑ 8 Dwayne Murphy	.05	.02
❑ 9 Roy Smith	.05	.02
❑ 10 Tony Gwynn	1.00	.45
❑ 11 Bob Ojeda	.05	.02
❑ 12 Jose Uribe	.05	.02
❑ 13 Bob Kearney	.05	.02
❑ 14 Julio Cruz	.05	.02
❑ 15 Eddie Whitson	.05	.02
❑ 16 Rick Schu	.05	.02
❑ 17 Mike Stenhouse	.05	.02
❑ 18 Brent Gaff	.05	.02
❑ 19 Rich Hebner	.05	.02
❑ 20 Lou Whitaker	.10	.05
❑ 21 George Bamberger MG	.05	.02
❑ 22 Duane Walker	.05	.02
❑ 23 Manny Lee	.05	.02
❑ 24 Len Barker	.05	.02
❑ 25 Willie Wilson	.05	.02
❑ 26 Frank DiPino	.05	.02
❑ 27 Ray Knight	.10	.05
❑ 28 Eric Davis	.20	.09
❑ 29 Tony Phillips	.05	.02
❑ 30 Eddie Murray	.40	.18
❑ 31 Jamie Easterly	.05	.02
❑ 32 Steve Yeager	.05	.02
❑ 33 Jeff Lahti	.05	.02
❑ 34 Ken Phelps	.05	.02
❑ 35 Jeff Reardon	.05	.02
❑ 36 Lance Parrish TL	.10	.05
❑ 37 Mark Thurmond	.05	.02

❑ 38 Glenn Hoffman	.05	.02
❑ 39 Dave Rucker	.05	.02
❑ 40 Ken Griffey	.10	.05
❑ 41 Brad Wellman	.05	.02
❑ 42 Geoff Zahn	.05	.02
❑ 43 Dave Engle	.05	.02
❑ 44 Lance McCullers	.05	.02
❑ 45 Damaso Garcia	.05	.02
❑ 46 Billy Hatcher	.05	.02
❑ 47 Juan Berenguer	.05	.02
❑ 48 Bill Almon	.05	.02
❑ 49 Rick Manning	.05	.02
❑ 50 Dan Quisenberry	.05	.02
❑ 51 Bobby Wine MG ERR	.05	.02

(Number of card on
back is actually 57)

❑ 52 Chris Welsh	.05	.02
❑ 53 Len Dykstra	.75	.35
❑ 54 John Franco	.40	.18
❑ 55 Fred Lynn	.10	.05
❑ 56 Tom Niedenfuer	.05	.02
❑ 57 Bill Doran	.05	.02

(See also 51)

❑ 58 Bill Krueger	.05	.02
❑ 59 Andre Thornton	.05	.02
❑ 60 Dwight Evans	.10	.05
❑ 61 Karl Best	.05	.02
❑ 62 Bob Boone	.05	.02
❑ 63 Ron Roenicke	.05	.02
❑ 64 Floyd Bannister	.05	.02
❑ 65 Dan Driessen	.05	.02
❑ 66 Bob Forsch TL	.05	.02
❑ 67 Carmelo Martinez	.05	.02
❑ 68 Ed Lynch	.05	.02
❑ 69 Luis Aguayo	.05	.02
❑ 70 Dave Winfield	.40	.18
❑ 71 Ken Schrom	.05	.02
❑ 72 Shawon Dunston	.10	.05
❑ 73 Randy O'Neal	.05	.02
❑ 74 Rance Mullinicks	.05	.02
❑ 75 Jose DeLeon	.05	.02
❑ 76 Dion James	.05	.02
❑ 77 Charlie Leibrandt	.05	.02
❑ 78 Bruce Benedict	.05	.02
❑ 79 Dave Schmidt	.05	.02
❑ 80 Darryl Strawberry	.40	.18
❑ 81 Gene Mauch MG	.10	.05
❑ 82 Tippy Martinez	.05	.02
❑ 83 Phil Garner	.10	.05
❑ 84 Curt Young	.05	.02
❑ 85 Tony Perez	.40	.18

(Eric Davis also
shown on card)

❑ 86 Tom Waddell	.05	.02
❑ 87 Candy Maldonado	.05	.02
❑ 88 Tom Nieto	.05	.02
❑ 89 Randy St.Claire	.05	.02
❑ 90 Garry Templeton	.05	.02
❑ 91 Steve Crawford	.05	.02
❑ 92 Al Cowens	.05	.02
❑ 93 Scot Thompson	.05	.02
❑ 94 Rich Bordi	.05	.02
❑ 95 Ozzie Virgil	.05	.02
❑ 96 Jim Clancy TL	.05	.02
❑ 97 Gary Gaetti	.10	.05
❑ 98 Dick Ruthven	.05	.02
❑ 99 Buddy Biancalana	.05	.02
❑ 100 Nolan Ryan	1.50	.70
❑ 101 Dave Bergman	.05	.02
❑ 102 Joe Orsulak	.05	.02
❑ 103 Luis Salazar	.05	.02
❑ 104 Sid Fernandez	.10	.05
❑ 105 Gary Ward	.05	.02
❑ 106 Ray Burris	.05	.02
❑ 107 Rafael Ramirez	.05	.02
❑ 108 Ted Power	.05	.02
❑ 109 Len Matuszek	.05	.02
❑ 110 Scott McGregor	.05	.02
❑ 111 Roger Craig MG	.05	.02
❑ 112 Bill Campbell	.05	.02
❑ 113 U.L. Washington	.05	.02
❑ 114 Mike C. Brown	.05	.02
❑ 115 Jay Howell	.05	.02
❑ 116 Brook Jacoby	.05	.02
❑ 117 Bruce Kison	.05	.02
❑ 118 Jerry Royster	.05	.02

☐ 119 Barry Bonnell	.05	.02
☐ 120 Steve Carlton	.40	.18
☐ 421 Nelson Simmons	.05	.02
☐ 122 Pete Filson	.05	.02
☐ 123 Greg Walker	.05	.02
☐ 124 Luis Sanchez	.05	.02
☐ 125 Dave Lopes	.10	.05
☐ 126 Mookie Wilson TL	.05	.02
☐ 127 Jack Howell	.05	.02
☐ 128 John Wathan	.05	.02
☐ 129 Jeff Dedmon	.05	.02
☐ 130 Alan Trammell	.20	.09
☐ 131 Checklist: 1-132	.10	.05
☐ 132 Razor Shines	.05	.02
☐ 133 Andy McGaffigan	.05	.02
☐ 134 Carney Lansford	.10	.05
☐ 135 Joe Niekro	.05	.02
☐ 136 Mike Hargrove	.10	.05
☐ 137 Charlie Moore	.05	.02
☐ 138 Mark Davis	.05	.02
☐ 139 Daryl Boston	.05	.02
☐ 140 John Candelaria	.05	.02
☐ 141 Chuck Cottier MG	.05	.02
See also 171		
☐ 142 Bob Jones	.05	.02
☐ 143 Dave Van Gorder	.05	.02
☐ 144 Doug Sisk	.05	.02
☐ 145 Pedro Guerrero	.10	.05
☐ 146 Jack Perconte	.05	.02
☐ 147 Larry Sheets	.05	.02
☐ 148 Mike Heath	.05	.02
☐ 149 Brett Butler	.10	.05
☐ 150 Joaquin Andujar	.05	.02
☐ 151 Dave Stapleton	.05	.02
☐ 152 Mike Morgan	.05	.02
☐ 153 Ricky Adams	.05	.02
☐ 154 Bert Roberge	.05	.02
☐ 155 Bobby Grich	.10	.05
☐ 156 Richard Dotson TL	.05	.02
☐ 157 Ron Hassey	.05	.02
☐ 158 Derrel Thomas	.05	.02
☐ 159 Orel Hershiser UER	.40	.18
(82 Alburquque)		
☐ 160 Chet Lemon	.05	.02
☐ 161 Lee Tunnell	.05	.02
☐ 162 Greg Gagne	.05	.02
☐ 163 Pete Ladd	.05	.02
☐ 164 Steve Balboni	.05	.02
☐ 165 Mike Davis	.05	.02
☐ 166 Dickie Thon	.05	.02
☐ 167 Zane Smith	.05	.02
☐ 168 Jeff Burroughs	.05	.02
☐ 169 George Wright	.05	.02
☐ 170 Gary Carter	.40	.18
☐ 171 Bob Rodgers MG ERR	.05	.02
Number of card on		
back actually 141)		
☐ 172 Jerry Reed	.05	.02
☐ 173 Wayne Gross	.05	.02
☐ 174 Brian Snyder	.05	.02
☐ 175 Steve Sax	.10	.05
☐ 176 Jay Tibbs	.05	.02
☐ 177 Joel Youngblood	.05	.02
☐ 178 Ivan DeJesus	.05	.02
☐ 179 Stu Cliburn	.05	.02
☐ 180 Don Mattingly	.75	.35
☐ 181 Al Nipper	.05	.02
☐ 182 Bobby Brown	.05	.02
☐ 183 Larry Andersen	.05	.02
☐ 184 Tim Laudner	.05	.02
☐ 185 Rollie Fingers	.40	.18
☐ 186 Jose Cruz TL	.05	.02
☐ 187 Scott Fletcher	.05	.02
☐ 188 Bob Dernier	.05	.02
☐ 189 Mike Mason	.05	.02
☐ 190 George Hendrick	.05	.02
☐ 191 Wally Backman	.05	.02
☐ 192 Milt Wilcox	.05	.02
☐ 193 Daryl Sconiers	.05	.02
☐ 194 Craig McMurtry	.05	.02
☐ 195 Dave Concepcion	.10	.05
☐ 196 Doyle Alexander	.05	.02
☐ 197 Enos Cabell	.05	.02
☐ 198 Ken Dixon	.05	.02
☐ 199 Dick Howser MG	.10	.05
☐ 200 Mike Schmidt	.60	.25

☐ 201 Vince Coleman RB	.10	.05
Most SB's rookie season		
☐ 202 Dwight Gooden RB	.10	.05
Youngest 20 game winner		
☐ 203 Keith Hernandez RB	.05	.02
Most game-winning RBI's		
☐ 204 Phil Niekro RB	.10	.05
Oldest shutout pitcher		
☐ 205 Tony Perez RB	.10	.05
Oldest grand slammer		
☐ 206 Pete Rose RB	.40	.18
Most lifetime hits		
☐ 207 Fernando Valenzuela RB	.10	.05
Most cons. innings start of season, no earned runs		
☐ 208 Ramon Romero	.05	.02
☐ 209 Randy Ready	.05	.02
☐ 210 Calvin Schiraldi	.05	.02
☐ 211 Ed Wojna	.05	.02
☐ 212 Chris Speier	.05	.02
☐ 213 Bob Shirley	.05	.02
☐ 214 Randy Bush	.05	.02
☐ 215 Frank White	.10	.05
☐ 216 Dwayne Murphy TL	.05	.02
☐ 217 Bill Scherrer	.05	.02
☐ 218 Randy Hunt	.05	.02
☐ 219 Dennis Lamp	.05	.02
☐ 220 Bob Horner	.05	.02
☐ 221 Dave Henderson	.05	.02
☐ 222 Craig Gerber	.05	.02
☐ 223 Atlee Hammaker	.05	.02
☐ 224 Cesar Cedeno	.10	.05
☐ 225 Ron Darling	.05	.02
☐ 226 Lee Lacy	.05	.02
☐ 227 Al Jones	.05	.02
☐ 228 Tom Lawless	.05	.02
☐ 229 Bill Gullickson	.05	.02
☐ 230 Terry Kennedy	.05	.02
☐ 231 Jim Frey MG	.05	.02
☐ 232 Rick Rhoden	.05	.02
☐ 233 Steve Lyons	.05	.02
☐ 234 Doug Corbett	.05	.02
☐ 235 Butch Wynegar	.05	.02
☐ 236 Frank Eufemia	.05	.02
☐ 237 Ted Simmons	.10	.05
☐ 238 Larry Parrish	.05	.02
☐ 239 Joel Skinner	.05	.02
☐ 240 Tommy John	.40	.18
☐ 241 Tony Fernandez	.05	.02
☐ 242 Rich Thompson	.05	.02
☐ 243 Johnny Grubb	.05	.02
☐ 244 Craig Lefferts	.05	.02
☐ 245 Jim Sundberg	.05	.02
☐ 246 Steve Carlton TL	.10	.05
☐ 247 Terry Harper	.05	.02
☐ 248 Spike Owen	.05	.02
☐ 249 Rob Deer	.10	.05
☐ 250 Dwight Gooden	.40	.18
☐ 251 Rich Dauer	.05	.02
☐ 252 Bobby Castillo	.05	.02
☐ 253 Dann Bilardello	.05	.02
☐ 254 Ozzie Guillen	.20	.09
☐ 255 Tony Armas	.05	.02
☐ 256 Kurt Kepshire	.05	.02
☐ 257 Doug DeCinces	.05	.02
☐ 258 Tim Burke	.05	.02
☐ 259 Dan Pasqua	.05	.02
☐ 260 Tony Pena	.05	.02
☐ 261 Bobby Valentine MG	.10	.05
☐ 262 Mario Ramirez	.05	.02
☐ 263 Checklist: 133-264	.10	.05
☐ 264 Darren Daulton	.75	.35
☐ 265 Ron Davis	.05	.02
☐ 266 Keith Moreland	.05	.02
☐ 267 Paul Molitor	.40	.18
☐ 268 Mike Scott	.05	.02
☐ 269 Dane Iorg	.05	.02
☐ 270 Jack Morris	.05	.02
☐ 271 Dave Collins	.05	.02
☐ 272 Tim Tolman	.05	.02
☐ 273 Jerry Willard	.05	.02
☐ 274 Ron Gardenhire	.05	.02
☐ 275 Charlie Hough	.10	.05
☐ 276 Willie Randolph TL	.05	.05

☐ 277 Jaime Cocanower	.05	.02
☐ 278 Sixto Lezcano	.05	.02
☐ 279 Al Pardo	.05	.02
☐ 280 Tim Raines	.10	.05
☐ 281 Steve Mura	.05	.02
☐ 282 Jerry Mumphrey	.05	.02
☐ 283 Mike Fischlin	.05	.02
☐ 284 Brian Dayett	.05	.02
☐ 285 Buddy Bell	.10	.05
☐ 286 Luis DeLeon	.05	.02
☐ 287 John Christensen	.05	.02
☐ 288 Don Aase	.05	.02
☐ 289 Johnnie LeMaster	.05	.02
☐ 290 Carlton Fisk	.40	.18
☐ 291 Tom Lasorda MG	.20	.09
☐ 292 Chuck Porter	.05	.02
☐ 293 Chris Chambliss	.10	.05
☐ 294 Danny Cox	.05	.02
☐ 295 Kirk Gibson	.10	.05
☐ 296 Geno Petralli	.05	.02
☐ 297 Tim Lollar	.05	.02
☐ 298 Craig Reynolds	.05	.02
☐ 299 Bryn Smith	.05	.02
☐ 300 George Brett	.75	.35
☐ 301 Dennis Rasmussen	.05	.02
☐ 302 Greg Gross	.05	.02
☐ 303 Curt Wardle	.05	.02
☐ 304 Mike Gallego	.10	.05
☐ 305 Phil Bradley	.05	.02
☐ 306 Terry Kennedy TL	.05	.02
☐ 307 Dave Sax	.05	.02
☐ 308 Ray Fontenot	.05	.02
☐ 309 John Shelby	.05	.02
☐ 310 Greg Minton	.05	.02
☐ 311 Dick Schofield	.05	.02
☐ 312 Tom Filer	.05	.02
☐ 313 Joe DeSa	.05	.02
☐ 314 Frank Pastore	.05	.02
☐ 315 Mookie Wilson	.05	.02
☐ 316 Sammy Khalifa	.05	.02
☐ 317 Ed Romero	.05	.02
☐ 318 Terry Whitfield	.05	.02
☐ 319 Rick Camp	.05	.02
☐ 320 Jim Rice	.10	.05
☐ 321 Earl Weaver MG	.40	.18
☐ 322 Bob Forsch	.05	.02
☐ 323 Jerry Davis	.05	.02
☐ 324 Dan Schatzeder	.05	.02
☐ 325 Juan Beniquez	.05	.02
☐ 326 Kent Tekulve	.05	.02
☐ 327 Mike Pagliarulo	.05	.02
☐ 328 Pete O'Brien	.05	.02
☐ 329 Kirby Puckett	1.25	.55
☐ 330 Rick Sutcliffe	.05	.02
☐ 331 Alan Ashby	.05	.02
☐ 332 Darryl Motley	.05	.02
☐ 333 Tom Henke	.10	.05
☐ 334 Ken Oberkfell	.05	.02
☐ 335 Don Sutton	.40	.18
☐ 336 Andre Thornton TL	.10	.05
☐ 337 Darnell Coles	.05	.02
☐ 338 Jorge Bell	.10	.05
☐ 339 Bruce Berenyi	.05	.02
☐ 340 Cal Ripken	1.50	.70
☐ 341 Frank Williams	.05	.02
☐ 342 Gary Redus	.05	.02
☐ 343 Carlos Diaz	.05	.02
☐ 344 Jim Wohlford	.05	.02
☐ 345 Donnie Moore	.05	.02
☐ 346 Bryan Little	.05	.02
☐ 347 Teddy Higuera	.10	.05
☐ 348 Cliff Johnson	.05	.02
☐ 349 Mark Clear	.05	.02
☐ 350 Jack Clark	.10	.05
☐ 351 Chuck Tanner MG	.05	.02
☐ 352 Harry Spilman	.05	.02
☐ 353 Keith Atherton	.05	.02
☐ 354 Tony Bernazard	.05	.02
☐ 355 Lee Smith	.20	.09
☐ 356 Mickey Hatcher	.05	.02
☐ 357 Ed VandeBerg	.05	.02
☐ 358 Rick Dempsey	.05	.02
☐ 359 Mike LaCoss	.05	.02
☐ 360 Lloyd Moseby	.05	.02
☐ 361 Shane Rawley	.05	.02
☐ 362 Tom Paciorek	.10	.05

☐ 363	Terry Forster	.05	.02
☐ 364	Reid Nichols	.05	.02
☐ 365	Mike Flanagan	.05	.02
☐ 366	Dave Concepcion TL	.10	.05
☐ 367	Aurelio Lopez	.05	.02
☐ 368	Greg Brock	.05	.02
☐ 369	Al Holland	.05	.02
☐ 370	Vince Coleman	.40	.18
☐ 371	Bill Stein	.05	.02
☐ 372	Ben Oglivie	.05	.02
☐ 373	Urbano Lugo	.05	.02
☐ 374	Terry Francona	.05	.02
☐ 375	Rich Gedman	.05	.02
☐ 376	Bill Dawley	.05	.02
☐ 377	Joe Carter	.40	.18
☐ 378	Bruce Bochte	.05	.02
☐ 379	Bobby Meacham	.05	.02
☐ 380	LaMarr Hoyt	.05	.02
☐ 381	Ray Miller MG	.05	.02
☐ 382	Ivan Calderon	.10	.05
☐ 383	Chris Brown	.05	.02
☐ 384	Steve Trout	.05	.02
☐ 385	Cecil Cooper	.10	.05
☐ 386	Cecil Fielder	.75	.35
☐ 387	Steve Kemp	.05	.02
☐ 388	Dickie Noles	.05	.02
☐ 389	Glenn Davis	.10	.05
☐ 390	Tom Seaver	.50	.23
☐ 391	Julio Franco	.05	.02
☐ 392	John Russell	.05	.02
☐ 393	Chris Pittaro	.05	.02
☐ 394	Checklist: 265-396	.10	.05
☐ 395	Scott Garrelts	.05	.02
☐ 396	Dwight Evans TL	.10	.05
☐ 397	Steve Buechele	.10	.05
☐ 398	Earnie Riles	.05	.02
☐ 399	Bill Swift	.05	.02
☐ 400	Rod Carew	.40	.18
☐ 401	Fernando Valenzuela TBC '81	.10	.05
☐ 402	Tom Seaver TBC '76	.10	.05
☐ 403	Willie Mays TBC '71	.20	.09
☐ 404	Frank Robinson TBC '66	.10	.05
☐ 405	Roger Maris TBC '61	.10	.05
☐ 406	Scott Sanderson	.05	.02
☐ 407	Sal Butera	.05	.02
☐ 408	Dave Smith	.05	.02
☐ 409	Paul Runge	.05	.02
☐ 410	Dave Kingman	.10	.05
☐ 411	Sparky Anderson MG	.20	.09
☐ 412	Jim Clancy	.05	.02
☐ 413	Tim Flannery	.05	.02
☐ 414	Tom Gorman	.05	.02
☐ 415	Hal McRae	.05	.02
☐ 416	Dennis Martinez	.10	.05
☐ 417	R.J. Reynolds	.05	.02
☐ 418	Alan Knicely	.05	.02
☐ 419	Frank Wills	.05	.02
☐ 420	Von Hayes	.05	.02
☐ 421	David Palmer	.05	.02
☐ 422	Mike Jorgensen	.05	.02
☐ 423	Dan Spillner	.05	.02
☐ 424	Rick Miller	.05	.02
☐ 425	Larry McWilliams	.05	.02
☐ 426	Charlie Moore TL	.05	.02
☐ 427	Joe Cowley	.05	.02
☐ 428	Max Venable	.05	.02
☐ 429	Greg Booker	.05	.02
☐ 430	Kent Hrbek	.10	.05
☐ 431	George Frazier	.05	.02
☐ 432	Mark Bailey	.05	.02
☐ 433	Chris Codiroli	.05	.02
☐ 434	Curt Wilkerson	.05	.02
☐ 435	Bill Caudill	.05	.02
☐ 436	Doug Flynn	.05	.02
☐ 437	Rick Mahler	.05	.02
☐ 438	Clint Hurdle	.05	.02
☐ 439	Rick Honeycutt	.05	.02
☐ 440	Alvin Davis	.05	.02
☐ 441	Whitey Herzog MG	.20	.09
☐ 442	Ron Robinson	.05	.02
☐ 443	Bill Buckner	.10	.05
☐ 444	Alex Trevino	.05	.02
☐ 445	Bert Blyleven	.10	.05
☐ 446	Lenn Sakata	.05	.02
☐ 447	Jerry Don Gleaton	.05	.02
☐ 448	Herm Winningham	.05	.02
☐ 449	Rod Scurry	.05	.02
☐ 450	Graig Nettles	.10	.05
☐ 451	Mark Brown	.05	.02
☐ 452	Bob Clark	.05	.02
☐ 453	Steve Jeltz	.05	.02
☐ 454	Burt Hooton	.05	.02
☐ 455	Willie Randolph	.10	.05
☐ 456	Dale Murphy TL	.10	.05
☐ 457	Mickey Tettleton	.40	.18
☐ 458	Kevin Bass	.05	.02
☐ 459	Luis Leal	.05	.02
☐ 460	Leon Durham	.05	.02
☐ 461	Walt Terrell	.05	.02
☐ 462	Domingo Ramos	.05	.02
☐ 463	Jim Gott	.05	.02
☐ 464	Ruppert Jones	.05	.02
☐ 465	Jesse Orosco	.05	.02
☐ 466	Tom Foley	.05	.02
☐ 467	Bob James	.05	.02
☐ 468	Mike Scioscia	.05	.02
☐ 469	Storm Davis	.05	.02
☐ 470	Bill Madlock	.05	.02
☐ 471	Bobby Cox MG	.10	.05
☐ 472	Joe Hesketh	.05	.02
☐ 473	Mark Brouhard	.05	.02
☐ 474	John Tudor	.05	.02
☐ 475	Juan Samuel	.05	.02
☐ 476	Ron Mathis	.05	.02
☐ 477	Mike Easler	.05	.02
☐ 478	Andy Hawkins	.05	.02
☐ 479	Bob Melvin	.05	.02
☐ 480	Oddibe McDowell	.05	.02
☐ 481	Scott Bradley	.05	.02
☐ 482	Rick Lysander	.05	.02
☐ 483	George Vukovich	.05	.02
☐ 484	Donnie Hill	.05	.02
☐ 485	Gary Matthews	.05	.02
☐ 486	Bobby Grich TL	.05	.02
☐ 487	Bret Saberhagen	.10	.05
☐ 488	Lou Thornton	.05	.02
☐ 489	Jim Winn	.05	.02
☐ 490	Jeff Leonard	.05	.02
☐ 491	Pascual Perez	.05	.02
☐ 492	Kelvin Chapman	.05	.02
☐ 493	Gene Nelson	.05	.02
☐ 494	Gary Roenicke	.05	.02
☐ 495	Mark Langston	.05	.02
☐ 496	Jay Johnstone	.10	.05
☐ 497	John Stuper	.05	.02
☐ 498	Tito Landrum	.05	.02
☐ 499	Bob L. Gibson	.05	.02
☐ 500	Rickey Henderson	.50	.23
☐ 501	Dave Johnson MG	.10	.05
☐ 502	Glen Cook	.05	.02
☐ 503	Mike Fitzgerald	.05	.02
☐ 504	Denny Walling	.05	.02
☐ 505	Jerry Koosman	.10	.05
☐ 506	Bill Russell	.05	.02
☐ 507	Steve Ontiveros	.10	.05
☐ 508	Alan Wiggins	.05	.02
☐ 509	Ernie Camacho	.05	.02
☐ 510	Wade Boggs	.40	.18
☐ 511	Ed Nunez	.05	.02
☐ 512	Thad Bosley	.05	.02
☐ 513	Ron Washington	.05	.02
☐ 514	Mike Jones	.05	.02
☐ 515	Darrell Evans	.10	.05
☐ 516	Greg Minton TL	.05	.02
☐ 517	Milt Thompson	.10	.05
☐ 518	Buck Martinez	.05	.02
☐ 519	Danny Darwin	.05	.02
☐ 520	Keith Hernandez	.10	.05
☐ 521	Nate Snell	.05	.02
☐ 522	Bob Bailor	.05	.02
☐ 523	Joe Price	.05	.02
☐ 524	Darrell Miller	.05	.02
☐ 525	Marvell Wynne	.05	.02
☐ 526	Charlie Lea	.05	.02
☐ 527	Checklist: 397-528	.10	.05
☐ 528	Terry Pendleton	.20	.09
☐ 529	Marc Sullivan	.05	.02
☐ 530	Rich Gossage	.10	.05
☐ 531	Tony LaRussa MG	.10	.05
☐ 532	Don Carman	.05	.02
☐ 533	Billy Sample	.05	.02
☐ 534	Jeff Calhoun	.05	.02
☐ 535	Toby Harrah	.05	.02
☐ 536	Jose Rijo	.05	.02
☐ 537	Mark Salas	.05	.02
☐ 538	Dennis Eckersley	.40	.18
☐ 539	Glenn Hubbard	.05	.02
☐ 540	Dan Petry	.05	.02
☐ 541	Jorge Orta	.05	.02
☐ 542	Don Schulze	.05	.02
☐ 543	Jerry Narron	.05	.02
☐ 544	Eddie Milner	.05	.02
☐ 545	Jimmy Key	.40	.18
☐ 546	Dave Henderson TL	.10	.05
☐ 547	Roger McDowell	.10	.05
☐ 548	Mike Young	.05	.02
☐ 549	Bob Welch	.05	.02
☐ 550	Tom Herr	.05	.02
☐ 551	Dave LaPoint	.05	.02
☐ 552	Marc Hill	.05	.02
☐ 553	Jim Morrison	.05	.02
☐ 554	Paul Householder	.05	.02
☐ 555	Hubie Brooks	.05	.02
☐ 556	John Denny	.05	.02
☐ 557	Gerald Perry	.05	.02
☐ 558	Tim Stoddard	.05	.02
☐ 559	Tommy Dunbar	.05	.02
☐ 560	Dave Righetti	.05	.02
☐ 561	Bob Lillis MG	.05	.02
☐ 562	Joe Beckwith	.05	.02
☐ 563	Alejandro Sanchez	.05	.02
☐ 564	Warren Brusstar	.05	.02
☐ 565	Tom Brunansky	.05	.02
☐ 566	Alfredo Griffin	.05	.02
☐ 567	Jeff Barkley	.05	.02
☐ 568	Donnie Scott	.05	.02
☐ 569	Jim Acker	.05	.02
☐ 570	Rusty Staub	.10	.05
☐ 571	Mike Jeffcoat	.05	.02
☐ 572	Paul Zuvella	.05	.02
☐ 573	Tom Hume	.05	.02
☐ 574	Ron Kittle	.05	.02
☐ 575	Mike Boddicker	.05	.02
☐ 576	Andre Dawson TL	.10	.05
☐ 577	Jerry Reuss	.05	.02
☐ 578	Lee Mazzilli	.05	.02
☐ 579	Jim Slaton	.05	.02
☐ 580	Willie McGee	.10	.05
☐ 581	Bruce Hurst	.05	.02
☐ 582	Jim Gantner	.05	.02
☐ 583	Al Bumbry	.05	.02
☐ 584	Brian Fisher	.05	.02
☐ 585	Garry Maddox	.05	.02
☐ 586	Greg Harris	.05	.02
☐ 587	Rafael Santana	.05	.02
☐ 588	Steve Lake	.05	.02
☐ 589	Sid Bream	.05	.02
☐ 590	Bob Knepper	.05	.02
☐ 591	Jackie Moore MG	.05	.02
☐ 592	Frank Tanana	.05	.02
☐ 593	Jesse Barfield	.10	.05
☐ 594	Chris Bando	.05	.02
☐ 595	Dave Parker	.10	.05
☐ 596	Onix Concepcion	.05	.02
☐ 597	Sammy Stewart	.05	.02
☐ 598	Jim Presley	.05	.02
☐ 599	Rick Aguilera	.40	.18
☐ 600	Dale Murphy	.40	.18
☐ 601	Gary Lucas	.05	.02
☐ 602	Mariano Duncan	.40	.18
☐ 603	Bill Laskey	.05	.02
☐ 604	Gary Pettis	.05	.02
☐ 605	Dennis Boyd	.05	.02
☐ 606	Hal McRae TL	.10	.05
☐ 607	Ken Dayley	.05	.05
☐ 608	Bruce Bochy	.05	.02
☐ 609	Barbaro Garbey	.05	.02
☐ 610	Ron Guidry	.10	.05
☐ 611	Gary Woods	.05	.02
☐ 612	Richard Dotson	.05	.02
☐ 613	Roy Smalley	.05	.02
☐ 614	Rick Waits	.05	.02
☐ 615	Johnny Ray	.05	.02
☐ 616	Glenn Brummer	.05	.02
☐ 617	Lonnie Smith	.05	.02
☐ 618	Jim Pankovits	.05	.02

❑ 619 Danny Heep	.05	.02
❑ 620 Bruce Sutter	.10	.05
❑ 621 John Felske MG	.05	.02
❑ 622 Gary Lavelle	.05	.02
❑ 623 Floyd Rayford	.05	.02
❑ 624 Steve McCatty	.05	.02
❑ 625 Bob Brenly	.05	.02
❑ 626 Roy Thomas	.05	.02
❑ 627 Ron Oester	.05	.02
❑ 628 Kirk McCaskill	.10	.05
❑ 629 Mitch Webster	.05	.02
❑ 630 Fernando Valenzuela	.10	.05
❑ 631 Steve Braun	.05	.02
❑ 632 Dave Von Ohlen	.05	.02
❑ 633 Jackie Gutierrez	.05	.02
❑ 634 Roy Lee Jackson	.05	.02
❑ 635 Jason Thompson	.05	.02
❑ 636 Lee Smith TL	.10	.05
❑ 637 Rudy Law	.05	.02
❑ 638 John Butcher	.05	.02
❑ 639 Bo Diaz	.05	.02
❑ 640 Jose Cruz	.10	.05
❑ 641 Wayne Tolleson	.05	.02
❑ 642 Ray Searage	.05	.02
❑ 643 Tom Brookens	.05	.02
❑ 644 Mark Gubicza	.05	.02
❑ 645 Dusty Baker	.10	.05
❑ 646 Mike Moore	.05	.02
❑ 647 Mel Hall	.05	.02
❑ 648 Steve Bedrosian	.05	.02
❑ 649 Ronn Reynolds	.05	.02
❑ 650 Dave Stieb	.05	.02
❑ 651 Billy Martin MG	.10	.05
❑ 652 Tom Browning	.05	.02
❑ 653 Jim Dwyer	.05	.02
❑ 654 Ken Howell	.05	.02
❑ 655 Manny Trillo	.05	.02
❑ 656 Brian Harper	.05	.02
❑ 657 Juan Agosto	.05	.02
❑ 658 Rob Wilfong	.05	.02
❑ 659 Checklist: 529-660	.10	.05
❑ 660 Steve Garvey	.20	.09
❑ 661 Roger Clemens	2.00	.90
❑ 662 Bill Schroeder	.05	.02
❑ 663 Neil Allen	.05	.02
❑ 664 Tim Corcoran	.05	.02
❑ 665 Alejandro Pena	.05	.02
❑ 666 Charlie Hough TL	.10	.05
❑ 667 Tim Teufel	.05	.02
❑ 668 Cecilio Guante	.05	.02
❑ 669 Ron Cey	.10	.05
❑ 670 Willie Hernandez	.05	.02
❑ 671 Lynn Jones	.05	.02
❑ 672 Rob Picciolo	.05	.02
❑ 673 Ernie Whitt	.05	.02
❑ 674 Pat Tabler	.05	.02
❑ 675 Claudell Washington	.05	.02
❑ 676 Matt Young	.05	.02
❑ 677 Nick Esasky	.05	.02
❑ 678 Dan Gladden	.05	.02
❑ 679 Britt Burns	.05	.02
❑ 680 George Foster	.10	.05
❑ 681 Dick Williams MG	.10	.05
❑ 682 Junior Ortiz	.05	.02
❑ 683 Andy Van Slyke	.10	.05
❑ 684 Bob McClure	.05	.02
❑ 685 Tim Wallach	.05	.02
❑ 686 Jeff Stone	.05	.02
❑ 687 Mike Trujillo	.05	.02
❑ 688 Larry Herndon	.05	.02
❑ 689 Dave Stewart	.10	.05
❑ 690 Ryne Sandberg UER	.50	.23
(No Topps logo on front)		
❑ 691 Mike Madden	.05	.02
❑ 692 Dale Berra	.05	.02
❑ 693 Tom Tellmann	.05	.02
❑ 694 Garth Iorg	.05	.02
❑ 695 Mike Smithson	.05	.02
❑ 696 Bill Russell TL	.10	.05
❑ 697 Bud Black	.05	.02
❑ 698 Brad Komminsk	.05	.02
❑ 699 Pat Corrales MG	.05	.02
❑ 700 Reggie Jackson	.50	.23
❑ 701 Keith Hernandez AS	.10	.05
❑ 702 Tom Herr AS	.05	.02

❑ 703 Tim Wallach AS	.05	.02
❑ 704 Ozzie Smith AS	.20	.09
❑ 705 Dale Murphy AS	.10	.05
❑ 706 Pedro Guerrero AS	.05	.02
❑ 707 Willie McGee AS	.05	.02
❑ 708 Gary Carter AS	.10	.05
❑ 709 Dwight Gooden AS	.10	.05
❑ 710 John Tudor AS	.05	.02
❑ 711 Jeff Reardon AS	.05	.02
❑ 712 Don Mattingly AS	.40	.18
❑ 713 Damaso Garcia AS	.05	.02
❑ 714 George Brett AS	.40	.18
❑ 715 Cal Ripken AS	.40	.18
❑ 716 Rickey Henderson AS	.10	.05
❑ 717 Dave Winfield AS	.10	.05
❑ 718 George Bell AS	.05	.02
❑ 719 Carlton Fisk AS	.10	.05
❑ 720 Bret Saberhagen AS	.05	.02
❑ 721 Ron Guidry AS	.10	.05
❑ 722 Dan Quisenberry AS	.05	.02
❑ 723 Marty Bystrom	.05	.02
❑ 724 Tim Hulett	.05	.02
❑ 725 Mario Soto	.05	.02
❑ 726 Rick Dempsey TL	.10	.05
❑ 727 David Green	.05	.02
❑ 728 Mike Marshall	.05	.02
❑ 729 Jim Beattie	.05	.02
❑ 730 Ozzie Smith	.50	.23
❑ 731 Don Robinson	.05	.02
❑ 732 Floyd Youmans	.05	.02
❑ 733 Ron Romanick	.05	.02
❑ 734 Marty Barrett	.05	.02
❑ 735 Dave Dravecky	.10	.05
❑ 736 Glenn Wilson	.05	.02
❑ 737 Pete Vuckovich	.05	.02
❑ 738 Andre Robertson	.05	.02
❑ 739 Dave Rozema	.05	.02
❑ 740 Lance Parrish	.10	.05
❑ 741 Pete Rose MG	.40	.18
❑ 742 Frank Viola	.10	.05
❑ 743 Pat Sheridan	.05	.02
❑ 744 Lary Sorensen	.05	.02
❑ 745 Willie Upshaw	.05	.02
❑ 746 Denny Gonzalez	.05	.02
❑ 747 Rick Cerone	.05	.02
❑ 748 Steve Henderson	.05	.02
❑ 749 Ed Jurak	.05	.02
❑ 750 Gorman Thomas	.05	.02
❑ 751 Howard Johnson	.10	.05
❑ 752 Mike Krukow	.05	.02
❑ 753 Dan Ford	.05	.02
❑ 754 Pat Clements	.05	.02
❑ 755 Harold Baines	.20	.09
❑ 756 Rick Rhoden TL	.05	.02
❑ 757 Darrell Porter	.10	.05
❑ 758 Dave Anderson	.05	.02
❑ 759 Moose Haas	.05	.02
❑ 760 Andre Dawson	.40	.18
❑ 761 Don Slaught	.05	.02
❑ 762 Eric Show	.05	.02
❑ 763 Terry Puhl	.05	.02
❑ 764 Kevin Gross	.05	.02
❑ 765 Don Baylor	.20	.09
❑ 766 Rick Langford	.05	.02
❑ 767 Jody Davis	.05	.02
❑ 768 Vern Ruhle	.05	.02
❑ 769 Harold Reynolds	.40	.18
❑ 770 Vida Blue	.10	.05
❑ 771 John McNamara MG	.05	.02
❑ 772 Brian Downing	.05	.02
❑ 773 Greg Pryor	.05	.02
❑ 774 Terry Leach	.05	.02
❑ 775 Al Oliver	.10	.05
❑ 776 Gene Garber	.05	.02
❑ 777 Wayne Krenchicki	.05	.02
❑ 778 Jerry Hairston	.05	.02
❑ 779 Rick Reuschel	.05	.02
❑ 780 Robin Yount	.40	.18
❑ 781 Joe Nolan	.05	.02
❑ 782 Ken Landreaux	.05	.02
❑ 783 Ricky Horton	.05	.02
❑ 784 Alan Bannister	.05	.02
❑ 785 Bob Stanley	.05	.02
❑ 786 Melvin Hatcher TL	.05	.02
❑ 787 Vance Law	.05	.02
❑ 788 Marty Castillo	.05	.02

❑ 789 Kurt Bevacqua	.05	.02
❑ 790 Phil Niekro	.40	.18
❑ 791 Checklist: 661-792	.10	.05
❑ 792 Charles Hudson	.05	.02

1986 Topps Tiffany

ROGER CLEMENS

	MINT	NRMT
COMP.FACT.SET (792)	100.00	45.00
COMMON CARD (1-792)	.40	.18

*STARS: 6X TO 12X BASIC CARDS
*ROOKIES: 6X TO 12X BASIC CARDS
STATED PRINT RUN 5000 SETS
DISTRIBUTED ONLY IN FACTORY SET FORM

1986 Topps Traded

BARRY BONDS

	MINT	NRMT
COMP.FACT.SET (132)	15.00	6.75
COMMON CARD (1T-132T)	.05	.02
MINOR STARS	.10	.05
SEMISTARS	.20	.09
UNLISTED STARS	.40	.18

❑ 1T Andy Allanson	.05	.02
❑ 2T Neil Allen	.05	.02
❑ 3T Joaquin Andujar	.05	.02
❑ 4T Paul Assenmacher	.05	.02
❑ 5T Scott Bailes	.05	.02
❑ 6T Don Baylor	.20	.09
❑ 7T Steve Bedrosian	.05	.02
❑ 8T Juan Beniquez	.05	.02
❑ 9T Juan Berenguer	.05	.02
❑ 10T Mike Bielecki	.05	.02
❑ 11T Barry Bonds	8.00	3.60
❑ 12T Bobby Bonilla	.60	.25
❑ 13T Juan Bonilla	.05	.02
❑ 14T Rich Bordi	.05	.02
❑ 15T Steve Boros MG	.05	.02
❑ 16T Rick Burleson	.05	.02
❑ 17T Bill Campbell	.05	.02
❑ 18T Tom Candiotti	.05	.02
❑ 19T John Cangelosi	.05	.02
❑ 20T Jose Canseco	5.00	2.20
❑ 21T Carmen Castillo	.05	.02
❑ 22T Rick Cerone	.05	.02
❑ 23T John Cerutti	.05	.02
❑ 24T Will Clark	1.25	.55
❑ 25T Mark Clear	.05	.02
❑ 26T Darnell Coles	.05	.02
❑ 27T Dave Collins	.05	.02

	MINT	NRMT
❏ 28T Tim Conroy	.05	.02
❏ 29T Joe Cowley	.05	.02
❏ 30T Joel Davis	.05	.02
❏ 31T Rob Deer	.05	.02
❏ 32T John Denny	.05	.02
❏ 33T Mike Easler	.05	.02
❏ 34T Mark Eichhorn	.05	.02
❏ 35T Steve Farr	.05	.02
❏ 36T Scott Fletcher	.05	.02
❏ 37T Terry Forster	.05	.02
❏ 38T Terry Francona	.05	.02
❏ 39T Jim Fregosi MG	.05	.02
❏ 40T Andres Galarraga	1.00	.45
❏ 41T Ken Griffey	.05	.02
❏ 42T Bill Gullickson	.05	.02
❏ 43T Jose Guzman	.05	.02
❏ 44T Moose Haas	.05	.02
❏ 45T Billy Hatcher	.05	.02
❏ 46T Mike Heath	.05	.02
❏ 47T Tom Hume	.05	.02
❏ 48T Pete Incaviglia	.40	.18
❏ 49T Dane Iorg	.05	.02
❏ 50T Bo Jackson	1.00	.45
❏ 51T Wally Joyner	.40	.18
❏ 52T Charlie Kerfeld	.05	.02
❏ 53T Eric King	.05	.02
❏ 54T Bob Kipper	.05	.02
❏ 55T Wayne Krenchicki	.05	.02
❏ 56T John Kruk	.40	.18
❏ 57T Mike LaCoss	.05	.02
❏ 58T Pete Ladd	.05	.02
❏ 59T Mike Laga	.05	.02
❏ 60T Hal Lanier MG	.05	.02
❏ 61T Dave LaPoint	.05	.02
❏ 62T Rudy Law	.05	.02
❏ 63T Rick Leach	.05	.02
❏ 64T Tim Leary	.05	.02
❏ 65T Dennis Leonard	.05	.02
❏ 66T Jim Leyland MG	.05	.02
❏ 67T Steve Lyons	.05	.02
❏ 68T Mickey Mahler	.05	.02
❏ 69T Candy Maldonado	.05	.02
❏ 70T Roger Mason	.05	.02
❏ 71T Bob McClure	.05	.02
❏ 72T Andy McGaffigan	.05	.02
❏ 73T Gene Michael MG	.05	.02
❏ 74T Kevin Mitchell	.40	.18
❏ 75T Omar Moreno	.05	.02
❏ 76T Jerry Mumphrey	.05	.02
❏ 77T Phil Niekro	.40	.18
❏ 78T Randy Niemann	.05	.02
❏ 79T Juan Nieves	.05	.02
❏ 80T Otis Nixon	.40	.18
❏ 81T Bob Ojeda	.05	.02
❏ 82T Jose Oquendo	.05	.02
❏ 83T Tom Paciorek	.10	.05
❏ 84T David Palmer	.05	.02
❏ 85T Frank Pastore	.05	.02
❏ 86T Lou Piniella MG	.10	.05
❏ 87T Dan Plesac	.05	.02
❏ 88T Darrell Porter	.10	.05
❏ 89T Rey Quinones	.05	.02
❏ 90T Gary Redus	.05	.02
❏ 91T Bip Roberts	.40	.18
❏ 92T Billy Joe Robidoux	.05	.02
❏ 93T Jeff D. Robinson	.05	.02
❏ 94T Gary Roenicke	.05	.02
❏ 95T Ed Romero	.05	.02
❏ 96T Argenis Salazar	.05	.02
❏ 97T Joe Sambito	.05	.02
❏ 98T Billy Sample	.05	.02
❏ 99T Dave Schmidt	.05	.02
❏ 100T Ken Schrom	.05	.02
❏ 101T Tom Seaver	.50	.23
❏ 102T Ted Simmons	.05	.02
❏ 103T Sammy Stewart	.05	.02
❏ 104T Kurt Stillwell	.05	.02
❏ 105T Franklin Stubbs	.05	.02
❏ 106T Dale Sveum	.05	.02
❏ 107T Chuck Tanner MG	.05	.02
❏ 108T Danny Tartabull	.10	.05
❏ 109T Tim Teufel	.05	.02
❏ 110T Bob Tewksbury	.10	.05
❏ 111T Andres Thomas	.05	.02
❏ 112T Milt Thompson	.05	.02
❏ 113T Robby Thompson	.10	.05
❏ 114T Jay Tibbs	.05	.02
❏ 115T Wayne Tolleson	.05	.02
❏ 116T Alex Trevino	.05	.02
❏ 117T Manny Trillo	.05	.02
❏ 118T Ed VandeBerg	.05	.02
❏ 119T Ozzie Virgil	.05	.02
❏ 120T Bob Walk	.05	.02
❏ 121T Gene Walter	.05	.02
❏ 122T Claudell Washington	.05	.02
❏ 123T Bill Wegman	.05	.02
❏ 124T Dick Williams MG	.10	.05
❏ 125T Mitch Williams	.10	.05
❏ 126T Bobby Witt	.20	.09
❏ 127T Todd Worrell	.40	.18
❏ 128T George Wright	.05	.02
❏ 129T Ricky Wright	.05	.02
❏ 130T Steve Yeager	.05	.02
❏ 131T Paul Zuvella	.05	.02
❏ 132T Checklist 1T-132T	.05	.02

1986 Topps Traded Tiffany

	MINT	NRMT
COMP.FACT.SET (132)	250.00	110.00
COMMON CARD (1T-132T)	.40	.18

*STARS: 6X TO 12X BASIC CARDS
*ROOKIES: 6X TO 12X BASIC CARDS
STATED PRINT RUN 5000 SETS
DISTRIBUTED ONLY IN FACTORY SET FORM

1987 Topps

	MINT	NRMT
COMPLETE SET (792)	15.00	6.75
COMP.HOBBY SET (792)	25.00	11.00
COMP.X-MAS.SET (792)	25.00	11.00
COMMON CARD (1-792)	.05	.02
MINOR STARS	.10	.05
UNLISTED STARS	.20	.09

SUBSET CARDS HALF VALUE OF BASE CARDS

❏ 1 Roger Clemens RB	.30	.14
Most K's 9-inning game		
❏ 2 Jim Deshaies RB	.05	.02
Most cons. K's, start of game		
❏ 3 Dwight Evans RB	.10	.05
Earliest home run		
❏ 4 Davey Lopes RB	.05	.02
Most steals season, 40-year-old		
❏ 5 Dave Righetti RB	.05	.02
Most saves season		
❏ 6 Ruben Sierra RB	.05	.02
Youngest player to switch hit HR's, game		
❏ 7 Todd Worrell RB	.05	.02
Most saves rookie season		
❏ 8 Terry Pendleton	.10	.05
❏ 9 Jay Tibbs	.05	.02
❏ 10 Cecil Cooper	.05	.02
❏ 11 Indians Team	.05	.02
(Mound conference)		
❏ 12 Jeff Sellers	.05	.02
❏ 13 Nick Esasky	.05	.02
❏ 14 Dave Stewart	.10	.05
❏ 15 Claudell Washington	.05	.02
❏ 16 Pat Clements	.05	.02
❏ 17 Pete O'Brien	.05	.02
❏ 18 Dick Howser MG	.05	.02
❏ 19 Matt Young	.05	.02
❏ 20 Gary Carter	.15	.07
❏ 21 Mark Davis	.05	.02
❏ 22 Doug DeCinces	.05	.02
❏ 23 Lee Smith	.15	.07
❏ 24 Tony Walker	.05	.02
❏ 25 Bert Blyleven	.10	.05
❏ 26 Greg Brock	.05	.02
❏ 27 Joe Cowley	.05	.02
❏ 28 Rick Dempsey	.05	.02
❏ 29 Jimmy Key	.10	.05
❏ 30 Tim Raines	.10	.05
❏ 31 Braves Team	.05	.02
(Glenn Hubbard and Rafael Ramirez)		
❏ 32 Tim Leary	.05	.02
❏ 33 Andy Van Slyke	.10	.05
❏ 34 Jose Rijo	.05	.02
❏ 35 Sid Bream	.05	.02
❏ 36 Eric King	.05	.02
❏ 37 Marvell Wynne	.05	.02
❏ 38 Dennis Leonard	.05	.02
❏ 39 Marty Barrett	.05	.02
❏ 40 Dave Righetti	.05	.02
❏ 41 Bo Diaz	.05	.02
❏ 42 Gary Redus	.05	.02
❏ 43 Gene Michael MG	.05	.02
❏ 44 Greg Harris	.05	.02
❏ 45 Jim Presley	.05	.02
❏ 46 Dan Gladden	.05	.02
❏ 47 Dennis Powell	.05	.02
❏ 48 Wally Backman	.05	.02
❏ 49 Terry Harper	.05	.02
❏ 50 Dave Smith	.05	.02
❏ 51 Mel Hall	.05	.02
❏ 52 Keith Atherton	.05	.02
❏ 53 Ruppert Jones	.05	.02
❏ 54 Bill Dawley	.05	.02
❏ 55 Tim Wallach	.05	.02
❏ 56 Brewers Team	.05	.02
(Mound conference)		
❏ 57 Scott Nielsen	.05	.02
❏ 58 Thad Bosley	.05	.02
❏ 59 Ken Dayley	.05	.02
❏ 60 Tony Pena	.05	.02
❏ 61 Bobby Thigpen	.10	.05
❏ 62 Bobby Meacham	.05	.02
❏ 63 Fred Toliver	.05	.02
❏ 64 Harry Spilman	.05	.02
❏ 65 Tom Browning	.05	.02
❏ 66 Marc Sullivan	.05	.02
❏ 67 Bill Swift	.05	.02
❏ 68 Tony LaRussa MG	.10	.05
❏ 69 Lonnie Smith	.05	.02
❏ 70 Charlie Hough	.05	.02
❏ 71 Mike Aldrete	.05	.02
❏ 72 Walt Terrell	.05	.02
❏ 73 Dave Anderson	.05	.02
❏ 74 Dan Pasqua	.05	.02
❏ 75 Ron Darling	.05	.02
❏ 76 Rafael Ramirez	.05	.02
❏ 77 Bryan Oelkers	.05	.02
❏ 78 Tom Foley	.05	.02
❏ 79 Juan Nieves	.05	.02
❏ 80 Wally Joyner	.20	.09
❏ 81 Padres Team	.05	.02
(Andy Hawkins and Terry Kennedy)		
❏ 82 Rob Murphy	.05	.02
❏ 83 Mike Davis	.05	.02
❏ 84 Steve Lake	.05	.02
❏ 85 Kevin Bass	.05	.02
❏ 86 Nate Snell	.05	.02
❏ 87 Mark Salas	.05	.02
❏ 88 Ed Wojna	.05	.02
❏ 89 Ozzie Guillen	.10	.05
❏ 90 Dave Stieb	.05	.02
❏ 91 Harold Reynolds	.10	.05
❏ 92A Urbano Lugo	.20	.09
ERR (no trademark)		
❏ 92B Urbano Lugo COR	.05	.02
❏ 93 Jim Leyland MG	.10	.05
❏ 94 Calvin Schiraldi	.05	.02

❏ 95	Oddibe McDowell	.05	.02
❏ 96	Frank Williams	.05	.02
❏ 97	Glenn Wilson	.05	.02
❏ 98	Bill Scherrer	.05	.02
❏ 99	Darryl Motley (Now with Braves on card front)	.05	.02
❏ 100	Steve Garvey	.15	.07
❏ 101	Carl Willis	.05	.02
❏ 102	Paul Zuvella	.05	.02
❏ 103	Rick Aguilera	.10	.05
❏ 104	Billy Sample	.05	.02
❏ 105	Floyd Youmans	.05	.02
❏ 106	Blue Jays Team (George Bell and Jesse Barfield)	.05	.02
❏ 107	John Butcher	.05	.02
❏ 108	Jim Gantner UER (Brewers logo reversed)	.05	.02
❏ 109	R.J. Reynolds	.05	.02
❏ 110	John Tudor	.05	.02
❏ 111	Alfredo Griffin	.05	.02
❏ 112	Alan Ashby	.05	.02
❏ 113	Neil Allen	.05	.02
❏ 114	Billy Beane	.05	.02
❏ 115	Donnie Moore	.05	.02
❏ 116	Bill Russell	.05	.02
❏ 117	Jim Beattie	.05	.02
❏ 118	Bobby Valentine MG	.05	.02
❏ 119	Ron Robinson	.05	.02
❏ 120	Eddie Murray	.20	.09
❏ 121	Kevin Romine	.05	.02
❏ 122	Jim Clancy	.05	.02
❏ 123	John Kruk	.20	.09
❏ 124	Ray Fontenot	.05	.02
❏ 125	Bob Brenly	.05	.02
❏ 126	Mike Loynd	.05	.02
❏ 127	Vance Law	.05	.02
❏ 128	Checklist 1-132	.05	.02
❏ 129	Rick Cerone	.05	.02
❏ 130	Dwight Gooden	.15	.07
❏ 131	Pirates Team (Sid Bream and Tony Pena)	.05	.02
❏ 132	Paul Assenmacher	.15	.07
❏ 133	Jose Oquendo	.05	.02
❏ 134	Rich Yett	.05	.02
❏ 135	Mike Easler	.05	.02
❏ 136	Ron Romanick	.05	.02
❏ 137	Jerry Willard	.05	.02
❏ 138	Roy Lee Jackson	.05	.02
❏ 139	Devon White	.25	.11
❏ 140	Bret Saberhagen	.10	.05
❏ 141	Herm Winningham	.05	.02
❏ 142	Rick Sutcliffe	.05	.02
❏ 143	Steve Boros MG	.05	.02
❏ 144	Mike Scioscia	.05	.02
❏ 145	Charlie Kerfeld	.05	.02
❏ 146	Tracy Jones	.05	.02
❏ 147	Randy Niemann	.05	.02
❏ 148	Dave Collins	.05	.02
❏ 149	Ray Searage	.05	.02
❏ 150	Wade Boggs	.20	.09
❏ 151	Mike LaCoss	.05	.02
❏ 152	Toby Harrah	.05	.02
❏ 153	Duane Ward	.10	.05
❏ 154	Tom O'Malley	.05	.02
❏ 155	Eddie Whitson	.05	.02
❏ 156	Mariners Team (Mound conference)	.05	.02
❏ 157	Danny Darwin	.05	.02
❏ 158	Tim Teufel	.05	.02
❏ 159	Ed Olwine	.05	.02
❏ 160	Julio Franco	.10	.05
❏ 161	Steve Ontiveros	.05	.02
❏ 162	Mike LaValliere	.05	.02
❏ 163	Kevin Gross	.05	.02
❏ 164	Sammy Khalifa	.05	.02
❏ 165	Jeff Reardon	.05	.02
❏ 166	Bob Boone	.10	.05
❏ 167	Jim Deshaies	.05	.02
❏ 168	Lou Piniella MG	.10	.05
❏ 169	Ron Washington	.05	.02
❏ 170	Bo Jackson	.40	.18
❏ 171	Chuck Cary	.05	.02
❏ 172	Ron Oester	.05	.02
❏ 173	Alex Trevino	.05	.02
❏ 174	Henry Cotto	.05	.02
❏ 175	Bob Stanley	.05	.02
❏ 176	Steve Buechele	.05	.02
❏ 177	Keith Moreland	.05	.02
❏ 178	Cecil Fielder	.15	.07
❏ 179	Bill Wegman	.05	.02
❏ 180	Chris Brown	.05	.02
❏ 181	Cardinals Team (Mound conference)	.05	.02
❏ 182	Lee Lacy	.05	.02
❏ 183	Andy Hawkins	.05	.02
❏ 184	Bobby Bonilla	.25	.11
❏ 185	Roger McDowell	.05	.02
❏ 186	Bruce Benedict	.05	.02
❏ 187	Mark Huismann	.05	.02
❏ 188	Tony Phillips	.05	.02
❏ 189	Joe Hesketh	.05	.02
❏ 190	Jim Sundberg	.05	.02
❏ 191	Charles Hudson	.05	.02
❏ 192	Cory Snyder	.05	.02
❏ 193	Roger Craig MG	.05	.02
❏ 194	Kirk McCaskill	.05	.02
❏ 195	Mike Pagliarulo	.05	.02
❏ 196	Randy O'Neal UER (Wrong ML career W-L totals)	.05	.02
❏ 197	Mark Bailey	.05	.02
❏ 198	Lee Mazzilli	.05	.02
❏ 199	Mariano Duncan	.05	.02
❏ 200	Pete Rose	.40	.18
❏ 201	John Cangelosi	.05	.02
❏ 202	Ricky Wright	.05	.02
❏ 203	Mike Kingery	.05	.02
❏ 204	Sammy Stewart	.05	.02
❏ 205	Graig Nettles	.10	.05
❏ 206	Twins Team (Frank Viola and Tim Laudner)	.05	.02
❏ 207	George Frazier	.05	.02
❏ 208	John Shelby	.05	.02
❏ 209	Rick Schu	.05	.02
❏ 210	Lloyd Moseby	.05	.02
❏ 211	John Morris	.05	.02
❏ 212	Mike Fitzgerald	.05	.02
❏ 213	Randy Myers	.20	.09
❏ 214	Omar Moreno	.05	.02
❏ 215	Mark Langston	.05	.02
❏ 216	B.J. Surhoff	.40	.18
❏ 217	Chris Codiroli	.05	.02
❏ 218	Sparky Anderson MG	.10	.05
❏ 219	Cecilio Guante	.05	.02
❏ 220	Joe Carter	.20	.09
❏ 221	Vern Ruhle	.05	.02
❏ 222	Denny Walling	.05	.02
❏ 223	Charlie Leibrandt	.05	.02
❏ 224	Wayne Tolleson	.05	.02
❏ 225	Mike Smithson	.05	.02
❏ 226	Max Venable	.05	.02
❏ 227	Jamie Moyer	.15	.07
❏ 228	Curt Wilkerson	.05	.02
❏ 229	Mike Birkbeck	.05	.02
❏ 230	Don Baylor	.10	.05
❏ 231	Giants Team (Bob Brenly and Jim Gott)	.05	.02
❏ 232	Reggie Williams	.05	.02
❏ 233	Russ Morman	.05	.02
❏ 234	Pat Sheridan	.05	.02
❏ 235	Alvin Davis	.05	.02
❏ 236	Tommy John	.10	.05
❏ 237	Jim Morrison	.05	.02
❏ 238	Bill Krueger	.05	.02
❏ 239	Juan Espino	.05	.02
❏ 240	Steve Balboni	.05	.02
❏ 241	Danny Heep	.05	.02
❏ 242	Rick Mahler	.05	.02
❏ 243	Whitey Herzog MG	.10	.05
❏ 244	Dickie Noles	.05	.02
❏ 245	Willie Upshaw	.05	.02
❏ 246	Jim Dwyer	.05	.02
❏ 247	Jeff Reed	.05	.02
❏ 248	Gene Walter	.05	.02
❏ 249	Jim Pankovits	.05	.02
❏ 250	Teddy Higuera	.05	.02
❏ 251	Rob Wilfong	.05	.02
❏ 252	Dennis Martinez	.10	.05
❏ 253	Eddie Milner	.05	.02
❏ 254	Bob Tewksbury	.10	.05
❏ 255	Juan Samuel	.05	.02
❏ 256	Royals Team (George Brett and Frank White)	.15	.07
❏ 257	Bob Forsch	.05	.02
❏ 258	Steve Yeager	.05	.02
❏ 259	Mike Greenwell	.20	.09
❏ 260	Vida Blue	.10	.05
❏ 261	Ruben Sierra	.20	.09
❏ 262	Jim Winn	.05	.02
❏ 263	Stan Javier	.05	.02
❏ 264	Checklist 133-264	.05	.02
❏ 265	Darrell Evans	.10	.05
❏ 266	Jeff Hamilton	.05	.02
❏ 267	Howard Johnson	.05	.02
❏ 268	Pat Corrales MG	.10	.05
❏ 269	Cliff Speck	.05	.02
❏ 270	Jody Davis	.05	.02
❏ 271	Mike G. Brown	.05	.02
❏ 272	Andres Galarraga	.20	.09
❏ 273	Gene Nelson	.05	.02
❏ 274	Jeff Hearron UER (Duplicate 1986 stat line on back)	.05	.02
❏ 275	LaMarr Hoyt	.05	.02
❏ 276	Jackie Gutierrez	.05	.02
❏ 277	Juan Agosto	.05	.02
❏ 278	Gary Pettis	.05	.02
❏ 279	Dan Plesac	.05	.02
❏ 280	Jeff Leonard	.05	.02
❏ 281	Reds Team (Pete Rose, Bo Diaz, and Bill Gullickson)	.20	.09
❏ 282	Jeff Calhoun	.05	.02
❏ 283	Doug Drabek	.20	.09
❏ 284	John Moses	.05	.02
❏ 285	Dennis Boyd	.05	.02
❏ 286	Mike Woodard	.05	.02
❏ 287	Dave Von Ohlen	.05	.02
❏ 288	Tito Landrum	.05	.02
❏ 289	Bob Kipper	.05	.02
❏ 290	Leon Durham	.05	.02
❏ 291	Mitch Williams	.10	.05
❏ 292	Franklin Stubbs	.05	.02
❏ 293	Bob Rodgers MG	.05	.02
❏ 294	Steve Jeltz	.05	.02
❏ 295	Len Dykstra	.15	.07
❏ 296	Andres Thomas	.05	.02
❏ 297	Don Schulze	.05	.02
❏ 298	Larry Herndon	.05	.02
❏ 299	Joel Davis	.05	.02
❏ 300	Reggie Jackson	.25	.11
❏ 301	Luis Aquino UER (No trademark never corrected)	.05	.02
❏ 302	Bill Schroeder	.05	.02
❏ 303	Juan Berenguer	.05	.02
❏ 304	Phil Garner	.05	.02
❏ 305	John Franco	.10	.05
❏ 306	Red Sox Team (Tom Seaver, John McNamara MG, and Rich Gedman)	.10	.05
❏ 307	Lee Guetterman	.05	.02
❏ 308	Don Slaught	.05	.02
❏ 309	Mike Young	.05	.02
❏ 310	Frank Viola	.05	.02
❏ 311	Rickey Henderson TBC '82	.10	.05
❏ 312	Reggie Jackson TBC '77	.20	.09
❏ 313	Roberto Clemente TBC '72	.25	.11
❏ 314	Carl Yastrzemski UER TBC '67 (Sic, 112 RBI's on back)	.20	.09
❏ 315	Maury Wills TBC '62	.10	.05
❏ 316	Brian Fisher	.05	.02
❏ 317	Clint Hurdle	.05	.02
❏ 318	Jim Fregosi MG	.05	.02
❏ 319	Greg Swindell	.20	.09
❏ 320	Barry Bonds	2.50	1.10

❑ 321	Mike Laga	.05	.02
❑ 322	Chris Bando	.05	.02
❑ 323	Al Newman	.05	.02
❑ 324	David Palmer	.05	.02
❑ 325	Garry Templeton	.05	.02
❑ 326	Mark Gubicza	.05	.02
❑ 327	Dale Sveum	.05	.02
❑ 328	Bob Welch	.05	.02
❑ 329	Ron Roenicke	.05	.02
❑ 330	Mike Scott	.05	.02
❑ 331	Mets Team	.10	.05
	(Gary Carter and Darryl Strawberry)		
❑ 332	Joe Price	.05	.02
❑ 333	Ken Phelps	.05	.02
❑ 334	Ed Correa	.05	.02
❑ 335	Candy Maldonado	.05	.02
❑ 336	Allan Anderson	.05	.02
❑ 337	Darrell Miller	.05	.02
❑ 338	Tim Conroy	.05	.02
❑ 339	Donnie Hill	.05	.02
❑ 340	Roger Clemens	.60	.25
❑ 341	Mike C. Brown	.05	.02
❑ 342	Bob James	.05	.02
❑ 343	Hal Lanier MG	.05	.02
❑ 344A	Joe Niekro	.05	.02
	(Copyright inside righthand border)		
❑ 344B	Joe Niekro	.05	.02
	(Copyright outside righthand border)		
❑ 345	Andre Dawson	.20	.09
❑ 346	Shawon Dunston	.05	.02
❑ 347	Mickey Brantley	.05	.02
❑ 348	Carmelo Martinez	.05	.02
❑ 349	Storm Davis	.05	.02
❑ 350	Keith Hernandez	.10	.05
❑ 351	Gene Garber	.05	.02
❑ 352	Mike Felder	.05	.02
❑ 353	Ernie Camacho	.05	.02
❑ 354	Jamie Quirk	.05	.02
❑ 355	Don Carman	.05	.02
❑ 356	White Sox Team	.05	.02
	(Mound conference)		
❑ 357	Steve Fireovid	.05	.02
❑ 358	Sal Butera	.05	.02
❑ 359	Doug Corbett	.05	.02
❑ 360	Pedro Guerrero	.05	.02
❑ 361	Mark Thurmond	.05	.02
❑ 362	Luis Quinones	.05	.02
❑ 363	Jose Guzman	.05	.02
❑ 364	Randy Bush	.05	.02
❑ 365	Rick Rhoden	.05	.02
❑ 366	Mark McGwire	6.00	2.70
❑ 367	Jeff Lahti	.05	.02
❑ 368	John McNamara MG	.05	.02
❑ 369	Brian Dayett	.05	.02
❑ 370	Fred Lynn	.10	.05
❑ 371	Mark Eichhorn	.05	.02
❑ 372	Jerry Mumphrey	.05	.02
❑ 373	Jeff Dedmon	.05	.02
❑ 374	Glenn Hoffman	.05	.02
❑ 375	Ron Guidry	.10	.05
❑ 376	Scott Bradley	.05	.02
❑ 377	John Henry Johnson	.05	.02
❑ 378	Rafael Santana	.05	.02
❑ 379	John Russell	.05	.02
❑ 380	Rich Gossage	.10	.05
❑ 381	Expos Team	.05	.02
	(Mound conference)		
❑ 382	Rudy Law	.05	.02
❑ 383	Ron Davis	.05	.02
❑ 384	Johnny Grubb	.05	.02
❑ 385	Orel Hershiser	.10	.05
❑ 386	Dickie Thon	.05	.02
❑ 387	T.R. Bryden	.05	.02
❑ 388	Geno Petralli	.05	.02
❑ 389	Jeff D. Robinson	.05	.02
❑ 390	Gary Matthews	.05	.02
❑ 391	Jay Howell	.05	.02
❑ 392	Checklist 265-396	.15	.02
❑ 393	Pete Rose MG	.15	.07
❑ 394	Mike Bielecki	.05	.02
❑ 395	Damaso Garcia	.05	.02
❑ 396	Tim Lollar	.05	.02
❑ 397	Greg Walker	.05	.02
❑ 398	Brad Havens	.05	.02
❑ 399	Curt Ford	.05	.02
❑ 400	George Brett	.40	.18
❑ 401	Billy Joe Robidoux	.05	.02
❑ 402	Mike Trujillo	.05	.02
❑ 403	Jerry Royster	.05	.02
❑ 404	Doug Sisk	.05	.02
❑ 405	Brook Jacoby	.05	.02
❑ 406	Yankees Team	.20	.09
	(Rickey Henderson and Don Mattingly)		
❑ 407	Jim Acker	.05	.02
❑ 408	John Mizerock	.05	.02
❑ 409	Milt Thompson	.05	.02
❑ 410	Fernando Valenzuela	.10	.05
❑ 411	Darnell Coles	.05	.02
❑ 412	Eric Davis	.15	.07
❑ 413	Moose Haas	.05	.02
❑ 414	Joe Orsulak	.05	.02
❑ 415	Bobby Witt	.10	.05
❑ 416	Tom Nieto	.05	.02
❑ 417	Pat Perry	.05	.02
❑ 418	Dick Williams MG	.05	.02
❑ 419	Mark Portugal	.10	.05
❑ 420	Will Clark	.60	.25
❑ 421	Jose DeLeon	.05	.02
❑ 422	Jack Howell	.05	.02
❑ 423	Jaime Cocanower	.05	.02
❑ 424	Chris Speier	.05	.02
❑ 425	Tom Seaver UER	.20	.09
	Earned Runs amount is wrong For 86 Red Sox and Career Also the ERA is wrong for 86 and career		
❑ 426	Floyd Rayford	.05	.02
❑ 427	Edwin Nunez	.05	.02
❑ 428	Bruce Bochy	.05	.02
❑ 429	Tim Pyznarski	.05	.02
❑ 430	Mike Schmidt	.30	.14
❑ 431	Dodgers Team	.05	.02
	(Mound conference)		
❑ 432	Jim Slaton	.05	.02
❑ 433	Ed Hearn	.05	.02
❑ 434	Mike Fischlin	.05	.02
❑ 435	Bruce Sutter	.05	.02
❑ 436	Andy Allanson	.05	.02
❑ 437	Ted Power	.05	.02
❑ 438	Kelly Downs	.05	.02
❑ 439	Karl Best	.05	.02
❑ 440	Willie McGee	.10	.05
❑ 441	Dave Leiper	.05	.02
❑ 442	Mitch Webster	.05	.02
❑ 443	John Felske MG	.05	.02
❑ 444	Jeff Russell	.05	.02
❑ 445	Dave Lopes	.05	.02
❑ 446	Chuck Finley	.25	.11
❑ 447	Bill Almon	.05	.02
❑ 448	Chris Bosio	.10	.05
❑ 449	Pat Dodson	.05	.02
❑ 450	Kirby Puckett	.40	.18
❑ 451	Joe Sambito	.05	.02
❑ 452	Dave Henderson	.05	.02
❑ 453	Scott Terry	.05	.02
❑ 454	Luis Salazar	.05	.02
❑ 455	Mike Boddicker	.05	.02
❑ 456	A's Team	.05	.02
	(Mound conference)		
❑ 457	Len Matuszek	.05	.02
❑ 458	Kelly Gruber	.25	.09
❑ 459	Dennis Eckersley	.20	.09
❑ 460	Darryl Strawberry	.15	.07
❑ 461	Craig McMurtry	.05	.02
❑ 462	Scott Fletcher	.05	.02
❑ 463	Tom Candiotti	.05	.02
❑ 464	Butch Wynegar	.05	.02
❑ 465	Todd Worrell	.10	.05
❑ 466	Kal Daniels	.05	.02
❑ 467	Randy St.Claire	.05	.02
❑ 468	George Bamberger MG	.05	.02
❑ 469	Mike Diaz	.05	.02
❑ 470	Dave Dravecky	.10	.05
❑ 471	Ronn Reynolds	.05	.02
❑ 472	Bill Doran	.05	.02
❑ 473	Steve Farr	.05	.02
❑ 474	Jerry Narron	.05	.02
❑ 475	Scott Garrelts	.05	.02
❑ 476	Danny Tartabull	.05	.02
❑ 477	Ken Howell	.05	.02
❑ 478	Tim Laudner	.05	.02
❑ 479	Bob Sebra	.05	.02
❑ 480	Jim Rice	.10	.05
❑ 481	Phillies Team	.05	.02
	(Glenn Wilson Juan Samuel and Von Hayes)		
❑ 482	Daryl Boston	.05	.02
❑ 483	Dwight Lowry	.05	.02
❑ 484	Jim Traber	.05	.02
❑ 485	Tony Fernandez	.05	.02
❑ 486	Otis Nixon	.15	.07
❑ 487	Dave Gumpert	.05	.02
❑ 488	Ray Knight	.05	.02
❑ 489	Bill Gullickson	.05	.02
❑ 490	Dale Murphy	.20	.09
❑ 491	Ron Karkovice	.10	.05
❑ 492	Mike Heath	.05	.02
❑ 493	Tom Lasorda MG	.10	.05
❑ 494	Barry Jones	.05	.02
❑ 495	Gorman Thomas	.05	.02
❑ 496	Bruce Bochte	.05	.02
❑ 497	Dale Mohorcic	.05	.02
❑ 498	Bob Kearney	.05	.02
❑ 499	Bruce Ruffin	.05	.02
❑ 500	Don Mattingly	.40	.18
❑ 501	Craig Lefferts	.05	.02
❑ 502	Dick Schofield	.05	.02
❑ 503	Larry Andersen	.05	.02
❑ 504	Mickey Hatcher	.05	.02
❑ 505	Bryn Smith	.05	.02
❑ 506	Orioles Team	.05	.02
	(Mound conference)		
❑ 507	Dave L. Stapleton	.05	.02
❑ 508	Scott Bankhead	.05	.02
❑ 509	Enos Cabell	.05	.02
❑ 510	Tom Henke	.10	.05
❑ 511	Steve Lyons	.05	.02
❑ 512	Dave Magadan	.10	.05
❑ 513	Carmen Castillo	.05	.02
❑ 514	Orlando Mercado	.05	.02
❑ 515	Willie Hernandez	.05	.02
❑ 516	Ted Simmons	.10	.05
❑ 517	Mario Soto	.05	.02
❑ 518	Gene Mauch MG	.05	.02
❑ 519	Curt Young	.05	.02
❑ 520	Jack Clark	.10	.05
❑ 521	Rick Reuschel	.05	.02
❑ 522	Checklist 397-528	.15	.02
❑ 523	Earnie Riles	.05	.02
❑ 524	Bob Shirley	.05	.02
❑ 525	Phil Bradley	.05	.02
❑ 526	Roger Mason	.05	.02
❑ 527	Jim Wohlford	.05	.02
❑ 528	Ken Dixon	.05	.02
❑ 529	Alvaro Espinoza	.05	.02
❑ 530	Tony Gwynn	.50	.23
❑ 531	Astros Team	.10	.05
	(Yogi Berra conference)		
❑ 532	Jeff Stone	.05	.02
❑ 533	Argenis Salazar	.05	.02
❑ 534	Scott Sanderson	.05	.02
❑ 535	Tony Armas	.05	.02
❑ 536	Terry Mulholland	.10	.05
❑ 537	Rance Mullinicks	.05	.02
❑ 538	Tom Niedenfuer	.05	.02
❑ 539	Reid Nichols	.05	.02
❑ 540	Terry Kennedy	.05	.02
❑ 541	Rafael Belliard	.05	.02
❑ 542	Ricky Horton	.05	.02
❑ 543	Dave Johnson MG	.10	.05
❑ 544	Zane Smith	.05	.02
❑ 545	Buddy Bell	.10	.05
❑ 546	Mike Morgan	.05	.02
❑ 547	Rob Deer	.05	.02
❑ 548	Bill Mooneyham	.05	.02
❑ 549	Bob Melvin	.05	.02
❑ 550	Pete Incaviglia	.10	.05
❑ 551	Frank Wills	.05	.02
❑ 552	Larry Sheets	.05	.02
❑ 553	Mike Maddux	.05	.02
❑ 554	Buddy Biancalana	.05	.02
❑ 555	Dennis Rasmussen	.05	.02
❑ 556	Angels Team	.05	.02

(Rene Lachemann CO, Mike Witt, and Bob Boone)

#	Player	Hi	Lo
557	John Cerutti	.05	.02
558	Greg Gagne	.05	.02
559	Lance McCullers	.05	.02
560	Glenn Davis	.05	.02
561	Rey Quinones	.05	.02
562	Bryan Clutterbuck	.05	.02
563	John Stefero	.05	.02
564	Larry McWilliams	.05	.02
565	Dusty Baker	.10	.05
566	Tim Hulett	.05	.02
567	Greg Mathews	.05	.02
568	Earl Weaver MG	.20	.09
569	Wade Rowdon	.05	.02
570	Sid Fernandez	.05	.02
571	Ozzie Virgil	.05	.02
572	Pete Ladd	.05	.02
573	Hal McRae	.10	.05
574	Manny Lee	.05	.02
575	Pat Tabler	.05	.02
576	Frank Pastore	.05	.02
577	Dann Bilardello	.05	.02
578	Billy Hatcher	.05	.02
579	Rick Burleson	.05	.02
580	Mike Krukow	.05	.02
581	Cubs Team	.05	.02

(Ron Cey and Steve Trout)

#	Player	Hi	Lo
582	Bruce Berenyi	.05	.02
583	Junior Ortiz	.05	.02
584	Ron Kittle	.05	.02
585	Scott Bailes	.05	.02
586	Ben Oglivie	.05	.02
587	Eric Plunk	.05	.02
588	Wallace Johnson	.05	.02
589	Steve Crawford	.05	.02
590	Vince Coleman	.15	.07
591	Spike Owen	.05	.02
592	Chris Welsh	.05	.02
593	Chuck Tanner MG	.05	.02
594	Rick Anderson	.05	.02
595	Keith Hernandez AS	.05	.02
596	Steve Sax AS	.05	.02
597	Mike Schmidt AS	.15	.07
598	Ozzie Smith AS	.15	.07
599	Tony Gwynn AS	.20	.09
600	Dave Parker AS	.05	.02
601	Darryl Strawberry AS	.10	.05
602	Gary Carter AS	.10	.05
603A	Dwight Gooden AS ERR (no trademark)	.15	.07
603B	Dwight Gooden AS COR	.15	.07
604	Fernando Valenzuela AS	.10	.05
605	Todd Worrell AS	.10	.05
606	Don Mattingly AS COR	.20	.09
606A	Don Mattingly AS ERR (no trademark)	.75	.35
607	Tony Bernazard AS	.05	.02
608	Wade Boggs AS	.10	.05
609	Cal Ripken AS	.20	.09
610	Jim Rice AS	.05	.02
611	Kirby Puckett AS	.20	.09
612	George Bell AS	.05	.02
613	Lance Parrish AS UER (Pitcher heading on back)	.10	.05
614	Roger Clemens AS	.20	.09
615	Teddy Higuera AS	.05	.02
616	Dave Righetti AS	.05	.02
617	Al Nipper	.05	.02
618	Tom Kelly MG	.05	.02
619	Jerry Reed	.05	.02
620	Jose Canseco	1.00	.45
621	Danny Cox	.05	.02
622	Glenn Braggs	.05	.02
623	Kurt Stillwell	.05	.02
624	Tim Burke	.05	.02
625	Mookie Wilson	.10	.05
626	Joel Skinner	.05	.02
627	Ken Oberkfell	.05	.02
628	Bob Walk	.05	.02
629	Larry Parrish	.05	.02
630	John Candelaria	.05	.02
631	Tigers Team (Mound conference)	.05	.02
632	Rob Woodward	.05	.02
633	Jose Uribe	.05	.02
634	Rafael Palmeiro	2.00	.90
635	Ken Schrom	.05	.02
636	Darren Daulton	.15	.07
637	Bip Roberts	.20	.09
638	Rich Bordi	.05	.02
639	Gerald Perry	.05	.02
640	Mark Clear	.05	.02
641	Domingo Ramos	.05	.02
642	Al Pulido	.05	.02
643	Ron Shepherd	.05	.02
644	John Denny	.05	.02
645	Dwight Evans	.10	.05
646	Mike Mason	.05	.02
647	Tom Lawless	.05	.02
648	Barry Larkin	1.00	.45
649	Mickey Tettleton	.05	.02
650	Hubie Brooks	.05	.02
651	Benny Distefano	.05	.02
652	Terry Forster	.05	.02
653	Kevin Mitchell	.15	.07
654	Checklist 529-660	.05	.02
655	Jesse Barfield	.05	.02
656	Rangers Team	.05	.02

(Bobby Valentine MG and Ricky Wright)

#	Player	Hi	Lo
657	Tom Niedenfuer	.05	.02
658	Robby Thompson	.10	.05
659	Aurelio Lopez	.05	.02
660	Bob Horner	.05	.02
661	Lou Whitaker	.10	.05
662	Frank DiPino	.05	.02
663	Cliff Johnson	.05	.02
664	Mike Marshall	.05	.02
665	Rod Scurry	.05	.02
666	Von Hayes	.05	.02
667	Ron Hassey	.05	.02
668	Juan Bonilla	.05	.02
669	Bud Black	.05	.02
670	Jose Cruz	.10	.05
671A	Ray Soff ERR (No D* before copyright line)	.05	.02
671B	Ray Soff COR (D* before copyright line)	.05	.02
672	Chili Davis	.15	.07
673	Don Sutton	.20	.09
674	Bill Campbell	.05	.02
675	Ed Romero	.05	.02
676	Charlie Moore	.05	.02
677	Bob Grich	.10	.05
678	Carney Lansford	.05	.02
679	Kent Hrbek	.10	.05
680	Ryne Sandberg	.25	.11
681	George Bell	.05	.02
682	Jerry Reuss	.05	.02
683	Gary Roenicke	.05	.02
684	Kent Tekulve	.05	.02
685	Jerry Hairston	.05	.02
686	Doyle Alexander	.05	.02
687	Alan Trammell	.15	.07
688	Juan Beniquez	.05	.02
689	Darrell Porter	.05	.02
690	Dane Iorg	.05	.02
691	Dave Parker	.10	.05
692	Frank White	.10	.05
693	Terry Puhl	.05	.02
694	Phil Niekro	.20	.09
695	Chico Walker	.05	.02
696	Gary Lucas	.05	.02
697	Ed Lynch	.05	.02
698	Ernie Whitt	.05	.02
699	Ken Landreaux	.05	.02
700	Dave Bergman	.05	.02
701	Willie Randolph	.10	.05
702	Greg Gross	.05	.02
703	Dave Schmidt	.05	.02
704	Jesse Orosco	.05	.02
705	Bruce Hurst	.05	.02
706	Rick Manning	.05	.02
707	Bob McClure	.05	.02
708	Scott McGregor	.05	.02
709	Dave Kingman	.10	.05
710	Gary Gaetti	.10	.05
711	Ken Griffey	.10	.05
712	Don Robinson	.05	.02
713	Tom Brookens	.05	.02
714	Dan Quisenberry	.05	.02
715	Bob Dernier	.05	.02
716	Rick Leach	.05	.02
717	Ed VandeBerg	.05	.02
718	Steve Carlton	.20	.09
719	Tom Hume	.05	.02
720	Richard Dotson	.05	.02
721	Tom Herr	.05	.02
722	Bob Knepper	.05	.02
723	Brett Butler	.10	.05
724	Greg Minton	.05	.02
725	George Hendrick	.05	.02
726	Frank Tanana	.05	.02
727	Mike Moore	.05	.02
728	Tippy Martinez	.05	.02
729	Tom Paciorek	.10	.05
730	Eric Show	.05	.02
731	Dave Concepcion	.10	.05
732	Manny Trillo	.05	.02
733	Bill Caudill	.05	.02
734	Bill Madlock	.10	.05
735	Rickey Henderson	.25	.11
736	Steve Bedrosian	.05	.02
737	Floyd Bannister	.05	.02
738	Jorge Orta	.05	.02
739	Chet Lemon	.05	.02
740	Rich Gedman	.05	.02
741	Paul Molitor	.20	.09
742	Andy McGaffigan	.05	.02
743	Dwayne Murphy	.05	.02
744	Roy Smalley	.05	.02
745	Glenn Hubbard	.05	.02
746	Bob Ojeda	.05	.02
747	Johnny Ray	.05	.02
748	Mike Flanagan	.05	.02
749	Ozzie Smith	.25	.11
750	Steve Trout	.05	.02
751	Garth Iorg	.05	.02
752	Dan Petry	.05	.02
753	Rick Honeycutt	.05	.02
754	Dave LaPoint	.05	.02
755	Luis Aguayo	.05	.02
756	Carlton Fisk	.20	.09
757	Nolan Ryan	.75	.35
758	Tony Bernazard	.05	.02
759	Joel Youngblood	.05	.02
760	Mike Witt	.05	.02
761	Greg Pryor	.05	.02
762	Gary Ward	.05	.02
763	Tim Flannery	.05	.02
764	Bill Buckner	.10	.05
765	Kirk Gibson	.10	.05
766	Don Aase	.05	.02
767	Ron Cey	.10	.05
768	Dennis Lamp	.05	.02
769	Steve Sax	.10	.05
770	Dave Winfield	.20	.09
771	Shane Rawley	.05	.02
772	Harold Baines	.10	.05
773	Robin Yount	.20	.09
774	Wayne Krenchicki	.05	.02
775	Joaquin Andujar	.05	.02
776	Tom Brunansky	.05	.02
777	Chris Chambliss	.10	.05
778	Jack Morris	.10	.05
779	Craig Reynolds	.05	.02
780	Andre Thornton	.05	.02
781	Atlee Hammaker	.05	.02
782	Brian Downing	.05	.02
783	Willie Wilson	.10	.05
784	Cal Ripken	.75	.35
785	Terry Francona	.05	.02
786	Jimy Williams MG	.05	.02
787	Alejandro Pena	.05	.02
788	Tim Stoddard	.05	.02
789	Dan Schatzeder	.05	.02
790	Julio Cruz	.05	.02
791	Lance Parrish UER (No trademark, never corrected)	.10	.05
792	Checklist 661-792	.05	.02

1987 Topps Tiffany

	MINT	NRMT
COMP.FACT.SET (792)	120.00	55.00
COMMON CARD (1-792)	.15	.07

*STARS: 3X TO 6X BASIC CARDS
*ROOKIES: 6X TO 12X BASIC CARDS
DISTRIBUTED ONLY IN FACTORY SET FORM

1987 Topps Rookies

	MINT	NRMT
COMPLETE SET (22)	12.00	5.50
COMMON PLAYER (1-22)	.25	.11
MINOR STARS	.50	.23

ONE PER RETAIL JUMBO PACK

☐ 1 Andy Allanson	.25	.11
☐ 2 John Cangelosi	.25	.11
☐ 3 Jose Canseco	5.00	2.20
☐ 4 Will Clark	2.50	1.10
☐ 5 Mark Eichhorn	.25	.11
☐ 6 Pete Incaviglia	.50	.23
☐ 7 Wally Joyner	.75	.35
☐ 8 Eric King	.25	.11
☐ 9 Dave Magadan	.50	.23
☐ 10 John Morris	.25	.11
☐ 11 Juan Nieves	.25	.11
☐ 12 Rafael Palmeiro	6.00	2.70
☐ 13 Billy Joe Robidoux	.25	.11
☐ 14 Bruce Ruffin	.25	.11
☐ 15 Ruben Sierra	.50	.23
☐ 16 Cory Snyder	.25	.11
☐ 17 Kurt Stillwell	.25	.11
☐ 18 Dale Sveum	.25	.11
☐ 19 Danny Tartabull	.50	.23
☐ 20 Andres Thomas	.25	.11
☐ 21 Robby Thompson	.50	.23
☐ 22 Todd Worrell	.50	.23

1987 Topps Traded

	MINT	NRMT
COMP.FACT.SET (132)	8.00	3.60
COMMON CARD (1T-132T)	.05	.02
MINOR STARS	.10	.05
UNLISTED STARS	.25	.11

☐ 1T Bill Almon	.05	.02
☐ 2T Scott Bankhead	.05	.02
☐ 3T Eric Bell	.05	.02
☐ 4T Juan Beniquez	.05	.02
☐ 5T Juan Berenguer	.05	.02
☐ 6T Greg Booker	.05	.02

☐ 7T Thad Bosley	.05	.02
☐ 8T Larry Bowa MG	.10	.05
☐ 9T Greg Brock	.05	.02
☐ 10T Bob Brower	.05	.02
☐ 11T Jerry Browne	.05	.02
☐ 12T Ralph Bryant	.05	.02
☐ 13T DeWayne Buice	.05	.02
☐ 14T Ellis Burks	.50	.23
☐ 15T Ivan Calderon	.05	.02
☐ 16T Jeff Calhoun	.05	.02
☐ 17T Casey Candaele	.05	.02
☐ 18T John Cangelosi	.05	.02
☐ 19T Steve Carlton	.25	.11
☐ 20T Juan Castillo	.05	.02
☐ 21T Rick Cerone	.05	.02
☐ 22T Ron Cey	.10	.05
☐ 23T John Christensen	.05	.02
☐ 24T David Cone	1.25	.55
☐ 25T Chuck Crim	.05	.02
☐ 26T Storm Davis	.05	.02
☐ 27T Andre Dawson	.25	.11
☐ 28T Rick Dempsey	.10	.05
☐ 29T Doug Drabek	.25	.11
☐ 30T Mike Dunne	.05	.02
☐ 31T Dennis Eckersley	.25	.11
☐ 32T Lee Elia MG	.05	.02
☐ 33T Brian Fisher	.05	.02
☐ 34T Terry Francona	.10	.05
☐ 35T Willie Fraser	.05	.02
☐ 36T Billy Gardner MG	.05	.02
☐ 37T Ken Gerhart	.05	.02
☐ 38T Dan Gladden	.05	.02
☐ 39T Jim Gott	.05	.02
☐ 40T Cecilio Guante	.05	.02
☐ 41T Albert Hall	.05	.02
☐ 42T Terry Harper	.05	.02
☐ 43T Mickey Hatcher	.05	.02
☐ 44T Brad Havens	.05	.02
☐ 45T Neal Heaton	.05	.02
☐ 46T Mike Henneman	.20	.09
☐ 47T Donnie Hill	.05	.02
☐ 48T Guy Hoffman	.05	.02
☐ 49T Brian Holton	.05	.02
☐ 50T Charles Hudson	.05	.02
☐ 51T Danny Jackson	.05	.02
☐ 52T Reggie Jackson	.40	.18
☐ 53T Chris James	.05	.02
☐ 54T Dion James	.05	.02
☐ 55T Stan Jefferson	.05	.02
☐ 56T Joe Johnson	.05	.02
☐ 57T Terry Kennedy	.05	.02
☐ 58T Mike Kingery	.05	.02
☐ 59T Ray Knight	.05	.02
☐ 60T Gene Larkin	.05	.02
☐ 61T Mike LaValliere	.05	.02
☐ 62T Jack Lazorko	.05	.02
☐ 63T Terry Leach	.05	.02
☐ 64T Tim Leary	.05	.02
☐ 65T Jim Lindeman	.05	.02
☐ 66T Steve Lombardozzi	.05	.02
☐ 67T Bill Long	.05	.02
☐ 68T Barry Lyons	.05	.02
☐ 69T Shane Mack	.10	.05
☐ 70T Greg Maddux	6.00	2.70
☐ 71T Bill Madlock	.10	.05
☐ 72T Joe Magrane	.05	.02
☐ 73T Dave Martinez	.10	.05
☐ 74T Fred McGriff	.40	.18

☐ 75T Mark McLemore	.10	.05
☐ 76T Kevin McReynolds	.05	.02
☐ 77T Dave Meads	.05	.02
☐ 78T Eddie Milner	.05	.02
☐ 79T Greg Minton	.05	.02
☐ 80T John Mitchell	.05	.02
☐ 81T Kevin Mitchell	.20	.09
☐ 82T Charlie Moore	.05	.02
☐ 83T Jeff Musselman	.05	.02
☐ 84T Gene Nelson	.05	.02
☐ 85T Graig Nettles	.10	.05
☐ 86T Al Newman	.05	.02
☐ 87T Reid Nichols	.05	.02
☐ 88T Tom Niedenfuer	.05	.02
☐ 89T Joe Niekro	.05	.02
☐ 90T Tom Nieto	.05	.02
☐ 91T Matt Nokes	.10	.05
☐ 92T Dickie Noles	.05	.02
☐ 93T Pat Pacillo	.05	.02
☐ 94T Lance Parrish	.10	.05
☐ 95T Tony Pena	.05	.02
☐ 96T Luis Polonia	.10	.05
☐ 97T Randy Ready	.05	.02
☐ 98T Jeff Reardon	.10	.05
☐ 99T Gary Redus	.05	.02
☐ 100T Jeff Reed	.05	.02
☐ 101T Rick Rhoden	.05	.02
☐ 102T Cal Ripken Sr. MG	.05	.02
☐ 103T Wally Ritchie	.05	.02
☐ 104T Jeff M. Robinson	.05	.02
☐ 105T Gary Roenicke	.05	.02
☐ 106T Jerry Royster	.05	.02
☐ 107T Mark Salas	.05	.02
☐ 108T Luis Salazar	.05	.02
☐ 109T Benny Santiago	.10	.05
☐ 110T Dave Schmidt	.05	.02
☐ 111T Kevin Seitzer	.25	.11
☐ 112T John Shelby	.05	.02
☐ 113T Steve Shields	.05	.02
☐ 114T John Smiley	.25	.11
☐ 115T Chris Speier	.05	.02
☐ 116T Mike Stanley	.25	.11
☐ 117T Terry Steinbach	.25	.11
☐ 118T Les Straker	.05	.02
☐ 119T Jim Sundberg	.05	.02
☐ 120T Danny Tartabull	.25	.11
☐ 121T Tom Trebelhorn MG	.05	.02
☐ 122T Dave Valle	.05	.02
☐ 123T Ed VandeBerg	.05	.02
☐ 124T Andy Van Slyke	.10	.05
☐ 125T Gary Ward	.05	.02
☐ 126T Alan Wiggins	.05	.02
☐ 127T Bill Wilkinson	.05	.02
☐ 128T Frank Williams	.05	.02
☐ 129T Matt Williams	1.50	.70
☐ 130T Jim Winn	.05	.02
☐ 131T Matt Young	.05	.02
☐ 132T Checklist 1T-132T	.05	.02

1987 Topps Traded Tiffany

	MINT	NRMT
COMP.FACT.SET (132)	70.00	32.00
COMMON CARD (1T-132T)	.15	.07

*STARS: 2.5X TO 5X BASIC CARDS
*ROOKIES: 3X TO 6X BASIC CARDS
DISTRIBUTED ONLY IN FACTORY SET FORM

1988 Topps

	MINT	NRMT
COMPLETE SET (792)	12.00	5.50
COMP.FACT.SET (792)	15.00	6.75
COMMON CARD (1-792)	.05	.02
MINOR STARS	.10	.05
UNLISTED STARS	.20	.09
SUBSET CARDS HALF VALUE OF BASE CARDS		

☐ 1	Vince Coleman RB 100 Steals for Third Cons. Season	.05	.02
☐ 2	Don Mattingly RB Six Grand Slams	.15	.07
☐ 3	Mark McGwire RB Rookie Homer Record (No white spot)	1.00	.45
☐ 3A	Mark McGwire RB Rookie Homer Record (White spot behind left foot)	1.00	.45
☐ 4	Eddie Murray RB Switch Home Runs, Two Straight Games (No caption on front)	.10	
☐ 4A	Eddie Murray RB Switch Home Runs, Two Straight Games (Caption in box on card front)	.40	.18
☐ 5	Phil Niekro RB Joe Niekro RB Brothers Win Record	.10	.05
☐ 6	Nolan Ryan RB 11th 200 K's Season	.20	.09
☐ 7	Benito Santiago RB 34-Game Hitting Streak Rookie Record	.05	.02
☐ 8	Kevin Elster	.05	.02
☐ 9	Andy Hawkins	.05	.02
☐ 10	Ryne Sandberg	.25	.11
☐ 11	Mike Young	.05	.02
☐ 12	Bill Schroeder	.05	.02
☐ 13	Andres Thomas	.05	.02
☐ 14	Sparky Anderson MG	.10	.05
☐ 15	Chili Davis	.15	.07
☐ 16	Kirk McCaskill	.05	.02
☐ 17	Ron Oester	.05	.02
☐ 18A	Al Leiter ERR (Photo actually Steve George, right ear visible)	.20	.09
☐ 18B	Al Leiter COR (Left ear visible)	.40	.18
☐ 19	Mark Davidson	.05	.02
☐ 20	Kevin Gross	.05	.02
☐ 21	Red Sox TL Wade Boggs and Spike Owen	.10	.05
☐ 22	Greg Swindell	.05	.02
☐ 23	Ken Landreaux	.05	.02
☐ 24	Jim Deshaies	.05	.02
☐ 25	Andres Galarraga	.20	.09
☐ 26	Mitch Williams	.05	.02
☐ 27	R.J. Reynolds	.05	.02
☐ 28	Jose Nunez	.05	.02
☐ 29	Argenis Salazar	.05	.02
☐ 30	Sid Fernandez	.05	.02

☐ 31	Bruce Bochy	.05	.02
☐ 32	Mike Morgan	.05	.02
☐ 33	Rob Deer	.05	.02
☐ 34	Ricky Horton	.05	.02
☐ 35	Harold Baines	.10	.05
☐ 36	Jamie Moyer	.05	.02
☐ 37	Ed Romero	.05	.02
☐ 38	Jeff Calhoun	.05	.02
☐ 39	Gerald Perry	.05	.02
☐ 40	Orel Hershiser	.10	.05
☐ 41	Bob Melvin	.05	.02
☐ 42	Bill Landrum	.05	.02
☐ 43	Dick Schofield	.05	.02
☐ 44	Lou Piniella MG	.10	.05
☐ 45	Kent Hrbek	.10	.05
☐ 46	Darnell Coles	.05	.02
☐ 47	Joaquin Andujar	.05	.02
☐ 48	Alan Ashby	.05	.02
☐ 49	Dave Clark	.05	.02
☐ 50	Hubie Brooks	.05	.02
☐ 51	Orioles TL Eddie Murray and Cal Ripken	.40	.18
☐ 52	Don Robinson	.05	.02
☐ 53	Curt Wilkerson	.05	.02
☐ 54	Jim Clancy	.05	.02
☐ 55	Phil Bradley	.05	.02
☐ 56	Ed Hearn	.05	.02
☐ 57	Tim Crews	.05	.02
☐ 58	Dave Magadan	.05	.02
☐ 59	Danny Cox	.05	.02
☐ 60	Rickey Henderson	.25	.11
☐ 61	Mark Knudson	.05	.02
☐ 62	Jeff Hamilton	.05	.02
☐ 63	Jimmy Jones	.05	.02
☐ 64	Ken Caminiti	.50	.23
☐ 65	Leon Durham	.05	.02
☐ 66	Shane Rawley	.05	.02
☐ 67	Ken Oberkfell	.05	.02
☐ 68	Dave Dravecky	.10	.05
☐ 69	Mike Hart	.05	.02
☐ 70	Roger Clemens	.50	.23
☐ 71	Gary Pettis	.05	.02
☐ 72	Dennis Eckersley	.10	.05
☐ 73	Randy Bush	.05	.02
☐ 74	Tom Lasorda MG	.20	.09
☐ 75	Joe Carter	.20	.09
☐ 76	Dennis Martinez	.10	.05
☐ 77	Tom O'Malley	.05	.02
☐ 78	Dan Petry	.05	.02
☐ 79	Ernie Whitt	.05	.02
☐ 80	Mark Langston	.05	.02
☐ 81	Reds TL Ron Robinson and John Franco	.05	.02
☐ 82	Darrel Akerfelds	.05	.02
☐ 83	Jose Oquendo	.05	.02
☐ 84	Cecilio Guante	.05	.02
☐ 85	Howard Johnson	.05	.02
☐ 86	Ron Karkovice	.05	.02
☐ 87	Mike Mason	.05	.02
☐ 88	Earnie Riles	.05	.02
☐ 89	Gary Thurman	.05	.02
☐ 90	Dale Murphy	.20	.09
☐ 91	Joey Cora	.20	.09
☐ 92	Len Matuszek	.05	.02
☐ 93	Bob Sebra	.05	.02
☐ 94	Chuck Jackson	.05	.02
☐ 95	Lance Parrish	.05	.02
☐ 96	Todd Benzinger	.05	.02
☐ 97	Scott Garrelts	.05	.02
☐ 98	Rene Gonzales	.05	.02
☐ 99	Chuck Finley	.15	.07
☐ 100	Jack Clark	.10	.05
☐ 101	Allan Anderson	.05	.02
☐ 102	Barry Larkin	.20	.09
☐ 103	Curt Young	.05	.02
☐ 104	Dick Williams MG	.10	.05
☐ 105	Jesse Orosco	.05	.02
☐ 106	Jim Walewander	.05	.02
☐ 107	Scott Bailes	.05	.02
☐ 108	Steve Lyons	.05	.02
☐ 109	Joel Skinner	.05	.02
☐ 110	Teddy Higuera	.05	.02
☐ 111	Expos TL Hubie Brooks and Vance Law	.05	.02

☐ 112	Les Lancaster	.05	.02
☐ 113	Kelly Gruber	.05	.02
☐ 114	Jeff Russell	.05	.02
☐ 115	Johnny Ray	.05	.02
☐ 116	Jerry Don Gleaton	.05	.02
☐ 117	James Steels	.05	.02
☐ 118	Bob Welch	.05	.02
☐ 119	Robbie Wine	.05	.02
☐ 120	Kirby Puckett	.30	.14
☐ 121	Checklist 1-132	.05	.02
☐ 122	Tony Bernazard	.05	.02
☐ 123	Tom Candiotti	.05	.02
☐ 124	Ray Knight	.05	.02
☐ 125	Bruce Hurst	.05	.02
☐ 126	Steve Jeltz	.05	.02
☐ 127	Jim Gott	.05	.02
☐ 128	Johnny Grubb	.05	.02
☐ 129	Greg Minton	.05	.02
☐ 130	Buddy Bell	.10	.05
☐ 131	Don Schulze	.05	.02
☐ 132	Donnie Hill	.05	.02
☐ 133	Greg Mathews	.05	.02
☐ 134	Chuck Tanner MG	.10	.05
☐ 135	Dennis Rasmussen	.05	.02
☐ 136	Brian Dayett	.05	.02
☐ 137	Chris Bosio	.05	.02
☐ 138	Mitch Webster	.05	.02
☐ 139	Jerry Browne	.05	.02
☐ 140	Jesse Barfield	.05	.02
☐ 141	Royals TL George Brett and Bret Saberhagen	.20	.09
☐ 142	Andy Van Slyke	.10	.05
☐ 143	Mickey Tettleton	.10	.05
☐ 144	Don Gordon	.05	.02
☐ 145	Bill Madlock	.10	.05
☐ 146	Donell Nixon	.05	.02
☐ 147	Bill Buckner	.10	.05
☐ 148	Carmelo Martinez	.05	.02
☐ 149	Ken Howell	.05	.02
☐ 150	Eric Davis	.10	.05
☐ 151	Bob Knepper	.05	.02
☐ 152	Jody Reed	.10	.05
☐ 153	John Habyan	.05	.02
☐ 154	Jeff Stone	.05	.02
☐ 155	Bruce Sutter	.10	.05
☐ 156	Gary Matthews	.05	.02
☐ 157	Atlee Hammaker	.05	.02
☐ 158	Tim Hulett	.05	.02
☐ 159	Brad Arnsberg	.05	.02
☐ 160	Willie McGee	.10	.05
☐ 161	Bryn Smith	.05	.02
☐ 162	Mark McLemore	.05	.02
☐ 163	Dale Mohorcic	.05	.02
☐ 164	Dave Johnson MG	.10	.05
☐ 165	Robin Yount	.20	.09
☐ 166	Rick Rodriguez	.05	.02
☐ 167	Rance Mulliniks	.05	.02
☐ 168	Barry Jones	.05	.02
☐ 169	Ross Jones	.05	.02
☐ 170	Rich Gossage	.10	.05
☐ 171	Cubs TL Shawon Dunston and Manny Trillo	.05	.02
☐ 172	Lloyd McClendon	.05	.02
☐ 173	Eric Plunk	.05	.02
☐ 174	Phil Garner	.05	.02
☐ 175	Kevin Bass	.05	.02
☐ 176	Jeff Reed	.05	.02
☐ 177	Frank Tanana	.05	.02
☐ 178	Dwayne Henry	.05	.02
☐ 179	Charlie Puleo	.05	.02
☐ 180	Terry Kennedy	.05	.02
☐ 181	David Cone	.25	.11
☐ 182	Ken Phelps	.05	.02
☐ 183	Tom Lawless	.05	.02
☐ 184	Ivan Calderon	.05	.02
☐ 185	Rick Rhoden	.05	.02
☐ 186	Rafael Palmeiro	.40	.18
☐ 187	Steve Kiefer	.05	.02
☐ 188	John Russell	.05	.02
☐ 189	Wes Gardner	.05	.02
☐ 190	Candy Maldonado	.05	.02
☐ 191	John Cerutti	.05	.02
☐ 192	Devon White	.10	.05

❑ 193	Brian Fisher	.05	.02
❑ 194	Tom Kelly MG	.05	.02
❑ 195	Dan Quisenberry	.05	.02
❑ 196	Dave Engle	.05	.02
❑ 197	Lance McCullers	.05	.02
❑ 198	Franklin Stubbs	.05	.02
❑ 199	Dave Meads	.05	.02
❑ 200	Wade Boggs	.20	.09
❑ 201	Rangers TL	.05	.02
	Bobby Valentine MG		
	Pete O'Brien,		
	Pete Incaviglia and		
	Steve Buechele		
❑ 202	Glenn Hoffman	.05	.02
❑ 203	Fred Toliver	.05	.02
❑ 204	Paul O'Neill	.15	.07
❑ 205	Nelson Liriano	.05	.02
❑ 206	Domingo Ramos	.05	.02
❑ 207	John Mitchell	.05	.02
❑ 208	Steve Lake	.05	.02
❑ 209	Richard Dotson	.05	.02
❑ 210	Willie Randolph	.10	.05
❑ 211	Frank DiPino	.05	.02
❑ 212	Greg Brock	.05	.02
❑ 213	Albert Hall	.05	.02
❑ 214	Dave Schmidt	.05	.02
❑ 215	Von Hayes	.05	.02
❑ 216	Jerry Reuss	.05	.02
❑ 217	Harry Spilman	.05	.02
❑ 218	Dan Schatzeder	.05	.02
❑ 219	Mike Stanley	.10	.05
❑ 220	Tom Henke	.05	.02
❑ 221	Rafael Belliard	.05	.02
❑ 222	Steve Farr	.05	.02
❑ 223	Stan Jefferson	.05	.02
❑ 224	Tom Trebelhorn MG	.05	.02
❑ 225	Mike Scioscia	.05	.02
❑ 226	Dave Lopes	.10	.05
❑ 227	Ed Correa	.05	.02
❑ 228	Wallace Johnson	.05	.02
❑ 229	Jeff Musselman	.05	.02
❑ 230	Pat Tabler	.05	.02
❑ 231	Pirates TL	.20	.09
	Barry Bonds and		
	Bobby Bonilla		
❑ 232	Bob James	.05	.02
❑ 233	Rafael Santana	.05	.02
❑ 234	Ken Dayley	.05	.02
❑ 235	Gary Ward	.05	.02
❑ 236	Ted Power	.05	.02
❑ 237	Mike Heath	.05	.02
❑ 238	Luis Polonia	.05	.02
❑ 239	Roy Smalley	.05	.02
❑ 240	Lee Smith	.10	.05
❑ 241	Damaso Garcia	.05	.02
❑ 242	Tom Niedenfuer	.05	.02
❑ 243	Mark Ryal	.05	.02
❑ 244	Jeff D. Robinson	.05	.02
❑ 245	Rich Gedman	.05	.02
❑ 246	Mike Campbell	.05	.02
❑ 247	Thad Bosley	.05	.02
❑ 248	Storm Davis	.05	.02
❑ 249	Mike Marshall	.05	.02
❑ 250	Nolan Ryan	.75	.35
❑ 251	Tom Foley	.05	.02
❑ 252	Bob Brower	.05	.02
❑ 253	Checklist 133-264	.05	.02
❑ 254	Lee Elia MG	.05	.02
❑ 255	Mookie Wilson	.10	.05
❑ 256	Ken Schrom	.05	.02
❑ 257	Jerry Royster	.05	.02
❑ 258	Ed Nunez	.05	.02
❑ 259	Ron Kittle	.05	.02
❑ 260	Vince Coleman	.10	.05
❑ 261	Giants TL	.05	.02
	(Five players)		
❑ 262	Drew Hall	.05	.02
❑ 263	Glenn Braggs	.05	.02
❑ 264	Les Straker	.05	.02
❑ 265	Bo Diaz	.05	.02
❑ 266	Paul Assenmacher	.05	.02
❑ 267	Billy Bean	.05	.02
❑ 268	Bruce Ruffin	.05	.02
❑ 269	Ellis Burks	.25	.11
❑ 270	Mike Witt	.05	.02
❑ 271	Ken Gerhart	.05	.02
❑ 272	Steve Ontiveros	.05	.02
❑ 273	Garth Iorg	.05	.02
❑ 274	Junior Ortiz	.05	.02
❑ 275	Kevin Seitzer	.10	.05
❑ 276	Luis Salazar	.05	.02
❑ 277	Alejandro Pena	.05	.02
❑ 278	Jose Cruz	.05	.02
❑ 279	Randy St.Claire	.05	.02
❑ 280	Pete Incaviglia	.05	.02
❑ 281	Jerry Hairston	.05	.02
❑ 282	Pat Perry	.05	.02
❑ 283	Phil Lombardi	.05	.02
❑ 284	Larry Bowa MG	.05	.02
❑ 285	Jim Presley	.05	.02
❑ 286	Chuck Crim	.05	.02
❑ 287	Manny Trillo	.05	.02
❑ 288	Pat Pacillo	.05	.02
	(Chris Sabo in		
	background of photo)		
❑ 289	Dave Bergman	.05	.02
❑ 290	Tony Fernandez	.10	.05
❑ 291	Astros TL	.05	.02
	Billy Hatcher		
	and Kevin Bass		
❑ 292	Carney Lansford	.10	.05
❑ 293	Doug Jones	.20	.09
❑ 294	Al Pedrique	.05	.02
❑ 295	Bert Blyleven	.10	.05
❑ 296	Floyd Rayford	.05	.02
❑ 297	Zane Smith	.05	.02
❑ 298	Milt Thompson	.05	.02
❑ 299	Steve Crawford	.05	.02
❑ 300	Don Mattingly	.40	.18
❑ 301	Bud Black	.05	.02
❑ 302	Jose Uribe	.05	.02
❑ 303	Eric Show	.05	.02
❑ 304	George Hendrick	.05	.02
❑ 305	Steve Sax	.10	.05
❑ 306	Billy Hatcher	.05	.02
❑ 307	Mike Trujillo	.05	.02
❑ 308	Lee Mazzilli	.05	.02
❑ 309	Bill Long	.05	.02
❑ 310	Tom Herr	.05	.02
❑ 311	Scott Sanderson	.05	.02
❑ 312	Joey Meyer	.05	.02
❑ 313	Bob McClure	.05	.02
❑ 314	Jimy Williams MG	.05	.02
❑ 315	Dave Parker	.10	.05
❑ 316	Jose Rijo	.05	.02
❑ 317	Tom Nieto	.05	.02
❑ 318	Mel Hall	.05	.02
❑ 319	Mike Loynd	.05	.02
❑ 320	Alan Trammell	.15	.07
❑ 321	White Sox TL	.10	.05
	Harold Baines and		
	Carlton Fisk		
❑ 322	Vicente Palacios	.05	.02
❑ 323	Rick Leach	.05	.02
❑ 324	Danny Jackson	.05	.02
❑ 325	Glenn Hubbard	.05	.02
❑ 326	Al Nipper	.05	.02
❑ 327	Larry Sheets	.05	.02
❑ 328	Greg Cadaret	.05	.02
❑ 329	Chris Speier	.05	.02
❑ 330	Eddie Whitson	.05	.02
❑ 331	Brian Downing	.05	.02
❑ 332	Jerry Reed	.05	.02
❑ 333	Wally Backman	.05	.02
❑ 334	Dave LaPoint	.05	.02
❑ 335	Claudell Washington	.05	.02
❑ 336	Ed Lynch	.05	.02
❑ 337	Jim Gantner	.05	.02
❑ 338	Brian Holton UER	.05	.02
	(1987 ERA .389,		
	should be 3.89)		
❑ 339	Kurt Stillwell	.05	.02
❑ 340	Jack Morris	.10	.05
❑ 341	Carmen Castillo	.05	.02
❑ 342	Larry Andersen	.05	.02
❑ 343	Greg Gagne	.05	.02
❑ 344	Tony LaRussa MG	.10	.05
❑ 345	Scott Fletcher	.05	.02
❑ 346	Vance Law	.05	.02
❑ 347	Joe Johnson	.05	.02
❑ 348	Jim Eisenreich	.20	.09
❑ 349	Bob Walk	.05	.02
❑ 350	Will Clark	.25	.11
❑ 351	Cardinals TL	.10	.05
	Red Schoendienst CO		
	and Tony Pena		
❑ 352	Bill Ripken	.05	.02
❑ 353	Ed Olwine	.05	.02
❑ 354	Marc Sullivan	.05	.02
❑ 355	Roger McDowell	.05	.02
❑ 356	Luis Aguayo	.05	.02
❑ 357	Floyd Bannister	.05	.02
❑ 358	Rey Quinones	.05	.02
❑ 359	Tim Stoddard	.05	.02
❑ 360	Tony Gwynn	.50	.23
❑ 361	Greg Maddux	1.00	.45
❑ 362	Juan Castillo	.05	.02
❑ 363	Willie Fraser	.05	.02
❑ 364	Nick Esasky	.05	.02
❑ 365	Floyd Youmans	.05	.02
❑ 366	Chet Lemon	.05	.02
❑ 367	Tim Leary	.05	.02
❑ 368	Gerald Young	.05	.02
❑ 369	Greg Harris	.05	.02
❑ 370	Jose Canseco	.40	.18
❑ 371	Joe Hesketh	.05	.02
❑ 372	Matt Williams	1.00	.45
❑ 373	Checklist 265-396	.05	.02
❑ 374	Doc Edwards MG	.05	.02
❑ 375	Tom Brunansky	.05	.02
❑ 376	Bill Wilkinson	.05	.02
❑ 377	Sam Horn	.05	.02
❑ 378	Todd Frohwirth	.05	.02
❑ 379	Rafael Ramirez	.05	.02
❑ 380	Joe Magrane	.05	.02
❑ 381	Angels TL	.10	.05
	Wally Joyner and		
	Jack Howell		
❑ 382	Keith A. Miller	.05	.02
❑ 383	Eric Bell	.05	.02
❑ 384	Neil Allen	.05	.02
❑ 385	Carlton Fisk	.20	.09
❑ 386	Don Mattingly AS	.15	.07
❑ 387	Willie Randolph AS	.05	.02
❑ 388	Wade Boggs AS	.10	.05
❑ 389	Alan Trammell AS	.10	.05
❑ 390	George Bell AS	.05	.02
❑ 391	Kirby Puckett AS	.20	.09
❑ 392	Dave Winfield AS	.20	.09
❑ 393	Matt Nokes AS	.05	.02
❑ 394	Roger Clemens AS	.20	.09
❑ 395	Jimmy Key AS	.05	.02
❑ 396	Tom Henke AS	.05	.02
❑ 397	Jack Clark AS	.10	.05
❑ 398	Juan Samuel AS	.05	.02
❑ 399	Tim Wallach AS	.05	.02
❑ 400	Ozzie Smith AS	.15	.07
❑ 401	Andre Dawson AS	.20	.09
❑ 402	Tony Gwynn AS	.20	.09
❑ 403	Tim Raines AS	.10	.05
❑ 404	Benny Santiago AS	.05	.02
❑ 405	Dwight Gooden AS	.10	.05
❑ 406	Shane Rawley AS	.05	.02
❑ 407	Steve Bedrosian AS	.05	.02
❑ 408	Dion James	.05	.02
❑ 409	Joel McKeon	.05	.02
❑ 410	Tony Pena	.05	.02
❑ 411	Wayne Tolleson	.05	.02
❑ 412	Randy Myers	.15	.07
❑ 413	John Christensen	.05	.02
❑ 414	John McNamara MG	.05	.02
❑ 415	Don Carman	.05	.02
❑ 416	Keith Moreland	.05	.02
❑ 417	Mark Ciardi	.05	.02
❑ 418	Joel Youngblood	.05	.02
❑ 419	Scott McGregor	.05	.02
❑ 420	Wally Joyner	.15	.07
❑ 421	Ed VandeBerg	.05	.02
❑ 422	Dave Concepcion	.10	.05
❑ 423	John Smiley	.10	.05
❑ 424	Dwayne Murphy	.05	.02
❑ 425	Jeff Reardon	.10	.05
❑ 426	Randy Ready	.05	.02
❑ 427	Paul Kilgus	.05	.02
❑ 428	John Shelby	.05	.02
❑ 429	Tigers TL	.10	.05
	Alan Trammell and		
	Kirk Gibson		

430	Glenn Davis	.05	.02
431	Casey Candaele	.05	.02
432	Mike Moore	.05	.02
433	Bill Pecota	.05	.02
434	Rick Aguilera	.10	.05
435	Mike Pagliarulo	.05	.02
436	Mike Bielecki	.05	.02
437	Fred Manrique	.05	.02
438	Rob Ducey	.05	.02
439	Dave Martinez	.05	.02
440	Steve Bedrosian	.05	.02
441	Rick Manning	.05	.02
442	Tom Bolton	.05	.02
443	Ken Griffey	.10	.05
444	Cal Ripken Sr. MG UER two copyrights	.05	.02
445	Mike Krukow	.05	.02
446	Doug DeCinces (Now with Cardinals on card front)	.05	.02
447	Jeff Montgomery	.20	.09
448	Mike Davis	.05	.02
449	Jeff M. Robinson	.05	.02
450	Barry Bonds	.50	.23
451	Keith Atherton	.05	.02
452	Willie Wilson	.05	.02
453	Dennis Powell	.05	.02
454	Marvell Wynne	.05	.02
455	Shawn Hillegas	.05	.02
456	Dave Anderson	.05	.02
457	Terry Leach	.05	.02
458	Ron Hassey	.05	.02
459	Yankees TL Dave Winfield and Willie Randolph	.20	.09
460	Ozzie Smith	.25	.11
461	Danny Darwin	.05	.02
462	Don Slaught	.05	.02
463	Fred McGriff	.20	.09
464	Jay Tibbs	.05	.02
465	Paul Molitor	.20	.09
466	Jerry Mumphrey	.05	.02
467	Don Aase	.05	.02
468	Darren Daulton	.10	.05
469	Jeff Dedmon	.05	.02
470	Dwight Evans	.10	.05
471	Donnie Moore	.05	.02
472	Robby Thompson	.05	.02
473	Joe Niekro	.05	.02
474	Tom Brookens	.05	.02
475	Pete Rose MG	.40	.18
476	Dave Stewart	.10	.05
477	Jamie Quirk	.05	.02
478	Sid Bream	.05	.02
479	Brett Butler	.10	.05
480	Dwight Gooden	.10	.05
481	Mariano Duncan	.05	.02
482	Mark Davis	.05	.02
483	Rod Booker	.05	.02
484	Pat Clements	.05	.02
485	Harold Reynolds	.10	.05
486	Pat Keedy	.05	.02
487	Jim Pankovits	.05	.02
488	Andy McGaffigan	.05	.02
489	Dodgers TL Pedro Guerrero and Fernando Valenzuela	.05	.02
490	Larry Parrish	.05	.02
491	B.J. Surhoff	.10	.05
492	Doyle Alexander	.05	.02
493	Mike Greenwell	.05	.02
494	Wally Ritchie	.05	.02
495	Eddie Murray	.20	.09
496	Guy Hoffman	.05	.02
497	Kevin Mitchell	.10	.05
498	Bob Boone	.10	.05
499	Eric King	.05	.02
500	Andre Dawson	.20	.09
501	Tim Birtsas	.05	.02
502	Dan Gladden	.05	.02
503	Junior Noboa	.05	.02
504	Bob Rodgers MG	.05	.02
505	Willie Upshaw	.05	.02
506	John Cangelosi	.05	.02
507	Mark Gubicza	.05	.02
508	Tim Teufel	.05	.02
509	Bill Dawley	.05	.02
510	Dave Winfield	.20	.09
511	Joel Davis	.05	.02
512	Alex Trevino	.05	.02
513	Tim Flannery	.05	.02
514	Pat Sheridan	.05	.02
515	Juan Nieves	.05	.02
516	Jim Sundberg	.05	.02
517	Ron Robinson	.05	.02
518	Greg Gross	.05	.02
519	Mariners TL Harold Reynolds and Phil Bradley	.05	.02
520	Dave Smith	.05	.02
521	Jim Dwyer	.05	.02
522	Bob Patterson	.05	.02
523	Gary Roenicke	.05	.02
524	Gary Lucas	.05	.02
525	Marty Barrett	.05	.02
526	Juan Berenguer	.05	.02
527	Steve Henderson	.05	.02
528A	Checklist 397-528 ERR (455 S. Carlton)	.20	.02
528B	Checklist 397-528 COR (455 S. Hillegas)	.10	.05
529	Tim Burke	.05	.02
530	Gary Carter	.15	.07
531	Rich Yett	.05	.02
532	Mike Kingery	.05	.02
533	John Farrell	.05	.02
534	John Wathan MG	.05	.02
535	Ron Guidry	.05	.02
536	John Morris	.05	.02
537	Steve Buechele	.05	.02
538	Bill Wegman	.05	.02
539	Mike LaValliere	.05	.02
540	Bret Saberhagen	.10	.05
541	Juan Beniquez	.05	.02
542	Paul Noce	.05	.02
543	Kent Tekulve	.05	.02
544	Jim Traber	.05	.02
545	Don Baylor	.10	.05
546	John Candelaria	.05	.02
547	Felix Fermin	.05	.02
548	Shane Mack	.05	.02
549	Braves TL Albert Hall, Dale Murphy, Ken Griffey and Dion James	.05	.02
550	Pedro Guerrero	.05	.02
551	Terry Steinbach	.10	.05
552	Mark Thurmond	.05	.02
553	Tracy Jones	.05	.02
554	Mike Smithson	.05	.02
555	Brook Jacoby	.05	.02
556	Stan Clarke	.05	.02
557	Craig Reynolds	.05	.02
558	Bob Ojeda	.05	.02
559	Ken Williams	.05	.02
560	Tim Wallach	.05	.02
561	Rick Cerone	.05	.02
562	Jim Lindeman	.05	.02
563	Jose Guzman	.05	.02
564	Frank Lucchesi MG	.05	.02
565	Lloyd Moseby	.05	.02
566	Charlie O'Brien	.05	.02
567	Mike Diaz	.05	.02
568	Chris Brown	.05	.02
569	Charlie Leibrandt	.05	.02
570	Jeffrey Leonard	.05	.02
571	Mark Williamson	.05	.02
572	Chris James	.05	.02
573	Bob Stanley	.05	.02
574	Graig Nettles	.10	.05
575	Don Sutton	.20	.09
576	Tommy Hinzo	.05	.02
577	Tom Browning	.05	.02
578	Gary Gaetti	.10	.05
579	Mets TL Gary Carter and Kevin McReynolds	.05	.02
580	Mark McGwire	2.00	.90
581	Tito Landrum	.05	.02
582	Mike Henneman	.10	.05
583	Dave Valle	.05	.02
584	Steve Trout	.05	.02
585	Ozzie Guillen	.05	.02
586	Bob Forsch	.05	.02
587	Terry Puhl	.05	.02
588	Jeff Parrett	.05	.02
589	Geno Petralli	.05	.02
590	George Bell	.05	.02
591	Doug Drabek	.05	.02
592	Dale Sveum	.05	.02
593	Bob Tewksbury	.05	.02
594	Bobby Valentine MG	.10	.05
595	Frank White	.10	.05
596	John Kruk	.10	.05
597	Gene Garber	.05	.02
598	Lee Lacy	.05	.02
599	Calvin Schiraldi	.05	.02
600	Mike Schmidt	.30	.14
601	Jack Lazorko	.05	.02
602	Mike Aldrete	.05	.02
603	Rob Murphy	.05	.02
604	Chris Bando	.05	.02
605	Kirk Gibson	.10	.05
606	Moose Haas	.05	.02
607	Mickey Hatcher	.05	.02
608	Charlie Kerfeld	.05	.02
609	Twins TL Gary Gaetti and Kent Hrbek	.10	.05
610	Keith Hernandez	.10	.05
611	Tommy John	.10	.05
612	Curt Ford	.05	.02
613	Bobby Thigpen	.05	.02
614	Herm Winningham	.05	.02
615	Jody Davis	.05	.02
616	Jay Aldrich	.05	.02
617	Oddibe McDowell	.05	.02
618	Cecil Fielder	.15	.07
619	Mike Dunne (Inconsistent design, black name on front)	.05	.02
620	Cory Snyder	.05	.02
621	Gene Nelson	.05	.02
622	Kal Daniels	.05	.02
623	Mike Flanagan	.05	.02
624	Jim Leyland MG	.10	.05
625	Frank Viola	.05	.02
626	Glenn Wilson	.05	.02
627	Joe Boever	.05	.02
628	Dave Henderson	.05	.02
629	Kelly Downs	.05	.02
630	Darrell Evans	.10	.05
631	Jack Howell	.05	.02
632	Steve Shields	.05	.02
633	Barry Lyons	.05	.02
634	Jose DeLeon	.05	.02
635	Terry Pendleton	.10	.05
636	Charles Hudson	.05	.02
637	Jay Bell	.50	.23
638	Steve Balboni	.05	.02
639	Brewers TL Glenn Braggs and Tony Muser CO	.05	.02
640	Garry Templeton (Inconsistent design, green border)	.05	.02
641	Rick Honeycutt	.05	.02
642	Bob Dernier	.05	.02
643	Rocky Childress	.05	.02
644	Terry McGriff	.05	.02
645	Matt Nokes	.05	.02
646	Checklist 529-660	.05	.02
647	Pascual Perez	.05	.02
648	Al Newman	.05	.02
649	DeWayne Buice	.05	.02
650	Cal Ripken	.75	.35
651	Mike Jackson	.20	.09
652	Bruce Benedict	.05	.02
653	Jeff Sellers	.05	.02
654	Roger Craig MG	.10	.05
655	Len Dykstra	.10	.05
656	Lee Guetterman	.05	.02
657	Gary Redus	.05	.02
658	Tim Conroy (Inconsistent design, name in white)	.05	.02
659	Bobby Meacham	.05	.02

☐ 660 Rick Reuschel	.05	.02
☐ 661 Nolan Ryan TBC '83	.20	.09
☐ 662 Jim Rice TBC '78	.05	.02
☐ 663 Ron Blomberg TBC '73	.05	.02
☐ 664 Bob Gibson TBC '68	.20	.09
☐ 665 Stan Musial TBC '63	.20	.09
☐ 666 Mario Soto	.05	.02
☐ 667 Luis Quinones	.05	.02
☐ 668 Walt Terrell	.05	.02
☐ 669 Phillies TL	.05	.02
Lance Parrish		
and Mike Ryan CO		
☐ 670 Dan Plesac	.05	.02
☐ 671 Tim Laudner	.05	.02
☐ 672 John Davis	.05	.02
☐ 673 Tony Phillips	.05	.02
☐ 674 Mike Fitzgerald	.05	.02
☐ 675 Jim Rice	.10	.05
☐ 676 Ken Dixon	.05	.02
☐ 677 Eddie Milner	.05	.02
☐ 678 Jim Acker	.05	.02
☐ 679 Darrell Miller	.05	.02
☐ 680 Charlie Hough	.10	.02
☐ 681 Bobby Bonilla	.15	.07
☐ 682 Jimmy Key	.10	.05
☐ 683 Julio Franco	.05	.02
☐ 684 Hal Lanier MG	.05	.02
☐ 685 Ron Darling	.05	.02
☐ 686 Terry Francona	.05	.02
☐ 687 Mickey Brantley	.05	.02
☐ 688 Jim Winn	.05	.02
☐ 689 Tom Pagnozzi	.05	.02
☐ 690 Jay Howell	.05	.02
☐ 691 Dan Pasqua	.05	.02
☐ 692 Mike Birkbeck	.05	.02
☐ 693 Benito Santiago	.05	.02
☐ 694 Eric Nolte	.05	.02
☐ 695 Shawon Dunston	.05	.02
☐ 696 Duane Ward	.05	.02
☐ 697 Steve Lombardozzi	.05	.02
☐ 698 Brad Havens	.05	.02
☐ 699 Padres TL	.10	.05
Benito Santiago		
and Tony Gwynn		
☐ 700 George Brett	.40	.18
☐ 701 Sammy Stewart	.05	.02
☐ 702 Mike Gallego	.05	.02
☐ 703 Bob Brenly	.05	.02
☐ 704 Dennis Boyd	.05	.02
☐ 705 Juan Samuel	.05	.02
☐ 706 Rick Mahler	.05	.02
☐ 707 Fred Lynn	.10	.05
☐ 708 Gus Polidor	.05	.02
☐ 709 George Frazier	.05	.02
☐ 710 Darryl Strawberry	.10	.05
☐ 711 Bill Gullickson	.05	.02
☐ 712 John Moses	.05	.02
☐ 713 Willie Hernandez	.05	.02
☐ 714 Jim Fregosi MG	.05	.02
☐ 715 Todd Worrell	.10	.05
☐ 716 Lenn Sakata	.05	.02
☐ 717 Jay Baller	.05	.02
☐ 718 Mike Felder	.05	.02
☐ 719 Denny Walling	.05	.02
☐ 720 Tim Raines	.10	.05
☐ 721 Pete O'Brien	.05	.02
☐ 722 Manny Lee	.05	.02
☐ 723 Bob Kipper	.05	.02
☐ 724 Danny Tartabull	.15	.02
☐ 725 Mike Boddicker	.05	.02
☐ 726 Alfredo Griffin	.05	.02
☐ 727 Greg Booker	.05	.02
☐ 728 Andy Allanson	.05	.02
☐ 729 Blue Jays TL	.10	.05
George Bell and		
Fred McGriff		
☐ 730 John Franco	.10	.05
☐ 731 Rick Schu	.05	.02
☐ 732 David Palmer	.05	.02
☐ 733 Spike Owen	.05	.02
☐ 734 Craig Lefferts	.05	.02
☐ 735 Kevin McReynolds	.05	.02
☐ 736 Matt Young	.05	.02
☐ 737 Butch Wynegar	.05	.02
☐ 738 Scott Bankhead	.05	.02
☐ 739 Daryl Boston	.05	.02

☐ 740 Rick Sutcliffe	.05	.02
☐ 741 Mike Easler	.05	.02
☐ 742 Mark Clear	.05	.02
☐ 743 Larry Herndon	.05	.02
☐ 744 Whitey Herzog MG	.10	.05
☐ 745 Bill Doran	.05	.02
☐ 746 Gene Larkin	.05	.02
☐ 747 Bobby Witt	.05	.02
☐ 748 Reid Nichols	.05	.02
☐ 749 Mark Eichhorn	.05	.02
☐ 750 Bo Jackson	.20	.09
☐ 751 Jim Morrison	.05	.02
☐ 752 Mark Grant	.05	.02
☐ 753 Danny Heep	.05	.02
☐ 754 Mike LaCoss	.05	.02
☐ 755 Ozzie Virgil	.05	.02
☐ 756 Mike Maddux	.05	.02
☐ 757 John Marzano	.05	.02
☐ 758 Eddie Williams	.10	.05
☐ 759 A's TL UER	1.00	.45
Mark McGwire		
and Jose Canseco		
(two copyrights)		
☐ 760 Mike Scott	.05	.02
☐ 761 Tony Armas	.05	.02
☐ 762 Scott Bradley	.05	.02
☐ 763 Doug Sisk	.05	.02
☐ 764 Greg Walker	.05	.02
☐ 765 Neal Heaton	.05	.02
☐ 766 Henry Cotto	.05	.02
☐ 767 Jose Lind	.05	.02
☐ 768 Dickie Noles	.05	.02
(Now with Tigers		
on card front)		
☐ 769 Cecil Cooper	.10	.05
☐ 770 Lou Whitaker	.10	.05
☐ 771 Ruben Sierra	.25	.11
☐ 772 Sal Butera	.05	.02
☐ 773 Frank Williams	.05	.02
☐ 774 Gene Mauch MG	.05	.02
☐ 775 Dave Stieb	.05	.02
☐ 776 Checklist 661-792	.05	.02
☐ 777 Lonnie Smith	.05	.02
☐ 778A Keith Comstock ERR	2.00	.90
(White "Padres")		
☐ 778B Keith Comstock COR	.05	.02
(Blue "Padres")		
☐ 779 Tom Glavine	1.00	.45
☐ 780 Fernando Valenzuela	.10	.05
☐ 781 Keith Hughes	.05	.02
☐ 782 Jeff Ballard	.05	.02
☐ 783 Ron Roenicke	.05	.02
☐ 784 Joe Sambito	.05	.02
☐ 785 Alvin Davis	.05	.02
☐ 786 Joe Price	.05	.02
(Inconsistent design,		
orange team name)		
☐ 787 Bill Almon	.05	.02
☐ 788 Ray Searage	.05	.02
☐ 789 Indians TL	.10	.05
Joe Carter and		
Cory Snyder		
☐ 790 Dave Righetti	.05	.02
☐ 791 Ted Simmons	.10	.05
☐ 792 John Tudor	.05	.02

1988 Topps Tiffany

	MINT	NRMT
COMP.FACT.SET (792)	100.00	45.00
COMMON CARD (1-792)	.15	.07
*STARS: 5X TO 10X BASIC CARDS		
*ROOKIES: 7.5X TO 15X BASIC CARDS		
DISTRIBUTED ONLY IN FACTORY SET FORM		

1988 Topps Rookies

	MINT	NRMT
COMPLETE SET (22)	25.00	11.00
COMMON PLAYER (1-22)	.25	.11
MINOR STARS	.50	.23
ONE PER RETAIL JUMBO PACK		

☐ 1 Bill Ripken	.25	.11
☐ 2 Ellis Burks	.75	.35
☐ 3 Mike Greenwell	.25	.11
☐ 4 DeWayne Buice	.25	.11
☐ 5 Devon White	.50	.23
☐ 6 Fred Manrique	.25	.11
☐ 7 Mike Henneman	.50	.23
☐ 8 Matt Nokes	.25	.11
☐ 9 Kevin Seitzer	.50	.23
☐ 10 B.J. Surhoff	.50	.23
☐ 11 Casey Candaele	.25	.11
☐ 12 Randy Myers	.60	.25
☐ 13 Mark McGwire	20.00	9.00
☐ 14 Luis Polonia	.25	.11
☐ 15 Terry Steinbach	.50	.23
☐ 16 Mike Dunne	.25	.11
☐ 17 Al Pedrique	.25	.11
☐ 18 Benito Santiago	.50	.23
☐ 19 Kelly Downs	.25	.11
☐ 20 Joe Magrane	.25	.11
☐ 21 Jerry Browne	.25	.11
☐ 22 Jeff Musselman	.25	.11

1988 Topps Traded

	MINT	NRMT
COMP.FACT.SET (132)	10.00	4.50
COMMON CARD (1T-132T)	.10	.05
MINOR STARS	.20	.09
SEMISTARS	.30	.14
UNLISTED STARS	.50	.23

☐ 1T Jim Abbott OLY	.50	.23
☐ 2T Juan Agosto	.10	.05
☐ 3T Luis Alicea	.20	.09
☐ 4T Roberto Alomar	3.00	1.35

	MINT	NRMT
❑ 5T Brady Anderson	1.00	.45
❑ 6T Jack Armstrong	.10	.05
❑ 7T Don August	.10	.05
❑ 8T Floyd Bannister	.10	.05
❑ 9T Bret Barberie OLY	.20	.09
❑ 10T Jose Bautista	.10	.05
❑ 11T Don Baylor	.20	.09
❑ 12T Tim Belcher	.20	.09
❑ 13T Buddy Bell	.20	.09
❑ 14T Andy Benes OLY	.50	.23
❑ 15T Damon Berryhill	.10	.05
❑ 16T Bud Black	.10	.05
❑ 17T Pat Borders	.20	.09
❑ 18T Phil Bradley	.10	.05
❑ 19T Jeff Branson OLY	.20	.09
❑ 20T Tom Brunansky	.10	.05
❑ 21T Jay Buhner	.75	.35
❑ 22T Brett Butler	.20	.09
❑ 23T Jim Campanis OLY	.10	.05
❑ 24T Sil Campusano	.10	.05
❑ 25T John Candelaria	.10	.05
❑ 26T Jose Cecena	.10	.05
❑ 27T Rick Cerone	.10	.05
❑ 28T Jack Clark	.20	.09
❑ 29T Kevin Coffman	.10	.05
❑ 30T Pat Combs OLY	.10	.05
❑ 31T Henry Cotto	.10	.05
❑ 32T Chili Davis	.30	.14
❑ 33T Mike Davis	.10	.05
❑ 34T Jose DeLeon	.10	.05
❑ 35T Richard Dotson	.10	.05
❑ 36T Cecil Espy	.10	.05
❑ 37T Tom Filer	.10	.05
❑ 38T Mike Fiore OLY	.10	.05
❑ 39T Ron Gant	.50	.23
❑ 40T Kirk Gibson	.50	.23
❑ 41T Rich Gossage	.20	.09
❑ 42T Mark Grace	2.00	.90
❑ 43T Alfredo Griffin	.10	.05
❑ 44T Ty Griffin OLY	.10	.05
❑ 45T Bryan Harvey	.20	.09
❑ 46T Ron Hassey	.10	.05
❑ 47T Ray Hayward	.10	.05
❑ 48T Dave Henderson	.10	.05
❑ 49T Tom Herr	.10	.05
❑ 50T Bob Horner	.10	.05
❑ 51T Ricky Horton	.10	.05
❑ 52T Jay Howell	.10	.05
❑ 53T Glenn Hubbard	.10	.05
❑ 54T Jeff Innis	.10	.05
❑ 55T Danny Jackson	.10	.05
❑ 56T Darrin Jackson	.20	.09
❑ 57T Roberto Kelly	.50	.23
❑ 58T Ron Kittle	.10	.05
❑ 59T Ray Knight	.10	.05
❑ 60T Vance Law	.10	.05
❑ 61T Jeffrey Leonard	.10	.05
❑ 62T Mike Macfarlane	.10	.05
❑ 63T Scotti Madison	.10	.05
❑ 64T Kirt Manwaring	.10	.05
❑ 65T Mark Marquess OLY CO	.10	.05
❑ 66T Tino Martinez OLY	2.50	1.10
❑ 67T Billy Masse OLY	.10	.05
❑ 68T Jack McDowell	.50	.23
❑ 69T Jack McKeon MG	.10	.05
❑ 70T Larry McWilliams	.10	.05
❑ 71T Mickey Morandini OLY	.50	.23
❑ 72T Keith Moreland	.10	.05
❑ 73T Mike Morgan	.10	.05
❑ 74T Charles Nagy OLY	.50	.23
❑ 75T Al Nipper	.10	.05
❑ 76T Russ Nixon MG	.10	.05
❑ 77T Jesse Orosco	.10	.05
❑ 78T Joe Orsulak	.10	.05
❑ 79T Dave Palmer	.10	.05
❑ 80T Mark Parent	.10	.05
❑ 81T Dave Parker	.20	.09
❑ 82T Dan Pasqua	.10	.05
❑ 83T Melido Perez	.10	.05
❑ 84T Steve Peters	.10	.05
❑ 85T Dan Petry	.10	.05
❑ 86T Gary Pettis	.10	.05
❑ 87T Jeff Pico	.10	.05
❑ 88T Jim Poole OLY	.20	.09
❑ 89T Ted Power	.10	.05
❑ 90T Rafael Ramirez	.10	.05
❑ 91T Dennis Rasmussen	.10	.05
❑ 92T Jose Rijo	.10	.05
❑ 93T Ernie Riles	.10	.05
❑ 94T Luis Rivera	.10	.05
❑ 95T Doug Robbins OLY	.10	.05
❑ 96T Frank Robinson MG	.30	.14
❑ 97T Cookie Rojas MG	.10	.05
❑ 98T Chris Sabo	.20	.09
❑ 99T Mark Salas	.10	.05
❑ 100T Luis Salazar	.10	.05
❑ 101T Rafael Santana	.10	.05
❑ 102T Nelson Santovenia	.10	.05
❑ 103T Mackey Sasser	.10	.05
❑ 104T Calvin Schiraldi	.10	.05
❑ 105T Mike Schooler	.10	.05
❑ 106T Scott Servais OLY	.10	.05
❑ 107T Dave Silvestri OLY	.10	.05
❑ 108T Don Slaught	.10	.05
❑ 109T Joe Slusarski OLY	.10	.05
❑ 110T Lee Smith	.20	.09
❑ 111T Pete Smith	.10	.05
❑ 112T Jim Snyder MG	.10	.05
❑ 113T Ed Sprague OLY	.50	.23
❑ 114T Pete Stanicek	.10	.05
❑ 115T Kurt Stillwell	.10	.05
❑ 116T Todd Stottlemyre	.50	.23
❑ 117T Bill Swift	.10	.05
❑ 118T Pat Tabler	.10	.05
❑ 119T Scott Terry	.10	.05
❑ 120T Mickey Tettleton	.20	.09
❑ 121T Dickie Thon	.10	.05
❑ 122T Jeff Treadway	.10	.05
❑ 123T Willie Upshaw	.10	.05
❑ 124T Robin Ventura OLY	4.00	1.80
❑ 125T Ron Washington	.10	.05
❑ 126T Walt Weiss	.50	.23
❑ 127T Bob Welch	.10	.05
❑ 128T David Wells	1.00	.45
❑ 129T Glenn Wilson	.10	.05
❑ 130T Ted Wood OLY	.10	.05
❑ 131T Don Zimmer MG	.20	.09
❑ 132T Checklist 1T-132T	.10	.05

1988 Topps Traded Tiffany

	MINT	NRMT
COMP.FACT.SET (132)	60.00	27.00
COMMON CARD (1T-132T)	.15	.07
*STARS: 2X TO 4X BASIC CARDS		
*ROOKIES: 3X TO 6X BASIC CARDS		
*OLY ROOKIES: 2X TO 4X BASIC CARDS		
DISTRIBUTED ONLY IN FACTORY SET FORM		

1989 Topps

	MINT	NRMT
COMPLETE SET (792)	12.00	5.50
COMP.FACT.SET (792)	20.00	9.00
COMMON CARD (1-792)	.05	.02
MINOR STARS	.10	.05
UNLISTED STARS	.20	.09

	MINT	NRMT
❑ 1 George Bell RB Slams 3 Opening Day HR's	.05	.02
❑ 2 Wade Boggs RB 200 Hits 6th Straight Season	.10	.05
❑ 3 Gary Carter RB Career Putouts Record	.05	.02
❑ 4 Andre Dawson RB	.10	.05

ERIC DAVIS

Logs Double Figures in HR and SB		
❑ 5 Orel Hershiser RB 59 Scoreless Innings	.10	.05
❑ 6 Doug Jones RB UER Earns His 15th Straight Save (Photo actually Chris Codiroli)	.05	.02
❑ 7 Kevin McReynolds RB Steals 21 Without Being Caught	.05	.02
❑ 8 Dave Eiland	.05	.02
❑ 9 Tim Teufel	.05	.02
❑ 10 Andre Dawson	.20	.09
❑ 11 Bruce Sutter	.05	.02
❑ 12 Dale Sveum	.05	.02
❑ 13 Doug Sisk	.05	.02
❑ 14 Tom Kelly MG	.05	.02
❑ 15 Robby Thompson	.05	.02
❑ 16 Ron Robinson	.05	.02
❑ 17 Brian Downing	.05	.02
❑ 18 Rick Rhoden	.05	.02
❑ 19 Greg Gagne	.05	.02
❑ 20 Steve Bedrosian	.05	.02
❑ 21 Chicago White Sox TL Greg Walker	.05	.02
❑ 22 Tim Crews	.05	.02
❑ 23 Mike Fitzgerald	.05	.02
❑ 24 Larry Andersen	.05	.02
❑ 25 Frank White	.10	.05
❑ 26 Dale Mohorcic	.05	.02
❑ 27A Orestes Destrade (F* next to copyright)	.05	.02
❑ 27B Orestes Destrade (E*F* next to copyright)	.05	.02
❑ 28 Mike Moore	.05	.02
❑ 29 Kelly Gruber	.05	.02
❑ 30 Dwight Gooden	.10	.05
❑ 31 Terry Francona	.05	.02
❑ 32 Dennis Rasmussen	.05	.02
❑ 33 B.J. Surhoff	.05	.02
❑ 34 Ken Williams	.05	.02
❑ 35 John Tudor UER (With Red Sox in '84, should be Pirates)	.05	.02
❑ 36 Mitch Webster	.05	.02
❑ 37 Bob Stanley	.05	.02
❑ 38 Paul Runge	.05	.02
❑ 39 Mike Maddux	.05	.02
❑ 40 Steve Sax	.05	.02
❑ 41 Terry Mulholland	.05	.02
❑ 42 Jim Eppard	.05	.02
❑ 43 Guillermo Hernandez	.05	.02
❑ 44 Jim Snyder MG	.05	.02
❑ 45 Kal Daniels	.05	.02
❑ 46 Mark Portugal	.05	.02
❑ 47 Carney Lansford	.05	.02
❑ 48 Tim Burke	.05	.02
❑ 49 Craig Biggio	.75	.35
❑ 50 George Bell	.05	.02
❑ 51 California Angels TL Mark McLemore	.05	.02
❑ 52 Bob Brenly	.05	.02
❑ 53 Ruben Sierra	.05	.02
❑ 54 Steve Trout	.05	.02
❑ 55 Julio Franco	.05	.02

☐ 56	Pat Tabler	.05	.02
☐ 57	Alejandro Pena	.05	.02
☐ 58	Lee Mazzilli	.05	.02
☐ 59	Mark Davis	.05	.02
☐ 60	Tom Brunansky	.05	.02
☐ 61	Neil Allen	.05	.02
☐ 62	Alfredo Griffin	.05	.02
☐ 63	Mark Clear	.05	.02
☐ 64	Alex Trevino	.05	.02
☐ 65	Rick Reuschel	.05	.02
☐ 66	Manny Trillo	.05	.02
☐ 67	Dave Palmer	.05	.02
☐ 68	Darrell Miller	.05	.02
☐ 69	Jeff Ballard	.05	.02
☐ 70	Mark McGwire	1.25	.55
☐ 71	Mike Boddicker	.05	.02
☐ 72	John Moses	.05	.02
☐ 73	Pascual Perez	.05	.02
☐ 74	Nick Leyva MG	.05	.02
☐ 75	Tom Henke	.05	.02
☐ 76	Terry Blocker	.05	.02
☐ 77	Doyle Alexander	.05	.02
☐ 78	Jim Sundberg	.05	.02
☐ 79	Scott Bankhead	.05	.02
☐ 80	Cory Snyder	.05	.02
☐ 81	Montreal Expos TL	.10	.05
	Tim Raines		
☐ 82	Dave Leiper	.05	.02
☐ 83	Jeff Blauser	.10	.05
☐ 84	Bill Bene FDP	.05	.02
☐ 85	Kevin McReynolds	.05	.02
☐ 86	Al Nipper	.05	.02
☐ 87	Larry Owen	.05	.02
☐ 88	Darryl Hamilton	.05	.02
☐ 89	Dave LaPoint	.05	.02
☐ 90	Vince Coleman UER	.05	.02
	(Wrong birth year)		
☐ 91	Floyd Youmans	.05	.02
☐ 92	Jeff Kunkel	.05	.02
☐ 93	Ken Howell	.05	.02
☐ 94	Chris Speier	.05	.02
☐ 95	Gerald Young	.05	.02
☐ 96	Rick Cerone	.05	.02
☐ 97	Greg Mathews	.05	.02
☐ 98	Larry Sheets	.05	.02
☐ 99	Sherman Corbett	.05	.02
☐ 100	Mike Schmidt	.30	.14
☐ 101	Les Straker	.05	.02
☐ 102	Mike Gallego	.05	.02
☐ 103	Tim Birtsas	.05	.02
☐ 104	Dallas Green MG	.05	.02
☐ 105	Ron Darling	.05	.02
☐ 106	Willie Upshaw	.05	.02
☐ 107	Jose DeLeon	.05	.02
☐ 108	Fred Manrique	.05	.02
☐ 109	Hipolito Pena	.05	.02
☐ 110	Paul Molitor	.20	.09
☐ 111	Cincinnati Reds TL	.05	.02
	Eric Davis		
	(Swinging bat)		
☐ 112	Jim Presley	.05	.02
☐ 113	Lloyd Moseby	.05	.02
☐ 114	Bob Kipper	.05	.02
☐ 115	Jody Davis	.05	.02
☐ 116	Jeff Montgomery	.10	.05
☐ 117	Dave Anderson	.05	.02
☐ 118	Checklist 1-132	.05	.02
☐ 119	Terry Puhl	.05	.02
☐ 120	Frank Viola	.05	.02
☐ 121	Garry Templeton	.05	.02
☐ 122	Lance Johnson	.10	.05
☐ 123	Spike Owen	.05	.02
☐ 124	Jim Traber	.05	.02
☐ 125	Mike Krukow	.05	.02
☐ 126	Sid Bream	.05	.02
☐ 127	Walt Terrell	.05	.02
☐ 128	Milt Thompson	.05	.02
☐ 129	Terry Clark	.05	.02
☐ 130	Gerald Perry	.05	.02
☐ 131	Dave Otto	.05	.02
☐ 132	Curt Ford	.05	.02
☐ 133	Bill Long	.05	.02
☐ 134	Don Zimmer MG	.05	.02
☐ 135	Jose Rijo	.05	.02
☐ 136	Joey Meyer	.05	.02
☐ 137	Geno Petralli	.05	.02
☐ 138	Wallace Johnson	.05	.02
☐ 139	Mike Flanagan	.05	.02
☐ 140	Shawon Dunston	.05	.02
☐ 141	Cleveland Indians TL	.05	.02
	Brook Jacoby		
☐ 142	Mike Diaz	.05	.02
☐ 143	Mike Campbell	.05	.02
☐ 144	Jay Bell	.15	.07
☐ 145	Dave Stewart	.10	.05
☐ 146	Gary Pettis	.05	.02
☐ 147	DeWayne Buice	.05	.02
☐ 148	Bill Pecota	.05	.02
☐ 149	Doug Dascenzo	.05	.02
☐ 150	Fernando Valenzuela	.10	.05
☐ 151	Terry McGriff	.05	.02
☐ 152	Mark Thurmond	.05	.02
☐ 153	Jim Pankovits	.05	.02
☐ 154	Don Carman	.05	.02
☐ 155	Marty Barrett	.05	.02
☐ 156	Dave Gallagher	.05	.02
☐ 157	Tom Glavine	.20	.09
☐ 158	Mike Aldrete	.05	.02
☐ 159	Pat Clements	.05	.02
☐ 160	Jeffrey Leonard	.05	.02
☐ 161	Gregg Olson FDP UER	.20	.09
	(Born Scribner, NE,		
	should be Omaha, NE)		
☐ 162	John Davis	.05	.02
☐ 163	Bob Forsch	.05	.02
☐ 164	Hal Lanier MG	.05	.02
☐ 165	Mike Dunne	.05	.02
☐ 166	Doug Jennings	.05	.02
☐ 167	Steve Searcy FS	.05	.02
☐ 168	Willie Wilson	.05	.02
☐ 169	Mike Jackson	.15	.07
☐ 170	Tony Fernandez	.05	.02
☐ 171	Atlanta Braves TL	.05	.02
	Andres Thomas		
☐ 172	Frank Williams	.05	.02
☐ 173	Mel Hall	.05	.02
☐ 174	Todd Burns	.05	.02
☐ 175	John Shelby	.05	.02
☐ 176	Jeff Parrett	.05	.02
☐ 177	Monty Fariss FDP	.05	.02
☐ 178	Mark Grant	.05	.02
☐ 179	Ozzie Virgil	.05	.02
☐ 180	Mike Scott	.05	.02
☐ 181	Craig Worthington	.05	.02
☐ 182	Bob McClure	.05	.02
☐ 183	Oddibe McDowell	.05	.02
☐ 184	John Costello	.05	.02
☐ 185	Claudell Washington	.05	.02
☐ 186	Pat Perry	.05	.02
☐ 187	Darren Daulton	.10	.05
☐ 188	Dennis Lamp	.05	.02
☐ 189	Kevin Mitchell	.10	.05
☐ 190	Mike Witt	.05	.02
☐ 191	Sil Campusano	.05	.02
☐ 192	Paul Mirabella	.05	.02
☐ 193	Sparky Anderson MG	.10	.05
	UER (553 Salazer)		
☐ 194	Greg W. Harris	.05	.02
☐ 195	Ozzie Guillen	.05	.02
☐ 196	Denny Walling	.05	.02
☐ 197	Neal Heaton	.05	.02
☐ 198	Danny Heep	.05	.02
☐ 199	Mike Schooler	.05	.02
☐ 200	George Brett	.40	.18
☐ 201	Blue Jays TL	.05	.02
	Kelly Gruber		
☐ 202	Brad Moore	.05	.02
☐ 203	Rob Ducey	.05	.02
☐ 204	Brad Havens	.05	.02
☐ 205	Dwight Evans	.10	.05
☐ 206	Roberto Alomar	.30	.14
☐ 207	Terry Leach	.05	.02
☐ 208	Tom Pagnozzi	.05	.02
☐ 209	Jeff Bittiger	.05	.02
☐ 210	Dale Murphy	.20	.09
☐ 211	Mike Pagliarulo	.05	.02
☐ 212	Scott Sanderson	.05	.02
☐ 213	Rene Gonzales	.05	.02
☐ 214	Charlie O'Brien	.05	.02
☐ 215	Kevin Gross	.05	.02
☐ 216	Jack Howell	.05	.02
☐ 217	Joe Price	.05	.02
☐ 218	Mike LaValliere	.05	.02
☐ 219	Jim Clancy	.05	.02
☐ 220	Gary Gaetti	.10	.05
☐ 221	Cecil Espy	.05	.02
☐ 222	Mark Lewis FDP	.10	.05
☐ 223	Jay Buhner	.20	.09
☐ 224	Tony LaRussa MG	.10	.05
☐ 225	Ramon Martinez	.25	.11
☐ 226	Bill Doran	.05	.02
☐ 227	John Farrell	.05	.02
☐ 228	Nelson Santovenia	.05	.02
☐ 229	Jimmy Key	.10	.05
☐ 230	Ozzie Smith	.25	.11
☐ 231	San Diego Padres TL	.20	.09
	Roberto Alomar		
	(Gary Carter at plate)		
☐ 232	Ricky Horton	.05	.02
☐ 233	Gregg Jefferies FS	.10	.05
☐ 234	Tom Browning	.05	.02
☐ 235	John Kruk	.05	.02
☐ 236	Charles Hudson	.05	.02
☐ 237	Glenn Hubbard	.05	.02
☐ 238	Eric King	.05	.02
☐ 239	Tim Laudner	.05	.02
☐ 240	Greg Maddux	.60	.25
☐ 241	Brett Butler	.10	.05
☐ 242	Ed VandeBerg	.05	.02
☐ 243	Bob Boone	.10	.05
☐ 244	Jim Acker	.05	.02
☐ 245	Jim Rice	.10	.05
☐ 246	Rey Quinones	.05	.02
☐ 247	Shawn Hillegas	.05	.02
☐ 248	Tony Phillips	.05	.02
☐ 249	Tim Leary	.05	.02
☐ 250	Cal Ripken	.75	.35
☐ 251	John Dopson	.05	.02
☐ 252	Billy Hatcher	.05	.02
☐ 253	Jose Alvarez	.05	.02
☐ 254	Tom Lasorda MG	.20	.09
☐ 255	Ron Guidry	.10	.05
☐ 256	Benny Santiago	.05	.02
☐ 257	Rick Aguilera	.10	.05
☐ 258	Checklist 133-264	.05	.02
☐ 259	Larry McWilliams	.05	.02
☐ 260	Dave Winfield	.20	.09
☐ 261	St.Louis Cardinals TL	.05	.02
	Tom Brunansky		
	(With Luis Alicea)		
☐ 262	Jeff Pico	.05	.02
☐ 263	Mike Felder	.05	.02
☐ 264	Rob Dibble	.10	.05
☐ 265	Kent Hrbek	.05	.02
☐ 266	Luis Aquino	.05	.02
☐ 267	Jeff M. Robinson	.05	.02
☐ 268	N. Keith Miller	.05	.02
☐ 269	Tom Bolton	.05	.02
☐ 270	Wally Joyner	.10	.05
☐ 271	Jay Tibbs	.05	.02
☐ 272	Ron Hassey	.05	.02
☐ 273	Jose Lind	.05	.02
☐ 274	Mark Eichhorn	.05	.02
☐ 275	Danny Tartabull UER	.05	.02
	(Born San Juan, PR		
	should be Miami, FL)		
☐ 276	Paul Kilgus	.05	.02
☐ 277	Mike Davis	.05	.02
☐ 278	Andy McGaffigan	.05	.02
☐ 279	Scott Bradley	.05	.02
☐ 280	Bob Knepper	.05	.02
☐ 281	Gary Redus	.05	.02
☐ 282	Cris Carpenter	.05	.02
☐ 283	Andy Allanson	.05	.02
☐ 284	Jim Leyland MG	.10	.05
☐ 285	John Candelaria	.05	.02
☐ 286	Darrin Jackson	.05	.02
☐ 287	Juan Nieves	.05	.02
☐ 288	Pat Sheridan	.05	.02
☐ 289	Ernie Whitt	.05	.02
☐ 290	John Franco	.10	.05
☐ 291	New York Mets TL	.05	.02
	Darryl Strawberry		
	(With Keith Hernandez		
	and Kevin McReynolds)		
☐ 292	Jim Corsi	.05	.02
☐ 293	Glenn Wilson	.05	.02
☐ 294	Juan Berenguer	.05	.02

295	Scott Fletcher	.05	.02
296	Ron Gant	.10	.05
297	Oswald Peraza	.05	.02
298	Chris James	.05	.02
299	Steve Ellsworth	.05	.02
300	Darryl Strawberry	.10	.05
301	Charlie Leibrandt	.05	.02
302	Gary Ward	.05	.02
303	Felix Fermin	.05	.02
304	Joel Youngblood	.05	.02
305	Dave Smith	.05	.02
306	Tracy Woodson	.05	.02
307	Lance McCullers	.05	.02
308	Ron Karkovice	.05	.02
309	Mario Diaz	.05	.02
310	Rafael Palmeiro	.25	.11
311	Chris Bosio	.05	.02
312	Tom Lawless	.05	.02
313	Dennis Martinez	.10	.05
314	Bobby Valentine MG	.05	.02
315	Greg Swindell	.05	.02
316	Walt Weiss	.05	.02
317	Jack Armstrong	.05	.02
318	Gene Larkin	.05	.02
319	Greg Booker	.05	.02
320	Lou Whitaker	.10	.05
321	Boston Red Sox TL	.05	.02
	Jody Reed		
322	John Smiley	.05	.02
323	Gary Thurman	.05	.02
324	Bob Milacki	.05	.02
325	Jesse Barfield	.05	.02
326	Dennis Boyd	.05	.02
327	Mark Lemke	.15	.07
328	Rick Honeycutt	.05	.02
329	Bob Melvin	.05	.02
330	Eric Davis	.10	.05
331	Curt Wilkerson	.05	.02
332	Tony Armas	.05	.02
333	Bob Ojeda	.05	.02
334	Steve Lyons	.05	.02
335	Dave Righetti	.05	.02
336	Steve Balboni	.05	.02
337	Calvin Schiraldi	.05	.02
338	Jim Adduci	.05	.02
339	Scott Bailes	.05	.02
340	Kirk Gibson	.10	.05
341	Jim Deshaies	.05	.02
342	Tom Brookens	.05	.02
343	Gary Sheffield FS	.50	.23
344	Tom Trebelhorn MG	.05	.02
345	Charlie Hough	.10	.05
346	Rex Hudler	.05	.02
347	John Cerutti	.05	.02
348	Ed Hearn	.05	.02
349	Ron Jones	.05	.02
350	Andy Van Slyke	.10	.05
351	San Fran. Giants TL	.05	.02
	Bob Melvin		
	(With Bill Fahey CO)		
352	Rick Schu	.05	.02
353	Marvell Wynne	.05	.02
354	Larry Parrish	.05	.02
355	Mark Langston	.05	.02
356	Kevin Elster	.05	.02
357	Jerry Reuss	.05	.02
358	Ricky Jordan	.10	.05
359	Tommy John	.10	.05
360	Ryne Sandberg	.25	.11
361	Kelly Downs	.05	.02
362	Jack Lazorko	.05	.02
363	Rich Yett	.05	.02
364	Rob Deer	.05	.02
365	Mike Henneman	.05	.02
366	Herm Winningham	.05	.02
367	Johnny Paredes	.05	.02
368	Brian Holton	.05	.02
369	Ken Caminiti	.20	.09
370	Dennis Eckersley	.15	.07
371	Manny Lee	.05	.02
372	Craig Lefferts	.05	.02
373	Tracy Jones	.05	.02
374	John Wathan MG	.05	.02
375	Terry Pendleton	.10	.05
376	Steve Lombardozzi	.05	.02
377	Mike Smithson	.05	.02
378	Checklist 265-396	.05	.02
379	Tim Flannery	.05	.02
380	Rickey Henderson	.25	.11
381	Baltimore Orioles TL	.05	.02
	Larry Sheets		
382	John Smoltz	.75	.35
383	Howard Johnson	.05	.02
384	Mark Salas	.05	.02
385	Von Hayes	.05	.02
386	Andres Galarraga AS	.10	.05
387	Ryne Sandberg AS	.15	.07
388	Bobby Bonilla AS	.10	.05
389	Ozzie Smith AS	.15	.07
390	Darryl Strawberry AS	.05	.02
391	Andre Dawson AS	.10	.05
392	Andy Van Slyke AS	.05	.02
393	Gary Carter AS	.10	.05
394	Orel Hershiser AS	.05	.02
395	Danny Jackson AS	.05	.02
396	Kirk Gibson AS	.10	.05
397	Don Mattingly AS	.15	.07
398	Julio Franco AS	.05	.02
399	Wade Boggs AS	.10	.05
400	Alan Trammell AS	.10	.05
401	Jose Canseco AS	.10	.05
402	Mike Greenwell AS	.05	.02
403	Kirby Puckett AS	.20	.09
404	Bob Boone AS	.05	.02
405	Roger Clemens AS	.20	.09
406	Frank Viola AS	.05	.02
407	Dave Winfield AS	.10	.05
408	Greg Walker	.05	.02
409	Ken Dayley	.05	.02
410	Jack Clark	.05	.02
411	Mitch Williams	.05	.02
412	Barry Lyons	.05	.02
413	Mike Kingery	.05	.02
414	Jim Fregosi MG	.05	.02
415	Rich Gossage	.10	.05
416	Fred Lynn	.05	.02
417	Mike LaCoss	.05	.02
418	Bob Dernier	.05	.02
419	Tom Filer	.05	.02
420	Joe Carter	.15	.07
421	Kirk McCaskill	.05	.02
422	Bo Diaz	.05	.02
423	Brian Fisher	.05	.02
424	Luis Polonia UER	.05	.02
	(Wrong birthdate)		
425	Jay Howell	.05	.02
426	Dan Gladden	.05	.02
427	Eric Show	.05	.02
428	Craig Reynolds	.05	.02
429	Minnesota Twins TL	.05	.02
	Greg Gagne		
	(Taking throw at 2nd)		
430	Mark Gubicza	.05	.02
431	Luis Rivera	.05	.02
432	Chad Kreuter	.05	.02
433	Albert Hall	.05	.02
434	Ken Patterson	.05	.02
435	Len Dykstra	.10	.05
436	Bobby Meacham	.05	.02
437	Andy Benes FDP	.25	.11
438	Greg Gross	.05	.02
439	Frank DiPino	.05	.02
440	Bobby Bonilla	.15	.07
441	Jerry Reed	.05	.02
442	Jose Oquendo	.05	.02
443	Rod Nichols	.05	.02
444	Moose Stubing MG	.05	.02
445	Matt Nokes	.05	.02
446	Rob Murphy	.05	.02
447	Donell Nixon	.05	.02
448	Eric Plunk	.05	.02
449	Carmelo Martinez	.05	.02
450	Roger Clemens	.50	.23
451	Mark Davidson	.05	.02
452	Israel Sanchez	.05	.02
453	Tom Prince	.05	.02
454	Paul Assenmacher	.05	.02
455	Johnny Ray	.05	.02
456	Tim Belcher	.05	.02
457	Mackey Sasser	.05	.02
458	Donn Pall	.05	.02
459	Seattle Mariners TL	.05	.02
	Dave Valle		
460	Dave Stieb	.05	.02
461	Buddy Bell	.10	.05
462	Jose Guzman	.05	.02
463	Steve Lake	.05	.02
464	Bryn Smith	.05	.02
465	Mark Grace	.20	.09
466	Chuck Crim	.05	.02
467	Jim Walewander	.05	.02
468	Henry Cotto	.05	.02
469	Jose Bautista	.05	.02
470	Lance Parrish	.05	.02
471	Steve Curry	.05	.02
472	Brian Harper	.05	.02
473	Don Robinson	.05	.02
474	Bob Rodgers MG	.05	.02
475	Dave Parker	.10	.05
476	Jon Perlman	.05	.02
477	Dick Schofield	.05	.02
478	Doug Drabek	.05	.02
479	Mike Macfarlane	.05	.02
480	Keith Hernandez	.10	.05
481	Chris Brown	.05	.02
482	Steve Peters	.05	.02
483	Mickey Hatcher	.05	.02
484	Steve Shields	.05	.02
485	Hubie Brooks	.05	.02
486	Jack McDowell	.10	.05
487	Scott Lusader	.05	.02
488	Kevin Coffman	.05	.02
	Now with Cubs		
489	Phila. Phillies TL	.10	.05
	Mike Schmidt		
490	Chris Sabo	.05	.02
491	Mike Birkbeck	.05	.02
492	Alan Ashby	.05	.02
493	Todd Benzinger	.05	.02
494	Shane Rawley	.05	.02
495	Candy Maldonado	.05	.02
496	Dwayne Henry	.05	.02
497	Pete Stanicek	.05	.02
498	Dave Valle	.05	.02
499	Don Heinkel	.05	.02
500	Jose Canseco	.25	.11
501	Vance Law	.05	.02
502	Duane Ward	.05	.02
503	Al Newman	.05	.02
504	Bob Walk	.05	.02
505	Pete Rose MG	.40	.18
506	Kurt Manwaring	.05	.02
507	Steve Farr	.05	.02
508	Wally Backman	.05	.02
509	Bud Black	.05	.02
510	Bob Horner	.05	.02
511	Richard Dotson	.05	.02
512	Donnie Hill	.05	.02
513	Jesse Orosco	.05	.02
514	Chet Lemon	.05	.02
515	Barry Larkin	.20	.09
516	Eddie Whitson	.05	.02
517	Greg Brock	.05	.02
518	Bruce Ruffin	.05	.02
519	New York Yankees TL	.05	.02
	Willie Randolph		
520	Rick Sutcliffe	.05	.02
521	Mickey Tettleton	.10	.05
522	Randy Kramer	.05	.02
523	Andres Thomas	.05	.02
524	Checklist 397-528	.05	.02
525	Chili Davis	.10	.05
526	Wes Gardner	.05	.02
527	Dave Henderson	.05	.02
528	Luis Medina	.05	.02
	(Lower left front has white triangle)		
529	Tom Foley	.05	.02
530	Nolan Ryan	.75	.35
531	Dave Hengel	.05	.02
532	Jerry Browne	.05	.02
533	Andy Hawkins	.05	.02
534	Doc Edwards MG	.05	.02
535	Todd Worrell UER	.05	.02
	(4 wins in '88, should be 5)		
536	Joel Skinner	.05	.02
537	Pete Smith	.05	.02

No.	Player	Price	Price
538	Juan Castillo	.05	.02
539	Barry Jones	.05	.02
540	Bo Jackson	.15	.07
541	Cecil Fielder	.05	.02
542	Todd Frohwirth	.05	.02
543	Damon Berryhill	.05	.02
544	Jeff Sellers	.05	.02
545	Mookie Wilson	.10	.05
546	Mark Williamson	.05	.02
547	Mark McLemore	.05	.02
548	Bobby Witt	.05	.02
549	Chicago Cubs TL	.05	.02
	Jamie Moyer		
	(Pitching)		
550	Orel Hershiser	.10	.05
551	Randy Ready	.05	.02
552	Greg Cadaret	.05	.02
553	Luis Salazar	.05	.02
554	Nick Esasky	.05	.02
555	Bert Blyleven	.10	.05
556	Bruce Fields	.05	.02
557	Keith A. Miller	.05	.02
558	Dan Pasqua	.05	.02
559	Juan Agosto	.05	.02
560	Tim Raines	.10	.05
561	Luis Aguayo	.05	.02
562	Danny Cox	.05	.02
563	Bill Schroeder	.05	.02
564	Russ Nixon MG	.05	.02
565	Jeff Russell	.05	.02
566	Al Pedrique	.05	.02
567	David Wells UER	.20	.09
	(Complete Pitching Recor)		
568	Mickey Brantley	.05	.02
569	German Jimenez	.05	.02
570	Tony Gwynn UER	.50	.23
	('88 average should be italicized as league leader)		
571	Billy Ripken	.05	.02
572	Atlee Hammaker	.05	.02
573	Jim Abbott FDP	.20	.09
574	Dave Clark	.05	.02
575	Juan Samuel	.05	.02
576	Greg Minton	.05	.02
577	Randy Bush	.05	.02
578	John Morris	.05	.02
579	Houston Astros TL	.05	.02
	Glenn Davis		
	(Batting stance)		
580	Harold Reynolds	.05	.02
581	Gene Nelson	.05	.02
582	Mike Marshall	.05	.02
583	Paul Gibson	.05	.02
584	Randy Velarde UER	.05	.02
	(Signed 1935, should be 1985)		
585	Harold Baines	.10	.05
586	Joe Boever	.05	.02
587	Mike Stanley	.05	.02
588	Luis Alicea	.05	.02
589	Dave Meads	.05	.02
590	Andres Galarraga	.20	.09
591	Jeff Musselman	.05	.02
592	John Cangelosi	.05	.02
593	Drew Hall	.05	.02
594	Jimy Williams MG	.05	.02
595	Teddy Higuera	.05	.02
596	Kurt Stillwell	.05	.02
597	Terry Taylor	.05	.02
598	Ken Gerhart	.05	.02
599	Tom Candiotti	.05	.02
600	Wade Boggs	.20	.09
601	Dave Dravecky	.05	.02
602	Devon White	.10	.05
603	Frank Tanana	.05	.02
604	Paul O'Neill	.05	.02
605A	Bob Welch ERR	2.00	.90
	(Missing line on back Complete M.L. Pitching Record)		
605B	Bob Welch COR	.05	.02
606	Rick Dempsey	.05	.02
607	Willie Ansley FDP	.05	.02
608	Phil Bradley	.05	.02
609	Detroit Tigers TL	.05	.02
	Frank Tanana		
	(With Alan Trammell and Mike Heath)		
610	Randy Myers	.10	.05
611	Don Slaught	.05	.02
612	Dan Quisenberry	.05	.02
613	Gary Varsho	.05	.02
614	Joe Hesketh	.05	.02
615	Robin Yount	.20	.09
616	Steve Rosenberg	.05	.02
617	Mark Parent	.05	.02
618	Rance Mulliniks	.05	.02
619	Checklist 529-660	.05	.02
620	Barry Bonds	.40	.18
621	Rick Mahler	.05	.02
622	Stan Javier	.05	.02
623	Fred Toliver	.05	.02
624	Jack McKeon MG	.05	.02
625	Eddie Murray	.20	.09
626	Jeff Reed	.05	.02
627	Greg A. Harris	.05	.02
628	Matt Williams	.20	.09
629	Pete O'Brien	.05	.02
630	Mike Greenwell	.05	.02
631	Dave Bergman	.05	.02
632	Bryan Harvey	.05	.02
633	Daryl Boston	.05	.02
634	Marvin Freeman	.05	.02
635	Willie Randolph	.10	.05
636	Bill Wilkinson	.05	.02
637	Carmen Castillo	.05	.02
638	Floyd Bannister	.05	.02
639	Oakland A's TL	.05	.02
	Walt Weiss		
640	Willie McGee	.10	.05
641	Curt Young	.05	.02
642	Argenis Salazar	.05	.02
643	Louie Meadows	.05	.02
644	Lloyd McClendon	.05	.02
645	Jack Morris	.10	.05
646	Kevin Bass	.05	.02
647	Randy Johnson	1.50	.70
648	Sandy Alomar FS	.25	.11
649	Stewart Cliburn	.05	.02
650	Kirby Puckett	.40	.18
651	Tom Niedenfuer	.05	.02
652	Rich Gedman	.05	.02
653	Tommy Barrett	.05	.02
654	Whitey Herzog MG	.05	.02
655	Dave Magadan	.05	.02
656	Ivan Calderon	.05	.02
657	Joe Magrane	.05	.02
658	R.J. Reynolds	.05	.02
659	Al Leiter	.20	.09
660	Will Clark	.20	.09
661	Dwight Gooden TBC84	.05	.02
662	Lou Brock TBC79	.20	.09
663	Hank Aaron TBC74	.20	.09
664	Gil Hodges TBC69	.15	.07
665A	Tony Oliva TBC64	2.00	.90
	ERR (fabricated card is enlarged version of Oliva's 64T card; Topps copyright missing)		
665B	Tony Oliva TBC64	.10	.05
	COR (fabricated card)		
666	Randy St.Claire	.05	.02
667	Dwayne Murphy	.05	.02
668	Mike Bielecki	.05	.02
669	L.A. Dodgers TL	.10	.05
	Orel Hershiser		
	(Mound celebration with Mike Scioscia)		
670	Kevin Seitzer	.05	.02
671	Jim Gantner	.05	.02
672	Allan Anderson	.05	.02
673	Don Baylor	.10	.05
674	Otis Nixon	.05	.02
675	Bruce Hurst	.05	.02
676	Ernie Riles	.05	.02
677	Dave Schmidt	.05	.02
678	Dion James	.05	.02
679	Willie Fraser	.05	.02
680	Gary Carter	.15	.07
681	Jeff D. Robinson	.05	.02
682	Rick Leach	.05	.02
683	Jose Cecena	.05	.02
684	Dave Johnson MG	.05	.02
685	Jeff Treadway	.05	.02
686	Scott Terry	.05	.02
687	Alvin Davis	.05	.02
688	Zane Smith	.05	.02
689A	Stan Jefferson	.05	.02
	(Pink triangle on front bottom left)		
689B	Stan Jefferson	.05	.02
	(Violet triangle on front bottom left)		
690	Doug Jones	.05	.02
691	Roberto Kelly UER	.05	.02
	(83 Oneonta)		
692	Steve Ontiveros	.05	.02
693	Pat Borders	.10	.05
694	Les Lancaster	.05	.02
695	Carlton Fisk	.20	.09
696	Don August	.05	.02
697A	Franklin Stubbs	.05	.02
	(Team name on front in white)		
697B	Franklin Stubbs	.05	.02
	(Team name on front in gray)		
698	Keith Atherton	.05	.02
699	Pittsburgh Pirates TL	.05	.02
	Al Pedrique		
	(Tony Gwynn sliding)		
700	Don Mattingly	.40	.18
701	Storm Davis	.05	.02
702	Jamie Quirk	.05	.02
703	Scott Garrelts	.05	.02
704	Carlos Quintana	.05	.02
705	Terry Kennedy	.05	.02
706	Pete Incaviglia	.05	.02
707	Steve Jeltz	.05	.02
708	Chuck Finley	.10	.05
709	Tom Herr	.05	.02
710	David Cone	.05	.02
711	Candy Sierra	.05	.02
712	Bill Swift	.05	.02
713	Ty Griffin FDP	.05	.02
714	Joe Morgan MG	.05	.02
715	Tony Pena	.05	.02
716	Wayne Tolleson	.05	.02
717	Jamie Moyer	.05	.02
718	Glenn Braggs	.05	.02
719	Danny Darwin	.05	.02
720	Tim Wallach	.05	.02
721	Ron Tingley	.05	.02
722	Todd Stottlemyre	.15	.07
723	Rafael Belliard	.05	.02
724	Jerry Don Gleaton	.05	.02
725	Terry Steinbach	.10	.05
726	Dickie Thon	.05	.02
727	Joe Orsulak	.05	.02
728	Charlie Puleo	.05	.02
729	Texas Rangers TL	.05	.02
	Steve Buechele		
	(Inconsistent design, team name on front surrounded by black, should be white)		
730	Danny Jackson	.05	.02
731	Mike Young	.05	.02
732	Steve Buechele	.05	.02
733	Randy Bockus	.05	.02
734	Jody Reed	.05	.02
735	Roger McDowell	.05	.02
736	Jeff Hamilton	.05	.02
737	Norm Charlton	.10	.05
738	Darnell Coles	.05	.02
739	Brook Jacoby	.05	.02
740	Dan Plesac	.05	.02
741	Ken Phelps	.05	.02
742	Mike Harkey FS	.05	.02
743	Mike Heath	.05	.02
744	Roger Craig MG	.05	.02
745	Fred McGriff	.20	.09
746	German Gonzalez UER	.05	.02
	(Wrong birthdate)		
747	Wil Tejada	.05	.02

		MINT	NRMT
☐ 748	Jimmy Jones	.05	.02
☐ 749	Rafael Ramirez	.05	.02
☐ 750	Bret Saberhagen	.10	.05
☐ 751	Ken Oberkfell	.05	.02
☐ 752	Jim Gott	.05	.02
☐ 753	Jose Uribe	.05	.02
☐ 754	Bob Brower	.05	.02
☐ 755	Mike Scioscia	.05	.02
☐ 756	Scott Medvin	.05	.02
☐ 757	Brady Anderson	.40	.18
☐ 758	Gene Walter	.05	.02
☐ 759	Milwaukee Brewers TL	.05	.02
	Rob Deer		
☐ 760	Lee Smith	.10	.05
☐ 761	Dante Bichette	.40	.18
☐ 762	Bobby Thigpen	.05	.02
☐ 763	Dave Martinez	.05	.02
☐ 764	Robin Ventura FDP	.75	.35
☐ 765	Glenn Davis	.05	.02
☐ 766	Cecilio Guante	.05	.02
☐ 767	Mike Capel	.05	.02
☐ 768	Bill Wegman	.05	.02
☐ 769	Junior Ortiz	.05	.02
☐ 770	Alan Trammell	.15	.07
☐ 771	Ron Kittle	.05	.02
☐ 772	Ron Oester	.05	.02
☐ 773	Keith Moreland	.05	.02
☐ 774	Frank Robinson MG	.20	.09
☐ 775	Jeff Reardon	.10	.05
☐ 776	Nelson Liriano	.05	.02
☐ 777	Ted Power	.05	.02
☐ 778	Bruce Benedict	.05	.02
☐ 779	Craig McMurtry	.05	.02
☐ 780	Pedro Guerrero	.05	.02
☐ 781	Greg Briley	.05	.02
☐ 782	Checklist 661-792	.05	.02
☐ 783	Trevor Wilson	.05	.02
☐ 784	Steve Avery FDP	.20	.09
☐ 785	Ellis Burks	.15	.07
☐ 786	Melido Perez	.05	.02
☐ 787	Dave West	.05	.02
☐ 788	Mike Morgan	.05	.02
☐ 789	Kansas City Royals TL	.20	.09
	Bo Jackson		
	(Throwing)		
☐ 790	Sid Fernandez	.05	.02
☐ 791	Jim Lindeman	.05	.02
☐ 792	Rafael Santana	.05	.02

1989 Topps Tiffany

	MINT	NRMT
COMP.FACT.SET (792)	100.00	45.00
COMMON CARD (1-792)	.20	.09
*STARS: 6X TO 12X BASIC CARDS		
*ROOKIES: 10X TO 20X BASIC CARDS		
DISTRIBUTED ONLY IN FACTORY SET FORM		

1989 Topps Traded

	MINT	NRMT
COMP.FACT.SET (132)	30.00	13.50
COMMON CARD (1T-132T)	.05	.02
MINOR STARS	.10	.05
UNLISTED STARS	.20	.09
☐ 1T	Don Aase	.05	.02
☐ 2T	Jim Abbott	.20	.09

		MINT	NRMT
☐ 3T	Kent Anderson	.05	.02
☐ 4T	Keith Atherton	.05	.02
☐ 5T	Wally Backman	.05	.02
☐ 6T	Steve Balboni	.05	.02
☐ 7T	Jesse Barfield	.05	.02
☐ 8T	Steve Bedrosian	.05	.02
☐ 9T	Todd Benzinger	.05	.02
☐ 10T	Geronimo Berroa	.05	.02
☐ 11T	Bert Blyleven	.10	.05
☐ 12T	Bob Boone	.05	.02
☐ 13T	Phil Bradley	.05	.02
☐ 14T	Jeff Brantley	.15	.07
☐ 15T	Kevin Brown	.40	.18
☐ 16T	Jerry Browne	.05	.02
☐ 17T	Chuck Cary	.05	.02
☐ 18T	Carmen Castillo	.05	.02
☐ 19T	Jim Clancy	.05	.02
☐ 20T	Jack Clark	.05	.02
☐ 21T	Bryan Clutterbuck	.05	.02
☐ 22T	Jody Davis	.05	.02
☐ 23T	Mike Devereaux	.05	.02
☐ 24T	Frank DiPino	.05	.02
☐ 25T	Benny Distefano	.05	.02
☐ 26T	John Dopson	.05	.02
☐ 27T	Len Dykstra	.10	.05
☐ 28T	Jim Eisenreich	.05	.02
☐ 29T	Nick Esasky	.05	.02
☐ 30T	Alvaro Espinoza	.05	.02
☐ 31T	Darrell Evans UER	.10	.05
	(Stat headings on back		
	are for a pitcher)		
☐ 32T	Junior Felix	.05	.02
☐ 33T	Felix Fermin	.05	.02
☐ 34T	Julio Franco	.05	.02
☐ 35T	Terry Francona	.10	.05
☐ 36T	Cito Gaston MG	.10	.05
☐ 37T	Bob Geren UER	.05	.02
	(Photo actually		
	Mike Fennell)		
☐ 38T	Tom Gordon	.20	.09
☐ 39T	Tommy Gregg	.05	.02
☐ 40T	Ken Griffey Sr.	.10	.05
☐ 41T	Ken Griffey Jr.	25.00	11.00
☐ 42T	Kevin Gross	.05	.02
☐ 43T	Lee Guetterman	.05	.02
☐ 44T	Mel Hall	.05	.02
☐ 45T	Erik Hanson	.10	.05
☐ 46T	Gene Harris	.05	.02
☐ 47T	Andy Hawkins	.05	.02
☐ 48T	Rickey Henderson	.25	.11
☐ 49T	Tom Herr	.05	.02
☐ 50T	Ken Hill	.20	.09
☐ 51T	Brian Holman	.05	.02
☐ 52T	Brian Holton	.05	.02
☐ 53T	Art Howe MG	.05	.02
☐ 54T	Ken Howell	.05	.02
☐ 55T	Bruce Hurst	.05	.02
☐ 56T	Chris James	.05	.02
☐ 57T	Randy Johnson	1.50	.70
☐ 58T	Jimmy Jones	.05	.02
☐ 59T	Terry Kennedy	.05	.02
☐ 60T	Paul Kilgus	.05	.02
☐ 61T	Eric King	.05	.02
☐ 62T	Ron Kittle	.05	.02
☐ 63T	John Kruk	.10	.05
☐ 64T	Randy Kutcher	.05	.02
☐ 65T	Steve Lake	.05	.02
☐ 66T	Mark Langston	.05	.02
☐ 67T	Dave LaPoint	.05	.02
☐ 68T	Rick Leach	.05	.02
☐ 69T	Terry Leach	.05	.02
☐ 70T	Jim Lefebvre MG	.05	.02
☐ 71T	Al Leiter	.20	.09
☐ 72T	Jeffrey Leonard	.05	.02
☐ 73T	Derek Lilliquist	.05	.02
☐ 74T	Rick Mahler	.05	.02
☐ 75T	Tom McCarthy	.05	.02
☐ 76T	Lloyd McClendon	.05	.02
☐ 77T	Lance McCullers	.05	.02
☐ 78T	Oddibe McDowell	.05	.02
☐ 79T	Roger McDowell	.05	.02
☐ 80T	Larry McWilliams	.05	.02
☐ 81T	Randy Milligan	.05	.02
☐ 82T	Mike Moore	.05	.02
☐ 83T	Keith Moreland	.05	.02
☐ 84T	Mike Morgan	.05	.02

		MINT	NRMT
☐ 85T	Jamie Moyer	.05	.02
☐ 86T	Rob Murphy	.05	.02
☐ 87T	Eddie Murray	.20	.09
☐ 88T	Pete O'Brien	.05	.02
☐ 89T	Gregg Olson	.05	.02
☐ 90T	Steve Ontiveros	.05	.02
☐ 91T	Jesse Orosco	.05	.02
☐ 92T	Spike Owen	.05	.02
☐ 93T	Rafael Palmeiro	.25	.11
☐ 94T	Clay Parker	.05	.02
☐ 95T	Jeff Parrett	.05	.02
☐ 96T	Lance Parrish	.05	.02
☐ 97T	Dennis Powell	.05	.02
☐ 98T	Rey Quinones	.05	.02
☐ 99T	Doug Rader MG	.05	.02
☐ 100T	Willie Randolph	.10	.05
☐ 101T	Shane Rawley	.05	.02
☐ 102T	Randy Ready	.05	.02
☐ 103T	Bip Roberts	.10	.05
☐ 104T	Kenny Rogers	.20	.09
☐ 105T	Ed Romero	.05	.02
☐ 106T	Nolan Ryan	1.50	.70
☐ 107T	Luis Salazar	.05	.02
☐ 108T	Juan Samuel	.05	.02
☐ 109T	Alex Sanchez	.05	.02
☐ 110T	Deion Sanders	.75	.35
☐ 111T	Steve Sax	.05	.02
☐ 112T	Rick Schu	.05	.02
☐ 113T	Dwight Smith	.10	.05
☐ 114T	Lonnie Smith	.05	.02
☐ 115T	Billy Spiers	.05	.02
☐ 116T	Kent Tekulve	.05	.02
☐ 117T	Walt Terrell	.05	.02
☐ 118T	Milt Thompson	.05	.02
☐ 119T	Dickie Thon	.05	.02
☐ 120T	Jeff Torborg MG	.05	.02
☐ 121T	Jeff Treadway	.05	.02
☐ 122T	Omar Vizquel	.50	.23
☐ 123T	Jerome Walton	.05	.02
☐ 124T	Gary Ward	.05	.02
☐ 125T	Claudell Washington	.05	.02
☐ 126T	Curt Wilkerson	.05	.02
☐ 127T	Eddie Williams	.05	.02
☐ 128T	Frank Williams	.05	.02
☐ 129T	Ken Williams	.05	.02
☐ 130T	Mitch Williams	.05	.02
☐ 131T	Steve Wilson	.05	.02
☐ 132T	Checklist 1T-132T	.05	.02

1989 Topps Traded Tiffany

	MINT	NRMT
COMP.FACT.SET (132)	350.00	160.00
COMMON CARD (1T-132T)	.20	.09
*STARS: 6X TO 12X BASIC CARDS		
*ROOKIES: 10X TO 20X BASIC CARDS		
DISTRIBUTED ONLY IN FACTORY SET FORM		

1990 Topps

	MINT	NRMT
COMPLETE SET (792)	20.00	9.00
COMP.FACT.SET (792)	25.00	11.00
COMP.X-MAS.SET (792)	25.00	11.00
COMMON CARD (1-792)	.05	.02
RYAN SALUTE (2-5)	.40	.18
MINOR STARS	.10	.05
UNLISTED-STARS	.20	.09
SUBSET CARDS HALF VALUE OF BASE		

CARDS
BEWARE COUNTERFEIT THOMAS NNOF

1	Nolan Ryan	.75	.35
2	Nolan Ryan Salute — New York Mets	.40	.18
3	Nolan Ryan Salute — California Angels	.40	.18
4	Nolan Ryan Salute — Houston Astros	.40	.18
5	Nolan Ryan Salute — Texas Rangers UER (Says Texas Stadium rather than Arlington Stadium)	.40	.18
6	Vince Coleman (50 consecutive SB's)	.05	.02
7	Rickey Henderson RB (40 career leadoff HR's)	.10	.05
8	Cal Ripken RB (20 or more homers for 8 consecutive years, record for shortstops)	.20	.09
9	Eric Plunk	.05	.02
10	Barry Larkin	.20	.09
11	Paul Gibson	.05	.02
12	Joe Girardi	.15	.07
13	Mark Williamson	.05	.02
14	Mike Fetters	.05	.02
15	Teddy Higuera	.05	.02
16	Kent Anderson	.05	.02
17	Kelly Downs	.05	.02
18	Carlos Quintana	.05	.02
19	Al Newman	.05	.02
20	Mark Gubicza	.05	.02
21	Jeff Torborg MG	.05	.02
22	Bruce Ruffin	.05	.02
23	Randy Velarde	.05	.02
24	Joe Hesketh	.05	.02
25	Willie Randolph	.10	.05
26	Don Slaught	.05	.02
27	Rick Leach	.05	.02
28	Duane Ward	.05	.02
29	John Cangelosi	.05	.02
30	David Cone	.20	.09
31	Henry Cotto	.05	.02
32	John Farrell	.05	.02
33	Greg Walker	.05	.02
34	Tony Fossas	.05	.02
35	Benito Santiago	.05	.02
36	John Costello	.05	.02
37	Domingo Ramos	.05	.02
38	Wes Gardner	.05	.02
39	Curt Ford	.05	.02
40	Jay Howell	.05	.02
41	Matt Williams	.20	.09
42	Jeff M. Robinson	.05	.02
43	Dante Bichette	.20	.09
44	Roger Salkeld FDP	.05	.02
45	Dave Parker (Born in Jackson, not Calhoun)	.10	.05
46	Rob Dibble	.05	.02
47	Brian Harper	.05	.02
48	Zane Smith	.05	.02
49	Tom Lawless	.05	.02
50	Glenn Davis	.05	.02
51	Doug Rader MG	.05	.02
52	Jack Daugherty	.05	.02
53	Mike LaCoss	.05	.02
54	Joel Skinner	.05	.02
55	Darrell Evans UER (HR total should be 414; not 424)	.10	.05
56	Franklin Stubbs	.05	.02
57	Greg Vaughn	.50	.23
58	Keith Miller	.05	.02
59	Ted Power	.05	.02
60	George Brett	.40	.18
61	Deion Sanders	.20	.09
62	Ramon Martinez	.15	.07
63	Mike Pagliarulo	.05	.02
64	Danny Darwin	.05	.02
65	Devon White	.05	.02
66	Greg Litton	.05	.02
67	Scott Sanderson	.05	.02
68	Dave Henderson	.05	.02
69	Todd Frohwirth	.05	.02
70	Mike Greenwell	.05	.02
71	Allan Anderson	.05	.02
72	Jeff Huson	.05	.02
73	Bob Milacki	.05	.02
74	Jeff Jackson FDP	.05	.02
75	Doug Jones	.05	.02
76	Dave Valle	.05	.02
77	Dave Bergman	.05	.02
78	Mike Flanagan	.05	.02
79	Ron Kittle	.05	.02
80	Jeff Russell	.05	.02
81	Bob Rodgers MG	.05	.02
82	Scott Terry	.05	.02
83	Hensley Meulens	.05	.02
84	Ray Searage	.05	.02
85	Juan Samuel	.05	.02
86	Paul Kilgus	.05	.02
87	Rick Luecken	.05	.02
88	Glenn Braggs	.05	.02
89	Clint Zavaras	.05	.02
90	Jack Clark	.10	.05
91	Steve Frey	.05	.02
92	Mike Stanley	.05	.02
93	Shawn Hillegas	.05	.02
94	Herm Winningham	.05	.02
95	Todd Worrell	.05	.02
96	Jody Reed	.05	.02
97	Curt Schilling	.60	.25
98	Jose Gonzalez	.05	.02
99	Rich Monteleone	.05	.02
100	Will Clark	.20	.09
101	Shane Rawley	.05	.02
102	Stan Javier	.05	.02
103	Marvin Freeman	.05	.02
104	Bob Knepper	.05	.02
105	Randy Myers	.10	.05
106	Charlie O'Brien	.05	.02
107	Fred Lynn	.05	.02
108	Rod Nichols	.05	.02
109	Roberto Kelly	.05	.02
110	Tommy Helms MG	.05	.02
111	Ed Whited	.05	.02
112	Glenn Wilson	.05	.02
113	Manny Lee	.05	.02
114	Mike Bielecki	.05	.02
115	Tony Pena	.05	.02
116	Floyd Bannister	.05	.02
117	Mike Sharperson	.05	.02
118	Erik Hanson	.05	.02
119	Billy Hatcher	.05	.02
120	John Franco	.10	.05
121	Robin Ventura	.20	.09
122	Shawn Abner	.05	.02
123	Rich Gedman	.05	.02
124	Dave Dravecky	.10	.05
125	Kent Hrbek	.10	.05
126	Randy Kramer	.05	.02
127	Mike Devereaux	.05	.02
128	Checklist 1	.05	.02
129	Ron Jones	.05	.02
130	Bert Blyleven	.10	.05
131	Matt Nokes	.05	.02
132	Lance Blankenship	.05	.02
133	Ricky Horton	.05	.02
134	Earl Cunningham FDP	.05	.02
135	Dave Magadan	.05	.02
136	Kevin Brown	.20	.09
137	Marty Pevey	.05	.02
138	Al Leiter	.20	.09
139	Greg Brock	.05	.02
140	Andre Dawson	.20	.09
141	John Hart MG	.05	.02
142	Jeff Wetherby	.05	.02
143	Rafael Belliard	.05	.02
144	Bud Black	.05	.02
145	Terry Steinbach	.05	.02
146	Rob Richie	.05	.02
147	Chuck Finley	.10	.05
148	Edgar Martinez	.20	.09
149	Steve Farr	.05	.02
150	Kirk Gibson	.10	.05
151	Rick Mahler	.05	.02
152	Lonnie Smith	.05	.02
153	Randy Milligan	.05	.02
154	Mike Maddux	.05	.02
155	Ellis Burks	.15	.07
156	Ken Patterson	.05	.02
157	Craig Biggio	.20	.09
158	Craig Lefferts	.05	.02
159	Mike Felder	.05	.02
160	Dave Righetti	.05	.02
161	Harold Reynolds	.05	.02
162	Todd Zeile	.10	.05
163	Phil Bradley	.05	.02
164	Jeff Juden FDP	.05	.02
165	Walt Weiss	.05	.02
166	Bobby Witt	.05	.02
167	Kevin Appier	.15	.07
168	Jose Lind	.05	.02
169	Richard Dotson	.05	.02
170	George Bell	.05	.02
171	Russ Nixon MG	.05	.02
172	Tom Lampkin	.05	.02
173	Tim Belcher	.05	.02
174	Jeff Kunkel	.05	.02
175	Mike Moore	.05	.02
176	Luis Quinones	.05	.02
177	Mike Henneman	.05	.02
178	Chris James	.05	.02
179	Brian Holton	.05	.02
180	Tim Raines	.10	.05
181	Juan Agosto	.05	.02
182	Mookie Wilson	.10	.05
183	Steve Lake	.05	.02
184	Danny Cox	.05	.02
185	Ruben Sierra	.05	.02
186	Dave LaPoint	.05	.02
187	Rick Wrona	.05	.02
188	Mike Smithson	.05	.02
189	Dick Schofield	.05	.02
190	Rick Reuschel	.05	.02
191	Pat Borders	.05	.02
192	Don August	.05	.02
193	Andy Benes	.20	.09
194	Glenallen Hill	.05	.02
195	Tim Burke	.05	.02
196	Gerald Young	.05	.02
197	Doug Drabek	.05	.02
198	Mike Marshall	.05	.02
199	Sergio Valdez	.05	.02
200	Don Mattingly	.40	.18
201	Cito Gaston MG	.05	.02
202	Mike Macfarlane	.05	.02
203	Mike Roesler	.05	.02
204	Bob Dernier	.05	.02
205	Mark Davis	.05	.02
206	Nick Esasky	.05	.02
207	Bob Ojeda	.05	.02
208	Brook Jacoby	.05	.02
209	Greg Mathews	.05	.02
210	Ryne Sandberg	.25	.11
211	John Cerutti	.05	.02
212	Joe Orsulak	.05	.02
213	Scott Bankhead	.05	.02
214	Terry Francona	.10	.05
215	Kirk McCaskill	.05	.02
216	Ricky Jordan	.05	.02
217	Don Robinson	.05	.02
218	Wally Backman	.05	.02
219	Donn Pall	.05	.02
220	Barry Bonds	.25	.11
221	Gary Mielke	.05	.02
222	Kurt Stillwell UER (Graduate misspelled as gradute)	.05	.02
223	Tommy Gregg	.05	.02
224	Delino DeShields	.20	.09
225	Jim Deshaies	.05	.02
226	Mickey Hatcher	.05	.02
227	Kevin Tapani	.10	.05
228	Dave Martinez	.05	.02
229	David Wells	.15	.07
230	Keith Hernandez	.10	.05
231	Jack McKeon MG	.05	.02
232	Darnell Coles	.05	.02
233	Ken Hill	.10	.05
234	Mariano Duncan	.05	.02
235	Jeff Reardon	.10	.05
236	Hal Morris	.05	.02
237	Kevin Ritz	.05	.02

238	Felix Jose	.05	.02
239	Eric Show	.05	.02
240	Mark Grace	.20	.09
241	Mike Krukow	.05	.02
242	Fred Manrique	.05	.02
243	Barry Jones	.05	.02
244	Bill Schroeder	.05	.02
245	Roger Clemens	.50	.23
246	Jim Eisenreich	.05	.02
247	Jerry Reed	.05	.02
248	Dave Anderson	.05	.02
249	Mike(Texas) Smith	.05	.02
250	Jose Canseco	.25	.11
251	Jeff Blauser	.05	.02
252	Otis Nixon	.10	.05
253	Mark Portugal	.05	.02
254	Francisco Cabrera	.05	.02
255	Bobby Thigpen	.05	.02
256	Marvell Wynne	.05	.02
257	Jose DeLeon	.05	.02
258	Barry Lyons	.05	.02
259	Lance McCullers	.05	.02
260	Eric Davis	.10	.05
261	Whitey Herzog MG	.10	.05
262	Checklist 2	.05	.02
263	Mel Stottlemyre Jr.	.05	.02
264	Bryan Clutterbuck	.05	.02
265	Pete O'Brien	.05	.02
266	German Gonzalez	.05	.02
267	Mark Davidson	.05	.02
268	Rob Murphy	.05	.02
269	Dickie Thon	.05	.02
270	Dave Stewart	.10	.05
271	Chet Lemon	.05	.02
272	Bryan Harvey	.05	.02
273	Bobby Bonilla	.10	.05
274	Mauro Gozzo	.05	.02
275	Mickey Tettleton	.10	.05
276	Gary Thurman	.05	.02
277	Lenny Harris	.05	.02
278	Pascual Perez	.05	.02
279	Steve Buechele	.05	.02
280	Lou Whitaker	.10	.05
281	Kevin Bass	.05	.02
282	Derek Lilliquist	.05	.02
283	Joey Belle	1.00	.45
284	Mark Gardner	.05	.02
285	Willie McGee	.10	.05
286	Lee Guetterman	.05	.02
287	Vance Law	.05	.02
288	Greg Briley	.05	.02
289	Norm Charlton	.05	.02
290	Robin Yount	.20	.09
291	Dave Johnson MG	.10	.05
292	Jim Gott	.05	.02
293	Mike Gallego	.05	.02
294	Craig McMurtry	.05	.02
295	Fred McGriff	.20	.09
296	Jeff Ballard	.05	.02
297	Tommy Herr	.05	.02
298	Dan Gladden	.05	.02
299	Adam Peterson	.05	.02
300	Bo Jackson	.25	.11
301	Don Aase	.05	.02
302	Marcus Lawton	.05	.02
303	Rick Cerone	.05	.02
304	Marty Clary	.05	.02
305	Eddie Murray	.20	.09
306	Tom Niedenfuer	.05	.02
307	Bip Roberts	.05	.02
308	Jose Guzman	.05	.02
309	Eric Yelding	.05	.02
310	Steve Bedrosian	.05	.02
311	Dwight Smith	.05	.02
312	Dan Quisenberry	.05	.02
313	Gus Polidor	.05	.02
314	Donald Harris FDP	.05	.02
315	Bruce Hurst	.05	.02
316	Carney Lansford	.10	.05
317	Mark Guthrie	.05	.02
318	Wallace Johnson	.05	.02
319	Dion James	.05	.02
320	Dave Stieb	.10	.05
321	Joe Morgan MG	.05	.02
322	Junior Ortiz	.05	.02
323	Willie Wilson	.05	.02
324	Pete Harnisch	.05	.02
325	Robby Thompson	.05	.02
326	Tom McCarthy	.05	.02
327	Ken Williams	.05	.02
328	Curt Young	.05	.02
329	Oddibe McDowell	.05	.02
330	Ron Darling	.05	.02
331	Juan Gonzalez	3.00	1.35
332	Paul O'Neill	.10	.05
333	Bill Wegman	.05	.02
334	Johnny Ray	.05	.02
335	Andy Hawkins	.05	.02
336	Ken Griffey Jr.	2.50	1.10
337	Lloyd McClendon	.05	.02
338	Dennis Lamp	.05	.02
339	Dave Clark	.05	.02
340	Fernando Valenzuela	.10	.05
341	Tom Foley	.05	.02
342	Alex Trevino	.05	.02
343	Frank Tanana	.05	.02
344	George Canale	.05	.02
345	Harold Baines	.10	.05
346	Jim Presley	.05	.02
347	Junior Felix	.05	.02
348	Gary Wayne	.05	.02
349	Steve Finley	.20	.09
350	Bret Saberhagen	.10	.05
351	Roger Craig MG	.05	.02
352	Bryn Smith	.05	.02
353	Sandy Alomar Jr.	.10	.05
	(Not listed as Jr. on card front)		
354	Stan Belinda	.05	.02
355	Marty Barrett	.05	.02
356	Randy Ready	.05	.02
357	Dave Weiss	.05	.02
358	Andres Thomas	.05	.02
359	Jimmy Jones	.05	.02
360	Paul Molitor	.20	.09
361	Randy McCament	.05	.02
362	Damon Berryhill	.05	.02
363	Dan Petry	.05	.02
364	Rolando Roomes	.05	.02
365	Ozzie Guillen	.05	.02
366	Mike Heath	.05	.02
367	Mike Morgan	.05	.02
368	Bill Doran	.05	.02
369	Todd Burns	.05	.02
370	Tim Wallach	.05	.02
371	Jimmy Key	.10	.05
372	Terry Kennedy	.05	.02
373	Alvin Davis	.05	.02
374	Steve Cummings	.05	.02
375	Dwight Evans	.10	.05
376	Checklist 3 UER	.05	.02
	(Higuera misalphabet-ized in Brewer list)		
377	Mickey Weston	.05	.02
378	Luis Salazar	.05	.02
379	Steve Rosenberg	.05	.02
380	Dave Winfield	.20	.09
381	Frank Robinson MG	.15	.07
382	Jeff Musselman	.05	.02
383	John Morris	.05	.02
384	Pat Combs	.05	.02
385	Fred McGriff AS	.10	.05
386	Julio Franco AS	.05	.02
387	Wade Boggs AS	.10	.05
388	Cal Ripken AS	.40	.18
389	Robin Yount AS	.10	.05
390	Ruben Sierra AS	.05	.02
391	Kirby Puckett AS	.20	.09
392	Carlton Fisk AS	.10	.05
393	Bret Saberhagen AS	.05	.02
394	Jeff Ballard AS	.05	.02
395	Jeff Russell AS	.05	.02
396	A.Bartlett Giamatti COMM MEM	.20	.09
397	Will Clark AS	.10	.05
398	Ryne Sandberg AS	.20	.09
399	Howard Johnson AS	.05	.02
400	Ozzie Smith AS	.10	.05
401	Kevin Mitchell AS	.05	.02
402	Eric Davis AS	.05	.02
403	Tony Gwynn AS	.10	.05
404	Craig Biggio AS	.10	.05
405	Mike Scott AS	.05	.02
406	Joe Magrane AS	.05	.02
407	Mark Davis AS	.05	.02
408	Trevor Wilson	.05	.02
409	Tom Brunansky	.05	.02
410	Joe Boever	.05	.02
411	Ken Phelps	.05	.02
412	Jamie Moyer	.05	.02
413	Brian DuBois	.05	.02
414A	Frank Thomas FDP	1000.00	450.00
	ERR (Name missing on card front)		
414B	F. Thomas FDP COR	3.00	1.35
415	Shawon Dunston	.05	.02
416	Dave Johnson (P)	.05	.02
417	Jim Gantner	.05	.02
418	Tom Browning	.05	.02
419	Beau Allred	.05	.02
420	Carlton Fisk	.20	.09
421	Greg Minton	.05	.02
422	Pat Sheridan	.05	.02
423	Fred Toliver	.05	.02
424	Jerry Reuss	.05	.02
425	Bill Landrum	.05	.02
426	Jeff Hamilton UER	.05	.02
	(Stats say he fanned 197 times in 1987, but he only had 147 at bats)		
427	Carmen Castillo	.05	.02
428	Steve Davis	.05	.02
429	Tom Kelly MG	.05	.02
430	Pete Incaviglia	.05	.02
431	Randy Johnson	.30	.14
432	Damaso Garcia	.05	.02
433	Steve Olin	.10	.05
434	Mark Carreon	.05	.02
435	Kevin Seitzer	.05	.02
436	Mel Hall	.05	.02
437	Les Lancaster	.05	.02
438	Greg Myers	.05	.02
439	Jeff Parrett	.05	.02
440	Alan Trammell	.15	.07
441	Bob Kipper	.05	.02
442	Jerry Browne	.05	.02
443	Cris Carpenter	.05	.02
444	Kyle Abbott FDP	.05	.02
445	Danny Jackson	.05	.02
446	Dan Pasqua	.05	.02
447	Atlee Hammaker	.05	.02
448	Greg Gagne	.05	.02
449	Dennis Rasmussen	.05	.02
450	Rickey Henderson	.25	.11
451	Mark Lemke	.05	.02
452	Luis DeLosSantos	.05	.02
453	Jody Davis	.05	.02
454	Jeff King	.05	.02
455	Jeffrey Leonard	.05	.02
456	Chris Gwynn	.05	.02
457	Gregg Jefferies	.10	.05
458	Bob McClure	.05	.02
459	Jim Lefebvre MG	.05	.02
460	Mike Scott	.05	.02
461	Carlos Martinez	.05	.02
462	Denny Walling	.05	.02
463	Drew Hall	.05	.02
464	Jerome Walton	.05	.02
465	Kevin Gross	.05	.02
466	Rance Mulliniks	.05	.02
467	Juan Nieves	.05	.02
468	Bill Ripken	.05	.02
469	John Kruk	.10	.05
470	Frank Viola	.10	.05
471	Mike Brumley	.05	.02
472	Jose Uribe	.05	.02
473	Joe Price	.05	.02
474	Rich Thompson	.05	.02
475	Bob Welch	.05	.02
476	Brad Komminsk	.05	.02
477	Willie Fraser	.05	.02
478	Mike LaValliere	.05	.02
479	Frank White	.10	.05
480	Sid Fernandez	.05	.02
481	Garry Templeton	.05	.02
482	Steve Carter	.05	.02
483	Alejandro Pena	.05	.02
484	Mike Fitzgerald	.05	.02

❑ 485	John Candelaria	.05	.02
❑ 486	Jeff Treadway	.05	.02
❑ 487	Steve Searcy	.05	.02
❑ 488	Ken Oberkfell	.05	.02
❑ 489	Nick Leyva MG	.05	.02
❑ 490	Dan Plesac	.05	.02
❑ 491	Dave Cochrane	.05	.02
❑ 492	Ron Oester	.05	.02
❑ 493	Jason Grimsley	.05	.02
❑ 494	Terry Puhl	.05	.02
❑ 495	Lee Smith	.10	.05
❑ 496	Cecil Espy UER	.05	.02
	('88 stats have 3 SB's, should be 33)		
❑ 497	Dave Schmidt	.05	.02
❑ 498	Rick Schu	.05	.02
❑ 499	Bill Long	.05	.02
❑ 500	Kevin Mitchell	.05	.02
❑ 501	Matt Young	.05	.02
❑ 502	Mitch Webster	.05	.02
❑ 503	Randy St.Claire	.05	.02
❑ 504	Tom O'Malley	.05	.02
❑ 505	Kelly Gruber	.05	.02
❑ 506	Tom Glavine	.20	.09
❑ 507	Gary Redus	.05	.02
❑ 508	Terry Leach	.05	.02
❑ 509	Tom Pagnozzi	.05	.02
❑ 510	Dwight Gooden	.10	.05
❑ 511	Clay Parker	.05	.02
❑ 512	Gary Pettis	.05	.02
❑ 513	Mark Eichhorn	.05	.02
❑ 514	Andy Allanson	.05	.02
❑ 515	Len Dykstra	.10	.05
❑ 516	Tim Leary	.05	.02
❑ 517	Roberto Alomar	.20	.09
❑ 518	Bill Krueger	.05	.02
❑ 519	Bucky Dent MG	.05	.02
❑ 520	Mitch Williams	.05	.02
❑ 521	Craig Worthington	.05	.02
❑ 522	Mike Dunne	.05	.02
❑ 523	Jay Bell	.10	.05
❑ 524	Daryl Boston	.05	.02
❑ 525	Wally Joyner	.10	.05
❑ 526	Checklist 4	.05	.02
❑ 527	Ron Hassey	.05	.02
❑ 528	Kevin Wickander UER	.05	.02
	(Monthly scoreboard strikeout total was 2.2, that was his innings pitched total)		
❑ 529	Greg A. Harris	.05	.02
❑ 530	Mark Langston	.05	.02
❑ 531	Ken Caminiti	.20	.09
❑ 532	Cecilio Guante	.05	.02
❑ 533	Tim Jones	.05	.02
❑ 534	Louie Meadows	.05	.02
❑ 535	John Smoltz	.20	.09
❑ 536	Bob Geren	.05	.02
❑ 537	Mark Grant	.05	.02
❑ 538	Bill Spiers UER	.05	.02
	(Photo actually George Canale)		
❑ 539	Neal Heaton	.05	.02
❑ 540	Danny Tartabull	.10	.05
❑ 541	Pat Perry	.05	.02
❑ 542	Darren Daulton	.10	.05
❑ 543	Nelson Liriano	.05	.02
❑ 544	Dennis Boyd	.05	.02
❑ 545	Kevin McReynolds	.05	.02
❑ 546	Kevin Hickey	.05	.02
❑ 547	Jack Howell	.05	.02
❑ 548	Pat Clements	.05	.02
❑ 549	Don Zimmer MG	.05	.02
❑ 550	Julio Franco	.05	.02
❑ 551	Tim Crews	.05	.02
❑ 552	Mike(Miss.) Smith	.05	.02
❑ 553	Scott Scudder UER	.05	.02
	(Cedar Rap1ds)		
❑ 554	Jay Buhner	.20	.09
❑ 555	Jack Morris	.10	.05
❑ 556	Gene Larkin	.05	.02
❑ 557	Jeff Innis	.05	.02
❑ 558	Rafael Ramirez	.05	.02
❑ 559	Andy McGaffigan	.05	.02
❑ 560	Steve Sax	.05	.02
❑ 561	Ken Dayley	.05	.02
❑ 562	Chad Kreuter	.05	.02
❑ 563	Alex Sanchez	.05	.02
❑ 564	Tyler Houston FDP	.15	.07
❑ 565	Scott Fletcher	.05	.02
❑ 566	Mark Knudson	.05	.02
❑ 567	Ron Gant	.10	.05
❑ 568	John Smiley	.05	.02
❑ 569	Ivan Calderon	.05	.02
❑ 570	Cal Ripken	.75	.35
❑ 571	Brett Butler	.10	.05
❑ 572	Greg W. Harris	.05	.02
❑ 573	Danny Heep	.05	.02
❑ 574	Bill Swift	.05	.02
❑ 575	Lance Parrish	.05	.02
❑ 576	Mike Dyer	.05	.02
❑ 577	Charlie Hayes	.05	.02
❑ 578	Joe Magrane	.05	.02
❑ 579	Art Howe MG	.05	.02
❑ 580	Joe Carter	.05	.02
❑ 581	Ken Griffey Sr.	.10	.05
❑ 582	Rick Honeycutt	.05	.02
❑ 583	Bruce Benedict	.05	.02
❑ 584	Phil Stephenson	.05	.02
❑ 585	Kal Daniels	.05	.02
❑ 586	Edwin Nunez	.05	.02
❑ 587	Lance Johnson	.05	.02
❑ 588	Rick Rhoden	.05	.02
❑ 589	Mike Aldrete	.05	.02
❑ 590	Ozzie Smith	.25	.11
❑ 591	Todd Stottlemyre	.10	.05
❑ 592	R.J. Reynolds	.05	.02
❑ 593	Scott Bradley	.05	.02
❑ 594	Luis Sojo	.05	.02
❑ 595	Greg Swindell	.05	.02
❑ 596	Jose DeJesus	.05	.02
❑ 597	Chris Bosio	.05	.02
❑ 598	Brady Anderson	.20	.09
❑ 599	Frank Williams	.05	.02
❑ 600	Darryl Strawberry	.10	.05
❑ 601	Luis Rivera	.05	.02
❑ 602	Scott Garrelts	.05	.02
❑ 603	Tony Armas	.05	.02
❑ 604	Ron Robinson	.05	.02
❑ 605	Mike Scioscia	.05	.02
❑ 606	Storm Davis	.05	.02
❑ 607	Steve Jeltz	.05	.02
❑ 608	Eric Anthony	.05	.02
❑ 609	Sparky Anderson MG	.10	.05
❑ 610	Pedro Guerrero	.05	.02
❑ 611	Walt Terrell	.05	.02
❑ 612	Dave Gallagher	.05	.02
❑ 613	Jeff Pico	.05	.02
❑ 614	Nelson Santovenia	.05	.02
❑ 615	Rob Deer	.05	.02
❑ 616	Brian Holman	.05	.02
❑ 617	Geronimo Berroa	.05	.02
❑ 618	Ed Whitson	.05	.02
❑ 619	Rob Ducey	.05	.02
❑ 620	Tony Castillo	.05	.02
❑ 621	Melido Perez	.05	.02
❑ 622	Sid Bream	.05	.02
❑ 623	Jim Corsi	.05	.02
❑ 624	Darrin Jackson	.05	.02
❑ 625	Roger McDowell	.05	.02
❑ 626	Bob Melvin	.05	.02
❑ 627	Jose Rijo	.05	.02
❑ 628	Candy Maldonado	.05	.02
❑ 629	Eric Hetzel	.05	.02
❑ 630	Gary Gaetti	.10	.05
❑ 631	John Wetteland	.20	.09
❑ 632	Scott Lusader	.05	.02
❑ 633	Dennis Cook	.05	.02
❑ 634	Luis Polonia	.05	.02
❑ 635	Brian Downing	.05	.02
❑ 636	Jesse Orosco	.05	.02
❑ 637	Craig Reynolds	.05	.02
❑ 638	Jeff Montgomery	.10	.05
❑ 639	Tony LaRussa MG	.10	.05
❑ 640	Rick Sutcliffe	.05	.02
❑ 641	Doug Strange	.05	.02
❑ 642	Jack Armstrong	.05	.02
❑ 643	Alfredo Griffin	.05	.02
❑ 644	Paul Assenmacher	.05	.02
❑ 645	Jose Oquendo	.05	.02
❑ 646	Checklist 5	.05	.02
❑ 647	Rex Hudler	.05	.02
❑ 648	Jim Clancy	.05	.02
❑ 649	Dan Murphy	.05	.02
❑ 650	Mike Witt	.05	.02
❑ 651	Rafael Santana	.05	.02
❑ 652	Mike Boddicker	.05	.02
❑ 653	John Moses	.05	.02
❑ 654	Paul Coleman FDP	.05	.02
❑ 655	Gregg Olson	.10	.05
❑ 656	Mackey Sasser	.05	.02
❑ 657	Terry Mulholland	.05	.02
❑ 658	Donell Nixon	.05	.02
❑ 659	Greg Cadaret	.05	.02
❑ 660	Vince Coleman	.05	.02
❑ 661	Dick Howser TBC'85	.05	.02
	UER (Seaver's 300th on 7/11/85, should be 8/4/85)		
❑ 662	Mike Schmidt TBC'80	.20	.09
❑ 663	Fred Lynn TBC'75	.05	.02
❑ 664	Johnny Bench TBC'70	.20	.09
❑ 665	Sandy Koufax TBC'65	.25	.11
❑ 666	Brian Fisher	.05	.02
❑ 667	Curt Wilkerson	.05	.02
❑ 668	Joe Oliver	.05	.02
❑ 669	Tom Lasorda MG	.20	.09
❑ 670	Dennis Eckersley	.15	.07
❑ 671	Bob Boone	.10	.05
❑ 672	Roy Smith	.05	.02
❑ 673	Joey Meyer	.05	.02
❑ 674	Spike Owen	.05	.02
❑ 675	Jim Abbott	.15	.07
❑ 676	Randy Kutcher	.05	.02
❑ 677	Jay Tibbs	.05	.02
❑ 678	Kirt Manwaring UER	.05	.02
	('88 Phoenix stats repeated)		
❑ 679	Gary Ward	.05	.02
❑ 680	Howard Johnson	.05	.02
❑ 681	Mike Schooler	.05	.02
❑ 682	Dann Bilardello	.05	.02
❑ 683	Kenny Rogers	.10	.05
❑ 684	Julio Machado	.05	.02
❑ 685	Tony Fernandez	.05	.02
❑ 686	Carmelo Martinez	.05	.02
❑ 687	Tim Birtsas	.05	.02
❑ 688	Milt Thompson	.05	.02
❑ 689	Rich Yett	.05	.02
❑ 690	Mark McGwire	1.00	.45
❑ 691	Chuck Cary	.05	.02
❑ 692	Sammy Sosa	6.00	2.70
❑ 693	Calvin Schiraldi	.05	.02
❑ 694	Mike Stanton	.05	.02
❑ 695	Tom Henke	.05	.02
❑ 696	B.J. Surhoff	.10	.05
❑ 697	Mike Davis	.05	.02
❑ 698	Omar Vizquel	.20	.09
❑ 699	Jim Leyland MG	.05	.02
❑ 700	Kirby Puckett	.30	.14
❑ 701	Bernie Williams	1.50	.70
❑ 702	Tony Phillips	.05	.02
❑ 703	Jeff Brantley	.05	.02
❑ 704	Chip Hale	.05	.02
❑ 705	Claudell Washington	.05	.02
❑ 706	Geno Petralli	.05	.02
❑ 707	Luis Aquino	.05	.02
❑ 708	Larry Sheets	.05	.02
❑ 709	Juan Berenguer	.05	.02
❑ 710	Von Hayes	.05	.02
❑ 711	Rick Aguilera	.10	.05
❑ 712	Todd Benzinger	.05	.02
❑ 713	Tim Drummond	.05	.02
❑ 714	Marquis Grissom	.25	.11
❑ 715	Greg Maddux	.50	.23
❑ 716	Steve Balboni	.05	.02
❑ 717	Ron Karkovice	.05	.02
❑ 718	Gary Sheffield	.20	.09
❑ 719	Wally Whitehurst	.05	.02
❑ 720	Andres Galarraga	.20	.09
❑ 721	Lee Mazzilli	.05	.02
❑ 722	Felix Fermin	.05	.02
❑ 723	Jeff D. Robinson	.05	.02
❑ 724	Juan Bell	.05	.02
❑ 725	Terry Pendleton	.10	.05
❑ 726	Gene Nelson	.05	.02
❑ 727	Pat Tabler	.05	.02
❑ 728	Jim Acker	.05	.02

❑ 729	Bobby Valentine MG	.05	.02
❑ 730	Tony Gwynn	.50	.23
❑ 731	Don Carman	.05	.02
❑ 732	Ernest Riles	.05	.02
❑ 733	John Dopson	.05	.02
❑ 734	Kevin Elster	.05	.02
❑ 735	Charlie Hough	.10	.05
❑ 736	Rick Dempsey	.05	.02
❑ 737	Chris Sabo	.05	.02
❑ 738	Gene Harris	.05	.02
❑ 739	Dale Sveum	.05	.02
❑ 740	Jesse Barfield	.05	.02
❑ 741	Steve Wilson	.05	.02
❑ 742	Ernie Whitt	.05	.02
❑ 743	Tom Candiotti	.05	.02
❑ 744	Kelly Mann	.05	.02
❑ 745	Hubie Brooks	.05	.02
❑ 746	Dave Smith	.05	.02
❑ 747	Randy Bush	.05	.02
❑ 748	Doyle Alexander	.05	.02
❑ 749	Mark Parent UER	.05	.02
	('87 BA .80,		
	should be .080)		
❑ 750	Dale Murphy	.20	.09
❑ 751	Steve Lyons	.05	.02
❑ 752	Tom Gordon	.05	.02
❑ 753	Chris Speier	.05	.02
❑ 754	Bob Walk	.05	.02
❑ 755	Rafael Palmeiro	.20	.09
❑ 756	Ken Howell	.05	.02
❑ 757	Larry Walker	1.50	.70
❑ 758	Mark Thurmond	.05	.02
❑ 759	Tom Trebelhorn MG	.05	.02
❑ 760	Wade Boggs	.20	.09
❑ 761	Mike Jackson	.05	.02
❑ 762	Doug Dascenzo	.05	.02
❑ 763	Dennis Martinez	.10	.05
❑ 764	Tim Teufel	.05	.02
❑ 765	Chili Davis	.10	.05
❑ 766	Brian Meyer	.05	.02
❑ 767	Tracy Jones	.05	.02
❑ 768	Chuck Crim	.05	.02
❑ 769	Greg Hibbard	.05	.02
❑ 770	Cory Snyder	.05	.02
❑ 771	Pete Smith	.05	.02
❑ 772	Jeff Reed	.05	.02
❑ 773	Dave Leiper	.05	.02
❑ 774	Ben McDonald	.10	.05
❑ 775	Andy Van Slyke	.10	.05
❑ 776	Charlie Leibrandt	.05	.02
❑ 777	Tim Laudner	.05	.02
❑ 778	Mike Jeffcoat	.05	.02
❑ 779	Lloyd Moseby	.05	.02
❑ 780	Orel Hershiser	.10	.05
❑ 781	Mario Diaz	.05	.02
❑ 782	Jose Alvarez	.05	.02
❑ 783	Checklist 6	.05	.02
❑ 784	Scott Bailes	.05	.02
❑ 785	Jim Rice	.10	.05
❑ 786	Eric King	.05	.02
❑ 787	Rene Gonzales	.05	.02
❑ 788	Frank DiPino	.05	.02
❑ 789	John Wathan MG	.05	.02
❑ 790	Gary Carter	.20	.09
❑ 791	Alvaro Espinoza	.05	.02
❑ 792	Gerald Perry	.05	.02

1990 Topps Tiffany

1990 Topps Traded

	MINT	NRMT
COMP.FACT.SET (792)	400.00	180.00
COMMON CARD (1-792)	.25	.11
*STARS: 7.5X TO 15X BASIC CARDS		
*ROOKIES: 10X TO 20X BASIC CARDS		
DISTRIBUTED ONLY IN FACTORY SET FORM		

1990 Topps Rookies

	MINT	NRMT
COMPLETE SET (33)	30.00	13.50
COMMON PLAYER (1-33)	.25	.11
MINOR STARS	.50	.23
ONE PER RETAIL JUMBO PACK		

❑ 1	Jim Abbott	.75	.35
❑ 2	Albert Belle	6.00	2.70
❑ 3	Andy Benes	1.00	.45
❑ 4	Greg Briley	.25	.11
❑ 5	Kevin Brown	1.00	.45
❑ 6	Mark Carreon	.25	.11
❑ 7	Mike Devereaux	.25	.11
❑ 8	Junior Felix	.25	.11
❑ 9	Bob Geren	.25	.11
❑ 10	Tom Gordon	.50	.23
❑ 11	Ken Griffey Jr.	20.00	9.00
❑ 12	Pete Harnisch	.25	.11
❑ 13	Greg W. Harris	.25	.11
❑ 14	Greg Hibbard	.25	.11
❑ 15	Ken Hill	.50	.23
❑ 16	Gregg Jefferies	.50	.23
❑ 17	Jeff King	.25	.11
❑ 18	Derek Lilliquist	.25	.11
❑ 19	Carlos Martinez	.25	.11
❑ 20	Ramon Martinez	.75	.35
❑ 21	Bob Milacki	.25	.11
❑ 22	Gregg Olson	.50	.23
❑ 23	Donn Pall	.25	.11
❑ 24	Kenny Rogers	.50	.23
❑ 25	Gary Sheffield	.75	.35
❑ 26	Dwight Smith	.25	.11
❑ 27	Billy Spiers	.25	.11
❑ 28	Omar Vizquel	1.00	.45
❑ 29	Jerome Walton	.25	.11
❑ 30	Dave West	.25	.11
❑ 31	John Wetteland	1.00	.45
❑ 32	Steve Wilson	.25	.11
❑ 33	Craig Worthington	.25	.11

	MINT	NRMT
COMPLETE SET (132)	3.00	1.35
COMMON CARD (1T-132T)	.05	.02
MINOR STARS	.10	.05
UNLISTED STARS	.20	.09
*GRAY AND WHITE BACKS: SAME VALUE		

❑ 1T	Darrel Akerfelds	.05	.02
❑ 2T	Sandy Alomar Jr.	.10	.05
❑ 3T	Brad Arnsberg	.05	.02
❑ 4T	Steve Avery	.05	.02
❑ 5T	Wally Backman	.05	.02
❑ 6T	Carlos Baerga	.20	.09
❑ 7T	Kevin Bass	.05	.02
❑ 8T	Willie Blair	.05	.02
❑ 9T	Mike Blowers	.10	.05
❑ 10T	Shawn Boskie	.05	.02
❑ 11T	Daryl Boston	.05	.02
❑ 12T	Dennis Boyd	.05	.02
❑ 13T	Glenn Braggs	.05	.02
❑ 14T	Hubie Brooks	.05	.02
❑ 15T	Tom Brunansky	.05	.02
❑ 16T	John Burkett	.05	.02
❑ 17T	Casey Candaele	.05	.02
❑ 18T	John Candelaria	.05	.02
❑ 19T	Gary Carter	.20	.09
❑ 20T	Joe Carter	.10	.05
❑ 21T	Rick Cerone	.05	.02
❑ 22T	Scott Coolbaugh	.05	.02
❑ 23T	Bobby Cox MG	.10	.05
❑ 24T	Mark Davis	.05	.02
❑ 25T	Storm Davis	.05	.02
❑ 26T	Edgar Diaz	.05	.02
❑ 27T	Wayne Edwards	.05	.02
❑ 28T	Mark Eichhorn	.05	.02
❑ 29T	Scott Erickson	.25	.11
❑ 30T	Nick Esasky	.05	.02
❑ 31T	Cecil Fielder	.10	.05
❑ 32T	John Franco	.10	.05
❑ 33T	Travis Fryman	.40	.18
❑ 34T	Bill Gullickson	.05	.02
❑ 35T	Darryl Hamilton	.05	.02
❑ 36T	Mike Harkey	.05	.02
❑ 37T	Bud Harrelson MG	.05	.02
❑ 38T	Billy Hatcher	.05	.02
❑ 39T	Keith Hernandez	.10	.05
❑ 40T	Joe Hesketh	.05	.02
❑ 41T	Dave Hollins	.20	.09
❑ 42T	Sam Horn	.05	.02
❑ 43T	Steve Howard	.05	.02
❑ 44T	Todd Hundley	.40	.18
❑ 45T	Jeff Huson	.05	.02
❑ 46T	Chris James	.05	.02
❑ 47T	Stan Javier	.05	.02
❑ 48T	Dave Justice	.60	.25
❑ 49T	Jeff Kaiser	.05	.02
❑ 50T	Dana Kiecker	.05	.02
❑ 51T	Joe Klink	.05	.02
❑ 52T	Brent Knackert	.05	.02
❑ 53T	Brad Komminsk	.05	.02
❑ 54T	Mark Langston	.05	.02
❑ 55T	Tim Layana	.05	.02
❑ 56T	Rick Leach	.05	.02
❑ 57T	Terry Leach	.05	.02
❑ 58T	Tim Leary	.05	.02
❑ 59T	Craig Lefferts	.05	.02
❑ 60T	Charlie Leibrandt	.05	.02
❑ 61T	Jim Leyritz	.25	.11
❑ 62T	Fred Lynn	.05	.02
❑ 63T	Kevin Maas	.10	.05
❑ 64T	Shane Mack	.05	.02
❑ 65T	Candy Maldonado	.05	.02
❑ 66T	Fred Manrique	.05	.02
❑ 67T	Mike Marshall	.05	.02
❑ 68T	Carmelo Martinez	.05	.02
❑ 69T	John Marzano	.05	.02
❑ 70T	Ben McDonald	.05	.02
❑ 71T	Jack McDowell	.05	.02
❑ 72T	John McNamara MG	.05	.02
❑ 73T	Orlando Mercado	.05	.02
❑ 74T	Stump Merrill MG	.05	.02
❑ 75T	Alan Mills	.05	.02
❑ 76T	Hal Morris	.05	.02
❑ 77T	Lloyd Moseby	.05	.02
❑ 78T	Randy Myers	.10	.05
❑ 79T	Tim Naehring	.10	.05

❑ 80T Junior Noboa	.05	.02
❑ 81T Matt Nokes	.05	.02
❑ 82T Pete O'Brien	.05	.02
❑ 83T John Olerud	.75	.35
❑ 84T Greg Olson	.05	.02
❑ 85T Junior Ortiz	.05	.02
❑ 86T Dave Parker	.10	
❑ 87T Rick Parker	.05	.02
❑ 88T Bob Patterson	.05	.02
❑ 89T Alejandro Pena	.05	.02
❑ 90T Tony Pena	.05	.02
❑ 91T Pascual Perez	.05	.02
❑ 92T Gerald Perry	.05	.02
❑ 93T Dan Petry	.05	.02
❑ 94T Gary Pettis	.05	.02
❑ 95T Tony Phillips	.05	.02
❑ 96T Lou Piniella MG	.10	
❑ 97T Luis Polonia	.05	.02
❑ 98T Jim Presley	.05	.02
❑ 99T Scott Radinsky	.05	.02
❑ 100T Willie Randolph	.10	.05
❑ 101T Jeff Reardon	.10	.05
❑ 102T Greg Riddoch MG	.05	.02
❑ 103T Jeff Robinson	.05	.02
❑ 104T Ron Robinson	.05	.02
❑ 105T Kevin Romine	.05	.02
❑ 106T Scott Ruskin	.05	.02
❑ 107T John Russell	.05	.02
❑ 108T Bill Sampen	.05	.02
❑ 109T Juan Samuel	.05	.02
❑ 110T Scott Sanderson	.05	.02
❑ 111T Jack Savage	.05	.02
❑ 112T Dave Schmidt	.05	.02
❑ 113T Red Schoendienst MG	.20	.09
❑ 114T Terry Shumpert	.05	.02
❑ 115T Matt Sinatro	.05	.02
❑ 116T Don Slaught	.05	.02
❑ 117T Bryn Smith	.05	.02
❑ 118T Lee Smith	.10	.05
❑ 119T Paul Sorrento	.15	.07
❑ 120T Franklin Stubbs UER	.05	.02
('84 says '99 and has		
the same stats as '89,		
'83 stats are missing)		
❑ 121T Russ Swan	.05	.02
❑ 122T Bob Tewksbury	.05	.02
❑ 123T Wayne Tolleson	.05	.02
❑ 124T John Tudor	.05	.02
❑ 125T Randy Veres	.05	.02
❑ 126T Hector Villanueva	.05	.02
❑ 127T Mitch Webster	.05	.02
❑ 128T Ernie Whitt	.05	.02
❑ 129T Frank Wills	.05	.02
❑ 130T Dave Winfield	.20	.09
❑ 131T Matt Young	.05	.02
❑ 132T Checklist 1T-132T	.05	.02

1990 Topps Traded Tiffany

	MINT	NRMT
COMP.FACT.SET (132)	30.00	13.50
COMMON CARD (1T-132T)	.25	.11

*STARS: 7.5X TO 15X BASIC CARDS
*ROOKIES: 10X TO 20X BASIC CARDS
DISTRIBUTED ONLY IN FACTORY SET FORM

1990 Topps Big

	MINT	NRMT
COMPLETE SET (330)	30.00	13.50
COMMON PLAYER (1-330)	.15	.07
MINOR STARS	.25	.11
SEMISTARS	.40	.18
UNLISTED STARS	.60	.25

❑ 1 Dwight Evans	.25	.11
❑ 2 Kirby Puckett	1.00	.45
❑ 3 Kevin Gross	.15	.07
❑ 4 Ron Hassey	.15	.07
❑ 5 Lloyd McClendon	.15	.07
❑ 6 Bo Jackson	.25	.11
❑ 7 Lonnie Smith	.15	.07
❑ 8 Alvaro Espinoza	.15	.07
❑ 9 Roberto Alomar	.60	.25
❑ 10 Glenn Braggs	.15	.07
❑ 11 David Cone	.60	.25
❑ 12 Claudell Washington	.15	.07
❑ 13 Pedro Guerrero	.15	.07
❑ 14 Todd Benzinger	.15	.07
❑ 15 Jeff Russell	.15	.07
❑ 16 Terry Kennedy	.15	.07
❑ 17 Kelly Gruber	.15	.07
❑ 18 Alfredo Griffin	.15	.07
❑ 19 Mark Grace	.60	.25
❑ 20 Dave Winfield	.60	.25
❑ 21 Bret Saberhagen	.25	.11
❑ 22 Roger Clemens	1.50	.70
❑ 23 Bob Walk	.15	.07
❑ 24 Dave Magadan	.15	.07
❑ 25 Spike Owen	.15	.07
❑ 26 Jody Davis	.15	.07
❑ 27 Kent Hrbek	.25	.11
❑ 28 Mark McGwire	3.00	1.35
❑ 29 Eddie Murray	.60	.25
❑ 30 Paul O'Neill	.25	.11
❑ 31 Jose DeLeon	.15	.07
❑ 32 Steve Lyons	.15	.07
❑ 33 Dan Plesac	.15	.07
❑ 34 Jack Howell	.15	.07
❑ 35 Greg Briley	.15	.07
❑ 36 Andy Hawkins	.15	.07
❑ 37 Cecil Espy	.15	.07
❑ 38 Rick Sutcliffe	.15	.07
❑ 39 Jack Clark	.25	.11
❑ 40 Dale Murphy	.60	.25
❑ 41 Mike Heath	.15	.07
❑ 42 Rick Honeycutt	.15	.07
❑ 43 Willie Randolph	.25	.11
❑ 44 Marty Barrett	.15	.07
❑ 45 Willie Wilson	.15	.07
❑ 46 Wallace Johnson	.15	.07
❑ 47 Greg Brock	.15	.07
❑ 48 Tom Browning	.15	.07
❑ 49 Gerald Young	.15	.07
❑ 50 Dennis Eckersley	.40	.18
❑ 51 Scott Garrelts	.15	.07
❑ 52 Gary Redus	.15	.07
❑ 53 Al Newman	.15	.07
❑ 54 Daryl Boston	.15	.07
❑ 55 Ron Oester	.15	.07
❑ 56 Danny Tartabull	.15	.07
❑ 57 Gregg Jefferies	.25	.11
❑ 58 Tom Foley	.15	.07
❑ 59 Robin Yount	.60	.25

❑ 60 Pat Borders	.15	.07
❑ 61 Mike Greenwell	.15	.07
❑ 62 Shawon Dunston	.15	.07
❑ 63 Steve Buechele	.15	.07
❑ 64 Dave Stewart	.25	.11
❑ 65 Jose Oquendo	.15	.07
❑ 66 Ron Gant	.25	.11
❑ 67 Mike Scioscia	.15	.07
❑ 68 Randy Velarde	.15	.07
❑ 69 Von Hayes	.15	.07
❑ 70 Tim Wallach	.15	.07
❑ 71 Eric Show	.15	.07
❑ 72 Eric Davis	.25	.11
❑ 73 Mike Gallego	.15	.07
❑ 74 Rob Deer	.15	.07
❑ 75 Ryne Sandberg	.75	.35
❑ 76 Kevin Seitzer	.15	.07
❑ 77 Wade Boggs	.60	.25
❑ 78 Greg Gagne	.15	.07
❑ 79 John Smiley	.15	.07
❑ 80 Ivan Calderon	.15	.07
❑ 81 Pete Incaviglia	.15	.07
❑ 82 Orel Hershiser	.25	.11
❑ 83 Carney Lansford	.25	.11
❑ 84 Mike Fitzgerald	.15	.07
❑ 85 Don Mattingly	1.25	.55
❑ 86 Chet Lemon	.15	.07
❑ 87 Rolando Roomes	.15	.07
❑ 88 Billy Spiers	.15	.07
❑ 89 Pat Tabler	.15	.07
❑ 90 Danny Heep	.15	.07
❑ 91 Andre Dawson	.60	.25
❑ 92 Randy Bush	.15	.07
❑ 93 Tony Gwynn	1.50	.70
❑ 94 Tom Brunansky	.15	.07
❑ 95 Johnny Ray	.15	.07
❑ 96 Matt Williams	.60	.25
❑ 97 Barry Lyons	.15	.07
❑ 98 Jeff Hamilton	.15	.07
❑ 99 Tom Glavine	.60	.25
❑ 100 Ken Griffey Sr.	.25	.11
❑ 101 Tom Henke	.15	.07
❑ 102 Dave Righetti	.15	.07
❑ 103 Paul Molitor	.60	.25
❑ 104 Mike LaValliere	.15	.07
❑ 105 Frank White	.25	.11
❑ 106 Bob Welch	.15	.07
❑ 107 Ellis Burks	.40	.18
❑ 108 Andres Galarraga	.60	.25
❑ 109 Mitch Williams	.15	.07
❑ 110 Checklist 1-110	.15	.07
❑ 111 Craig Biggio	.25	.11
❑ 112 Dave Stieb	.25	.11
❑ 113 Ron Darling	.15	.07
❑ 114 Bert Blyleven	.25	.11
❑ 115 Dickie Thon	.15	.07
❑ 116 Carlos Martinez	.15	.07
❑ 117 Jeff King	.15	.07
❑ 118 Terry Steinbach	.15	.07
❑ 119 Frank Tanana	.15	.07
❑ 120 Mark Lemke	.15	.07
❑ 121 Chris Sabo	.15	.07
❑ 122 Glenn Davis	.15	.07
❑ 123 Mel Hall	.15	.07
❑ 124 Jim Gantner	.15	.07
❑ 125 Benito Santiago	.15	.07
❑ 126 Milt Thompson	.15	.07
❑ 127 Rafael Palmeiro	.60	.25
❑ 128 Barry Bonds	.75	.35
❑ 129 Mike Bielecki	.15	.07
❑ 130 Lou Whitaker	.25	.11
❑ 131 Bob Ojeda	.15	.07
❑ 132 Dion James	.15	.07
❑ 133 Dennis Martinez	.25	.11
❑ 134 Fred McGriff	.60	.25
❑ 135 Terry Pendleton	.25	.11
❑ 136 Pat Combs	.15	.07
❑ 137 Kevin Mitchell	.15	.07
❑ 138 Marquis Grissom	.60	.25
❑ 139 Chris Bosio	.15	.07
❑ 140 Omar Vizquel	.60	.25
❑ 141 Steve Sax	.15	.07
❑ 142 Nelson Liriano	.15	.07
❑ 143 Kevin Elster	.15	.07
❑ 144 Dan Pasqua	.15	.07
❑ 145 Dave Smith	.15	.07

❑ 146 Craig Worthington	.15	.07	❑ 232 Mark Langston	.15	.07	
❑ 147 Dan Gladden	.15	.07	❑ 233 Wally Backman	.15	.07	
❑ 148 Oddibe McDowell	.15	.07	❑ 234 Jim Eisenreich	.15	.07	
❑ 149 Bip Roberts	.15	.07	❑ 235 Mike Schooler	.15	.07	
❑ 150 Randy Ready	.15	.07	❑ 236 Kevin Bass	.15	.07	
❑ 151 Dwight Smith	.15	.07	❑ 237 John Farrell	.15	.07	
❑ 152 Eddie Whitson	.15	.07	❑ 238 Kal Daniels	.15	.07	
❑ 153 George Bell	.15	.07	❑ 239 Tony Phillips	.15	.07	
❑ 154 Tim Raines	.25	.11	❑ 240 Todd Stottlemyre	.25	.11	
❑ 155 Sid Fernandez	.15	.07	❑ 241 Greg Olson	.15	.07	
❑ 156 Henry Cotto	.15	.07	❑ 242 Charlie Hough	.25	.11	
❑ 157 Harold Baines	.25	.11	❑ 243 Mariano Duncan	.15	.07	
❑ 158 Willie McGee	.15	.11	❑ 244 Bill Ripken	.15	.07	
❑ 159 Bill Doran	.15	.07	❑ 245 Joe Carter	.25	.11	
❑ 160 Steve Balboni	.15	.07	❑ 246 Tim Belcher	.15	.07	
❑ 161 Pete Smith	.15	.07	❑ 247 Roberto Kelly	.15	.07	
❑ 162 Frank Viola	.15	.07	❑ 248 Candy Maldonado	.15	.07	
❑ 163 Gary Sheffield	.60	.25	❑ 249 Mike Scott	.15	.07	
❑ 164 Bill Landrum	.15	.07	❑ 250 Ken Griffey Jr.	10.00	4.50	
❑ 165 Tony Fernandez	.15	.07	❑ 251 Nick Esasky	.15	.07	
❑ 166 Mike Heath	.15	.07	❑ 252 Tom Gordon	.25	.11	
❑ 167 Jody Reed	.15	.07	❑ 253 John Tudor	.15	.07	
❑ 168 Wally Joyner	.25	.11	❑ 254 Gary Gaetti	.25	.11	
❑ 169 Robby Thompson	.15	.07	❑ 255 Neal Heaton	.15	.07	
❑ 170 Ken Caminiti	.25	.11	❑ 256 Jerry Browne	.15	.07	
❑ 171 Nolan Ryan	2.50	1.10	❑ 257 Jose Rijo	.15	.07	
❑ 172 Ricky Jordan	.15	.07	❑ 258 Mike Boddicker	.15	.07	
❑ 173 Lance Blankenship	.15	.07	❑ 259 Brett Butler	.25	.11	
❑ 174 Dwight Gooden	.25	.11	❑ 260 Andy Benes	.60	.25	
❑ 175 Ruben Sierra	.15	.07	❑ 261 Kevin Brown	.60	.25	
❑ 176 Carlton Fisk	.60	.25	❑ 262 Hubie Brooks	.15	.07	
❑ 177 Garry Templeton	.15	.07	❑ 263 Randy Milligan	.15	.07	
❑ 178 Mike Devereaux	.25	.11	❑ 264 John Franco	.25	.11	
❑ 179 Mookie Wilson	.25	.11	❑ 265 Sandy Alomar Jr.	.25	.11	
❑ 180 Jeff Blauser	.15	.07	❑ 266 Dave Valle	.15	.07	
❑ 181 Scott Bradley	.15	.07	❑ 267 Jerome Walton	.25	.11	
❑ 182 Luis Salazar	.15	.07	❑ 268 Bob Boone	.25	.11	
❑ 183 Rafael Ramirez	.15	.07	❑ 269 Ken Howell	.15	.07	
❑ 184 Vince Coleman	.25	.11	❑ 270 Jose Canseco	.75	.35	
❑ 185 Doug Drabek	.15	.07	❑ 271 Joe Magrane	.15	.07	
❑ 186 Darryl Strawberry	.25	.11	❑ 272 Brian DuBois	.15	.07	
❑ 187 Tim Burke	.15	.07	❑ 273 Carlos Quintana	.15	.07	
❑ 188 Jesse Barfield	.15	.07	❑ 274 Lance Johnson	.15	.07	
❑ 189 Barry Larkin	.60	.25	❑ 275 Steve Bedrosian	.15	.07	
❑ 190 Alan Trammell	.40	.18	❑ 276 Brook Jacoby	.15	.07	
❑ 191 Steve Lake	.15	.07	❑ 277 Fred Lynn UER	.15	.07	
❑ 192 Derek Lilliquist	.15	.07	(Pirates logo			
❑ 193 Don Robinson	.15	.07	on card front)			
❑ 194 Kevin McReynolds	.15	.07	❑ 278 Jeff Ballard	.15	.07	
❑ 195 Melido Perez	.15	.07	❑ 279 Otis Nixon	.25	.11	
❑ 196 Jose Lind	.15	.07	❑ 280 Chili Davis	.25	.11	
❑ 197 Eric Anthony	.25	.11	❑ 281 Joe Oliver	.15	.07	
❑ 198 B.J. Surhoff	.25	.11	❑ 282 Brian Holman	.15	.07	
❑ 199 John Olerud	1.00	.45	❑ 283 Juan Samuel	.15	.07	
❑ 200 Mike Moore	.15	.07	❑ 284 Rick Aguilera	.25	.11	
❑ 201 Mark Gubicza	.15	.07	❑ 285 Jeff Reardon	.25	.11	
❑ 202 Phil Bradley	.15	.07	❑ 286 Sammy Sosa	10.00	4.50	
❑ 203 Ozzie Smith	.75	.35	❑ 287 Carmelo Martinez	.15	.07	
❑ 204 Greg Maddux	1.50	.70	❑ 288 Greg Swindell	.15	.07	
❑ 205 Julio Franco	.25	.11	❑ 289 Erik Hanson	.15	.07	
❑ 206 Tom Herr	.15	.07	❑ 290 Tony Pena	.15	.07	
❑ 207 Scott Fletcher	.15	.07	❑ 291 Pascual Perez	.15	.07	
❑ 208 Bobby Bonilla	.25	.11	❑ 292 Rickey Henderson	.60	.25	
❑ 209 Bob Geren	.15	.07	❑ 293 Kurt Stillwell	.15	.07	
❑ 210 Junior Felix	.15	.07	❑ 294 Todd Zeile	.25	.11	
❑ 211 Dick Schofield	.15	.07	❑ 295 Bobby Thigpen	.15	.07	
❑ 212 Jim Deshaies	.15	.07	❑ 296 Larry Walker	2.00	.90	
❑ 213 Jose Uribe	.15	.07	❑ 297 Rob Murphy	.15	.07	
❑ 214 John Kruk	.25	.11	❑ 298 Mitch Webster	.15	.07	
❑ 215 Ozzie Guillen	.15	.07	❑ 299 Devon White	.15	.07	
❑ 216 Howard Johnson	.25	.11	❑ 300 Len Dykstra	.25	.11	
❑ 217 Andy Van Slyke	.25	.11	❑ 301 Keith Hernandez	.25	.11	
❑ 218 Tim Laudner	.15	.07	❑ 302 Gene Larkin	.15	.07	
❑ 219 Manny Lee	.15	.07	❑ 303 Jeffrey Leonard	.15	.07	
❑ 220 Checklist 111-220	.15	.07	❑ 304 Jim Presley	.15	.07	
❑ 221 Cory Snyder	.15	.07	❑ 305 Lloyd Moseby	.15	.07	
❑ 222 Billy Hatcher	.15	.07	❑ 306 John Smoltz	.60	.25	
❑ 223 Bud Black	.15	.07	❑ 307 Sam Horn	.15	.07	
❑ 224 Will Clark	.60	.25	❑ 308 Greg Litton	.15	.07	
❑ 225 Kevin Tapani	.25	.11	❑ 309 Dave Henderson	.15	.07	
❑ 226 Mike Pagliarulo	.15	.07	❑ 310 Mark McLemore	.15	.07	
❑ 227 Dave Parker	.25	.11	❑ 311 Gary Pettis	.15	.07	
❑ 228 Ben McDonald	.15	.07	❑ 312 Mark Davis	.15	.07	
❑ 229 Carlos Baerga	.60	.25	❑ 313 Cecil Fielder	.25	.11	
❑ 230 Roger McDowell	.15	.07	❑ 314 Jack Armstrong	.15	.07	
❑ 231 Delino DeShields	.60	.25	❑ 315 Alvin Davis	.15	.07	

❑ 316 Doug Jones	.15	.07
❑ 317 Eric Yelding	.15	.07
❑ 318 Joe Orsulak	.15	.07
❑ 319 Chuck Finley	.25	.11
❑ 320 Glenn Wilson	.15	.07
❑ 321 Harold Reynolds	.15	.07
❑ 322 Teddy Higuera	.15	.07
❑ 323 Lance Parrish	.15	.07
❑ 324 Bruce Hurst	.15	.07
❑ 325 Dave West	.15	.07
❑ 326 Kirk Gibson	.25	.11
❑ 327 Cal Ripken	2.50	1.10
❑ 328 Rick Reuschel	.15	.07
❑ 329 Jim Abbott	.40	.18
❑ 330 Checklist 221-330	.15	.07

1990 Topps Debut '89

BEN McDONALD

	MINT	NRMT
COMP.FACT.SET (152)	50.00	22.00
COMMON CARD (1-152)	.15	.07
MINOR STARS	.25	.11
SEMISTARS	.50	.23

DISTRIBUTED ONLY IN FACTORY SET FORM

❑ 1 Jim Abbott	.50	.23
❑ 2 Beau Allred	.15	.07
❑ 3 Wilson Alvarez	.50	.23
❑ 4 Kent Anderson	.15	.07
❑ 5 Eric Anthony	.15	.07
❑ 6 Kevin Appier	.50	.23
❑ 7 Larry Arndt	.15	.07
❑ 8 John Barfield	.15	.07
❑ 9 Billy Bates	.15	.07
❑ 10 Kevin Batiste	.15	.07
❑ 11 Blaine Beatty	.15	.07
❑ 12 Stan Belinda	.15	.07
❑ 13 Juan Bell	.15	.07
❑ 14 Joey Belle	4.00	1.80
(Now known as Albert)		
❑ 15 Andy Benes	.75	.35
❑ 16 Mike Benjamin	.15	.07
❑ 17 Geronimo Berroa	.15	.07
❑ 18 Mike Blowers	.25	.11
❑ 19 Brian Brady	.15	.07
❑ 20 Francisco Cabrera	.15	.07
❑ 21 George Canale	.15	.07
❑ 22 Jose Cano	.15	.07
❑ 23 Steve Carter	.15	.07
❑ 24 Pat Combs	.15	.07
❑ 25 Scott Coolbaugh	.15	.07
❑ 26 Steve Cummings	.15	.07
❑ 27 Pete Dalena	.15	.07
❑ 28 Jeff Datz	.15	.07
❑ 29 Bobby Davidson	.15	.07
❑ 30 Drew Denson	.15	.07
❑ 31 Gary DiSarcina	.50	.23
❑ 32 Brian Dubois	.15	.07
❑ 33 Mike Dyer	.15	.07
❑ 34 Wayne Edwards	.15	.07
❑ 35 Junior Felix	.15	.07
❑ 36 Mike Fetters	.15	.07
❑ 37 Steve Finley	.75	.35
❑ 38 Darrin Fletcher	.25	.11
❑ 39 LaVel Freeman	.15	.07
❑ 40 Steve Frey	.15	.07
❑ 41 Mark Gardner	.15	.07
❑ 42 Joe Girardi	.50	.23

❏ 43	Juan Gonzalez	8.00	3.60			
❏ 44	Goose Gozzo	.15	.07			
❏ 45	Tommy Greene	.15	.07			
❏ 46	Ken Griffey Jr.	20.00	9.00			
❏ 47	Jason Grimsley	.15	.07			
❏ 48	Marquis Grissom	.75	.35			
❏ 49	Mark Guthrie	.15	.07			
❏ 50	Chip Hale	.15	.07			
❏ 51	Jack Hardy	.15	.07			
❏ 52	Gene Harris	.15	.07			
❏ 53	Mike Hartley	.15	.07			
❏ 54	Scott Hemond	.15	.07			
❏ 55	Xavier Hernandez	.15	.07			
❏ 56	Eric Hetzel	.15	.07			
❏ 57	Greg Hibbard	.15	.07			
❏ 58	Mark Higgins	.15	.07			
❏ 59	Glenallen Hill	.15	.07			
❏ 60	Chris Hoiles	.75	.35			
❏ 61	Shawn Holman	.15	.07			
❏ 62	Dann Howitt	.15	.07			
❏ 63	Mike Huff	.15	.07			
❏ 64	Terry Jorgensen	.15	.07			
❏ 65	David Justice	1.50	.70			
❏ 66	Jeff King	.15	.07			
❏ 67	Matt Kinzer	.15	.07			
❏ 68	Joe Kraemer	.15	.07			
❏ 69	Marcus Lawton	.15	.07			
❏ 70	Derek Lilliquist	.15	.07			
❏ 71	Scott Little	.15	.07			
❏ 72	Greg Litton	.15	.07			
❏ 73	Rick Luecken	.15	.07			
❏ 74	Julio Machado	.15	.07			
❏ 75	Tom Magrann	.15	.07			
❏ 76	Kelly Mann	.15	.07			
❏ 77	Randy McCament	.15	.07			
❏ 78	Ben McDonald	.15	.07			
❏ 79	Chuck McElroy	.15	.07			
❏ 80	Jeff McKnight	.15	.07			
❏ 81	Kent Mercker	.15	.07			
❏ 82	Matt Merullo	.15	.07			
❏ 83	Hensley Meulens	.15	.07			
❏ 84	Kevin Mmahat	.15	.07			
❏ 85	Mike Munoz	.15	.07			
❏ 86	Dan Murphy	.15	.07			
❏ 87	Jaime Navarro	.15	.07			
❏ 88	Randy Nosek	.15	.07			
❏ 89	John Olerud	2.00	.90			
❏ 90	Steve Olin	.25	.11			
❏ 91	Joe Oliver	.15	.07			
❏ 92	Francisco Oliveras	.15	.07			
❏ 93	Gregg Olson	.25	.11			
❏ 94	John Orton	.15	.07			
❏ 95	Dean Palmer	.75	.35			
❏ 96	Ramon Pena	.15	.07			
❏ 97	Jeff Peterek	.15	.07			
❏ 98	Marty Pevey	.15	.07			
❏ 99	Rusty Richards	.15	.07			
❏ 100	Jeff Richardson	.15	.07			
❏ 101	Rob Richie	.15	.07			
❏ 102	Kevin Ritz	.15	.07			
❏ 103	Rosario Rodriguez	.15	.07			
❏ 104	Mike Roesler	.15	.07			
❏ 105	Kenny Rogers	.25	.11			
❏ 106	Bobby Rose	.15	.07			
❏ 107	Alex Sanchez	.15	.07			
❏ 108	Deion Sanders	.75	.35			
❏ 109	Jeff Schaefer	.15	.07			
❏ 110	Jeff Schulz	.15	.07			
❏ 111	Mike Schwabe	.15	.07			
❏ 112	Dick Scott	.15	.07			
❏ 113	Scott Scudder	.15	.07			
❏ 114	Rudy Seanez	.15	.07			
❏ 115	Joe Skalski	.15	.07			
❏ 116	Dwight Smith	.15	.07			
❏ 117	Greg Smith	.15	.07			
❏ 118	Mike Smith	.15	.07			
❏ 119	Paul Sorrento	.50	.23			
❏ 120	Sammy Sosa	20.00	9.00			
❏ 121	Billy Spiers	.15	.07			
❏ 122	Mike Stanton	.15	.07			
❏ 123	Phil Stephenson	.15	.07			
❏ 124	Doug Strange	.15	.07			
❏ 125	Russ Swan	.15	.07			
❏ 126	Kevin Tapani	.25	.11			
❏ 127	Stu Tate	.15	.07			
❏ 128	Greg Vaughn	2.00	.90			

❏ 129	Robin Ventura	1.00	.45
❏ 130	Randy Veres	.15	.07
❏ 131	Jose Vizcaino	.50	.23
❏ 132	Omar Vizquel	1.00	.45
❏ 133	Larry Walker	4.00	1.80
❏ 134	Jerome Walton	.15	.07
❏ 135	Gary Wayne	.15	.07
❏ 136	Lenny Webster	.15	.07
❏ 137	Mickey Weston	.15	.07
❏ 138	Jeff Wetherby	.15	.07
❏ 139	John Wetteland	.75	.35
❏ 140	Ed Whited	.15	.07
❏ 141	Wally Whitehurst	.15	.07
❏ 142	Kevin Wickander	.15	.07
❏ 143	Dean Wilkins	.15	.07
❏ 144	Dana Williams	.15	.07
❏ 145	Paul Wilmet	.15	.07
❏ 146	Craig Wilson	.15	.07
❏ 147	Matt Winters	.15	.07
❏ 148	Eric Yelding	.15	.07
❏ 149	Clint Zavaras	.15	.07
❏ 150	Todd Zeile	.50	.23
❏ 151	Checklist Card	.15	.07
❏ 152	Checklist Card	.15	.07

1991 Topps

FRANK THOMAS

	MINT	NRMT
COMPLETE SET (792)	15.00	6.75
COMP.FACT.SET (792)	20.00	9.00
COMMON CARD (1-792)	.05	.02
MINOR STARS	.10	.05
UNLISTED STARS	.20	.09
SUBSET CARDS HALF VALUE OF BASE CARDS		

❏ 1	Nolan Ryan	.75	.35
❏ 2	George Brett RB	.20	.09
	Batting Title, 3 decades		
❏ 3	Carlton Fisk RB	.10	.05
	Catcher HR Record		
❏ 4	Kevin Maas RB	.05	.02
	Quickest to 10 HR's		
❏ 5	Cal Ripken RB	.20	.09
	Most cons. errorless games		
❏ 6	Nolan Ryan RB	.40	.18
	Oldest pitcher, no-hitter		
❏ 7	Ryne Sandberg RB	.20	.09
	Most cons. errorless games		
❏ 8	Bobby Thigpen RB	.05	.02
	Most saves, season		
❏ 9	Darrin Fletcher	.05	.02
❏ 10	Gregg Olson	.05	.02
❏ 11	Roberto Kelly	.05	.02
❏ 12	Paul Assenmacher	.05	.02
❏ 13	Mariano Duncan	.05	.02
❏ 14	Dennis Lamp	.05	.02
❏ 15	Von Hayes	.05	.02
❏ 16	Mike Heath	.05	.02
❏ 17	Jeff Brantley	.05	.02
❏ 18	Nelson Liriano	.05	.02
❏ 19	Jeff D. Robinson	.05	.02
❏ 20	Pedro Guerrero	.05	.02
❏ 21	Joe Morgan MG	.05	.02
❏ 22	Storm Davis	.05	.02
❏ 23	Jim Gantner	.05	.02
❏ 24	Dave Martinez	.05	.02
❏ 25	Tim Belcher	.05	.02

❏ 26	Luis Sojo UER	.05	.02
	(Born in Barquisimento, not Carquis)		
❏ 27	Bobby Witt	.05	.02
❏ 28	Alvaro Espinoza	.05	.02
❏ 29	Bob Walk	.05	.02
❏ 30	Gregg Jefferies	.05	.02
❏ 31	Colby Ward	.05	.02
❏ 32	Mike Simms	.05	.02
❏ 33	Barry Jones	.05	.02
❏ 34	Atlee Hammaker	.05	.02
❏ 35	Greg Maddux	.50	.23
❏ 36	Donnie Hill	.05	.02
❏ 37	Tom Bolton	.05	.02
❏ 38	Scott Bradley	.05	.02
❏ 39	Jim Neidinger	.05	.02
❏ 40	Kevin Mitchell	.05	.02
❏ 41	Ken Dayley	.05	.02
❏ 42	Chris Hoiles	.05	.02
❏ 43	Roger McDowell	.05	.02
❏ 44	Mike Felder	.05	.02
❏ 45	Chris Sabo	.05	.02
❏ 46	Tim Drummond	.05	.02
❏ 47	Brook Jacoby	.05	.02
❏ 48	Dennis Boyd	.05	.02
❏ 49A	Pat Borders ERR	.20	.09
	(40 steals at Kinston in '86)		
❏ 49B	Pat Borders COR	.05	.02
	(0 steals at Kinston in '86)		
❏ 50	Bob Welch	.05	.02
❏ 51	Art Howe MG	.05	.02
❏ 52	Francisco Oliveras	.05	.02
❏ 53	Mike Sharperson UER	.05	.02
	(Born in 1961, not 1960)		
❏ 54	Gary Mielke	.05	.02
❏ 55	Jeffrey Leonard	.05	.02
❏ 56	Jeff Parrett	.05	.02
❏ 57	Jack Howell	.05	.02
❏ 58	Mel Stottlemyre Jr.	.05	.02
❏ 59	Eric Yelding	.05	.02
❏ 60	Frank Viola	.05	.02
❏ 61	Stan Javier	.05	.02
❏ 62	Lee Guetterman	.05	.02
❏ 63	Milt Thompson	.05	.02
❏ 64	Tom Herr	.05	.02
❏ 65	Bruce Hurst	.05	.02
❏ 66	Terry Kennedy	.05	.02
❏ 67	Rick Honeycutt	.05	.02
❏ 68	Gary Sheffield	.20	.09
❏ 69	Steve Wilson	.05	.02
❏ 70	Ellis Burks	.10	.05
❏ 71	Jim Acker	.05	.02
❏ 72	Junior Ortiz	.05	.02
❏ 73	Craig Worthington	.05	.02
❏ 74	Shane Andrews	.05	.02
❏ 75	Jack Morris	.05	.02
❏ 76	Jerry Browne	.05	.02
❏ 77	Drew Hall	.05	.02
❏ 78	Geno Petralli	.05	.02
❏ 79	Frank Thomas	.75	.35
❏ 80A	Fernando Valenzuela ERR (104 earned runs in '90 tied for league lead)	.10	
❏ 80B	Fernando Valenzuela COR (104 earned runs in '90 led league, 20 CG's in 1986 now italicized)	.10	
❏ 81	Cito Gaston MG	.05	.02
❏ 82	Tom Glavine	.20	.09
❏ 83	Daryl Boston	.05	.02
❏ 84	Bob McClure	.05	.02
❏ 85	Jesse Barfield	.05	.02
❏ 86	Les Lancaster	.05	.02
❏ 87	Tracy Jones	.05	.02
❏ 88	Bob Tewksbury	.05	.02
❏ 89	Darren Daulton	.10	.05
❏ 90	Danny Tartabull	.05	.02
❏ 91	Greg Colbrunn	.05	.02
❏ 92	Danny Jackson	.05	.02
❏ 93	Ivan Calderon	.05	.02
❏ 94	John Dopson	.05	.02
❏ 95	Paul Molitor	.20	.09

❏ 96 Trevor Wilson	.05	.02	
❏ 97A Brady Anderson ERR	.20	.09	
(September, 2 RBI and			
3 hits, should be 3			
RBI and 14 hits)			
❏ 97B Brady Anderson COR	.20	.09	
❏ 98 Sergio Valdez	.05	.02	
❏ 99 Chris Gwynn	.05	.02	
❏ 100 Don Mattingly COR	.40	.18	
(101 hits in 1990)			
❏ 100A Don Mattingly ERR	1.00	.45	
(10 hits in 1990)			
❏ 101 Rob Ducey	.05	.02	
❏ 102 Gene Larkin	.05	.02	
❏ 103 Tim Costo	.05	.02	
❏ 104 Don Robinson	.05	.02	
❏ 105 Kevin McReynolds	.05	.02	
❏ 106 Ed Nunez	.05	.02	
❏ 107 Luis Polonia	.05	.02	
❏ 108 Matt Young	.05	.02	
❏ 109 Greg Riddoch MG	.05	.02	
❏ 110 Tom Henke	.05	.02	
❏ 111 Andres Thomas	.05	.02	
❏ 112 Frank DiPino	.05	.02	
❏ 113 Carl Everett	.50	.23	
❏ 114 Lance Dickson	.05	.02	
❏ 115 Hubie Brooks	.05	.02	
❏ 116 Mark Davis	.05	.02	
❏ 117 Dion James	.05	.02	
❏ 118 Tom Edens	.05	.02	
❏ 119 Carl Nichols	.05	.02	
❏ 120 Joe Carter	.10	.05	
❏ 121 Eric King	.05	.02	
❏ 122 Paul O'Neill	.05	.02	
❏ 123 Greg A. Harris	.05	.02	
❏ 124 Randy Bush	.05	.02	
❏ 125 Steve Bedrosian	.05	.02	
❏ 126 Bernard Gilkey	.10	.05	
❏ 127 Joe Price	.05	.02	
❏ 128 Travis Fryman	.20	.09	
(Front has SS			
back has SS-3B)			
❏ 129 Mark Eichhorn	.05	.02	
❏ 130 Ozzie Smith	.25	.11	
❏ 131A Checklist 1 ERR	.20	.09	
727 Phil Bradley			
❏ 131B Checklist 1 COR	.05	.02	
717 Phil Bradley			
❏ 132 Jamie Quirk	.05	.02	
❏ 133 Greg Briley	.05	.02	
❏ 134 Kevin Elster	.05	.02	
❏ 135 Jerome Walton	.05	.02	
❏ 136 Dave Schmidt	.05	.02	
❏ 137 Randy Ready	.05	.02	
❏ 138 Jamie Moyer	.05	.02	
❏ 139 Jeff Treadway	.05	.02	
❏ 140 Fred McGriff	.20	.09	
❏ 141 Nick Leyva MG	.05	.02	
❏ 142 Curt Wilkerson	.05	.02	
❏ 143 John Smiley	.05	.02	
❏ 144 Dave Henderson	.05	.02	
❏ 145 Lou Whitaker	.10	.05	
❏ 146 Dan Plesac	.05	.02	
❏ 147 Carlos Baerga	.10	.05	
❏ 148 Rey Palacios	.05	.02	
❏ 149 Al Osuna UER	.05	.02	
(Shown throwing right,			
but bio says lefty)			
❏ 150 Cal Ripken	.75	.35	
❏ 151 Tom Browning	.05	.02	
❏ 152 Mickey Hatcher	.05	.02	
❏ 153 Bryan Harvey	.05	.02	
❏ 154 Jay Buhner	.20	.09	
❏ 155A Dwight Evans ERR	.20	.09	
(Led league with			
162 games in '82)			
❏ 155B Dwight Evans COR	.10	.05	
(Tied for lead with			
162 games in '82)			
❏ 156 Carlos Martinez	.05	.02	
❏ 157 John Smoltz	.20	.09	
❏ 158 Jose Uribe	.05	.02	
❏ 159 Joe Boever	.05	.02	
❏ 160 Vince Coleman UER	.05	.02	
(Wrong birth year,			
born 9/22/60)			
❏ 161 Tim Leary	.05	.02	
❏ 162 Ozzie Canseco	.05	.02	
❏ 163 Dave Johnson	.05	.02	
❏ 164 Edgar Diaz	.05	.02	
❏ 165 Sandy Alomar Jr.	.10	.05	
❏ 166 Harold Baines	.05	.02	
❏ 167A Randy Tomlin ERR	.20	.09	
(Harrisburg)			
❏ 167B Randy Tomlin COR	.05	.02	
(Harrisburg)			
❏ 168 John Olerud	.15	.07	
❏ 169 Luis Aquino	.05	.02	
❏ 170 Carlton Fisk	.20	.09	
❏ 171 Tony LaRussa MG	.10	.05	
❏ 172 Pete Incaviglia	.05	.02	
❏ 173 Jason Grimsley	.05	.02	
❏ 174 Ken Caminiti	.20	.09	
❏ 175 Jack Armstrong	.05	.02	
❏ 176 John Orton	.05	.02	
❏ 177 Reggie Harris	.05	.02	
❏ 178 Dave Valle	.05	.02	
❏ 179 Pete Harnisch	.05	.02	
❏ 180 Tony Gwynn	.50	.23	
❏ 181 Duane Ward	.05	.02	
❏ 182 Junior Noboa	.05	.02	
❏ 183 Clay Parker	.05	.02	
❏ 184 Gary Green	.05	.02	
❏ 185 Joe Magrane	.05	.02	
❏ 186 Rod Booker	.05	.02	
❏ 187 Greg Cadaret	.05	.02	
❏ 188 Damon Berryhill	.05	.02	
❏ 189 Daryl Irvine	.05	.02	
❏ 190 Matt Williams	.20	.09	
❏ 191 Willie Blair	.05	.02	
❏ 192 Rob Deer	.05	.02	
❏ 193 Felix Fermin	.05	.02	
❏ 194 Xavier Hernandez	.05	.02	
❏ 195 Wally Joyner	.10	.05	
❏ 196 Jim Lefebvre	.05	.02	
❏ 197 Chris Nabholz	.05	.02	
❏ 198 R.J. Reynolds	.05	.02	
❏ 199 Mike Hartley	.05	.02	
❏ 200 Darryl Strawberry	.10	.05	
❏ 201 Tom Kelly MG	.05	.02	
❏ 202 Jim Leyritz	.10	.05	
❏ 203 Gene Harris	.05	.02	
❏ 204 Herm Winningham	.05	.02	
❏ 205 Mike Perez	.05	.02	
❏ 206 Carlos Quintana	.05	.02	
❏ 207 Gary Wayne	.05	.02	
❏ 208 Willie Wilson	.05	.02	
❏ 209 Ken Howell	.05	.02	
❏ 210 Lance Parrish	.05	.02	
❏ 211 Brian Barnes	.05	.02	
❏ 212 Steve Finley	.20	.09	
❏ 213 Frank Wills	.05	.02	
❏ 214 Joe Girardi	.10	.05	
❏ 215 Dave Smith	.05	.02	
❏ 216 Greg Gagne	.05	.02	
❏ 217 Chris Bosio	.05	.02	
❏ 218 Rick Parker	.05	.02	
❏ 219 Jack McDowell	.05	.02	
❏ 220 Tim Wallach	.05	.02	
❏ 221 Don Slaught	.05	.02	
❏ 222 Brian McRae	.10	.05	
❏ 223 Allan Anderson	.05	.02	
❏ 224 Juan Gonzalez	.75	.35	
❏ 225 Randy Johnson	.25	.11	
❏ 226 Alfredo Griffin	.05	.02	
❏ 227 Steve Avery UER	.05	.02	
(Pitched 13 games for			
Durham in 1989, not 2)			
❏ 228 Rex Hudler	.05	.02	
❏ 229 Rance Mulliniks	.05	.02	
❏ 230 Sid Fernandez	.05	.02	
❏ 231 Doug Rader MG	.05	.02	
❏ 232 Jose DeJesus	.05	.02	
❏ 233 Al Leiter	.10	.05	
❏ 234 Scott Erickson	.15	.07	
❏ 235 Dave Parker	.10	.05	
❏ 236A Frank Tanana ERR	.10	.05	
(Tied for lead with			
269 K's in '75)			
❏ 236B Frank Tanana COR	.05	.02	
(Led league with			
269 K's in '75)			
❏ 237 Rick Cerone	.05	.02	
❏ 238 Mike Dunne	.05	.02	
❏ 239 Darren Lewis	.10	.05	
❏ 240 Mike Scott	.05	.02	
❏ 241 Dave Clark UER	.05	.02	
(Career totals 19 HR			
and 5 3B, should			
be 22 and 3)			
❏ 242 Mike LaCoss	.05	.02	
❏ 243 Lance Johnson	.05	.02	
❏ 244 Mike Jeffcoat	.05	.02	
❏ 245 Kal Daniels	.05	.02	
❏ 246 Kevin Wickander	.05	.02	
❏ 247 Jody Reed	.05	.02	
❏ 248 Tom Gordon	.05	.02	
❏ 249 Bob Melvin	.05	.02	
❏ 250 Dennis Eckersley	.10	.05	
❏ 251 Mark Lemke	.05	.02	
❏ 252 Mel Rojas	.05	.02	
❏ 253 Garry Templeton	.05	.02	
❏ 254 Shawn Boskie	.05	.02	
❏ 255 Brian Downing	.05	.02	
❏ 256 Greg Hibbard	.05	.02	
❏ 257 Tom O'Malley	.05	.02	
❏ 258 Chris Hammond	.05	.02	
❏ 259 Hensley Meulens	.05	.02	
❏ 260 Harold Reynolds	.05	.02	
❏ 261 Bud Harrelson MG	.05	.02	
❏ 262 Tim Jones	.05	.02	
❏ 263 Checklist 2	.05	.02	
❏ 264 Dave Hollins	.15	.07	
❏ 265 Mark Gubicza	.05	.02	
❏ 266 Carmelo Castillo	.05	.02	
❏ 267 Mark Knudson	.05	.02	
❏ 268 Tom Brookens	.05	.02	
❏ 269 Joe Hesketh	.05	.02	
❏ 270 Mark McGwire COR	1.00	.45	
(1987 Slugging Pctg.			
listed as 618)			
❏ 270A Mark McGwire ERR	1.25	.55	
(1987 Slugging Pctg.			
listed as 618)			
❏ 271 Omar Olivares	.05	.02	
❏ 272 Jeff King	.05	.02	
❏ 273 Johnny Ray	.05	.02	
❏ 274 Ken Williams	.05	.02	
❏ 275 Alan Trammell	.15	.07	
❏ 276 Bill Swift	.05	.02	
❏ 277 Scott Coolbaugh	.05	.02	
❏ 278 Alex Fernandez UER	.10	.05	
(No '90 White Sox stats)			
❏ 279A Jose Gonzalez ERR	.05	.02	
(Photo actually			
Billy Bean)			
❏ 279B Jose Gonzalez COR	.05	.02	
❏ 280 Bret Saberhagen	.10	.05	
❏ 281 Larry Sheets	.05	.02	
❏ 282 Don Carman	.05	.02	
❏ 283 Marquis Grissom	.20	.09	
❏ 284 Billy Spiers	.05	.02	
❏ 285 Jim Abbott	.10	.05	
❏ 286 Ken Oberkfell	.05	.02	
❏ 287 Mark Grant	.05	.02	
❏ 288 Derrick May	.05	.02	
❏ 289 Tim Birtsas	.05	.02	
❏ 290 Steve Sax	.05	.02	
❏ 291 John Wathan MG	.05	.02	
❏ 292 Bud Black	.05	.02	
❏ 293 Jay Bell	.10	.05	
❏ 294 Mike Moore	.05	.02	
❏ 295 Rafael Palmeiro	.20	.09	
❏ 296 Mark Williamson	.05	.02	
❏ 297 Manny Lee	.05	.02	
❏ 298 Omar Vizquel	.20	.09	
❏ 299 Scott Radinsky	.05	.02	
❏ 300 Kirby Puckett	.30	.14	
❏ 301 Steve Farr	.05	.02	
❏ 302 Tim Teufel	.05	.02	
❏ 303 Mike Boddicker	.05	.02	
❏ 304 Kevin Reimer	.05	.02	
❏ 305 Mike Scioscia	.05	.02	
❏ 306A Lonnie Smith ERR	.20	.09	
(136 games in '90)			
❏ 306B Lonnie Smith COR	.05	.02	
(135 games in '90)			
❏ 307 Andy Benes	.10	.05	

308	Tom Pagnozzi	.05	.02
309	Norm Charlton	.05	.02
310	Gary Carter	.20	.09
311	Jeff Pico	.05	.02
312	Charlie Hayes	.05	.02
313	Ron Robinson	.05	.02
314	Gary Pettis	.05	.02
315	Roberto Alomar	.20	.09
316	Gene Nelson	.05	.02
317	Mike Fitzgerald	.05	.02
318	Rick Aguilera	.10	.05
319	Jeff McKnight	.05	.02
320	Tony Fernandez	.05	.02
321	Bob Rodgers MG	.05	.02
322	Terry Shumpert	.05	.02
323	Cory Snyder	.05	.02
324A	Ron Kittle ERR	.20	.09
	(Set another standard ...)		
324B	Ron Kittle COR	.05	.02
	(Tied another standard ...)		
325	Brett Butler	.10	.05
326	Ken Patterson	.05	.02
327	Ron Hassey	.05	.02
328	Walt Terrell	.05	.02
329	Dave Justice UER	.20	.09
	(Drafted third round on card, should say fourth pick)		
330	Dwight Gooden	.10	.05
331	Eric Anthony	.05	.02
332	Kenny Rogers	.05	.02
333	Chipper Jones FDP	5.00	2.20
334	Todd Benzinger	.05	.02
335	Mitch Williams	.05	.02
336	Matt Nokes	.05	.02
337A	Keith Comstock ERR	.20	.09
	(Cubs logo on front)		
337B	Keith Comstock COR	.05	.02
	(Mariners logo on front)		
338	Luis Rivera	.05	.02
339	Larry Walker	.30	.14
340	Ramon Martinez	.10	.05
341	John Moses	.05	.02
342	Mickey Morandini	.05	.02
343	Jose Oquendo	.05	.02
344	Jeff Russell	.05	.02
345	Len Dykstra	.10	.05
346	Jesse Orosco	.05	.02
347	Greg Vaughn	.20	.09
348	Todd Stottlemyre	.10	.05
349	Dave Gallagher	.05	.02
350	Glenn Davis	.05	.02
351	Joe Torre MG	.10	.05
352	Frank White	.10	.05
353	Tony Castillo	.05	.02
354	Sid Bream	.05	.02
355	Chili Davis	.05	.02
356	Mike Marshall	.05	.02
357	Jack Savage	.05	.02
358	Mark Parent	.05	.02
359	Chuck Cary	.05	.02
360	Tim Raines	.10	.05
361	Scott Garrelts	.05	.02
362	Hector Villanueva	.05	.02
363	Rick Mahler	.05	.02
364	Dan Pasqua	.05	.02
365	Mike Schooler	.05	.02
366A	Checklist 3 ERR	.20	.09
	19 Carl Nichols		
366B	Checklist 3 COR	.05	.02
	119 Carl Nichols		
367	Dave Walsh	.05	.02
368	Felix Jose	.05	.02
369	Steve Searcy	.05	.02
370	Kelly Gruber	.05	.02
371	Jeff Montgomery	.10	.05
372	Spike Owen	.05	.02
373	Darrin Jackson	.05	.02
374	Larry Casian	.05	.02
375	Tony Pena	.05	.02
376	Mike Harkey	.05	.02
377	Rene Gonzales	.05	.02
378A	Wilson Alvarez ERR	.50	.23
	('89 Port Charlotte and '90 Birmingham stat lines omitted)		
378B	Wilson Alvarez COR	.20	.09
	(Text still says 143 K's in 1988, whereas stats say 134)		
379	Randy Velarde	.05	.02
380	Willie McGee	.10	.05
381	Jim Leyland MG	.05	.02
382	Mackey Sasser	.05	.02
383	Pete Smith	.05	.02
384	Gerald Perry	.05	.02
385	Mickey Tettleton	.10	.05
386	Cecil Fielder AS	.05	.02
387	Julio Franco AS	.05	.02
388	Kelly Gruber AS	.05	.02
389	Alan Trammell AS	.10	.05
390	Jose Canseco AS	.10	.05
391	Rickey Henderson AS	.10	.05
392	Ken Griffey Jr. AS	.75	.35
393	Carlton Fisk AS	.10	.05
394	Bob Welch AS	.05	.02
395	Chuck Finley AS	.05	.02
396	Bobby Thigpen AS	.05	.02
397	Eddie Murray AS	.10	.05
398	Ryne Sandberg AS	.20	.09
399	Matt Williams AS	.10	.05
400	Barry Larkin AS	.10	.05
401	Barry Bonds AS	.20	.09
402	Darryl Strawberry AS	.05	.02
403	Bobby Bonilla AS	.05	.02
404	Mike Scioscia AS	.05	.02
405	Doug Drabek AS	.05	.02
406	Frank Viola AS	.05	.02
407	John Franco AS	.05	.02
408	Earnie Riles	.05	.02
409	Mike Stanley	.05	.02
410	Dave Righetti	.05	.02
411	Lance Blankenship	.05	.02
412	Dave Bergman	.05	.02
413	Terry Mulholland	.05	.02
414	Sammy Sosa	1.25	.55
415	Rick Sutcliffe	.05	.02
416	Randy Milligan	.05	.02
417	Bill Krueger	.05	.02
418	Nick Esasky	.05	.02
419	Jeff Reed	.05	.02
420	Bobby Thigpen	.05	.02
421	Alex Cole	.05	.02
422	Rick Reuschel	.05	.02
423	Rafael Ramirez UER	.05	.02
	(Born 1959, not 1958)		
424	Calvin Schiraldi	.05	.02
425	Andy Van Slyke	.10	.05
426	Joe Grahe	.05	.02
427	Rick Dempsey	.05	.02
428	John Barfield	.05	.02
429	Stump Merrill MG	.05	.02
430	Gary Gaetti	.05	.02
431	Paul Gibson	.05	.02
432	Delino DeShields	.10	.05
433	Pat Tabler	.05	.02
434	Julio Machado	.05	.02
435	Kevin Maas	.05	.02
436	Scott Bankhead	.05	.02
437	Doug Dascenzo	.05	.02
438	Vicente Palacios	.05	.02
439	Dickie Thon	.05	.02
440	George Bell	.05	.02
441	Zane Smith	.05	.02
442	Charlie O'Brien	.05	.02
443	Jeff Innis	.05	.02
444	Glenn Braggs	.05	.02
445	Greg Swindell	.05	.02
446	Craig Lefferts	.05	.02
447	John Burkett	.05	.02
448	Craig Lefferts	.05	.02
449	Juan Berenguer	.05	.02
450	Wade Boggs	.20	.09
451	Neal Heaton	.05	.02
452	Bill Schroeder	.05	.02
453	Lenny Harris	.05	.02
454A	Kevin Appier ERR	.20	.09
	('90 Omaha stat line omitted)		
454B	Kevin Appier COR	.10	.05
455	Walt Weiss	.05	.02
456	Charlie Leibrandt	.05	.02
457	Todd Hundley	.20	.09
458	Brian Holman	.05	.02
459	Tom Trebelhorn MG UER	.05	.02
	(Pitching and batting columns switched)		
460	Dave Steib	.05	.02
461	Robin Ventura	.20	.09
462	Steve Frey	.05	.02
463	Dwight Smith	.05	.02
464	Steve Buechele	.05	.02
465	Ken Griffey Sr.	.10	.05
466	Charles Nagy	.05	.02
467	Dennis Cook	.05	.02
468	Tim Hulett	.05	.02
469	Chet Lemon	.05	.02
470	Howard Johnson	.05	.02
471	Mike Lieberthal	.50	.23
472	Kirt Manwaring	.05	.02
473	Curt Young	.05	.02
474	Phil Plantier	.05	.02
475	Ted Higuera	.05	.02
476	Glenn Wilson	.05	.02
477	Mike Fetters	.05	.02
478	Kurt Stillwell	.05	.02
479	Bob Patterson UER	.05	.02
	(Has a decimal point between 7 and 9)		
480	Dave Magadan	.05	.02
481	Eddie Whitson	.05	.02
482	Tino Martinez	.20	.09
483	Mike Aldrete	.05	.02
484	Dave LaPoint	.05	.02
485	Terry Pendleton	.10	.05
486	Tommy Greene	.05	.02
487	Rafael Belliard	.05	.02
488	Jeff Manto	.05	.02
489	Bobby Valentine MG	.05	.02
490	Kirk Gibson	.10	.05
491	Kurt Miller	.05	.02
492	Ernie Whitt	.05	.02
493	Jose Rijo	.05	.02
494	Chris James	.05	.02
495	Charlie Hough	.10	.05
496	Marty Barrett	.05	.02
497	Ben McDonald	.05	.02
498	Mark Salas	.05	.02
499	Melido Perez	.05	.02
500	Will Clark	.20	.09
501	Mike Bielecki	.05	.02
502	Carney Lansford	.05	.02
503	Roy Smith	.05	.02
504	Julio Valera	.05	.02
505	Chuck Finley	.10	.05
506	Darnell Coles	.05	.02
507	Steve Jeltz	.05	.02
508	Mike York	.05	.02
509	Glenallen Hill	.05	.02
510	John Franco	.10	.05
511	Steve Balboni	.05	.02
512	Jose Mesa	.05	.02
513	Jerald Clark	.05	.02
514	Mike Stanton	.05	.02
515	Alvin Davis	.05	.02
516	Karl Rhodes	.05	.02
517	Joe Oliver	.05	.02
518	Cris Carpenter	.05	.02
519	Sparky Anderson MG	.10	.05
520	Mark Grace	.20	.09
521	Joe Orsulak	.05	.02
522	Stan Belinda	.05	.02
523	Rodney McCray	.05	.02
524	Darrel Akerfelds	.05	.02
525	Willie Randolph	.10	.05
526A	Moises Alou ERR	.50	.23
	(37 runs in 2 games for '90 Pirates)		
526B	Moises Alou COR	.20	.09
	(0 runs in 2 games for '90 Pirates)		
527A	Checklist 4 ERR	.20	.09
	105 Keith Miller 719 Kevin McReynolds		
527B	Checklist 4 COR	.05	.02
	105 Kevin McReynolds		

719 Keith Miller

Card	Hi	Lo
☐ 528 Dennis Martinez	.10	.05
☐ 529 Marc Newfield	.05	.02
☐ 530 Roger Clemens	.50	.23
☐ 531 Dave Rohde	.05	.02
☐ 532 Kirk McCaskill	.05	.02
☐ 533 Oddibe McDowell	.05	.02
☐ 534 Mike Jackson	.10	.05
☐ 535 Ruben Sierra UER	.05	.02
(Back reads 100 Runs amd 100 RBI's)		
☐ 536 Mike Witt	.05	.02
☐ 537 Jose Lind	.05	.02
☐ 538 Bip Roberts	.05	.02
☐ 539 Scott Terry	.05	.02
☐ 540 George Brett	.40	.18
☐ 541 Domingo Ramos	.05	.02
☐ 542 Rob Murphy	.05	.02
☐ 543 Junior Felix	.05	.02
☐ 544 Alejandro Pena	.05	.02
☐ 545 Dale Murphy	.20	.09
☐ 546 Jeff Ballard	.05	.02
☐ 547 Mike Pagliarulo	.05	.02
☐ 548 Jaime Navarro	.05	.02
☐ 549 John McNamara MG	.05	.02
☐ 550 Eric Davis	.10	.05
☐ 551 Bob Kipper	.05	.02
☐ 552 Jeff Hamilton	.05	.02
☐ 553 Joe Klink	.05	.02
☐ 554 Brian Harper	.05	.02
☐ 555 Turner Ward	.05	.02
☐ 556 Gary Ward	.05	.02
☐ 557 Wally Whitehurst	.05	.02
☐ 558 Otis Nixon	.10	.05
☐ 559 Adam Peterson	.05	.02
☐ 560 Greg Smith	.05	.02
☐ 561 Tim McIntosh	.05	.02
☐ 562 Jeff Kunkel	.05	.02
☐ 563 Brent Knackert	.05	.02
☐ 564 Dante Bichette	.05	.09
☐ 565 Craig Biggio	.20	.09
☐ 566 Craig Wilson	.05	.02
☐ 567 Dwayne Henry	.05	.02
☐ 568 Ron Karkovice	.05	.02
☐ 569 Curt Schilling	.20	.09
☐ 570 Barry Bonds	.25	.11
☐ 571 Pat Combs	.05	.02
☐ 572 Dave Anderson	.05	.02
☐ 573 Rich Rodriguez UER	.05	.02
(Stats drafted 4th, but bio says 9th round)		
☐ 574 John Marzano	.05	.02
☐ 575 Robin Yount	.20	.09
☐ 576 Jeff Kaiser	.05	.02
☐ 577 Bill Doran	.05	.02
☐ 578 Dave West	.05	.02
☐ 579 Roger Craig MG	.05	.02
☐ 580 Dave Stewart	.10	.05
☐ 581 Luis Quinones	.05	.02
☐ 582 Marty Clary	.05	.02
☐ 583 Tony Phillips	.05	.02
☐ 584 Kevin Brown	.15	.07
☐ 585 Pete O'Brien	.05	.02
☐ 586 Fred Lynn	.05	.02
☐ 587 Jose Offerman UER	.15	.07
(Text says he signed 7/24/86, but bio says 1988)		
☐ 588 Mark Whiten	.05	.02
☐ 589 Scott Ruskin	.05	.02
☐ 590 Eddie Murray	.20	.09
☐ 591 Ken Hill	.05	.02
☐ 592 B.J. Surhoff	.10	.05
☐ 593A Mike Walker ERR	.20	.09
('90 Canton-Akron stat line omitted)		
☐ 593B Mike Walker COR	.05	.02
☐ 594 Rich Garces	.05	.02
☐ 595 Bill Landrum	.05	.02
☐ 596 Ronnie Walden	.05	.02
☐ 597 Jerry Don Gleaton	.05	.02
☐ 598 Sam Horn	.05	.02
☐ 599A Greg Myers ERR	.20	.09
('90 Syracuse stat line omitted)		
☐ 599B Greg Myers COR	.05	.02
☐ 600 Bo Jackson	.10	.05
☐ 601 Bob Ojeda	.05	.02
☐ 602 Casey Candaele	.05	.02
☐ 603A Wes Chamberlain ERR	.20	.09
(Photo actually Louie Meadows)		
☐ 603B Wes Chamberlain COR	.05	.02
☐ 604 Billy Hatcher	.05	.02
☐ 605 Jeff Reardon	.10	.05
☐ 606 Jim Gott	.05	.02
☐ 607 Edgar Martinez	.20	.09
☐ 608 Todd Burns	.05	.02
☐ 609 Jeff Torborg MG	.05	.02
☐ 610 Andres Galarraga	.20	.09
☐ 611 Dave Eiland	.05	.02
☐ 612 Steve Lyons	.05	.02
☐ 613 Eric Show	.05	.02
☐ 614 Luis Salazar	.05	.02
☐ 615 Bert Blyleven	.10	.05
☐ 616 Todd Zeile	.10	.05
☐ 617 Bill Wegman	.05	.02
☐ 618 Sil Campusano	.05	.02
☐ 619 David Wells	.10	.05
☐ 620 Ozzie Guillen	.05	.02
☐ 621 Ted Power	.05	.02
☐ 622 Jack Daugherty	.05	.02
☐ 623 Jeff Blauser	.05	.02
☐ 624 Tom Candiotti	.05	.02
☐ 625 Terry Steinbach	.10	.05
☐ 626 Gerald Young	.05	.02
☐ 627 Tim Layana	.05	.02
☐ 628 Greg Litton	.05	.02
☐ 629 Wes Gardner	.05	.02
☐ 630 Dave Winfield	.20	.09
☐ 631 Mike Morgan	.05	.02
☐ 632 Lloyd Moseby	.05	.02
☐ 633 Kevin Tapani	.05	.02
☐ 634 Henry Cotto	.05	.02
☐ 635 Andy Hawkins	.05	.02
☐ 636 Geronimo Pena	.05	.02
☐ 637 Bruce Ruffin	.05	.02
☐ 638 Mike Macfarlane	.05	.02
☐ 639 Frank Robinson MG	.15	.07
☐ 640 Andre Dawson	.20	.09
☐ 641 Mike Henneman	.05	.02
☐ 642 Hal Morris	.05	.02
☐ 643 Jim Presley	.05	.02
☐ 644 Chuck Crim	.05	.02
☐ 645 Juan Samuel	.05	.02
☐ 646 Andujar Cedeno	.10	.05
☐ 647 Mark Portugal	.05	.02
☐ 648 Lee Stevens	.10	.05
☐ 649 Bill Sampen	.05	.02
☐ 650 Jack Clark	.10	.05
☐ 651 Alan Mills	.05	.02
☐ 652 Kevin Romine	.05	.02
☐ 653 Anthony Telford	.05	.02
☐ 654 Paul Sorrento	.10	.05
☐ 655 Erik Hanson	.05	.02
☐ 656A Checklist 5 ERR	.20	.09
348 Vicente Palacios		
381 Jose Lind		
537 Mike LaValliere		
665 Jim Leyland		
☐ 656B Checklist 5 ERR	.20	.09
433 Vicente Palacios (Palacios should be 438)		
537 Jose Lind		
665 Mike LaValliere		
381 Jim Leyland		
☐ 656C Checklist 5 COR	.20	.09
438 Vicente Palacios		
537 Jose Lind		
665 Mike LaValliere		
381 Jim Leyland		
☐ 657 Mike Kingery	.05	.02
☐ 658 Scott Aldred	.05	.02
☐ 659 Oscar Azocar	.05	.02
☐ 660 Lee Smith	.10	.05
☐ 661 Steve Lake	.05	.02
☐ 662 Ron Dibble	.05	.02
☐ 663 Greg Brock	.05	.02
☐ 664 John Farrell	.05	.02
☐ 665 Mike LaValliere	.05	.02
☐ 666 Danny Darwin	.05	.02
☐ 667 Kent Anderson	.05	.02
☐ 668 Bill Long	.05	.02
☐ 669 Lou Piniella MG	.10	.05
☐ 670 Rickey Henderson	.25	.11
☐ 671 Andy McGaffigan	.05	.02
☐ 672 Shane Mack	.05	.02
☐ 673 Greg Olson UER	.05	.02
(6 RBI in '88 at Tidewater and 2 RBI in '87, should be 48 and 15)		
☐ 674A Kevin Gross ERR	.20	.09
(89 BB with Phillies in '88 tied for league lead)		
☐ 674B Kevin Gross COR	.05	.02
(89 BB with Phillies in '88 led league)		
☐ 675 Tom Brunansky	.05	.02
☐ 676 Scott Chiamparino	.05	.02
☐ 677 Billy Ripken	.05	.02
☐ 678 Mark Davidson	.05	.02
☐ 679 Bill Bathe	.05	.02
☐ 680 David Cone	.10	.05
☐ 681 Jeff Schaefer	.05	.02
☐ 682 Ray Lankford	.20	.09
☐ 683 Derek Lilliquist	.05	.02
☐ 684 Milt Cuyler	.05	.02
☐ 685 Doug Drabek	.05	.02
☐ 686 Mike Gallego	.05	.02
☐ 687A John Cerutti ERR	.20	.09
(4.46 ERA in '90)		
☐ 687B John Cerutti COR	.05	.02
(4.76 ERA in '90)		
☐ 688 Rosario Rodriguez	.05	.02
☐ 689 John Kruk	.10	.05
☐ 690 Orel Hershiser	.10	.05
☐ 691 Mike Blowers	.05	.02
☐ 692A Efrain Valdez ERR	.20	.09
(Born 6/11/66)		
☐ 692B Efrain Valdez COR	.05	.02
(Born 7/11/66 and two lines of text added)		
☐ 693 Francisco Cabrera	.05	.02
☐ 694 Randy Veres	.05	.02
☐ 695 Kevin Seitzer	.05	.02
☐ 696 Steve Olin	.05	.02
☐ 697 Shawn Abner	.05	.02
☐ 698 Mark Guthrie	.05	.02
☐ 699 Jim Lefebvre MG	.05	.02
☐ 700 Jose Canseco	.25	.11
☐ 701 Pascual Perez	.05	.02
☐ 702 Tim Naehring	.05	.02
☐ 703 Juan Agosto	.05	.02
☐ 704 Devon White	.05	.02
☐ 705 Robby Thompson	.05	.02
☐ 706A Brad Arnsberg ERR	.20	.09
☐ 706B Brad Arnsberg COR	.05	.02
(62.2 IP in '90)		
☐ 707 Jim Eisenreich	.05	.02
☐ 708 John Mitchell	.05	.02
☐ 709 Matt Sinatro	.05	.02
☐ 710 Kent Hrbek	.10	.05
☐ 711 Jose DeLeon	.05	.02
☐ 712 Ricky Jordan	.05	.02
☐ 713 Scott Scudder	.05	.02
☐ 714 Marvell Wynne	.05	.02
☐ 715 Tim Burke	.05	.02
☐ 716 Bob Geren	.05	.02
☐ 717 Phil Bradley	.05	.02
☐ 718 Steve Crawford	.05	.02
☐ 719 Keith Miller	.05	.02
☐ 720 Cecil Fielder	.10	.05
☐ 721 Mark Lee	.05	.02
☐ 722 Wally Backman	.05	.02
☐ 723 Candy Maldonado	.05	.02
☐ 724 David Segui	.10	.05
☐ 725 Ron Gant	.20	.09
☐ 726 Phil Stephenson	.05	.02
☐ 727 Mookie Wilson	.10	.05
☐ 728 Scott Sanderson	.05	.02
☐ 729 Don Zimmer MG	.05	.02
☐ 730 Barry Larkin	.20	.09
☐ 731 Jeff Gray	.05	.02
☐ 732 Franklin Stubbs	.05	.02
☐ 733 Kelly Downs	.05	.02
☐ 734 John Russell	.05	.02

❏ 735	Ron Darling	.05	.02
❏ 736	Dick Schofield	.05	.02
❏ 737	Tim Crews	.05	.02
❏ 738	Mel Hall	.05	.02
❏ 739	Russ Swan	.05	.02
❏ 740	Ryne Sandberg	.25	.11
❏ 741	Jimmy Key	.10	
❏ 742	Tommy Gregg	.05	.02
❏ 743	Bryn Smith	.05	.02
❏ 744	Nelson Santovenia	.05	.02
❏ 745	Doug Jones	.05	.02
❏ 746	John Shelby	.05	.02
❏ 747	Tony Fossas	.05	.02
❏ 748	Al Newman	.05	.02
❏ 749	Greg W. Harris	.05	.02
❏ 750	Bobby Bonilla	.10	.05
❏ 751	Wayne Edwards	.05	.02
❏ 752	Kevin Bass	.05	.02
❏ 753	Paul Marak UER	.05	.02
	(Stats say drafted in Jan. but box says May)		
❏ 754	Bill Pecota	.05	.02
❏ 755	Mark Langston	.05	.02
❏ 756	Jeff Huson	.05	.02
❏ 757	Mark Gardner	.05	.02
❏ 758	Mike Devereaux	.05	.02
❏ 759	Bobby Cox MG	.05	.02
❏ 760	Benny Santiago	.05	.02
❏ 761	Larry Andersen	.05	.02
❏ 762	Mitch Webster	.05	.02
❏ 763	Dana Kiecker	.05	.02
❏ 764	Mark Carreon	.05	.02
❏ 765	Shawon Dunston	.05	.02
❏ 766	Jeff Robinson	.05	.02
❏ 767	Dan Wilson	.20	.09
❏ 768	Don Pall	.05	.02
❏ 769	Tim Sherrill	.05	.02
❏ 770	Jay Howell	.05	.02
❏ 771	Gary Redus UER	.05	.02
	(Born in Tanner, should say Athens)		
❏ 772	Kent Mercker UER	.05	.02
	(Born in Indianapolis, should say Dublin, Ohio)		
❏ 773	Tom Foley	.05	.02
❏ 774	Dennis Rasmussen	.05	.02
❏ 775	Julio Franco	.05	.02
❏ 776	Brent Mayne	.05	.02
❏ 777	John Candelaria	.05	.02
❏ 778	Dan Gladden	.05	.02
❏ 779	Carmelo Martinez	.05	.02
❏ 780A	Randy Myers ERR	.05	.02
	(15 career losses)		
❏ 780B	Randy Myers COR	.05	.02
	(19 career losses)		
❏ 781	Darryl Hamilton	.05	.02
❏ 782	Jim Deshaies	.05	.02
❏ 783	Joel Skinner	.05	.02
❏ 784	Willie Fraser	.05	.02
❏ 785	Scott Fletcher	.05	.02
❏ 786	Eric Plunk	.05	.02
❏ 787	Checklist 6	.05	.02
❏ 788	Bob Milacki	.05	.02
❏ 789	Tom Lasorda MG	.20	.09
❏ 790	Ken Griffey Jr.	1.50	.70
❏ 791	Mike Benjamin	.05	.02
❏ 792	Mike Greenwell	.05	.02

1991 Topps Tiffany

		MINT	NRMT
COMP.FACT.SET (792)		300.00	135.00
COMMON CARD (1-792)		.50	.23
*STARS: 15X TO 30X BASIC CARDS			
*ROOKIES: 12.5X TO 25X BASIC CARDS			
DISTRIBUTED ONLY IN FACTORY SET FORM			

1991 Topps Traded

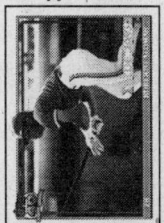

	MINT	NRMT
COMPLETE SET (132)	8.00	3.60
COMMON CARD (1T-132T)	.05	.02
MINOR STARS	.10	.05
UNLISTED STARS	.20	.09
*GRAY AND WHITE BACKS: SAME VALUE		

❏ 1T	Juan Agosto	.05	.02
❏ 2T	Roberto Alomar	.20	.09
❏ 3T	Wally Backman	.05	.02
❏ 4T	Jeff Bagwell	4.00	1.80
❏ 5T	Skeeter Barnes	.05	.02
❏ 6T	Steve Bedrosian	.05	.02
❏ 7T	Derek Bell	.20	.09
❏ 8T	George Bell	.10	.05
❏ 9T	Rafael Belliard	.05	.02
❏ 10T	Dante Bichette	.05	.02
❏ 11T	Bud Black	.05	.02
❏ 12T	Mike Boddicker	.05	.02
❏ 13T	Sid Bream	.05	.02
❏ 14T	Hubie Brooks	.05	.02
❏ 15T	Brett Butler	.10	.05
❏ 16T	Ivan Calderon	.05	.02
❏ 17T	John Candelaria	.05	.02
❏ 18T	Tom Candiotti	.05	.02
❏ 19T	Gary Carter	.20	.09
❏ 20T	Joe Carter	.10	.05
❏ 21T	Rick Cerone	.05	.02
❏ 22T	Jack Clark	.10	.05
❏ 23T	Vince Coleman	.05	.02
❏ 24T	Scott Coolbaugh	.05	.02
❏ 25T	Danny Cox	.05	.02
❏ 26T	Danny Darwin	.05	.02
❏ 27T	Chili Davis	.10	.05
❏ 28T	Glenn Davis	.05	.02
❏ 29T	Steve Decker	.05	.02
❏ 30T	Rob Deer	.05	.02
❏ 31T	Rich DeLucia	.05	.02
❏ 32T	John Dettmer USA	.05	.02
❏ 33T	Brian Downing	.05	.02
❏ 34T	Darren Dreifort USA	.50	.23
❏ 35T	Kirk Dressendorfer	.05	.02
❏ 36T	Jim Essian MG	.05	.02
❏ 37T	Dwight Evans	.10	.05
❏ 38T	Steve Farr	.05	.02
❏ 39T	Jeff Fassero	.10	.05
❏ 40T	Junior Felix	.05	.02
❏ 41T	Tony Fernandez	.05	.02
❏ 42T	Steve Finley	.20	.09
❏ 43T	Jim Fregosi MG	.05	.02
❏ 44T	Gary Gaetti	.10	.05
❏ 45T	Jason Giambi USA	2.00	.90
❏ 46T	Kirk Gibson	.10	.05
❏ 47T	Leo Gomez	.05	.02
❏ 48T	Luis Gonzalez	.50	.23
❏ 49T	Jeff Granger USA	.10	.05
❏ 50T	Todd Greene USA	.50	.23
❏ 51T	Jeffrey Hammonds USA	.75	.35
❏ 52T	Mike Hargrove MG	.05	.02

❏ 53T	Pete Harnisch	.05	.02
❏ 54T	Rick Helling USA UER	1.00	.45
	(Misspelled Hellings on card back)		
❏ 55T	Glenallen Hill	.05	.02
❏ 56T	Charlie Hough	.10	.05
❏ 57T	Pete Incaviglia	.05	.02
❏ 58T	Bo Jackson	.10	.05
❏ 59T	Danny Jackson	.05	.02
❏ 60T	Reggie Jefferson	.15	.07
❏ 61T	Charles Johnson USA	1.00	.45
❏ 62T	Jeff Johnson	.05	.02
❏ 63T	Todd Johnson USA	.05	.02
❏ 64T	Barry Jones	.05	.02
❏ 65T	Chris Jones	.05	.02
❏ 66T	Scott Kamieniecki	.05	.02
❏ 67T	Pat Kelly	.05	.02
❏ 68T	Darryl Kile	.20	.09
❏ 69T	Chuck Knoblauch	.20	.09
❏ 70T	Bill Krueger	.05	.02
❏ 71T	Scott Leius	.05	.02
❏ 72T	Donnie Leshnock USA	.05	.02
❏ 73T	Mark Lewis	.05	.02
❏ 74T	Candy Maldonado	.05	.02
❏ 75T	Jason McDonald USA	.05	.02
❏ 76T	Willie McGee	.10	.05
❏ 77T	Fred McGriff	.20	.09
❏ 78T	Billy McMillon USA	.05	.02
❏ 79T	Hal McRae MG	.05	.02
❏ 80T	Dan Melendez USA	.05	.02
❏ 81T	Orlando Merced	.05	.02
❏ 82T	Jack Morris	.10	.05
❏ 83T	Phil Nevin USA	.50	.23
❏ 84T	Otis Nixon	.10	.05
❏ 85T	Johnny Oates MG	.05	.02
❏ 86T	Bob Ojeda	.05	.02
❏ 87T	Mike Pagliarulo	.05	.02
❏ 88T	Dean Palmer	.10	.05
❏ 89T	Dave Parker	.10	.05
❏ 90T	Terry Pendleton	.10	.05
❏ 91T	Tony Phillips (P) USA	.05	.02
❏ 92T	Doug Piatt	.05	.02
❏ 93T	Ron Polk USA CO	.05	.02
❏ 94T	Tim Raines	.10	.05
❏ 95T	Willie Randolph	.10	.05
❏ 96T	Dave Righetti	.05	.02
❏ 97T	Ernie Riles	.05	.02
❏ 98T	Chris Roberts USA	.20	.09
❏ 99T	Jeff D. Robinson	.05	.02
❏ 100T	Jeff M. Robinson	.05	.02
❏ 101T	Ivan Rodriguez	4.00	1.80
❏ 102T	Steve Rodriguez USA	.05	.02
❏ 103T	Tom Runnells MG	.05	.02
❏ 104T	Scott Sanderson	.05	.02
❏ 105T	Bob Scanlan	.05	.02
❏ 106T	Pete Schourek	.10	.05
❏ 107T	Gary Scott	.05	.02
❏ 108T	Paul Shuey USA	.10	.05
❏ 109T	Doug Simons	.05	.02
❏ 110T	Dave Smith	.05	.02
❏ 111T	Cory Snyder	.05	.02
❏ 112T	Luis Sojo	.05	.02
❏ 113T	Kennie Steenstra USA	.05	.02
❏ 114T	Darryl Strawberry	.10	.05
❏ 115T	Franklin Stubbs	.05	.02
❏ 116T	Todd Taylor USA	.05	.02
❏ 117T	Wade Taylor	.05	.02
❏ 118T	Garry Templeton	.05	.02
❏ 119T	Mickey Tettleton	.10	.05
❏ 120T	Tim Teufel	.05	.02
❏ 121T	Mike Timlin	.05	.02
❏ 122T	David Tuttle USA	.05	.02
❏ 123T	Mo Vaughn	.40	.18
❏ 124T	Jeff Ware USA	.05	.02
❏ 125T	Devon White	.05	.02
❏ 126T	Mark Whiten	.05	.02
❏ 127T	Mitch Williams	.05	.02
❏ 128T	Craig Wilson USA	.05	.02
❏ 129T	Willie Wilson	.05	.02
❏ 130T	Chris Wimmer USA	.05	.02
❏ 131T	Ivan Zweig USA	.05	.02
❏ 132T	Checklist 1T-132T	.05	.02

1991 Topps Traded Tiffany

	MINT	NRMT
COMP.FACT.SET (132)	225.00	100.00
COMMON CARD (1T-132T)	.50	.23

*STARS: 15X TO 30X BASIC CARDS
*ROOKIES: 12.5X TO 25X BASIC CARDS
*USA ROOKIES: 6X TO 12X BASIC CARDS
DISTRIBUTED ONLY IN FACTORY SET FORM

1991 Topps Debut '90

	MINT	NRMT
COMPLETE SET (171)	20.00	9.00
COMMON CARD (1-171)	.15	.07
MINOR STARS	.25	.11
SEMISTARS	.50	.23

DISTRIBUTED ONLY IN FACTORY SET FORM

☐ 1	Paul Abbott	.15	.07
☐ 2	Steve Adkins	.15	.07
☐ 3	Scott Aldred	.15	.07
☐ 4	Gerald Alexander	.15	.07
☐ 5	Moises Alou	1.00	.45
☐ 6	Steve Avery	.25	.11
☐ 7	Oscar Azocar	.15	.07
☐ 8	Carlos Baerga	.25	.11
☐ 9	Kevin Baez	.15	.07
☐ 10	Jeff Baldwin	.15	.07
☐ 11	Brian Barnes	.15	.07
☐ 12	Kevin Bearse	.15	.07
☐ 13	Kevin Belcher	.15	.07
☐ 14	Mike Bell	.15	.07
☐ 15	Sean Berry	.25	.11
☐ 16	Joe Bitker	.15	.07
☐ 17	Willie Blair	.15	.07
☐ 18	Brian Bohanon	.15	.07
☐ 19	Mike Bordick	.25	.11
☐ 20	Shawn Boskie	.25	.11
☐ 21	Rod Brewer	.15	.07
☐ 22	Kevin D. Brown	.15	.07
☐ 23	Dave Burba	.60	.25
☐ 24	Jim Campbell	.15	.07
☐ 25	Ozzie Canseco	.15	.07
☐ 26	Chuck Carr	.15	.07
☐ 27	Larry Casian	.15	.07
☐ 28	Andujar Cedeno	.15	.07
☐ 29	Wes Chamberlain	.15	.07
☐ 30	Scott Chiamparino	.15	.07
☐ 31	Steve Chitren	.15	.07
☐ 32	Pete Coachman	.15	.07
☐ 33	Alex Cole	.15	.07
☐ 34	Jeff Conine	.60	.25
☐ 35	Scott Cooper	.15	.07
☐ 36	Milt Cuyler	.15	.07
☐ 37	Steve Decker	.15	.07
☐ 38	Rich DeLucia	.15	.07
☐ 39	Delino DeShields	.60	.25
☐ 40	Mark Dewey	.15	.07
☐ 41	Carlos Diaz	.15	.07
☐ 42	Lance Dickson	.15	.07
☐ 43	Narciso Elvira	.15	.07
☐ 44	Luis Encarnacion	.15	.07
☐ 45	Scott Erickson	.50	.23
☐ 46	Paul Faries	.15	.07
☐ 47	Howard Farmer	.15	.07
☐ 48	Alex Fernandez	.25	.11
☐ 49	Travis Fryman	.60	.25
☐ 50	Rich Garces	.15	.07
☐ 51	Carlos Garcia	.15	.07
☐ 52	Mike Gardiner	.15	.07
☐ 53	Bernard Gilkey	.25	.11
☐ 54	Tom Gilles	.15	.07
☐ 55	Jerry Goff	.15	.07
☐ 56	Leo Gomez	.15	.07
☐ 57	Luis Gonzalez	3.00	1.35
☐ 58	Joe Grahe	.15	.07
☐ 59	Craig Grebeck	.15	.07
☐ 60	Kip Gross	.15	.07
☐ 61	Eric Gunderson	.15	.07
☐ 62	Chris Hammond	.15	.07
☐ 63	Dave Hansen	.15	.07
☐ 64	Reggie Harris	.15	.07
☐ 65	Bill Haselman	.15	.07
☐ 66	Randy Hennis	.15	.07
☐ 67	Carlos Hernandez	.25	.11
☐ 68	Howard Hilton	.15	.07
☐ 69	Dave Hollins	.25	.11
☐ 70	Darren Holmes	.15	.07
☐ 71	John Hoover	.15	.07
☐ 72	Steve Howard	.15	.07
☐ 73	Thomas Howard	.15	.07
☐ 74	Todd Hundley	.60	.25
☐ 75	Daryl Irvine	.15	.07
☐ 76	Chris Jelic	.15	.07
☐ 77	Dana Kiecker	.15	.07
☐ 78	Brent Knackert	.15	.07
☐ 79	Jimmy Kremers	.15	.07
☐ 80	Jerry Kutzler	.15	.07
☐ 81	Ray Lankford	1.00	.45
☐ 82	Tim Layana	.15	.07
☐ 83	Terry Lee	.15	.07
☐ 84	Mark Leiter	.25	.11
☐ 85	Scott Leius	.15	.07
☐ 86	Mark Leonard	.15	.07
☐ 87	Darren Lewis	.25	.11
☐ 88	Scott Lewis	.15	.07
☐ 89	Jim Leyritz	.25	.11
☐ 90	Dave Liddell	.15	.07
☐ 91	Luis Lopez	.15	.07
☐ 92	Kevin Maas	.15	.07
☐ 93	Bob MacDonald	.15	.07
☐ 94	Carlos Maldonado	.15	.07
☐ 95	Chuck Malone	.15	.07
☐ 96	Ramon Manon	.15	.07
☐ 97	Jeff Manto	.15	.07
☐ 98	Paul Marak	.15	.07
☐ 99	Tino Martinez	1.00	.45
☐ 100	Derrick May	.15	.07
☐ 101	Brent Mayne	.15	.07
☐ 102	Paul McClellan	.15	.07
☐ 103	Rodney McCray	.15	.07
☐ 104	Tim McIntosh	.15	.07
☐ 105	Brian McRae	.25	.11
☐ 106	Jose Melendez	.15	.07
☐ 107	Orlando Merced	.15	.07
☐ 108	Alan Mills	.15	.07
☐ 109	Gino Minutelli	.15	.07
☐ 110	Mickey Morandini	.15	.07
☐ 111	Pedro Munoz	.15	.07
☐ 112	Chris Nabholz	.15	.07
☐ 113	Tim Naehring	.15	.07
☐ 114	Charles Nagy	.60	.25
☐ 115	Jim Neidlinger	.15	.07
☐ 116	Rafael Novoa	.15	.07
☐ 117	Jose Offerman	1.00	.45
☐ 118	Omar Olivares	.15	.07
☐ 119	Javier Ortiz	.15	.07
☐ 120	Al Osuna	.15	.07
☐ 121	Rick Parker	.15	.07
☐ 122	Dave Pavlas	.15	.07
☐ 123	Geronimo Pena	.15	.07
☐ 124	Mike Perez	.15	.07
☐ 125	Phil Plantier	.15	.07
☐ 126	Jim Poole	.15	.07
☐ 127	Tom Quinlan	.15	.07
☐ 128	Scott Radinsky	.15	.07
☐ 129	Darren Reed	.15	.07
☐ 130	Karl Rhodes	.15	.07
☐ 131	Jeff Richardson	.15	.07
☐ 132	Rich Rodriguez	.15	.07
☐ 133	Dave Rohde	.15	.07
☐ 134	Mel Rojas	.25	.11
☐ 135	Vic Rosario	.15	.07
☐ 136	Rich Rowland	.15	.07
☐ 137	Scott Ruskin	.15	.07
☐ 138	Bill Sampen	.15	.07
☐ 139	Andres Santana	.15	.07
☐ 140	David Segui	.25	.11
☐ 141	Jeff Shaw	.60	.25
☐ 142	Tim Sherrill	.15	.07
☐ 143	Terry Shumpert	.15	.07
☐ 144	Mike Simms	.15	.07
☐ 145	Daryl Smith	.15	.07
☐ 146	Luis Sojo	.15	.07
☐ 147	Steve Springer	.15	.07
☐ 148	Ray Stephens	.15	.07
☐ 149	Lee Stevens	.25	.11
☐ 150	Mel Stottlemyre Jr.	.15	.07
☐ 151	Glenn Sutko	.15	.07
☐ 152	Anthony Telford	.15	.07
☐ 153	Frank Thomas	10.00	4.50
☐ 154	Randy Tomlin	.15	.07
☐ 155	Brian Traxler	.15	.07
☐ 156	Efrain Valdez	.15	.07
☐ 157	Rafael Valdez	.15	.07
☐ 158	Julio Valera	.15	.07
☐ 159	Jim Vatcher	.15	.07
☐ 160	Hector Villanueva	.15	.07
☐ 161	Hector Wagner	.15	.07
☐ 162	Dave Walsh	.15	.07
☐ 163	Steve Wapnick	.15	.07
☐ 164	Colby Ward	.15	.07
☐ 165	Turner Ward	.15	.07
☐ 166	Terry Wells	.15	.07
☐ 167	Mark Whiten	.15	.07
☐ 168	Mike York	.15	.07
☐ 169	Cliff Young	.15	.07
☐ 170	Checklist Card	.15	.07
☐ 171	Checklist Card	.15	.07

1992 Topps

	MINT	NRMT
COMPLETE SET (792)	25.00	11.00
COMP.FACT.SET (802)	30.00	13.50
COMP.HOLIDAY SET (811)	35.00	16.00
COMMON CARD (1-792)	.05	.02
MINOR STARS	.10	.05
UNLISTED STARS	.20	.09

SUBSET CARDS HALF VALUE OF BASE CARDS

☐ 1	Nolan Ryan	.75	.35
☐ 2	Ricky Henderson RB	.10	.05
	Most career SB's		
	(Some cards have print		
	marks that show 1,991		
	on the front)		
☐ 3	Jeff Reardon RB	.05	.02
	10 seasons, 20 or more saves		
☐ 4	Nolan Ryan RB	.20	.09
	22 cons. 100 K seasons		
☐ 5	Dave Winfield RB	.10	.05
	Oldest player, cycle		
☐ 6	Brien Taylor	.05	.02
☐ 7	Jim Olander	.05	.02
☐ 8	Bryan Hickerson	.05	.02
☐ 9	Jon Farrell	.05	.02
☐ 10	Wade Boggs	.20	.09
☐ 11	Jack McDowell	.05	.02

12	Luis Gonzalez	.15	.07
13	Mike Scioscia	.05	.02
14	Wes Chamberlain	.05	.02
15	Dennis Martinez	.10	.05
16	Jeff Montgomery	.10	.05
17	Randy Milligan	.05	.02
18	Greg Cadaret	.05	.02
19	Jamie Quirk	.05	.02
20	Bip Roberts	.05	.02
21	Buck Rodgers MG	.05	.02
22	Bill Wegman	.05	.02
23	Chuck Knoblauch	.20	.09
24	Randy Myers	.10	.05
25	Ron Gant	.10	.05
26	Mike Bielecki	.05	.02
27	Juan Gonzalez	.50	.23
28	Mike Schooler	.05	.02
29	Mickey Tettleton	.05	.02
30	John Kruk	.10	.05
31	Bryn Smith	.05	.02
32	Chris Nabholz	.05	.02
33	Carlos Baerga	.25	.11
34	Jeff Juden	.05	.02
35	Dave Righetti	.05	.02
36	Scott Ruffcorn	.05	.02
37	Luis Polonia	.05	.02
38	Tom Candiotti	.05	.02
39	Greg Olson	.05	.02
40	Cal Ripken	2.00	.90
41	Craig Lefferts	.05	.02
42	Mike Macfarlane	.05	.02
43	Jose Lind	.05	.02
44	Rick Aguilera	.10	.05
45	Gary Carter	.20	.09
46	Steve Farr	.05	.02
47	Rex Hudler	.05	.02
48	Scott Scudder	.05	.02
49	Damon Berryhill	.05	.02
50	Ken Griffey Jr.	1.25	.55
51	Tom Runnells MG	.05	.02
52	Juan Bell	.05	.02
53	Tommy Gregg	.05	.02
54	David Wells	.10	.05
55	Rafael Palmeiro	.20	.09
56	Charlie O'Brien	.05	.02
57	Donn Pall	.05	.02
58	1992 Prospects C	.25	.11
	Brad Ausmus		
	Jim Campanis Jr.		
	Dave Nilsson		
	Doug Robbins		
59	Mo Vaughn	.25	.11
60	Tony Fernandez	.05	.02
61	Paul O'Neill	.10	.05
62	Gene Nelson	.05	.02
63	Randy Ready	.05	.02
64	Bob Kipper	.05	.02
65	Willie McGee	.05	.02
66	Scott Stahoviak	.05	.02
67	Luis Salazar	.05	.02
68	Marvin Freeman	.05	.02
69	Kenny Lofton	.25	.11
70	Gary Gaetti	.10	.05
71	Erik Hanson	.05	.02
72	Eddie Zosky	.05	.02
73	Brian Barnes	.05	.02
74	Scott Leius	.05	.02
75	Bret Saberhagen	.05	.02
76	Mike Gallego	.05	.02
77	Jack Armstrong	.05	.02
78	Ivan Rodriguez	.40	.18
79	Jesse Orosco	.05	.02
80	David Justice	.20	.09
81	Ced Landrum	.05	.02
82	Doug Simons	.05	.02
83	Tommy Greene	.05	.02
84	Leo Gomez	.05	.02
85	Jose DeLeon	.05	.02
86	Steve Finley	.10	.05
87	Bob MacDonald	.05	.02
88	Darrin Jackson	.05	.02
89	Neal Heaton	.05	.02
90	Robin Yount	.20	.09
91	Jeff Reed	.05	.02
92	Lenny Harris	.05	.02
93	Reggie Jefferson	.05	.05
94	Sammy Sosa	.60	.25
95	Scott Bailes	.05	.02
96	Tom McKinnon	.05	.02
97	Luis Rivera	.05	.02
98	Mike Harkey	.05	.02
99	Jeff Treadway	.05	.02
100	Jose Canseco	.25	.11
101	Omar Vizquel	.10	.05
102	Scott Kamieniecki	.05	.02
103	Ricky Jordan	.05	.02
104	Jeff Ballard	.05	.02
105	Felix Jose	.05	.02
106	Mike Boddicker	.05	.02
107	Dan Pasqua	.05	.02
108	Mike Timlin	.05	.02
109	Roger Craig MG	.05	.02
110	Ryne Sandberg	.25	.11
111	Mark Carreon	.05	.02
112	Oscar Azocar	.05	.02
113	Mike Greenwell	.05	.02
114	Mark Portugal	.05	.02
115	Terry Pendleton	.05	.02
116	Willie Randolph	.10	.05
117	Scott Terry	.05	.02
118	Chili Davis	.10	.05
119	Mark Gardner	.05	.02
120	Alan Trammell	.15	.07
121	Derek Bell	.05	.02
122	Gary Varsho	.05	.02
123	Bob Ojeda	.05	.02
124	Shawn Livsey	.05	.02
125	Chris Hoiles	.05	.02
126	1992 Prospects 1B	.25	.11
	Ryan Klesko		
	John Jaha		
	Rico Brogna		
	Dave Staton		
127	Carlos Quintana	.05	.02
128	Kurt Stillwell	.05	.02
129	Melido Perez	.05	.02
130	Alvin Davis	.05	.02
131	Checklist 1-132	.05	.02
132	Eric Show	.05	.02
133	Rance Mulliniks	.05	.02
134	Darryl Kile	.10	.05
135	Von Hayes	.05	.02
136	Bill Doran	.05	.02
137	Jeff D. Robinson	.05	.02
138	Monty Fariss	.05	.02
139	Jeff Innis	.05	.02
140	Mark Grace UER	.15	.07
	(Home Calie., should		
	be Calif.)		
141	Jim Leyland MG UER	.10	.05
	(No closed parenthesis		
	after East in 1991)		
142	Todd Van Poppel	.05	.02
143	Paul Gibson	.05	.02
144	Bill Swift	.05	.02
145	Danny Tartabull	.05	.02
146	Al Newman	.05	.02
147	Cris Carpenter	.05	.02
148	Anthony Young	.05	.02
149	Brian Bohanon	.05	.02
150	Roger Clemens UER	.50	.23
	(League leading ERA in		
	1990 not italicized)		
151	Jeff Hamilton	.05	.02
152	Charlie Leibrandt	.05	.02
153	Ron Karkovice	.05	.02
154	Hensley Meulens	.05	.02
155	Scott Bankhead	.05	.02
156	Manny Ramirez	2.00	.90
157	Keith Miller	.05	.02
158	Todd Frohwirth	.05	.02
159	Darrin Fletcher	.05	.02
160	Bobby Bonilla	.10	.05
161	Casey Candaele	.05	.02
162	Paul Faries	.05	.02
163	Dana Kiecker	.05	.02
164	Shane Mack	.05	.02
165	Mark Langston	.05	.02
166	Geronimo Pena	.05	.02
167	Andy Allanson	.05	.02
168	Dwight Smith	.05	.02
169	Chuck Crim	.05	.02
170	Alex Cole	.05	.02
171	Bill Plummer MG	.05	.02
172	Juan Berenguer	.05	.02
173	Brian Downing	.05	.02
174	Steve Frey	.05	.02
175	Orel Hershiser	.10	.05
176	Ramon Garcia	.05	.02
177	Dan Gladden	.05	.02
178	Jim Acker	.05	.02
179	1992 Prospects 2B	.05	.02
	Bobby DeJardin		
	Cesar Bernhardt		
	Armando Moreno		
	Andy Stankiewicz		
180	Kevin Mitchell	.10	.05
181	Hector Villanueva	.05	.02
182	Jeff Reardon	.05	.02
183	Brent Mayne	.05	.02
184	Jimmy Jones	.05	.02
185	Benito Santiago	.05	.02
186	Cliff Floyd	.25	.11
187	Ernie Riles	.05	.02
188	Jose Guzman	.05	.02
189	Junior Felix	.05	.02
190	Glenn Davis	.05	.02
191	Charlie Hough	.10	.05
192	Dave Fleming	.05	.02
193	Omar Olivares	.05	.02
194	Eric Karros	.20	.09
195	David Cone	.10	.05
196	Frank Castillo	.05	.02
197	Glenn Braggs	.05	.02
198	Scott Aldred	.05	.02
199	Jeff Blauser	.05	.02
200	Len Dykstra	.10	.05
201	Buck Showalter MG	.20	.09
202	Rick Honeycutt	.05	.02
203	Greg Myers	.05	.02
204	Trevor Wilson	.05	.02
205	Jay Howell	.05	.02
206	Luis Sojo	.05	.02
207	Jack Clark	.10	.05
208	Julio Machado	.05	.02
209	Lloyd McClendon	.05	.02
210	Ozzie Guillen	.05	.02
211	Jeremy Hernandez	.05	.02
212	Randy Velarde	.05	.02
213	Les Lancaster	.05	.02
214	Andy Mota	.05	.02
215	Rich Gossage	.10	.05
216	Brent Gates	.05	.02
217	Brian Harper	.05	.02
218	Mike Flanagan	.05	.02
219	Jerry Browne	.05	.02
220	Jose Rijo	.05	.02
221	Skeeter Barnes	.05	.02
222	Jaime Navarro	.05	.02
223	Mel Hall	.05	.02
224	Bret Barberie	.05	.02
225	Roberto Alomar	.20	.09
226	Pete Smith	.05	.02
227	Daryl Boston	.05	.02
228	Eddie Whitson	.05	.02
229	Shawn Boskie	.05	.02
230	Dick Schofield	.05	.02
231	Brian Drahman	.05	.02
232	John Smiley	.05	.02
233	Mitch Webster	.05	.02
234	Terry Steinbach	.05	.02
235	Jack Morris	.10	.05
236	Bill Pecota	.05	.02
237	Jose Hernandez	.05	.02
238	Greg Litton	.05	.02
239	Brian Holman	.05	.02
240	Andres Galarraga	.20	.09
241	Gerald Young	.05	.02
242	Mike Mussina	.30	.14
243	Alvaro Espinoza	.05	.02
244	Darren Daulton	.10	.05
245	John Smoltz	.15	.07
246	Jason Pruitt	.05	.02
247	Chuck Finley	.10	.05
248	Jim Gantner	.05	.02
249	Tony Fossas	.05	.02
250	Ken Griffey Sr.	.10	.05
251	Kevin Elster	.05	.02

252	Dennis Rasmussen	.05	.02
253	Terry Kennedy	.05	.02
254	Ryan Bowen	.05	.02
255	Robin Ventura	.10	.05
256	Mike Aldrete	.05	.02
257	Jeff Russell	.05	.02
258	Jim Lindeman	.05	.02
259	Ron Darling	.05	.02
260	Devon White	.05	.02
261	Tom Lasorda MG	.10	.05
262	Terry Lee	.05	.02
263	Bob Patterson	.05	.02
264	Checklist 133-264	.05	.02
265	Teddy Higuera	.05	.02
266	Roberto Kelly	.05	.02
267	Steve Bedrosian	.05	.02
268	Brady Anderson	.15	.07
269	Ruben Amaro	.05	.02
270	Tony Gwynn	.50	.23
271	Tracy Jones	.05	.02
272	Jerry Don Gleaton	.05	.02
273	Craig Grebeck	.05	.02
274	Bob Scanlan	.05	.02
275	Todd Zeile	.05	.02
276	Shawn Green	3.00	1.35
277	Scott Chiamparino	.05	.02
278	Darryl Hamilton	.05	.02
279	Jim Clancy	.05	.02
280	Carlos Martinez	.05	.02
281	Kevin Appier	.10	.05
282	John Wehner	.05	.02
283	Reggie Sanders	.10	.05
284	Gene Larkin	.05	.02
285	Bob Welch	.05	.02
286	Gilberto Reyes	.05	.02
287	Pete Schourek	.05	.02
288	Andujar Cedeno	.05	.02
289	Mike Morgan	.05	.02
290	Bo Jackson	.10	.05
291	Phil Garner MG	.05	.02
292	Ray Lankford	.20	.09
293	Mike Henneman	.05	.02
294	Dave Valle	.05	.02
295	Alonzo Powell	.05	.02
296	Tom Brunansky	.05	.02
297	Kevin Brown	.15	.07
298	Kelly Gruber	.05	.02
299	Charles Nagy	.10	.05
300	Don Mattingly	.40	.18
301	Kirk McCaskill	.05	.02
302	Joey Cora	.05	.02
303	Dan Plesac	.05	.02
304	Joe Oliver	.05	.02
305	Tom Glavine	.15	.07
306	Al Shirley	.15	.07
307	Bruce Ruffin	.05	.02
308	Craig Shipley	.05	.02
309	Dave Martinez	.05	.02
310	Jose Mesa	.05	.02
311	Henry Cotto	.05	.02
312	Mike LaValliere	.05	.02
313	Kevin Tapani	.05	.02
314	Jeff Huson	.05	.02
	(Shows Jose Canseco sliding into second)		
315	Juan Samuel	.05	.02
316	Curt Schilling	.15	.07
317	Mike Bordick	.05	.02
318	Steve Howe	.05	.02
319	Tony Phillips	.05	.02
320	George Bell	.05	.02
321	Lou Piniella MG	.10	.05
322	Tim Burke	.05	.02
323	Milt Thompson	.05	.02
324	Danny Darwin	.05	.02
325	Joe Orsulak	.05	.02
326	Eric King	.05	.02
327	Jay Buhner	.15	.07
328	Joel Johnston	.05	.02
329	Franklin Stubbs	.05	.02
330	Will Clark	.20	.09
331	Steve Lake	.05	.02
332	Chris Jones	.05	.02
333	Pat Tabler	.05	.02
334	Kevin Gross	.05	.02
335	Dave Henderson	.05	.02
336	Greg Anthony	.05	.02
337	Alejandro Pena	.05	.02
338	Shawn Abner	.05	.02
339	Tom Browning	.05	.02
340	Otis Nixon	.10	.05
341	Bob Geren	.05	.02
342	Tim Spehr	.05	.02
343	John Vander Wal	.05	.02
344	Jack Daugherty	.05	.02
345	Zane Smith	.05	.02
346	Rheal Cormier	.05	.02
347	Kent Hrbek	.10	.05
348	Rick Wilkins	.05	.02
349	Steve Lyons	.05	.02
350	Gregg Olson	.05	.02
351	Greg Riddoch MG	.05	.02
352	Ed Nunez	.05	.02
353	Braulio Castillo	.05	.02
354	Dave Bergman	.05	.02
355	Warren Newson	.05	.02
356	Luis Quinones	.05	.02
357	Mike Witt	.05	.02
358	Ted Wood	.05	.02
359	Mike Moore	.05	.02
360	Lance Parrish	.05	.02
361	Barry Jones	.05	.02
362	Javier Ortiz	.05	.02
363	John Candelaria	.05	.02
364	Glenallen Hill	.05	.02
365	Duane Ward	.05	.02
366	Checklist 265-396	.05	.02
367	Rafael Belliard	.05	.02
368	Bill Krueger	.05	.02
369	Steve Whitaker	.05	.02
370	Shawon Dunston	.05	.02
371	Dante Bichette	.15	.07
372	Kip Gross	.05	.02
373	Don Robinson	.05	.02
374	Bernie Williams	.20	.09
375	Bert Blyleven	.10	.05
376	Chris Donnels	.05	.02
377	Bob Zupcic	.05	.02
378	Joel Skinner	.05	.02
379	Steve Chitren	.05	.02
380	Barry Bonds	.25	.11
381	Sparky Anderson MG	.10	.05
382	Sid Fernandez	.05	.02
383	Dave Hollins	.05	.02
384	Mark Lee	.05	.02
385	Tim Wallach	.05	.02
386	Will Clark AS	.10	.05
387	Ryne Sandberg AS	.20	.09
388	Howard Johnson AS	.05	.02
389	Barry Larkin AS	.15	.07
390	Barry Bonds AS	.20	.09
391	Ron Gant AS	.05	.02
392	Bobby Bonilla AS	.05	.02
393	Craig Biggio AS	.10	.05
394	Dennis Martinez AS	.05	.02
395	Tom Glavine AS	.10	.05
396	Lee Smith AS	.05	.02
397	Cecil Fielder AS	.05	.02
398	Julio Franco AS	.05	.02
399	Wade Boggs AS	.10	.05
400	Cal Ripken AS	.20	.09
401	Jose Canseco AS	.10	.05
402	Joe Carter AS	.05	.02
403	Ruben Sierra AS	.05	.02
404	Matt Nokes AS	.05	.02
405	Roger Clemens AS	.20	.09
406	Jim Abbott AS	.05	.02
407	Bryan Harvey AS	.05	.02
408	Bob Milacki	.05	.02
409	Geno Petralli	.05	.02
410	Dave Stewart	.10	.05
411	Mike Jackson	.05	.02
412	Luis Aquino	.05	.02
413	Tim Teufel	.05	.02
414	Jeff Ware	.05	.02
415	Jim Deshaies	.05	.02
416	Ellis Burks	.05	.02
417	Allan Anderson	.05	.02
418	Alfredo Griffin	.05	.02
419	Wally Whitehurst	.05	.02
420	Sandy Alomar Jr.	.10	.05
421	Juan Agosto	.05	.02
422	Sam Horn	.05	.02
423	Jeff Fassero	.05	.02
424	Paul McClellan	.05	.02
425	Cecil Fielder	.10	.05
426	Tim Raines	.10	.05
427	Eddie Taubensee	.05	.02
428	Dennis Boyd	.05	.02
429	Tony LaRussa MG	.10	.05
430	Steve Sax	.05	.02
431	Tom Gordon	.05	.02
432	Billy Hatcher	.05	.02
433	Cal Eldred	.05	.02
434	Wally Backman	.05	.02
435	Mark Eichhorn	.05	.02
436	Mookie Wilson	.10	.05
437	Scott Servais	.05	.02
438	Mike Maddux	.05	.02
439	Chico Walker	.05	.02
440	Doug Drabek	.05	.02
441	Rob Deer	.05	.02
442	Dave West	.05	.02
443	Spike Owen	.05	.02
444	Tyrone Hill	.05	.02
445	Matt Williams	.15	.07
446	Mark Lewis	.05	.02
447	David Segui	.10	.05
448	Tom Pagnozzi	.05	.02
449	Jeff Johnson	.05	.02
450	Mark McGwire	1.00	.45
451	Tom Henke	.05	.02
452	Wilson Alvarez	.10	.05
453	Gary Redus	.05	.02
454	Darren Holmes	.05	.02
455	Pete O'Brien	.05	.02
456	Pat Combs	.05	.02
457	Hubie Brooks	.05	.02
458	Frank Tanana	.05	.02
459	Tom Kelly MG	.05	.02
460	Andre Dawson	.15	.07
461	Doug Jones	.05	.02
462	Rich Rodriguez	.05	.02
463	Mike Simms	.05	.02
464	Mike Jeffcoat	.05	.02
465	Barry Larkin	.15	.07
466	Stan Belinda	.05	.02
467	Lonnie Smith	.05	.02
468	Greg Harris	.05	.02
469	Jim Eisenreich	.05	.02
470	Pedro Guerrero	.05	.02
471	Jose DeJesus	.05	.02
472	Rich Rowland	.05	.02
473	1992 Prospects 3B UER	.20	.09
	Frank Bolick		
	Craig Paquette		
	Tom Redington		
	Paul Russo		
	(Line around top border)		
474	Mike Rossiter	.05	.02
475	Robby Thompson	.05	.02
476	Randy Bush	.05	.02
477	Greg Hibbard	.05	.02
478	Dale Sveum	.05	.02
479	Chito Martinez	.05	.02
480	Scott Sanderson	.05	.02
481	Tino Martinez	.20	.09
482	Jimmy Key	.10	.05
483	Terry Shumpert	.05	.02
484	Mike Hartley	.05	.02
485	Chris Sabo	.05	.02
486	Bob Walk	.05	.02
487	John Cerutti	.05	.02
488	Scott Cooper	.05	.02
489	Bobby Cox MG	.10	.05
490	Julio Franco	.05	.02
491	Jeff Brantley	.05	.02
492	Mike Devereaux	.05	.02
493	Jose Offerman	.10	.05
494	Gary Thurman	.05	.02
495	Carney Lansford	.05	.02
496	Joe Grahe	.05	.02
497	Andy Ashby	.10	.05
498	Gerald Perry	.05	.02
499	Dave Otto	.05	.02
500	Vince Coleman	.05	.02
501	Rob Mallicoat	.05	.02
502	Greg Briley	.05	.02

❏ 503	Pascual Perez	.05	.02
❏ 504	Aaron Sele	.30	.14
❏ 505	Bobby Thigpen	.05	.02
❏ 506	Todd Benzinger	.05	.02
❏ 507	Candy Maldonado	.05	.02
❏ 508	Bill Gullickson	.05	.02
❏ 509	Doug Dascenzo	.05	.02
❏ 510	Frank Viola	.05	.02
❏ 511	Kenny Rogers	.05	.02
❏ 512	Mike Heath	.05	.02
❏ 513	Kevin Bass	.05	.02
❏ 514	Kim Batiste	.05	.02
❏ 515	Delino DeShields	.10	.05
❏ 516	Ed Sprague	.05	.02
❏ 517	Jim Gott	.05	.02
❏ 518	Jose Melendez	.05	.02
❏ 519	Hal McRae MG	.05	.02
❏ 520	Jeff Bagwell	.40	.18
❏ 521	Joe Hesketh	.05	.02
❏ 522	Milt Cuyler	.05	.02
❏ 523	Shawn Hillegas	.05	.02
❏ 524	Don Slaught	.05	.02
❏ 525	Randy Johnson	.20	.09
❏ 526	Doug Piatt	.05	.02
❏ 527	Checklist 397-528	.05	.02
❏ 528	Steve Foster	.05	.02
❏ 529	Joe Girardi	.10	.05
❏ 530	Jim Abbott	.10	.05
❏ 531	Larry Walker	.20	.09
❏ 532	Mike Huff	.05	.02
❏ 533	Mackey Sasser	.05	.02
❏ 534	Benji Gil	.05	.02
❏ 535	Dave Stieb	.05	.02
❏ 536	Willie Wilson	.05	.02
❏ 537	Mark Leiter	.05	.02
❏ 538	Jose Uribe	.05	.02
❏ 539	Thomas Howard	.05	.02
❏ 540	Ben McDonald	.05	.02
❏ 541	Jose Tolentino	.05	.02
❏ 542	Keith Mitchell	.05	.02
❏ 543	Jerome Walton	.05	.02
❏ 544	Cliff Brantley	.05	.02
❏ 545	Andy Van Slyke	.10	.05
❏ 546	Paul Sorrento	.05	.02
❏ 547	Herm Winningham	.05	.02
❏ 548	Mark Guthrie	.05	.02
❏ 549	Joe Torre MG	.10	.05
❏ 550	Darryl Strawberry	.10	.05
❏ 551	1992 Prospects SS UER	1.50	.70
	Wilfredo Cordero		
	Chipper Jones		
	Manny Alexander		
	Alex Arias		
	(No line around top border)		
❏ 552	Dave Gallagher	.05	.02
❏ 553	Edgar Martinez	.15	.07
❏ 554	Donald Harris	.05	.02
❏ 555	Frank Thomas	.50	.23
❏ 556	Storm Davis	.05	.02
❏ 557	Dickie Thon	.05	.02
❏ 558	Scott Garrelts	.05	.02
❏ 559	Steve Olin	.05	.02
❏ 560	Rickey Henderson	.25	.11
❏ 561	Jose Vizcaino	.05	.02
❏ 562	Wade Taylor	.05	.02
❏ 563	Pat Borders	.05	.02
❏ 564	Jimmy Gonzalez	.05	.02
❏ 565	Lee Smith	.10	.05
❏ 566	Bill Sampen	.05	.02
❏ 567	Dean Palmer	.10	.05
❏ 568	Bryan Harvey	.05	.02
❏ 569	Tony Pena	.05	.02
❏ 570	Lou Whitaker	.10	.05
❏ 571	Randy Tomlin	.05	.02
❏ 572	Greg Vaughn	.15	.07
❏ 573	Kelly Downs	.05	.02
❏ 574	Steve Avery UER	.05	.02
	(Should be 13 games for Durham in 1989)		
❏ 575	Kirby Puckett	.30	.14
❏ 576	Heathcliff Slocumb	.05	.02
❏ 577	Kevin Seitzer	.05	.02
❏ 578	Lee Guetterman	.05	.02
❏ 579	Johnny Oates MG	.05	.02
❏ 580	Greg Maddux	.50	.23
❏ 581	Stan Javier	.05	.02
❏ 582	Vicente Palacios	.05	.02
❏ 583	Mel Rojas	.05	.02
❏ 584	Wayne Rosenthal	.05	.02
❏ 585	Lenny Webster	.05	.02
❏ 586	Rod Nichols	.05	.02
❏ 587	Mickey Morandini	.05	.02
❏ 588	Russ Swan	.05	.02
❏ 589	Mariano Duncan	.05	.02
❏ 590	Howard Johnson	.05	.02
❏ 591	1992 Prospects OF	.20	.09
	Jeromy Burnitz		
	Jacob Brumfield		
	Alan Cockrell		
	D.J. Dozier		
❏ 592	Denny Neagle	.15	.07
❏ 593	Steve Decker	.05	.02
❏ 594	Brian Barber	.05	.02
❏ 595	Bruce Hurst	.05	.02
❏ 596	Kent Mercker	.05	.02
❏ 597	Mike Magnante	.05	.02
❏ 598	Jody Reed	.05	.02
❏ 599	Steve Searcy	.05	.02
❏ 600	Paul Molitor	.20	.09
❏ 601	Dave Smith	.05	.02
❏ 602	Mike Fetters	.05	.02
❏ 603	Luis Mercedes	.05	.02
❏ 604	Chris Gwynn	.05	.02
❏ 605	Scott Erickson	.10	.05
❏ 606	Brook Jacoby	.05	.02
❏ 607	Todd Stottlemyre	.05	.02
❏ 608	Scott Bradley	.05	.02
❏ 609	Mike Hargrove MG	.10	.05
❏ 610	Eric Davis	.10	.05
❏ 611	Brian Hunter	.05	.02
❏ 612	Pat Kelly	.05	.02
❏ 613	Pedro Munoz	.05	.02
❏ 614	Al Osuna	.05	.02
❏ 615	Matt Merullo	.05	.02
❏ 616	Larry Andersen	.05	.02
❏ 617	Junior Ortiz	.05	.02
❏ 618	1992 Prospects OF	.05	.02
	Cesar Hernandez		
	Steve Hosey		
	Jeff McNeely		
	Dan Peltier		
❏ 619	Danny Jackson	.05	.02
❏ 620	George Brett	.40	.18
❏ 621	Dan Gakeler	.05	.02
❏ 622	Steve Buechele	.05	.02
❏ 623	Bob Tewksbury	.05	.02
❏ 624	Shawn Estes	.25	.11
❏ 625	Kevin McReynolds	.05	.02
❏ 626	Chris Haney	.05	.02
❏ 627	Mike Sharperson	.05	.02
❏ 628	Mark Williamson	.05	.02
❏ 629	Wally Joyner	.10	.05
❏ 630	Carlton Fisk	.20	.09
❏ 631	Armando Reynoso	.05	.02
❏ 632	Felix Fermin	.05	.02
❏ 633	Mitch Williams	.05	.02
❏ 634	Manuel Lee	.05	.02
❏ 635	Harold Baines	.10	.05
❏ 636	Greg Harris	.05	.02
❏ 637	Orlando Merced	.05	.02
❏ 638	Chris Bosio	.05	.02
❏ 639	Wayne Housie	.05	.02
❏ 640	Xavier Hernandez	.05	.02
❏ 641	David Howard	.05	.02
❏ 642	Tim Crews	.05	.02
❏ 643	Rick Cerone	.05	.02
❏ 644	Terry Leach	.05	.02
❏ 645	Deion Sanders	.20	.09
❏ 646	Craig Wilson	.05	.02
❏ 647	Marquis Grissom	.10	.05
❏ 648	Scott Fletcher	.05	.02
❏ 649	Norm Charlton	.05	.02
❏ 650	Jesse Barfield	.05	.02
❏ 651	Joe Slusarski	.05	.02
❏ 652	Bobby Rose	.05	.02
❏ 653	Dennis Lamp	.05	.02
❏ 654	Allen Watson	.05	.02
❏ 655	Brett Butler	.10	.05
❏ 656	1992 Prospects OF	.20	.09
	Rudy Pemberton		
	Henry Rodriguez		
	Lee Tinsley		
	Gerald Williams		
❏ 657	Dave Johnson	.05	.02
❏ 658	Checklist 529-660	.05	.02
❏ 659	Brian McRae	.05	.02
❏ 660	Fred McGriff	.15	.07
❏ 661	Bill Landrum	.05	.02
❏ 662	Juan Guzman	.05	.02
❏ 663	Greg Gagne	.05	.02
❏ 664	Ken Hill	.05	.02
❏ 665	Dave Haas	.05	.02
❏ 666	Tom Foley	.05	.02
❏ 667	Roberto Hernandez	.15	.07
❏ 668	Dwayne Henry	.05	.02
❏ 669	Jim Fregosi MG	.05	.02
❏ 670	Harold Reynolds	.05	.02
❏ 671	Mark Whiten	.05	.02
❏ 672	Eric Plunk	.05	.02
❏ 673	Todd Hundley	.10	.05
❏ 674	Mo Sanford	.05	.02
❏ 675	Bobby Witt	.05	.02
❏ 676	1992 Prospects P	.05	.02
	Sam Militello		
	Pat Mahomes		
	Turk Wendell		
	Roger Salkeld		
❏ 677	John Marzano	.05	.02
❏ 678	Joe Klink	.05	.02
❏ 679	Pete Incaviglia	.05	.02
❏ 680	Dale Murphy	.20	.09
❏ 681	Rene Gonzales	.05	.02
❏ 682	Andy Benes	.10	.05
❏ 683	Jim Poole	.05	.02
❏ 684	Trever Miller	.05	.02
❏ 685	Scott Livingstone	.05	.02
❏ 686	Rich DeLucia	.05	.02
❏ 687	Harvey Pulliam	.05	.02
❏ 688	Tim Belcher	.05	.02
❏ 689	Mark Lemke	.05	.02
❏ 690	John Franco	.10	.05
❏ 691	Walt Weiss	.05	.02
❏ 692	Scott Ruskin	.05	.02
❏ 693	Jeff King	.05	.02
❏ 694	Mike Gardiner	.05	.02
❏ 695	Gary Sheffield	.20	.09
❏ 696	Joe Boever	.05	.02
❏ 697	Mike Felder	.05	.02
❏ 698	John Habyan	.05	.02
❏ 699	Cito Gaston MG	.05	.02
❏ 700	Ruben Sierra	.20	.09
❏ 701	Scott Radinsky	.05	.02
❏ 702	Lee Stevens	.10	.05
❏ 703	Mark Wohlers	.05	.02
❏ 704	Curt Young	.05	.02
❏ 705	Dwight Evans	.10	.05
❏ 706	Rob Murphy	.05	.02
❏ 707	Gregg Jefferies	.05	.02
❏ 708	Tom Bolton	.05	.02
❏ 709	Chris James	.05	.02
❏ 710	Kevin Maas	.05	.02
❏ 711	Ricky Bones	.05	.02
❏ 712	Curt Wilkerson	.05	.02
❏ 713	Roger McDowell	.05	.02
❏ 714	Calvin Reese	.20	.09
❏ 715	Craig Biggio	.20	.09
❏ 716	Kirk Dressendorfer	.05	.02
❏ 717	Ken Dayley	.05	.02
❏ 718	B.J. Surhoff	.10	.05
❏ 719	Terry Mulholland	.05	.02
❏ 720	Kirk Gibson	.10	.05
❏ 721	Mike Pagliarulo	.05	.02
❏ 722	Walt Terrell	.05	.02
❏ 723	Jose Oquendo	.05	.02
❏ 724	Kevin Morton	.05	.02
❏ 725	Dwight Gooden	.10	.05
❏ 726	Kirt Manwaring	.05	.02
❏ 727	Chuck McElroy	.05	.02
❏ 728	Dave Burba	.05	.02
❏ 729	Art Howe MG	.05	.02
❏ 730	Ramon Martinez	.10	.05
❏ 731	Donnie Hill	.05	.02
❏ 732	Nelson Santovenia	.05	.02
❏ 733	Bob Melvin	.05	.02
❏ 734	Scott Hatteberg	.05	.02
❏ 735	Greg Swindell	.05	.02
❏ 736	Lance Johnson	.05	.02

☐ 737 Kevin Reimer .05 .02
☐ 738 Dennis Eckersley .10 .05
☐ 739 Rob Ducey .05 .02
☐ 740 Ken Caminiti .15 .07
☐ 741 Mark Gubicza .05 .02
☐ 742 Bill Spiers .05 .02
☐ 743 Darren Lewis .05 .02
☐ 744 Chris Hammond .05 .02
☐ 745 Dave Magadan .05 .02
☐ 746 Bernard Gilkey .10 .05
☐ 747 Willie Banks .05 .02
☐ 748 Matt Nokes .05 .02
☐ 749 Jerald Clark .05 .02
☐ 750 Travis Fryman .10 .05
☐ 751 Steve Wilson .05 .02
☐ 752 Billy Ripken .05 .02
☐ 753 Paul Assenmacher .05 .02
☐ 754 Charlie Hayes .05 .02
☐ 755 Alex Fernandez .10 .05
☐ 756 Gary Pettis .05 .02
☐ 757 Rob Dibble .05 .02
☐ 758 Tim Naehring .05 .02
☐ 759 Jeff Torborg MG .05 .02
☐ 760 Ozzie Smith .25 .11
☐ 761 Mike Fitzgerald .05 .02
☐ 762 John Burkett .05 .02
☐ 763 Kyle Abbott .05 .02
☐ 764 Tyler Green .05 .02
☐ 765 Pete Harnisch .05 .02
☐ 766 Mark Davis .05 .02
☐ 767 Kal Daniels .05 .02
☐ 768 Jim Thome .50 .23
☐ 769 Jack Howell .05 .02
☐ 770 Sid Bream .05 .02
☐ 771 Arthur Rhodes .05 .02
☐ 772 Garry Templeton UER .05 .02
(Stat heading in for pitchers)
☐ 773 Hal Morris .05 .02
☐ 774 Bud Black .05 .02
☐ 775 Ivan Calderon .05 .02
☐ 776 Doug Henry .05 .02
☐ 777 John Olerud .10 .05
☐ 778 Tim Leary .05 .02
☐ 779 Jay Bell .10 .05
☐ 780 Eddie Murray .20 .09
☐ 781 Paul Abbott .05 .02
☐ 782 Phil Plantier .05 .02
☐ 783 Joe Magrane .05 .02
☐ 784 Ken Patterson .05 .02
☐ 785 Albert Belle .20 .09
☐ 786 Royce Clayton .05 .02
☐ 787 Checklist 661-792 .05 .02
☐ 788 Mike Stanton .05 .02
☐ 789 Bobby Valentine MG .05 .02
☐ 790 Joe Carter .10 .05
☐ 791 Danny Cox .05 .02
☐ 792 Dave Winfield .20 .09

1992 Topps Gold

	MINT	NRMT
COMPLETE SET (792)	120.00	55.00
COMP.FACT.SET (733)	120.00	55.00
COMMON CARD (1-792)	.25	.11

*STARS: 6X TO 15X BASIC CARDS
*ROOKIES: 4X TO 10X BASIC CARDS
RANDOM INSERTS IN PACKS
TEN PER BASIC FACTORY SET

B.TAYLOR AUTO ONE PER GOLD FACT.SET
12,000 GOLD FACTORY SETS PRODUCED

☐ 131 Terry Mathews .50 .23
(Replaces Checklist 1)
☐ 264 Rod Beck 1.00 .45
(Replaces Checklist 2)
☐ 366 Tony Perezchica .50 .23
(Replaces Checklist 3)
☐ 527 Terry McDaniel .50 .23
(Replaces Checklist 4)
☐ 658 John Ramos .50 .23
(Replaces Checklist 5)
☐ 787 Brian Williams .50 .23
(Replaces Checklist 6)

1992 Topps Gold Winners

	MINT	NRMT
COMPLETE SET (792)	40.00	18.00
COMMON CARD (1-792)	.10	.05

*STARS: 1.25X TO 3X BASIC CARDS
*ROOKIES: 1.25X TO 3X BASIC CARDS
REDEEMED WITH WINNING GAME CARDS

☐ 131 Terry Mathews .15 .07
(Replaces Checklist 1)
☐ 264 Rod Beck .30 .14
(Replaces Checklist 2)
☐ 366 Tony Perezchica .15 .07
(Replaces Checklist 3)
☐ 527 Terry McDaniel .15 .07
(Replaces Checklist 4)
☐ 658 John Ramos .15 .07
(Replaces Checklist 5)
☐ 787 Brian Williams .15 .07
(Replaces Checklist 6)

1992 Topps Traded

	MINT	NRMT
COMP.FACT.SET (132)	120.00	55.00
COMMON CARD (1T-132T)	.10	.05
MINOR STARS	.20	.09
UNLISTED STARS	.40	.18

☐ 1T Willie Adams USA .10 .05
☐ 2T Jeff Alkire USA .10 .05
☐ 3T Felipe Alou MG .10 .05
☐ 4T Moises Alou 1.00 .45
☐ 5T Ruben Amaro .10 .05
☐ 6T Jack Armstrong .10 .05
☐ 7T Scott Bankhead .10 .05
☐ 8T Tim Belcher .10 .05
☐ 9T George Bell .10 .05
☐ 10T Freddie Benavides .10 .05
☐ 11T Todd Benzinger .10 .05
☐ 12T Joe Boever .10 .05
☐ 13T Ricky Bones .10 .05
☐ 14T Bobby Bonilla .20 .09
☐ 15T Hubie Brooks .10 .05
☐ 16T Jerry Browne .10 .05
☐ 17T Jim Bullinger .10 .05
☐ 18T Dave Burba .10 .05
☐ 19T Kevin Campbell .10 .05
☐ 20T Tom Candiotti .10 .05
☐ 21T Mark Carreon .10 .05
☐ 22T Gary Carter .40 .18
☐ 23T Archi Cianfrocco .10 .05
☐ 24T Phil Clark .10 .05
☐ 25T Chad Curtis .40 .18
☐ 26T Eric Davis .20 .09
☐ 27T Tim Davis USA .10 .05
☐ 28T Gary DiSarcina .10 .05
☐ 29T Darren Dreifort USA .20 .09
☐ 30T Mariano Duncan .10 .05
☐ 31T Mike Fitzgerald .10 .05
☐ 32T John Flaherty .10 .05
☐ 33T Darrin Fletcher .10 .05
☐ 34T Scott Fletcher .10 .05
☐ 35T Ron Fraser CO USA .10 .05
☐ 36T Andres Galarraga .40 .18
☐ 37T Dave Gallagher .10 .05
☐ 38T Mike Gallego .10 .05
☐ 39T Nomar Garciaparra USA 100.00 45.00
☐ 40T Jason Giambi USA 1.00 .45
☐ 41T Danny Gladden .10 .05
☐ 42T Rene Gonzales .10 .05
☐ 43T Jeff Granger USA .10 .05
☐ 44T Rick Greene USA .10 .05
☐ 45T Jeffrey Hammonds USA .40 .18
☐ 46T Charlie Hayes .10 .05
☐ 47T Von Hayes .10 .05
☐ 48T Rick Helling USA .40 .18
☐ 49T Butch Henry .10 .05
☐ 50T Carlos Hernandez .10 .05
☐ 51T Ken Hill .10 .05
☐ 52T Butch Hobson .10 .05
☐ 53T Vince Horsman .10 .05
☐ 54T Pete Incaviglia .10 .05
☐ 55T Gregg Jefferies .10 .05
☐ 56T Charles Johnson USA .75 .35
☐ 57T Doug Jones .10 .05
☐ 58T Brian Jordan 5.00 2.20
☐ 59T Wally Joyner .20 .09
☐ 60T Daron Kirkreit USA .10 .05
☐ 61T Bill Krueger .10 .05
☐ 62T Gene Lamont MG .10 .05
☐ 63T Jim Lefebvre MG .10 .05
☐ 64T Danny Leon .10 .05
☐ 65T Pat Listach .10 .05
☐ 66T Kenny Lofton 1.00 .45
☐ 67T Dave Martinez .10 .05
☐ 68T Derrick May .10 .05
☐ 69T Kirk McCaskill .10 .05
☐ 70T Chad McConnell USA .20 .09
☐ 71T Kevin McReynolds .10 .05
☐ 72T Rusty Meacham .10 .05
☐ 73T Keith Miller .10 .05
☐ 74T Kevin Mitchell .20 .09
☐ 75T Jason Moler USA .10 .05
☐ 76T Mike Morgan .10 .05
☐ 77T Jack Morris .20 .09
☐ 78T Calvin Murray USA .10 .05
☐ 79T Eddie Murray .40 .18
☐ 80T Randy Myers .10 .05
☐ 81T Denny Neagle .30 .14
☐ 82T Phil Nevin USA .40 .18
☐ 83T Dave Nilsson .20 .09
☐ 84T Junior Ortiz .10 .05
☐ 85T Donovan Osborne .10 .05
☐ 86T Bill Pecota .10 .05
☐ 87T Melido Perez .10 .05
☐ 88T Mike Perez .10 .05
☐ 89T Hipolito Pichardo .10 .05

❑ 90T Willie Randolph	.20	.09
❑ 91T Darren Reed	.10	.05
❑ 92T Bip Roberts	.10	.05
❑ 93T Chris Roberts USA	.10	.05
❑ 94T Steve Rodriguez USA	.10	.05
❑ 95T Bruce Ruffin	.10	.05
❑ 96T Scott Ruskin	.10	.05
❑ 97T Bret Saberhagen	.20	.09
❑ 98T Rey Sanchez	.10	.05
❑ 99T Steve Sax	.10	.05
❑ 100T Curt Schilling	.30	.14
❑ 101T Dick Schofield	.10	.05
❑ 102T Gary Scott	.10	.05
❑ 103T Kevin Seitzer	.10	.05
❑ 104T Frank Seminara	.10	.05
❑ 105T Gary Sheffield	.40	.18
❑ 106T John Smiley	.10	.05
❑ 107T Cory Snyder	.10	.05
❑ 108T Paul Sorrento	.10	.05
❑ 109T Sammy Sosa	4.00	1.80
❑ 110T Matt Stairs	2.50	1.10
❑ 111T Andy Stankiewicz	.10	.05
❑ 112T Kurt Stillwell	.10	.05
❑ 113T Rick Sutcliffe	.10	.05
❑ 114T Bill Swift	.10	.05
❑ 115T Jeff Tackett	.10	.05
❑ 116T Danny Tartabull	.10	.05
❑ 117T Eddie Taubensee	.20	.09
❑ 118T Dickie Thon	.10	.05
❑ 119T Michael Tucker USA	1.00	.45
❑ 120T Scooter Tucker	.10	.05
❑ 121T Marc Valdes USA	.10	.05
❑ 122T Julio Valera	.10	.05
❑ 123T Jason Varitek USA	3.00	1.35
❑ 124T Ron Villone USA	.10	.05
❑ 125T Frank Viola	.10	.05
❑ 126T B.J. Wallace USA	.20	.09
❑ 127T Dan Walters	.10	.05
❑ 128T Craig Wilson USA	.10	.05
❑ 129T Chris Wimmer USA	.10	.05
❑ 130T Dave Winfield	.40	.18
❑ 131T Herm Winningham	.10	.05
❑ 132T Checklist 1T-132T	.10	.05

1992 Topps Traded Gold

	MINT	NRMT
COMP.FACT.SET (132)	300.00	135.00
COMMON CARDS (1T-132T)	.25	.11

*GOLD: 1X TO 2X BASIC CARDS
GOLD SOLD ONLY IN FACTORY SET FORM

1992 Topps Debut '91

	MINT	NRMT
COMP.FACT.SET (194)	25.00	11.00
COMMON CARD (1-194)	.15	.07
MINOR STARS	.25	.11
SEMISTARS	.50	.23

DISTRIBUTED ONLY IN FACTORY SET FORM

❑ 1 Kyle Abbott	.15	.07
❑ 2 Dana Allison	.15	.07
❑ 3 Rich Amaral	.25	.11
❑ 4 Ruben Amaro	.15	.07
❑ 5 Andy Ashby	.25	.11
❑ 6 Jim Austin	.15	.07
❑ 7 Jeff Bagwell	5.00	2.20

❑ 8 Jeff Banister	.15	.07
❑ 9 Willie Banks	.15	.07
❑ 10 Bret Barberie	.15	.07
❑ 11 Kim Batiste	.15	.07
❑ 12 Chris Beasley	.15	.07
❑ 13 Rod Beck	.60	.25
❑ 14 Derek Bell	.25	.11
❑ 15 Esteban Beltre	.15	.07
❑ 16 Freddie Benavides	.15	.07
❑ 17 Ricky Bones	.15	.07
❑ 18 Denis Boucher	.15	.07
❑ 19 Ryan Bowen	.15	.07
❑ 20 Cliff Brantley	.15	.07
❑ 21 John Briscoe	.15	.07
❑ 22 Scott Brosius	.60	.25
❑ 23 Terry Bross	.15	.07
❑ 24 Jarvis Brown	.15	.07
❑ 25 Scott Bullett	.15	.07
❑ 26 Kevin Campbell	.15	.07
❑ 27 Amalio Carreno	.15	.07
❑ 28 Matias Carrillo	.15	.07
❑ 29 Jeff Carter	.15	.07
❑ 30 Vinny Castilla	5.00	2.20
❑ 31 Braulio Castillo	.15	.07
❑ 32 Frank Castro	.60	.25
❑ 33 Darrin Chapin	.15	.07
❑ 34 Mike Christopher	.15	.07
❑ 35 Mark Clark	.15	.07
❑ 36 Royce Clayton	.15	.07
❑ 37 Stu Cole	.15	.07
❑ 38 Gary Cooper	.15	.07
❑ 39 Archie Corbin	.15	.07
❑ 40 Rheal Cormier	.15	.07
❑ 41 Chris Cron	.15	.07
❑ 42 Mike Dalton	.15	.07
❑ 43 Mark Davis	.15	.07
❑ 44 Francisco de la Rosa	.15	.07
❑ 45 Chris Donnels	.15	.07
❑ 46 Brian Drahman	.15	.07
❑ 47 Tom Drees	.15	.07
❑ 48 Kirk Dressendorfer	.15	.07
❑ 49 Bruce Egloff	.15	.07
❑ 50 Cal Eldred	.25	.11
❑ 51 Jose Escobar	.15	.07
❑ 52 Tony Eusebio	.60	.25
❑ 53 Hector Fajardo	.15	.07
❑ 54 Monty Fariss	.15	.07
❑ 55 Jeff Fassero	.15	.07
❑ 56 Dave Fleming	.15	.07
❑ 57 Kevin Flora	.15	.07
❑ 58 Steve Foster	.15	.07
❑ 59 Dan Gakeler	.15	.07
❑ 60 Ramon Garcia	.15	.07
❑ 61 Chris Gardner	.15	.07
❑ 62 Jeff Gardner	.15	.07
❑ 63 Chris George	.15	.07
❑ 64 Ray Giannelli	.15	.07
❑ 65 Tom Goodwin	.25	.11
❑ 66 Mark Grater	.15	.07
❑ 67 Johnny Guzman	.15	.07
❑ 68 Juan Guzman	.15	.07
❑ 69 Dave Haas	.15	.07
❑ 70 Chris Haney	.15	.07
❑ 71 Shawn Hare	.15	.07
❑ 72 Donald Harris	.15	.07
❑ 73 Doug Henry	.15	.07
❑ 74 Pat Hentgen	.60	.25
❑ 75 Gil Heredia	.15	.07

❑ 76 Jeremy Hernandez	.15	.07
❑ 77 Jose Hernandez	.15	.07
❑ 78 Roberto Hernandez	.50	.23
❑ 79 Bryan Hickerson	.15	.07
❑ 80 Milt Hill	.15	.07
❑ 81 Vince Horsman	.15	.07
❑ 82 Wayne Housie	.15	.07
❑ 83 Chris Howard	.15	.07
❑ 84 David Howard	.15	.07
❑ 85 Mike Humphreys	.15	.07
❑ 86 Brian Hunter	.15	.07
❑ 87 Jim Hunter	.15	.07
❑ 88 Mike Ignasiak	.15	.07
❑ 89 Reggie Jefferson	.50	.23
❑ 90 Jeff Johnson	.15	.07
❑ 91 Joel Johnston	.15	.07
❑ 92 Calvin Jones	.15	.07
❑ 93 Chris Jones	.15	.07
❑ 94 Stacy Jones	.15	.07
❑ 95 Jeff Juden	.15	.07
❑ 96 Scott Kamieniecki	.15	.07
❑ 97 Eric Karros	1.00	.45
❑ 98 Pat Kelly	.15	.07
❑ 99 John Kiely	.15	.07
❑ 100 Darryl Kile	.25	.11
❑ 101 Wayne Kirby	.15	.07
❑ 102 Garland Kiser	.15	.07
❑ 103 Chuck Knoblauch	1.00	.45
❑ 104 Randy Knorr	.15	.07
❑ 105 Tom Kramer	.15	.07
❑ 106 Ced Landrum	.15	.07
❑ 107 Patrick Lennon	.15	.07
❑ 108 Jim Lewis	.15	.07
❑ 109 Mark Lewis	.25	.11
❑ 110 Doug Lindsey	.15	.07
❑ 111 Scott Livingstone	.15	.07
❑ 112 Kenny Lofton	2.00	.90
❑ 113 Ever Magallanes	.15	.07
❑ 114 Mike Magnante	.15	.07
❑ 115 Barry Manuel	.15	.07
❑ 116 Josias Manzanillo	.15	.07
❑ 117 Chito Martinez	.15	.07
❑ 118 Terry Mathews	.15	.07
❑ 119 Rob Maurer	.15	.07
❑ 120 Tim Mauser	.15	.07
❑ 121 Terry McDaniel	.15	.07
❑ 122 Rusty Meacham	.15	.07
❑ 123 Luis Mercedes	.15	.07
❑ 124 Paul Miller	.15	.07
❑ 125 Keith Mitchell	.15	.07
❑ 126 Bobby Moore	.15	.07
❑ 127 Kevin Morton	.15	.07
❑ 128 Andy Mota	.15	.07
❑ 129 Jose Mota	.15	.07
❑ 130 Mike Mussina	4.00	1.80
❑ 131 Jeff Mutis	.15	.07
❑ 132 Denny Neagle	.50	.23
❑ 133 Warren Newson	.15	.07
❑ 134 Jim Olander	.15	.07
❑ 135 Erik Pappas	.15	.07
❑ 136 Jorge Pedre	.15	.07
❑ 137 Yorkis Perez	.15	.07
❑ 138 Mark Petkovsek	.15	.07
❑ 139 Doug Piatt	.15	.07
❑ 140 Jeff Plympton	.15	.07
❑ 141 Harvey Pulliam	.15	.07
❑ 142 John Ramos	.15	.07
❑ 143 Mike Remlinger	.15	.07
❑ 144 Laddie Renfroe	.15	.07
❑ 145 Armando Reynoso	.15	.07
❑ 146 Arthur Rhodes	.15	.07
❑ 147 Pat Rice	.15	.07
❑ 148 Nikco Riesgo	.15	.07
❑ 149 Carlos Rodriguez	.15	.07
❑ 150 Ivan Rodriguez	5.00	2.20
❑ 151 Wayne Rosenthal	.15	.07
❑ 152 Rico Rossy	.15	.07
❑ 153 Stan Royer	.15	.07
❑ 154 Rey Sanchez	.15	.07
❑ 155 Reggie Sanders	.25	.11
❑ 156 Mo Sanford	.15	.07
❑ 157 Bob Scanlan	.15	.07
❑ 158 Pete Schourek	.15	.07
❑ 159 Gary Scott	.15	.07
❑ 160 Tim Scott	.15	.07
❑ 161 Tony Scruggs	.15	.07

162 Scott Servais	.15	.07
163 Doug Simons	.15	.07
164 Heathcliff Slocumb	.15	.07
165 Joe Slusarski	.15	.07
166 Tim Spehr	.15	.07
167 Ed Sprague	.15	.07
168 Jeff Tackett	.15	.07
169 Eddie Taubensee	.25	.11
170 Wade Taylor	.15	.07
171 Jim Thome	3.00	1.35
172 Mike Timlin	.60	.25
173 Jose Tolentino	.15	.07
174 John Vander Wal	.15	.07
175 Todd Van Poppel	.15	.07
176 Mo Vaughn	1.25	.55
177 Dave Wainhouse	.15	.07
178 Don Wakamatsu	.15	.07
179 Bruce Walton	.15	.07
180 Kevin Ward	.15	.07
181 Dave Weathers	.15	.07
182 Eric Wedge	.15	.07
183 John Wehner	.15	.07
184 Rick Wilkins	.25	.11
185 Bernie Williams	1.50	.70
186 Brian Williams	.15	.07
187 Ron Witmeyer	.15	.07
188 Mark Wohlers	.15	.07
189 Ted Wood	.15	.07
190 Anthony Young	.15	.07
191 Eddie Zosky	.15	.07
192 Bob Zupcic	.15	.07
193 Checklist 1	.15	.07
194 Checklist 2	.15	.07

1993 Topps

	MINT	NRMT
COMPLETE SET (825)	30.00	13.50
COMP.RETAIL.SET (838)	40.00	18.00
COMP.HOBBY.SET (847)	50.00	22.00
COMPLETE SERIES 1 (396)	15.00	6.75
COMPLETE SERIES 2 (429)	15.00	6.75
COMMON CARD (1-825)	.10	.05
MINOR STARS	.20	.09
UNLISTED STARS	.40	.18

1 Robin Yount	.30	.14
2 Barry Bonds	.50	.23
3 Ryne Sandberg	.50	.23
4 Roger Clemens	1.00	.45
5 Tony Gwynn	1.00	.45
6 Jeff Tackett	.10	.05
7 Pete Incaviglia	.10	.05
8 Mark Wohlers	.10	.05
9 Kent Hrbek	.20	.09
10 Will Clark	.30	.14
11 Eric Karros	.30	.14
12 Lee Smith	.20	.09
13 Esteban Beltre	.10	.05
14 Greg Briley	.10	.05
15 Marquis Grissom	.20	.09
16 Dan Plesac	.10	.05
17 Dave Hollins	.20	.09
18 Terry Steinbach	.10	.05
19 Ed Nunez	.10	.05
20 Tim Salmon	.40	.18
21 Luis Salazar	.10	.05
22 Jim Eisenreich	.10	.05
23 Todd Stottlemyre	.10	.05
24 Tim Naehring	.10	.05
25 John Franco	.20	.09
26 Skeeter Barnes	.10	.05
27 Carlos Garcia	.10	.05
28 Joe Orsulak	.10	.05
29 Dwayne Henry	.10	.05
30 Fred McGriff	.30	.14
31 Derek Lilliquist	.10	.05
32 Don Mattingly	.75	.35
33 B.J. Wallace	.10	.05
34 Juan Gonzalez	.75	.35
35 John Smoltz	.30	.14
36 Scott Servais	.10	.05
37 Lenny Webster	.10	.05
38 Chris James	.10	.05
39 Roger McDowell	.10	.05
40 Ozzie Smith	.50	.23
41 Alex Fernandez	.20	.09
42 Spike Owen	.10	.05
43 Ruben Amaro	.10	.05
44 Kevin Seitzer	.10	.05
45 Dave Fleming	.10	.05
46 Eric Fox	.10	.05
47 Bob Scanlan	.10	.05
48 Bert Blyleven	.20	.09
49 Brian McRae	.10	.05
50 Roberto Alomar	.40	.18
51 Mo Vaughn	.40	.18
52 Bobby Bonilla	.20	.09
53 Frank Tanana	.10	.05
54 Mike LaValliere	.10	.05
55 Mark McLemore	.10	.05
56 Chad Mottola	.10	.05
57 Norm Charlton	.10	.05
58 Jose Melendez	.10	.05
59 Carlos Martinez	.10	.05
60 Roberto Kelly	.10	.05
61 Gene Larkin	.10	.05
62 Rafael Belliard	.10	.05
63 Al Osuna	.10	.05
64 Scott Chiamparino	.10	.05
65 Brett Butler	.20	.09
66 John Burkett	.10	.05
67 Felix Jose	.10	.05
68 Omar Vizquel	.20	.09
69 John Vander Wal	.10	.05
70 Roberto Hernandez	.20	.09
71 Ricky Bones	.10	.05
72 Jeff Grotewold	.10	.05
73 Mike Moore	.10	.05
74 Steve Buechele	.10	.05
75 Juan Guzman	.20	.09
76 Kevin Appier	.20	.09
77 Junior Felix	.10	.05
78 Greg W. Harris	.10	.05
79 Dick Schofield	.10	.05
80 Cecil Fielder	.20	.09
81 Lloyd McClendon	.10	.05
82 David Segui	.10	.05
83 Reggie Sanders	.20	.09
84 Kurt Stillwell	.10	.05
85 Sandy Alomar Jr.	.20	.09
86 John Habyan	.10	.05
87 Kevin Reimer	.10	.05
88 Mike Stanton	.10	.05
89 Eric Anthony	.10	.05
90 Scott Erickson	.10	.05
91 Craig Colbert	.10	.05
92 Tom Pagnozzi	.10	.05
93 Pedro Astacio	.20	.09
94 Lance Johnson	.10	.05
95 Larry Walker	.40	.18
96 Russ Swan	.10	.05
97 Scott Fletcher	.10	.05
98 Derek Jeter	8.00	3.60
99 Mike Williams	.10	.05
100 Mark McGwire	2.00	.90
101 Jim Bullinger	.10	.05
102 Brian Hunter	.10	.05
103 Jody Reed	.10	.05
104 Mike Butcher	.10	.05
105 Gregg Jefferies	.20	.09
106 Howard Johnson	.10	.05
107 John Kiely	.10	.05
108 Jose Lind	.10	.05
109 Sam Horn	.10	.05
110 Barry Larkin	.40	.18
111 Bruce Hurst	.10	.05
112 Brian Barnes	.10	.05
113 Thomas Howard	.10	.05
114 Mel Hall	.10	.05
115 Robby Thompson	.10	.05
116 Mark Lemke	.10	.05
117 Eddie Taubensee	.10	.05
118 David Hulse	.10	.05
119 Pedro Munoz	.10	.05
120 Ramon Martinez	.20	.09
121 Todd Worrell	.10	.05
122 Joey Cora	.10	.05
123 Moises Alou	.20	.09
124 Franklin Stubbs	.10	.05
125 Pete O'Brien	.10	.05
126 Bob Ayrault	.10	.05
127 Carney Lansford	.10	.05
128 Kal Daniels	.10	.05
129 Joe Grahe	.10	.05
130 Jeff Montgomery	.20	.09
131 Dave Winfield	.30	.14
132 Preston Wilson	.75	.35
133 Steve Watson	.10	.05
134 Lee Guetterman	.10	.05
135 Mickey Tettleton	.10	.05
136 Jeff King	.10	.05
137 Alan Mills	.10	.05
138 Joe Oliver	.10	.05
139 Gary Gaetti	.20	.09
140 Gary Sheffield	.40	.18
141 Dennis Cook	.10	.05
142 Charlie Hayes	.10	.05
143 Jeff Huson	.10	.05
144 Kent Mercker	.10	.05
145 Eric Young	.40	.18
146 Scott Leius	.10	.05
147 Bryan Hickerson	.10	.05
148 Steve Finley	.20	.09
149 Rheal Cormier	.10	.05
150 Frank Thomas UER	.75	.35
(Categories leading league are italicized but not printed in red)		
151 Archi Cianfrocco	.10	.05
152 Rich DeLucia	.10	.05
153 Greg Vaughn	.20	.09
154 Wes Chamberlain	.10	.05
155 Dennis Eckersley	.20	.09
156 Sammy Sosa	1.25	.55
157 Gary DiSarcina	.10	.05
158 Kevin Koslofski	.10	.05
159 Doug Linton	.10	.05
160 Lou Whitaker	.20	.09
161 Chad McConnell	.10	.05
162 Joe Hesketh	.10	.05
163 Tim Wakefield	.20	.09
164 Leo Gomez	.10	.05
165 Jose Rijo	.10	.05
166 Tim Scott	.10	.05
167 Steve Olin UER	.10	.05
(Born 10/4/65 should say 10/10/65)		
168 Kevin Maas	.10	.05
169 Kenny Rogers	.10	.05
170 David Justice	.40	.18
171 John Jaha	.10	.05
172 Jeff Reboulet	.10	.05
173 Andres Galarraga	.40	.18
174 Randy Velarde	.10	.05
175 Kirk McCaskill	.10	.05
176 Darren Lewis	.10	.05
177 Lenny Harris	.10	.05
178 Jeff Fassero	.10	.05
179 Ken Griffey Jr.	2.00	.90
180 Darren Daulton	.20	.09
181 John Jaha	.10	.05
182 Ron Darling	.10	.05
183 Greg Maddux	1.00	.45
184 Damion Easley	.10	.05
185 Jack Morris	.20	.09
186 Mike Magnante	.10	.05
187 John Dopson	.10	.05
188 Sid Fernandez	.10	.05
189 Tony Phillips	.10	.05

❑ 190	Doug Drabek	.10	.05
❑ 191	Sean Lowe	.10	.05
❑ 192	Bob Milacki	.10	.05
❑ 193	Steve Foster	.10	.05
❑ 194	Jerald Clark	.10	.05
❑ 195	Pete Harnisch	.10	.05
❑ 196	Pat Kelly	.10	.05
❑ 197	Jeff Frye	.10	.05
❑ 198	Alejandro Pena	.10	.05
❑ 199	Junior Ortiz	.10	.05
❑ 200	Kirby Puckett	.60	.25
❑ 201	Jose Uribe	.10	.05
❑ 202	Mike Scioscia	.10	.05
❑ 203	Bernard Gilkey	.10	.05
❑ 204	Dan Pasqua	.10	.05
❑ 205	Gary Carter	.30	.14
❑ 206	Henry Cotto	.10	.05
❑ 207	Paul Molitor	.40	.18
❑ 208	Mike Hartley	.10	.05
❑ 209	Jeff Parrott	.10	.05
❑ 210	Mark Langston	.10	.05
❑ 211	Doug Dascenzo	.10	.05
❑ 212	Rick Reed	.10	.05
❑ 213	Candy Maldonado	.10	.05
❑ 214	Danny Darwin	.10	.05
❑ 215	Pat Howell	.10	.05
❑ 216	Mark Leiter	.10	.05
❑ 217	Kevin Mitchell	.10	.09
❑ 218	Ben McDonald	.10	.05
❑ 219	Bip Roberts	.10	.05
❑ 220	Benny Santiago	.10	.05
❑ 221	Carlos Baerga	.10	.05
❑ 222	Bernie Williams	.40	.18
❑ 223	Roger Pavlik	.10	.05
❑ 224	Sid Bream	.10	.05
❑ 225	Matt Williams	.30	.14
❑ 226	Willie Banks	.10	.05
❑ 227	Jeff Bagwell	.50	.23
❑ 228	Tom Goodwin	.10	.05
❑ 229	Mike Perez	.10	.05
❑ 230	Carlton Fisk	.40	.18
❑ 231	John Wetteland	.20	.09
❑ 232	Tino Martinez	.40	.18
❑ 233	Rick Greene	.10	.05
❑ 234	Tim McIntosh	.10	.05
❑ 235	Mitch Williams	.10	.05
❑ 236	Kevin Campbell	.10	.05
❑ 237	Jose Vizcaino	.10	.05
❑ 238	Chris Donnels	.10	.05
❑ 239	Mike Boddicker	.10	.05
❑ 240	John Olerud	.30	.14
❑ 241	Mike Gardiner	.10	.05
❑ 242	Charlie O'Brien	.10	.05
❑ 243	Rob Deer	.10	.05
❑ 244	Denny Neagle	.20	.09
❑ 245	Chris Sabo	.10	.05
❑ 246	Gregg Olson	.10	.05
❑ 247	Frank Seminara UER	.10	.05
	(Acquired 12/3/98)		
❑ 248	Scott Scudder	.10	.05
❑ 249	Tim Burke	.10	.05
❑ 250	Chuck Knoblauch	.40	.18
❑ 251	Mike Bielecki	.10	.05
❑ 252	Xavier Hernandez	.10	.05
❑ 253	Jose Guzman	.10	.05
❑ 254	Cory Snyder	.10	.05
❑ 255	Orel Hershiser	.20	.09
❑ 256	Wil Cordero	.10	.05
❑ 257	Luis Alicea	.10	.05
❑ 258	Mike Schooler	.10	.05
❑ 259	Craig Grebeck	.10	.05
❑ 260	Duane Ward	.10	.05
❑ 261	Bill Wegman	.10	.05
❑ 262	Mickey Morandini	.10	.05
❑ 263	Vince Horsman	.10	.05
❑ 264	Paul Sorrento	.10	.05
❑ 265	Andre Dawson	.30	.14
❑ 266	Rene Gonzales	.10	.05
❑ 267	Keith Miller	.10	.05
❑ 268	Derek Bell	.20	.09
❑ 269	Todd Stevenson	.10	.05
❑ 270	Frank Viola	.10	.05
❑ 271	Wally Whitehurst	.10	.05
❑ 272	Kurt Knudsen	.10	.05
❑ 273	Dan Walters	.10	.05
❑ 274	Rick Sutcliffe	.10	.05

❑ 275	Andy Van Slyke	.20	.09
❑ 276	Paul O'Neill	.20	.09
❑ 277	Mark Whiten	.10	.05
❑ 278	Chris Nabholz	.10	.05
❑ 279	Todd Burns	.10	.05
❑ 280	Tom Glavine	.30	.14
❑ 281	Butch Henry	.10	.05
❑ 282	Shane Mack	.10	.05
❑ 283	Mike Jackson	.20	.09
❑ 284	Henry Rodriguez	.20	.09
❑ 285	Bob Tewksbury	.10	.05
❑ 286	Ron Karkovice	.10	.05
❑ 287	Mike Gallego	.10	.05
❑ 288	Dave Cochrane	.10	.05
❑ 289	Jesse Orosco	.10	.05
❑ 290	Dave Stewart	.20	.09
❑ 291	Tommy Greene	.10	.05
❑ 292	Rey Sanchez	.10	.05
❑ 293	Rob Ducey	.10	.05
❑ 294	Brent Mayne	.10	.05
❑ 295	Dave Stieb	.10	.05
❑ 296	Luis Rivera	.10	.05
❑ 297	Jeff Innis	.10	.05
❑ 298	Scott Livingstone	.10	.05
❑ 299	Bob Patterson	.10	.05
❑ 300	Cal Ripken	1.50	.70
❑ 301	Cesar Hernandez	.10	.05
❑ 302	Randy Myers	.20	.09
❑ 303	Brook Jacoby	.10	.05
❑ 304	Melido Perez	.10	.05
❑ 305	Rafael Palmeiro	.40	.18
❑ 306	Damon Berryhill	.10	.05
❑ 307	Dan Serafini	.10	.05
❑ 308	Darryl Kile	.10	.05
❑ 309	J.T. Bruett	.10	.05
❑ 310	Dave Righetti	.10	.05
❑ 311	Jay Howell	.10	.05
❑ 312	Geronimo Pena	.10	.05
❑ 313	Greg Hibbard	.10	.05
❑ 314	Mark Gardner	.10	.05
❑ 315	Edgar Martinez	.30	.14
❑ 316	Dave Nilsson	.20	.09
❑ 317	Kyle Abbott	.10	.05
❑ 318	Willie Wilson	.10	.05
❑ 319	Paul Assenmacher	.10	.05
❑ 320	Tim Fortugno	.10	.05
❑ 321	Rusty Meacham	.10	.05
❑ 322	Pat Borders	.10	.05
❑ 323	Mike Greenwell	.10	.05
❑ 324	Willie Randolph	.20	.09
❑ 325	Bill Gullickson	.10	.05
❑ 326	Gary Varsho	.10	.05
❑ 327	Tim Hulett	.10	.05
❑ 328	Scott Ruskin	.10	.05
❑ 329	Mike Maddux	.10	.05
❑ 330	Danny Tartabull	.10	.05
❑ 331	Kenny Lofton	.40	.18
❑ 332	Geno Petralli	.10	.05
❑ 333	Otis Nixon	.10	.05
❑ 334	Jason Kendall	1.25	.55
❑ 335	Mark Portugal	.10	.05
❑ 336	Mike Pagliarulo	.10	.05
❑ 337	Kirt Manwaring	.10	.05
❑ 338	Bob Ojeda	.10	.05
❑ 339	Mark Clark	.10	.05
❑ 340	John Kruk	.20	.09
❑ 341	Mel Rojas	.10	.05
❑ 342	Erik Hanson	.10	.05
❑ 343	Doug Henry	.10	.05
❑ 344	Jack McDowell	.20	.09
❑ 345	Harold Baines	.20	.09
❑ 346	Chuck McElroy	.10	.05
❑ 347	Luis Sojo	.10	.05
❑ 348	Andy Stankiewicz	.10	.05
❑ 349	Hipolito Pichardo	.10	.05
❑ 350	Joe Carter	.20	.09
❑ 351	Ellis Burks	.20	.09
❑ 352	Pete Schourek	.10	.05
❑ 353	Bubby Groom	.10	.05
❑ 354	Jay Bell	.20	.09
❑ 355	Brady Anderson	.20	.09
❑ 356	Freddie Benavides	.10	.05
❑ 357	Phil Stephenson	.10	.05
❑ 358	Kevin Wickander	.10	.05
❑ 359	Mike Stanley	.10	.05
❑ 360	Ivan Rodriguez	.50	.23

❑ 361	Scott Bankhead	.10	.05
❑ 362	Luis Gonzalez	.20	.09
❑ 363	John Smiley	.10	.05
❑ 364	Trevor Wilson	.10	.05
❑ 365	Tom Candiotti	.10	.05
❑ 366	Craig Wilson	.10	.05
❑ 367	Steve Sax	.10	.05
❑ 368	Delino DeShields	.20	.09
❑ 369	Jaime Navarro	.10	.05
❑ 370	Dave Valle	.10	.05
❑ 371	Mariano Duncan	.10	.05
❑ 372	Rod Nichols	.10	.05
❑ 373	Mike Morgan	.10	.05
❑ 374	Julio Valera	.10	.05
❑ 375	Wally Joyner	.20	.09
❑ 376	Tom Henke	.10	.05
❑ 377	Herm Winningham	.10	.05
❑ 378	Orlando Merced	.10	.05
❑ 379	Mike Munoz	.10	.05
❑ 380	Todd Hundley	.30	.14
❑ 381	Mike Flanagan	.10	.05
❑ 382	Tim Belcher	.10	.05
❑ 383	Jerry Browne	.10	.05
❑ 384	Mike Benjamin	.10	.05
❑ 385	Jim Leyritz	.10	.05
❑ 386	Ray Lankford	.30	.14
❑ 387	Devon White	.10	.05
❑ 388	Jeremy Hernandez	.10	.05
❑ 389	Brian Harper	.10	.05
❑ 390	Wade Boggs	.40	.18
❑ 391	Derrick May	.10	.05
❑ 392	Travis Fryman	.20	.09
❑ 393	Ron Gant	.20	.09
❑ 394	Checklist 1-132	.10	.05
❑ 395	Checklist 133-264 UER	.10	.05
	(Eckersley)		
❑ 396	Checklist 265-396	.10	.05
❑ 397	George Brett	.75	.35
❑ 398	Bobby Witt	.10	.05
❑ 399	Daryl Boston	.10	.05
❑ 400	Bo Jackson	.20	.09
❑ 401	Fred McGriff	.40	.18
	Frank Thomas		
❑ 402	Ryne Sandberg	.20	.09
	Carlos Baerga		
❑ 403	Gary Sheffield	.20	.09
	Edgar Martinez		
❑ 404	Barry Larkin	.20	.09
	Travis Fryman		
❑ 405	Andy Van Slyke	.50	.23
	Ken Griffey Jr.		
❑ 406	Larry Walker	.40	.18
	Kirby Puckett		
❑ 407	Barry Bonds	.20	.09
	Joe Carter		
❑ 408	Darren Daulton	.20	.09
	Brian Harper		
❑ 409	Greg Maddux	.50	.23
	Roger Clemens		
❑ 410	Tom Glavine	.20	.09
	Dave Fleming		
❑ 411	Lee Smith	.20	.09
	Dennis Eckersley		
❑ 412	Jamie McAndrew	.10	.05
❑ 413	Pete Smith	.10	.05
❑ 414	Juan Guerrero	.10	.05
❑ 415	Todd Frohwirth	.10	.05
❑ 416	Randy Tomlin	.10	.05
❑ 417	B.J. Surhoff	.10	.05
❑ 418	Jim Gott	.10	.05
❑ 419	Mark Thompson	.10	.05
❑ 420	Kevin Tapani	.10	.05
❑ 421	Curt Schilling	.20	.09
❑ 422	J.T. Snow	.50	.23
❑ 423	1993 Prospects	.40	.18
	Ryan Klesko		
	Ivan Cruz		
	Bubba Smith		
	Larry Sutton		
❑ 424	John Valentin	.20	.09
❑ 425	Joe Girardi	.20	.09
❑ 426	Nigel Wilson	.10	.05
❑ 427	Bob MacDonald	.10	.05
❑ 428	Todd Zeile	.10	.05
❑ 429	Milt Cuyler	.10	.05
❑ 430	Eddie Murray	.40	.18

☐ 431	Rich Amaral	.10	.05
☐ 432	Pete Young	.10	.05
☐ 433	Roger Bailey and	.10	.05
	Tom Schmidt		
☐ 434	Jack Armstrong	.10	.05
☐ 435	Willie McGee	.20	.09
☐ 436	Greg W. Harris	.10	.05
☐ 437	Chris Hammond	.10	.05
☐ 438	Ritchie Moody	.10	.05
☐ 439	Bryan Harvey	.10	.05
☐ 440	Ruben Sierra	.20	.09
☐ 441	Don Lemon and	.10	.05
	Todd Pridy		
☐ 442	Kevin McReynolds	.10	.05
☐ 443	Terry Leach	.10	.05
☐ 444	David Nied	.10	.05
☐ 445	Dale Murphy	.30	.14
☐ 446	Luis Mercedes	.10	.05
☐ 447	Keith Shepherd	.10	.05
☐ 448	Ken Caminiti	.30	.14
☐ 449	James Austin	.10	.05
☐ 450	Darryl Strawberry	.20	.09
☐ 451	1993 Prospects	.20	.09
	Ramon Caraballo		
	Jon Shave		
	Brent Gates		
	Quinton McCracken		
☐ 452	Bob Wickman	.10	.05
☐ 453	Victor Cole	.10	.05
☐ 454	John Johnstone	.10	.05
☐ 455	Chili Davis	.20	.09
☐ 456	Scott Taylor	.10	.05
☐ 457	Tracy Woodson	.10	.05
☐ 458	David Wells	.20	.09
☐ 459	Derek Wallace	.10	.05
☐ 460	Randy Johnson	.40	.18
☐ 461	Steve Reed	.10	.05
☐ 462	Felix Fermin	.10	.05
☐ 463	Scott Aldred	.10	.05
☐ 464	Greg Colbrunn	.10	.05
☐ 465	Tony Fernandez	.20	.09
☐ 466	Mike Felder	.10	.05
☐ 467	Lee Stevens	.20	.09
☐ 468	Matt Whiteside	.10	.05
☐ 469	Dave Hansen	.10	.05
☐ 470	Rob Dibble	.10	.05
☐ 471	Dave Gallagher	.10	.05
☐ 472	Chris Gwynn	.10	.05
☐ 473	Dave Henderson	.10	.05
☐ 474	Ozzie Guillen	.10	.05
☐ 475	Jeff Reardon	.20	.09
☐ 476	Mark Voisard and	.10	.05
	Will Scalzitti		
☐ 477	Jimmy Jones	.10	.05
☐ 478	Greg Cadaret	.10	.05
☐ 479	Todd Pratt	.25	.11
☐ 480	Pat Listach	.10	.05
☐ 481	Ryan Luzinski	.10	.05
☐ 482	Darren Reed	.10	.05
☐ 483	Brian Griffiths	.10	.05
☐ 484	John Wehner	.10	.05
☐ 485	Glenn Davis	.10	.05
☐ 486	Eric Wedge	.10	.05
☐ 487	Jesse Hollins	.10	.05
☐ 488	Manuel Lee	.10	.05
☐ 489	Scott Fredrickson	.10	.05
☐ 490	Omar Olivares	.10	.05
☐ 491	Shawn Hare	.10	.05
☐ 492	Tom Lampkin	.10	.05
☐ 493	Jeff Nelson	.10	.05
☐ 494	1993 Prospects	.20	.09
	Kevin Young		
	Adell Davenport		
	Eduardo Perez		
	Lou Lucca		
☐ 495	Ken Hill	.10	.05
☐ 496	Reggie Jefferson	.20	.09
☐ 497	Matt Petersen and	.10	.05
	Willie Brown		
☐ 498	Bud Black	.10	.05
☐ 499	Chuck Crim	.10	.05
☐ 500	Jose Canseco	.50	.23
☐ 501	Johnny Oates MG	.20	.09
	Bobby Cox MG		
☐ 502	Butch Hobson MG	.10	.05
	Jim Lefebvre MG		
☐ 503	Buck Rodgers MG	.20	.09
	Tony Perez MG		
☐ 504	Gene Lamont MG	.20	.09
	Don Baylor MG		
☐ 505	Mike Hargrove MG	.20	.09
	Rene Lachemann MG		
☐ 506	Sparky Anderson MG	.20	.09
	Art Howe MG		
☐ 507	Hal McRae MG	.20	.09
	Tom Lasorda MG		
☐ 508	Phil Garner MG	.20	.09
	Felipe Alou MG		
☐ 509	Tom Kelly MG	.10	.05
	Jeff Torborg MG		
☐ 510	Buck Showalter MG	.20	.09
	Jim Fregosi MG		
☐ 511	Tony LaRussa MG	.20	.09
	Jim Leyland MG		
☐ 512	Lou Piniella MG	.20	.09
	Joe Torre MG		
☐ 513	Kevin Kennedy MG	.10	.05
	Jim Riggleman MG		
☐ 514	Cito Gaston MG	.10	.05
	Dusty Baker MG		
☐ 515	Greg Swindell	.10	.05
☐ 516	Alex Arias	.10	.05
☐ 517	Bill Pecota	.10	.05
☐ 518	Benji Grigsby UER	.10	.05
	(Misspelled Bengi		
	on card front)		
☐ 519	David Howard	.10	.05
☐ 520	Charlie Hough	.20	.09
☐ 521	Kevin Flora	.10	.05
☐ 522	Shane Reynolds	.20	.09
☐ 523	Doug Bochtler	.10	.05
☐ 524	Chris Hoiles	.10	.05
☐ 525	Scott Sanderson	.10	.05
☐ 526	Mike Sharperson	.10	.05
☐ 527	Mike Fetters	.10	.05
☐ 528	Paul Quantrill	.10	.05
☐ 529	1993 Prospects	1.25	.55
	Dave Silvestri		
	Chipper Jones		
	Benji Gil		
	Jeff Patzke		
☐ 530	Sterling Hitchcock	.40	.18
☐ 531	Joe Millette	.10	.05
☐ 532	Tom Brunansky	.10	.05
☐ 533	Frank Castillo	.10	.05
☐ 534	Randy Knorr	.10	.05
☐ 535	Jose Oquendo	.10	.05
☐ 536	Dave Haas	.10	.05
☐ 537	Jason Hutchins and	.10	.05
	Ryan Turner		
☐ 538	Jimmy Baron	.10	.05
☐ 539	Kerry Woodson	.10	.05
☐ 540	Ivan Calderon	.10	.05
☐ 541	Denis Boucher	.10	.05
☐ 542	Royce Clayton	.10	.05
☐ 543	Reggie Williams	.10	.05
☐ 544	Steve Decker	.10	.05
☐ 545	Dean Palmer	.10	.05
☐ 546	Hal Morris	.10	.05
☐ 547	Ryan Thompson	.10	.05
☐ 548	Lance Blankenship	.10	.05
☐ 549	Hensley Meulens	.10	.05
☐ 550	Scott Radinsky	.10	.05
☐ 551	Eric Young	.40	.18
☐ 552	Jeff Blauser	.10	.05
☐ 553	Andujar Cedeno	.10	.05
☐ 554	Arthur Rhodes	.10	.05
☐ 555	Terry Mulholland	.10	.05
☐ 556	Darryl Hamilton	.10	.05
☐ 557	Pedro Martinez	.75	.35
☐ 558	Ryan Whitman and	.10	.05
	Mark Skeels		
☐ 559	Jamie Arnold	.10	.05
☐ 560	Zane Smith	.10	.05
☐ 561	Matt Nokes	.10	.05
☐ 562	Bob Zupcic	.10	.05
☐ 563	Shawn Boskie	.10	.05
☐ 564	Mike Timlin	.10	.05
☐ 565	Jerald Clark	.10	.05
☐ 566	Rod Brewer	.10	.05
☐ 567	Mark Carreon	.10	.05
☐ 568	Andy Benes	.20	.09
☐ 569	Shawn Barton	.10	.05
☐ 570	Tim Wallach	.10	.05
☐ 571	Dave Mlicki	.10	.05
☐ 572	Trevor Hoffman	.40	.18
☐ 573	John Patterson	.10	.05
☐ 574	De Shawn Warren	.10	.05
☐ 575	Monty Fariss	.10	.05
☐ 576	1993 Prospects	.20	.09
	Darrell Sherman		
	Damon Buford		
	Cliff Floyd		
	Michael Moore		
☐ 577	Tim Costo	.10	.05
☐ 578	Dave Magadan	.10	.05
☐ 579	Neil Garret and	.10	.05
	Jason Bates		
☐ 580	Walt Weiss	.10	.05
☐ 581	Chris Haney	.10	.05
☐ 582	Shawn Abner	.10	.05
☐ 583	Marvin Freeman	.10	.05
☐ 584	Casey Candaele	.10	.05
☐ 585	Ricky Jordan	.10	.05
☐ 586	Jeff Tabaka	.10	.05
☐ 587	Manny Alexander	.10	.05
☐ 588	Mike Trombley	.10	.05
☐ 589	Carlos Hernandez	.10	.05
☐ 590	Cal Eldred	.10	.05
☐ 591	Alex Cole	.10	.05
☐ 592	Phil Plantier	.10	.05
☐ 593	Brett Merriman	.10	.05
☐ 594	Jerry Nielsen	.10	.05
☐ 595	Shawon Dunston	.10	.05
☐ 596	Jimmy Key	.20	.09
☐ 597	Gerald Perry	.10	.05
☐ 598	Rico Brogna	.20	.09
☐ 599	Clemente Nunez and	.10	.05
	Daniel Robinson		
☐ 600	Bret Saberhagen	.20	.09
☐ 601	Craig Shipley	.10	.05
☐ 602	Henry Mercedes	.10	.05
☐ 603	Jim Thome	.50	.23
☐ 604	Rod Beck	.20	.09
☐ 605	Chuck Finley	.20	.09
☐ 606	J. Owens	.10	.05
☐ 607	Dan Smith	.10	.05
☐ 608	Bill Doran	.10	.05
☐ 609	Lance Parrish	.10	.05
☐ 610	Dennis Martinez	.20	.09
☐ 611	Tom Gordon	.10	.05
☐ 612	Byron Mathews	.10	.05
☐ 613	Joel Adamson	.10	.05
☐ 614	Brian Williams	.10	.05
☐ 615	Steve Avery	.10	.05
☐ 616	1993 Prospects	.10	.05
	Matt Mieske		
	Tracy Sanders		
	Midre Cummings		
	Ryan Freeburg		
☐ 617	Craig Lefferts	.10	.05
☐ 618	Tony Pena	.10	.05
☐ 619	Billy Spiers	.10	.05
☐ 620	Todd Benzinger	.10	.05
☐ 621	Mike Kotarski and	.10	.05
	Greg Boyd		
☐ 622	Ben Rivera	.10	.05
☐ 623	Al Martin	.10	.05
☐ 624	Sam Militello UER	.10	.05
	(Profile says drafted		
	in 1988, bio says		
	drafted in 1990)		
☐ 625	Rick Aguilera	.10	.05
☐ 626	Dan Gladden	.10	.05
☐ 627	Andres Berumen	.10	.05
☐ 628	Kelly Gruber	.10	.05
☐ 629	Cris Carpenter	.10	.05
☐ 630	Mark Grace	.30	.14
☐ 631	Jeff Brantley	.10	.05
☐ 632	Chris Widger	.25	.11
☐ 633	Three Russians UER	.10	.05
	Rudolf Razijgaev		
	Eugneyi Puchkov		
	Ilya Bogatyrev		
	(Bogatyrev is a shortstop,		
	card has pitching header)		
☐ 634	Mo Sanford	.10	.05
☐ 635	Albert Belle	.40	.18

❏ 636 Tim Teufel	.10	.05	❏ 710 Mike Mussina	.40	.18	Aaron Taylor
❏ 637 Greg Myers	.10	.05	❏ 711 Scott Chiamparino	.10	.05	Gus Gandarillas
❏ 638 Brian Bohanon	.10	.05	❏ 712 Stan Javier	.10	.05	❏ 787 Mike Matthews	.10	.05
❏ 639 Mike Bordick	.10	.05	❏ 713 John Doherty	.10	.05	❏ 788 Mackey Sasser	.10	.05
❏ 640 Dwight Gooden	.20	.09	❏ 714 Kevin Gross	.10	.05	❏ 789 Jeff Conine UER	.10	.05
❏ 641 Pat Leahy and	.10	.05	❏ 715 Greg Gagne	.10	.05	(No inclusion of 1990
Gavin Baugh			❏ 716 Steve Cooke	.10	.05	stats in career total)
❏ 642 Milt Hill	.10	.05	❏ 717 Steve Farr	.10	.05	❏ 790 George Bell	.10	.05
❏ 643 Luis Aquino	.10	.05	❏ 718 Jay Buhner	.30	.14	❏ 791 Pat Rapp	.10	.05
❏ 644 Dante Bichette	.20	.09	❏ 719 Butch Henry	.10	.05	❏ 792 Joe Boever	.10	.05
❏ 645 Bobby Thigpen	.10	.05	❏ 720 David Cone	.30	.14	❏ 793 Jim Poole	.10	.05
❏ 646 Rich Scheid	.10	.05	❏ 721 Rick Wilkins	.10	.05	❏ 794 Andy Ashby	.20	.09
❏ 647 Brian Sackinsky	.10	.05	❏ 722 Chuck Carr	.10	.05	❏ 795 Deion Sanders	.30	.14
❏ 648 Ryan Hawblitzel	.10	.05	❏ 723 Kenny Felder	.10	.05	❏ 796 Scott Brosius	.10	.05
❏ 649 Tom Marsh	.10	.05	❏ 724 Guillermo Velasquez	.10	.05	❏ 797 Brad Pennington	.10	.05
❏ 650 Terry Pendleton	.10	.05	❏ 725 Billy Hatcher	.10	.05	❏ 798 Greg Blosser	.10	.05
❏ 651 Rafael Bournigal	.10	.05	❏ 726 Mike Veneziale and	.20	.09	❏ 799 Jim Edmonds	1.00	.45
❏ 652 Dave West	.10	.05	Ken Kendrena			❏ 800 Shawn Jeter	.10	.05
❏ 653 Steve Hosey	.10	.05	❏ 727 Jonathan Hurst	.10	.05	❏ 801 Jesse Levis	.10	.05
❏ 654 Gerald Williams	.10	.05	❏ 728 Steve Frey	.10	.05	❏ 802 Phil Clark UER	.10	.05
❏ 655 Scott Cooper	.10	.05	❏ 729 Mark Leonard	.10	.05	(Word "a" is missing in
❏ 656 Gary Scott	.10	.05	❏ 730 Charles Nagy	.20	.09	sentence beginning
❏ 657 Mike Harkey	.10	.05	❏ 731 Donald Harris	.10	.05	with "In 1992 ...")
❏ 658 1993 Prospects	.30	.14	❏ 732 Travis Buckley	.10	.05	❏ 803 Ed Pierce	.10	.05
Jeromy Burnitz			❏ 733 Tom Browning	.10	.05	❏ 804 Jose Valentin	.40	.18
Melvin Nieves			❏ 734 Anthony Young	.10	.05	❏ 805 Terry Jorgensen	.10	.05
Rich Becker			❏ 735 Steve Shifflett	.10	.05	❏ 806 Mark Hutton	.10	.05
Shon Walker			❏ 736 Jeff Russell	.10	.05	❏ 807 Troy Neel	.10	.05
❏ 659 Ed Sprague	.10	.05	❏ 737 Wilson Alvarez	.20	.09	❏ 808 Bret Boone	.20	.09
❏ 660 Alan Trammell	.30	.14	❏ 738 Lance Painter	.10	.05	❏ 809 Cris Colon	.10	.05
❏ 661 Garvin Alston and	.10	.05	❏ 739 Dave Weathers	.10	.05	❏ 810 Domingo Martinez	.10	.05
Michael Case			❏ 740 Len Dykstra	.20	.09	❏ 811 Javier Lopez	.40	.18
❏ 662 Donovan Osborne	.10	.05	❏ 741 Mike Devereaux	.10	.05	❏ 812 Matt Walbeck	.10	.05
❏ 663 Jeff Gardner	.10	.05	❏ 742 1993 Prospects	.10	.05	❏ 813 Dan Wilson	.20	.09
❏ 664 Calvin Jones	.10	.05	Rene Arocha			❏ 814 Scooter Tucker	.10	.05
❏ 665 Darrin Fletcher	.10	.05	Alan Embree			❏ 815 Billy Ashley	.10	.05
❏ 666 Glenallen Hill	.10	.05	Brien Taylor			❏ 816 Tim Laker	.10	.05
❏ 667 Jam Rosenbohm	.10	.05	Tim Crabtree			❏ 817 Bobby Jones	.20	.09
❏ 668 Scott Lewis	.10	.05	❏ 743 Dave Landaker	.10	.05	❏ 818 Brad Brink	.10	.05
❏ 669 Kip Yaughn	.10	.05	❏ 744 Chris George	.10	.05	❏ 819 William Pennyfeather	.10	.05
❏ 670 Julio Franco	.10	.05	❏ 745 Eric Davis	.20	.09	❏ 820 Stan Royer	.10	.05
❏ 671 Dave Martinez	.10	.05	❏ 746 Mark Strittmatter and	.20	.09	❏ 821 Doug Brocail	.10	.05
❏ 672 Kevin Bass	.10	.05	Lamarr Rogers			❏ 822 Kevin Rogers	.10	.05
❏ 673 Todd Van Poppel	.10	.05	❏ 747 Carl Willis	.10	.05	❏ 823 Checklist 397-540	.10	.05
❏ 674 Mark Gubicza	.10	.05	❏ 748 Stan Belinda	.10	.05	❏ 824 Checklist 541-691	.10	.05
❏ 675 Tim Raines	.20	.09	❏ 749 Scott Kamieniecki	.10	.05	❏ 825 Checklist 692-825	.10	.05
❏ 676 Rudy Seanez	.10	.05	❏ 750 Rickey Henderson	.50	.23	
❏ 677 Charlie Leibrandt	.10	.05	❏ 751 Eric Hillman	.10	.05	
❏ 678 Randy Milligan	.10	.05	❏ 752 Pat Hentgen	.30	.14	**1993 Topps Gold**
❏ 679 Kim Batiste	.10	.05	❏ 753 Jim Corsi	.10	.05	
❏ 680 Craig Biggio	.40	.18	❏ 754 Brian Jordan	.20	.09	
❏ 681 Darren Holmes	.10	.05	❏ 755 Bill Swift	.10	.05	
❏ 682 John Candelaria	.10	.05	❏ 756 Mike Henneman	.10	.05	
❏ 683 Jerry Stafford and	.20	.09	❏ 757 Harold Reynolds	.10	.05	
Eddie Christian			❏ 758 Sean Berry	.10	.05	
❏ 684 Pat Mahomes	.10	.05	❏ 759 Charlie Hayes	.10	.05	
❏ 685 Bob Walk	.10	.05	❏ 760 Luis Polonia	.10	.05	
❏ 686 Russ Springer	.10	.05	❏ 761 Darrin Jackson	.10	.05	
❏ 687 Tony Sheffield	.10	.05	❏ 762 Mark Lewis	.10	.05	
❏ 688 Dwight Smith	.10	.05	❏ 763 Rob Maurer	.10	.05	
❏ 689 Eddie Zosky	.10	.05	❏ 764 Willie Greene	.10	.05	
❏ 690 Bien Figueroa	.10	.05	❏ 765 Vince Coleman	.10	.05	
❏ 691 Jim Tatum	.10	.05	❏ 766 Todd Revenig	.10	.05	
❏ 692 Chad Kreuter	.10	.05	❏ 767 Rich Ireland	.10	.05	
❏ 693 Rich Rodriguez	.10	.05	❏ 768 Mike Macfarlane	.10	.05	
❏ 694 Shane Turner	.10	.05	❏ 769 Francisco Cabrera	.10	.05	
❏ 695 Kent Bottenfield	.10	.05	❏ 770 Robin Ventura	.20	.09	
❏ 696 Jose Mesa	.10	.05	❏ 771 Kevin Ritz	.10	.05	
❏ 697 Darrell Whitmore	.10	.05	❏ 772 Chito Martinez	.10	.05	
❏ 698 Ted Wood	.10	.05	❏ 773 Cliff Brantley	.10	.05	

	MINT	NRMT
COMPLETE GOLD SET (825)	70.00	32.00
COMPLETE SERIES 1 (396)	40.00	18.00
COMPLETE SERIES 2 (429)	30.00	13.50
COMMON CARD (1G-825G)	.15	.07

❏ 699 Chad Curtis	.20	.09	❏ 774 Curt Leskanic	.10	.05	*STARS: 1.25X TO 3X BASIC CARDS
❏ 700 Nolan Ryan	1.50	.70	❏ 775 Chris Bosio	.10	.05	*ROOKIES: 1.25X TO 3X BASIC CARDS
❏ 701 1993 Prospects	2.00	.90	❏ 776 Jose Offerman	.20	.09	GOLD CARDS 1 PER WAX PACK
Mike Piazza			❏ 777 Mark Guthrie	.10	.05	GOLD CARDS 3 PER RACK PACK
Brook Fordyce			❏ 778 Don Slaught	.10	.05	GOLD CARDS 5 PER JUMBO PACK
Carlos Delgado			❏ 779 Rich Monteleone	.10	.05	GOLD CARDS 10 PER FACTORY SET
Donnie Leshnock			❏ 780 Jim Abbott	.20	.09	
❏ 702 Tim Pugh	.10	.05	❏ 781 Jack Clark	.10	.05	
❏ 703 Jeff Kent	.20	.09	❏ 782 Reynol Mendoza and	.10	.05	❏ 394 Bernardo Brito	.25	.11
❏ 704 Jon Goodrich and	.20	.09	Dan Roman			Replaces Checklist 1
Danny Figueroa			❏ 783 Heathcliff Slocumb	.10	.05	❏ 395 Jim McNamara	.25	.11
❏ 705 Bob Welch	.10	.05	❏ 784 Jeff Branson	.10	.05	Replaces Checklist 2
❏ 706 Sherard Clinkscales	.10	.05	❏ 785 Kevin Brown	.30	.14	❏ 396 Rich Sauveur	.25	.11
❏ 707 Donn Pall	.10	.05	❏ 786 1993 Prospects	.20	.09	Replaces Checklist 3
❏ 708 Greg Olson	.10	.05	Mike Christopher			❏ 823 Keith Brown	.25	.11
❏ 709 Jeff Juden	.10	.05	Ken Ryan			

Replaces Checklist 4

❑ 824 Russ McGinnis .... .25 .11
Replaces Checklist 5

❑ 825 Mike Walker UER ...... .25 .11
(Card has 1993 Mariner
stats, should be 1992)
Replaces Checklist 6

1993 Topps Inaugural Marlins

	MINT	NRMT
COMP.FACT.SET (825)	150.00	70.00
COMMON CARD (1-825)	.15	.07

*STARS: 3X TO 6X BASIC CARDS
*ROOKIES: 3X TO 6X BASIC CARDS
DISTRIBUTED IN FACTORY SET FORM ONLY
NO MORE THAN 10,000 SETS PRODUCED

1993 Topps Inaugural Rockies

	MINT	NRMT
COMP.FACT.SET (825)	150.00	70.00
COMMON CARD (1-825)	.15	.07

*STARS: 3X TO 6X BASIC CARDS
*ROOKIES: 3X TO 6X BASIC CARDS
DISTRIBUTED IN FACTORY SET FORM ONLY
NO MORE THAN 10,000 SETS PRODUCED

1993 Topps Black Gold

	MINT	NRMT
COMPLETE SET (44)	10.00	4.50
COMPLETE SERIES 1 (22)	4.00	1.80
COMPLETE SERIES 2 (22)	6.00	2.70
COMMON CARD (1-44)	.10	.05

STATED ODDS 1:72 H/R, 1:12 J, 1:24 RACK
THREE PER FACTORY SET

❑ 1 Barry Bonds .... .75 .35
❑ 2 Will Clark .... .60 .25
❑ 3 Darren Daulton .... .25 .11
❑ 4 Andre Dawson .... .40 .18
❑ 5 Delino DeShields ...... .10 .05
❑ 6 Tom Glavine .... .40 .18
❑ 7 Marquis Grissom ...... .25 .11
❑ 8 Tony Gwynn .... 1.50 .70
❑ 9 Eric Karros .... .40 .18
❑ 10 Ray Lankford .... .40 .18

❑ 11 Barry Larkin .... .40 .18
❑ 12 Greg Maddux .... 1.50 .70
❑ 13 Fred McGriff .... .40 .18
❑ 14 Joe Oliver .... .10 .05
❑ 15 Terry Pendleton .... .10 .05
❑ 16 Bip Roberts .... .10 .05
❑ 17 Ryne Sandberg .... .75 .35
❑ 18 Gary Sheffield .... .60 .25
❑ 19 Lee Smith .... .25 .11
❑ 20 Ozzie Smith .... .75 .35
❑ 21 Andy Van Slyke .... .10 .05
❑ 22 Larry Walker .... .60 .25
❑ 23 Roberto Alomar .... .60 .25
❑ 24 Brady Anderson .... .40 .18
❑ 25 Carlos Baerga .... .10 .05
❑ 26 Joe Carter .... .25 .11
❑ 27 Roger Clemens .... 1.50 .70
❑ 28 Mike Devereaux .... .10 .05
❑ 29 Dennis Eckersley ...... .25 .11
❑ 30 Cecil Fielder .... .25 .11
❑ 31 Travis Fryman .... .25 .11
❑ 32 Juan Gonzalez UER .... 1.25 .55
(No copyright or
licensing on card)
❑ 33 Ken Griffey Jr. 3.00 1.35
❑ 34 Brian Harper .... .10 .05
❑ 35 Pat Listach .... .10 .05
❑ 36 Kenny Lofton .... .60 .25
❑ 37 Edgar Martinez .... .40 .18
❑ 38 Jack McDowell .... .10 .05
❑ 39 Mark McGwire 3.00 1.35
❑ 40 Kirby Puckett .... 1.00 .45
❑ 41 Mickey Tettleton ...... .10 .05
❑ 42 Frank Thomas UER .... 1.25 .55
(No copyright or
licensing on card)
❑ 43 Robin Ventura .... .25 .11
❑ 44 Dave Winfield .... .40 .18
❑ A Winner A 1-11 .... .50 .23
❑ B Winner B 12-22 .... .50 .23
❑ C Winner C 23-33 .... .75 .35
❑ D Winner D 34-44 .... .75 .35
❑ AB Winner AB 1-22 UER .. 1.00 .45
(Numbers 10 and 11
have the 1 missing)
❑ CD Winner C/D 23-44 .... 1.50 .70
❑ ABCD Winner ABCD 1-44 2.50 1.10

1993 Topps Traded

	MINT	NRMT
COMP.FACT.SET (132)	30.00	13.50
COMMON CARD (1T-132T)	.15	.07
MINOR STARS	.25	.11
UNLISTED STARS	.50	.23

❑ 1T Barry Bonds .... .60 .25
❑ 2T Rich Renteria .... .15 .07
❑ 3T Aaron Sele .... .50 .23
❑ 4T Carlton Loewer USA .. 1.50 .70
❑ 5T Erik Pappas .... .15 .07
❑ 6T Greg McMichael ...... .15 .07
❑ 7T Freddie Benavides .... .15 .07
❑ 8T Kirk Gibson .... .25 .11
❑ 9T Tony Fernandez .... .25 .11
❑ 10T Jay Gainer .... .15 .07
❑ 11T Orestes Destrade .... .15 .07
❑ 12T A.J. Hinch USA ...... 1.50 .70

❑ 13T Bobby Munoz .... .15 .07
❑ 14T Tom Henke .... .15 .07
❑ 15T Rob Butler .... .15 .07
❑ 16T Gary Wayne .... .15 .07
❑ 17T David McCarty .... .15 .07
❑ 18T Walt Weiss .... .15 .07
❑ 19T Todd Helton USA 15.00 6.75
❑ 20T Mark Whiten .... .15 .07
❑ 21T Ricky Gutierrez ...... .15 .07
❑ 22T Dustin Hermanson USA 1.50 .70
❑ 23T Sherman Obando .... .15 .07
❑ 24T Mike Piazza 2.50 1.10
❑ 25T Jeff Russell .... .15 .07
❑ 26T Jason Bere .... .15 .07
❑ 27T Jack Voigt .... .15 .07
❑ 28T Chris Bosio .... .15 .07
❑ 29T Phil Hiatt .... .15 .07
❑ 30T Matt Beaumont USA .. .15 .07
❑ 31T Andres Galarraga .... .50 .23
❑ 32T Greg Swindell .... .15 .07
❑ 33T Vinny Castilla .... 2.00 .90
❑ 34T Pat Clougherty USA .. .15 .07
❑ 35T Greg Briley .... .15 .07
❑ 36T Dallas Green MG ..... .15 .07
Davey Johnson MG
❑ 37T Tyler Green .... .15 .07
❑ 38T Craig Paquette ...... .15 .07
❑ 39T Danny Sheaffer ...... .15 .07
❑ 40T Jim Converse .... .15 .07
❑ 41T Terry Harvey USA .... .15 .07
❑ 42T Phil Plantier .... .15 .07
❑ 43T Doug Saunders ...... .15 .07
❑ 44T Benny Santiago ...... .15 .07
❑ 45T Dante Powell USA ... 1.50 .70
❑ 46T Jeff Parrett .... .15 .07
❑ 47T Wade Boggs .... .50 .23
❑ 48T Paul Molitor .... .50 .23
❑ 49T Turk Wendell .... .15 .07
❑ 50T David Wells .... .25 .11
❑ 51T Gary Sheffield .... .50 .23
❑ 52T Kevin Young .... .25 .11
❑ 53T Nelson Liriano .... .15 .07
❑ 54T Greg Maddux .... 1.25 .55
❑ 55T Derek Bell .... .25 .11
❑ 56T Matt Turner .... .15 .07
❑ 57T Charlie Nelson USA .. .15 .07
❑ 58T Mike Hampton .... .50 .23
❑ 59T Troy O'Leary .... 2.00 .90
❑ 60T Benji Gil .... .15 .07
❑ 61T Mitch Lyden .... .15 .07
❑ 62T J.T. Snow .... .50 .23
❑ 63T Damon Buford .... .15 .07
❑ 64T Gene Harris .... .15 .07
❑ 65T Randy Myers .... .25 .11
❑ 66T Felix Jose .... .25 .11
❑ 67T Todd Dunn USA ...... .15 .07
❑ 68T Jimmy Key .... .25 .11
❑ 69T Pedro Castellano .... .15 .07
❑ 70T Mark Merila USA ..... .15 .07
❑ 71T Rich Rodriguez ...... .15 .07
❑ 72T Matt Mieske .... .15 .07
❑ 73T Pete Incaviglia ...... .15 .07
❑ 74T Carl Everett .... .30 .14
❑ 75T Jim Abbott .... .25 .11
❑ 76T Luis Aquino .... .15 .07
❑ 77T Rene Arocha .... .15 .07
❑ 78T Jon Shave .... .15 .07
❑ 79T Todd Walker USA 4.00 1.80
❑ 80T Jack Armstrong ...... .15 .07
❑ 81T Jeff Richardson ..... .15 .07
❑ 82T Blas Minor .... .15 .07
❑ 83T Dave Winfield .... .30 .14
❑ 84T Paul O'Neill .... .25 .11
❑ 85T Steve Reich USA ..... .15 .07
❑ 86T Chris Hammond ..... .15 .07
❑ 87T Hilly Hathaway ...... .15 .07
❑ 88T Fred McGriff .... .30 .14
❑ 89T Dave Telgheder ..... .15 .07
❑ 90T Richie Lewis .... .15 .07
❑ 91T Brent Gates .... .15 .07
❑ 92T Andre Dawson .... .30 .14
❑ 93T Andy Barkett USA .... .15 .07
❑ 94T Doug Drabek .... .15 .07
❑ 95T Joe Klink .... .15 .07
❑ 96T Willie Blair .... .15 .07
❑ 97T Danny Graves USA ... .15 .07

	MINT	NRMT
98T Pat Meares	.15	.07
99T Mike Lansing	.25	.11
100T Marcos Armas	.15	.07
101T Darren Grass USA	.15	.07
102T Chris Jones	.15	.07
103T Ken Ryan	.15	.07
104T Ellis Burks	.25	.11
105T Roberto Kelly	.15	.07
106T Dave Magadan	.15	.07
107T Paul Wilson USA	.30	.14
108T Rob Natal	.15	.07
109T Paul Wagner	.15	.07
110T Jeromy Burnitz	.25	.11
111T Monty Fariss	.15	.07
112T Kevin Mitchell	.25	.11
113T Scott Pose	.15	.07
114T Dave Stewart	.25	.11
115T Russ Johnson USA	.50	.23
116T Armando Reynoso	.15	.07
117T Geronimo Berroa	.15	.07
118T Woody Williams	.30	.14
119T Tim Bogar	.15	.07
120T Bob Scafa USA	.15	.07
121T Henry Cotto	.15	.07
122T Gregg Jefferies	.15	.07
123T Norm Charlton	.15	.07
124T Bret Wagner USA	.50	.23
125T David Cone	.30	.14
126T Daryl Boston	.15	.07
127T Tim Wallach	.15	.07
128T Mike Martin USA	.15	.07
129T John Cummings	.15	.07
130T Ryan Bowen	.15	.07
131T John Powell USA	.15	.07
132T Checklist 1-132	.15	.07

1994 Topps

	MINT	NRMT
COMPLETE SET (792)	30.00	13.50
COMP.FACT.SET (808)	60.00	27.00
COMP.BAKER SET (818)	60.00	27.00
COMPLETE SERIES 1 (396)	15.00	6.75
COMPLETE SERIES 2 (396)	15.00	6.75
COMMON CARD (1-792)	.10	.05
MINOR STARS	.20	.09
UNLISTED STARS	.40	.18
SUBSET CARDS HALF VALUE OF BASE CARDS		
COMP.GOLD SET (792)	80.00	36.00
COMP.GOLD SERIES 1 (396)	40.00	18.00
COMP.GOLD SERIES 2 (396)	40.00	18.00
COMMON GOLD (1-792)	.15	.07

*GOLD STARS: 1.5X TO 4X HI COLUMN
*GOLD YOUNG STARS: 1.25X TO 3X HI
ONE GOLD PER PACK
TEN GOLD PER FACTORY SET

	MINT	NRMT
1 Mike Piazza	1.25	.55
2 Bernie Williams	.40	.18
3 Kevin Rogers	.10	.05
4 Paul Carey	.10	.05
5 Ozzie Guillen	.10	.05
6 Derrick May	.10	.05
7 Jose Mesa	.10	.05
8 Todd Hundley	.20	.09
9 Chris Haney	.10	.05
10 John Olerud	.20	.09
11 Anduja Cedeno	.10	.05
12 John Smiley	.10	.05
13 Phil Plantier	.10	.05
14 Willie Banks	.10	.05
15 Jay Bell	.20	.09
16 Doug Henry	.10	.05
17 Lance Blankenship	.10	.05
18 Greg W. Harris	.10	.05
19 Scott Livingstone	.10	.05
20 Bryan Harvey	.10	.05
21 Wil Cordero	.10	.05
22 Roger Pavlik	.10	.05
23 Mark Lemke	.10	.05
24 Jeff Nelson	.10	.05
25 Todd Zeile	.10	.05
26 Billy Hatcher	.10	.05
27 Joe Magrane	.10	.05
28 Tony Longmire	.10	.05
29 Omar Daal	.10	.05
30 Kirt Manwaring	.10	.05
31 Melido Perez	.10	.05
32 Tim Hulett	.10	.05
33 Jeff Schwartz	.10	.05
34 Nolan Ryan	1.50	.70
35 Jose Guzman	.10	.05
36 Felix Fermin	.10	.05
37 Jeff Innis	.10	.05
38 Brett Mayne	.10	.05
39 Huck Flener	.10	.05
40 Jeff Bagwell	.50	.23
41 Kevin Wickander	.10	.05
42 Ricky Gutierrez	.10	.05
43 Pat Mahomes	.10	.05
44 Jeff King	.10	.05
45 Cal Eldred	.10	.05
46 Craig Paquette	.10	.05
47 Richie Lewis	.10	.05
48 Tony Phillips	.10	.05
49 Armando Reynoso	.10	.05
50 Moises Alou	.20	.09
51 Manuel Lee	.10	.05
52 Otis Nixon	.10	.05
53 Billy Ashley	.10	.05
54 Mark Whiten	.10	.05
55 Jeff Russell	.10	.05
56 Chad Curtis	.10	.05
57 Kevin Stocker	.10	.05
58 Mike Jackson	.20	.09
59 Matt Nokes	.10	.05
60 Chris Bosio	.10	.05
61 Damon Buford	.10	.05
62 Tim Belcher	.10	.05
63 Glenallen Hill	.10	.05
64 Bill Wertz	.10	.05
65 Eddie Murray	.40	.18
66 Tom Gordon	.10	.05
67 Alex Gonzalez	.10	.05
68 Eddie Taubensee	.10	.05
69 Jacob Brumfield	.10	.05
70 Andy Benes	.20	.09
71 Rich Becker	.10	.05
72 Steve Cooke	.10	.05
73 Billy Spiers	.10	.05
74 Scott Brosius	.20	.09
75 Alan Trammell	.30	.14
76 Luis Aquino	.10	.05
77 Jerald Clark	.10	.05
78 Mel Rojas	.10	.05
79 Outfield Prospects	.10	.05
Billy Masse		
Stanton Cameron		
Tim Clark		
Craig McClure		
80 Jose Canseco	.50	.23
81 Greg McMichael	.10	.05
82 Brian Turang	.10	.05
83 Tom Urbani	.10	.05
84 Garret Anderson	.40	.18
85 Tony Pena	.10	.05
86 Ricky Jordan	.10	.05
87 Jim Gott	.10	.05
88 Pat Kelly	.10	.05
89 Bud Black	.10	.05
90 Robin Ventura	.20	.09
91 Rick Sutcliffe	.10	.05
92 Jose Bautista	.10	.05
93 Bob Ojeda	.10	.05
94 Phil Hiatt	.10	.05
95 Tim Pugh	.10	.05
96 Randy Knorr	.10	.05
97 Todd Jones	.10	.05
98 Ryan Thompson	.10	.05
99 Tim Mauser	.10	.05
100 Kirby Puckett	.60	.25
101 Mark Dewey	.10	.05
102 B.J. Surhoff	.20	.09
103 Sterling Hitchcock	.20	.09
104 Alex Arias	.10	.05
105 David Wells	.30	.14
106 Daryl Boston	.10	.05
107 Mike Stanton	.10	.05
108 Gary Redus	.10	.05
109 Delino DeShields	.10	.05
110 Lee Smith	.20	.09
111 Greg Litton	.10	.05
112 Frankie Rodriguez	.10	.05
113 Russ Springer	.10	.05
114 Mitch Williams	.10	.05
115 Eric Karros	.20	.09
116 Jeff Brantley	.10	.05
117 Jack Voigt	.10	.05
118 Jason Bere	.10	.05
119 Kevin Roberson	.10	.05
120 Jimmy Key	.20	.09
121 Reggie Jefferson	.10	.05
122 Jeromy Burnitz	.20	.09
123 Billy Brewer	.10	.05
124 Willie Canate	.10	.05
125 Greg Swindell	.10	.05
126 Hal Morris	.10	.05
127 Brad Ausmus	.10	.05
128 George Tsamis	.10	.05
129 Denny Neagle	.10	.05
130 Pat Listach	.10	.05
131 Steve Karsay	.10	.05
132 Bret Barberie	.10	.05
133 Mark Leiter	.10	.05
134 Greg Colbrunn	.10	.05
135 David Nied	.10	.05
136 Dean Palmer	.20	.09
137 Steve Avery	.10	.05
138 Bill Haselman	.10	.05
139 Tripp Cromer	.10	.05
140 Frank Viola	.10	.05
141 Rene Gonzales	.10	.05
142 Curt Schilling	.20	.09
143 Tim Wallach	.10	.05
144 Bobby Munoz	.10	.05
145 Brady Anderson	.20	.09
146 Rod Beck	.10	.05
147 Mike LaValliere	.10	.05
148 Greg Hibbard	.10	.05
149 Kenny Lofton	.40	.18
150 Dwight Gooden	.20	.09
151 Greg Gagne	.10	.05
152 Ray McDavid	.10	.05
153 Chris Donnels	.10	.05
154 Dan Wilson	.10	.05
155 Todd Stottlemyre	.10	.05
156 David McCarty	.10	.05
157 Paul Wagner	.10	.05
158 Shortstop Prospects	1.50	.70
Orlando Miller		
Brandon Wilson		
Derek Jeter		
Mike Neal		
159 Mike Fetters	.10	.05
160 Scott Lydy	.10	.05
161 Darrell Whitmore	.10	.05
162 Bob MacDonald	.10	.05
163 Vinny Castilla	.20	.09
164 Denis Boucher	.10	.05
165 Ivan Rodriguez	.50	.23
166 Ron Gant	.20	.09
167 Tim Davis	.10	.05
168 Steve Dixon	.10	.05
169 Scott Fletcher	.10	.05
170 Terry Mulholland	.10	.05
171 Greg Myers	.10	.05
172 Brett Butler	.20	.09
173 Bob Wickman	.10	.05
174 Dave Martinez	.10	.05

175	Fernando Valenzuela	.20	.09
176	Craig Grebeck	.10	.05
177	Shawn Boskie	.10	.05
178	Albie Lopez	.10	.05
179	Butch Huskey	.20	.09
180	George Brett	.75	.35
181	Juan Guzman	.10	.05
182	Eric Anthony	.10	.05
183	Rob Dibble	.10	.05
184	Craig Shipley	.10	.05
185	Kevin Tapani	.10	.05
186	Marcus Moore	.10	.05
187	Graeme Lloyd	.10	.05
188	Mike Bordick	.10	.05
189	Chris Hammond	.10	.05
190	Cecil Fielder	.20	.09
191	Curt Leskanic	.10	.05
192	Lou Frazier	.10	.05
193	Steve Dreyer	.10	.05
194	Javier Lopez	.30	.14
195	Edgar Martinez	.20	.09
196	Allen Watson	.10	.05
197	John Flaherty	.10	.05
198	Kurt Stillwell	.10	.05
199	Danny Jackson	.10	.05
200	Cal Ripken	1.50	.70
201	Mike Bell FDP	.10	.05
202	Alan Benes FDP	.10	.09
203	Matt Farner FDP	.10	.05
204	Jeff Granger	.10	.05
205	Brooks Kieschnick FDP	.10	.05
206	Jeremy Lee FDP	.20	.09
207	Charles Peterson FDP	.20	.09
208	Alan Rice FDP	.10	.05
209	Billy Wagner FDP	.50	.23
210	Kelly Wunsch FDP	.20	.09
211	Tom Candiotti	.10	.05
212	Domingo Jean	.10	.05
213	John Burkett	.10	.05
214	George Bell	.10	.05
215	Dan Plesac	.10	.05
216	Manny Ramirez	.75	.35
217	Mike Maddux	.10	.05
218	Kevin McReynolds	.10	.05
219	Pat Borders	.10	.05
220	Doug Drabek	.10	.05
221	Larry Luebbers	.10	.05
222	Trevor Hoffman	.20	.09
223	Pat Meares	.10	.05
224	Danny Miceli	.10	.05
225	Greg Vaughn	.20	.09
226	Scott Hemond	.10	.05
227	Pat Rapp	.10	.05
228	Kirk Gibson	.20	.09
229	Lance Painter	.10	.05
230	Larry Walker	.40	.18
231	Benji Gil	.10	.05
232	Mark Wohlers	.10	.05
233	Rich Amaral	.10	.05
234	Eric Pappas	.10	.05
235	Scott Cooper	.10	.05
236	Mike Butcher	.10	.05
237	Outfield Prospects	.60	.25
	Curtis Pride		
	Shawn Green		
	Mark Sweeney		
	Eddie Davis		
238	Kim Batiste	.10	.05
239	Paul Assenmacher	.10	.05
240	Will Clark	.40	.18
241	Jose Offerman	.20	.09
242	Todd Frohwirth	.10	.05
243	Tim Raines	.20	.09
244	Rick Wilkins	.10	.05
245	Bret Saberhagen	.20	.09
246	Thomas Howard	.10	.05
247	Stan Belinda	.10	.05
248	Rickey Henderson	.50	.23
249	Brian Williams	.10	.05
250	Barry Larkin	.40	.18
251	Jose Valentin	.10	.05
252	Lenny Webster	.10	.05
253	Blas Minor	.10	.05
254	Tim Teufel	.10	.05
255	Bobby Witt	.10	.05
256	Walt Weiss	.10	.05
257	Chad Kreuter	.10	.05
258	Roberto Mejia	.10	.05
259	Cliff Floyd	.20	.09
260	Julio Franco	.10	.05
261	Rafael Belliard	.10	.05
262	Marc Newfield	.10	.05
263	Gerald Perry	.10	.05
264	Ken Ryan	.10	.05
265	Chili Davis	.20	.09
266	Dave West	.10	.05
267	Royce Clayton	.10	.05
268	Pedro Martinez	.50	.23
269	Mark Hutton	.10	.05
270	Frank Thomas	.75	.35
271	Brad Pennington	.10	.05
272	Mike Harkey	.10	.05
273	Sandy Alomar Jr.	.20	.09
274	Dave Gallagher	.10	.05
275	Wally Joyner	.10	.05
276	Ricky Trlicek	.10	.05
277	Al Osuna	.10	.05
278	Calvin Reese	.30	.14
279	Kevin Higgins	.10	.05
280	Rick Aguilera	.10	.05
281	Orlando Merced	.10	.05
282	Mike Mohler	.10	.05
283	John Jaha	.10	.05
284	Rob Nen	.10	.05
285	Travis Fryman	.20	.09
286	Mark Thompson	.10	.05
287	Mike Lansing	.20	.09
288	Craig Lefferts	.10	.05
289	Damon Berryhill	.10	.05
290	Randy Johnson	.40	.18
291	Jeff Reed	.10	.05
292	Danny Darwin	.10	.05
293	J.T. Snow	.20	.09
294	Tyler Green	.10	.05
295	Chris Hoiles	.10	.05
296	Roger McDowell	.10	.05
297	Spike Owen	.10	.05
298	Salomon Torres	.10	.05
299	Wilson Alvarez	.20	.09
300	Ryne Sandberg	.50	.23
301	Derek Lilliquist	.10	.05
302	Howard Johnson	.10	.05
303	Greg Cadaret	.10	.05
304	Pat Hentgen	.20	.09
305	Craig Biggio	.40	.18
306	Scott Service	.10	.05
307	Melvin Nieves	.10	.05
308	Mike Trombley	.10	.05
309	Carlos Garcia	.10	.05
310	Robin Yount UER	.40	.18
	(listed with 111 triples in		
	1988; should be 11)		
311	Marcos Armas	.10	.05
312	Rich Rodriguez	.10	.05
313	Justin Thompson	.40	.18
314	Danny Sheaffer	.10	.05
315	Ken Hill	.10	.05
316	Pitching Prospects	.10	.05
	Chad Ogea		
	Duff Brumley		
	Terrell Wade		
	Chris Michalak		
317	Cris Carpenter	.10	.05
318	Jeff Blauser	.10	.05
319	Ted Power	.10	.05
320	Ozzie Smith	.50	.23
321	John Dopson	.10	.05
322	Chris Turner	.10	.05
323	Pete Incaviglia	.10	.05
324	Alan Mills	.10	.05
325	Jody Reed	.10	.05
326	Rich Monteleone	.10	.05
327	Mark Carreon	.10	.05
328	Donn Pall	.10	.05
329	Matt Walbeck	.10	.05
330	Charles Nagy	.20	.09
331	Jeff McKnight	.10	.05
332	Jose Lind	.10	.05
333	Mike Timlin	.10	.05
334	Doug Jones	.10	.05
335	Kevin Mitchell	.10	.05
336	Luis Lopez	.10	.05
337	Shane Mack	.10	.05
338	Randy Tomlin	.10	.05
339	Matt Mieske	.10	.05
340	Mark McGwire	2.00	.90
341	Nigel Wilson	.10	.05
342	Danny Gladden	.10	.05
343	Mo Sanford	.10	.05
344	Sean Berry	.10	.05
345	Kevin Brown	.20	.09
346	Greg Olson	.10	.05
347	Dave Magadan	.10	.05
348	Rene Arocha	.10	.05
349	Carlos Quintana	.10	.05
350	Jim Abbott	.20	.09
351	Gary DiSarcina	.10	.05
352	Ben Rivera	.10	.05
353	Carlos Hernandez	.10	.05
354	Darren Lewis	.10	.05
355	Harold Reynolds	.10	.05
356	Scott Ruffcorn	.10	.05
357	Mark Gubicza	.10	.05
358	Paul Sorrento	.10	.05
359	Anthony Young	.10	.05
360	Mark Grace	.30	.14
361	Rob Butler	.10	.05
362	Kevin Bass	.10	.05
363	Eric Helfand	.10	.05
364	Derek Bell	.20	.09
365	Scott Erickson	.20	.09
366	Al Martin	.10	.05
367	Ricky Bones	.10	.05
368	Jeff Branson	.10	.05
369	Third Base Prospects	.50	.23
	Luis Ortiz		
	David Bell		
	Jason Giambi		
	George Arias		
370	Benito Santiago	.10	.05
	(See also 379)		
371	John Doherty	.10	.05
372	Joe Girardi	.10	.05
373	Tim Scott	.10	.05
374	Marvin Freeman	.10	.05
375	Deion Sanders	.20	.09
376	Roger Salkeld	.10	.05
377	Bernard Gilkey	.10	.05
378	Tony Fossas	.10	.05
379	Mark McLemore UER	.10	.05
	(Card number is 370)		
380	Darren Daulton	.20	.09
381	Chuck Finley	.10	.05
382	Mitch Webster	.10	.05
383	Gerald Williams	.10	.05
384	Frank Thomas AS	.40	.18
	Fred McGriff AS		
385	Roberto Alomar AS	.20	.09
	Robby Thompson AS		
386	Wade Boggs AS	.10	.05
	Matt Williams AS		
387	Cal Ripken AS	.40	.18
	Jeff Blauser AS		
388	Ken Griffey Jr. AS	.50	.23
	Len Dykstra AS		
389	Juan Gonzalez AS	.40	.18
	David Justice AS		
390	George Belle AS	.20	.09
	Bobby Bonds AS		
391	Mike Stanley AS	.40	.18
	Mike Piazza AS		
392	Jack McDowell AS	.30	.14
	Greg Maddux AS		
393	Jimmy Key AS	.20	.09
	Tom Glavine AS		
394	Jeff Montgomery AS	.10	.05
	Randy Myers AS		
395	Checklist 1-198	.10	.05
396	Checklist 199-396	.10	.05
397	Tim Salmon	.40	.18
398	Todd Benzinger	.10	.05
399	Frank Castillo	.10	.05
400	Ken Griffey Jr.	2.00	.90
401	John Kruk	.20	.09
402	Dave Telgheder	.10	.05
403	Gary Gaetti	.20	.09
404	Jim Edmonds	.40	.18
405	Don Slaught	.10	.05

406	Jose Oquendo	.10	.05
407	Bruce Ruffin	.10	.05
408	Phil Clark	.10	.05
409	Joe Klink	.10	.05
410	Lou Whitaker	.20	.09
411	Kevin Seitzer	.10	.05
412	Darrin Fletcher	.10	.05
413	Kenny Rogers	.10	.05
414	Bill Pecota	.10	.05
415	Dave Fleming	.10	.05
416	Luis Alicea	.10	.05
417	Paul Quantrill	.10	.05
418	Damion Easley	.20	.09
419	Wes Chamberlain	.10	.05
420	Harold Baines	.20	.09
421	Scott Radinsky	.10	.05
422	Rey Sanchez	.10	.05
423	Junior Ortiz	.10	.05
424	Jeff Kent	.20	.09
425	Brian McRae	.10	.05
426	Ed Sprague	.10	.05
427	Tom Edens	.10	.05
428	Willie Greene	.10	.05
429	Bryan Hickerson	.10	.05
430	Dave Winfield	.40	.18
431	Pedro Astacio	.10	.05
432	Mike Gallego	.10	.05
433	Dave Burba	.10	.05
434	Bob Walk	.10	.05
435	Darryl Hamilton	.10	.05
436	Vince Horsman	.10	.05
437	Bob Natal	.10	.05
438	Mike Henneman	.10	.05
439	Willie Blair	.10	.05
440	Dennis Martinez	.20	.09
441	Dan Peltier	.10	.05
442	Tony Tarasco	.10	.05
443	John Cummings	.10	.05
444	Geronimo Pena	.10	.05
445	Aaron Sele	.20	.09
446	Stan Javier	.10	.05
447	Mike Williams	.10	.05
448	First Base Prospects	.30	.14
	Greg Pirkl		
	Roberto Petagine		
	D.J.Boston		
	Shawn Wooten		
449	Jim Poole	.10	.05
450	Carlos Baerga	.20	.09
451	Bob Scanlan	.10	.05
452	Lance Johnson	.10	.05
453	Eric Hillman	.10	.05
454	Keith Miller	.10	.05
455	Dave Stewart	.20	.09
456	Pete Harnisch	.10	.05
457	Roberto Kelly	.10	.05
458	Tim Worrell	.10	.05
459	Pedro Munoz	.10	.05
460	Orel Hershiser	.20	.09
461	Randy Velarde	.10	.05
462	Trevor Wilson	.10	.05
463	Jerry Goff	.10	.05
464	Bill Wegman	.10	.05
465	Dennis Eckersley	.20	.09
466	Jeff Conine	.10	.05
467	Joe Boever	.10	.05
468	Dante Bichette	.20	.09
469	Jeff Shaw	.10	.05
470	Rafael Palmeiro	.40	.18
471	Phil Leftwich	.10	.05
472	Jay Buhner	.10	.05
473	Bob Tewksbury	.10	.05
474	Tim Naehring	.10	.05
475	Tom Glavine	.40	.18
476	Dave Hollins	.10	.05
477	Arthur Rhodes	.10	.05
478	Joey Cora	.10	.05
479	Mike Morgan	.10	.05
480	Albert Belle	.40	.18
481	John Franco	.20	.09
482	Hipolito Pichardo	.10	.05
483	Duane Ward	.10	.05
484	Luis Gonzalez	.20	.09
485	Joe Oliver	.10	.05
486	Wally Whitehurst	.10	.05
487	Mike Benjamin	.10	.05
488	Eric Davis	.20	.09
489	Scott Kamieniecki	.10	.05
490	Kent Hrbek	.20	.09
491	John Hope	.10	.05
492	Jesse Orosco	.10	.05
493	Troy Neel	.10	.05
494	Ryan Bowen	.10	.05
495	Mickey Tettleton	.10	.05
496	Chris Jones	.10	.05
497	John Wetteland	.20	.09
498	David Hulse	.10	.05
499	Greg Maddux	1.00	.45
500	Bo Jackson	.40	.18
501	Donovan Osborne	.10	.05
502	Mike Greenwell	.10	.05
503	Steve Frey	.10	.05
504	Jim Eisenreich	.10	.05
505	Robby Thompson	.10	.05
506	Leo Gomez	.10	.05
507	Dave Staton	.10	.05
508	Wayne Kirby	.10	.05
509	Tim Bogar	.10	.05
510	David Cone	.30	.14
511	Devon White	.10	.05
512	Xavier Hernandez	.10	.05
513	Tim Costo	.10	.05
514	Gene Harris	.10	.05
515	Jack McDowell	.10	.05
516	Kevin Gross	.10	.05
517	Scott Leius	.10	.05
518	Lloyd McClendon	.10	.05
519	Alex Diaz	.10	.05
520	Wade Boggs	.40	.18
521	Bob Welch	.10	.05
522	Henry Cotto	.10	.05
523	Mike Moore	.10	.05
524	Tim Laker	.10	.05
525	Andres Galarraga	.40	.18
526	Jamie Moyer	.10	.05
527	Second Base Prospects	.20	.09
	Norberto Martin		
	Ruben Santana		
	Jason Hardtke		
	Chris Sexton		
528	Sid Bream	.10	.05
529	Erik Hanson	.10	.05
530	Ray Lankford	.20	.09
531	Rob Deer	.10	.05
532	Rod Correia	.10	.05
533	Roger Mason	.10	.05
534	Mike Devereaux	.10	.05
535	Jeff Montgomery	.10	.05
536	Dwight Smith	.10	.05
537	Jeremy Hernandez	.10	.05
538	Ellis Burks	.20	.09
539	Bobby Jones	.10	.05
540	Paul Molitor	.40	.18
541	Jeff Juden	.10	.05
542	Chris Sabo	.10	.05
543	Larry Casian	.10	.05
544	Jeff Gardner	.10	.05
545	Ramon Martinez	.20	.09
546	Paul O'Neill	.20	.09
547	Steve Hosey	.10	.05
548	Dave Nilsson	.10	.05
549	Ron Darling	.10	.05
550	Matt Williams	.30	.14
551	Jack Armstrong	.10	.05
552	Bill Krueger	.10	.05
553	Freddie Benavides	.10	.05
554	Jeff Fassero	.10	.05
555	Chuck Knoblauch	.40	.18
556	Guillermo Velasquez	.10	.05
557	Joel Johnston	.10	.05
558	Tom Lampkin	.10	.05
559	Todd Van Poppel	.10	.05
560	Gary Sheffield	.40	.18
561	Skeeter Barnes	.10	.05
562	Darren Holmes	.10	.05
563	John Vander Wal	.10	.05
564	Mike Ignasiak	.10	.05
565	Fred McGriff	.30	.14
566	Luis Polonia	.10	.05
567	Mike Perez	.10	.05
568	John Valentin	.20	.09
569	Mike Felder	.10	.05
570	Tommy Greene	.10	.05
571	David Segui	.20	.09
572	Roberto Hernandez	.10	.05
573	Steve Wilson	.10	.05
574	Willie McGee	.20	.09
575	Randy Myers	.10	.05
576	Darrin Jackson	.10	.05
577	Eric Plunk	.10	.05
578	Mike Macfarlane	.10	.05
579	Doug Brocail	.10	.05
580	Steve Finley	.20	.09
581	John Roper	.10	.05
582	Danny Cox	.10	.05
583	Chip Hale	.10	.05
584	Scott Bullett	.10	.05
585	Kevin Reimer	.10	.05
586	Brent Gates	.10	.05
587	Matt Turner	.10	.05
588	Rich Rowland	.10	.05
589	Kent Bottenfield	.10	.05
590	Marquis Grissom	.20	.09
591	Doug Strange	.10	.05
592	Jay Howell	.10	.05
593	Omar Vizquel	.20	.09
594	Rheal Cormier	.10	.05
595	Andre Dawson	.30	.14
596	Hilly Hathaway	.10	.05
597	Todd Pratt	.10	.05
598	Mike Mussina	.40	.18
599	Alex Fernandez	.10	.05
600	Don Mattingly	.75	.35
601	Frank Thomas ST	.40	.18
602	Ryne Sandberg ST	.30	.14
603	Wade Boggs ST	.40	.18
604	Cal Ripken ST	.75	.35
605	Barry Bonds ST	.40	.18
606	Ken Griffey Jr. ST	1.00	.45
607	Kirby Puckett ST	.40	.18
608	Darren Daulton ST	.10	.05
609	Paul Molitor ST	.20	.09
610	Terry Steinbach	.10	.05
611	Todd Worrell	.10	.05
612	Jim Thome	.40	.18
613	Mike McElroy	.10	.05
614	John Habyan	.10	.05
615	Sid Fernandez	.10	.05
616	Outfield Prospects	.20	.09
	Eddie Zambrano		
	Glenn Murray		
	Chad Mottola		
	Jermaine Allensworth		
617	Steve Bedrosian	.10	.05
618	Rob Ducey	.10	.05
619	Tom Browning	.10	.05
620	Tony Gwynn	1.00	.45
621	Carl Willis	.10	.05
622	Kevin Young	.10	.05
623	Rafael Novoa	.10	.05
624	Jerry Browne	.10	.05
625	Charlie Hough	.10	.05
626	Chris Gomez	.10	.05
627	Steve Reed	.10	.05
628	Kirk Rueter	.10	.05
629	Matt Whiteside	.10	.05
630	David Justice	.40	.18
631	Brad Holman	.10	.05
632	Brian Jordan	.20	.09
633	Scott Bankhead	.10	.05
634	Torey Lovullo	.10	.05
635	Len Dykstra	.20	.09
636	Ben McDonald	.10	.05
637	Steve Howe	.10	.05
638	Jose Vizcaino	.10	.05
639	Bill Swift	.20	.09
640	Darryl Strawberry	.20	.09
641	Steve Farr	.10	.05
642	Tom Kramer	.10	.05
643	Joe Orsulak	.10	.05
644	Tom Henke	.10	.05
645	Joe Carter	.20	.09
646	Ken Caminiti	.30	.14
647	Reggie Sanders	.20	.09
648	Andy Ashby	.10	.05
649	Derek Parks	.10	.05
650	Andy Van Slyke	.20	.09
651	Juan Bell	.10	.05

❑ 652	Roger Smithberg	.10	.05
❑ 653	Chuck Carr	.10	.05
❑ 654	Bill Gullickson	.10	.05
❑ 655	Charlie Hayes	.10	.05
❑ 656	Chris Nabholz	.10	.05
❑ 657	Karl Rhodes	.10	.05
❑ 658	Pete Smith	.10	.05
❑ 659	Bret Boone	.20	.09
❑ 660	Gregg Jefferies	.10	.05
❑ 661	Bob Zupcic	.10	.05
❑ 662	Steve Sax	.10	.05
❑ 663	Mariano Duncan	.10	.05
❑ 664	Jeff Tackett	.10	.05
❑ 665	Mark Langston	.10	.05
❑ 666	Steve Buechele	.10	.05
❑ 667	Candy Maldonado	.10	.05
❑ 668	Woody Williams	.10	.05
❑ 669	Tim Wakefield	.20	.09
❑ 670	Danny Tartabull	.10	.05
❑ 671	Charlie O'Brien	.10	.05
❑ 672	Felix Jose	.10	.05
❑ 673	Bobby Ayala	.10	.05
❑ 674	Scott Servais	.10	.05
❑ 675	Roberto Alomar	.40	.18
❑ 676	Pedro Martinez	.10	.05
❑ 677	Eddie Guardado	.10	.05
❑ 678	Mark Lewis	.10	.05
❑ 679	Jaime Navarro	.10	.05
❑ 680	Ruben Sierra	.10	.05
❑ 681	Rick Renteria	.10	.05
❑ 682	Storm Davis	.10	.05
❑ 683	Cory Snyder	.10	.05
❑ 684	Ron Karkovice	.10	.05
❑ 685	Juan Gonzalez	.75	.35
❑ 686	Catchers Prospects	.40	.18
	Chris Howard		
	Carlos Delgado		
	Jason Kendall		
	Paul Bako		
❑ 687	John Smoltz	.30	.14
❑ 688	Brian Dorsett	.10	.05
❑ 689	Omar Olivares	.10	.05
❑ 690	Mo Vaughn	.40	.18
❑ 691	Joe Grahe	.10	.05
❑ 692	Mickey Morandini	.10	.05
❑ 693	Tino Martinez	.40	.18
❑ 694	Brian Barnes	.10	.05
❑ 695	Mike Stanley	.10	.05
❑ 696	Mark Clark	.10	.05
❑ 697	Dave Hansen	.10	.05
❑ 698	Willie Wilson	.10	.05
❑ 699	Pete Schourek	.10	.05
❑ 700	Barry Bonds	.50	.23
❑ 701	Kevin Appier	.20	.09
❑ 702	Tony Fernandez	.20	.09
❑ 703	Darryl Kile	.10	.05
❑ 704	Archi Cianfrocco	.10	.05
❑ 705	Jose Rijo	.10	.05
❑ 706	Brian Harper	.10	.05
❑ 707	Zane Smith	.10	.05
❑ 708	Dave Henderson	.10	.05
❑ 709	Angel Miranda UER	.10	.05
	(no Topps logo on back)		
❑ 710	Orestes Destrade	.10	.05
❑ 711	Greg Gohr	.10	.05
❑ 712	Eric Young	.10	.05
❑ 713	Relief Pitchers	.10	.05
	Prospects		
	Todd Williams		
	Ron Watson		
	Kirk Bullinger		
	Mike Welch		
❑ 714	Tim Spehr	.10	.05
❑ 715	Hank Aaron 715 HR	.50	.23
❑ 716	Nate Minchey	.10	.05
❑ 717	Mike Blowers	.10	.05
❑ 718	Kent Mercker	.10	.05
❑ 719	Tom Pagnozzi	.10	.05
❑ 720	Roger Clemens	1.00	.45
❑ 721	Eduardo Perez	.10	.05
❑ 722	Milt Thompson	.10	.05
❑ 723	Gregg Olson	.10	.05
❑ 724	Kirk McCaskill	.10	.05
❑ 725	Sammy Sosa	1.25	.55
❑ 726	Alvaro Espinoza	.10	.05
❑ 727	Henry Rodriguez	.20	.09
❑ 728	Jim Leyritz	.20	.09
❑ 729	Steve Scarsone	.10	.05
❑ 730	Bobby Bonilla	.20	.09
❑ 731	Chris Gwynn	.10	.05
❑ 732	Al Leiter	.20	.09
❑ 733	Bip Roberts	.10	.05
❑ 734	Mark Portugal	.10	.05
❑ 735	Terry Pendleton	.10	.05
❑ 736	Dave Valle	.10	.05
❑ 737	Paul Kilgus	.10	.05
❑ 738	Greg A. Harris	.10	.05
❑ 739	Jon Ratliff DP	.10	.05
❑ 740	Kirk Presley DP	.10	.05
❑ 741	Josue Estrada DP	.20	.09
❑ 742	Wayne Gomes DP	.10	.05
❑ 743	Pat Watkins DP	.20	.09
❑ 744	Jamey Wright DP	.20	.09
❑ 745	Jay Powell DP	.30	.14
❑ 746	Ryan McGuire DP	.20	.09
❑ 747	Marc Barcelo DP	.20	.09
❑ 748	Sloan Smith DP	.10	.05
❑ 749	John Wasdin DP	.20	.09
❑ 750	Marc Valdes	.10	.05
❑ 751	Dan Ehler DP	.10	.05
❑ 752	Andre King DP	.10	.05
❑ 753	Greg Keagle DP	.10	.05
❑ 754	Jason Myers DP	.10	.05
❑ 755	Dax Winslett DP	.10	.05
❑ 756	Casey Whitten DP	.20	.09
❑ 757	Tony Fuduric DP	.10	.05
❑ 758	Greg Norton DP	.30	.14
❑ 759	Jeff D'Amico DP	.20	.09
❑ 760	Ryan Hancock DP	.10	.05
❑ 761	David Cooper DP	.10	.05
❑ 762	Kevin Orie DP	.25	.11
❑ 763	John O'Donoghue	.10	.05
	Mike Oquist		
❑ 764	Cory Bailey	.10	.05
	Scott Hatteberg		
❑ 765	Mark Holzemer	.10	.05
	Paul Swingle		
❑ 766	James Baldwin	.20	.09
	Rod Bolton		
❑ 767	Jerry Di Poto	.10	.05
	Julian Tavarez		
❑ 768	Danny Bautista	.10	.05
	Sean Bergman		
❑ 769	Bob Hamelin	.10	.05
	Joe Vitiello		
❑ 770	Mark Kiefer	.20	.09
	Troy O'Leary		
❑ 771	Denny Hocking	.20	.09
	Oscar Munoz		
❑ 772	Russ Davis	.20	.09
	Brien Taylor		
❑ 773	Kyle Abbott	.10	.05
	Miguel Jimenez		
❑ 774	Kevin King	.10	.05
	Eric Plantenberg		
❑ 775	Jon Shave	.10	.05
	Desi Wilson		
❑ 776	Domingo Cedeno	.10	.05
	Paul Spoljaric		
❑ 777	Chipper Jones	1.00	.45
	Ryan Klesko		
❑ 778	Steve Trachsel	.10	.05
	Turk Wendell		
❑ 779	Johnny Ruffin	.10	.05
	Jerry Spradlin		
❑ 780	Jason Bates	.10	.05
	John Burke		
❑ 781	Carl Everett	.20	.09
	Dave Weathers		
❑ 782	Gary Mota	.20	.09
	James Mouton		
❑ 783	Raul Mondesi	.40	.18
	Ben Van Ryn		
❑ 784	Gabe White	.20	.09
	Rondell White		
❑ 785	Brook Fordyce	.20	.09
	Bill Pulsipher		
❑ 786	Kevin Foster	.10	.05
	Gene Schall		
❑ 787	Rich Aude	.20	.09
	Midre Cummings		
❑ 788	Brian Barber	.20	.09
	Rich Batchelor		
❑ 789	Brian Johnson	.10	.05
	Scott Sanders		
❑ 790	Ricky Faneyte	.10	.05
	J.R. Phillips		
❑ 791	Checklist 3	.10	.05
❑ 792	Checklist 4	.10	.05

1994 Topps Black Gold

	MINT	NRMT
COMPLETE SET (44)	25.00	11.00
COMPLETE SERIES 1 (22)	15.00	6.75
COMPLETE SERIES 2 (22)	10.00	4.50
COMMON CARD (1-44)	.25	.11
STAT.ODDS 1:72H/R,1:18J,1:24RAC,1:36CEL		
THREE PER FACTORY SET		

❑ 1	Roberto Alomar	.75	.35
❑ 2	Carlos Baerga	.25	.11
❑ 3	Albert Belle	.75	.35
❑ 4	Joe Carter	.40	.18
❑ 5	Cecil Fielder	.40	.18
❑ 6	Travis Fryman	.40	.18
❑ 7	Juan Gonzalez	1.50	.70
❑ 8	Ken Griffey Jr.	4.00	1.80
❑ 9	Chris Hoiles	.25	.11
❑ 10	Randy Johnson	.75	.35
❑ 11	Kenny Lofton	.75	.35
❑ 12	Jack McDowell	.25	.11
❑ 13	Paul Molitor	.75	.35
❑ 14	Jeff Montgomery	.25	.11
❑ 15	John Olerud	.40	.18
❑ 16	Rafael Palmeiro	.50	.23
❑ 17	Kirby Puckett	1.50	.70
❑ 18	Cal Ripken	3.00	1.35
❑ 19	Tim Salmon	.75	.35
❑ 20	Mike Stanley	.25	.11
❑ 21	Frank Thomas	1.50	.70
❑ 22	Robin Ventura	.40	.18
❑ 23	Jeff Bagwell	1.00	.45
❑ 24	Jay Bell	.40	.18
❑ 25	Craig Biggio	.75	.35
❑ 26	Jeff Blauser	.25	.11
❑ 27	Barry Bonds	1.00	.45
❑ 28	Darren Daulton	.40	.18
❑ 29	Len Dykstra	.40	.18
❑ 30	Andres Galarraga	.75	.35
❑ 31	Ron Gant	.40	.18
❑ 32	Tom Glavine	.75	.35
❑ 33	Mark Grace	.25	.11
❑ 34	Marquis Grissom	.25	.11
❑ 35	Gregg Jefferies	.25	.11
❑ 36	David Justice	.75	.35
❑ 37	John Kruk	.40	.18
❑ 38	Greg Maddux	2.00	.90
❑ 39	Fred McGriff	.50	.23
❑ 40	Randy Myers	.25	.11
❑ 41	Mike Piazza	2.50	1.10
❑ 42	Sammy Sosa	2.50	1.10
❑ 43	Robby Thompson	.25	.11
❑ 44	Matt Williams	.50	.23
❑ A	Winner A 1-11	1.00	.45
❑ B	Winner B 12-22	1.00	.45
❑ C	Winner C 23-33	1.00	.45
❑ D	Winner D 34-44	1.00	.45
❑ AB	Winner AB 1-22	2.00	.90
❑ CD	Winner CD 23-44	2.00	.90
❑ ABCD	Winner ABCD 1-44	4.00	1.80

1994 Topps Traded

John Hudek

	MINT	NRMT
COMP.FACT.SET (140)	60.00	27.00
COMMON CARD (1T-132T)	.15	.07
MINOR STARS	.25	.11
UNLISTED STARS	.50	.23

❑ 1T Paul Wilson	.25	.11
❑ 2T Bill Taylor	.15	.07
❑ 3T Dan Wilson	.15	.07
❑ 4T Mark Smith	.15	.07
❑ 5T Toby Borland	.15	.07
❑ 6T Dave Clark	.15	.07
❑ 7T Dennis Martinez	.25	.11
❑ 8T Dave Gallagher	.15	.07
❑ 9T Josias Manzanillo	.15	.07
❑ 10T Brian Anderson	1.50	.70
❑ 11T Damon Berryhill	.15	.07
❑ 12T Alex Cole	.15	.07
❑ 13T Jacob Shumate	.25	.11
❑ 14T Oddibe McDowell	.15	.07
❑ 15T Willie Banks	.15	.07
❑ 16T Jerry Browne	.15	.07
❑ 17T Donnie Elliott	.15	.07
❑ 18T Ellis Burks	.25	.11
❑ 19T Chuck McElroy	.15	.07
❑ 20T Luis Polonia	.15	.07
❑ 21T Brian Harper	.15	.07
❑ 22T Mark Portugal	.15	.07
❑ 23T Dave Henderson	.15	.07
❑ 24T Mark Acre	.15	.07
❑ 25T Julio Franco	.15	.07
❑ 26T Darren Hall	.15	.07
❑ 27T Eric Anthony	.15	.07
❑ 28T Sid Fernandez	.15	.07
❑ 29T Rusty Greer	6.00	2.70
❑ 30T Riccardo Ingram	.15	.07
❑ 31T Gabe White	.15	.07
❑ 32T Tim Belcher	.15	.07
❑ 33T Terrence Long	2.00	.90
❑ 34T Mark Dalesandro	.15	.07
❑ 35T Mike Kelly	.15	.07
❑ 36T Jack Morris	.25	.11
❑ 37T Jeff Brantley	.15	.07
❑ 38T Larry Barnes	.25	.11
❑ 39T Brian R. Hunter	.15	.07
❑ 40T Otis Nixon	.15	.07
❑ 41T Bret Wagner	.15	.07
❑ 42T Pedro Martinez TR	.75	.35
Delino Deshields		
❑ 43T Heathcliff Slocumb	.15	.07
❑ 44T Ben Grieve	30.00	13.50
❑ 45T John Hudek	.15	.07
❑ 46T Shawon Dunston	.15	.07
❑ 47T Greg Colbrunn	.15	.07
❑ 48T Joey Hamilton	.50	.23
❑ 49T Marvin Freeman	.15	.07
❑ 50T Terry Mulholland	.15	.07
❑ 51T Keith Mitchell	.15	.07
❑ 52T Dwight Smith	.15	.07
❑ 53T Shawn Boskie	.15	.07
❑ 54T Kevin Witt	2.00	.90
❑ 55T Ron Gant	.25	.11
❑ 56T 1994 Prospects	1.50	.70
Trenidad Hubbard		
Jason Schmidt		
Larry Sutton		

Stephen Larkin		
❑ 57T Jody Reed	.15	.07
❑ 58T Rick Helling	.25	.11
❑ 59T John Powell	.25	.11
❑ 60T Eddie Murray	.50	.23
❑ 61T Joe Hall	.15	.07
❑ 62T Jorge Fabregas	.15	.07
❑ 63T Mike Mordecai	.15	.07
❑ 64T Ed Vosberg	.15	.07
❑ 65T Rickey Henderson	.60	.25
❑ 66T Tim Grieve	.15	.07
❑ 67T Jon Lieber	.15	.07
❑ 68T Chris Howard	.15	.07
❑ 69T Matt Walbeck	.15	.07
❑ 70T Chan Ho Park	5.00	2.20
❑ 71T Bryan Eversgerd	.15	.07
❑ 72T John Dettmer	.15	.07
❑ 73T Erik Hanson	.15	.07
❑ 74T Mike Thurman	.15	.07
❑ 75T Bobby Ayala	.15	.07
❑ 76T Rafael Palmeiro	.50	.23
❑ 77T Bret Boone	.25	.11
❑ 78T Paul Shuey	.15	.07
❑ 79T Kevin Foster	.15	.07
❑ 80T Dave Magadan	.15	.07
❑ 81T Bip Roberts	.15	.07
❑ 82T Howard Johnson	.15	.07
❑ 83T Xavier Hernandez	.15	.07
❑ 84T Ross Powell	.15	.07
❑ 85T Doug Million	.15	.07
❑ 86T Geronimo Berroa	.15	.07
❑ 87T Mark Farris	.25	.11
❑ 88T Butch Henry	.15	.07
❑ 89T Junior Felix	.15	.07
❑ 90T Bo Jackson	.25	.11
❑ 91T Hector Carrasco	.15	.07
❑ 92T Charlie O'Brien	.15	.07
❑ 93T Omar Vizquel	.25	.11
❑ 94T David Segui	.15	.07
❑ 95T Dustin Hermanson	.25	.11
❑ 96T Gar Finnvold	.15	.07
❑ 97T Dave Stevens	.15	.07
❑ 98T Corey Pointer	.15	.07
❑ 99T Felix Fermin	.15	.07
❑ 100T Lee Smith	.25	.11
❑ 101T Reid Ryan	.25	.11
❑ 102T Bobby Munoz	.15	.07
❑ 103T Deion Sanders TR	.25	.11
Roberto Kelly		
❑ 104T Turner Ward	.15	.07
❑ 105T W.VanLandingham	.15	.07
❑ 106T Vince Coleman	.15	.07
❑ 107T Stan Javier	.15	.07
❑ 108T Darrin Jackson	.15	.07
❑ 109T C.J. Nitkowski	.15	.07
❑ 110T Anthony Young	.15	.07
❑ 111T Kurt Miller	.15	.07
❑ 112T Paul Konerko	15.00	6.75
❑ 113T Walt Weiss	.15	.07
❑ 114T Daryl Boston	.15	.07
❑ 115T Will Clark	.50	.23
❑ 116T Matt Smith	.25	.11
❑ 117T Mark Leiter	.15	.07
❑ 118T Gregg Olson	.15	.07
❑ 119T Tony Pena	.15	.07
❑ 120T Jose Vizcaino	.15	.07
❑ 121T Rick White	.15	.07
❑ 122T Rich Rowland	.15	.07
❑ 123T Jeff Reboulet	.15	.07
❑ 124T Greg Hibbard	.15	.07
❑ 125T Chris Sabo	.25	.11
❑ 126T Doug Jones	.15	.07
❑ 127T Tony Fernandez	.25	.11
❑ 128T Carlos Reyes	.15	.07
❑ 129T Kevin Brown	.50	.23
❑ 130T Ryne Sandberg	1.00	.45
Farewell		
❑ 131T Ryne Sandberg	1.00	.45
Farewell		
❑ 132T Checklist 1-132	.15	.07

1994 Topps Traded Finest Inserts

	MINT	NRMT
COMPLETE SET (8)	5.00	2.20

	MINT	NRMT
COMMON CARD (1-8)	.30	.14
ONE SET PER TRADED FACTORY SET		

❑ 1 Greg Maddux	1.00	.45
❑ 2 Mike Piazza	1.25	.55
❑ 3 Matt Williams	.30	.14
❑ 4 Raul Mondesi	.40	.18
❑ 5 Ken Griffey Jr	2.00	.90
❑ 6 Kenny Lofton	.40	.18
❑ 7 Frank Thomas	.75	.35
❑ 8 Manny Ramirez	.75	.35

1995 Topps

Rafael Palmeiro

	MINT	NRMT
COMPLETE SET (660)	50.00	22.00
COMP.HOBBY SET (677)	80.00	36.00
COMP.RETAIL SET (677)	80.00	36.00
COMPLETE SERIES 1 (396)	25.00	11.00
COMPLETE SERIES 2 (264)	25.00	11.00
COMMON CARD (1-660)	.15	.07
MINOR STARS	.30	.14
UNLISTED STARS	.60	.25
COMP.CYBER.SET (396)	80.00	36.00
COMP.CYBER.SER.1 (198)	30.00	13.50
COMP.CYBER.SER.2 (198)	50.00	22.00
*CYBER.STARS: 1X TO 2.5X HI COLUMN		
*CYBER.YOUNG STARS: .75X TO 2X HI		
ONE CYBERSTATS CARD PER PACK		

❑ 1 Frank Thomas	1.25	.55
❑ 2 Mickey Morandini	.15	.07
❑ 3 Babe Ruth 100th B-Day	2.00	.90
❑ 4 Scott Cooper	.15	.07
❑ 5 David Cone	.40	.18
❑ 6 Jacob Shumate	.15	.07
❑ 7 Trevor Hoffman	.30	.14
❑ 8 Shane Mack	.15	.07
❑ 9 Delino DeShields	.15	.07
❑ 10 Matt Williams	.60	.25
❑ 11 Sammy Sosa	2.00	.90
❑ 12 Gary DiSarcina	.15	.07
❑ 13 Kenny Rogers	.15	.07
❑ 14 Jose Vizcaino	.15	.07
❑ 15 Lou Whitaker	.30	.14
❑ 16 Ron Darling	.15	.07
❑ 17 Dave Nilsson	.15	.07
❑ 18 Chris Hammond	.15	.07
❑ 19 Sid Bream	.15	.07
❑ 20 Denny Martinez	.30	.14
❑ 21 Orlando Merced	.15	.07

❏ 22	John Wetteland	.30	.14
❏ 23	Mike Devereaux	.15	.07
❏ 24	Rene Arocha	.15	.07
❏ 25	Jay Buhner	.30	.14
❏ 26	Darren Holmes	.15	.07
❏ 27	Hal Morris	.15	.07
❏ 28	Brian Buchanan	.30	.14
❏ 29	Keith Miller	.15	.07
❏ 30	Paul Molitor	.60	.25
❏ 31	Dave West	.15	.07
❏ 32	Tony Tarasco	.15	.07
❏ 33	Scott Sanders	.15	.07
❏ 34	Eddie Zambrano	.15	.07
❏ 35	Ricky Bones	.15	.07
❏ 36	John Valentin	.30	.14
❏ 37	Kevin Tapani	.15	.07
❏ 38	Tim Wallach	.15	.07
❏ 39	Darren Lewis	.15	.07
❏ 40	Travis Fryman	.30	.14
❏ 41	Mark Leiter	.15	.07
❏ 42	Jose Bautista	.15	.07
❏ 43	Pete Smith	.15	.07
❏ 44	Bret Barberie	.15	.07
❏ 45	Dennis Eckersley	.30	.14
❏ 46	Ken Hill	.15	.07
❏ 47	Chad Ogea	.15	.07
❏ 48	Pete Harnisch	.15	.07
❏ 49	James Baldwin	.30	.14
❏ 50	Mike Mussina	.60	.25
❏ 51	Al Martin	.15	.07
❏ 52	Mark Thompson	.15	.07
❏ 53	Matt Smith	.15	.07
❏ 54	Joey Hamilton	.30	.14
❏ 55	Edgar Martinez	.30	.14
❏ 56	John Smiley	.15	.07
❏ 57	Rey Sanchez	.15	.07
❏ 58	Mike Timlin	.15	.07
❏ 59	Ricky Bottalico	.15	.07
❏ 60	Jim Abbott	.30	.14
❏ 61	Mike Kelly	.15	.07
❏ 62	Brian Jordan	.30	.14
❏ 63	Ken Ryan	.15	.07
❏ 64	Matt Mieske	.15	.07
❏ 65	Rick Aguilera	.15	.07
❏ 66	Ismael Valdes	.30	.14
❏ 67	Royce Clayton	.15	.07
❏ 68	Junior Felix	.15	.07
❏ 69	Harold Reynolds	.15	.07
❏ 70	Juan Gonzalez	1.25	.55
❏ 71	Kelly Stinnett	.15	.07
❏ 72	Carlos Reyes	.15	.07
❏ 73	Dave Weathers	.15	.07
❏ 74	Mel Rojas	.15	.07
❏ 75	Doug Drabek	.15	.07
❏ 76	Charles Nagy	.30	.14
❏ 77	Tim Raines	.30	.14
❏ 78	Midre Cummings	.15	.07
❏ 79	First Base Prospects	.40	.18
	Gene Schall		
	Scott Talanoa		
	Harold Williams		
	Ray Brown		
❏ 80	Rafael Palmeiro	.60	.25
❏ 81	Charlie Hayes	.15	.07
❏ 82	Ray Lankford	.30	.14
❏ 83	Tim Davis	.15	.07
❏ 84	C.J. Nitkowski	.15	.07
❏ 85	Andy Ashby	.15	.07
❏ 86	Gerald Williams	.15	.07
❏ 87	Terry Shumpert	.15	.07
❏ 88	Heathcliff Slocumb	.15	.07
❏ 89	Domingo Cedeno	.15	.07
❏ 90	Mark Grace	.40	.18
❏ 91	Brad Woodall	.15	.07
❏ 92	Gar Finnvold	.15	.07
❏ 93	Jaime Navarro	.15	.07
❏ 94	Carlos Hernandez	.15	.07
❏ 95	Mark Langston	.15	.07
❏ 96	Chuck Carr	.15	.07
❏ 97	Mike Gardiner	.15	.07
❏ 98	Dave McCarty	.15	.07
❏ 99	Cris Carpenter	.15	.07
❏ 100	Barry Bonds	.75	.35
❏ 101	David Segui	.15	.07
❏ 102	Scott Brosius	.30	.14
❏ 103	Mariano Duncan	.15	.07

❏ 104	Kenny Lofton	.40	.18
❏ 105	Ken Caminiti	.40	.18
❏ 106	Darrin Jackson	.15	.07
❏ 107	Jim Poole	.15	.07
❏ 108	Wil Cordero	.15	.07
❏ 109	Danny Miceli	.15	.07
❏ 110	Walt Weiss	.15	.07
❏ 111	Tom Pagnozzi	.15	.07
❏ 112	Terrence Long	.40	.18
❏ 113	Bret Boone	.30	.14
❏ 114	Daryl Boston	.15	.07
❏ 115	Wally Joyner	.15	.07
❏ 116	Rob Butler	.15	.07
❏ 117	Rafael Belliard	.15	.07
❏ 118	Luis Lopez	.15	.07
❏ 119	Tony Fossas	.15	.07
❏ 120	Len Dykstra	.30	.14
❏ 121	Mike Morgan	.15	.07
❏ 122	Denny Hocking	.15	.07
❏ 123	Kevin Gross	.15	.07
❏ 124	Todd Benzinger	.15	.07
❏ 125	John Doherty	.15	.07
❏ 126	Eduardo Perez	.15	.07
❏ 127	Dan Smith	.15	.07
❏ 128	Joe Orsulak	.15	.07
❏ 129	Brent Gates	.15	.07
❏ 130	Jeff Conine	.15	.07
❏ 131	Doug Henry	.15	.07
❏ 132	Paul Sorrento	.15	.07
❏ 133	Mike Hampton	.15	.07
❏ 134	Tim Spehr	.15	.07
❏ 135	Julio Franco	.15	.07
❏ 136	Mike Dyer	.15	.07
❏ 137	Chris Sabo	.15	.07
❏ 138	Rheal Cormier	.15	.07
❏ 139	Paul Konerko	1.00	.45
❏ 140	Dante Bichette	.30	.14
❏ 141	Chuck McElroy	.15	.07
❏ 142	Mike Stanley	.15	.07
❏ 143	Bob Hamelin	.15	.07
❏ 144	Tommy Greene	.15	.07
❏ 145	John Smoltz	.40	.18
❏ 146	Ed Sprague	.15	.07
❏ 147	Ray McDavid	.15	.07
❏ 148	Otis Nixon	.15	.07
❏ 149	Turk Wendell	.15	.07
❏ 150	Chris James	.15	.07
❏ 151	Derek Parks	.15	.07
❏ 152	Jose Offerman	.30	.14
❏ 153	Tony Clark	.60	.25
❏ 154	Chad Curtis	.15	.07
❏ 155	Mark Portugal	.15	.07
❏ 156	Bill Pulsipher	.15	.07
❏ 157	Troy Neel	.15	.07
❏ 158	Dave Winfield	.60	.25
❏ 159	Bill Wegman	.15	.07
❏ 160	Benito Santiago	.15	.07
❏ 161	Jose Mesa	.15	.07
❏ 162	Luis Gonzalez	.15	.07
❏ 163	Alex Fernandez	.15	.07
❏ 164	Freddie Benavides	.15	.07
❏ 165	Ben McDonald	.15	.07
❏ 166	Blas Minor	.15	.07
❏ 167	Bret Wagner	.15	.07
❏ 168	Mac Suzuki	.30	.14
❏ 169	Roberto Mejia	.15	.07
❏ 170	Wade Boggs	.60	.25
❏ 171	Calvin Reese	.15	.07
❏ 172	Hipolito Pichardo	.15	.07
❏ 173	Kim Batiste	.15	.07
❏ 174	Darren Hall	.15	.07
❏ 175	Tom Glavine	.60	.25
❏ 176	Phil Plantier	.15	.07
❏ 177	Chris Howard	.15	.07
❏ 178	Karl Rhodes	.15	.07
❏ 179	LaTroy Hawkins	.15	.07
❏ 180	Raul Mondesi	.40	.18
❏ 181	Jeff Reed	.15	.07
❏ 182	Milt Cuyler	.15	.07
❏ 183	Jim Edmonds	.40	.18
❏ 184	Hector Fajardo	.15	.07
❏ 185	Jeff Kent	.30	.14
❏ 186	Wilson Alvarez	.30	.14
❏ 187	Geronimo Berroa	.15	.07
❏ 188	Billy Spiers	.15	.07
❏ 189	Derek Lilliquist	.15	.07

❏ 190	Craig Biggio	.60	.25
❏ 191	Roberto Hernandez	.15	.07
❏ 192	Bob Natal	.15	.07
❏ 193	Bobby Ayala	.15	.07
❏ 194	Travis Miller	.15	.07
❏ 195	Bob Tewksbury	.15	.07
❏ 196	Rondell White	.30	.14
❏ 197	Steve Cooke	.15	.07
❏ 198	Jeff Branson	.15	.07
❏ 199	Derek Jeter	2.00	.90
❏ 200	Tim Salmon	.60	.25
❏ 201	Steve Frey	.15	.07
❏ 202	Kent Mercker	.15	.07
❏ 203	Randy Johnson	.60	.25
❏ 204	Todd Worrell	.15	.07
❏ 205	Mo Vaughn	.60	.25
❏ 206	Howard Johnson	.15	.07
❏ 207	John Wasdin	.15	.07
❏ 208	Eddie Williams	.15	.07
❏ 209	Tim Belcher	.15	.07
❏ 210	Jeff Montgomery	.15	.07
❏ 211	Kirt Manwaring	.15	.07
❏ 212	Ben Grieve	1.50	.70
❏ 213	Pat Hentgen	.30	.14
❏ 214	Shawon Dunston	.15	.07
❏ 215	Mike Greenwell	.15	.07
❏ 216	Alex Diaz	.15	.07
❏ 217	Pat Mahomes	.15	.07
❏ 218	Dave Hansen	.15	.07
❏ 219	Kevin Rogers	.15	.07
❏ 220	Cecil Fielder	.30	.14
❏ 221	Andrew Lorraine	.15	.07
❏ 222	Jack Armstrong	.15	.07
❏ 223	Todd Hundley	.30	.14
❏ 224	Mark Acre	.15	.07
❏ 225	Darrell Whitmore	.15	.07
❏ 226	Randy Milligan	.15	.07
❏ 227	Wayne Kirby	.15	.07
❏ 228	Darryl Kile	.15	.07
❏ 229	Bob Zupcic	.15	.07
❏ 230	Jay Bell	.30	.14
❏ 231	Dustin Hermanson	.15	.07
❏ 232	Harold Baines	.30	.14
❏ 233	Alan Benes	.15	.07
❏ 234	Felix Fermin	.15	.07
❏ 235	Ellis Burks	.30	.14
❏ 236	Jeff Brantley	.15	.07
❏ 237	Outfield Prospects	.50	.23
	Brian Hunter		
	Jose Malave		
	Karim Garcia		
	Shane Pullen		
❏ 238	Matt Nokes	.15	.07
❏ 239	Ben Rivera	.15	.07
❏ 240	Joe Carter	.30	.14
❏ 241	Jeff Granger	.15	.07
❏ 242	Terry Pendelton	.15	.07
❏ 243	Melvin Nieves	.15	.07
❏ 244	Frankie Rodriguez	.15	.07
❏ 245	Darryl Hamilton	.15	.07
❏ 246	Brooks Kieschnick	.15	.07
❏ 247	Todd Hollandsworth	.15	.07
❏ 248	Joe Rosselli	.15	.07
❏ 249	Bill Gullickson	.15	.07
❏ 250	Chuck Knoblauch	.60	.25
❏ 251	Kurt Miller	.15	.07
❏ 252	Bobby Jones	.15	.07
❏ 253	Lance Blankenship	.15	.07
❏ 254	Matt Whiteside	.15	.07
❏ 255	Darrin Fletcher	.15	.07
❏ 256	Eric Plunk	.15	.07
❏ 257	Shane Reynolds	.30	.14
❏ 258	Norberto Martin	.15	.07
❏ 259	Mike Thurman	.15	.07
❏ 260	Andy Van Slyke	.30	.14
❏ 261	Dwight Smith	.15	.07
❏ 262	Allen Watson	.15	.07
❏ 263	Dan Wilson	.15	.07
❏ 264	Brent Mayne	.15	.07
❏ 265	Bip Roberts	.15	.07
❏ 266	Sterling Hitchcock	.30	.14
❏ 267	Alex Gonzalez	.15	.07
❏ 268	Greg Harris	.15	.07
❏ 269	Ricky Jordan	.15	.07
❏ 270	Johnny Ruffin	.15	.07
❏ 271	Mike Stanton	.15	.07

272	Rich Rowland	.15	.07
273	Steve Trachsel	.15	.07
274	Pedro Munoz	.15	.07
275	Ramon Martinez	.30	.14
276	Dave Henderson	.15	.07
277	Chris Gomez	.15	.07
278	Joe Grahe	.15	.07
279	Rusty Greer	.60	.25
280	John Franco	.30	.14
281	Mike Bordick	.15	.07
282	Jeff D'Amico	.30	.14
283	Dave Magadan	.15	.07
284	Tony Pena	.15	.07
285	Greg Swindell	.15	.07
286	Doug Million	.15	.07
287	Gabe White	.15	.07
288	Trey Beamon	.15	.07
289	Arthur Rhodes	.15	.07
290	Juan Guzman	.15	.07
291	Jose Oquendo	.15	.07
292	Willie Blair	.15	.07
293	Eddie Taubensee	.15	.07
294	Steve Howe	.15	.07
295	Greg Maddux	1.50	.70
296	Mike Macfarlane	.15	.07
297	Curt Schilling	.40	.18
298	Phil Clark	.15	.07
299	Woody Williams	.15	.07
300	Jose Canseco	.75	.35
301	Aaron Sele	.30	.14
302	Carl Willis	.15	.07
303	Steve Buechele	.15	.07
304	Dave Burba	.15	.07
305	Orel Hershiser	.30	.14
306	Damion Easley	.30	.14
307	Mike Henneman	.15	.07
308	Josias Manzanillo	.15	.07
309	Kevin Seitzer	.15	.07
310	Ruben Sierra	.15	.07
311	Bryan Harvey	.15	.07
312	Jim Thome	.60	.25
313	Ramon Castro	.30	.14
314	Lance Johnson	.15	.07
315	Marquis Grissom	.30	.14
316	Starting Pitcher	.40	.18
	Prospects		
	Terrell Wade		
	Juan Acevedo		
	Matt Arrandale		
	Eddie Priest		
317	Paul Wagner	.15	.07
318	Jamie Moyer	.15	.07
319	Todd Zeile	.15	.07
320	Chris Bosio	.15	.07
321	Steve Reed	.15	.07
322	Erik Hanson	.15	.07
323	Luis Polonia	.15	.07
324	Ryan Klesko	.30	.14
325	Kevin Appier	.30	.14
326	Jim Eisenreich	.15	.07
327	Randy Knorr	.15	.07
328	Craig Shipley	.15	.07
329	Tim Naehring	.15	.07
330	Randy Myers	.15	.07
331	Alex Cole	.15	.07
332	Jim Gott	.15	.07
333	Mike Jackson	.30	.14
334	John Flaherty	.15	.07
335	Chili Davis	.30	.14
336	Benji Gil	.15	.07
337	Jason Jacome	.15	.07
338	Stan Javier	.15	.07
339	Mike Fetters	.15	.07
340	Rich Renteria	.15	.07
341	Kevin Witt	.60	.25
342	Scott Servais	.15	.07
343	Craig Grebeck	.15	.07
344	Kirk Rueter	.15	.07
345	Don Slaught	.15	.07
346	Armando Benitez	.15	.07
347	Ozzie Smith	.75	.35
348	Mike Blowers	.15	.07
349	Armando Reynoso	.15	.07
350	Barry Larkin	.60	.25
351	Mike Williams	.15	.07
352	Scott Kamieniecki	.15	.07
353	Gary Gaetti	.30	.14
354	Todd Stottlemyre	.15	.07
355	Fred McGriff	.40	.18
356	Tim Mauser	.15	.07
357	Chris Gwynn	.15	.07
358	Frank Castillo	.15	.07
359	Jeff Reboulet	.15	.07
360	Roger Clemens	1.50	.70
361	Mark Carreon	.15	.07
362	Chad Kreuter	.15	.07
363	Mark Farris	.15	.07
364	Bob Welch	.15	.07
365	Dean Palmer	.30	.14
366	Jeromy Burnitz	.30	.14
367	B.J. Surhoff	.30	.14
368	Mike Butcher	.15	.07
369	Relief Pitcher	.30	.14
	Prospects		
	Brad Clontz		
	Steve Phoenix		
	Scott Gentile		
	Bucky Buckles		
370	Eddie Murray	.60	.25
371	Orlando Miller	.15	.07
372	Ron Karkovice	.15	.07
373	Richie Lewis	.15	.07
374	Lenny Webster	.15	.07
375	Jeff Tackett	.15	.07
376	Tom Urbani	.15	.07
377	Tino Martinez	.60	.25
378	Mark Dewey	.15	.07
379	Charles O'Brien	.15	.07
380	Terry Mulholland	.15	.07
381	Thomas Howard	.15	.07
382	Chris Haney	.15	.07
383	Billy Hatcher	.15	.07
384	Jeff Bagwell AS	.60	.25
	Frank Thomas AS		
385	Bret Boone AS	.15	.07
	Carlos Baerga AS		
386	Matt Williams AS	.40	.18
	Wade Boggs AS		
387	Wil Cordero AS	.60	.25
	Cal Ripken AS		
388	Barry Bonds AS	.75	.35
	Ken Griffey AS		
389	Tony Gwynn AS	.40	.18
	Albert Belle AS		
390	Dante Bichette AS	.40	.18
	Kirby Puckett AS		
391	Mike Piazza AS	.60	.25
	Mike Stanley AS		
392	Greg Maddux AS	.60	.25
	David Cone AS		
393	Danny Jackson AS	.15	.07
	Jimmy Key AS		
394	John Franco AS	.15	.07
	Lee Smith AS		
395	Checklist 1-198	.15	.07
396	Checklist 199-396	.15	.07
397	Ken Griffey Jr.	3.00	1.35
398	Rick Heiserman	.15	.07
399	Don Mattingly	1.25	.55
400	Henry Rodriguez	.30	.14
401	Lenny Harris	.15	.07
402	Ryan Thompson	.15	.07
403	Darren Oliver	.15	.07
404	Omar Vizquel	.30	.14
405	Jeff Bagwell	.75	.35
406	Doug Webb	.15	.07
407	Todd Van Poppel	.15	.07
408	Leo Gomez	.15	.07
409	Mark Whiten	.15	.07
410	Pedro Martinez	.15	.07
411	Reggie Sanders	.30	.14
412	Kevin Foster	.15	.07
413	Danny Tartabull	.15	.07
414	Jeff Blauser	.15	.07
415	Mike Magnante	.15	.07
416	Tom Candiotti	.15	.07
417	Rod Beck	.15	.07
418	Jody Reed	.15	.07
419	Vince Coleman	.15	.07
420	Danny Jackson	.15	.07
421	Ryan Nye	.30	.14
422	Larry Walker	.60	.25
423	Russ Johnson DP	.30	.14
424	Pat Borders	.15	.07
425	Lee Smith	.30	.14
426	Paul O'Neill	.30	.14
427	Devon White	.30	.14
428	Jim Bullinger	.15	.07
429	Starting Pitchers	.30	.14
	Prospects		
	Greg Hansell		
	Brian Sackinsky		
	Carey Paige		
	Rob Welch		
430	Steve Avery	.15	.07
431	Tony Gwynn	1.50	.70
432	Pat Meares	.15	.07
433	Bill Swift	.15	.07
434	David Wells	.40	.18
435	John Briscoe	.15	.07
436	Roger Pavlik	.15	.07
437	Jayson Peterson	.15	.07
438	Roberto Alomar	.60	.25
439	Billy Brewer	.15	.07
440	Gary Sheffield	.30	.14
441	Lou Frazier	.15	.07
442	Terry Steinbach	.15	.07
443	Jay Payton	.30	.14
444	Jason Bere	.15	.07
445	Denny Neagle	.30	.14
446	Andres Galarraga	.60	.25
447	Hector Carrasco	.15	.07
448	Bill Risley	.15	.07
449	Andy Benes	.30	.14
450	Jim Leyritz	.15	.07
451	Jose Oliva	.15	.07
452	Greg Vaughn	.30	.14
453	Rich Monteleone	.15	.07
454	Tony Eusebio	.15	.07
455	Chuck Finley	.30	.14
456	Kevin Brown	.40	.18
457	Joe Boever	.15	.07
458	Bobby Munoz	.15	.07
459	Bret Saberhagen	.30	.14
460	Kurt Abbott	.15	.07
461	Bobby Witt	.15	.07
462	Cliff Floyd	.30	.14
463	Mark Clark	.15	.07
464	Andujar Cedeno	.15	.07
465	Marvin Freeman	.15	.07
466	Mike Piazza	2.00	.90
467	Willie Greene	.15	.07
468	Pat Kelly	.15	.07
469	Carlos Delgado	.60	.25
470	Willie Banks	.15	.07
471	Matt Walbeck	.15	.07
472	Mark McGwire	3.00	1.35
473	McKay Christensen	.15	.07
474	Alan Trammell	.30	.14
475	Tom Gordon	.15	.07
476	Greg Colbrunn	.15	.07
477	Darren Daulton	.30	.14
478	Albie Lopez	.15	.07
479	Robin Ventura	.30	.14
480	Catcher Prospects	.50	.23
	Eddie Perez		
	Jason Kendall		
	Einar Diaz		
	Bret Hemphill		
481	Bryan Eversgerd	.15	.07
482	Dave Fleming	.15	.07
483	Scott Livingstone	.15	.07
484	Pete Schourek	.15	.07
485	Bernie Williams	.60	.25
486	Mark Lemke	.15	.07
487	Eric Karros	.30	.14
488	Scott Ruffcorn	.15	.07
489	Billy Ashley	.15	.07
490	Rico Brogna	.15	.07
491	John Burkett	.15	.07
492	Cade Gaspar	.30	.14
493	Jorge Fabregas	.15	.07
494	Greg Gagne	.15	.07
495	Doug Jones	.15	.07
496	Troy O'Leary	.30	.14
497	Pat Rapp	.15	.07
498	Butch Henry	.15	.07
499	John Olerud	.30	.14

❏ 500	John Hudek	.15	.07
❏ 501	Jeff King	.15	.07
❏ 502	Bobby Bonilla	.30	.14
❏ 503	Albert Belle	.60	.25
❏ 504	Rick Wilkins	.15	.07
❏ 505	John Jaha	.15	.07
❏ 506	Nigel Wilson	.15	.07
❏ 507	Sid Fernandez	.15	.07
❏ 508	Deion Sanders	.30	.14
❏ 509	Gil Heredia	.15	.07
❏ 510	Scott Elarton	1.00	.45
❏ 511	Melido Perez	.15	.07
❏ 512	Greg McMichael	.15	.07
❏ 513	Rusty Meacham	.15	.07
❏ 514	Shawn Green	.60	.25
❏ 515	Carlos Garcia	.15	.07
❏ 516	Dave Stevens	.15	.07
❏ 517	Eric Young	.15	.07
❏ 518	Omar Daal	.15	.07
❏ 519	Kirk Gibson	.30	.14
❏ 520	Spike Owen	.15	.07
❏ 521	Jacob Cruz	.50	.23
❏ 522	Sandy Alomar Jr.	.30	.14
❏ 523	Steve Bedrosian	.15	.07
❏ 524	Ricky Gutierrez	.15	.07
❏ 525	Dave Veres	.15	.07
❏ 526	Gregg Jefferies	.15	.07
❏ 527	Jose Valentin	.15	.07
❏ 528	Robb Nen	.15	.07
❏ 529	Jose Rijo	.15	.07
❏ 530	Sean Berry	.15	.07
❏ 531	Mike Gallego	.15	.07
❏ 532	Roberto Kelly	.15	.07
❏ 533	Kevin Stocker	.15	.07
❏ 534	Kirby Puckett	1.00	.45
❏ 535	Chipper Jones	1.50	.70
❏ 536	Russ Davis	.30	.14
❏ 537	Jon Lieber	.15	.07
❏ 538	Trey Moore	.30	.14
❏ 539	Joe Girardi	.15	.07
❏ 540	Second Base Prospects	.50	.23
	Quilvio Veras		
	Arquimedez Pozo		
	Miguel Cairo		
	Jason Camilli		
❏ 541	Tony Phillips	.15	.07
❏ 542	Brian Anderson	.30	.14
❏ 543	Ivan Rodriguez	.75	.35
❏ 544	Jeff Cirillo	.30	.14
❏ 545	Joey Cora	.15	.07
❏ 546	Chris Hoiles	.15	.07
❏ 547	Bernard Gilkey	.15	.07
❏ 548	Mike Lansing	.15	.07
❏ 549	Jimmy Key	.30	.14
❏ 550	Mark Wohlers	.15	.07
❏ 551	Chris Clemons	.30	.14
❏ 552	Vinny Castilla	.40	.18
❏ 553	Mark Guthrie	.15	.07
❏ 554	Mike Lieberthal	.15	.07
❏ 555	Tommy Davis	.15	.07
❏ 556	Robby Thompson	.15	.07
❏ 557	Danny Bautista	.15	.07
❏ 558	Will Clark	.60	.25
❏ 559	Rickey Henderson	.75	.35
❏ 560	Todd Jones	.15	.07
❏ 561	Jack McDowell	.15	.07
❏ 562	Carlos Rodriguez	.15	.07
❏ 563	Mark Eichhorn	.15	.07
❏ 564	Jeff Nelson	.15	.07
❏ 565	Eric Anthony	.15	.07
❏ 566	Randy Velarde	.15	.07
❏ 567	Javier Lopez	.30	.14
❏ 568	Kevin Mitchell	.15	.07
❏ 569	Steve Karsay	.15	.07
❏ 570	Brian Meadows	.30	.14
❏ 571	Rey Ordonez	1.25	.55
	Mike Metcalfe		
	Kevin Orie		
	Ray Holbert		
❏ 572	John Kruk	.30	.14
❏ 573	Scott Leius	.15	.07
❏ 574	John Patterson	.15	.07
❏ 575	Kevin Brown	.40	.18
❏ 576	Mike Moore	.15	.07
❏ 577	Manny Ramirez	.75	.35
❏ 578	Jose Lind	.15	.07

❏ 579	Derrick May	.15	.07
❏ 580	Cal Eldred	.15	.07
❏ 581	Third Base Prospects	.30	.14
	David Bell		
	Joel Chelmis		
	Lino Diaz		
	Aaron Boone		
❏ 582	J.T. Snow	.30	.14
❏ 583	Luis Sojo	.15	.07
❏ 584	Moises Alou	.30	.14
❏ 585	Dave Clark	.15	.07
❏ 586	Dave Hollins	.15	.07
❏ 587	Nomar Garciaparra	3.00	1.35
❏ 588	Cal Ripken	2.50	1.10
❏ 589	Pedro Astacio	.15	.07
❏ 590	J.R. Phillips	.15	.07
❏ 591	Jeff Frye	.15	.07
❏ 592	Bo Jackson	.30	.14
❏ 593	Steve Ontiveros	.15	.07
❏ 594	David Nied	.15	.07
❏ 595	Brad Ausmus	.15	.07
❏ 596	Carlos Baerga	.15	.07
❏ 597	James Mouton	.15	.07
❏ 598	Ozzie Guillen	.15	.07
❏ 599	Outfield Prospects	.60	.25
	Ozzie Timmons		
	Curtis Goodwin		
	Johnny Damon		
	Jeff Abbott		
❏ 600	Yorkis Perez	.15	.07
❏ 601	Rich Rodriguez	.15	.07
❏ 602	Mark McLemore	.15	.07
❏ 603	Jeff Fassero	.15	.07
❏ 604	John Roper	.15	.07
❏ 605	Mark Johnson	.15	.07
❏ 606	Wes Chamberlain	.15	.07
❏ 607	Felix Jose	.15	.07
❏ 608	Tony Longmire	.15	.07
❏ 609	Duane Ward	.15	.07
❏ 610	Brett Butler	.30	.14
❏ 611	William VanLandingham	.15	.07
❏ 612	Mickey Tettleton	.15	.07
❏ 613	Brady Anderson	.30	.14
❏ 614	Reggie Jefferson	.15	.07
❏ 615	Mike Kingery	.15	.07
❏ 616	Derek Bell	.30	.14
❏ 617	Scott Erickson	.15	.07
❏ 618	Bob Wickman	.15	.07
❏ 619	Phil Leftwich	.15	.07
❏ 620	David Justice	.60	.25
❏ 621	Paul Wilson	.75	.35
❏ 622	Pedro Martinez	.75	.35
❏ 623	Terry Mathews	.15	.07
❏ 624	Brian McRae	.15	.07
❏ 625	Bruce Ruffin	.15	.07
❏ 626	Steve Finley	.30	.14
❏ 627	Ron Gant	.15	.07
❏ 628	Rafael Bournigal	.15	.07
❏ 629	Darryl Strawberry	.30	.14
❏ 630	Luis Alicea	.15	.07
❏ 631	Orioles Prospects	.30	.14
	Mark Smith		
	Scott Klingenbeck		
❏ 632	Red Sox Prospects	.30	.14
	Cory Bailey		
	Scott Hatteberg		
❏ 633	Angels Prospects	.15	.07
	Todd Greene		
	Troy Percival		
❏ 634	White Sox Prospects	.15	.07
	Rod Bolton		
	Olmedo Saenz		
❏ 635	Indians Prospects	.30	.14
	Steve Kline		
	Herb Perry		
❏ 636	Tigers Prospects	.15	.07
	Sean Bergman		
	Shannon Penn		
❏ 637	Royals Prospects	.30	.14
	Joe Randa		
	Joe Vitiello		
❏ 638	Brewers Prospects	.15	.07
	Jose Mercedes		
	Duane Singleton		
❏ 639	Twins Prospects	.15	.07
	Marc Barcelo		

	Marty Cordova		
❏ 640	Yankees Prospects	.60	.25
	Andy Pettitte		
	Ruben Rivera		
❏ 641	Athletics Prospects	.30	.14
	Willie Adams		
	Scott Spiezio		
❏ 642	Mariners Prospects	.30	.14
	Eddy Diaz		
	Desi Relaford		
❏ 643	Rangers Prospects	.15	.07
	Terrell Lowery		
	Jon Shave		
❏ 644	Blue Jays Prospects	.15	.07
	Angel Martinez		
	Paul Spoljaric		
❏ 645	Braves Prospects	.30	.14
	Tony Graffanino		
	Damon Hollins		
❏ 646	Cubs Prospects	.30	.14
	Darron Cox		
	Doug Glanville		
❏ 647	Reds Prospects	.30	.14
	Tim Belk		
	Pat Watkins		
❏ 648	Rockies Prospects	.15	.07
	Rod Pedraza		
	Phil Schneider		
❏ 649	Marlins Prospects	.30	.14
	Vic Darensbourg		
	Marc Valdes		
❏ 650	Astros Prospects	.15	.07
	Rick Huisman		
	Roberto Petagine		
❏ 651	Dodgers Prospects	.50	.23
	Roger Cedeno		
	Ron Coomer		
❏ 652	Expos Prospects	.30	.14
	Shane Andrews		
	Carlos Perez		
❏ 653	Mets Prospects	.30	.14
	Jason Isringhausen		
	Chris Roberts		
❏ 654	Phillies Prospects	.30	.14
	Wayne Gomes		
	Kevin Jordan		
❏ 655	Pirates Prospects	.15	.07
	Esteban Loiaza		
	Steve Pegues		
❏ 656	Cardinals Prospects	.15	.07
	Terry Bradshaw		
	John Frascatore		
❏ 657	Padres Prospects	.30	.14
	Andres Berumen		
	Bryce Florie		
❏ 658	Giants Prospects	.30	.14
	Dan Carlson		
	Keith Williams		
❏ 659	Checklist	.15	.07
❏ 660	Checklist	.15	.07

1995 Topps Finest Inserts

	MINT	NRMT
COMPLETE SET (15)	60.00	27.00
COMMON CARD (1-15)	1.50	.70
SER.2 STAT.ODDS 1:36 HOB/RET, 1:20 JUM		

		MINT	NRMT
☐ 1	Jeff Bagwell	5.00	2.20
☐ 2	Albert Belle	4.00	1.80
☐ 3	Ken Griffey Jr.	20.00	9.00
☐ 4	Frank Thomas	8.00	3.60
☐ 5	Matt Williams	4.00	1.80
☐ 6	Dante Bichette	2.00	.90
☐ 7	Barry Bonds	5.00	2.20
☐ 8	Moises Alou	2.00	.90
☐ 9	Andres Galarraga	4.00	1.80
☐ 10	Kenny Lofton	3.00	1.35
☐ 11	Rafael Palmeiro	4.00	1.80
☐ 12	Tony Gwynn	10.00	4.50
☐ 13	Kirby Puckett	6.00	2.70
☐ 14	Jose Canseco	5.00	2.20
☐ 15	Jeff Conine	1.50	.70

1995 Topps League Leaders

	MINT	NRMT
COMPLETE SET (50)	50.00	22.00
COMPLETE SERIES 1 (25)	20.00	9.00
COMPLETE SERIES 2 (25)	30.00	13.50
COMMON CARD (LL1-LL50)	.50	.23
STATED ODDS 1:6 RETAIL, 1:3 JUMBO		

☐ LL1	Albert Belle	1.25	.55
☐ LL2	Kevin Mitchell	.50	.23
☐ LL3	Wade Boggs	1.25	.55
☐ LL4	Tony Gwynn	3.00	1.35
☐ LL5	Moises Alou	.75	.35
☐ LL6	Andres Galarraga	1.25	.55
☐ LL7	Matt Williams	1.25	.55
☐ LL8	Barry Bonds	1.50	.70
☐ LL9	Frank Thomas	2.50	1.10
☐ LL10	Jose Canseco	1.50	.70
☐ LL11	Jeff Bagwell	1.50	.70
☐ LL12	Kirby Puckett	2.00	.90
☐ LL13	Julio Franco	.50	.23
☐ LL14	Albert Belle	1.25	.55
☐ LL15	Fred McGriff	1.00	.45
☐ LL16	Kenny Lofton	1.00	.45
☐ LL17	Otis Nixon	.50	.23
☐ LL18	Brady Anderson	.75	.35
☐ LL19	Deion Sanders	.75	.35
☐ LL20	Chuck Carr	.50	.23
☐ LL21	Pat Hentgen	.75	.35
☐ LL22	Andy Benes	.75	.35
☐ LL23	Roger Clemens	3.00	1.35
☐ LL24	Greg Maddux	3.00	1.35
☐ LL25	Pedro Martinez	1.25	.55
☐ LL26	Paul O'Neill	.75	.35
☐ LL27	Jeff Bagwell	1.50	.70
☐ LL28	Frank Thomas	2.50	1.10
☐ LL29	Hal Morris	.50	.23
☐ LL30	Kenny Lofton	1.00	.45
☐ LL31	Ken Griffey Jr.	6.00	2.70
☐ LL32	Jeff Bagwell	1.50	.70
☐ LL33	Albert Belle	1.25	.55
☐ LL34	Fred McGriff	1.00	.45
☐ LL35	Cecil Fielder	.75	.35
☐ LL36	Matt Williams	1.25	.55
☐ LL37	Joe Carter	.75	.35
☐ LL38	Dante Bichette	.75	.35
☐ LL39	Frank Thomas	2.50	1.10
☐ LL40	Mike Piazza	4.00	1.80
☐ LL41	Craig Biggio	1.25	.55
☐ LL42	Vince Coleman	.50	.23

☐ LL43	Marquis Grissom	.75	.35
☐ LL44	Chuck Knoblauch	1.25	.55
☐ LL45	Darren Lewis	.50	.23
☐ LL46	Randy Johnson	1.25	.55
☐ LL47	Jose Rijo	.50	.23
☐ LL48	Chuck Finley	.75	.35
☐ LL49	Bret Saberhagen	.75	.35
☐ LL50	Kevin Appier	.75	.35

1995 Topps Traded

	MINT	NRMT
COMPLETE SET (165)	60.00	27.00
COMMON CARD (1T-165T)	.15	.07
MINOR STARS	.30	.14
UNLISTED STARS	.60	.25

☐ 1T	Frank Thomas ATB	.60	.25
☐ 2T	Ken Griffey Jr. ATB	1.50	.70
☐ 3T	Barry Bonds ATB	.40	.18
☐ 4T	Albert Belle ATB	.30	.14
☐ 5T	Cal Ripken ATB	1.25	.55
☐ 6T	Mike Piazza ATB	1.00	.45
☐ 7T	Tony Gwynn ATB	.75	.35
☐ 8T	Jeff Bagwell ATB	.60	.25
☐ 9T	Mo Vaughn ATB	.40	.18
☐ 10T	Matt Williams ATB	.30	.14
☐ 11T	Ray Durham	.30	.14
☐ 12T	Juan LeBron	6.00	2.70
	Card pictures Carlos Beltran instead of Juan LeBron		
☐ 13T	Shawn Green	.60	.25
☐ 14T	Kevin Gross	.15	.07
☐ 15T	Jon Nunnally	.15	.07
☐ 16T	Brian Maxcy	.15	.07
☐ 17T	Mark Kiefer	.15	.07
☐ 18T	Carlos Beltran UER	25.00	11.00
	Card pictures Juan LeBron instead of Carlos Beltran.		
☐ 19T	Mike Mimbs	.15	.07
☐ 20T	Larry Walker	.60	.25
☐ 21T	Chad Curtis	.15	.07
☐ 22T	Jeff Barry	.15	.07
☐ 23T	Joe Oliver	.15	.07
☐ 24T	Tomas Perez	.30	.14
☐ 25T	Michael Barrett	8.00	3.60
☐ 26T	Brian McRae	.15	.07
☐ 27T	Derek Bell	.30	.14
☐ 28T	Ray Durham	.30	.14
☐ 29T	Todd Williams	.15	.07
☐ 30T	Ryan Jaroncyk	.15	.07
☐ 31T	Todd Stevenson	.15	.07
☐ 32T	Mike Devereaux	.15	.07
☐ 33T	Rheal Cormier	.15	.07
☐ 34T	Benny Santiago	.15	.07
☐ 35T	Bobby Higginson	1.50	.70
☐ 36T	Jack McDowell	.15	.07
☐ 37T	Scott Karl	.15	.07
☐ 38T	Tony McKnight	.30	.14
☐ 39T	Brian Hunter	.30	.14
☐ 40T	Hideo Nomo	2.50	1.10
☐ 41T	Brett Butler	.30	.14
☐ 42T	Donovan Osborne	.15	.07
☐ 43T	Scott Karl	.15	.07
☐ 44T	Tony Phillips	.15	.07
☐ 45T	Marty Cordova	.15	.07
☐ 46T	Dave Mlicki	.15	.07
☐ 47T	Bronson Arroyo	1.50	.70

☐ 48T	John Burkett	.15	.07
☐ 49T	J.D. Smart	.50	.23
☐ 50T	Mickey Tettleton	.15	.07
☐ 51T	Todd Stottlemyre	.15	.07
☐ 52T	Mike Perez	.15	.07
☐ 53T	Terry Mulholland	.15	.07
☐ 54T	Edgardo Alfonzo	.60	.25
☐ 55T	Zane Smith	.15	.07
☐ 56T	Jacob Brumfield	.15	.07
☐ 57T	Andujar Cedeno	.15	.07
☐ 58T	Jose Parra	.15	.07
☐ 59T	Manny Alexander	.15	.07
☐ 60T	Tony Tarasco	.15	.07
☐ 61T	Orel Hershiser	.30	.14
☐ 62T	Tim Scott	.15	.07
☐ 63T	Felix Rodriguez	.15	.07
☐ 64T	Ken Hill	.15	.07
☐ 65T	Marquis Grissom	.30	.14
☐ 66T	Lee Smith	.30	.14
☐ 67T	Jason Bates	.15	.07
☐ 68T	Felipe Lira	.15	.07
☐ 69T	Alex Hernandez	1.50	.70
☐ 70T	Tony Fernandez	.30	.14
☐ 71T	Scott Radinsky	.15	.07
☐ 72T	Jose Canseco	.75	.35
☐ 73T	Mark Grudzielanek	.40	.18
☐ 74T	Ben Davis	10.00	4.50
☐ 75T	Jim Abbott	.30	.14
☐ 76T	Roger Bailey	.15	.07
☐ 77T	Gregg Jefferies	.15	.07
☐ 78T	Erik Hanson	.15	.07
☐ 79T	Brad Radke	1.50	.70
☐ 80T	Jaime Navarro	.15	.07
☐ 81T	John Wetteland	.30	.14
☐ 82T	Chad Fonville	.15	.07
☐ 83T	John Mabry	.15	.07
☐ 84T	Glenallen Hill	.15	.07
☐ 85T	Ken Caminiti	.40	.18
☐ 86T	Tom Goodwin	.15	.07
☐ 87T	Darren Bragg	.15	.07
☐ 88T	Pitching Prospects	3.00	1.35
	Pat Ahearne		
	Gary Rath		
	Larry Wimberly		
	Robbie Bell		
☐ 89T	Jeff Russell	.15	.07
☐ 90T	Dave Gallagher	.15	.07
☐ 91T	Steve Finley	.30	.14
☐ 92T	Vaughn Eshelman	.15	.07
☐ 93T	Kevin Jarvis	.15	.07
☐ 94T	Mark Gubicza	.15	.07
☐ 95T	Tim Wakefield	.30	.14
☐ 96T	Bob Tewksbury	.15	.07
☐ 97T	Sid Roberson	.15	.07
☐ 98T	Tom Henke	.15	.07
☐ 99T	Michael Tucker	.30	.14
☐ 100T	Jason Bates	.15	.07
☐ 101T	Otis Nixon	.15	.07
☐ 102T	Mark Whiten	.15	.07
☐ 103T	Dilson Torres	.15	.07
☐ 104T	Melvin Bunch	.15	.07
☐ 105T	Terry Pendleton	.15	.07
☐ 106T	Corey Jenkins	.60	.25
☐ 107T	Glenn Dishman	.30	.14
	Rob Grable		
☐ 108T	Reggie Taylor	2.00	.90
☐ 109T	Curtis Goodwin	.15	.07
☐ 110T	David Cone	.40	.18
☐ 111T	Antonio Osuna	.15	.07
☐ 112T	Paul Shuey	.15	.07
☐ 113T	Doug Jones	.15	.07
☐ 114T	Mark McLemore	.15	.07
☐ 115T	Kevin Ritz	.15	.07
☐ 116T	John Kruk	.30	.14
☐ 117T	Trevor Wilson	.15	.07
☐ 118T	Jerald Clark	.15	.07
☐ 119T	Julian Tavarez	.15	.07
☐ 120T	Tim Pugh	.15	.07
☐ 121T	Todd Zeile	.15	.07
☐ 122T	Prospects	10.00	4.50
	Mark Sweeney UER		
	George Arias		
	Richie Sexson		
	Brian Schneider		
☐ 123T	Bobby Witt	.15	.07
☐ 124T	Hideo Nomo	.75	.35

125T Joey Cora	.15	.07
126T Jim Scharrer	.15	.07
127T Paul Quantrill	.15	.07
128T Chipper Jones ROY	1.25	.55
129T Kenny James	.15	.07
130T Lyle Mouton	.60	.25
Mariano Rivera		
131T Tyler Green	.15	.07
132T Brad Clontz	.15	.07
133T Jon Nunnally	.15	.07
134T Dave Magadan	.15	.07
135T Al Leiter	.30	.14
136T Bret Barberie	.15	.07
137T Bill Swift	.15	.07
138T Scott Cooper	.15	.07
139T Roberto Kelly	.15	.07
140T Charlie Hayes	.15	.07
141T Pete Harnisch	.15	.07
142T Rich Amaral	.15	.07
143T Rudy Seanez	.15	.07
144T Pat Listach	.15	.07
145T Quilvio Veras	.15	.07
146T Jose Olmeda	.15	.07
147T Roberto Petagine	.15	.07
148T Kevin Brown	.40	.18
149T Phil Plantier	.15	.07
150T Carlos Perez	.30	.14
151T Pat Borders	.15	.07
152T Tyler Green	.15	.07
153T Stan Belinda	.15	.07
154T Dave Stewart	.30	.14
155T Andre Dawson	.40	.18
156T Frank Thomas AS	.60	.25
Fred McGriff UER		
(McGriff's team shown as Blue Jays)		
157T Carlos Baerga AS	.30	.14
Craig Biggio		
158T Wade Boggs AS	.30	.14
Matt Williams		
159T Cal Ripken AS	.60	.25
Ozzie Smith		
160T Ken Griffey Jr. AS	.75	.35
Tony Gwynn		
161T Albert Belle AS	.40	.18
Barry Bonds		
162T Kirby Puckett	.60	.25
Len Dykstra		
163T Ivan Rodriguez AS	.60	.25
Mike Piazza		
164T Randy Johnson AS	.60	.25
Hideo Nomo		
165T Checklist	.15	.07

1995 Topps Traded Power Boosters

	MINT	NRMT
COMPLETE SET (10)	120.00	55.00
COMMON CARD (1-10)	4.00	1.80
STATED ODDS 1:36		

1 Frank Thomas	12.00	5.50
2 Ken Griffey Jr.	30.00	13.50
3 Barry Bonds	6.00	2.70
4 Albert Belle	6.00	2.70
5 Cal Ripken	25.00	11.00
6 Mike Piazza	20.00	9.00
7 Tony Gwynn	15.00	6.75

8 Jeff Bagwell	8.00	3.60
9 Mo Vaughn	6.00	2.70
10 Matt Williams	4.00	1.80

1996 Topps

	MINT	NRMT
COMPLETE SET (440)	45.00	20.00
COMP HOBBY SET (449)	60.00	27.00
COMP CEREAL SET (444)	60.00	27.00
COMPLETE SERIES 1 (220)	30.00	13.50
COMPLETE SERIES 2 (220)	15.00	6.75
COMMON CARD (1-440)	.10	.05
MINOR STARS	.20	.09
UNLISTED STARS	.40	.18
SUBSET CARDS HALF VALUE OF BASE CARDS		
ONE LAST DAY MANTLE PER HOBBY SET		

1 Tony Gwynn STP	.40	.18
2 Mike Piazza STP	.60	.25
3 Greg Maddux STP	.60	.25
4 Jeff Bagwell STP	.40	.18
5 Larry Walker STP	.20	.09
6 Barry Larkin STP	.10	.05
7 Mickey Mantle	4.00	1.80
8 Tom Glavine STP UER	.20	.09
Won 21 games in June 95		
9 Craig Biggio STP	.20	.09
10 Barry Bonds STP	.30	.14
11 Heathcliff Slocumb STP	.10	.05
12 Matt Williams STP	.20	.09
13 Todd Helton	1.00	.45
14 Mark Redman	.10	.05
15 Michael Barrett	.50	.23
16 Ben Davis	.60	.25
17 Juan LeBron	.40	.18
18 Tony McKnight	.10	.05
19 Ryan Jaroncyk	.10	.05
20 Corey Jenkins	.10	.05
21 Jim Scharrer	.10	.05
22 Mark Bellhorn	.25	.11
23 Jarrod Washburn	.40	.18
24 Geoff Jenkins	1.00	.45
25 Sean Casey	15.00	6.75
26 Brett Tomko	.25	.11
27 Tony Fernandez	.10	.05
28 Rich Becker	.10	.05
29 Andujar Cedeno	.10	.05
30 Paul Molitor	.40	.18
31 Brent Gates	.10	.05
32 Glenallen Hill	.10	.05
33 Mike Macfarlane	.10	.05
34 Manny Alexander	.10	.05
35 Todd Zeile	.10	.05
36 Joe Girardi	.10	.05
37 Tony Tarasco	.10	.05
38 Tim Belcher	.10	.05
39 Tom Goodwin	.10	.05
40 Orel Hershiser	.20	.09
41 Tripp Cromer	.10	.05
42 Sean Bergman	.10	.05
43 Troy Percival	.10	.05
44 Kevin Stocker	.10	.05
45 Albert Belle	.40	.18
46 Tony Eusebio	.10	.05
47 Sid Roberson	.10	.05
48 Todd Hollandsworth	.10	.05

49 Mark Wohlers	.10	.05
50 Kirby Puckett	.60	.25
51 Darren Holmes	.10	.05
52 Ron Karkovice	.10	.05
53 Al Martin	.10	.05
54 Pat Rapp	.10	.05
55 Mark Grace	.30	.14
56 Greg Gagne	.10	.05
57 Stan Javier	.10	.05
58 Scott Sanders	.10	.05
59 J.T. Snow	.20	.09
60 David Justice	.40	.18
61 Royce Clayton	.10	.05
62 Kevin Foster	.10	.05
63 Tim Naehring	.10	.05
64 Orlando Miller	.10	.05
65 Mike Mussina	.40	.18
66 Jim Eisenreich	.10	.05
67 Felix Fermin	.10	.05
68 Bernie Williams	.40	.18
69 Robb Nen	.10	.05
70 Ron Gant	.10	.05
71 Felipe Lira	.10	.05
72 Jacob Brumfield	.10	.05
73 John Mabry	.10	.05
74 Mark Carreon	.10	.05
75 Carlos Baerga	.10	.05
76 Jim Dougherty	.10	.05
77 Ryan Thompson	.10	.05
78 Scott Leius	.10	.05
79 Roger Pavlik	.10	.05
80 Gary Sheffield	.20	.09
81 Julian Tavarez	.10	.05
82 Andy Ashby	.10	.05
83 Mark Lemke	.10	.05
84 Omar Vizquel	.20	.09
85 Darren Daulton	.20	.09
86 Mike Lansing	.10	.05
87 Rusty Greer	.20	.09
88 Dave Stevens	.10	.05
89 Jose Offerman	.20	.09
90 Tom Henke	.10	.05
91 Troy O'Leary	.20	.09
92 Michael Tucker	.10	.05
93 Marvin Freeman	.10	.05
94 Alex Diaz	.10	.05
95 John Wetteland	.20	.09
96 Cal Ripken 2131	2.00	.90
97 Mike Mimbs	.10	.05
98 Bobby Higginson	.20	.09
99 Edgardo Alfonzo	.40	.18
100 Frank Thomas	.75	.35
101 Steve Gibralter	.40	.18
Bob Abreu		
102 Brian Givens	.10	.05
T.J. Mathews		
103 Chris Pritchett	.10	.05
Trenidad Hubbard		
104 Eric Owens	.20	.09
Butch Huskey		
105 Doug Drabek	.10	.05
106 Tomas Perez	.10	.05
107 Mark Loiter	.10	.05
108 Joe Oliver	.10	.05
109 Tony Castillo	.10	.05
110 Checklist (1-110)	.10	.05
111 Kevin Seitzer	.10	.05
112 Pete Schourek	.10	.05
113 Sean Berry	.10	.05
114 Todd Stottlemyre	.10	.05
115 Joe Carter	.20	.09
116 Jeff King	.10	.05
117 Dan Wilson	.10	.05
118 Kurt Abbott	.10	.05
119 Lyle Mouton	.10	.05
120 Jose Rijo	.10	.05
121 Curtis Goodwin	.10	.05
122 Jose Valentin	.10	.05
123 Ellis Burks	.20	.09
124 David Cone	.30	.14
125 Eddie Murray	.40	.18
126 Brian Jordan	.20	.09
127 Darrin Fletcher	.10	.05
128 Curt Schilling	.30	.14
129 Ozzie Guillen	.10	.05
130 Kenny Rogers	.10	.05

131	Tom Pagnozzi	.10	.05
132	Garret Anderson	.20	.09
133	Bobby Jones	.10	.05
134	Chris Gomez	.10	.05
135	Mike Stanley	.10	.05
136	Hideo Nomo	.40	.18
137	Jon Nunnally	.10	.05
138	Tim Wakefield	.10	.05
139	Steve Finley	.20	.09
140	Ivan Rodriguez	.50	.23
141	Quilvio Veras	.10	.05
142	Mike Fetters	.10	.05
143	Mike Greenwell	.10	.05
144	Bill Pulsipher	.10	.05
145	Mark McGwire	2.00	.90
146	Frank Castillo	.10	.05
147	Greg Vaughn	.20	.09
148	Pat Hentgen	.20	.09
149	Walt Weiss	.10	.05
150	Randy Johnson	.40	.18
151	David Segui	.20	.09
152	Benji Gil	.10	.05
153	Tom Candiotti	.10	.05
154	Geronimo Berroa	.10	.05
155	John Franco	.20	.09
156	Jay Bell	.20	.09
157	Mark Gubicza	.10	.05
158	Hal Morris	.10	.05
159	Wilson Alvarez	.20	.09
160	Derek Bell	.20	.09
161	Ricky Bottalico	.10	.05
162	Bret Boone	.20	.09
163	Brad Radke	.20	.09
164	John Valentin	.20	.09
165	Steve Avery	.10	.05
166	Mark McLemore	.10	.05
167	Danny Jackson	.10	.05
168	Tino Martinez	.20	.09
169	Shane Reynolds	.10	.05
170	Terry Pendleton	.10	.05
171	Jim Edmonds	.30	.14
172	Esteban Loaiza	.20	.09
173	Ray Durham	.20	.09
174	Carlos Perez	.10	.05
175	Raul Mondesi	.20	.09
176	Steve Ontiveros	.10	.05
177	Chipper Jones	1.00	.45
178	Otis Nixon	.10	.05
179	John Burkett	.10	.05
180	Gregg Jefferies	.10	.05
181	Denny Martinez	.20	.09
182	Ken Caminiti	.20	.09
183	Doug Jones	.10	.05
184	Brian McRae	.10	.05
185	Don Mattingly	.75	.35
186	Mel Rojas	.10	.05
187	Marty Cordova	.10	.05
188	Vinny Castilla	.30	.14
189	John Smoltz	.30	.14
190	Travis Fryman	.20	.09
191	Chris Hoiles	.20	.09
192	Chuck Finley	.20	.09
193	Ryan Klesko	.20	.09
194	Alex Fernandez	.10	.05
195	Dante Bichette	.20	.09
196	Eric Karros	.20	.09
197	Roger Clemens	1.00	.45
198	Randy Myers	.10	.05
199	Tony Phillips	.10	.05
200	Cal Ripken	1.50	.70
201	Rod Beck	.10	.05
202	Chad Curtis	.10	.05
203	Jack McDowell	.10	.05
204	Gary Gaetti	.20	.09
205	Ken Griffey Jr.	2.00	.90
206	Ramon Martinez	.20	.09
207	Jeff Kent	.20	.09
208	Brad Ausmus	.10	.05
209	Devon White	.10	.05
210	Jason Giambi	.20	.09
211	Nomar Garciaparra	1.50	.70
212	Billy Wagner	.30	.14
213	Todd Greene	.20	.09
214	Paul Wilson	.10	.05
215	Johnny Damon	.30	.14
216	Alan Benes	.10	.05
217	Karim Garcia	.20	.09
218	Dustin Hermanson	.10	.05
219	Derek Jeter	1.25	.55
220	Checklist (111-220)	.10	.05
221	Kirby Puckett STP	.40	.18
222	Cal Ripken STP	.75	.35
223	Albert Belle STP	.20	.09
224	Randy Johnson STP	.20	.09
225	Wade Boggs STP	.20	.09
226	Carlos Baerga STP	.10	.05
227	Ivan Rodriguez STP	.30	.14
228	Mike Mussina STP	.20	.09
229	Frank Thomas STP	.40	.18
230	Ken Griffey Jr. STP	1.00	.45
231	Jose Mesa STP	.10	.05
232	Matt Morris	.25	.11
233	Craig Wilson	.25	.11
234	Alvie Shepherd	.10	.05
235	Randy Winn	.40	.18
236	David Yocum	.30	.14
237	Jason Brester	.25	.11
238	Shane Monahan	.25	.11
239	Brian McNichol	.25	.11
240	Reggie Taylor	.20	.09
241	Garrett Long	.20	.09
242	Jonathan Johnson	.20	.09
243	Jeff Liefer	.25	.11
244	Brian Powell	.20	.09
245	Brian Buchanan	.10	.05
246	Mike Piazza	1.25	.55
247	Edgar Martinez	.20	.09
248	Chuck Knoblauch	.40	.18
249	Andres Galarraga	.40	.18
250	Tony Gwynn	1.00	.45
251	Lee Smith	.20	.09
252	Sammy Sosa	1.25	.55
253	Jim Thome	.40	.18
254	Frank Rodriguez	.10	.05
255	Charlie Hayes	.10	.05
256	Bernard Gilkey	.10	.05
257	John Smiley	.10	.05
258	Brady Anderson	.20	.09
259	Rico Brogna	.10	.05
260	Kirt Manwaring	.10	.05
261	Len Dykstra	.20	.09
262	Tom Glavine	.40	.18
263	Vince Coleman	.10	.05
264	John Olerud	.20	.09
265	Orlando Merced	.10	.05
266	Kent Mercker	.10	.05
267	Terry Steinbach	.10	.05
268	Brian L. Hunter	.10	.05
269	Jeff Fassero	.10	.05
270	Jay Buhner	.20	.09
271	Jeff Brantley	.10	.05
272	Tim Raines	.20	.09
273	Jimmy Key	.20	.09
274	Mo Vaughn	.40	.18
275	Andre Dawson	.30	.14
276	Jose Mesa	.10	.05
277	Brett Butler	.20	.09
278	Luis Gonzalez	.20	.09
279	Steve Sparks	.10	.05
280	Chili Davis	.20	.09
281	Carl Everett	.20	.09
282	Jeff Cirillo	.20	.09
283	Thomas Howard	.10	.05
284	Paul O'Neill	.20	.09
285	Pat Meares	.10	.05
286	Mickey Tettleton	.20	.09
287	Rey Sanchez	.10	.05
288	Bip Roberts	.10	.05
289	Roberto Alomar	.40	.18
290	Ruben Sierra	.10	.05
291	John Flaherty	.10	.05
292	Bret Saberhagen	.20	.09
293	Barry Larkin	.40	.18
294	Sandy Alomar Jr.	.20	.09
295	Ed Sprague	.10	.05
296	Gary DiSarcina	.10	.05
297	Marquis Grissom	.10	.05
298	John Frascatore	.20	.09
299	Will Clark	.40	.18
300	Barry Bonds	.50	.23
301	Ozzie Smith UER	.50	.23
	Padres is listed as Padre		
302	Dave Nilsson	.10	.05
303	Pedro Martinez	.50	.23
304	Joey Cora	.10	.05
305	Rick Aguilera	.10	.05
306	Craig Biggio	.40	.18
307	Jose Vizcaino	.10	.05
308	Jeff Montgomery	.10	.05
309	Moises Alou	.20	.09
310	Robin Ventura	.20	.09
311	David Wells	.30	.14
312	Delino DeShields	.10	.05
313	Trevor Hoffman	.20	.09
314	Andy Benes	.20	.09
315	Deion Sanders	.20	.09
316	Jim Bullinger	.10	.05
317	John Jaha	.10	.05
318	Greg Maddux	1.00	.45
319	Tim Salmon	.30	.14
320	Ben McDonald	.10	.05
321	Sandy Martinez	.10	.05
322	Dan Miceli	.10	.05
323	Wade Boggs	.40	.18
324	Ismael Valdes	.20	.09
325	Juan Gonzalez	.75	.35
326	Charles Nagy	.20	.09
327	Ray Lankford	.20	.09
328	Mark Portugal	.10	.05
329	Bobby Bonilla	.20	.09
330	Reggie Sanders	.20	.09
331	Jamie Brewington	.10	.05
332	Aaron Sele	.20	.09
333	Pete Harnisch	.10	.05
334	Cliff Floyd	.20	.09
335	Cal Eldred	.10	.05
336	Jason Bates	.10	.05
337	Tony Clark	.40	.18
338	Jose Herrera	.10	.05
339	Alex Ochoa	.10	.05
340	Mark Loretta	.10	.05
341	Donne Wall	.10	.05
342	Jason Kendall	.40	.18
343	Shannon Stewart	.20	.09
344	Brooks Kieschnick	.10	.05
345	Chris Snopek	.10	.05
346	Ruben Rivera	.20	.09
347	Jeff Suppan	.10	.05
348	Phil Nevin	.10	.05
349	John Wasdin	.10	.05
350	Jay Payton	.10	.05
351	Tim Crabtree	.10	.05
352	Rick Krivda	.10	.05
353	Bob Wolcott	.10	.05
354	Jimmy Haynes	.10	.05
355	Herb Perry	.10	.05
356	Ryne Sandberg	.50	.23
357	Harold Baines	.20	.09
358	Chad Ogea	.10	.05
359	Lee Tinsley	.10	.05
360	Matt Williams	.40	.18
361	Randy Velarde	.10	.05
362	Jose Canseco	.50	.23
363	Larry Walker	.40	.18
364	Kevin Appier	.20	.09
365	Darryl Hamilton	.10	.05
366	Jose Lima	.30	.14
367	Javy Lopez	.20	.09
368	Dennis Eckersley	.20	.09
369	Jason Isringhausen	.20	.09
370	Mickey Morandini	.10	.05
371	Scott Cooper	.10	.05
372	Jim Abbott	.20	.09
373	Paul Sorrento	.10	.05
374	Chris Hammond	.10	.05
375	Lance Johnson	.10	.05
376	Kevin Brown	.30	.14
377	Luis Alicea	.10	.05
378	Andy Pettitte	.30	.14
379	Dean Palmer	.20	.09
380	Jeff Bagwell	.50	.23
381	Jaime Navarro	.10	.05
382	Rondell White	.20	.09
383	Erik Hanson	.10	.05
384	Pedro Munoz	.10	.05
385	Heathcliff Slocumb	.10	.05
386	Wally Joyner	.20	.09
387	Bob Tewksbury	.10	.05

		MINT	NRMT
☐ 388	David Bell	.10	.05
☐ 389	Fred McGriff	.30	.14
☐ 390	Mike Henneman	.10	.05
☐ 391	Robby Thompson	.10	.05
☐ 392	Norm Charlton	.10	.05
☐ 393	Cecil Fielder	.20	.09
☐ 394	Benito Santiago	.10	.05
☐ 395	Rafael Palmeiro	.40	.18
☐ 396	Ricky Bones	.10	.05
☐ 397	Rickey Henderson	.50	.23
☐ 398	C.J. Nitkowski	.10	.05
☐ 399	Shawon Dunston	.10	.05
☐ 400	Manny Ramirez	.50	.23
☐ 401	Bill Swift	.10	.05
☐ 402	Chad Fonville	.10	.05
☐ 403	Joey Hamilton	.10	.05
☐ 404	Alex Gonzalez	.10	.05
☐ 405	Roberto Hernandez	.10	.05
☐ 406	Jeff Blauser	.10	.05
☐ 407	LaTroy Hawkins	.10	.05
☐ 408	Greg Colbrunn	.10	.05
☐ 409	Todd Hundley	.20	.09
☐ 410	Glenn Dishman	.10	.05
☐ 411	Joe Vitiello	.10	.05
☐ 412	Todd Worrell	.10	.05
☐ 413	Wil Cordero	.10	.05
☐ 414	Ken Hill	.10	.05
☐ 415	Carlos Garcia	.10	.05
☐ 416	Bryan Rekar	.10	.05
☐ 417	Shawn Green	.40	.18
☐ 418	Tyler Green	.10	.05
☐ 419	Mike Blowers	.10	.05
☐ 420	Kenny Lofton	.30	.14
☐ 421	Denny Neagle	.10	.05
☐ 422	Jeff Conine	.10	.05
☐ 423	Mark Langston	.10	.05
☐ 424	Steve Cox	.50	.23
	Jesse Ibarra		
	Derrek Lee		
	Ron Wright		
☐ 425	Jim Bonnici	4.00	1.80
	Billy Owens		
	Richie Sexson		
	Daryle Ward		
☐ 426	Kevin Jordan	.20	.09
	Bobby Morris		
	Desi Relaford		
	Adam Riggs		
☐ 427	Tim Harkrider	.20	.09
	Rey Ordonez		
	Neifi Perez		
	Enrique Wilson		
☐ 428	Bartolo Colon	.40	.18
	Doug Million		
	Rafael Orellano		
	Ray Ricken		
☐ 429	Jeff D'Amico	.20	.09
	Marty Janzen		
	Gary Rath		
	Clint Sodowsky		
☐ 430	Matt Drews	.20	.09
	Rich Hunter		
	Matt Ruebel		
	Bret Wagner		
☐ 431	Jaime Bluma	.30	.14
	David Coggin		
	Steve Montgomery		
	Brandon Reed		
☐ 432	Mike Figga	.40	.18
	Raul Ibanez		
	Paul Konerko		
	Julio Mosquera		
☐ 433	Brian Barber	.20	.09
	Marc Kroon		
	Marc Valdes		
	Don Wengert		
☐ 434	George Arias	1.50	.70
	Chris Haas		
	Scott Rolen		
	Scott Spiezio		
☐ 435	Brian Banks	2.00	.90
	Vladimir Guerrero		
	Andruw Jones		
	Billy McMillon		
☐ 436	Roger Cedeno	1.50	.70
	Derrick Gibson		
	Ben Grieve		
	Shane Spencer		
☐ 437	Anton French	.25	.11
	Desmond Smith		
	DaRond Stovall		
	Keith Williams		
☐ 438	Michael Coleman	.50	.23
	Jacob Cruz		
	Richard Hidalgo		
	Charles Peterson		
☐ 439	Trey Beamon	.20	.09
	Yamil Benitez		
	Jermaine Dye		
	Angel Echevarria		
☐ 440	Checklist	.10	.05
☐ F7	Mickey Mantle Last Day	15.00	6.75

1996 Topps Classic Confrontations

	MINT	NRMT
COMPLETE SET (15)	6.00	2.70
COMMON CARD (CC1-CC15)	.15	.07
ONE PER SPECIAL SER.1 RETAIL PACK		

		MINT	NRMT
☐ CC1	Ken Griffey Jr.	1.50	.70
☐ CC2	Cal Ripken	1.25	.55
☐ CC3	Edgar Martinez	.15	.07
☐ CC4	Kirby Puckett	.50	.23
☐ CC5	Frank Thomas	.60	.25
☐ CC6	Barry Bonds	.40	.18
☐ CC7	Reggie Sanders	.15	.07
☐ CC8	Andres Galarraga	.30	.14
☐ CC9	Tony Gwynn	.75	.35
☐ CC10	Mike Piazza	1.00	.45
☐ CC11	Randy Johnson	.30	.14
☐ CC12	Mike Mussina	.30	.14
☐ CC13	Roger Clemens	.75	.35
☐ CC14	Tom Glavine	.30	.14
☐ CC15	Greg Maddux	.75	.35

1996 Topps Mantle

	MINT	NRMT
COMPLETE SET (19)	150.00	70.00
COMMON MANTLE (1-14)	8.00	3.60
COMMON MANTLE SP (15-19)	12.00	5.50
SER.1 STAT.ODDS 1:9 HOB, 1:6 RET, 1:2 JUM		
FOUR PER CEREAL FACT.SET		

		MINT	NRMT
☐ 1	Mickey Mantle 1951 Bowman	15.00	6.75
☐ 2	Mickey Mantle 1952 Topps	20.00	9.00
☐ 3	Mickey Mantle 1953 Topps	10.00	4.50
☐ 4	Mickey Mantle 1954 Bowman	8.00	3.60
☐ 5	Mickey Mantle 1955 Bowman	8.00	3.60
☐ 6	Mickey Mantle 1956 Topps	8.00	3.60
☐ 7	Mickey Mantle 1957 Topps	8.00	3.60
☐ 8	Mickey Mantle 1958 Topps	8.00	3.60
☐ 9	Mickey Mantle 1959 Topps	8.00	3.60
☐ 10	Mickey Mantle 1960 Topps	8.00	3.60
☐ 11	Mickey Mantle 1961 Topps	8.00	3.60
☐ 12	Mickey Mantle 1962 Topps	8.00	3.60
☐ 13	Mickey Mantle 1963 Topps	8.00	3.60
☐ 14	Mickey Mantle 1964 Topps	8.00	3.60
☐ 15	Mickey Mantle 1965 Topps	12.00	5.50
☐ 16	Mickey Mantle 1966 Topps	12.00	5.50
☐ 17	Mickey Mantle 1967 Topps	12.00	5.50
☐ 18	Mickey Mantle 1968 Topps	12.00	5.50
☐ 19	Mickey Mantle 1969 Topps	12.00	5.50

1996 Topps Mantle Case

	MINT	NRMT
COMPLETE SET (19)	800.00	350.00
COMMON MANTLE (1-14)	40.00	18.00
COMMON MANTLE SP (15-19)	50.00	22.00
ONE PER SER.2 HOBBY/JUMBO/VEND CASE		

		MINT	NRMT
☐ 1	Mickey Mantle 1951 Bowman	80.00	36.00
☐ 2	Mickey Mantle 1952 Topps	100.00	45.00
☐ 3	Mickey Mantle 1953 Topps	50.00	22.00

1996 Topps Mantle Finest

	MINT	NRMT
COMPLETE SET (19)	150.00	70.00
COMMON MANTLE (1-14)	8.00	3.60
COMMON MANTLE SP (15-19)	12.00	5.50
SER.2 STATED ODDS 1:18 RET, 1:12 ANCO		

		MINT	NRMT
☐ 1	Mickey Mantle 1951 Bowman	15.00	6.75
☐ 2	Mickey Mantle	20.00	9.00

1952 Topps

		MINT	NRMT
❑ 3 Mickey Mantle		10.00	4.50
1953 Topps			

1996 Topps Mantle Finest Refractors

	MINT	NRMT
COMPLETE SET (19)	500.00	220.00
COMMON MANTLE (1-14)	30.00	13.50
COMMON MANTLE SP (15-19)	40.00	18.00
SER.2 STATED ODDS 1:144 RET, 1:96 HOB		

❑ 1 Mickey Mantle	60.00	27.00
1951 Bowman		
❑ 2 Mickey Mantle	80.00	36.00
1952 Topps		
❑ 3 Mickey Mantle	40.00	18.00
1953 Topps		

1996 Topps Mantle Redemption

	MINT	NRMT
COMPLETE SET (19)	300.00	135.00
COMMON MANTLE (1-19)	15.00	6.75
SER.2 STATED ODDS 1:108 RET, 1:72 ANCO		

❑ 1 Mickey Mantle	30.00	13.50
1951 Bowman (2)		
❑ 2 Mickey Mantle	40.00	18.00
1952 Topps (1)		

❑ 3 Mickey Mantle	20.00	9.00
1953 Topps (4)		
❑ 4 Mickey Mantle	15.00	6.75
1954 Bowman (2)		
❑ 5 Mickey Mantle	15.00	6.75
1955 Bowman (3)		
❑ 6 Mickey Mantle	15.00	6.75
1956 Topps (2)		
❑ 7 Mickey Mantle	15.00	6.75
1957 Topps (2)		
❑ 8 Mickey Mantle	15.00	6.75
1958 Topps (2)		
❑ 9 Mickey Mantle	15.00	6.75
1959 Topps (3)		
❑ 10 Mickey Mantle	15.00	6.75
1960 Topps (3)		
❑ 11 Mickey Mantle	15.00	6.75
1961 Topps (3)		
❑ 12 Mickey Mantle	15.00	6.75
1962 Topps (3)		
❑ 13 Mickey Mantle	15.00	6.75
1963 Topps (3)		
❑ 14 Mickey Mantle	15.00	6.75
1964 Topps (6)		
❑ 15 Mickey Mantle	15.00	6.75
1965 Topps (3)		
❑ 16 Mickey Mantle	15.00	6.75
1966 Topps (10)		
❑ 17 Mickey Mantle	15.00	6.75
1967 Topps (10)		
❑ 18 Mickey Mantle	15.00	6.75
1968 Topps (10)		
❑ 19 Mickey Mantle	15.00	6.75
1969 Topps (4)		

1996 Topps Masters of the Game

	MINT	NRMT
COMPLETE SET (20)	30.00	13.50
COMMON CARD (1-20)	.50	.23
SER.1 STATED ODDS 1:18 HOBBY		
TWO PER HOBBY FACTORY SET		

❑ 1 Dennis Eckersley	.50	.23
❑ 2 Denny Martinez	.50	.23
❑ 3 Eddie Murray	1.50	.70
❑ 4 Paul Molitor	1.50	.70
❑ 5 Ozzie Smith	2.50	1.10
❑ 6 Rickey Henderson	2.50	1.10
❑ 7 Tim Raines	.50	.23
❑ 8 Lee Smith	.50	.23
❑ 9 Cal Ripken	8.00	3.60
❑ 10 Chili Davis	.50	.23
❑ 11 Wade Boggs	1.50	.70
❑ 12 Tony Gwynn	5.00	2.20
❑ 13 Don Mattingly	5.00	2.20
❑ 14 Bret Saberhagen	.50	.23
❑ 15 Kirby Puckett	4.00	1.80
❑ 16 Joe Carter	.50	.23
❑ 17 Roger Clemens	5.00	2.20
❑ 18 Barry Bonds	1.50	.70
❑ 19 Greg Maddux	5.00	2.20
❑ 20 Frank Thomas	4.00	1.80

1996 Topps Mystery Finest

	MINT	NRMT
COMPLETE SET (26)	150.00	70.00
COMMON CARD (M1-M26)	1.50	.70
SER.1 STATED ODDS 1:36 HOB/RET, 1:8 JUM		
*REF: 12.5X TO 30X BASE CARD HI		
REF.SER.1 ODDS 1:216 HOB/RET, 1:36 JUM		

❑ M1 Hideo Nomo	4.00	1.80
❑ M2 Greg Maddux	10.00	4.50
❑ M3 Randy Johnson	4.00	1.80
❑ M4 Chipper Jones	10.00	4.50
❑ M5 Marty Cordova	1.50	.70
❑ M6 Garret Anderson	2.00	.90
❑ M7 Cal Ripken	15.00	6.75
❑ M8 Kirby Puckett	6.00	2.70
❑ M9 Tony Gwynn	10.00	4.50
❑ M10 Manny Ramirez	5.00	2.20
❑ M11 Jim Edmonds	2.50	1.10
❑ M12 Mike Piazza	12.00	5.50
❑ M13 Barry Bonds	5.00	2.20
❑ M14 Raul Mondesi	2.00	.90
❑ M15 Sammy Sosa	12.00	5.50
❑ M16 Ken Griffey Jr.	20.00	9.00
❑ M17 Albert Belle	4.00	1.80
❑ M18 Dante Bichette	2.00	.90
❑ M19 Mo Vaughn	4.00	1.80
❑ M20 Jeff Bagwell	5.00	2.20
❑ M21 Frank Thomas	8.00	3.60
❑ M22 Hideo Nomo	4.00	1.80
❑ M23 Cal Ripken	15.00	6.75
❑ M24 Mike Piazza	12.00	5.50
❑ M25 Ken Griffey Jr.	20.00	9.00
❑ M26 Frank Thomas	8.00	3.60

1996 Topps Power Boosters

	MINT	NRMT
COMP.STAR POW.SET (11)	40.00	18.00
COMMON CARD (1-26)	1.00	.45
STR.PWR.SER.1 STAT.ODDS 1:36 RETAIL		
COMP.DRAFT PICKS SET (14)	120.00	55.00
COMMON DRAFT PICK (13-26)	2.00	.90
DRAFT PICK MINOR STARS	4.00	1.80
DP SER.1 STATED ODDS 1:36 HOBBY		
CARD #7 DOES NOT EXIST		

#	Player	MINT	NRMT
1	Tony Gwynn	10.00	4.50
2	Mike Piazza	12.00	5.50
3	Greg Maddux	10.00	4.50
4	Jeff Bagwell	5.00	2.20
5	Larry Walker	4.00	1.80
6	Barry Larkin	4.00	1.80
8	Tom Glavine	4.00	1.80
9	Craig Biggio	4.00	1.80
10	Barry Bonds	5.00	2.20
11	Heathcliff Slocumb	1.00	.45
12	Matt Williams	4.00	1.80
13	Todd Helton	15.00	6.75
14	Mark Redman	2.00	.90
15	Michael Barrett	8.00	3.60
16	Ben Davis	10.00	4.50
17	Juan LeBron	4.00	1.80
18	Tony McKnight	2.00	.90
19	Ryan Jaroncyk	2.00	.90
20	Corey Jenkins	2.00	.90
21	Jim Scharrer	2.00	.90
22	Mark Bellhorn	4.00	1.80
23	Jarrod Washburn	4.00	1.80
24	Geoff Jenkins	15.00	6.75
25	Sean Casey	60.00	27.00
26	Brett Tomko	4.00	1.80

1996 Topps Profiles

		MINT	NRMT
	COMPLETE SET (40)	40.00	18.00
	COMPLETE SERIES 1 (20)	30.00	13.50
	COMPLETE SERIES 2 (20)	10.00	4.50
	COMMON CARD (AL1-NL20)	.25	.11

STAT.ODDS 1:12 HOB/RET,1:6 JUM,1:8 ANCO
1 SER.1 AND 2 SER.2 PER HOB.FACT.SET

#	Player	MINT	NRMT
AL1	Roberto Alomar	1.00	.45
AL2	Carlos Baerga	.25	.11
AL3	Albert Belle	1.00	.45
AL4	Cecil Fielder	.25	.11
AL5	Ken Griffey Jr.	5.00	2.20
AL6	Randy Johnson	1.00	.45
AL7	Paul O'Neill	.50	.23
AL8	Cal Ripken	4.00	1.80
AL9	Frank Thomas	2.00	.90
AL10	Mo Vaughn	1.00	.45
AL11	Jay Buhner	.50	.23
AL12	Marty Cordova	.25	.11
AL13	Jim Edmonds	.75	.35
AL14	Juan Gonzalez	2.00	.90
AL15	Kenny Lofton	.75	.35
AL16	Edgar Martinez	.50	.23
AL17	Don Mattingly	2.50	1.10
AL18	Mark McGwire	5.00	2.20
AL19	Rafael Palmeiro	1.00	.45
AL20	Tim Salmon	.75	.35
NL1	Jeff Bagwell	1.25	.55
NL2	Derek Bell	.50	.23
NL3	Barry Bonds	1.25	.55
NL4	Greg Maddux	2.50	1.10
NL5	Fred McGriff	.75	.35
NL6	Raul Mondesi	.50	.23
NL7	Mike Piazza	3.00	1.35
NL8	Reggie Sanders	.50	.23
NL9	Sammy Sosa	3.00	1.35
NL10	Larry Walker	1.00	.45
NL11	Dante Bichette	.50	.23
NL12	Andres Galarraga	1.00	.45
NL13	Ron Gant	.25	.11
NL14	Tom Glavine	1.00	.45
NL15	Chipper Jones	2.50	1.10
NL16	David Justice	1.00	.45
NL17	Barry Larkin	1.00	.45
NL18	Hideo Nomo	1.00	.45
NL19	Gary Sheffield	.50	.23
NL20	Matt Williams	1.00	.45

1996 Topps Road Warriors

		MINT	NRMT
	COMPLETE SET (20)	12.00	5.50
	COMMON CARD (RW1-RW20)	.05	.02

ONE PER SPECIAL SER.2 RETAIL PACK

#	Player	MINT	NRMT
RW1	Derek Bell	.30	.14
RW2	Albert Belle	.75	.35
RW3	Craig Biggio	.75	.35
RW4	Barry Bonds	1.00	.45
RW5	Jay Buhner	.30	.14
RW6	Jim Edmonds	.50	.23
RW7	Gary Gaetti	.30	.14
RW8	Ron Gant	.25	.11
RW9	Edgar Martinez	.30	.14
RW10	Tino Martinez	.30	.14
RW11	Mark McGwire	4.00	1.80
RW12	Mike Piazza	3.00	1.35
RW13	Manny Ramirez	1.00	.45
RW14	Tim Salmon	.50	.23
RW15	Reggie Sanders	.30	.14
RW16	Frank Thomas	1.50	.70
RW17	John Valentin	.30	.14
RW18	Mo Vaughn	.75	.35
RW19	Robin Ventura	.30	.14
RW20	Matt Williams	.75	.35

1996 Topps Wrecking Crew

		MINT	NRMT
	COMPLETE SET (15)	70.00	32.00
	COMMON CARD (WC1-WC15)	1.50	.70

SER.2 STATED ODDS 1:18 HOBBY
ONE PER HOBBY FACTORY SET

#	Player	MINT	NRMT
WC1	Jeff Bagwell	5.00	2.20
WC2	Albert Belle	4.00	1.80
WC3	Barry Bonds	5.00	2.20
WC4	Jose Canseco	5.00	2.20
WC5	Joe Carter	2.00	.90
WC6	Cecil Fielder	1.50	.70
WC7	Ron Gant	1.50	.70
WC8	Juan Gonzalez	8.00	3.60
WC9	Ken Griffey Jr	20.00	9.00
WC10	Fred McGriff	2.50	1.10
WC11	Mark McGwire	20.00	9.00
WC12	Mike Piazza	12.00	5.50
WC13	Frank Thomas	8.00	3.60
WC14	Mo Vaughn	4.00	1.80
WC15	Matt Williams	4.00	1.80

1997 Topps

		MINT	NRMT
	COMPLETE SET (496)	50.00	22.00
	COMP.HOBBY.SET (497)	150.00	70.00
	COMPLETE SERIES 1 (276)	25.00	11.00
	COMPLETE SERIES 2 (220)	25.00	11.00
	COMMON CARD (1-496)	.10	.05
	MINOR STARS	.20	.09
	UNLISTED STARS	.40	.18

SUBSET CARDS HALF VALUE OF BASE CARDS
CARDS 7, 84 AND 277 DON'T EXIST
ELSTER AND FETTERS NUMBERED 61
CL 276 AND C.JONES NUMBERED 276

#	Player	MINT	NRMT
1	Barry Bonds	.50	.23
2	Tom Pagnozzi	.10	.05
3	Terrell Wade	.10	.05
4	Jose Valentin	.10	.05
5	Mark Clark	.10	.05
6	Brady Anderson	.20	.09
8	Wade Boggs	.40	.18
9	Scott Stahoviak	.10	.05
10	Andres Galarraga	.40	.18
11	Steve Avery	.10	.05
12	Rusty Greer	.20	.09
13	Derek Jeter	1.25	.55
14	Ricky Bottalico	.20	.09
15	Andy Ashby	.10	.05
16	Paul Shuey	.10	.05
17	F.P. Santangelo	.10	.05
18	Royce Clayton	.10	.05
19	Mike Mohler	.10	.05
20	Mike Piazza	1.25	.55
21	Jaime Navarro	.10	.05
22	Billy Wagner	.20	.09
23	Mike Timlin	.10	.05
24	Garret Anderson	.20	.09
25	Ben McDonald	.10	.05
26	Mel Rojas	.10	.05
27	John Burkett	.10	.05
28	Jeff King	.10	.05
29	Reggie Jefferson	.10	.05
30	Kevin Appier	.10	.05
31	Felipe Lira	.10	.05
32	Kevin Tapani	.10	.05
33	Mark Portugal	.10	.05
34	Carlos Garcia	.10	.05
35	Joey Cora	.10	.05
36	David Segui	.20	.09
37	Mark Grace	.30	.14
38	Erik Hanson	.10	.05
39	Jeff D'Amico	.10	.05
40	Jay Buhner	.20	.09
41	B.J. Surhoff	.20	.09

42	Jackie Robinson TRIB.....	2.00	.90
43	Roger Pavlik	.10	.05
44	Hal Morris		.05
45	Mariano Duncan	.10	.05
46	Harold Baines	.20	.09
47	Jorge Fabregas	.10	.05
48	Jose Herrera	.10	.05
49	Jeff Cirillo	.20	.09
50	Tom Glavine	.40	.18
51	Pedro Astacio	.10	.05
52	Mark Gardner	.10	.05
53	Arthur Rhodes	.10	.05
54	Troy O'Leary	.20	.09
55	Bip Roberts	.10	.05
56	Mike Lieberthal	.10	.05
57	Shane Andrews	.10	.05
58	Scott Karl	.10	.05
59	Gary DiSarcina	.10	.05
60	Andy Pettitte	.30	.14
61	Kevin Elster	.10	.05
62	Mark McGwire	2.00	.90
63	Dan Wilson	.10	.05
64	Mickey Morandini	.10	.05
65	Chuck Knoblauch	.40	.18
66	Tim Wakefield	.20	.09
67	Raul Mondesi	.20	.09
68	Todd Jones	.10	.05
69	Albert Belle	.40	.18
70	Trevor Hoffman	.20	.09
71	Eric Young	.20	.09
72	Robert Perez	.10	.05
73	Butch Huskey	.10	.05
74	Brian McRae	.10	.05
75	Jim Edmonds	.30	.14
76	Mike Henneman	.10	.05
77	Frank Rodriguez	.10	.05
78	Danny Tartabull	.10	.05
79	Robb Nen	.10	.05
80	Reggie Sanders	.20	.09
81	Ron Karkovice	.10	.05
82	Benito Santiago	.10	.05
83	Mike Lansing	.10	.05
84	Mike Fetters UER	.10	.05
	Card numbered 61		
85	Craig Biggio	.40	.18
86	Mike Bordick	.10	.05
87	Ray Lankford	.20	.09
88	Charles Nagy	.10	.05
89	Paul Wilson	.10	.05
90	John Wetteland	.10	.05
91	Tom Candiotti	.10	.05
92	Carlos Delgado	.40	.18
93	Derek Bell	.10	.05
94	Mark Lemke	.10	.05
95	Edgar Martinez	.20	.09
96	Rickey Henderson	.50	.23
97	Greg Myers	.10	.05
98	Jim Leyritz	.10	.05
99	Mark Johnson	.10	.05
100	Dwight Gooden HL	.10	.05
101	Al Leiter HL	.20	.09
102	John Mabry HL	.10	.05
103	Alex Ochoa HL	.10	.05
104	Mike Piazza HL	.60	.25
105	Jim Thome	.40	.18
106	Ricky Otero	.10	.05
107	Jamey Wright	.10	.05
108	Frank Thomas	.75	.35
109	Jody Reed	.10	.05
110	Orel Hershiser	.20	.09
111	Terry Steinbach	.10	.05
112	Mark Loretta	.10	.05
113	Turk Wendell	.10	.05
114	Marvin Benard	.10	.05
115	Kevin Brown	.30	.14
116	Robert Person	.10	.05
117	Joey Hamilton	.20	.09
118	Francisco Cordova	.10	.05
119	John Smiley	.10	.05
120	Travis Fryman	.20	.09
121	Jimmy Key	.10	.05
122	Tom Goodwin	.10	.05
123	Mike Greenwell	.10	.05
124	Juan Gonzalez	.75	.35
125	Pete Harnisch	.10	.05
126	Roger Cedeno	.20	.09
127	Ron Gant	.10	.05
128	Mark Langston	.20	.09
129	Tim Crabtree	.10	.05
130	Greg Maddux	1.00	.45
131	William VanLandingham	.10	.05
132	Wally Joyner	.20	.09
133	Randy Myers	.10	.05
134	John Valentin	.20	.09
135	Bret Boone	.20	.09
136	Bruce Ruffin	.10	.05
137	Chris Snopek	.10	.05
138	Paul Molitor	.40	.18
139	Mark McLemore	.10	.05
140	Rafael Palmeiro	.40	.18
141	Herb Perry	.10	.05
142	Luis Gonzalez	.20	.09
143	Doug Drabek	.10	.05
144	Ken Ryan	.10	.05
145	Todd Hundley	.20	.09
146	Ellis Burks	.20	.09
147	Ozzie Guillen	.10	.05
148	Rich Becker	.10	.05
149	Sterling Hitchcock	.10	.05
150	Bernie Williams	.40	.18
151	Mike Stanley	.10	.05
152	Roberto Alomar	.40	.18
153	Jose Mesa	.10	.05
154	Steve Trachsel	.10	.05
155	Alex Gonzalez	.10	.05
156	Troy Percival	.20	.09
157	John Smoltz	.30	.14
158	Pedro Martinez	.50	.23
159	Jeff Conine	.10	.05
160	Bernard Gilkey	.10	.05
161	Jim Eisenreich	.10	.05
162	Mickey Tettleton	.10	.05
163	Justin Thompson	.20	.09
164	Jose Offerman	.10	.05
165	Tony Phillips	.10	.05
166	Ismael Valdes	.20	.09
167	Ryne Sandberg	.50	.23
168	Matt Mieske	.10	.05
169	Geronimo Berroa	.10	.05
170	Otis Nixon	.10	.05
171	John Mabry	.10	.05
172	Shawn Dunston	.10	.05
173	Omar Vizquel	.20	.09
174	Chris Holles	.10	.05
175	Dwight Gooden	.20	.09
176	Wilson Alvarez	.10	.05
177	Todd Hollandsworth	.10	.05
178	Roger Salkeld	.10	.05
179	Rey Sanchez	.10	.05
180	Rey Ordonez	.20	.09
181	Denny Martinez	.20	.09
182	Ramon Martinez	.20	.09
183	Dave Nilsson	.10	.05
184	Marquis Grissom	.20	.09
185	Randy Velarde	.10	.05
186	Ron Coomer	.10	.05
187	Tino Martinez	.40	.18
188	Jeff Brantley	.10	.05
189	Steve Finley	.20	.09
190	Andy Benes	.20	.09
191	Terry Adams	.10	.05
192	Mike Blowers	.10	.05
193	Russ Davis	.20	.09
194	Darryl Hamilton	.10	.05
195	Jason Kendall	.30	.14
196	Johnny Damon	.20	.09
197	Dave Martinez	.10	.05
198	Mike Macfarlane	.10	.05
199	Norm Charlton	.10	.05
200	Doug Million	.25	.11
	Damian Moss		
	Bobby Rodgers		
201	Geoff Jenkins	.20	.09
	Raul Ibanez		
	Mike Cameron		
202	Sean Casey	1.25	.55
	Jim Bonnici		
	Dmitri Young		
203	Jed Hansen	.10	.05
	Homer Bush		
	Felipe Crespo		
204	Kevin Orie	.20	.09
	Gabe Alvarez		
	Aaron Boone		
205	Ben Davis	.20	.09
	Kevin Brown		
	Bobby Estalella		
206	Billy McMillon	.40	.18
	Bubba Trammell		
	Dante Powell		
207	Jarrod Washburn	.20	.09
	Marc Wilkins		
	Glendon Rusch		
208	Brian Hunter	.20	.09
209	Jason Giambi	.20	.09
210	Henry Rodriguez	.20	.09
211	Edgar Renteria	.20	.09
212	Edgardo Alfonzo	.30	.14
213	Fernando Vina	.10	.05
214	Shawn Green	.40	.18
215	Ray Durham	.20	.09
216	Joe Randa	.10	.05
217	Armando Reynoso	.10	.05
218	Eric Davis	.20	.09
219	Bob Tewksbury	.10	.05
220	Jacob Cruz	.10	.05
221	Glenallen Hill	.10	.05
222	Gary Gaetti	.20	.09
223	Donne Wall	.10	.05
224	Brad Clontz	.10	.05
225	Marty Janzen	.10	.05
226	Todd Worrell	.10	.05
227	John Franco	.20	.09
228	David Wells	.20	.09
229	Gregg Jefferies	.20	.09
230	Tim Naehring	.10	.05
231	Thomas Howard	.10	.05
232	Roberto Hernandez	.10	.05
233	Kevin Ritz	.10	.05
234	Julian Tavarez	.10	.05
235	Ken Hill	.10	.05
236	Greg Gagne	.10	.05
237	Bobby Chouinard	.10	.05
238	Joe Carter	.20	.09
239	Jermaine Dye	.20	.09
240	Antonio Osuna	.10	.05
241	Julio Franco	.20	.09
242	Mike Grace	.10	.05
243	Aaron Sele	.20	.09
244	David Justice	.40	.18
245	Sandy Alomar Jr.	.20	.09
246	Jose Canseco	.50	.23
247	Paul O'Neill	.20	.09
248	Sean Berry	.10	.05
249	Rick Bierbrodt	.50	.23
	Kevin Sweeney		
250	Larry Rodriguez	.25	.11
	Vladimir Nunez		
251	Ron Hartman	.25	.11
	David Hayman		
252	Alex Sanchez	.25	.11
	Matthew Quatraro		
253	Ronni Seberino	.25	.11
	Pablo Ortego		
254	Rex Hudler	.10	.05
255	Orlando Miller	.10	.05
256	Mariano Rivera	.20	.09
257	Brad Radke	.20	.09
258	Bobby Higginson	.20	.09
259	Jay Bell	.20	.09
260	Mark Grudzielanek	.20	.09
261	Lance Johnson	.10	.05
262	Ken Caminiti	.30	.14
263	J.T. Snow	.20	.09
264	Gary Sheffield	.20	.09
265	Darrin Fletcher	.10	.05
266	Eric Owens	.10	.05
267	Luis Castillo	.10	.05
268	Scott Rolen	.60	.25
269	Todd Noel	.25	.11
	John Oliver		
270	Robert Stratton	.50	.23
	Corey Lee		
271	Gil Meche	1.50	.70
	Matt Halloran		
272	Eric Milton	.75	.35
	Dermal Brown		
273	Josh Garrett	.25	.11

Chris Reitsma
- □ 274 A.J.Zapp .... .60 .25
  Jason Marquis
- □ 275 Checklist .... .10
- □ 276 Checklist .... .10 .05
- □ 277 Chipper Jones UER .... 1.00 .45
  incorrectly numbered 276
- □ 278 Orlando Merced .... .10 .05
- □ 279 Ariel Prieto .... .10 .05
- □ 280 Al Leiter .... .20 .09
- □ 281 Pat Meares .... .10 .05
- □ 282 Darryl Strawberry .... .20 .09
- □ 283 Jamie Moyer .... .10 .05
- □ 284 Scott Servais .... .10 .05
- □ 285 Delino DeShields .... .10 .05
- □ 286 Danny Graves .... .10 .05
- □ 287 Gerald Williams .... .10 .05
- □ 288 Todd Greene .... .10 .05
- □ 289 Rico Brogna .... .10 .05
- □ 290 Derrick Gibson .... .30 .14
- □ 291 Joe Girardi .... .10 .05
- □ 292 Darren Lewis .... .10 .05
- □ 293 Nomar Garciaparra .... 1.25 .55
- □ 294 Greg Colbrunn .... .10 .05
- □ 295 Jeff Bagwell .... .50 .23
- □ 296 Brent Gates .... .10 .05
- □ 297 Jose Vizcaino .... .10 .05
- □ 298 Alex Ochoa .... .10 .05
- □ 299 Sid Fernandez .... .10 .05
- □ 300 Ken Griffey Jr. .... 2.00 .90
- □ 301 Chris Gomez .... .10 .05
- □ 302 Wendell Magee .... .10 .05
- □ 303 Darren Oliver .... .10 .05
- □ 304 Mel Nieves .... .10 .05
- □ 305 Sammy Sosa .... 1.25 .55
- □ 306 George Arias .... .10 .05
- □ 307 Jack McDowell .... .10 .05
- □ 308 Stan Javier .... .10 .05
- □ 309 Kimera Bartee .... .10 .05
- □ 310 James Baldwin .... .20 .09
- □ 311 Rocky Coppinger .... .10 .05
- □ 312 Keith Lockhart .... .10 .05
- □ 313 C.J. Nitkowski .... .10 .05
- □ 314 Allen Watson .... .10 .05
- □ 315 Darryl Kile .... .10 .05
- □ 316 Amaury Telemaco .... .10 .05
- □ 317 Jason Isringhausen .... .10 .05
- □ 318 Manny Ramirez .... .50 .23
- □ 319 Terry Pendleton .... .10 .05
- □ 320 Tim Salmon .... .40 .18
- □ 321 Eric Karros .... .20 .09
- □ 322 Mark Whiten .... .10 .05
- □ 323 Rick Krivda .... .10 .05
- □ 324 Brett Butler .... .20 .09
- □ 325 Randy Johnson .... .40 .18
- □ 326 Eddie Taubensee .... .10 .05
- □ 327 Mark Leiter .... .10 .05
- □ 328 Kevin Gross .... .10 .05
- □ 329 Ernie Young .... .10 .05
- □ 330 Pat Hentgen .... .20 .09
- □ 331 Rondell White .... .20 .09
- □ 332 Bobby Witt .... .10 .05
- □ 333 Eddie Murray .... .40 .18
- □ 334 Tim Raines .... .20 .09
- □ 335 Jeff Fassero .... .10 .05
- □ 336 Chuck Finley .... .20 .09
- □ 337 Willie Adams .... .10 .05
- □ 338 Chan Ho Park .... .40 .18
- □ 339 Jay Powell .... .10 .05
- □ 340 Ivan Rodriguez .... .50 .23
- □ 341 Jermaine Allensworth .... .10 .05
- □ 342 Jay Payton .... .10 .05
- □ 343 T.J. Mathews .... .10 .05
- □ 344 Tony Batista .... .30 .14
- □ 345 Ed Sprague .... .10 .05
- □ 346 Jeff Kent .... .20 .09
- □ 347 Scott Erickson .... .20 .09
- □ 348 Jeff Suppan .... .10 .05
- □ 349 Pete Schourek .... .10 .05
- □ 350 Kenny Lofton .... .30 .14
- □ 351 Alan Benes .... .10 .05
- □ 352 Fred McGriff .... .30 .14
- □ 353 Charlie O'Brien .... .10 .05
- □ 354 Darren Bragg .... .10 .05
- □ 355 Alex Fernandez .... .10 .05
- □ 356 Al Martin .... .10 .05
- □ 357 Bob Wells .... .10 .05
- □ 358 Chad Mottola .... .10 .05
- □ 359 Devon White .... .20 .09
- □ 360 David Cone .... .30 .14
- □ 361 Bobby Jones .... .10 .05
- □ 362 Scott Sanders .... .10 .05
- □ 363 Karim Garcia .... .20 .09
- □ 364 Kirt Manwaring .... .10 .05
- □ 365 Chili Davis .... .20 .09
- □ 366 Mike Hampton .... .20 .09
- □ 367 Chad Ogea .... .10 .05
- □ 368 Curt Schilling .... .30 .14
- □ 369 Phil Nevin .... .10 .05
- □ 370 Roger Clemens .... 1.00 .45
- □ 371 Willie Greene .... .10 .05
- □ 372 Kenny Rogers .... .10 .05
- □ 373 Jose Rijo .... .10 .05
- □ 374 Bobby Bonilla .... .20 .09
- □ 375 Mike Mussina .... .40 .18
- □ 376 Curtis Pride .... .10 .05
- □ 377 Todd Walker .... .40 .18
- □ 378 Jason Bere .... .10 .05
- □ 379 Heathcliff Slocumb .... .10 .05
- □ 380 Dante Bichette .... .20 .09
- □ 381 Carlos Baerga .... .10 .05
- □ 382 Livan Hernandez .... .20 .09
- □ 383 Jason Schmidt .... .10 .05
- □ 384 Kevin Stocker .... .10 .05
- □ 385 Matt Williams .... .40 .18
- □ 386 Bartolo Colon .... .20 .09
- □ 387 Will Clark .... .40 .18
- □ 388 Dennis Eckersley .... .20 .09
- □ 389 Brooks Kieschnick .... .10 .05
- □ 390 Ryan Klesko .... .20 .09
- □ 391 Mark Carreon .... .10 .05
- □ 392 Tim Worrell .... .10 .05
- □ 393 Dean Palmer .... .20 .09
- □ 394 Wil Cordero .... .10 .05
- □ 395 Javy Lopez .... .20 .09
- □ 396 Rich Aurilia .... .20 .09
- □ 397 Greg Vaughn .... .20 .09
- □ 398 Vinny Castilla .... .30 .14
- □ 399 Jeff Montgomery .... .10 .05
- □ 400 Cal Ripken .... 1.50 .70
- □ 401 Walt Weiss .... .10 .05
- □ 402 Brad Ausmus .... .10 .05
- □ 403 Ruben Rivera .... .20 .09
- □ 404 Mark Wohlers .... .10 .05
- □ 405 Rick Aguilera .... .10 .05
- □ 406 Tony Clark .... .30 .14
- □ 407 Lyle Mouton .... .10 .05
- □ 408 Bill Pulsipher .... .10 .05
- □ 409 Jose Rosado .... .10 .05
- □ 410 Tony Gwynn .... 1.00 .45
- □ 411 Cecil Fielder .... .20 .09
- □ 412 John Flaherty .... .10 .05
- □ 413 Lenny Dykstra .... .20 .09
- □ 414 Ugueth Urbina .... .20 .09
- □ 415 Brian Jordan .... .20 .09
- □ 416 Bob Abreu .... .20 .09
- □ 417 Craig Paquette .... .10 .05
- □ 418 Sandy Martinez .... .10 .05
- □ 419 Jeff Blauser .... .10 .05
- □ 420 Barry Larkin .... .40 .18
- □ 421 Kevin Seitzer .... .10 .05
- □ 422 Tim Belcher .... .10 .05
- □ 423 Paul Sorrento .... .10 .05
- □ 424 Cal Eldred .... .10 .05
- □ 425 Robin Ventura .... .20 .09
- □ 426 John Olerud .... .20 .09
- □ 427 Bob Wolcott .... .10 .05
- □ 428 Matt Lawton .... .10 .05
- □ 429 Rod Beck .... .10 .05
- □ 430 Shane Reynolds .... .20 .09
- □ 431 Mike James .... .10 .05
- □ 432 Steve Wojciechowski .... .10 .05
- □ 433 Vladimir Guerrero .... .60 .25
- □ 434 Dustin Hermanson .... .10 .05
- □ 435 Marty Cordova .... .10 .05
- □ 436 Marc Newfield .... .10 .05
- □ 437 Todd Stottlemyre .... .10 .05
- □ 438 Jeffrey Hammonds .... .20 .09
- □ 439 Dave Stevens .... .10 .05
- □ 440 Hideo Nomo .... .40 .18
- □ 441 Mark Thompson .... .10 .05
- □ 442 Mark Lewis .... .10 .05
- □ 443 Quinton McCracken .... .10 .05
- □ 444 Cliff Floyd .... .20 .09
- □ 445 Denny Neagle .... .20 .09
- □ 446 John Jaha .... .10 .05
- □ 447 Mike Sweeney .... .20 .09
- □ 448 John Wasdin .... .10 .05
- □ 449 Chad Curtis .... .10 .05
- □ 450 Mo Vaughn .... .40 .18
- □ 451 Donovan Osborne .... .10 .05
- □ 452 Ruben Sierra .... .10 .05
- □ 453 Michael Tucker .... .10 .05
- □ 454 Kurt Abbott .... .10 .05
- □ 455 Andruw Jones UER .... .50 .23
  Birthdate is incorrectly listed
  as 1-22-67, should be 1-22-77
- □ 456 Shannon Stewart .... .20 .09
- □ 457 Scott Brosius .... .10 .05
- □ 458 Juan Guzman .... .10 .05
- □ 459 Ron Villone .... .10 .05
- □ 460 Moises Alou .... .20 .09
- □ 461 Larry Walker .... .40 .18
- □ 462 Eddie Murray SH .... .20 .09
- □ 463 Paul Molitor SH .... .20 .09
- □ 464 Hideo Nomo SH .... .20 .09
- □ 465 Barry Bonds SH .... .20 .09
- □ 466 Todd Hundley SH .... .10 .05
- □ 467 Rheal Cormier .... .10 .05
- □ 468 Jason Conti .... .75 .35
  Jhensy Sandoval
- □ 469 Rod Barajas .... .75 .35
  Jackie Rexrode
- □ 470 Cedric Bowers .... .75 .35
  Jared Sandberg
- □ 471 Chei Gunner .... .25 .11
  Paul Wilder
- □ 472 Mike Decelle .... .25 .11
  Marcus McCain
- □ 473 Todd Zeile .... .10 .05
- □ 474 Neifi Perez .... .20 .09
- □ 475 Jeromy Burnitz .... .20 .09
- □ 476 Trey Beamon .... .10 .05
- □ 477 Braden Looper .... .60 .25
  John Patterson
- □ 478 Danny Peoples .... .40 .18
  Jake Westbrook
- □ 479 Eric Chavez .... 1.50 .70
  Adam Eaton
- □ 480 Joe Lawrence .... 1.00 .45
  Pete Tucci
- □ 481 Kris Benson .... .60 .25
  Billy Koch
- □ 482 John Nicholson .... .30 .14
  Andy Prater
- □ 483 Mark Johnson .... .60 .25
  Mark Kotsay
- □ 484 Armando Benitez .... .10 .05
- □ 485 Mike Matheny .... .10 .05
- □ 486 Jeff Reed .... .10 .05
- □ 487 Mark Bellhorn .... .20 .09
  Russ Johnson
  Enrique Wilson
- □ 488 Ben Grieve .... .75 .35
  Richard Hidalgo
  Scott Morgan
- □ 489 Paul Konerko .... .40 .18
  Derrek Lee UER
  spelled Derek on back
  Ron Wright
- □ 490 Wes Helms .... .50 .23
  Bill Mueller
  Brad Seitzer
- □ 491 Jeff Abbott .... .20 .09
  Shane Monahan
  Edgard Velazquez
- □ 492 Jimmy Anderson .... .25 .11
  Ron Blazier
  Gerald Witasick
- □ 493 Darin Blood .... .30 .14
  Heath Murray
  Carl Pavano
- □ 494 Nelson Figueroa .... .25 .11
  Mark Redman
  Mike Villano
- □ 495 Checklist .... .10 .05
- □ 496 Checklist .... .10 .05
- □ NNO Derek Jeter AU 100.00 45.00

1997 Topps All-Stars

	MINT	NRMT
COMPLETE SET (22)	60.00	27.00
COMMON CARD (AS1-AS22)	1.50	.70
SER.1 STATED ODDS 1:18 HOB/RET, 1:6 JUM		

		MINT	NRMT
❑ AS1	Ivan Rodriguez	4.00	1.80
❑ AS2	Todd Hundley	1.50	.70
❑ AS3	Frank Thomas	6.00	2.70
❑ AS4	Andres Galarraga	3.00	1.35
❑ AS5	Chuck Knoblauch	3.00	1.35
❑ AS6	Eric Young	1.50	.70
❑ AS7	Jim Thome	3.00	1.35
❑ AS8	Chipper Jones	8.00	3.60
❑ AS9	Cal Ripken	12.00	5.50
❑ AS10	Barry Larkin	3.00	1.35
❑ AS11	Albert Belle	3.00	1.35
❑ AS12	Barry Bonds	4.00	1.80
❑ AS13	Ken Griffey Jr.	15.00	6.75
❑ AS14	Ellis Burks	1.50	.70
❑ AS15	Juan Gonzalez	6.00	2.70
❑ AS16	Gary Sheffield	1.50	.70
❑ AS17	Andy Pettitte	2.00	.90
❑ AS18	Tom Glavine	3.00	1.35
❑ AS19	Pat Hentgen	1.50	.70
❑ AS20	John Smoltz	2.00	.90
❑ AS21	Roberto Hernandez	1.50	.70
❑ AS22	Mark Wohlers	1.50	.70

1997 Topps Awesome Impact

	MINT	NRMT
COMPLETE SET (20)	100.00	45.00
COMMON CARD (AI1-AI20)	1.50	.70
SEMISTARS	3.00	1.35
UNLISTED STARS	5.00	2.20
SER.2 STATED ODDS 1:18 RETAIL		

		MINT	NRMT
❑ AI1	Jaime Bluma	1.50	.70
❑ AI2	Tony Clark	3.00	1.35
❑ AI3	Jermaine Dye	2.50	1.10
❑ AI4	Nomar Garciaparra	20.00	9.00
❑ AI5	Vladimir Guerrero	10.00	4.50
❑ AI6	Todd Hollandsworth	1.50	.70
❑ AI7	Derek Jeter	20.00	9.00
❑ AI8	Andruw Jones	8.00	3.60
❑ AI9	Chipper Jones	15.00	6.75
❑ AI10	Jason Kendall	3.00	1.35

		MINT	NRMT
❑ AI11	Brooks Kieschnick	1.50	.70
❑ AI12	Alex Ochoa	1.50	.70
❑ AI13	Rey Ordonez	2.50	1.10
❑ AI14	Neifi Perez	2.50	1.10
❑ AI15	Edgar Renteria	2.50	1.10
❑ AI16	Mariano Rivera	2.50	1.10
❑ AI17	Ruben Rivera	1.50	.70
❑ AI18	Scott Rolen	10.00	4.50
❑ AI19	Billy Wagner	2.50	1.10
❑ AI20	Todd Walker	5.00	2.20

1997 Topps Hobby Masters

	MINT	NRMT
COMPLETE SET (20)	110.00	50.00
COMPLETE SERIES 1 (10)	60.00	27.00
COMPLETE SERIES 2 (10)	50.00	22.00
COMMON CARD (HM1-HM20)	2.00	.90
STATED ODDS 1:36 HOBBY		

		MINT	NRMT
❑ HM1	Ken Griffey Jr.	15.00	6.75
❑ HM2	Cal Ripken	12.00	5.50
❑ HM3	Greg Maddux	8.00	3.60
❑ HM4	Albert Belle	3.00	1.35
❑ HM5	Tony Gwynn	8.00	3.60
❑ HM6	Jeff Bagwell	4.00	1.80
❑ HM7	Randy Johnson	3.00	1.35
❑ HM8	Raul Mondesi	2.00	.90
❑ HM9	Juan Gonzalez	6.00	2.70
❑ HM10	Kenny Lofton	2.00	.90
❑ HM11	Frank Thomas	6.00	2.70
❑ HM12	Mike Piazza	10.00	4.50
❑ HM13	Chipper Jones	8.00	3.60
❑ HM14	Brady Anderson	2.00	.90
❑ HM15	Ken Caminiti	2.00	.90
❑ HM16	Barry Bonds	4.00	1.80
❑ HM17	Mo Vaughn	3.00	1.35
❑ HM18	Derek Jeter	8.00	3.60
❑ HM19	Sammy Sosa	10.00	4.50
❑ HM20	Andres Galarraga	3.00	1.35

1997 Topps Inter-League Finest

	MINT	NRMT
COMPLETE SET (14)	60.00	27.00
COMMON CARD (ILM1-ILM14)	1.50	.70
UNLISTED STARS	3.00	1.35
SER.1 STATED ODDS 1:36 HOB/RET, 1:10		

JUM		
*REFRACTORS: 1.5X TO 4X HI COLUMN		
REF.SER.1 ODDS 1:216 HOB/RET, 1:56 JUM		

		MINT	NRMT
❑ ILM1	Mark McGwire	15.00	6.75
	Barry Bonds		
❑ ILM2	Tim Salmon	10.00	4.50
	Mike Piazza		
❑ ILM3	Ken Griffey Jr.	15.00	6.75
	Dante Bichette		
❑ ILM4	Juan Gonzalez	8.00	3.60
	Tony Gwynn		
❑ ILM5	Frank Thomas	15.00	6.75
	Sammy Sosa		
❑ ILM6	Albert Belle	4.00	1.80
	Barry Larkin		
❑ ILM7	Johnny Damon	1.50	.70
	Brian Jordan		
❑ ILM8	Paul Molitor	3.00	1.35
	Jeff King		
❑ ILM9	John Jaha	4.00	1.80
	Jeff Bagwell		
❑ ILM10	Bernie Williams		
	Todd Hundley		
❑ ILM11	Joe Carter	1.50	.70
	Henry Rodriguez		
❑ ILM12	Cal Ripken	12.00	5.50
	Gregg Jefferies		
❑ ILM13	Mo Vaughn	10.00	4.50
	Chipper Jones		
❑ ILM14	Travis Fryman	3.00	1.35
	Gary Sheffield		

1997 Topps Mantle

	MINT	NRMT
COMPLETE SET (16)	100.00	45.00
COMMON MANTLE (21-36)	6.00	2.70
SER.1 STATED ODDS 1:12 HOB/RET, 1:3 JUM		
COMP.FINEST SET (16)	100.00	45.00
COMMON FINEST (21-36)	6.00	2.70
FINEST SER.2 ODDS 1:24 HOB/RET, 1:6 JUM		
COMP.REF.SET (16)	400.00	180.00
COMMON REF. (21-36)	25.00	11.00
REF.SER.2 ODDS 1:216 HOB/RET, 1:60 JUM		

		MINT	NRMT
❑ 21	Mickey Mantle	6.00	2.70
	Hank Bauer		
	Yogi Berra		
	1953 Bowman		
❑ 22	Mickey Mantle	6.00	2.70
	1953 Bowman		
❑ 23	Mickey Mantle	6.00	2.70
	Yogi Berra		
	1957 Topps		
❑ 24	Mickey Mantle	6.00	2.70
	Hank Aaron		
	1958 Topps		
❑ 25	Mickey Mantle	6.00	2.70
	1958 Topps AS		
❑ 26	Mickey Mantle	6.00	2.70
	1959 Topps HL		
❑ 27	Mickey Mantle	6.00	2.70
	1959 Topps AS		
❑ 28	Mickey Mantle	6.00	2.70
	Ken Boyer		
	1960 Topps		
❑ 29	Mickey Mantle	6.00	2.70

		MINT	NRMT
❏ 30	Mickey Mantle .... 1960 Topps AS	6.00	2.70
❏ 31	Mickey Mantle .... 1961 Topps HL	6.00	2.70
❏ 32	Mickey Mantle .... 1961 Topps MVP	6.00	2.70
❏ 33	Mickey Mantle .... 1961 Topps AS	6.00	2.70

Willie Mays
1962 Topps
Hank Aaron and Ernie Banks
in background

		MINT	NRMT
❏ 34	Mickey Mantle .... 1962 Topps IA	6.00	2.70
❏ 35	Mickey Mantle .... 1962 AS	6.00	2.70
❏ 36	Mickey Mantle	6.00	2.70

Roger Maris
Al Kaline
Norm Cash
1964 Topps

1997 Topps Mays

	MINT	NRMT
COMPLETE SET (27)	80.00	36.00
COMMON MAYS (1-27)	4.00	1.80
SER.1 STATED ODDS 1:8 HOB/RET, 1:2 JUM		
COMP.FINEST SET (27)	80.00	36.00
COMMON FINEST (1-27)	4.00	1.80
*51-52 FINEST: 4X TO 1X LISTED CARDS		
FINEST SER.2 ODDS 1:20 HOB/RET,1:4 JUM		
COMP.REF.SET (27)	250.00	110.00
COMMON REF. (1-27)	10.00	4.50
*51-52 REF: 1X TO 2.5X LISTED CARDS		
REF.SER.2 ODDS 1:180 HOB/RET,1:48 JUM		

		MINT	NRMT
❏ 1	Willie Mays .... 1951 Bowman	8.00	3.60
❏ 2	Willie Mays .... 1952 Topps	6.00	2.70
❏ 3	Willie Mays .... 1953 Topps	4.00	1.80
❏ 4	Willie Mays .... 1954 Bowman	4.00	1.80
❏ 5	Willie Mays .... 1954 Topps	4.00	1.80
❏ 6	Willie Mays .... 1955 Bowman	4.00	1.80
❏ 7	Willie Mays .... 1955 Topps	4.00	1.80
❏ 8	Willie Mays .... 1956 Topps	4.00	1.80
❏ 9	Willie Mays .... 1957 Topps	4.00	1.80
❏ 10	Willie Mays .... 1958 Topps	4.00	1.80
❏ 11	Willie Mays .... 1959 Topps	4.00	1.80
❏ 12	Willie Mays .... 1960 Topps	4.00	1.80
❏ 13	Willie Mays .... 1960 Topps AS	4.00	1.80
❏ 14	Willie Mays .... 1961 Topps	4.00	1.80
❏ 15	Willie Mays .... 1961 Topps AS	4.00	1.80
❏ 16	Willie Mays .... 1962 Topps	4.00	1.80
❏ 17	Willie Mays .... 1963 Topps	4.00	1.80
❏ 18	Willie Mays .... 1964 Topps	4.00	1.80
❏ 19	Willie Mays .... 1965 Topps	4.00	1.80
❏ 20	Willie Mays .... 1966 Topps	4.00	1.80
❏ 21	Willie Mays .... 1967 Topps	4.00	1.80
❏ 22	Willie Mays .... 1968 Topps	4.00	1.80
❏ 23	Willie Mays .... 1969 Topps	4.00	1.80
❏ 24	Willie Mays .... 1970 Topps	4.00	1.80
❏ 25	Willie Mays .... 1971 Topps	4.00	1.80
❏ 26	Willie Mays .... 1972 Topps	4.00	1.80
❏ 27	Willie Mays .... 1973 Topps	4.00	1.80
❏ J261	Willie Mays 1952 Jumbo	10.00	4.50
❏ NNO	Willie Mays AU	100.00	45.00

1997 Topps Mays Autographs

	MINT	NRMT
COMMON CARD (1-27)	100.00	45.00
SER.1 ODDS 1:2400 HOB/RET, 1:625 JUMBO		

		MINT	NRMT
❏ 1	Willie Mays .... 1951 Bowman		
❏ 2	Willie Mays .... 1952 Topps		
❏ 3	Willie Mays .... 1953 Topps	100.00	45.00
❏ 4	Willie Mays .... 1954 Bowman	100.00	45.00
❏ 5	Willie Mays .... 1954 Topps	100.00	45.00
❏ 6	Willie Mays .... 1955 Bowman	100.00	45.00
❏ 7	Willie Mays .... 1955 Topps	100.00	45.00
❏ 8	Willie Mays .... 1956 Topps	100.00	45.00
❏ 9	Willie Mays .... 1957 Topps	100.00	45.00
❏ 10	Willie Mays .... 1958 Topps	100.00	45.00
❏ 11	Willie Mays .... 1959 Topps	100.00	45.00
❏ 12	Willie Mays .... 1960 Topps	100.00	45.00
❏ 13	Willie Mays .... 1960 Topps AS	100.00	45.00
❏ 14	Willie Mays .... 1961 Topps	100.00	45.00
❏ 15	Willie Mays .... 1961 Topps AS	100.00	45.00
❏ 16	Willie Mays .... 1962 Topps	100.00	45.00
❏ 17	Willie Mays .... 1963 Topps	100.00	45.00
❏ 18	Willie Mays .... 1964 Topps	100.00	45.00
❏ 19	Willie Mays .... 1965 Topps	100.00	45.00
❏ 20	Willie Mays .... 1966 Topps	100.00	45.00
❏ 21	Willie Mays .... 1967 Topps	100.00	45.00
❏ 22	Willie Mays .... 1968 Topps	100.00	45.00
❏ 23	Willie Mays .... 1969 Topps	100.00	45.00
❏ 24	Willie Mays .... 1970 Topps	100.00	45.00
❏ 25	Willie Mays .... 1971 Topps	100.00	45.00
❏ 26	Willie Mays .... 1972 Topps	100.00	45.00
❏ 27	Willie Mays .... 1973 Topps	100.00	45.00

1997 Topps Season's Best

	MINT	NRMT
COMPLETE SET (25)	25.00	11.00
COMMON CARD (SB1-SB25)	.50	.23
SER.2 STATED ODDS 1:6 HOB/RET, 1:1 JUM		

		MINT	NRMT
❏ SB1	Tony Gwynn	2.00	.90
❏ SB2	Frank Thomas	3.00	1.35
❏ SB3	Ellis Burks	.75	.35
❏ SB4	Paul Molitor	1.50	.70
❏ SB5	Chuck Knoblauch	1.50	.70
❏ SB6	Mark McGwire	8.00	3.60
❏ SB7	Brady Anderson	.75	.35
❏ SB8	Ken Griffey Jr.	8.00	3.60
❏ SB9	Albert Belle	1.50	.70
❏ SB10	Andres Galarraga	1.50	.70
❏ SB11	Andres Galarraga	1.50	.70
❏ SB12	Albert Belle	1.50	.70
❏ SB13	Juan Gonzalez	3.00	1.35
❏ SB14	Mo Vaughn	1.50	.70
❏ SB15	Rafael Palmeiro	1.50	.70
❏ SB16	John Smoltz	1.00	.45
❏ SB17	Andy Pettitte	1.00	.45
❏ SB18	Pat Hentgen	.75	.35
❏ SB19	Mike Mussina	1.50	.70
❏ SB20	Andy Benes	.75	.35
❏ SB21	Kenny Lofton	1.00	.45
❏ SB22	Tom Goodwin	.50	.23
❏ SB23	Otis Nixon	.50	.23
❏ SB24	Eric Young	.50	.23
❏ SB25	Lance Johnson	.50	.23

1997 Topps Sweet Strokes

	MINT	NRMT
COMPLETE SET (15)	40.00	18.00
COMMON CARD (SS1-SS15) ..	1.25	.55
SER.1 STATED ODDS 1:12 RETAIL		

		MINT	NRMT
❏ SS1	Roberto Alomar	2.00	.90
❏ SS2	Jeff Bagwell	2.50	1.10
❏ SS3	Albert Belle	2.00	.90
❏ SS4	Barry Bonds	2.50	1.10
❏ SS5	Mark Grace	1.50	.70

			MINT	NRMT
❏	SS6	Ken Griffey Jr.	10.00	4.50
❏	SS7	Tony Gwynn	5.00	2.20
❏	SS8	Chipper Jones	5.00	2.20
❏	SS9	Edgar Martinez	1.25	.55
❏	SS10	Mark McGwire	10.00	4.50
❏	SS11	Rafael Palmeiro	2.00	.90
❏	SS12	Mike Piazza	6.00	2.70
❏	SS13	Gary Sheffield	1.25	.55
❏	SS14	Frank Thomas	4.00	1.80
❏	SS15	Mo Vaughn	2.00	.90

1997 Topps Team Timber

	MINT	NRMT
COMPLETE SET (16)	50.00	22.00
COMMON CARD (TT1-TT16)	1.50	.70
SER.2 STATED ODDS 1:36 HOB/RET, 1:8 JUM		

❏	TT1	Ken Griffey Jr.	12.00	5.50
❏	TT2	Ken Caminiti	2.00	.90
❏	TT3	Bernie Williams	2.50	1.10
❏	TT4	Jeff Bagwell	3.00	1.35
❏	TT5	Frank Thomas	5.00	2.20
❏	TT6	Andres Galarraga	2.50	1.10
❏	TT7	Barry Bonds	3.00	1.35
❏	TT8	Rafael Palmeiro	2.50	1.10
❏	TT9	Brady Anderson	1.50	.70
❏	TT10	Juan Gonzalez	5.00	2.20
❏	TT11	Mo Vaughn	2.50	1.10
❏	TT12	Mark McGwire	12.00	5.50
❏	TT13	Gary Sheffield	2.00	.90
❏	TT14	Albert Belle	2.50	1.10
❏	TT15	Chipper Jones	6.00	2.70
❏	TT16	Mike Piazza	8.00	3.60

1998 Topps

	MINT	NRMT
COMPLETE SET (503)	50.00	22.00
COMPLETE SERIES 1 (282)	25.00	11.00
COMPLETE SERIES 2 (221)	25.00	11.00
COMP.HOBBY SET (511)	80.00	36.00
COMP.RETAIL SET (511)	80.00	36.00
COMMON CARD (1-504)	.10	.05
MINOR STARS	.15	.07
SEMISTARS	.25	.11
UNLISTED STARS	.40	.18
SUBSET CARDS HALF VALUE OF BASE CARDS		

COMP.MINTED SET (503)	700.00	325.00
COMP.MINTED SER.1 (282)	350.00	160.00
COMP.MINTED SER.2 (221)	350.00	160.00
COMMON MINTED (1-504)	1.00	.45
*MINTED STARS: 6X TO 12X HI COLUMN		
*MINTED YOUNG STARS: 5X TO 10X HI		
*MINTED ROOKIES/PROSPECTS: 4X TO 8X HI		
MINTED STATED ODDS: 1:8		
COMP.OPEN.DAY SET (165)	50.00	22.00
COMMON OPEN.DAY (1-165)	.20	.09
*OPEN.DAY STARS: 1X TO 2X HI COLUMN		
CARD NUMBER 7 DOES NOT EXIST		

❏	1	Tony Gwynn	1.00	.45
❏	2	Larry Walker	.40	.18
❏	3	Billy Wagner	.15	.07
❏	4	Denny Neagle	.10	.05
❏	5	Vladimir Guerrero	.50	.23
❏	6	Kevin Brown	.25	.11
❏	8	Mariano Rivera	.15	.07
❏	9	Tony Clark	.15	.07
❏	10	Deion Sanders	.15	.07
❏	11	Francisco Cordova	.10	.05
❏	12	Matt Williams	.40	.18
❏	13	Carlos Baerga	.10	.05
❏	14	Mo Vaughn	.40	.18
❏	15	Bobby Witt	.10	.05
❏	16	Matt Stairs	.10	.05
❏	17	Chan Ho Park	.15	.07
❏	18	Mike Bordick	.10	.05
❏	19	Michael Tucker	.10	.05
❏	20	Frank Thomas	.75	.35
❏	21	Roberto Clemente	1.00	.45
❏	22	Dmitri Young	.15	.07
❏	23	Steve Trachsel	.10	.05
❏	24	Jeff Kent	.15	.07
❏	25	Scott Rolen	.50	.23
❏	26	John Thomson	.10	.05
❏	27	Joe Vitiello	.10	.05
❏	28	Eddie Guardado	.10	.05
❏	29	Charlie Hayes	.10	.05
❏	30	Juan Gonzalez	.75	.35
❏	31	Garret Anderson	.15	.07
❏	32	John Jaha	.10	.05
❏	33	Omar Vizquel	.15	.07
❏	34	Brian Hunter	.10	.05
❏	35	Jeff Bagwell	.50	.23
❏	36	Mark Lemke	.10	.05
❏	37	Doug Glanville	.15	.07
❏	38	Dan Wilson	.10	.05
❏	39	Steve Cooke	.10	.05
❏	40	Chili Davis	.15	.07
❏	41	Mike Cameron	.15	.07
❏	42	F.P. Santangelo	.10	.05
❏	43	Brad Ausmus	.10	.05
❏	44	Gary DiSarcina	.10	.05
❏	45	Pat Hentgen	.10	.05
❏	46	Wilton Guerrero	.10	.05
❏	47	Devon White	.10	.05
❏	48	Danny Patterson	.10	.05
❏	49	Pat Meares	.10	.05
❏	50	Rafael Palmeiro	.40	.18
❏	51	Mark Gardner	.10	.05
❏	52	Jeff Blauser	.10	.05
❏	53	Dave Hollins	.10	.05
❏	54	Carlos Garcia	.10	.05
❏	55	Ben McDonald	.10	.05
❏	56	John Mabry	.10	.05
❏	57	Trevor Hoffman	.15	.07
❏	58	Tony Fernandez	.15	.07
❏	59	Rich Loiselle	.15	.07
❏	60	Mark Leiter	.10	.05
❏	61	Pat Kelly	.10	.05
❏	62	John Flaherty	.10	.05
❏	63	Roger Bailey	.10	.05
❏	64	Tom Gordon	.15	.07
❏	65	Ryan Klesko	.15	.07
❏	66	Darryl Hamilton	.10	.05
❏	67	Jim Eisenreich	.10	.05
❏	68	Butch Huskey	.10	.05
❏	69	Mark Grudzielanek	.10	.05
❏	70	Marquis Grissom	.10	.05
❏	71	Mark McLemore	.10	.05
❏	72	Gary Gaetti	.15	.07
❏	73	Greg Gagne	.10	.05
❏	74	Lyle Mouton	.10	.05
❏	75	Jim Edmonds	.15	.07
❏	76	Shawn Green	.40	.18
❏	77	Greg Vaughn	.15	.07
❏	78	Terry Adams	.10	.05
❏	79	Kevin Polcovich	.10	.05
❏	80	Troy O'Leary	.15	.07
❏	81	Jeff Shaw	.10	.05
❏	82	Rich Becker	.10	.05
❏	83	David Wells	.15	.07
❏	84	Steve Karsay	.10	.05
❏	85	Charles Nagy	.15	.07
❏	86	B.J. Surhoff	.10	.05
❏	87	Jamey Wright	.10	.05
❏	88	James Baldwin	.10	.05
❏	89	Edgardo Alfonzo	.25	.11
❏	90	Jay Buhner	.15	.07
❏	91	Brady Anderson	.15	.07
❏	92	Scott Servais	.10	.05
❏	93	Edgar Renteria	.10	.05
❏	94	Mike Lieberthal	.15	.07
❏	95	Rick Aguilera	.10	.05
❏	96	Walt Weiss	.15	.07
❏	97	Deivi Cruz	.10	.05
❏	98	Kurt Abbott	.10	.05
❏	99	Henry Rodriguez	.15	.07
❏	100	Mike Piazza	1.25	.55
❏	101	Bill Taylor	.10	.05
❏	102	Todd Zeile	.15	.07
❏	103	Rey Ordonez	.15	.07
❏	104	Willie Greene	.10	.05
❏	105	Tony Womack	.10	.05
❏	106	Mike Sweeney	.15	.07
❏	107	Jeffrey Hammonds	.10	.05
❏	108	Kevin Orie	.10	.05
❏	109	Alex Gonzalez	.10	.05
❏	110	Jose Canseco	.50	.23
❏	111	Paul Sorrento	.10	.05
❏	112	Joey Hamilton	.10	.05
❏	113	Brad Radke	.15	.07
❏	114	Steve Avery	.10	.05
❏	115	Esteban Loaiza	.10	.05
❏	116	Stan Javier	.10	.05
❏	117	Chris Gomez	.10	.05
❏	118	Royce Clayton	.10	.05
❏	119	Orlando Merced	.10	.05
❏	120	Kevin Appier	.15	.07
❏	121	Mel Nieves	.10	.05
❏	122	Joe Girardi	.10	.05
❏	123	Rico Brogna	.10	.05
❏	124	Kent Mercker	.10	.05
❏	125	Manny Ramirez	.50	.23
❏	126	Jeromy Burnitz	.15	.07
❏	127	Kevin Foster	.10	.05
❏	128	Matt Morris	.10	.05
❏	129	Jason Dickson	.10	.05
❏	130	Tom Glavine	.40	.18
❏	131	Wally Joyner	.15	.07
❏	132	Rick Reed	.10	.05
❏	133	Todd Jones	.10	.05
❏	134	Dave Martinez	.10	.05
❏	135	Sandy Alomar Jr.	.15	.07
❏	136	Mike Lansing	.10	.05
❏	137	Sean Berry	.10	.05
❏	138	Doug Jones	.10	.05
❏	139	Todd Stottlemyre	.10	.05
❏	140	Jay Bell	.15	.07
❏	141	Jaime Navarro	.10	.05
❏	142	Chris Hoiles	.10	.05

143	Joey Cora	.10	.05
144	Scott Spiezio	.10	.05
145	Joe Carter	.15	.07
146	Jose Guillen	.10	.05
147	Damion Easley	.15	.07
148	Lee Stevens	.10	.05
149	Alex Fernandez	.10	.05
150	Randy Johnson	.40	.18
151	J.T. Snow	.10	.05
152	Chuck Finley	.15	.07
153	Bernard Gilkey	.10	.05
154	David Segui	.10	.05
155	Dante Bichette	.10	.05
156	Kevin Stocker	.10	.05
157	Carl Everett	.15	.07
158	Jose Valentin	.10	.05
159	Pokey Reese	.10	.05
160	Derek Jeter	1.25	.55
161	Roger Pavlik	.10	.05
162	Mark Wohlers	.10	.05
163	Ricky Bottalico	.10	.05
164	Ozzie Guillen	.10	.05
165	Mike Mussina	.40	.18
166	Gary Sheffield	.15	.07
167	Hideo Nomo	.40	.18
168	Mark Grace	.25	.11
169	Aaron Sele	.10	.05
170	Darryl Kile	.10	.05
171	Shawn Estes	.10	.05
172	Vinny Castilla	.15	.07
173	Ron Coomer	.10	.05
174	Jose Rosado	.10	.05
175	Kenny Lofton	.25	.11
176	Jason Giambi	.15	.07
177	Hal Morris	.10	.05
178	Darren Bragg	.10	.05
179	Orel Hershiser	.15	.07
180	Ray Lankford	.15	.07
181	Hideki Irabu	.15	.07
182	Kevin Young	.10	.05
183	Javy Lopez	.15	.07
184	Jeff Montgomery	.10	.05
185	Mike Holtz	.10	.05
186	George Williams	.10	.05
187	Cal Eldred	.10	.05
188	Tom Candiotti	.10	.05
189	Glenallen Hill	.10	.05
190	Brian Giles	.15	.07
191	Dave Mlicki	.10	.06
192	Garrett Stephenson	.10	.05
193	Jeff Frye	.10	.05
194	Joe Oliver	.10	.05
195	Bob Hamelin	.10	.05
196	Luis Sojo	.10	.05
197	LaTroy Hawkins	.10	.05
198	Kevin Elster	.10	.05
199	Jeff Reed	.10	.05
200	Dennis Eckersley	.15	.07
201	Bill Mueller	.10	.05
202	Russ Davis	.15	.07
203	Armando Benitez	.10	.05
204	Quilvio Veras	.10	.05
205	Tim Naehring	.10	.05
206	Quinton McCracken	.10	.05
207	Raul Casanova	.10	.05
208	Matt Lawton	.10	.05
209	Luis Alicea	.10	.05
210	Luis Gonzalez	.15	.07
211	Allen Watson	.10	.05
212	Gerald Williams	.10	.05
213	David Bell	.10	.05
214	Todd Hollandsworth	.10	.05
215	Wade Boggs	.40	.18
216	Jose Mesa	.10	.05
217	Jamie Moyer	.10	.05
218	Darren Daulton	.15	.07
219	Mickey Morandini	.10	.05
220	Rusty Greer	.15	.07
221	Jim Bullinger	.10	.05
222	Jose Offerman	.10	.05
223	Matt Karchner	.10	.05
224	Woody Williams	.10	.05
225	Mark Loretta	.10	.05
226	Mike Hampton	.15	.07
227	Willie Adams	.10	.05
228	Scott Hatteberg	.10	.05
229	Rich Amaral	.10	.05
230	Terry Steinbach	.10	.05
231	Glendon Rusch	.10	.05
232	Bret Boone	.15	.07
233	Robert Person	.10	.05
234	Jose Hernandez	.10	.05
235	Doug Drabek	.10	.05
236	Jason McDonald	.10	.05
237	Chris Widger	.10	.05
238	Tom Martin	.10	.05
239	Dave Burba	.10	.05
240	Pete Rose Jr.	.15	.07
241	Bobby Ayala	.10	.05
242	Tim Wakefield	.10	.05
243	Dennis Springer	.10	.05
244	Tim Belcher	.10	.05
245	Jon Garland	.10	.05
	Geoff Goetz		
246	Glenn Davis	.25	.11
	Lance Berkman		
247	Vernon Wells	.25	.11
	Aaron Akin		
248	Adam Kennedy	.15	.07
	Jason Romano		
249	Jason Dellaero	.15	.07
	Troy Cameron		
250	Alex Sanchez	.15	.07
	Jared Sandberg		
251	Pablo Ortega	.10	.05
	James Manias		
252	Jason Conti	.25	.11
	Mike Stoner		
253	John Patterson	.15	.07
	Larry Rodriguez		
254	Adrian Beltre	.75	.35
	Ryan Minor		
	Aaron Boone		
255	Ben Grieve	.50	.23
	Brian Buchanan		
	Dermal Brown		
256	Kerry Wood	.50	.23
	Carl Pavano		
	Gil Meche		
257	David Ortiz	.15	.07
	Daryle Ward		
	Richie Sexson		
258	Randy Winn	.15	.07
	Juan Encarnacion		
	Andrew Vessel		
259	Kris Benson	.25	.11
	Travis Smith		
	Courtney Duncan		
260	Chad Hermansen	.75	.35
	Brent Butler		
	Warren Morris		
261	Ben Davis	.25	.11
	Eli Marrero		
	Ramon Hernandez		
262	Eric Chavez	.40	.18
	Russell Branyan		
	Russ Johnson		
263	Todd Dunwoody	.25	.11
	John Barnes		
	Ryan Jackson		
264	Matt Clement	.25	.11
	Roy Halladay		
	Brian Fuentes		
265	Randy Johnson SH	.15	.07
266	Kevin Brown SH	.15	.07
267	Ricardo Rincon SH	.10	.05
	Francisco Cordova		
268	Nomar Garciaparra SH	.60	.25
269	Tino Martinez SH	.15	.07
270	Chuck Knoblauch IL	.10	.05
271	Pedro Martinez IL	.25	.11
272	Denny Neagle IL	.10	.05
273	Juan Gonzalez IL	.40	.18
274	Andres Galarraga IL	.15	.07
275	Checklist	.10	.05
276	Checklist	.10	.05
277	Moises Alou WS	.15	.07
278	Sandy Alomar Jr. WS	.10	.05
279	Gary Sheffield WS	.15	.07
280	Matt Williams WS	.15	.07
281	Livan Hernandez WS	.10	.05
282	Chad Ogea WS	.10	.05
283	Marlins Champs	.10	.05
284	Tino Martinez	.15	.07
285	Roberto Alomar	.40	.18
286	Jeff King	.10	.05
287	Brian Jordan	.15	.07
288	Darin Erstad	.25	.11
289	Ken Caminiti	.15	.07
290	Jim Thome	.40	.18
291	Paul Molitor	.40	.18
292	Ivan Rodriguez	.50	.23
293	Bernie Williams	.40	.18
294	Todd Hundley	.15	.07
295	Andres Galarraga	.25	.11
296	Greg Maddux	1.00	.45
297	Edgar Martinez	.15	.07
298	Ron Gant	.15	.07
299	Steve Finley	.15	.07
300	Roger Clemens	1.00	.45
301	Rondell White	.15	.07
302	Barry Larkin	.40	.18
303	Robin Ventura	.15	.07
304	Jason Kendall	.15	.07
305	Chipper Jones	1.00	.45
306	John Franco	.15	.07
307	Sammy Sosa	1.25	.55
308	Troy Percival	.15	.07
309	Chuck Knoblauch	.15	.07
310	Ellis Burks	.15	.07
311	Al Martin	.10	.05
312	Tim Salmon	.25	.11
313	Moises Alou	.15	.07
314	Lance Johnson	.10	.05
315	Justin Thompson	.10	.05
316	Will Clark	.40	.18
317	Barry Bonds	.50	.23
318	Craig Biggio	.40	.18
319	John Smoltz	.25	.11
320	Cal Ripken	1.50	.70
321	Ken Griffey Jr.	2.00	.90
322	Paul O'Neill	.15	.07
323	Todd Helton	.50	.23
324	John Olerud	.15	.07
325	Mark McGwire	2.50	1.10
326	Jose Cruz Jr.	.15	.07
327	Jeff Cirillo	.15	.07
328	Dean Palmer	.15	.07
329	John Wetteland	.15	.07
330	Steve Finley	.15	.07
331	Albert Belle	.40	.18
332	Curt Schilling	.25	.11
333	Raul Mondesi	.15	.07
334	Andruw Jones	.40	.18
335	Nomar Garciaparra	1.25	.55
336	David Justice	.15	.07
337	Andy Pettitte	.15	.07
338	Pedro Martinez	.50	.23
339	Travis Miller	.10	.05
340	Chris Stynes	.10	.05
341	Gregg Jefferies	.10	.05
342	Jeff Fassero	.10	.05
343	Craig Counsell	.10	.05
344	Wilson Alvarez	.10	.05
345	Bip Roberts	.10	.05
346	Kelvim Escobar	.15	.07
347	Mark Bellhorn	.10	.05
348	Cory Lidle	.10	.05
349	Fred McGriff	.25	.11
350	Chuck Carr	.10	.05
351	Bob Abreu	.15	.07
352	Juan Guzman	.10	.05
353	Fernando Vina	.10	.05
354	Andy Benes	.15	.07
355	Dave Nilsson	.10	.05
356	Bobby Bonilla	.15	.07
357	Ismael Valdes	.10	.05
358	Carlos Perez	.10	.05
359	Kirk Rueter	.10	.05
360	Bartolo Colon	.15	.07
361	Mel Rojas	.10	.05
362	Johnny Damon	.15	.07
363	Geronimo Berroa	.10	.05
364	Reggie Sanders	.10	.05
365	Jermaine Allensworth	.10	.05
366	Orlando Cabrera	.10	.05
367	Jorge Fabregas	.10	.05
368	Scott Stahoviak	.10	.05

❑ 369 Ken Cloude	.10	.05
❑ 370 Donovan Osborne	.10	.05
❑ 371 Roger Cedeno	.15	.07
❑ 372 Neifi Perez	.15	.07
❑ 373 Chris Holt	.10	.05
❑ 374 Cecil Fielder	.15	.07
❑ 375 Marty Cordova	.10	.05
❑ 376 Tom Goodwin	.10	.05
❑ 377 Jeff Suppan	.10	.05
❑ 378 Jeff Brantley	.10	.05
❑ 379 Mark Langston	.10	.05
❑ 380 Shane Reynolds	.15	.07
❑ 381 Mike Fetters	.10	.05
❑ 382 Todd Greene	.10	.05
❑ 383 Ray Durham	.15	.07
❑ 384 Carlos Delgado	.40	.18
❑ 385 Jeff D'Amico	.10	.05
❑ 386 Brian McRae	.10	.05
❑ 387 Alan Benes	.10	.05
❑ 388 Heathcliff Slocumb	.10	.05
❑ 389 Eric Young	.10	.05
❑ 390 Travis Fryman	.15	.07
❑ 391 David Cone	.25	.11
❑ 392 Otis Nixon	.10	.05
❑ 393 Jeremi Gonzalez	.10	.05
❑ 394 Jeff Juden	.10	.05
❑ 395 Jose Vizcaino	.10	.05
❑ 396 Ugueth Urbina	.10	.05
❑ 397 Ramon Martinez	.10	.05
❑ 398 Robb Nen	.10	.05
❑ 399 Harold Baines	.15	.07
❑ 400 Delino DeShields	.10	.05
❑ 401 John Burkett	.10	.05
❑ 402 Sterling Hitchcock	.10	.05
❑ 403 Mark Clark	.10	.05
❑ 404 Terrell Wade	.10	.05
❑ 405 Scott Brosius	.15	.07
❑ 406 Chad Curtis	.10	.05
❑ 407 Brian Johnson	.10	.05
❑ 408 Roberto Kelly	.10	.05
❑ 409 Dave Dellucci	.30	.14
❑ 410 Michael Tucker	.10	.05
❑ 411 Mark Kotsay	.15	.07
❑ 412 Mark Lewis	.10	.05
❑ 413 Ryan McGuire	.10	.05
❑ 414 Shawon Dunston	.10	.05
❑ 415 Brad Rigby	.10	.05
❑ 416 Scott Erickson	.10	.05
❑ 417 Bobby Jones	.10	.05
❑ 418 Darren Oliver	.10	.05
❑ 419 John Smiley	.10	.05
❑ 420 T.J. Mathews	.10	.05
❑ 421 Dustin Hermanson	.10	.05
❑ 422 Mike Timlin	.10	.05
❑ 423 Willie Blair	.10	.05
❑ 424 Manny Alexander	.10	.05
❑ 425 Bob Tewksbury	.10	.05
❑ 426 Pete Schourek	.10	.05
❑ 427 Reggie Jefferson	.10	.05
❑ 428 Ed Sprague	.10	.05
❑ 429 Jeff Conine	.10	.05
❑ 430 Roberto Hernandez	.10	.05
❑ 431 Tom Pagnozzi	.10	.05
❑ 432 Jaret Wright	.15	.07
❑ 433 Livan Hernandez	.10	.05
❑ 434 Andy Ashby	.10	.05
❑ 435 Todd Dunn	.10	.05
❑ 436 Bobby Higginson	.15	.07
❑ 437 Rod Beck	.15	.07
❑ 438 Jim Leyritz	.10	.05
❑ 439 Matt Williams	.40	.18
❑ 440 Brett Tomko	.10	.05
❑ 441 Joe Randa	.10	.05
❑ 442 Chris Carpenter	.15	.07
❑ 443 Dennis Reyes	.10	.05
❑ 444 Al Leiter	.15	.07
❑ 445 Jason Schmidt	.10	.05
❑ 446 Ken Hill	.10	.05
❑ 447 Shannon Stewart	.15	.07
❑ 448 Enrique Wilson	.10	.05
❑ 449 Fernando Tatis	.40	.18
❑ 450 Jimmy Key	.15	.07
❑ 451 Darrin Fletcher	.10	.05
❑ 452 John Valentin	.15	.07
❑ 453 Kevin Tapani	.10	.05
❑ 454 Eric Karros	.15	.07

❑ 455 Jay Bell	.15	.07
❑ 456 Walt Weiss	.15	.07
❑ 457 Devon White	.10	.05
❑ 458 Carl Pavano	.10	.05
❑ 459 Mike Lansing	.10	.05
❑ 460 John Flaherty	.10	.05
❑ 461 Richard Hidalgo	.15	.07
❑ 462 Quinton McCracken	.10	.05
❑ 463 Karim Garcia	.10	.05
❑ 464 Miguel Cairo	.10	.05
❑ 465 Edwin Diaz	.10	.05
❑ 466 Bobby Smith	.10	.05
❑ 467 Yamil Benitez	.10	.05
❑ 468 Rich Butler	.25	.11
❑ 469 Ben Ford	.25	.11
❑ 470 Bubba Trammell	.10	.05
❑ 471 Brent Brede	.10	.05
❑ 472 Brooks Kieschnick	.10	.05
❑ 473 Carlos Castillo	.10	.05
❑ 474 Brad Radke SH	.10	.05
❑ 475 Roger Clemens SH	.40	.18
❑ 476 Curt Schilling SH	.15	.07
❑ 477 John Olerud SH	.10	.05
❑ 478 Mark McGwire SH	1.25	.55
❑ 479 Mike Piazza	1.00	.45
Ken Griffey Jr. IL		
❑ 480 Jeff Bagwell	.25	.11
Frank Thomas IL		
❑ 481 Chipper Jones	.60	.25
Nomar Garciaparra IL		
❑ 482 Larry Walker	.25	.11
Juan Gonzalez IL		
❑ 483 Gary Sheffield	.10	.05
Tino Martinez IL		
❑ 484 Derrick Gibson	.15	.07
Michael Coleman		
Norm Hutchins		
❑ 485 Braden Looper	.10	.05
Cliff Politte		
Brian Rose		
❑ 486 Eric Milton	.15	.07
Jason Marquis		
Corey Lee		
❑ 487 A.J. Hinch	.40	.18
Mark Osborne		
Robert Fick		
❑ 488 Aramis Ramirez	.60	.25
Alex Gonzalez		
Sean Casey		
❑ 489 Donnie Bridges	.25	.11
Tim Drew		
❑ 490 Ntema Ndungidi	.75	.35
Darnell McDonald		
❑ 491 Ryan Anderson	.75	.35
Mark Mangum		
❑ 492 J.J.Davis	1.50	.70
Troy Glaus		
❑ 493 Jayson Werth	.30	.14
Dan Reichert		
❑ 494 John Curtice	.60	.25
Michael Cuddyer		
❑ 495 Jack Cust	.75	.35
Jason Standridge		
❑ 496 Brian Anderson	.10	.05
❑ 497 Tony Saunders	.10	.05
❑ 498 Vladimir Nunez	.15	.07
Jhensy Sandoval		
❑ 499 Brad Penny	.15	.07
Nick Bierbrodt		
❑ 500 Dustin Carr	.25	.11
Luis Cruz		
❑ 501 Cedric Bowers	.15	.07
Marcus McCain		
❑ 502 Checklist	.10	.05
❑ 503 Checklist	.10	.05
❑ 504 Alex Rodriguez	2.50	1.10

1998 Topps Baby Boomers

MARK KOTSAY

	MINT	NRMT
COMPLETE SET (15)	50.00	22.00
COMMON CARD (BB1-BB15)	1.00	.45
SER.1 STATED ODDS 1:36 RETAIL		
❑ BB1 Derek Jeter	12.00	5.50
❑ BB2 Scott Rolen	6.00	2.70
❑ BB3 Nomar Garciaparra	12.00	5.50
❑ BB4 Jose Cruz Jr.	1.50	.70
❑ BB5 Darin Erstad	2.50	1.10
❑ BB6 Todd Helton	4.00	1.80
❑ BB7 Tony Clark	1.50	.70
❑ BB8 Jose Guillen	1.00	.45
❑ BB9 Andruw Jones	4.00	1.80
❑ BB10 Vladimir Guerrero	5.00	2.20
❑ BB11 Mark Kotsay	1.50	.70
❑ BB12 Todd Greene	1.00	.45
❑ BB13 Andy Pettitte	1.50	.70
❑ BB14 Jason Thompson	1.00	.45
❑ BB15 Alan Benes	1.00	.45

1998 Topps Clemente

	MINT	NRMT
COMPLETE SET (19)	110.00	50.00
COMPLETE SERIES 1 (10)	60.00	27.00
COMPLETE SERIES 2 (9)	50.00	22.00
COMMON CARD (1-19)	6.00	2.70
STATED ODDS 1:18		
ODD NUMBERS IN 1ST SERIES PACKS		
EVEN NUMBERS IN 2ND SERIES PACKS		
❑ 1 Roberto Clemente 1955	12.00	5.50
❑ 2 Roberto Clemente 1956	6.00	2.70
❑ 3 Roberto Clemente 1957	6.00	2.70
❑ 4 Roberto Clemente 1958	6.00	2.70
❑ 5 Roberto Clemente 1959	6.00	2.70
❑ 6 Roberto Clemente 1960	6.00	2.70
❑ 7 Roberto Clemente 1961	6.00	2.70
❑ 8 Roberto Clemente 1962	6.00	2.70
❑ 9 Roberto Clemente 1963	6.00	2.70
❑ 10 Roberto Clemente 1964	6.00	2.70
❑ 11 Roberto Clemente 1965	6.00	2.70
❑ 12 Roberto Clemente 1966	6.00	2.70
❑ 13 Roberto Clemente 1967	6.00	2.70
❑ 14 Roberto Clemente 1968	6.00	2.70
❑ 15 Roberto Clemente 1969	6.00	2.70
❑ 16 Roberto Clemente 1970	6.00	2.70
❑ 17 Roberto Clemente 1971	6.00	2.70
❑ 18 Roberto Clemente 1972	6.00	2.70
❑ 19 Roberto Clemente 1973	6.00	2.70

1998 Topps Clemente Finest

	MINT	NRMT
COMPLETE SET (19)	180.00	80.00
COMPLETE SERIES 1 (9)	80.00	36.00
COMPLETE SERIES 2 (10)	100.00	45.00
COMMON CARD (1-19)	12.00	5.50

STATED ODDS 1:72
COMP.REF.SET (19) 450.00 200.00
COMP.REF.SER.1 (9) 200.00 90.00
COMP.REF.SER.2 (10) 250.00 110.00
COMMON REF. (1-19) 30.00 13.50
*1955 REF: 1.25X TO 2.5X 1955 FINEST
REFRACTOR STATED ODDS 1:288
EVEN NUMBERS IN 1ST SERIES PACKS
ODD NUMBERS IN 2ND SERIES PACKS

❏ 1 Roberto Clemente 1955 25.00 11.00

1998 Topps Clemente Tribute

	MINT	NRMT
COMPLETE SET (5)	8.00	3.60
COMMON CARD (RC1-RC5)	2.00	.90

SER.1 STATED ODDS 1:12

❏ RC1 Roberto Clemente ...... 2.00 .90
  Picking Bat from Rack
❏ RC2 Roberto Clemente ...... 2.00 .90
  Posed batting shot
❏ RC3 Roberto Clemente ...... 2.00 .90
  Follow through on swing
❏ RC4 Roberto Clemente ...... 2.00 .90
  Portrait
❏ RC5 Roberto Clemente ...... 2.00 .90

1998 Topps Clout Nine

	MINT	NRMT
COMPLETE SET (9)	70.00	32.00
COMMON CARD (C1-C9)	1.00	.45

SER.2 STATED ODDS 1:72

❏ C1 Edgar Martinez ...... 2.00 .90
❏ C2 Mike Piazza 15.00 6.75
❏ C3 Frank Thomas 10.00 4.50
❏ C4 Craig Biggio 5.00 2.20
❏ C5 Vinny Castilla ...... 2.00 .90

❏ C6 Jeff Blauser ...... 1.00 .45
❏ C7 Barry Bonds 6.00 2.70
❏ C8 Ken Griffey Jr. 25.00 11.00
❏ C9 Larry Walker 5.00 2.20

1998 Topps Etch-A-Sketch

	MINT	NRMT
COMPLETE SET (9)	50.00	22.00
COMMON CARD (ES1-ES9)	2.00	.90

SER.1 STATED ODDS 1:36

❏ ES1 Albert Belle ...... 2.00 .90
❏ ES2 Barry Bonds 3.00 1.35
❏ ES3 Ken Griffey Jr. 12.00 5.50
❏ ES4 Greg Maddux 6.00 2.70
❏ ES5 Hideo Nomo ...... 2.00 .90
❏ ES6 Mike Piazza 8.00 3.60
❏ ES7 Cal Ripken 10.00 4.50
❏ ES8 Frank Thomas 5.00 2.20
❏ ES9 Mo Vaughn ...... 2.00 .90

1998 Topps Flashback

	MINT	NRMT
COMPLETE SET (10)	80.00	36.00
COMMON CARD (FB1-FB10)	2.50	1.10

SER.1 STATED ODDS 1:72

❏ FB1 Barry Bonds 8.00 3.60
❏ FB2 Ken Griffey Jr. 30.00 13.50
❏ FB3 Paul Molitor 6.00 2.70

❏ FB4 Randy Johnson 6.00 2.70
❏ FB5 Cal Ripken 25.00 11.00
❏ FB6 Tony Gwynn 15.00 6.75
❏ FB7 Kenny Lofton 4.00 1.80
❏ FB8 Gary Sheffield 2.50 1.10
❏ FB9 Deion Sanders 2.50 1.10
❏ FB10 Brady Anderson 2.50 1.10

1998 Topps Focal Points

	MINT	NRMT
COMPLETE SET (15)	120.00	55.00
COMMON CARD (FP1-FP15)	1.50	.70

SER.2 STATED ODDS 1:36 HOBBY

❏ FP1 Juan Gonzalez 8.00 3.60
❏ FP2 Nomar Garciaparra 12.00 5.50
❏ FP3 Jose Cruz Jr. ...... 1.50 .70
❏ FP4 Cal Ripken 15.00 6.75
❏ FP5 Ken Griffey Jr. 20.00 9.00
❏ FP6 Ivan Rodriguez 5.00 2.20
❏ FP7 Larry Walker 4.00 1.80
❏ FP8 Barry Bonds 5.00 2.20
❏ FP9 Roger Clemens 10.00 4.50
❏ FP10 Frank Thomas 8.00 3.60
❏ FP11 Chuck Knoblauch ...... 1.50 .70
❏ FP12 Mike Piazza 12.00 5.50
❏ FP13 Greg Maddux 10.00 4.50
❏ FP14 Vladimir Guerrero 5.00 2.20
❏ FP15 Andruw Jones 4.00 1.80

1998 Topps HallBound

	MINT	NRMT
COMPLETE SET (15)	100.00	45.00
COMMON CARD (HB1-HB15)	1.50	.70

SER.1 STATED ODDS 1:36 HOBBY

❏ HB1 Paul Molitor 4.00 1.80
❏ HB2 Tony Gwynn 10.00 4.50
❏ HB3 Wade Boggs 4.00 1.80
❏ HB4 Roger Clemens 10.00 4.50
❏ HB5 Dennis Eckersley ...... 1.50 .70
❏ HB6 Cal Ripken 15.00 6.75
❏ HB7 Greg Maddux 10.00 4.50
❏ HB8 Rickey Henderson 5.00 2.20
❏ HB9 Ken Griffey Jr. 20.00 9.00
❏ HB10 Frank Thomas 8.00 3.60
❏ HB11 Mark McGwire 25.00 11.00

		MINT	NRMT
❑ HB12	Barry Bonds 5.00		2.20
❑ HB13	Mike Piazza 12.00		5.50
❑ HB14	Juan Gonzalez 8.00		3.60
❑ HB15	Randy Johnson 4.00		1.80

1998 Topps Milestones

	MINT	NRMT
COMPLETE SET (10)	80.00	36.00
COMMON CARD (MS1-MS10)	1.25	.55
SER.2 STATED ODDS 1:36 RETAIL		

		MINT	NRMT
❑ MS1	Barry Bonds 4.00		1.80
❑ MS2	Roger Clemens 8.00		3.60
❑ MS3	Dennis Eckersley 1.25		.55
❑ MS4	Juan Gonzalez 6.00		2.70
❑ MS5	Ken Griffey Jr. 15.00		6.75
❑ MS6	Tony Gwynn 8.00		3.60
❑ MS7	Greg Maddux 8.00		3.60
❑ MS8	Mark McGwire 20.00		9.00
❑ MS9	Cal Ripken 12.00		5.50
❑ MS10	Frank Thomas 6.00		2.70

1998 Topps Mystery Finest

	MINT	NRMT
COMPLETE SET (20)	150.00	70.00
COMMON CARD (ILM1-ILM20)	2.00	.90
SER.1 STATED ODDS 1:36		
*REFRACTORS: 12.5X TO 30X BASE CARD HI		
REFRACTOR SER.1 STATED ODDS: 1:144		

		MINT	NRMT
❑ ILM1	Chipper Jones 12.00		5.50
❑ ILM2	Cal Ripken 20.00		9.00
❑ ILM3	Greg Maddux 12.00		5.50
❑ ILM4	Rafael Palmeiro 5.00		2.20
❑ ILM5	Todd Hundley 2.00		.90
❑ ILM6	Derek Jeter 15.00		6.75
❑ ILM7	John Olerud 2.00		.90
❑ ILM8	Tino Martinez 2.00		.90
❑ ILM9	Larry Walker 5.00		2.20
❑ ILM10	Ken Griffey Jr. 25.00		11.00
❑ ILM11	Andres Galarraga ... 3.00		1.35
❑ ILM12	Randy Johnson 5.00		2.20
❑ ILM13	Mike Piazza 15.00		6.75
❑ ILM14	Jim Edmonds 2.00		.90
❑ ILM15	Eric Karros 2.00		.90
❑ ILM16	Tim Salmon 3.00		1.35
❑ ILM17	Sammy Sosa 15.00		6.75

		MINT	NRMT
❑ ILM18	Frank Thomas 10.00		4.50
❑ ILM19	Mark Grace 3.00		1.35
❑ ILM20	Albert Belle 5.00		2.20

1998 Topps Mystery Finest Bordered

	MINT	NRMT
COMPLETE SET (20)	200.00	90.00
COMMON CARD (M1-M20)	2.00	.90
SER.2 STATED ODDS 1:36		
*BORDERED REF: 12.5X TO 30X BASE HI		
BORDERED REF.SER.2 ODDS 1:108		
*BORDERLESS: 10X TO 25X BASE CARD HI		
BORDERLESS SER.2 ODDS 1:72		
*BORDERLESS REF: 20X TO 50X BASE HI		
BORDERLESS REF.SER.2 ODDS 1:288		

		MINT	NRMT
❑ M1	Nomar Garciaparra ... 15.00		6.75
❑ M2	Chipper Jones 12.00		5.50
❑ M3	Scott Rolen 8.00		3.60
❑ M4	Albert Belle 5.00		2.20
❑ M5	Mo Vaughn 5.00		2.20
❑ M6	Jose Cruz Jr. 2.00		.90
❑ M7	Mark McGwire 30.00		13.50
❑ M8	Derek Jeter 15.00		6.75
❑ M9	Tony Gwynn 12.00		5.50
❑ M10	Frank Thomas 10.00		4.50
❑ M11	Tino Martinez 2.00		.90
❑ M12	Greg Maddux 12.00		5.50
❑ M13	Juan Gonzalez 10.00		4.50
❑ M14	Larry Walker 5.00		2.20
❑ M15	Mike Piazza 15.00		6.75
❑ M16	Cal Ripken 20.00		9.00
❑ M17	Jeff Bagwell 6.00		2.70
❑ M18	Andruw Jones 5.00		2.20
❑ M19	Barry Bonds 6.00		2.70
❑ M20	Ken Griffey Jr. 25.00		11.00

1998 Topps Rookie Class

	MINT	NRMT
COMPLETE SET (10)	10.00	4.50
COMMON CARD (R1-R10)	.50	.23
MINOR STARS	.75	.35
SEMISTARS	1.25	.55
UNLISTED STARS	2.00	.90
SER.2 STATED ODDS 1:12		

		MINT	NRMT
❑ R1	Travis Lee 1.25		.55
❑ R2	Richard Hidalgo ...... .75		.35
❑ R3	Todd Helton 2.50		1.10
❑ R4	Paul Konerko .... .75		.35
❑ R5	Mark Kotsay .... .75		.35
❑ R6	Derrek Lee .... .50		.23
❑ R7	Eli Marrero .... .50		.23
❑ R8	Fernando Tatis 2.00		.90
❑ R9	Juan Encarnacion .... .75		.35
❑ R10	Ben Grieve 2.00		.90

1999 Topps

	MINT	NRMT
COMPLETE SET (462)	55.00	25.00
COMP.HOBBY SET (462)	60.00	27.00
COMP.X-MAS SET (463)	60.00	27.00
COMPLETE SERIES 1 (241)	30.00	13.50
COMPLETE SERIES 2 (221)	25.00	11.00
COMMON CARD (1-6/6-463)	.10	.05
MINOR STARS	.15	.07
SEMISTARS	.25	.11
UNLISTED STARS	.40	.18
COMP.MCGWIRE HR SET (70)	1200.00	550.00
MCGWIRE 220 HR 1	50.00	22.00
MCGWIRE 220 HR 2-60	20.00	9.00
MCGWIRE 220 HR 61	40.00	18.00
MCGWIRE 220 HR 62	60.00	27.00
MCGWIRE 220 HR 63-69	20.00	9.00
MCGWIRE 220 HR 70	125.00	55.00
CARD 220 AVAIL.IN 70 VARIATIONS		
COMP.SOSA HR SET (66)	500.00	220.00
SOSA 461 HR 1	20.00	9.00
SOSA 461 HR 2-60	8.00	3.60
SOSA 461 HR 61	20.00	9.00
SOSA 461 HR 62	30.00	13.50
SOSA 461 HR 63-65	10.00	4.50
SOSA 461 HR 66	40.00	18.00
CARD 461 AVAILABLE IN 66 VARIATIONS		
CARD NUMBER 7 DOES NOT EXIST		
SER.1 SET INCLUDES 1 CARD 220 VARIA-		
TION		
SER.2 SET INCLUDES 1 CARD 461 VARIA-		
TION		

		MINT	NRMT
❑ 1	Roger Clemens 1.00		.45
❑ 2	Andres Galarraga ..... .25		.11
❑ 3	Scott Brosius .... .15		.07
❑ 4	John Flaherty .... .10		.05
❑ 5	Jim Leyritz .... .10		.05
❑ 6	Ray Durham .... .15		.07
❑ 8	Jose Vizcaino .... .10		.05
❑ 9	Will Clark .... .40		.18
❑ 10	David Wells .... .15		.07
❑ 11	Jose Guillen .... .10		.05
❑ 12	Scott Hatteberg ...... .10		.05
❑ 13	Edgardo Alfonzo ..... .25		.11
❑ 14	Mike Bordick .... .10		.05
❑ 15	Manny Ramirez .... .50		.23
❑ 16	Greg Maddux 1.00		.45
❑ 17	David Segui .... .10		.05
❑ 18	Darryl Strawberry .... .15		.07
❑ 19	Brad Radke .... .15		.07
❑ 20	Kerry Wood .... .40		.18
❑ 21	Matt Anderson .... .10		.05
❑ 22	Will Clark .... .10		.05
❑ 23	Mickey Morandini .... .10		.05
❑ 24	Paul Konerko .... .40		.18

❑ 25	Travis Lee	.25	.11
❑ 26	Ken Hill	.10	.05
❑ 27	Kenny Rogers	.10	.05
❑ 28	Paul Sorrento	.10	.05
❑ 29	Quilvio Veras	.10	.05
❑ 30	Todd Walker	.15	.07
❑ 31	Ryan Jackson	.10	.05
❑ 32	John Olerud	.15	.07
❑ 33	Doug Glanville	.15	.07
❑ 34	Nolan Ryan	2.00	.90
❑ 35	Ray Lankford	.15	.07
❑ 36	Mark Loretta	.10	.05
❑ 37	Jason Dickson	.10	.05
❑ 38	Sean Bergman	.10	.05
❑ 39	Quinton McCracken	.10	.05
❑ 40	Bartolo Colon	.15	.07
❑ 41	Brady Anderson	.15	.07
❑ 42	Chris Stynes	.10	.05
❑ 43	Jorge Posada	.10	.05
❑ 44	Justin Thompson	.10	.05
❑ 45	Johnny Damon	.15	.07
❑ 46	Armando Benitez	.10	.05
❑ 47	Brant Brown	.10	.05
❑ 48	Charlie Hayes	.10	.05
❑ 49	Darren Dreifort	.10	.05
❑ 50	Juan Gonzalez	.75	.35
❑ 51	Chuck Knoblauch	.15	.07
❑ 52	Todd Helton	.40	.18
❑ 53	Rick Reed	.10	.05
❑ 54	Chris Gomez	.10	.05
❑ 55	Gary Sheffield	.15	.07
❑ 56	Rod Beck	.15	.07
❑ 57	Rey Sanchez	.10	.05
❑ 58	Garret Anderson	.15	.07
❑ 59	Jimmy Haynes	.10	.05
❑ 60	Steve Woodard	.10	.05
❑ 61	Rondell White	.15	.07
❑ 62	Vladimir Guerrero	.50	.23
❑ 63	Eric Karros	.15	.07
❑ 64	Russ Davis	.10	.05
❑ 65	Mo Vaughn	.40	.18
❑ 66	Sammy Sosa	1.25	.55
❑ 67	Troy Percival	.15	.07
❑ 68	Kenny Lofton	.25	.11
❑ 69	Bill Taylor	.10	.05
❑ 70	Mark McGwire	2.50	1.10
❑ 71	Roger Cedeno	.15	.07
❑ 72	Javy Lopez	.15	.07
❑ 73	Damion Easley	.15	.07
❑ 74	Andy Pettitte	.15	.07
❑ 75	Tony Gwynn	1.00	.45
❑ 76	Ricardo Rincon	.10	.05
❑ 77	F.P. Santangelo	.10	.05
❑ 78	Jay Bell	.15	.07
❑ 79	Scott Servais	.10	.05
❑ 80	Jose Canseco	.50	.23
❑ 81	Roberto Hernandez	.10	.05
❑ 82	Todd Dunwoody	.10	.05
❑ 83	John Wetteland	.15	.07
❑ 84	Mike Caruso	.10	.05
❑ 85	Derek Jeter	1.25	.55
❑ 86	Aaron Sele	.15	.07
❑ 87	Jose Lima	.15	.07
❑ 88	Ryan Christenson	.10	.05
❑ 89	Jeff Cirillo	.15	.07
❑ 90	Jose Hernandez	.10	.05
❑ 91	Mark Kotsay	.10	.05
❑ 92	Darren Bragg	.10	.05
❑ 93	Albert Belle	.40	.18
❑ 94	Matt Lawton	.10	.05
❑ 95	Pedro Martinez	.50	.23
❑ 96	Greg Vaughn	.15	.07
❑ 97	Neifi Perez	.15	.07
❑ 98	Gerald Williams	.10	.05
❑ 99	Derek Bell	.15	.07
❑ 100	Ken Griffey Jr.	2.00	.90
❑ 101	David Cone	.25	.11
❑ 102	Brian Johnson	.10	.05
❑ 103	Dean Palmer	.15	.07
❑ 104	Javier Valentin	.10	.05
❑ 105	Trevor Hoffman	.15	.07
❑ 106	Butch Huskey	.10	.05
❑ 107	Dave Martinez	.10	.05
❑ 108	Billy Wagner	.15	.07
❑ 109	Shawn Green	.40	.18
❑ 110	Ben Grieve	.40	.18

❑ 111	Tom Goodwin	.10	.05
❑ 112	Jaret Wright	.15	.07
❑ 113	Aramis Ramirez	.25	.11
❑ 114	Dmitri Young	.15	.07
❑ 115	Hideki Irabu	.15	.07
❑ 116	Roberto Kelly	.10	.05
❑ 117	Jeff Fassero	.10	.05
❑ 118	Mark Clark UER	.10	.05
	1997 and Career Victory		
	totals are wrong		
❑ 119	Jason McDonald	.10	.05
❑ 120	Matt Williams	.40	.18
❑ 121	Dave Burba	.10	.05
❑ 122	Bret Saberhagen	.15	.07
❑ 123	Deivi Cruz	.10	.05
❑ 124	Chad Curtis	.10	.05
❑ 125	Scott Rolen	.50	.23
❑ 126	Lee Stevens	.10	.05
❑ 127	J.T. Snow	.15	.07
❑ 128	Rusty Greer	.15	.07
❑ 129	Brian Meadows	.10	.05
❑ 130	Jim Edmonds	.15	.07
❑ 131	Ron Gant	.15	.07
❑ 132	A.J. Hinch	.10	.05
❑ 133	Shannon Stewart	.15	.07
❑ 134	Brad Fullmer	.15	.07
❑ 135	Cal Eldred	.10	.05
❑ 136	Matt Walbeck	.10	.05
❑ 137	Carl Everett	.15	.07
❑ 138	Walt Weiss	.10	.05
❑ 139	Fred McGriff	.25	.11
❑ 140	Darin Erstad	.25	.11
❑ 141	Jose Valentin	.10	.05
❑ 142	Eric Young	.10	.05
❑ 143	Dan Wilson	.10	.05
❑ 144	Jeff Reed	.10	.05
❑ 145	Brett Tomko	.10	.05
❑ 146	Terry Steinbach	.10	.05
❑ 147	Seth Greisinger	.10	.05
❑ 148	Pat Meares	.10	.05
❑ 149	Livan Hernandez	.10	.05
❑ 150	Jeff Bagwell	.50	.23
❑ 151	Bob Wickman	.10	.05
❑ 152	Omar Vizquel	.15	.07
❑ 153	Eric Davis	.15	.07
❑ 154	Larry Sutton	.10	.05
❑ 155	Magglio Ordonez	.40	.18
❑ 156	Eric Milton	.10	.05
❑ 157	Darren Lewis	.10	.05
❑ 158	Rick Aguilera	.10	.05
❑ 159	Mike Lieberthal	.10	.05
❑ 160	Bob Hamelin	.10	.05
❑ 161	Brian Giles	.15	.07
❑ 162	Jeff Brantley	.10	.05
❑ 163	Gary DiSarcina	.10	.05
❑ 164	John Valentin	.15	.07
❑ 165	David Dellucci	.10	.05
❑ 166	Chan Ho Park	.15	.07
❑ 167	Masato Yoshii	.15	.07
❑ 168	Jason Schmidt	.10	.05
❑ 169	LaTroy Hawkins	.10	.05
❑ 170	Bret Boone	.15	.07
❑ 171	Jerry DiPoto	.10	.05
❑ 172	Mariano Rivera	.15	.07
❑ 173	Mike Cameron	.10	.05
❑ 174	Scott Erickson	.10	.05
❑ 175	Charles Johnson	.15	.07
❑ 176	Bobby Jones	.10	.05
❑ 177	Francisco Cordova	.10	.05
❑ 178	Todd Jones	.10	.05
❑ 179	Jeff Montgomery	.10	.05
❑ 180	Mike Mussina	.40	.18
❑ 181	Bob Abreu	.15	.07
❑ 182	Ismael Valdes	.10	.05
❑ 183	Andy Fox	.10	.05
❑ 184	Woody Williams	.10	.05
❑ 185	Denny Neagle	.15	.07
❑ 186	Jose Valentin	.10	.05
❑ 187	Darrin Fletcher	.10	.05
❑ 188	Gabe Alvarez	.15	.07
❑ 189	Eddie Taubensee	.10	.05
❑ 190	Edgar Martinez	.15	.07
❑ 191	Jason Kendall	.15	.07
❑ 192	Darryl Kile	.10	.05
❑ 193	Jeff King	.10	.05
❑ 194	Rey Ordonez	.15	.07

❑ 195	Andruw Jones	.40	.18
❑ 196	Tony Fernandez	.15	.07
❑ 197	Jamey Wright	.10	.05
❑ 198	B.J. Surhoff	.15	.07
❑ 199	Vinny Castilla	.15	.07
❑ 200	David Wells HL	.10	.05
❑ 201	Mark McGwire HL	1.25	.55
❑ 202	Sammy Sosa HL	.60	.25
❑ 203	Roger Clemens HL	.50	.23
❑ 204	Kerry Wood HL	.15	.07
❑ 205	Lance Berkman	.40	.18
	Mike Frank		
	Gabe Kapler		
❑ 206	Alex Escobar	.75	.35
	Ricky Ledee		
	Mike Stoner		
❑ 207	Peter Bergeron	.40	.18
	Jeremy Giambi		
	George Lombard		
❑ 208	Michael Barrett	.25	.11
	Ben Davis		
	Robert Fick		
❑ 209	Pat Cline	.15	.07
	Ramon Hernandez		
	Jayson Werth		
❑ 210	Bruce Chen	.15	.07
	Chris Enochs		
	Ryan Anderson		
❑ 211	Mike Lincoln	.15	.07
	Octavio Dotel		
	Brad Penny		
❑ 212	Chuck Abbott	.25	.11
	Brent Butler		
	Danny Klassen		
❑ 213	Chris C.Jones	.40	.18
	Jeff Urban		
❑ 214	Arturo McDowell	.40	.18
	Tony Torcato		
❑ 215	Josh McKinley	.40	.18
	Jason Tyner		
❑ 216	Matt Burch	.40	.18
	Seth Etheron		
	UER back Etherton		
❑ 217	Mamon Tucker	.50	.23
	Rick Elder		
❑ 218	J.M.Gold	.30	.14
	Ryan Mills		
❑ 219	Adam Brown	.50	.23
	Choo Freeman		
❑ 220A	Mark McGwire HR 1	50.00	22.00
❑ 220B	Mark McGwire HR 2	20.00	9.00
❑ 220C	Mark McGwire HR 3	20.00	9.00
❑ 220D	Mark McGwire HR 4	20.00	9.00
❑ 220E	Mark McGwire HR 5	20.00	9.00
❑ 220F	Mark McGwire HR 6	20.00	9.00
❑ 220G	Mark McGwire HR 7	20.00	9.00
❑ 220H	Mark McGwire HR 8	20.00	9.00
❑ 220I	Mark McGwire HR 9	20.00	9.00
❑ 220J	Mark McGwire HR 10	20.00	9.00
❑ 220K	Mark McGwire HR 11	20.00	9.00
❑ 220L	Mark McGwire HR 12	20.00	9.00
❑ 220M	Mark McGwire HR 13	20.00	9.00
❑ 220N	Mark McGwire HR 14	20.00	9.00
❑ 220O	Mark McGwire HR 15	20.00	9.00
❑ 220P	Mark McGwire HR 16	20.00	9.00
❑ 220Q	Mark McGwire HR 17	20.00	9.00
❑ 220R	Mark McGwire HR 18	20.00	9.00
❑ 220S	Mark McGwire HR 19	20.00	9.00
❑ 220T	Mark McGwire HR 20	20.00	9.00
❑ 220U	Mark McGwire HR 21	20.00	9.00
❑ 220V	Mark McGwire HR 22	20.00	9.00
❑ 220W	Mark McGwire HR 23	20.00	9.00
❑ 220X	Mark McGwire HR 24	20.00	9.00
❑ 220Y	Mark McGwire HR 25	20.00	9.00
❑ 220Z	Mark McGwire HR 26	20.00	9.00
❑ 220AA	Mark McGwire HR 27	20.00	9.00
❑ 220AB	Mark McGwire HR 28	20.00	9.00
❑ 220AC	Mark McGwire HR 29	20.00	9.00
❑ 220AD	Mark McGwire HR 30	20.00	9.00
❑ 220AE	Mark McGwire HR 31	20.00	9.00
❑ 220AF	Mark McGwire HR 32	20.00	9.00
❑ 220AG	Mark McGwire HR 33	20.00	9.00
❑ 220AH	Mark McGwire HR 34	20.00	9.00
❑ 220AI	Mark McGwire HR 35	20.00	9.00
❑ 220AJ	Mark McGwire HR 36	20.00	9.00
❑ 220AK	Mark McGwire HR 37	20.00	9.00

Card	Name		
220AL	Mark McGwire HR 38	20.00	9.00
220AM	Mark McGwire HR 39	20.00	9.00
220AN	Mark McGwire HR 40	20.00	9.00
220AO	Mark McGwire HR 41	20.00	9.00
220AP	Mark McGwire HR 42	20.00	9.00
220AQ	Mark McGwire HR 43	20.00	9.00
220AR	Mark McGwire HR 44	20.00	9.00
220AS	Mark McGwire HR 45	20.00	9.00
220AT	Mark McGwire HR 46	20.00	9.00
220AU	Mark McGwire HR 47	20.00	9.00
220AV	Mark McGwire HR 48	20.00	9.00
220AW	Mark McGwire HR 49	20.00	9.00
220AX	Mark McGwire HR 50	20.00	9.00
220AY	Mark McGwire HR 51	20.00	9.00
220AZ	Mark McGwire HR 52	20.00	9.00
220BB	Mark McGwire HR 53	20.00	9.00
220CC	Mark McGwire HR 54	20.00	9.00
220DD	Mark McGwire HR 55	20.00	9.00
220EE	Mark McGwire HR 56	20.00	9.00
220FF	Mark McGwire HR 57	20.00	9.00
220GG	Mark McGwire HR 58	20.00	9.00
220HH	Mark McGwire HR 59	20.00	9.00
220II	Mark McGwire HR 60	20.00	9.00
220JJ	Mark McGwire HR 61	40.00	18.00
220KK	Mark McGwire HR 62	60.00	27.00
220LL	Mark McGwire HR 63	20.00	9.00
220MM	Mark McGwire HR 64	20.00	9.00
220NN	Mark McGwire HR 65	20.00	9.00
220OO	Mark McGwire HR 66	20.00	9.00
220PP	Mark McGwire HR 67	20.00	9.00
220QQ	Mark McGwire HR 68	20.00	9.00
220RR	Mark McGwire HR 69	20.00	9.00
220SS	Mark McGwire HR 70	125.00	55.00
221	Larry Walker LL	.15	.07
222	Bernie Williams LL	.15	.07
223	Mark McGwire LL	1.25	.55
224	Ken Griffey Jr. LL	1.00	.45
225	Sammy Sosa LL	.60	.25
226	Juan Gonzalez LL	.40	.18
227	Dante Bichette LL	.10	.05
228	Alex Rodriguez LL	.60	.25
229	Sammy Sosa LL	.60	.25
230	Derek Jeter LL	.60	.25
231	Greg Maddux LL	.50	.23
232	Roger Clemens LL	.50	.23
233	Ricky Ledee WS	.10	.05
234	Chuck Knoblauch WS	.15	.07
235	Bernie Williams WS	.15	.07
236	Tino Martinez WS	.15	.07
237	Orlando Hernandez WS	.15	.07
238	Scott Brosius WS	.10	.05
239	Andy Pettitte WS	.10	.05
240	Mariano Rivera WS	.15	.07
241	Checklist 1	.10	.05
242	Checklist 2	.10	.05
243	Tom Glavine	.40	.18
244	Andy Benes	.10	.05
245	Sandy Alomar Jr.	.15	.07
246	Wilton Guerrero	.10	.05
247	Alex Gonzalez	.15	.07
248	Roberto Alomar	.40	.18
249	Ruben Rivera	.10	.05
250	Eric Chavez	.25	.11
251	Ellis Burks	.15	.07
252	Richie Sexson	.25	.11
253	Steve Finley	.15	.07
254	Dwight Gooden	.15	.07
255	Dustin Hermanson	.10	.05
256	Kirk Rueter	.10	.05
257	Steve Trachsel	.10	.05
258	Gregg Jefferies	.10	.05
259	Matt Stairs	.15	.07
260	Shane Reynolds	.15	.07
261	Gregg Olson	.10	.05
262	Kevin Tapani	.10	.05
263	Matt Morris	.10	.05
264	Carl Pavano	.10	.05
265	Nomar Garciaparra	1.25	.55
266	Kevin Young	.15	.07
267	Rick Helling	.10	.05
268	Matt Franco	.10	.05
269	Brian McRae	.10	.05
270	Cal Ripken	1.50	.70
271	Jeff Abbott	.10	.05
272	Tony Batista	.10	.05
273	Bill Simas	.10	.05
274	Brian Hunter	.10	.05
275	John Franco	.15	.07
276	Devon White	.10	.05
277	Rickey Henderson	.50	.23
278	Chuck Finley	.10	.05
279	Mike Blowers	.10	.05
280	Mark Grace	.25	.11
281	Randy Winn	.10	.05
282	Bobby Bonilla	.15	.07
283	David Justice	.15	.07
284	Shane Monahan	.10	.05
285	Kevin Brown	.25	.11
286	Todd Zeile	.15	.07
287	Al Martin	.10	.05
288	Troy O'Leary	.15	.07
289	Darryl Hamilton	.10	.05
290	Tino Martinez	.15	.07
291	David Ortiz	.10	.05
292	Tony Clark	.15	.07
293	Ryan Minor	.15	.07
294	Mark Leiter	.10	.05
295	Wally Joyner	.15	.07
296	Cliff Floyd	.15	.07
297	Shawn Estes	.10	.05
298	Pat Hentgen	.10	.05
299	Scott Elarton	.10	.05
300	Alex Rodriguez	1.25	.55
301	Ozzie Guillen	.10	.05
302	Hideo Nomo	.40	.18
303	Ryan McGuire	.10	.05
304	Brad Ausmus	.10	.05
305	Alex Gonzalez	.15	.07
306	Brian Jordan	.15	.07
307	John Jaha	.15	.07
308	Mark Grudzielanek	.10	.05
309	Juan Guzman	.10	.05
310	Tony Womack	.10	.05
311	Dennis Reyes	.10	.05
312	Marty Cordova	.10	.05
313	Ramiro Mendoza	.10	.05
314	Robin Ventura	.15	.07
315	Rafael Palmeiro	.40	.18
316	Ramon Martinez	.10	.05
317	Pedro Astacio	.10	.05
318	Dave Hollins	.10	.05
319	Tom Candiotti	.10	.05
320	Al Leiter	.15	.07
321	Rico Brogna	.10	.05
322	Reggie Jefferson	.10	.05
323	Bernard Gilkey	.10	.05
324	Jason Giambi	.15	.07
325	Craig Biggio	.40	.18
326	Troy Glaus	.40	.18
327	Delino DeShields	.10	.05
328	Fernando Vina	.10	.05
329	John Smoltz	.25	.11
330	Jeff Kent	.15	.07
331	Roy Halladay	.15	.07
332	Andy Ashby	.10	.05
333	Tim Wakefield	.10	.05
334	Roger Clemens	1.00	.45
335	Bernie Williams	.40	.18
336	Desi Relaford	.10	.05
337	John Burkett	.10	.05
338	Mike Hampton	.15	.07
339	Royce Clayton	.10	.05
340	Mike Piazza	1.25	.55
341	Jeremi Gonzalez	.10	.05
342	Mike Lansing	.10	.05
343	Jamie Moyer	.10	.05
344	Ron Coomer	.10	.05
345	Barry Larkin	.40	.18
346	Fernando Tatis	.40	.18
347	Chili Davis	.10	.05
348	Bobby Higginson	.15	.07
349	Hal Morris	.10	.05
350	Larry Walker	.40	.18
351	Carlos Guillen	.15	.07
352	Miguel Tejada	.15	.07
353	Travis Fryman	.15	.07
354	Jarrod Washburn	.10	.05
355	Chipper Jones	1.00	.45
356	Todd Stottlemyre	.10	.05
357	Henry Rodriguez	.15	.07
358	Eli Marrero	.10	.05
359	Alan Benes	.10	.05
360	Tim Salmon	.25	.11
361	Luis Gonzalez	.15	.07
362	Scott Spiezio	.10	.05
363	Chris Carpenter	.10	.05
364	Bobby Howry	.10	.05
365	Raul Mondesi	.15	.07
366	Ugueth Urbina	.10	.05
367	Tom Evans	.10	.05
368	Kerry Ligtenberg	.25	.11
369	Adrian Beltre	.40	.18
370	Ryan Klesko	.15	.07
371	Wilson Alvarez	.10	.05
372	John Thomson	.10	.05
373	Tony Saunders	.10	.05
374	Dave Mlicki	.10	.05
375	Ken Caminiti	.15	.07
376	Jay Buhner	.15	.07
377	Bill Mueller	.10	.05
378	Jeff Blauser	.10	.05
379	Edgar Renteria	.10	.05
380	Jim Thome	.40	.18
381	Joey Hamilton	.10	.05
382	Calvin Pickering	.15	.07
383	Marquis Grissom	.10	.05
384	Omar Daal	.10	.05
385	Curt Schilling	.25	.11
386	Jose Cruz Jr.	.15	.07
387	Chris Widger	.10	.05
388	Pete Harnisch	.10	.05
389	Charles Nagy	.15	.07
390	Tom Gordon	.15	.07
391	Bobby Smith	.10	.05
392	Derrick Gibson	.15	.07
393	Jeff Conine	.10	.05
394	Carlos Perez	.10	.05
395	Barry Bonds	.50	.23
396	Mark McLemore	.10	.05
397	Juan Encarnacion	.15	.07
398	Wade Boggs	.40	.18
399	Ivan Rodriguez	.50	.23
400	Moises Alou	.15	.07
401	Jeromy Burnitz	.15	.07
402	Sean Casey	.40	.18
403	Jose Offerman	.15	.07
404	Joe Fontenot	.10	.05
405	Kevin Millwood	.25	.11
406	Lance Johnson	.10	.05
407	Richard Hidalgo	.15	.07
408	Mike Jackson	.10	.05
409	Brian Anderson	.10	.05
410	Jeff Shaw	.10	.05
411	Preston Wilson	.15	.07
412	Todd Hundley	.15	.07
413	Jim Parque	.10	.05
414	Justin Baughman	.10	.05
415	Dante Bichette	.15	.07
416	Paul O'Neill	.15	.07
417	Miguel Cairo	.10	.05
418	Randy Johnson	.40	.18
419	Jesus Sanchez	.10	.05
420	Carlos Delgado	.40	.18
421	Ricky Ledee	.15	.07
422	Orlando Hernandez	.40	.18
423	Frank Thomas	.75	.35
424	Pokey Reese	.10	.05
425	Carlos Lee	.40	.18
	Mike Lowell		
	Kit Pellow		
426	Michael Cuddyer	.15	.07
	Mark DeRosa		
	Jerry Hairston Jr.		
427	Marlon Anderson	.15	.07
	Ron Belliard		
	Alex Cabrera		
428	Micah Bowie	.25	.11
	Phil Norton		
	Randy Wolf		
429	Jack Cressend	.25	.11
	Jason Rakers		
	John Rocker		
430	Ruben Mateo	.50	.23
	Scott Morgan		
	Mike Zywica		
431	Jason LaRue	.10	.05
	Matt LeCroy		
	Mitch Meluskey		

❑ 432 Gabe Kapler .... .40	.18
Armando Rios	
Fernando Seguignol	
❑ 433 Adam Kennedy .... .25	.11
Mickey Lopez	
Jackie Rexrode	
❑ 434 Jose Fernandez ...... .25	.11
Jeff Liefer	
Chris Truby	
❑ 435 Corey Koskie .... .25	.11
Doug Mientkiewicz	
Damon Minor	
❑ 436 Roosevelt Brown ..... .30	.14
Dernell Stenson	
Vernon Wells	
❑ 437 A.J. Burnett .... .40	.18
Billy Koch	
John Nicholson	
❑ 438 Matt Belisle .... .40	.18
Matt Roney	
Chris George	
❑ 439 Austin Kearns .... .50	.23
Chris George	
❑ 440 Nate Bump .... .40	.18
Nate Cornejo	
❑ 441 Brad Lidge .... .40	.18
Mike Nannini	
❑ 442 Matt Holliday .... .40	.18
Jeff Winchester	
❑ 443 Adam Everett .... .60	.25
Chip Ambres	
❑ 444 Pat Burrell 2.00	.90
Eric Valent	
❑ 445 Roger Clemens SK ... .50	.23
❑ 446 Kerry Wood SK .... .15	.07
❑ 447 Curt Schilling SK ..... .15	.07
❑ 448 Randy Johnson SK ... .15	.07
❑ 449 Pedro Martinez SK ... .25	.11
❑ 450 Jeff Bagwell AT 1.00	.45
Andres Galarraga	
Mark McGwire	
❑ 451 John Olerud AT .... .15	.07
Jim Thome	
Tino Martinez	
❑ 452 Alex Rodriguez AT .... .50	.23
Nomar Garciaparra	
Derek Jeter	
❑ 453 Vinny Castilla AT ...... .40	.18
Chipper Jones	
Scott Rolen	
❑ 454 Sammy Sosa AT ...... .75	.35
Ken Griffey Jr.	
Juan Gonzalez	
❑ 455 Barry Bonds AT .... .15	.07
Manny Ramirez	
Larry Walker	
❑ 456 Frank Thomas AT ..... .40	.18
Tim Salmon	
David Justice	
❑ 457 Travis Lee AT .... .15	.07
Todd Helton	
Ben Grieve	
❑ 458 Vladimir Guerrero AT ... .40	.18
Greg Vaughn	
Bernie Williams	
❑ 459 Mike Piazza AT .... .40	.18
Ivan Rodriguez	
Jason Kendall	
❑ 460 Roger Clemens AT .... .40	.18
Kerry Wood	
Greg Maddux	
❑ 461A Sammy Sosa HR 1 .. 20.00	9.00
❑ 461B Sammy Sosa HR 2 .. 8.00	3.60
❑ 461C Sammy Sosa HR 3 .. 8.00	3.60
❑ 461D Sammy Sosa HR 4 .. 8.00	3.60
❑ 461E Sammy Sosa HR 5 .. 8.00	3.60
❑ 461F Sammy Sosa HR 6 .. 8.00	3.60
❑ 461G Sammy Sosa HR 7 .. 8.00	3.60
❑ 461H Sammy Sosa HR 8 .. 8.00	3.60
❑ 461I Sammy Sosa HR 9 ... 8.00	3.60
❑ 461J Sammy Sosa HR 10 .. 8.00	3.60
❑ 461K Sammy Sosa HR 11 .. 8.00	3.60
❑ 461L Sammy Sosa HR 12 .. 8.00	3.60
❑ 461M Sammy Sosa HR 13 .. 8.00	3.60
❑ 461N Sammy Sosa HR 14 .. 8.00	3.60
❑ 461O Sammy Sosa HR 15 .. 8.00	3.60
❑ 461P Sammy Sosa HR 16 .. 8.00	3.60

❑ 461Q Sammy Sosa HR 17 ... 8.00	3.60
❑ 461R Sammy Sosa HR 18 ... 8.00	3.60
❑ 461S Sammy Sosa HR 19 ... 8.00	3.60
❑ 461T Sammy Sosa HR 20 ... 8.00	3.60
❑ 461U Sammy Sosa HR 21 ... 8.00	3.60
❑ 461V Sammy Sosa HR 22 ... 8.00	3.60
❑ 461W Sammy Sosa HR 23 ... 8.00	3.60
❑ 461X Sammy Sosa HR 24 ... 8.00	3.60
❑ 461Y Sammy Sosa HR 25 ... 8.00	3.60
❑ 461Z Sammy Sosa HR 26 ... 8.00	3.60
❑ 461AA Sammy Sosa HR 27 8.00	3.60
❑ 461AB Sammy Sosa HR 28 8.00	3.60
❑ 461AC Sammy Sosa HR 29 8.00	3.60
❑ 461AD Sammy Sosa HR 30 8.00	3.60
❑ 461AE Sammy Sosa HR 31 8.00	3.60
❑ 461AF Sammy Sosa HR 32 8.00	3.60
❑ 461AG Sammy Sosa HR 33 8.00	3.60
❑ 461AH Sammy Sosa HR 34 8.00	3.60
❑ 461AI Sammy Sosa HR 35 8.00	3.60
❑ 461AJ Sammy Sosa HR 36 8.00	3.60
❑ 461AK Sammy Sosa HR 37 8.00	3.60
❑ 461AL Sammy Sosa HR 38 8.00	3.60
❑ 461AM Sammy Sosa HR 39 8.00	3.60
❑ 461AN Sammy Sosa HR 40 8.00	3.60
❑ 461AO Sammy Sosa HR 41 8.00	3.60
❑ 461AP Sammy Sosa HR 42 8.00	3.60
❑ 461AR Sammy Sosa HR 43 8.00	3.60
❑ 461AS Sammy Sosa HR 44 8.00	3.60
❑ 461AT Sammy Sosa HR 45 8.00	3.60
❑ 461AU Sammy Sosa HR 46 8.00	3.60
❑ 461AV Sammy Sosa HR 47 8.00	3.60
❑ 461AW Sammy Sosa HR 48 8.00	3.60
❑ 461AX Sammy Sosa HR 49 8.00	3.60
❑ 461AY Sammy Sosa HR 50 8.00	3.60
❑ 461AZ Sammy Sosa HR 51 8.00	3.60
❑ 461BB Sammy Sosa HR 52 8.00	3.60
❑ 461CC Sammy Sosa HR 53 8.00	3.60
❑ 461DD Sammy Sosa HR 54 8.00	3.60
❑ 461EE Sammy Sosa HR 55 8.00	3.60
❑ 461FF Sammy Sosa HR 56 8.00	3.60
❑ 461GG Sammy Sosa HR 57 8.00	3.60
❑ 461HH Sammy Sosa HR 58 8.00	3.60
❑ 461II Sammy Sosa HR 59 .. 8.00	3.60
❑ 461JJ Sammy Sosa HR 60 .. 8.00	9.00
❑ 461KK Sammy Sosa HR 61 8.00	3.60
❑ 461LL Sammy Sosa HR 62 30.00	13.50
❑ 461MM Sammy Sosa HR 63 10.00	4.50
❑ 461NN Sammy Sosa HR 64 10.00	4.50
❑ 461OO Sammy Sosa HR 65 10.00	4.50
❑ 461PP Sammy Sosa HR 66 40.00	18.00
❑ 462 Checklist .... .10	.05
❑ 463 Checklist .... .10	.05

1999 Topps MVP Promotion

	MINT	NRMT
COMMON (1-6/8-199/243-460) 8.00		3.60

*STARS: 30X TO 80X BASIC CARDS
*YNG.STARS: 25X TO 60X BASIC CARDS
*RCS/DRAFT: 20X TO 50X BASIC CARDS
SER.1 ODDS 1:515 HOB, 1:142 HTA
SER.2 ODDS 1:504 HOB, 1:139 HTA, 1:504 RET
STATED PRINT RUN 100 SETS
MVP PARALLELS ARE UNNUMBERED
EXCHANGE DEADLINE: 12/31/99
PRIZE CARDS WILL MAIL OUT ON 2/15/00

❑ 35 Ray Lankford W 60.00	27.00
❑ 52 Todd Helton W 60.00	27.00
❑ 70 Mark McGwire W 250.00	110.00
❑ 96 Greg Vaughn W 60.00	27.00
❑ 101 David Cone W 60.00	27.00
❑ 125 Scott Rolen W 80.00	36.00
❑ 127 J.T. Snow W 60.00	27.00
❑ 139 Fred McGriff W 60.00	27.00
❑ 159 Mike Lieberthal W ... 60.00	27.00
❑ 198 B.J. Surhoff W 60.00	27.00
❑ 248 Roberto Alomar W .. 70.00	
❑ 265 Nomar Garciaparra W 150.00	70.00
❑ 290 Tino Martinez W 60.00	27.00
❑ 292 Tony Clark W 60.00	27.00
❑ 300 Alex Rodriguez W ... 150.00	70.00
❑ 315 Rafael Palmeiro W .. 60.00	27.00
❑ 340 Mike Piazza W 150.00	70.00
❑ 346 Fernando Tatis W 60.00	27.00
❑ 350 Larry Walker W 60.00	27.00
❑ 352 Miguel Tejada W 60.00	27.00
❑ 355 Chipper Jones W 120.00	55.00
❑ 360 Tim Salmon W 60.00	27.00
❑ 365 Raul Mondesi W 60.00	27.00
❑ 416 Paul O'Neill W 60.00	27.00
❑ 418 Randy Johnson W 60.00	27.00

1999 Topps Oversize

	MINT	NRMT
COMPLETE SERIES 1 (8)	25.00	11.00
COMPLETE SERIES 2 (8)	20.00	9.00
COMMON CARD (A1-B8)	.75	.35
UNLISTED STARS	1.25	.55
ONE PER HTA OR HOBBY BOX		

❑ A1 Roger Clemens 3.00	1.35
❑ A2 Greg Maddux 3.00	1.35
❑ A3 Kerry Wood 1.25	.55
❑ A4 Juan Gonzalez 2.50	1.10
❑ A5 Sammy Sosa 4.00	1.80
❑ A6 Mark McGwire 8.00	3.60
❑ A7 Ken Griffey Jr. 6.00	2.70
❑ A8 Ben Grieve 1.25	.55
❑ B1 Nomar Garciaparra .. 4.00	1.80
❑ B2 Cal Ripken 5.00	2.20
❑ B3 Alex Rodriguez 4.00	1.80
❑ B4 Mike Piazza 4.00	1.80
❑ B5 Larry Walker 1.25	.55
❑ B6 Chipper Jones 3.00	1.35
❑ B7 Barry Bonds 1.50	.70
❑ B8 Frank Thomas 2.50	1.10

1999 Topps All-Matrix

	MINT	NRMT
COMPLETE SET (30)	100.00	45.00
COMMON CARD (AM1-AM30)	1.25	.55
SEMISTARS	2.00	.90
UNLISTED STARS	3.00	1.35
SER.2 ODDS 1:18 HOB/RET, 1:5 HTA		

		MINT	NRMT
❏ AM1	Mark McGwire	20.00	9.00
❏ AM2	Sammy Sosa	10.00	4.50
❏ AM3	Ken Griffey Jr.	15.00	6.75
❏ AM4	Greg Vaughn	1.25	.55
❏ AM5	Albert Belle	3.00	1.35
❏ AM6	Vinny Castilla	1.25	.55
❏ AM7	Jose Canseco	4.00	1.80
❏ AM8	Juan Gonzalez	6.00	2.70
❏ AM9	Manny Ramirez	4.00	1.80
❏ AM10	Andres Galarraga	2.00	.90
❏ AM11	Rafael Palmeiro	3.00	1.35
❏ AM12	Alex Rodriguez	10.00	4.50
❏ AM13	Mo Vaughn	3.00	1.35
❏ AM14	Eric Chavez	2.00	.90
❏ AM15	Gabe Kapler	3.00	1.35
❏ AM16	Calvin Pickering	1.25	.55
❏ AM17	Ruben Mateo	3.00	1.35
❏ AM18	Roy Halladay	1.25	.55
❏ AM19	Jeremy Giambi	1.25	.55
❏ AM20	Alex Gonzalez	1.25	.55
❏ AM21	Ron Belliard	1.25	.55
❏ AM22	Marlon Anderson	1.25	.55
❏ AM23	Carlos Lee	1.25	.55
❏ AM24	Kerry Wood	3.00	1.35
❏ AM25	Roger Clemens	8.00	3.60
❏ AM26	Curt Schilling	2.00	.90
❏ AM27	Kevin Brown	2.00	.90
❏ AM28	Randy Johnson	3.00	1.35
❏ AM29	Pedro Martinez	4.00	1.80
❏ AM30	Orlando Hernandez	3.00	1.35

1999 Topps All-Topps Mystery Finest

	MINT	NRMT
COMPLETE SET (33)	300.00	135.00
COMMON CARD (M1-M33)	3.00	1.35
SEMISTARS	4.00	1.80
UNLISTED STARS	6.00	2.70
SER.2 ODDS 1:36 HOB/RET, 1:8 HTA		
*REFRACTORS: 1X TO 2.5X HI COLUMN		
SER.2 REF.ODDS 1:144 HOB/RET, 1:32 HTA		

		MINT	NRMT
❏ M1	Jeff Bagwell	8.00	3.60
❏ M2	Andres Galarraga	4.00	1.80
❏ M3	Mark McGwire	40.00	18.00
❏ M4	John Olerud	3.00	1.35
❏ M5	Jim Thome	6.00	2.70
❏ M6	Tino Martinez	3.00	1.35
❏ M7	Alex Rodriguez	20.00	9.00
❏ M8	Nomar Garciaparra	20.00	9.00
❏ M9	Derek Jeter	20.00	9.00
❏ M10	Vinny Castilla	3.00	1.35
❏ M11	Chipper Jones	15.00	6.75
❏ M12	Scott Rolen	6.00	2.70
❏ M13	Sammy Sosa	20.00	9.00
❏ M14	Ken Griffey Jr.	30.00	13.50
❏ M15	Juan Gonzalez	12.00	5.50
❏ M16	Barry Bonds	8.00	3.60
❏ M17	Manny Ramirez	8.00	3.60
❏ M18	Larry Walker	6.00	2.70

		MINT	NRMT
❏ M19	Frank Thomas	12.00	5.50
❏ M20	Tim Salmon	4.00	1.80
❏ M21	Dave Justice	3.00	1.35
❏ M22	Travis Lee	4.00	1.80
❏ M23	Todd Helton	6.00	2.70
❏ M24	Ben Grieve	6.00	2.70
❏ M25	Vladimir Guerrero	6.00	2.70
❏ M26	Greg Vaughn	3.00	1.35
❏ M27	Bernie Williams	6.00	2.70
❏ M28	Mike Piazza	20.00	9.00
❏ M29	Ivan Rodriguez	8.00	3.60
❏ M30	Jason Kendall	3.00	1.35
❏ M31	Roger Clemens	15.00	6.75
❏ M32	Kerry Wood	6.00	2.70
❏ M33	Greg Maddux	15.00	6.75

1999 Topps Autographs

	MINT	NRMT
COMPLETE SET (16)	900.00	400.00
COMPLETE SERIES 1 (8)	550.00	250.00
COMPLETE SERIES 2 (8)	350.00	160.00
COMMON CARD (A1-A16)	20.00	9.00
SER.1 ODDS 1:532 HOB, 1:146 HTA		
SER.2 ODDS 1:501 HOB, 1:138 HTA		

		MINT	NRMT
❏ A1	Roger Clemens	120.00	55.00
❏ A2	Chipper Jones	100.00	45.00
❏ A3	Scott Rolen	50.00	22.00
❏ A4	Alex Rodriguez	150.00	70.00
❏ A5	Andres Galarraga	25.00	11.00
❏ A6	Rondell White	20.00	9.00
❏ A7	Ben Grieve	30.00	13.50
❏ A8	Troy Glaus	30.00	13.50
❏ A9	Moises Alou	20.00	9.00
❏ A10	Barry Bonds	80.00	36.00
❏ A11	Vladimir Guerrero	50.00	22.00
❏ A12	Andruw Jones	40.00	18.00
❏ A13	Darin Erstad	25.00	11.00
❏ A14	Shawn Green	40.00	18.00
❏ A15	Eric Chavez	20.00	9.00
❏ A16	Pat Burrell	60.00	27.00

1999 Topps Hall of Fame Collection

	MINT	NRMT
COMPLETE SET (10)	20.00	9.00
COMMON CARD (HOF1-HOF10)	2.00	.90
SER.1 ODDS 1:12 HOB/RET, 1:3 HTA		

		MINT	NRMT
❏ HOF1	Mike Schmidt	3.00	1.35
❏ HOF2	Brooks Robinson	2.00	.90
❏ HOF3	Stan Musial	3.00	1.35
❏ HOF4	Willie McCovey	2.00	.90
❏ HOF5	Eddie Mathews	2.00	.90
❏ HOF6	Reggie Jackson	3.00	1.35
❏ HOF7	Ernie Banks	3.00	1.35
❏ HOF8	Whitey Ford	2.00	.90
❏ HOF9	Bob Feller	2.00	.90
❏ HOF10	Yogi Berra	3.00	1.35

1999 Topps Lords of the Diamond

	MINT	NRMT
COMPLETE SET (15)	60.00	27.00
COMMON CARD (LD1-LD15)	1.25	.55
SER.1 ODDS 1:18 HOB/RET, 1:5 HTA		

		MINT	NRMT
❏ LD1	Ken Griffey Jr.	10.00	4.50
❏ LD2	Chipper Jones	5.00	2.20
❏ LD3	Sammy Sosa	6.00	2.70
❏ LD4	Frank Thomas	4.00	1.80
❏ LD5	Mark McGwire	12.00	5.50
❏ LD6	Jeff Bagwell	2.50	1.10
❏ LD7	Alex Rodriguez	6.00	2.70
❏ LD8	Juan Gonzalez	4.00	1.80
❏ LD9	Barry Bonds	2.50	1.10
❏ LD10	Nomar Garciaparra	6.00	2.70
❏ LD11	Darin Erstad	1.25	.55
❏ LD12	Tony Gwynn	5.00	2.20
❏ LD13	Andres Galarraga	1.25	.55
❏ LD14	Mike Piazza	6.00	2.70
❏ LD15	Greg Maddux	5.00	2.20

1999 Topps New Breed

	MINT	NRMT
COMPLETE SET (15)	30.00	13.50
COMMON CARD (NB1-NB15)	.50	.23
SEMISTARS	1.00	.45
UNLISTED STARS	1.50	.70
SER.1 ODDS 1:18 HOB/RET, 1:5 HTA		

		MINT	NRMT
❏ NB1	Darin Erstad	1.00	.45
❏ NB2	Brad Fullmer	.50	.23
❏ NB3	Kerry Wood	1.50	.70
❏ NB4	Nomar Garciaparra	5.00	2.20
❏ NB5	Travis Lee	1.00	.45
❏ NB6	Scott Rolen	2.00	.90

	MINT	NRMT
❏ NB7 Todd Helton	1.50	.70
❏ NB8 Vladimir Guerrero	2.00	.90
❏ NB9 Derek Jeter	5.00	2.20
❏ NB10 Alex Rodriguez	5.00	2.20
❏ NB11 Ben Grieve	1.50	.70
❏ NB12 Andruw Jones	1.50	.70
❏ NB13 Paul Konerko	1.50	.70
❏ NB14 Aramis Ramirez	1.00	.45
❏ NB15 Adrian Beltre	1.50	.70

1999 Topps Picture Perfect

	MINT	NRMT
COMPLETE SET (10)	15.00	6.75
COMMON CARD (P1-P10)	.40	.18
UNLISTED STARS	.75	.35
SER.1 ODDS 1:8 HOB/RET, 1:2 HTA		
❏ P1 Ken Griffey Jr.	4.00	1.80
❏ P2 Kerry Wood	.75	.35
❏ P3 Pedro Martinez	1.00	.45
❏ P4 Mark McGwire	5.00	2.20
❏ P5 Greg Maddux	2.00	.90
❏ P6 Sammy Sosa	2.50	1.10
❏ P7 Greg Vaughn	.40	.18
❏ P8 Juan Gonzalez	1.50	.70
❏ P9 Jeff Bagwell	1.00	.45
❏ P10 Derek Jeter	2.50	1.10

1999 Topps Power Brokers

	MINT	NRMT
COMPLETE SET (20)	150.00	70.00
COMMON CARD (PB1-PB20)	2.00	.90
UNLISTED STARS	4.00	1.80
SER.1 ODDS 1:36 HOB/RET, 1:8 HTA		
*REFRACTORS: 1X TO 2.5X HI COLUMN		
SER.1 REF.ODDS 1:144 HOB/RET, 1:32 HTA		
❏ PB1 Mark McGwire	25.00	11.00
❏ PB2 Andres Galarraga	2.50	1.10
❏ PB3 Ken Griffey Jr.	20.00	9.00
❏ PB4 Sammy Sosa	12.00	5.50
❏ PB5 Juan Gonzalez	8.00	3.60
❏ PB6 Alex Rodriguez	12.00	5.50
❏ PB7 Frank Thomas	8.00	3.60
❏ PB8 Jeff Bagwell	5.00	2.20
❏ PB9 Vinny Castilla	2.00	.90

	MINT	NRMT
❏ PB10 Mike Piazza	12.00	5.50
❏ PB11 Greg Vaughn	2.00	.90
❏ PB12 Barry Bonds	5.00	2.20
❏ PB13 Mo Vaughn	4.00	1.80
❏ PB14 Jim Thome	4.00	1.80
❏ PB15 Larry Walker	4.00	1.80
❏ PB16 Chipper Jones	10.00	4.50
❏ PB17 Nomar Garciaparra	12.00	5.50
❏ PB18 Manny Ramirez	5.00	2.20
❏ PB19 Roger Clemens	10.00	4.50
❏ PB20 Kerry Wood	4.00	1.80

1999 Topps Record Numbers

	MINT	NRMT
COMPLETE SET (10)	20.00	9.00
COMMON CARD (RN1-RN10)	.50	.23
MINOR STARS	.50	
SER.2 ODDS 1:8 HOB/RET, 1:2 HTA		
❏ RN1 Mark McGwire	5.00	2.20
❏ RN2 Mike Piazza	2.50	1.10
❏ RN3 Curt Schilling	.50	.23
❏ RN4 Ken Griffey Jr.	4.00	1.80
❏ RN5 Sammy Sosa	2.50	1.10
❏ RN6 Nomar Garciaparra	2.50	1.10
❏ RN7 Kerry Wood	.75	.35
❏ RN8 Roger Clemens	2.00	.90
❏ RN9 Cal Ripken	3.00	1.35
❏ RN10 Mark McGwire	5.00	2.20

1999 Topps Record Numbers Gold

	MINT	NRMT
RANDOM INSERTS IN ALL SER.2 PACKS		
PRINT RUNS LISTED BELOW		
❏ RN1 Mark McGwire/70	250.00	110.00
❏ RN2 Mike Piazza/362	40.00	18.00
❏ RN3 Curt Schilling/319	8.00	3.60
❏ RN4 Ken Griffey Jr./350	60.00	27.00
❏ RN5 Sammy Sosa/20	400.00	180.00
❏ RN6 Nomar Garciaparra/30	400.00	180.00
❏ RN7 Kerry Wood/20	120.00	55.00
❏ RN8 Roger Clemens/20	300.00	135.00
❏ RN9 Cal Ripken/2632	25.00	11.00
❏ RN10 Mark McGwire/162	120.00	55.00

1999 Topps Ryan

	MINT	NRMT
COMPLETE SET (27)	150.00	70.00
COMPLETE SERIES 1 (14)	80.00	36.00
COMPLETE SERIES 2 (13)	80.00	36.00
COMMON CARD (1-27)	6.00	2.70
STATED ODDS 1:18 HOB/RET, 1:5 HTA		
RYAN AU SER.1 ODDS 1:4260 HOB, 1:1172 HTA		
RYAN AU SER.2 ODDS 1:5007 HOB		
ODD NUMBERS DISTRIBUTED IN SER.1		
EVEN NUMBERS DISTRIBUTED IN SER.2		
❏ 1 Nolan Ryan 1968	15.00	6.75
❏ 2 Nolan Ryan 1969	6.00	2.70
❏ 3 Nolan Ryan 1970	6.00	2.70
❏ 4 Nolan Ryan 1971	6.00	2.70
❏ 5 Nolan Ryan 1972	6.00	2.70
❏ 6 Nolan Ryan 1973	6.00	2.70
❏ 7 Nolan Ryan 1974	6.00	2.70
❏ 8 Nolan Ryan 1975	6.00	2.70
❏ 9 Nolan Ryan 1976	6.00	2.70
❏ 10 Nolan Ryan 1977	6.00	2.70
❏ 11 Nolan Ryan 1978	6.00	2.70
❏ 12 Nolan Ryan 1979	6.00	2.70
❏ 13 Nolan Ryan 1980	6.00	2.70
❏ 14 Nolan Ryan 1981	6.00	2.70
❏ 15 Nolan Ryan 1982	6.00	2.70
❏ 16 Nolan Ryan 1983	6.00	2.70
❏ 17 Nolan Ryan 1984	6.00	2.70
❏ 18 Nolan Ryan 1985	6.00	2.70
❏ 19 Nolan Ryan 1986	6.00	2.70
❏ 20 Nolan Ryan 1987	6.00	2.70
❏ 21 Nolan Ryan 1988	6.00	2.70
❏ 22 Nolan Ryan 1989	6.00	2.70
❏ 23 Nolan Ryan 1990	6.00	2.70
❏ 24 Nolan Ryan 1991	6.00	2.70
❏ 25 Nolan Ryan 1992	6.00	2.70
❏ 26 Nolan Ryan 1993	6.00	2.70
❏ 27 Nolan Ryan 1994	6.00	2.70

1999 Topps Ryan Autographs

	MINT	NRMT
COMMON CARD (1-27)	250.00	110.00
SER.1 ODDS 1:4260 HOB, 1:1172 HTA		
SER.2 ODDS 1:5007 HOB		
❏ 1 Nolan Ryan 1968	500.00	220.00

1999 Topps Ryan Finest

	MINT	NRMT
COMPLETE SET (27)	270.00	120.00
COMPLETE SERIES 1 (13)	120.00	55.00
COMPLETE SERIES 2 (14)	150.00	70.00
COMMON CARD (1-27)	12.00	5.50
STATED ODDS 1:72 HOB/RET, 1:16 HTA		
COMP.REF.SET (27)	550.00	250.00
COMP.REF.SER.1 (13)	300.00	135.00
COMP.REF.SER.2 (14)	350.00	160.00
*FINEST REF: 1.25X TO 2.5X FINEST		
REF.ODDS 1:288 HOB/RET, 1:76 HTA		
EVEN CARDS DISTRIBUTED IN SER.1		

ODD CARDS DISTRIBUTED IN SER.2

	MINT	NRMT
❏ 1 Nolan Ryan 1968	25.00	11.00

1999 Topps Traded

	MINT	NRMT
COMP.FACT SET (121)	40.00	18.00
COMMON CARD (T1-T121)	.15	.07
MINOR STARS	.25	.11
SEMISTARS	.40	.18
UNLISTED STARS	.60	.25
DISTRIBUTED ONLY IN FACTORY SET FORM		
❏ T1 Seth Etherton	.25	.11
❏ T2 Mark Harriger	.50	.23
❏ T3 Matt Wise	.50	.23
❏ T4 Carlos Hernandez	.50	.23
❏ T5 Julio Lugo	.50	.23
❏ T6 Mike Nannini	.25	.11
❏ T7 Justin Bowles	.50	.23
❏ T8 Mark Mulder	1.50	.70
❏ T9 Roberto Vaz	.50	.23
❏ T10 Felipe Lopez	1.50	.70
❏ T11 Matt Belisle	.50	.23
❏ T12 Micah Bowie	.40	.18
❏ T13 Ruben Quevedo	.75	.35
❏ T14 Jose Garcia	.75	.35
❏ T15 David Kelton	1.25	.55
❏ T16 Phil Norton	.25	.11
❏ T17 Corey Patterson	6.00	2.70
❏ T18 Ron Walker	.50	.23
❏ T19 Paul Hoover	.50	.23
❏ T20 Ryan Rupe	1.00	.45
❏ T21 J.D. Closser	1.00	.45
❏ T22 Rob Ryan	.50	.23
❏ T23 Steve Colyer	.75	.35
❏ T24 Bubba Crosby	.75	.35
❏ T25 Luke Prokopec	.50	.23
❏ T26 Matt Blank	.75	.35
❏ T27 Josh McKinley	.40	.18
❏ T28 Nate Bump	.25	.11
❏ T29 Giuseppe Chiaramonte	1.00	.45
❏ T30 Arturo McDowell	.50	.23
❏ T31 Tony Torcato	.50	.23
❏ T32 Dave Roberts	.75	.35
❏ T33 C.C. Sabathia	2.50	1.10
❏ T34 Sean Spencer	.50	.23
❏ T35 Chip Ambres	.60	.25
❏ T36 A.J. Burnett	.75	.35
❏ T37 Mo Bruce	.75	.35
❏ T38 Jason Tyner	.50	.23
❏ T39 Mamon Tucker	.50	.23
❏ T40 Sean Burroughs	5.00	2.20
❏ T41 Kevin Eberwein	.75	.35
❏ T42 Junior Herndon	.50	.23
❏ T43 Bryan Wolff	.50	.23
❏ T44 Pat Burrell	4.00	1.80
❏ T45 Eric Valent	1.25	.55
❏ T46 Carlos Pena	1.50	.70
❏ T47 Mike Zywica	.25	.11
❏ T48 Adam Everett	.60	.25
❏ T49 Juan Pena	.50	.23
❏ T50 Adam Dunn	1.50	.70
❏ T51 Austin Kearns	.75	.35
❏ T52 Jacobo Sequea	.50	.23
❏ T53 Choo Freeman	.60	.25
❏ T54 Jeff Winchester	.25	.11
❏ T55 Matt Burch	.25	.11
❏ T56 Chris George	.25	.11
❏ T57 Scott Mullen	.50	.23
❏ T58 Kit Pellow	.50	.23
❏ T59 Mark Quinn	2.50	1.10
❏ T60 Nate Cornejo	.50	.23
❏ T61 Ryan Mills	.25	.11
❏ T62 Kevin Beirne	.50	.23
❏ T63 Kip Wells	1.50	.70
❏ T64 Juan Rivera	1.25	.55
❏ T65 Alfonso Soriano	5.00	2.20
❏ T66 Josh Hamilton	6.00	2.70
❏ T67 Josh Girdley	1.00	.45
❏ T68 Kyle Snyder	1.00	.45
❏ T69 Mike Paradis	.50	.23
❏ T70 Jason Jennings	1.00	.45
❏ T71 David Walling	1.00	.45
❏ T72 Omar Ortiz	.50	.23
❏ T73 Jay Gehrke	.50	.23
❏ T74 Casey Burns	.50	.23
❏ T75 Carl Crawford	1.25	.55
❏ T76 Reggie Sanders	.15	.07
❏ T77 Will Clark	.60	.25
❏ T78 David Wells	.25	.11
❏ T79 Paul Konerko	.25	.11
❏ T80 Armando Benitez	.15	.07
❏ T81 Brant Brown	.15	.07
❏ T82 Mo Vaughn	.60	.25
❏ T83 Jose Canseco	.75	.35
❏ T84 Albert Belle	.60	.25
❏ T85 Dean Palmer	.25	.11
❏ T86 Greg Vaughn	.25	.11
❏ T87 Mark Clark	.15	.07
❏ T88 Pat Meares	.15	.07
❏ T89 Eric Davis	.25	.11
❏ T90 Brian Giles	.25	.11
❏ T91 Jeff Brantley	.15	.07
❏ T92 Bret Boone	.25	.11
❏ T93 Ron Gant	.25	.11
❏ T94 Mike Cameron	.15	.07
❏ T95 Charles Johnson	.25	.11
❏ T96 Denny Neagle	.25	.11
❏ T97 Brian Hunter	.15	.07
❏ T98 Jose Hernandez	.15	.07
❏ T99 Rick Aguilera	.15	.07
❏ T100 Tony Batista	.25	.11
❏ T101 Roger Cedeno	.25	.11
❏ T102 Creighton Gubanich	.15	.07
❏ T103 Tim Belcher	.15	.07
❏ T104 Bruce Aven	.15	.07
❏ T105 Brian Daubach	3.00	1.35
❏ T106 Ed Sprague	.15	.07
❏ T107 Michael Tucker	.15	.07
❏ T108 Homer Bush	.15	.07
❏ T109 Armando Reynoso	.15	.07
❏ T110 Brook Fordyce	.15	.07
❏ T111 Matt Mantei	.25	.11
❏ T112 Dave Mlicki	.15	.07
❏ T113 Kenny Rogers	.15	.07
❏ T114 Livan Hernandez	.15	.07
❏ T115 Butch Huskey	.15	.07
❏ T116 David Segui	.15	.07
❏ T117 Darryl Hamilton	.15	.07
❏ T118 Terry Mulholland	.15	.07
❏ T119 Randy Velarde	.15	.07
❏ T120 Bill Taylor	.15	.07
❏ T121 Kevin Appier	.25	.11

1999 Topps Traded Autographs

	MINT	NRMT
COMMON CARD (T1-T75)	10.00	4.50
ONE AUTO PER FACTORY SET		
❏ T1 Seth Etherton	10.00	4.50
❏ T2 Mark Harriger	10.00	4.50
❏ T3 Matt Wise	10.00	4.50
❏ T4 Carlos Hernandez	10.00	4.50
❏ T5 Julio Lugo	10.00	4.50
❏ T6 Mike Nannini	10.00	4.50
❏ T7 Justin Bowles	10.00	4.50
❏ T8 Mark Mulder	20.00	9.00
❏ T9 Roberto Vaz	10.00	4.50
❏ T10 Felipe Lopez	20.00	9.00
❏ T11 Matt Belisle	10.00	4.50
❏ T12 Micah Bowie	15.00	6.75
❏ T13 Ruben Quevedo	10.00	4.50
❏ T14 Jose Garcia	10.00	4.50
❏ T15 David Kelton	15.00	6.75
❏ T16 Phil Norton	10.00	4.50
❏ T17 Corey Patterson	60.00	27.00
❏ T18 Ron Walker	10.00	4.50
❏ T19 Paul Hoover	10.00	4.50
❏ T20 Ryan Rupe	15.00	6.75
❏ T21 J.D. Closser	15.00	6.75
❏ T22 Rob Ryan	10.00	4.50
❏ T23 Steve Colyer	10.00	4.50
❏ T24 Bubba Crosby	10.00	4.50
❏ T25 Luke Prokopec	10.00	4.50
❏ T26 Matt Blank	15.00	6.75
❏ T27 Josh McKinley	15.00	6.75
❏ T28 Nate Bump	10.00	4.50
❏ T29 Giuseppe Chiaramonte	15.00	6.75
❏ T30 Arturo McDowell	15.00	6.75
❏ T31 Tony Torcato	15.00	6.75
❏ T32 Dave Roberts	10.00	4.50
❏ T33 C.C. Sabathia	30.00	13.50
❏ T34 Sean Spencer	10.00	4.50
❏ T35 Chip Ambres	15.00	6.75
❏ T36 A.J. Burnett	15.00	6.75
❏ T37 Mo Bruce	10.00	4.50
❏ T38 Jason Tyner	15.00	6.75
❏ T39 Mamon Tucker	10.00	4.50
❏ T40 Sean Burroughs	60.00	27.00
❏ T41 Kevin Eberwein	10.00	4.50
❏ T42 Junior Herndon	10.00	4.50
❏ T43 Bryan Wolff	10.00	4.50
❏ T44 Pat Burrell	50.00	22.00
❏ T45 Eric Valent	25.00	11.00
❏ T46 Carlos Pena	20.00	9.00
❏ T47 Mike Zywica	10.00	4.50
❏ T48 Adam Everett	15.00	6.75
❏ T49 Juan Pena	10.00	4.50
❏ T50 Adam Dunn	20.00	9.00
❏ T51 Austin Kearns	20.00	9.00
❏ T52 Jacobo Sequea	10.00	4.50
❏ T53 Choo Freeman	15.00	6.75
❏ T54 Jeff Winchester	10.00	4.50
❏ T55 Matt Burch	10.00	4.50
❏ T56 Chris George	10.00	4.50
❏ T57 Scott Mullen	10.00	4.50
❏ T58 Kit Pellow	15.00	6.75
❏ T59 Mark Quinn	30.00	13.50
❏ T60 Nate Cornejo	15.00	6.75
❏ T61 Ryan Mills	10.00	4.50

		MINT	NRMT
❏ T62	Kevin Beirne	10.00	4.50
❏ T63	Kip Wells	20.00	9.00
❏ T64	Juan Rivera	15.00	6.75
❏ T65	Alfonso Soriano	60.00	27.00
❏ T66	Josh Hamilton	80.00	36.00
❏ T67	Josh Girdley	15.00	6.75
❏ T68	Kyle Snyder	15.00	6.75
❏ T69	Mike Paradis	10.00	4.50
❏ T70	Jason Jennings	15.00	6.75
❏ T71	David Walling	15.00	6.75
❏ T72	Omar Ortiz	10.00	4.50
❏ T73	Jay Gehrke	10.00	4.50
❏ T74	Casey Burns	10.00	4.50
❏ T75	Carl Crawford	15.00	6.75

2000 Topps

	MINT	NRMT
COMPLETE SERIES 1 (239)	25.00	11.00
COMMON CARD (1-6/8-240)	.10	.05
MINOR STARS	.15	.07
SEMISTARS	.25	.11
UNLISTED STARS	.40	.18
MCGWIRE MM SET (5)	15.00	6.75
MCGWIRE MM (236A-236E)	4.00	1.80
AARON MM SET (5)	8.00	3.60
AARON MM (237A-237E)	2.00	.90
RIPKEN MM SET (5)	12.00	5.50
RIPKEN MM (238A-238E)	3.00	1.35
BOGGS MM SET (5)	3.00	1.35
BOGGS MM (239A-239E)	.75	.35
GWYNN MM SET (5)	8.00	3.60
GWYNN MM (240A-240E)	2.00	.90

CARD NUMBER 7 DOES NOT EXIST
SER.1 INCLUDES ONLY 1 VERSION OF 236-240
MCGWIRE '85 ODDS 1:36 HOB/RET, 1:8 HTA

❏ 1	Mark McGwire	2.00	.90
❏ 2	Tony Gwynn	1.00	.45
❏ 3	Wade Boggs	.40	.18
❏ 4	Cal Ripken	1.50	.70
❏ 5	Matt Williams	.40	.18
❏ 6	Jay Buhner	.15	.07
❏ 7	Does Not Exist		
❏ 8	Jeff Conine	.10	.05
❏ 9	Todd Greene	.10	.05
❏ 10	Mike Lieberthal	.15	.07
❏ 11	Steve Avery	.10	.05
❏ 12	Bret Saberhagen	.15	.07
❏ 13	Magglio Ordonez	.40	.18
❏ 14	Brad Radke	.15	.07
❏ 15	Derek Jeter	1.25	.55
❏ 16	Javy Lopez	.15	.07
❏ 17	Russ Davis	.10	.05
❏ 18	Armando Benitez	.10	.05
❏ 19	B.J. Surhoff	.15	.07
❏ 20	Darryl Kile	.10	.05
❏ 21	Mark Lewis	.10	.05
❏ 22	Mike Williams	.10	.05
❏ 23	Mark McLemore	.10	.05
❏ 24	Sterling Hitchcock	.10	.05
❏ 25	Darin Erstad	.15	.07
❏ 26	Ricky Gutierrez	.10	.05
❏ 27	John Jaha	.10	.05
❏ 28	Homer Bush	.15	.07
❏ 29	Darrin Fletcher	.10	.05
❏ 30	Mark Grace	.25	.11
❏ 31	Fred McGriff	.25	.11
❏ 32	Omar Daal	.10	.05
❏ 33	Eric Karros	.15	.07
❏ 34	Orlando Cabrera	.10	.05
❏ 35	J.T. Snow	.10	.05
❏ 36	Luis Castillo	.10	.05
❏ 37	Rey Ordonez	.15	.07
❏ 38	Bob Abreu	.15	.07
❏ 39	Warren Morris	.10	.05
❏ 40	Juan Gonzalez	.75	.35
❏ 41	Mike Lansing	.10	.05
❏ 42	Chili Davis	.15	.07
❏ 43	Dean Palmer	.15	.07
❏ 44	Hank Aaron	1.00	.45
❏ 45	Jeff Bagwell	.50	.23
❏ 46	Jose Valentin	.10	.05
❏ 47	Shannon Stewart	.15	.07
❏ 48	Kent Bottenfield	.10	.05
❏ 49	Jeff Shaw	.10	.05
❏ 50	Sammy Sosa	1.25	.55
❏ 51	Randy Johnson	.40	.18
❏ 52	Benny Agbayani	.10	.05
❏ 53	Dante Bichette	.15	.07
❏ 54	Pete Harnisch	.10	.05
❏ 55	Frank Thomas	.75	.35
❏ 56	Jorge Posada	.10	.05
❏ 57	Todd Walker	.10	.05
❏ 58	Juan Encarnacion	.15	.07
❏ 59	Mike Sweeney	.10	.05
❏ 60	Pedro Martinez	.50	.23
❏ 61	Lee Stevens	.15	.07
❏ 62	Brian Giles	.15	.07
❏ 63	Chad Ogea	.10	.05
❏ 64	Ivan Rodriguez	.50	.23
❏ 65	Roger Cedeno	.15	.07
❏ 66	David Justice	.40	.18
❏ 67	Steve Trachsel	.10	.05
❏ 68	Eli Marrero	.10	.05
❏ 69	Dave Nilsson	.10	.05
❏ 70	Ken Caminiti	.15	.07
❏ 71	Tim Raines	.15	.07
❏ 72	Brian Jordan	.15	.07
❏ 73	Jeff Blauser	.10	.05
❏ 74	Bernard Gilkey	.10	.05
❏ 75	John Flaherty	.10	.05
❏ 76	Brent Mayne	.10	.05
❏ 77	Jose Vidro	.10	.05
❏ 78	David Bell	.10	.05
❏ 79	Bruce Aven	.10	.05
❏ 80	John Olerud	.15	.07
❏ 81	Juan Guzman	.10	.05
❏ 82	Woody Williams	.10	.05
❏ 83	Ed Sprague	.10	.05
❏ 84	Joe Girardi	.10	.05
❏ 85	Barry Larkin	.40	.18
❏ 86	Mike Caruso	.10	.05
❏ 87	Bobby Higginson	.10	.05
❏ 88	Roberto Kelly	.10	.05
❏ 89	Edgar Martinez	.15	.07
❏ 90	Mark Kotsay	.15	.07
❏ 91	Paul Sorrento	.10	.05
❏ 92	Eric Young	.10	.05
❏ 93	Carlos Delgado	.40	.18
❏ 94	Troy Glaus	.40	.18
❏ 95	Ben Grieve	.40	.18
❏ 96	Jose Lima	.15	.07
❏ 97	Garret Anderson	.15	.07
❏ 98	Luis Gonzalez	.15	.07
❏ 99	Carl Pavano	.10	.05
❏ 100	Alex Rodriguez	1.25	.55
❏ 101	Preston Wilson	.15	.07
❏ 102	Ron Gant	.15	.07
❏ 103	Brady Anderson	.15	.07
❏ 104	Rickey Henderson	.50	.23
❏ 105	Gary Sheffield	.15	.07
❏ 106	Mickey Morandini	.10	.05
❏ 107	Jim Edmonds	.15	.07
❏ 108	Kris Benson	.10	.05
❏ 109	Adrian Beltre	.15	.07
❏ 110	Alex Fernandez	.10	.05
❏ 111	Dan Wilson	.10	.05
❏ 112	Mark Clark	.10	.05
❏ 113	Greg Vaughn	.15	.07
❏ 114	Neifi Perez	.15	.07
❏ 115	Paul O'Neill	.15	.07
❏ 116	Jermaine Dye	.15	.05
❏ 117	Todd Jones	.10	.05
❏ 118	Terry Steinbach	.15	.07
❏ 119	Greg Norton	.10	.05
❏ 120	Curt Schilling	.25	.11
❏ 121	Todd Zeile	.15	.07
❏ 122	Edgardo Alfonzo	.25	.11
❏ 123	Ryan McGuire	.10	.05
❏ 124	Rich Aurilia	.10	.05
❏ 125	John Smoltz	.25	.11
❏ 126	Bob Wickman	.10	.05
❏ 127	Billy Wagner	.10	.05
❏ 128	Chuck Finley	.15	.07
❏ 129	Billy Wagner	.15	.07
❏ 130	Todd Hundley	.15	.07
❏ 131	Dwight Gooden	.15	.07
❏ 132	Russ Ortiz	.10	.05
❏ 133	Mike Lowell	.10	.05
❏ 134	Reggie Sanders	.15	.07
❏ 135	John Valentin	.10	.05
❏ 136	Brad Ausmus	.10	.05
❏ 137	Chad Kreuter	.10	.05
❏ 138	David Cone	.25	.11
❏ 139	Brook Fordyce	.10	.05
❏ 140	Roberto Alomar	.40	.18
❏ 141	Charles Nagy	.15	.07
❏ 142	Brian Hunter	.10	.05
❏ 143	Mike Mussina	.40	.18
❏ 144	Robin Ventura	.15	.07
❏ 145	Kevin Brown	.25	.11
❏ 146	Pat Hentgen	.10	.05
❏ 147	Ryan Klesko	.15	.07
❏ 148	Derek Bell	.15	.07
❏ 149	Andy Sheets	.10	.05
❏ 150	Larry Walker	.40	.18
❏ 151	Scott Williamson	.10	.05
❏ 152	Jose Offerman	.15	.07
❏ 153	Doug Mientkiewicz	.10	.05
❏ 154	John Snyder	.25	.11
❏ 155	Sandy Alomar Jr.	.15	.07
❏ 156	Joe Nathan	.10	.05
❏ 157	Lance Johnson	.10	.05
❏ 158	Odalis Perez	.10	.05
❏ 159	Hideo Nomo	.40	.18
❏ 160	Steve Finley	.10	.05
❏ 161	Dave Martinez	.10	.05
❏ 162	Matt Walbeck	.10	.05
❏ 163	Bill Spiers	.10	.05
❏ 164	Fernando Tatis	.25	.11
❏ 165	Kenny Lofton	.25	.11
❏ 166	Paul Byrd	.10	.05
❏ 167	Aaron Sele	.15	.07
❏ 168	Eddie Taubensee	.10	.05
❏ 169	Reggie Jefferson	.10	.05
❏ 170	Roger Clemens	1.00	.45
❏ 171	Francisco Cordova	.10	.05
❏ 172	Mike Bordick	.10	.05
❏ 173	Wally Joyner	.15	.07
❏ 174	Marvin Benard	.10	.05
❏ 175	Jason Kendall	.15	.07
❏ 176	Mike Stanley	.10	.05
❏ 177	Chad Allen	.10	.05
❏ 178	Carlos Beltran	.40	.18
❏ 179	Deivi Cruz	.10	.05
❏ 180	Chipper Jones	1.00	.45
❏ 181	Vladimir Guerrero	.50	.23
❏ 182	Dave Burba	.10	.05
❏ 183	Tom Goodwin	.10	.05
❏ 184	Brian Daubach	.10	.05
❏ 185	Jay Bell	.15	.07
❏ 186	Roy Halladay	.15	.07
❏ 187	Miguel Tejada	.15	.07
❏ 188	Armando Rios	.10	.05
❏ 189	Fernando Vina	.10	.05
❏ 190	Eric Davis	.15	.07
❏ 191	Henry Rodriguez	.10	.05
❏ 192	Joe McEwing	.15	.07
❏ 193	Jeff Kent	.15	.07
❏ 194	Mike Jackson	.10	.05
❏ 195	Mike Morgan	.10	.05
❏ 196	Jeff Montgomery	.10	.05
❏ 197	Jeff Zimmerman	.10	.05
❏ 198	Tony Fernandez	.10	.05
❏ 199	Jason Giambi	.25	.11
❏ 200	Jose Canseco	.50	.23
❏ 201	Alex Gonzalez	.10	.05
❏ 202	Jack Cust	.15	.07

Mike Colangelo
Dee Brown
❏ 203 Felipe Lopez .... 1.00 .45
Alfonso Soriano
Pablo Ozuna
❏ 204 Erubiel Durazo .... 1.00 .45
Pat Burrell
Nick Johnson
❏ 205 John Sneed .... .50 .23
Kip Wells
Matt Blank
❏ 206 Josh Kalinowski .... .50 .23
Michael Tejera
Chris Mears
❏ 207 Roosevelt Brown ...... 1.25 .55
Corey Patterson
Lance Berkman
❏ 208 Kit Pellow .... .15 .07
Kevin Barker
Russ Branyan
❏ 209 B.J. Garbe .... 1.50 .70
Larry Bigbie
❏ 210 Eric Munson .... 1.50 .70
Bobby Bradley
❏ 211 Josh Girdley .... .15 .07
Kyle Snyder
❏ 212 Chance Caple .... .50 .23
Jason Jennings
❏ 213 Ryan Christianson ...... .50 .23
Brett Myers
❏ 214 Jason Stumm .... .75 .35
Rob Purvis
❏ 215 David Walling .... .15 .07
Mike Paradis
❏ 216 Omar Ortiz .... .15 .07
Jay Gehrke
❏ 217 David Cone HL .... .10 .05
❏ 218 Jose Jimenez HL .... .10 .05
❏ 219 Chris Singleton HL ...... .10 .05
❏ 220 Fernando Tatis HL ...... .10 .05
❏ 221 Robin Ventura HL ...... .10 .05
❏ 222 Kevin Millwood DIV ...... .10 .05
❏ 223 Todd Pratt DIV .... .10 .05
❏ 224 Orlando Hernandez DIV .10 .05
❏ 225 Pedro Martinez DIV ...... .50 .23
❏ 226 Tom Glavine LCS .... .15 .07
❏ 227 Bernie Williams LCS .... .15 .07
❏ 228 Mariano Rivera LCS ...... .10 .05
❏ 229 Tony Gwynn 20CB ...... 1.00 .45
❏ 230 Wade Boggs 20CB ...... .15 .07
❏ 231 Lance Johnson CB ...... .10 .05
❏ 232 Mark McGwire 20CB .... 2.00 .90
❏ 233 Mark McGwire 20CB .... 2.00 .90
❏ 234 Rickey Henderson 20CB .50 .23
❏ 235 Roger Clemens 20CB .. 1.00 .45
❏ 236A M.McGwire MM 1st HR 5.00 2.20
❏ 236B M.McGwire MM 1987 HR 5.00 2.20
❏ 236C M.McGwire MM 62nd HR 5.00 2.20
❏ 236D M.McGwire MM 70th HR.. 5.00 2.20
❏ 236E M.McGwire MM 500th HR 5.00 2.20
❏ 237A H.Aaron MM 1st Career HR 2.00 .90
❏ 237B H.Aaron MM 1957 MVP 2.00 .90
❏ 237C H.Aaron MM 3000th Hit 2.00 .90
❏ 237D H.Aaron MM 715th HR 2.00 .90
❏ 237E H.Aaron MM 755th HR 2.00 .90
❏ 238A C.Ripken MM 1982 ROY .. 3.00 1.35
❏ 238B C.Ripken MM 1991 MVP .. 3.00 1.35
❏ 238C C.Ripken MM 2131 Game 3.00 1.35
❏ 238D C.Ripken MM Streak Ends 3.00 1.35
❏ 238E C.Ripken MM 400th HR 3.00 1.35
❏ 239A W.Boggs MM 1983 Batting .75 .35
❏ 239B W.Boggs MM 1988 Batting .75 .35
❏ 239C W.Boggs MM 2000th Hit.. .75 .35
❏ 239D W.Boggs MM 1996 Champs .75 .35
❏ 239E W.Boggs MM 3000th Hit.75 .35
❏ 240A T.Gwynn MM 1984 Batting 2.00 .90
❏ 240B T.Gwynn MM 1984 NLCS 2.00 .90

❏ 240C T.Gwynn MM 1995 Batting 2.00 .90
❏ 240D T.Gwynn MM 1998 NLCS 2.00 .90
❏ 240E T.Gwynn MM 3000th Hit 2.00 .90
❏ NNO Mark McGwire 85 Reprint 5.00 2.20

2000 Topps 20th Century Best Sequential

	MINT	NRMT
SER.1 STATED ODDS 1:869 HOBBY, 1:239 HTA		
PRINT RUNS LISTED BELOW		

❏ CB1 T.Gwynn AVG/339
❏ CB2 W.Boggs 2B/578
❏ CB3 L.Johnson 3B/117
❏ CB4 M.McGwire HR/522
❏ CB5 R.Henderson SB/1334 30.00 13.50
❏ CB6 R.Henderson RUN/2103 20.00 9.00
❏ CB7 R.Clemens WIN/247

2000 Topps MVP Promotion

	MINT	NRMT
COMMON CARD (1-6/8-201)....	8.00	3.60
*STARS: 30X TO 80X BASIC CARDS		
*YNG.STARS: 25X TO 60X BASIC CARDS		
SER.1 ODDS 1:510 HOB/RET, 1:140 HTA		
STATED PRINT RUN 100 SETS		
EXCHANGE DEADLINE 10/15/2000		
CARD NUMBERS 7 AND 44 DO NOT EXIST		
MVP PARALLELS ARE UNNUMBERED		

2000 Topps Oversize

	MINT	NRMT
COMPLETE SET (8)	20.00	9.00
COMMON CARD (1-18)	1.25	.55
ONE PER HOBBY BOX		

❏ 1 Mark McGwire 5.00 2.20

❏ 2 Hank Aaron 2.50 1.10
❏ 3 Derek Jeter 3.00 1.35
❏ 4 Sammy Sosa 3.00 1.35
❏ 5 Alex Rodriguez 3.00 1.35
❏ 6 Chipper Jones 2.50 1.10
❏ 7 Cal Ripken 4.00 1.80
❏ 8 Pedro Martinez .... 1.25 .55

2000 Topps 21st Century

	MINT	NRMT
COMPLETE SET (10)	12.00	5.50
COMMON CARD (C1-C10)	.40	.18
UNLISTED STARS	.75	.35
SER.1 STATED ODDS 1:18 HOB/RET, 1:5 HTA		

❏ C1 Ben Grieve .... .75 .35
❏ C2 Alex Gonzalez .... .50 .23
❏ C3 Derek Jeter 2.50 1.10
❏ C4 Sean Casey .... .75 .35
❏ C5 Nomar Garciaparra 2.50 1.10
❏ C6 Alex Rodriguez 2.50 1.10
❏ C7 Scott Rolen .... 1.00 .45
❏ C8 Andruw Jones .... .75 .35
❏ C9 Vladimir Guerrero ...... 1.00 .45
❏ C10 Todd Helton .... .75 .35

2000 Topps Aaron

	MINT	NRMT
COMPLETE SERIES 1 (12)	75.00	34.00
COMMON CARD (1-23)	6.00	2.70

		MINT	NRMT
❏ 1	Hank Aaron 1954	10.00	4.50
❏ 3	Hank Aaron 1956	6.00	2.70
❏ 5	Hank Aaron 1958	6.00	2.70
❏ 7	Hank Aaron 1960	6.00	2.70
❏ 9	Hank Aaron 1962	6.00	2.70
❏ 11	Hank Aaron 1964	6.00	2.70
❏ 13	Hank Aaron 1966	6.00	2.70
❏ 15	Hank Aaron 1968	6.00	2.70
❏ 17	Hank Aaron 1970	6.00	2.70
❏ 19	Hank Aaron 1972	6.00	2.70
❏ 21	Hank Aaron 1974	6.00	2.70
❏ 23	Hank Aaron 1976	6.00	2.70

2000 Topps Aaron Autograph Exchange

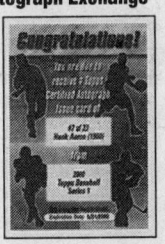

	MINT	NRMT
COMMON CARD (1-23)	175.00	80.00

SER.1 ODDS 1:4361 HOB/RET, 1:1199 HTA
EVEN YEAR CARDS DISTRIBUTED IN SER.1
EXCHANGE DEADLINE: 5/31/2000

2000 Topps Aaron Chrome

	MINT	NRMT
COMPLETE SERIES 1 (11)	80.00	36.00
COMMON CARD (2-22)	8.00	3.60

SER.1 STATED ODDS 1:72 HOB/RET, 1:16 HTA
*CHROME REF: 1.25X TO 3X CHROME
SER.1 CH.REF.ODDS 1:288 HOB/RET, 1:76 HTA
ODD YEAR CARDS DISTRIBUTED IN SER.1

2000 Topps All-Topps N.L. Team

	MINT	NRMT
COMPLETE SET (10)	10.00	4.50
COMMON CARD (AT1-AT10)	.40	.18
UNLISTED STARS	.60	.25

SER.1 STATED ODDS 1:12 HOB/RET, 1:3 HTA

❏ AT1	Greg Maddux	1.50	.70
❏ AT2	Mike Piazza	2.00	.90
❏ AT3	Mark McGwire	4.00	1.80
❏ AT4	Craig Biggio	.60	.25
❏ AT5	Chipper Jones	1.50	.70
❏ AT6	Barry Larkin	.60	.25
❏ AT7	Barry Bonds	.75	.35
❏ AT8	Andruw Jones	.60	.25
❏ AT9	Sammy Sosa	2.00	.90
❏ AT10	Larry Walker	.60	.25

2000 Topps Autographs

	MINT	NRMT
SER.1 GROUP A ODDS 1:7589 H/R, 1:2087 HTA
SER.1 GROUP B ODDS 1:4553 H/R, 1:1252 HTA
SER.1 GROUP C ODDS 1:1518 H/R, 1:417 HTA
SER.1 GROUP D ODDS 1:911 H/R, 1:250 HTA
SER.1 GROUP E ODDS 1:1138 H/R, 1:313 HTA

❏ TA1	Alex Rodriguez A	300.00	135.00
❏ TA2	Tony Gwynn A	200.00	90.00
❏ TA3	Vinny Castilla B	60.00	27.00
❏ TA4	Sean Casey		
❏ TA5	Shawn Green C	50.00	22.00
❏ TA6	Rey Ordonez C	50.00	22.00
❏ TA7	Matt Lawton C	15.00	6.75
❏ TA8	Tony Womack C	15.00	6.75
❏ TA9	Gabe Kapler D	25.00	11.00
❏ TA10	Pat Burrell D	50.00	22.00
❏ TA11	Preston Wilson D	30.00	13.50
❏ TA12	Troy Glaus D	30.00	13.50
❏ TA13	Carlos Beltran		
❏ TA14	Josh Girdley E	15.00	6.75
❏ TA15	B.J. Garbe E	30.00	13.50
❏ TA20	Vladimir Guerrero B	100.00	45.00
❏ TA27	Mike Sweeney D	25.00	11.00

2000 Topps Hands of Gold

	MINT	NRMT
COMPLETE SET (7)	10.00	4.50
COMMON CARD (HG1-HG7)	.40	.18
UNLISTED STARS	.75	.35

SER.1 STATED ODDS 1:18 HOB/RET, 1:5 HTA

❏ HG1	Barry Bonds	1.00	.45
❏ HG2	Ivan Rodriguez	1.00	.45
❏ HG3	Ken Griffey Jr.	4.00	1.80
❏ HG4	Roberto Alomar	.75	.35
❏ HG5	Tony Gwynn	2.00	.90
❏ HG6	Omar Vizquel	.50	.23
❏ HG7	Greg Maddux	2.00	.90

2000 Topps Perennial All-Stars

	MINT	NRMT
COMPLETE SET (10)	20.00	9.00
COMMON CARD (PA1-PA10)	1.00	.45

SER.1 STATED ODDS 1:18 HOB/RET, 1:5 HTA

❏ PA1	Ken Griffey Jr.	4.00	1.80
❏ PA2	Derek Jeter	2.50	1.10
❏ PA3	Sammy Sosa	2.50	1.10
❏ PA4	Cal Ripken	3.00	1.35
❏ PA5	Mike Piazza	2.50	1.10
❏ PA6	Nomar Garciaparra	2.50	1.10
❏ PA7	Jeff Bagwell	1.00	.45

		MINT	NRMT
☐ PA8	Barry Bonds	1.00	.45
☐ PA9	Alex Rodriguez	2.50	1.10
☐ PA10	Mark McGwire	4.00	1.80

2000 Topps Power Players

		MINT	NRMT
COMPLETE SET (20)		25.00	11.00
COMMON CARD (P1-P20)		.40	.18
UNLISTED STARS		.75	.35
SER.1 STATED ODDS 1:8 HOB/RET, 1:2 HTA			
☐ P1	Juan Gonzalez	1.50	.70
☐ P2	Ken Griffey Jr.	4.00	1.80
☐ P3	Mark McGwire	4.00	1.80
☐ P4	Nomar Garciaparra	2.50	1.10
☐ P5	Barry Bonds	1.00	.45
☐ P6	Mo Vaughn	.75	.35
☐ P7	Larry Walker	.75	.35
☐ P8	Alex Rodriguez	2.50	1.10
☐ P9	Jose Canseco	1.00	.45
☐ P10	Jeff Bagwell	1.00	.45
☐ P11	Manny Ramirez	1.00	.45
☐ P12	Albert Belle	.75	.35
☐ P13	Frank Thomas	1.50	.70
☐ P14	Mike Piazza	2.50	1.10
☐ P15	Chipper Jones	2.00	.90
☐ P16	Sammy Sosa	2.50	1.10
☐ P17	Vladimir Guerrero	1.00	.45
☐ P18	Scott Rolen	1.00	.45
☐ P19	Raul Mondesi	.50	.23
☐ P20	Derek Jeter	2.50	1.10

2000 Topps Stadium Relics

		MINT	NRMT
SER.1 STATED ODDS 1:165 HTA			
☐ SR1	Don Mattingly	200.00	90.00
☐ SR2	Carl Yastrzemski	150.00	70.00
☐ SR3	Ernie Banks	150.00	70.00
☐ SR4	Johnny Bench	200.00	90.00
☐ SR5	Willie Mays	250.00	110.00

1996 Topps Chrome

		MINT	NRMT
COMPLETE SET (165)		80.00	36.00
COMMON CARD (1-165)		.40	.18
MINOR STARS		.75	.35
UNLISTED STARS		1.50	.70
SUBSET CARDS HALF VALUE OF BASE CARDS			
☐ 1	Tony Gwynn STP	2.00	.90
☐ 2	Mike Piazza STP	2.50	1.10
☐ 3	Greg Maddux STP	2.00	.90
☐ 4	Jeff Bagwell STP	1.50	.70
☐ 5	Larry Walker STP	.75	.35
☐ 6	Barry Larkin STP	.40	.18
☐ 7	Mickey Mantle COMM	15.00	6.75
☐ 8	Tom Glavine STP	.75	.35
☐ 9	Craig Biggio STP	.75	.35
☐ 10	Barry Bonds STP	1.00	.45
☐ 11	Heathcliff Slocumb STP	.40	.18
☐ 12	Matt Williams STP	.75	.35
☐ 13	Todd Helton	8.00	3.60
☐ 14	Paul Molitor	1.50	.70
☐ 15	Glenallen Hill	.40	.18
☐ 16	Troy Percival	.75	.35
☐ 17	Albert Belle	1.50	.70
☐ 18	Mark Wohlers	.40	.18
☐ 19	Kirby Puckett	2.50	1.10
☐ 20	Mark Grace	1.00	.45
☐ 21	J.T. Snow	.75	.35
☐ 22	David Justice	1.50	.70
☐ 23	Mike Mussina	1.50	.70
☐ 24	Bernie Williams	1.50	.70
☐ 25	Ron Gant	.40	.18
☐ 26	Carlos Baerga	.40	.18
☐ 27	Gary Sheffield	.75	.35
☐ 28	Cal Ripken 2131	6.00	2.70
☐ 29	Frank Thomas	3.00	1.35
☐ 30	Kevin Seitzer	.40	.18
☐ 31	Joe Carter	.75	.35
☐ 32	Jeff King	.40	.18
☐ 33	David Cone	1.00	.45
☐ 34	Eddie Murray	1.50	.70
☐ 35	Brian Jordan	.75	.35
☐ 36	Garret Anderson	.75	.35
☐ 37	Hideo Nomo	1.50	.70
☐ 38	Steve Finley	.75	.35
☐ 39	Ivan Rodriguez	2.00	.90
☐ 40	Quivio Veras	.40	.18
☐ 41	Mark McGwire STP	8.00	3.60
☐ 42	Greg Vaughn	.75	.35
☐ 43	Randy Johnson	1.50	.70
☐ 44	David Segui	.75	.35
☐ 45	Derek Bell	.75	.35
☐ 46	John Valentin	.75	.35
☐ 47	Steve Avery	.40	.18
☐ 48	Tino Martinez	.75	.35
☐ 49	Shane Reynolds	.75	.35
☐ 50	Jim Edmonds	1.00	.45
☐ 51	Raul Mondesi	.75	.35
☐ 52	Chipper Jones	4.00	1.80
☐ 53	Gregg Jefferies	.40	.18
☐ 54	Ken Caminiti	.75	.35
☐ 55	Brian Anderson	.40	.18
☐ 56	Don Mattingly	3.00	1.35
☐ 57	Marty Cordova	.40	.18
☐ 58	Vinny Castilla	1.00	.45
☐ 59	John Smoltz	1.00	.45
☐ 60	Travis Fryman	.75	.35
☐ 61	Ryan Klesko	.75	.35
☐ 62	Alex Fernandez	.40	.18
☐ 63	Dante Bichette	.75	.35
☐ 64	Eric Karros	.75	.35
☐ 65	Roger Clemens	4.00	1.80
☐ 66	Randy Myers	.40	.18
☐ 67	Cal Ripken	6.00	2.70
☐ 68	Rod Beck	.40	.18
☐ 69	Jack McDowell	.40	.18
☐ 70	Ken Griffey Jr.	8.00	3.60
☐ 71	Ramon Martinez	.75	.35
☐ 72	Jason Giambi	.75	.35
☐ 73	Nomar Garciaparra FS	6.00	2.70
☐ 74	Billy Wagner	1.00	.45
☐ 75	Todd Greene	.40	.18
☐ 76	Paul Wilson	.40	.18
☐ 77	Johnny Damon	1.00	.45
☐ 78	Alan Benes	.40	.18
☐ 79	Karim Garcia FS	.75	.35
☐ 80	Derek Jeter FS	5.00	2.20
☐ 81	Kirby Puckett STP	1.50	.70
☐ 82	Cal Ripken STP	3.00	1.35
☐ 83	Albert Belle STP	.75	.35
☐ 84	Randy Johnson STP	.75	.35
☐ 85	Wade Boggs STP	.75	.35
☐ 86	Carlos Baerga STP	.40	.18
☐ 87	Ivan Rodriguez STP	1.00	.45
☐ 88	Mike Mussina STP	.75	.35
☐ 89	Frank Thomas STP	1.50	.70
☐ 90	Ken Griffey Jr. STP	4.00	1.80
☐ 91	Jose Mesa STP	.40	.18
☐ 92	Matt Morris	3.00	1.35
☐ 93	Mike Piazza	5.00	2.20
☐ 94	Edgar Martinez	.75	.35
☐ 95	Chuck Knoblauch	1.50	.70
☐ 96	Andres Galarraga	1.50	.70
☐ 97	Tony Gwynn	4.00	1.80
☐ 98	Lee Smith	.75	.35
☐ 99	Sammy Sosa	5.00	2.20
☐ 100	Jim Thome	1.50	.70
☐ 101	Bernard Gilkey	.40	.18
☐ 102	Brady Anderson	.75	.35
☐ 103	Rico Brogna	.40	.18
☐ 104	Len Dykstra	.75	.35
☐ 105	Tom Glavine	1.50	.70
☐ 106	John Olerud	.75	.35
☐ 107	Terry Steinbach	.40	.18
☐ 108	Brian Hunter	.40	.18
☐ 109	Jay Buhner	.75	.35
☐ 110	Mo Vaughn	1.50	.70
☐ 111	Jose Mesa	.40	.18
☐ 112	Brett Butler	.75	.35
☐ 113	Chili Davis	.75	.35
☐ 114	Paul O'Neill	.75	.35
☐ 115	Roberto Alomar	1.50	.70
☐ 116	Barry Larkin	1.50	.70
☐ 117	Marquis Grissom	.40	.18
☐ 118	Will Clark	1.50	.70
☐ 119	Barry Bonds	2.00	.90
☐ 120	Ozzie Smith	2.00	.90
☐ 121	Pedro Martinez	2.00	.90
☐ 122	Craig Biggio	1.50	.70
☐ 123	Moises Alou	.75	.35
☐ 124	Robin Ventura	.75	.35
☐ 125	Greg Maddux	4.00	1.80
☐ 126	Tim Salmon	1.00	.45
☐ 127	Wade Boggs	1.50	.70
☐ 128	Ismael Valdes	.75	.35
☐ 129	Juan Gonzalez	3.00	1.35
☐ 130	Ray Lankford	.75	.35
☐ 131	Bobby Bonilla	.75	.35
☐ 132	Reggie Sanders	.75	.35
☐ 133	Alex Ochoa	.40	.18
☐ 134	Mark Loretta	.40	.18
☐ 135	Jason Kendall	1.50	.70
☐ 136	Brooks Kieschnick	.40	.18
☐ 137	Chris Snopek	.40	.18
☐ 138	Ruben Rivera NOW	.75	.35
☐ 139	Jeff Suppan	.40	.18
☐ 140	John Wasdin	.40	.18
☐ 141	Jay Payton	.40	.18
☐ 142	Rick Krivda	.40	.18
☐ 143	Jimmy Haynes	.40	.18
☐ 144	Ryne Sandberg	2.00	.90

❏ 145 Matt Williams.............. 1.50 .70
❏ 146 Jose Canseco.............. 2.00 .90
❏ 147 Larry Walker.............. 1.50 .70
❏ 148 Kevin Appier................ .75 .35
❏ 149 Javy Lopez................... .75 .35
❏ 150 Dennis Eckersley........ .75 .35
❏ 151 Jason Isringhausen..... .75 .35
❏ 152 Dean Palmer............... .75 .35
❏ 153 Jeff Bagwell............... 2.00 .90
❏ 154 Rondell White............. .75 .35
❏ 155 Wally Joyner............... .75 .35
❏ 156 Fred McGriff.............. 1.00 .45
❏ 157 Cecil Fielder............... .75 .35
❏ 158 Rafael Palmeiro.......... 1.50 .70
❏ 159 Rickey Henderson...... 2.00 .90
❏ 160 Shawon Dunston........ .40 .18
❏ 161 Manny Ramirez.......... 2.00 .90
❏ 162 Alex Gonzalez............ .40 .18
❏ 163 Shawn Green.............. 1.50 .70
❏ 164 Kenny Lofton............. 1.00 .45
❏ 165 Jeff Conine................ .40 .18

1996 Topps Chrome Refractors

	MINT	NRMT
COMMON CARD (1-165)	4.00	1.80

*STARS: 4X TO 10X BASIC CARDS
*RC's/PROSPECTS: 1.5X TO 4X BASIC CARDS
STATED ODDS 1:12 HOBBY
CARDS 111-165 CONDITION SENSITIVE

1996 Topps Chrome Masters of the Game

	MINT	NRMT
COMPLETE SET (20)	60.00	27.00
COMMON CARD (1-20)	.50	.70

STATED ODDS 1:12 HOBBY
*REFRACTORS: 2.5X TO 6X BASE CARD HI
REF.STATED ODDS 1:36 HOBBY

❏ 1 Dennis Eckersley........ 1.50 .70
❏ 2 Denny Martinez........... 1.50 .70
❏ 3 Eddie Murray.............. 4.00 1.80
❏ 4 Paul Molitor............... 4.00 1.80
❏ 5 Ozzie Smith................ 5.00 2.20
❏ 6 Rickey Henderson....... 5.00 2.20
❏ 7 Tim Raines................. 1.50 .70

❏ 8 Lee Smith.................. 1.50 .70
❏ 9 Cal Ripken................. 15.00 6.75
❏ 10 Chili Davis................ 1.50 .70
❏ 11 Wade Boggs.............. 4.00 1.80
❏ 12 Tony Gwynn............. 10.00 4.50
❏ 13 Don Mattingly............ 8.00 3.60
❏ 14 Bret Saberhagen........ 1.50 .70
❏ 15 Kirby Puckett............ 6.00 2.70
❏ 16 Joe Carter............... 1.50 .70
❏ 17 Roger Clemens.......... 10.00 4.50
❏ 18 Barry Bonds.............. 5.00 2.20
❏ 19 Greg Maddux............. 10.00 4.50
❏ 20 Frank Thomas........... 8.00 3.60

1996 Topps Chrome Wrecking Crew

	MINT	NRMT
COMPLETE SET (15)	80.00	36.00
COMMON CARD (WC1-WC15)	2.00	.90

STATED ODDS 1:24 HOBBY
*REFRACTORS: 3X TO 8X BASE CARD HI
REF.STATED ODDS 1:72 HOBBY

❏ WC1 Jeff Bagwell............ 6.00 2.70
❏ WC2 Albert Belle............. 5.00 2.20
❏ WC3 Barry Bonds............ 6.00 2.70
❏ WC4 Jose Canseco.......... 6.00 2.70
❏ WC5 Joe Carter.............. 2.00 .90
❏ WC6 Cecil Fielder........... 2.00 .90
❏ WC7 Ron Gant................ 2.00 .90
❏ WC8 Juan Gonzalez......... 10.00 4.50
❏ WC9 Ken Griffey Jr......... 25.00 11.00
❏ WC10 Fred McGriff......... 3.00 1.35
❏ WC11 Mark McGwire....... 25.00 11.00
❏ WC12 Mike Piazza.......... 15.00 6.75
❏ WC13 Frank Thomas....... 10.00 4.50
❏ WC14 Mo Vaughn........... 5.00 2.20
❏ WC15 Matt Williams........ 5.00 2.20

1997 Topps Chrome

	MINT	NRMT
COMPLETE SET (165)	70.00	32.00
COMMON CARD (1-165)	.40	.18
MINOR STARS	.75	.35
UNLISTED STARS	1.50	.70

❏ 1 Barry Bonds............... 2.00 .90
❏ 2 Jose Valentin.............. .40 .18

❏ 3 Brady Anderson........... .75 .35
❏ 4 Wade Boggs............... 1.50 .70
❏ 5 Andres Galarraga........ 1.50 .70
❏ 6 Rusty Greer................ .75 .35
❏ 7 Derek Jeter............... 5.00 2.20
❏ 8 Ricky Bottalico........... .40 .18
❏ 9 Mike Piazza............... 5.00 2.20
❏ 10 Garret Anderson........ .75 .35
❏ 11 Jeff King.................. .40 .18
❏ 12 Kevin Appier............. .75 .35
❏ 13 Mark Grace.............. 1.00 .45
❏ 14 Jeff D'Amico............ .40 .18
❏ 15 Jay Buhner.............. .75 .35
❏ 16 Hal Morris............... .40 .18
❏ 17 Harold Baines........... .75 .35
❏ 18 Jeff Cirillo.............. .75 .35
❏ 19 Tom Glavine............. 1.50 .70
❏ 20 Andy Pettitte........... 1.00 .45
❏ 21 Mark McGwire.......... 8.00 3.60
❏ 22 Chuck Knoblauch....... 1.50 .70
❏ 23 Raul Mondesi............ .75 .35
❏ 24 Albert Belle............. 1.50 .70
❏ 25 Trevor Hoffman......... .75 .35
❏ 26 Eric Young............... .75 .35
❏ 27 Brian McRae............. .40 .18
❏ 28 Jim Edmonds............ 1.00 .45
❏ 29 Robb Nen................ .40 .18
❏ 30 Reggie Sanders......... .75 .35
❏ 31 Mike Lansing............ .40 .18
❏ 32 Craig Biggio............. 1.50 .70
❏ 33 Ray Lankford............ .75 .35
❏ 34 Charles Nagy............ .75 .35
❏ 35 Paul Wilson.............. .40 .18
❏ 36 John Wetteland......... .75 .35
❏ 37 Derek Bell.............. .75 .35
❏ 38 Edgar Martinez......... .75 .35
❏ 39 Rickey Henderson...... 2.00 .90
❏ 40 Jim Thome.............. 1.50 .70
❏ 41 Frank Thomas........... 3.00 1.35
❏ 42 Jackie Robinson........ 5.00 2.20
❏ 43 Terry Steinbach......... .40 .18
❏ 44 Kevin Brown............. 1.00 .45
❏ 45 Joey Hamilton........... .75 .35
❏ 46 Travis Fryman........... .75 .35
❏ 47 Juan Gonzalez........... 3.00 1.35
❏ 48 Ron Gant................ .40 .18
❏ 49 Greg Maddux............ 4.00 1.80
❏ 50 Wally Joyner............ .75 .35
❏ 51 John Valentin............ .75 .35
❏ 52 Bret Boone.............. .75 .35
❏ 53 Paul Molitor............. 1.50 .70
❏ 54 Rafael Palmeiro......... 1.50 .70
❏ 55 Todd Hundley............ .75 .35
❏ 56 Ellis Burks.............. .75 .35
❏ 57 Bernie Williams......... 1.50 .70
❏ 58 Roberto Alomar......... 1.50 .70
❏ 59 Jose Mesa.............. .40 .18
❏ 60 Troy Percival........... .40 .18
❏ 61 John Smoltz............. 1.00 .45
❏ 62 Jeff Conine............. .40 .18
❏ 63 Bernard Gilkey.......... .40 .18
❏ 64 Mickey Tettleton....... .40 .18
❏ 65 Justin Thompson........ .75 .35
❏ 66 Tony Phillips............ .40 .18
❏ 67 Ryne Sandberg.......... 2.00 .90
❏ 68 Geronimo Berroa........ .40 .18
❏ 69 Todd Hollandsworth..... .40 .18
❏ 70 Rey Ordonez............ .75 .35
❏ 71 Marquis Grissom........ .75 .35
❏ 72 Tino Martinez........... 1.50 .70
❏ 73 Steve Finley............ .75 .35
❏ 74 Andy Benes.............. .75 .35
❏ 75 Jason Kendall........... 1.00 .45
❏ 76 Johnny Damon........... .75 .35
❏ 77 Jason Giambi............ .75 .35
❏ 78 Henry Rodriguez........ .75 .35
❏ 79 Edgar Renteria......... .75 .35
❏ 80 Ray Durham............. .75 .35
❏ 81 Gregg Jefferies......... .40 .18
❏ 82 Roberto Hernandez..... .40 .18
❏ 83 Joe Carter.............. .75 .35
❏ 84 Jermaine Dye........... .75 .35
❏ 85 Julio Franco............ .75 .35
❏ 86 David Justice........... 1.50 .70
❏ 87 Jose Canseco............ 2.00 .90
❏ 88 Paul O'Neill............. .75 .35

☐ 89 Mariano Rivera	.75	.35
☐ 90 Bobby Higginson	.75	.35
☐ 91 Mark Grudzielanek	.75	.35
☐ 92 Lance Johnson	.40	.18
☐ 93 Ken Caminiti	1.00	.45
☐ 94 Gary Sheffield	.75	.35
☐ 95 Luis Castillo	.75	.35
☐ 96 Scott Rolen	2.50	1.10
☐ 97 Chipper Jones	4.00	1.80
☐ 98 Darryl Strawberry	.75	.35
☐ 99 Nomar Garciaparra	5.00	2.20
☐ 100 Jeff Bagwell	2.00	.90
☐ 101 Ken Griffey Jr.	8.00	3.60
☐ 102 Sammy Sosa	5.00	2.20
☐ 103 Jack McDowell	.40	.18
☐ 104 James Baldwin	.75	.35
☐ 105 Rocky Coppinger	.40	.18
☐ 106 Manny Ramirez	2.00	.90
☐ 107 Tim Salmon	1.50	.70
☐ 108 Eric Karros	.75	.35
☐ 109 Brett Butler	.75	.35
☐ 110 Randy Johnson	1.50	.70
☐ 111 Pat Hentgen	.75	.35
☐ 112 Rondell White	.75	.35
☐ 113 Eddie Murray	1.50	.70
☐ 114 Ivan Rodriguez	2.00	.90
☐ 115 Jermaine Allensworth	.40	.18
☐ 116 Ed Sprague	.40	.18
☐ 117 Kenny Lofton	1.00	.45
☐ 118 Alan Benes	.40	.18
☐ 119 Fred McGriff	1.00	.45
☐ 120 Alex Fernandez	.40	.18
☐ 121 Al Martin	.40	.18
☐ 122 Devon White	.40	.35
☐ 123 David Cone	1.00	.45
☐ 124 Karim Garcia	.75	.35
☐ 125 Chili Davis	.75	.35
☐ 126 Roger Clemens	4.00	1.80
☐ 127 Bobby Bonilla	.75	.35
☐ 128 Mike Mussina	1.50	.70
☐ 129 Todd Walker	1.50	.70
☐ 130 Dante Bichette	.75	.35
☐ 131 Carlos Baerga	.40	.18
☐ 132 Matt Williams	1.50	.70
☐ 133 Will Clark	1.50	.70
☐ 134 Dennis Eckersley	.75	.35
☐ 135 Ryan Klesko	.75	.35
☐ 136 Dean Palmer	.75	.35
☐ 137 Javy Lopez	.75	.35
☐ 138 Greg Vaughn	.75	.35
☐ 139 Vinny Castilla	1.00	.45
☐ 140 Cal Ripken	6.00	2.70
☐ 141 Ruben Rivera	.40	.18
☐ 142 Mark Wohlers	.40	.18
☐ 143 Tony Clark	1.00	.45
☐ 144 Jose Rosado	.40	.18
☐ 145 Tony Gwynn	4.00	1.80
☐ 146 Cecil Fielder	.75	.35
☐ 147 Brian Jordan	.75	.35
☐ 148 Bob Abreu	.75	.35
☐ 149 Barry Larkin	1.50	.70
☐ 150 Robin Ventura	.75	.35
☐ 151 John Olerud	.75	.35
☐ 152 Rod Beck	.40	.18
☐ 153 Vladimir Guerrero	2.50	1.10
☐ 154 Marty Cordova	.40	.18
☐ 155 Todd Stottlemyre	.40	.18
☐ 156 Hideo Nomo	1.50	.70
☐ 157 Denny Neagle	.75	.35
☐ 158 John Jaha	.40	.18
☐ 159 Mo Vaughn	1.50	.70
☐ 160 Andruw Jones	2.00	.90
☐ 161 Moises Alou	.75	.35
☐ 162 Larry Walker	1.50	.70
☐ 163 Eddie Murray SH	.75	.35
☐ 164 Paul Molitor SH	.75	.35
☐ 165 Checklist	.40	.18

1997 Topps Chrome Refractors

	MINT	NRMT
COMMON CARD (1-165)	3.00	1.35
*STARS: 3X TO 8X BASIC CARDS		
*YOUNG STARS: 2.5X TO 6X BASIC CARDS		

STATED ODDS 1:12
CONDITION SENSITIVE SET

1997 Topps Chrome All-Stars

	MINT	NRMT
COMPLETE SET (22)	120.00	55.00
COMMON CARD (AS1-AS22)	1.50	.70
STATED ODDS 1:24		
*REFRACTORS: 3X TO 8X BASE CARD HI		
REFRACTOR STATED ODDS 1:72		

☐ AS1 Ivan Rodriguez	6.00	2.70
☐ AS2 Todd Hundley	1.50	.70
☐ AS3 Frank Thomas	10.00	4.50
☐ AS4 Andres Galarraga	5.00	2.20
☐ AS5 Chuck Knoblauch	5.00	2.20
☐ AS6 Eric Young	1.50	.70
☐ AS7 Jim Thome	5.00	2.20
☐ AS8 Chipper Jones	12.00	5.50
☐ AS9 Cal Ripken	20.00	9.00
☐ AS10 Barry Larkin	5.00	2.20
☐ AS11 Albert Belle	5.00	2.20
☐ AS12 Barry Bonds	6.00	2.70
☐ AS13 Ken Griffey Jr.	25.00	11.00
☐ AS14 Ellis Burks	2.50	1.10
☐ AS15 Juan Gonzalez	10.00	4.50
☐ AS16 Gary Sheffield	2.50	1.10
☐ AS17 Andy Pettitte	3.00	1.35
☐ AS18 Tom Glavine	5.00	2.20
☐ AS19 Pat Hentgen	2.50	1.10
☐ AS20 John Smoltz	3.00	1.35
☐ AS21 Roberto Hernandez	1.50	.70
☐ AS22 Mark Wohlers	1.50	.70

1997 Topps Chrome Diamond Duos

	MINT	NRMT
COMPLETE SET (10)	100.00	45.00
COMMON CARD (DD1-DD10)	4.00	1.80
STATED ODDS 1:36		
*REFRACTORS: 1X TO 2.5X HI COLUMN		
REFRACTOR STATED ODDS 1:108		

☐ DD1 Chipper Jones Andruw Jones	12.00	5.50
☐ DD2 Derek Jeter Bernie Williams	12.00	5.50

☐ DD3 Ken Griffey Jr. Jay Buhner	20.00	9.00
☐ DD4 Kenny Lofton Manny Ramirez	5.00	2.20
☐ DD5 Jeff Bagwell Craig Biggio	5.00	2.20
☐ DD6 Juan Gonzalez Ivan Rodriguez	8.00	3.60
☐ DD7 Cal Ripken Brady Anderson	15.00	6.75
☐ DD8 Mike Piazza Hideo Nomo	12.00	5.50
☐ DD9 Andres Galarraga Dante Bichette	4.00	1.80
☐ DD10 Frank Thomas Albert Belle	8.00	3.60

1997 Topps Chrome Season's Best

	MINT	NRMT
COMPLETE SET (25)	100.00	45.00
COMMON CARD (1-25)	1.00	.45
STATED ODDS 1:18		
*REFRACTORS: 2.5X TO 6X BASE CARD HI		
REFRACTOR STATED ODDS 1:54		

☐ 1 Tony Gwynn	10.00	4.50
☐ 2 Frank Thomas	8.00	3.60
☐ 3 Ellis Burks	2.00	.90
☐ 4 Paul Molitor	4.00	1.80
☐ 5 Chuck Knoblauch	4.00	1.80
☐ 6 Mark McGwire	20.00	9.00
☐ 7 Brady Anderson	2.00	.90
☐ 8 Ken Griffey Jr.	20.00	9.00
☐ 9 Albert Belle	4.00	1.80
☐ 10 Andres Galarraga	4.00	1.80
☐ 11 Andres Galarraga	4.00	1.80
☐ 12 Albert Belle	4.00	1.80
☐ 13 Juan Gonzalez	8.00	3.60
☐ 14 Mo Vaughn	4.00	1.80
☐ 15 Rafael Palmeiro	4.00	1.80
☐ 16 John Smoltz	2.50	1.10
☐ 17 Andy Pettitte	2.50	1.10
☐ 18 Pat Hentgen	2.00	.90
☐ 19 Mike Mussina	4.00	1.80
☐ 20 Andy Benes	2.00	.90
☐ 21 Kenny Lofton	2.50	1.10
☐ 22 Tom Goodwin	1.00	.45
☐ 23 Otis Nixon	1.00	.45

❏ 24 Eric Young	1.00	.45
❏ 25 Lance Johnson	1.00	.45

1998 Topps Chrome

	MINT	NRMT
COMPLETE SET (503)	400.00	180.00
COMPLETE SERIES 1 (282)	200.00	90.00
COMPLETE SERIES 2 (221)	200.00	90.00
COMMON CARD (1-504)	.40	.18
MINOR STARS	.60	.25
SEMISTARS	1.00	.45
UNLISTED STARS	1.50	.70
COMMON (245-264/484-501)	1.00	.45
MINOR 245-264/484-501	1.50	.70
SEMIS 245-264/484-501	2.50	1.10

CARD NUMBER 7 DOES NOT EXIST

❏ 1 Tony Gwynn	4.00	1.80
❏ 2 Larry Walker	1.50	.70
❏ 3 Billy Wagner	.60	.25
❏ 4 Denny Neagle	.40	.18
❏ 5 Vladimir Guerrero	2.00	.90
❏ 6 Kevin Brown	1.00	.45
❏ 8 Mariano Rivera	.60	.25
❏ 9 Tony Clark	.60	.25
❏ 10 Deion Sanders	.60	.25
❏ 11 Francisco Cordova	.40	.18
❏ 12 Matt Williams	1.50	.70
❏ 13 Carlos Baerga	.40	.18
❏ 14 Mo Vaughn	1.50	.70
❏ 15 Bobby Witt	.40	.18
❏ 16 Matt Stairs	.60	.25
❏ 17 Chan Ho Park	.60	.25
❏ 18 Mike Bordick	.40	.18
❏ 19 Michael Tucker	.40	.18
❏ 20 Frank Thomas	3.00	1.35
❏ 21 Roberto Clemente	5.00	2.20
❏ 22 Dmitri Young	.60	.25
❏ 23 Steve Trachsel	.40	.18
❏ 24 Jeff Kent	.60	.25
❏ 25 Scott Rolen	2.00	.90
❏ 26 John Thomson	.40	.18
❏ 27 Joe Vitiello	.40	.18
❏ 28 Eddie Guardado	.40	.18
❏ 29 Charlie Hayes	.40	.18
❏ 30 Juan Gonzalez	3.00	1.35
❏ 31 Garret Anderson	.60	.25
❏ 32 John Jaha	.60	.25
❏ 33 Omar Vizquel	.60	.25
❏ 34 Brian Hunter	.40	.18
❏ 35 Jeff Bagwell	2.00	.90
❏ 36 Mark Lemke	.40	.18
❏ 37 Doug Glanville	.60	.25
❏ 38 Dan Wilson	.40	.18
❏ 39 Steve Cooke	.40	.18
❏ 40 Chili Davis	.60	.25
❏ 41 Mike Cameron	.60	.25
❏ 42 F.P. Santangelo	.40	.18
❏ 43 Brad Ausmus	.40	.18
❏ 44 Gary DiSarcina	.40	.18
❏ 45 Pat Hentgen	.40	.18
❏ 46 Wilton Guerrero	.40	.18
❏ 47 Devon White	.40	.18
❏ 48 Danny Patterson	.40	.18
❏ 49 Pat Meares	.40	.18
❏ 50 Rafael Palmeiro	1.50	.70
❏ 51 Mark Gardner	.40	.18

❏ 52 Jeff Blauser	.40	.18
❏ 53 Dave Hollins	.40	.18
❏ 54 Carlos Garcia	.40	.18
❏ 55 Ben McDonald	.40	.18
❏ 56 John Mabry	.40	.18
❏ 57 Trevor Hoffman	.60	.25
❏ 58 Tony Fernandez	.60	.25
❏ 59 Rich Loiselle	.40	.18
❏ 60 Mark Leiter	.40	.18
❏ 61 Pat Kelly	.40	.18
❏ 62 John Flaherty	.40	.18
❏ 63 Roger Bailey	.40	.18
❏ 64 Tom Gordon	.60	.25
❏ 65 Ryan Klesko	.60	.25
❏ 66 Darryl Hamilton	.40	.18
❏ 67 Jim Eisenreich	.40	.18
❏ 68 Butch Huskey	.40	.18
❏ 69 Mark Grudzielanek	.40	.18
❏ 70 Marquis Grissom	.40	.18
❏ 71 Mark McLemore	.40	.18
❏ 72 Gary Gaetti	.60	.25
❏ 73 Greg Gagne	.40	.18
❏ 74 Lyle Mouton	.40	.18
❏ 75 Jim Edmonds	.60	.25
❏ 76 Shawn Green	1.50	.70
❏ 77 Greg Vaughn	.60	.25
❏ 78 Terry Adams	.40	.18
❏ 79 Kevin Polcovich	.40	.18
❏ 80 Troy O'Leary	.40	.18
❏ 81 Jeff Shaw	.40	.18
❏ 82 Rich Becker	.40	.18
❏ 83 David Wells	.60	.25
❏ 84 Steve Karsay	.40	.18
❏ 85 Charles Nagy	.60	.25
❏ 86 B.J. Surhoff	.60	.25
❏ 87 Jimmy Haynes	.40	.18
❏ 88 James Baldwin	.40	.18
❏ 89 Edgardo Alfonzo	1.00	.45
❏ 90 Jay Buhner	.60	.25
❏ 91 Brady Anderson	.60	.25
❏ 92 Scott Servais	.40	.18
❏ 93 Edgar Renteria	.40	.18
❏ 94 Mike Lieberthal	.60	.25
❏ 95 Rick Aguilera	.40	.18
❏ 96 Walt Weiss	.40	.18
❏ 97 Delvi Cruz	.40	.18
❏ 98 Kurt Abbott	.40	.18
❏ 99 Henry Rodriguez	.60	.25
❏ 100 Mike Piazza	5.00	2.20
❏ 101 Billy Taylor	.40	.18
❏ 102 Todd Zeile	.60	.25
❏ 103 Rey Ordonez	.60	.25
❏ 104 Willie Greene	.40	.18
❏ 105 Tony Womack	.40	.18
❏ 106 Mike Sweeney	.60	.25
❏ 107 Jeffrey Hammonds	.40	.18
❏ 108 Kevin Orie	.40	.18
❏ 109 Alex Gonzalez	.40	.18
❏ 110 Jose Canseco	2.00	.90
❏ 111 Paul Sorrento	.40	.18
❏ 112 Joey Hamilton	.40	.18
❏ 113 Brad Radke	.60	.25
❏ 114 Steve Avery	.40	.18
❏ 115 Esteban Loaiza	.40	.18
❏ 116 Stan Javier	.40	.18
❏ 117 Chris Gomez	.40	.18
❏ 118 Royce Clayton	.40	.18
❏ 119 Orlando Merced	.40	.18
❏ 120 Kevin Appier	.60	.25
❏ 121 Mel Nieves	.40	.18
❏ 122 Joe Girardi	.40	.18
❏ 123 Rico Brogna	.40	.18
❏ 124 Kent Mercker	.40	.18
❏ 125 Manny Ramirez	2.00	.90
❏ 126 Jeromy Burnitz	.60	.25
❏ 127 Kevin Foster	.40	.18
❏ 128 Matt Morris	.40	.18
❏ 129 Jason Dickson	.40	.18
❏ 130 Tom Glavine	1.50	.70
❏ 131 Wally Joyner	.60	.25
❏ 132 Rick Reed	.40	.18
❏ 133 Todd Jones	.40	.18
❏ 134 Dave Martinez	.40	.18
❏ 135 Sandy Alomar Jr.	.60	.25
❏ 136 Mike Lansing	.40	.18
❏ 137 Sean Berry	.40	.18

❏ 138 Doug Jones	.40	.18
❏ 139 Todd Stottlemyre	.40	.18
❏ 140 Jay Bell	.60	.25
❏ 141 Jaime Navarro	.40	.18
❏ 142 Chris Hoiles	.40	.18
❏ 143 Joey Cora	.40	.18
❏ 144 Scott Spiezio	.40	.18
❏ 145 Joe Carter	.60	.25
❏ 146 Jose Guillen	.40	.18
❏ 147 Damion Easley	.60	.25
❏ 148 Lee Stevens	.40	.18
❏ 149 Alex Fernandez	.40	.18
❏ 150 Randy Johnson	1.50	.70
❏ 151 J.T. Snow	.60	.25
❏ 152 Chuck Finley	.60	.25
❏ 153 Bernard Gilkey	.40	.18
❏ 154 David Segui	.40	.18
❏ 155 Dante Bichette	.60	.25
❏ 156 Kevin Stocker	.40	.18
❏ 157 Carl Everett	.60	.25
❏ 158 Jose Valentin	.40	.18
❏ 159 Pokey Reese	.40	.18
❏ 160 Derek Jeter	5.00	2.20
❏ 161 Roger Pavlik	.40	.18
❏ 162 Mark Wohlers	.40	.18
❏ 163 Ricky Bottalico	.40	.18
❏ 164 Ozzie Guillen	.40	.18
❏ 165 Mike Mussina	1.50	.70
❏ 166 Gary Sheffield	.60	.25
❏ 167 Hideo Nomo	1.50	.70
❏ 168 Mark Grace	1.00	.45
❏ 169 Aaron Sele	.60	.25
❏ 170 Darryl Kile	.40	.18
❏ 171 Shawn Estes	.40	.18
❏ 172 Vinny Castilla	.60	.25
❏ 173 Ron Coomer	.40	.18
❏ 174 Jose Rosado	.40	.18
❏ 175 Kenny Lofton	1.00	.45
❏ 176 Jason Giambi	.60	.25
❏ 177 Hal Morris	.40	.18
❏ 178 Darren Bragg	.40	.18
❏ 179 Orel Hershiser	.60	.25
❏ 180 Ray Lankford	.60	.25
❏ 181 Hideki Irabu	.60	.25
❏ 182 Kevin Young	.60	.25
❏ 183 Javy Lopez	.60	.25
❏ 184 Jeff Montgomery	.40	.18
❏ 185 Mike Holtz	.40	.18
❏ 186 George Williams	.40	.18
❏ 187 Cal Eldred	.40	.18
❏ 188 Tom Candiotti	.40	.18
❏ 189 Glenallen Hill	.40	.18
❏ 190 Brian Giles	.60	.25
❏ 191 Dave Mlicki	.40	.18
❏ 192 Garrett Stephenson	.40	.18
❏ 193 Jeff Frye	.40	.18
❏ 194 Joe Oliver	.40	.18
❏ 195 Bob Hamelin	.40	.18
❏ 196 Luis Sojo	.40	.18
❏ 197 LaTroy Hawkins	.40	.18
❏ 198 Kevin Elster	.40	.18
❏ 199 Jeff Reed	.40	.18
❏ 200 Dennis Eckersley	.60	.25
❏ 201 Bill Mueller	.40	.18
❏ 202 Russ Davis	.40	.18
❏ 203 Armando Benitez	.40	.18
❏ 204 Quilvio Veras	.40	.18
❏ 205 Tim Naehring	.40	.18
❏ 206 Quinton McCracken	.40	.18
❏ 207 Raul Casanova	.40	.18
❏ 208 Matt Lawton	.40	.18
❏ 209 Luis Alicea	.40	.18
❏ 210 Luis Gonzalez	.60	.25
❏ 211 Allen Watson	.40	.18
❏ 212 Gerald Williams	.40	.18
❏ 213 David Bell	.40	.18
❏ 214 Todd Hollandsworth	.40	.18
❏ 215 Wade Boggs	1.50	.70
❏ 216 Jose Mesa	.40	.18
❏ 217 Jamie Moyer	.40	.18
❏ 218 Darren Daulton	.60	.25
❏ 219 Mickey Morandini	.40	.18
❏ 220 Rusty Greer	.60	.25
❏ 221 Jim Bullinger	.40	.18
❏ 222 Jose Offerman	.60	.25
❏ 223 Matt Karchner	.40	.18

❏ 224	Woody Williams	.40	.18
❏ 225	Mark Loretta	.40	.18
❏ 226	Mike Hampton	.60	.25
❏ 227	Willie Adams	.40	.18
❏ 228	Scott Hatteberg	.40	.18
❏ 229	Rich Amaral	.40	.18
❏ 230	Terry Steinbach	.40	.18
❏ 231	Glendon Rusch	.40	.18
❏ 232	Bret Boone	.60	.25
❏ 233	Robert Person	.40	.18
❏ 234	Jose Hernandez	.40	.18
❏ 235	Doug Drabek	.40	.18
❏ 236	Jason McDonald	.40	.18
❏ 237	Chris Widger	.40	.18
❏ 238	Tom Martin	.40	.18
❏ 239	Dave Burba	.40	.18
❏ 240	Pete Rose Jr.	.60	.25
❏ 241	Bobby Ayala	.40	.18
❏ 242	Tim Wakefield	.40	.18
❏ 243	Dennis Springer	.40	.18
❏ 244	Tim Belcher	.40	.18
❏ 245	Jon Garland	1.00	.45
	Geoff Goetz		
❏ 246	Glenn Davis	2.50	1.10
	Lance Berkman		
❏ 247	Vernon Wells	2.50	1.10
	Aaron Akin		
❏ 248	Adam Kennedy	1.50	.70
	Jason Romano		
❏ 249	Jason Dellaero	1.50	.70
	Troy Cameron		
❏ 250	Alex Sanchez	4.00	1.80
	Jared Sandberg		
❏ 251	Pablo Ortega	1.00	.45
	James Manias		
❏ 252	Jason Conti	2.50	1.10
	Mike Stoner		
❏ 253	John Patterson	1.50	.70
	Larry Rodriguez		
❏ 254	Adrian Beltre	8.00	3.60
	Ryan Minor		
	Aaron Boone		
❏ 255	Ben Grieve	4.00	1.80
	Brian Buchanan		
	Dermal Brown		
❏ 256	Kerrry Wood	4.00	1.80
	Carl Pavano		
	Gil Meche		
❏ 257	David Ortiz	1.50	.70
	Daryle Ward		
	Richie Sexson		
❏ 258	Randy Winn	1.50	.70
	Juan Encarnacion		
	Andrew Vessel		
❏ 259	Kris Benson	2.00	.90
	Travis Smith		
	Courtney Duncan		
❏ 260	Chad Hermansen	8.00	3.60
	Brent Butler		
	Warren Morris		
❏ 261	Ben Davis	2.50	1.10
	Eli Marrero		
	Ramon Hernandez		
❏ 262	Eric Chavez	4.00	1.80
	Russell Branyan		
	Russ Johnson		
❏ 263	Todd Dunwoody	2.00	.90
	John Barnes		
	Ryan Jackson		
❏ 264	Matt Clement	2.00	.90
	Roy Halladay		
	Brian Fuentes		
❏ 265	Randy Johnson SH	.60	.25
❏ 266	Kevin Brown SH	.60	.25
❏ 267	Ricardo Rincon SH	.40	.18
❏ 268	Nomar Garciaparra SH	2.50	1.10
❏ 269	Tino Martinez SH	.40	.18
❏ 270	Chuck Knoblauch IL	.40	.18
❏ 271	Pedro Martinez IL	1.00	.45
❏ 272	Denny Neagle IL	.40	.18
❏ 273	Juan Gonzalez IL	1.50	.70
❏ 274	Andres Galarraga IL	.60	.25
❏ 275	Checklist	.40	.18
❏ 276	Checklist	.40	.18
❏ 277	Moises Alou WS	.40	.18
❏ 278	Sandy Alomar Jr. WS	.60	.25
❏ 279	Gary Sheffield WS	.40	.18
❏ 280	Matt Williams WS	1.50	.70
❏ 281	Livan Hernandez WS	.40	.18
❏ 282	Chad Ogea WS	.40	.18
❏ 283	Marlins Champs	.60	.25
❏ 284	Tino Martinez	.60	.25
❏ 285	Roberto Alomar	1.50	.70
❏ 286	Jeff King	.40	.18
❏ 287	Brian Jordan	.60	.25
❏ 288	Darin Erstad	1.00	.45
❏ 289	Ken Caminiti	.60	.25
❏ 290	Jim Thome	1.50	.70
❏ 291	Paul Molitor	1.50	.70
❏ 292	Ivan Rodriguez	2.00	.90
❏ 293	Bernie Williams	1.50	.70
❏ 294	Todd Hundley	.60	.25
❏ 295	Andres Galarraga	1.00	.45
❏ 296	Greg Maddux	4.00	1.80
❏ 297	Edgar Martinez	.60	.25
❏ 298	Ron Gant	.60	.25
❏ 299	Derek Bell	.60	.25
❏ 300	Roger Clemens	4.00	1.80
❏ 301	Rondell White	.60	.25
❏ 302	Barry Larkin	.60	.25
❏ 303	Robin Ventura	.60	.25
❏ 304	Jason Kendall	.60	.25
❏ 305	Chipper Jones	4.00	1.80
❏ 306	John Franco	.40	.18
❏ 307	Sammy Sosa	5.00	2.20
❏ 308	Troy Percival	.40	.18
❏ 309	Chuck Knoblauch	.60	.25
❏ 310	Ellis Burks	.60	.25
❏ 311	Al Martin	.40	.18
❏ 312	Tim Salmon	1.00	.45
❏ 313	Moises Alou	.60	.25
❏ 314	Lance Johnson	.40	.18
❏ 315	Justin Thompson	.40	.18
❏ 316	Will Clark	1.50	.70
❏ 317	Barry Bonds	2.00	.90
❏ 318	Craig Biggio	1.50	.70
❏ 319	John Smoltz	1.00	.45
❏ 320	Cal Ripken	6.00	2.70
❏ 321	Ken Griffey Jr.	8.00	3.60
❏ 322	Paul O'Neill	.60	.25
❏ 323	Todd Helton	2.00	.90
❏ 324	John Olerud	.60	.25
❏ 325	Mark McGwire	10.00	4.50
❏ 326	Jose Cruz Jr.	.60	.25
❏ 327	Jeff Cirillo	.60	.25
❏ 328	Dean Palmer	.60	.25
❏ 329	John Wetteland	.40	.18
❏ 330	Steve Finley	.60	.25
❏ 331	Albert Belle	1.50	.70
❏ 332	Curt Schilling	1.00	.45
❏ 333	Raul Mondesi	.60	.25
❏ 334	Andruw Jones	1.50	.70
❏ 335	Nomar Garciaparra	5.00	2.20
❏ 336	David Justice	.60	.25
❏ 337	Andy Pettitte	.60	.25
❏ 338	Pedro Martinez	2.00	.90
❏ 339	Travis Miller	.40	.18
❏ 340	Chris Stynes	.40	.18
❏ 341	Gregg Jefferies	.40	.18
❏ 342	Jeff Fassero	.40	.18
❏ 343	Craig Counsell	.40	.18
❏ 344	Wilson Alvarez	.40	.18
❏ 345	Bip Roberts	.40	.18
❏ 346	Kelvim Escobar	.60	.25
❏ 347	Mark Bellhorn	.40	.18
❏ 348	Cory Lidle	.40	.18
❏ 349	Fred McGriff	1.00	.45
❏ 350	Chuck Carr	.40	.18
❏ 351	Bob Abreu	.60	.25
❏ 352	Juan Guzman	.40	.18
❏ 353	Fernando Vina	.40	.18
❏ 354	Andy Benes	.40	.18
❏ 355	Dave Nilsson	.40	.18
❏ 356	Bobby Bonilla	.60	.25
❏ 357	Ismael Valdes	.40	.18
❏ 358	Carlos Perez	.40	.18
❏ 359	Kirk Rueter	.40	.18
❏ 360	Bartolo Colon	.60	.25
❏ 361	Mel Rojas	.40	.18
❏ 362	Johnny Damon	.60	.25
❏ 363	Geronimo Berroa	.40	.18
❏ 364	Reggie Sanders	.40	.18
❏ 365	Jermaine Allensworth	.40	.18
❏ 366	Orlando Cabrera	.40	.18
❏ 367	Jorge Fabregas	.40	.18
❏ 368	Scott Stahoviak	.40	.18
❏ 369	Ken Cloude	.40	.18
❏ 370	Donovan Osborne	.40	.18
❏ 371	Roger Cedeno	.60	.25
❏ 372	Neifi Perez	.60	.25
❏ 373	Chris Holt	.40	.18
❏ 374	Cecil Fielder	.60	.25
❏ 375	Marty Cordova	.40	.18
❏ 376	Tom Goodwin	.40	.18
❏ 377	Jeff Suppan	.40	.18
❏ 378	Jeff Brantley	.40	.18
❏ 379	Mark Langston	.40	.18
❏ 380	Shane Reynolds	.60	.25
❏ 381	Mike Fetters	.40	.18
❏ 382	Todd Greene	.40	.18
❏ 383	Ray Durham	.60	.25
❏ 384	Carlos Delgado	1.50	.70
❏ 385	Jeff D'Amico	.40	.18
❏ 386	Brian McRae	.40	.18
❏ 387	Alan Benes	.40	.18
❏ 388	Heathcliff Slocumb	.40	.18
❏ 389	Eric Young	.40	.18
❏ 390	Travis Fryman	.60	.25
❏ 391	David Cone	1.00	.45
❏ 392	Otis Nixon	.40	.18
❏ 393	Jeremi Gonzalez	.40	.18
❏ 394	Jeff Juden	.40	.18
❏ 395	Jose Vizcaino	.40	.18
❏ 396	Ugueth Urbina	.40	.18
❏ 397	Ramon Martinez	.40	.18
❏ 398	Robb Nen	.40	.18
❏ 399	Harold Baines	.60	.25
❏ 400	Delino DeShields	.40	.18
❏ 401	John Burkett	.40	.18
❏ 402	Sterling Hitchcock	.40	.18
❏ 403	Mark Clark	.40	.18
❏ 404	Terrell Wade	.40	.18
❏ 405	Scott Brosius	.60	.25
❏ 406	Chad Curtis	.40	.18
❏ 407	Brian Johnson	.40	.18
❏ 408	Roberto Kelly	.40	.18
❏ 409	Dave Dellucci	2.50	1.10
❏ 410	Michael Tucker	.40	.18
❏ 411	Mark Kotsay	.60	.25
❏ 412	Mark Lewis	.40	.18
❏ 413	Ryan McGuire	.40	.18
❏ 414	Shawon Dunston	.40	.18
❏ 415	Brad Rigby	.40	.18
❏ 416	Scott Erickson	.40	.18
❏ 417	Bobby Jones	.40	.18
❏ 418	Darren Oliver	.40	.18
❏ 419	John Smiley	.40	.18
❏ 420	T.J. Mathews	.40	.18
❏ 421	Dustin Hermanson	.40	.18
❏ 422	Mike Timlin	.40	.18
❏ 423	Willie Blair	.40	.18
❏ 424	Manny Alexander	.40	.18
❏ 425	Bob Tewksbury	.40	.18
❏ 426	Pete Schourek	.40	.18
❏ 427	Reggie Jefferson	.40	.18
❏ 428	Ed Sprague	.40	.18
❏ 429	Jeff Conine	.40	.18
❏ 430	Roberto Hernandez	.40	.18
❏ 431	Tom Pagnozzi	.40	.18
❏ 432	Jaret Wright	.60	.25
❏ 433	Livan Hernandez	.60	.25
❏ 434	Andy Ashby	.40	.18
❏ 435	Todd Dunn	.40	.18
❏ 436	Bobby Higginson	.60	.25
❏ 437	Rod Beck	.60	.25
❏ 438	Jim Leyritz	.40	.18
❏ 439	Matt Williams	1.50	.70
❏ 440	Brett Tomko	.40	.18
❏ 441	Joe Randa	.40	.18
❏ 442	Chris Carpenter	.60	.25
❏ 443	Dennis Reyes	.40	.18
❏ 444	Al Leiter	.40	.18
❏ 445	Jason Schmidt	.40	.18
❏ 446	Ken Hill	.40	.18
❏ 447	Shannon Stewart	.60	.25
❏ 448	Enrique Wilson	.40	.18
❏ 449	Fernando Tatis	1.50	.70
❏ 450	Jimmy Key	.60	.25

	MINT	NRMT
☐ 451 Darrin Fletcher	.40	.18
☐ 452 John Valentin	.60	.25
☐ 453 Kevin Tapani	.40	.18
☐ 454 Eric Karros	.60	.25
☐ 455 Jay Bell	.60	.25
☐ 456 Walt Weiss	.60	.25
☐ 457 Devon White	.40	.18
☐ 458 Carl Pavano	.40	.18
☐ 459 Mike Lansing	.40	.18
☐ 460 John Flaherty	.40	.18
☐ 461 Richard Hidalgo	.60	.25
☐ 462 Quinton McCracken	.40	.18
☐ 463 Karim Garcia	.40	.18
☐ 464 Miguel Cairo	.40	.18
☐ 465 Edwin Diaz	.40	.18
☐ 466 Bobby Smith	.40	.18
☐ 467 Yamil Benitez	.40	.18
☐ 468 Rich Butler	2.00	.90
☐ 469 Ben Ford	1.50	.70
☐ 470 Bubba Trammell	.40	.18
☐ 471 Brent Brede	.40	.18
☐ 472 Brooks Kieschnick	.40	.18
☐ 473 Carlos Castillo	.40	.18
☐ 474 Brad Radke SH	.40	.18
☐ 475 Roger Clemens SH	2.00	.90
☐ 476 Curt Schilling SH	.60	.25
☐ 477 John Olerud SH	.40	.18
☐ 478 Mark McGwire SH	5.00	2.20
☐ 479 Mike Piazza IL	4.00	1.80
Ken Griffey Jr.		
☐ 480 Jeff Bagwell	1.50	.70
Frank Thomas		
☐ 481 Chipper Jones	2.50	1.10
Nomar Garciaparra IL		
☐ 482 Larry Walker IL	1.50	.70
Juan Gonzalez IL		
☐ 483 Gary Sheffield IL	.60	.25
Tino Martinez IL		
☐ 484 Derrick Gibson	1.50	.70
Michael Coleman		
Norm Hutchins		
☐ 485 Braden Looper	1.00	.45
Cliff Politte		
Brian Rose		
☐ 486 Eric Milton	1.50	.70
Jason Marquis		
Corey Lee		
☐ 487 A.J.Hinch	4.00	1.80
Mark Osborne		
Robert Fick		
☐ 488 Aramis Ramirez	6.00	2.70
Alex Gonzalez		
Sean Casey		
☐ 489 Donnie Bridges	2.50	1.10
Tim Drew		
☐ 490 Ntema Ndungidi	8.00	3.60
Darnell McDonald		
☐ 491 Ryan Anderson	8.00	3.60
Mark Mangum		
☐ 492 J.J.Davis	15.00	6.75
Troy Glaus		
☐ 493 Jayson Werth	2.50	1.10
Dan Reichert		
☐ 494 John Curtice	6.00	2.70
Michael Cuddyer		
☐ 495 Jack Cust	8.00	3.60
Jason Standridge		
☐ 496 Brian Anderson	.40	.18
☐ 497 Tony Saunders	.40	.18
☐ 498 Vladimir Nunez	1.50	.70
Jhensy Sandoval		
☐ 499 Brad Penny	1.50	.70
Nick Bierbrodt		
☐ 500 Dustin Carr	2.00	.90
Luis Cruz		
☐ 501 Cedric Bowers	1.50	.70
Marcus McCain		
☐ 502 Checklist	.40	.18
☐ 503 Checklist	.40	.18
☐ 504 Alex Rodriguez	5.00	2.20

1998 Topps Chrome Refractors

	MINT	NRMT
COMMON CARD (1-504)	4.00	1.80

*STARS: 4X TO 10X BASIC CARDS
*YNG.STARS: 2.5X TO 6X BASIC CARDS
*RC'S/PROSPECTS: 2X TO 4X BASIC
STATED ODDS 1:12
CARD NUMBER 7 DOES NOT EXIST

1998 Topps Chrome Baby Boomers

	MINT	NRMT
COMPLETE SET (15)	80.00	36.00
COMMON CARD (BB1-BB15)	1.50	.70
SER.1 STATED ODDS 1:24		
*REFRACTORS: 3X TO 8X BASE CARD HI		
REFRACTOR SER.1 STATED ODDS 1:72		
☐ BB1 Derek Jeter	20.00	9.00
☐ BB2 Scott Rolen	10.00	4.50
☐ BB3 Nomar Garciaparra	20.00	9.00
☐ BB4 Jose Cruz Jr.	2.50	1.10
☐ BB5 Darin Erstad	4.00	1.80
☐ BB6 Todd Helton	6.00	2.70
☐ BB7 Tony Clark	2.50	1.10
☐ BB8 Jose Guillen	1.50	.70
☐ BB9 Andruw Jones	6.00	2.70
☐ BB10 Vladimir Guerrero	8.00	3.60
☐ BB11 Mark Kotsay	2.50	1.10
☐ BB12 Todd Greene	1.50	.70
☐ BB13 Andy Pettitte	2.50	1.10
☐ BB14 Justin Thompson	1.50	.70
☐ BB15 Alan Benes	1.50	.70

1998 Topps Chrome Clout Nine

	MINT	NRMT
COMPLETE SET (9)	80.00	36.00
COMMON CARD (C1-C9)	1.50	.70
SER.2 STATED ODDS 1:24		
*REFRACTORS: 3X TO 8X BASE CARD HI		
REFRACTOR SER.2 STATED ODDS 1:72		
☐ C1 Edgar Martinez	2.50	1.10
☐ C2 Mike Piazza	20.00	9.00
☐ C3 Frank Thomas	12.00	5.50
☐ C4 Craig Biggio	6.00	2.70
☐ C5 Vinny Castilla	2.50	1.10
☐ C6 Jeff Blauser	1.50	.70
☐ C7 Barry Bonds	8.00	3.60
☐ C8 Ken Griffey Jr.	30.00	13.50
☐ C9 Larry Walker	6.00	2.70

1998 Topps Chrome Flashback

	MINT	NRMT
COMPLETE SET (10)	80.00	36.00
COMMON CARD (FB1-FB10)	2.50	1.10
SER.1 STATED ODDS 1:24		
*REFRACTORS: 3X TO 8X BASE CARD HI		
REFRACTOR SER.1 STATED ODDS 1:72		
☐ FB1 Barry Bonds	8.00	3.60
☐ FB2 Ken Griffey Jr.	30.00	13.50
☐ FB3 Paul Molitor	6.00	2.70
☐ FB4 Randy Johnson	6.00	2.70
☐ FB5 Cal Ripken	25.00	11.00
☐ FB6 Tony Gwynn	15.00	6.75
☐ FB7 Kenny Lofton	4.00	1.80
☐ FB8 Gary Sheffield	2.50	1.10
☐ FB9 Deion Sanders	2.50	1.10
☐ FB10 Brady Anderson	2.50	1.10

1998 Topps Chrome HallBound

	MINT	NRMT
COMPLETE SET (15)	200.00	90.00
COMMON CARD (HB1-HB15)	3.00	1.35
UNLISTED STARS	8.00	3.60
SER.1 STATED ODDS 1:24		
*REFRACTORS: .75X TO 2X HI COLUMN		
REFRACTOR SER.1 STATED ODDS 1:72		

		MINT	NRMT
❑ HB1	Paul Molitor	8.00	3.60
❑ HB2	Tony Gwynn	20.00	9.00
❑ HB3	Wade Boggs	8.00	3.60
❑ HB4	Roger Clemens	20.00	9.00
❑ HB5	Dennis Eckersley	3.00	1.35
❑ HB6	Cal Ripken	30.00	13.50
❑ HB7	Greg Maddux	20.00	9.00
❑ HB8	Rickey Henderson	10.00	4.50
❑ HB9	Ken Griffey Jr.	40.00	18.00
❑ HB10	Frank Thomas	15.00	6.75
❑ HB11	Mark McGwire	50.00	22.00
❑ HB12	Barry Bonds	10.00	4.50
❑ HB13	Mike Piazza	25.00	11.00
❑ HB14	Juan Gonzalez	15.00	6.75
❑ HB15	Randy Johnson	8.00	3.60

1998 Topps Chrome Milestones

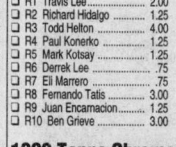

	MINT	NRMT
COMPLETE SET (10)	120.00	55.00
COMMON CARD (MS1-MS10)	2.50	1.10
SER.2 STATED ODDS 1:24		
*REFRACTORS: 3X TO 8X BASE CARD HI		
REFRACTOR SER.2 STATED ODDS 1:72		

❑ MS1	Barry Bonds	8.00	3.60
❑ MS2	Roger Clemens	15.00	6.75
❑ MS3	Dennis Eckersley	2.50	1.10
❑ MS4	Juan Gonzalez	12.00	5.50
❑ MS5	Ken Griffey Jr.	30.00	13.50
❑ MS6	Tony Gwynn	15.00	6.75
❑ MS7	Greg Maddux	15.00	6.75
❑ MS8	Mark McGwire	40.00	18.00
❑ MS9	Cal Ripken	25.00	11.00
❑ MS10	Frank Thomas	12.00	5.50

1998 Topps Chrome Rookie Class

	MINT	NRMT
COMPLETE SET (10)	20.00	9.00
COMMON CARD (R1-R10)	.75	.35
MINOR STARS	1.25	.55
SEMISTARS	2.00	.90
UNLISTED STARS	3.00	1.35
SER.2 STATED ODDS 1:12		
*REFRACTORS: .75X TO 2X HI COLUMN		
REFRACTOR SER.2 STATED ODDS 1:24		

❑ R1	Travis Lee	2.00	.90
❑ R2	Richard Hidalgo	1.25	.55
❑ R3	Todd Helton	4.00	1.80
❑ R4	Paul Konerko	1.25	.55
❑ R5	Mark Kotsay	1.25	.55
❑ R6	Derrek Lee	.75	.35
❑ R7	Eli Marrero	.75	.35
❑ R8	Fernando Tatis	3.00	1.35
❑ R9	Juan Encarnacion	1.25	.55
❑ R10	Ben Grieve	3.00	1.35

1999 Topps Chrome

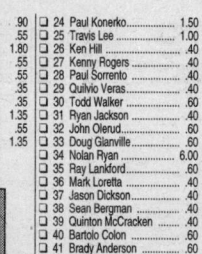

	MINT	NRMT
COMPLETE SET (462)	300.00	135.00
COMPLETE SERIES 1 (241)	150.00	70.00
COMPLETE SERIES 2 (221)	150.00	70.00
COMMON CARD (1-6/8-463)	.40	.18
MINOR STARS	.60	.25
SEMISTARS	1.00	.45
UNLISTED STARS	1.50	.70
COMMON PROSPECT (205-212)	1.50	.70
COMMON PROSPECT (425-437)	1.50	.70
COMP.MCGWIRE HR SET (70)	3000.00	
1350.00		
MCGWIRE 220 HR 1	80.00	36.00
MCGWIRE 220 HR 2-60	40.00	18.00
MCGWIRE 220 HR 61	80.00	36.00
MCGWIRE 220 HR 62	120.00	55.00
MCGWIRE 220 HR 63-69	60.00	27.00
MCGWIRE 220 HR 70	300.00	135.00
CARD 220 AVAILABLE IN 70 VARIATIONS		
COMP.SOSA HR SET (66)	1100.00	500.00
SOSA 461 HR 1	30.00	13.50
SOSA 461 HR 2-60	15.00	6.75
SOSA 461 HR 61	30.00	13.50
SOSA 461 HR 62	50.00	22.00
SOSA 461 HR 63-65	20.00	9.00
SOSA 461 HR 66	80.00	36.00
CARD 461 AVAILABLE IN 66 VARIATIONS		
CARD NUMBER 7 DOES NOT EXIST		
SER.1 SET INCLUDES 1 CARD 220 VARIA-TION		
SER.2 SET INCLUDES 1 CARD 461 VARIA-TION		

❑ 1	Roger Clemens	4.00	1.80
❑ 2	Andres Galarraga	1.00	.45
❑ 3	Scott Brosius	.60	.25
❑ 4	John Flaherty	.40	.18
❑ 5	Jim Leyritz	.40	.18
❑ 6	Ray Durham	.60	.25
❑ 8	Jose Vizcaino	.40	.18
❑ 9	Will Clark	1.50	.70
❑ 10	David Wells	.60	.25
❑ 11	Jose Guillen	.40	.18
❑ 12	Scott Hatteberg	.40	.18
❑ 13	Edgardo Alfonzo	1.00	.45
❑ 14	Mike Bordick	.40	.18
❑ 15	Manny Ramirez	2.00	.90
❑ 16	Greg Maddux	4.00	1.80
❑ 17	David Segui	.40	.18
❑ 18	Darryl Strawberry	.60	.25
❑ 19	Brad Radke	.60	.25
❑ 20	Kerry Wood	1.50	.70
❑ 21	Matt Anderson	.40	.18
❑ 22	Derrek Lee	.40	.18
❑ 23	Mickey Morandini	.49	.18

❑ 24	Paul Konerko	1.50	.70
❑ 25	Travis Lee	1.00	.45
❑ 26	Ken Hill	.40	.18
❑ 27	Kenny Rogers	.40	.18
❑ 28	Paul Sorrento	.40	.18
❑ 29	Quivilo Veras	.40	.18
❑ 30	Todd Walker	.60	.25
❑ 31	Ryan Jackson	.40	.18
❑ 32	John Olerud	.60	.25
❑ 33	Doug Glanville	.60	.25
❑ 34	Nolan Ryan	6.00	2.70
❑ 35	Ray Lankford	.60	.25
❑ 36	Mark Loretta	.40	.18
❑ 37	Jason Dickson	.40	.18
❑ 38	Sean Bergman	.40	.18
❑ 39	Quinton McCracken	.40	.18
❑ 40	Bartolo Colon	.60	.25
❑ 41	Brady Anderson	.60	.25
❑ 42	Chris Stynes	.40	.18
❑ 43	Jorge Posada	.60	.25
❑ 44	Justin Thompson	.40	.18
❑ 45	Johnny Damon	.60	.25
❑ 46	Armando Benitez	.40	.18
❑ 47	Brant Brown	.40	.18
❑ 48	Charlie Hayes	.40	.18
❑ 49	Darren Dreifort	.40	.18
❑ 50	Juan Gonzalez	3.00	1.35
❑ 51	Chuck Knoblauch	.60	.25
❑ 52	Todd Helton	1.50	.70
❑ 53	Rick Reed	.40	.18
❑ 54	Chris Gomez	.40	.18
❑ 55	Gary Sheffield	.60	.25
❑ 56	Rod Beck	.60	.25
❑ 57	Rey Sanchez	.40	.18
❑ 58	Garret Anderson	.60	.25
❑ 59	Jimmy Haynes	.40	.18
❑ 60	Steve Woodard	.40	.18
❑ 61	Rondell White	.60	.25
❑ 62	Vladimir Guerrero	2.00	.90
❑ 63	Eric Karros	.60	.25
❑ 64	Russ Davis	.40	.18
❑ 65	Mo Vaughn	1.50	.70
❑ 66	Sammy Sosa	5.00	2.20
❑ 67	Troy Percival	.60	.25
❑ 68	Kenny Lofton	1.00	.45
❑ 69	Bill Taylor	.40	.18
❑ 70	Mark McGwire	10.00	4.50
❑ 71	Roger Cedeno	.60	.25
❑ 72	Javy Lopez	.60	.25
❑ 73	Damion Easley	.40	.18
❑ 74	Andy Pettitte	.60	.25
❑ 75	Tony Gwynn	4.00	1.80
❑ 76	Ricardo Rincon	.40	.18
❑ 77	F.P. Santangelo	.40	.18
❑ 78	Jay Bell	.40	.18
❑ 79	Scott Servais	.40	.18
❑ 80	Jose Canseco	2.00	.90
❑ 81	Roberto Hernandez	.40	.18
❑ 82	Todd Dunwoody	.40	.18
❑ 83	John Wetteland	.60	.25
❑ 84	Mike Caruso	.40	.18
❑ 85	Derek Jeter	5.00	2.20
❑ 86	Aaron Sele	.60	.25
❑ 87	Jose Lima	.60	.25
❑ 88	Ryan Christenson	.40	.18
❑ 89	Jeff Cirillo	.60	.25
❑ 90	Jose Hernandez	.40	.18
❑ 91	Mark Kotsay	.40	.18
❑ 92	Darren Bragg	.40	.18
❑ 93	Albert Belle	1.50	.70
❑ 94	Matt Lawton	.40	.18
❑ 95	Pedro Martinez	2.00	.90
❑ 96	Greg Vaughn	.60	.25
❑ 97	Neifi Perez	.60	.25
❑ 98	Gerald Williams	.40	.18
❑ 99	Derek Bell	.60	.25
❑ 100	Ken Griffey Jr.	8.00	3.60
❑ 101	David Cone	1.00	.45
❑ 102	Brian Johnson	.40	.18
❑ 103	Dean Palmer	.40	.18
❑ 104	Javier Valentin	.40	.18
❑ 105	Trevor Hoffman	.60	.25
❑ 106	Butch Huskey	.40	.18
❑ 107	Dave Martinez	.40	.18
❑ 108	Billy Wagner	.60	.25
❑ 109	Shawn Green	1.50	.70

☐ 110	Ben Grieve	1.50	.70
☐ 111	Tom Goodwin	.40	.18
☐ 112	Jaret Wright	.60	.25
☐ 113	Aramis Ramirez	1.00	.45
☐ 114	Dmitri Young	.40	.25
☐ 115	Hideki Irabu	.60	.25
☐ 116	Roberto Kelly	.40	.18
☐ 117	Jeff Fassero	.40	.18
☐ 118	Mark Clark	.40	.18
☐ 119	Jason McDonald	.40	.18
☐ 120	Matt Williams	1.50	.70
☐ 121	Dave Burba	.40	.18
☐ 122	Bret Saberhagen	.60	.25
☐ 123	Deivi Cruz	.40	.18
☐ 124	Chad Curtis	.40	.18
☐ 125	Scott Rolen	2.00	.90
☐ 126	Lee Stevens	.40	.18
☐ 127	J.T. Snow	.60	.25
☐ 128	Rusty Greer	.60	.25
☐ 129	Brian Meadows	.40	.18
☐ 130	Jim Edmonds	.60	.25
☐ 131	Ron Gant	.60	.25
☐ 132	A.J. Hinch	.40	.18
☐ 133	Shannon Stewart	.60	.25
☐ 134	Brad Fullmer	.40	.18
☐ 135	Cal Eldred	.40	.18
☐ 136	Matt Walbeck	.40	.18
☐ 137	Carl Everett	.60	.25
☐ 138	Walt Weiss	.40	.18
☐ 139	Fred McGriff	1.00	.45
☐ 140	Darin Erstad	1.00	.45
☐ 141	Dave Nilsson	.40	.18
☐ 142	Eric Young	.40	.18
☐ 143	Dan Wilson	.40	.18
☐ 144	Jeff Reed	.40	.18
☐ 145	Brett Tomko	.40	.18
☐ 146	Terry Steinbach	.40	.18
☐ 147	Seth Greisinger	.40	.18
☐ 148	Pat Meares	.40	.18
☐ 149	Livan Hernandez	.40	.18
☐ 150	Jeff Bagwell	2.00	.90
☐ 151	Bob Wickman	.40	.18
☐ 152	Omar Vizquel	.60	.25
☐ 153	Eric Davis	.60	.25
☐ 154	Larry Sutton	.40	.18
☐ 155	Magglio Ordonez	1.50	.70
☐ 156	Eric Milton	.40	.18
☐ 157	Darren Lewis	.40	.18
☐ 158	Rick Aguilera	.40	.18
☐ 159	Mike Lieberthal	.60	.25
☐ 160	Robb Nen	.60	.25
☐ 161	Brian Giles	.60	.25
☐ 162	Jeff Brantley	.40	.18
☐ 163	Gary DiSarcina	.40	.18
☐ 164	John Valentin	.60	.25
☐ 165	Dave Dellucci	.40	.18
☐ 166	Chan Ho Park	.60	.25
☐ 167	Masato Yoshii	.40	.18
☐ 168	Jason Schmidt	.40	.18
☐ 169	LaTroy Hawkins	.40	.18
☐ 170	Bret Boone	.60	.25
☐ 171	Jerry DiPoto	.40	.18
☐ 172	Mariano Rivera	.60	.25
☐ 173	Mike Cameron	.40	.18
☐ 174	Scott Erickson	.40	.18
☐ 175	Charles Johnson	.60	.25
☐ 176	Bobby Jones	.40	.18
☐ 177	Francisco Cordova	.40	.18
☐ 178	Todd Jones	.40	.18
☐ 179	Jeff Montgomery	.40	.18
☐ 180	Mike Mussina	1.50	.70
☐ 181	Bob Abreu	.60	.25
☐ 182	Ismael Valdes	.40	.18
☐ 183	Andy Fox	.40	.18
☐ 184	Woody Williams	.40	.18
☐ 185	Denny Neagle	.40	.18
☐ 186	Jose Valentin	.40	.18
☐ 187	Darrin Fletcher	.40	.18
☐ 188	Gabe Alvarez	.40	.18
☐ 189	Eddie Taubensee	.40	.18
☐ 190	Edgar Martinez	.60	.25
☐ 191	Jason Kendall	.60	.25
☐ 192	Daryl Kile	.40	.18
☐ 193	Jeff King	.40	.18
☐ 194	Rey Ordonez	.40	.25
☐ 195	Andruw Jones	1.50	.70
☐ 196	Tony Fernandez	.60	.25
☐ 197	Jamey Wright	.40	.18
☐ 198	B.J. Surhoff	.60	.25
☐ 199	Vinny Castilla	.60	.25
☐ 200	David Wells HL	.40	.18
☐ 201	Mark McGwire HL	5.00	2.20
☐ 202	Sammy Sosa HL	2.50	1.10
☐ 203	Roger Clemens HL	2.00	.90
☐ 204	Kerry Wood HL	.60	.25
☐ 205	Gabe Kapler	2.50	1.10
	Lance Berkman		
	Mike Frank		
☐ 206	Alex Escobar	6.00	2.70
	Ricky Ledee		
	Mike Stoner		
☐ 207	Peter Bergeron	3.00	1.35
	Jeremy Giambi		
	George Lombard		
☐ 208	Michael Barrett	1.00	.45
	Ben Davis		
	Robert Fick		
☐ 209	Jayson Werth	.60	.25
	Ramon Hernandez		
	Pat Cline		
☐ 210	Ryan Anderson	2.00	.90
	Bruce Chen		
	Chris Enochs		
☐ 211	Brad Penny	.60	.25
	Octavio Dotel		
	Mike Lincoln		
☐ 212	Chuck Abbott	1.50	.70
	Brent Butler		
	Danny Klassen		
☐ 213	Chris C. Jones	3.00	1.35
	Jeff Urban		
☐ 214	Arturo McDonald	3.00	1.35
	Tony Torcato		
☐ 215	Josh McKinley	3.00	1.35
	Jason Tyner		
☐ 216	Matt Burch	3.00	1.35
	Seth Etheron		
☐ 217	Mamon Tucker	4.00	1.80
	Rick Elder		
☐ 218	J.M. Gold	3.00	1.35
	Ryan Mills		
☐ 219	Andy Brown	4.00	1.80
	Choo Freeman		
☐ 220A	Mark McGwire HR 1	80.00	36.00
☐ 220B	Mark McGwire HR 2	40.00	18.00
☐ 220C	Mark McGwire HR 3	40.00	18.00
☐ 220D	Mark McGwire HR 4	40.00	18.00
☐ 220E	Mark McGwire HR 5	40.00	18.00
☐ 220F	Mark McGwire HR 6	40.00	18.00
☐ 220G	Mark McGwire HR 7	40.00	18.00
☐ 220H	Mark McGwire HR 8	40.00	18.00
☐ 220I	Mark McGwire HR 9	40.00	18.00
☐ 220J	Mark McGwire HR 10	40.00	18.00
☐ 220K	Mark McGwire HR 11	40.00	18.00
☐ 220L	Mark McGwire HR 12	40.00	18.00
☐ 220M	Mark McGwire HR 13	40.00	18.00
☐ 220N	Mark McGwire HR 14	40.00	18.00
☐ 220O	Mark McGwire HR 15	40.00	18.00
☐ 220P	Mark McGwire HR 16	40.00	18.00
☐ 220Q	Mark McGwire HR 17	40.00	18.00
☐ 220R	Mark McGwire HR 18	40.00	18.00
☐ 220S	Mark McGwire HR 19	40.00	18.00
☐ 220T	Mark McGwire HR 20	40.00	18.00
☐ 220U	Mark McGwire HR 21	40.00	18.00
☐ 220V	Mark McGwire HR 22	40.00	18.00
☐ 220W	Mark McGwire HR 23	40.00	18.00
☐ 220X	Mark McGwire HR 24	40.00	18.00
☐ 220Y	Mark McGwire HR 25	40.00	18.00
☐ 220Z	Mark McGwire HR 26	40.00	18.00
☐ 220AA	Mark McGwire HR 27	40.00	18.00
☐ 220AB	Mark McGwire HR 28	40.00	18.00
☐ 220AC	Mark McGwire HR 29	40.00	18.00
☐ 220AD	Mark McGwire HR 30	40.00	18.00
☐ 220AE	Mark McGwire HR 31	40.00	18.00
☐ 220AF	Mark McGwire HR 32	40.00	18.00
☐ 220AG	Mark McGwire HR 33	40.00	18.00
☐ 220AH	Mark McGwire HR 34	40.00	18.00
☐ 220AI	Mark McGwire HR 35	40.00	18.00
☐ 220AJ	Mark McGwire HR 36	40.00	18.00
☐ 220AK	Mark McGwire HR 37	40.00	18.00
☐ 220AL	Mark McGwire HR 38	40.00	18.00
☐ 220AM	Mark McGwire HR 39	40.00	18.00
☐ 220AN	Mark McGwire HR 40	40.00	18.00
☐ 220AO	Mark McGwire HR 41	40.00	18.00
☐ 220AP	Mark McGwire HR 42	40.00	18.00
☐ 220AQ	Mark McGwire HR 43	40.00	18.00
☐ 220AR	Mark McGwire HR 44	40.00	18.00
☐ 220AS	Mark McGwire HR 45	40.00	18.00
☐ 220AT	Mark McGwire HR 46	40.00	18.00
☐ 220AU	Mark McGwire HR 47	40.00	18.00
☐ 220AV	Mark McGwire HR 48	40.00	18.00
☐ 220AW	Mark McGwire HR 49	40.00	18.00
☐ 220AX	Mark McGwire HR 50	40.00	18.00
☐ 220AY	Mark McGwire HR 51	40.00	18.00
☐ 220AZ	Mark McGwire HR 52	40.00	18.00
☐ 220BB	Mark McGwire HR 53	40.00	18.00
☐ 220CC	Mark McGwire HR 54	40.00	18.00
☐ 220DD	Mark McGwire HR 55	40.00	18.00
☐ 220EE	Mark McGwire HR 56	40.00	18.00
☐ 220FF	Mark McGwire HR 57	40.00	18.00
☐ 220GG	Mark McGwire HR 58	40.00	18.00
☐ 220HH	Mark McGwire HR 59	40.00	18.00
☐ 220II	Mark McGwire HR 60	40.00	18.00
☐ 220JJ	Mark McGwire HR 61	80.00	36.00
☐ 220KK	Mark McGwire HR 62	120.00	55.00
☐ 220LL	Mark McGwire HR 63	60.00	27.00
☐ 220MM	Mark McGwire HR 64	60.00	27.00
☐ 220NN	Mark McGwire HR 65	60.00	27.00
☐ 220OO	Mark McGwire HR 66	60.00	27.00
☐ 220PP	Mark McGwire HR 67	60.00	27.00
☐ 220QQ	Mark McGwire HR 68	60.00	27.00
☐ 220RR	Mark McGwire HR 69	60.00	27.00
☐ 220SS	Mark McGwire HR 70	300.00	135.00
☐ 221	Larry Walker LL	.60	.25
☐ 222	Bernie Williams LL	.60	.25
☐ 223	Mark McGwire LL	5.00	2.20
☐ 224	Ken Griffey Jr. LL	4.00	1.80
☐ 225	Sammy Sosa LL	2.50	1.10
☐ 226	Juan Gonzalez LL	1.50	.70
☐ 227	Dante Bichette LL	.40	.18
☐ 228	Alex Rodriguez LL	2.50	1.10
☐ 229	Sammy Sosa LL	2.50	1.10
☐ 230	Derek Jeter LL	2.50	1.10
☐ 231	Greg Maddux LL	2.00	.90
☐ 232	Roger Clemens LL	2.00	.90
☐ 233	Ricky Ledee WS	.40	.18
☐ 234	Chuck Knoblauch WS	.60	.25
☐ 235	Bernie Williams WS	.60	.25
☐ 236	Tino Martinez WS	.40	.18
☐ 237	Orlando Hernandez WS	.60	.25
☐ 238	Scott Brosius WS	.40	.18
☐ 239	Andy Pettitte WS	.40	.18
☐ 240	Mariano Rivera WS	.60	.25
☐ 241	Checklist	.40	.18
☐ 242	Checklist	.40	.18
☐ 243	Tom Glavine	1.50	.70
☐ 244	Andy Benes	.40	.18
☐ 245	Sandy Alomar Jr.	.60	.25
☐ 246	Wilton Guerrero	.40	.18
☐ 247	Alex Gonzalez	.60	.25
☐ 248	Roberto Alomar	1.50	.70
☐ 249	Ruben Rivera	.40	.18
☐ 250	Eric Chavez	1.00	.45
☐ 251	Ellis Burks	.60	.25
☐ 252	Richie Sexson	1.00	.45
☐ 253	Steve Finley	.60	.25
☐ 254	Dwight Gooden	.60	.25
☐ 255	Dustin Hermanson	.40	.18
☐ 256	Kirk Rueter	.40	.18
☐ 257	Steve Trachsel	.40	.18
☐ 258	Gregg Jefferies	.40	.18
☐ 259	Matt Stairs	.60	.25
☐ 260	Shane Reynolds	.60	.25
☐ 261	Gregg Olson	.40	.18
☐ 262	Kevin Tapani	.40	.18
☐ 263	Matt Morris	.40	.18
☐ 264	Carl Pavano	.40	.18
☐ 265	Nomar Garciaparra	5.00	2.20
☐ 266	Kevin Young	.40	.18
☐ 267	Rick Helling	.40	.18
☐ 268	Matt Franco	.40	.18
☐ 269	Brian McRae	.40	.18
☐ 270	Cal Ripken	6.00	2.70
☐ 271	Jeff Abbott	.40	.18
☐ 272	Tony Batista	.40	.18
☐ 273	Bill Simas	.40	.18
☐ 274	Brian Hunter	.40	.18
☐ 275	John Franco	.60	.25

☐ 276	Devon White	.40	.18
☐ 277	Rickey Henderson	2.00	.90
☐ 278	Chuck Finley	.60	.25
☐ 279	Mike Blowers	.40	.18
☐ 280	Mark Grace	1.00	.45
☐ 281	Randy Winn	.40	.18
☐ 282	Bobby Bonilla	.60	.25
☐ 283	David Justice	.60	.25
☐ 284	Shane Monahan	.40	.18
☐ 285	Kevin Brown	1.00	.45
☐ 286	Todd Zeile	.60	.25
☐ 287	Al Martin	.40	.18
☐ 288	Troy O'Leary	.60	.25
☐ 289	Darryl Hamilton	.40	.18
☐ 290	Tino Martinez	.60	.25
☐ 291	David Ortiz	.40	.18
☐ 292	Tony Clark	.60	.25
☐ 293	Ryan Minor	.40	.18
☐ 294	Mark Leiter	.40	.18
☐ 295	Wally Joyner	.60	.25
☐ 296	Cliff Floyd	.60	.25
☐ 297	Shawn Estes	.40	.18
☐ 298	Pat Hentgen	.40	.18
☐ 299	Scott Elarton	.40	.18
☐ 300	Alex Rodriguez	5.00	2.20
☐ 301	Ozzie Guillen	.40	.18
☐ 302	Hideo Nomo	1.50	.70
☐ 303	Ryan McGuire	.40	.18
☐ 304	Brad Ausmus	.40	.18
☐ 305	Alex Gonzalez	.60	.25
☐ 306	Brian Jordan	.60	.25
☐ 307	John Jaha	.60	.25
☐ 308	Mark Grudzielanek	.40	.18
☐ 309	Juan Guzman	.40	.18
☐ 310	Tony Womack	.40	.18
☐ 311	Dennis Reyes	.40	.18
☐ 312	Marty Cordova	.40	.18
☐ 313	Ramiro Mendoza	.40	.18
☐ 314	Robin Ventura	.40	.18
☐ 315	Rafael Palmeiro	1.50	.70
☐ 316	Ramon Martinez	.40	.18
☐ 317	Pedro Astacio	.40	.18
☐ 318	Dave Hollins	.40	.18
☐ 319	Tom Candiotti	.40	.18
☐ 320	Al Leiter	.60	.25
☐ 321	Rico Brogna	.40	.18
☐ 322	Reggie Jefferson	.40	.18
☐ 323	Bernard Gilkey	.40	.18
☐ 324	Jason Giambi	.60	.25
☐ 325	Craig Biggio	1.50	.70
☐ 326	Troy Glaus	1.50	.70
☐ 327	Delino DeShields	.40	.18
☐ 328	Fernando Vina	.40	.18
☐ 329	John Smoltz	1.00	.45
☐ 330	Jeff Kent	.60	.25
☐ 331	Roy Halladay	.60	.25
☐ 332	Andy Ashby	.40	.18
☐ 333	Tim Wakefield	.40	.18
☐ 334	Roger Clemens	4.00	1.80
☐ 335	Bernie Williams	1.50	.70
☐ 336	Desi Relaford	.40	.18
☐ 337	John Burkett	.40	.18
☐ 338	Mike Hampton	.60	.25
☐ 339	Royce Clayton	.40	.18
☐ 340	Mike Piazza	5.00	2.20
☐ 341	Jeremi Gonzalez	.40	.18
☐ 342	Mike Lansing	.40	.18
☐ 343	Jamie Moyer	.40	.18
☐ 344	Ron Coomer	.40	.18
☐ 345	Barry Larkin	1.50	.70
☐ 346	Fernando Tatis	1.50	.70
☐ 347	Chili Davis	.60	.25
☐ 348	Bobby Higginson	.40	.18
☐ 349	Hal Morris	.40	.18
☐ 350	Larry Walker	1.50	.70
☐ 351	Carlos Guillen	.40	.18
☐ 352	Miguel Tejada	.60	.25
☐ 353	Travis Fryman	.60	.25
☐ 354	Jarrod Washburn	.40	.18
☐ 355	Chipper Jones	4.00	1.80
☐ 356	Todd Stottlemyre	.40	.18
☐ 357	Henry Rodriguez	.60	.25
☐ 358	Eli Marrero	.40	.18
☐ 359	Alan Benes	.40	.18
☐ 360	Tim Salmon	1.00	.45
☐ 361	Luis Gonzalez	.60	.25
☐ 362	Scott Spiezio	.40	.18
☐ 363	Chris Carpenter	.40	.18
☐ 364	Bobby Howry	.40	.18
☐ 365	Raul Mondesi	.60	.25
☐ 366	Ugueth Urbina	.40	.18
☐ 367	Tom Evans	.40	.18
☐ 368	Kerry Ligtenberg	2.00	.90
☐ 369	Adrian Beltre	1.50	.70
☐ 370	Ryan Klesko	.60	.25
☐ 371	Wilson Alvarez	.40	.18
☐ 372	John Thomson	.40	.18
☐ 373	Tony Saunders	.40	.18
☐ 374	Dave Mlicki	.40	.18
☐ 375	Ken Caminiti	.60	.25
☐ 376	Jay Buhner	.60	.25
☐ 377	Bill Mueller	.40	.18
☐ 378	Jeff Blauser	.40	.18
☐ 379	Edgar Renteria	.40	.18
☐ 380	Jim Thome	1.50	.70
☐ 381	Joey Hamilton	.40	.18
☐ 382	Calvin Pickering	.60	.25
☐ 383	Marquis Grissom	.40	.18
☐ 384	Omar Daal	.40	.18
☐ 385	Curt Schilling	1.00	.45
☐ 386	Jose Cruz Jr.	.60	.25
☐ 387	Chris Widger	.40	.18
☐ 388	Pete Harnisch	.40	.18
☐ 389	Charles Nagy	.60	.25
☐ 390	Tom Gordon	.60	.25
☐ 391	Bobby Smith	.40	.18
☐ 392	Derrick Gibson	.60	.25
☐ 393	Jeff Conine	.40	.18
☐ 394	Carlos Perez	.40	.18
☐ 395	Barry Bonds	2.00	.90
☐ 396	Mark McLemore	.40	.18
☐ 397	Juan Encarnacion	.60	.25
☐ 398	Wade Boggs	1.50	.70
☐ 399	Ivan Rodriguez	2.00	.90
☐ 400	Moises Alou	.60	.25
☐ 401	Jeromy Burnitz	.60	.25
☐ 402	Sean Casey	1.50	.70
☐ 403	Jose Offerman	.40	.18
☐ 404	Joe Fontenot	.40	.18
☐ 405	Kevin Millwood	1.00	.45
☐ 406	Lance Johnson	.40	.18
☐ 407	Richard Hidalgo	.60	.25
☐ 408	Mike Jackson	.40	.18
☐ 409	Brian Anderson	.40	.18
☐ 410	Jeff Shaw	.40	.18
☐ 411	Preston Wilson	.60	.25
☐ 412	Todd Hundley	.60	.25
☐ 413	Jim Parque	.40	.18
☐ 414	Justin Baughman	.40	.18
☐ 415	Dante Bichette	.60	.25
☐ 416	Paul O'Neill	.60	.25
☐ 417	Miguel Cairo	.40	.18
☐ 418	Randy Johnson	1.50	.70
☐ 419	Jesus Sanchez	.40	.18
☐ 420	Carlos Delgado	1.50	.70
☐ 421	Ricky Ledee	.60	.25
☐ 422	Orlando Hernandez	1.50	.70
☐ 423	Frank Thomas	3.00	1.35
☐ 424	Pokey Reese	.60	.25
☐ 425	Carlos Lee	3.00	1.35
	Mike Lowell		
	Kit Pellow		
☐ 426	Michael Cuddyer	.60	.25
	Mark DeRosa		
	Jerry Hairston Jr.		
☐ 427	Marlon Anderson	.60	.25
	Ron Belliard		
	Orlando Cabrera		
☐ 428	Micah Bowie	2.00	.90
	Phil Norton		
	Randy Wolf		
☐ 429	Jack Cressend	1.50	.70
	Jason Rakers		
	John Rocker		
☐ 430	Ruben Mateo	3.00	1.35
	Scott Morgan		
	Mike Zywica		
☐ 431	Jason LaRue	.40	.18
	Matt LeCroy		
	Mitch Meluskey		
☐ 432	Gabe Kapler	2.50	1.10
	Armando Rios		
	Fernando Seguignol		
☐ 433	Adam Kennedy	1.50	.70
	Mickey Lopez		
	Jackie Rexrode		
☐ 434	Jose Fernandez	1.50	.70
	Jeff Liefer		
	Chris Truby		
☐ 435	Corey Koskie	1.50	.70
	Doug Mientkiewicz		
	Damon Minor		
☐ 436	Roosevelt Brown	2.50	1.10
	Dernell Stenson		
	Vernon Wells		
☐ 437	A.J. Burnett	3.00	1.35
	Billy Koch		
	John Nicholson		
☐ 438	Matt Belisle	3.00	1.35
	Matt Roney		
☐ 439	Austin Kearns	4.00	1.80
	Chris George		
☐ 440	Nate Bump	3.00	1.35
	Nate Cornejo		
☐ 441	Brad Lidge	3.00	1.35
	Mike Nannini		
☐ 442	Matt Holliday	4.00	1.80
	Jeff Winchester		
☐ 443	Adam Everett	4.00	1.80
	Chip Ambres		
☐ 444	Pat Burrell	15.00	6.75
	Eric Valent		
☐ 445	Roger Clemens SK	2.00	.90
☐ 446	Kerry Wood SK	.60	.25
☐ 447	Curt Schilling SK	.60	.25
☐ 448	Randy Johnson SK	.60	.25
☐ 449	Pedro Martinez SK	1.00	.45
☐ 450	Jeff Bagwell AT	4.00	1.80
	Andres Galarraga		
	Mark McGwire		
☐ 451	John Olerud AT	.60	.25
	Jim Thome		
	Tino Martinez		
☐ 452	Alex Rodriguez AT	2.00	.90
	Nomar Garciaparra		
	Derek Jeter		
☐ 453	Vinny Castilla AT	1.50	.70
	Chipper Jones		
	Scott Rolen		
☐ 454	Sammy Sosa AT	3.00	1.35
	Ken Griffey Jr.		
	Juan Gonzalez		
☐ 455	Barry Bonds AT	.60	.25
	Manny Ramirez		
	Larry Walker		
☐ 456	Frank Thomas AT	1.50	.70
	Tim Salmon		
	David Justice		
☐ 457	Travis Lee AT	.60	.25
	Todd Helton		
	Ben Grieve		
☐ 458	Vladimir Guerrero AT	1.50	.70
	Greg Vaughn		
	Bernie Williams		
☐ 459	Mike Piazza AT	1.50	.70
	Ivan Rodriguez		
	Jason Kendall		
☐ 460	Roger Clemens AT	1.50	.70
	Kerry Wood		
	Greg Maddux		
☐ 461A	Sammy Sosa HR 1	30.00	13.50
☐ 461B	Sammy Sosa HR 2	15.00	6.75
☐ 461C	Sammy Sosa HR 3	15.00	6.75
☐ 461D	Sammy Sosa HR 4	15.00	6.75
☐ 461E	Sammy Sosa HR 5	15.00	6.75
☐ 461F	Sammy Sosa HR 6	15.00	6.75
☐ 461G	Sammy Sosa HR 7	15.00	6.75
☐ 461H	Sammy Sosa HR 8	15.00	6.75
☐ 461I	Sammy Sosa HR 9	15.00	6.75
☐ 461J	Sammy Sosa HR 10	15.00	6.75
☐ 461K	Sammy Sosa HR 11	15.00	6.75
☐ 461L	Sammy Sosa HR 12	15.00	6.75
☐ 461M	Sammy Sosa HR 13	15.00	6.75
☐ 461N	Sammy Sosa HR 14	15.00	6.75
☐ 461O	Sammy Sosa HR 15	15.00	6.75
☐ 461P	Sammy Sosa HR 16	15.00	6.75
☐ 461Q	Sammy Sosa HR 17	15.00	6.75
☐ 461R	Sammy Sosa HR 18	15.00	6.75

❏ 461S Sammy Sosa HR 19	15.00	6.75
❏ 461T Sammy Sosa HR 20	15.00	6.75
❏ 461U Sammy Sosa HR 21	15.00	6.75
❏ 461V Sammy Sosa HR 22	15.00	6.75
❏ 461W Sammy Sosa HR 23	15.00	6.75
❏ 461X Sammy Sosa HR 24	15.00	6.75
❏ 461Y Sammy Sosa HR 25	15.00	6.75
❏ 461Z Sammy Sosa HR 26	15.00	6.75
❏ 461AA Sammy Sosa HR 27	15.00	6.75
❏ 461AB Sammy Sosa HR 28	15.00	6.75
❏ 461AC Sammy Sosa HR 29	15.00	6.75
❏ 461AD Sammy Sosa HR 30	15.00	6.75
❏ 461AE Sammy Sosa HR 31	15.00	6.75
❏ 461AF Sammy Sosa HR 32	15.00	6.75
❏ 461AG Sammy Sosa HR 33	15.00	6.75
❏ 461AH Sammy Sosa HR 34	15.00	6.75
❏ 461AI Sammy Sosa HR 35	15.00	6.75
❏ 461AJ Sammy Sosa HR 36	15.00	6.75
❏ 461AK Sammy Sosa HR 37	15.00	6.75
❏ 461AL Sammy Sosa HR 38	15.00	6.75
❏ 461AM Sammy Sosa HR 39	15.00	6.75
❏ 461AN Sammy Sosa HR 40	15.00	6.75
❏ 461AO Sammy Sosa HR 41	15.00	6.75
❏ 461AP Sammy Sosa HR 42	15.00	6.75
❏ 461AR Sammy Sosa HR 43	15.00	6.75
❏ 461AS Sammy Sosa HR 44	15.00	6.75
❏ 461AT Sammy Sosa HR 45	15.00	6.75
❏ 461AU Sammy Sosa HR 46	15.00	6.75
❏ 461AV Sammy Sosa HR 47	15.00	6.75
❏ 461AW Sammy Sosa HR 48	15.00	6.75
❏ 461AX Sammy Sosa HR 49	15.00	6.75
❏ 461AY Sammy Sosa HR 50	15.00	6.75
❏ 461AZ Sammy Sosa HR 51	15.00	6.75
❏ 461BB Sammy Sosa HR 52	15.00	6.75
❏ 461CC Sammy Sosa HR 53	15.00	6.75
❏ 461DD Sammy Sosa HR 54	15.00	6.75
❏ 461EE Sammy Sosa HR 55	15.00	6.75
❏ 461FF Sammy Sosa HR 56	15.00	6.75
❏ 461GG Sammy Sosa HR 57	15.00	6.75
❏ 461HH Sammy Sosa HR 58	15.00	6.75
❏ 461II Sammy Sosa HR 59	15.00	6.75
❏ 461JJ Sammy Sosa HR 60	15.00	6.75
❏ 461KK Sammy Sosa HR 61	30.00	13.50
❏ 461LL Sammy Sosa HR 62	50.00	22.00
❏ 461MM Sammy Sosa HR 63	20.00	9.00
❏ 461NN Sammy Sosa HR 64	20.00	9.00
❏ 461OO Sammy Sosa HR 65	20.00	9.00
❏ 461PP Sammy Sosa HR 66	80.00	36.00
❏ 462 Checklist	.40	.18
❏ 463 Checklist	.40	.18

1999 Topps Chrome Refractors

	MINT	NRMT
COMMON CARD (1-6/8-462)	4.00	1.80

*STARS: 4X TO 10X BASIC CARDS
*YNG.STARS: 3X TO 8X BASIC CARDS
*PROSPECTS: 1.5X TO 4X BASIC CARDS
*ROOKIES: 1.25X TO 3X BASIC CARDS

MCGWIRE 220 HR 1	300.00	135.00
MCGWIRE 220 HR 2-60	120.00	55.00
MCGWIRE 220 HR 61	300.00	135.00
MCGWIRE 220 HR 62	500.00	220.00
MCGWIRE 220 HR 63-69	150.00	70.00
MCGWIRE 220 HR 70	1200.00	550.00

CARD 220 AVAILABLE IN 70 VARIATIONS

SOSA 461 HR 1	80.00	36.00

SOSA 461 HR 2-60	40.00	18.00
SOSA 461 HR 61	80.00	36.00
SOSA 461 HR 62	120.00	55.00
SOSA 461 HR 63-65	60.00	27.00
SOSA 461 HR 66	300.00	135.00

CARD 461 AVAILABLE IN 66 VARIATIONS
SER.1 SET INCLUDES 1 CARD 220 VARIATION
SER.2 SET INCLUDES 1 CARD 461 VARIATION
REFRACTOR STATED ODDS 1:12
CARD NUMBER 7 DOES NOT EXIST

1999 Topps Chrome All-Etch

	MINT	NRMT
COMPLETE SET (30)	150.00	70.00
COMMON CARD (AE1-AE30)	1.50	.70
SEMISTARS	2.50	1.10
UNLISTED STARS	4.00	1.80

SER.2 STATED ODDS 1:6
*REFRACTORS: 1.25X TO 3X HI COLUMN
SER.2 REFRACTOR ODDS 1:24

❏ AE1 Mark McGwire	25.00	11.00
❏ AE2 Sammy Sosa	12.00	5.50
❏ AE3 Ken Griffey Jr.	20.00	9.00
❏ AE4 Greg Vaughn	1.50	.70
❏ AE5 Albert Belle	4.00	1.80
❏ AE6 Vinny Castilla	1.50	.70
❏ AE7 Jose Canseco	5.00	2.20
❏ AE8 Juan Gonzalez	8.00	3.60
❏ AE9 Manny Ramirez	5.00	2.20
❏ AE10 Andres Galarraga	2.50	1.10
❏ AE11 Rafael Palmeiro	4.00	1.80
❏ AE12 Alex Rodriguez	12.00	5.50
❏ AE13 Mo Vaughn	4.00	1.80
❏ AE14 Eric Chavez	2.50	1.10
❏ AE15 Gabe Kapler	4.00	1.80
❏ AE16 Calvin Pickering	1.50	.70
❏ AE17 Ruben Mateo	4.00	1.80
❏ AE18 Roy Halladay	1.50	.70
❏ AE19 Jeremy Giambi	1.50	.70
❏ AE20 Alex Gonzalez	1.50	.70
❏ AE21 Ron Belliard	1.50	.70
❏ AE22 Marlon Anderson	1.50	.70
❏ AE23 Carlos Lee	1.50	.70
❏ AE24 Kerry Wood	4.00	1.80
❏ AE25 Roger Clemens	10.00	4.50
❏ AE26 Curt Schilling	2.50	1.10
❏ AE27 Kevin Brown	2.50	1.10
❏ AE28 Randy Johnson	4.00	1.80
❏ AE29 Pedro Martinez	5.00	2.20
❏ AE30 Orlando Hernandez	4.00	1.80

1999 Topps Chrome Early Road to the Hall

Early Road
to the Hall

	MINT	NRMT
COMPLETE SET (10)	80.00	36.00
COMMON CARD (ER1-ER10)	5.00	2.20

SER.1 STATED ODDS 1:12
*REFRACTORS: 5X TO 12X BASIC ROAD
SER.1 REFRACTOR ODDS 1:944 HOBBY
REF.PRINT RUN 100 SERIAL #'d SETS

❏ ER1 Nomar Garciaparra	12.00	5.50
❏ ER2 Derek Jeter	12.00	5.50
❏ ER3 Alex Rodriguez	12.00	5.50
❏ ER4 Juan Gonzalez	8.00	3.60
❏ ER5 Ken Griffey Jr.	20.00	9.00
❏ ER6 Chipper Jones	10.00	4.50
❏ ER7 Vladimir Guerrero	5.00	2.20
❏ ER8 Jeff Bagwell	5.00	2.20
❏ ER9 Ivan Rodriguez	5.00	2.20
❏ ER10 Frank Thomas	8.00	3.60

1999 Topps Chrome Fortune 15

FORTUNE 15

	MINT	NRMT
COMPLETE SET (15)	120.00	55.00
COMMON CARD (FF1-FF15)	2.50	1.10
UNLISTED STARS	4.00	1.80

SER.2 STATED ODDS 1:12
*REFRACTORS: 5X TO 12X HI COLUMN
SER.2 REFRACTOR ODDS 1:627
REF.PRINT RUN 100 SERIAL #'d SETS

❏ FF1 Alex Rodriguez	12.00	5.50
❏ FF2 Nomar Garciaparra	12.00	5.50
❏ FF3 Derek Jeter	12.00	5.50
❏ FF4 Troy Glaus	4.00	1.80
❏ FF5 Ken Griffey Jr.	20.00	9.00
❏ FF6 Vladimir Guerrero	5.00	2.20
❏ FF7 Kerry Wood	4.00	1.80
❏ FF8 Eric Chavez	2.50	1.10
❏ FF9 Greg Maddux	10.00	4.50
❏ FF10 Mike Piazza	12.00	5.50
❏ FF11 Sammy Sosa	12.00	5.50
❏ FF12 Mark McGwire	25.00	11.00
❏ FF13 Ben Grieve	4.00	1.80
❏ FF14 Chipper Jones	10.00	4.50
❏ FF15 Manny Ramirez	5.00	2.20

1999 Topps Chrome Lords of the Diamond

LORDS of the
DIAMOND

	MINT	NRMT
COMPLETE SET (15)	60.00	27.00
COMMON CARD (LD1-LD15)	1.25	.55

SER.1 STATED ODDS 1:8
*REFRACTORS: 1.25X TO 3X BASIC LORDS
SER.1 REFRACTOR ODDS 1:24

❏ LD1 Ken Griffey Jr.	10.00	4.50

□ LD2 Chipper Jones	5.00	2.20
□ LD3 Sammy Sosa	6.00	2.70
□ LD4 Frank Thomas	4.00	1.80
□ LD5 Mark McGwire	12.00	5.50
□ LD6 Jeff Bagwell	2.50	1.10
□ LD7 Alex Rodriguez	6.00	2.70
□ LD8 Juan Gonzalez	4.00	1.80
□ LD9 Barry Bonds	2.50	1.10
□ LD10 Nomar Garciaparra	6.00	2.70
□ LD11 Darin Erstad	1.25	.55
□ LD12 Tony Gwynn	5.00	2.20
□ LD13 Andres Galarraga	.25	.55
□ LD14 Mike Piazza	6.00	2.70
□ LD15 Greg Maddux	5.00	2.20

1999 Topps Chrome New Breed

	MINT	NRMT
COMPLETE SET (15)	100.00	45.00
COMMON CARD (NB1-NB15)	1.50	.70
MINOR STARS	2.50	1.10
SEMISTARS	4.00	1.80
UNLISTED STARS	6.00	2.70

SER.1 STATED ODDS 1:24
*REFRACTORS: 1X TO 2.5X BASIC BREED
SER.1 REFRACTOR ODDS 1:72

□ NB1 Darin Erstad	4.00	1.80
□ NB2 Brad Fullmer	1.50	.70
□ NB3 Kerry Wood	6.00	2.70
□ NB4 Nomar Garciaparra	20.00	9.00
□ NB5 Travis Lee	6.00	2.70
□ NB6 Scott Rolen	8.00	3.60
□ NB7 Todd Helton	6.00	2.70
□ NB8 Vladimir Guerrero	8.00	3.60
□ NB9 Derek Jeter	20.00	9.00
□ NB10 Alex Rodriguez	20.00	9.00
□ NB11 Ben Grieve	6.00	2.70
□ NB12 Andruw Jones	6.00	2.70
□ NB13 Paul Konerko	2.50	1.10
□ NB14 Aramis Ramirez	4.00	1.80
□ NB15 Adrian Beltre	6.00	2.70

1999 Topps Chrome Record Numbers

	MINT	NRMT
COMPLETE SET (10)	150.00	70.00
COMMON CARD (RN1-RN10)	4.00	1.80

SER.2 STATED ODDS 1:36
*REFRACTORS: 1.25X TO 3X HI COLUMN
SER.2 REFRACTOR ODDS 1:144

□ RN1 Mark McGwire	40.00	18.00
□ RN2 Mike Piazza	20.00	9.00
□ RN3 Curt Schilling	4.00	1.80
□ RN4 Ken Griffey Jr.	30.00	13.50
□ RN5 Sammy Sosa	20.00	9.00
□ RN6 Nomar Garciaparra	20.00	9.00
□ RN7 Kerry Wood	4.00	1.80
□ RN8 Roger Clemens	15.00	6.75
□ RN9 Cal Ripken	25.00	11.00
□ RN10 Mark McGwire	40.00	18.00

1996 Topps Gallery

	MINT	NRMT
COMPLETE SET (180)	40.00	18.00
COMMON CARD (1-180)	.25	.11
MINOR STARS	.50	.23
UNLISTED STARS	1.00	.45
COMMON PPI (1-180)	2.00	.90

*PPI STARS: 6X TO 15X HI COLUMN
*PPI ROOKIES: 5X TO 12X HI
PPI STATED ODDS 1:8
PPI STAT.PRINT RUN 999 SERIAL #'d SETS
FIRST 100 PPI CARDS SENT TO PLAYERS
TOPPS ALSO DESTROYED 400 PPI SETS
MANTLE STATED ODDS 1:48

□ 1 Tom Glavine	1.00	.45
□ 2 Carlos Baerga	.25	.11
□ 3 Dante Bichette	.50	.23
□ 4 Mark Langston	.25	.11
□ 5 Ray Lankford	.50	.23
□ 6 Moises Alou	.50	.23
□ 7 Marquis Grissom	.25	.11
□ 8 Ramon Martinez	.50	.23
□ 9 Steve Finley	.50	.23
□ 10 Todd Hundley	.50	.23
□ 11 Brady Anderson	.50	.23
□ 12 John Valentin	.50	.23
□ 13 Heathcliff Slocumb	.25	.11
□ 14 Ruben Sierra	.25	.11
□ 15 Jeff Conine	.50	.23
□ 16 Jay Buhner	.50	.23
□ 17 Sammy Sosa	3.00	1.35
□ 18 Doug Drabek	.25	.11
□ 19 Jose Mesa	.25	.11
□ 20 Jeff King	.25	.11
□ 21 Mickey Tettleton	.25	.11
□ 22 Jeff Montgomery	.25	.11
□ 23 Alex Fernandez	.25	.11
□ 24 Greg Vaughn	.50	.23
□ 25 Chuck Finley	.50	.23
□ 26 Terry Steinbach	.25	.11
□ 27 Rod Beck	.25	.11
□ 28 Jack McDowell	.25	.11
□ 29 Mark Wohlers	.25	.11
□ 30 Len Dykstra	.50	.23
□ 31 Bernie Williams	1.00	.45
□ 32 Travis Fryman	.50	.23
□ 33 Jose Canseco	1.25	.55
□ 34 Ken Caminiti	.50	.23
□ 35 Devon White	.25	.11
□ 36 Bobby Bonilla	.50	.23
□ 37 Paul Sorrento	.25	.11

□ 38 Ryne Sandberg	1.25	.55
□ 39 Derek Bell	.50	.23
□ 40 Bobby Jones	.25	.11
□ 41 J.T. Snow	.50	.23
□ 42 Denny Neagle	.50	.23
□ 43 Tim Wakefield	.25	.11
□ 44 Andres Galarraga	1.00	.45
□ 45 David Segui	.50	.23
□ 46 Lee Smith	.50	.23
□ 47 Mel Rojas	.25	.11
□ 48 John Franco	.50	.23
□ 49 Pete Schourek	.25	.11
□ 50 John Wetteland	.50	.23
□ 51 Paul Molitor	1.00	.45
□ 52 Ivan Rodriguez	1.25	.55
□ 53 Chris Holles	.25	.11
□ 54 Mike Greenwell	.25	.11
□ 55 Orel Hershiser	.50	.23
□ 56 Brian McRae	.25	.11
□ 57 Geronimo Berroa	.25	.11
□ 58 Craig Biggio	1.00	.45
□ 59 David Justice	1.00	.45
□ 60 Lance Johnson	.25	.11
□ 61 Andy Ashby	.25	.11
□ 62 Randy Myers	.25	.11
□ 63 Gregg Jefferies	.25	.11
□ 64 Kevin Appier	.50	.23
□ 65 Rick Aguilera	.25	.11
□ 66 Shane Reynolds	.50	.23
□ 67 John Smoltz	.75	.35
□ 68 Ron Gant	.25	.11
□ 69 Eric Karros	.50	.23
□ 70 Jim Thome	1.00	.45
□ 71 Terry Pendleton	.25	.11
□ 72 Kenny Rogers	.25	.11
□ 73 Robin Ventura	.50	.23
□ 74 Dave Nilsson	.25	.11
□ 75 Brian Jordan	.50	.23
□ 76 Glenallen Hill	.25	.11
□ 77 Greg Colbrunn	.25	.11
□ 78 Roberto Alomar	1.00	.45
□ 79 Rickey Henderson	1.25	.55
□ 80 Carlos Garcia	.25	.11
□ 81 Dean Palmer	.50	.23
□ 82 Mike Stanley	.25	.11
□ 83 Hal Morris	.25	.11
□ 84 Wade Boggs	1.00	.45
□ 85 Chad Curtis	.25	.11
□ 86 Roberto Hernandez	.25	.11
□ 87 John Olerud	.50	.23
□ 88 Frank Castillo	.25	.11
□ 89 Rafael Palmeiro	1.00	.45
□ 90 Trevor Hoffman	.50	.23
□ 91 Marty Cordova	.25	.11
□ 92 Hideo Nomo	1.00	.45
□ 93 Johnny Damon	.75	.35
□ 94 Bill Pulsipher	.25	.11
□ 95 Garret Anderson	.50	.23
□ 96 Ray Durham	.50	.23
□ 97 Ricky Bottalico	.25	.11
□ 98 Carlos Perez	.25	.11
□ 99 Troy Percival	.50	.23
□ 100 Chipper Jones	2.50	1.10
□ 101 Esteban Loaiza	.25	.11
□ 102 John Mabry	.25	.11
□ 103 Jon Nunnally	.25	.11
□ 104 Andy Pettitte	.75	.35
□ 105 Lyle Mouton	.25	.11
□ 106 Jason Isringhausen	.50	.23
□ 107 Brian L.Hunter	.25	.11
□ 108 Quivlio Veras	.25	.11
□ 109 Jim Edmonds	.75	.35
□ 110 Ryan Klesko	.50	.23
□ 111 Pedro Martinez	1.25	.55
□ 112 Joey Hamilton	.25	.11
□ 113 Vinny Castilla	.75	.35
□ 114 Alex Gonzalez	.25	.11
□ 115 Raul Mondesi	.50	.23
□ 116 Rondell White	.50	.23
□ 117 Dan Miceli	.25	.11
□ 118 Tom Goodwin	.25	.11
□ 119 Bret Boone	.50	.23
□ 120 Shawn Green	1.00	.45
□ 121 Jeff Cirillo	.50	.23
□ 122 Rico Brogna	.25	.11
□ 123 Chris Gomez	.25	.11

☐ 124 Ismael Valdes	.50	.23
☐ 125 Javy Lopez	.50	.23
☐ 126 Manny Ramirez	1.25	.55
☐ 127 Paul Wilson	.25	.11
☐ 128 Billy Wagner	.75	.35
☐ 129 Eric Owens	.25	.11
☐ 130 Todd Greene	.25	.11
☐ 131 Karim Garcia	.50	.23
☐ 132 Jimmy Haynes	.25	.11
☐ 133 Michael Tucker	.25	.11
☐ 134 John Wasdin	.25	.11
☐ 135 Brooks Kieschnick	.25	.11
☐ 136 Alex Ochoa	.25	.11
☐ 137 Ariel Prieto	.25	.11
☐ 138 Tony Clark	1.00	.45
☐ 139 Mark Loretta	.25	.11
☐ 140 Rey Ordonez	1.00	.45
☐ 141 Chris Snopek	.25	.11
☐ 142 Roger Cedeno	.50	.23
☐ 143 Derek Jeter	3.00	1.35
☐ 144 Jeff Suppan	.25	.11
☐ 145 Greg Maddux	2.50	1.10
☐ 146 Ken Griffey Jr.	5.00	2.20
☐ 147 Tony Gwynn	2.50	1.10
☐ 148 Darren Daulton	.50	.23
☐ 149 Will Clark	1.00	.45
☐ 150 Mo Vaughn	1.00	.45
☐ 151 Reggie Sanders	.50	.23
☐ 152 Kirby Puckett	1.50	.70
☐ 153 Paul O'Neill	.50	.23
☐ 154 Tim Salmon	.75	.35
☐ 155 Mark McGwire	5.00	2.20
☐ 156 Barry Bonds	1.25	.55
☐ 157 Albert Belle	1.00	.45
☐ 158 Edgar Martinez	.50	.23
☐ 159 Mike Mussina	1.00	.45
☐ 160 Cecil Fielder	.50	.23
☐ 161 Kenny Lofton	.75	.35
☐ 162 Randy Johnson	1.00	.45
☐ 163 Juan Gonzalez	2.00	.90
☐ 164 Jeff Bagwell	1.25	.55
☐ 165 Joe Carter	.50	.23
☐ 166 Mike Piazza	3.00	1.35
☐ 167 Eddie Murray	1.00	.45
☐ 168 Cal Ripken	4.00	1.80
☐ 169 Barry Larkin	1.00	.45
☐ 170 Chuck Knoblauch	1.00	.45
☐ 171 Chili Davis	.50	.23
☐ 172 Fred McGriff	.75	.35
☐ 173 Matt Williams	1.00	.45
☐ 174 Roger Clemens	2.50	1.10
☐ 175 Frank Thomas	2.00	.90
☐ 176 Dennis Eckersley	.50	.23
☐ 177 Gary Sheffield	.50	.23
☐ 178 David Cone	.75	.35
☐ 179 Larry Walker	1.00	.45
☐ 180 Mark Grace	.75	.35
☐ NNO M. Mantle Masterpiece	20.00	9.00

1996 Topps Gallery Expressionists

	MINT	NRMT
COMPLETE SET (20)	80.00	36.00
COMMON CARD (1-20)	1.25	.55
STATED ODDS 1:24		
☐ 1 Mike Piazza	12.00	5.50

☐ 2 J.T. Snow	2.00	.90
☐ 3 Ken Griffey Jr.	9.00	
☐ 4 Kirby Puckett	6.00	2.70
☐ 5 Carlos Baerga	1.25	.55
☐ 6 Chipper Jones	10.00	4.50
☐ 7 Hideo Nomo	4.00	1.80
☐ 8 Mark McGwire	20.00	9.00
☐ 9 Gary Sheffield	2.00	.90
☐ 10 Randy Johnson	4.00	1.80
☐ 11 Ray Lankford	2.00	.90
☐ 12 Sammy Sosa	12.00	5.50
☐ 13 Denny Martinez	2.00	.90
☐ 14 Jose Canseco	5.00	2.20
☐ 15 Tony Gwynn	10.00	4.50
☐ 16 Edgar Martinez	2.00	.90
☐ 17 Reggie Sanders	2.00	.90
☐ 18 Andres Galarraga	4.00	1.80
☐ 19 Albert Belle	4.00	1.80
☐ 20 Barry Larkin	4.00	1.80

1996 Topps Gallery Photo Gallery

	MINT	NRMT
COMPLETE SET (15)	100.00	45.00
COMMON CARD (PG1-PG15)	1.25	.55
STATED ODDS 1:30		
☐ PG1 Eddie Murray	5.00	2.20
☐ PG2 Randy Johnson	5.00	2.20
☐ PG3 Cal Ripken	20.00	9.00
☐ PG4 Bret Boone	2.00	.90
☐ PG5 Frank Thomas	10.00	4.50
☐ PG6 Jeff Conine	1.25	.55
☐ PG7 Johnny Damon	3.00	1.95
☐ PG8 Roger Clemens	12.00	5.50
☐ PG9 Albert Belle	5.00	2.20
☐ PG10 Ken Griffey Jr.	25.00	11.00
☐ PG11 Kirby Puckett	8.00	3.60
☐ PG12 David Justice	5.00	2.20
☐ PG13 Bobby Bonilla	2.00	.90
☐ PG14 Colorado Rockies	5.00	2.20
☐ PG15 Atlanta Braves	5.00	2.20

1997 Topps Gallery

	MINT	NRMT
COMPLETE SET (180)	50.00	22.00
COMMON CARD (1-180)	.25	.11
MINOR STARS	.50	.23

UNLISTED STARS	1.00	.45
COMMON PPI (1-180)	5.00	2.20
*PPI STARS: 8X TO 20X HI COLUMN		
*PPI YNG.STARS: 6X TO 15X HI		
PPI STATED ODDS 1:12		
PPI STATED PRINT RUN 250 SETS		
☐ 1 Paul Molitor	1.00	.45
☐ 2 Devon White	.50	.23
☐ 3 Andres Galarraga	1.00	.45
☐ 4 Cal Ripken	4.00	1.80
☐ 5 Tony Gwynn	2.50	1.10
☐ 6 Mike Stanley	.25	.11
☐ 7 Orel Hershiser	.50	.23
☐ 8 Jose Canseco	1.25	.55
☐ 9 Chili Davis	.50	.23
☐ 10 Harold Baines	.50	.23
☐ 11 Rickey Henderson	1.25	.55
☐ 12 Darryl Strawberry	.50	.23
☐ 13 Todd Worrell	.25	.11
☐ 14 Cecil Fielder	.50	.23
☐ 15 Gary Gaetti	.50	.23
☐ 16 Bobby Bonilla	.50	.23
☐ 17 Will Clark	1.00	.45
☐ 18 Kevin Brown	.75	.35
☐ 19 Tom Glavine	1.00	.45
☐ 20 Wade Boggs	1.00	.45
☐ 21 Edgar Martinez	.50	.23
☐ 22 Lance Johnson	.25	.11
☐ 23 Gregg Jefferies	.25	.11
☐ 24 Big Roberts	.25	.11
☐ 25 Tony Phillips	.25	.11
☐ 26 Greg Maddux	2.50	1.10
☐ 27 Mickey Tettleton	.25	.11
☐ 28 Terry Steinbach	.25	.11
☐ 29 Ryne Sandberg	1.25	.55
☐ 30 Wally Joyner	.50	.23
☐ 31 Joe Carter	.50	.23
☐ 32 Ellis Burks	.50	.23
☐ 33 Fred McGriff	.75	.35
☐ 34 Barry Larkin	1.00	.45
☐ 35 John Franco	.50	.23
☐ 36 Rafael Palmeiro	1.00	.45
☐ 37 Mark McGwire	5.00	2.20
☐ 38 Ken Caminiti	.50	.35
☐ 39 David Cone	.75	.35
☐ 40 Julio Franco	.50	.23
☐ 41 Roger Clemens	2.50	1.10
☐ 42 Barry Bonds	1.25	.55
☐ 43 Dennis Eckersley	.50	.23
☐ 44 Eddie Murray	1.00	.45
☐ 45 Paul O'Neill	.50	.23
☐ 46 Craig Biggio	1.00	.45
☐ 47 Roberto Alomar	1.00	.45
☐ 48 Mark Grace	.75	.35
☐ 49 Matt Williams	1.00	.45
☐ 50 Jay Buhner	.50	.23
☐ 51 John Smoltz	.50	.23
☐ 52 Randy Johnson	.50	.23
☐ 53 Ramon Martinez	.50	.23
☐ 54 Curt Schilling	.75	.35
☐ 55 Gary Sheffield	.50	.23
☐ 56 Jack McDowell	.25	.11
☐ 57 Brady Anderson	.50	.23
☐ 58 Dante Bichette	.50	.23
☐ 59 Ron Gant	.25	.11
☐ 60 Alex Fernandez	.25	.11
☐ 61 Moises Alou	.25	.23
☐ 62 Travis Fryman	.50	.23
☐ 63 Dean Palmer	.50	.23
☐ 64 Todd Hundley	.50	.23
☐ 65 Jeff Brantley	.25	.11
☐ 66 Bernard Gilkey	.25	.11
☐ 67 Geronimo Berroa	.25	.11
☐ 68 John Wetteland	.50	.23
☐ 69 Robin Ventura	.50	.23
☐ 70 Ray Lankford	.50	.23
☐ 71 Kevin Appier	.50	.23
☐ 72 Larry Walker	1.00	.45
☐ 73 Juan Gonzalez	2.00	.90
☐ 74 Jeff King	.25	.11
☐ 75 Greg Vaughn	.50	.23
☐ 76 Steve Finley	.50	.23
☐ 77 Brian McRae	.25	.11
☐ 78 Paul Sorrento	.25	.11
☐ 79 Ken Griffey Jr.	5.00	2.20

☐ 80 Omar Vizquel	.50	.23
☐ 81 Jose Mesa	.25	.11
☐ 82 Albert Belle	1.00	.45
☐ 83 Glenallen Hill	.25	.11
☐ 84 Sammy Sosa	3.00	1.35
☐ 85 Andy Benes	.50	.23
☐ 86 David Justice	1.00	.45
☐ 87 Marquis Grissom	.50	.23
☐ 88 John Olerud	.50	.23
☐ 89 Tino Martinez	1.00	.45
☐ 90 Frank Thomas	2.00	.90
☐ 91 Raul Mondesi	.50	.23
☐ 92 Steve Trachsel	.25	.11
☐ 93 Jim Edmonds	.75	.35
☐ 94 Rusty Greer	.50	.23
☐ 95 Joey Hamilton	.50	.23
☐ 96 Ismael Valdes	.50	.23
☐ 97 Dave Nilsson	.25	.11
☐ 98 John Jaha	.25	.11
☐ 99 Alex Gonzalez	.25	.11
☐ 100 Javy Lopez	.50	.23
☐ 101 Ryan Klesko	.50	.23
☐ 102 Tim Salmon	1.00	.45
☐ 103 Bernie Williams	1.00	.45
☐ 104 Roberto Hernandez	.25	.11
☐ 105 Chuck Knoblauch	1.00	.45
☐ 106 Mike Lansing	.25	.11
☐ 107 Vinny Castilla	.75	.35
☐ 108 Reggie Sanders	.50	.23
☐ 109 Mo Vaughn	1.00	.45
☐ 110 Rondell White	.50	.23
☐ 111 Ivan Rodriguez	1.25	.55
☐ 112 Mike Mussina	1.00	.45
☐ 113 Carlos Baerga	.25	.11
☐ 114 Jeff Conine	.25	.11
☐ 115 Jim Thome	1.00	.45
☐ 116 Manny Ramirez	1.25	.55
☐ 117 Kenny Lofton	.75	.35
☐ 118 Wilson Alvarez	.50	.23
☐ 119 Eric Karros	.50	.23
☐ 120 Robb Nen	.25	.11
☐ 121 Mark Wohlers	.25	.11
☐ 122 Ed Sprague	.25	.11
☐ 123 Pat Hentgen	.50	.23
☐ 124 Juan Guzman	.50	.23
☐ 125 Derek Bell	.50	.23
☐ 126 Jeff Bagwell	1.25	.55
☐ 127 Eric Young	.50	.23
☐ 128 John Valentin	.50	.23
☐ 129 Al Martin UER	.25	.11
Picture of Javy Lopez		
☐ 130 Trevor Hoffman	.50	.23
☐ 131 Henry Rodriguez	.50	.23
☐ 132 Pedro Martinez	1.25	.55
☐ 133 Mike Piazza	3.00	1.35
☐ 134 Brian Jordan	.50	.23
☐ 135 Jose Valentin	.25	.11
☐ 136 Jeff Cirillo	.50	.23
☐ 137 Chipper Jones	2.50	1.10
☐ 138 Ricky Bottalico	.50	.23
☐ 139 Hideo Nomo	1.00	.45
☐ 140 Troy Percival	.50	.23
☐ 141 Rey Ordonez	.50	.23
☐ 142 Edgar Renteria	.50	.23
☐ 143 Luis Castillo	.50	.23
☐ 144 Vladimir Guerrero	1.50	.70
☐ 145 Jeff D'Amico	.25	.11
☐ 146 Andruw Jones	1.25	.55
☐ 147 Darin Erstad	1.00	.45
☐ 148 Bob Abreu	.50	.23
☐ 149 Carlos Delgado	1.00	.45
☐ 150 Jamey Wright	.25	.11
☐ 151 Nomar Garciaparra	3.00	1.35
☐ 152 Jason Kendall	.75	.35
☐ 153 Jermaine Allensworth	.25	.11
☐ 154 Scott Rolen	1.50	.70
☐ 155 Rocky Coppinger	.25	.11
☐ 156 Paul Wilson	.25	.11
☐ 157 Garret Anderson	.50	.23
☐ 158 Mariano Rivera	.25	.11
☐ 159 Ruben Rivera	.25	.11
☐ 160 Andy Pettitte	.75	.35
☐ 161 Derek Jeter	3.00	1.35
☐ 162 Neifi Perez	.50	.23
☐ 163 Ray Durham	.50	.23
☐ 164 James Baldwin	.50	.23

☐ 165 Marty Cordova	.25	.11
☐ 166 Tony Clark	.75	.35
☐ 167 Michael Tucker	.25	.11
☐ 168 Mike Sweeney	.50	.23
☐ 169 Johnny Damon	.50	.23
☐ 170 Jermaine Dye	.50	.23
☐ 171 Alex Ochoa	.25	.11
☐ 172 Jason Isringhausen	.25	.11
☐ 173 Mark Grudzielanek	.50	.23
☐ 174 Jose Rosado	.25	.11
☐ 175 Todd Hollandsworth	.25	.11
☐ 176 Alan Benes	.25	.11
☐ 177 Jason Giambi	.50	.23
☐ 178 Billy Wagner	.50	.23
☐ 179 Justin Thompson	.50	.23
☐ 180 Todd Walker	1.00	.45

1997 Topps Gallery Gallery of Heroes

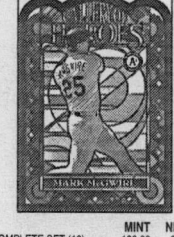

	MINT	NRMT
COMPLETE SET (10)	180.00	80.00
COMMON CARD (GH1-GH10)	8.00	3.60
STATED ODDS 1:36		

☐ GH1 Derek Jeter	25.00	11.00
☐ GH2 Chipper Jones	20.00	9.00
☐ GH3 Frank Thomas	15.00	6.75
☐ GH4 Ken Griffey Jr.	40.00	18.00
☐ GH5 Cal Ripken	30.00	13.50
☐ GH6 Mark McGwire	40.00	18.00
☐ GH7 Mike Piazza	25.00	11.00
☐ GH8 Jeff Bagwell	10.00	4.50
☐ GH9 Tony Gwynn	20.00	9.00
☐ GH10 Mo Vaughn	10.00	4.50

1997 Topps Gallery Peter Max Serigraphs

	MINT	NRMT
COMPLETE SET (10)	100.00	45.00
COMMON CARD (1-10)	3.00	1.35
UNLISTED STARS	5.00	2.20
STATED ODDS 1:24		

*AUTOGRAPHS: 8X TO 20X HI COLUMN
AUTOGRAPHS: RANDOM INS.IN PACKS
AUTO. PRINT RUN 40 SERIAL #'d SETS
AU'S SIGNED BY MAX BENEATH UV COATING

☐ 1 Derek Jeter	15.00	6.75
☐ 2 Albert Belle	5.00	2.20
☐ 3 Ken Caminiti	3.00	1.35
☐ 4 Chipper Jones	12.00	5.50
☐ 5 Ken Griffey Jr.	25.00	11.00
☐ 6 Frank Thomas	10.00	4.50
☐ 7 Cal Ripken	20.00	9.00
☐ 8 Mark McGwire	25.00	11.00
☐ 9 Barry Bonds	6.00	2.70
☐ 10 Mike Piazza	15.00	6.75

1997 Topps Gallery Photo Gallery

	MINT	NRMT
COMPLETE SET (16)	180.00	80.00
COMMON CARD (PG1-PG16)	2.00	.90
MINOR STARS	4.00	1.80
UNLISTED STARS	8.00	3.60
STATED ODDS 1:24		

☐ PG1 John Wetteland	2.00	.90
☐ PG2 Paul Molitor	8.00	3.60
☐ PG3 Eddie Murray	8.00	3.60
☐ PG4 Ken Griffey Jr.	40.00	18.00
☐ PG5 Chipper Jones	20.00	9.00
☐ PG6 Derek Jeter	25.00	11.00
☐ PG7 Frank Thomas	15.00	6.75
☐ PG8 Mark McGwire	40.00	18.00
☐ PG9 Kenny Lofton	6.00	2.70
☐ PG10 Gary Sheffield	4.00	1.80
☐ PG11 Mike Piazza	25.00	11.00
☐ PG12 Vinny Castilla	6.00	2.70
☐ PG13 Andres Galarraga	8.00	3.60
☐ PG14 Andy Pettitte	6.00	2.70
☐ PG15 Robin Ventura	4.00	1.80
☐ PG16 Barry Larkin	8.00	3.60

1998 Topps Gallery

	MINT	NRMT
COMPLETE SET (150)	55.00	25.00
COMMON CARD (1-150)	.25	.11
MINOR STARS	.40	.18
SEMISTARS	.60	.25
UNLISTED STARS	1.00	.45

☐ 1 Andruw Jones	1.00	.45
☐ 2 Fred McGriff	.60	.25
☐ 3 Wade Boggs	1.00	.45

☐ 4 Pedro Martinez	1.25	.55
☐ 5 Matt Williams	1.00	.45
☐ 6 Wilson Alvarez	.25	.11
☐ 7 Henry Rodriguez	.40	.18
☐ 8 Jay Bell	.40	.18
☐ 9 Marquis Grissom	.25	.11
☐ 10 Darryl Kile	.25	.11
☐ 11 Chuck Knoblauch	.40	.18
☐ 12 Kenny Lofton	.60	.25
☐ 13 Quinton McCracken	.25	.11
☐ 14 Andres Galarraga	.25	.11
☐ 15 Brian Jordan	.40	.18
☐ 16 Mike Lansing	.25	.11
☐ 17 Travis Fryman	.40	.18
☐ 18 Tony Saunders	.25	.11
☐ 19 Moises Alou	.40	.18
☐ 20 Travis Lee	.60	.25
☐ 21 Garret Anderson	.40	.18
☐ 22 Ken Caminiti	.40	.18
☐ 23 Pedro Astacio	.25	.11
☐ 24 Ellis Burks	.40	.18
☐ 25 Albert Belle	1.00	.45
☐ 26 Alan Benes	.25	.11
☐ 27 Jay Buhner	.40	.18
☐ 28 Derek Bell	.40	.18
☐ 29 Jeromy Burnitz	.40	.18
☐ 30 Kevin Appier	.40	.18
☐ 31 Jeff Cirillo	.40	.18
☐ 32 Bernard Gilkey	.25	.11
☐ 33 David Cone	.60	.25
☐ 34 Jason Dickson	.25	.11
☐ 35 Jose Cruz Jr.	.40	.18
☐ 36 Marty Cordova	.25	.11
☐ 37 Ray Durham	.40	.18
☐ 38 Jaret Wright	.40	.18
☐ 39 Billy Wagner	.40	.18
☐ 40 Roger Clemens	2.50	1.10
☐ 41 Juan Gonzalez	2.00	.90
☐ 42 Jeremi Gonzalez	.25	.11
☐ 43 Mark Grudzielanek	.25	.11
☐ 44 Tom Glavine	1.00	.45
☐ 45 Barry Larkin	1.00	.45
☐ 46 Lance Johnson	.25	.11
☐ 47 Bobby Higginson	.40	.18
☐ 48 Mike Mussina	1.00	.45
☐ 49 Al Martin	.25	.11
☐ 50 Mark McGwire	6.00	2.70
☐ 51 Todd Hundley	.40	.18
☐ 52 Ray Lankford	.40	.18
☐ 53 Jason Kendall	.40	.18
☐ 54 Javy Lopez	.40	.18
☐ 55 Ben Grieve	1.00	.45
☐ 56 Randy Johnson	1.00	.45
☐ 57 Jeff King	.25	.11
☐ 58 Mark Grace	.60	.25
☐ 59 Rusty Greer	.40	.18
☐ 60 Greg Maddux	2.50	1.10
☐ 61 Jeff Kent	.40	.18
☐ 62 Rey Ordonez	.40	.18
☐ 63 Hideo Nomo	1.00	.45
☐ 64 Charles Nagy	.40	.18
☐ 65 Rondell White	.40	.18
☐ 66 Todd Helton	1.25	.55
☐ 67 Jim Thome	1.00	.45
☐ 68 Denny Neagle	.25	.11
☐ 69 Ivan Rodriguez	1.25	.55
☐ 70 Vladimir Guerrero	1.25	.55
☐ 71 Jorge Posada	.25	.11
☐ 72 J.T. Snow	.40	.18
☐ 73 Reggie Sanders	.25	.11
☐ 74 Scott Rolen	1.25	.55
☐ 75 Robin Ventura	.40	.18
☐ 76 Mariano Rivera	.40	.18
☐ 77 Cal Ripken	4.00	1.80
☐ 78 Justin Thompson	.25	.11
☐ 79 Mike Piazza	3.00	1.35
☐ 80 Kevin Brown	.60	.25
☐ 81 Sandy Alomar Jr.	.40	.18
☐ 82 Craig Biggio	1.00	.45
☐ 83 Vinny Castilla	.40	.18
☐ 84 Eric Young	.25	.11
☐ 85 Bernie Williams	1.00	.45
☐ 86 Brady Anderson	.40	.18
☐ 87 Bobby Bonilla	.40	.18
☐ 88 Tony Clark	.40	.18
☐ 89 Dan Wilson	.25	.11

☐ 90 John Wetteland	.40	.18
☐ 91 Barry Bonds	1.25	.55
☐ 92 Chan Ho Park	.40	.18
☐ 93 Carlos Delgado	1.00	.45
☐ 94 David Justice	.40	.18
☐ 95 Chipper Jones	2.50	1.10
☐ 96 Shawn Estes	.25	.11
☐ 97 Jason Giambi	.40	.18
☐ 98 Ron Gant	.40	.18
☐ 99 John Olerud	.40	.18
☐ 100 Frank Thomas	2.00	.90
☐ 101 Jose Guillen	.25	.11
☐ 102 Brad Radke	.40	.18
☐ 103 Troy Percival	.40	.18
☐ 104 John Smoltz	.60	.25
☐ 105 Edgardo Alfonzo	.60	.25
☐ 106 Dante Bichette	.40	.18
☐ 107 Larry Walker	1.00	.45
☐ 108 John Valentin	.40	.18
☐ 109 Roberto Alomar	1.00	.45
☐ 110 Mike Cameron	.40	.18
☐ 111 Eric Davis	.40	.18
☐ 112 Johnny Damon	.40	.18
☐ 113 Darin Erstad	.60	.25
☐ 114 Omar Vizquel	.40	.18
☐ 115 Derek Jeter	3.00	1.35
☐ 116 Tony Womack	.25	.11
☐ 117 Edgar Renteria	.25	.11
☐ 118 Raul Mondesi	.40	.18
☐ 119 Tony Gwynn	2.50	1.10
☐ 120 Ken Griffey Jr.	5.00	2.20
☐ 121 Jim Edmonds	.40	.18
☐ 122 Brian Hunter	.25	.11
☐ 123 Neifi Perez	.40	.18
☐ 124 Dean Palmer	.40	.18
☐ 125 Alex Rodriguez	3.00	1.35
☐ 126 Tim Salmon	.60	.25
☐ 127 Curt Schilling	.60	.25
☐ 128 Kevin Orie	.25	.11
☐ 129 Andy Pettitte	.40	.18
☐ 130 Gary Sheffield	.60	.25
☐ 131 Jose Rosado	.25	.11
☐ 132 Manny Ramirez	1.25	.55
☐ 133 Rafael Palmeiro	1.00	.45
☐ 134 Sammy Sosa	3.00	1.35
☐ 135 Jeff Bagwell	1.25	.55
☐ 136 Delino DeShields	.25	.11
☐ 137 Ryan Klesko	.40	.18
☐ 138 Mo Vaughn	1.00	.45
☐ 139 Steve Finley	.40	.18
☐ 140 Nomar Garciaparra	3.00	1.35
☐ 141 Paul Molitor	1.00	.45
☐ 142 Pat Hentgen	.25	.11
☐ 143 Eric Karros	.40	.18
☐ 144 Bobby Jones	.25	.11
☐ 145 Tino Martinez	.40	.18
☐ 146 Matt Morris	.25	.11
☐ 147 Livan Hernandez	.25	.11
☐ 148 Edgar Martinez	.40	.18
☐ 149 Paul O'Neill	.40	.18
☐ 150 Checklist	.25	.11

1998 Topps Gallery Gallery Proofs

	MINT	NRMT
COMMON CARD (1-150)	10.00	4.50

*STARS: 15X TO 40X BASIC CARDS

*YNG.STARS: 12.5X TO 30X BASIC CARDS
STATED ODDS 1:34 HOBBY
STATED PRINT RUN 125 SERIAL #'d SETS

1998 Topps Gallery Player's Private Issue

	MINT	NRMT
COMMON CARD (1-150)	8.00	3.60

*STARS: 12.5X TO 30X BASIC CARDS
*YNG.STARS: 10X TO 25X BASIC CARDS
STATED ODDS 1:17 HOBBY
STATED PRINT RUN 250 SERIAL #'d SETS

1998 Topps Gallery Player's Private Issue Auction

	MINT	NRMT
COMPLETE SET (150)	100.00	45.00
COMMON CARD	.25	.11

*STARS: .75X TO 2X BASIC CARDS
ONE PER PACK
AUCTION CLOSED 10/16/98

1998 Topps Gallery Awards Gallery

	MINT	NRMT
COMPLETE SET (10)	100.00	45.00

*SINGLES: 2X TO 5X BASE CARD HI

STATED ODDS 1:24 HOBBY

	MINT	NRMT
☐ AG1 Ken Griffey Jr.	25.00	11.00
☐ AG2 Larry Walker	5.00	2.20
☐ AG3 Roger Clemens	12.00	5.50
☐ AG4 Pedro Martinez	6.00	2.70
☐ AG5 Nomar Garciaparra	15.00	6.75
☐ AG6 Scott Rolen	8.00	3.60
☐ AG7 Frank Thomas	10.00	4.50
☐ AG8 Tony Gwynn	12.00	5.50
☐ AG9 Mark McGwire	30.00	13.50
☐ AG10 Livan Hernandez	1.25	.55

1998 Topps Gallery Gallery of Heroes

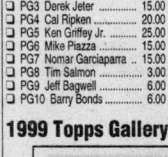

	MINT	NRMT
COMPLETE SET (15)	200.00	90.00
COMMON CARD (GH1-GH15)	2.50	1.10
STATED ODDS 1:24 HOBBY		
COMP.JUMBO SET (15)	150.00	70.00

*JUMBOS: 2X TO 5X BASE CARD HI
ONE OVERSIZED CARD PER HOBBY BOX

☐ GH1 Ken Griffey Jr.	30.00	13.50
☐ GH2 Derek Jeter	20.00	9.00
☐ GH3 Barry Bonds	8.00	3.60
☐ GH4 Alex Rodriguez	20.00	9.00
☐ GH5 Frank Thomas	12.00	5.50
☐ GH6 Nomar Garciaparra	20.00	9.00
☐ GH7 Mark McGwire	40.00	18.00
☐ GH8 Mike Piazza	20.00	9.00
☐ GH9 Cal Ripken	25.00	11.00
☐ GH10 Jose Cruz Jr.	2.50	1.10
☐ GH11 Jeff Bagwell	8.00	3.60
☐ GH12 Chipper Jones	15.00	6.75
☐ GH13 Juan Gonzalez	12.00	5.50
☐ GH14 Hideo Nomo	6.00	2.70
☐ GH15 Greg Maddux	15.00	6.75

1998 Topps Gallery Photo Gallery

	MINT	NRMT
COMPLETE SET (10)	100.00	45.00
COMMON CARD (PG1-PG10)	3.00	1.35
STATED ODDS 1:24 HOBBY		

☐ PG1 Alex Rodriguez	15.00	6.75
☐ PG2 Frank Thomas	10.00	4.50
☐ PG3 Derek Jeter	15.00	6.75
☐ PG4 Cal Ripken	20.00	9.00
☐ PG5 Ken Griffey Jr.	25.00	11.00
☐ PG6 Mike Piazza	15.00	6.75
☐ PG7 Nomar Garciaparra	15.00	6.75
☐ PG8 Tim Salmon	3.00	1.35
☐ PG9 Jeff Bagwell	6.00	2.70
☐ PG10 Barry Bonds	6.00	2.70

1999 Topps Gallery

NOMAR GARCIAPARRA

	MINT	NRMT
COMPLETE SET (150)	120.00	55.00
COMP.SET w/o SP's (100)	30.00	13.50
COMMON CARD (1-100)	.15	.07
MINOR STARS 1-100	.25	.11
SEMISTARS 1-100	.40	.18
UNLISTED STARS 1-100	.60	.25
COMMON CARD (101-150)	.50	.23
SEMISTARS 101-150	.75	.35
UNLISTED STARS 101-150	1.25	.55

CARDS 101-150 ONE PER PACK

☐ 1 Mark McGwire	4.00	1.80
☐ 2 Jim Thome	.60	.25
☐ 3 Bernie Williams	.60	.25
☐ 4 Larry Walker	.60	.25
☐ 5 Juan Gonzalez	1.25	.55
☐ 6 Ken Griffey Jr.	3.00	1.35
☐ 7 Raul Mondesi	.25	.11
☐ 8 Sammy Sosa	2.00	.90
☐ 9 Greg Maddux	1.50	.70
☐ 10 Jeff Bagwell	.75	.35
☐ 11 Vladimir Guerrero	.75	.35
☐ 12 Scott Rolen	.75	.35
☐ 13 Nomar Garciaparra	2.00	.90
☐ 14 Mike Piazza	2.00	.90
☐ 15 Travis Lee	.40	.18
☐ 16 Carlos Delgado	.40	.18
☐ 17 Darin Erstad	.40	.18
☐ 18 David Justice	.25	.11
☐ 19 Cal Ripken	2.50	1.10
☐ 20 Derek Jeter	2.00	.90
☐ 21 Tony Clark	.25	.11
☐ 22 Barry Larkin	.60	.25
☐ 23 Greg Vaughn	.25	.11
☐ 24 Jeff Kent	.25	.11
☐ 25 Wade Boggs	.60	.25
☐ 26 Andres Galarraga	.40	.18
☐ 27 Ken Caminiti	.25	.11
☐ 28 Jason Kendall	.25	.11
☐ 29 Todd Helton	.60	.25
☐ 30 Chuck Knoblauch	.25	.11
☐ 31 Roger Clemens	1.50	.70
☐ 32 Jeromy Burnitz	.25	.11
☐ 33 Javy Lopez	.25	.11
☐ 34 Roberto Alomar	.60	.25
☐ 35 Eric Karros	.25	.11
☐ 36 Brian Giles	.60	.25
☐ 37 Eric Davis	.25	.11
☐ 38 Rondell White	.25	.11
☐ 39 Dmitri Young	.25	.11
☐ 40 Ivan Rodriguez	.75	.35
☐ 41 Paul O'Neil	.25	.11
☐ 42 Jeff Cirillo	.25	.11
☐ 43 Kerry Wood	.60	.25
☐ 44 Albert Belle	.25	.11
☐ 45 Frank Thomas	1.25	.55
☐ 46 Manny Ramirez	.75	.35
☐ 47 Tom Glavine	.60	.25
☐ 48 Mo Vaughn	.60	.25
☐ 49 Jose Cruz Jr.	.25	.11
☐ 50 Sandy Alomar Jr.	.25	.11
☐ 51 Edgar Martinez	.25	.11
☐ 52 John Olerud	.25	.11
☐ 53 Todd Walker	.25	.11
☐ 54 Tim Salmon	.40	.18
☐ 55 Derek Bell	.25	.11
☐ 56 Matt Williams	.60	.25
☐ 57 Alex Rodriguez	2.00	.90
☐ 58 Rusty Greer	.25	.11
☐ 59 Vinny Castilla	.25	.11
☐ 60 Jason Giambi	.25	.11
☐ 61 Mark Grace	.40	.18
☐ 62 Jose Canseco	.75	.35
☐ 63 Gary Sheffield	.25	.11
☐ 64 Brad Fullmer	.15	.07
☐ 65 Trevor Hoffman	.25	.11
☐ 66 Mark Kotsay	.25	.11
☐ 67 Mike Mussina	.60	.25
☐ 68 Johnny Damon	.25	.11
☐ 69 Tino Martinez	.25	.11
☐ 70 Curt Schilling	.40	.18
☐ 71 Jay Buhner	.25	.11
☐ 72 Kenny Lofton	.40	.18
☐ 73 Randy Johnson	.60	.25
☐ 74 Kevin Brown	.40	.18
☐ 75 Brian Jordan	.25	.11
☐ 76 Craig Biggio	.60	.25
☐ 77 Barry Bonds	.75	.35
☐ 78 Tony Gwynn	1.50	.70
☐ 79 Jim Edmonds	.25	.11
☐ 80 Shawn Green	.60	.25
☐ 81 Todd Hundley	.25	.11
☐ 82 Cliff Floyd	.25	.11
☐ 83 Jose Guillen	.15	.07
☐ 84 Dante Bichette	.25	.11
☐ 85 Moises Alou	.25	.11
☐ 86 Chipper Jones	1.50	.70
☐ 87 Ray Lankford	.25	.11
☐ 88 Fred McGriff	.40	.18
☐ 89 Rod Beck	.25	.11
☐ 90 Dean Palmer	.25	.11
☐ 91 Pedro Martinez	.75	.35
☐ 92 Andruw Jones	.60	.25
☐ 93 Robin Ventura	.25	.11
☐ 94 Ugueth Urbina	.15	.07
☐ 95 Orlando Hernandez	.60	.25
☐ 96 Sean Casey	.25	.11
☐ 97 Denny Neagle	.15	.07
☐ 98 Troy Glaus	.60	.25
☐ 99 John Smoltz	.40	.18
☐ 100 Al Leiter	.25	.11
☐ 101 Ken Griffey Jr. MAS	6.00	2.70
☐ 102 Frank Thomas MAS	2.50	1.10
☐ 103 Mark McGwire MAS	8.00	3.60
☐ 104 Sammy Sosa MAS	4.00	1.80
☐ 105 Chipper Jones MAS	3.00	1.35
☐ 106 Alex Rodriguez MAS	4.00	1.80
☐ 107 Nomar Garciaparra MAS	4.00	1.80
☐ 108 Juan Gonzalez MAS	2.50	1.10
☐ 109 Derek Jeter MAS	4.00	1.80
☐ 110 Mike Piazza MAS	4.00	1.80
☐ 111 Barry Bonds MAS	1.50	.70
☐ 112 Tony Gwynn MAS	3.00	1.35
☐ 113 Cal Ripken MAS	5.00	2.20
☐ 114 Greg Maddux MAS	3.00	1.35
☐ 115 Roger Clemens MAS	3.00	1.35
☐ 116 Brad Fullmer ART	.50	.23
☐ 117 Kerry Wood ART	1.25	.55
☐ 118 Ben Grieve ART	1.25	.55
☐ 119 Todd Helton ART	1.25	.55
☐ 120 Kevin Millwood ART	.75	.35
☐ 121 Sean Casey ART	1.25	.55
☐ 122 Vladimir Guerrero ART	1.50	.70
☐ 123 Travis Lee ART	.75	.35
☐ 124 Troy Glaus ART	1.25	.55
☐ 125 Bartolo Colon ART	.50	.23
☐ 126 Andruw Jones ART	1.25	.55
☐ 127 Scott Rolen ART	1.50	.70
☐ 128 Alfonso Soriano APP	10.00	4.50
☐ 129 Nick Johnson APP	8.00	3.60
☐ 130 Matt Belisle APP	1.25	.55
☐ 131 Jorge Toca APP	2.50	1.10

☐ 132 Masao Kida APP	1.25	.55
☐ 133 Carlos Pena APP	2.50	1.10
☐ 134 Adrian Beltre APP	1.25	.55
☐ 135 Eric Chavez APP	.75	.35
☐ 136 Carlos Beltran APP	1.50	.70
☐ 137 Alex Gonzalez APP	.50	.23
☐ 138 Ryan Anderson APP	.50	.23
☐ 139 Ruben Mateo APP	1.25	.55
☐ 140 Bruce Chen APP	.50	.23
☐ 141 Pat Burrell APP	10.00	4.50
☐ 142 Michael Barrett APP	.75	.35
☐ 143 Carlos Lee APP	.50	.23
☐ 144 Mark Mulder APP	2.50	1.10
☐ 145 Choo Freeman APP	2.00	.90
☐ 146 Gabe Kapler APP	1.25	.55
☐ 147 Juan Encarnacion APP	.50	.23
☐ 148 Jeremy Giambi APP	.50	.23
☐ 149 Jason Tyner APP	1.50	.70
☐ 150 George Lombard APP	.50	.23

1999 Topps Gallery Player's Private Issue

	MINT	NRMT
COMPLETE SET (150)	2500.00	1100.00
COMMON CARD (1-150)	4.00	1.80

*STARS 1-100: 10X TO 25X BASIC CARDS
*YNG.STARS 1-100: 8X TO 20X BASIC CARDS
*MASTERS 101-115: 5X TO 12X BASIC
*ARTISANS 116-127: 4X TO 10X BASIC
*APPRENTICES 128-150: 4X TO 10X BASIC
*APP.RC'S 128-150: 1.5X TO 4X BASIC
STATED ODDS 1:17
STATED PRINT RUN 250 SERIAL #'d SETS

1999 Topps Gallery Press Plates

	MINT	NRMT
STATED ODDS 1:985
STATED PRINT RUN 4 DIFT.COLORED SETS
NO PRICING DUE TO SCARCITY

1999 Topps Gallery Autographs

	MINT	NRMT
STATED ODDS 1:209

☐ GA1 Troy Glaus	25.00	11.00
☐ GA2 Adrian Beltre	20.00	9.00
☐ GA3 Eric Chavez	15.00	6.75

1999 Topps Gallery Awards Gallery

	MINT	NRMT
COMPLETE SET (10)	50.00	22.00
COMMON CARD (AG1-AG10)	1.50	.70
UNLISTED STARS	2.50	1.10
STATED ODDS 1:12

☐ AG1 Kerry Wood	1.50	.70
☐ AG2 Ben Grieve	2.50	1.10
☐ AG3 Roger Clemens	6.00	2.70
☐ AG4 Tom Glavine	2.50	1.10
☐ AG5 Juan Gonzalez	5.00	2.20
☐ AG6 Sammy Sosa	8.00	3.60
☐ AG7 Ken Griffey Jr.	12.00	5.50
☐ AG8 Mark McGwire	15.00	6.75
☐ AG9 Bernie Williams	2.50	1.10
☐ AG10 Larry Walker	2.50	1.10

1999 Topps Gallery Exhibitions

	MINT	NRMT
COMPLETE SET (20)	250.00	110.00
COMMON CARD (E1-E20)	4.00	1.80
UNLISTED STARS	6.00	2.70
STATED ODDS 1:48

☐ E1 Sammy Sosa	20.00	9.00
☐ E2 Mark McGwire	40.00	18.00
☐ E3 Greg Maddux	15.00	6.75
☐ E4 Roger Clemens	15.00	6.75
☐ E5 Ben Grieve	6.00	2.70
☐ E6 Kerry Wood	6.00	2.70
☐ E7 Ken Griffey Jr	30.00	13.50
☐ E8 Tony Gwynn	15.00	6.75
☐ E9 Cal Ripken	25.00	11.00
☐ E10 Frank Thomas	12.00	5.50
☐ E11 Jeff Bagwell	8.00	3.60
☐ E12 Derek Jeter	20.00	9.00
☐ E13 Alex Rodriguez	20.00	9.00
☐ E14 Nomar Garciaparra	20.00	9.00
☐ E15 Manny Ramirez	8.00	3.60
☐ E16 Vladimir Guerrero	8.00	3.60
☐ E17 Darin Erstad	4.00	1.80
☐ E18 Scott Rolen	8.00	3.60
☐ E19 Mike Piazza	20.00	9.00
☐ E20 Andres Galarraga	4.00	1.80

1999 Topps Gallery Gallery of Heroes

	MINT	NRMT
COMPLETE SET (10)	100.00	45.00
COMMON CARD (GH1-GH10)	2.50	1.10
STATED ODDS 1:24

☐ GH1 Mark McGwire	25.00	11.00
☐ GH2 Sammy Sosa	12.00	5.50
☐ GH3 Ken Griffey Jr.	20.00	9.00
☐ GH4 Mike Piazza	12.00	5.50
☐ GH5 Derek Jeter	12.00	5.50
☐ GH6 Nomar Garciaparra	12.00	5.50
☐ GH7 Kerry Wood	2.50	1.10
☐ GH8 Ben Grieve	4.00	1.80
☐ GH9 Chipper Jones	10.00	4.50
☐ GH10 Alex Rodriguez	12.00	5.50

1999 Topps Gallery Heritage

	MINT	NRMT
COMPLETE SET (20)	400.00	180.00
COMMON CARD (TH1-TH20)	4.00	1.80
UNLISTED STARS	6.00	2.70
STATED ODDS 1:12
*PROOFS: .5X TO 1.25X HI COLUMN
PROOFS STATED ODDS 1:48

		MINT	NRMT
☐ TH1	Hank Aaron	30.00	13.50
☐ TH2	Ben Grieve	6.00	2.70
☐ TH3	Nomar Garciaparra	25.00	11.00
☐ TH4	Roger Clemens	20.00	9.00
☐ TH5	Travis Lee	4.00	1.80
☐ TH6	Tony Gwynn	20.00	9.00
☐ TH7	Alex Rodriguez	25.00	11.00
☐ TH8	Ken Griffey Jr.	40.00	18.00
☐ TH9	Derek Jeter	25.00	11.00
☐ TH10	Sammy Sosa	25.00	11.00
☐ TH11	Scott Rolen	10.00	4.50
☐ TH12	Chipper Jones	20.00	9.00
☐ TH13	Cal Ripken	30.00	13.50
☐ TH14	Kerry Wood	6.00	2.70
☐ TH15	Barry Bonds	10.00	4.50
☐ TH16	Juan Gonzalez	15.00	6.75
☐ TH17	Mike Piazza	25.00	11.00
☐ TH18	Greg Maddux	20.00	9.00
☐ TH19	Frank Thomas	15.00	6.75
☐ TH20	Mark McGwire	50.00	22.00

1998 Topps Gold Label Class 1

	MINT	NRMT
COMP.GOLD SET (100)	100.00	45.00
COMMON GOLD (1-100)	.40	.18
GOLD MINOR STARS	.60	.25
GOLD SEMISTARS	1.00	.45
GOLD UNLISTED STARS	1.50	.70
COMMON BLACK (1-100)	2.00	.90

*CLASS 1 BLACK: 2X TO 5X HI COLUMN
CLASS 1 BLACK STATED ODDS 1:8
COMMON RED (1-100) ..... 10.00 ..... 4.50
*CLASS 1 RED STARS: 10X TO 25X HI
*CLASS 1 RED RC's: 8X TO 20X HI
CLASS 1 RED STATED ODDS 1:99
CLASS 1 RED PRINT RUN 100 SERIAL #'d SETS
CLASS 1: FLAT GOLD TEXT ON FRONT
NINE DIFFERENT 1 OF 1 PARALLELS EXIST

☐ 1	Kevin Brown	1.00	.45
☐ 2	Greg Maddux	4.00	1.80
☐ 3	Albert Belle	1.50	.70
☐ 4	Andres Galarraga	1.00	.45
☐ 5	Craig Biggio	1.50	.70
☐ 6	Matt Williams	1.50	.70
☐ 7	Derek Jeter	5.00	2.20
☐ 8	Randy Johnson	1.50	.70
☐ 9	Jay Bell	.60	.25
☐ 10	Jim Thome	1.50	.70
☐ 11	Roberto Alomar	1.50	.70
☐ 12	Tom Glavine	1.50	.70
☐ 13	Reggie Sanders	.40	.18
☐ 14	Tony Gwynn	4.00	1.80
☐ 15	Mark McGwire	10.00	4.50
☐ 16	Jeromy Burnitz	.60	.25
☐ 17	Andruw Jones	1.50	.70
☐ 18	Jay Buhner	.60	.25
☐ 19	Robin Ventura	.60	.25
☐ 20	Jeff Bagwell	2.00	.90
☐ 21	Roger Clemens	4.00	1.80
☐ 22	Masato Yoshii	1.50	.70
☐ 23	Travis Fryman	.60	.25
☐ 24	Rafael Palmeiro	1.50	.70
☐ 25	Alex Rodriguez	5.00	2.20
☐ 26	Sandy Alomar Jr.	.60	.25
☐ 27	Chipper Jones	4.00	1.80
☐ 28	Rusty Greer	.60	.25
☐ 29	Cal Ripken	6.00	2.70
☐ 30	Tony Clark	.60	.25
☐ 31	Derek Bell	.60	.25
☐ 32	Fred McGriff	1.00	.45
☐ 33	Paul O'Neill	.60	.25
☐ 34	Moises Alou	.60	.25
☐ 35	Henry Rodriguez	.60	.25
☐ 36	Steve Finley	.60	.25
☐ 37	Marquis Grissom	.40	.18
☐ 38	Jason Giambi	.60	.25
☐ 39	Javy Lopez	.60	.25
☐ 40	Damion Easley	.60	.25
☐ 41	Mariano Rivera	.60	.25
☐ 42	Mo Vaughn	1.50	.70
☐ 43	Mike Mussina	1.50	.70
☐ 44	Jason Kendall	.60	.25
☐ 45	Pedro Martinez	2.00	.90
☐ 46	Frank Thomas	3.00	1.35
☐ 47	Jim Edmonds	.60	.25
☐ 48	Hideki Irabu	.60	.25
☐ 49	Eric Karros	.60	.25
☐ 50	Juan Gonzalez	3.00	1.35
☐ 51	Ellis Burks	.60	.25
☐ 52	Dean Palmer	.60	.25
☐ 53	Scott Rolen	2.00	.90
☐ 54	Raul Mondesi	.60	.25
☐ 55	Quinton McCracken	.40	.18
☐ 56	John Olerud	.60	.25
☐ 57	Ken Caminiti	.60	.25
☐ 58	Brian Jordan	.60	.25
☐ 59	Wade Boggs	1.50	.70
☐ 60	Mike Piazza	5.00	2.20
☐ 61	Darin Erstad	1.00	.45
☐ 62	Curt Schilling	.60	.25
☐ 63	David Justice	.60	.25
☐ 64	Kenny Lofton	1.00	.45
☐ 65	Barry Bonds	2.00	.90
☐ 66	Ray Lankford	.60	.25
☐ 67	Brian Hunter	.40	.18
☐ 68	Chuck Knoblauch	.60	.25
☐ 69	Vinny Castilla	.60	.25
☐ 70	Vladimir Guerrero	2.00	.90
☐ 71	Tim Salmon	1.00	.45
☐ 72	Larry Walker	1.50	.70
☐ 73	Paul Molitor	1.50	.70
☐ 74	Barry Larkin	1.50	.70
☐ 75	Edgar Martinez	.60	.25
☐ 76	Bernie Williams	1.50	.70
☐ 77	Dante Bichette	.60	.25
☐ 78	Nomar Garciaparra	5.00	2.20
☐ 79	Ben Grieve	1.50	.70
☐ 80	Ivan Rodriguez	2.00	.90
☐ 81	Todd Helton	2.00	.90
☐ 82	Ryan Klesko	.60	.25
☐ 83	Sammy Sosa	5.00	2.20
☐ 84	Travis Lee	1.00	.45
☐ 85	Jose Cruz Jr.	.60	.25
☐ 86	Mark Kotsay	.60	.25
☐ 87	Richard Hidalgo	.60	.25
☐ 88	Rondell White	.60	.25
☐ 89	Greg Vaughn	.60	.25
☐ 90	Gary Sheffield	.60	.25
☐ 91	Paul Konerko	.60	.25
☐ 92	Mark Grace	1.00	.45
☐ 93	Kevin Millwood	5.00	2.20
☐ 94	Manny Ramirez	2.00	.90
☐ 95	Tino Martinez	.60	.25
☐ 96	Brad Fullmer	.40	.18
☐ 97	Todd Walker	.60	.25
☐ 98	Carlos Delgado	1.50	.70
☐ 99	Kerry Wood	2.00	.90
☐ 100	Ken Griffey Jr.	8.00	3.60

1998 Topps Gold Label Class 2

	MINT	NRMT
COMP.GOLD SET (100)	200.00	90.00
COMMON GOLD (1-100)	.75	.35
GOLD MINOR STARS	1.25	.55
GOLD SEMISTARS	2.00	.90
GOLD UNLISTED STARS	3.00	1.35

CLASS 2 GOLD STATED ODDS 1:2
COMMON BLACK (1-100) ...... 3.00 ..... 1.35
*CLASS 2 BLACK: 1.5X TO 4X HI COLUMN

CLASS 2 BLACK STATED ODDS 1:16
COMMON RED (1-100) ..... 20.00 ..... 9.00
*CLASS 2 RED STARS: 10X TO 25X HI
*CLASS 2 RED RC's: 6X TO 15X HI
CLASS 2 RED STATED ODDS 1:198
CLASS 2 RED PRINT RUN 50 SERIAL #'d SETS
CLASS 2: SPARKLING SILVER TEXT ON FRONT

1998 Topps Gold Label Class 3

	MINT	NRMT
COMP.GOLD SET (100)	300.00	135.00
COMMON GOLD (1-100)	1.25	.55
GOLD MINOR STARS	2.00	.90
GOLD SEMISTARS	3.00	1.35
GOLD UNLISTED STARS	5.00	2.20

GOLD STATED ODDS 1:4
COMMON BLACK (1-100) ...... 5.00 ..... 2.20
*CLASS 3 BLACK: 1.5X TO 4X HI COLUMN
CLASS 3 BLACK STATED ODDS 1:32
COMMON RED (1-100) ..... 40.00 ..... 18.00
*CLASS 3 RED STARS: 12.5X TO 30X HI
*CLASS 3 RED RC's: 5X TO 12X HI
CLASS 3 RED STATED ODDS 1:396
CLASS 3 RED PRINT RUN 25 SERIAL #'d SETS
CLASS 3: SPARKLING GOLD TEXT ON FRONT

1998 Topps Gold Label Home Run Race

	MINT	NRMT
COMPLETE SET (4)	60.00	27.00
COMMON CARD (HR1-HR4)..	10.00	4.50
STATED ODDS 1:12 HTA		
*BLACK HR: 1.25X TO 3X HI COLUMN		
BLACK HR STATED ODDS 1:48		
*RED HR: 8X TO 20X HI COLUMN		
RED HR STATED ODDS 1:4055 HTA		
RED HR STATED PRINT RUN 61 SETS		

		MINT	NRMT
❑ HR1	Roger Maris	10.00	4.50
❑ HR2	Mark McGwire	25.00	11.00
❑ HR3	Ken Griffey Jr.	20.00	9.00
❑ HR4	Sammy Sosa	12.00	5.50

1999 Topps Gold Label
Class 1

	MINT	NRMT
COMP.GOLD SET (100)	80.00	36.00
COMMON GOLD (1-100)	.40	.18
GOLD MINOR STARS	.60	.25
GOLD SEMISTARS	1.00	.45
GOLD UNLISTED STARS	1.50	.70
COMMON BLACK (1-100)	1.50	.70
*CLASS 1 BLACK STARS: 1.5X TO 4X HI		
*CLASS 1 BLACK RC'S: 1.25X TO 3X HI		
CLASS 1 BLACK ODDS 1:12 RETAIL, 1:8 HTA		
COMMON RED (1-100)	8.00	3.60
*CLASS 1 RED STARS: 8X TO 20X HI		
*CLASS 1 RED RC'S: 8X TO 20X HI		
CLASS 1 RED ODDS 1:148 RETAIL, 1:118 HTA		
CLASS 1 RED PRINT RUN 100 SERIAL #'d SETS		
NINE DIFT.ONE TO ONE PARALLELS EXIST		
ONE TO ONE ODDS 1:1587 RETAIL, 1:1271 HTA		

❑ 1	Mike Piazza	5.00	2.20
❑ 2	Andres Galarraga	1.00	.45
❑ 3	Mark Grace	1.00	.45
❑ 4	Tony Clark	.80	.25
❑ 5	Jim Thome	1.50	.70
❑ 6	Tony Gwynn	4.00	1.80
❑ 7	Kelly Dransfeldt	1.00	.45
❑ 8	Eric Chavez	1.00	.45
❑ 9	Brian Jordan	.60	.25
❑ 10	Todd Hundley	.60	.25
❑ 11	Rondell White	.60	.25
❑ 12	Dmitri Young	.60	.25
❑ 13	Jeff Kent	.60	.25
❑ 14	Derek Bell	.60	.25
❑ 15	Todd Helton	1.50	.70
❑ 16	Chipper Jones	4.00	1.80
❑ 17	Albert Belle	1.50	.70
❑ 18	Barry Larkin	1.50	.70
❑ 19	Dante Bichette	.60	.25
❑ 20	Gary Sheffield	.60	.25
❑ 21	Cliff Floyd	.60	.25
❑ 22	Derek Jeter	5.00	2.20
❑ 23	Jason Giambi	.60	.25
❑ 24	Ray Lankford	.60	.25
❑ 25	Alex Rodriguez	5.00	2.20
❑ 26	Ruben Mateo	1.50	.70
❑ 27	Wade Boggs	1.50	.70
❑ 28	Carlos Delgado	1.50	.70
❑ 29	Tim Salmon	1.00	.45
❑ 30	Alfonso Soriano	6.00	2.70

❑ 31	Javy Lopez	.60	.25
❑ 32	Jason Kendall	.60	.25
❑ 33	Nick Johnson	5.00	2.20
❑ 34	A.J. Burnett	1.50	.70
❑ 35	Troy Glaus	1.50	.70
❑ 36	Pat Burrell	6.00	2.70
❑ 37	Jeff Cirillo	.60	.25
❑ 38	David Justice	.60	.25
❑ 39	Ivan Rodriguez	2.00	.90
❑ 40	Bernie Williams ..!	1.50	.70
❑ 41	Jay Buhner	.60	.25
❑ 42	Mo Vaughn	1.50	.70
❑ 43	Randy Johnson	1.50	.70
❑ 44	Pedro Martinez	2.00	.90
❑ 45	Larry Walker	1.50	.70
❑ 46	Todd Walker	.60	.25
❑ 47	Roberto Alomar	1.50	.70
❑ 48	Kevin Brown	1.00	.45
❑ 49	Mike Mussina	1.50	.70
❑ 50	Tom Glavine	1.50	.70
❑ 51	Curt Schilling	1.00	.45
❑ 52	Ken Caminiti	.60	.25
❑ 53	Brad Fullmer	.40	.18
❑ 54	Bobby Seay	1.00	.45
❑ 55	Orlando Hernandez	1.50	.70
❑ 56	Sean Casey	1.50	.70
❑ 57	Al Leiter	.60	.25
❑ 58	Sandy Alomar Jr	.60	.25
❑ 59	Mark Kotsay	.40	.18
❑ 60	Matt Williams	1.50	.70
❑ 61	Raul Mondesi	.60	.25
❑ 62	Joe Crede	2.00	.90
❑ 63	Jim Edmonds	.60	.25
❑ 64	Jose Cruz Jr.	.60	.25
❑ 65	Juan Gonzalez	3.00	1.35
❑ 66	Sammy Sosa	5.00	2.20
❑ 67	Cal Ripken	6.00	2.70
❑ 68	Vinny Castilla	.60	.25
❑ 69	Craig Biggio	1.50	.70
❑ 70	Mark McGwire	10.00	4.50
❑ 71	Greg Vaughn	.60	.25
❑ 72	Greg Maddux	4.00	1.80
❑ 73	Paul O'Neill	.60	.25
❑ 74	Scott Rolen	2.00	.90
❑ 75	Ben Grieve	1.50	.70
❑ 76	Vladimir Guerrero	2.00	.90
❑ 77	John Olerud	.60	.25
❑ 78	Eric Karros	.60	.25
❑ 79	Jeromy Burnitz	.60	.25
❑ 80	Jeff Bagwell	2.00	.90
❑ 81	Kenny Lofton	1.00	.45
❑ 82	Manny Ramirez	2.00	.90
❑ 83	Andruw Jones	1.50	.70
❑ 84	Travis Lee	1.00	.45
❑ 85	Darin Erstad	1.00	.45
❑ 86	Nomar Garciaparra	5.00	2.20
❑ 87	Frank Thomas	3.00	1.35
❑ 88	Moises Alou	1.50	.70
❑ 89	Tino Martinez	1.50	.70
❑ 90	Carlos Pena	1.50	.70
❑ 91	Shawn Green	1.50	.70
❑ 92	Rusty Greer	.60	.25
❑ 93	Matt Belisle	.75	.35
❑ 94	Adrian Beltre	1.50	.70
❑ 95	Roger Clemens	4.00	1.80
❑ 96	John Smoltz	1.00	.45
❑ 97	Mark Mulder	1.50	.70
❑ 98	Kerry Wood	1.50	.70
❑ 99	Barry Bonds	2.00	.90
❑ 100	Ken Griffey Jr.	8.00	3.60

1999 Topps Gold Label
Class 2

	MINT	NRMT
COMP.GOLD SET (100)	200.00	90.00
COMMON GOLD (1-100)	.60	.25
GOLD MINOR STARS	1.00	.45
GOLD SEMISTARS	1.50	.70
GOLD UNLISTED STARS	2.50	1.10
CLASS 2 GOLD ODDS 1:4 RETAIL, 1:2 HTA		
COMMON BLACK (1-100)	2.50	1.10
*CLASS 2 BLACK STARS: 1.5X TO 4X HI		
*CLASS 2 BLACK RC'S: 1.25X TO 3X HI		
CLASS 2 BLACK ODDS 1:24 RETAIL, 1:16 HTA		

	MINT	NRMT
COMMON RED (1-100)	15.00	6.75
*CLASS 2 RED STARS: 10X TO 25X HI		
*CLASS 2 RED RC'S: 8X TO 20X HI		
CLASS 2 RED ODDS 1:296 RETAIL, 1:237 HTA		
CLASS 2 RED PRINT RUN 50 SERIAL #'d SETS		

1999 Topps Gold Label
Class 3

	MINT	NRMT
COMP.GOLD SET (100)	300.00	135.00
COMMON GOLD (1-100)	1.00	.45
GOLD MINOR STARS	1.50	.70
GOLD SEMISTARS	2.50	1.10
GOLD UNLISTED STARS	4.00	1.80
GOLD STATED ODDS 1:8 RETAIL, 1:4 HTA		
COMMON BLACK (1-100)	4.00	1.80
*CLASS 3 BLACK RC'S: 1.25X TO 3X HI		
*CLASS 3 BLACK STARS: 1.5X TO 4X HI		
CLASS 3 BLACK ODDS 1:48 RETAIL, 1:32 HTA		
COMMON RED (1-100)	30.00	13.50
*CLASS 3 RED STARS: 12.5X TO 30X HI		
*CLASS 3 RED RC'S: 8X TO 20X HI		
CLASS 3 RED ODDS 1:591 RETAIL, 1:473 HTA		
CLASS 3 RED PRINT RUN 25 SERIAL #'d SETS		

1999 Topps Gold Label
Race to Aaron

	MINT	NRMT
COMPLETE SET (10)	100.00	45.00
COMMON CARD (RA1-RA10)	3.00	1.35

STATED ODDS 1:20 RETAIL, 1:12 HTA
*BLACK: 1X TO 2.5X HI COLUMN
BLACK ODDS 1:80 RETAIL, 1:48 HTA
*RED: 8X TO 20X HI COLUMN
RED ODDS 1:3343 RETAIL, 1:2695 HTA
RED PRINT RUN 44 SERIAL #'d SETS
AARON ONE TO ONE PARALLELS EXIST
ONE TO ONE'S NOT PRICED DUE TO
SCARCITY

RA1 Mark McGwire	25.00	11.00
RA2 Ken Griffey Jr.	20.00	9.00
RA3 Alex Rodriguez	12.00	5.50
RA4 Vladimir Guerrero	5.00	2.20
RA5 Albert Belle	3.00	1.35
RA6 Nomar Garciaparra	12.00	5.50
RA7 Ken Griffey Jr.	20.00	9.00
RA8 Alex Rodriguez	12.00	5.50
RA9 Juan Gonzalez	8.00	3.60
RA10 Barry Bonds	5.00	2.20

1996 Topps Laser

	MINT	NRMT
COMPLETE SET (128)	100.00	45.00
COMPLETE SERIES 1 (64)	50.00	22.00
COMPLETE SERIES 2 (64)	50.00	22.00
COMMON CARD (1-128)	.50	.23
MINOR STARS	1.00	.45
UNLISTED STARS		.90

1 Moises Alou	1.00	.45
2 Derek Bell	1.00	.45
3 Joe Carter	1.00	.45
4 Jeff Conine	.50	.23
5 Darren Daulton	1.00	.45
6 Jim Edmonds	1.50	.70
7 Ron Gant	.50	.23
8 Juan Gonzalez	5.00	2.20
9 Brian Jordan	1.00	.45
10 Ryan Klesko	1.00	.45
11 Paul Molitor	2.00	.90
12 Tony Phillips	.50	.23
13 Manny Ramirez	2.00	.90
14 Sammy Sosa	5.00	2.20
15 Devon White	1.00	.45
16 Bernie Williams	2.00	.90
17 Garrett Anderson	1.00	.45
18 Jay Bell	1.00	.45
19 Craig Biggio	2.00	.90
20 Bobby Bonilla	1.00	.45
21 Ken Caminiti	1.00	.45
22 Shawon Dunston	.50	.23
23 Mark Grace	1.50	.70
24 Gregg Jefferies	.50	.23
25 Jeff King	.50	.23
26 Javy Lopez	1.00	.45
27 Edgar Martinez	1.00	.45
28 Dean Palmer	1.00	.45
29 J.T. Snow	.50	.23
30 Mike Stanley	.50	.23
31 Terry Steinbach	.50	.23
32 Robin Ventura	1.00	.45
33 Roberto Alomar	2.00	.90
34 Jeff Bagwell	2.00	.90
35 Dante Bichette	1.00	.45
36 Wade Boggs	2.00	.90
37 Barry Bonds	2.00	.90
38 Jose Canseco	2.00	.90
39 Vinny Castilla	1.50	.70
40 Will Clark	2.00	.90
41 Marty Cordova	.50	.23
42 Ken Griffey Jr.	10.00	4.50
43 Tony Gwynn	2.00	.90
44 Rickey Henderson	2.00	.90
45 Chipper Jones	5.00	2.20
46 Mark McGwire	10.00	4.50
47 Brian McRae	.50	.23
48 Ryne Sandberg	2.00	.90
49 Andy Ashby	.50	.23
50 Alan Benes	.50	.23
51 Andy Benes	1.00	.45
52 Roger Clemens	5.00	2.20
53 Doug Drabek	.50	.23
54 Dennis Eckersley	1.00	.45
55 Tom Glavine	2.00	.90
56 Randy Johnson	2.00	.90
57 Mark Langston	.50	.23
58 Denny Martinez	1.00	.45
59 Jack McDowell	.50	.23
60 Hideo Nomo	2.00	.90
61 Shane Reynolds	.50	.23
62 John Smoltz	1.50	.70
63 Paul Wilson	.50	.23
64 Mark Wohlers	.50	.23
65 Shawn Green	2.00	.90
66 Marquis Grissom	.50	.23
67 Dave Hollins	.50	.23
68 Todd Hundley	1.00	.45
69 David Justice	2.00	.90
70 Eric Karros	1.00	.45
71 Ray Lankford	1.00	.45
72 Fred McGriff	1.50	.70
73 Hal Morris	.50	.23
74 Eddie Murray	2.00	.90
75 Paul O'Neill	1.00	.45
76 Rey Ordonez	1.00	.45
77 Reggie Sanders	1.00	.45
78 Gary Sheffield	2.00	.90
79 Jim Thome	2.00	.90
80 Rondell White	1.00	.45
81 Travis Fryman	1.00	.45
82 Derek Jeter	6.00	2.70
83 Chuck Knoblauch	2.00	.90
84 Barry Larkin	2.00	.90
85 Tino Martinez	1.00	.45
86 Raul Mondesi	1.00	.45
87 John Olerud	1.00	.45
88 Rafael Palmeiro	2.00	.90
89 Mike Piazza	6.00	2.70
90 Cal Ripken	8.00	3.60
91 Ivan Rodriguez	2.00	.90
92 Frank Thomas	5.00	2.20
93 John Valentin	1.00	.45
94 Mo Vaughn	2.00	.90
95 Quilvio Veras	.50	.23
96 Matt Williams	2.00	.90
97 Brady Anderson	1.00	.45
98 Carlos Baerga	.50	.23
99 Albert Belle	2.00	.90
100 Jay Buhner	1.00	.45
101 Johnny Damon	1.50	.70
102 Chili Davis	1.00	.45
103 Ray Durham	1.00	.45
104 Len Dykstra	1.00	.45
105 Cecil Fielder	1.00	.45
106 Andres Galarraga	2.00	.90
107 Brian L.Hunter	.50	.23
108 Kenny Lofton	2.00	.90
109 Kirby Puckett	3.00	1.35
110 Tim Salmon	1.50	.70
111 Greg Vaughn	1.00	.45
112 Larry Walker	2.00	.90
113 Rick Aguilera	.50	.23
114 Kevin Appier	1.00	.45
115 Kevin Brown	1.50	.70
116 David Cone	1.00	.45
117 Alex Fernandez	.50	.23
118 Chuck Finley	1.00	.45
119 Joey Hamilton	.50	.23
120 Jason Isringhausen	1.00	.45
121 Greg Maddux	6.00	2.70
122 Pedro Martinez	2.00	.90
123 Jose Mesa	.50	.23
124 Jeff Montgomery	.50	.23
125 Mike Mussina	2.00	.90
126 Randy Myers	.50	.23
127 Kenny Rogers	.50	.23
128 Ismael Valdes	1.00	.45

1996 Topps Laser Bright Spots

	MINT	NRMT
COMPLETE SET (16)	60.00	27.00
COMPLETE SERIES 1 (8)	25.00	11.00
COMPLETE SERIES 2 (8)	40.00	18.00
COMMON CARD (1-16)	2.50	1.10
STATED ODDS 1:20		

1 Brian L.Hunter	2.50	1.10
2 Derek Jeter	12.00	5.50
3 Jason Kendall	6.00	2.70
4 Brooks Kieschnick	2.50	1.10
5 Rey Ordonez	6.00	2.70
6 Jason Schmidt	2.50	1.10
7 Chris Snopek	2.50	1.10
8 Bob Wolcott	2.50	1.10
9 Alan Benes	2.50	1.10
10 Marty Cordova	2.50	1.10
11 Jimmy Haynes	2.50	1.10
12 Todd Hollandsworth	2.50	1.10
13 Derek Jeter	12.00	5.50
14 Chipper Jones	12.00	5.50
15 Hideo Nomo	6.00	2.70
16 Paul Wilson	2.50	1.10

1996 Topps Laser Power Cuts

	MINT	NRMT
COMPLETE SET (16)	120.00	55.00
COMPLETE SERIES 1 (8)	60.00	27.00
COMPLETE SERIES 2 (8)	60.00	27.00
COMMON CARD (1-16)	3.00	1.35
STATED ODDS 1:40		

1 Albert Belle	6.00	2.70
2 Jay Buhner	3.00	1.35
3 Fred McGriff	4.00	1.80
4 Mike Piazza	20.00	9.00

☐ 5 Tim Salmon	4.00	1.80
☐ 6 Frank Thomas	12.00	5.50
☐ 7 Mo Vaughn	6.00	2.70
☐ 8 Matt Williams	6.00	2.70
☐ 9 Jeff Bagwell	8.00	3.60
☐ 10 Barry Bonds	8.00	3.60
☐ 11 Jose Canseco	8.00	3.60
☐ 12 Cecil Fielder	3.00	1.35
☐ 13 Juan Gonzalez	12.00	5.50
☐ 14 Ken Griffey Jr.	30.00	13.50
☐ 15 Sammy Sosa	20.00	9.00
☐ 16 Larry Walker	6.00	2.70

1996 Topps Laser Stadium Stars

	MINT	NRMT
COMPLETE SET (16)	200.00	90.00
COMPLETE SERIES 1 (8)	100.00	45.00
COMPLETE SERIES 2 (8)	100.00	45.00
COMMON CARD (1-16)	4.00	1.80
UNLISTED STARS	8.00	3.60
STATED ODDS 1:60		

☐ 1 Carlos Baerga	4.00	1.80
☐ 2 Barry Bonds	8.00	3.60
☐ 3 Andres Galarraga	8.00	3.60
☐ 4 Ken Griffey Jr.	40.00	18.00
☐ 5 Barry Larkin	8.00	3.60
☐ 6 Raul Mondesi	5.00	2.20
☐ 7 Kirby Puckett	12.00	5.50
☐ 8 Cal Ripken	30.00	13.50
☐ 9 Will Clark	8.00	3.60
☐ 10 Roger Clemens	20.00	9.00
☐ 11 Tony Gwynn	20.00	9.00
☐ 12 Randy Johnson	8.00	3.60
☐ 13 Kenny Lofton	6.00	2.70
☐ 14 Edgar Martinez	5.00	2.20
☐ 15 Ryne Sandberg	8.00	3.60
☐ 16 Frank Thomas	20.00	9.00

1999 Topps Opening Day

	MINT	NRMT
COMPLETE SET (165)	45.00	20.00
COMMON CARD (1-165)	.20	.09
MINOR STARS	.30	.14
SEMISTARS	.50	.23
UNLISTED STARS	.75	.35

AARON AUTO STATED ODDS 1:29,642

☐ 1 Hank Aaron	2.50	1.10
☐ 2 Roger Clemens	2.00	.90
☐ 3 Andres Galarraga UER	.50	.23
Card erroneously numbered 2		
☐ 4 Scott Brosius	.30	.14
☐ 5 Ray Durham	.30	.14
☐ 6 Will Clark	.75	.35
☐ 7 David Wells	.30	.14
☐ 8 Jose Guillen	.20	.09
☐ 9 Edgardo Alfonzo	.50	.23
☐ 10 Manny Ramirez	1.00	.45
☐ 11 Greg Maddux	2.00	.90
☐ 12 David Segui	.20	.09
☐ 13 Darryl Strawberry	.30	.14
☐ 14 Brad Radke	.30	.14
☐ 15 Kerry Wood	.75	.35
☐ 16 Paul Konerko	.50	.23
☐ 17 Travis Lee	.50	.23
☐ 18 Kenny Rogers	.20	.09
☐ 19 Todd Walker	.30	.14
☐ 20 John Olerud	.30	.14
☐ 21 Nolan Ryan	4.00	1.80
☐ 22 Ray Lankford	.30	.14
☐ 23 Bartolo Colon	.30	.14
☐ 24 Brady Anderson	.30	.14
☐ 25 Jorge Posada	.20	.09
☐ 26 Justin Thompson	.20	.09
☐ 27 Juan Gonzalez	1.50	.70
☐ 28 Chuck Knoblauch	.30	.14
☐ 29 Todd Helton	.75	.35
☐ 30 Gary Sheffield	.30	.14
☐ 31 Rod Beck	.20	.09
☐ 32 Garret Anderson	.30	.14
☐ 33 Rondell White	.30	.14
☐ 34 Vladimir Guerrero	1.00	.45
☐ 35 Eric Karros	.30	.14
☐ 36 Mo Vaughn	.75	.35
☐ 37 Sammy Sosa	2.50	1.10
☐ 38 Kenny Lofton	.50	.23
☐ 39 Javy Lopez	.30	.14
☐ 40 Mark McGwire	5.00	2.20
☐ 41 Damion Easley	.30	.14
☐ 42 Andy Pettitte	.30	.14
☐ 43 Tony Gwynn	2.00	.90
☐ 44 Jay Bell	.30	.14
☐ 45 Jose Canseco	1.00	.45
☐ 46 John Wetteland	.30	.14
☐ 47 Mike Caruso	.20	.09
☐ 48 Derek Jeter	2.50	1.10
☐ 49 Aaron Sele	.30	.14
☐ 50 Jeff Cirillo	.30	.14
☐ 51 Mark Kotsay	.20	.09
☐ 52 Albert Belle	.75	.35
☐ 53 Matt Lawton	.20	.09
☐ 54 Pedro Martinez	1.00	.45
☐ 55 Greg Vaughn	.30	.14
☐ 56 Neifi Perez	.30	.14
☐ 57 Derek Bell	.30	.14
☐ 58 Ken Griffey Jr.	4.00	1.80
☐ 59 David Cone	.50	.23
☐ 60 Dean Palmer	.30	.14
☐ 61 Trevor Hoffman	.30	.14
☐ 62 Billy Wagner	.30	.14
☐ 63 Shawn Green	.75	.35
☐ 64 Ben Grieve	.75	.35
☐ 65 Tom Goodwin	.20	.09
☐ 66 Jaret Wright	.30	.14
☐ 67 Dmitri Young	.30	.14
☐ 68 Hideki Irabu	.30	.14
☐ 69 Jeff Fassero	.20	.09
☐ 70 Matt Williams	.75	.35
☐ 71 Bret Saberhagen	.30	.14
☐ 72 Chad Curtis	.20	.09
☐ 73 Scott Rolen	1.00	.45
☐ 74 J.T. Snow	.30	.14
☐ 75 Rusty Greer	.30	.14
☐ 76 Jim Edmonds	.30	.14
☐ 77 Ron Gant	.30	.14
☐ 78 A.J. Hinch	.20	.09
☐ 79 Shannon Stewart	.30	.14
☐ 80 Brad Fullmer	.20	.09
☐ 81 Matt Walbeck	.20	.09
☐ 82 Fred McGriff	.50	.23
☐ 83 Darin Erstad	.50	.23
☐ 84 Eric Young	.20	.09
☐ 85 Livan Hernandez	.20	.09
☐ 86 Jeff Bagwell	1.00	.45
☐ 87 Omar Vizquel	.30	.14
☐ 88 Eric Davis	.30	.14
☐ 89 Magglio Ordonez	.75	.35
☐ 90 John Valentin	.30	.14
☐ 91 Dave Dellucci	.20	.09
☐ 92 Chan Ho Park	.30	.14
☐ 93 Masato Yoshii	.30	.14
☐ 94 Bret Boone	.30	.14
☐ 95 Mariano Rivera	.30	.14
☐ 96 Bobby Jones	.20	.09
☐ 97 Francisco Cordova	.20	.09
☐ 98 Mike Mussina	.75	.35
☐ 99 Denny Neagle	.20	.09
☐ 100 Edgar Martinez	.30	.14
☐ 101 Jason Kendall	.30	.14
☐ 102 Jeff King	.20	.09
☐ 103 Rey Ordonez	.20	.09
☐ 104 Andruw Jones	.75	.35
☐ 105 Vinny Castilla	.30	.14
☐ 106 Troy Glaus	.75	.35
☐ 107 Tom Glavine	.75	.35
☐ 108 Moises Alou	.30	.14
☐ 109 Carlos Delgado	.75	.35
☐ 110 Raul Mondesi	.30	.14
☐ 111 Shane Reynolds	.30	.14
☐ 112 Jason Giambi	.30	.14
☐ 113 Jose Cruz Jr.	.30	.14
☐ 114 Ryan Klesko	.50	.23
☐ 115 Tim Salmon	.50	.23
☐ 116 Chipper Jones	2.00	.90
☐ 117 Andy Benes	.20	.09
☐ 118 John Smoltz	.50	.23
☐ 119 Jeromy Burnitz	.30	.14
☐ 120 Randy Johnson	.75	.35
☐ 121 Mark Grace	.50	.23
☐ 122 Henry Rodriguez	.30	.14
☐ 123 Ryan Klesko	.50	.23
☐ 124 Kevin Millwood	.50	.23
☐ 125 Sean Casey	.75	.35
☐ 126 Brian Jordan	.30	.14
☐ 127 Kevin Brown	.50	.23
☐ 128 Orlando Hernandez	.75	.35
☐ 129 Barry Bonds	1.00	.45
☐ 130 David Justice	.30	.14
☐ 131 Carlos Perez	.20	.09
☐ 132 Andy Ashby	.20	.09
☐ 133 Paul O'Neill	.30	.14
☐ 134 Curt Schilling	.50	.23
☐ 135 Alex Rodriguez	2.50	1.10
☐ 136 Cliff Floyd	.30	.14
☐ 137 Rafael Palmeiro	.75	.35
☐ 138 Nomar Garciaparra	2.50	1.10
☐ 139 Mike Piazza	2.50	1.10
☐ 140 Roberto Alomar	.75	.35
☐ 141 Todd Hundley	.30	.14
☐ 142 Jeff Kent	.30	.14
☐ 143 Larry Walker	.75	.35
☐ 144 Cal Ripken	3.00	1.35
☐ 145 Jay Buhner	.30	.14
☐ 146 Kevin Young	.30	.14
☐ 147 Ivan Rodriguez	1.00	.45
☐ 148 Al Leiter	.30	.14
☐ 149 Sandy Alomar Jr.	.30	.14
☐ 150 Bernie Williams	.75	.35
☐ 151 Ellis Burks	.30	.14
☐ 152 Wally Joyner	.30	.14
☐ 153 Bobby Higginson	.30	.14
☐ 154 Tony Clark	.30	.14
☐ 155 Larry Walker	.75	.35
☐ 156 Frank Thomas	1.50	.70
☐ 157 Tino Martinez	.30	.14
☐ 158 Jim Thome	.75	.35
☐ 159 Dante Bichette	.30	.14
☐ 160 David Wells HL	.20	.09
☐ 161 Roger Clemens HL	.75	.35
☐ 162 Kerry Wood HL	.30	.14
☐ 163 Mark McGwire HR 70	10.00	4.50
☐ 164 Sammy Sosa HR 66	6.00	2.70
☐ 165 Checklist	.20	.09
☐ NNO Hank Aaron AU	300.00	135.00

1999 Topps Opening Day Oversize

	MINT	NRMT
COMPLETE SET (3)	12.00	5.50
COMMON CARD (1-3)	3.00	1.35
ONE PER BOX		

☐ 1 Sammy Sosa	3.00	1.35
☐ 2 Mark McGwire	6.00	2.70
☐ 3 Ken Griffey Jr.	5.00	2.20

1997 Topps Stars

	MINT	NRMT
COMPLETE SET (125)	60.00	27.00
COMMON CARD (1-125)	.15	.07
MINOR STARS	.30	.14
UNLISTED STARS	.60	.25

☐ 1 Larry Walker	.60	.25
☐ 2 Tino Martinez	.60	.25
☐ 3 Cal Ripken	2.50	1.10
☐ 4 Ken Griffey Jr.	3.00	1.35
☐ 5 Chipper Jones	1.50	.70
☐ 6 David Justice	.60	.25
☐ 7 Mike Piazza	2.00	.90
☐ 8 Jeff Bagwell	.75	.35
☐ 9 Ron Gant	.15	.07
☐ 10 Sammy Sosa	2.00	.90
☐ 11 Tony Gwynn	1.50	.70
☐ 12 Carlos Baerga	.15	.07
☐ 13 Frank Thomas	1.25	.55
☐ 14 Moises Alou	.30	.14
☐ 15 Barry Larkin	.60	.25
☐ 16 Ivan Rodriguez	.75	.35
☐ 17 Greg Maddux	1.50	.70
☐ 18 Jim Edmonds	.40	.18
☐ 19 Jose Canseco	.75	.35
☐ 20 Rafael Palmeiro	.60	.25
☐ 21 Paul Molitor	.60	.25
☐ 22 Kevin Appier	.30	.14
☐ 23 Raul Mondesi	.30	.14
☐ 24 Lance Johnson	.15	.07
☐ 25 Edgar Martinez	.30	.14
☐ 26 Andres Galarraga	.60	.25
☐ 27 Mo Vaughn	.60	.25
☐ 28 Ken Caminiti	.40	.18
☐ 29 Cecil Fielder	.30	.14
☐ 30 Harold Baines	.30	.14
☐ 31 Roberto Alomar	.60	.25
☐ 32 Shawn Estes	.30	.14
☐ 33 Tom Glavine	.60	.25
☐ 34 Dennis Eckersley	.30	.14
☐ 35 Manny Ramirez	.75	.35
☐ 36 John Olerud	.30	.14
☐ 37 Juan Gonzalez	1.25	.55
☐ 38 Chuck Knoblauch	.60	.25
☐ 39 Albert Belle	.60	.25
☐ 40 Vinny Castilla	.40	.18
☐ 41 John Smoltz	.40	.18
☐ 42 Barry Bonds	.75	.35
☐ 43 Randy Johnson	.60	.25
☐ 44 Brady Anderson	.30	.14
☐ 45 Jeff Blauser	.15	.07
☐ 46 Craig Biggio	.60	.25
☐ 47 Jeff Conine	.15	.07
☐ 48 Marquis Grissom	.30	.14
☐ 49 Mark Grace	.40	.18
☐ 50 Roger Clemens	1.50	.70
☐ 51 Mark McGwire	3.00	1.35
☐ 52 Fred McGriff	.40	.18
☐ 53 Gary Sheffield	.30	.14
☐ 54 Bobby Jones	.15	.07
☐ 55 Eric Young	.30	.14
☐ 56 Robin Ventura	.30	.14
☐ 57 Wade Boggs	.60	.25
☐ 58 Joe Carter	.30	.14
☐ 59 Ryne Sandberg	.75	.35
☐ 60 Matt Williams	.60	.25
☐ 61 Todd Hundley	.30	.14
☐ 62 Dante Bichette	.30	.14
☐ 63 Chili Davis	.30	.14
☐ 64 Kenny Lofton	.40	.18
☐ 65 Jay Buhner	.30	.14
☐ 66 Will Clark	.60	.25
☐ 67 Travis Fryman	.30	.14
☐ 68 Pat Hentgen	.30	.14
☐ 69 Ellis Burks	.30	.14
☐ 70 Mike Mussina	.60	.25
☐ 71 Hideo Nomo	.60	.25
☐ 72 Sandy Alomar	.30	.14
☐ 73 Bobby Bonilla	.30	.14
☐ 74 Rickey Henderson	.75	.35
☐ 75 David Cone	.40	.18
☐ 76 Terry Steinbach	.15	.07
☐ 77 Pedro Martinez	.75	.35
☐ 78 Jim Thorne	.60	.25
☐ 79 Rod Beck	.15	.07
☐ 80 Randy Myers	.15	.07
☐ 81 Charles Nagy	.30	.14
☐ 82 Mark Wohlers	.15	.07
☐ 83 Paul O'Neill	.30	.14
☐ 84 Curt Schilling	.40	.18
☐ 85 Joey Cora	.15	.07
☐ 86 John Franco	.15	.07
☐ 87 Kevin Brown	.40	.18
☐ 88 Benito Santiago	.15	.07
☐ 89 Ray Lankford	.30	.14
☐ 90 Bernie Williams	.60	.25
☐ 91 Jason Dickson	.15	.07
☐ 92 Jeff Cirillo	.30	.14
☐ 93 Nomar Garciaparra	2.00	.90
☐ 94 Mariano Rivera	.30	.14
☐ 95 Javy Lopez	.30	.14
☐ 96 Tony Womack	2.00	.90
☐ 97 Jose Rosado	.15	.07
☐ 98 Denny Neagle	.30	.14
☐ 99 Darryl Kile	.15	.07
☐ 100 Justin Thompson	.30	.14
☐ 101 Juan Encarnacion	.30	.14
☐ 102 Brad Fullmer	.30	.14
☐ 103 Kris Benson	5.00	2.20
☐ 104 Todd Helton	1.25	.55
☐ 105 Paul Konerko	.60	.25
☐ 106 Travis Lee	6.00	2.70
☐ 107 Todd Greene	.15	.07
☐ 108 Mark Kotsay	2.50	1.10
☐ 109 Carl Pavano	.60	.25
☐ 110 Kerry Wood	12.00	5.50
☐ 111 Jason Romano	2.50	1.10
☐ 112 Geoff Goetz	1.25	.55
☐ 113 Scott Hodges	1.25	.55
☐ 114 Aaron Akin	1.00	.45
☐ 115 Vernon Wells	8.00	3.60
☐ 116 Chris Stowe	.75	.35
☐ 117 Brett Caradonna	1.50	.70
☐ 118 Adam Kennedy	4.00	1.80
☐ 119 Jayson Werth	4.00	1.80
☐ 120 Glenn Davis	1.50	.70
☐ 121 Troy Cameron	2.50	1.10
☐ 122 J.J. Davis	2.50	1.10
☐ 123 Jason Dellaoro	1.50	.70
☐ 124 Jason Standridge	3.00	1.35
☐ 125 Lance Berkman	8.00	3.60
☐ NNO Checklist	.15	.07

1997 Topps Stars Always Mint

	MINT	NRMT
COMMON CARD (1-125)	2.50	1.10
*STARS: 6X TO 15X BASIC CARDS		

*YOUNG STARS: 5X TO 12X BASIC CARDS
*ROOKIES: 1.5X TO 4X BASIC CARDS
STATED ODDS 1:12

1997 Topps Stars '97 All-Stars

	MINT	NRMT
COMPLETE SET (20)	300.00	135.00
COMMON CARD (AS1-AS20)	5.00	2.20
SEMISTARS	8.00	3.60
UNLISTED STARS	12.00	5.50
STATED ODDS 1:72		

☐ AS1 Greg Maddux	30.00	13.50
☐ AS2 Randy Johnson	12.00	5.50
☐ AS3 Tino Martinez	12.00	5.50
☐ AS4 Jeff Bagwell	15.00	6.75
☐ AS5 Ivan Rodriguez	15.00	6.75
☐ AS6 Mike Piazza	40.00	18.00
☐ AS7 Cal Ripken	50.00	22.00
☐ AS8 Ken Caminiti	8.00	3.60
☐ AS9 Tony Gwynn	30.00	13.50
☐ AS10 Edgar Martinez	5.00	2.20
☐ AS11 Craig Biggio	12.00	5.50
☐ AS12 Roberto Alomar	12.00	5.50
☐ AS13 Larry Walker	12.00	5.50
☐ AS14 Brady Anderson	5.00	2.20
☐ AS15 Barry Bonds	15.00	6.75
☐ AS16 Ken Griffey Jr.	60.00	27.00
☐ AS17 Ray Lankford	5.00	2.20
☐ AS18 Paul O'Neill	5.00	2.20
☐ AS19 Jeff Blauser	5.00	2.20
☐ AS20 Sandy Alomar	5.00	2.20

1997 Topps Stars All-Star Memories

	MINT	NRMT
COMPLETE SET (10)	80.00	36.00
COMMON CARD (ASM1-ASM10)	2.00	.90
STATED ODDS 1:24		

☐ ASM1 Cal Ripken	20.00	9.00
☐ ASM2 Jeff Conine	2.00	.90
☐ ASM3 Mike Piazza	15.00	6.75
☐ ASM4 Randy Johnson	5.00	2.20
☐ ASM5 Ken Griffey Jr.	25.00	11.00
☐ ASM6 Fred McGriff	3.00	1.35
☐ ASM7 Moises Alou	2.00	.90

	MINT	NRMT
ASM8 Hideo Nomo	5.00	2.20
ASM9 Larry Walker	5.00	2.20
ASM10 Sandy Alomar	2.00	.90

1997 Topps Stars Future All-Stars

	MINT	NRMT
COMPLETE SET (15)	50.00	22.00
COMMON CARD (FAS1-FAS15)	1.00	.45
SEMISTARS	2.00	.90
UNLISTED STARS	3.00	1.35
STATED ODDS 1:12		

FAS1 Derek Jeter	12.00	5.50
FAS2 Andruw Jones	5.00	2.20
FAS3 Vladimir Guerrero	6.00	2.70
FAS4 Scott Rolen	6.00	2.70
FAS5 Jose Guillen	2.00	.90
FAS6 Jose Cruz Jr.	3.00	1.35
FAS7 Darin Erstad	3.00	1.35
FAS8 Tony Clark	2.00	.90
FAS9 Scott Spiezio	1.00	.45
FAS10 Kevin Orie	1.00	.45
FAS11 Calvin Reese	1.50	.70
FAS12 Billy Wagner	1.50	.70
FAS13 Matt Morris	1.00	.45
FAS14 Jeremi Gonzalez	1.50	.70
FAS15 Hideki Irabu	3.00	1.35

1997 Topps Stars Rookie Reprints

	MINT	NRMT
COMPLETE SET (15)	60.00	27.00
COMMON CARD (1-15)	4.00	1.80
STATED ODDS 1:6		

1 Luis Aparicio	4.00	1.80
2 Richie Ashburn	4.00	1.80
3 Jim Bunning	4.00	1.80
4 Bob Feller	4.00	1.80
5 Rollie Fingers	4.00	1.80
6 Monte Irvin	4.00	1.80
7 Al Kaline	6.00	2.70
8 Ralph Kiner	4.00	1.80
9 Eddie Mathews	5.00	2.20
10 Hal Newhouser	4.00	1.80
11 Gaylord Perry	4.00	1.80
12 Robin Roberts	4.00	1.80
13 Brooks Robinson	5.00	2.20
14 Enos Slaughter	4.00	1.80
15 Earl Weaver	4.00	1.80

1997 Topps Stars Rookie Reprint Autographs

	MINT	NRMT
COMPLETE SET (14)	450.00	200.00
COMMON CARD (1/3-15)	20.00	9.00
STATED ODDS 1:30		
CARD NO.2 DOES NOT EXIST		

1 Luis Aparicio	40.00	18.00
3 Jim Bunning	50.00	22.00
4 Bob Feller	40.00	18.00
5 Rollie Fingers	25.00	11.00
6 Monte Irvin	20.00	9.00
7 Al Kaline	60.00	27.00
8 Ralph Kiner	30.00	13.50
9 Eddie Mathews	50.00	22.00
10 Hal Newhouser	20.00	9.00
11 Gaylord Perry	25.00	11.00
12 Robin Roberts	30.00	13.50
13 Brooks Robinson	50.00	22.00
14 Enos Slaughter	30.00	13.50
15 Earl Weaver	25.00	11.00

1998 Topps Stars

	MINT	NRMT
COMP.RED SET (150)	80.00	36.00
COMMON RED (1-150)	.40	.18
RED MINOR STARS	.60	.25
RED SEMISTARS	1.00	.45
RED UNLISTED STARS	1.50	.70
COMP.BRONZE SET (150)	80.00	36.00
COMMON BRONZE (1-150)	.40	.18
*BRONZE: SAME VALUE AS RED		
BRONZE PRINT RUN 9799 SERIAL #'d SETS		
COMP.SILVER SET (150)	200.00	90.00
COMMON SILVER (1-150)	.75	.35
*SILVER STARS: .75X TO 2X HI COLUMN		
*SILVER YOUNG STARS: .6X TO 1.5X HI		
SILVER: RANDOM INSERTS IN PACKS		
SILVER PRINT RUN 4399 SERIAL #'d SETS		
COMP.GOLD SET (150)	400.00	180.00
COMMON GOLD (1-150)	1.25	.55
*GOLD STARS: 1.25X TO 3X HI COLUMN		
*GOLD YOUNG STARS: 1X TO 2.5X HI		
GOLD STATED ODDS 1:2		
GOLD PRINT RUN 2299 SERIAL #'d SETS		
COMMON GOLD RBW (1-150)	10.00	4.50
*GOLD RBW.STARS: 10X TO 25X HI COL.		
*GOLD RBW.YNG.STARS: 8X TO 20X HI		
GOLD RAINBOW STATED ODDS 1:46		
GOLD RBW.PRINT RUN 99 SERIAL #'d SETS		
RED CARDS PRICED BELOW!		

1 Greg Maddux	4.00	1.80
2 Darryl Kile	.40	.18
3 Rod Beck	.60	.25
4 Ellis Burks	.60	.25
5 Gary Sheffield	.60	.25
6 David Ortiz	.40	.18
7 Marquis Grissom	.40	.18
8 Tony Womack	.40	.18
9 Mike Mussina	1.50	.70
10 Bernie Williams	1.50	.70
11 Andy Benes	.40	.18
12 Rusty Greer	.60	.25
13 Carlos Delgado	1.50	.70
14 Jim Edmonds	.60	.25
15 Raul Mondesi	.60	.25
16 Andres Galarraga	1.00	.45
17 Wade Boggs	1.50	.70
18 Paul O'Neill	.60	.25
19 Edgar Renteria	.40	.18
20 Tony Clark	.60	.25
21 Vladimir Guerrero	2.00	.90
22 Moises Alou	.60	.25
23 Bernard Gilkey	.40	.18
24 Lance Johnson	.40	.18
25 Ben Grieve	1.50	.70
26 Sandy Alomar Jr.	.60	.25
27 Ray Durham	.60	.25
28 Shawn Estes	.40	.18
29 David Segui	.40	.18
30 Javy Lopez	.60	.25
31 Steve Finley	.60	.25
32 Rey Ordonez	.60	.25
33 Derek Jeter	5.00	2.20
34 Henry Rodriguez	.40	.18
35 Mo Vaughn	1.50	.70
36 Richard Hidalgo	.60	.25
37 Omar Vizquel	.60	.25
38 Johnny Damon	.60	.25
39 Brian Hunter	.40	.18
40 Matt Williams	1.50	.70
41 Chuck Finley	.60	.25
42 Jeromy Burnitz	.60	.25
43 Livan Hernandez	.40	.18
44 Delino DeShields	.40	.18
45 Charles Nagy	.60	.25
46 Scott Rolen	2.00	.90
47 Neifi Perez	.60	.25
48 John Wetteland	.60	.25
49 Eric Milton	.40	.18
50 Mike Piazza	5.00	2.20
51 Cal Ripken	6.00	2.70
52 Mariano Rivera	.60	.25
53 Butch Huskey	.40	.18
54 Quinton McCracken	.40	.18
55 Jose Cruz Jr.	.60	.25
56 Brian Jordan	.60	.25

57 Hideo Nomo	1.50	.70
58 Masato Yoshii	1.00	.45
59 Cliff Floyd	.60	.25
60 Jose Guillen	.40	.18
61 Jeff Shaw	.40	.18
62 Edgar Martinez	.60	.25
63 Rondell White	.60	.25
64 Hal Morris	.40	.18
65 Barry Larkin	1.50	.70
66 Eric Young	.40	.18
67 Ray Lankford	.60	.25
68 Derek Bell	.60	.25
69 Charles Johnson	.60	.25
70 Robin Ventura	.60	.25
71 Chuck Knoblauch	.60	.25
72 Kevin Brown	1.00	.45
73 Jose Valentin	.40	.18
74 Jay Buhner	.60	.25
75 Tony Gwynn	4.00	1.80
76 Andy Pettitte	.60	.25
77 Edgardo Alfonzo	1.00	.45
78 Kerry Wood	2.00	.90
79 Darin Erstad	1.00	.45
80 Paul Konerko	.60	.25
81 Jason Kendall	.60	.25
82 Tino Martinez	.60	.25
83 Brad Radke	.60	.25
84 Jeff King	.40	.18
85 Travis Lee	1.00	.45
86 Jeff Kent	.60	.25
87 Trevor Hoffman	.60	.25
88 David Cone	1.00	.45
89 Jose Canseco	2.00	.90
90 Juan Gonzalez	3.00	1.35
91 Todd Hundley	.60	.25
92 John Valentin	.60	.25
93 Sammy Sosa	5.00	2.20
94 Jason Giambi	.60	.25
95 Chipper Jones	4.00	1.80
96 Jeff Blauser	.40	.18
97 Brad Fullmer	.40	.18
98 Derek Lee	.40	.18
99 Denny Neagle	.40	.18
100 Ken Griffey Jr.	8.00	3.60
101 David Justice	.60	.25
102 Tim Salmon	1.00	.45
103 J.T. Snow	.60	.25
104 Fred McGriff	1.00	.45
105 Brady Anderson	.60	.25
106 Larry Walker	1.50	.70
107 Jeff Cirillo	.60	.25
108 Andruw Jones	1.50	.70
109 Manny Ramirez	2.00	.90
110 Justin Thompson	.40	.18
111 Vinny Castilla	.60	.25
112 Chan Ho Park	.60	.25
113 Mark Grudzielanek	.40	.18
114 Mark Grace	.60	.25
115 Ken Caminiti	.60	.25
116 Ryan Klesko	.60	.25
117 Rafael Palmeiro	1.50	.70
118 Pat Hentgen	.40	.18
119 Eric Karros	.60	.25
120 Randy Johnson	1.50	.70
121 Roberto Alomar	1.50	.70
122 John Olerud	.60	.25
123 Paul Molitor	1.50	.70
124 Dean Palmer	.60	.25
125 Nomar Garciaparra	5.00	2.20
126 Curt Schilling	1.00	.45
127 Jay Bell	.60	.25
128 Craig Biggio	1.50	.70
129 Marty Cordova	.40	.18
130 Ivan Rodriguez	2.00	.90
131 Todd Helton	2.00	.90
132 Jim Thome	1.50	.70
133 Albert Belle	1.50	.70
134 Mike Lansing	.40	.18
135 Mark McGwire	10.00	4.50
136 Roger Clemens	4.00	1.80
137 Tom Glavine	1.50	.70
138 Ron Gant	.60	.25
139 Alex Rodriguez	5.00	2.20
140 Jeff Bagwell	2.00	.90
141 John Smoltz	1.00	.45
142 Kenny Lofton	1.00	.45
143 Dante Bichette	.60	.25
144 Pedro Martinez	2.00	.90
145 Barry Bonds	2.00	.90
146 Travis Fryman	.60	.25
147 Bobby Jones	.40	.18
148 Bobby Higginson	.60	.25
149 Reggie Sanders	.40	.18
150 Frank Thomas	3.00	1.35

1998 Topps Stars Galaxy Bronze

	MINT	NRMT
COMPLETE SET (10)	600.00	275.00
COMMON CARD (G1-G10)	15.00	6.75
UNLISTED STARS	40.00	18.00

BRONZE STATED ODDS 1:682
BRONZE PRINT RUN 100 SERIAL #'d SETS
SILVER STATED ODDS 1:910
*SILVER: .5X TO 1.2X HI COLUMN
SILVER PRINT RUN 75 SERIAL #'d SETS
*GOLD: .6X TO 1.5X HI COLUMN
GOLD STATED ODDS 1:1364
GOLD PRINT RUN 50 SERIAL #'d SETS
GOLD RAINBOW STATED ODDS 1:13643
GOLD RBW.PRINT RUN 5 SERIAL #'d SETS
BRONZE CARDS LISTED BELOW!

G1 Barry Bonds	50.00	22.00
G2 Jeff Bagwell	50.00	22.00
G3 Nomar Garciaparra	120.00	55.00
G4 Chipper Jones	100.00	45.00
G5 Ken Griffey Jr.	200.00	90.00
G6 Sammy Sosa	120.00	55.00
G7 Larry Walker	40.00	18.00
G8 Alex Rodriguez	120.00	55.00
G9 Craig Biggio	40.00	18.00
G10 Raul Mondesi	20.00	9.00

1998 Topps Stars Luminaries Bronze

	MINT	NRMT
COMPLETE SET (15)	1000.00	450.00
COMMON CARD (L1-L15)	15.00	6.75
SEMISTARS	25.00	11.00
UNLISTED STARS	30.00	13.50

BRONZE STATED ODDS 1:455
BRONZE PRINT RUN 100 SERIAL #'d SETS
*SILVER: .5X TO 1.2X HI COLUMN
SILVER STATED ODDS 1:606
SILVER PRINT RUN 75 SERIAL #'d SETS
*GOLD: .6X TO 1.5X HI COLUMN
GOLD STATED ODDS 1:910
GOLD PRINT RUN 50 SERIAL #'d SETS
GOLD RAINBOW STATED ODDS 1:9095
GOLD RBW.PRINT RUN 5 SERIAL #'d SETS

L1 Ken Griffey Jr.	200.00	90.00
L2 Mark McGwire	250.00	110.00
L3 Juan Gonzalez	80.00	36.00
L4 Tony Gwynn	100.00	45.00
L5 Frank Thomas	80.00	36.00
L6 Mike Piazza	120.00	55.00
L7 Chuck Knoblauch	20.00	9.00
L8 Kenny Lofton	25.00	11.00
L9 Barry Bonds	50.00	22.00
L10 Matt Williams	30.00	13.50
L11 Raul Mondesi	20.00	9.00
L12 Ivan Rodriguez	50.00	22.00
L13 Alex Rodriguez	120.00	55.00
L14 Nomar Garciaparra	120.00	55.00
L15 Ken Caminiti	20.00	9.00

1998 Topps Stars Rookie Reprints

	MINT	NRMT
COMPLETE SET (5)	40.00	18.00
COMMON CARD (1-5)	6.00	2.70
STATED ODDS 1:24		

1 Johnny Bench	10.00	4.50
2 Whitey Ford	6.00	2.70
3 Joe Morgan	6.00	2.70
4 Mike Schmidt	12.00	5.50
5 Carl Yastrzemski	10.00	4.50

1998 Topps Stars Rookie Reprints Autographs

	MINT	NRMT
COMPLETE SET (5)	400.00	180.00
COMMON CARD (1-5)	60.00	27.00
STATED ODDS 1:273		

1 Johnny Bench	100.00	45.00
2 Whitey Ford	60.00	27.00

		MINT	NRMT
❏ 3	Joe Morgan	60.00	27.00
❏ 4	Mike Schmidt	120.00	55.00
❏ 5	Carl Yastrzemski	100.00	45.00

1998 Topps Stars
Supernovas Bronze

	MINT	NRMT
COMPLETE SET (10)	250.00	110.00
COMMON CARD (S1-S10)	12.00	5.50
MINOR STARS	20.00	9.00
BRONZE STATED ODDS 1:682
BRONZE PRINT RUN 100 SERIAL #'d SETS
*SILVER: .5X TO 1.2X HI COLUMN
SILVER STATED ODDS 1:910
SILVER PRINT RUN 75 SERIAL #'d SETS
*GOLD: .6X TO 1.5X HI COLUMN
GOLD STATED ODDS 1:1364
GOLD PRINT RUN 50 SERIAL #'d SETS
GOLD RAINBOW STATED ODDS 1:13643
GOLD RBW.PRINT RUN 5 SERIAL #'d SETS

		MINT	NRMT
❏ S1	Ben Grieve	40.00	18.00
❏ S2	Travis Lee	30.00	13.50
❏ S3	Todd Helton	50.00	22.00
❏ S4	Adrian Beltre	40.00	18.00
❏ S5	Derek Lee	12.00	5.50
❏ S6	David Ortiz	12.00	5.50
❏ S7	Brad Fullmer	12.00	5.50
❏ S8	Mark Kotsay	20.00	9.00
❏ S9	Paul Konerko	20.00	9.00
❏ S10	Kerry Wood	40.00	18.00

1999 Topps Stars

	MINT	NRMT
COMPLETE SET (180)	120.00	55.00
COMMON CARD (1-180)	.50	.14
MINOR STARS	.50	.23
SEMISTARS	.75	.35
UNLISTED STARS	1.25	.55
THREE BASIC CARDS PER PACK
SUBSET CARDS HALF VALUE OF BASE CARDS
*FOIL STARS: 3X TO 8X BASIC CARDS
*FOIL ROOKIES: 2.5X TO 6X BASIC CARDS
FOIL ODDS 1:15
FOIL PRINT RUN 299 SERIAL #'d SETS

❏ 1	Ken Griffey Jr.	6.00	2.70
❏ 2	Chipper Jones	3.00	1.35
❏ 3	Mike Piazza	4.00	1.80
❏ 4	Nomar Garciaparra	4.00	1.80
❏ 5	Derek Jeter	4.00	1.80
❏ 6	Frank Thomas	2.50	1.10
❏ 7	Ben Grieve	1.25	.55
❏ 8	Mark McGwire	8.00	3.60
❏ 9	Sammy Sosa	4.00	1.80
❏ 10	Alex Rodriguez	4.00	1.80
❏ 11	Troy Glaus	1.25	.55
❏ 12	Eric Chavez	.75	.35
❏ 13	Kerry Wood	1.25	.55
❏ 14	Barry Bonds	1.50	.70
❏ 15	Vladimir Guerrero	1.50	.70
❏ 16	Albert Belle	1.25	.55
❏ 17	Juan Gonzalez	3.00	1.35
❏ 18	Roger Clemens	1.50	1.35
❏ 19	Ruben Mateo	1.25	.55
❏ 20	Cal Ripken	5.00	2.20
❏ 21	Darin Erstad	.75	.35
❏ 22	Jeff Bagwell	1.50	.70
❏ 23	Roy Halladay	.50	.23
❏ 24	Todd Helton	1.25	.55
❏ 25	Michael Barrett	.75	.35
❏ 26	Manny Ramirez	1.50	.70
❏ 27	Fernando Seguignol	.50	.23
❏ 28	Pat Burrell	5.00	2.20
❏ 29	Andruw Jones	1.25	.55
❏ 30	Randy Johnson	1.25	.55
❏ 31	Jose Canseco	1.50	.70
❏ 32	Brad Fullmer	.30	.14
❏ 33	Alex Escobar	2.50	1.10
❏ 34	Alfonso Soriano	5.00	2.20
❏ 35	Larry Walker	1.25	.55
❏ 36	Matt Clement	.50	.23
❏ 37	Mo Vaughn	1.25	.55
❏ 38	Bruce Chen	.50	.23
❏ 39	Travis Lee	.75	.35
❏ 40	Adrian Beltre	1.25	.55
❏ 41	Alex Gonzalez	.50	.23
❏ 42	Jason Tyner	.75	.35
❏ 43	George Lombard	.50	.23
❏ 44	Scott Rolen	1.50	.70
❏ 45	Mark Mulder	2.00	.90
❏ 46	Gabe Kapler	1.25	.55
❏ 47	Choo Freeman	1.00	.45
❏ 48	Tony Gwynn	3.00	1.35
❏ 49	A.J. Burnett	1.25	.55
❏ 50	Matt Belisle	.60	.25
❏ 51	Greg Maddux	3.00	1.35
❏ 52	John Smoltz	.75	.35
❏ 53	Mark Grace	.75	.35
❏ 54	Wade Boggs	1.25	.55
❏ 55	Bernie Williams	1.25	.55
❏ 56	Pedro Martinez	1.50	.70
❏ 57	Barry Larkin	1.25	.55
❏ 58	Orlando Hernandez	1.25	.55
❏ 59	Jason Kendall	.50	.23
❏ 60	Mark Kotsay	.30	.14
❏ 61	Jim Thome	1.25	.55
❏ 62	Gary Sheffield	.50	.23
❏ 63	Preston Wilson	.50	.23
❏ 64	Rafael Palmeiro	1.25	.55
❏ 65	David Wells	.50	.23
❏ 66	Shawn Green	1.25	.55
❏ 67	Tom Glavine	1.25	.55
❏ 68	Jeromy Burnitz	.50	.23
❏ 69	Kevin Brown	.75	.35
❏ 70	Rondell White	.50	.23
❏ 71	Roberto Alomar	1.25	.55
❏ 72	Cliff Floyd	.50	.23
❏ 73	Craig Biggio	1.25	.55
❏ 74	Greg Vaughn	.50	.23
❏ 75	Ivan Rodriguez	1.50	.70
❏ 76	Vinny Castilla	.50	.23
❏ 77	Todd Walker	.50	.23
❏ 78	Paul Konerko	.50	.23
❏ 79	Andy Brown	.75	.35
❏ 80	Todd Hundley	.50	.23
❏ 81	Dmitri Young	.50	.23
❏ 82	Tony Clark	.50	.23
❏ 83	Nick Johnson	4.00	1.80
❏ 84	Mike Caruso	.30	.14
❏ 85	David Ortiz	.30	.14
❏ 86	Matt Williams	1.25	.55
❏ 87	Raul Mondesi	.50	.23
❏ 88	Kenny Lofton	.75	.35
❏ 89	Miguel Tejada	.50	.23
❏ 90	Dante Bichette	.50	.23
❏ 91	Jorge Posada	.30	.14
❏ 92	Carlos Beltran	1.50	.70
❏ 93	Carlos Delgado	1.25	.55
❏ 94	Javy Lopez	.50	.23
❏ 95	Aramis Ramirez	.75	.35
❏ 96	Neifi Perez	.50	.23
❏ 97	Marlon Anderson	.30	.14
❏ 98	David Cone	.75	.35
❏ 99	Moises Alou	.50	.23
❏ 100	John Olerud	.50	.23
❏ 101	Tim Salmon	.75	.35
❏ 102	Jason Giambi	.50	.23
❏ 103	Sandy Alomar Jr.	.50	.23
❏ 104	Curt Schilling	.75	.35
❏ 105	Andres Galarraga	.75	.35
❏ 106	Rusty Greer	.50	.23
❏ 107	Bobby Seay	.75	.35
❏ 108	Eric Young	.30	.14
❏ 109	Brian Jordan	.50	.23
❏ 110	Eric Davis	.50	.23
❏ 111	Will Clark	1.25	.55
❏ 112	Andy Ashby	.30	.14
❏ 113	Edgardo Alfonzo	.75	.35
❏ 114	Paul O'Neill	.50	.23
❏ 115	Denny Neagle	.50	.14
❏ 116	Eric Karros	.50	.23
❏ 117	Ken Caminiti	.50	.23
❏ 118	Garret Anderson	.50	.23
❏ 119	Todd Stottlemyre	.30	.14
❏ 120	David Justice	.50	.23
❏ 121	Francisco Cordova	.30	.14
❏ 122	Robin Ventura	.50	.23
❏ 123	Mike Mussina	1.25	.55
❏ 124	Hideki Irabu	.50	.23
❏ 125	Justin Thompson	.30	.14
❏ 126	Mariano Rivera	.50	.23
❏ 127	Delino DeShields	.30	.14
❏ 128	Steve Finley	.50	.23
❏ 129	Jose Cruz Jr	.50	.23
❏ 130	Ray Lankford	.50	.23
❏ 131	Jim Edmonds	.50	.23
❏ 132	Charles Johnson	.50	.23
❏ 133	Al Leiter	.50	.23
❏ 134	Jose Offerman	.50	.23
❏ 135	Eric Milton	.30	.14
❏ 136	Dean Palmer	.50	.23
❏ 137	Johnny Damon	.50	.23
❏ 138	Andy Pettitte	.50	.23
❏ 139	Ray Durham	.50	.23
❏ 140	Ugueth Urbina	.30	.14
❏ 141	Marquis Grissom	.30	.14
❏ 142	Ryan Klesko	.50	.23
❏ 143	Brady Anderson	.50	.23
❏ 144	Bobby Higginson	.50	.23
❏ 145	Chuck Knoblauch	.50	.23
❏ 146	Rickey Henderson	1.50	.70
❏ 147	Kevin Millwood	.75	.35
❏ 148	Fred McGriff	.75	.35
❏ 149	Damion Easley	.50	.23
❏ 150	Tino Martinez	.50	.23
❏ 151	Greg Maddux LUM	1.50	.70
❏ 152	Scott Rolen LUM	1.25	.55
❏ 153	Pat Burrell LUM	1.50	.70
❏ 154	Roger Clemens LUM	1.50	.70
❏ 155	Albert Belle LUM	.50	.23
❏ 156	Troy Glaus LUM	.50	.23
❏ 157	Cal Ripken LUM	2.50	1.10
❏ 158	Alfonso Soriano LUM	1.50	.70
❏ 159	Manny Ramirez LUM	.75	.35
❏ 160	Eric Chavez LUM	.50	.23
❏ 161	Kerry Wood LUM	.50	.23
❏ 162	Tony Gwynn LUM	1.50	.70
❏ 163	Barry Bonds LUM	.75	.35
❏ 164	Ruben Mateo LUM	.50	.23
❏ 165	Todd Helton LUM	.50	.23
❏ 166	Darin Erstad LUM	.50	.23
❏ 167	Jeff Bagwell LUM	.75	.35
❏ 168	Juan Gonzalez LUM	1.25	.55
❏ 169	Mo Vaughn LUM	.50	.23
❏ 170	Vladimir Guerrero LUM	.75	.35
❏ 171	Nomar Garciaparra SUP	2.00	.90
❏ 172	Derek Jeter SUP	2.00	.90
❏ 173	Alex Rodriguez SUP	2.00	.90

	MINT	NRMT
❏ 174 Ben Grieve SUP .50		.23
❏ 175 Mike Piazza SUP 2.00		.90
❏ 176 Chipper Jones SUP 1.50		.70
❏ 177 Frank Thomas SUP 1.25		.55
❏ 178 Ken Griffey Jr. SUP 3.00		1.35
❏ 179 Sammy Sosa SUP 2.00		.90
❏ 180 Mark McGwire SUP 4.00		1.80

1999 Topps Stars One Star

	MINT	NRMT
COMPLETE SET (100)	40.00	18.00
COMMON CARD (1-100)	.20	.09
MINOR STARS	.30	.14
SEMISTARS	.50	.23
UNLISTED STARS	.75	.35

TWO PER PACK
*FOIL STARS: 6X TO 15X HI
*FOIL ROOKIES: 5X TO 12X HI
FOIL STATED ODDS 1:33
FOIL PRINT RUN 249 SERIAL #'d SETS

		MINT	NRMT
❏ 1	Ken Griffey Jr.	4.00	1.80
❏ 2	Chipper Jones	2.00	.90
❏ 3	Mike Piazza	2.50	1.10
❏ 4	Nomar Garciaparra	2.50	1.10
❏ 5	Derek Jeter	2.50	1.10
❏ 6	Frank Thomas	1.50	.70
❏ 7	Ben Grieve	.75	.35
❏ 8	Mark McGwire	5.00	2.20
❏ 9	Sammy Sosa	2.50	1.10
❏ 10	Alex Rodriguez	2.50	1.10
❏ 11	Troy Glaus	.75	.35
❏ 12	Eric Chavez	.50	.23
❏ 13	Kerry Wood	.75	.35
❏ 14	Barry Bonds	1.00	.45
❏ 15	Vladimir Guerrero	1.00	.45
❏ 16	Albert Belle	.75	.35
❏ 17	Juan Gonzalez	1.50	.70
❏ 18	Roger Clemens	2.00	.90
❏ 19	Ruben Mateo	.75	.35
❏ 20	Cal Ripken	3.00	1.35
❏ 21	Darin Erstad	.50	.23
❏ 22	Jeff Bagwell	1.00	.45
❏ 23	Roy Halladay	.30	.14
❏ 24	Todd Helton	.75	.35
❏ 25	Michael Barrett	.50	.23
❏ 26	Manny Ramirez	1.00	.45
❏ 27	Fernando Seguignol	.30	.14
❏ 28	Pat Burrell	3.00	1.35
❏ 29	Andruw Jones	.75	.35
❏ 30	Randy Johnson	.75	.35
❏ 31	Jose Canseco	1.00	.45
❏ 32	Brad Fullmer	.20	.09
❏ 33	Alex Escobar	1.50	.70
❏ 34	Alfonso Soriano	3.00	1.35
❏ 35	Larry Walker	.75	.35
❏ 36	Matt Clement	.30	.14
❏ 37	Mo Vaughn	.75	.35
❏ 38	Bruce Chen	.30	.14
❏ 39	Travis Lee	.50	.23
❏ 40	Adrian Beltre	.75	.35
❏ 41	Alex Gonzalez	.30	.14
❏ 42	Jason Tyner	.50	.23
❏ 43	George Lombard	.30	.14
❏ 44	Scott Rolen	1.00	.45
❏ 45	Mark Mulder	1.25	.55
❏ 46	Gabe Kapler	.75	.35
❏ 47	Choo Freeman	.60	.25
❏ 48	Tony Gwynn	2.00	.90
❏ 49	A.J. Burnett	.75	.35
❏ 50	Matt Belisle	.50	.23
❏ 51	Greg Maddux	2.00	.90
❏ 52	John Smoltz	.50	.23
❏ 53	Mark Grace	.50	.23
❏ 54	Wade Boggs	.75	.35
❏ 55	Bernie Williams	.75	.35
❏ 56	Pedro Martinez	1.00	.45
❏ 57	Barry Larkin	.75	.35
❏ 58	Orlando Hernandez	.75	.35
❏ 59	Jason Kendall	.30	.14
❏ 60	Mark Kotsay	.20	.09
❏ 61	Jim Thome	.75	.35
❏ 62	Gary Sheffield	.30	.14
❏ 63	Preston Wilson	.30	.14
❏ 64	Rafael Palmeiro	.75	.35
❏ 65	David Wells	.30	.14
❏ 66	Shawn Green	.75	.35
❏ 67	Tom Glavine	.75	.35
❏ 68	Jeromy Burnitz	.30	.14
❏ 69	Kevin Brown	.50	.23
❏ 70	Rondell White	.30	.14
❏ 71	Roberto Alomar	.75	.35
❏ 72	Cliff Floyd	.30	.14
❏ 73	Craig Biggio	.75	.35
❏ 74	Greg Vaughn	.30	.14
❏ 75	Ivan Rodriguez	1.00	.45
❏ 76	Vinny Castilla	.30	.14
❏ 77	Todd Walker	.30	.14
❏ 78	Paul Konerko	.30	.14
❏ 79	Andy Brown	.50	.23
❏ 80	Todd Hundley	.30	.14
❏ 81	Dmitri Young	.30	.14
❏ 82	Tony Clark	.30	.14
❏ 83	Nick Johnson	2.50	1.10
❏ 84	Mike Caruso	.20	.09
❏ 85	David Ortiz	.20	.09
❏ 86	Matt Williams	.75	.35
❏ 87	Raul Mondesi	.30	.14
❏ 88	Kenny Lofton	.50	.23
❏ 89	Miguel Tejada	.30	.14
❏ 90	Dante Bichette	.30	.14
❏ 91	Jorge Posada	.20	.09
❏ 92	Carlos Beltran	1.00	.45
❏ 93	Carlos Delgado	.75	.35
❏ 94	Javy Lopez	.30	.14
❏ 95	Aramis Ramirez	.50	.23
❏ 96	Neifi Perez	.30	.14
❏ 97	Marlon Anderson	.20	.09
❏ 98	David Cone	.50	.23
❏ 99	Moises Alou	.30	.14
❏ 100	John Olerud	.30	.14

1999 Topps Stars Two Star

	MINT	NRMT
COMPLETE SET (50)	30.00	13.50
COMMON CARD (1-50)	.20	.09
MINOR STARS	.30	.14
SEMISTARS	.50	.23
UNLISTED STARS	.75	.35

ONE PER PACK
*FOIL STARS: 8X TO 20X HI
*FOIL ROOKIES: 6X TO 15X HI
FOIL ODDS 1:82
FOIL PRINT RUN 199 SERIAL #'d SETS

		MINT	NRMT
❏ 1	Ken Griffey Jr.	4.00	1.80
❏ 2	Chipper Jones	2.00	.90
❏ 3	Mike Piazza	2.50	1.10
❏ 4	Nomar Garciaparra	2.50	1.10
❏ 5	Derek Jeter	2.50	1.10
❏ 6	Frank Thomas	1.50	.70
❏ 7	Ben Grieve	.75	.35
❏ 8	Mark McGwire	5.00	2.20
❏ 9	Sammy Sosa	2.50	1.10
❏ 10	Alex Rodriguez	2.50	1.10
❏ 11	Troy Glaus	.75	.35
❏ 12	Eric Chavez	.50	.23
❏ 13	Kerry Wood	.75	.35
❏ 14	Barry Bonds	1.00	.45
❏ 15	Vladimir Guerrero	1.00	.45
❏ 16	Albert Belle	.75	.35
❏ 17	Juan Gonzalez	1.50	.70
❏ 18	Roger Clemens	2.00	.90
❏ 19	Ruben Mateo	.75	.35
❏ 20	Cal Ripken	3.00	1.35
❏ 21	Darin Erstad	.50	.23
❏ 22	Jeff Bagwell	1.00	.45
❏ 23	Roy Halladay	.30	.14
❏ 24	Todd Helton	.75	.35
❏ 25	Michael Barrett	.50	.23
❏ 26	Manny Ramirez	1.00	.45
❏ 27	Fernando Seguignol	.30	.14
❏ 28	Pat Burrell	3.00	1.35
❏ 29	Andruw Jones	.75	.35
❏ 30	Randy Johnson	.75	.35
❏ 31	Jose Canseco	1.00	.45
❏ 32	Brad Fullmer	.20	.09
❏ 33	Alex Escobar	1.50	.70
❏ 34	Alfonso Soriano	3.00	1.35
❏ 35	Larry Walker	.75	.35
❏ 36	Matt Clement	.30	.14
❏ 37	Mo Vaughn	.75	.35
❏ 38	Bruce Chen	.30	.14
❏ 39	Travis Lee	.50	.23
❏ 40	Adrian Beltre	.75	.35
❏ 41	Alex Gonzalez	.30	.14
❏ 42	Jason Tyner	.50	.23
❏ 43	George Lombard	.30	.14
❏ 44	Scott Rolen	1.00	.45
❏ 45	Mark Mulder	1.25	.55
❏ 46	Gabe Kapler	.75	.35
❏ 47	Choo Freeman	.60	.25
❏ 48	Tony Gwynn	2.00	.90
❏ 49	A.J. Burnett	.75	.35
❏ 50	Matt Belisle	.50	.23

1999 Topps Stars Three Star

	MINT	NRMT
COMPLETE SET (20)	50.00	22.00
COMMON CARD (1-20)	1.00	.45
UNLISTED STARS	1.50	.70

*FOIL STARS: 8X TO 20X HI COLUMN
FOIL STATED ODDS 1:5
FOIL PRINT RUN 99 SERIAL #'d SETS

		MINT	NRMT
❏ 1	Ken Griffey Jr.	8.00	3.60
❏ 2	Chipper Jones	4.00	1.80

	MINT	NRMT
☐ 3 Mike Piazza	5.00	2.20
☐ 4 Nomar Garciaparra	5.00	2.20
☐ 5 Derek Jeter	5.00	2.20
☐ 6 Frank Thomas	3.00	1.35
☐ 7 Ben Grieve	1.50	.70
☐ 8 Mark McGwire	10.00	4.50
☐ 9 Sammy Sosa	5.00	2.20
☐ 10 Alex Rodriguez	5.00	2.20
☐ 11 Troy Glaus	1.50	.70
☐ 12 Eric Chavez	1.00	.45
☐ 13 Kerry Wood	1.50	.70
☐ 14 Barry Bonds	2.00	.90
☐ 15 Vladimir Guerrero	2.00	.90
☐ 16 Albert Belle	1.50	.70
☐ 17 Juan Gonzalez	3.00	1.35
☐ 18 Roger Clemens	4.00	1.80
☐ 19 Ruben Mateo	1.50	.70
☐ 20 Cal Ripken	6.00	2.70

1999 Topps Stars Four Star

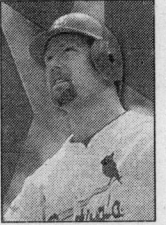

	MINT	NRMT
COMPLETE SET (10)	40.00	18.00
COMMON CARD (1-10)	1.50	.70
STATED ODDS 1:10		

*FOIL: 12.5X TO 30X HI COLUMN
FOIL STATED ODDS 1:1650
FOIL PRINT RUN 49 SERIAL #'d SETS

	MINT	NRMT
☐ 1 Ken Griffey Jr.	8.00	3.60
☐ 2 Chipper Jones	4.00	1.80
☐ 3 Mike Piazza	5.00	2.20
☐ 4 Nomar Garciaparra	5.00	2.20
☐ 5 Derek Jeter	5.00	2.20
☐ 6 Frank Thomas	3.00	1.35
☐ 7 Ben Grieve	1.50	.70
☐ 8 Mark McGwire	10.00	4.50
☐ 9 Sammy Sosa	5.00	2.20
☐ 10 Alex Rodriguez	5.00	2.20

1999 Topps Stars Bright Futures

	MINT	NRMT
COMPLETE SET (10)	50.00	22.00
COMMON CARD (BF1-BF10)	3.00	1.35
SEMISTARS	5.00	2.20
UNLISTED STARS	6.00	2.70
STATED ODDS 1:41		

STATED PRINT RUN 1999 SERIAL #'d SETS
*FOIL: 4X TO 10X HI COLUMN
FOIL ODDS 1:2702
FOIL PRINT RUN 30 SERIAL #'d SETS

	MINT	NRMT
☐ BF1 Troy Glaus	8.00	3.60
☐ BF2 Eric Chavez	5.00	2.20
☐ BF3 Adrian Beltre	6.00	2.70
☐ BF4 Michael Barrett	5.00	2.20
☐ BF5 Gabe Kapler	6.00	2.70
☐ BF6 Alex Gonzalez	3.00	1.35
☐ BF7 Matt Clement	3.00	1.35
☐ BF8 Pat Burrell	15.00	6.75
☐ BF9 Ruben Mateo	6.00	2.70
☐ BF10 Alfonso Soriano	15.00	6.75

1999 Topps Stars Galaxy

	MINT	NRMT
COMPLETE SET (10)	150.00	70.00
COMMON CARD (G1-G10)	4.00	1.80
UNLISTED STARS	5.00	2.20
STATED ODDS 1:41		

*FOIL: 4X TO 10X HI COLUMN
FOIL ODDS 1:2702
FOIL PRINT RUN 30 SERIAL #'d SETS

	MINT	NRMT
☐ G1 Mark McGwire	40.00	18.00
☐ G2 Roger Clemens	15.00	6.75
☐ G3 Nomar Garciaparra	20.00	9.00
☐ G4 Alex Rodriguez	20.00	9.00
☐ G5 Kerry Wood	5.00	2.20
☐ G6 Ben Grieve	4.00	1.80
☐ G7 Derek Jeter	20.00	9.00
☐ G8 Vladimir Guerrero	8.00	3.60
☐ G9 Ken Griffey Jr.	30.00	13.50
☐ G10 Sammy Sosa	20.00	9.00

1999 Topps Stars Rookie Reprints

	MINT	NRMT
COMPLETE SET (5)	80.00	36.00
COMMON CARD (1-5)	15.00	6.75
STATED ODDS 1:65		

	MINT	NRMT
☐ 1 Frank Robinson	15.00	6.75
☐ 2 Ernie Banks	20.00	9.00
☐ 3 Yogi Berra	20.00	9.00

	MINT	NRMT
☐ 4 Bob Gibson	15.00	6.75
☐ 5 Tom Seaver	25.00	11.00

1999 Topps Stars Rookie Reprints Autographs

	MINT	NRMT
STATED ODDS 1:406		
BANKS STATED ODDS 1:812		
☐ 1 Frank Robinson	80.00	36.00
☐ 2 Ernie Banks	100.00	45.00
☐ 3 Yogi Berra	100.00	45.00
☐ 4 Bob Gibson	80.00	36.00
☐ 5 Tom Seaver	120.00	55.00

1998 Topps Stars 'N Steel

	MINT	NRMT
COMPLETE SET (44)	180.00	80.00
COMMON CARD (1-44)	2.00	.90
SEMISTARS	3.00	1.35
UNLISTED STARS	5.00	2.20

*GOLD STARS: 1.5X TO 4X HI COLUMN
GOLD STATED ODDS 1:12
*HOLO.STARS: 5X TO 12X HI COLUMN
HOLOGRAPHIC STATED ODDS 1:40

	MINT	NRMT
☐ 1 Roberto Alomar	5.00	2.20
☐ 2 Jeff Bagwell	6.00	2.70
☐ 3 Albert Belle	5.00	2.20
☐ 4 Dante Bichette	2.00	.90
☐ 5 Barry Bonds	6.00	2.70
☐ 6 Jay Buhner	2.00	.90
☐ 7 Ken Caminiti	2.00	.90
☐ 8 Vinny Castilla	2.00	.90
☐ 9 Roger Clemens	12.00	5.50
☐ 10 Jose Cruz Jr.	2.00	.90
☐ 11 Andres Galarraga	3.00	1.35
☐ 12 Nomar Garciaparra	15.00	6.75
☐ 13 Juan Gonzalez	10.00	4.50
☐ 14 Mark Grace	3.00	1.35
☐ 15 Ken Griffey Jr.	25.00	11.00
☐ 16 Tony Gwynn	12.00	5.50
☐ 17 Todd Hundley	2.00	.90
☐ 18 Derek Jeter	15.00	6.75
☐ 19 Randy Johnson	5.00	2.20

		MINT	NRMT
❑ 20	Andruw Jones	5.00	2.20
❑ 21	Chipper Jones	12.00	5.50
❑ 22	David Justice	2.00	.90
❑ 23	Ray Lankford	2.00	.90
❑ 24	Barry Larkin	5.00	2.20
❑ 25	Kenny Lofton	3.00	1.35
❑ 26	Greg Maddux	12.00	5.50
❑ 27	Edgar Martinez	2.00	.90
❑ 28	Tino Martinez	2.00	.90
❑ 29	Mark McGwire	30.00	13.50
❑ 30	Paul Molitor	5.00	2.50
❑ 31	Rafael Palmeiro	5.00	2.20
❑ 32	Mike Piazza	15.00	6.75
❑ 33	Manny Ramirez	6.00	2.70
❑ 34	Cal Ripken	20.00	9.00
❑ 35	Ivan Rodriguez	6.00	2.70
❑ 36	Scott Rolen	6.00	2.70
❑ 37	Tim Salmon	3.00	1.35
❑ 38	Gary Sheffield	2.00	.90
❑ 39	Sammy Sosa	15.00	6.75
❑ 40	Frank Thomas	10.00	4.50
❑ 41	Jim Thome	5.00	2.20
❑ 42	Mo Vaughn	5.00	2.20
❑ 43	Larry Walker	5.00	2.20
❑ 44	Bernie Williams	5.00	2.20

1999 Topps Stars 'N Steel

	MINT	NRMT
COMPLETE SET (44)	150.00	70.00
COMMON CARD (1-44)	2.00	.90
SEMISTARS	3.00	1.35
UNLISTED STARS	5.00	2.20

		MINT	NRMT
❑ 1	Kerry Wood	5.00	2.20
❑ 2	Ben Grieve	5.00	2.20
❑ 3	Chipper Jones	12.00	5.50
❑ 4	Alex Rodriguez	15.00	6.75
❑ 5	Mo Vaughn	5.00	2.20
❑ 6	Bernie Williams	5.00	2.20
❑ 7	Juan Gonzalez	10.00	4.50
❑ 8	Vinny Castilla	2.00	.90
❑ 9	Tony Gwynn	12.00	5.50
❑ 10	Manny Ramirez	6.00	2.70
❑ 11	Raul Mondesi	2.00	.90
❑ 12	Roger Clemens	12.00	5.50
❑ 13	Darin Erstad	3.00	1.35
❑ 14	Barry Bonds	6.00	2.70
❑ 15	Cal Ripken	20.00	9.00
❑ 16	Barry Larkin	5.00	2.20
❑ 17	Scott Rolen	6.00	2.20
❑ 18	Albert Belle	5.00	2.20
❑ 19	Craig Biggio	5.00	2.20
❑ 20	Tony Clark	2.00	.90
❑ 21	Mark McGwire	30.00	13.50
❑ 22	Andres Galarraga	3.00	1.35
❑ 23	Kenny Lofton	3.00	1.35
❑ 24	Pedro Martinez	6.00	2.70
❑ 25	Paul O'Neill	2.00	.90
❑ 26	Ken Griffey Jr.	25.00	11.00
❑ 27	Travis Lee	3.00	1.35
❑ 28	Tim Salmon	3.00	1.35
❑ 29	Frank Thomas	10.00	4.50
❑ 30	Larry Walker	5.00	2.20
❑ 31	Moises Alou	2.00	.90
❑ 32	Vladimir Guerrero	6.00	2.70
❑ 33	Ivan Rodriguez	6.00	2.70
❑ 34	Derek Jeter	15.00	6.75
❑ 35	Greg Vaughn	2.00	.90
❑ 36	Gary Sheffield	2.00	.90
❑ 37	Carlos Delgado	5.00	2.20
❑ 38	Greg Maddux	12.00	5.50
❑ 39	Sammy Sosa	15.00	6.75
❑ 40	Mike Piazza	15.00	6.75
❑ 41	Nomar Garciaparra	15.00	6.75
❑ 42	Dante Bichette	2.00	.90
❑ 43	Jeff Bagwell	6.00	2.70
❑ 44	Jim Thome	5.00	2.20

1999 Topps Stars 'N Steel Gold

	MINT	NRMT
COMMON CARD (1-44)	6.00	2.70

*GOLD: 1.25X TO 3X BASIC CARDS
STATED ODDS 1:12

1999 Topps Stars 'N Steel Gold Domed Holographic

	MINT	NRMT
COMMON CARD (1-44)	12.00	5.50

*STARS: 2.5X TO 6X BASIC CARDS
STATED ODDS 1:24

1998 Topps SuperChrome

	MINT	NRMT
COMPLETE SET (36)	50.00	22.00
COMMON CARD (1-36)	.40	.18
SEMISTARS	.60	.25
UNLISTED STARS	1.00	.45

		MINT	NRMT
❑ 1	Tony Gwynn	2.50	1.10
❑ 2	Larry Walker	1.00	.45
❑ 3	Vladimir Guerrero	1.25	.55
❑ 4	Mo Vaughn	1.00	.45
❑ 5	Frank Thomas	2.00	.90
❑ 6	Barry Larkin	1.00	.45
❑ 7	Scott Rolen	1.25	.55
❑ 8	Juan Gonzalez	2.00	.90
❑ 9	Jeff Bagwell	1.25	.55
❑ 10	Ryan Klesko	.40	.18

		MINT	NRMT
❑ 11	Mike Piazza	3.00	1.35
❑ 12	Randy Johnson	1.00	.45
❑ 13	Derek Jeter	3.00	1.35
❑ 14	Gary Sheffield	.40	.18
❑ 15	Hideo Nomo	1.00	.45
❑ 16	Tino Martinez	.40	.18
❑ 17	Ivan Rodriguez	1.25	.55
❑ 18	Bernie Williams	1.00	.45
❑ 19	Greg Maddux	2.50	1.10
❑ 20	Roger Clemens	2.50	1.10
❑ 21	Roberto Clemente	2.50	1.10
❑ 22	Chipper Jones	2.50	1.10
❑ 23	Sammy Sosa	3.00	1.35
❑ 24	Tony Clark	.40	.18
❑ 25	Barry Bonds	1.25	.55
❑ 26	Craig Biggio	1.00	.45
❑ 27	Cal Ripken	4.00	1.80
❑ 28	Ken Griffey Jr.	5.00	2.20
❑ 29	Todd Helton	1.25	.55
❑ 30	Mark McGwire	6.00	2.70
❑ 31	Jose Cruz Jr.	.40	.18
❑ 32	Albert Belle	1.00	.45
❑ 33	Andruw Jones	1.00	.45
❑ 34	Nomar Garciaparra	3.00	1.35
❑ 35	Andy Pettitte	.40	.18
❑ 36	Alex Rodriguez	3.00	1.35

1998 Topps SuperChrome Refractors

	MINT	NRMT
COMMON CARD (1-36)	3.00	1.35

*STARS: 5X TO 12X BASIC CARDS
STATED ODDS 1:12

1999 Topps SuperChrome

	MINT	NRMT
COMPLETE SET (36)	60.00	27.00
COMMON CARD (1-36)	.75	.35
SEMISTARS	1.00	.45
UNLISTED STARS	1.50	.70

NO VARIATIONS EXIST ON CARDS 34 AND 35

		MINT	NRMT
❑ 1	Roger Clemens	4.00	1.80
❑ 2	Andres Galarraga	1.00	.45
❑ 3	Manny Ramirez	1.50	.70

		MINT	NRMT
❏ 4	Greg Maddux	4.00	1.80
❏ 5	Kerry Wood	1.50	.70
❏ 6	Travis Lee	1.00	.45
❏ 7	Nolan Ryan	8.00	3.60
❏ 8	Juan Gonzalez	3.00	1.35
❏ 9	Vladimir Guerrero	2.00	.90
❏ 10	Sammy Sosa	5.00	2.20
❏ 11	Mark McGwire	10.00	4.50
❏ 12	Javy Lopez	.75	.35
❏ 13	Tony Gwynn	4.00	1.80
❏ 14	Derek Jeter	5.00	2.20
❏ 15	Albert Belle	1.50	.70
❏ 16	Pedro Martinez	2.00	.90
❏ 17	Greg Vaughn	.75	.35
❏ 18	Ken Griffey Jr.	8.00	3.60
❏ 19	Ben Grieve	1.50	.70
❏ 20	Vinny Castilla	.75	.35
❏ 21	Moises Alou	.75	.35
❏ 22	Barry Bonds	2.00	.90
❏ 23	Nomar Garciaparra	5.00	2.20
❏ 24	Chipper Jones	4.00	1.80
❏ 25	Mike Piazza	5.00	2.20
❏ 26	Alex Rodriguez	5.00	2.20
❏ 27	Ivan Rodriguez	2.00	.90
❏ 28	Frank Thomas	3.00	1.35
❏ 29	Larry Walker	1.50	.70
❏ 30	Troy Glaus	1.50	.70
❏ 31	David Wells HL	.75	.35
❏ 32	Roger Clemens HL	2.00	.90
❏ 33	Kerry Wood HL	.75	.35
❏ 34	Mark McGwire HR 70	15.00	6.75
❏ 35	Sammy Sosa HR 66	10.00	4.50
❏ 36	Scott Brosius WS	.75	.35

1999 Topps SuperChrome Refractors

	MINT	NRMT
COMMON CARD (1-36)	4.00	1.80

*STARS: 2X TO 5X BASIC CARDS
*YOUNG STARS: 1.5X TO 4X BASIC CARDS
STATED ODDS 1:12

1998 Topps Tek

	MINT	NRMT
COMPLETE SET (90)	150.00	70.00
COMMON CARD (1-90)	.50	.23
MINOR STARS	.75	.35

SEMISTARS		1.25	.55
UNLISTED STARS		2.00	.90

NINETY PATTERN VARIATIONS AVAILABLE
ALL PATTERN VARIATIONS VALUED EQUALLY

❏ 1	Ben Grieve	2.00	.90
❏ 2	Kerry Wood	2.00	.90
❏ 3	Barry Bonds	2.50	1.10
❏ 4	John Olerud	.75	.35
❏ 5	Ivan Rodriguez	2.50	1.10
❏ 6	Frank Thomas	4.00	1.80
❏ 7	Bernie Williams	2.00	.90
❏ 8	Dante Bichette	.75	.35
❏ 9	Alex Rodriguez	6.00	2.70
❏ 10	Tom Glavine	2.00	.90
❏ 11	Eric Karros	.75	.35
❏ 12	Craig Biggio	2.00	.90
❏ 13	Mark McGwire	12.00	5.50
❏ 14	Derek Jeter	6.00	2.70
❏ 15	Nomar Garciaparra	6.00	2.70
❏ 16	Brady Anderson	.75	.35
❏ 17	Vladimir Guerrero	2.50	1.10
❏ 18	David Justice	.75	.35
❏ 19	Chipper Jones	5.00	2.20
❏ 20	Jim Edmonds	.75	.35
❏ 21	Roger Clemens	5.00	2.20
❏ 22	Mark Kotsay	.75	.35
❏ 23	Tony Gwynn	5.00	2.20
❏ 24	Todd Walker	.75	.35
❏ 25	Tino Martinez	.75	.35
❏ 26	Andruw Jones	2.00	.90
❏ 27	Sandy Alomar Jr.	.75	.35
❏ 28	Sammy Sosa	6.00	2.70
❏ 29	Gary Sheffield	.75	.35
❏ 30	Ken Griffey Jr.	10.00	4.50
❏ 31	Ramon Ramirez	2.00	.90
❏ 32	Curt Schilling	1.25	.55
❏ 33	Robin Ventura	.75	.35
❏ 34	Larry Walker	2.00	.90
❏ 35	Darin Erstad	1.25	.55
❏ 36	Todd Dunwoody	.50	.23
❏ 37	Paul O'Neill	.75	.35
❏ 38	Vinny Castilla	.75	.35
❏ 39	Randy Johnson	2.00	.90
❏ 40	Rafael Palmeiro	2.00	.90
❏ 41	Pedro Martinez	2.50	1.10
❏ 42	Derek Bell	.75	.35
❏ 43	Carlos Delgado	2.00	.90
❏ 44	Matt Williams	2.00	.90
❏ 45	Kenny Lofton	1.25	.55
❏ 46	Edgar Renteria	.50	.23
❏ 47	Albert Belle	2.00	.90
❏ 48	Jeromy Burnitz	.75	.35
❏ 49	Adrian Beltre	2.00	.90
❏ 50	Greg Maddux	5.00	2.20
❏ 51	Cal Ripken	8.00	3.60
❏ 52	Jason Kendall	.75	.35
❏ 53	Ellis Burks	.75	.35
❏ 54	Paul Molitor	2.00	.90
❏ 55	Moises Alou	.75	.35
❏ 56	Raul Mondesi	.75	.35
❏ 57	Barry Larkin	2.00	.90
❏ 58	Tony Clark	.75	.35
❏ 59	Travis Lee	1.25	.55
❏ 60	Juan Gonzalez	4.00	1.80
❏ 61	Troy Glaus	5.00	2.20
❏ 62	Jose Cruz Jr.	.75	.35
❏ 63	Paul Konerko	.75	.35
❏ 64	Edgar Martinez	.75	.35
❏ 65	Javy Lopez	.75	.35
❏ 66	Manny Ramirez	2.50	1.10
❏ 67	Roberto Alomar	2.00	.90
❏ 68	Ken Caminiti	.75	.35
❏ 69	Todd Helton	2.00	.90
❏ 70	Chuck Knoblauch	.75	.35
❏ 71	Kevin Brown	1.25	.55
❏ 72	Tim Salmon	1.25	.55
❏ 73	Orlando Hernandez	3.00	1.35
❏ 74	Jeff Bagwell	2.50	1.10
❏ 75	Brian Jordan	.75	.35
❏ 76	Derek Lee	.50	.23
❏ 77	Brad Fullmer	.50	.23
❏ 78	Mark Grace	1.25	.55
❏ 79	Jeff King	.50	.23
❏ 80	Mike Mussina	2.00	.90
❏ 81	Jay Buhner	.75	.35
❏ 82	Quinton McCracken	.50	.23
❏ 83	A.J. Hinch	.50	.23
❏ 84	Richard Hidalgo	.75	.35
❏ 85	Andres Galarraga	1.25	.55
❏ 86	Mike Piazza	6.00	2.70
❏ 87	Mo Vaughn	2.00	.90
❏ 88	Scott Rolen	2.50	1.10
❏ 89	Jim Thome	2.00	.90
❏ 90	Ray Lankford	.75	.35

1998 Topps Tek Diffractors

	MINT	NRMT
COMMON CARD (1-90)	3.00	1.35

*STARS: 2.5X TO 6X BASIC CARDS
*ROOKIES: 2X TO 5X BASIC CARDS
STATED ODDS 1:6
NINETY PATTERN VARIATIONS AVAILABLE
ALL PATTERN VARIATIONS VALUED EQUALLY

1999 Topps Tek

	MINT	NRMT
COMPLETE SET (90)	120.00	55.00
COMMON CARD (1A-45B)	.75	.35
SEMISTARS	1.00	.45
UNLISTED STARS	1.50	.70

CARD A IS HOME JERSEY VARIATION
CARD B IS AWAY JERSEY VARIATION

HOME A AND AWAY B CARDS EQUAL VALUE
THIRTY PATTERN VARIATIONS AVAILABLE
ALL PATTERN VARIATIONS VALUED EQUAL-
LY

		MINT	NRMT
❏ 1A	Ben Grieve	1.50	.70
❏ 1B	Ben Grieve Away	1.50	.70
❏ 2A	Andres Galarraga	1.00	.45
❏ 2B	Andres Galarraga Away	1.00	.45
❏ 3A	Travis Lee	1.00	.45
❏ 3B	Travis Lee Away	1.00	.45
❏ 4A	Larry Walker	1.50	.70
❏ 4B	Larry Walker Away	1.50	.70
❏ 5A	Ken Griffey Jr.	8.00	3.60
❏ 5B	Ken Griffey Jr. Away	8.00	3.60
❏ 6A	Sammy Sosa	5.00	2.20
❏ 6B	Sammy Sosa Away	5.00	2.20
❏ 7A	Mark McGwire	10.00	4.50
❏ 7B	Mark McGwire Away	10.00	4.50
❏ 8A	Roberto Alomar	1.50	.70
❏ 8B	Roberto Alomar Away	1.50	.70
❏ 9A	Wade Boggs	1.50	.70
❏ 9B	Wade Boggs Away	1.50	.70
❏ 10A	Troy Glaus	1.50	.70
❏ 10B	Troy Glaus Away	1.50	.70
❏ 11A	Craig Biggio	1.50	.70
❏ 11B	Craig Biggio Away	1.50	.70
❏ 12A	Kerry Wood	1.50	.70
❏ 12B	Kerry Wood Away	1.50	.70
❏ 13A	Vladimir Guerrero	2.00	.90
❏ 13B	Vladimir Guerrero Away	2.00	.90
❏ 14A	Albert Belle	1.50	.70
❏ 14B	Albert Belle Away	1.50	.70
❏ 15A	Mike Piazza	5.00	2.20
❏ 15B	Mike Piazza Away	5.00	2.20
❏ 16A	Chipper Jones	4.00	1.80
❏ 16B	Chipper Jones Away	4.00	1.80
❏ 17A	Randy Johnson	1.50	.70
❏ 17B	Randy Johnson Away	1.50	.70
❏ 18A	Adrian Beltre	1.50	.70
❏ 18B	Adrian Beltre Away	1.50	.70
❏ 19A	Barry Bonds	2.00	.90
❏ 19B	Barry Bonds Away	2.00	.90
❏ 20A	Jim Thome	1.50	.70
❏ 20B	Jim Thome Away	1.50	.70
❏ 21A	Greg Vaughn	.75	.35
❏ 21B	Greg Vaughn Away	.75	.35
❏ 22A	Scott Rolen	2.00	.90
❏ 22B	Scott Rolen Away	3.00	1.35
❏ 23A	Ivan Rodriguez	2.00	.90
❏ 23B	Ivan Rodriguez Away	2.00	.90
❏ 24A	Derek Jeter	5.00	2.20
❏ 24B	Derek Jeter Away	5.00	2.20
❏ 25A	Cal Ripken	6.00	2.70
❏ 25B	Cal Ripken Away	6.00	2.70
❏ 26A	Mark Grace	1.00	.45
❏ 26B	Mark Grace Away	1.00	.45
❏ 27A	Bernie Williams	1.50	.70
❏ 27B	Bernie Williams Away	1.50	.70
❏ 28A	Darin Erstad	1.00	.45
❏ 28B	Darin Erstad Away	1.00	.45
❏ 29A	Eric Chavez	1.00	.45
❏ 29B	Eric Chavez Away	1.00	.45
❏ 30A	Tom Glavine	1.50	.70
❏ 30B	Tom Glavine Away	1.50	.70
❏ 31A	Jeff Bagwell	2.00	.90
❏ 31B	Jeff Bagwell Away	2.00	.90
❏ 32A	Manny Ramirez	2.00	.90
❏ 32B	Manny Ramirez Away	2.00	.90
❏ 33A	Tino Martinez	.75	.35
❏ 33B	Tino Martinez Away	.75	.35
❏ 34A	Todd Helton	1.50	.70
❏ 34B	Todd Helton Away	1.50	.70
❏ 35A	Jason Kendall	.75	.35
❏ 35B	Jason Kendall Away	.75	.35
❏ 36A	Pat Burrell	5.00	2.20
❏ 36B	Pat Burrell Away	5.00	2.20
❏ 37A	Tony Gwynn	4.00	1.80
❏ 37B	Tony Gwynn Away	4.00	1.80
❏ 38A	Nomar Garciaparra	5.00	2.20
❏ 38B	Nomar Garciaparra Away	5.00	2.20
❏ 39A	Frank Thomas	3.00	1.35
❏ 39B	Frank Thomas Away	3.00	1.35
❏ 40A	Orlando Hernandez	1.50	.70
❏ 40B	Orlando Hernandez Away	1.50	.70
❏ 41A	Juan Gonzalez	3.00	1.35
❏ 41B	Juan Gonzalez Away	3.00	1.35
❏ 42A	Alex Rodriguez	5.00	2.20
❏ 42B	Alex Rodriguez Away	5.00	2.20
❏ 43A	Greg Maddux	4.00	1.80
❏ 43B	Greg Maddux Away	4.00	1.80
❏ 44A	Mo Vaughn	1.50	.70
❏ 44B	Mo Vaughn Away	1.50	.70
❏ 45A	Roger Clemens	4.00	1.80
❏ 45B	Roger Clemens Away	4.00	1.80

1999 Topps Tek Gold

	MINT	NRMT
COMMON CARD (1A-45B)	10.00	4.50

*STARS: 5X TO 12X BASIC CARDS
*ROOKIES: 4X TO 10X BASIC CARDS
STATED ODDS 1:15
10 SERIAL #'d SETS OF ALL 60 VARIATIONS

1999 Topps Tek Fantastek Phenoms

	MINT	NRMT
COMPLETE SET (10)	50.00	22.00
COMMON CARD (F1-F10)	2.50	1.10
SEMISTARS	4.00	1.80
UNLISTED STARS	6.00	2.70

STATED ODDS 1:18

❏ F1	Eric Chavez	4.00	1.80
❏ F2	Troy Glaus	6.00	2.70
❏ F3	Pat Burrell	15.00	6.75
❏ F4	Alex Gonzalez	2.50	1.10
❏ F5	Carlos Lee	2.50	1.10
❏ F6	Ruben Mateo	6.00	2.70
❏ F7	Carlos Beltran	8.00	3.60
❏ F8	Adrian Beltre	6.00	2.70
❏ F9	Bruce Chen	2.50	1.10
❏ F10	Ryan Anderson	2.50	1.10

1999 Topps Tek Teknicians

	MINT	NRMT
COMPLETE SET (10)	100.00	45.00
COMMON CARD (T1-T10)	2.00	.90
UNLISTED STARS	2.50	1.10

STATED ODDS 1:18

❏ T1	Ken Griffey Jr.	20.00	9.00

❏ T2	Mark McGwire	25.00	11.00
❏ T3	Kerry Wood	2.00	.90
❏ T4	Ben Grieve	2.50	1.10
❏ T5	Sammy Sosa	12.00	5.50
❏ T6	Derek Jeter	12.00	5.50
❏ T7	Alex Rodriguez	12.00	5.50
❏ T8	Roger Clemens	10.00	4.50
❏ T9	Nomar Garciaparra	12.00	5.50
❏ T10	Vladimir Guerrero	5.00	2.20

1995 UC3

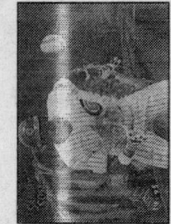

	MINT	NRMT
COMPLETE SET (147)	20.00	9.00
COMMON CARD (1-147)	.15	.07
MINOR STARS	.30	.14
UNLISTED STARS	.60	.25

SUBSET CARDS HALF VALUE OF BASE
CARDS

COMMON ART.PRF. (1-147)	3.00	1.35

*ART.PRF.STARS: 8X TO 20X HI COLUMN
*ART.PRF.ROOKIES: 5X TO 12X HI
AP STATED ODDS 1:36

❏ 1	Frank Thomas	1.25	.55
❏ 2	Wil Cordero	.15	.07
❏ 3	John Olerud	.30	.14
❏ 4	Deion Sanders	.30	.14
❏ 5	Mike Mussina	.60	.25
❏ 6	Mo Vaughn	.60	.25
❏ 7	Will Clark	.60	.25
❏ 8	Chili Davis	.30	.14
❏ 9	Jimmy Key	.30	.14
❏ 10	John Valentin	.30	.14
❏ 11	Tony Tarasco	.15	.07
❏ 12	Alan Trammell	.30	.14
❏ 13	David Cone	.40	.18
❏ 14	Tim Salmon	.60	.25
❏ 15	Danny Tartabull	.15	.07
❏ 16	Aaron Sele	.30	.14
❏ 17	Alex Fernandez	.15	.07
❏ 18	Barry Bonds	.75	.35
❏ 19	Andres Galarraga	.60	.25
❏ 20	Don Mattingly	1.25	.55
❏ 21	Kevin Appier	.30	.14
❏ 22	Paul Molitor	.60	.25
❏ 23	Omar Vizquel	.30	.14
❏ 24	Andy Benes	.30	.14
❏ 25	Rafael Palmeiro	.60	.25
❏ 26	Barry Larkin	.60	.25
❏ 27	Bernie Williams	.60	.25

❑ 28 Gary Sheffield	.30	.14
❑ 29 Wally Joyner	.30	.14
❑ 30 Wade Boggs	.60	.25
❑ 31 Rico Brogna	.15	.07
❑ 32 Ken Caminiti	.40	.18
❑ 33 Kirby Puckett	1.00	.45
❑ 34 Bobby Bonilla	.30	.14
❑ 35 Hal Morris	.15	.07
❑ 36 Moises Alou	.30	.14
❑ 37 Jim Thome	.60	.25
❑ 38 Chuck Knoblauch	.25	.11
❑ 39 Mike Piazza	2.00	.90
❑ 40 Travis Fryman	.30	.14
❑ 41 Rickey Henderson	.75	.35
❑ 42 Jack McDowell	.15	.07
❑ 43 Carlos Baerga	.15	.07
❑ 44 Gregg Jefferies	.15	.07
❑ 45 Kirk Gibson	.30	.14
❑ 46 Bret Saberhagen	.30	.14
❑ 47 Cecil Fielder	.30	.14
❑ 48 Manny Ramirez	.75	.35
❑ 49 Marquis Grissom	.15	.07
❑ 50 Dave Winfield	.60	.25
❑ 51 Mark McGwire	3.00	1.35
❑ 52 Dennis Eckersley	.30	.14
❑ 53 Robin Ventura	.30	.14
❑ 54 Ryan Klesko	.30	.14
❑ 55 Jeff Bagwell	.75	.35
❑ 56 Ozzie Smith	.75	.35
❑ 57 Brian McRae	.15	.07
❑ 58 Albert Belle	.60	.25
❑ 59 Darren Daulton	.30	.14
❑ 60 Jose Canseco	.75	.35
❑ 61 Greg Maddux	1.50	.70
❑ 62 Ben McDonald	.15	.07
❑ 63 Lenny Dykstra	.30	.14
❑ 64 Randy Johnson	.60	.25
❑ 65 Fred McGriff	.40	.18
❑ 66 Ray Lankford	.30	.14
❑ 67 Dave Justice	.60	.25
❑ 68 Paul O'Neill	.30	.14
❑ 69 Tony Gwynn	1.50	.70
❑ 70 Matt Williams	.60	.25
❑ 71 Dante Bichette	.30	.14
❑ 72 Craig Biggio	.60	.25
❑ 73 Ken Griffey Jr.	3.00	1.35
❑ 74 Juan Gonzalez	1.25	.55
❑ 75 Cal Ripken	2.50	1.10
❑ 76 Jay Bell	.30	.14
❑ 77 Joe Carter	.30	.14
❑ 78 Roberto Alomar	.60	.25
❑ 79 Mark Langston	.15	.07
❑ 80 Dave Hollins	.15	.07
❑ 81 Tom Glavine	.60	.25
❑ 82 Ivan Rodriguez	.75	.35
❑ 83 Mark Whiten	.15	.07
❑ 84 Raul Mondesi	.40	.18
❑ 85 Kenny Lofton	.40	.18
❑ 86 Ruben Sierra	.15	.07
❑ 87 Mark Grace	.40	.18
❑ 88 Royce Clayton	.15	.07
❑ 89 Billy Ashley	.15	.07
❑ 90 Larry Walker	.60	.25
❑ 91 Sammy Sosa	2.00	.90
❑ 92 Jason Bere	.15	.07
❑ 93 Bob Hamelin	.15	.07
❑ 94 Greg Vaughn	.30	.14
❑ 95 Roger Clemens	1.50	.70
❑ 96 Scott Ruffcorn	.15	.07
❑ 97 Hideo Nomo	1.50	.70
❑ 98 Michael Tucker	.15	.07
❑ 99 J.R. Phillips	.15	.07
❑ 100 Roberto Petagine	.15	.07
❑ 101 Chipper Jones	1.50	.70
❑ 102 Armando Benitez	.15	.07
❑ 103 Orlando Miller	.15	.07
❑ 104 Carlos Delgado	.60	.25
❑ 105 Jeff Cirillo	.30	.14
❑ 106 Shawn Green	.60	.25
❑ 107 Joe Randa	.15	.07
❑ 108 Vaughn Eshelman	.15	.07
❑ 109 Frank Rodriguez	.15	.07
❑ 110 Russ Davis	.30	.14
❑ 111 Todd Hollandsworth	.15	.07
❑ 112 Mark Grudzielanek	.40	.18
❑ 113 Jose Oliva	.15	.07
❑ 114 Ray Durham	.30	.14
❑ 115 Alex Rodriguez	2.50	1.10
❑ 116 Alex Gonzalez	.15	.07
❑ 117 Midre Cummings	.15	.07
❑ 118 Marty Cordova	.15	.07
❑ 119 John Mabry	.15	.07
❑ 120 Jason Jacome	.15	.07
❑ 121 Joe Vitiello	.15	.07
❑ 122 Charles Johnson	.30	.14
❑ 123 Cal Ripken ID	1.25	.55
❑ 124 Ken Griffey Jr. ID	1.50	.70
❑ 125 Frank Thomas ID	.60	.25
❑ 126 Mike Piazza ID	1.00	.45
❑ 127 Matt Williams ID	.30	.14
❑ 128 Barry Bonds ID	.40	.18
❑ 129 Greg Maddux ID	.75	.35
❑ 130 Randy Johnson ID	.30	.14
❑ 131 Albert Belle ID	.30	.14
❑ 132 Will Clark ID	.30	.14
❑ 133 Tony Gwynn ID	.60	.25
❑ 134 Manny Ramirez ID	.30	.14
❑ 135 Raul Mondesi ID	.15	.07
❑ 136 Mo Vaughn ID	.40	.18
❑ 137 Mark McGwire ID	.60	.25
❑ 138 Kirby Puckett ID	.60	.25
❑ 139 Don Mattingly ID	.60	.25
❑ 140 Carlos Baerga ID	.15	.07
❑ 141 Roger Clemens ID	.60	.25
❑ 142 Fred McGriff ID	.15	.07
❑ 143 Kenny Lofton ID	.30	.14
❑ 144 Jeff Bagwell ID	.60	.25
❑ 145 Larry Walker ID	.30	.14
❑ 146 Joe Carter ID	.15	.07
❑ 147 Rafael Palmeiro ID	.30	.14

1995 UC3 Clear Shots

	MINT	NRMT
COMPLETE SET (12)	60.00	27.00
COMMON PLAYER (CS1-CS12)	1.00	.45
SEMISTARS	2.50	1.10
STATED ODDS 1:24		

❑ CS1 Alex Rodriguez	20.00	9.00
❑ CS2 Shawn Green	4.00	1.80
❑ CS3 Hideo Nomo	8.00	3.60
❑ CS4 Charles Johnson	1.50	.70
❑ CS5 Orlando Miller	1.00	.45
❑ CS6 Billy Ashley	1.00	.45
❑ CS7 Carlos Delgado	4.00	1.80
❑ CS8 Cliff Floyd	1.50	.70
❑ CS9 Chipper Jones	15.00	6.75
❑ CS10 Alex Gonzalez	1.00	.45
❑ CS11 J.R. Phillips	1.00	.45
❑ CS12 Michael Tucker	1.50	.70
❑ PCS8 Cliff Floyd	2.00	.90
Promo		
❑ PCS10 Alex Gonzalez	1.00	.45
Promo		

1995 UC3 Cyclone Squad

	MINT	NRMT
COMPLETE SET (20)	20.00	9.00
COMMON CARD (CS1-CS20)	.40	.18
STATED ODDS 1:4		

❑ CS1 Frank Thomas	1.50	.70
❑ CS2 Ken Griffey Jr.	4.00	1.80
❑ CS3 Jeff Bagwell	1.00	.45
❑ CS4 Cal Ripken	3.00	1.35
❑ CS5 Barry Bonds	1.00	.45
❑ CS6 Mike Piazza	2.50	1.10
❑ CS7 Matt Williams	.75	.35
❑ CS8 Kirby Puckett	1.25	.55
❑ CS9 Jose Canseco	1.00	.45
❑ CS10 Will Clark	.75	.35
❑ CS11 Don Mattingly	.85	.35
❑ CS12 Albert Belle	.75	.35
❑ CS13 Tony Gwynn	2.00	.90
❑ CS14 Raul Mondesi	.50	.23
❑ CS15 Bobby Bonilla	.40	.18
❑ CS16 Rafael Palmeiro	.75	.35
❑ CS17 Fred McGriff	.50	.23
❑ CS18 Tim Salmon	.75	.35
❑ CS19 Kenny Lofton	.50	.23
❑ CS20 Joe Carter	.40	.18

1995 UC3 In Motion

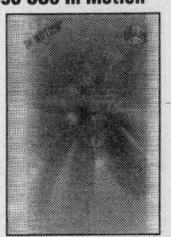

	MINT	NRMT
COMPLETE SET (10)	40.00	18.00
COMMON CARD (IM1-IM10)	1.50	.70
STATED ODDS 1:18		

❑ IM1 Cal Ripken	6.00	2.70
❑ IM2 Ken Griffey Jr.	8.00	3.60
❑ IM3 Frank Thomas	3.00	1.35
❑ IM4 Mike Piazza	5.00	2.20
❑ IM5 Barry Bonds	1.50	.70
❑ IM6 Matt Williams	1.50	.70
❑ IM7 Kirby Puckett	3.00	1.35
❑ IM8 Greg Maddux	4.00	1.80
❑ IM9 Don Mattingly	3.00	1.35
❑ IM10 Will Clark	1.50	.70

1997 UD3

	MINT	NRMT
COMPLETE SET (60)	50.00	22.00
COMMON CARD (1-60)	.50	.23
SEMISTARS	.75	.35
UNLISTED STARS	1.25	.55

❑ 1 Mark McGwire	6.00	2.70
❑ 2 Brady Anderson	.50	.23
❑ 3 Ken Griffey Jr.	6.00	2.70
❑ 4 Albert Belle	1.25	.55

		MINT	NRMT
❏ 5 Andres Galarraga	1.25		.55
❏ 6 Juan Gonzalez	2.50		1.10
❏ 7 Jay Buhner	.50		.23
❏ 8 Mo Vaughn	1.25		.55
❏ 9 Barry Bonds	1.50		.70
❏ 10 Gary Sheffield	.50		.23
❏ 11 Todd Hundley	.50		.23
❏ 12 Ellis Burks	.50		.23
❏ 13 Ken Caminiti	.75		.35
❏ 14 Vinny Castilla	.75		.35
❏ 15 Sammy Sosa	4.00		1.80
❏ 16 Frank Thomas	2.50		1.10
❏ 17 Rafael Palmeiro	1.25		.55
❏ 18 Mike Piazza	4.00		1.80
❏ 19 Matt Williams	1.25		.55
❏ 20 Eddie Murray	1.25		.55
❏ 21 Roger Clemens	3.00		1.35
❏ 22 Tim Salmon	1.25		.55
❏ 23 Robin Ventura	.50		.23
❏ 24 Ron Gant	.50		.23
❏ 25 Cal Ripken	5.00		2.20
❏ 26 Bernie Williams	1.25		.55
❏ 27 Hideo Nomo	1.25		.55
❏ 28 Ivan Rodriguez	1.50		.70
❏ 29 John Smoltz	.75		.35
❏ 30 Paul Molitor	1.25		.55
❏ 31 Greg Maddux	3.00		1.35
❏ 32 Raul Mondesi	.50		.23
❏ 33 Roberto Alomar	1.25		.55
❏ 34 Barry Larkin	1.25		.55
❏ 35 Tony Gwynn	3.00		1.35
❏ 36 Jim Thome	1.25		.55
❏ 37 Kenny Lofton	.75		.35
❏ 38 Jeff Bagwell	1.50		.70
❏ 39 Ozzie Smith	1.50		.70
❏ 40 Kirby Puckett	2.00		.90
❏ 41 Andruw Jones	1.50		.70
❏ 42 Vladimir Guerrero	2.00		.90
❏ 43 Edgar Renteria	.50		.23
❏ 44 Luis Castillo	.50		.23
❏ 45 Darin Erstad	1.25		.55
❏ 46 Nomar Garciaparra	4.00		1.80
❏ 47 Todd Greene	.50		.23
❏ 48 Jason Kendall	.75		.35
❏ 49 Rey Ordonez	.50		.23
❏ 50 Alex Rodriguez	4.00		1.80
❏ 51 Manny Ramirez	1.50		.70
❏ 52 Todd Walker	1.25		.55
❏ 53 Ruben Rivera	.50		.23
❏ 54 Andy Pettitte	.75		.35
❏ 55 Derek Jeter	4.00		1.80
❏ 56 Todd Hollandsworth	.50		.23
❏ 57 Rocky Coppinger	.50		.23
❏ 58 Scott Rolen	2.00		.90
❏ 59 Jermaine Dye	.50		.23
❏ 60 Chipper Jones	3.00		1.35

1997 UD3 Generation Next

	MINT	NRMT
COMPLETE SET (20)	120.00	55.00
COMMON CARD (1-20)	1.50	.70
MINOR STARS	2.50	1.10
UNLISTED STARS	6.00	2.70
STATED ODDS 1:11		
❏ GN1 Alex Rodriguez	20.00	9.00

		MINT	NRMT
❏ GN2 Vladimir Guerrero	10.00		4.50
❏ GN3 Luis Castillo	2.50		1.10
❏ GN4 Rey Ordonez	2.50		1.10
❏ GN5 Andruw Jones	8.00		3.60
❏ GN6 Darin Erstad	6.00		2.70
❏ GN7 Edgar Renteria	2.50		1.10
❏ GN8 Jason Kendall	3.00		1.35
❏ GN9 Jermaine Dye	2.50		1.10
❏ GN10 Chipper Jones	15.00		6.75
❏ GN11 Rocky Coppinger	1.50		.70
❏ GN12 Andy Pettitte	3.00		1.35
❏ GN13 Todd Greene	1.50		.70
❏ GN14 Todd Hollandsworth	1.50		.70
❏ GN15 Derek Jeter	20.00		9.00
❏ GN16 Ruben Rivera	1.50		.70
❏ GN17 Todd Walker	6.00		2.70
❏ GN18 Nomar Garciaparra	20.00		9.00
❏ GN19 Scott Rolen	10.00		4.50
❏ GN20 Manny Ramirez	8.00		3.60

1997 UD3 Marquee Attraction

	MINT	NRMT
COMPLETE SET (10)	300.00	135.00
COMMON CARD (MA1-MA10)	12.00	5.50
STATED ODDS 1:144		
❏ MA1 Ken Griffey Jr.	60.00	27.00
❏ MA2 Mark McGwire	60.00	27.00
❏ MA3 Juan Gonzalez	25.00	11.00
❏ MA4 Barry Bonds	15.00	6.75
❏ MA5 Frank Thomas	25.00	11.00
❏ MA6 Albert Belle	20.00	9.00
❏ MA7 Mike Piazza	40.00	18.00
❏ MA8 Cal Ripken	50.00	22.00
❏ MA9 Mo Vaughn	20.00	9.00
❏ MA10 Alex Rodriguez	40.00	18.00

1997 UD3 Superb Signatures

	MINT	NRMT
COMPLETE SET (4)	1000.00	450.00
COMMON CARD	50.00	22.00
STATED ODDS 1:1500		
❏ 1 Ken Caminiti	50.00	22.00
❏ 2 Ken Griffey Jr.	500.00	220.00
❏ 3 Vladimir Guerrero	150.00	70.00
❏ 4 Derek Jeter	250.00	110.00

1998 UD3

	MINT	NRMT
COMP.FUTURE FX SET (30)	80.00	36.00
COMMON FUTURE FX (1-30)	.75	.35
FUTURE FX MINOR STARS	1.25	.55
FUTURE FX SEMISTARS	2.00	.90
FUTURE FX UNLISTED STARS	3.00	1.35
FUTURE IMPACT FX ODDS 1:12		
COMP.POWER FX SET (30)	40.00	18.00
COMMON POWER FX (31-60)	.25	.11
POWER FX MINOR STARS	.40	.18
POWER FX SEMISTARS	.60	.25
POWER FX UNLISTED STARS	1.00	.45
POWER CORPS FX ODDS 1:1		
COMP.EST.FX SET (30)	60.00	27.00
COMMON EST.FX (61-90)	.60	.25
EST.FX MINOR STARS	1.00	.45
EST.FX SEMISTARS	1.50	.70
EST.FX UNLISTED STARS	2.50	1.10
ESTABLISHMENT FX ODDS 1:6		
COMP.FUTURE EMB.SET (30)	50.00	22.00
COM.FUTURE EMB. (91-120)	.50	.23
FUTURE EMB.MINOR STARS	.75	.35
FUTURE EMB.SEMISTARS	1.25	.55
FUTURE EMB.UNLISTED STARS	2.00	.90
FUTURE IMPACT EMBOSSED ODDS 1:6		
COMP.POWER EMB.SET (30)	60.00	27.00
COM.POWER EMB. (121-150)	.40	.18
POWER EMB.MINOR STARS	.60	.25
POWER EMB.SEMISTARS	1.00	.45
POWER EMB.UNLISTED STARS	1.50	.70
POWER CORPS EMBOSSED ODDS 1:4		
COMP.EST.EMB.SET (30)	20.00	9.00
COMMON EST.EMB. (151-180)	.20	.09
EST.EMB.MINOR STARS	.30	.14
EST.EMB.SEMISTARS	.50	.23
EST.EMB.UNLISTED STARS	.75	.35
ESTABLISHMENT EMBOSSED ODDS 1:1		
COMP.FUTURE RBW.SET (30)	25.00	11.00
COM.FUTURE RBW (181-210)	.25	.11
FUTURE RBW.MINOR STARS	.40	.18
FUTURE RBW.SEMISTARS	.60	.25
FUTURE RBW.UNLISTED STARS	1.00	.45
FUTURE IMPACT RAINBOW ODDS 1:1		
COMP.POWER RBW.SET (30)	200.00	90.00
COM.POWER RBW (211-240)	1.25	.55
POWER RBW.MINOR STARS	2.00	.90
POWER RBW.SEMISTARS	3.00	1.35
POWER RBW.UNLISTED STARS	5.00	2.20
POWER CORPS RAINBOW ODDS 1:12		
COMP.EST.RBW.SET (30)	200.00	90.00
COMMON EST.RBW (241-270)	2.00	.90
EST.RBW.MINOR STARS	3.00	1.35
EST.RBW.SEMISTARS	5.00	2.20
EST.RBW.UNLISTED STARS	8.00	3.60
ESTABLISHMENT RAINBOW ODDS 1:24		
❏ 1 Travis Lee FF	2.00	.90
❏ 2 A.J. Hinch FF	.75	.35
❏ 3 Mike Caruso FF	.75	.35
❏ 4 Miguel Tejada FF	1.25	.55
❏ 5 Brad Fullmer FF	.75	.35
❏ 6 Eric Milton FF	.75	.35
❏ 7 Mark Kotsay FF	1.25	.55
❏ 8 Darin Erstad FF	2.00	.90

❏ 9	Magglio Ordonez FF	10.00	4.50
❏ 10	Ben Grieve FF	1.25	.55
❏ 11	Brett Tomko FF	.75	.35
❏ 12	Mike Kinkade FF	3.00	1.35
❏ 13	Rolando Arrojo FF	3.00	1.35
❏ 14	Todd Helton FF	4.00	1.80
❏ 15	Scott Rolen FF	4.00	1.80
❏ 16	Bruce Chen FF	1.25	.55
❏ 17	Daryle Ward FF	1.25	.55
❏ 18	Jaret Wright FF	1.25	.55
❏ 19	Sean Casey FF	5.00	2.20
❏ 20	Paul Konerko FF	1.25	.55
❏ 21	Kerry Wood FF	3.00	1.35
❏ 22	Russell Branyan FF	1.25	.55
❏ 23	Gabe Alvarez FF	.75	.35
❏ 24	Juan Encarnacion FF	1.25	.55
❏ 25	Andruw Jones FF	3.00	1.35
❏ 26	Vladimir Guerrero FF	4.00	1.80
❏ 27	Eli Marrero FF	.75	.35
❏ 28	Matt Clement FF	1.25	.55
❏ 29	Gary Matthews Jr. FF	3.00	1.35
❏ 30	Derrek Lee FF	.75	.35
❏ 31	Ken Caminiti PF	.40	.18
❏ 32	Gary Sheffield PF	.40	.18
❏ 33	Jay Buhner PF	.40	.18
❏ 34	Ryan Klesko PF	.40	.18
❏ 35	Nomar Garciaparra PF	3.00	1.35
❏ 36	Vinny Castilla PF	.40	.18
❏ 37	Tony Clark PF	.40	.18
❏ 38	Sammy Sosa PF	3.00	1.35
❏ 39	Tino Martinez PF	.40	.18
❏ 40	Mike Piazza PF	3.00	1.35
❏ 41	Manny Ramirez PF	1.25	.55
❏ 42	Larry Walker PF	1.00	.45
❏ 43	Jose Cruz Jr. PF	.40	.18
❏ 44	Matt Williams PF	1.00	.45
❏ 45	Frank Thomas PF	2.00	.90
❏ 46	Jim Edmonds PF	.40	.18
❏ 47	Raul Mondesi PF	.40	.18
❏ 48	Alex Rodriguez PF	3.00	1.35
❏ 49	Albert Belle PF	1.00	.45
❏ 50	Mark McGwire PF	6.00	2.70
❏ 51	Tim Salmon PF	.60	.25
❏ 52	Andres Galarraga PF	.60	.25
❏ 53	Jeff Bagwell PF	1.25	.55
❏ 54	Jim Thome PF	1.00	.45
❏ 55	Barry Bonds PF	1.25	.55
❏ 56	Carlos Delgado PF	1.00	.45
❏ 57	Mo Vaughn PF	1.00	.45
❏ 58	Chipper Jones PF	2.50	1.10
❏ 59	Juan Gonzalez PF	2.00	.90
❏ 60	Ken Griffey Jr. PF	5.00	2.20
❏ 61	David Cone EF	1.50	.70
❏ 62	Hideo Nomo EF	2.50	1.10
❏ 63	Edgar Martinez EF	1.00	.45
❏ 64	Fred McGriff EF	1.50	.70
❏ 65	Cal Ripken EF	10.00	4.50
❏ 66	Todd Hundley EF	1.00	.45
❏ 67	Barry Larkin EF	2.50	1.10
❏ 68	Dennis Eckersley EF	1.00	.45
❏ 69	Randy Johnson EF	2.50	1.10
❏ 70	Paul Molitor EF	2.50	1.10
❏ 71	Eric Karros EF	1.00	.45
❏ 72	Rafael Palmeiro EF	2.50	1.10
❏ 73	Chuck Knoblauch EF	1.00	.45
❏ 74	Ivan Rodriguez EF	3.00	1.35
❏ 75	Greg Maddux EF	6.00	2.70
❏ 76	Dante Bichette EF	1.00	.45
❏ 77	Brady Anderson EF	1.00	.45
❏ 78	Craig Biggio EF	2.50	1.10
❏ 79	Derek Jeter EF	8.00	3.60
❏ 80	Roger Clemens EF	6.00	2.70
❏ 81	Roberto Alomar EF	2.50	1.10
❏ 82	Wade Boggs EF	2.50	1.10
❏ 83	Charles Johnson EF	1.00	.45
❏ 84	Mark Grace EF	1.50	.70
❏ 85	Kenny Lofton EF	.50	.23
❏ 86	Mike Piazza EF	2.50	1.10
❏ 87	Pedro Martinez EF	3.00	1.35
❏ 88	Curt Schilling EF	1.50	.70
❏ 89	Bernie Williams EF	2.50	1.10
❏ 90	Tony Gwynn EF	6.00	2.70
❏ 91	Travis Lee EF	1.25	.55
❏ 92	A.J. Hinch FE	.50	.23
❏ 93	Mike Caruso FE	.50	.23
❏ 94	Miguel Tejada FE	.75	.35
❏ 95	Brad Fullmer FE	.50	.23
❏ 96	Eric Milton FE	.50	.23
❏ 97	Mark Kotsay FE	.75	.35
❏ 98	Darin Erstad FE	1.25	.55
❏ 99	Magglio Ordonez FE	6.00	2.70
❏ 100	Ben Grieve FE	.75	.35
❏ 101	Brett Tomko FE	.50	.23
❏ 102	Mike Kinkade FE	2.00	.90
❏ 103	Rolando Arrojo FE	2.00	.90
❏ 104	Todd Helton FE	2.50	1.10
❏ 105	Scott Rolen FE	3.00	1.35
❏ 106	Bruce Chen FE	.75	.35
❏ 107	Daryle Ward FE	.75	.35
❏ 108	Jaret Wright FE	.75	.35
❏ 109	Sean Casey FE	3.00	1.35
❏ 110	Paul Konerko FE	.75	.35
❏ 111	Kerry Wood FE	2.00	.90
❏ 112	Russell Branyan FE	.50	.23
❏ 113	Gabe Alvarez FE	.50	.23
❏ 114	Juan Encarnacion FE	.75	.35
❏ 115	Andruw Jones FE	2.00	.90
❏ 116	Vladimir Guerrero FE	3.00	1.35
❏ 117	Eli Marrero FE	.50	.23
❏ 118	Matt Clement FE	.75	.35
❏ 119	Gary Matthews Jr. FE	2.00	.90
❏ 120	Derrek Lee FE	.50	.23
❏ 121	Ken Caminiti PE	.60	.25
❏ 122	Gary Sheffield PE	.60	.25
❏ 123	Jay Buhner PE	.60	.25
❏ 124	Ryan Klesko PE	.60	.25
❏ 125	Nomar Garciaparra PE	5.00	2.20
❏ 126	Vinny Castilla PE	.60	.25
❏ 127	Tony Clark PE	.60	.25
❏ 128	Sammy Sosa PE	5.00	2.20
❏ 129	Tino Martinez PE	.60	.25
❏ 130	Mike Piazza PE	5.00	2.20
❏ 131	Manny Ramirez PE	2.00	.90
❏ 132	Larry Walker PE	1.50	.70
❏ 133	Jose Cruz Jr. PE	.60	.25
❏ 134	Matt Williams PE	1.50	.70
❏ 135	Frank Thomas PE	3.00	1.35
❏ 136	Jim Edmonds PE	.60	.25
❏ 137	Raul Mondesi PE	.60	.25
❏ 138	Alex Rodriguez PE	5.00	2.20
❏ 139	Albert Belle PE	1.50	.70
❏ 140	Mark McGwire PE	10.00	4.50
❏ 141	Tim Salmon PE	.60	.25
❏ 142	Andres Galarraga PE	1.00	.45
❏ 143	Jeff Bagwell PE	2.00	.90
❏ 144	Jim Thome PE	1.50	.70
❏ 145	Barry Bonds PE	2.00	.90
❏ 146	Carlos Delgado PE	1.50	.70
❏ 147	Mo Vaughn PE	1.50	.70
❏ 148	Chipper Jones PE	4.00	1.80
❏ 149	Juan Gonzalez PE	3.00	1.35
❏ 150	Ken Griffey Jr. PE	8.00	3.60
❏ 151	David Cone EE	.50	.23
❏ 152	Hideo Nomo EE	.75	.35
❏ 153	Edgar Martinez EE	.30	.14
❏ 154	Fred McGriff EE	.50	.23
❏ 155	Cal Ripken EE	3.00	1.35
❏ 156	Todd Hundley EE	.30	.14
❏ 157	Barry Larkin EE	.75	.35
❏ 158	Dennis Eckersley EE	.30	.14
❏ 159	Randy Johnson EE	.75	.35
❏ 160	Paul Molitor EE	.75	.35
❏ 161	Eric Karros EE	.30	.14
❏ 162	Rafael Palmeiro EE	.75	.35
❏ 163	Chuck Knoblauch EE	.30	.14
❏ 164	Ivan Rodriguez EE	1.00	.45
❏ 165	Greg Maddux EE	2.00	.90
❏ 166	Dante Bichette EE	.30	.14
❏ 167	Brady Anderson EE	.30	.14
❏ 168	Craig Biggio EE	.75	.35
❏ 169	Derek Jeter EE	2.50	1.10
❏ 170	Roger Clemens EE	2.00	.90
❏ 171	Roberto Alomar EE	.75	.35
❏ 172	Wade Boggs EE	.75	.35
❏ 173	Charles Johnson EE	.30	.14
❏ 174	Mark Grace EE	.50	.23
❏ 175	Kenny Lofton EE	.75	.35
❏ 176	Mike Mussina EE	.75	.35
❏ 177	Pedro Martinez EE	1.00	.45
❏ 178	Curt Schilling EE	.50	.23
❏ 179	Bernie Williams EE	.75	.35
❏ 180	Tony Gwynn EE	2.00	.90
❏ 181	Travis Lee FR	.60	.25
❏ 182	A.J. Hinch FR	.25	.11
❏ 183	Mike Caruso FR	.25	.11
❏ 184	Miguel Tejada FR	.40	.18
❏ 185	Brad Fullmer FR	.25	.11
❏ 186	Eric Milton FR	.25	.11
❏ 187	Mark Kotsay FR	.40	.18
❏ 188	Darin Erstad FR	.60	.25
❏ 189	Magglio Ordonez FR	3.00	1.35
❏ 190	Ben Grieve FR	.40	.18
❏ 191	Brett Tomko FR	.25	.11
❏ 192	Mike Kinkade FR	.60	.25
❏ 193	Rolando Arrojo FR	1.00	.45
❏ 194	Todd Helton FR	1.25	.55
❏ 195	Scott Rolen FR	1.25	.55
❏ 196	Bruce Chen FR	.40	.18
❏ 197	Daryle Ward FR	.40	.18
❏ 198	Jaret Wright FR	.40	.18
❏ 199	Sean Casey FR	1.50	.70
❏ 200	Paul Konerko FR	.40	.18
❏ 201	Kerry Wood FR	1.00	.45
❏ 202	Russell Branyan FR	.40	.18
❏ 203	Gabe Alvarez FR	.25	.11
❏ 204	Juan Encarnacion FR	.40	.18
❏ 205	Andruw Jones FR	1.00	.45
❏ 206	Vladimir Guerrero FR	1.25	.55
❏ 207	Eli Marrero FR	.25	.11
❏ 208	Matt Clement FR	.40	.18
❏ 209	Gary Matthews Jr. FR	.75	.35
❏ 210	Derrek Lee FR	.25	.11
❏ 211	Ken Caminiti PR	2.00	.90
❏ 212	Gary Sheffield PR	2.00	.90
❏ 213	Jay Buhner PR	2.00	.90
❏ 214	Ryan Klesko PR	2.00	.90
❏ 215	Nomar Garciaparra PR	15.00	6.75
❏ 216	Vinny Castilla PR	2.00	.90
❏ 217	Tony Clark PR	2.00	.90
❏ 218	Sammy Sosa PR	15.00	6.75
❏ 219	Tino Martinez PR	2.00	.90
❏ 220	Mike Piazza PR	15.00	6.75
❏ 221	Manny Ramirez PR	6.00	2.70
❏ 222	Larry Walker PR	5.00	2.20
❏ 223	Jose Cruz Jr. PR	2.00	.90
❏ 224	Matt Williams PR	5.00	2.20
❏ 225	Frank Thomas PR	10.00	4.50
❏ 226	Jim Edmonds PR	2.00	.90
❏ 227	Raul Mondesi PR	2.00	.90
❏ 228	Alex Rodriguez PR	15.00	6.75
❏ 229	Albert Belle PR	5.00	2.20
❏ 230	Mark McGwire PR	30.00	13.50
❏ 231	Tim Salmon PR	3.00	1.35
❏ 232	Andres Galarraga PR	3.00	1.35
❏ 233	Jeff Bagwell PR	6.00	2.70
❏ 234	Jim Thome PR	5.00	2.20
❏ 235	Barry Bonds PR	6.00	2.70
❏ 236	Carlos Delgado PR	5.00	2.20
❏ 237	Mo Vaughn PR	5.00	2.20
❏ 238	Chipper Jones PR	12.00	5.50
❏ 239	Juan Gonzalez PR	10.00	4.50
❏ 240	Ken Griffey Jr. PR	25.00	11.00
❏ 241	David Cone PR	5.00	2.20
❏ 242	Hideo Nomo PR	8.00	3.60
❏ 243	Edgar Martinez PR	3.00	1.35
❏ 244	Fred McGriff PR	5.00	2.20
❏ 245	Cal Ripken PR	30.00	13.50
❏ 246	Todd Hundley PR	3.00	1.35
❏ 247	Barry Larkin PR	8.00	3.60
❏ 248	Dennis Eckersley PR	3.00	1.35
❏ 249	Randy Johnson PR	8.00	3.60
❏ 250	Paul Molitor PR	8.00	3.60
❏ 251	Eric Karros PR	3.00	1.35
❏ 252	Rafael Palmeiro PR	8.00	3.60
❏ 253	Chuck Knoblauch PR	3.00	1.35
❏ 254	Ivan Rodriguez PR	10.00	4.50
❏ 255	Greg Maddux PR	20.00	9.00
❏ 256	Dante Bichette PR	3.00	1.35
❏ 257	Brady Anderson PR	3.00	1.35
❏ 258	Craig Biggio PR	8.00	3.60
❏ 259	Derek Jeter PR	25.00	11.00
❏ 260	Roger Clemens PR	20.00	9.00
❏ 261	Roberto Alomar PR	8.00	3.60
❏ 262	Wade Boggs PR	8.00	3.60
❏ 263	Charles Johnson PR	3.00	1.35
❏ 264	Mark Grace PR	5.00	2.20
❏ 265	Kenny Lofton PR	5.00	2.20
❏ 266	Mike Mussina PR	8.00	3.60

- 267 Pedro Martinez ER .... 10.00 — 4.50
- 268 Curt Schilling ER .... 5.00 — 2.20
- 269 Bernie Williams ER .... 8.00 — 3.60
- 270 Tony Gwynn ER .... 20.00 — 9.00
- S1 Ken Griffey Jr. PE Sample 5.00 — 2.20

1998 UD3 Die Cuts

	MINT	NRMT
COMMON CARD (1-90)	2.00	.90

*DC'S 1-30: .6X TO 1.5X BASIC 1-30
*DC'S 31-60: 3X TO 8X BASIC 31-60
*DC'S 61-90: 1.25X TO 3X BASIC 61-90
1-90 PRINT RUN 2000 SERIAL #'d SETS

COMMON CARD 91-180	4.00	1.80

*DC'S 91-120: 1.5X TO 4X BASIC 91-120
*DC'S 121-150: 4X TO 10X BASIC 121-150
*DC'S 151-180: 8X TO 20X BASIC 151-180
91-180 PRINT RUN 1000 SERIAL #'d SETS

COMMON CARD (181-270)	15.00	6.75

*DC'S 181-210: 15X TO 40X BASIC 181-210
*RC'S 181-210: 10X TO 25X BASIC 181-210
*DC'S 211-240: 5X TO 12X BASIC 211-240
*DC'S 241-270: 3X TO 8X BASIC 241-270
181-270 PRINT RUN 100 SERIAL #'d SETS
RANDOM INSERTS IN PACKS

1999 UD Choice

	MINT	NRMT
COMPLETE SET (155)	20.00	9.00
COMMON CARD (1-155)	.10	.05
MINOR STARS	.15	.07
SEMISTARS	.25	.11
UNLISTED STARS	.40	.18

MURRAY BAT LISTED W/UD APH 500 CLUB

- 1 Gabe Kapler .... .40 — .18
- 2 Jin Ho Cho .... .15 — .07
- 3 Matt Anderson .... .10 — .05
- 4 Ricky Ledee .... .15 — .07
- 5 Bruce Chen .... .15 — .07
- 6 Alex Gonzalez .... .15 — .07
- 7 Ryan Minor .... .15 — .07
- 8 Michael Barrett .... .25 — .11
- 9 Carlos Beltran .... .50 — .23
- 10 Ramon E.Martinez .... .10 — .05
- 11 Dermal Brown .... .15 — .07
- 12 Robert Fick .... .15 — .07
- 13 Preston Wilson .... .15 — .07
- 14 Orlando Hernandez .... .40 — .18
- 15 Troy Glaus .... .40 — .18
- 16 Calvin Pickering .... .15 — .07
- 17 Corey Koskie .... .10 — .05
- 18 Fernando Seguignol .... .15 — .07
- 19 Carlos Guillen .... .15 — .07
- 20 Kevin Witt .... .10 — .05
- 21 Mike Kinkade .... .10 — .05
- 22 Eric Chavez .... .25 — .11
- 23 Mike Lowell .... .10 — .05
- 24 Adrian Beltre .... .40 — .18
- 25 George Lombard .... .15 — .07
- 26 Jeremy Giambi .... .15 — .07
- 27 J.D. Drew .... .60 — .25
- 28 Mark McGwire CG .. 1.25 — .55
- 29 Kerry Wood CG .... .15 — .07
- 30 David Wells CG .... .10 — .05
- 31 Gonzalez CG .... .40 — .18

- 32 Randy Johnson CG .... .15 — .07
- 33 Derek Jeter CG .... .60 — .25
- 34 Tony Gwynn CG .... .50 — .23
- 35 Greg Maddux CG .... .50 — .23
- 36 Cal Ripken CG .... .75 — .35
- 37 Ken Griffey Jr. CG .... 1.00 — .45
- 38 Bartolo Colon CG .... .15 — .07
- 39 Troy Glaus CG .... .15 — .07
- 40 Ben Grieve CG .... .15 — .07
- 41 Roger Clemens CG .... .50 — .23
- 42 Chipper Jones CG .... .50 — .23
- 43 Scott Rolen CG .... .40 — .18
- 44 Nomar Garciaparra CG .. .60 — .25
- 45 Sammy Sosa CG .... .60 — .25
- 46 Tim Salmon .... .25 — .11
- 47 Darin Erstad .... .25 — .11
- 48 Chuck Finley .... .15 — .07
- 49 Garret Anderson .... .15 — .07
- 50 Matt Williams .... .40 — .18
- 51 Jay Bell .... .15 — .07
- 52 Travis Lee .... .25 — .11
- 53 Andruw Jones .... .40 — .18
- 54 Andres Galarraga .... .25 — .11
- 55 Chipper Jones .... 1.00 — .45
- 56 Greg Maddux .... 1.00 — .45
- 57 Javy Lopez .... .15 — .07
- 58 Cal Ripken .... 1.50 — .70
- 59 Brady Anderson .... .15 — .07
- 60 Rafael Palmeiro .... .40 — .18
- 61 B.J. Surhoff .... .15 — .07
- 62 Nomar Garciaparra .. 1.25 — .55
- 63 Troy O'Leary .... .15 — .07
- 64 Pedro Martinez .... .50 — .23
- 65 Jason Varitek .... .15 — .07
- 66 Kerry Wood .... .40 — .18
- 67 Sammy Sosa .... 1.25 — .55
- 68 Mark Grace .... .25 — .11
- 69 Mickey Morandini .... .10 — .05
- 70 Albert Belle .... .40 — .18
- 71 Mike Caruso .... .10 — .05
- 72 Frank Thomas .... .75 — .35
- 73 Sean Casey .... .40 — .18
- 74 Pete Harnisch .... .10 — .05
- 75 Dmitri Young .... .15 — .07
- 76 Manny Ramirez .... .50 — .23
- 77 Omar Vizquel .... .15 — .07
- 78 Travis Fryman .... .15 — .07
- 79 Jim Thome .... .40 — .18
- 80 Kenny Lofton .... .25 — .11
- 81 Todd Helton .... .40 — .18
- 82 Larry Walker .... .40 — .18
- 83 Vinny Castilla .... .15 — .07
- 84 Gabe Alvarez .... .10 — .05
- 85 Tony Clark .... .15 — .07
- 86 Damion Easley .... .10 — .05
- 87 Livan Hernandez .... .10 — .05
- 88 Mark Kotsay .... .15 — .07
- 89 Cliff Floyd .... .15 — .07
- 90 Jeff Bagwell .... .50 — .23
- 91 Moises Alou .... .15 — .07
- 92 Randy Johnson .... .40 — .18
- 93 Craig Biggio .... .40 — .18
- 94 Larry Sutton .... .10 — .05
- 95 Dean Palmer .... .15 — .07
- 96 Johnny Damon .... .15 — .07
- 97 Charles Johnson .... .15 — .07
- 98 Gary Sheffield .... .15 — .07
- 99 Raul Mondesi .... .15 — .07
- 100 Mark Grudzielanek .... .10 — .05
- 101 Jeromy Burnitz .... .10 — .05
- 102 Jeff Cirillo .... .10 — .05
- 103 Jose Valentin .... .10 — .05
- 104 Mark Loretta .... .10 — .05
- 105 Todd Walker .... .15 — .07
- 106 David Ortiz .... .40 — .18
- 107 Brad Radke .... .15 — .07
- 108 Brad Fullmer .... .10 — .05
- 109 Rondell White .... .15 — .07
- 110 Vladimir Guerrero .... .50 — .23
- 111 Mike Piazza .... 1.25 — .55
- 112 Brian McRae .... .10 — .05
- 113 John Olerud .... .15 — .07
- 114 Rey Ordonez .... .15 — .07
- 115 Derek Jeter .... 1.25 — .55
- 116 Bernie Williams .... .40 — .18
- 117 David Wells .... .15 — .07

- 118 Paul O'Neill .... .15 — .07
- 119 Tino Martinez .... .15 — .07
- 120 A.J. Hinch .... .10 — .05
- 121 Jason Giambi .... .15 — .07
- 122 Miguel Tejada .... .15 — .07
- 123 Ben Grieve .... .40 — .18
- 124 Scott Rolen .... .50 — .23
- 125 Desi Relaford .... .10 — .05
- 126 Bobby Abreu .... .15 — .07
- 127 Jose Guillen .... .10 — .05
- 128 Jason Kendall .... .15 — .07
- 129 Aramis Ramirez .... .25 — .11
- 130 Mark McGwire .... 2.50 — 1.10
- 131 Ray Lankford .... .15 — .07
- 132 Eli Marrero .... .10 — .05
- 133 Wally Joyner .... .15 — .07
- 134 Greg Vaughn .... .15 — .07
- 135 Trevor Hoffman .... .15 — .07
- 136 Kevin Brown .... .25 — .11
- 137 Tony Gwynn .... 1.00 — .45
- 138 Bill Mueller .... .10 — .05
- 139 Ellis Burks .... .15 — .07
- 140 Barry Bonds .... .50 — .23
- 141 Robb Nen .... .10 — .05
- 142 Ken Griffey Jr. .... 2.00 — .90
- 143 Alex Rodriguez .... 1.25 — .55
- 144 Jay Buhner .... .15 — .07
- 145 Edgar Martinez .... .15 — .07
- 146 Rolando Arrojo .... .10 — .05
- 147 Robert Smith .... .10 — .05
- 148 Quinton McCracken .... .10 — .05
- 149 Ivan Rodriguez .... .50 — .23
- 150 Will Clark .... .40 — .18
- 151 Mark McLemore .... .10 — .05
- 152 Juan Gonzalez .... .75 — .35
- 153 Jose Cruz Jr. .... .10 — .05
- 154 Carlos Delgado .... .40 — .18
- 155 Roger Clemens .... 1.00 — .45

1999 UD Choice Prime Choice Reserve

	MINT	NRMT
COMMON CARD (1-155)	5.00	2.20

*STARS: 20X TO 50X BASIC CARDS
*YNG.STARS: 15X TO 40X BASIC
RANDOM INSERTS IN PACKS
STATED PRINT RUN 100 SERIAL #'d SETS

1999 UD Choice Mini Bobbing Head

	MINT	NRMT
COMPLETE SET (30)	25.00	11.00
COMMON CARD (B1-B30)	.50	.23
UNLISTED STARS	1.00	.45

STATED ODDS 1:5

- B1 Randy Johnson .... 1.00 — .45
- B2 Troy Glaus .... 1.00 — .45
- B3 Chipper Jones .... 2.50 — 1.10
- B4 Cal Ripken .... 4.00 — 1.80
- B5 Nomar Garciaparra .. 3.00 — 1.35
- B6 Pedro Martinez .... 1.25 — .55
- B7 Kerry Wood .... 1.00 — .45
- B8 Sammy Sosa .... 3.00 — 1.35
- B9 Frank Thomas .... 2.00 — .90

❏ B10 Paul Konerko	1.00	.45
❏ B11 Omar Vizquel	.50	.23
❏ B12 Kenny Lofton	.60	.25
❏ B13 Gabe Kapler	1.00	.45
❏ B14 Adrian Beltre	1.00	.45
❏ B15 Orlando Hernandez	1.00	.45
❏ B16 Derek Jeter	3.00	1.35
❏ B17 Mike Piazza	3.00	1.35
❏ B18 Tino Martinez	.50	.23
❏ B19 Ben Grieve	1.00	.45
❏ B20 Rickey Henderson	1.25	.55
❏ B21 Scott Rolen	1.25	.55
❏ B22 Aramis Ramirez	.60	.25
❏ B23 Greg Vaughn	.50	.23
❏ B24 Tony Gwynn	2.50	1.10
❏ B25 Barry Bonds	1.25	.55
❏ B26 Alex Rodriguez	3.00	1.35
❏ B27 Ken Griffey Jr.	5.00	2.20
❏ B28 Mark McGwire	6.00	2.70
❏ B29 J.D. Drew	1.50	.70
❏ B30 Juan Gonzalez	2.00	.90

1999 UD Choice StarQuest

	MINT	NRMT
COMP. BLUE SET (30)	20.00	9.00
COMMON BLUE (1-30)	.25	.11
SEMISTARS	.40	.18
UNLISTED STARS	.60	.25

ONE BLUE PER PACK
*GREEN: 1X TO 2.5X HI COLUMN
GREEN STATED ODDS 1:8
*RED: 2.5X TO 6X HI COLUMN
RED STATED ODDS 1:23
*GOLD: 30X TO 80X HI COLUMN
GOLD RANDOM INSERTS IN PACKS
GOLD PRINT RUN 100 SERIAL #'d SETS
BLUE FOIL CARDS PRICED BELOW

❏ 1 Ken Griffey Jr.	3.00	1.35
❏ 2 Sammy Sosa	2.00	.90
❏ 3 Alex Rodriguez	2.00	.90
❏ 4 Derek Jeter	2.00	.90
❏ 5 Troy Glaus	.60	.25
❏ 6 Mike Piazza	2.00	.90
❏ 7 Barry Bonds	.75	.35
❏ 8 Tony Gwynn	1.50	.70
❏ 9 Juan Gonzalez	1.25	.55
❏ 10 Chipper Jones	1.50	.70

❏ 11 Greg Maddux	1.50	.70
❏ 12 Randy Johnson	.60	.25
❏ 13 Roger Clemens	1.50	.70
❏ 14 Ben Grieve	.60	.25
❏ 15 Nomar Garciaparra	2.00	.90
❏ 16 Travis Lee	.40	.18
❏ 17 Frank Thomas	1.25	.55
❏ 18 Vladimir Guerrero	.75	.35
❏ 19 Scott Rolen	.75	.35
❏ 20 Ivan Rodriguez	.75	.35
❏ 21 Cal Ripken	2.50	1.10
❏ 22 Mark McGwire	4.00	1.80
❏ 23 Jeff Bagwell	.75	.35
❏ 24 Tony Clark	.25	.11
❏ 25 Kerry Wood	.60	.25
❏ 26 Kenny Lofton	.40	.18
❏ 27 Adrian Beltre	.60	.25
❏ 28 Larry Walker	.60	.25
❏ 29 Curt Schilling	.40	.18
❏ 30 Jim Thome	.60	.25

1999 UD Choice Yard Work

	MINT	NRMT
COMPLETE SET (30)	80.00	36.00
COMMON CARD (Y1-Y30)	.75	.35
SEMISTARS	1.25	.55
UNLISTED STARS	2.00	.90

STATED ODDS 1:13

❏ Y1 Andres Galarraga	1.25	.55
❏ Y2 Chipper Jones	5.00	2.20
❏ Y3 Rafael Palmeiro	2.00	.90
❏ Y4 Nomar Garciaparra	6.00	2.70
❏ Y5 Sammy Sosa	6.00	2.70
❏ Y6 Frank Thomas	4.00	1.80
❏ Y7 J.D. Drew	2.50	1.10
❏ Y8 Albert Belle	2.00	.90
❏ Y9 Jim Thome	2.00	.90
❏ Y10 Manny Ramirez	2.50	1.10
❏ Y11 Larry Walker	2.00	.90
❏ Y12 Vinny Castilla	.75	.35
❏ Y13 Tony Clark	.75	.35
❏ Y14 Jeff Bagwell	2.50	1.10
❏ Y15 Moises Alou	.75	.35
❏ Y16 Dean Palmer	.75	.35
❏ Y17 Gary Sheffield	.75	.35
❏ Y18 Vladimir Guerrero	2.50	1.10
❏ Y19 Mike Piazza	6.00	2.70
❏ Y20 Tino Martinez	.75	.35
❏ Y21 Ben Grieve	2.00	.90
❏ Y22 Greg Vaughn	.75	.35
❏ Y23 Ken Caminiti	.75	.35
❏ Y24 Barry Bonds	2.50	1.10
❏ Y25 Ken Griffey Jr.	10.00	4.50
❏ Y26 Alex Rodriguez	6.00	2.70
❏ Y27 Mark McGwire	12.00	5.50
❏ Y28 Juan Gonzalez	4.00	1.80
❏ Y29 Jose Canseco	2.50	1.10
❏ Y30 Jose Cruz Jr.	.75	.35

1999 UD Ionix

	MINT	NRMT
COMPLETE SET (90)	250.00	110.00
COMP. SET w/o SP's (60)	50.00	22.00
COMMON CARD (1-60)	.30	.14

MINOR STARS	.50	.23
SEMISTARS	.75	.35
UNLISTED STARS	1.25	.55
COMMON TECH (61-90)	2.00	.90
TECH SEMISTARS	2.50	1.10
TECH UNLISTED STARS	4.00	1.80

TECH STATED ODDS 1:4
F.ROB BAT LISTED W/UD APH 500 CLUB

❏ 1 Troy Glaus	1.25	.55
❏ 2 Darin Erstad	.75	.35
❏ 3 Travis Lee	.75	.35
❏ 4 Matt Williams	1.25	.55
❏ 5 Chipper Jones	3.00	1.35
❏ 6 Greg Maddux	3.00	1.35
❏ 7 Andruw Jones	1.25	.55
❏ 8 Andres Galarraga	.75	.35
❏ 9 Tom Glavine	1.25	.55
❏ 10 Cal Ripken	5.00	2.20
❏ 11 Ryan Minor	.50	.23
❏ 12 Nomar Garciaparra	4.00	1.80
❏ 13 Mo Vaughn	1.25	.55
❏ 14 Pedro Martinez	1.50	.70
❏ 15 Sammy Sosa	4.00	1.80
❏ 16 Kerry Wood	1.25	.55
❏ 17 Albert Belle	1.25	.55
❏ 18 Frank Thomas	2.50	1.10
❏ 19 Sean Casey	1.25	.55
❏ 20 Kenny Lofton	.75	.35
❏ 21 Manny Ramirez	1.50	.70
❏ 22 Jim Thome	1.25	.55
❏ 23 Bartolo Colon	.50	.23
❏ 24 Jaret Wright	.50	.23
❏ 25 Larry Walker	1.25	.55
❏ 26 Tony Clark	.50	.23
❏ 27 Gabe Kapler	1.25	.55
❏ 28 Edgar Renteria	.30	.14
❏ 29 Randy Johnson	1.25	.55
❏ 30 Craig Biggio	1.25	.55
❏ 31 Jeff Bagwell	1.50	.70
❏ 32 Moises Alou	.50	.23
❏ 33 Johnny Damon	.50	.23
❏ 34 Adrian Beltre	1.25	.55
❏ 35 Jeromy Burnitz	.50	.23
❏ 36 Todd Walker	.50	.23
❏ 37 Corey Koskie	.30	.14
❏ 38 Vladimir Guerrero	1.50	.70
❏ 39 Mike Piazza	4.00	1.80
❏ 40 Hideo Nomo	1.25	.55
❏ 41 Derek Jeter	4.00	1.80
❏ 42 Tino Martinez	.50	.23
❏ 43 Orlando Hernandez	1.25	.55
❏ 44 Ben Grieve	1.25	.55
❏ 45 Rickey Henderson	1.50	.70
❏ 46 Scott Rolen	1.50	.70
❏ 47 Curt Schilling	.75	.35
❏ 48 Aramis Ramirez	.75	.35
❏ 49 Tony Gwynn	3.00	1.35
❏ 50 Kevin Brown	.75	.35
❏ 51 Barry Bonds	1.50	.70
❏ 52 Ken Griffey Jr.	6.00	2.70
❏ 53 Alex Rodriguez	4.00	1.80
❏ 54 Mark McGwire	8.00	3.60
❏ 55 J.D. Drew	2.00	.90
❏ 56 Rolando Arrojo	.30	.14
❏ 57 Ivan Rodriguez	1.50	.70
❏ 58 Juan Gonzalez	2.50	1.10
❏ 59 Roger Clemens	3.00	1.35

	MINT	NRMT
60 Jose Cruz Jr.	.50	.23
61 Travis Lee TECH	2.50	1.10
62 Andres Galarraga TECH	2.50	1.10
63 Andruw Jones TECH	4.00	1.80
64 Chipper Jones TECH	10.00	4.50
65 Greg Maddux TECH	10.00	4.50
66 Cal Ripken TECH	15.00	6.75
67 Nomar Garciaparra TECH	12.00	5.50
68 Mo Vaughn TECH	4.00	1.80
69 Sammy Sosa TECH	12.00	5.50
70 Frank Thomas TECH	8.00	3.60
71 Kerry Wood TECH	4.00	1.80
72 Kenny Lofton TECH	2.50	1.10
73 Manny Ramirez TECH	5.00	2.20
74 Larry Walker TECH	4.00	1.80
75 Jeff Bagwell TECH	5.00	2.20
76 Randy Johnson TECH	4.00	1.80
77 Paul Molitor TECH	4.00	1.80
78 Derek Jeter TECH	12.00	5.50
79 Tino Martinez TECH	2.00	.90
80 Mike Piazza TECH	12.00	5.50
81 Ben Grieve TECH	4.00	1.80
82 Scott Rolen TECH	5.00	2.20
83 Mark McGwire TECH	25.00	11.00
84 Tony Gwynn TECH	10.00	4.50
85 Barry Bonds TECH	5.00	2.20
86 Ken Griffey Jr. TECH	20.00	9.00
87 Alex Rodriguez TECH	12.00	5.50
88 Juan Gonzalez TECH	8.00	3.60
89 Roger Clemens TECH	10.00	4.50
90 J.D. Drew TECH	5.00	2.20
S100 Ken Griffey Jr. Sample	4.00	1.80

1999 UD Ionix Reciprocal

	MINT	NRMT
COMMON CARD (1-60)	3.00	1.35

*RECIP.1-60: 4X TO 10X BASIC 1-60
RECIP.1-60 PRINT RUN 750 SERIAL #'d SETS

	MINT	NRMT
COMMON CARD (61-90)	15.00	6.75

*TECH RECIP: 3X TO 8X BASIC TECH
TECH RECIP.PRINT RUN 100 SERIAL #'d SETS
RANDOM INSERTS IN PACKS

1999 UD Ionix Cyber

	MINT	NRMT
COMPLETE SET (25)	800.00	350.00

	MINT	NRMT
COMMON CARD (C1-C25)	10.00	4.50
UNLISTED STARS	15.00	6.75
STATED ODDS 1:53		
C1 Ken Griffey Jr.	80.00	36.00
C2 Cal Ripken	60.00	27.00
C3 Frank Thomas	30.00	13.50
C4 Greg Maddux	40.00	18.00
C5 Mike Piazza	50.00	22.00
C6 Alex Rodriguez	50.00	22.00
C7 Chipper Jones	40.00	18.00
C8 Derek Jeter	50.00	22.00
C9 Mark McGwire	100.00	45.00
C10 Juan Gonzalez	30.00	13.50
C11 Kerry Wood	15.00	6.75
C12 Tony Gwynn	40.00	18.00
C13 Scott Rolen	20.00	9.00
C14 Nomar Garciaparra	50.00	22.00
C15 Roger Clemens	40.00	18.00
C16 Sammy Sosa	50.00	22.00
C17 Travis Lee	10.00	4.50
C18 Ben Grieve	15.00	6.75
C19 Jeff Bagwell	20.00	9.00
C20 Ivan Rodriguez	20.00	9.00
C21 Barry Bonds	20.00	9.00
C22 J.D. Drew	20.00	9.00
C23 Kenny Lofton	10.00	4.50
C24 Andruw Jones	15.00	6.75
C25 Vladimir Guerrero	20.00	9.00

1999 UD Ionix HoloGrFX

	MINT	NRMT
COMPLETE SET (10)	2000.00	900.00
COMMON CARD (HG1-HG10)	120.00	55.00
STATED ODDS 1:1500		
HG1 Ken Griffey Jr.	300.00	135.00
HG2 Cal Ripken	250.00	110.00
HG3 Frank Thomas	120.00	55.00
HG4 Greg Maddux	150.00	70.00
HG5 Mike Piazza	200.00	90.00
HG6 Alex Rodriguez	200.00	90.00
HG7 Chipper Jones	150.00	70.00
HG8 Derek Jeter	200.00	90.00
HG9 Mark McGwire	400.00	180.00
HG10 Juan Gonzalez	120.00	55.00

1999 UD Ionix Hyper

	MINT	NRMT
COMPLETE SET (20)	200.00	90.00
COMMON CARD (H1-H20)	2.50	1.10
UNLISTED STARS	4.00	1.80
STATED ODDS 1:9		
H1 Ken Griffey Jr.	20.00	9.00
H2 Cal Ripken	15.00	6.75
H3 Frank Thomas	8.00	3.60
H4 Greg Maddux	10.00	4.50
H5 Mike Piazza	12.00	5.50
H6 Alex Rodriguez	12.00	5.50
H7 Chipper Jones	10.00	4.50
H8 Derek Jeter	12.00	5.50
H9 Mark McGwire	25.00	11.00
H10 Juan Gonzalez	8.00	3.60
H11 Kerry Wood	4.00	1.80
H12 Tony Gwynn	10.00	4.50
H13 Scott Rolen	5.00	2.20
H14 Nomar Garciaparra	12.00	5.50
H15 Roger Clemens	10.00	4.50
H16 Sammy Sosa	12.00	5.50
H17 Travis Lee	2.50	1.10
H18 Ben Grieve	4.00	1.80
H19 Jeff Bagwell	5.00	2.20
H20 J.D. Drew	5.00	2.20

1999 UD Ionix Nitro

	MINT	NRMT
COMPLETE SET (10)	120.00	55.00
COMMON CARD (N1-N10)	5.00	2.20
STATED ODDS 1:18		
N1 Ken Griffey Jr.	20.00	9.00
N2 Cal Ripken	15.00	6.75
N3 Frank Thomas	8.00	3.60
N4 Greg Maddux	10.00	4.50
N5 Mike Piazza	12.00	5.50
N6 Alex Rodriguez	12.00	5.50
N7 Chipper Jones	10.00	4.50
N8 Derek Jeter	12.00	5.50
N9 Mark McGwire	25.00	11.00
N10 J.D. Drew	5.00	2.20

1999 UD Ionix Warp Zone

	MINT	NRMT
COMPLETE SET (15)	1000.00	450.00

COMMON CARD (WZ1-WZ15) 15.00   6.75
STATED ODDS 1:216

		MINT	NRMT
☐	WZ1 Ken Griffey Jr.	120.00	55.00
☐	WZ2 Cal Ripken	100.00	45.00
☐	WZ3 Frank Thomas	50.00	22.00
☐	WZ4 Greg Maddux	60.00	27.00
☐	WZ5 Mike Piazza	80.00	36.00
☐	WZ6 Alex Rodriguez	80.00	36.00
☐	WZ7 Chipper Jones	60.00	27.00
☐	WZ8 Derek Jeter	60.00	36.00
☐	WZ9 Mark McGwire	150.00	70.00
☐	WZ10 Juan Gonzalez	50.00	22.00
☐	WZ11 Kerry Wood	15.00	6.75
☐	WZ12 Tony Gwynn	60.00	27.00
☐	WZ13 Scott Rolen	30.00	13.50
☐	WZ14 Nomar Garciaparra	80.00	36.00
☐	WZ15 J.D. Drew	30.00	13.50

1991 Ultra

	MINT	NRMT
COMPLETE SET (400)	20.00	9.00
COMMON CARD (1-400)	.10	.05
MINOR STARS	.20	.09
UNLISTED STARS	.40	.18

☐ 1 Steve Avery	.10	.05
☐ 2 Jeff Blauser	.10	.05
☐ 3 Francisco Cabrera	.10	.05
☐ 4 Ron Gant	.20	.09
☐ 5 Tom Glavine	.40	.18
☐ 6 Tommy Gregg	.10	.05
☐ 7 Dave Justice	.40	.18
☐ 8 Oddibe McDowell	.10	.05
☐ 9 Greg Olson	.10	.05
☐ 10 Terry Pendleton	.20	.09
☐ 11 Lonnie Smith	.10	.05
☐ 12 John Smoltz	.40	.18
☐ 13 Jeff Treadway	.10	.05
☐ 14 Glenn Davis	.10	.05
☐ 15 Mike Devereaux	.10	.05
☐ 16 Leo Gomez	.10	.05
☐ 17 Chris Hoiles	.10	.05
☐ 18 Dave Johnson	.10	.05
☐ 19 Ben McDonald	.10	.05
☐ 20 Randy Milligan	.10	.05
☐ 21 Gregg Olson	.10	.05
☐ 22 Joe Orsulak	.10	.05
☐ 23 Bill Ripken	.10	.05
☐ 24 Cal Ripken	1.50	.70
☐ 25 David Segui	.10	.05
☐ 26 Craig Worthington	.10	.05
☐ 27 Wade Boggs	.40	.18
☐ 28 Tom Bolton	.10	.05
☐ 29 Tom Brunansky	.10	.05
☐ 30 Ellis Burks	.20	.05
☐ 31 Roger Clemens	1.00	.45
☐ 32 Mike Greenwell	.10	.05
☐ 33 Greg A. Harris	.10	.05
☐ 34 Daryl Irvine	.10	.05
☐ 35 Mike Marshall UER	.10	.05
(1990 in stats is		
shown as 990)		
☐ 36 Tim Naehring	.10	.05
☐ 37 Tony Pena	.10	.05
☐ 38 Phil Plantier	.10	.05
☐ 39 Carlos Quintana	.10	.05

☐ 40 Jeff Reardon	.20	.09
☐ 41 Jody Reed	.10	.05
☐ 42 Luis Rivera	.10	.05
☐ 43 Jim Abbott	.20	.09
☐ 44 Chuck Finley	.20	.09
☐ 45 Bryan Harvey	.10	.05
☐ 46 Donnie Hill	.10	.05
☐ 47 Jack Howell	.10	.05
☐ 48 Wally Joyner	.20	.09
☐ 49 Mark Langston	.10	.05
☐ 50 Kirk McCaskill	.10	.05
☐ 51 Lance Parrish	.10	.05
☐ 52 Dick Schofield	.10	.05
☐ 53 Lee Stevens	.20	.09
☐ 54 Dave Winfield	.40	.18
☐ 55 George Bell	.10	.05
☐ 56 Damon Berryhill	.10	.05
☐ 57 Mike Bielecki	.10	.05
☐ 58 Andre Dawson	.40	.18
☐ 59 Shawon Dunston	.10	.05
☐ 60 Joe Girardi UER	.20	.09
(Bats right, LH hitter		
shown is Doug Dascenzo)		
☐ 61 Mark Grace	.40	.18
☐ 62 Mike Harkey	.10	.05
☐ 63 Les Lancaster	.10	.05
☐ 64 Greg Maddux	1.00	.45
☐ 65 Derrick May	.10	.05
☐ 66 Ryne Sandberg	.50	.23
☐ 67 Luis Salazar	.10	.05
☐ 68 Dwight Smith	.10	.05
☐ 69 Hector Villanueva	.10	.05
☐ 70 Jerome Walton	.10	.05
☐ 71 Mitch Williams	.10	.05
☐ 72 Carlton Fisk	.40	.18
☐ 73 Scott Fletcher	.10	.05
☐ 74 Ozzie Guillen	.10	.05
☐ 75 Greg Hibbard	.10	.05
☐ 76 Lance Johnson	.10	.05
☐ 77 Steve Lyons	.10	.05
☐ 78 Jack McDowell	.10	.05
☐ 79 Dan Pasqua	.10	.05
☐ 80 Melido Perez	.10	.05
☐ 81 Tim Raines	.20	.09
☐ 82 Sammy Sosa	2.50	1.10
☐ 83 Cory Snyder	.10	.05
☐ 84 Bobby Thigpen	.10	.05
☐ 85 Frank Thomas	1.50	.70
(Card says he is		
an outfielder)		
☐ 86 Robin Ventura	.40	.18
☐ 87 Todd Benzinger	.10	.05
☐ 88 Glenn Braggs	.10	.05
☐ 89 Tom Browning UER	.10	.05
(Front photo actually		
Norm Charlton)		
☐ 90 Norm Charlton	.10	.05
Norm Charlton)		
☐ 91 Eric Davis	.20	.09
☐ 92 Rob Dibble	.10	.05
☐ 93 Bill Doran	.10	.05
☐ 94 Mariano Duncan UER	.10	.05
(Right back photo		
is Billy Hatcher)		
☐ 95 Billy Hatcher	.10	.05
☐ 96 Barry Larkin	.40	.18
☐ 97 Randy Myers	.10	.05
☐ 98 Hal Morris	.10	.05
☐ 99 Joe Oliver	.10	.05
☐ 100 Paul O'Neill	.20	.09
☐ 101 Jeff Reed	.10	.05
(See also 104)		
☐ 102 Jose Rijo	.20	.09
☐ 103 Chris Sabo	.10	.05
(See also 106)		
☐ 104 Beau Allred UER	.10	.05
(Card number is 101)		
☐ 105 Sandy Alomar Jr.	.20	.09
☐ 106 Carlos Baerga UER	.10	.05
(Card number is 103)		
☐ 107 Albert Belle	.50	.23
☐ 108 Jerry Browne	.10	.05
☐ 109 Tom Candiotti	.10	.05
☐ 110 Alex Cole	.10	.05
☐ 111 John Farrell	.10	.05
(See also 114)		
☐ 112 Felix Fermin	.10	.05

☐ 113 Brook Jacoby	.10	.05
☐ 114 Chris James UER	.10	.05
(Card number is 111)		
☐ 115 Doug Jones	.10	.05
☐ 116 Steve Olin	.10	.05
(See also 119)		
☐ 117 Greg Swindell	.10	.05
☐ 118 Turner Ward	.10	.05
☐ 119 Mitch Webster UER	.10	.05
(Card number is 116)		
☐ 120 Dave Bergman	.10	.05
☐ 121 Cecil Fielder	.20	.09
☐ 122 Travis Fryman	.40	.18
☐ 123 Mike Henneman	.10	.05
☐ 124 Lloyd Moseby	.10	.05
☐ 125 Dan Petry	.10	.05
☐ 126 Tony Phillips	.10	.05
☐ 127 Mark Salas	.10	.05
☐ 128 Frank Tanana	.10	.05
☐ 129 Alan Trammell	.30	.14
☐ 130 Lou Whitaker	.20	.09
☐ 131 Eric Anthony	.10	.05
☐ 132 Craig Biggio	.40	.18
☐ 133 Ken Caminiti	.40	.18
☐ 134 Casey Candaele	.10	.05
☐ 135 Andujar Cedeno	.10	.05
☐ 136 Mark Davidson	.10	.05
☐ 137 Jim Deshaies	.10	.05
☐ 138 Mark Portugal	.10	.05
☐ 139 Rafael Ramirez	.10	.05
☐ 140 Mike Scott	.10	.05
☐ 141 Eric Yelding	.10	.05
☐ 142 Gerald Young	.10	.05
☐ 143 Kevin Appier	.20	.09
☐ 144 George Brett	.75	.35
☐ 145 Jeff Conine	.40	.18
☐ 146 Jim Eisenreich	.10	.05
☐ 147 Tom Gordon	.10	.05
☐ 148 Mark Gubicza	.10	.05
☐ 149 Bo Jackson	.20	.09
☐ 150 Brent Mayne	.10	.05
☐ 151 Mike Macfarlane	.10	.05
☐ 152 Brian McRae	.20	.09
☐ 153 Jeff Montgomery	.20	.09
☐ 154 Bret Saberhagen	.20	.09
☐ 155 Kevin Seitzer	.10	.05
☐ 156 Terry Shumpert	.10	.05
☐ 157 Kurt Stillwell	.10	.05
☐ 158 Danny Tartabull	.10	.05
☐ 159 Tim Belcher	.10	.05
☐ 160 Kal Daniels	.10	.05
☐ 161 Alfredo Griffin	.10	.05
☐ 162 Lenny Harris	.10	.05
☐ 163 Jay Howell	.10	.05
☐ 164 Ramon Martinez	.20	.09
☐ 165 Mike Morgan	.10	.05
☐ 166 Eddie Murray	.40	.18
☐ 167 Jose Offerman	.30	.14
☐ 168 Juan Samuel	.10	.05
☐ 169 Mike Scioscia	.10	.05
☐ 170 Mike Sharperson	.10	.05
☐ 171 Darryl Strawberry	.20	.09
☐ 172 Greg Brock	.10	.05
☐ 173 Chuck Crim	.10	.05
☐ 174 Jim Gantner	.10	.05
☐ 175 Ted Higuera	.10	.05
☐ 176 Mark Knudson	.10	.05
☐ 177 Tim McIntosh	.10	.05
☐ 178 Paul Molitor	.40	.18
☐ 179 Dan Plesac	.10	.05
☐ 180 Gary Sheffield	.40	.18
☐ 181 Bill Spiers	.10	.05
☐ 182 B.J. Surhoff	.20	.09
☐ 183 Greg Vaughn	.40	.18
☐ 184 Robin Yount	.40	.18
☐ 185 Rick Aguilera	.20	.09
☐ 186 Greg Gagne	.10	.05
☐ 187 Dan Gladden	.10	.05
☐ 188 Brian Harper	.10	.05
☐ 189 Kent Hrbek	.20	.09
☐ 190 Gene Larkin	.10	.05
☐ 191 Shane Mack	.10	.05
☐ 192 Pedro Munoz	.10	.05
☐ 193 Al Newman	.10	.05
☐ 194 Junior Ortiz	.10	.05
☐ 195 Kirby Puckett	.60	.25

❏ 196 Kevin Tapani	.10	.05
❏ 197 Dennis Boyd	.10	.05
❏ 198 Tim Burke	.10	.05
❏ 199 Ivan Calderon	.10	.05
❏ 200 Delino DeShields	.20	.09
❏ 201 Mike Fitzgerald	.10	.05
❏ 202 Steve Frey	.10	.05
❏ 203 Andres Galarraga	.40	.18
❏ 204 Marquis Grissom	.40	.18
❏ 205 Dave Martinez	.10	.05
❏ 206 Dennis Martinez	.20	.09
❏ 207 Junior Noboa	.10	.05
❏ 208 Spike Owen	.10	.05
❏ 209 Scott Ruskin	.10	.05
❏ 210 Tim Wallach	.10	.05
❏ 211 Daryl Boston	.10	.05
❏ 212 Vince Coleman	.10	.05
❏ 213 David Cone	.20	.09
❏ 214 Ron Darling	.10	.05
❏ 215 Kevin Elster	.10	.05
❏ 216 Sid Fernandez	.10	.05
❏ 217 John Franco	.20	.09
❏ 218 Dwight Gooden	.10	.05
❏ 219 Tom Herr	.10	.05
❏ 220 Todd Hundley	.40	.18
❏ 221 Gregg Jefferies	.10	.05
❏ 222 Howard Johnson	.10	.05
❏ 223 Dave Magadan	.10	.05
❏ 224 Kevin McReynolds	.10	.05
❏ 225 Keith Miller	.10	.05
❏ 226 Mackey Sasser	.10	.05
❏ 227 Frank Viola	.10	.05
❏ 228 Jesse Barfield	.10	.05
❏ 229 Greg Cadaret	.10	.05
❏ 230 Alvaro Espinoza	.10	.05
❏ 231 Bob Geren	.10	.05
❏ 232 Lee Guetterman	.10	.05
❏ 233 Mel Hall	.10	.05
❏ 234 Andy Hawkins UER	.10	.05
(Back center photo		
is not him)		
❏ 235 Roberto Kelly	.10	.05
❏ 236 Tim Leary	.10	.05
❏ 237 Jim Leyritz	.20	.09
❏ 238 Kevin Maas	.10	.05
❏ 239 Don Mattingly	.75	.35
❏ 240 Hensley Meulens	.10	.05
❏ 241 Eric Plunk	.10	.05
❏ 242 Steve Sax	.10	.05
❏ 243 Todd Burns	.10	.05
❏ 244 Jose Canseco	.50	.23
❏ 245 Dennis Eckersley	.20	.09
❏ 246 Mike Gallego	.10	.05
❏ 247 Dave Henderson	.10	.05
❏ 248 Rickey Henderson	.50	.23
❏ 249 Rick Honeycutt	.10	.05
❏ 250 Carney Lansford	.10	.05
❏ 251 Mark McGwire	2.00	.90
❏ 252 Mike Moore	.10	.05
❏ 253 Terry Steinbach	.20	.09
❏ 254 Dave Stewart	.20	.09
❏ 255 Walt Weiss	.10	.05
❏ 256 Bob Welch	.10	.05
❏ 257 Curt Young	.10	.05
❏ 258 Wes Chamberlain	.10	.05
❏ 259 Pat Combs	.10	.05
❏ 260 Darren Daulton	.20	.09
❏ 261 Jose DeJesus	.10	.05
❏ 262 Len Dykstra	.20	.09
❏ 263 Charlie Hayes	.10	.05
❏ 264 Von Hayes	.10	.05
❏ 265 Ken Howell	.10	.05
❏ 266 John Kruk	.20	.09
❏ 267 Roger McDowell	.10	.05
❏ 268 Mickey Morandini	.10	.05
❏ 269 Terry Mulholland	.10	.05
❏ 270 Dale Murphy	.40	.18
❏ 271 Randy Ready	.10	.05
❏ 272 Dickie Thon	.10	.05
❏ 273 Stan Belinda	.10	.05
❏ 274 Jay Bell	.20	.09
❏ 275 Barry Bonds	.50	.23
❏ 276 Bobby Bonilla	.20	.09
❏ 277 Doug Drabek	.10	.05
❏ 278 Carlos Garcia	.10	.05
❏ 279 Neal Heaton	.10	.05

❏ 280 Jeff King	.10	.05
❏ 281 Bill Landrum	.10	.05
❏ 282 Mike LaValliere	.10	.05
❏ 283 Jose Lind	.10	.05
❏ 284 Orlando Merced	.20	.09
❏ 285 Gary Redus	.10	.05
❏ 286 Don Slaught	.10	.05
❏ 287 Andy Van Slyke	.20	.09
❏ 288 Jose DeLeon	.10	.05
❏ 289 Pedro Guerrero	.10	.05
❏ 290 Ray Lankford	.40	.18
❏ 291 Joe Magrane	.10	.05
❏ 292 Jose Oquendo	.10	.05
❏ 293 Tom Pagnozzi	.10	.05
❏ 294 Bryn Smith	.10	.05
❏ 295 Lee Smith	.20	.09
❏ 296 Ozzie Smith UER	.50	.23
(Born 12-26, 54,		
should have hyphen)		
❏ 297 Milt Thompson	.10	.05
❏ 298 Craig Wilson	.10	.05
❏ 299 Todd Zeile	.20	.09
❏ 300 Shawn Abner	.10	.05
❏ 301 Andy Benes	.20	.09
❏ 302 Paul Faries	.10	.05
❏ 303 Tony Gwynn	1.00	.45
❏ 304 Greg W. Harris	.10	.05
❏ 305 Thomas Howard	.10	.05
❏ 306 Bruce Hurst	.10	.05
❏ 307 Craig Lefferts	.10	.05
❏ 308 Fred McGriff	.40	.18
❏ 309 Dennis Rasmussen	.10	.05
❏ 310 Bip Roberts	.10	.05
❏ 311 Benito Santiago	.10	.05
❏ 312 Garry Templeton	.10	.05
❏ 313 Ed Whitson	.10	.05
❏ 314 Dave Anderson	.10	.05
❏ 315 Kevin Bass	.10	.05
❏ 316 Jeff Brantley	.10	.05
❏ 317 John Burkett	.10	.05
❏ 318 Will Clark	.40	.18
❏ 319 Steve Decker	.10	.05
❏ 320 Scott Garrelts	.10	.05
❏ 321 Terry Kennedy	.10	.05
❏ 322 Mark Leonard	.10	.05
❏ 323 Darren Lewis	.20	.09
❏ 324 Greg Litton	.10	.05
❏ 325 Willie McGee	.20	.09
❏ 326 Kevin Mitchell	.10	.05
❏ 327 Don Robinson	.10	.05
❏ 328 Andres Santana	.10	.05
❏ 329 Robby Thompson	.10	.05
❏ 330 Jose Uribe	.10	.05
❏ 331 Matt Williams	.40	.18
❏ 332 Scott Bradley	.10	.05
❏ 333 Henry Cotto	.10	.05
❏ 334 Alvin Davis	.10	.05
❏ 335 Ken Griffey Sr.	.20	.09
❏ 336 Ken Griffey Jr.	3.00	1.35
❏ 337 Erik Hanson	.10	.05
❏ 338 Brian Holman	.10	.05
❏ 339 Randy Johnson	.50	.23
❏ 340 Edgar Martinez UER	.40	.18
(Listed as playing SS)		
❏ 341 Tino Martinez	.40	.18
❏ 342 Pete O'Brien	.10	.05
❏ 343 Harold Reynolds	.10	.05
❏ 344 Dave Valle	.10	.05
❏ 345 Omar Vizquel	.40	.18
❏ 346 Brad Arnsberg	.10	.05
❏ 347 Kevin Brown	.30	.14
❏ 348 Julio Franco	.10	.05
❏ 349 Jeff Huson	.10	.05
❏ 350 Rafael Palmeiro	.40	.18
❏ 351 Geno Petralli	.10	.05
❏ 352 Gary Pettis	.10	.05
❏ 353 Kenny Rogers	.10	.05
❏ 354 Jeff Russell	.10	.05
❏ 355 Nolan Ryan	1.50	.70
❏ 356 Ruben Sierra	.10	.05
❏ 357 Bobby Witt	.10	.05
❏ 358 Roberto Alomar	.40	.18
❏ 359 Pat Borders	.10	.05
❏ 360 Joe Carter UER	.20	.09
(Reverse negative		
on back photo)		

❏ 361 Kelly Gruber	.10	.05
❏ 362 Tom Henke	.10	.05
❏ 363 Glenallen Hill	.10	.05
❏ 364 Jimmy Key	.20	.09
❏ 365 Manny Lee	.10	.05
❏ 366 Rance Mulliniks	.10	.05
❏ 367 John Olerud UER	.30	.14
(Throwing left on card;		
back has throws right;		
he does throw lefty)		
❏ 368 Dave Stieb	.10	.05
❏ 369 Duane Ward	.10	.05
❏ 370 David Wells	.20	.09
❏ 371 Mark Whiten	.20	.09
❏ 372 Mookie Wilson	.20	.09
❏ 373 Willie Banks MLP	.10	.05
❏ 374 Steve Carter MLP	.10	.05
❏ 375 Scott Chiamparino MLP	.10	.05
❏ 376 Steve Chitren MLP	.10	.05
❏ 377 Darrin Fletcher MLP	.10	.05
❏ 378 Rich Garces MLP	.10	.05
❏ 379 Reggie Jefferson MLP	.30	.14
❏ 380 Eric Karros MLP	.75	.35
❏ 381 Pat Kelly MLP	.10	.05
❏ 382 Chuck Knoblauch MLP	.40	.18
❏ 383 Denny Neagle MLP	.40	.18
❏ 384 Dan Opperman MLP	.10	.05
❏ 385 John Ramos MLP	.10	.05
❏ 386 Henry Rodriguez MLP	.75	.35
❏ 387 Mo Vaughn MLP	.75	.35
❏ 388 Gerald Williams MLP	.10	.05
❏ 389 Mike York MLP	.10	.05
❏ 390 Eddie Zosky MLP	.10	.05
❏ 391 Barry Bonds EP	.40	.18
❏ 392 Cecil Fielder EP	.20	.09
❏ 393 Rickey Henderson EP	.20	.09
❏ 394 Dave Justice EP	.20	.09
❏ 395 Nolan Ryan EP	.75	.35
❏ 396 Bobby Thigpen EP	.10	.05
❏ 397 Gregg Jefferies CL	.10	.05
❏ 398 Von Hayes CL	.10	.05
❏ 399 Terry Kennedy CL	.10	.05
❏ 400 Nolan Ryan CL	.40	.18

1991 Ultra Gold

BARRY BONDS
PITTSBURGH PIRATES • OUTFIELD

	MINT	NRMT
COMPLETE SET (10)	10.00	4.50
*SINGLES: 1X TO 2X BASE CARD HI		
RANDOM INSERTS IN FOIL PACKS		

❏ 1 Barry Bonds	1.00	.45
❏ 2 Will Clark	.75	.35
❏ 3 Doug Drabek	.25	.11
❏ 4 Ken Griffey Jr.	6.00	2.70
❏ 5 Rickey Henderson	1.00	.45
❏ 6 Bo Jackson	.40	.18
❏ 7 Ramon Martinez	.40	.18
❏ 8 Kirby Puckett UER	1.25	.55
(Boggs won 1988		
batting title, so		
Puckett didn't win		
consecutive titles)		
❏ 9 Chris Sabo	.25	.11
❏ 10 Ryne Sandberg UER	1.00	.45
(Johnson and Hornsby		
didn't hit 40 homers		
in 1990, Fielder did		
hit 51 in '90)		

1991 Ultra Update

JUAN GUZMAN BLUE JAYS
PITCHER

	MINT	NRMT
COMP. FACT. SET (120)	50.00	22.00
COMMON CARD (1-120)	.25	.11
MINOR STARS	.50	.23
SEMISTARS	.50	.23
UNLISTED STARS	1.00	.45

☐ 1 Dwight Evans	.50	.23
☐ 2 Chito Martinez	.25	.11
☐ 3 Bob Melvin	.25	.11
☐ 4 Mike Mussina	6.00	2.70
☐ 5 Jack Clark	.50	.23
☐ 6 Dana Kiecker	.25	.11
☐ 7 Steve Lyons	.25	.11
☐ 8 Gary Gaetti	.50	.23
☐ 9 Dave Gallagher	.25	.11
☐ 10 Dave Parker	.50	.23
☐ 11 Luis Polonia	.25	.11
☐ 12 Luis Sojo	.25	.11
☐ 13 Wilson Alvarez	1.00	.45
☐ 14 Alex Fernandez	.50	.23
☐ 15 Craig Grebeck	.25	.11
☐ 16 Ron Karkovice	.25	.11
☐ 17 Warren Newson	.25	.11
☐ 18 Scott Radinsky	.25	.11
☐ 19 Glenallen Hill	.25	.11
☐ 20 Charles Nagy	1.00	.45
☐ 21 Mark Whiten	.25	.11
☐ 22 Milt Cuyler	.25	.11
☐ 23 Paul Gibson	.25	.11
☐ 24 Mickey Tettleton	.50	.23
☐ 25 Todd Benzinger	.25	.11
☐ 26 Storm Davis	.25	.11
☐ 27 Kirk Gibson	.50	.23
☐ 28 Bill Pecota	.25	.11
☐ 29 Gary Thurman	.25	.11
☐ 30 Darryl Hamilton	.25	.11
☐ 31 Jaime Navarro	.25	.11
☐ 32 Willie Randolph	.50	.23
☐ 33 Bill Wegman	.25	.11
☐ 34 Randy Bush	.25	.11
☐ 35 Chili Davis	.50	.23
☐ 36 Scott Erickson	.50	.23
☐ 37 Chuck Knoblauch	1.50	.70
☐ 38 Scott Leius	.25	.11
☐ 39 Jack Morris	.50	.23
☐ 40 John Habyan	.25	.11
☐ 41 Pat Kelly	.25	.11
☐ 42 Matt Nokes	.25	.11
☐ 43 Scott Sanderson	.25	.11
☐ 44 Bernie Williams	5.00	2.20
☐ 45 Harold Baines	.50	.23
☐ 46 Brook Jacoby	.25	.11
☐ 47 Earnest Riles	.25	.11
☐ 48 Willie Wilson	.25	.11
☐ 49 Jay Buhner	1.00	.45
☐ 50 Rich DeLucia	.25	.11
☐ 51 Mike Jackson	.50	.23
☐ 52 Bill Krueger	.25	.11
☐ 53 Bill Swift	.25	.11
☐ 54 Brian Downing	.25	.11
☐ 55 Juan Gonzalez	15.00	6.75
☐ 56 Dean Palmer	2.00	.90
☐ 57 Kevin Reimer	.25	.11
☐ 58 Ivan Rodriguez	12.00	5.50
☐ 59 Tom Candiotti	.25	.11

☐ 60 Juan Guzman	.50	.23
☐ 61 Bob MacDonald	.25	.11
☐ 62 Greg Myers	.25	.11
☐ 63 Ed Sprague	.25	.11
☐ 64 Devon White	.25	.11
☐ 65 Rafael Belliard	.25	.11
☐ 66 Juan Berenguer	.25	.11
☐ 67 Brian R. Hunter	.25	.11
☐ 68 Kent Mercker	.25	.11
☐ 69 Otis Nixon	.50	.23
☐ 70 Danny Jackson	.25	.11
☐ 71 Chuck McElroy	.25	.11
☐ 72 Gary Scott	.25	.11
☐ 73 Heathcliff Slocumb	1.00	.45
☐ 74 Chico Walker	.25	.11
☐ 75 Rick Wilkins	.25	.11
☐ 76 Chris Hammond	.25	.11
☐ 77 Luis Quinones	.25	.11
☐ 78 Herm Winningham	.25	.11
☐ 79 Jeff Bagwell	15.00	6.75
☐ 80 Jim Corsi	.25	.11
☐ 81 Steve Finley	1.00	.45
☐ 82 Luis Gonzalez	2.50	1.10
☐ 83 Pete Harnisch	.25	.11
☐ 84 Darryl Kile	1.00	.45
☐ 85 Brett Butler	.50	.23
☐ 86 Gary Carter	1.00	.45
☐ 87 Tim Crews	.25	.11
☐ 88 Orel Hershiser	.50	.23
☐ 89 Bob Ojeda	.25	.11
☐ 90 Bret Barberie	.25	.11
☐ 91 Barry Jones	.25	.11
☐ 92 Gilberto Reyes	.25	.11
☐ 93 Larry Walker	2.00	.90
☐ 94 Hubie Brooks	.25	.11
☐ 95 Tim Burke	.25	.11
☐ 96 Rick Cerone	.25	.11
☐ 97 Jeff Innis	.25	.11
☐ 98 Wally Backman	.25	.11
☐ 99 Tommy Greene	.25	.11
☐ 100 Ricky Jordan	.25	.11
☐ 101 Mitch Williams	.25	.11
☐ 102 John Smiley	.25	.11
☐ 103 Randy Tomlin	.25	.11
☐ 104 Gary Varsho	.25	.11
☐ 105 Cris Carpenter	.25	.11
☐ 106 Ken Hill	.25	.11
☐ 107 Felix Jose	.25	.11
☐ 108 Omar Olivares	.25	.11
☐ 109 Gerald Perry	.25	.11
☐ 110 Jerald Clark	.25	.11
☐ 111 Tony Fernandez	.25	.11
☐ 112 Darrin Jackson	.25	.11
☐ 113 Mike Maddux	.25	.11
☐ 114 Tim Teufel	.25	.11
☐ 115 Bud Black	.25	.11
☐ 116 Kelly Downs	.25	.11
☐ 117 Mike Felder	.25	.11
☐ 118 Willie McGee	.50	.23
☐ 119 Trevor Wilson	.25	.11
☐ 120 Checklist 1-120	.25	.11

1992 Ultra

BRIAN McRAE
KANSAS CITY ROYALS • OUTFIELD

	MINT	NRMT
COMPLETE SET (600)	30.00	13.50
COMPLETE SERIES 1 (300)	20.00	9.00
COMPLETE SERIES 2 (300)	10.00	4.50

COMMON CARD (1-600)	.10	.05
MINOR STARS	.20	.09
UNLISTED STARS	.40	.18

☐ 1 Glenn Davis	.10	.05
☐ 2 Mike Devereaux	.10	.05
☐ 3 Dwight Evans	.20	.09
☐ 4 Leo Gomez	.20	.09
☐ 5 Chris Hoiles	.10	.05
☐ 6 Sam Horn	.10	.05
☐ 7 Chito Martinez	.10	.05
☐ 8 Randy Milligan	.10	.05
☐ 9 Mike Mussina	.60	.25
☐ 10 Billy Ripken	.10	.05
☐ 11 Cal Ripken	1.50	.70
☐ 12 Tom Brunansky	.10	.05
☐ 13 Ellis Burks	.20	.09
☐ 14 Jack Clark	.20	.09
☐ 15 Roger Clemens	1.00	.45
☐ 16 Mike Greenwell	.10	.05
☐ 17 Joe Hesketh	.10	.05
☐ 18 Tony Pena	.10	.05
☐ 19 Carlos Quintana	.10	.05
☐ 20 Jeff Reardon	.20	.09
☐ 21 Jody Reed	.10	.05
☐ 22 Luis Rivera	.10	.05
☐ 23 Mo Vaughn	.50	.23
☐ 24 Gary DiSarcina	.10	.05
☐ 25 Chuck Finley	.20	.09
☐ 26 Gary Gaetti	.20	.09
☐ 27 Bryan Harvey	.10	.05
☐ 28 Lance Parrish	.10	.05
☐ 29 Luis Polonia	.10	.05
☐ 30 Dick Schofield	.10	.05
☐ 31 Luis Sojo	.10	.05
☐ 32 Wilson Alvarez	.20	.09
☐ 33 Carlton Fisk	.40	.18
☐ 34 Craig Grebeck	.10	.05
☐ 35 Ozzie Guillen	.10	.05
☐ 36 Greg Hibbard	.10	.05
☐ 37 Charlie Hough	.20	.09
☐ 38 Lance Johnson	.10	.05
☐ 39 Ron Karkovice	.10	.05
☐ 40 Jack McDowell	.20	.09
☐ 41 Donn Pall	.10	.05
☐ 42 Melido Perez	.10	.05
☐ 43 Tim Raines	.20	.09
☐ 44 Frank Thomas	1.00	.45
☐ 45 Sandy Alomar Jr.	.20	.09
☐ 46 Carlos Baerga	.40	.18
☐ 47 Albert Belle	.40	.18
☐ 48 Jerry Browne UER	.10	.05
(Reversed negative on card back)		
☐ 49 Felix Fermin	.10	.05
☐ 50 Reggie Jefferson UER	.20	.09
(Born 1968, not 1966)		
☐ 51 Mark Lewis	.10	.05
☐ 52 Carlos Martinez	.10	.05
☐ 53 Steve Olin	.10	.05
☐ 54 Jim Thome	1.00	.45
☐ 55 Mark Whiten	.10	.05
☐ 56 Dave Bergman	.10	.05
☐ 57 Milt Cuyler	.10	.05
☐ 58 Rob Deer	.20	.09
☐ 59 Cecil Fielder	.20	.09
☐ 60 Travis Fryman	.20	.09
☐ 61 Scott Livingstone	.10	.05
☐ 62 Tony Phillips	.10	.05
☐ 63 Mickey Tettleton	.10	.05
☐ 64 Alan Trammell	.30	.14
☐ 65 Lou Whitaker	.20	.09
☐ 66 Kevin Appier	.20	.09
☐ 67 Mike Boddicker	.10	.05
☐ 68 George Brett	.75	.35
☐ 69 Jim Eisenreich	.10	.05
☐ 70 Mark Gubicza	.10	.05
☐ 71 David Howard	.10	.05
☐ 72 Joel Johnston	.10	.05
☐ 73 Mike Macfarlane	.10	.05
☐ 74 Brent Mayne	.10	.05
☐ 75 Brian McRae	.10	.05
☐ 76 Jeff Montgomery	.20	.09
☐ 77 Danny Tartabull	.10	.05
☐ 78 Don August	.10	.05
☐ 79 Dante Bichette	.30	.14

80	Ted Higuera	.10	.05
81	Paul Molitor	.40	.18
82	Jaime Navarro	.10	.05
83	Gary Sheffield	.40	.18
84	Bill Spiers	.10	.05
85	B.J. Surhoff	.20	.09
86	Greg Vaughn	.30	.14
87	Robin Yount	.40	.18
88	Rick Aguilera	.20	.09
89	Chili Davis	.20	.09
90	Scott Erickson	.20	.09
91	Brian Harper	.10	.05
92	Kent Hrbek	.20	.09
93	Chuck Knoblauch	.40	.18
94	Scott Leius	.10	.05
95	Shane Mack	.10	.05
96	Mike Pagliarulo	.10	.05
97	Kirby Puckett	.60	.25
98	Kevin Tapani	.10	.05
99	Jesse Barfield	.10	.05
100	Alvaro Espinoza	.10	.05
101	Mel Hall	.10	.05
102	Pat Kelly	.10	.05
103	Roberto Kelly	.20	.09
104	Kevin Maas	.10	.05
105	Don Mattingly	.75	.35
106	Hensley Meulens	.10	.05
107	Matt Nokes	.10	.05
108	Steve Sax	.20	.09
109	Harold Baines	.20	.09
110	Jose Canseco	.50	.23
111	Ron Darling	.10	.05
112	Mike Gallego	.10	.05
113	Dave Henderson	.10	.05
114	Rickey Henderson	.50	.23
115	Mark McGwire	2.00	.90
116	Terry Steinbach	.10	.05
117	Dave Stewart	.20	.09
118	Todd Van Poppel	.10	.05
119	Bob Welch	.10	.05
120	Greg Briley	.10	.05
121	Jay Buhner	.30	.14
122	Rick DeLucia	.10	.05
123	Ken Griffey Jr.	2.50	1.10
124	Erik Hanson	.10	.05
125	Randy Johnson	.40	.18
126	Edgar Martinez	.30	.14
127	Tino Martinez	.40	.18
128	Pete O'Brien	.10	.05
129	Harold Reynolds	.10	.05
130	Dave Valle	.10	.05
131	Julio Franco	.10	.05
132	Juan Gonzalez	1.00	.45
133	Jeff Huson	.20	.09
	(Shows Jose Canseco sliding into second)		
134	Mike Jeffcoat	.10	.05
135	Terry Mathews	.10	.05
136	Rafael Palmeiro	.40	.18
137	Dean Palmer	.20	.09
138	Geno Petralli	.10	.05
139	Ivan Rodriguez	.75	.35
140	Jeff Russell	.10	.05
141	Nolan Ryan	1.50	.70
142	Ruben Sierra	.40	.18
143	Roberto Alomar	.40	.18
144	Pat Borders	.10	.05
145	Joe Carter	.20	.09
146	Kelly Gruber	.10	.05
147	Jimmy Key	.20	.09
148	Manny Lee	.10	.05
149	Rance Mulliniks	.10	.05
150	Greg Myers	.10	.05
151	John Olerud	.20	.09
152	Dave Stieb	.10	.05
153	Todd Stottlemyre	.20	.09
154	Duane Ward	.10	.05
155	Devon White	.10	.05
156	Eddie Zosky	.10	.05
157	Steve Avery	.20	.09
158	Rafael Belliard	.10	.05
159	Jeff Blauser	.10	.05
160	Sid Bream	.10	.05
161	Ron Gant	.20	.09
162	Tom Glavine	.30	.14
163	Brian Hunter	.10	.05
164	Dave Justice	.40	.18
165	Mark Lemke	.10	.05
166	Greg Olson	.10	.05
167	Terry Pendleton	.10	.05
168	Lonnie Smith	.10	.05
169	John Smoltz	.30	.14
170	Mike Stanton	.10	.05
171	Jeff Treadway	.10	.05
172	Paul Assenmacher	.10	.05
173	George Bell	.10	.05
174	Shawon Dunston	.10	.05
175	Mark Grace	.30	.14
176	Danny Jackson	.10	.05
177	Les Lancaster	.10	.05
178	Greg Maddux	1.00	.45
179	Luis Salazar	.10	.05
180	Rey Sanchez	.10	.05
181	Ryne Sandberg	.50	.23
182	Jose Vizcaino	.10	.05
183	Chico Walker	.10	.05
184	Jerome Walton	.10	.05
185	Glenn Braggs	.10	.05
186	Tom Browning	.10	.05
187	Rob Dibble	.10	.05
188	Bill Doran	.10	.05
189	Chris Hammond	.10	.05
190	Billy Hatcher	.10	.05
191	Barry Larkin	.30	.14
192	Hal Morris	.10	.05
193	Joe Oliver	.10	.05
194	Paul O'Neill	.20	.09
195	Jeff Reed	.10	.05
196	Jose Rijo	.10	.05
197	Chris Sabo	.10	.05
198	Jeff Bagwell	.75	.35
199	Craig Biggio	.40	.18
200	Ken Caminiti	.30	.14
201	Andujar Cedeno	.10	.05
202	Steve Finley	.20	.09
203	Luis Gonzalez	.30	.14
204	Pete Harnisch	.10	.05
205	Xavier Hernandez	.10	.05
206	Darryl Kile	.20	.09
207	Al Osuna	.10	.05
208	Curt Schilling	.30	.14
209	Brett Butler	.20	.09
210	Kal Daniels	.10	.05
211	Lenny Harris	.10	.05
212	Stan Javier	.10	.05
213	Ramon Martinez	.20	.09
214	Roger McDowell	.10	.05
215	Jose Offerman	.20	.09
216	Juan Samuel	.10	.05
217	Mike Scioscia	.10	.05
218	Mike Sharperson	.10	.05
219	Darryl Strawberry	.20	.09
220	Delino DeShields	.20	.09
221	Tom Foley	.10	.05
222	Steve Frey	.10	.05
223	Dennis Martinez	.20	.09
224	Spike Owen	.10	.05
225	Gilberto Reyes	.10	.05
226	Tim Wallach	.10	.05
227	Daryl Boston	.10	.05
228	Tim Burke	.10	.05
229	Vince Coleman	.10	.05
230	David Cone	.20	.09
231	Kevin Elster	.10	.05
232	Dwight Gooden	.20	.09
233	Todd Hundley	.10	.05
234	Jeff Innis	.10	.05
235	Howard Johnson ►	.10	.05
236	Dave Magadan	.10	.05
237	Mackey Sasser	.10	.05
238	Anthony Young	.10	.05
239	Wes Chamberlain	.10	.05
240	Darren Daulton	.20	.09
241	Len Dykstra	.20	.09
242	Tommy Greene	.10	.05
243	Charlie Hayes	.10	.05
244	Dave Hollins	.20	.09
245	Ricky Jordan	.10	.05
246	John Kruk	.20	.09
247	Mickey Morandini	.10	.05
248	Terry Mulholland	.10	.05
249	Dale Murphy	.40	.18
250	Jay Bell	.20	.09
251	Barry Bonds	.50	.23
252	Steve Buechele	.10	.05
253	Doug Drabek	.10	.05
254	Mike LaValliere	.10	.05
255	Jose Lind	.10	.05
256	Lloyd McClendon	.10	.05
257	Orlando Merced	.10	.05
258	Don Slaught	.10	.05
259	John Smiley	.10	.05
260	Zane Smith	.10	.05
261	Randy Tomlin	.10	.05
262	Andy Van Slyke	.20	.09
263	Pedro Guerrero	.10	.05
264	Felix Jose	.10	.05
265	Ray Lankford	.40	.18
266	Omar Olivares	.10	.05
267	Jose Oquendo	.10	.05
268	Tom Pagnozzi	.10	.05
269	Bryn Smith	.10	.05
270	Lee Smith UER	.20	.09
	(1991 record listed as 61-61)		
271	Ozzie Smith UER	.50	.23
	(Comma before year of birth on card back)		
272	Milt Thompson	.10	.05
273	Todd Zeile	.10	.05
274	Andy Benes	.20	.09
275	Jerald Clark	.10	.05
276	Tony Fernandez	.10	.05
277	Tony Gwynn	1.00	.45
278	Greg W. Harris	.10	.05
279	Thomas Howard	.10	.05
280	Bruce Hurst	.10	.05
281	Mike Maddux	.10	.05
282	Fred McGriff	.30	.14
283	Benito Santiago	.10	.05
284	Kevin Bass	.10	.05
285	Jeff Brantley	.10	.05
286	John Burkett	.10	.05
287	Will Clark	.40	.18
288	Royce Clayton	.10	.05
289	Steve Decker	.10	.05
290	Kelly Downs	.10	.05
291	Mike Felder	.10	.05
292	Darren Lewis	.10	.05
293	Kirt Manwaring	.10	.05
294	Willie McGee	.20	.09
295	Robby Thompson	.10	.05
296	Matt Williams	.30	.14
297	Trevor Wilson	.10	.05
298	Checklist 1-100	.10	.05
299	Checklist 101-200	.10	.05
300	Checklist 201-300	.10	.05
301	Brady Anderson	.30	.14
302	Todd Frohwirth	.10	.05
303	Ben McDonald	.10	.05
304	Mark McLemore	.10	.05
305	Jose Mesa	.10	.05
306	Bob Milacki	.10	.05
307	Gregg Olson	.20	.09
308	David Segui	.10	.05
309	Rick Sutcliffe	.10	.05
310	Jeff Tackett	.10	.05
311	Wade Boggs	.40	.18
312	Scott Cooper	.10	.05
313	John Flaherty	.10	.05
314	Wayne Housie	.10	.05
315	Peter Hoy	.10	.05
316	John Marzano	.10	.05
317	Tim Naehring	.10	.05
318	Phil Plantier	.40	.18
319	Frank Viola	.10	.05
320	Matt Young	.10	.05
321	Jim Abbott	.20	.09
322	Hubie Brooks	.10	.05
323	Chad Curtis	.40	.18
324	Alvin Davis	.10	.05
325	Junior Felix	.10	.05
326	Von Hayes	.10	.05
327	Mark Langston	.20	.09
328	Scott Lewis	.10	.05
329	Don Robinson	.10	.05
330	Bobby Rose	.10	.05
331	Lee Stevens	.20	.09

332	George Bell	.10	.05
333	Esteban Beltre	.10	.05
334	Joey Cora	.10	.05
335	Alex Fernandez	.20	.09
336	Roberto Hernandez	.30	.14
337	Mike Huff	.10	.05
338	Kirk McCaskill	.10	.05
339	Dan Pasqua	.10	.05
340	Scott Radinsky	.10	.05
341	Steve Sax	.10	.05
342	Bobby Thigpen	.10	.05
343	Robin Ventura	.20	.09
344	Jack Armstrong	.10	.05
345	Alex Cole	.10	.05
346	Dennis Cook	.10	.05
347	Glenallen Hill	.10	.05
348	Thomas Howard	.10	.05
349	Brook Jacoby	.10	.05
350	Kenny Lofton	.50	.23
351	Charles Nagy	.20	.09
352	Rod Nichols	.10	.05
353	Junior Ortiz	.10	.05
354	Dave Otto	.10	.05
355	Tony Perezchica	.10	.05
356	Scott Scudder	.10	.05
357	Paul Sorrento	.10	.05
358	Skeeter Barnes	.10	.05
359	Mark Carreon	.10	.05
360	John Doherty	.10	.05
361	Dan Gladden	.10	.05
362	Bill Gullickson	.10	.05
363	Shawn Hare	.10	.05
364	Mike Henneman	.10	.05
365	Chad Kreuter	.10	.05
366	Mark Leiter	.10	.05
367	Mike Munoz	.10	.05
368	Kevin Ritz	.10	.05
369	Mark Davis	.10	.05
370	Tom Gordon	.10	.05
371	Chris Gwynn	.10	.05
372	Gregg Jefferies	.10	.05
373	Wally Joyner	.20	.09
374	Kevin McReynolds	.10	.05
375	Keith Miller	.10	.05
376	Rico Rossy	.10	.05
377	Curtis Wilkerson	.10	.05
378	Ricky Bones	.10	.05
379	Chris Bosio	.10	.05
380	Cal Eldred	.10	.05
381	Scott Fletcher	.10	.05
382	Jim Gantner	.10	.05
383	Darryl Hamilton	.10	.05
384	Doug Henry	.10	.05
385	Pat Listach	.10	.05
386	Tim McIntosh	.10	.05
387	Edwin Nunez	.10	.05
388	Dan Plesac	.10	.05
389	Kevin Seitzer	.10	.05
390	Franklin Stubbs	.10	.05
391	William Suero	.10	.05
392	Bill Wegman	.10	.05
393	Willie Banks	.10	.05
394	Jarvis Brown	.10	.05
395	Greg Gagne	.10	.05
396	Mark Guthrie	.10	.05
397	Bill Krueger	.10	.05
398	Pat Mahomes	.10	.05
399	Pedro Munoz	.10	.05
400	John Smiley	.10	.05
401	Gary Wayne	.10	.05
402	Lenny Webster	.10	.05
403	Carl Willis	.10	.05
404	Greg Cadaret	.10	.05
405	Steve Farr	.10	.05
406	Mike Gallego	.10	.05
407	Charlie Hayes	.10	.05
408	Steve Howe	.10	.05
409	Dion James	.10	.05
410	Jeff Johnson	.10	.05
411	Tim Leary	.10	.05
412	Jim Leyritz	.10	.05
413	Melido Perez	.10	.05
414	Scott Sanderson	.10	.05
415	Andy Stankiewicz	.10	.05
416	Mike Stanley	.10	.05
417	Danny Tartabull	.10	.05
418	Lance Blankenship	.10	.05
419	Mike Bordick	.10	.05
420	Scott Brosius	.50	.23
421	Dennis Eckersley	.20	.09
422	Scott Hemond	.10	.05
423	Carney Lansford	.20	.09
424	Henry Mercedes	.10	.05
425	Mike Moore	.10	.05
426	Gene Nelson	.10	.05
427	Randy Ready	.10	.05
428	Bruce Walton	.10	.05
429	Willie Wilson	.10	.05
430	Rich Amaral	.10	.05
431	Dave Cochrane	.10	.05
432	Henry Cotto	.10	.05
433	Calvin Jones	.10	.05
434	Kevin Mitchell	.20	.09
435	Clay Parker	.10	.05
436	Omar Vizquel	.20	.09
437	Dave Fleming	.10	.05
438	Kevin Brown	.30	.14
439	John Cangelosi	.10	.05
440	Brian Downing	.10	.05
441	Monty Fariss	.10	.05
442	Jose Guzman	.10	.05
443	Donald Harris	.10	.05
444	Kevin Reimer	.10	.05
445	Kenny Rogers	.10	.05
446	Wayne Rosenthal	.10	.05
447	Dickie Thon	.10	.05
448	Derek Bell	.20	.09
449	Juan Guzman	.10	.05
450	Tom Henke	.10	.05
451	Candy Maldonado	.10	.05
452	Jack Morris	.20	.09
453	David Wells	.20	.09
454	Dave Winfield	.40	.18
455	Juan Berenguer	.10	.05
456	Damon Berryhill	.10	.05
457	Mike Bielecki	.10	.05
458	Marvin Freeman	.10	.05
459	Charlie Leibrandt	.10	.05
460	Kent Mercker	.10	.05
461	Otis Nixon	.20	.09
462	Alejandro Pena	.10	.05
463	Ben Rivera	.10	.05
464	Deion Sanders	.40	.18
465	Mark Wohlers	.10	.05
466	Shawn Boskie	.10	.05
467	Frank Castillo	.10	.05
468	Andre Dawson	.30	.14
469	Joe Girardi	.20	.09
470	Chuck McElroy	.10	.05
471	Mike Morgan	.10	.05
472	Ken Patterson	.10	.05
473	Bob Scanlan	.10	.05
474	Gary Scott	.10	.05
475	Dave Smith	.10	.05
476	Sammy Sosa	1.25	.55
477	Hector Villanueva	.10	.05
478	Scott Bankhead	.10	.05
479	Tim Belcher	.10	.05
480	Freddie Benavides	.10	.05
481	Jacob Brumfield	.10	.05
482	Norm Charlton	.10	.05
483	Dwayne Henry	.10	.05
484	Dave Martinez	.10	.05
485	Bip Roberts	.10	.05
486	Reggie Sanders	.20	.09
487	Greg Swindell	.10	.05
488	Ryan Bowen	.10	.05
489	Casey Candaele	.10	.05
490	Juan Guerrero UER	.10	.05
	(photo on front is Andujar Cedeno)		
491	Pete Incaviglia	.10	.05
492	Jeff Juden	.10	.05
493	Rob Murphy	.10	.05
494	Mark Portugal	.10	.05
495	Rafael Ramirez	.10	.05
496	Scott Servais	.10	.05
497	Ed Taubensee	.20	.09
498	Brian Williams	.10	.05
499	Todd Benzinger	.10	.05
500	John Candelaria	.10	.05
501	Tom Candiotti	.10	.05
502	Tim Crews	.10	.05
503	Eric Davis	.20	.09
504	Jim Gott	.10	.05
505	Dave Hansen	.10	.05
506	Carlos Hernandez	.10	.05
507	Orel Hershiser	.20	.09
508	Eric Karros	.40	.18
509	Bob Ojeda	.10	.05
510	Steve Wilson	.10	.05
511	Moises Alou	.40	.18
512	Bret Barberie	.10	.05
513	Ivan Calderon	.10	.05
514	Gary Carter	.40	.18
515	Archi Cianfrocco	.10	.05
516	Jeff Fassero	.10	.05
517	Darrin Fletcher	.10	.05
518	Marquis Grissom	.20	.09
519	Chris Haney	.10	.05
520	Ken Hill	.10	.05
521	Chris Nabholz	.10	.05
522	Bill Sampen	.10	.05
523	John Vander Wal	.10	.05
524	Dave Wainhouse	.10	.05
525	Larry Walker	.40	.18
526	John Wetteland	.20	.09
527	Bobby Bonilla	.20	.09
528	Sid Fernandez	.10	.05
529	John Franco	.20	.09
530	Dave Gallagher	.10	.05
531	Paul Gibson	.10	.05
532	Eddie Murray	.40	.18
533	Junior Noboa	.10	.05
534	Charlie O'Brien	.10	.05
535	Bill Pecota	.10	.05
536	Willie Randolph	.20	.09
537	Bret Saberhagen	.20	.09
538	Dick Schofield	.10	.05
539	Pete Schourek	.10	.05
540	Ruben Amaro	.10	.05
541	Andy Ashby	.20	.09
542	Kim Batiste	.10	.05
543	Cliff Brantley	.10	.05
544	Mariano Duncan	.10	.05
545	Jeff Grotewold	.10	.05
546	Barry Jones	.10	.05
547	Julio Peguero	.10	.05
548	Curt Schilling	.30	.14
549	Mitch Williams	.10	.05
550	Stan Belinda	.10	.05
551	Scott Bullett	.10	.05
552	Cecil Espy	.10	.05
553	Jeff King	.10	.05
554	Roger Mason	.10	.05
555	Paul Miller	.10	.05
556	Denny Neagle	.30	.14
557	Vicente Palacios	.10	.05
558	Bob Patterson	.10	.05
559	Tom Prince	.10	.05
560	Gary Redus	.10	.05
561	Gary Varsho	.10	.05
562	Juan Agosto	.10	.05
563	Cris Carpenter	.10	.05
564	Mark Clark	.10	.05
565	Jose DeLeon	.10	.05
566	Rich Gedman	.10	.05
567	Bernard Gilkey	.20	.09
568	Rex Hudler	.10	.05
569	Tim Jones	.10	.05
570	Donovan Osborne	.10	.05
571	Mike Perez	.10	.05
572	Gerald Perry	.10	.05
573	Bob Tewksbury	.10	.05
574	Todd Worrell	.10	.05
575	Dave Eiland	.10	.05
576	Jeremy Hernandez	.10	.05
577	Craig Lefferts	.10	.05
578	Jose Melendez	.10	.05
579	Randy Myers	.20	.09
580	Gary Pettis	.10	.05
581	Rich Rodriguez	.10	.05
582	Gary Sheffield	.40	.18
583	Craig Shipley	.10	.05
584	Kurt Stillwell	.10	.05
585	Tim Teufel	.10	.05
586	Rod Beck	.40	.18
587	Dave Burba	.10	.05
588	Craig Colbert	.10	.05

		MINT	NRMT
❏ 589	Bryan Hickerson	.10	.05
❏ 590	Mike Jackson	.20	.09
❏ 591	Mark Leonard	.10	.05
❏ 592	Jim McNamara	.10	.05
❏ 593	John Patterson	.10	.05
❏ 594	Dave Righetti	.10	.05
❏ 595	Cory Snyder	.10	.05
❏ 596	Bill Swift	.10	.05
❏ 597	Ted Wood	.10	.05
❏ 598	Checklist 301-400	.10	.05
❏ 599	Checklist 401-500	.10	.05
❏ 600	Checklist 501-600	.10	.05

1992 Ultra All-Rookies

	MINT	NRMT
COMPLETE SET (10)	12.00	5.50
COMMON CARD (1-10)	.50	.23
SER.2 STATED ODDS 1:13		

		MINT	NRMT
❏ 1	Eric Karros	2.00	.90
❏ 2	Andy Stankiewicz	.50	.23
❏ 3	Gary DiSarcina	.50	.23
❏ 4	Archi Cianfrocco	.50	.23
❏ 5	Jim McNamara	.50	.23
❏ 6	Chad Curtis	2.00	.90
❏ 7	Kenny Lofton	5.00	2.20
❏ 8	Reggie Sanders	1.00	.45
❏ 9	Pat Mahomes	.50	.23
❏ 10	Donovan Osborne	.50	.23

1992 Ultra All-Stars

	MINT	NRMT
COMPLETE SET (20)	25.00	11.00
COMMON CARD (1-20)	.25	.11
SER.2 STATED ODDS 1:6.5		

		MINT	NRMT
❏ 1	Mark McGwire	6.00	2.70
❏ 2	Roberto Alomar	1.25	.55
❏ 3	Cal Ripken Jr.	5.00	2.20
❏ 4	Wade Boggs	1.25	.55
❏ 5	Mickey Tettleton	.25	.11
❏ 6	Ken Griffey Jr.	8.00	3.60
❏ 7	Roberto Kelly	.25	.11
❏ 8	Kirby Puckett	2.00	.90
❏ 9	Frank Thomas	3.00	1.35
❏ 10	Jack McDowell	.25	.11
❏ 11	Will Clark	1.25	.55
❏ 12	Ryne Sandberg	1.50	.70
❏ 13	Barry Larkin	.75	.35
❏ 14	Gary Sheffield	1.25	.55
❏ 15	Tom Pagnozzi	.25	.11
❏ 16	Barry Bonds	1.50	.70
❏ 17	Deion Sanders	1.25	.55
❏ 18	Darryl Strawberry	.50	.23
❏ 19	David Cone	.50	.23
❏ 20	Tom Glavine	.75	.35

1992 Ultra Award Winners

TERRY PENDLETON

	MINT	NRMT
COMPLETE SET (25)	50.00	22.00
COMMON CARD (1-25)	.50	.23
RANDOM INSERTS IN SER.1 PACKS		

		MINT	NRMT
❏ 1	Jack Morris	1.00	.45
❏ 2	Chuck Knoblauch	1.50	.70
❏ 3	Jeff Bagwell	4.00	1.80
❏ 4	Terry Pendleton	.50	.23
❏ 5	Cal Ripken	8.00	3.60
❏ 6	Roger Clemens	5.00	2.20
❏ 7	Tom Glavine	1.25	.55
❏ 8	Tom Pagnozzi	.50	.23
❏ 9	Ozzie Smith	2.50	1.10
❏ 10	Andy Van Slyke	1.00	.45
❏ 11	Barry Bonds	2.50	1.10
❏ 12	Tony Gwynn	5.00	2.20
❏ 13	Matt Williams	1.25	.55
❏ 14	Will Clark	1.50	.70
❏ 15	Robin Ventura	1.00	.45
❏ 16	Mark Langston	.50	.23
❏ 17	Tony Pena	.50	.23
❏ 18	Devon White	.50	.23
❏ 19	Don Mattingly	4.00	1.80
❏ 20	Roberto Alomar	1.50	.70
❏ 21A	Cal Ripken ERR (Reversed negative on card back)	15.00	6.75
❏ 21B	Cal Ripken COR	8.00	3.60
❏ 22	Ken Griffey Jr.	12.00	5.50
❏ 23	Kirby Puckett	3.00	1.35
❏ 24	Greg Maddux	5.00	2.20
❏ 25	Ryne Sandberg	2.50	1.10

1992 Ultra Gwynn

TONY GWYNN

	MINT	NRMT
COMPLETE SET (10)	10.00	4.50
COMMON GWYNN (1-10)	1.00	.45

RANDOM INSERTS IN SER.1 PACKS
COMMON MAIL-IN (S1-S2) ...... 1.00 .45
MAIL-IN CARDS AVAIL.VIA WRAPPER EXCH.

		MINT	NRMT
❏ 1	Tony Gwynn (Leaping and catching ball at outfield wall)	1.00	.45
❏ 2	Tony Gwynn (Batting stance, brown Padres' uniform)	1.00	.45
❏ 3	Tony Gwynn (Awaiting flyball, glove above head)	1.00	.45
❏ 4	Tony Gwynn (Follow-through on swing)	1.00	.45
❏ 5	Tony Gwynn (Leading off base; crouching at the knees)	1.00	.45
❏ 6	Tony Gwynn (Posed with silver bat and Gold Glove trophy)	1.00	.45
❏ 7	Tony Gwynn (Bunting)	1.00	.45
❏ 8	Tony Gwynn (Full body shot; swinging)	1.00	.45
❏ 9	Tony Gwynn (Taking off for first)	1.00	.45
❏ 10	Tony Gwynn (Batting, following through, sunglasses on)	1.00	.45
❏ S1	Tony Gwynn EXCH (Batting)	1.00	.45
❏ S2	Tony Gwynn EXCH (Fielding)	1.00	.45
❏ AU	Tony Gwynn AU (Autographed with certified signature)	100.00	45.00

1993 Ultra

	MINT	NRMT
COMPLETE SET (650)	30.00	13.50
COMPLETE SERIES 1 (300)	15.00	6.75
COMPLETE SERIES 2 (350)	15.00	6.75
COMMON CARD (1-650)	.15	.07
MINOR STARS	.30	.14
UNLISTED STARS	.60	.25

		MINT	NRMT
❏ 1	Steve Avery	.15	.07
❏ 2	Rafael Belliard	.15	.07
❏ 3	Damon Berryhill	.15	.07
❏ 4	Sid Bream	.15	.07
❏ 5	Ron Gant	.30	.14
❏ 6	Tom Glavine	.40	.18
❏ 7	Ryan Klesko	.60	.25
❏ 8	Mark Lemke	.15	.07
❏ 9	Javier Lopez	.60	.25
❏ 10	Greg Olson	.15	.07
❏ 11	Terry Pendleton	.15	.07
❏ 12	Deion Sanders	.40	.18
❏ 13	Mike Stanton	.15	.07
❏ 14	Paul Assenmacher	.15	.07
❏ 15	Steve Buechele	.15	.07
❏ 16	Frank Castillo	.15	.07
❏ 17	Shawon Dunston	.15	.07
❏ 18	Mark Grace	.40	.18
❏ 19	Derrick May	.15	.07

❑ 20	Chuck McElroy	.15	.07
❑ 21	Mike Morgan	.15	.07
❑ 22	Bob Scanlan	.15	.07
❑ 23	Dwight Smith	.15	.07
❑ 24	Sammy Sosa	2.00	.90
❑ 25	Rick Wilkins	.15	.07
❑ 26	Tim Belcher	.15	.07
❑ 27	Jeff Branson	.15	.07
❑ 28	Bill Doran	.15	.07
❑ 29	Chris Hammond	.15	.07
❑ 30	Barry Larkin	.60	.25
❑ 31	Hal Morris	.15	.07
❑ 32	Joe Oliver	.15	.07
❑ 33	Jose Rijo	.15	.07
❑ 34	Bip Roberts	.15	.07
❑ 35	Chris Sabo	.15	.07
❑ 36	Reggie Sanders	.30	.14
❑ 37	Craig Biggio	.60	.25
❑ 38	Ken Caminiti	.40	.18
❑ 39	Steve Finley	.30	.14
❑ 40	Luis Gonzalez	.30	.14
❑ 41	Juan Guerrero	.15	.07
❑ 42	Pete Harnisch	.15	.07
❑ 43	Xavier Hernandez	.15	.07
❑ 44	Doug Jones	.15	.07
❑ 45	Al Osuna	.15	.07
❑ 46	Eddie Taubensee	.15	.07
❑ 47	Scooter Tucker	.15	.07
❑ 48	Brian Williams	.15	.07
❑ 49	Pedro Astacio	.30	.14
❑ 50	Rafael Bournigal	.15	.07
❑ 51	Brett Butler	.30	.14
❑ 52	Tom Candiotti	.15	.07
❑ 53	Eric Davis	.30	.14
❑ 54	Lenny Harris	.15	.07
❑ 55	Orel Hershiser	.30	.14
❑ 56	Eric Karros	.40	.18
❑ 57	Pedro Martinez	1.25	.55
❑ 58	Roger McDowell	.15	.07
❑ 59	Jose Offerman	.30	.14
❑ 60	Mike Piazza	3.00	1.35
❑ 61	Moises Alou	.30	.14
❑ 62	Kent Bottenfield	.15	.07
❑ 63	Archi Cianfrocco	.15	.07
❑ 64	Greg Colbrunn	.15	.07
❑ 65	Wil Cordero	.15	.07
❑ 66	Delino DeShields	.30	.14
❑ 67	Darrin Fletcher	.15	.07
❑ 68	Ken Hill	.15	.07
❑ 69	Chris Nabholz	.15	.07
❑ 70	Mel Rojas	.15	.07
❑ 71	Larry Walker	.60	.25
❑ 72	Sid Fernandez	.15	.07
❑ 73	John Franco	.30	.14
❑ 74	Dave Gallagher	.15	.07
❑ 75	Todd Hundley	.40	.18
❑ 76	Howard Johnson	.15	.07
❑ 77	Jeff Kent	.30	.14
❑ 78	Eddie Murray	.60	.25
❑ 79	Bret Saberhagen	.30	.14
❑ 80	Chico Walker	.15	.07
❑ 81	Anthony Young	.15	.07
❑ 82	Kyle Abbott	.15	.07
❑ 83	Ruben Amaro	.15	.07
❑ 84	Juan Bell	.15	.07
❑ 85	Wes Chamberlain	.15	.07
❑ 86	Darren Daulton	.30	.14
❑ 87	Mariano Duncan	.15	.07
❑ 88	Dave Hollins	.15	.07
❑ 89	Ricky Jordan	.15	.07
❑ 90	John Kruk	.30	.14
❑ 91	Mickey Morandini	.15	.07
❑ 92	Terry Mulholland	.15	.07
❑ 93	Ben Rivera	.15	.07
❑ 94	Mike Williams	.15	.07
❑ 95	Stan Belinda	.15	.07
❑ 96	Jay Bell	.30	.14
❑ 97	Jeff King	.15	.07
❑ 98	Mike LaValliere	.15	.07
❑ 99	Lloyd McClendon	.15	.07
❑ 100	Orlando Merced	.15	.07
❑ 101	Zane Smith	.15	.07
❑ 102	Randy Tomlin	.15	.07
❑ 103	Andy Van Slyke	.30	.14
❑ 104	Tim Wakefield	.30	.14
❑ 105	John Wehner	.15	.07
❑ 106	Bernard Gilkey	.15	.07
❑ 107	Brian Jordan	.30	.14
❑ 108	Ray Lankford	.40	.18
❑ 109	Donovan Osborne	.15	.07
❑ 110	Tom Pagnozzi	.15	.07
❑ 111	Mike Perez	.15	.07
❑ 112	Lee Smith	.30	.14
❑ 113	Ozzie Smith	.75	.35
❑ 114	Bob Tewksbury	.15	.07
❑ 115	Todd Zeile	.15	.07
❑ 116	Andy Benes	.30	.14
❑ 117	Greg W. Harris	.15	.07
❑ 118	Darrin Jackson	.15	.07
❑ 119	Fred McGriff	.40	.18
❑ 120	Rich Rodriguez	.15	.07
❑ 121	Frank Seminara	.15	.07
❑ 122	Gary Sheffield	.60	.25
❑ 123	Craig Shipley	.15	.07
❑ 124	Kurt Stillwell	.15	.07
❑ 125	Dan Walters	.15	.07
❑ 126	Rod Beck	.30	.14
❑ 127	Mike Benjamin	.15	.07
❑ 128	Jeff Brantley	.15	.07
❑ 129	John Burkett	.15	.07
❑ 130	Will Clark	.60	.25
❑ 131	Royce Clayton	.15	.07
❑ 132	Steve Hosey	.15	.07
❑ 133	Mike Jackson	.30	.14
❑ 134	Darren Lewis	.15	.07
❑ 135	Kirt Manwaring	.15	.07
❑ 136	Bill Swift	.15	.07
❑ 137	Robby Thompson	.15	.07
❑ 138	Brady Anderson	.30	.14
❑ 139	Glenn Davis	.15	.07
❑ 140	Leo Gomez	.15	.07
❑ 141	Chito Martinez	.15	.07
❑ 142	Ben McDonald	.15	.07
❑ 143	Alan Mills	.15	.07
❑ 144	Mike Mussina	.60	.25
❑ 145	Gregg Olson	.15	.07
❑ 146	David Segui	.15	.07
❑ 147	Jeff Tackett	.15	.07
❑ 148	Jack Clark	.15	.07
❑ 149	Scott Cooper	.15	.07
❑ 150	Danny Darwin	.15	.07
❑ 151	John Dopson	.15	.07
❑ 152	Mike Greenwell	.15	.07
❑ 153	Tim Naehring	.15	.07
❑ 154	Tony Pena	.15	.07
❑ 155	Paul Quantrill	.15	.07
❑ 156	Mo Vaughn	.60	.25
❑ 157	Frank Viola	.30	.14
❑ 158	Bob Zupcic	.15	.07
❑ 159	Chad Curtis	.30	.14
❑ 160	Gary DiSarcina	.15	.07
❑ 161	Damion Easley	.30	.14
❑ 162	Chuck Finley	.30	.14
❑ 163	Tim Fortugno	.15	.07
❑ 164	Rene Gonzales	.15	.07
❑ 165	Joe Grahe	.15	.07
❑ 166	Mark Langston	.15	.07
❑ 167	John Orton	.15	.07
❑ 168	Luis Polonia	.15	.07
❑ 169	Julio Valera	.15	.07
❑ 170	Wilson Alvarez	.30	.14
❑ 171	George Bell	.30	.14
❑ 172	Joey Cora	.15	.07
❑ 173	Alex Fernandez	.30	.14
❑ 174	Lance Johnson	.15	.07
❑ 175	Ron Karkovice	.15	.07
❑ 176	Jack McDowell	.30	.14
❑ 177	Scott Radinsky	.15	.07
❑ 178	Tim Raines	.30	.14
❑ 179	Steve Sax	.15	.07
❑ 180	Bobby Thigpen	.15	.07
❑ 181	Frank Thomas	1.25	.55
❑ 182	Sandy Alomar Jr.	.30	.14
❑ 183	Carlos Baerga	.30	.14
❑ 184	Felix Fermin	.15	.07
❑ 185	Thomas Howard	.15	.07
❑ 186	Mark Lewis	.15	.07
❑ 187	Derek Lilliquist	.15	.07
❑ 188	Carlos Martinez	.15	.07
❑ 189	Charles Nagy	.30	.14
❑ 190	Scott Scudder	.15	.07
❑ 191	Paul Sorrento	.15	.07
❑ 192	Jim Thome	.75	.35
❑ 193	Mark Whiten	.15	.07
❑ 194	Milt Cuyler UER (Reversed negative on card front)	.15	.07
❑ 195	Rob Deer	.15	.07
❑ 196	John Doherty	.15	.07
❑ 197	Travis Fryman	.30	.14
❑ 198	Dan Gladden	.15	.07
❑ 199	Mike Henneman	.15	.07
❑ 200	John Kiely	.15	.07
❑ 201	Chad Kreuter	.15	.07
❑ 202	Scott Livingstone	.15	.07
❑ 203	Tony Phillips	.15	.07
❑ 204	Alan Trammell	.40	.18
❑ 205	Mike Boddicker	.15	.07
❑ 206	George Brett	1.25	.55
❑ 207	Tom Gordon	.15	.07
❑ 208	Mark Gubicza	.15	.07
❑ 209	Gregg Jefferies	.15	.07
❑ 210	Wally Joyner	.30	.14
❑ 211	Kevin Koslofski	.15	.07
❑ 212	Brent Mayne	.15	.07
❑ 213	Brian McRae	.15	.07
❑ 214	Kevin McReynolds	.15	.07
❑ 215	Rusty Meacham	.15	.07
❑ 216	Steve Shifflett	.15	.07
❑ 217	James Austin	.15	.07
❑ 218	Cal Eldred	.15	.07
❑ 219	Darryl Hamilton	.15	.07
❑ 220	Doug Henry	.15	.07
❑ 221	John Jaha	.15	.07
❑ 222	Dave Nilsson	.30	.14
❑ 223	Jesse Orosco	.15	.07
❑ 224	B.J. Surhoff	.30	.14
❑ 225	Greg Vaughn	.30	.14
❑ 226	Bill Wegman	.15	.07
❑ 227	Robin Yount UER (Born in Illinois, not in Virginia)	.40	.18
❑ 228	Rick Aguilera	.15	.07
❑ 229	J.T. Bruett	.15	.07
❑ 230	Scott Erickson	.15	.07
❑ 231	Kent Hrbek	.30	.14
❑ 232	Terry Jorgensen	.15	.07
❑ 233	Scott Leius	.15	.07
❑ 234	Pat Mahomes	.15	.07
❑ 235	Pedro Munoz	.15	.07
❑ 236	Kirby Puckett	1.00	.45
❑ 237	Kevin Tapani	.15	.07
❑ 238	Lenny Webster	.15	.07
❑ 239	Carl Willis	.15	.07
❑ 240	Mike Gallego	.15	.07
❑ 241	John Habyan	.15	.07
❑ 242	Pat Kelly	.15	.07
❑ 243	Kevin Maas	.15	.07
❑ 244	Don Mattingly	1.25	.55
❑ 245	Hensley Meulens	.15	.07
❑ 246	Sam Militello	.15	.07
❑ 247	Matt Nokes	.15	.07
❑ 248	Melido Perez	.15	.07
❑ 249	Andy Stankiewicz	.15	.07
❑ 250	Randy Velarde	.15	.07
❑ 251	Bob Wickman	.15	.07
❑ 252	Bernie Williams	.60	.25
❑ 253	Lance Blankenship	.15	.07
❑ 254	Mike Bordick	.15	.07
❑ 255	Jerry Browne	.15	.07
❑ 256	Ron Darling	.15	.07
❑ 257	Dennis Eckersley	.30	.14
❑ 258	Rickey Henderson	.75	.35
❑ 259	Vince Horsman	.15	.07
❑ 260	Troy Neel	.15	.07
❑ 261	Jeff Parrett	.15	.07
❑ 262	Terry Steinbach	.15	.07
❑ 263	Bob Welch	.15	.07
❑ 264	Bobby Witt	.15	.07
❑ 265	Rich Amaral	.15	.07
❑ 266	Bret Boone	.30	.14
❑ 267	Jay Buhner	.40	.18
❑ 268	Dave Fleming	.15	.07
❑ 269	Randy Johnson	.60	.25
❑ 270	Edgar Martinez	.40	.18
❑ 271	Mike Schooler	.15	.07
❑ 272	Russ Swan	.15	.07
❑ 273	Dave Valle	.15	.07

274	Omar Vizquel	.30	.14
275	Kerry Woodson	.15	.07
276	Kevin Brown	.40	.18
277	Julio Franco	.15	.07
278	Jeff Frye	.15	.07
279	Juan Gonzalez	1.25	.55
280	Jeff Huson	.15	.07
281	Rafael Palmeiro	.60	.25
282	Dean Palmer	.30	.14
283	Roger Pavlik	.15	.07
284	Ivan Rodriguez	.75	.35
285	Kenny Rogers	.15	.07
286	Derek Bell	.30	.14
287	Pat Borders	.15	.07
288	Joe Carter	.30	.14
289	Bob MacDonald	.15	.07
290	Jack Morris	.30	.14
291	John Olerud	.40	.18
292	Ed Sprague	.15	.07
293	Todd Stottlemyre	.15	.07
294	Mike Timlin	.15	.07
295	Duane Ward	.15	.07
296	David Wells	.30	.14
297	Devon White	.15	.07
298	Ray Lankford CL	.30	.14
299	Bobby Witt CL	.15	.07
300	Mike Piazza CL	.60	.25
301	Steve Bedrosian	.15	.07
302	Jeff Blauser	.15	.07
303	Francisco Cabrera	.15	.07
304	Marvin Freeman	.15	.07
305	Brian Hunter	.15	.07
306	David Justice	.60	.25
307	Greg Maddux	1.50	.70
308	Greg McMichael	.15	.07
309	Kent Mercker	.15	.07
310	Otis Nixon	.15	.07
311	Pete Smith	.15	.07
312	John Smoltz	.40	.18
313	Jose Guzman	.15	.07
314	Mike Harkey	.15	.07
315	Greg Hibbard	.15	.07
316	Candy Maldonado	.15	.07
317	Randy Myers	.30	.14
318	Dan Plesac	.15	.07
319	Rey Sanchez	.15	.07
320	Ryne Sandberg	.75	.35
321	Tommy Shields	.15	.07
322	Jose Vizcaino	.15	.07
323	Matt Walbeck	.15	.07
324	Willie Wilson	.15	.07
325	Tom Browning	.15	.07
326	Tim Costo	.15	.07
327	Rob Dibble	.15	.07
328	Steve Foster	.15	.07
329	Roberto Kelly	.15	.07
330	Randy Milligan	.15	.07
331	Kevin Mitchell	.30	.14
332	Tim Pugh	.15	.07
333	Jeff Reardon	.30	.14
334	John Roper	.15	.07
335	Juan Samuel	.15	.07
336	John Smiley	.15	.07
337	Dan Wilson	.30	.14
338	Scott Aldred	.15	.07
339	Andy Ashby	.30	.14
340	Freddie Benavides	.15	.07
341	Dante Bichette	.30	.14
342	Willie Blair	.15	.07
343	Daryl Boston	.15	.07
344	Vinny Castilla	.75	.35
345	Jerald Clark	.15	.07
346	Alex Cole	.15	.07
347	Andres Galarraga	.60	.25
348	Joe Girardi	.30	.14
349	Ryan Hawblitzel	.15	.07
350	Charlie Hayes	.15	.07
351	Butch Henry	.15	.07
352	Darren Holmes	.15	.07
353	Dale Murphy	.40	.18
354	David Nied	.15	.07
355	Jeff Parrett	.15	.07
356	Steve Reed	.15	.07
357	Bruce Ruffin	.15	.07
358	Danny Sheaffer	.15	.07
359	Bryn Smith	.15	.07
360	Jim Tatum	.15	.07
361	Eric Young	.60	.25
362	Gerald Young	.15	.07
363	Luis Aquino	.15	.07
364	Alex Arias	.15	.07
365	Jack Armstrong	.15	.07
366	Bret Barberie	.15	.07
367	Ryan Bowen	.15	.07
368	Greg Briley	.15	.07
369	Cris Carpenter	.15	.07
370	Chuck Carr	.15	.07
371	Jeff Conine	.15	.07
372	Steve Decker	.15	.07
373	Orestes Destrade	.15	.07
374	Monty Fariss	.15	.07
375	Junior Felix	.15	.07
376	Chris Hammond	.15	.07
377	Bryan Harvey	.15	.07
378	Trevor Hoffman	.60	.25
379	Charlie Hough	.30	.14
380	Joe Klink	.15	.07
381	Richie Lewis	.15	.07
382	Dave Magadan	.15	.07
383	Bob McClure	.15	.07
384	Scott Pose	.15	.07
385	Rich Renteria	.15	.07
386	Benito Santiago	.15	.07
387	Walt Weiss	.15	.07
388	Nigel Wilson	.15	.07
389	Eric Anthony	.15	.07
390	Jeff Bagwell	.75	.35
391	Andujar Cedeno	.15	.07
392	Doug Drabek	.15	.07
393	Darryl Kile	.15	.07
394	Mark Portugal	.15	.07
395	Karl Rhodes	.15	.07
396	Scott Servais	.15	.07
397	Greg Swindell	.15	.07
398	Tom Goodwin	.15	.07
399	Kevin Gross	.15	.07
400	Carlos Hernandez	.15	.07
401	Ramon Martinez	.30	.14
402	Raul Mondesi	.60	.25
403	Jody Reed	.15	.07
404	Mike Sharperson	.15	.07
405	Cory Snyder	.15	.07
406	Darryl Strawberry	.30	.14
407	Rick Trlicek	.15	.07
408	Tim Wallach	.15	.07
409	Todd Worrell	.15	.07
410	Tavo Alvarez	.15	.07
411	Sean Berry	.15	.07
412	Frank Bolick	.15	.07
413	Cliff Floyd	.30	.14
414	Mike Gardiner	.15	.07
415	Marquis Grissom	.30	.14
416	Tim Laker	.15	.07
417	Mike Lansing	.30	.14
418	Dennis Martinez	.30	.14
419	John Vander Wal	.15	.07
420	John Wetteland	.30	.14
421	Rondell White	.40	.18
422	Bobby Bonilla	.30	.14
423	Jeromy Burnitz	.30	.14
424	Vince Coleman	.15	.07
425	Mike Draper	.15	.07
426	Tony Fernandez	.30	.14
427	Dwight Gooden	.30	.14
428	Jeff Innis	.15	.07
429	Bobby Jones	.15	.07
430	Mike Maddux	.15	.07
431	Charlie O'Brien	.15	.07
432	Joe Orsulak	.15	.07
433	Pete Schourek	.15	.07
434	Frank Tanana	.15	.07
435	Ryan Thompson	.30	.14
436	Kim Batiste	.15	.07
437	Mark Davis	.15	.07
438	Jose DeLeon	.15	.07
439	Len Dykstra	.30	.14
440	Jim Eisenreich	.15	.07
441	Tommy Greene	.15	.07
442	Pete Incaviglia	.15	.07
443	Danny Jackson	.15	.07
444	Todd Pratt	.40	.18
445	Curt Schilling	.30	.14
446	Milt Thompson	.15	.07
447	David West	.15	.07
448	Mitch Williams	.15	.07
449	Steve Cooke	.15	.07
450	Carlos Garcia	.15	.07
451	Al Martin	.15	.07
452	Blas Minor	.15	.07
453	Dennis Moeller	.15	.07
454	Denny Neagle	.30	.14
455	Don Slaught	.15	.07
456	Lonnie Smith	.15	.07
457	Paul Wagner	.15	.07
458	Bob Walk	.15	.07
459	Kevin Young	.30	.14
460	Rene Arocha	.15	.07
461	Brian Barber	.15	.07
462	Rheal Cormier	.15	.07
463	Gregg Jefferies	.15	.07
464	Joe Magrane	.15	.07
465	Omar Olivares	.15	.07
466	Geronimo Pena	.15	.07
467	Allen Watson	.15	.07
468	Mark Whiten	.15	.07
469	Derek Bell	.30	.14
470	Phil Clark	.15	.07
471	Pat Gomez	.15	.07
472	Tony Gwynn	1.50	.70
473	Jeremy Hernandez	.15	.07
474	Bruce Hurst	.15	.07
475	Phil Plantier	.15	.07
476	Scott Sanders	.15	.07
477	Tim Scott	.15	.07
478	Darrell Sherman	.15	.07
479	Guillermo Velasquez	.15	.07
480	Tim Worrell	.15	.07
481	Todd Benzinger	.15	.07
482	Bud Black	.15	.07
483	Barry Bonds	.75	.35
484	Dave Burba	.15	.07
485	Bryan Hickerson	.15	.07
486	Dave Martinez	.15	.07
487	Willie McGee	.30	.14
488	Jeff Reed	.15	.07
489	Kevin Rogers	.15	.07
490	Matt Williams	.40	.18
491	Trevor Wilson	.15	.07
492	Harold Baines	.30	.14
493	Mike Devereaux	.15	.07
494	Todd Frohwirth	.15	.07
495	Chris Hoiles	.15	.07
496	Luis Mercedes	.15	.07
497	Sherman Obando	.15	.07
498	Brad Pennington	.15	.07
499	Harold Reynolds	.15	.07
500	Arthur Rhodes	.15	.07
501	Cal Ripken	2.50	1.10
502	Rick Sutcliffe	.15	.07
503	Fernando Valenzuela	.30	.14
504	Mark Williamson	.15	.07
505	Scott Bankhead	.15	.07
506	Greg Blosser	.15	.07
507	Ivan Calderon	.15	.07
508	Roger Clemens	1.50	.70
509	Andre Dawson	.40	.18
510	Scott Fletcher	.15	.07
511	Greg A. Harris	.15	.07
512	Billy Hatcher	.15	.07
513	Bob Melvin	.15	.07
514	Carlos Quintana	.15	.07
515	Luis Rivera	.15	.07
516	Jeff Russell	.15	.07
517	Ken Ryan	.15	.07
518	Chili Davis	.30	.14
519	Jim Edmonds	1.50	.70
520	Gary Gaetti	.30	.14
521	Torey Lovullo	.15	.07
522	Troy Percival	.40	.18
523	Tim Salmon	.60	.25
524	Scott Sanderson	.15	.07
525	J.T. Snow	.75	.35
526	Jerome Walton	.15	.07
527	Jason Bere	.15	.07
528	Rod Bolton	.15	.07
529	Ellis Burks	.30	.14
530	Carlton Fisk	.60	.25
531	Craig Grebeck	.15	.07

532 Ozzie Guillen	.15	.07
533 Roberto Hernandez	.30	.14
534 Bo Jackson	.30	.14
535 Kirk McCaskill	.15	.07
536 Dave Stieb	.15	.07
537 Robin Ventura	.30	.14
538 Albert Belle	.60	.25
539 Mike Bielecki	.15	.07
540 Glenallen Hill	.15	.07
541 Reggie Jefferson	.30	.14
542 Kenny Lofton	.60	.25
543 Jeff Mutis	.15	.07
544 Junior Ortiz	.15	.07
545 Manny Ramirez	2.00	.90
546 Jeff Treadway	.15	.07
547 Kevin Wickander	.15	.07
548 Cecil Fielder	.30	.14
549 Kirk Gibson	.30	.14
550 Greg Gohr	.15	.07
551 David Haas	.15	.07
552 Bill Krueger	.15	.07
553 Mike Moore	.15	.07
554 Mickey Tettleton	.15	.07
555 Lou Whitaker	.30	.14
556 Kevin Appier	.30	.14
557 Billy Brewer	.15	.07
558 David Cone	.40	.18
559 Greg Gagne	.15	.07
560 Mark Gardner	.15	.07
561 Phil Hiatt	.15	.07
562 Felix Jose	.15	.07
563 Jose Lind	.15	.07
564 Mike Macfarlane	.15	.07
565 Keith Miller	.15	.07
566 Jeff Montgomery	.30	.14
567 Hipolito Pichardo	.15	.07
568 Ricky Bones	.15	.07
569 Tom Brunansky	.15	.07
570 Joe Kmak	.15	.07
571 Pat Listach	.15	.07
572 Graeme Lloyd	.15	.07
573 Carlos Maldonado	.15	.07
574 Josias Manzanillo	.15	.07
575 Matt Mieske	.15	.07
576 Kevin Reimer	.15	.07
577 Bill Spiers	.15	.07
578 Dickie Thon	.15	.07
579 Willie Banks	.15	.07
580 Jim Deshaies	.15	.07
581 Mark Guthrie	.15	.07
582 Brian Harper	.15	.07
583 Chuck Knoblauch	.60	.25
584 Gene Larkin	.15	.07
585 Shane Mack	.15	.07
586 David McCarty	.15	.07
587 Mike Pagliarulo	.15	.07
588 Mike Trombley	.15	.07
589 Dave Winfield	.40	.18
590 Jim Abbott	.30	.14
591 Wade Boggs	.60	.25
592 Russ Davis	.15	.07
593 Steve Farr	.15	.07
594 Steve Howe	.15	.07
595 Mike Humphreys	.15	.07
596 Jimmy Key	.30	.14
597 Jim Leyritz	.15	.07
598 Bobby Munoz	.15	.07
599 Paul O'Neill	.30	.14
600 Spike Owen	.15	.07
601 Mike Stanley	.15	.07
602 Danny Tartabull	.30	.14
603 Scott Brosius	.30	.14
604 Storm Davis	.15	.07
605 Eric Fox	.15	.07
606 Rich Gossage	.30	.14
607 Scott Hemond	.15	.07
608 Dave Henderson	.15	.07
609 Mark McGwire	3.00	1.35
610 Mike Mohler	.15	.07
611 Edwin Nunez	.15	.07
612 Kevin Seitzer	.15	.07
613 Ruben Sierra	.15	.07
614 Chris Bosio	.15	.07
615 Norm Charlton	.15	.07
616 Jim Converse	.15	.07
617 John Cummings	.15	.07

618 Mike Felder	.15	.07
619 Ken Griffey Jr.	3.00	1.35
620 Mike Hampton	.60	.25
621 Erik Hanson	.15	.07
622 Bill Haselman	.15	.07
623 Tino Martinez	.60	.25
624 Lee Tinsley	.15	.07
625 Fernando Vina	.40	.18
626 David Wainhouse	.15	.07
627 Jose Canseco	.75	.35
628 Benji Gil	.15	.07
629 Tom Henke	.15	.07
630 David Hulse	.15	.07
631 Manuel Lee	.15	.07
632 Craig Lefferts	.15	.07
633 Robb Nen	.40	.18
634 Gary Redus	.15	.07
635 Bill Ripken	.15	.07
636 Nolan Ryan	2.50	1.10
637 Dan Smith	.15	.07
638 Matt Whiteside	.15	.07
639 Roberto Alomar	.60	.25
640 Juan Guzman	.15	.07
641 Pat Hentgen	.40	.18
642 Darrin Jackson	.15	.07
643 Randy Knorr	.15	.07
644 Domingo Martinez	.15	.07
645 Paul Molitor	.60	.25
646 Dick Schofield	.15	.07
647 Dave Stewart	.30	.14
648 Rey Sanchez CL	.15	.07
649 Jeremy Hernandez CL	.15	.07
650 Junior Ortiz CL	.15	.07

1993 Ultra All-Rookies

	MINT	NRMT
COMPLETE SET (10)	15.00	6.75
COMMON CARD (1-10)	.50	.23
SER.2 STATED ODDS 1:18		
1 Rene Arocha	.50	.23
2 Jeff Conine	.50	.23
3 Phil Hiatt	.50	.23
4 Mike Lansing	.75	.35
5 Al Martin	.50	.23
6 David Neid	.50	.23
7 Mike Piazza	12.00	5.50
8 Tim Salmon	2.00	.90
9 J.T. Snow	2.00	.90
10 Kevin Young	.75	.35

1993 Ultra All-Stars

	MINT	NRMT
COMPLETE SET (20)	40.00	18.00
COMMON CARD (1-20)	.75	.35
SER.2 STATED ODDS 1:9		
1 Darren Daulton	1.00	.45
2 Will Clark	2.00	.90
3 Ryne Sandberg	3.00	1.35
4 Barry Larkin	2.00	.90
5 Gary Sheffield	2.00	.90
6 Barry Bonds	3.00	1.35
7 Ray Lankford	1.50	.70
8 Larry Walker	2.00	.90
9 Greg Maddux	6.00	2.70
10 Lee Smith	1.00	.45
11 Ivan Rodriguez	3.00	1.35
12 Mark McGwire	12.00	5.50
13 Carlos Baerga	.75	.35
14 Cal Ripken	10.00	4.50
15 Edgar Martinez	1.50	.70
16 Juan Gonzalez	5.00	2.20
17 Ken Griffey Jr.	12.00	5.50
18 Kirby Puckett	4.00	1.80
19 Frank Thomas	5.00	2.20
20 Mike Mussina	2.00	.90

1993 Ultra Award Winners

	MINT	NRMT
COMPLETE SET (25)	40.00	18.00
COMMON CARD (1-25)	.50	.23
RANDOM INSERTS IN SER.1 PACKS		
1 Greg Maddux	6.00	2.70
2 Tom Pagnozzi	.50	.23
3 Mark Grace	1.50	.70
4 Jose Lind	.50	.23
5 Terry Pendleton	.50	.23
6 Ozzie Smith	3.00	1.35
7 Barry Bonds	3.00	1.35
8 Andy Van Slyke	.50	.23
9 Larry Walker	2.00	.90
10 Mark Langston	.50	.23
11 Ivan Rodriguez	3.00	1.35
12 Don Mattingly	5.00	2.20
13 Roberto Alomar	2.00	.90
14 Robin Ventura	1.00	.45
15 Cal Ripken	10.00	4.50
16 Ken Griffey	12.00	5.50
17 Kirby Puckett	4.00	1.80
18 Devon White	.50	.23
19 Pat Listach	.50	.23
20 Eric Karros	1.50	.70
21 Pat Borders	.50	.23
22 Greg Maddux	6.00	2.70
23 Dennis Eckersley	1.00	.45
24 Barry Bonds	3.00	1.35
25 Gary Sheffield	2.00	.90

1993 Ultra Eckersley

	MINT	NRMT
COMPLETE SET (10)	4.00	1.80
COMMON CARD (1-10)	.50	.23
RANDOM INSERTS IN SER.1 PACKS		
COMMON MAIL-IN (11-12)	1.00	.45
MAIL-IN CARDS. DIST.VIA WRAPPER EXCH.		

	MINT	NRMT
❑ 1 Dennis Eckersley Perfection	.50	.23
❑ 2 Dennis Eckersley The Kid	.50	.23
❑ 3 Dennis Eckersley The Warrior	.50	.23
❑ 4 Dennis Eckersley Beantown Blazer	.50	.23
❑ 5 Dennis Eckersley Eckspeak	.50	.23
❑ 6 Dennis Eckersley Down to Earth	.50	.23
❑ 7 Dennis Eckersley Wrigley Bound	.50	.23
❑ 8 Dennis Eckersley No Relief	.50	.23
❑ 9 Dennis Eckersley In Control	.50	.23
❑ 10 Dennis Eckersley Simply the Best	.50	.23
❑ 11 Dennis Eckersley Reign of Perfection	1.00	.45
❑ 12 Dennis Eckersley Leaving His Mark	1.00	.45
❑ P1 Dennis Eckersley Promo with Paul Mullan	4.00	1.80
❑ AU Dennis Eckersley AU (Certified autograph)	40.00	18.00

1993 Ultra Home Run Kings

	MINT	NRMT
COMPLETE SET (10)	15.00	6.75
COMMON CARD (1-10)	1.00	.45
RANDOM INSERTS IN PACKS		
❑ 1 Juan Gonzalez	6.00	2.70
❑ 2 Mark McGwire	15.00	6.75
❑ 3 Cecil Fielder	1.50	.70
❑ 4 Fred McGriff	2.00	.90
❑ 5 Albert Belle	2.50	1.10
❑ 6 Barry Bonds	4.00	1.80
❑ 7 Joe Carter	1.50	.70
❑ 8 Gary Sheffield	2.50	1.10
❑ 9 Darren Daulton	1.50	.70
❑ 10 Dave Hollins	1.00	.45

1993 Ultra Performers

	MINT	NRMT
COMPLETE SET (10)	25.00	11.00
COMMON CARD (1-660)	.50	.23
SETS DISTRIBUTED VIA MAIL-IN OFFER		
❑ 1 Barry Bonds	2.00	.90
❑ 2 Juan Gonzalez	3.00	1.35
❑ 3 Ken Griffey Jr.	8.00	3.60
❑ 4 Eric Karros	1.25	.55
❑ 5 Pat Listach	.50	.23
❑ 6 Greg Maddux	4.00	1.80
❑ 7 David Nied	.50	.23
❑ 8 Gary Sheffield	2.00	.90
❑ 9 J.T. Snow	1.50	.70
❑ 10 Frank Thomas	3.00	1.35

1993 Ultra Strikeout Kings

	MINT	NRMT
COMPLETE SET (5)	20.00	9.00
COMMON CARD (1-5)	1.00	.45
SER.2 STATED ODDS 1:37		
❑ 1 Roger Clemens	10.00	4.50
❑ 2 Juan Guzman	1.00	.45
❑ 3 Randy Johnson	2.50	1.10
❑ 4 Nolan Ryan	15.00	6.75
❑ 5 John Smoltz	2.00	.90

1994 Ultra

	MINT	NRMT
COMPLETE SET (600)	40.00	18.00
COMPLETE SERIES 1 (300)	20.00	9.00
COMPLETE SERIES 2 (300)	20.00	9.00
COMMON CARD (1-600)	.15	.07
MINOR STARS	.30	.14
UNLISTED STARS	.60	.25
❑ 1 Jeffrey Hammonds	.30	.14
❑ 2 Chris Hoiles	.15	.07
❑ 3 Ben McDonald	.15	.07
❑ 4 Mark McLemore	.15	.07
❑ 5 Alan Mills	.15	.07
❑ 6 Jamie Moyer	.15	.07
❑ 7 Brad Pennington	.15	.07
❑ 8 Jim Poole	.15	.07
❑ 9 Cal Ripken Jr.	2.50	1.10
❑ 10 Jack Voigt	.15	.07
❑ 11 Roger Clemens	1.50	.70
❑ 12 Danny Darwin	.15	.07
❑ 13 Andre Dawson	.40	.18
❑ 14 Scott Fletcher	.15	.07
❑ 15 Greg A Harris	.15	.07
❑ 16 Billy Hatcher	.15	.07
❑ 17 Jeff Russell	.15	.07
❑ 18 Aaron Sele	.30	.14
❑ 19 Mo Vaughn	.60	.25
❑ 20 Mike Butcher	.15	.07
❑ 21 Rod Correia	.15	.07
❑ 22 Steve Frey	.15	.07
❑ 23 Phil Leftwich	.15	.07
❑ 24 Torey Lovullo	.15	.07
❑ 25 Ken Patterson	.15	.07
❑ 26 Eduardo Perez UER (listed as a Twin instead of Angel)	.15	.07
❑ 27 Tim Salmon	.60	.25
❑ 28 J.T. Snow	.30	.14
❑ 29 Chris Turner	.15	.07
❑ 30 Wilson Alvarez	.30	.14
❑ 31 Jason Bere	.15	.07
❑ 32 Joey Cora	.15	.07
❑ 33 Alex Fernandez	.15	.07
❑ 34 Roberto Hernandez	.15	.07
❑ 35 Lance Johnson	.15	.07
❑ 36 Ron Karkovice	.15	.07
❑ 37 Kirk McCaskill	.15	.07
❑ 38 Jeff Schwarz	.15	.07
❑ 39 Frank Thomas	1.25	.55
❑ 40 Sandy Alomar Jr.	.30	.14
❑ 41 Albert Belle	.60	.25
❑ 42 Felix Fermin	.15	.07
❑ 43 Wayne Kirby	.15	.07
❑ 44 Tom Kramer	.15	.07
❑ 45 Kenny Lofton	.60	.25
❑ 46 Jose Mesa	.15	.07
❑ 47 Eric Plunk	.15	.07
❑ 48 Paul Sorrento	.15	.07
❑ 49 Jim Thome	.60	.25
❑ 50 Bill Wertz	.15	.07
❑ 51 John Doherty	.15	.07
❑ 52 Cecil Fielder	.30	.14
❑ 53 Travis Fryman	.15	.07
❑ 54 Chris Gomez	.15	.07
❑ 55 Mike Henneman	.15	.07
❑ 56 Chad Kreuter	.15	.07
❑ 57 Bob MacDonald	.15	.07
❑ 58 Mike Moore	.15	.07
❑ 59 Tony Phillips	.15	.07
❑ 60 Lou Whitaker	.30	.14
❑ 61 Kevin Appier	.30	.14
❑ 62 Greg Gagne	.15	.07
❑ 63 Chris Gwynn	.15	.07
❑ 64 Bob Hamelin	.15	.07
❑ 65 Chris Haney	.15	.07
❑ 66 Phil Hiatt	.15	.07
❑ 67 Felix Jose	.15	.07
❑ 68 Jose Lind	.15	.07
❑ 69 Mike Macfarlane	.15	.07
❑ 70 Jeff Montgomery	.15	.07
❑ 71 Hipolito Pichardo	.15	.07
❑ 72 Juan Bell	.15	.07
❑ 73 Cal Eldred	.15	.07
❑ 74 Darryl Hamilton	.15	.07
❑ 75 Doug Henry	.15	.07
❑ 76 Mike Ignasiak	.15	.07

77	John Jaha	.15	.07
78	Graeme Lloyd	.15	.07
79	Angel Miranda	.15	.07
80	Dave Nilsson	.15	.07
81	Troy O'Leary	.30	.14
82	Kevin Reimer	.15	.07
83	Willie Banks	.15	.07
84	Larry Casian	.15	.07
85	Scott Erickson	.30	.14
86	Eddie Guardado	.15	.07
87	Kent Hrbek	.30	.14
88	Terry Jorgensen	.15	.07
89	Chuck Knoblauch	.60	.25
90	Pat Meares	.15	.07
91	Mike Trombley	.15	.07
92	Dave Winfield	.60	.25
93	Wade Boggs	.60	.25
94	Scott Kamieniecki	.15	.07
95	Pat Kelly	.15	.07
96	Jimmy Key	.30	.14
97	Jim Leyritz	.30	.14
98	Bobby Munoz	.15	.07
99	Paul O'Neill	.30	.14
100	Melido Perez	.15	.07
101	Mike Stanley	.15	.07
102	Danny Tartabull	.15	.07
103	Bernie Williams	.60	.25
104	Kurt Abbott	.15	.07
105	Mike Bordick	.15	.07
106	Ron Darling	.15	.07
107	Brent Gates	.15	.07
108	Miguel Jimenez	.15	.07
109	Steve Karsay	.15	.07
110	Scott Lydy	.15	.07
111	Mark McGwire	3.00	1.35
112	Troy Neel	.15	.07
113	Craig Paquette	.15	.07
114	Bob Welch	.15	.07
115	Bobby Witt	.15	.07
116	Rich Amaral	.15	.07
117	Mike Blowers	.15	.07
118	Jay Buhner	.30	.14
119	Dave Fleming	.15	.07
120	Ken Griffey Jr.	3.00	1.35
121	Tino Martinez	.60	.25
122	Marc Newfield	.15	.07
123	Ted Power	.15	.07
124	Mackey Sasser	.15	.07
125	Omar Vizquel	.30	.14
126	Kevin Brown	.30	.14
127	Juan Gonzalez	1.25	.55
128	Tom Henke	.15	.07
129	David Holse	.15	.07
130	Dean Palmer	.30	.14
131	Roger Pavlik	.15	.07
132	Ivan Rodriguez	.75	.35
133	Kenny Rogers	.15	.07
134	Doug Strange	.15	.07
135	Pat Borders	.15	.07
136	Joe Carter	.30	.14
137	Darnell Coles	.15	.07
138	Pat Hentgen	.30	.14
139	Al Leiter	.30	.14
140	Paul Molitor	.60	.25
141	John Olerud	.30	.14
142	Ed Sprague	.15	.07
143	Dave Stewart	.30	.14
144	Mike Timlin	.15	.07
145	Duane Ward	.15	.07
146	Devon White	.15	.07
147	Steve Avery	.15	.07
148	Steve Bedrosian	.15	.07
149	Damon Berryhill	.15	.07
150	Jeff Blauser	.15	.07
151	Tom Glavine	.60	.25
152	Chipper Jones	1.50	.70
153	Mark Lemke	.15	.07
154	Fred McGriff	.40	.18
155	Greg McMichael	.15	.07
156	Deion Sanders	.30	.14
157	John Smoltz	.40	.18
158	Mark Wohlers	.15	.07
159	Jose Bautista	.15	.07
160	Steve Buechele	.15	.07
161	Mike Harkey	.15	.07
162	Greg Hibbard	.15	.07
163	Chuck McElroy	.15	.07
164	Mike Morgan	.15	.07
165	Kevin Roberson	.15	.07
166	Ryne Sandberg	.75	.35
167	Jose Vizcaino	.15	.07
168	Rick Wilkins	.15	.07
169	Willie Wilson	.15	.07
170	Willie Greene	.15	.07
171	Roberto Kelly	.15	.07
172	Larry Luebbers	.15	.07
173	Kevin Mitchell	.15	.07
174	Joe Oliver	.15	.07
175	John Roper	.15	.07
176	Johnny Ruffin	.15	.07
177	Reggie Sanders	.30	.14
178	John Smiley	.15	.07
179	Jerry Spradlin	.15	.07
180	Freddie Benavides	.15	.07
181	Dante Bichette	.30	.14
182	Willie Blair	.15	.07
183	Kent Bottenfield	.15	.07
184	Jerald Clark	.15	.07
185	Joe Girardi	.15	.07
186	Roberto Mejia	.15	.07
187	Steve Reed	.15	.07
188	Armando Reynoso	.15	.07
189	Bruce Ruffin	.15	.07
190	Eric Young	.15	.07
191	Luis Aquino	.15	.07
192	Bret Barberie	.15	.07
193	Ryan Bowen	.15	.07
194	Chuck Carr	.15	.07
195	Orestes Destrade	.15	.07
196	Richie Lewis	.15	.07
197	Dave Magadan	.15	.07
198	Bob Natal	.15	.07
199	Gary Sheffield	.60	.25
200	Matt Turner	.15	.07
201	Darrell Whitmore	.15	.07
202	Eric Anthony	.15	.07
203	Jeff Bagwell	.75	.35
204	Andujar Cedeno	.15	.07
205	Luis Gonzalez	.30	.14
206	Xavier Hernandez	.15	.07
207	Doug Jones	.15	.07
208	Darryl Kile	.15	.07
209	Scott Servais	.15	.07
210	Greg Swindell	.15	.07
211	Brian Williams	.15	.07
212	Pedro Astacio	.15	.07
213	Brett Butler	.30	.14
214	Omar Daal	.15	.07
215	Jim Gott	.15	.07
216	Raul Mondesi	.60	.25
217	Jose Offerman	.30	.14
218	Mike Piazza	2.00	.90
219	Cory Snyder	.15	.07
220	Tim Wallach	.15	.07
221	Todd Worrell	.15	.07
222	Moises Alou	.30	.14
223	Sean Berry	.15	.07
224	Wil Cordero	.15	.07
225	Jeff Fassero	.15	.07
226	Darrin Fletcher	.15	.07
227	Cliff Floyd	.30	.14
228	Marquis Grissom	.30	.14
229	Ken Hill	.15	.07
230	Mike Lansing	.30	.14
231	Kirk Rueter	.15	.07
232	John Wetteland	.30	.14
233	Rondell White	.30	.14
234	Tim Bogar	.15	.07
235	Jeromy Burnitz	.30	.14
236	Dwight Gooden	.30	.14
237	Todd Hundley	.30	.14
238	Jeff Kent	.30	.14
239	Josias Manzanillo	.15	.07
240	Joe Orsulak	.15	.07
241	Ryan Thompson	.15	.07
242	Kim Batiste	.15	.07
243	Darren Daulton	.30	.14
244	Tommy Greene	.15	.07
245	Dave Hollins	.15	.07
246	Pete Incaviglia	.15	.07
247	Danny Jackson	.15	.07
248	Ricky Jordan	.15	.07
249	John Kruk	.30	.14
250	Mickey Morandini	.15	.07
251	Terry Mulholland	.15	.07
252	Ben Rivera	.15	.07
253	Kevin Stocker	.15	.07
254	Jay Bell	.30	.14
255	Steve Cooke	.15	.07
256	Jeff King	.15	.07
257	Al Martin	.15	.07
258	Danny Miceli	.15	.07
259	Blas Minor	.15	.07
260	Don Slaught	.15	.07
261	Paul Wagner	.15	.07
262	Tim Wakefield	.30	.14
263	Kevin Young	.15	.07
264	Rene Arocha	.15	.07
265	Richard Batchelor	.15	.07
266	Gregg Jefferies	.15	.07
267	Brian Jordan	.30	.14
268	Jose Oquendo	.15	.07
269	Donovan Osborne	.15	.07
270	Erik Pappas	.15	.07
271	Mike Perez	.15	.07
272	Bob Tewksbury	.15	.07
273	Mark Whiten	.15	.07
274	Todd Zeile	.15	.07
275	Andy Ashby	.15	.07
276	Brad Ausmus	.15	.07
277	Phil Clark	.15	.07
278	Jeff Gardner	.15	.07
279	Ricky Gutierrez	.15	.07
280	Tony Gwynn	1.50	.70
281	Tim Mauser	.15	.07
282	Scott Sanders	.15	.07
283	Frank Seminara	.15	.07
284	Wally Whitehurst	.15	.07
285	Rod Beck	.15	.07
286	Barry Bonds	.75	.35
287	Dave Burba	.15	.07
288	Mark Carreon	.15	.07
289	Royce Clayton	.15	.07
290	Darren Jackson	.30	.14
291	Darren Lewis	.15	.07
292	Kirt Manwaring	.15	.07
293	Dave Martinez	.15	.07
294	Billy Swift	.15	.07
295	Salomon Torres	.15	.07
296	Matt Williams	.40	.18
297	Checklist 1-75	.15	.07
298	Checklist 76-150	.15	.07
299	Checklist 151-225	.15	.07
300	Checklist 226-300	.15	.07
301	Brady Anderson	.30	.14
302	Harold Baines	.30	.14
303	Damon Buford	.15	.07
304	Mike Devereaux	.15	.07
305	Sid Fernandez	.15	.07
306	Rick Krivda	.15	.07
307	Mike Mussina	.60	.25
308	Rafael Palmeiro	.60	.25
309	Arthur Rhodes	.15	.07
310	Chris Sabo	.15	.07
311	Lee Smith	.30	.14
312	Gregg Zaun	.15	.07
313	Scott Cooper	.15	.07
314	Mike Greenwell	.15	.07
315	Tim Naehring	.15	.07
316	Otis Nixon	.15	.07
317	Paul Quantrill	.15	.07
318	John Valentin	.30	.14
319	Dave Valle	.15	.07
320	Frank Viola	.15	.07
321	Brian Anderson	.40	.18
322	Garret Anderson	.60	.25
323	Chad Curtis	.15	.07
324	Chili Davis	.30	.14
325	Gary DiSarcina	.15	.07
326	Damion Easley	.30	.14
327	Jim Edmonds	.60	.25
328	Chuck Finley	.30	.14
329	Joe Grahe	.15	.07
330	Bo Jackson	.30	.14
331	Mark Langston	.30	.14
332	Harold Reynolds	.15	.07
333	James Baldwin	.30	.14
334	Ray Durham	1.00	.45

#	Player			#	Player			#	Player		
335	Julio Franco	.15	.07	421	Anthony Manahan	.15	.07	507	Todd Jones	.15	.07
336	Craig Grebeck	.15	.07	422	Edgar Martinez	.30	.14	508	Orlando Miller	.15	.07
337	Ozzie Guillen	.15	.07	423	Keith Mitchell	.15	.07	509	James Mouton	.15	.07
338	Joe Hall	.15	.07	424	Roger Salkeld	.15	.07	510	Roberto Petagine	.15	.07
339	Darrin Jackson	.15	.07	425	Mac Suzuki	.30	.14	511	Shane Reynolds	.30	.14
340	Jack McDowell	.15	.07	426	Dan Wilson	.15	.07	512	Mitch Williams	.15	.07
341	Tim Raines	.30	.14	427	Duff Brumley	.15	.07	513	Billy Ashley	.15	.07
342	Robin Ventura	.30	.14	428	Jose Canseco	.75	.35	514	Tom Candiotti	.15	.07
343	Carlos Baerga	.30	.14	429	Will Clark	.60	.25	515	Delino DeShields	.15	.07
344	Derek Lilliquist	.15	.07	430	Steve Dreyer	.15	.07	516	Kevin Gross	.15	.07
345	Dennis Martinez	.30	.14	431	Rick Helling	.30	.14	517	Orel Hershiser	.30	.14
346	Jack Morris	.30	.14	432	Chris James	.15	.07	518	Eric Karros	.30	.14
347	Eddie Murray	.60	.25	433	Matt Whiteside	.15	.07	519	Ramon Martinez	.30	.14
348	Chris Nabholz	.15	.07	434	Roberto Alomar	.60	.25	520	Chan Ho Park	1.00	.45
349	Charles Nagy	.30	.14	435	Scott Brow	.15	.07	521	Henry Rodriguez	.30	.14
350	Chad Ogea	.15	.07	436	Domingo Cedeno	.15	.07	522	Joey Eischen	.15	.07
351	Manny Ramirez	1.25	.55	437	Carlos Delgado	.60	.25	523	Rod Henderson	.15	.07
352	Omar Vizquel	.30	.14	438	Juan Guzman	.15	.07	524	Pedro Martinez	.75	.35
353	Tim Belcher	.15	.07	439	Paul Spoljaric	.15	.07	525	Mel Rojas	.15	.07
354	Eric Davis	.30	.14	440	Todd Stottlemyre	.15	.07	526	Larry Walker	.60	.25
355	Kirk Gibson	.30	.14	441	Woody Williams	.15	.07	527	Gabe White	.15	.07
356	Rick Greene	.15	.07	442	David Justice	.60	.25	528	Bobby Bonilla	.30	.14
357	Mickey Tettleton	.15	.07	443	Mike Kelly	.15	.07	529	Jonathan Hurst	.15	.07
358	Alan Trammell	.40	.18	444	Ryan Klesko	.30	.14	530	Bobby Jones	.15	.07
359	David Wells	.40	.18	445	Javier Lopez	.40	.18	531	Kevin McReynolds	.15	.07
360	Stan Belinda	.15	.07	446	Greg Maddux	1.50	.70	532	Bill Pulsipher	.30	.14
361	Vince Coleman	.15	.07	447	Kent Mercker	.15	.07	533	Bret Saberhagen	.30	.14
362	David Cone	.40	.18	448	Charlie O'Brien	.15	.07	534	David Segui	.15	.07
363	Gary Gaetti	.30	.14	449	Terry Pendleton	.15	.07	535	Pete Smith	.15	.07
364	Tom Gordon	.15	.07	450	Mike Stanton	.15	.07	536	Kelly Stinnett	.15	.07
365	Dave Henderson	.15	.07	451	Tony Tarasco	.15	.07	537	Dave Telgheder	.15	.07
366	Wally Joyner	.30	.14	452	Terrell Wade	.15	.07	538	Quilvio Veras	.30	.14
367	Brent Mayne	.15	.07	453	Willie Banks	.15	.07	539	Jose Vizcaino	.15	.07
368	Brian McRae	.15	.07	454	Shawon Dunston	.15	.07	540	Pete Walker	.15	.07
369	Michael Tucker	.40	.18	455	Mark Grace	.40	.18	541	Ricky Bottalico	.30	.14
370	Ricky Bones	.15	.07	456	Jose Guzman	.15	.07	542	Wes Chamberlain	.15	.07
371	Brian Harper	.15	.07	457	Jose Hernandez	.15	.07	543	Mariano Duncan	.15	.07
372	Tyrone Hill	.15	.07	458	Glenallen Hill	.15	.07	544	Lenny Dykstra	.30	.14
373	Mark Kiefer	.15	.07	459	Blaise Ilsley	.15	.07	545	Jim Eisenreich	.15	.07
374	Pat Listach	.15	.07	460	Brooks Kieschnick	.15	.07	546	Phil Geisler	.15	.07
375	Mike Matheny	.15	.07	461	Derrick May	.15	.07	547	Wayne Gomes	.15	.07
376	Jose Mercedes	.15	.07	462	Randy Myers	.15	.07	548	Doug Jones	.15	.07
377	Jody Reed	.15	.07	463	Karl Rhodes	.15	.07	549	Jeff Juden	.15	.07
378	Kevin Seitzer	.15	.07	464	Sammy Sosa	2.00	.90	550	Mike Lieberthal	.15	.07
379	B.J. Surhoff	.30	.14	465	Steve Trachsel	.15	.07	551	Tony Longmire	.15	.07
380	Greg Vaughn	.30	.14	466	Anthony Young	.15	.07	552	Tom Marsh	.15	.07
381	Turner Ward	.15	.07	467	Eddie Zambrano	.15	.07	553	Bobby Munoz	.15	.07
382	Wes Weger	.15	.07	468	Bret Boone	.30	.14	554	Curt Schilling	.30	.14
383	Bill Wegman	.15	.07	469	Tom Browning	.15	.07	555	Carlos Garcia	.15	.07
384	Rick Aguilera	.15	.07	470	Hector Carrasco	.15	.07	556	Ravelo Manzanillo	.15	.07
385	Rich Becker	.15	.07	471	Rob Dibble	.15	.07	557	Orlando Merced	.15	.07
386	Alex Cole	.15	.07	472	Erik Hanson	.15	.07	558	Will Pennyfeather	.15	.07
387	Steve Dunn	.15	.07	473	Thomas Howard	.15	.07	559	Zane Smith	.15	.07
388	Keith Garagozzo	.15	.07	474	Barry Larkin	.60	.25	560	Andy Van Slyke	.30	.14
389	LaTroy Hawkins	.40	.18	475	Hal Morris	.15	.07	561	Rick White	.15	.07
390	Shane Mack	.15	.07	476	Jose Rijo	.15	.07	562	Luis Alicea	.15	.07
391	David McCarty	.15	.07	477	John Burke	.15	.07	563	Brian Barber	.15	.07
392	Pedro Munoz	.15	.07	478	Ellis Burks	.30	.14	564	Clint Davis	.15	.07
393	Derek Parks	.15	.07	479	Marvin Freeman	.15	.07	565	Bernard Gilkey	.15	.07
394	Kirby Puckett	1.00	.45	480	Andres Galarraga	.60	.25	566	Ray Lankford	.30	.14
395	Kevin Tapani	.15	.07	481	Greg W. Harris	.15	.07	567	Tom Pagnozzi	.15	.07
396	Matt Walbeck	.15	.07	482	Charlie Hayes	.15	.07	568	Ozzie Smith	.75	.35
397	Jim Abbott	.30	.14	483	Darren Holmes	.15	.07	569	Rick Sutcliffe	.15	.07
398	Mike Gallego	.15	.07	484	Howard Johnson	.15	.07	570	Allen Watson	.15	.07
399	Xavier Hernandez	.15	.07	485	Marcus Moore	.15	.07	571	Dmitri Young	.30	.14
400	Don Mattingly	1.25	.55	486	David Nied	.15	.07	572	Derek Bell	.30	.14
401	Terry Mulholland	.15	.07	487	Mark Thompson	.15	.07	573	Andy Benes	.30	.14
402	Matt Nokes	.15	.07	488	Walt Weiss	.15	.07	574	Archi Cianfrocco	.15	.07
403	Luis Polonia	.15	.07	489	Kurt Abbott	.15	.07	575	Joey Hamilton	.60	.25
404	Bob Wickman	.15	.07	490	Matias Carrillo	.15	.07	576	Gene Harris	.15	.07
405	Mark Acre	.15	.07	491	Jeff Conine	.15	.07	577	Trevor Hoffman	.30	.14
406	Fausto Cruz	.15	.07	492	Chris Hammond	.15	.07	578	Tim Hyers	.15	.07
407	Dennis Eckersley	.30	.14	493	Bryan Harvey	.15	.07	579	Brian Johnson	.15	.07
408	Rickey Henderson	.75	.35	494	Charlie Hough	.15	.07	580	Keith Lockhart	.15	.07
409	Stan Javier	.15	.07	495	Yorkis Perez	.15	.07	581	Pedro A. Martinez	.15	.07
410	Carlos Reyes	.15	.07	496	Pat Rapp	.15	.07	582	Ray McDavid	.15	.07
411	Ruben Sierra	.15	.07	497	Benito Santiago	.15	.07	583	Phil Plantier	.15	.07
412	Terry Steinbach	.15	.07	498	David Weathers	.15	.07	584	Bip Roberts	.15	.07
413	Bill Taylor	.15	.07	499	Craig Biggio	.60	.25	585	Dave Staton	.15	.07
414	Todd Van Poppel	.15	.07	500	Ken Caminiti	.40	.18	586	Todd Benzinger	.15	.07
415	Eric Anthony	.15	.07	501	Doug Drabek	.15	.07	587	John Burkett	.15	.07
416	Bobby Ayala	.15	.07	502	Tony Eusebio	.15	.07	588	Bryan Hickerson	.15	.07
417	Chris Bosio	.15	.07	503	Steve Finley	.30	.14	589	Willie McGee	.30	.14
418	Tim Davis	.15	.07	504	Pete Harnisch	.15	.07	590	John Patterson	.15	.07
419	Randy Johnson	.60	.25	505	Brian L. Hunter	.30	.14	591	Mark Portugal	.15	.07
420	Kevin King	.15	.07	506	Domingo Jean	.15	.07	592	Kevin Rogers	.15	.07

		MINT	NRMT
❏ 593	Joe Rosselli	.15	.07
❏ 594	Steve Soderstrom	.15	.07
❏ 595	Robby Thompson	.15	.07
❏ 596	125th Anniversary Card	.15	.07
❏ 597	Checklist	.15	.07
❏ 598	Checklist	.15	.07
❏ 599	Checklist	.15	.07
❏ 600	Checklist	.15	.07
❏ P243	Darren Daulton Promo	2.00	.90
❏ P249	John Kruk Promo	2.00	.90

1994 Ultra All-Rookies

	MINT	NRMT
COMPLETE SET (10)	8.00	3.60
COMMON CARD (1-10)	.50	.23
MINOR STARS	1.25	.55

RANDOM INSERTS IN ALL SER.2 PACKS
*JUMBOS: 1X TO 2X HI COLUMN
ONE JUMBO SET PER HOBBY CASE

		MINT	NRMT
❏ 1	Kurt Abbott	.50	.23
❏ 2	Carlos Delgado	2.00	.90
❏ 3	Cliff Floyd	1.25	.55
❏ 4	Jeffrey Hammonds	1.25	.55
❏ 5	Ryan Klesko	1.25	.55
❏ 6	Javier Lopez	1.50	.70
❏ 7	Raul Mondesi	2.00	.90
❏ 8	James Mouton	.50	.23
❏ 9	Chan Ho Park	1.50	.70
❏ 10	Dave Staton	.50	.23

1994 Ultra All-Stars

	MINT	NRMT
COMPLETE SET (20)	15.00	6.75
COMMON CARD (1-20)	.25	.11

RANDOM INSERTS IN ALL SER.2 PACKS

		MINT	NRMT
❏ 1	Chris Hoiles	.25	.11
❏ 2	Frank Thomas	2.00	.90
❏ 3	Roberto Alomar	1.00	.45
❏ 4	Cal Ripken Jr.	4.00	1.80
❏ 5	Robin Ventura	.50	.23
❏ 6	Albert Belle	1.00	.45
❏ 7	Juan Gonzalez	2.00	.90
❏ 8	Ken Griffey Jr.	5.00	2.20
❏ 9	John Olerud	.50	.23
❏ 10	Jack McDowell	.25	.11
❏ 11	Mike Piazza	3.00	1.35

		MINT	NRMT
❏ 12	Fred McGriff	.75	.35
❏ 13	Ryne Sandberg	1.25	.55
❏ 14	Jay Bell	.50	.23
❏ 15	Matt Williams	.75	.35
❏ 16	Barry Bonds	1.25	.55
❏ 17	Lenny Dykstra	.50	.23
❏ 18	David Justice	1.00	.45
❏ 19	Tom Glavine	1.00	.45
❏ 20	Greg Maddux	2.50	1.10

1994 Ultra Award Winners

	MINT	NRMT
COMPLETE SET (25)	15.00	6.75
COMMON CARD (1-25)	.25	.11

RANDOM INSERTS IN ALL SER.1 PACKS

		MINT	NRMT
❏ 1	Ivan Rodriguez	1.25	.55
❏ 2	Don Mattingly	1.50	.70
❏ 3	Roberto Alomar	1.00	.45
❏ 4	Robin Ventura	.50	.23
❏ 5	Omar Vizquel	.50	.23
❏ 6	Ken Griffey Jr.	5.00	2.20
❏ 7	Kenny Lofton	1.00	.45
❏ 8	Devon White	.25	.11
❏ 9	Mark Langston	.25	.11
❏ 10	Kirt Manwaring	.25	.11
❏ 11	Mark Grace	.75	.35
❏ 12	Robby Thompson	.25	.11
❏ 13	Matt Williams	.75	.35
❏ 14	Jay Bell	.50	.23
❏ 15	Barry Bonds	1.25	.55
❏ 16	Marquis Grissom	.25	.11
❏ 17	Larry Walker	1.00	.45
❏ 18	Greg Maddux	2.50	1.10
❏ 19	Frank Thomas	2.00	.90
❏ 20	Barry Bonds	1.25	.55
❏ 21	Paul Molitor	1.00	.45
❏ 22	Jack McDowell	.25	.11
❏ 23	Greg Maddux	2.50	1.10
❏ 24	Tim Salmon	1.00	.45
❏ 25	Mike Piazza	3.00	1.35

1994 Ultra Career Achievement

	MINT	NRMT
COMPLETE SET (5)	10.00	4.50
COMMON CARD (1-5)	1.00	.45

RANDOM INSERTS IN ALL SER.2 PACKS

		MINT	NRMT
❏ 1	Joe Carter	1.00	.45
❏ 2	Paul Molitor	2.00	.90
❏ 3	Cal Ripken Jr.	8.00	3.60
❏ 4	Ryne Sandberg	2.50	1.10
❏ 5	Dave Winfield	2.00	.90

1994 Ultra Firemen

	MINT	NRMT
COMPLETE SET (10)	5.00	2.20
COMMON CARD (1-10)	.50	.23

SER.1 STATED ODDS 1:11

		MINT	NRMT
❏ 1	Jeff Montgomery	.50	.23
❏ 2	Duane Ward	.50	.23
❏ 3	Tom Henke	.50	.23
❏ 4	Roberto Hernandez	.50	.23
❏ 5	Dennis Eckersley	.75	.35
❏ 6	Randy Myers	.50	.23
❏ 7	Rod Beck	.50	.23
❏ 8	Bryan Harvey	.50	.23
❏ 9	John Wetteland	.75	.35
❏ 10	Mitch Williams	.50	.23

1994 Ultra Hitting Machines

	MINT	NRMT
COMPLETE SET (10)	12.00	5.50
COMMON CARD (1-10)	.25	.11

RANDOM INSERTS IN ALL SER.2 PACKS

		MINT	NRMT
❏ 1	Roberto Alomar	1.00	.45
❏ 2	Carlos Baerga	.25	.11
❏ 3	Barry Bonds	1.25	.55
❏ 4	Andres Galarraga	1.00	.45
❏ 5	Juan Gonzalez	2.00	.90
❏ 6	Tony Gwynn	2.50	1.10
❏ 7	Paul Molitor	1.00	.45
❏ 8	John Olerud	.50	.23
❏ 9	Mike Piazza	3.00	1.35
❏ 10	Frank Thomas	2.00	.90

1994 Ultra Home Run Kings

	MINT	NRMT
COMPLETE SET (12)	80.00	36.00

COMMON CARD (1-12) .... 1.50   .70
RANDOM INS.IN SER.1 FOIL/JUMBO PACKS

☐ 1 Juan Gonzalez	10.00	4.50
☐ 2 Ken Griffey Jr.	25.00	11.00
☐ 3 Frank Thomas	10.00	4.50
☐ 4 Albert Belle	4.00	1.80
☐ 5 Rafael Palmeiro	4.00	1.80
☐ 6 Joe Carter	1.50	.70
☐ 7 Barry Bonds	6.00	2.70
☐ 8 David Justice	4.00	1.80
☐ 9 Matt Williams	2.00	.90
☐ 10 Fred McGriff	2.00	.90
☐ 11 Ron Gant	1.50	.70
☐ 12 Mike Piazza	15.00	6.75

1994 Ultra League Leaders

N.L. Batting Average

	MINT	NRMT
COMPLETE SET (10)	5.00	2.20
COMMON CARD (1-10)	3.00	1.35
RANDOM INSERTS IN ALL SER.1 PACKS		

☐ 1 John Olerud	.50	.23
☐ 2 Rafael Palmeiro	1.50	.70
☐ 3 Kenny Lofton	1.50	.70
☐ 4 Jack McDowell	.25	.11
☐ 5 Randy Johnson	.50	.23
☐ 6 Andres Galarraga	1.50	.70
☐ 7 Lenny Dykstra	.50	.23
☐ 8 Chuck Carr	.25	.11
☐ 9 Tom Glavine	1.50	.70
☐ 10 Jose Rijo	.25	.11

1994 Ultra On-Base Leaders

	MINT	NRMT
COMPLETE SET (12)	120.00	55.00
COMMON CARD (1-12)	.05	.02
RANDOM INSERTS IN SER.2 JUMBO PACKS		

☐ 1 Roberto Alomar	10.00	4.50
☐ 2 Barry Bonds	10.00	4.50
☐ 3 Lenny Dykstra	6.00	2.70
☐ 4 Andres Galarraga	10.00	4.50
☐ 5 Mark Grace	6.00	2.70
☐ 6 Ken Griffey Jr.	50.00	22.00
☐ 7 Gregg Jefferies	3.00	1.35

☐ 8 Orlando Merced	3.00	1.35
☐ 9 Paul Molitor	10.00	4.50
☐ 10 John Olerud	6.00	2.70
☐ 11 Tony Phillips	3.00	1.35
☐ 12 Frank Thomas	25.00	11.00

1994 Ultra Phillies Finest

	MINT	NRMT
COMPLETE SET (20)	10.00	4.50
COMPLETE SERIES 1 (10)	5.00	2.20
COMPLETE SERIES 2 (10)	5.00	2.20
COMMON DAULTON (1-5/11-15)	.50	.23
COMMON KRUK (6-10/16-20)	.50	.23
RANDOM INSERTS IN ALL PACKS		
COMMON MAIL-IN (M1-M4) ...	1.00	.45
MAIL-IN CARDS DIST.VIA WRAPPER EXCH.		

☐ 1 Darren Daulton .... .50		.23
(Standing behind home plate)		
☐ 2 Darren Daulton .... .50		.23
(Swinging at a pitch)		
☐ 3 Darren Daulton .... .50		.23
(Blocking home plate)		
☐ 4 Darren Daulton .... .50		.23
(Just completed swing and is headed for first)		
☐ 5 Darren Daulton .... .50		.23
(Looking skyward after connecting with a pitch)		
☐ 6 John Kruk .... .50		.23
(Swinging at a pitch)		
☐ 7 John Kruk .... .50		.23
(Fielding)		
☐ 8 John Kruk .... .50		.23
(Just completed a swing)		
☐ 9 John Kruk .... .50		.23
(On deck)		
☐ 10 John Kruk .... .50		.23
(Breaking out of batters box)		
☐ 11 Darren Daulton .... .50		.23
(Looking skyward after swing)		
☐ 12 Darren Daulton .... .50		.23
☐ 13 Darren Daulton .... .50		.23
(Anticipating throw home)		
☐ 14 Darren Daulton .... .50		.23

(Standing at home with ball in hand)		
☐ 15 Darren Daulton .... .50		.23
(Running up first base line with in catching gear)		
☐ 16 John Kruk .... .50		.23
(Follow through of swing)		
☐ 17 John Kruk .... .50		.23
(Waiting on deck)		
☐ 18 John Kruk .... .50		.23
(Follow through from first base dugout angle)		
☐ 19 John Kruk .... .50		.23
(Swinging at pitch) chest high)		
☐ 20 John Kruk .... .50		.23
(Looking out toward left field afer swinging)		
☐ M1 Darren Daulton 1.00		.45
(About to throw down to second base)		
☐ M2 John Kruk 1.00		.45
(Fielding position)		
☐ M3 Darren Daulton 1.00		.45
(Awaiting pitch)		
☐ M4 John Kruk 1.00		.45
(Running)		
☐ AU1 Darren Daulton 30.00		13.50
Certified Autograph		
☐ AU2 John Kruk 30.00		13.50
Certified Autograph		

1994 Ultra RBI Kings

	MINT	NRMT
COMPLETE SET (12)	80.00	36.00
COMMON CARD (1-12)	2.00	.90
RANDOM INS.IN SER.1 JUMBO PACKS		

☐ 1 Albert Belle	6.00	2.70
☐ 2 Frank Thomas	12.00	5.50
☐ 3 Joe Carter	3.00	1.35
☐ 4 Juan Gonzalez	12.00	5.50
☐ 5 Cecil Fielder	2.00	.90
☐ 6 Carlos Baerga	2.00	.90
☐ 7 Barry Bonds	8.00	3.60
☐ 8 David Justice	6.00	2.70
☐ 9 Ron Gant	2.00	.90
☐ 10 Mike Piazza	20.00	9.00
☐ 11 Matt Williams	4.00	1.80
☐ 12 Darren Daulton	3.00	1.35

1994 Ultra Rising Stars

	MINT	NRMT
COMPLETE SET (12)	80.00	36.00
COMMON CARD (1-12)	2.50	1.10
RANDOM INS.IN SER.2 FOIL/JUMBO PACKS		

☐ 1 Carlos Baerga	2.50	1.10
☐ 2 Jeff Bagwell	8.00	3.60
☐ 3 Albert Belle	8.00	3.60
☐ 4 Cliff Floyd	4.00	1.80
☐ 5 Travis Fryman	4.00	1.80
☐ 6 Marquis Grissom	2.50	1.10

		MINT	NRMT
☐ 7	Kenny Lofton	8.00	3.60
☐ 8	John Olerud	4.00	1.80
☐ 9	Mike Piazza	25.00	11.00
☐ 10	Kirk Rueter	2.50	1.10
☐ 11	Tim Salmon	8.00	3.60
☐ 12	Aaron Sele	4.00	1.80

1994 Ultra Second Year Standouts

	MINT	NRMT
COMPLETE SET (10)	10.00	4.50
COMMON CARD (1-10)	.25	.11
SER.1 STATED ODDS 1:11		

		MINT	NRMT
☐ 1	Jason Bere	.25	.11
☐ 2	Brent Gates	.25	.11
☐ 3	Jeffrey Hammonds	.50	.23
☐ 4	Tim Salmon	1.00	.45
☐ 5	Aaron Sele	.50	.23
☐ 6	Chuck Carr	.25	.11
☐ 7	Jeff Conine	.25	.11
☐ 8	Greg McMichael	.25	.11
☐ 9	Mike Piazza	8.00	3.60
☐ 10	Kevin Stocker	.25	.11

1994 Ultra Strikeout Kings

	MINT	NRMT
COMPLETE SET (5)	5.00	2.20
COMMON CARD (1-5)	.25	.11

SER.2 STATED ODDS 1:7

☐ 1	Randy Johnson	1.00	.45
☐ 2	Mark Langston	.25	.11
☐ 3	Greg Maddux	2.50	1.10
☐ 4	Jose Rijo	.25	.11
☐ 5	John Smoltz	.75	.35

1995 Ultra

	MINT	NRMT
COMPLETE SET (450)	30.00	13.50
COMPLETE SERIES 1 (250)	18.00	8.00
COMPLETE SERIES 2 (200)	12.00	5.50
COMMON CARD (1-450)	.15	.07
MINOR STARS	.30	.14
UNLISTED STARS	.60	.25
COMP.G.MED.SET (450)	110.00	50.00
COMP.G.MED.SER.1 (250)	60.00	27.00
COMP.G.MED.SER.2 (200)	50.00	22.00
COMMON G.MED. (1-450)	.30	.14
*G.MED.STARS: 1.5X TO 4X HI COLUMN		
*G.MED.YOUNG STARS: 1.25X TO 3X HI		
ONE GOLD MEDALLION PER PACK		

☐ 1	Brady Anderson	.30	.14
☐ 2	Sid Fernandez	.15	.07
☐ 3	Jeffrey Hammonds	.30	.14
☐ 4	Chris Hoiles	.15	.07
☐ 5	Ben McDonald	.15	.07
☐ 6	Mike Mussina	.60	.25
☐ 7	Rafael Palmeiro	.60	.25
☐ 8	Jack Voigt	.15	.07
☐ 9	Wes Chamberlain	.15	.07
☐ 10	Roger Clemens	1.50	.70
☐ 11	Chris Howard	.15	.07
☐ 12	Tim Naehring	.15	.07
☐ 13	Otis Nixon	.15	.07
☐ 14	Rich Rowland	.15	.07
☐ 15	Ken Ryan	.15	.07
☐ 16	John Valentin	.30	.14
☐ 17	Mo Vaughn	.60	.25
☐ 18	Brian Anderson	.30	.14
☐ 19	Chili Davis	.30	.14
☐ 20	Damion Easley	.30	.14
☐ 21	Jim Edmonds	.40	.18
☐ 22	Mark Langston	.15	.07
☐ 23	Tim Salmon	.60	.25
☐ 24	J.T. Snow	.30	.14
☐ 25	Chris Turner	.15	.07
☐ 26	Wilson Alvarez	.30	.14
☐ 27	Joey Cora	.15	.07
☐ 28	Alex Fernandez	.15	.07
☐ 29	Roberto Hernandez	.15	.07
☐ 30	Lance Johnson	.15	.07
☐ 31	Ron Karkovice	.15	.07
☐ 32	Kirk McCaskill	.15	.07
☐ 33	Tim Raines	.30	.14
☐ 34	Frank Thomas	1.25	.55
☐ 35	Sandy Alomar Jr.	.30	.14
☐ 36	Albert Belle	.60	.25
☐ 37	Mark Clark	.15	.07
☐ 38	Kenny Lofton	.40	.18
☐ 39	Eddie Murray	.60	.25
☐ 40	Eric Plunk	.15	.07
☐ 41	Manny Ramirez	.75	.35
☐ 42	Jim Thome	.60	.25
☐ 43	Omar Vizquel	.30	.14

☐ 44	Danny Bautista	.15	.07
☐ 45	Junior Felix	.15	.07
☐ 46	Cecil Fielder	.30	.14
☐ 47	Chris Gomez	.15	.07
☐ 48	Chad Kreuter	.15	.07
☐ 49	Mike Moore	.15	.07
☐ 50	Tony Phillips	.15	.07
☐ 51	Alan Trammell	.30	.14
☐ 52	David Wells	.40	.18
☐ 53	Kevin Appier	.30	.14
☐ 54	Billy Brewer	.15	.07
☐ 55	David Cone	.40	.18
☐ 56	Greg Gagne	.15	.07
☐ 57	Bob Hamelin	.15	.07
☐ 58	Jose Lind	.15	.07
☐ 59	Brent Mayne	.15	.07
☐ 60	Brian McRae	.15	.07
☐ 61	Terry Shumpert	.15	.07
☐ 62	Ricky Bones	.15	.07
☐ 63	Mike Fetters	.15	.07
☐ 64	Darryl Hamilton	.15	.07
☐ 65	John Jaha	.15	.07
☐ 66	Graeme Lloyd	.15	.07
☐ 67	Matt Mieske	.15	.07
☐ 68	Kevin Seitzer	.15	.07
☐ 69	Jose Valentin	.15	.07
☐ 70	Turner Ward	.15	.07
☐ 71	Rick Aguilera	.15	.07
☐ 72	Rich Becker	.15	.07
☐ 73	Alex Cole	.15	.07
☐ 74	Scott Leius	.15	.07
☐ 75	Pat Meares	.15	.07
☐ 76	Kirby Puckett	1.00	.45
☐ 77	Dave Stevens	.15	.07
☐ 78	Kevin Tapani	.15	.07
☐ 79	Matt Walbeck	.15	.07
☐ 80	Wade Boggs	.60	.25
☐ 81	Scott Kamieniecki	.15	.07
☐ 82	Pat Kelly	.15	.07
☐ 83	Jimmy Key	.30	.14
☐ 84	Paul O'Neill	.30	.14
☐ 85	Luis Polonia	.15	.07
☐ 86	Mike Stanley	.15	.07
☐ 87	Danny Tartabull	.15	.07
☐ 88	Bob Wickman	.15	.07
☐ 89	Mark Acre	.15	.07
☐ 90	Geronimo Berroa	.15	.07
☐ 91	Mike Bordick	.15	.07
☐ 92	Ron Darling	.15	.07
☐ 93	Stan Javier	.15	.07
☐ 94	Mark McGwire	3.00	1.35
☐ 95	Troy Neel	.15	.07
☐ 96	Ruben Sierra	.30	.14
☐ 97	Terry Steinbach	.15	.07
☐ 98	Eric Anthony	.15	.07
☐ 99	Chris Bosio	.15	.07
☐ 100	Dave Fleming	.15	.07
☐ 101	Ken Griffey Jr.	3.00	1.35
☐ 102	Reggie Jefferson	.15	.07
☐ 103	Randy Johnson	.60	.25
☐ 104	Edgar Martinez	.30	.14
☐ 105	Bill Risley	.15	.07
☐ 106	Dan Wilson	.15	.07
☐ 107	Cris Carpenter	.15	.07
☐ 108	Will Clark	.60	.25
☐ 109	Juan Gonzalez	1.25	.55
☐ 110	Rusty Greer	.60	.25
☐ 111	David Hulse	.15	.07
☐ 112	Roger Pavlik	.15	.07
☐ 113	Ivan Rodriguez	.75	.35
☐ 114	Doug Strange	.15	.07
☐ 115	Matt Whiteside	.15	.07
☐ 116	Roberto Alomar	.60	.25
☐ 117	Brad Cornett	.15	.07
☐ 118	Carlos Delgado	.60	.25
☐ 119	Alex Gonzalez	.30	.14
☐ 120	Darren Hall	.15	.07
☐ 121	Pat Hentgen	.30	.14
☐ 122	Paul Molitor	.60	.25
☐ 123	Ed Sprague	.15	.07
☐ 124	Devon White	.30	.14
☐ 125	Tom Glavine	.60	.25
☐ 126	David Justice	.60	.25
☐ 127	Roberto Kelly	.15	.07
☐ 128	Mark Lemke	.15	.07
☐ 129	Greg Maddux	1.50	.70

130	Greg McMichael	.15	.07
131	Kent Mercker	.15	.07
132	Charlie O'Brien	.15	.07
133	John Smoltz	.40	.18
134	Willie Banks	.15	.07
135	Steve Buechele	.15	.07
136	Kevin Foster	.15	.07
137	Glenallen Hill	.15	.07
138	Rey Sanchez	.15	.07
139	Sammy Sosa	2.00	.90
140	Steve Trachsel	.15	.07
141	Rick Wilkins	.15	.07
142	Jeff Brantley	.15	.07
143	Hector Carrasco	.15	.07
144	Kevin Jarvis	.15	.07
145	Barry Larkin	.60	.25
146	Chuck McElroy	.15	.07
147	Jose Rijo	.15	.07
148	Johnny Ruffin	.15	.07
149	Deion Sanders	.30	.14
150	Eddie Taubensee	.15	.07
151	Dante Bichette	.30	.14
152	Ellis Burks	.30	.14
153	Joe Girardi	.15	.07
154	Charlie Hayes	.15	.07
155	Mike Kingery	.15	.07
156	Steve Reed	.15	.07
157	Kevin Ritz	.15	.07
158	Bruce Ruffin	.15	.07
159	Eric Young	.15	.07
160	Kurt Abbott	.15	.07
161	Chuck Carr	.15	.07
162	Chris Hammond	.15	.07
163	Bryan Harvey	.15	.07
164	Terry Mathews	.15	.07
165	Yorkis Perez	.15	.07
166	Pat Rapp	.15	.07
167	Gary Sheffield	.30	.14
168	Dave Weathers	.15	.07
169	Jeff Bagwell	.75	.35
170	Ken Caminiti	.40	.18
171	Doug Drabek	.15	.07
172	Steve Finley	.30	.14
173	John Hudek	.15	.07
174	Todd Jones	.15	.07
175	James Mouton	.15	.07
176	Shane Reynolds	.30	.14
177	Scott Servais	.15	.07
178	Tom Candiotti	.15	.07
179	Omar Daal	.15	.07
180	Darren Dreifort	.30	.14
181	Eric Karros	.30	.14
182	Ramon J.Martinez	.30	.14
183	Raul Mondesi	.40	.18
184	Henry Rodriguez	.30	.14
185	Todd Worrell	.15	.07
186	Moises Alou	.30	.14
187	Sean Berry	.15	.07
188	Wil Cordero	.15	.07
189	Jeff Fassero	.15	.07
190	Darrin Fletcher	.15	.07
191	Butch Henry	.15	.07
192	Ken Hill	.15	.07
193	Mel Rojas	.15	.07
194	John Wetteland	.30	.14
195	Bobby Bonilla	.30	.14
196	Rico Brogna	.15	.07
197	Bobby Jones	.15	.07
198	Jeff Kent	.30	.14
199	Josias Manzanillo	.15	.07
200	Kelly Stinnett	.15	.07
201	Ryan Thompson	.15	.07
202	Jose Vizcaino	.15	.07
203	Lenny Dykstra	.30	.14
204	Jim Eisenreich	.15	.07
205	Dave Hollins	.15	.07
206	Mike Lieberthal	.15	.07
207	Mickey Morandini	.15	.07
208	Bobby Munoz	.15	.07
209	Curt Schilling	.40	.18
210	Heathcliff Slocumb	.15	.07
211	David West	.40	.18
212	Dave Clark	.15	.07
213	Steve Cooke	.15	.07
214	Midre Cummings	.15	.07
215	Carlos Garcia	.15	.07
216	Jeff King	.15	.07
217	Jon Lieber	.15	.07
218	Orlando Merced	.15	.07
219	Don Slaught	.15	.07
220	Rick White	.15	.07
221	Rene Arocha	.15	.07
222	Bernard Gilkey	.15	.07
223	Brian Jordan	.30	.14
224	Tom Pagnozzi	.15	.07
225	Vicente Palacios	.15	.07
226	Geronimo Pena	.15	.07
227	Ozzie Smith	.75	.35
228	Allen Watson	.15	.07
229	Mark Whiten	.15	.07
230	Brad Ausmus	.15	.07
231	Derek Bell	.30	.14
232	Andy Benes	.15	.07
233	Tony Gwynn	1.50	.70
234	Joey Hamilton	.30	.14
235	Luis Lopez	.15	.07
236	Pedro A.Martinez	.15	.07
237	Scott Sanders	.15	.07
238	Eddie Williams	.15	.07
239	Rod Beck	.15	.07
240	Dave Burba	.15	.07
241	Darren Lewis	.15	.07
242	Kirt Manwaring	.15	.07
243	Mark Portugal	.15	.07
244	Darryl Strawberry	.30	.14
245	Robby Thompson	.15	.07
246	Wm.VanLandingham	.15	.07
247	Matt Williams	.60	.25
248	Checklist	.15	.07
249	Checklist	.15	.07
250	Checklist	.15	.07
251	Harold Baines	.30	.14
252	Bret Barberie	.15	.07
253	Armando Benitez	.15	.07
254	Mike Devereaux	.15	.07
255	Leo Gomez	.15	.07
256	Jamie Moyer	.15	.07
257	Arthur Rhodes	.15	.07
258	Cal Ripken	2.50	1.10
259	Luis Alicea	.15	.07
260	Jose Canseco	.75	.35
261	Scott Cooper	.15	.07
262	Andre Dawson	.40	.18
263	Mike Greenwell	.15	.07
264	Aaron Sele	.30	.14
265	Garret Anderson	.30	.14
266	Chad Curtis	.15	.07
267	Gary DiSarcina	.15	.07
268	Chuck Finley	.30	.14
269	Rex Hudler	.15	.07
270	Andrew Lorraine	.15	.07
271	Spike Owen	.15	.07
272	Lee Smith	.30	.14
273	Jason Bere	.15	.07
274	Ozzie Guillen	.15	.07
275	Norberto Martin	.15	.07
276	Scott Ruffcorn	.15	.07
277	Robin Ventura	.30	.14
278	Carlos Baerga	.30	.14
279	Jason Grimsley	.15	.07
280	Dennis Martinez	.30	.14
281	Charles Nagy	.30	.14
282	Paul Sorrento	.15	.07
283	Dave Winfield	.60	.25
284	John Doherty	.15	.07
285	Travis Fryman	.30	.14
286	Kirk Gibson	.30	.14
287	Lou Whitaker	.30	.14
288	Gary Gaetti	.30	.14
289	Tom Gordon	.15	.07
290	Mark Gubicza	.15	.07
291	Wally Joyner	.15	.07
292	Mike Macfarlane	.15	.07
293	Jeff Montgomery	.15	.07
294	Jeff Cirillo	.30	.14
295	Cal Eldred	.15	.07
296	Pat Listach	.15	.07
297	Jose Mercedes	.15	.07
298	Dave Nilsson	.15	.07
299	Duane Singleton	.15	.07
300	Greg Vaughn	.30	.14
301	Scott Erickson	.30	.14
302	Denny Hocking	.15	.07
303	Chuck Knoblauch	.60	.25
304	Pat Mahomes	.15	.07
305	Pedro Munoz	.15	.07
306	Erik Schullstrom	.15	.07
307	Jim Abbott	.30	.14
308	Tony Fernandez	.30	.14
309	Sterling Hitchcock	.30	.14
310	Jim Leyritz	.15	.07
311	Don Mattingly	1.25	.55
312	Jack McDowell	.15	.07
313	Melido Perez	.15	.07
314	Bernie Williams	.60	.25
315	Scott Brosius	.30	.14
316	Dennis Eckersley	.30	.14
317	Brent Gates	.15	.07
318	Rickey Henderson	.75	.35
319	Steve Karsay	.15	.07
320	Steve Ontiveros	.15	.07
321	Bill Taylor	.15	.07
322	Todd Van Poppel	.15	.07
323	Bob Welch	.15	.07
324	Bobby Ayala	.15	.07
325	Mike Blowers	.15	.07
326	Jay Buhner	.30	.14
327	Felix Fermin	.15	.07
328	Tino Martinez	.60	.25
329	Marc Newfield	.15	.07
330	Greg Pirkl	.15	.07
331	Alex Rodriguez	2.50	1.10
332	Kevin Brown	.40	.18
333	John Burkett	.15	.07
334	Jeff Frye	.15	.07
335	Kevin Gross	.15	.07
336	Dean Palmer	.30	.14
337	Joe Carter	.30	.14
338	Shawn Green	.60	.25
339	Juan Guzman	.15	.07
340	Mike Huff	.15	.07
341	Al Leiter	.30	.14
342	John Olerud	.30	.14
343	Dave Stewart	.30	.14
344	Todd Stottlemyre	.15	.07
345	Steve Avery	.15	.07
346	Jeff Blauser	.15	.07
347	Chipper Jones	1.50	.70
348	Mike Kelly	.15	.07
349	Ryan Klesko	.30	.14
350	Javier Lopez	.30	.14
351	Fred McGriff	.40	.18
352	Jose Oliva	.15	.07
353	Terry Pendleton	.15	.07
354	Mike Stanton	.15	.07
355	Tony Tarasco	.15	.07
356	Mark Wohlers	.15	.07
357	Jim Bullinger	.15	.07
358	Shawon Dunston	.15	.07
359	Mark Grace	.40	.18
360	Derrick May	.15	.07
361	Randy Myers	.15	.07
362	Karl Rhodes	.15	.07
363	Bret Boone	.30	.14
364	Brian Dorsett	.15	.07
365	Ron Gant	.30	.14
366	Brian R.Hunter	.15	.07
367	Hal Morris	.15	.07
368	Jack Morris	.30	.14
369	John Roper	.15	.07
370	Reggie Sanders	.30	.14
371	Pete Schourek	.15	.07
372	John Smiley	.15	.07
373	Marvin Freeman	.15	.07
374	Andres Galarraga	.60	.25
375	Mike Munoz	.15	.07
376	David Nied	.15	.07
377	Walt Weiss	.15	.07
378	Greg Colbrunn	.15	.07
379	Jeff Conine	.15	.07
380	Charles Johnson	.30	.14
381	Kurt Miller	.15	.07
382	Robb Nen	.15	.07
383	Benito Santiago	.15	.07
384	Craig Biggio	.60	.25
385	Tony Eusebio	.15	.07
386	Luis Gonzalez	.15	.07
387	Brian L.Hunter	.30	.14

❑ 388 Darryl Kile	.15	.07
❑ 389 Orlando Miller	.15	.07
❑ 390 Phil Plantier	.15	.07
❑ 391 Greg Swindell	.15	.07
❑ 392 Billy Ashley	.15	.07
❑ 393 Pedro Astacio	.15	.07
❑ 394 Brett Butler	.30	.14
❑ 395 Delino DeShields	.15	.07
❑ 396 Orel Hershiser	.30	.14
❑ 397 Garey Ingram	.15	.07
❑ 398 Chan Ho Park	.60	.25
❑ 399 Mike Piazza	2.00	.90
❑ 400 Ismael Valdes	.30	.14
❑ 401 Tim Wallach	.15	.07
❑ 402 Cliff Floyd	.30	.14
❑ 403 Marquis Grissom	.30	.14
❑ 404 Mike Lansing	.15	.07
❑ 405 Pedro Martinez	.75	.35
❑ 406 Kirk Rueter	.15	.07
❑ 407 Tim Scott	.15	.07
❑ 408 Jeff Shaw	.15	.07
❑ 409 Larry Walker	.60	.25
❑ 410 Rondell White	.30	.14
❑ 411 John Franco	.30	.14
❑ 412 Todd Hundley	.30	.14
❑ 413 Jason Jacome	.15	.07
❑ 414 Joe Orsulak	.15	.07
❑ 415 Bret Saberhagen	.30	.14
❑ 416 David Segui	.15	.07
❑ 417 Darren Daulton	.30	.14
❑ 418 Mariano Duncan	.15	.07
❑ 419 Tommy Greene	.15	.07
❑ 420 Gregg Jefferies	.15	.07
❑ 421 John Kruk	.30	.14
❑ 422 Kevin Stocker	.15	.07
❑ 423 Jay Bell	.30	.14
❑ 424 Al Martin	.15	.07
❑ 425 Denny Neagle	.30	.14
❑ 426 Zane Smith	.15	.07
❑ 427 Andy Van Slyke	.30	.14
❑ 428 Paul Wagner	.15	.07
❑ 429 Tom Henke	.15	.07
❑ 430 Danny Jackson	.15	.07
❑ 431 Ray Lankford	.30	.14
❑ 432 John Mabry	.15	.07
❑ 433 Bob Tewksbury	.15	.07
❑ 434 Todd Zeile	.15	.07
❑ 435 Andy Ashby	.15	.07
❑ 436 Andujar Cedeno	.15	.07
❑ 437 Donnie Elliott	.15	.07
❑ 438 Bryce Florie	.15	.07
❑ 439 Trevor Hoffman	.30	.14
❑ 440 Melvin Nieves	.15	.07
❑ 441 Bip Roberts	.15	.07
❑ 442 Barry Bonds	.75	.35
❑ 443 Royce Clayton	.15	.07
❑ 444 Mike Jackson	.30	.14
❑ 445 John Patterson	.15	.07
❑ 446 J.R. Phillips	.15	.07
❑ 447 Bill Swift	.15	.07
❑ 448 Checklist	.15	.07
❑ 449 Checklist	.15	.07
❑ 450 Checklist	.15	.07

1995 Ultra All-Rookies

	MINT	NRMT
COMPLETE SET (10)	5.00	2.20

COMMON CARD (1-10)	.25	.11
SER.2 STATED ODDS 1:5		
*GOLD MEDAL: 2X TO 5X BASE CARD HI		
GM SER.2 STATED ODDS 1:50		

❑ 1 Cliff Floyd	.50	.23
❑ 2 Chris Gomez	.25	.11
❑ 3 Rusty Greer	1.25	.55
❑ 4 Bob Hamelin	.25	.11
❑ 5 Joey Hamilton	.50	.23
❑ 6 John Hudek	.25	.11
❑ 7 Ryan Klesko	.50	.23
❑ 8 Raul Mondesi	.75	.35
❑ 9 Manny Ramirez	1.50	.70
❑ 10 Steve Trachsel	.25	.11

1995 Ultra All-Stars

	MINT	NRMT
COMPLETE SET (20)	20.00	9.00
COMMON CARD (1-20)	.50	.23
SER.2 STATED ODDS 1:4		
*GOLD MEDAL: 1.25X TO 3X BASE CARD HI		
GM SER.2 STATED ODDS 1:40		

❑ 1 Moises Alou	.50	.23
❑ 2 Albert Belle	1.00	.45
❑ 3 Craig Biggio	1.00	.45
❑ 4 Wade Boggs	1.00	.45
❑ 5 Barry Bonds	1.25	.55
❑ 6 David Cone	.75	.35
❑ 7 Ken Griffey Jr.	5.00	2.20
❑ 8 Tony Gwynn	2.00	.90
❑ 9 Chuck Knoblauch	1.00	.45
❑ 10 Barry Larkin	.75	.35
❑ 11 Kenny Lofton	.75	.35
❑ 12 Greg Maddux	2.50	1.10
❑ 13 Fred McGriff	.75	.35
❑ 14 Paul O'Neill	.50	.23
❑ 15 Mike Piazza	3.00	1.35
❑ 16 Kirby Puckett	2.00	.90
❑ 17 Cal Ripken	4.00	1.80
❑ 18 Ivan Rodriguez	1.25	.55
❑ 19 Frank Thomas	2.00	.90
❑ 20 Matt Williams	1.00	.45

1995 Ultra Award Winners

	MINT	NRMT
COMPLETE SET (25)	20.00	9.00

COMMON CARD (1-25)	.25	.11
SER.1 STATED ODDS 1:4		
*GOLD MEDAL: 1.25X TO 3X HI COLUMN		
GM SER.1 STATED ODDS 1:40		

❑ 1 Ivan Rodriguez	1.25	.55
❑ 2 Don Mattingly	2.00	.90
❑ 3 Roberto Alomar	1.00	.45
❑ 4 Wade Boggs	1.00	.45
❑ 5 Omar Vizquel	.50	.23
❑ 6 Ken Griffey Jr.	5.00	2.20
❑ 7 Kenny Lofton	.75	.35
❑ 8 Devon White	.50	.23
❑ 9 Mark Langston	.25	.11
❑ 10 Tom Pagnozzi	.25	.11
❑ 11 Jeff Bagwell	1.25	.55
❑ 12 Craig Biggio	1.00	.45
❑ 13 Matt Williams	1.00	.45
❑ 14 Barry Larkin	1.00	.45
❑ 15 Barry Bonds	1.25	.55
❑ 16 Marquis Grissom	.50	.23
❑ 17 Darren Lewis	.25	.11
❑ 18 Greg Maddux	2.50	1.10
❑ 19 Frank Thomas	2.00	.90
❑ 20 Jeff Bagwell	1.25	.55
❑ 21 David Cone	.75	.35
❑ 22 Greg Maddux	2.50	1.10
❑ 23 Bob Hamelin	.25	.11
❑ 24 Raul Mondesi	.75	.35
❑ 25 Moises Alou	.50	.23

1995 Ultra Gold Medallion Rookies

	MINT	NRMT
COMPLETE SET (20)	8.00	3.60
COMMON CARD (M1-M20)	.25	.11
SEMISTARS	.50	.23
UNLISTED STARS	1.00	.45
SET DIST.VIA MAIL-IN WRAPPER OFFER		

❑ M1 Manny Alexander	.25	.11
❑ M2 Edgardo Alfonzo	1.00	.45
❑ M3 Jason Bates	.25	.11
❑ M4 Andres Berumen	.25	.11
❑ M5 Darren Bragg	.25	.11
❑ M6 Jamie Brewington	.25	.11
❑ M7 Jason Christiansen	.25	.11
❑ M8 Brad Clontz	.25	.11
❑ M9 Marty Cordova	.50	.23
❑ M10 Johnny Damon	.50	.23
❑ M11 Vaughn Eshelman	.25	.11
❑ M12 Chad Fonville	.25	.11
❑ M13 Curtis Goodwin	.25	.11
❑ M14 Tyler Green	.25	.11
❑ M15 Bobby Higginson	1.50	.70
❑ M16 Jason Isringhausen	.30	.14
❑ M17 Hideo Nomo	2.50	1.10
❑ M18 Jon Nunnally	.25	.11
❑ M19 Carlos Perez	.30	.14
❑ M20 Julian Tavarez	.25	.11

1995 Ultra Golden Prospects

	MINT	NRMT
COMPLETE SET (10)	12.00	5.50

	MINT	NRMT
COMMON CARD (1-10)	.50	.23
SEMISTARS	1.00	.45
SER.1 STATED ODDS 1:8 HOBBY		
*GOLD MEDAL: 1X TO 2X HI COLUMN		
GM SER.1 STATED ODDS 1:80		

❑ 1	James Baldwin	.75	.35
❑ 2	Alan Benes	.50	.23
❑ 3	Armando Benitez	.50	.23
❑ 4	Ray Durham	.75	.35
❑ 5	LaTroy Hawkins	.50	.23
❑ 6	Brian L.Hunter	.75	.35
❑ 7	Derek Jeter	6.00	2.70
❑ 8	Charles Johnson	.75	.35
❑ 9	Alex Rodriguez	6.00	2.70
❑ 10	Michael Tucker	.75	.35

1995 Ultra Hitting Machines

	MINT	NRMT
COMPLETE SET (10)	12.00	5.50
COMMON CARD (1-10)	.50	.23
SER.2 STATED ODDS 1:8 RETAIL		
*GOLD MEDAL: 1.25X TO 3X BASE CARD HI		
GM SER.2 STATED ODDS 1:80 RETAIL		

❑ 1	Jeff Bagwell	1.25	.55
❑ 2	Albert Belle	1.00	.45
❑ 3	Dante Bichette	.50	.23
❑ 4	Barry Bonds	1.25	.55
❑ 5	Jose Canseco	1.25	.55
❑ 6	Ken Griffey Jr.	5.00	2.20
❑ 7	Tony Gwynn	2.00	.90
❑ 8	Fred McGriff	.75	.35
❑ 9	Mike Piazza	3.00	1.35
❑ 10	Frank Thomas	2.00	.90

1995 Ultra Home Run Kings

	MINT	NRMT
COMPLETE SET (10)	30.00	13.50
COMMON CARD (1-10)	1.00	.45
SER.1 STATED ODDS 1:8 RETAIL		
*GOLD MEDAL: 3X TO 8X BASE CARD HI		
GM SER.1 STATED ODDS 1:80 RETAIL		

❑ 1	Ken Griffey Jr.	12.00	5.50
❑ 2	Frank Thomas	5.00	2.20

❑ 3	Albert Belle	2.50	1.10
❑ 4	Jose Canseco	3.00	1.35
❑ 5	Cecil Fielder	1.00	.45
❑ 6	Matt Williams	2.50	1.10
❑ 7	Jeff Bagwell	3.00	1.35
❑ 8	Barry Bonds	3.00	1.35
❑ 9	Fred McGriff	1.50	.70
❑ 10	Andres Galarraga	2.50	1.10
❑ S8	Barry Bonds Sample	3.00	1.35

1995 Ultra League Leaders

	MINT	NRMT
COMPLETE SET (10)	6.00	2.70
COMMON CARD (1-10)	.25	.11
SER.1 STATED ODDS 1:3		
*GOLD MEDAL: 1.25X TO 3X BASE CARD HI		
GM SER.1 STATED ODDS 1:30		

❑ 1	Paul O'Neill	.25	.11
❑ 2	Kenny Lofton	.50	.23
❑ 3	Jimmy Key	.25	.11
❑ 4	Randy Johnson	.75	.35
❑ 5	Lee Smith	.25	.11
❑ 6	Tony Gwynn	2.50	1.10
❑ 7	Craig Biggio	.75	.35
❑ 8	Greg Maddux	2.50	1.10
❑ 9	Andy Benes	.25	.11
❑ 10	John Franco	.25	.11

1995 Ultra On-Base Leaders

	MINT	NRMT
COMPLETE SET (10)	40.00	18.00
COMMON CARD (1-10)	2.00	.90
SER.2 STATED ODDS 1:8 JUMBO		
*GOLD MEDAL: 5X TO 12X BASE CARD HI		
GM SER.2 STATED ODDS 1:80 JUMBO		

❑ 1	Jeff Bagwell	5.00	2.20
❑ 2	Albert Belle	4.00	1.80
❑ 3	Craig Biggio	4.00	1.80
❑ 4	Wade Boggs	4.00	1.80
❑ 5	Barry Bonds	5.00	2.20
❑ 6	Will Clark	4.00	1.80
❑ 7	Tony Gwynn	10.00	4.50
❑ 8	David Justice	4.00	1.80
❑ 9	Paul O'Neill	2.00	.90
❑ 10	Frank Thomas	8.00	3.60

1995 Ultra Power Plus

	MINT	NRMT
COMPLETE SET (6)	50.00	22.00
COMMON CARD (1-6)	4.00	1.80
SER.1 STATED ODDS 1:37		
*GOLD MEDAL: 5X TO 12X BASE CARD HI		
GM SER.1 STATED ODDS 1:370		

❑ 1	Albert Belle	4.00	1.80
❑ 2	Ken Griffey Jr.	20.00	9.00
❑ 3	Frank Thomas	8.00	3.60
❑ 4	Jeff Bagwell	5.00	2.20
❑ 5	Barry Bonds	5.00	2.20
❑ 6	Matt Williams	4.00	1.80

1995 Ultra RBI Kings

	MINT	NRMT
COMPLETE SET (10)	50.00	22.00
COMMON CARD (1-10)	1.00	.45
SER.1 STATED ODDS 1:11 JUMBO		
*GOLD MEDAL: 5X TO 12X BASE CARD HI		
GM SER.1 STATED ODDS 1:110 JUMBO		

❑ 1	Kirby Puckett	8.00	3.60
❑ 2	Joe Carter	2.00	.90
❑ 3	Albert Belle	4.00	1.80
❑ 4	Frank Thomas	10.00	4.50
❑ 5	Julio Franco	1.00	.45
❑ 6	Jeff Bagwell	6.00	2.70
❑ 7	Matt Williams	4.00	1.80
❑ 8	Dante Bichette	2.00	.90

□ 9 Fred McGriff 2.50 1.10
□ 10 Mike Piazza............ 12.00 5.50

1995 Ultra Rising Stars

	MINT	NRMT
COMPLETE SET (9)	60.00	27.00
COMMON CARD (1-9)	3.00	1.35

SER.2 STATED ODDS 1:37
*GOLD MEDAL: 8X TO 20X BASE CARD HI
GM SER.2 STATED ODDS 1:370

□ 1 Moises Alou 3.00 1.35
□ 2 Jeff Bagwell 8.00 3.60
□ 3 Albert Belle 6.00 2.70
□ 4 Juan Gonzalez 12.00 5.50
□ 5 Chuck Knoblauch 6.00 2.70
□ 6 Kenny Lofton 4.00 1.80
□ 7 Raul Mondesi 4.00 1.80
□ 8 Mike Piazza 20.00 9.00
□ 9 Frank Thomas 12.00 5.50

1995 Ultra Second Year Standouts

	MINT	NRMT
COMPLETE SET (15)	10.00	4.50
COMMON CARD (1-15)	.50	.23

SER.1 STATED ODDS 1:6
*GOLD MEDAL: 3X TO 8X BASE CARD HI
GM SER.1 STATED ODDS 1:60

□ 1 Cliff Floyd .... 1.00 .45
□ 2 Chris Gomez .... .50 .23
□ 3 Rusty Greer .... 2.00 .90
□ 4 Darren Hall .... .50 .23
□ 5 Bob Hamelin .... .50 .23
□ 6 Joey Hamilton .... 1.00 .45
□ 7 Jeffrey Hammonds .... 1.00 .45
□ 8 John Hudek .... .50 .23
□ 9 Ryan Klesko .... 1.00 .45
□ 10 Raul Mondesi .... 1.50 .70
□ 11 Manny Ramirez 2.50 1.10
□ 12 Bill Risley .... .50 .23
□ 13 Steve Trachsel ...... .50 .23
□ 14 W.VanLandingham ... .50 .23
□ 15 Rondell White .... 1.00 .45

1995 Ultra Strikeout Kings

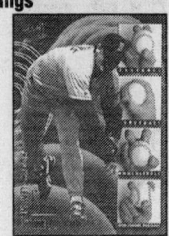

	MINT	NRMT
COMPLETE SET (6)	5.00	2.20
COMMON CARD (1-6)	.25	.11

SER.2 STATED ODDS 1:5
*GOLD MEDAL: 1X TO 2X HI COLUMN
GM SER.2 STATED ODDS 1:50

□ 1 Andy Benes .... .75 .35
□ 2 Roger Clemens .... 2.00 .90
□ 3 Randy Johnson .... 1.00 .45
□ 4 Greg Maddux .... 2.00 .90
□ 5 Pedro Martinez ...... 1.00 .45
□ 6 Jose Rijo .... .25 .11

1996 Ultra

	MINT	NRMT
COMPLETE SET (600)	60.00	27.00
COMPLETE SERIES 1 (300)	30.00	13.50
COMPLETE SERIES 2 (300)	30.00	13.50
COMMON CARD (1-600)	.15	.07
MINOR STARS	.30	.14
UNLISTED STARS	.60	.25

SUBSET CARDS HALF VALUE OF BASE CARDS

□ 1 Manny Alexander ...... .15 .07
□ 2 Brady Anderson ...... .30 .14
□ 3 Bobby Bonilla .... .30 .14
□ 4 Scott Erickson ...... .30 .14
□ 5 Curtis Goodwin ...... .15 .07
□ 6 Chris Hoiles .... .15 .07
□ 7 Doug Jones .... .15 .07
□ 8 Jeff Manto .... .15 .07
□ 9 Mike Mussina .... .60 .25
□ 10 Rafael Palmeiro ..... .60 .25
□ 11 Cal Ripken 2.50 1.10
□ 12 Rick Aguilera ...... .15 .07
□ 13 Luis Alicea .... .15 .07
□ 14 Stan Belinda .... .15 .07
□ 15 Jose Canseco .... .75 .35
□ 16 Roger Clemens ...... 1.50 .70
□ 17 Mike Greenwell ...... .15 .07
□ 18 Mike Macfarlane .... .15 .07
□ 19 Tim Naehring .... .15 .07
□ 20 Troy O'Leary .... .30 .14
□ 21 John Valentin ...... .30 .14
□ 22 Mo Vaughn .... .60 .25
□ 23 Tim Wakefield ...... .15 .07
□ 24 Brian Anderson ...... .15 .07
□ 25 Garret Anderson ...... .30 .14
□ 26 Chili Davis .... .30 .14
□ 27 Gary DiSarcina ...... .15 .07
□ 28 Jim Edmonds .... .40 .18
□ 29 Jorge Fabregas ...... .15 .07
□ 30 Chuck Finley .... .30 .14
□ 31 Mark Langston ...... .15 .07
□ 32 Troy Percival ...... .30 .14
□ 33 Tim Salmon .... .40 .18
□ 34 Lee Smith .... .30 .14
□ 35 Wilson Alvarez ...... .15 .07
□ 36 Ray Durham .... .30 .14
□ 37 Alex Fernandez ...... .15 .07
□ 38 Ozzie Guillen ...... .15 .07
□ 39 Roberto Hernandez ... .15 .07
□ 40 Lance Johnson ...... .15 .07
□ 41 Ron Karkovice ...... .15 .07
□ 42 Lyle Mouton .... .15 .07
□ 43 Tim Raines .... .30 .14
□ 44 Frank Thomas .... 1.25 .55
□ 45 Carlos Baerga ...... .15 .07
□ 46 Albert Belle .... .60 .25
□ 47 Orel Hershiser ...... .30 .14
□ 48 Kenny Lofton .... .40 .18
□ 49 Dennis Martinez .... .30 .14
□ 50 Jose Mesa .... .15 .07
□ 51 Eddie Murray .... .60 .25
□ 52 Chad Ogea .... .15 .07
□ 53 Manny Ramirez ...... .75 .35
□ 54 Jim Thome .... .60 .25
□ 55 Omar Vizquel .... .30 .14
□ 56 Dave Winfield ...... .60 .25
□ 57 Chad Curtis .... .15 .07
□ 58 Cecil Fielder ...... .30 .14
□ 59 John Flaherty ...... .15 .07
□ 60 Travis Fryman ...... .30 .14
□ 61 Chris Gomez .... .15 .07
□ 62 Bob Higginson ...... .30 .14
□ 63 Felipe Lira .... .15 .07
□ 64 Brian Maxcy .... .15 .07
□ 65 Alan Trammell ...... .40 .18
□ 66 Lou Whitaker .... .30 .14
□ 67 Kevin Appier .... .30 .14
□ 68 Gary Gaetti .... .30 .14
□ 69 Tom Goodwin .... .15 .07
□ 70 Tom Gordon .... .15 .07
□ 71 Jason Jacome .... .15 .07
□ 72 Wally Joyner .... .30 .14
□ 73 Brent Mayne .... .15 .07
□ 74 Jeff Montgomery .... .15 .07
□ 75 Jon Nunnally .... .15 .07
□ 76 Joe Vitiello .... .15 .07
□ 77 Ricky Bones .... .15 .07
□ 78 Jeff Cirillo .... .30 .14
□ 79 Mike Fetters .... .15 .07
□ 80 Darryl Hamilton .... .15 .07
□ 81 David Hulse .... .15 .07
□ 82 Dave Nilsson .... .15 .07
□ 83 Kevin Seitzer ...... .15 .07
□ 84 Steve Sparks .... .15 .07
□ 85 B.J. Surhoff .... .30 .14
□ 86 Jose Valentin ...... .15 .07
□ 87 Greg Vaughn .... .30 .14
□ 88 Marty Cordova ...... .15 .07
□ 89 Chuck Knoblauch .... .60 .25
□ 90 Pat Meares .... .15 .07
□ 91 Pedro Munoz .... .15 .07
□ 92 Kirby Puckett ...... 1.00 .45
□ 93 Brad Radke .... .30 .14
□ 94 Scott Stahoviak .... .15 .07
□ 95 Dave Stevens .... .15 .07
□ 96 Mike Trombley ...... .15 .07
□ 97 Matt Walbeck .... .15 .07
□ 98 Wade Boggs .... .60 .25
□ 99 Russ Davis .... .15 .07
□ 100 Jim Leyritz .... .15 .07
□ 101 Don Mattingly ...... 1.25 .55
□ 102 Jack McDowell ...... .15 .07
□ 103 Paul O'Neill .... .30 .14
□ 104 Andy Pettitte ...... .40 .18
□ 105 Mariano Rivera .... .40 .18
□ 106 Ruben Sierra .... .15 .07
□ 107 Darryl Strawberry ... .30 .14
□ 108 John Wetteland .... .15 .07
□ 109 Bernie Williams .... .60 .25
□ 110 Geronimo Berroa .... .15 .07

111	Scott Brosius	.30	.14
112	Dennis Eckersley	.30	.14
113	Brent Gates	.15	.07
114	Rickey Henderson	.75	.35
115	Mark McGwire	3.00	1.35
116	Ariel Prieto	.15	.07
117	Terry Steinbach	.15	.07
118	Todd Stottlemyre	.15	.07
119	Todd Van Poppel	.15	.07
120	Steve Wojciechowski	.15	.07
121	Rich Amaral	.15	.07
122	Bobby Ayala	.15	.07
123	Mike Blowers	.15	.07
124	Chris Bosio	.15	.07
125	Joey Cora	.15	.07
126	Ken Griffey Jr.	3.00	1.35
127	Randy Johnson	.60	.25
128	Edgar Martinez	.30	.14
129	Tino Martinez	.30	.14
130	Alex Rodriguez	2.00	.90
131	Dan Wilson	.15	.07
132	Will Clark	.60	.25
133	Jeff Frye	.15	.07
134	Benji Gil	.15	.07
135	Juan Gonzalez	1.25	.55
136	Rusty Greer	.30	.14
137	Mark McLemore	.15	.07
138	Roger Pavlik	.15	.07
139	Ivan Rodriguez	.75	.35
140	Kenny Rogers	.15	.07
141	Mickey Tettleton	.15	.07
142	Roberto Alomar	.60	.25
143	Joe Carter	.30	.14
144	Tony Castillo	.15	.07
145	Alex Gonzalez	.15	.07
146	Shawn Green	.60	.25
147	Pat Hentgen	.30	.14
148	Sandy Martinez	.15	.07
149	Paul Molitor	.60	.25
150	John Olerud	.30	.14
151	Ed Sprague	.15	.07
152	Jeff Blauser	.15	.07
153	Brad Clontz	.15	.07
154	Tom Glavine	.60	.25
155	Marquis Grissom	.15	.07
156	Chipper Jones	1.50	.70
157	David Justice	.60	.25
158	Ryan Klesko	.30	.14
159	Javier Lopez	.30	.14
160	Greg Maddux	1.50	.70
161	John Smoltz	.40	.18
162	Mark Wohlers	.15	.07
163	Jim Bullinger	.15	.07
164	Frank Castillo	.15	.07
165	Shawon Dunston	.15	.07
166	Kevin Foster	.15	.07
167	Luis Gonzalez	.30	.14
168	Mark Grace	.40	.18
169	Rey Sanchez	.15	.07
170	Scott Servais	.15	.07
171	Sammy Sosa	2.00	.90
172	Ozzie Timmons	.15	.07
173	Steve Trachsel	.15	.07
174	Bret Boone	.30	.14
175	Jeff Branson	.15	.07
176	Jeff Brantley	.15	.07
177	Dave Burba	.15	.07
178	Ron Gant	.15	.07
179	Barry Larkin	.60	.25
180	Darren Lewis	.15	.07
181	Mark Portugal	.15	.07
182	Reggie Sanders	.30	.14
183	Pete Schourek	.15	.07
184	John Smiley	.15	.07
185	Jason Bates	.15	.07
186	Dante Bichette	.30	.14
187	Ellis Burks	.30	.14
188	Vinny Castilla	.40	.18
189	Andres Galarraga	.60	.25
190	Darren Holmes	.15	.07
191	Armando Reynoso	.15	.07
192	Kevin Ritz	.15	.07
193	Bill Swift	.15	.07
194	Larry Walker	.60	.25
195	Kurt Abbott	.15	.07
196	John Burkett	.15	.07
197	Greg Colbrunn	.15	.07
198	Jeff Conine	.15	.07
199	Andre Dawson	.40	.18
200	Chris Hammond	.15	.07
201	Charles Johnson	.30	.14
202	Robb Nen	.15	.07
203	Terry Pendleton	.15	.07
204	Quilvio Veras	.15	.07
205	Jeff Bagwell	.75	.35
206	Derek Bell	.30	.14
207	Doug Drabek	.15	.07
208	Tony Eusebio	.15	.07
209	Mike Hampton	.30	.14
210	Brian L. Hunter	.15	.07
211	Todd Jones	.15	.07
212	Orlando Miller	.15	.07
213	James Mouton	.15	.07
214	Shane Reynolds	.30	.14
215	Dave Veres	.15	.07
216	Billy Ashley	.15	.07
217	Brett Butler	.30	.14
218	Chad Fonville	.15	.07
219	Todd Hollandsworth	.15	.07
220	Eric Karros	.30	.14
221	Ramon Martinez	.30	.14
222	Raul Mondesi	.30	.14
223	Hideo Nomo	.60	.25
224	Mike Piazza	2.00	.90
225	Kevin Tapani	.15	.07
226	Ismael Valdes	.30	.14
227	Todd Worrell	.15	.07
228	Moises Alou	.15	.07
229	Wil Cordero	.15	.07
230	Jeff Fassero	.15	.07
231	Darrin Fletcher	.15	.07
232	Mike Lansing	.15	.07
233	Pedro Martinez	.75	.35
234	Carlos Perez	.15	.07
235	Mel Rojas	.15	.07
236	David Segui	.30	.14
237	Tony Tarasco	.15	.07
238	Rondell White	.30	.14
239	Edgardo Alfonzo	.60	.25
240	Rico Brogna	.15	.07
241	Carl Everett	.30	.14
242	Todd Hundley	.30	.14
243	Butch Huskey	.15	.07
244	Jason Isringhausen	.30	.14
245	Bobby Jones	.15	.07
246	Jeff Kent	.30	.14
247	Bill Pulsipher	.15	.07
248	Jose Vizcaino	.15	.07
249	Ricky Bottalico	.15	.07
250	Darren Daulton	.30	.14
251	Jim Eisenreich	.15	.07
252	Tyler Green	.15	.07
253	Charlie Hayes	.15	.07
254	Gregg Jefferies	.15	.07
255	Tony Longmire	.15	.07
256	Michael Mimbs	.15	.07
257	Mickey Morandini	.15	.07
258	Paul Quantrill	.15	.07
259	Heathcliff Slocumb	.15	.07
260	Jay Bell	.30	.14
261	Jacob Brumfield	.15	.07
262	Angelo Encarnacion	.15	.07
263	John Ericks	.15	.07
264	Mark Johnson	.15	.07
265	Esteban Loaiza	.15	.07
266	Al Martin	.15	.07
267	Orlando Merced	.15	.07
268	Dan Miceli	.15	.07
269	Denny Neagle	.30	.14
270	Brian Barber	.15	.07
271	Scott Cooper	.15	.07
272	Tripp Cromer	.15	.07
273	Bernard Gilkey	.15	.07
274	Tom Henke	.15	.07
275	Brian Jordan	.30	.14
276	John Mabry	.15	.07
277	Tom Pagnozzi	.15	.07
278	Mark Petkovsek	.15	.07
279	Ozzie Smith	.75	.35
280	Andy Ashby	.15	.07
281	Brad Ausmus	.15	.07
282	Ken Caminiti	.30	.14
283	Glenn Dishman	.15	.07
284	Tony Gwynn	1.50	.70
285	Joey Hamilton	.15	.07
286	Trevor Hoffman	.30	.14
287	Phil Plantier	.15	.07
288	Jody Reed	.15	.07
289	Eddie Williams	.15	.07
290	Barry Bonds	.75	.35
291	Jamie Brewington	.15	.07
292	Mark Carreon	.15	.07
293	Royce Clayton	.15	.07
294	Glenallen Hill	.15	.07
295	Mark Leiter	.15	.07
296	Kirt Manwaring	.15	.07
297	J.R. Phillips	.15	.07
298	Deion Sanders	.30	.14
299	Wm. VanLandingham	.15	.07
300	Matt Williams	.60	.25
301	Roberto Alomar	.60	.25
302	Armando Benitez	.15	.07
303	Mike Devereaux	.15	.07
304	Jeffrey Hammonds	.30	.14
305	Jimmy Haynes	.15	.07
306	Scott McClain	.15	.07
307	Kent Mercker	.15	.07
308	Randy Myers	.15	.07
309	B.J. Surhoff	.30	.14
310	Tony Tarasco	.15	.07
311	David Wells	.40	.18
312	Wil Cordero	.15	.07
313	Alex Delgado	.15	.07
314	Tom Gordon	.15	.07
315	Dwayne Hosey	.15	.07
316	Jose Malave	.15	.07
317	Kevin Mitchell	.15	.07
318	Jamie Moyer	.15	.07
319	Aaron Sele	.30	.14
320	Heathcliff Slocumb	.15	.07
321	Mike Stanley	.15	.07
322	Jeff Suppan	.15	.07
323	Jim Abbott	.30	.14
324	George Arias	.15	.07
325	Todd Greene	.15	.07
326	Bryan Harvey	.15	.07
327	J.T. Snow	.30	.14
328	Randy Velarde	.15	.07
329	Tim Wallach	.15	.07
330	Harold Baines	.15	.07
331	Jason Bere	.15	.07
332	Darren Lewis	.15	.07
333	Norberto Martin	.15	.07
334	Tony Phillips	.15	.07
335	Bill Simas	.15	.07
336	Chris Snopek	.15	.07
337	Kevin Tapani	.15	.07
338	Danny Tartabull	.15	.07
339	Robin Ventura	.30	.14
340	Sandy Alomar Jr.	.30	.14
341	Julio Franco	.15	.07
342	Jack McDowell	.15	.07
343	Charles Nagy	.30	.14
344	Julian Tavarez	.15	.07
345	Kimera Bartee	.15	.07
346	Greg Keagle	.15	.07
347	Mark Lewis	.15	.07
348	Jose Lima	.40	.18
349	Melvin Nieves	.15	.07
350	Mark Parent	.15	.07
351	Eddie Williams	.15	.07
352	Johnny Damon	.40	.18
353	Sal Fasano	.15	.07
354	Mark Gubicza	.15	.07
355	Bob Hamelin	.15	.07
356	Chris Haney	.15	.07
357	Keith Lockhart	.15	.07
358	Mike Macfarlane	.15	.07
359	Jose Offerman	.30	.14
360	Bip Roberts	.15	.07
361	Michael Tucker	.15	.07
362	Chuck Carr	.15	.07
363	Bobby Hughes	.15	.07
364	John Jaha	.15	.07
365	Mark Loretta	.15	.07
366	Mike Matheny	.15	.07
367	Ben McDonald	.15	.07
368	Matt Mieske	.15	.07

❏ 369	Angel Miranda	.15	.07
❏ 370	Fernando Vina	.15	.07
❏ 371	Rick Aguilera	.15	.07
❏ 372	Rich Becker	.15	.07
❏ 373	LaTroy Hawkins	.15	.07
❏ 374	Dave Hollins	.15	.07
❏ 375	Roberto Kelly	.15	.07
❏ 376	Matt Lawton	.75	.35
❏ 377	Paul Molitor	.60	.25
❏ 378	Dan Naulty	.15	.07
❏ 379	Rich Robertson	.15	.07
❏ 380	Frank Rodriguez	.15	.07
❏ 381	David Cone	.40	.18
❏ 382	Mariano Duncan	.15	.07
❏ 383	Andy Fox	.15	.07
❏ 384	Joe Girardi	.15	.07
❏ 385	Dwight Gooden	.30	.14
❏ 386	Derek Jeter	2.00	.90
❏ 387	Pat Kelly	.15	.07
❏ 388	Jimmy Key	.30	.14
❏ 389	Matt Luke	.15	.07
❏ 390	Tino Martinez	.30	.14
❏ 391	Jeff Nelson	.15	.07
❏ 392	Melido Perez	.15	.07
❏ 393	Tim Raines	.30	.14
❏ 394	Ruben Rivera	.30	.14
❏ 395	Kenny Rogers	.15	.07
❏ 396	Tony Batista	1.25	.55
❏ 397	Allen Battle	.15	.07
❏ 398	Mike Bordick	.15	.07
❏ 399	Steve Cox	.15	.07
❏ 400	Jason Giambi	.30	.14
❏ 401	Doug Johns	.15	.07
❏ 402	Pedro Munoz	.15	.07
❏ 403	Phil Plantier	.15	.07
❏ 404	Scott Spiezio	.15	.07
❏ 405	George Williams	.15	.07
❏ 406	Ernie Young	.15	.07
❏ 407	Darren Bragg	.15	.07
❏ 408	Jay Buhner	.30	.14
❏ 409	Norm Charlton	.15	.07
❏ 410	Russ Davis	.15	.07
❏ 411	Sterling Hitchcock	.15	.07
❏ 412	Edwin Hurtado	.15	.07
❏ 413	Raul Ibanez	.15	.07
❏ 414	Mike Jackson	.30	.14
❏ 415	Luis Sojo	.15	.07
❏ 416	Paul Sorrento	.15	.07
❏ 417	Bob Wolcott	.15	.07
❏ 418	Damon Buford	.15	.07
❏ 419	Kevin Gross	.15	.07
❏ 420	Darryl Hamilton UER	.15	.07
❏ 421	Mike Henneman	.15	.07
❏ 422	Ken Hill	.15	.07
❏ 423	Dean Palmer	.30	.14
❏ 424	Bobby Witt	.15	.07
❏ 425	Tilson Brito	.15	.07
❏ 426	Giovanni Carrara	.15	.07
❏ 427	Domingo Cedeno	.15	.07
❏ 428	Felipe Crespo	.15	.07
❏ 429	Carlos Delgado	.60	.25
❏ 430	Juan Guzman	.15	.07
❏ 431	Erik Hanson	.15	.07
❏ 432	Marty Janzen	.15	.07
❏ 433	Otis Nixon	.15	.07
❏ 434	Robert Perez	.15	.07
❏ 435	Paul Quantrill	.15	.07
❏ 436	Bill Risley	.15	.07
❏ 437	Steve Avery	.15	.07
❏ 438	Jermaine Dye	.30	.14
❏ 439	Mark Lemke	.15	.07
❏ 440	Marty Malloy	.15	.07
❏ 441	Fred McGriff	.40	.18
❏ 442	Greg McMichael	.15	.07
❏ 443	Wonderful Monds	.15	.07
❏ 444	Eddie Perez	.15	.07
❏ 445	Jason Schmidt	.15	.07
❏ 446	Terrell Wade	.15	.07
❏ 447	Terry Adams	.15	.07
❏ 448	Scott Bullett	.15	.07
❏ 449	Robin Jennings	.15	.07
❏ 450	Doug Jones	.15	.07
❏ 451	Brooks Kieschnick	.15	.07
❏ 452	Dave Magadan	.15	.07
❏ 453	Jason Maxwell	.15	.07
❏ 454	Brian McRae	.15	.07
❏ 455	Rodney Myers	.15	.07
❏ 456	Jaime Navarro	.15	.07
❏ 457	Ryne Sandberg	.75	.35
❏ 458	Vince Coleman	.15	.07
❏ 459	Eric Davis	.30	.14
❏ 460	Steve Gibralter	.15	.07
❏ 461	Thomas Howard	.15	.07
❏ 462	Mike Kelly	.15	.07
❏ 463	Hal Morris	.15	.07
❏ 464	Eric Owens	.15	.07
❏ 465	Jose Rijo	.15	.07
❏ 466	Chris Sabo	.15	.07
❏ 467	Eddie Taubensee	.15	.07
❏ 468	Trenidad Hubbard	.15	.07
❏ 469	Curt Leskanic	.15	.07
❏ 470	Quinton McCracken	.15	.07
❏ 471	Jayhawk Owens	.15	.07
❏ 472	Steve Reed	.15	.07
❏ 473	Bryan Rekar	.15	.07
❏ 474	Bruce Ruffin	.15	.07
❏ 475	Bret Saberhagen	.30	.14
❏ 476	Walt Weiss	.15	.07
❏ 477	Eric Young	.15	.07
❏ 478	Kevin Brown	.40	.18
❏ 479	Al Leiter	.30	.14
❏ 480	Pat Rapp	.15	.07
❏ 481	Gary Sheffield	.30	.14
❏ 482	Devon White	.30	.14
❏ 483	Bob Abreu	.40	.18
❏ 484	Sean Berry	.15	.07
❏ 485	Craig Biggio	.60	.25
❏ 486	Jim Dougherty	.15	.07
❏ 487	Richard Hidalgo	.30	.14
❏ 488	Darryl Kile	.15	.07
❏ 489	Derrick May	.15	.07
❏ 490	Greg Swindell	.15	.07
❏ 491	Rick Wilkins	.15	.07
❏ 492	Mike Blowers	.15	.07
❏ 493	Tom Candiotti	.15	.07
❏ 494	Roger Cedeno	.30	.14
❏ 495	Delino DeShields	.15	.07
❏ 496	Greg Gagne	.15	.07
❏ 497	Karim Garcia	.30	.14
❏ 498	Wilton Guerrero	.50	.23
❏ 499	Chan Ho Park	.40	.18
❏ 500	Isreal Alcantara	.15	.07
❏ 501	Shane Andrews	.15	.07
❏ 502	Yamil Benitez	.15	.07
❏ 503	Cliff Floyd	.30	.14
❏ 504	Mark Grudzielanek	.15	.07
❏ 505	Ryan McGuire	.15	.07
❏ 506	Sherman Obando	.15	.07
❏ 507	Jose Paniagua	.15	.07
❏ 508	Henry Rodriguez	.30	.14
❏ 509	Kirk Rueter	.15	.07
❏ 510	Juan Acevedo	.15	.07
❏ 511	John Franco	.30	.14
❏ 512	Bernard Gilkey	.15	.07
❏ 513	Lance Johnson	.15	.07
❏ 514	Rey Ordonez	.60	.25
❏ 515	Robert Person	.15	.07
❏ 516	Paul Wilson	.15	.07
❏ 517	Toby Borland	.15	.07
❏ 518	David Doster	.15	.07
❏ 519	Lenny Dykstra	.30	.14
❏ 520	Sid Fernandez	.15	.07
❏ 521	Mike Grace	.15	.07
❏ 522	Rich Hunter	.15	.07
❏ 523	Benito Santiago	.15	.07
❏ 524	Gene Schall	.15	.07
❏ 525	Curt Schilling	.40	.18
❏ 526	Kevin Sefcik	.15	.07
❏ 527	Lee Tinsley	.15	.07
❏ 528	David West	.15	.07
❏ 529	Mark Whiten	.15	.07
❏ 530	Todd Zeile	.15	.07
❏ 531	Carlos Garcia	.15	.07
❏ 532	Charlie Hayes	.15	.07
❏ 533	Jason Kendall	.60	.25
❏ 534	Jeff King	.15	.07
❏ 535	Mike Kingery	.15	.07
❏ 536	Nelson Liriano	.15	.07
❏ 537	Dan Plesac	.15	.07
❏ 538	Paul Wagner	.15	.07
❏ 539	Luis Alicea	.15	.07
❏ 540	David Bell	.15	.07
❏ 541	Alan Benes	.15	.07
❏ 542	Andy Benes	.30	.14
❏ 543	Mike Busby	.15	.07
❏ 544	Royce Clayton	.15	.07
❏ 545	Dennis Eckersley	.30	.14
❏ 546	Gary Gaetti	.30	.14
❏ 547	Ron Gant	.15	.07
❏ 548	Aaron Holbert	.15	.07
❏ 549	Ray Lankford	.30	.14
❏ 550	T.J. Mathews	.15	.07
❏ 551	Willie McGee	.30	.14
❏ 552	Miguel Mejia	.15	.07
❏ 553	Todd Stottlemyre	.15	.07
❏ 554	Sean Bergman	.15	.07
❏ 555	Willie Blair	.15	.07
❏ 556	Andujar Cedeno	.15	.07
❏ 557	Steve Finley	.30	.14
❏ 558	Rickey Henderson	.75	.35
❏ 559	Wally Joyner	.30	.14
❏ 560	Scott Livingstone	.15	.07
❏ 561	Marc Newfield	.15	.07
❏ 562	Bob Tewksbury	.15	.07
❏ 563	Fernando Valenzuela	.30	.14
❏ 564	Rod Beck	.15	.07
❏ 565	Doug Creek	.15	.07
❏ 566	Shawon Dunston	.15	.07
❏ 567	Osvaldo Fernandez	.15	.07
❏ 568	Stan Javier	.15	.07
❏ 569	Marcus Jensen	.15	.07
❏ 570	Steve Scarsone	.15	.07
❏ 571	Robby Thompson	.15	.07
❏ 572	Allen Watson	.15	.07
❏ 573	Roberto Alomar STA	.30	.14
❏ 574	Jeff Bagwell STA	.60	.25
❏ 575	Albert Belle STA	.30	.14
❏ 576	Wade Boggs STA	.30	.14
❏ 577	Barry Bonds STA	.40	.18
❏ 578	Juan Gonzalez STA	.60	.25
❏ 579	Ken Griffey Jr. STA	1.50	.70
❏ 580	Tony Gwynn STA	.75	.35
❏ 581	Randy Johnson STA	.30	.14
❏ 582	Chipper Jones STA	.75	.35
❏ 583	Barry Larkin STA	.15	.07
❏ 584	Kenny Lofton STA	.30	.14
❏ 585	Greg Maddux STA	.75	.35
❏ 586	Raul Mondesi STA	.15	.07
❏ 587	Mike Piazza STA	1.00	.45
❏ 588	Cal Ripken STA	1.25	.55
❏ 589	Tim Salmon STA	.15	.07
❏ 590	Frank Thomas STA	.60	.25
❏ 591	Mo Vaughn STA	.30	.14
❏ 592	Matt Williams STA	.30	.14
❏ 593	Marty Cordova RAW	.15	.07
❏ 594	Jim Edmonds RAW	.15	.07
❏ 595	Cliff Floyd RAW	.15	.07
❏ 596	Chipper Jones RAW	.75	.35
❏ 597	Ryan Klesko RAW	.15	.07
❏ 598	Raul Mondesi RAW	.15	.07
❏ 599	Manny Ramirez RAW	.60	.25
❏ 600	Ruben Rivera RAW	.15	.07
❏ DD1	C. Ripken Diamond Dust	40.00	18.00
	Issued through dealers Serial numbered to 2131		
❏ DD2	C. Ripken Diamond Dust	30.00	13.50
	Issued through a wrapper redemption		

1996 Ultra Gold Medallion

	MINT	NRMT
COMPLETE SET (600)	200.00	90.00
COMPLETE SERIES 1 (300)	100.00	45.00
COMPLETE SERIES 2 (300)	100.00	45.00
COMMON CARD (1-600)	.25	.11
*STARS: 1.5X TO 4X BASIC CARDS		
*ROOKIES: 1.25X TO 3X BASIC CARDS		
ONE PER PACK		

1996 Ultra Call to the Hall

	MINT	NRMT
COMPLETE SET (10)	80.00	36.00
COMMON CARD (1-10)	1.50	.70
SER.2 STATED ODDS 1:24		
*GOLD MEDAL: 5X TO 12X BASE CARD HI		
GM SER.2 STATED ODDS 1:240		

☐ 1 Barry Bonds	5.00	2.20
☐ 2 Ken Griffey Jr.	20.00	9.00
☐ 3 Tony Gwynn	10.00	4.50
☐ 4 Rickey Henderson	5.00	2.20
☐ 5 Greg Maddux	10.00	4.50
☐ 6 Eddie Murray	1.50	.70
☐ 7 Cal Ripken	15.00	6.75
☐ 8 Ryne Sandberg	4.00	1.80
☐ 9 Ozzie Smith	5.00	2.20
☐ 10 Frank Thomas	8.00	3.60

1996 Ultra Checklists

	MINT	NRMT
COMPLETE SERIES 1 (10)	10.00	4.50
COMPLETE SERIES 2 (10)	8.00	3.60
COMMON CARD (A1-B10)	.40	.18
*GOLD MEDAL: 1X TO 2.5X BASE CARD HI		
GM STATED ODDS 1:40		

☐ A1 Jeff Bagwell	1.25	.55
☐ A2 Barry Bonds	1.00	.45
☐ A3 Juan Gonzalez	1.50	.70
☐ A4 Ken Griffey Jr.	4.00	1.80
☐ A5 Chipper Jones	2.00	.90
☐ A6 Mike Piazza	2.50	1.10
☐ A7 Manny Ramirez	1.00	.45
☐ A8 Cal Ripken	3.00	1.35
☐ A9 Frank Thomas	1.50	.70
☐ A10 Matt Williams	.75	.35
☐ B1 Albert Belle	.75	.35

☐ B2 Cecil Fielder	.40	.18
☐ B3 Ken Griffey Jr.	4.00	1.80
☐ B4 Tony Gwynn	2.00	.90
☐ B5 Derek Jeter	2.00	.90
☐ B6 Jason Kendall	.75	.35
☐ B7 Ryan Klesko	.40	.18
☐ B8 Greg Maddux	2.00	.90
☐ B9 Cal Ripken	3.00	1.35
☐ B10 Frank Thomas	1.50	.70

1996 Ultra Diamond Producers

	MINT	NRMT
COMPLETE SET (12)	60.00	27.00
COMMON CARD (1-12)	3.00	1.35
SER.1 STATED ODDS 1:20		
*GOLD MEDAL: 4X TO 10X BASE CARD HI		
GM SER.1 STATED ODDS 1:200		

☐ 1 Albert Belle	3.00	1.35
☐ 2 Barry Bonds	4.00	1.80
☐ 3 Ken Griffey Jr.	15.00	6.75
☐ 4 Tony Gwynn	8.00	3.60
☐ 5 Greg Maddux	8.00	3.60
☐ 6 Hideo Nomo	3.00	1.35
☐ 7 Mike Piazza	10.00	4.50
☐ 8 Kirby Puckett	6.00	2.70
☐ 9 Cal Ripken	12.00	5.50
☐ 10 Frank Thomas	6.00	2.70
☐ 11 Mo Vaughn	3.00	1.35
☐ 12 Matt Williams	3.00	1.35

1996 Ultra Fresh Foundations

	MINT	NRMT
COMPLETE SET (10)	3.00	1.35
COMMON CARD (1-10)	.15	.07
SER.1 STATED ODDS 1:3		
*GOLD MEDAL: .75X TO 2X BASE CARD HI		
GM SER.1 STATED ODDS 1:30		

☐ 1 Garret Anderson	.25	.11
☐ 2 Marty Cordova	.15	.07
☐ 3 Jim Edmonds	.40	.18
☐ 4 Brian L.Hunter	.15	.07
☐ 5 Chipper Jones	1.50	.70
☐ 6 Ryan Klesko	.25	.11
☐ 7 Raul Mondesi	.25	.11

1996 Ultra Golden Prospects

	MINT	NRMT
COMPLETE SET (10)	5.00	2.20
COMMON CARD (1-10)	.25	.11
SER.1 STATED ODDS 1:5 HOBBY		
*GOLD MEDAL: 1.5X TO 4X BASE CARD HI		
GM SER.1 STATED ODDS 1:50 HOBBY		

☐ 1 Yamil Benitez	.25	.11
☐ 2 Alberto Castillo	.25	.11
☐ 3 Roger Cedeno	.50	.23
☐ 4 Johnny Damon	1.00	.45
☐ 5 Micah Franklin	.25	.11
☐ 6 Jason Giambi	.50	.23
☐ 7 Jose Herrera	.25	.11
☐ 8 Derek Jeter	5.00	2.20
☐ 9 Kevin Jordan	.25	.11
☐ 10 Ruben Rivera	.50	.23

1996 Ultra Golden Prospects Hobby

	MINT	NRMT
COMPLETE SET (15)	80.00	36.00
COMMON CARD (1-15)	2.00	.90
SER.2 STATED ODDS 1:72 HOBBY		
*GOLD MEDAL: .75X TO 2X HI COLUMN		
GM SER.2 STATED ODDS 1:720 HOBBY		

☐ 1 Bob Abreu	15.00	6.75
☐ 2 Israel Alcantara	2.00	.90
☐ 3 Tony Batista	8.00	3.60
☐ 4 Mike Cameron	6.00	2.70
☐ 5 Steve Cox	2.00	.90
☐ 6 Jermaine Dye	10.00	4.50
☐ 7 Wilton Guerrero	3.00	1.35
☐ 8 Richard Hidalgo	6.00	2.70
☐ 9 Raul Ibanez	2.00	.90
☐ 10 Marty Janzen	2.00	.90
☐ 11 Robin Jennings	2.00	.90
☐ 12 Jason Maxwell	2.00	.90
☐ 13 Scott McClain	2.00	.90
☐ 14 Wonderful Monds	2.00	.90
☐ 15 Chris Singleton	20.00	9.00

1996 Ultra Hitting Machines

	MINT	NRMT
COMPLETE SET (10)	250.00	110.00
COMMON CARD (1-10)	10.00	4.50
UNLISTED STARS	15.00	6.75

SER.2 STATED ODDS 1:288
*GOLD MEDAL: .75X TO 2X HI COLUMN
GM SER.2 STATED ODDS 1:2880

		MINT	NRMT
❏ 1	Albert Belle	15.00	6.75
❏ 2	Barry Bonds	20.00	9.00
❏ 3	Juan Gonzalez	30.00	13.50
❏ 4	Ken Griffey Jr.	80.00	36.00
❏ 5	Edgar Martinez	10.00	4.50
❏ 6	Rafael Palmeiro	15.00	6.75
❏ 7	Mike Piazza	50.00	22.00
❏ 8	Tim Salmon	12.00	5.50
❏ 9	Frank Thomas	30.00	13.50
❏ 10	Matt Williams	15.00	6.75

1996 Ultra Home Run Kings

	MINT	NRMT
COMPLETE SET (12)	60.00	27.00
COMMON CARD (1-12)	1.50	.70

SER.1 STATED ODDS 1:75
*GOLD MEDAL: 25X TO 60X BASE CARD HI
GM SER.1 STATED ODDS 1:750
*REDEMPTION: 2.5X TO 6X BASE CARD HI
ONE RDMP.CARD VIA MAIL PER HR CARD

		MINT	NRMT
❏ 1	Albert Belle	4.00	1.80
❏ 2	Dante Bichette	1.50	.70
❏ 3	Barry Bonds	5.00	2.20
❏ 4	Jose Canseco	5.00	2.20
❏ 5	Juan Gonzalez	8.00	3.60
❏ 6	Ken Griffey Jr.	20.00	9.00
❏ 7	Mark McGwire	20.00	9.00
❏ 8	Manny Ramirez	5.00	2.20
❏ 9	Tim Salmon	2.50	1.10
❏ 10	Frank Thomas	8.00	3.60
❏ 11	Mo Vaughn	4.00	1.80
❏ 12	Matt Williams	4.00	1.80

1996 Ultra On-Base Leaders

	MINT	NRMT
COMPLETE SET (10)	5.00	2.20
COMMON CARD (1-10)	.50	.23

SER.2 STATED ODDS 1:4
*GOLD MEDAL: 1X TO 2.5X BASE CARD HI
GM SER.2 STATED ODDS 1:40

		MINT	NRMT
❏ 1	Wade Boggs	.75	.35
❏ 2	Barry Bonds	1.00	.45
❏ 3	Tony Gwynn	2.00	.90
❏ 4	Rickey Henderson	1.00	.45
❏ 5	Chuck Knoblauch	.75	.35
❏ 6	Edgar Martinez	.50	.23
❏ 7	Mike Piazza	2.50	1.10
❏ 8	Tim Salmon	.60	.25
❏ 9	Frank Thomas	1.50	.70
❏ 10	Jim Thome	.75	.35

1996 Ultra Power Plus

	MINT	NRMT
COMPLETE SET (12)	25.00	11.00
COMMON CARD (1-12)	1.00	.45

SER.1 STATED ODDS 1:10
*GOLD MEDAL: 2.5X TO 6X BASE CARD HI
GM SER.1 STATED ODDS 1:100

		MINT	NRMT
❏ 1	Jeff Bagwell	2.50	1.10
❏ 2	Barry Bonds	2.50	1.10
❏ 3	Ken Griffey Jr.	10.00	4.50
❏ 4	Raul Mondesi	1.00	.45
❏ 5	Rafael Palmeiro	2.00	.90
❏ 6	Mike Piazza	6.00	2.70
❏ 7	Manny Ramirez	2.50	1.10
❏ 8	Tim Salmon	1.50	.70
❏ 9	Reggie Sanders	1.00	.45
❏ 10	Frank Thomas	4.00	1.80
❏ 11	Larry Walker	2.00	.90
❏ 12	Matt Williams	2.00	.90

1996 Ultra Prime Leather

	MINT	NRMT
COMPLETE SET (18)	25.00	11.00
COMMON CARD (1-18)	.50	.23

SER.1 STATED ODDS 1:8

*GOLD MEDAL: 2.5X TO 6X BASE CARD HI
GM SER.1 STATED ODDS 1:80

		MINT	NRMT
❏ 1	Ivan Rodriguez	2.50	1.10
❏ 2	Will Clark	2.00	.90
❏ 3	Roberto Alomar	2.00	.90
❏ 4	Cal Ripken	8.00	3.60
❏ 5	Wade Boggs	2.00	.90
❏ 6	Ken Griffey Jr.	10.00	4.50
❏ 7	Kenny Lofton	1.50	.70
❏ 8	Kirby Puckett	4.00	1.80
❏ 9	Tim Salmon	1.50	.70
❏ 10	Mike Piazza	6.00	2.70
❏ 11	Mark Grace	1.50	.70
❏ 12	Craig Biggio	2.00	.90
❏ 13	Barry Larkin	2.00	.90
❏ 14	Matt Williams	2.00	.90
❏ 15	Barry Bonds	2.50	1.10
❏ 16	Tony Gwynn	5.00	2.20
❏ 17	Brian McRae	.50	.23
❏ 18	Raul Mondesi	1.00	.45
❏ S4	Cal Ripken Jr Promo	.50	.23

1996 Ultra Rawhide

	MINT	NRMT
COMPLETE SET (10)	15.00	6.75
COMMON CARD (1-10)	1.00	.45

SER.2 STATED ODDS 1:8
*GOLD MEDAL: 1.5X TO 4X BASE CARD HI
GM SER.2 STATED ODDS 1:80

		MINT	NRMT
❏ 1	Roberto Alomar	1.25	.55
❏ 2	Barry Bonds	1.25	.55
❏ 3	Mark Grace	1.00	.45
❏ 4	Ken Griffey Jr.	6.00	2.70
❏ 5	Kenny Lofton	1.00	.45
❏ 6	Greg Maddux	3.00	1.35
❏ 7	Raul Mondesi	1.00	.45
❏ 8	Mike Piazza	4.00	1.80
❏ 9	Cal Ripken	5.00	2.20
❏ 10	Matt Williams	1.25	.55

1996 Ultra RBI Kings

	MINT	NRMT
COMPLETE SET (10)	30.00	13.50
COMMON CARD (1-10)	1.50	.70

SER.1 STATED ODDS 1:5 RETAIL
*GOLD MEDAL: 5X TO 12X BASE CARD HI
GM SER.1 STATED ODDS 1:50 RETAIL

	MINT	NRMT
COMPLETE SET (10)	4.00	1.80
COMMON CARD (1-10)	.25	.11
SER.2 STATED ODDS 1:4		
*GOLD MEDAL: .75X TO 2X BASE CARD HI		
GM SER.2 STATED ODDS 1:40		
☐ 1 Garret Anderson	.40	.18
☐ 2 Marty Cordova	.25	.11
☐ 3 Jim Edmonds	.60	.25
☐ 4 Cliff Floyd	.40	.18
☐ 5 Brian L.Hunter	.25	.11
☐ 6 Chipper Jones	2.00	.90
☐ 7 Ryan Klesko	.40	.18
☐ 8 Hideo Nomo	.75	.35
☐ 9 Manny Ramirez	1.00	.45
☐ 10 Rondell White	.40	.18

☐ 1 Derek Bell	1.50	.70
☐ 2 Albert Belle	4.00	1.80
☐ 3 Dante Bichette	1.50	.70
☐ 4 Barry Bonds	5.00	2.20
☐ 5 Jim Edmonds	2.50	1.10
☐ 6 Manny Ramirez	5.00	2.20
☐ 7 Reggie Sanders	1.50	.70
☐ 8 Sammy Sosa	12.00	5.50
☐ 9 Frank Thomas	8.00	3.60
☐ 10 Mo Vaughn	4.00	1.80

1996 Ultra Respect

	MINT	NRMT
COMPLETE SET (10)	60.00	27.00
COMMON CARD (1-10)	1.50	.70
SER.2 STATED ODDS 1:18		
*GOLD MEDAL: 4X TO 10X BASE CARD HI		
GM SER.2 STATED ODDS 1:180		
☐ 1 Joe Carter	1.50	.70
☐ 2 Ken Griffey Jr.	15.00	6.75
☐ 3 Tony Gwynn	8.00	3.60
☐ 4 Greg Maddux	8.00	3.60
☐ 5 Eddie Murray	3.00	1.35
☐ 6 Kirby Puckett	5.00	2.20
☐ 7 Cal Ripken	12.00	5.50
☐ 8 Ryne Sandberg	4.00	1.80
☐ 9 Frank Thomas	6.00	2.70
☐ 10 Mo Vaughn	3.00	1.35

1996 Ultra Rising Stars

1996 Ultra Season Crowns

	MINT	NRMT
COMPLETE SET (10)	30.00	13.50
COMMON CARD (1-10)	.60	.23
SER.1 STATED ODDS 1:10		
*GOLD MEDAL: 2.5X TO 6X BASE CARD HI		
GM SER.1 STATED ODDS 1:100		
☐ 1 Barry Bonds	2.50	1.10
☐ 2 Tony Gwynn	5.00	2.20
☐ 3 Randy Johnson	1.50	.70
☐ 4 Kenny Lofton	1.00	.45
☐ 5 Greg Maddux	5.00	2.20
☐ 6 Edgar Martinez	.50	.23
☐ 7 Hideo Nomo	1.50	.70
☐ 8 Cal Ripken	8.00	3.60
☐ 9 Frank Thomas	4.00	1.80
☐ 10 Tim Wakefield	.50	.23

1996 Ultra Thunderclap

	MINT	NRMT
COMPLETE SET (20)	500.00	220.00
COMMON CARD (1-20)	8.00	3.60
SEMISTARS	12.00	5.50
UNLISTED STARS	20.00	9.00
SER.2 STATED ODDS 1:72 RETAIL		
*GOLD MEDAL: 1.25X TO 3X HI COLUMN		
GM SER.2 STATED ODDS 1:720 RETAIL		

☐ 1 Albert Belle	20.00	9.00
☐ 2 Barry Bonds	25.00	11.00
☐ 3 Bobby Bonilla	8.00	3.60
☐ 4 Jose Canseco	25.00	11.00
☐ 5 Joe Carter	8.00	3.60
☐ 6 Will Clark	12.00	5.50
☐ 7 Andre Dawson	12.00	5.50
☐ 8 Cecil Fielder	8.00	3.60
☐ 9 Andres Galarraga	20.00	9.00
☐ 10 Juan Gonzalez	40.00	18.00
☐ 11 Ken Griffey Jr.	100.00	45.00
☐ 12 Fred McGriff	12.00	5.50
☐ 13 Mark McGwire	100.00	45.00
☐ 14 Eddie Murray	20.00	9.00
☐ 15 Rafael Palmeiro	20.00	9.00
☐ 16 Kirby Puckett	40.00	18.00
☐ 17 Cal Ripken	80.00	36.00
☐ 18 Ryne Sandberg	30.00	13.50
☐ 19 Frank Thomas	40.00	18.00
☐ 20 Matt Williams	20.00	9.00

1997 Ultra

	MINT	NRMT
COMPLETE SET (553)	60.00	27.00
COMPLETE SERIES 1 (300)	30.00	13.50
COMPLETE SERIES 2 (253)	30.00	13.50
COMMON CARD (1-450)	.15	.07
MINOR STARS	.30	.14
UNLISTED STARS	.60	.25
COMMON CARD (451-553)	.20	.09
MINOR STARS 451-553	.40	.18
UNLISTED STARS 451-553	.75	.35
CARDS 451-553 ARE HOBBY ONLY		

☐ 1 Roberto Alomar	.60	.25
☐ 2 Brady Anderson	.30	.14
☐ 3 Rocky Coppinger	.15	.07
☐ 4 Jeffrey Hammonds	.30	.14
☐ 5 Chris Holles	.15	.07
☐ 6 Eddie Murray	.60	.25
☐ 7 Mike Mussina	.60	.25
☐ 8 Jimmy Myers	.15	.07
☐ 9 Randy Myers	.15	.07
☐ 10 Arthur Rhodes	.15	.07
☐ 11 Cal Ripken	2.50	1.10
☐ 12 Jose Canseco	.75	.35
☐ 13 Roger Clemens	1.50	.70
☐ 14 Tom Gordon	.15	.07
☐ 15 Jose Malave	.15	.07
☐ 16 Tim Naehring	.15	.07
☐ 17 Troy O'Leary	.30	.14
☐ 18 Bill Selby	.15	.07
☐ 19 Heathcliff Slocumb	.15	.07
☐ 20 Mike Stanley	.15	.07
☐ 21 Mo Vaughn	.60	.25
☐ 22 Garret Anderson	.30	.14
☐ 23 George Arias	.15	.07
☐ 24 Chili Davis	.30	.14
☐ 25 Jim Edmonds	.40	.18
☐ 26 Darin Erstad	.60	.25
☐ 27 Chuck Finley	.30	.14
☐ 28 Todd Greene	.15	.07
☐ 29 Troy Percival	.30	.14
☐ 30 Tim Salmon	.60	.25
☐ 31 Jeff Schmidt	.15	.07
☐ 32 Randy Velarde	.15	.07
☐ 33 Shad Williams	.15	.07

#	Player	Price 1	Price 2
34	Wilson Alvarez	.30	.14
35	Harold Baines	.30	.14
36	James Baldwin	.30	.14
37	Mike Cameron	.30	.14
38	Ray Durham	.30	.14
39	Ozzie Guillen	.15	.07
40	Roberto Hernandez	.15	.07
41	Darren Lewis	.15	.07
42	Jose Munoz	.15	.07
43	Tony Phillips	.15	.07
44	Frank Thomas	1.25	.55
45	Sandy Alomar Jr.	.30	.14
46	Albert Belle	.60	.25
47	Mark Carreon	.15	.07
48	Julio Franco	.30	.14
49	Orel Hershiser	.30	.14
50	Kenny Lofton	.40	.18
51	Jack McDowell	.15	.07
52	Jose Mesa	.15	.07
53	Charles Nagy	.30	.14
54	Manny Ramirez	.75	.35
55	Julian Tavarez	.15	.07
56	Omar Vizquel	.30	.14
57	Raul Casanova	.15	.07
58	Tony Clark	.40	.18
59	Travis Fryman	.30	.14
60	Bob Higginson	.30	.14
61	Melvin Nieves	.15	.07
62	Curtis Pride	.15	.07
63	Justin Thompson	.30	.14
64	Alan Trammell	.30	.14
65	Kevin Appier	.30	.14
66	Johnny Damon	.30	.14
67	Keith Lockhart	.15	.07
68	Jeff Montgomery	.15	.07
69	Jose Offerman	.15	.07
70	Bip Roberts	.15	.07
71	Jose Rosado	.15	.07
72	Chris Stynes	.15	.07
73	Mike Sweeney	.30	.14
74	Jeff Cirillo	.30	.14
75	Jeff D'Amico	.15	.07
76	John Jaha	.15	.07
77	Scott Karl	.15	.07
78	Mike Matheny	.15	.07
79	Ben McDonald	.15	.07
80	Matt Mieske	.15	.07
81	Marc Newfield	.15	.07
82	Dave Nilsson	.15	.07
83	Jose Valentin	.15	.07
84	Fernando Vina	.15	.07
85	Rick Aguilera	.15	.07
86	Marty Cordova	.60	.25
87	Chuck Knoblauch	.60	.25
88	Matt Lawton	.30	.14
89	Pat Meares	.15	.07
90	Paul Molitor	.60	.25
91	Greg Myers	.15	.07
92	Dan Naulty	.15	.07
93	Kirby Puckett	1.00	.45
94	Frank Rodriguez	.15	.07
95	Wade Boggs	.60	.25
96	Cecil Fielder	.30	.14
97	Joe Girardi	.15	.07
98	Dwight Gooden	.30	.14
99	Derek Jeter	2.00	.90
100	Tino Martinez	.60	.25
101	Ramiro Mendoza	.50	.23
102	Andy Pettitte	.40	.18
103	Mariano Rivera	.30	.14
104	Ruben Rivera	.15	.07
105	Kenny Rogers	.15	.07
106	Darryl Strawberry	.30	.14
107	Bernie Williams	.60	.25
108	Tony Batista	.40	.18
109	Geronimo Berroa	.15	.07
110	Bobby Chouinard	.15	.07
111	Brent Gates	.15	.07
112	Jason Giambi	.30	.14
113	Damon Mashore	.15	.07
114	Mark McGwire	3.00	1.35
115	Scott Spiezio	.15	.07
116	John Wasdin	.15	.07
117	Steve Wojciechowski	.15	.07
118	Ernie Young	.15	.07
119	Norm Charlton	.15	.07
120	Joey Cora	.15	.07
121	Ken Griffey Jr.	3.00	1.35
122	Sterling Hitchcock	.30	.14
123	Raul Ibanez	.15	.07
124	Randy Johnson	.60	.25
125	Edgar Martinez	.30	.14
126	Alex Rodriguez	2.00	.90
127	Matt Wagner	.15	.07
128	Bob Wells	.15	.07
129	Dan Wilson	.15	.07
130	Will Clark	.60	.25
131	Kevin Elster	.15	.07
132	Juan Gonzalez	1.25	.55
133	Rusty Greer	.30	.14
134	Darryl Hamilton	.15	.07
135	Mike Henneman	.15	.07
136	Ken Hill	.15	.07
137	Mark McLemore	.15	.07
138	Dean Palmer	.30	.14
139	Roger Pavlik	.15	.07
140	Ivan Rodriguez	.75	.35
141	Joe Carter	.30	.14
142	Carlos Delgado	.60	.25
143	Alex Gonzalez	.15	.07
144	Juan Guzman	.15	.07
145	Pat Hentgen	.30	.14
146	Marty Janzen	.15	.07
147	Otis Nixon	.15	.07
148	Charlie O'Brien	.15	.07
149	John Olerud	.30	.14
150	Robert Perez	.15	.07
151	Jermaine Dye	.15	.07
152	Tom Glavine	.60	.25
153	Andruw Jones	.75	.35
154	Chipper Jones	1.50	.70
155	Ryan Klesko	.30	.14
156	Javier Lopez	.30	.14
157	Greg Maddux	1.50	.70
158	Fred McGriff	.40	.18
159	Wonderful Monds	.15	.07
160	John Smoltz	.40	.18
161	Terrel Wade	.15	.07
162	Mark Wohlers	.15	.07
163	Brant Brown	.30	.14
164	Mark Grace	.40	.18
165	Tyler Houston	.15	.07
166	Robin Jennings	.15	.07
167	Jason Maxwell	.15	.07
168	Ryne Sandberg	.75	.35
169	Sammy Sosa	2.00	.90
170	Amaury Telemaco	.15	.07
171	Steve Trachsel	.15	.07
172	Pedro Valdes	.15	.07
173	Tim Belk	.15	.07
174	Bret Boone	.30	.14
175	Jeff Brantley	.15	.07
176	Eric Davis	.30	.14
177	Barry Larkin	.60	.25
178	Chad Mottola	.15	.07
179	Mark Portugal	.15	.07
180	Reggie Sanders	.30	.14
181	John Smiley	.15	.07
182	Eddie Taubensee	.15	.07
183	Dante Bichette	.30	.14
184	Ellis Burks	.30	.14
185	Andres Galarraga	.60	.25
186	Curt Leskanic	.15	.07
187	Quinton McCracken	.15	.07
188	Jeff Reed	.15	.07
189	Kevin Ritz	.15	.07
190	Walt Weiss	.15	.07
191	Jamey Wright	.30	.14
192	Eric Young	.30	.14
193	Kevin Brown	.40	.18
194	Luis Castillo	.30	.14
195	Jeff Conine	.15	.07
196	Andre Dawson	.40	.18
197	Charles Johnson	.30	.14
198	Al Leiter	.30	.14
199	Ralph Milliard	.15	.07
200	Robb Nen	.15	.07
201	Edgar Renteria	.30	.14
202	Gary Sheffield	.30	.14
203	Bob Abreu	.30	.14
204	Jeff Bagwell	.75	.35
205	Derek Bell	.30	.14
206	Sean Berry	.15	.07
207	Richard Hidalgo	.30	.14
208	Todd Jones	.15	.07
209	Darryl Kile	.15	.07
210	Orlando Miller	.15	.07
211	Shane Reynolds	.30	.14
212	Billy Wagner	.30	.14
213	Donne Wall	.15	.07
214	Roger Cedeno	.30	.14
215	Greg Gagne	.15	.07
216	Karim Garcia	.30	.14
217	Wilton Guerrero	.15	.07
218	Todd Hollandsworth	.15	.07
219	Ramon Martinez	.30	.14
220	Raul Mondesi	.30	.14
221	Hideo Nomo	.60	.25
222	Chan Ho Park	.60	.25
223	Mike Piazza	2.00	.90
224	Ismael Valdes	.30	.14
225	Moises Alou	.30	.14
226	Derek Aucoin	.15	.07
227	Yamil Benitez	.15	.07
228	Jeff Fassero	.15	.07
229	Darrin Fletcher	.15	.07
230	Mark Grudzielanek	.30	.14
231	Barry Manuel	.15	.07
232	Pedro Martinez	.75	.35
233	Henry Rodriguez	.30	.14
234	Ugueth Urbina	.30	.14
235	Rondell White	.30	.14
236	Carlos Baerga	.15	.07
237	John Franco	.30	.14
238	Bernard Gilkey	.15	.07
239	Todd Hundley	.30	.14
240	Butch Huskey	.15	.07
241	Jason Isringhausen	.15	.07
242	Lance Johnson	.15	.07
243	Bobby Jones	.15	.07
244	Alex Ochoa	.15	.07
245	Rey Ordonez	.30	.14
246	Paul Wilson	.15	.07
247	Ron Blazier	.15	.07
248	David Doster	.15	.07
249	Jim Eisenreich	.15	.07
250	Mike Grace	.15	.07
251	Mike Lieberthal	.15	.07
252	Wendell Magee	.15	.07
253	Mickey Morandini	.15	.07
254	Ricky Otero	.15	.07
255	Scott Rolen	1.00	.45
256	Curt Schilling	.40	.18
257	Todd Zeile	.15	.07
258	Jermaine Allensworth	.15	.07
259	Trey Beamon	.15	.07
260	Carlos Garcia	.15	.07
261	Mark Johnson	.15	.07
262	Jason Kendall	.40	.18
263	Jeff King	.15	.07
264	Al Martin	.15	.07
265	Denny Neagle	.30	.14
266	Matt Ruebel	.15	.07
267	Marc Wilkins	.15	.07
268	Alan Benes	.30	.14
269	Dennis Eckersley	.30	.14
270	Ron Gant	.30	.14
271	Aaron Holbert	.15	.07
272	Brian Jordan	.30	.14
273	Ray Lankford	.30	.14
274	John Mabry	.15	.07
275	T.J. Mathews	.15	.07
276	Ozzie Smith	.75	.35
277	Todd Stottlemyre	.15	.07
278	Mark Sweeney	.15	.07
279	Andy Ashby	.15	.07
280	Steve Finley	.30	.14
281	John Flaherty	.15	.07
282	Chris Gomez	.15	.07
283	Tony Gwynn	1.50	.70
284	Joey Hamilton	.30	.14
285	Rickey Henderson	.75	.35
286	Trevor Hoffman	.30	.14
287	Jason Thompson	.15	.07
288	Fernando Valenzuela	.30	.14
289	Greg Vaughn	.30	.14
290	Barry Bonds	.75	.35
291	Jay Canizaro	.15	.07

292	Jacob Cruz	.15	.07
293	Shawon Dunston	.15	.07
294	Shawn Estes	.30	.14
295	Mark Gardner	.15	.07
296	Marcus Jensen	.15	.07
297	Bill Mueller	.75	.35
298	Chris Singleton	.75	.35
299	Allen Watson	.15	.07
300	Matt Williams	.60	.25
301	Rod Beck	.15	.07
302	Jay Bell	.30	.14
303	Shawon Dunston	.15	.07
304	Reggie Jefferson	.15	.07
305	Darren Oliver	.15	.07
306	Benito Santiago	.15	.07
307	Gerald Williams	.15	.07
308	Damon Buford	.15	.07
309	Jeromy Burnitz	.30	.14
310	Sterling Hitchcock	.30	.14
311	Dave Hollins	.15	.07
312	Mel Rojas	.15	.07
313	Robin Ventura	.30	.14
314	David Wells	.30	.14
315	Cal Eldred	.30	.14
316	Gary Gaetti	.30	.14
317	John Hudek	.15	.07
318	Brian Johnson	.15	.07
319	Denny Neagle	.30	.14
320	Larry Walker	.60	.25
321	Russ Davis	.30	.14
322	Delino DeShields	.15	.07
323	Charlie Hayes	.15	.07
324	Jermaine Dye	.30	.14
325	John Ericks	.15	.07
326	Jeff Fassero	.15	.07
327	Nomar Garciaparra	2.00	.90
328	Willie Greene	.15	.07
329	Greg McMichael	.15	.07
330	Damion Easley	.30	.14
331	Ricky Bones	.15	.07
332	John Burkett	.15	.07
333	Royce Clayton	.15	.07
334	Greg Colbrunn	.15	.07
335	Tony Eusebio	.15	.07
336	Gregg Jefferies	.15	.07
337	Wally Joyner	.30	.14
338	Jim Leyritz	.15	.07
339	Paul O'Neill	.30	.14
340	Bruce Ruffin	.15	.07
341	Michael Tucker	.15	.07
342	Andy Benes	.30	.14
343	Craig Biggio	.60	.25
344	Rex Hudler	.15	.07
345	Brad Radke	.30	.14
346	Deion Sanders	.30	.14
347	Moises Alou	.30	.14
348	Brad Ausmus	.15	.07
349	Armando Benitez	.15	.07
350	Mark Gubicza	.15	.07
351	Terry Steinbach	.15	.07
352	Mark Whiten	.15	.07
353	Ricky Bottalico	.30	.14
354	Brian Giles	2.00	.90
355	Eric Karros	.30	.14
356	Jimmy Key	.15	.07
357	Carlos Perez	.15	.07
358	Alex Fernandez	.30	.14
359	J.T. Snow	.30	.14
360	Bobby Bonilla	.30	.14
361	Scott Brosius	.30	.14
362	Greg Swindell	.15	.07
363	Jose Vizcaino	.15	.07
364	Matt Williams	.60	.25
365	Darren Daulton	.30	.14
366	Shane Andrews	.15	.07
367	Jim Eisenreich	.15	.07
368	Ariel Prieto	.15	.07
369	Bob Tewksbury	.15	.07
370	Mike Bordick	.15	.07
371	Rheal Cormier	.15	.07
372	Cliff Floyd	.30	.14
373	David Justice	.60	.25
374	John Wetteland	.30	.14
375	Mike Blowers	.15	.07
376	Jose Canseco	.75	.35
377	Roger Clemens	1.50	.70
378	Kevin Mitchell	.15	.07
379	Todd Zeile	.15	.07
380	Jim Thome	.60	.25
381	Turk Wendell	.15	.07
382	Rico Brogna	.15	.07
383	Eric Davis	.30	.14
384	Mike Lansing	.15	.07
385	Devon White	.30	.14
386	Marquis Grissom	.30	.14
387	Todd Worrell	.15	.07
388	Jeff Kent	.30	.14
389	Mickey Tettleton	.15	.07
390	Steve Avery	.15	.07
391	David Cone	.40	.18
392	Scott Cooper	.15	.07
393	Lee Stevens	.30	.14
394	Kevin Elster	.15	.07
395	Tom Goodwin	.15	.07
396	Shawn Green	.50	.25
397	Pete Harnisch	.15	.07
398	Eddie Murray	.50	.25
399	Joe Randa	.15	.07
400	Scott Sanders	.15	.07
401	John Valentin	.30	.14
402	Todd Jones	.15	.07
403	Terry Adams	.15	.07
404	Brian Hunter	.30	.14
405	Pat Listach	.15	.07
406	Kenny Lofton	.40	.18
407	Mark Wohlers	.15	.07
408	Ed Sprague	.15	.07
409	Rich Becker	.15	.07
410	Edgardo Alfonzo	.40	.18
411	Albert Belle	.60	.25
412	Jeff King	.15	.07
413	Kirt Manwaring	.15	.07
414	Jason Schmidt	.15	.07
415	Allen Watson	.15	.07
416	Lee Tinsley	.15	.07
417	Brett Butler	.30	.14
418	Carlos Garcia	.15	.07
419	Mark Lemke	.15	.07
420	Jaime Navarro	.15	.07
421	David Segui	.30	.14
422	Ruben Sierra	.15	.07
423	B.J. Surhoff	.30	.14
424	Julian Tavarez	.15	.07
425	Billy Taylor	.15	.07
426	Ken Caminiti	.40	.18
427	Chuck Carr	.15	.07
428	Benji Gil	.15	.07
429	Terry Mulholland	.15	.07
430	Mike Stanton	.15	.07
431	Wil Cordero	.15	.07
432	Chili Davis	.30	.14
433	Mariano Duncan	.15	.07
434	Orlando Merced	.15	.07
435	Kent Mercker	.15	.07
436	John Olerud	.30	.14
437	Quilvio Veras	.15	.07
438	Mike Fetters	.15	.07
439	Glenallen Hill	.15	.07
440	Bill Swift	.15	.07
441	Tim Wakefield	.30	.14
442	Pedro Astacio	.15	.07
443	Vinny Castilla	.40	.18
444	Doug Drabek	.15	.07
445	Alan Embree	.15	.07
446	Lee Smith	.30	.14
447	Darryl Hamilton	.15	.07
448	Brian McRae	.15	.07
449	Mike Timlin	.15	.07
450	Bob Wickman	.15	.07
451	Jason Dickson	.20	.09
452	Chad Curtis	.20	.09
453	Mark Leiter	.15	.07
454	Damon Berryhill	.20	.09
455	Kevin Orie	.20	.09
456	Dave Burba	.15	.07
457	Chris Holt	.20	.09
458	Ricky Ledee	2.00	.90
459	Mike Devereaux	.15	.07
460	Pokey Reese	.40	.18
461	Tim Raines	.20	.09
462	Ryan Jones	.20	.09
463	Shane Mack	.20	.09
464	Darren Dreifort	.40	.18
465	Mark Parent	.20	.09
466	Mark Portugal	.20	.09
467	Dante Powell	.40	.18
468	Craig Grebeck	.20	.09
469	Ron Villone	.20	.09
470	Dmitri Young	.40	.18
471	Shannon Stewart	.40	.18
472	Rick Helling	.40	.18
473	Bill Haselman	.20	.09
474	Albie Lopez	.20	.09
475	Glendon Rusch	.20	.09
476	Derrick May	.20	.09
477	Chad Ogea	.20	.09
478	Kirk Rueter	.20	.09
479	Chris Hammond	.20	.09
480	Russ Johnson	.20	.09
481	James Mouton	.20	.09
482	Mike Macfarlane	.20	.09
483	Scott Ruffcorn	.20	.09
484	Jeff Frye	.20	.09
485	Richie Sexson	.75	.35
486	Emil Brown	.50	.23
487	Desi Wilson	.20	.09
488	Brent Gates	.20	.09
489	Tony Graffanino	.20	.09
490	Dan Miceli	.20	.09
491	Orlando Cabrera	.50	.23
492	Tony Womack	.75	.35
493	Jerome Walton	.20	.09
494	Mark Thompson	.20	.09
495	Jose Guillen	.50	.23
496	Willie Blair	.20	.09
497	T.J. Staton	.50	.23
498	Scott Kamieniecki	.20	.09
499	Vince Coleman	.20	.09
500	Jeff Abbott	.20	.09
501	Chris Widger	.20	.09
502	Kevin Tapani	.20	.09
503	Carlos Castillo	.50	.23
504	Luis Gonzalez	.40	.18
505	Tim Belcher	.20	.09
506	Armando Reynoso	.20	.09
507	Jamie Moyer	.20	.09
508	Randall Simon	.75	.35
509	Vladimir Guerrero	1.25	.55
510	Wady Almonte	.40	.18
511	Dustin Hermanson	.20	.09
512	Deivi Cruz	.75	.35
513	Luis Alicea	.20	.09
514	Felix Heredia	.40	.18
515	Don Slaught	.20	.09
516	Shigetoshi Hasegawa	.40	.18
517	Matt Walbeck	.20	.09
518	David Arias-Ortiz	1.25	.55
519	Brady Raggio	.20	.09
520	Rudy Pemberton	.20	.09
521	Wayne Kirby	.20	.09
522	Calvin Maduro	.20	.09
523	Mark Lewis	.20	.09
524	Mike Jackson	.20	.09
525	Sid Fernandez	.20	.09
526	Mike Bielecki	.20	.09
527	Bubba Trammell	.75	.35
528	Brent Brede	.20	.09
529	Matt Morris	.40	.18
530	Joe Borowski	.20	.09
531	Orlando Miller	.20	.09
532	Jim Bullinger	.20	.09
533	Robert Person	.20	.09
534	Doug Glanville	.50	.23
535	Terry Pendleton	.20	.09
536	Jorge Posada	.40	.18
537	Marc Sagmoen	.20	.09
538	Fernando Tatis	3.00	1.35
539	Aaron Sele	.40	.18
540	Brian Banks	.20	.09
541	Derrek Lee	.50	.23
542	John Wasdin	.20	.09
543	Justin Towle	.60	.25
544	Pat Cline	.40	.18
545	Dave Magadan	.20	.09
546	Jeff Blauser	.20	.09
547	Phil Nevin	.20	.09
548	Todd Walker	.75	.35
549	Eli Marrero	.20	.09

		MINT	NRMT
❏ 550	Bartolo Colon	.40	.18
❏ 551	Jose Cruz Jr.	1.50	.70
❏ 552	Todd Dunwoody	.40	.18
❏ 553	Hideki Irabu	1.25	.55
❏ P11	Cal Ripken Promo	4.00	1.80
	Three Card Strip		

1997 Ultra Gold Medallion

	MINT	NRMT
COMPLETE SET (553)	270.00	120.00
COMPLETE SERIES 1 (300)	150.00	70.00
COMPLETE SERIES 2 (253)	120.00	55.00
COMMON CARD (1-450)	.25	.11
COMMON CARD (451-553)	.30	.14
*STARS: 1.5X TO 4X BASIC CARDS		
*ROOKIES: .75X TO 2X BASIC CARDS		
ONE PER PACK		
MEDALLIONS: DIFT.PHOTOS FROM BASE CARDS		

1997 Ultra Platinum Medallion

	MINT	NRMT
COMMON CARD (1-553)	5.00	2.20
*STARS 1-450: 12.5X TO 30X BASIC CARDS		
*STARS 451-553: 10X TO 25X BASIC CARDS		
*ROOKIES 1-450: 6X TO 15X BASIC CARDS		
*ROOKIES: 451-553: 5X TO 12X BASIC CARDS		
STATED ODDS 1:100		
STATED PRINT RUN LESS THAN 200 SETS		
MEDALLIONS: DIFT.PHOTOS FROM BASE CARDS		

1997 Ultra Autographstix Emeralds

		MINT	NRMT
❏ 1	Alex Ochoa	5.00	2.20
❏ 2	Todd Walker	6.00	2.70
❏ 3	Scott Rolen	12.00	5.50
❏ 4	Darin Erstad	10.00	4.50
❏ 5	Alex Rodriguez	25.00	11.00
❏ 6	Todd Hollandsworth	5.00	2.20

1997 Ultra Baseball Rules

		MINT	NRMT
COMPLETE SET (10)		120.00	55.00
COMMON CARD (1-10)		1.50	.70
SER.1 STATED ODDS 1:36 RETAIL			
❏ 1	Barry Bonds	5.00	2.20
❏ 2	Ken Griffey Jr.	25.00	11.00
❏ 3	Derek Jeter	12.00	5.50
❏ 4	Chipper Jones	12.00	5.50
❏ 5	Greg Maddux	15.00	6.75
❏ 6	Mark McGwire	25.00	11.00
❏ 7	Troy Percival	1.50	.70
❏ 8	Mike Piazza	15.00	6.75
❏ 9	Cal Ripken	20.00	9.00
❏ 10	Frank Thomas	12.00	5.50

1997 Ultra Checklists

		MINT	NRMT
COMPLETE SERIES 1 (10)		8.00	3.60
COMPLETE SERIES 2 (10)		12.00	5.50
COMMON CARD (A1-B10)		.25	.11
STATED ODDS 1:4 HOBBY			
❏ A1	Dante Bichette	.25	.11
❏ A2	Barry Bonds	.75	.35
❏ A3	Ken Griffey Jr.	3.00	1.35
❏ A4	Greg Maddux	2.00	.90
❏ A5	Mark McGwire	3.00	1.35
❏ A6	Mike Piazza	2.00	.90
❏ A7	Cal Ripken	2.00	.90
❏ A8	John Smoltz	.40	.18
❏ A9	Sammy Sosa	2.00	.90
❏ A10	Frank Thomas	1.25	.55
❏ B1	Andruw Jones	1.00	.45
❏ B2	Ken Griffey Jr.	3.00	1.35
❏ B3	Frank Thomas	1.25	.55
❏ B4	Alex Rodriguez	2.00	.90
❏ B5	Cal Ripken	2.00	.90
❏ B6	Mike Piazza	2.00	.90
❏ B7	Greg Maddux	2.00	.90
❏ B8	Chipper Jones	1.50	.70
❏ B9	Derek Jeter	2.00	.90
❏ B10	Juan Gonzalez	1.25	.55

1997 Ultra Diamond Producers

		MINT	NRMT
COMPLETE SET (12)		500.00	220.00
COMMON CARD (1-12)		10.00	4.50
UNLISTED STARS		15.00	6.75
SER.1 STATED ODDS 1:288			
❏ 1	Jeff Bagwell	20.00	9.00
❏ 2	Barry Bonds	20.00	9.00
❏ 3	Ken Griffey Jr.	80.00	36.00
❏ 4	Chipper Jones	40.00	18.00
❏ 5	Kenny Lofton	10.00	4.50
❏ 6	Greg Maddux	40.00	18.00
❏ 7	Mark McGwire	80.00	36.00
❏ 8	Mike Piazza	50.00	22.00
❏ 9	Cal Ripken	60.00	27.00
❏ 10	Alex Rodriguez	50.00	22.00
❏ 11	Frank Thomas	30.00	13.50
❏ 12	Matt Williams	15.00	6.75

1997 Ultra Double Trouble

		MINT	NRMT
COMPLETE SET (20)		12.00	5.50
COMMON CARD (1-20)		.25	.11
UNLISTED STARS		.50	.23
SER.1 STATED ODDS 1:4			
❏ 1	Roberto Alomar	2.00	.90
	Cal Ripken		
❏ 2	Mo Vaughn	.60	.25

	Jose Canseco	
❏ 3	Jim Edmonds .... .50	.23
	Tim Salmon	
❏ 4	Harold Baines 1.00	.45
	Frank Thomas	
❏ 5	Albert Belle .... .50	.23
	Kenny Lofton	
❏ 6	Marty Cordova .... .50	.23
	Chuck Knoblauch	
❏ 7	Derek Jeter 1.50	.70
	Andy Pettitte	
❏ 8	Jason Giambi 2.50	1.10
	Mark McGwire	
❏ 9	Ken Griffey Jr. 3.00	1.35
	Alex Rodriguez	
❏ 10	Juan Gonzalez 1.00	.45
	Will Clark	
❏ 11	Greg Maddux 1.50	.70
	Chipper Jones	
❏ 12	Mark Grace 1.50	.70
	Sammy Sosa	
❏ 13	Dante Bichette .... .50	.23
	Andres Galarraga	
❏ 14	Jeff Bagwell .... .60	.25
	Derek Bell	
❏ 15	Hideo Nomo 1.50	.70
	Mike Piazza	
❏ 16	Henry Rodriguez .... .25	.11
	Moises Alou	
❏ 17	Rey Ordonez .... .25	.11
	Alex Ochoa	
❏ 18	Ray Lankford .... .25	.11
	Ron Gant	
❏ 19	Tony Gwynn 1.25	.55
	Rickey Henderson	
❏ 20	Barry Bonds .... .60	.25
	Matt Williams	

1997 Ultra Fame Game

	MINT	NRMT
COMPLETE SET (18)	70.00	32.00
COMMON CARD (1-18)	2.00	.90
SER.2 STATED ODDS 1:8 HOBBY		

❏ 1 Ken Griffey Jr.	12.00	5.50
❏ 2 Frank Thomas	5.00	2.20
❏ 3 Alex Rodriguez	8.00	3.60
❏ 4 Cal Ripken	10.00	4.50
❏ 5 Mike Piazza	8.00	3.60
❏ 6 Greg Maddux	6.00	2.70
❏ 7 Derek Jeter	6.00	2.70
❏ 8 Jeff Bagwell	3.00	1.35
❏ 9 Juan Gonzalez	5.00	2.20
❏ 10 Albert Belle	2.50	1.10
❏ 11 Tony Gwynn	6.00	2.70
❏ 12 Mark McGwire	12.00	5.50
❏ 13 Andy Pettitte	2.00	.90
❏ 14 Kenny Lofton	2.00	.90
❏ 15 Roberto Alomar	2.50	1.10
❏ 16 Ryne Sandberg	3.00	1.35
❏ 17 Barry Bonds	3.00	1.35
❏ 18 Eddie Murray	2.50	1.10

1997 Ultra Fielder's Choice

	MINT	NRMT
COMPLETE SET (18)	250.00	110.00

	MINT	NRMT
COMMON CARD (1-18)	4.00	1.80
SEMISTARS	8.00	3.60
UNLISTED STARS	12.00	5.50
SER.1 STATED ODDS 1:144		

❏ 1 Roberto Alomar	12.00	5.50
❏ 2 Jeff Bagwell	15.00	6.75
❏ 3 Wade Boggs	12.00	5.50
❏ 4 Barry Bonds	15.00	6.75
❏ 5 Mark Grace	8.00	3.60
❏ 6 Ken Griffey Jr.	60.00	27.00
❏ 7 Marquis Grissom	4.00	1.80
❏ 8 Charles Johnson	8.00	3.60
❏ 9 Chuck Knoblauch	12.00	5.50
❏ 10 Barry Larkin	12.00	5.50
❏ 11 Kenny Lofton	6.00	3.60
❏ 12 Greg Maddux	30.00	13.50
❏ 13 Raul Mondesi	8.00	3.60
❏ 14 Rey Ordonez	4.00	1.80
❏ 15 Cal Ripken	50.00	22.00
❏ 16 Alex Rodriguez	40.00	18.00
❏ 17 Ivan Rodriguez	15.00	6.75
❏ 18 Matt Williams	12.00	5.50

1997 Ultra Golden Prospects

	MINT	NRMT
COMPLETE SET (10)	6.00	2.70
COMMON CARD (1-10)	.40	.18
SER.2 STATED ODDS 1:4 HOBBY		

❏ 1 Andruw Jones	1.25	.55
❏ 2 Vladimir Guerrero	1.25	.55
❏ 3 Todd Walker	.75	.35
❏ 4 Karim Garcia	.40	.18
❏ 5 Kevin Orie	.40	.18
❏ 6 Brian Giles	.40	.18
❏ 7 Jason Dickson	.40	.18
❏ 8 Jose Guillen	.50	.23
❏ 9 Ruben Rivera	.40	.18
❏ 10 Derrek Lee	.50	.23

1997 Ultra Hitting Machines

	MINT	NRMT
COMPLETE SET (18)	200.00	90.00
COMMON CARD (1-18)	4.00	1.80
SER.2 STATED ODDS 1:36 HOBBY		

❏ 1 Andruw Jones	6.00	2.70
❏ 2 Ken Griffey Jr.	30.00	13.50
❏ 3 Frank Thomas	12.00	5.50
❏ 4 Alex Rodriguez	20.00	9.00
❏ 5 Cal Ripken	25.00	11.00
❏ 6 Mike Piazza	20.00	9.00
❏ 7 Derek Jeter	15.00	6.75
❏ 8 Albert Belle	6.00	2.70
❏ 9 Tony Gwynn	15.00	6.75
❏ 10 Jeff Bagwell	8.00	3.60
❏ 11 Mark McGwire	30.00	13.50
❏ 12 Kenny Lofton	4.00	1.80
❏ 13 Manny Ramirez	8.00	3.60
❏ 14 Roberto Alomar	6.00	2.70
❏ 15 Ryne Sandberg	8.00	3.60
❏ 16 Eddie Murray	6.00	2.70
❏ 17 Sammy Sosa	20.00	9.00
❏ 18 Ken Caminiti	4.00	1.80

1997 Ultra Home Run Kings

	MINT	NRMT
COMPLETE SET (12)	100.00	45.00
COMMON CARD (1-12)	2.50	1.10
SER.1 STATED ODDS 1:36 HOBBY		

❏ 1 Albert Balle	5.00	2.20
❏ 2 Barry Bonds	6.00	2.70
❏ 3 Juan Gonzalez	10.00	4.50
❏ 4 Ken Griffey Jr.	25.00	11.00
❏ 5 Todd Hundley	2.50	1.10
❏ 6 Ryan Klesko	2.50	1.10
❏ 7 Mark McGwire	25.00	11.00
❏ 8 Mike Piazza	15.00	6.75
❏ 9 Sammy Sosa	15.00	6.75
❏ 10 Frank Thomas	10.00	4.50
❏ 11 Mo Vaughn	5.00	2.20
❏ 12 Matt Williams	5.00	2.20

1997 Ultra Leather Shop

	MINT	NRMT
COMPLETE SET (12)	20.00	9.00
COMMON CARD (1-12)	.75	.35
SER.2 STATED ODDS 1:6 HOBBY		

❏ 1 Ken Griffey Jr.	5.00	2.20
❏ 2 Alex Rodriguez	3.00	1.35
❏ 3 Cal Ripken	4.00	1.80

		MINT	NRMT
❑ 4	Derek Jeter	3.00	1.35
❑ 5	Juan Gonzalez	2.00	.90
❑ 6	Tony Gwynn	2.50	1.10
❑ 7	Jeff Bagwell	1.00	.45
❑ 8	Roberto Alomar	1.00	.45
❑ 9	Ryne Sandberg	1.25	.55
❑ 10	Ken Caminiti	.75	.35
❑ 11	Kenny Lofton	.75	.35
❑ 12	John Smoltz	.75	.35

1997 Ultra Power Plus

		MINT	NRMT
COMPLETE SERIES 1 (12)		80.00	36.00
COMMON CARD (A1-A12)		3.00	1.35
SER.1 STATED ODDS 1:24			
COMPLETE SERIES 2 (12)		30.00	13.50
COMMON CARD (B1-B12)		1.25	.55
SER.2 STATED ODDS 1:8 HOBBY			
❑ A1	Jeff Bagwell	3.00	1.35
❑ A2	Barry Bonds	4.00	1.80
❑ A3	Juan Gonzalez	6.00	2.70
❑ A4	Ken Griffey Jr.	15.00	6.75
❑ A5	Chipper Jones	8.00	3.60
❑ A6	Mark McGwire	15.00	6.75
❑ A7	Mike Piazza	10.00	4.50
❑ A8	Cal Ripken	12.00	5.50
❑ A9	Alex Rodriguez	10.00	4.50
❑ A10	Sammy Sosa	10.00	4.50
❑ A11	Frank Thomas	6.00	2.70
❑ A12	Matt Williams	3.00	1.35
❑ B1	Ken Griffey Jr.	6.00	2.70
❑ B2	Frank Thomas	2.50	1.10
❑ B3	Alex Rodriguez	4.00	1.80
❑ B4	Cal Ripken	5.00	2.20
❑ B5	Mike Piazza	4.00	1.80
❑ B6	Chipper Jones	4.00	1.80
❑ B7	Albert Belle	1.50	.70
❑ B8	Juan Gonzalez	2.50	1.10
❑ B9	Jeff Bagwell	1.25	.55
❑ B10	Mark McGwire	6.00	2.70
❑ B11	Mo Vaughn	1.50	.70
❑ B12	Barry Bonds	1.50	.70

1997 Ultra RBI Kings

	MINT	NRMT
COMPLETE SET (10)	40.00	18.00
COMMON CARD (1-10)	1.50	.70
SER.1 STATED ODDS 1:18		

		MINT	NRMT
❑ 1	Jeff Bagwell	3.00	1.35
❑ 2	Albert Belle	3.00	1.35
❑ 3	Dante Bichette	1.50	.70
❑ 4	Barry Bonds	4.00	1.80
❑ 5	Jay Buhner	1.50	.70
❑ 6	Juan Gonzalez	6.00	2.70
❑ 7	Ken Griffey Jr.	15.00	6.75
❑ 8	Sammy Sosa	10.00	4.50
❑ 9	Frank Thomas	6.00	2.70
❑ 10	Mo Vaughn	3.00	1.35

1997 Ultra Rookie Reflections

	MINT	NRMT
COMPLETE SET (10)	4.00	1.80
COMMON CARD (1-10)	.25	.11
SER.1 STATED ODDS 1:4		

		MINT	NRMT
❑ 1	James Baldwin	.40	.18
❑ 2	Jermaine Dye	.40	.18
❑ 3	Darin Erstad	.75	.35
❑ 4	Todd Hollandsworth	.25	.11
❑ 5	Derek Jeter	2.50	1.10
❑ 6	Jason Kendall	.50	.23
❑ 7	Alex Ochoa	.25	.11
❑ 8	Rey Ordonez	.40	.18
❑ 9	Edgar Renteria	.40	.18
❑ 10	Scott Rolen	1.50	.70

1997 Ultra Season Crowns

		MINT	NRMT
COMPLETE SET (12)		15.00	6.75
COMMON CARD (1-12)		.50	.23
SER.1 STATED ODDS 1:8			
❑ 1	Albert Belle	1.00	.45
❑ 2	Dante Bichette	.50	.23
❑ 3	Barry Bonds	1.25	.55
❑ 4	Kenny Lofton	.75	.35
❑ 5	Edgar Martinez	.50	.23
❑ 6	Mark McGwire	6.00	2.70
❑ 7	Andy Pettitte	.75	.35
❑ 8	Mike Piazza	3.00	1.35
❑ 9	Alex Rodriguez	3.00	1.35
❑ 10	John Smoltz	.75	.35
❑ 11	Sammy Sosa	4.00	1.80
❑ 12	Frank Thomas	2.50	1.10

1997 Ultra Starring Role

		MINT	NRMT
COMPLETE SET (12)		500.00	220.00
COMMON CARD (1-12)		15.00	6.75
SER.2 STATED ODDS 1:288 HOBBY			
❑ 1	Andruw Jones	20.00	9.00
❑ 2	Ken Griffey Jr.	80.00	36.00
❑ 3	Frank Thomas	30.00	13.50
❑ 4	Alex Rodriguez	50.00	22.00
❑ 5	Cal Ripken	60.00	27.00
❑ 6	Mike Piazza	50.00	22.00
❑ 7	Greg Maddux	40.00	18.00
❑ 8	Chipper Jones	40.00	18.00
❑ 9	Derek Jeter	50.00	22.00
❑ 10	Juan Gonzalez	30.00	13.50
❑ 11	Albert Belle	20.00	9.00
❑ 12	Tony Gwynn	40.00	18.00

1997 Ultra Thunderclap

		MINT	NRMT
COMPLETE SET (10)		80.00	36.00
COMMON CARD (1-660)		3.00	1.35
SER.2 STATED ODDS 1:18 HOBBY			
❑ 1	Barry Bonds	4.00	1.80
❑ 2	Mo Vaughn	4.00	1.80
❑ 3	Mark McGwire	15.00	6.75
❑ 4	Jeff Bagwell	3.00	1.35
❑ 5	Juan Gonzalez	6.00	2.70
❑ 6	Alex Rodriguez	10.00	4.50

		MINT	NRMT
❑ 7	Chipper Jones	8.00	3.60
❑ 8	Ken Griffey Jr.	15.00	6.75
❑ 9	Mike Piazza	10.00	4.50
❑ 10	Frank Thomas	6.00	2.70

1997 Ultra Top 30

		MINT	NRMT
COMPLETE SET (30)		40.00	18.00
COMMON CARD (1-30)		.40	.18
SER.2 STATED ODDS 1:1 RETAIL			
COMP.G.MED.SET (30)		250.00	110.00
*GOLD MED: 4X TO 10X BASE CARD HI			
G.MED SER.2 STATED ODDS 1:18 RETAIL			

❑ 1	Andruw Jones	1.25	.55
❑ 2	Ken Griffey	4.00	1.80
❑ 3	Frank Thomas	1.50	.70
❑ 4	Alex Rodriguez	2.50	1.10
❑ 5	Cal Ripken	3.00	1.35
❑ 6	Mike Piazza	2.50	1.10
❑ 7	Greg Maddux	2.00	.90
❑ 8	Chipper Jones	2.00	.90
❑ 9	Derek Jeter	2.50	1.10
❑ 10	Juan Gonzalez	1.50	.70
❑ 11	Albert Belle	.75	.35
❑ 12	Tony Gwynn	2.00	.90
❑ 13	Jeff Bagwell	.75	.35
❑ 14	Mark McGwire	4.00	1.80
❑ 15	Andy Pettitte	.50	.23
❑ 16	Mo Vaughn	.75	.35
❑ 17	Kenny Lofton	.50	.23
❑ 18	Manny Ramirez	1.00	.45
❑ 19	Roberto Alomar	.75	.35
❑ 20	Ryne Sandberg	1.00	.45
❑ 21	Hideo Nomo	.75	.35
❑ 22	Barry Bonds	1.00	.45
❑ 23	Eddie Murray	.50	.23
❑ 24	Ken Caminiti	.50	.23
❑ 25	John Smoltz	.50	.23
❑ 26	Pat Hentgen	.40	.18
❑ 27	Todd Hollandsworth	.40	.18
❑ 28	Matt Williams	.75	.35
❑ 29	Bernie Williams	.75	.35
❑ 30	Brady Anderson	.40	.18

1998 Ultra

		MINT	NRMT
COMPLETE SET (501)		250.00	110.00
COMPLETE SERIES 1 (250)		150.00	70.00

COMPLETE SERIES 2 (251)	100.00	45.00
COMP.SER.1 w/o SP's (210)	15.00	6.75
COMP.SER.2 w/o SP's (226)	15.00	6.75
COMMON 1 (1-220/246-250)	.15	.07
COMMON 2 (251-475/501)	.15	.07
MINOR STARS	.25	.11
SEMISTARS	.40	.18
UNLISTED STARS	.60	.25
CHECKLISTS ODDS 1:4		
COMMON SC (211-220)	2.50	1.10
SEASON CROWN ODDS 1:12		
COMMON PROS (221-245)	.75	.35
PROS MINOR STARS 221-245	1.25	.55
PROS SEMISTARS 221-245	2.00	.90
PROSPECTS ODDS 1:4		
COMMON PZ (476-500)	.75	.35
PZ SEMISTARS 476-500	1.25	.55
PZ UNLISTED STARS 476-500	2.00	.90
PIZZAZZ ODDS 1:4		
MASTERPIECE 1 OF 1 PARALLELS EXIST		

❑ 1	Ken Griffey Jr.	3.00	1.35
❑ 2	Matt Morris	.15	.07
❑ 3	Roger Clemens	1.50	.70
❑ 4	Matt Williams	.60	.25
❑ 5	Roberto Hernandez	.15	.07
❑ 6	Rondell White	.25	.11
❑ 7	Tim Salmon	.40	.18
❑ 8	Brad Radke	.25	.11
❑ 9	Brett Butler	.25	.11
❑ 10	Carl Everett	.25	.11
❑ 11	Chili Davis	.25	.11
❑ 12	Chuck Finley	.25	.11
❑ 13	Darryl Kile	.15	.07
❑ 14	Deivi Cruz	.15	.07
❑ 15	Gary Gaetti	.25	.11
❑ 16	Matt Stairs	.25	.11
❑ 17	Pat Meares	.15	.07
❑ 18	Will Cunnane	.15	.07
❑ 19	Steve Woodard	.15	.07
❑ 20	Andy Ashby	.15	.07
❑ 21	Bobby Higginson	.25	.11
❑ 22	Brian Jordan	.25	.11
❑ 23	Craig Biggio	.60	.25
❑ 24	Jim Edmonds	.25	.11
❑ 25	Ryan McGuire	.15	.07
❑ 26	Scott Hatteberg	.15	.07
❑ 27	Willie Greene	.15	.07
❑ 28	Albert Belle	.60	.25
❑ 29	Ellis Burks	.25	.11
❑ 30	Hideo Nomo	.60	.25
❑ 31	Jeff Bagwell	.75	.35
❑ 32	Kevin Brown	.40	.18
❑ 33	Nomar Garciaparra	2.00	.90
❑ 34	Pedro Martinez	.75	.35
❑ 35	Raul Mondesi	.25	.11
❑ 36	Ricky Bottalico	.15	.07
❑ 37	Shawn Estes	.15	.07
❑ 38	Otis Nixon	.15	.07
❑ 39	Terry Steinbach	.15	.07
❑ 40	Tom Glavine	.25	.11
❑ 41	Todd Dunwoody	.15	.07
❑ 42	Deion Sanders	.25	.11
❑ 43	Gary Sheffield	.25	.11
❑ 44	Mike Lansing	.15	.07
❑ 45	Mike Lieberthal	.15	.07
❑ 46	Paul Sorrento	.15	.07
❑ 47	Paul O'Neil	.25	.11
❑ 48	Tom Goodwin	.15	.07
❑ 49	Andruw Jones	.60	.25
❑ 50	Barry Bonds	.75	.35
❑ 51	Bernie Williams	.60	.25
❑ 52	Jeremi Gonzalez	.15	.07
❑ 53	Mike Piazza	2.00	.90
❑ 54	Russ Davis	.25	.11
❑ 55	Vinny Castilla	.25	.11
❑ 56	Rod Beck	.25	.11
❑ 57	Andres Galarraga	.40	.18
❑ 58	Ben McDonald	.15	.07
❑ 59	Billy Wagner	.25	.11
❑ 60	Charles Johnson	.25	.11
❑ 61	Fred McGriff	.40	.18
❑ 62	Dean Palmer	.25	.11
❑ 63	Frank Thomas	1.25	.55
❑ 64	Ismael Valdes	.15	.07
❑ 65	Mark Bellhorn	.15	.07

❑ 66	Jeff King	.15	.07
❑ 67	John Wetteland	.25	.11
❑ 68	Mark Grace	.40	.18
❑ 69	Mark Kotsay	.25	.11
❑ 70	Scott Rolen	.75	.35
❑ 71	Todd Hundley	.25	.11
❑ 72	Todd Worrell	.15	.07
❑ 73	Wilson Alvarez	.15	.07
❑ 74	Bobby Jones	.15	.07
❑ 75	Jose Canseco	.75	.35
❑ 76	Kevin Appier	.25	.11
❑ 77	Neifi Perez	.25	.11
❑ 78	Paul Molitor	.60	.25
❑ 79	Quivio Veras	.15	.07
❑ 80	Randy Johnson	.60	.25
❑ 81	Glendon Rusch	.15	.07
❑ 82	Curt Schilling	.40	.18
❑ 83	Alex Rodriguez	2.00	.90
❑ 84	Rey Ordonez	.25	.11
❑ 85	Jeff Juden	.15	.07
❑ 86	Mike Cameron	.25	.11
❑ 87	Ryan Klesko	.25	.11
❑ 88	Trevor Hoffman	.25	.11
❑ 89	Chuck Knoblauch	.25	.11
❑ 90	Larry Walker	.60	.25
❑ 91	Mark McLemore	.15	.07
❑ 92	B.J. Surhoff	.25	.11
❑ 93	Darren Daulton	.25	.11
❑ 94	Ray Durham	.25	.11
❑ 95	Sammy Sosa	2.00	.90
❑ 96	Eric Young	.15	.07
❑ 97	Gerald Williams	.15	.07
❑ 98	Javy Lopez	.25	.11
❑ 99	John Smiley	.15	.07
❑ 100	Juan Gonzalez	1.25	.55
❑ 101	Shawn Green	.60	.25
❑ 102	Charles Nagy	.25	.11
❑ 103	David Justice	.25	.11
❑ 104	Joey Hamilton	.15	.07
❑ 105	Pat Hentgen	.15	.07
❑ 106	Raul Casanova	.15	.07
❑ 107	Tony Phillips	.15	.07
❑ 108	Tony Gwynn	1.50	.70
❑ 109	Will Clark	.60	.25
❑ 110	Jason Giambi	.25	.11
❑ 111	Jay Bell	.25	.11
❑ 112	Johnny Damon	.25	.11
❑ 113	Alan Benes	.15	.07
❑ 114	Jeff Suppan	.15	.07
❑ 115	Kevin Polcovich	.15	.07
❑ 116	Shigetoshi Hasegawa	.25	.11
❑ 117	Steve Finley	.25	.11
❑ 118	Tony Clark	.25	.11
❑ 119	David Cone	.40	.18
❑ 120	Jose Guillen	.15	.07
❑ 121	Kevin Millwood	2.00	.90
❑ 122	Greg Maddux	1.50	.70
❑ 123	Dave Nilsson	.15	.07
❑ 124	Hideki Irabu	.25	.11
❑ 125	Jason Kendall	.25	.11
❑ 126	Jim Thome	.60	.25
❑ 127	Delino DeShields	.15	.07
❑ 128	Edgar Renteria	.15	.07
❑ 129	Edgardo Alfonzo	.40	.18
❑ 130	J.T. Snow	.25	.11
❑ 131	Jeff Abbott	.15	.07
❑ 132	Jeffrey Hammonds	.15	.07
❑ 133	Todd Greene	.15	.07
❑ 134	Vladimir Guerrero	.75	.35
❑ 135	Jay Buhner	.25	.11
❑ 136	Jeff Cirillo	.25	.11
❑ 137	Jeromy Burnitz	.25	.11
❑ 138	Mickey Morandini	.15	.07
❑ 139	Tino Martinez	.25	.11
❑ 140	Jeff Shaw	.15	.07
❑ 141	Rafael Palmeiro	.60	.25
❑ 142	Bobby Bonilla	.25	.11
❑ 143	Cal Ripken	2.50	1.10
❑ 144	Chad Fox	.15	.07
❑ 145	Dante Bichette	.25	.11
❑ 146	Dennis Eckersley	.25	.11
❑ 147	Mariano Rivera	.25	.11
❑ 148	Mo Vaughn	.60	.25
❑ 149	Reggie Sanders	.15	.07
❑ 150	Derek Jeter	2.00	.90
❑ 151	Rusty Greer	.25	.11

152	Brady Anderson	.25	.11
153	Brett Tomko	.15	.07
154	Jaime Navarro	.15	.07
155	Kevin Orie	.15	.07
156	Roberto Alomar	.60	.25
157	Edgar Martinez	.25	.11
158	John Olerud	.25	.11
159	John Smoltz	.40	.18
160	Ryne Sandberg	.75	.35
161	Billy Taylor	.15	.07
162	Chris Holt	.15	.07
163	Damion Easley	.25	.11
164	Darin Erstad	.40	.18
165	Joe Carter	.25	.11
166	Kelvim Escobar	.25	.11
167	Ken Caminiti	.25	.11
168	Pokey Reese	.25	.11
169	Ray Lankford	.25	.11
170	Livan Hernandez	.15	.07
171	Steve Kline	.15	.07
172	Tom Gordon	.25	.11
173	Travis Fryman	.25	.11
174	Al Martin	.15	.07
175	Andy Pettitte	.25	.11
176	Jeff Kent	.25	.11
177	Jimmy Key	.25	.11
178	Mark Grudzielanek	.15	.07
179	Tony Saunders	.15	.07
180	Barry Larkin	.60	.25
181	Bubba Trammell	.15	.07
182	Carlos Delgado	.60	.25
183	Carlos Baerga	.15	.07
184	Derek Bell	.25	.11
185	Henry Rodriguez	.25	.11
186	Jason Dickson	.15	.07
187	Ron Gant	.25	.11
188	Tony Womack	.15	.07
189	Justin Thompson	.15	.07
190	Fernando Tatis	.60	.25
191	Mark Wohlers	.15	.07
192	Takashi Kashiwada	.25	.11
193	Garret Anderson	.25	.11
194	Jose Cruz Jr.	.25	.11
195	Ricardo Rincon	.15	.07
196	Tim Naehring	.15	.07
197	Moises Alou	.25	.11
198	Eric Karros	.25	.11
199	John Jaha	.25	.11
200	Marty Cordova	.15	.07
201	Ken Hill	.15	.07
202	Chipper Jones	1.50	.70
203	Kenny Lofton	.40	.18
204	Mike Mussina	.60	.25
205	Manny Ramirez	.75	.35
206	Todd Hollandsworth	.15	.07
207	Cecil Fielder	.25	.11
208	Mark McGwire	4.00	1.80
209	Jim Leyritz	.15	.07
210	Ivan Rodriguez	.75	.35
211	Jeff Bagwell SC	3.00	1.35
212	Barry Bonds SC	3.00	1.35
213	Roger Clemens SC	6.00	2.70
214	Nomar Garciaparra SC	8.00	3.60
215	Ken Griffey Jr. SC	12.00	5.50
216	Tony Gwynn SC	6.00	2.70
217	Randy Johnson SC	2.50	1.10
218	Mark McGwire SC	15.00	6.75
219	Scott Rolen SC	3.00	1.35
220	Frank Thomas SC	5.00	2.20
221	Matt Perisho PROS	.75	.35
222	Wes Helms PROS	.75	.35
223	Dave Dellucci PROS	1.50	.70
224	Todd Helton PROS	4.00	1.80
225	Brian Rose PROS	.75	.35
226	Aaron Boone PROS	.75	.35
227	Keith Foulke PROS	.75	.35
228	Homer Bush PROS	.75	.35
229	Shannon Stewart PROS	1.25	.55
230	Richard Hidalgo PROS	1.25	.55
231	Russ Johnson PROS	.75	.35
232	Henry Blanco PROS	.75	.35
233	Paul Konerko PROS	1.25	.55
234	Antone Williamson PROS	.75	.35
235	Shane Bowers PROS	.75	.35
236	Jose Vidro PROS	.75	.35
237	Derek Wallace PROS	.75	.35
238	Ricky Ledee PROS	1.25	.55
239	Ben Grieve PROS	3.00	1.35
240	Lou Collier PROS	.75	.35
241	Derrek Lee PROS	.75	.35
242	Ruben Rivera PROS	.75	.35
243	Jorge Velandia PROS	.75	.35
244	Andrew Vessel PROS	.75	.35
245	Chris Carpenter PROS	1.25	.55
246	Ken Griffey Jr. CL	1.50	.70
247	Alex Rodriguez CL	1.00	.45
248	Diamond Ink CL	.15	.07
249	Frank Thomas CL	.60	.25
250	Cal Ripken CL	1.25	.55
251	Carlos Perez	.15	.07
252	Larry Sutton	.15	.07
253	Gary Sheffield	.25	.11
254	Wally Joyner	.25	.11
255	Todd Stottlemyre	.15	.07
256	Nerio Rodriguez	.15	.07
257	Charles Johnson	.25	.11
258	Pedro Astacio	.15	.07
259	Cal Eldred	.15	.07
260	Chili Davis	.25	.11
261	Freddy Garcia	.15	.07
262	Bobby Witt	.15	.07
263	Michael Coleman	.25	.11
264	Mike Caruso	.15	.07
265	Mike Lansing	.15	.07
266	Dennis Reyes	.15	.07
267	F.P. Santangelo	.15	.07
268	Darryl Hamilton	.15	.07
269	Mike Fetters	.15	.07
270	Charlie Hayes	.15	.07
271	Royce Clayton	.15	.07
272	Doug Drabek	.15	.07
273	James Baldwin	.15	.07
274	Brian Hunter	.15	.07
275	Chan Ho Park	.25	.11
276	John Franco	.15	.07
277	David Wells	.25	.11
278	Eli Marrero	.15	.07
279	Kerry Wood	.75	.35
280	Donnie Sadler	.15	.07
281	Scott Winchester	.25	.11
282	Hal Morris	.15	.07
283	Brad Fullmer	.25	.11
284	Bernard Gilkey	.15	.07
285	Ramiro Mendoza	.15	.07
286	Kevin Brown	.40	.18
287	David Segui	.15	.07
288	Willie McGee	.25	.11
289	Darren Oliver	.15	.07
290	Antonio Alfonseca	.15	.07
291	Eric Davis	.25	.11
292	Mickey Morandini	.15	.07
293	Frank Catalanotto	.25	.11
294	Derek Lee	.15	.07
295	Todd Zeile	.15	.07
296	Chuck Knoblauch	.25	.11
297	Wilson Delgado	.15	.07
298	Bobby Bonilla	.25	.11
299	Orel Hershiser	.15	.07
300	Ozzie Guillen	.15	.07
301	Aaron Sele	.15	.07
302	Joe Carter	.25	.11
303	Darryl Kile	.15	.07
304	Shane Reynolds	.25	.11
305	Todd Dunn	.15	.07
306	Bob Abreu	.25	.11
307	Doug Strange	.15	.07
308	Jose Canseco	.75	.35
309	Lance Johnson	.15	.07
310	Harold Baines	.25	.11
311	Todd Pratt	.15	.07
312	Greg Colbrunn	.15	.07
313	Masato Yoshii	.40	.18
314	Felix Heredia	.15	.07
315	Dennis Martinez	.25	.11
316	Geronimo Berroa	.15	.07
317	Darren Lewis	.15	.07
318	Bill Ripken	.15	.07
319	Enrique Wilson	.15	.07
320	Alex Ochoa	.15	.07
321	Doug Glanville	.25	.11
322	Mike Stanley	.15	.07
323	Gerald Williams	.15	.07
324	Pedro Martinez	.75	.35
325	Jaret Wright	.25	.11
326	Terry Pendleton	.25	.11
327	LaTroy Hawkins	.15	.07
328	Emil Brown	.15	.07
329	Walt Weiss	.25	.11
330	Omar Vizquel	.25	.11
331	Carl Everett	.25	.11
332	Fernando Vina	.15	.07
333	Mike Blowers	.15	.07
334	Dwight Gooden	.15	.07
335	Mark Lewis	.15	.07
336	Jim Leyritz	.15	.07
337	Kenny Lofton	.40	.18
338	John Halama	.60	.25
339	Jose Valentin	.15	.07
340	Desi Relaford	.15	.07
341	Dante Powell	.15	.07
342	Ed Sprague	.15	.07
343	Reggie Jefferson	.15	.07
344	Mike Hampton	.25	.11
345	Marquis Grissom	.15	.07
346	Heathcliff Slocumb	.15	.07
347	Francisco Cordova	.15	.07
348	Ken Cloude	.15	.07
349	Benito Santiago	.15	.07
350	Denny Neagle	.15	.07
351	Sean Casey	1.00	.45
352	Robb Nen	.15	.07
353	Orlando Merced	.15	.07
354	Adrian Brown	.15	.07
355	Gregg Jefferies	.15	.07
356	Otis Nixon	.15	.07
357	Michael Tucker	.15	.07
358	Eric Milton	.15	.07
359	Travis Fryman	.25	.11
360	Gary DiSarcina	.15	.07
361	Mario Valdez	.15	.07
362	Craig Counsell	.15	.07
363	Jose Offerman	.25	.11
364	Tony Fernandez	.15	.07
365	Jason McDonald	.15	.07
366	Sterling Hitchcock	.15	.07
367	Donovan Osborne	.15	.07
368	Troy Percival	.25	.11
369	Henry Rodriguez	.15	.07
370	Dmitri Young	.15	.07
371	Jay Powell	.15	.07
372	Jeff Conine	.15	.07
373	Orlando Cabrera	.15	.07
374	Butch Huskey	.15	.07
375	Mike Lowell	.60	.25
376	Kevin Young	.15	.07
377	Jamie Moyer	.15	.07
378	Jeff D'Amico	.15	.07
379	Scott Erickson	.15	.07
380	Magglio Ordonez	2.00	.90
381	Melvin Nieves	.15	.07
382	Ramon Martinez	.15	.07
383	A.J. Hinch	.25	.11
384	Jeff Brantley	.15	.07
385	Kevin Elster	.15	.07
386	Allen Watson	.15	.07
387	Moises Alou	.25	.11
388	Jeff Blauser	.15	.07
389	Pete Harnisch	.15	.07
390	Shane Andrews	.15	.07
391	Rico Brogna	.15	.07
392	Stan Javier	.15	.07
393	David Howard	.15	.07
394	Darryl Strawberry	.25	.11
395	Kent Mercker	.15	.07
396	Juan Encarnacion	.25	.11
397	Sandy Alomar Jr.	.25	.11
398	Al Leiter	.25	.11
399	Tony Graffanino	.15	.07
400	Terry Adams	.15	.07
401	Bruce Aven	.15	.07
402	Derrick Gibson	.15	.07
403	Jose Cabrera	.15	.07
404	Rich Becker	.15	.07
405	David Ortiz	.15	.07
406	Brian McRae	.15	.07
407	Bobby Estalella	.15	.07
408	Bill Mueller	.15	.07
409	Dennis Eckersley	.25	.11

❑ 410 Sandy Martinez	.15	.07	
❑ 411 Jose Vizcaino	.15	.07	
❑ 412 Jermaine Allensworth	.15	.07	
❑ 413 Miguel Tejada	.25	.11	
❑ 414 Turner Ward	.15	.07	
❑ 415 Glenallen Hill	.15	.07	
❑ 416 Lee Stevens	.15	.07	
❑ 417 Cecil Fielder	.25	.11	
❑ 418 Ruben Sierra	.15	.07	
❑ 419 Jon Nunnally	.15	.07	
❑ 420 Rod Myers	.15	.07	
❑ 421 Dustin Hermanson	.15	.07	
❑ 422 James Mouton	.15	.07	
❑ 423 Dan Wilson	.15	.07	
❑ 424 Roberto Kelly	.15	.07	
❑ 425 Antonio Osuna	.15	.07	
❑ 426 Jacob Cruz	.15	.07	
❑ 427 Brent Mayne	.15	.07	
❑ 428 Matt Karchner	.15	.07	
❑ 429 Damian Jackson	.15	.07	
❑ 430 Roger Cedeno	.25	.11	
❑ 431 Rickey Henderson	.75	.35	
❑ 432 Joe Randa	.15	.07	
❑ 433 Greg Vaughn	.25	.11	
❑ 434 Andres Galarraga	.40	.18	
❑ 435 Rod Beck	.15	.07	
❑ 436 Curtis Goodwin	.15	.07	
❑ 437 Brad Ausmus	.15	.07	
❑ 438 Bob Hamelin	.15	.07	
❑ 439 Todd Walker	.25	.11	
❑ 440 Scott Brosius	.25	.11	
❑ 441 Len Dykstra	.25	.11	
❑ 442 Abraham Nunez	.15	.07	
❑ 443 Brian Johnson	.15	.07	
❑ 444 Randy Myers	.15	.07	
❑ 445 Bret Boone	.25	.11	
❑ 446 Oscar Henriquez	.15	.07	
❑ 447 Mike Sweeney	.25	.11	
❑ 448 Kenny Rogers	.15	.07	
❑ 449 Mark Langston	.15	.07	
❑ 450 Luis Gonzalez	.25	.11	
❑ 451 John Burkett	.15	.07	
❑ 452 Bip Roberts	.15	.07	
❑ 453 Travis Lee	.40	.18	
❑ 454 Felix Rodriguez	.15	.07	
❑ 455 Andy Benes	.15	.07	
❑ 456 Willie Blair	.15	.07	
❑ 457 Brian Anderson	.15	.07	
❑ 458 Jay Bell	.25	.11	
❑ 459 Matt Williams	.60	.25	
❑ 460 Devon White	.15	.07	
❑ 461 Karim Garcia	.15	.07	
❑ 462 Jorge Fabregas	.15	.07	
❑ 463 Wilson Alvarez	.15	.07	
❑ 464 Roberto Hernandez	.15	.07	
❑ 465 Tony Saunders	.15	.07	
❑ 466 Rolando Arrojo	.60	.25	
❑ 467 Wade Boggs	.60	.25	
❑ 468 Fred McGriff	.40	.18	
❑ 469 Paul Sorrento	.15	.07	
❑ 470 Kevin Stocker	.15	.07	
❑ 471 Bubba Trammell	.15	.07	
❑ 472 Quinton McCracken	.15	.07	
❑ 473 Ken Griffey Jr. CL	1.50	.70	
❑ 474 Cal Ripken CL	1.25	.55	
❑ 475 Frank Thomas CL	.60	.25	
❑ 476 Ken Griffey Jr. PZ	10.00	4.50	
❑ 477 Cal Ripken PZ	8.00	3.60	
❑ 478 Frank Thomas PZ	4.00	1.80	
❑ 479 Alex Rodriguez PZ	6.00	2.70	
❑ 480 Nomar Garciaparra PZ	6.00	2.70	
❑ 481 Derek Jeter PZ	6.00	2.70	
❑ 482 Andruw Jones PZ	2.00	.90	
❑ 483 Chipper Jones PZ	5.00	2.20	
❑ 484 Greg Maddux PZ	5.00	2.20	
❑ 485 Mike Piazza PZ	6.00	2.70	
❑ 486 Juan Gonzalez PZ	4.00	1.80	
❑ 487 Jose Cruz Jr. PZ	.75	.35	
❑ 488 Jaret Wright PZ	.75	.35	
❑ 489 Hideo Nomo PZ	2.00	.90	
❑ 490 Scott Rolen PZ	2.50	1.10	
❑ 491 Tony Gwynn PZ	5.00	2.20	
❑ 492 Roger Clemens PZ	5.00	2.20	
❑ 493 Darin Erstad PZ	1.25	.55	
❑ 494 Mark McGwire PZ	12.00	5.50	
❑ 495 Jeff Bagwell PZ	2.50	1.10	

❑ 496 Mo Vaughn PZ	2.00	.90	
❑ 497 Albert Belle PZ	2.00	.90	
❑ 498 Kenny Lofton PZ	1.25	.55	
❑ 499 Ben Grieve PZ	2.00	.90	
❑ 500 Barry Bonds PZ	2.50	1.10	
❑ 501 Mike Piazza PZ	5.00	2.20	
❑ S100 Alex Rodriguez AU/750	150.00	70.00	

1998 Ultra Gold Medallion

	MINT	NRMT
COMPLETE SET (501)	400.00	180.00
COMPLETE SERIES 1 (250)	200.00	90.00
COMPLETE SERIES 2 (251)	200.00	90.00
COMMON CARD (1-501)	.50	.23

*STARS: 1.5X TO 4X BASIC CARDS
*YOUNG STARS: 1.25X TO 3X BASIC CARDS
*ROOKIES: 1X TO 2.5X BASIC CARDS
*SEASON CROWNS: .4X TO 1X BASIC SC
*PROSPECTS: .3X TO .8X BASIC PROSPECTS
*CHECKLISTS: 1.5X TO 4X BASIC CL'S
*PIZZAZZ: .5X TO 1.2X BASIC PIZZAZZ
SUBSETS ARE NOT SP'S IN G.MED SET
ONE PER HOBBY PACK

1998 Ultra Platinum Medallion

	MINT	NRMT
COMMON CARD (1-501)	10.00	4.50

*STARS: 25X TO 60X BASIC CARDS
*YNG.STARS: 20X TO 50X BASIC CARDS
*ROOKIES: 12.5X TO 30X BASIC CARDS
*SEASON CROWNS: 3 TO 8X BASIC SC
*PROSPECTS: 4X TO 10X BASIC PROSP.
*CHECKLISTS: 25X TO 60X BASIC CL'S
*PIZZAZZ: 4X TO 10X BASIC PIZZAZZ
RANDOM INSERTS IN HOBBY PACKS
SER.1 PRINT RUN 100 SERIAL #'d SETS
SER.2 PRINT RUN 98 SERIAL #'d SETS
SUBSETS ARE NOT SP'S IN PLAT.MED SET

1998 Ultra Artistic Talents

	MINT	NRMT
COMPLETE SET (18)	80.00	36.00

	MINT	NRMT
COMMON CARD (1-18)	1.25	.55
SER.1 STATED ODDS 1:8		

❑ 1 Ken Griffey Jr.	10.00	4.50	
❑ 2 Andruw Jones	2.00	.90	
❑ 3 Alex Rodriguez	6.00	2.70	
❑ 4 Frank Thomas	4.00	1.80	
❑ 5 Cal Ripken	8.00	3.60	
❑ 6 Derek Jeter	6.00	2.70	
❑ 7 Chipper Jones	5.00	2.20	
❑ 8 Greg Maddux	5.00	2.20	
❑ 9 Mike Piazza	6.00	2.70	
❑ 10 Albert Belle	2.00	.90	
❑ 11 Darin Erstad	1.25	.55	
❑ 12 Juan Gonzalez	4.00	1.80	
❑ 13 Jeff Bagwell	2.50	1.10	
❑ 14 Tony Gwynn	5.00	2.20	
❑ 15 Mark McGwire	12.00	5.50	
❑ 16 Scott Rolen	3.00	1.35	
❑ 17 Barry Bonds	2.50	1.10	
❑ 18 Kenny Lofton	1.25	.55	

1998 Ultra Back to the Future

	MINT	NRMT
COMPLETE SET (15)	20.00	9.00
COMMON CARD (1-15)	.30	.14
SER.1 STATED ODDS 1:6		

❑ 1 Andruw Jones	1.25	.55	
❑ 2 Alex Rodriguez	4.00	1.80	
❑ 3 Derek Jeter	4.00	1.80	
❑ 4 Darin Erstad	.75	.35	
❑ 5 Mike Cameron	.50	.23	
❑ 6 Scott Rolen	2.00	.90	
❑ 7 Nomar Garciaparra	4.00	1.80	
❑ 8 Hideki Irabu	.50	.23	
❑ 9 Jose Cruz Jr.	.50	.23	
❑ 10 Vladimir Guerrero	1.50	.70	
❑ 11 Mark Kotsay	.50	.23	
❑ 12 Tony Womack	.30	.14	
❑ 13 Jason Dickson	.30	.14	
❑ 14 Jose Guillen	.30	.14	
❑ 15 Tony Clark	.50	.23	

1998 Ultra Big Shots

	MINT	NRMT
COMPLETE SET (15)	12.00	5.50

	MINT	NRMT
COMMON CARD (1-15)	.30	.14
SER.1 STATED ODDS 1:4		

☐ 1 Ken Griffey Jr.	4.00	1.80
☐ 2 Frank Thomas	1.50	.70
☐ 3 Chipper Jones	2.00	.90
☐ 4 Albert Belle	.75	.35
☐ 5 Juan Gonzalez	1.50	.70
☐ 6 Jeff Bagwell	1.00	.45
☐ 7 Mark McGwire	5.00	2.20
☐ 8 Barry Bonds	1.00	.45
☐ 9 Manny Ramirez	1.00	.45
☐ 10 Mo Vaughn	.75	.35
☐ 11 Matt Williams	.75	.35
☐ 12 Jim Thome	.75	.35
☐ 13 Tino Martinez	.30	.14
☐ 14 Mike Piazza	2.50	1.10
☐ 15 Tony Clark	.30	.14

1998 Ultra Diamond Immortals

	MINT	NRMT
COMPLETE SET (15)	800.00	350.00
COMMON CARD (1-15)	8.00	3.60
UNLISTED STARS	20.00	9.00
SER.2 STATED ODDS 1:288		

☐ 1 Ken Griffey Jr.	100.00	45.00
☐ 2 Frank Thomas	40.00	18.00
☐ 3 Alex Rodriguez	60.00	27.00
☐ 4 Cal Ripken	80.00	36.00
☐ 5 Mike Piazza	60.00	27.00
☐ 6 Mark McGwire	120.00	55.00
☐ 7 Greg Maddux	50.00	22.00
☐ 8 Andruw Jones	20.00	9.00
☐ 9 Chipper Jones	50.00	22.00
☐ 10 Derek Jeter	60.00	27.00
☐ 11 Tony Gwynn	50.00	22.00
☐ 12 Juan Gonzalez	40.00	18.00
☐ 13 Jose Cruz Jr.	8.00	3.60
☐ 14 Roger Clemens	50.00	22.00
☐ 15 Barry Bonds	25.00	11.00

1998 Ultra Diamond Producers

	MINT	NRMT
COMPLETE SET (15)	750.00	350.00
COMMON CARD (1-15)	8.00	3.60

	MINT	NRMT
UNLISTED STARS	20.00	9.00
SER.1 STATED ODDS 1:288		
CONDITION SENSITIVE SET		

☐ 1 Ken Griffey Jr.	100.00	45.00
☐ 2 Andruw Jones	20.00	9.00
☐ 3 Alex Rodriguez	60.00	27.00
☐ 4 Frank Thomas	40.00	18.00
☐ 5 Cal Ripken	80.00	36.00
☐ 6 Derek Jeter	60.00	27.00
☐ 7 Chipper Jones	50.00	22.00
☐ 8 Greg Maddux	50.00	22.00
☐ 9 Mike Piazza	60.00	27.00
☐ 10 Juan Gonzalez	40.00	18.00
☐ 11 Jeff Bagwell	25.00	11.00
☐ 12 Tony Gwynn	50.00	22.00
☐ 13 Mark McGwire	120.00	55.00
☐ 14 Barry Bonds	25.00	11.00
☐ 15 Jose Cruz Jr.	8.00	3.60

1998 Ultra Double Trouble

	MINT	NRMT
COMPLETE SET (20)	12.00	5.50
COMMON CARD (1-20)	.25	.11
SEMISTARS	.40	.18
UNLISTED STARS	.60	.25
SER.1 STATED ODDS 1:4		

☐ 1 Ken Griffey Jr. Alex Rodriguez	4.00	1.80
☐ 2 Vladimir Guerrero Pedro Martinez	1.00	.45
☐ 3 Andruw Jones Kenny Lofton	.60	.25
☐ 4 Chipper Jones Greg Maddux	2.00	.90
☐ 5 Derek Jeter Tino Martinez	2.00	.90
☐ 6 Frank Thomas Albert Belle	1.25	.55
☐ 7 Cal Ripken Roberto Alomar	2.50	1.10
☐ 8 Mike Piazza Hideo Nomo	2.00	.90
☐ 9 Darin Erstad Jason Dickson	.40	.18
☐ 10 Juan Gonzalez Ivan Rodriguez	1.50	.70
☐ 11 Jeff Bagwell Darryl Kile UER front by Kyle	.75	.35
☐ 12 Tony Gwynn Steve Finley	1.50	.70
☐ 13 Mark McGwire Ray Lankford	4.00	1.80
☐ 14 Barry Bonds Jeff Kent	.75	.35
☐ 15 Andy Pettitte Bernie Williams	.60	.25
☐ 16 Mo Vaughn Nomar Garciaparra	2.00	.90
☐ 17 Matt Williams Jim Thome	.60	.25
☐ 18 Hideki Irabu Mariano Rivera	.25	.11
☐ 19 Roger Clemens Jose Cruz Jr.	1.50	.70
☐ 20 Manny Ramirez David Justice	.75	.35

1998 Ultra Fall Classics

	MINT	NRMT
COMPLETE SET (15)	120.00	55.00
COMMON CARD (1-15)	4.00	1.80
SER.1 STATED ODDS 1:18		

☐ 1 Ken Griffey Jr.	20.00	9.00
☐ 2 Andruw Jones	4.00	1.80
☐ 3 Alex Rodriguez	12.00	5.50
☐ 4 Frank Thomas	8.00	3.60
☐ 5 Cal Ripken	15.00	6.75
☐ 6 Derek Jeter	12.00	5.50
☐ 7 Chipper Jones	10.00	4.50
☐ 8 Greg Maddux	10.00	4.50
☐ 9 Mike Piazza	12.00	5.50
☐ 10 Albert Belle	4.00	1.80
☐ 11 Juan Gonzalez	8.00	3.60
☐ 12 Jeff Bagwell	5.00	2.20
☐ 13 Tony Gwynn	10.00	4.50
☐ 14 Mark McGwire	25.00	11.00
☐ 15 Barry Bonds	5.00	2.20

1998 Ultra Kid Gloves

	MINT	NRMT
COMPLETE SET (12)	20.00	9.00
COMMON CARD (1-12)	.50	.23
SER.1 STATED ODDS 1:8		

#	Player	MINT	NRMT
1	Andruw Jones	1.25	.55
2	Alex Rodriguez	4.00	1.80
3	Derek Jeter	4.00	1.80
4	Chipper Jones	3.00	1.35
5	Darin Erstad	.75	.35
6	Todd Walker	.50	.23
7	Scott Rolen	2.00	.90
8	Nomar Garciaparra	4.00	1.80
9	Jose Cruz Jr.	.50	.23
10	Charles Johnson	.50	.23
11	Rey Ordonez	.50	.23
12	Vladimir Guerrero	1.50	.70

7	Mark McGwire	8.00	3.60
8	Barry Bonds	1.50	.70
9	Scott Rolen	2.00	.90
10	Mo Vaughn	1.25	.55
11	Andruw Jones	1.25	.55
12	Chipper Jones	3.00	1.35
13	Tino Martinez	.50	.23
14	Mike Piazza	4.00	1.80
15	Tony Clark	.50	.23
16	Jose Cruz Jr.	.50	.23
17	Nomar Garciaparra	4.00	1.80
18	Cal Ripken	5.00	2.20
19	Alex Rodriguez	4.00	1.80
20	Derek Jeter	4.00	1.80

8	Greg Maddux	40.00	18.00
9	Mike Piazza	50.00	22.00
10	Albert Belle	15.00	6.75
11	Darin Erstad	10.00	4.50
12	Juan Gonzalez	30.00	13.50
13	Jeff Bagwell	20.00	9.00
14	Tony Gwynn	40.00	18.00
15	Roberto Alomar	15.00	6.75
16	Barry Bonds	20.00	9.00
17	Kenny Lofton	10.00	4.50
18	Jose Cruz Jr.	6.00	2.70

1998 Ultra Millennium Men

	MINT	NRMT
COMPLETE SET (15)	150.00	70.00
COMMON CARD (1-15)	2.00	.90
SER.2 STATED ODDS 1:35 HOBBY		

#	Player	MINT	NRMT
1	Jose Cruz Jr.	2.00	.90
2	Ken Griffey Jr.	25.00	11.00
3	Cal Ripken	20.00	9.00
4	Derek Jeter	15.00	6.75
5	Andruw Jones	5.00	2.20
6	Alex Rodriguez	15.00	6.75
7	Chipper Jones	12.00	5.50
8	Scott Rolen	8.00	3.60
9	Nomar Garciaparra	15.00	6.75
10	Frank Thomas	10.00	4.50
11	Mike Piazza	15.00	6.75
12	Greg Maddux	12.00	5.50
13	Juan Gonzalez	10.00	4.50
14	Ben Grieve	5.00	2.20
15	Jaret Wright	2.00	.90

1998 Ultra Notables

	MINT	NRMT
COMPLETE SET (20)	40.00	18.00
COMMON CARD (1-20)	.50	.23
SER.2 STATED ODDS 1:4		

#	Player	MINT	NRMT
1	Frank Thomas	2.50	1.10
2	Ken Griffey Jr.	6.00	2.70
3	Edgar Renteria	.50	.23
4	Albert Belle	1.25	.55
5	Juan Gonzalez	2.50	1.10
6	Jeff Bagwell	1.50	.70

1998 Ultra Power Plus

	MINT	NRMT
COMPLETE SET (10)	120.00	55.00
COMMON CARD (1-10)	2.50	1.10
SER.1 STATED ODDS 1:36		

#	Player	MINT	NRMT
1	Ken Griffey Jr.	30.00	13.50
2	Andruw Jones	6.00	2.70
3	Alex Rodriguez	20.00	9.00
4	Frank Thomas	12.00	5.50
5	Mike Piazza	20.00	9.00
6	Albert Belle	6.00	2.70
7	Juan Gonzalez	12.00	5.50
8	Jeff Bagwell	8.00	3.60
9	Barry Bonds	8.00	3.60
10	Jose Cruz Jr.	2.50	1.10

1998 Ultra Prime Leather

	MINT	NRMT
COMPLETE SET (18)	600.00	275.00
COMMON CARD (1-18)	6.00	2.70
SEMISTARS	10.00	4.50
UNLISTED STARS	15.00	6.75
SER.1 STATED ODDS 1:144		

#	Player	MINT	NRMT
1	Ken Griffey Jr.	80.00	36.00
2	Andruw Jones	15.00	6.75
3	Alex Rodriguez	50.00	22.00
4	Frank Thomas	30.00	13.50
5	Cal Ripken	60.00	27.00
6	Derek Jeter	50.00	22.00
7	Chipper Jones	40.00	18.00

1998 Ultra Rocket to Stardom

	MINT	NRMT
COMPLETE SET (15)	30.00	13.50
COMMON CARD (1-15)	1.00	.45
MINOR STARS	1.50	.70
SEMISTARS	2.50	1.10
UNLISTED STARS	4.00	1.80
SER.2 STATED ODDS 1:20		

#	Player	MINT	NRMT
1	Ben Grieve	4.00	1.80
2	Magglio Ordonez	10.00	4.50
3	Travis Lee	2.50	1.10
4	Mike Caruso	1.00	.45
5	Brian Rose	1.00	.45
6	Brad Fullmer	1.00	.45
7	Michael Coleman	1.50	.70
8	Juan Encarnacion	1.50	.70
9	Karim Garcia	1.00	.45
10	Todd Helton	5.00	2.20
11	Richard Hidalgo	1.50	.70
12	Paul Konerko	1.50	.70
13	Rod Myers	1.00	.45
14	Jaret Wright	1.50	.70
15	Miguel Tejada	1.50	.70

1998 Ultra Ticket Studs

	MINT	NRMT
COMPLETE SET (15)	600.00	275.00
COMMON CARD (1-15)	6.00	2.70
SEMISTARS	10.00	4.50
UNLISTED STARS	15.00	6.75
SER.2 STATED ODDS 1:144		

#	Player	MINT	NRMT
1	Travis Lee	10.00	4.50
2	Tony Gwynn	40.00	18.00

			MINT	NRMT
❑ 3	Scott Rolen		20.00	9.00
❑ 4	Nomar Garciaparra		50.00	22.00
❑ 5	Mike Piazza		50.00	22.00
❑ 6	Mark McGwire		100.00	45.00
❑ 7	Ken Griffey Jr.		80.00	36.00
❑ 8	Juan Gonzalez		30.00	13.50
❑ 9	Jose Cruz Jr.		6.00	2.70
❑ 10	Frank Thomas		30.00	13.50
❑ 11	Derek Jeter		50.00	22.00
❑ 12	Chipper Jones		40.00	18.00
❑ 13	Cal Ripken		60.00	27.00
❑ 14	Andruw Jones		15.00	6.75
❑ 15	Alex Rodriguez		50.00	22.00

1998 Ultra Top 30

		MINT	NRMT
COMPLETE SET (30)		40.00	18.00
COMMON CARD (1-30)		.40	.18
ONE PER SER.2 RETAIL PACK			
❑ 1 Barry Bonds		1.00	.45
❑ 2 Ivan Rodriguez		1.00	.45
❑ 3 Kenny Lofton		.50	.23
❑ 4 Albert Belle		.75	.35
❑ 5 Mo Vaughn		.75	.35
❑ 6 Jeff Bagwell		1.00	.45
❑ 7 Mark McGwire		5.00	2.20
❑ 8 Darin Erstad		.50	.23
❑ 9 Roger Clemens		2.00	.90
❑ 10 Tony Gwynn		2.00	.90
❑ 11 Scott Rolen		1.25	.55
❑ 12 Hideo Nomo		.75	.35
❑ 13 Juan Gonzalez		1.50	.70
❑ 14 Mike Piazza		2.50	1.10
❑ 15 Greg Maddux		2.00	.90
❑ 16 Chipper Jones		2.00	.90
❑ 17 Andruw Jones		.75	.35
❑ 18 Derek Jeter		2.50	1.10
❑ 19 Nomar Garciaparra		2.50	1.10
❑ 20 Alex Rodriguez		2.50	1.10
❑ 21 Frank Thomas		1.50	.70
❑ 22 Cal Ripken		3.00	1.35
❑ 23 Ken Griffey Jr.		4.00	1.80
❑ 24 Jose Cruz Jr.		.40	.18
❑ 25 Jaret Wright		.40	.18
❑ 26 Travis Lee		.50	.23
❑ 27 Wade Boggs		.75	.35
❑ 28 Chuck Knoblauch		.40	.18
❑ 29 Joe Carter		.40	.18
❑ 30 Ben Grieve		.75	.35

1998 Ultra Win Now

	MINT	NRMT
COMPLETE SET (20)	400.00	180.00
COMMON CARD (1-20)	4.00	1.80
SEMISTARS	6.00	2.70
UNLISTED STARS	10.00	4.50
SER.2 STATED ODDS 1:72		
❑ 1 Alex Rodriguez	30.00	13.50
❑ 2 Andruw Jones	10.00	4.50
❑ 3 Cal Ripken	40.00	18.00
❑ 4 Chipper Jones	25.00	11.00
❑ 5 Darin Erstad	6.00	2.70
❑ 6 Derek Jeter	30.00	13.50
❑ 7 Frank Thomas	20.00	9.00

			MINT	NRMT
❑ 8	Greg Maddux		25.00	11.00
❑ 9	Hideo Nomo		10.00	4.50
❑ 10	Jeff Bagwell		12.00	5.50
❑ 11	Jose Cruz Jr.		4.00	1.80
❑ 12	Juan Gonzalez		20.00	9.00
❑ 13	Ken Griffey Jr.		50.00	22.00
❑ 14	Mark McGwire		60.00	27.00
❑ 15	Mike Piazza		30.00	13.50
❑ 16	Mo Vaughn		10.00	4.50
❑ 17	Nomar Garciaparra		30.00	13.50
❑ 18	Roger Clemens		25.00	11.00
❑ 19	Scott Rolen		12.00	5.50
❑ 20	Tony Gwynn		25.00	11.00

1999 Ultra

	MINT	NRMT
COMPLETE SET (250)	100.00	45.00
COMP.SET w/o SP's (215)	20.00	9.00
COMMON CARD (1-215)	.15	.07
MINOR STARS	.25	.11
SEMISTARS	.40	.18
UNLISTED STARS	.60	.25
COMMON SC (216-225)	1.00	.45
SC UNLISTED STARS	1.50	.70
SEASON CROWN STATED ODDS 1:8		
COMMON PROSPECT (226-250)	1.50	.70
PROSPECT MINOR STARS	2.00	.90
PROSPECT SEMISTARS	3.00	1.35
PROSPECT UNLISTED STARS	4.00	1.80
PROSPECT STATED ODDS 1:4		
❑ 1 Greg Maddux	1.50	.70
❑ 2 Greg Vaughn	.25	.11
❑ 3 John Wetteland	.25	.11
❑ 4 Tino Martinez	.25	.11
❑ 5 Todd Walker	.25	.11
❑ 6 Troy O'Leary	.15	.07
❑ 7 Barry Larkin	.60	.25
❑ 8 Mike Lansing	.15	.07
❑ 9 Delino DeShields	.15	.07
❑ 10 Brett Tomko	.15	.07
❑ 11 Carlos Perez	.15	.07
❑ 12 Mark Langston	.15	.07
❑ 13 Jamie Moyer	.15	.07
❑ 14 Jose Guillen	.15	.07
❑ 15 Bartolo Colon	.25	.11
❑ 16 Brady Anderson	.25	.11
❑ 17 Walt Weiss	.15	.07
❑ 18 Shane Reynolds	.25	.11
❑ 19 David Segui	.15	.07

			MINT	NRMT
❑ 20	Vladimir Guerrero		.75	.35
❑ 21	Freddy Garcia		.15	.07
❑ 22	Carl Everett		.25	.11
❑ 23	Jose Cruz Jr.		.25	.11
❑ 24	David Ortiz		.15	.07
❑ 25	Andruw Jones		.60	.25
❑ 26	Darren Lewis		.15	.07
❑ 27	Ray Lankford		.25	.11
❑ 28	Wally Joyner		.25	.11
❑ 29	Charles Johnson		.25	.11
❑ 30	Derek Jeter		2.00	.90
❑ 31	Sean Casey		.60	.25
❑ 32	Bobby Bonilla		.25	.11
❑ 33	Todd Zeile		.25	.11
❑ 34	Todd Helton		.60	.25
❑ 35	David Wells		.25	.11
❑ 36	Darin Erstad		.40	.18
❑ 37	Ivan Rodriguez		.75	.35
❑ 38	Antonio Osuna		.15	.07
❑ 39	Mickey Morandini		.15	.07
❑ 40	Rusty Greer		.25	.11
❑ 41	Rod Beck		.25	.11
❑ 42	Larry Sutton		.15	.07
❑ 43	Edgar Renteria		.25	.11
❑ 44	Otis Nixon		.15	.07
❑ 45	Eli Marrero		.15	.07
❑ 46	Reggie Jefferson		.15	.07
❑ 47	Trevor Hoffman		.25	.11
❑ 48	Andres Galarraga		.40	.18
❑ 49	Scott Brosius		.25	.11
❑ 50	Vinny Castilla		.25	.11
❑ 51	Brett Boone		.25	.11
❑ 52	Masato Yoshii		.25	.11
❑ 53	Matt Williams		.60	.25
❑ 54	Robin Ventura		.25	.11
❑ 55	Jay Powell		.15	.07
❑ 56	Dean Palmer		.25	.11
❑ 57	Eric Milton		.15	.07
❑ 58	Willie McGee		.25	.11
❑ 59	Tony Gwynn		1.50	.70
❑ 60	Tom Gordon		.25	.11
❑ 61	Dante Bichette		.25	.11
❑ 62	Jaret Wright		.25	.11
❑ 63	Devon White		.15	.07
❑ 64	Frank Thomas		1.25	.55
❑ 65	Mike Piazza		2.00	.90
❑ 66	Jose Offerman		.25	.11
❑ 67	Pat Meares		.15	.07
❑ 68	Brian Meadows		.15	.07
❑ 69	Nomar Garciaparra		2.00	.90
❑ 70	Mark McGwire		4.00	1.80
❑ 71	Tony Graffanino		.15	.07
❑ 72	Ken Griffey Jr.		3.00	1.35
❑ 73	Ken Caminiti		.25	.11
❑ 74	Todd Jones		.15	.07
❑ 75	A.J. Hinch		.15	.07
❑ 76	Marquis Grissom		.15	.07
❑ 77	Jay Buhner		.25	.11
❑ 78	Albert Belle		.60	.25
❑ 79	Brian Anderson		.15	.07
❑ 80	Quinton McCracken		.15	.07
❑ 81	Omar Vizquel		.25	.11
❑ 82	Todd Stottlemyre		.15	.07
❑ 83	Cal Ripken		2.50	1.10
❑ 84	Magglio Ordonez		.60	.25
❑ 85	John Olerud		.25	.11
❑ 86	Hal Morris		.15	.07
❑ 87	Derek Lee		.15	.07
❑ 88	Doug Glanville		.25	.11
❑ 89	Marty Cordova		.15	.07
❑ 90	Kevin Brown		.40	.18
❑ 91	Kevin Young		.25	.11
❑ 92	Rico Brogna		.15	.07
❑ 93	Wilson Alvarez		.15	.07
❑ 94	Bob Wickman		.15	.07
❑ 95	Jim Thome		.60	.25
❑ 96	Mike Mussina		.60	.25
❑ 97	Al Leiter		.25	.11
❑ 98	Travis Lee		.40	.18
❑ 99	Jeff King		.15	.07
❑ 100	Kerry Wood		.60	.25
❑ 101	Cliff Floyd		.25	.11
❑ 102	Jose Valentin		.15	.07
❑ 103	Manny Ramirez		.75	.35
❑ 104	Butch Huskey		.15	.07
❑ 105	Scott Erickson		.15	.07

❏ 106 Ray Durham	.25	.11
❏ 107 Johnny Damon	.25	.11
❏ 108 Craig Counsell	.15	.07
❏ 109 Rolando Arrojo	.15	.07
❏ 110 Bob Abreu	.25	.11
❏ 111 Tony Womack	.15	.07
❏ 112 Mike Stanley	.15	.07
❏ 113 Kenny Lofton	.40	.18
❏ 114 Eric Davis	.25	.11
❏ 115 Jeff Conine	.15	.07
❏ 116 Carlos Baerga	.15	.07
❏ 117 Rondell White	.25	.11
❏ 118 Billy Wagner	.25	.11
❏ 119 Ed Sprague	.15	.07
❏ 120 Jason Schmidt	.15	.07
❏ 121 Edgar Martinez	.25	.11
❏ 122 Travis Fryman	.25	.11
❏ 123 Armando Benitez	.15	.07
❏ 124 Matt Stairs	.15	.07
❏ 125 Roberto Hernandez	.15	.07
❏ 126 Jay Bell	.25	.11
❏ 127 Justin Thompson	.15	.07
❏ 128 John Jaha	.15	.07
❏ 129 Mike Caruso	.15	.07
❏ 130 Miguel Tejada	.25	.11
❏ 131 Geoff Jenkins	.25	.11
❏ 132 Wade Boggs	.60	.25
❏ 133 Andy Benes	.15	.07
❏ 134 Aaron Sele	.25	.11
❏ 135 Bret Saberhagen	.25	.11
❏ 136 Mariano Rivera	.25	.11
❏ 137 Neifi Perez	.25	.11
❏ 138 Paul Konerko	.60	.25
❏ 139 Barry Bonds	.75	.35
❏ 140 Garret Anderson	.25	.11
❏ 141 Bernie Williams	.60	.25
❏ 142 Gary Sheffield	.25	.11
❏ 143 Rafael Palmeiro	.60	.25
❏ 144 Orel Hershiser	.25	.11
❏ 145 Craig Biggio	.60	.25
❏ 146 Dmitri Young	.25	.11
❏ 147 Damion Easley	.25	.11
❏ 148 Henry Rodriguez	.25	.11
❏ 149 Brad Radke	.25	.11
❏ 150 Pedro Martinez	.75	.35
❏ 151 Mike Lieberthal	.25	.11
❏ 152 Jim Leyritz	.15	.07
❏ 153 Chuck Knoblauch	.25	.11
❏ 154 Darryl Kile	.15	.07
❏ 155 Brian Jordan	.25	.11
❏ 156 Chipper Jones	1.50	.70
❏ 157 Pete Harnisch	.15	.07
❏ 158 Moises Alou	.25	.11
❏ 159 Ismael Valdes	.15	.07
❏ 160 Stan Javier	.15	.07
❏ 161 Mark Grace	.40	.18
❏ 162 Jason Giambi	.25	.11
❏ 163 Chuck Finley	.25	.11
❏ 164 Juan Encarnacion	.25	.11
❏ 165 Chan Ho Park	.25	.11
❏ 166 Randy Johnson	.60	.25
❏ 167 J.T. Snow	.25	.11
❏ 168 Tim Salmon	.40	.18
❏ 169 Brian L.Hunter	.15	.07
❏ 170 Rickey Henderson	.75	.35
❏ 171 Cal Eldred	.15	.07
❏ 172 Curt Schilling	.40	.18
❏ 173 Alex Rodriguez	2.00	.90
❏ 174 Dustin Hermanson	.15	.07
❏ 175 Mike Hampton	.25	.11
❏ 176 Shawn Green	.60	.25
❏ 177 Roberto Alomar	.60	.25
❏ 178 Sandy Alomar Jr.	.25	.11
❏ 179 Larry Walker	.60	.25
❏ 180 Mo Vaughn	.60	.25
❏ 181 Raul Mondesi	.25	.11
❏ 182 Hideki Irabu	.25	.11
❏ 183 Jim Edmonds	.25	.11
❏ 184 Shawn Estes	.15	.07
❏ 185 Tony Clark	.25	.11
❏ 186 Dan Wilson	.15	.07
❏ 187 Michael Tucker	.15	.07
❏ 188 Jeff Shaw	.15	.07
❏ 189 Mark Grudzielanek	.15	.07
❏ 190 Roger Clemens	1.50	.70
❏ 191 Juan Gonzalez	1.25	.55

❏ 192 Sammy Sosa	2.00	.90
❏ 193 Troy Percival	.15	.07
❏ 194 Robb Nen	.15	.07
❏ 195 Bill Mueller	.15	.07
❏ 196 Ben Grieve	.60	.25
❏ 197 Luis Gonzalez	.25	.11
❏ 198 Will Clark	.60	.25
❏ 199 Jeff Cirillo	.25	.11
❏ 200 Scott Rolen	.75	.35
❏ 201 Reggie Sanders	.15	.07
❏ 202 Fred McGriff	.40	.18
❏ 203 Denny Neagle	.15	.07
❏ 204 Brad Fullmer	.15	.07
❏ 205 Royce Clayton	.15	.07
❏ 206 Jose Canseco	.75	.35
❏ 207 Jeff Bagwell	.75	.35
❏ 208 Hideo Nomo	.60	.25
❏ 209 Karim Garcia	.15	.07
❏ 210 Kenny Rogers	.15	.07
❏ 211 Kerry Wood CL	.25	.11
❏ 212 Alex Rodriguez CL	1.00	.45
❏ 213 Cal Ripken CL	1.25	.55
❏ 214 Frank Thomas CL	.60	.25
❏ 215 Ken Griffey Jr. CL	1.50	.70
❏ 216 Alex Rodriguez SC	5.00	2.20
❏ 217 Greg Maddux SC	4.00	1.80
❏ 218 Juan Gonzalez SC	3.00	1.35
❏ 219 Ken Griffey Jr. SC	8.00	3.60
❏ 220 Kerry Wood SC	1.50	.70
❏ 221 Mark McGwire SC	10.00	4.50
❏ 222 Mike Piazza SC	5.00	2.20
❏ 223 Rickey Henderson SC	2.00	.90
❏ 224 Sammy Sosa SC	5.00	2.20
❏ 225 Travis Lee SC	1.00	.45
❏ 226 Gabe Alvarez PROS	1.50	.70
❏ 227 Matt Anderson PROS	1.50	.70
❏ 228 Adrian Beltre PROS	4.00	1.80
❏ 229 Orlando Cabrera PROS	1.50	.70
❏ 230 Orl. Hernandez PROS	4.00	1.80
❏ 231 Aramis Ramirez PROS	3.00	1.35
❏ 232 Troy Glaus PROS	5.00	2.20
❏ 233 Gabe Kapler PROS	4.00	1.80
❏ 234 Jeremy Giambi PROS	2.00	.90
❏ 235 Derrick Gibson PROS	2.00	.90
❏ 236 Carlton Loewer PROS	1.50	.70
❏ 237 Mike Frank PROS	1.50	.70
❏ 238 Carlos Guillen PROS	1.50	.70
❏ 239 Alex Gonzalez PROS	2.00	.90
❏ 240 Enrique Wilson PROS	1.50	.70
❏ 241 J.D. Drew PROS	8.00	3.60
❏ 242 Bruce Chen PROS	2.00	.90
❏ 243 Ryan Minor PROS	2.00	.90
❏ 244 Preston Wilson PROS	2.00	.90
❏ 245 Josh Booty PROS	1.50	.70
❏ 246 Luis Ordaz PROS	1.50	.70
❏ 247 George Lombard PROS	2.00	.90
❏ 248 Matt Clement PROS	2.00	.90
❏ 249 Eric Chavez PROS	3.00	1.35
❏ 250 Corey Koskie PROS	1.50	.70

1999 Ultra Gold Medallion

	MINT	NRMT
COMPLETE SET (250)	500.00	220.00
COMMON CARD (1-215)	.50	.23
*STARS: 1.5X TO 4X BASIC CARDS
*YOUNG STARS: 1.25X TO 3X BASIC CARDS
ONE PER HOBBY PACK

COMMON SC (216-225) 5.00 2.20
SEASON CROWN STATED ODDS 1:80 HOBBY
COMMON PROSPECT (226-250) 4.00 1.80
*PROSPECTS: 1X TO 2.5X BASIC PROSPECTS
PROSPECT STATED ODDS 1:40 HOBBY

1999 Ultra Masterpiece

RANDOM INSERTS IN HOBBY PACKS
STATED PRINT RUN 1 SERIAL #'d SET
NOT PRICED DUE TO SCARCITY

1999 Ultra Platinum Medallion

	MINT	NRMT
COMMON CARD (1-215)	8.00	3.60
*STARS: 20X TO 50X BASIC CARDS
*YNG.STARS: 15X TO 40X BASIC CARDS
BASIC 1-215 PRINT RUN 99 SERIAL #'d SETS
| COMMON SC (216-225) | 40.00 | 18.00 |
*SC STARS: 15X TO 40X BASIC SC
SEAS.CROWN PRINT RUN 50 SERIAL #'d SETS
| COMMON PROSPECT (226-250) | 12.00 | 5.50 |
*PROSPECTS: 3X TO 8X BASIC PROSPECTS
PROSPECT PRINT RUN 65 SERIAL #'d SETS
RANDOM INSERTS IN HOBBY PACKS

1999 Ultra The Book On

	MINT	NRMT
COMPLETE SET (20)	50.00	22.00
COMMON CARD (1-20)	1.00	.45

	MINT	NRMT
UNLISTED STARS	1.50	.70
SER.1 STATED ODDS 1:6		
❏ 1 Kerry Wood	1.50	.70
❏ 2 Ken Griffey Jr.	8.00	3.60
❏ 3 Frank Thomas	3.00	1.35
❏ 4 Albert Belle	1.50	.70
❏ 5 Juan Gonzalez	3.00	1.35
❏ 6 Jeff Bagwell	2.00	.90
❏ 7 Mark McGwire	4.00	4.50
❏ 8 Barry Bonds	2.00	.90
❏ 9 Andruw Jones	1.50	.70
❏ 10 Mo Vaughn	1.50	.70
❏ 11 Scott Rolen	2.50	1.10
❏ 12 Travis Lee	1.00	.45
❏ 13 Tony Gwynn	4.00	1.80
❏ 14 Greg Maddux	4.00	1.80
❏ 15 Mike Piazza	5.00	2.20
❏ 16 Chipper Jones	4.00	1.80
❏ 17 Nomar Garciaparra	5.00	2.20
❏ 18 Cal Ripken	6.00	2.70
❏ 19 Derek Jeter	5.00	2.20
❏ 20 Alex Rodriguez	5.00	2.20

1999 Ultra Damage Inc.

	MINT	NRMT
COMPLETE SET (15)	300.00	135.00
COMMON CARD (1-15)	8.00	2.20
UNLISTED STARS	8.00	3.60
SER.1 STATED ODDS 1:72		
❏ 1 Alex Rodriguez	25.00	11.00
❏ 2 Greg Maddux	20.00	9.00
❏ 3 Cal Ripken	30.00	13.50
❏ 4 Chipper Jones	20.00	9.00
❏ 5 Derek Jeter	25.00	11.00
❏ 6 Frank Thomas	15.00	6.75
❏ 7 Juan Gonzalez	15.00	6.75
❏ 8 Ken Griffey Jr.	40.00	18.00
❏ 9 Kerry Wood	8.00	3.60
❏ 10 Mark McGwire	50.00	22.00
❏ 11 Mike Piazza	25.00	11.00
❏ 12 Nomar Garciaparra	25.00	11.00
❏ 13 Scott Rolen	10.00	4.50
❏ 14 Tony Gwynn	20.00	9.00
❏ 15 Travis Lee	5.00	2.20

1999 Ultra Diamond Producers

	MINT	NRMT
COMPLETE SET (10)	600.00	275.00
COMMON CARD (1-10)	15.00	6.75
SER.1 STATED ODDS 1:288		
❏ 1 Ken Griffey Jr.	100.00	45.00
❏ 2 Frank Thomas	40.00	18.00
❏ 3 Alex Rodriguez	60.00	27.00
❏ 4 Cal Ripken	80.00	36.00
❏ 5 Mike Piazza	60.00	27.00
❏ 6 Mark McGwire	120.00	55.00
❏ 7 Greg Maddux	50.00	22.00
❏ 8 Kerry Wood	15.00	6.75
❏ 9 Chipper Jones	50.00	22.00
❏ 10 Derek Jeter	60.00	27.00

1999 Ultra RBI Kings

	MINT	NRMT
COMPLETE SET (30)	30.00	13.50
COMMON CARD (1-30)	.40	.18
SEMISTARS	.50	.23
UNLISTED STARS	.75	.35
ONE PER RETAIL PACK		
❏ 1 Rafael Palmeiro	.75	.35
❏ 2 Mo Vaughn	.75	.35
❏ 3 Ivan Rodriguez	1.00	.45
❏ 4 Barry Bonds	1.00	.45
❏ 5 Albert Belle	.75	.35
❏ 6 Jeff Bagwell	1.00	.45
❏ 7 Mark McGwire	5.00	2.20
❏ 8 Darin Erstad	.50	.23
❏ 9 Manny Ramirez	1.00	.45
❏ 10 Chipper Jones	2.00	.90
❏ 11 Jim Thome	.75	.35
❏ 12 Scott Rolen	1.00	.45
❏ 13 Tony Gwynn	2.00	.90
❏ 14 Juan Gonzalez	1.50	.70
❏ 15 Mike Piazza	2.50	1.10
❏ 16 Sammy Sosa	2.50	1.10
❏ 17 Andruw Jones	.75	.35
❏ 18 Derek Jeter	2.50	1.10
❏ 19 Nomar Garciaparra	2.50	1.10
❏ 20 Alex Rodriguez	2.50	1.10
❏ 21 Frank Thomas	1.50	.70
❏ 22 Cal Ripken	3.00	1.35
❏ 23 Ken Griffey Jr.	4.00	1.80
❏ 24 Travis Lee	.50	.23
❏ 25 Paul O'Neill	.40	.18
❏ 26 Greg Vaughn	.40	.18
❏ 27 Andres Galarraga	.50	.23
❏ 28 Tino Martinez	.40	.18
❏ 29 Jose Canseco	1.00	.45
❏ 30 Ben Grieve	.75	.35

1999 Ultra Thunderclap

	MINT	NRMT
COMPLETE SET (15)	150.00	70.00
COMMON CARD (1-15)	2.50	1.10
UNLISTED STARS	4.00	1.80
SER.1 STATED ODDS 1:36		
❏ 1 Alex Rodriguez	12.00	5.50
❏ 2 Andruw Jones	4.00	1.80
❏ 3 Cal Ripken	15.00	6.75
❏ 4 Chipper Jones	10.00	4.50
❏ 5 Darin Erstad	2.50	1.10
❏ 6 Derek Jeter	12.00	5.50
❏ 7 Frank Thomas	8.00	3.60
❏ 8 Jeff Bagwell	5.00	2.20
❏ 9 Juan Gonzalez	8.00	3.60
❏ 10 Ken Griffey Jr.	20.00	9.00
❏ 11 Mark McGwire	25.00	11.00
❏ 12 Mike Piazza	12.00	5.50
❏ 13 Travis Lee	2.50	1.10
❏ 14 Nomar Garciaparra	12.00	5.50
❏ 15 Scott Rolen	5.00	2.20

1999 Ultra World Premiere

	MINT	NRMT
COMPLETE SET (15)	25.00	11.00
COMMON CARD (1-15)	1.00	.45
MINOR STARS	1.50	.70
SEMISTARS	2.50	1.10
UNLISTED STARS	3.00	1.35
SER.1 STATED ODDS 1:18		
❏ 1 Gabe Alvarez	1.00	.45
❏ 2 Kerry Wood	3.00	1.35
❏ 3 Orlando Hernandez	3.00	1.35
❏ 4 Mike Caruso	1.00	.45
❏ 5 Matt Anderson	1.00	.45
❏ 6 Randall Simon	1.00	.45
❏ 7 Adrian Beltre	3.00	1.35
❏ 8 Scott Elarton	1.00	.45
❏ 9 Karim Garcia	1.00	.45
❏ 10 Mike Frank	1.00	.45
❏ 11 Richard Hidalgo	1.50	.70
❏ 12 Paul Konerko	1.50	.70
❏ 13 Travis Lee	2.50	1.10
❏ 14 J.D. Drew	6.00	2.70
❏ 15 Miguel Tejada	1.50	.70

2000 Ultra

	MINT	NRMT
COMPLETE SET (300)	250.00	110.00
COMP.SET w/o SP's (250)	25.00	11.00
COMMON CARD (1-250)	.15	.07
MINOR STARS 1-250	.25	.11
SEMISTARS 1-250	.40	.18
COMMON PROSPECT (251-300)	1.50	.70
PROSPECT STATED ODDS 1:4		

1	Alex Rodriguez	2.00	.90
2	Shawn Green	.60	.25
3	Magglio Ordonez	.40	.18
4	Tony Gwynn	1.50	.70
5	Joe McEwing	.25	.11
6	Jose Rosado	.15	.07
7	Sammy Sosa	2.00	.90
8	Gary Sheffield	.25	.11
9	Mickey Morandini	.15	.07
10	Mo Vaughn	.50	.23
11	Todd Hollandsworth	.15	.07
12	Tom Gordon	.25	.11
13	Charles Johnson	.25	.11
14	Derek Bell	.25	.11
15	Kevin Young	.25	.11
16	Jay Buhner	.25	.11
17	J.T. Snow	.25	.11
18	Jay Bell	.15	.07
19	John Rocker	.15	.07
20	Ivan Rodriguez	.75	.35
21	Pokey Reese	.25	.11
22	Paul O'Neill	.25	.11
23	Ronnie Belliard	.15	.07
24	Ryan Rupe	.15	.07
25	Travis Fryman	.25	.11
26	Trot Nixon	.25	.11
27	Wally Joyner	.25	.11
28	Andy Pettitte	.25	.11
29	Dan Wilson	.15	.07
30	Orlando Hernandez	.50	.23
31	Dmitri Young	.15	.07
32	Edgar Renteria	.15	.07
33	Eric Karros	.15	.07
34	Fernando Seguignol	.25	.11
35	Jason Kendall	.25	.11
36	Jeff Shaw	.25	.11
37	Matt Lawton	.15	.07
38	Robin Ventura	.25	.11
39	Scott Williamson	.15	.07
40	Ben Grieve	.50	.23
41	Billy Wagner	.25	.11
42	Javy Lopez	.25	.11
43	Joe Randa	.15	.07
44	Neifi Perez	.15	.07
45	David Justice	.25	.11
46	Ray Durham	.25	.11
47	Dustin Hermanson	.15	.07
48	Andres Galarraga	.25	.11
49	Brad Fullmer	.15	.07
50	Nomar Garciaparra	2.00	.90
51	David Cone	.40	.18
52	David Nilsson	.15	.07
53	David Wells	.25	.11
54	Miguel Tejada	.25	.11
55	Ismael Valdes	.15	.07
56	Jose Lima	.25	.11
57	Juan Encarnacion	.25	.11
58	Fred McGriff	.40	.18
59	Kenny Rogers	.15	.07
60	Vladimir Guerrero	.75	.35
61	Benito Santiago	.25	.11
62	Chris Singleton	.25	.11
63	Carlos Lee	.25	.11
64	Sean Casey	.50	.23
65	Tom Goodwin	.15	.07
66	Todd Hundley	.25	.11
67	Ellis Burks	.25	.11
68	Tim Hudson	.75	.35
69	Matt Stairs	.15	.07
70	Chipper Jones	1.50	.70
71	Craig Biggio	.50	.23
72	Brian Rose	.15	.07
73	Carlos Delgado	.50	.23
74	Eddie Taubensee	.15	.07
75	John Smoltz	.40	.18
76	Ken Caminiti	.25	.11
77	Rafael Palmeiro	.60	.25
78	Sidney Ponson	.25	.11
79	Todd Helton	.50	.23
80	Juan Gonzalez	1.25	.55
81	Bruce Aven	.15	.07
82	Desi Relaford	.15	.07
83	Johnny Damon	.25	.11
84	Albert Belle	.50	.23
85	Mark McGwire	3.00	1.35
86	Rico Brogna	.15	.07
87	Tom Glavine	.50	.23
88	Harold Baines	.25	.11
89	Chad Allen	.15	.07
90	Barry Bonds	.75	.35
91	Mark Grace	.40	.18
92	Paul Byrd	.15	.07
93	Roberto Alomar	.60	.25
94	Roberto Hernandez	.25	.11
95	Steve Finley	.25	.11
96	Bret Boone	.25	.11
97	Charles Nagy	.15	.07
98	Eric Chavez	.25	.11
99	Jamie Moyer	.15	.07
100	Ken Griffey Jr.	3.00	1.35
101	J.D. Drew	.75	.35
102	Todd Stottlemyre	.15	.07
103	Tony Fernandez	.25	.11
104	Jeromy Burnitz	.25	.11
105	Jeremy Giambi	.15	.07
106	Livan Hernandez	.15	.07
107	Marlon Anderson	.15	.07
108	Troy Glaus	.50	.23
109	Troy O'Leary	.25	.11
110	Scott Rolen	.75	.35
111	Bernard Gilkey	.15	.07
112	Brady Anderson	.25	.11
113	Chuck Knoblauch	.25	.11
114	Jeff Weaver	.25	.11
115	B.J. Surhoff	.25	.11
116	Alex Gonzalez	.25	.11
117	Vinny Castilla	.25	.11
118	Tim Salmon	.40	.18
119	Brian Jordan	.25	.11
120	Corey Koskie	.25	.11
121	Dean Palmer	.25	.11
122	Gabe Kapler	.25	.11
123	Jim Edmonds	.25	.11
124	John Jaha	.25	.11
125	Mark Grudzielanek	.15	.07
126	Mike Bordick	.15	.07
127	Mike Lieberthal	.15	.07
128	Pete Harnisch	.15	.07
129	Russ Ortiz	.25	.11
130	Kevin Brown	.40	.18
131	Troy Percival	.15	.07
132	Alex Gonzalez	.15	.07
133	Bartolo Colon	.15	.07
134	John Valentin	.15	.07
135	Jose Hernandez	.15	.07
136	Marquis Grissom	.25	.11
137	Wade Boggs	.60	.25
138	Dante Bichette	.25	.11
139	Bobby Higginson	.15	.07
140	Frank Thomas	1.25	.55
141	Geoff Jenkins	.25	.11
142	Jason Giambi	.15	.07
143	Jeff Cirillo	.15	.07
144	Andruw Jones Jr.	.25	.11
145	Luis Gonzalez	.25	.11
146	Preston Wilson	.25	.11
147	Carlos Beltran	.60	.25
148	Greg Vaughn	.25	.11
149	Carlos Febles	.15	.07
150	Jose Canseco	.75	.35
151	Kris Benson	.15	.07
152	Chuck Finley	.15	.07
153	Michael Barrett	.25	.11
154	Rey Ordonez	.25	.11
155	Adrian Beltre	.40	.18
156	Andruw Jones	.60	.25
157	Barry Larkin	.50	.23
158	Brian Giles	.25	.11
159	Carl Everett	.25	.11
160	Manny Ramirez	.75	.35
161	Darryl Kile	.15	.07
162	Edgar Martinez	.25	.11
163	Jeff Kent	.25	.11
164	Matt Williams	.50	.23
165	Mike Piazza	2.00	.90
166	Pedro Martinez	.75	.35
167	Ray Lankford	.25	.11
168	Roger Cedeno	.25	.11
169	Ron Coomer	.15	.07
170	Cal Ripken	2.50	1.10
171	Jose Offerman	.25	.11
172	Kenny Lofton	.25	.11
173	Kent Bottenfield	.15	.07
174	Kevin Millwood	.40	.18
175	Omar Daal	.25	.11
176	Orlando Cabrera	.15	.07
177	Pat Hentgen	.25	.11
178	Tino Martinez	.25	.11
179	Tony Clark	.25	.11
180	Roger Clemens	1.50	.70
181	Brad Radke	.25	.11
182	Darin Erstad	.25	.11
183	Jose Jimenez	.15	.07
184	Jim Thome	.50	.23
185	John Wetteland	.25	.11
186	Justin Thompson	.15	.07
187	John Halama	.15	.07
188	Lee Stevens	.15	.07
189	Miguel Cairo	.15	.07
190	Mike Mussina	.60	.25
191	Raul Mondesi	.25	.11
192	Armando Rios	.15	.07
193	Trevor Hoffman	.25	.11
194	Tony Batista	.25	.11
195	Will Clark	.50	.23
196	Brad Ausmus	.15	.07
197	Chili Davis	.25	.11
198	Cliff Floyd	.25	.11
199	Curt Schilling	.40	.18
200	Derek Jeter	2.00	.90
201	Henry Rodriguez	.15	.07
202	Jose Cruz Jr.	.25	.11
203	Omar Vizquel	.25	.11
204	Randy Johnson	.60	.25
205	Reggie Sanders	.15	.07
206	Al Leiter	.25	.11
207	Damion Easley	.15	.07
208	David Bell	.15	.07
209	Fernando Tatis	.25	.11
210	Kerry Wood	.50	.23
211	Kevin Appier	.15	.07
212	Mariano Rivera	.25	.11
213	Mike Caruso	.15	.07
214	Moises Alou	.25	.11
215	Randy Winn	.15	.07
216	Roy Halladay	.15	.07
217	Shannon Stewart	.25	.11
218	Todd Walker	.25	.11
219	Jim Parque	.15	.07
220	Travis Lee	.15	.07
221	Andy Ashby	.15	.07
222	Ed Sprague	.15	.07
223	Larry Walker	.60	.25
224	Rick Helling	.15	.07
225	Rusty Greer	.25	.11
226	Todd Zeile	.25	.11
227	Freddy Garcia	.75	.35
228	Hideo Nomo	.50	.23
229	Marty Cordova	.15	.07
230	Greg Maddux	1.50	.70
231	Rondell White	.25	.11
232	Paul Konerko	.25	.11
233	Warren Morris	.15	.07
234	Bernie Williams	.60	.25
235	Bobby Abreu	.25	.11
236	John Olerud	.25	.11
237	Doug Glanville	.15	.07
238	Eric Young	.15	.07
239	Robb Nen	.25	.11
240	Jeff Bagwell	.75	.35

		MINT	NRMT
❏ 241	Sterling Hitchcock	.15	.07
❏ 242	Todd Greene	.15	.07
❏ 243	Bill Mueller	.15	.07
❏ 244	Rickey Henderson	.75	.35
❏ 245	Chan Ho Park	.25	.11
❏ 246	Jason Schmidt	.15	.07
❏ 247	Jeff Zimmerman	.25	.11
❏ 248	Jermaine Dye	.25	.11
❏ 249	Randall Simon	.25	.11
❏ 250	Richie Sexson	.40	.18
❏ 251	Micah Bowie PROS	1.50	.70
❏ 252	Joe Nathan PROS	1.50	.70
❏ 253	Chris Woodward PROS	1.50	.70
❏ 254	Lance Berkman PROS	3.00	1.35
❏ 255	Ruben Mateo PROS	4.00	1.80
❏ 256	Russell Branyan PROS	3.00	1.35
❏ 257	Randy Wolf PROS	2.00	.90
❏ 258	A.J. Burnett PROS	2.50	1.10
❏ 259	Mark Quinn PROS	4.00	1.80
❏ 260	Buddy Carlyle PROS	1.50	.70
❏ 261	Ben Davis PROS	4.00	1.80
❏ 262	Yamid Haad PROS	1.50	.70
❏ 263	Mike Colangelo PROS	1.50	.70
❏ 264	Rick Ankiel PROS	20.00	9.00
❏ 265	Jacque Jones PROS	2.00	.90
❏ 266	Kelly Dransfeldt PROS	1.50	.70
❏ 267	Matt Riley PROS	8.00	3.60
❏ 268	Adam Kennedy PROS	2.00	.90
❏ 269	Octavio Dotel PROS	2.00	.90
❏ 270	Francisco Cordero PROS	1.50	.70
❏ 271	Wilton Veras PROS	6.00	2.70
❏ 272	Calvin Pickering PROS	2.00	.90
❏ 273	Alex Sanchez PROS	1.50	.70
❏ 274	Tony Armas Jr. PROS	3.00	1.35
❏ 275	Pat Burrell PROS	10.00	4.50
❏ 276	Chad Meyers PROS	1.50	.70
❏ 277	Ben Petrick PROS	2.50	1.10
❏ 278	Ramon Hernandez PROS	1.50	.70
❏ 279	Ed Yarnall PROS	2.00	.90
❏ 280	Erubiel Durazo PROS	10.00	4.50
❏ 281	Vernon Wells PROS	3.00	1.35
❏ 282	Gary Matthews Jr. PROS	1.50	.70
❏ 283	Kip Wells PROS	2.50	1.10
❏ 284	Peter Bergeron PROS	2.50	1.10
❏ 285	Travis Dawkins PROS	2.50	1.10
❏ 286	Jorge Toca PROS	2.50	1.10
❏ 287	Cole Liniak PROS	1.50	.70
❏ 288	Chad Hermansen PROS	2.00	.90
❏ 289	Eric Gagné PROS	3.00	1.35
❏ 290	Chad Hutchinson PROS	3.00	1.35
❏ 291	Eric Munson PROS	10.00	4.50
❏ 292	Wiki Gonzalez PROS	2.00	.90
❏ 293	Alfonso Soriano PROS	10.00	4.50
❏ 294	Trent Durrington PROS	1.50	.70
❏ 295	Ben Molina PROS	1.50	.70
❏ 296	Aaron Myette PROS	2.00	.90
❏ 297	Wily Pena PROS	6.00	2.70
❏ 298	Kevin Barker PROS	1.50	.70
❏ 299	Geoff Blum PROS	1.50	.70
❏ 300	Josh Beckett PROS	10.00	4.50
❏ S1	Alex Rodriguez Sample	2.00	.90

2000 Ultra Gold Medallion

	MINT	NRMT
COMPLETE SET (300)	500.00	220.00
COMMON CARD (1-250)	.50	.23

*STARS 1-250: 1.5X TO 4X BASIC CARDS
*YNG.STARS 1-250: 1.25X TO 3X BASIC CARDS 1-250 ONE PER HOBBY PACK
COMMON PROSPECT (251-300)
*PROSPECTS: .75X TO 2X BASIC CARDS
PROSPECTS STATED ODDS 1:24 HOBBY

2000 Ultra Masterpiece

	MINT	NRMT
RANDOM INSERTS IN PACKS
STATED PRINT RUN 1 SERIAL #'d SET
NO PRICING DUE TO SCARCITY

2000 Ultra Platinum Medallion

	MINT	NRMT
COMMON CARD (1-250)	12.00	5.50

*STARS 1-250: 30X TO 80X BASIC CARDS
*YNG.STARS 1-250: 25X TO 60X BASIC CARDS 1-250 PRINT RUN 50 SERIAL #'d SETS
COMMON PROSPECT (251-300) 25.00 11.00
*PROSPECTS: 6X TO 15X BASIC CARDS
PROSPECT PRINT RUN 25 SERIAL #'d SETS
RANDOM INSERTS IN HOBBY PACKS

2000 Ultra Club 3000

	MINT	NRMT
COMPLETE SET (3)	10.00	4.50
COMMON CARD	3.00	1.35

STATED ODDS 1:24
ACTUAL CARDS ARE ALL UNNUMBERED

❏ 1	Wade Boggs	3.00	1.35
❏ 2	Tony Gwynn	5.00	2.20
❏ 3	Carl Yastrzemski	4.00	1.80

2000 Ultra Club 3000 Memorabilia

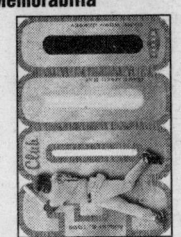

	MINT	NRMT
RANDOM INSERTS IN PACKS
PRINT RUNS LISTED BELOW
ACTUAL CARDS ARE ALL UNNUMBERED

❏ 1	W.Boggs Bat/250	100.00	45.00
❏ 2	W.Boggs Hat/100	120.00	55.00
❏ 3	W.Boggs Jersey/440	80.00	36.00
❏ 4	W.Boggs Bat/Jersey/100	150.00	70.00
❏ 5	W.Boggs Bat/Hat/Jersey/25		
❏ 6	T.Gwynn Bat/260	150.00	70.00
❏ 7	T.Gwynn Hat/115	200.00	90.00
❏ 8	T.Gwynn Jersey/450	120.00	55.00
❏ 9	T.Gwynn Bat/Jersey/100	250.00	110.00
❏ 10	T.Gwynn Bat/Hat/Jersey/25		
❏ 11	C.Yastrzemski Bat/250	150.00	70.00
❏ 12	C.Yastrzemski Hat/100	200.00	90.00
❏ 13	C.Yastrzemski Jersey/440	120.00	55.00
❏ 14	C.Yastrzemski Bat/Jersey/100	250.00	110.00
❏ 15	C.Yastrzemski Bat/Hat/Jersey/25		

2000 Ultra Crunch Time

	MINT	NRMT
COMPLETE SET (15)	200.00	90.00
COMMON CARD (1-15)	5.00	2.20
STATED ODDS 1:72

❏ 1	Nomar Garciaparra	20.00	9.00
❏ 2	Ken Griffey Jr.	30.00	13.50
❏ 3	Mark McGwire	30.00	13.50
❏ 4	Alex Rodriguez	20.00	9.00
❏ 5	Derek Jeter	20.00	9.00
❏ 6	Sammy Sosa	20.00	9.00
❏ 7	Mike Piazza	20.00	9.00
❏ 8	Cal Ripken Jr.	25.00	11.00
❏ 9	Frank Thomas	12.00	5.50
❏ 10	Juan Gonzalez	12.00	5.50
❏ 11	J.D. Drew	6.00	2.70

		MINT	NRMT
❏ 12	Greg Maddux	15.00	6.75
❏ 13	Tony Gwynn	15.00	6.75
❏ 14	Vladimir Guerrero	8.00	3.60
❏ 15	Ben Grieve	5.00	2.20

2000 Ultra Diamond Mine

FRANK THOMAS

	MINT	NRMT
COMPLETE SET (15)	30.00	13.50
COMMON CARD (1-15)	1.25	.55
STATED ODDS 1:6		

		MINT	NRMT
❏ 1	Greg Maddux	2.50	1.10
❏ 2	Mark McGwire	5.00	2.20
❏ 3	Ken Griffey Jr.	5.00	2.20
❏ 4	Cal Ripken	4.00	1.80
❏ 5	Nomar Garciaparra	3.00	1.35
❏ 6	Mike Piazza	3.00	1.35
❏ 7	Alex Rodriguez	3.00	1.35
❏ 8	Frank Thomas	2.00	.90
❏ 9	Juan Gonzalez	2.00	.90
❏ 10	Derek Jeter	3.00	1.35
❏ 11	Tony Gwynn	2.50	1.10
❏ 12	Chipper Jones	2.50	1.10
❏ 13	Sammy Sosa	3.00	1.35
❏ 14	Roger Clemens	2.50	1.10
❏ 15	Vladimir Guerrero	1.25	.55

2000 Ultra Feel the Game

	MINT	NRMT
STATED ODDS 1:168		
CARD NUMBER 12 DOES NOT EXIST		

		MINT	NRMT
❏ 1	A.Rodriguez Jersey	150.00	70.00
❏ 2	C.Jones Jersey	120.00	55.00
❏ 3	R.Alomar Btg.Glove	100.00	45.00
❏ 4	G.Maddux Jersey	120.00	55.00
❏ 5	P.Martinez Jersey	100.00	45.00
❏ 6	C.Ripken Jersey	200.00	90.00
❏ 7	R.Ventura Jersey	50.00	22.00
❏ 8	J.D.Drew Jersey	60.00	27.00
❏ 9	R.Johnson Jersey	100.00	45.00
❏ 10	S.Rolen Jersey	80.00	36.00
❏ 11	K.Millwood Jersey	50.00	22.00
❏ 13	T.Gwynn Btg.Glove	100.00	45.00
❏ 14	C.Schilling Jersey	40.00	18.00
❏ 15	E.Martinez Btg.Glove	40.00	18.00

2000 Ultra Fresh Ink

	MINT	NRMT
RANDOM INSERTS IN PACKS		
PRINT RUNS LISTED BELOW		

		MINT	NRMT
❏ 1	Bob Abreu/200	30.00	13.50
❏ 2	Chad Allen/975	10.00	4.50
❏ 3	Marlon Anderson/975	10.00	4.50
❏ 4	Rick Ankiel/500	80.00	36.00
❏ 5	Glen Barker/975	10.00	4.50
❏ 6	Michael Barrett/975	15.00	6.75
❏ 7	Carlos Beltran/975	30.00	13.50
❏ 8	Adrian Beltre/900	15.00	6.75
❏ 9	Peter Bergeron/1000	15.00	6.75
❏ 10	Wade Boggs/250	80.00	36.00
❏ 11	Barry Bonds/250	80.00	36.00
❏ 12	Pat Burrell/600	40.00	18.00
❏ 13	Roger Cedeno/500	20.00	9.00
❏ 14	Eric Chavez/900	15.00	6.75
❏ 15	Bruce Chen/600	15.00	6.75
❏ 16	Johnny Damon/975	15.00	6.75
❏ 17	Ben Davis/1000	15.00	6.75
❏ 18	Carlos Delgado/275	40.00	18.00
❏ 19	Einar Diaz/975	10.00	4.50
❏ 20	Octavio Dotel/950	15.00	6.75
❏ 21	J.D. Drew/600	50.00	22.00
❏ 22	Scott Elarton/1000	10.00	4.50
❏ 23	Freddy Garcia/500	40.00	18.00
❏ 24	Jeremy Giambi/975	10.00	4.50
❏ 25	Troy Glaus/500	30.00	13.50
❏ 26	Shawn Green/350	50.00	22.00
❏ 27	Tony Gwynn/245	120.00	55.00
❏ 28	Richard Hidalgo/500	15.00	6.75
❏ 29	Bobby Higginson/975	15.00	6.75
❏ 30	Tim Hudson/975	20.00	9.00
❏ 31	Norm Hutchins/1000	10.00	4.50
❏ 32	Derek Jeter/95	300.00	135.00
❏ 33	Randy Johnson/240	80.00	36.00
❏ 34	Gabe Kapler/725	25.00	11.00
❏ 35	Jason Kendall/375	25.00	11.00
❏ 36	Paul Konerko/500	20.00	9.00
❏ 37	Matt Lawton/1000	10.00	4.50
❏ 38	Carlos Lee/900	15.00	6.75
❏ 39	Jose Macias/1000	10.00	4.50
❏ 40	Greg Maddux/225	150.00	70.00
❏ 41	Kevin Millwood/500	40.00	18.00
❏ 42	Warren Morris/1000	15.00	6.75
❏ 43	Eric Munson/900	40.00	18.00
❏ 44	Heath Murray/925	10.00	4.50
❏ 45	Joe Nathan/1000	10.00	4.50
❏ 46	Magglio Ordonez/335	30.00	13.50
❏ 47	Angel Pena/1000	10.00	4.50
❏ 48	Cal Ripken/300	250.00	110.00
❏ 49	Alex Rodriguez/350	200.00	90.00
❏ 50	Scott Rolen/250	60.00	27.00
❏ 51	Ryan Rupe/1000	10.00	4.50
❏ 52	Curt Schilling/375	30.00	13.50
❏ 53	Randall Simon/1000	10.00	4.50
❏ 54	Alfonso Soriano/975	40.00	18.00
❏ 55	Shannon Stewart/275	25.00	11.00
❏ 56	Miguel Tejada/1000	15.00	6.75
❏ 57	Frank Thomas/150	150.00	70.00
❏ 58	Jeff Weaver/1000	15.00	6.75
❏ 59	Randy Wolf/1000	15.00	6.75
❏ 60	Ed Yarnall/1000	15.00	6.75
❏ 61	Kevin Young/1000	10.00	4.50
❏ 62	Wade Boggs	1000.00	450.00

Tony Gwynn
Nolan Ryan 100

2000 Ultra Swing Kings

	MINT	NRMT
COMPLETE SET (10)	60.00	27.00
COMMON CARD (1-10)	5.00	2.20
STATED ODDS 1:24		

		MINT	NRMT
❏ 1	Cal Ripken	10.00	4.50
❏ 2	Nomar Garciaparra	8.00	3.60
❏ 3	Frank Thomas	5.00	2.20
❏ 4	Tony Gwynn	6.00	2.70
❏ 5	Ken Griffey Jr.	12.00	5.50
❏ 6	Chipper Jones	6.00	2.70
❏ 7	Mark McGwire	12.00	5.50
❏ 8	Sammy Sosa	8.00	3.60
❏ 9	Derek Jeter	8.00	3.60
❏ 10	Alex Rodriguez	8.00	3.60

2000 Ultra Talented

ULTRA TALENTED

	MINT	NRMT
COMPLETE SET (10)	800.00	350.00
COMMON CARD (1-10)	30.00	13.50
RANDOM INSERTS IN HOBBY PACKS		
STATED PRINT RUN 100 SERIAL #'d SETS		

		MINT	NRMT
❏ 1	Sammy Sosa	100.00	45.00
❏ 2	Derek Jeter	100.00	45.00
❏ 3	Alex Rodriguez	100.00	45.00
❏ 4	Mike Piazza	100.00	45.00
❏ 5	Ken Griffey Jr.	150.00	70.00
❏ 6	Nomar Garciaparra	100.00	45.00
❏ 7	Mark McGwire	150.00	70.00
❏ 8	Cal Ripken	120.00	55.00
❏ 9	Frank Thomas	60.00	27.00
❏ 10	J.D. Drew	30.00	13.50

2000 Ultra World Premiere

	MINT	NRMT
COMPLETE SET (10)	20.00	9.00
COMMON CARD (1-10)	1.00	.45
STATED ODDS 1:12		

		MINT	NRMT
❏ 1	Ruben Mateo	2.00	.90
❏ 2	Lance Berkman	1.50	.70

❏ 3 Octavio Dotel	1.00	.45
❏ 4 Ben Davis	2.00	.90
❏ 5 Warren Morris	1.50	.70
❏ 6 Carlos Beltran	2.50	1.10
❏ 7 Rick Ankiel	8.00	3.60
❏ 8 Adam Kennedy	1.00	.45
❏ 9 Tim Hudson	2.00	.90
❏ 10 Jorge Toca	1.00	.45

1989 Upper Deck

Orel Hershiser

	MINT	NRMT
COMPLETE SET (800)	200.00	90.00
COMP.FACT.SET (800)	250.00	110.00
COMMON CARD (1-800)	.20	.09
MINOR STARS	.30	.14
SEMISTARS	.50	.23
UNLISTED STARS	.75	.35

❏ 1 Ken Griffey Jr.	150.00	70.00
❏ 2 Luis Medina	.20	.09
❏ 3 Tony Chance	.20	.09
❏ 4 Dave Otto	.20	.09
❏ 5 Sandy Alomar Jr. UER	1.00	.45
(Born 6/16/66, should be 6/18/66)		
❏ 6 Rolando Roomes	.20	.09
❏ 7 Dave West	.20	.09
❏ 8 Cris Carpenter	.20	.09
❏ 9 Gregg Jefferies	.30	.14
❏ 10 Doug Dascenzo	.20	.09
❏ 11 Ron Jones	.20	.09
❏ 12 Luis DeLosSantos	.20	.09
❏ 13 Gary Sheffield COR	2.50	1.10
❏ 13A Gary Sheffield ERR	3.00	1.35
(SS upside down on card front)		
❏ 14 Mike Harkey	.20	.09
❏ 15 Lance Blankenship	.20	.09
❏ 16 William Brennan	.20	.09
❏ 17 John Smoltz	4.00	1.80
❏ 18 Ramon Martinez	1.00	.45
❏ 19 Mark Lemke	.50	.23
❏ 20 Juan Bell	.20	.09
❏ 21 Rey Palacios	.20	.09
❏ 22 Felix Jose	.20	.09
❏ 23 Van Snider	.20	.09
❏ 24 Dante Bichette	2.00	.90
❏ 25 Randy Johnson	10.00	4.50
❏ 26 Carlos Quintana	.20	.09
❏ 27 Star Rookie CL	.20	.09

❏ 28 Mike Schooler	.20	.09
❏ 29 Randy St.Claire	.20	.09
❏ 30 Jerald Clark	.20	.09
❏ 31 Kevin Gross	.20	.09
❏ 32 Dan Firova	.20	.09
❏ 33 Jeff Calhoun	.20	.09
❏ 34 Tommy Hinzo	.20	.09
❏ 35 Ricky Jordan	.30	.14
❏ 36 Larry Parrish	.20	.09
❏ 37 Bret Saberhagen UER	.30	.14
(Hit total 931, should be 1031)		
❏ 38 Mike Smithson	.20	.09
❏ 39 Dave Dravecky	.30	.14
❏ 40 Ed Romero	.20	.09
❏ 41 Jeff Musselman	.20	.09
❏ 42 Ed Hearn	.20	.09
❏ 43 Rance Mullinks	.20	.09
❏ 44 Jim Eisenreich	.20	.09
❏ 45 Sil Campusano	.20	.09
❏ 46 Mike Krukow	.20	.09
❏ 47 Paul Gibson	.20	.09
❏ 48 Mike LaCoss	.20	.09
❏ 49 Larry Herndon	.20	.09
❏ 50 Scott Garrelts	.20	.09
❏ 51 Dwayne Henry	.20	.09
❏ 52 Jim Acker	.20	.09
❏ 53 Steve Sax	.20	.09
❏ 54 Pete O'Brien	.20	.09
❏ 55 Paul Runge	.20	.09
❏ 56 Rick Rhoden	.20	.09
❏ 57 John Dopson	.20	.09
❏ 58 Casey Candaele UER	.20	.09
(No stats for Astros for '88 season)		
❏ 59 Dave Righetti	.20	.09
❏ 60 Joe Hesketh	.20	.09
❏ 61 Frank DiPino	.20	.09
❏ 62 Tim Laudner	.20	.09
❏ 63 Jamie Moyer	.20	.09
❏ 64 Fred Toliver	.20	.09
❏ 65 Mitch Webster	.20	.09
❏ 66 John Tudor	.20	.09
❏ 67 John Cangelosi	.20	.09
❏ 68 Mike Devereaux	.20	.09
❏ 69 Brian Fisher	.20	.09
❏ 70 Mike Marshall	.20	.09
❏ 71 Zane Smith	.20	.09
❏ 72A Brian Holton ERR	1.00	.45
(Photo actually Shawn Hillegas)		
❏ 72B Brian Holton COR	.30	.14
❏ 73 Jose Guzman	.20	.09
❏ 74 Rick Mahler	.20	.09
❏ 75 John Shelby	.20	.09
❏ 76 Jim Deshaies	.20	.09
❏ 77 Bobby Meacham	.20	.09
❏ 78 Bryn Smith	.20	.09
❏ 79 Joaquin Andujar	.20	.09
❏ 80 Richard Dotson	.20	.09
❏ 81 Charlie Lea	.20	.09
❏ 82 Calvin Schiraldi	.20	.09
❏ 83 Les Straker	.20	.09
❏ 84 Les Lancaster	.20	.09
❏ 85 Allan Anderson	.20	.09
❏ 86 Junior Ortiz	.20	.09
❏ 87 Jesse Orosco	.20	.09
❏ 88 Felix Fermin	.20	.09
❏ 89 Dave Anderson	.20	.09
❏ 90 Rafael Belliard UER	.20	.09
(Born '61, not '51)		
❏ 91 Franklin Stubbs	.20	.09
❏ 92 Cecil Espy	.20	.09
❏ 93 Albert Hall	.20	.09
❏ 94 Tim Leary	.20	.09
❏ 95 Mitch Williams	.20	.09
❏ 96 Tracy Jones	.20	.09
❏ 97 Danny Darwin	.20	.09
❏ 98 Gary Ward	.20	.09
❏ 99 Neal Heaton	.20	.09
❏ 100 Jim Pankovits	.20	.09
❏ 101 Bill Doran	.20	.09
❏ 102 Tim Wallach	.20	.09
❏ 103 Joe Magrane	.20	.09
❏ 104 Ozzie Virgil	.20	.09
❏ 105 Alvin Davis	.20	.09

❏ 106 Tom Brookens	.20	.09
❏ 107 Shawon Dunston	.20	.09
❏ 108 Tracy Woodson	.20	.09
❏ 109 Nelson Liriano	.20	.09
❏ 110 Devon White UER	.30	.14
(Doubles total 46, should be 56)		
❏ 111 Steve Balboni	.20	.09
❏ 112 Buddy Bell	.30	.14
❏ 113 German Jimenez	.20	.09
❏ 114 Ken Dayley	.20	.09
❏ 115 Andres Galarraga	.75	.35
❏ 116 Mike Scioscia	.20	.09
❏ 117 Gary Pettis	.20	.09
❏ 118 Ernie Whitt	.20	.09
❏ 119 Bob Boone	.30	.14
❏ 120 Ryne Sandberg	1.00	.45
❏ 121 Bruce Benedict	.20	.09
❏ 122 Hubie Brooks	.20	.09
❏ 123 Mike Moore	.20	.09
❏ 124 Wallace Johnson	.20	.09
❏ 125 Bob Horner	.20	.09
❏ 126 Chili Davis	.30	.14
❏ 127 Manny Trillo	.20	.09
❏ 128 Chet Lemon	.20	.09
❏ 129 John Cerutti	.20	.09
❏ 130 Orel Hershiser	.30	.14
❏ 131 Terry Pendleton	.20	.09
❏ 132 Jeff Blauser	.20	.09
❏ 133 Mike Fitzgerald	.20	.09
❏ 134 Henry Cotto	.20	.09
❏ 135 Gerald Young	.20	.09
❏ 136 Luis Salazar	.20	.09
❏ 137 Alejandro Pena	.20	.09
❏ 138 Jack Howell	.20	.09
❏ 139 Tony Fernandez	.20	.09
❏ 140 Mark Grace	.75	.35
❏ 141 Ken Caminiti	1.00	.45
❏ 142 Mike Jackson	.50	.23
❏ 143 Larry McWilliams	.20	.09
❏ 144 Andres Thomas	.20	.09
❏ 145 Nolan Ryan 3X	3.00	1.35
❏ 146 Mike Davis	.20	.09
❏ 147 DeWayne Buice	.20	.09
❏ 148 Jody Davis	.20	.09
❏ 149 Jesse Barfield	.20	.09
❏ 150 Matt Nokes	.20	.09
❏ 151 Jerry Reuss	.20	.09
❏ 152 Rick Cerone	.20	.09
❏ 153 Storm Davis	.20	.09
❏ 154 Marvell Wynne	.20	.09
❏ 155 Will Clark	.75	.35
❏ 156 Luis Aguayo	.20	.09
❏ 157 Willie Upshaw	.20	.09
❏ 158 Randy Bush	.20	.09
❏ 159 Ron Darling	.20	.09
❏ 160 Kal Daniels	.20	.09
❏ 161 Spike Owen	.20	.09
❏ 162 Luis Polonia	.20	.09
❏ 163 Kevin Mitchell UER	.30	.14
('88/min HR's 18/52, should be 19/53)		
❏ 164 Dave Gallagher	.20	.09
❏ 165 Benito Santiago	.20	.09
❏ 166 Greg Gagne	.20	.09
❏ 167 Ken Phelps	.20	.09
❏ 168 Sid Fernandez	.20	.09
❏ 169 Bo Diaz	.20	.09
❏ 170 Cory Snyder	.20	.09
❏ 171 Eric Show	.20	.09
❏ 172 Robby Thompson	.20	.09
❏ 173 Marty Barrett	.20	.09
❏ 174 Dave Henderson	.20	.09
❏ 175 Ozzie Guillen	.20	.09
❏ 176 Barry Lyons	.20	.09
❏ 177 Kelvin Torve	.20	.09
❏ 178 Don Slaught	.20	.09
❏ 179 Steve Lombardozzi	.20	.09
❏ 180 Chris Sabo	.20	.09
❏ 181 Jose Uribe	.20	.09
❏ 182 Shane Mack	.20	.09
❏ 183 Ron Karkovice	.20	.09
❏ 184 Todd Benzinger	.20	.09
❏ 185 Dave Stewart	.30	.14
❏ 186 Julio Franco	.20	.09
❏ 187 Ron Robinson	.20	.09

188	Wally Backman	.20	.09
189	Randy Velarde	.20	.09
190	Joe Carter	.50	.23
191	Bob Welch	.20	.09
192	Kelly Paris	.20	.09
193	Chris Brown	.20	.09
194	Rick Reuschel	.20	.09
195	Roger Clemens	2.00	.90
196	Dave Concepcion	.30	.14
197	Al Newman	.20	.09
198	Brook Jacoby	.20	.09
199	Mookie Wilson	.30	.14
200	Don Mattingly	1.50	.70
201	Dick Schofield	.20	.09
202	Mark Gubicza	.20	.09
203	Gary Gaetti	.30	.14
204	Dan Pasqua	.20	.09
205	Andre Dawson	.75	.35
206	Chris Speier	.20	.09
207	Kent Tekulve	.20	.09
208	Rod Scurry	.20	.09
209	Scott Bailes	.20	.09
210	Rickey Henderson UER (Throws Right)	1.00	.45
211	Harold Baines	.30	.14
212	Tony Armas	.20	.09
213	Kent Hrbek	.30	.14
214	Darrin Jackson	.20	.09
215	George Brett	1.50	.70
216	Rafael Santana	.20	.09
217	Andy Allanson	.20	.09
218	Brett Butler	.30	.14
219	Steve Jeltz	.20	.09
220	Jay Buhner	.75	.35
221	Bo Jackson	.50	.23
222	Angel Salazar	.20	.09
223	Kirk McCaskill	.20	.09
224	Steve Lyons	.20	.09
225	Bert Blyleven	.30	.14
226	Scott Bradley	.20	.09
227	Bob Melvin	.20	.09
228	Ron Kittle	.20	.09
229	Phil Bradley	.20	.09
230	Tommy John	.30	.14
231	Greg Walker	.20	.09
232	Juan Berenguer	.20	.09
233	Pat Tabler	.20	.09
234	Terry Clark	.20	.09
235	Rafael Palmeiro	1.00	.45
236	Paul Zuvella	.20	.09
237	Willie Randolph	.30	.14
238	Bruce Fields	.20	.09
239	Mike Aldrete	.20	.09
240	Lance Parrish	.20	.09
241	Greg Maddux	3.00	1.35
242	John Moses	.20	.09
243	Melido Perez	.20	.09
244	Willie Wilson	.20	.09
245	Mark McLemore	.20	.09
246	Von Hayes	.20	.09
247	Matt Williams	.75	.35
248	John Candelaria UER (Listed as Yankee for part of '87, should be Mets)	.20	.09
249	Harold Reynolds	.20	.09
250	Greg Swindell	.20	.09
251	Juan Agosto	.20	.09
252	Mike Felder	.20	.09
253	Vince Coleman	.20	.09
254	Larry Sheets	.20	.09
255	George Bell	.20	.09
256	Terry Steinbach	.30	.14
257	Jack Armstrong	.20	.09
258	Dickie Thon	.20	.09
259	Ray Knight	.20	.09
260	Darryl Strawberry	.30	.14
261	Doug Sisk	.20	.09
262	Alex Trevino	.20	.09
263	Jeffrey Leonard	.20	.09
264	Tom Henke	.20	.09
265	Ozzie Smith	1.00	.45
266	Dave Bergman	.20	.09
267	Tony Phillips	.20	.09
268	Mark Davis	.20	.09
269	Kevin Elster	.20	.09
270	Barry Larkin	.75	.35
271	Manny Lee	.20	.09
272	Tom Brunansky	.20	.09
273	Craig Biggio	4.00	1.80
274	Jim Gantner	.20	.09
275	Eddie Murray	.75	.35
276	Jeff Reed	.20	.09
277	Tim Teufel	.20	.09
278	Rick Honeycutt	.20	.09
279	Guillermo Hernandez	.20	.09
280	John Kruk	.30	.14
281	Luis Alicea	.20	.09
282	Jim Clancy	.20	.09
283	Billy Ripken	.20	.09
284	Craig Reynolds	.20	.09
285	Robin Yount	.75	.35
286	Jimmy Jones	.20	.09
287	Ron Oester	.20	.09
288	Terry Leach	.20	.09
289	Dennis Eckersley	.50	.23
290	Alan Trammell	.50	.23
291	Jimmy Key	.30	.14
292	Chris Bosio	.20	.09
293	Jose DeLeon	.20	.09
294	Jim Traber	.20	.09
295	Mike Scott	.20	.09
296	Roger McDowell	.20	.09
297	Garry Templeton	.20	.09
298	Doyle Alexander	.20	.09
299	Nick Esasky	.20	.09
300	Mark McGwire UER (Doubles total 52, should be 51)	6.00	2.70
301	Darryl Hamilton	.20	.09
302	Dave Smith	.20	.09
303	Rick Sutcliffe	.20	.09
304	Dave Stapleton	.20	.09
305	Alan Ashby	.20	.09
306	Pedro Guerrero	.20	.09
307	Ron Guidry	.30	.14
308	Steve Farr	.20	.09
309	Curt Ford	.20	.09
310	Claudell Washington	.20	.09
311	Tom Prince	.20	.09
312	Chad Kreuter	.20	.09
313	Ken Oberkfell	.20	.09
314	Jerry Browne	.20	.09
315	R.J. Reynolds	.20	.09
316	Scott Bankhead	.20	.09
317	Milt Thompson	.20	.09
318	Mario Diaz	.20	.09
319	Bruce Ruffin	.20	.09
320	Dave Valle	.20	.09
321A	Gary Varsho ERR (Back photo actually Mike Bielecki bunting)	2.00	.90
321B	Gary Varsho COR (In road uniform)	.20	.09
322	Paul Mirabella	.20	.09
323	Chuck Jackson	.20	.09
324	Drew Hall	.20	.09
325	Don August	.20	.09
326	Israel Sanchez	.20	.09
327	Denny Walling	.20	.09
328	Joel Skinner	.20	.09
329	Danny Tartabull	.20	.09
330	Tony Pena	.20	.09
331	Jim Sundberg	.20	.09
332	Jeff D. Robinson	.20	.09
333	Oddibe McDowell	.20	.09
334	Jose Lind	.20	.09
335	Paul Kilgus	.20	.09
336	Juan Samuel	.20	.09
337	Mike Campbell	.20	.09
338	Mike Maddux	.20	.09
339	Darnell Coles	.20	.09
340	Bob Dernier	.20	.09
341	Rafael Ramirez	.20	.09
342	Scott Sanderson	.20	.09
343	B.J. Surhoff	.30	.14
344	Billy Hatcher	.20	.09
345	Pat Perry	.20	.09
346	Jack Clark	.20	.09
347	Gary Thurman	.20	.09
348	Tim Jones	.20	.09
349	Dave Winfield	.75	.35
350	Frank White	.30	.14
351	Dave Collins	.20	.09
352	Jack Morris	.30	.14
353	Eric Plunk	.20	.09
354	Leon Durham	.20	.09
355	Ivan DeJesus	.20	.09
356	Brian Holman	.20	.09
357A	Dale Murphy ERR (Front has reverse negative)	25.00	11.00
357B	Dale Murphy COR	.30	.14
358	Mark Portugal	.20	.09
359	Andy McGaffigan	.20	.09
360	Tom Glavine	.75	.35
361	Keith Moreland	.20	.09
362	Todd Stottlemyre	.50	.23
363	Dave Leiper	.20	.09
364	Cecil Fielder	.30	.14
365	Carmelo Martinez	.20	.09
366	Dwight Evans	.30	.14
367	Kevin McReynolds	.20	.09
368	Rich Gedman	.20	.09
369	Len Dykstra	.30	.14
370	Jody Reed	.20	.09
371	Jose Canseco UER (Strikeout total 391, should be 491)	1.00	.45
372	Rob Murphy	.20	.09
373	Mike Henneman	.20	.09
374	Walt Weiss	.20	.09
375	Rob Dibble	.30	.14
376	Kirby Puckett (Mark McGwire in background)	1.50	.70
377	Dennis Martinez	.30	.14
378	Ron Gant	.30	.14
379	Brian Harper	.20	.09
380	Nelson Santovenia	.20	.09
381	Lloyd Moseby	.20	.09
382	Lance McCullers	.20	.09
383	Dave Stieb	.20	.09
384	Tony Gwynn	2.00	.90
385	Mike Flanagan	.20	.09
386	Bob Ojeda	.20	.09
387	Bruce Hurst	.20	.09
388	Dave Magadan	.20	.09
389	Wade Boggs	.75	.35
390	Gary Carter	.50	.23
391	Frank Tanana	.20	.09
392	Curt Young	.20	.09
393	Jeff Treadway	.20	.09
394	Darrell Evans	.30	.14
395	Glenn Hubbard	.20	.09
396	Chuck Cary	.20	.09
397	Frank Viola	.20	.09
398	Jeff Parrett	.20	.09
399	Terry Blocker	.20	.09
400	Dan Gladden	.20	.09
401	Louie Meadows	.20	.09
402	Tim Raines	.30	.14
403	Joey Meyer	.20	.09
404	Larry Andersen	.20	.09
405	Rex Hudler	.20	.09
406	Mike Schmidt	1.25	.55
407	John Franco	.20	.09
408	Brady Anderson	2.00	.90
409	Don Carman	.20	.09
410	Eric Davis	.30	.14
411	Bob Stanley	.20	.09
412	Pete Smith	.20	.09
413	Jim Rice	.30	.14
414	Bruce Sutter	.20	.09
415	Oil Can Boyd	.20	.09
416	Ruben Sierra	.30	.14
417	Mike LaValliere	.20	.09
418	Steve Buechele	.20	.09
419	Gary Redus	.20	.09
420	Scott Fletcher	.20	.09
421	Dale Sveum	.20	.09
422	Bob Knepper	.20	.09
423	Luis Rivera	.20	.09
424	Ted Higuera	.20	.09
425	Kevin Bass	.20	.09
426	Ken Gerhart	.20	.09
427	Shane Rawley	.20	.09
428	Paul O'Neill	.30	.14

❏ 429	Joe Orsulak	.20	.09
❏ 430	Jackie Gutierrez	.20	.09
❏ 431	Gerald Perry	.20	.09
❏ 432	Mike Greenwell	.20	.09
❏ 433	Jerry Royster	.20	.09
❏ 434	Ellis Burks	.50	.23
❏ 435	Ed Olwine	.20	.09
❏ 436	Dave Rucker	.20	.09
❏ 437	Charlie Hough	.30	.14
❏ 438	Bob Walk	.20	.09
❏ 439	Bob Brower	.20	.09
❏ 440	Barry Bonds	1.50	.70
❏ 441	Tom Foley	.20	.09
❏ 442	Rob Deer	.20	.09
❏ 443	Glenn Davis	.20	.09
❏ 444	Dave Martinez	.20	.09
❏ 445	Bill Wegman	.20	.09
❏ 446	Lloyd McClendon	.20	.09
❏ 447	Dave Schmidt	.20	.09
❏ 448	Darren Daulton	.30	.14
❏ 449	Frank Williams	.20	.09
❏ 450	Don Aase	.20	.09
❏ 451	Lou Whitaker	.30	.14
❏ 452	Rich Gossage	.30	.14
❏ 453	Ed Whitson	.20	.09
❏ 454	Jim Walewander	.20	.09
❏ 455	Damon Berryhill	.20	.09
❏ 456	Tim Burke	.20	.09
❏ 457	Barry Jones	.20	.09
❏ 458	Joel Youngblood	.20	.09
❏ 459	Floyd Youmans	.20	.09
❏ 460	Mark Salas	.20	.09
❏ 461	Jeff Russell	.20	.09
❏ 462	Darnell Miller	.20	.09
❏ 463	Jeff Kunkel	.20	.09
❏ 464	Sherman Corbett	.20	.09
❏ 465	Curtis Wilkerson	.20	.09
❏ 466	Bud Black	.20	.09
❏ 467	Cal Ripken	3.00	1.35
❏ 468	John Farrell	.20	.09
❏ 469	Terry Kennedy	.20	.09
❏ 470	Tom Candiotti	.20	.09
❏ 471	Roberto Alomar	1.25	.55
❏ 472	Jeff M. Robinson	.20	.09
❏ 473	Vance Law	.20	.09
❏ 474	Randy Ready UER	.20	.09
	(Strikeout total 136, should be 115)		
❏ 475	Walt Terrell	.20	.09
❏ 476	Kelly Downs	.20	.09
❏ 477	Johnny Paredes	.20	.09
❏ 478	Shawn Hillegas	.20	.09
❏ 479	Bob Brenly	.20	.09
❏ 480	Otis Nixon	.30	.14
❏ 481	Johnny Ray	.20	.09
❏ 482	Geno Petralli	.20	.09
❏ 483	Stu Cliburn	.20	.09
❏ 484	Pete Incaviglia	.20	.09
❏ 485	Brian Downing	.20	.09
❏ 486	Jeff Stone	.20	.09
❏ 487	Carmen Castillo	.20	.09
❏ 488	Tom Niedenfuer	.20	.09
❏ 489	Jay Bell	.50	.23
❏ 490	Rick Schu	.20	.09
❏ 491	Jeff Pico	.20	.09
❏ 492	Mark Parent	.20	.09
❏ 493	Eric King	.20	.09
❏ 494	Al Nipper	.20	.09
❏ 495	Andy Hawkins	.20	.09
❏ 496	Daryl Boston	.20	.09
❏ 497	Ernie Riles	.20	.09
❏ 498	Pascual Perez	.20	.09
❏ 499	Bill Long UER	.20	.09
	(Games started total 70, should be 44)		
❏ 500	Kirt Manwaring	.20	.09
❏ 501	Chuck Crim	.20	.09
❏ 502	Candy Maldonado	.20	.09
❏ 503	Dennis Lamp	.20	.09
❏ 504	Glenn Braggs	.20	.09
❏ 505	Joe Price	.20	.09
❏ 506	Ken Williams	.20	.09
❏ 507	Bill Pecota	.20	.09
❏ 508	Rey Quinones	.20	.09
❏ 509	Jeff Bittiger	.20	.09
❏ 510	Kevin Seitzer	.20	.09
❏ 511	Steve Bedrosian	.20	.09
❏ 512	Todd Worrell	.30	.14
❏ 513	Chris James	.20	.09
❏ 514	Jose Oquendo	.20	.09
❏ 515	David Palmer	.20	.09
❏ 516	John Smiley	.20	.09
❏ 517	Dave Clark	.20	.09
❏ 518	Mike Dunne	.20	.09
❏ 519	Ron Washington	.20	.09
❏ 520	Bob Kipper	.20	.09
❏ 521	Lee Smith	.30	.14
❏ 522	Juan Castillo	.20	.09
❏ 523	Don Robinson	.20	.09
❏ 524	Kevin Romine	.20	.09
❏ 525	Paul Molitor	.75	.35
❏ 526	Mark Langston	.20	.09
❏ 527	Donnie Hill	.20	.09
❏ 528	Larry Owen	.20	.09
❏ 529	Jerry Reed	.20	.09
❏ 530	Jack McDowell	.30	.14
❏ 531	Greg Mathews	.20	.09
❏ 532	John Russell	.20	.09
❏ 533	Dan Quisenberry	.20	.09
❏ 534	Greg Gross	.20	.09
❏ 535	Danny Cox	.20	.09
❏ 536	Terry Francona	.30	.14
❏ 537	Andy Van Slyke	.30	.14
❏ 538	Mel Hall	.20	.09
❏ 539	Jim Gott	.20	.09
❏ 540	Doug Jones	.20	.09
❏ 541	Craig Lefferts	.20	.09
❏ 542	Mike Boddicker	.20	.09
❏ 543	Greg Brock	.20	.09
❏ 544	Atlee Hammaker	.20	.09
❏ 545	Tom Bolton	.20	.09
❏ 546	Mike Macfarlane	.20	.09
❏ 547	Rich Renteria	.20	.09
❏ 548	John Davis	.20	.09
❏ 549	Floyd Bannister	.20	.09
❏ 550	Mickey Brantley	.20	.09
❏ 551	Duane Ward	.20	.09
❏ 552	Dan Petry	.20	.09
❏ 553	Mickey Tettleton UER	.30	.14
	(Walks total 175, should be 136)		
❏ 554	Rick Leach	.20	.09
❏ 555	Mike Witt	.20	.09
❏ 556	Sid Bream	.20	.09
❏ 557	Bobby Witt	.20	.09
❏ 558	Tommy Herr	.20	.09
❏ 559	Randy Milligan	.20	.09
❏ 560	Jose Cecena	.20	.09
❏ 561	Mackey Sasser	.20	.09
❏ 562	Carney Lansford	.30	.14
❏ 563	Rick Aguilera	.30	.14
❏ 564	Ron Hassey	.20	.09
❏ 565	Dwight Gooden	.30	.14
❏ 566	Paul Assenmacher	.20	.09
❏ 567	Neil Allen	.20	.09
❏ 568	Jim Morrison	.20	.09
❏ 569	Mike Pagliarulo	.20	.09
❏ 570	Ted Simmons	.30	.14
❏ 571	Mark Thurmond	.20	.09
❏ 572	Fred McGriff	.75	.35
❏ 573	Wally Joyner	.30	.14
❏ 574	Jose Bautista	.20	.09
❏ 575	Kelly Gruber	.20	.09
❏ 576	Cecilio Guante	.20	.09
❏ 577	Mark Davidson	.20	.09
❏ 578	Bobby Bonilla UER	.50	.23
	(Total steals 2 in '87, should be 3)		
❏ 579	Mike Stanley	.20	.09
❏ 580	Gene Larkin	.20	.09
❏ 581	Stan Javier	.20	.09
❏ 582	Howard Johnson	.20	.09
❏ 583A	Mike Gallego ERR	1.00	.45
	(Front reversed negative)		
❏ 583B	Mike Gallego COR	.75	.35
❏ 584	David Cone	.75	.35
❏ 585	Doug Jennings	.20	.09
❏ 586	Charles Hudson	.20	.09
❏ 587	Dion James	.20	.09
❏ 588	Al Leiter	.75	.35
❏ 589	Charlie Puleo	.20	.09
❏ 590	Roberto Kelly	.30	.14
❏ 591	Thad Bosley	.20	.09
❏ 592	Pete Stanicek	.20	.09
❏ 593	Pat Borders	.30	.14
❏ 594	Bryan Harvey	.20	.09
❏ 595	Jeff Ballard	.20	.09
❏ 596	Jeff Reardon	.30	.14
❏ 597	Doug Drabek	.20	.09
❏ 598	Edwin Correa	.20	.09
❏ 599	Keith Atherton	.20	.09
❏ 600	Dave LaPoint	.20	.09
❏ 601	Don Baylor	.30	.14
❏ 602	Tom Pagnozzi	.20	.09
❏ 603	Tim Flannery	.20	.09
❏ 604	Gene Walter	.20	.09
❏ 605	Dave Parker	.30	.14
❏ 606	Mike Diaz	.20	.09
❏ 607	Chris Gwynn	.20	.09
❏ 608	Odell Jones	.20	.09
❏ 609	Carlton Fisk	.75	.35
❏ 610	Jay Howell	.20	.09
❏ 611	Tim Crews	.20	.09
❏ 612	Keith Hernandez	.30	.14
❏ 613	Willie Fraser	.20	.09
❏ 614	Jim Eppard	.20	.09
❏ 615	Jeff Hamilton	.20	.09
❏ 616	Kurt Stillwell	.20	.09
❏ 617	Tom Browning	.20	.09
❏ 618	Jeff Montgomery	.30	.14
❏ 619	Jose Rijo	.20	.09
❏ 620	Jamie Quirk	.20	.09
❏ 621	Willie McGee	.30	.14
❏ 622	Mark Grant UER	.20	.09
	(Glove on wrong hand)		
❏ 623	Bill Swift	.20	.09
❏ 624	Orlando Mercado	.20	.09
❏ 625	John Costello	.20	.09
❏ 626	Jose Gonzalez	.20	.09
❏ 627A	Bill Schroeder ERR	1.00	.45
	(Back photo actually Ronn Reynolds buckling shin guards)		
❏ 627B	Bill Schroeder COR	.75	.35
❏ 628A	Fred Manrique ERR	.75	.35
	(Back photo actually Ozzie Guillen throwing)		
❏ 628B	Fred Manrique COR	.20	.09
	(Swinging bat on back)		
❏ 629	Ricky Horton	.20	.09
❏ 630	Dan Plesac	.20	.09
❏ 631	Alfredo Griffin	.20	.09
❏ 632	Chuck Finley	.30	.14
❏ 633	Kirk Gibson	.30	.14
❏ 634	Randy Myers	.20	.09
❏ 635	Greg Minton	.20	.09
❏ 636A	Herm Winningham	.75	.35
	ERR (W1nningham on back)		
❏ 636B	Herm Winningham COR	.20	.09
❏ 637	Charlie Leibrandt	.20	.09
❏ 638	Tim Birtsas	.20	.09
❏ 639	Bill Buckner	.30	.14
❏ 640	Danny Jackson	.20	.09
❏ 641	Greg Booker	.20	.09
❏ 642	Jim Presley	.20	.09
❏ 643	Gene Nelson	.20	.09
❏ 644	Rod Booker	.20	.09
❏ 645	Dennis Rasmussen	.20	.09
❏ 646	Juan Nieves	.20	.09
❏ 647	Bobby Thigpen	.20	.09
❏ 648	Tim Belcher	.20	.09
❏ 649	Mike Young	.20	.09
❏ 650	Ivan Calderon	.20	.09
❏ 651	Oswaldo Peraza	.20	.09
❏ 652A	Pat Sheridan ERR	2.00	.90
	(No position on front)		
❏ 652B	Pat Sheridan COR	.20	.09
❏ 653	Mike Morgan	.20	.09
❏ 654	Mike Heath	.20	.09
❏ 655	Jay Tibbs	.20	.09
❏ 656	Fernando Valenzuela	.30	.14
❏ 657	Lee Mazzilli	.20	.09
❏ 658	Frank Viola AL CY	.20	.09
❏ 659A	Jose Canseco AL MVP	.30	.14
	(Eagle logo in black)		
❏ 659B	Jose Canseco AL MVP	.30	.14

(Eagle logo in blue)
❏ 660	Walt Weiss AL ROY	.20	.09
❏ 661	Orel Hershiser NL CY	.30	.14
❏ 662	Kirk Gibson NL MVP	.20	.09
❏ 663	Chris Sabo NL ROY	.20	.09
❏ 664	Dennis Eckersley	.20	.09

ALCS MVP
❏ 665	Orel Hershiser	.30	.14

NLCS MVP
❏ 666	Kirk Gibson WS	.75	.35
❏ 667	Orel Hershiser WS MVP	.30	.14
❏ 668	Wally Joyner TC	.20	.09
❏ 669	Nolan Ryan TC	1.00	.45
❏ 670	Jose Canseco TC	.30	.14
❏ 671	Fred McGriff TC	.30	.14
❏ 672	Dale Murphy TC	.30	.14
❏ 673	Paul Molitor TC	.30	.14
❏ 674	Ozzie Smith TC	.50	.23
❏ 675	Ryne Sandberg TC	.50	.23
❏ 676	Kirk Gibson TC	.20	.09
❏ 677	Andres Galarraga TC	.30	.14
❏ 678	Will Clark TC	.30	.14
❏ 679	Cory Snyder TC	.20	.09
❏ 680	Alvin Davis TC	.20	.09
❏ 681	Darryl Strawberry TC	.20	.09
❏ 682	Cal Ripken TC	1.00	.45
❏ 683	Tony Gwynn TC	.75	.35
❏ 684	Mike Schmidt TC	.30	.14
❏ 685	Andy Van Slyke TC UER	.20	.09

(96 Junior Ortiz)
❏ 686	Ruben Sierra TC	.20	.09
❏ 687	Wade Boggs TC	.30	.14
❏ 688	Eric Davis TC	.20	.09
❏ 689	George Brett TC	.75	.35
❏ 690	Alan Trammell TC	.30	.14
❏ 691	Frank Viola TC	.20	.09
❏ 692	Harold Baines TC	.20	.09
❏ 693	Don Mattingly TC	.50	.23
❏ 694	Checklist 1-100	.20	.09
❏ 695	Checklist 101-200	.20	.09
❏ 696	Checklist 201-300	.20	.09
❏ 697	Checklist 301-400	.20	.09
❏ 698	Checklist 401-500 UER	.20	.09

(467 Cal Ripken Jr.)
❏ 699	Checklist 501-600 UER	.20	.09

(543 Greg Booker)
❏ 700	Checklist 601-700	.20	.09
❏ 701	Checklist 701-800	.20	.09
❏ 702	Jesse Barfield	.20	.09
❏ 703	Walt Terrell	.20	.09
❏ 704	Dickie Thon	.20	.09
❏ 705	Al Leiter	.75	.35
❏ 706	Dave LaPoint	.20	.09
❏ 707	Charlie Hayes	.75	.35
❏ 708	Andy Hawkins	.20	.09
❏ 709	Mickey Hatcher	.20	.09
❏ 710	Lance McCullers	.20	.09
❏ 711	Ron Kittle	.20	.09
❏ 712	Bert Blyleven	.30	.14
❏ 713	Rick Dempsey	.20	.09
❏ 714	Ken Williams	.20	.09
❏ 715	Steve Rosenberg	.20	.09
❏ 716	Joe Skalski	.20	.09
❏ 717	Spike Owen	.20	.09
❏ 718	Todd Burns	.20	.09
❏ 719	Kevin Gross	.20	.09
❏ 720	Tommy Herr	.20	.09
❏ 721	Rob Ducey	.20	.09
❏ 722	Gary Green	.20	.09
❏ 723	Gregg Olson	.75	.35
❏ 724	Greg W. Harris	.20	.09
❏ 725	Craig Worthington	.20	.09
❏ 726	Tom Howard	.20	.09
❏ 727	Dale Mohorcic	.20	.09
❏ 728	Rich Yett	.20	.09
❏ 729	Mel Hall	.20	.09
❏ 730	Floyd Youmans	.20	.09
❏ 731	Lonnie Smith	.20	.09
❏ 732	Wally Backman	.20	.09
❏ 733	Trevor Wilson	.20	.09
❏ 734	Jose Alvarez	.20	.09
❏ 735	Bob Milacki	.20	.09
❏ 736	Tom Gordon	.75	.35
❏ 737	Wally Whitehurst	.20	.09
❏ 738	Mike Aldrete	.20	.09
❏ 739	Keith Miller	.20	.09

❏ 740	Randy Milligan	.20	.09
❏ 741	Jeff Parrett	.20	.09
❏ 742	Steve Finley	2.00	.90
❏ 743	Junior Felix	.20	.09
❏ 744	Pete Harnisch	1.00	.45
❏ 745	Bill Spiers	.20	.09
❏ 746	Hensley Meulens	.20	.09
❏ 747	Juan Bell	.20	.09
❏ 748	Steve Sax	.20	.09
❏ 749	Phil Bradley	.20	.09
❏ 750	Rey Quinones	.20	.09
❏ 751	Tommy Gregg	.20	.09
❏ 752	Kevin Brown	1.50	.70
❏ 753	Derek Lilliquist	.20	.09
❏ 754	Todd Zeile	1.00	.45
❏ 755	Jim Abbott	.75	.35

(Triple exposure)
❏ 756	Ozzie Canseco	.20	.09
❏ 757	Nick Esasky	.20	.09
❏ 758	Mike Moore	.20	.09
❏ 759	Rob Murphy	.20	.09
❏ 760	Rick Mahler	.20	.09
❏ 761	Fred Lynn	.20	.09
❏ 762	Kevin Blankenship	.20	.09
❏ 763	Eddie Murray	.75	.35
❏ 764	Steve Searcy	.20	.09
❏ 765	Jerome Walton	.75	.35
❏ 766	Erik Hanson	.30	.14
❏ 767	Bob Boone	.75	.35
❏ 768	Edgar Martinez	.75	.35
❏ 769	Jose DeJesus	.20	.09
❏ 770	Greg Briley	.20	.09
❏ 771	Steve Peters	.20	.09
❏ 772	Rafael Palmeiro	1.00	.45
❏ 773	Jack Clark	.30	.14
❏ 774	Nolan Ryan	3.00	1.35

(Throwing football)
❏ 775	Lance Parrish	.20	.09
❏ 776	Joe Girardi	.75	.35
❏ 777	Willie Randolph	.30	.14
❏ 778	Mitch Williams	.20	.09
❏ 779	Dennis Cook	.20	.09
❏ 780	Dwight Smith	.30	.14
❏ 781	Lenny Harris	.30	.14
❏ 782	Torey Lovullo	.20	.09
❏ 783	Norm Charlton	.20	.09
❏ 784	Chris Brown	.20	.09
❏ 785	Todd Benzinger	.20	.09
❏ 786	Shane Rawley	.20	.09
❏ 787	Omar Vizquel	2.50	1.10
❏ 788	LaVel Freeman	.20	.09
❏ 789	Jeffrey Leonard	.20	.09
❏ 790	Eddie Williams	.20	.09
❏ 791	Jamie Moyer	.20	.09
❏ 792	Bruce Hurst UER	.20	.09

(Workd Series)
❏ 793	Julio Franco	.20	.09
❏ 794	Claudell Washington	.20	.09
❏ 795	Jody Davis	.20	.09
❏ 796	Oddibe McDowell	.20	.09
❏ 797	Paul Kilgus	.20	.09
❏ 798	Tracy Jones	.20	.09
❏ 799	Steve Wilson	.20	.09
❏ 800	Pete O'Brien	.20	.09

1990 Upper Deck

Kevin Maas

	MINT	NRMT
COMPLETE SET (800)	30.00	13.50
COMP.FACT.SET (800)	30.00	13.50
COMMON CARD (1-800)	.10	.05
MINOR STARS	.20	.09
UNLISTED STARS	.40	.18

❏ 1	Star Rookie Checklist	.10	.05
❏ 2	Randy Nosek	.10	.05
❏ 3	Tom Drees UER	.10	.05

(11th line, hulred,
should be hurled)
❏ 4	Curt Young	.10	.05
❏ 5	Devon White TC	.10	.05
❏ 6	Luis Salazar	.10	.05
❏ 7	Von Hayes TC	.10	.05
❏ 8	Jose Bautista	.10	.05
❏ 9	Marquis Grissom	.50	.23
❏ 10	Orel Hershiser TC	.10	.05
❏ 11	Rick Aguilera	.20	.09
❏ 12	Benito Santiago TC	.10	.05
❏ 13	Deion Sanders	.40	.18
❏ 14	Marvell Wynne	.10	.05
❏ 15	Dave West	.10	.05
❏ 16	Bobby Bonilla TC	.10	.05
❏ 17	Sammy Sosa	10.00	4.50
❏ 18	Steve Sax TC	.10	.05
❏ 19	Jack Howell	.10	.05
❏ 20	Mike Schmidt Special	.60	.25

UER (Suprising,
should be surprising)
❏ 21	Robin Ventura UER	.40	.18

(Samta Maria)
❏ 22	Brian Meyer	.10	.05
❏ 23	Blaine Beatty	.10	.05
❏ 24	Ken Griffey Jr. TC	1.25	.55
❏ 25	Greg Vaughn UER	.75	.35

(Association misspelled
as assiocation)
❏ 26	Xavier Hernandez	.10	.05
❏ 27	Jason Grimsley	.10	.05
❏ 28	Eric Anthony UER	.10	.05

(Ashville, should
be Asheville)
❏ 29	Tim Raines TC UER	.10	.05

(Wallach listed before Walker)
❏ 30	David Wells	.30	.14
❏ 31	Hal Morris	.10	.05
❏ 32	Bo Jackson TC	.20	.09
❏ 33	Kelly Mann	.10	.05
❏ 34	Nolan Ryan Special	.75	.35
❏ 35	Scott Service UER	.10	.05

(Born Cincinatti on
7/27/67, should be
Cincinnati 2/27)
❏ 36	Mark McGwire TC	1.00	.45
❏ 37	Tino Martinez	.50	.23
❏ 38	Chili Davis	.20	.09
❏ 39	Scott Sanderson	.10	.05
❏ 40	Kevin Mitchell TC	.10	.05
❏ 41	Lou Whitaker TC	.10	.05
❏ 42	Scott Coolbaugh UER	.10	.05

(Definately)
❏ 43	Jose Cano UER	.10	.05

(Born 9/7/62, should
be 3/7/62)
❏ 44	Jose Vizcaino	.30	.14
❏ 45	Bob Hamelin	.40	.18
❏ 46	Jose Offerman UER	.75	.35

(Posesses)
❏ 47	Kevin Blankenship	.10	.05
❏ 48	Kirby Puckett TC	.40	.18
❏ 49	Tommy Greene UER	.10	.05

(Livest, should be
liveliest)
❏ 50	Will Clark Special	.20	.09

UER (Perenial, should
be perennial)
❏ 51	Rob Nelson	.10	.05
❏ 52	Chris Hammond UER	.10	.05

(Chatanooga)
❏ 53	Joe Carter TC	.10	.05
❏ 54A	Ben McDonald ERR	2.00	.90

(No Rookie designation
on card front)
❏ 54B	Ben McDonald COR	.30	.14

❑ 55 Andy Benes UER	.40	.18
(Whichita)		
❑ 56 John Olerud	1.25	.55
❑ 57 Roger Clemens TC	.50	.23
❑ 58 Tony Armas	.10	.05
❑ 59 George Canale	.10	.05
❑ 60A Mickey Tettleton TC	2.00	.90
ERR (683 Jamie Weston)		
❑ 60B Mickey Tettleton TC	.10	.05
COR (683 Mickey Weston)		
❑ 61 Mike Stanton	.10	.05
❑ 62 Dwight Gooden TC	.10	.05
❑ 63 Kent Mercker UER	.10	.05
(Albuquerque)		
❑ 64 Francisco Cabrera	.10	.05
❑ 65 Steve Avery UER	.10	.05
(Born NJ, should be MI,		
Merker should be Mercker)		
❑ 66 Jose Canseco	.50	.23
❑ 67 Matt Merullo	.10	.05
❑ 68 Vince Coleman TC UER	.10	.05
(Guerrero)		
❑ 69 Ron Karkovice	.10	.05
❑ 70 Kevin Maas	.20	.09
❑ 71 Dennis Cook UER	.10	.05
(Shown with righty		
glove on card back)		
❑ 72 Juan Gonzalez UER	5.00	2.20
(135 games for Tulsa		
in '89, should be 133)		
❑ 73 Andre Dawson TC	.20	.09
❑ 74 Dean Palmer UER	1.00	.45
(Permanent misspelled		
as perminant)		
❑ 75 Bo Jackson Special	.20	.09
UER (Monsterous,		
should be monstrous)		
❑ 76 Rob Richie	.10	.05
❑ 77 Bobby Rose UER	.10	.05
(Pickin, should		
be pick in)		
❑ 78 Brian DuBois UER	.10	.05
(Commiting)		
❑ 79 Ozzie Guillen TC	.10	.05
❑ 80 Gene Nelson	.10	.05
❑ 81 Bob McClure	.10	.05
❑ 82 Julio Franco TC	.10	.05
❑ 83 Greg Minton	.10	.05
❑ 84 John Smoltz TC UER	.20	.09
(Oddibe not Oddibe)		
❑ 85 Willie Fraser	.10	.05
❑ 86 Neal Heaton	.10	.05
❑ 87 Kevin Tapani UER	.20	.09
(24th line has excpet,		
should be except)		
❑ 88 Mike Scott TC	.10	.05
❑ 89A Jim Gott ERR	2.50	1.10
(Photo actually		
Rick Reed)		
❑ 89B Jim Gott COR	.10	.05
❑ 90 Lance Johnson	.10	.05
❑ 91 Robin Yount TC UER	.20	.09
(Checklist on back has		
178 Rob Deer and		
176 Mike Felder)		
❑ 92 Jeff Parrett	.10	.05
❑ 93 Julio Machado UER	.10	.05
(Valenzuelan, should		
be Venezuelan)		
❑ 94 Ron Jones	.10	.05
❑ 95 George Bell TC	.10	.05
❑ 96 Jerry Reuss	.10	.05
❑ 97 Brian Fisher	.10	.05
❑ 98 Kevin Ritz UER	.10	.05
(Amercian)		
❑ 99 Barry Larkin TC	.20	.09
❑ 100 Checklist 1-100	.10	.05
❑ 101 Gerald Perry	.10	.05
❑ 102 Kevin Appier	.30	.14
❑ 103 Julio Franco	.10	.05
❑ 104 Craig Biggio	.40	.18
❑ 105 Bo Jackson UER	.20	.09
('89 BA wrong,		
should be .256)		
❑ 106 Junior Felix	.10	.05
❑ 107 Mike Harkey	.10	.05

❑ 108 Fred McGriff	.40	.18
❑ 109 Rick Sutcliffe	.10	.05
❑ 110 Pete O'Brien	.10	.05
❑ 111 Kelly Gruber	.10	.05
❑ 112 Dwight Evans	.20	.09
❑ 113 Pat Borders	.10	.05
❑ 114 Dwight Gooden	.20	.09
❑ 115 Kevin Batiste	.10	.05
❑ 116 Eric Davis	.20	.09
❑ 117 Kevin Mitchell UER	.10	.05
(Career HR total 99,		
should be 100)		
❑ 118 Ron Oester	.10	.05
❑ 119 Brett Butler	.20	.09
❑ 120 Danny Jackson	.10	.05
❑ 121 Tommy Gregg	.10	.05
❑ 122 Ken Caminiti	.40	.18
❑ 123 Kevin Brown	.40	.18
❑ 124 George Brett UER	.75	.35
(133 runs, should		
be 1300)		
❑ 125 Mike Scott	.10	.05
❑ 126 Cory Snyder	.10	.05
❑ 127 George Bell	.10	.05
❑ 128 Mark Grace	.40	.18
❑ 129 Devon White	.10	.05
❑ 130 Tony Fernandez	.10	.05
❑ 131 Don Aase	.10	.05
❑ 132 Rance Mulliniks	.10	.05
❑ 133 Marty Barrett	.10	.05
❑ 134 Nelson Liriano	.10	.05
❑ 135 Mark Carreon	.10	.05
❑ 136 Candy Maldonado	.10	.05
❑ 137 Tim Birtsas	.10	.05
❑ 138 Tom Brookens	.10	.05
❑ 139 John Franco	.10	.05
❑ 140 Mike LaCoss	.10	.05
❑ 141 Jeff Treadway	.10	.05
❑ 142 Pat Tabler	.10	.05
❑ 143 Darrell Evans	.20	.09
❑ 144 Rafael Ramirez	.10	.05
❑ 145 Oddibe McDowell UER	.10	.05
(Misspelled Odibbe)		
❑ 146 Brian Downing	.10	.05
❑ 147 Curt Wilkerson	.10	.05
❑ 148 Ernie Whitt	.10	.05
❑ 149 Bill Schroeder	.10	.05
❑ 150 Domingo Ramos UER	.10	.05
(Says throws right,		
but shows him		
throwing lefty)		
❑ 151 Rick Honeycutt	.10	.05
❑ 152 Don Slaught	.10	.05
❑ 153 Mitch Webster	.10	.05
❑ 154 Tony Phillips	.10	.05
❑ 155 Paul Kilgus	.10	.05
❑ 156 Ken Griffey Jr. UER	6.00	2.70
(Simultaniously)		
❑ 157 Gary Sheffield	.40	.18
❑ 158 Wally Backman	.10	.05
❑ 159 B.J. Surhoff	.10	.05
❑ 160 Louie Meadows	.10	.05
❑ 161 Paul O'Neill	.20	.09
❑ 162 Jeff McKnight	.10	.05
❑ 163 Alvaro Espinoza	.10	.05
❑ 164 Scott Scudder	.10	.05
❑ 165 Jeff Reed	.10	.05
❑ 166 Gregg Jefferies	.20	.09
❑ 167 Barry Larkin	.40	.18
❑ 168 Gary Carter	.40	.18
❑ 169 Robby Thompson	.10	.05
❑ 170 Rolando Roomes	.10	.05
❑ 171 Mark McGwire UER	2.00	.90
(Total games 427 and		
hits 479, should be		
467 and 427)		
❑ 172 Steve Sax	.10	.05
❑ 173 Mark Williamson	.10	.05
❑ 174 Mitch Williams	.10	.05
❑ 175 Brian Holton	.10	.05
❑ 176 Rob Deer	.10	.05
❑ 177 Tim Raines	.20	.09
❑ 178 Mike Felder	.10	.05
❑ 179 Harold Reynolds	.10	.05
❑ 180 Terry Francona	.10	.05
❑ 181 Chris Sabo	.20	.09

❑ 182 Darryl Strawberry	.20	.09
❑ 183 Willie Randolph	.20	.09
❑ 184 Bill Ripken	.10	.05
❑ 185 Mackey Sasser	.10	.05
❑ 186 Todd Benzinger	.10	.05
❑ 187 Kevin Elster UER	.10	.05
(16 homers in 1989,		
should be 10)		
❑ 188 Jose Uribe	.10	.05
❑ 189 Tom Browning	.10	.05
❑ 190 Keith Miller	.10	.05
❑ 191 Don Mattingly	.75	.35
❑ 192 Dave Parker	.20	.09
❑ 193 Roberto Kelly UER	.10	.05
(96 RBI, should be 62)		
❑ 194 Phil Bradley	.10	.05
❑ 195 Ron Hassey	.10	.05
❑ 196 Gerald Young	.10	.05
❑ 197 Hubie Brooks	.10	.05
❑ 198 Bill Doran	.10	.05
❑ 199 Al Newman	.10	.05
❑ 200 Checklist 101-200	.10	.05
❑ 201 Terry Puhl	.10	.05
❑ 202 Frank DiPino	.10	.05
❑ 203 Jim Clancy	.10	.05
❑ 204 Bob Ojeda	.10	.05
❑ 205 Alex Trevino	.10	.05
❑ 206 Dave Henderson	.10	.05
❑ 207 Henry Cotto	.10	.05
❑ 208 Rafael Belliard UER	.10	.05
(Born 1961, not 1951)		
❑ 209 Stan Javier	.10	.05
❑ 210 Jerry Reed	.10	.05
❑ 211 Doug Dascenzo	.10	.05
❑ 212 Andres Thomas	.10	.05
❑ 213 Greg Maddux	1.00	.45
❑ 214 Mike Schooler	.10	.05
❑ 215 Lonnie Smith	.10	.05
❑ 216 Jose Rijo	.10	.05
❑ 217 Greg Gagne	.10	.05
❑ 218 Jim Gantner	.10	.05
❑ 219 Allan Anderson	.10	.05
❑ 220 Rick Mahler	.10	.05
❑ 221 Jim Deshaies	.10	.05
❑ 222 Keith Hernandez	.20	.09
❑ 223 Vince Coleman	.10	.05
❑ 224 David Cone	.40	.18
❑ 225 Ozzie Smith	.50	.23
❑ 226 Matt Nokes	.10	.05
❑ 227 Barry Bonds	.50	.23
❑ 228 Felix Jose	.10	.05
❑ 229 Dennis Powell	.10	.05
❑ 230 Mike Gallego	.10	.05
❑ 231 Shawon Dunston UER	.10	.05
('89 stats are		
Andre Dawson's)		
❑ 232 Ron Gant	.20	.09
❑ 233 Omar Vizquel	.40	.18
❑ 234 Derek Lilliquist	.10	.05
❑ 235 Erik Hanson	.10	.05
❑ 236 Kirby Puckett UER	.60	.25
(824 games, should		
be 924)		
❑ 237 Bill Spiers	.10	.05
❑ 238 Dan Gladden	.10	.05
❑ 239 Bryan Clutterbuck	.10	.05
❑ 240 John Moses	.10	.05
❑ 241 Ron Darling	.10	.05
❑ 242 Joe Magrane	.10	.05
❑ 243 Dave Magadan	.10	.05
❑ 244 Pedro Guerrero UER	.10	.05
(Misspelled Guerrero)		
❑ 245 Glenn Davis	.10	.05
❑ 246 Terry Steinbach	.10	.05
❑ 247 Fred Lynn	.10	.05
❑ 248 Gary Redus	.10	.05
❑ 249 Ken Williams	.10	.05
❑ 250 Sid Bream	.10	.05
❑ 251 Bob Welch UER	.10	.05
(2587 career strike-		
outs, should be 1587)		
❑ 252 Bill Buckner	.10	.05
❑ 253 Carney Lansford	.20	.09
❑ 254 Paul Molitor	.40	.18
❑ 255 Jose DeJesus	.10	.05
❑ 256 Orel Hershiser	.20	.09

☐ 257 Tom Brunansky	.10	.05
☐ 258 Mike Davis	.10	.05
☐ 259 Jeff Ballard	.10	.05
☐ 260 Scott Terry	.10	.05
☐ 261 Sid Fernandez	.10	.05
☐ 262 Mike Marshall	.10	.05
☐ 263 Howard Johnson UER	.10	.05
(192 SO, should be 592)		
☐ 264 Kirk Gibson UER	.20	.09
(659 runs, should be 669)		
☐ 265 Kevin McReynolds	.10	.05
☐ 266 Cal Ripken	1.50	.70
☐ 267 Ozzie Guillen UER	.10	.05
(Career triples 27, should be 29)		
☐ 268 Jim Traber	.10	.05
☐ 269 Bobby Thigpen UER	.10	.05
(31 saves in 1989, should be 34)		
☐ 270 Joe Orsulak	.10	.05
☐ 271 Bob Boone	.20	.09
☐ 272 Dave Stewart UER	.20	.09
(Totals wrong due to omission of '86 stats)		
☐ 273 Tim Wallach	.10	.05
☐ 274 Luis Aquino UER	.10	.05
(Says throws lefty, but shows him throwing righty)		
☐ 275 Mike Moore	.10	.05
☐ 276 Tony Pena	.10	.05
☐ 277 Eddie Murray UER	.40	.18
(Several typos in career total stats)		
☐ 278 Milt Thompson	.10	.05
☐ 279 Alejandro Pena	.10	.05
☐ 280 Ken Dayley	.10	.05
☐ 281 Carmen Castillo	.10	.05
☐ 282 Tom Henke	.10	.05
☐ 283 Mickey Hatcher	.10	.05
☐ 284 Roy Smith	.10	.05
☐ 285 Manny Lee	.10	.05
☐ 286 Dan Pasqua	.10	.05
☐ 287 Larry Sheets	.10	.05
☐ 288 Garry Templeton	.10	.05
☐ 289 Eddie Williams	.10	.05
☐ 290 Brady Anderson UER	.40	.18
(Home: Silver Springs, not Silver Springs)		
☐ 291 Spike Owen	.10	.05
☐ 292 Storm Davis	.10	.05
☐ 293 Chris Bosio	.10	.05
☐ 294 Jim Eisenreich	.10	.05
☐ 295 Don August	.10	.05
☐ 296 Jeff Hamilton	.10	.05
☐ 297 Mickey Tettleton	.20	.09
☐ 298 Mike Scioscia	.10	.05
☐ 299 Kevin Hickey	.10	.05
☐ 300 Checklist 201-300	.10	.05
☐ 301 Shawn Abner	.10	.05
☐ 302 Kevin Bass	.10	.05
☐ 303 Bip Roberts	.10	.05
☐ 304 Joe Girardi	.30	.14
☐ 305 Danny Darwin	.10	.05
☐ 306 Mike Heath	.10	.05
☐ 307 Mike Macfarlane	.10	.05
☐ 308 Ed Whitson	.10	.05
☐ 309 Tracy Jones	.10	.05
☐ 310 Scott Fletcher	.10	.05
☐ 311 Darnell Coles	.10	.05
☐ 312 Mike Brumley	.10	.05
☐ 313 Bill Swift	.10	.05
☐ 314 Charlie Hough	.20	.09
☐ 315 Jim Presley	.10	.05
☐ 316 Luis Polonia	.10	.05
☐ 317 Mike Morgan	.10	.05
☐ 318 Lee Guetterman	.10	.05
☐ 319 Jose Oquendo	.10	.05
☐ 320 Wayne Tolleson	.10	.05
☐ 321 Jody Reed	.10	.05
☐ 322 Damon Berryhill	.10	.05
☐ 323 Roger Clemens	1.00	.45
☐ 324 Ryne Sandberg	.50	.23
☐ 325 Benito Santiago UER	.10	.05
(Misspelled Santago		

on card back)		
☐ 326 Bret Saberhagen UER	.20	.09
(1140 hits, should be 1240; 56 CG, should be 52)		
☐ 327 Lou Whitaker	.20	.09
☐ 328 Dave Gallagher	.10	.05
☐ 329 Mike Pagliarulo	.10	.05
☐ 330 Doyle Alexander	.10	.05
☐ 331 Jeffrey Leonard	.10	.05
☐ 332 Torey Lovullo	.10	.05
☐ 333 Pete Incaviglia	.10	.05
☐ 334 Rickey Henderson	.50	.23
☐ 335 Rafael Palmeiro	.40	.18
☐ 336 Ken Hill	.20	.09
☐ 337 Dave Winfield UER	.40	.18
(1418 RBI, should be 1438)		
☐ 338 Alfredo Griffin	.10	.05
☐ 339 Andy Hawkins	.10	.05
☐ 340 Ted Power	.10	.05
☐ 341 Steve Wilson	.10	.05
☐ 342 Jack Clark UER	.20	.09
(916 BB, should be 1006; 1142 SO, should be 1130)		
☐ 343 Ellis Burks	.30	.14
☐ 344 Tony Gwynn UER	1.00	.45
(Doubles stats on card back are wrong)		
☐ 345 Jerome Walton UER	.10	.05
(Total At Bats 476, should be 475)		
☐ 346 Roberto Alomar UER	.40	.18
(61 doubles, should be 51)		
☐ 347 Carlos Martinez UER	.10	.05
(Born 8/11/64, should be 8/11/65)		
☐ 348 Chet Lemon	.10	.05
☐ 349 Willie Wilson	.10	.05
☐ 350 Greg Walker	.10	.05
☐ 351 Tom Bolton	.10	.05
☐ 352 German Gonzalez	.10	.05
☐ 353 Harold Baines	.20	.09
☐ 354 Mike Greenwell	.10	.05
☐ 355 Ruben Sierra	.40	.18
☐ 356 Andres Galarraga	.40	.18
☐ 357 Andre Dawson	.40	.18
☐ 358 Jeff Brantley	.10	.05
☐ 359 Mike Bielecki	.10	.05
☐ 360 Ken Oberkfell	.10	.05
☐ 361 Kurt Stillwell	.10	.05
☐ 362 Brian Holman	.10	.05
☐ 363 Kevin Seitzer UER	.10	.05
(Career triples total does not add up)		
☐ 364 Alvin Davis	.10	.05
☐ 365 Tom Gordon	.10	.05
☐ 366 Bobby Bonilla UER	.20	.09
(Two steals in 1987, should be 3)		
☐ 367 Carlton Fisk	.40	.18
☐ 368 Steve Carter UER	.10	.05
(Charlotesville)		
☐ 369 Joel Skinner	.10	.05
☐ 370 John Cangelosi	.10	.05
☐ 371 Cecil Espy	.10	.05
☐ 372 Gary Wayne	.10	.05
☐ 373 Jim Rice	.20	.09
☐ 374 Mike Dyer	.10	.05
☐ 375 Joe Carter	.20	.09
☐ 376 Dwight Smith	.10	.05
☐ 377 John Wetteland	.40	.18
☐ 378 Earnie Riles	.10	.05
☐ 379 Otis Nixon	.20	.09
☐ 380 Vance Law	.10	.05
☐ 381 Dave Bergman	.10	.05
☐ 382 Frank White	.20	.09
☐ 383 Scott Bradley	.10	.05
☐ 384 Israel Sanchez UER	.10	.05
(Totals don't include '89 stats)		
☐ 385 Gary Pettis	.10	.05
☐ 386 Donn Pall	.10	.05
☐ 387 John Smiley	.10	.05

☐ 388 Tom Candiotti	.10	.05
☐ 389 Junior Ortiz	.10	.05
☐ 390 Steve Lyons	.10	.05
☐ 391 Brian Harper	.10	.05
☐ 392 Fred Manrique	.10	.05
☐ 393 Lee Smith	.20	.09
☐ 394 Jeff Kunkel	.10	.05
☐ 395 Claudell Washington	.10	.05
☐ 396 John Tudor	.10	.05
☐ 397 Terry Kennedy UER	.10	.05
(Career totals all wrong)		
☐ 398 Lloyd McClendon	.10	.05
☐ 399 Craig Lefferts	.10	.05
☐ 400 Checklist 301-400	.10	.05
☐ 401 Keith Moreland	.10	.05
☐ 402 Rich Gedman	.10	.05
☐ 403 Jeff D. Robinson	.10	.05
☐ 404 Randy Ready	.10	.05
☐ 405 Rick Cerone	.10	.05
☐ 406 Jeff Blauser	.10	.05
☐ 407 Larry Andersen	.10	.05
☐ 408 Joe Boever	.10	.05
☐ 409 Felix Fermin	.10	.05
☐ 410 Glenn Wilson	.10	.05
☐ 411 Rex Hudler	.10	.05
☐ 412 Mark Grant	.10	.05
☐ 413 Dennis Martinez	.20	.09
☐ 414 Darrin Jackson	.10	.05
☐ 415 Mike Aldrete	.10	.05
☐ 416 Roger McDowell	.10	.05
☐ 417 Jeff Reardon	.20	.09
☐ 418 Darren Daulton	.20	.09
☐ 419 Tim Laudner	.10	.05
☐ 420 Don Carman	.10	.05
☐ 421 Lloyd Moseby	.10	.05
☐ 422 Doug Drabek	.10	.05
☐ 423 Lenny Harris UER	.10	.05
(Walks 2 in '89, should be 20)		
☐ 424 Jose Lind	.10	.05
☐ 425 Dave Johnson (P)	.10	.05
☐ 426 Jerry Browne	.10	.05
☐ 427 Eric Yelding	.10	.05
☐ 428 Brad Komminsk	.10	.05
☐ 429 Jody Davis	.10	.05
☐ 430 Mariano Duncan	.10	.05
☐ 431 Mark Davis	.10	.05
☐ 432 Nelson Santovenia	.10	.05
☐ 433 Bruce Hurst	.10	.05
☐ 434 Jeff Huson	.10	.05
☐ 435 Chris James	.10	.05
☐ 436 Mark Guthrie	.10	.05
☐ 437 Charlie Hayes	.10	.05
☐ 438 Shane Rawley	.10	.05
☐ 439 Dickie Thon	.10	.05
☐ 440 Juan Berenguer	.10	.05
☐ 441 Kevin Romine	.10	.05
☐ 442 Bill Landrum	.10	.05
☐ 443 Todd Frohwirth	.10	.05
☐ 444 Craig Worthington	.10	.05
☐ 445 Fernando Valenzuela	.20	.09
☐ 446 Joey Belle	1.50	.70
☐ 447 Ed Whited UER	.10	.05
(Ashville, should be Asheville)		
☐ 448 Dave Smith	.10	.05
☐ 449 Dave Clark	.10	.05
☐ 450 Juan Agosto	.10	.05
☐ 451 Dave Valle	.10	.05
☐ 452 Kent Hrbek	.20	.09
☐ 453 Von Hayes	.10	.05
☐ 454 Gary Gaetti	.20	.09
☐ 455 Greg Briley	.10	.05
☐ 456 Glenn Braggs	.10	.05
☐ 457 Kirt Manwaring	.10	.05
☐ 458 Mel Hall	.10	.05
☐ 459 Brook Jacoby	.10	.05
☐ 460 Pat Sheridan	.10	.05
☐ 461 Rob Murphy	.10	.05
☐ 462 Jimmy Key	.20	.09
☐ 463 Nick Esasky	.10	.05
☐ 464 Rob Ducey	.10	.05
☐ 465 Carlos Quintana UER	.10	.05
(International)		
☐ 466 Larry Walker	2.50	1.10

❏ 467	Todd Worrell	.10	.05
❏ 468	Kevin Gross	.10	.05
❏ 469	Terry Pendleton	.20	.09
❏ 470	Dave Martinez	.10	.05
❏ 471	Gene Larkin	.10	.05
❏ 472	Len Dykstra UER	.20	.09
	('89 and total runs understated by 10)		
❏ 473	Barry Lyons	.10	.05
❏ 474	Terry Mulholland	.10	.05
❏ 475	Chip Hale	.10	.05
❏ 476	Jesse Barfield	.10	.05
❏ 477	Dan Plesac	.10	.05
❏ 478A	Scott Garrelts ERR	2.00	.90
	(Photo actually Bill Bathe)		
❏ 478B	Scott Garrelts COR	.10	.05
❏ 479	Dave Righetti	.10	.05
❏ 480	Gus Polidor UER	.10	.05
	(Wearing 14 on front, but 10 on back)		
❏ 481	Mookie Wilson	.20	.09
❏ 482	Luis Rivera	.10	.05
❏ 483	Mike Flanagan	.10	.05
❏ 484	Dennis Boyd	.10	.05
❏ 485	John Cerutti	.10	.05
❏ 486	John Costello	.10	.05
❏ 487	Pascual Perez	.10	.05
❏ 488	Tommy Herr	.10	.05
❏ 489	Tom Foley	.10	.05
❏ 490	Curt Ford	.10	.05
❏ 491	Steve Lake	.10	.05
❏ 492	Tim Teufel	.10	.05
❏ 493	Randy Bush	.10	.05
❏ 494	Mike Jackson	.20	.09
❏ 495	Steve Jeltz	.10	.05
❏ 496	Paul Gibson	.10	.05
❏ 497	Steve Balboni	.10	.05
❏ 498	Bud Black	.10	.05
❏ 499	Dale Sveum	.10	.05
❏ 500	Checklist 401-500	.10	.05
❏ 501	Tim Jones	.10	.05
❏ 502	Mark Portugal	.10	.05
❏ 503	Ivan Calderon	.10	.05
❏ 504	Rick Rhoden	.10	.05
❏ 505	Willie McGee	.20	.09
❏ 506	Kirk McCaskill	.10	.05
❏ 507	Dave LaPoint	.10	.05
❏ 508	Jay Howell	.10	.05
❏ 509	Johnny Ray	.10	.05
❏ 510	Dave Anderson	.10	.05
❏ 511	Chuck Crim	.10	.05
❏ 512	Joe Hesketh	.10	.05
❏ 513	Dennis Eckersley	.30	.14
❏ 514	Greg Brock	.10	.05
❏ 515	Tim Burke	.10	.05
❏ 516	Frank Tanana	.10	.05
❏ 517	Jay Bell	.20	.09
❏ 518	Guillermo Hernandez	.10	.05
❏ 519	Randy Kramer UER	.10	.05
	(Codiroli misspelled as Codoroli)		
❏ 520	Charles Hudson	.10	.05
❏ 521	Jim Corsi	.10	.05
	(Word %%originally- is misspelled on back)		
❏ 522	Steve Rosenberg	.10	.05
❏ 523	Cris Carpenter	.10	.05
❏ 524	Matt Winters	.10	.05
❏ 525	Melido Perez	.10	.05
❏ 526	Chris Gwynn UER	.10	.05
	(Albequerque)		
❏ 527	Bert Blyleven UER	.20	.09
	(Games career total is wrong, should be 644)		
❏ 528	Chuck Cary	.10	.05
❏ 529	Daryl Boston	.10	.05
❏ 530	Dale Mohorcic	.10	.05
❏ 531	Geronimo Berroa	.10	.05
❏ 532	Edgar Martinez	.40	.18
❏ 533	Dale Murphy	.40	.18
❏ 534	Jay Buhner	.40	.18
❏ 535	John Smoltz UER	.40	.18
	(HEA Stadium)		
❏ 536	Andy Van Slyke	.20	.09
❏ 537	Mike Henneman	.10	.05
❏ 538	Miguel Garcia	.10	.05
❏ 539	Frank Williams	.10	.05
❏ 540	R.J. Reynolds	.10	.05
❏ 541	Shawn Hillegas	.10	.05
❏ 542	Walt Weiss	.10	.05
❏ 543	Greg Hibbard	.10	.05
❏ 544	Nolan Ryan	1.50	.70
❏ 545	Todd Zeile	.20	.09
❏ 546	Hensley Meulens	.10	.05
❏ 547	Tim Belcher	.10	.05
❏ 548	Mike Witt	.10	.05
❏ 549	Greg Cadaret UER	.10	.05
	(Aquiring, should be Acquiring)		
❏ 550	Franklin Stubbs	.10	.05
❏ 551	Tony Castillo	.10	.05
❏ 552	Jeff M. Robinson	.10	.05
❏ 553	Steve Olin	.20	.09
❏ 554	Alan Trammell	.30	.14
❏ 555	Wade Boggs 4X	.40	.18
	(Bo Jackson in background)		
❏ 556	Will Clark	.40	.18
❏ 557	Jeff King	.10	.05
❏ 558	Mike Fitzgerald	.10	.05
❏ 559	Ken Howell	.10	.05
❏ 560	Bob Kipper	.10	.05
❏ 561	Scott Bankhead	.10	.05
❏ 562A	Jeff Innis ERR	2.00	.90
	(Photo actually David West)		
❏ 562B	Jeff Innis COR	.10	.05
❏ 563	Randy Johnson	.60	.25
❏ 564	Wally Whitehurst	.10	.05
❏ 565	Gene Harris	.10	.05
❏ 566	Norm Charlton	.10	.05
❏ 567	Robin Yount UER	.20	.09
	(7602 career hits, should be 2606)		
❏ 568	Joe Oliver UER	.10	.05
	(Fl.orida)		
❏ 569	Mark Parent	.10	.05
❏ 570	John Farrell UER	.10	.05
	(Loss total added wrong)		
❏ 571	Tom Glavine	.40	.18
❏ 572	Rod Nichols	.10	.05
❏ 573	Jack Morris	.20	.09
❏ 574	Greg Swindell	.10	.05
❏ 575	Steve Searcy	.10	.05
❏ 576	Ricky Jordan	.10	.05
❏ 577	Matt Williams	.40	.18
❏ 578	Mike LaValliere	.10	.05
❏ 579	Bryn Smith	.10	.05
❏ 580	Bruce Ruffin	.10	.05
❏ 581	Randy Myers	.20	.09
❏ 582	Rick Wrona	.10	.05
❏ 583	Juan Samuel	.10	.05
❏ 584	Les Lancaster	.10	.05
❏ 585	Jeff Musselman	.10	.05
❏ 586	Rob Dibble	.10	.05
❏ 587	Eric Show	.10	.05
❏ 588	Jesse Orosco	.10	.05
❏ 589	Herm Winningham	.10	.05
❏ 590	Andy Allanson	.10	.05
❏ 591	Dion James	.10	.05
❏ 592	Carmelo Martinez	.10	.05
❏ 593	Luis Quinones	.10	.05
❏ 594	Dennis Rasmussen	.10	.05
❏ 595	Rich Yett	.10	.05
❏ 596	Bob Walk	.10	.05
❏ 597A	Andy McGaffigan ERR	.20	.09
	(Photo actually Rich Thompson)		
❏ 597B	Andy McGaffigan COR	.10	.05
❏ 598	Billy Hatcher	.10	.05
❏ 599	Bob Knepper	.10	.05
❏ 600	Checklist 501-600 UER	.10	.05
	(599 Bob Kneppers)		
❏ 601	Joey Cora	.20	.09
❏ 602	Steve Finley	.40	.18
❏ 603	Kal Daniels UER	.10	.05
	(12 hits in '87, should be 123; 335 runs, should be 235)		
❏ 604	Gregg Olson	.20	.09
❏ 605	Dave Stieb	.20	.09
❏ 606	Kenny Rogers	.20	.09
	(Shown catching football)		
❏ 607	Zane Smith	.10	.05
❏ 608	Bob Geren UER	.10	.05
	(Origionally)		
❏ 609	Chad Kreuter	.10	.05
❏ 610	Mike Smithson	.10	.05
❏ 611	Jeff Wetherby	.10	.05
❏ 612	Gary Mielke	.10	.05
❏ 613	Pete Smith	.10	.05
❏ 614	Jack Daugherty UER	.10	.05
	(Born 7/30/60, should be 7/3/60)		
❏ 615	Lance McCullers	.10	.05
❏ 616	Don Robinson	.10	.05
❏ 617	Jose Guzman	.10	.05
❏ 618	Steve Bedrosian	.10	.05
❏ 619	Jamie Moyer	.10	.05
❏ 620	Atlee Hammaker	.10	.05
❏ 621	Rick Luecken UER	.10	.05
	(Innings pitched wrong)		
❏ 622	Greg W. Harris	.10	.05
❏ 623	Pete Harnisch	.10	.05
❏ 624	Jerald Clark	.10	.05
❏ 625	Jack McDowell UER	.10	.05
	(Career totals for Games and GS don't include 1987 season)		
❏ 626	Frank Viola	.10	.05
❏ 627	Teddy Higuera	.10	.05
❏ 628	Marty Pevey	.10	.05
❏ 629	Bill Wegman	.10	.05
❏ 630	Eric Plunk	.10	.05
❏ 631	Drew Hall	.10	.05
❏ 632	Doug Jones	.10	.05
❏ 633	Geno Petralli UER	.10	.05
	(Sacremento)		
❏ 634	Jose Alvarez	.10	.05
❏ 635	Bob Milacki	.10	.05
❏ 636	Bobby Witt	.10	.05
❏ 637	Trevor Wilson	.10	.05
❏ 638	Jeff Russell UER	.10	.05
	(Shutout stats wrong)		
❏ 639	Mike Krukow	.10	.05
❏ 640	Rick Leach	.10	.05
❏ 641	Dave Schmidt	.10	.05
❏ 642	Terry Leach	.10	.05
❏ 643	Calvin Schiraldi	.10	.05
❏ 644	Bob Melvin	.10	.05
❏ 645	Jim Abbott	.30	.14
❏ 646	Jaime Navarro	.10	.05
❏ 647	Mark Langston UER	.10	.05
	(Several errors in stats totals)		
❏ 648	Juan Nieves	.10	.05
❏ 649	Damaso Garcia	.10	.05
❏ 650	Charlie O'Brien	.10	.05
❏ 651	Eric King	.10	.05
❏ 652	Mike Boddicker	.10	.05
❏ 653	Duane Ward	.10	.05
❏ 654	Bob Stanley	.10	.05
❏ 655	Sandy Alomar Jr.	.20	.09
❏ 656	Danny Tartabull UER	.10	.05
	(395 BB, should be 295)		
❏ 657	Randy McCament	.10	.05
❏ 658	Charlie Leibrandt	.10	.05
❏ 659	Dan Quisenberry	.10	.05
❏ 660	Paul Assenmacher	.10	.05
❏ 661	Walt Terrell	.10	.05
❏ 662	Tim Leary	.10	.05
❏ 663	Randy Milligan	.10	.05
❏ 664	Bo Diaz	.10	.05
❏ 665	Mark Lemke UER	.10	.05
	(Richmond misspelled as Rachmond)		
❏ 666	Jose Gonzalez	.10	.05
❏ 667	Chuck Finley UER	.20	.09
	(Born 11/16/62, should be 11/26/62)		
❏ 668	John Kruk	.20	.09
❏ 669	Dick Schofield	.10	.05
❏ 670	Tim Crews	.10	.05
❏ 671	John Dopson	.10	.05
❏ 672	John Orton	.10	.05
❏ 673	Eric Hetzel	.10	.05

❏ 674 Lance Parrish	.10	.05
❏ 675 Ramon Martinez	.30	.14
❏ 676 Mark Gubicza	.10	.05
❏ 677 Greg Litton	.10	.05
❏ 678 Greg Mathews	.10	.05
❏ 679 Dave Dravecky	.20	.09
❏ 680 Steve Farr	.10	.05
❏ 681 Mike Devereaux	.20	.09
❏ 682 Ken Griffey Sr.	.20	.09
❏ 683A Mickey Weston ERR	2.00	.90
(Listed as Jamie on card)		
❏ 683B Mickey Weston COR	.10	.05
(Technically still an error as birthdate is listed as 3/26/81)		
❏ 684 Jack Armstrong	.10	.05
❏ 685 Steve Buechele	.10	.05
❏ 686 Bryan Harvey	.10	.05
❏ 687 Lance Blankenship	.10	.05
❏ 688 Dante Bichette	.40	.18
❏ 689 Todd Burns	.10	.05
❏ 690 Dan Petry	.10	.05
❏ 691 Kent Anderson	.10	.05
❏ 692 Todd Stottlemyre	.20	.09
❏ 693 Wally Joyner UER	.20	.09
(Several stats errors)		
❏ 694 Mike Rochford	.10	.05
❏ 695 Floyd Bannister	.10	.05
❏ 696 Rick Reuschel	.10	.05
❏ 697 Jose DeLeon	.10	.05
❏ 698 Jeff Montgomery	.20	.09
❏ 699 Kelly Downs	.10	.05
❏ 700A Checklist 601-700	2.00	.90
(683 Jamie Weston)		
❏ 700B Checklist 601-700	.10	.05
(683 Mickey Weston)		
❏ 701 Jim Gott	.10	.05
❏ 702 Rookie Threats	.50	.23
Delino DeShields		
Marquis Grissom		
Larry Walker		
❏ 703 Alejandro Pena	.10	.05
❏ 704 Willie Randolph	.20	.09
❏ 705 Tim Leary	.10	.05
❏ 706 Chuck McElroy	.10	.05
❏ 707 Gerald Perry	.10	.05
❏ 708 Tom Brunansky	.20	.09
❏ 709 John Franco	.20	.09
❏ 710 Mark Davis	.10	.05
❏ 711 David Justice	1.00	.45
❏ 712 Storm Davis	.10	.05
❏ 713 Scott Ruskin	.10	.05
❏ 714 Glenn Braggs	.10	.05
❏ 715 Kevin Bearse	.10	.05
❏ 716 Jose Nunez	.10	.05
❏ 717 Tim Layana	.10	.05
❏ 718 Greg Myers	.10	.05
❏ 719 Pete O'Brien	.10	.05
❏ 720 John Candelaria	.10	.05
❏ 721 Craig Grebeck	.10	.05
❏ 722 Shawn Boskie	.10	.05
❏ 723 Jim Leyritz	.50	.23
❏ 724 Bill Sampen	.10	.05
❏ 725 Scott Radinsky	.10	.05
❏ 726 Todd Hundley	.50	.23
❏ 727 Scott Hemond	.10	.05
❏ 728 Lenny Webster	.10	.05
❏ 729 Jeff Reardon	.20	.09
❏ 730 Mitch Webster	.10	.05
❏ 731 Brian Bohanon	.10	.05
❏ 732 Rick Parker	.10	.05
❏ 733 Terry Shumpert	.10	.05
❏ 734A Ryan's 6th No-Hitter	2.50	1.10
(No stripe on front)		
❏ 734B Ryan's 6th No-Hitter	.75	.35
(stripe added on card front for 300th win)		
❏ 735 John Burkett	.10	.05
❏ 736 Derrick May	.20	.09
❏ 737 Carlos Baerga	.40	.18
❏ 738 Greg Smith	.10	.05
❏ 739 Scott Sanderson	.10	.05
❏ 740 Joe Kraemer	.10	.05
❏ 741 Hector Villanueva	.10	.05
❏ 742 Mike Fetters	.10	.05

❏ 743 Mark Gardner	.10	.05
❏ 744 Matt Nokes	.10	.05
❏ 745 Dave Winfield	.40	.18
❏ 746 Delino DeShields	.40	.18
❏ 747 Dann Howitt	.10	.05
❏ 748 Tony Pena	.10	.05
❏ 749 Oil Can Boyd	.10	.05
❏ 750 Mike Benjamin	.10	.05
❏ 751 Alex Cole	.10	.05
❏ 752 Eric Gunderson	.10	.05
❏ 753 Howard Farmer	.10	.05
❏ 754 Joe Carter	.20	.09
❏ 755 Ray Lankford	.75	.35
❏ 756 Sandy Alomar Jr.	.20	.09
❏ 757 Alex Sanchez	.10	.05
❏ 758 Nick Esasky	.10	.05
❏ 759 Stan Belinda	.10	.05
❏ 760 Jim Presley	.10	.05
❏ 761 Gary DiSarcina	.30	.14
❏ 762 Wayne Edwards	.10	.05
❏ 763 Pat Combs	.10	.05
❏ 764 Mickey Pina	.10	.05
❏ 765 Wilson Alvarez	.30	.14
❏ 766 Dave Parker	.20	.09
❏ 767 Mike Blowers	.20	.09
❏ 768 Tony Phillips	.10	.05
❏ 769 Pascual Perez	.10	.05
❏ 770 Gary Pettis	.10	.05
❏ 771 Fred Lynn	.10	.05
❏ 772 Mel Rojas	.20	.09
❏ 773 David Segui	.50	.23
❏ 774 Gary Carter	.40	.18
❏ 775 Rafael Valdez	.10	.05
❏ 776 Glenallen Hill	.10	.05
❏ 777 Keith Hernandez	.20	.09
❏ 778 Billy Hatcher	.10	.05
❏ 779 Marty Clary	.10	.05
❏ 780 Candy Maldonado	.10	.05
❏ 781 Mike Marshall	.10	.05
❏ 782 Billy Joe Robidoux	.10	.05
❏ 783 Mark Langston	.10	.05
❏ 784 Paul Sorrento	.30	.14
❏ 785 Dave Hollins	.40	.18
❏ 786 Cecil Fielder	.20	.09
❏ 787 Matt Young	.10	.05
❏ 788 Jeff Huson	.10	.05
❏ 789 Lloyd Moseby	.10	.05
❏ 790 Ron Kittle	.10	.05
❏ 791 Hubie Brooks	.10	.05
❏ 792 Craig Lefferts	.10	.05
❏ 793 Kevin Bass	.10	.05
❏ 794 Bryn Smith	.10	.05
❏ 795 Juan Samuel	.10	.05
❏ 796 Sam Horn	.10	.05
❏ 797 Randy Myers	.20	.09
❏ 798 Chris James	.10	.05
❏ 799 Bill Gullickson	.10	.05
❏ 800 Checklist 701-800	.10	.05

1990 Upper Deck Jackson Heroes

	MINT	NRMT
COMPLETE SET (10)	15.00	6.75
COMMON REGGIE (1-9)	1.50	.70
RANDOM INSERTS IN HI SERIES		
❏ 1 Reggie Jackson	1.50	.70

1969 Emerging Superstar		
❏ 2 Reggie Jackson	1.50	.70
1973 An MVP Year		
❏ 3 Reggie Jackson	1.50	.70
1977 Mr. October		
❏ 4 Reggie Jackson	1.50	.70
1978 vs. Bob Welch		
❏ 5 Reggie Jackson	1.50	.70
1982 Under the Halo		
❏ 6 Reggie Jackson	1.50	.70
1984 500 Homers		
❏ 7 Reggie Jackson	1.50	.70
1986 Moving Up the List		
❏ 8 Reggie Jackson	1.50	.70
1987 A Great Career Ends		
❏ 9 Jackson Heroes art/CL	1.50	.70
❏ NNO Reggie Jackson	3.00	1.35
Header Card		
❏ AU1 Reggie Jackson AU	100.00	45.00
(Signed and Numbered out of 2500)		

1991 Upper Deck

Frank Thomas

	MINT	NRMT
COMPLETE SET (800)	20.00	9.00
COMPLETE LO SET (700)	16.00	7.25
COMPLETE HI SET (100)	4.00	1.80
COMMON CARD (1-800)	.05	.02
MINOR STARS	.10	.05
UNLISTED STARS	.20	.09

❏ 1 Star Rookie Checklist	.05	.02
❏ 2 Phil Plantier	16.00	7.25
❏ 3 D.J. Dozier	.05	.02
❏ 4 Dave Hansen	.05	.02
❏ 5 Maurice Vaughn	.40	.18
❏ 6 Leo Gomez	.05	.02
❏ 7 Scott Aldred	.05	.02
❏ 8 Scott Chiamparino	.05	.02
❏ 9 Lance Dickson	.05	.02
❏ 10 Sean Berry	.10	.05
❏ 11 Bernie Williams	.50	.23
❏ 12 Brian Barnes UER	.05	.02
(Photo either not him or in wrong jersey)		
❏ 13 Narciso Elvira	.05	.02
❏ 14 Mike Gardiner	.05	.02
❏ 15 Greg Colbrunn	.05	.02
❏ 16 Bernard Gilkey	.10	.05
❏ 17 Mark Lewis	.05	.02
❏ 18 Mickey Morandini	.20	.09
❏ 19 Charles Nagy	.20	.09
❏ 20 Geronimo Pena	.10	.05
❏ 21 Henry Rodriguez	.50	.23
❏ 22 Scott Cooper	.05	.02
❏ 23 Andujar Cedeno UER	.05	.02
(Shown batting left, back says right)		
❏ 24 Eric Karros	.50	.23
❏ 25 Steve Decker UER	.05	.02
(Lewis-Clark State College, not Lewis and Clark)		
❏ 26 Kevin Belcher	.05	.02
❏ 27 Jeff Conine	.20	.09
❏ 28 Dave Stewart TC	.05	.02
❏ 29 Carlton Fisk TC	.10	.05

30	Rafael Palmeiro TC	.10	.05
31	Chuck Finley TC	.05	.02
32	Harold Reynolds TC	.05	.02
33	Bret Saberhagen TC	.05	.02
34	Gary Gaetti TC	.05	.02
35	Scott Leius	.05	.02
36	Neal Heaton	.05	.02
37	Terry Lee	.05	.02
38	Gary Redus	.05	.02
39	Barry Jones	.05	.02
40	Chuck Knoblauch	.20	.09
41	Larry Andersen	.05	.02
42	Darryl Hamilton	.05	.02
43	Mike Greenwell TC	.05	.02
44	Kelly Gruber TC	.05	.02
45	Jack Morris TC	.05	.02
46	Sandy Alomar Jr. TC	.05	.02
47	Gregg Olson TC	.05	.02
48	Dave Parker TC	.05	.02
49	Roberto Kelly TC	.05	.02
50	Top Prospect Checklist	.05	.02
51	Kyle Abbott	.05	.02
52	Jeff Juden	.05	.02
53	Todd Van Poppel UER	.05	.02
	(Born Arlington and attended John Martin HS, should say Hinsdale and James Martin HS)		
54	Steve Karsay	.25	.11
55	Chipper Jones	4.00	1.80
56	Chris Johnson UER	.05	.02
	(Called Tim on back)		
57	John Ericks	.05	.02
58	Gary Scott	.05	.02
59	Kiki Jones	.05	.02
60	Wil Cordero	.15	.07
61	Royce Clayton	.15	.07
62	Tim Costo	.05	.02
63	Roger Salkeld	.05	.02
64	Brook Fordyce	.05	.02
65	Mike Mussina	1.25	.55
66	Dave Staton	.05	.02
67	Mike Lieberthal	.50	.23
68	Kurt Miller	.05	.02
69	Dan Peltier	.05	.02
70	Greg Blosser	.05	.02
71	Reggie Sanders	.25	.11
72	Brent Mayne	.05	.02
73	Rico Brogna	.15	.07
74	Willie Banks	.05	.02
75	Len Brutcher	.05	.02
76	Pat Kelly	.05	.02
77	Chris Sabo TC	.05	.02
78	Ramon Martinez TC	.10	.05
79	Matt Williams TC	.10	.05
80	Roberto Alomar TC	.10	.05
81	Glenn Davis TC	.05	.02
82	Ron Gant TC	.05	.02
83	Cecil Fielder FEAT	.05	.02
84	Orlando Merced	.05	.02
85	Domingo Ramos	.05	.02
86	Tom Bolton	.05	.02
87	Andres Santana	.05	.02
88	John Dopson	.05	.02
89	Kenny Williams	.05	.02
90	Marty Barrett	.05	.02
91	Tom Pagnozzi	.05	.02
92	Carmelo Martinez	.05	.02
93	Bobby Thigpen SAVE	.05	.02
94	Barry Bonds TC	.20	.09
95	Gregg Jefferies TC	.05	.02
96	Tim Wallach TC	.05	.02
97	Len Dykstra TC	.05	.02
98	Pedro Guerrero TC	.05	.02
99	Mark Grace TC	.10	.05
100	Checklist 1-100	.05	.02
101	Kevin Elster	.05	.02
102	Tom Brookens	.05	.02
103	Mackey Sasser	.05	.02
104	Felix Fermin	.05	.02
105	Kevin McReynolds	.05	.02
106	Dave Stieb	.05	.02
107	Jeffrey Leonard	.05	.02
108	Dave Henderson	.05	.02
109	Sid Bream	.05	.02
110	Henry Cotto	.05	.02
111	Shawon Dunston	.05	.02
112	Mariano Duncan	.05	.02
113	Joe Girardi	.10	.05
114	Billy Hatcher	.05	.02
115	Greg Maddux	.50	.23
116	Jerry Browne	.05	.02
117	Juan Samuel	.05	.02
118	Steve Olin	.05	.02
119	Alfredo Griffin	.05	.02
120	Mitch Webster	.05	.02
121	Joel Skinner	.05	.02
122	Frank Viola	.05	.02
123	Cory Snyder	.05	.02
124	Howard Johnson	.05	.02
125	Carlos Baerga	.10	.05
126	Tony Fernandez	.05	.02
127	Dave Stewart	.10	.05
128	Jay Buhner	.20	.09
129	Mike LaValliere	.05	.02
130	Scott Bradley	.05	.02
131	Tony Phillips	.05	.02
132	Ryne Sandberg	.25	.11
133	Paul O'Neill	.10	.05
134	Mark Grace	.20	.09
135	Chris Sabo	.05	.02
136	Ramon Martinez	.10	.05
137	Brook Jacoby	.05	.02
138	Candy Maldonado	.05	.02
139	Mike Scioscia	.05	.02
140	Chris James	.05	.02
141	Craig Worthington	.05	.02
142	Manny Lee	.05	.02
143	Tim Raines	.10	.05
144	Sandy Alomar Jr.	.10	.05
145	John Olerud	.15	.07
146	Ozzie Canseco	.10	.05
	(With Jose)		
147	Pat Borders	.05	.02
148	Harold Reynolds	.05	.02
149	Tom Henke	.05	.02
150	R.J. Reynolds	.05	.02
151	Mike Gallego	.05	.02
152	Bobby Bonilla	.10	.05
153	Terry Steinbach	.10	.05
154	Barry Bonds	.25	.11
155	Jose Canseco	.25	.11
156	Gregg Jefferies	.05	.02
157	Matt Williams	.20	.09
158	Craig Biggio	.20	.09
159	Daryl Boston	.05	.02
160	Ricky Jordan	.05	.02
161	Stan Belinda	.05	.02
162	Ozzie Smith	.25	.11
163	Tom Brunansky	.05	.02
164	Todd Zeile	.10	.05
165	Mike Greenwell	.05	.02
166	Kal Daniels	.05	.02
167	Kent Hrbek	.10	.05
168	Franklin Stubbs	.05	.02
169	Dick Schofield	.05	.02
170	Junior Ortiz	.05	.02
171	Hector Villanueva	.05	.02
172	Dennis Eckersley	.10	.05
173	Mitch Williams	.05	.02
174	Mark McGwire	1.00	.45
175	Fernando Valenzuela 3X	.10	.05
176	Gary Carter	.20	.09
177	Dave Magadan	.05	.02
178	Robby Thompson	.05	.02
179	Bob Ojeda	.05	.02
180	Ken Caminiti	.05	.02
181	Don Slaught	.05	.02
182	Luis Rivera	.05	.02
183	Jay Bell	.10	.05
184	Jody Reed	.05	.02
185	Wally Backman	.05	.02
186	Dave Martinez	.05	.02
187	Luis Polonia	.05	.02
188	Shane Mack	.05	.02
189	Spike Owen	.05	.02
190	Scott Bailes	.05	.02
191	John Russell	.05	.02
192	Walt Weiss	.05	.02
193	Jose Oquendo	.05	.02
194	Carney Lansford	.10	.05
195	Jeff Huson	.05	.02
196	Keith Miller	.05	.02
197	Eric Yelding	.05	.02
198	Ron Darling	.05	.02
199	John Kruk	.10	.05
200	Checklist 101-200	.05	.02
201	John Shelby	.05	.02
202	Bob Geren	.05	.02
203	Lance McCullers	.05	.02
204	Alvaro Espinoza	.05	.02
205	Mark Salas	.05	.02
206	Mike Pagliarulo	.05	.02
207	Jose Uribe	.05	.02
208	Jim Deshaies	.05	.02
209	Ron Karkovice	.05	.02
210	Rafael Ramirez	.05	.02
211	Donnie Hill	.05	.02
212	Brian Harper	.05	.02
213	Jack Howell	.05	.02
214	Wes Gardner	.05	.02
215	Tim Burke	.05	.02
216	Doug Jones	.05	.02
217	Hubie Brooks	.05	.02
218	Tom Candiotti	.05	.02
219	Gerald Perry	.05	.02
220	Jose DeLeon	.05	.02
221	Wally Whitehurst	.05	.02
222	Alan Mills	.05	.02
223	Alan Trammell	.15	.07
224	Dwight Gooden	.15	.07
225	Travis Fryman	.20	.09
226	Joe Carter	.10	.05
227	Julio Franco	.05	.02
228	Craig Lefferts	.05	.02
229	Gary Pettis	.05	.02
230	Dennis Rasmussen	.05	.02
231A	Brian Downing ERR	.05	.02
	(No position on front)		
231B	Brian Downing COR	.15	.07
	(DH on front)		
232	Carlos Quintana	.05	.02
233	Gary Gaetti	.10	.05
234	Mark Langston	.05	.02
235	Tim Wallach	.05	.02
236	Greg Swindell	.05	.02
237	Eddie Murray	.20	.09
238	Jeff Manto	.05	.02
239	Lenny Harris	.05	.02
240	Jesse Orosco	.05	.02
241	Scott Lusader	.05	.02
242	Sid Fernandez	.05	.02
243	Jim Leyritz	.10	.05
244	Cecil Fielder	.10	.05
245	Darryl Strawberry	.10	.05
246	Frank Thomas UER	.75	.35
	(Comiskey Park misspelled Comisky)		
247	Kevin Mitchell	.05	.02
248	Lance Johnson	.05	.02
249	Rick Reuschel	.05	.02
250	Mark Portugal	.05	.02
251	Derek Lilliquist	.05	.02
252	Brian Holman	.05	.02
253	Rafael Valdez UER	.05	.02
	(Born 4/17/68, should be 12/17/67)		
254	B.J. Surhoff	.10	.05
255	Tony Gwynn	.50	.23
256	Andy Van Slyke	.10	.05
257	Todd Stottlemyre	.05	.02
258	Jose Lind	.05	.02
259	Greg Myers	.05	.02
260	Jeff Ballard	.05	.02
261	Bobby Thigpen	.05	.02
262	Jimmy Kremers	.05	.02
263	Robin Ventura	.20	.09
264	John Smoltz	.20	.09
265	Sammy Sosa	1.25	.55
266	Gary Sheffield	.20	.09
267	Len Dykstra	.10	.05
268	Bill Spiers	.05	.02
269	Charlie Hayes	.05	.02
270	Brett Butler	.10	.05
271	Bip Roberts	.05	.02
272	Rob Deer	.05	.02
273	Fred Lynn	.05	.02
274	Dave Parker	.10	.05

❏ 275	Andy Benes	.10	.05
❏ 276	Glenallen Hill	.05	.02
❏ 277	Steve Howard	.05	.02
❏ 278	Doug Drabek	.05	.02
❏ 279	Joe Oliver	.05	.02
❏ 280	Todd Benzinger	.05	.02
❏ 281	Eric King	.05	.02
❏ 282	Jim Presley	.05	.02
❏ 283	Ken Patterson	.05	.02
❏ 284	Jack Daugherty	.05	.02
❏ 285	Ivan Calderon	.05	.02
❏ 286	Edgar Diaz	.05	.02
❏ 287	Kevin Bass	.05	.02
❏ 288	Don Carman	.05	.02
❏ 289	Greg Brock	.05	.02
❏ 290	John Franco	.10	.05
❏ 291	Joey Cora	.05	.02
❏ 292	Bill Wegman	.05	.02
❏ 293	Eric Show	.05	.02
❏ 294	Scott Bankhead	.05	.02
❏ 295	Garry Templeton	.05	.02
❏ 296	Mickey Tettleton	.10	.05
❏ 297	Luis Sojo	.05	.02
❏ 298	Jose Rijo	.05	.02
❏ 299	Dave Johnson	.05	.02
❏ 300	Checklist 201-300	.05	.02
❏ 301	Mark Grant	.05	.02
❏ 302	Pete Harnisch	.05	.02
❏ 303	Greg Olson	.05	.02
❏ 304	Anthony Telford	.05	.02
❏ 305	Lonnie Smith	.05	.02
❏ 306	Chris Hoiles	.05	.02
❏ 307	Bryn Smith	.05	.02
❏ 308	Mike Devereaux	.05	.02
❏ 309A	Milt Thompson ERR	.20	.09
	(Under yr information has print dot)		
❏ 309B	Milt Thompson COR	.05	.02
	(Under yr information says 86)		
❏ 310	Bob Melvin	.05	.02
❏ 311	Luis Salazar	.05	.02
❏ 312	Ed Whitson	.05	.02
❏ 313	Charlie Hough	.10	.05
❏ 314	Dave Clark	.05	.02
❏ 315	Eric Gunderson	.05	.02
❏ 316	Dan Petry	.05	.02
❏ 317	Dante Bichette UER	.20	.09
	(Assists misspelled as assists)		
❏ 318	Mike Heath	.05	.02
❏ 319	Damon Berryhill	.05	.02
❏ 320	Walt Terrell	.05	.02
❏ 321	Scott Fletcher	.05	.02
❏ 322	Dan Plesac	.05	.02
❏ 323	Jack McDowell	.05	.02
❏ 324	Paul Molitor	.20	.09
❏ 325	Ozzie Guillen	.05	.02
❏ 326	Gregg Olson	.05	.02
❏ 327	Pedro Guerrero	.05	.02
❏ 328	Bob Milacki	.05	.02
❏ 329	John Tudor UER	.05	.02
	('90 Cardinals, should be '90 Dodgers)		
❏ 330	Steve Finley UER	.20	.09
	(Born 3/12/65, should be 5/12)		
❏ 331	Jack Clark	.10	.05
❏ 332	Jerome Walton	.05	.02
❏ 333	Andy Hawkins	.05	.02
❏ 334	Derrick May	.05	.02
❏ 335	Roberto Alomar	.20	.09
❏ 336	Jack Morris	.10	.05
❏ 337	Dave Winfield	.20	.09
❏ 338	Steve Searcy	.05	.02
❏ 339	Chili Davis	.10	.05
❏ 340	Larry Sheets	.05	.02
❏ 341	Ted Higuera	.05	.02
❏ 342	David Segui	.10	.05
❏ 343	Greg Cadaret	.05	.02
❏ 344	Robin Yount	.20	.09
❏ 345	Nolan Ryan	.75	.35
❏ 346	Ray Lankford	.20	.09
❏ 347	Cal Ripken	.75	.35
❏ 348	Lee Smith	.10	.05
❏ 349	Brady Anderson	.20	.09
❏ 350	Frank DiPino	.05	.02
❏ 351	Hal Morris	.05	.02
❏ 352	Deion Sanders	.10	.05
❏ 353	Barry Larkin	.20	.09
❏ 354	Don Mattingly	.40	.18
❏ 355	Eric Davis	.10	.05
❏ 356	Jose Offerman	.15	.07
❏ 357	Mel Rojas	.10	.05
❏ 358	Rudy Seanez	.05	.02
❏ 359	Oil Can Boyd	.05	.02
❏ 360	Nelson Liriano	.05	.02
❏ 361	Ron Gant	.10	.05
❏ 362	Howard Farmer	.05	.02
❏ 363	David Justice	.20	.09
❏ 364	Delino DeShields	.10	.05
❏ 365	Steve Avery	.05	.02
❏ 366	David Cone	.10	.05
❏ 367	Lou Whitaker	.10	.05
❏ 368	Von Hayes	.05	.02
❏ 369	Frank Tanana	.05	.02
❏ 370	Tim Teufel	.05	.02
❏ 371	Randy Myers	.05	.02
❏ 372	Roberto Kelly	.05	.02
❏ 373	Jack Armstrong	.05	.02
❏ 374	Kelly Gruber	.05	.02
❏ 375	Kevin Maas	.05	.02
❏ 376	Randy Johnson	.25	.11
❏ 377	David West	.05	.02
❏ 378	Brent Knackert	.05	.02
❏ 379	Rick Honeycutt	.05	.02
❏ 380	Kevin Gross	.05	.02
❏ 381	Tom Foley	.05	.02
❏ 382	Jeff Blauser	.05	.02
❏ 383	Scott Ruskin	.05	.02
❏ 384	Andres Thomas	.05	.02
❏ 385	Dennis Martinez	.10	.05
❏ 386	Mike Henneman	.05	.02
❏ 387	Felix Jose	.05	.02
❏ 388	Alejandro Pena	.05	.02
❏ 389	Chet Lemon	.05	.02
❏ 390	Craig Wilson	.05	.02
❏ 391	Chuck Crim	.05	.02
❏ 392	Mel Hall	.05	.02
❏ 393	Mark Knudson	.05	.02
❏ 394	Norm Charlton	.05	.02
❏ 395	Mike Felder	.05	.02
❏ 396	Tim Layana	.05	.02
❏ 397	Steve Frey	.05	.02
❏ 398	Bill Doran	.05	.02
❏ 399	Dion James	.05	.02
❏ 400	Checklist 301-400	.05	.02
❏ 401	Ron Hassey	.05	.02
❏ 402	Don Robinson	.05	.02
❏ 403	Gene Nelson	.05	.02
❏ 404	Terry Kennedy	.05	.02
❏ 405	Todd Burns	.05	.02
❏ 406	Roger McDowell	.05	.02
❏ 407	Bob Kipper	.05	.02
❏ 408	Darren Daulton	.10	.05
❏ 409	Chuck Cary	.05	.02
❏ 410	Bruce Ruffin	.05	.02
❏ 411	Juan Berenguer	.05	.02
❏ 412	Gary Ward	.05	.02
❏ 413	Al Newman	.05	.02
❏ 414	Danny Jackson	.05	.02
❏ 415	Greg Gagne	.05	.02
❏ 416	Tom Herr	.05	.02
❏ 417	Jeff Parrett	.05	.02
❏ 418	Jeff Reardon	.10	.05
❏ 419	Mark Lemke	.05	.02
❏ 420	Charlie O'Brien	.05	.02
❏ 421	Willie Randolph	.05	.02
❏ 422	Steve Bedrosian	.05	.02
❏ 423	Mike Moore	.05	.02
❏ 424	Jeff Brantley	.05	.02
❏ 425	Bob Welch	.05	.02
❏ 426	Terry Mulholland	.05	.02
❏ 427	Willie Blair	.05	.02
❏ 428	Darrin Fletcher	.05	.02
❏ 429	Mike Witt	.05	.02
❏ 430	Joe Boever	.05	.02
❏ 431	Tom Gordon	.05	.02
❏ 432	Pedro Munoz	.05	.02
❏ 433	Kevin Seitzer	.05	.02
❏ 434	Kevin Tapani	.05	.02
❏ 435	Bret Saberhagen	.10	.05
❏ 436	Ellis Burks	.10	.05
❏ 437	Chuck Finley	.10	.05
❏ 438	Mike Boddicker	.05	.02
❏ 439	Francisco Cabrera	.05	.02
❏ 440	Todd Hundley	.20	.09
❏ 441	Kelly Downs	.05	.02
❏ 442	Dann Howitt	.05	.02
❏ 443	Scott Garrelts	.05	.02
❏ 444	Rickey Henderson 3X	.25	.11
❏ 445	Will Clark	.20	.09
❏ 446	Ben McDonald	.05	.02
❏ 447	Dale Murphy	.20	.09
❏ 448	Dave Righetti	.05	.02
❏ 449	Dickie Thon	.05	.02
❏ 450	Ted Power	.05	.02
❏ 451	Scott Coolbaugh	.05	.02
❏ 452	Dwight Smith	.05	.02
❏ 453	Pete Incaviglia	.05	.02
❏ 454	Andre Dawson	.20	.09
❏ 455	Ruben Sierra	.20	.09
❏ 456	Andres Galarraga	.20	.09
❏ 457	Alvin Davis	.05	.02
❏ 458	Tony Castillo	.05	.02
❏ 459	Pete O'Brien	.05	.02
❏ 460	Charlie Leibrandt	.05	.02
❏ 461	Vince Coleman	.05	.02
❏ 462	Steve Sax	.05	.02
❏ 463	Omar Olivares	.05	.02
❏ 464	Oscar Azocar	.05	.02
❏ 465	Joe Magrane	.05	.02
❏ 466	Karl Rhodes	.05	.02
❏ 467	Benito Santiago	.05	.02
❏ 468	Joe Klink	.05	.02
❏ 469	Sil Campusano	.05	.02
❏ 470	Mark Parent	.05	.02
❏ 471	Shawn Boskie UER	.05	.02
	(Depleted misspelled as depleated)		
❏ 472	Kevin Brown	.15	.07
❏ 473	Rick Sutcliffe	.05	.02
❏ 474	Rafael Palmeiro	.20	.09
❏ 475	Mike Harkey	.05	.02
❏ 476	Jaime Navarro	.05	.02
❏ 477	Marquis Grissom UER	.20	.09
	(DeShields misspelled as DeSheilds)		
❏ 478	Marty Clary	.05	.02
❏ 479	Greg Briley	.05	.02
❏ 480	Tom Glavine	.20	.09
❏ 481	Lee Guetterman	.05	.02
❏ 482	Rex Hudler	.05	.02
❏ 483	Dave LaPoint	.05	.02
❏ 484	Terry Pendleton	.10	.05
❏ 485	Jesse Barfield	.05	.02
❏ 486	Jose DeJesus	.05	.02
❏ 487	Paul Abbott	.05	.02
❏ 488	Ken Howell	.05	.02
❏ 489	Greg W. Harris	.05	.02
❏ 490	Roy Smith	.05	.02
❏ 491	Paul Assenmacher	.05	.02
❏ 492	Geno Petralli	.05	.02
❏ 493	Steve Wilson	.05	.02
❏ 494	Kevin Reimer	.05	.02
❏ 495	Bill Long	.05	.02
❏ 496	Mike Jackson	.10	.05
❏ 497	Oddibe McDowell	.05	.02
❏ 498	Bill Swift	.05	.02
❏ 499	Jeff Treadway	.05	.02
❏ 500	Checklist 401-500	.05	.02
❏ 501	Gene Larkin	.05	.02
❏ 502	Bob Boone	.10	.05
❏ 503	Allan Anderson	.05	.02
❏ 504	Luis Aquino	.05	.02
❏ 505	Mark Guthrie	.05	.02
❏ 506	Joe Orsulak	.05	.02
❏ 507	Dana Kiecker	.05	.02
❏ 508	Dave Gallagher	.05	.02
❏ 509	Greg A. Harris	.05	.02
❏ 510	Mark Williamson	.05	.02
❏ 511	Casey Candaele	.05	.02
❏ 512	Mookie Wilson	.10	.05
❏ 513	Dave Smith	.05	.02
❏ 514	Chuck Carr	.05	.02
❏ 515	Glenn Wilson	.05	.02
❏ 516	Mike Fitzgerald	.05	.02
❏ 517	Devon White	.05	.02

Card		
☐ 518 Dave Hollins	.05	.02
☐ 519 Mark Eichhorn	.05	.02
☐ 520 Otis Nixon	.10	.05
☐ 521 Terry Shumpert	.05	.02
☐ 522 Scott Erickson	.15	.07
☐ 523 Danny Tartabull	.05	.02
☐ 524 Orel Hershiser	.10	.05
☐ 525 George Brett	.40	.18
☐ 526 Greg Vaughn	.20	.09
☐ 527 Tim Naehring	.05	.02
☐ 528 Curt Schilling	.20	.09
☐ 529 Chris Bosio	.05	.02
☐ 530 Sam Horn	.05	.02
☐ 531 Mike Scott	.05	.02
☐ 532 George Bell	.05	.02
☐ 533 Eric Anthony	.05	.02
☐ 534 Julio Valera	.05	.02
☐ 535 Glenn Davis	.05	.02
☐ 536 Larry Walker UER	.30	.14
(Should have comma after Expos in text)		
☐ 537 Pat Combs	.05	.02
☐ 538 Chris Nabholz	.05	.02
☐ 539 Kirk McCaskill	.05	.02
☐ 540 Randy Ready	.05	.02
☐ 541 Mark Gubicza	.05	.02
☐ 542 Rick Aguilera	.10	.05
☐ 543 Brian McRae	.10	.05
☐ 544 Kirby Puckett	.30	.14
☐ 545 Bo Jackson	.10	.05
☐ 546 Wade Boggs	.20	.09
☐ 547 Tim McIntosh	.05	.02
☐ 548 Randy Milligan	.05	.02
☐ 549 Dwight Evans	.10	.05
☐ 550 Billy Ripken	.05	.02
☐ 551 Erik Hanson	.05	.02
☐ 552 Lance Parrish	.05	.02
☐ 553 Tino Martinez	.20	.09
☐ 554 Jim Abbott	.10	.05
☐ 555 Ken Griffey Jr.	1.50	.70
(Second most votes for 1991 All-Star Game)		
☐ 556 Milt Cuyler	.05	.02
☐ 557 Mark Leonard	.05	.02
☐ 558 Jay Howell	.05	.02
☐ 559 Lloyd Moseby	.05	.02
☐ 560 Chris Gwynn	.05	.02
☐ 561 Mark Whiten	.05	.02
☐ 562 Harold Baines	.10	.05
☐ 563 Junior Felix	.05	.02
☐ 564 Darren Lewis	.10	.05
☐ 565 Fred McGriff	.20	.09
☐ 566 Kevin Appier	.10	.05
☐ 567 Luis Gonzalez	.50	.23
☐ 568 Frank White	.10	.05
☐ 569 Juan Agosto	.05	.02
☐ 570 Mike Macfarlane	.05	.02
☐ 571 Bert Blyleven	.10	.05
☐ 572 Ken Griffey Sr.	.50	.23
Ken Griffey Jr.		
☐ 573 Lee Stevens	.10	.05
☐ 574 Edgar Martinez	.20	.09
☐ 575 Wally Joyner	.10	.05
☐ 576 Tim Belcher	.05	.02
☐ 577 John Burkett	.05	.02
☐ 578 Mike Morgan	.05	.02
☐ 579 Paul Gibson	.05	.02
☐ 580 Jose Vizcaino	.05	.02
☐ 581 Duane Ward	.05	.02
☐ 582 Scott Sanderson	.05	.02
☐ 583 David Wells	.10	.05
☐ 584 Willie McGee	.10	.05
☐ 585 John Cerutti	.05	.02
☐ 586 Danny Darwin	.05	.02
☐ 587 Kurt Stillwell	.05	.02
☐ 588 Rich Gedman	.05	.02
☐ 589 Mark Davis	.05	.02
☐ 590 Bill Gullickson	.05	.02
☐ 591 Matt Young	.05	.02
☐ 592 Bryan Harvey	.05	.02
☐ 593 Omar Vizquel	.20	.09
☐ 594 Scott Lewis	.05	.02
☐ 595 Dave Valle	.05	.02
☐ 596 Tim Crews	.05	.02
☐ 597 Mike Bielecki	.05	.02
☐ 598 Mike Sharperson	.05	.02
☐ 599 Dave Bergman	.05	.02
☐ 600 Checklist 501-600	.05	.02
☐ 601 Steve Lyons	.05	.02
☐ 602 Bruce Hurst	.05	.02
☐ 603 Donn Pall	.05	.02
☐ 604 Jim Vatcher	.05	.02
☐ 605 Dan Pasqua	.05	.02
☐ 606 Kenny Rogers	.05	.02
☐ 607 Jeff Schulz	.05	.02
☐ 608 Brad Arnsberg	.05	.02
☐ 609 Willie Wilson	.05	.02
☐ 610 Jamie Moyer	.05	.02
☐ 611 Ron Oester	.05	.02
☐ 612 Dennis Cook	.05	.02
☐ 613 Rick Mahler	.05	.02
☐ 614 Bill Landrum	.05	.02
☐ 615 Scott Scudder	.05	.02
☐ 616 Tom Edens	.05	.02
☐ 617 1917 Revisited	.10	.05
(White Sox in vintage uniforms)		
☐ 618 Jim Gantner	.05	.02
☐ 619 Darrel Akerfelds	.05	.02
☐ 620 Ron Robinson	.05	.02
☐ 621 Scott Radinsky	.05	.02
☐ 622 Pete Smith	.05	.02
☐ 623 Melido Perez	.05	.02
☐ 624 Jerald Clark	.05	.02
☐ 625 Carlos Martinez	.05	.02
☐ 626 Wes Chamberlain	.05	.02
☐ 627 Bobby Witt	.05	.02
☐ 628 Ken Dayley	.05	.02
☐ 629 John Barfield	.05	.02
☐ 630 Bob Tewksbury	.05	.02
☐ 631 Glenn Braggs	.05	.02
☐ 632 Jim Neidlinger	.05	.02
☐ 633 Tom Browning	.05	.02
☐ 634 Kirk Gibson	.10	.05
☐ 635 Rob Dibble	.05	.02
☐ 636 Rickey Henderson SB	.25	.11
Lou Brock		
May 1, 1991 on front		
☐ 636A Rickey Henderson SB	.25	.11
Lou Brock		
no date on card		
☐ 637 Jeff Montgomery	.10	.05
☐ 638 Mike Schooler	.05	.02
☐ 639 Storm Davis	.05	.02
☐ 640 Rich Rodriguez	.05	.02
☐ 641 Phil Bradley	.05	.02
☐ 642 Kent Mercker	.05	.02
☐ 643 Carlton Fisk	.20	.09
☐ 644 Mike Bell	.05	.02
☐ 645 Alex Fernandez	.10	.05
☐ 646 Juan Gonzalez	.75	.35
☐ 647 Ken Hill	.05	.02
☐ 648 Jeff Russell	.05	.02
☐ 649 Chuck Malone	.05	.02
☐ 650 Steve Buechele	.05	.02
☐ 651 Mike Benjamin	.05	.02
☐ 652 Tony Pena	.05	.02
☐ 653 Trevor Wilson	.05	.02
☐ 654 Alex Cole	.05	.02
☐ 655 Roger Clemens	.50	.23
☐ 656 Mark McGwire BASH	.50	.23
☐ 657 Joe Grahe	.05	.02
☐ 658 Jim Eisenreich	.05	.02
☐ 659 Dan Gladden	.05	.02
☐ 660 Steve Farr	.05	.02
☐ 661 Bill Sampen	.05	.02
☐ 662 Dave Rohde	.05	.02
☐ 663 Mark Gardner	.05	.02
☐ 664 Mike Simms	.05	.02
☐ 665 Moises Alou	.20	.09
☐ 666 Mickey Hatcher	.05	.02
☐ 667 Jimmy Key	.10	.05
☐ 668 John Wetteland	.05	.02
☐ 669 John Smiley	.05	.02
☐ 670 Jim Acker	.05	.02
☐ 671 Pascual Perez	.05	.02
☐ 672 Reggie Harris UER	.05	.02
(Opportunity misspelled as opportunty)		
☐ 673 Matt Nokes	.05	.02
☐ 674 Rafael Novoa	.05	.02
☐ 675 Hensley Meulens	.05	.02
☐ 676 Jeff M. Robinson	.05	.02
☐ 677 Ground Breaking	.10	.05
(New Comiskey Park; Carlton Fisk and Robin Ventura)		
☐ 678 Johnny Ray	.05	.02
☐ 679 Greg Hibbard	.05	.02
☐ 680 Paul Sorrento	.10	.05
☐ 681 Mike Marshall	.05	.02
☐ 682 Jim Clancy	.05	.02
☐ 683 Rob Murphy	.05	.02
☐ 684 Dave Schmidt	.05	.02
☐ 685 Jeff Gray	.05	.02
☐ 686 Mike Hartley	.05	.02
☐ 687 Jeff King	.05	.02
☐ 688 Stan Javier	.05	.02
☐ 689 Bob Walk	.05	.02
☐ 690 Jim Gott	.05	.02
☐ 691 Mike LaCoss	.05	.02
☐ 692 John Farrell	.05	.02
☐ 693 Tim Leary	.05	.02
☐ 694 Mike Walker	.05	.02
☐ 695 Eric Plunk	.05	.02
☐ 696 Mike Fetters	.05	.02
☐ 697 Wayne Edwards	.05	.02
☐ 698 Tim Drummond	.05	.02
☐ 699 Willie Fraser	.05	.02
☐ 700 Checklist 601-700	.05	.02
☐ 701 Mike Heath	.05	.02
☐ 702 Rookie Threats	.50	.23
Luis Gonzalez		
Karl Rhodes		
Jeff Bagwell		
☐ 703 Jose Mesa	.05	.02
☐ 704 Dave Smith	.05	.02
☐ 705 Danny Darwin	.05	.02
☐ 706 Rafael Belliard	.05	.02
☐ 707 Rob Murphy	.05	.02
☐ 708 Terry Pendleton	.10	.05
☐ 709 Mike Pagliarulo	.05	.02
☐ 710 Sid Bream	.05	.02
☐ 711 Junior Felix	.05	.02
☐ 712 Dante Bichette	.20	.09
☐ 713 Kevin Gross	.05	.02
☐ 714 Luis Sojo	.05	.02
☐ 715 Bob Ojeda	.05	.02
☐ 716 Julio Machado	.05	.02
☐ 717 Steve Farr	.05	.02
☐ 718 Franklin Stubbs	.05	.02
☐ 719 Mike Boddicker	.05	.02
☐ 720 Willie Randolph	.10	.05
☐ 721 Willie McGee	.10	.05
☐ 722 Chili Davis	.05	.02
☐ 723 Danny Jackson	.05	.02
☐ 724 Cory Snyder	.05	.02
☐ 725 MVP Lineup	.20	.09
Andre Dawson		
George Bell		
Ryne Sandberg		
☐ 726 Rob Deer	.05	.02
☐ 727 Rich DeLucia	.05	.02
☐ 728 Mike Perez	.05	.02
☐ 729 Mickey Tettleton	.10	.05
☐ 730 Mike Blowers	.05	.02
☐ 731 Gary Gaetti	.05	.02
☐ 732 Brett Butler	.10	.05
☐ 733 Dave Parker	.10	.05
☐ 734 Eddie Zosky	.05	.02
☐ 735 Jack Clark	.10	.05
☐ 736 Jack Morris	.10	.05
☐ 737 Kirk Gibson	.05	.02
☐ 738 Steve Bedrosian	.05	.02
☐ 739 Candy Maldonado	.05	.02
☐ 740 Matt Young	.05	.02
☐ 741 Rich Garces	.05	.02
☐ 742 George Bell	.05	.02
☐ 743 Deion Sanders	.10	.05
☐ 744 Bo Jackson	.10	.05
☐ 745 Luis Mercedes	.05	.02
☐ 746 Reggie Jefferson UER	.15	.07
(Throwing left on card; back has throws right)		
☐ 747 Pete Incaviglia	.05	.02
☐ 748 Chris Hammond	.05	.02
☐ 749 Mike Stanton	.05	.02
☐ 750 Scott Sanderson	.05	.02

		MINT	NRMT
☐ 751	Paul Faries	.05	.02
☐ 752	Al Osuna	.05	.02
☐ 753	Steve Chitren	.05	.02
☐ 754	Tony Fernandez	.05	.02
☐ 755	Jeff Bagwell UER	2.50	1.10
	(Strikeout and walk		
	totals reversed)		
☐ 756	Kirk Dressendorfer	.05	.02
☐ 757	Glenn Davis	.05	.02
☐ 758	Gary Carter	.20	.09
☐ 759	Zane Smith	.05	.02
☐ 760	Vance Law	.05	.02
☐ 761	Denis Boucher	.05	.02
☐ 762	Turner Ward	.05	.02
☐ 763	Roberto Alomar	.20	.09
☐ 764	Albert Belle	.25	.11
☐ 765	Joe Carter	.10	.05
☐ 766	Pete Schourek	.10	.05
☐ 767	Heathcliff Slocumb	.20	.09
☐ 768	Vince Coleman	.05	.02
☐ 769	Mitch Williams	.05	.02
☐ 770	Brian Downing	.05	.02
☐ 771	Dana Allison	.05	.02
☐ 772	Pete Harnisch	.05	.02
☐ 773	Tim Raines	.10	.05
☐ 774	Darryl Kile	.05	.02
☐ 775	Fred McGriff	.20	.09
☐ 776	Dwight Evans	.10	.05
☐ 777	Joe Slusarski	.05	.02
☐ 778	Dave Righetti	.05	.02
☐ 779	Jeff Hamilton	.05	.02
☐ 780	Ernest Riles	.05	.02
☐ 781	Ken Dayley	.05	.02
☐ 782	Eric King	.05	.02
☐ 783	Devon White	.05	.02
☐ 784	Beau Allred	.05	.02
☐ 785	Mike Timlin	.05	.02
☐ 786	Ivan Calderon	.05	.02
☐ 787	Hubie Brooks	.05	.02
☐ 788	Juan Agosto	.05	.02
☐ 789	Barry Jones	.05	.02
☐ 790	Wally Backman	.05	.02
☐ 791	Jim Presley	.05	.02
☐ 792	Charlie Hough	.10	.05
☐ 793	Larry Andersen	.05	.02
☐ 794	Steve Finley	.20	.09
☐ 795	Shawn Abner	.05	.02
☐ 796	Jeff M. Robinson	.05	.02
☐ 797	Joe Bitker	.05	.02
☐ 798	Eric Show	.05	.02
☐ 799	Bud Black	.05	.02
☐ 800	Checklist 701-800	.05	.02
☐ HH1	Hank Aaron Hologram	1.50	.70
☐ SP1	Michael Jordan SP	15.00	6.75
	(Shown batting in		
	White Sox uniform)		
☐ SP2	Rickey Henderson SP	1.50	.70
	Nolan Ryan		
	May 1, 1991 Records		

☐ 19	Hank Aaron	.50	.23
	1954 Rookie Year		
☐ 20	Hank Aaron	.50	.23
	1957 MVP		
☐ 21	Hank Aaron	.50	.23
	1966 Move to Atlanta		
☐ 22	Hank Aaron	.50	.23
	1970 3,000 Hits		
☐ 23	Hank Aaron	.50	.23
	1974 715 Homers		
☐ 24	Hank Aaron	.50	.23
	1975 Return to Milwaukee		
☐ 25	Hank Aaron	.50	.23
	1976 755 Homers		
☐ 26	Hank Aaron	.50	.23
	1982 Hall of Fame		
☐ 27	Checklist 19-27	.50	.23
☐ NNO	Title/Header card SP	1.00	.45
☐ AU3	Hank Aaron AU	150.00	70.00
	(Signed and Numbered		
	out of 2500)		

1991 Upper Deck Heroes of Baseball

	MINT	NRMT
COMPLETE SET (4)	20.00	9.00
COMMON CARD (H1-H4)	5.00	2.20
RANDOM INSERTS IN HEROES FOIL		

☐ H1	Harmon Killebrew	5.00	2.20
☐ H2	Gaylord Perry	5.00	2.20
☐ H3	Ferguson Jenkins	5.00	2.20
☐ H4	Harmon Killebrew ART	5.00	2.20
	Ferguson Jenkins		
	Gaylord Perry		
☐ AU1	Harmon Killebrew AU	50.00	22.00
	3000		
☐ AU2	Gaylord Perry AU	50.00	22.00
	3000		
☐ AU3	Fergie Jenkins AU	50.00	22.00
	3000		

1991 Upper Deck Aaron Heroes

	MINT	NRMT
COMPLETE SET (10)	5.00	2.20
COMMON AARON (19-27)	.50	.23
RANDOM INSERTS IN HI SERIES		

1991 Upper Deck Ryan Heroes

	MINT	NRMT
COMPLETE SET (10)	5.00	2.20
COMMON RYAN (10-18)	.50	.23
RANDOM INSERTS IN LO SERIES		

☐ 10	Nolan Ryan	.50	.23
	Tom Seaver		
	Jerry Koosman		
	1968 Victory 1		
☐ 11	Nolan Ryan	.50	.23
	1973 A Career Year		
☐ 12	Nolan Ryan	.50	.23
	1975 Double Milestone		
☐ 13	Nolan Ryan	.50	.23
	1979 Back Home		
☐ 14	Nolan Ryan	.50	.23
	1981 All Time Leader		
☐ 15	Nolan Ryan	.50	.23
	1989 5,000 K's		
☐ 16	Nolan Ryan	.50	.23
	1990 6th No-Hitter		
☐ 17	Nolan Ryan	.50	.23
	1990 And Still Counting		
☐ 18	Nolan Ryan	.50	.23
	Checklist Card		
	Vernon Wells drawing		
	with 5 poses of Ryan		
	including each team		
	he played for		
☐ NNO	Baseball Heroes SP	1.00	.45
	(Header card)		
☐ AU2	Nolan Ryan AU	300.00	135.00
	(Signed and Numbered		
	out of 2500)		

1991 Upper Deck Silver Sluggers

	MINT	NRMT
COMPLETE SET (18)	15.00	6.75
COMMON CARD (SS1-SS18)	.50	.23
ONE PER LO OR HI JUMBO PACK		

☐ SS1	Julio Franco	.50	.23
☐ SS2	Alan Trammell	1.00	.45
☐ SS3	Rickey Henderson	2.00	.90
☐ SS4	Jose Canseco	2.00	.90
☐ SS5	Barry Bonds	2.00	.90
☐ SS6	Eddie Murray	1.25	.55
☐ SS7	Kelly Gruber	.50	.23
☐ SS8	Ryne Sandberg	2.00	.90
☐ SS9	Darryl Strawberry	.75	.35
☐ SS10	Ellis Burks	.75	.35
☐ SS11	Lance Parrish	.50	.23
☐ SS12	Cecil Fielder	.75	.35
☐ SS13	Matt Williams	1.00	.45
☐ SS14	Dave Parker	.75	.35
☐ SS15	Bobby Bonilla	.75	.35
☐ SS16	Don Robinson	.50	.23
☐ SS17	Benito Santiago	.50	.23
☐ SS18	Barry Larkin	1.25	.55

1991 Upper Deck Final Edition

	MINT	NRMT
COMP.FACT.SET (100)	12.00	5.50
COMMON CARD (1F-100F)	.05	.02
MINOR STARS	.10	.05
UNLISTED STARS	.20	.09

☐ 1F	Ryan Klesko CL	.20	.09

Dean Palmer

Reggie Sanders

❑	2F Pedro Martinez	8.00	3.60
❑	3F Lance Dickson	.05	.02
❑	4F Royce Clayton	.15	.07
❑	5F Scott Bryant	.05	.02
❑	6F Dan Wilson	.20	.09
❑	7F Dmitri Young	.25	.11
❑	8F Ryan Klesko	.40	.18
❑	9F Tom Goodwin	.10	.05
❑	10F Rondell White	.40	.18
❑	11F Reggie Sanders	.20	.09
❑	12F Todd Van Poppel	.05	.02
❑	13F Arthur Rhodes	.10	.05
❑	14F Eddie Zosky	.05	.02
❑	15F Gerald Williams	.05	.02
❑	16F Robert Eenhoorn	.05	.02
❑	17F Jim Thome	1.00	.45
❑	18F Marc Newfield	.05	.02
❑	19F Kerwin Moore	.05	.02
❑	20F Jeff McNeely	.05	.02
❑	21F Frankie Rodriguez	.10	.05
❑	22F Andy Mota	.05	.02
❑	23F Chris Haney	.05	.02
❑	24F Kenny Lofton	.60	.25
❑	25F Dave Nilsson	.40	.18
❑	26F Derek Bell	.20	.09
❑	27F Frank Castillo	.05	.02
❑	28F Candy Maldonado	.05	.02
❑	29F Chuck McElroy	.05	.02
❑	30F Chito Martinez	.05	.02
❑	31F Steve Howe	.05	.02
❑	32F Freddie Benavides	.05	.02
❑	33F Scott Kamieniecki	.05	.02
❑	34F Denny Neagle	.20	.09
❑	35F Mike Humphreys	.05	.02
❑	36F Mike Remlinger	.05	.02
❑	37F Scott Coolbaugh	.05	.02
❑	38F Darren Lewis	.05	.02
❑	39F Thomas Howard	.05	.02
❑	40F John Candelaria	.05	.02
❑	41F Todd Benzinger	.05	.02
❑	42F Wilson Alvarez	.20	.09
❑	43F Patrick Lennon	.05	.02
❑	44F Rusty Meacham	.05	.02
❑	45F Ryan Bowen	.05	.02
❑	46F Rick Wilkins	.05	.02
❑	47F Ed Sprague	.05	.02
❑	48F Bob Scanlan	.05	.02
❑	49F Tom Candiotti	.05	.02
❑	50F Dennis Martinez (Perfecto)	.05	.02
❑	51F Oil Can Boyd	.05	.02
❑	52F Glenallen Hill	.05	.02
❑	53F Scott Livingstone	.05	.02
❑	54F Brian R. Hunter	.05	.02
❑	55F Ivan Rodriguez	2.00	.90
❑	56F Keith Mitchell	.05	.02
❑	57F Roger McDowell	.05	.02
❑	58F Otis Nixon	.10	.05
❑	59F Juan Bell	.05	.02
❑	60F Bill Krueger	.05	.02
❑	61F Chris Donnels	.05	.02
❑	62F Tommy Greene	.05	.02
❑	63F Doug Simons	.05	.02
❑	64F Andy Ashby	.20	.09
❑	65F Anthony Young	.05	.02
❑	66F Kevin Morton	.05	.02
❑	67F Bret Barberie	.05	.02

❑	68F Scott Servais	.05	.02
❑	69F Ron Darling	.05	.02
❑	70F Tim Burke	.05	.02
❑	71F Vicente Palacios	.05	.02
❑	72F Gerald Alexander	.05	.02
❑	73F Reggie Jefferson	.15	.07
❑	74F Dean Palmer	.10	.05
❑	75F Mark Whiten	.05	.02
❑	76F Randy Tomlin	.05	.02
❑	77F Mark Wohlers	.10	.05
❑	78F Brook Jacoby	.05	.02
❑	79F Ken Griffey Jr. CL	.40	.18
	Ryne Sandberg		
❑	80F Jack Morris AS	.05	.02
❑	81F Sandy Alomar Jr. AS	.05	.02
❑	82F Cecil Fielder AS	.05	.02
❑	83F Roberto Alomar AS	.05	.02
❑	84F Wade Boggs AS	.10	.05
❑	85F Cal Ripken AS	.40	.18
❑	86F Rickey Henderson AS	.10	.05
❑	87F Ken Griffey Jr. AS	.75	.35
❑	88F Dave Henderson AS	.05	.02
❑	89F Danny Tartabull AS	.05	.02
❑	90F Tom Glavine AS	.10	.05
❑	91F Benito Santiago AS	.05	.02
❑	92F Will Clark AS	.10	.05
❑	93F Ryne Sandberg AS	.20	.09
❑	94F Chris Sabo AS	.05	.02
❑	95F Ozzie Smith AS	.20	.09
❑	96F Ivan Calderon AS	.05	.02
❑	97F Tony Gwynn AS	.25	.11
❑	98F Andre Dawson AS	.10	.05
❑	99F Bobby Bonilla AS	.05	.02
❑	100F Checklist 1-100	.05	.02

1992 Upper Deck

	MINT	NRMT
COMPLETE SET (800)	15.00	6.75
COMP.FACT.SET (800)	20.00	9.00
COMPLETE LO SET (700)	12.00	5.50
COMPLETE HI SET (100)	3.00	1.35
COMMON CARD (1-800)	.05	.02
MINOR STARS	.10	.05
UNLISTED STARS	.20	.09
SUBSET CARDS HALF VALUE OF BASE CARDS		
COMP.COLLEGE POY SET (3)	2.00	.90
COLL.POY: RANDOM INSERTS IN HI PACKS		

❑	1 Ryan Klesko CL	.40	.18
	Jim Thome		
❑	2 Royce Clayton SR	.05	.02
❑	3 Brian Jordan SR	.60	.25
❑	4 Dave Fleming SR	.05	.02
❑	5 Jim Thome SR	.50	.23
❑	6 Jeff Juden SR	.05	.02
❑	7 Roberto Hernandez SR	.15	.07
❑	8 Kyle Abbott SR	.05	.02
❑	9 Chris George SR	.05	.02
❑	10 Rob Maurer SR	.05	.02
❑	11 Donald Harris SR	.05	.02
❑	12 Ted Wood SR	.05	.02
❑	13 Patrick Lennon SR	.05	.02
❑	14 Willie Banks SR	.05	.02
❑	15 Roger Salkeld SR UER (Bill was his grandfather, not his father)	.05	.02

❑	16 Wil Cordero SR	.05	.02
❑	17 Arthur Rhodes SR	.05	.02
❑	18 Pedro Martinez SR	1.50	.70
❑	19 Andy Ashby SR	.10	.05
❑	20 Tom Goodwin SR	.05	.02
❑	21 Braulio Castillo SR	.05	.02
❑	22 Todd Van Poppel SR	.05	.02
❑	23 Brian Williams SR	.05	.02
❑	24 Ryan Klesko SR	.20	.09
❑	25 Kenny Lofton SR	.25	.11
❑	26 Derek Bell SR	.10	.05
❑	27 Reggie Sanders SR	.10	.05
❑	28 Dave Winfield's 400th	.10	.05
❑	29 David Justice TC	.10	.05
❑	30 Rob Dibble TC	.05	.02
❑	31 Craig Biggio TC	.10	.05
❑	32 Eddie Murray TC	.10	.05
❑	33 Fred McGriff TC	.10	.05
❑	34 Willie McGee TC	.05	.02
❑	35 Shawon Dunston TC	.05	.02
❑	36 Delino DeShields TC	.05	.02
❑	37 Howard Johnson TC	.05	.02
❑	38 John Kruk TC	.05	.02
❑	39 Doug Drabek TC	.05	.02
❑	40 Todd Zeile TC	.05	.02
❑	41 Steve Avery TC	.05	.02
	Playoff Perfection		
❑	42 Jeremy Hernandez	.05	.02
❑	43 Doug Henry	.05	.02
❑	44 Chris Donnels	.05	.02
❑	45 Mo Sanford	.05	.02
❑	46 Scott Kamieniecki	.05	.02
❑	47 Mark Lemke	.05	.02
❑	48 Steve Farr	.05	.02
❑	49 Francisco Oliveras	.05	.02
❑	50 Ced Landrum	.05	.02
❑	51 Rondell White CL	.20	.09
	Mark Newfield		
❑	52 Eduardo Perez TP	.05	.02
❑	53 Tom Nevers TP	.05	.02
❑	54 David Zancanaro TP	.05	.02
❑	55 Shawn Green TP	3.00	1.35
❑	56 Mark Wohlers TP	.05	.02
❑	57 Dan Nilsson TP	.10	.05
❑	58 Dmitri Young TP	.20	.09
❑	59 Ryan Hawblitzel TP	.05	.02
❑	60 Raul Mondesi TP	.40	.18
❑	61 Rondell White TP	.20	.09
❑	62 Steve Hosey TP	.05	.02
❑	63 Manny Ramirez TP	2.00	.90
❑	64 Marc Newfield TP	.05	.02
❑	65 Jeromy Burnitz TP	.20	.09
❑	66 Mark Smith TP	.05	.02
❑	67 Joey Hamilton TP	.25	.11
❑	68 Tyler Green TP	.05	.02
❑	69 Jon Farrell TP	.05	.02
❑	70 Kurt Miller TP	.05	.02
❑	71 Jeff Plympton TP	.05	.02
❑	72 Dan Wilson TP	.10	.05
❑	73 Joe Vitiello TP	.05	.02
❑	74 Rico Brogna TP	.10	.05
❑	75 David McCarty TP	.05	.02
❑	76 Bob Wickman TP	.05	.02
❑	77 Carlos Rodriguez TP	.05	.02
❑	78 Jim Abbott	.05	.02
	Stay In School		
❑	79 Ramon Martinez	.50	.23
	Pedro Martinez		
❑	80 Kevin Mitchell	.05	.02
	Keith Mitchell		
❑	81 Sandy Alomar Jr.	.20	.09
	Roberto Alomar		
❑	82 Cal Ripken	.50	.23
	Billy Ripken		
❑	83 Tony Gwynn	.20	.09
	Chris Gwynn		
❑	84 Dwight Gooden	.15	.07
	Gary Sheffield		
❑	85 Ken Griffey Jr.	.60	.25
	Ken Griffey Jr.		
	Craig Griffey		
❑	86 Jim Abbott TC	.05	.02
❑	87 Frank Thomas TC	.25	.11
❑	88 Danny Tartabull TC	.05	.02
❑	89 Scott Erickson TC	.05	.02
❑	90 Rickey Henderson TC	.10	.05

No.	Player	Price	Price
91	Edgar Martinez TC	.10	.05
92	Nolan Ryan TC	.20	.09
93	Ben McDonald TC	.05	.02
94	Ellis Burks TC	.05	.02
95	Greg Swindell TC	.05	.02
96	Cecil Fielder TC	.05	.02
97	Greg Vaughn TC	.05	.02
98	Kevin Maas TC	.05	.02
99	Dave Stieb TC	.05	.02
100	Checklist 1-100	.05	.02
101	Joe Oliver	.05	.02
102	Hector Villanueva	.05	.02
103	Ed Whitson	.05	.02
104	Danny Jackson	.05	.02
105	Chris Hammond	.05	.02
106	Ricky Jordan	.05	.02
107	Kevin Bass	.05	.02
108	Darrin Fletcher	.05	.02
109	Junior Ortiz	.05	.02
110	Tom Bolton	.05	.02
111	Jeff King	.05	.02
112	Dave Magadan	.05	.02
113	Mike LaValliere	.05	.02
114	Hubie Brooks	.05	.02
115	Jay Bell	.10	.05
116	David Wells	.10	.05
117	Jim Leyritz	.05	.02
118	Manuel Lee	.05	.02
119	Alvaro Espinoza	.05	.02
120	B.J. Surhoff	.10	.05
121	Hal Morris	.05	.02
122	Shawon Dawson	.05	.02
123	Chris Sabo	.05	.02
124	Andre Dawson	.15	.07
125	Eric Davis	.10	.05
126	Chili Davis	.10	.05
127	Dale Murphy	.20	.09
128	Kirk McCaskill	.05	.02
129	Terry Mulholland	.05	.02
130	Rick Aguilera	.10	.05
131	Vince Coleman	.05	.02
132	Andy Van Slyke	.10	.05
133	Gregg Jefferies	.05	.02
134	Barry Bonds	.25	.11
135	Dwight Gooden	.10	.05
136	Dave Stieb	.05	.02
137	Albert Belle	.20	.09
138	Teddy Higuera	.05	.02
139	Jesse Barfield	.05	.02
140	Pat Borders	.05	.02
141	Bip Roberts	.05	.02
142	Rob Dibble	.05	.02
143	Mark Grace	.15	.07
144	Barry Larkin	.15	.07
145	Ryne Sandberg	.25	.11
146	Scott Erickson	.10	.05
147	Luis Polonia	.05	.02
148	John Burkett	.05	.02
149	Luis Sojo	.05	.02
150	Dickie Thon	.05	.02
151	Walt Weiss	.05	.02
152	Mike Scioscia	.05	.02
153	Mark McGwire	1.00	.45
154	Matt Williams	.15	.07
155	Rickey Henderson	.25	.11
156	Sandy Alomar Jr.	.10	.05
157	Brian McRae	.05	.02
158	Harold Baines	.10	.05
159	Kevin Appier	.10	.05
160	Felix Fermin	.05	.02
161	Leo Gomez	.05	.02
162	Craig Biggio	.20	.09
163	Ben McDonald	.20	.09
164	Randy Johnson	.20	.09
165	Cal Ripken	.75	.35
166	Frank Thomas	.50	.23
167	Delino DeShields	.10	.05
168	Greg Gagne	.05	.02
169	Ron Karkovice	.05	.02
170	Charlie Leibrandt	.05	.02
171	Dave Righetti	.05	.02
172	Dave Henderson	.05	.02
173	Steve Decker	.05	.02
174	Darryl Strawberry	.10	.05
175	Will Clark	.20	.09
176	Ruben Sierra	.05	.02

No.	Player	Price	Price
177	Ozzie Smith	.25	.11
178	Charles Nagy	.10	.05
179	Gary Pettis	.05	.02
180	Kirk Gibson	.05	.02
181	Randy Milligan	.05	.02
182	Dave Valle	.05	.02
183	Chris Hoiles	.05	.02
184	Tony Phillips	.05	.02
185	Brady Anderson	.15	.07
186	Scott Fletcher	.05	.02
187	Gene Larkin	.05	.02
188	Lance Johnson	.05	.02
189	Greg Olson	.05	.02
190	Melido Perez	.05	.02
191	Lenny Harris	.05	.02
192	Terry Kennedy	.05	.02
193	Mike Gallego	.05	.02
194	Willie McGee	.10	.05
195	Juan Samuel	.05	.02
196	Jeff Huson	.10	.05
	(Shows Jose Canseco sliding into second)		
197	Alex Cole	.05	.02
198	Ron Robinson	.05	.02
199	Joel Skinner	.05	.02
200	Checklist 101-200	.05	.02
201	Kevin Reimer	.05	.02
202	Stan Belinda	.05	.02
203	Pat Tabler	.05	.02
204	Jose Guzman	.05	.02
205	Jose Lind	.05	.02
206	Spike Owen	.05	.02
207	Joe Orsulak	.05	.02
208	Charlie Hayes	.05	.02
209	Mike Devereaux	.05	.02
210	Mike Fitzgerald	.05	.02
211	Willie Randolph	.10	.05
212	Rod Nichols	.05	.02
213	Mike Boddicker	.05	.02
214	Bill Spiers	.05	.02
215	Steve Olin	.05	.02
216	David Howard	.05	.02
217	Gary Varsho	.05	.02
218	Mike Harkey	.05	.02
219	Luis Aquino	.05	.02
220	Chuck McElroy	.05	.02
221	Doug Drabek	.05	.02
222	Dave Winfield	.20	.09
223	Rafael Palmeiro	.20	.09
224	Joe Carter	.10	.05
225	Bobby Bonilla	.10	.05
226	Ivan Calderon	.05	.02
227	Gregg Olson	.05	.02
228	Tim Wallach	.05	.02
229	Terry Pendleton	.05	.02
230	Gilberto Reyes	.05	.02
231	Carlos Baerga	.20	.09
232	Greg Vaughn	.15	.07
233	Bret Saberhagen	.05	.02
234	Gary Sheffield	.20	.09
235	Mark Lewis	.05	.02
236	George Bell	.10	.05
237	Danny Tartabull	.45	.20
238	Willie Wilson	.05	.02
239	Doug Dascenzo	.05	.02
240	Bill Pecota	.05	.02
241	Julio Franco	.05	.02
242	Ed Sprague	.05	.02
243	Juan Gonzalez	.50	.23
244	Chuck Finley	.05	.02
245	Ivan Rodriguez	.40	.18
246	Len Dykstra	.05	.02
247	Dennis Eckersley	.10	.05
248	Dwight Evans	.10	.05
249	Larry Walker	.20	.09
250	Billy Ripken	.05	.02
251	Mickey Tettleton	.05	.02
252	Tony Pena	.05	.02
253	Benito Santiago	.05	.02
254	Kirby Puckett	.30	.14
255	Cecil Fielder	.20	.09
256	Howard Johnson	.05	.02
257	Andujar Cedeno	.05	.02
258	Jose Rijo	.05	.02
259	Al Osuna	.05	.02
260	Todd Hundley	.10	.05

No.	Player	Price	Price
261	Orel Hershiser	.10	.05
262	Ray Lankford	.20	.09
263	Robin Ventura	.10	.05
264	Felix Jose	.05	.02
265	Eddie Murray	.20	.09
266	Kevin Mitchell	.10	.05
267	Gary Carter	.20	.09
268	Mike Benjamin	.05	.02
269	Dick Schofield	.05	.02
270	Jose Uribe	.05	.02
271	Pete Incaviglia	.05	.02
272	Tony Fernandez	.05	.02
273	Alan Trammell	.15	.07
274	Tony Gwynn	.50	.23
275	Mike Greenwell	.05	.02
276	Jeff Bagwell	.40	.18
277	Frank Viola	.05	.02
278	Randy Myers	.10	.05
279	Ken Caminiti	.05	.02
280	Bill Doran	.05	.02
281	Dan Pasqua	.05	.02
282	Alfredo Griffin	.05	.02
283	Jose Oquendo	.05	.02
284	Kal Daniels	.05	.02
285	Bobby Thigpen	.05	.02
286	Robby Thompson	.05	.02
287	Mark Eichhorn	.05	.02
288	Mike Felder	.05	.02
289	Dave Gallagher	.05	.02
290	Dave Anderson	.05	.02
291	Mel Hall	.05	.02
292	Jerald Clark	.05	.02
293	Al Newman	.05	.02
294	Rob Deer	.05	.02
295	Matt Nokes	.05	.02
296	Jack Armstrong	.05	.02
297	Jim Deshaies	.05	.02
298	Jeff Innis	.05	.02
299	Jeff Reed	.05	.02
300	Checklist 201-300	.05	.02
301	Lonnie Smith	.05	.02
302	Jimmy Key	.10	.05
303	Junior Felix	.05	.02
304	Mike Heath	.05	.02
305	Mark Langston	.10	.05
306	Greg W. Harris	.05	.02
307	Brett Butler	.10	.05
308	Luis Rivera	.05	.02
309	Bruce Ruffin	.05	.02
310	Paul Faries	.05	.02
311	Terry Leach	.05	.02
312	Scott Scudder	.25	.11
313	Scott Leius	.05	.02
314	Harold Reynolds	.05	.02
315	Jack Morris	.10	.05
316	David Segui	.10	.05
317	Bill Gullickson	.05	.02
318	Todd Frohwirth	.05	.02
319	Mark Leiter	.05	.02
320	Jeff M. Robinson	.05	.02
321	Gary Gaetti	.10	.05
322	John Smoltz	.15	.07
323	Andy Benes	.10	.05
324	Kelly Gruber	.05	.02
325	Jim Abbott	.15	.07
326	John Kruk	.10	.05
327	Kevin Seitzer	.05	.02
328	Darrin Jackson	.05	.02
329	Kurt Stillwell	.05	.02
330	Mike Maddux	.05	.02
331	Dennis Eckersley	.10	.05
332	Dan Gladden	.05	.02
333	Jose Canseco	.25	.11
334	Ken Hrbek	.05	.02
335	Ken Griffey Sr.	.10	.05
336	Greg Swindell	.05	.02
337	Trevor Wilson	.05	.02
338	Sam Horn	.05	.02
339	Mike Henneman	.05	.02
340	Jerry Browne	.05	.02
341	Glenn Braggs	.05	.02
342	Tom Glavine	.15	.07
343	Wally Joyner	.10	.05
344	Fred McGriff	.15	.07
345	Ron Gant	.10	.05
346	Ramon Martinez	.10	.05

347	Wes Chamberlain	.05	.02
348	Terry Shumpert	.05	.02
349	Tim Teufel	.05	.02
350	Wally Backman	.05	.02
351	Joe Girardi	.10	.05
352	Devon White	.05	.02
353	Greg Maddux	.50	.23
354	Ryan Bowen	.05	.02
355	Roberto Alomar	.20	.09
356	Don Mattingly	.40	.18
357	Pedro Guerrero	.05	.02
358	Steve Sax	.05	.02
359	Joey Cora	.05	.02
360	Jim Gantner	.05	.02
361	Brian Barnes	.05	.02
362	Kevin McReynolds	.05	.02
363	Bret Barberie	.05	.02
364	David Cone	.10	.05
365	Dennis Martinez	.10	.05
366	Brian Hunter	.05	.02
367	Edgar Martinez	.15	.07
368	Steve Finley	.10	.05
369	Greg Briley	.05	.02
370	Jeff Blauser	.05	.02
371	Todd Stottlemyre	.10	.05
372	Luis Gonzalez	.15	.07
373	Rick Wilkins	.05	.02
374	Darryl Kile	.10	.05
375	John Olerud	.10	.05
376	Lee Smith	.10	.05
377	Kevin Maas	.05	.02
378	Dante Bichette	.15	.07
379	Tom Pagnozzi	.05	.02
380	Mike Flanagan	.05	.02
381	Charlie O'Brien	.05	.02
382	Dave Martinez	.05	.02
383	Keith Miller	.05	.02
384	Scott Ruskin	.05	.02
385	Kevin Elster	.05	.02
386	Alvin Davis	.05	.02
387	Casey Candaele	.05	.02
388	Pete O'Brien	.05	.02
389	Jeff Treadway	.05	.02
390	Scott Bradley	.05	.02
391	Mookie Wilson	.10	.05
392	Jimmy Jones	.05	.02
393	Candy Maldonado	.05	.02
394	Eric Yelding	.05	.02
395	Tom Henke	.05	.02
396	Franklin Stubbs	.05	.02
397	Milt Thompson	.05	.02
398	Mark Carreon	.05	.02
399	Randy Velarde	.05	.02
400	Checklist 301-400	.05	.02
401	Omar Vizquel	.10	.05
402	Joe Boever	.05	.02
403	Bill Krueger	.05	.02
404	Jody Reed	.05	.02
405	Mike Schooler	.05	.02
406	Jason Grimsley	.05	.02
407	Greg Myers	.05	.02
408	Randy Ready	.05	.02
409	Mike Timlin	.05	.02
410	Mitch Williams	.05	.02
411	Garry Templeton	.05	.02
412	Greg Cadaret	.05	.02
413	Donnie Hill	.05	.02
414	Wally Whitehurst	.05	.02
415	Scott Sanderson	.05	.02
416	Thomas Howard	.05	.02
417	Neal Heaton	.05	.02
418	Charlie Hough	.10	.05
419	Jack Howell	.05	.02
420	Greg Hibbard	.05	.02
421	Carlos Quintana	.05	.02
422	Kim Batiste	.05	.02
423	Paul Molitor	.20	.09
424	Ken Griffey Jr.	1.25	.55
425	Phil Plantier	.15	.07
426	Denny Neagle	.15	.07
427	Von Hayes	.05	.02
428	Shane Mack	.05	.02
429	Darren Daulton	.10	.05
430	Dwayne Henry	.05	.02
431	Lance Parrish	.05	.02
432	Mike Humphreys	.05	.02
433	Tim Burke	.05	.02
434	Bryan Harvey	.05	.02
435	Pat Kelly	.05	.02
436	Ozzie Guillen	.05	.02
437	Bruce Hurst	.05	.02
438	Sammy Sosa	.60	.25
439	Dennis Rasmussen	.05	.02
440	Ken Patterson	.05	.02
441	Jay Buhner	.15	.07
442	Pat Combs	.05	.02
443	Wade Boggs	.20	.09
444	George Brett	.40	.18
445	Mo Vaughn	.25	.11
446	Chuck Knoblauch	.20	.09
447	Tom Candiotti	.05	.02
448	Mark Portugal	.05	.02
449	Mickey Morandini	.05	.02
450	Duane Ward	.05	.02
451	Otis Nixon	.10	.05
452	Bob Welch	.05	.02
453	Rusty Meacham	.05	.02
454	Keith Mitchell	.05	.02
455	Marquis Grissom	.10	.05
456	Robin Yount	.20	.09
457	Harvey Pulliam	.05	.02
458	Jose DeLeon	.05	.02
459	Mark Gubicza	.05	.02
460	Darryl Hamilton	.05	.02
461	Tom Browning	.05	.02
462	Monty Fariss	.05	.02
463	Jerome Walton	.05	.02
464	Paul O'Neil	.10	.05
465	Dean Palmer	.10	.05
466	Travis Fryman	.10	.05
467	John Smiley	.05	.02
468	Lloyd Moseby	.05	.02
469	John Wehner	.05	.02
470	Skeeter Barnes	.05	.02
471	Steve Chitren	.05	.02
472	Kent Mercker	.05	.02
473	Terry Steinbach	.05	.02
474	Andres Galarraga	.20	.09
475	Steve Avery	.05	.02
476	Tom Gordon	.05	.02
477	Cal Eldred	.05	.02
478	Omar Olivares	.05	.02
479	Julio Machado	.05	.02
480	Bob Milacki	.05	.02
481	Les Lancaster	.05	.02
482	John Candelaria	.05	.02
483	Brian Downing	.05	.02
484	Roger McDowell	.05	.02
485	Scott Scudder	.05	.02
486	Zane Smith	.05	.02
487	John Cerutti	.05	.02
488	Steve Buechele	.05	.02
489	Paul Gibson	.05	.02
490	Curtis Wilkerson	.05	.02
491	Marvin Freeman	.05	.02
492	Tom Foley	.05	.02
493	Juan Berenguer	.05	.02
494	Ernest Riles	.05	.02
495	Sid Bream	.05	.02
496	Chuck Crim	.05	.02
497	Mike Macfarlane	.05	.02
498	Dale Sveum	.05	.02
499	Storm Davis	.05	.02
500	Checklist 401-500	.05	.02
501	Jeff Reardon	.10	.05
502	Shawn Abner	.05	.02
503	Tony Fossas	.05	.02
504	Cory Snyder	.05	.02
505	Matt Young	.05	.02
506	Allan Anderson	.05	.02
507	Mark Lee	.05	.02
508	Gene Nelson	.05	.02
509	Mike Pagliarulo	.05	.02
510	Rafael Belliard	.05	.02
511	Jay Howell	.05	.02
512	Bob Tewksbury	.05	.02
513	Mike Morgan	.05	.02
514	John Franco	.10	.05
515	Kevin Gross	.05	.02
516	Lou Whitaker	.10	.05
517	Orlando Merced	.05	.02
518	Todd Benzinger	.05	.02
519	Gary Redus	.05	.02
520	Walt Terrell	.05	.02
521	Jack Clark	.10	.05
522	Dave Parker	.10	.05
523	Tim Naehring	.05	.02
524	Mark Whiten	.05	.02
525	Ellis Burks	.10	.05
526	Frank Castillo	.05	.02
527	Brian Harper	.05	.02
528	Brook Jacoby	.05	.02
529	Rick Sutcliffe	.05	.02
530	Joe Klink	.05	.02
531	Terry Bross	.05	.02
532	Jose Offerman	.10	.05
533	Todd Zeile	.05	.02
534	Eric Karros	.20	.09
535	Anthony Young	.05	.02
536	Milt Cuyler	.05	.02
537	Randy Tomlin	.05	.02
538	Scott Livingstone	.05	.02
539	Jim Eisenreich	.05	.02
540	Don Slaught	.05	.02
541	Scott Cooper	.05	.02
542	Joe Grahe	.05	.02
543	Tom Brunansky	.05	.02
544	Eddie Zosky	.05	.02
545	Roger Clemens	.50	.23
546	David Justice	.20	.09
547	Dave Stewart	.10	.05
548	David West	.05	.02
549	Dave Smith	.05	.02
550	Dan Plesac	.05	.02
551	Alex Fernandez	.10	.05
552	Bernard Gilkey	.10	.05
553	Jack McDowell	.10	.05
554	Tino Martinez	.20	.09
555	Bo Jackson	.20	.09
556	Bernie Williams	.20	.09
557	Mark Gardner	.05	.02
558	Glenallen Hill	.05	.02
559	Oil Can Boyd	.05	.02
560	Chris James	.05	.02
561	Scott Servais	.05	.02
562	Rey Sanchez	.05	.02
563	Paul McClellan	.05	.02
564	Andy Mota	.05	.02
565	Darren Lewis	.05	.02
566	Jose Melendez	.05	.02
567	Tommy Greene	.05	.02
568	Rich Rodriguez	.05	.02
569	Heathcliff Slocumb	.05	.02
570	Joe Hesketh	.05	.02
571	Carlton Fisk	.20	.09
572	Erik Hanson	.05	.02
573	Wilson Alvarez	.10	.05
574	Rheal Cormier	.05	.02
575	Tim Raines	.10	.05
576	Bobby Witt	.05	.02
577	Roberto Kelly	.15	.07
578	Kevin Brown	.05	.02
579	Chris Nabholz	.05	.02
580	Jesse Orosco	.05	.02
581	Jeff Brantley	.05	.02
582	Rafael Ramirez	.05	.02
583	Kelly Downs	.05	.02
584	Mike Simms	.05	.02
585	Mike Remlinger	.05	.02
586	Dave Hollins	.10	.05
587	Larry Andersen	.05	.02
588	Mike Gardiner	.05	.02
589	Craig Lefferts	.05	.02
590	Paul Assenmacher	.05	.02
591	Bryn Smith	.05	.02
592	Donn Pall	.05	.02
593	Mike Jackson	.10	.05
594	Scott Radinsky	.05	.02
595	Brian Holman	.05	.02
596	Geronimo Pena	.05	.02
597	Mike Jeffcoat	.05	.02
598	Carlos Martinez	.05	.02
599	Geno Petralli	.05	.02
600	Checklist 501-600	.05	.02
601	Jerry Don Gleaton	.05	.02
602	Adam Peterson	.05	.02
603	Craig Grebeck	.05	.02
604	Mark Guthrie	.05	.02

❑ 605	Frank Tanana	.05	.02
❑ 606	Hensley Meulens	.05	.02
❑ 607	Mark Davis	.05	.02
❑ 608	Eric Plunk	.05	.02
❑ 609	Mark Williamson	.05	.02
❑ 610	Lee Guetterman	.05	.02
❑ 611	Bobby Rose	.05	.02
❑ 612	Bill Wegman	.05	.02
❑ 613	Mike Hartley	.05	.02
❑ 614	Chris Beasley	.05	.02
❑ 615	Chris Bosio	.05	.02
❑ 616	Henry Cotto	.05	.02
❑ 617	Chico Walker	.05	.02
❑ 618	Russ Swan	.05	.02
❑ 619	Bob Walk	.05	.02
❑ 620	Bill Swift	.05	.02
❑ 621	Warren Newson	.05	.02
❑ 622	Steve Bedrosian	.05	.02
❑ 623	Ricky Bones	.05	.02
❑ 624	Kevin Tapani	.05	.02
❑ 625	Juan Guzman	.05	.02
❑ 626	Jeff Johnson	.05	.02
❑ 627	Jeff Montgomery	.10	.05
❑ 628	Ken Hill	.05	.02
❑ 629	Gary Thurman	.05	.02
❑ 630	Steve Howe	.05	.02
❑ 631	Jose DeJesus	.05	.02
❑ 632	Kirk Dressendorfer	.05	.02
❑ 633	Jaime Navarro	.05	.02
❑ 634	Lee Stevens	.10	.05
❑ 635	Pete Harnisch	.05	.02
❑ 636	Bill Landrum	.05	.02
❑ 637	Rich DeLucia	.05	.02
❑ 638	Luis Salazar	.05	.02
❑ 639	Rob Murphy	.05	.02
❑ 640	Jose Canseco CL	.20	.09
	Rickey Henderson		
❑ 641	Roger Clemens DS	.20	.09
❑ 642	Jim Abbott DS	.05	.02
❑ 643	Travis Fryman DS	.05	.02
❑ 644	Jesse Barfield DS	.05	.02
❑ 645	Cal Ripken DS	.40	.18
❑ 646	Wade Boggs DS	.10	.05
❑ 647	Cecil Fielder DS	.05	.02
❑ 648	Rickey Henderson DS	.10	.05
❑ 649	Jose Canseco DS	.10	.05
❑ 650	Ken Griffey Jr. DS	1.00	.45
❑ 651	Kenny Rogers	.05	.02
❑ 652	Luis Mercedes	.05	.02
❑ 653	Mike Stanton	.05	.02
❑ 654	Glenn Davis	.05	.02
❑ 655	Nolan Ryan	.75	.35
❑ 656	Reggie Jefferson	.10	.05
❑ 657	Javier Ortiz	.05	.02
❑ 658	Greg A. Harris	.05	.02
❑ 659	Mariano Duncan	.05	.02
❑ 660	Jeff Shaw	.05	.02
❑ 661	Mike Moore	.05	.02
❑ 662	Chris Haney	.05	.02
❑ 663	Joe Slusarski	.05	.02
❑ 664	Wayne Housie	.05	.02
❑ 665	Carlos Garcia	.05	.02
❑ 666	Bob Ojeda	.05	.02
❑ 667	Bryan Hickerson	.05	.02
❑ 668	Tim Belcher	.05	.02
❑ 669	Ron Darling	.05	.02
❑ 670	Rex Hudler	.05	.02
❑ 671	Sid Fernandez	.05	.02
❑ 672	Chito Martinez	.05	.02
❑ 673	Pete Schourek	.05	.02
❑ 674	Armando Reynoso	.05	.02
❑ 675	Mike Mussina	.30	.14
❑ 676	Kevin Morton	.05	.02
❑ 677	Norm Charlton	.05	.02
❑ 678	Danny Darwin	.05	.02
❑ 679	Eric King	.05	.02
❑ 680	Ted Power	.05	.02
❑ 681	Barry Jones	.05	.02
❑ 682	Carney Lansford	.10	.05
❑ 683	Mel Rojas	.05	.02
❑ 684	Rick Honeycutt	.05	.02
❑ 685	Jeff Fassero	.05	.02
❑ 686	Cris Carpenter	.05	.02
❑ 687	Tim Crews	.05	.02
❑ 688	Scott Terry	.05	.02
❑ 689	Chris Gwynn	.05	.02

❑ 690	Gerald Perry	.05	.02
❑ 691	John Barfield	.05	.02
❑ 692	Bob Melvin	.05	.02
❑ 693	Juan Agosto	.05	.02
❑ 694	Alejandro Pena	.05	.02
❑ 695	Jeff Russell	.05	.02
❑ 696	Carmelo Martinez	.05	.02
❑ 697	Bud Black	.05	.02
❑ 698	Dave Otto	.05	.02
❑ 699	Billy Hatcher	.05	.02
❑ 700	Checklist 601-700	.05	.02
❑ 701	Clemente Nunez	.10	.05
❑ 702	Rookie Threats	.05	.02
	Mark Clark		
	Donovan Osborne		
	Brian Jordan		
❑ 703	Mike Morgan	.05	.02
❑ 704	Keith Miller	.05	.02
❑ 705	Kurt Stillwell	.05	.02
❑ 706	Damon Berryhill	.05	.02
❑ 707	Von Hayes	.05	.02
❑ 708	Rick Sutcliffe	.05	.02
❑ 709	Hubie Brooks	.05	.02
❑ 710	Ryan Turner	.05	.02
❑ 711	Barry Bonds CL	.10	.05
	Andy Van Slyke		
❑ 712	Jose Rijo DS	.05	.02
❑ 713	Tom Glavine DS	.10	.05
❑ 714	Shawon Dunston DS	.05	.02
❑ 715	Andy Van Slyke DS	.05	.02
❑ 716	Ozzie Smith DS	.20	.09
❑ 717	Tony Gwynn DS	.20	.09
❑ 718	Will Clark DS	.10	.05
❑ 719	Marquis Grissom DS	.05	.02
❑ 720	Howard Johnson DS	.05	.02
❑ 721	Barry Bonds DS	.20	.09
❑ 722	Kirk McCaskill	.05	.02
❑ 723	Sammy Sosa	1.25	.55
❑ 724	George Bell	.05	.02
❑ 725	Gregg Jefferies	.05	.02
❑ 726	Gary DiSarcina	.05	.02
❑ 727	Mike Bordick	.05	.02
❑ 728	Eddie Murray	.10	.05
	400 Home Run Club		
❑ 729	Rene Gonzales	.05	.02
❑ 730	Mike Bielecki	.05	.02
❑ 731	Calvin Jones	.05	.02
❑ 732	Jack Morris	.10	.05
❑ 733	Frank Viola	.05	.02
❑ 734	Dave Winfield	.20	.09
❑ 735	Kevin Mitchell	.05	.02
❑ 736	Bill Swift	.05	.02
❑ 737	Dan Gladden	.05	.02
❑ 738	Mike Jackson	.05	.02
❑ 739	Mark Carreon	.05	.02
❑ 740	Kirt Manwaring	.05	.02
❑ 741	Randy Myers	.10	.05
❑ 742	Kevin McReynolds	.05	.02
❑ 743	Steve Sax	.05	.02
❑ 744	Wally Joyner	.10	.05
❑ 745	Gary Sheffield	.20	.09
❑ 746	Danny Tartabull	.10	.05
❑ 747	Julio Valera	.05	.02
❑ 748	Denny Neagle	.15	.07
❑ 749	Lance Blankenship	.05	.02
❑ 750	Mike Gallego	.05	.02
❑ 751	Bret Saberhagen	.10	.05
❑ 752	Ruben Amaro	.05	.02
❑ 753	Eddie Murray	.20	.09
❑ 754	Kyle Abbott	.05	.02
❑ 755	Bobby Bonilla	.10	.05
❑ 756	Eric Davis	.10	.05
❑ 757	Eddie Taubensee	.10	.05
❑ 758	Andres Galarraga	.20	.09
❑ 759	Pete Incaviglia	.05	.02
❑ 760	Tom Candiotti	.05	.02
❑ 761	Tim Belcher	.05	.02
❑ 762	Ricky Bones	.05	.02
❑ 763	Bip Roberts	.05	.02
❑ 764	Pedro Munoz	.05	.02
❑ 765	Greg Swindell	.05	.02
❑ 766	Kenny Lofton	.25	.11
❑ 767	Gary Carter	.20	.09
❑ 768	Charlie Hayes	.05	.02
❑ 769	Dickie Thon	.05	.02
❑ 770	Donovan Osborne DD CL	.05	.02

❑ 771	Bret Boone DD	.20	.09
❑ 772	Archi Cianfrocco DD	.05	.02
❑ 773	Mark Clark DD	.05	.02
❑ 774	Chad Curtis DD	.25	.11
❑ 775	Pat Listach DD	.05	.02
❑ 776	Pat Mahomes DD	.05	.02
❑ 777	Donovan Osborne DD	.05	.02
❑ 778	John Patterson DD	.05	.02
❑ 779	Andy Stankiewicz DD	.05	.02
❑ 780	Turk Wendell DD	.10	.05
❑ 781	Bill Krueger	.05	.02
❑ 782	Rickey Henderson	.10	.05
	Grand Theft		
❑ 783	Kevin Seitzer	.05	.02
❑ 784	Dave Martinez	.05	.02
❑ 785	John Smiley	.05	.02
❑ 786	Matt Stairs	.30	.14
❑ 787	Scott Scudder	.05	.02
❑ 788	John Wetteland	.10	.05
❑ 789	Jack Armstrong	.05	.02
❑ 790	Ken Hill	.05	.02
❑ 791	Dick Schofield	.05	.02
❑ 792	Mariano Duncan	.05	.02
❑ 793	Bill Pecota	.05	.02
❑ 794	Mike Kelly	.10	.05
❑ 795	Willie Randolph	.10	.05
❑ 796	Butch Henry	.05	.02
❑ 797	Carlos Hernandez	.05	.02
❑ 798	Doug Jones	.05	.02
❑ 799	Melido Perez	.05	.02
❑ 800	Checklist 701-800	.05	.02
❑ HH2	Ted Williams Hologram	2.00	.90
	(Top left corner says		
	91 Upper Deck 92)		
❑ SP3	Deion Sanders FB/BB	.50	.23
❑ SP4	Tom Selleck	1.00	.45
	Frank Thomas SP		
	(Mr. Baseball)		

1992 Upper Deck Bench/Morgan Heroes

	MINT	NRMT
COMPLETE SET (10)	10.00	4.50
COMMON BENCH/MORG (37-45)	1.00	
	.45	

RANDOM INSERTS IN HI SERIES PACKS

❑ 37	Johnny Bench	1.00	.45
	1968 Rookie-of-the-Year		
❑ 38	Johnny Bench	1.00	.45
	1968-77		
	Ten Straight Gold Gloves		
❑ 39	Johnny Bench	1.00	.45
	1970 and 1972 MVP		
❑ 40	Joe Morgan	1.00	.45
	1965 Rookie Year		
❑ 41	Joe Morgan	1.00	.45
	1975-76 Back-to-Back MVP		
❑ 42	Joe Morgan	1.00	.45
	1980-83		
	The Golden Years		
❑ 43	Johnny Bench	1.00	.45
	Joe Morgan		
	1972-79		
	Big Red Machine		
❑ 44	Johnny Bench	1.00	.45
	Joe Morgan		

1989 and 1990 Hall of Fame

	MINT	NRMT
45 Checklist-Heroes 37-45...	1.00	.45
NNO Baseball Heroes SP.	2.50	1.10
(Header card)		
AU5 Johnny Bench and ..	120.00	55.00
Joe Morgan AU		
(Signed and Numbered of 2500)		

1992 Upper Deck Heroes of Baseball

	MINT	NRMT
COMPLETE SET (4)	6.00	2.70
COMMON CARD (H5-H8)	.50	.23
RANDOM INSERTS IN HEROES FOIL		
H5 Vida Blue	.50	.23
H6 Lou Brock	3.00	1.35
H7 Rollie Fingers	1.00	.45
H8 Vida Blue ART	2.00	.90
Lou Brock		
Rollie Fingers		
AU5 Vida Blue AU/3000	10.00	4.50
AU6 Lou Brock AU/3000	50.00	22.00
AU7 R.Fingers AU/3000	20.00	9.00

1992 Upper Deck Home Run Heroes

	MINT	NRMT
COMPLETE SET (26)	12.00	5.50
COMMON CARD (HR1-HR26)	.25	.11
ONE PER LO SERIES JUMBO		
HR1 Jose Canseco	.75	.35
HR2 Cecil Fielder	.40	.18
HR3 Howard Johnson	.25	.11
HR4 Cal Ripken	2.00	.90
HR5 Matt Williams	.60	.25
HR6 Joe Carter	.40	.18
HR7 Ron Gant	.40	.18
HR8 Frank Thomas	1.50	.70
HR9 Andre Dawson	.60	.25
HR10 Fred McGriff	.60	.25
HR11 Danny Tartabull	.25	.11
HR12 Chili Davis	.40	.18
HR13 Albert Belle	.75	.35
HR14 Jack Clark	.25	.11
HR15 Paul O'Neill	.40	.18
HR16 Darryl Strawberry	.40	.18
HR17 Dave Winfield	.75	.35
HR18 Jay Buhner	.60	.25
HR19 Juan Gonzalez	1.50	.70
HR20 Greg Vaughn	.60	.25
HR21 Barry Bonds	.75	.35
HR22 Matt Nokes	.25	.11
HR23 John Kruk	.40	.18
HR24 Ivan Calderon	.25	.11
HR25 Jeff Bagwell	1.25	.55
HR26 Todd Zeile	.25	.11

1992 Upper Deck Scouting Report

	MINT	NRMT
COMPLETE SET (25)	15.00	6.75
COMMON CARD (SR1-SR25)	.50	.23
MINOR STARS	1.00	.45
UNLISTED STARS	1.50	.70
ONE PER HI SERIES JUMBO		
SR1 Andy Ashby	1.00	.45
SR2 Willie Banks	.50	.23
SR3 Kim Batiste	.50	.23
SR4 Derek Bell	1.00	.45
SR5 Archi Cianfrocco	.50	.23
SR6 Royce Clayton	.50	.23
SR7 Gary DiSarcina	.50	.23
SR8 Dave Fleming	.50	.23
SR9 Butch Henry	.50	.23
SR10 Todd Hundley	1.00	.45
SR11 Brian Jordan	1.50	.70
SR12 Eric Karros	1.50	.70
SR13 Pat Listach	.50	.23
SR14 Scott Livingstone	.50	.23
SR15 Kenny Lofton	3.00	1.35
SR16 Pat Mahomes	.50	.23
SR17 Denny Neagle	1.25	.55
SR18 Dave Nilsson	1.00	.45
SR19 Donovan Osborne	.50	.23
SR20 Reggie Sanders	1.00	.45
SR21 Andy Stankiewicz	.50	.23
SR22 Jim Thome	6.00	2.70
SR23 Julio Valera	.50	.23
SR24 Mark Wohlers	.50	.23
SR25 Anthony Young	.50	.23

1992 Upper Deck Williams Best

	MINT	NRMT
COMPLETE SET (20)	25.00	11.00
COMMON CARD (T1-T20)	.25	.11
RANDOM INSERTS IN HI SERIES		
T1 Wade Boggs	1.00	.45
T2 Barry Bonds	1.25	.55
T3 Jose Canseco	1.25	.55
T4 Will Clark	1.00	.45
T5 Cecil Fielder	.50	.23
T6 Tony Gwynn	2.50	1.10
T7 Rickey Henderson	1.25	.55
T8 Fred McGriff	.75	.35
T9 Kirby Puckett	1.50	.70
T10 Ruben Sierra	.25	.11
T11 Roberto Alomar	1.00	.45
T12 Jeff Bagwell	2.00	.90
T13 Albert Belle	1.00	.45
T14 Juan Gonzalez	2.50	1.10
T15 Ken Griffey Jr.	6.00	2.70
T16 Chris Hoiles	.25	.11
T17 David Justice	1.00	.45
T18 Phil Plantier	.25	.11
T19 Frank Thomas	2.50	1.10
T20 Robin Ventura	.50	.23

1992 Upper Deck Williams Heroes

	MINT	NRMT
COMPLETE SET (10)	6.00	2.70
COMMON T.WILLIAMS (28-36)	.50	.23
RANDOM INSERTS IN LO SERIES PACKS		
28 Ted Williams	.50	.23
1939 Rookie Year		
29 Ted Williams	.50	.23
1941 .406 BA		
30 Ted Williams	.50	.23
1942 Triple Crown Year		
31 Ted Williams	.50	.23
1946 and 1949 MVP		
32 Ted Williams	.50	.23
1947 2nd Triple Crown		
33 Ted Williams	.50	.23
1950s Player of the Decade		
34 Ted Williams	.50	.23
1960 500 Home Run Club		
35 Ted Williams	.50	.23
1966 Hall of Fame		
36 Baseball Heroes CL	.50	.23
NNO Baseball Heroes SP	2.00	.90
(Header card)		
AU4 Ted Williams	400.00	180.00
(Signed and Numbered of 2500)		

1993 Upper Deck

	MINT	NRMT
COMPLETE SET (840)	30.00	13.50
COMP.FACT.SET (840)	40.00	18.00
COMPLETE SERIES 1 (420)	15.00	6.75
COMPLETE SERIES 2 (420)	15.00	6.75
COMMON CARD (1-840)	.10	.05
MINOR STARS	.20	.09
UNLISTED STARS	.40	.18
SUBSET CARDS HALF VALUE OF BASE		

CARDS
SP CARDS STATED ODDS 1:72

❏ 1 Tim Salmon CL	.30	.14
❏ 2 Mike Piazza SR	2.00	.90
❏ 3 Rene Arocha SR	.10	.05
❏ 4 Willie Greene SR	.10	.05
❏ 5 Manny Alexander	.10	.05
❏ 6 Dan Wilson	.20	.09
❏ 7 Dan Smith	.10	.05
❏ 8 Kevin Rogers	.10	.05
❏ 9 Kurt Miller SR	.10	.05
❏ 10 Joe Vitko	.10	.05
❏ 11 Tim Costo	.10	.05
❏ 12 Alan Embree SR	.10	.05
❏ 13 Jim Tatum SR	.10	.05
❏ 14 Cris Colon	.10	.05
❏ 15 Steve Hosey	.10	.05
❏ 16 Sterling Hitchcock SR	.40	.18
❏ 17 Dave Mlicki	.10	.05
❏ 18 Jessie Hollins	.10	.05
❏ 19 Bobby Jones SR	.20	.09
❏ 20 Kurt Miller	.10	.05
❏ 21 Melvin Nieves SR	.10	.05
❏ 22 Billy Ashley SR	.10	.05
❏ 23 J.T. Snow SR	.50	.23
❏ 24 Chipper Jones SR	1.25	.55
❏ 25 Tim Salmon SR	.40	.18
❏ 26 Tim Pugh SR	.10	.05
❏ 27 David Nied SR	.10	.05
❏ 28 Mike Trombley	.10	.05
❏ 29 Javier Lopez SR	.40	.18
❏ 30 Jim Abbott CL CL	.10	.05
❏ 31 Jim Abbott CH	.10	.05
❏ 32 Dale Murphy CH	.20	.09
❏ 33 Tony Pena CH	.10	.05
❏ 34 Kirby Puckett CH	.40	.18
❏ 35 Harold Reynolds CH	.10	.05
❏ 36 Cal Ripken CH	.75	.35
❏ 37 Nolan Ryan CH	.75	.35
❏ 38 Ryne Sandberg CH	.30	.14
❏ 39 Dave Stewart CH	.10	.05
❏ 40 Dave Winfield CH	.20	.09
❏ 41 Joe Carter CL	.40	.18
Mark McGwire		
❏ 42 Blockbuster Trade	.40	.18
Joe Carter		
Roberto Alomar		
❏ 43 Brew Crew	.40	.18
Paul Molitor		
Pat Listach		
Robin Yount		
❏ 44 Iron and Steel	.40	.18
Cal Ripken		
Brady Anderson		
❏ 45 Youthful Tribe	.20	.09
Albert Belle		
Sandy Alomar Jr.		
Jim Thome		
Carlos Baerga		
Kenny Lofton		
❏ 46 Motown Mashers	.20	.09
Cecil Fielder		
Mickey Tettleton		
❏ 47 Yankee Pride	.20	.09
Roberto Kelly		
Don Mattingly		
❏ 48 Boston Cy Sox	.20	.09
Frank Viola		
Roger Clemens		
❏ 49 Bash Brothers	.20	.09
Ruben Sierra		
Mark McGwire		
❏ 50 Twin Titles	.40	.18
Kent Hrbek		
Kirby Puckett		
❏ 51 Southside Sluggers	.40	.18
Robin Ventura		
Frank Thomas		
❏ 52 Latin Stars	.40	.18
Juan Gonzalez		
Jose Canseco		
Ivan Rodriguez		
Rafael Palmeiro		
❏ 53 Lethal Lefties	.10	.05
Mark Langston		
Jim Abbott		
Chuck Finley		
❏ 54 Royal Family	.10	.05
Wally Joyner		
Gregg Jefferies		
George Brett		
❏ 55 Pacific Sock Exchange	.50	.23
Kevin Mitchell		
Ken Griffey Jr.		
Jay Buhner		
❏ 56 George Brett	.75	.35
❏ 57 Scott Cooper	.10	.05
❏ 58 Mike Maddux	.10	.05
❏ 59 Rusty Meacham	.10	.05
❏ 60 Wil Cordero	.10	.05
❏ 61 Tim Teufel	.10	.05
❏ 62 Jeff Montgomery	.20	.09
❏ 63 Scott Livingstone	.10	.05
❏ 64 Doug Dascenzo	.10	.05
❏ 65 Bret Boone	.20	.09
❏ 66 Tim Wakefield	.20	.09
❏ 67 Curt Schilling	.20	.09
❏ 68 Frank Tanana	.10	.05
❏ 69 Len Dykstra	.20	.09
❏ 70 Derek Lilliquist	.10	.05
❏ 71 Anthony Young	.10	.05
❏ 72 Hipolito Pichardo	.10	.05
❏ 73 Rod Beck	.20	.09
❏ 74 Kent Hrbek	.20	.09
❏ 75 Tom Glavine	.30	.14
❏ 76 Kevin Brown	.30	.14
❏ 77 Chuck Finley	.10	.05
❏ 78 Bob Walk	.10	.05
❏ 79 Rheal Cormier UER	.10	.05
(Born in New Brunswick,		
not British Columbia)		
❏ 80 Rick Sutcliffe	.10	.05
❏ 81 Harold Baines	.20	.09
❏ 82 Lee Smith	.20	.09
❏ 83 Geno Petralli	.10	.05
❏ 84 Jose Oquendo	.10	.05
❏ 85 Mark Gubicza	.10	.05
❏ 86 Mickey Tettleton	.10	.05
❏ 87 Bobby Witt	.10	.05
❏ 88 Mark Lewis	.10	.05
❏ 89 Kevin Appier	.20	.09
❏ 90 Mike Stanton	.10	.05
❏ 91 Rafael Belliard	.10	.05
❏ 92 Kenny Rogers	.10	.05
❏ 93 Randy Velarde	.10	.05
❏ 94 Luis Sojo	.10	.05
❏ 95 Mark Letter	.10	.05
❏ 96 Jody Reed	.10	.05
❏ 97 Pete Harnisch	.10	.05
❏ 98 Tom Candiotti	.10	.05
❏ 99 Mark Portugal	.10	.05
❏ 100 Dave Valle	.10	.05
❏ 101 Shawon Dunston	.10	.05
❏ 102 B.J. Surhoff	.20	.09
❏ 103 Jay Bell	.20	.09
❏ 104 Sid Bream	.10	.05
❏ 105 Frank Thomas CL	.40	.18
❏ 106 Mike Morgan	.10	.05
❏ 107 Bill Doran	.10	.05
❏ 108 Lance Blankenship	.10	.05
❏ 109 Mark Lemke	.10	.05
❏ 110 Brian Harper	.10	.05
❏ 111 Brady Anderson	.20	.09
❏ 112 Bip Roberts	.10	.05
❏ 113 Mitch Williams	.10	.05
❏ 114 Craig Biggio	.40	.18
❏ 115 Eddie Murray	.40	.18
❏ 116 Matt Nokes	.10	.05
❏ 117 Lance Parrish	.10	.05
❏ 118 Bill Swift	.10	.05
❏ 119 Jeff Innis	.10	.05
❏ 120 Mike LaValliere	.10	.05
❏ 121 Hal Morris	.10	.05
❏ 122 Walt Weiss	.10	.05
❏ 123 Ivan Rodriguez	.50	.23
❏ 124 Andy Van Slyke	.20	.09
❏ 125 Roberto Alomar	.40	.18
❏ 126 Robby Thompson	.10	.05
❏ 127 Sammy Sosa	1.25	.55
❏ 128 Mark Langston	.10	.05
❏ 129 Jerry Browne	.10	.05
❏ 130 Chuck McElroy	.10	.05
❏ 131 Frank Viola	.10	.05
❏ 132 Leo Gomez	.10	.05
❏ 133 Ramon Martinez	.20	.09
❏ 134 Don Mattingly	.75	.35
❏ 135 Roger Clemens	1.00	.45
❏ 136 Rickey Henderson	.50	.23
❏ 137 Darren Daulton	.20	.09
❏ 138 Ken Hill	.10	.05
❏ 139 Ozzie Guillen	.10	.05
❏ 140 Jerald Clark	.10	.05
❏ 141 Dave Fleming	.10	.05
❏ 142 Delino DeShields	.20	.09
❏ 143 Matt Williams	.30	.14
❏ 144 Larry Walker	.40	.18
❏ 145 Ruben Sierra	.10	.05
❏ 146 Ozzie Smith	.50	.23
❏ 147 Chris Sabo	.10	.05
❏ 148 Carlos Hernandez	.10	.05
❏ 149 Pat Borders	.10	.05
❏ 150 Orlando Merced	.10	.05
❏ 151 Royce Clayton	.10	.05
❏ 152 Kurt Stillwell	.10	.05
❏ 153 Dave Hollins	.10	.05
❏ 154 Mike Greenwell	.10	.05
❏ 155 Nolan Ryan	1.50	.70
❏ 156 Felix Jose	.10	.05
❏ 157 Junior Felix	.10	.05
❏ 158 Derek Bell	.20	.09
❏ 159 Steve Buechele	.10	.05
❏ 160 John Burkett	.10	.05
❏ 161 Pat Howell	.10	.05
❏ 162 Milt Cuyler	.10	.05
❏ 163 Terry Pendleton	.20	.09
❏ 164 Jack Morris	.20	.09
❏ 165 Tony Gwynn	1.00	.45
❏ 166 Deion Sanders	.30	.14
❏ 167 Mike Devereaux	.10	.05
❏ 168 Ron Darling	.10	.05
❏ 169 Orel Hershiser	.20	.09
❏ 170 Mike Jackson	.20	.09
❏ 171 Doug Jones	.10	.05
❏ 172 Dan Walters	.10	.05
❏ 173 Darren Lewis	.10	.05
❏ 174 Carlos Baerga	.10	.05
❏ 175 Ryne Sandberg	.50	.23
❏ 176 Gregg Jefferies	.10	.05
❏ 177 John Jaha	.10	.05
❏ 178 Luis Polonia	.10	.05
❏ 179 Kirt Manwaring	.10	.05
❏ 180 Mike Magnante	.10	.05
❏ 181 Billy Ripken	.10	.05
❏ 182 Mike Moore	.10	.05
❏ 183 Eric Anthony	.10	.05
❏ 184 Lenny Harris	.10	.05
❏ 185 Tony Pena	.10	.05
❏ 186 Mike Felder	.10	.05
❏ 187 Greg Olson	.10	.05
❏ 188 Rene Gonzales	.10	.05
❏ 189 Mike Bordick	.10	.05
❏ 190 Mel Rojas	.10	.05
❏ 191 Todd Frohwirth	.10	.05
❏ 192 Darryl Hamilton	.10	.05
❏ 193 Mike Fetters	.10	.05
❏ 194 Omar Olivares	.10	.05
❏ 195 Tony Phillips	.10	.05
❏ 196 Paul Sorrento	.10	.05
❏ 197 Trevor Wilson	.10	.05

198	Kevin Gross	.10	.05
199	Ron Karkovice	.10	.05
200	Brook Jacoby	.10	.05
201	Mariano Duncan	.10	.05
202	Dennis Cook	.10	.05
203	Daryl Boston	.10	.05
204	Mike Perez	.10	.05
205	Manuel Lee	.10	.05
206	Steve Olin	.10	.05
207	Charlie Hough	.20	.09
208	Scott Scudder	.10	.05
209	Charlie O'Brien	.10	.05
210	Barry Bonds CL	.40	.18
211	Jose Vizcaino	.10	.05
212	Scott Leius	.10	.05
213	Kevin Mitchell	.20	.09
214	Brian Barnes	.10	.05
215	Pat Kelly	.10	.05
216	Chris Hammond	.10	.05
217	Rob Deer	.10	.05
218	Cory Snyder	.10	.05
219	Gary Carter	.30	.14
220	Danny Darwin	.10	.05
221	Tom Gordon	.10	.05
222	Gary Sheffield	.40	.18
223	Joe Carter	.20	.09
224	Jay Buhner	.30	.14
225	Jose Offerman	.20	.09
226	Jose Rijo	.10	.05
227	Mark Whiten	.10	.05
228	Randy Milligan	.10	.05
229	Bud Black	.10	.05
230	Gary DiSarcina	.10	.05
231	Steve Finley	.20	.09
232	Dennis Martinez	.20	.09
233	Mike Mussina	.40	.18
234	Joe Oliver	.10	.05
235	Chad Curtis	.20	.09
236	Shane Mack	.10	.05
237	Jaime Navarro	.10	.05
238	Brian McRae	.10	.05
239	Chili Davis	.20	.09
240	Jeff King	.10	.05
241	Dean Palmer	.20	.09
242	Danny Tartabull	.10	.05
243	Charles Nagy	.20	.09
244	Ray Lankford	.30	.14
245	Barry Larkin	.40	.18
246	Steve Avery	.10	.05
247	John Kruk	.20	.09
248	Derrick May	.10	.05
249	Stan Javier	.10	.05
250	Roger McDowell	.10	.05
251	Dan Gladden	.10	.05
252	Wally Joyner	.20	.09
253	Pat Listach	.10	.05
254	Chuck Knoblauch	.40	.18
255	Sandy Alomar Jr.	.20	.09
256	Jeff Bagwell	.50	.23
257	Andy Stankiewicz	.10	.05
258	Darrin Jackson	.10	.05
259	Brett Butler	.20	.09
260	Joe Orsulak	.10	.05
261	Andy Benes	.20	.09
262	Kenny Lofton	.40	.18
263	Robin Ventura	.20	.09
264	Ron Gant	.20	.09
265	Ellis Burks	.20	.09
266	Juan Guzman	.10	.05
267	Wes Chamberlain	.10	.05
268	John Smiley	.10	.05
269	Franklin Stubbs	.10	.05
270	Tom Browning	.10	.05
271	Dennis Eckersley	.20	.09
272	Carlton Fisk	.40	.18
273	Lou Whitaker	.20	.09
274	Phil Plantier	.10	.05
275	Bobby Bonilla	.20	.09
276	Ben McDonald	.10	.05
277	Bob Zupcic	.10	.05
278	Terry Steinbach	.10	.05
279	Terry Mulholland	.10	.05
280	Lance Johnson	.10	.05
281	Willie McGee	.20	.09
282	Bret Saberhagen	.20	.09
283	Randy Myers	.20	.09
284	Randy Tomlin	.10	.05
285	Mickey Morandini	.10	.05
286	Brian Williams	.10	.05
287	Tino Martinez	.40	.18
288	Jose Melendez	.10	.05
289	Jeff Huson	.10	.05
290	Joe Grahe	.10	.05
291	Mel Hall	.10	.05
292	Otis Nixon	.10	.05
293	Todd Hundley	.30	.14
294	Casey Candaele	.10	.05
295	Kevin Seitzer	.10	.05
296	Eddie Taubensee	.10	.05
297	Moises Alou	.20	.09
298	Scott Radinsky	.10	.05
299	Thomas Howard	.10	.05
300	Kyle Abbott	.10	.05
301	Omar Vizquel	.20	.09
302	Keith Miller	.10	.05
303	Rick Aguilera	.10	.05
304	Bruce Hurst	.10	.05
305	Ken Caminiti	.30	.14
306	Mike Pagliarulo	.10	.05
307	Frank Seminara	.10	.05
308	Andre Dawson	.30	.14
309	Jose Lind	.10	.05
310	Joe Boever	.10	.05
311	Jeff Parrett	.10	.05
312	Alan Mills	.10	.05
313	Kevin Tapani	.10	.05
314	Darryl Kile	.10	.05
315	Will Clark CL	.20	.09
316	Mike Sharperson	.10	.05
317	John Orton	.10	.05
318	Bob Tewksbury	.10	.05
319	Xavier Hernandez	.10	.05
320	Paul Assenmacher	.10	.05
321	John Franco	.20	.09
322	Mike Timlin	.10	.05
323	Jose Guzman	.10	.05
324	Pedro Martinez	.75	.35
325	Bill Spiers	.10	.05
326	Melido Perez	.10	.05
327	Mike Macfarlane	.10	.05
328	Ricky Bones	.10	.05
329	Scott Bankhead	.10	.05
330	Rich Rodriguez	.10	.05
331	Geronimo Pena	.10	.05
332	Bernie Williams	.40	.18
333	Paul Molitor	.40	.18
334	Carlos Garcia	.10	.05
335	David Cone	.30	.14
336	Randy Johnson	.40	.18
337	Pat Mahomes	.10	.05
338	Erik Hanson	.10	.05
339	Duane Ward	.10	.05
340	Al Martin	.10	.05
341	Pedro Munoz	.10	.05
342	Greg Colbrunn	.10	.05
343	Julio Valera	.10	.05
344	John Olerud	.30	.14
345	George Bell	.20	.09
346	Devon White	.10	.05
347	Donovan Osborne	.20	.09
348	Mark Gardner	.10	.05
349	Zane Smith	.10	.05
350	Wilson Alvarez	.20	.09
351	Kevin Koslofski	.10	.05
352	Roberto Hernandez	.20	.09
353	Glenn Davis	.10	.05
354	Reggie Sanders	.20	.09
355	Ken Griffey Jr.	2.00	.90
356	Marquis Grissom	.20	.09
357	Jack McDowell	.20	.09
358	Jimmy Key	.10	.05
359	Stan Belinda	.10	.05
360	Gerald Williams	.10	.05
361	Sid Fernandez	.10	.05
362	Alex Fernandez	.20	.09
363	John Smoltz	.30	.14
364	Travis Fryman	.20	.09
365	Jose Canseco	.50	.23
366	David Justice	.40	.18
367	Pedro Astacio	.20	.09
368	Tim Belcher	.10	.05
369	Steve Sax	.10	.05
370	Gary Gaetti	.20	.09
371	Jeff Frye	.10	.05
372	Bob Wickman	.10	.05
373	Ryan Thompson	.10	.05
374	David Hulse	.10	.05
375	Cal Eldred	.10	.05
376	Ryan Klesko	.40	.18
377	Damion Easley	.20	.09
378	John Kiely	.10	.05
379	Jim Bullinger	.10	.05
380	Brian Bohanon	.10	.05
381	Rod Brewer	.10	.05
382	Fernando Ramsey	.10	.05
383	Sam Militello	.10	.05
384	Arthur Rhodes	.10	.05
385	Eric Karros	.30	.14
386	Rico Brogna	.20	.09
387	John Valentin	.20	.09
388	Kerry Woodson	.10	.05
389	Ben Rivera	.10	.05
390	Matt Whiteside	.10	.05
391	Henry Rodriguez	.20	.09
392	John Wetteland	.20	.09
393	Kent Mercker	.10	.05
394	Bernard Gilkey	.10	.05
395	Doug Henry	.10	.05
396	Mo Vaughn	.40	.18
397	Scott Erickson	.10	.05
398	Bill Gullickson	.10	.05
399	Mark Guthrie	.10	.05
400	Dave Martinez	.10	.05
401	Jeff Kent	.20	.09
402	Chris Hoiles	.10	.05
403	Mike Henneman	.10	.05
404	Chris Nabholz	.10	.05
405	Tom Pagnozzi	.10	.05
406	Kelly Gruber	.10	.05
407	Bob Welch	.10	.05
408	Frank Castillo	.10	.05
409	John Dopson	.10	.05
410	Steve Farr	.10	.05
411	Henry Cotto	.10	.05
412	Bob Patterson	.10	.05
413	Todd Stottlemyre	.10	.05
414	Greg A. Harris	.10	.05
415	Denny Neagle	.20	.09
416	Bill Wegman	.10	.05
417	Willie Wilson	.10	.05
418	Terry Leach	.10	.05
419	Willie Randolph	.20	.09
420	Mark McGwire CL	.40	.18
421	Calvin Murray CL	.10	.05
422	Pete Janicki TP	.10	.05
423	Todd Jones TP	.10	.05
424	Mike Neill TP	.10	.05
425	Carlos Delgado TP	.40	.18
426	Jose Oliva TP	.10	.05
427	Tyrone Hill TP	.10	.05
428	Dmitri Young TP	.40	.18
429	Derek Wallace TP	.10	.05
430	Michael Moore TP	.10	.05
431	Cliff Floyd TP	.20	.09
432	Calvin Murray TP	.10	.05
433	Manny Ramirez TP	1.25	.55
434	Marc Newfield TP	.10	.05
435	Charles Johnson TP	.40	.18
436	Butch Huskey TP	.30	.14
437	Brad Pennington TP	.10	.05
438	Ray McDavid TP	.10	.05
439	Chad McConnell TP	.10	.05
440	Midre Cummings TP	.10	.05
441	Benji Gil TP	.10	.05
442	Frankie Rodriguez TP	.10	.05
443	Chad Mottola TP	.10	.05
444	John Burke TP	.10	.05
445	Michael Tucker TP	.40	.18
446	Rick Greene TP	.10	.05
447	Rich Becker TP	.20	.09
448	Mike Robertson TP	.10	.05
449	Derek Jeter TP	8.00	3.60
450	Ivan Rodriguez CL	.20	.09
	David McCarty		
451	Jim Abbott IN	.10	.05
452	Jeff Bagwell IN	.30	.14
453	Jason Bere IN	.10	.05
454	Delino DeShields IN	.10	.05

455	Travis Fryman IN	.10	
456	Alex Gonzalez IN	.20	.09
457	Phil Hiatt IN	.10	.05
458	Dave Hollins IN	.10	.05
459	Chipper Jones IN	.60	.25
460	David Justice IN	.20	.09
461	Ray Lankford IN	.20	.09
462	David McCarty IN	.10	.05
463	Mike Mussina IN	.20	.09
464	Jose Offerman IN	.10	.05
465	Dean Palmer IN	.10	.05
466	Geronimo Pena IN	.10	.05
467	Eduardo Perez IN	.10	.05
468	Ivan Rodriguez IN	.30	.14
469	Reggie Sanders IN	.20	.09
470	Bernie Williams IN	.40	.18
471	Barry Bonds CL	.40	.18
	Matt Williams		
	Will Clark		
472	Strike Force	.40	.18
	Greg Maddux		
	Steve Avery		
	John Smoltz		
	Tom Glavine		
473	Red October	.10	.05
	Jose Rijo		
	Rob Dibble		
	Roberto Kelly		
	Reggie Sanders		
	Barry Larkin		
474	Four Corners	.30	.14
	Gary Sheffield		
	Phil Plantier		
	Tony Gwynn		
	Fred McGriff		
475	Shooting Stars	.10	.05
	Doug Drabek		
	Craig Biggio		
	Jeff Bagwell		
476	Giant Sticks	.30	.14
	Will Clark		
	Barry Bonds		
	Matt Williams		
477	Boyhood Friends	.20	.09
	Eric Davis		
	Darryl Strawberry		
478	Rock Solid Foundation	.30	.14
	Dante Bichette		
	David Nied		
	Andres Galarraga		
479	Inaugural Catch	.10	.05
	Dave Magadan		
	Orestes Destrade		
	Bret Barberie		
	Jeff Conine		
480	Steel City Champions	.10	.05
	Tim Wakefield		
	Andy Van Slyke		
	Jay Bell		
481	Les Grandes Etoiles	.20	.09
	Marquis Grissom		
	Delino DeShields		
	Dennis Martinez		
	Larry Walker		
482	Runnin' Redbirds	.20	.09
	Geronimo Pena		
	Ray Lankford		
	Ozzie Smith		
	Bernard Gilkey		
483	Ivy Leaguers	.20	.09
	Randy Myers		
	Ryne Sandberg		
	Mark Grace		
484	Big Apple Power Switch	.20	.09
	Eddie Murray		
	Howard Johnson		
	Bobby Bonilla		
485	Hammers and Nails	.10	.05
	John Kruk		
	Dave Hollins		
	Darren Daulton		
	Len Dykstra		
486	Barry Bonds AW	.40	.18
487	Dennis Eckersley AW	.10	.05
488	Greg Maddux AW	.50	.23
489	Dennis Eckersley AW	.10	.05
490	Eric Karros AW	.10	.05
491	Pat Listach AW	.10	.05
492	Gary Sheffield AW	.20	.09
493	Mark McGwire AW	1.00	.45
494	Gary Sheffield AW	.20	.09
495	Edgar Martinez AW	.20	.09
496	Fred McGriff AW	.20	.09
497	Juan Gonzalez AW	.40	.18
498	Darren Daulton AW	.10	.05
499	Cecil Fielder AW	.10	.05
500	Brent Gates CL	.10	.05
501	Tavo Alvarez DD	.10	.05
502	Rod Bolton	.10	.05
503	John Cummings DD	.10	.05
504	Brent Gates DD	.10	.05
505	Tyler Green	.10	.05
506	Jose Martinez DD	.10	.05
507	Troy Percival	.30	.14
508	Kevin Stocker DD	.10	.05
509	Matt Walbeck DD	.10	.05
510	Rondell White DD	.30	.14
511	Billy Ripken	.10	.05
512	Mike Moore	.10	.05
513	Jose Lind	.10	.05
514	Chito Martinez	.10	.05
515	Jose Guzman	.10	.05
516	Kim Batiste	.10	.05
517	Jeff Tackett	.10	.05
518	Charlie Hough	.20	.09
519	Marvin Freeman	.10	.05
520	Carlos Martinez	.10	.05
521	Eric Young	.40	.18
522	Pete Incaviglia	.10	.05
523	Scott Fletcher	.10	.05
524	Orestes Destrade	.10	.05
525	Ken Griffey Jr. CL	.40	.18
526	Ellis Burks	.20	.09
527	Juan Samuel	.10	.05
528	Dave Magadan	.10	.05
529	Jeff Parrett	.10	.05
530	Bill Krueger	.10	.05
531	Frank Bolick	.10	.05
532	Alan Trammell	.30	.14
533	Walt Weiss	.10	.05
534	David Cone	.30	.14
535	Greg Maddux	1.00	.45
536	Kevin Young	.20	.09
537	Dave Hansen	.10	.05
538	Alex Cole	.10	.05
539	Greg Hibbard	.10	.05
540	Gene Larkin	.10	.05
541	Jeff Reardon	.20	.09
542	Felix Jose	.10	.05
543	Jimmy Key	.20	.09
544	Reggie Jefferson	.20	.09
545	Gregg Jefferies	.20	.09
546	Dave Stewart	.20	.09
547	Tim Wallach	.10	.05
548	Spike Owen	.10	.05
549	Tommy Greene	.10	.05
550	Fernando Valenzuela	.20	.09
551	Rich Amaral	.10	.05
552	Bret Barberie	.10	.05
553	Edgar Martinez	.30	.14
554	Jim Abbott	.20	.09
555	Frank Thomas	.75	.35
556	Wade Boggs	.40	.18
557	Tom Henke	.10	.05
558	Milt Thompson	.10	.05
559	Lloyd McClendon	.10	.05
560	Vinny Castilla	.50	.23
561	Ricky Jordan	.10	.05
562	Andujar Cedeno	.10	.05
563	Greg Vaughn	.20	.09
564	Cecil Fielder	.20	.09
565	Kirby Puckett	.60	.25
566	Mark McGwire	2.00	.90
567	Barry Bonds	.50	.23
568	Jody Reed	.10	.05
569	Todd Zeile	.10	.05
570	Mark Carreon	.10	.05
571	Joe Girardi	.10	.05
572	Luis Gonzalez	.20	.09
573	Dave Grace	.30	.14
574	Rafael Palmeiro	.40	.18
575	Darryl Strawberry	.20	.09
576	Will Clark	.40	.18
577	Fred McGriff	.30	.14
578	Kevin Reimer	.10	.05
579	Dave Righetti	.10	.05
580	Juan Bell	.10	.05
581	Jeff Brantley	.10	.05
582	Brian Hunter	.10	.05
583	Tim Naehring	.10	.05
584	Glenallen Hill	.10	.05
585	Cal Ripken	1.50	.70
586	Albert Belle	.40	.18
587	Robin Yount	.30	.14
588	Chris Bosio	.10	.05
589	Pete Smith	.10	.05
590	Chuck Carr	.10	.05
591	Jeff Blauser	.10	.05
592	Kevin McReynolds	.10	.05
593	Andres Galarraga	.40	.18
594	Kevin Maas	.10	.05
595	Eric Davis	.20	.09
596	Brian Jordan	.20	.09
597	Tim Raines	.10	.05
598	Rick Wilkins	.10	.05
599	Steve Cooke	.10	.05
600	Mike Gallego	.10	.05
601	Mike Munoz	.10	.05
602	Luis Rivera	.10	.05
603	Junior Ortiz	.10	.05
604	Brent Mayne	.10	.05
605	Luis Alicea	.10	.05
606	Damon Berryhill	.10	.05
607	Dave Henderson	.10	.05
608	Kirk McCaskill	.10	.05
609	Jeff Fassero	.10	.05
610	Mike Harkey	.10	.05
611	Francisco Cabrera	.10	.05
612	Rey Sanchez	.10	.05
613	Scott Servais	.10	.05
614	Darrin Fletcher	.10	.05
615	Felix Fermin	.10	.05
616	Kevin Seitzer	.10	.05
617	Bob Scanlan	.10	.05
618	Billy Hatcher	.10	.05
619	John Vander Wal	.10	.05
620	Joe Hesketh	.10	.05
621	Hector Villanueva	.10	.05
622	Randy Milligan	.10	.05
623	Tony Tarasco	.10	.05
624	Russ Swan	.10	.05
625	Willie Wilson	.10	.05
626	Frank Tanana	.10	.05
627	Pete O'Brien	.10	.05
628	Lenny Webster	.10	.05
629	Mark Clark	.10	.05
630	Roger Clemens CL	.40	.18
631	Alex Arias	.10	.05
632	Chris Gwynn	.10	.05
633	Tom Bolton	.10	.05
634	Greg Briley	.10	.05
635	Kent Bottenfield	.10	.05
636	Kelly Downs	.10	.05
637	Manuel Lee	.10	.05
638	Al Leiter	.20	.09
639	Jeff Gardner	.10	.05
640	Mike Gardiner	.10	.05
641	Mark Gardner	.10	.05
642	Jeff Branson	.10	.05
643	Paul Wagner	.10	.05
644	Sean Berry	.10	.05
645	Phil Hiatt	.20	.09
646	Kevin Mitchell	.20	.09
647	Charlie Hayes	.10	.05
648	Jim Deshaies	.10	.05
649	Dan Pasqua	.10	.05
650	Mike Maddux	.10	.05
651	Domingo Martinez	.10	.05
652	Greg McMichael	.10	.05
653	Eric Wedge	.10	.05
654	Mark Whiten	.10	.05
655	Roberto Kelly	.10	.05
656	Julio Franco	.10	.05
657	Gene Harris	.10	.05
658	Pete Schourek	.10	.05
659	Mike Bielecki	.10	.05
660	Ricky Gutierrez	.10	.05
661	Chris Hammond	.10	.05

☐ 662 Tim Scott	.10	.05
☐ 663 Norm Charlton	.10	.05
☐ 664 Doug Drabek	.10	.05
☐ 665 Dwight Gooden	.20	.09
☐ 666 Jim Gott	.10	.05
☐ 667 Randy Myers	.20	.09
☐ 668 Darren Holmes	.10	.05
☐ 669 Tim Spehr	.10	.05
☐ 670 Bruce Ruffin	.10	.05
☐ 671 Bobby Thigpen	.10	.05
☐ 672 Tony Fernandez	.20	.09
☐ 673 Darrin Jackson	.10	.05
☐ 674 Gregg Olson	.10	.05
☐ 675 Rob Dibble	.10	.05
☐ 676 Howard Johnson	.10	.05
☐ 677 Mike Lansing	.20	.09
☐ 678 Charlie Leibrandt	.10	.05
☐ 679 Kevin Bass	.10	.05
☐ 680 Hubie Brooks	.10	.05
☐ 681 Scott Brosius	.20	.09
☐ 682 Randy Knorr	.10	.05
☐ 683 Dante Bichette	.20	.09
☐ 684 Bryan Harvey	.10	.05
☐ 685 Greg Gohr	.10	.05
☐ 686 Willie Banks	.10	.05
☐ 687 Robb Nen	.30	.14
☐ 688 Mike Scioscia	.10	.05
☐ 689 John Farrell	.10	.05
☐ 690 John Candelaria	.10	.05
☐ 691 Damon Buford	.10	.05
☐ 692 Todd Worrell	.10	.05
☐ 693 Pat Hentgen	.30	.14
☐ 694 John Smiley	.10	.05
☐ 695 Greg Swindell	.10	.05
☐ 696 Derek Bell	.20	.09
☐ 697 Terry Jorgensen	.10	.05
☐ 698 Jimmy Jones	.10	.05
☐ 699 David Wells	.20	.09
☐ 700 Dave Martinez	.10	.05
☐ 701 Steve Bedrosian	.10	.05
☐ 702 Jeff Russell	.10	.05
☐ 703 Joe Magrane	.10	.05
☐ 704 Matt Mieske	.10	.05
☐ 705 Paul Molitor	.40	.18
☐ 706 Dale Murphy	.30	.14
☐ 707 Steve Howe	.10	.05
☐ 708 Greg Gagne	.10	.05
☐ 709 Dave Eiland	.10	.05
☐ 710 David West	.10	.05
☐ 711 Luis Aquino	.10	.05
☐ 712 Joe Orsulak	.10	.05
☐ 713 Eric Plunk	.10	.05
☐ 714 Mike Felder	.10	.05
☐ 715 Joe Klink	.10	.05
☐ 716 Lonnie Smith	.10	.05
☐ 717 Monty Fariss	.10	.05
☐ 718 Craig Lefferts	.10	.05
☐ 719 John Habyan	.10	.05
☐ 720 Willie Blair	.10	.05
☐ 721 Darnell Coles	.10	.05
☐ 722 Mark Williamson	.10	.05
☐ 723 Bryn Smith	.10	.05
☐ 724 Greg W. Harris	.10	.05
☐ 725 Graeme Lloyd	.10	.05
☐ 726 Cris Carpenter	.10	.05
☐ 727 Chico Walker	.10	.05
☐ 728 Tracy Woodson	.10	.05
☐ 729 Jose Uribe	.10	.05
☐ 730 Stan Javier	.10	.05
☐ 731 Jay Howell	.10	.05
☐ 732 Freddie Benavides	.10	.05
☐ 733 Jeff Reboulet	.10	.05
☐ 734 Scott Sanderson	.10	.05
☐ 735 Ryne Sandberg CL	.30	.14
☐ 736 Archi Cianfrocco	.10	.05
☐ 737 Daryl Boston	.10	.05
☐ 738 Craig Grebeck	.10	.05
☐ 739 Doug Dascenzo	.10	.05
☐ 740 Gerald Young	.10	.05
☐ 741 Candy Maldonado	.10	.05
☐ 742 Joey Cora	.10	.05
☐ 743 Don Slaught	.10	.05
☐ 744 Steve Decker	.10	.05
☐ 745 Blas Minor	.10	.05
☐ 746 Storm Davis	.10	.05
☐ 747 Carlos Quintana	.10	.05

☐ 748 Vince Coleman	.10	.05
☐ 749 Todd Burns	.10	.05
☐ 750 Steve Frey	.10	.05
☐ 751 Ivan Calderon	.10	.05
☐ 752 Steve Reed	.10	.05
☐ 753 Danny Jackson	.10	.05
☐ 754 Jeff Conine	.10	.05
☐ 755 Juan Gonzalez	.75	.35
☐ 756 Mike Kelly	.10	.05
☐ 757 John Doherty	.10	.05
☐ 758 Jack Armstrong	.10	.05
☐ 759 John Wehner	.10	.05
☐ 760 Scott Bankhead	.10	.05
☐ 761 Jim Tatum	.10	.05
☐ 762 Scott Pose	.10	.05
☐ 763 Andy Ashby	.20	.09
☐ 764 Ed Sprague	.10	.05
☐ 765 Harold Baines	.20	.09
☐ 766 Kirk Gibson	.20	.09
☐ 767 Troy Neel	.10	.05
☐ 768 Dick Schofield	.10	.05
☐ 769 Dickie Thon	.10	.05
☐ 770 Butch Henry	.10	.05
☐ 771 Junior Felix	.10	.05
☐ 772 Ken Ryan	.10	.05
☐ 773 Trevor Hoffman	.40	.18
☐ 774 Phil Plantier	.25	.11
☐ 775 Bo Jackson	.20	.09
☐ 776 Benito Santiago	.10	.05
☐ 777 Andre Dawson	.30	.14
☐ 778 Bryan Hickerson	.10	.05
☐ 779 Dennis Moeller	.10	.05
☐ 780 Ryan Bowen	.10	.05
☐ 781 Eric Fox	.10	.05
☐ 782 Joe Kmak	.10	.05
☐ 783 Mike Hampton	.40	.18
☐ 784 Darrell Sherman	.10	.05
☐ 785 J.T. Snow	.40	.18
☐ 786 Dave Winfield	.30	.14
☐ 787 Jim Austin	.10	.05
☐ 788 Craig Shipley	.10	.05
☐ 789 Greg Myers	.10	.05
☐ 790 Todd Benzinger	.10	.05
☐ 791 Cory Snyder	.10	.05
☐ 792 David Segui	.10	.05
☐ 793 Armando Reynoso	.10	.05
☐ 794 Chili Davis	.10	.05
☐ 795 Dave Nilsson	.20	.09
☐ 796 Paul O'Neill	.20	.09
☐ 797 Jarald Clark	.10	.05
☐ 798 Jose Mesa	.10	.05
☐ 799 Brain Holman	.10	.05
☐ 800 Jim Eisenreich	.10	.05
☐ 801 Mark McLemore	.10	.05
☐ 802 Luis Sojo	.10	.05
☐ 803 Harold Reynolds	.10	.05
☐ 804 Dan Plesac	.10	.05
☐ 805 Dave Stieb	.10	.05
☐ 806 Tom Brunansky	.10	.05
☐ 807 Kelly Gruber	.10	.05
☐ 808 Bob Ojeda	.10	.05
☐ 809 Dave Burba	.10	.05
☐ 810 Joe Boever	.10	.05
☐ 811 Jeremy Hernandez	.10	.05
☐ 812 Tim Salmon TC	.25	.11
☐ 813 Jeff Bagwell TC	.30	.14
☐ 814 Dennis Eckersley TC	.10	.05
☐ 815 Roberto Alomar TC	.20	.09
☐ 816 Steve Avery TC	.10	.05
☐ 817 Pat Listach TC	.10	.05
☐ 818 Gregg Jefferies TC	.10	.05
☐ 819 Sammy Sosa TC	.60	.25
☐ 820 Darryl Strawberry TC	.10	.05
☐ 821 Dennis Martinez TC	.10	.05
☐ 822 Robby Thompson TC	.10	.05
☐ 823 Albert Belle TC	.20	.09
☐ 824 Randy Johnson TC	.20	.09
☐ 825 Nigel Wilson TC	.10	.05
☐ 826 Bobby Bonilla TC	.10	.05
☐ 827 Glenn Davis TC	.10	.05
☐ 828 Gary Sheffield TC	.20	.09
☐ 829 Darren Daulton TC	.10	.05
☐ 830 Jay Bell TC	.10	.05
☐ 831 Juan Gonzalez TC	.40	.18
☐ 832 Andre Dawson TC	.20	.09
☐ 833 Hal Morris TC	.10	.05

☐ 834 David Nied TC	.10	.05
☐ 835 Felix Jose TC	.10	.05
☐ 836 Travis Fryman TC	.10	.05
☐ 837 Shane Mack TC	.10	.05
☐ 838 Robin Ventura TC	.20	.09
☐ 839 Danny Tartabull TC	.10	.05
☐ 840 Roberto Alomar CL	.20	.09
☐ SP5 George Brett	1.00	.45
Robin Yount		
3,000th Hit		
☐ SP6 Nolan Ryan	2.00	.90

1993 Upper Deck Gold

	MINT	NRMT
COMP.FACT.SET (840)	200.00	90.00
COMMON CARD (1-840)	.25	.11

*GOLD HOLOGRAM: 2X TO 5X BASIC CARDS
GOLD DIST.ONLY IN FACT.SET FORM
ONE GOLD SET PER 20 CT FACT.SET CASE

1993 Upper Deck Clutch Performers

	MINT	NRMT
COMPLETE SET (20)	20.00	9.00
COMMON CARD (R1-R20)	.25	.11
SER.2 STAT.ODDS 1:9 RET, 1:1 RED JUMBO		

☐ R1 Roberto Alomar	1.00	.45
☐ R2 Wade Boggs	1.00	.45
☐ R3 Barry Bonds	1.25	.55
☐ R4 Jose Canseco	1.25	.55
☐ R5 Joe Carter	.50	.23
☐ R6 Will Clark	1.00	.45
☐ R7 Roger Clemens	2.50	1.10
☐ R8 Dennis Eckersley	.50	.23
☐ R9 Cecil Fielder	.50	.23
☐ R10 Juan Gonzalez	2.00	.90
☐ R11 Ken Griffey Jr.	5.00	2.20
☐ R12 Rickey Henderson	1.25	.55
☐ R13 Barry Larkin	1.00	.45
☐ R14 Don Mattingly	2.00	.90
☐ R15 Fred McGriff	.75	.35
☐ R16 Terry Pendleton	.25	.11
☐ R17 Kirby Puckett	1.50	.70
☐ R18 Ryne Sandberg	1.25	.55
☐ R19 John Smoltz	.75	.35
☐ R20 Frank Thomas	2.00	.90

1993 Upper Deck Fifth Anniversary

	MINT	NRMT
COMPLETE SET (15)	20.00	9.00
COMMON CARD (A1-A15)	.25	.11
SER.2 STATED ODDS 1:9 HOBBY		

☐ A1 Ken Griffey Jr.	5.00	2.20
☐ A2 Gary Sheffield	1.00	.45
☐ A3 Roberto Alomar	1.00	.45
☐ A4 Jim Abbott	.50	.23
☐ A5 Nolan Ryan	4.00	1.80
☐ A6 Juan Gonzalez	2.00	.90
☐ A7 David Justice	1.00	.45
☐ A8 Carlos Baerga	.25	.11
☐ A9 Reggie Jackson	1.00	.45

	MINT	NRMT
❏ A10 Eric Karros	.75	.35
❏ A11 Chipper Jones	4.00	1.80
❏ A12 Ivan Rodriguez	1.25	.55
❏ A13 Pat Listach	.25	.11
❏ A14 Frank Thomas	2.00	.90
❏ A15 Tim Salmon	1.00	.45

1993 Upper Deck Future Heroes

	MINT	NRMT
COMPLETE SET (10)	12.00	5.50
COMMON CARD (55-63)	.25	.11
SER.2 STATED ODDS 1:9		

❏ 55 Roberto Alomar	1.00	.45
❏ 56 Barry Bonds	1.25	.55
❏ 57 Roger Clemens	2.50	1.10
❏ 58 Juan Gonzalez	2.00	.90
❏ 59 Ken Griffey Jr.	5.00	2.20
❏ 60 Mark McGwire	5.00	2.20
❏ 61 Kirby Puckett	1.50	.70
❏ 62 Frank Thomas	2.00	.90
❏ 63 Checklist	.25	.11
❏ NNO Header Card SP	.75	.35

1993 Upper Deck Home Run Heroes

	MINT	NRMT
COMPLETE SET (28)	15.00	6.75
COMMON CARD (HR1-HR28)	.25	.11

ONE PER SER.1 JUMBO PACK

❏ HR1 Juan Gonzalez	2.00	.90
❏ HR2 Mark McGwire	5.00	2.20
❏ HR3 Cecil Fielder	.50	.23
❏ HR4 Fred McGriff	.75	.35
❏ HR5 Albert Belle	1.00	.45
❏ HR6 Barry Bonds	1.25	.55
❏ HR7 Joe Carter	.50	.23
❏ HR8 Darren Daulton	.50	.23
❏ HR9 Ken Griffey Jr.	5.00	2.20
❏ HR10 Dave Hollins	.25	.11
❏ HR11 Ryne Sandberg	1.25	.55
❏ HR12 George Bell	.25	.11
❏ HR13 Danny Tartabull	.25	.11
❏ HR14 Mike Devereaux	.25	.11
❏ HR15 Greg Vaughn	.50	.23
❏ HR16 Larry Walker	1.00	.45
❏ HR17 David Justice	.50	.23
❏ HR18 Terry Pendleton	.25	.11
❏ HR19 Eric Karros	.75	.35
❏ HR20 Ray Lankford	.75	.35
❏ HR21 Matt Williams	.75	.35
❏ HR22 Eric Anthony	.25	.11
❏ HR23 Bobby Bonilla	.50	.23
❏ HR24 Kirby Puckett	1.50	.70
❏ HR25 Mike Macfarlane	.25	.11
❏ HR26 Tom Brunansky	.25	.11
❏ HR27 Paul O'Neill	.50	.23
❏ HR28 Gary Gaetti	.50	.23

1993 Upper Deck Iooss Collection

	MINT	NRMT
COMPLETE SET (27)	25.00	11.00
COMMON CARD (WI1-WI27)	.25	.11
SER.1 STATED ODDS 1:9 RET, 1:5 JUM		

❏ WI1 Tim Salmon	1.00	.45
❏ WI2 Jeff Bagwell	1.50	.70
❏ WI3 Mark McGwire	6.00	2.70
❏ WI4 Roberto Alomar	1.00	.45
❏ WI5 Steve Avery	.25	.11
❏ WI6 Paul Molitor	1.00	.45
❏ WI7 Ozzie Smith	1.50	.70
❏ WI8 Mark Grace	.75	.35
❏ WI9 Eric Karros	.75	.35
❏ WI10 Delino DeShields	.25	.11
❏ WI11 Will Clark	1.00	.45
❏ WI12 Albert Belle	1.00	.45
❏ WI13 Ken Griffey Jr.	6.00	2.70
❏ WI14 Howard Johnson	.25	.11
❏ WI15 Cal Ripken Jr.	5.00	2.20
❏ WI16 Fred McGriff	.75	.35
❏ WI17 Darren Daulton	.50	.23
❏ WI18 Andy Van Slyke	.25	.11
❏ WI19 Nolan Ryan	5.00	2.20
❏ WI20 Wade Boggs	1.00	.45
❏ WI21 Barry Larkin	1.00	.45
❏ WI22 George Brett	2.00	.90
❏ WI23 Cecil Fielder	.50	.23
❏ WI24 Kirby Puckett	2.00	.90
❏ WI25 Frank Thomas	2.00	.90
❏ WI26 Don Mattingly	2.00	.90
❏ NNO Title Card	.50	.23
Iooss Header		

1993 Upper Deck Mays Heroes

	MINT	NRMT
COMPLETE SET (10)	3.00	1.35
COMMON CARD (46-54(HDR))	.50	.23
SER.1 STATED ODDS 1:9		

❏ 46 Willie Mays	.50	.23
1951 Rookie-of-the-Year		
❏ 47 Willie Mays	.50	.23
1954 The Catch		
❏ 48 Willie Mays	.50	.23
1956-57 30-30 Club		
❏ 49 Willie Mays	.50	.23
1961 Four-Homer Game		
❏ 50 Willie Mays	.50	.23
1965 Most Valuable Player		
❏ 51 Willie Mays	.50	.23
1969 600-Home Run Club		
❏ 52 Willie Mays	.50	.23
1972 New York Homecoming		
❏ 53 Willie Mays	.50	.23
1979 Hall of Fame		
❏ 54 Baseball Heroes CL	.50	.23
Vernon Wells Portrait		
❏ NNO0 Baseball Heroes SP	.50	.23
(Header card)		

1993 Upper Deck On Deck

	MINT	NRMT
COMPLETE SET (25)	20.00	9.00
COMMON CARD (D1-D25)	.25	.11
SER.2 STAT.ODDS 1:1 RED/BLUE JUMBO		

❏ D1 Jim Abbott	.50	.23
❏ D2 Roberto Alomar	1.00	.45
❏ D3 Carlos Baerga	.25	.11
❏ D4 Albert Belle	1.00	.45
❏ D5 Wade Boggs	1.00	.45
❏ D6 George Brett	2.00	.90
❏ D7 Jose Canseco	1.25	.55
❏ D8 Will Clark	1.00	.45
❏ D9 Roger Clemens	2.50	1.10
❏ D10 Dennis Eckersley	.50	.23
❏ D11 Cecil Fielder	.50	.23
❏ D12 Juan Gonzalez	2.00	.90
❏ D13 Ken Griffey Jr.	5.00	2.20

❏ D14 Tony Gwynn	2.50	1.10
❏ D15 Bo Jackson	.50	.23
❏ D16 Chipper Jones	4.00	1.80
❏ D17 Eric Karros	.75	.35
❏ D18 Mark McGwire	5.00	2.20
❏ D19 Kirby Puckett	1.50	.70
❏ D20 Nolan Ryan	4.00	1.80
❏ D21 Tim Salmon	1.00	.45
❏ D22 Ryne Sandberg	1.25	.55
❏ D23 Darryl Strawberry	.50	.23
❏ D24 Frank Thomas	2.00	.90
❏ D25 Andy Van Slyke	.25	.11

1993 Upper Deck Season Highlights

	MINT	NRMT
COMPLETE SET (20)	100.00	45.00
COMMON CARD (HI1-HI20)	2.00	.90

STATED ODDS 1:9 HOBBY SEASON HL

❏ HI1 Roberto Alomar	8.00	3.60
❏ HI2 Steve Avery	2.00	.90
❏ HI3 Harold Baines	3.00	1.35
❏ HI4 Damon Berryhill	2.00	.90
❏ HI5 Barry Bonds	8.00	3.60
❏ HI6 Bret Boone	3.00	1.35
❏ HI7 George Brett	15.00	6.75
❏ HI8 Francisco Cabrera	2.00	.90
❏ HI9 Ken Griffey Jr.	40.00	18.00
❏ HI10 Rickey Henderson	8.00	3.60
❏ HI11 Kenny Lofton	8.00	3.60
❏ HI12 Mickey Morandini	2.00	.90
❏ HI13 Eddie Murray	8.00	3.60
❏ HI14 David Nied	2.00	.90
❏ HI15 Jeff Reardon	3.00	1.35
❏ HI16 Bip Roberts	2.00	.90
❏ HI17 Nolan Ryan	40.00	18.00
❏ HI18 Ed Sprague	2.00	.90
❏ HI19 Dave Winfield	4.00	1.80
❏ HI20 Robin Yount	4.00	1.80

1993 Upper Deck Then And Now

	MINT	NRMT
COMPLETE SET (18)	40.00	18.00
COMPLETE SERIES 1 (9)	15.00	6.75
COMPLETE SERIES 2 (9)	25.00	11.00
COMMON CARD (TN1-TN18)	.50	.23

STATED ODDS 1:27 HOBBY

❏ TN1 Wade Boggs	1.50	.70
❏ TN2 George Brett	4.00	1.80
❏ TN3 Rickey Henderson	2.00	.90
❏ TN4 Cal Ripken	8.00	3.60
❏ TN5 Nolan Ryan	8.00	3.60
❏ TN6 Ryne Sandberg	2.50	1.10
❏ TN7 Ozzie Smith	2.50	1.10
❏ TN8 Darryl Strawberry	.75	.35
❏ TN9 Dave Winfield	1.00	.45
❏ TN10 Dennis Eckersley	.75	.35
❏ TN11 Tony Gwynn	5.00	2.20
❏ TN12 Howard Johnson	.50	.23
❏ TN13 Don Mattingly	4.00	1.80
❏ TN14 Eddie Murray	1.50	.70
❏ TN15 Robin Yount	1.00	.45
❏ TN16 Reggie Jackson	2.50	1.10
❏ TN17 Mickey Mantle	12.00	5.50
❏ TN18 Willie Mays	6.00	2.70

1993 Upper Deck Triple Crown

	MINT	NRMT
COMPLETE SET (10)	12.00	5.50
COMMON CARD (TC1-TC10)	1.00	.45

STATED ODDS 1:15 HOBBY

❏ TC1 Barry Bonds	1.25	.55
❏ TC2 Jose Canseco	1.50	.70
❏ TC3 Will Clark	1.50	.70
❏ TC4 Ken Griffey Jr.	5.00	2.20
❏ TC5 Fred McGriff	1.00	.45
❏ TC6 Kirby Puckett	1.50	.70
❏ TC7 Cal Ripken Jr.	4.00	1.80
❏ TC8 Gary Sheffield	1.50	.70
❏ TC9 Frank Thomas	2.00	.90
❏ TC10 Larry Walker	1.50	.70

1994 Upper Deck

	MINT	NRMT
COMPLETE SET (550)	50.00	22.00
COMPLETE SERIES 1 (280)	30.00	13.50
COMPLETE SERIES 2 (270)	20.00	9.00
COMMON CARD (1-550)	.15	.07
MINOR STARS	.30	.14
UNLISTED STARS	.60	.25
SUBSET CARDS HALF VALUE OF BASE		

CARDS
GRIFFEY/MANTLE AU INSERTS IN SER.1 RET.
A.RODRIGUEZ AU INSERT IN SER.2 RET.

❏ 1 Brian Anderson	.40	.18
❏ 2 Shane Andrews	.15	.07
❏ 3 James Baldwin	.30	.14
❏ 4 Rich Becker	.15	.07
❏ 5 Greg Blosser	.15	.07
❏ 6 Ricky Bottalico	.30	.14
❏ 7 Midre Cummings	.15	.07
❏ 8 Carlos Delgado	.60	.25
❏ 9 Steve Dreyer	.15	.07
❏ 10 Joey Eischen	.15	.07
❏ 11 Carl Everett	.30	.14
❏ 12 Cliff Floyd UER	.30	.14
(text indicates he throws left; should be right)		
❏ 13 Alex Gonzalez	.15	.07
❏ 14 Jeff Granger	.15	.07
❏ 15 Shawn Green	1.00	.45
❏ 16 Brian L. Hunter	.30	.14
❏ 17 Butch Huskey	.30	.14
❏ 18 Mark Hutton	.15	.07
❏ 19 Michael Jordan	10.00	4.50
❏ 20 Steve Karsay	.15	.07
❏ 21 Jeff McNeely	.15	.07
❏ 22 Marc Newfield	.15	.07
❏ 23 Manny Ramirez	1.25	.55
❏ 24 Alex Rodriguez	15.00	6.75
❏ 25 Scott Ruffcorn UER	.15	.07
(photo on back is Robert Ellis)		
❏ 26 Paul Spoljaric UER	.15	.07
(Expos logo on back)		
❏ 27 Salomon Torres	.15	.07
❏ 28 Steve Trachsel	.15	.07
❏ 29 Chris Turner	.15	.07
❏ 30 Gabe White	.15	.07
❏ 31 Randy Johnson FT	.30	.14
❏ 32 John Wetteland FT	.15	.07
❏ 33 Mike Piazza FT	1.00	.45
❏ 34 Rafael Palmeiro FT	.30	.14
❏ 35 Roberto Alomar FT	.30	.14
❏ 36 Matt Williams FT	.30	.14
❏ 37 Travis Fryman FT	.15	.07
❏ 38 Barry Bonds FT	.60	.25
❏ 39 Marquis Grissom FT	.15	.07
❏ 40 Albert Belle FT	.30	.14
❏ 41 Steve Avery FUT	.15	.07
❏ 42 Jason Bere FUT	.15	.07
❏ 43 Alex Fernandez FUT	.15	.07
❏ 44 Mike Mussina FUT	.30	.14
❏ 45 Aaron Sele FUT	.15	.07
❏ 46 Rod Beck FUT	.15	.07
❏ 47 Mike Piazza FUT	1.00	.45
❏ 48 John Olerud FUT	.15	.07
❏ 49 Carlos Baerga FUT	.15	.07
❏ 50 Gary Sheffield FUT	.30	.14
❏ 51 Travis Fryman FUT	.15	.07
❏ 52 Juan Gonzalez FUT	.60	.25
❏ 53 Ken Griffey Jr. FUT	1.50	.70
❏ 54 Tim Salmon FUT	.30	.14
❏ 55 Frank Thomas FUT	.60	.25
❏ 56 Tony Phillips	.15	.07
❏ 57 Julio Franco	.15	.07
❏ 58 Kevin Mitchell	.15	.07
❏ 59 Raul Mondesi	.60	.25
❏ 60 Rickey Henderson	.75	.35
❏ 61 Jay Buhner	.30	.14
❏ 62 Bill Swift	.15	.07
❏ 63 Brady Anderson	.30	.14
❏ 64 Ryan Klesko	.30	.14
❏ 65 Darren Daulton	.30	.14
❏ 66 Damion Easley	.15	.07
❏ 67 Mark McGwire	3.00	1.35
❏ 68 John Roper	.15	.07
❏ 69 Dave Telgheder	.15	.07
❏ 70 David Nied	.15	.07
❏ 71 Mo Vaughn	.60	.25
❏ 72 Tyler Green	.15	.07
❏ 73 Dave Magadan	.15	.07
❏ 74 Chili Davis	.30	.14
❏ 75 Archi Cianfrocco	.15	.07
❏ 76 Joe Girardi	.15	.07
❏ 77 Chris Hoiles	.15	.07

78	Ryan Bowen	.15	.07
79	Greg Gagne	.15	.07
80	Aaron Sele	.30	.14
81	Dave Winfield	.60	.25
82	Chad Curtis	.15	.07
83	Andy Van Slyke	.30	.14
84	Kevin Stocker	.15	.07
85	Deion Sanders	.30	.14
86	Bernie Williams	.60	.25
87	John Smoltz	.40	.18
88	Ruben Santana	.15	.07
89	Dave Stewart	.30	.14
90	Don Mattingly	1.25	.55
91	Joe Carter	.30	.14
92	Ryne Sandberg	.75	.35
93	Chris Gomez	.15	.07
94	Tino Martinez	.60	.25
95	Terry Pendleton	.15	.07
96	Andre Dawson	.40	.18
97	Wil Cordero	.15	.07
98	Kent Hrbek	.30	.14
99	John Olerud	.30	.14
100	Kirt Manwaring	.15	.07
101	Tim Bogar	.15	.07
102	Mike Mussina	.60	.25
103	Nigel Wilson	.15	.07
104	Ricky Gutierrez	.15	.07
105	Roberto Mejia	.15	.07
106	Tom Pagnozzi	.15	.07
107	Mike Macfarlane	.15	.07
108	Jose Bautista	.15	.07
109	Luis Ortiz	.15	.07
110	Brent Gates	.15	.07
111	Tim Salmon	.60	.25
112	Wade Boggs	.60	.25
113	Tripp Cromer	.15	.07
114	Denny Hocking	.15	.07
115	Carlos Baerga	.30	.14
116	J.R. Phillips	.15	.07
117	Bo Jackson	.30	.14
118	Lance Johnson	.15	.07
119	Bobby Jones	.15	.07
120	Bobby Witt	.15	.07
121	Ron Karkovice	.15	.07
122	Jose Vizcaino	.15	.07
123	Danny Darwin	.15	.07
124	Eduardo Perez	.15	.07
125	Brian Looney	.15	.07
126	Pat Hentgen	.30	.14
127	Frank Viola	.15	.07
128	Darren Holmes	.15	.07
129	Wally Whitehurst	.15	.07
130	Matt Walbeck	.15	.07
131	Albert Belle	.60	.25
132	Steve Cooke	.15	.07
133	Kevin Appier	.30	.14
134	Joe Oliver	.15	.07
135	Benji Gil	.15	.07
136	Steve Buechele	.15	.07
137	Devon White	.15	.07
138	Sterling Hitchcock UER (two losses for career; should be four)	.30	.14
139	Phil Leftwich	.15	.07
140	Jose Canseco	.75	.35
141	Rick Aguilera	.15	.07
142	Rod Beck	.15	.07
143	Jose Rijo	.15	.07
144	Tom Glavine	.60	.25
145	Phil Plantier	.15	.07
146	Jason Bere	.30	.14
147	Jamie Moyer	.15	.07
148	Wes Chamberlain	.15	.07
149	Glenallen Hill	.15	.07
150	Mark Whiten	.15	.07
151	Bret Barberie	.15	.07
152	Chuck Knoblauch	.60	.25
153	Trevor Hoffman	.30	.14
154	Rick Wilkins	.15	.07
155	Juan Gonzalez	1.25	.55
156	Ozzie Guillen	.15	.07
157	Jim Eisenreich	.15	.07
158	Pedro Astacio	.15	.07
159	Joe Magrane	.15	.07
160	Ryan Thompson	.15	.07
161	Jose Lind	.15	.07
162	Jeff Conine	.15	.07
163	Todd Benzinger	.15	.07
164	Roger Salkeld	.15	.07
165	Gary DiSarcina	.15	.07
166	Kevin Gross	.15	.07
167	Charlie Hayes	.15	.07
168	Tim Costo	.15	.07
169	Wally Joyner	.30	.14
170	Johnny Ruffin	.15	.07
171	Kirk Rueter	.15	.07
172	Lenny Dykstra	.30	.14
173	Ken Hill	.15	.07
174	Mike Bordick	.15	.07
175	Billy Hall	.15	.07
176	Rob Butler	.15	.07
177	Jay Bell	.30	.14
178	Jeff Kent	.30	.14
179	David Wells	.40	.18
180	Dean Palmer	.30	.14
181	Mariano Duncan	.15	.07
182	Orlando Merced	.15	.07
183	Brett Butler	.30	.14
184	Milt Thompson	.15	.07
185	Chipper Jones	1.50	.70
186	Paul O'Neill	.30	.14
187	Mike Greenwell	.15	.07
188	Harold Baines	.30	.14
189	Todd Stottlemyre	.15	.07
190	Jeromy Burnitz	.30	.14
191	Rene Arocha	.15	.07
192	Jeff Fassero	.15	.07
193	Robby Thompson	.15	.07
194	Greg W. Harris	.15	.07
195	Todd Van Poppel	.30	.14
196	Jose Guzman	.15	.07
197	Shane Mack	.15	.07
198	Carlos Garcia	.15	.07
199	Kevin Roberson	.15	.07
200	David McCarty	.15	.07
201	Alan Trammell	.40	.18
202	Chuck Carr	.15	.07
203	Tommy Greene	.15	.07
204	Wilson Alvarez	.30	.14
205	Dwight Gooden	.30	.14
206	Tony Tarasco	.15	.07
207	Darren Lewis	.15	.07
208	Eric Karros	.30	.14
209	Chris Hammond	.15	.07
210	Jeffrey Hammonds	.30	.14
211	Rich Amaral	.15	.07
212	Danny Tartabull	.30	.14
213	Jeff Russell	.15	.07
214	Dave Staton	.30	.14
215	Kenny Lofton	.60	.25
216	Manuel Lee	.15	.07
217	Brian Koelling	.15	.07
218	Scott Lydy	.15	.07
219	Tony Gwynn	1.50	.70
220	Cecil Fielder	.30	.14
221	Royce Clayton	.15	.07
222	Reggie Sanders	.30	.14
223	Brian Jordan	.30	.14
224	Ken Griffey Jr.	3.00	1.35
225	Fred McGriff	.40	.18
226	Felix Jose	.15	.07
227	Brad Pennington	.15	.07
228	Chris Bosio	.15	.07
229	Mike Stanley	.15	.07
230	Willie Greene	.15	.07
231	Alex Fernandez	.15	.07
232	Brad Ausmus	.15	.07
233	Darrell Whitmore	.15	.07
234	Marcus Moore	.15	.07
235	Allen Watson	.15	.07
236	Jose Offerman	.30	.14
237	Rondell White	.30	.14
238	Jeff King	.15	.07
239	Luis Alicea	.15	.07
240	Dan Wilson	.15	.07
241	Ed Sprague	.15	.07
242	Todd Hundley	.30	.14
243	Al Martin	.15	.07
244	Mike Lansing	.30	.14
245	Ivan Rodriguez	.75	.35
246	Dave Fleming	.15	.07
247	John Doherty	.15	.07
248	Mark McLemore	.15	.07
249	Bob Hamelin	.15	.07
250	Curtis Pride	.15	.07
251	Zane Smith	.15	.07
252	Eric Young	.15	.07
253	Brian McRae	.15	.07
254	Tim Raines	.30	.14
255	Javier Lopez	.40	.18
256	Melvin Nieves	.15	.07
257	Randy Myers	.15	.07
258	Willie McGee	.30	.14
259	Jimmy Key UER (birthdate missing on back)	.30	.14
260	Tom Candiotti	.15	.07
261	Eric Davis	.30	.14
262	Craig Paquette	.15	.07
263	Robin Ventura	.30	.14
264	Pat Kelly	.15	.07
265	Gregg Jefferies	.15	.07
266	Cory Snyder	.15	.07
267	David Justice HFA	.30	.14
268	Sammy Sosa HFA	1.00	.45
269	Barry Larkin HFA	.30	.14
270	Andres Galarraga HFA	.30	.14
271	Gary Sheffield HFA	.30	.14
272	Jeff Bagwell HFA	.30	.14
273	Mike Piazza HFA	1.00	.45
274	Larry Walker HFA	.30	.14
275	John Kruk HFA	.15	.07
276	Bobby Bonilla HFA	.15	.07
277	Jay Bell HFA	.15	.07
278	Ozzie Smith HFA	.60	.25
279	Tony Gwynn HFA	.75	.35
280	Barry Bonds HFA	.60	.25
281	Cal Ripken Jr. HFA	1.25	.55
282	Mo Vaughn HFA	.40	.18
283	Tim Salmon HFA	.30	.14
284	Frank Thomas HFA	.60	.25
285	Albert Belle HFA	.30	.14
286	Cecil Fielder HFA	.15	.07
287	Wally Joyner HFA	.15	.07
288	Greg Vaughn HFA	.15	.07
289	Kirby Puckett HFA	.60	.25
290	Don Mattingly HFA	.40	.18
291	Terry Steinbach HFA	.15	.07
292	Ken Griffey Jr. HFA	1.50	.70
293	Juan Gonzalez HFA	.60	.25
294	Paul Molitor HFA	.30	.14
295	Tavo Alvarez UDCA	.15	.07
296	Matt Brunson UDC	.15	.07
297	Shawn Green UDC	.30	.14
298	Alex Rodriguez UDC	2.50	1.10
299	Shannon Stewart UDCA	.60	.25
300	Frank Thomas	1.25	.55
301	Mickey Tettleton	.15	.07
302	Pedro Munoz	.15	.07
303	Jose Valentin	.15	.07
304	Orestes Destrade	.15	.07
305	Pat Listach	.15	.07
306	Scott Brosius	.30	.14
307	Kurt Miller	.15	.07
308	Rob Dibble	.15	.07
309	Mike Blowers	.15	.07
310	Jim Abbott	.30	.14
311	Mike Jackson	.15	.07
312	Craig Biggio	.60	.25
313	Kurt Abbott	.15	.07
314	Chuck Finley	.30	.14
315	Andres Galarraga	.60	.25
316	Mike Moore	.15	.07
317	Doug Strange	.15	.07
318	Pedro Martinez	.75	.35
319	Kevin McReynolds	.15	.07
320	Greg Maddux	1.50	.70
321	Mike Henneman	.15	.07
322	Scott Leius	.15	.07
323	John Franco	.30	.14
324	Jeff Blauser	.15	.07
325	Kirby Puckett	1.00	.45
326	Darryl Hamilton	.15	.07
327	John Smiley	.15	.07
328	Derrick May	.15	.07
329	Jose Vizcaino	.15	.07
330	Randy Johnson	.60	.25
331	Jack Morris	.30	.14
332	Graeme Lloyd	.15	.07

333	Dave Valle	.15	.07
334	Greg Myers	.15	.07
335	John Wetteland	.30	.14
336	Jim Gott	.15	.07
337	Tim Naehring	.15	.07
338	Mike Kelly	.15	.07
339	Jeff Montgomery	.15	.07
340	Rafael Palmeiro	.60	.25
341	Eddie Murray	.60	.25
342	Xavier Hernandez	.15	.07
343	Bobby Munoz	.15	.07
344	Bobby Bonilla	.30	.14
345	Travis Fryman	.30	.14
346	Steve Finley	.15	.07
347	Chris Sabo	.15	.07
348	Armando Reynoso	.15	.07
349	Ramon Martinez	.30	.14
350	Will Clark	.60	.25
351	Moises Alou	.30	.14
352	Jim Thome	.60	.25
353	Bob Tewksbury	.15	.07
354	Andujar Cedeno	.15	.07
355	Orel Hershiser	.30	.14
356	Mike Devereaux	.15	.07
357	Mike Perez	.15	.07
358	Dennis Martinez	.30	.14
359	Dave Nilsson	.15	.07
360	Ozzie Smith	.75	.35
361	Eric Anthony	.15	.07
362	Scott Sanders	.15	.07
363	Paul Sorrento	.15	.07
364	Tim Belcher	.15	.07
365	Dennis Eckersley	.30	.14
366	Mel Rojas	.15	.07
367	Tom Henke	.15	.07
368	Randy Tomlin	.15	.07
369	B.J. Surhoff	.30	.14
370	Larry Walker	.60	.25
371	Joey Cora	.15	.07
372	Mike Harkey	.15	.07
373	John Valentin	.30	.14
374	Doug Jones	.15	.07
375	David Justice	.60	.25
376	Vince Coleman	.15	.07
377	David Hulse	.15	.07
378	Kevin Seitzer	.15	.07
379	Pete Harnisch	.15	.07
380	Ruben Sierra	.30	.14
381	Mark Lewis	.15	.07
382	Bip Roberts	.15	.07
383	Paul Wagner	.15	.07
384	Stan Javier	.15	.07
385	Barry Larkin	.60	.25
386	Mark Portugal	.15	.07
387	Roberto Kelly	.15	.07
388	Andy Benes	.30	.14
389	Felix Fermin	.15	.07
390	Marquis Grissom	.30	.14
391	Troy Neel	.15	.07
392	Chad Kreuter	.15	.07
393	Gregg Olson	.15	.07
394	Charles Nagy	.30	.14
395	Jack McDowell	.30	.14
396	Luis Gonzalez	.30	.14
397	Benito Santiago	.15	.07
398	Chris James	.15	.07
399	Terry Mulholland	.15	.07
400	Barry Bonds	.75	.35
401	Joe Grahe	.15	.07
402	Duane Ward	.15	.07
403	John Burkett	.15	.07
404	Scott Servais	.15	.07
405	Bryan Harvey	.15	.07
406	Bernard Gilkey	.15	.07
407	Greg McMichael	.15	.07
408	Tim Wallach	.15	.07
409	Ken Caminiti	.40	.18
410	John Kruk	.30	.14
411	Darrin Jackson	.15	.07
412	Mike Gallego	.15	.07
413	David Cone	.40	.18
414	Lou Whitaker	.30	.14
415	Sandy Alomar Jr.	.30	.14
416	Bill Wegman	.15	.07
417	Pat Borders	.15	.07
418	Roger Pavlik	.15	.07
419	Pete Smith	.15	.07
420	Steve Avery	.15	.07
421	David Segui	.30	.07
422	Rheal Cormier	.15	.07
423	Harold Reynolds	.15	.07
424	Edgar Martinez	.30	.14
425	Cal Ripken Jr.	2.50	1.10
426	Jaime Navarro	.15	.07
427	Sean Berry	.15	.07
428	Bret Saberhagen	.30	.14
429	Bob Welch	.15	.07
430	Juan Guzman	.15	.07
431	Cal Eldred	.15	.07
432	Dave Hollins	.15	.07
433	Sid Fernandez	.15	.07
434	Willie Banks	.15	.07
435	Darryl Kile	.15	.07
436	Henry Rodriguez	.30	.14
437	Tony Fernandez	.30	.14
438	Walt Weiss	.15	.07
439	Kevin Tapani	.15	.07
440	Mark Grace	.40	.18
441	Brian Harper	.15	.07
442	Kent Mercker	.15	.07
443	Anthony Young	.15	.07
444	Todd Zeile	.15	.07
445	Greg Vaughn	.30	.14
446	Ray Lankford	.30	.14
447	Dave Weathers	.15	.07
448	Bret Boone	.30	.14
449	Charlie Hough	.15	.07
450	Roger Clemens	1.50	.70
451	Mike Morgan	.15	.07
452	Doug Drabek	.15	.07
453	Danny Jackson	.15	.07
454	Dante Bichette	.30	.14
455	Roberto Alomar	.60	.25
456	Ben McDonald	.15	.07
457	Kenny Rogers	.15	.07
458	Bill Gullickson	.15	.07
459	Darrin Fletcher	.15	.07
460	Curt Schilling	.30	.14
461	Billy Hatcher	.15	.07
462	Howard Johnson	.15	.07
463	Mickey Morandini	.15	.07
464	Frank Castillo	.15	.07
465	Delino DeShields	.15	.07
466	Gary Gaetti	.30	.14
467	Steve Farr	.15	.07
468	Roberto Hernandez	.15	.07
469	Jack Armstrong	.15	.07
470	Paul Molitor	.60	.25
471	Melido Perez	.15	.07
472	Greg Hibbard	.15	.07
473	Jody Reed	.15	.07
474	Tom Gordon	.15	.07
475	Gary Sheffield	.60	.25
476	John Jaha	.15	.07
477	Shawon Dunston	.15	.07
478	Reggie Jefferson	.15	.07
479	Don Slaught	.15	.07
480	Jeff Bagwell	.75	.35
481	Tim Pugh	.15	.07
482	Kevin Young	.15	.07
483	Ellis Burks	.30	.14
484	Greg Swindell	.15	.07
485	Mark Langston	.30	.14
486	Omar Vizquel	.30	.14
487	Kevin Brown	.30	.14
488	Terry Steinbach	.15	.07
489	Mark Lemke	.15	.07
490	Matt Williams	.40	.18
491	Pete Incaviglia	.15	.07
492	Karl Rhodes	.15	.07
493	Shawn Green	.60	.25
494	Hal Morris	.15	.07
495	Derek Bell	.30	.14
496	Luis Polonia	.15	.07
497	Otis Nixon	.15	.07
498	Ron Darling	.15	.07
499	Mitch Williams	.15	.07
500	Mike Piazza	2.00	.90
501	Pat Meares	.15	.07
502	Scott Cooper	.15	.07
503	Scott Erickson	.30	.14
504	Jeff Juden	.15	.07
505	Lee Smith	.30	.14
506	Bobby Ayala	.15	.07
507	Dave Henderson	.15	.07
508	Erik Hanson	.15	.07
509	Bob Wickman	.15	.07
510	Sammy Sosa	2.00	.90
511	Hector Carrasco	.15	.07
512	Tim Davis	.15	.07
513	Joey Hamilton DD	.60	.25
514	Robert Eenhoorn	.15	.07
515	Jorge Fabregas	.15	.07
516	Tim Hyers	.15	.07
517	John Hudek DD	.15	.07
518	James Mouton DD	.15	.07
519	Herbert Perry DD	.15	.07
520	Chan Ho Park DD	1.00	.45
521	W. Van Landingham DD	.15	.07
522	Paul Shuey DD	.15	.07
523	Ryan Hancock DD	.15	.07
524	Billy Wagner TP	.75	.35
525	Jason Giambi	.40	.18
526	Jose Silva TP	.15	.07
527	Terrell Wade TP	.15	.07
528	Todd Dunn TP	.15	.07
529	Alan Benes TP	.30	.14
530	Brooks Kieschnick TP	.15	.07
531	Todd Hollandsworth TP	.40	.18
532	Brad Fullmer TP	1.00	.45
533	Steve Soderstrom TP	.15	.07
534	Daron Kirkreit	.15	.07
535	Arquimedez Pozo TP	.30	.14
536	Charles Johnson TP	.30	.14
537	Preston Wilson	.60	.25
538	Alex Ochoa	.15	.07
539	Derrek Lee TP	.50	.23
540	Wayne Gomes TP	.15	.07
541	Jermaine Allensworth TP	.30	.14
542	Mike Bell TP	.15	.07
543	Trot Nixon TP	1.25	.55
544	Pokey Reese	.40	.18
545	Neifi Perez TP	.75	.35
546	Johnny Damon TP	.60	.25
547	Matt Brunson TP	.15	.07
548	LaTroy Hawkins TP	.40	.18
549	Eddie Pearson TP	.30	.14
550	Derek Jeter TP	2.50	1.10
A298	Alex Rodriguez AU	150.00	70.00
P224	Ken Griffey Jr. Promo	3.00	1.35
GM1	Ken Griffey Jr. AU	1500.00	700.00
	Mickey Mantle AU/1000		
KG1	Ken Griffey Jr. AU/1000	300.00	135.00
MM1	Mickey Mantle AU/1000	600.00	275.00

1994 Upper Deck Electric Diamond

	MINT	NRMT
COMPLETE SET (550)	100.00	45.00
COMPLETE SERIES 1 (280)	60.00	27.00
COMPLETE SERIES 2 (270)	40.00	18.00
COMMON CARD (1-550)	.20	.09

*STARS: .75X TO 2X BASIC CARDS
*RC's: .6X TO 1.5X BASIC CARDS
ONE PER PACK/TWO PER MINI JUMBO

1994 Upper Deck Diamond Collection

	MINT	NRMT
COMPLETE SET (30)	200.00	90.00
COMPLETE CENTRAL (10)	100.00	45.00
COMPLETE EAST (10)	40.00	18.00
COMPLETE WEST (10)	60.00	27.00
COMMON CARD	1.50	.70
SEMISTARS	3.00	1.35
UNLISTED STARS	5.00	2.20
SER.1 STATED ODDS 1:18 HOBBY REGIONAL		
❑ C1 Jeff Bagwell	6.00	2.70
❑ C2 Michael Jordan	30.00	13.50
❑ C3 Barry Larkin	5.00	2.20
❑ C4 Kirby Puckett	8.00	3.60
❑ C5 Manny Ramirez	10.00	4.50
❑ C6 Ryne Sandberg	6.00	2.70
❑ C7 Ozzie Smith	6.00	2.70
❑ C8 Frank Thomas	10.00	4.50
❑ C9 Andy Van Slyke	1.50	.70
❑ C10 Robin Yount	5.00	2.20
❑ E1 Roberto Alomar	5.00	2.20
❑ E2 Roger Clemens	12.00	5.50
❑ E3 Lenny Dykstra	1.50	.70
❑ E4 Cecil Fielder	1.50	.70
❑ E5 Cliff Floyd	1.50	.70
❑ E6 Dwight Gooden	4.00	1.80
❑ E7 David Justice	5.00	2.20
❑ E8 Don Mattingly	10.00	4.50
❑ E9 Cal Ripken Jr.	20.00	9.00
❑ E10 Gary Sheffield	5.00	2.20
❑ W1 Barry Bonds	6.00	2.70
❑ W2 Andres Galarraga	5.00	2.20
❑ W3 Juan Gonzalez	10.00	4.50
❑ W4 Ken Griffey Jr.	25.00	11.00
❑ W5 Tony Gwynn	12.00	5.50
❑ W6 Rickey Henderson	10.00	4.50
❑ W7 Bo Jackson	4.00	1.80
❑ W8 Mark McGwire	25.00	11.00
❑ W9 Mike Piazza	15.00	6.75
❑ W10 Tim Salmon	5.00	2.20

1994 Upper Deck Griffey Jumbos

	MINT	NRMT
COMPLETE SET (4)	20.00	9.00
COMMON GRIFFEY (CL1-CL4)	4.00	1.80

		MINT	NRMT
ONE PER SEALED SER.1 HOBBY FOIL BOX			
❑ CL1 Numerical CL TP		4.00	1.80
❑ CL2 Alphabetical CL DP		5.00	2.20
❑ CL3 Team CL		6.00	2.70
❑ CL4 Insert CL SP		8.00	3.60

1994 Upper Deck Mantle Heroes

	MINT	NRMT
COMPLETE SET (10)	100.00	45.00
COMMON CARD (64-72/HDR)	12.00	5.50
SER.2 STATED ODDS 1:35		
❑ 64 Mickey Mantle	12.00	5.50
1951 The Early Years		
❑ 65 Mickey Mantle	12.00	5.50
1953 Tape-Measure Home Runs		
❑ 66 Mickey Mantle	12.00	5.50
1956 Triple Crown Season		
❑ 67 Mickey Mantle	12.00	5.50
1957 Second Consecutive MVP		
❑ 68 Mickey Mantle	12.00	5.50
1961 Chasing the Babe		
❑ 69 Mickey Mantle	12.00	5.50
1964 Series Home Run Record		
❑ 70 Mickey Mantle	12.00	5.50
1967 500th Home Run		
❑ 71 Mickey Mantle	12.00	5.50
1974 Hall of Fame		
❑ 72 Mickey Mantle	12.00	5.50
Checklist		
❑ NNO0 Mickey Mantle	12.00	5.50
Header Card		

1994 Upper Deck Mantle's Long Shots

	MINT	NRMT
COMPLETE SET (21)	40.00	18.00
COMMON CARD (MM1-MM21)	.50	.23
SER.1 STATED ODDS 1:18 RETAIL		
ONE SET VIA MAIL PER SILVER TRADE CARD		
COMP.ELEC.DIAM.SET (21)	50.00	22.00

		MINT	NRMT
*ELEC.DIAMOND: 1.5X TO 4X BASE CARD HI			
ONE ED SET VIA MAIL PER BLUE TRD.CARD			
TRADES: RANDOM INS.IN SER.1 HOB.PACKS			
❑ MM1 Jeff Bagwell		2.50	1.10
❑ MM2 Albert Belle		2.00	.90
❑ MM3 Barry Bonds		2.50	1.10
❑ MM4 Jose Canseco		2.50	1.10
❑ MM5 Joe Carter		1.00	.45
❑ MM6 Carlos Delgado		2.00	.90
❑ MM7 Cecil Fielder		.50	.23
❑ MM8 Cliff Floyd		.50	.23
❑ MM9 Juan Gonzalez		4.00	1.80
❑ MM10 Ken Griffey Jr.		10.00	4.50
❑ MM11 David Justice		2.00	.90
❑ MM12 Fred McGriff		1.50	.70
❑ MM13 Mark McGwire		10.00	4.50
❑ MM14 Dean Palmer		1.00	.45
❑ MM15 Mike Piazza		6.00	2.70
❑ MM16 Manny Ramirez		2.50	1.10
❑ MM17 Frank Thomas		4.00	1.80
❑ MM18 Frank Thomas		4.00	1.80
❑ MM19 Mo Vaughn		2.00	.90
❑ MM20 Matt Williams		1.50	.70
❑ MM21 Mickey Mantle		15.00	6.75
❑ NNO Mickey Mantle		6.00	2.70
Silver Trade			
❑ NNO Mickey Mantle		12.00	5.50
Blue ED Trade			

1994 Upper Deck Next Generation

	MINT	NRMT
COMPLETE SET (18)	80.00	36.00
COMMON CARD (1-18)	1.00	.45
SER.2 STATED ODDS 1:20 RETAIL		
ONE SET VIA MAIL PER TRADE CARD		
❑ 1 Roberto Alomar	4.00	1.80
❑ 2 Carlos Delgado	4.00	1.80
❑ 3 Cliff Floyd	1.50	.70
❑ 4 Alex Gonzalez	1.00	.45
❑ 5 Juan Gonzalez	8.00	3.60
❑ 6 Ken Griffey Jr.	20.00	9.00
❑ 7 Jeffrey Hammonds	1.00	.45
❑ 8 Michael Jordan	20.00	9.00
❑ 9 David Justice	2.50	1.10
❑ 10 Ryan Klesko	1.50	.70
❑ 11 Javier Lopez	2.50	1.10
❑ 12 Raul Mondesi	4.00	1.80
❑ 13 Mike Piazza	12.00	5.50
❑ 14 Kirby Puckett	6.00	2.70
❑ 15 Manny Ramirez	8.00	3.60
❑ 16 Alex Rodriguez	30.00	13.50
❑ 17 Tim Salmon	4.00	1.80
❑ 18 Gary Sheffield	1.50	.70
❑ NNO Expired NG Trade Card	4.00	1.80
❑ NNO Expired NG Trade Card	4.00	1.80

1994 Upper Deck Next Generation Electric Diamond

	MINT	NRMT
COMPLETE SET (18)	100.00	45.00

*SINGLES: 3X TO 8X BASE CARD HI
ONE ED SET VIA MAIL PER ED TRADE CARD
TRADES: RANDOM INSERTS IN SER.2
HOBBY*

1995 Upper Deck

	MINT	NRMT
COMPLETE SET (450)	80.00	36.00
COMPLETE SERIES 1 (225)	40.00	18.00
COMPLETE SERIES 2 (225)	40.00	18.00
COMMON CARD (1-450)	.15	.07
MINOR STARS	.30	.14
UNLISTED STARS	.60	.25
SUBSET CARDS HALF VALUE OF BASE CARDS		
COMP.TRADE SET (45)	20.00	9.00
COMMON TRADE (451T-495T)	.25	.11
TRADE SEMISTARS	.50	.23
NINE TRADE CARDS PER TRADE EXCH.CARD		
COMP.TRADE EXCH.SET (5)	4.00	1.80
COMMON TRADE EXCH. (1-5)	1.00	.45
TRD.EXCH: RANDOM INS.IN SER.2 PACKS		
COMP.ED SET (450)	110.00	50.00
COMP.ED SER.1 (225)	50.00	22.00
COMP.ED SER.2 (225)	60.00	27.00
COMMON ELEC.DIAM. (1-450)	.25	.11
*ED STARS: 1.25X TO 3X HI COLUMN		
*ED RC's/PROSPECTS: 1X TO 2.5X HI ONE ED PER RETAIL PACK		
COMMON ED GOLD (1-450)	4.00	1.80
*ED GOLD STARS: 10X TO 25X HI COLUMN		
*ED GOLD RC's/PROSPECTS: 6X TO 15X HI ED GOLD STATED ODDS 1:35 RETAIL JUMBO AUS WERE REDEEMED W/WRAP-PERS		

❏ 1 Ruben Rivera	.30	.14
❏ 2 Bill Pulsipher	.15	.07
❏ 3 Ben Grieve	1.50	.70
❏ 4 Curtis Goodwin	.15	.07
❏ 5 Damon Hollins	.15	.07
❏ 6 Todd Greene	.30	.14
❏ 7 Glenn Williams	.30	.14
❏ 8 Bret Wagner	.15	.07
❏ 9 Karim Garcia	.50	.23
❏ 10 Nomar Garciaparra	3.00	1.35
❏ 11 Raul Casanova	.15	.07
❏ 12 Matt Smith	.15	.07
❏ 13 Paul Wilson	.15	.07
❏ 14 Jason Isringhausen	.30	.14
❏ 15 Reid Ryan	.30	.14
❏ 16 Lee Smith	.30	.14
❏ 17 Chili Davis	.30	.14
❏ 18 Brian Anderson	.30	.14
❏ 19 Gary DiSarcina	.15	.07
❏ 20 Bo Jackson	.30	.14
❏ 21 Chuck Finley	.30	.14
❏ 22 Darryl Kile	.15	.07
❏ 23 Shane Reynolds	.30	.14
❏ 24 Tony Eusebio	.15	.07
❏ 25 Craig Biggio	.60	.25
❏ 26 Doug Drabek	.15	.07
❏ 27 Brian L. Hunter	.30	.14
❏ 28 James Mouton	.15	.07
❏ 29 Geronimo Berroa	.15	.07
❏ 30 Rickey Henderson	.75	.35
❏ 31 Steve Karsay	.15	.07
❏ 32 Steve Ontiveros	.15	.07
❏ 33 Ernie Young	.15	.07
❏ 34 Dennis Eckersley	.30	.14
❏ 35 Mark McGwire	3.00	1.35
❏ 36 Dave Stewart	.30	.14
❏ 37 Pat Hentgen	.30	.14
❏ 38 Carlos Delgado	.60	.25
❏ 39 Joe Carter	.30	.14
❏ 40 Roberto Alomar	.60	.25
❏ 41 John Olerud	.30	.14
❏ 42 Devon White	.30	.14
❏ 43 Roberto Kelly	.15	.07
❏ 44 Jeff Blauser	.15	.07
❏ 45 Fred McGriff	.40	.18
❏ 46 Tom Glavine	.60	.25
❏ 47 Mike Kelly	.15	.07
❏ 48 Javier Lopez	.30	.14
❏ 49 Greg Maddux	1.50	.70
❏ 50 Matt Mieske	.15	.07
❏ 51 Troy O'Leary	.30	.14
❏ 52 Jeff Cirillo	.30	.14
❏ 53 Cal Eldred	.15	.07
❏ 54 Pat Listach	.15	.07
❏ 55 Jose Valentin	.15	.07
❏ 56 John Mabry	.15	.07
❏ 57 Bob Tewksbury	.15	.07
❏ 58 Brian Jordan	.30	.14
❏ 59 Gregg Jefferies	.30	.14
❏ 60 Ozzie Smith	.75	.35
❏ 61 Geronimo Pena	.15	.07
❏ 62 Mark Whiten	.15	.07
❏ 63 Rey Sanchez	.15	.07
❏ 64 Willie Banks	.15	.07
❏ 65 Mark Grace	.40	.18
❏ 66 Randy Myers	.15	.07
❏ 67 Steve Trachsel	.15	.07
❏ 68 Derrick May	.15	.07
❏ 69 Brett Butler	.30	.14
❏ 70 Eric Karros	.30	.14
❏ 71 Tim Wallach	.15	.07
❏ 72 Delino DeShields	.15	.07
❏ 73 Darren Dreifort	.30	.14
❏ 74 Orel Hershiser	.30	.14
❏ 75 Billy Ashley	.15	.07
❏ 76 Sean Berry	.15	.07
❏ 77 Ken Hill	.15	.07
❏ 78 John Wetteland	.30	.14
❏ 79 Moises Alou	.30	.14
❏ 80 Cliff Floyd	.30	.14
❏ 81 Marquis Grissom	.30	.14
❏ 82 Larry Walker	.60	.25
❏ 83 Rondell White	.30	.14
❏ 84 William VanLandingham	.15	.07
❏ 85 Matt Williams	.60	.25
❏ 86 Rod Beck	.15	.07
❏ 87 Darren Lewis	.15	.07
❏ 88 Robby Thompson	.15	.07
❏ 89 Darryl Strawberry	.30	.14
❏ 90 Kenny Lofton	.40	.18
❏ 91 Charles Nagy	.30	.14
❏ 92 Sandy Alomar Jr.	.30	.14
❏ 93 Mark Clark	.15	.07
❏ 94 Dennis Martinez	.30	.14
❏ 95 Dave Winfield	.60	.25
❏ 96 Jim Thome	.60	.25
❏ 97 Manny Ramirez	.75	.35
❏ 98 Goose Gossage	.30	.14
❏ 99 Tino Martinez	.60	.25
❏ 100 Ken Griffey Jr.	3.00	1.35
❏ 101 Greg Maddux ANA	.75	.35
❏ 102 Randy Johnson ANA	.30	.14
❏ 103 Barry Bonds ANA	.40	.18
❏ 104 Juan Gonzalez ANA	.60	.25
❏ 105 Frank Thomas ANA	.60	.25
❏ 106 Matt Williams ANA	.30	.14
❏ 107 Paul Molitor ANA	.30	.14
❏ 108 Fred McGriff ANA	.15	.07
❏ 109 Carlos Baerga ANA	.15	.07
❏ 110 Ken Griffey Jr. ANA	1.50	.70
❏ 111 Reggie Jefferson	.15	.07
❏ 112 Randy Johnson	.60	.25
❏ 113 Marc Newfield	.15	.07
❏ 114 Robb Nen	.15	.07
❏ 115 Jeff Conine	.15	.07
❏ 116 Kurt Abbott	.15	.07
❏ 117 Charlie Hough	.15	.07
❏ 118 Dave Weathers	.15	.07
❏ 119 Juan Castillo	.15	.07
❏ 120 Bret Saberhagen	.30	.14
❏ 121 Rico Brogna	.15	.07
❏ 122 John Franco	.30	.14
❏ 123 Todd Hundley	.15	.07
❏ 124 Jason Jacome	.15	.07
❏ 125 Bobby Jones	.15	.07
❏ 126 Bret Barberie	.15	.07
❏ 127 Ben McDonald	.15	.07
❏ 128 Harold Baines	.30	.14
❏ 129 Jeffrey Hammonds	.30	.14
❏ 130 Mike Mussina	.60	.25
❏ 131 Chris Hoiles	.15	.07
❏ 132 Brady Anderson	.30	.14
❏ 133 Eddie Williams	.15	.07
❏ 134 Andy Benes	.15	.07
❏ 135 Tony Gwynn	1.50	.70
❏ 136 Bip Roberts	.15	.07
❏ 137 Joey Hamilton	.30	.14
❏ 138 Luis Lopez	.15	.07
❏ 139 Ray McDavid	.15	.07
❏ 140 Lenny Dykstra	.30	.14
❏ 141 Mariano Duncan	.15	.07
❏ 142 Fernando Valenzuela	.30	.14
❏ 143 Bobby Munoz	.15	.07
❏ 144 Kevin Stocker	.15	.07
❏ 145 John Kruk	.30	.14
❏ 146 Jon Lieber	.15	.07
❏ 147 Zane Smith	.15	.07
❏ 148 Steve Cooke	.15	.07
❏ 149 Andy Van Slyke	.30	.14
❏ 150 Jay Bell	.30	.14
❏ 151 Carlos Garcia	.15	.07
❏ 152 John Dettmer	.15	.07
❏ 153 Darren Oliver	.15	.07
❏ 154 Dean Palmer	.30	.14
❏ 155 Otis Nixon	.15	.07
❏ 156 Rusty Greer	.60	.25
❏ 157 Rick Helling	.15	.07
❏ 158 Jose Canseco	.75	.35
❏ 159 Roger Clemens	1.50	.70
❏ 160 Andre Dawson	.40	.18
❏ 161 Mo Vaughn	.60	.25
❏ 162 Aaron Sele	.15	.07
❏ 163 John Valentin	.15	.07
❏ 164 Brian R. Hunter	.15	.07
❏ 165 Bret Boone	.30	.14
❏ 166 Hector Carrasco	.15	.07
❏ 167 Pete Schourek	.15	.07
❏ 168 Willie Greene	.15	.07
❏ 169 Kevin Mitchell	.15	.07
❏ 170 Deion Sanders	.30	.14
❏ 171 John Roper	.15	.07
❏ 172 Charlie Hayes	.15	.07
❏ 173 David Nied	.15	.07
❏ 174 Ellis Burks	.30	.14
❏ 175 Dante Bichette	.30	.14
❏ 176 Marvin Freeman	.15	.07
❏ 177 Eric Young	.15	.07
❏ 178 David Cone	.40	.18
❏ 179 Greg Gagne	.15	.07
❏ 180 Bob Hamelin	.15	.07
❏ 181 Wally Joyner	.30	.14
❏ 182 Jeff Montgomery	.15	.07
❏ 183 Jose Lind	.15	.07
❏ 184 Chris Gomez	.15	.07
❏ 185 Travis Fryman	.30	.14

186	Kirk Gibson	.30	.14
187	Mike Moore	.15	.07
188	Lou Whitaker	.30	.14
189	Sean Bergman	.15	.07
190	Shane Mack	.15	.07
191	Rick Aguilera	.15	.07
192	Denny Hocking	.15	.07
193	Chuck Knoblauch	.60	.25
194	Kevin Tapani	.15	.07
195	Kent Hrbek	.15	.07
196	Ozzie Guillen	.15	.07
197	Wilson Alvarez	.30	.14
198	Tim Raines	.30	.14
199	Scott Ruffcorn	.15	.07
200	Michael Jordan	3.00	1.35
201	Robin Ventura	.30	.14
202	Jason Bere	.15	.07
203	Darrin Jackson	.15	.07
204	Russ Davis	.30	.14
205	Jimmy Key	.30	.14
206	Jack McDowell	.15	.07
207	Jim Abbott	.30	.14
208	Paul O'Neill	.30	.14
209	Bernie Williams	.60	.25
210	Don Mattingly	1.25	.55
211	Orlando Miller	.15	.07
212	Alex Gonzalez	.15	.07
213	Terrell Wade	.15	.07
214	Jose Oliva	.15	.07
215	Alex Rodriguez	2.50	1.10
216	Garret Anderson	.30	.14
217	Alan Benes	.15	.07
218	Armando Benitez	.15	.07
219	Dustin Hermanson	.15	.07
220	Charles Johnson	.30	.14
221	Julian Tavarez	.15	.07
222	Jason Giambi	.30	.14
223	LaTroy Hawkins	.15	.07
224	Todd Hollandsworth	.15	.07
225	Derek Jeter	2.00	.90
226	Hideo Nomo	1.50	.70
227	Tony Clark	.60	.25
228	Roger Cedeno	.15	.07
229	Scott Stahoviak	.15	.07
230	Michael Tucker	.30	.14
231	Joe Rosselli	.15	.07
232	Antonio Osuna	.15	.07
233	Bobby Higginson	1.00	.45
234	Mark Grudzielanek	.40	.18
235	Ray Durham	.30	.14
236	Frank Rodriguez	.15	.07
237	Quilvio Veras	.15	.07
238	Darren Bragg	.15	.07
239	Ugueth Urbina	.15	.07
240	Jason Bates	.15	.07
241	David Bell	.15	.07
242	Ron Villone	.15	.07
243	Joe Randa	.15	.07
244	Carlos Perez	.30	.14
245	Brad Clontz	.15	.07
246	Steve Rodriguez	.15	.07
247	Joe Vitiello	.15	.07
248	Ozzie Timmons	.15	.07
249	Rudy Pemberton	.15	.07
250	Marty Cordova	.15	.07
251	Tony Graffanino	.15	.07
252	Mark Johnson	.15	.07
253	Tomas Perez	.30	.14
254	Jimmy Hurst	.15	.07
255	Edgardo Alfonzo	.60	.25
256	Jose Malave	.15	.07
257	Brad Radke	1.00	.45
258	Jon Nunnally	.15	.07
259	Dilson Torres	.15	.07
260	Esteban Loaiza	.15	.07
261	Freddy Garcia	.15	.07
262	Don Wengert	.15	.07
263	Robert Person	.15	.07
264	Tim Unroe	.15	.07
265	Juan Acevedo	.15	.07
266	Eduardo Perez	.15	.07
267	Tony Phillips	.15	.07
268	Jim Edmonds	.40	.18
269	Jorge Fabregas	.15	.07
270	Tim Salmon	.60	.25
271	Mark Langston	.15	.07
272	J.T. Snow	.30	.14
273	Phil Plantier	.15	.07
274	Derek Bell	.30	.14
275	Jeff Bagwell	.75	.35
276	Luis Gonzalez	.15	.07
277	John Hudek	.15	.07
278	Todd Stottlemyre	.15	.07
279	Mark Acre	.15	.07
280	Ruben Sierra	.15	.07
281	Mike Bordick	.15	.07
282	Ron Darling	.15	.07
283	Brent Gates	.15	.07
284	Todd Van Poppel	.15	.07
285	Paul Molitor	.60	.25
286	Ed Sprague	.15	.07
287	Juan Guzman	.15	.07
288	David Cone	.40	.18
289	Shawn Green	.60	.25
290	Marquis Grissom	.30	.14
291	Kent Mercker	.15	.07
292	Steve Avery	.15	.07
293	Chipper Jones	1.50	.70
294	John Smoltz	.40	.18
295	David Justice	.60	.25
296	Ryan Klesko	.30	.14
297	Joe Oliver	.15	.07
298	Ricky Bones	.15	.07
299	John Jaha	.15	.07
300	Greg Vaughn	.30	.14
301	Dave Nilsson	.15	.07
302	Kevin Seitzer	.15	.07
303	Bernard Gilkey	.15	.07
304	Allen Battle	.15	.07
305	Ray Lankford	.30	.14
306	Tom Pagnozzi	.15	.07
307	Allen Watson	.15	.07
308	Danny Jackson	.15	.07
309	Ken Hill	.15	.07
310	Todd Zeile	.15	.07
311	Kevin Roberson	.15	.07
312	Steve Buechele	.15	.07
313	Rick Wilkins	.15	.07
314	Kevin Foster	.15	.07
315	Sammy Sosa	2.00	.90
316	Howard Johnson	.15	.07
317	Greg Hansell	.15	.07
318	Pedro Astacio	.15	.07
319	Rafael Bournigal	.15	.07
320	Mike Piazza	2.00	.90
321	Ramon Martinez	.30	.14
322	Raul Mondesi	.40	.18
323	Ismael Valdes	.30	.14
324	Wil Cordero	.15	.07
325	Tony Tarasco	.15	.07
326	Roberto Kelly	.15	.07
327	Jeff Fassero	.15	.07
328	Mike Lansing	.15	.07
329	Pedro Martinez	.75	.35
330	Kirk Rueter	.15	.07
331	Glenallen Hill	.15	.07
332	Kirt Manwaring	.15	.07
333	Royce Clayton	.15	.07
334	J.R. Phillips	.15	.07
335	Barry Bonds	.75	.35
336	Mark Portugal	.15	.07
337	Terry Mulholland	.15	.07
338	Omar Vizquel	.30	.14
339	Carlos Baerga	.15	.07
340	Albert Belle	.60	.25
341	Eddie Murray	.60	.25
342	Wayne Kirby	.15	.07
343	Chad Ogea	.15	.07
344	Tim Davis	.15	.07
345	Jay Buhner	.30	.14
346	Bobby Ayala	.15	.07
347	Mike Blowers	.15	.07
348	Dave Fleming	.15	.07
349	Edgar Martinez	.30	.14
350	Andre Dawson	.40	.18
351	Darrell Whitmore	.15	.07
352	Chuck Carr	.15	.07
353	John Burkett	.15	.07
354	Chris Hammond	.15	.07
355	Gary Sheffield	.30	.14
356	Pat Rapp	.15	.07
357	Greg Colbrunn	.15	.07
358	David Segui	.30	.14
359	Jeff Kent	.30	.14
360	Bobby Bonilla	.30	.14
361	Pete Harnisch	.15	.07
362	Ryan Thompson	.15	.07
363	Jose Vizcaino	.15	.07
364	Brett Butler	.30	.14
365	Cal Ripken Jr.	2.50	1.10
366	Rafael Palmeiro	.60	.25
367	Leo Gomez	.15	.07
368	Andy Van Slyke	.30	.14
369	Arthur Rhodes	.15	.07
370	Ken Caminiti	.40	.18
371	Steve Finley	.30	.14
372	Melvin Nieves	.15	.07
373	Andujar Cedeno	.15	.07
374	Trevor Hoffman	.30	.14
375	Fernando Valenzuela	.30	.14
376	Ricky Bottalico	.15	.07
377	Dave Hollins	.15	.07
378	Charlie Hayes	.15	.07
379	Tommy Greene	.15	.07
380	Darren Daulton	.30	.14
381	Curt Schilling	.40	.18
382	Midre Cummings	.15	.07
383	Al Martin	.15	.07
384	Jeff King	.15	.07
385	Orlando Merced	.15	.07
386	Denny Neagle	.30	.14
387	Don Slaught	.15	.07
388	Dave Clark	.15	.07
389	Kevin Gross	.15	.07
390	Will Clark	.60	.25
391	Ivan Rodriguez	.75	.35
392	Benji Gil	.15	.07
393	Jeff Frye	.15	.07
394	Kenny Rogers	.15	.07
395	Juan Gonzalez	1.25	.55
396	Mike Macfarlane	.15	.07
397	Lee Tinsley	.15	.07
398	Tim Naehring	.15	.07
399	Tim Vanegmond	.15	.07
400	Mike Greenwell	.15	.07
401	Ken Ryan	.15	.07
402	John Smiley	.15	.07
403	Tim Pugh	.15	.07
404	Reggie Sanders	.30	.14
405	Barry Larkin	.60	.25
406	Hal Morris	.15	.07
407	Jose Rijo	.15	.07
408	Lance Painter	.15	.07
409	Joe Girardi	.15	.07
410	Andres Galarraga	.60	.25
411	Mike Kingery	.15	.07
412	Roberto Mejia	.15	.07
413	Walt Weiss	.15	.07
414	Bill Swift	.15	.07
415	Larry Walker	.60	.25
416	Billy Brewer	.15	.07
417	Pat Borders	.15	.07
418	Tom Gordon	.15	.07
419	Kevin Appier	.30	.14
420	Gary Gaetti	.30	.14
421	Greg Gohr	.15	.07
422	Felipe Lira	.15	.07
423	John Doherty	.15	.07
424	Chad Curtis	.15	.07
425	Cecil Fielder	.30	.14
426	Alan Trammell	.30	.14
427	David McCarty	.15	.07
428	Scott Erickson	.30	.14
429	Pat Mahomes	.15	.07
430	Kirby Puckett	1.00	.45
431	Dave Stevens	.15	.07
432	Pedro Munoz	.15	.07
433	Chris Sabo	.15	.07
434	Alex Fernandez	.15	.07
435	Frank Thomas	1.25	.55
436	Roberto Hernandez	.15	.07
437	Lance Johnson	.15	.07
438	Jim Abbott	.30	.14
439	John Wetteland	.30	.14
440	Melido Perez	.15	.07
441	Tony Fernandez	.30	.14
442	Pat Kelly	.15	.07
443	Mike Stanley	.15	.07

	MINT	NRMT
❏ 444 Danny Tartabull	.15	.07
❏ 445 Wade Boggs	.60	.25
❏ 446 Robin Yount	.60	.25
❏ 447 Ryne Sandberg	.75	.35
❏ 448 Nolan Ryan	2.50	1.10
❏ 449 George Brett	1.25	.55
❏ 450 Mike Schmidt	1.00	.45
❏ 451 Jim Abbott TRADE	.25	.16
❏ 452 Danny Tartabull TRADE	.25	.11
❏ 453 Ariel Prieto TRADE	.25	.11
❏ 454 Scott Cooper TRADE	.25	.11
❏ 455 Tom Henke TRADE	.25	.11
❏ 456 Todd Zeile TRADE	.25	.11
❏ 457 Brian McRae TRADE	.25	.11
❏ 458 Luis Gonzalez TRADE	.25	.11
❏ 459 Jaime Navarro TRADE	.25	.11
❏ 460 Todd Worrell TRADE	.25	.11
❏ 461 Roberto Kelly TRADE	.25	.11
❏ 462 Chad Fonville TRADE	.25	.11
❏ 463 Shane Andrews TRADE	.25	.11
❏ 464 David Segui TRADE	.35	.16
❏ 465 Deion Sanders TRADE	.35	.16
❏ 466 Orel Hershiser TRADE	.35	.16
❏ 467 Ken Hill TRADE	.25	.11
❏ 468 Andy Benes TRADE	.25	.11
❏ 469 Terry Pendleton TRADE	.25	.11
❏ 470 Bobby Bonilla TRADE	.35	.16
❏ 471 Scott Erickson TRADE	.25	.16
❏ 472 Kevin Brown TRADE	.50	.23
❏ 473 Glenn Dishman TRADE	.25	.11
❏ 474 Phil Plantier TRADE	.25	.11
❏ 475 Gregg Jefferies TRADE	.25	.11
❏ 476 Tyler Green TRADE	.25	.11
❏ 477 H. Slocumb TRADE	.25	.11
❏ 478 Mark Whiten TRADE	.25	.11
❏ 479 Mickey Tettleton TRADE	.25	.11
❏ 480 Tim Wakefield TRADE	.35	.16
❏ 481 V. Eshelman TRADE	.25	.11
❏ 482 Rick Aguilera TRADE	.25	.11
❏ 483 Erik Hanson TRADE	.25	.11
❏ 484 Willie McGee TRADE	.35	.16
❏ 485 Troy O'Leary TRADE	.25	.16
❏ 486 Benito Santiago TRADE	.25	.11
❏ 487 Darren Lewis TRADE	.25	.11
❏ 488 Dave Burba TRADE	.25	.11
❏ 489 Ron Gant TRADE	.25	.11
❏ 490 Bret Saberhagen TRADE	.35	.16
❏ 491 Vinny Castilla TRADE	.35	.16
❏ 492 Frank Rodriguez TRADE	.35	.16
❏ 493 Andy Pettitte TRADE	5.00	2.20
❏ 494 Ruben Sierra TRADE	.25	.11
❏ 495 David Cone TRADE	.50	.23
❏ J159 R. Clemens Jumbo AU	50.00	22.00
❏ J215 A. Rodriguez Jumbo AU	80.00	36.00
❏ P100 Ken Griffey Jr. Promo	3.00	1.35

1995 Upper Deck Autographs

	MINT	NRMT
COMPLETE SET (5)	250.00	110.00
COMMON CARD	25.00	11.00
SER.2 STATED ODDS 1:72 HOBBY		
❏ 1 Roger Clemens	60.00	27.00
❏ 2 Reggie Jackson	40.00	18.00
❏ 3 Willie Mays	100.00	45.00
❏ 4 Raul Mondesi	25.00	11.00
❏ 5 Frank Robinson	40.00	18.00

1995 Upper Deck Checklists

	MINT	NRMT
COMPLETE SET (10)	15.00	6.75
COMPLETE SERIES 1 (5)	6.00	2.70
COMPLETE SERIES 2 (5)	10.00	4.50
COMMON CARD (1-5)	.75	.35
STATED ODDS 1:17 ALL PACKS		
❏ 1A Montreal Expos	.75	.35
❏ 2A Fred McGriff	1.25	.55
❏ 3A John Valentin	1.00	.45
❏ 4A Kenny Rogers	.75	.35
❏ 5A Greg Maddux	5.00	2.20
❏ 1B Cecil Fielder	1.00	.45
❏ 2B Tony Gwynn	5.00	2.20
❏ 3B Greg Maddux	5.00	2.20
❏ 4B Randy Johnson	1.50	.70
❏ 5B Mike Schmidt	2.50	1.10

1995 Upper Deck Predictor Award Winners

	MINT	NRMT
COMPLETE SET (40)	60.00	27.00
COMPLETE SERIES 1 (20)	40.00	18.00
COMPLETE SERIES 2 (20)	25.00	11.00
COMMON CARD (H1-H40)	.50	.23
STATED ODDS 1:30 HOBBY		
COMP.SER.1 EXCH.SET (20)	15.00	6.75
COMP.SER.2 EXCH.SET (20)	10.00	4.50
*AW EXCH.CARDS: .4X TO .8X BASE CARD HI		
ONE EXCH.SET VIA MAIL PER PRED.WINNER		
❏ H1 Albert Belle MVP	2.00	.90
❏ H2 Juan Gonzalez MVP	4.00	1.80
❏ H3 Ken Griffey Jr. MVP	10.00	4.50
❏ H4 Kirby Puckett MVP	3.00	1.35
❏ H5 Frank Thomas MVP	4.00	1.80
❏ H6 Jeff Bagwell MVP	2.50	1.10
❏ H7 Barry Bonds MVP	2.50	1.10
❏ H8 Mike Piazza MVP	6.00	2.70
❏ H9 Matt Williams MVP	2.00	.90
❏ H10 MVP Wild Card W (M.Vaughn/B.Larkin)	.50	.23
❏ H11 Armando Benitez ROY	.50	.23
❏ H12 Alex Gonzalez ROY	.50	.23
❏ H13 Shawn Green ROY	2.00	.90
❏ H14 Derek Jeter ROY	8.00	3.60
❏ H15 Alex Rodriguez ROY	8.00	3.60
❏ H16 Alan Benes ROY	.50	.23
❏ H17 Brian L.Hunter ROY	1.00	.45
❏ H18 Charles Johnson ROY	1.00	.45
❏ H19 Jose Oliva ROY	.50	.23
❏ H20 ROY Wild Card	.50	.23
❏ H21 Cal Ripken MVP	8.00	3.60
❏ H22 Don Mattingly MVP	4.00	1.80
❏ H23 Roberto Alomar MVP	2.00	.90
❏ H24 Kenny Lofton MVP	1.50	.70
❏ H25 Will Clark MVP	2.00	.90
❏ H26 Mark McGwire MVP	10.00	4.50
❏ H27 Greg Maddux MVP	5.00	2.20
❏ H28 Fred McGriff MVP	1.50	.70
❏ H29 Andres Galarraga MVP	2.00	.90
❏ H30 Jose Canseco MVP	2.50	1.10
❏ H31 Ray Durham ROY	1.00	.45
❏ H32 Mark Grudzielanek ROY	1.50	.70
❏ H33 Scott Ruffcorn ROY	.50	.23
❏ H34 Michael Tucker ROY	1.00	.45
❏ H35 Garret Anderson ROY	1.00	.45
❏ H36 Darren Bragg ROY	.50	.23
❏ H37 Quilvio Veras ROY	.50	.23
❏ H38 Hideo Nomo ROY W	3.00	1.35
❏ H39 Chipper Jones ROY	5.00	2.20
❏ H40 Marty Cordova ROY W	.50	.23

1995 Upper Deck Predictor League Leaders

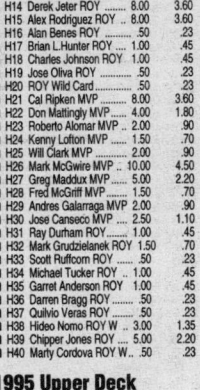

	MINT	NRMT
COMPLETE SET (60)	80.00	36.00
COMPLETE SERIES 1 (30)	50.00	22.00
COMPLETE SERIES 2 (30)	30.00	13.50
COMMON CARD (R1-R60)	.50	.23
STATED ODDS 1:30 RET, 1:17 ANCO		
COMP.SER.1 EXCH.SET (30)	20.00	9.00
COMP.SER.2 EXCH.SET (30)	12.00	5.50
*LL EXCH.CARDS: .4X TO .8X BASE CARD HI		
ONE EXCH.SET VIA MAIL PER PRED.WINNER		
❏ R1 Albert Belle HR W	2.00	.90
❏ R2 Jose Canseco HR	2.50	1.10
❏ R3 Juan Gonzalez HR	4.00	1.80
❏ R4 Ken Griffey Jr. HR	10.00	4.50
❏ R5 Frank Thomas HR	4.00	1.80
❏ R6 Jeff Bagwell HR	2.50	1.10
❏ R7 Barry Bonds HR	2.50	1.10
❏ R8 Fred McGriff HR	1.50	.70
❏ R9 Matt Williams HR	2.00	.90
❏ R10 HR WC W (Bichette)	.50	.23
❏ R11 Albert Belle RBI W	2.00	.90
❏ R12 Joe Carter RBI	1.00	.45
❏ R13 Cecil Fielder RBI	1.00	.45
❏ R14 Kirby Puckett RBI	4.00	1.80
❏ R15 Frank Thomas RBI	4.00	1.80
❏ R16 Jeff Bagwell RBI	2.50	1.10
❏ R17 Barry Bonds RBI	2.50	1.10
❏ R18 Mike Piazza RBI	6.00	2.70
❏ R19 Matt Williams RBI	2.00	.90
❏ R20 RBI WC W (M.Vaughn)	.50	.23
❏ R21 Wade Boggs BAT	2.00	.90
❏ R22 Kenny Lofton BAT	1.50	.70
❏ R23 Paul Molitor BAT	2.00	.90

		MINT	NRMT
R24	Paul O'Neill BAT	1.00	.45
R25	Frank Thomas BAT	4.00	1.80
R26	Jeff Bagwell BAT	2.50	1.10
R27	Tony Gwynn BAT W	5.00	2.20
R28	Gregg Jefferies BAT	.50	.23
R29	Hal Morris BAT	.50	.23
R30	Batting WC W (E.Martinez)	.50	.23
R31	Joe Carter HR	1.00	.45
R32	Cecil Fielder HR	1.00	.45
R33	Rafael Palmeiro HR	2.00	.90
R34	Larry Walker HR	2.00	.90
R35	Manny Ramirez HR	2.50	1.10
R36	Tim Salmon HR	2.00	.90
R37	Mike Piazza HR	6.00	2.70
R38	Andres Galarraga HR	2.00	.90
R39	David Justice HR	2.00	.90
R40	Gary Sheffield HR	1.00	.45
R41	Juan Gonzalez RBI	4.00	1.80
R42	Jose Canseco RBI	2.50	1.10
R43	Will Clark RBI	2.00	.90
R44	Rafael Palmeiro RBI	2.00	.90
R45	Ken Griffey Jr. RBI	10.00	4.50
R46	Ruben Sierra RBI	.50	.23
R47	Larry Walker RBI	2.00	.90
R48	Fred McGriff RBI	1.50	.70
R49	Dante Bichette RBI W	1.00	.45
R50	Darren Daulton RBI	1.00	.45
R51	Will Clark BAT	2.00	.90
R52	Ken Griffey Jr. BAT	10.00	4.50
R53	Don Mattingly BAT	5.00	2.20
R54	John Olerud BAT	1.00	.45
R55	Kirby Puckett BAT	2.00	.90
R56	Raul Mondesi BAT	1.50	.70
R57	Moises Alou BAT	1.00	.45
R58	Bret Boone BAT	1.00	.45
R59	Albert Belle BAT	2.00	.90
R60	Mike Piazza BAT	6.00	2.70

1995 Upper Deck Ruth Heroes

	MINT	NRMT
COMPLETE SET (10)	120.00	55.00
COMMON CARD (73-81/HDR)	15.00	6.75
SER.2 STATED ODDS 1:34 HOBBY/RETAIL		

		MINT	NRMT
73	Babe Ruth	15.00	6.75
	1914-18 Pitching Career		
74	Babe Ruth	15.00	6.75
	1919 Move to Outfield		
75	Babe Ruth	15.00	6.75
	1920 Renaissance Man		
76	Babe Ruth	15.00	6.75
	1923 House that Ruth Built		
77	Babe Ruth	15.00	6.75
	1927 60-home run Season		
78	Babe Ruth	15.00	6.75
	1928 Three Homers in Game 4		
79	Babe Ruth	15.00	6.75
	1932 The Called Shot		
80	Babe Ruth	15.00	6.75
	1930-35 Milestones		
81	Babe Ruth	15.00	6.75
	1935 The Last Hurrah		
NNO	Babe Ruth Header Card	15.00	6.75
	An American Hero		

1995 Upper Deck Special Edition

	MINT	NRMT
COMPLETE SET (270)	160.00	70.00
COMPLETE SERIES 1 (135)	80.00	36.00
COMPLETE SERIES 2 (135)	80.00	36.00
COMMON CARD (1-270)	.40	.18
MINOR STARS	.60	.25
SEMISTARS	1.00	.45
UNLISTED STARS	1.50	.70
ONE PER HOBBY PACK		
COMP.SE GOLD SET (270)	1600.00	700.00
COMP.SE GOLD SER.1 (135)	800.00	350.00
COMP.SE GOLD SER.2 (135)	800.00	350.00
COMMON SE GOLD (1-270)	3.00	1.35
*SE GOLD STARS: 10X TO 8X HI COLUMN		
*SE GOLD RC's/PROSP: 2X TO 5X HI		
SE GOLD STATED ODDS 1:35 HOBBY		

		MINT	NRMT
1	Cliff Floyd	.60	.25
2	Wil Cordero	.40	.18
3	Pedro Martinez	2.00	.90
4	Larry Walker	1.50	.70
5	Derek Jeter	5.00	2.20
6	Mike Stanley	.40	.18
7	Melido Perez	.40	.18
8	Jim Leyritz	.40	.18
9	Danny Tartabull	.40	.18
10	Wade Boggs	1.50	.70
11	Ryan Klesko	.60	.25
12	Steve Avery	.40	.18
13	Damon Hollins	.40	.18
14	Chipper Jones	4.00	1.80
15	David Justice	1.50	.70
16	Glenn Williams	.60	.25
17	Jose Oliva	.40	.18
18	Terrell Wade	.40	.18
19	Alex Fernandez	.40	.18
20	Frank Thomas	3.00	1.35
21	Ozzie Guillen	.40	.18
22	Roberto Hernandez	.40	.18
23	Albie Lopez	.40	.18
24	Eddie Murray	1.50	.70
25	Albert Belle	1.50	.70
26	Omar Vizquel	.60	.25
27	Carlos Baerga	.40	.18
28	Jose Rijo	.40	.18
29	Hal Morris	.40	.18
30	Reggie Sanders	.60	.25
31	Jack Morris	.60	.25
32	Raul Mondesi	1.00	.45
33	Karim Garcia	2.00	.90
34	Todd Hollandsworth	.40	.18
35	Mike Piazza	5.00	2.20
36	Chan Ho Park	1.50	.70
37	Ramon Martinez	.60	.25
38	Kenny Rogers	.40	.18
39	Will Clark	1.50	.70
40	Juan Gonzalez	3.00	1.35
41	Ivan Rodriguez	2.00	.90
42	Charlton Miller	.40	.18
43	John Hudek	.40	.18
44	Luis Gonzalez	.40	.18
45	Jeff Bagwell	2.00	.90
46	Cal Ripken	6.00	2.70
47	Mike Oquist	.40	.18
48	Armando Benitez	.40	.18
49	Ben McDonald	.40	.18
50	Rafael Palmeiro	1.50	.70
51	Curtis Goodwin	.40	.18
52	Vince Coleman	.40	.18
53	Tom Gordon	.40	.18
54	Mike Macfarlane	.40	.18
55	Brian McRae	.40	.18
56	Matt Smith	.40	.18
57	David Segui	.60	.25
58	Paul Wilson	.40	.18
59	Bill Pulsipher	.40	.18
60	Bobby Bonilla	.60	.25
61	Jeff Kent	.60	.25
62	Ryan Thompson	.40	.18
63	Jason Isringhausen	.60	.25
64	Ed Sprague	.40	.18
65	Paul Molitor	1.50	.70
66	Juan Guzman	.40	.18
67	Alex Gonzalez	.40	.18
68	Shawn Green	1.50	.70
69	Mark Portugal	.40	.18
70	Barry Bonds	2.00	.90
71	Robby Thompson	.40	.18
72	Royce Clayton	.40	.18
73	Ricky Bottalico	.40	.18
74	Doug Jones	.40	.18
75	Darren Daulton	.60	.25
76	Gregg Jefferies	.40	.18
77	Scott Cooper	.40	.18
78	Nomar Garciaparra	8.00	3.60
79	Ken Ryan	.40	.18
80	Mike Greenwell	.40	.18
81	LaTroy Hawkins	.40	.18
82	Rich Becker	.40	.18
83	Scott Erickson	.60	.25
84	Pedro Munoz	.40	.18
85	Kirby Puckett	3.00	1.35
86	Orlando Merced	.40	.18
87	Jeff King	.40	.18
88	Midre Cummings	.40	.18
89	Bernard Gilkey	.40	.18
90	Ray Lankford	.60	.25
91	Todd Zeile	.40	.18
92	Alan Benes	.40	.18
93	Bret Wagner	.40	.18
94	Rene Arocha	.40	.18
95	Cecil Fielder	.60	.25
96	Alan Trammell	.60	.25
97	Tony Phillips	.40	.18
98	Junior Felix	.40	.18
99	Brian Harper	.40	.18
100	Greg Vaughn	.40	.18
101	Ricky Bones	.40	.18
102	Walt Weiss	.40	.18
103	Lance Painter	.40	.18
104	Roberto Mejia	.40	.18
105	Andres Galarraga	1.50	.70
106	Todd Van Poppel	.40	.18
107	Ben Grieve	4.00	1.80
108	Brent Gates	.40	.18
109	Jason Giambi	.60	.25
110	Ruben Sierra	.60	.25
111	Terry Steinbach	.40	.18
112	Chris Hammond	.40	.18
113	Charles Johnson	.60	.25
114	Jesus Tavarez	.40	.18
115	Gary Sheffield	.60	.25
116	Chuck Carr	.40	.18
117	Bobby Ayala	.40	.18
118	Randy Johnson	1.50	.70
119	Edgar Martinez	.60	.25
120	Alex Rodriguez	6.00	2.70
121	Kevin Foster	.40	.18
122	Kevin Roberson	.40	.18
123	Sammy Sosa	5.00	2.20
124	Steve Trachsel	.40	.18
125	Eduardo Perez	.40	.18
126	Tim Salmon	1.50	.70
127	Todd Greene	.40	.18
128	Jorge Fabregas	.40	.18
129	Mark Langston	.40	.18
130	Mitch Williams	.40	.18
131	Raul Casanova	.60	.25
132	Mel Nieves	.40	.18
133	Andy Benes	.60	.25
134	Dustin Hermanson	.40	.18

		MINT	NRMT
☐ 135	Trevor Hoffman	.60	.25
☐ 136	Mark Grudzielanek	1.00	.45
☐ 137	Ugueth Urbina	.40	.18
☐ 138	Moises Alou	.60	.25
☐ 139	Roberto Kelly	.40	.18
☐ 140	Rondell White	.60	.25
☐ 141	Paul O'Neill	.60	.25
☐ 142	Jimmy Key	.40	.25
☐ 143	Jack McDowell	.40	.18
☐ 144	Ruben Rivera	.60	.25
☐ 145	Don Mattingly	3.00	1.35
☐ 146	John Wetteland	.60	.25
☐ 147	Tom Glavine	1.50	.70
☐ 148	Marquis Grissom	.60	.25
☐ 149	Javier Lopez	.60	.25
☐ 150	Fred McGriff	1.00	.45
☐ 151	Greg Maddux	4.00	1.80
☐ 152	Chris Sabo	.40	.18
☐ 153	Ray Durham	.60	.25
☐ 154	Robin Ventura	.60	.25
☐ 155	Jim Abbott	.60	.25
☐ 156	Jimmy Hurst	.40	.18
☐ 157	Tim Raines	.60	.25
☐ 158	Dennis Martinez	.60	.25
☐ 159	Kenny Lofton	1.00	.45
☐ 160	Dave Winfield	1.50	.70
☐ 161	Manny Ramirez	2.00	.90
☐ 162	Jim Thome	1.50	.70
☐ 163	Barry Larkin	1.50	.70
☐ 164	Bret Boone	.60	.25
☐ 165	Deion Sanders	.60	.25
☐ 166	Ron Gant	.40	.18
☐ 167	Benito Santiago	.40	.18
☐ 168	Hideo Nomo	4.00	1.80
☐ 169	Billy Ashley	.40	.18
☐ 170	Roger Cedeno	.40	.18
☐ 171	Ismael Valdes	.60	.25
☐ 172	Eric Karros	.60	.25
☐ 173	Rusty Greer	1.50	.70
☐ 174	Rick Helling	.60	.25
☐ 175	Nolan Ryan	6.00	2.70
☐ 176	Dean Palmer	.60	.25
☐ 177	Phil Plantier	.40	.18
☐ 178	Darryl Kile	.40	.18
☐ 179	Derek Bell	.60	.25
☐ 180	Doug Drabek	.40	.18
☐ 181	Craig Biggio	1.50	.70
☐ 182	Kevin Brown	1.00	.45
☐ 183	Harold Baines	.60	.25
☐ 184	Jeffrey Hammonds	.60	.25
☐ 185	Chris Hoiles	.40	.18
☐ 186	Mike Mussina	1.50	.70
☐ 187	Bob Hamelin	.40	.18
☐ 188	Jeff Montgomery	.40	.18
☐ 189	Michael Tucker	.60	.25
☐ 190	George Brett	3.00	1.35
☐ 191	Edgardo Alfonzo	1.50	.70
☐ 192	Brett Butler	.60	.25
☐ 193	Bobby Jones	.60	.25
☐ 194	Todd Hundley	.60	.25
☐ 195	Bret Saberhagen	.60	.25
☐ 196	Pat Hentgen	.60	.25
☐ 197	Roberto Alomar	1.50	.70
☐ 198	David Cone	1.00	.45
☐ 199	Carlos Delgado	1.50	.70
☐ 200	Joe Carter	.60	.25
☐ 201	Wm. VanLandingham	.40	.18
☐ 202	Rod Beck	.40	.18
☐ 203	J.R. Phillips	.40	.18
☐ 204	Darren Lewis	.40	.18
☐ 205	Matt Williams	1.50	.70
☐ 206	Lenny Dykstra	.60	.25
☐ 207	Dave Hollins	.40	.18
☐ 208	Mike Schmidt	2.50	1.10
☐ 209	Charlie Hayes	.40	.18
☐ 210	Mo Vaughn	1.50	.70
☐ 211	Jose Malave	.40	.18
☐ 212	Roger Clemens	4.00	1.80
☐ 213	Jose Canseco	2.00	.90
☐ 214	Mark Whiten	.40	.18
☐ 215	Marty Cordova	.40	.18
☐ 216	Rick Aguilera	.40	.18
☐ 217	Kevin Tapani	.60	.25
☐ 218	Chuck Knoblauch	1.50	.70
☐ 219	Al Martin	.40	.18
☐ 220	Jay Bell	.60	.25

		MINT	NRMT
☐ 221	Carlos Garcia	.40	.18
☐ 222	Freddy Garcia	.40	.18
☐ 223	Jon Lieber	.40	.18
☐ 224	Danny Jackson	.40	.18
☐ 225	Ozzie Smith	2.00	.90
☐ 226	Brian Jordan	.60	.25
☐ 227	Ken Hill	.40	.18
☐ 228	Scott Cooper	.40	.18
☐ 229	Chad Curtis	.40	.18
☐ 230	Lou Whitaker	.60	.25
☐ 231	Kirk Gibson	.60	.25
☐ 232	Travis Fryman	.60	.25
☐ 233	Jose Valentin	.40	.18
☐ 234	Dave Nilsson	.40	.18
☐ 235	Cal Eldred	.40	.18
☐ 236	Matt Mieske	.40	.18
☐ 237	Bill Swift	.40	.18
☐ 238	Marvin Freeman	.40	.18
☐ 239	Jason Bates	.40	.18
☐ 240	Larry Walker	1.50	.70
☐ 241	Dave Nied	.40	.18
☐ 242	Dante Bichette	.60	.25
☐ 243	Dennis Eckersley	.60	.25
☐ 244	Todd Stottlemyre	.40	.18
☐ 245	Rickey Henderson	2.00	.90
☐ 246	Geronimo Berroa	.40	.18
☐ 247	Mark McGwire	8.00	3.60
☐ 248	Quilvio Veras	.40	.18
☐ 249	Terry Pendleton	.40	.18
☐ 250	Andre Dawson	1.00	.45
☐ 251	Jeff Conine	.40	.18
☐ 252	Kurt Abbott	.40	.18
☐ 253	Jay Buhner	.60	.25
☐ 254	Darren Bragg	.40	.18
☐ 255	Ken Griffey Jr.	8.00	3.60
☐ 256	Tino Martinez	1.50	.70
☐ 257	Mark Grace	1.00	.45
☐ 258	Ryne Sandberg	2.00	.90
☐ 259	Randy Myers	.40	.18
☐ 260	Howard Johnson	.40	.18
☐ 261	Lee Smith	.60	.25
☐ 262	J.T. Snow	.60	.25
☐ 263	Chili Davis	.60	.25
☐ 264	Chuck Finley	.40	.18
☐ 265	Eddie Williams	.40	.18
☐ 266	Joey Hamilton	.40	.18
☐ 267	Ken Caminiti	1.00	.45
☐ 268	Andujar Cedeno	.40	.18
☐ 269	Steve Finley	.60	.25
☐ 270	Tony Gwynn	4.00	1.80

1995 Upper Deck Steal of a Deal

		MINT	NRMT
COMPLETE SET (15)		80.00	36.00
COMMON CARD (SD1-SD15)		1.50	.70
SER.1 STATED ODDS 1:34 ALL PACKS			
☐ SD1	Mike Piazza	20.00	9.00
☐ SD2	Fred McGriff	4.00	1.80
☐ SD3	Kenny Lofton	4.00	1.80
☐ SD4	Jose Oliva	1.50	.70
☐ SD5	Jeff Bagwell	6.00	2.70
☐ SD6	Roberto Alomar Joe Carter	6.00	2.70
☐ SD7	Steve Karsay	1.50	.70
☐ SD8	Ozzie Smith	6.00	2.70

		MINT	NRMT
☐ SD9	Dennis Eckersley	2.50	1.10
☐ SD10	Jose Canseco	6.00	2.70
☐ SD11	Carlos Baerga	1.50	.70
☐ SD12	Cecil Fielder	2.50	1.10
☐ SD13	Don Mattingly	10.00	4.50
☐ SD14	Bret Boone	2.50	1.10
☐ SD15	Michael Jordan	30.00	13.50

1996 Upper Deck

		MINT	NRMT
COMPLETE SET (480)		70.00	32.00
COMP.FACT.SET (510)		80.00	36.00
COMPLETE SERIES 1 (240)		40.00	18.00
COMPLETE SERIES 2 (240)		30.00	13.50
COMMON CARD (1-480)		.15	.07
MINOR STARS		.30	.14
UNLISTED STARS		.60	.25

SUBSET CARDS HALF VALUE OF BASE CARDS

		MINT	NRMT
COMP.UPDATE SET (30)		10.00	4.50
COMMON UPDATE (481U-510U)		.25	.11

ONE UPDATE SET PER FACTORY SET
ONE UPDATE SET PER SER.2 WRAP.OFFER

		MINT	NRMT
☐ 1	Cal Ripken 2131	4.00	1.80
☐ 2	Eddie Murray 3000 Hits	.60	.25
☐ 3	Mark Wohlers	.15	.07
☐ 4	David Justice	.60	.25
☐ 5	Chipper Jones	1.50	.70
☐ 6	Javier Lopez	.30	.14
☐ 7	Mark Lemke	.15	.07
☐ 8	Marquis Grissom	.15	.07
☐ 9	Tom Glavine	.60	.25
☐ 10	Greg Maddux	1.50	.70
☐ 11	Manny Alexander	.15	.07
☐ 12	Curtis Goodwin	.15	.07
☐ 13	Scott Erickson	.30	.14
☐ 14	Chris Hoiles	.15	.07
☐ 15	Rafael Palmeiro	.60	.25
☐ 16	Rick Krivda	.15	.07
☐ 17	Jeff Manto	.15	.07
☐ 18	Mo Vaughn	.60	.25
☐ 19	Tim Wakefield	.15	.07
☐ 20	Roger Clemens	1.50	.70
☐ 21	Tim Naehring	.15	.07
☐ 22	Troy O'Leary	.30	.14
☐ 23	Mike Greenwell	.15	.07
☐ 24	Stan Belinda	.15	.07
☐ 25	John Valentin	.30	.14
☐ 26	J.T. Snow	.30	.14
☐ 27	Gary DiSarcina	.15	.07
☐ 28	Mark Langston	.15	.07
☐ 29	Brian Anderson	.15	.07
☐ 30	Jim Edmonds	.40	.18
☐ 31	Garret Anderson	.30	.14
☐ 32	Orlando Palmeiro	.15	.07
☐ 33	Brian McRae	.15	.07
☐ 34	Kevin Foster	.15	.07
☐ 35	Sammy Sosa	2.00	.90
☐ 36	Todd Zeile	.15	.07
☐ 37	Jim Bullinger	.15	.07
☐ 38	Luis Gonzalez	.30	.14
☐ 39	Lyle Mouton	.15	.07
☐ 40	Ray Durham	.30	.14
☐ 41	Ozzie Guillen	.15	.07
☐ 42	Alex Fernandez	.15	.07
☐ 43	Brian Keyser	.15	.07

44	Robin Ventura	.30	.14
45	Reggie Sanders	.30	.14
46	Pete Schourek	.15	.07
47	John Smiley	.15	.07
48	Jeff Brantley	.15	.07
49	Thomas Howard	.15	.07
50	Bret Boone	.30	.14
51	Kevin Jarvis	.15	.07
52	Jeff Branson	.15	.07
53	Carlos Baerga	.15	.07
54	Jim Thome	.60	.25
55	Manny Ramirez	.75	.35
56	Omar Vizquel	.30	.14
57	Jose Mesa	.15	.07
58	Julian Tavarez UER	.15	.07
59	Orel Hershiser	.30	.14
60	Larry Walker	.60	.25
61	Brett Saberhagen	.30	.14
62	Vinny Castilla	.40	.18
63	Eric Young	.15	.07
64	Bryan Rekar	.15	.07
65	Andres Galarraga	.60	.25
66	Steve Reed	.15	.07
67	Chad Curtis	.15	.07
68	Bobby Higginson	.30	.14
69	Phil Nevin	.15	.07
70	Cecil Fielder	.30	.14
71	Felipe Lira	.15	.07
72	Chris Gomez	.15	.07
73	Charles Johnson	.30	.14
74	Quilvio Veras	.15	.07
75	Jeff Conine	.15	.07
76	John Burkett	.15	.07
77	Greg Colbrunn	.15	.07
78	Terry Pendleton	.15	.07
79	Shane Reynolds	.30	.14
80	Jeff Bagwell	.75	.35
81	Orlando Miller	.15	.07
82	Mike Hampton	.30	.14
83	James Mouton	.15	.07
84	Brian L. Hunter	.15	.07
85	Derek Bell	.30	.14
86	Kevin Appier	.30	.14
87	Joe Vitiello	.15	.07
88	Wally Joyner	.30	.14
89	Michael Tucker	.15	.07
90	Johnny Damon	.40	.18
91	Jon Nunnally	.15	.07
92	Jason Jacome	.15	.07
93	Chad Fonville	.15	.07
94	Chan Ho Park	.40	.18
95	Hideo Nomo	.60	.25
96	Ismael Valdes	.30	.14
97	Greg Gagne	.15	.07
98	Diamondbacks-Devil Rays	.60	.25
99	Raul Mondesi	.30	.14
100	Dave Winfield YH	.30	.14
101	Dennis Eckersley YH	.15	.07
102	Andre Dawson YH	.15	.07
103	Dennis Martinez YH	.15	.07
104	Lance Parrish YH	.15	.07
105	Eddie Murray YH	.30	.14
106	Alan Trammell YH	.15	.07
107	Lou Whitaker YH	.15	.07
108	Ozzie Smith YH	.60	.25
109	Paul Molitor YH	.30	.14
110	Rickey Henderson YH	.40	.18
111	Tim Raines YH	.15	.07
112	Harold Baines YH	.15	.07
113	Lee Smith YH	.15	.07
114	Fernando Valenzuela YH	.15	.07
115	Cal Ripken YH	1.25	.55
116	Tony Gwynn YH	.75	.35
117	Wade Boggs	.60	.25
118	Todd Hollandsworth	.15	.07
119	Dave Nilsson	.15	.07
120	Jose Valentin	.15	.07
121	Steve Sparks	.15	.07
122	Chuck Carr	.15	.07
123	John Jaha	.15	.07
124	Scott Karl	.15	.07
125	Chuck Knoblauch	.60	.25
126	Brad Radke	.30	.14
127	Pat Meares	.15	.07
128	Ron Coomer	.15	.07
129	Pedro Munoz	.15	.07
130	Kirby Puckett	1.00	.45
131	David Segui	.30	.14
132	Mark Grudzielanek	.15	.07
133	Mike Lansing	.15	.07
134	Sean Berry	.15	.07
135	Rondell White	.30	.14
136	Pedro Martinez	.75	.35
137	Carl Everett	.30	.14
138	Dave Mlicki	.15	.07
139	Bill Pulsipher	.15	.07
140	Jason Isringhausen	.30	.14
141	Rico Brogna	.15	.07
142	Edgardo Alfonzo	.60	.25
143	Jeff Kent	.30	.14
144	Andy Pettitte	.40	.18
145	Mike Piazza BO	1.00	.45
146	Cliff Floyd BO	.15	.07
147	Jason Isringhausen BO	.15	.07
148	Tim Wakefield BO	.15	.07
149	Chipper Jones BO	.75	.35
150	Hideo Nomo BO	.30	.14
151	Mark McGwire BO	1.50	.70
152	Ron Gant BO	.15	.07
153	Gary Gaetti BO	.15	.07
154	Don Mattingly	1.25	.55
155	Paul O'Neil	.30	.14
156	Derek Jeter	2.00	.90
157	Joe Girardi	.15	.07
158	Ruben Sierra	.15	.07
159	Jorge Posada	.30	.14
160	Geronimo Berroa	.15	.07
161	Steve Ontiveros	.15	.07
162	George Williams	.15	.07
163	Doug Johns	.15	.07
164	Ariel Prieto	.15	.07
165	Scott Brosius	.30	.14
166	Mike Bordick	.15	.07
167	Tyler Green	.15	.07
168	Mickey Morandini	.15	.07
169	Darren Daulton	.30	.14
170	Gregg Jefferies	.15	.07
171	Jim Eisenreich	.15	.07
172	Heathcliff Slocumb	.15	.07
173	Kevin Stocker	.15	.07
174	Esteban Loaiza	.30	.14
175	Jeff King	.15	.07
176	Mark Johnson	.15	.07
177	Denny Neagle	.30	.14
178	Orlando Merced	.15	.07
179	Carlos Garcia	.15	.07
180	Brian Jordan	.30	.14
181	Mike Morgan	.15	.07
182	Mark Petkovsek	.15	.07
183	Bernard Gilkey	.15	.07
184	John Mabry	.15	.07
185	Tom Henke	.15	.07
186	Glenn Dishman	.15	.07
187	Andy Ashby	.15	.07
188	Bip Roberts	.15	.07
189	Melvin Nieves	.15	.07
190	Ken Caminiti	.30	.14
191	Brad Ausmus	.15	.07
192	Deion Sanders	.30	.14
193	Jamie Brewington	.15	.07
194	Glenallen Hill	.15	.07
195	Barry Bonds	.75	.35
196	Wm. Van Landingham	.15	.07
197	Mark Carreon	.15	.07
198	Royce Clayton	.15	.07
199	Joey Cora	.15	.07
200	Ken Griffey Jr.	3.00	1.35
201	Jay Buhner	.30	.14
202	Alex Rodriguez	2.00	.90
203	Norm Charlton	.15	.07
204	Andy Benes	.30	.14
205	Edgar Martinez	.30	.14
206	Juan Gonzalez	1.25	.55
207	Will Clark	.60	.25
208	Kevin Gross	.15	.07
209	Roger Pavlik	.15	.07
210	Ivan Rodriguez	.75	.35
211	Rusty Greer	.30	.14
212	Angel Martinez	.15	.07
213	Tomas Perez	.15	.07
214	Alex Gonzalez	.15	.07
215	Joe Carter	.30	.14
216	Shawn Green	.60	.25
217	Edwin Hurtado	.15	.07
218	Edgar Martinez / Tony Pena CL	.30	.14
219	Chipper Jones / Barry Larkin CL	.60	.25
220	Orel Hershiser CL	.15	.07
221	Mike Devereaux CL	.15	.07
222	Tom Glavine CL	.30	.14
223	Karim Garcia	.30	.14
224	Arquimedez Pozo	.15	.07
225	Billy Wagner	.40	.18
226	John Wasdin	.15	.07
227	Jeff Suppan	.15	.07
228	Steve Gibralter	.15	.07
229	Jimmy Haynes	.15	.07
230	Ruben Rivera	.30	.14
231	Chris Snopek	.15	.07
232	Alex Ochoa	.15	.07
233	Shannon Stewart	.30	.14
234	Quinton McCracken	.15	.07
235	Trey Beamon	.15	.07
236	Billy McMillon	.15	.07
237	Steve Cox	.15	.07
238	George Arias	.15	.07
239	Jose Herrera	.15	.07
240	Todd Greene	.15	.07
241	Jason Kendall	.60	.25
242	Brooks Kieschnick	.15	.07
243	Osvaldo Fernandez	.15	.07
244	Livan Hernandez	1.00	.45
245	Rey Ordonez	.60	.25
246	Mike Grace	.15	.07
247	Jay Canizaro	.15	.07
248	Bob Wolcott	.15	.07
249	Jermaine Dye	.30	.14
250	Jason Schmidt	.15	.07
251	Mike Sweeney	1.25	.55
252	Marcus Jensen	.15	.07
253	Mendy Lopez	.15	.07
254	Wilton Guerrero	.50	.23
255	Paul Wilson	.15	.07
256	Edgar Renteria	.30	.14
257	Richard Hidalgo	.30	.14
258	Bob Abreu	.40	.18
259	Robert Smith	.50	.23
260	Sal Fasano	.15	.07
261	Enrique Wilson	.30	.14
262	Rich Hunter	.15	.07
263	Sergio Nunez	.15	.07
264	Dan Serafini	.15	.07
265	David Doster	.15	.07
266	Ryan McGuire	.15	.07
267	Scott Spiezio	.15	.07
268	Rafael Orellano	.15	.07
269	Steve Avery	.15	.07
270	Fred McGriff	.40	.18
271	John Smoltz	.40	.18
272	Ryan Klesko	.30	.14
273	Jeff Blauser	.15	.07
274	Brad Clontz	.15	.07
275	Roberto Alomar	.60	.25
276	B.J. Surhoff	.30	.14
277	Jeffrey Hammonds	.15	.07
278	Brady Anderson	.30	.14
279	Bobby Bonilla	.30	.14
280	Cal Ripken	2.50	1.10
281	Mike Mussina	.60	.25
282	Wil Cordero	.15	.07
283	Mike Stanley	.15	.07
284	Aaron Sele	.30	.14
285	Jose Canseco	.75	.35
286	Tom Gordon	.15	.07
287	Heathcliff Slocumb	.15	.07
288	Lee Smith	.30	.14
289	Troy Percival	.30	.14
290	Tim Salmon	.40	.18
291	Chuck Finley	.30	.14
292	Jim Abbott	.30	.14
293	Chili Davis	.30	.14
294	Steve Trachsel	.15	.07
295	Mark Grace	.40	.18
296	Rey Sanchez	.15	.07
297	Scott Servais	.15	.07
298	Jaime Navarro	.15	.07
299	Frank Castillo	.15	.07

#	Name	MINT	NRMT
300	Frank Thomas	1.25	.55
301	Jason Bere	.15	.07
302	Danny Tartabull	.15	.07
303	Darren Lewis	.15	.07
304	Roberto Hernandez	.15	.07
305	Tony Phillips	.15	.07
306	Wilson Alvarez	.15	.07
307	Jose Rijo	.15	.07
308	Hal Morris	.15	.07
309	Mark Portugal	.15	.07
310	Barry Larkin	.60	.25
311	Dave Burba	.15	.07
312	Ed Taubensee	.15	.07
313	Sandy Alomar Jr.	.30	.14
314	Dennis Martinez	.30	.14
315	Albert Belle	.60	.25
316	Eddie Murray	.60	.25
317	Charles Nagy	.30	.14
318	Chad Ogea	.15	.07
319	Kenny Lofton	.40	.18
320	Dante Bichette	.30	.14
321	Armando Reynoso	.15	.07
322	Walt Weiss	.15	.07
323	Ellis Burks	.30	.14
324	Kevin Ritz	.15	.07
325	Bill Swift	.15	.07
326	Jason Bates	.15	.07
327	Tony Clark	.60	.25
328	Travis Fryman	.30	.14
329	Mark Parent	.15	.07
330	Alan Trammell	.40	.18
331	C.J. Nitkowski	.15	.07
332	Jose Lima	.40	.18
333	Phil Plantier	.15	.07
334	Kurt Abbott	.15	.07
335	Andre Dawson	.40	.18
336	Chris Hammond	.15	.07
337	Robb Nen	.15	.07
338	Pat Rapp	.15	.07
339	Al Leiter	.30	.14
340	Gary Sheffield UER	.30	.14
	(HR total says 17)		
341	Todd Jones	.15	.07
342	Doug Drabek	.15	.07
343	Greg Swindell	.15	.07
344	Tony Eusebio	.15	.07
345	Craig Biggio	.60	.25
346	Darryl Kile	.15	.07
347	Mike Macfarlane	.15	.07
348	Jeff Montgomery	.15	.07
349	Chris Haney	.15	.07
350	Bip Roberts	.15	.07
351	Tom Goodwin	.15	.07
352	Mark Gubicza	.15	.07
353	Joe Randa	.15	.07
354	Ramon Martinez	.30	.14
355	Eric Karros	.30	.14
356	Delino DeShields	.15	.07
357	Brett Butler	.30	.14
358	Todd Worrell	.15	.07
359	Mike Blowers	.15	.07
360	Mike Piazza	2.00	.90
361	Ben McDonald	.15	.07
362	Ricky Bones	.15	.07
363	Greg Vaughn	.30	.14
364	Matt Mieske	.15	.07
365	Kevin Seitzer	.15	.07
366	Jeff Cirillo	.30	.14
367	LaTroy Hawkins	.15	.07
368	Frank Rodriguez	.15	.07
369	Rick Aguilera	.15	.07
370	Roberto Alomar BG	.30	.14
371	Albert Belle BG	.30	.14
372	Wade Boggs BG	.30	.14
373	Barry Bonds BG	.40	.18
374	Roger Clemens BG	.75	.35
375	Dennis Eckersley BG	.15	.07
376	Ken Griffey Jr. BG	1.50	.70
377	Tony Gwynn BG	.75	.35
378	Rickey Henderson BG	.40	.18
379	Greg Maddux BG	.75	.35
380	Fred McGriff BG	.15	.07
381	Paul Molitor BG	.30	.14
382	Eddie Murray BG	.30	.14
383	Mike Piazza BG	1.00	.45
384	Kirby Puckett BG	.60	.25
385	Cal Ripken BG	1.25	.55
386	Ozzie Smith BG	.60	.25
387	Frank Thomas BG	.60	.25
388	Matt Walbeck	.15	.07
389	Dave Stevens	.15	.07
390	Marty Cordova	.15	.07
391	Darrin Fletcher	.15	.07
392	Cliff Floyd	.30	.14
393	Mel Rojas	.15	.07
394	Shane Andrews	.15	.07
395	Moises Alou	.30	.14
396	Carlos Perez	.15	.07
397	Jeff Fassero	.15	.07
398	Bobby Jones	.15	.07
399	Todd Hundley	.30	.14
400	John Franco	.30	.14
401	Jose Vizcaino	.15	.07
402	Bernard Gilkey	.15	.07
403	Pete Harnisch	.15	.07
404	Pat Kelly	.15	.07
405	David Cone	.30	.14
406	Bernie Williams	.60	.25
407	John Wetteland	.30	.14
408	Scott Kamieniecki	.15	.07
409	Tim Raines	.15	.07
410	Wade Boggs	.60	.25
411	Terry Steinbach	.15	.07
412	Jason Giambi	.30	.14
413	Todd Van Poppel	.15	.07
414	Pedro Munoz	.15	.07
415	Eddie Murray SBT	.30	.14
416	Dennis Eckersley SBT	.15	.07
417	Bip Roberts SBT	.15	.07
418	Glenallen Hill SBT	.15	.07
419	John Hudek SBT	.15	.07
420	Derek Bell SBT	.15	.07
421	Larry Walker SBT	.30	.14
422	Greg Maddux SBT	.75	.35
423	Ken Caminiti SBT	.15	.07
424	Brent Gates	.15	.07
425	Mark McGwire	3.00	1.35
426	Mark Whiten	.15	.07
427	Sid Fernandez	.15	.07
428	Ricky Bottalico	.15	.07
429	Mike Mimbs	.15	.07
430	Lenny Dykstra	.30	.14
431	Todd Zeile	.15	.07
432	Benito Santiago	.15	.07
433	Danny Miceli	.15	.07
434	Al Martin	.15	.07
435	Jay Bell	.30	.14
436	Charlie Hayes	.15	.07
437	Mike Kingery	.15	.07
438	Paul Wagner	.15	.07
439	Tom Pagnozzi	.15	.07
440	Ozzie Smith	.75	.35
441	Ray Lankford	.30	.14
442	Dennis Eckersley	.30	.14
443	Ron Gant	.15	.07
444	Alan Benes	.15	.07
445	Rickey Henderson	.75	.35
446	Jody Reed	.15	.07
447	Trevor Hoffman	.30	.14
448	Andujar Cedeno	.15	.07
449	Steve Finley	.15	.07
450	Tony Gwynn	1.50	.70
451	Joey Hamilton	.15	.07
452	Mark Leiter	.15	.07
453	Rod Beck	.15	.07
454	Kirt Manwaring	.15	.07
455	Matt Williams	.60	.25
456	Robby Thompson	.15	.07
457	Shawon Dunston	.15	.07
458	Russ Davis	.15	.07
459	Paul Sorrento	.15	.07
460	Randy Johnson	.60	.25
461	Chris Bosio	.15	.07
462	Luis Sojo	.15	.07
463	Sterling Hitchcock	.15	.07
464	Benji Gil	.15	.07
465	Mickey Tettleton	.15	.07
466	Mark McLemore	.15	.07
467	Darryl Hamilton	.15	.07
468	Ken Hill	.15	.07
469	Dean Palmer	.30	.14
470	Carlos Delgado	.60	.25
471	Ed Sprague	.15	.07
472	Otis Nixon	.15	.07
473	Pat Hentgen	.30	.14
474	Juan Guzman	.15	.07
475	John Olerud	.30	.14
476	Buck Showalter CL	.15	.07
477	Bobby Cox CL	.15	.07
478	Tommy Lasorda CL	.30	.14
479	Buck Showalter CL	.15	.07
480	Sparky Anderson CL	.30	.14
481U	Randy Myers	.25	.11
482U	Kent Mercker	.25	.11
483U	David Wells	.75	.35
484U	Kevin Mitchell	.25	.11
485U	Randy Velarde	.25	.11
486U	Ryne Sandberg	1.50	.70
487U	Doug Jones	.25	.11
488U	Terry Adams	.25	.11
489U	Kevin Tapani	.25	.11
490U	Harold Baines	.50	.23
491U	Eric Davis	.50	.23
492U	Julio Franco	.25	.11
493U	Jack McDowell	.25	.11
494U	Devon White	.50	.23
495U	Kevin Brown	.75	.35
496U	Rick Wilkins	.25	.11
497U	Sean Berry	.25	.11
498U	Keith Lockhart	.25	.11
499U	Mark Loretta	.25	.11
500U	Paul Molitor	1.25	.55
501U	Roberto Kelly	.25	.11
502U	Lance Johnson	.25	.11
503U	Tino Martinez	.50	.23
504U	Kenny Rogers	.25	.11
505U	Todd Stottlemyre	.25	.11
506U	Gary Gaetti	.50	.23
507U	Royce Clayton	.25	.11
508U	Andy Benes	.50	.23
509U	Wally Joyner	.50	.23
510U	Erik Hanson	.25	.11

1996 Upper Deck Blue Chip Prospects

		MINT	NRMT
COMPLETE SET (20)		150.00	70.00
COMMON CARD (BC1-BC20)		4.00	1.80
SEMISTARS		6.00	2.70
UNLISTED STARS		10.00	4.50
SER.1 STATED ODDS 1:72			
BC1	Hideo Nomo	10.00	4.50
BC2	Johnny Damon	6.00	2.70
BC3	Jason Isringhausen	6.00	2.70
BC4	Bill Pulsipher	4.00	1.80
BC5	Marty Cordova	4.00	1.80
BC6	Michael Tucker	4.00	1.80
BC7	John Wasdin	4.00	1.80
BC8	Karim Garcia	6.00	2.70
BC9	Ruben Rivera	6.00	2.70
BC10	Chipper Jones	25.00	11.00
BC11	Billy Wagner	6.00	2.70
BC12	Brooks Kieschnick	4.00	1.80
BC13	Alan Benes	4.00	1.80
BC14	Roger Cedeno	6.00	2.70
BC15	Alex Rodriguez	30.00	13.50
BC16	Jason Schmidt	4.00	1.80
BC17	Derek Jeter	30.00	13.50

	MINT	NRMT
❑ BC18 Brian L.Hunter	4.00	1.80
❑ BC19 Garret Anderson	6.00	2.70
❑ BC20 Manny Ramirez	12.00	5.50

1996 Upper Deck Diamond Destiny

	MINT	NRMT
COMPLETE SET (40)	120.00	55.00
COMMON CARD (DD1-DD40)	1.00	.45

ONE PER UD TECH RETAIL PACK
*GOLD DD: 20X TO 50X BASE CARD HI
GOLD DD STATED ODDS 1:143 UD TECH
*SILVER DD: 6X TO 15X BASE CARD HI
SILVER DD STATED ODDS 1:35 UD TECH

		MINT	NRMT
❑ DD1	Chipper Jones	8.00	3.60
❑ DD2	Fred McGriff	1.50	.70
❑ DD3	John Smoltz	1.50	.70
❑ DD4	Ryan Klesko	1.00	.45
❑ DD5	Greg Maddux	8.00	3.60
❑ DD6	Cal Ripken	12.00	5.50
❑ DD7	Roberto Alomar	2.00	.90
❑ DD8	Eddie Murray	2.00	.90
❑ DD9	Brady Anderson	1.00	.45
❑ DD10	Mo Vaughn	2.00	.90
❑ DD11	Roger Clemens	8.00	3.60
❑ DD12	Darin Erstad	8.00	3.60
❑ DD13	Sammy Sosa	10.00	4.50
❑ DD14	Frank Thomas	6.00	2.70
❑ DD15	Barry Larkin	2.00	.90
❑ DD16	Albert Belle	2.00	.90
❑ DD17	Manny Ramirez	4.00	1.80
❑ DD18	Kenny Lofton	1.50	.70
❑ DD19	Dante Bichette	1.00	.45
❑ DD20	Gary Sheffield	1.00	.45
❑ DD21	Jeff Bagwell	4.00	1.80
❑ DD22	Hideo Nomo	2.00	.90
❑ DD23	Mike Piazza	10.00	4.50
❑ DD24	Kirby Puckett	5.00	2.20
❑ DD25	Paul Molitor	2.00	.90
❑ DD26	Chuck Knoblauch	2.00	.90
❑ DD27	Wade Boggs	2.00	.90
❑ DD28	Derek Jeter	10.00	4.50
❑ DD29	Rey Ordonez	1.00	.45
❑ DD30	Mark McGwire	15.00	6.75
❑ DD31	Ozzie Smith	4.00	1.80
❑ DD32	Tony Gwynn	8.00	3.60
❑ DD33	Barry Bonds	2.00	.90
❑ DD34	Matt Williams	2.00	.90
❑ DD35	Ken Griffey Jr.	15.00	6.75
❑ DD36	Jay Buhner	1.00	.45
❑ DD37	Randy Johnson	2.00	.90
❑ DD38	Alex Rodriguez	10.00	4.50
❑ DD39	Juan Gonzalez	6.00	2.70
❑ DD40	Joe Carter	1.00	.45

1996 Upper Deck Future Stock Prospects

	MINT	NRMT
COMPLETE SET (20)	8.00	3.60
COMMON CARD (FS1-FS20)	1.00	.45

SER.1 STATED ODDS 1:6 HOB/RET

		MINT	NRMT
❑ FS1	George Arias	1.00	.45
❑ FS2	Brian Barber	1.00	.45

		MINT	NRMT
❑ FS3	Trey Beamon	1.00	.45
❑ FS4	Yamil Benitez	1.00	.45
❑ FS5	Jamie Brewington	1.00	.45
❑ FS6	Tony Clark	2.50	1.10
❑ FS7	Steve Cox	1.00	.45
❑ FS8	Carlos Delgado	3.00	1.35
❑ FS9	Chad Fonville	1.00	.45
❑ FS10	Alex Ochoa	1.00	.45
❑ FS11	Curtis Goodwin	1.00	.45
❑ FS12	Todd Greene	1.00	.45
❑ FS13	Jimmy Haynes	1.00	.45
❑ FS14	Quinton McCracken	1.00	.45
❑ FS15	Billy McMillon	1.00	.45
❑ FS16	Chan Ho Park	2.00	.90
❑ FS17	Arquimedez Pozo	1.00	.45
❑ FS18	Chris Snopek	1.00	.45
❑ FS19	Shannon Stewart	1.25	.55
❑ FS20	Jeff Suppan	1.00	.45

1996 Upper Deck Gameface

	MINT	NRMT
COMPLETE SET (10)	12.00	5.50
COMMON CARD (GF1-GF10)	.60	.25

ONE PER SPECIAL SER.2 RETAIL PACK

		MINT	NRMT
❑ GF1	Ken Griffey Jr.	3.00	1.35
❑ GF2	Frank Thomas	1.25	.55
❑ GF3	Barry Bonds	.75	.35
❑ GF4	Albert Belle	.60	.25
❑ GF5	Cal Ripken	2.50	1.10
❑ GF6	Mike Piazza	2.00	.90
❑ GF7	Chipper Jones	1.50	.70
❑ GF8	Matt Williams	.60	.25
❑ GF9	Hideo Nomo	.60	.25
❑ GF10	Greg Maddux	1.50	.70

1996 Upper Deck Hot Commodities

	MINT	NRMT
COMPLETE SET (20)	150.00	70.00
COMMON CARD (HC1-HC20)	4.00	1.80

SER.2 STATED ODDS 1:36 HOB/RET/ANCO

		MINT	NRMT
❑ HC1	Ken Griffey Jr.	30.00	13.50
❑ HC2	Hideo Nomo	6.00	2.70
❑ HC3	Roberto Alomar	6.00	2.70
❑ HC4	Paul Wilson	4.00	1.80

		MINT	NRMT
❑ HC5	Albert Belle	6.00	2.70
❑ HC6	Manny Ramirez	8.00	3.60
❑ HC7	Kirby Puckett	10.00	4.50
❑ HC8	Johnny Damon	5.00	2.20
❑ HC9	Randy Johnson	6.00	2.70
❑ HC10	Greg Maddux	15.00	6.75
❑ HC11	Chipper Jones	15.00	6.75
❑ HC12	Barry Bonds	8.00	3.60
❑ HC13	Mo Vaughn	6.00	2.70
❑ HC14	Mike Piazza	20.00	9.00
❑ HC15	Cal Ripken	25.00	11.00
❑ HC16	Tim Salmon	5.00	2.20
❑ HC17	Sammy Sosa	20.00	9.00
❑ HC18	Kenny Lofton	5.00	2.20
❑ HC19	Tony Gwynn	15.00	6.75
❑ HC20	Frank Thomas	12.00	5.50

1996 Upper Deck V.J. Lovero Showcase

	MINT	NRMT
COMPLETE SET (19)	25.00	11.00
COMMON CARD (VJ1-VJ19)	.50	.23

SER.2 STATED ODDS 1:6 HOB/RET,1:3 ANCO

		MINT	NRMT
❑ VJ1	Jim Abbott	.50	.23
❑ VJ2	Hideo Nomo	1.50	.70
❑ VJ3	Derek Jeter	5.00	2.20
❑ VJ4	Barry Bonds	2.00	.90
❑ VJ5	Greg Maddux	4.00	1.80
❑ VJ6	Mark McGwire	8.00	3.60
❑ VJ7	Jose Canseco	2.00	.90
❑ VJ8	Ken Caminiti	.50	.23
❑ VJ9	Raul Mondesi	.50	.23
❑ VJ10	Ken Griffey Jr.	8.00	3.60
❑ VJ11	Jay Buhner	.50	.23
❑ VJ12	Randy Johnson	1.50	.70
❑ VJ13	Roger Clemens	4.00	1.80
❑ VJ14	Brady Anderson	.50	.23
❑ VJ15	Frank Thomas	3.00	1.35
❑ VJ16	Garret Anderson	1.50	.70
❑ VJ17	Jim Edmonds Tim Salmon Mike Piazza	5.00	2.20
❑ VJ17	Mike Piazza	.50	2.20
❑ VJ18	Dante Bichette	.50	.23
❑ VJ19	Tony Gwynn	4.00	1.80

1996 Upper Deck Nomo Highlights

	MINT	NRMT
COMPLETE SET (5)	20.00	9.00
COMMON CARD (1-5)	5.00	2.20
SER.2 STATED ODDS 1:24		

			MINT	NRMT
❑	1	Hideo Nomo	5.00	2.20
		Dodgers at Giants		
		First Career Start		
❑	2	Hideo Nomo	5.00	2.20
❑	3	Hideo Nomo	5.00	2.20
		1995 All-Star Game		
❑	4	Hideo Nomo	5.00	2.20
		Dodgers at Giants		
		One-Hitter		
❑	5	Hideo Nomo	5.00	2.20
		Dodgers at Padres		
		Season-Ending Performance		

1996 Upper Deck Power Driven

	MINT	NRMT
COMPLETE SET (20)	120.00	55.00
COMMON CARD (PD1-PD20)	2.50	1.10
SER.1 STATED ODDS 1:36 HOB/RET		

❑	PD1	Albert Belle	6.00	2.70
❑	PD2	Barry Bonds	8.00	3.60
❑	PD3	Jay Buhner	3.00	1.35
❑	PD4	Jose Canseco	8.00	3.60
❑	PD5	Cecil Fielder	2.50	1.10
❑	PD6	Juan Gonzalez	12.00	5.50
❑	PD7	Ken Griffey Jr.	30.00	13.50
❑	PD8	Eric Karros	3.00	1.35
❑	PD9	Fred McGriff	4.00	1.80
❑	PD10	Mark McGwire	30.00	13.50
❑	PD11	Rafael Palmeiro	6.00	2.70
❑	PD12	Mike Piazza	20.00	9.00
❑	PD13	Manny Ramirez	8.00	3.60
❑	PD14	Tim Salmon	4.00	1.80
❑	PD15	Reggie Sanders	3.00	1.35
❑	PD16	Sammy Sosa	20.00	9.00
❑	PD17	Frank Thomas	12.00	5.50
❑	PD18	Mo Vaughn	6.00	2.70
❑	PD19	Larry Walker	6.00	2.70
❑	PD20	Matt Williams	6.00	2.70

1996 Upper Deck Predictor Hobby

	MINT	NRMT
COMPLETE SERIES 1 (30)	40.00	18.00
COMPLETE SERIES 2 (30)	30.00	13.50
COMMON CARD (H1-H60)	1.00	.45
STATED ODDS 1:12 HOBBY		
COMP.AL PLAY.EXCH.SET (10)	20.00	9.00
COMP.AL PITCH.EXCH.SET (10)	6.00	2.70
COMP.AL ROOK.EXCH.SET (10)	8.00	3.60
COMP.NL PLAY.EXCH.SET (10)	12.00	5.50
COMP.NL PITCH.EXCH.SET (10)	8.00	3.60
COMP.NL ROOK.EXCH.SET (10)	6.00	2.70
*EXCH.CARDS: .6X TO 1.5X BASE CARD HI		
ONE EXCH.SET VIA MAIL PER PRED.WINNER		

❑	H1	Albert Belle	2.00	.90
❑	H2	Kenny Lofton	1.50	.70
❑	H3	Rafael Palmeiro	2.00	.90
❑	H4	Ken Griffey Jr.	10.00	4.50
❑	H5	Tim Salmon	1.50	.70
❑	H6	Cal Ripken	8.00	3.60
❑	H7	Mark McGwire W	10.00	4.50
❑	H8	Frank Thomas W	4.00	1.80
❑	H9	Mo Vaughn W	2.00	.90
❑	H10	Player of Month LS W	1.00	.45
❑	H11	Roger Clemens	5.00	2.20
❑	H12	David Cone	1.50	.70
❑	H13	Jose Mesa	1.00	.45
❑	H14	Randy Johnson	2.00	.90
❑	H15	Chuck Finley	1.25	.55
❑	H16	Mike Mussina	2.00	.90
❑	H17	Kevin Appier	1.25	.55
❑	H18	Kenny Rogers	1.00	.45
❑	H19	Lee Smith	1.25	.55
❑	H20	Pitcher of Month LS W	1.00	.45
❑	H21	George Arias	1.00	.45
❑	H22	Jose Herrera	1.00	.45
❑	H23	Tony Clark	2.00	.90
❑	H24	Todd Greene	1.00	.45
❑	H25	Derek Jeter W	5.00	2.20
❑	H26	Arquimedez Pozo	1.00	.45
❑	H27	Matt Lawton	2.00	.90
❑	H28	Shannon Stewart	1.25	.55
❑	H29	Chris Snopek	1.00	.45
❑	H30	Most Rookie Hits LS	1.00	.45
❑	H31	Jeff Bagwell W	2.50	1.10
❑	H32	Dante Bichette	1.25	.55
❑	H33	Barry Bonds W	2.50	1.10
❑	H34	Tony Gwynn W	5.00	2.20
❑	H35	Chipper Jones	5.00	2.20
❑	H36	Eric Karros	1.25	.55
❑	H37	Barry Larkin	2.00	.90
❑	H38	Mike Piazza	6.00	2.70
❑	H39	Matt Williams	2.00	.90
❑	H40	Long Shot Card	1.00	.45
❑	H41	Osvaldo Fernandez	1.00	.45
❑	H42	Tom Glavine	2.00	.90
❑	H43	Jason Isringhausen	1.25	.55
❑	H44	Greg Maddux	5.00	2.20
❑	H45	Pedro Martinez	2.50	1.10
❑	H46	Hideo Nomo	2.00	.90
❑	H47	Pete Schourek	1.00	.45
❑	H48	Paul Wilson	1.00	.45
❑	H49	Mark Wohlers	1.00	.45
❑	H50	Long Shot Card	1.00	.45
❑	H51	Bob Abreu	1.50	.70
❑	H52	Trey Beamon	1.00	.45
❑	H53	Yamil Benitez	1.00	.45
❑	H54	Roger Cedeno	1.25	.55
❑	H55	Todd Hollandsworth	1.00	.45
❑	H56	Marvin Benard	1.00	.45
❑	H57	Jason Kendall	2.00	.90
❑	H58	Brooks Kieschnick	1.00	.45
❑	H59	Rey Ordonez W	2.00	.90
❑	H60	Long Shot Card	1.00	.45

1996 Upper Deck Predictor Retail

	MINT	NRMT
COMPLETE SERIES 1 (30)	60.00	27.00
COMPLETE SERIES 2 (30)	30.00	13.50
COMMON CARD (R1-R60)	.75	.35
STATED ODDS 1:12 RETAIL		
COMP.AL HR EXCH.SET (10)	20.00	9.00
COMP.AL RBI EXCH.SET (10)	15.00	6.75
COMP.AL AVG.EXCH.SET (10)	15.00	6.75
COMP.NL HR EXCH.SET (10)	10.00	4.50
COMP.NL RBI EXCH.SET (10)	8.00	3.60
COMP.NL AVG.EXCH.SET (10)	10.00	4.50
*EXCH.CARDS: .6X TO 1.5X BASE CARD HI		
ONE EXCH.SET VIA MAIL PER PRED.WINNER		

❑	R1	Albert Belle W	1.50	.70
❑	R2	Jay Buhner W	1.00	.45
❑	R3	Juan Gonzalez	3.00	1.35
❑	R4	Ken Griffey Jr.	8.00	3.60
❑	R5	Mark McGwire W	8.00	3.60
❑	R6	Rafael Palmeiro	1.50	.70
❑	R7	Tim Salmon	1.25	.55
❑	R8	Frank Thomas	3.00	1.35
❑	R9	Mo Vaughn W	1.50	.70
❑	R10	Monthly HR Ldr LS W	.75	.35
❑	R11	Albert Belle W	1.50	.70
❑	R12	Jay Buhner	1.00	.45
❑	R13	Jim Edmonds	1.25	.55
❑	R14	Cecil Fielder	.75	.35
❑	R15	Ken Griffey Jr.	8.00	3.60
❑	R16	Edgar Martinez	1.00	.45
❑	R17	Manny Ramirez	2.00	.90
❑	R18	Frank Thomas	3.00	1.35
❑	R19	Mo Vaughn W	1.50	.70
❑	R20	Monthly RBI Ldr LS W	.75	.35
❑	R21	Roberto Alomar W	1.50	.70
❑	R22	Carlos Baerga	.75	.35
❑	R23	Wade Boggs	1.50	.70
❑	R24	Ken Griffey Jr.	8.00	3.60
❑	R25	Chuck Knoblauch	1.50	.70
❑	R26	Kenny Lofton	1.25	.55
❑	R27	Edgar Martinez	1.00	.45
❑	R28	Tim Salmon	1.25	.55
❑	R29	Frank Thomas	3.00	1.35
❑	R30	Monthly Hits Ldr Longshot W	.75	.35
❑	R31	Dante Bichette	1.00	.45
❑	R32	Barry Bonds W	2.00	.90
❑	R33	Ron Gant	.75	.35
❑	R34	Chipper Jones	4.00	1.80
❑	R35	Fred McGriff	1.25	.55
❑	R36	Mike Piazza	5.00	2.20
❑	R37	Sammy Sosa	5.00	2.20
❑	R38	Larry Walker	1.50	.70
❑	R39	Matt Williams	1.50	.70
❑	R40	Long Shot Card	.75	.35

	MINT	NRMT
❑ R41 Jeff Bagwell W	2.00	.90
❑ R42 Dante Bichette W	1.00	.45
❑ R43 Barry Bonds W	2.00	.90
❑ R44 Jeff Conine	.75	.35
❑ R45 Andres Galarraga	1.50	.70
❑ R46 Mike Piazza	5.00	2.20
❑ R47 Reggie Sanders	1.00	.45
❑ R48 Sammy Sosa	5.00	2.20
❑ R49 Matt Williams	1.50	.70
❑ R50 Long Shot Card	.75	.35
❑ R51 Jeff Bagwell	2.00	.90
❑ R52 Derek Bell	1.00	.45
❑ R53 Dante Bichette	1.00	.45
❑ R54 Craig Biggio	1.50	.70
❑ R55 Barry Bonds	2.00	.90
❑ R56 Bret Boone	1.00	.45
❑ R57 Tony Gwynn	4.00	1.80
❑ R58 Barry Larkin	1.50	.70
❑ R59 Mike Piazza W	5.00	2.20
❑ R60 Long Shot Card	.75	.35

1996 Upper Deck Ripken Collection

	MINT	NRMT
COMPLETE SET (23)	120.00	55.00
COMMON COLC (1-4/9-12)	3.00	1.35
COMMON UD (5-8/13-17)	6.00	2.70
COMMON SP (18-22)	12.00	5.50
HEADER CARD (CCH)	3.00	1.35

CARDS 1-4 STATED ODDS 1:12 CC SER.1
CARDS 5-8 STATED ODDS 1:24 UD SER.1
CARDS 9-12 STATED ODDS 1:12 CC SER.2
CARDS13-17 STATED ODDS 1:24 UD SER.2
CARDS18-22 STATED ODDS 1:45 SP

❑ 1 Cal Ripken COLC	3.00	1.35
After playing in 2,131 consecutive games		
❑ 2 Cal Ripken COLC	3.00	1.35
Barry Bonds 1995 All-Star Game		
❑ 3 Cal Ripken COLC	3.00	1.35
300th home run		
❑ 4 Cal Ripken COLC	3.00	1.35
Chasing Pop-up 1994		
❑ 5 Cal Ripken UD	6.00	2.70
Running to first 1995		
❑ 6 Cal Ripken UD	6.00	2.70
Brian McRae sliding into second 1992		
❑ 7 Cal Ripken UD	6.00	2.70
1992 Roberto Clemente Award		
❑ 8 Cal Ripken UD	6.00	2.70
Batting pose 1991		
❑ 9 Cal Ripken COLC	3.00	1.35
Batting follow-through 1991		
❑ 10 Cal Ripken COLC	3.00	1.35
1991 1st Gold Glove		
❑ 11 Cal Ripken COLC	3.00	1.35
Midway through swing 1991		
❑ 12 Cal Ripken.COLC	3.00	1.35
Fielding and throwing Ball		
❑ 13 Cal Ripken UD	6.00	2.70
Black uniform top in field 1990		
❑ 14 Cal Ripken UD	6.00	2.70
Batting follow-through 1987		
❑ 15 Cal Ripken UD	6.00	2.70
In Backswing 1986		
❑ 16 Cal Ripken UD	6.00	2.70
Midway through swing 1984		
❑ 17 Cal Ripken UD	6.00	2.70
Ball about to enter glove 1983		
❑ 18 Cal Ripken SP	12.00	5.50
Throwing 1983		
❑ 19 Cal Ripken SP	12.00	5.50
Batting, Orange Uniform 1983		
❑ 20 Cal Ripken SP	12.00	5.50
Batting follow-through 1982		
❑ 21 Cal Ripken SP	12.00	5.50
Fielding at third Mark Belanger in background 1981		
❑ 22 Cal Ripken SP	12.00	5.50
Eddie Murray 1981		
❑ NNO Cal Ripken Header COLC	4.00	1.80

1996 Upper Deck Run Producers

	MINT	NRMT
COMPLETE SET (20)	200.00	90.00
COMMON CARD (RP1-RP20)	4.00	1.80

SER.2 ODDS 1:72 HOB/RET, 1:36 ANCO
CONDITION SENSITIVE SET
THIS SET PRICED IN NRMT CONDITION

❑ RP1 Albert Belle	8.00	3.60
❑ RP2 Dante Bichette	4.00	1.80
❑ RP3 Barry Bonds	8.00	3.60
❑ RP4 Jay Buhner	4.00	1.80
❑ RP5 Jose Canseco	8.00	3.60
❑ RP6 Juan Gonzalez	20.00	9.00
❑ RP7 Ken Griffey Jr.	40.00	18.00
❑ RP8 Tony Gwynn	20.00	9.00
❑ RP9 Kenny Lofton	8.00	3.60
❑ RP10 Edgar Martinez	4.00	1.80
❑ RP11 Fred McGriff	6.00	2.70
❑ RP12 Mark McGwire	40.00	18.00
❑ RP13 Rafael Palmeiro	6.00	2.70
❑ RP14 Mike Piazza	25.00	11.00
❑ RP15 Manny Ramirez	8.00	3.60
❑ RP16 Tim Salmon	8.00	3.60
❑ RP17 Sammy Sosa	20.00	9.00
❑ RP18 Frank Thomas	20.00	9.00
❑ RP19 Mo Vaughn	8.00	3.60
❑ RP20 Matt Williams	4.00	1.80

1997 Upper Deck

	MINT	NRMT
COMP.MASTER SET (550)	210.00	95.00
COMPLETE SET (490)	115.00	52.50
COMPLETE SERIES 1 (240)	35.00	16.00
COMPLETE SERIES 2 (250)	80.00	36.00
COMP.SER.2 w/o GHL (240)	20.00	9.00
COMMON (1-240/271-520)	.15	.07
J.ROBINSON TRIB. (1-9)	.50	.23
MINOR STARS	.30	.14
UNLISTED STARS	.60	.25

SUBSET CARDS HALF VALUE OF BASE CARDS

	MINT	NRMT
COMP.UPDATE SET (30)	75.00	34.00
COMMON UPDATE (241-270)	.75	.35
UPDATE MINOR STARS	1.25	.55
UPDATE SEMISTARS	2.00	.90
UPDATE UNLISTED	3.00	1.35

ONE UPD.SET VIA MAIL PER 10 SER.1 WRAP.

	MINT	NRMT
COMP.TRADE SET (30)	25.00	11.00
COMMON TRADE (521-550)	.40	.18
TRADE MINOR STARS	.75	.35
TRADE UNLISTED STARS	1.50	.70

ONE TRD.SET VIA MAIL PER 10 SER.2 WRAP.
COMP.SET (490) EXCLUDES UPD/TRD SETS

❑ 1 Jackie Robinson	.50	.23
The Beginnings		
❑ 2 Jackie Robinson	.50	.23
Breaking the Barrier		
❑ 3 Jackie Robinson	.50	.23
The MVP Season, 1949		
❑ 4 Jackie Robinson	.50	.23
1951 season		
❑ 5 Jackie Robinson	.50	.23
1952 and 1953 seasons		
❑ 6 Jackie Robinson	.50	.23
1954 season		
❑ 7 Jackie Robinson	.50	.23
1955 season		
❑ 8 Jackie Robinson	.50	.23
1956 season		
❑ 9 Jackie Robinson	.50	.23
Hall of Fame		
❑ 10 Chipper Jones	1.50	.70
❑ 11 Marquis Grissom	.30	.14
❑ 12 Jermaine Dye	.30	.14
❑ 13 Mark Lemke	.15	.07
❑ 14 Terrell Wade	.15	.07
❑ 15 Fred McGriff	.40	.18
❑ 16 Tom Glavine	.60	.25
❑ 17 Mark Wohlers	.15	.07
❑ 18 Randy Myers	.15	.07
❑ 19 Roberto Alomar	.60	.25
❑ 20 Cal Ripken	2.50	1.10
❑ 21 Rafael Palmeiro	.60	.25
❑ 22 Mike Mussina	.60	.25
❑ 23 Brady Anderson	.30	.14
❑ 24 Jose Canseco	.75	.35
❑ 25 Mo Vaughn	.60	.25
❑ 26 Roger Clemens	1.50	.70
❑ 27 Tim Naehring	.15	.07
❑ 28 Jeff Suppan	.15	.07
❑ 29 Troy Percival	.30	.14
❑ 30 Sammy Sosa	2.00	.90
❑ 31 Amaury Telemaco	.15	.07
❑ 32 Rey Sanchez	.15	.07

33	Scott Servais	.15	.07
34	Steve Trachsel	.15	.07
35	Mark Grace	.40	.18
36	Wilson Alvarez	.30	.14
37	Harold Baines	.30	.14
38	Tony Phillips	.15	.07
39	James Baldwin	.30	.14
40	Frank Thomas UER	1.25	.55
	Bio information is Ken Griffey Jr.'s		
41	Lyle Mouton	.15	.07
42	Chris Snopek	.15	.07
43	Hal Morris	.15	.07
44	Eric Davis	.30	.14
45	Barry Larkin	.60	.25
46	Reggie Sanders	.30	.14
47	Pete Schourek	.15	.07
48	Lee Smith	.30	.14
49	Charles Nagy	.30	.14
50	Albert Belle	.60	.25
51	Julio Franco	.30	.14
52	Kenny Lofton	.40	.18
53	Orel Hershiser	.30	.14
54	Omar Vizquel	.30	.14
55	Eric Young	.30	.14
56	Curtis Leskanic	.15	.07
57	Quinton McCracken	.15	.07
58	Kevin Ritz	.15	.07
59	Walt Weiss	.15	.07
60	Dante Bichette	.30	.14
61	Mark Lewis	.15	.07
62	Tony Clark	.40	.18
63	Travis Fryman	.30	.14
64	John Smoltz SF	.30	.14
65	Greg Maddux SF	.75	.35
66	Tom Glavine SF	.30	.14
67	Mike Mussina SF	.30	.14
68	Andy Pettitte SF	.15	.07
69	Mariano Rivera SF	.15	.07
70	Hideo Nomo SF	.30	.14
71	Kevin Brown SF	.15	.07
72	Randy Johnson SF	.30	.14
73	Felipe Lira	.15	.07
74	Kimera Bartee	.15	.07
75	Alan Trammell	.30	.14
76	Kevin Brown	.40	.18
77	Edgar Renteria	.30	.14
78	Al Leiter	.30	.14
79	Charles Johnson	.30	.14
80	Andre Dawson	.40	.18
81	Billy Wagner	.30	.14
82	Donne Wall	.15	.07
83	Jeff Bagwell	.75	.35
84	Keith Lockhart	.15	.07
85	Jeff Montgomery	.15	.07
86	Tom Goodwin	.15	.07
87	Tim Belcher	.15	.07
88	Mike Macfarlane	.15	.07
89	Joe Randa	.15	.07
90	Brett Butler	.30	.14
91	Todd Worrell	.15	.07
92	Todd Hollandsworth	.15	.07
93	Ismael Valdes	.30	.14
94	Hideo Nomo	.60	.25
95	Mike Piazza	2.00	.90
96	Jeff Cirillo	.30	.14
97	Ricky Bones	.15	.07
98	Fernando Vina	.15	.07
99	Ben McDonald	.15	.07
100	John Jaha	.15	.07
101	Mark Loretta	.15	.07
102	Paul Molitor	.60	.25
103	Rick Aguilera	.15	.07
104	Marty Cordova	.15	.07
105	Kirby Puckett	1.00	.45
106	Dan Naulty	.15	.07
107	Frank Rodriguez	.15	.07
108	Shane Andrews	.15	.07
109	Henry Rodriguez	.30	.14
110	Mark Grudzielanek	.30	.14
111	Pedro Martinez	.75	.35
112	Ugueth Urbina	.30	.14
113	David Segui	.15	.07
114	Rey Ordonez	.30	.14
115	Bernard Gilkey	.15	.07
116	Butch Huskey	.15	.07
117	Paul Wilson	.15	.07
118	Alex Ochoa	.15	.07
119	John Franco	.30	.14
120	Dwight Gooden	.30	.14
121	Ruben Rivera	.15	.07
122	Andy Pettitte	.40	.18
123	Tino Martinez	.60	.25
124	Bernie Williams	.60	.25
125	Wade Boggs	.60	.25
126	Paul O'Neill	.30	.14
127	Scott Brosius	.30	.14
128	Ernie Young	.15	.07
129	Doug Johns	.15	.07
130	Geronimo Berroa	.15	.07
131	Jason Giambi	.30	.14
132	John Wasdin	.15	.07
133	Jim Eisenreich	.15	.07
134	Ricky Otero	.15	.07
135	Ricky Bottalico	.30	.14
136	Mark Langston DG	.15	.07
137	Greg Maddux DG	.75	.35
138	Ivan Rodriguez DG	.40	.18
139	Charles Johnson DG	.15	.07
140	J.T. Snow DG	.15	.07
141	Mark Grace DG	.15	.07
142	Roberto Alomar DG	.30	.14
143	Craig Biggio DG	.30	.14
144	Ken Caminiti DG	.15	.07
145	Matt Williams DG	.30	.14
146	Omar Vizquel DG	.15	.07
147	Cal Ripken DG	1.25	.55
148	Ozzie Smith DG	.60	.25
149	Rey Ordonez DG	.15	.07
150	Ken Griffey Jr. DG	1.50	.70
151	Devon White DG	.15	.07
152	Barry Bonds DG	.30	.14
153	Kenny Lofton DG	.30	.14
154	Mickey Morandini	.15	.07
155	Gregg Jefferies	.15	.07
156	Curt Schilling	.40	.18
157	Jason Kendall	.40	.18
158	Francisco Cordova	.15	.07
159	Dennis Eckersley	.30	.14
160	Ron Gant	.15	.07
161	Ozzie Smith	.75	.35
162	Brian Jordan	.30	.14
163	John Mabry	.15	.07
164	Andy Ashby	.15	.07
165	Steve Finley	.30	.14
166	Fernando Valenzuela	.30	.14
167	Archi Cianfrocco	.15	.07
168	Wally Joyner	.30	.14
169	Greg Vaughn	.30	.14
170	Barry Bonds	.75	.35
171	William VanLandingham	.15	.07
172	Marvin Benard	.15	.07
173	Rich Aurilia	.30	.14
174	Jay Canizaro	.15	.07
175	Ken Griffey Jr.	3.00	1.35
176	Bob Wells	.15	.07
177	Jay Buhner	.30	.14
178	Sterling Hitchcock	.30	.14
179	Edgar Martinez	.30	.14
180	Rusty Greer	.30	.14
181	Dave Nilsson GI	.15	.07
182	Larry Walker GI	.30	.14
183	Edgar Renteria GI	.15	.07
184	Rey Ordonez GI	.15	.07
185	Rafael Palmeiro GI	.30	.14
186	Osvaldo Fernandez GI	.15	.07
187	Raul Mondesi GI	.15	.07
188	Manny Ramirez GI	.40	.18
189	Sammy Sosa GI	1.00	.45
190	Devon White GI	.15	.07
191	Hideo Nomo GI	.30	.14
192	Hideo Nomo GI	.30	.14
193	Mac Suzuki GI	.15	.07
194	Chan Ho Park GI	.30	.14
195	Fernando Valenzuela GI	.15	.07
196	Andruw Jones GI	.40	.18
197	Vinny Castilla GI	.15	.07
198	Dennis Martinez GI	.15	.07
199	Ruben Rivera GI	.15	.07
200	Juan Gonzalez GI	.60	.25
201	Roberto Alomar GI	.30	.14
202	Edgar Martinez GI	.15	.07
203	Ivan Rodriguez GI	.40	.18
204	Carlos Delgado GI	.30	.14
205	Andres Galarraga GI	.30	.14
206	Ozzie Guillen GI	.15	.07
207	Midre Cummings GI	.15	.07
208	Roger Pavlik	.15	.07
209	Darren Oliver	.15	.07
210	Dean Palmer	.30	.14
211	Ivan Galarraga	.75	.35
212	Otis Nixon	.15	.07
213	Pat Hentgen	.30	.14
214	Ozzie Smith / Andre Dawson / Kirby Puckett HL/CL (1-27)	.30	.14
215	Barry Bonds / Gary Sheffield / Brady Anderson HL/CL (28-54)	.30	.14
216	Ken Caminiti SH CL	.15	.07
217	John Smoltz SH CL	.30	.14
218	Eric Young SH CL	.15	.07
219	Juan Gonzalez SH CL	.60	.25
220	Eddie Murray SH CL	.30	.14
221	Tommy Lasorda SH CL	.15	.07
222	Paul Molitor SH CL	.30	.14
223	Luis Castillo	.30	.14
224	Justin Thompson	.30	.14
225	Rocky Coppinger	.15	.07
226	Jermaine Allensworth	.15	.07
227	Jeff D'Amico	.15	.07
228	Jamey Wright	.15	.07
229	Scott Rolen	1.00	.45
230	Darin Erstad	.60	.25
231	Marty Janzen	.15	.07
232	Jacob Cruz	.15	.07
233	Raul Ibanez	.15	.07
234	Nomar Garciaparra	2.00	.90
235	Todd Walker	.60	.25
236	Brian Giles	2.00	.90
237	Matt Beech	.15	.07
238	Mike Cameron	.30	.14
239	Jose Paniagua	.15	.07
240	Andruw Jones	.75	.35
241	Brant Brown UPD	1.25	.55
242	Robin Jennings UPD	.75	.35
243	Willie Adams UPD	.75	.35
244	Ken Caminiti UPD	2.00	.90
245	Brian Jordan UPD	1.25	.55
246	Chipper Jones UPD	8.00	3.60
247	Juan Gonzalez UPD	6.00	2.70
248	Bernie Williams UPD	3.00	1.35
249	Roberto Alomar UPD	3.00	1.35
250	Bernie Williams UPD	3.00	1.35
251	David Wells UPD	1.25	.55
252	Cecil Fielder UPD	1.25	.55
253	Darryl Strawberry UPD	1.25	.55
254	Andy Pettitte UPD	2.00	.90
255	Javier Lopez UPD	1.25	.55
256	Gary Gaetti UPD	.75	.35
257	Ron Gant UPD	.75	.35
258	Brian Jordan UPD	1.25	.55
259	John Smoltz UPD	1.25	.55
260	Greg Maddux UPD	8.00	3.60
261	Tom Glavine UPD	3.00	1.35
262	Andruw Jones UPD	4.00	1.80
263	Greg Maddux UPD	8.00	3.60
264	David Cone UPD	2.00	.90
265	Jim Leyritz UPD	.75	.35
266	Andy Pettitte UPD	2.00	.90
267	John Wetteland UPD	.75	.55
268	Dario Veras UPD	1.25	.55
269	Neifi Perez UPD	1.25	.55
270	Bill Mueller UPD	4.00	1.80
271	Vladimir Guerrero	1.00	.45
272	Dmitri Young	.30	.14
273	Nerio Rodriguez	.30	.14
274	Kevin Orie	.15	.07
275	Felipe Crespo	.15	.07
276	Danny Graves	.15	.07
277	Rod Myers	.15	.07
278	Felix Heredia	.30	.14
279	Ralph Milliard	.15	.07
280	Greg Norton	.15	.07
281	Derek Wallace	.15	.07
282	Trot Nixon	.30	.14
283	Bobby Chouinard	.15	.07

#	Player	Price 1	Price 2
284	Jay Witasick	.15	.07
285	Travis Miller	.15	.07
286	Brian Bevil	.15	.07
287	Bobby Estalella	.15	.07
288	Steve Soderstrom	.15	.07
289	Mark Langston	.30	.14
290	Tim Salmon	.60	.25
291	Jim Edmonds	.40	.18
292	Garret Anderson	.30	.14
293	George Arias	.15	.07
294	Gary DiSarcina	.15	.07
295	Chuck Finley	.30	.14
296	Todd Greene	.15	.07
297	Randy Velarde	.15	.07
298	David Justice	.60	.25
299	Ryan Klesko	.30	.14
300	John Smoltz	.40	.18
301	Javier Lopez	.30	.14
302	Greg Maddux	1.50	.70
303	Denny Neagle	.30	.14
304	B.J. Surhoff	.30	.14
305	Chris Hoiles	.15	.07
306	Eric Davis	.30	.14
307	Scott Erickson	.30	.14
308	Mike Bordick	.15	.07
309	John Valentin	.30	.14
310	Heathcliff Slocumb	.15	.07
311	Tom Gordon	.15	.07
312	Mike Stanley	.15	.07
313	Reggie Jefferson	.15	.07
314	Darren Bragg	.15	.07
315	Troy O'Leary	.30	.14
316	John Mabry SH CL	.15	.07
317	Mark Whiten SH CL	.15	.07
318	Edgar Martinez SH CL	.15	.07
319	Alex Rodriguez SH CL	1.00	.45
320	Mark McGwire SH CL	1.50	.70
321	Hideo Nomo SH CL	.30	.14
322	Todd Hundley SH CL	.15	.07
323	Barry Bonds SH CL	.30	.14
324	Andruw Jones SH CL	.40	.18
325	Payne Sandberg	.75	.35
326	Brian McRae	.15	.07
327	Frank Castillo	.15	.07
328	Shawon Dunston	.15	.07
329	Ray Durham	.30	.14
330	Robin Ventura	.30	.14
331	Ozzie Guillen	.15	.07
332	Roberto Hernandez	.15	.07
333	Albert Belle	.60	.25
334	Dave Martinez	.15	.07
335	Willie Greene	.15	.07
336	Jeff Brantley	.15	.07
337	Kevin Jarvis	.15	.07
338	John Smiley	.15	.07
339	Eddie Taubensee	.15	.07
340	Bret Boone	.15	.07
341	Kevin Seitzer	.15	.07
342	Jack McDowell	.15	.07
343	Sandy Alomar Jr.	.30	.14
344	Chad Curtis	.15	.07
345	Manny Ramirez	.75	.35
346	Chad Ogea	.15	.07
347	Jim Thome	.60	.25
348	Mark Thompson	.15	.07
349	Ellis Burks	.30	.14
350	Andres Galarraga	.60	.25
351	Vinny Castilla	.40	.18
352	Kirt Manwaring	.15	.07
353	Larry Walker	.60	.25
354	Omar Olivares	.15	.07
355	Bobby Higginson	.30	.14
356	Melvin Nieves	.15	.07
357	Brian Johnson	.15	.07
358	Devon White	.30	.14
359	Jeff Conine	.15	.07
360	Gary Sheffield	.30	.14
361	Robb Nen	.15	.07
362	Mike Hampton	.30	.14
363	Bob Abreu	.30	.14
364	Luis Gonzalez	.30	.14
365	Derek Bell	.30	.14
366	Sean Berry	.15	.07
367	Craig Biggio	.60	.25
368	Darryl Kile	.15	.07
369	Shane Reynolds	.30	.14
370	Jeff Bagwell CF	.30	.14
371	Ron Gant CF	.15	.07
372	Andy Benes CF	.15	.07
373	Gary Gaetti CF	.15	.07
374	Ramon Martinez CF	.15	.07
375	Raul Mondesi CF	.30	.14
376	Steve Finley CF	.15	.07
377	Ken Caminiti CF	.15	.07
378	Tony Gwynn CF	.75	.35
379	Dario Veras	.40	.18
380	Andy Pettitte CF	.15	.07
381	Ruben Rivera CF	.15	.07
382	David Cone CF	.30	.14
383	Roberto Alomar CF	.30	.14
384	Edgar Martinez CF	.15	.07
385	Ken Griffey Jr. CF	1.50	.70
386	Mark McGwire CF	1.50	.70
387	Rusty Greer CF	.15	.07
388	Jose Rosado	.15	.07
389	Kevin Appier	.30	.14
390	Johnny Damon	.30	.14
391	Jose Offerman	.30	.14
392	Michael Tucker	.15	.07
393	Craig Paquette	.15	.07
394	Bip Roberts	.15	.07
395	Ramon Martinez	.30	.14
396	Greg Gagne	.15	.07
397	Chan Ho Park	.60	.25
398	Karim Garcia	.30	.14
399	Wilton Guerrero	.15	.07
400	Eric Karros	.30	.14
401	Raul Mondesi	.30	.14
402	Matt Mieske	.15	.07
403	Mike Fetters	.15	.07
404	Dave Nilsson	.15	.07
405	Jose Valentin	.15	.07
406	Scott Karl	.15	.07
407	Marc Newfield	.15	.07
408	Cal Eldred	.15	.07
409	Rich Becker	.30	.14
410	Terry Steinbach	.15	.07
411	Chuck Knoblauch	.60	.25
412	Pat Meares	.15	.07
413	Brad Radke	.30	.14
414	Kirby Puckett UER	1.00	.45
	Card numbered 415		
415	Andruw Jones GHL SP	3.00	1.35
416	Chipper Jones GHL SP	6.00	2.70
417	Mo Vaughn GHL SP	2.00	.90
418	Frank Thomas GHL SP	5.00	2.20
419	Albert Belle GHL SP	2.00	.90
420	Mark McGwire GHL SP	12.00	5.50
421	Derek Jeter GHL SP	8.00	3.60
422	Alex Rodriguez GHL SP	8.00	3.60
423	Juan Gonzalez GHL SP	5.00	2.20
424	Ken Griffey Jr. GHL SP	12.00	5.50
425	Rondell White	.30	.14
426	Darrin Fletcher	.15	.07
427	Cliff Floyd	.30	.14
428	Mike Lansing	.15	.07
429	F.P. Santangelo	.15	.07
430	Todd Hundley	.30	.14
431	Mark Clark	.15	.07
432	Pete Harnisch	.15	.07
433	Jason Isringhausen	.15	.07
434	Bobby Jones	.15	.07
435	Lance Johnson	.15	.07
436	Carlos Baerga	.15	.07
437	Mariano Duncan	.15	.07
438	David Cone	.40	.18
439	Mariano Rivera	.30	.14
440	Derek Jeter	2.00	.90
441	Joe Girardi	.15	.07
442	Charlie Hayes	.15	.07
443	Tim Raines	.30	.14
444	Darryl Strawberry	.30	.14
445	Cecil Fielder	.30	.14
446	Ariel Prieto	.15	.07
447	Tony Batista	.40	.18
448	Brent Gates	.15	.07
449	Scott Spiezio	.15	.07
450	Mark McGwire	3.00	1.35
451	Don Wengert	.15	.07
452	Mike Lieberthal	.15	.07
453	Lenny Dykstra	.30	.14
454	Rex Hudler	.15	.07
455	Darren Daulton	.30	.14
456	Kevin Stocker	.15	.07
457	Trey Beamon	.15	.07
458	Midre Cummings	.15	.07
459	Mark Johnson	.15	.07
460	Al Martin	.15	.07
461	Kevin Elster	.15	.07
462	Jon Lieber	.15	.07
463	Jason Schmidt	.15	.07
464	Paul Wagner	.15	.07
465	Andy Benes	.30	.14
466	Alan Benes	.15	.07
467	Royce Clayton	.15	.07
468	Gary Gaetti	.15	.07
469	Curt Lyons	.15	.07
470	Eugene Kingsale DD	.30	.14
471	Damian Jackson DD	.15	.07
472	Wendell Magee DD	.15	.07
473	Kevin L. Brown DD	.15	.07
474	Raul Casanova DD	.15	.07
475	Ramiro Mendoza DD	.50	.23
476	Todd Dunn DD	.15	.07
477	Chad Mottola DD	.15	.07
478	Andy Larkin DD	.15	.07
479	Jaime Bluma DD	.15	.07
480	Mac Suzuki DD	.15	.07
481	Brian Banks DD	.15	.07
482	Desi Wilson DD	.15	.07
483	Einar Diaz DD	.15	.07
484	Tom Pagnozzi	.15	.07
485	Ray Lankford	.30	.14
486	Todd Stottlemyre	.15	.07
487	Donovan Osborne	.15	.07
488	Trevor Hoffman	.30	.14
489	Chris Gomez	.15	.07
490	Ken Caminiti	.40	.18
491	John Flaherty	.15	.07
492	Tony Gwynn	1.50	.70
493	Joey Hamilton	.30	.14
494	Rickey Henderson	.75	.35
495	Glenallen Hill	.15	.07
496	Rod Beck	.15	.07
497	Osvaldo Fernandez	.15	.07
498	Rick Wilkins	.15	.07
499	Joey Cora	.15	.07
500	Alex Rodriguez	2.00	.90
501	Randy Johnson	.60	.25
502	Paul Sorrento	.15	.07
503	Dan Wilson	.15	.07
504	Jamie Moyer	.15	.07
505	Will Clark	.60	.25
506	Mickey Tettleton	.15	.07
507	John Burkett	.15	.07
508	Ken Hill	.15	.07
509	Mark McLemore	.15	.07
510	Juan Gonzalez	1.25	.55
511	Bobby Witt	.15	.07
512	Carlos Delgado	.60	.25
513	Alex Gonzalez	.15	.07
514	Shawn Green	.60	.25
515	Joe Carter	.30	.14
516	Juan Guzman	.15	.07
517	Charlie O'Brien	.15	.07
518	Ed Sprague	.15	.07
519	Mike Timlin	.15	.07
520	Roger Clemens	1.50	.70
521	Eddie Murray TRADE	1.50	.70
522	Jason Dickson TRADE	.40	.18
523	Jim Leyritz TRADE	.15	.07
524	Michael Tucker TRADE	.40	.18
525	Kenny Lofton TRADE	.75	.35
526	Jimmy Key TRADE	.75	.35
527	Mel Rojas TRADE	.40	.18
528	Deion Sanders TRADE	.75	.35
529	Bartolo Colon TRADE	.75	.35
530	Matt Williams TRADE	1.50	.70
531	Marquis Grissom TRADE	.75	.35
532	David Justice TRADE	1.50	.70
533	Bubba Trammell TRADE	1.50	.70
534	Moises Alou TRADE	.75	.35
535	Bobby Bonilla TRADE	.75	.35
536	Alex Fernandez TRADE	.40	.18
537	Jay Bell TRADE	.75	.35
538	Chili Davis TRADE	.75	.35
539	Jeff King TRADE	.40	.18
540	Todd Zeile TRADE	.40	.18

		MINT	NRMT
❏ 541	John Olerud TRADE	.75	.35
❏ 542	Jose Guillen TRADE	.75	.35
❏ 543	Derek Lee TRADE	.75	.35
❏ 544	Dante Powell TRADE	.75	.35
❏ 545	J.T. Snow TRADE	.75	.35
❏ 546	Jeff Kent TRADE	.75	.35
❏ 547	Jose Cruz Jr. TRADE	5.00	2.20
❏ 548	John Wetteland TRADE	.75	.35
❏ 549	Orlando Merced TRADE	.40	.18
❏ 550	Hideki Irabu TRADE	3.00	1.35

1997 Upper Deck Amazing Greats

		MINT	NRMT
COMPLETE SET (20)		350.00	160.00
COMMON CARD (AG1-AG20)		6.00	2.70
UNLISTED STARS		10.00	4.50
SER.1 STATED ODDS 1:69			
❏ AG1	Ken Griffey Jr.	50.00	22.00
❏ AG2	Roberto Alomar	10.00	4.50
❏ AG3	Alex Rodriguez	30.00	13.50
❏ AG4	Paul Molitor	10.00	4.50
❏ AG5	Chipper Jones	25.00	11.00
❏ AG6	Tony Gwynn	10.00	4.50
❏ AG7	Kenny Lofton	6.00	2.70
❏ AG8	Albert Belle	10.00	4.50
❏ AG9	Matt Williams	10.00	4.50
❏ AG10	Frank Thomas	20.00	9.00
❏ AG11	Greg Maddux	25.00	11.00
❏ AG12	Sammy Sosa	30.00	13.50
❏ AG13	Kirby Puckett	15.00	6.75
❏ AG14	Jeff Bagwell	12.00	5.50
❏ AG15	Cal Ripken	40.00	18.00
❏ AG16	Manny Ramirez	12.00	5.50
❏ AG17	Barry Bonds	12.00	5.50
❏ AG18	Mo Vaughn	10.00	4.50
❏ AG19	Eddie Murray	25.00	11.00
❏ AG20	Mike Piazza	30.00	13.50

1997 Upper Deck Blue Chip Prospects

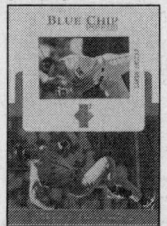

	MINT	NRMT
COMPLETE SET (20)	300.00	135.00
COMMON CARD (BC1-BC20)	4.00	1.80
MINOR STARS	8.00	3.60
UNLISTED STARS	15.00	6.75
RANDOM INSERTS IN SER.2 PACKS		

STATED PRINT RUN 500 SETS

		MINT	NRMT
❏ BC1	Andruw Jones	20.00	9.00
❏ BC2	Derek Jeter	50.00	22.00
❏ BC3	Scott Rolen	25.00	11.00
❏ BC4	Manny Ramirez	20.00	9.00
❏ BC5	Todd Walker	15.00	6.75
❏ BC6	Rocky Coppinger	4.00	1.80
❏ BC7	Nomar Garciaparra	50.00	22.00
❏ BC8	Darin Erstad	15.00	6.75
❏ BC9	Jermaine Dye	8.00	3.60
❏ BC10	Vladimir Guerrero	25.00	11.00
❏ BC11	Edgar Renteria	8.00	3.60
❏ BC12	Bob Abreu	8.00	3.60
❏ BC13	Karim Garcia	8.00	3.60
❏ BC14	Jeff D'Amico	4.00	1.80
❏ BC15	Chipper Jones	40.00	18.00
❏ BC16	Todd Hollandsworth	4.00	1.80
❏ BC17	Andy Pettitte	10.00	4.50
❏ BC18	Ruben Rivera	4.00	1.80
❏ BC19	Jason Kendall	10.00	4.50
❏ BC20	Alex Rodriguez	50.00	22.00

1997 Upper Deck Game Jersey

		MINT	NRMT
SER.1 STATED ODDS 1:800			
❏ GJ1	Ken Griffey Jr.	500.00	220.00
❏ GJ2	Tony Gwynn	150.00	70.00
❏ GJ3	Rey Ordonez	120.00	55.00

1997 Upper Deck Hot Commodities

		MINT	NRMT
COMPLETE SET (20)		100.00	45.00
COMMON CARD (HC1-HC20)		1.50	.70
SER.2 STATED ODDS 1:13			
❏ HC1	Alex Rodriguez	6.00	2.70
❏ HC2	Andruw Jones	2.50	1.10
❏ HC3	Derek Jeter	5.00	2.20
❏ HC4	Frank Thomas	4.00	1.80
❏ HC5	Ken Griffey Jr.	10.00	4.50
❏ HC6	Chipper Jones	5.00	2.20
❏ HC7	Juan Gonzalez	4.00	1.80
❏ HC8	Cal Ripken	8.00	3.60
❏ HC9	John Smoltz	1.50	.70
❏ HC10	Mark McGwire	10.00	4.50
❏ HC11	Barry Bonds	2.50	1.10
❏ HC12	Albert Belle	2.00	.90
❏ HC13	Mike Piazza	6.00	2.70
❏ HC14	Manny Ramirez	2.50	1.10
❏ HC15	Mo Vaughn	2.00	.90
❏ HC16	Tony Gwynn	5.00	2.20
❏ HC17	Vladimir Guerrero	3.00	1.35
❏ HC18	Hideo Nomo	2.00	.90
❏ HC19	Greg Maddux	6.00	2.70
❏ HC20	Kirby Puckett	3.00	1.35

1997 Upper Deck Long Distance Connection

		MINT	NRMT
COMPLETE SET (20)		150.00	70.00
COMMON CARD (LD1-LD20)		2.50	1.10
SER.2 STATED ODDS 1:35			
❏ LD1	Mark McGwire	25.00	11.00
❏ LD2	Brady Anderson	4.00	1.80
❏ LD3	Ken Griffey Jr.	25.00	11.00
❏ LD4	Albert Belle	5.00	2.20
❏ LD5	Juan Gonzalez	10.00	4.50
❏ LD6	Andres Galarraga	5.00	2.20
❏ LD7	Jay Buhner	4.00	1.80
❏ LD8	Mo Vaughn	5.00	2.20
❏ LD9	Barry Bonds	6.00	2.70
❏ LD10	Gary Sheffield	4.00	1.80
❏ LD11	Todd Hundley	2.50	1.10
❏ LD12	Frank Thomas	10.00	4.50
❏ LD13	Sammy Sosa	15.00	6.75
❏ LD14	Rafael Palmeiro	5.00	2.20
❏ LD15	Alex Rodriguez	15.00	6.75
❏ LD16	Mike Piazza	15.00	6.75
❏ LD17	Ken Caminiti	5.00	2.20
❏ LD18	Chipper Jones	12.00	5.50
❏ LD19	Manny Ramirez	6.00	2.70
❏ LD20	Andy Jones	5.00	2.20

1997 Upper Deck Memorable Moments

	MINT	NRMT
COMPLETE SERIES 1 (10)	15.00	6.75
COMPLETE SERIES 2 (10)	15.00	6.75
COMMON CARD (A1-B10)	.60	.25
ONE PER CC1 AND CC2 6-CARD RETAIL PACK		
❏ A1	Andruw Jones	.75	.35
❏ A2	Chipper Jones	1.50	.70
❏ A3	Cal Ripken	2.50	1.10

	MINT	NRMT
❏ A4 Frank Thomas	1.25	.55
❏ A5 Manny Ramirez	.75	.35
❏ A6 Mike Piazza	2.00	.90
❏ A7 Mark McGwire	3.00	1.35
❏ A8 Barry Bonds	.75	.35
❏ A9 Ken Griffey Jr.	3.00	1.35
❏ A10 Alex Rodriguez	2.00	.90
❏ B1 Ken Griffey Jr.	3.00	1.35
❏ B2 Albert Belle	.60	.25
❏ B3 Derek Jeter	2.00	.90
❏ B4 Greg Maddux	1.50	.70
❏ B5 Tony Gwynn	1.50	.70
❏ B6 Ryne Sandberg	.75	.35
❏ B7 Juan Gonzalez	1.25	.55
❏ B8 Roger Clemens	1.50	.70
❏ B9 Jose Cruz Jr.	1.50	.70
❏ B10 Mo Vaughn	.60	.25

1997 Upper Deck Power Package

	MINT	NRMT
COMPLETE SET (20)	100.00	45.00
COMMON CARD (PP1-PP20)	2.00	.90
SER.1 STATED ODDS 1:24		

	MINT	NRMT
❏ PP1 Ken Griffey Jr.	20.00	9.00
❏ PP2 Joe Carter	3.00	1.35
❏ PP3 Rafael Palmeiro	4.00	1.80
❏ PP4 Jay Buhner	3.00	1.35
❏ PP5 Sammy Sosa	12.00	5.50
❏ PP6 Fred McGriff	4.00	1.80
❏ PP7 Jeff Bagwell	4.00	1.80
❏ PP8 Albert Belle	4.00	1.80
❏ PP9 Matt Williams	4.00	1.80
❏ PP10 Mark McGwire	20.00	9.00
❏ PP11 Gary Sheffield	3.00	1.35
❏ PP12 Tim Salmon	4.00	1.80
❏ PP13 Ryan Klesko	2.00	.90
❏ PP14 Manny Ramirez	5.00	2.20
❏ PP15 Mike Piazza	12.00	5.50
❏ PP16 Barry Bonds	5.00	2.20
❏ PP17 Mo Vaughn	4.00	1.80
❏ PP18 Jose Canseco	4.00	1.80
❏ PP19 Juan Gonzalez	8.00	3.60
❏ PP20 Frank Thomas	8.00	3.60

1997 Upper Deck Predictor

	MINT	NRMT
COMPLETE SET (30)	30.00	13.50
COMMON CARD (1-30)	.40	.18
*SCRATCHED SINGLES: .25X TO .6X BASE HI		
*EXCHANGED WINNERS: 1.25X TO 3X BASE HI		
SER.2 STATED ODDS 1:5		

	MINT	NRMT
❏ 1 Andruw Jones L	1.25	.55
❏ 2 Chipper Jones L	2.00	.90
❏ 3 Greg Maddux W	2.00	.90
Complete Game Shutout		
❏ 4 Fred McGriff W	.50	.23
4 Hits/2HR/3B		
❏ 5 John Smoltz W	.50	.23
Complete Game Shutout		
❏ 6 Brady Anderson W	.40	.18
Leadoff HR		
❏ 7 Cal Ripken W	3.00	1.35
Grand Slam		
❏ 8 Mo Vaughn W	.75	.35
3HR/6RBI		
❏ 9 Sammy Sosa L	3.00	1.35
❏ 10 Albert Belle W	.75	.35
Grand Slam/9th HR		
❏ 11 Frank Thomas L	2.00	.90
❏ 12 Kenny Lofton W	.50	.23
5 Hits		
❏ 13 Jim Thome W	.75	.35
❏ 14 Dante Bichette W	.40	.18
6RBI		
❏ 15 Andres Galarraga L	.75	.35
❏ 16 Gary Sheffield L	.40	.18
❏ 17 Hideo Nomo W	.75	.35
Base Hit		
❏ 18 Mike Piazza W	2.50	1.10
Steal/9th HR		
❏ 19 Derek Jeter W	2.50	1.10
2HR		
❏ 20 Bernie Williams L	.75	.35
❏ 21 Mark McGwire W	4.00	1.80
Grand Slam/4HR		
❏ 22 Ken Caminiti W	.50	.23
5RBI's		
❏ 23 Tony Gwynn W	2.00	.90
2 2B/3RBI		
❏ 24 Barry Bonds W	1.00	.45
5RBI's		
❏ 25 Jay Buhner W	.40	.18
5RBI's		
❏ 26 Ken Griffey Jr. W	4.00	1.80
3HR's		
❏ 27 Alex Rodriguez W	2.50	1.10
Cycle		
❏ 28 Juan Gonzalez W	1.50	.70
5RBI's		
❏ 29 Dean Palmer W	.40	.18
2HR's/5RBI's		
❏ 30 Roger Clemens W	2.00	.90
Complete Game Shutout		

1997 Upper Deck Rock Solid Foundation

	MINT	NRMT
COMPLETE SET (20)	40.00	18.00
COMMON CARD (RS1-RS20)	1.00	.45
SER.1 STATED ODDS 1:7		

	MINT	NRMT
❏ RS1 Alex Rodriguez	10.00	4.50
❏ RS2 Rey Ordonez	1.50	.70
❏ RS3 Derek Jeter	8.00	3.60
❏ RS4 Darin Erstad	3.00	1.35
❏ RS5 Chipper Jones	8.00	3.60
❏ RS6 Johnny Damon	1.50	.70
❏ RS7 Ryan Klesko	1.50	.70
❏ RS8 Charles Johnson	1.50	.70
❏ RS9 Andy Pettitte	2.00	.90
❏ RS10 Manny Ramirez	4.00	1.80
❏ RS11 Ivan Rodriguez	4.00	1.80
❏ RS12 Jason Kendall	2.00	.90
❏ RS13 Rondell White	1.50	.70
❏ RS14 Alex Ochoa	1.00	.45
❏ RS15 Javier Lopez	1.50	.70
❏ RS16 Pedro Martinez	4.00	1.80
❏ RS17 Carlos Delgado	3.00	1.35
❏ RS18 Paul Wilson	1.00	.45
❏ RS19 Alan Benes	1.00	.45
❏ RS20 Raul Mondesi	1.50	.70

1997 Upper Deck Run Producers

	MINT	NRMT
COMPLETE SET (24)	250.00	110.00
COMMON CARD (RP1-RP24)	4.00	1.80
SEMISTARS	5.00	2.20
UNLISTED STARS	8.00	3.60
SER.2 STATED ODDS 1:69		
CONDITION SENSITIVE SET		

	MINT	NRMT
❏ RP1 Ken Griffey Jr.	40.00	18.00
❏ RP2 Barry Bonds	10.00	4.50
❏ RP3 Albert Belle	8.00	3.60
❏ RP4 Mark McGwire	40.00	18.00
❏ RP5 Frank Thomas	15.00	6.75
❏ RP6 Juan Gonzalez	15.00	6.75
❏ RP7 Brady Anderson	4.00	1.80
❏ RP8 Andres Galarraga	8.00	3.60
❏ RP9 Rafael Palmeiro	8.00	3.60
❏ RP10 Alex Rodriguez	25.00	11.00
❏ RP11 Jay Buhner	4.00	1.80
❏ RP12 Gary Sheffield	4.00	1.80
❏ RP13 Sammy Sosa	25.00	11.00
❏ RP14 Dante Bichette	4.00	1.80
❏ RP15 Mike Piazza	25.00	11.00
❏ RP16 Manny Ramirez	10.00	4.50
❏ RP17 Kenny Lofton	5.00	2.20
❏ RP18 Mo Vaughn	8.00	3.60
❏ RP19 Tim Salmon	8.00	3.60
❏ RP20 Chipper Jones	20.00	9.00
❏ RP21 Jim Thome	8.00	3.60
❏ RP22 Ken Caminiti	5.00	2.20
❏ RP23 Jeff Bagwell	10.00	4.50
❏ RP24 Paul Molitor	8.00	3.60

1997 Upper Deck Star Attractions

	MINT	NRMT
COMPLETE SET (20)	30.00	13.50
COMMON CARD (1-20)	.75	.35
1-10 ONE PER UD MADNESS RETAIL PACK		
11-20 ONE PER CC MADNESS RETAIL PACK		

	MINT	NRMT
❏ 1 Ken Griffey Jr.	4.00	1.80

1998 Upper Deck

		MINT	NRMT
	COMPLETE SET (751)	225.00	100.00
	COMPLETE SERIES 1 (270)	50.00	22.00
	COMPLETE SERIES 2 (270)	50.00	22.00
	COMPLETE SERIES 3 (211)	125.00	55.00
	COMMON (1-600/631-750)	.15	.07
	MINOR STARS	.25	.11
	SEMISTARS	.40	.18
	UNLISTED STARS	.60	.25
	COMMON (601-630)	1.00	.45
	EP SEMISTARS	1.25	.55
	EP UNLISTED STARS	2.00	.90

❏ 2	Barry Bonds	1.00	.45
❏ 3	Jeff Bagwell	.75	.35
❏ 4	Nomar Garciaparra	2.00	.90
❏ 5	Tony Gwynn	2.00	.90
❏ 6	Roger Clemens	2.00	.90
❏ 7	Chipper Jones	2.00	.90
❏ 8	Tino Martinez	.75	.35
❏ 9	Albert Belle	.75	.35
❏ 10	Kenny Lofton	.75	.35
❏ 11	Alex Rodriguez	2.50	1.10
❏ 12	Mark McGwire	4.00	1.80
❏ 13	Cal Ripken	3.00	1.35
❏ 14	Larry Walker	.75	.35
❏ 15	Mike Piazza	2.50	1.10
❏ 16	Frank Thomas	1.50	.70
❏ 17	Juan Gonzalez	1.50	.70
❏ 18	Greg Maddux	2.00	.90
❏ 19	Jose Cruz Jr.	.75	.35
❏ 20	Mo Vaughn	.75	.35

1997 Upper Deck Ticket To Stardom

		MINT	NRMT
	COMPLETE SET (20)	100.00	45.00
	COMMON CARD (TS1-TS20)	1.50	.70
	MINOR STARS	3.00	1.35
	UNLISTED STARS	6.00	2.70
	SER.1 STATED ODDS 1:34		

❏ TS1	Chipper Jones	15.00	6.75
❏ TS2	Jermaine Dye	3.00	1.35
❏ TS3	Rey Ordonez	3.00	1.35
❏ TS4	Alex Ochoa	1.50	.70
❏ TS5	Derek Jeter	20.00	9.00
❏ TS6	Ruben Rivera	1.50	.70
❏ TS7	Billy Wagner	3.00	1.35
❏ TS8	Jason Kendall	5.00	2.20
❏ TS9	Darin Erstad	6.00	2.70
❏ TS10	Alex Rodriguez	20.00	9.00
❏ TS11	Bob Abreu	3.00	1.35
❏ TS12	Richard Hidalgo	3.00	1.35
❏ TS13	Karim Garcia	3.00	1.35
❏ TS14	Andruw Jones	8.00	3.60
❏ TS15	Carlos Delgado	6.00	2.70
❏ TS16	Rocky Coppinger	1.50	.70
❏ TS17	Jeff D'Amico	1.50	.70
❏ TS18	Johnny Damon	3.00	1.35
❏ TS19	John Wasdin	1.50	.70
❏ TS20	Manny Ramirez	8.00	3.60

❏ 1	Tino Martinez HIST	.15	.07
❏ 2	Jimmy Key HIST	.15	.07
❏ 3	Jay Buhner HIST	.15	.07
❏ 4	Mark Gardner HIST	.15	.07
❏ 5	Greg Maddux HIST	.75	.35
❏ 6	Pedro Martinez HIST	.40	.18
❏ 7	Hideo Nomo HIST	.25	.11
❏ 8	Sammy Sosa HIST	1.00	.45
❏ 9	Mark McGwire GHL	4.00	1.80
❏ 10	Ken Griffey Jr. GHL	3.00	1.35
❏ 11	Larry Walker GHL	.60	.25
❏ 12	Tino Martinez GHL	.25	.11
❏ 13	Mike Piazza GHL	2.00	.90
❏ 14	Jose Cruz Jr. GHL	.25	.11
❏ 15	Tony Gwynn GHL	1.50	.70
❏ 16	Greg Maddux GHL	1.50	.70
❏ 17	Roger Clemens GHL	1.50	.70
❏ 18	Alex Rodriguez GHL	2.00	.90
❏ 19	Shigetoshi Hasegawa	.25	.11
❏ 20	Eddie Murray	.60	.25
❏ 21	Jason Dickson	.15	.07
❏ 22	Darin Erstad	.40	.18
❏ 23	Chuck Finley	.25	.11
❏ 24	Dave Hollins	.15	.07
❏ 25	Garret Anderson	.25	.11
❏ 26	Michael Tucker	.15	.07
❏ 27	Kenny Lofton	.40	.18
❏ 28	Javier Lopez	.25	.11
❏ 29	Fred McGriff	.40	.18
❏ 30	Greg Maddux	1.50	.70
❏ 31	Jeff Blauser	.15	.07
❏ 32	John Smoltz	.40	.18
❏ 33	Mark Wohlers	.15	.07
❏ 34	Scott Erickson	.15	.07
❏ 35	Jimmy Key	.15	.07
❏ 36	Harold Baines	.25	.11
❏ 37	Randy Myers	.25	.11
❏ 38	B.J. Surhoff	.25	.11
❏ 39	Eric Davis	.25	.11
❏ 40	Rafael Palmeiro	.60	.25
❏ 41	Jeffrey Hammonds	.25	.11
❏ 42	Mo Vaughn	.60	.25
❏ 43	Darren Bragg	.15	.07
❏ 44	Tim Naehring	.15	.07
❏ 45	Darren Bragg	.15	.07
❏ 46	Aaron Sele	.25	.11
❏ 47	Troy O'Leary	.25	.11
❏ 48	John Valentin	.25	.11
❏ 49	Doug Glanville	.25	.11
❏ 50	Ryne Sandberg	.75	.35
❏ 51	Steve Trachsel	.15	.07
❏ 52	Mark Grace	.40	.18
❏ 53	Kevin Foster	.15	.07

❏ 54	Kevin Tapani	.15	.07
❏ 55	Kevin Orie	.15	.07
❏ 56	Lyle Mouton	.15	.07
❏ 57	Ray Durham	.25	.11
❏ 58	Jaime Navarro	.15	.07
❏ 59	Mike Cameron	.25	.11
❏ 60	Albert Belle	.60	.25
❏ 61	Doug Drabek	.15	.07
❏ 62	Chris Snopek	.15	.07
❏ 63	Ed Taubensee	.15	.07
❏ 64	Terry Pendleton	.25	.11
❏ 65	Barry Larkin	.60	.25
❏ 66	Willie Greene	.15	.07
❏ 67	Deion Sanders	.25	.11
❏ 68	Pokey Reese	.15	.07
❏ 69	Jeff Shaw	.15	.07
❏ 70	Jim Thome	.60	.25
❏ 71	Orel Hershiser	.25	.11
❏ 72	Omar Vizquel	.25	.11
❏ 73	Brian Giles	.25	.11
❏ 74	David Justice	.25	.11
❏ 75	Bartolo Colon	.25	.11
❏ 76	Sandy Alomar Jr.	.25	.11
❏ 77	Neifi Perez	.25	.11
❏ 78	Dante Bichette	.25	.11
❏ 79	Vinny Castilla	.25	.11
❏ 80	Eric Young	.15	.07
❏ 81	Quinton McCracken	.15	.07
❏ 82	Jamey Wright	.15	.07
❏ 83	John Thomson	.15	.07
❏ 84	Damion Easley	.25	.11
❏ 85	Justin Thompson	.25	.11
❏ 86	Willie Blair	.15	.07
❏ 87	Raul Casanova	.15	.07
❏ 88	Bobby Higginson	.25	.11
❏ 89	Bubba Trammell	.15	.07
❏ 90	Tony Clark	.25	.11
❏ 91	Livan Hernandez	.15	.07
❏ 92	Charles Johnson	.15	.07
❏ 93	Edgar Renteria	.25	.11
❏ 94	Alex Fernandez	.15	.07
❏ 95	Gary Sheffield	.25	.11
❏ 96	Moises Alou	.25	.11
❏ 97	Tony Saunders	.15	.07
❏ 98	Robb Nen	.15	.07
❏ 99	Darryl Kile	.15	.07
❏ 100	Craig Biggio	.60	.25
❏ 101	Chris Holt	.15	.07
❏ 102	Bob Abreu	.25	.11
❏ 103	Luis Gonzalez	.25	.11
❏ 104	Billy Wagner	.25	.11
❏ 105	Brad Ausmus	.15	.07
❏ 106	Chili Davis	.25	.11
❏ 107	Tim Belcher	.15	.07
❏ 108	Dean Palmer	.25	.11
❏ 109	Jeff King	.15	.07
❏ 110	Jose Rosado	.15	.07
❏ 111	Mike Macfarlane	.15	.07
❏ 112	Jay Bell	.25	.11
❏ 113	Todd Worrell	.15	.07
❏ 114	Chan Ho Park	.25	.11
❏ 115	Raul Mondesi	.25	.11
❏ 116	Brett Butler	.25	.11
❏ 117	Greg Gagne	.15	.07
❏ 118	Hideo Nomo	.60	.25
❏ 119	Todd Zeile	.25	.11
❏ 120	Eric Karros	.25	.11
❏ 121	Cal Eldred	.15	.07
❏ 122	Jeff D'Amico	.15	.07
❏ 123	Antone Williamson	.15	.07
❏ 124	Doug Jones	.15	.07
❏ 125	Dave Nilsson	.15	.07
❏ 126	Gerald Williams	.15	.07
❏ 127	Fernando Vina	.15	.07
❏ 128	Ron Coomer	.15	.07
❏ 129	Matt Lawton	.15	.07
❏ 130	Paul Molitor	.60	.25
❏ 131	Todd Walker	.25	.11
❏ 132	Rick Aguilera	.15	.07
❏ 133	Brad Radke	.25	.11
❏ 134	Bob Tewksbury	.15	.07
❏ 135	Vladimir Guerrero	.75	.35
❏ 136	Tony Gwynn DG	.75	.35
❏ 137	Roger Clemens DG	.75	.35
❏ 138	Dennis Eckersley DG	.15	.07
❏ 139	Brady Anderson DG	.15	.07

140	Ken Griffey Jr. DG	1.50	.70
141	Derek Jeter DG	1.00	.45
142	Ken Caminiti DG	.15	.07
143	Frank Thomas DG	.60	.25
144	Barry Bonds DG	.40	.18
145	Cal Ripken DG	1.25	.55
146	Alex Rodriguez DG	1.00	.45
147	Greg Maddux DG	.75	.35
148	Kenny Lofton DG	.25	.11
149	Mike Piazza DG	1.00	.45
150	Mark McGwire DG	2.00	.90
151	Andruw Jones DG	.25	.11
152	Rusty Greer DG	.15	.07
153	F.P. Santangelo DG	.15	.07
154	Mike Lansing	.15	.07
155	Lee Smith	.25	.11
156	Carlos Perez	.15	.07
157	Pedro Martinez	.75	.35
158	Ryan McGuire	.15	.07
159	F.P. Santangelo	.15	.07
160	Rondell White	.25	.11
161	Takashi Kashiwada	.40	.18
162	Butch Huskey	.25	.11
163	Edgardo Alfonzo	.40	.18
164	John Franco	.25	.11
165	Todd Hundley	.25	.11
166	Rey Ordonez	.25	.11
167	Armando Reynoso	.15	.07
168	John Olerud	.25	.11
169	Bernie Williams	.60	.25
170	Andy Pettitte	.25	.11
171	Wade Boggs	.60	.25
172	Paul O'Neill	.25	.11
173	Cecil Fielder	.25	.11
174	Charlie Hayes	.15	.07
175	David Cone	.40	.18
176	Hideki Irabu	.25	.11
177	Mark Bellhorn	.15	.07
178	Steve Karsay	.15	.07
179	Damon Mashore	.15	.07
180	Jason McDonald	.15	.07
181	Scott Spiezio	.15	.07
182	Ariel Prieto	.15	.07
183	Jason Giambi	.25	.11
184	Wendell Magee	.15	.07
185	Rico Brogna	.15	.07
186	Garrett Stephenson	.15	.07
187	Wayne Gomes	.15	.07
188	Ricky Bottalico	.15	.07
189	Mickey Morandini	.15	.07
190	Mike Lieberthal	.25	.11
191	Kevin Polcovich	.15	.07
192	Francisco Cordova	.15	.07
193	Kevin Young	.25	.11
194	Jon Lieber	.15	.07
195	Kevin Elster	.15	.07
196	Tony Womack	.25	.11
197	Lou Collier	.15	.07
198	Mike Difelice	.15	.07
199	Gary Gaetti	.25	.11
200	Dennis Eckersley	.25	.11
201	Alan Benes	.15	.07
202	Willie McGee	.25	.11
203	Ron Gant	.25	.11
204	Fernando Valenzuela	.25	.11
205	Mark McGwire	4.00	1.80
206	Archi Cianfrocco	.15	.07
207	Andy Ashby	.15	.07
208	Steve Finley	.25	.11
209	Quilvio Veras	.15	.07
210	Ken Caminiti	.25	.11
211	Rickey Henderson	.75	.35
212	Joey Hamilton	.15	.07
213	Derrek Lee	.15	.07
214	Bill Mueller	.15	.07
215	Shawn Estes	.15	.07
216	J.T. Snow	.25	.11
217	Mark Gardner	.15	.07
218	Terry Mulholland	.15	.07
219	Dante Powell	.15	.07
220	Jeff Kent	.25	.11
221	Jamie Moyer	.15	.07
222	Joey Cora	.15	.07
223	Jeff Fassero	.15	.07
224	Dennis Martinez	.25	.11
225	Ken Griffey Jr.	3.00	1.35
226	Edgar Martinez	.25	.11
227	Russ Davis	.25	.11
228	Dan Wilson	.15	.07
229	Will Clark	.60	.25
230	Ivan Rodriguez	.75	.35
231	Benji Gil	.15	.07
232	Lee Stevens	.15	.07
233	Mickey Tettleton	.15	.07
234	Julio Santana	.15	.07
235	Rusty Greer	.25	.11
236	Bobby Witt	.15	.07
237	Ed Sprague	.15	.07
238	Pat Hentgen	.15	.07
239	Kelvim Escobar	.25	.11
240	Joe Carter	.25	.11
241	Carlos Delgado	.25	.11
242	Shannon Stewart	.25	.11
243	Benito Santiago	.15	.07
244	Tino Martinez	.25	.11
245	Ken Griffey Jr. SH	1.50	.70
246	Kevin Brown SH	.25	.11
247	Ryne Sandberg SH	.40	.18
248	Mo Vaughn SH	.25	.11
249	Darryl Hamilton SH	.15	.07
250	Randy Johnson SH	.25	.11
251	Steve Finley SH	.15	.07
252	Bobby Higginson SH	.15	.07
253	Brett Tomko	.15	.07
254	Mark Kotsay	.25	.11
255	Jose Guillen	.25	.11
256	Eli Marrero	.15	.07
257	Dennis Reyes	.15	.07
258	Richie Sexson	.40	.18
259	Pat Cline	.25	.11
260	Todd Helton	.75	.35
261	Juan Melo	.15	.07
262	Matt Morris	.25	.11
263	Jeremi Gonzalez	.15	.07
264	Jeff Abbott	.15	.07
265	Aaron Boone	.15	.07
266	Todd Dunwoody	.15	.07
267	Jaret Wright	.25	.11
268	Derrick Gibson	.25	.11
269	Mario Valdez	.15	.07
270	Fernando Tatis	.60	.25
271	Craig Counsell	.15	.07
272	Brad Rigby	.15	.07
273	Danny Clyburn	.15	.07
274	Brian Rose	.15	.07
275	Miguel Tejada	.25	.11
276	Jason Varitek	.25	.11
277	Dave Dellucci	.50	.23
278	Michael Coleman	.25	.11
279	Adam Riggs	.15	.07
280	Ben Grieve	.60	.25
281	Brad Fullmer	.15	.07
282	Ken Cloude	.15	.07
283	Tom Evans	.15	.07
284	Kevin Millwood	2.00	.90
285	Paul Konerko	.25	.11
286	Juan Encarnacion	.25	.11
287	Chris Carpenter	.25	.11
288	Tom Fordham	.15	.07
289	Gary DiSarcina	.15	.07
290	Tim Salmon	.40	.18
291	Troy Percival	.25	.11
292	Todd Greene	.15	.07
293	Ken Hill	.15	.07
294	Dennis Springer	.15	.07
295	Jim Edmonds	.25	.11
296	Allen Watson	.15	.07
297	Brian Anderson	.15	.07
298	Keith Lockhart	.15	.07
299	Tom Glavine	.60	.25
300	Chipper Jones	1.50	.70
301	Randall Simon	.25	.11
302	Mark Lemke	.15	.07
303	Ryan Klesko	.25	.11
304	Denny Neagle	.15	.07
305	Andruw Jones	.60	.25
306	Mike Mussina	.60	.25
307	Brady Anderson	.25	.11
308	Chris Hoiles	.15	.07
309	Mike Bordick	.15	.07
310	Cal Ripken	2.50	1.10
311	Geronimo Berroa	.15	.07
312	Armando Benitez	.15	.07
313	Roberto Alomar	.60	.25
314	Tim Wakefield	.15	.07
315	Reggie Jefferson	.15	.07
316	Jeff Frye	.15	.07
317	Scott Hatteberg	.15	.07
318	Steve Avery	.15	.07
319	Robinson Checo	.15	.07
320	Nomar Garciaparra	2.00	.90
321	Lance Johnson	.15	.07
322	Tyler Houston	.15	.07
323	Mark Clark	.15	.07
324	Terry Adams	.15	.07
325	Sammy Sosa	2.00	.90
326	Scott Servais	.15	.07
327	Manny Alexander	.15	.07
328	Norberto Martin	.15	.07
329	Scott Eyre	.15	.07
330	Frank Thomas	1.25	.55
331	Robin Ventura	.25	.11
332	Matt Karchner	.15	.07
333	Keith Foulke	.15	.07
334	James Baldwin	.15	.07
335	Chris Stynes	.15	.07
336	Bret Boone	.25	.11
337	Jon Nunnally	.15	.07
338	Dave Burba	.15	.07
339	Eduardo Perez	.15	.07
340	Reggie Sanders	.15	.07
341	Mike Remlinger	.15	.07
342	Pat Watkins	.15	.07
343	Chad Ogea	.15	.07
344	John Smiley	.15	.07
345	Kenny Lofton	.40	.18
346	Jose Mesa	.15	.07
347	Charles Nagy	.25	.11
348	Enrique Wilson	.15	.07
349	Bruce Aven	.15	.07
350	Manny Ramirez	.75	.35
351	Jerry DiPoto	.15	.07
352	Ellis Burks	.25	.11
353	Kirt Manwaring	.15	.07
354	Vinny Castilla	.25	.11
355	Larry Walker	.60	.25
356	Kevin Ritz	.15	.07
357	Pedro Astacio	.15	.07
358	Scott Sanders	.15	.07
359	Deivi Cruz	.15	.07
360	Brian L. Hunter	.15	.07
361	Pedro Martinez HM	.40	.18
362	Tom Glavine HM	.25	.11
363	Willie McGee HM	.15	.07
364	J.T. Snow HM	.15	.07
365	Rusty Greer HM	.15	.07
366	Mike Grace HM	.15	.07
367	Tony Clark HM	.25	.11
368	Ben Grieve HM	.40	.18
369	Gary Sheffield HM	.15	.07
370	Joe Oliver	.15	.07
371	Todd Jones	.15	.07
372	Frank Catalanotto	.25	.11
373	Brian Moehler	.15	.07
374	Cliff Floyd	.25	.11
375	Bobby Bonilla	.25	.11
376	Al Leiter	.15	.07
377	Josh Booty	.15	.07
378	Darren Daulton	.25	.11
379	Jay Powell	.15	.07
380	Felix Heredia	.15	.07
381	Jim Eisenreich	.15	.07
382	Richard Hidalgo	.25	.11
383	Mike Hampton	.25	.11
384	Shane Reynolds	.25	.11
385	Jeff Bagwell	.75	.35
386	Derek Bell	.25	.11
387	Ricky Gutierrez	.15	.07
388	Bill Spiers	.15	.07
389	Jose Offerman	.25	.11
390	Johnny Damon	.25	.11
391	Jermaine Dye	.25	.11
392	Jeff Montgomery	.15	.07
393	Glendon Rusch	.15	.07
394	Mike Sweeney	.25	.11
395	Kevin Appier	.25	.11
396	Joe Vitiello	.15	.07
397	Ramon Martinez	.15	.07

398	Darren Dreifort	.15	.07
399	Wilton Guerrero	.15	.07
400	Mike Piazza	2.00	.90
401	Eddie Murray	.60	.25
402	Ismael Valdes	.15	.07
403	Todd Hollandsworth	.15	.07
404	Mark Loretta	.15	.07
405	Jeromy Burnitz	.25	.11
406	Jeff Cirillo	.25	.11
407	Scott Karl	.15	.07
408	Mike Matheny	.15	.07
409	Jose Valentin	.15	.07
410	John Jaha	.25	.11
411	Terry Steinbach	.15	.07
412	Toni Hunter	.15	.07
413	Pat Meares	.15	.07
414	Marty Cordova	.15	.07
415	Jaret Wright PH	.15	.07
416	Mike Mussina PH	.25	.11
417	John Smoltz PH	.25	.11
418	Devon White PH	.15	.07
419	Denny Neagle PH	.15	.07
420	Livan Hernandez PH	.15	.07
421	Kevin Brown PH	.25	.11
422	Marquis Grissom PH	.15	.07
423	Mike Mussina PH	.25	.11
424	Eric Davis PH	.15	.07
425	Tony Fernandez PH	.15	.07
426	Moises Alou PH	.15	.07
427	Sandy Alomar Jr. PH	.15	.07
428	Gary Sheffield PH	.15	.07
429	Jaret Wright PH	.15	.07
430	Livan Hernandez PH	.15	.07
431	Chad Ogea PH	.15	.07
432	Edgar Renteria PH	.15	.07
433	LaTroy Hawkins	.15	.07
434	Rich Robertson	.15	.07
435	Chuck Knoblauch	.25	.11
436	Jose Vidro	.15	.07
437	Dustin Hermanson	.15	.07
438	Jim Bullinger	.15	.07
439	Orlando Cabrera	.15	.07
440	Vladimir Guerrero	.75	.35
441	Ugueth Urbina	.15	.07
442	Brian McRae	.15	.07
443	Matt Franco	.15	.07
444	Bobby Jones	.15	.07
445	Bernard Gilkey	.15	.07
446	Dave Mlicki	.15	.07
447	Brian Bohanon	.15	.07
448	Mel Rojas	.15	.07
449	Tim Raines	.25	.11
450	Derek Jeter	2.00	.90
451	Roger Clemens UE	.35	.15
452	Nomar Garciaparra UE	1.00	.45
453	Mike Piazza UE	1.00	.45
454	Mark McGwire UE	2.00	.90
455	Ken Griffey Jr. UE	1.50	.70
456	Larry Walker UE	.25	.11
457	Alex Rodriguez UE	1.00	.45
458	Tony Gwynn UE	.75	.35
459	Frank Thomas UE	.60	.25
460	Tino Martinez	.25	.11
461	Chad Curtis	.15	.07
462	Ramiro Mendoza	.15	.07
463	Joe Girardi	.15	.07
464	David Wells	.25	.11
465	Mariano Rivera	.25	.11
466	Willie Adams	.15	.07
467	George Williams	.15	.07
468	Dave Telgheder	.15	.07
469	Dave Magadan	.15	.07
470	Matt Stairs	.25	.11
471	Bill Taylor	.15	.07
472	Jimmy Haynes	.15	.07
473	Gregg Jefferies	.15	.07
474	Midre Cummings	.15	.07
475	Curt Schilling	.40	.18
476	Mike Grace	.15	.07
477	Mark Leiter	.15	.07
478	Matt Beech	.15	.07
479	Scott Rolen	.75	.35
480	Jason Kendall	.25	.11
481	Esteban Loaiza	.15	.07
482	Jermaine Allensworth	.15	.07
483	Mark Smith	.15	.07
484	Jason Schmidt	.15	.07
485	Jose Guillen	.15	.07
486	Al Martin	.15	.07
487	Delino DeShields	.15	.07
488	Todd Stottlemyre	.15	.07
489	Brian Jordan	.25	.11
490	Ray Lankford	.25	.11
491	Matt Morris	.15	.07
492	Royce Clayton	.15	.07
493	John Mabry	.15	.07
494	Wally Joyner	.25	.11
495	Trevor Hoffman	.25	.11
496	Chris Gomez	.15	.07
497	Sterling Hitchcock	.15	.07
498	Pete Smith	.15	.07
499	Greg Vaughn	.25	.11
500	Tony Gwynn	1.50	.70
501	Will Cunnane	.15	.07
502	Darryl Hamilton	.15	.07
503	Brian Johnson	.15	.07
504	Kirk Rueter	.15	.07
505	Barry Bonds	.75	.35
506	Osvaldo Fernandez	.15	.07
507	Stan Javier	.15	.07
508	Julian Tavarez	.15	.07
509	Rich Aurilia	.15	.07
510	Alex Rodriguez	2.00	.90
511	David Segui	.15	.07
512	Rich Amaral	.15	.07
513	Raul Ibanez	.15	.07
514	Jay Buhner	.25	.11
515	Randy Johnson	.60	.25
516	Heathcliff Slocumb	.15	.07
517	Tony Saunders	.15	.07
518	Kevin Elster	.15	.07
519	John Burkett	.15	.07
520	Juan Gonzalez	1.25	.55
521	John Wetteland	.25	.11
522	Domingo Cedeno	.15	.07
523	Darren Oliver	.15	.07
524	Roger Pavlik	.15	.07
525	Jose Cruz Jr.	.25	.11
526	Woody Williams	.15	.07
527	Alex Gonzalez	.15	.07
528	Robert Person	.15	.07
529	Juan Guzman	.15	.07
530	Roger Clemens	1.50	.70
531	Shawn Green	.60	.25
532	Francisco Cordova SH / Ricardo Rincon / Mark Smith	.15	.07
533	Nomar Garciaparra SH	1.00	.45
534	Roger Clemens SH	.75	.35
535	Mark McGwire SH	2.00	.90
536	Larry Walker SH	.25	.11
537	Mike Piazza SH	1.00	.45
538	Curt Schilling SH	.15	.07
539	Tony Gwynn SH	.75	.35
540	Ken Griffey Jr. SH	1.50	.70
541	Carl Pavano	.15	.07
542	Shane Monahan	.15	.07
543	Gabe Kapler	2.00	.90
544	Eric Milton	.15	.07
545	Gary Matthews Jr.	.50	.23
546	Mike Kinkade	.40	.18
547	Ryan Christenson	.25	.11
548	Corey Koskie	.60	.25
549	Norm Hutchins	.15	.07
550	Russell Branyan	.25	.11
551	Masato Yoshii	.40	.18
552	Jesus Sanchez	.40	.18
553	Anthony Sanders	.15	.07
554	Edwin Diaz	.15	.07
555	Gabe Alvarez	.15	.07
556	Carlos Lee	1.25	.55
557	Mike Darr	.25	.11
558	Kerry Wood	.75	.35
559	Carlos Guillen	.15	.07
560	Sean Casey	1.00	.45
561	Manny Aybar	.25	.11
562	Octavio Dotel	.25	.11
563	Jarrod Washburn	.15	.07
564	Mark L. Johnson	.15	.07
565	Ramon Hernandez	.25	.11
566	Rich Butler	.40	.18
567	Mike Caruso	.15	.07
568	Cliff Politte	.15	.07
569	Scott Elarton	.15	.07
570	Magglio Ordonez	2.00	.90
571	Adam Butler	.25	.11
572	Marlon Anderson	.25	.11
573	Julio Ramirez	1.00	.45
574	Darron Ingram	.50	.23
575	Bruce Chen	.25	.11
576	Steve Woodard	.15	.07
577	Hiram Bocachica	.15	.07
578	Kevin Witt	.15	.07
579	Javier Vazquez	.15	.07
580	Alex Gonzalez	.25	.11
581	Brian Powell	.15	.07
582	Wes Helms	.15	.07
583	Ron Wright	.15	.07
584	Rafael Medina	.15	.07
585	Daryle Ward	.25	.11
586	Geoff Jenkins	.25	.11
587	Preston Wilson	.25	.11
588	Jim Chamblee	.15	.07
589	Mike Lowell	.60	.25
590	A.J. Hinch	.15	.07
591	Francisco Cordova	.40	.18
592	Rolando Arrojo	.60	.25
593	Braden Looper	.15	.07
594	Sidney Ponson	.25	.11
595	Matt Clement	.25	.11
596	Carlton Loewer	.15	.07
597	Brian Meadows	.15	.07
598	Danny Klassen	.15	.07
599	Larry Sutton	.15	.07
600	Travis Lee	.40	.18
601	Randy Johnson EP	2.00	.90
602	Greg Maddux EP	5.00	2.20
603	Roger Clemens EP	5.00	2.20
604	Jaret Wright EP	.75	.35
605	Mike Piazza EP	6.00	2.70
606	Tino Martinez EP	.75	.35
607	Frank Thomas EP	4.00	1.80
608	Mo Vaughn EP	2.00	.90
609	Todd Helton EP	2.50	1.10
610	Mark McGwire EP	12.00	5.50
611	Jeff Bagwell EP	2.50	1.10
612	Travis Lee EP	1.25	.55
613	Scott Rolen EP	2.50	1.10
614	Cal Ripken EP	8.00	3.60
615	Chipper Jones EP	5.00	2.20
616	Nomar Garciaparra EP	6.00	2.70
617	Alex Rodriguez EP	6.00	2.70
618	Derek Jeter EP	6.00	2.70
619	Tony Gwynn EP	5.00	2.20
620	Ken Griffey Jr. EP	10.00	4.50
621	Kenny Lofton EP	1.25	.55
622	Juan Gonzalez EP	4.00	1.80
623	Jose Cruz Jr. EP	.75	.35
624	Larry Walker EP	2.00	.90
625	Barry Bonds EP	2.50	1.10
626	Ben Grieve EP	2.00	.90
627	Andruw Jones EP	2.00	.90
628	Vladimir Guerrero EP	2.50	1.10
629	Paul Konerko EP	.75	.35
630	Paul Molitor EP	2.00	.90
631	Cecil Fielder EP	.25	.11
632	Jack McDowell EP	.15	.07
633	Mike James EP	.15	.07
634	Brian Anderson EP	.15	.07
635	Jay Bell EP	.25	.11
636	Devon White EP	.15	.07
637	Andy Stankiewicz EP	.15	.07
638	Tony Batista EP	.15	.07
639	Omar Daal EP	.15	.07
640	Matt Williams EP	.60	.25
641	Brent Brede EP	.15	.07
642	Jorge Fabregas EP	.15	.07
643	Karim Garcia EP	.15	.07
644	Felix Rodriguez EP	.15	.07
645	Andy Benes EP	.25	.11
646	Willie Blair EP	.15	.07
647	Jeff Suppan EP	.15	.07
648	Yamil Benitez EP	.15	.07
649	Walt Weiss EP	.25	.11
650	Andres Galarraga EP	.40	.18
651	Doug Drabek EP	.15	.07
652	Ozzie Guillen EP	.15	.07
653	Joe Carter EP	.25	.11

❑ 654 Dennis Eckersley	.25	.11
❑ 655 Pedro Martinez	.75	.35
❑ 656 Jim Leyritz	.15	.07
❑ 657 Henry Rodriguez	.25	.11
❑ 658 Rod Beck	.25	.11
❑ 659 Mickey Morandini	.15	.07
❑ 660 Jeff Blauser	.15	.07
❑ 661 Ruben Sierra	.15	.07
❑ 662 Mike Sirotka	.15	.07
❑ 663 Pete Harnisch	.15	.07
❑ 664 Damian Jackson	.15	.07
❑ 665 Dmitri Young	.15	.11
❑ 666 Steve Cooke	.15	.07
❑ 667 Geronimo Berroa	.15	.07
❑ 668 Shawon Dunston	.15	.07
❑ 669 Mike Jackson	.25	.11
❑ 670 Travis Fryman	.25	.11
❑ 671 Dwight Gooden	.15	.07
❑ 672 Paul Assenmacher	.15	.07
❑ 673 Eric Plunk	.15	.07
❑ 674 Mike Lansing	.15	.07
❑ 675 Darryl Kile	.15	.07
❑ 676 Luis Gonzalez	.25	.11
❑ 677 Frank Castillo	.15	.07
❑ 678 Joe Randa	.15	.07
❑ 679 Bip Roberts	.15	.07
❑ 680 Derrek Lee	.15	.07
❑ 681 Mike Piazza SP	5.00	2.20
New York Mets		
❑ 681A Mike Piazza SP	5.00	2.20
Florida Marlins		
❑ 682 Sean Berry	.15	.07
❑ 683 Ramon Garcia	.15	.07
❑ 684 Carl Everett	.25	.11
❑ 685 Moises Alou	.25	.11
❑ 686 Hal Morris	.15	.07
❑ 687 Jeff Conine	.15	.07
❑ 688 Gary Sheffield	.25	.11
❑ 689 Jose Vizcaino	.15	.07
❑ 690 Charles Johnson	.25	.11
❑ 691 Bobby Bonilla	.25	.11
❑ 692 Marquis Grissom	.15	.07
❑ 693 Alex Ochoa	.15	.07
❑ 694 Mike Morgan	.15	.07
❑ 695 Orlando Merced	.15	.07
❑ 696 David Ortiz	.15	.07
❑ 697 Brent Gates	.15	.07
❑ 698 Otis Nixon	.15	.07
❑ 699 Trey Moore	.15	.07
❑ 700 Derrick May	.15	.07
❑ 701 Rich Becker	.15	.07
❑ 702 Al Leiter	.25	.11
❑ 703 Chili Davis	.25	.11
❑ 704 Scott Brosius	.25	.11
❑ 705 Chuck Knoblauch	.25	.11
❑ 706 Kenny Rogers	.15	.07
❑ 707 Mike Blowers	.15	.07
❑ 708 Mike Fetters	.15	.07
❑ 709 Tom Candiotti	.15	.07
❑ 710 Rickey Henderson	.75	.35
❑ 711 Bob Abreu	.25	.11
❑ 712 Mark Lewis	.15	.07
❑ 713 Doug Glanville	.25	.11
❑ 714 Desi Relaford	.15	.07
❑ 715 Kent Mercker	.15	.07
❑ 716 Kevin Brown	.40	.18
❑ 717 James Mouton	.15	.07
❑ 718 Mark Langston	.15	.07
❑ 719 Greg Myers	.15	.07
❑ 720 Orel Hershiser	.25	.07
❑ 721 Charlie Hayes	.15	.07
❑ 722 Robb Nen	.15	.07
❑ 723 Glenallen Hill	.15	.07
❑ 724 Tony Saunders	.15	.07
❑ 725 Wade Boggs	.60	.25
❑ 726 Kevin Stocker	.15	.07
❑ 727 Wilson Alvarez	.15	.07
❑ 728 Albie Lopez	.15	.07
❑ 729 Dave Martinez	.15	.07
❑ 730 Fred McGriff	.40	.18
❑ 731 Quinton McCracken	.15	.07
❑ 732 Bryan Rekar	.15	.07
❑ 733 Paul Sorrento	.15	.07
❑ 734 Roberto Hernandez	.15	.07
❑ 735 Bubba Trammell	.15	.07
❑ 736 Miguel Cairo	.15	.07

❑ 737 John Flaherty	.15	.07
❑ 738 Terrell Wade	.15	.07
❑ 739 Roberto Kelly	.15	.07
❑ 740 Mark McLemore	.15	.07
❑ 741 Danny Patterson	.15	.07
❑ 742 Aaron Sele	.25	.11
❑ 743 Tony Fernandez	.25	.11
❑ 744 Randy Myers	.25	.11
❑ 745 Jose Canseco	.75	.35
❑ 746 Darrin Fletcher	.15	.07
❑ 747 Mike Stanley	.15	.07
❑ 748 Marquis Grissom SH CL	.15	.07
❑ 749 Fred McGriff SH CL	.25	.11
❑ 750 Travis Lee SH CL	.25	.11

1998 Upper Deck 10th Anniversary Preview

Mike Piazza

	MINT	NRMT
COMPLETE SET (60)	120.00	55.00
COMMON CARD (1-60)	.50	.23
SER.1 STATED ODDS 1:5		

❑ 1 Greg Maddux	6.00	2.70
❑ 2 Mike Mussina	2.50	1.10
❑ 3 Roger Clemens	6.00	2.70
❑ 4 Hideo Nomo	2.50	1.10
❑ 5 David Cone	1.50	.70
❑ 6 Tom Glavine	2.50	1.10
❑ 7 Andy Pettitte	1.00	.45
❑ 8 Jimmy Key	1.00	.45
❑ 9 Randy Johnson	2.50	1.10
❑ 10 Dennis Eckersley	1.00	.45
❑ 11 Lee Smith	1.00	.45
❑ 12 John Franco	1.00	.45
❑ 13 Randy Myers	1.00	.45
❑ 14 Mike Piazza	8.00	3.60
❑ 15 Ivan Rodriguez	3.00	1.35
❑ 16 Todd Hundley	1.00	.45
❑ 17 Sandy Alomar Jr.	1.00	.45
❑ 18 Frank Thomas	5.00	2.20
❑ 19 Rafael Palmeiro	2.50	1.10
❑ 20 Mark McGwire	15.00	6.75
❑ 21 Mo Vaughn	2.50	1.10
❑ 22 Fred McGriff	1.50	.70
❑ 23 Andres Galarraga	1.50	.70
❑ 24 Mark Grace	1.50	.70
❑ 25 Jeff Bagwell	3.00	1.35
❑ 26 Roberto Alomar	2.50	1.10
❑ 27 Chuck Knoblauch	1.00	.45
❑ 28 Ryne Sandberg	3.00	1.35
❑ 29 Eric Young	.50	.23
❑ 30 Craig Biggio	2.50	1.10
❑ 31 Carlos Baerga	.50	.23
❑ 32 Robin Ventura	1.00	.45
❑ 33 Matt Williams	2.50	1.10
❑ 34 Wade Boggs	2.50	1.10
❑ 35 Dean Palmer	1.00	.45
❑ 36 Chipper Jones	6.00	2.70
❑ 37 Vinny Castilla	1.00	.45
❑ 38 Ken Caminiti	1.00	.45
❑ 39 Omar Vizquel	1.00	.45
❑ 40 Cal Ripken	10.00	4.50
❑ 41 Derek Jeter	8.00	3.60
❑ 42 Alex Rodriguez	8.00	3.60
❑ 43 Barry Larkin	2.50	1.10
❑ 44 Mark Grudzielanek	.50	.23
❑ 45 Albert Belle	2.50	1.10

❑ 46 Manny Ramirez	3.00	1.35
❑ 47 Jose Canseco	3.00	1.35
❑ 48 Ken Griffey Jr.	12.00	5.50
❑ 49 Juan Gonzalez	5.00	2.20
❑ 50 Kenny Lofton	1.50	.70
❑ 51 Sammy Sosa	8.00	3.60
❑ 52 Larry Walker	2.50	1.10
❑ 53 Gary Sheffield	1.00	.45
❑ 54 Rickey Henderson	3.00	1.35
❑ 55 Tony Gwynn	6.00	2.70
❑ 56 Barry Bonds	3.00	1.35
❑ 57 Paul Molitor	2.50	1.10
❑ 58 Edgar Martinez	1.00	.45
❑ 59 Chili Davis	1.00	.45
❑ 60 Eddie Murray	2.50	1.10

1998 Upper Deck A Piece of the Action 1

	MINT	NRMT
SER.1 STATED ODDS 1:2500		
MULTI-COLOR PATCHES CARRY PREMIUMS		

❑ 1 Jay Buhner Bat	50.00	22.00
❑ 2 Tony Gwynn Bat	200.00	90.00
❑ 3 Tony Gwynn Jersey	250.00	110.00
❑ 4 Todd Hollandsworth Bat	40.00	18.00
❑ 5 Todd Hollandsworth Jersey	50.00	22.00
❑ 6 Greg Maddux Jersey	300.00	135.00
❑ 7 Alex Rodriguez Bat	250.00	110.00
❑ 8 Alex Rodriguez Jersey	300.00	135.00
❑ 9 Gary Sheffield Bat	50.00	22.00
❑ 10 Gary Sheffield Jersey	60.00	27.00

1998 Upper Deck A Piece of the Action 2

	MINT	NRMT
SER.2 STATED ODDS 1:2500		
STATED PRINT RUN 225 SETS		

❑ AJ Andruw Jones	200.00	90.00
❑ GS Gary Sheffield	100.00	45.00
❑ JB Jay Buhner	80.00	36.00
❑ RA Roberto Alomar	150.00	70.00

1998 Upper Deck A Piece of the Action 3

RANDOM INSERTS IN SER.3 PACKS
PRINT RUNS LISTED BELOW

		MINT	NRMT
❏ BG	Ben Grieve/200	150.00	70.00
❏ JC	Jose Cruz Jr./200	80.00	36.00
❏ KG	Ken Griffey Jr./300	600.00	275.00
❏ TL	Travis Lee/200	100.00	45.00
❏ KGS	Ken Griffey Jr. AU/24	5000.00	2200.00

1998 Upper Deck All-Star Credentials

		MINT	NRMT
COMPLETE SET (30)		120.00	55.00
COMMON CARD (AS1-AS30)		1.00	.45
SER.3 STATED ODDS 1:9			
❏ AS1	Ken Griffey Jr.	12.00	5.50
❏ AS2	Travis Lee	1.50	.70
❏ AS3	Ben Grieve	2.50	1.10
❏ AS4	Jose Cruz Jr.	1.00	.45
❏ AS5	Andruw Jones	2.50	1.10
❏ AS6	Craig Biggio	2.50	1.10
❏ AS7	Hideo Nomo	2.50	1.10
❏ AS8	Cal Ripken	10.00	4.50
❏ AS9	Jaret Wright	1.00	.45
❏ AS10	Mark McGwire	15.00	6.75
❏ AS11	Derek Jeter	8.00	3.60
❏ AS12	Scott Rolen	4.00	1.80
❏ AS13	Jeff Bagwell	3.00	1.35
❏ AS14	Manny Ramirez	3.00	1.35
❏ AS15	Alex Rodriguez	8.00	3.60
❏ AS16	Chipper Jones	6.00	2.70
❏ AS17	Larry Walker	2.50	1.10
❏ AS18	Barry Bonds	3.00	1.35
❏ AS19	Tony Gwynn	6.00	2.70
❏ AS20	Mike Piazza	8.00	3.60
❏ AS21	Roger Clemens	6.00	2.70
❏ AS22	Greg Maddux	6.00	2.70
❏ AS23	Jim Thome	2.50	1.10
❏ AS24	Tino Martinez	1.00	.45
❏ AS25	Nomar Garciaparra	8.00	3.60
❏ AS26	Juan Gonzalez	5.00	2.20
❏ AS27	Kenny Lofton	1.50	.70
❏ AS28	Randy Johnson	2.50	1.10
❏ AS29	Todd Helton	2.50	1.10
❏ AS30	Frank Thomas	5.00	2.20

1998 Upper Deck Amazing Greats

		MINT	NRMT
COMPLETE SET (30)		600.00	275.00
COMMON CARD (AG1-AG30)		5.00	2.20
SEMISTARS		8.00	3.60
UNLISTED STARS		12.00	5.50
STATED PRINT RUN 2000 SETS			
*DIE CUT STARS: 1X TO 2.5X HI COLUMN			
DIE CUT PRINT RUN 250 SERIAL #'d SETS			
RANDOM INSERTS IN SER.1 PACKS			
❏ AG1	Ken Griffey Jr.	60.00	27.00
❏ AG2	Derek Jeter	40.00	18.00
❏ AG3	Alex Rodriguez	40.00	18.00
❏ AG4	Paul Molitor	12.00	5.50
❏ AG5	Jeff Bagwell	15.00	6.75
❏ AG6	Larry Walker	12.00	5.50
❏ AG7	Kenny Lofton	8.00	3.60
❏ AG8	Cal Ripken	50.00	22.00
❏ AG9	Juan Gonzalez	25.00	11.00
❏ AG10	Chipper Jones	30.00	13.50
❏ AG11	Greg Maddux	30.00	13.50
❏ AG12	Roberto Alomar	12.00	5.50
❏ AG13	Mike Piazza	40.00	18.00
❏ AG14	Andres Galarraga	8.00	3.60
❏ AG15	Barry Bonds	15.00	6.75
❏ AG16	Andy Pettitte	5.00	2.20
❏ AG17	Nomar Garciaparra	40.00	18.00
❏ AG18	Tino Martinez	5.00	2.20
❏ AG19	Tony Gwynn	30.00	13.50
❏ AG20	Frank Thomas	25.00	11.00
❏ AG21	Roger Clemens	30.00	13.50
❏ AG22	Sammy Sosa	40.00	18.00
❏ AG23	Jose Cruz Jr.	5.00	2.20
❏ AG24	Manny Ramirez	15.00	6.75
❏ AG25	Mark McGwire	80.00	36.00
❏ AG26	Randy Johnson	12.00	5.50
❏ AG27	Mo Vaughn	12.00	5.50
❏ AG28	Gary Sheffield	5.00	2.20
❏ AG29	Andruw Jones	12.00	5.50
❏ AG30	Albert Belle	12.00	5.50

1998 Upper Deck Blue Chip Prospects

		MINT	NRMT
COMPLETE SET (30)		300.00	135.00
COMMON CARD (BC1-BC30)		3.00	1.35

		MINT	NRMT
MINOR STARS		5.00	2.20
SEMISTARS		8.00	3.60
UNLISTED STARS		12.00	5.50
RANDOM INSERTS IN SER.2 PACKS			
STATED PRINT RUN 2000 SETS			
❏ BC1	Nomar Garciaparra	40.00	18.00
❏ BC2	Scott Rolen	15.00	6.75
❏ BC3	Jason Dickson	3.00	1.35
❏ BC4	Darin Erstad	8.00	3.60
❏ BC5	Brad Fullmer	3.00	1.35
❏ BC6	Jaret Wright	5.00	2.20
❏ BC7	Justin Thompson	3.00	1.35
❏ BC8	Matt Morris	3.00	1.35
❏ BC9	Fernando Tatis	12.00	5.50
❏ BC10	Alex Rodriguez	40.00	18.00
❏ BC11	Todd Helton	12.00	5.50
❏ BC12	Andy Pettitte	5.00	2.20
❏ BC13	Jose Cruz Jr.	5.00	2.20
❏ BC14	Mark Kotsay	5.00	2.20
❏ BC15	Derek Jeter	40.00	18.00
❏ BC16	Paul Konerko	5.00	2.20
❏ BC17	Todd Dunwoody	3.00	1.35
❏ BC18	Vladimir Guerrero	15.00	6.75
❏ BC19	Miguel Tejada	5.00	2.20
❏ BC20	Chipper Jones	30.00	13.50
❏ BC21	Kevin Orie	3.00	1.35
❏ BC22	Juan Encarnacion	5.00	2.20
❏ BC23	Brian Rose	3.00	1.35
❏ BC24	Livan Hernandez	3.00	1.35
❏ BC25	Andruw Jones	12.00	5.50
❏ BC26	Brian Giles	5.00	2.20
❏ BC27	Brett Tomko	3.00	1.35
❏ BC28	Jose Guillen	3.00	1.35
❏ BC29	Aaron Boone	3.00	1.35
❏ BC30	Ben Grieve	12.00	5.50

1998 Upper Deck Clearly Dominant

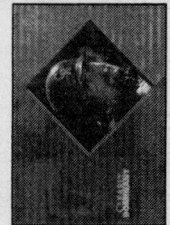

		MINT	NRMT
COMPLETE SET (30)		1500.00	700.00
COMMON CARD (CD1-CD30)		10.00	4.50
SEMISTARS		15.00	6.75
UNLISTED STARS		25.00	11.00
RANDOM INSERTS IN SER.2 PACKS			
STATED PRINT RUN 250 SERIAL #'d SETS			
❏ CD1	Mark McGwire	200.00	90.00
❏ CD2	Derek Jeter	100.00	45.00
❏ CD3	Alex Rodriguez	100.00	45.00
❏ CD4	Paul Molitor	25.00	11.00
❏ CD5	Jeff Bagwell	40.00	18.00
❏ CD6	Ivan Rodriguez	40.00	18.00
❏ CD7	Kenny Lofton	15.00	6.75
❏ CD8	Cal Ripken	120.00	55.00
❏ CD9	Albert Belle	25.00	11.00
❏ CD10	Chipper Jones	80.00	36.00
❏ CD11	Gary Sheffield	15.00	6.75
❏ CD12	Roberto Alomar	25.00	11.00
❏ CD13	Mo Vaughn	25.00	11.00
❏ CD14	Andres Galarraga	15.00	6.75
❏ CD15	Nomar Garciaparra	100.00	45.00
❏ CD16	Randy Johnson	25.00	11.00
❏ CD17	Mike Mussina	25.00	11.00
❏ CD18	Greg Maddux	80.00	36.00
❏ CD19	Tony Gwynn	80.00	36.00
❏ CD20	Frank Thomas	60.00	27.00

		MINT	NRMT
❑ CD21	Roger Clemens	80.00	36.00
❑ CD22	Dennis Eckersley	15.00	6.75
❑ CD23	Juan Gonzalez	60.00	27.00
❑ CD24	Tino Martinez	15.00	6.75
❑ CD25	Andruw Jones	25.00	11.00
❑ CD26	Larry Walker	25.00	11.00
❑ CD27	Ken Caminiti	15.00	6.75
❑ CD28	Mike Piazza	100.00	45.00
❑ CD29	Barry Bonds	40.00	18.00
❑ CD30	Ken Griffey Jr.	150.00	70.00

1998 Upper Deck Destination Stardom

	MINT	NRMT
COMPLETE SET (60)	150.00	70.00
COMMON CARD (DS1-DS60)	.75	.35
MINOR STARS	1.25	.55
SEMISTARS	2.00	.90
UNLISTED STARS	3.00	1.35
SER.3 STATED ODDS 1:5		
❑ DS1 Travis Lee	2.00	.90
❑ DS2 Nomar Garciaparra	10.00	4.50
❑ DS3 Alex Gonzalez	1.25	.55
❑ DS4 Richard Hidalgo	1.25	.55
❑ DS5 Jaret Wright	1.25	.55
❑ DS6 Mike Kinkade	3.00	1.35
❑ DS7 Matt Morris	.75	.35
❑ DS8 Gary Matthews Jr.	3.00	1.35
❑ DS9 Brett Tomko	.75	.35
❑ DS10 Todd Helton	4.00	1.80
❑ DS11 Scott Elarton	.75	.35
❑ DS12 Scott Rolen	4.00	1.80
❑ DS13 Jose Cruz Jr.	1.25	.55
❑ DS14 Jarrod Washburn	.75	.35
❑ DS15 Sean Casey	5.00	2.20
❑ DS16 Magglio Ordonez	10.00	4.50
❑ DS17 Gabe Alvarez	.75	.35
❑ DS18 Todd Dunwoody	.75	.35
❑ DS19 Kevin Witt	.75	.35
❑ DS20 Ben Grieve	3.00	1.35
❑ DS21 Daryle Ward	.75	.55
❑ DS22 Matt Clement	1.25	.55
❑ DS23 Carlton Loewer	.75	.35
❑ DS24 Javier Vazquez	.75	.35
❑ DS25 Paul Konerko	1.25	.55
❑ DS26 Preston Wilson	1.25	.55
❑ DS27 Wes Helms	.75	.35
❑ DS28 Derek Jeter	10.00	4.50
❑ DS29 Corey Koskie	3.00	1.35
❑ DS30 Russell Branyan	1.25	.55
❑ DS31 Vladimir Guerrero	4.00	1.80
❑ DS32 Ryan Christenson	1.25	.55
❑ DS33 Carlos Lee	6.00	2.70
❑ DS34 Dave Dellucci	3.00	1.35
❑ DS35 Bruce Chen	1.25	.55
❑ DS36 Ricky Ledee	1.25	.55
❑ DS37 Ron Wright	.75	.35
❑ DS38 Derrek Lee	.75	.35
❑ DS39 Miguel Tejada	1.25	.55
❑ DS40 Brad Fullmer	.75	.35
❑ DS41 Rich Butler	2.00	.90
❑ DS42 Chris Carpenter	1.25	.55
❑ DS43 Alex Rodriguez	10.00	4.50
❑ DS44 Darron Ingram	3.00	1.35
❑ DS45 Kerry Wood	4.00	1.80
❑ DS46 Jason Varitek	1.25	.55
❑ DS47 Ramon Hernandez	.75	.35
❑ DS48 Aaron Boone	.75	.35
❑ DS49 Juan Encarnacion	1.25	.55
❑ DS50 A.J. Hinch	.75	.35
❑ DS51 Mike Lowell	3.00	1.35
❑ DS52 Fernando Tatis	3.00	1.35
❑ DS53 Jose Guillen	.75	.35
❑ DS54 Mike Caruso	.75	.35
❑ DS55 Carl Pavano	.75	.35
❑ DS56 Chris Clemons	.75	.35
❑ DS57 Mark L. Johnson	.75	.35
❑ DS58 Ken Cloude	.75	.35
❑ DS59 Rolando Arrojo	5.00	2.20
❑ DS60 Mark Kotsay	1.25	.55

1998 Upper Deck Griffey Home Run Chronicles

Griffey holds fifth homer in air as Mariners win. April 6, 1998

	MINT	NRMT
COMPLETE SET (56)	220.00	100.00
COMPLETE SERIES 1 (30)	120.00	55.00
COMPLETE SERIES 2 (26)	100.00	45.00
COMMON GRIFFEY (1-56)	5.00	2.20
SER.1 AND 2 STATED ODDS 1:9		
❑ 1 Ken Griffey Jr. — April 1	5.00	2.20
❑ 2 Ken Griffey Jr. — April 1	5.00	2.20
❑ 3 Ken Griffey Jr. — April 4	5.00	2.20
❑ 4 Ken Griffey Jr. — April 5	5.00	2.20
❑ 5 Ken Griffey Jr. — April 6	5.00	2.20
❑ 6 Ken Griffey Jr. — April 8	5.00	2.20
❑ 7 Ken Griffey Jr. — April 16	5.00	2.20
❑ 8 Ken Griffey Jr. — April 17	5.00	2.20
❑ 9 Ken Griffey Jr. — April 21	5.00	2.20
❑ 10 Ken Griffey Jr. — April 23	5.00	2.20
❑ 11 Ken Griffey Jr. — April 25	5.00	2.20
❑ 12 Ken Griffey Jr. — April 25	5.00	2.20
❑ 13 Ken Griffey Jr. — April 25	5.00	2.20
❑ 14 Ken Griffey Jr. — May 2	5.00	2.20
❑ 15 Ken Griffey Jr. — May 9	5.00	2.20
❑ 16 Ken Griffey Jr. — May 12	5.00	2.20
❑ 17 Ken Griffey Jr. — May 14	5.00	2.20
❑ 18 Ken Griffey Jr. — May 15	5.00	2.20
❑ 19 Ken Griffey Jr. — May 18	5.00	2.20
❑ 20 Ken Griffey Jr. — May 20	5.00	2.20
❑ 21 Ken Griffey Jr. — May 22	5.00	2.20
❑ 22 Ken Griffey Jr. — May 25	5.00	2.20
❑ 23 Ken Griffey Jr. — May 27	5.00	2.20
❑ 24 Ken Griffey Jr. — May 30	5.00	2.20
❑ 25 Ken Griffey Jr. — June 2	5.00	2.20
❑ 26 Ken Griffey Jr. — June 10	5.00	2.20
❑ 27 Ken Griffey Jr. — June 14	5.00	2.20
❑ 28 Ken Griffey Jr. — June 20	5.00	2.20
❑ 29 Ken Griffey Jr. Jay Buhner — June 22	5.00	2.20
❑ 30 Ken Griffey Jr. — July 5	5.00	2.20
❑ 31 Ken Griffey Jr. — July 25	5.00	2.20
❑ 32 Ken Griffey Jr. — July 26	5.00	2.20
❑ 33 Ken Griffey Jr. — August 2	5.00	2.20
❑ 34 Ken Griffey Jr.#[August 7	5.00	2.20
❑ 35 Ken Griffey Jr. — August 8	5.00	2.20
❑ 36 Ken Griffey Jr. — August 10	5.00	2.20
❑ 37 Ken Griffey Jr. — August 12	5.00	2.20
❑ 38 Ken Griffey Jr.#[August 15	5.00	2.20
❑ 39 Ken Griffey Jr. — August 17	5.00	2.20
❑ 40 Ken Griffey Jr. — August 17	5.00	2.20
❑ 41 Ken Griffey Jr. — August 23	5.00	2.20
❑ 42 Ken Griffey Jr. — August 25	5.00	2.20
❑ 43 Ken Griffey Jr. — August 25	5.00	2.20
❑ 44 Ken Griffey Jr. — August 31	5.00	2.20
❑ 45 Ken Griffey Jr. — September 1	5.00	2.20
❑ 46 Ken Griffey Jr. — September 1	5.00	2.20
❑ 47 Ken Griffey Jr. — September 4	5.00	2.20
❑ 48 Ken Griffey Jr. — September 4	5.00	2.20
❑ 49 Ken Griffey Jr. — September 5	5.00	2.20
❑ 50 Ken Griffey Jr. — September 7	5.00	2.20
❑ 51 Ken Griffey Jr. — September 15	5.00	2.20
❑ 52 Ken Griffey Jr. — September 15	5.00	2.20
❑ 53 Ken Griffey Jr. — September 19	5.00	2.20
❑ 54 Ken Griffey Jr. — September 22	5.00	2.20
❑ 55 Ken Griffey Jr. — September 22	5.00	2.20
❑ 56 Ken Griffey Jr. — September 27	5.00	2.20

1998 Upper Deck National Pride

	MINT	NRMT
COMPLETE SET (42)	250.00	110.00
COMMON CARD (NP1-NP42)	2.50	1.10
MINOR STARS	4.00	1.80
SEMISTARS	6.00	2.70
UNLISTED STARS	10.00	4.50
SER.1 STATED ODDS 1:23		
❑ NP1 Dave Nilsson	2.50	1.10
❑ NP2 Larry Walker	10.00	4.50
❑ NP3 Edgar Renteria	2.50	1.10
❑ NP4 Jose Canseco	12.00	5.50
❑ NP5 Rey Ordonez	4.00	1.80

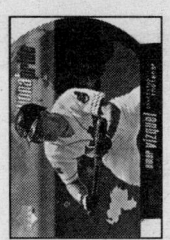

Card		MINT	NRMT
NP6	Rafael Palmeiro	10.00	4.50
NP7	Livan Hernandez	2.50	1.10
NP8	Andruw Jones	10.00	4.50
NP9	Manny Ramirez	12.00	5.50
NP10	Sammy Sosa	30.00	13.50
NP11	Raul Mondesi	4.00	1.80
NP12	Moises Alou	4.00	1.80
NP13	Pedro Martinez	12.00	5.50
NP14	Vladimir Guerrero	12.00	5.50
NP15	Chili Davis	4.00	1.80
NP16	Hideo Nomo	10.00	4.50
NP17	Hideki Irabu	4.00	1.80
NP18	Shigetoshi Hasegawa	4.00	1.80
NP19	Takashi Kashiwada	4.00	1.80
NP20	Chan Ho Park	4.00	1.80
NP21	Fernando Valenzuela	4.00	1.80
NP22	Vinny Castilla	4.00	1.80
NP23	Armando Reynoso	2.50	1.10
NP24	Karim Garcia	2.50	1.10
NP25	Marvin Benard	2.50	1.10
NP26	Mariano Rivera	4.00	1.80
NP27	Juan Gonzalez	20.00	9.00
NP28	Roberto Alomar	10.00	4.50
NP29	Ivan Rodriguez	12.00	5.50
NP30	Carlos Delgado	10.00	4.50
NP31	Bernie Williams	10.00	4.50
NP32	Edgar Martinez	4.00	1.80
NP33	Frank Thomas	20.00	9.00
NP34	Barry Bonds	12.00	5.50
NP35	Mike Piazza	30.00	13.50
NP36	Chipper Jones	25.00	11.00
NP37	Cal Ripken	40.00	18.00
NP38	Alex Rodriguez	30.00	13.50
NP39	Ken Griffey Jr.	50.00	22.00
NP40	Andres Galarraga	6.00	2.70
NP41	Omar Vizquel	4.00	1.80
NP42	Ozzie Guillen	2.50	1.10

1998 Upper Deck Prime Nine

	MINT	NRMT
COMPLETE SET (60)	250.00	110.00
COMMON GRIFFEY (1-7)	8.00	3.60
COMMON PIAZZA (8-14)	5.00	2.20
COMMON F.THOMAS (15-21)	3.00	1.35
COMMON MCGWIRE (22-28)	10.00	4.50
COMMON RIPKEN (29-35)	6.00	2.70
COMMON J.GONZALEZ (36-42)	3.00	1.35
COMMON GWYNN (43-49)	4.00	1.80
COMMON BONDS (50-55)	2.00	.90
COMMON MADDUX (56-60)	4.00	1.80
SER.2 STATED ODDS 1:5		

Card			MINT	NRMT
PN1	Ken Griffey Jr.	1989-92	8.00	3.60
PN2	Ken Griffey Jr.	1993	8.00	3.60
PN3	Ken Griffey Jr.	1994	8.00	3.60
PN4	Ken Griffey Jr.	1995	8.00	3.60
PN5	Ken Griffey Jr.	1996	8.00	3.60
PN6	Ken Griffey Jr.	1997	8.00	3.60
PN7	Ken Griffey Jr.	1997	8.00	3.60
PN8	Mike Piazza	1991	5.00	2.20
PN9	Mike Piazza	1992	5.00	2.20
PN10	Mike Piazza	1993	5.00	2.20
PN11	Mike Piazza	1994	5.00	2.20
PN12	Mike Piazza	1995	5.00	2.20
PN13	Mike Piazza	1996	5.00	2.20
PN14	Mike Piazza	1997	5.00	2.20
PN15	Frank Thomas	1991	3.00	1.35
PN16	Frank Thomas	1992	3.00	1.35
PN17	Frank Thomas	1993	3.00	1.35
PN18	Frank Thomas	1994	3.00	1.35
PN19	Frank Thomas	1995	3.00	1.35
PN20	Frank Thomas	1996	3.00	1.35
PN21	Frank Thomas	1996	3.00	1.35
PN22	Mark McGwire	1987	10.00	4.50
PN23	Mark McGwire	1988-90	10.00	4.50
PN24	Mark McGwire	1992	10.00	4.50
PN25	Mark McGwire	1995-96	10.00	4.50
PN26	Mark McGwire	1997	10.00	4.50
PN27	Mark McGwire	1997	10.00	4.50
PN28	Mark McGwire	1997	10.00	4.50
PN29	Cal Ripken	1982	6.00	2.70
PN30	Cal Ripken	1983	6.00	2.70
PN31	Cal Ripken	1989	6.00	2.70
PN32	Cal Ripken	1991	6.00	2.70
PN33	Cal Ripken	1995	6.00	2.70
PN34	Cal Ripken	1996	6.00	2.70
PN35	Cal Ripken	1997	6.00	2.70
PN36	Juan Gonzalez	1992	3.00	1.35
PN37	Juan Gonzalez	1993	3.00	1.35
PN38	Juan Gonzalez	1994	3.00	1.35
PN39	Juan Gonzalez	1995	3.00	1.35
PN40	Juan Gonzalez	1996	3.00	1.35
PN41	Juan Gonzalez	1996	3.00	1.35
PN42	Juan Gonzalez	1997	3.00	1.35
PN43	Tony Gwynn	1984	4.00	1.80
PN44	Tony Gwynn	1987-89	4.00	1.80
PN45	Tony Gwynn	1990-93	4.00	1.80
PN46	Tony Gwynn	1994	4.00	1.80
PN47	Tony Gwynn	1997	4.00	1.80
PN48	Tony Gwynn	1997	4.00	1.80
PN49	Tony Gwynn	1997	4.00	1.80
PN50	Barry Bonds	1986-92	2.00	.90
PN51	Barry Bonds	1990-93	2.00	.90
PN52	Barry Bonds	1993	2.00	.90
PN53	Barry Bonds	1994	2.00	.90
PN54	Barry Bonds	1996	2.00	.90
PN55	Barry Bonds	1997	2.00	.90
PN56	Greg Maddux	1992	4.00	1.80
PN57	Greg Maddux	1993-94	4.00	1.80
PN58	Greg Maddux	1995	4.00	1.80
PN59	Greg Maddux	1996	4.00	1.80
PN60	Greg Maddux	1997	4.00	1.80

1998 Upper Deck Retrospectives

	MINT	NRMT
COMPLETE SET (30)	250.00	110.00
COMMON CARD (1-30)	2.50	1.10
SER.3 STATED ODDS 1:24		

Card		MINT	NRMT
1	Dennis Eckersley	2.50	1.10
2	Rickey Henderson	8.00	3.60
3	Harold Baines	2.50	1.10
4	Cal Ripken	25.00	11.00
5	Tony Gwynn	15.00	6.75
6	Wade Boggs	6.00	2.70
7	Orel Hershiser	2.50	1.10
8	Joe Carter	2.50	1.10
9	Roger Clemens	15.00	6.75
10	Barry Bonds	8.00	3.60
11	Mark McGwire	40.00	18.00
12	Greg Maddux	15.00	6.75
13	Fred McGriff	4.00	1.80
14	Rafael Palmeiro	6.00	2.70
15	Craig Biggio	6.00	2.70
16	Brady Anderson	2.50	1.10
17	Randy Johnson	6.00	2.70
18	Gary Sheffield	2.50	1.10
19	Albert Belle	6.00	2.70
20	Ken Griffey Jr.	30.00	13.50
21	Juan Gonzalez	12.00	5.50

		MINT	NRMT
❏ 22	Larry Walker	6.00	2.70
❏ 23	Tino Martinez	2.50	1.10
❏ 24	Frank Thomas	12.00	5.50
❏ 25	Jeff Bagwell	8.00	3.60
❏ 26	Kenny Lofton	4.00	1.80
❏ 27	Mo Vaughn	6.00	2.70
❏ 28	Mike Piazza	20.00	9.00
❏ 29	Alex Rodriguez	20.00	9.00
❏ 30	Chipper Jones	15.00	6.75

1998 Upper Deck Rookie Edition Preview

star rookie

	MINT	NRMT
COMPLETE SET (10)	10.00	4.50
COMMON CARD (1-10)	.40	.18
RANDOM INSERTS IN SER.2 PACKS		

		MINT	NRMT
❏ 1	Nomar Garciaparra	3.00	1.35
❏ 2	Scott Rolen	1.50	.70
❏ 3	Mark Kotsay	.40	.18
❏ 4	Todd Helton	1.00	.45
❏ 5	Paul Konerko	.40	.18
❏ 6	Juan Encarnacion	.40	.18
❏ 7	Brad Fullmer	.40	.18
❏ 8	Miguel Tejada	.40	.18
❏ 9	Richard Hidalgo	.40	.18
❏ 10	Ben Grieve	1.00	.45

1998 Upper Deck Tape Measure Titans

	MINT	NRMT
COMPLETE SET (30)	250.00	110.00
COMMON CARD (1-30)	2.50	1.10
SER.2 STATED ODDS 1:23		

		MINT	NRMT
❏ 1	Mark McGwire	40.00	18.00
❏ 2	Andres Galarraga	4.00	1.80
❏ 3	Jeff Bagwell	8.00	3.60
❏ 4	Larry Walker	6.00	2.70
❏ 5	Frank Thomas	12.00	5.50
❏ 6	Rafael Palmeiro	6.00	2.70
❏ 7	Nomar Garciaparra	20.00	9.00
❏ 8	Mo Vaughn	6.00	2.70
❏ 9	Albert Belle	6.00	2.70
❏ 10	Ken Griffey Jr.	30.00	13.50
❏ 11	Manny Ramirez	8.00	3.60
❏ 12	Jim Thome	6.00	2.70
❏ 13	Tony Clark	2.50	1.10

		MINT	NRMT
❏ 14	Juan Gonzalez	12.00	5.50
❏ 15	Mike Piazza	20.00	9.00
❏ 16	Jose Canseco	8.00	3.60
❏ 17	Jay Buhner	2.50	1.10
❏ 18	Alex Rodriguez	20.00	9.00
❏ 19	Jose Cruz Jr.	2.50	1.10
❏ 20	Tino Martinez	2.50	1.10
❏ 21	Carlos Delgado	6.00	2.70
❏ 22	Andruw Jones	6.00	2.70
❏ 23	Chipper Jones	15.00	6.75
❏ 24	Fred McGriff	4.00	1.80
❏ 25	Matt Williams	6.00	2.70
❏ 26	Sammy Sosa	20.00	9.00
❏ 27	Vinny Castilla	2.50	1.10
❏ 28	Tim Salmon	4.00	1.80
❏ 29	Ken Caminiti	2.50	1.10
❏ 30	Barry Bonds	8.00	3.60

1998 Upper Deck Unparalleled

	MINT	NRMT
COMPLETE SET (20)	500.00	220.00
COMMON CARD (1-20)	5.00	2.20
SEMISTARS	8.00	3.60
UNLISTED STARS	12.00	5.50
SER.3 STATED ODDS 1:72 HOBBY		

		MINT	NRMT
❏ 1	Ken Griffey Jr.	60.00	27.00
❏ 2	Travis Lee	8.00	3.60
❏ 3	Ben Grieve	12.00	5.50
❏ 4	Jose Cruz Jr.	5.00	2.20
❏ 5	Nomar Garciaparra	40.00	18.00
❏ 6	Hideo Nomo	12.00	5.50
❏ 7	Kenny Lofton	8.00	3.60
❏ 8	Cal Ripken	50.00	22.00
❏ 9	Roger Clemens	30.00	13.50
❏ 10	Mike Piazza	40.00	18.00
❏ 11	Jeff Bagwell	15.00	6.75
❏ 12	Chipper Jones	30.00	13.50
❏ 13	Greg Maddux	30.00	13.50
❏ 14	Randy Johnson	12.00	5.50
❏ 15	Alex Rodriguez	40.00	18.00
❏ 16	Barry Bonds	15.00	6.75
❏ 17	Frank Thomas	25.00	11.00
❏ 18	Juan Gonzalez	25.00	11.00
❏ 19	Tony Gwynn	30.00	13.50
❏ 20	Mark McGwire	80.00	36.00

1999 Upper Deck

	MINT	NRMT
COMPLETE SET (525)	110.00	50.00
COMPLETE SERIES 1 (255)	60.00	27.00
COMPLETE SERIES 2 (270)	50.00	22.00
COMMON (19-255/293-535)	.15	.07
MINOR STARS	.25	.11
SEMISTARS	.40	.18
UNLISTED STARS	.60	.25
COMMON SER.1 SR (1-18)	.50	.23
SER.1 SR MINOR STARS	1.00	.45
SER.1 SR SEMISTARS	1.50	.70
COMMON SER.2 SR (266-292)	.25	.11
SER.2 SR MINOR STARS	.50	.23
SER.2 SR SEMISTARS	.75	.35
SER.2 SR UNLISTED STARS	1.25	.55
CARDS 256-265 DO NOT EXIST		
GRIFFEY 89 AU SEEDED IN SER.1 PACKS		

		MINT	NRMT
❏ 1	Troy Glaus SR	2.50	1.10
❏ 2	Adrian Beltre SR	2.50	1.10
❏ 3	Matt Anderson SR	.50	.23
❏ 4	Eric Chavez SR	1.50	.70
❏ 5	Jin Ho Cho SR	1.00	.45
❏ 6	Robert Smith SR	.50	.23
❏ 7	George Lombard SR	1.00	.45
❏ 8	Mike Kinkade SR	.50	.23
❏ 9	Seth Greisinger SR	.50	.23
❏ 10	J.D. Drew SR	4.00	1.80
❏ 11	Aramis Ramirez SR	1.50	.70
❏ 12	Carlos Guillen SR	.50	.23
❏ 13	Justin Baughman SR	.50	.23
❏ 14	Jim Parque SR	.50	.23
❏ 15	Ryan Jackson SR	.50	.23
❏ 16	Ramon E.Martinez SR	.50	.23
❏ 17	Orlando Hernandez SR..	2.00	.90
❏ 18	Jeremy Giambi SR	1.00	.45
❏ 19	Gary DiSarcina	.15	.07
❏ 20	Darin Erstad	.40	.18
❏ 21	Troy Glaus	.60	.25
❏ 22	Chuck Finley	.25	.11
❏ 23	Dave Hollins	.15	.07
❏ 24	Troy Percival	.25	.11
❏ 25	Tim Salmon	.40	.18
❏ 26	Brian Anderson	.15	.07
❏ 27	Jay Bell	.25	.11
❏ 28	Andy Benes	.25	.11
❏ 29	Brent Brede	.15	.07
❏ 30	David Dellucci	.15	.07
❏ 31	Karim Garcia	.15	.07
❏ 32	Travis Lee	.40	.18
❏ 33	Andres Galarraga	.25	.11
❏ 34	Ryan Klesko	.25	.11
❏ 35	Keith Lockhart	.15	.07
❏ 36	Kevin Millwood	.40	.18
❏ 37	Denny Neagle	.25	.11
❏ 38	John Smoltz	.40	.18
❏ 39	Michael Tucker	.15	.07
❏ 40	Walt Weiss	.15	.07
❏ 41	Dennis Martinez	.25	.11
❏ 42	Javy Lopez	.25	.11
❏ 43	Brady Anderson	.25	.11
❏ 44	Harold Baines	.25	.11
❏ 45	Mike Bordick	.15	.07
❏ 46	Roberto Alomar	.60	.25
❏ 47	Scott Erickson	.15	.07
❏ 48	Mike Mussina	.60	.25
❏ 49	Cal Ripken	2.50	1.10
❏ 50	Darren Bragg	.15	.07
❏ 51	Dennis Eckersley	.25	.11
❏ 52	Nomar Garciaparra	2.00	.90
❏ 53	Scott Hatteberg	.15	.07
❏ 54	Troy O'Leary	.25	.11
❏ 55	Bret Saberhagen	.25	.11
❏ 56	John Valentin	.15	.07
❏ 57	Rod Beck	.25	.11
❏ 58	Jeff Blauser	.15	.07
❏ 59	Brant Brown	.15	.07
❏ 60	Mark Clark	.15	.07
❏ 61	Mark Grace	.40	.18
❏ 62	Kevin Tapani	.15	.07
❏ 63	Henry Rodriguez	.15	.07
❏ 64	Mike Cameron	.15	.07
❏ 65	Mike Caruso	.15	.07
❏ 66	Ray Durham	.25	.11
❏ 67	Jaime Navarro	.15	.07
❏ 68	Magglio Ordonez	.60	.25

69	Mike Sirotka	.15	.07
70	Sean Casey	.60	.25
71	Barry Larkin	.60	.25
72	Jon Nunnally	.15	.07
73	Paul Konerko	.60	.25
74	Chris Stynes	.15	.07
75	Brett Tomko	.15	.07
76	Dmitri Young	.25	.11
77	Sandy Alomar Jr.	.25	.11
78	Bartolo Colon	.25	.11
79	Travis Fryman	.25	.11
80	Brian Giles	.25	.11
81	David Justice	.25	.11
82	Omar Vizquel	.25	.11
83	Jaret Wright	.25	.11
84	Jim Thome	.60	.25
85	Charles Nagy	.25	.11
86	Pedro Astacio	.15	.07
87	Todd Helton	.60	.25
88	Darryl Kile	.15	.07
89	Mike Lansing	.15	.07
90	Neifi Perez	.25	.11
91	John Thomson	.15	.07
92	Larry Walker	.60	.25
93	Tony Clark	.25	.11
94	Deivi Cruz	.15	.07
95	Damion Easley	.25	.11
96	Brian L.Hunter	.15	.07
97	Todd Jones	.15	.07
98	Brian Moehler	.15	.07
99	Gabe Alvarez	.15	.07
100	Craig Counsell	.15	.07
101	Cliff Floyd	.25	.11
102	Livan Hernandez	.15	.07
103	Andy Larkin	.15	.07
104	Derrek Lee	.15	.07
105	Brian Meadows	.15	.07
106	Moises Alou	.25	.11
107	Sean Berry	.15	.07
108	Craig Biggio	.60	.25
109	Ricky Gutierrez	.15	.07
110	Mike Hampton	.25	.11
111	Jose Lima	.25	.11
112	Billy Wagner	.25	.11
113	Hal Morris	.15	.07
114	Johnny Damon	.25	.11
115	Jeff King	.15	.07
116	Jeff Montgomery	.15	.07
117	Glendon Rusch	.15	.07
118	Larry Sutton	.15	.07
119	Bobby Bonilla	.25	.11
120	Jim Eisenreich	.15	.07
121	Eric Karros	.25	.11
122	Matt Luke	.15	.07
123	Ramon Martinez	.25	.11
124	Gary Sheffield	.25	.11
125	Eric Young	.15	.07
126	Charles Johnson	.25	.11
127	Jeff Cirillo	.25	.11
128	Marquis Grissom	.25	.11
129	Jeromy Burnitz	.25	.11
130	Bob Wickman	.15	.07
131	Scott Karl	.15	.07
132	Mark Loretta	.15	.07
133	Fernando Vina	.15	.07
134	Matt Lawton	.15	.07
135	Pat Meares	.15	.07
136	Eric Milton	.15	.07
137	Paul Molitor	.60	.25
138	David Ortiz	.25	.07
139	Todd Walker	.25	.11
140	Shane Andrews	.15	.07
141	Brad Fullmer	.15	.07
142	Vladimir Guerrero	.75	.35
143	Dustin Hermanson	.15	.07
144	Ryan McGuire	.15	.07
145	Ugueth Urbina	.15	.07
146	John Franco	.25	.11
147	Butch Huskey	.15	.07
148	Bobby Jones	.25	.11
149	John Olerud	.25	.11
150	Rey Ordonez	.25	.11
151	Mike Piazza	2.00	.90
152	Hideo Nomo	.60	.25
153	Masato Yoshii	.15	.11
154	Derek Jeter	2.00	.90
155	Chuck Knoblauch	.25	.11
156	Paul O'Neill	.25	.11
157	Andy Pettitte	.25	.11
158	Mariano Rivera	.25	.11
159	Darryl Strawberry	.25	.11
160	David Wells	.25	.11
161	Jorge Posada	.15	.07
162	Ramiro Mendoza	.15	.07
163	Miguel Tejada	.25	.11
164	Ryan Christenson	.15	.07
165	Rickey Henderson	.75	.35
166	A.J. Hinch	.15	.07
167	Ben Grieve	.60	.25
168	Kenny Rogers	.15	.07
169	Matt Stairs	.25	.11
170	Bob Abreu	.25	.11
171	Rico Brogna	.15	.07
172	Doug Glanville	.25	.11
173	Mike Grace	.15	.07
174	Desi Relaford	.15	.07
175	Scott Rolen	.75	.35
176	Jose Guillen	.15	.07
177	Francisco Cordova	.15	.07
178	Al Martin	.15	.07
179	Jason Schmidt	.15	.07
180	Turner Ward	.15	.07
181	Kevin Young	.25	.11
182	Mark McGwire	4.00	1.80
183	Delino DeShields	.15	.07
184	Eli Marrero	.15	.07
185	Tom Lampkin	.15	.07
186	Ray Lankford	.25	.11
187	Willie McGee	.25	.11
188	Matt Morris	.15	.07
189	Andy Ashby	.15	.07
190	Kevin Brown	.40	.18
191	Ken Caminiti	.25	.11
192	Trevor Hoffman	.25	.11
193	Wally Joyner	.25	.11
194	Greg Vaughn	.25	.11
195	Quilvio Veras	.15	.07
196	Shawn Estes	.15	.07
197	Orel Hershiser	.25	.11
198	Jeff Kent	.25	.11
199	Bill Mueller	.15	.07
200	J.T. Snow	.25	.11
201	Robb Nen	.15	.07
202	Ken Cloude	.15	.07
203	Russ Davis	.15	.07
204	Jeff Fassero	.15	.07
205	Ken Griffey Jr.	3.00	1.35
206	Shane Monahan	.15	.07
207	David Segui	.15	.07
208	Dan Wilson	.15	.07
209	Wilson Alvarez	.15	.07
210	Wade Boggs	.25	.11
211	Miguel Cairo	.15	.07
212	Bubba Trammell	.15	.07
213	Quinton McCracken	.15	.07
214	Paul Sorrento	.15	.07
215	Kevin Stocker	.15	.07
216	Will Clark	.60	.25
217	Rusty Greer	.25	.11
218	Rick Helling	.15	.07
219	Mark McLemore	.15	.07
220	Ivan Rodriguez	.75	.35
221	John Wetteland	.25	.11
222	Jose Canseco	.75	.35
223	Roger Clemens	1.50	.70
224	Carlos Delgado	.60	.25
225	Darrin Fletcher	.15	.07
226	Alex Gonzalez	.25	.11
227	Jose Cruz Jr.	.25	.11
228	Shannon Stewart	.25	.11
229	Rolando Arrojo FF	.15	.07
230	Livan Hernandez FF	.15	.07
231	Orlando Hernandez FF	.60	.25
232	Raul Mondesi FF	.25	.11
233	Moises Alou FF	.25	.11
234	Pedro Martinez FF	.75	.35
235	Sammy Sosa FF	2.00	.90
236	Vladimir Guerrero FF	.75	.35
237	Bartolo Colon FF	.25	.11
238	Miguel Tejada FF	.25	.11
239	Ismael Valdes FF	.15	.07
240	Mariano Rivera FF	.25	.11
241	Jose Cruz Jr. FF	.25	.11
242	Juan Gonzalez FF	1.25	.55
243	Ivan Rodriguez FF	.75	.35
244	Sandy Alomar Jr. FF	.25	.11
245	Roberto Alomar FF	.60	.25
246	Magglio Ordonez FF	.60	.25
247	Kerry Wood SH CL	.60	.25
248	Mark McGwire SH CL	4.00	1.80
249	David Wells SH CL	.25	.11
250	Rolando Arrojo SH CL	.15	.07
251	Ken Griffey Jr. SH CL	3.00	1.35
252	Trevor Hoffman SH CL	.25	.11
253	Travis Lee SH CL	.40	.18
254	Roberto Alomar SH CL	.60	.25
255	Sammy Sosa SH CL	2.00	.90
266	Pat Burrell SR	5.00	2.20
267	Shea Hillenbrand SR	.75	.35
268	Robert Fick SR	.50	.23
269	Roy Halladay SR	.50	.23
270	Ruben Mateo SR	1.25	.55
271	Bruce Chen SR	.50	.23
272	Angel Pena SR	.25	.11
273	Michael Barrett SR	.75	.35
274	Kevin Witt SR	.50	.23
275	Damon Minor SR	.25	.11
276	Ryan Minor SR	.50	.23
277	A.J. Pierzynski SR	.25	.11
278	A.J. Burnett SR	1.25	.55
279	Dermal Brown SR	.50	.23
280	Joe Lawrence SR	.50	.23
281	Derrick Gibson SR	.50	.23
282	Carlos Febles SR	.50	.23
283	Chris Haas SR	.25	.11
284	Cesar King SR	.25	.11
285	Calvin Pickering SR	.50	.23
286	Mitch Meluskey SR	.25	.11
287	Carlos Beltran SR	1.50	.70
288	Ron Belliard SR	.25	.11
289	Jerry Hairston Jr. SR	.50	.23
290	Fernando Seguignol SR	.50	.23
291	Kris Benson SR	.50	.23
292	Chad Hutchinson SR	1.50	.70
293	Jarrod Washburn SR	.15	.07
294	Jason Dickson	.15	.07
295	Mo Vaughn	.60	.25
296	Garret Anderson	.25	.11
297	Jim Edmonds	.25	.11
298	Ken Hill	.15	.07
299	Shigetoshi Hasegawa	.15	.07
300	Todd Stottlemyre	.15	.07
301	Randy Johnson	.60	.25
302	Omar Daal	.15	.07
303	Steve Finley	.25	.11
304	Matt Williams	.60	.25
305	Danny Klassen	.15	.07
306	Tony Batista	.15	.07
307	Brian Jordan	.25	.11
308	Greg Maddux	1.50	.70
309	Chipper Jones	1.50	.70
310	Bret Boone	.25	.11
311	Ozzie Guillen	.15	.07
312	John Rucker	.40	.18
313	Tom Glavine	.60	.25
314	Andruw Jones	.60	.25
315	Albert Belle	.60	.25
316	Charles Johnson	.25	.11
317	Will Clark	.60	.25
318	B.J. Surhoff	.25	.11
319	Delino DeShields	.15	.07
320	Heathcliff Slocumb	.15	.07
321	Sidney Ponson	.15	.07
322	Juan Guzman	.15	.07
323	Reggie Jefferson	.15	.07
324	Mark Portugal	.15	.07
325	Tim Wakefield	.15	.07
326	Jason Varitek	.25	.11
327	Jose Offerman	.25	.11
328	Pedro Martinez	.75	.35
329	Trot Nixon	.25	.11
330	Kerry Wood	.60	.25
331	Sammy Sosa	2.00	.90
332	Glenallen Hill	.15	.07
333	Gary Gaetti	.25	.11
334	Mickey Morandini	.15	.07
335	Benito Santiago	.15	.07
336	Jeff Blauser	.15	.07

❑ 337 Frank Thomas	1.25	.55
❑ 338 Paul Konerko	.25	.11
❑ 339 Jaime Navarro	.15	.07
❑ 340 Carlos Lee	.25	.11
❑ 341 Brian Simmons	.15	.07
❑ 342 Mark Johnson	.15	.07
❑ 343 Jeff Abbott	.15	.07
❑ 344 Steve Avery	.15	.07
❑ 345 Mike Cameron	.15	.07
❑ 346 Michael Tucker	.15	.07
❑ 347 Greg Vaughn	.25	.11
❑ 348 Hal Morris	.15	.07
❑ 349 Pete Harnisch	.15	.07
❑ 350 Denny Neagle	.15	.07
❑ 351 Manny Ramirez	.75	.35
❑ 352 Roberto Alomar	.60	.25
❑ 353 Dwight Gooden	.25	.11
❑ 354 Kenny Lofton	.40	.18
❑ 355 Mike Jackson	.15	.07
❑ 356 Charles Nagy	.25	.11
❑ 357 Enrique Wilson	.15	.07
❑ 358 Russ Branyan	.25	.11
❑ 359 Richie Sexson	.40	.18
❑ 360 Vinny Castilla	.25	.11
❑ 361 Dante Bichette	.25	.11
❑ 362 Kirt Manwaring	.15	.07
❑ 363 Darryl Hamilton	.15	.07
❑ 364 Jamey Wright	.15	.07
❑ 365 Curtis Leskanic	.15	.07
❑ 366 Jeff Reed	.15	.07
❑ 367 Bobby Higginson	.25	.11
❑ 368 Justin Thompson	.15	.07
❑ 369 Brad Ausmus	.15	.07
❑ 370 Dean Palmer	.25	.11
❑ 371 Gabe Kapler	.60	.25
❑ 372 Juan Encarnacion	.25	.11
❑ 373 Karim Garcia	.15	.07
❑ 374 Alex Gonzalez	.25	.11
❑ 375 Braden Looper	.15	.07
❑ 376 Preston Wilson	.25	.11
❑ 377 Todd Dunwoody	.15	.07
❑ 378 Alex Fernandez	.15	.07
❑ 379 Mark Kotsay	.15	.07
❑ 380 Matt Mantei	.25	.11
❑ 381 Ken Caminiti	.25	.11
❑ 382 Scott Elarton	.15	.07
❑ 383 Jeff Bagwell	.75	.35
❑ 385 Derek Bell	.25	.11
❑ 385 Ricky Gutierrez	.15	.07
❑ 386 Richard Hidalgo	.25	.11
❑ 387 Shane Reynolds	.15	.07
❑ 388 Carl Everett	.25	.11
❑ 389 Scott Service	.15	.07
❑ 390 Jeff Suppan	.15	.07
❑ 391 Joe Randa	.15	.07
❑ 392 Kevin Appier	.25	.11
❑ 393 Shane Halter	.15	.07
❑ 394 Chad Kreuter	.15	.07
❑ 395 Mike Sweeney	.25	.11
❑ 396 Kevin Brown	.40	.18
❑ 397 Devon White	.15	.07
❑ 398 Todd Hollandsworth	.15	.07
❑ 399 Todd Hundley	.25	.11
❑ 400 Chan Ho Park	.25	.11
❑ 401 Mark Grudzielanek	.15	.07
❑ 402 Raul Mondesi	.25	.11
❑ 403 Ismael Valdes	.15	.07
❑ 404 Rafael Roque	.15	.07
❑ 405 Sean Berry	.15	.07
❑ 406 Kevin Barker	.15	.07
❑ 407 Dave Nilsson	.15	.07
❑ 408 Geoff Jenkins	.25	.11
❑ 409 Jim Abbott	.25	.11
❑ 410 Bobby Hughes	.15	.07
❑ 411 Corey Koskie	.15	.07
❑ 412 Rick Aguilera	.15	.07
❑ 413 LaTroy Hawkins	.15	.07
❑ 414 Ron Coomer	.15	.07
❑ 415 Denny Hocking	.15	.07
❑ 416 Marty Cordova	.15	.07
❑ 417 Terry Steinbach	.15	.07
❑ 418 Rondell White	.25	.11
❑ 419 Wilton Guerrero	.15	.07
❑ 420 Shane Andrews	.15	.07
❑ 421 Orlando Cabrera	.15	.07
❑ 422 Carl Pavano	.15	.07

❑ 423 Javier Vazquez	.15	.07
❑ 424 Chris Widger	.15	.07
❑ 425 Robin Ventura	.25	.11
❑ 426 Rickey Henderson	.75	.35
❑ 427 Al Leiter	.25	.11
❑ 428 Bobby Jones	.15	.07
❑ 429 Brian McRae	.15	.07
❑ 430 Roger Cedeno	.25	.11
❑ 431 Bobby Bonilla	.25	.11
❑ 432 Edgardo Alfonzo	.40	.18
❑ 433 Bernie Williams	.60	.25
❑ 434 Ricky Ledee	.25	.11
❑ 435 Chili Davis	.25	.11
❑ 436 Tino Martinez	.25	.11
❑ 437 Scott Brosius	.25	.11
❑ 438 David Cone	.40	.18
❑ 439 Joe Girardi	.15	.07
❑ 440 Roger Clemens	1.50	.70
❑ 441 Chad Curtis	.15	.07
❑ 442 Hideki Irabu	.25	.11
❑ 443 Jason Giambi	.25	.11
❑ 444 Scott Spiezio	.15	.07
❑ 445 Tony Phillips	.15	.07
❑ 446 Ramon Hernandez	.15	.07
❑ 447 Mike Macfarlane	.15	.07
❑ 448 Tom Candiotti	.15	.07
❑ 449 Billy Taylor	.15	.07
❑ 450 Bobby Estalella	.15	.07
❑ 451 Curt Schilling	.40	.18
❑ 452 Carlton Loewer	.15	.07
❑ 453 Marlon Anderson	.15	.07
❑ 454 Kevin Jordan	.15	.07
❑ 455 Ron Gant	.25	.11
❑ 456 Chad Ogea	.15	.07
❑ 457 Abraham Nunez	.15	.07
❑ 458 Jason Kendall	.25	.11
❑ 459 Pat Meares	.15	.07
❑ 460 Brant Brown	.15	.07
❑ 461 Brian Giles	.25	.11
❑ 462 Chad Hermansen	.25	.11
❑ 463 Freddy Garcia	.15	.07
❑ 464 Edgar Renteria	.15	.07
❑ 465 Fernando Tatis	.60	.25
❑ 466 Eric Davis	.15	.07
❑ 467 Darren Bragg	.15	.07
❑ 468 Donovan Osborne	.15	.07
❑ 469 Manny Aybar	.15	.07
❑ 470 Jose Jimenez	.25	.11
❑ 471 Kent Mercker	.15	.07
❑ 472 Reggie Sanders	.15	.07
❑ 473 Ruben Rivera	.15	.07
❑ 474 Tony Gwynn	1.50	.70
❑ 475 Jim Leyritz	.15	.07
❑ 476 Chris Gomez	.15	.07
❑ 477 Matt Clement	.25	.11
❑ 478 Carlos Hernandez	.15	.07
❑ 479 Sterling Hitchcock	.15	.07
❑ 480 Ellis Burks	.15	.07
❑ 481 Barry Bonds	.75	.35
❑ 482 Marvin Benard	.15	.07
❑ 483 Kirk Rueter	.15	.07
❑ 484 F.P. Santangelo	.15	.07
❑ 485 Stan Javier	.15	.07
❑ 486 Jeff Kent	.25	.11
❑ 487 Alex Rodriguez	2.00	.90
❑ 488 Tom Lampkin	.15	.07
❑ 489 Jose Mesa	.15	.07
❑ 490 Jay Buhner	.25	.11
❑ 491 Edgar Martinez	.25	.11
❑ 492 Butch Huskey	.15	.07
❑ 493 John Mabry	.15	.07
❑ 494 Jamie Moyer	.15	.07
❑ 495 Roberto Hernandez	.15	.07
❑ 496 Tony Saunders	.15	.07
❑ 497 Fred McGriff	.40	.18
❑ 498 Dave Martinez	.15	.07
❑ 499 Jose Canseco	.75	.35
❑ 500 Rolando Arrojo	.15	.07
❑ 501 Esteban Yan	.15	.07
❑ 502 Juan Gonzalez	1.25	.55
❑ 503 Rafael Palmeiro	.60	.25
❑ 504 Aaron Sele	.15	.07
❑ 505 Royce Clayton	.15	.07
❑ 506 Todd Zeile	.25	.11
❑ 507 Tom Goodwin	.15	.07
❑ 508 Lee Stevens	.15	.07

❑ 509 Esteban Loaiza	.15	.07
❑ 510 Joey Hamilton	.15	.07
❑ 511 Homer Bush	.15	.07
❑ 512 Willie Greene	.15	.07
❑ 513 Shawn Green	.60	.25
❑ 514 David Wells	.25	.11
❑ 515 Kelvim Escobar	.15	.07
❑ 516 Tony Fernandez	.25	.11
❑ 517 Pat Hentgen	.15	.07
❑ 518 Mark McGwire AR	2.00	.90
❑ 519 Ken Griffey Jr. AR	1.50	.70
❑ 520 Sammy Sosa AR	1.00	.45
❑ 521 Juan Gonzalez AR	.60	.25
❑ 522 J.D. Drew AR	.60	.25
❑ 523 Chipper Jones AR	.75	.35
❑ 524 Alex Rodriguez AR	1.00	.45
❑ 525 Mike Piazza AR	1.00	.45
❑ 526 Nomar Garciaparra AR	1.00	.45
❑ 527 Mark McGwire SH CL	2.00	.90
❑ 528 Sammy Sosa SH CL	1.00	.45
❑ 529 Scott Brosius SH CL	.15	.07
❑ 530 Cal Ripken SH CL	1.25	.55
❑ 531 Barry Bonds SH CL	.40	.18
❑ 532 Roger Clemens SH CL	.75	.35
❑ 533 Ken Griffey Jr. SH CL	1.50	.70
❑ 534 Alex Rodriguez SH CL	1.00	.45
❑ 535 Curt Schilling SH CL	.25	.11
❑ NNO K.Griffey Jr. '89 AU/100	1500.00	700.00

1999 Upper Deck Exclusives Level 1

	MINT	NRMT
COMMON (1-255/266-535)	5.00	2.20

*STARS: 12.5X TO 30X BASIC CARDS
*YNG.STARS: 10X TO 25X BASIC CARDS
*SER.1 STAR ROOK: 4X TO 10X BASIC SR
*SER.2 STAR ROOK: 6X TO 15X BASIC SR
CARDS 256-265 DO NOT EXIST
RANDOM INSERTS IN ALL HOBBY PACKS
STATED PRINT RUN 100 SERIAL #'d SETS

1999 Upper Deck Exclusives Level 2

	MINT	NRMT
COMMON CARD (266-535)	30.00	13.50

SER.1 PRINT RUN 1 SERIAL #'d SET
SER.2 PRINT RUN 10 SERIAL #'d SETS
RANDOM INSERTS IN ALL HOBBY PACKS

1999 Upper Deck 10th Anniversary Team

	MINT	NRMT
COMPLETE SET (30)	50.00	22.00
COMMON CARD (X1-X30)	.50	.23
MINOR STARS	.75	.35
UNLISTED STARS	1.50	.70

SER.1 STATED ODDS 1:4
*DOUBLES: 1.5X TO 4X HI COLUMN
DOUBLES RANDOM INSERTS IN SER.1 PACKS
DOUBLES PRINT RUN 4000 SERIAL #'d SETS
*TRIPLES: 10X TO 25X HI COLUMN
TRIPLES RANDOM INSERTS IN SER.1 PACKS
TRIPLES PRINT RUN 100 SERIAL #'d SETS
HR'S RANDOM INSERTS IN SER.1 PACKS
HOME RUN PRINT RUN 1 SERIAL #'d SET
HR'S NOT PRICED DUE TO SCARCITY

❏ X1	Mike Piazza	4.00	1.80
❏ X2	Mark McGwire	8.00	3.60
❏ X3	Roberto Alomar	1.50	.70
❏ X4	Chipper Jones	3.00	1.35
❏ X5	Cal Ripken	5.00	2.20
❏ X6	Ken Griffey Jr.	6.00	2.70
❏ X7	Barry Bonds	1.50	.70
❏ X8	Tony Gwynn	3.00	1.35
❏ X9	Nolan Ryan	6.00	2.70
❏ X10	Randy Johnson	1.50	.70
❏ X11	Dennis Eckersley	.75	.35
❏ X12	Ivan Rodriguez	1.50	.70
❏ X13	Frank Thomas	2.50	1.10
❏ X14	Craig Biggio	1.50	.70
❏ X15	Wade Boggs	1.50	.70
❏ X16	Alex Rodriguez	4.00	1.80
❏ X17	Albert Belle	1.50	.70
❏ X18	Juan Gonzalez	2.50	1.10
❏ X19	Rickey Henderson	1.50	.70
❏ X20	Greg Maddux	3.00	1.35
❏ X21	Tom Glavine	1.50	.70
❏ X22	Randy Myers	.50	.23
❏ X23	Sandy Alomar Jr.	.75	.35
❏ X24	Jeff Bagwell	1.50	.70
❏ X25	Derek Jeter	4.00	1.80
❏ X26	Matt Williams	1.50	.70
❏ X27	Kenny Lofton	.45	
❏ X28	Sammy Sosa	4.00	1.80
❏ X29	Larry Walker	1.50	.70
❏ X30	Roger Clemens	3.00	1.35

1999 Upper Deck A Piece of History

SER.1 STATED ODDS 1:15,000
B.RUTH AU NOT PRICED DUE TO SCARCITY

❏ PH	Babe Ruth	1600.00	700.00
❏ LCPH	Babe Ruth AU/3		

1999 Upper Deck A Piece of History 500 Club

RANDOM INSERTS IN 1999-2000 UD BRANDS
PRINT RUN APPROXIMATELY 350 SETS

		MINT	NRMT
❏ BR	Babe Ruth/50	3500.00	1600.00
❏ EB	Ernie Banks	250.00	110.00
❏ EM	Eddie Mathews	300.00	135.00
❏ EM	Eddie Murray	250.00	110.00
❏ FR	Frank Robinson	200.00	90.00
❏ HA	Hank Aaron	600.00	275.00
❏ HK	Harmon Killebrew	300.00	135.00
❏ JF	Jimmie Foxx	300.00	135.00
❏ MM	Mickey Mantle	1200.00	550.00
❏ MO	Mel Ott	250.00	110.00
❏ MS	Mike Schmidt	350.00	160.00
❏ RJ	Reggie Jackson	500.00	220.00
❏ TW	Ted Williams	800.00	350.00
❏ WM	Willie Mays	350.00	160.00
❏ WM	Willie McCovey	300.00	135.00

1999 Upper Deck A Piece of History 500 Club Autographs

		MINT	NRMT

RANDOM INSERTS IN 1999-2000 UD BRANDS
PRINT RUNS LISTED BELOW

❏ EBAU	Ernie Banks/14	1000.00	450.00
❏ EMAU	Eddie Mathews/41	500.00	220.00
❏ FRAU	Frank Robinson/20	800.00	350.00
❏ HAAU	Hank Aaron/44	1200.00	550.00
❏ HKAU	Harmon Killebrew/3		
❏ MSAU	Mike Schmidt/20	1200.00	550.00
❏ RJAU	Reggie Jackson/44		
❏ TWAU	Ted Williams/9		
❏ WMAU	Willie Mays/24	1200.00	550.00
❏ WMAU	Willie McCovey/44	500.00	220.00

1999 Upper Deck Crowning Glory

		MINT	NRMT
COMPLETE SET (3)		80.00	36.00
COMMON CARD (CG1-CG3)		15.00	6.75

RANDOM INSERTS IN SER.1 PACKS
*DOUBLES: .75X TO 2X HI COLUMN
DOUBLES RANDOM INSERTS IN SER.1 PACKS
DOUBLES PRINT RUN 1000 SERIAL #'d SETS
*TRIPLES: 5X TO 12X HI COLUMN
TRIPLES RANDOM INSERTS IN SER.1 PACKS
TRIPLES PRINT RUN 25 SERIAL #'d SETS
HR'S RANDOM INSERTS IN SER.1 PACKS

HOME RUNS PRINT RUN 1 SERIAL #'d SET
HOME RUNS NOT PRICED DUE TO SCARCITY

❏ CG1	Roger Clemens Kerry Wood	15.00	6.75
❏ CG2	Mark McGwire Barry Bonds	30.00	13.50
❏ CG3	Ken Griffey Jr. Mark McGwire	40.00	18.00

1999 Upper Deck Forte

	MINT	NRMT
COMPLETE SET (30)	250.00	110.00
COMMON CARD (F1-F30)	3.00	1.35
UNLISTED STARS	5.00	2.20

SER.2 STATED ODDS 1:23
*DOUBLES: .6X TO 1.5X HI COLUMN
DOUBLES RANDOM INSERTS IN SER.2 PACKS
DOUBLES PRINT RUN 2000 SERIAL #'d SETS
*TRIPLES: 2.5X TO 6X HI COLUMN
TRIPLES RANDOM INSERTS IN SER.2 PACKS
TRIPLES PRINT RUN 100 SERIAL #'d SETS
QUADS RANDOM INSERTS IN SER.2 PACKS
QUADRUPLES PRINT RUN 10 SERIAL #'d SETS
QUADRUPLES NOT PRICED DUE TO SCARCITY

❏ F1	Darin Erstad	3.00	1.35
❏ F2	Troy Glaus	5.00	2.20
❏ F3	Mo Vaughn	5.00	2.20
❏ F4	Greg Maddux	12.00	5.50
❏ F5	Andres Galarraga	3.00	1.35
❏ F6	Chipper Jones	12.00	5.50
❏ F7	Cal Ripken	20.00	9.00
❏ F8	Albert Belle	5.00	2.20
❏ F9	Nomar Garciaparra	15.00	6.75
❏ F10	Sammy Sosa	15.00	6.75
❏ F11	Kerry Wood	5.00	2.20
❏ F12	Frank Thomas	10.00	4.50
❏ F13	Jim Thome	5.00	2.20
❏ F14	Jeff Bagwell	6.00	2.70
❏ F15	Vladimir Guerrero	6.00	2.70
❏ F16	Mike Piazza	15.00	6.75
❏ F17	Derek Jeter	15.00	6.75
❏ F18	Ben Grieve	5.00	2.20
❏ F19	Eric Chavez	3.00	1.35
❏ F20	Scott Rolen	6.00	2.70

❏ F21 Mark McGwire	30.00	13.50
❏ F22 J.D. Drew	6.00	2.70
❏ F23 Tony Gwynn	12.00	5.50
❏ F24 Barry Bonds	6.00	2.70
❏ F25 Alex Rodriguez	15.00	6.75
❏ F26 Ken Griffey Jr.	25.00	11.00
❏ F27 Ivan Rodriguez	6.00	2.70
❏ F28 Juan Gonzalez	10.00	4.50
❏ F29 Roger Clemens	12.00	5.50
❏ F30 Andruw Jones	5.00	2.20

1999 Upper Deck Game Jersey

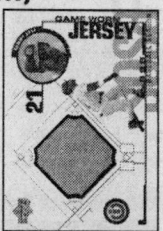

	MINT	NRMT
H1 AND HR1 CARDS DIST.IN SER.1 PACKS		
H2 AND HR2 CARDS DIST.IN SER.2 PACKS		
H STATED ODDS 1:288 HOBBY		
HR STATED ODDS 1:2500 HOBBY/RETAIL		
AU PRINT RUNS LISTED BELOW		

❏ AB Adrian Beltre H1	80.00	36.00
❏ AR Alex Rodriguez HR1	300.00	135.00
❏ BF Brad Fullmer H2	50.00	22.00
❏ BG Ben Grieve H1	80.00	36.00
❏ BT Bubba Trammell H2	50.00	22.00
❏ CJ Charles Johnson HR1	50.00	22.00
❏ CJ Chipper Jones H2	150.00	70.00
❏ DE Darin Erstad H1	80.00	36.00
❏ EC Eric Chavez H2	60.00	27.00
❏ FT Frank Thomas HR2	250.00	110.00
❏ GM Greg Maddux HR2	250.00	110.00
❏ IR Ivan Rodriguez H1	120.00	55.00
❏ JD J.D. Drew H2	120.00	55.00
❏ JG Juan Gonzalez HR1	200.00	90.00
❏ JR Ken Griffey Jr. HR2	400.00	180.00
❏ KG Ken Griffey Jr. H1	400.00	180.00
❏ KW Kerry Wood HR1	100.00	45.00
❏ MP Mike Piazza HR1	300.00	135.00
❏ MR Manny Ramirez H2	120.00	55.00
❏ NRA Nolan Ryan Astros H2	400.00	180.00
❏ NRB Nolan Ryan Rangers HR2	500.00	220.00
❏ SS Sammy Sosa H2	250.00	110.00
❏ TH Todd Helton H2	80.00	36.00
❏ TGW Tony Gwynn H2	120.00	55.00
❏ TL Travis Lee H1	50.00	22.00
❏ JDS J.Drew AU/8 H2		
❏ JRS Ken Griffey Jr. AU/24 H2	5000.00	2200.00
❏ KGAU Ken Griffey Jr. AU/24 H1	5000.00	2200.00
❏ KWAU Kerry Wood AU/34 HR1	1200.00	550.00
❏ NRAS NolanRyanAstrosAU/34 H2	5000.00	2200.00

1999 Upper Deck Immaculate Perception

	MINT	NRMT
COMPLETE SET (27)	300.00	135.00
COMMON CARD (I1-I27)	2.50	1.10

SEMISTARS	4.00	1.80
UNLISTED STARS	6.00	2.70
SER.1 STATED ODDS 1:23		
*DOUBLES: 1X TO 2.5X HI COLUMN		
DOUBLES RANDOM INSERTS IN SER.1 PACKS		
DOUBLES PRINT RUN 1000 SERIAL #'d SETS		
*TRIPLES: 6X TO 15X HI COLUMN		
TRIPLES RANDOM INSERTS IN SER.1 PACKS		
TRIPLES PRINT RUN 25 SERIAL #'d SETS		
HR'S RANDOM INSERTS IN SER.1 PACKS		
HOME RUNS PRINT RUN 1 SERIAL #'d SET		
HOME RUNS NOT PRICED DUE TO SCARCITY		

❏ I1 Jeff Bagwell	8.00	3.60
❏ I2 Craig Biggio	6.00	2.70
❏ I3 Barry Bonds	8.00	3.60
❏ I4 Roger Clemens	15.00	6.75
❏ I5 Jose Cruz Jr.	2.50	1.10
❏ I6 Nomar Garciaparra	20.00	9.00
❏ I7 Tony Clark	2.50	1.10
❏ I8 Ben Grieve	6.00	2.70
❏ I9 Ken Griffey Jr.	30.00	13.50
❏ I10 Tony Gwynn	15.00	6.75
❏ I11 Randy Johnson	6.00	2.70
❏ I12 Chipper Jones	15.00	6.75
❏ I13 Travis Lee	4.00	1.80
❏ I14 Kenny Lofton	4.00	1.80
❏ I15 Greg Maddux	15.00	6.75
❏ I16 Mark McGwire	40.00	18.00
❏ I17 Hideo Nomo	6.00	2.70
❏ I18 Mike Piazza	20.00	9.00
❏ I19 Manny Ramirez	8.00	3.60
❏ I20 Cal Ripken	25.00	11.00
❏ I21 Alex Rodriguez	20.00	9.00
❏ I22 Scott Rolen	8.00	3.60
❏ I23 Frank Thomas	12.00	5.50
❏ I24 Kerry Wood	6.00	2.70
❏ I25 Larry Walker	6.00	2.70
❏ I26 Vinny Castilla	2.50	1.10
❏ I27 Derek Jeter	20.00	9.00

1999 Upper Deck Textbook Excellence

	MINT	NRMT
COMPLETE SET (30)	50.00	22.00
COMMON CARD (T1-T30)	.75	.35
SEMISTARS	1.00	.45

UNLISTED STARS	1.50	.70
SER.2 STATED ODDS 1:4		
*DOUBLES: 2X TO 5X HI COLUMN		
DOUBLES RANDOM INSERTS IN SER.2 PACKS		
DOUBLES PRINT RUN 2000 SERIAL #'d SETS		
*TRIPLES: 8X TO 20X HI COLUMN		
TRIPLES RANDOM INSERTS IN SER.2 PACKS		
TRIPLES PRINT RUN 100 SERIAL #'d SETS		
QUADS RANDOM INSERTS IN SER.2 PACKS		
QUADRUPLES PRINT RUN 10 SERIAL #'d SETS		
QUADRUPLES NOT PRICED DUE TO SCARCITY		

❏ T1 Mo Vaughn	1.50	.70
❏ T2 Greg Maddux	4.00	1.80
❏ T3 Chipper Jones	4.00	1.80
❏ T4 Andruw Jones	1.50	.70
❏ T5 Cal Ripken	6.00	2.70
❏ T6 Albert Belle	1.50	.70
❏ T7 Roberto Alomar	1.50	.70
❏ T8 Nomar Garciaparra	5.00	2.20
❏ T9 Kerry Wood	1.50	.70
❏ T10 Sammy Sosa	5.00	2.20
❏ T11 Greg Vaughn	.75	.35
❏ T12 Jeff Bagwell	2.00	.90
❏ T13 Kevin Brown	1.00	.45
❏ T14 Vladimir Guerrero	2.00	.90
❏ T15 Mike Piazza	5.00	2.20
❏ T16 Bernie Williams	1.50	.70
❏ T17 Derek Jeter	5.00	2.20
❏ T18 Ben Grieve	1.50	.70
❏ T19 Eric Chavez	1.00	.45
❏ T20 Scott Rolen	2.00	.90
❏ T21 Mark McGwire	10.00	4.50
❏ T22 David Wells	.75	.35
❏ T23 J.D. Drew	2.00	.90
❏ T24 Tony Gwynn	4.00	1.80
❏ T25 Barry Bonds	2.00	.90
❏ T26 Alex Rodriguez	5.00	2.20
❏ T27 Ken Griffey Jr.	8.00	3.60
❏ T28 Juan Gonzalez	3.00	1.35
❏ T29 Ivan Rodriguez	2.00	.90
❏ T30 Roger Clemens	4.00	1.80

1999 Upper Deck View to a Thrill

	MINT	NRMT
COMPLETE SET (30)	100.00	45.00
COMMON CARD (V1-V30)	1.00	.45
SEMISTARS	1.50	.70
UNLISTED STARS	2.50	1.10
SER.2 STATED ODDS 1:7		
*DOUBLES: 1.25X TO 3X HI COLUMN		
DOUBLES RANDOM INSERTS IN SER.2 PACKS		
DOUBLES PRINT RUN 2000 SERIAL #'d SETS		
*TRIPLES: 5X TO 12X HI COLUMN		
TRIPLES RANDOM INSERTS IN SER.2 PACKS		
TRIPLES PRINT RUN 100 SERIAL #'d SETS		
QUADS RANDOM INSERTS IN SER.2 PACKS		
QUADRUPLES PRINT RUN 10 SERIAL #'d SETS		
QUADRUPLES NOT PRICED DUE TO SCARCITY		

		MINT	NRMT
V1	Mo Vaughn	2.50	1.10
V2	Darin Erstad	1.50	.70
V3	Travis Lee	1.50	.70
V4	Chipper Jones	6.00	2.70
V5	Greg Maddux	6.00	2.70
V6	Gabe Kapler	2.50	1.10
V7	Cal Ripken	10.00	4.50
V8	Nomar Garciaparra	8.00	3.60
V9	Kerry Wood	2.50	1.10
V10	Frank Thomas	5.00	2.20
V11	Manny Ramirez	3.00	1.35
V12	Larry Walker	2.50	1.10
V13	Tony Clark	1.00	.45
V14	Jeff Bagwell	3.00	1.35
V15	Craig Biggio	2.50	1.35
V16	Vladimir Guerrero	3.00	1.35
V17	Mike Piazza	8.00	3.60
V18	Bernie Williams	2.50	1.10
V19	Derek Jeter	8.00	3.60
V20	Ben Grieve	2.50	1.10
V21	Eric Chavez	1.50	.70
V22	Scott Rolen	3.00	1.35
V23	Mark McGwire	15.00	6.75
V24	Tony Gwynn	6.00	2.70
V25	Barry Bonds	3.00	1.35
V26	Ken Griffey Jr.	12.00	5.50
V27	Alex Rodriguez	8.00	3.60
V28	J.D. Drew	3.00	1.35
V29	Juan Gonzalez	5.00	2.20
V30	Roger Clemens	6.00	2.70

1999 Upper Deck Wonder Years

	MINT	NRMT
COMPLETE SET (30)	100.00	45.00
COMMON CARD (W1-W30)	1.00	.45
SEMISTARS	1.50	.70

SER.1 STATED ODDS 1:7
*DOUBLES: 1.25X TO 3X HI COLUMN
DOUBLES RANDOM INSERTS IN SER.1 PACKS
DOUBLES PRINT RUN 2000 SERIAL #'d SETS
*TRIPLES: 10X TO 25X HI COLUMN
TRIPLES RANDOM INSERTS IN SER.1 PACKS
TRIPLES PRINT RUN 50 SERIAL #'d SETS
HR'S RANDOM INSERTS IN SER.1 PACKS
HOME RUNS PRINT RUN 1 SERAIL #'d SET
HOME RUNS NOT PRICED DUE TO SCARCITY

W1	Kerry Wood	2.50	1.10
W2	Travis Lee	1.50	.70
W3	Jeff Bagwell	3.00	1.35
W4	Barry Bonds	3.00	1.35
W5	Roger Clemens	6.00	2.70
W6	Jose Cruz Jr.	1.00	.45
W7	Andres Galarraga	1.50	.70
W8	Nomar Garciaparra	8.00	3.60
W9	Juan Gonzalez	5.00	2.20
W10	Ken Griffey Jr.	12.00	5.50
W11	Tony Gwynn	6.00	2.70
W12	Derek Jeter	8.00	3.60
W13	Randy Johnson	6.00	2.70
W14	Andruw Jones	2.50	1.10
W15	Chipper Jones	6.00	2.70
W16	Kenny Lofton	1.50	.70
W17	Greg Maddux	6.00	2.70
W18	Tino Martinez	1.00	.45
W19	Mark McGwire	15.00	6.75
W20	Paul Molitor	2.50	1.10
W21	Mike Piazza	8.00	3.60
W22	Manny Ramirez	3.00	1.35
W23	Cal Ripken	10.00	4.50
W24	Alex Rodriguez	8.00	3.60
W25	Sammy Sosa	8.00	3.60
W26	Frank Thomas	5.00	2.20
W27	Mo Vaughn	2.50	1.10
W28	Larry Walker	2.50	1.10
W29	Scott Rolen	3.00	1.35
W30	Ben Grieve	2.50	1.10

2000 Upper Deck

	MINT	NRMT
COMPLETE SERIES 1 (270)	50.00	22.00
COMMON CARD (28-270)	.15	.07
MINOR STARS	.25	.11
SEMISTARS	.40	.18
UNLISTED STARS	.60	.25
COMMON SR (1-28)	.50	.23
SR MINOR STARS	.75	.35
SR SEMISTARS	1.00	.45

SR CARDS ARE NOT SHORTPRINTED
AARON BAT LISTED W/UD APH 500 CLUB

1	Rick Ankiel SR	8.00	3.60
2	Vernon Wells SR	1.00	.45
3	Ryan Anderson SR	.50	.23
4	Ed Yarnall SR	.75	.35
5	Brian McNichol SR	.50	.23
6	Ben Petrick SR	.75	.35
7	Kip Wells SR	.75	.35
8	Eric Munson SR	3.00	1.35
9	Matt Riley SR	2.00	.90
10	Peter Bergeron SR	.50	.23
11	Eric Gagne SR	.50	.23
12	Ramon Ortiz SR	.50	.23
13	Josh Beckett SR	2.50	1.10
14	Alfonso Soriano SR	2.50	1.10
15	Jorge Toca SR	.50	.23
16	Buddy Carlyle SR	.50	.23
17	Chad Hermansen SR	.75	.35
18	Matt Perisho SR	.50	.23
19	Tomokazu Ohka SR	1.00	.45
20	Jacque Jones SR	.50	.23
21	Josh Paul SR	.50	.23
22	Dermal Brown SR	.75	.35
23	Adam Kennedy SR	.75	.35
24	Chad Harville SR	.50	.23
25	Calvin Murray SR	.50	.23
26	Chad Meyers SR	.50	.23
27	Brian Cooper SR	.50	.23
28	Troy Glaus	.60	.25
29	Ben Molina	.15	.07
30	Troy Percival	.25	.11
31	Ken Hill	.15	.07
32	Chuck Finley	.25	.11
33	Todd Greene	.15	.07
34	Tim Salmon	.40	.18
35	Gary DiSarcina	.15	.07
36	Luis Gonzalez	.25	.11
37	Tony Womack	.15	.07
38	Omar Daal	.15	.07
39	Randy Johnson	.60	.25
40	Erubiel Durazo	1.50	.70
41	Jay Bell	.25	.11
42	Steve Finley	.25	.11
43	Travis Lee	.25	.11
44	Greg Maddux	2.00	.90
45	Bret Boone	.25	.11
46	Brian Jordan	.25	.11
47	Kevin Millwood	.40	.18
48	Odalis Perez	.15	.07
49	Javy Lopez	.25	.11
50	John Smoltz	.40	.18
51	Bruce Chen	.15	.07
52	Albert Belle	.60	.25
53	Jerry Hairston Jr.	.25	.11
54	Will Clark	.60	.25
55	Sidney Ponson	.15	.07
56	Charles Johnson	.25	.11
57	Cal Ripken	2.50	1.10
58	Ryan Minor	.15	.07
59	Mike Mussina	.60	.25
60	Tom Gordon	.15	.07
61	Jose Offerman	.25	.11
62	Trot Nixon	.25	.11
63	Pedro Martinez	.75	.35
64	John Valentin	.15	.07
65	Jason Varitek	.15	.07
66	Juan Pena	.15	.07
67	Troy O'Leary	.15	.07
68	Sammy Sosa	2.00	.90
69	Henry Rodriguez	.25	.11
70	Kyle Farnsworth	.15	.07
71	Glenallen Hill	.15	.07
72	Lance Johnson	.15	.07
73	Mickey Morandini	.15	.07
74	Jon Lieber	.15	.07
75	Kevin Tapani	.15	.07
76	Carlos Lee	.25	.11
77	Ray Durham	.15	.07
78	Jim Parque	.25	.11
79	Bob Howry	.15	.07
80	Magglio Ordonez	.60	.25
81	Paul Konerko	.25	.11
82	Mike Caruso	.15	.07
83	Chris Singleton	.25	.11
84	Sean Casey	.60	.25
85	Barry Larkin	.60	.25
86	Pokey Reese	.25	.11
87	Eddie Taubensee	.15	.07
88	Scott Williamson	.25	.11
89	Jason LaRue	.15	.07
90	Aaron Boone	.15	.07
91	Jeffrey Hammonds	.15	.07
92	Omar Vizquel	.25	.11
93	Manny Ramirez	.75	.35
94	Kenny Lofton	.40	.18
95	Jaret Wright	.25	.11
96	Einar Diaz	.15	.07
97	Charles Nagy	.25	.11
98	David Justice	.25	.11
99	Richie Sexson	.40	.18
100	Steve Karsay	.15	.07
101	Todd Helton	.60	.25
102	Dante Bichette	.25	.11
103	Larry Walker	.60	.25
104	Pedro Astacio	.15	.07
105	Neifi Perez	.25	.11
106	Brian Bohanon	.15	.07
107	Edgard Clemente	.15	.07
108	Dave Veres	.15	.07
109	Gabe Kapler	.25	.11
110	Juan Encarnacion	.25	.11
111	Jeff Weaver	.25	.11
112	Damion Easley	.25	.11
113	Justin Thompson	.15	.07
114	Brad Ausmus	.15	.07
115	Frank Catalanotto	.15	.07
116	Todd Jones	.25	.11
117	Preston Wilson	.25	.11
118	Cliff Floyd	.25	.11
119	Mike Lowell	.15	.07
120	Antonio Alfonseca	.15	.07
121	Alex Gonzalez	.25	.11
122	Braden Looper	.15	.07
123	Bruce Aven	.15	.07
124	Richard Hidalgo	.25	.11
125	Mitch Meluskey	.15	.07
126	Jeff Bagwell	.75	.35

☐ 127 Jose Lima	.25	.11
☐ 128 Derek Bell	.25	.11
☐ 129 Billy Wagner	.25	.11
☐ 130 Shane Reynolds	.25	.11
☐ 131 Moises Alou	.25	.11
☐ 132 Carlos Beltran	.60	.25
☐ 133 Carlos Febles	.25	.11
☐ 134 Jermaine Dye	.15	.07
☐ 135 Jeremy Giambi	.25	.11
☐ 136 Joe Randa	.15	.07
☐ 137 Jose Rosado	.15	.07
☐ 138 Chad Kreuter	.15	.07
☐ 139 Jose Vizcaino	.15	.07
☐ 140 Adrian Beltre	.40	.18
☐ 141 Kevin Brown	.40	.18
☐ 142 Ismael Valdes	.25	.11
☐ 143 Angel Pena	.25	.11
☐ 144 Chan Ho Park	.25	.11
☐ 145 Mark Grudzielanek	.15	.07
☐ 146 Jeff Shaw	.15	.07
☐ 147 Geoff Jenkins	.15	.07
☐ 148 Jeromy Burnitz	.25	.11
☐ 149 Hideo Nomo	.60	.25
☐ 150 Ron Belliard	.15	.07
☐ 151 Sean Berry	.15	.07
☐ 152 Mark Loretta	.15	.07
☐ 153 Steve Woodard	.15	.07
☐ 154 Joe Mays	.15	.07
☐ 155 Eric Milton	.15	.07
☐ 156 Corey Koskie	.15	.07
☐ 157 Ron Coomer	.15	.07
☐ 158 Brad Radke	.25	.11
☐ 159 Terry Steinbach	.25	.11
☐ 160 Cristian Guzman	.15	.07
☐ 161 Vladimir Guerrero	.75	.35
☐ 162 Wilton Guerrero	.15	.07
☐ 163 Michael Barrett	.15	.07
☐ 164 Chris Widger	.15	.07
☐ 165 Fernando Seguignol	.25	.11
☐ 166 Ugueth Urbina	.25	.11
☐ 167 Dustin Hermanson	.15	.07
☐ 168 Kenny Rogers	.15	.07
☐ 169 Edgardo Alfonzo	.40	.18
☐ 170 Orel Hershiser	.25	.11
☐ 171 Robin Ventura	.25	.11
☐ 172 Octavio Dotel	.25	.11
☐ 173 Rickey Henderson	.75	.35
☐ 174 Roger Cedeno	.25	.11
☐ 175 John Olerud	.25	.11
☐ 176 Derek Jeter	2.00	.90
☐ 177 Tino Martinez	.25	.11
☐ 178 Orlando Hernandez	.60	.25
☐ 179 Chuck Knoblauch	.25	.11
☐ 180 Bernie Williams	.25	.11
☐ 181 Chili Davis	.25	.11
☐ 182 David Cone	.40	.18
☐ 183 Ricky Ledee	.25	.11
☐ 184 Paul O'Neill	.25	.11
☐ 185 Jason Giambi	.25	.11
☐ 186 Eric Chavez	.40	.18
☐ 187 Matt Stairs	.25	.11
☐ 188 Miguel Tejada	.25	.11
☐ 189 Olmedo Saenz	.15	.07
☐ 190 Tim Hudson	.75	.35
☐ 191 John Jaha	.15	.07
☐ 192 Randy Velarde	.15	.07
☐ 193 Rico Brogna	.25	.11
☐ 194 Mike Lieberthal	.25	.11
☐ 195 Marlon Anderson	.15	.07
☐ 196 Bobby Abreu	.25	.11
☐ 197 Ron Gant	.25	.11
☐ 198 Randy Wolf	.15	.07
☐ 199 Desi Relaford	.15	.07
☐ 200 Doug Glanville	.25	.11
☐ 201 Warren Morris	.15	.07
☐ 202 Kris Benson	.25	.11
☐ 203 Kevin Young	.25	.11
☐ 204 Brian Giles	.25	.11
☐ 205 Jason Schmidt	.15	.07
☐ 206 Ed Sprague	.15	.07
☐ 207 Francisco Cordova	.15	.07
☐ 208 Mark McGwire	4.00	1.80
☐ 209 Jose Jimenez	.15	.07
☐ 210 Fernando Tatis	.40	.18
☐ 211 Kent Bottenfield	.15	.07
☐ 212 Eli Marrero	.15	.07

☐ 213 Edgar Renteria	.15	.07
☐ 214 Joe McEwing	.25	.11
☐ 215 J.D. Drew	.75	.35
☐ 216 Tony Gwynn	1.50	.70
☐ 217 Gary Matthews Jr.	.15	.07
☐ 218 Eric Owens	.15	.07
☐ 219 Damian Jackson	.15	.07
☐ 220 Reggie Sanders	.25	.11
☐ 221 Trevor Hoffman	.25	.11
☐ 222 Ben Davis	.40	.18
☐ 223 Shawn Estes	.15	.07
☐ 224 F.P. Santangelo	.15	.07
☐ 225 Livan Hernandez	.15	.07
☐ 226 Ellis Burks	.25	.11
☐ 227 J.T. Snow	.25	.11
☐ 228 Jeff Kent	.25	.11
☐ 229 Robb Nen	.25	.11
☐ 230 Marvin Benard	.15	.07
☐ 231 Ken Griffey Jr.	3.00	1.35
☐ 232 John Halama	.25	.11
☐ 233 Gil Meche	.25	.11
☐ 234 David Bell	.15	.07
☐ 235 Brian Hunter	.15	.07
☐ 236 Jay Buhner	.25	.11
☐ 237 Edgar Martinez	.25	.11
☐ 238 Jose Mesa	.15	.07
☐ 239 Wilson Alvarez	.15	.07
☐ 240 Wade Boggs	.60	.25
☐ 241 Fred McGriff	.40	.18
☐ 242 Jose Canseco	.75	.35
☐ 243 Kevin Stocker	.15	.07
☐ 244 Roberto Hernandez	.25	.11
☐ 245 Bubba Trammell	.25	.11
☐ 246 John Flaherty	.15	.07
☐ 247 Ivan Rodriguez	.75	.35
☐ 248 Rusty Greer	.25	.11
☐ 249 Rafael Palmeiro	.60	.25
☐ 250 Jeff Zimmerman	.25	.11
☐ 251 Royce Clayton	.15	.07
☐ 252 Todd Zeile	.25	.11
☐ 253 John Wetteland	.25	.11
☐ 254 Ruben Mateo	.60	.25
☐ 255 Kelvim Escobar	.15	.07
☐ 256 David Wells	.25	.11
☐ 257 Shawn Green	.60	.25
☐ 258 Homer Bush	.25	.11
☐ 259 Shannon Stewart	.25	.11
☐ 260 Carlos Delgado	.60	.25
☐ 261 Roy Halladay	.15	.07
☐ 262 Fernando Tatis SH CL	.15	.07
☐ 263 Jose Jimenez SH CL	.15	.07
☐ 264 Tony Gwynn SH CL	.75	.35
☐ 265 Wade Boggs SH CL	.25	.11
☐ 266 Cal Ripken SH CL	1.25	.55
☐ 267 David Cone SH CL	.25	.11
☐ 268 Mark McGwire SH CL	2.00	.90
☐ 269 Pedro Martinez SH CL	.40	.18
☐ 270 N. Garciaparra SH CL	1.00	.45

2000 Upper Deck Exclusives Gold

	MINT	NRMT
RANDOM INSERTS IN HOBBY PACKS		
STATED PRINT RUN 1 SERIAL #'d SET		
NOT PRICED DUE TO SCARCITY		

2000 Upper Deck Exclusives Silver

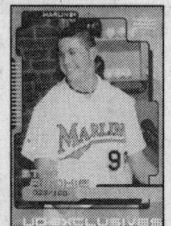

	MINT	NRMT
COMMON CARD (1-270)	5.00	2.20
*STARS: 12.5X TO 30X BASIC CARDS		
*YNG.STARS: 10X TO 25X BASIC CARDS		
*STAR ROOKIES: 5X TO 12X BASIC SR		
RANDOM INSERTS IN HOBBY PACKS		
STATED PRINT RUN 100 SERIAL #'d SETS		

2000 Upper Deck 2K Plus

	MINT	NRMT
COMPLETE SET (12)	60.00	27.00
COMMON CARD (2K1-2K12)	2.00	.90
SER.1 STATED ODDS 1:23		
*DIE CUTS: 4X TO 10X HI COLUMN		
DIE CUTS RANDOM INSERTS IN SER.1 HOBBY		
DIE CUTS PRINT RUN 100 SERIAL #'d SETS		
GOLD DIE CUTS RANDOM IN SER.1 HOBBY		
GOLD DIE CUT PRINT RUN 1 SERIAL #'d SET		
GOLD DC NOT PRICED DUE TO SCARCITY		

☐ 2K1 Ken Griffey Jr.	15.00	6.75
☐ 2K2 J.D. Drew	3.00	1.35
☐ 2K3 Derek Jeter	10.00	4.50
☐ 2K4 Nomar Garciaparra	10.00	4.50
☐ 2K5 Pat Burrell	6.00	2.70
☐ 2K6 Ruben Mateo	2.00	.90
☐ 2K7 Carlos Beltran	2.50	1.10
☐ 2K8 Vladimir Guerrero	4.00	1.80
☐ 2K9 Scott Rolen	4.00	1.80
☐ 2K10 Chipper Jones	8.00	3.60
☐ 2K11 Alex Rodriguez	10.00	4.50
☐ 2K12 Magglio Ordonez	3.00	1.35

2000 Upper Deck Faces of the Game

	MINT	NRMT
COMPLETE SET (20)	80.00	36.00
COMMON CARD (F1-F20)	2.00	.90
SER.1 STATED ODDS 1:11		
*DIE CUTS: 5X TO 12X HI COLUMN		
DIE CUTS RANDOM INSERTS IN SER.1 HOBBY		

		MINT	NRMT
☐ TG	Troy Glaus H	60.00	27.00
☐ TH	Todd Helton HR	60.00	27.00
☐ VG	Vladimir Guerrero HR	100.00	45.00
☐ AR-S	Alex Rodriguez AU/3 HR		
☐ DJ-S	Derek Jeter AU/2 HR		
☐ JR-S	K.Griffey AU/24 H EXCH		
☐ MR-S	Manny Ramirez AU/24 H		

2000 Upper Deck Game Jersey Patch

MINT NRMT
SER.1 STATED ODDS 1:10,000

☐ M-TG	Troy Glaus		
☐ P-AR	Alex Rodriguez		
☐ P-CJ	Chipper Jones	600.00	275.00
☐ P-CR	Cal Ripken		
☐ P-CY	Tom Glavine		
☐ P-DJ	Derek Jeter		
☐ P-FT	Frank Thomas		
☐ P-GK	Gabe Kapler		
☐ P-GM	Greg Maddux	600.00	275.00
☐ P-GV	Greg Vaughn		
☐ P-JB	Jeff Bagwell	500.00	220.00
☐ P-JC	Jose Canseco		
☐ P-JR	Ken Griffey Jr.		
☐ P-MP	Mike Piazza	750.00	350.00
☐ P-MR	Manny Ramirez		
☐ P-PM	Pedro Martinez		
☐ P-TH	Todd Helton		
☐ P-VG	Vladimir Guerrero		

2000 Upper Deck Game Jersey Patch 1 of 1's

MINT NRMT
RANDOM INSERTS IN SER.1 PACKS
STATED PRINT RUN 1 SET
NOT PRICED DUE TO SCARCITY

☐ AR-1	Alex Rodriguez
☐ CR-1	Cal Ripken
☐ DJ-1	Derek Jeter
☐ GK-1	Gabe Kapler
☐ JB-1	Jeff Bagwell
☐ JC-1	Jose Canseco
☐ JR-1	Ken Griffey Jr.
☐ MP-1	Mike Piazza
☐ MR-1	Manny Ramirez

2000 Upper Deck Hit Brigade

		MINT	NRMT
COMPLETE SET (15)		30.00	13.50
COMMON CARD (H1-H15)		1.00	.45

SER.1 STATED ODDS 1:18
*DIE CUTS: 10X TO 25X HI COLUMN
DIE CUTS RANDOM INSERTS IN SER.1
DIE CUTS PRINT RUN 100 SERIAL #'d SETS
GOLD DIE CUTS RANDOM IN SER.1 PACKS
GOLD DIE CUT PRINT RUN 1 SERIAL #'d SET
GOLD DC NOT PRICED DUE TO SCARCITY

DIE CUTS PRINT RUN 100 SERIAL #'d SETS
GOLD DIE CUTS RANDOM IN SER.1
GOLD DIE CUT PRINT RUN 1 SERIAL #'d SET
GOLD DC NOT PRICED DUE TO SCARCITY

☐ F1	Ken Griffey Jr.	12.00	5.50
☐ F2	Mark McGwire	12.00	5.50
☐ F3	Sammy Sosa	8.00	3.60
☐ F4	Alex Rodriguez	8.00	3.60
☐ F5	Manny Ramirez	3.00	1.35
☐ F6	Derek Jeter	8.00	3.60
☐ F7	Jeff Bagwell	3.00	1.35
☐ F8	Roger Clemens	6.00	2.70
☐ F9	Scott Rolen	3.00	1.35
☐ F10	Tony Gwynn	6.00	2.70
☐ F11	Nomar Garciaparra	8.00	3.60
☐ F12	Randy Johnson	2.50	1.10
☐ F13	Greg Maddux	6.00	2.70
☐ F14	Mike Piazza	8.00	3.60
☐ F15	Frank Thomas	5.00	2.20
☐ F16	Cal Ripken	10.00	4.50
☐ F17	Ivan Rodriguez	3.00	1.35
☐ F18	Mo Vaughn	2.00	.90
☐ F19	Chipper Jones	6.00	2.70
☐ F20	Sean Casey	2.00	.90

2000 Upper Deck Game Jersey

MINT NRMT
H STATED ODDS 1:288 HOBBY
HR STATED ODDS 1:2500 HOBBY/RETAIL
AU PRINT RUNS LISTED BELOW
AU EXCHANGE DEADLINE 7/15/00

☐ AR	Alex Rodriguez H	300.00	135.00
☐ CJ	Chipper Jones HR	150.00	70.00
☐ CR	Cal Ripken HR	250.00	110.00
☐ CY	Tom Glavine H	100.00	45.00
☐ DJ	Derek Jeter H	400.00	180.00
☐ FT	Frank Thomas H	150.00	70.00
☐ GK	Gabe Kapler HR	60.00	27.00
☐ GM	Greg Maddux HR	150.00	70.00
☐ GV	Greg Vaughn HR	50.00	22.00
☐ JB	Jeff Bagwell H	120.00	55.00
☐ JC	Jose Canseco H	150.00	70.00
☐ JR	Ken Griffey Jr. H	400.00	180.00
☐ MP	Mike Piazza H	250.00	110.00
☐ MR	Manny Ramirez HR	100.00	45.00
☐ PM	Pedro Martinez H	120.00	55.00

☐ H1	Ken Griffey Jr.	6.00	2.70
☐ H2	Tony Gwynn	3.00	1.35
☐ H3	Alex Rodriguez	4.00	1.80
☐ H4	Derek Jeter	4.00	1.80
☐ H5	Mike Piazza	4.00	1.80
☐ H6	Sammy Sosa	4.00	1.80
☐ H7	Juan Gonzalez	2.50	1.10
☐ H8	Scott Rolen	1.50	.70
☐ H9	Nomar Garciaparra	4.00	1.80
☐ H10	Barry Bonds	1.50	.70
☐ H11	Craig Biggio	1.00	.45
☐ H12	Chipper Jones	3.00	1.35
☐ H13	Frank Thomas	2.50	1.10
☐ H14	Larry Walker	1.25	.55
☐ H15	Mark McGwire	6.00	2.70

2000 Upper Deck Power MARK

		MINT	NRMT
COMPLETE SET (10)		80.00	36.00
COMMON CARD (MC1-MC10)		10.00	4.50

SER.1 STATED ODDS 1:23
DIE CUTS: 3X TO 8X HI COLUMN
DIE CUTS RANDOM INSERTS IN SER.1
HOBBY
DIE CUTS PRINT RUN 100 SERIAL #'d SETS
GOLD DIE CUTS RANDOM IN SER.1 HOBBY
GOLD DIE CUT PRINT RUN 1 SERIAL #'d SET
GOLD DC NOT PRICED DUE TO SCARCITY

☐ MC1	Mark McGwire	10.00	4.50
☐ MC2	Mark McGwire	10.00	4.50
☐ MC3	Mark McGwire	10.00	4.50
☐ MC4	Mark McGwire	10.00	4.50
☐ MC5	Mark McGwire	10.00	4.50
☐ MC6	Mark McGwire	10.00	4.50
☐ MC7	Mark McGwire	10.00	4.50
☐ MC8	Mark McGwire	10.00	4.50
☐ MC9	Mark McGwire	10.00	4.50
☐ MC10	Mark McGwire	10.00	4.50

2000 Upper Deck Power Rally

		MINT	NRMT
COMPLETE SET (15)		40.00	18.00
COMMON CARD (P1-P15)		1.25	.55

SER.1 STATED ODDS 1:11
*DIE CUTS: 8X TO 20X HI COLUMN

DIE CUTS RANDOM INSERTS IN SER.1 PACKS
DIE CUTS PRINT RUN 100 SERIAL #'d SETS
GOLD DIE CUTS RANDOM IN SER.1 PACKS
GOLD DIE CUT PRINT RUN 1 SERIAL #'d SET
GOLD DC NOT PRICED DUE TO SCARCITY

		MINT	NRMT
☐ P1	Ken Griffey Jr.	8.00	3.60
☐ P2	Mark McGwire	8.00	3.60
☐ P3	Sammy Sosa	5.00	2.20
☐ P4	Jose Canseco	2.00	.90
☐ P5	Juan Gonzalez	3.00	1.35
☐ P6	Bernie Williams	1.50	.70
☐ P7	Jeff Bagwell	2.00	.90
☐ P8	Chipper Jones	4.00	1.80
☐ P9	Vladimir Guerrero	2.00	.90
☐ P10	Mo Vaughn	1.25	.55
☐ P11	Derek Jeter	5.00	2.20
☐ P12	Mike Piazza	5.00	2.20
☐ P13	Barry Bonds	2.00	.90
☐ P14	Alex Rodriguez	5.00	2.20
☐ P15	Nomar Garciaparra	5.00	2.20

2000 Upper Deck PowerDeck Inserts

		MINT	NRMT
COMMON CARD (PD1-PD11)		8.00	3.60

SER.1 1-8 STATED ODDS 1:23
SER.1 8-11 STATED ODDS 1:287

		MINT	NRMT
☐ PD1	Ken Griffey Jr.	15.00	6.75
☐ PD2	Cal Ripken	12.00	5.50
☐ PD3	Mark McGwire	15.00	6.75
☐ PD4	Tony Gwynn	8.00	3.60
☐ PD5	Roger Clemens	8.00	3.60
☐ PD6	Alex Rodriguez EXCH		
☐ PD7	Sammy Sosa	10.00	4.50
☐ PD8	Derek Jeter	10.00	4.50
☐ PD9	Ken Griffey Jr. SP	50.00	22.00
☐ PD10	Mark McGwire SP	50.00	22.00
☐ PD11	Reggie Jackson SP	25.00	11.00

2000 Upper Deck Statitude

		MINT	NRMT
COMPLETE SET (30)		40.00	18.00
COMMON CARD (S1-S30)		.50	.23

SER.1 STATED ODDS 1:4

☐ S1	Mo Vaughn	1.00	.45
☐ S2	Matt Williams	1.00	.45
☐ S3	Travis Lee	.50	.23
☐ S4	Chipper Jones	3.00	1.35
☐ S5	Greg Maddux	3.00	1.35
☐ S6	Gabe Kapler	.50	.23
☐ S7	Cal Ripken	5.00	2.20
☐ S8	Nomar Garciaparra	4.00	1.80
☐ S9	Sammy Sosa	4.00	1.80
☐ S10	Frank Thomas	2.50	1.10
☐ S11	Manny Ramirez	1.50	.70
☐ S12	Larry Walker	1.25	.55
☐ S13	Ivan Rodriguez	1.50	.70
☐ S14	Jeff Bagwell	1.50	.70
☐ S15	Craig Biggio	1.00	.45
☐ S16	Vladimir Guerrero	1.50	.70
☐ S17	Mike Piazza	4.00	1.80
☐ S18	Bernie Williams	1.25	.55
☐ S19	Derek Jeter	4.00	1.80
☐ S20	Jose Canseco	1.50	.70
☐ S21	Eric Chavez	.50	.23
☐ S22	Scott Rolen	1.50	.70
☐ S23	Mark McGwire	6.00	2.70
☐ S24	Tony Gwynn	3.00	1.35
☐ S25	Barry Bonds	1.50	.70
☐ S26	Ken Griffey Jr.	6.00	2.70
☐ S27	Alex Rodriguez	4.00	1.80
☐ S28	J.D. Drew	1.25	.55
☐ S29	Juan Gonzalez	2.50	1.10
☐ S30	Roger Clemens	3.00	1.35

1999 Upper Deck Black Diamond

		MINT	NRMT
COMPLETE SET (120)		120.00	55.00
COMP.SET w/o DD's (90)		40.00	18.00
COMMON CARD (1-90)		.20	.09
MINOR STARS 1-90		.30	.14
SEMISTARS 1-90		.50	.23
UNLISTED STARS 1-90		.75	.35
COMMON DIAM.DEB (91-120)		1.50	.70
DD MINOR STARS		2.50	1.10
DD SEMISTARS		4.00	1.80

DIAMOND DEBUT STATED ODDS 1:4

☐ 1	Darin Erstad	.50	.23
☐ 2	Tim Salmon	.50	.23
☐ 3	Jim Edmonds	.30	.14
☐ 4	Matt Williams	.75	.35
☐ 5	David Dellucci	.20	.09
☐ 6	Jay Bell	.30	.14
☐ 7	Andres Galarraga	.50	.23
☐ 8	Chipper Jones	2.00	.90
☐ 9	Greg Maddux	2.00	.90
☐ 10	Andruw Jones	.75	.35
☐ 11	Cal Ripken	3.00	1.35
☐ 12	Rafael Palmeiro	.75	.35
☐ 13	Brady Anderson	.30	.14
☐ 14	Mike Mussina	.75	.35
☐ 15	Nomar Garciaparra	2.50	1.10
☐ 16	Mo Vaughn	.75	.35
☐ 17	Pedro Martinez	1.00	.45
☐ 18	Sammy Sosa	2.50	1.10
☐ 19	Henry Rodriguez	.30	.14
☐ 20	Frank Thomas	1.50	.70
☐ 21	Magglio Ordonez	.75	.35
☐ 22	Albert Belle	.75	.35
☐ 23	Paul Konerko	.75	.35
☐ 24	Sean Casey	.75	.35
☐ 25	Jim Thome	.75	.35
☐ 26	Kenny Lofton	.50	.23
☐ 27	Sandy Alomar Jr.	.30	.14
☐ 28	Jaret Wright	.30	.14
☐ 29	Larry Walker	.75	.35
☐ 30	Todd Helton	.75	.35
☐ 31	Vinny Castilla	.30	.14
☐ 32	Tony Clark	.30	.14
☐ 33	Damion Easley	.20	.09
☐ 34	Mark Kotsay	.20	.09
☐ 35	Derrek Lee	.30	.14
☐ 36	Moises Alou	.30	.14
☐ 37	Jeff Bagwell	1.00	.45
☐ 38	Craig Biggio	.75	.35
☐ 39	Randy Johnson	.75	.35
☐ 40	Dean Palmer	.30	.14
☐ 41	Johnny Damon	.30	.14
☐ 42	Chan Ho Park	.30	.14
☐ 43	Raul Mondesi	.30	.14
☐ 44	Gary Sheffield	.30	.14
☐ 45	Jeromy Burnitz	.30	.14
☐ 46	Marquis Grissom	.20	.09
☐ 47	Jeff Cirillo	.20	.09
☐ 48	Paul Molitor	.75	.35
☐ 49	Todd Walker	.30	.14
☐ 50	Vladimir Guerrero	1.00	.45
☐ 51	Brad Fullmer	.20	.09
☐ 52	Mike Piazza	2.50	1.10
☐ 53	Hideo Nomo	.75	.35
☐ 54	Carlos Baerga	.30	.14
☐ 55	John Olerud	.30	.14
☐ 56	Derek Jeter	2.50	1.10
☐ 57	Hideki Irabu	.30	.14
☐ 58	Tino Martinez	.30	.14
☐ 59	Bernie Williams	.75	.35
☐ 60	Miguel Tejada	.30	.14
☐ 61	Ben Grieve	.75	.35
☐ 62	Jason Giambi	.30	.14
☐ 63	Scott Rolen	1.00	.45
☐ 64	Doug Glanville	.30	.14
☐ 65	Desi Relaford	.20	.09
☐ 66	Tony Womack	.20	.09
☐ 67	Jason Kendall	.30	.14
☐ 68	Jose Guillen	.20	.09
☐ 69	Tony Gwynn	2.00	.90
☐ 70	Ken Caminiti	.30	.14
☐ 71	Greg Vaughn	.50	.23
☐ 72	Kevin Brown	.50	.23
☐ 73	Barry Bonds	1.00	.45
☐ 74	J.T. Snow	.30	.14
☐ 75	Jeff Kent	.30	.14
☐ 76	Ken Griffey Jr.	4.00	1.80
☐ 77	Alex Rodriguez	2.50	1.10
☐ 78	Edgar Martinez	.30	.14
☐ 79	Jay Buhner	.30	.14
☐ 80	Mark McGwire	5.00	2.20
☐ 81	Delino DeShields	.20	.09
☐ 82	Brian Jordan	.30	.14
☐ 83	Quinton McCracken	.20	.09
☐ 84	Fred McGriff	.50	.23
☐ 85	Juan Gonzalez	1.50	.70
☐ 86	Ivan Rodriguez	1.00	.45
☐ 87	Will Clark	.75	.35
☐ 88	Roger Clemens	2.00	.90
☐ 89	Jose Cruz Jr.	.30	.14
☐ 90	Babe Ruth	5.00	2.20

		MINT	NRMT
☐ 91	Troy Glaus DD	6.00	2.70
☐ 92	Jarrod Washburn DD	1.50	.70
☐ 93	Travis Lee DD	4.00	1.80
☐ 94	Bruce Chen DD	2.50	1.10
☐ 95	Mike Caruso DD	1.50	.70
☐ 96	Jim Parque DD	1.50	.70
☐ 97	Kerry Wood DD	5.00	2.20
☐ 98	Jeremy Giambi DD	2.50	1.10
☐ 99	Matt Anderson DD	1.50	.70
☐ 100	Seth Greisinger DD	1.50	.70
☐ 101	Gabe Alvarez DD	1.50	.70
☐ 102	Rafael Medina DD	1.50	.70
☐ 103	Daryle Ward DD	2.50	1.10
☐ 104	Alex Cora DD	1.50	.70
☐ 105	Adrian Beltre DD	5.00	2.20
☐ 106	Geoff Jenkins DD	2.50	1.10
☐ 107	Eric Milton DD	1.50	.70
☐ 108	Carl Pavano DD	1.50	.70
☐ 109	Eric Chavez DD	4.00	1.80
☐ 110	Orlando Hernandez DD	5.00	2.20
☐ 111	A.J. Hinch DD	1.50	.70
☐ 112	Carlton Loewer DD	1.50	.70
☐ 113	Aramis Ramirez DD	4.00	1.80
☐ 114	Cliff Politte DD	1.50	.70
☐ 115	Matt Clement DD	2.50	1.10
☐ 116	Alex Gonzalez DD	2.50	1.10
☐ 117	J.D. Drew DD	10.00	4.50
☐ 118	Shane Monahan DD	1.50	.70
☐ 119	Rolando Arrojo DD	1.50	.70
☐ 120	George Lombard DD	2.50	1.10

1999 Upper Deck Black Diamond Double

	MINT	NRMT
COMMON CARD (1-120)	1.25	.55

*STARS: 2.5X TO 6X BASIC CARDS
*DIAM.DEB: .6X TO 1.2X BASIC DIAM.DEB.
RANDOM INSERTS IN PACKS
1-90 PRINT RUN 3000 SERIAL #'d SETS
91-120 PRINT RUN 2500 SERIAL #'d SETS
GRIFFEY, MCGWIRE AND SOSA ARE SP'S

☐ 18	Sammy Sosa/1998	25.00	11.00
☐ 76	Ken Griffey Jr./1998	40.00	18.00
☐ 80	Mark McGwire/1998	50.00	22.00
☐ 117	J.D. Drew DD	50.00	22.00

1999 Upper Deck Black Diamond Triple

	MINT	NRMT
COMMON CARD (1-120)	2.00	.90

*STARS: 4X TO 10X BASIC CARDS
*DIAM.DEB: 1X TO 2.5X BASIC DIAM.DEB.
RANDOM INSERTS IN PACKS
1-90 PRINT RUN 1500 SERIAL #'d SETS
91-120 PRINT RUN 1000 SERIAL #'d SETS
GRIFFEY, MCGWIRE AND SOSA ARE SP'S

☐ 18	Sammy Sosa/273	60.00	27.00
☐ 76	Ken Griffey Jr./350	80.00	36.00
☐ 80	Mark McGwire/457	100.00	45.00
☐ 117	J.D. Drew DD	100.00	45.00

1999 Upper Deck Black Diamond Quadruple

	MINT	NRMT
COMMON CARD (1-120)	6.00	2.70

*STARS: 12.5X TO 30X BASIC CARDS
*DIAM.DEB: 2.5X TO 6X BASIC DIAM.DEB.
RANDOM INSERTS IN PACKS
1-90 PRINT RUN 150 SERIAL #'d SETS
91-120 PRINT RUN 100 SERIAL #'d SETS
GRIFFEY, MCGWIRE AND SOSA ARE SP'S

☐ 18	Sammy Sosa/66	150.00	70.00
☐ 76	Ken Griffey Jr./56	250.00	110.00
☐ 80	Mark McGwire/70	300.00	135.00
☐ 117	J.D. Drew DD	250.00	110.00

1999 Upper Deck Black Diamond A Piece of History

	MINT	NRMT
RANDOM INSERTS IN PACKS		
☐ BW	Bernie Williams	80.00	36.00
☐ JG	Juan Gonzalez	120.00	55.00
☐ MM	Mark McGwire	600.00	275.00
☐ MV	Mo Vaughn	60.00	27.00
☐ SS	Sammy Sosa	250.00	110.00
☐ TG	Tony Gwynn	150.00	70.00

1999 Upper Deck Black Diamond Dominance

	MINT	NRMT
COMPLETE SET (30)	400.00	180.00
COMMON CARD (D1-D30)	2.00	.90
MINOR STARS	3.00	1.35
SEMISTARS	5.00	2.20
UNLISTED STARS	8.00	3.60

RANDOM INSERTS IN PACKS
STATED PRINT RUN 1500 SERIAL #'d SETS
PARALLEL EMERALD ONE OF ONE'S EXIST

☐ D1	Kerry Wood	8.00	3.60
☐ D2	Derek Jeter	25.00	11.00
☐ D3	Alex Rodriguez	25.00	11.00
☐ D4	Frank Thomas	15.00	6.75
☐ D5	Jeff Bagwell	10.00	4.50
☐ D6	Mo Vaughn	8.00	3.60
☐ D7	Ivan Rodriguez	10.00	4.50
☐ D8	Cal Ripken	30.00	13.50
☐ D9	Rolando Arrojo	2.00	.90
☐ D10	Chipper Jones	20.00	9.00
☐ D11	Kenny Lofton	5.00	2.20
☐ D12	Paul Konerko	8.00	3.60
☐ D13	Mike Piazza	25.00	11.00
☐ D14	Ben Grieve	8.00	3.60
☐ D15	Nomar Garciaparra	25.00	11.00
☐ D16	Travis Lee	5.00	2.20
☐ D17	Scott Rolen	10.00	4.50
☐ D18	Juan Gonzalez	15.00	6.75
☐ D19	Tony Gwynn	20.00	9.00
☐ D20	Tony Clark	3.00	1.35
☐ D21	Roger Clemens	20.00	9.00
☐ D22	Sammy Sosa	25.00	11.00
☐ D23	Larry Walker	8.00	3.60
☐ D24	Ken Griffey Jr.	40.00	18.00
☐ D25	Mark McGwire	50.00	22.00
☐ D26	Barry Bonds	10.00	4.50
☐ D27	Vladimir Guerrero	10.00	4.50
☐ D28	Tino Martinez	3.00	1.35
☐ D29	Greg Maddux	20.00	9.00
☐ D30	Babe Ruth	50.00	22.00

1999 Upper Deck Black Diamond Mystery Numbers

	MINT	NRMT
COMPLETE SET (30)	1000.00	450.00
COMMON CARD (M1-M30)	2.50	1.10

RANDOM INSERTS IN HOBBY PACKS
PRINT RUNS LISTED BELOW
SCARCE EMERALD PARALLELS EXIST

		MINT	NRMT
❏ M1	Babe Ruth/100	200.00	90.00
❏ M2	Ken Griffey Jr./200	150.00	70.00
❏ M3	Kerry Wood/300	20.00	9.00
❏ M4	Mark McGwire/400	120.00	55.00
❏ M5	Alex Rodriguez/500	60.00	27.00
❏ M6	Chipper Jones/600	40.00	18.00
❏ M7	Nomar Garciaparra/700	50.00	22.00
❏ M8	Derek Jeter/800	50.00	22.00
❏ M9	Mike Piazza/900	50.00	22.00
❏ M10	Roger Clemens/1000	30.00	13.50
❏ M11	Greg Maddux/1100	30.00	13.50
❏ M12	Scott Rolen/1200	15.00	6.75
❏ M13	Cal Ripken/1300	50.00	22.00
❏ M14	Ben Grieve/1400	8.00	3.60
❏ M15	Troy Glaus/1500	10.00	4.50
❏ M16	Sammy Sosa/1600	30.00	13.50
❏ M17	Darin Erstad/1700	4.00	1.80
❏ M18	Juan Gonzalez/1800	20.00	9.00
❏ M19	Pedro Martinez/1900	12.00	5.50
❏ M20	Larry Walker/2000	8.00	3.60
❏ M21	Vladimir Guerrero/2100	10.00	4.50
❏ M22	Jeff Bagwell/2200	10.00	4.50
❏ M23	Jaret Wright/2300	2.50	1.10
❏ M24	Travis Lee/2400	2.50	1.10
❏ M25	Barry Bonds/2500	8.00	3.60
❏ M26	Orlando Hernandez/2600	5.00	2.20
❏ M27	Frank Thomas/2700	12.00	5.50
❏ M28	Tony Gwynn/2800	15.00	6.75
❏ M29	Andres Galarraga/2900	3.00	1.35
❏ M30	Craig Biggio/3000	5.00	2.20

2000 Upper Deck Black Diamond

	MINT	NRMT
COMPLETE SET (120)	150.00	70.00
COMP.SET w/o SP's (90)	40.00	18.00
COMMON CARD (1-90)	.20	.09
MINOR STARS	.30	.14
SEMISTARS	.50	.23
COMMON DD (91-120)	1.50	.70

DD STATED ODDS 1:4
REGGIE BAT LISTED W/UD APH 500 CLUB

❏ 1	Darin Erstad	.30	.14
❏ 2	Tim Salmon	.50	.23
❏ 3	Mo Vaughn	.60	.25
❏ 4	Matt Williams	.60	.25
❏ 5	Travis Lee	.30	.14
❏ 6	Randy Johnson	.75	.35
❏ 7	Tom Glavine	.60	.25
❏ 8	Chipper Jones	2.00	.90
❏ 9	Greg Maddux	2.00	.90
❏ 10	Andruw Jones	.75	.35
❏ 11	Brian Jordan	.30	.14
❏ 12	Cal Ripken	3.00	1.35
❏ 13	Albert Belle	.60	.25
❏ 14	Mike Mussina	.75	.35
❏ 15	Nomar Garciaparra	2.50	1.10
❏ 16	Troy O'Leary	.30	.14
❏ 17	Pedro Martinez	1.00	.45
❏ 18	Sammy Sosa	2.50	1.10
❏ 19	Henry Rodriguez	.20	.09
❏ 20	Frank Thomas	1.50	.70
❏ 21	Magglio Ordonez	.50	.23
❏ 22	Greg Vaughn	.30	.14
❏ 23	Barry Larkin	.60	.25
❏ 24	Sean Casey	.60	.25
❏ 25	Jim Thome	.60	.25
❏ 26	Kenny Lofton	.30	.14
❏ 27	Roberto Alomar	.75	.35
❏ 28	Manny Ramirez	1.00	.45
❏ 29	Larry Walker	.75	.35
❏ 30	Todd Helton	.60	.25
❏ 31	Gabe Kapler	.50	.23
❏ 32	Tony Clark	.30	.14
❏ 33	Dean Palmer	.30	.14
❏ 34	Cliff Floyd	.30	.14
❏ 35	Alex Gonzalez	.30	.14
❏ 36	Moises Alou	.30	.14
❏ 37	Jeff Bagwell	1.00	.45
❏ 38	Craig Biggio	.60	.25
❏ 39	Richard Hidalgo	.30	.14
❏ 40	Carlos Beltran	.75	.35
❏ 41	Johnny Damon	.30	.14
❏ 42	Adrian Beltre	.50	.23
❏ 43	Gary Sheffield	.//	.14
❏ 44	Kevin Brown	.50*	.23
❏ 45	Jeromy Burnitz	.30	.14
❏ 46	Jeff Cirillo	.30	.14
❏ 47	Joe Mays	.30	.14
❏ 48	Todd Walker	.30	.14
❏ 49	Vladimir Guerrero	1.00	.45
❏ 50	Michael Barrett	.30	.14
❏ 51	Rickey Henderson	1.00	.45
❏ 52	Mike Piazza	2.50	1.10
❏ 53	Robin Ventura	.30	.14
❏ 54	John Olerud	.30	.14
❏ 55	Edgardo Alfonzo	.50	.23
❏ 56	Derek Jeter	2.50	1.10
❏ 57	Orlando Hernandez	.60	.25
❏ 58	Tino Martinez	.30	.14
❏ 59	Bernie Williams	.75	.35
❏ 60	Roger Clemens	2.00	.90
❏ 61	Eric Chavez	.30	.14
❏ 62	Ben Grieve	.60	.25
❏ 63	Jason Giambi	.30	.14
❏ 64	Scott Rolen	.60	.25
❏ 65	Bobby Abreu	.30	.14
❏ 66	Curt Schilling	.50	.23
❏ 67	Mike Lieberthal	.30	.14
❏ 68	Warren Morris	.30	.14
❏ 69	Brian Giles	.30	.14
❏ 70	Eric Owens	.20	.09
❏ 71	Tony Gwynn	2.00	.90
❏ 72	Reggie Sanders	.30	.14
❏ 73	Barry Bonds	1.00	.45
❏ 74	J.T. Snow	.30	.14
❏ 75	Jeff Kent	.30	.14
❏ 76	Ken Griffey Jr.	4.00	1.80
❏ 77	Alex Rodriguez	2.50	1.10
❏ 78	Edgar Martinez	.30	.14
❏ 79	Jay Buhner	.30	.14
❏ 80	Mark McGwire	4.00	1.80
❏ 81	J.D. Drew	1.00	.45
❏ 82	Eric Davis	.30	.14
❏ 83	Fernando Tatis	.30	.14
❏ 84	Wade Boggs	.75	.35
❏ 85	Fred McGriff	.50	.23
❏ 86	Juan Gonzalez	1.50	.70
❏ 87	Ivan Rodriguez	1.00	.45
❏ 88	Rafael Palmeiro	.75	.35
❏ 89	Shawn Green	.75	.35
❏ 90	Carlos Delgado	.60	.25
❏ 91	Pat Burrell DD	8.00	3.60
❏ 92	Eric Munson DD	8.00	3.60
❏ 93	Jorge Toca DD	2.00	.90
❏ 94	Rick Ankiel DD	15.00	6.75
❏ 95	Tony Armas Jr. DD	2.50	1.10
❏ 96	Byung-Hyun Kim DD	3.00	1.35
❏ 97	Alfonso Soriano DD	8.00	3.60
❏ 98	Mark Quinn DD	3.00	1.35
❏ 99	Ryan Rupe DD	1.50	.70
❏ 100	Adam Kennedy DD	1.50	.70
❏ 101	Jeff Weaver DD	2.00	.90
❏ 102	Ramon Ortiz DD	1.50	.70
❏ 103	Eugene Kingsale DD	1.50	.70
❏ 104	Josh Beckett DD	8.00	3.60
❏ 105	Eric Gagne DD	2.50	1.10
❏ 106	Peter Bergeron DD	2.00	.90
❏ 107	Erubiel Durazo DD	8.00	3.60
❏ 108	Chad Meyers DD	1.50	.70
❏ 109	Kip Wells DD	2.00	.90
❏ 110	Chad Harville DD	1.50	.70
❏ 111	Matt Riley DD	6.00	2.70
❏ 112	Ben Petrick DD	2.00	.90
❏ 113	Ed Yarnall DD	1.50	.70
❏ 114	Calvin Murray DD	1.50	.70
❏ 115	Vernon Wells DD	2.50	1.10
❏ 116	A.J. Burnett DD	2.00	.90
❏ 117	Jacque Jones DD	1.50	.70
❏ 118	Francisco Cordero DD	1.50	.70
❏ 119	Tomokazu Ohka DD	3.00	1.35
❏ 120	Julio Ramirez DD	1.50	.70

2000 Upper Deck Black Diamond Final Cut

	MINT	NRMT
COMMON CARD (1-120)	6.00	2.70

*STARS 1-90: 12.5X TO 30X BASIC CARDS
*YNG.STARS 1-90: 10X TO 25X BASIC CARDS
*DIAM.DEB 91-120: 2.5X TO 6X BASIC DD
RANDOM INSERTS IN PACKS
STATED PRINT RUN 100 SERIAL #'d SETS

2000 Upper Deck Black Diamond Reciprocal Cut

MOISES ALOU

	MINT	NRMT
COMMON CARD (1-90)	1.00	.45

*STARS 1-90: 2X TO 5X BASIC CARDS
*YNG.STARS 1-90: 1.5X TO 4X BASIC CARDS
CARDS 1-90 STATED ODDS 1:7

	MINT	NRMT
COMMON DD (91-120)	2.50	1.10

*DIAM.DEB 91-120: .6X TO 1.5X BASIC DD
DD 91-120 STATED ODDS 1:12

2000 Upper Deck Black Diamond A Piece of History

	MINT	NRMT

STATED ODDS 1:179 HOBBY, 1:359 RETAIL

		MINT	NRMT
❑ AB	Albert Belle	60.00	27.00
❑ AJ	Andruw Jones	60.00	27.00
❑ AR	Alex Rodriguez	200.00	90.00
❑ BB	Barry Bonds	80.00	36.00
❑ CJ	Chipper Jones	120.00	55.00
❑ DE	Darin Erstad	50.00	22.00
❑ DJ	Derek Jeter	250.00	110.00
❑ IR	Ivan Rodriguez	80.00	36.00
❑ JC	Jose Canseco	100.00	45.00
❑ JR	Ken Griffey Jr.	300.00	135.00
❑ MP	Mike Piazza	120.00	55.00
❑ MV	Mo Vaughn	50.00	22.00
❑ RM	Raul Mondesi	40.00	18.00
❑ SR	Scott Rolen	80.00	36.00
❑ TG	Tony Gwynn	100.00	45.00
❑ TH	Todd Helton	50.00	22.00
❑ TL	Travis Lee	40.00	18.00
❑ VG	Vladimir Guerrero	80.00	36.00
❑ CAL	Cal Ripken	200.00	90.00

2000 Upper Deck Black Diamond A Piece of History Double

	MINT	NRMT
STATED ODDS 1:1079 HOBBY		

2000 Upper Deck Black Diamond A Piece of History Triple

	MINT	NRMT
RANDOM INSERTS IN PACKS		
STATED PRINT RUN 1 SERIAL #'d SET		
NO PRICING DUE TO SCARCITY		

2000 Upper Deck Black Diamond Barrage

		MINT	NRMT
COMPLETE SET (10)		60.00	27.00
COMMON CARD (B1-B10)		4.00	1.80
STATED ODDS 1:29			
❑ B1	Mark McGwire	15.00	6.75
❑ B2	Ken Griffey Jr.	15.00	6.75
❑ B3	Sammy Sosa	10.00	4.50
❑ B4	Jeff Bagwell	4.00	1.80
❑ B5	Juan Gonzalez	6.00	2.70
❑ B6	Alex Rodriguez	10.00	4.50
❑ B7	Manny Ramirez	4.00	1.80
❑ B8	Ivan Rodriguez	4.00	1.80
❑ B9	Chipper Jones	8.00	3.60
❑ B10	Mike Piazza	10.00	4.50

2000 Upper Deck Black Diamond Constant Threat

	MINT	NRMT
COMPLETE SET (10)	60.00	27.00
COMMON CARD (T1-T10)	4.00	1.80
STATED ODDS 1:29		

		MINT	NRMT
❑ T1	Ken Griffey Jr.	15.00	6.75
❑ T2	Vladimir Guerrero	4.00	1.80
❑ T3	Alex Rodriguez	10.00	4.50
❑ T4	Sammy Sosa	10.00	4.50
❑ T5	Juan Gonzalez	6.00	2.70
❑ T6	Derek Jeter	10.00	4.50
❑ T7	Nomar Garciaparra	10.00	4.50
❑ T8	Barry Bonds	4.00	1.80
❑ T9	Chipper Jones	8.00	3.60
❑ T10	Mike Piazza	10.00	4.50

2000 Upper Deck Black Diamond Diamonation

		MINT	NRMT
COMPLETE SET (10)		15.00	6.75
COMMON CARD (D1-D10)		.75	.35
STATED ODDS 1:4			
❑ D1	Ken Griffey Jr.	5.00	2.20
❑ D2	Randy Johnson	1.00	.45
❑ D3	Mark McGwire	5.00	2.20
❑ D4	Manny Ramirez	1.25	.55
❑ D5	Scott Rolen	1.25	.55
❑ D6	Bernie Williams	1.00	.45
❑ D7	Roger Clemens	2.50	1.10
❑ D8	Mo Vaughn	.75	.35
❑ D9	Frank Thomas	2.00	.90
❑ D10	Sean Casey	.75	.35

2000 Upper Deck Black Diamond Diamond Gallery

		MINT	NRMT
COMPLETE SET (10)		50.00	22.00
COMMON CARD (G1-G10)		3.00	1.35
STATED ODDS 1:14			
❑ G1	Derek Jeter	8.00	3.60
❑ G2	Alex Rodriguez	8.00	3.60
❑ G3	Nomar Garciaparra	8.00	3.60
❑ G4	Cal Ripken	10.00	4.50
❑ G5	Sammy Sosa	8.00	3.60
❑ G6	Tony Gwynn	6.00	2.70
❑ G7	Mark McGwire	12.00	5.50
❑ G8	Roger Clemens	6.00	2.70
❑ G9	Greg Maddux	6.00	2.70
❑ G10	Pedro Martinez	3.00	1.35

2000 Upper Deck Black Diamond DiamondMight

		MINT	NRMT
COMPLETE SET (10)		40.00	18.00
COMMON CARD (M1-M10)		2.50	1.10
STATED ODDS 1:14			
❑ M1	Ken Griffey Jr.	10.00	4.50
❑ M2	Mark McGwire	10.00	4.50
❑ M3	Sammy Sosa	6.00	2.70
❑ M4	Manny Ramirez	2.50	1.10
❑ M5	Jeff Bagwell	2.50	1.10
❑ M6	Frank Thomas	4.00	1.80
❑ M7	Mike Piazza	6.00	2.70
❑ M8	Juan Gonzalez	4.00	1.80
❑ M9	Barry Bonds	2.50	1.10
❑ M10	Alex Rodriguez	6.00	2.70

2000 Upper Deck Black Diamond Diamonds in the Rough

		MINT	NRMT
COMPLETE SET (10)		25.00	11.00
COMMON CARD (R1-R10)		1.00	.45
STATED ODDS 1:9			
❑ R1	Pat Burrell	5.00	2.20
❑ R2	Eric Munson	5.00	2.20
❑ R3	Alfonso Soriano	5.00	2.20
❑ R4	Ruben Mateo	2.00	.90
❑ R5	A.J. Burnett	1.25	.55

❏ R6 Ben Davis	2.00	.90
❏ R7 Lance Berkman	1.50	.70
❏ R8 Ed Yarnall	1.00	.45
❏ R9 Rick Ankiel	10.00	4.50
❏ R10 Ryan Bradley	1.00	.45

1999 Upper Deck Century Legends

	MINT	NRMT
COMPLETE SET (131)	40.00	18.00
COMMON CARD (1-135)	.15	.07
MINOR STARS	.25	.11
SEMISTARS	.40	.18
UNLISTED STARS	.60	.25

CARDS 11, 25, 26 AND 126 DO NOT EXIST
FOXX BAT LISTED W/UD APH 500 CLUB

❏ 1 Babe Ruth	3.00	1.35
❏ 2 Willie Mays	1.50	.70
❏ 3 Ty Cobb	1.50	.70
❏ 4 Walter Johnson	.75	.35
❏ 5 Hank Aaron	1.50	.70
❏ 6 Lou Gehrig	2.00	.90
❏ 7 Christy Mathewson	.60	.25
❏ 8 Ted Williams	1.50	.70
❏ 9 Rogers Hornsby	.60	.25
❏ 10 Stan Musial	1.00	.45
❏ 12 Grover Alexander	.60	.25
❏ 13 Honus Wagner	.75	.35
❏ 14 Cy Young	.75	.35
❏ 15 Jimmie Foxx	.75	.35
❏ 16 Johnny Bench	.75	.35
❏ 17 Mickey Mantle	3.00	1.35
❏ 18 Josh Gibson	1.00	.45
❏ 19 Satchel Paige	1.00	.45
❏ 20 Roberto Clemente	1.50	.70
❏ 21 Warren Spahn	.60	.25
❏ 22 Frank Robinson	.60	.25
❏ 23 Lefty Grove	.40	.18
❏ 24 Eddie Collins	.40	.18
❏ 27 Tris Speaker	.60	.25
❏ 28 Mike Schmidt	1.00	.45
❏ 29 Napoleon Lajoie	.25	.11
❏ 30 Steve Carlton	.75	.35
❏ 31 Bob Gibson	.60	.25
❏ 32 Tom Seaver	.75	.35
❏ 33 George Sisler	.25	.11
❏ 34 Barry Bonds	.75	.35
❏ 35 Joe Jackson NNO UER.	1.00	.45
❏ 36 Bob Feller	.60	.25
❏ 37 Hank Greenberg	.60	.25
❏ 38 Ernie Banks	.75	.35
❏ 39 Greg Maddux	1.50	.70
❏ 40 Yogi Berra	1.00	.45
❏ 41 Nolan Ryan	2.50	1.10
❏ 42 Mel Ott	.60	.25
❏ 43 Al Simmons	.25	.11
❏ 44 Jackie Robinson	1.50	.70
❏ 45 Carl Hubbell	.25	.11
❏ 46 Charley Gehringer	.25	.11
❏ 47 Buck Leonard	.25	.11
❏ 48 Reggie Jackson	.75	.35
❏ 49 Tony Gwynn	1.50	.70
❏ 50 Roy Campanella	1.00	.45
❏ 51 Ken Griffey Jr.	3.00	1.35
❏ 52 Barry Bonds	.75	.35
❏ 53 Roger Clemens	1.50	.70

❏ 54 Tony Gwynn	1.50	.70
❏ 55 Cal Ripken	2.50	1.10
❏ 56 Greg Maddux	1.50	.70
❏ 57 Frank Thomas	1.25	.55
❏ 58 Mark McGwire	4.00	1.80
❏ 59 Mike Piazza	2.00	.90
❏ 60 Wade Boggs	.60	.25
❏ 61 Alex Rodriguez	2.00	.90
❏ 62 Juan Gonzalez	1.25	.55
❏ 63 Mo Vaughn	.60	.25
❏ 64 Albert Belle	.60	.25
❏ 65 Sammy Sosa	2.00	.90
❏ 66 Nomar Garciaparra	2.00	.90
❏ 67 Derek Jeter	2.00	.90
❏ 68 Kevin Brown	.40	.18
❏ 69 Jose Canseco	.75	.35
❏ 70 Randy Johnson	.60	.25
❏ 71 Tom Glavine	.60	.25
❏ 72 Barry Larkin	.60	.25
❏ 73 Curt Schilling	.40	.18
❏ 74 Moises Alou	.25	.11
❏ 75 Fred McGriff	.40	.18
❏ 76 Pedro Martinez	.75	.35
❏ 77 Andres Galarraga	.40	.18
❏ 78 Will Clark	.60	.25
❏ 79 Larry Walker	.60	.25
❏ 80 Ivan Rodriguez	.75	.35
❏ 81 Chipper Jones	1.50	.70
❏ 82 Jeff Bagwell	.75	.35
❏ 83 Craig Biggio	.60	.25
❏ 84 Kerry Wood	.25	.11
❏ 85 Roberto Alomar	.60	.25
❏ 86 Vinny Castilla	.25	.11
❏ 87 Kenny Lofton	.40	.18
❏ 88 Rafael Palmeiro	.60	.25
❏ 89 Manny Ramirez	.75	.35
❏ 90 David Wells	.25	.11
❏ 91 Mark Grace	.40	.18
❏ 92 Bernie Williams	.60	.25
❏ 93 David Cone	.40	.18
❏ 94 John Olerud	.25	.11
❏ 95 John Smoltz	.40	.18
❏ 96 Tino Martinez	.25	.11
❏ 97 Raul Mondesi	.25	.11
❏ 98 Gary Sheffield	.25	.11
❏ 99 Orel Hershiser	.25	.11
❏ 100 Rickey Henderson	.75	.35
❏ 101 J.D. Drew 21CP	1.00	.45
❏ 102 Troy Glaus 21CP	.60	.25
❏ 103 Nomar Garciaparra 21CP	2.00	.90
❏ 104 Scott Rolen 21CP	.75	.35
❏ 105 Ryan Minor 21CP	.25	.11
❏ 106 Travis Lee 21CP	.40	.18
❏ 107 Roy Halladay 21CP	.25	.11
❏ 108 Carlos Beltran 21CP	.75	.35
❏ 109 Alex Rodriguez 21CP	2.00	.90
❏ 110 Eric Chavez 21CP	.40	.18
❏ 111 Vladimir Guerrero 21CP	.75	.35
❏ 112 Ben Grieve 21CP	.60	.25
❏ 113 Kerry Wood 21CP	.60	.25
❏ 114 Alex Gonzalez 21CP	.25	.11
❏ 115 Darin Erstad 21CP	.40	.18
❏ 116 Derek Jeter 21CP	2.00	.90
❏ 117 Jaret Wright 21CP	.25	.11
❏ 118 Jose Cruz Jr. 21CP	.25	.11
❏ 119 Chipper Jones 21CP	1.50	.70
❏ 120 Gabe Kapler 21CP	.25	.11
❏ 121 Satchel Paige MEM	1.00	.45
❏ 122 Willie Mays MEM	1.50	.70
❏ 123 Roberto Clemente MEM	1.50	.70
❏ 124 Lou Gehrig MEM	2.00	.90
❏ 125 Mark McGwire MEM	4.00	1.80
❏ 127 Bob Gibson MEM	.60	.25
❏ 128 Johnny VanderMeer MEM .07		.15
❏ 129 Walter Johnson MEM	.75	.35
❏ 130 Ty Cobb MEM	1.50	.70
❏ 131 Don Larsen MEM	.25	.11
❏ 132 Jackie Robinson MEM	2.00	.90
❏ 133 Tom Seaver MEM	.75	.35
❏ 134 Johnny Bench MEM	.75	.35
❏ 135 Frank Robinson MEM	.60	.25
❏ S1 Babe Ruth Sample	4.00	1.80

1999 Upper Deck Century Legends Century Collection

	MINT	NRMT
COMMON CARD (1-135)	8.00	3.60

*STARS: 20X TO 50X BASIC CARDS
*21ST CENT: 15X TO 40X BASIC CARDS
RANDOM INSERTS IN HOBBY PACKS
STATED PRINT RUN 100 SERIAL #'d SETS
CARDS 11, 25, 26 AND 126 DO NOT EXIST

1999 Upper Deck Century Legends All-Century Team

	MINT	NRMT
COMPLETE SET (10)	60.00	27.00
COMMON CARD (AC1-AC10)	4.00	1.80

STATED ODDS 1:23

❏ AC1 Babe Ruth	15.00	6.75
❏ AC2 Ty Cobb	8.00	3.60
❏ AC3 Willie Mays	8.00	3.60
❏ AC4 Lou Gehrig	10.00	4.50
❏ AC5 Jackie Robinson	8.00	3.60
❏ AC6 Mike Schmidt	4.00	1.80
❏ AC7 Ernie Banks	4.00	1.80
❏ AC8 Johnny Bench	4.00	1.80
❏ AC9 Cy Young	4.00	1.80
❏ AC10 Lineup Sheet	10.00	4.50

1999 Upper Deck Century Legends Artifacts

	MINT	NRMT

RANDOM INSERTS IN PACKS
NO PRICING AVAILABLE DUE TO SCARCITY
ONE OF ONE MEMORABILIA EXCHANGE CARDS

❏ 1900 Ty Cobb Framed Cut	
❏ 1910 Babe Ruth Framed Cut	
❏ 1920 Rogers Hornsby Framed Cut	
❏ 1930 Satchel Paige Framed Cut	
❏ 1950 Hank Aaron	

Willie Mays
Mickey Mantle AU Balls
❑ 1960 Ernie Banks
Bob Gibson
Johnny Bench AU Balls
❑ 1970 Tom Seaver
Mike Schmidt
Steve Carlton AU Balls
❑ 1980 Nolan Ryan
Ken Griffey Jr. AU Balls
❑ 1990 Ken Griffey Jr. AU Jersey

1999 Upper Deck Century Legends Epic Milestones

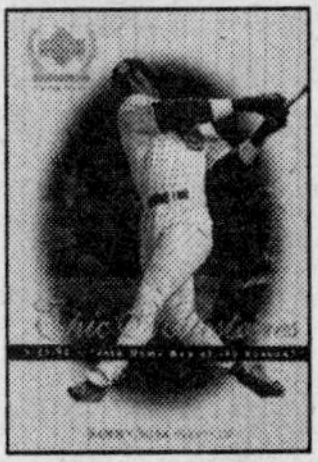

	MINT	NRMT
COMPLETE SET (9)	40.00	18.00
COMMON CARD (EM2-EM10)	2.50	1.10

STATED ODDS 1:12
CARD EM1 DOES NOT EXIST

❑ EM2 Jackie Robinson	6.00	2.70
❑ EM3 Nolan Ryan	10.00	4.50
❑ EM4 Mark McGwire	12.00	5.50
❑ EM5 Roger Clemens	5.00	2.20
❑ EM6 Sammy Sosa	6.00	2.70
❑ EM7 Cal Ripken	8.00	3.60
❑ EM8 Rickey Henderson	2.50	1.10
❑ EM9 Hank Aaron	5.00	2.20
❑ EM10 Barry Bonds	2.50	1.10

1999 Upper Deck Century Legends Epic Signatures

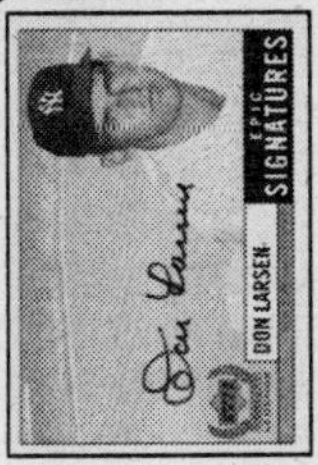

	MINT	NRMT
COMPLETE SET (30)	2000.00	900.00
COMMON CARD	20.00	9.00

STATED ODDS 1:24
*STICKER EXCH.CARDS: .1X TO .25X REAL AU
EXCHANGE DEADLINE 12/31/99

❑ AR Alex Rodriguez	200.00	90.00
❑ BB Barry Bonds	80.00	36.00
❑ BD Bucky Dent	20.00	9.00
❑ BF Bob Feller	25.00	11.00
❑ BG Bob Gibson	25.00	11.00
❑ BM Bill Mazeroski	20.00	9.00
❑ BT Bobby Thomson	20.00	9.00
❑ CF Carlton Fisk	40.00	18.00
❑ CFX Carlton Fisk EXCH	20.00	9.00
❑ DL Don Larsen	20.00	9.00
❑ EB Ernie Banks	40.00	18.00
❑ FR Frank Robinson	40.00	18.00
❑ FT Frank Thomas	175.00	80.00
❑ GM Greg Maddux	150.00	70.00
❑ HK Harmon Killebrew	40.00	18.00
❑ JB Johnny Bench	80.00	36.00
❑ JBX Johnny Bench EXCH	20.00	9.00
❑ JG Juan Gonzalez	80.00	36.00
❑ JR Ken Griffey Jr.	300.00	135.00
❑ MS Mike Schmidt	60.00	27.00
❑ NR Nolan Ryan	400.00	180.00
❑ RJ Reggie Jackson	150.00	70.00
❑ SC Steve Carlton	40.00	18.00
❑ SM Stan Musial	80.00	36.00
❑ SR Ken Griffey Sr.	20.00	9.00
❑ TG Tony Gwynn	100.00	45.00
❑ TS Tom Seaver	80.00	36.00
❑ VG Vladimir Guerrero	40.00	18.00
❑ WS Warren Spahn	40.00	18.00
❑ YB Yogi Berra	50.00	22.00
❑ YBX Yogi Berra EXCH	20.00	9.00
❑ EMA Eddie Mathews	40.00	18.00
❑ WMC Willie McCovey	40.00	18.00
❑ WMCX Willie McCovey EXCH	20.00	9.00

1999 Upper Deck Century Legends Epic Signatures Century

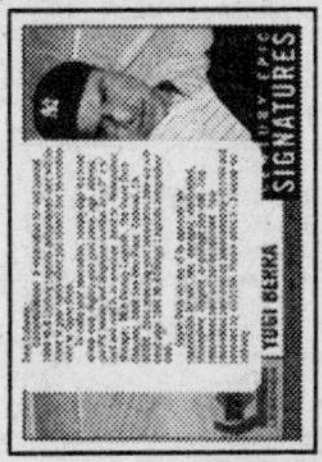

	MINT	NRMT
COMMON CARD	50.00	22.00

RANDOM INSERTS IN PACKS
STATED PRINT RUN 100 SERIAL #'d SETS
*STICKER EXCH.CARDS: .1X TO .25X REAL AU
EXCHANGE DEADLINE 12/31/99

❑ AR Alex Rodriguez	400.00	180.00
❑ BB Barry Bonds	150.00	70.00
❑ BD Bucky Dent	50.00	22.00
❑ BF Bob Feller	80.00	36.00
❑ BG Bob Gibson	100.00	45.00
❑ BM Bill Mazeroski	50.00	22.00
❑ BT Bobby Thomson	50.00	22.00
❑ CF Carlton Fisk	100.00	45.00
❑ CFX Carlton Fisk EXCH	50.00	22.00
❑ DL Don Larsen	50.00	22.00
❑ EB Ernie Banks	120.00	55.00
❑ FR Frank Robinson	100.00	45.00
❑ FT Frank Thomas	250.00	110.00
❑ GM Greg Maddux	300.00	135.00
❑ HK Harmon Killebrew	100.00	45.00
❑ JB Johnny Bench	150.00	70.00
❑ JBX Johnny Bench EXCH	50.00	22.00
❑ JG Juan Gonzalez	200.00	90.00
❑ JR Ken Griffey Jr.	600.00	275.00
❑ MS Mike Schmidt	150.00	70.00
❑ NR Nolan Ryan	600.00	275.00
❑ RJ Reggie Jackson	300.00	135.00
❑ SC Steve Carlton	120.00	55.00
❑ SM Stan Musial	200.00	90.00
❑ SR Ken Griffey Sr.	50.00	22.00
❑ TG Tony Gwynn	250.00	110.00
❑ TS Tom Seaver	150.00	70.00
❑ TW Ted Williams	1000.00	450.00
❑ VG Vladimir Guerrero	100.00	45.00
❑ WM Willie Mays	300.00	135.00
❑ WS Warren Spahn	100.00	45.00
❑ YB Yogi Berra	150.00	70.00
❑ YBX Yogi Berra EXCH	50.00	22.00
❑ EMA Eddie Mathews	100.00	45.00
❑ WMC Willie McCovey	80.00	36.00
❑ WMCX Willie McCovey EXCH	50.00	22.00

1999 Upper Deck Century Legends Jerseys of the Century

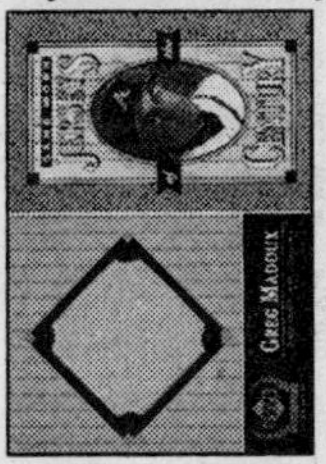

	MINT	NRMT
COMMON CARD	120.00	55.00

STATED ODDS 1:418

❑ DW Dave Winfield	120.00	55.00
❑ EM Eddie Murray	120.00	55.00
❑ GB George Brett	200.00	90.00
❑ GM Greg Maddux	250.00	110.00
❑ MS Mike Schmidt	200.00	90.00
❑ NR Nolan Ryan	600.00	275.00
❑ OZ Ozzie Smith	150.00	70.00
❑ RC Roger Clemens	250.00	110.00
❑ TG Tony Gwynn	200.00	90.00

1999 Upper Deck Century Legends Legendary Cuts

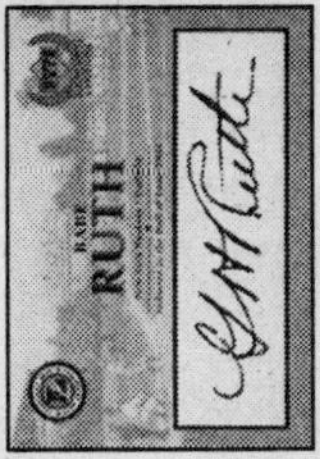

MINT NRMT

RANDOM INSERTS IN PACKS
NO PRICING AVAILABLE DUE TO SCARCITY

❑ BR Babe Ruth
❑ CY Cy Young
❑ LG Lefty Grove
❑ MO Mel Ott
❑ RC Roy Campanella
❑ SP Satchel Paige
❑ TY Ty Cobb
❑ WJ Walter Johnson
❑ XX Jimmie Foxx

1999 Upper Deck Century Legends Memorable Shots

	MINT	NRMT
COMPLETE SET (10)	40.00	18.00
COMMON CARD (1-10)	1.00	.45
SEMISTARS	1.50	.70
STATED ODDS 1:12		

		MINT	NRMT
❏ HR1	Babe Ruth	12.00	5.50
❏ HR2	Bobby Thomson	1.00	.45
❏ HR3	Kirk Gibson	1.00	.45
❏ HR4	Carlton Fisk	1.50	.70
❏ HR5	Bill Mazeroski	1.00	.45
❏ HR6	Bucky Dent	1.00	.45
❏ HR7	Mark McGwire	10.00	4.50
❏ HR8	Mickey Mantle	10.00	4.50
❏ HR9	Joe Carter	1.00	.45
❏ HR10	Mark McGwire	10.00	4.50

1999 Upper Deck Century Legends MVPs

	MINT	NRMT
RANDOM INSERTS IN PACKS		
STATED PRINT RUN 1 SERIAL #'d SET		
NO PRICING AVAILABLE DUE TO SCARCITY		
CARDS PARALLEL BASIC 1999 UD MVP		
BRAND		

❏ C1 Mo Vaughn
❏ C2 Troy Glaus
❏ C3 Darin Erstad
❏ C4 Randy Johnson
❏ C5 Travis Lee
❏ C6 Chipper Jones
❏ C7 Greg Maddux
❏ C8 Tom Glavine
❏ C9 John Smoltz
❏ C10 Cal Ripken
❏ C11 Charles Johnson
❏ C12 Albert Belle
❏ C13 Nomar Garciaparra
❏ C14 Pedro Martinez
❏ C15 Kerry Wood
❏ C16 Sammy Sosa
❏ C17 Mark Grace
❏ C18 Frank Thomas

❏ C19 Paul Konerko
❏ C20 Ray Durham
❏ C21 Denny Neagle
❏ C22 Sean Casey
❏ C23 Barry Larkin
❏ C24 Roberto Alomar
❏ C25 Kenny Lofton
❏ C26 Travis Fryman
❏ C27 Jim Thome
❏ C28 Manny Ramirez
❏ C29 Vinny Castilla
❏ C30 Todd Helton
❏ C31 Dante Bichette
❏ C32 Larry Walker
❏ C33 Gabe Kapler
❏ C34 Dean Palmer
❏ C35 Tony Clark
❏ C36 Juan Encarnacion
❏ C37 Alex Gonzalez
❏ C38 Preston Wilson
❏ C39 Derek Lee
❏ C40 Ken Caminiti
❏ C41 Jeff Bagwell
❏ C42 Moises Alou
❏ C43 Craig Biggio
❏ C44 Carlos Beltran
❏ C45 Jeremy Giambi
❏ C46 Johnny Damon
❏ C47 Kevin Brown
❏ C48 Chan Ho Park
❏ C49 Raul Mondesi
❏ C50 Gary Sheffield
❏ C51 Sean Berry
❏ C52 Jeromy Burnitz
❏ C53 Brad Radke
❏ C54 Eric Milton
❏ C55 Todd Walker
❏ C56 Vladimir Guerrero
❏ C57 Rondell White
❏ C58 Mike Piazza
❏ C59 Rickey Henderson
❏ C60 Rey Ordonez
❏ C61 Derek Jeter
❏ C62 Bernie Williams
❏ C63 Paul O'Neill
❏ C64 Scott Brosius
❏ C65 Tino Martinez
❏ C66 Roger Clemens
❏ C67 Orlando Hernandez
❏ C68 Ben Grieve
❏ C69 Eric Chavez
❏ C70 Jason Giambi
❏ C71 Curt Schilling
❏ C72 Scott Rolen
❏ C73 Pat Burrell
❏ C74 Jason Kendall
❏ C75 Aramis Ramirez
❏ C76 Mark McGwire
❏ C77 J.D. Drew
❏ C78 Edgar Renteria
❏ C79 Tony Gwynn
❏ C80 Sterling Hitchcock
❏ C81 Ruben Rivera
❏ C82 Trevor Hoffman
❏ C83 Barry Bonds
❏ C84 Ellis Burks
❏ C85 Robb Nen
❏ C86 Ken Griffey Jr.
❏ C87 Alex Rodriguez
❏ C88 Carlos Guillen
❏ C89 Edgar Martinez
❏ C90 Jose Canseco
❏ C91 Rolando Arrojo
❏ C92 Wade Boggs
❏ C93 Fred McGriff
❏ C94 Juan Gonzalez
❏ C95 Ivan Rodriguez
❏ C96 Rafael Palmeiro
❏ C97 David Wells
❏ C98 Roy Halladay
❏ C99 Carlos Delgado
❏ C100 Jose Cruz Jr.

1999 Upper Deck Challengers for 70

	MINT	NRMT
COMPLETE SET (90)	40.00	18.00
COMMON CARD (1-90)	.15	.07
MINOR STARS	.25	.11
SEMISTARS	.40	.18
UNLISTED STARS	.60	.25
MCGWIRE HRH (46-71)	2.00	.90
KILLEBREW BAT LISTED W/UD APH 500 CLUB		

		MINT	NRMT
❏ 1	Mark McGwire	4.00	1.80
❏ 2	Sammy Sosa	2.00	.90
❏ 3	Ken Griffey Jr.	3.00	1.35
❏ 4	Alex Rodriguez	2.00	.90
❏ 5	Albert Belle	.60	.25
❏ 6	Mo Vaughn	.60	.25
❏ 7	Mike Piazza	2.00	.90
❏ 8	Frank Thomas	1.25	.55
❏ 9	Juan Gonzalez	1.25	.55
❏ 10	Barry Bonds	.75	.35
❏ 11	Rafael Palmeiro	.60	.25
❏ 12	Jose Canseco	.75	.35
❏ 13	Nomar Garciaparra	2.00	.90
❏ 14	Carlos Delgado	.60	.25
❏ 15	Brian Jordan	.25	.11
❏ 16	Vladimir Guerrero	.75	.35
❏ 17	Vinny Castilla	.25	.11
❏ 18	Chipper Jones	1.50	.70
❏ 19	Jeff Bagwell	.75	.35
❏ 20	Moises Alou	.25	.11
❏ 21	Tony Clark	.25	.11
❏ 22	Jim Thome	.60	.25
❏ 23	Tino Martinez	.25	.11
❏ 24	Greg Vaughn	.25	.11
❏ 25	Javy Lopez	.25	.11
❏ 26	Jeromy Burnitz	.25	.11
❏ 27	Cal Ripken	2.50	1.10
❏ 28	Manny Ramirez	.75	.35
❏ 29	Darin Erstad	.40	.18
❏ 30	Ken Caminiti	.25	.11
❏ 31	Edgar Martinez	.25	.11
❏ 32	Ivan Rodriguez	.75	.35
❏ 33	Larry Walker	.60	.25
❏ 34	Todd Helton	.60	.25
❏ 35	Andruw Jones	.60	.25
❏ 36	Ray Lankford	.25	.11
❏ 37	Travis Lee	.40	.18
❏ 38	Raul Mondesi	.25	.11
❏ 39	Scott Rolen	.75	.35
❏ 40	Ben Grieve	.60	.25
❏ 41	J.D. Drew	1.00	.45
❏ 42	Troy Glaus	.60	.25
❏ 43	Eric Chavez	.40	.18
❏ 44	Gabe Kapler	.60	.25
❏ 45	Michael Barrett	.40	.18
❏ 46	Mark McGwire HRH	2.00	.90
❏ 47	Jose Canseco HRH	.40	.18
❏ 48	Greg Vaughn HRH	.15	.07
❏ 49	Albert Belle HRH	.25	.11
❏ 50	Mark McGwire HRH	2.00	.90
❏ 51	Vinny Castilla HRH	.15	.07
❏ 52	Vladimir Guerrero HRH	.40	.18
❏ 53	Andres Galarraga HRH	.25	.11
❏ 54	Rafael Palmeiro HRH	.25	.11
❏ 55	Juan Gonzalez HRH	.75	.35

❏ 56 Ken Griffey Jr. HRH	1.50	.70
❏ 57 Barry Bonds HRH	.40	.18
❏ 58 Mo Vaughn HRH	.25	.11
❏ 59 Nomar Garciaparra HRH	1.00	.45
❏ 60 Tino Martinez HRH	.15	.07
❏ 61 Mark McGwire HRH	2.00	.90
❏ 62 Mark McGwire HRH	2.00	.90
❏ 63 Mark McGwire HRH	2.00	.90
❏ 64 Mark McGwire HRH	2.00	.90
❏ 65 Mark McGwire HRH	2.00	.90
❏ 66 Sammy Sosa HRH	1.00	.45
❏ 67 Mark McGwire HRH	2.00	.90
❏ 68 Mark McGwire HRH	2.00	.90
❏ 69 Mark McGwire HRH	2.00	.90
❏ 70 Mark McGwire HRH	2.00	.90
❏ 71 Mark McGwire HRH	2.00	.90
❏ 72 Scott Brosius HRH	.15	.07
❏ 73 Tony Gwynn HRH	.75	.35
❏ 74 Chipper Jones HRH	.75	.35
❏ 75 Jeff Bagwell HRH	.40	.18
❏ 76 Moises Alou HRH	.15	.07
❏ 77 Manny Ramirez HRH	.40	.18
❏ 78 Carlos Delgado HRH	.25	.11
❏ 79 Kerry Wood HRH	.25	.11
❏ 80 Ken Griffey Jr. HRH	1.50	.70
❏ 81 Cal Ripken HRH	1.25	.55
❏ 82 Alex Rodriguez HRH	1.00	.45
❏ 83 Barry Bonds HRH	.40	.18
❏ 84 Ken Griffey Jr. HRH	1.50	.70
❏ 85 Travis Lee HRH	.25	.11
❏ 86 George Lombard HRH	.15	.07
❏ 87 Michael Barrett HRH	.25	.11
❏ 88 Jeremy Giambi HRH	.15	.07
❏ 89 Troy Glaus HRH	.25	.11
❏ 90 J.D. Drew HRH	.60	.25

1999 Upper Deck Challengers for 70 Challengers Edition

	MINT	NRMT
COMMON CARD (1-90)	2.00	.90

*STARS: 5X TO 12X BASIC CARDS
*YNG.STARS: 4X TO 10X BASIC CARDS
RANDOM INSERTS IN PACKS
STATED PRINT RUN 600 SERIAL #'d SETS

1999 Upper Deck Challengers for 70 Challengers Inserts

	MINT	NRMT
	25.00	11.00
COMPLETE SET (30)	25.00	11.00
COMMON CARD (C1-C30)	.25	.11
SEMISTARS	.40	.18
UNLISTED STARS	.60	.25
ONE PER PACK		
COMMON PARALLEL (C1-C30)	12.00	5.50

*PARALLEL STARS: 20X TO 50X HI COLUMN
*PARALLEL YNG.STARS: 15X TO 40X HI
PARALLEL: RANDOM INSERTS IN PACKS
PARALLEL PRINT RUN 70 SERIAL #'d SETS

❏ C1 Mark McGwire	4.00	1.80
❏ C2 Sammy Sosa	2.00	.90
❏ C3 Ken Griffey Jr.	3.00	1.35
❏ C4 Alex Rodriguez	2.00	.90
❏ C5 Albert Belle	.60	.25
❏ C6 Mo Vaughn	.60	.25
❏ C7 Mike Piazza	2.00	.90
❏ C8 Frank Thomas	1.25	.55
❏ C9 Juan Gonzalez	1.25	.55
❏ C10 Barry Bonds	.75	.35
❏ C11 Rafael Palmeiro	.60	.25
❏ C12 Nomar Garciaparra	2.00	.90
❏ C13 Vladimir Guerrero	.75	.35
❏ C14 Vinny Castilla	.25	.11
❏ C15 Chipper Jones	1.50	.70
❏ C16 Jeff Bagwell	.75	.35
❏ C17 Moises Alou	.25	.11
❏ C18 Tony Clark	.25	.11
❏ C19 Jim Thome	.60	.25
❏ C20 Tino Martinez	.25	.11
❏ C21 Greg Vaughn	.25	.11
❏ C22 Manny Ramirez	.75	.35
❏ C23 Darin Erstad	.40	.18
❏ C24 Ken Caminiti	.25	.11
❏ C25 Ivan Rodriguez	.75	.35
❏ C26 Andruw Jones	.75	.35
❏ C27 Travis Lee	.40	.18
❏ C28 Scott Rolen	.75	.35
❏ C29 Ben Grieve	.60	.25
❏ C30 J.D. Drew	1.00	.45

1999 Upper Deck Challengers for 70 Longball Legends

	MINT	NRMT
COMPLETE SET (30)	300.00	135.00
COMMON CARD (L1-L30)	2.50	1.10
SEMISTARS	4.00	1.80
UNLISTED STARS	6.00	2.70
STATED ODDS 1:39		

❏ L1 Ken Griffey Jr.	30.00	13.50
❏ L2 Mark McGwire	40.00	18.00
❏ L3 Sammy Sosa	20.00	9.00
❏ L4 Cal Ripken	25.00	11.00
❏ L5 Barry Bonds	8.00	3.60
❏ L6 Larry Walker	6.00	2.70
❏ L7 Fred McGriff	4.00	1.80
❏ L8 Alex Rodriguez	20.00	9.00
❏ L9 Frank Thomas	12.00	5.50
❏ L10 Juan Gonzalez	12.00	5.50
❏ L11 Jeff Bagwell	8.00	3.60
❏ L12 Mo Vaughn	6.00	2.70
❏ L13 Albert Belle	6.00	2.70
❏ L14 Mike Piazza	20.00	9.00
❏ L15 Vladimir Guerrero	8.00	3.60
❏ L16 Chipper Jones	15.00	6.75
❏ L17 Ken Caminiti	2.50	1.10
❏ L18 Rafael Palmeiro	6.00	2.70
❏ L19 Nomar Garciaparra	20.00	9.00
❏ L20 Jim Thome	6.00	2.70
❏ L21 Edgar Martinez	2.50	1.10
❏ L22 Ivan Rodriguez	8.00	3.60
❏ L23 Andres Galarraga	4.00	1.80
❏ L24 Scott Rolen	8.00	3.60
❏ L25 Darin Erstad	4.00	1.80
❏ L26 Moises Alou	2.50	1.10
❏ L27 J.D. Drew	8.00	3.60
❏ L28 Andruw Jones	6.00	2.70
❏ L29 Manny Ramirez	8.00	3.60
❏ L30 Tino Martinez	2.50	1.10

1999 Upper Deck Challengers for 70 Mark on History

	MINT	NRMT
COMPLETE SET (25)	100.00	45.00
COMMON CARD (M1-M25)	5.00	2.20
STATED ODDS 1:5		
COMMON PARALLEL (M1-M25)	80.00	36.00

*PARALLEL HR70: 6X TO 15X BASE HR70
PARALLEL: RANDOM INSERTS IN PACKS
PARALLEL PRINT RUN 70 SERIAL #'d SETS

❏ M1 Mark McGwire 1	5.00	2.20
❏ M2 Mark McGwire 2	5.00	2.20
❏ M3 Mark McGwire 10	5.00	2.20
❏ M4 Mark McGwire 12	5.00	2.20
❏ M5 Mark McGwire 16	5.00	2.20
❏ M6 Mark McGwire 24	5.00	2.20
❏ M7 Mark McGwire 25	5.00	2.20
❏ M8 Mark McGwire 39	5.00	2.20
❏ M9 Mark McGwire 40	5.00	2.20
❏ M10 Mark McGwire 44	5.00	2.20
❏ M11 Mark McGwire 49	5.00	2.20
❏ M12 Mark McGwire 50	5.00	2.20
❏ M13 Mark McGwire 57	5.00	2.20
❏ M14 Mark McGwire 57	5.00	2.20
❏ M15 Mark McGwire 60	5.00	2.20
❏ M16 Mark McGwire 61	5.00	2.20
❏ M17 Mark McGwire 62	5.00	2.20
❏ M18 Mark McGwire 63	5.00	2.20
❏ M19 Mark McGwire 64	5.00	2.20
❏ M20 Mark McGwire 65	5.00	2.20
❏ M21 Mark McGwire 66	5.00	2.20
❏ M22 Mark McGwire 67	5.00	2.20
❏ M23 Mark McGwire 68	5.00	2.20
❏ M24 Mark McGwire 69	5.00	2.20
❏ M25 Mark McGwire 70	10.00	4.50

1999 Upper Deck Challengers for 70 Swinging for the Fences

	MINT	NRMT
COMPLETE SET (15)	100.00	45.00
COMMON CARD (S1-S15)	2.00	.90
UNLISTED STARS	3.00	1.35
STATED ODDS 1:19		

	MINT	NRMT
☐ S1 Ken Griffey Jr.	15.00	6.75
☐ S2 Mark McGwire	20.00	9.00
☐ S3 Sammy Sosa	10.00	4.50
☐ S4 Alex Rodriguez	10.00	4.50
☐ S5 Nomar Garciaparra	10.00	4.50
☐ S6 J.D. Drew	4.00	1.80
☐ S7 Vladimir Guerrero	4.00	1.80
☐ S8 Ben Grieve	3.00	1.35
☐ S9 Chipper Jones	8.00	3.60
☐ S10 Gabe Kapler	3.00	1.35
☐ S11 Travis Lee	2.00	.90
☐ S12 Todd Helton	3.00	1.35
☐ S13 Juan Gonzalez	6.00	2.70
☐ S14 Mike Piazza	10.00	4.50
☐ S15 Mo Vaughn	3.00	1.35

1999 Upper Deck Challengers for 70 Swinging for the Fences Autographed

	MINT	NRMT
RANDOM INSERTS IN PACKS		
2700 TOTAL CARDS SIGNED		
☐ AR Alex Rodriguez EXCH	200.00	90.00
☐ GK Gabe Kapler	25.00	11.00
☐ JR Ken Griffey Jr.	400.00	180.00
☐ TH Todd Helton	30.00	13.50
☐ TL Travis Lee	20.00	9.00
☐ VG Vladimir Guerrero	50.00	22.00

1999 Upper Deck Encore

	MINT	NRMT
COMPLETE SET (180)	300.00	135.00
COMP.SET w/o SP's (90)	30.00	13.50
COMMON CARD (1-90)	.20	.09
MINOR STARS 1-90	.30	.14
SEMISTARS 1-90	.50	.23
UNLISTED STARS 1-90	.75	.35
COMMON SR (91-135)	1.00	.45
SR MINOR STARS	2.00	.90
SR SEMISTARS	3.00	1.35
SR UNLISTED STARS	4.00	1.80
SR STATED ODDS 1:4		
COMMON HO (136-165)	.75	.35

HO SEMISTARS	1.00	.45
HO UNLISTED STARS	1.50	.70
HO STATED ODDS 1:6		
COMMON SG (166-180)	1.00	.45
SG UNLISTED STARS	1.25	.55
SG STATED ODDS 1:8		
☐ 1 Darin Erstad	.50	.23
☐ 2 Mo Vaughn	.75	.35
☐ 3 Travis Lee	.50	.23
☐ 4 Randy Johnson	.75	.35
☐ 5 Matt Williams	.75	.35
☐ 6 John Smoltz	.50	.23
☐ 7 Greg Maddux	2.00	.90
☐ 8 Chipper Jones	2.00	.90
☐ 9 Tom Glavine	.75	.35
☐ 10 Andruw Jones	.75	.35
☐ 11 Cal Ripken	3.00	1.35
☐ 12 Mike Mussina	.75	.35
☐ 13 Albert Belle	.75	.35
☐ 14 Nomar Garciaparra	2.50	1.10
☐ 15 Jose Offerman	.30	.14
☐ 16 Pedro Martinez	1.00	.45
☐ 17 Trot Nixon	.30	.14
☐ 18 Kerry Wood	.75	.35
☐ 19 Sammy Sosa	2.50	1.10
☐ 20 Frank Thomas	1.50	.70
☐ 21 Paul Konerko	.30	.14
☐ 22 Sean Casey	.75	.35
☐ 23 Barry Larkin	.75	.35
☐ 24 Greg Vaughn	.30	.14
☐ 25 Travis Fryman	.30	.14
☐ 26 Jaret Wright	.30	.14
☐ 27 Jim Thome	.75	.35
☐ 28 Manny Ramirez	1.00	.45
☐ 29 Roberto Alomar	.75	.35
☐ 30 Kenny Lofton	.50	.23
☐ 31 Todd Helton	.75	.35
☐ 32 Larry Walker	.75	.35
☐ 33 Vinny Castilla	.30	.14
☐ 34 Dante Bichette	.30	.14
☐ 35 Tony Clark	.30	.14
☐ 36 Dean Palmer	.30	.14
☐ 37 Gabe Kapler	.75	.35
☐ 38 Juan Encarnacion	.30	.14
☐ 39 Alex Gonzalez	.30	.14
☐ 40 Preston Wilson	.30	.14
☐ 41 Mark Kotsay	.20	.09
☐ 42 Moises Alou	.30	.14
☐ 43 Craig Biggio	.75	.35
☐ 44 Ken Caminiti	.30	.14
☐ 45 Jeff Bagwell	1.00	.45
☐ 46 Johnny Damon	.30	.14
☐ 47 Gary Sheffield	.30	.14
☐ 48 Kevin Brown	.50	.23
☐ 49 Raul Mondesi	.30	.14
☐ 50 Jeff Cirillo	.30	.14
☐ 51 Jeromy Burnitz	.30	.14
☐ 52 Todd Walker	.30	.14
☐ 53 Corey Koskie	.20	.09
☐ 54 Brad Fullmer	.20	.09
☐ 55 Vladimir Guerrero	1.00	.45
☐ 56 Mike Piazza	2.50	1.10
☐ 57 Robin Ventura	.30	.14
☐ 58 Rickey Henderson	.50	.23
☐ 59 Derek Jeter	2.50	1.10
☐ 60 Paul O'Neill	.30	.14
☐ 61 Bernie Williams	.75	.35

☐ 62 Tino Martinez	.30	.14
☐ 63 Roger Clemens	2.00	.90
☐ 64 Ben Grieve	.75	.35
☐ 65 Jason Giambi	.30	.14
☐ 66 Bob Abreu	.30	.14
☐ 67 Scott Rolen	1.00	.45
☐ 68 Curt Schilling	.50	.23
☐ 69 Marlon Anderson	.20	.09
☐ 70 Kevin Young	.30	.14
☐ 71 Jason Kendall	.30	.14
☐ 72 Brian Giles	.30	.14
☐ 73 Mark McGwire	5.00	2.20
☐ 74 Fernando Tatis	.75	.35
☐ 75 Eric Davis	.30	.14
☐ 76 Trevor Hoffman	.30	.14
☐ 77 Tony Gwynn	2.00	.90
☐ 78 Matt Clement	.30	.14
☐ 79 Robb Nen	.20	.09
☐ 80 Barry Bonds	1.00	.45
☐ 81 Ken Griffey Jr.	4.00	1.80
☐ 82 Alex Rodriguez	2.50	1.10
☐ 83 Wade Boggs	.75	.35
☐ 84 Fred McGriff	.50	.23
☐ 85 Jose Canseco	1.00	.45
☐ 86 Ivan Rodriguez	1.00	.45
☐ 87 Juan Gonzalez	1.50	.70
☐ 88 Rafael Palmeiro	.75	.35
☐ 89 Carlos Delgado	.75	.35
☐ 90 David Wells	.30	.14
☐ 91 Troy Glaus SR	5.00	2.20
☐ 92 Adrian Beltre SR	4.00	1.80
☐ 93 Matt Anderson SR	1.00	.45
☐ 94 Eric Chavez SR	3.00	1.35
☐ 95 Jeff Weaver SR	5.00	2.20
☐ 96 Warren Morris SR	2.00	.90
☐ 97 George Lombard SR	2.00	.90
☐ 98 Mike Kinkade SR	1.00	.45
☐ 99 Kyle Farnsworth SR	2.50	1.10
☐ 100 J.D. Drew SR	8.00	3.60
☐ 101 Jose McEwing SR	8.00	3.60
☐ 102 Carlos Guillen SR	1.00	.45
☐ 103 Kelly Dransfeldt SR	2.50	1.10
☐ 104 Eric Munson SR	30.00	13.50
☐ 105 Armando Rios SR	1.00	.45
☐ 106 Ramon E.Martinez SR	1.00	.45
☐ 107 Orlando Hernandez SR	4.00	1.80
☐ 108 Jeremy Giambi SR	2.00	.90
☐ 109 Pat Burrell SR	20.00	9.00
☐ 110 Shea Hillenbrand SR	2.50	1.10
☐ 111 Billy Koch SR	2.00	.90
☐ 112 Roy Halladay SR	2.00	.90
☐ 113 Ruben Mateo SR	4.00	1.80
☐ 114 Bruce Chen SR	2.00	.90
☐ 115 Angel Pena SR	1.00	.45
☐ 116 Michael Barrett SR	3.00	1.35
☐ 117 Kevin Witt SR	1.00	.45
☐ 118 Damon Minor SR	1.00	.45
☐ 119 Ryan Minor SR	2.00	.90
☐ 120 A.J. Pierzynski SR	1.00	.45
☐ 121 A.J. Burnett SR	5.00	2.20
☐ 122 Cristian Guzman SR	1.00	.45
☐ 123 Joe Lawrence SR	1.00	.45
☐ 124 Derrick Gibson SR	2.00	.90
☐ 125 Carlos Febles SR	2.00	.90
☐ 126 Chris Haas SR	1.00	.45
☐ 127 Cesar King SR	1.00	.45
☐ 128 Calvin Pickering SR	1.00	.45
☐ 129 Mitch Meluskey SR	1.00	.45
☐ 130 Carlos Beltran SR	6.00	2.70
☐ 131 Ron Belliard SR	2.00	.90
☐ 132 Jerry Hairston Jr. SR	2.00	.90
☐ 133 Fernando Seguignol SR	2.00	.90
☐ 134 Kris Benson SR	2.00	.90
☐ 135 Chad Hutchinson SR	6.00	2.70
☐ 136 Ken Griffey Jr. HO	8.00	3.60
☐ 137 Mark McGwire HO	10.00	4.50
☐ 138 Sammy Sosa HO	5.00	2.20
☐ 139 Albert Belle HO	1.50	.70
☐ 140 Mo Vaughn HO	1.50	.70
☐ 141 Alex Rodriguez HO	5.00	2.20
☐ 142 Manny Ramirez HO	2.00	.90
☐ 143 J.D. Drew HO	2.00	.90
☐ 144 Juan Gonzalez HO	3.00	1.35
☐ 145 Vladimir Guerrero HO	2.00	.90
☐ 146 Fernando Tatis HO	1.50	.70
☐ 147 Mike Piazza HO	5.00	2.20

		MINT	NRMT
❏ 148	Barry Bonds HO	2.00	.90
❏ 149	Ivan Rodriguez HO	2.00	.90
❏ 150	Jeff Bagwell HO	2.00	.90
❏ 151	Raul Mondesi HO	.75	.35
❏ 152	Nomar Garciaparra HO	5.00	2.20
❏ 153	Jose Canseco HO	2.00	.90
❏ 154	Greg Vaughn HO	.75	.35
❏ 155	Scott Rolen HO	2.00	.90
❏ 156	Vinny Castilla HO	.75	.35
❏ 157	Troy Glaus HO	1.50	.70
❏ 158	Craig Biggio HO	1.50	.70
❏ 159	Tino Martinez HO	.75	.35
❏ 160	Jim Thome HO	1.50	.70
❏ 161	Frank Thomas HO	3.00	1.35
❏ 162	Tony Clark HO	.75	.35
❏ 163	Ben Grieve HO	1.50	.70
❏ 164	Matt Williams HO	1.50	.70
❏ 165	Derek Jeter HO	5.00	2.20
❏ 166	Ken Griffey Jr. SG	6.00	2.70
❏ 167	Tony Gwynn SG	3.00	1.35
❏ 168	Mike Piazza SG	4.00	1.80
❏ 169	Mark McGwire SG	8.00	3.60
❏ 170	Sammy Sosa SG	4.00	1.80
❏ 171	Juan Gonzalez SG	2.50	1.10
❏ 172	Mo Vaughn SG	1.00	.45
❏ 173	Derek Jeter SG	4.00	1.80
❏ 174	Bernie Williams SG	1.25	.55
❏ 175	Ivan Rodriguez SG	1.50	.70
❏ 176	Barry Bonds SG	1.50	.70
❏ 177	Scott Rolen SG	2.00	.90
❏ 178	Larry Walker SG	1.25	.55
❏ 179	Chipper Jones SG	3.00	1.35
❏ 180	Alex Rodriguez SG	4.00	1.80

1999 Upper Deck Encore FX Gold

	MINT	NRMT
COMMON CARD (1-180)	6.00	2.70

*STARS 1-90: 12.5X TO 30X BASIC 1-90
*YNG.STARS 1-90: 10X TO 25X BASIC 1-90
*STAR ROOKIES: 1.5X TO 4X BASIC SR
*HOMER ODYSSEY: 3X TO 8X BASIC HO
*STROKES OF GENIUS: 4X TO 10X BASIC SG
RANDOM INSERTS IN PACKS
STATED PRINT RUN 125 SERIAL #'d SETS

1999 Upper Deck Encore 2K Countdown

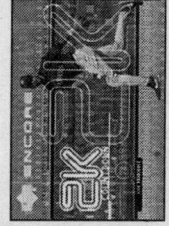

	MINT	NRMT
COMPLETE SET (10)	30.00	13.50
COMMON CARD (2K1-2K10)	1.50	.70
STATED ODDS 1:11		

		MINT	NRMT
❏ 2K1	Ken Griffey Jr.	6.00	2.70
❏ 2K2	Derek Jeter	4.00	1.80
❏ 2K3	Mike Piazza	4.00	1.80
❏ 2K4	J.D. Drew	1.50	.70
❏ 2K5	Vladimir Guerrero	1.50	.70
❏ 2K6	Chipper Jones	3.00	1.35
❏ 2K7	Alex Rodriguez	4.00	1.80
❏ 2K8	Nomar Garciaparra	4.00	1.80
❏ 2K9	Mark McGwire	8.00	3.60
❏ 2K10	Sammy Sosa	4.00	1.80

1999 Upper Deck Encore Batting Practice Caps

	MINT	NRMT
STATED ODDS 1:750		

		MINT	NRMT
❏ C-BB	Barry Bonds	120.00	55.00
❏ C-BH	Frank Thomas	150.00	70.00
❏ C-CB	Carlos Beltran	80.00	36.00
❏ C-DP	Dean Palmer	40.00	18.00
❏ C-EC	Eric Chavez	50.00	22.00
❏ C-GK	Gabe Kapler	60.00	27.00
❏ C-GV	Greg Vaughn	60.00	27.00
❏ C-JD	J.D. Drew	120.00	55.00
❏ C-JK	Jason Kendall	60.00	27.00
❏ C-TC	Tony Clark	50.00	22.00
❏ C-TG	Tony Gwynn	150.00	70.00
❏ C-TH	Todd Helton	60.00	27.00
❏ C-TW	Todd Walker	40.00	18.00
❏ C-VC	Vinny Castilla	60.00	27.00
❏ C-VG	Vladimir Guerrero	100.00	45.00

1999 Upper Deck Encore Driving Forces

	MINT	NRMT
COMPLETE SET (15)	100.00	45.00
COMMON CARD (D1-D15)	2.50	1.10
UNLISTED STARS	3.00	1.35
STATED ODDS 1:23		
FX GOLD RANDOM INSERTS IN PACKS		
FX GOLD PRINT RUN 10 SERIAL #'d SETS		

FX GOLD NOT PRICED DUE TO SCARCITY

		MINT	NRMT
❏ D1	Ken Griffey Jr.	15.00	6.75
❏ D2	Mark McGwire	20.00	9.00
❏ D3	Sammy Sosa	10.00	4.50
❏ D4	Albert Belle	3.00	1.35
❏ D5	Alex Rodriguez	10.00	4.50
❏ D6	Mo Vaughn	3.00	1.35
❏ D7	Juan Gonzalez	6.00	2.70
❏ D8	Jeff Bagwell	4.00	1.80
❏ D9	Mike Piazza	10.00	4.50
❏ D10	Frank Thomas	6.00	2.70
❏ D11	Barry Bonds	4.00	1.80
❏ D12	Vladimir Guerrero	4.00	1.80
❏ D13	Chipper Jones	8.00	3.60
❏ D14	Tony Gwynn	8.00	3.60
❏ D15	J.D. Drew	4.00	1.80

1999 Upper Deck Encore McGwired

	MINT	NRMT
COMPLETE SET (10)	80.00	36.00
COMMON CARD (MC1-MC10)	10.00	4.50
STATED ODDS 1:23		
*FX GOLD: 1X TO 2.5X HI COLUMN		
FX GOLD RANDOM INSERTS IN PACKS		
FX GOLD PRINT RUN 500 SERIAL #'d SETS		

		MINT	NRMT
❏ MC1	Mark McGwire / Carl Pavano	15.00	6.75
❏ MC2	Mark McGwire / Mike Morgan	10.00	4.50
❏ MC3	Mark McGwire / Steve Trachsel	10.00	4.50
❏ MC4	Mark McGwire / Ramon Martinez	10.00	4.50
❏ MC5	Mark McGwire / Willie Blair	10.00	4.50
❏ MC6	Mark McGwire / Scott Elarton	10.00	4.50
❏ MC7	Mark McGwire / Jim Parque	10.00	4.50
❏ MC8	Mark McGwire / Livan Hernandez	10.00	4.50
❏ MC9	Mark McGwire / Rafael Roque	10.00	4.50
❏ MC10	Mark McGwire / Jaret Wright	10.00	4.50

1999 Upper Deck Encore Pure Excitement

	MINT	NRMT
COMPLETE SET (30)	100.00	45.00
COMMON CARD (1-30)	1.00	.45
SEMISTARS	1.25	.55
UNLISTED STARS	2.00	.90
STATED ODDS 1:7		

		MINT	NRMT
❏ P1	Mo Vaughn	2.00	.90
❏ P2	Darin Erstad	1.25	.55
❏ P3	Travis Lee	1.25	.55
❏ P4	Chipper Jones	5.00	2.20
❏ P5	Greg Maddux	5.00	2.20
❏ P6	Gabe Kapler	2.00	.90
❏ P7	Cal Ripken	8.00	3.60

		MINT	NRMT
❑ P8	Nomar Garciaparra	6.00	2.70
❑ P9	Kerry Wood	2.00	.90
❑ P10	Frank Thomas	4.00	1.80
❑ P11	Manny Ramirez	2.50	1.10
❑ P12	Larry Walker	2.00	.90
❑ P13	Tony Clark	1.00	.45
❑ P14	Jeff Bagwell	2.50	1.10
❑ P15	Craig Biggio	2.00	.90
❑ P16	Vladimir Guerrero	2.50	1.10
❑ P17	Mike Piazza	6.00	2.70
❑ P18	Bernie Williams	2.00	.90
❑ P19	Derek Jeter	6.00	2.70
❑ P20	Ben Grieve	2.00	.90
❑ P21	Eric Chavez	1.25	.55
❑ P22	Scott Rolen	2.50	1.10
❑ P23	Mark McGwire	12.00	5.50
❑ P24	Tony Gwynn	5.00	2.20
❑ P25	Barry Bonds	2.50	1.10
❑ P26	Ken Griffey Jr.	10.00	4.50
❑ P27	Alex Rodriguez	6.00	2.70
❑ P28	J.D. Drew	2.50	1.10
❑ P29	Juan Gonzalez	4.00	1.80
❑ P30	Roger Clemens	5.00	2.20

1999 Upper Deck Encore Rookie Encore

	MINT	NRMT
COMPLETE SET (10)	25.00	11.00
COMMON CARD (R1-R10)	1.25	.55
SEMISTARS	2.00	.90
UNLISTED STARS	3.00	1.35
STATED ODDS 1:23		
*FX GOLD: 1.25X TO 3X HI COLUMN		
FX GOLD RANDOM INSERTS IN PACKS		
FX GOLD PRINT RUN 500 SERIAL #'d SETS		

		MINT	NRMT
❑ R1	J.D. Drew	5.00	2.20
❑ R2	Eric Chavez	2.00	.90
❑ R3	Gabe Kapler	3.00	1.35
❑ R4	Bruce Chen	1.25	.55
❑ R5	Carlos Beltran	4.00	1.80
❑ R6	Troy Glaus	3.00	1.35
❑ R7	Roy Halladay	1.25	.55
❑ R8	Adrian Beltre	3.00	1.35
❑ R9	Michael Barrett	2.00	.90
❑ R10	Pat Burrell	10.00	4.50

1999 Upper Deck Encore UD Authentics

		MINT	NRMT
STATED ODDS 1:288			
❑ JD	J.D. Drew	50.00	22.00
❑ JR	Ken Griffey Jr.	400.00	180.00
❑ MB	Michael Barrett	15.00	6.75
❑ NG	Nomar Garciaparra	120.00	55.00
❑ PB	Pat Burrell	50.00	22.00
❑ TG	Troy Glaus	30.00	13.50

1999 Upper Deck Encore Upper Realm

	MINT	NRMT
COMPLETE SET (15)	60.00	27.00
COMMON CARD (U1-U15)	1.25	.55
UNLISTED STARS	1.50	.70
STATED ODDS 1:11		

		MINT	NRMT
❑ U1	Ken Griffey Jr.	8.00	3.60
❑ U2	Mark McGwire	10.00	4.50
❑ U3	Sammy Sosa	5.00	2.20
❑ U4	Tony Gwynn	4.00	1.80
❑ U5	Alex Rodriguez	5.00	2.20
❑ U6	Juan Gonzalez	3.00	1.35
❑ U7	J.D. Drew	2.00	.90
❑ U8	Roger Clemens	4.00	1.80
❑ U9	Greg Maddux	4.00	1.80
❑ U10	Randy Johnson	1.50	.70
❑ U11	Mo Vaughn	1.25	.55
❑ U12	Derek Jeter	5.00	2.20
❑ U13	Vladimir Guerrero	2.00	.90
❑ U14	Cal Ripken	6.00	2.70
❑ U15	Nomar Garciaparra	5.00	2.20

1999 Upper Deck HoloGrFX

	MINT	NRMT
COMPLETE SET (60)	30.00	13.50
COMMON CARD (1-60)	.30	.14
UNLISTED STARS	.75	.35
PRODUCT DISTRIBUTED ONLY TO RETAIL		
MCCOVEY BAT LISTED W/UD APH 500 CLUB		

		MINT	NRMT
❑ 1	Mo Vaughn	.75	.35

		MINT	NRMT
❑ 2	Troy Glaus	.75	.35
❑ 3	Tim Salmon		
❑ 4	Randy Johnson	.75	.35
❑ 5	Travis Lee		
❑ 6	Chipper Jones	2.00	.90
❑ 7	Greg Maddux	2.00	.90
❑ 8	Andruw Jones	.75	.35
❑ 9	Tom Glavine	.75	.35
❑ 10	Cal Ripken	3.00	1.35
❑ 11	Albert Belle	.75	.35
❑ 12	Nomar Garciaparra	2.50	1.10
❑ 13	Pedro Martinez	1.00	.45
❑ 14	Sammy Sosa	2.50	1.10
❑ 15	Frank Thomas	1.50	.70
❑ 16	Greg Vaughn	.30	.14
❑ 17	Kenny Lofton		
❑ 18	Jim Thome	.75	.35
❑ 19	Manny Ramirez	1.00	.45
❑ 20	Todd Helton	.75	.35
❑ 21	Larry Walker	.75	.35
❑ 22	Tony Clark	.30	.14
❑ 23	Mark Kotsay	.30	.14
❑ 24	Jeff Bagwell	1.00	.45
❑ 25	Craig Biggio	.75	.35
❑ 26	Ken Caminiti	.30	.14
❑ 27	Carlos Beltran	1.00	.45
❑ 28	Jeremy Giambi	.30	.14
❑ 29	Raul Mondesi	.30	.14
❑ 30	Kevin Brown		
❑ 31	Jeromy Burnitz	.30	.14
❑ 32	Corey Koskie	.30	.14
❑ 33	Todd Walker	.30	.14
❑ 34	Vladimir Guerrero	1.00	.45
❑ 35	Mike Piazza	2.50	1.10
❑ 36	Robin Ventura	.30	.14
❑ 37	Derek Jeter	2.50	1.10
❑ 38	Roger Clemens	2.00	.90
❑ 39	Bernie Williams	.75	.35
❑ 40	Orlando Hernandez	.75	.35
❑ 41	Ben Grieve	.75	.35
❑ 42	Eric Chavez		
❑ 43	Scott Rolen	1.00	.45
❑ 44	Pat Burrell	6.00	2.70
❑ 45	Warren Morris	.30	.14
❑ 46	Jason Kendall	.30	.14
❑ 47	Mark McGwire	5.00	2.20
❑ 48	J.D. Drew	1.25	.55
❑ 49	Tony Gwynn	2.00	.90
❑ 50	Trevor Hoffman	.30	.14
❑ 51	Barry Bonds	1.00	.45
❑ 52	Ken Griffey Jr.	4.00	1.80
❑ 53	Alex Rodriguez	2.50	1.10
❑ 54	Jose Canseco	1.00	.45
❑ 55	Juan Gonzalez	1.50	.70
❑ 56	Ivan Rodriguez	1.00	.45
❑ 57	Rafael Palmeiro	.75	.35
❑ 58	David Wells	.30	.14
❑ 59	Carlos Delgado	.75	.35
❑ 60	Ken Griffey Jr. Sample	3.00	1.35

1999 Upper Deck HoloGrFX AuSOME

	MINT	NRMT
COMPLETE SET (60)	300.00	135.00
COMMON CARD (1-60)	2.00	.90

*STARS: 2.5X TO 6X BASIC CARDS
*RC's: 1X TO 2.5X BASIC CARDS
STATED ODDS 1:8

1999 Upper Deck HoloGrFX Future Fame

	MINT	NRMT
COMPLETE SET (6)	60.00	27.00
COMMON CARD (F1-F6)	8.00	3.60
STATED ODDS 1:32		
*GOLD: 2X TO 5X HI COLUMN		
GOLD STATED ODDS 1:432		

☐ F1 Tony Gwynn	8.00	3.60
☐ F2 Cal Ripken	12.00	5.50
☐ F3 Mark McGwire	20.00	9.00
☐ F4 Ken Griffey Jr.	15.00	6.75
☐ F5 Greg Maddux	8.00	3.60
☐ F6 Roger Clemens	8.00	3.60

1999 Upper Deck HoloGrFX Launchers

	MINT	NRMT
COMPLETE SET (15)	40.00	18.00
COMMON CARD (L1-L15)	1.00	.45
STATED ODDS 1:4		
*GOLD: 2.5X TO 6X HI COLUMN		
GOLD STATED ODDS 1:105		

| ☐ L1 Mark McGwire | 8.00 | 3.60 |

☐ L2 Ken Griffey Jr.	6.00	2.70
☐ L3 Sammy Sosa	4.00	1.80
☐ L4 J.D. Drew	1.50	.70
☐ L5 Mo Vaughn	1.00	.45
☐ L6 Juan Gonzalez	2.50	1.10
☐ L7 Mike Piazza	4.00	1.80
☐ L8 Alex Rodriguez	4.00	1.80
☐ L9 Chipper Jones	3.00	1.35
☐ L10 Nomar Garciaparra	4.00	1.80
☐ L11 Vladimir Guerrero	1.50	.70
☐ L12 Albert Belle	1.00	.45
☐ L13 Barry Bonds	1.50	.70
☐ L14 Frank Thomas	2.50	1.10
☐ L15 Jeff Bagwell	1.50	.70

1999 Upper Deck HoloGrFX StarView

	MINT	NRMT
COMPLETE SET (9)	40.00	18.00
COMMON CARD (S1-S9)	5.00	2.20
STATED ODDS 1:16		
*GOLD: 2X TO 5X HI COLUMN		
GOLD STATED ODDS 1:210		

☐ S1 Mark McGwire	12.00	5.50
☐ S2 Ken Griffey Jr.	10.00	4.50
☐ S3 Sammy Sosa	6.00	2.70
☐ S4 Nomar Garciaparra	6.00	2.70
☐ S5 Roger Clemens	5.00	2.20
☐ S6 Greg Maddux	5.00	2.20
☐ S7 Mike Piazza	6.00	2.70
☐ S8 Alex Rodriguez	6.00	2.70
☐ S9 Chipper Jones	5.00	2.20

1999 Upper Deck HoloGrFX UD Authentics

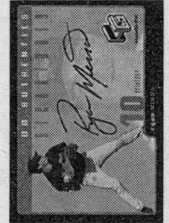

	MINT	NRMT
COMMON CARD (1-12)	10.00	4.50
STATED ODDS 1:431		

☐ AG Alex Gonzalez	15.00	6.75
☐ BC Bruce Chen	20.00	9.00
☐ CB Carlos Beltran	40.00	18.00
☐ CJ Chipper Jones	120.00	55.00
☐ CK Corey Koskie	12.00	5.50
☐ GK Gabe Kapler	25.00	11.00
☐ GL George Lombard	15.00	6.75
☐ JD J.D. Drew	50.00	22.00

☐ JR Ken Griffey Jr.	400.00	180.00
☐ MK Mike Kinkade	10.00	4.50
☐ RM Ryan Minor	20.00	9.00
☐ SM Shane Monahan	10.00	4.50

1999 Upper Deck MVP

	MINT	NRMT
COMPLETE SET (220)	25.00	11.00
COMMON CARD (1-220)	.10	.05
MINOR STARS	.15	.07
SEMISTARS	.25	.11
UNLISTED STARS	.40	.18
SCHMIDT BAT LISTED W/UD APH 500 CLUB		

☐ 1 Mo Vaughn	.40	.18
☐ 2 Tim Belcher	.10	.05
☐ 3 Jack McDowell	.10	.05
☐ 4 Troy Glaus	.40	.18
☐ 5 Darin Erstad	.25	.11
☐ 6 Tim Salmon	.25	.11
☐ 7 Jim Edmonds	.40	.18
☐ 8 Randy Johnson	.40	.18
☐ 9 Steve Finley	.15	.07
☐ 10 Travis Lee	.25	.11
☐ 11 Matt Williams	.40	.18
☐ 12 Todd Stottlemyre	.10	.05
☐ 13 Jay Bell	.15	.07
☐ 14 David Dellucci	.10	.05
☐ 15 Chipper Jones	1.00	.45
☐ 16 Andruw Jones	.40	.18
☐ 17 Greg Maddux	1.00	.45
☐ 18 Tom Glavine	.40	.18
☐ 19 Javy Lopez	.15	.07
☐ 20 Brian Jordan	.15	.07
☐ 21 George Lombard	.15	.07
☐ 22 John Smoltz	.25	.11
☐ 23 Cal Ripken	1.50	.70
☐ 24 Charles Johnson	.15	.07
☐ 25 Albert Belle	.40	.18
☐ 26 Brady Anderson	.15	.07
☐ 27 Mike Mussina	.40	.18
☐ 28 Calvin Pickering	.15	.07
☐ 29 Ryan Minor	.15	.07
☐ 30 Jerry Hairston Jr.	.15	.07
☐ 31 Nomar Garciaparra	1.25	.55
☐ 32 Pedro Martinez	.50	.23
☐ 33 Jason Varitek	.15	.07
☐ 34 Troy O'Leary	.15	.07
☐ 35 Donnie Sadler	.10	.05
☐ 36 Mark Portugal	.10	.05
☐ 37 John Valentin	.15	.07
☐ 38 Kerry Wood	.40	.18
☐ 39 Sammy Sosa	1.25	.55
☐ 40 Mark Grace	.25	.11
☐ 41 Henry Rodriguez	.15	.07
☐ 42 Rod Beck	.15	.07
☐ 43 Benito Santiago	.10	.05
☐ 44 Kevin Tapani	.10	.05
☐ 45 Frank Thomas	.75	.35
☐ 46 Mike Caruso	.10	.05
☐ 47 Magglio Ordonez	.40	.18
☐ 48 Paul Konerko	.15	.07
☐ 49 Ray Durham	.15	.07
☐ 50 Jim Parque	.10	.05
☐ 51 Carlos Lee	.15	.07
☐ 52 Denny Neagle	.10	.05
☐ 53 Pete Harnisch	.10	.05

#	Player	MINT	NRMT
54	Michael Tucker	.10	.05
55	Sean Casey	.40	.18
56	Eddie Taubensee	.10	.05
57	Barry Larkin	.40	.18
58	Pokey Reese	.10	.05
59	Sandy Alomar Jr.	.15	.07
60	Roberto Alomar	.40	.18
61	Bartolo Colon	.15	.07
62	Kenny Lofton	.25	.11
63	Omar Vizquel	.15	.07
64	Travis Fryman	.15	.07
65	Jim Thome	.40	.18
66	Manny Ramirez	.50	.23
67	Jaret Wright	.15	.07
68	Darryl Kile	.15	.05
69	Kirt Manwaring	.10	.05
70	Vinny Castilla	.15	.07
71	Todd Helton	.40	.18
72	Dante Bichette	.15	.07
73	Larry Walker	.40	.18
74	Derrick Gibson	.15	.07
75	Gabe Kapler	.40	.18
76	Dean Palmer	.15	.07
77	Matt Anderson	.10	.05
78	Bobby Higginson	.15	.07
79	Damion Easley	.15	.07
80	Tony Clark	.15	.07
81	Juan Encarnacion	.15	.07
82	Livan Hernandez	.10	.05
83	Alex Gonzalez	.15	.07
84	Preston Wilson	.15	.07
85	Derrek Lee	.15	.07
86	Mark Kotsay	.10	.05
87	Todd Dunwoody	.10	.05
88	Cliff Floyd	.15	.07
89	Ken Caminiti	.15	.07
90	Jeff Bagwell	.50	.23
91	Moises Alou	.15	.07
92	Craig Biggio	.40	.18
93	Billy Wagner	.15	.07
94	Richard Hidalgo	.15	.07
95	Derek Bell	.15	.07
96	Hipolito Pichardo	.10	.05
97	Jeff King	.15	.05
98	Carlos Beltran	.50	.23
99	Jeremy Giambi	.15	.07
100	Larry Sutton	.10	.05
101	Johnny Damon	.15	.07
102	Dee Brown	.15	.07
103	Kevin Brown	.25	.11
104	Chan Ho Park	.15	.07
105	Raul Mondesi	.15	.07
106	Eric Karros	.15	.07
107	Adrian Beltre	.40	.18
108	Devon White	.10	.05
109	Gary Sheffield	.15	.07
110	Sean Berry	.10	.05
111	Alex Ochoa	.10	.05
112	Marquis Grissom	.10	.05
113	Fernando Vina	.10	.05
114	Jeff Cirillo	.15	.07
115	Geoff Jenkins	.15	.07
116	Jeromy Burnitz	.15	.07
117	Brad Radke	.15	.07
118	Eric Milton	.10	.05
119	A.J. Pierzynski	.15	.07
120	Todd Walker	.15	.07
121	David Ortiz	.10	.05
122	Corey Koskie	.15	.05
123	Vladimir Guerrero	.50	.23
124	Rondell White	.15	.07
125	Brad Fullmer	.10	.05
126	Ugueth Urbina	.10	.05
127	Dustin Hermanson	.10	.05
128	Michael Barrett	.25	.11
129	Fernando Seguignol	.15	.07
130	Mike Piazza	1.25	.55
131	Rickey Henderson	.50	.23
132	Rey Ordonez	.15	.07
133	John Olerud	.15	.07
134	Robin Ventura	.15	.07
135	Hideo Nomo	.40	.18
136	Mike Kinkade	.10	.05
137	Al Leiter	.15	.07
138	Brian McRae	.10	.05
139	Derek Jeter	1.25	.55
140	Bernie Williams	.40	.18
141	Paul O'Neill	.15	.07
142	Scott Brosius	.15	.07
143	Tino Martinez	.15	.07
144	Roger Clemens	1.00	.45
145	Orlando Hernandez	.40	.18
146	Mariano Rivera	.15	.07
147	Ricky Ledee	.15	.07
148	A.J. Hinch	.10	.05
149	Ben Grieve	.40	.18
150	Eric Chavez	.25	.11
151	Miguel Tejada	.15	.07
152	Matt Stairs	.15	.07
153	Ryan Christenson	.10	.05
154	Jason Giambi	.15	.07
155	Curt Schilling	.25	.11
156	Scott Rolen	.50	.23
157	Pat Burrell	2.00	.90
158	Doug Glanville	.15	.07
159	Bobby Abreu	.15	.07
160	Rico Brogna	.10	.05
161	Ron Gant	.15	.07
162	Jason Kendall	.15	.07
163	Aramis Ramirez	.25	.11
164	Jose Guillen	.15	.05
165	Emil Brown	.10	.05
166	Pat Meares	.10	.05
167	Kevin Young	.15	.07
168	Brian Giles	.15	.07
169	Mark McGwire	2.50	1.10
170	J.D. Drew	.60	.25
171	Edgar Renteria	.10	.05
172	Fernando Tatis	.40	.18
173	Matt Morris	.15	.07
174	Eli Marrero	.10	.05
175	Ray Lankford	.15	.07
176	Tony Gwynn	1.00	.45
177	Sterling Hitchcock	.10	.05
178	Ruben Rivera	.10	.05
179	Wally Joyner	.15	.07
180	Trevor Hoffman	.15	.07
181	Jim Leyritz	.10	.05
182	Carlos Hernandez	.10	.05
183	Barry Bonds	.50	.23
184	Ellis Burks	.15	.07
185	F.P. Santangelo	.10	.05
186	J.T. Snow	.15	.07
187	Ramon E.Martinez	.15	.07
188	Jeff Kent	.15	.07
189	Robb Nen	.10	.05
190	Ken Griffey Jr.	2.00	.90
191	Alex Rodriguez	1.25	.55
192	Shane Monahan	.10	.05
193	Carlos Guillen	.10	.05
194	Edgar Martinez	.15	.07
195	David Segui	.10	.05
196	Jose Mesa	.10	.05
197	Jose Canseco	.50	.23
198	Rolando Arrojo	.10	.05
199	Wade Boggs	.40	.18
200	Fred McGriff	.25	.11
201	Quinton McCracken	.10	.05
202	Bobby Smith	.10	.05
203	Bubba Trammell	.10	.05
204	Juan Gonzalez	.75	.35
205	Ivan Rodriguez	.50	.23
206	Rafael Palmeiro	.40	.18
207	Royce Clayton	.10	.05
208	Rick Helling	.10	.05
209	Todd Zeile	.15	.07
210	Rusty Greer	.15	.07
211	David Wells	.15	.07
212	Roy Halladay	.15	.07
213	Carlos Delgado	.40	.18
214	Darrin Fletcher	.10	.05
215	Shawn Green	.40	.18
216	Kevin Witt	.10	.05
217	Jose Cruz Jr.	.15	.07
218	Ken Griffey Jr. CL	1.00	.45
219	Sammy Sosa CL	.60	.25
220	Mark McGwire CL	1.25	.55
S3	Ken Griffey Jr. Sample	3.00	1.35

1999 Upper Deck MVP Gold Script

	MINT	NRMT
COMMON CARD (1-220)	6.00	2.70

*STARS: 25X TO 60X BASIC CARDS
*YNG.STARS: 20X TO 50X BASIC CARDS
*ROOKIES: 15X TO 40X BASIC CARDS
RANDOM INSERTS IN HOBBY PACKS
STATED PRINT RUN 100 SERIAL #'d SETS

1999 Upper Deck MVP Silver Script

	MINT	NRMT
COMPLETE SET (220)	150.00	70.00
COMMON CARD (1-220)	.25	.11

*STARS: 1.5X TO 4X BASIC CARDS
*ROOKIES: 1.5X TO 4X BASIC CARDS
STATED ODDS 1:2

S3	Ken Griffey Jr. Sample .. 3.00	1.35

1999 Upper Deck MVP Super Script

	MINT	NRMT
COMMON CARD (1-220)	20.00	9.00

*STARS: 80X TO 200X BASIC CARDS
*YNG.STARS: 60X TO 150X BASIC CARDS
*ROOKIES: 40X TO 100X BASIC CARDS
RANDOM INSERTS IN HOBBY PACKS
STATED PRINT RUN 25 SERIAL #'d SETS

1999 Upper Deck MVP Dynamics

	MINT	NRMT
COMPLETE SET (15)	120.00	55.00
COMMON CARD (D1-D15)	2.50	1.10

STATED ODDS 1:28

#	Player	MINT	NRMT
D1	Ken Griffey Jr.	15.00	6.75
D2	Alex Rodriguez	10.00	4.50
D3	Nomar Garciaparra	10.00	4.50
D4	Mike Piazza	10.00	4.50
D5	Mark McGwire	20.00	9.00
D6	Sammy Sosa	10.00	4.50

	MINT	NRMT
COMPLETE SET (15)	25.00	11.00
COMMON CARD (P1-P15)	.75	.35
STATED ODDS 1:9		
❑ P1 Mark McGwire	6.00	2.70
❑ P2 Sammy Sosa	3.00	1.35
❑ P3 Ken Griffey Jr.	5.00	2.20
❑ P4 Alex Rodriguez	3.00	1.35
❑ P5 Juan Gonzalez	2.00	.90
❑ P6 Nomar Garciaparra	3.00	1.35
❑ P7 Vladimir Guerrero	1.25	.55
❑ P8 Chipper Jones	2.50	1.10
❑ P9 Albert Belle	.75	.35
❑ P10 Frank Thomas	2.00	.90
❑ P11 Mike Piazza	3.00	1.35
❑ P12 Jeff Bagwell	1.25	.55
❑ P13 Manny Ramirez	1.25	.55
❑ P14 Mo Vaughn	.75	.35
❑ P15 Barry Bonds	1.25	.55

1999 Upper Deck MVP ProSign

	MINT	NRMT
COMMON CARD	10.00	4.50
STATED ODDS 1:216 RETAIL		
❑ AG Alex Gonzalez	15.00	6.75
❑ AN Abraham Nunez	10.00	4.50
❑ BC Bruce Chen	15.00	6.75
❑ BF Brad Fullmer	15.00	6.75
❑ BG Ben Grieve	40.00	18.00
❑ CB Carlos Beltran	50.00	22.00
❑ CG Chris Gomez	10.00	4.50
❑ CJ Chipper Jones		
❑ CK Corey Koskie	15.00	6.75
❑ CP Calvin Pickering	20.00	9.00
❑ DG Derrick Gibson	20.00	9.00
❑ EC Eric Chavez	25.00	11.00
❑ GK Gabe Kapler	30.00	13.50
❑ GL George Lombard	20.00	9.00
❑ IR Ivan Rodriguez		
❑ JG Jeremy Giambi	20.00	9.00
❑ JP Jim Parque	10.00	4.50
❑ JR Ken Griffey Jr.		
❑ KW Kevin Witt	10.00	4.50
❑ MA Matt Anderson	15.00	6.75
❑ ML Mike Lincoln	10.00	4.50
❑ NG Nomar Garciaparra		
❑ RB Russ Branyan	20.00	9.00
❑ RH Richard Hidalgo	15.00	6.75
❑ RL Ricky Ledee	20.00	9.00
❑ RM Ryan Minor	20.00	9.00
❑ RR Ruben Rivera	10.00	4.50
❑ SH Shea Hillenbrand	15.00	6.75
❑ SK Scott Karl	10.00	4.50
❑ SM Shane Monahan	10.00	4.50
❑ JRA Jason Rakers	10.00	4.50
❑ MLO Mike Lowell	15.00	6.75

1999 Upper Deck MVP Scout's Choice

	MINT	NRMT
COMPLETE SET (15)	12.00	5.50
COMMON CARD (SC1-SC15)	.50	.23

❑ D7 Chipper Jones	8.00	3.60
❑ D8 Mo Vaughn	2.50	1.10
❑ D9 Tony Gwynn	8.00	3.60
❑ D10 Vladimir Guerrero	4.00	1.80
❑ D11 Derek Jeter	10.00	4.50
❑ D12 Jeff Bagwell	4.00	1.80
❑ D13 Cal Ripken	12.00	5.50
❑ D14 Juan Gonzalez	6.00	2.70
❑ D15 J.D. Drew	4.00	1.80

1999 Upper Deck MVP Game Used Souvenirs

	MINT	NRMT
COMPLETE SET (9)	1000.00	450.00
COMMON CARD	40.00	18.00
STATED ODDS 1:144 HOBBY		
❑ GUBB Barry Bonds	80.00	36.00
❑ GUCJ Chipper Jones	100.00	45.00
❑ GUCR Cal Ripken	150.00	70.00
❑ GUJB Jeff Bagwell	60.00	27.00
❑ GUJD J.D. Drew	80.00	36.00
❑ GUKG Ken Griffey Jr.	200.00	90.00
❑ GUMP Mike Piazza	80.00	36.00
❑ GUMV Mo Vaughn	40.00	18.00
❑ GUSR Scott Rolen	60.00	27.00
❑ GAKG K. Griffey Jr. AU/24	4000.00	1800.00
❑ GACJ Chipper Jones AU/10		

1999 Upper Deck MVP Power Surge

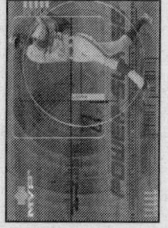

	MINT	NRMT
SEMISTARS	.75	.35
UNLISTED STARS	1.25	.55
STATED ODDS 1:9		
❑ SC1 J.D. Drew	2.00	.90
❑ SC2 Ben Grieve	1.25	.55
❑ SC3 Troy Glaus	1.25	.55
❑ SC4 Gabe Kapler	1.25	.55
❑ SC5 Carlos Beltran	1.50	.70
❑ SC6 Aramis Ramirez	.75	.35
❑ SC7 Pat Burrell	4.00	1.80
❑ SC8 Kerry Wood	1.25	.55
❑ SC9 Ryan Minor	.50	.23
❑ SC10 Todd Helton	1.25	.55
❑ SC11 Eric Chavez	.75	.35
❑ SC12 Russ Branyan	.50	.23
❑ SC13 Travis Lee	.75	.35
❑ SC14 Ruben Mateo	1.25	.55
❑ SC15 Roy Halladay	.50	.23

1999 Upper Deck MVP Super Tools

	MINT	NRMT
COMPLETE SET (15)	60.00	27.00
COMMON CARD (T1-T15)	1.25	.55
UNLISTED STARS	2.00	.90
STATED ODDS 1:14		
❑ T1 Ken Griffey Jr.	10.00	4.50
❑ T2 Alex Rodriguez	6.00	2.70
❑ T3 Sammy Sosa	6.00	2.70
❑ T4 Derek Jeter	6.00	2.70
❑ T5 Vladimir Guerrero	2.50	1.10
❑ T6 Ben Grieve	2.00	.90
❑ T7 Mike Piazza	6.00	2.70
❑ T8 Kenny Lofton	1.25	.55
❑ T9 Barry Bonds	2.50	1.10
❑ T10 Darin Erstad	1.25	.55
❑ T11 Nomar Garciaparra	6.00	2.70
❑ T12 Cal Ripken	8.00	3.60
❑ T13 J.D. Drew	2.50	1.10
❑ T14 Larry Walker	2.00	.90
❑ T15 Chipper Jones	5.00	2.20

1999 Upper Deck MVP Swing Time

	MINT	NRMT
COMPLETE SET (12)	20.00	9.00

	MINT	NRMT
COMMON CARD (S1-S12)	1.00	.45
STATED ODDS 1:6		

		MINT	NRMT
☐ S1 Ken Griffey Jr.		4.00	1.80
☐ S2 Mark McGwire		5.00	2.20
☐ S3 Sammy Sosa		2.50	1.10
☐ S4 Tony Gwynn		2.00	.90
☐ S5 Alex Rodriguez		2.50	1.10
☐ S6 Nomar Garciaparra		2.50	1.10
☐ S7 Barry Bonds		1.00	.45
☐ S8 Frank Thomas		1.50	.70
☐ S9 Chipper Jones		2.00	.90
☐ S10 Ivan Rodriguez		1.00	.45
☐ S11 Mike Piazza		2.50	1.10
☐ S12 Derek Jeter		2.50	1.10

1999 Upper Deck Ovation

	MINT	NRMT
COMPLETE SET (90)	150.00	70.00
COMP.SET w/o SP's (60)	30.00	13.50
COMMON CARD (1-60)	.20	.09
MINOR STARS	.30	.14
SEMISTARS	.50	.23
UNLISTED STARS	.75	.35
COMMON WP (61-80)	1.00	.45
WP MINOR STARS	1.50	.70
WP SEMISTARS	2.50	1.10
WP STATED ODDS 1:3.5		
COMMON SS (81-90)	5.00	2.20
SS STATED ODDS 1:6		

MANTLE BAT LISTED W/UD APH 500 CLUB
1 OF 1 MANTLE LEGENDARY CUT CARD
EXISTS

			MINT	NRMT
☐ 1 Ken Griffey Jr.			4.00	1.80
☐ 2 Rondell White			.30	.14
☐ 3 Tony Clark			.30	.14
☐ 4 Barry Bonds			1.00	.45
☐ 5 Larry Walker			.75	.35
☐ 6 Greg Vaughn			.30	.14
☐ 7 Mark Grace			.50	.23
☐ 8 John Olerud			.30	.14
☐ 9 Matt Williams			.75	.35
☐ 10 Craig Biggio			.75	.35
☐ 11 Quinton McCracken			.20	.09
☐ 12 Kerry Wood			.75	.35
☐ 13 Derek Jeter			2.50	1.10
☐ 14 Frank Thomas			1.50	.70

		MINT	NRMT
☐ 15 Tino Martinez		.30	.14
☐ 16 Albert Belle		.75	.35
☐ 17 Ben Grieve		.75	.35
☐ 18 Cal Ripken		3.00	1.35
☐ 19 Johnny Damon		.30	.14
☐ 20 Jose Cruz Jr.		.30	.14
☐ 21 Barry Larkin		.75	.35
☐ 22 Jason Giambi		.30	.14
☐ 23 Sean Casey		.75	.35
☐ 24 Scott Rolen		1.00	.45
☐ 25 Jim Thome		.75	.35
☐ 26 Curt Schilling		.50	.23
☐ 27 Moises Alou		.30	.14
☐ 28 Alex Rodriguez		2.50	1.10
☐ 29 Mark Kotsay		.20	.09
☐ 30 Darin Erstad		.50	.23
☐ 31 Mike Mussina		.75	.35
☐ 32 Todd Walker		.30	.14
☐ 33 Nomar Garciaparra		2.50	1.10
☐ 34 Vladimir Guerrero		1.00	.45
☐ 35 Jeff Bagwell		1.00	.45
☐ 36 Mark McGwire		5.00	2.20
☐ 37 Travis Lee		.50	.23
☐ 38 Dean Palmer		.30	.14
☐ 39 Fred McGriff		.50	.23
☐ 40 Sammy Sosa		2.50	1.10
☐ 41 Mike Piazza		2.50	1.10
☐ 42 Andres Galarraga		.50	.23
☐ 43 Pedro Martinez		1.00	.45
☐ 44 Juan Gonzalez		1.50	.70
☐ 45 Greg Maddux		2.00	.90
☐ 46 Jeromy Burnitz		.30	.14
☐ 47 Roger Clemens		2.00	.90
☐ 48 Vinny Castilla		.30	.14
☐ 49 Kevin Brown		.50	.23
☐ 50 Mo Vaughn		.75	.35
☐ 51 Raul Mondesi		.30	.14
☐ 52 Randy Johnson		.75	.35
☐ 53 Ray Lankford		.30	.14
☐ 54 Jaret Wright		.30	.14
☐ 55 Tony Gwynn		2.00	.90
☐ 56 Chipper Jones		2.00	.90
☐ 57 Gary Sheffield		.30	.14
☐ 58 Ivan Rodriguez		1.00	.45
☐ 59 Kenny Lofton		.50	.23
☐ 60 Jason Kendall		.30	.14
☐ 61 J.D. Drew WP		6.00	2.70
☐ 62 Gabe Kapler WP		3.00	1.35
☐ 63 Adrian Beltre WP		4.00	1.80
☐ 64 Carlos Beltran WP		5.00	2.20
☐ 65 Eric Chavez WP		2.50	1.10
☐ 66 Mike Lowell WP		1.00	.45
☐ 67 Troy Glaus WP		4.00	1.80
☐ 68 George Lombard WP		.50	.70
☐ 69 Alex Gonzalez WP		1.50	.70
☐ 70 Mike Kinkade WP		1.00	.45
☐ 71 Jeremy Giambi WP		1.50	.70
☐ 72 Bruce Chen WP		1.50	.70
☐ 73 Preston Wilson WP		1.50	.70
☐ 74 Kevin Witt WP		1.00	.45
☐ 75 Carlos Guillen WP		1.00	.45
☐ 76 Ryan Minor WP		1.50	.70
☐ 77 Corey Koskie WP		1.00	.45
☐ 78 Robert Fick WP		1.50	.70
☐ 79 Michael Barrett WP		2.50	1.10
☐ 80 Calvin Pickering WP		1.50	.70
☐ 81 Ken Griffey Jr. SS		12.00	5.50
☐ 82 Mark McGwire SS		15.00	6.75
☐ 83 Cal Ripken SS		10.00	4.50
☐ 84 Derek Jeter SS		8.00	3.60
☐ 85 Chipper Jones SS		6.00	2.70
☐ 86 Nomar Garciaparra SS		8.00	3.60
☐ 87 Sammy Sosa SS		8.00	3.60
☐ 88 Juan Gonzalez SS		5.00	2.20
☐ 89 Mike Piazza SS		8.00	3.60
☐ 90 Alex Rodriguez SS		8.00	3.60
☐ MICL M.Mantle Legendary Cut/1			

1999 Upper Deck Ovation Standing Ovation

	MINT	NRMT
COMMON CARD (1-90)	2.50	1.10

*STARS 1-60: 5X TO 12X BASIC 1-60
*YNG.STARS 1-60: 4X TO 10X BASIC 1-60
*WP CARDS 61-80: 1X TO 2.5X BASIC WP
*SS CARDS 81-90: 1.5X TO 4X BASIC SS
RANDOM INSERTS IN PACKS
STATED PRINT RUN 500 SERIAL #'d SETS

1999 Upper Deck Ovation A Piece of History

	MINT	NRMT
STATED ODDS 1:247		

		MINT	NRMT
☐ AR Alex Rodriguez		300.00	135.00
☐ BB Barry Bonds		150.00	70.00
☐ BG Ben Grieve		80.00	36.00
☐ BW Bernie Williams		100.00	45.00
☐ CJ Chipper Jones		150.00	70.00
☐ CR Cal Ripken		400.00	180.00
☐ DJ Derek Jeter		300.00	135.00
☐ JG Juan Gonzalez		120.00	55.00
☐ MP Mike Piazza		250.00	110.00
☐ NG Nomar Garciaparra		250.00	110.00
☐ SS Sammy Sosa		250.00	110.00
☐ TG Tony Gwynn		150.00	70.00
☐ VG Vladimir Guerrero		120.00	55.00
☐ KGJ Ken Griffey Jr.		500.00	220.00
☐ BGAU B. Grieve Bat AU/25		1200.00	550.00
☐ KWAU Kerry Wood Ball AU/25			

1999 Upper Deck Ovation Curtain Calls

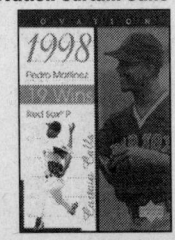

	MINT	NRMT
COMPLETE SET (20)	100.00	45.00
COMMON CARD (R1-R20)	1.00	.45
SEMISTARS	1.50	.70
UNLISTED STARS	2.50	1.10
STATED ODDS 1:8		

		MINT	NRMT
☐ R1	Mark McGwire	15.00	6.75
☐ R2	Sammy Sosa	8.00	3.60
☐ R3	Ken Griffey Jr.	12.00	5.50
☐ R4	Alex Rodriguez	8.00	3.60
☐ R5	Roger Clemens	6.00	2.70
☐ R6	Cal Ripken	10.00	4.50
☐ R7	Barry Bonds	3.00	1.35
☐ R8	Kerry Wood	1.50	.70
☐ R9	Nomar Garciaparra	8.00	3.60
☐ R10	Derek Jeter	8.00	3.60
☐ R11	Juan Gonzalez	5.00	2.20
☐ R12	Greg Maddux	6.00	2.70
☐ R13	Pedro Martinez	3.00	1.35
☐ R14	David Wells	1.00	.45
☐ R15	Moises Alou	1.00	.45
☐ R16	Tony Gwynn	6.00	2.70
☐ R17	Albert Belle	2.00	.90
☐ R18	Mike Piazza	8.00	3.60
☐ R19	Ivan Rodriguez	3.00	1.35
☐ R20	Randy Johnson	2.50	1.10

1999 Upper Deck Ovation Major Production

	MINT	NRMT
COMPLETE SET (20)	400.00	180.00
COMMON CARD (1-20)	6.00	2.70
UNLISTED STARS	10.00	4.50
STATED ODDS 1:45		

		MINT	NRMT
☐ S1	Mike Piazza	30.00	13.50
☐ S2	Mark McGwire	60.00	27.00
☐ S3	Chipper Jones	25.00	11.00
☐ S4	Cal Ripken	40.00	18.00
☐ S5	Ken Griffey Jr.	50.00	22.00
☐ S6	Barry Bonds	12.00	5.50
☐ S7	Tony Gwynn	25.00	11.00
☐ S8	Randy Johnson	10.00	4.50
☐ S9	Ivan Rodriguez	12.00	5.50
☐ S10	Frank Thomas	20.00	9.00
☐ S11	Alex Rodriguez	30.00	13.50
☐ S12	Albert Belle	10.00	4.50
☐ S13	Juan Gonzalez	20.00	9.00
☐ S14	Greg Maddux	25.00	11.00
☐ S15	Jeff Bagwell	12.00	5.50
☐ S16	Derek Jeter	30.00	13.50
☐ S17	Matt Williams	10.00	4.50
☐ S18	Kenny Lofton	6.00	2.70
☐ S19	Sammy Sosa	30.00	13.50
☐ S20	Roger Clemens	25.00	11.00

1999 Upper Deck Ovation ReMarkable Moments

	MINT	NRMT
COMPLETE SET (15)	200.00	90.00
COMMON CARD (1-5)	6.00	2.70

	MINT	NRMT
CARDS 1-5 STATED ODDS 1:9		
COMMON CARD (6-10)	15.00	6.75
CARDS 6-10 STATED ODDS 1:25		
COMMON CARD (11-15)	30.00	13.50
CARDS 11-15 STATED ODDS 1:99		

		MINT	NRMT
☐ MM1	Mark McGwire HR 1	6.00	2.70
☐ MM2	Mark McGwire HR 4	6.00	2.70
☐ MM3	Mark McGwire HR 7	6.00	2.70
☐ MM4	Mark McGwire HR 13	6.00	2.70
☐ MM5	Mark McGwire HR 14	6.00	2.70
☐ MM6	Mark McGwire HR 16	15.00	6.75
☐ MM7	Mark McGwire HR 20	15.00	6.75
☐ MM8	Mark McGwire HR 38	15.00	6.75
☐ MM9	Mark McGwire HR 49	15.00	6.75
☐ MM10	Mark McGwire HR 50	15.00	6.75
☐ MM11	Mark McGwire HR 57	30.00	13.50
☐ MM12	Mark McGwire HR 60	30.00	13.50
☐ MM13	Mark McGwire HR 61	30.00	13.50
☐ MM14	Mark McGwire HR 62	30.00	13.50
☐ MM15	Mark McGwire HR 70	30.00	13.50

1999 Upper Deck PowerDeck

	MINT	NRMT
COMPLETE SET (25)	130.00	57.50
COMMON CD (1-25)	2.50	1.10
ONE PER PACK		

		MINT	NRMT
☐ 1	Ken Griffey Jr.	15.00	6.75
☐ 2	Mark McGwire	20.00	9.00
☐ 3	Cal Ripken	12.00	5.50
☐ 4	Sammy Sosa	10.00	4.50
☐ 5	Derek Jeter	10.00	4.50

		MINT	NRMT
☐ 6	Mike Piazza	10.00	4.50
☐ 7	Nomar Garciaparra	10.00	4.50
☐ 8	Greg Maddux	8.00	3.60
☐ 9	Tony Gwynn	8.00	3.60
☐ 10	Roger Clemens	8.00	3.60
☐ 11	Scott Rolen	4.00	1.80
☐ 12	Alex Rodriguez	10.00	4.50
☐ 13	Manny Ramirez	4.00	1.80
☐ 14	Chipper Jones	8.00	3.60
☐ 15	Juan Gonzalez	6.00	2.70
☐ 16	Ivan Rodriguez	4.00	1.80
☐ 17	Frank Thomas	6.00	2.70
☐ 18	Mo Vaughn	2.50	1.10
☐ 19	Barry Bonds	4.00	1.80
☐ 20	Vladimir Guerrero	4.00	1.80
☐ 21	Jose Canseco	4.00	1.80
☐ 22	Jeff Bagwell	4.00	1.80
☐ 23	Pedro Martinez	4.00	1.80
☐ 24	Gabe Kapler	2.50	1.10
☐ 25	J.D. Drew	5.00	2.20

1999 Upper Deck PowerDeck Auxiliary

	MINT	NRMT
COMPLETE SET (25)	25.00	11.00
COMMON CARD (AUX1-AUX25)	.50	.23
APPROXIMATELY TWO PER PACK		
1 OF 1 GOLD PARALLELS EXIST		
NO 1 OF 1 PRICING DUE TO SCARCITY		

1999 Upper Deck PowerDeck A Season To Remember

	MINT	NRMT
ONE PER BOX		

		MINT	NRMT
☐ 1	Mark McGwire	10.00	4.50
	Wade Boggs		
	Tony Gwynn		
	Ken Griffey Jr.		
	Sammy Sosa		
	David Cone		
	Cal Ripken		

1999 Upper Deck PowerDeck Most Valuable Performances

	MINT	NRMT
COMPLETE SET (7)	350.00	160.00
COMMON CD (M1-M7)	20.00	9.00

STATED ODDS 1:287
*AUXILIARY: 75% VALUE OF CD'S
AUXILIARY STATED ODDS 1:287
1 OF 1 AUXILIARY GOLD CARDS EXIST
1 OF 1 AUX.GOLD TOO SCARCE TO PRICE
CD'S LISTED BELOW!

			MINT	NRMT
❑	M1	Sammy Sosa	50.00	22.00
❑	M2	Barry Bonds	20.00	9.00
❑	M3	Cal Ripken	60.00	27.00
❑	M4	Juan Gonzalez	30.00	13.50
❑	M5	Ken Griffey Jr.	80.00	36.00
❑	M6	Roger Clemens	40.00	18.00
❑	M7	Mark McGwire	100.00	45.00

1999 Upper Deck PowerDeck Powerful Moments

	MINT	NRMT
COMPLETE SET (6)	60.00	27.00
COMMON CARD (P1-P6)	10.00	4.50

STATED ODDS 1:7
*AUXILIARY: 75% VALUE OF CD'S
AUXILIARY STATED ODDS 1:7
1 OF 1 AUXILIARY GOLD CARDS EXIST
1 OF 1 AUX.GOLD TOO SCARCE TO PRICE
CD'S LISTED BELOW!

			MINT	NRMT
❑	P1	Mark McGwire	20.00	9.00
❑	P2	Sammy Sosa	10.00	4.50
❑	P3	Cal Ripken	12.00	5.50
❑	P4	Ken Griffey Jr.	15.00	6.75
❑	P5	Derek Jeter	10.00	4.50
❑	P6	Alex Rodriguez	10.00	4.50

1999 Upper Deck PowerDeck Time Capsule

	MINT	NRMT
COMPLETE SET (6)	100.00	45.00
COMMON CARD (R1-R6)	6.00	2.70

STATED ODDS 1:23
*AUXILIARY: 75% VALUE OF CD'S
AUXILIARY STATED ODDS 1:23
1 OF 1 AUXILIARY GOLD CARDS EXIST
1 OF 1 AUX.GOLD TOO SCARCE TO PRICE
CD'S LISTED BELOW!

			MINT	NRMT
❑	R1	Ken Griffey Jr.	25.00	11.00
❑	R2	Mike Piazza	15.00	6.75
❑	R3	Mark McGwire	30.00	13.50
❑	R4	Derek Jeter	15.00	6.75
❑	R5	Jose Canseco	6.00	2.70
❑	R6	Nomar Garciaparra	15.00	6.75

1998 Upper Deck Retro

	MINT	NRMT
COMPLETE SET (129)	60.00	27.00
COMMON CARD (1-81/83-130)	.20	.09
MINOR STARS	.30	.14
SEMISTARS	.50	.23
UNLISTED STARS	.75	.35

CARD NUMBER 82 DOES NOT EXIST

❑ 1 Jim Edmonds	.30	.14	
❑ 2 Darin Erstad	.50	.23	
❑ 3 Tim Salmon	.50	.23	
❑ 4 Jay Bell	.30	.14	
❑ 5 Matt Williams	.75	.35	
❑ 6 Andres Galarraga	.50	.23	
❑ 7 Andruw Jones	.75	.35	
❑ 8 Chipper Jones	2.00	.90	
❑ 9 Greg Maddux	2.00	.90	
❑ 10 Rafael Palmeiro	.75	.35	
❑ 11 Cal Ripken	3.00	1.35	
❑ 12 Brooks Robinson	.75	.35	
❑ 13 Nomar Garciaparra	2.50	1.10	
❑ 14 Pedro Martinez	1.00	.45	
❑ 15 Mo Vaughn	.75	.35	
❑ 16 Ernie Banks	1.00	.45	
❑ 17 Mark Grace	.50	.23	
❑ 18 Gary Matthews Sr.	.30	.14	
❑ 19 Sammy Sosa	2.50	1.10	
❑ 20 Albert Belle	.75	.35	
❑ 21 Carlton Fisk	.75	.35	
❑ 22 Frank Thomas	1.50	.70	
❑ 23 Ken Griffey Sr.	.30	.14	
❑ 24 Paul Konerko	.30	.14	
❑ 25 Barry Larkin	.75	.35	
❑ 26 Sean Casey	1.25	.55	
❑ 27 Tony Perez	.30	.14	
❑ 28 Bob Feller	.75	.35	
❑ 29 Kenny Lofton	.50	.23	
❑ 30 Manny Ramirez	.75	.35	
❑ 31 Jim Thome	.75	.35	
❑ 32 Omar Vizquel	.30	.14	
❑ 33 Dante Bichette	.30	.14	
❑ 34 Larry Walker	.75	.35	
❑ 35 Tony Clark	.30	.14	
❑ 36 Damion Easley	.30	.14	
❑ 37 Cliff Floyd	.30	.14	
❑ 38 Livan Hernandez	.20	.09	
❑ 39 Jeff Bagwell	1.00	.45	
❑ 40 Craig Biggio	.75	.35	
❑ 41 Al Kaline	.75	.35	
❑ 42 Johnny Damon	.30	.14	
❑ 43 Dean Palmer	.30	.14	
❑ 44 Charles Johnson	.30	.14	
❑ 45 Eric Karros	.30	.14	
❑ 46 Gaylord Perry	.50	.23	
❑ 47 Raul Mondesi	.30	.14	
❑ 48 Gary Sheffield	.30	.14	
❑ 49 Eddie Mathews	.75	.35	
❑ 50 Warren Spahn	.75	.35	
❑ 51 Jeromy Burnitz	.30	.14	
❑ 52 Jeff Cirillo	.30	.14	
❑ 53 Marquis Grissom	.20	.09	
❑ 54 Paul Molitor	.75	.35	
❑ 55 Kirby Puckett	1.25	.55	
❑ 56 Brad Radke	.30	.14	
❑ 57 Todd Walker	.30	.14	
❑ 58 Vladimir Guerrero	1.00	.45	
❑ 59 Brad Fullmer	.20	.09	
❑ 60 Rondell White	.30	.14	
❑ 61 Bobby Jones	.20	.09	
❑ 62 Hideo Nomo	.75	.35	
❑ 63 Mike Piazza	2.50	1.10	
❑ 64 Tom Seaver	1.00	.45	
❑ 65 Frank Thomas	.20	.09	
❑ 66 Yogi Berra	1.00	.45	
❑ 67 Derek Jeter	2.50	1.10	
❑ 68 Tino Martinez	.30	.14	
❑ 69 Paul O'Neill	.30	.14	
❑ 70 Andy Pettitte	.30	.14	
❑ 71 Rollie Fingers	.50	.23	
❑ 72 Rickey Henderson	1.00	.45	
❑ 73 Matt Stairs	.30	.14	
❑ 74 Scott Rolen	1.00	.45	
❑ 75 Curt Schilling	.50	.23	
❑ 76 Jose Guillen	.20	.09	
❑ 77 Jason Kendall	.30	.14	
❑ 78 Lou Brock	.75	.35	
❑ 79 Bob Gibson	.75	.35	
❑ 80 Ray Lankford	.30	.14	
❑ 81 Ken Griffey Jr.	5.00	2.20	
❑ 83 Kevin Brown	.50	.23	
❑ 84 Ken Caminiti	.30	.14	
❑ 85 Tony Gwynn	2.00	.90	
❑ 86 Greg Vaughn	.30	.14	
❑ 87 Barry Bonds	1.00	.45	
❑ 88 Willie Stargell	.50	.23	
❑ 89 Willie McCovey	.75	.35	
❑ 90 Ken Griffey Jr.	4.00	1.80	
❑ 91 Randy Johnson	.75	.35	
❑ 92 Alex Rodriguez	2.50	1.10	
❑ 93 Quinton McCracken	.20	.09	
❑ 94 Fred McGriff	.50	.23	
❑ 95 Juan Gonzalez	1.50	.70	
❑ 96 Ivan Rodriguez	1.00	.45	
❑ 97 Nolan Ryan	3.00	1.35	
❑ 98 Jose Canseco	1.00	.45	
❑ 99 Roger Clemens	2.00	.90	
❑ 100 Jose Cruz Jr.	.30	.14	
❑ 101 Justin Thompson FUT	.30	.14	
❑ 102 Dave Dellucci FUT	.60	.25	
❑ 103 Travis Lee FUT	.50	.23	
❑ 104 Troy Glaus FUT	3.00	1.35	
❑ 105 Kerry Wood FUT	1.00	.45	
❑ 106 Mike Caruso FUT	.20	.09	
❑ 107 Jim Parque FUT	.50	.23	
❑ 108 Brett Tomko FUT	.20	.09	
❑ 109 Russell Branyan FUT	.30	.14	
❑ 110 Jaret Wright FUT	.30	.14	
❑ 111 Todd Helton FUT	1.00	.45	
❑ 112 Gabe Alvarez FUT	.20	.09	
❑ 113 Matt Anderson FUT	.75	.35	
❑ 114 Alex Gonzalez FUT	.30	.14	
❑ 115 Mark Kotsay FUT	.30	.14	
❑ 116 Derek Lee FUT	.20	.09	
❑ 117 Richard Hidalgo FUT	.30	.14	
❑ 118 Adrian Beltre FUT	.75	.35	
❑ 119 Geoff Jenkins FUT	.30	.14	
❑ 120 Eric Milton FUT	.20	.09	
❑ 121 Brad Fullmer FUT	.20	.09	
❑ 122 Vladimir Guerrero FUT	1.00	.45	
❑ 123 Carl Pavano FUT	.20	.09	
❑ 124 Orlando Hernandez FUT	2.00	.90	
❑ 125 Ben Grieve FUT	.75	.35	
❑ 126 A.J. Hinch FUT	.20	.09	
❑ 127 Matt Clement FUT	.30	.14	
❑ 128 Gary Matthews Jr. FUT	.60	.25	

❏ 129 Aramis Ramirez FUT	.75	.35
❏ 130 Rolando Arrojo FUT	.75	.35

1998 Upper Deck Retro Big Boppers

	MINT	NRMT
COMPLETE SET (30)	600.00	275.00
COMMON CARD (BB1-BB30)	5.00	2.20
SEMISTARS	8.00	3.60
UNLISTED STARS	12.00	5.50
RANDOM INSERTS IN PACKS		
STATED PRINT RUN 500 SERIAL #'d SETS		

❏ BB1 Darin Erstad	8.00	3.60
❏ BB2 Rafael Palmeiro	12.00	5.50
❏ BB3 Cal Ripken	50.00	22.00
❏ BB4 Nomar Garciaparra	40.00	18.00
❏ BB5 Mo Vaughn	12.00	5.50
❏ BB6 Frank Thomas	25.00	11.00
❏ BB7 Albert Belle	12.00	5.50
❏ BB8 Jim Thome	12.00	5.50
❏ BB9 Manny Ramirez	15.00	6.75
❏ BB10 Tony Clark	5.00	2.20
❏ BB11 Tino Martinez	5.00	2.20
❏ BB12 Ben Grieve	12.00	5.50
❏ BB13 Ken Griffey Jr.	60.00	27.00
❏ BB14 Alex Rodriguez	40.00	18.00
❏ BB15 Jay Buhner	5.00	2.20
❏ BB16 Juan Gonzalez	25.00	11.00
❏ BB17 Jose Cruz Jr.	5.00	2.20
❏ BB18 Jose Canseco	15.00	6.75
❏ BB19 Travis Lee	8.00	3.60
❏ BB20 Chipper Jones	30.00	13.50
❏ BB21 Andres Galarraga	8.00	3.60
❏ BB22 Andruw Jones	12.00	5.50
❏ BB23 Sammy Sosa	40.00	18.00
❏ BB24 Vinny Castilla	5.00	2.20
❏ BB25 Larry Walker	12.00	5.50
❏ BB26 Jeff Bagwell	15.00	6.75
❏ BB27 Gary Sheffield	5.00	2.20
❏ BB28 Mike Piazza	40.00	18.00
❏ BB29 Mark McGwire	80.00	36.00
❏ BB30 Barry Bonds	15.00	6.75

1998 Upper Deck Retro Groovy Kind of Glove

	MINT	NRMT
COMPLETE SET (30)	200.00	90.00

COMMON CARD (G1-G30)	1.50	.70
STATED ODDS 1:7		

❏ G1 Roberto Alomar	4.00	1.80
❏ G2 Cal Ripken	15.00	6.75
❏ G3 Nomar Garciaparra	12.00	5.50
❏ G4 Frank Thomas	8.00	3.60
❏ G5 Robin Ventura	1.50	.70
❏ G6 Omar Vizquel	1.50	.70
❏ G7 Kenny Lofton	2.50	1.10
❏ G8 Ben Grieve	4.00	1.80
❏ G9 Alex Rodriguez	12.00	5.50
❏ G10 Ken Griffey Jr.	20.00	9.00
❏ G11 Ivan Rodriguez	5.00	2.20
❏ G12 Travis Lee	2.50	1.10
❏ G13 Matt Williams	4.00	1.80
❏ G14 Greg Maddux	10.00	4.50
❏ G15 Andres Galarraga	2.50	1.10
❏ G16 Andruw Jones	4.00	1.80
❏ G17 Kerry Wood	4.00	1.80
❏ G18 Mark Grace	2.50	1.10
❏ G19 Craig Biggio	4.00	1.80
❏ G20 Charles Johnson	1.50	.70
❏ G21 Raul Mondesi	1.50	.70
❏ G22 Mike Piazza	12.00	5.50
❏ G23 Rey Ordonez	1.50	.70
❏ G24 Derek Jeter	12.00	5.50
❏ G25 Scott Rolen	6.00	2.70
❏ G26 Mark McGwire	25.00	11.00
❏ G27 Ken Caminiti	1.50	.70
❏ G28 Tony Gwynn	10.00	4.50
❏ G29 J.T. Snow	1.50	.70
❏ G30 Barry Bonds	5.00	2.20

1998 Upper Deck Retro Lunchboxes

	MINT	NRMT
COMPLETE SET (6)	100.00	45.00
COMMON LUNCHBOX (1-6)	3.00	1.35

❏ 1 Nomar Garciaparra	15.00	6.75
❏ 2 Ken Griffey Jr.	25.00	11.00
❏ 3 Chipper Jones	12.00	5.50
❏ 4 Travis Lee	3.00	1.35
❏ 5 Mark McGwire	30.00	13.50
❏ 6 Cal Ripken	20.00	9.00

1998 Upper Deck Retro New Frontier

	MINT	NRMT
COMPLETE SET (30)	120.00	55.00
COMMON CARD (NF1-NF30)	2.50	1.10
SEMISTARS	4.00	1.80
UNLISTED STARS	6.00	2.70
RANDOM INSERTS IN PACKS		
STATED PRINT RUN 1000 SERIAL #'d SETS		

❏ NF1 Justin Baughman	3.00	1.35
❏ NF2 David Dellucci	6.00	2.70
❏ NF3 Travis Lee	4.00	1.80
❏ NF4 Troy Glaus	20.00	9.00
❏ NF5 Mike Caruso	2.50	1.10
❏ NF6 Jim Parque	4.00	1.80
❏ NF7 Kerry Wood	8.00	3.60
❏ NF8 Brett Tomko	2.50	1.10
❏ NF9 Russell Branyan	3.00	1.35
❏ NF10 Jaret Wright	3.00	1.35
❏ NF11 Todd Helton	8.00	3.60
❏ NF12 Gabe Alvarez	2.50	1.10
❏ NF13 Matt Anderson	6.00	2.70
❏ NF14 Alex Gonzalez	3.00	1.35
❏ NF15 Mark Kotsay	3.00	1.35
❏ NF16 Derrek Lee	2.50	1.10
❏ NF17 Richard Hidalgo	3.00	1.35
❏ NF18 Adrian Beltre	6.00	2.70
❏ NF19 Geoff Jenkins	3.00	1.35
❏ NF20 Eric Milton	2.50	1.10
❏ NF21 Brad Fullmer	2.50	1.10
❏ NF22 Vladimir Guerrero	10.00	4.50
❏ NF23 Carl Pavano	2.50	1.10
❏ NF24 Orlando Hernandez	10.00	4.50
❏ NF25 Ben Grieve	6.00	2.70
❏ NF26 A.J. Hinch	2.50	1.10
❏ NF27 Matt Clement	3.00	1.35
❏ NF28 Gary Matthews Jr.	6.00	2.70
❏ NF29 Aramis Ramirez	6.00	2.70
❏ NF30 Rolando Arrojo	6.00	2.70

1998 Upper Deck Retro Quantum Leap

	MINT	NRMT
COMPLETE SET (30)	5000.00	2200.00
COMMON CARD (Q1-Q30)	80.00	36.00
RANDOM INSERTS IN PACKS		
STATED PRINT RUN 50 SERIAL #'d SETS		

❏ Q1 Darin Erstad	50.00	22.00
❏ Q2 Cal Ripken	300.00	135.00
❏ Q3 Nomar Garciaparra	250.00	110.00
❏ Q4 Frank Thomas	150.00	70.00
❏ Q5 Kenny Lofton	50.00	22.00
❏ Q6 Ben Grieve	80.00	36.00
❏ Q7 Ken Griffey Jr.	400.00	180.00
❏ Q8 Alex Rodriguez	250.00	110.00
❏ Q9 Juan Gonzalez	150.00	70.00
❏ Q10 Jose Cruz Jr.	30.00	13.50
❏ Q11 Roger Clemens	200.00	90.00
❏ Q12 Travis Lee	50.00	22.00
❏ Q13 Chipper Jones	200.00	90.00
❏ Q14 Greg Maddux	200.00	90.00
❏ Q15 Kerry Wood	80.00	36.00
❏ Q16 Jeff Bagwell	100.00	45.00
❏ Q17 Mike Piazza	250.00	110.00
❏ Q18 Scott Rolen	100.00	45.00
❏ Q19 Mark McGwire	500.00	220.00

		MINT	NRMT
Q20	Tony Gwynn	200.00	90.00
Q21	Larry Walker	80.00	36.00
Q22	Derek Jeter	250.00	110.00
Q23	Sammy Sosa	250.00	110.00
Q24	Barry Bonds	100.00	45.00
Q25	Mo Vaughn	80.00	36.00
Q26	Roberto Alomar	80.00	36.00
Q27	Todd Helton	80.00	36.00
Q28	Ivan Rodriguez	100.00	45.00
Q29	Vladimir Guerrero	100.00	45.00
Q30	Albert Belle	80.00	36.00

1998 Upper Deck Retro Sign of the Times

	MINT	NRMT
COMMON CARD (AK-WIS)	10.00	4.50
MINOR STARS	20.00	9.00
STATED ODDS 1:36		

		MINT	NRMT
AK	Al Kaline/600	60.00	27.00
BF	Bob Feller/600	40.00	18.00
BR	Brooks Robinson/300	60.00	27.00
CF	Carlton Fisk/600	50.00	22.00
EB	Ernie Banks/300	60.00	27.00
EM	Eddie Mathews/600	60.00	27.00
FT	Frank Thomas/600	20.00	9.00
GP	Gaylord Perry/1000	40.00	18.00
JC	Jose Cruz Jr./300	40.00	18.00
KP	Kirby Puckett/450	120.00	55.00
KW	Kerry Wood/200	80.00	36.00
LB	Lou Brock/300	60.00	27.00
NR	Nolan Ryan/500	300.00	135.00
PK	Paul Konerko/750	30.00	13.50
RB	Russell Branyan/750	25.00	11.00
RF	Rollie Fingers/600	40.00	18.00
SR	Scott Rolen/300	60.00	27.00
TG	Tony Gwynn/200	150.00	70.00
TP	Tony Perez/600	40.00	18.00
TS	Tom Seaver/300	80.00	36.00
WM	Willie McCovey/600	50.00	22.00
WS	Warren Spahn/600	60.00	27.00
YB	Yogi Berra/150	120.00	55.00
BGI	Bob Gibson/300	60.00	27.00
BGR	Ben Grieve/300	30.00	13.50
GMJ	Gary Matthews Jr./750	30.00	13.50
GMS	Gary Matthews Sr./600	30.00	13.50
KGJ	Ken Griffey Jr./100	600.00	275.00
KGS	Ken Griffey Sr./600	40.00	18.00
TLE	Travis Lee/300	30.00	13.50
WIS	Willie Stargell/600	50.00	22.00

1998 Upper Deck Retro Time Capsule

	MINT	NRMT
COMPLETE SET (50)	150.00	70.00
COMMON CARD (TC1-TC50)	.60	.25
STATED ODDS 1:2		

		MINT	NRMT
TC1	Mike Mussina	2.50	1.10
TC2	Rafael Palmeiro	2.50	1.10
TC3	Cal Ripken	10.00	4.50
TC4	Nomar Garciaparra	8.00	3.60
TC5	Pedro Martinez	3.00	1.35
TC6	Mo Vaughn	2.50	1.10
TC7	Albert Belle	2.50	1.10

TC8	Frank Thomas	5.00	2.20
TC9	David Justice	1.00	.45
TC10	Kenny Lofton	1.50	.70
TC11	Manny Ramirez	3.00	1.35
TC12	Jim Thome	2.50	1.10
TC13	Derek Jeter	8.00	3.60
TC14	Tino Martinez	1.00	.45
TC15	Ben Grieve	2.50	1.10
TC16	Rickey Henderson	3.00	1.35
TC17	Ken Griffey Jr.	12.00	5.50
TC18	Randy Johnson	2.50	1.10
TC19	Alex Rodriguez	8.00	3.60
TC20	Wade Boggs	2.50	1.10
TC21	Fred McGriff	1.50	.70
TC22	Juan Gonzalez	5.00	2.20
TC23	Ivan Rodriguez	3.00	1.35
TC24	Nolan Ryan	12.00	5.50
TC25	Jose Canseco	3.00	1.35
TC26	Roger Clemens	6.00	2.70
TC27	Jose Cruz Jr.	1.00	.45
TC28	Travis Lee	1.50	.70
TC29	Matt Williams	2.50	1.10
TC30	Andres Galarraga	1.50	.70
TC31	Andruw Jones	2.50	1.10
TC32	Chipper Jones	6.00	2.70
TC33	Greg Maddux	6.00	2.70
TC34	Kerry Wood	2.50	1.10
TC35	Barry Larkin	2.50	1.10
TC36	Dante Bichette	1.00	.45
TC37	Larry Walker	2.50	1.10
TC38	Livan Hernandez	.60	.25
TC39	Jeff Bagwell	3.00	1.35
TC40	Craig Biggio	2.50	1.10
TC41	Charles Johnson	1.00	.45
TC42	Gary Sheffield	1.00	.45
TC43	Marquis Grissom	.60	.25
TC44	Mike Piazza	8.00	3.60
TC45	Scott Rolen	4.00	1.80
TC46	Curt Schilling	1.50	.70
TC47	Mark McGwire	15.00	6.75
TC48	Ken Caminiti	1.00	.45
TC49	Tony Gwynn	6.00	2.70
TC50	Barry Bonds	3.00	1.35

1999 Upper Deck Retro

	MINT	NRMT
COMPLETE SET (110)	40.00	18.00
COMMON CARD (1-110)	.20	.09
MINOR STARS	.30	.14
SEMISTARS	.50	.23

UNLISTED STARS		.75	.35
T.WILLIAMS BAT LISTED W/UD APH 500 CLUB			

1	Mo Vaughn	.75	.35
2	Troy Glaus	.75	.35
3	Tim Salmon	.50	.23
4	Randy Johnson	.75	.35
5	Travis Lee	.50	.23
6	Matt Williams	.75	.35
7	Greg Maddux	2.00	.90
8	Chipper Jones	2.00	.90
9	Andruw Jones	.75	.35
10	Tom Glavine	.75	.35
11	Javy Lopez	.30	.14
12	Albert Belle	.75	.35
13	Cal Ripken	3.00	1.35
14	Brady Anderson	.30	.14
15	Nomar Garciaparra	2.50	1.10
16	Pedro Martinez	1.00	.45
17	Sammy Sosa	2.50	1.10
18	Mark Grace	.50	.23
19	Frank Thomas	1.50	.70
20	Ray Durham	.30	.14
21	Sean Casey	.75	.35
22	Greg Vaughn	.30	.14
23	Barry Larkin	.75	.35
24	Manny Ramirez	1.00	.45
25	Jim Thome	.75	.35
26	Jaret Wright	.30	.14
27	Kenny Lofton	.50	.23
28	Larry Walker	.75	.35
29	Todd Helton	.75	.35
30	Vinny Castilla	.30	.14
31	Tony Clark	.30	.14
32	Juan Encarnacion	.30	.14
33	Dean Palmer	.30	.14
34	Mark Kotsay	.20	.09
35	Alex Gonzalez	.30	.14
36	Shane Reynolds	.30	.14
37	Ken Caminiti	.30	.14
38	Jeff Bagwell	1.00	.45
39	Craig Biggio	.75	.35
40	Carlos Febles	.30	.14
41	Carlos Beltran	1.00	.45
42	Jeremy Giambi	.30	.14
43	Raul Mondesi	.30	.14
44	Adrian Beltre	.75	.35
45	Kevin Brown	.50	.23
46	Jeromy Burnitz	.30	.14
47	Jeff Cirillo	.30	.14
48	Corey Koskie	.20	.09
49	Todd Walker	.30	.14
50	Vladimir Guerrero	1.00	.45
51	Michael Barrett	.50	.23
52	Mike Piazza	2.50	1.10
53	Robin Ventura	.50	.23
54	Edgardo Alfonzo	.50	.23
55	Derek Jeter	2.50	1.10
56	Roger Clemens	2.00	.90
57	Tino Martinez	.30	.14
58	Orlando Hernandez	.75	.35
59	Chuck Knoblauch	.30	.14
60	Bernie Williams	.75	.35
61	Eric Chavez	.50	.23
62	Ben Grieve	.75	.35
63	Jason Giambi	.30	.14
64	Scott Rolen	1.00	.45
65	Curt Schilling	.50	.23
66	Bobby Abreu	.30	.14
67	Jason Kendall	.30	.14
68	Kevin Young	.30	.14
69	Mark McGwire	5.00	2.20
70	J.D. Drew	1.25	.55
71	Eric Davis	.30	.14
72	Tony Gwynn	2.00	.90
73	Trevor Hoffman	.30	.14
74	Barry Bonds	1.00	.45
75	Robb Nen	.20	.09
76	Ken Griffey Jr.	4.00	1.80
77	Alex Rodriguez	2.50	1.10
78	Jay Buhner	.30	.14
79	Carlos Guillen	.20	.09
80	Jose Canseco	1.00	.45
81	Bobby Smith	.20	.09
82	Juan Gonzalez	1.50	.70

	MINT	NRMT
☐ 83 Ivan Rodriguez	1.00	.45
☐ 84 Rafael Palmeiro	.75	.35
☐ 85 Rick Helling	.20	.09
☐ 86 Jose Cruz Jr.	.30	.14
☐ 87 David Wells	.30	.14
☐ 88 Carlos Delgado	.75	.35
☐ 89 Nolan Ryan	4.00	1.80
☐ 90 George Brett	1.50	.70
☐ 91 Robin Yount	.75	.35
☐ 92 Paul Molitor	.75	.35
☐ 93 Dave Winfield	.75	.35
☐ 94 Steve Garvey	.50	.23
☐ 95 Ozzie Smith	1.00	.45
☐ 96 Ted Williams	3.00	1.35
☐ 97 Don Mattingly	1.50	.70
☐ 98 Mickey Mantle	4.00	1.80
☐ 99 Harmon Killebrew	.75	.35
☐ 100 Rollie Fingers	.50	.23
☐ 101 Kirk Gibson	.30	.14
☐ 102 Bucky Dent	.30	.14
☐ 103 Willie Mays	2.00	.90
☐ 104 Babe Ruth	4.00	1.80
☐ 105 Gary Carter	.50	.23
☐ 106 Reggie Jackson	1.00	.45
☐ 107 Frank Robinson	.75	.35
☐ 108 Ernie Banks	1.00	.45
☐ 109 Eddie Murray	.75	.35
☐ 110 Mike Schmidt	1.50	.70

1999 Upper Deck Retro Gold

	MINT	NRMT
COMMON CARD (1-110)	3.00	1.35

*ACTIVE STARS 1-88: 6X TO 15X BASIC
*RETIRED STARS 89-110: 10X TO 25X BASIC
RANDOM INSERTS IN PACKS
STATED PRINT RUN 250 SERIAL #'d SETS

1999 Upper Deck Retro Platinum

	MINT	NRMT

RANDOM INSERTS IN PACKS
STATED PRINT RUN 1 SERIAL #'d SET
NOT PRICED DUE TO SCARCITY

1999 Upper Deck Retro Distant Replay

	MINT	NRMT
COMPLETE SET (15)	60.00	27.00
COMMON CARD (D1-D15)	2.50	1.10

STATED ODDS 1:8
*LEVEL 2: 5X TO 12X HI COLUMN
LEVEL 2 RANDOM INSERTS IN PACKS
LEVEL 2 PRINT RUN 100 SERIAL #'d SETS

☐ D1 Ken Griffey Jr.	10.00	4.50
☐ D2 Mark McGwire	12.00	5.50
☐ D3 Cal Ripken	8.00	3.60
☐ D4 Greg Maddux	5.00	2.20
☐ D5 Nomar Garciaparra	6.00	2.70
☐ D6 Roger Clemens	5.00	2.20
☐ D7 Alex Rodriguez	6.00	2.70
☐ D8 Frank Thomas	4.00	1.80
☐ D9 Mike Piazza	6.00	2.70
☐ D10 Chipper Jones	5.00	2.20
☐ D11 Juan Gonzalez	4.00	1.80
☐ D12 Tony Gwynn	5.00	2.20
☐ D13 Barry Bonds	2.50	1.10
☐ D14 Ivan Rodriguez	2.50	1.10
☐ D15 Derek Jeter	6.00	2.70

1999 Upper Deck Retro Inkredible

	MINT	NRMT

STATED ODDS 1:24
EXCHANGE DEADLINE 4/15/2000

☐ AP Angel Pena	10.00	4.50
☐ BD Bucky Dent	15.00	6.75
☐ BW Bernie Williams	60.00	27.00
☐ CJ Chipper Jones	100.00	45.00
☐ DE Darin Erstad	25.00	11.00
☐ DM Don Mattingly	100.00	45.00
☐ DW Dave Winfield	40.00	18.00
☐ EM Eddie Murray EXCH	100.00	45.00
☐ FL Fred Lynn	20.00	9.00
☐ GB George Brett	150.00	70.00
☐ GK Gabe Kapler	25.00	11.00
☐ HK Harmon Killebrew	40.00	18.00
☐ IR Ivan Rodriguez	60.00	27.00
☐ JR Ken Griffey Jr.	400.00	180.00
☐ KG Kirk Gibson	20.00	9.00
☐ MR Manny Ramirez	80.00	36.00
☐ NR Nolan Ryan	300.00	135.00
☐ OZ Ozzie Smith	50.00	22.00
☐ PB Pat Burrell	40.00	18.00
☐ PM Paul Molitor	50.00	22.00
☐ PO Paul O'Neill	30.00	13.50
☐ RF Rollie Fingers	20.00	9.00
☐ RG Rusty Greer	15.00	6.75
☐ RY Robin Yount	100.00	45.00
☐ SC Sean Casey EXCH	30.00	13.50
☐ SG Steve Garvey	20.00	9.00
☐ TC Tony Clark	15.00	6.75
☐ TG Tony Gwynn	120.00	55.00
☐ CBE Carlos Beltran	30.00	13.50

1999 Upper Deck Retro Inkredible Level 2

	MINT	NRMT

RANDOM INSERTS IN PACKS
PRINT RUNS LISTED BELOW

EXCHANGE DATE 4/15/2000

☐ AP Angel Pena/36	25.00	11.00
☐ BD Bucky Dent/20	100.00	45.00
☐ BW Bernie Williams/51	120.00	55.00
☐ CJ Chipper Jones/10		
☐ DE Darin Erstad/17	120.00	55.00
☐ DM Don Mattingly/23	600.00	275.00
☐ DW Dave Winfield/31	200.00	90.00
☐ EM Eddie Murray/33 EXCH	200.00	90.00
☐ FL Fred Lynn/5	120.00	55.00
☐ GB George Brett/5		
☐ GK Gabe Kapler/23	150.00	70.00
☐ HK Harmon Killebrew/3		
☐ IR Ivan Rodriguez/7		
☐ JR Ken Griffey Jr./24	1500.00	700.00
☐ KG Kirk Gibson/23	120.00	55.00
☐ MR Manny Ramirez/24	300.00	135.00
☐ NR Nolan Ryan/34	1500.00	700.00
☐ OZ Ozzie Smith/1		
☐ PB Pat Burrell/76	150.00	70.00
☐ PM Paul Molitor/4		
☐ PO Paul O'Neill/21	120.00	55.00
☐ RF Rollie Fingers/34	80.00	36.00
☐ RG Rusty Greer/29	80.00	36.00
☐ RY Robin Yount/19	300.00	135.00
☐ SC Sean Casey/21 EXCH	200.00	90.00
☐ SG Steve Garvey/6		
☐ TC Tony Clark/17	100.00	45.00
☐ TG Tony Gwynn/19	500.00	220.00
☐ CBE Carlos Beltran/36	150.00	70.00

1999 Upper Deck Retro Lunchboxes

	MINT	NRMT
COMPLETE SET (17)	400.00	180.00
COMMON BOX	12.00	5.50

ONE DUAL PLAYER BOX PER 12-CT CASE

☐ 1 Roger Clemens	12.00	5.50
☐ 2 Ken Griffey Jr.	25.00	11.00
☐ 3 Mickey Mantle	25.00	11.00
☐ 4 Mark McGwire	30.00	13.50
☐ 5 Mike Piazza	15.00	6.75
☐ 6 Alex Rodriguez	15.00	6.75
☐ 7 Babe Ruth	25.00	11.00
☐ 8 Sammy Sosa	15.00	6.75
☐ 9 Ted Williams	20.00	9.00
☐ 10 Ken Griffey Jr.	40.00	18.00

		MINT	NRMT
	Mickey Mantle		
☐ 11	Ken Griffey Jr.	40.00	18.00
	Mark McGwire		
☐ 12	K.Griffey Jr.	40.00	18.00
	Babe Ruth		
☐ 13	Ken Griffey Jr.	40.00	18.00
	Ted Williams		
☐ 14	Mickey Mantle	40.00	18.00
	Babe Ruth		
☐ 15	Mark McGwire	40.00	18.00
	Mickey Mantle		
☐ 16	Mark McGwire	40.00	18.00
	Babe Ruth		
☐ 17	Mark McGwire	40.00	18.00
	Ted Williams		

1999 Upper Deck Retro Old School/New School

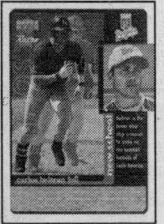

	MINT	NRMT
COMPLETE SET (30)	300.00	135.00
COMMON CARD (S1-S30)	2.00	.90
SEMISTARS	3.00	1.35
UNLISTED STARS	5.00	2.20

STATED PRINT RUN 1000 SERIAL #'d SETS
*LEVEL 2 STARS: 3X TO 8X HI COLUMN
*LEVEL 2 ROOKIES: 2X TO 5X HI COL
STATED PRINT RUN 50 SERIAL #'d SETS
RANDOM INSERTS IN PACKS

☐ S1	Ken Griffey Jr.	25.00	11.00
☐ S2	Alex Rodriguez	15.00	6.75
☐ S3	Frank Thomas	10.00	4.50
☐ S4	Cal Ripken	20.00	9.00
☐ S5	Chipper Jones	12.00	5.50
☐ S6	Craig Biggio	5.00	2.20
☐ S7	Greg Maddux	12.00	5.50
☐ S8	Jeff Bagwell	6.00	2.70
☐ S9	Juan Gonzalez	10.00	4.50
☐ S10	Mark McGwire	30.00	13.50
☐ S11	Mike Piazza	15.00	6.75
☐ S12	Mo Vaughn	5.00	2.20
☐ S13	Roger Clemens	12.00	5.50
☐ S14	Sammy Sosa	15.00	6.75
☐ S15	Tony Gwynn	12.00	5.50
☐ S16	Gabe Kapler	5.00	2.20
☐ S17	J.D. Drew	8.00	3.60
☐ S18	Pat Burrell	20.00	9.00
☐ S19	Roy Halladay	2.00	.90
☐ S20	Jeff Weaver	5.00	2.20
☐ S21	Troy Glaus	5.00	2.20
☐ S22	Vladimir Guerrero	6.00	2.70
☐ S23	Michael Barrett	3.00	1.35
☐ S24	Carlos Beltran	6.00	2.70
☐ S25	Scott Rolen	6.00	2.70
☐ S26	Nomar Garciaparra	15.00	6.75
☐ S27	Warren Morris	2.00	.90
☐ S28	Alex Gonzalez	2.00	.90
☐ S29	Kyle Farnsworth	5.00	2.20
☐ S30	Derek Jeter	15.00	6.75

1999 Upper Deck Retro Throwback Attack

	MINT	NRMT
COMPLETE SET (15)	60.00	27.00
COMMON CARD (T1-T15)	1.25	.55

throwback attack

MARK McGWIRE

STATED ODDS 1:5
LEVEL 2: 2.5X TO 6X HI COLUMN
LEVEL 2 RANDOM INSERTS IN PACKS
LEVEL 2 PRINT RUN 500 SERIAL #'d SETS

☐ T1	Ken Griffey Jr.	8.00	3.60
☐ T2	Mark McGwire	10.00	4.50
☐ T3	Sammy Sosa	5.00	2.20
☐ T4	Roger Clemens	4.00	1.80
☐ T5	J.D. Drew	2.00	.90
☐ T6	Alex Rodriguez	5.00	2.20
☐ T7	Greg Maddux	4.00	1.80
☐ T8	Mike Piazza	5.00	2.20
☐ T9	Juan Gonzalez	3.00	1.35
☐ T10	Mo Vaughn	1.25	.55
☐ T11	Cal Ripken	6.00	2.70
☐ T12	Frank Thomas	3.00	1.35
☐ T13	Nomar Garciaparra	5.00	2.20
☐ T14	Vladimir Guerrero	2.00	.90
☐ T15	Tony Gwynn	4.00	1.80

1998 Upper Deck Special F/X

	MINT	NRMT
COMPLETE SET (150)	60.00	27.00
COMMON CARD (1-150)	.25	.11
MINOR STARS	.40	.18
SEMISTARS	.60	.25
UNLISTED STARS	1.00	.45

DISTRIBUTED ONLY IN RETAIL OUTLETS

☐ 1	Ken Griffey Jr. GHL	5.00	2.20
☐ 2	Mark McGwire GHL	6.00	2.70
☐ 3	Alex Rodriguez GHL	3.00	1.35
☐ 4	Larry Walker GHL	1.00	.45
☐ 5	Tino Martinez GHL	.40	.18
☐ 6	Mike Piazza GHL	3.00	1.35
☐ 7	Jose Cruz Jr. GHL	.40	.18
☐ 8	Greg Maddux GHL	2.50	1.10
☐ 9	Tony Gwynn GHL	2.50	1.10
☐ 10	Roger Clemens GHL	2.50	1.10
☐ 11	Jason Dickson	.25	.11
☐ 12	Darin Erstad	.60	.25
☐ 13	Chuck Finley	.40	.18
☐ 14	Dave Hollins	.25	.11
☐ 15	Garret Anderson	.40	.18
☐ 16	Michael Tucker	.25	.11
☐ 17	Javier Lopez	.40	.18
☐ 18	John Smoltz	.60	.25
☐ 19	Mark Wohlers	.25	.11
☐ 20	Greg Maddux	2.50	1.10
☐ 21	Scott Erickson	.25	.11
☐ 22	Jimmy Key	.40	.18
☐ 23	B.J. Surhoff	.40	.18
☐ 24	Eric Davis	.40	.18
☐ 25	Rafael Palmeiro	1.00	.45
☐ 26	Tim Naehring	.25	.11
☐ 27	Darren Bragg	.25	.11
☐ 28	Troy O'Leary	.40	.18
☐ 29	John Valentin	.40	.18
☐ 30	Mo Vaughn	1.00	.45
☐ 31	Mark Grace	.60	.25
☐ 32	Kevin Foster	.25	.11
☐ 33	Kevin Tapani	.25	.11
☐ 34	Kevin Orie	.25	.11
☐ 35	Albert Belle	1.00	.45
☐ 36	Ray Durham	.40	.18
☐ 37	Jaime Navarro	.25	.11
☐ 38	Mike Cameron	.40	.18
☐ 39	Eddie Taubensee	.25	.11
☐ 40	Barry Larkin	1.00	.45
☐ 41	Willie Greene	.25	.11
☐ 42	Jeff Shaw	.25	.11
☐ 43	Omar Vizquel	.40	.18
☐ 44	Brian Giles	.40	.18
☐ 45	Jim Thome	1.00	.45
☐ 46	David Justice	.40	.18
☐ 47	Sandy Alomar Jr.	.40	.18
☐ 48	Neifi Perez	.40	.18
☐ 49	Dante Bichette	.40	.18
☐ 50	Vinny Castilla	.40	.18
☐ 51	John Thomson	.25	.11
☐ 52	Damion Easley	.25	.11
☐ 53	Justin Thompson	.25	.11
☐ 54	Bobby Higginson	.40	.18
☐ 55	Tony Clark	.40	.18
☐ 56	Charles Johnson	.40	.18
☐ 57	Edgar Renteria	.25	.11
☐ 58	Alex Fernandez	.25	.11
☐ 59	Gary Sheffield	.40	.18
☐ 60	Livan Hernandez	.25	.11
☐ 61	Craig Biggio	1.00	.45
☐ 62	Chris Holt	.25	.11
☐ 63	Billy Wagner	.40	.18
☐ 64	Brad Ausmus	.25	.11
☐ 65	Dean Palmer	.40	.18
☐ 66	Tim Belcher	.25	.11
☐ 67	Jeff King	.25	.11
☐ 68	Jose Rosado	.25	.11
☐ 69	Chan Ho Park	.40	.18
☐ 70	Raul Mondesi	.40	.18
☐ 71	Hideo Nomo	1.00	.45
☐ 72	Todd Zeile	.40	.18
☐ 73	Eric Karros	.40	.18
☐ 74	Cal Eldred	.25	.11
☐ 75	Jeff D'Amico	.25	.11
☐ 76	Doug Jones	.25	.11
☐ 77	Dave Nilsson	.25	.11
☐ 78	Todd Walker	.40	.18
☐ 79	Rick Aguilera	.25	.11
☐ 80	Paul Molitor	1.00	.45
☐ 81	Brad Radke	.40	.18
☐ 82	Vladimir Guerrero	1.25	.55
☐ 83	Carlos Perez	.25	.11
☐ 84	F.P. Santangelo	.25	.11
☐ 85	Rondell White	.40	.18
☐ 86	Butch Huskey	.25	.11
☐ 87	Edgardo Alfonzo	.60	.25
☐ 88	John Franco	.25	.11
☐ 89	John Olerud	.40	.18
☐ 90	Todd Hundley	.40	.18
☐ 91	Bernie Williams	1.00	.45
☐ 92	Andy Pettitte	.40	.18
☐ 93	Paul O'Neill	.40	.18
☐ 94	David Cone	.60	.25
☐ 95	Jason Giambi	.25	.11
☐ 96	Damon Mashore	.25	.11
☐ 97	Scott Spiezio	.25	.11
☐ 98	Ariel Prieto	.25	.11
☐ 99	Rico Brogna	.25	.11
☐ 100	Mike Lieberthal	.40	.18
☐ 101	Garrett Stephenson	.25	.11
☐ 102	Ricky Bottalico	.25	.11
☐ 103	Kevin Polcovich	.25	.11
☐ 104	Jon Lieber	.25	.11

☐ 105	Kevin Young	.40	.18
☐ 106	Tony Womack	.25	.11
☐ 107	Gary Gaetti	.40	.18
☐ 108	Alan Benes	.25	.11
☐ 109	Willie McGee	.40	.18
☐ 110	Mark McGwire	6.00	2.70
☐ 111	Ron Gant	.40	.18
☐ 112	Andy Ashby	.25	.11
☐ 113	Steve Finley	.40	.18
☐ 114	Quilvio Veras	.25	.11
☐ 115	Ken Caminiti	.40	.18
☐ 116	Joey Hamilton	.25	.11
☐ 117	Bill Mueller	.25	.11
☐ 118	Mark Gardner	.25	.11
☐ 119	Shawn Estes	.25	.11
☐ 120	J.T. Snow	.40	.18
☐ 121	Dante Powell	.25	.11
☐ 122	Jeff Kent	.40	.18
☐ 123	Jamie Moyer	.25	.11
☐ 124	Joey Cora	.25	.11
☐ 125	Ken Griffey Jr.	5.00	2.20
☐ 126	Jeff Fassero	.25	.11
☐ 127	Edgar Martinez	.40	.18
☐ 128	Will Clark	1.00	.45
☐ 129	Lee Stevens	.25	.11
☐ 130	Ivan Rodriguez	1.25	.55
☐ 131	Rusty Greer	.40	.18
☐ 132	Ed Sprague	.25	.11
☐ 133	Pat Hentgen	.25	.11
☐ 134	Shannon Stewart	.40	.18
☐ 135	Carlos Delgado	1.00	.45
☐ 136	Brett Tomko	.25	.11
☐ 137	Jose Guillen	.25	.11
☐ 138	Eli Marrero	.25	.11
☐ 139	Dennis Reyes	.25	.11
☐ 140	Mark Kotsay	.40	.18
☐ 141	Richie Sexson	.60	.25
☐ 142	Todd Helton	1.25	.55
☐ 143	Jeremi Gonzalez	.25	.11
☐ 144	Jeff Abbott	.25	.11
☐ 145	Matt Morris	.25	.11
☐ 146	Aaron Boone	.25	.11
☐ 147	Todd Dunwoody	.25	.11
☐ 148	Mario Valdez	.25	.11
☐ 149	Fernando Tatis	1.00	.45
☐ 150	Jaret Wright	.40	.18

1998 Upper Deck Special F/X Power Zone

	MINT	NRMT
COMPLETE SET (20)	80.00	36.00
COMMON CARD (PZ1-PZ20)	1.00	.45
SEMISTARS	1.50	.70
UNLISTED STARS	2.50	1.10
STATED ODDS 1:7		

☐ PZ1	Jose Cruz Jr.	1.00	.45
☐ PZ2	Frank Thomas	5.00	2.20
☐ PZ3	Juan Gonzalez	5.00	2.20
☐ PZ4	Mike Piazza	8.00	3.60
☐ PZ5	Mark McGwire	15.00	6.75
☐ PZ6	Barry Bonds	3.00	1.35
☐ PZ7	Greg Maddux	6.00	2.70
☐ PZ8	Alex Rodriguez	8.00	3.60
☐ PZ9	Nomar Garciaparra	8.00	3.60
☐ PZ10	Ken Griffey Jr.	12.00	5.50
☐ PZ11	John Smoltz	1.50	.70

1998 Upper Deck Special F/X Power Zone OctoberBest

	MINT	NRMT
COMPLETE SET (15)	200.00	90.00
COMMON CARD (PZ1-PZ15)	3.00	1.35
SEMISTARS	5.00	2.20
UNLISTED STARS	8.00	3.60
STATED ODDS 1:34		

☐ PZ1	Frank Thomas	15.00	6.75
☐ PZ2	Juan Gonzalez	15.00	6.75
☐ PZ3	Mike Piazza	25.00	11.00
☐ PZ4	Mark McGwire	50.00	22.00
☐ PZ5	Jeff Bagwell	10.00	4.50
☐ PZ6	Barry Bonds	10.00	4.50
☐ PZ7	Ken Griffey Jr.	40.00	18.00
☐ PZ8	John Smoltz	5.00	2.20
☐ PZ9	Andruw Jones	8.00	3.60
☐ PZ10	Greg Maddux	20.00	9.00
☐ PZ11	Sandy Alomar Jr.	3.00	1.35
☐ PZ12	Roberto Alomar	8.00	3.60
☐ PZ13	Chipper Jones	20.00	9.00
☐ PZ14	Kenny Lofton	5.00	2.20
☐ PZ15	Tom Glavine	8.00	3.60

1998 Upper Deck Special F/X Power Zone Power Driven

	MINT	NRMT
COMPLETE SET (10)	200.00	90.00
COMMON CARD (PZ1-PZ10)	4.00	1.80
UNLISTED STARS	10.00	4.50
STATED ODDS 1:69 SPECIAL F/X		

☐ PZ1	Frank Thomas	20.00	9.00

☐ PZ12	Andruw Jones	2.50	1.10
☐ PZ13	Sandy Alomar Jr.	1.00	.45
☐ PZ14	Roberto Alomar	2.50	1.10
☐ PZ15	Chipper Jones	6.00	2.70
☐ PZ16	Kenny Lofton	1.50	.70
☐ PZ17	Larry Walker	2.50	1.10
☐ PZ18	Jeff Bagwell	3.00	1.35
☐ PZ19	Mo Vaughn	2.50	1.10
☐ PZ20	Tom Glavine	2.50	1.10

1998 Upper Deck Special F/X Power Zone Superstar Xcitement

	MINT	NRMT
COMPLETE SET (10)	800.00	350.00
COMMON CARD (PZ1-PZ10)	12.00	5.50
RANDOM INSERTS IN SPECIAL F/X PACKS		
STATED PRINT RUN 250 SERIAL #'d SETS		

☐ PZ1	Jose Cruz Jr.	15.00	6.75
☐ PZ2	Frank Thomas	60.00	27.00
☐ PZ3	Juan Gonzalez	60.00	27.00
☐ PZ4	Mike Piazza	100.00	45.00
☐ PZ5	Mark McGwire	200.00	90.00
☐ PZ6	Barry Bonds	40.00	18.00
☐ PZ7	Greg Maddux	80.00	36.00
☐ PZ8	Alex Rodriguez	100.00	45.00
☐ PZ9	Nomar Garciaparra	100.00	45.00
☐ PZ10	Ken Griffey Jr.	150.00	70.00

1999 Upper Deck Ultimate Victory

	MINT	NRMT
COMPLETE SET (180)	300.00	135.00
COMP. SET w/o SP's (120)	40.00	18.00
COMMON CARD (1-120)	.20	.09
MINOR STARS	.30	.14
SEMISTARS	.50	.23
UNLISTED STARS	.75	.35
COMMON SP (121-150)	2.00	.90
SP STATED ODDS 1:4		
COMMON MCGWIRE (151-180)	2.00	.90
MCGWIRE 151-180 STATED ODDS 1:4		

☐ 1	Troy Glaus	.75	.35
☐ 2	Tim Salmon	.50	.23
☐ 3	Mo Vaughn	.75	.35
☐ 4	Garret Anderson	.30	.14
☐ 5	Darin Erstad	.50	.23
☐ 6	Randy Johnson	.75	.35
☐ 7	Matt Williams	.75	.35
☐ 8	Travis Lee	.50	.23
☐ 9	Jay Bell	.30	.14
☐ 10	Steve Finley	.30	.14
☐ 11	Luis Gonzalez	.30	.14
☐ 12	Greg Maddux	2.00	.90
☐ 13	Chipper Jones	2.00	.90
☐ 14	Javy Lopez	.30	.14
☐ 15	Tom Glavine	.75	.35
☐ 16	John Smoltz	.50	.23
☐ 17	Cal Ripken	3.00	1.35
☐ 18	Charles Johnson	.30	.14
☐ 19	Albert Belle	.75	.35
☐ 20	Mike Mussina	.75	.35

☐ 21 Pedro Martinez	1.00	.45
☐ 22 Nomar Garciaparra	2.50	1.10
☐ 23 Jose Offerman	.30	.14
☐ 24 Sammy Sosa	2.50	1.10
☐ 25 Mark Grace	.50	.23
☐ 26 Kerry Wood	.75	.35
☐ 27 Frank Thomas	1.50	.70
☐ 28 Ray Durham	.30	.14
☐ 29 Paul Konerko	.30	.14
☐ 30 Pete Harnisch	.20	.09
☐ 31 Greg Vaughn	.30	.14
☐ 32 Sean Casey	.75	.35
☐ 33 Manny Ramirez	1.00	.45
☐ 34 Jim Thome	.75	.35
☐ 35 Sandy Alomar Jr.	.30	.14
☐ 36 Roberto Alomar	.75	.35
☐ 37 Travis Fryman	.30	.14
☐ 38 Kenny Lofton	.50	.23
☐ 39 Omar Vizquel	.30	.14
☐ 40 Larry Walker	.75	.35
☐ 41 Todd Helton	.75	.35
☐ 42 Vinny Castilla	.30	.14
☐ 43 Tony Clark	.30	.14
☐ 44 Juan Encarnacion	.30	.14
☐ 45 Dean Palmer	.30	.14
☐ 46 Damion Easley	.30	.14
☐ 47 Mark Kotsay	.20	.09
☐ 48 Cliff Floyd	.30	.14
☐ 49 Jeff Bagwell	1.00	.45
☐ 50 Ken Caminiti	.30	.14
☐ 51 Craig Biggio	.75	.35
☐ 52 Moises Alou	.30	.14
☐ 53 Johnny Damon	.30	.14
☐ 54 Larry Sutton	.20	.09
☐ 55 Kevin Brown	.50	.23
☐ 56 Adrian Beltre	.75	.35
☐ 57 Raul Mondesi	.30	.14
☐ 58 Gary Sheffield	.30	.14
☐ 59 Jeromy Burnitz	.30	.14
☐ 60 Sean Berry	.20	.09
☐ 61 Jeff Cirillo	.30	.14
☐ 62 Brad Radke	.30	.14
☐ 63 Todd Walker	.30	.14
☐ 64 Matt Lawton	.20	.09
☐ 65 Vladimir Guerrero	1.00	.45
☐ 66 Rondell White	.30	.14
☐ 67 Dustin Hermanson	.20	.09
☐ 68 Mike Piazza	2.50	1.10
☐ 69 Rickey Henderson	.75	.35
☐ 70 Robin Ventura	.30	.14
☐ 71 John Olerud	.30	.14
☐ 72 Derek Jeter	2.50	1.10
☐ 73 Roger Clemens	2.00	.90
☐ 74 Orlando Hernandez	.75	.35
☐ 75 Paul O'Neill	.30	.14
☐ 76 Bernie Williams	.75	.35
☐ 77 Chuck Knoblauch	.30	.14
☐ 78 Tino Martinez	.30	.14
☐ 79 Jason Giambi	.30	.14
☐ 80 Ben Grieve	.75	.35
☐ 81 Matt Stairs	.30	.14
☐ 82 Scott Rolen	1.00	.45
☐ 83 Ron Gant	.30	.14
☐ 84 Bobby Abreu	.30	.14
☐ 85 Curt Schilling	.50	.23
☐ 86 Brian Giles	.30	.14
☐ 87 Jason Kendall	.30	.14
☐ 88 Kevin Young	.30	.14
☐ 89 Mark McGwire	5.00	2.20
☐ 90 Fernando Tatis	.30	.14
☐ 91 Ray Lankford	.30	.14
☐ 92 Eric Davis	.30	.14
☐ 93 Tony Gwynn	2.00	.90
☐ 94 Reggie Sanders	.20	.09
☐ 95 Wally Joyner	.30	.14
☐ 96 Trevor Hoffman	.30	.14
☐ 97 Robb Nen	.20	.09
☐ 98 Barry Bonds	1.00	.45
☐ 99 Jeff Kent	.30	.14
☐ 100 J.T. Snow	.30	.14
☐ 101 Ellis Burks	.30	.14
☐ 102 Ken Griffey Jr.	4.00	1.80
☐ 103 Alex Rodriguez	2.50	1.10
☐ 104 Jay Buhner	.30	.14
☐ 105 Edgar Martinez	.30	.14
☐ 106 David Bell	.20	.09

☐ 107 Bobby Smith	.20	.09
☐ 108 Wade Boggs	.75	.35
☐ 109 Fred McGriff	.50	.23
☐ 110 Rolando Arrojo	.20	.09
☐ 111 Jose Canseco	1.00	.45
☐ 112 Ivan Rodriguez	1.00	.45
☐ 113 Juan Gonzalez	1.50	.70
☐ 114 Rafael Palmeiro	.75	.35
☐ 115 Rusty Greer	.30	.14
☐ 116 Todd Zeile	.30	.14
☐ 117 Jose Cruz Jr.	.30	.14
☐ 118 Carlos Delgado	.75	.35
☐ 119 Shawn Green	.75	.35
☐ 120 David Wells	.30	.14
☐ 121 Eric Munson	20.00	9.00
☐ 122 Lance Berkman SP	2.50	1.10
☐ 123 Ed Yarnall SP	2.50	1.10
☐ 124 Jacque Jones SP	2.50	1.10
☐ 125 Kyle Farnsworth SP	4.00	1.80
☐ 126 Ryan Ruge SP	2.50	1.10
☐ 127 Jeff Weaver SP	4.00	1.80
☐ 128 Gabe Kapler SP	3.00	1.35
☐ 129 Alex Gonzalez SP	2.50	1.10
☐ 130 Randy Wolf SP	2.50	1.10
☐ 131 Ben Davis SP	2.50	1.10
☐ 132 Carlos Beltran SP	5.00	2.20
☐ 133 Jim Morris SP	2.00	.90
☐ 134 Jeff Zimmerman SP	4.00	1.80
☐ 135 Bruce Aven SP	2.00	.90
☐ 136 Alfonso Soriano SP	15.00	6.75
☐ 137 Tim Hudson SP	8.00	3.60
☐ 138 Josh Beckett SP	20.00	9.00
☐ 139 Michael Barrett SP	2.50	1.10
☐ 140 Eric Chavez SP	2.50	1.10
☐ 141 Pat Burrell SP	15.00	6.75
☐ 142 Kris Benson SP	2.50	1.10
☐ 143 J.D. Drew SP	6.00	2.70
☐ 144 Matt Clement SP	2.50	1.10
☐ 145 Rick Ankiel SP	40.00	18.00
☐ 146 Vernon Wells SP	3.00	1.35
☐ 147 Ruben Mateo SP UER	3.00	1.35
Card is misnumbered		
☐ 148 Roy Halladay SP	2.50	1.10
☐ 149 Joe McEwing SP	6.00	2.70
☐ 150 Freddy Garcia SP	15.00	6.75
☐ 151 Mark McGwire MM	2.00	.90
☐ 152 Mark McGwire MM	2.00	.90
☐ 153 Mark McGwire MM	2.00	.90
☐ 154 Mark McGwire MM	2.00	.90
☐ 155 Mark McGwire MM	2.00	.90
☐ 156 Mark McGwire MM	2.00	.90
☐ 157 Mark McGwire MM	2.00	.90
☐ 158 Mark McGwire MM	2.00	.90
☐ 159 Mark McGwire MM	2.00	.90
☐ 160 Mark McGwire MM	2.00	.90
☐ 161 Mark McGwire MM	2.00	.90
☐ 162 Mark McGwire MM	2.00	.90
☐ 163 Mark McGwire MM	2.00	.90
☐ 164 Mark McGwire MM	2.00	.90
☐ 165 Mark McGwire MM	2.00	.90
☐ 166 Mark McGwire MM	2.00	.90
☐ 167 Mark McGwire MM	2.00	.90
☐ 168 Mark McGwire MM	2.00	.90
☐ 169 Mark McGwire MM	2.00	.90
☐ 170 Mark McGwire MM	2.00	.90
☐ 171 Mark McGwire MM	2.00	.90
☐ 172 Mark McGwire MM	2.00	.90
☐ 173 Mark McGwire MM	2.00	.90
☐ 174 Mark McGwire MM	2.00	.90
☐ 175 Mark McGwire MM	2.00	.90
☐ 176 Mark McGwire MM	2.00	.90
☐ 177 Mark McGwire MM	2.00	.90
☐ 178 Mark McGwire MM	2.00	.90
☐ 179 Mark McGwire MM	2.00	.90
☐ 180 Mark McGwire MM	2.00	.90

*PARALLEL 121-150: .6X TO 1.5X BASE121-
150
STATED ODDS 1:12

1999 Upper Deck Ultimate Victory Parallel 1 of 1

	MINT	NRMT
RANDOM INSERTS IN PACKS
STATED PRINT RUN 1 SERIAL #'d SET
NOT PRICED DUE TO SCARCITY

1999 Upper Deck Ultimate Victory Parallel 100

	MINT	NRMT
COMMON CARD (1-180)	5.00	2.20
COMMON MCGWIRE (151-180)	40.00	18.00
*PARA 121-150: 1.5X TO 4X BASIC 121-150
RANDOM INSERTS IN PACKS
STATED PRINT RUN 100 SERIAL #'d SETS

1999 Upper Deck Ultimate Victory Parallel

	MINT	NRMT
COMMON CARD (1-180)	1.50	.70
COMMON MCGWIRE (151-180)	10.00	4.50
*PARALLEL 1-120: 3X TO 8X BASIC 1-120

1999 Upper Deck Ultimate Victory Bleacher Reachers

	MINT	NRMT
COMPLETE SET (11)	60.00	27.00
COMMON CARD (BR1-BR11)	3.00	1.35

COMMON CARD (1-180) 5.00 2.20
COMMON MCGWIRE (151-180) 40.00 18.00
*PARALLEL 1-120: 10X TO 25X BASIC 1-120

STATED ODDS 1:23

		MINT	NRMT
☐ BR1	Ken Griffey Jr.	12.00	5.50
☐ BR2	Mark McGwire	15.00	6.75
☐ BR3	Sammy Sosa	8.00	3.60
☐ BR4	Barry Bonds	3.00	1.35
☐ BR5	Nomar Garciaparra	8.00	3.60
☐ BR6	Juan Gonzalez	5.00	2.20
☐ BR7	Jose Canseco	3.00	1.35
☐ BR8	Manny Ramirez	3.00	1.35
☐ BR9	Mike Piazza	8.00	3.60
☐ BR10	Jeff Bagwell	3.00	1.35
☐ BR11	Alex Rodriguez	8.00	3.60

1999 Upper Deck Ultimate Victory Fame-Used Memorabilia

	MINT	NRMT

RANDOM INSERTS IN PACKS
350 OF EACH CARD EXCEPT HOF CARD
HOF PRINT RUN 99 SERIAL #'d CARDS

☐ GB	George Brett	150.00	70.00
☐ NR	Nolan Ryan	400.00	180.00
☐ OC	Orlando Cepeda	50.00	22.00
☐ RY	Robin Yount	100.00	45.00
☐ HOF	Nolan Ryan	1200.00	550.00
	George Brett		
	Robin Yount		
	Orlando Cepeda		

1999 Upper Deck Ultimate Victory Frozen Ropes

	MINT	NRMT
COMPLETE SET (10)	60.00	27.00
COMMON CARD (F1-F10)	2.00	.90

STATED ODDS 1:23

☐ F1	Ken Griffey Jr.	12.00	5.50
☐ F2	Mark McGwire	15.00	6.75
☐ F3	Sammy Sosa	8.00	3.60
☐ F4	Derek Jeter	8.00	3.60
☐ F5	Tony Gwynn	6.00	2.70
☐ F6	Nomar Garciaparra	8.00	3.60
☐ F7	Alex Rodriguez	8.00	3.60
☐ F8	Mike Piazza	8.00	3.60
☐ F9	Mo Vaughn	2.00	.90
☐ F10	Craig Biggio	2.00	.90

1999 Upper Deck Ultimate Victory STATure

	MINT	NRMT
COMPLETE SET (15)	30.00	13.50
COMMON CARD (S1-S15)	1.00	.45

STATED ODDS 1:6

☐ S1	Ken Griffey Jr.	4.00	1.80
☐ S2	Mark McGwire	5.00	2.20
☐ S3	Sammy Sosa	2.50	1.10
☐ S4	Nomar Garciaparra	2.50	1.10
☐ S5	Roger Clemens	2.00	.90
☐ S6	Greg Maddux	2.00	.90
☐ S7	Alex Rodriguez	2.50	1.10
☐ S8	Derek Jeter	2.50	1.10
☐ S9	Juan Gonzalez	1.50	.70
☐ S10	Manny Ramirez	1.00	.45
☐ S11	Mike Piazza	2.50	1.10
☐ S12	Tony Gwynn	2.00	.90
☐ S13	Chipper Jones	2.00	.90
☐ S14	Pedro Martinez	1.00	.45
☐ S15	Frank Thomas	1.50	.70

1999 Upper Deck Ultimate Victory Tribute 1999

	MINT	NRMT
COMPLETE SET (4)	15.00	6.75
COMMON CARD (T1-T4)	1.50	.70

STATED ODDS 1:11

☐ T1	Nolan Ryan	10.00	4.50
☐ T2	Robin Yount	3.00	1.35
☐ T3	George Brett	4.00	1.80
☐ T4	Orlando Cepeda	1.50	.70

1999 Upper Deck Ultimate Victory Ultimate Competitors

	MINT	NRMT
COMPLETE SET (12)	80.00	36.00
COMMON CARD (U1-U12)	2.00	.90
UNLISTED STARS	3.00	1.35

STATED ODDS 1:23

☐ U1	Ken Griffey Jr.	15.00	6.75
☐ U2	Roger Clemens	8.00	3.60
☐ U3	Scott Rolen	4.00	1.80
☐ U4	Greg Maddux	8.00	3.60
☐ U5	Mark McGwire	20.00	9.00
☐ U6	Derek Jeter	10.00	4.50
☐ U7	Randy Johnson	3.00	1.35
☐ U8	Cal Ripken	12.00	5.50
☐ U9	Craig Biggio	3.00	1.35
☐ U10	Kevin Brown	2.00	.90
☐ U11	Chipper Jones	8.00	3.60
☐ U12	Vladimir Guerrero	4.00	1.80

1999 Upper Deck Ultimate Victory Ultimate Hit Men

	MINT	NRMT
COMPLETE SET (8)	30.00	13.50
COMMON CARD (H1-H8)	2.00	.90

STATED ODDS 1:23

☐ H1	Tony Gwynn	5.00	2.20
☐ H2	Cal Ripken	8.00	3.60
☐ H3	Wade Boggs	2.00	.90
☐ H4	Larry Walker	2.00	.90
☐ H5	Alex Rodriguez	6.00	2.70
☐ H6	Derek Jeter	6.00	2.70
☐ H7	Ivan Rodriguez	2.50	1.10
☐ H8	Ken Griffey Jr.	10.00	4.50

1999 Upper Deck Victory

	MINT	NRMT
COMPLETE SET (470)	60.00	27.00
COMMON CARD (1-470)	.10	.05
MINOR STARS	.15	.07
SEMISTARS	.20	.09
UNLISTED STARS	.30	.14
COMMON MCGWIRE (421-450)	.50	.23

ONE MCGWIRE 421-450 PER PACK
SUBSET CARDS HALF VALUE OF BASE CARDS

☐ 1	Anaheim Angels TC	.10	.05
☐ 2	Mark Harriger	.25	.11
☐ 3	Mo Vaughn PT	.15	.07
☐ 4	Darin Erstad BP	.15	.07

□			
□ 5	Troy Glaus	.30	.14
□ 6	Tim Salmon	.20	.09
□ 7	Mo Vaughn	.30	.14
□ 8	Darin Erstad	.20	.09
□ 9	Garret Anderson	.15	.07
□ 10	Todd Greene	.10	.05
□ 11	Troy Percival	.15	.07
□ 12	Chuck Finley	.15	.07
□ 13	Jason Dickson	.10	.05
□ 14	Jim Edmonds	.15	.07
□ 15	Arizona Diamondbacks TC	.10	.05
□ 16	Randy Johnson	.30	.14
□ 17	Matt Williams	.30	.14
□ 18	Travis Lee	.20	.09
□ 19	Jay Bell	.15	.07
□ 20	Tony Womack	.10	.05
□ 21	Steve Finley	.15	.07
□ 22	Bernard Gilkey	.10	.05
□ 23	Tony Batista	.10	.05
□ 24	Todd Stottlemyre	.10	.05
□ 25	Omar Daal	.10	.05
□ 26	Atlanta Braves TC	.10	.05
□ 27	Bruce Chen	.15	.07
□ 28	George Lombard	.15	.07
□ 29	Chipper Jones PT	.40	.18
□ 30	Chipper Jones BP	.40	.18
□ 31	Greg Maddux	.75	.35
□ 32	Chipper Jones	.75	.35
□ 33	Javy Lopez	.15	.07
□ 34	Tom Glavine	.30	.14
□ 35	John Smoltz	.20	.09
□ 36	Andruw Jones	.30	.14
□ 37	Brian Jordan	.15	.07
□ 38	Walt Weiss	.10	.05
□ 39	Bret Boone	.15	.07
□ 40	Andres Galarraga	.20	.09
□ 41	Baltimore Orioles TC	.10	.05
□ 42	Ryan Minor	.15	.07
□ 43	Jerry Hairston Jr.	.15	.07
□ 44	Calvin Pickering	.15	.07
□ 45	Cal Ripken HM	.60	.25
□ 46	Cal Ripken	1.25	.55
□ 47	Charles Johnson	.15	.07
□ 48	Albert Belle	.30	.14
□ 49	Delino DeShields	.10	.05
□ 50	Mike Mussina	.30	.14
□ 51	Scott Erickson	.10	.05
□ 52	Brady Anderson	.15	.07
□ 53	B.J. Surhoff	.15	.07
□ 54	Harold Baines	.15	.07
□ 55	Will Clark	.30	.14
□ 56	Boston Red Sox TC	.10	.05
□ 57	Shea Hillenbrand	.25	.11
□ 58	Trot Nixon	.15	.07
□ 59	Jin Ho Cho	.15	.07
□ 60	Nomar Garciaparra PT	.50	.23
□ 61	Nomar Garciaparra BP	.50	.23
□ 62	Pedro Martinez	.40	.18
□ 63	Nomar Garciaparra	1.00	.45
□ 64	Jose Offerman	.15	.07
□ 65	Jason Varitek	.15	.07
□ 66	Darren Lewis	.10	.05
□ 67	Troy O'Leary	.15	.07
□ 68	Donnie Sadler	.10	.05
□ 69	John Valentin	.15	.07
□ 70	Tim Wakefield	.10	.05
□ 71	Bret Saberhagen	.15	.07
□ 72	Chicago Cubs TC	.10	.05

□ 73	Kyle Farnsworth	.25	.11
□ 74	Sammy Sosa PT	.50	.23
□ 75	Sammy Sosa BP	.50	.23
□ 76	Sammy Sosa HM	.50	.23
□ 77	Kerry Wood HM	.15	.07
□ 78	Sammy Sosa	1.00	.45
□ 79	Mark Grace	.20	.09
□ 80	Kerry Wood	.30	.14
□ 81	Kevin Tapani	.10	.05
□ 82	Benito Santiago	.10	.05
□ 83	Gary Gaetti	.15	.07
□ 84	Mickey Morandini	.10	.05
□ 85	Glenallen Hill	.10	.05
□ 86	Henry Rodriguez	.15	.07
□ 87	Rod Beck	.10	.05
□ 88	Chicago White Sox TC	.10	.05
□ 89	Carlos Lee	.25	.11
□ 90	Mark Johnson	.10	.05
□ 91	Frank Thomas PT	.30	.14
□ 92	Frank Thomas	.60	.25
□ 93	Jim Parque	.10	.05
□ 94	Mike Sirotka	.10	.05
□ 95	Mike Caruso	.10	.05
□ 96	Ray Durham	.15	.07
□ 97	Magglio Ordonez	.30	.14
□ 98	Paul Konerko	.20	.09
□ 99	Bob Howry	.10	.05
□ 100	Brian Simmons	.10	.05
□ 101	Jaime Navarro	.10	.05
□ 102	Cincinnati Reds TC	.10	.05
□ 103	Denny Neagle	.15	.07
□ 104	Pete Harnisch	.10	.05
□ 105	Greg Vaughn	.15	.07
□ 106	Brett Tomko	.10	.05
□ 107	Mike Cameron	.10	.05
□ 108	Sean Casey	.30	.14
□ 109	Aaron Boone	.10	.05
□ 110	Michael Tucker	.10	.05
□ 111	Dmitri Young	.15	.07
□ 112	Barry Larkin	.30	.14
□ 113	Cleveland Indians TC	.10	.05
□ 114	Russ Branyan	.15	.07
□ 115	Jim Thome PT	.15	.07
□ 116	Manny Ramirez PT	.20	.09
□ 117	Manny Ramirez	.40	.18
□ 118	Jim Thome	.30	.14
□ 119	David Justice	.15	.07
□ 120	Sandy Alomar Jr.	.15	.07
□ 121	Roberto Alomar	.30	.14
□ 122	Jaret Wright	.15	.07
□ 123	Bartolo Colon	.15	.07
□ 124	Travis Fryman	.15	.07
□ 125	Kenny Lofton	.20	.09
□ 126	Omar Vizquel	.15	.07
□ 127	Colorado Rockies TC	.10	.05
□ 128	Derrick Gibson	.15	.07
□ 129	Larry Walker BP	.15	.07
□ 130	Larry Walker	.30	.14
□ 131	Dante Bichette	.15	.07
□ 132	Todd Helton	.30	.14
□ 133	Neifi Perez	.15	.07
□ 134	Vinny Castilla	.15	.07
□ 135	Darryl Kile	.10	.05
□ 136	Pedro Astacio	.10	.05
□ 137	Darryl Hamilton	.10	.05
□ 138	Mike Lansing	.10	.05
□ 139	Kirt Manwaring	.10	.05
□ 140	Detroit Tigers TC	.10	.05
□ 141	Jeff Weaver	.30	.14
□ 142	Gabe Kapler	.30	.14
□ 143	Tony Clark PT	.10	.05
□ 144	Tony Clark	.15	.07
□ 145	Juan Encarnacion	.15	.07
□ 146	Dean Palmer	.15	.07
□ 147	Damion Easley	.10	.05
□ 148	Bobby Higginson	.15	.07
□ 149	Karim Garcia	.10	.05
□ 150	Justin Thompson	.10	.05
□ 151	Matt Anderson	.10	.05
□ 152	Willie Blair	.10	.05
□ 153	Brian Hunter	.10	.05
□ 154	Florida Marlins TC	.10	.05
□ 155	Alex Gonzalez	.15	.07
□ 156	Mark Kotsay	.15	.05
□ 157	Livan Hernandez	.10	.05
□ 158	Cliff Floyd	.15	.07

□ 159	Todd Dunwoody	.10	.05
□ 160	Alex Fernandez	.10	.05
□ 161	Matt Mantei	.15	.07
□ 162	Derrek Lee	.10	.05
□ 163	Kevin Orie	.10	.05
□ 164	Craig Counsell	.10	.05
□ 165	Rafael Medina	.10	.05
□ 166	Houston Astros TC	.10	.05
□ 167	Daryle Ward	.15	.07
□ 168	Mitch Meluskey	.15	.07
□ 169	Jeff Bagwell PT	.20	.09
□ 170	Jeff Bagwell	.40	.18
□ 171	Ken Caminiti	.15	.07
□ 172	Craig Biggio	.30	.14
□ 173	Derek Bell	.15	.07
□ 174	Moises Alou	.15	.07
□ 175	Billy Wagner	.15	.07
□ 176	Shane Reynolds	.15	.07
□ 177	Carl Everett	.15	.07
□ 178	Scott Elarton	.10	.05
□ 179	Richard Hidalgo	.15	.07
□ 180	Kansas City Royals TC	.10	.05
□ 181	Carlos Beltran	.40	.18
□ 182	Carlos Febles	.15	.07
□ 183	Jeremy Giambi	.15	.07
□ 184	Johnny Damon	.15	.07
□ 185	Joe Randa	.10	.05
□ 186	Jeff King	.10	.05
□ 187	Hipolito Pichardo	.10	.05
□ 188	Kevin Appier	.15	.07
□ 189	Chad Kreuter	.10	.05
□ 190	Rey Sanchez	.10	.05
□ 191	Larry Sutton	.10	.05
□ 192	Jeff Montgomery	.10	.05
□ 193	Jermaine Dye	.15	.07
□ 194	Los Angeles Dodgers TC	.10	.05
□ 195	Adam Riggs	.10	.05
□ 196	Angel Pena	.10	.05
□ 197	Todd Hundley	.15	.07
□ 198	Kevin Brown	.20	.09
□ 199	Ismael Valdes	.10	.05
□ 200	Chan Ho Park	.15	.07
□ 201	Adrian Beltre	.30	.14
□ 202	Mark Grudzielanek	.10	.05
□ 203	Raul Mondesi	.15	.07
□ 204	Gary Sheffield	.15	.07
□ 205	Eric Karros	.15	.07
□ 206	Devon White	.10	.05
□ 207	Milwaukee Brewers TC	.10	.05
□ 208	Ron Belliard	.15	.07
□ 209	Rafael Roque	.15	.07
□ 210	Jeromy Burnitz	.15	.07
□ 211	Fernando Vina	.10	.05
□ 212	Scott Karl	.10	.05
□ 213	Jim Abbott	.15	.07
□ 214	Sean Berry	.10	.05
□ 215	Marquis Grissom	.10	.05
□ 216	Geoff Jenkins	.15	.07
□ 217	Jeff Cirillo	.15	.07
□ 218	Dave Nilsson	.10	.05
□ 219	Jose Valentin	.10	.05
□ 220	Minnesota Twins TC	.10	.05
□ 221	Corey Koskie	.15	.07
□ 222	Cristian Guzman	.15	.07
□ 223	A.J. Pierzynski	.15	.07
□ 224	David Ortiz	.10	.05
□ 225	Brad Radke	.15	.07
□ 226	Todd Walker	.15	.07
□ 227	Matt Lawton	.10	.05
□ 228	Rick Aguilera	.10	.05
□ 229	Eric Milton	.10	.05
□ 230	Marty Cordova	.10	.05
□ 231	Torii Hunter	.15	.07
□ 232	Ron Coomer	.10	.05
□ 233	LaTroy Hawkins	.10	.05
□ 234	Montreal Expos TC	.10	.05
□ 235	Fernando Seguignol	.15	.07
□ 236	Michael Barrett	.20	.09
□ 237	Vladimir Guerrero BP	.20	.09
□ 238	Vladimir Guerrero	.40	.18
□ 239	Brad Fullmer	.15	.07
□ 240	Rondell White	.15	.07
□ 241	Ugueth Urbina	.10	.05
□ 242	Dustin Hermanson	.10	.05
□ 243	Orlando Cabrera	.10	.05
□ 244	Wilton Guerrero	.10	.05

❑ 245 Carl Pavano	.10	.05
❑ 246 Javier Vazquez	.10	.05
❑ 247 Chris Widger	.10	.05
❑ 248 New York Mets TC	.10	.05
❑ 249 Mike Kinkade	.10	.05
❑ 250 Octavio Dotel	.15	.07
❑ 251 Mike Piazza PT	.50	.23
❑ 252 Mike Piazza	1.00	.45
❑ 253 Rickey Henderson	.40	.18
❑ 254 Edgardo Alfonzo	.20	.09
❑ 255 Robin Ventura	.15	.07
❑ 256 Al Leiter	.15	.07
❑ 257 Brian McRae	.10	.05
❑ 258 Rey Ordonez	.15	.07
❑ 259 Bobby Bonilla	.15	.07
❑ 260 Orel Hershiser	.15	.07
❑ 261 John Olerud	.15	.07
❑ 262 New York Yankees TC	.10	.05
❑ 263 Ricky Ledee	.15	.07
❑ 264 Bernie Williams BP	.15	.07
❑ 265 Derek Jeter BP	.50	.23
❑ 266 Scott Brosius HM	.10	.05
❑ 267 Derek Jeter	1.00	.45
❑ 268 Roger Clemens	.75	.35
❑ 269 Orlando Hernandez	.30	.14
❑ 270 Scott Brosius	.15	.07
❑ 271 Paul O'Neill	.15	.07
❑ 272 Bernie Williams	.30	.14
❑ 273 Chuck Knoblauch	.15	.07
❑ 274 Tino Martinez	.15	.07
❑ 275 Mariano Rivera	.15	.07
❑ 276 Jorge Posada	.10	.05
❑ 277 Oakland Athletics TC	.10	.05
❑ 278 Eric Chavez	.20	.09
❑ 279 Ben Grieve HM	.15	.07
❑ 280 Jason Giambi	.15	.07
❑ 281 John Jaha	.15	.07
❑ 282 Miguel Tejada	.15	.07
❑ 283 Ben Grieve	.30	.14
❑ 284 Matt Stairs	.15	.07
❑ 285 Ryan Christenson	.10	.05
❑ 286 A.J. Hinch	.10	.05
❑ 287 Kenny Rogers	.10	.05
❑ 288 Tom Candiotti	.10	.05
❑ 289 Scott Spiezio	.10	.05
❑ 290 Philadelphia Phillies TC	.10	.05
❑ 291 Pat Burrell	1.25	.55
❑ 292 Marlon Anderson	.10	.05
❑ 293 Scott Rolen BP	.30	.14
❑ 294 Scott Rolen	.40	.18
❑ 295 Doug Glanville	.15	.07
❑ 296 Rico Brogna	.10	.05
❑ 297 Ron Gant	.15	.07
❑ 298 Bobby Abreu	.15	.07
❑ 299 Desi Relaford	.10	.05
❑ 300 Curt Schilling	.20	.09
❑ 301 Chad Ogea	.10	.05
❑ 302 Kevin Jordan	.10	.05
❑ 303 Carlton Loewer	.10	.05
❑ 304 Pittsburgh Pirates TC	.10	.05
❑ 305 Kris Benson	.15	.07
❑ 306 Brian Giles	.15	.07
❑ 307 Jason Kendall	.15	.07
❑ 308 Jose Guillen	.10	.05
❑ 309 Pat Meares	.10	.05
❑ 310 Brant Brown	.10	.05
❑ 311 Kevin Young	.15	.07
❑ 312 Ed Sprague	.10	.05
❑ 313 Francisco Cordova	.10	.05
❑ 314 Aramis Ramirez	.20	.09
❑ 315 Freddy Garcia	.10	.05
❑ 316 St. Louis Cardinals TC	.10	.05
❑ 317 J.D. Drew	.50	.23
❑ 318 Chad Hutchinson	.50	.23
❑ 319 Mark McGwire PT	.75	.35
❑ 320 J.D. Drew PT	.30	.14
❑ 321 Mark McGwire	.75	.35
❑ 322 Mark McGwire HM	.75	.35
❑ 323 Mark McGwire	1.50	.70
❑ 324 Fernando Tatis	.30	.14
❑ 325 Edgar Renteria	.15	.07
❑ 326 Ray Lankford	.15	.07
❑ 327 Willie McGee	.15	.07
❑ 328 Ricky Bottalico	.10	.05
❑ 329 Eli Marrero	.10	.05
❑ 330 Matt Morris	.10	.05
❑ 331 Eric Davis	.15	.07
❑ 332 Darren Bragg	.10	.05
❑ 333 San Diego Padres TC	.10	.05
❑ 334 Matt Clement	.15	.07
❑ 335 Ben Davis	.20	.09
❑ 336 Gary Matthews Jr.	.10	.05
❑ 337 Tony Gwynn BP	.40	.18
❑ 338 Tony Gwynn HM	.40	.18
❑ 339 Tony Gwynn	.75	.35
❑ 340 Reggie Sanders	.10	.05
❑ 341 Ruben Rivera	.10	.05
❑ 342 Wally Joyner	.15	.07
❑ 343 Sterling Hitchcock	.10	.05
❑ 344 Carlos Hernandez	.10	.05
❑ 345 Andy Ashby	.10	.05
❑ 346 Trevor Hoffman	.15	.07
❑ 347 Chris Gomez	.10	.05
❑ 348 Jim Leyritz	.10	.05
❑ 349 San Francisco Giants TC	.10	.05
❑ 350 Armando Rios	.10	.05
❑ 351 Barry Bonds PT	.20	.09
❑ 352 Barry Bonds BP	.20	.09
❑ 353 Barry Bonds HM	.20	.09
❑ 354 Robb Nen	.10	.05
❑ 355 Bill Mueller	.10	.05
❑ 356 Barry Bonds	.40	.18
❑ 357 Jeff Kent	.15	.07
❑ 358 J.T. Snow	.15	.07
❑ 359 Ellis Burks	.15	.07
❑ 360 F.P. Santangelo	.10	.05
❑ 361 Marvin Benard	.10	.05
❑ 362 Stan Javier	.10	.05
❑ 363 Shawn Estes	.10	.05
❑ 364 Seattle Mariners TC	.10	.05
❑ 365 Carlos Guillen	.10	.05
❑ 366 Ken Griffey Jr. PT	.75	.35
❑ 367 Alex Rodriguez PT	.50	.23
❑ 368 Ken Griffey Jr. BP	.75	.35
❑ 369 Alex Rodriguez BP	.50	.23
❑ 370 Ken Griffey Jr. HM	.75	.35
❑ 371 Alex Rodriguez HM	.50	.23
❑ 372 Ken Griffey Jr.	1.50	.70
❑ 373 Alex Rodriguez	1.00	.45
❑ 374 Jay Buhner	.10	.05
❑ 375 Edgar Martinez	.15	.07
❑ 376 Jeff Fassero	.10	.05
❑ 377 David Bell	.10	.05
❑ 378 David Segui	.10	.05
❑ 379 Russ Davis	.10	.05
❑ 380 Dan Wilson	.10	.05
❑ 381 Jamie Moyer	.10	.05
❑ 382 Tampa Bay Devil Rays TC	.10	.05
❑ 383 Roberto Hernandez	.10	.05
❑ 384 Bobby Smith	.10	.05
❑ 385 Wade Boggs	.30	.14
❑ 386 Fred McGriff	.15	.07
❑ 387 Rolando Arrojo	.10	.05
❑ 388 Jose Canseco	.40	.18
❑ 389 Wilson Alvarez	.10	.05
❑ 390 Kevin Stocker	.10	.05
❑ 391 Miguel Cairo	.10	.05
❑ 392 Quinton McCracken	.10	.05
❑ 393 Texas Rangers TC	.10	.05
❑ 394 Ruben Mateo	.30	.14
❑ 395 Cesar King	.10	.05
❑ 396 Juan Gonzalez PT	.30	.14
❑ 397 Juan Gonzalez BP	.30	.14
❑ 398 Ivan Rodriguez	.40	.18
❑ 399 Juan Gonzalez	.60	.25
❑ 400 Rafael Palmeiro	.30	.14
❑ 401 Rick Helling	.10	.05
❑ 402 Aaron Sele	.15	.07
❑ 403 John Wetteland	.15	.07
❑ 404 Rusty Greer	.15	.07
❑ 405 Todd Zeile	.15	.07
❑ 406 Royce Clayton	.10	.05
❑ 407 Tom Goodwin	.10	.05
❑ 408 Toronto Blue Jays TC	.10	.05
❑ 409 Kevin Witt	.10	.05
❑ 410 Roy Halladay	.15	.07
❑ 411 Jose Cruz Jr.	.15	.07
❑ 412 Carlos Delgado	.30	.14
❑ 413 Willie Greene	.10	.05
❑ 414 Shawn Green	.30	.14
❑ 415 Homer Bush	.10	.05
❑ 416 Shannon Stewart	.15	.07
❑ 417 David Wells	.15	.07
❑ 418 Kelvim Escobar	.10	.05
❑ 419 Joey Hamilton	.10	.05
❑ 420 Alex Gonzalez	.15	.07
❑ 421 Mark McGwire MM	.50	.23
❑ 422 Mark McGwire MM	.50	.23
❑ 423 Mark McGwire MM	.50	.23
❑ 424 Mark McGwire MM	.50	.23
❑ 425 Mark McGwire MM	.50	.23
❑ 426 Mark McGwire MM	.50	.23
❑ 427 Mark McGwire MM	.50	.23
❑ 428 Mark McGwire MM	.50	.23
❑ 429 Mark McGwire MM	.50	.23
❑ 430 Mark McGwire MM	.50	.23
❑ 431 Mark McGwire MM	.50	.23
❑ 432 Mark McGwire MM	.50	.23
❑ 433 Mark McGwire MM	.50	.23
❑ 434 Mark McGwire MM	.50	.23
❑ 435 Mark McGwire MM	.50	.23
❑ 436 Mark McGwire MM	.50	.23
❑ 437 Mark McGwire MM	.50	.23
❑ 438 Mark McGwire MM	.50	.23
❑ 439 Mark McGwire MM	.50	.23
❑ 440 Mark McGwire MM	.50	.23
❑ 441 Mark McGwire MM	.50	.23
❑ 442 Mark McGwire MM	.50	.23
❑ 443 Mark McGwire MM	.50	.23
❑ 444 Mark McGwire MM	.50	.23
❑ 445 Mark McGwire MM	.50	.23
❑ 446 Mark McGwire MM	.50	.23
❑ 447 Mark McGwire MM	.50	.23
❑ 448 Mark McGwire MM	.50	.23
❑ 449 Mark McGwire MM	.50	.23
❑ 450 Mark McGwire MM	.50	.23
❑ 451 Chipper Jones RF	.40	.18
❑ 452 Cal Ripken RF	.60	.25
❑ 453 Roger Clemens RF	.40	.18
❑ 454 Wade Boggs RF	.15	.07
❑ 455 Greg Maddux RF	.40	.18
❑ 456 Frank Thomas RF	.30	.14
❑ 457 Jeff Bagwell RF	.20	.09
❑ 458 Mike Piazza RF	.50	.23
❑ 459 Randy Johnson RF	.15	.07
❑ 460 Mo Vaughn RF	.15	.07
❑ 461 Mark McGwire RF	.75	.35
❑ 462 Rickey Henderson RF	.20	.09
❑ 463 Barry Bonds RF	.20	.09
❑ 464 Tony Gwynn RF	.40	.18
❑ 465 Ken Griffey Jr. RF	.75	.35
❑ 466 Alex Rodriguez RF	.50	.23
❑ 467 Sammy Sosa RF	.50	.23
❑ 468 Juan Gonzalez RF	.30	.14
❑ 469 Kevin Brown RF	.15	.07
❑ 470 Fred McGriff RF	.15	.07

1995 Zenith

	MINT	NRMT
COMPLETE SET (150)	40.00	18.00
COMMON CARD (1-150)	.20	.09
MINOR STARS	.40	.18
UNLISTED STARS	.75	.35
❑ 1 Albert Belle	.75	.35
❑ 2 Alex Fernandez	.20	.09
❑ 3 Andy Benes	.40	.18
❑ 4 Barry Larkin	.75	.35
❑ 5 Barry Bonds	1.00	.45
❑ 6 Ben McDonald	.20	.09

□ 7 Bernard Gilkey .20 .09
□ 8 Billy Ashley .20 .09
□ 9 Bobby Bonilla .40 .18
□ 10 Bret Saberhagen .40 .18
□ 11 Brian Jordan .40 .18
□ 12 Cal Ripken 3.00 1.35
□ 13 Carlos Baerga .20 .09
□ 14 Carlos Delgado .75 .35
□ 15 Cecil Fielder .40 .18
□ 16 Chili Davis .40 .18
□ 17 Chuck Knoblauch .75 .35
□ 18 Craig Biggio .75 .35
□ 19 Danny Tartabull .20 .09
□ 20 Dante Bichette .40 .18
□ 21 Darren Daulton .40 .18
□ 22 David Justice .75 .35
□ 23 Dave Winfield .75 .35
□ 24 David Cone .60 .25
□ 25 Dean Palmer .40 .18
□ 26 Deion Sanders .40 .18
□ 27 Dennis Eckersley .40 .18
□ 28 Derek Bell .40 .18
□ 29 Don Mattingly 1.50 .70
□ 30 Edgar Martinez .40 .18
□ 31 Eric Karros .40 .18
□ 32 James Mouton .20 .09
□ 33 Frank Thomas 1.50 .70
□ 34 Fred McGriff .60 .25
□ 35 Gary Sheffield .40 .18
□ 36 Gary Gaetti .40 .18
□ 37 Greg Maddux 2.00 .90
□ 38 Gregg Jefferies .20 .09
□ 39 Ivan Rodriguez 1.00 .45
□ 40 Kenny Rogers .20 .09
□ 41 J.T. Snow .40 .18
□ 42 Hal Morris .20 .09
□ 43 Eddie Murray 3000th Hit .40 .18
□ 44 Javier Lopez .40 .18
□ 45 Jay Bell .40 .18
□ 46 Jeff Conine .20 .09
□ 47 Jeff Bagwell 1.00 .45
□ 48 Hideo Nomo Japanese 2.00 .90
□ 49 Jeff Kent .40 .18
□ 50 Jeff King .20 .09
□ 51 Jim Thome .75 .35
□ 52 Jimmy Key .40 .18
□ 53 Joe Carter .40 .18
□ 54 John Valentin .40 .18
□ 55 John Olerud .40 .18
□ 56 Jose Canseco 1.00 .45
□ 57 Jose Rijo .20 .09
□ 58 Jose Offerman .40 .18
□ 59 Juan Gonzalez 1.50 .70
□ 60 Ken Caminiti .60 .25
□ 61 Ken Griffey Jr. 4.00 1.80
□ 62 Kenny Lofton .60 .25
□ 63 Kevin Appier .40 .18
□ 64 Kevin Seitzer .20 .09
□ 65 Kirby Puckett 1.25 .55
□ 66 Kirk Gibson .40 .18
□ 67 Larry Walker .75 .35
□ 68 Lenny Dykstra .40 .18
□ 69 Manny Ramirez 1.00 .45
□ 70 Mark Grace .60 .25
□ 71 Mark McGwire 4.00 1.80
□ 72 Marquis Grissom .40 .18
□ 73 Jim Edmonds .60 .25
□ 74 Matt Williams .75 .35
□ 75 Mike Mussina .75 .35
□ 76 Mike Piazza 2.50 1.10
□ 77 Mo Vaughn .75 .35
□ 78 Moises Alou .40 .18
□ 79 Ozzie Smith 1.00 .45
□ 80 Paul O'Neill .40 .18
□ 81 Paul Molitor .75 .35
□ 82 Rafael Palmeiro .75 .35
□ 83 Randy Johnson .75 .35
□ 84 Raul Mondesi .60 .25
□ 85 Ray Lankford .40 .18
□ 86 Reggie Sanders .40 .18
□ 87 Rickey Henderson 1.00 .45
□ 88 Rico Brogna .20 .09
□ 89 Roberto Alomar .75 .35
□ 90 Robin Ventura .40 .18
□ 91 Roger Clemens 2.00 .90
□ 92 Ron Gant .20 .09

□ 93 Rondell White .40 .18
□ 94 Royce Clayton .20 .09
□ 95 Ruben Sierra .20 .09
□ 96 Rusty Greer .75 .35
□ 97 Ryan Klesko .40 .18
□ 98 Sammy Sosa 2.50 1.10
□ 99 Shawon Dunston .20 .09
□ 100 Steve Ontiveros .20 .09
□ 101 Tim Naehring .20 .09
□ 102 Tim Salmon .75 .35
□ 103 Tino Martinez .75 .35
□ 104 Tony Gwynn 2.00 .90
□ 105 Travis Fryman .40 .18
□ 106 Vinny Castilla .60 .25
□ 107 Wade Boggs .75 .35
□ 108 Wally Joyner .40 .18
□ 109 Wil Cordero .20 .09
□ 110 Will Clark .75 .35
□ 111 Chipper Jones 2.00 .90
□ 112 Armando Benitez .20 .09
□ 113 Curtis Goodwin .20 .09
□ 114 Gabe White .20 .09
□ 115 Vaughn Eshelman .20 .09
□ 116 Marty Cordova .20 .09
□ 117 Dustin Hermanson .20 .09
□ 118 Rich Becker .20 .09
□ 119 Ray Durham .40 .18
□ 120 Shane Andrews .20 .09
□ 121 Scott Ruffcorn .20 .09
□ 122 Mark Grudzielanek .60 .25
□ 123 James Baldwin .40 .18
□ 124 Carlos Perez .40 .18
□ 125 Julian Tavarez .20 .09
□ 126 Joe Vitiello .20 .09
□ 127 Jason Bates .20 .09
□ 128 Edgardo Alfonzo .75 .35
□ 129 Juan Acevedo .20 .09
□ 130 Bill Pulsipher .20 .09
□ 131 Bob Higginson 2.00 .90
□ 132 Russ Davis .40 .18
□ 133 Charles Johnson .40 .18
□ 134 Derek Jeter 2.50 1.10
□ 135 Orlando Miller .20 .09
□ 136 LaTroy Hawkins .20 .09
□ 137 Brian L.Hunter .40 .18
□ 138 Roberto Petagine .20 .09
□ 139 Midre Cummings .20 .09
□ 140 Garret Anderson .40 .18
□ 141 Ugueth Urbina .20 .09
□ 142 Antonio Osuna .20 .09
□ 143 Michael Tucker .40 .18
□ 144 Benji Gil .20 .09
□ 145 Jon Nunnally .20 .09
□ 146 Alex Rodriguez 3.00 1.35
□ 147 Todd Hollandsworth .20 .09
□ 148 Alex Gonzalez .20 .09
□ 149 Hideo Nomo 2.00 .90
□ 150 Shawn Green .75 .35

1995 Zenith All-Star Salute

	MINT	NRMT
COMPLETE SET (18)	50.00	22.00
COMMON CARD (1-18)	.50	.23

STATED ODDS 1:6

□ 1 Cal Ripken 8.00 3.60
□ 2 Frank Thomas 4.00 1.80
□ 3 Mike Piazza 6.00 2.70
□ 4 Kirby Puckett 4.00 1.80
□ 5 Manny Ramirez 2.50 1.10
□ 6 Tony Gwynn 5.00 2.20
□ 7 Hideo Nomo 3.00 1.35
□ 8 Matt Williams 2.00 .90
□ 9 Randy Johnson 2.00 .90
□ 10 Raul Mondesi 1.50 .70
□ 11 Albert Belle 2.00 .90
□ 12 Ivan Rodriguez 2.50 1.10
□ 13 Barry Bonds 2.50 1.10
□ 14 Carlos Baerga .50 .23
□ 15 Ken Griffey Jr. 10.00 4.50
□ 16 Jeff Conine .50 .23
□ 17 Frank Thomas 4.00 1.80
□ 18 Cal Ripken 6.00 2.70
Barry Bonds

1995 Zenith Rookie Roll Call

	MINT	NRMT
COMPLETE SET (18)	150.00	70.00
COMMON CARD (1-18)	2.50	1.10
MINOR STARS	5.00	2.20
SEMISTARS	8.00	3.60
STATED ODDS 1:24		

□ 1 Alex Rodriguez 40.00 18.00
□ 2 Derek Jeter 40.00 18.00
□ 3 Chipper Jones 30.00 13.50
□ 4 Shawn Green 15.00 6.75
□ 5 Todd Hollandsworth 2.50 1.10
□ 6 Bill Pulsipher 2.50 1.10
□ 7 Hideo Nomo 15.00 6.75
□ 8 Ray Durham 5.00 2.20
□ 9 Curtis Goodwin 2.50 1.10
□ 10 Brian L.Hunter 5.00 2.20
□ 11 Julian Tavarez 2.50 1.10
□ 12 Marty Cordova UER 2.50 1.10
Kevin Maas pictured
□ 13 Michael Tucker 5.00 2.20
□ 14 Edgardo Alfonzo 15.00 6.75
□ 15 LaTroy Hawkins 2.50 1.10
□ 16 Carlos Perez 5.00 2.20
□ 17 Charles Johnson 5.00 2.20
□ 18 Benji Gil 2.50 1.10

1995 Zenith Z-Team

	MINT	NRMT
COMPLETE SET (18)	300.00	135.00
COMMON CARD (1-18)	8.00	3.60
STATED ODDS 1:72		

□ 1 Cal Ripken 50.00 22.00
□ 2 Ken Griffey Jr. 60.00 27.00
□ 3 Frank Thomas 30.00 13.50
□ 4 Matt Williams 12.00 5.50
□ 5 Mike Piazza UER 40.00 18.00

(Card says started at first base
Piazza is a catcher)

		MINT	NRMT
❏ 6	Barry Bonds	12.00	5.50
❏ 7	Raul Mondesi	10.00	4.50
❏ 8	Greg Maddux	40.00	18.00
❏ 9	Jeff Bagwell	12.00	5.50
❏ 10	Manny Ramirez	12.00	5.50
❏ 11	Larry Walker	12.00	5.50
❏ 12	Tony Gwynn	30.00	13.50
❏ 13	Will Clark	12.00	5.50
❏ 14	Albert Belle	12.00	5.50
❏ 15	Kenny Lofton	10.00	4.50
❏ 16	Rafael Palmeiro	12.00	5.50
❏ 17	Don Mattingly	20.00	9.00
❏ 18	Carlos Baerga	8.00	3.60

1996 Zenith

	MINT	NRMT
COMPLETE SET (150)	30.00	13.50
COMMON CARD (1-150)	.15	.07
MINOR STARS	.30	.14
UNLISTED STARS	.60	.25
SUBSET CARDS HALF VALUE OF BASE CARDS		

❏ 1	Ken Griffey Jr.	3.00	1.35
❏ 2	Ozzie Smith	.75	.35
❏ 3	Greg Maddux	1.50	.70
❏ 4	Rondell White	.30	.14
❏ 5	Mark McGwire	3.00	1.35
❏ 6	Jim Thome	.60	.25
❏ 7	Ivan Rodriguez	.75	.35
❏ 8	Marc Newfield	.15	.07
❏ 9	Travis Fryman	.30	.14
❏ 10	Fred McGriff	.40	.18
❏ 11	Shawn Green	.60	.25
❏ 12	Mike Piazza	2.00	.90
❏ 13	Dante Bichette	.30	.14
❏ 14	Tino Martinez	.30	.14
❏ 15	Sterling Hitchcock	.15	.07
❏ 16	Ryne Sandberg	.75	.35
❏ 17	Rico Brogna	.15	.07
❏ 18	Roberto Alomar	.60	.25
❏ 19	Barry Larkin	.60	.25
❏ 20	Bernie Williams	.60	.25
❏ 21	Gary Sheffield	.30	.14
❏ 22	Frank Thomas	1.25	.55
❏ 23	Gregg Jefferies	.15	.07
❏ 24	Jeff Bagwell	.75	.35
❏ 25	Marty Cordova	.15	.07

❏ 26	Jim Edmonds	.40	.18
❏ 27	Jay Bell	.30	.14
❏ 28	Ben McDonald	.15	.07
❏ 29	Barry Bonds	.75	.35
❏ 30	Mo Vaughn	.60	.25
❏ 31	Johnny Damon	.40	.18
❏ 32	Dean Palmer	.30	.14
❏ 33	Ismael Valdes	.30	.14
❏ 34	Manny Ramirez	.75	.35
❏ 35	Edgar Martinez	.30	.14
❏ 36	Cecil Fielder	.30	.14
❏ 37	Ryan Klesko	.30	.14
❏ 38	Ray Lankford	.30	.14
❏ 39	Tim Salmon	.40	.18
❏ 40	Joe Carter	.30	.14
❏ 41	Jason Isringhausen	.30	.14
❏ 42	Rickey Henderson	.75	.35
❏ 43	Lenny Dykstra	.30	.14
❏ 44	Andre Dawson	.40	.18
❏ 45	Paul O'Neill	.30	.14
❏ 46	Ray Durham	.30	.14
❏ 47	Raul Mondesi	.30	.14
❏ 48	Jay Buhner	.30	.14
❏ 49	Eddie Murray	.60	.25
❏ 50	Henry Rodriguez	.30	.14
❏ 51	Hal Morris	.15	.07
❏ 52	Mike Mussina	.60	.25
❏ 53	Wally Joyner	.30	.14
❏ 54	Will Clark	.60	.25
❏ 55	Chipper Jones	1.50	.70
❏ 56	Brian Jordan	.30	.14
❏ 57	Larry Walker	.60	.25
❏ 58	Wade Boggs	.60	.25
❏ 59	Melvin Nieves	.15	.07
❏ 60	Charles Johnson	.30	.14
❏ 61	Juan Gonzalez	1.25	.55
❏ 62	Carlos Delgado	.60	.25
❏ 63	Reggie Sanders	.30	.14
❏ 64	Brian L.Hunter	.15	.07
❏ 65	Edgardo Alfonzo	.60	.25
❏ 66	Kenny Lofton	.40	.25
❏ 67	Paul Molitor	.60	.25
❏ 68	Mike Bordick	.15	.07
❏ 69	Garret Anderson	.30	.14
❏ 70	Orlando Merced	.15	.07
❏ 71	Craig Biggio	.60	.25
❏ 72	Chuck Knoblauch	.60	.25
❏ 73	Mark Grace	.40	.18
❏ 74	Jack McDowell	.15	.07
❏ 75	Randy Johnson	.60	.25
❏ 76	Cal Ripken	2.50	1.10
❏ 77	Matt Williams	.60	.25
❏ 78	Benji Gil	.15	.07
❏ 79	Moises Alou	.30	.14
❏ 80	Robin Ventura	.30	.14
❏ 81	Greg Vaughn	.30	.14
❏ 82	Carlos Baerga	.15	.07
❏ 83	Roger Clemens	1.50	.70
❏ 84	Hideo Nomo	.60	.25
❏ 85	Pedro Martinez	.75	.35
❏ 86	John Valentin	.30	.14
❏ 87	Andres Galarraga	.60	.25
❏ 88	Andy Pettitte	.40	.18
❏ 89	Derek Bell	.30	.14
❏ 90	Kirby Puckett	1.00	.45
❏ 91	Tony Gwynn	1.50	.70
❏ 92	Brady Anderson	.30	.14
❏ 93	Derek Jeter	2.00	.90
❏ 94	Michael Tucker	.15	.07
❏ 95	Albert Belle	.60	.25
❏ 96	David Cone	.40	.18
❏ 97	J.T. Snow	.30	.14
❏ 98	Tom Glavine	.60	.25
❏ 99	Alex Rodriguez	2.00	.90
❏ 100	Sammy Sosa	2.00	.90
❏ 101	Karim Garcia	.30	.14
❏ 102	Alan Benes	.15	.07
❏ 103	Chad Mottola	.15	.07
❏ 104	Robin Jennings	.15	.07
❏ 105	Bob Abreu	.40	.18
❏ 106	Tony Clark	.60	.25
❏ 107	George Arias	.15	.07
❏ 108	Jermaine Dye	.30	.14
❏ 109	Jeff Suppan	.15	.07
❏ 110	Ralph Milliard	.15	.07
❏ 111	Ruben Rivera	.30	.14

❏ 112	Billy Wagner	.40	.18
❏ 113	Jason Kendall	.60	.25
❏ 114	Mike Grace	.15	.07
❏ 115	Edgar Renteria	.30	.14
❏ 116	Jason Schmidt	.15	.07
❏ 117	Paul Wilson	.15	.07
❏ 118	Rey Ordonez	.60	.25
❏ 119	Rocky Coppinger	.60	.25
❏ 120	Wilton Guerrero	.50	.23
❏ 121	Brooks Kieschnick	.15	.07
❏ 122	Raul Casanova	.15	.07
❏ 123	Alex Ochoa	.15	.07
❏ 124	Chan Ho Park	.40	.18
❏ 125	John Wasdin	.15	.07
❏ 126	Eric Owens	.15	.07
❏ 127	Justin Thompson	.30	.14
❏ 128	Chris Snopek	.15	.07
❏ 129	Terrell Wade	.15	.07
❏ 130	Darin Erstad	5.00	2.20
❏ 131	Albert Belle HON	.30	.14
❏ 132	Cal Ripken HON	1.25	.55
❏ 133	Frank Thomas HON	.60	.25
❏ 134	Greg Maddux HON	.75	.35
❏ 135	Ken Griffey Jr. HON	1.50	.70
❏ 136	Mo Vaughn HON	.30	.14
❏ 137	Chipper Jones HON	.75	.35
❏ 138	Mike Piazza HON	1.00	.45
❏ 139	Ryan Klesko HON	.15	.07
❏ 140	Hideo Nomo HON	.30	.14
❏ 141	Roberto Alomar HON	.30	.14
❏ 142	Manny Ramirez HON	.60	.25
❏ 143	Gary Sheffield HON	.15	.07
❏ 144	Barry Bonds HON	.40	.18
❏ 145	Matt Williams HON	.30	.14
❏ 146	Jim Edmonds HON	.15	.07
❏ 147	Derek Jeter HON	1.00	.45
❏ 148	Sammy Sosa HON	1.00	.45
❏ 149	Kirby Puckett HON	.30	.14
❏ 150	Tony Gwynn HON	.75	.35

1996 Zenith Artist's Proofs

	MINT	NRMT
COMMON CARD (1-150)	3.00	1.35
*STARS: 10X TO 25X BASIC CARDS		
*ROOKIES: 3X TO 8X BASIC CARDS		
STATED ODDS 1:35		

1996 Zenith Diamond Club

	MINT	NRMT
COMPLETE SET (20)	200.00	90.00
COMMON CARD (1-20)	3.00	1.35
STATED ODDS 1:24		
❑ 1 Albert Belle	5.00	2.20
❑ 2 Mo Vaughn	5.00	2.20
❑ 3 Ken Griffey Jr.	25.00	11.00
❑ 4 Mike Piazza	15.00	6.75
❑ 5 Cal Ripken	20.00	9.00
❑ 6 Jermaine Dye	3.00	1.35
❑ 7 Jeff Bagwell	6.00	2.70
❑ 8 Frank Thomas	10.00	4.50
❑ 9 Alex Rodriguez	15.00	6.75
❑ 10 Ryan Klesko	3.00	1.35
❑ 11 Roberto Alomar	5.00	2.20
❑ 12 Sammy Sosa	15.00	6.75
❑ 13 Matt Williams	5.00	2.20
❑ 14 Gary Sheffield	3.00	1.35
❑ 15 Ruben Rivera	3.00	1.35
❑ 16 Darin Erstad	20.00	9.00
❑ 17 Randy Johnson	5.00	2.20
❑ 18 Greg Maddux	12.00	5.50
❑ 19 Karim Garcia	3.00	1.35
❑ 20 Chipper Jones	12.00	5.50

1996 Zenith Diamond Club Parallel

	MINT	NRMT
COMPLETE SET (20)	1000.00	450.00
*SINGLES: 15X TO 40X BASE CARD HI		
STATED ODDS 1:350		

1996 Zenith Mozaics

	MINT	NRMT
COMPLETE SET (25)	100.00	45.00
COMMON CARD (1-25)	1.50	.70
SEMISTARS	2.50	1.10
STATED ODDS 1:10		
❑ 1 Greg Maddux	8.00	3.60
Chipper Jones		
Ryan Klesko		
❑ 2 Juan Gonzalez	5.00	2.20
Will Clark		
Ivan Rodriguez		
❑ 3 Frank Thomas	5.00	2.20
Robin Ventura		
Ray Durham		
❑ 4 Matt Williams	3.00	1.35
Barry Bonds		
Osvaldo Fernandez		
❑ 5 Ken Griffey Jr.	15.00	6.75
Randy Johnson		
Alex Rodriguez		
❑ 6 Sammy Sosa	8.00	3.60
Ryne Sandberg		
Mark Grace		
❑ 7 Jim Edmonds	6.00	2.70
Tim Salmon		
Garret Anderson		
❑ 8 Cal Ripken	10.00	4.50
Roberto Alomar		
Mike Mussina		
❑ 9 Mo Vaughn	6.00	2.70
Roger Clemens		

	MINT	NRMT
John Valentin		
❑ 10 Barry Larkin	2.50	1.10
Reggie Sanders		
Hal Morris		
❑ 11 Ray Lankford	6.00	2.70
Brian Jordan		
Ozzie Smith		
❑ 12 Dante Bichette	6.00	2.70
Larry Walker		
Andres Galarraga		
❑ 13 Mike Piazza	8.00	3.60
Hideo Nomo		
Raul Mondesi		
❑ 14 Ben McDonald	1.50	.70
Greg Vaughn		
Kevin Seitzer		
❑ 15 Joe Carter	3.00	1.35
Carlos Delgado		
Alex Gonzalez		
❑ 16 Gary Sheffield	6.00	2.70
Charles Johnson		
Jeff Conine		
❑ 17 Rondell White	3.00	1.35
Moises Alou		
Henry Rodriguez		
❑ 18 Albert Belle	3.00	1.35
Manny Ramirez		
Carlos Baerga		
❑ 19 Kirby Puckett	4.00	1.80
Paul Molitor		
Chuck Knoblauch		
❑ 20 Tony Gwynn	6.00	2.70
Rickey Henderson *		
Wally Joyner		
❑ 21 Mark McGwire	12.00	5.50
Mike Bordick		
Scott Brosius		
❑ 22 Paul O'Neill	6.00	2.70
Bernie Williams		
Wade Boggs		
❑ 23 Jay Bell	3.00	1.35
Orlando Merced		
Jason Kendall		
❑ 24 Rico Brogna	1.50	.70
Paul Wilson		
Jason Isringhausen		
❑ 25 Jeff Bagwell	3.00	1.35
Craig Biggio		
Derek Bell		

1996 Zenith Z-Team

	MINT	NRMT
COMPLETE SET (18)	300.00	135.00
COMMON CARD (1-18)	8.00	3.60
STATED ODDS 1:72		
❑ 1 Ken Griffey Jr.	50.00	22.00
❑ 2 Albert Belle	10.00	4.50
❑ 3 Cal Ripken	40.00	18.00
❑ 4 Frank Thomas	25.00	11.00
❑ 5 Greg Maddux	30.00	13.50
❑ 6 Mo Vaughn	10.00	4.50
❑ 7 Chipper Jones	25.00	11.00
❑ 8 Mike Piazza	30.00	13.50
❑ 9 Ryan Klesko	8.00	3.60
❑ 10 Hideo Nomo	10.00	4.50
❑ 11 Roberto Alomar	10.00	4.50
❑ 12 Manny Ramirez	10.00	4.50
❑ 13 Gary Sheffield	8.00	3.60
❑ 14 Barry Bonds	10.00	4.50
❑ 15 Matt Williams	10.00	4.50
❑ 16 Jim Edmonds	10.00	4.50
❑ 17 Kirby Puckett	15.00	6.75
❑ 18 Sammy Sosa	25.00	11.00

1997 Zenith

	MINT	NRMT
COMPLETE SET (50)	40.00	18.00
COMMON CARD (1-50)	.40	.18
SEMISTARS	.60	.25
UNLISTED STARS	.75	.35
❑ 1 Frank Thomas	1.50	.70
❑ 2 Tony Gwynn	2.00	.90
❑ 3 Jeff Bagwell	1.00	.45
❑ 4 Paul Molitor	.75	.35
❑ 5 Roberto Alomar	.75	.35
❑ 6 Mike Piazza	2.50	1.10
❑ 7 Albert Belle	.75	.35
❑ 8 Greg Maddux	2.00	.90
❑ 9 Barry Larkin	.75	.35
❑ 10 Tony Clark	.60	.25
❑ 11 Larry Walker	.75	.35
❑ 12 Chipper Jones	2.00	.90
❑ 13 Juan Gonzalez	1.50	.70
❑ 14 Barry Bonds	1.00	.45
❑ 15 Ivan Rodriguez	1.00	.45
❑ 16 Sammy Sosa	2.50	1.10
❑ 17 Derek Jeter	2.50	1.10
❑ 18 Hideo Nomo	.75	.35
❑ 19 Roger Clemens	2.00	.90
❑ 20 Ken Griffey Jr.	4.00	1.80
❑ 21 Andy Pettitte	.60	.25
❑ 22 Alex Rodriguez	2.50	1.10
❑ 23 Tino Martinez	.75	.35
❑ 24 Bernie Williams	.75	.35
❑ 25 Ken Caminiti	.60	.25
❑ 26 John Smoltz	.60	.25
❑ 27 Javier Lopez	.60	.25
❑ 28 Mark McGwire	4.00	1.80
❑ 29 Gary Sheffield	.60	.25
❑ 30 David Justice	.75	.35
❑ 31 Randy Johnson	.75	.35
❑ 32 Chuck Knoblauch	.75	.35
❑ 33 Mike Mussina	.75	.35
❑ 34 Deion Sanders	.60	.25
❑ 35 Cal Ripken	3.00	1.35
❑ 36 Darin Erstad	.75	.35
❑ 37 Kenny Lofton	.60	.25
❑ 38 Jay Buhner	.60	.25
❑ 39 Brady Anderson	.60	.25
❑ 40 Edgar Martinez	.60	.25
❑ 41 Mo Vaughn	.75	.35
❑ 42 Ryne Sandberg	1.00	.45
❑ 43 Andruw Jones	1.00	.45
❑ 44 Nomar Garciaparra	2.50	1.10
❑ 45 Hideki Irabu	1.25	.55
❑ 46 Wilton Guerrero	.40	.18
❑ 47 Jose Cruz Jr.	1.50	.70
❑ 48 Vladimir Guerrero	1.25	.55
❑ 49 Scott Rolen	1.25	.55
❑ 50 Jose Guillen	.60	.25

1997 Zenith 8 x 10

	MINT	NRMT
COMPLETE SET (24)	40.00	18.00
COMMON CARD (1-24)	.50	.23
ONE PER PACK		
COMP.DUFEX SET (24)	80.00	36.00
*DUFEX SINGLES : 1X TO 2.5X BASE CARD HI		
ONE DUFEX PER PACK		

❏ 1 Frank Thomas	2.00	.90
❏ 2 Tony Gwynn	2.50	1.10
❏ 3 Jeff Bagwell	.75	.35
❏ 4 Ken Griffey Jr.	5.00	2.20
❏ 5 Mike Piazza	3.00	1.35
❏ 6 Greg Maddux	2.50	1.10
❏ 7 Ken Caminiti	.50	.23
❏ 8 Albert Belle	.75	.35
❏ 9 Ivan Rodriguez	1.00	.45
❏ 10 Sammy Sosa	4.00	1.80
❏ 11 Mark McGwire	5.00	2.20
❏ 12 Roger Clemens	2.50	1.10
❏ 13 Alex Rodriguez	3.00	1.35
❏ 14 Chipper Jones	2.50	1.10
❏ 15 Juan Gonzalez	2.00	.90
❏ 16 Barry Bonds	1.00	.45
❏ 17 Derek Jeter	3.00	1.35
❏ 18 Hideo Nomo	.75	.35
❏ 19 Cal Ripken	4.00	1.80
❏ 20 Hideki Irabu	.75	.35
❏ 21 Andruw Jones	1.50	.70
❏ 22 Nomar Garciaparra	3.00	1.35
❏ 23 Vladimir Guerrero	1.50	.70
❏ 24 Scott Rolen	2.00	.90

1997 Zenith V-2

	MINT	NRMT
COMPLETE SET (8)	200.00	90.00
COMMON CARD (1-8)	12.00	5.50
STATED ODDS 1:47		

❏ 1 Ken Griffey Jr.	50.00	22.00
❏ 2 Andruw Jones	12.00	5.50
❏ 3 Frank Thomas	20.00	9.00
❏ 4 Mike Piazza	30.00	13.50
❏ 5 Alex Rodriguez	30.00	13.50
❏ 6 Cal Ripken	40.00	18.00
❏ 7 Derek Jeter	30.00	13.50
❏ 8 Vladimir Guerrero	15.00	6.75

1997 Zenith Z-Team

	MINT	NRMT
COMPLETE SET (9)	350.00	160.00
COMMON CARD (1-9)	15.00	6.75
RANDOM INSERTS IN PACKS		
STATED PRINT RUN 1000 SERIAL #'d SETS		

❏ 1 Ken Griffey Jr.	80.00	36.00
❏ 2 Larry Walker	15.00	6.75
❏ 3 Frank Thomas	30.00	13.50
❏ 4 Alex Rodriguez	50.00	22.00
❏ 5 Mike Piazza	50.00	22.00
❏ 6 Cal Ripken	60.00	27.00
❏ 7 Derek Jeter	50.00	22.00
❏ 8 Andruw Jones	20.00	9.00
❏ 9 Roger Clemens	40.00	18.00

1998 Zenith

	MINT	NRMT
COMPLETE SET (100)	100.00	45.00
COMMON CARD (1-100)	.30	.14
MINOR STARS	.50	.23
SEMISTARS	.75	.35
UNLISTED STARS	1.25	.55

❏ 1 Larry Walker	1.25	.55
❏ 2 Ken Griffey Jr.	6.00	2.70
❏ 3 Cal Ripken	5.00	2.20
❏ 4 Sammy Sosa	4.00	1.80
❏ 5 Andruw Jones	1.25	.55
❏ 6 Frank Thomas	2.50	1.10
❏ 7 Tony Gwynn	3.00	1.35
❏ 8 Rafael Palmeiro	1.25	.55
❏ 9 Tim Salmon	.75	.35
❏ 10 Randy Johnson	1.25	.55
❏ 11 Juan Gonzalez	2.50	1.10
❏ 12 Greg Maddux	3.00	1.35
❏ 13 Vladimir Guerrero	1.50	.70
❏ 14 Mike Piazza	4.00	1.80
❏ 15 Andres Galarraga	.75	.35
❏ 16 Alex Rodriguez	4.00	1.80
❏ 17 Derek Jeter	4.00	1.80
❏ 18 Nomar Garciaparra	4.00	1.80
❏ 19 Ivan Rodriguez	1.50	.70
❏ 20 Chipper Jones	3.00	1.35

❏ 21 Barry Larkin	1.25	.55
❏ 22 Mo Vaughn	1.25	.55
❏ 23 Albert Belle	1.25	.55
❏ 24 Scott Rolen	1.50	.55
❏ 25 Sandy Alomar Jr.	.50	.23
❏ 26 Roberto Alomar	1.25	.55
❏ 27 Andy Pettitte	.50	.23
❏ 28 Chuck Knoblauch	.50	.23
❏ 29 Jeff Bagwell	1.50	.70
❏ 30 Mike Mussina	1.25	.55
❏ 31 Fred McGriff	.75	.35
❏ 32 Roger Clemens	3.00	1.35
❏ 33 Rusty Greer	.50	.23
❏ 34 Edgar Martinez	.50	.23
❏ 35 Paul Molitor	1.25	.55
❏ 36 Mark Grace	.75	.35
❏ 37 Darin Erstad	.75	.35
❏ 38 Kenny Lofton	.75	.35
❏ 39 Tom Glavine	1.25	.55
❏ 40 Javier Lopez	.50	.23
❏ 41 Will Clark	1.25	.55
❏ 42 Tino Martinez	.50	.23
❏ 43 Raul Mondesi	.50	.23
❏ 44 Brady Anderson	.50	.23
❏ 45 Chan Ho Park	.50	.23
❏ 46 Jason Giambi	.50	.23
❏ 47 Manny Ramirez	1.50	.70
❏ 48 Jay Buhner	.50	.23
❏ 49 Dante Bichette	.50	.23
❏ 50 Jose Cruz Jr.	.50	.23
❏ 51 Charles Johnson	.50	.23
❏ 52 Bernard Gilkey	.30	.14
❏ 53 Johnny Damon	.50	.23
❏ 54 David Justice	.50	.23
❏ 55 Justin Thompson	.30	.14
❏ 56 Bobby Higginson	.50	.23
❏ 57 Todd Hundley	.50	.23
❏ 58 Gary Sheffield	.50	.23
❏ 59 Barry Bonds	1.50	.70
❏ 60 Mark McGwire	8.00	3.60
❏ 61 John Smoltz	.75	.35
❏ 62 Tony Clark	.50	.23
❏ 63 Brian Jordan	.50	.23
❏ 64 Jason Kendall	.50	.23
❏ 65 Mariano Rivera	.50	.23
❏ 66 Pedro Martinez	1.50	.70
❏ 67 Jim Thome	1.25	.55
❏ 68 Neifi Perez	.50	.23
❏ 69 Kevin Brown	.75	.35
❏ 70 Hideo Nomo	1.25	.55
❏ 71 Craig Biggio	1.25	.55
❏ 72 Bernie Williams	1.25	.55
❏ 73 Jose Guillen	.30	.14
❏ 74 Ken Caminiti	.50	.23
❏ 75 Livan Hernandez	.30	.14
❏ 76 Ray Lankford	.50	.23
❏ 77 Jim Edmonds	.50	.23
❏ 78 Matt Williams	1.25	.55
❏ 79 Mark Kotsay	.50	.23
❏ 80 Moises Alou	.50	.23
❏ 81 Antone Williamson	.30	.14
❏ 82 Jaret Wright	.50	.23
❏ 83 Jacob Cruz	.30	.14
❏ 84 Abraham Nunez	.30	.14
❏ 85 Raul Ibanez	.30	.14
❏ 86 Miguel Tejada	.50	.23
❏ 87 Derrek Lee	.30	.14
❏ 88 Juan Encarnacion	.50	.23
❏ 89 Todd Helton	1.50	.70
❏ 90 Travis Lee	.75	.35
❏ 91 Ben Grieve	1.25	.55
❏ 92 Ryan McGuire	.30	.14
❏ 93 Richard Hidalgo	.50	.23
❏ 94 Paul Konerko	.50	.23
❏ 95 Shannon Stewart	.50	.23
❏ 96 Homer Bush	.30	.14
❏ 97 Lou Collier	.30	.14
❏ 98 Jeff Abbott	.30	.14
❏ 99 Brett Tomko	.30	.14
❏ 100 Fernando Tatis	1.25	.55

1998 Zenith Z-Gold

	MINT	NRMT
COMMON CARD (1-100)	10.00	4.50

*STARS: 12.5X TO 30X BASIC CARDS
*YNG.STARS: 10X TO 25X BASIC CARDS
RANDOM INSERTS IN PACKS
STATED PRINT RUN 100 SERIAL #'d SETS

1998 Zenith Z-Silver

	MINT	NRMT
COMMON CARD (1-100)	1.50	.70

*STARS: 2X TO 5X BASIC CARDS
*YNG.STARS: 1.5X TO 4X BASIC CARDS
STATED ODDS 1:7

1998 Zenith 5 x 7

	MINT	NRMT
COMPLETE SET (80)	120.00	55.00
COMMON CARD (1-80)	.40	.18
MINOR STARS	.60	.25
SEMISTARS	1.00	.45
UNLISTED STARS	1.50	.70
COMP.SLIT-BACK SET (80)	25.00	11.00
COMMON SLIT-BACK (1-80)	.10	.05

*SLIT-BACK CARDS: .1X TO .25X HI COLUMN
THREE CARDS PER PACK
CONDITION SENSITIVE SET
PRICES BELOW ARE FOR MT UNCUT CARDS
SLIT CARD MUST BE CLEAN RAZOR CUT
BACK

□			
□ 1	Nomar Garciaparra	5.00	2.20
□ 2	Andres Galarraga	1.00	.45
□ 3	Greg Maddux	4.00	1.80
□ 4	Frank Thomas	3.00	1.35
□ 5	Mark McGwire	10.00	4.50
□ 6	Rafael Palmeiro	1.50	.70
□ 7	John Smoltz	1.00	.45
□ 8	Jeff Bagwell	2.00	.90
□ 9	Andruw Jones	1.50	.70
□ 10	Rusty Greer	.60	.25
□ 11	Paul Molitor	1.50	.70
□ 12	Bernie Williams	1.50	.70
□ 13	Kenny Lofton	1.00	.45
□ 14	Alex Rodriguez	5.00	2.20
□ 15	Derek Jeter	5.00	2.20
□ 16	Scott Rolen	2.00	.90
□ 17	Albert Belle	1.50	.70
□ 18	Mo Vaughn	1.50	.70
□ 19	Chipper Jones	4.00	1.80
□ 20	Chuck Knoblauch	.60	.25
□ 21	Mike Piazza	5.00	2.20
□ 22	Tony Gwynn	4.00	1.80
□ 23	Juan Gonzalez	3.00	1.35
□ 24	Andy Pettitte	.60	.25
□ 25	Tim Salmon	1.00	.45
□ 26	Brady Anderson	.60	.25
□ 27	Mike Mussina	1.50	.70
□ 28	Edgar Martinez	.60	.25
□ 29	Jose Guillen	.40	.18
□ 30	Hideo Nomo	1.50	.70
□ 31	Jim Thome	1.50	.70
□ 32	Mark Grace	1.00	.45
□ 33	Darin Erstad	1.00	.45
□ 34	Bobby Higginson	.60	.25
□ 35	Ivan Rodriguez	2.00	.90
□ 36	Todd Hundley	.60	.25
□ 37	Sandy Alomar Jr.	.60	.25
□ 38	Gary Sheffield	.60	.25
□ 39	David Justice	.60	.25
□ 40	Ken Griffey Jr.	8.00	3.60
□ 41	Vladimir Guerrero	2.00	.90
□ 42	Larry Walker	1.50	.70
□ 43	Barry Bonds	2.00	.90
□ 44	Randy Johnson	1.50	.70
□ 45	Roger Clemens	4.00	1.80
□ 46	Raul Mondesi	.60	.25
□ 47	Tino Martinez	.60	.25
□ 48	Jason Giambi	.60	.25
□ 49	Matt Williams	1.50	.70
□ 50	Cal Ripken	6.00	2.70
□ 51	Barry Larkin	1.50	.70
□ 52	Jim Edmonds	.60	.25
□ 53	Ken Caminiti	.60	.25
□ 54	Sammy Sosa	5.00	2.20
□ 55	Tony Clark	.60	.25
□ 56	Manny Ramirez	1.50	.70
□ 57	Bernard Gilkey	.40	.18
□ 58	Jose Cruz Jr.	.60	.25
□ 59	Brian Jordan	.60	.25
□ 60	Kevin Brown	1.00	.45
□ 61	Craig Biggio	1.50	.70
□ 62	Javier Lopez	.60	.25
□ 63	Jay Buhner	.60	.25
□ 64	Roberto Alomar	1.50	.70
□ 65	Justin Thompson	.40	.18
□ 66	Todd Helton	2.00	.90
□ 67	Travis Lee	1.00	.45
□ 68	Paul Konerko	.60	.25
□ 69	Jaret Wright	.60	.25
□ 70	Ben Grieve	1.50	.70
□ 71	Juan Encarnacion	.60	.25
□ 72	Ryan McGuire	.40	.18
□ 73	Derrek Lee	.40	.18
□ 74	Abraham Nunez	.40	.18
□ 75	Richard Hidalgo	.60	.25
□ 76	Miguel Tejada	.60	.25
□ 77	Jacob Cruz	.40	.18
□ 78	Homer Bush	.40	.18
□ 79	Jeff Abbott	.40	.18
□ 80	Lou Collier	.40	.18

1998 Zenith 5 x 7 Gold Impulse

	MINT	NRMT
COMMON CARD (1-80)	10.00	4.50

*STARS: 10X TO 25X BASIC 5 x 7'S
*YNG.STARS: 8X TO 20X BASIC 5 x 7'S
*SLIT-BACKS: 3X TO 8X BASIC 5 x 7'S
STATED PRINT RUN 100 SERIAL #'d SETS
RANDOM INSERTS IN PACKS
CONDITION SENSITIVE SET
SLIT CARD MUST BE CLEAN RAZOR CUT
BACK

1998 Zenith 5 x 7 Impulse

	MINT	NRMT
COMMON CARD (1-80)	1.50	.70

*STARS: 1.5X TO 4X BASIC 5 x 7'S
*YNG.STARS: 1.25X TO 3X BASIC 5 x 7'S
*SLIT-BACKS: 4X TO 1X BASIC 5 x 7'S
STATED ODDS 1:7
CONDITION SENSITIVE SET
SLIT CARD MUST BE CLEAN RAZOR CUT
BACK

1998 Zenith Epix

	MINT	NRMT
COMMON CARD (E1-E24)	2.00	.90

*PURPLE CARDS: .6X TO 1.5X ORANGE

*EMERALD CARDS: 1.25X TO 3X ORANGE
STATED ODDS 1:11
LESS THAN 30 EMERALD MOMENTS PRINTED
ONLY ORANGE CARDS LISTED BELOW!
USE MULTIPLIERS FOR EMERALD/PURPLE

1998 Zenith Raising the Bar

	MINT	NRMT
COMPLETE SET (15)	250.00	110.00
COMMON CARD (1-15)	6.00	2.70
STATED ODDS 1:25		

		MINT	NRMT
❏ 1	Ken Griffey Jr.	30.00	13.50
❏ 2	Frank Thomas	12.00	5.50
❏ 3	Alex Rodriguez	20.00	9.00
❏ 4	Tony Gwynn	15.00	6.75
❏ 5	Mike Piazza	20.00	9.00
❏ 6	Ivan Rodriguez	8.00	3.60
❏ 7	Cal Ripken	25.00	11.00
❏ 8	Greg Maddux	15.00	6.75
❏ 9	Hideo Nomo	6.00	2.70
❏ 10	Mark McGwire	40.00	18.00
❏ 11	Juan Gonzalez	12.00	5.50
❏ 12	Andruw Jones	6.00	2.70
❏ 13	Jeff Bagwell	8.00	3.60
❏ 14	Chipper Jones	15.00	6.75
❏ 15	Nomar Garciaparra	20.00	9.00

1998 Zenith Rookie Thrills

	MINT	NRMT
COMPLETE SET (15)	40.00	18.00
COMMON CARD (1-15)	1.25	.55
STATED ODDS 1:25		

		MINT	NRMT
❏ 1	Travis Lee	3.00	1.35
❏ 2	Juan Encarnacion	2.00	.90
❏ 3	Derrek Lee	1.25	.55

❏ 4	Raul Ibanez	1.25	.55
❏ 5	Ryan McGuire	1.25	.55
❏ 6	Todd Helton	5.00	2.20
❏ 7	Jacob Cruz	1.25	.55
❏ 8	Abraham Nunez	1.25	.55
❏ 9	Paul Konerko	2.00	.90
❏ 10	Ben Grieve	5.00	2.20
❏ 11	Jeff Abbott	1.25	.55
❏ 12	Richard Hidalgo	2.00	.90
❏ 13	Jaret Wright	2.00	.90
❏ 14	Lou Collier	1.25	.55
❏ 15	Miguel Tejada	2.00	.90

1998 Zenith Z-Team

	MINT	NRMT
COMPLETE SET (18)	300.00	135.00
COMMON CARD (1-18)	5.00	2.20
UNLISTED STARS	8.00	3.60
CARDS 1-9 STATED ODDS 1:35		
CARDS 10-18 STATED ODDS 1:58		
*GOLD: 1.25X TO 3X HI COLUMN		
GOLD STATED ODDS 1:175		

		MINT	NRMT
❏ 1	Frank Thomas	15.00	6.75
❏ 2	Ken Griffey Jr.	40.00	18.00

❏ 3	Mike Piazza	25.00	11.00
❏ 4	Cal Ripken	30.00	13.50
❏ 5	Alex Rodriguez	25.00	11.00
❏ 6	Greg Maddux	20.00	9.00
❏ 7	Derek Jeter	25.00	11.00
❏ 8	Chipper Jones	20.00	9.00
❏ 9	Roger Clemens	20.00	9.00
❏ 10	Ben Grieve	8.00	3.60
❏ 11	Derrek Lee	5.00	2.20
❏ 12	Jose Cruz Jr.	5.00	2.20
❏ 13	Nomar Garciaparra	25.00	11.00
❏ 14	Travis Lee	5.00	2.20
❏ 15	Todd Helton	8.00	3.60
❏ 16	Paul Konerko	5.00	2.20
❏ 17	Miguel Tejada	5.00	2.20
❏ 18	Scott Rolen	10.00	4.50

1998 Zenith Z-Team 5 x 7

	MINT	NRMT
COMPLETE SET (9)	300.00	135.00
COMMON CARD (1-9)	25.00	11.00
*SLIT-BACKS: .1X TO .25X HI COLUMN		
STATED ODDS 1:35		
CONDITION SENSITIVE SET		
PRICES BELOW ARE FOR MT UNCUT CARDS		
SLIT CARD MUST BE CLEAN RAZOR CUT		
BACK		

		MINT	NRMT
❏ 1	Frank Thomas	25.00	11.00
❏ 2	Ken Griffey Jr.	60.00	27.00
❏ 3	Mike Piazza	40.00	18.00
❏ 4	Cal Ripken	50.00	22.00
❏ 5	Alex Rodriguez	40.00	18.00
❏ 6	Greg Maddux	30.00	13.50
❏ 7	Derek Jeter	40.00	18.00
❏ 8	Chipper Jones	30.00	13.50
❏ 9	Roger Clemens	30.00	13.50

Acknowledgments

Each year we refine the process of developing the most accurate and up-to-date information for this book. I believe this year's Price Guide is our best yet. Thanks again to all the contributors nationwide (listed below) as well as our staff here in Dallas.

Those who have worked closely with us on this and many other books have again proven themselves invaluable: Frank and Vivian Baining, David Berman, Pat Blandford, Levi Bleam and Jim Fleck (707 Sportscards), Peter Brennan, Ray Bright, Card Collectors Co., Cartophilium (Andrew Pywowarczuk), Dwight Chapin, Barry Colla, Bill and Diane Dodge, Dan Even, David Festberg, Fleer/SkyBox (Rich Bradley and Julian McCracken), Steve Freedman, Gervise Ford, Larry and Jeff Fritsch, Tony Galovich, Georgia Music and Sports (Dick DeCourcey), Dick Gilkeson, Steve Gold (AU Sports), Bill Goodwin (St. Louis Baseball Cards), Mike and Howard Gordon, George Grauer, Steve Green (STB Sports), John Greenwald, Greg's Cards, Bill Henderson, Jerry and Etta Hersh, Mike Hersh, Neil Hoppenworth, Hunt Action, Jay and Mary Kasper (Jay's Emporium), Jerry Katz, Pete Kennedy, David Kohler (SportsCards Plus), Paul Lewicki, Robert Lifsen (Robert Edward Auction), Lew Lipset (Four Base Hits), Mike Livingston (University Trading Cards), Mark Macrae, Bill Madden, Bill Mastro, Dr.William McAvoy, Michael McDonald, Mid-Atlantic Sports Cards (Bill Bossert), Gary Mills, Ernie Montella, Brian Morris, Mike Mosier (Columbia City Collectibles Co.), B.A. Murry, Ralph Nozaki, Mike O'Brien, Oldies and Goodies (Nigel Spill), Oregon Trail Auctions, Pacific Trading Cards (Mike Cramer and Mike Monson), Jack Pollard, Jeff Prillaman, Pat Quinn, Jerald Reichstein (Fabulous Cardboard), Tom Reid, Gavin Riley, Clifton Rouse, John Rumierz, Kevin Savage (Sports Gallery), Gary Sawatski, Mike Schechter, Barry Sloate, John E. Spalding, Phil Spector, Frank Steele, Murvin Sterling, Lee Temanson, Topps (Marty Appel, Brian Parkinson), Ed Twombly (New England Bullpen), Upper Deck (Terry Melia, Justin Kanoya), Wayne Varner, Rob Veres, Bill Vizas, Bill Wesslund (Portland Sports Card Co.), Kit Young and Bob Ivanjack (Kit Young Cards), Rick Young, Ted Zanidakis, Robert Zanze (Z-Cards and Sports), Bill Zimpleman and Dean Zindler. Finally we give a special acknowledgment to the late Dennis W. Eckes, "Mr. Sport Americana." The success of the Beckett Price Guides has always been the result of a team effort.

It is very difficult to be "accurate" — one can only do one's best. But this job is especially difficult since we're shooting at a moving target: Prices are fluctuating all the time. Having several full-time pricing experts has definitely proven to be better than just one, and I thank all of them for working together to provide you, our readers, with the most accurate prices possible.

Many people have provided price input, illustrative material, checklist verifications, errata, and/or background information. We should like to individually thank AbD Cards (Dale Wesolewski), Action Card Sales, Jerry Adamic, Johnny and Sandy Adams, Mehdi Ahlei, Alex's MVP Cards & Comics, Doug Allen (Round Tripper Sportscards), Will Allison, Dennis Anderson, Ed Anderson, Shane Anderson, Bruce W. Andrews, Ellis Anmuth, Tom Antonowicz, Alan Applegate, Ric Apter, Jason Arasate, Clyde Archer, Randy Archer, Matt Argento, Burl Armstrong, Neil Armstrong (World Series Cards), Todd Armstrong, B and J Sportscards, Jeremy Bachman, Shawn Bailey, Ball Four Cards (Frank and Steve Pemper), Bob Bartosz, Nathan Basford, Carl Berg, Beulah Sports (Jeff Blatt), George Birsic, B.J. Sportscollectables, David Boedicker (The Wild Pitch Inc.), Bob Boffa, Louis Bollman, Tim Bond (Tim's Cards & Comics), Andrew Bosarge, Brian W. Bottles, Terry Boyd, Dan

Brandenberry, Bill Brandt, Jeff Breitenfield, John Brigandi, John Broggi, Chuck Brooks, Dan Bruner, Lesha Bundrick, Michael Bunker, John E. Burick, Ed Burkey Jr., Bubba Bennett, Virgil Burns, Greg Bussineau, David Byer, California Card Co., Capital Cards, Danny Cariseo, Carl Carlson (C.T.S.), Jim Carr, Patrick Carroll, Ira Cetron, Don Chaffee, Michael Chan, Sandy Chan, Ric Chandgie, Ray Cherry, Bigg Wayne Christian, Josh Chidester, Dick Cianciotto, Michael and Abe Citron, Dr. Jeffrey Clair, Derrick F. Clark, Mike Clark, Bill Cochran, Don Coe, Michael Cohen, Tom Cohoon (Cardboard Dreams), Collection de Sport AZ (Ronald Villaneuve), Gary Collett, Andrew T. Collier, Charles A. Collins, Curt Cooter, Steven Cooter, Pedro Cortes, Rick Cosmen (RC Card Co.), Lou Costanzo (Champion Sports), Mike Coyne, Paul and Ryan Crabb, Tony Craig (T.C. Card Co.), Kevin Crane, Taylor Crane, Scott Crump, Brian Cunningham, Allen Custer, Donald L. Cutler, Eugene C. Dalager, Dave Dame, Brett Daniel, Tony Daniele III, Scott Dantio, Roy Datema, John Davidson, Travis Deaton, Dee's Baseball Cards (Dee Robinson), Joe Delgrippo, Mike DeLuca, Tim DelVecchio, Steve Dempski, John Derossett, Mark Diamond, Gilberto Diaz Jr., Ken Dinerman (California Cruizers), Cliff Dolgins, Discount Dorothy, Walter J. Dodds Sr., Bill Dodson, Richard Dolloff (Dolloff Coin Center), Joe Donato, Jerry Dong, Pat Dorsey, Ron Dorsey, Double Play Baseball Cards, Richard Duglin (Baseball Cards-N-More), The Dugout, Joe Drelich, Kyle Dunbar, B.M. Dungan, Ken Edick (Home Plate of Utah), Randall Edwards, Rick Einhorn, Mark Ely, Brad Englehardt, Todd Entenman, Doak Ewing, Bryan Failing, R.J. Faletti, Terry Falkner, Mike and Chris Fanning, John Fedak, Stephen A. Ferradino, Tom Ferrara, Dick Fields, Louis Fineberg, Jay Finglass, L.V. Fischer, Bob Flitter, Fremont Fong, Perry Fong, Craig Frank, Mark Franke, Walter Franklin, Ron Frasier, Tom Freeman, Bob Frye, Bill Fusaro, Chris Gala, Ray Garner, David Garza, David Gaumer, Georgetown Card Exchange, Richard Gibson Jr., Glenn A. Giesey, David Giove, Dick Goddard, Alvin Goldblum, Brian Goldner, Jeff Goldstein, Ron Gomez, Rich Gove, Jay and Jan Gringsby, Joseph Griffin, Mike Grimm, Bob Grissett, Neil Gubitz (What-A-Card), Gerry Guenther, Hall's Nostalgia, Hershell Hanks, Gregg Hara, Zac Hargis, Todd Harrell, Steve Hart, Floyd Haynes (H and H Baseball Cards), Ben Heckert, Kevin Heffner, Kevin Heimbigner, Dennis Heitland, Joel Hellman, Arthur W. Henkel, Hit and Run Cards (Jon, David, and Kirk Peterson), Gary Holcomb, Lyle Holcomb, Rich Hovorka, John Howard, Mark Hromalik, H.P. Hubert, Dennis Hughes, Harold Hull, Johnny Hustle Card Co., Tom Imboden, Chris Imbriaco, John Inouye, Vern Isenberg, Dale Jackson, Marshall Jackson, Mike Jardina, Hal Jarvis, Paul Jastrzembski, Jeff's Sports Cards, David Jenkins, Donn Jennings Cards, George Johnson, Robe Johnson, Stephen Jones, Al Julian, Chuck Juliana, Dave Jurgensmeier, John Just, Robert Just, Nick Kardoulias, Scott Kashner, Frank J. Katen, Mark Kauffman, Allan Kaye, Rick Keplinger, Sam Kessler, Kevin's Kards, Larry B. Killian, Kingdom Collectibles, Inc., John Klassnik, Steve Kloloack, Philip C. Klutts, Don Knutsen, Steven Koenigsberg, Mike Kohlas, Gregg Kohn, Bob and Bryan Kornfield, Blake Krier, Neil Krohn, Scott Ku, Thomas Kunnecke, Gary Lambert, Matthew Lancaster (MC's Card and Hobby), Jason Lassic, Allan Latawiec, Howard Lau, Gerald A. Lavelle, Dan Lavin, Richard S. Lawrence, William Lawrence, Brent Lee, W.H. Lee, Morley Leeking, Ronald Lenhardt, Brian Lentz, Irv Lerner, Larry and Sally Levine, Lisa Licitra, James Litopoulos, Larry Loeschen (A and J Sportscards), Neil Lopez, Allan Lowenberg, Kendall Loyd (Orlando Sportscards South), Steve Love, Robert Luce, David Macaray, Jim Macie, Joe Maddigan, David Madison, Rob Maerten, Frank Magaha, Pepter Maltin, Pierre Marceau, Brian Marcy, Paul Marchant, Jim Marsh, Rich Markus, Bob Marquette, Brad L. Marten, Ronald L. Martin, Scott Martinez, Frank J.

Masi, Duane Matthes, James S. Maxwell Jr., Michael McCormick, Paul McCormick, McDag Productions Inc., Bob McDonald, Steve McHenry, Tony McLaughlin, Mendal Mearkle, Carlos Medina, Ken Melanson, William Mendel, Eric Meredith, Blake Meyer (Lone Star Sportscards), Tim Meyer, Joe Michalowicz, Lee Milazzo, Jimmy Milburn, Cary S. Miller, David (Otis) Miller, Eldon Miller, George Miller, Wayne Miller, Dick Millerd, Frank Mineo, Mitchell's Baseball Cards, Perry Miyashita, Douglas Mo, John Morales, William Munn, Mark Murphy, John Musacchio, Robert Nappe, National Sportscard Exchange, Steve Novella, Roger Neufeldt, Bud Obermeyer, Francisco Ochoa, John O'Hara, Glenn Olson, Steve Olson, Mike Orth, Ron Oser, Luther Owen, Earle Parrish, Clay Pasternack, Mickey Payne, Michael Perrotta, Doug and Zachary Perry, Tom Pfirrmann, Don Phlong, Bob Pirro, George Pollitt, Don Prestia, Coy Priest, Loran Pulver, Bob Ragonese, Richard H. Ranck, Bryan Rappaport, Don and Tom Ras, Robert M. Ray, R.W. Ray, Phil Regli, Glenn Renick, Rob Resnick, John Revell, Carson Ritchey, Bill Rodman, Craig Roehrig, David H. Rogers, Michael H. Rosen, Martin Rotunno, Michael Runyan, Mark Rush, George Rusnak, Mark Russell, Mike Sablow, Terry Sack, Thomas Salem, Jennifer Salems, Barry Sanders, Everett Sands, Jon Sands, Tony Scarpa, John Schad, Dave Schau (Baseball Cards), Bruce M. Schwartz, Keith A. Schwartz, Charlie Seaver, Tom Shanyfelt, Steven C. Sharek, Masa Shinohara, Eddie Silard (Eddie's Sports Den), Sam Silheet, Mike Slepcevic, Art Smith, Ben Smith, Michael Smith, Lynn and Todd Solt, Jerry Sorice, Don Spagnolo, Carl Specht, Sports Card Fan-Attic, The Sport Hobbyist, Dauer Stackpole, Norm Stapleton, Bill Steinberg, Bob Stern, Lisa Stellato (Never Enough Cards), Jason Stern, Andy Stoltz, Bill Stone, Ted Straka, Tim Strandberg (East Texas Sports Cards), Edward Strauss, Strike Three, Richard Strobino, Kevin Struss, Dr. Richard Swales, Paul Taglione, George Tahinos, Ian Taylor, Lyle Telfer, The Thirdhand Shoppe, Scott A. Thomas, Brent Thornton, Paul Thornton, Carl N. Thrower, Jim Thurtell, John Tomko, Bud Tompkins (Minnesota Connection), Philip J. Tremont, Ralph Triplette, Mike Trotta, Umpire's Choice Inc., Eric Unglaub, Hoyt Vanderpool, Nathan Voss, Steven Wagman, Jonathan Waldman, Terry Walker, T. Wall, Gary A. Walter, Mark Weber, Joe and John Weisenburger (The Wise Guys), Brian Wentz, Richard West, Mike Wheat, Richard Wiercinski, Don Williams (Robin's Nest of Dolls), Jeff Williams, John Williams, Kent Williams, Craig Williamson, Opry Winston, Brandon Witz, Rich Wojtasick, John Wolf Jr., Jay Wolt (Cavalcade of Sports), Carl Womack, Pete Wooten, Peter Yee, Wes Young, Mark Zubrensky and Tim Zwick.

Every year we make active solicitations for expert input. We are particularly appreciative of help (however extensive or cursory) provided for this volume. We receive many inquiries, comments and questions regarding material within this book. In fact, each and every one is read and digested. Time constraints, however, prevent us from personally replying. But keep sharing your knowledge. Your letters and input are part of the "big picture" of hobby information we can pass along to readers in our books and magazines. Even though we cannot respond to each letter, you are making significant contributions to the hobby through your interest and comments.

The effort to continually refine and improve this book also involves a growing number of people and types of expertise on our home team. Our company boasts a substantial Sports Data Publishing team, which strengthens our ability to provide comprehensive analysis of the marketplace. SDP capably handled numerous technical details and provided able assistance in the preparation of this edition.

Our baseball analysts played a major part in compiling this year's book, traveling thousands of miles during the past year to attend sports card shows

and visit card shops around the United States and Canada. The Beckett baseball specialists are, Rich Klein, Grant Sandground (Senior Price Guide Editor) and Evan Thompson. Their pricing analysis and careful proofreading were key contributions to the accuracy of this annual.

Grant Sandground's coordination and reconciling of prices as Beckett Baseball Card Monthly Price Guide Editor helped immeasurably. Rich Klein, as research analyst, contributed detailed pricing analysis and hours of proofing. They were ably assisted by Vicky Vyers, who helped enter new sets and pricing information, and ably handled administration of our contributor Price Guide surveys. Card librarian Brad Grmela handled the ever-growing quantity of cards we need organized for efforts such as this.

The effort was led by the Senior Manager of Sport Data Publishing Dan Hitt. They were ably assisted by the rest of the Price Guide analysts: Wayne Grove, Denny Parsons,Scott Prusha, Rob Springs and Bill Sutherland.

The price gathering and analytical talents of this fine group of hobbyists have helped make our Beckett team stronger, while making this guide and its companion monthly Price Guide more widely recognized as the hobby's most reliable and relied upon sources of pricing information.

The whole Beckett Publications team has my thanks for jobs well done. Thank you, everyone.

Notes

Notes

Notes